YEARBOOK OF LABOUR STATISTICS
Time series

ANNUAIRE DES STATISTIQUES DU TRAVAIL
Séries chronologiques

ANUARIO DE ESTADISTICAS DEL TRABAJO
Series cronológicas

2009

YEARBOOK
OF LABOUR
STATISTICS
Time series

ANNUAIRE
DES STATISTIQUES
DU TRAVAIL
Séries chronologiques

ANUARIO
DE ESTADISTICAS
DEL TRABAJO
Series cronológicas

68th ISSUE
68ᵉ ÉDITION
68.ª EDICIÓN

INTERNATIONAL LABOUR OFFICE   GENEVA
BUREAU INTERNATIONAL DU TRAVAIL   GENÈVE
OFICINA INTERNACIONAL DEL TRABAJO   GINEBRA

ISBN   978-92-2-022238-6

ISSN   0084-3857

ILO publications can be obtained through major booksellers or ILO local offices in many countries, or direct from ILO Publications, International Labour Office, CH-1211 Geneva 22, Switzerland. A catalogue or list of new publications will be sent free of charge from the above address.

Les publications du BIT peuvent être obtenues dans les principales librairies ou les bureaux locaux du BIT dans de nombreux pays, ou sur demande adressée directement à Publications du BIT, Bureau international du Travail, CH-1211 Genève 22, Suisse, lequel enverra également sur demande un catalogue ou une liste des nouvelles publications.

Las publicaciones de la OIT pueden obtenerse en las principales librerías o en oficinas locales de la OIT en muchos países o pidiéndolas a: Publicaciones de la OIT, Oficina Internacional del Trabajo, CH-1211 Ginebra 22, Suiza, que también puede enviar a quienes lo soliciten un catálogo o una lista de nuevas publicaciones.

Printed by the International Labour
Office, Geneva, Switzerland

Imprimé par le Bureau international
du Travail, Genève, Suisse

Impreso por la Oficina Internacional
del Trabajo, Ginebra, Suiza

Contents

IX	**Preface**	
XV	Signs and symbols used in the tables	
XVI	Types of data sources	

1	**Chapter 1**	**Economically active population**
3	Explanatory notes	
9	Table 1A	Total and economically active population, by age group
33	Table 1B	Economically active population, by level of education and age group

75	**Chapter 2**	**Employment**
77	Explanatory notes	
87	Table 2A	General level
99	Table 2B	Total employment, by economic activity
197	Table 2C	Total employment, by occupation
257	Table 2D	Total employment, by status in employment
293	Table 2E	Paid employment, by economic activity
381	Table 2F	Paid employment in manufacturing

449	**Chapter 3**	**Unemployment**
451	Explanatory notes	
461	Table 3A	General level
479	Table 3B	Unemployment, by age group
555	Table 3C	Unemployment, by level of education
605	Table 3D	Unemployment, by economic activity
669	Table 3E	Unemployment, by occupation

719	**Chapter 4**	**Hours of work**
721	Explanatory notes	
727	Table 4A	Hours of work, by economic activity
805	Table 4B	Hours of work in manufacturing

875	**Chapter 5**	**Wages**
877	Explanatory notes	
885	Table 5A	Wages, by economic activity
959	Table 5B	Wages in manufacturing

1037	**Chapter 6**	**Labour cost**
1039	Explanatory notes	
1045	Table 6A	Labour cost in manufacturing

1065	**Chapter 7**	**Consumer prices**
1067	Explanatory notes	
1073	Table 7A	General indices
1083	Table 7B	General indices, excluding shelter
1087	Table 7C	Food indices
1097	Table 7D	Electricity, gas and other fuels indices
1103	Table 7E	Clothing indices
1113	Table 7F	Rent indices

1123	**Chapter 8**	**Occupational injuries**
1125	Explanatory notes	
1131	Synoptic table	
1139	Table 8A	Cases of injury with lost workdays, by economic activity
1277	Table 8B	Rates of occupational injuries, by economic activity
1339	Table 8C	Days lost, by economic activity

1359	**Chapter 9**	**Strikes and lockouts**
1361	Explanatory notes	
1367	Table 9A	Strikes and lockouts, by economic activity
1381	Table 9B	Workers involved, by economic activity
1397	Table 9C	Days not worked, by economic activity
1413	Table 9D	Rates of days not worked, by economic activity

1419	**Appendix**	
	Classifications used in the Yearbook	
1421		International Standard Industrial Classification of all Economic Activities (ISIC - Rev. 2, 1968)
1427		International Standard Industrial Classification of all Economic Activities (ISIC - Rev. 3)
1432		International Standard Industrial Classification of all Economic Activities (ISIC - Rev. 4)
1438		International Classification by Status in Employment (ICSE - 1993)
1444		International Standard Classification of Occupations (ISCO - 1968)
1450		International Standard Classification of Occupations (ISCO - 88)
1456		International Standard Classification of Education (ISCED-76)
1459		International Standard Classification of Education (ISCED-97)
1463	References	
1467	Order of arrangement of countries, areas and territories	

1473	**Index (countries, areas and territories included in each table)**	

Table des matières

XI	**Préface**	
XV	Signes et symboles utilisés dans les tableaux	
XVI	Types de sources de données	

1	**Chapitre 1**	**Population active**
5	Notes explicatives	
9	Tableau 1A	Population totale et population active par groupe d'âge
33	Tableau 1B	Population active, par niveau d'instruction et groupe d'âge

75	**Chapitre 2**	**Emploi**
80	Notes explicatives	
87	Tableau 2A	Niveau général
99	Tableau 2B	Emploi total, par activité économique
197	Tableau 2C	Emploi total, par profession
257	Tableau 2D	Emploi total, par situation dans la profession
293	Tableau 2E	Emploi rémunéré, par activité économique
381	Tableau 2F	Emploi rémunéré dans les industries manufacturières

449	**Chapitre 3**	**Chômage**
454	Notes explicatives	
461	Tableau 3A	Niveau général
479	Tableau 3B	Chômage, par groupe d'âge
555	Tableau 3C	Chômage, par niveau d'instruction
605	Tableau 3D	Chômage, par activité économique
669	Tableau 3E	Chômage, par profession

719	**Chapitre 4**	**Durée du travail**
723	Notes explicatives	
727	Tableau 4A	Durée du travail, par activité économique
805	Tableau 4B	Durée du travail dans les industries manufacturières

875	**Chapitre 5**	**Salaires**
879	Notes explicatives	
885	Tableau 5A	Salaires, par activité économique
959	Tableau 5B	Salaires dans les industries manufacturières

1037	**Chapitre 6**	**Coût de la main-d'œuvre**
1041	Notes explicatives	
1045	Tableau 6A	Coût de la main-d'œuvre dans les industries manufacturières

1065	**Chapitre 7**	**Prix à la consommation**
1069	Notes explicatives	
1073	Tableau 7A	Indices généraux
1083	Tableau 7B	Indices généraux, non compris l'habitation
1087	Tableau 7C	Indices de l'alimentation
1097	Tableau 7D	Indices de l'électricité, gaz et autres combustibles
1103	Tableau 7E	Indices de l'habillement
1113	Tableau 7F	Indices du loyer

1123	**Chapitre 8**	**Lésions professionnelles**
1127	Notes explicatives	
1131	Tableau synoptique	
1139	Tableau 8A	Cas de lésion avec perte de journées de travail, par activité économique
1277	Tableau 8B	Taux de lésions professionnelles, par activité économique
1339	Tableau 8C	Journées perdues, par activité économique

1359	**Chapitre 9**	**Grèves et lock-out**
1363	Notes explicatives	
1367	Tableau 9A	Grèves et lock-out, par activité économique
1381	Tableau 9B	Travailleurs impliqués, par activité économique
1397	Tableau 9C	Journées non effectuées, par activité économique
1413	Tableau 9D	Taux de journées non effectuées, par activité économique

1419	**Annexe**	
	Classifications utilisées dans l'Annuaire	
1423		Classification internationale type, par industrie, de toutes les branches d'activité économique (CITI - Rév. 2, 1968)
1428		Classification internationale type, par industrie, de toutes les branches d'activité économique (CITI - Rév. 3)
1434		Classification internationale type, par industrie, de toutes les branches d'activité économique (CITI - Rév. 4)
1440		Classification internationale d'après la situation dans la profession (CISP - 1993)
1446		Classification internationale type des professions (CITP - 1968)
1452		Classification internationale type des professions (CITP - 88)
1457		Classification internationale type de l'éducation (CITE-76)
1460		Classification internationale type de l'éducation (CITE-97)
1463	Références	
1467	Ordre de présentation des pays, zones et territoires	

1473	**Index (pays, zones ou territoires compris dans chaque tableau)**	

Índice general

XIII   **Prefacio**

XV   Signos y símbolos utilizados en los cuadros

XVI   Tipos de fuentes de datos

1   **Capítulo 1**   **Población económicamente activa**

7   Notas explicativas

9   Cuadro 1A   Población total y población económicamente activa, por grupo de edad

33   Cuadro 1B   Población económicamente activa, por nivel de educación y grupo de edad

75   **Capítulo 2**   **Empleo**

83   Notas explicativas

87   Cuadro 2A   Nivel general

99   Cuadro 2B   Empleo total, por actividad económica

197   Cuadro 2C   Empleo total, por ocupación

257   Cuadro 2D   Empleo total, por situación en el empleo

293   Cuadro 2E   Empleo remunerado, por actividad económica

381   Cuadro 2F   Empleo remunerado en las industrias manufactureras

449   **Capítulo 3**   **Desempleo**

457   Notas explicativas

461   Cuadro 3A   Nivel general

479   Cuadro 3B   Desempleo, por grupo de edad

555   Cuadro 3C   Desempleo, por nivel de educación

605   Cuadro 3D   Desempleo, por actividad económica

669   Cuadro 3E   Desempleo, por ocupación

719   **Capítulo 4**   **Horas de trabajo**

725   Notas explicativas

727   Cuadro 4A   Horas de trabajo, por actividad económica

805   Cuadro 4B   Horas de trabajo en las industrias manufactureras

875   **Capítulo 5**   **Salarios**

882   Notas explicativas

885   Cuadro 5A   Salarios, por actividad económica

959   Cuadro 5B   Salarios en las industrias manufactureras

1037   **Capítulo 6**   **Costo de la mano de obra**

1043   Notas explicativas

1045   Cuadro 6A   Costo de la mano de obra en las industrias manufactureras

1065   **Capítulo 7**   **Precios al consumidor**

1071   Notas explicativas

1073   Cuadro 7A   Índices generales

1083   Cuadro 7B   Índices generales excl. la habitación

1087   Cuadro 7C   Índices de la alimentación

1097   Cuadro 7D   Índices de la electricidad, gas y otros combustibles

1103   Cuadro 7E   Índices del vestido

1113   Cuadro 7F   Índices del alquiler

1123   **Capítulo 8**   **Lesiones profesionales**

1129   Notas explicativas

1131   Cuadro sinóptico

1139   Cuadro 8A   Casos de lesión con pérdida de días de trabajo, por actividad económica

1277   Cuadro 8B   Tasas de lesiones mortales, por actividad económica

1339   Cuadro 8C   Días de trabajo perdidos, por actividad económica

1359   **Capítulo 9**   **Huelgas y cierres patronales**

1365   Notas explicativas

1367   Cuadro 9A   Huelgas y cierres patronales, por actividad económica

1381   Cuadro 9B   Trabajadores implicados, por actividad económica

1397   Cuadro 9C   Días no trabajados, por actividad económica

1413   Cuadro 9D   Tasas de días no trabajados, por actividad económica

1419   **Apéndice**

Clasificaciones empleadas en el Anuario

1425   Clasificación Industrial Internacional Uniforme de Todas las Actividades Económicas (CIIU - Rev. 2, 1968)

1430   Clasificación Industrial Internacional Uniforme de Todas las Actividades Económicas (CIIU - Rev. 3)

1436   Clasificación Industrial Internacional Uniforme de Todas las Actividades Económicas (CIIU - Rev. 4)

1442   Clasificación Internacional de la Situación en el Empleo (CISE - 1993)

1448   Clasificación Internacional Uniforme de Ocupaciones (CIUO - 1968)

1454   Clasificación Internacional Uniforme de Ocupaciones (CIUO - 88)

1458   Clasificación Internacional Normalizada de la Educación (CINE-76)

1461   Clasificación internacional Normalizada de la Educación (CINE-97)

1463   Referencias

1467   Orden de presentación de los países, áreas y territorios

1473   **Índice (países, áreas y territorios incluidos en cada cuadro)**

Preface

The Yearbook of Labour Statistics is a publication of the International Labour Office, prepared by the Department of Statistics. The 2009 issue presents the principal labour statistics for over 190 countries, areas or territories. Most of the tables cover the ten years from 1999-2008. However, not all countries are in a position to provide the ILO with series covering the whole period; for some, figures may not be available until several years after the reference year. The data published in this edition of the *Yearbook* are those available in the ILO at 30 September 2009.

Because of the voluminous size of the Yearbook (i) the series with no available data for at least one of the past five years; and (ii) the series containing data for one year only that have been published in previous issues of the Yearbook, are not presented in the printed publication. These series, however, are disseminated online at http://laborsta.ilo.org.

The figures have been drawn mainly from information sent to the ILO by national statistical services, or taken from official publications. They have not been adjusted by the ILO to conform with the international recommendations on labour statistics. Nevertheless, reporting agencies were requested to supply information conforming as closely as possible to the international standards.

Where available, separate data by sex are shown in the tables on the economically active population, employment, unemployment, hours of work, wages and occupational injuries.

The annual data on consumer price indices, which also appear in the *Bulletin of Labour Statistics* with monthly, quarterly or half-yearly frequency, are identified in the corresponding tables of the present *Yearbook* by the symbol "B" (see Chapter 7).

N.B. As certain statistical series may have been revised retroactively by the countries for a number of reasons, users should always use the most recent edition of the *Yearbook*.

Arrangement of material

The subjects are grouped in nine chapters, each with an explanatory note briefly indicating the main characteristics of the different types of data published.

The type of source for the series is shown as a code in parenthesis following the name of the country. The explanations of the codes are provided on page XVI.

The coverage of the series in terms of groups of workers or types of data is shown on the first line of the table, where relevant. Additional information concerning the coverage may be shown as footnotes.

The countries appear by continent in accordance with the table "Order of arrangement of countries, areas and territories" given in the Appendix.

Base period of indices

For the series of consumer price indices, a uniform base (2000=100) has been adopted in the *Yearbook* in accordance with the practice followed by the statistical services of the United Nations and the specialized agencies. If data are available only for periods after 2000, the indices are shown in *italics*, usually with the first calendar year for which the figures are available as the base period. When a series has been interrupted and replaced by a new series, the latter is linked to the former if the two series are sufficiently comparable; otherwise it is published on a new base. The break in continuity is indicated by a vertical line separating the two series and an explanatory footnote where appropriate. The base year for indices of employment and wages is indicated

in the notes to the series, and the figures are printed in *italics*.

Methodology

Information on the scope of the statistics, their definitions and the methods used by the national statistical services in establishing the data published in the *Yearbook of Labour Statistics* and in the *Bulletin of Labour Statistics* is given in the series *Sources and Methods: Labour Statistics* (formerly *Statistical Sources and Methods*).

Ten volumes have been issued: *1 - Consumer price indices; 2 - Employment, wages, hours of work and labour cost (establishment surveys); 3 - Economically active population, employment, unemployment and hours of work (household surveys); 4 - Employment, unemployment, wages and hours of work (administrative records and related sources); 5 - Total and economically active population, employment and unemployment (population censuses); 6 - Household income and expenditure surveys; 7 - Strikes and lockouts; 8 - Occupational injuries; 9 - Transition countries;* and *10 - Estimates and projections of the economically active population 1950-2010.* These publications, which complement the brief explanations given in the tables, should enable a better understanding of the data and facilitate their international comparison.

A list of ILO documents dealing with the methodology recommended for the compilation of labour statistics is given in the Appendix (see "References").

Classifications used in the Yearbook

Data are published wherever possible according to the latest versions of the international standard classifications: the *International Standard Industrial Classification of all Economic Activities (ISIC) Revision 4;* the *International Classification of Status in Employment (ISCE-93)* and the *International Standard Classification of Education (ISCED-97),* and the previous version of the *International Standard Classification of Occupations (ISCO-88).* If statistics are not available according to the latest classifications, the former classifications continue to be used. The classifications are given in the Appendix.

If the data shown according to the latest version of the classification are not available for the full ten years presented in the *Yearbook,* the data for the earlier years are given according to the previous version, and the two series are shown side-by-side, with a vertical bar separating them. In this case the codes for the new classification are given in the right-hand column, while those for the old one are given in the left.

The revised classifications differ in general structure from the previous versions, so that direct comparisons are not always possible. For this reason, the ILO Department of Statistics has not attempted to convert data from one version to another.

The groups, divisions or categories of each classification that are used in the tables are shown as codes, with an indication of the classification to which they refer. The name corresponding to each code is given in the Appendix.

N.B. A new version of the *International Standard Classification of Occupations (ISCO-08)* was adopted in 2007. Information about the classification can be found at http://www.ilo.org/public/english/bureau/stat/isco/isco08/index.htm

Acknowledgement

The International Labour Office wishes to express its gratitude to the national statistical services for their valuable collaboration in providing the statistics shown in this *Yearbook*.

Other regular statistical publications

Yearbook of Labour Statistics: Country Profiles (published annually): This publication shows the latest available statistics (without time series) for each of over 190 countries, areas and territories, grouped into five main tables comprising statistics on (i) the number of workers and the percentage of women who are in the economically active population, employment and unemployment by age group, branch of economic activity (industry), occupation, status in employment and level of education; (ii) total population, activity rates and unemployment rates by sex and broad age groups; (iii) number of workers in paid employment, their average hours of work and earnings, by sex and branch of economic activity (industry); (iv) the rates of fatal and non-fatal injuries by sex and branch of economic activity (industry); as well as the number of strikes and lockouts, the number of workers involved and the number of days not worked by branch of economic activity (industry); and (v) consumer price indices by expenditure groups. It also includes a Supplement with global and regional estimates on the economically active population, employment and unemployment.

Bulletin of Labour Statistics (published 6-monthly): Monthly, quarterly, half-yearly and annual data on employment, unemployment, hours of work, wages and consumer prices for the last four years are published in the *Bulletin of Labour Statistics*. The *Bulletin* also features articles of professional interest to labour statisticians.

Occupational Wages and Hours of Work and Retail Food Prices, Statistics from the ILO October Inquiry (published annually): This publication presents data on occupational wages and hours of work and retail food prices collected by the ILO each year through its October Inquiry.

CD-ROMs containing longer time series are available annually for the *Yearbook of Labour Statistics* and for the *Occupational Wages and Hours of Work and Retail Food Prices, Statistics from the ILO October Inquiry*.

For viewing and downloading data:
http://laborsta.ilo.org

Please visit the Department of Statistics' web site:
http://www.ilo.org/stat

For further information, please contact:
Department of Statistics
International Labour Office
CH-1211 Geneva 22
Switzerland

Fax: + 41 22 799 6957
Tel: + 41 22 799 8631
E-mail: STAT@ilo.org

Préface

L'*Annuaire des statistiques du travail* est une publication du Bureau international du Travail, préparée par le Département de statistique. L'édition de 2009 présente les principales statistiques du travail pour quelque 190 pays, zones ou territoires. La plupart des tableaux couvrent les dix années 1999-2008. Néanmoins, certains pays ne sont pas en mesure de fournir au BIT des séries qui couvrent la totalité de cette période; pour quelques-uns, les données ne seront peut-être disponibles que plusieurs années après l'année de référence. Les données publiées dans cette édition de l'*Annuaire* sont celles disponibles au BIT le 30 septembre 2009.

Compte tenu de la taille volumineuse de l'Annuaire, les séries pour lesquelles les données ne sont pas disponibles pour au moins l'une des cinq dernières années et celles contenant des données pour une année seulement et qui ont été publiées dans les éditions précédentes de l'Annuaire, ne sont pas présentées dans cette publication. Cependant ces séries sont diffusées en ligne sur http://laborsta.ilo.org.

Les données présentées proviennent principalement d'informations communiquées au BIT par les services statistiques nationaux ou de publications officielles. Ces données n'ont pas été ajustées par le BIT pour leur assurer une parfaite conformité avec les recommandations internationales en matière de statistiques du travail. Il faut noter cependant que les services statistiques nationaux ont été invités à fournir des renseignements aussi conformes que possible aux normes internationales existantes.

Dans la mesure du possible, des données séparées par sexe sont présentées dans les tableaux sur la population active, l'emploi, le chômage, la durée du travail, les salaires et les lésions professionnelles.

Les données annuelles sur les indices des prix à la consommation qui sont également diffusées avec des données mensuelles, trimestrielles ou semestrielles dans le *Bulletin des statistiques du travail* sont identifiées dans les tableaux correspondants de l'*Annuaire* par le symbole «B» (voir chapitre 7).

N.B. Etant donné que certaines séries statistiques pourraient avoir été révisées rétroactivement par les pays pour diverses raisons, il est recommandé aux utilisateurs de toujours consulter l'édition la plus récente de l'*Annuaire*.

Disposition des sujets traités

Les différents sujets traités dans cet *Annuaire* sont groupés en neuf chapitres dont chacun comprend une note explicative où sont indiquées brièvement les principales caractéristiques des divers types de données publiées dans les tableaux.

Le type de source pour les séries apparaît sous forme d'un code entre parenthèses placé après le nom du pays. Les explications concernant les codes figurent en page XVI.

La portée des séries en termes de groupes de travailleurs et de types de données apparaît sur la première ligne du tableau lorsque c'est possible. Des informations supplémentaires concernant la portée peuvent être signalées en notes de bas de page.

Les pays sont présentés par continent, selon la liste figurant au tableau «Ordre de présentation des pays, zones et territoires».

Période de base des indices

Pour les séries de prix à la consommation, une base uniforme (100 en 2000) a été adoptée dans l'*Annuaire*, conformément à la pratique suivie par les services statistiques des Nations Unies et des institutions spécialisées. Lorsque des données ne sont disponibles que pour des périodes postérieures à 2000, les indices, imprimés en *italique*, sont généralement présentés avec, pour période de base, la première année civile pour laquelle des chiffres sont disponibles. Lorsqu'une série est interrompue et remplacée par une nouvelle série, cette dernière est enchaînée à la précédente dans la mesure où ces deux séries sont suffisamment comparables, ou publiée sur une nouvelle base dans le cas contraire; cette discontinuité dans l'homogénéité des séries est indiquée par un trait vertical séparant les deux séries et par une note explicative de bas de page. La base des séries d'emploi et de salaires en nombres-indices est indiquée dans les notes aux séries et les chiffres sont imprimés en *italique*.

Méthodologie

Des renseignements sur la portée des statistiques, leur définition et les méthodes utilisées par les services statistiques nationaux lors de l'établissement des séries générales publiées dans l'*Annuaire des statistiques du travail* et dans le *Bulletin des statistiques du travail* sont présentés dans une série de publications intitulée *Sources et méthodes: statistiques du travail* (précédemment *Sources et méthodes statistiques*).

Dix volumes sont déjà disponibles, à savoir: 1. *Indices des prix à la consommation*; 2. *Emploi, salaires, durée du travail et coût de la main d'œuvre (enquêtes auprès des établissements)*; 3. *Population active, emploi, chômage et durée du travail (enquêtes auprès des ménages)*; 4. *Emploi, chômage, salaires et durée du travail (documents administratifs et sources assimilées)*; 5. *Population totale et population active, emploi et chômage (recensements de population)*; 6. *Enquêtes sur le revenu et les dépenses des ménages*; 7. *Grèves et lock-out*; 8. *Lésions professionnelles*; 9. *Pays en transition* et 10. *Evaluations et projections de la population active 1950-2010*. Ces publications complètent les renseignements succincts qui figurent dans les notes explicatives aux tableaux et devraient permettre une bonne compréhension des séries et une meilleure comparaison sur le plan international.

Une liste des documents du BIT traitant des méthodes statistiques recommandées pour l'établissement des statistiques du travail est fournie dans l'annexe du présent *Annuaire* (voir «*Références*»).

Classifications utilisées dans l'Annuaire

Les données sont publiées, lorsque c'est possible, selon les versions les plus récentes des classifications internationales types suivantes: la *Classification internationale type, par industrie, de toutes les activités économiques (CITI), révision 4*; la *Classification internationale d'après la situation dans la profession (CISP-93)* et la *Classification internationale type de l'éducation (CITE-97)* et la version antérieure de la *Classification internationale type des professions (CITP-88)*. Si les statistiques ne sont pas disponibles selon les dernières classifications, on continue d'utiliser les anciennes classifications. Les diverses classifications sont présentées dans l'Annexe.

Si, pour l'ensemble de la décennie présentée dans l'*Annuaire*, les données produites ne sont pas disponibles selon la version la plus récente, celles des premières années sont données selon la version antérieure et les deux séries apparaissent côte à côte, une ligne verticale marquant la séparation entre les deux versions. Dans ce cas-là, les codes de la nouvelle classification apparaissent dans la colonne de droite tandis que ceux de l'ancienne classification occupent celle de gauche.

La structure générale des classifications révisées diffère de celle des versions précédentes de sorte que les comparaisons directes ne sont pas toujours possibles. C'est pourquoi le Département de statistique du BIT a renoncé à convertir les données d'une version à l'autre.

Les groupes, branches et catégories de chaque classification apparaissent dans les tableaux sous forme de codes avec indication de la classification utilisée. Le nom correspondant à chaque code est donné dans l'Annexe.

NB La nouvelle version de la *Classification internationale type des professions (CITP-08)* a été adoptée en 2007. Les informations concernant cette classification peuvent être consultées à l'adresse:
http://www.ilo.org/public/english/bureau/stat/isco/isco08/index.htm

Remerciements

Le Bureau international du Travail tient à exprimer sa gratitude aux services statistiques nationaux des différents pays pour leur précieuse collaboration dans la transmission des données présentées dans cet *Annuaire*.

Autres publications statistiques régulières

Annuaire des statistiques du travail : Profils des pays (publié annuellement) : cette publication présente les dernières statistiques disponibles sous un nouveau format (sans séries chronologiques) pour plus de 190 pays, zones et territoires, groupées en cinq tableaux principaux incluant des données sur : (i) le nombre de travailleurs et le pourcentage des femmes dans la population active, emploi et chômage, classés par groupe d'âge, activité économique (industrie), profession, niveau d'instruction, et situation dans la profession; (ii) la population totale, le taux d'activité et le taux de chômage par sexe et grands groupes d'âge; (iii) le nombre de personnes ayant un emploi rémunéré, leur durée moyenne du travail et leurs salaires par sexe et activité économique (industrie); (iv) le taux des lésions professionnelles mortelles et non mortelles par sexe et activité économique (industrie), ainsi que le nombre de grèves et lock-out, de travailleurs impliqués et des journées non effectuées, par activité économique (industrie); (v) et les indices des prix à la consommation par groupes de dépenses. Il inclut également un Supplément avec des estimations globales et régionales sur la population active, l'emploi et le chômage.

Bulletin des statistiques du travail (publié semestriellement) : cette publication présente les données mensuelles, trimestrielles, semestrielles et annuelles sur l'emploi, le chômage, les heures de travail, les salaires et les prix à la consommation pour les 4 dernières années. Le *Bulletin* propose également des articles professionnels dédiés aux statisticiens du travail.

Salaires et Durée du travail par profession et Prix de détail de produits alimentaires, Statistiques de l'Enquête d'octobre du BIT (publiée annuellement) : cette publication présente les données sur les salaires et la durée du travail par profession et sur les prix au détail des produits alimentaires collectés par le BIT chaque année au travers de l'Enquête d'octobre.

Des CD-ROMs, qui contiennent les séries chronologiques plus complètes, sont disponibles chaque année pour l'*Annuaire des Statistiques du Travail* et pour les *Salaires et Durée du travail par profession et Prix de détail de produits alimentaires, Statistiques de l'Enquête d'octobre du BIT.*

Pour visualiser et télécharger les données:
http://laborsta.ilo.org

Pour visiter le site Web du Département de statistique:
http://www.ilo.org/stat

Pour tout renseignement complémentaire, s'adresser à:

Département de statistique
Bureau international du Travail
CH-1211 Genève 22
Suisse

Fax: + 41-22-799 6957
Tél.:   + 41-22-799 8631
E-mail: STAT@ilo.org

Prefacio

El *Anuario de Estadísticas del Trabajo* es una publicación de la Oficina Internacional del Trabajo, preparada por el Departamento de Estadística. La edición de 2009 presenta las principales estadísticas del trabajo para unos 190 países, áreas y territorios. La mayoría de los cuadros abarcan los diez años que van de 1999-2008. Sin embargo, no todos los países proporcionan series que abarcan todo el período; para algunos, las cifras están disponibles varios años después del año al que se refieren. Los datos que se publican en esta edición del *Anuario* son aquellos que estaban disponibles en la OIT al 30 de septiembre de 2009.

A causa del tamaño voluminoso del Anuario (i) las series sin datos disponibles para al menos uno de los cinco años pasados; y (ii) las series que contienen datos para sólo un año que han sido publicadas en las publicaciones anteriores del Anuario, no son presentadas en la publicación impresa. Estas series, sin embargo, son diseminadas en línea en http://laborsta.ilo.org.

Las cifras provienen, en su mayor parte, de las informaciones que los servicios estadísticos nacionales envían a la Oficina, o de publicaciones oficiales de cada país. La OIT no efectúa ningún ajuste, de acuerdo con las recomendaciones internacionales en materia de estadísticas del trabajo. Sin embargo, siempre se pide a los servicios estadísticos que suministren datos conformes, en lo posible, con las normas internacionales existentes.

Cuando la información existe, se muestran datos separados por sexo en los cuadros de la población económicamente activa, empleo, desempleo, horas de trabajo, salarios y lesiones profesionales.

Cuando existen datos de índices de precios al consumidor de manera mensual, trimestral o semestral, y que se publican en el *Boletín de Estadísticas del Trabajo,* los datos anuales correspondientes publicados en el *Anuario* se identifican con el símbolo «B» (véase el capítulo 7).

N.B.: Como ciertas series estadísticas podrían haber sido revisadas retroactivamente por los países por razones diferentes, se recomienda a los usuarios que siempre utilicen la edición más reciente del *Anuario.*

Disposición de los temas tratados

Los temas se hallan agrupados en nueve capítulos, cada uno de los cuales se introduce con una nota explicativa que indica brevemente las principales características de las diversas clases de datos publicados.

La fuente de las series se indica a continuación del nombre del país mediante un código entre paréntesis. Las explicaciones de estos códigos figuran en la página XVI.

Si corresponde, el alcance de las series, en cuanto a los grupos de trabajadores abarcados y a los tipos de datos, figura en la primera línea del cuadro. Otras informaciones pertinentes sobre el alcance pueden indicarse en notas de pie de página.

Los países se presentan por continentes, según el cuadro «Orden de presentación de los países, áreas y territorios», que se encuentra en el Apéndice.

Período base de los índices

Para las series sobre los índices de precios al consumidor, el *Anuario* ha adoptado una base uniforme (2000 = 100), de conformidad con la práctica seguida por los servicios estadísticos de las Naciones Unidas y las instituciones especializadas. Cuando sólo se dispone de datos para períodos posteriores a 2000, los índices, impresos en *itálicas,* se presentan generalmente tomando como período base el primer año civil para el cual se dispone de cifras. Si una serie queda interrumpida y se sustituye por otra nueva, esta última serie se enlaza con la anterior cuando existe suficiente comparabilidad entre las series; en caso contrario, se publica sobre una nueva base. Esta discontinuidad en las series se indica con una raya vertical entre las dos series y una nota explicativa al pie de la página. El año base para los índices de empleo y salarios se indica en las notas de las series y las cifras se imprimen en *itálicas.*

Metodología

El ámbito de las estadísticas, sus definiciones y los métodos utilizados por los servicios nacionales de estadística para producir los datos que se publican en el *Anuario de Estadísticas del Trabajo* y en el *Boletín de Estadísticas del Trabajo* se describen en la serie de publicaciones titulada *Fuentes y Métodos: Estadísticas del Trabajo* (anteriormente *Fuentes y métodos estadísticos).*

Hasta la fecha se han publicado diez volúmenes: 1 - *Indices de los precios al consumidor;* 2 - *Empleo, salarios, horas de trabajo y costo de la mano de obra (encuestas de establecimientos);* 3 - *Población económicamente activa, empleo, desempleo y horas de trabajo (encuestas de hogares);* 4 - *Empleo, desempleo, salarios y horas de trabajo (registros administrativos y fuentes relacionadas);* 5 - *Población total y población económicamente activa, empleo y desempleo (censos de población);* 6 - *Encuestas sobre los ingresos y gastos de los hogares;* 7 - *Huelgas y cierres patronales;* 8 - *Lesiones profesionales;* 9 - *Países en transición,* y 10 - *Evaluaciones y proyecciones de la población económicamente activa 1950-2010.* Estas publicaciones complementan las breves indicaciones dadas en las notas explicativas de los cuadros y permiten comprender mejor las series y facilitar su comparación internacional.

En el Apéndice figura una lista de documentos de la Oficina Internacional del Trabajo que tratan de los métodos estadísticos recomendados para compilar estadísticas del trabajo (véase «*Referencias*»).

Clasificaciones utilizadas en el Anuario

Los datos se ajustan en lo posible a la última versión de las clasificaciones internacionales, es decir: la *Clasificación Internacional Industrial Uniforme de Todas las Actividades Económicas (CIIU), Revisión 4;* la *Clasificación Internacional de la Situación en el Empleo (CISE-93)* y la *Clasificación Internacional Normalizada de la Educación (CINE-97)* y la versión anterior de la *Clasificación Internacional Uniforme de Ocupaciones (CIUO-88).* Si los datos estadísticos clasificándolos según la anterior. Las diversas clasificaciones figuran en el Apéndice.

Si no es posible presentar los datos según la última versión de una clasificación para todos los años de la década del *Anuario,* los que corresponden a años anteriores figuran según la versión previa, mostrándose las dos series una junto a la otra, con una línea vertical de separación entre ambas. En tales casos los códigos de la nueva clasificación figuran a la derecha de cada columna, y en la izquierda los de la antigua.

Como la estructura general de las clasificaciones revisadas difiere de las versiones anteriores, no siempre es posible compararlas directamente. Por tal motivo el Departamento de Estadística de la OIT no ha tratado de convertir los datos de una versión en otra.

Los grupos, divisiones o categorías de cada clasificación utilizada se indican en forma codificada, con mención de la clasificación a la que corresponden. El nombre de cada código figura en el Apéndice, así como el texto integral de cada una de las clasificaciones.

NB La nueva versión de la *Clasificación Internacional Uniforme de Ocupaciones (CIUO-08)* ha sido adoptada en *2007. Se pueden consultar las informaciones relativas a esta clasificación en:*
http://www.ilo.org/public/english/bureau/stat/isco/isco08/index.htm

Agradecimiento

La Oficina Internacional del Trabajo desea expresar su gratitud a los servicios estadísticos de los diferentes países por su preciosa colaboración en el suministro de los datos presentados en este *Anuario.*

Otras publicaciones estadísticas regulares

Anuario de Estadísticas del Trabajo: Perfiles de los países (publicados anualmente): esta publicación presenta un nuevo formato de las últimas estadísticas (sin las series cronológicas) para más de 190 países, áreas y territorios, agrupadas en cinco cuadros principales que abarcan: (i) el número de personas y el porcentaje de mujeres en la población activa, el empleo y el desempleo, clasificados por grupo de edad, rama de actividad económica, ocupación, nivel de educación y situación en el empleo; (ii) la población total, las tasas de actividad y de desempleo por sexo y grandes grupos de edad; (iii) el número de personas con un empleo asalariado, sus horas promedio de trabajo y sus salarios, por sexo y rama de actividad económica; (iv) las tasas de lesiones mortales y no mortales por sexo y rama de actividad económica; así como el número de huelgas y cierres patronales, de trabajadores implicados y de días no trabajados, por rama de actividad económica; y (v) los índices de precios al consumidor por grupos de gastos. También incluye un Suplemento con estimaciones globales y regionales sobre la población económicamente active, el empleo y el desempleo.

Boletín de Estadísticas del Trabajo (publicado 2 veces por año): contiene datos mensuales, trimestrales, semestrales y datos anuales sobre el empleo, el desempleo, las horas de trabajo, los salarios y el índice de los precios al consumo durante los cuatro últimos años. *El Boletín* también publica artículos de interés profesional en estadistas de trabajo.

Salarios y Horas de Trabajo por Ocupación y Precios al por menor de artículos alimenticios, Estadísticas de la Encuesta de octubre de la OIT (publicados anualmente): esta publicación presenta datos sobre salarios y horas de trabajo por ocupación y los precios de artículos alimenticios al detalle reunidos por la OIT cada año durante la Encuesta de octubre.

Los CD-ROMs que contienen mas completas series cronológicas están disponibles anualmente para el *Anuario de Estadística de Trabajo* y para los *Salarios y Horas de Trabajo por Ocupación y Precios al por menor de artículos alimenticios, Estadísticas de la Encuesta de octubre de la OIT.*

Para visualizar y bajar datos:
http://laborsta.ilo.org

El sitio Web del Departamento de Estadística:
http://www.ilo.org/stat

Para más información, diríjase a:

Departamento de Estadística
Oficina Internacional del Trabajo
CH-1211 Ginebra 22
Suiza

Fax:	+ 41-22-799.6957
Tel.:	+ 41-22-799.8631
Correo electrónico:	STAT@ilo.org

Signs and symbols used in the tables

.	Not available
...	Not applicable
*	Provisional
-	Insignificant, less than half the unit used or sampling variability too high
0	Nil
— or |	A line placed between two years indicates that the figures above and below it are not strictly comparable or that a new series begins immediately after the line (see footnotes)
∅	Mean of the observations
B	Series published in the *ILO Bulletin of Labour Statistics* (refers to Chapter 7 only)

Indices in *italics* : indices based on a year other than 2000

Decimal figures are separated by a point

Signes et symboles utilisés dans les tableaux

.	Pas disponible
...	Ne s'applique pas
*	Provisoire
-	Négligeable, inférieur à la moitié de l'unité retenue, ou variabilité d'échantillonnage trop grande
0	Nul
— ou |	Un filet entre deux années indique que les chiffres places au-dessus et au-dessous ne sont pas strictement comparables ou qu'une nouvelle série commence immédiatement après le filet (voir les notes de bas de page)
∅	Moyenne des observations
B	Séries publiées dans le *Bulletin de statistiques du travail du BIT* (ne se réfère qu'au chapitre 7)

Indices en *italique* : indices ayant comme base une autre année que 2000

Dans les tableaux, un point sépare les unités des décimales

Signos y símbolos utilizados en los cuadros

.	No disponible
...	No se aplica
*	Provisional
-	Despreciable, inferior a la mitad de la unidad utilizada, o con variabilidad muestral demasiado grande
0	Nula
— o |	Una raya entre dos años indica que las cifras que están encima no son estrictamente comparables con las que están abajo, o que una nueva serie comienza inmediatamente después de la raya (véanse notas al pie de la página correspondiente)
∅	Promedio de observaciones
B	Series publicadas en el *Boletín de Estadísticas de Trabajo de la OIT* (se refiere solamente al capítulo 7)

Índices en *itálica* : índices que no tienen por base el año 2000

En los cuadros, un punto separa las unidades de los decimales

	Types of data sources	Types de sources de données	Tipos de fuentes de datos
A	**Population census**	**Recensement de la population**	**Censo de población**
B	**Household survey**	**Enquête auprès des ménages**	**Encuesta de hogares**
BA	Labour force survey	Enquête sur la main-d'oeuvre	Encuesta de la fuerza de trabajo
BB	Household income and/or expenditure survey	Enquête sur les revenus et/ou les dépenses des ménages	Encuesta sobre ingresos y/o gastos de los hogares
C	**Establishment census**	**Recensement des établissements**	**Censo de establecimientos**
CA	Labour-related establishment Census	Recensement des établissements, relatif au travail	Censo de establecimientos relacionado con el trabajo
CB	Industrial or commercial census	Recensement industriel ou commercial	Censo industrial o comercial
D	**Establishment survey**	**Enquête auprès des établissements**	**Encuesta de establecimientos**
DA	Labour-related establishment survey	Enquête auprès des établissements, relative au travail	Encuesta de establecimientos relacionada con el trabajo
DB	Industrial or commercial survey	Enquête industrielle ou commerciale	Encuesta industrial o comercial
E	**Official estimates**	**Estimations officielles**	**Estimaciones oficiales**
F	**Administrative records and related sources**	**Fichiers administratifs et sources connexes**	**Registros administrativos y fuentes relacionadas**
FA	Insurance records	Fichiers des assurances	Registros de seguros
FB	Employment office records	Fichiers des bureaux de placement	Registros de oficinas de colocación
FC	Tax records	Fichiers fiscaux	Registros fiscales
FD	Administrative reports	Rapports administratifs	Informes administrativos
FE	Collective agreements	Conventions collectives	Convenios colectivos
FF	Labour inspectorate records	Fichiers d'inspection du travail	Registros de inspección del trabajo
FG	Labour relations records	Fichiers des relations du travail	Registros de relaciones laborales
FH	Records of employers' or workers' organizations	Fichiers des organisations d'employeurs ou de travailleurs	Registros de organizaciones de empleadores o trabajadores
G	**Regular collection of consumer prices**	**Collecte régulière des prix à la consommation**	**Recolección periódica de precios al consumidor**
H	**Special data collection**	**Collecte spéciale de données**	**Recolección especial de datos**
I	**Legislation**	**Législation**	**Legislación**
Z	**Source unknown**	**Source inconnue**	**Fuente ignorada**

Economically active population

Population active

Población económicamente activa

Economically active population

The *economically active population* are all those persons who during the specified reference period are classified either as employed or as unemployed, i.e. who supply labour[1]. If the reference period is short, e.g. a day or a week, the terms 'labour force' or 'currently active population' are frequently used. If the reference period is long, e.g. a year, then the term 'usually active population' may be used.

The statistics presented in Tables 1A and 1B are mostly results from the latest available Population Census (A), or from a recent Labour force sample survey (BA), as indicated by the code to the right of the country name[2] but may in some cases be based on official estimates (E).

The coverage of the statistics presented differs between countries because of the treatment of groups such as armed forces, members of religious orders, persons who contribute to family enterprises without pay, persons seeking their first job, seasonal workers or persons engaged in part-time economic activities. In certain countries, all or some of these groups are excluded from the economically active population. It should be noted that the economically active population does not include students and retired persons who do not work or seek work, persons occupied solely in domestic duties in their own households, persons living entirely on their own means, and persons wholly dependent upon others. In practice for most countries the statistics will also exclude persons living in collective households, such as prisons and convents.

The comparability of the statistics for different countries therefore will be limited by details of the definitions used and groups covered, as well as by differences in the methods of collection, classification and tabulation of the basic data. The reference period may also be an important factor of difference: in some countries statistics on the economically active population refer to the **actual** position of each individual on the day of the census or surveyor during a brief, specific period, such as the week immediately prior to the census or survey date; while in others the data recorded refer to the **usual** position of each person, generally without an explicit reference to a given period of time. Note also that the age range specified for collecting information about the economically active population will differ between countries[3].

Table 1A

Total and economically active population, by age group

This table presents statistics on the economically active population and its relation to the total population, by sex and age groups. The lower and/or upper age limits used when collecting information relevant for inclusion in the economically active population are indicated in parentheses to the right of the country name, e.g.: (15+) means that persons aged 15 years and above are included, (15-74) means persons aged 15 to 74 years are included, (.) means that the age limits are not available and (...) means that age limits are *not applicable*. Two types of totals appear for most countries. From the first type (penultimate line of each table)

specific activity rates, indicated *in italics*, can be obtained, i.e. ratios (expressed in per cent) of the economically active population aged *15 years and over* to the total population of the corresponding age groups. In **bold** in the last line of each table the *crude activity rates* are presented, i.e. ratios (expressed in per cent) of the total economically active population to the total population which includes persons who do not belong to the working-age population.

In interpreting the crude activity rates, i.e. the ratios of the total economically active population to the total population of all ages, it should be recalled that the relative size of the population in each sex-age group (and in particular those under 15 years of age) will affect the crude activity rate shown. Countries with many young (or old) people who are mainly inactive will have l+ower crude activity rates than countries with relatively few young (old) people. The effects of differences in the definitions of the economically active population used in the various countries referred to above should also be taken into account. They may in particular influence the comparability of the activity rates for women, because in many countries a relatively large number of women work without pay on family farms or in other family enterprises, and countries differ in the criteria adopted and the procedures used for determining the extent to which such workers are to be counted among the economically active. Certain countries only include contributing family workers who work more than one-third of a normal work day. In some countries the relevant questions may be formulated so that many, especially women, do not respond in a way that signals that they are to be considered as economically active. Activity rates for young people also should be compared with caution, owing to variations among countries in the treatment of contributing family workers, of unemployed persons not previously employed, and of students engaged in part-time economic activities.

It should be noted that the statistics for a particular year and country are published only in one issue of the *Yearbook*. However, the country name, the year for which the latest statistics are available and the issue in which they appeared will be indicated in subsequent issues[4].

Table 1B

Economically active population, by level of education and age group

Table 1B shows the distribution of the economically active population, according to the highest *level of education* attained, by *sex and age group*, for the latest available year. It has been designed to permit the comparison of the levels of education attained by these different groups of the population within a country, as well as the comparison of the educational attainment of the economically active population in different countries. The levels indicated in the table's heading refer to the *International Standard Classification of Education* of UNESCO, either the 1976 or the 1997 version, depending on the statistics that have been supplied for the countries.

Because most persons obtain their education while young quite different educational systems may have applied to persons in different age groups even within a country, and some may also have been educated abroad. It may therefore be difficult to establish homogeneous groups for educational attainment for the population, and comparisons between age groups may not be very precise. In addition, for many countries it can be difficult to establish correspondences between their national classification and ISCED, especially with respect to technical or professional training programmes, short-term programmes and adult-oriented programmes (ranging around levels 3 and 5 of ISCED76 and levels 3, 4 and 5 of ISCED97). For programmes leading to a university-type diploma difficulties may arise when, for example, only one diploma is awarded; or when the first diploma is awarded following a number of years which exceeds the standard duration of first stage of tertiary education programmes (as may be the case e.g. for medical studies). Therefore the duration and contents of national programmes grouped together into the same ISCED level may only be approximately comparable between countries or between age groups for the same country.

The criterion used to determine the 'level of education attained' differs between countries, but tends to be one of the following: (i) has completed the programme, (ii) has attended the programme, or (iii) has obtained the requisite diploma at the end of the programme. It is the first criterion which has been recommended by ISCED and which seems to be the most frequently used.

Abridged presentations of the 1976 and 1997 versions of the *International Standard Classifications of Education (ISCED)* can be found in the appendix on classifications.

As for table 1A it should be noted that the statistics for a particular year and country are published only in one issue of the *Yearbook*. However, the country name, the year for which the latest statistics are available and the issue in which they appeared will be indicated in subsequent issues.

Notes

[1] For the definition of 'employed persons' see the introduction to Chapter 2. For the definition of 'unemployed persons' see the introduction to Chapter 3.

[2] For further information about the codes used as well as on sources and coverage of the statistics, see "Signs and symbols used in the tables".

[3] Information on the scope, definitions and methods of calculation for the statistics from many countries are presented in ILO: *Sources and Methods: Labour Statistics*, Vol.3, third edition: "Economically active population, employment, unemployment and hours of work (Household surveys)", third edition (Geneva, 2003) and Vol. 5: "Total and economically active population, employment and unemployment (population censuses)", second edition (Geneva,1996). Updated descriptions can be found at the web site: http://laborsta.ilo.org.

[4] In 1990 ILO published *Year Book of Labour Statistics, Retrospective Edition on Population Censuses*, 1945-89. The statistics presented there cover 184 countries, areas and territories throughout the world and presents data on the economically active population by age-group, status in employment, industry and occupation, derived from 559 population censuses carried out since 1945. It can be ordered from ILO Publications, International Labour Office, CH-1211 Geneva 22, Switzerland.

Population active

La *population active* comprend toutes les personnes qui, durant une période de référence spécifiée, sont considérées comme pourvues d'un emploi ou au chômage, c'est-à-dire qui constituent la main-d'oeuvre[1]. Si la période de référence est courte, et porte par exemple sur un jour ou une semaine, on utilise plus fréquemment les termes de « population active du moment » ou encore « main-d'œuvre ». Si la période de référence est longue, telle qu'une année, on utilise les termes de « population habituellement active ».

Les données présentées dans les Tableaux 1A et 1B proviennent généralement du dernier recensement disponible sur la main-d'œuvre ou de la dernière enquête par sondage de la main-d'œuvre, respectivement identifiées par le code (A) ou (BA) à droite du nom de pays[2]; dans certains cas, les données proviennent de statistiques officielles et sont identifiées sous le code (E).

La portée des données présentées varie selon les pays car certains groupes, tels que les membres des forces armées, les membres des institutions religieuses, les personnes collaborant à l'entreprise familiale sans rémunération, les personnes en quête d'un premier emploi, les travailleurs saisonniers ou les personnes qui ont une activité à temps partiel, ne sont pas classés de la même manière dans tous les pays. Dans certains pays, tous ces groupes ou une partie seulement sont considérés comme inactifs. Il convient de noter que les données sur la population active ne comprennent pas les étudiants, les personnes occupées exclusivement aux travaux ménagers de leur propre ménage, les rentiers et les personnes entièrement à la charge d'autrui. Concrètement, pour la plupart des pays, les données sur la population active ne comprennent pas les membres de ménages collectifs, tels que les pensionnaires d'institutions pénitentiaires et des couvents.

La comparabilité des données est donc affectée par les différences que présentent les définitions utilisées, les groupes de population couverts et les méthodes de rassemblement, de classification et de tabulation des données de base. La période de référence peut également constituer un élément important de différence : dans certains pays, les données relatives à la population active se rapportent à la situation **effective** de chaque individu le jour du recensement ou de l'enquête, ou pendant une brève période déterminée, telle que la semaine précédant immédiatement la date du recensement ou de l'enquête ; dans d'autres pays, les données recueillies ont trait à la situation **habituelle** de chaque individu et ne se rapportent pas à une période déterminée. En outre, tous les pays ne prévoient pas de limite d'âge dans la définition de la population active[3].

Tableau 1A

Population totale et population active, par groupe d'âge

Le tableau 1A fournit des données sur la population active et son rapport à la population totale, par sexe et par groupe d'âge. Les limites d'âge inférieure et/ou supérieure retenues pour l'inclusion dans la population active sont indiquées entre parenthèses à droite du nom du pays. Ainsi, (15 +) signifie que les personnes âgées de 15 ans et plus sont incluses ; (15-74) veut dire que les personnes âgées de 15 à 74 ans sont incluses ; (.) signifie que les limites d'âge *ne sont pas disponibles* ; et (...) que les limites d'âge *ne s'appliquent pas*. Deux types de totaux sont, pour la plupart des pays, présentés : les premiers (avant-dernière ligne de chaque tableau) sont indiqués en *italique* et permettent d'obtenir *les taux d'activité spécifiques*, c'est-à-dire les rapports (exprimés en pourcentage) de la population active âgée de 15 ans et plus à la population totale des groupes d'âge correspondants; les seconds (indiqués en **caractères gras** à la dernière ligne de chaque tableau) présentent *les taux d'activité bruts*, c'est-à-dire les rapports (exprimés en pourcentage) de la population active totale à la population totale, y compris les personnes qui n'appartiennent pas à la population en âge de travailler.

En analysant les taux d'activité bruts, c'est-à-dire les rapports de la population active totale à la population totale de tous les âges, il convient de rappeler que la proportion de la population dans chaque groupe d'âge, selon le sexe (en particulier le groupe de moins de 15 ans) influencera le taux d'activité brute indiqué. Les pays avec une population jeune (ou âgée) importante, généralement considérée comme inactive, obtiendront des taux d'activité bruts inférieurs aux pays qui ont peu de jeunes gens (ou de personnes âgées). Il convient également de tenir compte des différences dans les critères utilisés pour déterminer qui compose la population active des pays mentionnés. Ces différences peuvent en effet affecter la comparaison des taux d'activité des femmes, car dans beaucoup de pays, un nombre relativement élevé de femmes aident, sans rémunération, aux travaux de l'exploitation familiale, agricole ou autre. Or, les pays n'utilisent pas tous les mêmes critères pour déterminer dans quelle mesure cette catégorie doit être considérée comme entrant dans la population active. Certains pays ne prennent en compte les travailleurs familiaux collaborant à l'entreprise familiale que s'ils ont travaillé plus d'un tiers de la journée normale de travail. Dans certains pays, les questions peuvent être formulées de telle sorte que nombre de personnes, en particulier les femmes, ne répondent pas de manière à indiquer qu'elles devraient être considérées comme actives. Il convient également de se montrer prudent dans la comparaison des taux d'activité des jeunes gens, en raison du fait que les travailleurs familiaux collaborant à l'entreprise familiale, les chômeurs n'ayant jamais travaillé et les étudiants qui ont une activité à temps partiel, ne sont pas comptabilisés de la même manière par tous les pays.

Il convient de souligner que les statistiques relatives à une année ou à un pays spécifiques ne sont publiées que dans l'Annuaire des statistiques du travail correspondant. Cependant, le pays, l'année à laquelle se rapportent les données disponibles et la publication dans laquelle ils figureront seront indiqués dans les Annuaires ultérieurs[4].

Population active, par niveau d'instruction et groupe d'âge

Le tableau 1B présente la répartition de la population active selon le niveau d'instruction le plus élevé, par sexe et par groupe d'âge pour la dernière année disponible. Ce tableau permet de comparer les niveaux d'instruction par sexe et par groupe d'âge de la population aux niveaux national et international. Les niveaux indiqués dans ce tableau sont issus de la Classification internationale type de l'Education (CITE) de l'UNESCO, dans sa version de 1976 ou de 1997, selon les données communiquées par les pays.

Parce que la plupart des personnes acquièrent une instruction lorsqu'elles sont jeunes, plusieurs systèmes éducatifs peuvent concerner différents groupes d'âge; certaines personnes ont aussi pu étudier à l'étranger. Il peut par conséquent s'avérer difficile d'établir des groupes homogènes en terme de niveau d'instruction et les correspondances entre groupes d'âge peuvent être peu précises. En outre, nombre de pays éprouvent des difficultés à établir des correspondances entre leur classification nationale et la CITE, particulièrement pour les programmes à contenu de formation technique ou professionnelle, ceux de courte durée et ceux destinés aux adultes (aux limites des catégories 3 et 5 de la Classification de 1976 et aux niveaux 3, 4 et 5 de la Classification de 1997). Pour les programmes menant à un diplôme de type universitaire, des confusions entre les niveaux 6 et 7 peuvent être observées lorsque par exemple le cursus ne comporte qu'un diplôme ou lorsque le premier diplôme s'obtient après une durée d'études plus longue que la durée type (comme cela est le cas pour les études médicales). Par conséquent, les durées et contenus des programmes nationaux classés dans un même niveau de la CITE ne sont pas strictement comparables entre pays ou entre différents groupes d'âge au sein d'un même pays.

Le critère utilisé pour déterminer le niveau d'instruction diffère selon les pays mais tend en général, à être l'un des trois suivants : a) a complété le programme, b) a fréquenté le programme, c) est diplômé au terme de ce programme. Le premier type de critère, conforme aux directives de la CITE, semble être celui le plus fréquemment utilisé.

Des versions abrégées de la Classification internationale type de l'Education (CITE), 1976 et 1997, sont présentées en annexe.

Comme pour le Tableau 1A, il convient de souligner que les statistiques relatives à une année ou à un pays spécifiques ne sont publiées que dans l'Annuaire des statistiques du travail correspondant. Cependant, le pays, l'année à laquelle se rapportent les données disponibles et la publication dans laquelle ils figureront seront indiqués dans les Annuaires ultérieurs.

Notes

[1] Pour les définitions des « personnes pourvues d'un emploi » et des « chômeurs », voir les notes explicatives des chapitres 2 et 3.

[2] Pour de plus amples informations concernant la source et la portée des données, voir les « Signes et symboles utilisés dans les tableaux ».

[3] Pour les renseignements sur la portée, les définitions et les méthodes de calcul utilisées pour les diverses séries nationales, voir BIT : Sources et méthodes statistiques, vol. 3: « Population active, emploi, chômage et durée du travail et coût de la main d'œuvre (enquêtes auprès des ménages) », troisième édition, (Genève, 2003) et vol. 5, « population totale et population active, emploi et chômage » (recensements de population), deuxième édition (Genève, 1996). Les dernières descriptions se trouvent sur le site : http://laborsta.ilo.org.

[4] En 1990, le BIT a publié *l'Annuaire des statistiques du travail : édition rétrospective sur les recensements de population, 1945-1989*. Les données statistiques qui y figurent portent sur 184 pays, zones et territoires du monde entier et sur la population active par groupe d'âge, par situation dans la profession, par branches d'activité économique et par professions, et proviennent de 559 recensements de population effectués depuis 1945. Cette publication peut être commandée au service des publications du BIT, Bureau international du Travail, CH-1211 Genève 22, Suisse.

Población económicamente activa

La *población económicamente activa* la constituyen todas aquellas personas que durante el período de referencia especificado pueden clasificarse como personas con empleo o como personas desempleadas, es decir, que aportan trabajo[1]. Si el período de referencia es corto, por ejemplo un día o una semana, se utilizan con frecuencia los términos «fuerza de trabajo» o «población actualmente activa». Si el período de referencia es largo, por ejemplo un año, puede utilizarse el término «población habitualmente activa».

Las estadísticas que aparecen en los cuadros 1A y 1B son, en su mayoría, el resultado del último censo de población disponible (A), o de la última encuesta por muestra de la fuerza de trabajo (BA), tal como indica el código que figura a la derecha del nombre del país[2], pero en algunos casos pueden estar basadas en estimaciones oficiales (E).

El campo de cobertura de las estadísticas presentadas difiere entre países debido al tratamiento de ciertos grupos, como fuerzas armadas, hermandades religiosas, personas que trabajan en empresas familiares sin sueldo, personas en busca de un primer empleo, trabajadores estacionales o personas ocupadas en actividades económicas a tiempo parcial. En ciertos países no se incluyen en la población económicamente activa a todos o a algunos de estos grupos. Cabe destacar que la población económicamente activa no abarca a estudiantes ni personas jubiladas que no trabajan ni buscan empleo, a las personas que sólo realizan labores domésticas en su propio hogar, rentistas, y a las totalmente dependientes de otras. En la práctica, en la mayor parte de los países las estadísticas no incluyen a las personas que viven en colectividades, como prisiones o conventos. Así pues, la comparabilidad de las estadísticas de los distintos países se ve limitada por los detalles de las definiciones utilizadas y de los grupos que abarcan, así como por diferencias en los métodos de recolección, clasificación y tabulación de los datos básicos. El período de referencia también puede constituir un factor importante de disparidad: en algunos países, las estadísticas sobre la población económicamente activa se refieren a la situación **real** de cada individuo el día del censo o de la encuesta o durante un breve período específico, como la semana inmediatamente anterior a la fecha del censo o la encuesta; mientras que otras sólo registran la situación **habitual** de cada persona, generalmente sin ninguna referencia explícita a un período determinado. También cabe señalar que el intervalo de edad especificado para recopilar información sobre la población económicamente activa varía según los países[3].

Cuadro 1A

Población total y población económicamente activa, por grupo de edad

Este cuadro presenta estadísticas sobre la población económicamente activa y su relación con la población total, por sexo y grupo de edad. Los límites de edad inferiores y/o superiores que se utilizan en la recopilación de información sobre la población económicamente activa están indicados entre paréntesis a la derecha del nombre del país. Por ejemplo: (+ 15) significa que se incluyen las personas de 15 años de edad y más; (15-74), que se incluyen las personas con edades comprendidas entre 15 y 74 años; (.) que los límites de edad no *están disponibles*; (...), que *no se aplican límites de edad*. Para la mayoría de los países se dan dos totales: del primero (penúltima línea de cada cuadro, en cursiva), se pueden obtener *tasas de actividad específica*, es decir razones (expresadas en porcentajes) entre la población económicamente activa de *15 años de edad y más* y la población total del mismo grupo de edad. En la última línea decada cuadro se presentan, **en negrita**, *las tasas brutas de actividad*, es decir razones (expresadas en porcentajes) entre el total de la población económicamente activa y la población total de todos los grupos de edad, comprendidas las personas que no tienen la edad de trabajar.

Al interpretar las tasas brutas de actividad, es decir el porcentaje de la población total de toda edad que es económicamente activa, cabe recordar que la dimensión relativa de cada grupo de edad, por sexo (y en particular del de menos de 15 años de edad), influye en las tasas brutas de actividad que se presentan. Los países con muchos jóvenes (o viejos), en su mayoría inactivos, presentarán tasas brutas de actividad menores que los países con menos jóvenes (viejos). También cabe tener presente las repercusiones de las distintas definiciones, según los países, de la población económicamente activa. Pueden afectar específicamente a la comparabilidad entre tasas de actividad relativas a las mujeres, porque en muchos países un número relativamente elevado de mujeres trabaja sin remuneración como ayudas familiares en establecimientos agrícolas o industriales familiares, y porque difieren los criterios de los distintos países para determinar hasta qué punto estos trabajadores familiares forman parte de la población económicamente activa. Ciertos países sólo incluyen a los trabajadores familiares que trabajan más de un tercio de las horas normales de trabajo por día. En algunos países, las preguntas correspondientes pueden formularse de manera que, muchos encuestados, especialmente mujeres, parecen responder de tal modo que no se las considera económicamente activas. También deben compararse con precaución las tasas de actividad de los jóvenes, en virtud del diferente tratamiento que dan los países a los trabajadores familiares no remunerados, los desempleados sin empleo anterior, y los estudiantes con una actividad económica a tiempo parcial.

Cabe señalar que las estadísticas correspondientes a un año y país en particular aparecen únicamente en el *Anuario* correspondiente. No obstante, en futuras ediciones se indicará el nombre del país, el año de las últimas estadísticas disponibles y la edición en la que aparecen[4].

Cuadro 1B

Población económicamente activa, por nivel de educación y grupo de edad

El cuadro 1B muestra, para *cada sexo y grupo de edad* la distribución de la población económicamente activa según *el nivel de educación* más elevado, para el último año disponible. Se ha diseñado de modo que permite la comparación entre los niveles de educación alcanzados por estos diferentes grupos de la población en un mismo país, así como entre el nivel de instrucción de la población económicamente activa de los distintos países. Los niveles que se indican en el título del cuadro corresponden a la *Clasificación Internacional Normalizada de la Educación (CINE)* de la UNESCO, ya sea en su versión de 1976 o de 1997, según de las estadísticas que han facilitado los países.

Dado que la mayoría de las personas reciben su educación mientras son jóvenes, cabe que se hayan aplicado distintos sistemas de educación a personas de distintos grupos de edad incluso en un mismo país, o que algunas hayan recibido la educación en el extranjero. Por consiguiente, puede ser difícil establecer grupos homogéneos de nivel de instrucción para la población, y las comparaciones entre grupos de edad pueden resultar no muy precisas. Además, muchos países pueden encontrar dificultades a la hora de establecer correspondencias entre sus clasificaciones nacionales y la CINE, especialmente con respecto a los programas de formación profesional o técnica, los programas de breve duración y los de educación de adultos (que se sitúan alrededor de los niveles 3 y 5 de la CINE 76 y de los niveles 3, 4 y 5 de la CINE 97). Para los programas que culminan en la obtención de un diploma o título de tipo universitario pueden plantearse dificultades cuando, por ejemplo, sólo se otorga un diploma o cuando el primer diploma sólo se obtiene tras haber cursado un cierto número de años que superan la duración media de la primera etapa de los programas de estudios superiores (como es el caso de, por ejemplo, las profesiones médicas). Por consiguiente, la duración y el contenido de los programas nacionales agrupados en el mismo nivel de la CINE pueden ser comparables sólo aproximadamente, ya sea entre países o entre grupos de edad de un mismo país.

El criterio utilizado para determinar el « Nivel de educación » difiere entre los países, pero suele ser uno de los siguientes: i) han completado el programa; ii) han asistido a los cursos del programa; iii) han obtenido el diploma que culmina el programa. La CINE recomienda el primer criterio, que parece ser el más utilizado.

En el apéndice de clasificaciones figuran presentaciones abreviadas de las versiones de 1976 y 1997 de la *Clasificación Internacional Normalizada de la Educación (CINE)*.

En lo que se refiere al cuadro 1A, cabe señalar que las estadísticas para un año y país en particular aparecen únicamente en el *Anuario* correspondiente. No obstante, en futuras ediciones se indicará el nombre del país, el año de las últimas estadísticas disponibles y la edición en la que aparecen.

Notes

[1] Para la definición de «personas con empleo» véase la introducción al capítulo 2. Para la definición de «personas desempleadas» véase la introducción al capítulo 3.

[2] Para más información sobre los códigos utilizados, así como sobre las fuentes y campos que abarcan las estadísticas, véase «signos y símbolos utilizados en los cuadrose».

[3] Para información sobre el alcance, definiciones y métodos de cálculo de las estadísticas de muchos países véase OIT: Fuentes y métodos estadísticos, volumen 3, tercera edición: «Población económicamente activa, empleo, desempleo y horas de trabajo (Encuesta de hogares)» (Ginebra, 2003) y volumen 5, segunda edición: «Población total y población económicamente activa, empleo y desempleo (censos de población)» (Ginebra, 1996). Todas las descripciones actualizadas se encuentran en el sitio web: http://laborsta.ilo.org.

[4] En 1990 la OIT publicó el *Anuario de estadísticas del trabajo, Edición retrospectiva sobre los censos de población, 1945-1989*. El estudio presenta estadísticas de 184 países, zonas y territorios de todo el mundo, que incluyen datos estadísticos sobre la población económicamente activa por grupo de edad, situación en la ocupación, industria y ocupación, provenientes de 559 censos de población realizados desde 1945. Puede encargarse al Departamento de Publicaciones de la OIT, Oficina Internacional del Trabajo, CH-1211, Ginebra, 22, Suiza.

ECONOMICALLY ACTIVE POPULATION

POPULATION ACTIVE

POBLACION ECONOMICAMENTE ACTIVA

1A

Total and economically active population by age group

Population totale et population active par groupe d'âge

Población total y población económicamente activa por grupo de edad

Thousands — Milliers — Millares

	Total			Men - Hommes - Hombres			Women - Femmes - Mujeres		
	Total population / Population totale / Población total	Active population / Population active / Población activa	Activity rate / Taux d'activité / Tasa de actividad %	Total population / Population totale / Población total	Active population / Population active / Población activa	Activity rate / Taux d'activité / Tasa de actividad %	Total population / Population totale / Población total	Active population / Population active / Población activa	Activity rate / Taux d'activité / Tasa de actividad %

AFRICA - AFRIQUE - AFRICA

Botswana (2006) BA (12+) [1] [2]

Total	**1 702.8**	**653.2**	*38.4*	**798.5**	**332.6**	*41.7*	**904.4**	**320.6**	*35.4*
Total (15+)	*1 089.1*	*640.2*	*58.8*	*489.4*	*324.6*	*66.3*	*599.7*	*315.7*	*52.6*
0-11	409.2	.	.	207.1	.	.	202.1	.	.
12-14	204.5	12.9	*6.3*	101.9	8.0	*7.9*	102.6	4.9	*4.7*
15-19	178.5	40.2	*22.5*	88.1	24.3	*27.5*	90.4	16.1	*17.8*
20-24	169.4	105.0	*62.0*	77.5	53.0	*68.4*	91.8	52.0	*56.6*
25-29	147.2	107.9	*73.3*	68.1	53.9	*79.1*	79.0	54.0	*68.3*
30-34	119.9	90.5	*75.4*	52.9	43.5	*82.4*	67.1	46.9	*70.0*
35-39	97.3	74.2	*76.3*	43.9	36.4	*83.0*	53.4	37.8	*70.8*
40-44	80.3	58.9	*73.4*	33.3	26.4	*79.5*	47.0	32.5	*69.1*
45-49	71.3	51.8	*72.7*	30.4	25.5	*84.0*	40.9	26.3	*64.3*
50-54	56.6	38.3	*67.7*	25.1	19.6	*78.2*	31.5	18.7	*59.4*
55-59	39.5	24.9	*63.1*	17.4	13.2	*75.9*	22.1	11.7	*53.0*
60-74	81.1	48.4	*59.6*	34.8	28.7	*82.4*	46.4	19.7	*42.5*
75+	47.4	-	.	17.8	-	.	29.7	-	.
?	0.6	-	.	0.2	-	.	0.4	-	.

Egypt (V-XI.2007) BA [3]

Total	**73 424.0**	**24 402.8**	*33.2*	**37 532.4**	**18 631.6**	*49.6*	**35 891.6**	**5 771.2**	*16.1*
Total (15+)	*50 600.2*	*24 250.9*	*47.9*	*25 819.3*	*18 511.2*	*71.7*	*24 780.9*	*5 739.7*	*23.2*
0-14	22 823.8	151.9	*0.7*	11 713.1	120.4	*1.0*	11 110.7	31.5	*0.3*
15-19	8 692.8	1 730.8	*19.9*	4 629.4	1 336.3	*28.9*	4 063.4	394.5	*9.7*
20-24	7 405.0	3 684.3	*49.8*	4 130.6	2 733.7	*66.2*	3 274.4	950.6	*29.0*
25-29	5 495.5	3 317.4	*60.4*	2 630.3	2 473.6	*94.0*	2 865.2	843.8	*29.4*
30-34	9 001.1	5 547.7	*61.6*	4 215.6	4 144.3	*98.3*	4 785.5	1 403.4	*29.3*
40-44	8 617.8	5 468.6	*63.5*	4 222.3	4 115.8	*97.5*	4 395.5	1 352.8	*30.8*
50-54	6 211.6	3 517.5	*56.6*	3 213.4	2 854.9	*88.8*	2 998.2	662.6	*22.1*
60-64	2 033.0	592.7	*29.2*	1 070.9	508.7	*47.5*	962.1	84.0	*8.7*
65+	3 143.4	391.9	*12.5*	1 706.8	343.9	*20.1*	1 436.6	48.0	*3.3*

Maroc (2008) BA (15+)

Total	**31 177.4**	**11 458.5**	*36.8*	**15 391.2**	**8 344.3**	*54.2*	**15 786.2**	**3 114.2**	*19.7*
Total (15+)	*22 270.1*	*11 267.2*	*50.6*	*10 851.1*	*8 234.7*	*75.9*	*11 419.0*	*3 032.4*	*26.6*
0-14	8 907.3	191.3	*2.1*	4 540.1	109.5	*2.4*	4 367.2	81.8	*1.9*
15-24	6 321.9	2 461.8	*38.9*	3 165.4	1 789.0	*56.5*	3 156.5	672.7	*21.3*
25-34	5 177.1	3 229.1	*62.4*	2 482.9	2 357.7	*95.0*	2 694.3	871.4	*32.3*
35-44	3 958.0	2 468.2	*62.4*	1 876.0	1 802.1	*96.1*	2 082.1	666.1	*32.0*
45-59	4 215.2	2 446.4	*58.0*	2 039.8	1 786.3	*87.6*	2 175.4	660.0	*30.3*
60+	2 597.8	661.7	*25.5*	1 287.2	499.6	*38.8*	1 310.6	162.1	*12.4*

Mauritius (2008) BA (16+) [3] [4]

Total	.	**559.4**	.	.	**355.6**	.	.	**203.8**	.
16-19	82.4	19.1	*23.2*	42.9	12.0	*28.0*	39.5	7.1	*18.0*
20-24	89.1	55.0	*61.7*	45.7	32.3	*70.7*	43.4	22.7	*52.3*
25-29	106.9	80.8	*75.6*	54.0	49.8	*92.2*	52.9	31.0	*58.6*
30-34	101.9	80.1	*78.6*	50.3	48.9	*97.2*	51.6	31.2	*60.5*
35-39	90.5	70.0	*77.3*	44.9	43.1	*96.0*	45.6	26.9	*59.0*
40-44	100.9	76.6	*75.9*	50.3	48.5	*96.4*	50.6	28.1	*55.5*
45-49	94.1	67.7	*71.9*	47.1	44.8	*95.1*	47.0	22.9	*48.7*
50-54	80.6	54.9	*68.1*	40.0	37.0	*92.5*	40.6	17.9	*44.1*
55-59	67.9	38.9	*57.3*	33.1	27.8	*84.0*	34.8	11.1	*31.9*
60-64	44.8	9.4	*21.0*	20.8	6.3	*30.3*	24.0	3.1	*12.9*
65-69	29.4	4.0	*13.6*	13.2	2.9	*22.0*	16.2	1.1	*6.8*
70-74	23.9	2.0	*8.4*	10.2	1.5	*14.7*	13.7	0.5	*3.6*
75+	32.6	0.9	*2.8*	12.0	0.7	*5.8*	20.6	0.2	*1.0*

Explanations and sources: see p. 3.

[1] Incl. armed forces, Excl. conscripts. [2] Excl. discouraged job seekers. [3] Excl. armed forces. [4] "De jure" population.

Explications et sources: voir p. 5.

[1] Y compris les forces armées, Excl. conscrits [2] Non compris les travailleurs découragés. [3] Non compris les forces armées. [4] Population "de jure".

Explicaciones y fuentes: véase p. 7.

[1] Incl. las fuerzas armadas, excl. los conscriptos. [2] Excl. los trabajadores desalentados. [3] Excl. las fuerzas armadas. [4] Población "de jure".

1A ECONOMICALLY ACTIVE POPULATION

POPULATION ACTIVE

POBLACION ECONOMICAMENTE ACTIVA

Total and economically active population by age group

Population totale et population active par groupe d'âge

Población total y población económicamente activa por grupo de edad

Thousands · Milliers · Millares

	Total			Men - Hommes - Hombres			Women - Femmes - Mujeres		
	Total population / Population totale / Población total	Active population / Population active / Población activa	Activity rate / Taux d'activité / Tasa de actividad %	Total population / Population totale / Población total	Active population / Population active / Población activa	Activity rate / Taux d'activité / Tasa de actividad %	Total population / Population totale / Población total	Active population / Population active / Población activa	Activity rate / Taux d'activité / Tasa de actividad %
South Africa (2008) BA (15-64) [1] [2]									
Total	**48 683.0**	**17 788.0**	*36.5*	**23 443.0**	**9 589.0**	*40.9*	**25 240.0**	**8 199.0**	*32.5*
Total (15+)	*33 012.0*	*17 788.0*	*53.9*	*15 516.8*	*9 589.0*	*61.8*	*17 495.2*	*8 199.0*	*46.9*
0-9	10 393.9	.	.	5 260.8	.	.	5 133.1	.	.
10-14	5 277.1	.	.	2 665.4	.	.	2 611.7	.	.
15-19	5 152.5	465.3	9.0	2 596.4	255.5	9.8	2 556.2	209.7	8.2
20-24	4 784.8	2 553.4	53.4	2 369.8	1 395.7	58.9	2 415.1	1 157.7	47.9
25-29	4 366.4	3 268.4	74.9	2 121.4	1 777.4	83.8	2 245.0	1 490.9	66.4
30-34	3 913.5	3 053.7	78.0	1 893.4	1 660.6	87.7	2 020.1	1 393.0	69.0
35-39	3 144.0	2 485.4	79.1	1 456.7	1 295.1	88.9	1 687.2	1 190.3	70.5
40-44	2 392.8	1 834.1	76.7	1 083.7	952.2	87.9	1 309.1	881.8	67.4
45-49	2 239.3	1 635.9	73.1	1 008.6	855.9	84.9	1 230.6	780.0	63.4
50-54	1 941.7	1 269.3	65.4	869.4	686.5	79.0	1 072.3	582.8	54.4
55-59	1 568.2	845.2	53.9	699.7	468.7	67.0	868.6	376.5	43.3
60-64	1 248.6	377.5	30.2	548.2	241.2	44.0	700.5	136.3	19.5
65+	2 260.2	.	.	869.6	.	.	1 390.6	.	.

AMERICA - AMÉRIQUE - AMERICA

	Total population	Active population	Activity rate %	Total population	Active population	Activity rate %	Total population	Active population	Activity rate %
Argentina (IV-VI.2008) BA (10+) [2] [3]									
Total	.	**11 177**		.	.		.	.	
Aruba (X.2007) BA (15+) [4] [5]									
Total	.	**54.729**		.	**28.571**		.	**26.081**	
Total (15+)	*82.671*	*54.729*	*66.2*	*38.800*	*28.571*	*73.6*	*43.871*	*26.081*	*59.4*
15-19	7.325	1.784	24.4	3.708	1.031	27.8	3.617	0.753	20.8
20-24	5.930	4.145	69.9	2.949	2.282	77.4	2.981	1.863	62.5
25-29	6.252	5.359	85.7	2.967	2.714	91.5	3.285	2.645	80.5
30-34	7.285	6.253	85.8	3.427	3.259	95.1	3.858	2.994	77.6
35-39	8.863	7.563	85.3	4.168	3.885	93.2	4.695	3.678	78.3
40-44	9.558	8.378	87.7	4.513	4.161	92.2	5.045	4.217	83.6
45-49	9.559	8.342	87.3	4.526	4.081	90.2	5.033	4.261	84.7
50-54	7.833	6.116	78.1	3.610	3.241	89.8	4.223	2.875	68.1
55-59	6.110	4.288	70.2	2.865	2.370	82.7	3.245	1.918	59.1
60-64	4.573	1.828	40.0	2.117	1.110	52.4	2.456	0.718	29.2
65-69	3.446	0.425	12.3	1.564	0.300	19.2	1.882	0.125	6.6
70-74	2.637	0.171	6.5	1.093	0.137	12.5	1.544	0.034	2.2
75+	3.300	0.077	2.3	1.293	-	.	2.007	-	.
Barbados (2008) BA (15+) [6]									
Total	.	**143.8**		.	**73.7**		.	**70.1**	
Belize (V.2008) BA (14+) [7]									
Total	.	**124.6**		.	.		.	.	
Bolivia (2007) BA (10+) [2] [8]									
Total	**9 902.6**	**4 927.4**	*49.8*	**4 786.7**	**2 699.3**	*56.4*	**5 115.9**	**2 228.0**	*43.6*
Brasil (IX.2007) BA (10+) [2] [5]									
Total	**159 360.8**	**98 845.6**	*62.0*	**77 052.2**	**55 754.1**	*72.4*	**82 308.6**	**43 091.5**	*52.4*
Total (15+)	*141 512.5*	*97 039.0*	*68.6*	*67 870.7*	*54 548.0*	*80.4*	*73 641.8*	*42 491.0*	*57.7*
10-14	17 848.3	1 806.5	10.1	9 181.6	1 206.0	13.1	8 666.7	600.5	6.9
15-19	17 226.0	8 610.7	50.0	8 813.5	5 113.8	58.0	8 412.4	3 496.9	41.6
20-24	16 882.0	13 079.8	77.5	8 411.2	7 332.4	87.2	8 470.8	5 747.4	67.8
25-29	16 158.1	13 344.7	82.6	7 846.4	7 313.3	93.2	8 311.7	6 031.4	72.6
30-34	14 645.9	12 298.5	84.0	7 031.2	6 698.9	95.3	7 614.7	5 599.6	73.5
35-39	13 587.9	11 323.3	83.3	6 524.6	6 173.8	94.6	7 063.3	5 149.5	72.9
40-44	13 317.8	11 039.2	82.9	6 414.6	6 033.6	94.1	6 903.2	5 005.7	72.5
45-49	11 612.2	9 154.7	78.8	5 457.0	4 986.2	91.4	6 155.3	4 168.4	67.7
50-54	10 018.6	7 149.4	71.4	4 737.9	4 081.9	86.2	5 280.6	3 067.4	58.1
55-59	8 109.6	4 949.3	61.0	3 795.5	2 928.3	77.2	4 314.1	2 021.0	46.8
60-64	6 163.6	2 938.9	47.7	2 851.1	1 868.8	65.5	3 312.5	1 070.1	32.3
65-69	4 913.7	1 608.6	32.7	2 256.3	1 028.7	45.6	2 657.4	580.0	21.8
70-74	3 612.0	832.4	23.0	1 605.7	538.3	33.5	2 006.3	294.2	14.7
75+	5 265.2	709.5	13.5	2 125.7	450.0	21.2	3 139.5	259.5	8.3

Explanations and sources: see p. 3.

[1] Excl. armed forces and conscripts. [2] "De jure" population. [3] 31 Urban agglomerations. [4] "De facto" population. [5] Included armed forces and conscripts. [6] Excl. armed forces. [7] Incl. the armed forces. [8] Incl. armed forces, Excl. conscripts.

Explications et sources: voir p. 5.

[1] Non compris les forces armées et les conscrits. [2] Population "de jure". [3] 31 agglomérations urbaines. [4] Population "de facto". [5] Y compris les forces armées et les conscrits. [6] Non compris les forces armées. [7] Y compris les forces armées. [8] Y compris les forces armées, Excl. conscrits

Explicaciones y fuentes: véase p. 7.

[1] Excl. las fuerzas armadas y los conscriptos. [2] Población "de jure". [3] 31 aglomerados úrbanos. [4] Población "de facto". [5] Incluye las fuezas armadas y los conscriptos. [6] Excl. las fuerzas armadas. [7] Incl. las fuerzas armadas. [8] Incl. las fuerzas armadas, excl. los conscriptos.

ECONOMICALLY ACTIVE POPULATION

POPULATION ACTIVE

POBLACION ECONOMICAMENTE ACTIVA

1A

Total and economically active population by age group

Population totale et population active par groupe d'âge

Población total y población económicamente activa por grupo de edad

Thousands — Milliers — Millares

	Total			Men - Hommes - Hombres			Women - Femmes - Mujeres		
	Total population / Population totale / Población total	Active population / Population active / Población activa	Activity rate / Taux d'activité / Tasa de actividad %	Total population / Population totale / Población total	Active population / Population active / Población activa	Activity rate / Taux d'activité / Tasa de actividad %	Total population / Population totale / Población total	Active population / Population active / Población activa	Activity rate / Taux d'activité / Tasa de actividad %
Canada (2008) BA (15+) [1] [2] [3]									
Total	.	**18 245.1**	.	.	**9 654.0**	.	.	**8 591.2**	.
Total (15+)	*26 924.7*	*18 245.0*	*67.8*	*13 251.8*	*9 654.0*	*72.9*	*13 673.0*	*8 591.0*	*62.8*
15-19	2 157.1	1 207.1	56.0	1 103.8	601.4	54.5	1 053.3	605.7	57.5
20-24	2 218.8	1 742.5	78.5	1 128.6	912.1	80.8	1 090.2	830.4	76.2
25-29	2 255.2	1 940.8	86.1	1 133.2	1 025.2	90.5	1 121.9	915.6	81.6
30-34	2 209.3	1 921.0	87.0	1 106.3	1 026.9	92.8	1 103.1	894.1	81.1
35-39	2 257.7	1 980.0	87.7	1 112.1	1 039.9	93.5	1 145.6	940.1	82.1
40-44	2 534.1	2 234.7	88.2	1 283.4	1 188.9	92.6	1 250.8	1 045.8	83.6
45-49	2 661.7	2 332.2	87.6	1 317.2	1 201.7	91.2	1 344.6	1 130.5	84.1
50-54	2 505.1	2 096.7	83.7	1 252.4	1 104.9	88.2	1 252.7	991.8	79.2
55-59	2 115.4	1 511.8	71.5	1 040.9	802.7	77.1	1 074.4	709.1	66.0
60-64	1 767.2	849.6	48.1	866.6	479.6	55.3	900.6	370.0	41.1
65+	4 243.1	428.6	10.1	1 907.3	270.7	14.2	2 335.8	157.9	6.8
Cayman Islands (X.2008) BA (15+) [4]									
Total	**57.009**	**38.999**	**68.4**	**28.264**	**20.128**	**71.2**	**28.745**	**18.871**	**65.6**
Total (15+)	*46.375*	*38.999*	*84.1*	*23.016*	*20.127*	*87.4*	*23.361*	*18.871*	*80.8*
0-14	10.633	.	.	5.247	.	.	5.386	.	.
15-19	2.603	0.791	30.4	1.310	0.375	28.6	1.293	0.416	32.2
20-24	2.771	2.315	83.5	1.382	1.171	84.7	1.390	1.143	82.2
25-34	12.630	11.844	93.8	6.152	5.805	94.4	6.479	6.039	93.2
35-44	12.669	12.049	95.1	6.594	6.435	97.6	6.075	5.614	92.4
45-54	8.585	7.829	91.2	4.051	3.948	97.5	4.534	3.881	85.6
55-64	4.243	3.339	78.7	2.252	1.847	82.0	1.991	1.492	74.9
65+	2.874	0.832	28.9	1.275	0.546	42.8	1.599	0.286	17.9
Colombia (2008) BA (10+) [5] [6]									
Total	**43 258.6**	**19 671.4**	**45.5**	**21 333.6**	**11 644.0**	**54.6**	**21 925.0**	**8 027.4**	**36.6**
0-11	10 069.4	6.6	0.1	5 169.7	4.9	0.1	4 899.8	1.7	-
12-17	5 461.6	690.5	12.6	2 895.0	479.8	16.6	2 566.6	210.7	8.2
18-24	5 151.9	3 255.6	63.2	2 486.1	1 856.4	74.7	2 665.8	1 399.2	52.5
25-55	17 148.0	13 633.1	79.5	8 250.8	7 862.3	95.3	8 897.1	5 770.8	64.9
56+	5 427.8	2 085.6	38.4	2 532.1	1 440.6	56.9	2 895.7	645.0	22.3
Costa Rica (VII.2008) BA (12+) [4]									
Total	**4 533.2**	**2 059.6**	**45.4**	**2 246.5**	**1 283.0**	**57.1**	**2 286.7**	**776.6**	**34.0**
Total (15+)	*3 368.1*	*2 051.5*	*60.9*	*1 631.5*	*1 277.3*	*78.3*	*1 736.6*	*774.2*	*44.6*
0-11	725.8	.	.	385.9	.	.	339.9	.	.
12-14	439.2	8.1	1.8	229.1	5.7	2.5	210.1	2.4	1.1
15-19	454.8	131.1	28.8	237.7	88.2	37.1	217.1	43.0	19.8
20-24	447.6	311.9	69.7	227.7	190.2	83.5	219.9	121.7	55.3
25-29	368.0	285.6	77.6	174.4	164.5	94.3	193.6	121.1	62.5
30-34	323.0	253.5	78.5	153.9	151.1	98.2	169.1	102.4	60.6
35-39	284.0	218.9	77.1	131.0	128.5	98.1	153.0	90.4	59.1
40-44	314.4	239.3	76.1	149.9	146.1	97.4	164.4	93.2	56.7
45-49	289.3	215.6	74.5	137.6	132.6	96.4	151.7	83.0	54.7
50-54	253.7	171.6	67.7	119.7	109.3	91.3	134.0	62.3	46.5
55-59	185.7	106.8	57.5	86.4	75.0	86.8	99.3	31.8	32.0
60-64	128.8	60.7	47.1	65.0	46.9	72.1	63.8	13.8	21.6
65-69	98.9	27.2	27.5	46.1	21.9	47.5	52.7	5.3	10.0
70-74	78.0	12.2	15.6	38.0	9.3	24.4	40.1	2.9	7.2
75+	134.5	11.6	8.6	59.1	9.6	16.3	75.3	2.0	2.6
?	7.7	5.6	73.0	5.0	4.1	81.8	2.7	1.5	56.6

Explanations and sources: see p. 3.

[1] "De facto" population. [2] Excl. full-time members of the armed forces. [3] Excl. residents of the Territories and indigenous persons living on reserves. [4] "De jure" population. [5] Excl. armed forces. [6] From 2001, figures revised on the basis of the 2005 census results.

Explications et sources: voir p. 5.

[1] Population "de facto". [2] Non compris les membres à temps complet des forces armées. [3] Non compris les habitants des "Territoires" et les populations indigènes vivant dans les réserves. [4] Population "de jure". [5] Non compris les forces armées. [6] A partir de 2001, données révisées sur la base des résultats du recensement de 2005.

Explicaciones y fuentes: véase p. 7.

[1] Población "de facto". [2] Excl. los miembros a tiempo completo de las fuerzas armadas. [3] Excl. a los habitantes de los "Territorios" y a las poblaciones indígenas que viven en reservas. [4] Población "de jure". [5] Excl. las fuerzas armadas. [6] A partir de 2001, datos revisados de acuerdocon los resultados del censo de 2005.

ECONOMICALLY ACTIVE POPULATION

POPULATION ACTIVE

POBLACION ECONOMICAMENTE ACTIVA

Total and economically active population by age group

Population totale et population active par groupe d'âge

Población total y población económicamente activa por grupo de edad

	Thousands			Milliers			Millares		
	Total			**Men - Hommes - Hombres**			**Women - Femmes - Mujeres**		
	Total population	Active population	Activity rate	Total population	Active population	Activity rate	Total population	Active population	Activity rate
	Population totale	Population active	Taux d'activité	Population totale	Population active	Taux d'activité	Population totale	Population active	Taux d'activité
	Población total	Población activa	Tasa de actividad	Población total	Población activa	Tasa de actividad	Población total	Población activa	Tasa de actividad
			%			%			%
Cuba (II-IV.2008) BA									
Total	11 236.1	5 027.9	44.7	5 627.9	3 115.1	55.4	5 608.2	1 912.8	34.1
Total (15+)	9 233.8	5 027.9	54.5	4 608.2	3 115.1	67.6	4 645.6	1 912.8	41.2
0-14	1 982.3			1 019.8			962.5		
15-19	820.2	146.9	17.9	422.6	94.3	22.3	397.6	52.6	13.2
20-24	805.6	478.4	59.4	415.6	280.5	67.5	390.0	197.9	50.8
25-29	667.5	441.8	66.2	345.8	264.7	76.5	321.7	177.1	55.1
30-34	796.7	604.4	75.9	408.4	369.0	90.4	388.3	235.3	60.6
35-39	1 043.9	804.5	77.1	528.4	484.2	91.6	515.6	320.3	62.1
40-44	1 085.8	851.0	78.4	541.1	501.5	92.7	544.7	349.5	64.2
45-49	872.7	656.1	75.2	431.1	394.3	91.5	441.5	261.8	59.3
50-54	636.8	489.1	76.8	310.5	295.8	95.3	326.4	193.3	59.2
55-59	616.1	361.9	58.7	301.2	275.7	91.5	314.8	86.2	27.4
60-64	539.4	114.0	21.1	259.4	88.1	34.0	280.0	25.9	9.2
65-69	432.9	47.3	10.9	220.6	38.0	17.2	232.4	9.2	4.0
70-74	337.4	18.1	5.4	162.7	15.7	9.7	174.7	2.4	1.4
75+	578.8	14.4	2.5	260.8	13.2	5.1	318.0	1.2	0.4
Chile (X-XII.2008) BA (15+) [1]									
Total	16 825.6	7 285.1	43.3	8 328.5	4 546.1	54.6	8 497.1	2 739.0	32.2
Total (15+)	12 933.1	7 285.1	56.3	6 347.1	4 546.1	71.6	6 586.0	2 739.0	41.6
0-9	2 418.7			1 235.8			1 182.9		
10-14	1 473.8			745.6			728.2		
15-19	1 525.2	228.6	15.0	792.4	145.9	18.4	732.8	82.7	11.3
20-24	1 344.9	747.1	55.6	701.3	476.3	67.9	643.6	270.8	42.1
25-29	1 070.9	812.1	75.8	542.5	477.1	87.9	528.4	335.0	63.4
30-34	1 012.1	792.5	78.3	497.3	472.3	95.0	514.9	320.3	62.2
35-39	1 136.8	884.1	77.8	558.1	534.5	95.8	578.7	349.6	60.4
40-44	1 228.9	942.3	76.7	597.3	572.4	95.8	631.6	369.9	58.6
45-49	1 148.6	857.3	74.6	553.5	523.0	94.5	595.1	334.3	56.2
50-54	1 090.7	784.4	71.9	532.6	493.1	92.6	558.1	291.3	52.2
55-59	835.2	548.7	65.7	411.8	359.3	87.2	423.4	189.5	44.8
60-64	750.4	382.0	50.9	363.0	270.7	74.6	387.4	111.3	28.7
65-69	602.2	187.1	31.1	290.0	139.7	48.2	312.3	47.4	15.2
70-74	439.2	66.8	15.2	196.4	48.1	24.5	242.8	18.7	7.7
75+	748.1	52.1	7.0	311.0	33.8	10.9	437.1	18.3	4.2
República Dominicana (2008) BA (10+) [2]									
Total	.	4 256.4	.	.	2 573.9	.	.	1 682.6	.
10-14		35.4			26.7			8.7	
15-19		343.7			229.1			114.6	
20-24		625.4			361.4			264.0	
25-29		562.6			319.2			243.4	
30-34		546.0			308.3			237.7	
35-39		540.0			305.4			234.6	
40-44		511.5			298.9			212.6	
45-49		351.8			206.2			145.6	
50-54		297.7			193.2			104.5	
55-59		179.4			120.8			58.5	
60-64		115.1			88.2			26.9	
65+		147.6			116.3			31.3	
Ecuador (XII.2008) BA (10+) [3] [4]									
Total	9 202.3	4 383.5	47.6	4 470.7	2 517.9	56.3	4 731.7	1 865.6	39.4
El Salvador (XII.2007) BA (10+) [5]									
Total	6 098.7	2 585.7	42.4	2 875.2	1 528.4	53.2	3 223.5	1 057.3	32.8
0-9	1 212.0			628.5			583.5		
10-15	781.8	86.6	11.1	399.5	64.6	16.2	382.3	21.9	5.7
16-19	648.6	225.8	34.8	328.0	162.8	49.6	320.6	62.9	19.6
20-24	506.9	318.2	62.8	236.6	198.8	84.0	270.3	119.5	44.2
25-29	463.4	335.1	72.3	205.4	192.8	93.8	258.0	142.4	55.2
30-34	406.7	316.5	77.8	179.6	171.8	95.6	227.1	144.8	63.8
35-39	372.5	293.2	78.7	162.3	155.1	95.6	210.3	138.1	65.7
40-44	336.9	265.1	78.7	141.3	135.5	95.9	195.6	129.6	66.2
45-49	282.6	208.6	73.8	122.5	115.7	94.4	160.1	92.9	58.0
50-54	257.6	181.1	70.3	115.2	105.9	91.9	142.4	75.2	52.8
55-59	199.2	130.1	65.3	93.5	82.0	87.6	105.6	48.1	45.5
60-64	176.7	91.4	51.7	75.4	56.3	74.6	101.2	35.1	34.7
65-69	141.1	58.2	41.2	58.2	35.9	61.6	82.8	22.3	26.9
70+	312.8	75.9	24.3	129.1	51.3	39.8	183.7	24.6	13.4

Explanations and sources: see p. 3.

[1] "De facto" population. [2] Excl. armed forces. [3] "De jure" population. [4] Urban areas. [5] Incl. the armed forces.

Explications et sources: voir p. 5.

[1] Population "de facto". [2] Non compris les forces armées. [3] Population "de jure". [4] Régions urbaines. [5] Y compris les forces armées.

Explicaciones y fuentes: véase p. 7.

[1] Población "de facto". [2] Excl. las fuerzas armadas. [3] Población "de jure". [4] Areas urbanas. [5] Incl. las fuerzas armadas.

ECONOMICALLY ACTIVE POPULATION
POPULATION ACTIVE
POBLACION ECONOMICAMENTE ACTIVA

Total and economically active population by age group

Population totale et population active par groupe d'âge

Población total y población económicamente activa por grupo de edad

Thousands — Milliers — Millares

	Total			Men - Hommes - Hombres			Women - Femmes - Mujeres		
	Total population / Population totale / Población total	Active population / Population active / Población activa	Activity rate / Taux d'activité / Tasa de actividad %	Total population / Population totale / Población total	Active population / Population active / Población activa	Activity rate / Taux d'activité / Tasa de actividad %	Total population / Population totale / Población total	Active population / Population active / Población activa	Activity rate / Taux d'activité / Tasa de actividad %
Haïti (2005) E (15+)									
Total	**9 292.3**	**3 676.3**	*39.6*	**4 596.6**	**1 945.5**	*42.3*	**4 695.7**	**1 730.8**	*36.9*
Total (15+)	*5 759.7*	*3 676.3*	*63.8*	*2 799.6*	*1 945.5*	*69.5*	*2 960.1*	*1 730.8*	*58.5*
0-9	2 413.3	.	.	1 229.5			1 183.8		
10-14	1 119.3	.	.	567.5	.		551.8		
15-19	1 055.5	221.5	21.0	531.9	123.6	23.2	523.7	97.9	18.7
20-24	957.9	504.7	52.7	475.7	271.9	57.2	482.2	232.8	48.3
25-29	734.1	550.2	74.9	356.9	294.1	82.4	377.2	256.1	67.9
30-34	574.5	480.0	83.5	274.7	246.7	89.8	299.8	233.3	77.8
35-39	511.7	443.1	86.6	246.6	229.6	93.1	265.1	213.5	80.5
40-44	445.0	389.8	87.6	215.3	201.2	93.5	229.7	188.5	82.1
45-49	362.3	315.9	87.2	176.4	163.5	92.6	185.8	152.4	82.0
50-54	305.2	258.2	84.6	146.9	133.8	91.1	158.3	124.4	78.6
55-59	227.4	182.0	80.0	106.7	94.6	88.6	120.7	87.4	72.4
60-64	202.2	145.5	72.0	95.5	78.6	82.3	106.7	66.9	62.7
65-69	159.8	94.4	59.1	73.3	53.3	72.8	86.5	41.1	47.5
70-74	111.9	54.1	48.3	50.5	32.3	63.9	61.4	21.8	35.6
75+	112.2	37.0	33.0	49.2	22.3	45.3	62.9	14.7	23.4
Jamaica (2008) BA (14+) [1]									
Total	.	**1 302.4**	.	.	**711.1**	.	.	**591.3**	.
14-19	.	45.9	.	.	27.1	.	.	18.8	.
20-24	.	144.2	.	.	81.2	.	.	63.0	.
25-34	.	364.1	.	.	189.4	.	.	174.7	.
35-44	.	360.4	.	.	187.7	.	.	172.7	.
45-54	.	209.4	.	.	114.4	.	.	95.0	.
55-64	.	110.7	.	.	66.7	.	.	44.0	.
65+	.	67.7	.	.	44.6	.	.	23.1	.
Martinique (VI .2008) BA (15+) [2]									
Total	.	**161.6**	.	.	**77.1**	.	.	**84.5**	.
Total (15+)	*310.6*	*161.6*	*52.0*	*140.2*	*77.1*	*55.0*	*170.4*	*84.5*	*49.6*
15-19	30.7	2.0	6.5	15.8	1.4	8.7	11.2	0.6	4.2
20-24	21.6	11.0	51.1	10.5	6.0	57.3	11.2	5.1	45.3
25-29	17.3	13.3	77.1	7.6	6.1	79.4	9.6	7.2	75.2
30-34	23.6	19.0	80.4	10.0	8.5	84.6	13.6	10.5	77.3
35-39	31.6	24.9	78.7	13.7	11.5	84.3	18.0	13.4	74.4
40-44	33.9	28.3	83.4	15.3	13.0	84.9	18.6	15.3	82.2
45-49	31.1	25.5	81.9	14.0	12.1	85.9	17.0	13.4	78.5
50-54	26.0	19.4	74.6	12.0	10.0	82.8	14.0	9.4	67.5
55-59	23.0	12.9	56.2	10.5	6.2	58.6	12.5	6.8	54.2
60-64	18.7	4.6	24.5	8.4	2.1	25.3	10.3	2.5	23.9
65-69	15.8	0.4	2.8	7.3	0.2	2.6	8.5	0.3	2.9
70-74	14.2	0.1	1.0	6.1	0.1	1.3	8.1	0.1	0.8
75+	23.0	0.1	0.3	8.9	0.0	0.3	14.1	0.0	0.2
México (IV-VI.2008) BA (14+) [3]									
Total	**106 572.9**	**45 460.0**	*42.7*	**51 265.3**	**28 329.1**	*55.3*	**55 307.6**	**17 130.9**	*31.0*
Total (15+)	*74 683.7*	*45 121.5*	*60.4*	*35 023.2*	*28 090.8*	*80.2*	*39 660.5*	*17 030.7*	*42.9*
0-9	20 664.4	.	.	10 438.7			10 225.7		
10-14	11 224.8	338.5	3.0	5 803.4	238.3	4.1	5 421.5	100.2	1.8
15-19	10 851.2	3 904.9	36.0	5 387.0	2 578.4	47.9	5 464.2	1 326.5	24.3
20-24	8 895.4	5 511.5	62.0	4 202.7	3 345.2	79.6	4 692.6	2 166.2	46.2
25-29	7 802.6	5 582.2	71.5	3 622.7	3 404.7	94.0	4 180.0	2 177.5	52.1
30-34	7 744.9	5 631.7	72.7	3 592.7	3 454.3	96.1	4 152.2	2 177.4	52.4
35-39	7 678.7	5 704.5	74.3	3 544.4	3 419.2	96.5	4 134.3	2 285.3	55.3
40-44	6 892.3	5 171.8	75.0	3 193.1	3 065.1	96.0	3 699.3	2 106.7	56.9
45-49	5 919.8	4 331.9	73.2	2 739.8	2 601.5	95.0	3 180.0	1 730.4	54.4
50-54	4 915.6	3 327.5	67.7	2 328.2	2 136.3	91.8	2 587.5	1 191.2	46.0
55-59	3 857.4	2 392.5	62.0	1 826.3	1 583.6	86.7	2 031.0	808.9	39.8
60-64	3 149.9	1 515.5	48.1	1 436.9	1 027.9	71.5	1 713.0	487.6	28.5
65-69	2 333.8	952.6	40.8	1 110.6	686.3	61.8	1 223.2	266.2	21.8
70-74	1 861.2	586.7	31.5	822.7	415.2	50.5	1 038.5	171.6	16.5
75+	2 755.4	497.5	18.1	1 207.0	365.5	30.3	1 548.4	131.9	8.5
?	25.4	10.6	41.9	9.2	7.5	80.8	16.1	3.2	19.6

Explanations and sources: see p. 3.
[1] Excl. armed forces. [2] "De facto" population. [3] "De jure" population.

Explications et sources: voir p. 5.
[1] Non compris les forces armées. [2] Population "de facto". [3] Population "de jure".

Explicaciones y fuentes: véase p. 7.
[1] Excl. las fuerzas armadas. [2] Población "de facto". [3] Población "de jure".

ECONOMICALLY ACTIVE POPULATION

Total and economically active population by age group

Thousands

POPULATION ACTIVE

Population totale et population active par groupe d'âge

Milliers

POBLACION ECONOMICAMENTE ACTIVA

Población total y población económicamente activa por grupo de edad

Millares

	Total			Men - Hommes - Hombres			Women - Femmes - Mujeres		
	Total population / Population totale / Población total	Active population / Population active / Población activa	Activity rate / Taux d'activité / Tasa de actividad %	Total population / Population totale / Población total	Active population / Population active / Población activa	Activity rate / Taux d'activité / Tasa de actividad %	Total population / Population totale / Población total	Active population / Population active / Población activa	Activity rate / Taux d'activité / Tasa de actividad %
Netherlands Antilles (2008) BA (15+) [1]									
Total	**138.6**	**63.0**	*45.5*	**63.1**	**30.8**	*48.9*	**75.6**	**32.2**	*42.6*
Total (15+)	*108.5*	*63.0*	*58.1*	*47.8*	*30.8*	*64.5*	*60.7*	*32.2*	*53.0*
0-9	19.6	.	.	10.0	.	.	9.6	.	.
10-14	10.4	.	.	5.3	.	.	5.1	.	.
15-19	10.7	1.4	*13.3*	5.4	0.8	*14.4*	5.3	0.6	*12.2*
20-24	7.4	4.0	*54.5*	3.5	2.0	*58.0*	3.9	2.0	*51.3*
25-29	7.2	5.8	*79.5*	3.1	2.7	*87.7*	4.1	3.0	*73.4*
30-34	8.1	6.8	*83.7*	3.6	3.3	*91.1*	4.5	3.5	*77.8*
35-39	10.2	8.7	*85.3*	4.5	4.1	*90.9*	5.7	4.6	*80.9*
40-44	11.2	9.7	*86.9*	4.9	4.5	*92.0*	6.3	5.2	*83.0*
45-49	11.8	9.9	*84.1*	5.1	4.7	*91.1*	6.7	5.2	*78.7*
50-54	10.1	7.8	*77.7*	4.4	3.9	*88.4*	5.7	3.9	*69.4*
55-59	8.8	5.6	*63.3*	3.8	2.9	*75.9*	5.0	2.7	*53.7*
60-64	7.2	2.1	*29.4*	3.1	1.3	*40.4*	4.1	0.9	*21.0*
65-69	5.6	0.7	*12.9*	2.6	0.5	*17.9*	3.0	0.3	*8.7*
70-74	4.0	0.3	*6.3*	1.5	0.2	*11.9*	2.5	0.1	*2.8*
75+	6.2	0.1	*2.4*	2.3	0.1	*5.5*	3.9	0.0	*0.4*
Nicaragua (2007) BA (10+)									
Total	.	**2 185.7**		.	**1 372.9**		.	**812.8**	
Panamá (VIII.2008) BA (15+)									
Total	.	**1 416.2**		.	**877.2**		.	**539.5**	
Total (15+)	*2 224.4*	*1 416.6*	*63.7*	*1 083.4*	*877.2*	*81.0*	*1 141.0*	*539.5*	*47.3*
15-19	287.3	92.8	*32.3*	148.0	66.8	*45.1*	139.3	26.0	*18.7*
20-24	254.8	176.9	*69.4*	130.5	114.8	*88.0*	124.3	62.0	*49.9*
25-29	229.6	180.0	*78.4*	109.0	106.2	*97.4*	120.6	73.8	*61.2*
30-34	215.6	173.6	*80.5*	106.5	103.7	*97.4*	109.1	69.9	*64.1*
35-39	219.0	177.0	*80.8*	100.7	99.4	*98.7*	118.2	77.6	*65.7*
40-44	195.9	157.4	*80.3*	94.7	92.6	*97.8*	101.2	64.8	*64.0*
45-49	180.1	143.7	*79.8*	85.4	82.2	*96.3*	94.7	61.4	*64.8*
50-54	150.0	116.4	*77.6*	75.4	70.6	*93.6*	74.6	45.9	*61.5*
55-59	124.2	80.8	*65.1*	59.0	53.8	*91.2*	65.3	27.0	*41.3*
60-64	112.4	54.2	*48.2*	56.6	39.6	*70.0*	55.8	14.7	*26.3*
65-69	85.0	29.6	*34.8*	40.1	21.3	*53.1*	44.9	8.4	*18.7*
70-74	63.3	17.1	*27.0*	28.4	13.2	*46.5*	34.9	3.9	*11.2*
75+	107.2	17.1	*16.0*	49.1	13.0	*26.5*	58.1	4.1	*7.1*
Paraguay (X-XII.2008) BA (10+) [1] [2]									
Total	**6 163.913**	**2 981.126**	*48.4*	**3 069.097**	**1 810.287**	*59.0*	**3 094.816**	**1 170.839**	*37.8*
Total (15+)	*4 077.591*	*2 834.077*	*69.5*	*2 003.848*	*1 708.708*	*85.3*	*2 073.743*	*1 125.369*	*54.3*
0-9	1 333.904			682.209			651.695		
10-14	752.418	147.049	*19.5*	383.040	101.579	*26.5*	369.378	45.470	*12.3*
15-19	704.900	348.095	*49.4*	354.843	222.734	*62.8*	350.057	125.361	*35.8*
20-24	515.428	378.033	*73.3*	252.704	221.989	*87.8*	262.724	156.044	*59.4*
25-29	472.218	377.497	*79.9*	232.279	223.760	*96.3*	239.939	153.737	*64.1*
30-34	381.535	308.042	*80.7*	184.482	181.243	*98.2*	197.053	126.799	*64.3*
35-39	367.317	303.015	*82.5*	186.298	180.998	*97.2*	181.019	122.017	*67.4*
40-44	319.442	264.035	*82.7*	160.787	157.442	*97.9*	158.655	106.593	*67.2*
45-49	284.553	228.961	*80.5*	137.815	133.085	*96.6*	146.738	95.876	*65.3*
50-54	266.333	211.846	*79.5*	134.828	125.743	*93.3*	131.505	86.103	*65.5*
55-59	210.087	147.976	*70.4*	102.945	91.968	*89.3*	107.142	56.008	*52.3*
60-64	186.188	121.914	*65.5*	96.940	78.041	*80.5*	89.248	43.873	*49.2*
65-69	125.857	67.063	*53.3*	58.466	45.400	*77.7*	67.391	21.663	*32.1*
70-74	94.863	45.380	*47.8*	39.780	26.074	*65.5*	55.083	19.306	*35.0*
75+	148.870	32.220	*21.6*	61.681	20.231	*32.8*	87.189	11.989	*13.8*

Explanations and sources: see p. 3.
[1] "De facto" population. [2] Excl. armed forces and conscripts.

Explications et sources: voir p. 5.
[1] Population "de facto". [2] Non compris les forces armées et les conscrits.

Explicaciones y fuentes: véase p. 7.
[1] Población "de facto". [2] Excl. las fuerzas armadas y los conscriptos.

ECONOMICALLY ACTIVE POPULATION

Total and economically active population by age group
Thousands

POPULATION ACTIVE

Population totale et population active par groupe d'âge
Milliers

POBLACION ECONOMICAMENTE ACTIVA

Población total y población económicamente activa por grupo de edad
Millares

1A

	Total			Men - Hommes - Hombres			Women - Femmes - Mujeres		
	Total population / Population totale / Población total	Active population / Population active / Población activa	Activity rate / Taux d'activité / Tasa de actividad %	Total population / Population totale / Población total	Active population / Population active / Población activa	Activity rate / Taux d'activité / Tasa de actividad %	Total population / Population totale / Población total	Active population / Population active / Población activa	Activity rate / Taux d'activité / Tasa de actividad %
Perú (2008) BA (14+) [1] [2]									
Total	**8 580.0**	**4 554.6**	*53.1*	**4 064.9**	**2 426.2**	*59.7*	**4 515.2**	**2 128.5**	*47.1*
Total (15+)	*6 465.2*	*4 530.6*	*70.1*	*2 997.9*	*2 414.9*	*80.6*	*3 467.3*	*2 115.7*	*61.0*
0-9	1 391.8	.	.	703.6	.	.	359.6	.	.
10-14	723.0	24.1	*3.3*	363.4	11.3	*3.1*	415.6	12.8	*3.6*
15-19	787.3	341.2	*43.3*	371.7	169.7	*45.6*	452.5	171.6	*41.3*
20-24	852.1	623.5	*73.2*	399.6	330.8	*82.8*	398.6	292.7	*64.7*
25-29	739.9	613.6	*82.9*	341.3	314.3	*92.1*	336.9	299.3	*75.1*
30-34	668.9	572.9	*85.6*	332.1	319.3	*96.1*	312.1	253.7	*75.3*
35-39	550.4	460.5	*83.7*	238.3	231.9	*97.3*	301.2	228.6	*73.3*
40-44	569.0	483.7	*85.0*	267.8	261.2	*97.5*	259.2	222.6	*73.9*
45-49	491.9	425.6	*86.5*	232.6	227.0	*97.6*	259.9	198.6	*76.6*
50-54	449.6	366.4	*81.5*	189.7	181.5	*95.7*	199.0	184.8	*71.1*
55-59	376.6	260.3	*69.1*	177.6	147.8	*83.2*	165.0	112.5	*56.5*
60-64	308.5	194.3	*63.0*	143.4	111.7	*77.8*	106.3	82.7	*50.1*
65-69	214.3	103.3	*48.2*	108.0	60.4	*55.9*	90.6	42.9	*40.4*
70-74	172.5	49.9	*28.9*	81.9	36.1	*44.1*	170.3	13.9	*15.3*
75+	284.2	35.2	*12.4*	113.9	23.4	*20.5*		11.8	*6.9*
Puerto Rico (2008) BA (16+) [3]									
Total	.	**1 366**	.	.	**756**	.	.	**610**	.
16-19	258	33	*12.8*	131	21	*16.0*	128	12	*9.4*
20-24	259	126	*48.6*	125	74	*59.2*	134	52	*38.8*
25-34	481	344	*71.5*	213	180	*84.5*	268	164	*61.2*
35-44	500	353	*70.6*	223	189	*84.8*	277	163	*58.8*
45-54	524	315	*60.1*	232	170	*73.3*	292	145	*49.7*
55-64	472	156	*33.1*	209	94	*45.0*	264	62	*23.5*
65+	555	41	*7.4*	244	28	*11.5*	311	13	*4.2*
Trinidad and Tobago (2008) BA (15+)									
Total	.	**626.6**	.	.	**366.3**	.	.	**260.3**	.
Total (15+)	*987.1*	*626.8*	*63.5*	*491.6*	*366.4*	*74.5*	*495.5*	*260.4*	*52.6*
15-19	103.1	26.1	*25.3*	53.6	16.6	*31.0*	49.5	9.5	*19.2*
20-24	120.4	90.4	*75.1*	61.2	51.7	*84.5*	59.2	38.7	*65.4*
25-29	105.8	88.7	*83.8*	51.8	49.2	*95.0*	54.0	39.5	*73.1*
30-34	91.5	77.0	*84.2*	46.7	44.9	*96.1*	44.8	32.1	*71.7*
35-39	84.2	71.7	*85.2*	41.7	40.2	*96.4*	42.5	31.5	*74.1*
40-44	89.6	73.7	*82.3*	45.2	42.6	*94.2*	44.4	31.1	*70.0*
45-49	89.9	71.6	*79.6*	44.4	41.5	*93.5*	45.5	30.1	*66.2*
50-54	84.3	63.1	*74.9*	44.0	39.6	*90.0*	40.3	23.5	*58.3*
55-59	57.4	37.3	*65.0*	28.2	23.1	*81.9*	29.2	14.2	*48.6*
60-64	53.5	17.7	*33.1*	26.2	10.8	*41.2*	27.3	6.9	*25.3*
65+	107.4	9.5	*8.8*	48.6	6.2	*12.8*	58.8	3.3	*5.6*
Turks and Caicos Islands (2007) BA (15+)									
Total	**34.862**	**20.711**	*59.4*	.	.	.	.	.	.
United States (2008) BA (16+) [4]									
Total	.	**154 287**	.	.	**82 520**	.	.	**71 767**	.
16-19	17 075	6 858	*40.2*	8 660	3 472	*40.1*	8 415	3 385	*40.2*
20-24	20 409	15 174	*74.3*	10 249	8 065	*78.7*	10 160	7 109	*70.0*
25-29	20 815	17 293	*83.1*	10 451	9 431	*90.2*	10 363	7 862	*75.9*
30-34	19 179	16 039	*83.6*	9 548	8 871	*92.9*	9 631	7 168	*74.4*
35-39	20 537	17 218	*83.8*	10 142	9 404	*92.7*	10 395	7 814	*75.2*
40-44	21 162	17 843	*84.3*	10 425	9 568	*91.8*	10 737	8 275	*77.1*
45-49	22 644	18 870	*83.3*	11 108	9 962	*89.7*	11 536	8 908	*77.2*
50-54	21 316	17 133	*80.4*	10 404	8 966	*86.2*	10 912	8 167	*74.8*
55-59	18 444	13 480	*73.1*	8 929	7 035	*78.8*	9 515	6 445	*67.7*
60-64	15 047	8 135	*54.1*	7 194	4 310	*59.9*	7 852	3 825	*48.7*
65-69	11 242	3 451	*30.7*	5 246	1 866	*35.6*	5 995	1 585	*26.4*
70-74	8 639	1 534	*17.8*	3 912	858	*21.9*	4 728	676	*14.3*
75+	17 281	1 258	*7.3*	6 844	711	*10.4*	10 437	547	*5.2*
Venezuela, Rep. Bolivariana de (VII-XII.2008) BA (15+) [2] [4]									
Total	**27 849.4**	**12 736.1**	*45.7*	**13 965.2**	**7 770.8**	*55.6*	**13 884.2**	**4 965.2**	*35.8*
Total (15+)	*19 526.4*	*12 736.0*	*65.2*	*9 714.2*	*7 770.8*	*80.0*	*9 812.1*	*4 965.2*	*50.6*
0-14	8 323.0	.	.	4 251.0	.	.	4 072.0	.	.
15-24	5 264.7	2 383.9	*45.3*	2 672.5	1 558.2	*58.3*	2 592.3	825.7	*31.9*
25-44	8 053.8	6 597.8	*81.9*	4 025.8	3 865.8	*96.0*	4 028.0	2 732.0	*67.8*
45-64	4 684.7	3 343.8	*71.4*	2 312.4	2 061.1	*89.1*	2 372.3	1 282.8	*54.1*
65+	1 523.1	410.4	*26.9*	703.6	285.7	*40.6*	819.5	124.8	*15.2*

Explanations and sources: see p. 3.
[1] Metropolitan Lima. [2] "De jure" population. [3] Non-institutional civilian population. [4] Excl. armed forces.

Explications et sources: voir p. 5.
[1] Lima métropolitaine. [2] Population "de jure". [3] Population civile non institutionnelle. [4] Non compris les forces armées.

Explicaciones y fuentes: véase p. 7.
[1] Lima metropolitana. [2] Población "de jure". [3] Población civil no institucional. [4] Excl. las fuerzas armadas.

1A

ECONOMICALLY ACTIVE POPULATION	POPULATION ACTIVE	POBLACION ECONOMICAMENTE ACTIVA
Total and economically active population by age group	Population totale et population active par groupe d'âge	Población total y población económicamente activa por grupo de edad
Thousands	Milliers	Millares

			Total	Men - Hommes - Hombres			Women - Femmes - Mujeres		
	Total population / Population totale / Población total	Active population / Population active / Población activa	Activity rate / Taux d'activité / Tasa de actividad %	Total population / Population totale / Población total	Active population / Population active / Población activa	Activity rate / Taux d'activité / Tasa de actividad %	Total population / Population totale / Población total	Active population / Population active / Población activa	Activity rate / Taux d'activité / Tasa de actividad %

ASIA - ASIE - ASIA

Armenia (2008) E (16-62) [1][2]

Total	·	1 194.6	·	·	599.6	·	·	595.0	·

Azerbaijan (2008) BA (15+) [2][3]

Total	8 730.3	4 317.4	49.5	4 313.0	2 205.2	51.1	4 417.3	2 112.2	47.8
Total (15+)	6 752.7	4 317.4	63.9	3 260.3	2 205.2	67.6	3 492.4	2 112.2	60.5
0-9	1 277.1	·	·	686.7	·	·	590.4	·	·
10-14	700.5	·	·	366.0	·	·	334.5	·	·
15-19	913.3	180.0	19.7	468.7	83.3	17.8	444.6	96.7	21.7
20-24	894.5	464.7	52.0	457.1	252.4	55.2	437.4	212.3	48.5
25-29	748.0	559.3	74.8	376.1	287.8	76.5	371.9	271.5	73.0
30-34	637.6	598.4	93.9	307.4	301.3	98.0	330.2	297.1	90.0
35-39	618.7	555.2	89.7	291.8	282.9	96.9	326.9	272.3	83.3
40-49	1 348.1	1 225.3	90.9	637.4	626.5	98.3	710.7	598.8	84.3
50-54	509.3	386.4	75.9	244.6	186.3	76.2	264.7	200.1	75.6
55-59	317.0	208.8	65.9	150.2	127.8	85.1	166.8	81.0	48.6
60-64	176.4	93.8	53.2	81.3	44.6	54.9	95.1	49.2	51.7
65+	589.8	45.5	7.7	245.7	12.3	5.0	344.1	33.2	9.6

Georgia (2008) BA (15+) [3][4]

Total	·	1 917.8	·	·	1 028.0	·	·	889.7	·
15-19	·	44.2	·	·	29.2	·	·	15.0	·
20-24	·	155.7	·	·	95.2	·	·	60.5	·
25-29	·	183.2	·	·	109.5	·	·	73.7	·
30-34	·	189.0	·	·	111.1	·	·	77.9	·
35-39	·	188.5	·	·	99.7	·	·	88.8	·
40-44	·	192.9	·	·	101.1	·	·	91.7	·
45-49	·	213.7	·	·	110.6	·	·	103.0	·
50-54	·	203.2	·	·	103.0	·	·	100.2	·
55-59	·	181.9	·	·	91.4	·	·	90.5	·
60-64	·	112.4	·	·	58.4	·	·	54.1	·
65+	·	253.1	·	·	118.8	·	·	134.3	·

Hong Kong, China (2008) BA (15+) [5]

Total	6 893.8	3 648.9	52.9	3 261.3	1 949.4	59.8	3 632.5	1 699.5	46.8
Total (15+)	5 994.0	3 649.0	60.9	2 796.3	1 949.4	69.7	3 197.6	1 699.6	53.2
0-9	502.3	·	·	261.5	·	·	240.8	·	·
10-14	397.7	·	·	203.6	·	·	194.0	·	·
15-19	442.7	56.4	12.7	227.4	29.6	13.0	215.3	26.7	12.4
20-24	457.9	310.1	67.7	217.1	142.8	65.8	240.8	167.3	69.5
25-29	527.6	476.6	90.3	228.6	215.5	94.3	299.1	261.1	87.3
30-34	541.3	471.0	87.0	229.0	221.1	96.6	312.3	249.9	80.0
35-39	574.3	478.2	83.3	239.9	231.5	96.5	334.4	246.8	73.8
40-44	620.6	504.4	81.3	276.4	265.0	95.9	344.2	239.5	69.6
45-49	666.5	523.2	78.5	319.3	301.7	94.5	347.1	221.6	63.8
50-54	584.6	421.4	72.1	289.4	260.0	89.8	295.2	161.4	54.7
55-59	455.2	266.3	58.5	227.5	173.9	76.4	227.7	92.3	40.5
60-64	300.6	98.1	32.6	153.5	73.0	47.6	147.0	25.1	17.1
65-69	222.3	27.4	12.3	116.3	22.2	19.1	106.0	5.2	4.9
70-74	229.7	10.9	4.7	112.3	9.1	8.1	117.4	1.7	1.4
75+	370.7	5.0	1.3	159.6	4.0	2.5	211.1	1.0	0.5

Explanations and sources: see p. 3.

[1] "De jure" population. [2] Excl. armed forces and conscripts. [3] "De facto" population. [4] Excl. armed forces. [5] Excl. marine, military and institutional populations.

Explications et sources: voir p. 5.

[1] Population "de jure". [2] Non compris les forces armées et les conscrits. [3] Population "de facto". [4] Non compris les forces armées. [5] Non compris le personnel militaire, de la marine et la population institutionnelle.

Explicaciones y fuentes: véase p. 7.

[1] Población "de jure". [2] Excl. las fuerzas armadas y los conscriptos. [3] Población "de facto". [4] Excl. las fuerzas armadas. [5] Excl. el personal militar y de la marina, y la población institucional.

ECONOMICALLY ACTIVE POPULATION

Total and economically active population by age group

Thousands

POPULATION ACTIVE

Population totale et population active par groupe d'âge

Milliers

POBLACION ECONOMICAMENTE ACTIVA

Población total y población económicamente activa por grupo de edad

Millares

	Total			Men - Hommes - Hombres			Women - Femmes - Mujeres		
	Total population	Active population	Activity rate	Total population	Active population	Activity rate	Total population	Active population	Activity rate
	Population totale	Population active	Taux d'activité	Population totale	Population active	Taux d'activité	Population totale	Population active	Taux d'activité
	Población total	Población activa	Tasa de actividad %	Población total	Población activa	Tasa de actividad %	Población total	Población activa	Tasa de actividad %
Indonesia (2008) BA (15+) [1]									
Total	.	**111 947.3**	.	.	**69 144.3**	.	.	**42 802.9**	.
Total (15+)	166 641.1	111 947.3	67.2	82 841.2	69 144.3	83.5	83 799.9	42 802.9	51.1
15-19	22 901.1	8 154.3	35.6	11 854.5	4 816.3	40.6	11 046.6	3 338.0	30.2
20-24	19 538.4	13 429.6	68.7	9 657.3	8 103.7	83.9	9 881.1	5 325.9	53.9
25-29	20 619.1	15 372.0	74.6	10 122.0	9 659.3	95.4	10 497.1	5 712.7	54.4
30-34	19 462.2	14 652.8	75.3	9 502.5	9 255.2	97.4	9 959.7	5 397.6	54.2
35-39	17 986.5	14 054.3	78.1	8 837.9	8 667.1	98.1	9 148.7	5 387.2	58.9
40-44	15 686.1	12 512.7	79.8	7 805.9	7 645.6	97.9	7 880.2	4 867.1	61.8
45-49	13 496.4	10 868.0	80.5	6 760.1	6 584.8	97.4	6 736.3	4 283.2	63.6
50-54	11 168.5	8 760.3	78.4	5 782.3	5 497.9	95.1	5 386.3	3 262.5	60.6
55-59	7 871.9	5 713.5	72.6	4 076.0	3 597.6	88.3	3 795.9	2 115.8	55.7
60-64	6 062.9	3 723.0	61.4	2 946.4	2 304.5	78.2	3 116.5	1 418.5	45.5
65-69	4 620.2	2 472.9	53.5	2 238.7	1 549.4	69.2	2 381.5	923.5	38.8
70-74	3 479.2	1 324.7	38.1	1 561.0	833.5	53.4	1 918.2	491.2	25.6
75+	3 748.4	909.2	24.3	1 696.6	629.4	37.1	2 051.8	279.8	13.6
Iran, Islamic Rep. of (2008) BA (10+)									
Total	**71 249**	**22 892**	**32.1**	**36 015**	**18 834**	**52.3**	**35 234**	**4 058**	**11.5**
Total (15+)	54 091	22 729	42.0	27 181	18 714	68.8	26 908	4 016	14.9
0-9	10 949		.	5 600	.	.	5 348	.	.
10-14	6 209	163	2.6	3 233	121	3.7	2 976	42	1.4
15-19	8 450	1 431	16.9	4 424	1 157	26.2	4 027	275	6.8
20-24	8 073	3 394	42.0	4 050	2 692	66.5	4 022	703	17.5
25-29	6 676	3 744	56.1	3 356	2 960	88.2	3 320	784	23.6
30-34	5 119	2 874	56.1	2 454	2 312	94.2	2 666	562	21.1
35-39	4 995	2 842	56.9	2 447	2 328	95.1	2 548	514	20.2
40-44	4 607	2 534	55.0	2 290	2 123	92.7	2 316	411	17.7
45-49	4 312	2 223	51.6	2 169	1 901	87.6	2 143	321	15.0
50-54	3 638	1 563	43.0	1 808	1 357	75.1	1 830	206	11.3
55-59	2 602	931	35.8	1 317	815	61.9	1 284	116	9.0
60-64	1 931	537	27.8	959	468	48.8	972	69	7.1
65+	3 688	656	17.8	1 907	601	31.5	1 780	55	3.1
Israel (2008) BA (15+) [2]									
Total	.	**2 957.1**	.	.	**1 579.9**	.	.	**1 377.2**	.
Total (15+)	5 233.0	2 957.0	56.5	2 549.5	1 579.8	62.0	2 683.4	1 377.3	51.3
15-17	356.7	28.7	8.0	182.7	16.6	9.1	174.0	12.1	7.0
18-24	805.1	338.8	42.1	410.0	161.6	39.4	395.1	177.2	44.8
25-34	1 089.0	837.4	76.9	548.5	448.3	81.7	540.5	389.1	72.0
35-44	878.2	703.2	80.1	435.2	376.4	86.5	442.9	326.8	73.8
45-54	753.8	584.3	77.5	363.4	306.0	84.2	390.4	278.4	71.3
55-59	356.1	242.5	68.1	170.0	131.5	77.4	186.1	111.0	59.6
60-64	279.2	146.0	52.3	133.1	85.8	64.5	146.1	60.2	41.2
65-69	190.6	45.8	24.0	87.1	31.2	35.8	103.5	14.6	14.1
70+	524.3	30.3	5.8	219.5	22.4	10.2	304.8	7.9	2.6
Japan (2008) BA (15+) [1]									
Total	**127 710**	**66 500**	**52.1**	**62 260**	**38 880**	**62.4**	**65 450**	**27 620**	**42.2**
Total (15+)	110 490	66 500	60.2	53 440	38 880	72.8	57 080	27 610	48.4
0-14	17 210		.	8 820	.	.	8 390		.
15-19	6 190	1 000	16.2	3 170	510	16.1	3 020	490	16.2
20-24	7 140	4 950	69.3	3 660	2 530	69.1	3 470	2 420	69.7
25-29	7 670	6 540	85.3	3 910	3 690	94.4	3 760	2 860	76.1
30-34	9 070	7 350	81.0	4 600	4 440	96.5	4 470	2 910	65.1
35-39	9 570	7 750	81.0	4 840	4 680	96.7	4 730	3 070	64.9
40-44	8 350	7 030	84.2	4 210	4 080	96.9	4 150	2 950	71.1
45-49	7 770	6 690	86.1	3 900	3 780	96.9	3 870	2 920	75.5
50-54	7 860	6 580	83.7	3 920	3 750	95.7	3 940	2 820	71.6
55-59	9 940	7 650	77.0	4 920	4 550	92.5	5 030	3 100	61.6
60-64	8 870	5 300	59.8	4 330	3 310	76.4	4 540	1 980	43.6
65-69	7 960	2 980	37.4	3 810	1 890	49.6	4 160	1 080	26.0
70-74	6 960	1 540	22.1	3 210	980	30.5	3 750	560	14.9
75+	13 140	1 140	8.7	4 960	690	13.9	8 190	450	5.5

Explanations and sources: see p. 3.
[1] "De facto" population. [2] Excl. armed forces.

Explications et sources: voir p. 5.
[1] Population "de facto". [2] Non compris les forces armées.

Explicaciones y fuentes: véase p. 7.
[1] Población "de facto". [2] Excl. las fuerzas armadas.

1A

ECONOMICALLY ACTIVE POPULATION	POPULATION ACTIVE	POBLACION ECONOMICAMENTE ACTIVA
Total and economically active population by age group	Population totale et population active par groupe d'âge	Población total y población económicamente activa por grupo de edad
Thousands	Milliers	Millares

	Total			Men - Hommes - Hombres			Women - Femmes - Mujeres		
	Total population / Population totale / Población total	Active population / Population active / Población activa	Activity rate / Taux d'activité / Tasa de actividad %	Total population / Population totale / Población total	Active population / Population active / Población activa	Activity rate / Taux d'activité / Tasa de actividad %	Total population / Population totale / Población total	Active population / Population active / Población activa	Activity rate / Taux d'activité / Tasa de actividad %
Kazakhstan (2008) BA (15+) [1][2]									
Total	.	**8 415.0**	.	.	**4 244.2**	.	.	**4 170.9**	.
Total (15+)	*11 831.4*	*8 415.1*	*71.1*	*5 576.4*	*4 244.2*	*76.1*	*6 255.3*	*4 171.1*	*66.7*
15-19	1 346.7	307.7	22.8	690.0	174.8	25.3	656.7	132.8	20.2
20-24	1 435.4	998.0	69.5	740.2	539.2	72.8	695.2	458.9	66.0
25-29	1 354.6	1 246.1	92.0	680.5	650.3	95.6	674.2	595.8	88.4
30-34	1 357.4	1 264.6	93.2	653.0	624.5	95.6	704.4	640.0	90.9
35-39	998.1	944.1	94.6	478.1	465.6	97.4	520.0	478.5	92.0
40-44	1 030.2	969.8	94.1	493.1	473.2	96.0	537.1	496.6	92.5
45-49	1 144.4	1 072.2	93.7	544.2	519.8	95.5	600.2	552.5	92.1
50-54	928.9	841.2	90.6	430.2	400.1	93.0	498.8	441.2	88.5
55-59	638.7	507.9	79.5	276.2	246.5	89.2	362.6	261.4	72.1
60-64	401.1	168.0	41.9	155.1	100.4	64.7	246.0	67.7	27.5
65-69	477.3	61.4	12.9	201.4	32.1	15.9	275.9	29.3	10.6
70+	718.6	34.1	4.7	234.4	17.7	7.6	484.2	16.4	3.4
Korea, Republic of (2008) BA (15+) [1][2]									
Total	.	**24 347**	.	.	**14 208**	.	.	**10 139**	.
Total (15+)	*39 599*	*24 348*	*61.5*						
15-19	3 238	212	6.5						
20-24	2 681	1 343	50.1						
25-29	3 903	2 844	72.9						
30-34	3 876	2 842	73.3						
35-39	4 373	3 361	76.9						
40-44	4 116	3 316	80.6						
45-49	4 237	3 374	79.6						
50-54	3 557	2 682	75.4						
55-59	2 534	1 706	67.3						
60-64	2 046	1 127	55.1						
65+	5 038	1 541	30.6						
Kuwait (2005) A (15+)									
Total	**2 193.7**	**1 146.4**	*52.3*	**1 300.3**	**858.0**	*66.0*	**893.3**	**288.4**	*32.3*
Total (15+)	*1 646.6*	*1 146.4*	*69.6*	*1 017.0*	*858.0*	*84.4*	*629.6*	*288.4*	*45.8*
0-9	380.2			196.7			183.5		
10-14	166.9			86.7			80.2		
15-19	156.0	9.6	6.2	80.7	7.9	9.7	75.3	1.8	2.4
20-24	200.2	122.1	61.0	113.6	87.0	76.5	86.5	35.1	40.6
25-29	280.4	235.2	83.9	175.7	167.6	95.4	104.6	67.6	64.6
30-34	269.5	231.2	85.8	172.3	167.6	97.2	97.1	63.6	65.5
35-39	237.9	203.8	85.7	154.6	151.2	97.8	83.2	52.5	63.1
40-44	177.8	146.8	82.5	114.9	111.7	97.2	62.9	35.1	55.8
45-49	128.9	99.0	76.8	84.7	79.4	93.7	44.2	19.7	44.4
50-54	82.2	54.9	66.7	53.9	46.5	86.2	28.3	8.4	29.7
55-59	48.6	27.0	55.6	30.3	23.7	78.3	18.3	3.3	18.2
60-64	28.3	10.8	38.2	16.5	9.9	60.0	11.8	0.9	7.8
65+	36.8	6.1	16.4	19.6	5.7	28.8	17.2	0.4	2.3
Liban (2007) B (15+)									
Total	**3 759.1**	**1 228.8**	*32.7*	**1 857.7**	**921.6**	*49.6*	**1 901.5**	**307.1**	*16.2*
Total (15+)	*2 831.2*	*1 228.8*	*43.4*	*1 377.0*	*921.6*	*66.9*	*1 454.2*	*307.1*	*21.1*
0-4	261.0			136.5			124.5		
5-9	312.9			160.6			152.3		
10-14	354.0			183.6			170.4		
15-19	363.6	58.5	16.1	196.0	48.9	24.9	167.6	9.7	5.8
20-24	367.8	166.2	45.2	191.5	113.7	59.4	176.3	52.5	29.8
25-29	305.9	198.9	65.0	148.3	131.8	88.8	157.6	67.1	42.6
30-34	276.8	175.7	63.5	132.1	123.9	93.8	144.7	51.8	35.8
35-39	249.6	139.6	55.9	111.8	106.0	94.8	137.7	33.5	24.3
40-44	233.0	121.8	52.3	102.4	92.4	90.2	130.6	29.4	22.5
45-49	208.8	112.7	54.0	95.6	87.9	91.9	113.2	24.8	22.0
50-54	179.9	86.9	48.3	84.1	70.5	83.8	95.8	16.5	17.2
55-59	143.4	65.2	45.5	67.0	54.5	81.3	76.4	10.7	14.0
60-64	140.0	49.9	35.6	65.7	41.6	63.4	74.3	8.2	11.1
65-69	122.0	28.8	23.6	59.9	26.8	44.7	62.1	2.0	3.2
70-74	105.3	13.7	13.0	53.3	13.0	24.4	52.0	0.7	1.3
75+	135.2	10.9	8.1	69.3	10.8	15.5	65.9	0.2	0.2

Explanations and sources: see p. 3.
[1] Excl. armed forces and conscripts. [2] "De facto" population.

Explications et sources: voir p. 5.
[1] Non compris les forces armées et les conscrits. [2] Population "de facto".

Explicaciones y fuentes: véase p. 7.
[1] Excl. las fuerzas armadas y los conscriptos. [2] Población "de facto".

ECONOMICALLY ACTIVE POPULATION

Total and economically active population by age group

Thousands

POPULATION ACTIVE

Population totale et population active par groupe d'âge

Milliers

POBLACION ECONOMICAMENTE ACTIVA

Población total y población económicamente activa por grupo de edad

Millares

	Total			Men - Hommes - Hombres			Women - Femmes - Mujeres		
	Total population	Active population	Activity rate	Total population	Active population	Activity rate	Total population	Active population	Activity rate
	Population totale	Population active	Taux d'activité	Population totale	Population active	Taux d'activité	Population totale	Population active	Taux d'activité
	Población total	Población activa	Tasa de actividad %	Población total	Población activa	Tasa de actividad %	Población total	Población activa	Tasa de actividad %
Macau, China (2008) BA (14+) [1] [2]									
Total	**535.3**	**333.0**	*62.2*	**263.5**	**178.0**	*67.6*	**271.8**	**155.1**	*57.1*
0-13	63.9	.	.	33.2	.	.	30.7	.	.
14-19	49.0	6.7	*13.7*	25.1	3.5	*13.9*	23.9	3.2	*13.4*
20-24	51.1	39.4	*77.1*	24.5	18.8	*76.7*	26.5	20.5	*77.4*
25-29	43.0	40.2	*93.5*	20.3	19.8	*97.5*	22.7	20.5	*90.3*
30-34	43.7	40.9	*93.6*	20.9	20.5	*98.1*	22.8	20.4	*89.5*
35-39	48.8	44.7	*91.6*	22.3	21.9	*98.2*	26.5	22.8	*86.0*
40-44	49.3	43.8	*88.8*	22.5	21.8	*96.9*	26.8	22.1	*82.5*
45-49	53.9	45.7	*84.8*	27.1	25.8	*95.2*	26.9	20.0	*74.3*
50-54	46.8	37.8	*80.8*	25.2	23.1	*91.7*	21.6	14.7	*68.1*
55-59	30.2	20.7	*68.5*	15.9	12.9	*81.1*	14.3	7.7	*53.8*
60-64	18.6	9.1	*48.9*	10.0	6.7	*67.0*	8.6	2.3	*26.7*
65-69	10.2	2.1	*20.6*	5.3	1.6	*30.2*	4.9	0.5	*10.2*
70-74	9.1	1.1	*12.1*	4.1	0.9	*22.0*	5.0	0.3	*6.0*
75+	17.7	0.9	*5.1*	7.0	0.8	*11.4*	10.7	0.1	*0.9*
Malaysia (2008) BA (15-64) [2] [3]									
Total	.	**11 028.1**	.	.	**7 074.6**	.	.	**3 953.5**	.
15-19	.	478.8	.	.	294.6	.	.	184.3	.
20-24	.	1 619.5	.	.	965.0	.	.	654.5	.
25-29	.	1 831.5	.	.	1 097.4	.	.	734.1	.
30-34	.	1 578.3	.	.	989.9	.	.	588.5	.
35-39	.	1 437.9	.	.	934.7	.	.	503.2	.
40-44	.	1 328.2	.	.	872.2	.	.	456.0	.
45-49	.	1 132.6	.	.	764.4	.	.	368.2	.
50-54	.	882.5	.	.	612.4	.	.	270.1	.
55-59	.	482.7	.	.	350.0	.	.	132.8	.
60-64	.	256.0	.	.	194.1	.	.	61.8	.
Mongolia (XII.2008) E (16+) [2]									
Total	**2 645.5**	**1 071.6**	*40.5*	**1 291.1**	**525.0**	*40.7*	**1 354.5**	**546.6**	*40.4*
0-15	796.6	0.1	-	402.7	0.1	-	393.9	0.0	.
16-19	243.6	75.0	*30.8*	121.5	38.3	*31.6*	122.1	36.7	*30.0*
20-24	278.8	150.6	*54.0*	135.8	73.9	*54.4*	143.0	76.8	*53.7*
25-29	236.5	165.2	*69.8*	114.5	83.5	*73.0*	122.0	81.6	*66.9*
30-34	218.6	169.0	*77.3*	106.2	83.4	*78.5*	112.4	85.6	*76.1*
35-39	196.3	154.6	*78.7*	94.7	75.0	*79.2*	101.7	79.6	*78.3*
40-44	177.4	133.1	*75.0*	85.1	62.3	*73.3*	92.4	70.7	*76.6*
45-49	154.7	112.8	*72.9*	73.7	52.8	*71.6*	81.0	60.0	*74.1*
50-54	110.8	69.2	*62.4*	52.6	33.0	*62.8*	58.2	36.1	*62.0*
55-59	71.9	37.7	*52.4*	33.9	19.7	*58.0*	38.0	18.0	*47.5*
60+	160.3	4.4	*2.8*	70.5	2.9	*4.1*	89.8	1.5	*1.7*
Philippines (X.2008) BA (15+) [4] [5]									
Total	**88 910**	**37 058**	*41.7*	**44 690**	**22 872**	*51.2*	**44 220**	**14 187**	*32.1*
Total (15+)	*58 180*	*37 058*	*63.7*	*28 990*	*22 872*	*78.9*	*29 191*	*14 186*	*48.6*
0-14	30 728	.	.	15 700	.	.	15 028	.	.
15-24	17 699	7 953	*44.9*	8 999	5 000	*55.6*	8 700	2 953	*33.9*
25-34	13 323	9 805	*73.6*	6 643	6 258	*94.2*	6 680	3 547	*53.1*
35-44	10 547	8 274	*78.4*	5 300	5 088	*96.0*	5 246	3 186	*60.7*
45-54	7 894	6 262	*79.3*	3 947	3 728	*94.5*	3 947	2 534	*64.2*
55-64	4 864	3 300	*67.8*	2 386	1 941	*81.3*	2 479	1 359	*54.8*
65+	3 849	1 463	*38.0*	1 714	857	*50.0*	2 136	606	*28.4*
?	4	1	*25.0*	1	-	.	3	1	*33.3*
Qatar (III.2007) BA (15+)									
Total	.	**831.9**	.	.	**728.3**	.	.	**103.6**	.
Total (15+)	*977.0*	*831.9*	*85.1*	*767.1*	*728.3*	*94.9*	*209.9*	*103.6*	*49.3*
15-19	50.5	9.2	*18.3*	29.2	8.1	*27.8*	21.4	1.1	*5.4*
20-24	139.3	119.0	*85.4*	109.4	102.6	*93.8*	29.9	16.3	*54.7*
25-29	185.7	171.9	*92.6*	148.1	146.8	*99.2*	37.6	25.1	*66.7*
30-34	181.1	168.4	*93.0*	148.1	147.6	*99.7*	33.0	20.8	*63.1*
35-39	128.3	115.8	*90.2*	100.1	99.8	*99.7*	28.2	16.1	*56.9*
40-44	102.8	92.4	*89.9*	82.1	81.6	*99.4*	20.7	10.8	*52.2*
45-49	82.5	72.1	*87.4*	65.2	64.2	*98.4*	17.2	7.9	*46.1*
50-54	52.6	45.9	*87.3*	43.4	42.0	*96.9*	9.2	3.9	*42.0*
55-59	30.9	25.3	*82.0*	26.1	24.6	*94.4*	4.8	0.7	*14.4*
60-64	11.0	6.8	*62.1*	7.5	6.3	*83.7*	3.4	0.5	*14.8*
65+	12.4	5.0	*40.3*	8.0	4.7	*59.1*	4.5	0.3	*6.9*

Explanations and sources: see p. 3.

[1] Excl. armed forces and conscripts. [2] "De jure" population. [3] Excl. armed forces. [4] "De facto" population. [5] Excl. regular military living in barracks.

Explications et sources: voir p. 5.

[1] Non compris les forces armées et les conscrits. [2] Population "de jure". [3] Non compris les forces armées. [4] Population "de facto". [5] Non compris les militaires de carrière vivant dans des casernes.

Explicaciones y fuentes: véase p. 7.

[1] Excl. las fuerzas armadas y los conscriptos. [2] Población "de jure". [3] Excl. las fuerzas armadas. [4] Población "de facto". [5] Excl. los militares profesionales que viven en casernas.

ECONOMICALLY ACTIVE POPULATION

Total and economically active population by age group

Thousands

POPULATION ACTIVE

Population totale et population active par groupe d'âge

Milliers

POBLACION ECONOMICAMENTE ACTIVA

Población total y población económicamente activa por grupo de edad

Millares

	Total			Men - Hommes - Hombres			Women - Femmes - Mujeres		
	Total population / Population totale / Población total	Active population / Population active / Población activa	Activity rate / Taux d'activité / Tasa de actividad	Total population / Population totale / Población total	Active population / Population active / Población activa	Activity rate / Taux d'activité / Tasa de actividad	Total population / Population totale / Población total	Active population / Population active / Población activa	Activity rate / Taux d'activité / Tasa de actividad
			%			%			%
Saudi Arabia (2008) BA (15+)									
Total		**8 374.9**			**7 087.6**			**1 287.3**	
15-19		62.0			54.8			7.2	
20-24		703.5			551.9			151.6	
25-29		1 470.0			1 173.7			296.4	
30-34		1 764.3			1 432.8			331.5	
35-39		1 537.4			1 279.2			258.1	
40-44		1 164.0			1 027.5			136.5	
45-49		771.7			707.8			63.9	
50-54		465.7			438.8			26.8	
55-59		247.4			236.6			10.8	
60-64		97.9			95.3			2.6	
65+		91.1			89.3			1.8	
Singapore (VI.2008) BA (15+) [1]									
Total		**1 928.3**			**1 093.2**			**835.1**	
Total (15+)	*2 938.7*	*1 928.4*	*65.6*	*1 437.3*	*1 093.3*	*76.1*	*1 501.6*	*835.1*	*55.6*
15-19	266.7	34.2	12.8	138.6	19.3	13.9	128.2	14.9	11.6
20-24	221.0	147.0	66.5	114.6	75.7	66.1	106.4	71.3	67.0
25-29	235.9	209.2	88.7	112.6	105.1	93.3	123.3	104.2	84.5
30-34	274.1	242.9	88.6	126.5	124.1	98.1	147.6	118.8	80.5
35-39	308.2	263.9	85.6	148.2	144.8	97.7	160.0	119.0	74.4
40-44	314.4	262.1	83.4	153.3	149.4	97.5	161.2	112.7	69.9
45-49	316.2	261.9	82.8	160.2	154.8	96.6	156.0	107.2	68.7
50-54	290.1	224.9	77.5	144.8	134.7	93.0	145.3	90.1	62.0
55-59	228.1	152.0	66.6	115.3	97.9	84.9	112.8	54.1	48.0
60-64	160.3	78.2	48.8	79.5	51.5	64.8	80.8	26.7	33.0
65+	323.7	52.1	16.1	143.7	36.0	25.1	180.0	16.1	8.9
Sri Lanka (2008) BA (10+) [2]									
Total		**7 568.7**			**4 836.4**			**2 732.3**	
10-14		17.6			10.7			6.9	
15-19		303.0			195.3			107.7	
20-24		851.9			512.1			339.8	
25-29		913.1			585.3			327.8	
30-39		1 764.7			1 130.1			634.6	
40+		3 718.4			2 402.8			1 315.6	
Syrian Arab Republic (2007) BA (15+)									
Total	**19 644**	**5 400**	**27.5**	**10 042**	**4 553**	**45.3**	**9 602**	**847**	**8.8**
Total (15+)	*12 205*	*5 400*	*44.2*	*6 188*	*4 553*	*73.6*	*6 017*	*847*	*14.1*
0-9	5 159			2 669			2 490		
10-14	2 280			1 185			1 095		
15-19	2 205	489	22.2	1 132	427	37.7	1 073	63	5.8
20-24	1 908	865	45.3	989	703	71.1	919	162	17.7
25-29	1 531	837	54.6	739	672	90.9	792	165	20.8
30-34	1 251	704	56.3	602	578	96.0	649	126	19.4
35-39	1 175	665	56.6	574	554	96.5	601	111	18.5
40-44	1 028	579	56.3	509	487	95.7	519	91	17.6
45-49	817	442	54.1	409	382	93.4	408	60	14.6
50-54	690	342	49.6	353	305	86.5	337	37	11.0
55-59	479	215	44.8	248	197	79.5	231	17	7.6
60-64	409	120	29.5	220	114	51.6	189	7	3.7
65+	712	143	20.1	413	136	32.8	299	7	2.4
Taiwan, China (2008) BA (15+) [3]									
Total	**22 943**	**10 853**	**47.3**						
Total (15+)	*18 967*	*10 853*	*57.2*						
0-14	3 892								
15-24	3 235	931	28.8						
25-44	7 499	6 250	83.3						
45-64	5 842	3 481	59.6						
65+	2 391	191	8.0						

Explanations and sources: see p. 3.

[1] The data refer to the residents (Singapore citizens and permanent residents) aged 15 years and over. [2] Excl. Northern and Eastern provinces. [3] Excl. armed forces.

Explications et sources: voir p. 5.

[1] Les données se réfèrent aux résidents (citoyens de Singapour et résidents permanents) âgés de 15 ans et plus. [2] Non compris les provinces du Nord et de l'Est. [3] Non compris les forces armées.

Explicaciones y fuentes: véase p. 7.

[1] Los datos se refieren a los residentes (ciudadanos de Singapur y residentes permanentes) de 15 años y más. [2] Excl. las provincias del Norte y del Este. [3] Excl. las fuerzas armadas.

ECONOMICALLY ACTIVE POPULATION

Total and economically active population by age group

Thousands

POPULATION ACTIVE

Population totale et population active par groupe d'âge

Milliers

POBLACION ECONOMICAMENTE ACTIVA

Población total y población económicamente activa por grupo de edad

Millares

1A

	Total			Men - Hommes - Hombres			Women - Femmes - Mujeres		
	Total population	Active population	Activity rate	Total population	Active population	Activity rate	Total population	Active population	Activity rate
	Population totale	Population active	Taux d'activité	Population totale	Population active	Taux d'activité	Population totale	Population active	Taux d'activité
	Población total	Población activa	Tasa de actividad	Población total	Población activa	Tasa de actividad	Población total	Población activa	Tasa de actividad
			%			%			%
Thailand (VII-IX.2008) BA (15+) [1]									
Total	**66 511.7**	**38 344.7**	*57.7*	**32 686.7**	**20 691.1**	*63.3*	**33 825.0**	**17 653.6**	*52.2*
Total (15+)	*52 237.5*	*38 344.6*	*73.4*	*25 389.8*	*20 691.1*	*81.5*	*26 847.6*	*17 653.5*	*65.8*
0-14	14 274.2	.	.	7 296.9	.	.	6 977.3	.	.
15-19	5 269.0	1 413.1	*26.8*	2 693.5	916.2	*34.0*	2 575.6	496.9	*19.3*
20-24	5 253.8	3 742.0	*71.2*	2 677.4	2 150.6	*80.3*	2 576.4	1 591.4	*61.8*
25-29	5 335.3	4 687.6	*87.9*	2 698.0	2 537.1	*94.0*	2 637.3	2 150.5	*81.5*
30-34	5 421.8	4 909.1	*90.5*	2 691.3	2 587.5	*96.1*	2 730.4	2 321.6	*85.0*
35-39	5 567.5	5 119.3	*91.9*	2 695.1	2 619.8	*97.2*	2 872.4	2 499.5	*87.0*
40-49	10 511.5	9 489.6	*90.3*	5 079.6	4 915.1	*96.8*	5 431.9	4 574.5	*84.2*
50-59	7 462.1	6 172.6	*82.7*	3 572.5	3 315.0	*92.8*	3 889.6	2 857.6	*73.5*
60+	7 416.5	2 811.3	*37.9*	3 282.4	1 649.8	*50.3*	4 134.0	1 161.5	*28.1*
United Arab Emirates (II.2008) BA (15+)									
Total	**3 503.345**	**1 923.214**	*54.9*	**2 157.706**	**1 531.424**	*71.0*	**1 345.639**	**391.790**	*29.1*
Total (15+)	*2 650.474*	*1 923.214*	*72.6*	*1 713.637*	*1 531.424*	*89.4*	*936.837*	*391.790*	*41.8*
0-9	583.096	.	.	301.853	.	.	281.243	.	.
10-14	269.775	.	.	142.216	.	.	127.559	.	.
15-19	229.886	23.477	*10.2*	119.069	16.801	*14.1*	110.817	6.676	*6.0*
20-24	343.987	233.472	*67.9*	195.354	162.114	*83.0*	148.633	71.358	*48.0*
25-29	483.399	404.289	*83.6*	292.456	288.292	*98.6*	190.943	115.997	*60.7*
30-34	468.278	390.838	*83.5*	309.452	307.706	*99.4*	158.826	83.132	*52.3*
35-39	400.254	336.746	*84.1*	282.930	280.796	*99.2*	117.324	55.950	*47.7*
40-44	282.138	228.959	*81.2*	201.630	198.855	*98.6*	80.508	30.104	*37.4*
45-49	191.408	148.836	*77.8*	135.129	131.697	*97.5*	56.279	17.139	*30.5*
50-54	121.818	91.259	*74.9*	88.661	83.751	*94.5*	33.157	7.508	*22.6*
55-59	66.355	46.439	*70.0*	49.479	43.642	*88.2*	16.876	2.797	*16.6*
60-64	27.590	13.673	*49.6*	17.968	12.751	*71.0*	9.622	0.922	*9.6*
65-69	15.652	3.692	*23.6*	10.652	3.562	*33.4*	5.000	0.130	*2.6*
70-74	10.004	1.009	*10.1*	5.779	0.945	*16.4*	4.225	0.064	*1.5*
75+	9.705	0.525	*5.4*	5.078	0.512	*10.1*	4.627	0.013	*0.3*
West Bank and Gaza Strip (2008) BA (10+)									
Total	**3 718.101**	**886.828**	*23.9*	**1 884.616**	**725.491**	*38.5*	**1 833.485**	**161.337**	*8.8*
Total (15+)	*2 024.190*	*874.197*	*43.2*	*1 021.341*	*715.005*	*70.0*	*1 002.851*	*159.192*	*15.9*
0-9	1 209.380	.	.	616.889	.	.	592.492	.	.
10-14	484.569	12.633	*2.6*	246.404	10.488	*4.3*	238.165	2.144	*0.9*
15-19	403.906	63.585	*15.7*	205.466	59.674	*29.0*	198.440	3.911	*2.0*
20-24	325.457	143.801	*44.2*	166.775	112.555	*67.5*	158.682	31.245	*19.7*
25-29	273.031	155.273	*56.9*	139.671	121.769	*87.2*	133.360	33.504	*25.1*
30-34	231.099	135.304	*58.5*	117.491	110.714	*94.2*	113.608	24.590	*21.6*
35-39	193.428	113.881	*58.9*	98.759	94.109	*95.3*	94.669	19.771	*20.9*
40-44	160.575	97.583	*60.8*	83.175	80.705	*97.0*	77.400	16.878	*21.8*
45-49	125.360	71.598	*57.1*	64.756	58.936	*91.0*	60.604	12.662	*20.9*
50-54	86.257	43.484	*50.4*	43.837	36.842	*84.0*	42.421	6.643	*15.7*
55-59	65.135	27.750	*42.6*	31.909	22.280	*69.8*	33.226	5.470	*16.5*
60-64	49.377	10.362	*21.0*	22.237	8.376	*37.7*	27.140	1.986	*7.3*
65-69	39.065	6.204	*15.9*	16.824	4.949	*29.4*	22.241	1.255	*5.6*
70-74	32.399	3.254	*10.0*	13.750	2.424	*17.6*	18.650	0.830	*4.5*
75+	39.062	2.116	*5.4*	16.674	1.670	*10.0*	22.388	0.447	*2.0*
?	0.039	0.002	*5.1*	0.017	0.002	*11.8*	0.022	-	.

Explanations and sources: see p. 3.

[1] Excl. armed forces.

Explications et sources: voir p. 5.

[1] Non compris les forces armées.

Explicaciones y fuentes: véase p. 7.

[1] Excl. las fuerzas armadas.

1A

ECONOMICALLY ACTIVE POPULATION

Total and economically active population by age group

Thousands

POPULATION ACTIVE

Population totale et population active par groupe d'âge

Milliers

POBLACION ECONOMICAMENTE ACTIVA

Población total y población económicamente activa por grupo de edad

Millares

	Total			Men - Hommes - Hombres			Women - Femmes - Mujeres		
	Total population / Population totale / Población total	Active population / Population active / Población activa	Activity rate / Taux d'activité / Tasa de actividad	Total population / Population totale / Población total	Active population / Population active / Población activa	Activity rate / Taux d'activité / Tasa de actividad	Total population / Population totale / Población total	Active population / Population active / Población activa	Activity rate / Taux d'activité / Tasa de actividad
			%			%			%
EUROPE - EUROPE - EUROPA									
Austria (2008) BA (15+) [1] [2]									
Total	**8 220.0**	**4 252.3**	*51.7*	**4 001.2**	**2 303.9**	*57.6*	**4 218.8**	**1 948.4**	*46.2*
Total (15+)	*6 951.8*	*4 252.3*	*61.2*	*3 351.6*	*2 303.9*	*68.7*	*3 600.1*	*1 948.4*	*54.1*
0-9	805.0	.	.	412.5	.	.	392.5	.	.
10-14	463.2	.	.	237.1	.	.	226.2	.	.
15-19	487.2	222.4	*45.7*	244.0	120.8	*49.5*	243.2	101.6	*41.8*
20-24	506.3	381.2	*75.3*	250.7	198.8	*79.3*	255.6	182.4	*71.4*
25-29	541.0	459.0	*84.8*	271.1	245.3	*90.5*	270.0	213.7	*79.2*
30-34	537.8	474.4	*88.2*	267.7	255.7	*95.5*	270.1	218.7	*81.0*
35-39	641.4	575.7	*89.8*	320.0	306.3	*95.7*	321.3	269.4	*83.9*
40-44	712.3	641.6	*90.1*	360.0	342.4	*95.1*	352.4	299.1	*84.9*
45-49	665.8	586.0	*88.0*	335.6	312.5	*93.1*	330.2	273.5	*82.8*
50-54	556.2	452.9	*81.4*	275.3	239.5	*87.0*	280.9	213.4	*76.0*
55-59	489.5	296.7	*60.6*	239.7	175.6	*73.3*	249.8	121.0	*48.5*
60-64	438.5	92.0	*21.0*	211.1	62.3	*29.5*	227.3	29.7	*13.1*
65-69	470.4	39.9	*8.5*	221.8	24.9	*11.2*	248.6	15.0	*6.0*
70-74	294.4	16.9	*5.7*	132.5	10.4	*7.8*	161.9	6.5	*4.0*
75+	610.9	13.5	*2.2*	222.1	9.2	*4.2*	388.8	4.3	*1.1*
Belarus (2008) E (16+) [3] [4]									
Total	**9 671.9**	**4 638.1**	*48.0*	**4 511.6**	**2 188.7**	*48.5*	**5 160.3**	**2 449.4**	*47.5*
Belgique (2008) BA (15+) [3] [5]									
Total	**10 707.6**	**4 779.6**	*44.6*	**5 245.8**	**2 631.2**	*50.2*	**5 461.8**	**2 148.4**	*39.3*
Total (15+)	*8 903.6*	*4 779.6*	*53.7*	*4 323.8*	*2 631.2*	*60.9*	*4 579.8*	*2 148.4*	*46.9*
0-14	1 804.0	.	.	922.0	.	.	882.0	.	.
15-19	653.0	62.8	*9.6*	333.2	39.9	*12.0*	319.8	22.9	*7.2*
20-24	644.8	370.7	*57.5*	323.6	196.4	*60.7*	321.1	174.3	*54.3*
25-29	687.8	605.3	*88.0*	344.5	317.4	*92.1*	343.3	287.9	*83.9*
30-34	686.7	621.0	*90.4*	346.2	330.0	*95.3*	340.5	291.0	*85.5*
35-39	759.5	673.2	*88.6*	384.2	363.7	*94.7*	375.3	309.5	*82.5*
40-44	806.5	708.3	*87.8*	409.2	383.8	*93.8*	397.3	324.5	*81.7*
45-49	807.4	684.7	*84.8*	406.9	374.9	*92.1*	400.5	309.8	*77.4*
50-54	745.8	558.1	*74.8*	373.6	320.2	*85.7*	372.1	237.9	*63.9*
55-59	678.9	356.9	*52.6*	339.0	212.8	*62.8*	339.9	144.1	*42.4*
60-64	602.9	105.6	*17.5*	296.3	69.6	*23.5*	306.6	36.1	*11.8*
65-69	460.6	16.8	*3.6*	218.9	12.1	*5.5*	241.7	4.7	*1.9*
70-74	451.3	7.3	*1.6*	205.5	5.4	*2.6*	245.7	1.9	*0.8*
75+	918.4	8.8	*1.0*	342.6	5.0	*1.5*	575.8	3.8	*0.7*
Bosnia and Herzegovina (2008) BA (15+)									
Total	**3 211**	**1 162**	*36.2*	**1 566**	**729**	*46.6*	**1 645**	**433**	*26.3*
Total (15+)	*2 649*	*1 163*	*43.9*	*1 278*	*729*	*57.0*	*1 370*	*434*	*31.7*
0-14	563	.	.	289	.	.	274	.	.
15-24	447	148	*33.1*	236	94	*39.8*	211	54	*25.6*
25-49	1 096	752	*68.6*	541	461	*85.2*	555	291	*52.4*
50-64	577	234	*40.6*	271	155	*57.2*	305	79	*25.9*
65+	529	29	*5.5*	230	19	*8.3*	299	10	*3.3*
Bulgaria (2008) BA (15+) [3] [6]									
Total	**7 640.2**	**3 560.4**	*46.6*	**3 699.7**	**1 896.8**	*51.3*	**3 940.5**	**1 663.6**	*42.2*
Total (15+)	*6 616.9*	*3 560.2*	*53.8*	*3 173.9*	*1 896.8*	*59.8*	*3 443.0*	*1 663.7*	*48.3*
0-9	581.6	.	.	299.1	.	.	282.5	.	.
10-14	441.8	.	.	226.7	.	.	215.1	.	.
15-19	534.2	40.7	*7.6*	280.1	25.5	*9.1*	254.1	15.3	*6.0*
20-24	464.2	260.1	*56.0*	231.7	148.5	*64.1*	232.5	111.6	*48.0*
25-29	421.8	337.8	*80.1*	228.4	201.4	*88.2*	193.4	136.4	*70.5*
30-34	521.6	443.8	*85.1*	261.1	236.0	*90.4*	260.5	207.8	*79.8*
35-39	578.7	506.3	*87.5*	287.1	259.9	*90.5*	291.6	246.5	*84.5*
40-44	563.4	502.9	*89.3*	287.0	260.8	*90.9*	276.4	242.1	*87.6*
45-49	641.8	558.3	*87.0*	315.7	277.9	*88.0*	326.1	280.4	*86.0*
50-54	459.5	375.1	*81.6*	217.0	182.1	*83.9*	242.5	193.0	*79.6*
55-59	500.3	338.4	*67.6*	232.0	167.8	*72.3*	268.3	170.6	*63.6*
60-64	483.9	141.2	*29.2*	222.2	98.9	*44.5*	261.7	42.3	*16.2*
65-69	416.2	35.4	*8.5*	184.3	23.9	*13.0*	231.9	11.5	*5.0*
70-74	401.1	13.3	*3.3*	173.2	9.1	*5.3*	227.9	4.3	*1.9*
75+	630.2	6.9	*1.1*	254.1	5.0	*2.0*	376.1	1.9	*0.5*

Explanations and sources: see p. 3.

[1] "De facto" population. [2] Excl. conscripts on compulsory military service. [3] "De jure" population. [4] Excl. armed forces. [5] Incl. professional army. [6] Incl. armed forces, Excl. conscripts.

Explications et sources: voir p. 5.

[1] Population "de facto". [2] Non compris conscrits ceux du contingent. [3] Population "de jure". [4] Non compris les forces armées. [5] Y compris les militaires de carrière. [6] Y compris les forces armées, Excl. conscrits

Explicaciones y fuentes: véase p. 7.

[1] Población "de facto". [2] Excl. los conscriptos del servicio obligatorio. [3] Población "de jure". [4] Excl. las fuerzas armadas. [5] Incl. los militares profesionales. [6] Incl. las fuerzas armadas, excl. los conscriptos.

ECONOMICALLY ACTIVE POPULATION

POPULATION ACTIVE

POBLACION ECONOMICAMENTE ACTIVA

1A

Total and economically active population by age group

Thousands

Population totale et population active par groupe d'âge

Milliers

Población total y población económicamente activa por grupo de edad

Millares

	Total			Men - Hommes - Hombres			Women - Femmes - Mujeres		
	Total population	Active population	Activity rate	Total population	Active population	Activity rate	Total population	Active population	Activity rate
	Population totale	Population active	Taux d'activité	Population totale	Population active	Taux d'activité	Population totale	Population active	Taux d'activité
	Población total	Población activa	Tasa de actividad	Población total	Población activa	Tasa de actividad	Población total	Población activa	Tasa de actividad
			%			%			%
Croatia (2008) BA (15+) [1] [2]									
Total	**4 231.2**	**1 784.8**	*42.2*	**2 003.8**	**973.0**	*48.6*	**2 227.4**	**811.8**	*36.4*
Total (15+)	*3 680.1*	*1 784.9*	*48.5*	*1 732.5*	*973.0*	*56.2*	*1 947.9*	*811.8*	*41.7*
10-14	545.0	.	.	267.8	.	.	277.2	.	.
15-19	256.0	35.1	*13.7*	128.5	20.3	*15.8*	127.6	14.8	*11.6*
20-24	265.9	145.9	*54.9*	140.9	89.4	*63.4*	125.1	56.5	*45.2*
25-29	226.0	192.0	*85.0*	120.3	108.2	*89.9*	105.7	83.8	*79.3*
30-34	196.7	173.3	*88.1*	101.4	94.8	*93.5*	95.3	78.5	*82.4*
35-39	235.2	202.7	*86.2*	109.8	98.3	*89.5*	125.4	104.4	*83.3*
40-44	286.3	242.0	*84.5*	140.3	123.6	*88.1*	146.0	118.4	*81.1*
45-49	334.5	267.0	*79.8*	161.9	134.6	*83.1*	172.6	132.4	*76.7*
50-54	361.3	250.0	*69.2*	178.7	136.1	*76.2*	182.5	113.8	*62.4*
55-59	325.1	163.3	*50.2*	162.4	106.7	*65.7*	162.8	56.6	*34.8*
60-64	254.8	61.9	*24.3*	112.6	37.1	*32.9*	142.3	24.8	*17.4*
65-69	270.2	25.1	*9.3*	117.8	11.3	*9.6*	152.4	13.8	*9.1*
70-74	263.7	18.6	*7.1*	113.3	8.8	*7.8*	150.4	9.8	*6.5*
75+	404.4	8.0	*2.0*	144.6	3.8	*2.6*	259.8	4.2	*1.6*
Cyprus (2008) BA (15+) [1] [2] [3]									
Total	**758.3**	**397.4**	*52.4*	**371.4**	**219.2**	*59.0*	**386.9**	**178.2**	*46.1*
Total (15+)	*618.9*	*397.4*	*64.2*	*299.8*	*219.2*	*73.1*	*319.1*	*178.2*	*55.8*
0-9	86.5	.	.	44.5	.	.	42.0	.	.
10-14	52.9	.	.	27.1	.	.	25.8	.	.
15-19	44.5	4.9	*10.9*	20.7	2.7	*13.1*	23.8	2.2	*9.1*
20-24	48.9	34.1	*69.7*	22.6	16.0	*70.6*	26.3	18.1	*69.0*
25-29	65.9	56.6	*85.9*	32.6	28.5	*87.4*	33.3	28.1	*84.5*
30-34	59.3	54.2	*91.5*	29.7	28.8	*97.1*	29.6	25.4	*85.9*
35-39	55.5	48.3	*87.1*	27.2	26.1	*95.8*	28.3	22.3	*78.8*
40-44	56.7	49.5	*87.3*	27.8	26.6	*95.6*	28.9	22.9	*79.4*
45-49	57.2	48.9	*85.4*	28.7	27.5	*95.8*	28.5	21.4	*75.0*
50-54	50.7	40.9	*80.7*	25.1	23.3	*92.8*	25.6	17.6	*68.8*
55-59	46.8	32.0	*68.4*	23.0	19.5	*85.0*	23.8	12.5	*52.4*
60-64	38.3	16.2	*42.2*	18.5	10.8	*58.1*	19.8	5.4	*27.4*
65-69	32.2	6.3	*19.6*	15.7	5.0	*32.2*	16.5	1.3	*7.7*
70-74	24.9	3.0	*11.9*	11.6	2.4	*21.0*	13.3	0.5	*3.9*
75+	38.0	2.4	*6.3*	16.5	1.9	*11.5*	21.5	0.5	*2.4*
Czech Republic (2008) BA (15+) [1] [2]									
Total	**10 421.8**	**5 232.3**	*50.2*	**5 107.2**	**2 965.8**	*58.1*	**5 314.6**	**2 266.5**	*42.6*
Total (15+)	*8 943.7*	*5 232.3*	*58.5*	*4 348.4*	*2 965.8*	*68.2*	*4 595.3*	*2 266.5*	*49.3*
0-9	959.4	.	.	489.5	.	.	469.9	.	.
10-14	518.8	.	.	269.3	.	.	249.5	.	.
15-19	640.9	47.2	*7.4*	328.4	27.6	*8.4*	312.6	19.6	*6.3*
20-24	702.3	371.1	*52.8*	362.5	220.3	*60.8*	339.8	150.8	*44.4*
25-29	796.3	629.2	*79.0*	410.1	372.8	*90.9*	386.2	256.5	*66.4*
30-34	938.2	767.3	*81.8*	480.8	465.5	*96.8*	457.3	301.8	*66.0*
35-39	768.9	684.7	*89.1*	395.3	385.8	*97.6*	373.6	298.9	*80.0*
40-44	710.8	666.7	*93.8*	364.0	351.3	*96.5*	346.8	315.4	*91.0*
45-49	648.7	607.2	*93.6*	329.0	311.4	*94.6*	319.6	295.8	*92.5*
50-54	741.3	664.7	*89.7*	368.2	337.6	*91.7*	373.1	327.1	*87.7*
55-59	767.4	535.7	*69.8*	373.0	316.2	*84.8*	394.3	219.5	*55.7*
60-64	695.8	189.0	*27.2*	328.0	133.6	*40.7*	367.8	55.5	*15.1*
65-69	496.4	47.3	*9.5*	220.0	29.2	*13.3*	276.4	18.1	*6.5*
70-74	368.8	14.4	*3.9*	153.8	9.0	*5.9*	215.1	5.4	*2.5*
75+	668.1	7.9	*1.2*	235.3	5.5	*2.3*	432.8	2.4	*0.6*
Denmark (2008) BA (15-66) [2] [4]									
Total	.	**2 925.8**	.	.	**1 544.4**	.	.	**1 381.4**	.
Total (15+)	*3 735.8*	*2 925.8*	*78.3*	*1 883.6*	*1 544.4*	*82.0*	*1 852.2*	*1 381.4*	*74.6*
15-19	337.0	221.9	*65.8*	172.9	112.4	*65.0*	164.1	109.5	*66.7*
20-24	307.8	247.6	*80.5*	156.9	130.9	*83.4*	150.9	116.8	*77.4*
25-29	316.7	277.6	*87.7*	158.9	144.2	*90.8*	157.8	133.4	*84.5*
30-34	365.0	333.1	*91.3*	183.1	174.4	*95.2*	181.9	158.7	*87.3*
35-39	385.9	357.2	*92.6*	195.5	186.8	*95.6*	190.5	170.4	*89.5*
40-44	428.8	391.6	*91.3*	217.6	206.8	*95.0*	211.1	184.7	*87.5*
45-49	382.1	346.0	*90.5*	193.2	178.3	*92.3*	188.9	167.7	*88.7*
50-54	362.3	317.1	*87.5*	182.1	165.8	*91.0*	180.1	151.3	*84.0*
55-59	353.8	289.5	*81.8*	176.7	153.3	*86.8*	177.1	136.2	*76.9*
60-64	364.6	125.6	*34.5*	179.7	78.8	*43.9*	184.9	46.8	*25.3*
65-66	131.8	18.6	*14.1*	67.0	12.7	*19.0*	64.9	5.9	*9.1*

Explanations and sources: see p. 3.

[1] Incl. armed forces, Excl. conscripts. [2] "De jure" population. [3] Government-controlled area. [4] Included armed forces and conscripts.

Explications et sources: voir p. 5.

[1] Y compris les forces armées, Excl. conscrits [2] Population "de jure". [3] Région sous contrôle gouvernemental. [4] Y compris les forces armées et les conscrits.

Explicaciones y fuentes: véase p. 7.

[1] Incl. las fuerzas armadas, excl. los conscriptos. [2] Población "de jure". [3] Area controlada por el gobierno. [4] Incluye las fuezas armadas y los conscriptos.

1A ECONOMICALLY ACTIVE POPULATION — POPULATION ACTIVE — POBLACION ECONOMICAMENTE ACTIVA

Total and economically active population by age group — Thousands

Population totale et population active par groupe d'âge — Milliers

Población total y población económicamente activa por grupo de edad — Millares

	Total			Men - Hommes - Hombres			Women - Femmes - Mujeres		
	Total population / Population totale / Población total	Active population / Population active / Población activa	Activity rate / Taux d'activité / Tasa de actividad %	Total population / Population totale / Población total	Active population / Population active / Población activa	Activity rate / Taux d'activité / Tasa de actividad %	Total population / Population totale / Población total	Active population / Population active / Población activa	Activity rate / Taux d'activité / Tasa de actividad %
España (2008) BA (16+) [1][2]									
Total	**45 328.7**	**22 848.2**	*50.4*	**22 411.6**	**13 031.7**	*58.1*	**22 917.1**	**9 816.5**	*42.8*
0-9	4 598.3	.	.	2 364.2	.	.	2 234.0	.	.
10-15	2 522.7	.	.	1 295.2	.	.	1 227.4	.	.
16-19	1 840.6	535.6	*29.1*	946.1	310.0	*32.8*	894.6	225.5	*25.2*
20-24	2 749.5	1 872.4	*68.1*	1 404.6	1 020.7	*72.7*	1 345.0	851.7	*63.3*
25-29	3 595.2	3 108.5	*86.5*	1 850.2	1 666.6	*90.1*	1 745.0	1 441.9	*82.6*
30-34	4 054.4	3 569.7	*88.0*	2 102.8	1 996.2	*94.9*	1 951.6	1 573.5	*80.6*
35-39	3 860.4	3 307.1	*85.7*	1 988.9	1 880.5	*94.6*	1 871.4	1 426.5	*76.2*
40-44	3 638.5	3 065.1	*84.2*	1 846.0	1 732.1	*93.8*	1 792.5	1 333.0	*74.4*
45-49	3 318.1	2 703.9	*81.5*	1 660.1	1 533.1	*92.4*	1 658.0	1 170.8	*70.6*
50-54	2 868.9	2 131.8	*74.3*	1 419.5	1 255.0	*88.4*	1 449.4	876.8	*60.5*
55-59	2 531.7	1 544.6	*61.0*	1 238.8	972.8	*78.5*	1 293.0	571.8	*44.2*
60-64	2 336.0	850.9	*36.4*	1 125.0	566.3	*50.3*	1 211.0	284.6	*23.5*
65-69	1 906.5	117.0	*6.1*	872.5	73.2	*8.4*	1 034.0	43.8	*4.2*
70-74	1 899.7	28.1	*1.5*	867.0	17.2	*2.0*	1 032.8	11.0	*1.1*
75+	3 608.2	13.7	*0.4*	1 430.7	7.9	*0.6*	2 177.5	5.8	*0.3*
Estonia (2008) BA (15-74) [2][3]									
Total	**1 340.9**	**694.9**	*51.8*	**617.4**	**351.2**	*56.9*	**723.5**	**343.7**	*47.5*
Total (15+)	*1 142.2*	*694.9*	*60.8*	*515.2*	*351.3*	*68.2*	*627.1*	*343.8*	*54.8*
0-9	133.7	.	.	68.9	.	.	64.8	.	.
10-14	65.0	.	.	33.4	.	.	31.6	.	.
15-19	97.3	12.7	*13.1*	49.9	7.0	*14.0*	47.4	5.7	*12.0*
20-24	106.2	70.4	*66.3*	54.0	38.8	*71.8*	52.2	31.6	*60.6*
25-29	97.4	81.1	*83.3*	49.4	48.0	*97.2*	48.0	33.1	*69.0*
30-34	92.3	80.8	*87.5*	46.2	43.8	*94.8*	46.1	37.1	*80.5*
35-39	92.8	83.1	*89.5*	45.7	43.3	*94.7*	47.1	39.7	*84.2*
40-44	87.3	79.9	*91.5*	41.9	39.0	*93.0*	45.4	40.9	*90.2*
45-49	96.3	87.3	*90.6*	45.3	40.6	*89.7*	51.1	46.8	*91.6*
50-54	91.7	78.6	*85.7*	41.8	35.6	*85.3*	50.0	43.0	*86.0*
55-59	85.9	67.4	*78.4*	37.7	29.8	*79.0*	48.2	37.7	*78.2*
60-64	64.3	30.0	*46.7*	27.0	14.6	*54.1*	37.3	15.4	*41.3*
65-69	71.6	17.8	*24.9*	27.8	7.7	*27.7*	43.8	10.1	*23.1*
70-74	59.6	5.8	*9.7*	21.2	3.1	*14.6*	38.4	2.7	*7.0*
75+	99.3	.	.	27.2	.	.	72.0	.	.
?	0.2	.	.	0.1	.	.	0.1	.	.
Finland (2008) BA (15-74) [4][5]									
Total	**5 313.4**	**2 725.6**	*51.3*	**2 604.2**	**1 421.6**	*54.6*	**2 709.2**	**1 304.0**	*48.1*
Total (15+)	*4 420.5*	*2 725.6*	*61.7*	*2 148.3*	*1 421.6*	*66.2*	*2 272.2*	*1 304.0*	*57.4*
0-9	579.8	.	.	296.5	.	.	283.4	.	.
10-14	313.0	.	.	159.5	.	.	153.6	.	.
15-19	332.5	118.9	*35.8*	169.7	60.0	*35.3*	162.8	58.9	*36.2*
20-24	326.4	243.7	*74.7*	166.9	129.9	*77.8*	159.4	113.8	*71.4*
25-29	337.5	286.6	*84.9*	173.1	157.8	*91.1*	164.4	128.8	*78.3*
30-34	329.0	287.5	*87.4*	168.9	157.4	*93.2*	160.1	130.2	*81.3*
35-39	318.0	286.3	*90.0*	162.5	154.8	*95.3*	155.6	131.4	*84.5*
40-44	370.9	337.3	*91.0*	188.2	172.2	*91.5*	182.6	165.1	*90.4*
45-49	376.2	340.8	*90.6*	189.8	172.0	*90.6*	186.4	168.8	*90.6*
50-54	384.4	335.7	*87.3*	192.1	165.6	*86.2*	192.3	170.1	*88.5*
55-59	399.1	299.7	*75.1*	198.8	149.2	*75.1*	200.4	150.5	*75.1*
60-64	362.8	155.0	*42.7*	177.9	79.2	*44.5*	184.9	75.8	*41.0*
65-69	254.2	25.2	*9.9*	119.8	17.0	*14.2*	134.4	8.2	*6.1*
70-74	213.5	8.9	*4.2*	95.6	6.5	*6.8*	117.9	2.4	*2.0*
75+	415.9	.	.	145.0	.	.	270.9	.	.

Explanations and sources: see p. 3.

[1] Excl. compulsory military service. [2] "De facto" population. [3] Incl. armed forces, Excl. conscripts. [4] "De jure" population. [5] Included armed forces and conscripts.

Explications et sources: voir p. 5.

[1] Non compris les militaires du contingent. [2] Population "de facto". [3] Y compris les forces armées, Excl. conscrits [4] Population "de jure". [5] Y compris les forces armées et les conscrits.

Explicaciones y fuentes: véase p. 7.

[1] Excl. a los militares en servicio obligatorio. [2] Población "de facto". [3] Incl. las fuerzas armadas, excl. los conscriptos. [4] Población "de jure". [5] Incluye las fuezas armadas y los conscriptos.

ECONOMICALLY ACTIVE POPULATION

POPULATION ACTIVE

POBLACION ECONOMICAMENTE ACTIVA

Total and economically active population by age group

Thousands

Population totale et population active par groupe d'âge

Milliers

Población total y población económicamente activa por grupo de edad

Millares

	Total			Men - Hommes - Hombres			Women - Femmes - Mujeres		
	Total population	Active population	Activity rate	Total population	Active population	Activity rate	Total population	Active population	Activity rate
	Population totale	Population active	Taux d'activité	Population totale	Population active	Taux d'activité	Population totale	Population active	Taux d'activité
	Población total	Población activa	Tasa de actividad	Población total	Población activa	Tasa de actividad	Población total	Población activa	Tasa de actividad
			%			%			%
France (2008) BA (15+) [1]									
Total	.	**27 983.5**	.	.	**14 687.9**	.	.	**13 295.6**	.
Total (15+)	49 805.6	27 983.3	56.2	23 783.9	14 688.0	61.8	26 021.6	13 295.6	51.1
15-19	3 744.2	601.4	16.1	1 899.5	367.7	19.4	1 844.6	233.8	12.7
20-24	3 762.5	2 342.6	62.3	1 865.3	1 240.1	66.5	1 897.2	1 102.5	58.1
25-29	3 841.7	3 338.1	86.9	1 889.7	1 759.6	93.1	1 952.0	1 578.6	80.9
30-34	3 850.0	3 448.1	89.6	1 903.9	1 834.8	96.4	1 946.1	1 613.2	82.9
35-39	4 308.3	3 895.0	90.4	2 130.6	2 051.0	96.3	2 177.6	1 844.0	84.7
40-44	4 326.6	3 907.7	90.3	2 119.5	2 032.1	95.9	2 207.1	1 875.7	85.0
45-49	4 253.8	3 814.6	89.7	2 082.8	1 963.7	94.3	2 171.0	1 850.8	85.3
50-54	4 104.0	3 488.5	85.0	1 990.4	1 801.9	90.5	2 113.6	1 686.6	79.8
55-59	4 092.6	2 421.9	59.2	1 988.6	1 233.4	62.0	2 104.0	1 188.6	56.5
60-64	3 405.0	577.7	17.0	1 646.9	314.0	19.1	1 758.1	263.7	15.0
65-69	2 346.9	98.1	4.2	1 107.6	59.3	5.4	1 239.3	38.8	3.1
70-74	2 382.1	30.8	1.3	1 063.2	19.7	1.9	1 318.9	11.1	0.8
75+	5 034.8	17.5	0.3	1 914.2	9.9	0.5	3 120.6	7.7	0.2
?	353.1	1.3	0.4	181.7	0.8	0.4	171.5	0.5	0.3
Germany (2008) BA (15+) [2] [3]									
Total	**82 135**	**41 875**	**51.0**	**40 231**	**22 878**	**56.9**	**41 904**	**18 997**	**45.3**
Total (15+)	71 215	41 874	58.8	34 629	22 879	66.1	36 588	18 997	51.9
0-9	7 052	.	.	3 596	.	.	3 456	.	.
10-14	3 867	.	.	2 007	.	.	1 860	.	.
15-19	4 655	1 514	32.5	2 425	862	35.5	2 230	652	29.2
20-24	4 878	3 497	71.7	2 517	1 880	74.7	2 361	1 617	68.5
25-29	4 948	4 033	81.5	2 486	2 156	86.7	2 462	1 877	76.2
30-34	4 683	4 007	85.6	2 357	2 229	94.6	2 326	1 777	76.4
35-39	5 822	5 134	88.2	2 956	2 839	96.0	2 866	2 295	80.1
40-44	7 232	6 491	89.8	3 686	3 524	95.6	3 547	2 967	83.6
45-49	6 572	5 855	89.1	3 310	3 119	94.2	3 262	2 737	83.9
50-54	5 837	4 978	85.3	2 910	2 644	90.9	2 927	2 334	79.7
55-59	5 402	4 065	75.2	2 664	2 218	83.3	2 738	1 847	67.5
60-64	4 363	1 651	37.8	2 146	1 001	46.6	2 217	651	29.4
65-69	5 404	413	7.6	2 566	254	9.9	2 839	160	5.6
70-74	4 499	164	3.6	2 084	106	5.1	2 415	58	2.4
75+	6 920	72	1.0	2 522	47	1.9	4 398	25	0.6
Greece (IV-VI.2008) BA (15+) [1] [4]									
Total	**10 776.1**	**4 939.7**	**45.8**	**5 297.7**	**2 925.5**	**55.2**	**5 478.4**	**2 014.2**	**36.8**
Total (15+)	9 230.1	4 939.7	53.5	4 502.6	2 925.5	65.0	4 727.5	2 014.2	42.6
0-9	950.1	.	.	483.6	.	.	466.4	.	.
10-14	596.0	.	.	311.5	.	.	284.5	.	.
15-19	557.1	48.8	8.8	275.3	28.5	10.3	281.8	20.3	7.2
20-24	594.4	299.8	50.4	303.8	168.3	55.4	290.6	131.5	45.2
25-29	782.7	659.9	84.3	408.2	373.6	91.5	374.5	286.2	76.4
30-34	835.2	712.2	85.3	423.8	412.1	97.2	411.4	300.1	72.9
35-39	828.6	710.2	85.7	430.9	418.6	97.1	397.7	291.7	73.3
40-44	847.6	718.5	84.8	414.6	403.3	97.3	432.9	315.2	72.8
45-49	764.4	614.7	80.4	379.9	362.3	95.4	384.5	252.4	65.6
50-54	735.2	522.2	71.0	359.1	318.6	88.7	376.1	203.6	54.1
55-59	634.7	360.1	56.7	309.0	236.5	76.5	325.8	123.7	38.0
60-64	648.3	207.8	32.0	310.6	140.9	45.4	337.7	66.9	19.8
65-69	529.1	53.1	10.0	232.2	38.0	16.4	296.9	15.1	5.1
70-74	570.3	21.8	3.8	263.6	16.3	6.2	306.7	5.5	1.8
75+	902.5	10.6	1.2	391.7	8.4	2.2	510.8	2.2	0.4
Hungary (2008) BA (15-74) [1] [4]									
Total	.	**4 208.6**	.	.	**2 285.1**	.	.	**1 923.5**	.
Total (15+)	7 710.2	4 208.6	54.6	3 688.6	2 285.1	62.0	4 021.6	1 923.5	47.8
15-19	600.5	26.2	4.4	304.5	17.3	5.7	296.0	8.9	3.0
20-24	627.7	280.7	44.7	314.3	159.8	50.8	313.4	120.9	38.6
25-29	729.3	570.4	78.2	370.5	326.8	88.2	358.8	243.6	67.9
30-34	821.5	652.5	79.4	413.4	384.6	93.0	408.1	267.9	65.6
35-39	742.0	618.9	83.4	376.5	345.4	91.7	365.5	273.5	74.8
40-44	597.3	508.8	85.2	295.7	263.1	89.0	301.6	245.7	81.5
45-49	622.1	507.1	81.5	297.5	248.7	83.6	324.6	258.4	79.6
50-54	802.4	599.2	74.7	386.9	293.7	75.9	415.5	305.5	73.5
55-59	694.7	339.8	48.9	318.9	186.0	58.3	375.8	153.8	40.9
60-64	556.7	74.3	13.3	243.2	41.7	17.1	313.5	32.6	10.4
65-69	513.2	24.5	4.8	214.7	13.9	6.5	298.5	10.6	3.6
70-74	402.8	6.2	1.5	152.5	4.1	2.7	250.3	2.1	0.8

Explanations and sources: see p. 3.

[1] "De facto" population. [2] Included armed forces and conscripts. [3] "De jure" population. [4] Excl. conscripts.

Explications et sources: voir p. 5.

[1] Population "de facto". [2] Y compris les forces armées et les conscrits. [3] Population "de jure". [4] Non compris les conscrits.

Explicaciones y fuentes: véase p. 7.

[1] Población "de facto". [2] Incluye las fuerzas armadas y los conscriptos. [3] Población "de jure". [4] Excl. los conscriptos.

1A   ECONOMICALLY ACTIVE POPULATION

POPULATION ACTIVE

POBLACION ECONOMICAMENTE ACTIVA

Total and economically active population by age group

Population totale et population active par groupe d'âge

Población total y población económicamente activa por grupo de edad

Thousands — Milliers — Millares

	Total			Men - Hommes - Hombres			Women - Femmes - Mujeres		
	Total population Population totale Población total	Active population Population active Población activa	Activity rate Taux d'activité Tasa de actividad %	Total population Population totale Población total	Active population Population active Población activa	Activity rate Taux d'activité Tasa de actividad %	Total population Population totale Población total	Active population Population active Población activa	Activity rate Taux d'activité Tasa de actividad %
Iceland (2008) BA (16-74) [1]									
Total	.	**184.1**	.	.	**100.4**	.	.	**83.7**	.
16-19	18.5	13.9	75.1	9.6	6.8	70.8	8.9	7.1	79.8
20-24	21.7	17.7	81.6	11.3	9.4	83.2	10.4	8.4	80.8
25-29	23.8	20.2	84.9	12.5	11.6	92.8	11.3	8.5	75.2
30-34	21.6	19.6	90.7	11.4	10.8	94.7	10.3	8.7	84.5
35-39	21.5	19.6	91.2	11.4	11.0	96.5	10.1	8.6	85.1
40-44	22.4	20.3	90.6	11.5	11.0	95.7	10.9	9.4	86.2
45-49	22.5	20.5	91.1	11.7	11.0	94.0	10.8	9.5	88.0
50-54	20.5	18.8	91.7	10.6	10.2	96.2	9.9	8.6	86.9
55-59	17.6	15.9	90.3	9.1	8.6	94.5	8.5	7.3	85.9
60-64	14.1	11.0	78.0	7.2	6.1	84.7	7.0	4.8	68.6
65-69	10.1	5.1	50.5	4.9	2.9	59.2	5.1	2.2	43.1
70-74	8.6	1.5	17.4	4.1	0.9	22.0	4.5	0.6	13.3
Ireland (IV-VI.2008) BA (15+) [2]									
Total	**4 422.1**	**2 223.9**	*50.3*	**2 206.4**	**1 264.9**	*57.3*	**2 215.6**	**959.1**	*43.3*
Total (15+)	*3 510.2*	*2 224.0*	*63.4*	*1 739.2*	*1 264.9*	*72.7*	*1 770.7*	*959.1*	*54.2*
0-9	631.1			323.1			308.0		
10-14	280.9			144.1			136.8		
15-19	283.9	69.2	24.4	144.6	37.1	25.7	139.3	32.1	23.0
20-24	334.3	249.6	74.7	165.9	131.1	79.0	168.4	118.5	70.4
25-29	416.7	358.8	86.1	209.4	191.9	91.6	207.2	167.0	80.6
30-34	367.0	307.0	83.7	185.3	172.2	92.9	181.7	134.8	74.2
35-39	342.0	280.5	82.0	173.9	162.6	93.5	168.1	117.9	70.1
40-44	310.2	248.1	80.0	155.8	143.4	92.0	154.4	104.8	67.9
45-49	286.1	230.2	80.5	143.3	130.8	91.3	142.7	99.4	69.7
50-54	257.2	194.0	75.4	129.1	112.1	86.8	128.0	81.9	64.0
55-59	232.0	145.7	62.8	117.0	88.2	75.4	115.0	57.4	49.9
60-64	199.2	94.0	47.2	100.4	60.5	60.3	98.8	33.4	33.8
65-69	148.8	27.0	18.1	73.6	18.7	25.4	75.2	8.3	11.0
70-74	120.8	11.6	9.6	57.5	9.2	16.0	63.3	2.4	3.8
75+	212.0	8.3	3.9	83.4	7.1	8.5	128.6	1.2	0.9
Italy (2008) BA (15+) [3] [4]									
Total	**59 336.4**	**25 096.6**	*42.3*	**28 848.7**	**14 884.0**	*51.6*	**30 487.7**	**10 212.7**	*33.5*
Total (15+)	*50 956.1*	*25 096.6*	*49.3*	*24 543.2*	*14 884.0*	*60.6*	*26 412.9*	*10 212.6*	*38.7*
0-9	5 683.7			2 913.0			2 770.7		
10-14	2 696.6			1 392.6			1 304.0		
15-19	2 977.3	327.7	11.0	1 529.3	205.5	13.4	1 448.0	122.2	8.4
20-24	3 092.2	1 549.4	50.1	1 568.1	907.7	57.9	1 524.1	641.8	42.1
25-29	3 602.6	2 604.7	72.3	1 810.6	1 463.4	80.8	1 792.1	1 141.2	63.7
30-34	4 434.0	3 572.9	80.6	2 234.9	2 046.4	91.6	2 199.0	1 526.6	69.4
35-39	4 799.1	3 907.4	81.4	2 419.1	2 270.8	93.9	2 380.0	1 636.6	68.8
40-44	4 896.7	3 934.7	80.4	2 457.5	2 304.4	93.8	2 439.3	1 630.3	66.8
45-49	4 340.9	3 412.0	78.6	2 158.9	2 021.2	93.6	2 181.9	1 390.9	63.7
50-54	3 874.5	2 842.0	73.4	1 910.3	1 714.6	89.8	1 964.2	1 127.4	57.4
55-59	3 741.7	1 839.1	49.2	1 828.8	1 140.5	62.4	1 912.8	698.5	36.5
60-64	3 422.8	706.2	20.6	1 656.0	496.7	30.0	1 766.8	209.5	11.9
65-69	3 277.5	254.6	7.8	1 546.3	196.3	12.7	1 731.2	58.3	3.4
70-74	2 877.6	94.2	3.3	1 303.2	74.0	5.7	1 574.4	20.2	1.3
75+	5 619.2	51.7	0.9	2 120.1	42.5	2.0	3 499.2	9.2	0.3
Latvia (2008) BA (15-74) [2] [3]									
Total	**2 270.9**	**1 215.8**	*53.5*	**1 046.9**	**621.8**	*59.4*	**1 224.0**	**594.0**	*48.5*
Total (15+)	*1 958.6*	*1 215.8*	*62.1*	*887.2*	*621.8*	*70.1*	*1 071.4*	*594.0*	*55.4*
0-9	203.4			102.2			101.2		
10-14	108.9			57.5			51.4		
15-19	167.5	22.0	13.1	85.5	14.4	16.8	82.1	7.6	9.2
20-24	186.0	130.0	69.9	94.6	73.9	78.1	91.4	56.2	61.4
25-29	163.2	142.9	87.6	83.0	78.5	94.5	80.1	64.4	80.4
30-34	158.2	137.0	86.6	80.0	73.8	92.3	78.2	63.2	80.8
35-39	159.4	147.0	92.2	79.3	75.2	94.8	80.1	71.8	89.6
40-44	157.1	143.6	91.4	76.6	71.1	92.8	80.5	72.5	90.1
45-49	172.3	153.8	89.3	82.0	72.9	88.9	90.3	80.8	89.6
50-54	152.9	132.0	86.3	70.5	62.7	88.9	82.4	69.4	84.2
55-59	139.4	112.3	80.5	61.4	52.3	85.2	78.1	60.0	76.8
60-64	111.7	47.0	42.0	46.6	22.2	47.8	65.2	24.7	37.9
65-69	127.7	34.9	27.3	49.4	16.9	34.3	78.3	18.0	22.9
70-74	100.9	13.4	13.3	35.2	7.9	22.4	65.7	5.5	8.4
75+	162.2			43.3			118.9		

Explanations and sources: see p. 3.

[1] Excl. armed forces and conscripts. [2] "De jure" population. [3] Excl. conscripts. [4] "De facto" population.

Explications et sources: voir p. 5.

[1] Non compris les forces armées et les conscrits. [2] Population "de jure". [3] Non compris les conscrits. [4] Population "de facto".

Explicaciones y fuentes: véase p. 7.

[1] Excl. las fuerzas armadas y los conscriptos. [2] Población "de jure". [3] Excl. los conscriptos. [4] Población "de facto".

ECONOMICALLY ACTIVE POPULATION

Total and economically active population by age group

Thousands

POPULATION ACTIVE

Population totale et population active par groupe d'âge

Milliers

POBLACION ECONOMICAMENTE ACTIVA

Población total y población económicamente activa por grupo de edad

Millares

	Total			Men - Hommes - Hombres			Women - Femmes - Mujeres		
	Total population / Population totale / Población total	Active population / Population active / Población activa	Activity rate / Taux d'activité / Tasa de actividad %	Total population / Population totale / Población total	Active population / Population active / Población activa	Activity rate / Taux d'activité / Tasa de actividad %	Total population / Population totale / Población total	Active population / Population active / Población activa	Activity rate / Taux d'activité / Tasa de actividad %
Lithuania (2008) BA (15+) [1] [2]									
Total	**3 366.4**	**1 614.3**	*48.0*	**1 567.0**	**818.1**	*52.2*	**1 799.4**	**796.1**	*44.2*
Total (15+)	*2 849.4*	*1 614.3*	*56.7*	*1 301.9*	*818.1*	*62.8*	*1 547.5*	*796.1*	*51.4*
0-9	321.8	.	.	162.9	.	.	158.9	.	.
10-14	195.2	.	.	102.3	.	.	93.0	.	.
15-19	261.5	13.8	*5.3*	133.3	8.2	*6.2*	128.2	5.6	*4.4*
20-24	273.3	150.8	*55.2*	139.3	88.2	*63.4*	134.1	62.6	*46.7*
25-29	230.0	189.4	*82.4*	117.5	100.3	*85.3*	112.5	89.2	*79.2*
30-34	223.0	191.1	*85.7*	111.2	98.1	*88.2*	111.8	93.0	*83.2*
35-39	246.1	216.4	*87.9*	121.1	108.6	*89.7*	125.0	107.8	*86.2*
40-44	251.2	221.1	*88.0*	122.4	108.7	*88.8*	128.7	112.4	*87.3*
45-49	266.6	232.1	*87.1*	126.3	110.9	*87.8*	140.3	121.2	*86.4*
50-54	214.7	174.4	*81.2*	99.0	82.7	*83.5*	115.6	91.7	*79.3*
55-59	192.3	131.9	*68.6*	84.7	62.9	*74.3*	107.6	69.0	*64.1*
60-64	157.6	62.6	*39.7*	65.8	31.8	*48.4*	91.9	30.7	*33.4*
65-69	164.2	22.9	*14.0*	64.0	13.7	*21.4*	100.1	9.2	*9.2*
70-74	145.5	5.8	*4.0*	51.5	2.9	*5.5*	93.9	3.0	*3.2*
75+	223.5	1.9	*0.9*	65.8	1.0	*1.6*	157.8	0.9	*0.6*
Luxembourg (2008) BA (15+) [3]									
Total	**475.1**	**218.1**	*45.9*	**235.8**	**123.3**	*52.3*	**239.2**	**94.8**	*39.6*
Total (15+)	*388.1*	*218.1*	*56.2*	*191.2*	*123.3*	*64.5*	*196.9*	*94.8*	*48.2*
0-9	54.7	.	.	28.8	.	.	25.8	.	.
10-14	32.3	.	.	15.8	.	.	16.5	.	.
15-19	28.0	2.5	*9.0*	14.2	1.7	*12.0*	13.8	0.8	*6.0*
20-24	27.8	14.8	*53.0*	14.1	7.5	*53.6*	13.8	7.2	*52.4*
25-29	32.5	26.8	*82.6*	16.2	13.7	*85.0*	16.3	13.1	*80.2*
30-34	35.3	30.6	*86.7*	17.6	17.0	*96.6*	17.7	13.6	*76.9*
35-39	39.3	34.0	*86.6*	19.6	19.4	*99.0*	19.7	14.6	*74.1*
40-44	41.3	34.6	*84.0*	21.0	19.9	*94.6*	20.2	14.7	*72.9*
45-49	37.4	31.0	*82.8*	19.1	17.9	*94.1*	18.4	13.0	*71.0*
50-54	32.7	25.2	*77.0*	16.5	15.2	*92.0*	16.2	10.0	*61.7*
55-59	27.9	14.6	*52.2*	14.4	8.6	*59.8*	13.6	6.0	*44.2*
60-64	22.5	3.4	*15.1*	11.4	2.0	*17.5*	11.1	1.4	*12.7*
65+	63.3	0.6	*0.9*	27.2	0.3	*0.9*	36.1	0.3	*0.9*
Macedonia, The Former Yugoslav Rep. of (2008) BA (15+)									
Total	.	**919.4**	.	.	**561.7**	.	.	**357.7**	.
Total (15+)	*1 633.3*	*919.4*	*56.3*	*816.8*	*561.7*	*68.8*	*816.6*	*357.7*	*43.8*
15-19	159.3	25.9	*16.2*	82.0	16.8	*20.5*	77.4	9.1	*11.7*
20-24	165.0	90.6	*54.9*	84.6	55.4	*65.5*	80.4	35.2	*43.8*
25-29	161.6	124.6	*77.1*	83.2	74.7	*89.7*	78.4	49.9	*63.7*
30-34	153.3	122.5	*79.9*	78.2	73.9	*94.5*	75.1	48.6	*64.7*
35-39	147.7	120.1	*81.3*	74.8	71.4	*95.5*	73.0	48.8	*66.8*
40-44	149.4	119.9	*80.3*	75.9	70.2	*92.6*	73.6	49.7	*67.6*
45-49	144.6	113.7	*78.6*	73.5	67.9	*92.4*	71.1	45.8	*64.4*
50-54	139.4	99.3	*71.2*	70.7	60.9	*86.1*	68.7	38.4	*55.9*
55-59	123.3	67.8	*55.0*	60.1	45.7	*76.0*	63.1	22.1	*35.0*
60-64	91.1	27.2	*29.8*	43.5	19.5	*44.8*	47.6	7.6	*16.1*
65+	198.5	7.8	*3.9*	90.3	5.3	*5.9*	108.3	2.5	*2.3*
Malta (2008) BA (15+)									
Total	**413.6**	**171.4**	*41.4*	**205.6**	**113.9**	*55.4*	**208.1**	**57.5**	*27.6*
Total (15+)	*347.3*	*171.4*	*49.3*	*171.6*	*113.9*	*66.4*	*175.7*	*57.5*	*32.7*
0-9	39.4	.	.	20.1	.	.	19.3	.	.
10-14	27.0	.	.	13.9	.	.	13.1	.	.
15-19	30.2	9.1	*30.3*	15.2	4.9	*32.4*	14.9	4.2	*28.1*
20-24	28.0	21.2	*75.7*	14.6	11.5	*79.1*	13.4	9.7	*72.1*
25-29	29.1	24.7	*84.9*	15.2	14.6	*96.1*	13.9	10.1	*72.6*
30-34	31.9	24.8	*77.6*	16.4	15.8	*96.5*	15.5	8.9	*57.6*
35-39	24.5	17.0	*69.6*	12.2	11.7	*96.3*	12.3	5.3	*43.1*
40-44	27.0	19.2	*71.1*	14.3	13.5	*94.8*	12.8	5.7	*44.6*
45-49	29.3	18.3	*62.5*	14.4	13.2	*91.7*	14.9	5.1	*34.3*
50-54	30.8	18.1	*58.9*	15.9	13.9	*87.3*	14.9	4.3	*28.6*
55-59	29.1	13.7	*47.0*	14.3	10.6	*74.0*	14.8	3.1	*20.9*
60-64	30.2	4.3	*14.1*	14.8	3.3	*22.5*	15.4	0.9	*6.0*
65-69	16.6	0.6	*3.5*	7.6	0.5	*6.6*	9.0	0.1	*0.9*
70-74	16.3	0.3	*2.0*	7.2	0.3	*3.7*	9.2	0.1	*0.6*
75+	24.3	0.0	*0.1*	9.6	0.0	-	14.7	0.0	*0.2*

Explanations and sources: see p. 3.
[1] Excl. conscripts. [2] "De facto" population. [3] "De jure" population.

Explications et sources: voir p. 5.
[1] Non compris les conscrits. [2] Population "de facto". [3] Population "de jure".

Explicaciones y fuentes: véase p. 7.
[1] Excl. los conscriptos. [2] Población "de facto". [3] Población "de jure".

1A

ECONOMICALLY ACTIVE POPULATION	POPULATION ACTIVE	POBLACION ECONOMICAMENTE ACTIVA
Total and economically active population by age group	Population totale et population active par groupe d'âge	Población total y población económicamente activa por grupo de edad
Thousands	Milliers	Millares

	Total			Men - Hommes - Hombres			Women - Femmes - Mujeres		
	Total population / Population totale / Población total	Active population / Population active / Población activa	Activity rate / Taux d'activité / Tasa de actividad	Total population / Population totale / Población total	Active population / Population active / Población activa	Activity rate / Taux d'activité / Tasa de actividad	Total population / Population totale / Población total	Active population / Population active / Población activa	Activity rate / Taux d'activité / Tasa de actividad
			%			%			%
Moldova, Republic of (2008) BA (15+) [1]									
Total	.	**1 302.8**	.	.	**658.8**	.	.	**644.0**	.
15-19		32.8			20.1			12.8	
20-24		107.1			58.8			48.3	
25-29		125.7			65.5			60.2	
30-34		140.2			73.0			67.2	
35-39		148.0			70.1			77.9	
40-44		169.1			78.3			90.8	
45-49		214.7			102.9			111.8	
50-54		151.3			72.1			79.2	
55-59		133.2			72.4			60.7	
60-64		40.1			23.5			16.6	
65+		40.7			22.0			18.7	
Netherlands (2008) BA (15+)									
Total	.	**8 718**	.	.	**4 726**	.	.	**3 992**	.
Total (15+)	*13 275*	*8 717*	*65.7*	*6 536*	*4 723*	*72.3*	*6 739*	*3 991*	*59.2*
15-19	998	649	*65.0*	509	331	*65.0*	489	318	*65.0*
20-24	975	797	*81.7*	492	408	*82.9*	483	389	*80.5*
25-29	978	877	*89.7*	488	458	*93.9*	489	419	*85.7*
30-34	1 007	910	*90.4*	502	481	*95.8*	505	429	*85.0*
35-39	1 244	1 111	*89.3*	623	596	*95.7*	621	515	*82.9*
40-44	1 288	1 142	*88.7*	651	614	*94.3*	638	528	*82.8*
45-49	1 251	1 085	*86.7*	629	583	*92.7*	622	501	*80.5*
50-54	1 140	933	*81.8*	572	515	*90.0*	568	418	*73.6*
55-59	1 078	752	*69.8*	542	440	*81.2*	535	312	*58.3*
60-64	1 011	347	*34.3*	507	217	*42.8*	504	130	*25.8*
65-69	677	68	*10.0*	328	47	*14.3*	349	21	*6.0*
70-74	637	32	*5.0*	305	23	*7.5*	332	21	*6.0*
75+	991	14	*1.4*	388	10	*2.6*	604	3	*0.5*
Norway (2008) BA (15-74) [1]									
Total	.	**2 591**	.	.	**1 370**	.	.	**1 222**	.
Total (15+)	*3 505*	*2 591*	*73.9*	*1 777*	*1 369*	*77.0*	*1 728*	*1 222*	*70.7*
15-19	317	158	*49.8*	163	79	*48.5*	154	79	*51.3*
20-24	290	222	*76.6*	148	116	*78.4*	142	106	*74.6*
25-29	300	260	*86.7*	154	136	*88.3*	146	124	*84.9*
30-34	320	286	*89.4*	163	150	*92.0*	157	136	*86.6*
35-39	363	327	*90.1*	185	174	*94.1*	178	153	*86.0*
40-44	355	319	*89.9*	183	169	*92.3*	172	150	*87.2*
45-49	327	291	*89.0*	167	154	*92.2*	160	137	*85.6*
50-54	312	268	*85.9*	158	140	*88.6*	154	128	*83.1*
55-59	293	234	*79.9*	148	124	*83.8*	145	110	*75.9*
60-64	284	170	*59.9*	143	94	*65.7*	141	76	*53.9*
65-69	193	47	*24.4*	94	27	*28.7*	99	20	*20.2*
70-74	151	9	*6.0*	71	6	*8.5*	80	3	*3.8*
Poland (2008) BA (15+) [2][3]									
Total	.	**17 011**	.	.	**9 317**	.	.	**7 694**	.
Total (15+)	*31 373*	*17 011*	*54.2*	*14 868*	*9 317*	*62.7*	*16 509*	*7 693*	*46.6*
15-19	2 572	198	*7.7*	1 315	114	*8.7*	1 257	83	*6.6*
20-24	2 831	1 589	*56.1*	1 405	879	*62.6*	1 427	710	*49.8*
25-29	3 042	2 528	*83.1*	1 523	1 389	*91.2*	1 520	1 139	*74.9*
30-34	2 873	2 466	*85.8*	1 439	1 349	*93.7*	1 435	1 117	*77.8*
35-39	2 460	2 168	*88.1*	1 231	1 160	*94.2*	1 230	1 008	*82.0*
40-44	2 317	2 013	*86.9*	1 157	1 057	*91.4*	1 160	956	*82.4*
45-49	2 653	2 171	*81.8*	1 306	1 116	*85.5*	1 347	1 055	*78.3*
50-54	2 984	2 120	*71.0*	1 443	1 117	*77.4*	1 541	1 003	*65.1*
55-59	2 703	1 154	*42.7*	1 278	747	*58.5*	1 425	406	*28.5*
60-64	1 830	358	*19.6*	836	241	*28.8*	994	117	*11.8*
65-69	1 463	137	*9.4*	614	82	*13.4*	849	56	*6.6*
70-74	1 363	67	*4.9*	530	40	*7.5*	833	27	*3.2*
75+	2 282	42	*1.8*	791	26	*3.3*	1 491	16	*1.1*

Explanations and sources: see p. 3.
[1] "De jure" population. [2] Excl. conscripts. [3] "De facto" population.

Explications et sources: voir p. 5.
[1] Population "de jure". [2] Non compris les conscrits. [3] Population "de facto".

Explicaciones y fuentes: véase p. 7.
[1] Población "de jure". [2] Excl. los conscriptos. [3] Población "de facto".

ECONOMICALLY ACTIVE POPULATION

Total and economically active population by age group

Thousands

POPULATION ACTIVE

Population totale et population active par groupe d'âge

Milliers

POBLACION ECONOMICAMENTE ACTIVA

Población total y población económicamente activa por grupo de edad

Millares

	Total			Men - Hommes - Hombres			Women - Femmes - Mujeres		
	Total population	Active population	Activity rate	Total population	Active population	Activity rate	Total population	Active population	Activity rate
	Population totale	Population active	Taux d'activité	Population totale	Population active	Taux d'activité	Population totale	Population active	Taux d'activité
	Población total	Población activa	Tasa de actividad	Población total	Población activa	Tasa de actividad	Población total	Población activa	Tasa de actividad
			%			%			%
Portugal (2008) BA (15+) [1]									
Total	**10 622.7**	**5 624.9**	*53.0*	**5 141.3**	**2 991.4**	*58.2*	**5 481.3**	**2 633.4**	*48.0*
Total (15+)	*8 998.2*	*5 624.7*	*62.5*	*4 308.3*	*2 991.5*	*69.4*	*4 689.9*	*2 633.4*	*56.2*
0-9	1 092.0	.	.	560.9	.	.	531.1	.	.
10-14	532.6	.	.	272.1	.	.	260.5	.	.
15-19	578.4	90.9	*15.7*	295.6	54.9	*18.6*	282.8	36.0	*12.7*
20-24	642.9	416.6	*64.8*	327.9	222.0	*67.7*	314.9	194.6	*61.8*
25-29	763.8	673.5	*88.2*	386.0	349.5	*90.5*	377.7	324.1	*85.8*
30-34	863.7	790.8	*91.6*	435.1	414.0	*95.2*	428.7	376.8	*87.9*
35-39	798.4	725.7	*90.9*	400.0	378.9	*94.7*	398.4	346.8	*87.0*
40-44	784.8	697.4	*88.9*	387.0	367.3	*94.9*	397.8	330.1	*83.0*
45-49	769.7	669.6	*87.0*	377.2	350.5	*92.9*	392.5	319.1	*81.3*
50-54	686.5	550.9	*80.2*	332.2	299.0	*90.0*	354.3	251.8	*71.1*
55-59	670.0	425.2	*63.5*	323.0	234.0	*72.4*	347.0	191.2	*55.1*
60-64	587.0	258.2	*44.0*	271.6	140.7	*51.8*	315.4	117.5	*37.3*
65-69	499.7	132.2	*26.5*	228.3	71.9	*31.5*	271.4	60.3	*22.2*
70-74	495.0	96.2	*19.4*	216.1	54.0	*25.0*	279.0	42.2	*15.1*
75+	858.3	97.7	*11.4*	328.3	54.8	*16.7*	530.0	42.9	*8.1*
Roumanie (2008) BA (15+) [1]									
Total	**21 516.5**	**9 944.7**	*46.2*	**10 484.3**	**5 526.7**	*52.7*	**11 032.3**	**4 418.0**	*40.0*
Total (15+)	*18 244.2*	*9 944.7*	*54.5*	*8 805.1*	*5 526.7*	*62.8*	*9 439.0*	*4 418.0*	*46.8*
0-14	3 272.4	.	.	1 679.1	.	.	1 593.2	.	.
15-19	1 457.0	190.8	*13.1*	743.4	126.0	*17.0*	713.6	64.8	*9.1*
20-24	1 678.4	762.6	*45.4*	858.7	449.0	*52.3*	819.8	313.6	*38.3*
25-29	1 697.7	1 260.1	*74.2*	868.9	688.1	*79.2*	828.8	572.0	*69.0*
30-34	1 742.7	1 408.2	*80.8*	893.2	780.3	*87.4*	849.5	627.9	*73.9*
35-39	1 779.8	1 475.6	*82.9*	902.5	819.0	*90.8*	877.4	656.6	*74.8*
40-44	1 405.5	1 165.1	*82.9*	705.8	634.5	*89.9*	699.7	530.6	*75.8*
45-49	1 335.5	1 060.4	*79.4*	660.2	577.6	*87.5*	675.4	482.9	*71.5*
50-54	1 544.1	1 072.2	*69.4*	746.1	600.6	*80.5*	798.0	471.6	*59.1*
55-59	1 403.2	738.6	*52.6*	663.7	436.3	*65.7*	739.6	302.3	*40.9*
60-64	998.2	323.8	*32.4*	458.6	182.2	*39.7*	539.7	141.6	*26.2*
65-69	971.8	263.9	*27.2*	423.3	124.9	*29.5*	548.5	139.0	*25.3*
70-74	920.4	223.4	*24.3*	382.7	108.2	*28.3*	537.7	115.2	*21.4*
75+	1 309.7	-	.	498.1	-	.	811.5	-	.
Russian Federation (2008) BA (15-72) [1]									
Total	**141 956**	**75 756**	*53.4*	**65 679**	**38 681**	*58.9*	**76 277**	**37 076**	*48.6*
Total (15+)	*120 997*	*75 757*	*62.6*	*54 942*	*38 679*	*70.4*	*66 055*	*37 074*	*56.1*
0-9	14 133	.	.	7 249	.	.	6 884	.	.
10-14	6 826	.	.	3 488	.	.	3 338	.	.
15-19	9 734	1 728	*17.8*	4 967	1 031	*20.8*	4 767	696	*14.6*
20-24	12 668	8 335	*65.8*	6 410	4 600	*71.8*	6 258	3 735	*59.7*
25-29	11 684	9 812	*84.0*	5 857	5 282	*90.2*	5 827	4 530	*77.7*
30-34	10 586	9 355	*88.4*	5 234	4 871	*93.1*	5 352	4 483	*83.8*
35-39	9 778	8 766	*89.7*	4 815	4 458	*92.6*	4 963	4 308	*86.8*
40-44	9 602	9 257	*96.4*	4 630	4 506	*97.3*	4 972	4 751	*95.6*
45-49	11 819	10 882	*92.1*	5 571	5 180	*93.0*	6 248	5 702	*91.3*
50-54	11 072	9 169	*82.8*	5 026	4 306	*85.7*	6 046	4 863	*80.4*
55-59	9 475	5 729	*60.5*	4 126	3 063	*74.2*	5 349	2 665	*49.8*
60-64	5 336	1 554	*29.1*	2 197	830	*37.8*	3 139	724	*23.1*
65+	19 243	1 170	*6.1*	6 109	552	*9.0*	13 134	617	*4.7*
San Marino (XII.2008) E (15+)									
Total	.	**22.708**	.	.	**13.164**	.	.	**9.544**	.
15-19	.	0.177	.	.	0.128	.	.	0.049	.
20-24	.	1.056	.	.	0.620	.	.	0.436	.
25-29	.	2.210	.	.	1.232	.	.	0.978	.
30-34	.	3.413	.	.	1.896	.	.	1.517	.
35-39	.	4.089	.	.	2.426	.	.	1.663	.
40-44	.	4.040	.	.	2.367	.	.	1.673	.
45-49	.	3.281	.	.	1.918	.	.	1.363	.
50-54	.	2.346	.	.	1.345	.	.	1.001	.
55-59	.	1.674	.	.	0.998	.	.	0.676	.
60-64	.	0.361	.	.	0.198	.	.	0.163	.
65-69	.	0.039	.	.	0.019	.	.	0.020	.
70-74	.	0.015	.	.	0.013	.	.	0.002	.
75+	.	0.007	.	.	0.004	.	.	0.003	.

Explanations and sources: see p. 3.

[1] "De jure" population.

Explications et sources: voir p. 5.

[1] Population "de jure".

Explicaciones y fuentes: véase p. 7.

[1] Población "de jure".

1A ECONOMICALLY ACTIVE POPULATION / POPULATION ACTIVE / POBLACION ECONOMICAMENTE ACTIVA

Total and economically active population by age group — Population totale et population active par groupe d'âge — Población total y población económicamente activa por grupo de edad

Thousands — Milliers — Millares

	Total — Population totale — Población total	Active population — Population active — Población activa	Activity rate — Taux d'activité — Tasa de actividad %	Total population — Population totale — Población total	Active population — Population active — Población activa	Activity rate — Taux d'activité — Tasa de actividad %	Total population — Population totale — Población total	Active population — Population active — Población activa	Activity rate — Taux d'activité — Tasa de actividad %
	Total			**Men - Hommes - Hombres**			**Women - Femmes - Mujeres**		
Serbia (X.2008) BA (15+)									
Total	7 528.3	3 267.1	43.4	3 646.5	1 828.8	50.2	3 881.8	1 438.3	37.1
Total (15+)	6 350.3	3 267.1	51.4	3 030.2	1 828.8	60.4	3 320.1	1 438.3	43.3
0-9	712.1			366.7			345.4		
10-14	465.8			242.7			223.2		
15-19	433.0	63.8	14.7	225.1	39.8	17.7	207.9	24.0	11.5
20-24	465.1	228.0	49.0	236.5	133.8	56.6	228.6	94.2	41.2
25-29	462.5	343.7	74.3	245.8	202.1	82.2	216.6	141.6	65.4
30-34	441.5	371.4	84.1	218.9	200.8	91.7	222.6	170.6	76.7
35-39	437.8	385.4	88.0	215.7	204.5	94.8	222.1	180.9	81.4
40-44	466.0	393.9	84.5	226.7	207.4	91.5	239.3	186.5	77.9
45-49	531.8	425.7	80.1	250.3	218.1	87.2	281.5	207.6	73.7
50-54	628.7	447.5	71.2	307.4	246.3	80.1	321.3	201.2	62.6
55-59	640.1	323.6	50.6	309.6	203.6	65.8	330.5	119.9	36.3
60-64	429.7	111.2	25.9	194.1	73.6	37.9	235.6	37.6	15.9
65-69	425.2	75.4	17.7	189.1	41.9	22.2	236.1	33.4	14.1
70-74	419.5	56.3	13.4	184.8	32.2	17.4	234.7	24.1	10.3
75+	569.5	41.2	7.2	226.2	24.5	10.8	343.3	16.7	4.9
Slovakia (2008) BA (15+)									
Total	.	2 691.2	.	.	1 488.3	.	.	1 202.8	.
Total (15+)	4 536.8	2 691.3	59.3	2 180.0	1 488.3	68.3	2 357.3	1 203.1	51.0
15-19	395.3	28.7	7.3	201.9	18.4	9.1	193.5	10.3	5.3
20-24	439.4	241.1	54.9	224.1	142.0	63.4	215.3	99.1	46.0
25-29	466.4	384.6	82.5	237.9	224.2	94.2	228.6	160.4	70.2
30-34	453.3	388.2	85.6	230.8	220.3	95.5	222.5	167.9	75.5
35-39	370.9	337.6	91.0	187.8	181.5	96.6	183.1	156.1	85.3
40-44	377.4	350.2	92.8	189.2	176.9	93.5	188.2	173.3	92.1
45-49	387.1	351.8	90.9	193.1	177.7	92.0	194.0	174.0	89.7
50-54	404.5	346.9	85.8	197.5	174.0	88.1	207.0	172.9	83.5
55-59	350.3	206.7	59.0	166.5	131.6	79.0	183.9	75.2	40.9
60-64	249.0	45.0	18.1	111.3	35.0	31.4	137.7	10.0	7.3
65-69	203.1	7.5	3.7	85.1	5.1	6.0	118.1	2.4	2.0
70-74	165.7	2.2	1.3	64.3	1.1	1.7	101.4	1.1	1.1
75+	274.4	0.8	0.3	90.5	0.5	0.6	184.0	0.4	0.2
Slovenia (IV-VI.2008) BA (15+) [1] [2]									
Total	2 026	1 033	51.0	1 001	559	55.9	1 025	474	46.2
Total (15+)	1 745	1 033	59.2	856	559	65.3	889	474	53.3
0-9	188			95			889		
10-14	93			49			93		
15-19	115	20	17.2	59	12	19.9	55	8	14.1
20-24	141	85	60.6	76	51	66.8	65	35	53.5
25-29	149	132	88.6	76	70	91.8	73	62	85.2
30-34	146	136	93.2	76	71	94.4	73	65	92.0
35-39	154	143	92.9	80	75	93.4	73	68	92.5
40-44	155	144	92.8	80	76	94.3	74	68	91.1
45-49	158	144	91.2	79	73	91.7	78	71	90.8
50-54	149	120	80.1	74	60	81.1	75	59	79.2
55-59	150	70	47.0	78	49	63.0	71	21	29.4
60-64	104	19	18.1	48	11	23.2	56	8	13.4
65-69	97	10	10.0	47	6	12.2	50	4	8.0
70-74	89	7	8.0	34	4	10.7	56	4	6.3
75+	139	4	3.1	48	2	3.6	91	3	2.7
Suisse (IV-VI.2008) BA (15+) [3]									
Total	.	4 375	.	.	2 356	.	.	2 020	.
Total (15+)	6 417	4 375	68.2	3 122	2 356	75.5	3 295	2 020	61.3
15-19	455	248	54.5	230	131	56.9	224	117	52.0
20-24	452	361	79.9	231	183	79.3	221	178	80.5
25-29	484	436	90.1	242	224	92.9	242	212	87.4
30-34	513	459	89.6	261	256	97.9	252	204	80.9
35-39	587	528	90.0	288	282	98.2	299	246	82.2
40-44	647	580	89.6	317	307	96.9	330	273	82.6
45-49	593	539	90.9	308	294	95.5	286	246	86.0
50-54	519	458	88.2	263	246	93.4	256	212	82.9
55-59	477	397	83.2	240	216	90.0	237	181	76.4
60-64	446	251	56.3	218	145	66.8	228	106	46.3
65-69	351	66	18.8	153	38	25.0	198	28	14.1
70-74	293	28	9.7	129	18	14.2	164	10	6.2
75+	601	24	4.0	242	14	6.0	359	10	2.7

Explanations and sources: see p. 3.
[1] Excl. conscripts. [2] "De facto" population. [3] Excl. armed forces and conscripts.

Explications et sources: voir p. 5.
[1] Non compris les conscrits. [2] Population "de facto". [3] Non compris les forces armées et les conscrits.

Explicaciones y fuentes: véase p. 7.
[1] Excl. los conscriptos. [2] Población "de facto". [3] Excl. las fuerzas armadas y los conscriptos.

ECONOMICALLY ACTIVE POPULATION

POPULATION ACTIVE

POBLACION ECONOMICAMENTE ACTIVA

Total and economically active population by age group

Population totale et population active par groupe d'âge

Población total y población económicamente activa por grupo de edad

Thousands — Milliers — Millares

	Total			Men - Hommes - Hombres			Women - Femmes - Mujeres		
	Total population / Population totale / Población total	Active population / Population active / Población activa	Activity rate / Taux d'activité / Tasa de actividad %	Total population / Population totale / Población total	Active population / Population active / Población activa	Activity rate / Taux d'activité / Tasa de actividad %	Total population / Population totale / Población total	Active population / Population active / Población activa	Activity rate / Taux d'activité / Tasa de actividad %
Sweden (2008) BA (15-74) [1]									
Total	.	**4 898**	.	.	**2 574**	.	.	**2 324**	.
Total (15+)	*6 880*	*4 896*	*71.2*	*3 478*	*2 573*	*74.0*	*3 400*	*2 325*	*68.4*
15-19	639	217	34.0	329	99	30.1	310	118	38.1
20-24	568	416	73.2	290	223	76.9	277	193	69.7
25-29	557	480	86.2	285	257	90.2	272	224	82.4
30-34	587	537	91.5	300	284	94.7	288	253	87.8
35-39	625	578	92.5	318	303	95.3	307	276	89.9
40-44	673	621	92.3	344	326	94.8	329	295	89.7
45-49	595	539	90.6	302	280	92.7	292	259	88.7
50-54	582	514	88.3	294	265	90.1	288	249	86.5
55-59	592	495	83.6	297	257	86.5	295	238	80.7
60-64	629	396	63.0	315	212	67.3	314	184	58.6
65-69	471	81	17.2	233	51	21.9	238	30	12.6
70-74	362	22	6.1	171	16	9.4	190	6	3.2
Turkey (2008) BA (15+) [2]									
Total	.	**23 805**	.	.	**17 475**	.	.	**6 330**	.
Total (15+)	*50 772*	*23 805*	*46.9*	*24 917*	*17 475*	*70.1*	*25 855*	*6 330*	*24.5*
15-19	6 151	1 681	27.3	3 209	1 177	36.7	2 942	504	17.1
20-24	5 340	2 701	50.6	2 408	1 728	71.8	2 932	973	33.2
25-29	6 350	3 979	62.7	3 161	2 918	92.3	3 189	1 061	33.3
30-34	5 664	3 598	63.5	2 864	2 715	94.8	2 800	883	31.5
35-39	5 221	3 324	63.7	2 617	2 480	94.8	2 604	844	32.4
40-44	4 615	2 832	61.4	2 331	2 177	93.4	2 284	655	28.7
45-49	4 185	2 209	52.8	2 099	1 694	80.7	2 086	515	24.7
50-54	3 536	1 500	42.4	1 766	1 141	64.6	1 770	359	20.3
55-59	2 782	894	32.1	1 374	663	48.3	1 408	231	16.4
60-64	2 120	523	24.7	996	375	37.7	1 124	148	13.2
65+	4 808	564	11.7	2 092	407	19.5	2 716	157	5.8
Ukraine (2008) BA (15-70) [3]									
Total	.	**22 397.4**	.	.	**11 618.6**	.	.	**10 778.8**	.
United Kingdom (IV-VI.2008) BA (16+)									
Total	**60 540**	**31 118**	*51.4*	**29 755**	**16 872**	*56.7*	**30 786**	**14 246**	*46.3*
0-9	7 071	.	.	3 617	.	.	3 454	.	.
10-15	3 687	.	.	1 896	.	.	1 790	.	.
16-19	3 898	1 698	43.6	1 997	873	43.7	1 901	824	43.3
20-24	4 137	3 097	74.9	2 100	1 679	80.0	2 037	1 418	69.6
25-29	4 044	3 429	84.8	2 021	1 864	92.2	2 023	1 565	77.4
30-34	3 805	3 228	84.8	1 886	1 775	94.1	1 919	1 453	75.7
35-39	4 425	3 743	84.6	2 184	2 025	92.7	2 369	1 718	76.7
40-44	4 691	4 029	85.9	2 323	2 145	92.3	2 369	1 884	79.5
45-49	4 318	3 731	86.4	2 127	1 940	91.2	2 191	1 791	81.7
50-54	3 782	3 126	82.7	1 867	1 629	87.3	1 915	1 498	78.2
55-59	3 627	2 635	72.6	1 784	1 428	80.0	1 843	1 207	65.5
60-64	3 604	1 694	47.0	1 759	1 056	60.0	1 845	637	34.5
65-69	2 733	471	17.2	1 315	295	22.4	1 418	176	12.4
70-74	2 365	167	7.1	1 107	112	10.1	1 258	55	4.4
75+	4 355	70	1.6	1 772	51	2.9	2 583	20	0.8

Explanations and sources: see p. 3.

[1] "De jure" population. [2] Excl. armed forces. [3] "De facto" population.

Explications et sources: voir p. 5.

[1] Population "de jure". [2] Non compris les forces armées. [3] Population "de facto".

Explicaciones y fuentes: véase p. 7.

[1] Población "de jure". [2] Excl. las fuerzas armadas. [3] Población "de facto".

1A

ECONOMICALLY ACTIVE POPULATION	POPULATION ACTIVE	POBLACION ECONOMICAMENTE ACTIVA
Total and economically active population by age group	Population totale et population active par groupe d'âge	Población total y población económicamente activa por grupo de edad
Thousands	Milliers	Millares

	Total			Men - Hommes - Hombres			Women - Femmes - Mujeres		
	Total population	Active population	Activity rate	Total population	Active population	Activity rate	Total population	Active population	Activity rate
	Population totale	Population active	Taux d'activité	Population totale	Population active	Taux d'activité	Population totale	Population active	Taux d'activité
	Población total	Población activa	Tasa de actividad	Población total	Población activa	Tasa de actividad	Población total	Población activa	Tasa de actividad
			%			%			%

OCEANIA - OCÉANIE - OCEANIA

Australia (2008) BA (15+) [1] [2]

	Total population	Active population	Activity rate	Total population	Active population	Activity rate	Total population	Active population	Activity rate
Total	**21 343.9**	**11 211.4**	52.5	**10 595.4**	**6 116.1**	57.7	**10 748.5**	**5 095.2**	47.4
Total (15+)	*17 207.7*	*11 211.4*	*65.2*	*8 473.2*	*6 116.1*	*72.2*	*8 734.5*	*5 095.2*	*58.3*
0-9	2 733.4	.	.	1 402.1	.	.	1 331.2	.	.
10-14	1 402.9	.	.	720.0	.	.	682.8	.	.
15-19	1 462.0	842.2	57.6	749.4	426.3	56.9	712.5	416.0	58.4
20-24	1 502.8	1 219.5	81.1	760.4	640.0	84.2	742.4	579.4	78.0
25-29	1 489.0	1 247.9	83.8	749.7	684.9	91.4	739.3	563.1	76.2
30-34	1 456.6	1 202.1	82.5	725.7	674.4	92.9	731.0	527.6	72.2
35-39	1 583.1	1 294.7	81.8	784.2	723.7	92.3	798.9	571.0	71.5
40-44	1 509.4	1 276.9	84.6	749.2	682.0	91.0	760.2	594.9	78.2
45-49	1 544.7	1 309.6	84.8	764.3	687.2	89.9	780.5	622.4	79.7
50-54	1 409.0	1 138.2	80.8	698.1	607.1	87.0	710.9	531.1	74.7
55-59	1 285.2	878.7	68.4	638.7	484.5	75.9	646.5	394.1	61.0
60-64	1 126.7	540.7	48.0	563.8	326.9	58.0	562.9	213.8	38.0
65-69	834.7	176.2	21.1	413.5	116.8	28.3	421.2	59.4	14.1
70+	2 004.3	84.7	4.2	876.1	62.2	7.1	1 128.2	22.5	2.0

New Zealand (2008) BA (15+) [1] [2]

	Total population	Active population	Activity rate	Total population	Active population	Activity rate	Total population	Active population	Activity rate
Total	**4 271.1**	**2 283.2**	53.5	**2 093.3**	**1 214.8**	58.0	**2 177.8**	**1 068.4**	49.1
Total (15+)	*3 381.5*	*2 283.2*	*67.5*	*1 637.5*	*1 214.8*	*74.2*	*1 743.9*	*1 068.3*	*61.3*
0-9	587.9	.	.	301.1	.	.	286.9	.	.
10-14	301.5	.	.	154.6	.	.	146.9	.	.
15-19	322.5	172.9	53.6	164.7	89.7	54.5	157.8	83.1	52.7
20-24	297.3	216.1	72.7	150.2	115.5	76.9	147.1	100.6	68.4
25-29	273.6	223.9	81.8	134.4	120.6	89.7	139.2	103.3	74.2
30-34	271.4	222.1	81.8	129.7	119.4	92.1	141.6	102.7	72.5
35-39	312.5	256.7	82.1	148.7	136.2	91.6	163.9	120.6	73.6
40-44	314.2	267.5	85.1	151.5	137.6	90.8	162.7	129.9	79.8
45-49	319.5	276.1	86.4	155.1	142.3	91.7	164.3	133.9	81.5
50-54	276.7	237.4	85.8	135.8	122.7	90.4	140.9	114.7	81.4
55-59	244.3	196.7	80.5	120.5	105.3	87.4	123.8	91.3	73.7
60-64	211.2	135.4	64.1	103.9	77.3	74.4	107.3	58.0	54.1
65-69	166.4	54.0	32.5	81.0	32.2	39.8	85.4	21.9	25.6
70-74	126.1	17.3	13.7	60.4	11.3	18.7	65.7	6.0	9.1
75+	245.8	7.1	2.9	101.6	4.7	4.6	144.2	2.3	1.6

Explanations and sources: see p. 3.
[1] Excl. armed forces. [2] "De jure" population.

Explications et sources: voir p. 5.
[1] Non compris les forces armées. [2] Population "de jure".

Explicaciones y fuentes: véase p. 7.
[1] Excl. las fuerzas armadas. [2] Población "de jure".

By level of education and age group

Par niveau d'instruction et groupe d'âge

Por nivel de educación y grupo de edad

	Thousands / Milliers / Millares										
ISCED 1976 CITE Total	X	0	1	2	3	5	6	7	9	?	
CINE 1997 Total	X	0	1	2	3	4	5A	5B	6	?	

AFRICA-AFRIQUE-AFRICA

Botswana (BA) (2006) [1][2]

Total - Total - Total
ISCED-76 - CITE-76 - CINE-76

	Total	X	0	1	2	3	5	6	7	9	?
Total	653.2	100.9[3]	.	171.4	187.5	169.1[4]	.	.	.	.	24.3
12-14	12.9	0.5[3]	.	1.1	0.1	-[4]	.	.	.	.	11.3
15-19	40.3	1.7[3]	.	5.9	16.6	6.0[4]	.	.	.	.	10.3
20-24	105.0	4.8[3]	.	13.3	47.6	39.0[4]	.	.	.	.	0.4
25-29	107.9	4.3[3]	.	13.4	47.4	42.6[4]	.	.	.	.	0.2
30-34	90.5	6.2[3]	.	20.4	29.5	33.9[4]	.	.	.	.	0.4
35-39	74.2	8.2[3]	.	26.0	19.1	20.2[4]	.	.	.	.	0.6
40-44	58.9	10.6[3]	.	24.0	12.3	11.8[4]	.	.	.	.	0.3
45-49	51.8	15.4[3]	.	20.5	7.7	8.0[4]	.	.	.	.	0.3
50-54	38.3	13.0[3]	.	17.0	4.3	3.8[4]	.	.	.	.	0.1
55-59	24.9	9.1[3]	.	11.7	2.0	1.9[4]	.	.	.	.	0.1
60-64	15.3	7.8[3]	.	5.9	0.4	0.9[4]	.	.	.	.	0.3
65-69	33.1	19.2[3]	.	12.2	0.6	0.9[4]	.	.	.	.	0.2

Men - Hommes - Hombres
ISCED-76 - CITE-76 - CINE-76

	Total	X	0	1	2	3	5	6	7	9	?
Total	332.6	64.6[3]	.	84.8	82.5	86.2[4]	.	.	.	.	14.6
12-14	9.5	0.4[3]	.	1.0	-	1.5[4]	.	.	.	.	6.6
15-19	33.5	1.4[3]	.	4.2	9.2	11.9[4]	.	.	.	.	6.9
20-24	59.3	3.2[3]	.	9.1	23.7	23.2[4]	.	.	.	.	0.1
25-29	53.3	3.3[3]	.	8.6	21.1	20.1[4]	.	.	.	.	0.1
30-34	39.0	4.9[3]	.	9.5	11.8	12.7[4]	.	.	.	.	0.2
35-39	30.9	4.8[3]	.	12.2	6.8	6.9[4]	.	.	.	.	0.3
40-44	24.8	6.2[3]	.	9.4	4.1	5.1[4]	.	.	.	.	0.1
45-49	22.8	8.7[3]	.	9.5	2.7	2.0[4]	.	.	.	.	-
50-54	18.9	8.3[3]	.	7.3	1.7	1.6[4]	.	.	.	.	0.1
55-59	12.5	5.7[3]	.	5.3	0.8	0.6[4]	.	.	.	.	0.1
60-64	8.5	5.2[3]	.	2.2	0.3	0.5[4]	.	.	.	.	0.3
65-69	19.6	12.6[3]	.	6.6	0.3	-[4]	.	.	.	.	0.1

Women - Femmes - Mujeres
ISCED-76 - CITE-76 - CINE-76

	Total	X	0	1	2	3	5	6	7	9	?
Total	320.6	36.3[3]	.	86.6	105.0	82.3[4]	.	.	.	.	9.8
12-14	4.9	0.1[3]	.	0.1	0.1	-[4]	.	.	.	.	4.7
15-19	16.1	0.3[3]	.	1.7	7.4	3.2[4]	.	.	.	.	3.4
20-24	52.0	1.6[3]	.	4.3	23.8	22.0[4]	.	.	.	.	0.3
25-29	54.0	1.0[3]	.	4.8	26.2	21.9[4]	.	.	.	.	0.1
30-34	46.9	1.4[3]	.	10.9	17.7	16.7[4]	.	.	.	.	0.2
35-39	37.8	3.4[3]	.	13.9	12.4	7.8[4]	.	.	.	.	0.4
40-44	32.5	4.4[3]	.	14.6	8.2	5.0[4]	.	.	.	.	0.2
45-49	26.3	6.8[3]	.	11.0	5.0	3.3[4]	.	.	.	.	0.3
50-54	18.7	4.7[3]	.	9.7	2.6	1.6[4]	.	.	.	.	0.1
55-59	11.7	3.4[3]	.	6.4	1.2	0.6[4]	.	.	.	.	0.1
60-64	6.7	2.6[3]	.	3.7	0.1	0.3[4]	.	.	.	.	0.1
65-69	13.0	6.6[3]	.	5.6	0.3	0.4[4]	.	.	.	.	0.1

South Africa (BA) (2008) [5][6]

Total - Total - Total
ISCED-97 - CITE-97 - CINE-97

	Total	X	0	1	2	3	4	5A	5B	6	?
Total	17 787.981	671.148	2 802.157[7]	.	11 580.144[8]	.	1 614.483	640.991[9]	.	283.706	195.351
15-19	465.252	3.598	84.198[7]	.	369.08[8]	.	4.731	0.487[9]	.	.	3.158
20-24	2 553.375	17.623	234.94[7]	.	2 079.808[8]	.	155.809	37.704[9]	.	11.999	15.491
25-29	3 268.355	31.466	285.77[7]	.	2 508.082[8]	.	295.829	95.086[9]	.	22.133	29.99
30-34	3 053.652	53.481	346.897[7]	.	2 169.231[8]	.	319.99	101.195[9]	.	33.853	29.004
35-39	2 485.367	68.937	386.771[7]	.	1 587.648[8]	.	271.508	99.123[9]	.	44.511	26.869
40-44	1 834.074	83.088	375.309[7]	.	1 018.473[8]	.	193.406	89.893[9]	.	54.348	19.556
45-49	1 635.904	111.592	398.615[7]	.	809.926[8]	.	156.611	86.933[9]	.	44.969	27.258
50-54	1 269.344	133.694	355.393[7]	.	542.32[8]	.	117.439	62.096[9]	.	36.467	21.935
55-59	845.186	109.162	238.51[7]	.	346.093[8]	.	69.31	44.688[9]	.	23.726	13.698
60-64	377.471	58.507	95.755[7]	.	149.483[8]	.	29.85	23.785[9]	.	11.699	8.393

Explanatory notes: see p. 3.

[1] Persons aged 12 years and over. [2] Totals include persons still attending school. [3] Levels X-0. [4] Levels 3-7. [5] Persons aged 15 to 64 years. [6] Excl. armed forces and conscripts. [7] Levels 0-1. [8] Levels 2-3. [9] Levels 5A-5B.

Notes explicatives: voir p. 5.

[1] Personnes âgées de 12 ans et plus. [2] Les totaux incluent les personnes encore en cours d'études. [3] Niveaux X-0. [4] Niveaux 3-7. [5] Personnes âgées de 15 à 64 ans. [6] Non compris les forces armées et les conscrits. [7] Niveaux 0-1. [8] Niveaux 2-3. [9] Niveaux 5A-5B.

Notas explicativas: véase p. 7.

[1] Personas de 12 años y más. [2] Los totales incluyen a las personas que siguen estudiando. [3] Niveles X-0. [4] Niveles 3-7. [5] Personas de 15 a 64 años. [6] Excl. las fuerzas armadas y los conscriptos. [7] Niveles 0-1. [8] Niveles 2-3. [9] Niveles 5A-5B

1B

ECONOMICALLY ACTIVE POPULATION
By level of education and age group

POPULATION ACTIVE
Par niveau d'instruction et groupe d'âge

POBLACION ECONOMICAMENTE ACTIVA
Por nivel de educación y grupo de edad

Thousands — Milliers — Millares

| ISCED 1976 / CITE | Total | X | 0 | 1 | 2 | 3 | 5 | 6 | 7 | 9 | ? |
CINE 1997	Total	X	0	1	2	3	4	5A	5B	6	?

South Africa (BA) (2008) [1] [2]

Men - Hommes - Hombres
ISCED-97 - CITE-97 - CINE-97

Age	Total	X	0	1	2	3	4	5A	5B	6	?
Total	9 588.981	351.805		1 626.588 [3]		6 224.046 [4]	757.151	326.761 [5]		167.126	135.504
15-19	255.532	2.161		56.912 [3]		191.553 [4]	2.295	0.31 [5]			2.301
20-24	1 395.687	13.395		166.683 [3]		1 125.66 [4]	61.18	13.186 [5]		5.412	10.172
25-29	1 777.435	17.077		191.723 [3]		1 353.141 [4]	139.264	45.969 [5]		10.644	19.617
30-34	1 660.646	35.01		221.05 [3]		1 164.298 [4]	154.384	48.742 [5]		16.473	20.689
35-39	1 295.113	36.165		206.704 [3]		829.816 [4]	131.609	45.204 [5]		25.482	20.132
40-44	952.24	36.849		194.693 [3]		535.487 [4]	95.921	47.343 [5]		29.537	12.41
45-49	855.92	51.249		208.967 [3]		424.308 [4]	75.909	47.18 [5]		29.576	18.73
50-54	686.519	63.763		189.555 [3]		310.019 [4]	49.989	33.032 [5]		24.42	15.742
55-59	468.713	57.395		127.109 [3]		195.781 [4]	32.337	29.258 [5]		17.506	9.327
60-64	241.176	38.74		63.192 [3]		93.984 [4]	14.262	16.536 [5]		8.078	6.384

Women - Femmes - Mujeres
ISCED-97 - CITE-97 - CINE-97

Age	Total	X	0	1	2	3	4	5A	5B	6	?
Total	8 199.001	319.343		1 175.57 [3]		5 356.098 [4]	857.332	314.23 [5]		116.58	59.847
15-19	209.72	1.437		27.286 [3]		177.527 [4]	2.436	0.178 [5]			0.856
20-24	1 157.687	4.228		68.257 [3]		954.148 [4]	94.629	24.518 [5]		6.588	5.319
25-29	1 490.921	14.389		94.047 [3]		1 154.94 [4]	156.565	49.117 [5]		11.49	10.373
30-34	1 393.006	18.471		125.847 [3]		1 004.933 [4]	165.607	52.453 [5]		17.381	8.315
35-39	1 190.254	32.772		180.067 [3]		757.832 [4]	139.899	53.919 [5]		19.029	6.737
40-44	881.834	46.24		180.616 [3]		482.986 [4]	97.485	42.55 [5]		24.811	7.146
45-49	779.984	60.343		189.648 [3]		385.618 [4]	80.702	39.752 [5]		15.393	8.528
50-54	582.825	69.931		165.838 [3]		232.301 [4]	67.45	29.064 [5]		12.048	6.193
55-59	376.474	51.767		111.401 [3]		150.313 [4]	36.972	15.429 [5]		6.221	4.371
60-64	136.295	19.766		32.563 [3]		55.499 [4]	15.588	7.249 [5]		3.621	2.009

AMERICA-AMÉRIQUE-AMERICA

Brasil (BA) (2007) [6] [7]

Total - Total - Total
ISCED-97 - CITE-97 - CINE-97

Age	Total	X	0	1	2	3	4	5A	5B	6	?
Total	98 846	7 961	10 865	23 442	17 593		29 708 [8]			9 042 [9]	235
10-14	1 807	80	559	1 098	69		- [8]			- [9]	1
15-19	8 611	156	390	2 338	3 740		1 937 [8]			3 [9]	1
20-24	13 080	289	526	2 082	2 905		6 743 [8]			509 [9]	47
25-29	13 345	478	782	2 505	2 259		5 777 [8]			1 513 [9]	27
30-34	12 299	664	1 035	2 983	2 020		4 158 [8]			1 404 [9]	30
35-39	11 323	759	1 111	2 875	1 964		3 363 [8]			1 217 [9]	34
40-44	11 039	936	1 262	2 768	1 746		2 937 [8]			1 365 [9]	34
45-49	9 155	931	1 302	2 348	1 252		2 148 [8]			1 155 [9]	25
50-54	7 149	927	1 260	1 824	827		1 421 [8]			880 [9]	19
55-59	4 949	880	1 083	1 269	443		718 [8]			550 [9]	10
60-64	2 939	747	726	694	218		302 [8]			250 [9]	5
65-69	1 609	493	425	360	89		123 [8]			119 [9]	3
70-74	832	294	228	177	37		52 [8]			44 [9]	-
75+	709	326	174	121	23		28 [8]			35 [9]	1

Men - Hommes - Hombres
ISCED-97 - CITE-97 - CINE-97

Age	Total	X	0	1	2	3	4	5A	5B	6	?
Total	55 754	5 087	6 914	14 275	10 231		15 137 [8]			3 993 [9]	117
10-14	1 206	66	419	686	35		- [8]			- [9]	1
15-19	5 114	118	321	1 660	2 092		887 [8]			1 [9]	35
20-24	7 332	217	386	1 398	1 796		3 333 [8]			186 [9]	16
25-29	7 313	343	540	1 543	1 334		2 942 [8]			601 [9]	11
30-34	6 699	454	666	1 748	1 148		2 089 [8]			579 [9]	15
35-39	6 174	472	694	1 666	1 113		1 696 [8]			518 [9]	14
40-44	6 034	604	744	1 579	996		1 530 [8]			568 [9]	11
45-49	4 986	572	764	1 284	728		1 125 [8]			505 [9]	8
50-54	4 082	546	744	1 072	488		798 [8]			430 [9]	3
55-59	2 928	515	637	779	276		417 [8]			303 [9]	1
60-64	1 869	474	464	448	135		184 [8]			163 [9]	1
65-69	1 029	310	276	226	53		80 [8]			82 [9]	1
70-74	538	194	144	114	21		36 [8]			31 [9]	-
75+	450	202	115	73	15		19 [8]			26 [9]	-

Explanatory notes: see p. 3.

[1] Persons aged 15 to 64 years. [2] Excl. armed forces and conscripts. [3] Levels 0-1. [4] Levels 2-3. [5] Levels 5A-5B. [6] Persons aged 10 years and over. [7] Sep. [8] Levels 3-4. [9] Levels 5-6.

Notes explicatives: voir p. 5.

[1] Personnes âgées de 15 à 64 ans. [2] Non compris les forces armées et les conscrits. [3] Niveaux 0-1. [4] Niveaux 2-3. [5] Niveaux 5A-5B. [6] Personnes âgées de 10 ans et plus. [7] Sept. [8] Niveaux 3-4. [9] Niveaux 5-6.

Notas explicativas: véase p. 7.

[1] Personas de 15 a 64 años. [2] Excl. las fuerzas armadas y los conscriptos. [3] Niveles 0-1. [4] Niveles 2-3. [5] Niveles 5A-5B [6] Personas de 10 años y más. [7] Sept. [8] Niveles 3-4. [9] Niveles 5-6.

ECONOMICALLY ACTIVE POPULATION

By level of education and age group

POPULATION ACTIVE

Par niveau d'instruction et groupe d'âge

POBLACION ECONOMICAMENTE ACTIVA

Por nivel de educación y grupo de edad

	Thousands / Milliers / Millares										
ISCED 1976	Total	X	0	1	2	3	5	6	7	9	?
CITE / CINE 1997	Total	X	0	1	2	3	4	5A	5B	6	?
Brasil (BA) (2007) [1][2]											
Women - Femmes - Mujeres											
ISCED-97 - CITE-97 - CINE-97											
Total	43 091	2 874	3 951	9 167	7 362	14 572 [3]	.	5 049 [4]	.	.	118
10-14	601	14	140	412	34	- [3]	.	- [4]	.	.	-
15-19	3 497	38	69	679	1 648	1 050 [3]	.	1 [4]	.	.	12
20-24	5 747	72	140	684	1 108	3 410 [3]	.	322 [4]	.	.	10
25-29	6 031	136	242	962	924	2 835 [3]	.	913 [4]	.	.	18
30-34	5 600	210	370	1 234	873	2 069 [3]	.	824 [4]	.	.	19
35-39	5 149	287	417	1 209	851	1 667 [3]	.	699 [4]	.	.	19
40-44	5 006	332	518	1 188	750	1 407 [3]	.	796 [4]	.	.	14
45-49	4 168	359	539	1 064	524	1 022 [3]	.	650 [4]	.	.	10
50-54	3 067	381	516	752	339	623 [3]	.	450 [4]	.	.	7
55-59	2 021	365	445	491	167	301 [3]	.	247 [4]	.	.	4
60-64	1 070	273	262	246	83	118 [3]	.	87 [4]	.	.	2
65-69	580	182	149	133	36	43 [3]	.	37 [4]	.	.	-
70-74	294	101	85	63	16	17 [3]	.	13 [4]	.	.	
75+	260	125	59	48	7	10 [3]	.	9 [4]	.	.	1
Canada (BA) (2008) [5][6][7]											
Total - Total - Total											
ISCED-97 - CITE-97 - CINE-97											
Total	18 245.1	463.9 [8]	.	.	1 999.0	5 228.6	2 075.6	4 265.9 [9]	4 212.1	.	.
15-19	1 207.1	48.4 [8]	.	.	628.7	483.5	16.1	- [9]	29.0	.	.
20-24	1 742.5	19.4 [8]	.	.	154.7	839.7	148.6	199.0 [9]	381.1	.	.
25-29	1 940.8	18.8 [8]	.	.	109.6	499.6	226.4	564.6 [9]	521.9	.	.
30-34	1 921.0	21.7 [8]	.	.	104.5	427.9	225.4	602.5 [9]	539.1	.	.
35-39	1 980.0	24.1 [8]	.	.	115.1	459.8	224.1	638.3 [9]	518.6	.	.
40-44	2 234.7	36.8 [8]	.	.	170.9	550.1	276.9	601.3 [9]	598.7	.	.
45-49	2 332.2	53.2 [8]	.	.	205.3	644.1	317.7	527.4 [9]	584.5	.	.
50-54	2 096.7	63.5 [8]	.	.	206.1	592.9	269.9	468.3 [9]	496.1	.	.
55-59	1 511.8	66.9 [8]	.	.	153.3	414.1	199.0	363.4 [9]	315.1	.	.
60-64	849.6	63.4 [8]	.	.	93.2	217.6	115.6	200.4 [9]	159.3	.	.
65+	428.6	47.7 [8]	.	.	57.6	99.5	55.9	99.3 [9]	68.6	.	.
Men - Hommes - Hombres											
ISCED-97 - CITE-97 - CINE-97											
Total	9 654.0	296.1 [8]	.	.	1 184.7	2 778.1	1 380.6	2 140.8 [9]	1 873.7	.	.
15-19	601.4	27.5 [8]	.	.	314.9	235.7	11.0	- [9]	11.8	.	.
20-24	912.1	13.0 [8]	.	.	100.3	465.8	92.8	74.4 [9]	165.8	.	.
25-29	1 025.2	14.4 [8]	.	.	76.4	301.3	146.9	244.0 [9]	242.3	.	.
30-34	1 026.9	13.6 [8]	.	.	74.3	259.8	153.6	274.0 [9]	251.5	.	.
35-39	1 039.9	16.3 [8]	.	.	73.3	258.3	148.5	313.2 [9]	230.2	.	.
40-44	1 188.9	25.4 [8]	.	.	110.9	292.9	181.6	317.5 [9]	260.6	.	.
45-49	1 201.7	33.3 [8]	.	.	131.1	312.7	206.7	269.5 [9]	248.4	.	.
50-54	1 104.9	40.3 [8]	.	.	123.8	280.5	187.8	251.5 [9]	221.0	.	.
55-59	802.7	38.1 [8]	.	.	88.0	204.6	132.4	203.9 [9]	135.8	.	.
60-64	479.6	39.6 [8]	.	.	55.6	108.2	79.2	123.1 [9]	73.8	.	.
65+	270.7	34.6 [8]	.	.	36.1	58.2	40.0	69.3 [9]	32.4	.	.
Women - Femmes - Mujeres											
ISCED-97 - CITE-97 - CINE-97											
Total	8 591.2	167.8 [8]	.	.	814.3	2 450.5	695.0	2 125.1 [9]	2 338.5	.	.
15-19	605.7	20.9 [8]	.	.	313.8	247.8	5.2	- [9]	17.2	.	.
20-24	830.4	6.5 [8]	.	.	54.3	373.9	55.8	124.6 [9]	215.3	.	.
25-29	915.6	4.3 [8]	.	.	33.2	198.3	79.5	320.6 [9]	279.6	.	.
30-34	894.1	8.1 [8]	.	.	30.2	168.1	71.7	328.5 [9]	287.5	.	.
35-39	940.1	7.8 [8]	.	.	41.8	201.5	75.6	325.1 [9]	288.4	.	.
40-44	1 045.8	11.4 [8]	.	.	60.0	257.2	95.3	283.8 [9]	338.2	.	.
45-49	1 130.5	19.9 [8]	.	.	74.2	331.3	111.0	257.9 [9]	336.2	.	.
50-54	991.8	23.2 [8]	.	.	82.3	312.3	82.0	216.9 [9]	275.1	.	.
55-59	709.1	28.8 [8]	.	.	65.3	209.5	66.6	159.5 [9]	179.4	.	.
60-64	370.0	23.8 [8]	.	.	37.7	109.4	36.4	77.3 [9]	85.5	.	.
65+	157.9	13.1 [8]	.	.	21.5	41.3	15.9	29.9 [9]	36.2	.	.
Cayman Islands (BA) (2008) [5][10]											
Total - Total - Total											
ISCED-97 - CITE-97 - CINE-97											
Total	38.999	0.225 [11]	.	1.959	5.043	13.528	3.134	7.909 [9]	6.855	.	0.345
Men - Hommes - Hombres											
ISCED-97 - CITE-97 - CINE-97											
Total	20.128	0.104 [11]	.	1.169	3.068	7.154	1.693	3.778 [9]	2.908	.	0.254

Explanatory notes: see p. 3.

[1] Persons aged 10 years and over. [2] Sep. [3] Levels 3-4. [4] Levels 5-6. [5] Persons aged 15 years and over. [6] Excl. residents of the Territories and indigenous persons living on reserves. [7] Excl. full-time members of the armed forces. [8] Levels X-1. [9] Levels 5A and 6. [10] Oct. [11] Levels X-0.

Notes explicatives: voir p. 5.

[1] Personnes âgées de 10 ans et plus. [2] Sept. [3] Niveaux 3-4. [4] Niveaux 5-6. [5] Personnes âgées de 15 ans et plus. [6] Non compris les habitants des "Territoires" et les populations indigènes vivant dans les réserves. [7] Non compris les membres à temps complet des forces armées. [8] Niveaux X-1. [9] Niveaux 5A et 6. [10] Oct. [11] Niveaux X-0.

Notas explicativas: véase p. 7.

[1] Personas de 10 años y más. [2] Sept. [3] Niveles 3-4. [4] Niveles 5-6. [5] Personas de 15 años y más. [6] Excl. a los habitantes de los "Territorios" y a las poblaciones indígenas que viven en reservas. [7] Excl. los miembros a tiempo completo de las fuerzas armadas. [8] Niveles X-1. [9] Niveles 5A y 6. [10] Oct. [11] Niveles X-0.

1B ECONOMICALLY ACTIVE POPULATION — POPULATION ACTIVE — POBLACION ECONOMICAMENTE ACTIVA

By level of education and age group — Par niveau d'instruction et groupe d'âge — Por nivel de educación y grupo de edad

Thousands — Milliers — Millares

ISCED 1976 CITE	Total	X	0	1	2	3	5	6	7	9	?
CINE 1997	**Total**	**X**	**0**	**1**	**2**	**3**	**4**	**5A**	**5B**	**6**	**?**
Cayman Islands (BA) (2008) [1][2]											
Women - Femmes - Mujeres — ISCED-97 - CITE-97 - CINE-97											
Total	18.871	0.121 [3]	.	0.791	1.974	6.374	1.442	4.131 [4]	3.947		0.091
Costa Rica (BA) (2008) [5][6]											
Total - Total - Total — ISCED-97 - CITE-97 - CINE-97											
Total	2 059.6	48.1	1.1	785.2	349.9	382.0	112.2	173.2	140.9	57.9	9.1
0-9	0.1	0.1	-	-	-	-	-	-	-	-	-
10-14	8.1	0.3	-	5.9	2.1	-	-	-	-	-	-
15-19	131.1	0.3	-	57.9	42.1	27.4	2.8	0.1	-	-	0.1
20-24	311.9	2.6	0.2	86.6	62.5	88.3	38.3	24.3	7.1	0.7	1.2
25-29	285.6	3.9	-	87.2	47.7	57.8	21.3	35.5	23.6	7.9	0.7
30-34	253.5	4.5	0.3	89.3	41.9	44.6	11.9	25.6	25.4	8.7	1.2
35-39	218.9	4.5	0.3	89.2	37.4	36.5	7.1	17.6	16.7	8.6	0.8
40-44	239.3	4.4	0.3	96.4	40.0	39.2	9.0	21.2	19.3	8.6	0.8
45-49	215.6	5.3	-	76.9	32.9	39.8	9.8	22.2	19.7	8.3	0.6
50-54	171.6	5.6	-	76.8	20.7	27.9	6.1	12.8	13.6	7.0	1.1
55-59	106.8	5.0	-	52.3	13.1	11.2	3.1	7.9	8.4	5.5	0.3
60-64	60.7	4.7	-	34.4	6.0	6.4	1.0	3.5	3.1	1.4	0.3
65-69	27.2	2.5	-	16.4	2.6	1.3	0.4	1.2	1.7	0.4	0.8
70-74	12.2	2.1	-	7.9	-	0.7	-	0.4	0.3	0.8	-
75+	11.6	2.1	-	6.3	0.6	0.5	0.3	0.7	1.1	-	-
?	5.6	0.1	-	1.6	0.2	0.2	1.1	0.2	0.9	-	1.3
Men - Hommes - Hombres — ISCED-97 - CITE-97 - CINE-97											
Total	1 283.0	34.6	0.4	550.4	225.8	216.7	65.0	84.7	67.3	31.1	7.0
0-9	0.1	0.1	-	-	-	-	-	-	-	-	-
10-14	5.7	0.3	-	4.1	1.5	-	-	-	-	-	-
15-19	88.2	0.3	-	42.1	30.1	13.9	1.4	0.1	-	-	0.1
20-24	190.2	2.1	0.2	63.7	42.0	50.6	19.9	8.4	2.3	0.1	0.8
25-29	164.5	2.3	-	59.9	29.9	32.9	12.1	16.3	7.5	3.4	0.1
30-34	151.1	3.5	0.2	62.1	27.1	24.0	6.3	12.9	9.7	4.1	1.2
35-39	128.5	3.2	-	60.0	21.8	19.3	3.4	8.1	7.7	4.5	0.6
40-44	146.1	3.3	-	65.0	25.0	21.3	6.1	10.1	10.7	3.8	0.7
45-49	132.6	3.9	-	52.4	19.5	23.3	6.3	11.9	11.2	3.9	0.2
50-54	109.3	4.1	-	51.7	12.9	16.8	4.6	7.3	6.6	4.3	0.9
55-59	75.0	2.8	-	37.9	8.4	7.8	2.3	4.9	6.0	4.7	0.3
60-64	46.9	3.5	-	26.7	4.7	5.0	0.9	2.6	2.1	1.1	0.3
65-69	21.9	1.8	-	12.5	2.3	1.3	0.4	0.8	1.7	0.4	0.8
70-74	9.3	1.3	-	6.3	-	0.2	-	0.4	0.3	0.8	-
75+	9.6	1.8	-	4.9	0.6	0.3	0.3	0.7	1.1	-	-
?	4.1	0.1	-	1.1	0.1	0.2	1.1	0.1	0.4	-	1.1
Women - Femmes - Mujeres — ISCED-97 - CITE-97 - CINE-97											
Total	776.6	13.6	0.7	234.8	124.1	165.2	47.2	88.5	73.6	26.8	2.1
0-9	-	-	-	-	-	-	-	-	-	-	-
10-14	2.4	-	-	1.8	0.6	-	-	-	-	-	-
15-19	43.0	-	-	15.8	12.0	13.6	1.5	-	-	-	-
20-24	121.7	0.5	-	22.9	20.6	37.6	18.4	15.9	4.8	0.6	0.1
25-29	121.1	1.5	-	27.3	17.8	24.9	9.2	19.2	16.1	4.5	0.4
30-34	102.4	1.0	0.1	27.2	14.9	20.6	5.6	12.8	15.7	4.6	0.6
35-39	90.4	1.4	0.3	29.3	15.7	17.3	3.7	9.5	9.0	4.2	-
40-44	93.2	1.1	0.3	31.4	15.0	18.0	2.9	11.1	8.6	4.8	0.2
45-49	83.0	1.4	-	24.5	13.4	16.6	3.5	10.3	8.5	4.4	0.1
50-54	62.3	1.5	-	25.1	7.8	11.2	1.5	5.4	7.0	2.7	0.5
55-59	31.8	2.3	-	14.4	4.7	3.4	0.8	3.0	2.4	0.8	0.2
60-64	13.8	1.1	-	7.7	1.3	1.4	0.1	0.9	1.0	0.2	-
65-69	5.3	0.7	-	3.9	0.3	0.1	-	0.4	-	-	-
70-74	2.9	0.8	-	1.6	-	0.5	-	-	-	-	-
75+	2.0	0.3	-	1.4	-	0.3	-	-	-	-	-
?	1.5	-	-	0.5	0.2	-	-	0.1	0.5	-	0.2

Explanatory notes: see p. 3.

[1] Persons aged 15 years and over. [2] Oct. [3] Levels X-0. [4] Levels 5A and 6. [5] Persons aged 12 years and over. [6] July of each year.

Notes explicatives: voir p. 5.

[1] Personnes âgées de 15 ans et plus. [2] Oct. [3] Niveaux X-0. [4] Niveaux 5A et 6. [5] Personnes âgées de 12 ans et plus. [6] Juillet de chaque année.

Notas explicativas: véase p. 7.

[1] Personas de 15 años y más. [2] Oct. [3] Niveles X-0. [4] Niveles 5A y 6. [5] Personas de 12 años y más. [6] Julio de cada año.

ECONOMICALLY ACTIVE POPULATION

By level of education and age group

POPULATION ACTIVE

Par niveau d'instruction et groupe d'âge

POBLACION ECONOMICAMENTE ACTIVA

Por nivel de educación y grupo de edad

Thousands — Milliers — Millares

ISCED 1976 CITE / CINE 1997	Total	X	0	1	2	3	5 / 4	6 / 5A	7 / 5B	9 / 6	?

Cuba (BA) (2008) [1]

Total - Total - Total
ISCED-97 - CITE-97 - CINE-97

Age	Total	X	0	1	2	3	4	5A	5B	6	?
Total	5 027.9	.	94.7	306.3	1 353.4	1 547.1	998.8	727.6 [2]	.	.	.
17-19	146.9	.	0.6	3.4	41.7	64.5	36.7	- [2]	.	.	.
20-24	478.4	.	2.4	10.8	95.9	201.5	138.9	28.9 [2]	.	.	.
25-29	441.8	.	2.5	17.2	108.1	157.9	86.5	69.6 [2]	.	.	.
30-34	604.4	.	4.6	24.7	161.2	211.4	119.4	83.1 [2]	.	.	.
35-39	804.5	.	7.3	35.9	217.1	252.7	171.0	120.5 [2]	.	.	.
40-44	851.0	.	9.0	42.5	239.7	253.0	167.8	139.0 [2]	.	.	.
45-49	656.1	.	12.3	43.1	181.9	179.7	125.9	113.2 [2]	.	.	.
50-54	489.1	.	14.0	43.6	149.3	122.8	75.8	83.6 [2]	.	.	.
55-59	361.9	.	18.2	47.2	113.3	73.3	53.3	56.6 [2]	.	.	.
60-64	114.0	.	9.5	18.2	30.4	19.5	15.0	21.4 [2]	.	.	.
65-69	47.3	.	5.6	9.5	10.3	7.3	5.6	9.0 [2]	.	.	.
70-74	18.1	.	3.5	5.1	3.0	2.7	2.1	1.7 [2]	.	.	.
75+	14.4	.	5.2	5.1	1.5	0.8	0.8	1.0 [2]	.	.	.

Men - Hommes - Hombres
ISCED-97 - CITE-97 - CINE-97

Age	Total	X	0	1	2	3	4	5A	5B	6	?
Total	3 115.1	.	79.5	235.8	978.9	937.0	522.2	361.7 [2]	.	.	.
17-19	94.3	.	0.6	3.0	33.5	38.2	19.0	- [2]	.	.	.
20-24	280.4	.	2.3	9.2	78.6	108.6	72.4	9.3 [2]	.	.	.
25-29	264.7	.	2.4	15.4	86.2	89.0	42.8	28.9 [2]	.	.	.
30-34	369.1	.	4.2	20.1	122.8	127.2	60.1	34.7 [2]	.	.	.
35-39	484.2	.	6.5	29.0	158.8	150.8	86.9	52.2 [2]	.	.	.
40-44	501.5	.	7.2	32.5	161.6	150.0	83.5	66.7 [2]	.	.	.
45-49	394.3	.	10.2	28.4	119.6	111.6	64.2	60.3 [2]	.	.	.
50-54	295.8	.	10.3	29.0	95.8	79.1	38.2	43.4 [2]	.	.	.
55-59	275.7	.	14.8	37.4	86.6	57.7	37.9	41.3 [2]	.	.	.
60-64	88.1	.	7.9	14.7	23.4	15.7	11.0	15.4 [2]	.	.	.
65-69	38.1	.	5.1	7.5	8.0	6.2	4.2	7.1 [2]	.	.	.
70-74	15.7	.	3.0	4.8	2.7	2.3	1.4	1.5 [2]	.	.	.
75+	13.2	.	5.0	4.8	1.3	0.6	0.6	0.9 [2]	.	.	.

Women - Femmes - Mujeres
ISCED-97 - CITE-97 - CINE-97

Age	Total	X	0	1	2	3	4	5A	5B	6	?
Total	1 912.8	.	15.2	70.5	374.5	610.1	476.6	365.9 [2]	.	.	.
17-19	52.6	.	-	0.4	8.2	26.3	17.7	- [2]	.	.	.
20-24	198.0	.	0.1	1.6	17.3	92.9	66.5	19.6 [2]	.	.	.
25-29	177.1	.	0.1	1.8	21.9	68.9	43.7	40.7 [2]	.	.	.
30-34	235.3	.	0.4	4.6	38.4	84.2	59.3	48.4 [2]	.	.	.
35-39	320.3	.	0.8	6.9	58.3	101.9	84.1	68.3 [2]	.	.	.
40-44	349.5	.	1.8	10.0	78.1	103.0	84.3	72.3 [2]	.	.	.
45-49	261.8	.	2.1	14.7	62.3	68.1	61.7	52.9 [2]	.	.	.
50-54	193.3	.	3.7	14.6	53.5	43.7	37.6	40.2 [2]	.	.	.
55-59	86.2	.	3.4	9.8	26.7	15.6	15.4	15.3 [2]	.	.	.
60-64	25.9	.	1.6	3.5	7.0	3.8	4.0	6.0 [2]	.	.	.
65-69	9.2	.	0.5	2.0	2.3	1.1	1.4	1.9 [2]	.	.	.
70-74	2.4	.	0.5	0.3	0.3	0.4	0.7	0.2 [2]	.	.	.
75+	1.2	.	0.2	0.3	0.2	0.2	0.2	0.1 [2]	.	.	.

Chile (BA) (2008) [3] [4]

Total - Total - Total
ISCED-76 - CITE-76 - CINE-76

Age	Total	X	0	1	2	3	5	6	7	9	?
Total	7 285.1	72.1	0.5	1 748.8 [5]	.	3 564.0	658.3	1 229.9 [6]	.	11.5	.
15-19	228.6	0.5	-	41.4 [5]	.	178.2	4.0	4.4 [6]	.	0.1	.
20-24	747.1	0.7	-	59.6 [5]	.	499.8	76.5	110.2 [6]	.	0.3	.
25-29	812.1	0.7	0.1	87.3 [5]	.	425.3	103.9	194.2 [6]	.	0.6	.
30-34	792.5	1.7	-	121.4 [5]	.	394.9	100.4	173.3 [6]	.	0.9	.
35-39	884.1	2.4	-	187.2 [5]	.	439.5	108.7	143.0 [6]	.	3.3	.
40-44	942.3	6.2	-	231.4 [5]	.	457.1	102.5	143.6 [6]	.	1.5	.
45-49	857.3	6.7	0.1	251.9 [5]	.	405.3	69.4	122.6 [6]	.	1.2	.
50-54	784.4	8.6	0.1	241.3 [5]	.	345.6	52.4	135.2 [6]	.	1.2	.
55-59	548.7	10.7	-	208.6 [5]	.	195.4	21.7	110.9 [6]	.	1.3	.
60-64	382.0	12.1	0.3	167.8 [5]	.	131.4	12.2	57.4 [6]	.	0.8	.
65-69	187.1	9.1	-	93.6 [5]	.	58.1	4.4	21.7 [6]	.	0.3	.
70-74	66.8	6.9	-	33.1 [5]	.	18.0	0.8	8.0 [6]	.	-	.
75+	52.1	6.0	-	24.2 [5]	.	15.2	1.4	5.3 [6]	.	-	.

Explanatory notes: see p. 3.

[1] February - April [2] Levels 5-6. [3] Persons aged 15 years and over. [4] Fourth quarter. [5] Levels 1-2. [6] Levels 6-7.

Notes explicatives: voir p. 5.

[1] Février - Avril [2] Niveaux 5-6. [3] Personnes âgées de 15 ans et plus. [4] Quatrième trimestre. [5] Niveaux 1-2. [6] Niveaux 6-7.

Notas explicativas: véase p. 7.

[1] Febrero - Abril [2] Niveles 5-6. [3] Personas de 15 años y más. [4] Cuarto trimestre. [5] Niveles 1-2. [6] Niveles 6-7.

ECONOMICALLY ACTIVE POPULATION

By level of education and age group

POPULATION ACTIVE

Par niveau d'instruction et groupe d'âge

POBLACION ECONOMICAMENTE ACTIVA

Por nivel de educación y grupo de edad

		Thousands				Milliers				Millares		
ISCED 1976 CITE	Total	X	0	1	2	3	5	6	7	9	?
CINE 1997	Total	X	0	1	2	3	4	5A	5B	6	?

Chile (BA) (2008) [1][2]

Men - Hommes - Hombres
ISCED-76 - CITE-76 - CINE-76

	Total	X	0	1	2	3	5	6	7	9	?
Total	4 546.1	52.9	0.3	1 207.9[3]		2 230.2	342.0	704.1[4]		8.7	
15-19	145.9	0.5	-	33.8[3]		107.5	1.3	2.8[4]		0.1	
20-24	476.3	0.7	-	47.1[3]		331.5	43.1	53.6[4]		0.3	
25-29	477.1	0.7	-	60.5[3]		257.7	54.4	103.7[4]		0.1	
30-34	472.3	1.6	-	87.4[3]		242.0	49.7	90.8[4]		0.9	
35-39	534.5	1.9	-	127.5[3]		258.6	58.5	85.4[4]		2.6	
40-44	572.4	4.5	-	149.2[3]		276.6	53.5	87.5[4]		1.1	
45-49	523.0	4.5	-	169.2[3]		250.0	30.5	68.2[4]		0.7	
50-54	493.1	7.5	-	157.8[3]		221.5	28.1	77.2[4]		1.0	
55-59	359.3	7.2	-	144.0[3]		130.1	10.9	66.1[4]		1.0	
60-64	270.7	8.0	0.3	121.9[3]		91.8	7.7	40.2[4]		0.8	
65-69	139.7	7.0	-	69.7[3]		41.5	3.6	17.7[4]		0.3	
70-74	48.1	5.1	-	25.2[3]		11.0	0.4	6.5[4]		-	
75+	33.8	3.7	-	14.7[3]		10.6	0.3	4.5[4]		-	

Women - Femmes - Mujeres
ISCED-76 - CITE-76 - CINE-76

	Total	X	0	1	2	3	5	6	7	9	?
Total	2 739.0	19.2	0.3	540.9[3]		1 333.7	316.2	525.9[4]		2.8	
15-19	82.7	-	-	7.6[3]		70.8	2.7	1.7[4]		-	
20-24	270.8	-	-	12.5[3]		168.3	33.4	56.6[4]		-	
25-29	335.0	-	0.1	26.8[3]		167.7	49.5	90.5[4]		0.5	
30-34	320.3	0.1	-	34.0[3]		152.9	50.7	82.5[4]		0.0	
35-39	349.6	0.5	-	59.7[3]		180.9	50.2	57.5[4]		0.7	
40-44	369.9	1.7	-	82.2[3]		180.5	49.0	56.1[4]		0.4	
45-49	334.3	2.2	0.1	82.7[3]		155.4	39.0	54.5[4]		0.5	
50-54	291.3	1.0	0.1	83.5[3]		124.1	24.3	58.0[4]		0.2	
55-59	189.5	3.6	-	64.6[3]		65.4	10.8	44.8[4]		0.3	
60-64	111.3	4.1	-	45.9[3]		39.6	4.5	17.2[4]		0.1	
65-69	47.4	2.1	-	23.8[3]		16.6	0.8	4.0[4]		-	
70-74	18.7	1.7	-	7.9[3]		7.1	0.4	1.6[4]		-	
75+	18.3	2.3	-	9.4[3]		4.6	1.1	0.8[4]		-	

República Dominicana (BA) (2007) [5]

Total - Total - Total
ISCED-76 - CITE-76 - CINE-76

	Total	X	0	1	2	3	5	6	7	9	?
Total	4 204.8	283.2[6]		1 790.1	1 362.1[7]			769.5[8]			
0-9	2.6	-[6]		2.6	-[7]			-[8]			
10-14	50.8	2.5[6]		47.3	1.0[7]			-[8]			
15-19	346.7	8.1[6]		146.9	176.5[7]			15.2[8]			
20-24	606.1	13.8[6]		162.5	290.9[7]			138.8[8]			
25-29	580.0	22.1[6]		184.6	214.0[7]			159.3[8]			
30-34	542.4	19.3[6]		222.6	186.7[7]			113.8[8]			
35-39	506.0	26.9[6]		209.9	174.2[7]			95.0[8]			
40-44	473.8	33.8[6]		212.2	140.4[7]			87.4[8]			
45-49	357.2	28.7[6]		171.1	85.5[7]			71.9[8]			
50-54	287.6	39.4[6]		148.7	51.9[7]			47.6[8]			
55-59	173.2	25.5[6]		103.5	21.8[7]			22.4[8]			
60+	278.4	63.1[6]		178.2	19.0[7]			18.0[8]			
?	2.6	-[6]		2.6	-[7]			-[8]			

México (BA) (2008) [9][10]

Total - Total - Total
ISCED-97 - CITE-97 - CINE-97

	Total	X	0	1	2	3	4	5A	5B	6	?
Total	45 460.0	2 486.5		13 471.1	12 569.6	6 791.2	2 311.4	7 062.3	211.9	537.1	18.9
14-14	338.5	3.5		164.5	170.4	0.0	0.0	0.0	0.0	0.0	0.2
15-19	3 904.9	51.2		767.5	2 003.1	961.1	65.3	53.6	2.8	0.0	0.3
20-24	5 511.5	64.5		888.8	1 792.8	1 475.8	217.6	1 018.0	46.0	6.1	1.7
25-29	5 582.2	117.3		1 123.9	1 661.3	999.9	223.1	1 375.0	36.0	44.9	0.8
30-34	5 631.7	136.3		1 420.8	1 740.4	862.9	284.4	1 076.0	32.4	76.6	1.9
35-39	5 704.5	153.1		1 474.8	1 798.6	839.3	399.3	931.5	29.8	75.6	2.7
40-44	5 171.8	198.0		1 532.1	1 328.1	726.4	409.4	861.5	30.0	85.5	1.0
45-49	4 331.9	257.6		1 613.9	855.1	453.2	301.9	739.6	19.3	90.2	0.9
50-54	3 327.5	282.6		1 414.7	571.6	256.7	204.2	519.5	7.3	68.1	2.8
55-59	2 392.5	311.3		1 176.9	342.4	120.4	121.2	265.0	4.8	49.7	0.8
60-64	1 515.5	276.1		802.2	164.2	60.3	54.0	127.6	1.9	26.7	2.5
65-69	952.6	243.1		514.9	85.9	18.1	16.3	65.1	0.3	7.5	1.3
70-74	586.7	182.7		322.5	37.3	10.4	10.1	18.6	0.2	4.4	0.6
75+	497.5	208.1		248.8	16.6	6.3	4.5	10.6	0.1	1.8	0.6
?	10.6	1.1		4.8	1.9	0.6	0.0	0.5	1.0	0.1	0.8

Explanatory notes: see p. 3.

[1] Persons aged 15 years and over. [2] Fourth quarter. [3] Levels 1-2. [4] Levels 6-7. [5] Persons aged 10 years and over. [6] Levels X-0. [7] Levels 2-5. [8] Levels 6-9. [9] Persons aged 14 years and over. [10] Second quarter.

Notes explicatives: voir p. 5.

[1] Personnes âgées de 15 ans et plus. [2] Quatrième trimestre. [3] Niveaux 1-2. [4] Niveaux 6-7. [5] Personnes âgées de 10 ans et plus. [6] Niveaux X-0. [7] Niveaux 2-5. [8] Niveaux 6-9. [9] Personnes âgées de 14 ans et plus. [10] Deuxième trimestre.

Notas explicativas: véase p. 7.

[1] Personas de 15 años y más. [2] Cuarto trimestre. [3] Niveles 1-2. [4] Niveles 6-7. [5] Personas de 10 años y más. [6] Niveles X-0. [7] Niveles 2-5. [8] Niveles 6-9. [9] Personas de 14 años y más. [10] Segundo trimestre.

ECONOMICALLY ACTIVE POPULATION

By level of education and age group

POPULATION ACTIVE

Par niveau d'instruction et groupe d'âge

POBLACION ECONOMICAMENTE ACTIVA

Por nivel de educación y grupo de edad

Thousands						Milliers				Millares			
ISCED 1976 CITE	Total	X	0	1	2	3	5	6	7	9	?		
CINE 1997	Total	X	0	1	2	3	4	5A	5B	6	?		

México (BA) (2008) [1] [2]

Men - Hommes - Hombres
ISCED-97 - CITE-97 - CINE-97

	Total	X	0	1	2	3	4	5A	5B	6	?
Total	28 329.0	1 534.0	.	8 879.0	8 177.0	4 339.0	838.0	4 108.0	105.0	334.0	11.9
14-14	238.3	3.2	.	125.0	109.9	0.0	0.0	0.0	0.0	0.0	0.2
15-19	2 578.4	39.3	.	563.9	1 363.1	553.2	30.4	26.9	1.6	0.0	0.0
20-24	3 345.2	46.7	.	615.4	1 181.3	880.0	95.0	503.9	20.4	1.5	1.1
25-29	3 404.7	79.6	.	757.8	1 072.1	639.6	97.4	717.8	20.1	19.8	0.5
30-34	3 454.3	98.5	.	924.6	1 138.8	553.2	105.0	571.4	15.7	46.7	0.4
35-39	3 419.2	98.0	.	900.3	1 141.3	541.7	131.1	540.4	17.0	47.6	1.9
40-44	3 065.1	104.7	.	932.1	830.0	503.0	125.3	507.4	13.6	48.2	0.7
45-49	2 601.5	143.3	.	976.4	542.4	317.6	90.9	461.7	10.8	57.9	0.5
50-54	2 136.3	164.2	.	917.6	369.5	191.0	72.5	373.1	1.7	44.8	1.9
55-59	1 583.6	169.0	.	799.5	224.6	86.3	52.8	213.3	1.7	36.2	0.2
60-64	1 027.9	164.6	.	553.9	108.6	42.8	24.9	110.2	1.4	20.1	1.5
65-69	686.3	162.3	.	377.2	60.0	15.9	7.3	56.4	0.3	5.8	1.1
70-74	415.2	119.6	.	237.9	24.9	9.6	2.9	15.5	0.2	4.0	0.5
75+	365.5	140.5	.	194.5	10.2	5.2	2.9	10.0	0.1	1.6	0.6
?	7.5	1.1	.	3.4	0.7	0.3	0.0	0.1	1.0	0.1	0.7

Women - Femmes - Mujeres
ISCED-97 - CITE-97 - CINE-97

	Total	X	0	1	2	3	4	5A	5B	6	?
Total	17 130.9	952.0	.	4 591.6	4 392.2	2 451.8	1 472.9	2 954.2	106.3	203.0	7.0
14-14	100.2	0.3	.	39.5	60.4	0.0	0.0	0.0	0.0	0.0	0.0
15-19	1 326.5	11.9	.	203.6	640.0	408.0	34.9	26.7	1.2	0.0	0.3
20-24	2 166.2	17.8	.	273.4	611.6	595.8	122.6	514.1	25.6	4.6	0.6
25-29	2 177.5	37.8	.	366.0	589.2	360.2	125.6	657.3	15.9	25.1	0.3
30-34	2 177.4	37.7	.	496.3	601.6	309.7	179.4	504.6	16.7	29.9	1.6
35-39	2 285.3	55.1	.	574.6	657.3	297.6	268.2	391.1	12.8	28.0	0.7
40-44	2 106.7	93.3	.	600.0	498.1	223.3	284.1	354.0	16.4	37.3	0.3
45-49	1 730.4	114.3	.	637.5	312.7	135.6	211.0	278.0	8.5	32.3	0.4
50-54	1 191.2	118.4	.	497.1	202.1	65.7	131.7	146.4	5.6	23.3	0.9
55-59	808.9	142.3	.	377.4	117.8	34.1	68.4	51.8	3.1	13.5	0.6
60-64	487.6	111.5	.	248.3	55.6	17.5	29.1	17.5	0.5	6.7	1.0
65-69	266.2	80.8	.	137.7	25.9	2.2	9.0	8.7	0.0	1.7	0.2
70-74	171.6	63.0	.	84.6	12.4	0.8	7.2	3.1	0.0	0.4	0.1
75+	131.9	67.6	.	54.3	6.5	1.1	1.7	0.6	0.0	0.2	0.0
?	3.2	0.0	.	1.3	1.2	0.2	0.0	0.4	0.0	0.0	0.1

Panamá (BA) (2008) [3] [4]

Total - Total - Total
ISCED-97 - CITE-97 - CINE-97

	Total	X	0	1	2	3	4	5A	5B	6	?
Total	1 416.7	30.9	.	343.6	262.9	427.0	1.2	351.1 [5]	.	.	.
15-19	92.8	0.3	.	19.7	34.0	36.2	0.1	2.6 [5]	.	.	.
20-24	176.9	1.0	.	22.6	29.8	78.3	0.1	45.0 [5]	.	.	.
25-29	180.0	1.7	.	27.3	30.8	60.8	0.1	59.3 [5]	.	.	.
30-34	173.6	1.9	.	33.0	31.3	53.4	0.2	53.7 [5]	.	.	.
35-39	177.0	1.5	.	40.1	33.4	55.1	0.3	46.7 [5]	.	.	.
40-44	157.4	1.4	.	38.1	29.9	43.6	0.2	44.2 [5]	.	.	.
45-49	143.7	1.9	.	34.0	26.5	43.1	0.1	38.0 [5]	.	.	.
50-54	116.4	2.2	.	33.2	18.7	28.6	0.1	33.8 [5]	.	.	.
55-59	80.8	2.5	.	33.2	14.3	14.9	-	16.0 [5]	.	.	.
60-64	54.2	4.7	.	25.6	8.6	7.9	-	7.5 [5]	.	.	.
65-69	29.6	4.5	.	16.8	2.7	2.9	-	2.7 [5]	.	.	.
70-74	17.1	3.2	.	10.3	1.5	1.4	-	0.6 [5]	.	.	.
75+	17.1	4.2	.	9.9	1.4	0.7	-	1.0 [5]	.	.	.

Men - Hommes - Hombres
ISCED-97 - CITE-97 - CINE-97

	Total	X	0	1	2	3	4	5A	5B	6	?
Total	877.2	22.8	.	249.7	179.5	266.1	0.8	158.3 [5]	.	.	.
15-19	66.8	0.3	.	16.8	26.1	23.0	-	0.7 [5]	.	.	.
20-24	114.8	0.8	.	18.7	22.6	53.4	0.1	19.2 [5]	.	.	.
25-29	106.2	1.2	.	21.7	21.5	37.6	-	24.2 [5]	.	.	.
30-34	103.7	1.2	.	24.7	21.5	33.5	0.2	22.6 [5]	.	.	.
35-39	99.4	1.1	.	26.6	20.8	32.6	-	18.3 [5]	.	.	.
40-44	92.6	0.8	.	25.5	19.7	25.3	0.2	21.1 [5]	.	.	.
45-49	82.2	1.2	.	22.9	16.7	24.6	0.1	16.7 [5]	.	.	.
50-54	70.6	1.5	.	22.3	12.2	17.0	0.1	17.5 [5]	.	.	.
55-59	53.8	1.9	.	23.6	9.1	9.5	-	9.7 [5]	.	.	.
60-64	39.6	3.6	.	18.8	5.8	6.0	-	5.3 [5]	.	.	.
65-69	21.3	3.4	.	12.3	1.8	2.1	-	1.7 [5]	.	.	.
70-74	13.2	2.4	.	8.3	1.1	1.0	-	0.4 [5]	.	.	.
75+	13.0	3.3	.	7.6	0.8	0.5	-	0.8 [5]	.	.	.

Explanatory notes: see p. 3.

[1] Persons aged 14 years and over. [2] Second quarter. [3] Persons aged 15 years and over. [4] Aug. [5] Levels 5-6.

Notes explicatives: voir p. 5.

[1] Personnes âgées de 14 ans et plus. [2] Deuxième trimestre. [3] Personnes âgées de 15 ans et plus. [4] Août. [5] Niveaux 5-6.

Notas explicativas: véase p. 7.

[1] Personas de 14 años y más. [2] Segundo trimestre. [3] Personas de 15 años y más. [4] Agosto. [5] Niveles 5-6.

ECONOMICALLY ACTIVE POPULATION	POPULATION ACTIVE	POBLACION ECONOMICAMENTE ACTIVA
By level of education and age group	Par niveau d'instruction et groupe d'âge	Por nivel de educación y grupo de edad
Thousands	Milliers	Millares

ISCED 1976 CITE	Total	X	0	1	2	3	5	6	7	9	?
CINE 1997	Total	X	0	1	2	3	4	5A	5B	6	?

Panamá (BA) (2008) [1] [2]

Women - Femmes - Mujeres
ISCED-97 - CITE-97 - CINE-97

Age	Total	X	0	1	2	3	4	5A	5B	6	?
Total	539.5	8.1	.	93.8	83.4	160.9	0.4	192.8 [3]	.	.	.
15-19	26.0	-	.	2.9	7.9	13.2	0.1	2.0 [3]	.	.	.
20-24	62.0	0.2	.	4.0	7.2	25.0	-	25.7 [3]	.	.	.
25-29	73.8	0.5	.	5.5	9.4	23.3	0.1	35.1 [3]	.	.	.
30-34	69.9	0.7	.	8.3	9.9	19.9	-	31.1 [3]	.	.	.
35-39	77.6	0.4	.	13.5	12.6	22.5	0.2	28.4 [3]	.	.	.
40-44	64.8	0.6	.	12.5	10.2	18.3	-	23.1 [3]	.	.	.
45-49	61.4	0.7	.	11.1	9.8	18.5	-	21.3 [3]	.	.	.
50-54	45.9	0.7	.	10.8	6.5	11.6	-	16.3 [3]	.	.	.
55-59	27.0	0.6	.	9.6	5.2	5.4	-	6.3 [3]	.	.	.
60-64	14.7	1.1	.	6.8	2.7	1.9	-	2.2 [3]	.	.	.
65-69	8.4	1.1	.	4.5	0.9	0.9	-	1.0 [3]	.	.	.
70-74	3.9	0.7	.	2.0	0.4	0.4	-	0.3 [3]	.	.	.
75+	4.1	0.9	.	2.3	0.6	0.2	-	0.2 [3]	.	.	.

Paraguay (BA) (2008) [4] [5] [6]

Total - Total - Total
ISCED-97 - CITE-97 - CINE-97

Age	Total	X	0	1	2	3	4	5A	5B	6	?
Total	2 981.126	72.822	0.478	1 340.830	463.030	661.612 [7]	.	301.156	135.526	3.304	2.368
10-14	147.049	0.404	0.478	118.189	27.978	- [7]	.	-	-	-	-
15-19	348.095	2.858	-	96.783	124.253	117.363 [7]	.	4.834	2.004	-	-
20-24	378.033	1.294	-	93.548	57.155	148.428 [7]	.	57.624	19.153	-	0.831
25-29	377.497	3.636	-	114.522	45.235	118.329 [7]	.	62.839	32.082	0.854	-
30-34	308.042	4.080	-	120.671	43.449	69.246 [7]	.	42.397	27.828	-	0.371
35-39	303.015	6.757	-	123.791	45.428	64.687 [7]	.	43.459	18.154	0.164	0.575
40-44	264.035	5.109	-	136.273	33.714	46.420 [7]	.	27.072	15.274	-	0.173
45-49	228.961	6.351	-	125.602	31.914	33.617 [7]	.	20.238	10.825	0.205	0.209
50-54	211.846	10.508	-	125.071	23.587	25.130 [7]	.	21.423	5.314	0.813	-
55-59	147.976	8.702	-	97.125	12.873	17.449 [7]	.	9.080	1.967	0.780	-
60-64	121.914	8.072	-	82.036	9.824	13.016 [7]	.	7.741	1.225	-	-
65+	144.663	15.051	-	107.219	7.620	7.927 [7]	.	4.449	1.700	0.488	0.209

Men - Hommes - Hombres
ISCED-97 - CITE-97 - CINE-97

Age	Total	X	0	1	2	3	4	5A	5B	6	?
Total	1 810.287	39.095	0.192	827.559	316.904	416.544 [7]	.	154.059	52.225	2.596	1.113
10-14	101.579	0.404	0.192	81.720	19.263	- [7]	.	-	-	-	-
15-19	222.734	2.516	-	67.209	84.901	63.652 [7]	.	3.071	1.385	-	-
20-24	221.989	0.522	-	60.544	36.321	92.861 [7]	.	24.549	6.670	-	0.522
25-29	223.760	2.812	-	70.119	29.696	76.290 [7]	.	31.870	12.663	0.310	-
30-34	181.243	2.191	-	68.763	28.771	47.612 [7]	.	24.046	9.860	-	-
35-39	180.998	3.099	-	74.246	31.467	44.666 [7]	.	21.840	5.680	-	-
40-44	157.442	2.832	-	78.814	26.370	30.964 [7]	.	13.586	4.703	-	0.173
45-49	133.085	2.880	-	72.182	22.083	19.475 [7]	.	9.659	6.392	0.205	0.209
50-54	125.743	6.408	-	72.245	15.890	15.366 [7]	.	12.283	2.738	0.813	-
55-59	91.968	4.037	-	61.733	9.081	11.656 [7]	.	4.194	0.487	0.780	-
60-64	78.041	3.988	-	50.843	7.697	9.793 [7]	.	5.508	0.212	-	-
65+	91.705	7.406	-	69.141	5.364	4.209 [7]	.	3.453	1.435	0.488	0.209

Women - Femmes - Mujeres
ISCED-97 - CITE-97 - CINE-97

Age	Total	X	0	1	2	3	4	5A	5B	6	?
Total	1 170.839	33.727	0.286	513.271	146.126	245.068 [7]	.	147.097	83.301	0.708	1.255
10-14	45.470	.	0.286	36.469	8.715	- [7]	.	-	-	-	-
15-19	125.361	0.342	-	29.574	39.352	53.711 [7]	.	1.763	0.619	-	-
20-24	156.044	0.772	-	33.004	20.834	55.567 [7]	.	33.075	12.483	-	0.309
25-29	153.737	0.824	-	44.403	15.539	42.039 [7]	.	30.969	19.419	0.544	-
30-34	126.799	1.889	-	51.908	14.678	21.634 [7]	.	18.351	17.968	-	0.371
35-39	122.017	3.658	-	49.545	13.961	20.021 [7]	.	21.619	12.474	0.164	0.575
40-44	106.593	2.277	-	57.459	7.344	15.456 [7]	.	13.486	10.571	-	-
45-49	95.876	3.471	-	53.420	9.831	14.142 [7]	.	10.579	4.433	-	-
50-54	86.103	4.100	-	52.826	7.697	9.764 [7]	.	9.140	2.576	-	-
55-59	56.008	4.665	-	35.392	3.792	5.793 [7]	.	4.886	1.480	-	-
60-64	43.873	4.084	-	31.193	2.127	3.223 [7]	.	2.233	1.013	-	-
65+	52.958	7.645	-	38.078	2.256	3.718 [7]	.	0.996	0.265	-	-

Explanatory notes: see p. 3.

[1] Persons aged 15 years and over. [2] Aug. [3] Levels 5-6. [4] Persons aged 10 years and over. [5] Excl. armed forces and conscripts. [6] Fourth quarter. [7] Levels 3-4.

Notes explicatives: voir p. 5.

[1] Personnes âgées de 15 ans et plus. [2] Août. [3] Niveaux 5-6. [4] Personnes âgées de 10 ans et plus. [5] Non compris les forces armées et les conscrits. [6] Quatrième trimestre. [7] Niveaux 3-4.

Notas explicativas: véase p. 7.

[1] Personas de 15 años y más. [2] Agosto. [3] Niveles 5-6. [4] Personas de 10 años y más. [5] Excl. las fuerzas armadas y los conscriptos. [6] Cuarto trimestre. [7] Niveles 3-4.

ECONOMICALLY ACTIVE POPULATION

POPULATION ACTIVE

POBLACION ECONOMICAMENTE ACTIVA

1B

By level of education and age group

Par niveau d'instruction et groupe d'âge

Por nivel de educación y grupo de edad

	Thousands — Milliers — Millares										
ISCED 1976 / CITE	Total	X	0	1	2	3	5	6	7	9	?
CINE 1997	Total	X	0	1	2	3	4	5A	5B	6	?
Perú (BA) (2008) [1][2]											
Total - Total - Total — ISCED-97 - CITE-97 - CINE-97											
Total	4 554.6	.	48.5	525.5	661.7	1 541.1 [3]	.	869.3	807.9	100.7	.
14-14	24.1	.	-	3.4	20.7	- [3]	.	-	-	-	.
15-19	341.2	.	-	14.3	126.9	163.8 [3]	.	18.1	18.1	-	.
20-24	623.5	.	0.7	19.6	84.5	278.4 [3]	.	112.0	128.3	-	.
25-29	613.6	.	0.3	43.1	59.3	220.8 [3]	.	134.1	153.1	2.8	.
30-34	572.9	.	1.8	36.3	72.7	199.2 [3]	.	120.6	134.2	8.2	.
35-39	460.5	.	3.1	34.0	51.3	163.8 [3]	.	94.6	102.5	11.2	.
40-44	483.7	.	1.5	45.5	59.6	157.5 [3]	.	97.1	105.0	17.6	.
45-49	425.6	.	4.6	61.1	47.2	129.8 [3]	.	89.0	73.2	20.9	.
50-54	366.4	.	6.3	63.9	50.7	105.0 [3]	.	82.0	48.7	9.8	.
55-59	260.3	.	5.7	63.5	43.7	52.8 [3]	.	57.5	25.1	12.1	.
60-64	194.3	.	9.3	64.2	23.5	38.1 [3]	.	34.2	13.1	12.0	.
65-69	103.3	.	6.7	37.5	11.4	21.3 [3]	.	15.8	4.5	6.2	.
70-74	49.9	.	2.8	20.5	7.4	9.0 [3]	.	8.2	2.0	-	.
75+	35.2	.	5.9	18.6	2.9	1.7 [3]	.	6.2	-	-	.
Men - Hommes - Hombres — ISCED-97 - CITE-97 - CINE-97											
Total	2 426.2	.	8.7	221.7	357.5	878.2 [3]	.	472.4	429.6	58.0	.
14-14	11.3	.	-	2.0	9.3	- [3]	.	-	-	-	.
15-19	169.7	.	-	7.7	64.5	80.0 [3]	.	6.5	10.9	-	.
20-24	330.8	.	-	8.7	51.2	151.0 [3]	.	56.0	63.9	-	.
25-29	314.3	.	0.3	14.4	36.4	123.3 [3]	.	58.5	80.4	0.9	.
30-34	319.3	.	0.4	20.2	34.8	122.9 [3]	.	64.7	71.1	5.2	.
35-39	231.9	.	1.7	13.4	26.4	88.1 [3]	.	45.7	53.3	3.4	.
40-44	261.2	.	-	16.0	26.2	99.2 [3]	.	52.4	58.3	9.1	.
45-49	227.0	.	-	19.7	23.9	72.5 [3]	.	57.4	39.3	14.3	.
50-54	181.5	.	0.7	24.9	24.3	59.6 [3]	.	42.6	23.8	5.7	.
55-59	147.8	.	0.7	24.8	25.0	34.8 [3]	.	40.0	15.6	6.9	.
60-64	111.7	.	0.3	25.9	17.6	26.1 [3]	.	23.0	9.3	9.5	.
65-69	60.4	.	0.9	18.5	8.7	13.6 [3]	.	13.2	2.5	3.0	.
70-74	36.1	.	1.8	13.9	6.3	5.6 [3]	.	7.3	1.3	-	.
75+	23.4	.	1.9	11.7	2.9	1.7 [3]	.	5.2	-	-	.
Women - Femmes - Mujeres — ISCED-97 - CITE-97 - CINE-97											
Total	2 128.5	.	39.8	303.8	304.2	662.8 [3]	.	396.9	378.2	42.7	.
14-14	12.8	.	-	1.4	11.4	- [3]	.	-	-	-	.
15-19	171.6	.	-	6.7	62.3	83.8 [3]	.	11.6	7.2	-	.
20-24	292.7	.	0.7	10.8	33.4	127.4 [3]	.	56.0	64.4	-	.
25-29	299.3	.	-	28.7	22.9	97.5 [3]	.	75.6	72.7	1.9	.
30-34	253.7	.	1.4	16.2	37.8	76.3 [3]	.	55.8	63.1	3.0	.
35-39	228.6	.	1.4	20.6	24.9	75.6 [3]	.	48.9	49.3	7.8	.
40-44	222.6	.	1.5	29.5	33.5	58.3 [3]	.	44.6	46.7	8.5	.
45-49	198.6	.	4.6	41.4	23.3	57.3 [3]	.	31.6	33.8	6.5	.
50-54	184.8	.	5.5	39.0	26.5	45.4 [3]	.	39.4	24.9	4.1	.
55-59	112.5	.	5.0	38.6	18.7	18.0 [3]	.	17.5	9.5	5.2	.
60-64	82.7	.	9.0	38.3	5.8	12.1 [3]	.	11.2	3.8	2.5	.
65-69	42.9	.	5.8	19.1	2.6	7.7 [3]	.	2.6	2.0	3.1	.
70-74	13.9	.	1.0	6.7	1.1	3.4 [3]	.	0.9	0.7	-	.
75+	11.8	.	3.9	6.9	-	- [3]	.	1.0	-	-	.
Trinidad and Tobago (BA) (2008) [4]											
Total - Total - Total — ISCED-76 - CITE-76 - CINE-76											
Total	626.6	1.9 [5]	.	158.4	394.6 [6]	.	69.8 [7]	.	.	1.6	-
Men - Hommes - Hombres — ISCED-76 - CITE-76 - CINE-76											
Total	366.3	1.1 [5]	.	103.3	230.7 [6]	.	30.0 [7]	.	.	1.0	-
Women - Femmes - Mujeres — ISCED-76 - CITE-76 - CINE-76											
Total	260.3	0.8 [5]	.	55.1	163.9 [6]	.	39.8 [7]	.	.	0.6	
United States (BA) (2008) [8][9]											
Total - Total - Total — ISCED-76 - CITE-76 - CINE-76											
Total	132 255	12 166 [10]	.	.	.	38 263	36 718	29 266	15 842	.	.
Men - Hommes - Hombres — ISCED-76 - CITE-76 - CINE-76											
Total	70 982	7 790 [10]	.	.	.	21 364	18 217	15 249	8 363	.	.

Explanatory notes: see p. 3.

[1] Persons aged 14 years and over. [2] Metropolitan Lima. [3] Levels 3-4. [4] Persons aged 15 years and over. [5] Levels X-0. [6] Levels 2-3. [7] Levels 5-7. [8] Excl. armed forces. [9] Persons aged 25 years and over. [10] Levels X-2.

Notes explicatives: voir p. 5.

[1] Personnes âgées de 14 ans et plus. [2] Lima métropolitaine. [3] Niveaux 3-4. [4] Personnes âgées de 15 ans et plus. [5] Niveaux X-0. [6] Niveaux 2-3. [7] Niveaux 5-7. [8] Non compris les forces armées. [9] Personnes âgées de 25 ans et plus. [10] Niveaux X-2.

Notas explicativas: véase p. 7.

[1] Personas de 14 años y más. [2] Lima metropolitana. [3] Niveles 3-4. [4] Personas de 15 años y más. [5] Niveles X-0. [6] Niveles 2-3. [7] Niveles 5-7. [8] Excl. las fuerzas armadas. [9] Personas de 25 años y más. [10] Niveles X-2.

1B — ECONOMICALLY ACTIVE POPULATION / POPULATION ACTIVE / POBLACION ECONOMICAMENTE ACTIVA

By level of education and age group — Par niveau d'instruction et groupe d'âge — Por nivel de educación y grupo de edad

Thousands — Milliers — Millares

	Total	X	0	1	2	3	5 / 4	6 / 5A	7 / 5B	9 / 6	?
ISCED 1976 / CITE / CINE 1997 Total		X	0	1	2	3	5 / 4	6 / 5A	7 / 5B	9 / 6	?

United States (BA) (2008) [1][2]

Women - Femmes - Mujeres
ISCED-76 - CITE-76 - CINE-76

	Total	X	0	1	2	3	5/4	6/5A	7/5B	9/6	?
Total	61 273	4 376 [3]				16 899	18 501	14 017	7 480		

ASIA-ASIE-ASIA

Armenia (BA) (2007) [4][5]

Total - Total - Total
ISCED-97 - CITE-97 - CINE-97

	Total	X	0	1	2	3	5/4	6/5A	7/5B	9/6	?
Total	1 659.4	2.3 [6]	.	36.0	139.2	682.4	419.5	51.2	324.5	4.3	.
16-19	67.3	. [6]	.	0.9	11.2	48.1	5.4	1.7	-	-	.
20-24	199.8	- [6]	.	1.1	17.6	90.8	43.3	9.1	37.0	0.9	.
25-29	183.9	0.2 [6]	.	0.4	16.0	76.8	36.3	3.7	49.2	1.3	.
30-34	161.7	0.1 [6]	.	0.1	11.5	67.4	38.3	7.2	36.9	0.3	.
35-39	148.2	- [6]	.	0.3	9.9	57.4	45.6	5.6	29.3	0.2	.
40-44	197.1	- [6]	.	0.6	10.2	77.2	61.1	6.4	41.4	0.1	.
45-49	231.4	- [6]	.	1.7	11.0	97.2	75.4	6.4	39.4	0.3	.
50-54	176.3	- [6]	.	0.8	12.8	69.2	51.3	4.1	37.7	0.4	.
55-59	116.5	0.5 [6]	.	1.4	10.1	40.0	34.5	4.1	25.9	-	.
60-64	52.0	- [6]	.	2.7	5.8	16.8	11.4	1.3	14.0	-	.
65-69	60.8	- [6]	.	7.8	9.7	23.2	10.3	1.1	8.4	0.2	.
70-74	35.9	- [6]	.	8.9	7.4	12.3	3.9	0.4	2.8	0.2	.
75+	28.4	- [6]	.	9.2	6.1	5.9	2.6	0.2	2.5	0.4	.

Men - Hommes - Hombres
ISCED-97 - CITE-97 - CINE-97

	Total	X	0	1	2	3	5/4	6/5A	7/5B	9/6	?
Total	838.3	0.7 [6]	.	17.9	85.7	361.0	186.3	25.2	159.3	2.1	.
16-19	30.9	- [6]	.	0.7	6.9	20.7	1.5	1.0	-	-	.
20-24	110.9	- [6]	.	0.9	12.5	61.6	14.9	5.1	15.0	0.9	.
25-29	106.9	0.2 [6]	.	0.2	12.6	49.9	15.6	2.1	25.8	0.6	.
30-34	88.9	0.1 [6]	.	0.1	7.7	40.7	18.0	3.8	18.6	-	.
35-39	68.8	- [6]	.	0.3	6.7	27.7	18.5	2.1	13.6	-	.
40-44	89.3	- [6]	.	-	6.8	33.9	25.6	2.9	20.1	0.1	.
45-49	106.7	- [6]	.	1.4	7.1	43.0	33.9	3.1	18.3	-	.
50-54	89.9	- [6]	.	0.5	7.1	35.1	25.3	1.4	20.4	0.1	.
55-59	55.7	- [6]	.	0.4	5.1	20.2	16.2	2.2	11.7	-	.
60-64	27.6	- [6]	.	1.5	2.8	8.0	7.5	0.6	7.3	-	.
65-69	30.5	- [6]	.	3.5	4.1	11.2	5.6	0.5	5.4	0.2	.
70-74	17.8	- [6]	.	4.0	3.4	6.1	1.6	0.4	2.1	0.2	.
75+	14.3	0.4 [6]	.	4.5	3.0	2.9	2.0	0.2	1.2	-	.

Women - Femmes - Mujeres
ISCED-97 - CITE-97 - CINE-97

	Total	X	0	1	2	3	5/4	6/5A	7/5B	9/6	?
Total	821.1	1.7 [6]	.	18.0	53.4	321.5	233.2	26.0	165.2	2.2	.
16-19	36.4	- [6]	.	0.2	4.3	27.4	3.9	0.7	-	-	.
20-24	88.9	- [6]	.	0.2	5.1	29.2	28.4	4.0	22.0	-	.
25-29	77.0	- [6]	.	0.2	3.4	26.9	20.7	1.6	23.5	0.7	.
30-34	72.8	- [6]	.	-	3.8	26.7	20.3	3.4	18.3	0.3	.
35-39	79.4	- [6]	.	-	3.2	29.6	27.1	3.5	15.7	0.2	.
40-44	107.7	- [6]	.	0.5	3.4	43.4	35.5	3.5	21.4	-	.
45-49	124.7	- [6]	.	0.3	3.9	54.3	41.4	3.3	21.1	0.3	.
50-54	86.4	- [6]	.	0.3	5.7	34.1	26.0	2.7	17.3	0.3	.
55-59	60.8	0.5 [6]	.	1.0	5.0	19.8	18.4	1.9	14.2	-	.
60-64	24.4	- [6]	.	1.3	3.0	8.8	3.9	0.8	6.7	-	.
65-69	30.2	- [6]	.	4.3	5.6	12.0	4.7	0.6	3.0	-	.
70-74	18.1	- [6]	.	4.9	4.0	6.2	2.3	-	0.7	-	.
75+	14.2	1.1 [6]	.	4.7	3.1	3.0	0.6	-	1.3	0.4	.

Explanatory notes: see p. 3.

[1] Excl. armed forces. [2] Persons aged 25 years and over. [3] Levels X-2. [4] Incl. armed forces, Excl. conscripts. [5] Persons aged 16 years and over. [6] Levels X-0.

Notes explicatives: voir p. 5.

[1] Non compris les forces armées. [2] Personnes âgées de 25 ans et plus. [3] Niveaux X-2. [4] Y compris les forces armées, Excl. conscrits [5] Personnes âgées de 16 ans et plus. [6] Niveaux X-0.

Notas explicativas: véase p. 7.

[1] Excl. las fuerzas armadas. [2] Personas de 25 años y más. [3] Niveles X-2. [4] Incl. las fuerzas armadas, excl. los conscriptos. [5] Personas de 16 años y más. [6] Niveles X-0.

ECONOMICALLY ACTIVE POPULATION

By level of education and age group

POPULATION ACTIVE

Par niveau d'instruction et groupe d'âge

POBLACION ECONOMICAMENTE ACTIVA

Por nivel de educación y grupo de edad

1B

Thousands — Milliers — Millares

	ISCED 1976 Total	X	0	1	2	3	5	6	7	9	?
CITE CINE 1997	Total	X	0	1	2	3	4	5A	5B	6	?

Azerbaijan (BA) (2008) [1] [2]

Total - Total - Total
ISCED-97 - CITE-97 - CINE-97

Total	4 317.4	16.1 [3]	.	.	108.8	2 659.6	625.4	907.5 [4]	.	.	.
15-19	180.0	1.1 [3]	.	.	34.4	134.4	10.0	0.1 [4]	.	.	.
20-24	464.7	- [3]	.	.	9.3	343.9	60.8	50.7 [4]	.	.	.
25-29	559.3	1.2 [3]	.	.	7.0	326.8	68.2	156.1 [4]	.	.	.
30-34	598.4	1.0 [3]	.	.	6.7	352.9	76.2	161.6 [4]	.	.	.
35-39	555.2	- [3]	.	.	9.9	324.4	87.9	133.0 [4]	.	.	.
40-44	633.2	0.7 [3]	.	.	10.6	400.1	93.7	128.1 [4]	.	.	.
45-49	592.1	- [3]	.	.	7.4	372.6	92.5	119.6 [4]	.	.	.
50-54	386.4	- [3]	.	.	11.3	230.3	67.9	76.9 [4]	.	.	.
55-59	208.8	1.1 [3]	.	.	2.1	115.3	42.6	47.7 [4]	.	.	.
60-64	93.8	5.6 [3]	.	.	7.1	41.6	18.2	21.3 [4]	.	.	.
65+	45.5	5.4 [3]	.	.	3.0	17.3	7.4	12.4 [4]	.	.	.

Men - Hommes - Hombres
ISCED-97 - CITE-97 - CINE-97

Total	2 205.2	3.8 [3]	.	.	38.8	1 341.5	302.3	518.8 [4]	.	.	.
15-19	83.3	- [3]	.	.	20.8	54.7	7.7	0.1 [4]	.	.	.
20-24	252.4	- [3]	.	.	3.8	196.6	24.1	27.9 [4]	.	.	.
25-29	287.8	0.7 [3]	.	.	2.2	174.5	27.0	83.4 [4]	.	.	.
30-34	301.3	- [3]	.	.	2.3	170.4	40.3	88.3 [4]	.	.	.
35-39	282.9	- [3]	.	.	4.1	173.5	35.6	69.7 [4]	.	.	.
40-44	318.5	0.7 [3]	.	.	0.8	184.8	50.4	81.8 [4]	.	.	.
45-49	308.0	- [3]	.	.	1.1	189.4	43.7	73.8 [4]	.	.	.
50-54	186.3	- [3]	.	.	2.6	102.5	38.3	42.9 [4]	.	.	.
55-59	127.8	- [3]	.	.	0.4	68.7	24.8	33.9 [4]	.	.	.
60-64	44.6	2.4 [3]	.	.	0.7	21.8	7.0	12.7 [4]	.	.	.
65+	12.3	- [3]	.	.	-	4.6	3.4	4.3 [4]	.	.	.

Women - Femmes - Mujeres
ISCED-97 - CITE-97 - CINE-97

Total	2 112.2	12.3 [3]	.	.	70.0	1 318.1	323.1	388.7 [4]	.	.	.
15-19	96.7	1.1 [3]	.	.	13.6	79.7	2.3	- [4]	.	.	.
20-24	212.3	- [3]	.	.	5.5	147.3	36.7	22.8 [4]	.	.	.
25-29	271.5	0.5 [3]	.	.	4.8	152.3	41.2	72.7 [4]	.	.	.
30-34	297.1	1.0 [3]	.	.	4.4	182.5	35.9	73.3 [4]	.	.	.
35-39	272.3	- [3]	.	.	5.8	150.9	52.3	63.3 [4]	.	.	.
40-44	314.7	- [3]	.	.	9.8	215.3	43.3	46.3 [4]	.	.	.
45-49	284.1	- [3]	.	.	6.3	183.2	48.8	45.8 [4]	.	.	.
50-54	200.1	- [3]	.	.	8.7	127.8	29.6	34.0 [4]	.	.	.
55-59	81.0	1.1 [3]	.	.	1.7	46.6	17.8	13.8 [4]	.	.	.
60-64	49.2	3.2 [3]	.	.	6.4	19.8	11.2	8.6 [4]	.	.	.
65+	33.2	5.4 [3]	.	.	3.0	12.7	4.0	8.1 [4]	.	.	.

Hong Kong, China (BA) (2008) [1] [5]

Total - Total - Total
ISCED-97 - CITE-97 - CINE-97

Total	3 648.9	30.0	.	439.8	603.0	1 429.0	188.3	187.6	609.5	161.7	.
15-19	56.4	-	.	-	8.6	37.2	4.2	3.6	2.7	-	.
20-24	310.1	-	.	4.7	29.9	150.1	19.9	30.5	71.5	3.4	.
25-29	476.6	-	.	10.9	47.9	200.8	28.5	30.1	131.8	26.4	.
30-34	471.0	-	.	14.1	63.6	191.9	26.5	27.3	113.6	33.7	.
35-39	478.2	0.6	.	20.1	75.0	205.6	22.9	24.2	97.8	32.0	.
40-44	504.4	2.0	.	37.7	90.8	218.9	29.1	23.1	75.9	26.9	.
45-49	523.2	3.9	.	82.5	109.1	202.3	26.9	22.6	56.6	19.3	.
50-54	421.4	7.5	.	119.3	91.1	126.4	18.0	15.0	32.1	12.1	.
55-59	266.3	7.2	.	95.5	61.4	65.1	7.8	7.4	16.0	5.9	.
60-64	98.1	4.7	.	38.8	19.7	22.1	2.7	2.7	6.1	1.3	.
65-69	27.4	1.8	.	10.2	4.2	5.8	1.1	0.5	3.4	-	.
70-74	10.9	1.1	.	4.1	1.2	2.0	0.5	-	1.6	-	.
75+	5.0	0.9	.	1.9	-	0.7	-	-	0.5	-	.

Explanatory notes: see p. 3.

[1] Persons aged 15 years and over. [2] Excl. armed forces and conscripts. [3] Levels X-1. [4] Levels 5A, 5B and 6. [5] Excl. marine, military and institutional populations.

Notes explicatives: voir p. 5.

[1] Personnes âgées de 15 ans et plus. [2] Non compris les forces armées et les conscrits. [3] Niveaux X-1. [4] Niveaux 5A, 5B et 6. [5] Non compris le personnel militaire, de la marine et la population institutionnelle.

Notas explicativas: véase p. 7.

[1] Personas de 15 años y más. [2] Excl. las fuerzas armadas y los conscriptos. [3] Niveles X-1. [4] Niveles 5A, 5B y 6. [5] Excl. el personal militar y de la marina, y la población institucional.

ECONOMICALLY ACTIVE POPULATION
By level of education and age group

POPULATION ACTIVE
Par niveau d'instruction et groupe d'âge

POBLACION ECONOMICAMENTE ACTIVA
Por nivel de educación y grupo de edad

Thousands — Milliers — Millares

ISCED 1976 CITE	Total	X	0	1	2	3	5	6	7	9	?
CINE 1997	Total	X	0	1	2	3	4	5A	5B	6	?

Hong Kong, China (BA) (2008) [1] [2]

Men - Hommes - Hombres
ISCED-97 - CITE-97 - CINE-97

Age	Total	X	0	1	2	3	4	5A	5B	6	?
Total	1 949.4	12.5	.	235.7	376.1	731.5	90.1	91.0	314.6	97.8	.
15-19	29.6	-	.	-	6.3	19.0	1.6	1.5	1.2	-	.
20-24	142.8	-	.	-	16.7	71.9	7.9	13.7	30.2	1.9	.
25-29	215.5	-	.	1.7	26.2	90.3	10.7	14.0	59.7	13.0	.
30-34	221.1	-	.	3.0	36.1	88.6	10.2	12.3	53.4	17.5	.
35-39	231.5	-	.	6.8	43.8	95.1	9.3	10.6	47.3	18.6	.
40-44	265.0	0.9	.	15.4	53.8	108.5	13.7	11.7	43.3	17.6	.
45-49	301.7	1.1	.	42.9	68.6	110.4	15.8	12.4	36.7	13.8	.
50-54	260.0	3.1	.	67.3	59.8	78.8	12.2	8.0	21.6	9.2	.
55-59	173.9	3.0	.	57.2	44.1	44.2	5.1	4.1	11.5	4.7	.
60-64	73.0	2.1	.	27.7	15.5	17.6	2.2	1.9	5.0	1.0	.
65-69	22.2	1.0	.	8.1	3.7	4.9	0.8	-	3.0	-	.
70-74	9.1	0.7	.	3.5	1.2	1.7	0.5	-	1.4	-	.
75+	4.0	-	.	1.6	-	0.7	-	-	-	-	.

Women - Femmes - Mujeres
ISCED-97 - CITE-97 - CINE-97

Age	Total	X	0	1	2	3	4	5A	5B	6	?
Total	1 699.5	17.5	.	204.1	226.8	697.5	98.2	96.5	294.9	63.9	.
15-19	26.7	-	.	-	2.3	18.2	2.6	2.2	1.5	-	.
20-24	167.3	-	.	4.3	13.1	78.2	11.9	16.8	41.3	1.6	.
25-29	261.1	-	.	9.3	21.8	110.5	17.9	16.1	72.0	13.4	.
30-34	249.9	-	.	11.1	27.5	103.3	16.3	15.1	60.2	16.2	.
35-39	246.8	-	.	13.3	31.3	110.5	13.6	13.7	50.5	13.5	.
40-44	239.5	1.2	.	22.3	36.9	110.5	15.4	11.4	32.5	9.3	.
45-49	221.6	2.9	.	39.5	40.5	92.0	11.1	10.1	19.9	5.5	.
50-54	161.4	4.4	.	51.9	31.3	47.6	5.8	7.0	10.5	2.9	.
55-59	92.3	4.2	.	38.3	17.3	20.9	2.7	3.3	4.5	1.2	.
60-64	25.1	2.6	.	11.1	4.2	4.5	0.5	0.8	1.2	-	.
65-69	5.2	0.8	.	2.1	0.5	0.9	-	-	-	-	.
70-74	1.7	-	.	0.6	-	-	-	-	-	-	.
75+	1.0	-	.	-	-	-	-	-	-	-	.

Indonesia (BA) (2008) [2] [3]

Total - Total - Total
ISCED-76 - CITE-76 - CINE-76

Age	Total	X	0	1	2	3	5	6	7	9	?
Total	111 947.3	5 571.3	13 552.7	38 856.9	21 013.2	24 965.7	1 468.1	1 766.4	4 752.9	.	.
15-19	8 154.3	81.0	532.1	2 819.6	2 791.3	1 918.0	11.7	0.4	0.0	.	.
20-24	13 429.6	120.1	626.3	3 262.2	3 318.6	5 211.7	263.9	278.4	348.4	.	.
25-29	15 372.0	159.2	891.7	4 393.8	3 650.4	4 553.5	283.9	431.1	1 008.5	.	.
30-34	14 652.8	207.1	1 041.7	5 230.7	3 025.6	3 868.0	196.0	306.9	777.0	.	.
35-39	14 054.3	344.3	1 320.0	5 105.2	2 744.3	3 429.3	163.5	218.2	729.4	.	.
40-44	12 512.7	575.9	1 681.7	4 652.7	1 808.4	2 672.8	184.0	190.9	746.4	.	.
45-49	10 868.0	741.3	1 988.9	4 440.3	1 302.1	1 492.3	157.2	143.2	602.6	.	.
50-54	8 760.3	781.1	1 834.2	3 620.1	1 009.5	952.8	109.1	100.2	353.3	.	.
55-59	5 713.5	636.7	1 331.3	2 365.2	619.8	506.0	70.0	54.9	129.7	.	.
60-64	3 723.0	672.3	984.0	1 426.9	351.3	209.4	18.7	25.1	35.3	.	.
65-69	2 472.9	536.1	689.1	885.6	224.2	101.0	7.4	12.9	16.6	.	.
70-74	1 324.7	404.4	378.8	387.3	105.5	39.1	2.1	2.9	4.7	.	.
75+	909.2	311.9	252.7	267.3	62.4	12.0	0.7	1.3	0.9	.	.

Men - Hommes - Hombres
ISCED-76 - CITE-76 - CINE-76

Age	Total	X	0	1	2	3	5	6	7	9	?
Total	69 144.3	2 441.6	7 782.5	24 090.0	13 693.2	16 826.0	586.4	912.7	2 812.0	.	.
15-19	4 816.3	44.2	377.6	1 788.0	1 595.0	1 005.9	5.6	0.0	0.0	.	.
20-24	8 103.7	61.6	408.3	2 125.2	2 074.0	3 109.9	83.2	103.9	137.6	.	.
25-29	9 659.3	83.0	554.1	2 731.4	2 433.8	3 055.2	108.3	199.0	494.6	.	.
30-34	9 255.2	93.6	619.0	3 179.5	1 999.4	2 699.9	75.0	156.7	432.0	.	.
35-39	8 667.1	134.9	681.3	2 960.6	1 836.5	2 422.4	64.6	120.5	446.2	.	.
40-44	7 645.6	223.0	834.7	2 718.7	1 237.7	1 959.1	72.1	110.3	489.8	.	.
45-49	6 584.8	310.6	1 039.9	2 649.2	893.7	1 143.0	59.2	86.4	402.6	.	.
50-54	5 497.9	346.6	1 024.5	2 295.7	708.3	740.8	54.6	65.8	261.4	.	.
55-59	3 597.6	275.4	761.8	1 556.5	432.7	392.4	42.0	35.3	101.5	.	.
60-64	2 304.5	283.6	590.5	964.5	233.5	169.5	13.8	20.4	28.7	.	.
65-69	1 549.4	235.7	432.0	624.2	145.1	82.6	6.1	10.7	13.0	.	.
70-74	833.5	182.2	264.1	282.5	62.9	33.9	1.3	2.9	3.7	.	.
75+	629.4	167.1	194.6	213.9	40.4	11.1	0.5	0.8	0.9	.	.

Explanatory notes: see p. 3.
[1] Excl. marine, military and institutional populations. [2] Persons aged 15 years and over. [3] August.

Notes explicatives: voir p. 5.
[1] Non compris le personnel militaire, de la marine et la population institutionnelle. [2] Personnes âgées de 15 ans et plus. [3] Août.

Notas explicativas: véase p. 7.
[1] Excl. el personal militar y de la marina, y la población institucional. [2] Personas de 15 años y más. [3] Agosto.

ECONOMICALLY ACTIVE POPULATION

By level of education and age group

POPULATION ACTIVE

Par niveau d'instruction et groupe d'âge

POBLACION ECONOMICAMENTE ACTIVA

Por nivel de educación y grupo de edad

1B

	Thousands / Milliers / Millares										
ISCED 1976 CITE	Total	X	0	1	2	3	5	6	7	9	?
CINE 1997	Total	X	0	1	2	3	4	5A	5B	6	?
Indonesia (BA) (2008) [1][2]											
Women - Femmes - Mujeres											
ISCED-76 - CITE-76 - CINE-76											
Total	42 802.9	3 129.8	5 770.2	14 766.9	7 320.0	8 139.7	881.7	853.8	1 940.9	.	.
15-19	3 338.0	36.8	154.6	1 031.6	1 196.3	912.1	6.1	0.4	0.0	.	.
20-24	5 325.9	58.5	218.0	1 137.0	1 244.6	2 101.7	180.6	174.5	210.8	.	.
25-29	5 712.7	76.2	337.6	1 662.4	1 216.4	1 498.2	175.7	232.2	514.0	.	.
30-34	5 397.6	113.5	422.7	2 051.2	1 026.2	1 168.0	120.9	150.2	345.0	.	.
35-39	5 387.2	209.4	638.7	2 144.6	907.9	1 006.8	99.0	97.7	283.2	.	.
40-44	4 867.1	352.8	846.9	1 934.0	570.7	713.7	111.8	80.7	256.5	.	.
45-49	4 283.2	430.7	949.0	1 791.2	408.3	349.3	98.0	56.7	200.0	.	.
50-54	3 262.5	434.5	809.7	1 324.3	301.2	212.0	54.4	34.4	91.9	.	.
55-59	2 115.8	361.3	569.5	808.7	187.0	113.5	28.0	19.6	28.2	.	.
60-64	1 418.5	388.7	393.5	462.4	117.8	39.9	5.0	4.6	6.6	.	.
65-69	923.5	300.4	257.1	261.4	79.1	18.3	1.3	2.2	3.7	.	.
70-74	491.2	222.2	114.8	104.7	42.5	5.2	0.7	0.1	1.1	.	.
75+	279.8	144.8	58.1	53.3	22.0	0.8	0.2	0.5	0.0	.	.
Iran, Islamic Rep. of (BA) (2008) [3]											
Total - Total - Total											
ISCED-97 - CITE-97 - CINE-97											
Total	22 893	.	.	7 026	5 406	5 790	.	2 922	1 355	32	362
Men - Hommes - Hombres											
ISCED-97 - CITE-97 - CINE-97											
Total	18 835	.	.	6 077	4 977	4 789	.	1 743	905	26	318
Women - Femmes - Mujeres											
ISCED-97 - CITE-97 - CINE-97											
Total	4 058	.	.	951	428	1 001	.	1 179	450	5	44
Israel (BA) (2008) [2][4]											
Total - Total - Total											
ISCED-97 - CITE-97 - CINE-97											
Total	2 957.1	13.7	1.3	164.5	212.3	1 206.8	.	844.7	453.7	35.2	.
15-17	28.7	0.0	0.1	3.0	22.6	2.9	.	0.0	0.0	0.0	.
18-24	338.8	0.7	0.2	12.1	25.3	260.6	.	10.7	27.1	0.0	.
25-34	837.4	2.3	0.4	29.6	38.5	358.5	.	273.7	123.8	3.7	.
35-44	703.2	4.7	0.3	33.4	40.1	260.6	.	228.3	119.7	10.3	.
45-54	584.3	3.1	0.1	39.4	47.9	194.1	.	185.4	101.5	7.8	.
55-64	388.5	2.3	0.0	36.3	32.5	107.8	.	125.1	70.0	9.8	.
65+	76.1	-	0.0	10.6	5.5	22.3	.	21.4	11.5	3.6	.
Men - Hommes - Hombres											
ISCED-97 - CITE-97 - CINE-97											
Total	1 579.9	6.5	-	123.7	149.5	653.4	.	394.1	217.0	22.8	.
15-17	16.6	0.0	-	2.2	11.9	2.4	.	0.0	0.0	0.0	.
18-24	161.6	-	-	10.3	18.7	122.2	.	2.7	6.2	0.0	.
25-34	448.3	-	-	24.2	30.6	212.4	.	113.5	60.6	2.2	.
35-44	376.4	-	-	26.3	30.4	140.9	.	107.5	61.0	6.0	.
45-54	306.0	-	-	28.7	31.2	101.1	.	88.8	47.0	5.1	.
55-64	217.4	-	-	24.1	22.3	58.5	.	66.1	36.1	6.2	.
65+	53.6	-	0.0	7.8	4.5	16.0	.	15.4	6.0	3.3	.
Women - Femmes - Mujeres											
ISCED-97 - CITE-97 - CINE-97											
Total	1 377.2	7.2	-	40.8	62.8	553.4	.	450.6	236.6	12.4	.
15-17	12.1	0.0	-	-	10.7	-	.	0.0	0.0	0.0	.
18-24	177.2	-	-	-	6.6	138.4	.	7.9	20.9	0.0	.
25-34	389.1	-	-	5.4	8.0	146.1	.	160.2	63.1	-	.
35-44	326.8	3.1	-	7.1	9.7	119.7	.	120.9	58.7	4.3	.
45-54	278.4	-	-	10.6	16.7	93.0	.	96.6	54.5	2.7	.
55-64	171.2	-	-	12.3	10.3	49.4	.	59.0	33.9	3.6	.
65+	22.5	-	0.0	2.8	-	6.3	.	6.0	5.5	-	.
Japan (BA) (2008) [2][5]											
Total - Total - Total											
ISCED-76 - CITE-76 - CINE-76											
Total	63 830	50	.	37 410 [6]	.	.	10 680	15 740 [7]	.	.	.
15-24	4 670	0	.	2 830 [6]	.	.	1 000	830 [7]	.	.	.
25-34	13 520	10	.	6 070 [6]	.	.	3 090	4 360 [7]	.	.	.
35-44	14 530	10	.	7 540 [6]	.	.	2 960	4 040 [7]	.	.	.
45-54	13 030	10	.	7 340 [6]	.	.	2 150	3 530 [7]	.	.	.
55-64	12 420	10	.	8 950 [6]	.	.	1 150	2 310 [7]	.	.	.
65+	5 660	10	.	4 670 [6]	.	.	330	660 [7]	.	.	.

Explanatory notes: see p. 3.

[1] August. [2] Persons aged 15 years and over. [3] Persons aged 10 years and over. [4] Excl. armed forces. [5] Refer only to persons graduated from school. [6] Levels 1-3. [7] Levels 6-7.

Notes explicatives: voir p. 5.

[1] Août. [2] Personnes âgées de 15 ans et plus. [3] Personnes âgées de 10 ans et plus. [4] Non compris les forces armées. [5] Se rapportent seulement aux personnes diplômées de l'école. [6] Niveaux 1-3. [7] Niveaux 6-7.

Notas explicativas: véase p. 7.

[1] Agosto. [2] Personas de 15 años y más. [3] Personas de 10 años y más. [4] Excl. las fuerzas armadas. [5] Se refieren solamente a las personas con diploma. [6] Niveles 1-3. [7] Niveles 6-7.

1B — ECONOMICALLY ACTIVE POPULATION / POPULATION ACTIVE / POBLACION ECONOMICAMENTE ACTIVA

By level of education and age group — Par niveau d'instruction et groupe d'âge — Por nivel de educación y grupo de edad

Thousands — Milliers — Millares

	Total	X	0	1	2	3	5 / 4	6 / 5A	7 / 5B	9 / 6	?
ISCED 1976 / CITE	Total	X	0	1	2	3	5	6	7	9	?
CINE 1997	Total	X	0	1	2	3	4	5A	5B	6	?

Japan (BA) (2008) [1][2]

Men - Hommes - Hombres — ISCED-76 - CITE-76 - CINE-76

	Total	X	0	1	2	3	5	6	7	9	?
Total	37 360	30	.	21 770[3]	.	.	3 740	11 850[4]	.	.	.
15-24	2 340	0	.	1 600[3]	.	.	330	410[4]	.	.	.
25-34	7 910	10	.	3 850[3]	.	.	1 160	2 900[4]	.	.	.
35-44	8 610	0	.	4 410[3]	.	.	1 050	3 160[4]	.	.	.
45-54	7 390	10	.	3 970[3]	.	.	610	2 810[4]	.	.	.
55-64	7 520	10	.	5 110[3]	.	.	430	1 990[4]	.	.	.
65+	3 580	0	.	2 840[3]	.	.	160	580[4]	.	.	.

Women - Femmes - Mujeres — ISCED-76 - CITE-76 - CINE-76

	Total	X	0	1	2	3	5	6	7	9	?
Total	26 470	20	.	15 640[3]	.	.	6 940	3 890[4]	.	.	.
15-24	2 330	0	.	1 230[3]	.	.	670	420[4]	.	.	.
25-34	5 610	0	.	2 220[3]	.	.	1 930	1 470[4]	.	.	.
35-44	5 920	10	.	3 140[3]	.	.	1 910	880[4]	.	.	.
45-54	5 630	0	.	3 370[3]	.	.	1 540	720[4]	.	.	.
55-64	4 890	0	.	3 850[3]	.	.	720	320[4]	.	.	.
65+	2 080	10	.	1 830[3]	.	.	170	80[4]	.	.	.

Kazakhstan (BA) (2008) [1][5]

Total - Total - Total — ISCED-97 - CITE-97 - CINE-97

	Total	X	0	1	2	3	4	5A	5B	6	?
Total	8 415.0	.	.	382.9	2 645.3	3 149.4	288.9	.	1 948.7	.	.

Men - Hommes - Hombres — ISCED-97 - CITE-97 - CINE-97

	Total	X	0	1	2	3	4	5A	5B	6	?
Total	4 244.2	.	.	211.4	1 405.0	1 629.7	131.9	.	866.3	.	.

Women - Femmes - Mujeres — ISCED-97 - CITE-97 - CINE-97

	Total	X	0	1	2	3	4	5A	5B	6	?
Total	4 170.9	.	.	171.5	1 240.3	1 519.7	157.0	.	1 082.4	.	.

Macau, China (BA) (2008) [5][6]

Total - Total - Total — ISCED-97 - CITE-97 - CINE-97

	Total	X	0	1	2	3	4	5A	5B	6	?
Total	333.0	4.5	11.4	56.9	99.9	90.9	.	57.3	12.1	.	0.1
14-19	6.7	0.0	0.2	1.4	2.8	2.1	.	0.0	0.1	.	0.0
20-24	39.4	0.1	0.2	2.6	10.1	17.5	.	7.3	1.6	.	-
25-29	40.2	-	0.2	2.3	8.9	11.1	.	15.6	2.1	.	-
30-34	40.9	0.1	0.3	3.2	12.8	11.4	.	10.9	2.0	.	0.0
35-39	44.7	0.2	0.7	5.4	15.6	11.3	.	9.3	2.1	.	-
40-44	43.8	0.5	1.3	7.7	15.4	11.5	.	6.0	1.5	.	0.0
45-49	45.7	0.8	2.0	10.4	14.9	12.7	.	3.8	1.2	.	0.0
50-54	37.8	1.2	3.0	11.7	10.5	8.5	.	2.3	0.7	.	0.0
55-59	20.7	0.7	1.8	7.6	6.0	3.0	.	1.1	0.5	.	0.0
60-64	9.1	0.5	1.0	3.4	2.1	1.3	.	0.6	0.2	.	0.0
65-69	2.1	0.1	0.2	0.7	0.4	0.4	.	0.3	0.1	.	0.0
70-74	1.1	0.1	0.2	0.3	0.3	0.1	.	0.2	0.1	.	0.0
75+	0.9	0.2	0.2	0.2	0.2	0.1	.	0.1	-	.	0.0

Men - Hommes - Hombres — ISCED-97 - CITE-97 - CINE-97

	Total	X	0	1	2	3	4	5A	5B	6	?
Total	178.0	1.8	6.1	31.4	54.2	49.4	.	28.9	6.1	.	-
14-19	3.5	0.0	0.1	0.9	1.6	0.8	.	0.0	0.1	.	-
20-24	18.8	0.0	0.1	1.8	5.5	8.4	.	2.6	0.5	.	0.0
25-29	19.8	0.0	0.2	1.2	4.5	5.4	.	7.2	1.2	.	-
30-34	20.5	0.1	0.2	1.8	6.4	5.9	.	5.0	1.1	.	0.0
35-39	21.9	0.1	0.3	2.1	7.4	5.8	.	5.2	1.0	.	-
40-44	21.8	0.2	0.4	3.4	7.2	6.3	.	3.4	0.8	.	0.0
45-49	25.8	0.3	1.1	5.3	8.4	7.7	.	2.3	0.7	.	0.0
50-54	23.1	0.3	1.6	6.8	7.0	5.4	.	1.5	0.4	.	0.0
55-59	12.9	0.3	0.9	4.6	3.9	2.3	.	0.8	0.2	.	0.0
60-64	6.7	0.2	0.7	2.6	1.7	1.0	.	0.5	0.1	.	0.0
65-69	1.6	-	0.2	0.5	0.3	0.4	.	0.2	-	.	0.0
70-74	0.9	-	0.2	0.2	0.2	0.1	.	0.1	0.1	.	0.0
75+	0.8	0.2	0.2	0.2	0.1	0.1	.	0.1	-	.	0.0

Explanatory notes: see p. 3.

[1] Persons aged 15 years and over. [2] Refer only to persons graduated from school. [3] Levels 1-3. [4] Levels 6-7. [5] Excl. armed forces and conscripts. [6] Persons aged 14 years and over.

Notes explicatives: voir p. 5.

[1] Personnes âgées de 15 ans et plus. [2] Se rapportent seulement aux personnes diplômées de l'école. [3] Niveaux 1-3. [4] Niveaux 6-7. [5] Non compris les forces armées et les conscrits. [6] Personnes âgées de 14 ans et plus.

Notas explicativas: véase p. 7.

[1] Personas de 15 años y más. [2] Se refieren solamente de las personas con diploma. [3] Niveles 1-3. [4] Niveles 6-7. [5] Excl. las fuerzas armadas y los conscriptos. [6] Personas de 14 años y más.

ECONOMICALLY ACTIVE POPULATION

By level of education and age group

Thousands

POPULATION ACTIVE

Par niveau d'instruction et groupe d'âge

Milliers

POBLACION ECONOMICAMENTE ACTIVA

Por nivel de educación y grupo de edad

Millares

ISCED 1976 CITE	Total	X	0	1	2	3	5	6	7	9	?
CINE 1997	**Total**	**X**	**0**	**1**	**2**	**3**	**4**	**5A**	**5B**	**6**	**?**

Macau, China (BA) (2008) [1,2]

Women - Femmes - Mujeres
ISCED-97 - CITE-97 - CINE-97

Age	Total	X	0	1	2	3	4	5A	5B	6	?
Total	155.1	2.7	5.2	25.5	45.7	41.5	.	28.4	6.0	.	-
14-19	3.2	0.0	0.1	0.5	0.8	1.3	.	0.0	0.1	.	0.0
20-24	20.5	0.1	0.1	0.8	4.6	9.2	.	4.7	1.1	.	0.0
25-29	20.5	-	0.1	1.1	4.3	5.7	.	8.4	0.8	.	-
30-34	20.4	0.1	0.1	1.5	6.4	5.6	.	5.9	0.9	.	0.0
35-39	22.8	0.2	0.4	3.3	8.2	5.5	.	4.1	1.1	.	0.0
40-44	22.1	0.3	0.9	4.3	8.1	5.2	.	2.6	0.7	.	0.0
45-49	20.0	0.5	0.9	5.1	6.5	5.0	.	1.5	0.5	.	0.0
50-54	14.7	0.8	1.4	4.9	3.4	3.0	.	0.7	0.3	.	0.0
55-59	7.7	0.4	0.9	3.0	2.1	0.7	.	0.3	0.3	.	0.0
60-64	2.3	0.3	0.3	0.8	0.5	0.3	.	0.1	0.1	.	0.0
65-69	0.5	-	0.1	0.1	0.1	-	.	-	-	.	0.0
70-74	0.3	0.1	-	0.1	0.1	-	.	-	0.0	.	0.0
75+	0.1	0.1	0.0	0.0	-	0.0	.	-	0.0	.	0.0

Malaysia (BA) (2008) [3,4]

Total - Total - Total
ISCED-97 - CITE-97 - CINE-97

Age	Total	X	0	1	2	3	4	5A	5B	6	?
Total	11 028.1	489.0	.	2 016.7	6 180.4 [5]	.	.	2 342.0 [6]	.	.	.
15-19	478.8	20.4	.	77.0	363.5 [5]	.	.	18.0 [6]	.	.	.
20-24	1 619.5	22.2	.	129.6	1 063.3 [5]	.	.	404.5 [6]	.	.	.
25-29	1 831.5	32.9	.	170.0	1 048.6 [5]	.	.	580.0 [6]	.	.	.
30-34	1 578.3	42.3	.	213.3	922.7 [5]	.	.	400.1 [6]	.	.	.
35-39	1 437.9	55.2	.	225.3	847.1 [5]	.	.	310.2 [6]	.	.	.
40-44	1 328.2	65.9	.	248.6	750.7 [5]	.	.	262.9 [6]	.	.	.
45-49	1 132.6	66.6	.	297.6	577.6 [5]	.	.	190.8 [6]	.	.	.
50-54	882.5	73.7	.	297.3	385.9 [5]	.	.	125.6 [6]	.	.	.
55-59	482.7	60.9	.	220.3	166.1 [5]	.	.	35.4 [6]	.	.	.
60-64	256.0	48.9	.	137.6	55.0 [5]	.	.	14.5 [6]	.	.	.

Men - Hommes - Hombres
ISCED-97 - CITE-97 - CINE-97

Age	Total	X	0	1	2	3	4	5A	5B	6	?
Total	7 074.6	269.6	.	1 404.4	4 134.4 [5]	.	.	1 266.1 [6]	.	.	.
15-19	294.6	12.2	.	50.1	223.6 [5]	.	.	8.8 [6]	.	.	.
20-24	965.0	14.9	.	91.5	666.9 [5]	.	.	191.7 [6]	.	.	.
25-29	1 097.4	22.1	.	119.0	682.5 [5]	.	.	273.7 [6]	.	.	.
30-34	989.9	27.5	.	147.3	607.7 [5]	.	.	207.4 [6]	.	.	.
35-39	934.7	32.5	.	152.7	575.3 [5]	.	.	174.2 [6]	.	.	.
40-44	872.2	33.7	.	165.5	512.7 [5]	.	.	160.3 [6]	.	.	.
45-49	764.4	34.2	.	201.2	405.9 [5]	.	.	123.1 [6]	.	.	.
50-54	612.4	37.5	.	204.1	283.5 [5]	.	.	87.2 [6]	.	.	.
55-59	350.0	28.8	.	163.3	130.3 [5]	.	.	27.5 [6]	.	.	.
60-64	194.1	26.2	.	109.8	46.0 [5]	.	.	12.2 [6]	.	.	.

Women - Femmes - Mujeres
ISCED-97 - CITE-97 - CINE-97

Age	Total	X	0	1	2	3	4	5A	5B	6	?
Total	3 953.5	219.4	.	612.2	2 046.0 [5]	.	.	1 075.9 [6]	.	.	.
15-19	184.3	8.2	.	26.9	139.9 [5]	.	.	9.2 [6]	.	.	.
20-24	654.5	7.2	.	38.1	396.4 [5]	.	.	212.8 [6]	.	.	.
25-29	734.1	10.8	.	51.0	366.0 [5]	.	.	306.3 [6]	.	.	.
30-34	588.5	14.8	.	65.9	315.0 [5]	.	.	192.7 [6]	.	.	.
35-39	503.2	22.7	.	72.7	271.8 [5]	.	.	136.0 [6]	.	.	.
40-44	456.0	32.3	.	83.2	238.1 [5]	.	.	102.5 [6]	.	.	.
45-49	368.2	32.4	.	96.5	171.6 [5]	.	.	67.7 [6]	.	.	.
50-54	270.1	36.1	.	93.2	102.4 [5]	.	.	38.4 [6]	.	.	.
55-59	132.8	32.1	.	57.0	35.7 [5]	.	.	7.9 [6]	.	.	.
60-64	61.8	22.7	.	27.8	9.1 [5]	.	.	2.3 [6]	.	.	.

Philippines (BA) (2008) [7,8,9]

Total - Total - Total
ISCED-97 - CITE-97 - CINE-97

Age	Total	X	0	1	2	3	4	5A	5B	6	?
Total	37 058	654	5 645 [10]	.	5 884	4 913	9 605	4 919	5 438 [11]	.	.
15-24	7 953	64	963 [10]	.	923	1 552	2 534	1 102	816 [11]	.	.
25-34	9 805	111	1 019 [10]	.	1 047	1 238	2 825	1 578	1 988 [11]	.	.
35-44	8 274	129	1 081 [10]	.	1 387	1 001	2 251	1 160	1 266 [11]	.	.
45-54	6 262	132	1 147 [10]	.	1 304	686	1 359	751	883 [11]	.	.
55-64	3 300	112	850 [10]	.	844	316	505	266	407 [11]	.	.
65+	1 463	107	585 [10]	.	379	120	131	62	79 [11]	.	.
?	1	1	- [10]	.	-	-	-	-	- [11]	.	.

Explanatory notes: see p. 3.

[1] Persons aged 14 years and over. [2] Excl. armed forces and conscripts. [3] Persons aged 15 to 64 years. [4] Excl. armed forces. [5] Levels 2-3. [6] Levels 5-6. [7] Persons aged 15 years and over. [8] Excl. regular military living in barracks. [9] Oct. [10] Levels 0-1. [11] Levels 5B and 6.

Notes explicatives: voir p. 5.

[1] Personnes âgées de 14 ans et plus. [2] Non compris les forces armées et les conscrits. [3] Personnes âgées de 15 à 64 ans. [4] Non compris les forces armées. [5] Niveaux 2-3. [6] Niveaux 5-6. [7] Personnes âgées de 15 ans et plus. [8] Non compris les militaires de carrière vivant dans des casernes. [9] Oct. [10] Niveaux 0-1. [11] Niveaux 5B et 6.

Notas explicativas: véase p. 7.

[1] Personas de 14 años y más. [2] Excl. las fuerzas armadas y los conscriptos. [3] Personas de 15 a 64 años. [4] Excl. las fuerzas armadas. [5] Niveles 2-3. [6] Niveles 5-6. [7] Personas de 15 años y más. [8] Excl. los militares profesionales que viven en casernas. [9] Oct. [10] Niveles 0-1. [11] Niveles 5B y 6.

1B

ECONOMICALLY ACTIVE POPULATION	POPULATION ACTIVE	POBLACION ECONOMICAMENTE ACTIVA
By level of education and age group	Par niveau d'instruction et groupe d'âge	Por nivel de educación y grupo de edad
Thousands	Milliers	Millares

ISCED 1976 / CITE	Total	X	0	1	2	3	5	6	7	9	?
CINE 1997	**Total**	**X**	**0**	**1**	**2**	**3**	**4**	**5A**	**5B**	**6**	**?**

Philippines (BA) (2008) [1][2][3]

Men - Hommes - Hombres — ISCED-97 - CITE-97 - CINE-97

Age	Total	X	0	1	2	3	5/4	6/5A	7/5B	9/6	?
Total	22 872	409	3 952 [4]		3 769	3 276	6 028	3 010	2 428 [5]		
15-24	5 000	49	788 [4]		702	1 109	1 454	584	314 [5]		
25-34	6 258	74	786 [4]		772	857	1 876	1 014	879 [5]		
35-44	5 088	83	783 [4]		855	636	1 424	719	589 [5]		
45-54	3 728	79	720 [4]		752	418	858	485	417 [5]		
55-64	1 941	64	525 [4]		473	194	331	167	186 [5]		
65+	857	59	349 [4]		216	63	84	41	44 [5]		
?	-	-	- [4]		-	-	-	-	- [5]		

Women - Femmes - Mujeres — ISCED-97 - CITE-97 - CINE-97

Age	Total	X	0	1	2	3	5/4	6/5A	7/5B	9/6	?
Total	14 187	246	1 693 [4]		2 115	1 637	3 578	1 909	3 009 [5]		
15-24	2 953	15	174 [4]		222	443	1 080	517	502 [5]		
25-34	3 547	37	233 [4]		275	381	949	564	1 109 [5]		
35-44	3 186	45	298 [4]		532	365	827	441	677 [5]		
45-54	2 534	54	427 [4]		552	268	501	267	466 [5]		
55-64	1 359	48	324 [4]		370	122	175	99	221 [5]		
65+	606	48	236 [4]		164	57	47	21	34 [5]		
?	1	-	- [4]		-	-	-	-	- [5]		

Singapore (BA) (2008) [6][7]

Total - Total - Total — ISCED-97 - CITE-97 - CINE-97

Age	Total	X	0	1	2	3	5/4	6/5A	7/5B	9/6	?
Total	1 928.3	262.0 [8]			205.0	452.8	510.0 [9]			498.4	
15-19	34.2	0.4 [8]			4.1	14.4	15.3 [9]			-	
20-24	147.0	1.7 [8]			5.8	28.8	90.4 [9]			20.3	
25-29	209.2	2.7 [8]			7.9	31.6	74.5 [9]			92.6	
30-34	242.9	6.1 [8]			11.7	39.9	71.9 [9]			113.2	
35-39	263.9	14.8 [8]			15.5	58.6	72.6 [9]			102.3	
40-44	262.1	29.2 [8]			30.2	70.0	58.9 [9]			73.7	
45-49	261.9	47.0 [8]			38.5	77.4	52.0 [9]			46.9	
50-54	224.9	55.3 [8]			38.2	66.9	38.6 [9]			25.8	
55-59	152.0	42.4 [8]			31.3	42.2	21.6 [9]			14.6	
60-64	78.2	30.3 [8]			14.8	17.3	9.6 [9]			6.1	
65+	52.1	32.0 [8]			6.9	5.7	4.5 [9]			2.9	

Men - Hommes - Hombres — ISCED-97 - CITE-97 - CINE-97

Age	Total	X	0	1	2	3	5/4	6/5A	7/5B	9/6	?
Total	1 093.2	156.1 [8]			131.1	236.2	292.5 [9]			277.3	
15-19	19.3	0.3 [8]			2.1	7.4	9.5 [9]			-	
20-24	75.7	0.8 [8]			3.2	16.4	51.6 [9]			3.7	
25-29	105.1	1.7 [8]			4.8	16.5	39.4 [9]			42.6	
30-34	124.1	3.4 [8]			6.5	18.9	38.0 [9]			57.4	
35-39	144.8	8.5 [8]			8.3	27.6	40.4 [9]			60.0	
40-44	149.4	17.9 [8]			16.9	33.6	33.2 [9]			47.8	
45-49	154.8	28.0 [8]			25.4	40.0	31.5 [9]			29.9	
50-54	134.7	33.0 [8]			25.5	34.8	23.3 [9]			18.1	
55-59	97.9	23.9 [8]			21.9	25.7	15.7 [9]			10.6	
60-64	51.5	18.3 [8]			10.9	10.7	6.7 [9]			4.9	
65+	36.0	20.2 [8]			5.6	4.6	3.4 [9]			2.3	

Women - Femmes - Mujeres — ISCED-97 - CITE-97 - CINE-97

Age	Total	X	0	1	2	3	5/4	6/5A	7/5B	9/6	?
Total	835.1	105.9 [8]			73.9	216.6	217.5 [9]			221.2	
15-19	14.9	- [8]			2.0	6.9	5.8 [9]			-	
20-24	71.3	0.9 [8]			2.5	12.4	38.8 [9]			16.6	
25-29	104.2	1.0 [8]			3.0	15.1	35.1 [9]			50.0	
30-34	118.8	2.7 [8]			5.2	21.1	33.9 [9]			55.8	
35-39	119.0	6.3 [8]			7.2	31.0	32.2 [9]			42.3	
40-44	112.7	11.3 [8]			13.3	36.4	25.7 [9]			25.9	
45-49	107.2	19.0 [8]			13.1	37.5	20.5 [9]			17.1	
50-54	90.1	22.3 [8]			12.7	32.1	15.3 [9]			7.7	
55-59	54.1	18.4 [8]			9.4	16.4	5.9 [9]			4.0	
60-64	26.7	12.1 [8]			4.0	6.6	3.0 [9]			1.1	
65+	16.1	11.8 [8]			1.4	1.1	1.2 [9]			0.6	

Sri Lanka (BA) (2008) [10][11]

Total - Total - Total — ISCED-97 - CITE-97 - CINE-97

Age	Total	X	0	1	2	3	5/4	6/5A	7/5B	9/6	?
Total	7 568.7	1 472.7 [8]			3 603.6	1 222.4 [12]		1 270.1 [13]			

Explanatory notes: see p. 3.

[1] Persons aged 15 years and over. [2] Excl. regular military living in barracks. [3] Oct. [4] Levels 0-1. [5] Levels 5B and 6. [6] The data refer to the residents (Singapore citizens and permanent residents) aged 15 years and over. [7] June. [8] Levels X-1. [9] Levels 4-5. [10] Persons aged 10 years and over. [11] Excl. Northern and Eastern provinces. [12] Levels 3-4. [13] Levels 5-6.

Notes explicatives: voir p. 5.

[1] Personnes âgées de 15 ans et plus. [2] Non compris les militaires de carrière vivant dans des casernes. [3] Oct. [4] Niveaux 0-1. [5] Niveaux 5B et 6. [6] Les données se réfèrent aux résidents (citoyens de Singapour et résidents permanents) âgés de 15 ans et plus. [7] Juin. [8] Niveaux X-1. [9] Niveaux 4-5. [10] Personnes âgées de 10 ans et plus. [11] Non compris les provinces du Nord et de l'Est. [12] Niveaux 3-4. [13] Niveaux 5-6.

Notas explicativas: véase p. 7.

[1] Personas de 15 años y más. [2] Excl. los militares profesionales que viven en casernas. [3] Oct. [4] Niveles 0-1. [5] Niveles 5B y 6. [6] Los datos se refieren a los residentes (ciudadanos de Singapur y residentes permanentes) de 15 años y más. [7] Junio. [8] Niveles X-1. [9] Niveles 4-5. [10] Personas de 10 años y más. [11] Excl. las provincias del Norte y del Este. [12] Niveles 3-4. [13] Niveles 5-6.

ECONOMICALLY ACTIVE POPULATION

By level of education and age group

POPULATION ACTIVE

Par niveau d'instruction et groupe d'âge

POBLACION ECONOMICAMENTE ACTIVA

Por nivel de educación y grupo de edad

1B

	Thousands / Milliers / Millares										
ISCED 1976 CITE	Total	X	0	1	2	3	5	6	7	9	?
CINE 1997	Total	X	0	1	2	3	4	5A	5B	6	?

Sri Lanka (BA) (2008) [1] [2]

Men - Hommes - Hombres
ISCED-97 - CITE-97 - CINE-97

Total	4 836.4	915.1 [3]	.	.	2 483.4	787.2 [4]	.	652.8 [5]	.	.	.

Women - Femmes - Mujeres
ISCED-97 - CITE-97 - CINE-97

Total	2 732.3	557.6 [3]	.	.	1 120.2	435.2 [4]	.	617.3 [5]	.	.	.

Syrian Arab Republic (BA) (2007) [6]

Total - Total - Total
ISCED-97 - CITE-97 - CINE-97

Total	5 400.8	401.8	568.2	2 159.0	793.6	572.8	495.6	409.1 [7]	.	.	0.5

Men - Hommes - Hombres
ISCED-97 - CITE-97 - CINE-97

Total	4 553.7	321.6	526.8	1 990.4	698.9	450.0	277.4	288.2 [7]	.	.	0.4

Women - Femmes - Mujeres
ISCED-97 - CITE-97 - CINE-97

Total	847.1	80.1	41.3	168.6	94.7	122.8	218.6	120.9 [7]	.	.	-

Taiwan, China (BA) (2008) [6] [8]

Total - Total - Total
ISCED-76 - CITE-76 - CINE-76

Total	10 853	.	.	2 660 [9]	.	921	2 912	1 850	2 509		

West Bank and Gaza Strip (BA) (2008) [1]

Total - Total - Total
ISCED-76 - CITE-76 - CINE-76

Total	886.828	73.472	.	166.574	284.178	138.010	.	138.358	73.171	13.066	.
10-14	12.633	3.041	.	8.494	1.098	-	.	-	-	-	.
15-19	63.585	2.747	.	13.744	38.935	7.770	.	0.008	0.382	-	.
20-24	143.801	4.716	.	18.418	49.819	29.377	.	26.933	14.385	0.153	.
25-29	155.273	7.119	.	24.886	48.834	21.881	.	39.041	11.467	2.046	.
30-34	135.304	9.323	.	23.790	48.815	19.453	.	23.638	7.880	2.406	.
35-39	113.881	8.680	.	23.629	34.105	21.861	.	14.475	8.563	2.568	.
40-44	97.583	8.034	.	21.270	26.902	15.079	.	12.170	11.837	2.291	.
45-49	71.598	8.361	.	15.096	16.186	10.414	.	10.286	9.655	1.600	.
50-54	43.484	6.500	.	8.654	10.662	5.770	.	5.833	4.888	1.177	.
55-59	27.750	5.213	.	4.679	5.999	4.094	.	4.104	3.024	0.637	.
60-64	10.362	3.547	.	2.109	1.574	1.548	.	0.744	0.753	0.087	.
65-69	6.204	2.547	.	0.703	1.130	0.538	.	0.917	0.297	0.072	.
70-74	3.254	2.195	.	0.657	0.044	0.209	.	-	-	0.028	.
75+	2.116	1.450	.	0.445	0.077	0.017	.	0.089	0.039	-	.

Men - Hommes - Hombres
ISCED-76 - CITE-76 - CINE-76

Total	725.491	54.958	.	149.645	259.245	124.927	.	81.060	46.217	9.438	.
10-14	10.491	2.562	.	6.936	0.990	-	.	-	-	-	.
15-19	59.674	2.524	.	13.094	36.999	6.978	.	-	0.080	-	.
20-24	112.555	4.286	.	17.515	45.947	26.823	.	10.638	7.318	0.030	.
25-29	121.769	6.477	.	23.069	44.378	20.070	.	20.091	6.384	1.300	.
30-34	110.714	7.780	.	20.973	43.516	17.375	.	14.459	4.945	1.670	.
35-39	94.109	6.778	.	20.338	30.549	19.694	.	9.316	5.514	1.920	.
40-44	80.705	5.831	.	19.063	24.406	13.705	.	8.398	7.863	1.440	.
45-49	58.936	5.359	.	13.268	14.544	9.535	.	7.840	7.171	1.220	.
50-54	36.842	4.234	.	7.524	9.757	5.139	.	4.959	4.093	1.140	.
55-59	22.280	3.056	.	4.190	5.532	3.498	.	3.506	1.927	0.570	.
60-64	8.376	2.111	.	1.953	1.430	1.430	.	0.744	0.622	0.090	.
65-69	4.949	1.430	.	0.655	1.076	0.538	.	0.917	0.261	0.070	.
70-74	2.424	1.499	.	0.635	0.044	0.125	.	0.120	-	-	.
75+	1.670	1.031	.	0.434	0.077	0.017	.	0.071	0.039	-	.

Explanatory notes: see p. 3.

[1] Persons aged 10 years and over. [2] Excl. Northern and Eastern provinces. [3] Levels X-1. [4] Levels 3-4. [5] Levels 5-6. [6] Persons aged 15 years and over. [7] Levels 5A, 5B and 6. [8] Excl. armed forces. [9] Levels 1-2.

Notes explicatives: voir p. 5.

[1] Personnes âgées de 10 ans et plus. [2] Non compris les provinces du Nord et de l'Est. [3] Niveaux X-1. [4] Niveaux 3-4. [5] Niveaux 5-6. [6] Personnes âgées de 15 ans et plus. [7] Niveaux 5A, 5B et 6. [8] Non compris les forces armées. [9] Niveaux 1-2.

Notas explicativas: véase p. 7.

[1] Personas de 10 años y más. [2] Excl. las provincias del Norte y del Este. [3] Niveles X-1. [4] Niveles 3-4. [5] Niveles 5-6. [6] Personas de 15 años y más. [7] Niveles 5A, 5B y 6. [8] Excl. las fuerzas armadas. [9] Niveles 1-2.

1B — ECONOMICALLY ACTIVE POPULATION / POPULATION ACTIVE / POBLACION ECONOMICAMENTE ACTIVA

By level of education and age group / Par niveau d'instruction et groupe d'âge / Por nivel de educación y grupo de edad

Thousands — Milliers — Millares

ISCED 1976 – CITE	Total	X	0	1	2	3	5	6	7	9	?
CINE 1997	Total	X	0	1	2	3	4	5A	5B	6	?

West Bank and Gaza Strip (BA) (2008) [1]

Women - Femmes - Mujeres
ISCED-76 - CITE-76 - CINE-76

Age	Total	X	0	1	2	3	5	6	7	9	?
Total	161.337	18.513	.	16.929	24.932	13.082	.	57.297	26.953	3.627	.
10-14	2.144	0.479	.	1.558	0.107	-	.	-	-	-	.
15-19	3.911	0.223	.	0.650	1.935	0.792	.	0.008	0.302	-	.
20-24	31.245	0.429	.	0.903	3.872	2.554	.	16.294	7.067	0.126	.
25-29	33.504	0.642	.	1.817	4.456	1.810	.	18.950	5.083	0.745	.
30-34	24.590	1.543	.	2.817	5.298	2.078	.	9.179	2.935	0.740	.
35-39	19.771	1.902	.	3.292	3.555	2.166	.	5.159	3.049	0.648	.
40-44	16.878	2.203	.	2.207	2.496	1.374	.	3.772	3.974	0.853	.
45-49	12.662	3.002	.	1.829	1.641	0.879	.	2.446	2.485	0.381	.
50-54	6.643	2.266	.	1.130	0.905	0.631	.	0.875	0.795	0.041	.
55-59	5.470	2.157	.	0.489	0.467	0.596	.	0.598	1.097	0.065	.
60-64	1.986	1.437	.	0.156	0.144	0.118	.	-	0.131	-	.
65-69	1.255	1.117	.	0.049	0.054	-	.	-	0.035	-	.
70-74	0.830	0.696	.	0.023	-	0.084	.	.	-	-	0.028
75+	0.447	0.418	.	0.011	-	-	.	0.017	-	-	.

EUROPE-EUROPE-EUROPA

Austria (BA) (2008) [2][3]

Total - Total - Total
ISCED-97 - CITE-97 - CINE-97

Age	Total	X	0	1	2	3	4	5A	5B	6	?
Total	4 252.3	.	760.2 [4]	.	.	2 236.6	472.6	380.2	307.6	72.4	.
15-19	222.4	.	169.2 [4]	.	.	46.8	4.9	-	0.1	-	.
20-24	381.2	.	53.7 [4]	.	.	238.2	73.7	6.4	6.9	0.3	.
25-29	459.0	.	45.1 [4]	.	.	256.0	75.4	52.6	26.3	1.3	.
30-34	474.4	.	46.0 [4]	.	.	245.6	70.2	70.0	33.4	7.7	.
35-39	575.7	.	66.3 [4]	.	.	309.3	74.8	67.3	44.6	11.1	.
40-44	641.6	.	88.3 [4]	.	.	363.0	62.8	59.5	55.2	10.0	.
45-49	586.0	.	84.9 [4]	.	.	329.6	52.9	45.6	54.6	14.6	.
50-54	452.9	.	95.6 [4]	.	.	237.5	29.8	36.9	42.0	8.7	.
55-59	296.7	.	62.9 [4]	.	.	152.0	19.5	21.1	29.8	8.6	.
60-64	92.0	.	21.0 [4]	.	.	36.9	6.1	13.9	7.6	5.9	.
65-69	39.9	.	12.0 [4]	.	.	15.6	1.6	3.4	4.3	2.7	.
70-74	16.9	.	8.4 [4]	.	.	3.5	0.4	1.3	2.0	1.0	.
75+	13.5	.	6.8 [4]	.	.	2.7	0.4	2.2	0.8	0.6	.

Men - Hommes - Hombres
ISCED-97 - CITE-97 - CINE-97

Age	Total	X	0	1	2	3	4	5A	5B	6	?
Total	2 303.9	.	351.1 [4]	.	.	1 276.1	217.1	207.0	190.2	50.1	.
15-19	120.8	.	98.2 [4]	.	.	20.4	1.2	-	-	-	.
20-24	198.8	.	30.5 [4]	.	.	133.2	29.4	2.8	2.1	-	.
25-29	245.3	.	25.5 [4]	.	.	148.2	31.8	25.5	11.9	0.8	.
30-34	255.7	.	20.4 [4]	.	.	145.2	32.1	35.3	18.0	4.3	.
35-39	306.3	.	25.2 [4]	.	.	175.8	33.3	36.4	27.3	6.5	.
40-44	342.4	.	36.2 [4]	.	.	200.1	31.0	31.0	35.8	7.4	.
45-49	312.5	.	28.3 [4]	.	.	183.5	27.8	24.2	36.2	10.5	.
50-54	239.5	.	33.8 [4]	.	.	135.7	14.3	23.2	25.7	5.7	.
55-59	175.6	.	27.7 [4]	.	.	95.3	10.5	13.8	20.7	5.9	.
60-64	62.3	.	10.6 [4]	.	.	25.4	4.4	9.8	6.4	5.3	.
65-69	24.9	.	6.3 [4]	.	.	9.1	0.8	2.3	4.0	2.4	.
70-74	10.4	.	4.2 [4]	.	.	2.3	0.4	1.2	1.5	0.6	.
75+	9.2	.	4.3 [4]	.	.	2.0	0.2	1.5	0.6	0.6	.

Women - Femmes - Mujeres
ISCED-97 - CITE-97 - CINE-97

Age	Total	X	0	1	2	3	4	5A	5B	6	?
Total	1 948.4	.	409.0 [4]	.	.	960.6	255.5	173.2	117.4	22.3	.
15-19	101.6	.	71.0 [4]	.	.	26.4	3.7	-	0.1	-	.
20-24	182.4	.	23.2 [4]	.	.	105.0	44.2	3.6	4.8	0.3	.
25-29	213.7	.	19.6 [4]	.	.	107.8	43.6	27.2	14.5	0.5	.
30-34	218.7	.	25.6 [4]	.	.	100.4	38.1	34.7	15.4	3.3	.
35-39	269.4	.	41.1 [4]	.	.	133.4	41.6	30.9	17.4	4.5	.
40-44	299.1	.	52.1 [4]	.	.	162.9	31.8	28.5	19.4	2.6	.
45-49	273.5	.	56.6 [4]	.	.	146.1	25.2	21.4	18.4	4.1	.
50-54	213.4	.	61.9 [4]	.	.	101.8	15.5	13.6	16.3	3.0	.
55-59	121.0	.	35.1 [4]	.	.	56.7	8.9	7.2	9.1	2.7	.
60-64	29.7	.	10.5 [4]	.	.	11.5	1.7	4.0	1.2	0.6	.
65-69	15.0	.	5.8 [4]	.	.	6.5	0.8	1.2	0.3	0.3	.
70-74	6.5	.	4.2 [4]	.	.	1.2	0.1	0.1	0.5	0.4	.
75+	4.3	.	2.5 [4]	.	.	0.7	0.2	0.7	0.2	-	.

Explanatory notes: see p. 3. Notes explicatives: voir p. 5. Notas explicativas: véase p. 7.

1 Persons aged 10 years and over. 2 Excl. conscripts on compulsory military service. 3 Persons aged 15 years and over. 4 Levels 0-2.

1 Personnes âgées de 10 ans et plus. 2 Non compris conscrits ceux du contingent. 3 Personnes âgées de 15 ans et plus. 4 Niveaux 0-2.

1 Personas de 10 años y más. 2 Excl. los conscriptos del servicio obligatorio. 3 Personas de 15 años y más. 4 Niveles 0-2.

ECONOMICALLY ACTIVE POPULATION

By level of education and age group

POPULATION ACTIVE

Par niveau d'instruction et groupe d'âge

POBLACION ECONOMICAMENTE ACTIVA

Por nivel de educación y grupo de edad

	Thousands / Milliers / Millares										
ISCED 1976 CITE	Total	X	0	1	2	3	5	6	7	9	?
CINE 1997	Total	X	0	1	2	3	4	5A	5B	6	?

Belgique (BA) (2008) [1] [2]

Total - Total - Total
ISCED-97 - CITE-97 - CINE-97

Total	4 779.6	114.1	242.5	733.8	550.6	1 260.2	132.7	845.7	869.6	30.4	.
15-19	62.8	1.7	5.4	26.8	11.3	15.8	1.6	0.1	0.1	-	.
20-24	370.7	7.3	10.6	52.1	63.0	120.6	17.0	53.6	46.4	-	.
25-29	605.3	12.6	10.7	59.8	78.1	154.1	21.3	129.4	137.0	2.3	.
30-34	621.0	11.6	17.6	59.1	79.5	152.2	20.3	127.4	147.8	5.5	.
35-39	673.2	16.0	21.3	77.8	94.8	174.4	20.3	132.5	130.8	5.4	.
40-44	708.3	16.0	33.8	106.5	88.4	191.3	17.9	122.8	127.7	4.1	.
45-49	684.7	13.8	45.2	133.0	65.9	180.3	13.2	120.9	108.1	4.3	.
50-54	558.1	18.1	46.5	120.8	38.0	151.2	10.9	87.9	81.4	3.3	.
55-59	356.9	11.2	33.6	73.4	23.5	92.1	7.2	52.3	60.8	2.8	.
60-64	105.6	3.7	12.5	19.5	7.0	22.3	2.1	15.4	21.1	2.0	.
65-69	16.8	1.0	2.7	2.4	0.8	3.2	0.0	2.0	4.4	0.3	.
70-74	7.3	0.2	1.4	1.7	0.3	0.7	0.2	0.9	1.5	0.4	.
75+	8.8	0.8	1.2	1.0	0.2	1.8	0.7	0.6	2.5	-	.

Men - Hommes - Hombres
ISCED-97 - CITE-97 - CINE-97

Total	2 631.2	69.5	143.8	453.8	308.5	730.2	69.5	351.2	483.4	21.2	.
15-19	39.9	1.1	4.1	16.7	7.6	9.4	0.9	-	0.1	-	.
20-24	196.4	3.9	5.9	33.0	37.1	71.3	9.2	17.5	18.5	-	.
25-29	317.4	7.8	6.9	39.4	46.2	91.6	11.3	50.8	62.0	1.3	.
30-34	330.0	7.5	11.9	40.3	44.5	88.7	10.7	49.1	73.4	3.7	.
35-39	363.7	11.2	12.5	47.4	53.0	101.7	10.5	53.2	71.1	3.3	.
40-44	383.8	9.4	19.7	64.6	46.2	108.7	9.2	52.0	71.6	2.5	.
45-49	374.9	8.0	25.8	81.5	34.3	98.6	6.6	52.0	65.3	2.9	.
50-54	320.2	10.5	27.3	73.5	20.7	87.0	5.6	39.7	53.1	2.7	.
55-59	212.8	7.1	18.9	42.0	13.6	55.5	3.7	26.1	43.6	2.3	.
60-64	69.6	2.2	7.8	12.1	4.3	13.9	0.9	8.7	18.0	1.8	.
65-69	12.1	0.6	1.7	1.5	0.6	2.1	0.0	1.5	3.7	0.3	.
70-74	5.4	0.2	0.9	0.8	0.3	0.5	0.2	0.7	1.4	0.4	.
75+	5.0	-	0.4	1.0	0.2	1.2	0.7	-	1.6	-	.

Women - Femmes - Mujeres
ISCED-97 - CITE-97 - CINE-97

Total	2 148.4	44.6	98.7	280.0	242.0	530.0	63.2	494.5	386.2	9.2	.
15-19	22.9	0.7	1.3	10.0	3.7	6.5	0.7	0.1	-	-	.
20-24	174.3	3.4	4.6	19.1	25.9	49.3	7.8	36.1	28.0	-	.
25-29	287.9	4.8	3.8	20.4	31.9	62.5	10.0	78.6	75.0	1.0	.
30-34	291.0	4.1	5.7	18.8	34.9	63.5	9.7	78.3	74.3	1.8	.
35-39	309.5	4.8	8.8	30.4	41.8	72.7	9.8	79.3	59.7	2.1	.
40-44	324.5	6.6	14.1	41.8	42.2	82.6	8.7	70.8	56.1	1.6	.
45-49	309.8	5.9	19.4	51.5	31.6	81.7	6.6	68.9	42.8	1.4	.
50-54	237.9	7.7	19.2	47.2	17.3	64.2	5.3	48.2	28.2	0.6	.
55-59	144.1	4.1	14.7	31.4	9.9	36.6	3.5	26.3	17.2	0.5	.
60-64	36.1	1.6	4.7	7.5	2.7	8.5	1.2	6.7	3.1	0.2	.
65-69	4.7	0.3	1.0	0.9	0.2	1.1	-	0.4	0.7	-	.
70-74	1.9	-	0.5	0.9	-	0.3	-	0.2	0.1	-	.
75+	3.8	0.8	0.8	-	-	0.6	-	0.6	0.9	-	.

Bulgaria (BA) (2008) [2] [3]

Total - Total - Total
ISCED-97 - CITE-97 - CINE-97

Total	3 560.4	87.5 [4]	.	.	498.7	2 097.2 [5]	.	736.8 [6]	140.2	.	.
15-19	40.7	5.1 [4]	.	.	12.0	23.6 [5]	.	- [6]	-	.	.
20-24	260.1	8.7 [4]	.	.	24.8	204.4 [5]	.	19.5 [6]	2.8	.	.
25-29	337.8	12.8 [4]	.	.	35.7	195.3 [5]	.	88.9 [6]	5.1	.	.
30-34	443.8	9.0 [4]	.	.	59.4	246.5 [5]	.	117.8 [6]	11.1	.	.
35-39	506.3	9.6 [4]	.	.	61.6	303.3 [5]	.	110.9 [6]	20.9	.	.
40-44	502.9	8.6 [4]	.	.	58.5	306.6 [5]	.	107.3 [6]	21.9	.	.
45-49	558.3	10.8 [4]	.	.	67.5	342.9 [5]	.	111.7 [6]	25.4	.	.
50-54	375.1	7.7 [4]	.	.	63.8	206.6 [5]	.	72.9 [6]	24.1	.	.
55-59	338.4	8.6 [4]	.	.	66.6	179.0 [5]	.	65.5 [6]	18.6	.	.
60-64	141.2	3.8 [4]	.	.	32.1	69.3 [5]	.	28.7 [6]	7.3	.	.
65-69	35.4	1.8 [4]	.	.	9.6	13.8 [5]	.	8.0 [6]	2.3	.	.
70-74	13.3	0.5 [4]	.	.	4.4	4.2 [5]	.	3.7 [6]	0.6	.	.
75+	6.9	0.6 [4]	.	.	2.7	1.7 [5]	.	1.8 [6]	-	.	.

Explanatory notes: see p. 3.

[1] Incl. professional army. [2] Persons aged 15 years and over. [3] Excl. conscripts. [4] Levels X-1. [5] Levels 3-4. [6] Levels 5A and 6.

Notes explicatives: voir p. 5.

[1] Y compris les militaires de carrière. [2] Personnes âgées de 15 ans et plus. [3] Non compris les conscrits. [4] Niveaux X-1. [5] Niveaux 3-4. [6] Niveaux 5A et 6.

Notas explicativas: véase p. 7.

[1] Incl. los militares profesionales. [2] Personas de 15 años y más. [3] Excl. los conscriptos. [4] Niveles X-1. [5] Niveles 3-4. [6] Niveles 5A y 6.

ECONOMICALLY ACTIVE POPULATION

By level of education and age group

POPULATION ACTIVE

Par niveau d'instruction et groupe d'âge

POBLACION ECONOMICAMENTE ACTIVA

Por nivel de educación y grupo de edad

		Thousands				Milliers				Millares	
ISCED 1976 CITE	Total	X	0	1	2	3	5	6	7	9	?
CINE 1997	Total	X	0	1	2	3	4	5A	5B	6	?

Bulgaria (BA) (2008) [1][2]

Men - Hommes - Hombres
ISCED-97 - CITE-97 - CINE-97

Age	Total	X	0	1	2	3	4/5	5A/6	5B/7	6/9	?
Total	1 896.8	50.8[3]	.	.	290.0	1 191.8[4]	.	322.1[5]	42.2	.	.
15-19	25.5	3.4[3]	.	.	7.8	14.3[4]	.	-[5]		.	.
20-24	148.5	5.8[3]	.	.	15.0	119.1[4]	.	7.5[5]	1.2	.	.
25-29	201.4	8.6[3]	.	.	22.7	128.0[4]	.	40.6[5]	1.6	.	.
30-34	236.0	4.9[3]	.	.	33.3	148.3[4]	.	47.0[5]	2.6	.	.
35-39	259.9	5.8[3]	.	.	37.1	165.9[4]	.	45.3[5]	5.8	.	.
40-44	260.8	4.5[3]	.	.	32.0	169.1[4]	.	45.6[5]	9.7	.	.
45-49	277.9	5.3[3]	.	.	36.3	182.5[4]	.	47.1[5]	6.8	.	.
50-54	182.1	3.9[3]	.	.	34.9	109.5[4]	.	29.0[5]	4.8	.	.
55-59	167.8	4.7[3]	.	.	36.1	92.0[4]	.	30.5[5]	4.5	.	.
60-64	98.9	2.6[3]	.	.	23.9	49.6[4]	.	18.8[5]	4.1	.	.
65-69	23.9	0.9[3]	.	.	5.8	9.8[4]	.	6.4[5]	1.1	.	.
70-74	9.1	0.2[3]	.	.	3.0	2.5[4]	.	3.1[5]	0.2	.	.
75+	5.0	0.2[3]	.	.	2.1	1.4[4]	.	1.3[5]	-	.	.

Women - Femmes - Mujeres
ISCED-97 - CITE-97 - CINE-97

Age	Total	X	0	1	2	3	4/5	5A/6	5B/7	6/9	?
Total	1 663.6	36.7[3]	.	.	208.7	905.4[4]	.	414.7[5]	98.0	.	.
15-19	15.3	1.7[3]	.	.	4.3	9.3[4]	.	-[5]		.	.
20-24	111.6	2.9[3]	.	.	9.8	85.4[4]	.	12.0[5]	1.6	.	.
25-29	136.4	4.2[3]	.	.	13.0	67.3[4]	.	48.4[5]	3.5	.	.
30-34	207.8	4.1[3]	.	.	26.1	98.2[4]	.	70.9[5]	8.6	.	.
35-39	246.5	3.8[3]	.	.	24.5	137.4[4]	.	65.6[5]	15.1	.	.
40-44	242.1	4.2[3]	.	.	26.5	137.5[4]	.	61.7[5]	12.2	.	.
45-49	280.4	5.5[3]	.	.	31.2	160.4[4]	.	64.6[5]	18.7	.	.
50-54	193.0	3.7[3]	.	.	28.9	97.1[4]	.	43.9[5]	19.4	.	.
55-59	170.6	3.9[3]	.	.	30.5	87.0[4]	.	35.0[5]	14.1	.	.
60-64	42.3	1.2[3]	.	.	8.2	19.7[4]	.	9.9[5]	3.2	.	.
65-69	11.5	0.9[3]	.	.	3.8	3.9[4]	.	1.7[5]	1.2	.	.
70-74	4.3	0.3[3]	.	.	1.4	1.7[4]	.	0.6[5]	0.3	.	.
75+	1.9	0.4[3]	.	.	0.6	0.4[4]	.	0.5[5]	-	.	.

Croatia (BA) (2008) [1][6]

Total - Total - Total
ISCED-97 - CITE-97 - CINE-97

Age	Total	X	0	1	2	3	4/5	5A/6	5B/7	6/9	?
Total	1 784.8	7.6[7]	.	52.5	267.6	1 123.7[4]	.	203.4	124.8	-	.
15-19	35.0	-[7]	.	-	4.0	30.8[4]	.	-	-	-	.
20-24	145.9	-[7]	.	-	8.5	127.2[4]	.	4.7	4.8	-	.
25-29	192.0	-[7]	.	-	12.4	132.1[4]	.	31.2	15.5	-	.
30-34	173.3	-[7]	.	-	19.0	117.8[4]	.	22.5	12.5	-	.
35-39	202.7	-[7]	.	-	26.6	133.6[4]	.	27.2	13.8	-	.
40-44	242.0	-[7]	.	-	40.5	161.0[4]	.	24.9	12.6	-	.
45-49	267.0	-[7]	.	4.0	45.4	162.0[4]	.	31.7	21.3	-	.
50-54	250.0	-[7]	.	8.8	48.2	149.9[4]	.	22.8	18.1	-	.
55-59	163.3	-[7]	.	8.2	33.8	80.5[4]	.	22.9	17.0	-	.
60-64	61.9	-[7]	.	5.9	12.6	23.4[4]	.	11.8	7.5	-	.
65-69	25.1	-[7]	.	10.9	5.8	-[4]	.	-	-	-	.
70-74	18.6	-[7]	.	7.1	6.5	-[4]	.	-	-	-	.
75+	8.0	-[7]	.	-	4.2	-[4]	.	-	-	-	.

Men - Hommes - Hombres
ISCED-97 - CITE-97 - CINE-97

Age	Total	X	0	1	2	3	4/5	5A/6	5B/7	6/9	?
Total	973.0	3.1[7]	.	25.3	132.5	654.3[4]	.	92.8	61.2	-	.
15-19	20.3	-[7]	.	-	-	17.8[4]	.	-	-	-	.
20-24	89.4	-[7]	.	-	6.2	79.2[4]	.	-	-	-	.
25-29	108.2	-[7]	.	-	8.5	81.9[4]	.	10.6	6.5	-	.
30-34	94.8	-[7]	.	-	12.0	66.0[4]	.	9.5	5.8	-	.
35-39	98.3	-[7]	.	-	15.0	66.3[4]	.	10.5	5.8	-	.
40-44	123.6	-[7]	.	-	19.4	84.8[4]	.	11.9	5.6	-	.
45-49	134.6	-[7]	.	-	18.0	86.5[4]	.	15.2	11.6	-	.
50-54	136.1	-[7]	.	4.6	21.3	90.0[4]	.	10.1	8.6	-	.
55-59	106.7	-[7]	.	4.6	18.0	59.7[4]	.	13.8	9.9	-	.
60-64	37.1	-[7]	.	-	5.1	17.9[4]	.	7.0	-	-	.
65-69	11.3	-[7]	.	-	-	2.9[4]	.	-	-	-	.
70-74	8.8	-[7]	.	3.3	2.6	-[4]	.	-	-	-	.
75+	3.8	-[7]	.	-	-	-[4]	.	-	-	-	.

Explanatory notes: see p. 3.

[1] Persons aged 15 years and over. [2] Excl. conscripts. [3] Levels X-1. [4] Levels 3-4. [5] Levels 5A and 6. [6] Incl. armed forces, Excl. conscripts. [7] Levels X-0.

Notes explicatives: voir p. 5.

[1] Personnes âgées de 15 ans et plus. [2] Non compris les conscrits. [3] Niveaux X-1. [4] Niveaux 3-4. [5] Niveaux 5A et 6. [6] Y compris les forces armées, Excl. conscrits [7] Niveaux X-0.

Notas explicativas: véase p. 7.

[1] Personas de 15 años y más. [2] Excl. los conscriptos. [3] Niveles X-1. [4] Niveles 3-4. [5] Niveles 5A y 6. [6] Incl. las fuerzas armadas, excl. los conscriptos. [7] Niveles X-0.

ECONOMICALLY ACTIVE POPULATION

By level of education and age group

POPULATION ACTIVE

Par niveau d'instruction et groupe d'âge

POBLACION ECONOMICAMENTE ACTIVA

Por nivel de educación y grupo de edad

	Thousands / Milliers / Millares										
ISCED 1976 CITE — Total		X	0	1	2	3	5	6	7	9	?
CINE 1997 — Total		X	0	1	2	3	4	5A	5B	6	?

Croatia (BA) (2008) [1] [2]

Women - Femmes - Mujeres
ISCED-97 - CITE-97 - CINE-97

	Total	X	0	1	2	3	4	5A	5B	6	?
Total	811.8	4.5 [3]	.	27.3	135.1	469.3 [4]	.	110.5	63.6	-	.
15-19	14.8	- [3]	.	-	-	13.0 [4]	.	-	-	-	.
20-24	56.5	- [3]	.	-	2.3	48.0 [4]	.	-	-	-	.
25-29	83.8	- [3]	.	-	3.9	50.2 [4]	.	20.6	9.0	-	.
30-34	78.5	- [3]	.	-	6.9	51.8 [4]	.	13.0	6.7	-	.
35-39	104.4	- [3]	.	-	11.5	67.3 [4]	.	16.7	8.0	-	.
40-44	118.4	- [3]	.	-	21.2	76.2 [4]	.	13.0	7.0	-	.
45-49	132.4	- [3]	.	-	27.4	75.4 [4]	.	16.5	9.6	-	.
50-54	113.8	- [3]	.	4.2	26.9	60.0 [4]	.	12.7	9.4	-	.
55-59	56.6	- [3]	.	3.6	15.9	20.8 [4]	.	8.9	7.1	-	.
60-64	24.8	- [3]	.	-	7.5	5.5 [4]	.	4.8	-	-	.
65-69	13.8	- [3]	.	8.0	-	- [4]	.	-	-	-	.
70-74	9.8	- [3]	.	3.8	3.9	- [4]	.	-	-	-	.
75+	4.2	- [3]	.	-	-	- [4]	.	-	-	-	.

Cyprus (BA) (2008) [1] [2] [5]

Total - Total - Total
ISCED-97 - CITE-97 - CINE-97

	Total	X	0	1	2	3	4	5A	5B	6	?
Total	397.4	5.3 [3]	.	47.3	37.4	154.8	6.1	91.4	53.0	2.2	.
15-19	4.9	0.1 [3]	.	0.7	1.5	2.5	0.1	-	0.0	-	.
20-24	34.1	0.2 [3]	.	1.3	3.6	17.3	0.3	7.0	4.5	-	.
25-29	56.6	0.2 [3]	.	1.9	5.3	19.6	0.7	19.9	9.1	0.0	.
30-34	54.2	0.1 [3]	.	2.1	3.9	21.0	1.0	15.8	9.9	0.4	.
35-39	48.3	0.1 [3]	.	2.2	4.4	19.5	1.4	11.4	9.0	0.4	.
40-44	49.5	0.1 [3]	.	3.0	6.1	23.3	0.7	9.5	6.6	0.3	.
45-49	48.9	0.3 [3]	.	6.2	4.7	21.1	0.7	9.6	5.8	0.4	.
50-54	40.9	0.5 [3]	.	9.1	3.2	13.6	0.5	9.3	4.5	0.3	.
55-59	32.0	0.7 [3]	.	10.1	2.4	9.9	0.5	5.8	2.5	0.2	.
60-64	16.2	1.3 [3]	.	5.6	1.7	4.8	0.1	1.9	0.7	0.1	.
65-69	6.3	0.8 [3]	.	2.5	0.6	1.1	0.1	1.0	0.2	0.1	.
70-74	3.0	0.5 [3]	.	1.6	0.1	0.5	-	0.2	0.0	-	.
75+	2.4	0.5 [3]	.	1.1	0.1	0.6	-	-	0.1	-	.

Men - Hommes - Hombres
ISCED-97 - CITE-97 - CINE-97

	Total	X	0	1	2	3	4	5A	5B	6	?
Total	219.2	3.2 [3]	.	30.3	20.2	93.9	1.5	46.3	22.3	1.5	.
15-19	2.7	0.1 [3]	.	0.7	0.8	1.1	-	-	-	-	.
20-24	16.0	0.1 [3]	.	1.1	2.1	11.0	0.2	0.7	0.9	-	.
25-29	28.5	0.2 [3]	.	1.2	3.4	11.7	0.2	8.4	3.5	-	.
30-34	28.8	0.1 [3]	.	1.5	2.0	13.2	0.1	7.5	4.1	0.3	.
35-39	26.1	0.0 [3]	.	1.5	1.9	11.6	0.2	6.4	4.3	0.2	.
40-44	26.6	0.1 [3]	.	1.5	2.6	13.5	0.1	5.6	2.9	0.2	.
45-49	27.5	0.2 [3]	.	3.7	1.9	12.3	0.2	6.2	2.6	0.3	.
50-54	23.3	0.4 [3]	.	5.2	1.7	8.3	0.2	5.3	2.1	0.2	.
55-59	19.5	0.3 [3]	.	5.8	1.8	6.0	0.3	3.9	1.2	0.2	.
60-64	10.8	0.7 [3]	.	3.7	1.4	3.3	0.0	1.3	0.4	0.1	.
65-69	5.0	0.5 [3]	.	2.0	0.5	1.0	-	0.8	0.1	0.1	.
70-74	2.4	0.3 [3]	.	1.4	0.1	0.5	-	0.2	0.0	-	.
75+	1.9	0.3 [3]	.	0.9	0.1	0.6	-	-	0.1	-	.

Women - Femmes - Mujeres
ISCED-97 - CITE-97 - CINE-97

	Total	X	0	1	2	3	4	5A	5B	6	?
Total	178.2	2.1 [3]	.	17.0	17.2	60.9	4.6	45.1	30.6	0.7	.
15-19	2.2	- [3]	.	0.1	0.6	1.3	0.1	-	0.0	-	.
20-24	18.1	0.1 [3]	.	0.2	1.5	6.3	0.2	6.3	3.6	-	.
25-29	28.1	- [3]	.	0.7	1.9	7.9	0.5	11.5	5.6	0.0	.
30-34	25.4	- [3]	.	0.6	1.9	7.8	0.9	8.3	5.8	0.1	.
35-39	22.3	0.1 [3]	.	0.7	2.5	7.8	1.3	5.1	4.7	0.2	.
40-44	22.9	- [3]	.	1.5	3.5	9.9	0.5	3.8	3.6	0.1	.
45-49	21.4	0.2 [3]	.	2.4	2.8	8.8	0.5	3.4	3.2	0.1	.
50-54	17.6	0.1 [3]	.	3.8	1.5	5.4	0.3	4.1	2.4	0.1	.
55-59	12.5	0.3 [3]	.	4.3	0.6	3.9	0.2	1.9	1.3	-	.
60-64	5.4	0.6 [3]	.	1.9	0.3	1.5	0.1	0.6	0.3	-	.
65-69	1.3	0.3 [3]	.	0.5	0.1	0.1	0.1	0.2	0.1	-	.
70-74	0.5	0.2 [3]	.	0.2	-	0.1	-	-	0.0	-	.
75+	0.5	0.3 [3]	.	0.2	-	0.0	-	-	-	-	.

Explanatory notes: see p. 3.

[1] Incl. armed forces, Excl. conscripts. [2] Persons aged 15 years and over. [3] Levels X-0. [4] Levels 3-4. [5] Government-controlled area.

Notes explicatives: voir p. 5.

[1] Y compris les forces armées, Excl. conscrits [2] Personnes âgées de 15 ans et plus. [3] Niveaux X-0. [4] Niveaux 3-4. [5] Région sous contrôle gouvernemental.

Notas explicativas: véase p. 7.

[1] Incl. las fuerzas armadas, excl. los conscriptos. [2] Personas de 15 años y más. [3] Niveles X-0. [4] Niveles 3-4. [5] Area controlada por el gobierno.

1B ECONOMICALLY ACTIVE POPULATION / POPULATION ACTIVE / POBLACION ECONOMICAMENTE ACTIVA

By level of education and age group / Par niveau d'instruction et groupe d'âge / Por nivel de educación y grupo de edad

Thousands / Milliers / Millares

ISCED 1976 CITE / CINE 1997		Total	X	0	1	2	3	5 / 4	6 / 5A	7 / 5B	9 / 6	?
ISCED 1976	Total		X	0	1	2	3	5	6	7	9	?
CINE 1997	Total		X	0	1	2	3	4	5A	5B	6	?

Czech Republic (BA) (2008) [1]

Total - Total - Total
ISCED-97 - CITE-97 - CINE-97

Age	Total	X	0	1	2	3	4	5A	5B	6	?
Total	5 232.3	357.5[2]				4 071.4[3]		802.6[4]			
15-19	47.2	15.5[2]				31.7[3]		-[4]			
20-24	371.1	25.3[2]				327.3[3]		18.5[4]			
25-29	629.2	28.9[2]				466.1[3]		134.2[4]			
30-34	767.3	36.4[2]				615.8[3]		115.1[4]			
35-39	684.7	29.5[2]				562.6[3]		92.1[4]			
40-44	666.7	37.3[2]				525.0[3]		104.3[4]			
45-49	607.2	42.0[2]				467.4[3]		97.7[4]			
50-54	664.7	68.6[2]				494.5[3]		101.4[4]			
55-59	535.7	55.2[2]				403.8[3]		76.7[4]			
60-64	189.0	12.2[2]				137.9[3]		39.0[4]			
65-69	47.3	4.7[2]				27.6[3]		15.0[4]			
70-74	14.4	1.1[2]				8.7[3]		4.6[4]			
75+	7.9	0.9[2]				2.9[3]		4.1[4]			

Men - Hommes - Hombres
ISCED-97 - CITE-97 - CINE-97

Age	Total	X	0	1	2	3	4	5A	5B	6	?
Total	2 965.8	151.4[2]				2 355.5[3]		458.3[4]			
15-19	27.6	8.7[2]				18.9[3]		-[4]			
20-24	220.3	17.5[2]				197.4[3]		5.4[4]			
25-29	372.8	19.6[2]				292.9[3]		60.3[4]			
30-34	465.5	18.1[2]				377.4[3]		70.1[4]			
35-39	385.8	16.2[2]				313.5[3]		55.8[4]			
40-44	351.3	13.7[2]				280.3[3]		57.1[4]			
45-49	311.4	12.0[2]				245.0[3]		54.2[4]			
50-54	337.6	17.3[2]				261.6[3]		58.7[4]			
55-59	316.2	21.1[2]				244.5[3]		50.5[4]			
60-64	133.6	6.0[2]				99.4[3]		28.1[4]			
65-69	29.2	0.7[2]				17.1[3]		11.4[4]			
70-74	9.0	0.0[2]				5.5[3]		3.4[4]			
75+	5.5	0.4[2]				1.8[3]		3.2[4]			

Women - Femmes - Mujeres
ISCED-97 - CITE-97 - CINE-97

Age	Total	X	0	1	2	3	4	5A	5B	6	?
Total	2 266.5	206.1[2]				1 715.9[3]		344.3[4]			
15-19	19.6	6.7[2]				12.8[3]		-[4]			
20-24	150.8	7.8[2]				129.9[3]		13.1[4]			
25-29	256.5	9.3[2]				173.2[3]		73.9[4]			
30-34	301.8	18.3[2]				238.5[3]		45.0[4]			
35-39	298.9	13.4[2]				249.2[3]		36.4[4]			
40-44	315.4	23.6[2]				244.7[3]		47.1[4]			
45-49	295.8	30.0[2]				222.4[3]		43.4[4]			
50-54	327.1	51.3[2]				232.9[3]		42.7[4]			
55-59	219.5	34.0[2]				159.3[3]		26.2[4]			
60-64	55.5	6.2[2]				38.4[3]		10.8[4]			
65-69	18.1	3.9[2]				10.5[3]		3.6[4]			
70-74	5.4	1.0[2]				3.2[3]		1.1[4]			
75+	2.4	0.5[2]				1.1[3]		0.9[4]			

España (BA) (2008) [5][6]

Total - Total - Total
ISCED-97 - CITE-97 - CINE-97

Age	Total	X	0	1	2	3	4	5A	5B	6	?
Total	22 848.2	107.9[7]		3 496.6	6 497.1	5 477.1	15.8	4 759.8	2 321.4	172.6	
16-19	535.6	0.5[7]		141.2	283.4	105.3	0.1	0.2	4.8	-	
20-24	1 872.4	3.0[7]		222.5	666.3	594.1	1.1	195.9	189.3	0.2	
25-29	3 108.5	11.6[7]		211.6	818.5	863.1	5.8	775.3	416.8	5.8	
30-34	3 569.7	14.9[7]		268.0	902.6	885.5	3.1	981.1	496.7	17.6	
35-39	3 307.1	15.3[7]		294.2	966.2	803.1	1.6	811.4	392.9	22.4	
40-44	3 065.1	12.5[7]		326.8	939.4	763.8	1.8	652.5	333.4	34.9	
45-49	2 703.9	13.3[7]		429.3	860.8	626.9	1.0	519.1	224.9	28.6	
50-54	2 131.8	11.1[7]		565.0	543.2	456.2	0.8	396.5	133.7	25.2	
55-59	1 544.6	11.7[7]		575.7	341.4	255.3	0.4	259.4	84.4	16.2	
60-64	850.9	11.8[7]		394.3	160.3	106.6	0.1	126.0	37.2	14.7	
65-69	117.0	0.8[7]		50.9	13.2	11.9	-	29.8	5.7	4.6	
70-74	28.1	1.2[7]		11.4	1.4	2.8	-	8.5	0.9	1.9	
75+	13.7	0.1[7]		5.6	0.3	2.5	-	4.1	0.7	0.3	

Explanatory notes: see p. 3.

[1] Persons aged 15 years and over. [2] Levels X-2. [3] Levels 3-4. [4] Levels 5-6. [5] Excl. compulsory military service. [6] Persons aged 16 years and over. [7] Levels X-0.

Notes explicatives: voir p. 5.

[1] Personnes âgées de 15 ans et plus. [2] Niveaux X-2. [3] Niveaux 3-4. [4] Niveaux 5-6. [5] Non compris les militaires du contingent. [6] Personnes âgées de 16 ans et plus. [7] Niveaux X-0.

Notas explicativas: véase p. 7.

[1] Personas de 15 años y más. [2] Niveles X-2. [3] Niveles 3-4. [4] Niveles 5-6. [5] Excl. a los militares en servicio obligatorio. [6] Personas de 16 años y más. [7] Niveles X-0.

ECONOMICALLY ACTIVE POPULATION

POPULATION ACTIVE

POBLACION ECONOMICAMENTE ACTIVA

1B

By level of education and age group

Par niveau d'instruction et groupe d'âge

Por nivel de educación y grupo de edad

	Thousands / Milliers / Millares										
ISCED 1976 Total	X	0	1	2	3	5	6	7	9	?	
CITE CINE 1997 Total	X	0	1	2	3	4	5A	5B	6	?	

España (BA) (2008) [1] [2]

Men - Hommes - Hombres
ISCED-97 - CITE-97 - CINE-97

	Total	X	0	1	2	3	4	5A	5B	6	?
Total	13 031.7	70.1 [3]	.	2 236.0	4 026.1	2 980.8	9.1	2 234.9	1 369.6	105.1	.
16-19	310.0	0.5 [3]	.	96.9	162.0	48.2	0.1	-	2.3	-	.
20-24	1 020.7	1.7 [3]	.	153.5	414.2	297.4	0.5	60.0	93.5	-	.
25-29	1 666.6	6.7 [3]	.	133.7	515.0	463.7	3.2	312.3	229.5	2.4	.
30-34	1 996.2	10.7 [3]	.	180.7	590.1	492.8	1.8	439.7	269.8	10.6	.
35-39	1 880.5	11.6 [3]	.	192.2	614.9	445.3	1.1	376.1	228.2	11.3	.
40-44	1 732.1	7.0 [3]	.	204.7	560.3	417.5	1.1	319.1	204.2	18.2	.
45-49	1 533.1	10.6 [3]	.	253.4	510.4	340.8	0.3	253.2	148.4	16.2	.
50-54	1 255.0	7.3 [3]	.	344.9	320.4	259.2	0.5	212.3	94.3	16.1	.
55-59	972.8	5.7 [3]	.	371.8	224.3	144.1	0.4	150.1	64.4	11.9	.
60-64	566.3	7.8 [3]	.	265.3	105.9	63.8	0.1	81.3	29.9	12.3	.
65-69	73.2	0.4 [3]	.	30.3	7.6	5.8	-	21.2	3.9	4.0	.
70-74	17.2	0.1 [3]	.	6.0	0.7	1.5	-	6.3	0.8	1.8	.
75+	7.9	0.0 [3]	.	2.9	0.2	0.6	-	3.4	0.5	0.3	.

Women - Femmes - Mujeres
ISCED-97 - CITE-97 - CINE-97

	Total	X	0	1	2	3	4	5A	5B	6	?
Total	9 816.5	37.8 [3]	.	1 260.5	2 471.0	2 496.3	6.7	2 525.0	951.8	67.5	.
16-19	225.5	- [3]	.	44.4	121.4	57.0	-	0.2	2.5	-	.
20-24	851.7	1.3 [3]	.	69.1	252.1	296.7	0.6	135.9	95.8	0.2	.
25-29	1 441.9	4.9 [3]	.	78.0	303.4	399.3	2.6	463.0	187.2	3.4	.
30-34	1 573.5	4.2 [3]	.	87.3	312.5	392.7	1.4	541.3	226.9	7.0	.
35-39	1 426.5	3.7 [3]	.	102.0	351.3	357.9	0.5	435.3	164.7	11.1	.
40-44	1 333.0	5.5 [3]	.	122.1	379.0	346.3	0.7	333.4	129.2	16.7	.
45-49	1 170.8	2.8 [3]	.	175.9	350.4	286.1	0.7	266.0	76.5	12.4	.
50-54	876.8	3.9 [3]	.	220.1	222.8	196.9	0.2	184.2	39.4	9.1	.
55-59	571.8	6.0 [3]	.	203.9	117.2	111.2	-	109.3	20.0	4.3	.
60-64	284.6	3.9 [3]	.	129.0	54.4	42.7	-	44.7	7.3	2.4	.
65-69	43.8	0.4 [3]	.	20.6	5.6	6.1	-	8.7	1.8	0.6	.
70-74	11.0	1.1 [3]	.	5.4	0.6	1.3	-	2.2	0.2	0.1	.
75+	5.8	0.1 [3]	.	2.7	0.1	1.9	-	0.7	0.3	-	.

Estonia (BA) (2008) [4] [5]

Total - Total - Total
ISCED-97 - CITE-97 - CINE-97

	Total	X	0	1	2	3	4	5A	5B	6	?
Total	694.9	5.0 [6]	.	.	71.6	338.8	44.6	153.5	79.0	2.1	.
15-19	12.7	1.1 [6]	.	.	7.8	3.7	-	-	-	-	.
20-24	70.4	1.3 [6]	.	.	11.4	44.1	3.7	5.5	4.4	-	.
25-29	81.1	- [6]	.	.	10.8	33.7	6.1	18.9	10.5	-	.
30-34	80.8	- [6]	.	.	9.9	39.2	3.6	17.9	9.6	-	.
35-39	83.1	- [6]	.	.	4.0	46.9	3.2	18.3	10.1	-	.
40-44	79.9	- [6]	.	.	4.2	40.5	6.4	19.2	9.5	-	.
45-49	87.3	- [6]	.	.	5.4	40.5	8.0	22.8	10.1	-	.
50-54	78.6	- [6]	.	.	5.7	37.9	7.0	17.1	10.7	-	.
55-59	67.4	- [6]	.	.	6.9	29.4	4.9	16.5	9.4	-	.
60-64	30.0	- [6]	.	.	3.1	13.3	1.2	8.9	3.1	-	.
65-69	17.8	- [6]	.	.	2.0	7.6	-	5.6	1.4	-	.
70-74	5.8	- [6]	.	.	-	2.0	-	2.8	-	-	.

Men - Hommes - Hombres
ISCED-97 - CITE-97 - CINE-97

	Total	X	0	1	2	3	4	5A	5B	6	?
Total	351.2	3.1 [6]	.	.	45.2	193.8	17.5	63.2	26.7	1.4	.
15-19	6.9	- [6]	.	.	4.3	1.8	-	-	-	-	.
20-24	38.8	- [6]	.	.	8.7	24.3	1.9	1.6	1.4	-	.
25-29	48.0	- [6]	.	.	7.2	22.2	2.9	10.0	5.1	-	.
30-34	43.8	- [6]	.	.	6.3	23.7	0.9	8.2	4.4	-	.
35-39	43.3	- [6]	.	.	2.6	29.8	1.0	6.8	2.8	-	.
40-44	39.0	- [6]	.	.	2.6	24.6	2.3	7.4	2.0	-	.
45-49	40.6	- [6]	.	.	3.1	22.6	2.9	8.4	3.4	-	.
50-54	35.6	- [6]	.	.	3.6	19.7	2.7	6.5	2.8	-	.
55-59	29.8	- [6]	.	.	3.5	14.2	2.3	6.2	3.4	-	.
60-64	14.6	- [6]	.	.	2.0	7.0	-	4.2	0.8	-	.
65-69	7.7	- [6]	.	.	1.0	3.1	-	2.4	0.3	-	.
70-74	3.1	- [6]	.	.	-	1.0	-	1.4	-	-	.

Explanatory notes: see p. 3.

[1] Excl. compulsory military service. [2] Persons aged 16 years and over. [3] Levels X-0. [4] Incl. armed forces, Excl. conscripts. [5] Persons aged 15 to 74 years. [6] Levels X-1.

Notes explicatives: voir p. 5.

[1] Non compris les militaires du contingent. [2] Personnes âgées de 16 ans et plus. [3] Niveaux X-0. [4] Y compris les forces armées, Excl. conscrits [5] Personnes âgées de 15 à 74 ans. [6] Niveaux X-1.

Notas explicativas: véase p. 7.

[1] Excl. a los militares en servicio obligatorio. [2] Personas de 16 años y más. [3] Niveles X-0. [4] Incl. las fuerzas armadas, excl. los conscriptos. [5] Personas de 15 a 74 años. [6] Niveles X-1.

1B

ECONOMICALLY ACTIVE POPULATION	POPULATION ACTIVE	POBLACION ECONOMICAMENTE ACTIVA
By level of education and age group	Par niveau d'instruction et groupe d'âge	Por nivel de educación y grupo de edad
Thousands	Milliers	Millares

ISCED 1976 CITE / CINE 1997		Total	X	0	1	2	3	5	6	7	9	?
ISCED 1976 CITE	Total		X	0	1	2	3	5	6	7	9	?
CINE 1997	Total		X	0	1	2	3	4	5A	5B	6	?

Estonia (BA) (2008) [1] [2]

Women - Femmes - Mujeres
ISCED-97 - CITE-97 - CINE-97

Age	Total	X	0	1	2	3	4	5A	5B	6	?
Total	343.7	1.9 [3]	.	.	26.4	145.0	27.1	90.4	52.3	0.7	.
15-19	5.7	- [3]	.	.	3.5	2.0	-	-	-	-	.
20-24	31.6	- [3]	.	.	2.7	19.9	1.7	3.9	2.9	-	.
25-29	33.1	- [3]	.	.	3.6	11.5	3.3	9.0	5.3	-	.
30-34	37.1	- [3]	.	.	3.6	15.5	2.8	9.7	5.2	-	.
35-39	39.7	- [3]	.	.	1.4	17.1	2.2	11.5	7.3	-	.
40-44	40.9	- [3]	.	.	1.6	16.0	4.0	11.7	7.5	-	.
45-49	46.8	- [3]	.	.	2.3	18.0	5.1	14.4	6.7	-	.
50-54	43.0	- [3]	.	.	2.1	18.2	4.3	10.6	7.8	-	.
55-59	37.7	- [3]	.	.	3.4	15.2	2.6	10.3	6.1	-	.
60-64	15.4	- [3]	.	.	1.1	6.3	-	4.7	2.3	-	.
65-69	10.1	- [3]	.	.	1.0	4.5	-	3.2	1.1	-	.
70-74	2.7	- [3]	.	.	-	1.0	-	1.4	-	-	.

Finland (BA) (2008) [2] [4]

Total - Total - Total
ISCED-97 - CITE-97 - CINE-97

Age	Total	X	0	1	2	3	4	5A	5B	6	?
Total	2 725.6	.	525.4 [5]	.	.	1 232.1 [6]	14.5	546.4	377.7	29.5	.
15-19	118.9	.	103.0 [5]	.	.	16.0 [6]	-	-	-	-	.
20-24	243.7	.	36.8 [5]	.	.	197.7 [6]	0.1	8.8	0.3	-	.
25-29	286.6	.	32.3 [5]	.	.	157.5 [6]	1.1	93.2	2.0	0.4	.
30-34	287.5	.	26.9 [5]	.	.	124.4 [6]	2.2	102.0	29.3	2.7	.
35-39	286.3	.	35.3 [5]	.	.	116.2 [6]	2.3	73.1	54.8	4.5	.
40-44	337.3	.	37.2 [5]	.	.	146.8 [6]	2.6	73.6	72.7	4.4	.
45-49	340.8	.	45.9 [5]	.	.	154.7 [6]	2.8	60.8	71.9	4.7	.
50-54	335.7	.	63.4 [5]	.	.	145.9 [6]	1.8	55.6	64.2	4.8	.
55-59	299.7	.	78.1 [5]	.	.	116.9 [6]	1.5	44.9	54.5	3.8	.
60-64	155.0	.	52.6 [5]	.	.	48.6 [6]	0.1	27.2	23.2	3.2	.
65-69	25.2	.	9.1 [5]	.	.	5.6 [6]	-	5.5	4.2	0.7	.
70-74	8.9	.	4.7 [5]	.	.	1.6 [6]	-	1.7	0.6	0.2	.

Men - Hommes - Hombres
ISCED-97 - CITE-97 - CINE-97

Age	Total	X	0	1	2	3	4	5A	5B	6	?
Total	1 421.6	.	308.1 [5]	.	.	684.8 [6]	6.6	258.5	146.2	17.3	.
15-19	60.0	.	50.7 [5]	.	.	9.3 [6]	-	-	-	-	.
20-24	129.9	.	24.2 [5]	.	.	103.9 [6]	-	1.6	0.3	-	.
25-29	157.8	.	22.8 [5]	.	.	95.5 [6]	0.6	37.2	1.5	0.2	.
30-34	157.4	.	17.9 [5]	.	.	81.1 [6]	1.0	45.5	10.6	1.3	.
35-39	154.8	.	23.4 [5]	.	.	70.1 [6]	1.2	37.0	20.9	2.2	.
40-44	172.2	.	23.6 [5]	.	.	83.7 [6]	1.4	34.7	26.5	2.3	.
45-49	172.0	.	29.8 [5]	.	.	81.3 [6]	0.9	30.8	26.1	3.1	.
50-54	165.6	.	35.2 [5]	.	.	75.5 [6]	0.6	27.7	23.3	3.3	.
55-59	149.2	.	43.2 [5]	.	.	55.9 [6]	0.8	23.6	23.4	2.3	.
60-64	79.2	.	27.8 [5]	.	.	23.7 [6]	0.1	15.1	10.5	2.0	.
65-69	17.0	.	6.0 [5]	.	.	4.0 [6]	-	3.9	2.7	0.4	.
70-74	6.5	.	3.5 [5]	.	.	0.9 [6]	-	1.4	0.5	0.2	.

Women - Femmes - Mujeres
ISCED-97 - CITE-97 - CINE-97

Age	Total	X	0	1	2	3	4	5A	5B	6	?
Total	1 303.7	.	217.1 [5]	.	.	547.3 [6]	7.9	287.7	231.5	12.2	.
15-19	58.9	.	52.3 [5]	.	.	6.7 [6]	-	-	-	-	.
20-24	113.8	.	12.7 [5]	.	.	93.8 [6]	0.1	7.2	.	-	.
25-29	128.6	.	9.5 [5]	.	.	62.1 [6]	0.5	55.8	0.6	0.2	.
30-34	130.2	.	8.9 [5]	.	.	43.3 [6]	1.2	56.5	18.8	1.5	.
35-39	131.4	.	11.9 [5]	.	.	46.1 [6]	1.1	36.1	33.9	2.3	.
40-44	165.1	.	13.5 [5]	.	.	63.1 [6]	1.2	38.9	46.3	2.0	.
45-49	168.8	.	16.1 [5]	.	.	73.4 [6]	1.9	30.1	45.8	1.6	.
50-54	170.1	.	28.3 [5]	.	.	70.4 [6]	1.2	27.8	40.9	1.5	.
55-59	150.5	.	34.9 [5]	.	.	61.0 [6]	0.7	21.3	31.1	1.5	.
60-64	75.8	.	24.8 [5]	.	.	25.0 [6]	-	12.1	12.7	1.2	.
65-69	8.2	.	3.2 [5]	.	.	1.6 [6]	-	1.6	1.5	0.3	.
70-74	2.4	.	1.2 [5]	.	.	0.7 [6]	-	0.3	0.1	-	.

Explanatory notes: see p. 3.

[1] Incl. armed forces, Excl. conscripts. [2] Persons aged 15 to 74 years. [3] Levels X-1. [4] Included armed forces and conscripts. [5] Levels 0-2. [6] Levels 3-4.

Notes explicatives: voir p. 5.

[1] Y compris les forces armées, Excl. conscrits [2] Personnes âgées de 15 à 74 ans. [3] Niveaux X-1. [4] Y compris les forces armées et les conscrits. [5] Niveaux 0-2. [6] Niveaux 3-4.

Notas explicativas: véase p. 7.

[1] Incl. las fuerzas armadas, excl. los conscriptos. [2] Personas de 15 a 74 años. [3] Niveles X-1. [4] Incluye las fuerzas armadas y los conscriptos. [5] Niveles 0-2. [6] Niveles 3-4.

ECONOMICALLY ACTIVE POPULATION

By level of education and age group

POPULATION ACTIVE

Par niveau d'instruction et groupe d'âge

POBLACION ECONOMICAMENTE ACTIVA

Por nivel de educación y grupo de edad

Thousands — Milliers — Millares

ISCED 1976 / CITE / CINE 1997	Total	X	0	1	2	3	5 / 4	6 / 5A	7 / 5B	9 / 6	?

France (BA) (2008) [1]

Total - Total - Total
ISCED-97 - CITE-97 - CINE-97

	Total	X	0	1	2	3	4	5A	5B	6	?
Total	27 983.5	0.8	72.3	1 893.4	5 068.2	12 510.6	24.8	4 741.1	3 473.5	198.8	.
15-19	601.4	0.2	-	9.3	310.5	273.4	-	4.6	3.5	-	.
20-24	2 342.6	0.5	1.9	42.7	385.0	1 284.4	0.9	293.4	333.9	-	.
25-29	3 338.1	-	3.0	73.9	423.0	1 419.8	2.2	796.0	610.4	9.8	.
30-34	3 448.1	0.2	4.0	81.6	405.9	1 455.0	1.7	864.1	611.0	24.8	.
35-39	3 895.0	-	5.7	147.2	618.1	1 703.3	3.2	815.6	563.3	38.6	.
40-44	3 907.7	-	10.3	204.2	738.1	1 866.0	6.9	567.8	470.9	43.5	.
45-49	3 814.6	-	13.5	279.4	863.9	1 826.8	2.6	446.9	360.1	21.3	.
50-54	3 488.5	-	14.3	441.2	811.4	1 492.7	5.0	403.7	293.3	27.0	.
55-59	2 421.9	-	10.3	448.4	412.4	990.8	2.2	365.0	177.9	14.8	.
60-64	577.7	-	8.0	126.5	74.8	158.9	-	150.1	42.8	16.5	.
65-69	98.1	-	0.5	18.7	16.1	29.4	-	26.5	5.0	1.8	.
70-74	30.8	-	0.8	13.5	4.4	5.8	-	5.0	1.4	-	.
75+	17.5	-	-	6.8	3.4	4.2	-	2.4	-	0.6	.
?	1.3	-	-	0.1	1.2	-	-	-	-	-	.

Men - Hommes - Hombres
ISCED-97 - CITE-97 - CINE-97

	Total	X	0	1	2	3	4	5A	5B	6	?
Total	14 687.9	0.4	34.9	976.5	2 819.0	6 912.9	7.2	2 273.2	1 545.7	118.2	.
15-19	367.7	-	-	7.2	206.1	151.4	-	1.2	1.9	-	.
20-24	1 240.1	0.2	0.1	32.1	242.5	718.5	-	108.4	138.4	-	.
25-29	1 759.6	-	1.3	51.6	268.6	819.7	0.1	338.8	273.5	6.1	.
30-34	1 834.8	0.2	1.1	52.9	260.3	826.7	0.5	391.8	285.3	16.0	.
35-39	2 051.0	-	3.6	81.1	355.5	936.7	1.5	384.5	263.8	24.3	.
40-44	2 032.1	-	4.7	114.9	391.8	999.8	1.4	286.4	214.4	18.7	.
45-49	1 963.7	-	7.3	143.4	431.0	998.9	1.1	219.3	150.2	12.6	.
50-54	1 801.9	-	6.2	222.1	418.6	803.6	2.6	214.2	119.9	14.7	.
55-59	1 233.4	-	3.5	190.9	200.5	544.0	-	207.3	76.0	11.1	.
60-64	314.0	-	6.4	64.0	32.6	86.9	-	93.4	18.5	12.2	.
65-69	59.3	-	0.5	6.0	7.4	20.1	-	20.6	2.9	1.8	.
70-74	19.7	-	0.2	7.6	2.4	3.7	-	4.8	1.0	-	.
75+	9.9	-	-	2.8	1.2	2.8	-	2.4	-	0.6	.
?	0.8	-	-	0.1	0.7	-	-	-	-	-	.

Women - Femmes - Mujeres
ISCED-97 - CITE-97 - CINE-97

	Total	X	0	1	2	3	4	5A	5B	6	?
Total	13 295.6	0.4	37.4	916.9	2 249.1	5 597.7	17.6	2 468.0	1 927.9	80.6	.
15-19	233.8	0.2	-	2.2	104.4	122.1	-	3.4	1.6	-	.
20-24	1 102.5	0.2	1.8	10.6	142.6	565.9	0.9	185.0	195.5	-	.
25-29	1 578.6	-	1.7	22.3	154.4	600.1	2.2	457.2	336.9	3.7	.
30-34	1 613.2	-	2.9	28.7	145.6	628.3	1.2	472.2	325.6	8.8	.
35-39	1 844.0	-	2.1	66.1	262.6	766.6	1.6	431.1	299.6	14.3	.
40-44	1 875.7	-	5.6	89.4	346.3	866.2	5.5	281.5	256.5	24.8	.
45-49	1 850.8	-	6.2	136.0	432.9	827.9	1.5	227.6	209.9	8.7	.
50-54	1 686.6	-	8.1	219.0	392.8	689.1	2.4	189.5	173.4	12.3	.
55-59	1 188.6	-	6.7	257.5	211.9	446.8	2.2	157.7	101.9	3.7	.
60-64	263.7	-	1.6	62.5	42.2	72.0	-	56.6	24.3	4.4	.
65-69	38.8	-	-	12.8	8.7	9.3	-	5.9	2.2	-	.
70-74	11.1	-	0.6	5.9	2.0	2.0	-	0.2	0.4	-	.
75+	7.7	-	-	4.0	2.2	1.4	-	-	-	-	.
?	0.5	-	-	-	0.5	-	-	-	-	-	.

Germany (BA) (2008) [1][2]

Total - Total - Total
ISCED-97 - CITE-97 - CINE-97

	Total	X	0	1	2	3	4	5A	5B	6	?
Total	38 734	874 [3]	.	.	4 815	19 902	2 945	5 980	3 580	537	101
15-19	1 348	114 [3]	.	.	1 036	192	-	-	-	-	-
20-24	3 145	64 [3]	.	.	683	1 972	259	64	96	-	7
25-29	3 694	65 [3]	.	.	321	1 906	526	612	249	13	5
30-34	3 700	82 [3]	.	.	299	1 734	435	780	308	53	9
35-39	4 794	104 [3]	.	.	384	2 449	438	861	462	81	14
40-44	6 084	136 [3]	.	.	482	3 175	518	990	666	98	19
45-49	5 475	121 [3]	.	.	496	2 927	365	856	611	85	14
50-54	4 618	86 [3]	.	.	435	2 491	224	780	518	71	14
55-59	3 707	65 [3]	.	.	383	2 019	121	635	405	66	12
60-64	1 526	29 [3]	.	.	180	759	40	295	174	44	-
65-69	408	5 [3]	.	.	64	179	12	71	58	19	-
70-74	163	- [3]	.	.	33	72	-	26	22	-	-
75+	72	- [3]	.	.	19	28	-	10	10	-	-

Explanatory notes: see p. 3.

[1] Persons aged 15 years and over. [2] Included armed forces and conscripts. [3] Levels X-1.

Notes explicatives: voir p. 5.

[1] Personnes âgées de 15 ans et plus. [2] Y compris les forces armées et les conscrits. [3] Niveaux X-1.

Notas explicativas: véase p. 7.

[1] Personas de 15 años y más. [2] Incluye las fuerzas armadas y los conscriptos. [3] Niveles X-1.

1B

ECONOMICALLY ACTIVE POPULATION	POPULATION ACTIVE	POBLACION ECONOMICAMENTE ACTIVA
By level of education and age group	Par niveau d'instruction et groupe d'âge	Por nivel de educación y grupo de edad
Thousands	Milliers	Millares

ISCED 1976 / CITE	Total	X	0	1	2	3	5	6	7	9	?
CINE 1997	**Total**	**X**	**0**	**1**	**2**	**3**	**4**	**5A**	**5B**	**6**	**?**

Germany (BA) (2008) [1][2]

Men - Hommes - Hombres
ISCED-97 - CITE-97 - CINE-97

Age	Total	X	0	1	2	3	4	5A	5B	6	?
Total	21 188	514[3]	.	.	2 444	10 786	1 371	3 471	2 168	380	56
15-19	770	66[3]	.	.	607	95	-	-	-	-	-
20-24	1 680	45[3]	.	.	410	1 068	98	23	33	-	-
25-29	1 965	44[3]	.	.	197	1 094	223	279	118	6	-
30-34	2 059	50[3]	.	.	177	1 000	201	420	177	29	5
35-39	2 657	62[3]	.	.	196	1 339	213	509	278	52	9
40-44	3 315	80[3]	.	.	227	1 687	242	591	408	70	10
45-49	2 924	64[3]	.	.	214	1 535	172	503	366	63	7
50-54	2 456	46[3]	.	.	177	1 287	116	454	319	50	7
55-59	2 034	35[3]	.	.	137	1 069	71	399	265	52	7
60-64	923	17[3]	.	.	65	442	23	208	129	38	-
65-69	251	-[3]	.	.	19	103	8	57	48	14	-
70-74	105	-[3]	.	.	10	47	-	20	19	-	-
75+	47	-[3]	.	.	7	19	-	8	8	-	-

Women - Femmes - Mujeres
ISCED-97 - CITE-97 - CINE-97

Age	Total	X	0	1	2	3	4	5A	5B	6	?
Total	17 546	360[3]	.	.	2 371	9 116	1 574	2 509	1 412	158	46
15-19	578	48[3]	.	.	429	98	-	-	-	-	-
20-24	1 464	19[3]	.	.	273	904	162	41	63	-	-
25-29	1 729	20[3]	.	.	123	811	302	333	130	7	-
30-34	1 640	32[3]	.	.	122	733	234	360	131	24	-
35-39	2 137	43[3]	.	.	188	1 110	225	352	185	29	6
40-44	2 769	55[3]	.	.	255	1 487	276	399	258	29	9
45-49	2 551	57[3]	.	.	282	1 392	193	353	246	22	7
50-54	2 162	40[3]	.	.	257	1 203	108	326	199	21	7
55-59	1 673	30[3]	.	.	247	950	50	236	140	14	-
60-64	603	12[3]	.	.	116	317	17	88	45	7	-
65-69	157	-[3]	.	.	45	76	4	14	11	5	-
70-74	58	-[3]	.	.	23	24	-	6	3	-	-
75+	25	-[3]	.	.	12	9	-	2	2	-	-

Greece (BA) (2008) [2][4][5]

Total - Total - Total
ISCED-97 - CITE-97 - CINE-97

Age	Total	X	0	1	2	3	4	5A	5B	6	?
Total	4 939.7	46.4[6]	.	934.1	557.8	1 634.5	460.0	904.1	378.6	24.2	.
15-19	48.8	-[6]	.	8.5	14.9	24.7	0.5	-	0.1	-	.
20-24	299.8	2.0[6]	.	24.2	34.5	148.4	39.8	25.2	25.4	0.2	.
25-29	659.9	2.2[6]	.	52.2	68.9	221.3	107.0	129.6	78.1	0.5	.
30-34	712.2	2.2[6]	.	67.0	83.1	259.1	93.0	135.3	68.0	4.6	.
35-39	710.2	4.0[6]	.	74.8	96.9	270.6	64.2	139.9	56.0	3.8	.
40-44	718.5	3.8[6]	.	105.0	92.6	244.2	54.3	147.8	67.0	3.8	.
45-49	614.7	3.8[6]	.	137.5	66.4	207.6	45.0	111.6	39.0	3.7	.
50-54	522.2	5.0[6]	.	169.4	45.8	139.6	29.8	103.7	26.7	2.2	.
55-59	360.1	6.0[6]	.	143.2	33.6	77.8	17.5	68.8	11.2	2.0	.
60-64	207.8	5.9[6]	.	109.5	16.5	31.5	7.6	29.7	5.2	1.9	.
65-69	53.1	4.3[6]	.	27.9	3.4	5.6	0.7	8.7	1.5	1.0	.
70-74	21.8	4.3[6]	.	10.5	0.8	2.3	0.3	3.4	0.2	0.1	.
75+	10.6	3.0[6]	.	4.3	0.4	1.8	0.3	0.5	-	0.3	.

Men - Hommes - Hombres
ISCED-97 - CITE-97 - CINE-97

Age	Total	X	0	1	2	3	4	5A	5B	6	?
Total	2 925.5	27.3[6]	.	590.4	387.6	1 005.9	220.7	463.8	213.8	16.0	.
15-19	28.5	-[6]	.	5.8	10.5	12.0	-	-	0.1	-	.
20-24	168.3	1.3[6]	.	18.2	25.6	92.0	14.9	5.5	10.8	-	.
25-29	373.6	1.4[6]	.	41.1	52.5	143.4	47.6	50.4	37.0	0.4	.
30-34	412.1	1.3[6]	.	48.1	61.1	157.0	43.3	62.9	35.9	2.6	.
35-39	418.6	2.8[6]	.	49.5	64.2	171.8	29.8	68.3	29.7	2.6	.
40-44	403.3	2.0[6]	.	62.6	59.9	137.9	25.9	72.0	40.6	2.4	.
45-49	362.3	2.8[6]	.	77.3	45.2	122.1	24.2	61.7	26.2	2.8	.
50-54	318.6	2.4[6]	.	100.7	29.1	87.7	15.9	62.0	19.4	1.4	.
55-59	236.5	3.5[6]	.	88.8	24.3	51.5	11.6	47.3	8.4	1.1	.
60-64	140.9	2.5[6]	.	68.0	12.0	22.9	6.3	23.1	4.5	1.7	.
65-69	38.0	2.6[6]	.	18.3	2.5	4.7	0.6	7.3	1.2	0.9	.
70-74	16.3	2.4[6]	.	8.3	0.4	1.7	0.3	2.9	0.2	0.1	.
75+	8.4	2.1[6]	.	3.7	0.4	1.4	0.3	0.5	-	-	.

Explanatory notes: see p. 3.

[1] Included armed forces and conscripts. [2] Persons aged 15 years and over. [3] Levels X-1. [4] Excl. conscripts. [5] Second quarter of each year. [6] Levels X-0.

Notes explicatives: voir p. 5.

[1] Y compris les forces armées et les conscrits. [2] Personnes âgées de 15 ans et plus. [3] Niveaux X-1. [4] Non compris les conscrits. [5] Deuxième trimestre de chaque année. [6] Niveaux X-0.

Notas explicativas: véase p. 7.

[1] Incluye las fuezas armadas y los conscriptos. [2] Personas de 15 años y más. [3] Niveles X-1. [4] Excl. los conscriptos. [5] Segundo trimestre de cada año. [6] Niveles X-0.

ECONOMICALLY ACTIVE POPULATION

By level of education and age group

POPULATION ACTIVE

Par niveau d'instruction et groupe d'âge

POBLACION ECONOMICAMENTE ACTIVA

Por nivel de educación y grupo de edad

	Thousands				Milliers				Millares			
ISCED 1976	Total	X	0	1	2	3	5	6	7	9	?
CITE CINE 1997	Total	X	0	1	2	3	4	5A	5B	6	?

Greece (BA) (2008) [1] [2] [3]

Women - Femmes - Mujeres
ISCED-97 - CITE-97 - CINE-97

Total	2 014.2	19.1 [4]	.	343.7	170.2	628.6	239.2	440.4	164.9	8.2	.
15-19	20.3	- [4]	.	2.7	4.4	12.7	0.5	-	-	-	.
20-24	131.5	0.7 [4]	.	6.0	8.9	56.4	24.9	19.8	14.6	0.2	.
25-29	286.2	0.8 [4]	.	11.2	16.4	77.9	59.4	79.2	41.2	0.1	.
30-34	300.1	0.8 [4]	.	19.0	22.0	102.2	49.6	72.4	32.1	2.0	.
35-39	291.7	1.2 [4]	.	25.3	32.8	98.8	34.4	71.6	26.4	1.2	.
40-44	315.2	1.8 [4]	.	42.3	32.7	106.4	28.4	75.8	26.5	1.4	.
45-49	252.4	0.9 [4]	.	60.2	21.2	85.5	20.8	49.9	12.8	0.9	.
50-54	203.6	2.6 [4]	.	68.7	16.7	52.0	13.9	41.7	7.3	0.8	.
55-59	123.7	2.5 [4]	.	54.5	9.3	26.3	5.9	21.5	2.9	0.9	.
60-64	66.9	3.3 [4]	.	41.5	4.6	8.6	1.3	6.6	0.7	0.2	.
65-69	15.1	1.7 [4]	.	9.6	0.9	0.9	0.2	1.3	0.4	0.2	.
70-74	5.5	1.9 [4]	.	2.1	0.3	0.6	-	0.6	-	-	.
75+	2.2	0.8 [4]	.	0.6	-	0.4	-	-	-	0.3	.

Hungary (BA) (2008) [2] [5]

Total - Total - Total
ISCED-97 - CITE-97 - CINE-97

Total	4 208.6	.	.	18.9	576.1	2 588.4	103.0	29.4	873.8	19.1	.
15-19	26.2	.	.	0.7	13.7	11.8	0.0	0.0	0.0	0.0	.
20-24	280.8	.	.	1.3	43.3	195.4	5.3	6.0	29.4	0.0	.
25-29	570.4	.	.	2.6	55.0	335.9	14.0	8.7	153.8	0.5	.
30-34	652.5	.	.	2.2	74.4	399.2	23.2	4.3	146.9	2.2	.
35-39	618.9	.	.	2.1	74.0	393.0	19.8	4.2	122.2	3.6	.
40-44	508.7	.	.	1.8	69.4	325.9	8.2	1.6	99.3	2.5	.
45-49	507.1	.	.	3.0	72.4	313.0	9.5	2.0	104.9	2.2	.
50-54	599.2	.	.	2.7	98.4	368.2	14.8	2.0	109.5	3.7	.
55-59	339.8	.	.	1.5	55.8	199.3	6.1	0.5	75.0	1.6	.
60-64	74.3	.	.	0.5	12.5	36.2	2.0	0.0	22.3	0.8	.
65-69	24.5	.	.	0.2	5.6	9.2	0.1	0.0	7.7	1.6	.
70-74	6.2	.	.	0.3	1.7	1.1	0.0	0.0	2.8	0.4	.

Men - Hommes - Hombres
ISCED-97 - CITE-97 - CINE-97

Total	2 285.1	.	.	11.5	297.9	1 490.8	57.6	10.5	404.3	12.7	.
15-19	17.3	.	.	0.7	9.0	7.6	-	-	-	-	.
20-24	159.9	.	.	0.9	29.8	113.2	2.9	3.1	9.9	0.0	.
25-29	326.8	.	.	2.2	36.6	208.7	7.7	3.1	68.5	0.0	.
30-34	384.6	.	.	1.4	48.4	245.3	13.3	1.9	72.8	1.5	.
35-39	345.4	.	.	1.4	41.0	227.5	11.1	1.4	61.2	1.8	.
40-44	263.1	.	.	1.1	34.9	180.9	4.2	0.3	40.0	1.7	.
45-49	248.7	.	.	1.5	28.7	167.3	5.6	0.4	43.5	1.7	.
50-54	293.7	.	.	1.4	35.1	199.0	8.0	0.2	47.3	2.6	.
55-59	186.0	.	.	0.6	25.8	115.6	3.6	0.0	39.3	1.1	.
60-64	41.7	.	.	0.2	4.1	20.7	0.9	0.0	15.0	0.8	.
65-69	13.9	.	.	-	3.5	4.7	0.1	0.0	4.6	1.1	.
70-74	4.1	.	.	0.2	0.9	0.4	0.0	0.0	2.2	0.4	.

Women - Femmes - Mujeres
ISCED-97 - CITE-97 - CINE-97

Total	1 923.5	.	.	7.4	278.2	1 097.5	45.4	19.0	469.5	6.5	.
15-19	8.9	.	.	0.1	4.6	4.2	0.0	0.0	0.0	0.0	.
20-24	120.9	.	.	0.4	13.5	82.2	2.3	2.9	19.5	0.0	.
25-29	243.6	.	.	0.4	18.4	127.2	6.3	5.6	85.3	0.4	.
30-34	267.9	.	.	0.8	26.0	153.9	10.0	2.5	74.1	0.7	.
35-39	273.6	.	.	0.7	33.1	165.6	8.6	2.8	61.0	1.9	.
40-44	245.7	.	.	0.7	34.5	145.1	4.0	1.3	59.3	0.8	.
45-49	258.4	.	.	1.5	43.7	145.8	3.8	1.7	61.4	0.5	.
50-54	305.5	.	.	1.3	63.3	169.2	6.8	1.8	62.2	1.0	.
55-59	153.8	.	.	0.9	30.0	83.8	2.5	0.5	35.7	0.5	.
60-64	32.6	.	.	0.4	8.3	15.5	1.1	0.0	7.2	0.0	.
65-69	10.6	.	.	0.2	2.1	4.5	-	0.0	3.1	0.6	.
70-74	2.1	.	.	0.1	0.8	0.6	0.0	0.0	0.6	0.0	.

Explanatory notes: see p. 3.

[1] Persons aged 15 years and over. [2] Excl. conscripts. [3] Second quarter of each year. [4] Levels X-0. [5] Persons aged 15 to 74 years.

Notes explicatives: voir p. 5.

[1] Personnes âgées de 15 ans et plus. [2] Non compris les conscrits. [3] Deuxième trimestre de chaque année. [4] Niveaux X-0. [5] Personnes âgées de 15 à 74 ans.

Notas explicativas: véase p. 7.

[1] Personas de 15 años y más. [2] Excl. los conscriptos. [3] Segundo trimestre de cada año. [4] Niveles X-0. [5] Personas de 15 a 74 años.

1B

ECONOMICALLY ACTIVE POPULATION	POPULATION ACTIVE	POBLACION ECONOMICAMENTE ACTIVA
By level of education and age group	Par niveau d'instruction et groupe d'âge	Por nivel de educación y grupo de edad

		Thousands				Milliers				Millares	
ISCED 1976 CITE	Total	X	0	1	2	3	5	6	7	9	?
CINE 1997	Total	X	0	1	2	3	4	5A	5B	6	?

Ireland (BA) (2008) [1]

Total - Total - Total
ISCED-97 - CITE-97 - CINE-97

	Total	X	0	1	2	3	4	5A	5B	6	?
Total	2 177.0	3.1	.	170.3	334.2	602.8	229.3	494.9	256.0	8.8	77.7
15-19	69.2	-	.	3.2	27.9	34.3	1.7	-	-	-	1.1
20-24	249.6	-	.	4.0	23.7	115.5	26.8	46.0	22.0	-	11.3
25-29	358.8	-	.	7.6	29.7	98.7	40.4	112.6	47.9	-	20.5
30-34	307.0	-	.	10.8	30.4	75.7	33.9	90.0	48.7	1.1	15.8
35-39	280.5	-	.	12.6	41.2	67.1	32.9	74.1	40.6	2.4	8.9
40-44	248.1	-	.	14.9	45.7	63.7	29.9	54.1	32.4	1.0	6.1
45-49	230.2	-	.	20.6	46.1	59.2	23.5	46.3	26.8	1.2	6.4
50-54	194.0	-	.	28.6	42.9	45.4	17.9	35.5	18.6	-	4.0
55-59	145.7	-	.	37.0	28.7	28.1	13.9	23.2	11.9	-	2.3
60-64	94.0	-	.	30.9	17.9	15.2	8.3	12.8	6.4	-	1.5
65-69	-	-	.	-	-	-	-	-	-	-	-
70-74	-	-	.	-	-	-	-	-	-	-	-
75+	-	-	.	-	-	-	-	-	-	-	-

Men - Hommes - Hombres
ISCED-97 - CITE-97 - CINE-97

	Total	X	0	1	2	3	4	5A	5B	6	?
Total	1 229.9	2.3	.	121.2	227.0	334.8	134.5	240.3	115.9	5.6	48.3
15-19	37.1	-	.	2.2	15.7	17.8	-	0.0	-	-	-
20-24	131.1	-	.	3.1	18.1	64.4	14.0	17.7	7.9	-	5.7
25-29	191.9	-	.	5.7	21.2	59.0	25.0	47.7	19.6	-	13.0
30-34	172.2	-	.	8.3	22.5	44.4	22.4	41.2	21.8	-	10.6
35-39	162.6	-	.	9.0	29.1	39.0	19.1	38.4	20.0	1.8	5.8
40-44	143.4	-	.	10.4	31.8	34.7	17.8	28.3	15.7	-	3.9
45-49	130.8	-	.	14.3	31.0	29.3	13.0	24.8	13.5	-	4.0
50-54	112.1	-	.	18.9	28.6	23.6	10.5	19.2	8.5	-	2.1
55-59	88.2	-	.	26.6	17.6	14.7	7.5	14.0	5.8	-	1.7
60-64	60.5	-	.	23.0	11.5	8.0	4.7	8.9	2.9	-	-
65-69	-	-	.	-	-	-	-	-	-	-	-
70-74	-	-	.	-	-	-	-	-	-	-	-
75+	-	-	.	-	-	-	-	-	-	-	-

Women - Femmes - Mujeres
ISCED-97 - CITE-97 - CINE-97

	Total	X	0	1	2	3	4	5A	5B	6	?
Total	947.2	-	.	49.0	107.1	268.0	94.9	254.6	140.2	3.2	29.4
15-19	32.1	-	.	1.0	12.2	16.5	1.3	-	-	-	-
20-24	118.5	-	.	-	5.5	51.5	12.8	28.3	14.1	-	5.5
25-29	167.0	-	.	2.0	8.5	39.7	15.4	64.9	28.4	-	7.5
30-34	134.8	-	.	2.5	7.9	31.2	11.5	48.8	26.9	-	5.2
35-39	117.9	-	.	3.6	12.1	28.2	13.8	35.6	20.7	-	3.1
40-44	104.8	-	.	4.5	14.0	28.9	12.1	25.8	16.7	-	2.2
45-49	99.4	-	.	6.3	15.1	29.9	10.5	21.5	13.3	-	2.4
50-54	81.9	-	.	9.7	14.3	21.8	7.4	16.3	10.2	-	1.9
55-59	57.4	-	.	10.4	11.1	13.5	6.4	9.2	6.0	-	-
60-64	33.4	-	.	8.0	6.4	7.2	3.7	3.9	3.5	0.0	-
65-69	-	-	.	-	-	-	-	-	-	-	-
70-74	-	-	.	-	-	-	-	-	-	-	-
75+	-	-	.	-	-	-	-	-	-	-	-

Italy (BA) (2008) [1]

Total - Total - Total
ISCED-97 - CITE-97 - CINE-97

	Total	X	0	1	2	3	4	5A	5B	6	?
Total	25 096.6	218.9	.	1 464.6	8 093.8	10 832.8	312.5	3 999.0	120.3	54.8	.
15-19	327.7	1.0	.	9.3	201.9	115.4	0.1	.	.	.	.
20-24	1 549.4	3.9	.	19.0	441.1	989.4	17.4	78.4	0.3	.	.
25-29	2 604.7	15.5	.	35.4	670.8	1 310.4	44.3	517.7	9.4	1.2	.
30-34	3 572.9	22.6	.	67.1	1 004.3	1 667.7	69.8	712.0	17.1	12.4	.
35-39	3 907.4	26.1	.	95.9	1 280.7	1 682.4	70.3	712.4	22.3	17.4	.
40-44	3 934.7	26.8	.	138.3	1 479.4	1 630.3	58.2	564.2	24.8	12.8	.
45-49	3 412.0	32.3	.	178.4	1 289.9	1 410.9	26.9	451.3	17.1	5.3	.
50-54	2 842.0	32.4	.	276.3	970.4	1 101.6	17.3	425.1	15.4	3.5	.
55-59	1 839.1	27.4	.	320.9	514.8	642.1	6.3	317.5	9.4	0.7	.
60-64	706.2	17.8	.	195.5	157.8	195.7	1.6	133.9	3.3	0.8	.
65-69	254.6	7.4	.	78.7	55.8	61.2	0.1	50.2	0.9	0.3	.
70-74	94.2	3.4	.	33.7	19.0	16.5	.	21.1	0.4	0.0	.
75+	51.7	2.4	.	16.3	8.1	9.3	.	15.2	0.0	0.3	.

Explanatory notes: see p. 3.
[1] Persons aged 15 years and over.

Notes explicatives: voir p. 5.
[1] Personnes âgées de 15 ans et plus.

Notas explicativas: véase p. 7.
[1] Personas de 15 años y más.

ECONOMICALLY ACTIVE POPULATION

By level of education and age group

POPULATION ACTIVE

Par niveau d'instruction et groupe d'âge

POBLACION ECONOMICAMENTE ACTIVA

Por nivel de educación y grupo de edad

	Thousands — Milliers — Millares										
ISCED 1976 CITE	Total	X	0	1	2	3	5	6	7	9	?
CINE 1997	Total	X	0	1	2	3	4	5A	5B	6	?

Italy (BA) (2008) [1]

Men - Hommes - Hombres
ISCED-97 - CITE-97 - CINE-97

	Total	X	0	1	2	3	4	5A	5B	6	?
Total	14 884.0	148.7	.	1 003.4	5 435.3	6 153.7	130.9	1 926.6	56.8	28.7	.
15-19	205.5	0.8	.	6.7	135.1	62.9	0.1	.	.	.	.
20-24	907.7	3.0	.	15.5	290.6	566.0	8.9	23.3	0.3	.	.
25-29	1 463.4	11.2	.	26.6	457.2	732.9	22.3	207.6	4.8	0.8	.
30-34	2 046.4	15.6	.	50.9	701.3	946.9	27.2	291.1	8.1	5.2	.
35-39	2 270.8	15.5	.	72.6	856.2	944.2	31.9	331.9	9.8	8.6	.
40-44	2 304.4	20.0	.	97.6	980.3	897.4	21.1	268.6	11.1	8.2	.
45-49	2 021.2	24.0	.	114.7	859.4	773.1	8.9	232.2	6.7	2.1	.
50-54	1 714.6	20.2	.	173.7	644.1	632.0	7.1	228.0	7.8	1.7	.
55-59	1 140.5	16.7	.	205.5	337.5	395.3	2.8	177.1	4.9	0.7	.
60-64	496.7	13.3	.	142.5	111.2	133.7	0.6	92.6	2.1	0.8	.
65-69	196.3	4.6	.	58.7	42.1	47.5	.	42.6	0.7	0.2	.
70-74	74.0	2.1	.	25.2	14.1	14.1	.	18.0	0.4	0.0	.
75+	42.5	1.7	.	13.0	6.2	7.6	.	13.6	0.0	0.3	.

Women - Femmes - Mujeres
ISCED-97 - CITE-97 - CINE-97

	Total	X	0	1	2	3	4	5A	5B	6	?
Total	10 212.7	70.2	.	461.3	2 658.5	4 679.2	181.5	2 072.4	63.5	26.1	.
15-19	122.2	0.2	.	2.5	66.8	52.6	0.0	.	.	.	.
20-24	641.8	0.9	.	3.4	150.4	423.4	8.5	55.1	0.0	.	.
25-29	1 141.2	4.3	.	8.8	213.6	577.5	22.0	310.1	4.6	0.4	.
30-34	1 526.6	7.0	.	16.1	303.0	720.8	42.6	420.9	8.9	7.2	.
35-39	1 636.6	10.6	.	23.2	424.5	738.2	38.4	380.4	12.4	8.8	.
40-44	1 630.3	6.7	.	40.6	499.1	732.9	37.1	295.7	13.7	4.6	.
45-49	1 390.9	8.3	.	63.7	430.5	637.8	18.0	219.1	10.3	3.2	.
50-54	1 127.4	12.2	.	102.7	326.3	469.5	10.2	197.1	7.6	1.8	.
55-59	698.5	10.6	.	115.4	177.3	246.8	3.5	140.5	4.6	.	.
60-64	209.5	4.5	.	52.9	46.5	62.0	1.0	41.3	1.2	0.1	.
65-69	58.3	2.8	.	20.1	13.7	13.7	0.1	7.6	0.1	0.2	.
70-74	20.2	1.3	.	8.5	4.9	2.4	.	3.1	.	.	.
75+	9.2	0.7	.	3.3	1.9	1.7	.	1.6	.	.	.

Latvia (BA) (2008) [2][3]

Total - Total - Total
ISCED-97 - CITE-97 - CINE-97

	Total	X	0	1	2	3	4	5A	5B	6	?
Total	1 215.8	.	.	7.0	154.5	668.0	68.0	312.1 [4]	.	4.5	.
15-19	22.0	.	.	-	13.9	6.4	-	- [4]	.	-	.
20-24	130.0	.	.	-	23.8	82.6	2.4	20.2 [4]	.	-	.
25-29	142.9	.	.	-	23.1	65.7	8.1	44.0 [4]	.	-	.
30-34	137.0	.	.	-	22.9	68.4	6.6	36.8 [4]	.	-	.
35-39	147.0	.	.	-	12.6	89.4	5.6	38.9 [4]	.	-	-
40-44	143.6	.	.	-	7.6	84.6	9.6	40.5 [4]	.	-	.
45-49	153.8	.	.	-	8.8	93.3	12.0	39.2 [4]	.	-	.
50-54	132.0	.	.	-	10.1	77.2	10.3	33.7 [4]	.	-	.
55-59	112.3	.	.	-	15.8	58.8	7.8	29.3 [4]	.	-	.
60-64	47.0	.	.	-	8.6	22.7	2.5	12.3 [4]	.	-	.
65-69	34.9	.	.	-	5.3	14.7	1.8	12.1 [4]	.	-	.
70-74	13.4	.	.	-	2.0	4.3	-	5.1 [4]	.	-	.

Men - Hommes - Hombres
ISCED-97 - CITE-97 - CINE-97

	Total	X	0	1	2	3	4	5A	5B	6	?
Total	621.8	.	.	5.0	104.2	363.4	28.3	117.4 [4]	.	2.3	.
15-19	14.4	.	.	-	9.4	3.8	-	. [4]	.	-	.
20-24	73.9	.	.	-	18.3	45.6	-	7.7 [4]	.	-	.
25-29	78.5	.	.	-	15.4	40.7	3.6	17.2 [4]	.	-	.
30-34	73.8	.	.	-	16.1	38.8	3.5	13.2 [4]	.	-	.
35-39	75.2	.	.	-	9.6	49.5	2.1	13.8 [4]	.	-	.
40-44	71.1	.	.	-	4.6	48.0	3.3	14.7 [4]	.	-	.
45-49	72.9	.	.	-	6.1	48.4	5.1	13.0 [4]	.	-	.
50-54	62.7	.	.	-	6.7	39.9	3.9	11.9 [4]	.	-	.
55-59	52.3	.	.	-	9.2	28.9	3.0	10.8 [4]	.	-	.
60-64	22.2	.	.	-	4.6	11.1	-	5.6 [4]	.	-	.
65-69	16.9	.	.	-	3.2	6.4	-	6.2 [4]	.	-	.
70-74	7.9	.	.	-	-	2.3	-	3.1 [4]	.	-	.

Explanatory notes: see p. 3.

[1] Persons aged 15 years and over. [2] Persons aged 15 to 74 years. [3] Excl. conscripts. [4] Levels 5.

Notes explicatives: voir p. 5.

[1] Personnes âgées de 15 ans et plus. [2] Personnes âgées de 15 à 74 ans. [3] Non compris les conscrits. [4] Niveaux 5.

Notas explicativas: véase p. 7.

[1] Personas de 15 años y más. [2] Personas de 15 a 74 años. [3] Excl. los conscriptos. [4] Niveles 5.

ECONOMICALLY ACTIVE POPULATION
By level of education and age group

POPULATION ACTIVE
Par niveau d'instruction et groupe d'âge

POBLACION ECONOMICAMENTE ACTIVA
Por nivel de educación y grupo de edad

ISCED 1976 CITE		Thousands — Milliers — Millares										
ISCED 1976	Total	X	0	1	2	3	5	6	7	9	?
CINE 1997	Total	X	0	1	2	3	4	5A	5B	6	?

Latvia (BA) (2008) [1][2]

Women - Femmes - Mujeres
ISCED-97 - CITE-97 - CINE-97

	Total	X	0	1	2	3	4	5A	5B	6	?
Total	594.0	.	.	1.9	50.3	304.6	39.7	194.7[3]	.	2.2	.
15-19	7.6	.	.	-	4.5	2.6	-	[3]	.	-	.
20-24	56.2	.	.	-	5.6	37.0	-	12.5[3]	.	-	.
25-29	64.4	.	.	-	7.7	25.1	4.5	26.8[3]	.	-	.
30-34	63.2	.	.	-	6.8	29.5	3.2	23.6[3]	.	-	.
35-39	71.8	.	.	-	3.0	39.9	3.6	25.1[3]	.	-	.
40-44	72.5	.	.	-	3.0	36.6	6.3	25.8[3]	.	-	.
45-49	80.8	.	.	-	2.7	44.9	6.9	26.2[3]	.	-	.
50-54	69.4	.	.	-	3.5	37.3	6.4	21.7[3]	.	-	.
55-59	60.0	.	.	-	6.5	29.9	4.8	18.5[3]	.	-	.
60-64	24.7	.	.	-	4.0	11.6	-	6.7[3]	.	-	.
65-69	18.0	.	.	-	2.1	8.3	-	5.9[3]	.	-	.
70-74	5.5	.	.	-	-	2.0	-	1.9[3]	.	-	.

Lithuania (BA) (2008) [2][4]

Total - Total - Total
ISCED-97 - CITE-97 - CINE-97

	Total	X	0	1	2	3	4	5A	5B	6	?
Total	1 614.3	.	.	7.3	102.4	581.2	379.6	390.3	148.5	4.9	.
15-19	13.8	.	.	0.7	5.9	6.7	0.3	0.0	0.3	0.0	.
20-24	150.8	.	.	1.6	15.4	86.5	10.0	19.1	18.1	0.0	.
25-29	189.4	.	.	0.3	15.8	67.9	14.4	57.9	32.8	0.2	.
30-34	191.1	.	.	0.4	21.5	68.6	17.2	54.2	28.5	0.8	.
35-39	216.4	.	.	0.2	7.8	77.1	54.3	51.3	25.2	0.6	.
40-44	221.1	.	.	-	5.1	79.1	74.0	47.8	14.6	0.5	.
45-49	232.1	.	.	0.1	4.7	78.1	82.0	52.7	13.6	0.9	.
50-54	174.4	.	.	-	5.8	55.3	60.9	44.2	7.6	0.6	.
55-59	131.9	.	.	0.3	10.2	39.0	44.0	32.7	5.3	0.5	.
60-64	62.6	.	.	1.3	5.5	18.0	16.6	19.0	1.8	0.4	.
65-69	22.9	.	.	1.5	4.1	3.9	4.7	8.3	0.4	0.1	.
70-74	5.8	.	.	0.9	0.5	0.7	1.0	2.2	0.2	0.3	.
75+	1.9	.	.	0.1	0.2	0.2	0.3	0.9	0.1	-	.

Men - Hommes - Hombres
ISCED-97 - CITE-97 - CINE-97

	Total	X	0	1	2	3	4	5A	5B	6	?
Total	818.1	.	.	4.6	66.3	347.5	176.2	161.4	59.4	2.7	.
15-19	8.2	.	.	0.6	4.3	3.1	0.1	0.0	0.1	0.0	.
20-24	88.2	.	.	1.3	11.5	55.2	5.3	7.0	8.0	0.0	.
25-29	100.3	.	.	-	10.4	41.8	6.5	25.6	16.0	0.0	.
30-34	98.1	.	.	0.4	13.2	42.3	8.4	20.7	12.8	0.4	.
35-39	108.6	.	.	0.1	5.1	47.2	28.6	18.7	8.7	0.2	.
40-44	108.7	.	.	-	3.7	46.4	34.1	19.2	5.0	0.3	.
45-49	110.9	.	.	0.1	2.5	43.6	36.9	22.4	4.9	0.6	.
50-54	82.7	.	.	-	3.1	32.2	27.2	18.3	1.5	0.4	.
55-59	62.9	.	.	0.1	5.6	22.7	19.1	13.8	1.5	0.2	.
60-64	31.8	.	.	0.7	4.1	9.9	7.2	8.7	0.9	0.3	.
65-69	13.7	.	.	0.9	2.3	2.7	2.5	5.3	0.1	-	.
70-74	2.9	.	.	0.4	0.4	0.3	0.4	1.0	0.1	0.2	.
75+	1.0	.	.	0.0	0.2	0.1	-	0.7	-	-	.

Women - Femmes - Mujeres
ISCED-97 - CITE-97 - CINE-97

	Total	X	0	1	2	3	4	5A	5B	6	?
Total	796.1	.	.	2.7	36.1	233.7	203.3	229.0	89.0	2.2	.
15-19	5.6	.	.	0.1	1.5	3.6	0.1	0.0	0.2	0.0	.
20-24	62.6	.	.	0.3	3.9	31.4	4.7	12.1	10.1	0.0	.
25-29	89.2	.	.	0.3	5.4	26.2	7.9	32.4	16.9	0.2	.
30-34	93.0	.	.	0.0	8.3	26.4	8.8	33.5	15.7	0.4	.
35-39	107.8	.	.	0.1	2.7	29.8	25.7	32.6	16.5	0.3	.
40-44	112.4	.	.	0.0	1.4	32.8	39.9	28.6	9.6	0.2	.
45-49	121.2	.	.	0.0	2.2	34.5	45.1	30.2	8.8	0.3	.
50-54	91.7	.	.	0.0	2.7	23.1	33.7	25.9	6.1	0.3	.
55-59	69.0	.	.	0.2	4.6	16.3	24.9	18.9	3.8	0.3	.
60-64	30.7	.	.	0.6	1.4	8.0	9.5	10.4	0.9	0.1	.
65-69	9.2	.	.	0.6	1.9	1.1	2.2	3.0	0.3	0.1	.
70-74	3.0	.	.	0.5	0.1	0.4	0.6	1.2	0.1	0.1	.
75+	0.9	.	.	0.1	0.1	0.1	0.2	0.3	0.1	-	.

Explanatory notes: see p. 3.

[1] Persons aged 15 to 74 years. [2] Excl. conscripts. [3] Levels 5.
[4] Persons aged 15 years and over.

Notes explicatives: voir p. 5.

[1] Personnes âgées de 15 à 74 ans. [2] Non compris les conscrits.
[3] Niveaux 5. [4] Personnes âgées de 15 ans et plus.

Notas explicativas: véase p. 7.

[1] Personas de 15 a 74 años. [2] Excl. los conscriptos. [3] Niveles 5.
[4] Personas de 15 años y más.

ECONOMICALLY ACTIVE POPULATION / POPULATION ACTIVE / POBLACION ECONOMICAMENTE ACTIVA

1B

By level of education and age group / **Par niveau d'instruction et groupe d'âge** / **Por nivel de educación y grupo de edad**

Thousands — Milliers — Millares

ISCED 1976 CITE / CINE 1997	Total	X	0	1	2	3	5 / 4	6 / 5A	7 / 5B	9 / 6	?

Luxembourg (BA) (2008) [1]

Total - Total - Total
ISCED-97 - CITE-97 - CINE-97

Age	Total	X	0	1	2	3	4	5A	5B	6	?
Total	218.1	.	8.2	20.5	32.0	83.7	6.8	18.6	44.4	3.9	.
15-19	2.5	.	0.0	0.0	2.0	0.5	0.0	0.0	0.0	0.0	.
20-24	14.8	.	0.0	0.8	3.8	8.4	0.1	0.8	0.8	0.0	.
25-29	26.8	.	0.2	1.1	3.7	10.6	0.8	3.2	7.0	0.2	.
30-34	30.6	.	0.5	2.7	2.8	11.4	0.5	3.7	8.3	0.7	.
35-39	34.0	.	1.0	3.8	4.9	12.1	0.9	2.7	8.2	0.3	.
40-44	34.6	.	1.3	3.5	4.4	13.9	1.4	2.2	7.1	0.8	.
45-49	31.0	.	1.5	4.0	5.2	11.3	1.0	1.9	5.3	0.9	.
50-54	25.2	.	2.3	2.9	3.1	9.3	1.5	2.3	3.5	0.4	.
55-59	14.6	.	0.9	1.5	1.7	5.1	0.5	1.3	3.1	0.4	.
60-64	3.4	.	0.3	0.3	0.4	0.8	0.1	0.4	0.9	0.3	.
65+	0.6	.	0.0	0.1	0.1	0.2	0.0	0.1	0.2	0.0	.

Men - Hommes - Hombres
ISCED-97 - CITE-97 - CINE-97

Age	Total	X	0	1	2	3	4	5A	5B	6	?
Total	123.3	.	4.5	11.8	17.5	47.8	4.3	8.6	26.2	2.7	.
15-19	1.7	.	0.0	0.0	1.4	0.3	0.0	0.0	0.0	0.0	.
20-24	7.5	.	0.0	0.4	2.3	4.1	0.0	0.4	0.4	0.0	.
25-29	13.7	.	0.1	0.7	2.3	5.9	0.3	1.0	3.5	0.0	.
30-34	17.0	.	0.4	1.6	1.7	6.7	0.2	1.7	4.0	0.7	.
35-39	19.5	.	0.7	2.2	2.5	7.1	0.5	1.1	5.1	0.2	.
40-44	19.9	.	0.5	1.8	2.5	8.1	1.0	1.1	4.4	0.4	.
45-49	17.9	.	0.8	2.3	2.7	6.4	0.7	1.0	3.5	0.6	.
50-54	15.2	.	1.5	1.7	1.4	5.5	1.1	1.3	2.4	0.3	.
55-59	8.6	.	0.5	0.9	0.5	3.3	0.3	0.7	2.2	0.2	.
60-64	2.0	.	0.1	0.1	0.1	0.4	0.0	0.2	0.7	0.2	.
65+	0.3	.	0.0	0.0	0.0	0.1	0.0	0.0	0.1	0.0	.

Women - Femmes - Mujeres
ISCED-97 - CITE-97 - CINE-97

Age	Total	X	0	1	2	3	4	5A	5B	6	?
Total	94.8	.	3.6	8.7	14.6	35.9	2.6	10.0	18.2	1.2	.
15-19	0.8	.	0.0	0.0	0.6	0.2	0.0	0.0	0.0	0.0	.
20-24	7.2	.	0.0	0.4	1.5	4.3	0.1	0.4	0.4	0.0	.
25-29	13.1	.	0.2	0.4	1.4	4.7	0.5	2.2	3.6	0.1	.
30-34	13.6	.	0.2	1.0	1.1	4.7	0.3	2.0	4.3	0.0	.
35-39	14.6	.	0.3	1.6	2.4	5.0	0.4	1.6	3.1	0.1	.
40-44	14.7	.	0.8	1.6	1.9	5.8	0.4	1.1	2.7	0.4	.
45-49	13.0	.	0.7	1.7	2.6	4.9	0.3	0.9	1.8	0.3	.
50-54	10.0	.	0.9	1.2	1.6	3.8	0.3	1.0	1.1	0.1	.
55-59	6.0	.	0.5	0.6	1.2	1.8	0.2	0.6	0.9	0.2	.
60-64	1.4	.	0.1	0.1	0.3	0.4	0.0	0.2	0.2	0.0	.
65+	0.3	.	0.0	0.1	0.1	0.1	0.0	0.0	0.1	0.0	.

Malta (BA) (2008) [1]

Total - Total - Total
ISCED-97 - CITE-97 - CINE-97

Age	Total	X	0	1	2	3	4	5A	5B	6	?
Total	171.4	.	0.4	19.2	86.0	15.7	20.0	29.7	.	0.4	.
15-19	9.1	.	.	0.5	7.1	1.0	0.5	0.0	.	.	.
20-24	21.2	.	.	0.3	10.8	3.5	3.5	3.1	.	.	.
25-29	24.7	.	.	0.2	11.5	2.6	3.5	6.8	.	0.1	.
30-34	24.8	.	.	0.3	11.9	3.2	3.0	6.3	.	.	.
35-39	17.0	.	.	0.2	9.2	1.7	2.6	3.2	.	0.0	.
40-44	19.2	.	.	1.0	10.9	1.5	2.5	3.2	.	0.1	.
45-49	18.3	.	0.0	2.3	11.4	0.7	1.7	2.0	.	0.0	.
50-54	18.1	.	0.1	5.8	7.6	0.7	1.6	2.3	.	0.1	.
55-59	13.7	.	0.1	6.3	4.2	0.5	0.8	1.8	.	.	.
60-64	4.3	.	0.1	1.7	1.3	0.3	0.2	0.7	.	0.0	.
65-69	0.6	.	0.0	0.3	0.0	0.0	0.0	0.2	.	.	.
70-74	0.3	.	0.0	0.2	0.0	0.0	0.0	0.1	.	.	.
75+	0.0	.	0.0	.	.	.	.	0.0	.	.	.

Men - Hommes - Hombres
ISCED-97 - CITE-97 - CINE-97

Age	Total	X	0	1	2	3	4	5A	5B	6	?
Total	113.9	.	0.3	15.3	59.1	7.7	14.9	16.4	.	0.2	.
15-19	4.9	.	.	0.2	4.1	0.4	0.2	.	.	.	.
20-24	11.5	.	.	0.2	6.4	1.3	2.3	1.3	.	.	.
25-29	14.6	.	.	0.2	7.6	1.3	2.4	3.2	.	0.1	.
30-34	15.8	.	.	0.3	8.5	1.5	2.2	3.4	.	.	.
35-39	11.7	.	.	0.1	6.4	0.9	2.2	2.0	.	0.0	.
40-44	13.5	.	.	0.8	7.8	0.9	2.1	1.8	.	0.1	.
45-49	13.2	.	0.0	1.8	8.2	0.4	1.3	1.4	.	0.0	.
50-54	13.9	.	0.1	4.6	5.9	0.4	1.3	1.6	.	0.1	.
55-59	10.6	.	0.1	5.3	3.0	0.4	0.6	1.0	.	.	.
60-64	3.3	.	0.1	1.4	1.0	0.2	0.2	0.4	.	0.0	.
65-69	0.5	.	0.0	0.3	0.0	0.0	0.0	0.1	.	.	.
70-74	0.3	.	0.0	0.1	0.0	0.0	0.0	0.1	.	.	.
75+	0.0	.	0.0	.	.	.	.	0.0	.	.	.

Explanatory notes: see p. 3.
[1] Persons aged 15 years and over.

Notes explicatives: voir p. 5.
[1] Personnes âgées de 15 ans et plus.

Notas explicativas: véase p. 7.
[1] Personas de 15 años y más.

ILO YEARBOOK OF LABOUR STATISTICS 2009 — ANNUAIRE DES STATISTIQUES DU TRAVAIL DU BIT 2009 — ANUARIO DE ESTADISTICAS DEL TRABAJO DEL OIT 2009

63

1B

ECONOMICALLY ACTIVE POPULATION	POPULATION ACTIVE	POBLACION ECONOMICAMENTE ACTIVA
By level of education and age group	Par niveau d'instruction et groupe d'âge	Por nivel de educación y grupo de edad

		Thousands						Milliers			Millares	
ISCED 1976 CITE	Total	X	0	1	2	3	5	6	7	9	?
CINE 1997	Total	X	0	1	2	3	4	5A	5B	6	?

Malta (BA) (2008) [1]

Women - Femmes - Mujeres
ISCED-97 - CITE-97 - CINE-97

	Total	X	0	1	2	3	4	5A	5B	6	?
Total	57.5	.	0.1	3.9	26.9	8.1	5.1	13.3	.	0.1	.
15-19	4.2	.	.	0.3	3.0	0.6	0.3	0.0	.	.	.
20-24	9.7	.	.	0.1	4.3	2.2	1.2	1.8	.	.	.
25-29	10.1	.	.	0.1	3.9	1.3	1.1	3.6	.	0.0	.
30-34	8.9	.	.	0.1	3.4	1.7	0.8	2.9	.	.	.
35-39	5.3	.	.	0.1	2.8	0.8	0.4	1.2	.	0.0	.
40-44	5.7	.	.	0.2	3.1	0.6	0.4	1.3	.	0.1	.
45-49	5.1	.	0.0	0.5	3.2	0.3	0.4	0.6	.	0.0	.
50-54	4.3	.	0.0	1.2	1.7	0.3	0.3	0.7	.	0.0	.
55-59	3.1	.	0.0	1.0	1.1	0.1	0.2	0.7	.	.	.
60-64	0.9	.	0.0	0.3	0.2	0.1	0.0	0.2	.	0.0	.
65-69	0.1	.	0.0	0.0	0.0	0.0	0.0	0.0	.	.	.
70-74	0.1	.	0.0	0.0	0.0	0.0	0.0	0.0	.	.	.
75+	0.0	.	0.0	.	.	.	.	0.0	.	.	.

Netherlands (BA) (2008) [1]

Total - Total - Total
ISCED-97 - CITE-97 - CINE-97

	Total	X	0	1	2	3	4	5A	5B	6	?
Total	8 457	52	46	408	1 763	3 345	286	2 326	171	59	.
15-19	601	-	-	89	368	136	.	5	-	-	.
20-24	764	8	-	16	154	458	10	112	5	-	.
25-29	856	10	3	18	105	361	14	325	14	5	.
30-34	891	8	4	22	114	358	20	333	22	10	.
35-39	1 089	6	6	34	173	453	36	345	26	11	.
40-44	1 116	6	7	38	195	470	48	314	31	8	.
45-49	1 060	6	7	48	207	410	55	291	27	9	.
50-54	910	4	7	54	182	323	45	269	21	6	.
55-59	727	2	5	53	161	240	37	206	17	6	.
60-64	332	-	3	26	73	104	16	98	7	3	.
65-69	65	-	-	5	17	18	2	19	-	-	.
70-74	30	-	-	2	11	9	-	7	-	-	.
75+	14	-	-	-	4	4	-	3	-	-	.

Men - Hommes - Hombres
ISCED-97 - CITE-97 - CINE-97

	Total	X	0	1	2	3	4	5A	5B	6	?
Total	4 594	32	31	240	980	1 770	153	1 252	95	41	.
15-19	306	-	-	53	190	61	-	2	-	-	.
20-24	391	4	-	10	99	227	5	42	3	-	.
25-29	448	5	2	14	68	193	8	148	7	3	.
30-34	472	5	2	15	72	186	12	164	11	6	.
35-39	588	4	4	23	101	235	18	184	13	7	.
40-44	604	4	5	23	113	240	23	174	16	6	.
45-49	572	4	5	25	113	211	27	166	16	6	.
50-54	503	3	5	28	94	176	26	154	12	5	.
55-59	425	-	4	29	76	147	21	130	12	5	.
60-64	207	-	2	16	36	70	10	65	5	2	.
65-69	44	-	-	3	10	13	2	15	-	-	.
70-74	22	-	-	-	7	7	-	6	-	-	.
75+	10	-	-	-	3	4	-	2	-	-	.

Women - Femmes - Mujeres
ISCED-97 - CITE-97 - CINE-97

	Total	X	0	1	2	3	4	5A	5B	6	?
Total	3 863	20	16	168	783	1 575	133	1 074	76	18	.
15-19	295	-	-	36	178	75	-	3	-	-	.
20-24	373	4	-	6	55	231	5	70	2	-	.
25-29	408	5	-	4	38	168	6	176	7	2	.
30-34	419	3	2	7	42	173	8	169	11	4	.
35-39	502	2	2	12	72	218	18	161	13	4	.
40-44	512	2	2	15	82	230	25	139	15	2	.
45-49	488	-	3	23	94	200	28	125	11	3	.
50-54	407	-	2	26	88	147	19	114	8	-	.
55-59	302	-	2	24	85	93	16	76	5	-	.
60-64	125	-	-	10	37	34	6	33	2	-	.
65-69	20	-	-	2	7	5	-	5	-	-	.
70-74	8	-	-	2	4	2	-	-	-	-	.
75+	3	-	-	-	-	-	-	-	-	-	.

Explanatory notes: see p. 3.
[1] Persons aged 15 years and over.

Notes explicatives: voir p. 5.
[1] Personnes âgées de 15 ans et plus.

Notas explicativas: véase p. 7.
[1] Personas de 15 años y más.

ECONOMICALLY ACTIVE POPULATION / POPULATION ACTIVE / POBLACION ECONOMICAMENTE ACTIVA

By level of education and age group / Par niveau d'instruction et groupe d'âge / Por nivel de educación y grupo de edad

Thousands — Milliers — Millares

ISCED 1976 CITE	Total	X	0	1	2	3	5	6	7	9	?
CINE 1997	Total	X	0	1	2	3	4	5A	5B	6	?

Norway (BA) (2008) [1]

Total - Total - Total
ISCED-97 - CITE-97 - CINE-97

	Total	X	0	1	2	3	4	5A	5B	6	?
Total	2 591	.	11	1	558	1 062	80	865 [2]	.	15	.
15-19	158	.	7	-	130	21	-	- [2]	.	-	.
20-24	222	.	-	-	65	123	4	30 [2]	.	-	.
25-29	260	.	1	-	44	99	7	110 [2]	.	-	.
30-34	286	.	1	-	31	108	8	137 [2]	.	1	.
35-39	327	.	1	-	46	123	13	143 [2]	.	2	.
40-44	319	.	1	-	55	132	14	114 [2]	.	3	.
45-49	291	.	-	-	68	114	11	94 [2]	.	4	.
50-54	268	.	-	-	43	124	9	90 [2]	.	2	.
55-59	234	.	-	-	34	112	9	77 [2]	.	2	.
60-64	170	.	-	-	31	80	3	55 [2]	.	1	.
65-69	47	.	-	-	8	23	1	15 [2]	.	1	.
70-74	9	.	-	-	2	5	-	2 [2]	.	-	.

Men - Hommes - Hombres
ISCED-97 - CITE-97 - CINE-97

	Total	X	0	1	2	3	4	5A	5B	6	?
Total	1 370	.	5	1	305	595	53	401 [2]	.	9	.
15-19	79	.	3	-	66	10	-	- [2]	.	-	.
20-24	116	.	-	-	42	62	3	10 [2]	.	-	.
25-29	136	.	-	-	27	57	6	45 [2]	.	-	.
30-34	150	.	1	-	18	67	5	58 [2]	.	1	.
35-39	174	.	-	-	27	73	8	65 [2]	.	1	.
40-44	169	.	-	-	30	73	10	54 [2]	.	2	.
45-49	154	.	-	-	34	67	7	43 [2]	.	2	.
50-54	140	.	-	-	23	66	6	43 [2]	.	1	.
55-59	124	.	-	-	15	62	6	39 [2]	.	2	.
60-64	94	.	-	-	17	42	2	33 [2]	.	1	.
65-69	27	.	-	-	4	11	1	9 [2]	.	1	.
70-74	6	.	-	-	1	3	-	2 [2]	.	-	.

Women - Femmes - Mujeres
ISCED-97 - CITE-97 - CINE-97

	Total	X	0	1	2	3	4	5A	5B	6	?
Total	1 222	.	6	1	252	467	26	464 [2]	.	5	.
15-19	79	.	4	-	64	11	-	- [2]	.	-	.
20-24	106	.	-	-	24	61	1	20 [2]	.	-	.
25-29	124	.	-	-	16	41	1	65 [2]	.	-	.
30-34	136	.	-	-	13	41	3	79 [2]	.	-	.
35-39	153	.	-	-	19	49	5	77 [2]	.	1	.
40-44	150	.	-	-	25	60	5	60 [2]	.	1	.
45-49	137	.	-	-	34	46	4	51 [2]	.	1	.
50-54	128	.	-	-	20	58	3	46 [2]	.	1	.
55-59	110	.	-	-	19	49	3	38 [2]	.	-	.
60-64	76	.	-	-	14	38	1	22 [2]	.	-	.
65-69	20	.	-	-	3	11	-	5 [2]	.	-	.
70-74	3	.	-	-	1	1	-	1 [2]	.	-	.

Poland (BA) (2008) [3][4]

Total - Total - Total
ISCED-97 - CITE-97 - CINE-97

	Total	X	0	1	2	3	4	5A	5B	6	?
Total	17 011	.	.	1 619 [5]	.	10 893	659	3 839 [6]	.	.	.
15-19	198	.	.	94 [5]	.	104	-	- [6]	.	.	.
20-24	1 589	.	.	115 [5]	.	1 198	82	194 [6]	.	.	.
25-29	2 529	.	.	125 [5]	.	1 329	119	956 [6]	.	.	.
30-34	2 466	.	.	149 [5]	.	1 426	91	800 [6]	.	.	.
35-39	2 168	.	.	152 [5]	.	1 449	59	509 [6]	.	.	.
40-44	2 013	.	.	150 [5]	.	1 437	68	358 [6]	.	.	.
45-49	2 171	.	.	170 [5]	.	1 567	96	338 [6]	.	.	.
50-54	2 120	.	.	280 [5]	.	1 420	95	325 [6]	.	.	.
55-59	1 154	.	.	193 [5]	.	709	36	215 [6]	.	.	.
60-64	358	.	.	82 [5]	.	178	11	87 [6]	.	.	.
65+	246	.	.	109 [5]	.	77	-	58 [6]	.	.	.

Explanatory notes: see p. 3.

[1] Persons aged 15 to 74 years. [2] Levels 5. [3] Persons aged 15 years and over. [4] Excl. regular military living in barracks and conscripts. [5] Levels 1-2. [6] Levels 5A, 5B and 6.

Notes explicatives: voir p. 5.

[1] Personnes âgées de 15 à 74 ans. [2] Niveaux 5. [3] Personnes âgées de 15 ans et plus. [4] Non compris les militaires de carrière vivant dans des casernes et les conscrits. [5] Niveaux 1-2. [6] Niveaux 5A, 5B et 6.

Notas explicativas: véase p. 7.

[1] Personas de 15 a 74 años. [2] Niveles 5. [3] Personas de 15 años y más. [4] Excl. los militares profesionales que viven en casernas y los conscriptos. [5] Niveles 1-2. [6] Niveles 5A, 5B y 6.

ECONOMICALLY ACTIVE POPULATION	POPULATION ACTIVE	POBLACION ECONOMICAMENTE ACTIVA
By level of education and age group	Par niveau d'instruction et groupe d'âge	Por nivel de educación y grupo de edad

		Thousands				Milliers				Millares		
ISCED 1976 CITE	Total	X	0	1	2	3	5	6	7	9	?
CINE 1997	Total	X	0	1	2	3	4	5A	5B	6	?

Poland (BA) (2008) [1] [2]

Men - Hommes - Hombres
ISCED-97 - CITE-97 - CINE-97

Total	9 317	.	.	986 [3]	.	6 481	195	1 655 [4]			
15-19	114	.	.	65 [3]	.	49	-	- [4]			
20-24	879	.	.	86 [3]	.	698	35	60 [4]			
25-29	1 389	.	.	94 [3]	.	858	46	391 [4]			
30-34	1 349	.	.	93 [3]	.	882	29	344 [4]			
35-39	1 160	.	.	91 [3]	.	838	12	218 [4]			
40-44	1 057	.	.	85 [3]	.	811	16	145 [4]			
45-49	1 116	.	.	92 [3]	.	866	24	135 [4]			
50-54	1 117	.	.	151 [3]	.	806	18	142 [4]			
55-59	747	.	.	120 [3]	.	494	10	124 [4]			
60-64	241	.	.	50 [3]	.	129	-	58 [4]			
65+	148	.	.	58 [3]	.	49	-	39 [4]			

Women - Femmes - Mujeres
ISCED-97 - CITE-97 - CINE-97

Total	7 694	.	.	634 [3]	.	4 412	464	2 184 [4]			
15-19	83	.	.	29 [3]	.	54	-	- [4]			
20-24	710	.	.	29 [3]	.	500	47	134 [4]			
25-29	1 139	.	.	31 [3]	.	470	72	565 [4]			
30-34	1 117	.	.	56 [3]	.	543	62	456 [4]			
35-39	1 008	.	.	60 [3]	.	611	47	290 [4]			
40-44	956	.	.	65 [3]	.	626	52	214 [4]			
45-49	1 055	.	.	78 [3]	.	701	73	203 [4]			
50-54	1 003	.	.	129 [3]	.	614	77	183 [4]			
55-59	406	.	.	73 [3]	.	215	26	91 [4]			
60-64	117	.	.	32 [3]	.	49	8	29 [4]			
65+	99	.	.	51 [3]	.	28	-	19 [4]			

Portugal (BA) (2008) [1]

Total - Total - Total
ISCED-97 - CITE-97 - CINE-97

Total	5 624.9	267.8 [5]	.	2 519.6	1 143.8	823.1	36.3	673.2	98.2	62.8	.
15-19	90.9	0.1 [5]	.	29.7	47.8	12.8	0.4	-	-	-	.
20-24	416.6	1.4 [5]	.	85.0	156.4	122.6	5.6	41.6	2.2	1.8	.
25-29	673.5	4.4 [5]	.	125.4	201.6	157.8	7.0	157.7	11.8	7.9	.
30-34	790.8	8.8 [5]	.	254.4	178.4	160.5	7.2	151.3	21.9	8.4	.
35-39	725.7	16.2 [5]	.	312.0	146.9	121.7	3.5	98.3	14.2	12.8	.
40-44	697.4	17.5 [5]	.	368.1	129.4	81.8	3.6	70.5	14.5	12.1	.
45-49	669.6	24.1 [5]	.	367.6	123.9	74.6	1.6	59.8	10.1	7.8	.
50-54	550.7	23.3 [5]	.	334.5	79.5	51.8	2.3	42.2	11.8	5.4	.
55-59	425.2	22.9 [5]	.	279.7	52.7	25.1	2.7	31.2	7.0	3.8	.
60-64	258.2	28.6 [5]	.	178.9	19.9	10.5	1.2	14.0	3.1	2.0	.
65-69	132.2	34.2 [5]	.	85.6	4.1	3.0	0.4	3.3	1.1	0.4	.
70-74	96.2	39.1 [5]	.	52.6	1.2	0.5	0.1	2.1	0.3	0.4	.
75+	97.7	47.0 [5]	.	46.0	2.1	0.5	0.6	1.0	0.3	0.1	.

Men - Hommes - Hombres
ISCED-97 - CITE-97 - CINE-97

Total	2 991.4	118.5 [5]	.	1 458.4	642.5	419.6	18.7	257.0	44.4	32.5	.
15-19	54.9	0.1 [5]	.	20.6	27.7	6.3	0.2	-	-	-	.
20-24	222.0	1.4 [5]	.	58.4	88.9	59.7	2.5	10.0	0.6	0.5	.
25-29	349.5	2.9 [5]	.	83.1	120.9	78.6	3.7	51.8	4.8	3.7	.
30-34	414.0	6.4 [5]	.	150.8	101.0	80.5	3.2	57.7	10.0	4.4	.
35-39	378.9	12.9 [5]	.	171.1	83.2	60.8	1.7	36.5	6.5	6.2	.
40-44	367.3	11.8 [5]	.	207.1	65.0	41.4	2.3	28.5	5.3	6.0	.
45-49	350.5	14.0 [5]	.	196.2	68.2	36.4	1.0	26.2	4.3	4.3	.
50-54	299.0	10.1 [5]	.	188.7	41.4	30.6	1.5	18.0	5.5	3.0	.
55-59	234.0	6.9 [5]	.	160.8	27.8	14.4	1.1	15.9	4.5	2.5	.
60-64	140.7	6.9 [5]	.	103.0	12.6	7.6	0.7	7.3	1.6	1.2	.
65-69	71.9	12.0 [5]	.	50.3	3.2	2.3	0.2	2.6	0.9	0.4	.
70-74	54.0	14.4 [5]	.	35.9	1.1	0.5	0.1	1.6	0.3	0.3	.
75+	54.8	18.7 [5]	.	32.6	1.5	0.4	0.4	0.9	0.2	0.1	.

Explanatory notes: see p. 3.

[1] Persons aged 15 years and over. [2] Excl. regular military living in barracks and conscripts. [3] Levels 1-2. [4] Levels 5A, 5B and 6. [5] Levels X-0.

Notes explicatives: voir p. 5.

[1] Personnes âgées de 15 ans et plus. [2] Non compris les militaires de carrière vivant dans des casernes et les conscrits. [3] Niveaux 1-2. [4] Niveaux 5A, 5B et 6. [5] Niveaux X-0.

Notas explicativas: véase p. 7.

[1] Personas de 15 años y más. [2] Excl. los militares profesionales que viven en casernas y los conscriptos. [3] Niveles 1-2. [4] Niveles 5A, 5B y 6. [5] Niveles X-0.

ECONOMICALLY ACTIVE POPULATION

By level of education and age group

POPULATION ACTIVE

Par niveau d'instruction et groupe d'âge

POBLACION ECONOMICAMENTE ACTIVA

Por nivel de educación y grupo de edad

ISCED 1976 CITE	Thousands / Milliers / Millares										
ISCED 1976	Total	X	0	1	2	3	5	6	7	9	?
CINE 1997	Total	X	0	1	2	3	4	5A	5B	6	?

Portugal (BA) (2008) [1]

Women - Femmes - Mujeres
ISCED-97 - CITE-97 - CINE-97

	Total	X	0	1	2	3	4	5A	5B	6	?
Total	2 633.4	149.4 [2]	.	1 061.2	501.4	403.5	17.6	416.1	53.9	30.3	.
15-19	36.0	- [2]	.	9.2	20.0	6.4	0.3	-	-	-	.
20-24	194.6	- [2]	.	26.7	67.5	62.8	3.0	31.6	1.6	1.3	.
25-29	324.1	1.6 [2]	.	42.1	80.7	79.1	3.3	106.0	7.0	4.2	.
30-34	376.8	2.5 [2]	.	103.5	77.5	80.0	4.0	93.6	11.9	4.0	.
35-39	346.8	3.3 [2]	.	140.9	63.7	60.9	1.8	61.9	7.6	6.8	.
40-44	330.1	5.7 [2]	.	161.0	64.4	40.5	1.2	42.0	9.2	6.1	.
45-49	319.1	10.2 [2]	.	171.4	55.7	38.3	0.6	33.7	5.8	3.5	.
50-54	251.8	13.2 [2]	.	145.7	38.1	21.1	0.8	24.2	6.3	2.3	.
55-59	191.2	16.0 [2]	.	119.1	24.8	10.7	1.5	15.3	2.4	1.4	.
60-64	117.5	21.7 [2]	.	75.9	7.3	2.9	0.6	6.8	1.5	0.9	.
65-69	60.3	22.2 [2]	.	35.5	0.9	0.7	0.2	0.7	0.3	-	.
70-74	42.2	24.7 [2]	.	16.7	0.1	-	-	0.5	-	0.1	.
75+	42.9	28.4 [2]	.	13.5	0.6	0.1	0.3	-	0.1	-	.

Russian Federation (BA) (2008) [3]

Total - Total - Total
ISCED-97 - CITE-97 - CINE-97

	Total	X	0	1	2	3	4	5A	5B	6	?
Total	75 756	.	.	447	3 788	16 411	14 205	19 860	1 302	19 744	.
15-19	1 728	.	.	39	352	785	319	173	58	2	.
20-24	8 335	.	.	34	460	1 987	1 620	2 004	515	1 715	.
25-29	9 812	.	.	43	450	1 828	1 737	2 182	217	3 356	.
30-34	9 355	.	.	36	468	1 924	1 727	2 335	148	2 717	.
35-39	8 766	.	.	22	316	1 771	1 718	2 396	110	2 434	.
40-44	9 257	.	.	29	298	1 879	1 891	2 642	76	2 443	.
45-49	10 882	.	.	44	353	2 418	2 135	3 148	79	2 706	.
50-54	9 169	.	.	46	421	2 107	1 675	2 705	53	2 162	.
55-59	5 729	.	.	37	388	1 237	1 008	1 613	35	1 410	.
60-64	1 554	.	.	25	114	287	236	402	7	483	.
65-72	1 170	.	.	93	168	187	138	262	5	316	.

Men - Hommes - Hombres
ISCED-97 - CITE-97 - CINE-97

	Total	X	0	1	2	3	4	5A	5B	6	?
Total	38 681	.	.	253	2 328	9 303	8 997	8 212	611	8 977	.
15-19	1 031	.	.	29	223	464	214	74	27	1	.
20-24	4 600	.	.	23	334	1 225	1 088	945	228	757	.
25-29	5 282	.	.	31	294	1 127	1 130	1 051	121	1 528	.
30-34	4 871	.	.	23	301	1 096	1 098	1 021	75	1 258	.
35-39	4 458	.	.	17	189	1 022	1 064	1 003	47	1 117	.
40-44	4 506	.	.	16	176	1 002	1 181	1 033	33	1 065	.
45-49	5 180	.	.	26	207	1 305	1 282	1 160	36	1 165	.
50-54	4 306	.	.	23	228	1 091	1 004	974	20	964	.
55-59	3 063	.	.	24	244	718	684	679	16	699	.
60-64	830	.	.	11	62	167	164	169	4	252	.
65-72	552	.	.	32	70	87	87	102	3	172	.

Women - Femmes - Mujeres
ISCED-97 - CITE-97 - CINE-97

	Total	X	0	1	2	3	4	5A	5B	6	?
Total	37 076	.	.	194	1 459	7 108	5 208	11 648	691	10 767	.
15-19	696	.	.	10	129	321	105	99	31	2	.
20-24	3 735	.	.	10	126	763	532	1 059	286	959	.
25-29	4 530	.	.	12	156	701	607	1 131	95	1 828	.
30-34	4 483	.	.	13	167	829	629	1 314	73	1 460	.
35-39	4 308	.	.	5	127	749	654	1 393	62	1 317	.
40-44	4 751	.	.	13	122	877	710	1 609	43	1 378	.
45-49	5 702	.	.	18	146	1 113	853	1 987	44	1 541	.
50-54	4 863	.	.	23	192	1 016	671	1 731	33	1 198	.
55-59	2 665	.	.	13	145	520	324	934	19	711	.
60-64	724	.	.	14	52	120	72	232	2	231	.
65-72	617	.	.	61	98	100	51	159	2	144	.

Explanatory notes: see p. 3.
[1] Persons aged 15 years and over. [2] Levels X-0. [3] Persons aged 15 to 72 years.

Notes explicatives: voir p. 5.
[1] Personnes âgées de 15 ans et plus. [2] Niveaux X-0. [3] Personnes âgées de 15 à 72 ans.

Notas explicativas: véase p. 7.
[1] Personas de 15 años y más. [2] Niveles X-0. [3] Personas de 15 a 72 años.

1B

ECONOMICALLY ACTIVE POPULATION	POPULATION ACTIVE	POBLACION ECONOMICAMENTE ACTIVA
By level of education and age group	Par niveau d'instruction et groupe d'âge	Por nivel de educación y grupo de edad
Thousands	Milliers	Millares

ISCED 1976 / CITE	Total	X	0	1	2	3	5	6	7	9	?
CINE 1997	Total	X	0	1	2	3	4	5A	5B	6	?

San Marino (E) (2008) [1] [2]

Total - Total - Total — ISCED-97 - CITE-97 - CINE-97

Age	Total	X	0	1	2	3	4	5A	5B	6	?
Total	22.708	0.029	.	1.847	8.218	9.219[3]	.	2.243	0.531	.	0.621
15-19	0.177	-	.	0.002	0.079	0.091[3]	.	-	-	.	0.005
20-24	1.056	-	.	0.037	0.262	0.669[3]	.	0.006	0.043	.	0.039
25-29	2.210	0.002	.	0.075	0.577	1.095[3]	.	0.245	0.126	.	0.090
30-34	3.413	0.002	.	0.135	1.013	1.601[3]	.	0.468	0.087	.	0.107
35-39	4.089	0.001	.	0.190	1.463	1.733[3]	.	0.520	0.084	.	0.098
40-44	4.040	0.002	.	0.271	1.718	1.556[3]	.	0.344	0.050	.	0.099
45-49	3.281	0.002	.	0.233	1.476	1.191[3]	.	0.230	0.070	.	0.079
50-54	2.346	-	.	0.296	0.965	0.784[3]	.	0.209	0.051	.	0.041
55-59	1.674	0.011	.	0.473	0.545	0.428[3]	.	0.172	0.017	.	0.028
60-64	0.361	0.007	.	0.122	0.100	0.062[3]	.	0.040	0.003	.	0.027
65-69	0.039	-	.	0.011	0.013	0.007[3]	.	0.004	-	.	0.004
70-74	0.015	-	.	0.002	0.004	0.002[3]	.	0.003	-	.	0.004
75+	0.007	0.002	.	-	0.003	-[3]	.	0.002	-	.	-

Men - Hommes - Hombres — ISCED-97 - CITE-97 - CINE-97

Age	Total	X	0	1	2	3	4	5A	5B	6	?
Total	13.164	0.022	.	1.327	5.207	4.874[3]	.	1.132	0.194	.	0.408
15-19	0.128	-	.	0.002	0.061	0.060[3]	.	-	-	.	0.005
20-24	0.620	-	.	0.030	0.173	0.381[3]	.	0.002	0.012	.	0.022
25-29	1.232	0.002	.	0.060	0.374	0.619[3]	.	0.076	0.044	.	0.057
30-34	1.896	0.002	.	0.104	0.656	0.834[3]	.	0.201	0.035	.	0.064
35-39	2.426	-	.	0.151	1.010	0.918[3]	.	0.253	0.030	.	0.064
40-44	2.367	0.002	.	0.217	1.092	0.781[3]	.	0.189	0.015	.	0.071
45-49	1.918	0.002	.	0.178	0.921	0.597[3]	.	0.141	0.025	.	0.054
50-54	1.345	-	.	0.197	0.556	0.418[3]	.	0.126	0.021	.	0.027
55-59	0.998	0.010	.	0.314	0.313	0.227[3]	.	0.104	0.011	.	0.019
60-64	0.198	0.004	.	0.067	0.043	0.033[3]	.	0.032	0.001	.	0.018
65-69	0.019	-	.	0.006	0.003	0.004[3]	.	0.003	-	.	0.003
70-74	0.013	-	.	0.001	0.003	0.002[3]	.	0.003	-	.	0.004
75+	0.004	-	.	-	0.002	-[3]	.	0.002	-	.	-

Women - Femmes - Mujeres — ISCED-97 - CITE-97 - CINE-97

Age	Total	X	0	1	2	3	4	5A	5B	6	?
Total	9.544	0.007	.	0.520	3.011	4.345[3]	.	1.111	0.337	.	0.213
15-19	0.049	-	.	-	0.018	0.031[3]	.	-	-	.	-
20-24	0.436	-	.	0.007	0.089	0.288[3]	.	0.004	0.031	.	0.017
25-29	0.978	-	.	0.015	0.203	0.476[3]	.	0.169	0.082	.	0.033
30-34	1.517	-	.	0.031	0.357	0.767[3]	.	0.267	0.052	.	0.043
35-39	1.663	0.001	.	0.039	0.453	0.815[3]	.	0.267	0.054	.	0.034
40-44	1.673	-	.	0.054	0.626	0.775[3]	.	0.155	0.035	.	0.028
45-49	1.363	-	.	0.055	0.555	0.594[3]	.	0.089	0.045	.	0.025
50-54	1.001	-	.	0.099	0.409	0.366[3]	.	0.083	0.030	.	0.014
55-59	0.676	0.001	.	0.159	0.232	0.201[3]	.	0.068	0.006	.	0.009
60-64	0.163	0.003	.	0.055	0.057	0.029[3]	.	0.008	0.002	.	0.009
65-69	0.020	-	.	0.005	0.010	0.003[3]	.	0.001	-	.	0.001
70-74	0.002	-	.	0.001	0.001	-[3]	.	-	-	.	-
75+	0.003	0.002	.	-	0.001	-[3]	.	-	-	.	-

Slovakia (BA) (2008) [1] [4]

Total - Total - Total — ISCED-97 - CITE-97 - CINE-97

Age	Total	X	0	1	2	3	4	5A	5B	6	?
Total	2 700.4	.	0.2	2.7	163.6	2 106.6[3]	.	400.0	20.0	7.3	:
15-19	30.0	.	-	1.0	7.0	22.0[3]	.	-	-	-	:
20-24	231.0	.	.	-	12.3	197.7[3]	.	19.5	1.5	-	:
25-29	381.6	.	.	-	13.2	285.7[3]	.	80.0	2.4	0.3	:
30-34	395.9	.	.	-	18.6	316.5[3]	.	58.2	2.1	0.6	:
35-39	341.2	.	.	-	12.7	276.5[3]	.	49.2	1.9	1.0	:
40-44	347.8	.	-	0.2	18.1	276.3[3]	.	48.6	4.0	0.6	:
45-49	350.9	.	0.2	0.6	18.2	278.3[3]	.	50.0	2.5	1.1	:
50-54	348.8	.	-	0.3	38.1	256.6[3]	.	50.2	2.8	0.7	:
55-59	214.8	.	-	0.6	20.7	158.4[3]	.	31.7	2.1	1.4	:
60-64	47.3	.	-	-	3.6	33.3[3]	.	9.1	0.5	0.8	:
65-69	8.2	.	-	-	0.9	4.1[3]	.	2.4	0.3	0.5	:
70-74	2.1	.	-	-	0.3	0.9[3]	.	0.8	-	0.2	:
75+	0.8	.	-	-	-	0.4[3]	.	0.3	-	0.1	:

Explanatory notes: see p. 3.

[1] Persons aged 15 years and over. [2] Dec. [3] Levels 3-4. [4] Fourth quarter.

Notes explicatives: voir p. 5.

[1] Personnes âgées de 15 ans et plus. [2] Déc. [3] Niveaux 3-4. [4] Quatrième trimestre.

Notas explicativas: véase p. 7.

[1] Personas de 15 años y más. [2] Dic. [3] Niveles 3-4. [4] Cuarto trimestre.

ECONOMICALLY ACTIVE POPULATION

By level of education and age group

POPULATION ACTIVE

Par niveau d'instruction et groupe d'âge

POBLACION ECONOMICAMENTE ACTIVA

Por nivel de educación y grupo de edad

1B

	Thousands / Milliers / Millares										
ISCED 1976 CITE	Total	X	0	1	2	3	5	6	7	9	?
CINE 1997	Total	X	0	1	2	3	4	5A	5B	6	?

Slovakia (BA) (2008) [1] [2]

Men - Hommes - Hombres
ISCED-97 - CITE-97 - CINE-97

	Total	X	0	1	2	3	4	5A	5B	6	?
Total	1 499.1	.	0.2	1.3	77.2	1 201.6 [3]	.	206.6	6.9	5.3	.
15-19	19.1	.	-	0.6	4.9	13.6 [3]	.	-	-	-	.
20-24	138.0	.	-	-	9.1	121.0 [3]	.	6.7	1.3	-	.
25-29	224.0	.	-	-	7.2	177.7 [3]	.	38.1	1.0	-	.
30-34	224.9	.	-	-	10.7	182.2 [3]	.	30.2	1.4	0.6	.
35-39	184.5	.	-	-	6.6	150.6 [3]	.	25.8	0.8	0.7	.
40-44	176.2	.	-	-	8.0	143.3 [3]	.	24.1	0.7	0.2	.
45-49	177.1	.	0.2	0.4	6.5	142.7 [3]	.	26.4	0.4	0.6	.
50-54	175.2	.	-	0.2	11.9	134.5 [3]	.	27.8	0.2	0.7	.
55-59	135.5	.	-	0.1	9.5	105.0 [3]	.	19.1	0.7	1.1	.
60-64	37.0	.	-	-	2.4	27.6 [3]	.	5.9	0.3	0.7	.
65-69	5.6	.	-	-	0.4	3.0 [3]	.	1.7	0.1	0.4	.
70-74	1.4	.	-	-	0.1	0.5 [3]	.	0.7	-	0.2	.
75+	0.4	.	-	-	-	- [3]	.	0.3	-	0.1	.

Women - Femmes - Mujeres
ISCED-97 - CITE-97 - CINE-97

	Total	X	0	1	2	3	4	5A	5B	6	?
Total	1 201.3	.	-	1.4	86.4	905.0 [3]	.	193.4	13.1	2.0	.
15-19	10.8	.	-	0.4	2.1	8.4 [3]	.	-	-	-	.
20-24	93.0	.	-	-	3.2	76.8 [3]	.	12.8	0.2	-	.
25-29	157.6	.	-	-	6.0	108.1 [3]	.	41.9	1.4	0.3	.
30-34	171.0	.	-	-	7.9	134.3 [3]	.	28.0	0.7	-	.
35-39	156.7	.	-	-	6.1	125.9 [3]	.	23.4	1.0	0.2	.
40-44	171.6	.	-	0.2	10.1	133.0 [3]	.	24.6	3.3	0.4	.
45-49	173.8	.	-	0.2	11.8	135.6 [3]	.	23.6	2.1	0.5	.
50-54	173.6	.	-	0.2	26.3	122.1 [3]	.	22.4	2.6	-	.
55-59	79.3	.	-	0.4	11.2	53.4 [3]	.	12.6	1.4	0.3	.
60-64	10.3	.	-	-	1.2	5.7 [3]	.	3.2	0.1	0.2	.
65-69	2.5	.	-	-	0.5	1.0 [3]	.	0.7	0.1	0.1	.
70-74	0.7	.	-	-	0.2	0.4 [3]	.	0.1	-	-	.
75+	0.4	.	-	-	-	0.4 [3]	.	-	-	-	.

Slovenia (BA) (2008) [1] [4] [5]

Total - Total - Total
ISCED-97 - CITE-97 - CINE-97

	Total	X	0	1	2	3	4	5A	5B	6	?
Total	1 745	.	20	61	396	973 [3]	.	148	129	18	.
15-19	115	.	1	6	88	20 [3]	.	-	-	-	.
20-24	141	.	-	-	14	121 [3]	.	3	2	-	.
25-29	149	.	-	-	7	97 [3]	.	17	26	2	.
30-34	146	.	-	-	15	86 [3]	.	18	24	2	.
35-39	153	.	1	2	22	92 [3]	.	16	17	2	.
40-44	155	.	-	1	23	101 [3]	.	15	11	2	.
45-49	158	.	2	3	27	92 [3]	.	19	12	3	.
50-54	149	.	1	5	31	85 [3]	.	15	10	2	.
55-59	150	.	-	5	37	86 [3]	.	11	8	1	.
60-64	104	.	-	4	25	56 [3]	.	11	6	-	.
65-69	97	.	2	6	28	47 [3]	.	9	5	-	.
70-74	89	.	4	7	30	39 [3]	.	6	2	-	.
75+	139	.	6	21	49	51 [3]	.	7	4	1	.

Men - Hommes - Hombres
ISCED-97 - CITE-97 - CINE-97

	Total	X	0	1	2	3	4	5A	5B	6	?
Total	856	.	8	24	157	537 [3]	.	63	57	9	.
15-19	59	.	-	3	46	10 [3]	.	-	-	-	.
20-24	76	.	-	-	9	64 [3]	.	1	-	-	.
25-29	76	.	-	-	4	57 [3]	.	5	8	-	.
30-34	76	.	-	-	10	47 [3]	.	9	8	1	.
35-39	80	.	1	1	11	53 [3]	.	7	6	-	.
40-44	80	.	-	-	10	57 [3]	.	6	5	1	.
45-49	79	.	-	2	10	52 [3]	.	7	5	2	.
50-54	74	.	-	2	12	46 [3]	.	6	6	-	.
55-59	78	.	-	2	13	51 [3]	.	6	5	-	.
60-64	48	.	-	2	8	29 [3]	.	5	4	-	.
65-69	47	.	-	3	8	27 [3]	.	4	4	-	.
70-74	34	.	1	2	7	19 [3]	.	3	2	-	.
75+	48	.	2	5	9	25 [3]	.	4	3	-	.

Explanatory notes: see p. 3.

[1] Persons aged 15 years and over. [2] Fourth quarter. [3] Levels 3-4. [4] Excl. conscripts. [5] Second quarter.

Notes explicatives: voir p. 5.

[1] Personnes âgées de 15 ans et plus. [2] Quatrième trimestre. [3] Niveaux 3-4. [4] Non compris les conscrits. [5] Deuxième trimestre.

Notas explicativas: véase p. 7.

[1] Personas de 15 años y más. [2] Cuarto trimestre. [3] Niveles 3-4. [4] Excl. los conscriptos. [5] Segundo trimestre.

1B — ECONOMICALLY ACTIVE POPULATION / POPULATION ACTIVE / POBLACION ECONOMICAMENTE ACTIVA

By level of education and age group / Par niveau d'instruction et groupe d'âge / Por nivel de educación y grupo de edad

		Thousands / Milliers / Millares									
ISCED 1976 CITE	Total	X	0	1	2	3	5	6	7	9	?
CINE 1997	Total	X	0	1	2	3	4	5A	5B	6	?
Slovenia (BA) (2008) [1,2,3]											
Women - Femmes - Mujeres ISCED-97 - CITE-97 - CINE-97											
Total	889	.	12	38	239	435 [4]	.	85	72	9	.
15-19	55	.	-	3	42	10 [4]	.	-	-	-	.
20-24	65	.	-	-	5	57 [4]	.	1	2	-	.
25-29	73	.	-	-	3	39 [4]	.	12	18	-	.
30-34	70	.	-	-	6	38 [4]	.	9	16	1	.
35-39	73	.	-	-	11	40 [4]	.	10	11	1	.
40-44	74	.	-	-	13	44 [4]	.	9	6	1	.
45-49	78	.	-	1	16	40 [4]	.	12	7	1	.
50-54	75	.	-	2	19	39 [4]	.	9	4	1	.
55-59	71	.	-	3	24	35 [4]	.	5	3	-	.
60-64	56	.	-	2	17	27 [4]	.	6	3	-	.
65-69	50	.	-	3	20	20 [4]	.	4	1	-	.
70-74	55	.	3	5	23	19 [4]	.	3	-	-	.
75+	91	.	4	16	41	26 [4]	.	3	-	-	.
Suisse (BA) (2008) [1,5,6]											
Total - Total - Total ISCED-97 - CITE-97 - CINE-97											
Total	4 375.374	.	.	139.068	506.061	2 213.445	122.967	833.755	434.871	120.04	5 [7]
15-24	608.466	.	.	36.165	226.906	302.186	13.223	21.2	8 [7]	. [8]	. [8]
25-39	1 423.86	.	.	35.044	85.645	681.767	46.661	376.888	155.524	41.083	. [8]
40-54	1 576.766	.	.	43.829	122.269	820.828	43.86	303.62	190.757	49.024	3 [8]
55-64	647.722	.	.	18.655	55.662	351.497	17.208	111.91	68.775	23.185	. [8]
65+	118.56	.	.	5.375	15.578	57.168	2 [7]	20.136	11.562	6.6	. [8]
Men - Hommes - Hombres ISCED-97 - CITE-97 - CINE-97											
Total	2 355.631	.	.	67.046	253.52	1 078.013	65.051	505.888	297.391	85.913	3 [7]
15-24	314.368	.	.	15.016	132.79	145.829	7 [7]	9 [7]	4 [7]	. [8]	. [8]
25-39	762.295	.	.	17.831	41.175	342.552	22.558	209.742	101.309	26.754	. [8]
40-54	846.517	.	.	21.655	50.945	387.406	25.018	195.193	129.812	34.582	. [8]
55-64	361.519	.	.	10.134	22.422	172.031	9.495	76.206	52.04	18.89	. [8]
65+	70.933	.	.	2 [7]	6 [7]	30.194	. [8]	15.478	9.864	5.688	. [8]
Women - Femmes - Mujeres ISCED-97 - CITE-97 - CINE-97											
Total	2 019.743	.	.	72.022	252.541	1 135.433	57.917	327.867	137.48	34.127	2 [7]
15-24	294.098	.	.	21.15	94.116	156.357	6 [7]	12 [7]	4 [7]	. [8]	. [8]
25-39	661.565	.	.	17.213	44.471	339.215	24.103	167.146	54.215	14.329	. [8]
40-54	730.249	.	.	22.173	71.324	433.421	18.842	108.427	60.944	14.442	. [8]
55-64	286.204	.	.	8.521	33.24	179.465	7.713	35.704	16.736	4 [7]	. [8]
65+	47.627	.	.	3 [7]	9.391	26.974	. [8]	4.657	2 [7]	. [8]	. [8]
Sweden (BA) (2008) [9]											
Total - Total - Total ISCED-97 - CITE-97 - CINE-97											
Total	4 898	.	.	174	563	2 300	321	1 033	404	52	50
15-19	217	.	.	-	153	32	-	-	-	-	32
20-24	416	.	.	2	44	290	40	14	20	-	6
25-29	480	.	.	5	35	211	33	150	42	1	3
30-34	537	.	.	5	31	237	29	187	40	6	2
35-39	578	.	.	8	34	275	43	158	50	8	2
40-44	621	.	.	10	46	319	56	127	53	8	1
45-49	539	.	.	10	56	270	40	107	49	7	1
50-54	514	.	.	11	73	238	36	97	52	7	-
55-59	495	.	.	36	55	222	26	98	51	6	-
60-64	396	.	.	66	32	167	15	74	37	5	1
65-69	81	.	.	15	4	30	4	16	7	3	1
70-74	22	.	.	4	1	7	-	6	2	1	-

Explanatory notes: see p. 3.

[1] Persons aged 15 years and over. [2] Excl. conscripts. [3] Second quarter. [4] Levels 3-4. [5] Excluding armed forces and seasonal/border workers. [6] Second quarter of each year. [7] Relative statistical reliability. [8] Not indicated due to lack of statistical reliability. [9] Persons aged 15 to 74 years.

Notes explicatives: voir p. 5.

[1] Personnes âgées de 15 ans et plus. [2] Non compris les conscrits. [3] Deuxième trimestre. [4] Niveaux 3-4. [5] Non compris les forces armées et les travailleurs saisonniers et frontaliers. [6] Deuxième trimestre de chaque année. [7] Fiabilité statistique relative. [8] Non indiqué en raison du manque de fiabilité statistique. [9] Personnes âgées de 15 à 74 ans.

Notas explicativas: véase p. 7.

[1] Personas de 15 años y más. [2] Excl. los conscriptos. [3] Segundo trimestre. [4] Niveles 3-4. [5] Excluidas las fuerzas armadas y excl. a los trabajadores temporales y fronterizos. [6] Segundo trimestre de cada año. [7] Confiabilidad estadística relativa. [8] No se indica por la falta de confiabilidad estadística. [9] Personas de 15 a 74 años.

ECONOMICALLY ACTIVE POPULATION

By level of education and age group

POPULATION ACTIVE

Par niveau d'instruction et groupe d'âge

POBLACION ECONOMICAMENTE ACTIVA

Por nivel de educación y grupo de edad

1B

ISCED 1976 / CITE / CINE 1997	Thousands / Milliers / Millares	X / X	0 / 0	1 / 1	2 / 2	3 / 3	5 / 4	6 / 5A	7 / 5B	9 / 6	? / ?

Sweden (BA) (2008) [1]

Men - Hommes - Hombres
ISCED-97 - CITE-97 - CINE-97

Age	Total	X	0	1	2	3	5/4	6/5A	7/5B	9/6	?
Total	2 574	.	.	107	330	1 263	193	458	163	37	24
15-19	99	.	.	-	71	15	-	-	-	-	13
20-24	223	.	.	2	28	160	17	5	9	-	3
25-29	257	.	.	4	22	124	17	63	23	-	3
30-34	284	.	.	3	19	139	15	81	21	4	1
35-39	303	.	.	3	22	154	26	69	23	5	1
40-44	326	.	.	5	29	173	36	58	20	5	1
45-49	280	.	.	4	36	147	27	45	16	5	-
50-54	265	.	.	5	50	119	25	44	16	5	-
55-59	257	.	.	26	34	115	19	43	16	5	-
60-64	212	.	.	42	16	90	9	37	14	3	1
65-69	51	.	.	10	2	21	2	9	4	3	1
70-74	16	.	.	3	1	5	-	5	1	1	-

Women - Femmes - Mujeres
ISCED-97 - CITE-97 - CINE-97

Age	Total	X	0	1	2	3	5/4	6/5A	7/5B	9/6	?
Total	2 324	.	.	67	234	1 037	128	575	241	16	26
15-19	118	.	.	-	82	17	-	-	-	-	19
20-24	193	.	.	1	16	130	23	9	11	-	2
25-29	224	.	.	2	13	87	16	86	19	1	1
30-34	253	.	.	3	11	98	14	105	19	2	1
35-39	276	.	.	5	12	121	17	89	27	3	-
40-44	295	.	.	5	17	146	20	70	34	3	-
45-49	259	.	.	6	20	123	13	62	33	2	-
50-54	249	.	.	6	23	119	11	53	36	2	-
55-59	238	.	.	10	21	107	8	55	35	2	-
60-64	184	.	.	24	16	77	6	37	22	1	1
65-69	30	.	.	5	2	9	1	7	3	1	-
70-74	6	.	.	1	-	2	-	1	1	-	-

Turkey (BA) (2008) [2][3]

Total - Total - Total
ISCED-97 - CITE-97 - CINE-97

Age	Total	X	0	1	2	3	5/4	6/5A	7/5B	9/6	?
Total	23 805	1 023	.	9 215	3 707	5 246 [4]	.	3 504 [5]	.	.	1110
15-19	1 681	31	.	1	998	437 [4]	.	11 [5]	.	.	203
20-24	2 701	40	.	506	579	986 [4]	.	453 [5]	.	.	137
25-29	3 979	49	.	1 245	521	1 193 [4]	.	905 [5]	.	.	66
30-34	3 597	59	.	1 518	402	895 [4]	.	662 [5]	.	.	61
35-39	3 327	88	.	1 613	426	604 [4]	.	519 [5]	.	.	77
40-44	2 832	99	.	1 442	365	480 [4]	.	369 [5]	.	.	77
45-49	2 210	115	.	1 166	216	390 [4]	.	239 [5]	.	.	84
50-54	1 500	130	.	796	118	172 [4]	.	192 [5]	.	.	92
55-59	893	133	.	463	49	59 [4]	.	94 [5]	.	.	95
60-64	523	111	.	240	22	21 [4]	.	43 [5]	.	.	86
65+	562	168	.	225	11	9 [4]	.	17 [5]	.	.	132

Men - Hommes - Hombres
ISCED-97 - CITE-97 - CINE-97

Age	Total	X	0	1	2	3	5/4	6/5A	7/5B	9/6	?
Total	17 476	335	.	7 153	3 080	4 006 [4]	.	2 222 [5]	.	.	680
15-19	1 177	12	.	-	748	290 [4]	.	5 [5]	.	.	122
20-24	1 728	12	.	343	437	643 [4]	.	214 [5]	.	.	79
25-29	2 919	23	.	950	462	919 [4]	.	518 [5]	.	.	47
30-34	2 715	25	.	1 164	349	721 [4]	.	415 [5]	.	.	41
35-39	2 481	30	.	1 216	379	469 [4]	.	342 [5]	.	.	45
40-44	2 177	32	.	1 118	325	399 [4]	.	256 [5]	.	.	47
45-49	1 696	34	.	914	196	332 [4]	.	175 [5]	.	.	45
50-54	1 140	33	.	648	106	150 [4]	.	157 [5]	.	.	46
55-59	662	35	.	390	47	55 [4]	.	84 [5]	.	.	51
60-64	375	32	.	210	20	19 [4]	.	40 [5]	.	.	54
65+	406	67	.	200	11	9 [4]	.	16 [5]	.	.	103

Women - Femmes - Mujeres
ISCED-97 - CITE-97 - CINE-97

Age	Total	X	0	1	2	3	5/4	6/5A	7/5B	9/6	?
Total	6 329	688	.	2 062	627	1 240 [4]	.	1 282 [5]	.	.	430
15-19	504	19	.	1	250	147 [4]	.	6 [5]	.	.	81
20-24	973	28	.	163	142	343 [4]	.	239 [5]	.	.	58
25-29	1 060	26	.	295	59	274 [4]	.	387 [5]	.	.	19
30-34	882	34	.	354	53	174 [4]	.	247 [5]	.	.	20
35-39	846	58	.	397	47	135 [4]	.	177 [5]	.	.	32
40-44	655	67	.	324	40	81 [4]	.	113 [5]	.	.	30
45-49	514	81	.	252	20	58 [4]	.	64 [5]	.	.	39
50-54	360	97	.	148	12	22 [4]	.	35 [5]	.	.	46
55-59	231	98	.	73	2	4 [4]	.	10 [5]	.	.	44
60-64	148	79	.	30	2	2 [4]	.	3 [5]	.	.	32
65+	156	101	.	25	-	- [4]	.	1 [5]	.	.	29

Explanatory notes: see p. 3.
[1] Persons aged 15 to 74 years. [2] Excl. armed forces. [3] Persons aged 15 years and over. [4] Levels 3-4. [5] Levels 5-6.

Notes explicatives: voir p. 5.
[1] Personnes âgées de 15 à 74 ans. [2] Non compris les forces armées. [3] Personnes âgées de 15 ans et plus. [4] Niveaux 3-4. [5] Niveaux 5-6.

Notas explicativas: véase p. 7.
[1] Personas de 15 a 74 años. [2] Excl. las fuerzas armadas. [3] Personas de 15 años y más. [4] Niveles 3-4. [5] Niveles 5-6.

ECONOMICALLY ACTIVE POPULATION
By level of education and age group

POPULATION ACTIVE
Par niveau d'instruction et groupe d'âge

POBLACION ECONOMICAMENTE ACTIVA
Por nivel de educación y grupo de edad

		Thousands / Milliers / Millares									
ISCED 1976 / CITE	Total	X	0	1	2	3	5	6	7	9	?
CINE 1997	Total	X	0	1	2	3	4	5A	5B	6	?
Ukraine (E) (2008) [1]											
Total - Total - Total											
ISCED-76 - CITE-76 - CINE-76											
Total	22 397.4			147.0	1 880.0	10 131.1	5 033.0	5 206.3 [2]			
Men - Hommes - Hombres											
ISCED-76 - CITE-76 - CINE-76											
Total	11 618.6			60.2	1 044.7	6 013.6	2 054.7	2 445.4 [2]			
Women - Femmes - Mujeres											
ISCED-76 - CITE-76 - CINE-76											
Total	10 778.8			86.8	835.3	4 117.5	2 978.3	2 760.9 [2]			
United Kingdom (BA) (2008) [3] [4]											
Total - Total - Total											
ISCED-76 - CITE-76 - CINE-76											
Total	31 118	2 838 [5]			3 976	14 160	2 902	7 038 [2]		197	7
16-19	1 698	180 [5]			163	1 319	24	3 [2]		10	-
20-24	3 097	205 [5]			354	1 791	176	551 [2]		21	-
25-29	3 429	163 [5]			430	1 418	264	1 126 [2]		26	-
30-34	3 228	167 [5]			396	1 262	286	1 092 [2]		25	-
35-39	3 743	233 [5]			488	1 636	362	1 001 [2]		24	-
40-44	4 029	276 [5]			502	1 847	457	918 [2]		29	-
45-49	3 731	344 [5]			438	1 740	402	787 [2]		21	-
50-54	3 126	366 [5]			417	1 290	363	674 [2]		17	-
55-59	2 635	382 [5]			373	1 064	315	488 [2]		13	-
60-64	1 694	321 [5]			296	610	194	266 [2]		6	-
65-69	471	115 [5]			72	144	44	93 [2]		3	-
70-74	167	55 [5]			34	32	13	29 [2]		2	3
75+	70	31 [5]			13	9	4	10 [2]		-	2
Men - Hommes - Hombres											
ISCED-76 - CITE-76 - CINE-76											
Total	16 872	1 624 [5]			2 376	7 671	1 352	3 718 [2]		126	5
16-19	873	105 [5]			105	647	9	2 [2]		6	-
20-24	1 679	136 [5]			227	976	81	252 [2]		8	-
25-29	1 864	106 [5]			276	794	126	543 [2]		18	-
30-34	1 775	114 [5]			260	696	151	539 [2]		16	-
35-39	2 025	148 [5]			303	866	165	527 [2]		16	-
40-44	2 145	165 [5]			303	955	204	498 [2]		19	-
45-49	1 940	187 [5]			250	882	188	420 [2]		13	-
50-54	1 629	181 [5]			227	698	154	359 [2]		11	-
55-59	1 428	174 [5]			184	620	146	295 [2]		9	-
60-64	1 056	191 [5]			168	409	96	188 [2]		5	-
65-69	295	66 [5]			38	102	23	65 [2]		2	-
70-74	112	30 [5]			25	21	8	23 [2]		2	3
75+	51	22 [5]			10	7	2	8 [2]		-	-
Women - Femmes - Mujeres											
ISCED-76 - CITE-76 - CINE-76											
Total	14 246	1 214 [5]			1 600	6 489	1 550	3 320 [2]		71	2
16-19	824	74 [5]			58	672	15	1 [2]		4	-
20-24	1 418	70 [5]			127	815	95	298 [2]		12	-
25-29	1 565	57 [5]			154	624	138	584 [2]		8	-
30-34	1 453	54 [5]			136	565	136	553 [2]		9	-
35-39	1 718	85 [5]			185	769	197	475 [2]		8	-
40-44	1 884	111			199	892	252	420 [2]		10	-
45-49	1 791	157 [5]			188	858	214	367 [2]		7	-
50-54	1 498	185 [5]			190	592	210	315 [2]		6	-
55-59	1 207	208 [5]			189	444	169	193 [2]		4	-
60-64	637	130 [5]			128	202	98	78 [2]		1	-
65-69	176	50 [5]			35	42	21	28 [2]		-	-
70-74	55	25 [5]			9	11	5	6 [2]		-	-
75+	20	9 [5]			3	2	1	2 [2]		-	1

Explanatory notes: see p. 3.

[1] Persons aged 15-70 years. [2] Levels 6-7. [3] Persons aged 16 years and over. [4] Second quarter. [5] Levels X-1.

Notes explicatives: voir p. 5.

[1] Personnes âgées de 15 à 70 ans. [2] Niveaux 6-7. [3] Personnes âgées de 16 ans et plus. [4] Deuxième trimestre. [5] Niveaux X-1.

Notas explicativas: véase p. 7.

[1] Personas de 15 á 70 años. [2] Niveles 6-7. [3] Personas de 16 años y más. [4] Segundo trimestre. [5] Niveles X-1.

ECONOMICALLY ACTIVE POPULATION
By level of education and age group

POPULATION ACTIVE
Par niveau d'instruction et groupe d'âge

POBLACION ECONOMICAMENTE ACTIVA
Por nivel de educación y grupo de edad

Thousands — Milliers — Millares

ISCED 1976 CITE		X	0	1	2	3	5	6	7	9	?
ISCED 1976	Total	X	0	1	2	3	5	6	7	9	?
CINE 1997	Total	X	0	1	2	3	4	5A	5B	6	?

OCEANIA-OCÉANIE-OCEANIA

Australia (BA) (2008) [1][2][3]

Total - Total - Total
ISCED-97 - CITE-97 - CINE-97

	Total	X	0	1	2	3	4	5A	5B	6	?
Total	10 744.3	589.5 [4]	.	.	2 343.9	3 788.1	386.6	2 621.9 [5]	1 014.3	.	.
15-19	842.6	112.5 [4]	.	.	379.4	337.4	7.0	0.8 [5]	5.4	.	.
20-24	1 205.9	21.2 [4]	.	.	167.9	664.8	49.1	204.8 [5]	98.2	.	.
25-29	1 223.3	28.4 [4]	.	.	157.7	451.0	46.9	416.7 [5]	122.6	.	.
30-34	1 179.1	26.9 [4]	.	.	150.7	448.0	46.7	388.3 [5]	118.6	.	.
35-39	1 269.2	38.9 [4]	.	.	244.8	426.7	46.2	374.7 [5]	138.0	.	.
40-44	1 261.2	55.3 [4]	.	.	302.5	379.1	51.6	337.7 [5]	135.0	.	.
45-49	1 294.7	74.4 [4]	.	.	318.1	398.0	53.5	313.7 [5]	137.0	.	.
50-54	1 119.7	73.3 [4]	.	.	277.0	326.6	37.5	281.6 [5]	123.7	.	.
55-59	878.0	89.5 [4]	.	.	231.1	232.6	33.9	201.8 [5]	89.0	.	.
60-64	470.4	69.1 [4]	.	.	114.6	123.9	14.2	101.9 [5]	46.8	.	.

Men - Hommes - Hombres
ISCED-97 - CITE-97 - CINE-97

	Total	X	0	1	2	3	4	5A	5B	6	?
Total	5 841.9	358.3 [4]	.	.	1 204.2	2 341.6	189.4	1 291.3 [5]	457.1	.	.
15-19	425.4	60.8 [4]	.	.	194.6	164.4	3.1	0.8 [5]	1.7	.	.
20-24	635.3	16.2 [4]	.	.	109.8	364.7	26.6	77.4 [5]	40.7	.	.
25-29	678.5	19.4 [4]	.	.	99.5	281.7	26.5	197.0 [5]	54.4	.	.
30-34	670.2	17.8 [4]	.	.	97.3	284.1	25.0	192.2 [5]	53.7	.	.
35-39	711.9	25.3 [4]	.	.	126.5	278.3	23.3	188.6 [5]	69.9	.	.
40-44	675.2	36.3 [4]	.	.	138.7	239.8	23.6	174.8 [5]	61.7	.	.
45-49	682.5	46.2 [4]	.	.	152.4	251.2	25.1	150.1 [5]	57.4	.	.
50-54	594.2	40.6 [4]	.	.	125.2	223.9	15.4	143.9 [5]	45.1	.	.
55-59	490.2	51.5 [4]	.	.	104.5	166.1	14.0	108.9 [5]	45.2	.	.
60-64	278.6	43.9 [4]	.	.	55.7	87.5	6.8	57.5 [5]	27.2	.	.

Women - Femmes - Mujeres
ISCED-97 - CITE-97 - CINE-97

	Total	X	0	1	2	3	4	5A	5B	6	?
Total	4 902.4	231.2 [4]	.	.	1 139.7	1 446.5	197.2	1 330.6 [5]	557.3	.	.
15-19	417.2	51.7 [4]	.	.	184.8	173.0	4.0	- [5]	3.7	.	.
20-24	570.6	5.0 [4]	.	.	58.1	300.1	22.5	127.4 [5]	57.5	.	.
25-29	544.8	9.0 [4]	.	.	58.2	169.3	20.4	219.7 [5]	68.1	.	.
30-34	509.0	9.1 [4]	.	.	53.3	164.0	21.7	196.1 [5]	64.8	.	.
35-39	557.3	13.6 [4]	.	.	118.4	148.4	22.9	186.0 [5]	68.1	.	.
40-44	586.0	18.7 [4]	.	.	163.8	139.3	28.0	162.9 [5]	73.3	.	.
45-49	612.3	28.3 [4]	.	.	165.7	146.8	28.3	163.6 [5]	79.6	.	.
50-54	525.5	32.7 [4]	.	.	151.8	102.8	22.1	137.6 [5]	78.6	.	.
55-59	387.9	38.0 [4]	.	.	126.6	66.5	20.0	92.9 [5]	43.8	.	.
60-64	191.8	25.2 [4]	.	.	58.9	36.3	7.4	44.4 [5]	19.6	.	.

New Zealand (BA) (2008) [1][2]

Total - Total - Total
ISCED-97 - CITE-97 - CINE-97

	Total	X	0	1	2	3	4	5A	5B	6	?
Total	2 283.2	.	.	-	408.5	702.2	238.1	371.8	310.6	145.3	106.7
15-19	172.9	.	.	.	48.5	107.9	2.1	2.1	7.5	-	4.6
20-24	216.1	.	.	.	32.5	93.4	12.0	35.1	26.6	5.0	11.4
25-29	223.9	.	.	.	29.5	58.5	18.4	58.4	29.9	18.0	11.2
30-34	222.1	.	.	.	25.4	62.2	20.2	56.1	27.3	21.0	9.8
35-39	256.7	.	.	.	36.1	72.1	30.2	52.2	33.2	20.9	12.0
40-44	267.5	.	.	.	47.4	74.1	32.8	42.4	37.8	17.8	15.0
45-49	276.1	.	.	.	48.0	77.3	37.7	40.9	43.4	16.9	11.9
50-54	237.4	.	.	.	44.6	63.6	28.3	36.5	37.4	16.9	10.1
55-59	196.7	.	.	.	40.0	48.0	26.8	25.6	33.5	14.1	8.6
60-64	135.4	.	.	.	33.9	28.8	19.2	15.1	21.8	9.3	7.3
65-69	54.0	.	.	.	15.1	11.1	7.8	4.8	8.4	3.4	3.4
70-74	17.3	.	.	.	5.2	3.9	2.0	1.3	2.6	1.4	-
75+	7.1	.	.	-	2.3	1.3	-	1.1	1.0	-	-

Explanatory notes: see p. 3.

[1] Excl. armed forces. [2] Persons aged 15 years and over. [3] May. [4] Levels X-1. [5] Levels 5A and 6.

Notes explicatives: voir p. 5.

[1] Non compris les forces armées. [2] Personnes âgées de 15 ans et plus. [3] Mai. [4] Niveaux X-1. [5] Niveaux 5A et 6.

Notas explicativas: véase p. 7.

[1] Excl. las fuerzas armadas. [2] Personas de 15 años y más. [3] Mayo. [4] Niveles X-1. [5] Niveles 5A y 6.

ECONOMICALLY ACTIVE POPULATION

By level of education and age group

POPULATION ACTIVE

Par niveau d'instruction et groupe d'âge

POBLACION ECONOMICAMENTE ACTIVA

Por nivel de educación y grupo de edad

		Thousands			Milliers			Millares			
ISCED 1976 CITE	Total	X	0	1	2	3	5	6	7	9	?
CINE 1997	Total	X	0	1	2	3	4	5A	5B	6	?

New Zealand (BA) (2008) [1][2]

Men - Hommes - Hombres
ISCED-97 - CITE-97 - CINE-97

	Total	X	0	1	2	3	4	5A	5B	6	?
Total	1 214.8	.	.	-	231.7	337.0	206.2	188.2	123.6	73.5	54.6
15-19	89.7	.	.	.	28.4	53.3	1.8	1.3	2.6	-	2.0
20-24	115.5	.	.	.	22.9	48.3	9.8	14.0	11.9	2.2	6.5
25-29	120.6	.	.	.	18.7	31.4	15.1	28.0	14.2	7.1	6.1
30-34	119.4	.	.	.	15.5	30.4	17.7	27.8	12.0	10.1	5.8
35-39	136.2	.	.	.	19.8	34.7	26.3	25.0	14.5	9.7	6.1
40-44	137.6	.	.	.	24.6	31.4	28.0	21.8	14.3	10.6	6.8
45-49	142.3	.	.	.	26.7	33.0	33.1	20.9	14.5	8.4	5.7
50-54	122.7	.	.	.	23.2	28.2	24.5	19.9	13.6	8.3	5.1
55-59	105.3	.	.	.	19.5	22.7	23.9	15.3	12.2	7.5	4.2
60-64	77.3	.	.	.	18.3	15.0	16.6	9.1	8.6	6.0	3.7
65-69	32.2	.	.	.	8.5	5.6	7.3	3.2	3.7	1.9	1.9
70-74	11.3	.	.	.	3.9	2.2	1.7	1.1	-	1.3	-
75+	4.7	.	.	-	1.6	-	-	-	-	-	-

Women - Femmes - Mujeres
ISCED-97 - CITE-97 - CINE-97

	Total	X	0	1	2	3	4	5A	5B	6	?
Total	1 068.4	.	.	-	176.8	365.2	31.9	183.6	187.0	71.8	52.2
15-19	83.1	.	.	.	20.1	54.6	-	-	4.9	-	2.5
20-24	100.6	.	.	.	9.6	45.1	2.2	21.2	14.7	2.8	4.9
25-29	103.3	.	.	.	10.8	27.1	3.4	30.4	15.6	10.9	5.1
30-34	102.7	.	.	.	9.9	31.8	2.6	28.3	15.2	10.9	4.0
35-39	120.6	.	.	.	16.3	37.4	3.8	27.2	18.7	11.2	5.9
40-44	129.9	.	.	.	22.8	42.7	4.8	20.6	23.6	7.2	8.2
45-49	133.9	.	.	.	21.3	44.3	4.6	20.0	28.9	8.5	6.2
50-54	114.7	.	.	.	21.4	35.4	3.8	16.6	23.8	8.6	5.0
55-59	91.4	.	.	.	20.5	25.3	2.8	10.4	21.4	6.6	4.4
60-64	58.0	.	.	.	15.6	13.8	2.6	6.0	13.2	3.3	3.6
65-69	21.9	.	.	.	6.6	5.5	-	1.6	4.7	1.5	1.5
70-74	6.0	.	.	.	1.2	1.7	-	-	1.9	-	-
75+	2.3	.	.	-	-	-	-	-	-	-	-

Explanatory notes: see p. 3.

[1] Excl. armed forces. [2] Persons aged 15 years and over.

Notes explicatives: voir p. 5.

[1] Non compris les forces armées. [2] Personnes âgées de 15 ans et plus.

Notas explicativas: véase p. 7.

[1] Excl. las fuerzas armadas. [2] Personas de 15 años y más.

Employment

Emploi

Empleo

Employment

Employment is defined as follows in the Resolution concerning statistics of the economically active population, employment, unemployment and underemployment, adopted by the Thirteenth International Conference of Labour Statisticians (Geneva, 1982):

(1) The "employed" comprise all persons above a specific age who during a specified brief period, either one week or one day, were in the following categories:

(a) "paid employment":
(a1) "at work": persons who during the reference period performed some work for wage or salary, in cash or in kind;
(a2) "with a job but not at work" : persons who, having already worked in their present job, were temporarily not at work during the reference period and had a formal attachment to their job.
This formal job attachment should be determined in the light of national circumstances, according to one or more of the following criteria:
(i) the continued receipt of wage or salary;
(ii) an assurance of return to work following the end of the contingency, or an agreement as to the date of return;
(iii) the elapsed duration of absence from the job which, wherever relevant, may be that duration for which workers can receive compensation benefits without obligations to accept other jobs.

(b) "self-employment" :
(b1) "at work": persons who during the reference period performed some work for profit or family gain, in cash or in kind;
(b2) "with an enterprise but not at work": persons with an enterprise, which may be a business enterprise, a farm or a service undertaking, who were temporarily not at work during the reference period for any specific reason.

(2) For operational purposes, the notion "some work" may be interpreted as work for at least one hour.

(3) Persons temporarily not at work because of illness or injury, holiday or vacation, strike or lockout, educational or training leave, maternity or parental leave, reduction in economic activity, temporary disorganization or suspension of work due to such reasons as bad weather, mechanical or electrical breakdown, or shortage of raw materials or fuels, or other temporary absence with or without leave should be considered as in paid employment provided they had a formal job attachment.

(4) Employers, own-account workers and members of producers' cooperatives should be considered as in self-employment and classified as "at work" or "not at work", as the case may be.

(5) Unpaid family workers at work should be considered as in self-employment irrespective of the number of hours worked during the reference period. Countries which prefer for special reasons to set a minimum time criterion for the inclusion of unpaid family workers among the employed should identify and separately classify those who worked less than the prescribed time.

(6) Persons engaged in the production of economic goods and services for own and household consumption should be considered as in self-employment if such production comprises an important contribution to the total consumption of the house-hold.

(7) Apprentices who received pay in cash or in kind should be considered in paid employment and classified as "at work" or "not at work" on the same basis as other persons in paid employment.

(8) Students, homemakers and others mainly engaged in non-economic activities during the reference period, who at the same time were in paid employment or self-employment as defined in subparagraph (1) above should be considered as employed on the same basis as other categories of employed persons and be identified separately, where possible.

(9) Members of the armed forces should be included among persons in paid employment. The armed forces should include both the regular and temporary members as specified in the most recent revision of the *International Standard Classification of Occupations (ISCO)*.

National definitions of employment may in a number of cases differ from the recommended international standard definition.[1]

As the data in tables 2B to 2F of this *Yearbook* attest to, a large and ever increasing number of countries can and do rearrange national classifications by branch of economic activity (industry), occupation and status in employment to the international standard classification schemes, including the most recent revisions. When a country has adopted the latest revision within the 10-year time series presented, the earlier and latest version of the data are presented side by side separated by a thick vertical line in between the relevant years of implementation.

The classification according to main economic activity carried out where work is performed *(industry)* is fundamentally different from that according to main type of duties performed *(occupation)*. In the former, all persons working in a given establishment are classified under the same industry irrespective of their particular occupations. The latter, on the other hand, brings together individuals working in similar types of work, irrespective of where the work is performed. As indicated in the tables, most countries have supplied data on the basis of the *International Standard Industrial Classification of all Economic Activities ISIC Rev.2, ISIC Rev.3* or ISIC Rev.4 and the International Standard Classification of *Occupations, ISCO-68* or *ISCO-88* (see Appendix).

Where the data are given according to national classifications, it should be borne in mind that the industrial and occupational classifications used by the different countries present many points of divergence. The actual content of industrial or occupational groups may differ from one country to another owing to variations in definitions and methods of tabulation. Classification into broad groups may also obscure fundamental differences in the industrial or occupational patterns of the various countries.

The *International Classification of Status in Employment (ICSE)* classifies jobs with respect to the type of explicit or implicit contract of employment the person has with other persons or organizations. The basic criteria to define groups of the classification are the type of economic risk and the type of authority over establishments and other workers which the job incumbent has or will have.

Up to 1993 the main ICSE groups were *employers, own-account workers, employees, members of producers' cooperatives, and unpaid family workers.* ICSE was revised and expanded in 1993, in a way which left the titles of these main groups basically unchanged, except for the last group now called *contributing family workers*. The content of the group *own-account workers* was enlarged, however, to include persons working in a family enterprise with the same degree of commitment as the head of enterprise. These people, usually women, were formerly considered unpaid family workers in the old ICSE. The revised ICSE also makes the distinctions between groups clearer.

Experience has shown that frequently because of the way countries measure "status in employment", the content of the groups is not easily comparable. For example, in most countries managers and directors of incorporated enterprises are classified as *employees*, while in some others they are classified as *employers*. Another example is that family members who regularly receive remuneration as wages, salary, commission, piece-rates or pay in kind, are mainly classified as *employees*, but some countries classify them as *contributing family workers*. Another important difference affecting the comparability of the number of *contributing family workers* arises from the fact that some countries are not able to measure such persons as in employment at all. Many countries cannot distinguish between *own-account workers* and *employers* in their basic observations, so only the sum of these two groups can be presented. Some countries which have few *members of producers' cooperatives* may group them with *employees*, while others group them with *own-account workers*.

It should be recalled that the purpose of international classification schemes is not to supersede national classifications but to provide a framework for the international comparison of national statistics. Many countries, particularly those developing classifications for the first time, or revising existing schemes, use international schemes as a central framework.

In general, employment data are obtained from four main sources, namely, household sample surveys, establishment censuses or surveys, official national estimates, or administrative records of social insurance schemes.

These four main sources of employment statistics, presented in Chapter 2, are identified in the tables by codes in parentheses to the right of the country name. These codes (BA), (DA), (E) and (FA) are described below: Source (BA). Labour force sample surveys.

These are a source of regular information on both the total labour force and its components (employed and unemployed persons) and the total inactive population.

For total employment, these surveys cover all status groups, that is, not only employees (wage earners and salaried employees), including paid family workers, but also employers, own-account workers, members of producers' cooperatives, contributing family workers and workers not classifiable by status. The data generally relate to employment during a specified brief period, either one week or one day. Usually, no distinction is made between persons employed full time and those working less than full time.

Source (DA). *Establishment surveys*. This source provides data on the number of workers on establishment payrolls for a specified payroll period or working day in this period. In general, there are two types of establishment statistics.

The first type covers *all establishments of a given importance*, e.g. those fulfilling certain conditions, such as having more than a certain number of

employees, having an annual output of more than a certain value, etc. The data thus obtained may be subject to some bias owing to the exclusion of establishments which are below the minimum size fixed for the series. Moreover, a shift of employment from small to large establishments will be reflected in a rising trend in the series. Provided that this minimum is small, the scope of these series is usually very wide and they can furnish a close approximation of the fluctuations in paid employment.

The second type of statistics relates to *a sample of establishments*. The chief difficulty with such statistics is to ensure that the sample of establishments remains representative of the whole. For example, changes in industrial structure, the growth and decline of individual establishments, general population movements and pronounced changes in the levels of activity in some sectors of the economy tend to introduce a cumulative bias in this sample which may become appreciable after several years.

In certain countries where statistics of the first type *(all establishments of a given importance)* are available only at annual or longer intervals, they may be combined either by linking or by interpolation with statistics of the second type *(samples of establishments)* which are available more frequently.

Source (E). *Official estimates*. These statistics are official estimates provided by national authorities. Such estimates are usually based on combined information drawn from one or more of the other sources described here.

Source (FA). *Social insurance statistics*. This source covers the working population protected by sickness, accident or unemployment insurance schemes, or the like. The number of contributors or of contributions paid provides a measure of the number of insured persons in employment (unemployed persons being exempt from the obligation to pay contributions). Persons working a very short time, receiving very low pay or who are above a certain age, are sometimes excluded from these statistics. In addition to changes in the actual number of persons employed, employment statistics based on social insurance records may also reflect changes in cover- age of particular industrial, occupational or status groups.

Table 2A

Employment: General level

The employment series shown in this summary table cover, in principle all major divisions of economic activity and all sectors of activity. They refer, as far as is possible, to all status categories of persons in employment. For certain series some component categories may not be fully represented. The worker coverage is indicated in the table at the centre of the page for each series as *total employment, all persons engaged,* and *employees*. The inclusion or exclusion of data on the armed forces, which varies by country, is indicated in the footnotes, where known.

Table 2B

Total employment, by economic activity

This table presents absolute figures on the distribution of the employed by economic activity, according to either ISIC Rev.2, ISIC Rev.3 or ISIC Rev.4, or to two out of three versions side by side, in cases where the latest revision of this international classification has been introduced during the 10-year time series covered in the *Yearbook*.

Table 2C

Total employment, by occupation

This table presents absolute figures on the distribution of the employed by occupation, according to either ISCO-68 or ISCO-88, or to both versions side by side, in cases where the later revision of this international classification has been introduced during the 10-year time series covered in the *Yearbook*.

Table 2D

Total employment, by status in employment

This employment series covers, in principle, the total number of persons in employment for all status groups, according to the *International Classification of Status in Employment 1993 (ICSE-93)*.

Table 2E

Paid employment, by economic activity

The data on employment shown in this table cover all available series of paid employment which should relate solely to employees (wage earners and salaried employees) in employment and preferably be derived from an establishment survey. However, data on paid employment can also be derived from other sources (for example a labour force survey or administrative records) and may in some cases have a different worker coverage which is indicated in the table at the centre of the page for each series.

Table 2F

Paid employment in manufacturing

This table presents data on paid employment in manufacturing as a whole and for all components of this category of economic activity where available, according either to the three-digit level of ISIC Rev2., or to the division level of ISIC Rev.3 (divisions 15 to 37) or ISIC Rev.4 (divisions 10 to 33). Where data are available according to both revisions of this international classification within the 10-year time series covered in the *Yearbook* these are presented side by side.

The number of persons in paid employment by economic activity presented in the tables of this chapter is obtained, as far as possible, from identical sources as the data given in the corresponding tables on hours of work (Chapter 4) and wages (Chapter 5).

When comparing data on employment shown in the six tables of this chapter, due regard should be given not only to differences in sources of data but also to the differences in scope and coverage of the statistics shown. Details on status groups and divisions of economic activity covered or omitted, or on geographic coverage and alternate dates of reference are given in each table nd its footnotes.

Abridged versions of the *International Standard Industrial Classification of all Economic Activities (ISIC Rev2, ISIC Rev. 3 and ISIC Rev.4)*, the *International Standard Classification of Occupations (ISCO-1968 and ISCO-1988)* and the *International Classification of Status in Employment (ICSE-1993)* are shown in the Appendix.

Note

[1] For information on the differences in scope, definitions and methods of calculation, etc., used for the national series, see ILO: Sources and Methods: Labour Statistics (formerly Statistical Sources and Methods), Vol. 2: "Employment, wages, hours of work and labour cost (establishment surveys)", second edition (Geneva, 1995); Vol. 3: "Economically active population, employment, unemployment and hours of work (household surveys)" second edition (Geneva, 1990); Vol. 4 : "Employment, unemployment, wages and hours of work (Administrative records and related sources)" (Geneva, 1989).

Emploi

L'emploi est défini de la manière suivante dans la Résolution concernant les statistiques de la population active, de l'emploi, du chômage et du sous-emploi adoptée par la treizième Conférence internationale des statisticiens du travail (Genève, 1982):

1) Les « personnes pourvues d'un emploi » comprennent toutes les personnes ayant dépassé un âge spécifié qui se trouvaient, durant une brève période de référence spécifiée telle qu'une semaine ou un jour, dans les catégories suivantes:

a) « emploi salarié »:

a1) « personnes au travail »: personnes qui, durant la période de référence, ont effectué un travail moyennant un salaire ou un traitement en espèces ou en nature;

a2) « personnes qui ont un emploi mais qui ne sont pas au travail »: personnes qui, ayant déjà travaillé dans leur emploi actuel, en étaient absentes durant la période de référence et avaient un lien formel avec leur emploi.

Ce lien formel avec l'emploi devrait être déterminé à la lumière des circonstances nationales, par référence à l'un ou plusieurs des critères suivants:

i) le service ininterrompu du salaire ou du traitement;

ii) une assurance de retour au travail à la fin de la situation d'exception ou un accord sur la date de retour;

iii) la durée de l'absence du travail qui, le cas échéant, peut être la durée pendant laquelle les travailleurs peuvent recevoir une indemnisation sans obligation d'accepter d'autres emplois qui leur seraient éventuellement proposés.

b) « emploi non salarié »:

b1) « personnes au travail »: personnes qui, durant la période de référence, ont effectué un travail en vue d'un bénéfice ou d'un gain familial, en espèces ou en nature;

b2) « personnes ayant une entreprise mais n'étant pas au travail »: personnes qui, durant la période de référence, avaient une entreprise qui peut être une entreprise industrielle, un commerce, une exploitation agricole ou une entreprise de prestations de services, mais n'étaient temporairement pas au travail pour toute raison spécifique.

2) Dans la pratique, on peut interpréter la notion de « travail effectué au cours de la période de référence » comme étant un travail d'une durée d'une heure au moins.

3) Les personnes temporairement absentes de leur travail pour raison de maladie ou d'accident, de congé ou de vacances, de conflit du travail ou de grève, de congé-éducation ou formation, de congé-maternité ou parental, de mauvaise conjoncture économique ou de suspension temporaire du travail due à des causes telles que: conditions météorologiques défavorables, incidents mécaniques ou électriques, pénurie de matières premières ou de combustibles, ou toute autre cause d'absence temporaire avec ou sans autorisation, devraient être considérées comme pourvues d'un emploi salarié, à condition qu'elles aient un lien formel avec leur emploi.

4) Les employeurs, les personnes travaillant à leur propre compte et les membres des coopératives de producteurs devraient être considérés comme travailleurs non salariés et classés comme « étant au travail » ou « n'étant pas au travail », selon le cas.

5) Les travailleurs familiaux non rémunérés devraient être considérés comme travailleurs non salariés indépendamment du nombre d'heures de travail effectué durant la période de référence. Les pays qui, pour des raisons particulières, préféraient choisir comme critère une durée minimale de temps de travail pour inclure les travailleurs familiaux non rémunérés parmi les personnes pourvues d'un emploi devraient identifier et classer séparément les personnes de cette catégorie qui ont travaillé moins que le temps prescrit.

6) Les personnes engagées dans la production de biens et services pour leur propre consommation ou celle du ménage devraient être considérées comme travailleurs non salariés si une telle production apporte une importante contribution à la consommation totale du ménage.

7) Les apprentis qui ont reçu une rétribution en espèces ou en nature devraient être considérés comme personnes pourvues d'un emploi salarié et classés comme « étant au travail » ou « n'étant pas au travail » sur la même base que les autres catégories de personnes pourvues d'un emploi salarié.

8) Les étudiants, les personnes s'occupant du foyer et autres personnes principalement engagées dans des activités non économiques durant la période de référence et qui étaient en même temps pourvues d'un emploi salarié ou non salarié comme défini au sous-paragraphe (1) ci-dessus devraient être considérées comme ayant un emploi, sur la même base que les autres catégories de personnes ayant un emploi, et être identifiés séparément lorsque cela est possible.

9) Les membres des forces armées devraient être inclus parmi les personnes pourvues d'un emploi salarié. Elles devraient comprendre aussi bien les membres permanents que les membres temporaires, comme spécifié dans la plus récente révision de la *Classification internationale type des professions (CITP)*.

Dans un certain nombre de cas, les définitions nationales de l'emploi peuvent s'écarter de la définition internationale type recommandée[1].

Comme cela apparaît dans les tableaux 2B à 2F de cet *Annuaire*, un nombre croissant de pays ont pu adapter leurs classifications par branches d'activité économique, professions et situation dans la profession aux structures des classifications internationales, y compris celles ayant été révisées récemment. Lorsqu'un pays a adopté l'une de ces classifications révisées, au cours de la période décennale publiée dans cet *Annuaire*, les données sont publiées selon l'ancienne et la nouvelle classifications de part et d'autre d'une barre verticale marquant l'introduction d'une nouvelle classification.

La classification selon l'activité économique principale (industrie) est fondamentalement différente de celle selon les principales tâches accomplies (profession). Dans la première, toutes les personnes travaillant dans un établissement donné sont classées dans la même industrie quelles que soient leurs professions. Par contre, dans la seconde, sont regroupées dans une même catégorie toutes les personnes accomplissant le même genre de travail quel que soit le lieu où ce travail est effectué. La plupart des pays ont transmis les données sur la base de la *Classification internationale type, par industrie, de toutes les branches d'activité économique CITI Rév. 2, CITI Rév. 3 ou CITI Rév.. 4* et la *Classification internationale type des professions CITP-68 ou CITP-88* (voir annexe).

Lorsque les données sont présentées selon les classifications nationales, industrielles ou professionnelles, il faut noter que cela tient essentiellement aux nombreuses divergences par rapport aux classifications internationales. La teneur des groupes d'industries ou de professions peut également varier d'un pays à un autre du fait des différentes définitions ou méthodes de classification. De plus, des classifications selon les groupes agrégés peuvent aussi cacher des différences fondamentales dans les systèmes industriels ou professionnels des différents pays.

La *Classification internationale d'après la situation dans la profession (CISP)* classe les emplois eu égard au type de contrat explicite ou implicite d'une personne avec d'autres personnes ou organisations. Les critères de base retenus pour définir les groupes sont la nature du risque économique encouru ou la nature du contrôle qu'exercent ou exerceront les titulaires sur les entreprises et sur d'autres salariés.

Jusqu'en 1993, les principaux groupes de la CISP étaient les suivants: *employeur; personne travaillant pour son propre compte; salarié; travailleur familial non rémunéré et membre d'une coopérative de producteurs.* En 1993, la CISP a été révisée et élargie, mais d'une manière telle que les titres de ces principaux groupes n'ont pas été modifiés à l'exception du dernier qui est devenu *travailleurs familiaux collaborant à l'entreprise familiale.* Le contenu du groupe *personnes travaillant pour leur propre compte* a cependant été élargi pour inclure les personnes travaillant dans l'entreprise familiale avec les mêmes responsabilités que le chef de l'entreprise. Ces personnes, généralement des femmes, étaient classées « travailleurs familiaux non rémunérés » dans l'ancienne classification. La CISP révisée a également clarifié les distinctions entre les groupes.

L'expérience a montré que fréquemment, compte tenu de la manière dont les pays mesuraient la « situation dans la profession », la teneur des groupes n'était pas facilement comparable. Par exemple, dans la plupart des pays les propriétaires-gérants d'entreprises constituées en sociétés sont classés dans le groupe des *salariés*, alors qu'ils le seront dans celui des *employeurs* dans d'autres pays. Il en est de même pour les travailleurs familiaux qui, percevant régulièrement leur rémunération sous forme de salaire, traitement, primes, rémunération aux pièces ou paiements en nature, sont généralement classés comme *salariés* mais, dans d'autres pays, comme *travailleurs familiaux collaborant à l'entreprise familiale.* Une autre difficulté, quant à la comparabilité du nombre de ces *travailleurs familiaux*, vient du fait que certains pays ne sont pas en mesure de les dénombrer en tant que personnes ayant un emploi. Beaucoup de pays ne pouvant pas distinguer *les personnes travaillant pour leur propre compte* des *employeurs* dans leurs observations de base, seule la somme de ces deux catégories est disponible. Certains pays ayant peu de travailleurs membres de coopératives de production peuvent les agréger au groupe des salariés, alors que d'autres le feront avec celui des *personnes travaillant à leur propre compte.*

Il faut toutefois rappeler que l'objectif des classifications internationales n'est pas de se substituer aux nationales mais de donner un cadre général à la comparaison internationale de ces données. De plus, beaucoup de pays utilisent ces classifications internationales comme cadre lors de l'élaboration ou la révision de leurs classifications.

En général, les données sur l'emploi sont obtenues à partir de quatre sources principales, à savoir: les enquêtes par sondage auprès des ménages, les enquêtes auprès des établissements ou les recensements, les évaluations officielles et les registres administratifs provenant des régimes d'assurances sociales.

Ces quatre sources principales des statistiques d'emploi sont identifiées dans les tableaux de ce chapitre par des codes, entre parenthèses à la droite du nom de pays. Ces codes, définis ci-dessous sont les suivants: (BA), (DA), (E) et (FA).

Source (BA). *Enquêtes par sondage sur la main-d'œuvre.* C'est une source d'informations régulières tant sur la main-d'œuvre totale et ses sous-groupes (personnes occupées et chômeurs) que sur la population inactive totale.

Pour ce qui est de l'emploi total, ces enquêtes couvrent toutes les personnes occupées appartenant à toutes les catégories de *situation dans la profession*, c'est-à-dire non seulement les salariés (ouvriers et employés), y compris les travailleurs familiaux rémunérés mais également les employeurs, les personnes travaillant pour leur propre compte, les membres de coopératives de producteurs, les travailleurs familiaux collaborant à l'entreprise familiale et les travailleurs inclassables selon la situation dans la profession.

Source (DA). *Enquêtes auprès des établissements.* Cette source couvre les travailleurs inscrits sur les bordereaux de salaires au cours d'une période de paie déterminée ou d'un jour de travail de cette période. En général, on distingue deux types d'enquêtes auprès des établissements.

Le premier type de statistiques englobe *tous les établissements d'une importance déterminée*, c'est-à-dire ceux qui répondent à certains critères (par exemple les entreprises qui occupent plus d'un certain nombre de salariés; celles dont la production annuelle est supérieure à une certaine valeur, etc.). Les données ainsi rassemblées peuvent être sujettes à des écarts systématiques provenant de l'élimination d'établissements qui n'atteignent pas la limite minimale fixée pour ces séries; de plus, un déplacement de l'emploi des petits établissements vers les grands établissements se traduira par une tendance d'augmentation des séries. Toutefois, lorsque la limite minimale est fixée assez bas, le champ de telles séries est généralement très étendu et ces statistiques reflètent assez fidèlement les fluctuations de l'emploi.

Les statistiques du second type reposent sur un *échantillon d'établissements.* Dans de telles séries, la difficulté principale consiste à conserver aux établissements sélectionnés un caractère représentatif. Par exemple, des variations de la structure industrielle, le développement ou le déclin d'établissements particuliers, le mouvement général de la population ou des changements marqués dans l'activité de certains secteurs économiques ont tendance à introduire un écart systématique cumulatif dans l'échantillon qui, au bout de quelques années, peut devenir sensible.

Dans certains pays où les statistiques du premier type (tous les établissements d'une importance déterminée) ne sont disponibles que tous les ans ou à des intervalles plus longs, elles peuvent être combinées, soit par enchaînement, soit par interpolation, avec les statistiques du second type *(échantillon d'établissements)* plus fréquemment disponibles.

Source (E). *Evaluations officielles.* Ces statistiques sont des évaluations officielles fournies par les autorités nationales. De telles estimations sont généralement basées sur une combinaison d'informations tirées d'une ou plusieurs sources mentionnées dans ce texte.

Source (FA). *Statistiques d'assurances sociales.* Cette source couvre les personnes occupées, protégées par l'assurance maladie, accident ou chômage, ou par un régime analogue. Le nombre de cotisants ou de cotisations versées fournit une mesure des effectifs assurés et occupés (les chômeurs étant dispensés du paiement de leur cotisation). Les personnes travaillant durant une très courte période, qui sont très peu rémunérées ou qui sont au-dessus d'un certain âge, sont quelquefois omises de ces statistiques. Outre les changements intervenant dans le nombre effectif de personnes occupées, les statistiques de l'emploi fondées sur les registres des assurances sociales peuvent également refléter des modifications de portée pour certains groupes classés selon la branche d'activité économique, la profession ou la situation dans la profession.

Tableau 2A

Emploi: niveau général

Les séries d'emploi présentées dans ce tableau couvrent, en principe, toutes les branches d'activité économique ainsi que tous les secteurs. Elles couvrent, autant que possible, toutes les catégories de personnes, quelle que soit leur situation dans la profession. Cependant, il arrive que pour certaines séries, certaines composantes ne sont pas entièrement représentées. Pour chaque série, la catégorie de travailleurs concernés *(emploi total, effectif occupé ou salariés)* est indiquée au centre de la page. L'inclusion ou non de données sur les forces armées varie selon le pays et, dans la mesure du possible, cela est indiqué dans les notes de bas de page.

Tableau 2B

Emploi total, par activité économique

Ce tableau présente (en nombres absolus) la répartition de la main-d'œuvre occupée par activité économique, selon la CITI Rév. 2, la CITI Rév. 3 *ou la CITI Rév. 4*, ou selon deux des trois versions dans tous les cas où la révision postérieure de cette classification internationale a été introduite au cours de la période décennale couverte par l'*Annuaire*.

Tableau 2C

Emploi total, par profession

Ce tableau présente (en nombres absolus) la répartition de la main-d'œuvre occupée par profession, selon la CITP-68 ou CITP-88, ou selon l'une et l'autre versions, dans tous les cas où la révision postérieure de cette classification internationale a été introduite au cours de la période décennale couverte par l'*Annuaire*.

Tableau 2D

Emploi total, par situation dans la profession

Ce tableau présente la répartition de la main-d'œuvre occupée selon la situation dans la profession telle que définie dans la *Classification internationale d'après la situation dans la profession 1993 (CISP-93)*.

Tableau 2E

Emploi rémunéré, par activité économique

Dans ce tableau, les séries sur l'emploi rémunéré visent seulement les salariés (ouvriers et employés) et sont essentiellement dérivées d'enquêtes auprès des établissements. Cependant, de telles séries peuvent être dérivées d'autres sources (par exemple, enquêtes sur la main-d'œuvre, sources administratives) et concerner d'autres catégories de personnes occupées; dans ce dernier cas, cela est indiqué pour chaque série au centre de la page.

Tableau 2F

Emploi rémunéré dans les industries manufacturières

Ce tableau présente des données pour l'ensemble des industries manufacturières et ses composantes, à savoir par classe d'industrie de la CITI Rév. 2 (indicatifs à trois chiffres) ou par divisions de la CITI Rév. 3 (indicatifs à deux chiffres 15 à 37) ou de la CITI Rév. 4 (indicatifs à deux chiffres 10 à 33). Dans tous les cas où la révision postérieure été introduite au cours de la période décennale couverte par l'*Annuaire*, les données apparaissent successivement selon l'une et l'autre versions de la CITI.

Les données sur l'emploi rémunéré par activité économique, publiées dans ces tableaux, sont, autant que possible, dérivées des mêmes enquêtes que celles relatives à la durée du travail et aux salaires publiées dans les tableaux correspondants des chapitres 4 et 5.

Lorsque l'on compare les données de l'emploi présentées dans les six tableaux de ce chapitre, il convient de prêter une attention particulière non seulement aux différences entre les sources des données, mais égale- ment entre les portées des statistiques publiées. Des indications détaillées sont fournies dans chaque tableau ainsi que dans les notes de bas de page sur les situations dans la profession et sur les branches d'activité économique couvertes, de même que sur la portée géographique et les périodes de référence des séries.

Des versions abrégées des classifications internationales suivantes sont présentées dans l'annexe:
— *Classification internationale type, par industrie, de toutes les branches d'activité économique (CITI Rév. 2, CITI Rév. 3 et CITI Rév. 4)*
— *Classification internationale type des professions (CITP-68 et CITP-88)*
— *Classification internationale d'après la situation dans la profession (CISP-93).*

Note

[1] Pour des renseignements sur les différences de portée, définitions et méthodes de calcul, etc., utilisées pour les diverses séries nationales, voir BIT: *Sources et méthodes: statistiques du travail* (précédemment *Sources et méthodes statistiques*), vol. 2 «Emploi, salaires, durée du travail et coût de la main-d'œuvre (enquête auprès des établissements)», deuxième édition (Genève, 1995); vol. 3 «Population active, emploi, chômage, et durée du travail (enquêtes auprès des ménages)», deuxième édition (Genève, 1991); vol. 4 «Emploi, chômage, salaires et durée du travail (documents administratifs et sources assimilées)» (Genève, 1989). Les volumes 3 et 4 sont disponibles sous forme brochée uniquement en anglais, mais une édition française non brochée peut être obtenue sur demande auprès du Département de statistique.

Empleo

La Resolución sobre estadísticas de la población económicamente activa, del empleo, del desempleo y del subempleo, adoptada por la decimotercera Conferencia Internacional de Estadísticos del Trabajo (Ginebra, 1982), define el empleo como sigue:

1) Se considerará como «personas con empleo» a todas las personas que tengan más de cierta edad especificada y que durante un breve período de referencia, tal como una semana o un día, estuvieran en cualquiera de las siguientes categorías:
a) Con «empleo asalariado»:
   a1) «trabajando»: personas que durante el período de referencia hayan realizado algún trabajo por un sueldo o salario en metálico o en especie;
   a2) «con empleo pero sin trabajar»: personas que, habiendo trabajado en su empleo actual, no estaban trabajando temporalmente durante el período de referencia y mantenían un vínculo formal con su empleo. Este vínculo formal al empleo debería determinarse en función de las circunstancias nacionales, de acuerdo con uno o más de los siguientes criterios:
      i) pago ininterrumpido de sueldos o salarios;
      ii) garantía de reintegración en el empleo al término de la contingencia o un acuerdo respecto de la fecha de reintegración;
      iii) duración de la ausencia del trabajo, la cual, cuando sea el caso, puede ser aquella por la que los trabajadores pueden percibir una compensación social sin obligación de aceptar otros trabajos.
b) Con «empleo independiente»:
   b1) «trabajando»: las personas que durante el período de referencia hayan realizado algún trabajo para obtener beneficios o ganancia familiar, en metálico o en especie;
   b2) «con una empresa pero sin trabajar»: las personas que, teniendo una empresa -sea industrial, comercial, de explotación agrícola o de prestación de servicios-, estaban temporalmente ausentes del trabajo durante el período de referencia por cualquier razón específica.

2) Por razones prácticas, la noción «algún trabajo» debe interpretarse como una hora de trabajo por lo menos.

3) Las personas ausentes de su trabajo temporalmente por causa de enfermedad o accidente, días festivos o vacaciones, huelga, paro de empleadores, licencia de estudios o de forma- ción profesional, licencia de maternidad o paternidad, coyuntura económica difícil, desorganización suspensión temporal del trabajo por razones tales como mal tiempo, averías mecánicas o eléctricas, escasez de materias primas o combustibles, u otras ausencias temporales con o sin licencia, deberían considerarse como personas con empleo asalariado, siempre que mantuvieran un vínculo formal con su empleo.

4) Debería considerarse como personas con empleo independiente a los empleadores, trabajadores por cuenta propia y miembros de cooperativas de producción, y clasificarse «trabajando» o «con empleo pero sin trabajar», según sea el caso.

5) Debería considerarse como personas con empleo independiente a los trabajadores familiares no remunerados que estén trabajando, sin consideración al número de horas trabajadas durante el período de referencia. Los países que, por razones particulares, prefieren introducir un criterio de tiempo mínimo de trabajo como condición para incluir a los trabajadores familiares no remunerados entre las personas con empleo, deberían identificar y clasificar aparte a los que trabajan menos del tiempo prescrito.

6) Las personas ocupadas en la producción de bienes y servicios económicos para consumo propio o del hogar, deberían considerarse como personas con empleo independiente, si dicha producción constituye una aportación importante al consumo total del hogar.

7) Los aprendices que hayan recibido una retribución en metálico o en especie deberían considerarse como personas con empleo asalariado y clasificarse como «trabajando» o «con empleo pero sin trabajar», sobre las mismas bases que las demás personas con empleo asalariado.

8) Los estudiantes, trabajadores del hogar y otros dedicados principalmente a actividades no económicas durante el período de referencia y que al mismo tiempo tenían un empleo asalariado o un empleo independiente, según definiciones en el subpárrafo 1) anterior, deberían considerarse como personas con empleo, sobre las mismas bases que las otras categorías de personas con empleo y, si fuese posible, clasificarse aparte.

9) Los miembros de las fuerzas armadas deberían figurar entre las personas con empleo asalariado. Las fuerzas armadas incluirían los miembros permanentes y temporales, como se ha especificado en la última edición revisada de la *Clasificación Internacional Uniforme de Ocupaciones (CIUO)*.

Las definiciones nacionales de empleo pueden diferir en algunos casos de la definición internacional estándar recomendada[1].

Los datos de los cuadros 2B a 2F de este *Anuario* confirman que un número cada vez más elevado de países están en condiciones o en vías de adaptar sus clasificaciones nacionales de ramas de actividad, Ocupaciones y situación en el empleo a las normas internacionales de clasificación, comprendidas las revisiones más recientes. Cuando un país adopta la última revisión en el curso de la década abarcada por las series, éstas se presentan según la última versión y la anterior, una junto a otra, separadas por una línea vertical, a partir del año en que comenzó a aplicarse la última revisión.

La clasificación de la principal actividad económica que se desarrolla en el lugar de trabajo (industria) difiere fundamentalmente de la que se refiere a la clase principal de tareas que se llevan a cabo (ocupación). En la antigua presentación, todas las personas que trabajaban en el mismo establecimiento se clasificaban en la misma industria, con independencia de sus ocupaciones. En la actual, por el contrario, se reúnen los individuos que desempeñan el mismo tipo de trabajo, con independencia del lugar en que lo realizan. Como lo indican los cuadros correspondientes, la mayoría de los países ha comunicado datos sobre la industria según la *Clasificación Internacional Industrial Uniforme de Todas las Actividades Económicas, CIIU Rev.2, CIIU Rev.3 o CIIU Rev.4* y los relativos a las ocupaciones según la *Clasificación Internacional Uniforme de Ocupaciones, CIUO-68 o CIUO-88* (véase Apéndice).

Cuando los datos se dan según las clasificaciones nacionales, cabe tener presente que las clasificaciones industriales y de ocupaciones de los diversos países presentan varios puntos divergentes. En efecto, en cada país el contenido real de los grupos de industrias o de ocupaciones puede variar en función de las distintas definiciones y métodos de tabulación utilizados. La clasificación en grupos muy amplios puede también ocultar diferencias fundamentales de las características industriales o de ocupación propias de cada país.

La *Clasificación Internacional de la Situación en el Empleo (CISE)* clasifica los empleos en relación con el tipo de contrato de empleo, tácito o expreso, entre una persona y otras personas u organizaciones. El criterio básico para definir los grupos de clasificación son la clase de riesgo económico y el tipo de autoridad ejercida por los trabajadores sobre los establecimientos y otros trabajadores, en virtud del empleo que tienen o tendrán.

Hasta 1993, los principales grupos de la CISE eran «empleadores», «trabajadores por cuenta propia», «empleados», «miembros de cooperativas de productores» y «trabajadores familiares no remunerados». En 1993 se revisó y amplió la CISE sin modificar los títulos de estos grupos principales, salvo el último de los mencionados que ahora se llama trabajadores familiares contribuyentes. Se amplió el contenido de los trabajadores por cuenta propia para que comprenda a las personas que trabajan en empresas familiares con la misma dedicación que el jefe de la empresa. Estas personas, generalmente mujeres, se consideraban antes como trabajadores familiares no remunerados. La CISE revisada también distingue los grupos con mayor claridad.

La experiencia demuestra que con frecuencia las distintas formas de medir la «situación en el empleo» de los países impide que el contenido de los grupos pueda compararse con facilidad. Por ejemplo, la mayoría de los países clasifican los gerentes y directores de empresas no personales como «empleadores». Otro ejemplo son los trabajadores familiares que perciben periódicamente una remuneración, como sueldo o salario, comisión, pago a destajo o en especie, que la mayoría clasifica como «empleados» pero algunos países los incluyen entre los «trabajadores familiares contribuyentes». Otro importante factor que afecta la comparabilidad del número de estos trabajadores familiares es que algunos países no pueden medir a estas personas en la medida que no tienen ninguna clase de empleo. Muchos países no pueden distinguir entre «trabajadores por cuenta propia» y «empleadores» y por tal motivo presentan la suma de ambos. Entre los países donde el número de cooperativas de productores es muy escaso, algunos incluyen a sus miembros entre los «empleados» mientras que en otros entre los «trabajadores por cuenta propia».

Cabe recordar que el objetivo de los sistemas internacionales de clasificación no es sustituir las clasificaciones de cada país sino constituir un marco que facilite las comparaciones internacionales de las estadísticas nacionales. Muchos países, sobre todo los que elaboran clasificaciones por primera vez o las revisan, utilizan los sistemas internacionales como marco central.

En general, las cuatro fuentes principales de los datos sobre el empleo son las encuestas por muestra a los hogares, los censos o encuestas de establecimientos, las estimaciones oficiales y los registros administrativos de los regímenes de seguridad social.

En los cuadros de este capítulo, las cuatro fuentes mencionadas se señalan por los códigos entre paréntesis (BA), (DA), (E) y (FA), a la derecha del nombre del país, como se describe a continuación:

Fuente (BA). *Encuesta de la fuerza de trabajo*. Es una fuente de información periódica tanto sobre el total de la fuerza de trabajo y sus componentes (empleo y desempleo) como sobre la población inactiva total.

Con respecto al empleo total, estas encuestas abarcan todos los grupos de situación, es decir, no sólo los asalariados (obreros y empleados), comprendidos los trabajadores familiares remunerados, sino también los empleadores, trabajadores por cuenta propia, miembros de cooperativas de productores, trabajadores familiares contribuyentes y otros no clasificables por su situación en el empleo. Los datos por lo general se refieren al empleo durante un breve período determinado (una semana o un día). Habitualmente no se distingue entre personas empleadas a tiempo completo y quienes trabajan menos horas.

Fuente (DA). *Encuesta de establecimientos relacionada con el trabajo*. Esta fuente permite obtener datos sobre el número de trabajadores que figuran en las nóminas de salarios de los establecimientos en un período de pago determinado o un día de este último. Habitualmente se distinguen dos tipos de estadísticas de establecimientos.

El primero abarca todos los de una cierta importancia, como los que ocupan más de un cierto número de asalariados, o los que tienen una producción anual que supera un cierto valor, etc. Los datos así obtenidos pueden presentar un sesgo, o distorsión, debido a la exclusión de los establecimientos que no alcanzan los mínimos fijados. Más aún, con tendencia ascendente, las series reflejarán un desplazamiento del empleo de los pequeños establecimientos hacia los grandes. Cuando el mínimo es bajo, se supone que el ámbito de estas series será muy amplio y permitirá obtener una aproximación muy estrecha de la fluctuación del empleo remunerado.

El segundo tipo se relaciona con una *muestra de establecimientos*. Su principal dificultad es asegurar que la muestra siga siendo representativa del conjunto. Así, por ejemplo, la transformación de la estructura industrial, el auge y la decadencia de establecimientos individuales, la evolución demográfica y las considerables variaciones de los niveles de actividad de algunos sectores económicos contribuyen a una distorsión acumulativa de la muestra que puede llegar a ser importante al cabo de varios años.

Con respecto al primer tipo de estadísticas *(todos los establecimientos de una cierta importancia)*, las de ciertos países, donde sólo se pueden obtener para períodos de un año o más, se las puede combinar con estadísticas del segundo tipo *(muestras de establecimientos)*, que es posible obtener para períodos más breves, mediante enlaces (encadenamiento) o interpolaciones.

Fuente (E). *Estimaciones oficiales*. Estas estadísticas se fundan en las estimaciones oficiales comunicadas por autoridades nacionales que, por lo general, se combinan con informaciones provenientes de una o más de las otras fuentes que aquí se describen.

Fuente (FA). *Registros de seguros*. Esta fuente abarca la población cubierta por regímenes de seguros de salud, accidente, paro y semejantes. El número de contribuyentes o de contribuciones pagadas da una medida del número de personas aseguradas con empleo (las personas sin empleo están exentas del pago de contribuciones). Con frecuencia se excluyen de estas estadísticas las personas que han trabajado muy poco tiempo, las que perciben pagos muy escasos y las mayores de una cierta edad. Además de la evolución del número de personas con empleo, las estadísticas basadas en datos de los registros de seguros también pueden reflejar modificaciones del alcance de la cobertura de ciertos grupos industriales, de ocupaciones o de situación en el empleo.

Cuadro 2A

Empleo: nivel general

Las series de empleo de este cuadro resumido abarcan,

en principio, todas las grandes divisiones de actividad económica y todos los sectores de actividad. Se refieren, en la medida de lo posible, a toda clase de situación en el empleo. Para ciertas series algunas categorías pueden no estar plenamente representadas. Los trabajadores abarcados se indican en el cuadro al centro de cada página para cada serie como *Empleo total, Todas las personas que trabajan* y *Asalariados*. La inclusión o exclusión de datos sobre las fuerzas armadas varía según los países y si se conoce este hecho se señala en las notas de pie de página.

Cuadro 2B

Empleo total, por actividad económica

En este cuadro se presentan cifras absolutas de la distribución del empleo por actividad económica, siguiendo sea la CIIU Rev.2, la CIIU Rev.3 o la CIIU Rev.4 o dos de las tres versiones, lado a lado, cuando la última de ellas se ha introducido en el curso de la década que abarcan las series del *Anuario*.

Cuadro 2C

Empleo total, por ocupación

En este cuadro se presentan cifras absolutas de la distribución del empleo por ocupación, siguiendo sea la CIUO-68, sea la CIUO-88 o ambas, lado a lado, cuando la revisión posterior de esta clasificación internacional ha sido introducida en el curso de la década que abarcan las series del *Anuario*.

Cuadro 2D

Empleo total, por situación en el empleo

Estas series abarcan en principio el número total de personas con empleo para todos los grupos de la *Clasificación Internacional de la Situación en el Empleo (CISE-93)*.

Cuadro 2E

Empleo remunerado, por actividad económica

Los datos de este cuadro abarcan todas las series disponibles sobre empleo remunerado que sólo se refieran a los asalariados (obreros y empleados) y que provengan, de preferencia, de una encuesta de establecimientos. Sin embargo, los datos sobre empleo remunerado también pueden tener otras fuentes (como por ejemplo encuestas sobre la fuerza de trabajo o registros administrativos) y, en algunos casos, que se indican para cada serie en el centro de la página, diferente alcance de los trabajadores abarcados.

Cuadro 2F

Empleo remunerado en las industrias manufactureras

Este cuadro contiene datos sobre el empleo remunerado de las industrias manufactureras en su conjunto y, de ser posible, para todos los componentes de esta categoría de clasificación, siguiendo sea la CIIU Rev.2 a niveles de codificación de tres dígitos, sea la CIIU Rev.3 (códigos 15 a 37) o CIIU Rev. 4 (códigos 10 a 33). Si en el curso de los diez años de las series del *Anuario* se dispone de datos según ambas versiones, se les presenta lado a lado.

El número de personas con empleo remunerado por actividad económica de los cuadros de este capítulo tiene, en la medida de lo posible, la misma fuente que los datos que figuran en los cuadros correspondientes a las horas de trabajo (capítulo 4) y a los salarios (capítulo 5). Al comparar los datos sobre el empleo que figuran en los seis cuadros de este capítulo, se deberán tener en cuenta no sólo las diferentes fuentes sino también las diferencias de ámbito y alcance de las estadísticas presentadas. Detalles sobre los grupos de situación en el empleo y las divisiones de actividad económica que se omiten o se incluyen, y otros sobre el alcance geográfico y las fechas alternas de los períodos de referencia, se dan en cada cuadro y sus notas de pie de página.

En el Apéndice figuran versiones abreviadas de la *Clasificación Internacional Industrial Uniforme de Todas las Actividades Económicas (CIIU Rev.2, CIIU Rev.3 y CIIU Rev.4)*, la *Clasificación Internacional Uniforme de Ocupaciones (CIUO-68 y CIUO-88)* y la *Clasificación Internacional de la Situación en el Empleo (CISE-1993)*.

Nota

[1] Para más amplias informaciones sobre el diferente alcance de las definiciones, métodos de cálculo, etc., de las series nacionales, véanse OIT: *Fuentes y Métodos: Estadísticas del Trabajo* (anteriormente *Fuentes y Métodos Estadísticos*), vol. 2: «Empleo, salarios, horas de trabajo y costo de la mano de obra (encuestas de establecimientos)», segunda edición (Ginebra 1995); vol. 3: «Población económicamente activa, empleo, desempleo y horas de trabajo (encuestas de hogares)», segunda edición (Ginebra, 1990); vol. 4: «Empleo, desempleo, salarios y horas de trabajo (registros administrativos y fuentes conexas)» (Ginebra, 1989).

	Thousands / Milliers / Millares									
	1999	2000	2001	2002	2003	2004	2005	2006	2007	2008

AFRICA-AFRIQUE-AFRICA

Algérie (BA) [1][2]
Total employment - Emploi total - Empleo total

	1999	2000	2001	2002	2003	2004	2005	2006	2007	2008
Total	.	.	6 228.8	.	6 684.1	7 798.4	8 181.5	8 868.8	8 594.2	.
M-H	.	.	5 345.2	.	5 751.0	6 439.2	6 988.1	7 371.9	7 247.4	.
W-F-M	.	.	883.6	.	933.0	1 356.1	1 193.4	1 496.9	1 346.9	.

Botswana (BA) [3][4]
Total employment - Emploi total - Empleo total

	1999	2000	2001	2002	2003	2004	2005	2006	2007	2008
Total	.	483.4	.	.	462.4	.	.	539.2	.	.
M-H	.	269.4	.	.	245.4	.	.	281.8	.	.
W-F-M	.	214.0	.	.	217.0	.	.	257.4	.	.

Egypt (BA) [3][5][6]
Total employment - Emploi total - Empleo total

	1999	2000	2001	2002	2003	2004	2005	2006	2007	2008
Total	16 750.2	17 203.3	17 556.7	17 856.2	18 118.6	18 717.4	19 341.7	20 444.0	21 723.8	.
M-H	13 611.0	13 958.5	14 361.1	14 550.7	14 651.7	14 936.4	15 592.7	16 559.0	17 089.5	.
W-F-M	3 139.2	3 244.8	3 195.6	3 305.5	3 466.9	3 781.0	3 749.0	3 884.2	4 634.3	.

Madagascar (B) [7][8]
Total employment - Emploi total - Empleo total

	1999	2000	2001	2002	2003	2004	2005	2006	2007	2008
Total	.	.	.	.	8 098.5	.	9 570.4	.	.	.
M-H	.	.	.	.	4 135.7	.	4 841.8	.	.	.
W-F-M	.	.	.	.	3 962.8	.	4 728.6	.	.	.

Mali (BA) [1]
Total employment - Emploi total - Empleo total

	1999	2000	2001	2002	2003	2004	2005	2006	2007	2008
Total	.	.	.	.	.	2 370.8	.	.	.	.
M-H	.	.	.	.	.	1 388.3	.	.	.	.
W-F-M	.	.	.	.	.	982.5	.	.	.	.

Maroc (BA) [1]
Total employment - Emploi total - Empleo total

	1999	2000	2001	2002	2003	2004	2005	2006	2007	2008
Total	.	.	9 329.8 [9]	9 487.5 [9]	9 602.8	9 821.9	9 913.3	9 927.7	10 056.2	10 189.3
M-H	.	.	6 914.1 [9]	7 100.6 [9]	7 074.8	7 155.0	7 240.7	7 233.3	7 323.7	7 453.5
W-F-M	.	.	2 415.7 [9]	2 387.0 [9]	2 528.0	2 666.9	2 672.6	2 694.4	2 732.6	2 735.8

Mauritius (BA) [3][10]
Total employment - Emploi total - Empleo total

	1999	2000	2001	2002	2003	2004	2005	2006	2007	2008
Total	.	.	.	.	.	487.0	490.4	499.1	502.1 [11]	519.0
M-H	.	.	.	.	.	327.9	329.1	332.5	335.0 [11]	341.0
W-F-M	.	.	.	.	.	159.1	161.3	166.6	167.1 [11]	178.0

Mauritius (E)
Total employment - Emploi total - Empleo total

	1999	2000	2001	2002	2003	2004	2005	2006	2007	2008
Total	.	485.9	493.6	493.8	500.4	504.5	507.2	515.3	523.7	543.0
M-H	.	323.2	326.4	328.6	332.4	336.9	338.5	340.5	347.1	355.7
W-F-M	.	162.7	167.2	165.2	168.0	167.6	168.7	174.8	176.6	187.3

Namibia (BA) [12]
Total employment - Emploi total - Empleo total

	1999	2000	2001	2002	2003	2004	2005	2006	2007	2008
Total	.	431.849	406.771	.	.	385.329	.	.	.	.
M-H	.	226.828	223.015	.	.	216.651	.	.	.	.
W-F-M	.	205.021	183.756	.	.	168.678	.	.	.	.

Réunion (E) [1][13]
Total employment - Emploi total - Empleo total

	1999	2000	2001	2002	2003	2004	2005	2006	2007	2008
Total	180.6	188.9	196.8	202.3	205.7	207.6	213.2	220.7	233.2	.

Sao Tomé-et-Principe (E) [1]
Total employment - Emploi total - Empleo total

	1999	2000	2001	2002	2003	2004	2005	2006	2007	2008
Total	.	37.518	43.980	44.474	45.846	42.955	44.314	44.397	.	.
M-H	.	24.475	28.472	27.201	28.492	27.160	27.831	27.671	.	.
W-F-M	.	13.043	15.508	17.273	17.354	15.795	16.482	16.726	.	.

Sénégal (B) [1]
Total employment - Emploi total - Empleo total

	1999	2000	2001	2002	2003	2004	2005	2006	2007	2008
Total	.	.	.	.	.	.	3 152.9	.	.	.
M-H	.	.	.	.	.	.	2 048.1	.	.	.
W-F-M	.	.	.	.	.	.	1 104.8	.	.	.

Sierra Leone (BA) [14]
Total employment - Emploi total - Empleo total

	1999	2000	2001	2002	2003	2004	2005	2006	2007	2008
Total	.	.	.	.	.	1 900.6	.	.	.	.
M-H	.	.	.	.	.	874.7	.	.	.	.
W-F-M	.	.	.	.	.	1 025.9	.	.	.	.

South Africa (BA) [5][15]
Total employment - Emploi total - Empleo total

	1999	2000	2001	2002	2003	2004	2005	2006	2007	2008
Total	.	12 238	11 181	11 296	11 424	11 643	12 301	12 800	13 234	13 713
M-H	.	6 943	6 442	6 614	6 613	6 772	7 055	7 320	7 554	7 672
W-F-M	.	5 295	4 739	4 678	4 810	4 866	5 242	5 480	5 668	6 041

Explanatory notes: see p. 77.

[1] Persons aged 15 years and over. [2] Sep. of each year. [3] Excl. armed forces. [4] Persons aged 12 years and over. [5] Persons aged 15 to 64 years. [6] May and Nov. [7] Persons aged 6 years and over. [8] Excl. armed forces and conscripts. [9] Persons aged 7 years and over. [10] Persons aged 16 years and over. [11] Prior to 2007: persons aged 15 years and over. [12] Persons aged 15 to 69 years. [13] December. [14] Persons aged 10 years and over. [15] Prior to 2008: persons aged 15 years and over; September of each year.

Notes explicatives: voir p. 80.

[1] Personnes âgées de 15 ans et plus. [2] Sept. de chaque année. [3] Non compris les forces armées. [4] Personnes âgées de 12 ans et plus. [5] Personnes âgées de 15 à 64 ans. [6] Mai et nov. [7] Personnes âgées de 6 ans et plus. [8] Non compris les forces armées et les conscrits. [9] Personnes âgées de 7 ans et plus. [10] Personnes âgées de 16 ans et plus. [11] Avant 2006: personnes âgées de 15 ans et plus. [12] Personnes âgées de 15 à 69 ans. [13] Décembre. [14] Personnes âgées de 10 ans et plus. [15] Avant 2008: personnes agées de 15 ans et plus; septembre de chaque année.

Notas explicativas: véase p. 83.

[1] Personas de 15 años y más. [2] Sept. de cada año. [3] Excl. las fuerzas armadas. [4] Personas de 12 años y más. [5] Personas de 15 a 64 años. [6] Mayo y nov. [7] Personas de 6 años y más. [8] Excl. las fuerzas armadas y los conscriptos. [9] Personas de 7 años y más. [10] Personas de 16 años y más. [11] Antes de 2006: personas de 15 años y más. [12] Personas de 15 a 69 años. [13] Diciembre. [14] Personas de 10 años y más. [15] Antes de 2008: personas de 15 años y más; Septiembre de cada año.

EMPLOYMENT — EMPLOI — EMPLEO

General level — Niveau général — Nivel general

	Thousands — Milliers — Millares									
	1999	2000	2001	2002	2003	2004	2005	2006	2007	2008
Saint Helena (A) [1][2]				Total employment - Emploi total - Empleo total						
Total										2.130
M-H										1.174
W-F-M										0.956
Sudan (E) [3]				Total employment - Emploi total - Empleo total						
Total									9 300	
Tanzania, United Republic of (BA) [4]				Total employment - Emploi total - Empleo total						
Total								17 944.6		
M-H								8 779.8		
W-F-M								9 164.7		
Tunisie (BA) [4][5]				Total employment - Emploi total - Empleo total						
Total	2 635.0	2 704.9	2 788.8	2 852.0	2 951.2	2 854.7	2 926.7			
M-H	1 992.1	2 039.5	2 095.4	2 134.2	2 205.8					
W-F-M	642.9	665.4	693.4	717.8	745.4					

AMERICA-AMÉRIQUE-AMERICA

	1999	2000	2001	2002	2003	2004	2005	2006	2007	2008
Antigua and Barbuda (E) [4]				Total employment - Emploi total - Empleo total						
Total			33.801	34.431	35.074	35.728	36.395	37.074	37.765	38.470
M-H			16.976	17.293	17.615	17.944	18.279	18.620	18.967	19.321
W-F-M			16.825	17.139	17.459	17.784	18.116	18.454	18.798	19.149
Argentina (BA) [3][6][7]				Total employment - Emploi total - Empleo total						
Total	8 285.2	8 261.7	8 143.4	8 016.1	8 956.2 [8]	9 415.0	9 638.7	10 040.5 [9]	10 116.0 [10]	10 279.0 [10]
M-H	4 971.4	4 942.0	4 832.4	4 653.6	5 150.9 [8]	5 446.9	5 557.3	5 786.7 [9]		
W-F-M	3 313.8	3 319.8	3 310.9	3 362.5	3 805.3 [8]	3 968.0	4 081.4	4 253.8 [9]		
Aruba (BA) [4][11]				Total employment - Emploi total - Empleo total						
Total								51.605		
M-H								27.210		
W-F-M								24.396		
Bahamas (BA) [4][12][13]				Total employment - Emploi total - Empleo total						
Total	145.35		153.32	152.69	154.97	158.34	160.53	166.51 [14]	171.49	
M-H	77.25		79.08	78.41	79.14	81.74	82.79	85.97 [14]	89.61	
W-F-M	68.11		74.23	74.28	75.83	76.56	77.74	80.54 [14]	81.89	
Barbados (BA) [4][12]				Total employment - Emploi total - Empleo total						
Total	125.2	129.0	130.9	128.6	129.5	132.0	133.5	130.9	133.0	132.2
M-H	67.2	68.0	68.9	67.7	67.4	68.3	69.5	67.9	69.7	68.7
W-F-M	58.0	61.0	61.9	60.9	62.0	63.8	64.0	63.1	63.3	63.5
Belize (BA) [12][13][15]				Total employment - Emploi total - Empleo total						
Total	77.755		85.869	84.720			98.589 [16]	102.234	111.835	114.465 [14]
M-H	53.680		58.546	58.582			64.878 [16]	67.909	72.381	
W-F-M	24.075		27.323	26.138			33.711 [16]	34.325	39.454	
Bermuda (CA) [17]				Total employment - Emploi total - Empleo total						
Total	37.849	38.017	37.597	37.815	37.686	38.363	38.947	39.686	39.851	
M-H	19.197	19.310	19.301	19.411	19.520	19.937	20.257	20.730	20.727	
W-F-M	18.652	18.707	18.296	18.404	18.166	18.426	18.690	18.956	19.124	
Bolivia (BA) [3][18]				Total employment - Emploi total - Empleo total						
Total	3 637.9	3 637.0	3 884.3	3 824.9		4 194.8	4 257.2	4 550.3	4 672.4	
M-H	2 000.5	2 032.2	2 128.4	2 160.2		2 283.0	2 356.0	2 505.6	2 577.0	
W-F-M	1 637.4	1 604.9	1 755.8	1 664.8		1 911.7	1 901.1	2 044.7	2 095.4	
Brasil (BA) [3][19]				Total employment - Emploi total - Empleo total						
Total	71 676.0		76 098.3	78 958.9	80 163.5 [20]	84 596.3	87 189.4	89 318.0	90 786.0	
M-H	42 813.0		45 126.8	46 334.2	46 935.1 [20]	49 242.0	50 493.7	51 400.0	52 363.0	
W-F-M	28 864.0		30 971.6	32 624.6	33 228.4 [20]	35 354.3	36 695.7	37 918.0	38 423.0	

Explanatory notes: see p. 77.

[1] Persons aged 15 to 69 years. [2] Feb. [3] Persons aged 10 years and over. [4] Persons aged 15 years and over. [5] 1999-2003: figures revised on the basis of the 2004 census results. [6] 31 Urban agglomerations. [7] Second semester. [8] Methodology revised; data not strictly comparable; Prior to 2003: May and October. [9] Prior to 2006: 28 urban agglomerations. [10] Second quarter. [11] Oct. [12] Excl. armed forces. [13] April of each year. [14] May. [15] Persons aged 14 years and over. [16] Incl. the armed forces. [17] Aug. of each year. [18] Excl. conscripts. [19] Sep. of each year. [20] Prior to 2003: Excl. rural population of Rondônia, Acre, Amazonas, Roraima, Pará and Amapá.

Notes explicatives: voir p. 80.

[1] Personnes âgées de 15 à 69 ans. [2] Fév. [3] Personnes âgées de 10 ans et plus. [4] Personnes âgées de 15 ans et plus. [5] 1999-2003: données révisées sur la base des résultats du Recensement de 2004. [6] 31 agglomérations urbaines. [7] Second semestre. [8] Méthodologie révisée; les données ne sont pas strictement comparables; Avant 2003: mai et octobre. [9] Avant 2006: 28 agglomérations urbaines. [10] Deuxième trimestre. [11] Oct. [12] Non compris les forces armées. [13] Avril de chaque année. [14] Mai. [15] Personnes âgées de 14 ans et plus. [16] Y compris les forces armées. [17] Août de chaque année. [18] Non compris les conscrits. [19] Sept. de chaque année. [20] Avant 2003: Non compris la population rurale de Rondônia, Acre, Amazonas, Roraima, Pará et Amapá.

Notas explicativas: véase p. 83.

[1] Personas de 15 a 69 años. [2] Feb. [3] Personas de 10 años y más. [4] Personas de 15 años y más. [5] 1999-2003: datos revisados de acuerdo con los resultados del Censo de 2004. [6] 31 aglomerados urbanos. [7] Segundo semestre. [8] Metodología revisada; los datos no son estrictamente comparables; antes de 2003: mayo y octubre. [9] Antes de 2006: 28 aglomerados úrbanos [10] Segundo trimestre. [11] Oct. [12] Excl. las fuerzas armadas. [13] Abril de cada año. [14] Mayo. [15] Personas de 14 años y más. [16] Incl. las fuerzas armadas. [17] Agosto de cada año. [18] Excl. los conscriptos. [19] Sept. de cada año. [20] Antes de 2003: Excl. la población rural de Rondonia, Acre, Amazonas, Roraima, Pará y Amapá.

EMPLOYMENT — EMPLOI — EMPLEO

General level — Niveau général — Nivel general

	Thousands			Milliers				Millares		
	1999	2000	2001	2002	2003	2004	2005	2006	2007	2008
Canada (BA) [1] [2] [3]				*Total employment - Emploi total - Empleo total*						
Total	14 406.7	14 764.2	14 946.2	15 310.4	15 672.3	15 947.0	16 169.7	16 484.3	16 866.4	17 125.8
M-H	7 797.2	7 973.9	8 035.8	8 184.4	8 348.1	8 480.6	8 594.7	8 727.1	8 888.9	9 021.3
W-F-M	6 609.6	6 790.4	6 910.3	7 126.0	7 324.2	7 466.4	7 575.0	7 757.2	7 977.5	8 104.5
Cayman Islands (BA) [1] [4] [5]				*Total employment - Emploi total - Empleo total*						
Total	.	.	25.862	27.354	28.827	28.947 [6]	35.464	35.016 [6]	36.026	37.450
M-H	.	.	.	13.752	13.840	14.455 [6]	18.628	18.408 [6]	18.806	19.355
W-F-M	.	.	.	13.602	14.987	14.492 [6]	16.836	16.608 [6]	17.220	18.094
Colombia (BA) [7] [8] [9]				*Total employment - Emploi total - Empleo total*						
Total	.	.	15 813.5	15 844.3	16 650.1	16 704.0	17 154.9	16 680.9	17 076.5	17 425.7
M-H	.	.	9 658.1	9 689.2	10 106.6	10 196.8	10 491.3	10 189.9	10 399.9	10 611.0
W-F-M	.	.	6 155.4	6 155.1	6 543.5	6 507.2	6 663.6	6 490.9	6 676.5	6 814.7
Costa Rica (BA) [10] [11]				*Total employment - Emploi total - Empleo total*						
Total	1 300.1	1 318.6	1 552.9	1 586.5	1 640.4	1 653.9	1 776.9	1 829.9	1 925.7	1 957.7
M-H	879.6	902.5	1 013.0	1 037.5	1 069.0	1 093.6	1 153.9	1 172.6	1 222.6	1 229.5
W-F-M	420.5	416.1	539.9	549.0	571.4	560.3	623.0	657.3	703.1	728.2
Cuba (BA) [1] [12]				*Total employment - Emploi total - Empleo total*						
Total	4 359.4	4 379.3	4 505.1	4 558.2	4 607.0	4 641.7	4 722.5	4 754.6	4 867.7	4 948.2 [13]
M-H	2 814.5	2 819.8	2 906.3	2 926.8	2 945.8	2 955.7	2 998.5	2 985.8	3 016.0	3 073.0 [13]
W-F-M	1 544.9	1 559.5	1 598.8	1 631.4	1 661.2	1 686.0	1 724.0	1 768.8	1 851.7	1 875.2 [13]
Chile (BA) [1] [14]				*Total employment - Emploi total - Empleo total*						
Total	5 404.5	5 381.5	5 479.4	5 531.3	5 675.1	5 862.9	5 905.0	6 411.0 [15]	6 566.1	6 740.4
M-H	3 603.6	3 600.5	3 663.7	3 697.0	3 749.7	3 816.1	3 840.2	4 130.2 [15]	4 188.3	4 239.4
W-F-M	1 800.9	1 781.0	1 815.8	1 834.3	1 925.4	2 046.8	2 064.8	2 280.8 [15]	2 377.7	2 501.0
República Dominicana (BA) [9]				*Total employment - Emploi total - Empleo total*						
Total	2 979.5	3 041.1	3 001.7	3 105.5	3 093.0	3 212.8	3 279.1	3 469.9	3 550.9	3 654.0
M-H	2 069.9	2 027.9	2 010.7	2 055.2	2 053.1	2 148.4	2 175.4	2 272.0	2 336.8	2 355.6
W-F-M	909.6	1 013.2	991.1	1 050.3	1 039.9	1 064.4	1 103.7	1 197.9	1 214.1	1 298.4
Ecuador (BA) [9] [16] [17]				*Total employment - Emploi total - Empleo total*						
Total	3 226.1	3 376.1	3 673.2 [18]	3 459.4	3 531.2	3 858.5	3 891.9	4 031.6	4 032.7 [12]	4 063.1 [12]
M-H	1 978.3	2 078.2	2 211.7 [18]	2 131.7	2 138.4	2 288.5	2 327.8	2 416.5	2 365.2 [12]	2 375.8 [12]
W-F-M	1 247.8	1 297.9	1 461.6 [18]	1 327.7	1 392.4	1 570.1	1 564.0	1 615.1	1 667.6 [12]	1 687.2 [12]
El Salvador (BA) [9] [12]				*Total employment - Emploi total - Empleo total*						
Total	2 182.5	2 198.9	2 275.2	2 219.6	2 280.7	2 253.6	2 283.6	2 337.1	2 419.2	.
M-H	1 294.5	1 301.2	1 354.3	1 292.0	1 328.2	1 332.7	1 330.6	1 342.0	1 401.8	.
W-F-M	888.1	897.8	920.9	927.6	952.5	920.9	952.9	995.1	1 017.3	.
Greenland (E) [1] [19]				*Total employment - Emploi total - Empleo total*						
Total	23.282	22.912	23.672	24.074	23.916	24.197	24.819	.	.	.
M-H	11.774	11.636	11.936	12.247	12.110	12.209	12.583	.	.	.
W-F-M	11.508	11.176	11.736	11.827	11.806	11.988	12.236	.	.	.
Guadeloupe (E) [8]				*Total employment - Emploi total - Empleo total*						
Total	124.4	126.3	131.8	134.4	135.7	136.6	138.2	138.1	147.0	.
Guatemala (BA) [8] [9]				*Total employment - Emploi total - Empleo total*						
Total	.	4 511.6	.	4 769.4	4 893.2	4 834.0	.	5 390.5 [15]	.	.
M-H	.	2 913.0	.	3 064.9	3 074.9	3 149.2	.	3 338.7 [15]	.	.
W-F-M	.	1 598.5	.	1 704.5	1 818.3	1 684.8	.	2 051.8 [15]	.	.
Guyane française (BA) [1] [20]				*Total employment - Emploi total - Empleo total*						
Total	.	.	.	44.236	43.451	.	.	.	.	.
M-H	.	.	.	25.834	25.511	.	.	.	.	.
W-F-M	.	.	.	18.402	17.940	.	.	.	.	.
Guyane française (E) [1]				*Total employment - Emploi total - Empleo total*						
Total	43.370	46.076	47.513	49.481	50.483	50.201	50.313	51.871	54.695	.
Honduras (BA) [8] [9]				*Total employment - Emploi total - Empleo total*						
Total	2 299.0 [21]	.	2 288.7	2 351.1	2 426.1	2 439.0	2 543.5	2 724.4	2 836.1	.
M-H	1 472.1 [21]	.	1 535.9	1 593.0	1 610.9	1 638.1	1 736.5	1 788.7	1 848.7	.
W-F-M	826.9 [21]	.	752.8	758.0	815.3	800.9	807.0	935.7	987.4	.

Explanatory notes: see p. 77.

[1] Persons aged 15 years and over. [2] Excl. residents of the Territories and indigenous persons living on reserves. [3] Excl. full-time members of the armed forces. [4] Excl. armed forces and conscripts. [5] Oct. [6] April. [7] From 2001, figures revised on the basis of the 2005 census results. [8] Excl. armed forces. [9] Persons aged 10 years and over. [10] Persons aged 12 years and over. [11] July of each year. [12] Dec. [13] February - April [14] Fourth quarter of each year. [15] Methodology revised; data not strictly comparable. [16] Urban areas. [17] Nov. of each year. [18] July. [19] Jan. of each year. [20] June of each year. [21] March.

Notes explicatives: voir p. 80.

[1] Personnes âgées de 15 ans et plus. [2] Non compris les habitants des "Territoires" et les populations indigènes vivant dans les réserves. [3] Non compris les membres à temps complet des forces armées. [4] Non compris les forces armées et les conscrits. [5] Oct. [6] Avril. [7] A partir de 2001, données révisées sur la base des résultats du recensement de 2005. [8] Non compris les forces armées. [9] Personnes âgées de 10 ans et plus. [10] Personnes âgées de 12 ans et plus. [11] Juillet de chaque année. [12] Déc. [13] Février - Avril [14] Quatrième trimestre de chaque année. [15] Méthodologie révisée; les données ne sont pas strictement comparables. [16] Régions urbaines. [17] Nov. de chaque année. [18] Juillet. [19] Jan. de chaque année. [20] Juin de chaque année. [21] Mars.

Notas explicativas: véase p. 83.

[1] Personas de 15 años y más. [2] Excl. a los habitantes de los "Territorios" y a las poblaciones indígenas que viven en reservas. [3] Excl. los miembros a tiempo completo de las fuerzas armadas. [4] Excl. las fuerzas armadas y los conscriptos. [5] Oct. [6] Abril. [7] A partir de 2001, datos revisados de acuerdo con los resultados del censo de 2005. [8] Excl. las fuerzas armadas. [9] Personas de 10 años y más. [10] Personas de 12 años y más. [11] Julio de cada año. [12] Dic. [13] Febrero - Abril [14] Cuarto trimestre de cada año. [15] Metodología revisada; los datos no son estrictamente comparables. [16] Areas urbanas. [17] Nov. de cada año. [18] Julio. [19] Ene. de cada año. [20] Junio de cada año. [21] Marzo.

EMPLOYMENT / EMPLOI / EMPLEO

General level / Niveau général / Nivel general

	Thousands			Milliers				Millares		
	1999	2000	2001	2002	2003	2004	2005	2006	2007	2008
Jamaica (BA) [1]				*Total employment - Emploi total - Empleo total*						
Total	936.8	935.6	942.3	1 025.9	1 056.6	1 058.7	1 091.7	1 129.5	1 170.2	1 167.8
M-H	551.9	552.5	556.6	596.3	615.3	613.9	629.3	649.8	670.4	658.3
W-F-M	384.9	383.1	385.7	429.6	441.2	444.8	462.4	479.7	499.8	509.5
Martinique (E) [2]				*Total employment - Emploi total - Empleo total*						
Total	115.4	121.2	120.4	122.1	123.4	123.3	125.3	126.4	139.2	.
México (BA) [1][3]				*Total employment - Emploi total - Empleo total*						
Total	37 279.9	38 044.5	38 065.8	38 939.7	39 221.5	40 561.0	40 791.8	42 197.8	42 906.7	43 866.7
M-H	24 805.7	25 014.1	25 055.1	25 422.8	25 713.5	26 138.0	25 853.1	26 597.9	26 840.6	27 401.7
W-F-M	12 474.2	13 030.4	13 010.6	13 516.8	13 508.0	14 423.0	14 938.7	15 599.9	16 066.0	16 465.0
Netherlands Antilles (BA) [2][4][5]				*Total employment - Emploi total - Empleo total*						
Total	.	50.1	47.7	49.1	52.1	51.5	51.3	52.1	54.0	56.5
M-H	.	25.7	24.5	25.2	26.6	25.3	25.3	26.0	26.7	28.4
W-F-M	.	24.4	23.1	23.9	25.5	26.2	26.0	26.0	27.4	28.2
Nicaragua (BA) [6]				*Total employment - Emploi total - Empleo total*						
Total	.	.	.	.	1 917.0	1 973.1	2 080.9	2 089.8	2 078.8	.
M-H	.	.	.	.	1 178.5	1 239.3	1 296.6	1 303.5	1 307.0	.
W-F-M	.	.	.	.	738.4	733.8	784.3	786.3	771.8	.
Panamá (BA) [2][7]				*Total employment - Emploi total - Empleo total*						
Total	961.4	940.1	984.2	1 049.5	1 080.5	1 134.7	1 188.3	1 210.7	1 264.0	1 333.8
M-H	638.0	625.0	659.2	687.6	703.3	734.3	755.7	777.5	799.1	837.0
W-F-M	323.4	315.1	325.1	362.0	377.2	400.4	432.6	433.1	464.9	496.8
Paraguay (BA) [6][8]				*Total employment - Emploi total - Empleo total*						
Total	.	2 413.6 [9]	.	2 259.7	2 350.6	2 617.7	2 560.6	2 553.7 [10]	2 716.4	2 810.5
M-H	.	1 491.4 [9]	.	1 431.3	1 461.0	1 598.2	1 561.7	1 592.9 [10]	1 653.6	1 726.4
W-F-M	.	922.3 [9]	.	828.4	889.6	1 019.5	998.9	960.8 [10]	1 062.8	1 084.1
Perú (BA) [1][11]				*Total employment - Emploi total - Empleo total*						
Total	.	.	.	3 338.9 [8]	3 703.0 [12]	3 652.5	3 529.0	3 851.2	4 163.7	4 246.7
M-H	.	.	.	1 834.1 [8]	2 074.6 [12]	2 054.0	1 981.3	2 133.6	2 269.0	2 294.8
W-F-M	.	.	.	1 504.7 [8]	1 628.4 [12]	1 598.5	1 547.7	1 717.6	1 894.7	1 951.8
Perú (BA) [1][13]				*Total employment - Emploi total - Empleo total*						
Total	7 211.2	7 128.4	7 619.9	7 578.2 [8]	8 165.7 [8]	8 238.6	8 216.0	8 694.0	9 197.8	9 445.9
M-H	3 980.4	4 067.6	4 232.6	4 234.2 [8]	4 537.0 [8]	4 616.2	4 562.8	4 821.9	5 015.0	5 143.2
W-F-M	3 230.8	3 060.7	3 387.3	3 344.0 [8]	3 628.8 [8]	3 622.4	3 653.2	3 872.1	4 182.8	4 302.7
Puerto Rico (BA) [14][15]				*Total employment - Emploi total - Empleo total*						
Total	1 142	1 162	1 134	1 170	1 201	1 226	1 250	1 253	1 241	1 209
M-H	665	670	652	665	676	690	697	695	677	659
W-F-M	477	492	482	502	525	537	553	558	564	550
Saint Lucia (BA) [2]				*Total employment - Emploi total - Empleo total*						
Total	59.850	63.470	.	58.525	63.868	62.265	.	.	.	.
M-H	31.830	35.030	.	32.105	36.475	34.838	.	.	.	.
W-F-M	28.020	28.440	.	26.420	27.393	27.428	.	.	.	.
Trinidad and Tobago (BA) [2]				*Total employment - Emploi total - Empleo total*						
Total	489.4	503.1	514.1	525.1	534.1	562.3	574.0	586.2	587.8	597.6
M-H	310.1	316.9	326.0	329.0	330.6	342.0	343.6	348.5	354.2	353.5
W-F-M	179.3	186.2	188.1	196.1	203.5	220.3	230.4	237.7	233.6	245.9
Turks and Caicos Islands (BA) [2]				*Total employment - Emploi total - Empleo total*						
Total	.	.	10.180	11.473	14.051	15.161	17.442	18.195	19.587	.
M-H	.	.	.	.	8.439	8.957	10.346	10.936	12.214	.
W-F-M	.	.	.	.	5.612	6.204	7.093	7.259	7.373	.
United States (BA) [14][16]				*Total employment - Emploi total - Empleo total*						
Total	133 488	135 208	135 073	136 485	137 736	139 252	141 730	144 427	146 047	145 362
M-H	71 446	72 293	72 080	72 903	73 332	74 524	75 973	77 502	78 254	77 486
W-F-M	62 042	62 915	62 992	63 582	64 404	64 728	65 757	66 925	67 792	67 876
Uruguay (BA) [1][17]				*Total employment - Emploi total - Empleo total*						
Total	1 082.1	1 067.6	1 076.2	1 038.3	1 032.0	1 077.9	1 114.5	1 413.5 [18]	1 482.1	.
M-H	623.7	613.4	617.7	597.9	589.7	617.3	620.1	822.4 [18]	852.9	.
W-F-M	458.4	454.2	458.5	440.4	442.3	460.6	494.4	591.0 [18]	629.1	.

Explanatory notes: see p. 77.

[1] Persons aged 14 years and over. [2] Persons aged 15 years and over. [3] Second quarter of each year. [4] Curaçao. [5] Oct. of each year. [6] Persons aged 10 years and over. [7] Aug. of each year. [8] Fourth quarter. [9] Year beginning in September of year indicated. [10] November 2006 - february 2007. [11] Metropolitan Lima. [12] May-Dec. [13] Urban areas. [14] Persons aged 16 years and over. [15] Civilian labour force employed. [16] Excl. armed forces. [17] Excl. conscripts. [18] Prior to 2006: urban areas.

Notes explicatives: voir p. 80.

[1] Personnes âgées de 14 ans et plus. [2] Personnes âgées de 15 ans et plus. [3] Deuxième trimestre de chaque année. [4] Curaçao. [5] Oct. de chaque année. [6] Personnes âgées de 10 ans et plus. [7] Août de chaque année. [8] Quatrième trimestre. [9] Année commençant en septembre de l'année indiquée. [10] Novembre 2006 - février 2007. [11] Lima métropolitaine. [12] Mai-déc. [13] Régions urbaines. [14] Personnes âgées de 16 ans et plus. [15] Main-d'oeuvre civile occupée. [16] Non compris les forces armées. [17] Non compris les conscrits. [18] Avant 2006: régions urbaines.

Notas explicativas: véase p. 83.

[1] Personas de 14 años y más. [2] Personas de 15 años y más. [3] Segundo trimestre de cada año. [4] Curaçao. [5] Oct. de cada año. [6] Personas de 10 años y más. [7] Agosto de cada año. [8] Cuarto trimestre. [9] Año que comienza en septiembre del año indicado. [10] Noviembre 2006 - febrero 2007. [11] Lima metropolitana. [12] Mayo-dic. [13] Areas urbanas. [14] Personas de 16 años y más. [15] Fuerza de trabajo civil ocupada. [16] Excl. las fuerzas armadas. [17] Excl. los conscriptos. [18] Antes de 2006: areas urbanas.

EMPLOYMENT / EMPLOI / EMPLEO

General level / Niveau général / Nivel general

	Thousands / Milliers / Millares									
	1999	2000	2001	2002	2003	2004	2005	2006	2007	2008
Venezuela, Rep. Bolivariana de (BA) [1][2][3]				Total employment - Emploi total - Empleo total						
Total	8 741.6	8 960.9	9 685.6	9 786.2	9 993.8	10 417.6	10 734.0	11 116.9	11 491.9	11 863.1
M-H	5 610.3	5 722.8	5 995.7	6 029.7	6 140.7	6 403.4	6 620.8	6 894.0	7 073.0	7 264.4
W-F-M	3 131.3	3 238.1	3 689.9	3 756.5	3 853.1	4 014.2	4 113.1	4 223.0	4 418.9	4 598.6

ASIA-ASIE-ASIA

	1999	2000	2001	2002	2003	2004	2005	2006	2007	2008
Afghanistan (BA) [2]				Total employment - Emploi total - Empleo total						
Total	.	.	.	.	.	.	3 932.5	.	.	.
M-H	.	.	.	.	.	.	2 102.3	.	.	.
W-F-M	.	.	.	.	.	.	1 830.2	.	.	.
Armenia (BA) [4][5]				Total employment - Emploi total - Empleo total						
Total	.	.	.	.	.	.	.	.	1 188.5	.
M-H	.	.	.	.	.	.	.	.	654.6	.
W-F-M	.	.	.	.	.	.	.	.	533.9	.
Armenia (E) [1]				Total employment - Emploi total - Empleo total						
Total	1 298.2	1 277.7	1 264.9	1 106.4 [6]	1 107.6	1 081.7	1 097.8	1 092.4	1 085.3	.
M-H	689.4	696.8	682.9	578.5 [6]	581.8	584.2	597.1	593.0	589.3	.
W-F-M	608.8	580.9	582.0	527.9 [6]	525.8	497.5	500.7	499.4	496.0	.
Azerbaijan (BA) [2][7]				Total employment - Emploi total - Empleo total						
Total	.	.	.	.	3 377.8	.	.	3 985.9	4 014.0	4 056.0
M-H	.	.	.	.	1 975.6	.	.	2 105.7	2 020.5	2 048.3
W-F-M	.	.	.	.	1 402.2	.	.	1 880.2	1 993.5	2 007.7
Azerbaijan (E) [2]				Total employment - Emploi total - Empleo total						
Total	3 702.8	3 704.5	3 715.0	3 726.5	3 747.0	3 809.1	3 850.2	3 973.0	4 041.1	4 056.0
M-H	1 936.6	1 937.5	1 945.0	1 948.0	1 959.7	1 995.8	2 017.4	2 054.1	2 028.5	2 048.3
W-F-M	1 766.2	1 767.0	1 770.0	1 778.5	1 787.3	1 813.3	1 832.8	1 918.9	1 985.6	2 007.7
China (E) [8][9][10]				Total employment - Emploi total - Empleo total						
Total	713 940	720 850	730 250	737 400	744 320	752 000	758 250	764 000	769 900	774 800
Georgia (BA) [1][2]				Total employment - Emploi total - Empleo total						
Total	1 732.6	1 839.3	1 877.7	1 839.2	1 814.5	1 783.3	1 744.6	1 747.3	1 704.3	1 601.9
M-H	884.8	946.9	966.7	954.1	957.5	926.5	915.2	920.4	888.1	855.6
W-F-M	847.8	892.4	911.0	885.1	857.0	856.8	829.4	826.8	816.2	746.3
Hong Kong, China (BA) [2][11]				Total employment - Emploi total - Empleo total						
Total	3 112.1	3 207.3	3 252.9	3 218.4	3 190.6	3 273.5	3 336.6	3 400.8	3 483.8	3 518.8
M-H	1 816.5	1 854.5	1 845.7	1 794.0	1 764.3	1 800.8	1 822.6	1 840.4	1 869.0	1 870.0
W-F-M	1 295.6	1 352.8	1 407.3	1 424.4	1 426.3	1 472.7	1 514.0	1 560.4	1 614.8	1 648.8
Indonesia (BA) [2][12]				Total employment - Emploi total - Empleo total						
Total	88 817	89 838	90 807	91 647	92 811	93 722	93 958 [13]	95 457	99 930	102 553
M-H	54 908	55 439	57 131	58 583	59 500	60 582	61 439 [13]	61 977	63 148	63 899
W-F-M	33 908	34 399	33 676	33 064	33 311	33 141	32 519 [13]	33 480	36 782	38 653
Iran, Islamic Rep. of (BA) [14]				Total employment - Emploi total - Empleo total						
Total	.	.	.	.	.	.	20 619	20 841	21 092	.
M-H	.	.	.	.	.	.	16 660	16 872	17 230	.
W-F-M	.	.	.	.	.	.	3 962	3 970	3 862	.
Israel (BA) [1][2]				Total employment - Emploi total - Empleo total						
Total	2 136.7	2 221.2	2 264.9	2 284.4	2 330.2	2 400.8	2 493.6	2 573.6	2 682.0	2 776.7
M-H	1 176.2	1 211.7	1 236.1	1 238.0	1 257.6	1 300.3	1 339.9	1 383.6	1 441.9	1 489.1
W-F-M	960.5	1 009.5	1 028.6	1 046.4	1 072.6	1 100.5	1 153.7	1 190.0	1 240.1	1 287.6
Japan (BA) [2]				Total employment - Emploi total - Empleo total						
Total	64 620	64 460	64 120	63 300	63 160	63 290	63 560	63 820	64 120	63 850
M-H	38 310	38 180	37 830	37 360	37 190	37 130	37 230	37 300	37 530	37 290
W-F-M	26 320	26 300	26 290	25 940	25 970	26 160	26 330	26 520	26 590	26 560
Kazakhstan (BA) [2]				Total employment - Emploi total - Empleo total						
Total	.	.	6 699	6 709	6 985	7 182	7 261	7 404	7 631	7 857
M-H	.	.	3 470	3 486	3 618	3 719	3 764	3 809	3 923	4 018
W-F-M	.	.	3 229	3 223	3 367	3 463	3 497	3 595	3 708	3 840

Explanatory notes: see p. 77.

[1] Excl. armed forces. [2] Persons aged 15 years and over. [3] Second semester. [4] Incl. armed forces, Excl. conscripts. [5] Persons aged 16 years and over. [6] Methodology revised; data not strictly comparable. [7] Excl. armed forces and conscripts. [8] Excl. armed forces and reemployed retired persons. [9] Whole national economy. [10] Dec. of each year. [11] Excl. marine, military and institutional populations. [12] Aug. of each year. [13] Nov. [14] Persons aged 10 years and over.

Notes explicatives: voir p. 80.

[1] Non compris les forces armées. [2] Personnes âgées de 15 ans et plus. [3] Second semestre. [4] Y compris les forces armées, Excl. conscrits [5] Personnes âgées de 16 ans et plus. [6] Méthodologie révisée; les données ne sont pas strictement comparables. [7] Non compris les forces armées et les conscrits. [8] Non compris les forces armées et les retraités réemployés. [9] Ensemble de l'économie nationale. [10] Déc. de chaque année. [11] Non compris le personnel militaire, de la marine et la population institutionnelle. [12] Août de chaque année. [13] Nov. [14] Personnes âgées de 10 ans et plus.

Notas explicativas: véase p. 83.

[1] Excl. las fuerzas armadas. [2] Personas de 15 años y más. [3] Segundo semestre. [4] Incl. las fuerzas armadas, excl. los conscriptos. [5] Personas de 16 años y más. [6] Metodología revisada; los datos no son estrictamente comparables. [7] Excl. las fuerzas armadas y los conscriptos. [8] Excl. las fuerzas armadas y los jubilados que trabajan. [9] Toda la economía nacional. [10] Dic. de cada año. [11] Excl. el personal militar y de la marina, y la población institucional. [12] Agosto de cada año. [13] Nov. [14] Personas de 10 años y más.

EMPLOYMENT EMPLOI EMPLEO

General level Niveau général Nivel general

	Thousands			Milliers				Millares		
	1999	2000	2001	2002	2003	2004	2005	2006	2007	2008
Korea, Republic of (BA) [1][2]				Total employment - Emploi total - Empleo total						
Total	20 281	21 156 [3]	21 572	22 169	22 139	22 557	22 856	23 151	23 433	23 577
M-H	11 978	12 387 [3]	12 581	12 944	13 031	13 193	13 330	13 444	13 607	13 703
W-F-M	8 303	8 769 [3]	8 991	9 225	9 108	9 364	9 526	9 706	9 826	9 874
Kyrgyzstan (BA) [2][4]				Total employment - Emploi total - Empleo total						
Total				1 850.1	1 930.5	1 991.2	2 077.1	2 096.1	2 152.7	
M-H				1 051.4	1 083.8	1 140.7	1 195.9	1 214.4	1 251.7	
W-F-M				798.7	846.7	850.5	881.2	881.6	901.1	
Kyrgyzstan (E)				Total employment - Emploi total - Empleo total						
Total	1 764.3	1 768.4	1 787.0	1 807.1	1 837.0	1 879.9	1 931.8			
Liban (B) [2]				Total employment - Emploi total - Empleo total						
Total						1 108.1			1 118.4	
M-H						850.1			842.4	
W-F-M						258.1			276.0	
Macau, China (BA) [5][6]				Total employment - Emploi total - Empleo total						
Total	196.1	195.3	205.0	204.9	205.4	219.1	237.5	265.1	300.4	323.0
M-H	104.2	103.2	108.0	106.4	108.3	115.2	124.3	141.6	160.5	172.3
W-F-M	91.9	92.1	96.9	98.5	97.1	103.9	113.2	123.5	139.8	150.7
Malaysia (BA) [1][7]				Total employment - Emploi total - Empleo total						
Total	8 837.8	9 269.2	9 357.0	9 542.6	9 869.7	9 979.5	10 045.4	10 275.4	10 538.1	10 659.6
M-H	5 851.2	5 973.5	6 055.9	6 141.8	6 323.6	6 390.4	6 470.5	6 618.6	6 747.1	6 851.1
W-F-M	2 986.6	3 295.7	3 301.1	3 400.8	3 546.1	3 589.1	3 574.8	3 656.8	3 791.0	3 808.5
Mongolia (E) [8][9]				Total employment - Emploi total - Empleo total						
Total	813.6	809.0	832.3	870.8	926.5	950.5	968.3	1 009.9	1 024.1	1 041.7
M-H	427.0	416.9	424.6	440.2	468.8	467.1	478.4	491.8	504.2	512.7
W-F-M	386.6	392.1	407.7	430.6	457.7	483.4	488.9	518.1	519.9	529.0
Pakistan (BA) [1][10][11]				Total employment - Emploi total - Empleo total						
Total	37 296	36 847	37 481	38 882	39 852	42 009	42 916	46 952	47 651	
M-H	32 099	31 688	32 233	33 189	34 017	34 903	35 573	37 808	38 118	
W-F-M	5 197	5 159	5 248	5 693	5 835	7 106	7 243	9 144	9 533	
Philippines (BA) [2][12]				Total employment - Emploi total - Empleo total						
Total	27 742	27 452	29 156	30 062	30 635	31 613	32 313	32 636	33 560	34 089
M-H	17 253	17 193	17 923	18 306	18 873	19 646	19 910	20 013	20 542	20 959
W-F-M	10 489	10 259	11 232	11 756	11 762	11 968	12 403	12 622	13 018	13 129
Philippines (CA) [13]				Total employment - Emploi total - Empleo total						
Total	2 853.9		2 418.9		2 428.8		2 742.8			
M-H	1 683.7		1 413.5		1 393.9		1 552.4			
W-F-M	1 170.1		1 005.4		1 034.9		1 190.4			
Qatar (BA) [2][14]				Total employment - Emploi total - Empleo total						
Total			310.291					529.304	827.583	
M-H			266.371					452.599	726.752	
W-F-M			43.920					76.705	100.831	
Saudi Arabia (BA) [2]				Total employment - Emploi total - Empleo total						
Total	5 592.854	5 713.345	5 808.617	5 913.010				7 522.985 [15]	7 766.343	7 956.832
M-H	4 800.625	4 943.511	5 027.718	5 115.826				6 461.490 [15]	6 664.018	6 837.240
W-F-M	792.233	769.834	780.899	797.184				1 061.495 [15]	1 102.325	1 119.592
Singapore (BA) [16][17]				Total employment - Emploi total - Empleo total						
Total	1 518.3		1 582.5 [18]	1 573.7	1 605.4	1 632.1		1 796.7 [18]	1 803.2	1 852.0
M-H	912.1		938.4 [18]	937.7	948.7	960.8		1 036.5 [18]	1 038.4	1 053.6
W-F-M	606.2		644.0 [18]	636.0	656.6	671.3		760.2 [18]	764.8	798.5
Sri Lanka (BA) [19][20]				Total employment - Emploi total - Empleo total						
Total	6 082.6	6 310.1	6 235.6	6 519.4	7 012.8 [21]	7 394.0 [22]	7 518.0	7 105.3	7 041.9	7 174.7
M-H	4 107.5	4 241.5	4 248.9	4 395.2	4 833.5 [21]	5 049.4 [22]	5 134.8	4 610.6	4 653.1	4 663.3
W-F-M	1 975.2	2 068.7	1 986.7	2 124.3	2 179.3 [21]	2 344.6 [22]	2 383.2	2 494.7	2 388.8	2 511.4

Explanatory notes: see p. 77.

[1] Excl. armed forces. [2] Persons aged 15 years and over. [3] Estimates based on the 2000 Population Census results. [4] Nov. of each year. [5] Persons aged 14 years and over. [6] Excl. armed forces and conscripts. [7] Persons aged 15 to 64 years. [8] Persons aged 16 years and over. [9] Dec. of each year. [10] Persons aged 10 years and over. [11] Jan. [12] Excl. regular military living in barracks. [13] Establishments with 20 or more persons employed. [14] March of each year. [15] April. [16] The data refer to the residents (Singapore citizens and permanent residents) aged 15 years and over. [17] June. [18] Methodology revised; data not strictly comparable. [19] Persons aged 10 years and over. [20] Excl. Northern and Eastern provinces. [21] Excl. Northern province. [22] Excl. Mullativu and Killinochchi districts.

Notes explicatives: voir p. 80.

[1] Non compris les forces armées. [2] Personnes âgées de 15 ans et plus. [3] Estimations basées sur les résultats du Recensement de la population de 2000. [4] Nov. de chaque année. [5] Personnes âgées de 14 ans et plus. [6] Non compris les forces armées et les conscrits. [7] Personnes âgées de 15 à 64 ans. [8] Personnes âgées de 16 ans et plus. [9] Déc. de chaque année. [10] Personnes âgées de 10 ans et plus. [11] Janv. [12] Non compris les militaires de carrière vivant dans des casernes. [13] Etablissements occupant 20 personnes et plus. [14] Mars de chaque année. [15] Avril. [16] Les données se réfèrent aux résidents (citoyens de Singapour et résidents permanents) âgés de 15 ans et plus. [17] Juin. [18] Méthodologie révisée; les données ne sont pas strictement comparables. [19] Personnes âgées de 10 ans et plus. [20] Non compris les provinces du Nord et de l'Est. [21] Non compris la province du Nord. [22] Non compris les provinces de Mullativu et Killinochchi.

Notas explicativas: véase p. 83.

[1] Excl. las fuerzas armadas. [2] Personas de 15 años y más. [3] Estimaciones basadas en los resultados del Censo de población de 2000. [4] Nov. de cada año. [5] Personas de 14 años y más. [6] Excl. las fuerzas armadas y los conscriptos. [7] Personas de 15 a 64 años. [8] Personas de 16 años y más. [9] Dic. de cada año. [10] Personas de 10 años y más. [11] Enero. [12] Excl. los militares profesionales que viven en casernas. [13] Establecimientos con 20 y más trabajadores. [14] Marzo de cada año. [15] Abril. [16] Los datos se refieren a los residentes (ciudadanos de Singapur y residentes permanentes) de 15 años y más. [17] Junio. [18] Metodología revisada; los datos no son estrictamente comparables. [19] Personas de 10 años y más. [20] Excl. las provincias del Norte y del Este. [21] Excl. la provincia del Norte. [22] Excl. las provincias de Mullativu y Killinocchchi.

Thousands — Milliers — Millares

	1999	2000	2001	2002	2003	2004	2005	2006	2007	2008
Syrian Arab Republic (BA) [1]				Total employment - Emploi total - Empleo total						
Total	.	.	4 730.0	4 821.8 |	4 468.9 [2]	4 339.3	4 693.5	4 859.9	4 946.0	.
M-H	.	.	3 926.0	3 933.4 |	3 708.2 [2]	3 709.8	4 063.1	4 229.7	4 316.4	
W-F-M	.	.	804.0	888.4 |	760.7 [2]	629.5	630.4	630.2	629.6	
Taiwan, China (BA) [1][3]				Total employment - Emploi total - Empleo total						
Total	9 385	9 491	9 383	9 454	9 573	9 786	9 942	10 111	10 294	10 403
M-H	5 624	5 670	5 553	5 547	5 579	5 680	5 752	5 810	5 868	5 902
W-F-M	3 761	3 821	3 830	3 907	3 994	4 106	4 190	4 301	4 426	4 501
Tajikistan (BA) [1]				Total employment - Emploi total - Empleo total						
Total	1 737.0	1 745.5	.	1 857.1	1 884.8	2 452.6	2 111.7	2 137.0		.
M-H	.	.	.	.	.	1 441.7	.	.		
W-F-M	.	.	.	.	.	1 010.8	.	.		
Thailand (BA) [1][3][4]				Total employment - Emploi total - Empleo total						
Total	32 087.1	33 001.0 |	33 483.7 [5]	34 262.9	34 677.1	35 711.6	36 302.4	36 344.5	37 122.0	37 836.6
M-H	17 721.1	18 164.9 |	18 471.1 [5]	18 872.1	19 081.5	19 698.8	19 470.3	19 638.2	19 976.7	20 405.0
W-F-M	14 365.9	14 836.1 |	15 012.7 [5]	15 390.8	15 595.6	16 012.8	16 832.1	16 706.3	17 145.3	17 431.6
United Arab Emirates (BA) [1][6]				Total employment - Emploi total - Empleo total						
Total	.	.	.	.	.	.	.	.	.	1 846.150
M-H	.	.	.	.	.	.	.	.	.	1 501.293
W-F-M	.	.	.	.	.	.	.	.	.	344.857
Uzbekistan (E) [1]				Total employment - Emploi total - Empleo total						
Total	8 885	9 000	9 100	9 300	.	9 900	10 200	.	.	.
Viet Nam (BA) [1][7]				Total employment - Emploi total - Empleo total						
Total	38 119.9	38 367.6	39 000.3	40 162.3	41 175.7	42 315.6 |	42 526.9	43 338.9	44 173.8	44 915.8
M-H	19 028.5	19 292.1	19 743.7	20 355.6	20 959.2	21 649.3	.	.	.	.
W-F-M	19 091.4	19 075.5	19 256.5	19 806.7	20 216.5	20 666.3	.	.	.	.
West Bank and Gaza Strip (BA) [1]				Total employment - Emploi total - Empleo total						
Total	588.000	597.440 |	504.786 [8]	476.661	564.571	578.439	632.939	666.375	665.620	647.022
M-H	502.000	504.220 |	427.889 [8]	398.778	467.371	473.755	527.806	546.000	538.019	525.696
W-F-M	86.000	93.220 |	76.897 [8]	77.883	97.200	104.683	105.132	120.375	127.602	121.326

EUROPE-EUROPE-EUROPA

	1999	2000	2001	2002	2003	2004	2005	2006	2007	2008
Austria (BA) [1][9]				Total employment - Emploi total - Empleo total						
Total	3 762.3	3 776.5	3 799.6	3 835.7	3 798.4 |	3 744.0 [10]	3 824.4	3 928.3	4 027.9	4 090.0
M-H	2 139.7	2 145.6	2 142.5	2 139.0	2 101.8 |	2 061.5 [10]	2 095.2	2 147.5	2 208.5	2 222.1
W-F-M	1 622.7	1 631.0	1 657.1	1 696.7	1 696.6 |	1 682.5 [10]	1 729.2	1 780.7	1 819.4	1 867.9
Belarus (DA) [11]				Total employment - Emploi total - Empleo total						
Total	4 442.0	4 441.0	4 417.4	4 380.8	4 339.3	4 316.3	4 349.8	4 401.9 |	4 445.3 [2]	4 638.1
M-H	2 127.8	2 113.9	2 085.0	2 056.9	2 033.8	2 029.0	2 049.2	2 078.1 |	2 099.8 [2]	2 188.7
W-F-M	2 314.2	2 327.1	2 332.4	2 323.9	2 305.5	2 287.3	2 300.6	2 323.8 |	2 345.5 [2]	2 449.4
Belgique (BA) [1][12]				Total employment - Emploi total - Empleo total						
Total	4 006.9 [13]	4 092.2	4 051.2	4 069.8	4 070.4	4 139.2	4 235.3	4 264.0	4 380.3	4 445.9
M-H	2 321.4 [13]	2 367.6	2 346.3	2 339.2	2 317.0	2 354.3	2 386.8	2 391.6	2 443.7	2 460.7
W-F-M	1 685.5 [13]	1 724.5	1 704.9	1 730.7	1 753.4	1 784.9	1 848.5	1 872.4	1 936.6	1 985.2
Bosnia and Herzegovina (BA) [1]				Total employment - Emploi total - Empleo total						
Total	.	.	.	.	.	.	.	811	850	890
M-H	.	.	.	.	.	.	.	528	557	573
W-F-M	.	.	.	.	.	.	.	283	292	317
Bulgaria (BA) [1][14]				Total employment - Emploi total - Empleo total						
Total	.	.	2 751.5 [15]	2 800.5 [15]	2 834.0	2 922.2	2 980.0	3 110.0	3 252.6	3 360.7
M-H	.	.	1 431.1 [15]	1 469.1 [15]	1 500.0	1 550.7	1 591.4	1 652.8	1 731.5	1 792.9
W-F-M	.	.	1 320.4 [15]	1 331.4 [15]	1 334.0	1 371.5	1 388.7	1 457.2	1 521.1	1 567.8
Croatia (BA) [1][16]				Total employment - Emploi total - Empleo total						
Total	1 491.6	1 553.0	1 469.5	1 527.2	1 536.4	1 562.7	1 572.9	1 586.4	1 614.4	1 635.6
M-H	802.2	848.7	818.9	842.5	850.5	866.4	867.0	868.1	897.3	905.1
W-F-M	689.5	704.3	650.6	684.7	685.9	696.4	705.9	718.3	717.1	730.5

Explanatory notes: see p. 77.

[1] Persons aged 15 years and over. [2] Methodology revised; data not strictly comparable. [3] Excl. armed forces. [4] Third quarter. [5] Prior to 2001: persons aged 13 years and over [6] February. [7] July of each year. [8] Prior to 2001: persons aged 10 years and over. [9] Excl. conscripts on compulsory military service. [10] Prior to 2004: incl. conscripts. [11] Persons aged 16 years and over. [12] Incl. professional army. [13] Prior to 1999: April of each year. [14] Excl. conscripts. [15] June. [16] Incl. armed forces, Excl. conscripts.

Notes explicatives: voir p. 80.

[1] Personnes âgées de 15 ans et plus. [2] Méthodologie révisée; les données ne sont pas strictement comparables. [3] Non compris les forces armées. [4] Troisième trimestre. [5] Avant 2001: personnes agées de 13 ans et pl us. [6] Février. [7] Juillet de chaque année. [8] Avant 2001: personnes agées de 10 ans et plus. [9] Non compris conscrits ceux du contingent. [10] Avant 2004: y compris les conscrits. [11] Personnes âgées de 16 ans et plus. [12] Y compris les militaires de carrière. [13] Avant 1999: avril de chaque année. [14] Non compris les conscrits. [15] Juin. [16] Y compris les forces armées, Excl. conscrits

Notas explicativas: véase p. 83.

[1] Personas de 15 años y más. [2] Metodología revisada; los datos no son estrictamente comparables. [3] Excl. las fuerzas armadas. [4] Tercer trimestre. [5] Antes de 2001: personas de 13 años y más. [6] Febrero. [7] Julio de cada año. [8] Antes de 2001: personas de 10 años y más. [9] Excl. los conscriptos del servicio obligatorio. [10] Antes de 2004: incl. los conscriptos. [11] Personas de 16 años y más. [12] Incl. los militares profesionales. [13] Antes de 1999: abril de cada año. [14] Excl. los conscriptos. [15] Junio. [16] Incl. las fuerzas armadas, excl. los conscriptos.

EMPLOYMENT   EMPLOI   EMPLEO

General level   Niveau général   Nivel general

	Thousands					Milliers			Millares	
	1999	2000	2001	2002	2003	2004	2005	2006	2007	2008
Cyprus (BA) [1] [2] [3]				Total employment - Emploi total - Empleo total						
Total	279.2	288.6	309.5	315.3	327.1	338.0	348.0	357.3	377.9	382.9
M-H	172.9	176.1	176.2	176.8	181.6	190.8	197.3	200.4	209.5	212.2
W-F-M	106.3	112.5	133.3	138.6	145.5	147.2	150.7	156.9	168.5	170.6
Czech Republic (BA) [3]				Total employment - Emploi total - Empleo total						
Total	4 764	4 732	4 728	4 765	4 733	4 707	4 764	4 828	4 922	5 002
M-H	2 694	2 676	2 674	2 700	2 686	2 663	2 706	2 742	2 806	2 863
W-F-M	2 070	2 056	2 054	2 065	2 047	2 044	2 059	2 086	2 116	2 139
Denmark (BA) [4] [5]				Total employment - Emploi total - Empleo total						
Total	2 707.0	2 722.1	2 725.1	2 715.3	2 692.5	2 720.1	2 732.8	2 786.6	2 778.6	2 827.4
M-H	1 463.0	1 458.1	1 456.3	1 449.3	1 447.8	1 451.6	1 456.1	1 482.3	1 476.1	1 497.3
W-F-M	1 244.0	1 263.9	1 268.9	1 265.9	1 244.6	1 268.5	1 276.6	1 304.3	1 302.6	1 330.1
España (BA) [6] [7]				Total employment - Emploi total - Empleo total						
Total	14 689.8	15 505.9	16 146.3	16 630.3	17 295.9	17 970.8	18 973.2 [8]	19 747.6	20 356.0	20 257.6
M-H	9 433.8	9 821.1	10 150.5	10 365.0	10 652.9	10 934.3	11 388.8 [8]	11 742.5	11 987.3	11 720.7
W-F-M	5 256.0	5 684.8	5 995.8	6 265.3	6 643.1	7 036.5	7 584.4 [8]	8 005.1	8 368.8	8 536.9
Estonia (BA) [9] [10]				Total employment - Emploi total - Empleo total						
Total	579.3	572.5	577.7	585.5	594.3	595.5	607.4	646.3	655.3	656.5
M-H	294.2	291.1	293.9	297.5	302.5	299.1	300.5	322.9	330.0	330.9
W-F-M	285.1	281.4	283.8	288.1	291.8	296.4	306.9	323.3	325.4	325.6
Finland (BA) [4] [9]				Total employment - Emploi total - Empleo total						
Total	2 317	2 356	2 388	2 393	2 385	2 387	2 421	2 466	2 512	2 553
M-H	1 227	1 248	1 261	1 249	1 247	1 250	1 263	1 288	1 310	1 337
W-F-M	1 090	1 108	1 127	1 144	1 138	1 137	1 158	1 178	1 202	1 217
France (BA) [3] [11] [12]				Total employment - Emploi total - Empleo total						
Total	22 672.1 [12]	23 261.5	23 759.0	23 942.0	24 695.8 [11]	24 800.3	24 978.0	25 133.5	25 565.2	25 913.2
M-H	12 550.2 [12]	12 843.5	13 105.0	13 103.0	13 302.9 [11]	13 315.7	13 350.0	13 381.5	13 521.9	13 670.2
W-F-M	10 121.9 [12]	10 417.9	10 654.0	10 839.0	11 392.9 [11]	11 484.7	11 628.0	11 752.0	12 043.3	12 243.0
Germany (BA) [3]				Total employment - Emploi total - Empleo total						
Total	36 402	36 604 [13]	36 816	36 536 [14]	36 172 [13]	35 659 [15]	36 566 [8]	37 322	38 163	38 734
M-H	20 659	20 680 [13]	20 629	20 336 [14]	19 996 [13]	19 681 [15]	20 135 [8]	20 462	20 890	21 188
W-F-M	15 743	15 924 [13]	16 187	16 200 [14]	16 176 [13]	15 978 [15]	16 432 [8]	16 860	17 272	17 546
Gibraltar (DA) [16]				Total employment - Emploi total - Empleo total						
Total	12.9	13.4	13.9	14.3	15.4	16.0	16.9	18.5	19.7	.
M-H	7.9	8.1	8.4	8.5	9.0	9.4	9.8	10.8	11.6	.
W-F-M	5.1	5.3	5.6	5.7	6.4	6.6	7.1	7.7	8.1	.
Greece (BA) [3] [10] [17]				Total employment - Emploi total - Empleo total						
Total	4 040.4	4 097.9	4 103.2	4 190.2	4 286.6	4 330.5	4 382.1	4 452.8	4 520.0	4 582.5
M-H	2 554.1	2 577.7	2 582.2	2 622.5	2 666.1	2 680.2	2 705.8	2 725.7	2 762.0	2 788.8
W-F-M	1 486.2	1 520.2	1 521.0	1 567.7	1 620.5	1 650.3	1 676.2	1 727.1	1 758.0	1 793.7
Hungary (BA) [9] [10]				Total employment - Emploi total - Empleo total						
Total	3 811.5	3 849.1	3 859.5	3 870.6 [18]	3 921.9	3 900.4	3 901.5	3 930.1	3 926.2	3 879.4
M-H	2 103.1	2 122.4	2 130.6	2 112.5 [18]	2 126.5	2 117.3	2 116.1	2 137.4	2 143.0	2 110.8
W-F-M	1 708.4	1 726.7	1 728.9	1 758.1 [18]	1 795.4	1 783.1	1 785.4	1 792.7	1 783.2	1 768.6
Iceland (BA) [19] [20]				Total employment - Emploi total - Empleo total						
Total	153.3	156.4	159.0	156.7	156.9	156.1	161.3	169.6	177.2	178.6
M-H	82.2	83.6	85.0	83.0	82.4	82.5	85.7	92.0	96.6	97.1
W-F-M	71.2	72.8	74.0	73.8	74.6	73.6	75.6	77.5	80.7	81.5
Ireland (BA) [3] [17]				Total employment - Emploi total - Empleo total						
Total	1 591.1	1 670.7	1 716.5	1 760.6	1 790.1	1 834.6	1 931.6	2 021.1	2 101.6	2 108.5
M-H	947.3	989.9	1 013.9	1 026.2	1 039.3	1 065.0	1 113.3	1 166.7	1 201.5	1 186.9
W-F-M	643.9	680.8	702.5	734.4	750.9	769.6	818.4	854.5	900.1	921.6
Italy (BA) [3]				Total employment - Emploi total - Empleo total						
Total	20 864	21 225	21 634	21 922	22 133	22 404 [8]	22 563	22 988	23 222	23 405
M-H	13 330	13 461	13 574	13 685	13 769	13 622 [8]	13 738	13 939	14 057	14 064
W-F-M	7 533	7 764	8 060	8 236	8 365	8 783 [8]	8 825	9 049	9 165	9 341

Explanatory notes: see p. 77.

[1] Incl. armed forces, Excl. conscripts. [2] Government-controlled area. [3] Persons aged 15 years and over. [4] Included armed forces and conscripts. [5] Persons aged 15 to 66 years. [6] Excl. compulsory military service. [7] Persons aged 16 years and over. [8] Methodology revised; data not strictly comparable. [9] Persons aged 15 to 74 years. [10] Excl. conscripts. [11] Prior to 2003: March of each year. [12] Jan. [13] May. [14] Prior to 2002: April of each year. [15] March. [16] Oct. of each year. [17] Second quarter of each year. [18] Estimates based on the 2001 Population Census results. [19] Persons aged 16 to 74 years. [20] Excl. armed forces and conscripts.

Notes explicatives: voir p. 80.

[1] Y compris les forces armées, Excl. conscrits [2] Région sous contrôle gouvernemental. [3] Personnes âgées de 15 ans et plus. [4] Y compris les forces armées et les conscrits. [5] Personnes âgées de 15 à 66 ans. [6] Non compris les militaires du contingent. [7] Personnes âgées de 16 ans et plus. [8] Méthodologie révisée; les données ne sont pas strictement comparables. [9] Personnes âgées de 15 à 74 ans. [10] Non compris les conscrits. [11] Avant 2003: mars de chaque année. [12] Janv. [13] Mai. [14] Avant 2002: avril de chaque année. [15] Mars. [16] Oct. de chaque année. [17] Deuxième trimestre de chaque année. [18] Estimations basées sur les résultats du Recensement de la population de 2001. [19] Personnes âgées de 16 à 74 ans. [20] Non compris les forces armées et les conscrits.

Notas explicativas: véase p. 83.

[1] Incl. las fuerzas armadas, excl. los conscriptos. [2] Area controlada por el gobierno. [3] Personas de 15 años y más. [4] Incluye las fuezas armadas y los conscriptos. [5] Personas de 15 a 66 años. [6] Excl. a los militares en servicio obligatorio. [7] Personas de 16 años y más. [8] Metodología revisada; los datos no son estrictamente comparables. [9] Personas de 15 a 74 años. [10] Excl. los conscriptos. [11] Antes de 2003: marzo de cada año. [12] Enero. [13] Mayo. [14] Antes del 2002: abril de cada año. [15] Marzo. [16] Oct. de cada año. [17] Segundo trimestre de cada año. [18] Estimaciones basadas en los resultados del Censo de población de 2001. [19] Personas de 16 a 74 años. [20] Excl. las fuerzas armadas y los conscriptos.

EMPLOYMENT / EMPLOI / EMPLEO

General level / Niveau général / Nivel general

2A

	Thousands / Milliers / Millares									
	1999	2000	2001	2002	2003	2004	2005	2006	2007	2008
Jersey (E) [1]				Total employment - Emploi total - Empleo total						
Total	49.6	49.8	50.1	50.3	49.7	49.6	50.2	51.8	53.0	53.5
Jersey (FD) [1]				Total employment - Emploi total - Empleo total						
Total	42.3	42.5	42.6	42.5	41.6	41.3	41.9	42.9	44.4	.
Latvia (BA) [2][3]				Total employment - Emploi total - Empleo total						
Total	968.5	941.1	962.1 |	989.0 [4]	1 006.9	1 017.7	1 035.9	1 087.6	1 119.0	1 124.1
M-H	502.9	479.7	486.4 |	504.6 [4]	516.6	521.8	534.1	559.2	573.5	571.5
W-F-M	465.6	461.4	475.7 |	484.3 [4]	490.2	495.9	501.8	528.5	545.5	552.6
Liechtenstein (E)				Total employment - Emploi total - Empleo total						
Total	25.343	26.797	28.783	28.814	29.055	29.533	30.757	.	.	.
M-H	.	.	.	.	.	.	18.698	.	.	.
W-F-M	.	.	.	.	.	.	12.059	.	.	.
Lithuania (BA) [3][5]				Total employment - Emploi total - Empleo total						
Total	1 456.5	1 397.8	1 351.8	1 405.9	1 438.0	1 436.3	1 473.9	1 499.0	1 534.2	1 520.0
M-H	729.2	686.5	664.5	707.8	726.2	733.8	750.9	755.8	777.7	768.7
W-F-M	727.4	711.3	687.3	698.1	711.8	702.5	723.0	743.2	756.5	751.4
Luxembourg (BA) [5]				Total employment - Emploi total - Empleo total						
Total	.	.	.	.	.	.	.	195.4	204.3	207.8
M-H	.	.	.	.	.	.	.	111.1	114.1	118.4
W-F-M	.	.	.	.	.	.	.	84.3	90.2	89.4
Luxembourg (E)				Total employment - Emploi total - Empleo total						
Total	249.9	263.8	278.4	286.5	291.8	298.5	307.3	319.1	333.2	348.7
Macedonia, The Former Yugoslav Rep. of (BA) [5]				Total employment - Emploi total - Empleo total						
Total	545.222	549.846	599.308	561.341	545.108	522.995 [6]	545.253	570.404	590.234	609.015
M-H	.	.	357.266	342.779	327.283	320.640 [6]	332.179	351.974	358.835	373.483
W-F-M	.	.	242.042	218.562	217.825	202.355 [6]	213.074	218.431	231.399	235.532
Malta (BA) [5]				Total employment - Emploi total - Empleo total						
Total	.	145.2	145.6	148.4	147.0	148.6	148.5	152.5	155.5	161.0
M-H	.	101.4	103.6	102.1	101.2	103.8	102.8	104.4	104.4	107.5
W-F-M	.	43.8	42.0	46.3	45.9	44.8	46.0	48.1	51.1	53.5
Moldova, Republic of (BA) [5]				Total employment - Emploi total - Empleo total						
Total	1 494.4	1 514.6	1 499.0	1 505.1	1 356.5	1 316.0	1 318.7	1 257.3	1 247.2	1 251.0
M-H	739.1	747.4	736.5	730.9	661.3	631.5	629.7	628.6	621.5	628.8
W-F-M	755.3	767.2	762.5	774.2	695.2	684.6	689.0	628.7	625.7	622.3
Montenegro (BA) [7][8]				Total employment - Emploi total - Empleo total						
Total	.	.	.	.	.	.	178.8			
M-H	.	.	.	.	.	.	105.6			
W-F-M	.	.	.	.	.	.	73.2			
Netherlands (BA) [5]				Total employment - Emploi total - Empleo total						
Total	7 613	7 798	7 953	8 018	7 991	7 928	7 958	8 108	8 310	8 457
M-H	4 382	4 459	4 522	4 526	4 480	4 432	4 421	4 475	4 548	4 594
W-F-M	3 231	3 339	3 431	3 492	3 511	3 495	3 537	3 633	3 763	3 863
Norway (BA) [2]				Total employment - Emploi total - Empleo total						
Total	2 259	2 269	2 278	2 286	2 269	2 276	2 289 |	2 362 [9]	2 443	2 524
M-H	1 209	1 212	1 214	1 210	1 198	1 201	1 211 |	1 251 [9]	1 289	1 332
W-F-M	1 050	1 057	1 064	1 076	1 071	1 074	1 078 |	1 111 [9]	1 154	1 192
Poland (BA) [5][10]				Total employment - Emploi total - Empleo total						
Total	14 747 [11]	14 526	14 207	13 782	13 617	13 795	14 116	14 594	15 241	15 800
M-H	8 132 [11]	8 004	7 797	7 529	7 432	7 566	7 809	8 081	8 403	8 718
W-F-M	6 624 [11]	6 522	6 410	6 253	6 185	6 230	6 307	6 513	6 838	7 082
Portugal (BA) [5]				Total employment - Emploi total - Empleo total						
Total	4 921.6	5 032.9	5 121.7	5 145.6	5 127.7	5 127.5	5 122.6	5 159.5	5 169.7	5 197.8
M-H	2 720.5	2 777.2	2 819.2	2 824.7	2 796.8	2 788.8	2 765.4	2 789.7	2 789.3	2 797.1
W-F-M	2 201.1	2 255.7	2 302.0	2 320.9	2 330.9	2 338.6	2 357.2	2 369.8	2 380.4	2 400.7
Roumanie (BA) [5]				Total employment - Emploi total - Empleo total						
Total	10 775.7	10 763.8	10 696.9 |	9 234.1 [12]	9 222.5	9 157.6	9 146.6	9 313.3	9 353.3	9 369.1
M-H	5 799.1	5 772.2	5 719.3 |	5 031.5 [12]	5 056.7	4 980.0	5 011.2	5 074.0	5 116.3	5 157.4
W-F-M	4 976.6	4 991.6	4 977.6 |	4 202.6 [12]	4 165.7	4 177.5	4 135.4	4 239.3	4 237.0	4 211.7

Explanatory notes: see p. 77.

[1] December. [2] Persons aged 15 to 74 years. [3] Excl. conscripts. [4] Prior to 2002: persons aged 15 years and over. [5] Persons aged 15 years and over. [6] Prior to 2004: April of each year. [7] Persons aged 15 to 64 years. [8] Oct. of each year. [9] Prior to 2006: persons aged 16 to 74 years. [10] Excl. regular military living in barracks and conscripts. [11] First and fourth quarters. [12] Estimates based on the 2002 Population Census results.

Notes explicatives: voir p. 80.

[1] Décembre. [2] Personnes âgées de 15 à 74 ans. [3] Non compris les conscrits. [4] Avant 2002: personnes agées de 15 ans et plus. [5] Personnes âgées de 15 ans et plus. [6] Avant 2004: Avril de chaque année. [7] Personnes âgées de 15 à 64 ans. [8] Oct. de chaque année. [9] Avant 2006: personnes âgées de 16 à 74 ans. [10] Non compris les militaires de carrière vivant dans des casernes et les conscrits. [11] Premier et quatrième trimestres. [12] Estimations basées sur les résultats du Recensement de la population de 2002.

Notas explicativas: véase p. 83.

[1] Diciembre. [2] Personas de 15 a 74 años. [3] Excl. los conscriptos. [4] Antes de 2002: personas de 15 años y más. [5] Personas de 15 años y más. [6] Antes de 2004: Abril de cada año. [7] Personas de 15 a 64 años. [8] Oct. de cada año. [9] Antes de 2006: personas de 16 a 74 años. [10] Excl. los militares profesionales que viven en casernas y los conscriptos. [11] Primero y cuarto trimestres. [12] Estimaciones basadas en los resultados del Censo de población de 2002.

2A

<table>
<tr><td></td><td>EMPLOYMENT</td><td>EMPLOI</td><td>EMPLEO</td></tr>
<tr><td></td><td>General level</td><td>Niveau général</td><td>Nivel general</td></tr>
</table>

	Thousands / Milliers / Millares									
	1999	2000	2001	2002	2003	2004	2005	2006	2007	2008
Russian Federation (BA) [1]				Total employment - Emploi total - Empleo total						
Total	62 945	65 070	65 123	66 659	66 432	67 275	68 169	68 855	70 570	70 965
M-H	32 570	33 574	33 504	34 014	33 827	34 181	34 549	34 695	35 650	36 139
W-F-M	30 375	31 496	31 619	32 645	32 605	33 094	33 620	34 160	34 920	34 826
San Marino (E) [2][3]				Total employment - Emploi total - Empleo total						
Total	18.667	18.644	19.112	19.249	19.340	19.890	20.124	20.695	21.483	21.995
M-H	11.319	11.163	11.404	11.483	11.480	11.768	11.902	12.219	12.667	12.967
W-F-M	7.348	7.481	7.708	7.766	7.860	8.122	8.222	8.476	8.816	9.028
Serbia (BA) [2][4]				Total employment - Emploi total - Empleo total						
Total						2 930.8	2 733.4	2 630.7	2 655.7	2 821.7
M-H						1 708.9	1 635.0	1 554.7	1 545.8	1 611.3
W-F-M						1 222.0	1 098.4	1 076.0	1 110.0	1 210.4
Slovakia (BA) [2][5][6]				Total employment - Emploi total - Empleo total						
Total	2 132.1	2 101.7	2 123.7	2 127.0	2 164.6	2 170.4	2 216.2	2 301.4	2 357.3	2 433.8
M-H	1 163.7	1 137.3	1 145.8	1 156.8	1 177.1	1 193.7	1 233.0	1 291.1	1 321.6	1 363.7
W-F-M	968.4	964.4	977.9	970.2	987.5	976.7	983.1	1 010.3	1 035.6	1 070.0
Slovenia (BA) [2][7]				Total employment - Emploi total - Empleo total						
Total	892	894	914	922	896	946	947	969	994	990
M-H	482	481	497	500	488	511	512	521	542	540
W-F-M	410	413	417	423	409	434	435	448	451	450
Suisse (BA) [2][7][8]				Total employment - Emploi total - Empleo total						
Total	3 862	3 879	3 938	3 965	3 963	3 959	3 974	4 051	4 122	4 229
M-H	2 157	2 172	2 190	2 175	2 177	2 173	2 172	2 214	2 259	2 289
W-F-M	1 705	1 707	1 748	1 790	1 786	1 786	1 802	1 837	1 863	1 940
Suisse (E) [9]				Total employment - Emploi total - Empleo total						
Total	4 038	4 080	4 146	4 171	4 156	4 169	4 201	4 304	4 413	4 495
M-H	2 280	2 301	2 328	2 321	2 307	2 315	2 331	2 385	2 447	2 472
W-F-M	1 759	1 779	1 818	1 850	1 848	1 854	1 870	1 919	1 966	2 023
Sweden (BA) [10][11]				Total employment - Emploi total - Empleo total						
Total	4 068	4 159	4 239	4 244	4 234	4 213	4 263 [12]	4 341	4 541	4 593
M-H	2 121	2 167	2 203	2 197	2 191	2 186	2 225 [12]	2 273	2 390	2 422
W-F-M	1 946	1 992	2 036	2 047	2 043	2 027	2 038 [12]	2 067	2 150	2 171
Turkey (BA) [2][13]				Total employment - Emploi total - Empleo total						
Total	21 413	21 581 [14]	21 524	21 354	21 147	21 791	22 046	22 330	20 738	21 194
M-H	15 257	15 780 [14]	15 555	15 232	15 256	16 023	16 346	16 520	15 382	15 598
W-F-M	6 157	5 801 [14]	5 969	6 122	5 891	5 768	5 700	5 810	5 356	5 595
Ukraine (BA) [15]				Total employment - Emploi total - Empleo total						
Total	19 947.8	20 175.0	19 971.5	20 091.2	20 163.3	20 295.7	20 680.0	20 730.4	20 904.7	20 972.3
M-H	10 043.7	10 318.1	10 176.7	10 189.9	10 199.7	10 288.8	10 604.5	10 675.6	10 764.8	10 849.7
W-F-M	9 904.1	9 856.9	9 794.8	9 901.3	9 963.6	10 006.9	10 075.5	10 054.8	10 139.9	10 122.6
United Kingdom (BA) [16][17]				Total employment - Emploi total - Empleo total						
Total	27 023	27 399	27 643	27 852	28 132	28 365	28 665	28 926	29 100	29 475
M-H	14 692	14 859	14 961	15 033	15 256	15 327	15 468	15 578	15 747	15 904
W-F-M	12 331	12 540	12 681	12 819	12 876	13 038	13 198	13 348	13 353	13 572

OCEANIA-OCÉANIE-OCEANIA

	1999	2000	2001	2002	2003	2004	2005	2006	2007	2008
Australia (BA) [2][13]				Total employment - Emploi total - Empleo total						
Total	8 720.2	8 951.3	9 060.8	9 245.8	9 464.9	9 623.3	9 968.6	10 218.3	10 512.3	10 740.5
M-H	4 917.6	5 006.0	5 031.7	5 131.0	5 225.6	5 331.0	5 488.0	5 605.6	5 769.9	5 879.2
W-F-M	3 802.6	3 945.3	4 029.1	4 114.8	4 239.4	4 292.3	4 480.6	4 612.8	4 742.4	4 861.3
New Zealand (BA) [2][13]				Total employment - Emploi total - Empleo total						
Total	1 766.3	1 800.0	1 845.8	1 906.2	1 955.6	2 024.1	2 084.6	2 134.7	2 174.5	2 188.2
M-H	963.1	981.6	1 001.7	1 035.5	1 056.8	1 095.6	1 120.1	1 146.3	1 165.0	1 164.9
W-F-M	803.3	818.4	844.1	870.6	898.8	928.5	964.6	988.4	1 009.5	1 023.2

Explanatory notes: see p. 77.

[1] Persons aged 15 to 72 years. [2] Persons aged 15 years and over. [3] Dec. [4] Oct. [5] Excl. conscripts. [6] Excl. persons on child-care leave. [7] Second quarter of each year. [8] Excluding armed forces and seasonal/border workers. [9] Civilian labour force employed. [10] Incl. professional army; excl. compulsory military service. [11] Persons aged 15 to 74 years; prior to 2007: 16 to 64 years. [12] Methodology revised; data not strictly comparable. [13] Excl. armed forces. [14] Estimates based on the 2000 Population Census results. Prior to 2000: persons aged 12 years and over. [15] Persons aged 15-70 years. [16] Persons aged 16 years and over. [17] Second quarter.

Notes explicatives: voir p. 80.

[1] Personnes âgées de 15 à 72 ans. [2] Personnes âgées de 15 ans et plus. [3] Déc. [4] Oct. [5] Non compris les conscrits. [6] Non compris les personnes en congé parental. [7] Deuxième trimestre de chaque année. [8] Non compris les forces armées et les travailleurs saisonniers et frontaliers. [9] Main-d'oeuvre civile occupée. [10] Y compris les militaires de carrière; non compris les militaires du contingent. [11] Personnes âgées de 15 à 74 ans; avant 2007: 16 à 64 ans. [12] Méthodologie révisée; les données ne sont pas strictement comparables. [13] Non compris les forces armées. [14] Estimations basées sur les résultats du Recensement de la population de 2000. Avant 2000: personnes âgées de 12 ans et plus. [15] Personnes âgées de 15 à 70 ans. [16] Personnes âgées de 16 ans et plus. [17] Deuxième trimestre.

Notas explicativas: véase p. 83.

[1] Personas de 15 a 72 años. [2] Personas de 15 años y más. [3] Dic. [4] Oct. [5] Excl. los conscriptos. [6] Excl. las personas con licencia parental. [7] Segundo trimestre de cada año. [8] Excluidas las fuerzas armadas y excl. a los trabajadores temporales y fronterizos. [9] Fuerza de trabajo civil ocupada. [10] Incl. los militares profesionales; excl. los militares en servicio obligatorio. [11] Personas de 15 a 74 años; antes de 2007: 16 a 64 años. [12] Metodología revisada; los datos no son estrictamente comparables. [13] Excl. las fuerzas armadas. [14] Estimaciones basadas en los resultados del Censo de población de 2000. Antes de 2000: personas de 12 años y más. [15] Personas de 15 á 70 años. [16] Personas de 16 años y más. [17] Segundo trimestre.

General level   Niveau général   Nivel general

	Thousands				Milliers				Millares		
	1999	2000	2001	2002	2003	2004	2005	2006	2007	2008	
Polynésie française (BA) [1]				Total employment - Emploi total - Empleo total							
Total	55.215	58.054	59.203	61.889	63.156	63.385	66.134	68.256	69.291	.	
M-H	32.202	33.451	34.449	35.595	36.507	36.320	37.997	39.064	39.704	.	
W-F-M	23.013	24.603	24.754	26.294	26.649	27.065	28.137	29.192	29.587	.	

Explanatory notes: see p. 77.
[1] Persons aged 15 years and over.

Notes explicatives: voir p. 80.
[1] Personnes âgées de 15 ans et plus.

Notas explicativas: véase p. 83.
[1] Personas de 15 años y más.

| Total employment, by economic activity | Emploi total, par activité économique | Empleo total, por actividad económica |

Thousands				Milliers			Millares		
1999	2000	2001	2002	2003	2004	2005	2006	2007	2008

AFRICA-AFRIQUE-AFRICA

Botswana (BA) [1][2]   Total employment - Emploi total - Empleo total

Total - Total - Total
ISIC 3 - CITI 3 - CIIU 3

	1999	2000	2001	2002	2003	2004	2005	2006	2007	2008
Total	.	483.4	.	.	462.4	.	.	539.2	.	.
A-B	.	95.3	.	.	98.1	.	.	161.4	.	.
C	.	11.2	.	.	13.8	.	.	14.2	.	.
D	.	42.6	.	.	44.6	.	.	36.0	.	.
E	.	2.2	.	.	4.4	.	.	4.2	.	.
F	.	44.9	.	.	41.9	.	.	27.6	.	.
G	.	63.6	.	.	61.7	.	.	77.4	.	.
H	.	9.9	.	.	14.7	.	.	14.7	.	.
I	.	13.8	.	.	12.6	.	.	16.1	.	.
J	.	4.3	.	.	4.9	.	.	8.4	.	.
K	.	17.8	.	.	14.3	.	.	25.3	.	.
L	.	73.2	.	.	67.2	.	.	60.2	.	.
M	.	43.0	.	.	38.7	.	.	43.2	.	.
N	.	12.2	.	.	14.0	.	.	14.0	.	.
O	.	22.0	.	.	9.6	.	.	10.6	.	.
P	.	21.2	.	.	21.6	.	.	25.2	.	.
Q	.	0.3	.	.	0.2	.	.	0.9	.	.
X	.	6.0	.	.	-	.	.	-	.	.

Men - Hommes - Hombres
ISIC 3 - CITI 3 - CIIU 3

	1999	2000	2001	2002	2003	2004	2005	2006	2007	2008
Total	.	269.4	.	.	245.4	.	.	281.8	.	.
A-B	.	58.9	.	.	70.1	.	.	98.8	.	.
C	.	10.0	.	.	11.3	.	.	12.5	.	.
D	.	19.8	.	.	18.3	.	.	16.0	.	.
E	.	2.0	.	.	3.5	.	.	2.6	.	.
F	.	39.0	.	.	35.7	.	.	23.1	.	.
G	.	25.3	.	.	20.9	.	.	27.9	.	.
H	.	2.4	.	.	3.8	.	.	3.8	.	.
I	.	10.8	.	.	9.4	.	.	10.5	.	.
J	.	2.0	.	.	1.5	.	.	3.0	.	.
K	.	11.7	.	.	9.2	.	.	15.6	.	.
L	.	47.6	.	.	36.2	.	.	34.5	.	.
M	.	18.3	.	.	14.2	.	.	15.2	.	.
N	.	4.4	.	.	4.5	.	.	5.4	.	.
O	.	11.0	.	.	4.0	.	.	5.2	.	.
P	.	2.8	.	.	2.4	.	.	7.2	.	.
Q	.	0.2	.	.	0.2	.	.	0.5	.	.
X	.	3.1	.	.	-	.	.	-	.	.

Women - Femmes - Mujeres
ISIC 3 - CITI 3 - CIIU 3

	1999	2000	2001	2002	2003	2004	2005	2006	2007	2008
Total	.	214.0	.	.	217.0	.	.	257.4	.	.
A-B	.	36.4	.	.	28.0	.	.	62.6	.	.
C	.	1.2	.	.	2.5	.	.	1.7	.	.
D	.	22.8	.	.	26.2	.	.	20.0	.	.
E	.	0.2	.	.	0.9	.	.	1.5	.	.
F	.	5.9	.	.	6.2	.	.	4.5	.	.
G	.	38.3	.	.	40.7	.	.	49.5	.	.
H	.	7.4	.	.	10.9	.	.	10.9	.	.
I	.	3.0	.	.	3.2	.	.	5.6	.	.
J	.	2.3	.	.	3.4	.	.	5.4	.	.
K	.	6.1	.	.	5.1	.	.	9.7	.	.
L	.	25.7	.	.	31.0	.	.	25.6	.	.
M	.	24.3	.	.	24.5	.	.	28.1	.	.
N	.	7.8	.	.	9.5	.	.	8.6	.	.
O	.	11.0	.	.	5.5	.	.	5.3	.	.
P	.	18.4	.	.	19.2	.	.	18.0	.	.
Q	.	0.1	.	.	-	.	.	0.4	.	.
X	.	2.9	.	.	-	.	.	-	.	.

Explanatory notes: see p. 77.   Notes explicatives: voir p. 80.   Notas explicativas: véase p. 83.

[1] Excl. armed forces. [2] Persons aged 12 years and over.   [1] Non compris les forces armées. [2] Personnes âgées de 12 ans et plus.   [1] Excl. las fuerzas armadas. [2] Personas de 12 años y más.

EMPLOYMENT EMPLOI EMPLEO

Total employment, by economic activity Emploi total, par activité économique Empleo total, por actividad económica

	Thousands				Milliers				Millares	
	1999	2000	2001	2002	2003	2004	2005	2006	2007	2008

Egypt (BA) [1][2][3] Total employment - Emploi total - Empleo total

Total - Total - Total
ISIC 3 - CITI 3 - CIIU 3

	1999	2000	2001	2002	2003	2004	2005	2006	2007	2008
Total	16 750.2	17 203.3	17 556.7	17 856.2	18 118.6	18 717.4	19 341.7	20 443.6	21 723.8	.
A	4 684.4	5 000.5	4 901.5	4 800.4	5 250.1	5 820.5	5 816.4	6 208.9	6 744.2	.
B	122.6	96.7	109.1	113.4	161.2	137.7	157.6	161.8	144.8	.
C	47.5	47.4	59.5	44.5	32.0	32.0	29.0	53.3	35.5	.
D	2 207.6	2 048.2	2 115.0	2 070.7	1 976.9	2 085.1	2 229.7	2 380.8	2 412.2	.
E	207.0	209.2	210.2	241.8	228.7	218.5	245.3	250.4	282.3	.
F	1 320.1	1 358.6	1 348.4	1 315.1	1 341.0	1 399.5	1 649.8	1 822.9	2 078.1	.
G	2 020.2	2 006.9	2 125.6	2 302.7	2 161.1	2 252.0	2 141.2	2 171.9	2 307.0	.
H	299.6	269.0	324.7	337.3	291.3	334.4	366.4	411.4	370.8	.
I	1 060.2	1 126.0	1 142.2	1 132.9	1 145.3	1 171.4	1 322.7	1 357.3	1 452.4	.
J	185.2	185.6	199.4	219.5	199.9	195.8	169.2	175.0	194.9	.
K	273.0	313.4	337.9	342.4	347.2	355.1	400.5	431.8	451.7	.
L	1 631.7	1 825.1	1 886.8	1 945.5	2 025.1	1 926.2	1 849.5	1 901.7	1 974.5	.
M	1 764.5	1 790.4	1 819.8	1 962.7	1 969.1	1 845.5	1 908.2	1 969.9	2 079.8	.
N	531.1	532.2	566.5	594.5	545.6	503.3	503.3	545.5	573.1	.
O	356.5	342.7	353.9	379.5	408.8	404.5	464.8	507.5	538.8	.
P	38.0	49.3	52.8	51.9	33.8	34.4	52.6	45.0	51.6	.
Q	-	-	-	-	-	-	2.7	2.5	1.0	.
X	0.9	1.9	3.4	1.4	1.5	1.5	34.3	46.2	34.1	.

Men - Hommes - Hombres
ISIC 3 - CITI 3 - CIIU 3

	1999	2000	2001	2002	2003	2004	2005	2006	2007	2008
Total	13 611.0	13 958.5	14 361.1	14 550.7	14 651.7	14 936.4	15 592.7	16 559.4	17 089.5	.
A	3 688.1	3 722.5	3 883.6	3 888.2	3 898.4	4 061.8	4 071.2	4 529.7	4 587.7	.
B	117.1	96.7	108.8	112.2	159.3	136.5	156.7	160.5	144.2	.
C	46.4	45.7	58.1	41.3	30.0	31.3	27.3	49.5	34.8	.
D	1 897.8	1 870.2	1 835.6	1 786.5	1 810.7	1 898.7	2 077.7	2 188.3	2 190.4	.
E	188.3	191.3	194.8	220.1	208.6	203.1	227.1	229.2	245.9	.
F	1 299.8	1 332.2	1 323.2	1 279.7	1 313.1	1 377.3	1 634.7	1 806.9	2 051.5	.
G	1 741.8	1 803.2	1 903.2	2 050.4	1 941.4	2 032.8	1 951.8	1 964.6	2 048.8	.
H	257.2	257.4	271.4	287.2	276.5	320.2	357.4	394.5	358.5	.
I	1 019.6	1 066.3	1 078.7	1 060.2	1 093.5	1 114.9	1 276.4	1 300.7	1 398.6	.
J	143.6	142.0	152.6	160.5	152.0	148.5	129.0	133.7	145.1	.
K	239.0	268.9	299.5	287.9	298.2	307.0	347.0	374.6	389.1	.
L	1 292.2	1 444.1	1 495.6	1 523.2	1 579.7	1 520.0	1 446.7	1 475.8	1 515.1	.
M	1 061.7	1 064.6	1 107.5	1 178.3	1 190.4	1 118.8	1 133.6	1 140.8	1 165.8	.
N	255.2	296.5	297.2	301.1	293.6	258.3	244.4	261.2	261.5	.
O	333.5	314.0	315.8	337.0	376.7	376.1	434.6	472.5	486.5	.
P	28.8	41.7	33.2	35.5	28.4	29.7	43.6	34.3	36.6	.
Q	-	-	-	-	-	-	1.9	2.1	0.5	.
X	0.9	1.1	2.3	1.4	1.2	1.4	31.6	40.6	28.6	.

Women - Femmes - Mujeres
ISIC 3 - CITI 3 - CIIU 3

	1999	2000	2001	2002	2003	2004	2005	2006	2007	2008
Total	3 139.2	3 244.8	3 195.6	3 305.5	3 466.9	3 781.0	3 749.0	3 884.2	4 634.3	.
A	996.3	1 278.0	1 017.9	912.2	1 351.7	1 758.7	1 743.4	1 679.2	2 153.5	.
B	5.5	-	0.3	1.2	1.9	1.2	0.9	1.3	0.6	.
C	1.0	1.7	1.4	3.2	2.0	0.7	1.7	3.8	0.7	.
D	309.8	178.0	279.4	284.2	166.2	186.4	152.0	192.5	221.8	.
E	18.7	17.9	15.4	21.7	20.1	15.4	18.2	21.2	36.4	.
F	20.3	26.4	25.2	35.4	27.9	22.2	15.1	16.0	26.6	.
G	278.4	203.7	222.4	252.2	219.7	219.2	189.4	207.3	258.2	.
H	42.4	11.6	53.3	50.1	14.8	14.2	9.0	16.9	12.3	.
I	40.6	59.7	63.5	72.7	51.8	56.5	46.3	56.6	53.8	.
J	41.6	43.6	46.8	59.0	47.9	47.3	40.2	41.3	49.8	.
K	34.0	44.5	38.4	54.5	49.0	48.1	53.5	57.2	62.6	.
L	339.5	381.0	391.2	422.3	445.4	406.2	402.8	425.9	459.4	.
M	702.8	725.8	712.3	784.4	778.7	726.7	774.6	829.1	914.0	.
N	275.9	235.7	269.3	293.4	252.0	245.0	259.1	284.3	311.6	.
O	23.0	28.7	38.1	42.5	32.1	28.4	30.2	35.0	52.0	.
P	9.2	7.6	19.6	16.4	5.4	4.7	9.0	10.7	15.0	.
Q	-	-	-	-	-	-	0.8	0.4	0.5	.
X	-	0.8	1.1	-	0.3	0.1	2.7	5.6	5.5	.

Explanatory notes: see p. 77.

[1] Persons aged 15 to 64 years. [2] Excl. armed forces. [3] May and Nov.

Notes explicatives: voir p. 80.

[1] Personnes âgées de 15 à 64 ans. [2] Non compris les forces armées. [3] Mai et nov.

Notas explicativas: véase p. 83.

[1] Personas de 15 a 64 años. [2] Excl. las fuerzas armadas. [3] Mayo y nov.

Total employment, by economic activity
Emploi total, par activité économique
Empleo total, por actividad económica

Thousands   Milliers   Millares

	1999	2000	2001	2002	2003	2004	2005	2006	2007	2008
Madagascar (B) [1][2]					Total employment - Emploi total - Empleo total					
Total - Total - Total										
ISIC 3 - CITI 3 - CIIU 3										
Total	.	.	.	.	8 098.5	.	9 570.4	.	.	.
A	.	.	.	.	6 228.5	.	7 745.3	.	.	.
B	.	.	.	.	87.5	.	99.0	.	.	.
C	.	.	.	.	14.2	.	18.8	.	.	.
D	.	.	.	.	449.3	.	267.5	.	.	.
E	.	.	.	.	18.6	.	27.5	.	.	.
F	.	.	.	.	60.6	.	13.0	.	.	.
G	.	.	.	.	420.5	.	470.5	.	.	.
H	.	.	.	.	47.7	.	63.9	.	.	.
I	.	.	.	.	117.1	.	86.3	.	.	.
J	.	.	.	.	.	.	4.1	.	.	.
J-K	.	.	.	.	5.7	.	.	.	.	.
K	.	.	.	.	.	.	-	.	.	.
L	.	.	.	.	205.7	.	202.4	.	.	.
M	.	.	.	.	66.2	.	44.5	.	.	.
N	.	.	.	.	14.4	.	9.9	.	.	.
O	.	.	.	.	362.6	.	517.7	.	.	.
Men - Hommes - Hombres										
ISIC 3 - CITI 3 - CIIU 3										
Total	.	.	.	.	4 135.7	.	4 841.8	.	.	.
A	.	.	.	.	3 110.1	.	3 875.7	.	.	.
B	.	.	.	.	61.8	.	68.1	.	.	.
C	.	.	.	.	4.5	.	10.4	.	.	.
D	.	.	.	.	227.0	.	205.3	.	.	.
E	.	.	.	.	18.1	.	21.4	.	.	.
F	.	.	.	.	54.6	.	12.0	.	.	.
G	.	.	.	.	167.7	.	173.9	.	.	.
H	.	.	.	.	21.0	.	30.5	.	.	.
I	.	.	.	.	108.1	.	80.8	.	.	.
J	.	.	.	.	.	.	2.7	.	.	.
J-K	.	.	.	.	4.4	.	.	.	.	.
K	.	.	.	.	.	.	-	.	.	.
L	.	.	.	.	144.3	.	133.6	.	.	.
M	.	.	.	.	33.1	.	18.5	.	.	.
N	.	.	.	.	8.8	.	5.1	.	.	.
O	.	.	.	.	172.3	.	203.8	.	.	.
Women - Femmes - Mujeres										
ISIC 3 - CITI 3 - CIIU 3										
Total	.	.	.	.	3 962.8	.	4 728.6	.	.	.
A	.	.	.	.	3 118.4	.	3 869.6	.	.	.
B	.	.	.	.	25.8	.	30.9	.	.	.
C	.	.	.	.	9.7	.	8.5	.	.	.
D	.	.	.	.	222.3	.	62.2	.	.	.
E	.	.	.	.	0.5	.	6.1	.	.	.
F	.	.	.	.	6.0	.	0.9	.	.	.
G	.	.	.	.	252.9	.	296.6	.	.	.
H	.	.	.	.	26.7	.	33.5	.	.	.
I	.	.	.	.	9.1	.	5.4	.	.	.
J	.	.	.	.	.	.	1.4	.	.	.
J-K	.	.	.	.	1.3	.	.	.	.	.
K	.	.	.	.	.	.	-	.	.	.
L	.	.	.	.	61.3	.	68.8	.	.	.
M	.	.	.	.	33.1	.	26.0	.	.	.
N	.	.	.	.	5.6	.	4.8	.	.	.
O	.	.	.	.	190.2	.	313.9	.	.	.
Mali (BA) [3]							Total employment - Emploi total - Empleo total			
Total - Total - Total										
ISIC 3 - CITI 3 - CIIU 3										
Total	.	.	.	.	.	.	2 370.8	.	.	.
A	.	.	.	.	.	.	949.4	.	.	.
B	.	.	.	.	.	.	35.2	.	.	.
C	.	.	.	.	.	.	11.4	.	.	.
D	.	.	.	.	.	.	272.5	.	.	.
E	.	.	.	.	.	.	5.1	.	.	.
F	.	.	.	.	.	.	102.1	.	.	.
G	.	.	.	.	.	.	668.1	.	.	.
H	.	.	.	.	.	.	7.6	.	.	.
I	.	.	.	.	.	.	55.3	.	.	.
J	.	.	.	.	.	.	4.4	.	.	.
K	.	.	.	.	.	.	4.0	.	.	.
L	.	.	.	.	.	.	39.9	.	.	.
M	.	.	.	.	.	.	53.9	.	.	.
N	.	.	.	.	.	.	20.9	.	.	.
O	.	.	.	.	.	.	35.3	.	.	.
P	.	.	.	.	.	.	103.9	.	.	.
Q	.	.	.	.	.	.	0.9	.	.	.

Explanatory notes: see p. 77.   Notes explicatives: voir p. 80.   Notas explicativas: véase p. 83.

[1] Persons aged 6 years and over. [2] Excl. armed forces and conscripts. [3] Persons aged 15 years and over.

[1] Personnes âgées de 6 ans et plus. [2] Non compris les forces armées et les conscrits. [3] Personnes âgées de 15 ans et plus.

[1] Personas de 6 años y más. [2] Excl. las fuerzas armadas y los conscriptos. [3] Personas de 15 años y más.

EMPLOYMENT	EMPLOI	EMPLEO
Total employment, by economic activity	Emploi total, par activité économique	Empleo total, por actividad económica
Thousands	Milliers	Millares

	1999	2000	2001	2002	2003	2004	2005	2006	2007	2008

Mali (BA) [1]

Total employment - Emploi total - Empleo total

Men - Hommes - Hombres
ISIC 3 - CITI 3 - CIIU 3

	1999	2000	2001	2002	2003	2004	2005	2006	2007	2008
Total						1 388.3				
A						657.7				
B						33.3				
C						8.4				
D						136.1				
E						5.1				
F						97.5				
G						266.1				
H						1.4				
I						51.8				
J						4.4				
K						3.5				
L						33.3				
M						35.6				
N						11.4				
O						23.8				
P						18.8				
Q						-				

Women - Femmes - Mujeres
ISIC 3 - CITI 3 - CIIU 3

	1999	2000	2001	2002	2003	2004	2005	2006	2007	2008
Total						982.5				
A						291.7				
B						2.0				
C						3.0				
D						136.4				
E						0.0				
F						4.7				
G						402.1				
H						6.3				
I						3.5				
J						0.0				
K						0.6				
L						6.6				
M						18.3				
N						9.5				
O						11.5				
P						85.1				
Q						0.9				

Maroc (BA) [1]

Total employment - Emploi total - Empleo total

Total - Total - Total
ISIC 3 - CITI 3 - CIIU 3

	1999	2000	2001	2002	2003	2004	2005	2006	2007	2008
Total				9 487.5 [2]	9 602.8	9 821.9	9 913.3	9 927.7	10 056.2	
A-B				4 209.4 [2]	4 212.0	4 497.4	4 505.2	4 303.3	4 235.1	
C				50.8 [2]	54.5	40.6	41.8	39.9	48.4	
D				1 171.3 [2]	1 192.4	1 178.0	1 153.9	1 142.0	1 191.3	
E				37.3 [2]	39.0	31.2	31.7	42.8	39.4	
F				647.6 [2]	650.5	662.0	705.4	789.6	838.9	
G				1 371.3 [2]	1 228.5					
G-H						1 613.0	1 656.9	1 602.3	1 637.0	
H				174.9 [2]	181.8					
I				331.9 [2]	342.7	347.4	380.3	394.7	401.9	
J-K				115.3 [2]	123.3	116.0	130.2	152.4	171.9	
L				502.6 [2]	485.7					
L-Q						1 328.9	1 301.4	1 449.5	1 478.7	
M-Q				871.1 [2]	1 085.0					
X				4.1 [2]	7.2	7.2	6.5	11.1	13.7	

Men - Hommes - Hombres
ISIC 3 - CITI 3 - CIIU 3

	1999	2000	2001	2002	2003	2004	2005	2006	2007	2008
Total				7 100.6 [2]	7 074.8	7 155.0	7 240.7	7 233.3	7 323.7	
A-B				2 845.9 [2]	2 775.1	2 887.3	2 864.4	2 651.8	2 596.3	
C				49.1 [2]	52.4	39.4	41.1	39.3	47.4	
D				730.8 [2]	732.7	740.5	739.5	760.8	791.2	
E				33.7 [2]	36.1	27.9	29.0	39.2	34.5	
F				640.7 [2]	644.2	656.8	699.4	783.1	832.4	
G				1 282.4 [2]	1 132.1					
G-H						1 476.7	1 519.5	1 461.6	1 484.4	
H				152.0 [2]	151.1					
I				312.5 [2]	321.1	323.9	350.1	367.7	371.9	
J-K				77.7 [2]	81.5	77.5	91.2	105.0	118.9	
L				414.8 [2]	397.7					
L-Q						919.1	902.1	1 016.2	1 035.8	
M-Q				558.2 [2]	745.2					
X				2.8 [2]	5.5	5.9	4.6	8.6	10.7	

Explanatory notes: see p. 77.	Notes explicatives: voir p. 80.	Notas explicativas: véase p. 83.
[1] Persons aged 15 years and over. [2] Persons aged 7 years and over.	[1] Personnes âgées de 15 ans et plus. [2] Personnes âgées de 7 ans et plus.	[1] Personas de 15 años y más. [2] Personas de 7 años y más.

Total employment, by economic activity — **Emploi total, par activité économique** — **Empleo total, por actividad económica**

Thousands — Milliers — Millares

Maroc (BA) [1]
Women - Femmes - Mujeres
ISIC 3 - CITI 3 - CIIU 3

Total employment - Emploi total - Empleo total

	1999	2000	2001	2002	2003	2004	2005	2006	2007	2008
Total	.	.	.	2 387.0 [2]	2 528.0	2 666.9	2 672.6	2 694.4	2 732.6	.
A-B	.	.	.	1 363.4 [2]	1 436.9	1 610.3	1 640.8	1 651.6	1 638.8	.
C	.	.	.	1.8 [2]	2.1	1.2	0.7	0.6	0.9	.
D	.	.	.	440.5 [2]	459.7	437.5	414.4	381.2	400.1	.
E	.	.	.	3.6 [2]	2.8	3.3	2.8	3.6	4.9	.
F	.	.	.	6.9 [2]	6.3	5.2	6.0	6.5	6.4	.
G	.	.	.	88.9 [2]	96.4					.
G-H	.	.	.			137.4	136.3	140.8	152.6	.
H	.	.	.	22.9 [2]	30.7					.
I	.	.	.	19.4 [2]	21.6	23.5	30.2	27.1	29.9	.
J-K	.	.	.	37.6 [2]	41.9	38.5	39.1	47.4	53.0	.
L	.	.	.	87.9 [2]	88.0					.
L-Q	.	.	.			409.8	399.3	433.3	442.9	.
M-Q	.	.	.	312.9 [2]	339.8					.
X	.	.	.	1.3 [2]	1.7	1.3	1.9	2.5	3.0	.

Mauritius (BA) [3][4]
Total - Total - Total
ISIC 3 - CITI 3 - CIIU 3

Total employment - Emploi total - Empleo total

	1999	2000	2001	2002	2003	2004	2005	2006	2007	2008
Total	.	.	.	.	.	487.0	490.4	499.1 |	502.1 [5]	519.0
A	.	.	.	.	.	42.7	43.0	41.4 |	40.0 [5]	40.8
B	.	.	.	.	.	6.1	6.0	6.7 |	5.7 [5]	5.3
C	.	.	.	.	.	0.2	0.3	0.4 |	0.3 [5]	0.5
D	.	.	.	.	.	109.1	103.7	105.3 |	102.2 [5]	102.2
E	.	.	.	.	.	3.5	3.8	3.5 |	4.1 [5]	3.7
F	.	.	.	.	.	50.5	51.1	51.1 |	55.5 [5]	57.7
G	.	.	.	.	.	73.3	68.6	69.6 |	71.3 [5]	71.6
H	.	.	.	.	.	27.3	34.3	35.1 |	34.8 [5]	37.1
I	.	.	.	.	.	33.2	34.5	34.9 |	35.9 [5]	38.3
J	.	.	.	.	.	9.9	10.0	9.9 |	10.3 [5]	13.4
K	.	.	.	.	.	17.9	20.9	21.7 |	21.5 [5]	26.4
L	.	.	.	.	.	36.0	36.4	37.9 |	34.7 [5]	34.0
M	.	.	.	.	.	27.9	28.3	28.4 |	28.9 [5]	30.1
N	.	.	.	.	.	15.3	16.2	15.8 |	18.1 [5]	16.6
O	.	.	.	.	.	14.9	15.8	17.2 |	16.5 [5]	19.8
P	.	.	.	.	.	17.8	16.7	18.6 |	18.8 [5]	19.1
Q	.	.	.	.	.	0.2	0.2	0.3 |	0.5 [5]	0.3
X	.	.	.	.	.	1.2	0.6	1.3 |	3.0 [5]	2.1

Men - Hommes - Hombres
ISIC 3 - CITI 3 - CIIU 3

	1999	2000	2001	2002	2003	2004	2005	2006	2007	2008
Total	.	.	.	.	.	327.9	329.1	332.5 |	335.0 [5]	341.0
A	.	.	.	.	.	30.4	29.5	28.5 |	28.0 [5]	28.1
B	.	.	.	.	.	5.4	5.2	6.1 |	5.0 [5]	4.7
C	.	.	.	.	.	0.1	0.3	0.3 |	0.2 [5]	0.3
D	.	.	.	.	.	60.8	58.4	60.9 |	60.6 [5]	59.6
E	.	.	.	.	.	3.2	3.7	3.3 |	3.5 [5]	3.2
F	.	.	.	.	.	49.4	50.1	50.3 |	54.7 [5]	56.1
G	.	.	.	.	.	48.6	44.6	43.2 |	43.9 [5]	44.8
H	.	.	.	.	.	19.8	23.2	23.4 |	23.2 [5]	24.6
I	.	.	.	.	.	29.0	30.2	30.0 |	30.8 [5]	32.7
J	.	.	.	.	.	5.9	6.0	5.5 |	5.8 [5]	6.7
K	.	.	.	.	.	13.2	15.6	15.2 |	14.5 [5]	17.5
L	.	.	.	.	.	28.1	28.1	29.7 |	27.3 [5]	25.1
M	.	.	.	.	.	11.7	12.5	13.0 |	12.8 [5]	13.1
N	.	.	.	.	.	7.9	7.3	7.6 |	8.7 [5]	8.0
O	.	.	.	.	.	10.5	11.1	11.7 |	10.7 [5]	12.6
P	.	.	.	.	.	2.6	2.7	2.6 |	2.7 [5]	2.2
Q	.	.	.	.	.	0.2	0.1	0.2 |	0.4 [5]	0.2
X	.	.	.	.	.	1.1	0.5	1.0 |	2.2 [5]	1.5

Explanatory notes: see p. 77.

[1] Persons aged 15 years and over. [2] Persons aged 7 years and over. [3] Excl. armed forces. [4] Persons aged 16 years and over. [5] Prior to 2007: persons aged 15 years and over.

Notes explicatives: voir p. 80.

[1] Personnes âgées de 15 ans et plus. [2] Personnes âgées de 7 ans et plus. [3] Non compris les forces armées. [4] Personnes âgées de 16 ans et plus. [5] Avant 2006: personnes âgées de 15 ans et plus.

Notas explicativas: véase p. 83.

[1] Personas de 15 años y más. [2] Personas de 7 años y más. [3] Excl. las fuerzas armadas. [4] Personas de 16 años y más. [5] Antes de 2006: personas de 15 años y más.

EMPLOYMENT

Total employment, by economic activity

EMPLOI

Emploi total, par activité économique

EMPLEO

Empleo total, por actividad económica

	Thousands					Milliers			Millares	
	1999	2000	2001	2002	2003	2004	2005	2006	2007	2008

Mauritius (BA) [1] [2]

Total employment - Emploi total - Empleo total

Women - Femmes - Mujeres
ISIC 3 - CITI 3 - CIIU 3

	1999	2000	2001	2002	2003	2004	2005	2006	2007	2008
Total	.	.	.	.	.	159.1	161.3	166.6	167.1 [3]	178.0
A	.	.	.	.	.	12.3	13.5	12.9	12.0 [3]	12.7
B	.	.	.	.	.	0.7	0.8	0.6	0.7 [3]	0.6
C	.	.	.	.	.	0.1	0.0	0.1	0.1 [3]	0.2
D	.	.	.	.	.	48.3	45.3	44.4	41.6 [3]	42.6
E	.	.	.	.	.	0.3	0.1	0.2	0.6 [3]	0.5
F	.	.	.	.	.	1.1	1.0	0.8	0.8 [3]	1.6
G	.	.	.	.	.	24.7	24.0	26.4	27.4 [3]	26.8
H	.	.	.	.	.	7.5	11.1	11.7	11.6 [3]	12.5
I	.	.	.	.	.	4.2	4.3	4.9	5.1 [3]	5.6
J	.	.	.	.	.	4.0	4.0	4.4	4.5 [3]	6.7
K	.	.	.	.	.	4.7	5.3	6.5	7.0 [3]	8.9
L	.	.	.	.	.	7.9	8.3	8.2	7.4 [3]	8.9
M	.	.	.	.	.	16.2	15.8	15.4	16.1 [3]	17.0
N	.	.	.	.	.	7.4	8.9	8.2	9.4 [3]	8.6
O	.	.	.	.	.	4.4	4.7	5.5	5.8 [3]	7.2
P	.	.	.	.	.	15.2	14.0	16.0	16.1 [3]	16.9
Q	.	.	.	.	.	-	0.1	0.1	0.1 [3]	0.1
X	.	.	.	.	.	0.1	0.1	0.3	0.8 [3]	0.6

Mauritius (E)

Total employment - Emploi total - Empleo total

Total - Total - Total
ISIC 3 - CITI 3 - CIIU 3

	1999	2000	2001	2002	2003	2004	2005	2006	2007	2008
Total	485.9	493.6	493.8	500.4	504.5	507.2	515.3	523.7	543.0	
A-B	59.0	57.5	50.1	49.5	49.0	48.6	47.9	47.3	46.8	
C	1.3	1.3	1.3	0.3	0.3	0.3	0.3	0.2	0.2	
D	139.2	140.7	136.8	132.0	125.7	120.1	120.9	122.5	122.0	
E	3.0	3.0	3.1	3.0	3.0	3.0	3.0	3.0	3.1	
F	45.1	45.8	46.3	48.0	49.1	47.2	48.4	49.7	52.5	
G	62.8	64.7	67.4	71.3	74.8	76.6	78.8	78.4	80.8	
H	23.6	25.1	26.3	27.4	28.4	30.9	31.6	32.1	36.1	
I	31.5	32.4	34.1	34.9	35.9	36.5	36.9	37.4	39.2	
J	7.2	7.4	7.4	7.8	7.9	8.8	9.4	10.6	12.5	
K	14.6	15.1	15.7	16.6	18.1	20.0	21.1	24.7	28.4	
L	35.1	36.2	38.2	39.2	39.0	39.4	39.6	39.1	39.6	
M	22.0	22.6	23.6	25.1	26.2	27.1	28.4	28.8	29.3	
N	13.3	13.0	13.4	14.0	14.5	15.0	15.0	15.6	16.4	
O	28.2	28.8	30.1	31.3	33.1	33.7	34.0	34.3	36.1	

Men - Hommes - Hombres
ISIC 3 - CITI 3 - CIIU 3

	1999	2000	2001	2002	2003	2004	2005	2006	2007	2008
Total	323.2	326.4	328.6	332.4	336.9	338.5	340.5	347.1	355.7	
A-B	41.8	40.7	36.4	36.3	35.9	35.8	35.2	35.2	34.1	
C	1.2	1.2	1.2	0.2	0.2	0.2	0.2	0.2	0.2	
D	69.9	70.4	70.3	68.5	67.7	67.0	66.3	68.4	68.9	
E	2.8	2.8	2.9	2.8	2.8	2.8	2.8	2.8	2.9	
F	44.5	45.2	45.7	47.4	48.5	46.5	47.6	48.9	51.7	
G	43.0	43.8	45.2	47.3	49.3	49.5	50.1	50.1	50.6	
H	17.1	18.2	19.1	19.6	20.4	22.1	22.3	22.6	24.6	
I	28.5	28.9	30.4	31.0	31.7	32.1	32.3	32.7	33.9	
J	4.3	4.4	4.4	4.5	4.5	4.8	5.1	5.8	6.5	
K	10.8	11.1	11.1	11.7	12.3	13.4	14.1	15.5	17.4	
L	28.3	28.8	30.2	30.8	30.6	30.7	30.6	30.3	30.4	
M	11.3	11.2	11.4	11.9	12.1	12.2	12.7	12.9	12.5	
N	7.0	6.9	7.1	7.3	7.5	7.8	7.5	7.9	8.0	
O	12.7	12.8	13.2	13.1	13.4	13.6	13.7	13.8	14.1	

Women - Femmes - Mujeres
ISIC 3 - CITI 3 - CIIU 3

	1999	2000	2001	2002	2003	2004	2005	2006	2007	2008
Total	162.7	167.2	165.2	168.0	167.6	168.7	174.8	176.6	187.3	
A-B	17.2	16.8	13.7	13.2	13.1	12.8	12.7	12.1	12.7	
C	0.1	0.1	0.1	0.1	0.1	0.1	0.1	0.0	0.1	
D	69.3	70.3	66.5	63.5	57.5	53.1	54.6	54.1	53.1	
E	0.2	0.2	0.2	0.2	0.2	0.2	0.2	0.2	0.2	
F	0.6	0.6	0.6	0.6	0.6	0.7	0.8	0.8	0.8	
G	19.8	20.9	22.2	24.0	25.5	27.1	28.7	28.3	30.2	
H	6.5	6.9	7.2	7.8	8.0	8.8	9.3	9.5	11.5	
I	3.0	3.5	3.7	3.9	4.2	4.4	4.6	4.7	5.3	
J	2.9	3.0	3.0	3.3	3.4	4.0	4.3	4.8	6.0	
K	3.8	4.0	4.6	4.9	5.8	6.6	7.0	9.2	11.0	
L	6.8	7.4	8.0	8.4	8.4	8.7	9.0	8.8	9.2	
M	10.7	11.4	12.2	13.2	14.1	14.9	15.7	15.9	16.8	
N	6.3	6.1	6.3	6.7	7.0	7.2	7.5	7.7	8.4	
O	15.5	16.0	16.9	18.2	19.7	20.1	20.3	20.5	22.0	

Explanatory notes: see p. 77.

[1] Excl. armed forces. [2] Persons aged 16 years and over. [3] Prior to 2007: persons aged 15 years and over.

Notes explicatives: voir p. 80.

[1] Non compris les forces armées. [2] Personnes âgées de 16 ans et plus. [3] Avant 2006: personnes âgées de 15 ans et plus.

Notas explicativas: véase p. 83.

[1] Excl. las fuerzas armadas. [2] Personas de 16 años y más. [3] Antes de 2006: personas de 15 años y más.

Total employment, by economic activity
Emploi total, par activité économique
Empleo total, por actividad económica

	Thousands							Milliers		Millares
	1999	2000	2001	2002	2003	2004	2005	2006	2007	2008

Namibia (BA) [1] Total employment - Emploi total - Empleo total

Total - Total - Total
ISIC 3 - CITI 3 - CIIU 3

	1999	2000	2001	2002	2003	2004	2005	2006	2007	2008
Total	.	431.849	.	.	.	385.329	.	.	.	.
A	.	126.459	.	.	.	102.636	.	.	.	.
B	.	7.800	.	.	.	12.720	.	.	.	.
C	.	3.868	.	.	.	7.562	.	.	.	.
D	.	22.922	.	.	.	23.755	.	.	.	.
E	.	4.193	.	.	.	6.151	.	.	.	.
F	.	21.788	.	.	.	19.605	.	.	.	.
G	.	38.902	.	.	.	53.895	.	.	.	.
H	.	7.677	.	.	.	13.132	.	.	.	.
I	.	14.308	.	.	.	15.861	.	.	.	.
J	.	4.933	.	.	.	7.582	.	.	.	.
K	.	39.318	.	.	.	9.375	.	.	.	.
L	.	24.419	.	.	.	30.685	.	.	.	.
M	.	30.538	.	.	.	31.168	.	.	.	.
N	.	13.135	.	.	.	14.010	.	.	.	.
O	.	46.289	.	.	.	12.632	.	.	.	.
P	.	22.210	.	.	.	24.081	.	.	.	.
Q	.	0.327	.	.	.	0.072	.	.	.	.
X	.	2.765	.	.	.	0.407	.	.	.	.

Men - Hommes - Hombres
ISIC 3 - CITI 3 - CIIU 3

	1999	2000	2001	2002	2003	2004	2005	2006	2007	2008
Total	.	226.828	.	.	.	216.651	.	.	.	.
A	.	69.782	.	.	.	64.991	.	.	.	.
B	.	4.725	.	.	.	7.933	.	.	.	.
C	.	3.154	.	.	.	5.909	.	.	.	.
D	.	11.375	.	.	.	12.082	.	.	.	.
E	.	3.709	.	.	.	5.031	.	.	.	.
F	.	20.740	.	.	.	18.296	.	.	.	.
G	.	17.220	.	.	.	27.004	.	.	.	.
H	.	3.006	.	.	.	5.889	.	.	.	.
I	.	12.243	.	.	.	12.744	.	.	.	.
J	.	2.489	.	.	.	3.506	.	.	.	.
K	.	17.880	.	.	.	5.280	.	.	.	.
L	.	15.372	.	.	.	20.216	.	.	.	.
M	.	11.742	.	.	.	12.313	.	.	.	.
N	.	2.993	.	.	.	3.533	.	.	.	.
O	.	24.324	.	.	.	7.480	.	.	.	.
P	.	4.754	.	.	.	4.067	.	.	.	.
Q	.	0.155	.	.	.	0.072	.	.	.	.
X	.	1.166	.	.	.	0.305	.	.	.	.

Women - Femmes - Mujeres
ISIC 3 - CITI 3 - CIIU 3

	1999	2000	2001	2002	2003	2004	2005	2006	2007	2008
Total	.	205.021	.	.	.	168.678	.	.	.	.
A	.	56.677	.	.	.	37.645	.	.	.	.
B	.	3.075	.	.	.	4.787	.	.	.	.
C	.	0.713	.	.	.	1.653	.	.	.	.
D	.	11.548	.	.	.	11.673	.	.	.	.
E	.	0.484	.	.	.	1.120	.	.	.	.
F	.	1.048	.	.	.	1.309	.	.	.	.
G	.	21.683	.	.	.	26.891	.	.	.	.
H	.	4.671	.	.	.	7.243	.	.	.	.
I	.	2.065	.	.	.	3.117	.	.	.	.
J	.	2.444	.	.	.	4.076	.	.	.	.
K	.	21.437	.	.	.	4.095	.	.	.	.
L	.	9.047	.	.	.	10.469	.	.	.	.
M	.	18.797	.	.	.	18.855	.	.	.	.
N	.	10.143	.	.	.	10.477	.	.	.	.
O	.	21.965	.	.	.	5.152	.	.	.	.
P	.	17.456	.	.	.	20.014	.	.	.	.
Q	.	0.172	.	.	.	0.000	.	.	.	.
X	.	1.599	.	.	.	0.102	.	.	.	.

Sénégal (B) [2] Total employment - Emploi total - Empleo total

Total - Total - Total
ISIC 3 - CITI 3 - CIIU 3

	1999	2000	2001	2002	2003	2004	2005	2006	2007	2008
Total	.	.	.	.	.	.	.	3 152.9	.	.
A	.	.	.	.	.	.	.	986.5	.	.
B	.	.	.	.	.	.	.	76.9	.	.
C	.	.	.	.	.	.	.	14.1	.	.
D	.	.	.	.	.	.	.	245.4	.	.
E	.	.	.	.	.	.	.	21.8	.	.
F	.	.	.	.	.	.	.	186.6	.	.
G	.	.	.	.	.	.	.	785.9	.	.
H	.	.	.	.	.	.	.	28.6	.	.
I	.	.	.	.	.	.	.	141.7	.	.
J	.	.	.	.	.	.	.	16.7	.	.
L-N	.	.	.	.	.	.	.	157.7	.	.
Q	.	.	.	.	.	.	.	7.0	.	.
X	.	.	.	.	.	.	.	484.0	.	.

Explanatory notes: see p. 77. Notes explicatives: voir p. 80. Notas explicativas: véase p. 83.

[1] Persons aged 15 to 69 years. [2] Persons aged 15 years and over. [1] Personnes âgées de 15 à 69 ans. [2] Personnes âgées de 15 ans et plus. [1] Personas de 15 a 69 años. [2] Personas de 15 años y más.

EMPLOYMENT — EMPLOI — EMPLEO

Total employment, by economic activity — Emploi total, par activité économique — Empleo total, por actividad económica

Thousands — Milliers — Millares

	1999	2000	2001	2002	2003	2004	2005	2006	2007	2008

Sénégal (B) [1]

Total employment - Emploi total - Empleo total

Men - Hommes - Hombres
ISIC 3 - CITI 3 - CIIU 3

	1999	2000	2001	2002	2003	2004	2005	2006	2007	2008
Total	.	.	.	.	.	.	.	2 048.1	.	.
A								631.9		
B								66.5		
C								11.5		
D								203.7		
E								18.5		
F								179.7		
G								388.0		
H								12.2		
I								135.9		
J								11.8		
L-N								118.7		
Q								3.3		
X								266.5		

Women - Femmes - Mujeres
ISIC 3 - CITI 3 - CIIU 3

	1999	2000	2001	2002	2003	2004	2005	2006	2007	2008
Total	.	.	.	.	.	.	.	1 104.8	.	.
A								354.6		
B								10.4		
C								2.6		
D								41.7		
E								3.3		
F								6.9		
G								397.9		
H								16.4		
I								5.8		
J								4.9		
L-N								39.0		
Q								3.7		
X								217.5		

South Africa (BA) [2][3]

Total employment - Emploi total - Empleo total

Total - Total - Total
ISIC 3 - CITI 3 - CIIU 3

	1999	2000	2001	2002	2003	2004	2005	2006	2007	2008
Total	12 238	11 181	11 296	11 424	11 643	12 301	12 800	13 234	13 713
A-B	1 914	1 178	1 420	1 212	1 063	925	1 088	1 164	776
C	603	554	559	552	405	411	398	455	328
D	1 578	1 620	1 633	1 550	1 714	1 706	1 737	1 799	1 961
E	94	94	84	91	99	100	119	116	94
F	683	634	605	664	824	935	1 024	1 066	1 141
G-H	2 476	2 454	2 194	2 429	2 542	3 024	3 055	2 952	3 141
I	582	546	574	537	563	616	611	596	767
J-K	976	1 035	1 084	1 098	1 147	1 296	1 309	1 340	1 646
L-O	2 084	1 989	2 043	2 180	2 185	2 192	2 319	2 452	2 624
P	1 146	1 034	1 029	1 075	1 075	1 067	1 108	1 244	1 232
X	103	42	72	34	26	29	33	51	3

Men - Hommes - Hombres
ISIC 3 - CITI 3 - CIIU 3

	1999	2000	2001	2002	2003	2004	2005	2006	2007	2008
Total	6 943	6 442	6 614	6 613	6 772	7 055	7 320	7 554	7 672
A-B	1 062	832	941	847	703	608	662	798	520
C	585	535	536	529	394	388	375	419	292
D	1 020	1 047	1 082	1 028	1 117	1 113	1 146	1 231	1 331
E	79	82	67	69	74	77	95	68	69
F	633	575	546	584	747	858	911	947	1 027
G-H	1 272	1 240	1 122	1 237	1 347	1 543	1 581	1 496	1 561
I	495	452	470	425	441	491	487	460	615
J-K	587	581	677	662	697	739	760	781	910
L-O	931	907	925	996	1 006	1 000	1 055	1 027	1 086
P	216	166	210	217	229	217	223	299	260
X	63	25	39	19	16	22	25	29	2

Women - Femmes - Mujeres
ISIC 3 - CITI 3 - CIIU 3

	1999	2000	2001	2002	2003	2004	2005	2006	2007	2008
Total	5 295	4 739	4 678	4 810	4 866	5 242	5 480	5 668	6 041
A-B	852	346	479	365	359	317	426	366	257
C	17	19	23	24	11	23	23	36	36
D	558	574	551	521	597	593	591	567	630
E	15	12	17	22	25	23	24	48	25
F	50	59	59	81	77	77	113	119	114
G-H	1 203	1 214	1 072	1 192	1 195	1 479	1 474	1 455	1 580
I	87	95	104	112	121	125	123	135	152
J-K	389	454	406	436	450	556	550	558	736
L-O	1 154	1 082	1 115	1 184	1 175	1 192	1 264	1 422	1 538
P	930	868	819	858	845	850	884	945	972
X	41	17	33	15	10	7	8	22	2

Explanatory notes: see p. 77.

Notes explicatives: voir p. 80.

Notas explicativas: véase p. 83.

[1] Persons aged 15 years and over. [2] Persons aged 15 to 64 years. [3] Prior to 2008: persons aged 15 years and over; September of each year.

[1] Personnes âgées de 15 ans et plus. [2] Personnes âgées de 15 à 64 ans. [3] Avant 2008: personnes agées de 15 ans et plus; septembre de chaque année.

[1] Personas de 15 años y más. [2] Personas de 15 a 64 años. [3] Antes de 2008: personas de 15 años y más; Septiembre de cada año.

Total employment, by economic activity
Emploi total, par activité économique
Empleo total, por actividad económica

	1999	2000	2001	2002	2003	2004	2005	2006	2007	2008	

Thousands   Milliers   Millares

Saint Helena (A) [1] [2]   Total employment - Emploi total - Empleo total

Total - Total - Total
ISIC 3 - CITI 3 - CIIU 3

	2008
Total	2.130
A	0.122
B	0.033
C	0.008
D	0.115
E	0.113
F	0.190
G	0.385
H	0.036
I	0.237
J	0.020
K	0.185
L	0.157
M	0.112
N	0.178
O	0.217
P	0.017
Q	0.005
X	-

Men - Hommes - Hombres
ISIC 3 - CITI 3 - CIIU 3

	2008
Total	1.174
A	0.107
B	0.032
C	0.006
D	0.090
E	0.113
F	0.189
G	0.145
H	0.013
I	0.188
J	0.004
K	0.059
L	0.067
M	0.015
N	0.020
O	0.114
P	0.007
Q	0.005
X	-

Women - Femmes - Mujeres
ISIC 3 - CITI 3 - CIIU 3

	2008
Total	0.956
A	0.015
B	0.001
C	0.002
D	0.025
E	-
F	0.001
G	0.240
H	0.023
I	0.049
J	0.016
K	0.126
L	0.090
M	0.097
N	0.158
O	0.103
P	0.010
Q	-
X	-

Explanatory notes: see p. 77.   Notes explicatives: voir p. 80.   Notas explicativas: véase p. 83.

[1] Persons aged 15 to 69 years. [2] Feb.   [1] Personnes âgées de 15 à 69 ans. [2] Fév.   [1] Personas de 15 a 69 años. [2] Feb.

**Total employment,
by economic activity**

**Emploi total,
par activité économique**

**Empleo total,
por actividad económica**

	1999	2000	2001	2002	2003	2004	2005	2006	2007	2008
	Thousands				Milliers				Millares	

Tanzania, United Republic of (BA) [1]   Total employment - Emploi total - Empleo total

Total - Total - Total
ISIC 3 - CITI 3 - CIIU 3

								2006		
Total								17 944.6		
A								13 185.1		
B								209.6		
C								104.9		
D								565.1		
E								17.0		
F								211.5		
G								1 572.7		
H								377.5		
I								258.1		
J								17.5		
K								82.0		
L								184.7		
M								225.6		
N								105.2		
O								126.5		
P								701.5		

Men - Hommes - Hombres
ISIC 3 - CITI 3 - CIIU 3

								2006		
Total								8 779.8		
A								6 064.8		
B								184.6		
C								90.8		
D								332.9		
E								13.5		
F								204.8		
G								907.7		
H								98.5		
I								245.0		
J								11.3		
K								69.0		
L								157.4		
M								126.9		
N								46.1		
O								88.3		
P								138.2		

Women - Femmes - Mujeres
ISIC 3 - CITI 3 - CIIU 3

								2006		
Total								9 164.7		
A								7 120.3		
B								25.0		
C								14.1		
D								232.2		
E								3.5		
F								6.7		
G								665.0		
H								279.0		
I								13.1		
J								6.2		
K								13.0		
L								27.3		
M								98.7		
N								59.1		
O								38.2		
P								563.3		

Explanatory notes: see p. 77.
[1] Persons aged 15 years and over.

Notes explicatives: voir p. 80.
[1] Personnes âgées de 15 ans et plus.

Notas explicativas: véase p. 83.
[1] Personas de 15 años y más.

**Total employment,
by economic activity**

**Emploi total,
par activité économique**

**Empleo total,
por actividad económica**

	Thousands				Milliers				Millares	
	1999	2000	2001	2002	2003	2004	2005	2006	2007	2008

AMERICA-AMÉRIQUE-AMERICA

Antigua and Barbuda (E) [1]　　　　Total employment - Emploi total - Empleo total

Total - Total - Total
ISIC 3 - CITI 3 - CIIU 3

	1999	2000	2001	2002	2003	2004	2005	2006	2007	2008
Total	.	.	33.801	34.431	35.074	35.728	36.395	37.074	37.765	38.470
A	.	.	0.693	0.706	0.719	0.733	0.746	0.760	0.774	0.789
B	.	.	0.255	0.260	0.265	0.270	0.275	0.280	0.285	0.290
C	.	.	0.106	0.108	0.110	0.112	0.114	0.116	0.118	0.121
D	.	.	1.541	1.570	1.599	1.629	1.659	1.690	1.722	1.754
E	.	.	0.514	0.524	0.533	0.543	0.553	0.564	0.574	0.585
F	.	.	3.125	3.183	3.243	3.303	3.365	3.428	3.491	3.557
G	.	.	4.847	4.937	5.030	5.123	5.219	5.316	5.415	5.516
H	.	.	5.081	5.176	5.272	5.371	5.471	5.573	5.677	5.783
I	.	.	2.814	2.866	2.920	2.974	3.030	3.086	3.144	3.203
J	.	.	1.050	1.070	1.090	1.110	1.131	1.152	1.173	1.195
K	.	.	1.463	1.490	1.518	1.546	1.575	1.605	1.635	1.665
L	.	.	4.381	4.463	4.546	4.631	4.717	4.805	4.895	4.986
M	.	.	1.719	1.751	1.784	1.817	1.851	1.885	1.921	1.956
N	.	.	1.718	1.750	1.783	1.816	1.850	1.884	1.919	1.955
O	.	.	2.686	2.736	2.787	2.839	2.892	2.946	3.001	3.057
P	.	.	1.305	1.329	1.354	1.379	1.405	1.431	1.458	1.485
Q	.	.	0.503	0.512	0.522	0.532	0.542	0.552	0.562	0.572

Men - Hommes - Hombres
ISIC 3 - CITI 3 - CIIU 3

	1999	2000	2001	2002	2003	2004	2005	2006	2007	2008
Total	.	.	16.976	17.293	17.615	17.944	18.279	18.620	18.967	19.321
A	.	.	0.495	0.504	0.514	0.523	0.533	0.543	0.553	0.563
B	.	.	0.253	0.258	0.263	0.267	0.272	0.277	0.283	0.288
C	.	.	0.087	0.089	0.090	0.092	0.094	0.095	0.097	0.099
D	.	.	0.926	0.943	0.961	0.979	0.997	1.016	1.035	1.054
E	.	.	0.420	0.428	0.436	0.444	0.452	0.461	0.469	0.478
F	.	.	3.004	3.060	3.117	3.175	3.235	3.295	3.356	3.419
G	.	.	2.272	2.314	2.358	2.402	2.446	2.492	2.538	2.586
H	.	.	2.045	2.083	2.122	2.162	2.202	2.243	2.285	2.327
I	.	.	1.829	1.863	1.898	1.933	1.969	2.006	2.044	2.082
J	.	.	0.319	0.325	0.331	0.337	0.343	0.350	0.356	0.363
K	.	.	0.803	0.818	0.833	0.849	0.865	0.881	0.897	0.914
L	.	.	2.108	2.147	2.187	2.228	2.270	2.312	2.355	2.399
M	.	.	0.395	0.402	0.410	0.418	0.425	0.433	0.441	0.450
N	.	.	0.300	0.306	0.311	0.317	0.323	0.329	0.335	0.341
O	.	.	1.175	1.197	1.219	1.242	1.265	1.289	1.313	1.337
P	.	.	0.238	0.242	0.247	0.252	0.256	0.261	0.266	0.271
Q	.	.	0.307	0.313	0.319	0.325	0.331	0.337	0.343	0.349

Women - Femmes - Mujeres
ISIC 3 - CITI 3 - CIIU 3

	1999	2000	2001	2002	2003	2004	2005	2006	2007	2008
Total	.	.	16.825	17.139	17.459	17.784	18.116	18.454	18.798	19.149
A	.	.	0.198	0.202	0.205	0.209	0.213	0.217	0.221	0.225
B	.	.	0.002	0.002	0.002	0.002	0.002	0.002	0.002	0.002
C	.	.	0.019	0.019	0.020	0.020	0.020	0.021	0.021	0.022
D	.	.	0.615	0.626	0.638	0.650	0.662	0.675	0.687	0.700
E	.	.	0.094	0.096	0.098	0.099	0.101	0.103	0.105	0.107
F	.	.	0.121	0.123	0.126	0.128	0.130	0.133	0.135	0.138
G	.	.	2.575	2.623	2.672	2.722	2.773	2.824	2.877	2.931
H	.	.	3.036	3.093	3.150	3.209	3.269	3.330	3.392	3.455
I	.	.	0.985	1.003	1.022	1.041	1.061	1.080	1.101	1.121
J	.	.	0.731	0.745	0.759	0.773	0.787	0.802	0.817	0.832
K	.	.	0.660	0.672	0.685	0.698	0.711	0.724	0.737	0.751
L	.	.	2.273	2.315	2.359	2.403	2.447	2.493	2.540	2.587
M	.	.	1.324	1.349	1.374	1.399	1.426	1.452	1.479	1.507
N	.	.	1.418	1.444	1.471	1.499	1.527	1.555	1.584	1.614
O	.	.	1.511	1.539	1.568	1.597	1.627	1.657	1.688	1.720
P	.	.	1.067	1.087	1.107	1.128	1.149	1.170	1.192	1.214
Q	.	.	0.196	0.200	0.203	0.207	0.211	0.215	0.219	0.223

Explanatory notes: see p. 77.	Notes explicatives: voir p. 80.	Notas explicativas: véase p. 83.
[1] Persons aged 15 years and over.	[1] Personnes âgées de 15 ans et plus.	[1] Personas de 15 años y más.

Total employment, by economic activity
Emploi total, par activité économique
Empleo total, por actividad económica

	Thousands						Milliers			Millares	
	1999	2000	2001	2002	2003	2004	2005	2006	2007	2008

Argentina (BA) [1] [2] [3]   Total employment - Emploi total - Empleo total

Total - Total - Total
ISIC 3 - CITI 3 - CIIU 3

	1999	2000	2001	2002	2003	2004	2005	2006	2007	2008
Total	8 285.2	8 261.7	8 143.4	8 016.1	8 956.2 [4]	9 415.0	9 638.7	10 040.5 [5]	.	.
A	56.9	49.7	60.5	70.6	118.1 [4]	97.7	99.8	72.9 [5]	.	.
B	4.8	5.6	7.1	7.7	6.1 [4]	11.2	7.4	9.0 [5]	.	.
C	15.1	15.5	19.6	21.0	28.3 [4]	33.2	30.9	39.8 [5]	.	.
D	1 199.3	1 155.4	1 132.0	1 055.6	1 230.9 [4]	1 360.4	1 359.7	1 410.7 [5]	.	.
E	51.3	48.4	52.1	42.5	47.2 [4]	44.0	48.9	44.1 [5]	.	.
F	689.9	654.1	583.2	497.4	632.9 [4]	731.7	823.0	884.7 [5]	.	.
G	1 640.2	1 683.3	1 658.0	1 543.9	1 830.8 [4]	1 945.7	1 951.8	2 018.6 [5]	.	.
H	236.1	254.8	274.7	233.9	246.2 [4]	321.1	315.6	380.8 [5]	.	.
I	668.2	674.4	655.9	602.3	588.8 [4]	648.0	648.9	644.0 [5]	.	.
J	200.6	207.1	198.3	186.2	148.8 [4]	143.7	162.9	189.4 [5]	.	.
K	634.9	600.4	569.7	556.0	656.3 [4]	676.4	742.7	809.8 [5]	.	.
L	642.8	633.5	659.6	780.0	790.8 [4]	772.9	728.6	768.7 [5]	.	.
M	607.2	625.8	646.4	723.3	748.9 [4]	712.3	736.4	806.8 [5]	.	.
N	487.1	474.5	443.0	496.4	649.1 [4]	652.5	628.3	590.2 [5]	.	.
O	483.0	484.8	514.6	580.9	494.6 [4]	529.9	580.9	546.7 [5]	.	.
P	638.6	655.2	639.1	592.0	676.5 [4]	702.4	741.0	797.0 [5]	.	.
Q	2.0	2.5	1.4	2.7	4.3 [4]	-	3.5	2.2 [5]	.	.
X	27.4	36.6	28.1	23.8	57.6 [4]	31.8	28.4	25.0 [5]	.	.

Men - Hommes - Hombres
ISIC 3 - CITI 3 - CIIU 3

	1999	2000	2001	2002	2003	2004	2005	2006	2007	2008
Total	4 971.4	4 942.0	4 832.4	4 653.6	5 150.9 [4]	5 446.9	5 557.3	5 786.7 [5]	.	.
A	49.4	42.0	51.1	55.1	81.3 [4]	65.7	74.5	59.2 [5]	.	.
B	4.8	5.6	7.1	7.2	5.2 [4]	8.4	6.4	8.2 [5]	.	.
C	13.0	14.9	18.7	18.2	25.6 [4]	30.6	23.2	34.1 [5]	.	.
D	872.2	846.8	817.6	760.3	828.8 [4]	925.4	947.2	988.3 [5]	.	.
E	44.8	40.7	40.9	34.7	34.9 [4]	33.8	44.0	38.1 [5]	.	.
F	673.2	634.2	570.9	486.9	616.9 [4]	717.8	801.1	854.8 [5]	.	.
G	1 067.2	1 074.7	1 051.2	989.2	1 180.2 [4]	1 230.0	1 227.0	1 263.5 [5]	.	.
H	127.5	142.2	158.5	131.6	149.9 [4]	167.6	171.2	213.9 [5]	.	.
I	578.3	589.4	574.1	524.2	510.0 [4]	561.5	548.3	557.4 [5]	.	.
J	117.5	128.8	116.6	108.4	92.8 [4]	92.0	93.0	95.9 [5]	.	.
K	387.8	381.8	348.3	342.9	445.4 [4]	436.2	459.4	528.3 [5]	.	.
L	400.9	389.2	400.4	457.2	486.0 [4]	466.2	429.7	444.4 [5]	.	.
M	117.7	138.0	150.4	167.9	155.2 [4]	154.9	174.6	185.9 [5]	.	.
N	155.6	153.9	150.4	156.4	188.9 [4]	196.6	173.8	163.5 [5]	.	.
O	302.0	294.7	321.3	346.2	264.4 [4]	287.6	311.2	317.1 [5]	.	.
P	42.2	40.7	44.3	55.8	45.1 [4]	53.1	56.4	18.2 [5]	.	.
Q	0.1	1.2	0.2	0.1	2.0 [4]	-	2.1	2.0 [5]	.	.
X	17.3	23.3	10.7	11.1	38.3 [4]	19.5	14.3	13.9 [5]	.	.

Women - Femmes - Mujeres
ISIC 3 - CITI 3 - CIIU 3

	1999	2000	2001	2002	2003	2004	2005	2006	2007	2008
Total	3 313.8	3 319.8	3 310.9	3 362.5	3 805.3 [4]	3 968.0	4 081.4	4 253.8 [5]	.	.
A	7.5	7.7	9.4	15.5	36.8 [4]	32.0	25.3	13.6 [5]	.	.
B	-	0.0	0.0	0.5	0.9 [4]	2.9	1.0	0.8 [5]	.	.
C	2.2	0.6	1.0	2.7	2.7 [4]	2.6	7.7	5.7 [5]	.	.
D	327.1	308.6	314.4	295.3	402.1 [4]	435.0	412.5	422.3 [5]	.	.
E	6.5	7.7	11.2	7.7	12.3 [4]	10.2	5.0	6.0 [5]	.	.
F	16.6	19.9	12.3	10.5	16.0 [4]	14.0	21.9	29.9 [5]	.	.
G	573.0	608.6	606.8	554.7	650.6 [4]	715.7	724.8	755.2 [5]	.	.
H	108.7	112.7	116.3	102.3	96.3 [4]	153.5	144.3	167.0 [5]	.	.
I	89.9	85.0	81.8	78.1	78.8 [4]	86.4	100.6	86.6 [5]	.	.
J	83.1	78.3	81.7	77.9	56.0 [4]	51.8	69.8	93.5 [5]	.	.
K	247.1	218.7	221.3	213.1	210.9 [4]	240.2	283.3	281.5 [5]	.	.
L	241.9	244.3	259.1	322.7	304.7 [4]	306.7	299.0	324.3 [5]	.	.
M	489.5	487.8	496.0	555.4	593.7 [4]	557.4	561.8	620.9 [5]	.	.
N	331.5	320.6	292.7	340.0	460.2 [4]	455.9	454.5	426.7 [5]	.	.
O	180.9	190.1	193.4	234.7	230.2 [4]	242.3	269.7	229.6 [5]	.	.
P	596.3	614.5	594.8	536.2	631.4 [4]	649.3	684.6	778.8 [5]	.	.
Q	1.9	1.3	1.2	2.6	2.4 [4]	-	1.4	0.2 [5]	.	.
X	10.1	13.3	17.4	12.7	19.3 [4]	12.4	14.2	11.2 [5]	.	.

Explanatory notes: see p. 77.

[1] Persons aged 10 years and over. [2] 31 Urban agglomerations. [3] Second semester. [4] Methodology revised; data not strictly comparable; Prior to 2003: May and October. [5] Prior to 2006: 28 urban agglomerations.

Notes explicatives: voir p. 80.

[1] Personnes âgées de 10 ans et plus. [2] 31 agglomérations urbaines. [3] Second semestre. [4] Méthodologie révisée; les données ne sont pas strictement comparables; Avant 2003: mai et octobre. [5] Avant 2006: 28 agglomérations urbaines.

Notas explicativas: véase p. 83.

[1] Personas de 10 años y más. [2] 31 aglomerados úrbanos. [3] Segundo semestre. [4] Metodología revisada; los datos no son estrictamente comparables; antes de 2003: mayo y octubre. [5] Antes de 2006: 28 aglomerados úrbanos

Total employment, by economic activity
Emploi total, par activité économique
Empleo total, por actividad económica

Thousands   Milliers   Millares

	1999	2000	2001	2002	2003	2004	2005	2006	2007	2008
Aruba (BA) [1][2]				Total employment - Emploi total - Empleo total						
Total - Total - Total										
ISIC 3 - CITI 3 - CIIU 3										
Total	.	.	.	.	.	.	.	.	51.607	.
A	.	.	.	.	.	.	.	.	0.352	.
B	.	.	.	.	.	.	.	.	-	.
C	.	.	.	.	.	.	.	.	0.017	.
D	.	.	.	.	.	.	.	.	3.246	.
E	.	.	.	.	.	.	.	.	0.699	.
F	.	.	.	.	.	.	.	.	6.500	.
G	.	.	.	.	.	.	.	.	7.283	.
H	.	.	.	.	.	.	.	.	8.712	.
I	.	.	.	.	.	.	.	.	2.832	.
J	.	.	.	.	.	.	.	.	1.905	.
K	.	.	.	.	.	.	.	.	6.811	.
L	.	.	.	.	.	.	.	.	3.983	.
M	.	.	.	.	.	.	.	.	1.589	.
N	.	.	.	.	.	.	.	.	3.177	.
O	.	.	.	.	.	.	.	.	3.218	.
P	.	.	.	.	.	.	.	.	1.163	.
Q	.	.	.	.	.	.	.	.	0.033	.
X	.	.	.	.	.	.	.	.	0.087	.
Men - Hommes - Hombres										
ISIC 3 - CITI 3 - CIIU 3										
Total	.	.	.	.	.	.	.	.	27.209	.
A	.	.	.	.	.	.	.	.	0.256	.
B	.	.	.	.	.	.	.	.	-	.
C	.	.	.	.	.	.	.	.	0.017	.
D	.	.	.	.	.	.	.	.	2.627	.
E	.	.	.	.	.	.	.	.	0.646	.
F	.	.	.	.	.	.	.	.	5.665	.
G	.	.	.	.	.	.	.	.	3.126	.
H	.	.	.	.	.	.	.	.	3.593	.
I	.	.	.	.	.	.	.	.	1.961	.
J	.	.	.	.	.	.	.	.	0.516	.
K	.	.	.	.	.	.	.	.	3.453	.
L	.	.	.	.	.	.	.	.	2.059	.
M	.	.	.	.	.	.	.	.	0.632	.
N	.	.	.	.	.	.	.	.	0.835	.
O	.	.	.	.	.	.	.	.	1.689	.
P	.	.	.	.	.	.	.	.	0.071	.
Q	.	.	.	.	.	.	.	.	-	.
X	.	.	.	.	.	.	.	.	0.063	.
Women - Femmes - Mujeres										
ISIC 3 - CITI 3 - CIIU 3										
Total	.	.	.	.	.	.	.	.	24.398	.
A	.	.	.	.	.	.	.	.	0.096	.
B	.	.	.	.	.	.	.	.	-	.
C	.	.	.	.	.	.	.	.	-	.
D	.	.	.	.	.	.	.	.	0.619	.
E	.	.	.	.	.	.	.	.	0.053	.
F	.	.	.	.	.	.	.	.	0.835	.
G	.	.	.	.	.	.	.	.	4.157	.
H	.	.	.	.	.	.	.	.	5.119	.
I	.	.	.	.	.	.	.	.	0.871	.
J	.	.	.	.	.	.	.	.	1.389	.
K	.	.	.	.	.	.	.	.	3.358	.
L	.	.	.	.	.	.	.	.	1.924	.
M	.	.	.	.	.	.	.	.	0.957	.
N	.	.	.	.	.	.	.	.	2.342	.
O	.	.	.	.	.	.	.	.	1.529	.
P	.	.	.	.	.	.	.	.	1.092	.
Q	.	.	.	.	.	.	.	.	0.033	.
X	.	.	.	.	.	.	.	.	0.024	.
Bahamas (BA) [1][3][4]				Total employment - Emploi total - Empleo total						
Total - Total - Total										
ISIC 3 - CITI 3 - CIIU 3										
Total	145.35	.	153.31	152.69	154.97	158.34	160.53	165.51 [5]	171.49	.
A-B	5.84	.	6.42	5.64	4.64	7.01	5.59	4.16 [5]	3.94	.
C,E	1.75	.	2.33	2.46	2.18	2.58	2.01	2.41 [5]	2.97	.
D	5.91	.	6.24	6.16	6.77	6.18	7.60	7.37 [5]	6.42	.
F	16.54	.	17.46	16.76	15.54	16.67	18.91	20.61 [5]	21.34	.
G	19.96	.	21.93	22.02	23.84	26.91	23.89	24.49 [5]	24.89	.
H	23.30	.	25.52	25.69	27.92	23.77	29.10	26.66 [5]	27.41	.
I	10.31	.	10.87	11.60	11.79	10.34	10.69	11.18 [5]	13.28	.
J-K	13.35	.	16.33	16.48	15.60	17.58	16.18	18.34 [5]	20.18	.
L-P	47.78	.	45.58	45.17	46.25	47.16	46.04	50.80 [5]	50.69	.
X	0.63	.	0.67	0.73	0.45	0.17	0.54	0.50 [5]	0.39	.

Explanatory notes: see p. 77.   Notes explicatives: voir p. 80.   Notas explicativas: véase p. 83.

[1] Persons aged 15 years and over. [2] Oct. [3] Excl. armed forces. [4] April of each year. [5] May.

[1] Personnes âgées de 15 ans et plus. [2] Oct. [3] Non compris les forces armées. [4] Avril de chaque année. [5] Mai.

[1] Personas de 15 años y más. [2] Oct. [3] Excl. las fuerzas armadas. [4] Abril de cada año. [5] Mayo.

EMPLOYMENT — EMPLOI — EMPLEO

Total employment, by economic activity — Emploi total, par activité économique — Empleo total, por actividad económica

	Thousands — Milliers — Millares									
	1999	2000	2001	2002	2003	2004	2005	2006	2007	2008
Bahamas (BA) [1][2][3]					Total employment - Emploi total - Empleo total					
Men - Hommes - Hombres ISIC 3 - CITI 3 - CIIU 3										
Total	77.25	.	79.08	78.41	79.14	81.74	82.79	85.97 [4]	89.61	.
A-B	5.20	.	5.38	4.41	4.18	6.67	5.30	3.77 [4]	3.74	.
C.E	1.36	.	1.88	1.93	1.50	1.85	1.58	1.95 [4]	2.33	.
D	3.38	.	3.46	4.11	4.03	3.83	4.82	4.92 [4]	4.05	.
F	15.76	.	16.14	16.14	14.74	15.80	18.14	19.42 [4]	19.93	.
G	8.85	.	10.48	10.52	12.05	13.00	11.23	12.04 [4]	12.84	.
H	9.63	.	10.80	10.89	11.99	9.18	11.38	10.83 [4]	11.53	.
I	6.83	.	6.99	7.09	7.89	6.79	7.21	7.29 [4]	9.32	.
J-K	5.30	.	6.38	6.46	5.68	6.93	6.33	7.88 [4]	7.97	.
L-P	20.52	.	17.16	16.62	16.75	17.62	16.43	17.63 [4]	17.67	.
X	0.43	.	0.44	0.26	0.34	0.14	0.37	0.25 [4]	0.25	.
Women - Femmes - Mujeres ISIC 3 - CITI 3 - CIIU 3										
Total	68.11	.	74.23	74.28	75.83	76.56	77.74	80.54 [4]	81.89	.
A-B	0.64	.	1.04	1.24	0.46	0.34	0.27	0.39 [4]	0.20	.
C.E	0.39	.	0.45	0.53	0.69	0.73	0.43	0.46 [4]	0.64	.
D	2.54	.	2.78	2.05	2.74	2.35	2.78	2.45 [4]	2.37	.
F	0.78	.	1.32	0.62	0.81	0.87	0.77	1.19 [4]	1.42	.
G	11.11	.	11.45	11.50	11.79	13.91	12.67	12.45 [4]	12.05	.
H	13.67	.	14.72	14.80	15.94	14.59	17.72	15.83 [4]	15.88	.
I	3.48	.	3.88	4.51	3.90	3.55	3.48	3.89 [4]	3.96	.
J-K	8.06	.	9.95	10.02	9.92	10.65	9.85	10.46 [4]	12.21	.
L-P	27.26	.	28.42	28.56	29.50	29.55	29.61	33.18 [4]	33.02	.
X	0.21	.	0.23	0.48	0.11	0.04	0.17 [1]	0.25 [4]	0.15	.
Bolivia (BA) [5][6]					Total employment - Emploi total - Empleo total					
Total - Total - Total ISIC 3 - CITI 3 - CIIU 3										
Total	3 637.9	3 637.0	3 884.3	3 824.9	.	4 194.8	4 257.2	4 550.3	4 672.4	.
A [7]	1 438.6	1 403.9	1 713.8	1 616.3	.	1 447.8	1 629.8	1 785.0	1 673.2	.
B [8]	14.8	10.9	2.9	4.9	.	23.8	13.8	12.4	13.5	.
C	52.7	50.9	49.3	37.9	.	90.9	71.0	55.5	72.4	.
D	414.6	367.3	357.2	427.4	.	470.4	465.5	477.8	514.9	.
E	8.1	18.2	11.4	8.1	.	14.5	13.9	13.0	15.4	.
F	212.5	240.0	191.4	205.8	.	284.9	275.3	248.1	316.3	.
G	590.1	581.9	573.9	543.2	.	689.0	629.3	647.3	673.8	.
H	141.7	141.8	155.3	176.3	.	236.6	171.4	186.7	159.3	.
I	181.1	156.4	180.3	175.8	.	205.6	256.3	251.5	272.4	.
J	17.5	18.2	20.1	17.3	.	16.2	13.1	23.3	28.0	.
K	73.6	98.2	105.6	78.2	.	93.1	104.6	152.0	136.9	.
L	82.1	80.0	69.6	75.4	.	93.5	91.0	115.2	152.3	.
M	168.8	163.7	156.4	149.1	.	159.4	192.7	217.9	222.9	.
N	66.8	54.6	60.2	62.4	.	74.7	64.0	96.9	109.3	.
O	81.8	105.5	100.9	115.8	.	158.0	153.0	147.5	149.0	.
P	92.0	138.2	134.9	127.5	.	133.8	108.3	119.6	160.7	.
Q	1.2	3.6	0.6	3.6	.	2.6	4.0	0.5	1.9	.
Men - Hommes - Hombres ISIC 3 - CITI 3 - CIIU 3										
Total	2 000.5	2 032.2	2 128.4	2 160.2	.	2 283.0	2 356.0	2 505.6	2 577.0	.
A [7]	783.0	804.7	967.9	964.7	.	787.1	887.9	981.8	871.5	.
B [8]	12.9	10.2	2.0	3.1	.	21.8	11.8	8.8	13.1	.
C	43.8	46.7	45.6	34.1	.	85.7	59.9	50.8	70.6	.
D	241.2	225.6	210.5	263.4	.	275.5	295.2	279.9	331.4	.
E	7.4	16.3	8.3	6.8	.	13.3	11.0	12.6	13.1	.
F	209.8	233.7	185.1	195.4	.	274.4	253.9	245.1	310.3	.
G	218.7	217.4	220.2	206.9	.	272.1	244.0	257.1	266.7	.
H	36.6	32.5	39.9	40.5	.	42.0	38.5	48.0	33.8	.
I	171.4	142.3	159.9	163.3	.	189.5	231.2	216.9	242.2	.
J	9.1	14.2	15.5	10.2	.	9.3	4.1	13.6	17.3	.
K	45.2	73.2	71.3	51.3	.	61.8	65.6	101.2	94.1	.
L	62.3	61.0	55.2	58.0	.	69.5	62.5	81.3	107.7	.
M	88.6	73.2	66.2	69.5	.	72.3	91.4	93.6	92.0	.
N	20.7	22.4	28.7	22.2	.	29.4	21.7	33.8	39.9	.
O	45.1	50.8	45.7	54.4	.	72.6	70.6	72.3	66.5	.
P	3.4	8.1	5.8	14.4	.	5.7	3.1	8.2	5.9	.
Q	1.2	2.0	0.6	1.8	.	1.1	3.8	0.5	0.3	.

Explanatory notes: see p. 77.

[1] Excl. armed forces. [2] Persons aged 15 years and over. [3] April of each year. [4] May. [5] Persons aged 10 years and over. [6] Excl. conscripts. [7] Excl. forestry. [8] Incl. forestry.

Notes explicatives: voir p. 80.

[1] Non compris les forces armées. [2] Personnes âgées de 15 ans et plus. [3] Avril de chaque année. [4] Mai. [5] Personnes âgées de 10 ans et plus. [6] Non compris les conscrits. [7] Non compris la sylviculture. [8] Y compris la sylviculture.

Notas explicativas: véase p. 83.

[1] Excl. las fuerzas armadas. [2] Personas de 15 años y más. [3] Abril de cada año. [4] Mayo. [5] Personas de 10 años y más. [6] Excl. los conscriptos. [7] Excl. la silvicultura. [8] Incl. silvicultura.

Total employment, by economic activity — **Emploi total, par activité économique** — **Empleo total, por actividad económica**

Thousands — Milliers — Millares

	1999	2000	2001	2002	2003	2004	2005	2006	2007	2008
Bolivia (BA) [1][2]				Total employment - Emploi total - Empleo total						
Women - Femmes - Mujeres										
ISIC 3 - CITI 3 - CIIU 3										
Total	1 637.4	1 604.9	1 755.8	1 664.8	.	1 911.7	1 901.1	2 044.7	2 095.4	.
A [3]	655.6	598.6	745.9	651.6	.	660.8	741.9	803.2	801.5	.
B [4]	1.9	1.6	0.9	1.8	.	2.0	2.0	3.6	0.2	.
C	8.8	6.4	3.7	3.8	.	5.2	11.2	4.7	1.7	.
D	173.4	141.2	146.8	163.9	.	194.9	170.3	197.9	183.6	.
E	0.8	1.6	3.0	1.3	.	1.2	2.9	0.4	2.3	.
F	2.7	8.0	6.3	10.4	.	10.5	21.4	3.0	5.9	.
G	371.3	362.7	353.7	336.3	.	416.9	385.4	390.2	406.9	.
H	105.0	109.1	115.5	135.8	.	194.6	132.8	138.7	125.5	.
I	9.6	14.4	20.4	12.5	.	16.1	25.1	34.6	30.2	.
J	8.5	6.4	4.7	7.2	.	6.8	9.1	9.8	10.9	.
K	28.4	24.1	34.3	26.9	.	31.3	39.0	50.8	42.7	.
L	19.9	19.3	14.4	17.4	.	24.0	28.6	33.9	44.4	.
M	80.2	91.5	90.3	79.6	.	87.1	101.3	124.3	131.0	.
N	46.1	30.5	31.5	40.2	.	45.3	42.4	63.1	69.6	.
O	36.8	56.2	55.1	61.3	.	85.3	82.4	75.2	82.6	.
P	88.5	130.0	129.1	113.1	.	128.1	105.2	111.4	154.9	.
Q	-	1.6	-	1.7	.	1.5	0.2	-	1.7	.
Brasil (BA) [1][5]				Total employment - Emploi total - Empleo total						
Total - Total - Total										
ISIC 3 - CITI 3 - CIIU 3										
Total	.	.	.	78 959	80 163 [6]	84 596	87 189	89 318	90 786	.
A	.	.	.	15 953	16 225 [6]	17 330	17 387	16 864	16 207	.
B	.	.	.	324	343 [6]	404	444	400	372	.
C	.	.	.	254	313 [6]	325	318	343	379	.
D	.	.	.	10 678	10 877 [6]	11 724	12 336	12 497	13 105	.
E	.	.	.	314	332 [6]	354	359	396	363	.
F	.	.	.	5 616	5 220 [6]	5 354	5 642	5 837	6 107	.
G	.	.	.	13 553	14 216 [6]	14 653	15 503	15 748	16 309	.
H	.	.	.	2 932	2 893 [6]	3 023	3 187	3 395	3 351	.
I	.	.	.	3 692	3 725 [6]	3 894	3 967	4 064	4 374	.
J	.	.	.	983	1 025 [6]	1 000	1 007	1 071	1 181	.
K	.	.	.	4 261	4 494 [6]	4 720	4 937	5 431	5 499	.
L	.	.	.	3 871	3 990 [6]	4 204	4 267	4 452	4 504	.
M	.	.	.	4 304	4 354 [6]	4 569	4 684	4 856	5 052	.
N	.	.	.	2 759	2 818 [6]	2 840	2 977	3 162	3 327	.
O	.	.	.	3 148	2 982 [6]	3 498	3 301	3 800	3 711	.
P	.	.	.	6 110	6 155 [6]	6 472	6 666	6 782	6 732	.
Q	.	.	.	5	4 [6]	4	7	4	3	.
X	.	.	.	202	198 [6]	227	198	218	209	.
Men - Hommes - Hombres										
ISIC 3 - CITI 3 - CIIU 3										
Total	.	.	.	46 334	46 935 [6]	49 242	50 494	51 400	52 363	.
A	.	.	.	10 601	10 929 [6]	11 715	11 582	11 226	10 934	.
B	.	.	.	291	299 [6]	348	373	345	316	.
C	.	.	.	236	285 [6]	303	293	314	343	.
D	.	.	.	6 764	6 840 [6]	7 370	7 687	7 831	8 320	.
E	.	.	.	259	273 [6]	300	299	325	297	.
F	.	.	.	5 468	5 098 [6]	5 220	5 494	5 665	5 921	.
G	.	.	.	8 533	8 924 [6]	9 044	9 566	9 637	9 959	.
H	.	.	.	1 501	1 459 [6]	1 518	1 587	1 644	1 615	.
I	.	.	.	3 291	3 301 [6]	3 428	3 442	3 535	3 780	.
J	.	.	.	523	541 [6]	524	501	539	603	.
K	.	.	.	2 831	2 986 [6]	3 067	3 287	3 541	3 520	.
L	.	.	.	2 504	2 519 [6]	2 637	2 634	2 766	2 778	.
M	.	.	.	922	933 [6]	990	1 037	1 054	1 127	.
N	.	.	.	652	689 [6]	686	702	760	764	.
O	.	.	.	1 342	1 282 [6]	1 450	1 370	1 556	1 491	.
P	.	.	.	433	403 [6]	432	453	460	418	.
Q	.	.	.	3	2 [6]	2	3	1	2	.
X	.	.	.	179	175 [6]	207	183	199	174	.

Explanatory notes: see p. 77.

[1] Persons aged 10 years and over. [2] Excl. conscripts. [3] Excl. forestry. [4] Incl. forestry. [5] Sep. of each year. [6] Prior to 2003: Excl. rural population of Rondônia, Acre, Amazonas, Roraima, Pará and Amapá.

Notes explicatives: voir p. 80.

[1] Personnes âgées de 10 ans et plus. [2] Non compris les conscrits. [3] Non compris la sylviculture. [4] Y compris la sylviculture. [5] Sept. de chaque année. [6] Avant 2003: Non compris la population rurale de Rondônia, Acre, Amazonas, Roraima, Pará et Amapá.

Notas explicativas: véase p. 83.

[1] Personas de 10 años y más. [2] Excl. los conscriptos. [3] Excl. la silvicultura. [4] Incl. silvicultura. [5] Sept. de cada año. [6] Antes de 2003: Excl. la población rural de Rondonia, Acre, Amazonas, Roraima, Pará y Amapá.

2B

**Total employment,
by economic activity**

**Emploi total,
par activité économique**

**Empleo total,
por actividad económica**

	1999	2000	2001	2002	2003	2004	2005	2006	2007	2008
	Thousands				Milliers				Millares	

Brasil (BA) [1] [2] — Total employment - Emploi total - Empleo total

Women - Femmes - Mujeres
ISIC 3 - CITI 3 - CIIU 3

	1999	2000	2001	2002	2003	2004	2005	2006	2007	2008
Total	.	.	.	32 625	33 228 [3]	35 354	36 696	37 918	38 423	
A	.	.	.	5 351	5 297 [3]	5 615	5 805	5 638	5 273	
B	.	.	.	33	44 [3]	56	71	54	56	
C	.	.	.	19	28 [3]	22	25	28	36	
D	.	.	.	3 914	4 038 [3]	4 354	4 649	4 665	4 785	
E	.	.	.	54	59 [3]	54	60	71	65	
F	.	.	.	148	122 [3]	134	148	172	186	
G	.	.	.	5 020	5 292 [3]	5 609	5 937	6 110	6 350	
H	.	.	.	1 431	1 434 [3]	1 505	1 600	1 751	1 736	
I	.	.	.	401	423 [3]	466	525	529	594	
J	.	.	.	459	485 [3]	476	506	531	578	
K	.	.	.	1 430	1 508 [3]	1 653	1 650	1 890	1 979	
L	.	.	.	1 367	1 471 [3]	1 567	1 633	1 685	1 726	
M	.	.	.	3 382	3 421 [3]	3 579	3 647	3 802	3 925	
N	.	.	.	2 107	2 129 [3]	2 154	2 275	2 402	2 563	
O	.	.	.	1 806	1 700 [3]	2 049	1 932	2 245	2 220	
P	.	.	.	5 677	5 752 [3]	6 040	6 214	6 322	6 313	
Q	.	.	.	2	2 [3]	2	4	2	1	
X	.	.	.	23	23 [3]	20	16	18	36	

Canada (BA) [4] [5] [6] — Total employment - Emploi total - Empleo total

Total - Total - Total
ISIC 3 - CITI 3 - CIIU 3

	1999	2000	2001	2002	2003	2004	2005	2006	2007	2008
Total	14 406.7	14 764.2	14 946.2	15 310.4	15 672.3	15 947.0	16 169.7	16 484.3	16 866.4	17 125.8
A	483.2	454.2	393.2	396.7	406.5	394.9	408.7	405.4	393.1	376.8
B	32.5	33.2	29.7	28.8	29.4	30.1	30.9	30.5	28.8	26.1
C	154.1	160.1	179.3	170.2	178.1	187.6	210.7	240.6	254.7	264.2
D	2 264.7	2 249.4	2 229.0	2 285.9	2 275.2	2 292.1	2 207.4	2 193.1	2 116.0	2 040.9
E	114.3	114.9	124.4	131.9	130.5	133.3	125.3	122.0	138.0	151.8
F	766.9	803.0	820.7	858.0	898.3	943.2	1 012.4	1 069.7	1 133.5	1 232.2
G	2 481.5	2 548.7	2 621.1	2 664.7	2 729.9	2 771.8	2 839.9	2 891.8	2 947.4	2 951.1
H	913.6	938.2	943.2	985.1	1 005.5	1 012.4	1 004.5	1 015.0	1 069.4	1 073.5
I	970.1	1 123.4	1 152.7	1 118.2	1 141.7	1 156.3	1 153.8	1 097.1	1 125.0	1 148.2
J	620.4	608.1	635.7	652.2	649.5	682.9	707.0	745.0	760.2	786.1
K	1 642.7	1 731.2	1 774.3	1 812.5	1 884.5	1 928.0	1 991.8	2 071.1	2 142.7	2 176.0
L	774.5	769.9	783.0	786.7	817.1	824.2	830.5	834.1	862.1	923.7
M	970.7	974.1	981.6	1 007.4	1 027.1	1 035.7	1 106.1	1 158.4	1 183.2	1 192.8
N	1 436.0	1 514.0	1 540.4	1 617.3	1 679.2	1 733.4	1 734.6	1 785.5	1 846.1	1 903.4
O	683.1	660.3	671.7	719.3	742.4	754.7	741.7	817.1	868.3	866.6
P	96.5	78.6	63.8	73.5	75.4	65.2	61.9	59.2	59.5	72.8
Q	1.9	2.7	2.4	2.2	1.9	-	2.5	3.3	2.5	2.0

Men - Hommes - Hombres
ISIC 3 - CITI 3 - CIIU 3

	1999	2000	2001	2002	2003	2004	2005	2006	2007	2008
Total	7 797.2	7 973.9	8 035.8	8 184.4	8 348.1	8 480.6	8 594.7	8 727.1	8 888.9	9 021.3
A	345.3	332.2	291.1	289.7	299.2	288.5	295.7	290.3	281.0	274.2
B	28.1	27.1	24.4	24.7	25.0	25.1	26.1	25.9	23.7	21.6
C	130.8	132.3	149.9	141.6	148.2	155.7	175.5	192.3	205.4	214.0
D	1 609.9	1 624.0	1 605.7	1 627.6	1 614.6	1 641.8	1 581.2	1 552.5	1 501.1	1 444.2
E	86.6	89.0	92.9	99.2	102.0	97.7	93.2	92.5	99.0	115.6
F	688.6	718.9	734.7	774.4	804.9	835.9	905.4	946.8	996.9	1 087.3
G	1 374.2	1 397.8	1 444.4	1 448.7	1 490.2	1 515.6	1 533.4	1 555.6	1 577.0	1 578.0
H	368.9	381.4	381.8	390.3	408.2	402.2	402.4	402.2	433.9	433.0
I	702.9	780.6	789.3	778.9	786.0	788.6	792.2	779.8	796.4	807.1
J	216.2	218.3	225.9	244.2	236.3	246.3	254.4	275.8	276.0	306.8
K	906.5	952.0	974.3	1 003.6	1 028.8	1 064.7	1 100.3	1 145.6	1 197.9	1 213.5
L	416.4	408.4	416.1	417.4	421.9	424.6	425.8	426.1	429.7	453.2
M	350.0	344.6	340.9	344.1	366.5	354.4	379.4	410.4	414.0	405.9
N	270.0	286.3	277.9	287.5	298.5	317.5	310.1	312.8	322.2	342.4
O	296.7	275.7	282.0	306.6	311.8	317.5	313.9	344.7	373.0	359.6
P	5.6	4.4	3.7	4.7	4.8	3.7	4.7	4.2	2.9	2.5
Q	0.4	0.9	0.8	2.2	1.9	-	0.8	2.3	-	-

Explanatory notes: see p. 77.

[1] Persons aged 10 years and over. [2] Sep. of each year. [3] Prior to 2003: Excl. rural population of Rondônia, Acre, Amazonas, Roraima, Pará and Amapá. [4] Persons aged 15 years and over. [5] Excl. residents of the Territories and indigenous persons living on reserves. [6] Excl. full-time members of the armed forces.

Notes explicatives: voir p. 80.

[1] Personnes âgées de 10 ans et plus. [2] Sept. de chaque année. [3] Avant 2003: Non compris la population rurale de Rondônia, Acre, Amazonas, Roraima, Pará et Amapá. [4] Personnes âgées de 15 ans et plus. [5] Non compris les habitants des "Territoires" et les populations indigènes vivant dans les réserves. [6] Non compris les membres à temps complet des forces armées.

Notas explicativas: véase p. 83.

[1] Personas de 10 años y más. [2] Sept. de cada año. [3] Antes de 2003: Excl. la población rural de Rondonia, Acre, Amazonas, Roraima, Pará y Amapá. [4] Personas de 15 años y más. [5] Excl. a los habitantes de los "Territorios" y a las poblaciones indígenas que viven en reservas. [6] Excl. los miembros a tiempo completo de las fuerzas armadas.

Total employment, by economic activity

Emploi total, par activité économique

Empleo total, por actividad económica

	Thousands			Milliers			Millares		
	1999	2000	2001	2002	2003	2004	2005	2006	2007	2008

Canada (BA) [1] [2] [3]

Total employment - Emploi total - Empleo total

Women - Femmes - Mujeres
ISIC 3 - CITI 3 - CIIU 3

	1999	2000	2001	2002	2003	2004	2005	2006	2007	2008
Total	6 609.6	6 790.4	6 910.3	7 126.0	7 324.2	7 466.4	7 575.0	7 757.2	7 977.5	8 104.5
A	137.9	122.0	102.0	107.0	107.3	106.4	112.9	115.0	112.1	102.6
B	4.4	6.1	5.4	4.0	4.4	5.0	4.8	4.6	5.0	4.5
C	23.2	27.8	29.4	28.6	30.0	32.0	35.2	48.3	49.4	50.2
D	654.8	625.4	623.3	658.3	660.6	650.4	626.2	640.6	614.9	596.7
E	27.7	25.9	31.5	32.7	28.5	35.6	32.1	29.5	39.1	36.1
F	78.2	84.1	86.0	83.6	93.4	107.3	107.0	122.9	136.6	144.8
G	1 107.3	1 150.9	1 176.7	1 216.0	1 239.7	1 256.2	1 306.4	1 336.2	1 370.4	1 373.1
H	544.7	556.8	561.4	594.7	597.3	610.1	602.1	612.8	635.5	640.4
I	267.2	342.9	363.4	339.3	355.7	367.7	361.6	317.3	328.6	341.1
J	404.1	389.8	409.8	408.1	413.3	436.6	452.6	469.1	484.2	479.4
K	736.2	779.3	800.0	808.9	855.7	863.3	891.5	925.5	944.8	962.5
L	358.1	361.6	366.9	369.3	395.2	399.6	404.8	408.0	432.4	470.5
M	620.7	629.5	640.7	663.3	660.6	681.3	726.7	748.0	769.1	787.0
N	1 166.0	1 227.7	1 262.5	1 329.8	1 380.7	1 415.9	1 424.5	1 472.7	1 523.9	1 561.0
O	386.5	384.6	389.7	412.7	430.6	437.2	427.8	472.5	495.3	507.0
P	90.9	74.2	60.0	68.8	70.6	61.5	57.2	55.0	56.7	70.3
Q	1.5	1.8	1.6	-	-	-	1.7	1.0	-	-

Cayman Islands (BA) [1] [4] [5]

Total employment - Emploi total - Empleo total

Total - Total - Total
ISIC 3 - CITI 3 - CIIU 3

	1999	2000	2001	2002	2003	2004	2005	2006	2007	2008
Total	.	.	.	.	.	.	35.464	35.016 [6]	35.081	37.450
A-B	.	.	.	.	.	.	0.597	0.805 [6]	0.639	0.697
C-D	.	.	.	.	.	.	.	.	.	0.790
C,E	.	.	.	.	.	.	0.478	0.726 [6]	0.550	.
D	.	.	.	.	.	.	0.336	0.383 [6]	0.658	.
E	.	.	.	.	.	.	.	.	.	0.553
F	.	.	.	.	.	.	7.059	6.344 [6]	5.646	5.796
G	.	.	.	.	.	.	5.200	4.232 [6]	3.619	4.732
H	.	.	.	.	.	.	2.903	3.779 [6]	3.499	4.300
I	.	.	.	.	.	.	1.619	1.477 [6]	2.004	1.687
J	.	.	.	.	.	.	3.092	3.205 [6]	3.332	3.773
K	.	.	.	.	.	.	4.289	4.443 [6]	4.200	5.020
L	.	.	.	.	.	.	1.953	2.380 [6]	2.509	2.095
M-N	.	.	.	.	.	.	2.895	2.421 [6]	2.833	2.971
O	.	.	.	.	.	.	1.711	1.817 [6]	2.008	1.912
P	.	.	.	.	.	.	3.120	3.004 [6]	2.786	2.752
Q	.	.	.	.	.	.	-	- [6]	0.018	-
X	.	.	.	.	.	.	0.210	- [6]	0.780	0.370

Men - Hommes - Hombres
ISIC 3 - CITI 3 - CIIU 3

	1999	2000	2001	2002	2003	2004	2005	2006	2007	2008
Total	.	.	.	.	.	.	18.628	18.408 [6]	18.305	19.355
A-B	.	.	.	.	.	.	0.490	0.645 [6]	0.592	0.590
C-D	.	.	.	.	.	.	.	.	.	0.644
C,E	.	.	.	.	.	.	0.421	0.644 [6]	0.399	.
D	.	.	.	.	.	.	0.182	0.222 [6]	0.519	.
E	.	.	.	.	.	.	.	.	.	0.360
F	.	.	.	.	.	.	6.712	5.994 [6]	5.227	5.340
G	.	.	.	.	.	.	2.780	2.282 [6]	1.786	2.108
H	.	.	.	.	.	.	1.181	1.598 [6]	1.588	2.108
I	.	.	.	.	.	.	0.893	0.863 [6]	0.999	0.935
J	.	.	.	.	.	.	1.031	0.956 [6]	1.195	1.416
K	.	.	.	.	.	.	2.002	2.121 [6]	2.084	2.520
L	.	.	.	.	.	.	1.040	1.163 [6]	1.526	1.140
M-N	.	.	.	.	.	.	0.749	0.571 [6]	0.696	0.683
O	.	.	.	.	.	.	0.813	1.088 [6]	1.150	0.962
P	.	.	.	.	.	.	0.188	0.261 [6]	0.168	0.323
Q	.	.	.	.	.	.	-	- [6]	-	-
X	.	.	.	.	.	.	0.146	- [6]	0.375	0.228

Explanatory notes: see p. 77.

[1] Persons aged 15 years and over. [2] Excl. residents of the Territories and indigenous persons living on reserves. [3] Excl. full-time members of the armed forces. [4] Excl. armed forces and conscripts. [5] Oct. [6] April.

Notes explicatives: voir p. 80.

[1] Personnes âgées de 15 ans et plus. [2] Non compris les habitants des "Territoires" et les populations indigènes vivant dans les réserves. [3] Non compris les membres à temps complet des forces armées. [4] Non compris les forces armées et les conscrits. [5] Oct. [6] Avril.

Notas explicativas: véase p. 83.

[1] Personas de 15 años y más. [2] Excl. a los habitantes de los "Territorios" y a las poblaciones indígenas que viven en reservas. [3] Excl. los miembros a tiempo completo de las fuerzas armadas. [4] Excl. las fuerzas armadas y los conscriptos. [5] Oct. [6] Abril.

Total employment, by economic activity   **Emploi total, par activité économique**   **Empleo total, por actividad económica**

Thousands   Milliers   Millares

	1999	2000	2001	2002	2003	2004	2005	2006	2007	2008
Cayman Islands (BA) [1][2][3]						Total employment - Emploi total - Empleo total				
Women - Femmes - Mujeres										
ISIC 3 - CITI 3 - CIIU 3										
Total							16.836	16.608 [4]	16.776	18.094
A-B							0.107	0.160 [4]	0.047	0.107
C-D										0.147
C.E							0.057	0.082 [4]	0.151	
D							0.154	0.161 [4]	0.140	
E										0.193
F							0.347	0.350 [4]	0.419	0.456
G							2.420	1.950 [4]	1.834	2.624
H							1.722	2.181 [4]	1.911	2.192
I							0.726	0.614 [4]	1.005	0.753
J							2.061	2.249 [4]	2.137	2.357
K							2.287	2.322 [4]	2.115	2.500
L							0.913	1.217 [4]	0.983	0.955
M-N							2.146	1.850 [4]	2.137	2.288
O							0.898	0.729 [4]	0.858	0.951
P							2.932	2.743 [4]	2.617	2.430
Q							-	- [4]	0.018	-
X							0.066	- [4]	0.404	0.142
Colombia (BA) [5][6][7]						Total employment - Emploi total - Empleo total				
Total - Total - Total										
ISIC 3 - CITI 3 - CIIU 3										
Total				15 844.3	16 650.1	16 704.0	17 154.9	16 680.9	17 076.5	17 425.7
A				3 169.3	3 413.0	3 304.7	3 735.1	2 059.2	3 035.0	3 054.5
C				276.1	203.1	188.0	130.6	102.0	103.2	149.1
D				2 051.1	2 134.9	2 283.3	2 253.1	1 998.0	2 361.4	2 335.6
E				68.9	65.0	68.2	83.7	62.9	83.7	78.7
F				825.8	766.4	781.4	846.3	755.2	905.1	878.5
G				4 015.9	4 249.6	4 163.7	4 253.1	3 646.5	4 344.4	4 605.3
I				1 054.1	1 173.5	1 248.8	1 153.0	1 097.9	1 450.1	1 467.4
J				188.8	200.4	213.5	221.9	204.8	222.2	219.6
K				640.1	713.0	745.5	792.4	811.2	995.7	1 146.8
N				3 546.3	3 728.2	3 702.6	3 684.7	3 183.0	3 567.3	3 463.3
X				7.8	3.1	4.4	0.8	2 760.1	8.5	26.9
Men - Hommes - Hombres										
ISIC 3 - CITI 3 - CIIU 3										
Total				9 689.2	10 106.6	10 196.8	10 491.3	10 189.9	10 399.9	10 611.0
A				2 828.9	2 958.1	2 888.2	3 193.6	1 805.7	2 645.3	2 654.4
C				214.7	160.2	168.3	110.2	88.3	95.4	142.0
D				1 109.6	1 149.3	1 215.0	1 230.1	1 135.6	1 347.9	1 355.6
E				57.9	53.0	56.2	64.1	46.0	70.9	63.3
F				792.0	745.0	755.0	823.3	723.3	872.8	852.1
G				2 239.0	2 300.0	2 289.8	2 260.8	1 996.2	2 346.9	2 438.5
I				924.6	1 055.9	1 094.5	987.5	907.7	1 180.3	1 178.9
J				88.1	96.5	108.8	109.1	113.1	106.4	111.5
K				409.7	449.0	473.8	512.7	505.5	560.1	650.5
N				1 020.3	1 139.2	1 144.4	1 199.2	1 028.8	1 167.2	1 146.7
X				4.4	0.5	2.8	0.6	1 839.7	6.7	17.5
Women - Femmes - Mujeres										
ISIC 3 - CITI 3 - CIIU 3										
Total				6 155.1	6 543.5	6 507.2	6 663.6	6 490.9	6 676.5	6 814.7
A				340.4	454.9	416.5	541.5	253.5	389.7	400.1
C				61.3	42.9	19.8	20.4	13.7	7.8	7.1
D				941.6	985.5	1 068.3	1 023.0	862.4	1 013.5	980.0
E				11.1	12.0	12.0	19.6	16.9	12.7	15.4
F				33.8	21.4	26.4	23.0	32.0	32.3	26.4
G				1 776.9	1 949.6	1 873.9	1 992.3	1 650.3	1 997.5	2 166.8
I				129.6	117.6	154.3	165.5	190.2	269.8	288.5
J				100.7	104.0	104.7	112.8	91.7	115.8	108.2
K				230.5	264.0	271.6	279.8	305.7	435.6	496.3
N				2 525.9	2 589.0	2 558.2	2 485.5	2 154.2	2 400.1	2 316.6
X				3.4	2.6	1.6	0.2	920.4	1.7	9.4

Explanatory notes: see p. 77.

[1] Persons aged 15 years and over. [2] Excl. armed forces and conscripts. [3] Oct. [4] April. [5] From 2001, figures revised on the basis of the 2005 census results. [6] Excl. armed forces. [7] Persons aged 10 years and over.

Notes explicatives: voir p. 80.

[1] Personnes âgées de 15 ans et plus. [2] Non compris les forces armées et les conscrits. [3] Oct. [4] Avril. [5] A partir de 2001, données révisées sur la base des résultats du recensement de 2005. [6] Non compris les forces armées. [7] Personnes âgées de 10 ans et plus.

Notas explicativas: véase p. 83.

[1] Personas de 15 años y más. [2] Excl. las fuerzas armadas y los conscriptos. [3] Oct. [4] Abril. [5] A partir de 2001, datos revisados de acuerdocon los resultados del censo de 2005. [6] Excl. las fuerzas armadas. [7] Personas de 10 años y más.

Total employment,
by economic activity

Emploi total,
par activité économique

Empleo total,
por actividad económica

	Thousands				Milliers				Millares	
	1999	2000	2001	2002	2003	2004	2005	2006	2007	2008

Costa Rica (BA) [1][2] Total employment - Emploi total - Empleo total

Total - Total - Total
ISIC 3 - CITI 3 - CIIU 3

	1999	2000	2001	2002	2003	2004	2005	2006	2007	2008
Total	1 300.1	1 318.6	1 552.9	1 586.5	1 640.4	1 653.9	1 776.9	1 829.9	1 925.7	1 957.7
A	250.2	262.0	234.3	242.7	239.8	237.3	260.5	247.0	244.8	235.1
B	6.3	7.2	7.6	8.8	8.6	8.1	9.5	9.3	9.8	6.6
C	2.1	2.6	1.8	2.3	2.2	3.6	4.0	4.7	2.6	2.2
D	204.0	190.3	232.9	226.3	230.1	229.5	242.7	243.9	251.6	239.5
E	13.2	10.9	19.6	21.9	22.1	23.6	20.5	22.0	21.1	28.0
F	82.6	89.7	107.9	106.6	109.6	107.3	115.7	126.7	151.8	152.4
G	203.9	204.3	292.9	303.4	322.4	329.9	332.2	352.1	366.5	377.6
H	64.7	62.6	85.1	82.5	89.9	91.4	98.0	97.8	108.3	100.3
I	74.6	78.8	86.0	90.2	94.0	96.3	111.9	118.5	125.7	143.0
J	20.4	23.9	29.2	32.0	35.5	36.7	36.2	38.2	49.5	53.3
K	5.4	5.4	92.7	103.2	101.2	102.0	103.0	108.2	121.6	137.6
L	.	.	73.3	71.9	76.3	78.5	81.4	86.5	88.7	93.8
L,O	158.9	162.6	.	.	.	.	.	.	.	.
M	65.4	74.7	85.0	91.9	98.4	95.9	104.1	108.4	110.7	112.6
N	55.8	51.9	59.4	53.0	49.2	51.3	62.7	62.5	64.0	64.7
O	.	.	60.9	58.5	72.1	62.9	64.9	65.9	72.7	81.1
P	83.5	81.4	75.6	83.4	79.3	90.8	121.2	131.2	128.6	119.0
Q	2.2	1.5	2.2	2.5	2.4	3.9	2.0	2.6	1.1	2.7
X	6.9	8.9	5.6	5.5	7.2	5.0	6.5	4.5	6.6	8.3

Men - Hommes - Hombres
ISIC 3 - CITI 3 - CIIU 3

	1999	2000	2001	2002	2003	2004	2005	2006	2007	2008
Total	879.6	902.5	1 013.0	1 037.5	1 069.0	1 093.6	1 153.9	1 172.6	1 222.6	1 229.5
A	230.5	239.7	214.3	220.5	217.1	215.6	231.3	218.6	209.8	205.1
B	6.2	7.0	7.3	8.4	7.9	7.2	8.9	8.7	9.0	6.2
C	1.9	2.4	1.6	2.1	2.0	2.9	3.2	4.1	2.3	1.8
D	133.4	125.6	148.2	151.6	153.3	162.1	170.4	166.9	170.6	155.3
E	11.8	9.3	15.8	16.5	17.9	19.8	17.8	17.5	16.7	21.9
F	81.6	87.5	104.0	104.5	108.3	105.0	113.0	124.7	146.5	148.3
G	126.1	128.8	193.2	197.3	211.8	218.7	215.2	227.5	237.3	242.8
H	30.4	29.6	40.9	36.1	38.9	41.6	41.9	41.8	44.3	41.7
I	66.9	69.9	76.1	81.4	82.6	84.9	97.8	104.0	108.8	119.6
J	12.9	15.2	18.5	20.8	21.2	24.2	22.7	23.3	25.8	26.3
K	3.8	3.0	58.3	65.0	66.6	70.6	73.0	73.4	84.3	88.7
L	.	.	46.4	44.2	47.5	47.6	53.2	55.8	54.6	58.6
L,O	115.1	121.9	.	.	.	.	.	.	.	.
M	21.2	23.3	25.1	26.7	28.2	27.4	29.7	30.6	34.3	31.0
N	24.7	23.6	20.7	20.9	17.5	20.0	25.9	23.8	23.3	23.1
O	.	.	31.6	29.7	34.8	29.8	33.9	34.1	35.9	43.5
P	6.9	8.3	5.7	5.9	6.9	9.3	10.1	14.2	14.1	8.4
Q	1.4	1.3	1.5	1.9	1.7	2.2	0.6	0.9	0.8	1.2
X	4.9	6.3	3.9	4.1	4.9	4.2	5.5	2.7	4.1	6.1

Women - Femmes - Mujeres
ISIC 3 - CITI 3 - CIIU 3

	1999	2000	2001	2002	2003	2004	2005	2006	2007	2008
Total	420.5	416.1	539.9	549.0	571.4	560.3	623.0	657.3	703.1	728.2
A	19.7	22.4	20.0	22.3	22.7	21.7	29.2	28.4	34.9	30.0
B	0.1	0.2	0.3	0.4	0.7	0.8	0.6	0.5	0.9	0.4
C	0.2	0.2	0.2	0.2	0.3	0.7	0.8	0.6	0.3	0.4
D	70.6	64.7	84.7	74.7	76.7	66.8	72.3	77.0	81.0	84.3
E	1.4	1.6	3.8	5.4	4.2	3.8	2.7	4.6	4.4	6.1
F	1.0	2.2	3.8	2.1	1.4	2.3	2.8	2.0	5.3	4.1
G	77.7	75.5	99.6	106.0	110.6	111.3	117.0	124.7	129.2	134.8
H	34.4	33.0	45.1	46.4	51.0	49.8	56.2	56.0	64.0	58.6
I	7.7	8.9	9.9	8.9	11.5	11.3	14.1	14.5	16.9	23.5
J	7.5	8.7	10.8	11.2	14.4	12.5	13.5	14.9	23.7	27.1
K	1.6	2.4	34.5	38.2	34.7	31.4	30.0	34.8	37.3	48.8
L	.	.	26.9	27.7	28.8	30.9	28.2	30.7	34.1	35.2
L,O	43.7	40.7	.	.	.	.	.	.	.	.
M	44.2	51.4	59.0	65.1	70.2	68.6	74.4	77.8	76.4	81.5
N	31.1	28.2	38.7	32.1	31.8	31.3	36.8	38.7	40.7	41.6
O	.	.	29.3	28.8	37.3	33.1	31.0	31.7	36.8	37.6
P	76.6	73.1	69.9	77.5	72.4	81.5	111.1	116.9	114.4	110.6
Q	0.8	0.2	0.6	0.7	0.6	1.7	1.5	1.7	0.4	1.5
X	2.0	2.7	1.7	1.3	2.3	0.8	1.0	1.8	2.6	2.3

Cuba (BA) [3][4] Total employment - Emploi total - Empleo total

Total - Total - Total
ISIC 2 - CITI 2 - CIIU 2

	1999	2000	2001	2002	2003	2004	2005	2006	2007	2008
Total	4 359.4	4 379.3	4 505.1	4 558.2	4 607.0	4 641.7	4 722.5	4 754.6	4 867.7	4 948.2 [5]
1	1 182.2	1 187.6	975.6	987.2	997.7	982.4	956.3	951.9	912.3	919.1 [5]
2	42.6	42.8	18.1	18.3	18.5	27.6	26.2	22.0	25.7	26.7 [5]
3	426.8	428.7	595.6	602.7	609.1	573.1	565.6	525.1	523.3	543.1 [5]
4	85.0	85.4	63.6	64.3	65.0	62.6	67.4	72.7	85.0	79.8 [5]
5	277.8	279.1	233.1	235.8	238.3	236.7	243.4	242.4	243.7	245.2 [5]
6	479.6	481.8	622.8	630.2	636.9	610.3	617.8	603.1	613.6	610.2 [5]
7	240.6	241.7	253.1	256.1	258.8	278.2	280.7	275.3	289.3	301.4 [5]
8	149.8	150.5	146.6	148.3	149.9	104.0	105.2	116.6	111.4	123.0 [5]
9	1 474.9	1 481.7	1 596.6	1 615.5	1 632.7	1 766.8	1 859.9	1 945.5	2 063.4	2 099.7 [5]

Explanatory notes: see p. 77. Notes explicatives: voir p. 80. Notas explicativas: véase p. 83.

[1] Persons aged 12 years and over. [2] July of each year. [3] Persons aged 15 years and over. [4] Dec. [5] February - April

[1] Personnes âgées de 12 ans et plus. [2] Juillet de chaque année. [3] Personnes âgées de 15 ans et plus. [4] Déc. [5] Février - Avril

[1] Personas de 12 años y más. [2] Julio de cada año. [3] Personas de 15 años y más. [4] Dic. [5] Febrero - Abril

**Total employment,
by economic activity** **Emploi total,
par activité économique** **Empleo total,
por actividad económica**

	Thousands				Milliers			Millares		
	1999	2000	2001	2002	2003	2004	2005	2006	2007	2008

Cuba (BA) [1] [2]   **Total employment - Emploi total - Empleo total**

Men - Hommes - Hombres
ISIC 2 - CITI 2 - CIIU 2

Total	2 814.5	2 819.8	2 906.3	2 926.8	2 945.8	2 955.7	2 998.5	2 985.8	3 016.0	3 073.0 [3]
1	963.1	966.4	828.4	836.9	844.7	811.7	794.2	786.3	753.5	759.0 [3]
2	35.7	35.9	14.9	15.0	15.2	22.2	21.6	17.8	20.6	22.7 [3]
3	287.0	287.7	401.3	404.4	407.2	396.7	396.8	359.6	362.1	382.4 [3]
4	63.9	64.1	47.0	47.4	47.8	47.6	50.4	53.7	62.7	59.1 [3]
5	230.3	231.2	196.3	198.3	200.1	199.1	206.8	204.4	203.6	208.4 [3]
6	263.1	263.2	359.8	361.7	363.6	362.6	364.2	353.0	354.3	347.7 [3]
7	179.3	179.8	188.8	190.4	192.0	210.9	213.3	207.5	217.0	227.1 [3]
8	84.1	84.2	80.4	80.8	81.1	47.8	50.4	55.5	50.7	57.9 [3]
9	708.0	707.4	789.5	791.8	794.0	857.1	900.8	948.0	991.4	1 008.7 [3]

Women - Femmes - Mujeres
ISIC 2 - CITI 2 - CIIU 2

Total	1 544.9	1 559.5	1 598.8	1 631.4	1 661.2	1 686.0	1 724.0	1 768.8	1 851.7	1 875.2 [3]
1	219.1	221.2	147.2	150.2	153.0	170.7	162.1	165.6	158.8	160.1 [3]
2	6.9	6.9	3.2	3.2	3.3	5.4	4.6	4.2	5.1	4.0 [3]
3	139.7	141.1	194.3	198.3	201.9	176.4	168.8	165.5	161.2	160.7 [3]
4	21.1	21.3	16.6	16.9	17.2	15.0	17.0	19.0	22.3	20.7 [3]
5	47.4	47.9	36.8	37.5	38.2	37.6	36.6	38.0	40.1	36.8 [3]
6	216.6	218.6	263.1	268.4	273.3	247.7	253.6	250.1	259.3	262.5 [3]
7	61.3	61.9	64.3	65.6	66.8	67.3	67.4	67.8	72.3	74.3 [3]
8	65.7	66.3	66.2	67.5	68.8	56.2	54.8	61.1	60.7	65.1 [3]
9	767.0	774.3	807.1	823.6	838.7	909.7	959.1	997.5	1 072.0	1 091.0 [3]

Chile (BA) [1] [4]   **Total employment - Emploi total - Empleo total**

Total - Total - Total
ISIC 2 - CITI 2 - CIIU 2

Total	5 404.5	5 381.5	5 479.4	5 531.3	5 675.1	5 862.9	5 905.0	6 411.0 [5]	6 566.1	6 740.4
1	780.1	777.0	745.4	746.6	771.8	783.2	777.1	823.6 [5]	808.3	789.7
2	73.3	70.3	71.7	69.8	71.9	73.8	74.3	87.0 [5]	93.0	99.6
3	775.5	754.2	781.8	780.4	797.2	805.1	775.0	838.0 [5]	857.0	865.4
4	28.5	28.4	33.2	29.5	31.2	31.9	34.8	38.3 [5]	40.1	38.2
5	388.6	406.1	424.2	439.9	427.4	473.0	471.3	530.0 [5]	545.0	583.6
6	1 027.2	995.5	1 028.9	1 073.1	1 066.8	1 127.5	1 114.8	1 266.4 [5]	1 285.0	1 330.7
7	403.2	430.2	439.0	444.8	483.3	461.2	471.5	519.4 [5]	538.6	561.5
8	390.4	425.8	414.2	430.9	453.5	472.6	521.2	551.6 [5]	618.4	626.5
9	1 537.7	1 494.2	1 541.0	1 516.2	1 572.1	1 634.7	1 665.1	1 757.2 [5]	1 780.2	1 845.3

Men - Hommes - Hombres
ISIC 2 - CITI 2 - CIIU 2

Total	3 603.6	3 600.5	3 663.7	3 697.0	3 749.7	3 816.1	3 840.2	4 130.2 [5]	4 188.3	4 239.4
1	696.7	695.3	661.3	660.1	677.6	671.3	657.8	691.2 [5]	674.7	653.1
2	70.4	68.4	69.3	66.1	68.3	69.9	71.1	80.9 [5]	89.3	95.4
3	568.2	552.2	567.2	581.0	594.6	581.4	566.4	614.6 [5]	631.0	620.7
4	23.7	23.3	27.9	26.1	27.4	25.7	28.0	32.9 [5]	34.5	30.4
5	376.8	397.2	412.2	426.1	411.1	456.1	452.3	506.2 [5]	520.7	555.4
6	558.6	550.4	571.3	592.0	564.1	594.6	589.5	641.7 [5]	643.0	654.6
7	354.9	371.0	379.2	384.8	410.7	391.3	391.8	437.6 [5]	454.2	470.3
8	247.4	270.0	250.9	261.7	281.3	297.6	321.6	342.9 [5]	378.9	373.8
9	706.9	672.7	724.3	699.1	714.7	728.2	761.9	782.3 [5]	761.5	785.7

Women - Femmes - Mujeres
ISIC 2 - CITI 2 - CIIU 2

Total	1 800.9	1 781.0	1 815.8	1 834.3	1 925.4	2 046.8	2 064.8	2 280.8 [5]	2 377.4	2 501.0
1	83.3	81.6	84.2	86.5	94.2	111.9	119.3	132.4 [5]	133.5	136.6
2	2.9	1.9	2.3	3.7	3.7	3.9	3.2	6.1 [5]	3.7	4.2
3	207.3	201.9	214.6	199.4	202.6	223.7	208.6	223.4 [5]	225.9	244.6
4	4.8	5.0	5.3	3.5	3.8	6.2	6.8	5.4 [5]	5.6	7.8
5	11.8	8.9	12.0	13.7	16.3	16.9	19.0	23.3 [5]	24.2	28.2
6	468.6	445.1	457.6	481.1	502.7	532.9	525.4	624.7 [5]	641.9	676.1
7	48.4	59.2	59.8	60.0	72.6	69.9	79.7	81.8 [5]	84.4	91.1
8	143.0	155.8	163.3	169.2	172.2	175.0	199.6	208.7 [5]	239.4	252.7
9	830.9	821.5	816.6	817.1	857.4	906.5	903.3	974.8 [5]	1 018.7	1 059.6

Explanatory notes: see p. 77.

[1] Persons aged 15 years and over. [2] Dec. [3] February - April
[4] Fourth quarter of each year. [5] Methodology revised; data not
strictly comparable.

Notes explicatives: voir p. 80.

[1] Personnes âgées de 15 ans et plus. [2] Déc. [3] Février - Avril
[4] Quatrième trimestre de chaque année. [5] Méthodologie révisée;
les données ne sont pas strictement comparables.

Notas explicativas: véase p. 83.

[1] Personas de 15 años y más. [2] Dic. [3] Febrero - Abril [4] Cuarto
trimestre de cada año. [5] Metodología revisada; los datos no son
estrictamente comparables.

Total employment, by economic activity
Emploi total, par activité économique
Empleo total, por actividad económica

Thousands — Milliers — Millares

	1999	2000	2001	2002	2003	2004	2005	2006	2007	2008	

República Dominicana (BA) [1]

Total employment - Emploi total - Empleo total

Total - Total - Total
ISIC 2 - CITI 2 - CIIU 2   ISIC 3 - CITI 3 - CIIU 3

ISIC 2	1999	2000	2001	2002	2003	2004	2005	2006	2007	2008	ISIC 3
Total	2 979.5	3 041.1	3 001.7	3 105.5	3 098.4	3 212.8	3 279.1	3 469.9	3 550.9	.	Total
1	522.7	483.5	443.6	494.5	426.0	.	.	.	.	.	A-B
2	7.5	6.0	7.1	6.8	.	469.1	467.1	503.8	502.3	.	A
3	519.0	519.4	461.1	441.3	.	7.1	11.3	11.6	12.8	.	B
4	13.2	24.0	27.3	24.3	7.3	4.8	5.9	3.5	6.0	.	C
5	214.1	190.9	198.4	182.8	456.0	494.5	486.9	489.8	494.5	.	D
6	794.7	820.6	819.8	828.7	26.4	26.7	26.2	26.6	30.8	.	E
7	218.4	187.5	217.8	230.0	220.2	213.2	213.5	241.2	246.9	.	F
8	37.9	57.3	53.5	62.3	641.2	653.5	708.5	722.1	732.4	.	G
9	651.8	752.4	764.7	833.6	169.8	180.1	191.9	213.4	222.3	.	H
					239.4	232.8	238.5	248.2	257.5	.	I
					63.7	55.7	62.3	66.1	73.5	.	J
					.	97.3	97.3	87.0	94.0	.	K
					710.7	140.8	147.5	.	.	.	K,M-N
					137.7	145.6	150.8	149.1	152.6	.	L
					.	101.2	104.0	152.3	169.9	.	M
					.	233.1	214.3	103.2	96.4	.	N
					.	156.6	151.6	270.5	263.0	.	O
					-	0.7	1.5	180.6	194.6	.	P
					-	-	-	0.9	1.5	.	Q

Men - Hommes - Hombres
ISIC 2 - CITI 2 - CIIU 2   ISIC 3 - CITI 3 - CIIU 3

ISIC 2	1999	2000	2001	2002	2003	2004	2005	2006	2007	2008	ISIC 3
Total	2 069.9	2 027.9	2 010.7	2 055.2	2 069.5	2 148.4	2 175.4	2 272.0	2 336.8	.	Total
1	497.4	457.3	425.3	474.5	408.2	.	.	.	.	.	A-B
2	6.0	5.5	5.5	6.5	.	448.5	436.2	478.5	477.0	.	A
3	341.8	324.8	305.0	289.6	.	7.1	11.3	11.6	12.7	.	B
4	13.0	18.6	21.9	19.9	7.3	4.7	5.8	3.1	5.8	.	C
5	208.7	186.9	192.8	177.7	310.9	345.7	335.6	332.1	345.1	.	D
6	494.7	518.5	497.9	495.6	21.2	20.1	17.2	21.2	22.1	.	E
7	204.6	170.0	209.9	210.2	213.7	205.4	207.1	236.0	239.4	.	F
8	19.2	27.6	25.5	13.3	425.0	432.5	460.7	477.3	487.2	.	G
9	286.1	318.2	327.3	349.5	86.1	90.2	88.6	100.4	104.5	.	H
					217.9	205.8	215.5	230.1	234.4	.	I
					31.4	28.9	34.5	31.8	33.1	.	J
					.	65.4	66.3	60.6	62.6	.	K
					250.6	94.9	103.6	.	.	.	K,M-N
					97.3	43.9	44.2	95.0	105.8	.	L
					.	28.5	29.2	42.1	55.4	.	M
					.	108.9	100.3	27.1	28.2	.	N
					-	17.3	18.9	110.0	103.9	.	O
					-	0.4	0.5	15.0	19.5	.	P
					-	-	-	-	0.2	.	Q

Women - Femmes - Mujeres
ISIC 2 - CITI 2 - CIIU 2   ISIC 3 - CITI 3 - CIIU 3

ISIC 2	1999	2000	2001	2002	2003	2004	2005	2006	2007	2008	ISIC 3
Total	909.6	1 013.2	991.1	1 050.3	1 029.0	1 064.4	1 103.7	1 197.9	1 214.1	.	Total
1	25.4	25.5	18.4	20.0	17.8	.	.	.	.	.	A-B
2	1.3	0.5	1.6	0.2	.	20.6	30.9	25.3	25.2	.	A
3	177.2	194.6	156.1	151.7	.	-	-	-	0.2	.	B
4	5.4	5.4	4.4	4.4	.	0.1	0.1	0.5	0.2	.	C
5	5.4	4.1	5.5	5.0	145.1	148.7	151.3	157.6	149.5	.	D
6	300.1	302.3	322.2	315.6	5.2	6.6	9.0	5.5	8.7	.	E
7	13.8	17.5	18.7	19.7	6.5	7.8	6.4	5.2	7.4	.	F
8	18.7	29.7	28.0	31.0	216.2	221.0	247.8	244.8	245.3	.	G
9	365.7	434.9	437.2	484.6	83.8	89.8	103.3	113.0	117.8	.	H
					21.5	27.0	23.0	18.1	23.1	.	I
					32.3	26.8	27.8	34.3	40.5	.	J
					.	31.9	31.1	26.4	31.4	.	K
					460.1	45.9	43.9	.	.	.	K,M-N
					40.5	101.7	106.7	54.1	46.8	.	L
					.	72.7	74.8	110.2	114.5	.	M
					.	124.1	114.0	76.2	68.2	.	N
					-	139.3	132.7	160.5	159.0	.	O
					-	0.2	1.0	165.6	175.1	.	P
					-	-	-	0.9	1.3	.	Q

Explanatory notes: see p. 77.   Notes explicatives: voir p. 80.   Notas explicativas: véase p. 83.

[1] Persons aged 10 years and over.   [1] Personnes âgées de 10 ans et plus.   [1] Personas de 10 años y más.

**Total employment,
by economic activity**

**Emploi total,
par activité économique**

**Empleo total,
por actividad económica**

	Thousands				Milliers				Millares	
	1999	2000	2001	2002	2003	2004	2005	2006	2007	2008

Ecuador (BA) [1] [2] [3] Total employment - Emploi total - Empleo total

Total - Total - Total
ISIC 3 - CITI 3 - CIIU 3

Total	3 226.1	3 376.1	3 673.2 ⁴	3 459.4	3 531.2	3 858.5	3 891.9	4 031.6	.	.
A	193.0	237.6	239.8 ⁴	261.2	276.7	320.8	273.5	285.0	.	.
B	48.0	50.8	42.3 ⁴	35.6	46.0	37.5	51.1	48.9	.	.
C	11.4	20.1	18.3 ⁴	22.3	20.4	16.1	10.7	15.8	.	.
D	506.5	526.3	610.6 ⁴	501.5	487.8	539.0	537.2	555.5	.	.
E	21.2	20.1	27.8 ⁴	14.0	17.0	22.9	18.8	19.4	.	.
F	215.5	239.7	234.9 ⁴	240.5	239.9	248.7	258.7	290.1	.	.
G	850.1	897.4	1 026.7 ⁴	971.5	1 000.8	1 096.2	1 099.0	1 151.8	.	.
H	176.1	145.2	158.2 ⁴	147.4	131.3	171.1	190.8	225.4	.	.
I	219.3	211.6	244.6 ⁴	222.3	233.2	264.7	280.1	292.3	.	.
J	49.7	43.4	33.5 ⁴	46.4	51.8	49.1	51.9	47.9	.	.
K	105.7	134.8	158.2 ⁴	155.0	154.9	189.8	199.7	200.7	.	.
L	127.1	138.5	159.9 ⁴	146.1	181.7	173.9	168.2	170.3	.	.
M	218.0	221.8	211.4 ⁴	238.8	234.4	263.0	258.9	281.0	.	.
N	98.9	106.9	99.8 ⁴	118.6	116.5	137.8	132.0	116.0	.	.
O	142.7	166.8	154.2 ⁴	121.0	174.5	176.1	158.7	162.9	.	.
P	242.3	214.5	232.1 ⁴	217.0	163.4	150.4	201.7	167.7	.	.
Q	0.6	0.5	1.4 ⁴	0.4	1.0	1.4	0.7	0.9	.	.
X	-	-	19.6 ⁴	-	-					

Men - Hommes - Hombres
ISIC 3 - CITI 3 - CIIU 3

Total	1 978.3	2 078.2	2 211.7 ⁴	2 131.7	.	2 288.5	2 327.8	2 416.5	.	.
A	161.5	186.4	186.7 ⁴	204.8	.	247.5	218.7	222.8	.	.
B	46.4	45.1	38.9 ⁴	30.3	.	34.2	38.4	42.2	.	.
C	10.0	18.1	16.6 ⁴	20.0	.	14.6	10.6	14.2	.	.
D	337.3	347.1	388.0 ⁴	331.2	.	335.6	361.4	368.3	.	.
E	17.7	17.2	22.6 ⁴	12.3	.	17.3	15.4	15.7	.	.
F	205.3	230.9	227.7 ⁴	226.0	.	239.9	249.4	278.2	.	.
G	506.3	515.8	583.1 ⁴	547.9	.	589.5	597.3	623.0	.	.
H	69.4	61.5	57.0 ⁴	65.6	.	62.2	71.0	85.3	.	.
I	195.9	188.8	216.5 ⁴	196.8	.	233.9	244.6	251.7	.	.
J	29.8	20.2	16.4 ⁴	24.1	.	26.3	26.2	25.2	.	.
K	79.3	90.3	108.2 ⁴	125.2	.	138.0	144.1	146.7	.	.
L	98.2	109.5	117.2 ⁴	109.5	.	124.9	125.6	126.4	.	.
M	84.8	83.4	81.4 ⁴	104.1	.	100.6	91.7	100.2	.	.
N	33.5	35.8	35.3 ⁴	43.3	.	47.4	46.9	42.3	.	.
O	87.5	110.9	86.0 ⁴	72.1	.	68.5	65.0	64.6	.	.
P	14.9	16.9	22.5 ⁴	18.2	.	7.0	20.9	9.7	.	.
Q	0.3	0.5	0.3 ⁴	0.4	.	1.2	0.4	-	.	.
X	-	-	7.4 ⁴	-	.					

Women - Femmes - Mujeres
ISIC 3 - CITI 3 - CIIU 3

Total	1 247.8	1 297.9	1 461.6 ⁴	1 327.7	.	1 570.1	1 564.0	1 615.1	.	.
A	31.5	51.2	53.1 ⁴	56.4	.	73.3	54.8	62.2	.	.
B	1.5	5.7	3.4 ⁴	5.4	.	3.3	12.7	6.8	.	.
C	1.4	2.0	1.7 ⁴	2.3	.	1.5	0.1	1.6	.	.
D	169.2	179.7	222.6 ⁴	170.3	.	203.4	175.7	187.2	.	.
E	3.5	3.4	5.2 ⁴	1.6	.	5.6	3.4	3.6	.	.
F	10.2	8.3	7.2 ⁴	14.5	.	8.8	9.4	11.9	.	.
G	343.8	382.8	443.6 ⁴	423.6	.	506.7	501.6	528.8	.	.
H	106.7	83.8	101.2 ⁴	81.8	.	108.9	119.8	140.1	.	.
I	23.4	22.6	28.2 ⁴	25.5	.	30.9	35.5	40.7	.	.
J	20.0	23.3	17.1 ⁴	22.2	.	22.8	25.7	22.7	.	.
K	26.4	44.5	50.1 ⁴	29.8	.	51.8	55.6	54.0	.	.
L	28.8	29.0	42.6 ⁴	36.7	.	49.0	42.6	43.9	.	.
M	133.2	138.4	130.1 ⁴	134.7	.	162.4	167.2	180.7	.	.
N	65.4	69.2	64.5 ⁴	75.2	.	90.4	85.1	73.7	.	.
O	55.1	55.9	68.1 ⁴	48.9	.	107.6	93.7	98.2	.	.
P	227.5	197.1	209.7 ⁴	198.8	.	143.4	180.8	158.0	.	.
Q	0.3	0.1	1.0 ⁴	-	.	0.2	0.3	0.9	.	.
X	-	-	12.2 ⁴	-	.	-	-	-		

El Salvador (BA) [1] [5] Total employment - Emploi total - Empleo total

Total - Total - Total
ISIC 3 - CITI 3 - CIIU 3

Total	2 182.5	2 198.9	2 275.2	2 219.6	2 280.7	2 253.6	2 283.6	2 337.1	2 419.2	.
A	466.8	459.1	483.5	421.7	389.6	415.5	444.4	427.8	422.3	.
B	16.1	16.0	12.4	14.7	26.3	15.5	12.1	13.0	13.5	.
C	1.7	1.5	2.8	3.2	2.0	1.6	2.2	2.0	3.7	.
D	409.3	410.4	400.5	399.3	405.2	377.7	369.2	368.4	403.6	.
E	8.1	8.3	10.1	9.8	5.7	9.2	6.4	9.0	10.2	.
F	125.6	112.5	123.4	125.3	147.2	145.2	129.4	157.7	148.4	.
G-H	555.1	578.3	619.4	633.4	655.7	659.7	674.1	698.8	720.6	.
I	96.2	103.6	105.3	95.1	102.9	112.2	106.5	104.7	103.2	.
J-K	81.0	83.1	93.2	90.2	99.2	92.0	108.2	100.0	114.4	.
L	108.6	117.2	90.4	92.5	93.9	87.8	88.4	92.1	98.7	.
M	71.6	66.1	81.7	86.9	76.6	77.6	85.7	81.7	90.0	.
N-O	134.4	146.7	144.2	143.0	169.0	153.1	158.7	164.9	178.4	.
P	106.8	95.1	106.7	94.9	106.4	105.9	98.3	117.0	111.7	.
X	1.2	1.1	1.4	9.6	1.1	0.7	-	-	0.4	.

Explanatory notes: see p. 77. Notes explicatives: voir p. 80. Notas explicativas: véase p. 83.

[1] Persons aged 10 years and over. [2] Urban areas. [3] Nov. of each year. [4] July. [5] Dec.

[1] Personnes âgées de 10 ans et plus. [2] Régions urbaines. [3] Nov. de chaque année. [4] Juillet. [5] Déc.

[1] Personas de 10 años y más. [2] Areas urbanas. [3] Nov. de cada año. [4] Julio. [5] Dic.

| **Total employment,**
by economic activity | **Emploi total,**
par activité économique | **Empleo total,**
por actividad económica |

Thousands			Milliers				Millares		
1999	2000	2001	2002	2003	2004	2005	2006	2007	2008

El Salvador (BA) [1] [2] — Total employment - Emploi total - Empleo total

Men - Hommes - Hombres
ISIC 3 - CITI 3 - CIIU 3

	1999	2000	2001	2002	2003	2004	2005	2006	2007	2008
Total	1 294.5	1 301.2	1 354.3	1 292.0	1 328.2	1 332.7	1 330.6	1 342.0	1 401.8	.
A	426.3	426.6	447.2	398.1	355.8	386.3	399.3	381.7	385.2	.
B	14.7	14.7	11.1	13.6	23.4	13.7	11.3	11.6	11.6	.
C	1.7	1.5	2.8	3.2	1.9	1.5	2.2	2.0	3.7	.
D	198.6	193.9	200.2	187.1	200.7	183.9	181.1	185.4	201.3	.
E	7.7	8.0	9.8	8.5	4.9	8.0	5.5	7.8	9.2	.
F	121.3	110.9	120.3	120.7	144.1	140.8	127.0	152.7	144.6	.
G-H	220.5	232.9	245.3	246.0	259.2	270.2	277.1	273.0	288.3	.
I	88.7	95.6	93.5	86.7	92.4	100.5	95.7	96.6	94.7	.
J-K	50.1	56.6	58.3	57.6	66.3	67.1	73.7	64.0	76.3	.
L	79.0	81.8	65.7	66.1	68.1	65.4	62.4	67.0	73.2	.
M	25.3	24.4	29.7	33.6	29.1	26.9	27.3	28.9	34.0	.
N-O	49.7	47.1	60.4	53.4	69.6	58.4	58.3	60.2	65.5	.
P	10.1	6.3	8.8	8.8	12.1	9.4	9.7	11.2	13.8	.
X	0.5	0.9	1.2	8.8	0.7	0.6	-	-	0.4	.

Women - Femmes - Mujeres
ISIC 3 - CITI 3 - CIIU 3

	1999	2000	2001	2002	2003	2004	2005	2006	2007	2008
Total	888.1	897.8	920.9	927.6	952.5	920.9	952.9	995.1	1 017.3	.
A	40.4	32.5	36.3	23.7	33.8	29.2	45.1	46.1	37.1	.
B	1.3	1.2	1.3	1.1	2.9	1.8	0.8	1.4	2.0	.
C	-	-	-	0.1	0.1	0.1	0.0	-	-	.
D	210.7	216.5	200.4	212.2	204.5	193.8	188.1	183.1	202.3	.
E	0.4	0.3	0.3	1.4	0.7	1.2	0.9	1.2	1.0	.
F	4.4	1.6	3.1	4.7	3.1	4.4	2.3	5.0	3.8	.
G-H	334.5	345.5	374.1	387.4	396.6	389.5	397.0	425.8	432.3	.
I	7.5	8.0	11.8	8.4	10.5	11.7	10.8	8.2	8.6	.
J-K	30.9	26.5	34.9	32.6	32.8	24.9	34.5	36.0	38.0	.
L	29.5	35.4	24.8	26.4	25.8	22.4	26.0	25.2	25.5	.
M	46.2	41.7	52.0	53.3	47.5	50.7	58.4	52.8	56.0	.
N-O	84.7	99.6	83.8	89.6	99.4	94.7	100.3	104.6	112.9	.
P	96.7	88.7	97.9	86.1	94.3	96.5	88.6	105.8	97.9	.
X	0.7	0.2	0.3	0.8	0.4	0.1	-	-	-	.

Guatemala (BA) [1] [3] — Total employment - Emploi total - Empleo total

Total - Total - Total
ISIC 3 - CITI 3 - CIIU 3

	1999	2000	2001	2002	2003	2004	2005	2006	2007	2008
Total	.	.	.	.	.	.	.	5 390.5	.	.
A-B	.	.	.	.	.	.	.	1 791.4	.	.
C	.	.	.	.	.	.	.	7.5	.	.
D	.	.	.	.	.	.	.	854.8	.	.
E	.	.	.	.	.	.	.	12.4	.	.
F	.	.	.	.	.	.	.	354.9	.	.
G-H	.	.	.	.	.	.	.	1 226.9	.	.
I	.	.	.	.	.	.	.	160.7	.	.
J-K	.	.	.	.	.	.	.	176.1	.	.
L	.	.	.	.	.	.	.	115.5	.	.
M	.	.	.	.	.	.	.	219.8	.	.
N-O	.	.	.	.	.	.	.	457.4	.	.
Q	.	.	.	.	.	.	.	13.2	.	.

Men - Hommes - Hombres
ISIC 3 - CITI 3 - CIIU 3

	1999	2000	2001	2002	2003	2004	2005	2006	2007	2008
Total	.	.	.	.	.	.	.	3 338.7	.	.
A-B	.	.	.	.	.	.	.	1 462.6	.	.
C	.	.	.	.	.	.	.	7.3	.	.
D	.	.	.	.	.	.	.	438.5	.	.
E	.	.	.	.	.	.	.	11.1	.	.
F	.	.	.	.	.	.	.	349.1	.	.
G-H	.	.	.	.	.	.	.	522.3	.	.
I	.	.	.	.	.	.	.	146.6	.	.
J-K	.	.	.	.	.	.	.	129.3	.	.
L	.	.	.	.	.	.	.	87.7	.	.
M	.	.	.	.	.	.	.	73.2	.	.
N-O	.	.	.	.	.	.	.	103.2	.	.
Q	.	.	.	.	.	.	.	8.0	.	.

Explanatory notes: see p. 77.
[1] Persons aged 10 years and over. [2] Dec. [3] Excl. armed forces.

Notes explicatives: voir p. 80.
[1] Personnes âgées de 10 ans et plus. [2] Déc. [3] Non compris les forces armées.

Notas explicativas: véase p. 83.
[1] Personas de 10 años y más. [2] Dic. [3] Excl. las fuerzas armadas.

EMPLOYMENT   EMPLOI   EMPLEO

Total employment, by economic activity   Emploi total, par activité économique   Empleo total, por actividad económica

Thousands   Milliers   Millares

	1999	2000	2001	2002	2003	2004	2005	2006	2007	2008
Guatemala (BA) [1][2]				Total employment - Emploi total - Empleo total						
Women - Femmes - Mujeres										
ISIC 3 - CITI 3 - CIIU 3										
Total	.	.	.	.	.	.	.	2 051.8	.	.
A-B	.	.	.	.	.	.	.	328.8	.	.
C	.	.	.	.	.	.	.	0.2	.	.
D	.	.	.	.	.	.	.	416.3	.	.
E	.	.	.	.	.	.	.	1.3	.	.
F	.	.	.	.	.	.	.	5.8	.	.
G-H	.	.	.	.	.	.	.	704.6	.	.
I	.	.	.	.	.	.	.	14.1	.	.
J-K	.	.	.	.	.	.	.	46.9	.	.
L	.	.	.	.	.	.	.	27.8	.	.
M	.	.	.	.	.	.	.	146.6	.	.
N-O	.	.	.	.	.	.	.	354.2	.	.
Q	.	.	.	.	.	.	.	5.2	.	.
Honduras (BA) [1][2]				Total employment - Emploi total - Empleo total						
Total - Total - Total										
ISIC 2 - CITI 2 - CIIU 2										
Total	2 299.0 [3]	.	2 288.7	2 351.1	2 426.1	2 439.0	2 543.5	2 724.4	2 836.1	.
1	806.1 [3]	.	845.2	912.6	906.3	851.1	997.2	989.0	979.9	.
2	3.8 [3]	.	5.1	5.1	5.8	6.4	6.2	6.4	7.1	.
3	376.9 [3]	.	367.2	374.6	381.2	385.5	378.1	406.6	421.2	.
4	8.2 [3]	.	11.5	10.5	9.6	10.0	11.0	11.2	12.4	.
5	117.8 [3]	.	123.6	122.5	122.8	143.5	135.5	165.6	189.2	.
6	489.1 [3]	.	462.8	469.6	495.9	514.5	503.8	584.4	603.6	.
7	56.0 [3]	.	71.7	75.2	79.1	82.8	87.4	87.7	106.1	.
8	49.9 [3]	.	66.6	63.2	73.3	69.5	81.7	85.5	94.9	.
9	391.1 [3]	.	334.4	316.7	352.1	373.6	337.8	386.2	419.4	.
0	- [3]	.	0.7	1.0	-	2.0	4.7	1.6	2.3	.
Men - Hommes - Hombres										
ISIC 2 - CITI 2 - CIIU 2										
Total	1 472.1 [3]	.	1 535.9	1 593.0	1 610.9	1 638.1	1 736.5	1 788.7	1 848.7	.
1	732.5 [3]	.	792.7	845.2	835.7	793.6	891.2	890.0	881.3	.
2	2.3 [3]	.	5.0	4.5	5.6	6.2	5.8	5.9	6.5	.
3	180.2 [3]	.	181.6	180.5	177.8	199.0	194.2	205.4	210.7	.
4	6.6 [3]	.	9.9	8.8	8.1	8.5	9.4	8.9	10.6	.
5	114.3 [3]	.	119.8	119.3	120.3	140.9	133.5	160.7	186.1	.
6	182.3 [3]	.	206.9	220.3	226.5	241.9	252.1	257.6	261.7	.
7	51.8 [3]	.	63.5	65.9	70.8	73.6	76.7	77.2	94.8	.
8	31.2 [3]	.	41.2	40.7	45.6	43.7	53.9	54.7	60.7	.
9	170.8 [3]	.	114.7	107.3	120.5	129.9	116.2	127.1	134.7	.
0	- [3]	.	0.6	0.7	-	0.9	3.7	1.1	1.7	.
Women - Femmes - Mujeres										
ISIC 2 - CITI 2 - CIIU 2										
Total	826.9 [3]	.	752.8	758.0	815.3	800.9	807.0	935.7	987.4	.
1	73.6 [3]	.	52.5	67.4	70.7	57.5	106.1	99.0	98.6	.
2	1.5 [3]	.	0.1	0.6	0.2	0.2	0.5	0.5	0.6	.
3	196.6 [3]	.	185.6	194.2	203.4	186.5	183.9	201.2	210.6	.
4	1.6 [3]	.	1.7	1.7	1.5	1.5	1.6	2.3	1.8	.
5	3.5 [3]	.	3.8	3.3	2.5	2.6	2.0	4.9	3.0	.
6	306.8 [3]	.	255.9	249.3	269.3	272.6	251.8	326.8	341.9	.
7	4.2 [3]	.	8.1	9.3	8.3	9.2	10.7	10.4	11.3	.
8	18.7 [3]	.	25.5	22.4	27.7	25.9	27.9	30.8	34.2	.
9	220.3 [3]	.	219.6	209.5	231.6	243.7	221.5	259.2	284.7	.
0	- [3]	.	0.1	0.3	-	1.1	1.0	0.5	0.6	.
Jamaica (BA) [4]				Total employment - Emploi total - Empleo total						
Total - Total - Total										
ISIC 2 - CITI 2 - CIIU 2										
Total	936.8	935.6	942.3	1 025.9	1 056.5	1 058.7	1 091.7	1 129.5	1 170.2	1 167.8
1	192.5	194.5	195.2	205.8	215.0	195.6	197.2	206.1	206.1	222.6
2	4.7	4.7	5.2	4.5	4.7	5.3	4.8	6.4	8.8	9.2
3	81.3	65.8	69.1	69.4	73.9	72.3	73.2	73.6	71.6	68.6
4	6.4	5.6	6.4	6.7	7.0	6.5	5.4	7.1	9.3	9.0
5	75.7	82.4	80.5	96.4	98.5	109.2	110.1	113.1	121.3	106.1
6	200.2	204.8	214.7	219.5	227.7	248.6	260.8	272.4	262.3	265.2
7	56.8	57.6	60.6	71.3	71.3	77.2	78.4	79.3	80.6	81.3
8	56.0	55.9	46.4	65.0	71.0	58.3	55.7	59.3	71.1	77.8
9	261.1	261.4	261.9	283.9	285.6	285.3	303.4	310.4	337.2	326.6
0	2.1	2.9	2.3	3.4	1.8	0.4	2.7	1.8	1.9	1.4

Explanatory notes: see p. 77.   Notes explicatives: voir p. 80.   Notas explicativas: véase p. 83.

[1] Excl. armed forces. [2] Persons aged 10 years and over. [3] March. [4] Persons aged 14 years and over.

[1] Non compris les forces armées. [2] Personnes âgées de 10 ans et plus. [3] Mars. [4] Personnes âgées de 14 ans et plus.

[1] Excl. las fuerzas armadas. [2] Personas de 10 años y más. [3] Marzo. [4] Personas de 14 años y más.

Total employment, by economic activity
Emploi total, par activité économique
Empleo total, por actividad económica

	Thousands							Milliers					Millares	
	1999	2000	2001	2002	2003	2004	2005	2006	2007	2008

Jamaica (BA) [1]   Total employment - Emploi total - Empleo total

Men - Hommes - Hombres
ISIC 2 - CITI 2 - CIIU 2

	1999	2000	2001	2002	2003	2004	2005	2006	2007	2008
Total	551.9	552.5	556.6	596.3	615.3	613.9	629.3	649.8	670.4	658.3
1	158.3	159.1	158.2	163.4	176.0	156.5	158.1	166.2	165.6	172.9
2	4.4	4.1	4.7	3.8	4.2	4.6	4.2	5.8	8.0	7.7
3	56.6	47.6	50.0	48.2	51.0	53.8	56.3	57.5	51.8	47.5
4	5.2	3.8	4.9	5.3	5.8	4.8	3.4	4.8	6.3	6.5
5	73.1	79.2	78.0	91.8	95.1	106.0	105.3	109.9	115.0	101.1
6	74.2	82.0	83.3	83.6	84.5	92.5	94.7	97.4	97.9	96.5
7	44.9	46.2	47.2	57.8	57.9	63.6	63.5	63.3	64.0	63.3
8	28.4	25.9	21.8	29.9	34.8	28.3	26.8	26.1	34.9	38.3
9	105.9	103.5	106.7	111.1	104.8	103.9	115.5	118.2	126.1	123.8
0	0.9	1.1	1.8	1.4	1.2	0.2	1.5	0.6	0.8	0.7

Women - Femmes - Mujeres
ISIC 2 - CITI 2 - CIIU 2

	1999	2000	2001	2002	2003	2004	2005	2006	2007	2008
Total	384.9	383.1	385.7	429.6	441.2	444.8	462.4	479.7	499.8	509.5
1	34.2	35.4	37.0	42.4	39.0	39.1	39.1	39.9	40.5	49.7
2	0.3	0.6	0.5	0.7	0.5	0.7	0.6	0.6	0.8	1.5
3	24.7	18.2	19.1	21.2	22.9	18.5	16.9	16.1	19.8	21.1
4	1.2	1.8	1.5	1.4	1.2	1.7	2.0	2.3	3.0	2.5
5	2.6	3.2	2.5	4.6	3.4	3.2	4.8	3.2	6.3	5.0
6	126.0	122.8	131.4	135.9	143.2	156.1	166.1	175.0	164.4	168.7
7	11.9	11.4	13.4	13.5	13.4	13.9	14.9	16.0	16.6	18.0
8	27.6	30.0	24.6	35.1	36.2	30.0	28.9	33.2	36.2	39.5
9	155.2	157.9	155.2	172.8	180.8	181.4	187.9	192.2	211.1	202.8
0	1.2	1.5	0.5	2.0	0.6	0.2	1.2	1.2	1.1	0.7

México (BA) [1][2]   Total employment - Emploi total - Empleo total

Total - Total - Total
ISIC 3 - CITI 3 - CIIU 3

	1999	2000	2001	2002	2003	2004	2005	2006	2007	2008
Total	37 279.9	38 044.5	38 065.8	38 939.7	39 221.5	40 561.0	40 791.8	42 197.8	42 906.7	43 866.7
A	7 494.6	6 539.6	6 548.2	6 659.2	6 213.6	6 301.0	5 898.1	5 865.7	5 630.1	5 628.9
B	151.0	154.9	146.2	139.7	169.9	151.8	161.8	167.3	142.3	129.6
C	125.4	156.3	129.2	143.0	136.4	167.2	193.5	164.1	185.9	183.2
D	7 106.7	7 442.7	7 252.2	6 957.7	6 820.6	7 100.1	6 910.6	7 078.7	7 129.6	7 228.1
E	189.8	187.6	194.9	195.3	213.5	235.3	186.1	186.3	220.4	206.2
F	2 057.6	2 449.4	2 304.7	2 408.3	2 623.3	2 574.3	3 181.1	3 452.5	3 585.8	3 641.2
G	7 971.6	8 342.3	8 668.2	9 071.7	9 198.6	9 719.6	9 332.8	9 594.9	9 820.8	9 974.4
H	1 719.9	1 800.6	1 949.5	2 021.8	2 128.4	2 285.7	2 438.3	2 514.9	2 670.6	2 836.7
I	1 689.7	1 723.8	1 764.7	1 782.4	1 825.1	1 827.2	1 846.5	2 001.4	1 943.0	2 034.4
J	296.1	294.8	282.4	288.1	283.1	285.6	307.2	362.6	403.6	405.8
K	1 035.8	1 172.9	1 213.0	1 262.6	1 315.5	1 432.8	1 828.5	1 925.3	2 049.6	2 189.2
L	1 694.5	1 742.7	1 687.2	1 790.6	1 819.8	1 798.3	1 916.9	2 032.1	2 041.2	2 172.0
M	1 697.4	1 887.0	1 979.9	2 027.4	2 033.4	2 171.3	2 181.1	2 252.4	2 319.3	2 326.0
N	1 003.7	1 064.8	1 044.6	1 094.8	1 118.7	1 211.7	1 136.2	1 161.3	1 212.6	1 252.8
O	1 262.8	1 232.5	1 139.1	1 255.6	1 358.5	1 370.3	1 327.7	1 369.4	1 373.9	1 469.4
P	1 628.4	1 699.5	1 626.2	1 699.8	1 826.8	1 768.4	1 693.5	1 756.4	1 858.3	1 851.8
Q	0.0	1.7	0.7	0.0	0.0	2.8	3.6	2.8	7.2	3.8
X	154.8	151.4	135.1	141.7	136.4	157.7	248.2	309.7	312.2	333.0

Men - Hommes - Hombres
ISIC 3 - CITI 3 - CIIU 3

	1999	2000	2001	2002	2003	2004	2005	2006	2007	2008
Total	24 805.7	25 014.1	25 055.1	25 422.8	25 713.5	26 138.0	25 853.1	26 597.9	26 840.6	27 401.7
A	6 410.8	5 651.3	5 773.2	5 834.2	5 520.1	5 508.3	5 187.2	5 141.3	4 938.0	4 971.8
B	144.6	147.0	134.2	127.2	155.9	143.1	145.3	157.2	134.4	121.0
C	114.8	138.0	116.6	122.1	122.3	150.3	168.7	147.9	164.8	162.3
D	4 540.7	4 670.7	4 505.5	4 295.8	4 278.8	4 457.0	4 244.1	4 357.5	4 400.5	4 448.3
E	165.6	157.0	164.4	165.0	180.2	195.4	158.1	150.2	182.4	174.1
F	2 017.7	2 382.9	2 238.3	2 339.9	2 568.9	2 488.6	3 076.8	3 352.0	3 473.8	3 522.1
G	4 956.4	5 129.2	5 352.9	5 527.6	5 608.0	5 760.4	5 269.7	5 380.2	5 389.5	5 483.6
H	782.5	824.5	877.9	898.9	953.5	999.0	1 041.3	1 041.9	1 142.4	1 177.4
I	1 503.3	1 563.4	1 568.7	1 607.2	1 671.8	1 662.8	1 680.2	1 802.8	1 742.0	1 820.8
J	175.2	152.0	171.6	167.8	157.0	163.8	159.1	190.8	215.8	209.3
K	667.8	773.4	816.2	830.1	877.3	962.9	1 180.4	1 245.0	1 322.3	1 378.2
L	1 165.9	1 170.3	1 143.5	1 207.3	1 238.3	1 198.4	1 246.7	1 329.6	1 316.2	1 386.9
M	720.1	773.4	807.0	811.3	828.8	893.6	845.5	846.2	910.2	916.9
N	358.2	366.1	365.0	388.5	396.8	401.6	380.7	366.4	372.3	411.4
O	787.3	806.0	715.5	779.5	813.7	823.2	741.3	736.9	781.5	837.3
P	171.2	192.4	196.6	206.9	236.4	204.7	154.5	142.9	144.6	151.2
Q	0.0	0.4	0.6	0.0	0.0	0.8	2.3	0.9	3.1	3.5
X	123.6	116.1	107.4	113.4	105.7	124.3	171.4	208.2	206.8	225.6

Explanatory notes: see p. 77.   Notes explicatives: voir p. 80.   Notas explicativas: véase p. 83.

[1] Persons aged 14 years and over. [2] Second quarter of each year.   [1] Personnes âgées de 14 ans et plus. [2] Deuxième trimestre de chaque année.   [1] Personas de 14 años y más. [2] Segundo trimestre de cada año.

Total employment, by economic activity   **Emploi total, par activité économique**   **Empleo total, por actividad económica**

	Thousands				Milliers				Millares	
	1999	2000	2001	2002	2003	2004	2005	2006	2007	2008

México (BA) [1][2]   Total employment - Emploi total - Empleo total

Women - Femmes - Mujeres
ISIC 3 - CITI 3 - CIIU 3

	1999	2000	2001	2002	2003	2004	2005	2006	2007	2008
Total	12 474.2	13 030.4	13 010.6	13 516.8	13 508.0	14 423.0	14 938.7	15 599.9	16 066.0	16 465.0
A	1 083.9	888.3	774.9	825.1	693.5	792.6	710.9	724.4	692.1	657.1
B	6.4	7.8	12.0	12.6	14.0	8.7	16.5	10.1	7.9	8.7
C	10.7	18.3	12.6	20.9	14.1	16.8	24.7	16.2	21.1	20.9
D	2 566.0	2 772.1	2 746.7	2 661.9	2 541.8	2 643.1	2 666.6	2 721.2	2 729.2	2 779.8
E	24.1	30.6	30.5	30.2	33.2	39.9	28.0	36.1	38.0	32.1
F	39.9	66.5	66.3	68.3	54.4	85.7	104.3	100.5	112.0	119.1
G	3 015.2	3 213.1	3 315.3	3 544.1	3 590.6	3 959.3	4 063.1	4 214.7	4 431.4	4 490.8
H	937.5	976.0	1 071.6	1 122.9	1 174.9	1 286.7	1 397.0	1 473.1	1 528.1	1 659.3
I	186.4	160.4	196.0	175.2	153.3	164.4	166.3	198.6	201.0	213.5
J	120.9	142.8	110.9	120.3	126.0	121.8	148.2	171.7	187.8	196.6
K	368.0	399.5	396.8	432.5	438.2	469.9	648.2	680.2	727.3	811.0
L	528.5	572.5	543.6	583.3	581.5	600.0	670.2	702.5	725.1	785.1
M	977.3	1 113.6	1 172.9	1 216.1	1 204.6	1 277.7	1 335.6	1 406.2	1 409.2	1 409.1
N	645.5	698.8	679.6	706.3	721.9	810.1	755.6	794.9	840.3	841.5
O	475.5	426.5	423.5	476.0	544.8	547.0	586.4	632.5	592.4	632.1
P	1 457.2	1 507.1	1 429.5	1 492.9	1 590.5	1 563.7	1 539.0	1 613.5	1 713.7	1 700.6
Q	0.0	1.3	0.1	0.0	0.0	2.0	1.3	1.9	4.1	0.3
X	31.2	35.2	27.6	28.3	30.7	33.4	76.8	101.5	105.4	107.5

Netherlands Antilles (BA) [3][4][5]   Total employment - Emploi total - Empleo total

Total - Total - Total
ISIC 3 - CITI 3 - CIIU 3

	1999	2000	2001	2002	2003	2004	2005	2006	2007	2008
Total	.	52.2	.	49.1	52.1	51.5	51.3	52.1	54.0	56.5
A-B	.	0.6	.	0.4	0.5	0.4	0.5	0.5	0.7	0.6
C	.	0.1	.	0.1	0.1	0.1	0.1	0.0	0.1	0.1
D	.	4.7	.	4.1	4.1	3.9	3.4	3.5	3.8	3.9
E	.	0.9	.	0.8	0.8	0.7	0.7	0.8	0.8	0.8
F	.	3.7	.	3.6	3.7	3.5	3.7	3.9	4.0	5.1
G	.	9.9	.	8.9	9.7	9.7	9.7	9.5	9.2	9.8
H	.	3.7	.	3.4	3.8	4.0	4.1	4.2	4.4	4.5
I	.	4.0	.	3.3	3.4	3.2	3.1	3.1	3.5	4.1
J	.	3.5	.	3.3	3.4	3.5	3.7	3.9	4.1	4.1
K	.	4.0	.	4.2	4.7	4.8	5.0	5.2	5.6	6.0
L	.	5.0	.	4.5	4.7	4.3	4.4	4.8	5.3	4.7
M	.	2.9	.	2.1	2.0	2.2	2.3	2.6	2.8	2.5
N	.	4.3	.	4.2	4.4	4.4	4.3	4.4	4.6	4.4
O	.	3.3	.	3.7	4.3	4.2	3.9	3.6	3.3	3.6
P	.	1.7	.	2.2	2.7	2.4	2.4	2.0	1.8	2.1
Q	.	0.1	.	0.0	0.1	0.1	0.1	0.1	0.1	0.0

Nicaragua (BA) [6]   Total employment - Emploi total - Empleo total

Total - Total - Total
ISIC 3 - CITI 3 - CIIU 3

	1999	2000	2001	2002	2003	2004	2005	2006	2007	2008
Total	.	.	.	.	1 917.0	1 973.1	2 080.9	2 089.8	.	.
A	.	.	.	.	568.3	586.3	588.1	593.6	.	.
B	.	.	.	.	17.1	11.6	13.1	15.5	.	.
C	.	.	.	.	4.6	5.6	5.4	6.7	.	.
D	.	.	.	.	254.5	254.8	302.3	289.2	.	.
E	.	.	.	.	12.5	6.9	9.2	6.5	.	.
F	.	.	.	.	72.6	95.3	92.6	100.8	.	.
G	.	.	.	.	388.0	392.6	419.3	409.1	.	.
H	.	.	.	.	60.4	73.9	61.7	72.0	.	.
I	.	.	.	.	73.4	80.0	88.1	89.0	.	.
J	.	.	.	.	14.9	16.8	17.0	15.9	.	.
K	.	.	.	.	36.2	43.9	53.0	54.0	.	.
L	.	.	.	.	57.0	68.3	70.8	73.7	.	.
M	.	.	.	.	85.2	86.6	89.0	94.5	.	.
N	.	.	.	.	50.8	55.8	51.4	54.3	.	.
O	.	.	.	.	92.8	84.9	91.8	89.2	.	.
P	.	.	.	.	123.5	106.2	118.7	117.4	.	.
Q	.	.	.	.	5.2	3.6	9.2	8.1	.	.

Explanatory notes: see p. 77.   Notes explicatives: voir p. 80.   Notas explicativas: véase p. 83.

[1] Persons aged 14 years and over. [2] Second quarter of each year. [3] Persons aged 15 years and over. [4] Curaçao. [5] Oct. of each year. [6] Persons aged 10 years and over.

[1] Personnes âgées de 14 ans et plus. [2] Deuxième trimestre de chaque année. [3] Personnes âgées de 15 ans et plus. [4] Curaçao. [5] Oct. de chaque année. [6] Personnes âgées de 10 ans et plus.

[1] Personas de 14 años y más. [2] Segundo trimestre de cada año. [3] Personas de 15 años y más. [4] Curaçao. [5] Oct. de cada año. [6] Personas de 10 años y más.

Total employment, by economic activity — Emploi total, par activité économique — Empleo total, por actividad económica

	Thousands — Milliers — Millares									
	1999	2000	2001	2002	2003	2004	2005	2006	2007	2008

Nicaragua (BA) [1]

Total employment - Emploi total - Empleo total

Men - Hommes - Hombres
ISIC 3 - CITI 3 - CIIU 3

	1999	2000	2001	2002	2003	2004	2005	2006	2007	2008
Total	.	.	.	.	1 178.5	1 239.3	1 296.6	1 303.5	.	.
A	.	.	.	.	492.6	509.2	523.6	528.7	.	.
B	.	.	.	.	15.9	11.0	12.2	14.5	.	.
C	.	.	.	.	3.8	4.8	4.2	5.9	.	.
D	.	.	.	.	134.4	135.5	157.5	153.1	.	.
E	.	.	.	.	10.0	6.1	7.4	5.3	.	.
F	.	.	.	.	70.6	94.3	90.9	99.1	.	.
G	.	.	.	.	183.7	199.1	201.0	195.6	.	.
H	.	.	.	.	16.7	20.9	16.3	18.1	.	.
I	.	.	.	.	68.6	74.6	80.6	82.3	.	.
J	.	.	.	.	7.3	8.1	8.8	7.5	.	.
K	.	.	.	.	26.1	33.9	40.4	42.1	.	.
L	.	.	.	.	37.7	44.5	47.4	44.6	.	.
M	.	.	.	.	23.9	26.8	28.6	28.5	.	.
N	.	.	.	.	18.0	19.5	18.7	19.6	.	.
O	.	.	.	.	50.2	32.3	34.4	33.0	.	.
P	.	.	.	.	16.7	16.7	18.4	22.6	.	.
Q	.	.	.	.	2.6	2.1	5.9	3.1	.	.

Women - Femmes - Mujeres
ISIC 3 - CITI 3 - CIIU 3

	1999	2000	2001	2002	2003	2004	2005	2006	2007	2008
Total	.	.	.	.	738.4	733.8	784.3	786.3	.	.
A	.	.	.	.	75.6	77.2	64.5	64.9	.	.
B	.	.	.	.	1.2	0.6	0.9	1.0	.	.
C	.	.	.	.	0.8	0.8	1.2	0.8	.	.
D	.	.	.	.	120.1	119.3	144.8	136.1	.	.
E	.	.	.	.	2.5	0.7	1.8	1.2	.	.
F	.	.	.	.	2.0	1.0	1.7	1.7	.	.
G	.	.	.	.	204.3	193.5	218.3	213.5	.	.
H	.	.	.	.	43.7	53.0	45.4	53.9	.	.
I	.	.	.	.	4.8	5.4	7.5	6.7	.	.
J	.	.	.	.	7.5	8.7	8.3	8.4	.	.
K	.	.	.	.	10.2	10.0	12.6	11.9	.	.
L	.	.	.	.	19.3	23.8	23.4	29.1	.	.
M	.	.	.	.	61.3	59.7	60.4	66.0	.	.
N	.	.	.	.	32.9	36.4	32.6	34.7	.	.
O	.	.	.	.	42.6	52.6	57.3	56.2	.	.
P	.	.	.	.	106.8	89.6	100.3	94.8	.	.
Q	.	.	.	.	2.7	1.5	3.3	5.0	.	.

Panamá (BA) [2] [3]

Total employment - Emploi total - Empleo total

Total - Total - Total
ISIC 3 - CITI 3 - CIIU 3

	1999	2000	2001	2002	2003	2004	2005	2006	2007	2008
Total	961.4	940.1	984.2	1 049.5	1 080.5	1 134.7	1 188.3	1 210.7	1 264.0	1 333.8
A	157.2	149.8	166.6	171.5	179.2	172.3	176.8	183.1	176.5	176.5
B	10.4	9.7	11.2	10.6	9.7	9.4	9.5	9.9	9.8	9.1
C	0.9	0.8	1.8	1.6	1.0	0.7	1.0	2.3	3.6	3.3
D	94.0	86.9	88.5	96.3	96.6	100.4	104.3	105.2	109.6	114.1
E	7.0	6.4	9.6	8.6	8.8	8.4	7.7	8.5	8.1	6.9
F	73.0	69.2	70.5	71.8	79.6	90.6	91.1	102.8	122.4	136.7
G	182.7	180.1	181.8	193.2	194.2	207.2	226.9	229.6	240.7	258.6
H	39.5	34.6	42.4	47.9	53.3	61.1	69.6	64.5	69.5	70.8
I	73.0	71.7	78.0	81.7	85.8	89.4	91.3	90.8	91.9	100.9
J	23.9	26.4	22.7	22.5	21.5	25.0	24.3	26.4	28.8	28.4
K	39.4	37.5	34.3	42.0	44.6	54.1	61.7	62.6	67.0	71.7
L	68.1	70.3	69.4	69.6	73.8	73.7	69.4	70.3	79.6	78.7
M	50.2	55.7	57.6	61.4	64.2	66.8	64.9	62.7	65.3	74.6
N	30.8	32.2	36.5	38.7	37.8	43.2	47.6	48.3	50.6	55.1
O	57.5	54.7	57.0	70.1	65.3	62.2	71.6	68.0	63.8	70.0
P	51.2	53.2	55.9	61.9	64.0	69.4	70.0	74.9	76.1	77.4
Q	2.4	0.9	0.5	0.2	1.0	0.7	0.6	0.8	0.7	0.9

Men - Hommes - Hombres
ISIC 3 - CITI 3 - CIIU 3

	1999	2000	2001	2002	2003	2004	2005	2006	2007	2008
Total	638.0	625.0	659.2	687.6	703.3	734.3	755.7	777.5	799.1	837.0
A	151.4	144.8	157.7	161.3	165.9	161.0	158.5	164.1	161.2	157.7
B	10.0	9.3	10.3	10.0	9.0	8.8	9.1	9.5	9.4	8.6
C	0.9	0.7	1.6	1.6	1.0	0.7	1.0	2.0	3.4	2.9
D	64.2	61.8	64.2	66.7	68.4	67.7	69.4	72.8	71.5	73.5
E	5.8	5.3	7.4	7.2	7.6	7.5	6.5	6.7	5.8	4.8
F	70.4	66.8	67.5	68.9	76.6	88.8	87.8	99.2	117.8	133.1
G	113.7	113.0	117.3	119.8	119.1	130.2	138.3	143.5	142.8	151.4
H	18.1	17.1	19.2	20.8	24.2	26.7	28.5	25.0	27.2	27.7
I	62.2	60.1	67.3	70.6	75.4	76.4	79.5	77.9	79.5	89.3
J	10.0	11.6	9.5	9.4	8.4	9.1	9.5	11.2	11.3	10.9
K	25.8	24.2	23.6	28.3	28.5	32.1	39.0	40.3	41.3	42.1
L	41.1	41.8	41.7	41.9	43.0	42.8	40.3	41.8	46.4	46.0
M	17.4	18.9	18.3	18.8	19.3	21.9	21.8	20.3	22.2	25.4
N	11.7	11.1	14.3	14.1	14.7	14.9	15.2	15.9	16.0	16.6
O	27.8	30.5	33.3	40.4	35.0	37.1	42.1	39.2	34.4	38.2
P	5.7	7.6	5.7	7.5	7.0	8.0	9.0	7.6	8.5	8.6
Q	1.6	0.5	0.2	0.2	0.5	0.7	0.1	0.6	0.4	0.3

Explanatory notes: see p. 77.

[1] Persons aged 10 years and over. [2] Persons aged 15 years and over. [3] Aug. of each year.

Notes explicatives: voir p. 80.

[1] Personnes âgées de 10 ans et plus. [2] Personnes âgées de 15 ans et plus. [3] Août de chaque année.

Notas explicativas: véase p. 83.

[1] Personas de 10 años y más. [2] Personas de 15 años y más. [3] Agosto de cada año.

EMPLOYMENT — EMPLOI — EMPLEO

Total employment, by economic activity — Emploi total, par activité économique — Empleo total, por actividad económica

Thousands — Milliers — Millares

Panamá (BA) [1][2]

Women - Femmes - Mujeres
ISIC 3 - CITI 3 - CIIU 3

Total employment - Emploi total - Empleo total

	1999	2000	2001	2002	2003	2004	2005	2006	2007	2008
Total	323.4	315.1	325.1	362.0	377.2	400.4	432.6	433.2	464.9	496.8
A	5.7	5.0	8.9	10.2	13.3	11.3	18.3	19.0	15.2	18.9
B	0.4	0.4	0.8	0.6	0.7	0.7	0.5	0.4	0.4	0.5
C	-	-	0.2	-	-	-	-	0.3	0.2	0.4
D	29.8	25.1	24.2	29.6	28.2	32.7	34.9	32.4	38.1	40.6
E	1.1	1.2	2.3	1.5	1.2	0.9	1.3	1.8	2.3	2.0
F	2.5	2.4	3.0	2.9	3.1	1.8	3.3	3.6	4.6	3.6
G	69.0	67.0	64.5	73.4	75.2	77.1	88.6	86.0	98.0	107.3
H	21.4	17.4	23.1	27.0	29.1	34.5	41.1	39.5	42.3	43.1
I	10.8	11.6	10.8	11.1	10.5	13.0	11.7	12.9	12.4	11.6
J	13.9	14.8	13.2	13.1	13.2	15.9	14.8	15.2	17.5	17.5
K	13.6	13.3	10.8	13.6	16.1	22.0	22.7	22.4	25.7	29.6
L	27.0	28.6	27.7	27.6	30.8	30.9	29.0	28.5	33.2	32.7
M	32.8	36.9	39.3	42.6	44.9	44.8	43.1	42.4	43.1	49.2
N	19.1	21.1	22.2	24.5	23.2	28.3	32.4	32.4	34.6	38.5
O	29.8	24.3	23.7	29.7	30.3	25.1	29.5	28.9	29.4	31.9
P	45.4	45.6	50.2	54.4	56.9	61.3	61.0	67.3	67.7	68.8
Q	0.8	0.3	0.2	-	0.5	0.1	0.4	0.2	0.3	0.6

Paraguay (BA) [3][4]

Total employment - Emploi total - Empleo total

Total - Total - Total
ISIC 3 - CITI 3 - CIIU 3

	2007	2008
Total	2 716.4	2 810.5
A-B	800.6	745.2
C	8.6	6.6
D	319.3	340.2
E	8.8	10.8
F	154.9	174.1
G-H	639.5	673.8
I	101.5	118.4
J-K	104.2	120.8
L-Q	578.4	620.0
X	0.6	0.6

Men - Hommes - Hombres
ISIC 3 - CITI 3 - CIIU 3

	2007	2008
Total	1 653.6	1 726.4
A-B	551.2	537.2
C	8.6	6.4
D	226.7	238.4
E	8.0	8.8
F	153.9	173.5
G-H	355.4	364.4
I	85.7	101.5
J-K	65.7	78.5
L-Q	198.1	217.7
X	0.2	-

Women - Femmes - Mujeres
ISIC 3 - CITI 3 - CIIU 3

	2007	2008
Total	1 062.8	1 084.1
A-B	249.4	208.0
C		0.2
D	92.5	101.8
E	0.8	2.0
F	1.0	0.6
G-H	284.1	309.5
I	15.8	16.9
J-K	38.6	42.3
L-Q	380.3	402.3
X	0.4	0.6

Explanatory notes: see p. 77.

[1] Persons aged 15 years and over. [2] Aug. of each year. [3] Persons aged 10 years and over. [4] Fourth quarter.

Notes explicatives: voir p. 80.

[1] Personnes âgées de 15 ans et plus. [2] Août de chaque année. [3] Personnes âgées de 10 ans et plus. [4] Quatrième trimestre.

Notas explicativas: véase p. 83.

[1] Personas de 15 años y más. [2] Agosto de cada año. [3] Personas de 10 años y más. [4] Cuarto trimestre.

Total employment,
by economic activity

Emploi total,
par activité économique

Empleo total,
por actividad económica

	Thousands			Milliers				Millares		
	1999	2000	2001	2002	2003	2004	2005	2006	2007	2008

Perú (BA) [1] [2]   Total employment - Emploi total - Empleo total

Total - Total - Total
ISIC 3 - CITI 3 - CIIU 3

	1999	2000	2001	2002	2003	2004	2005	2006	2007	2008
Total	.	.	.	3 338.9 [3]	3 703.0 [4]	3 652.0	3 529.0	3 851.2	4 163.7	4 246.3
A	.	.	.	26.7 [3]	38.4 [4]	38.1	37.4	38.6	41.8	33.7
B	.	.	.	8.0 [3]	14.5 [4]	4.1	7.5	8.0	6.7	4.3
C	.	.	.	5.1 [3]	3.1 [4]	16.7	16.1	18.8	22.3	21.3
D	.	.	.	520.6 [3]	503.6 [4]	608.3	575.0	628.1	728.0	725.3
E	.	.	.	9.1 [3]	8.5 [4]	5.2	11.4	9.5	9.0	8.6
F	.	.	.	191.9 [3]	251.3 [4]	230.5	180.9	240.6	245.9	251.7
G	.	.	.	804.7 [3]	900.9 [4]	855.4	828.5	891.4	901.3	932.1
H	.	.	.	258.7 [3]	293.6 [4]	272.6	256.8	276.3	271.7	300.3
I	.	.	.	291.0 [3]	344.2 [4]	309.9	319.6	364.5	404.1	449.7
J	.	.	.	34.9 [3]	37.6 [4]	32.5	48.7	47.5	40.1	62.2
K	.	.	.	249.2 [3]	312.0 [4]	255.1	211.8	270.0	306.3	289.7
L	.	.	.	155.8 [3]	149.0 [4]	139.2	152.5	176.0	205.7	167.4
M	.	.	.	189.2 [3]	204.5 [4]	223.1	234.5	206.3	250.2	258.9
N	.	.	.	96.4 [3]	89.7 [4]	116.6	95.7	96.4	131.1	145.6
O	.	.	.	268.8 [3]	282.4 [4]	283.6	314.8	286.5	309.1	321.7
P	.	.	.	228.8 [3]	268.5 [4]	258.3	237.9	291.9	289.1	271.5
Q	.	.	.	- [3]	1.2 [4]	2.7	-	0.7	1.2	2.2
X	.	.	.	- [3]	- [4]	-	-	-	-	-

Men - Hommes - Hombres
ISIC 3 - CITI 3 - CIIU 3

	1999	2000	2001	2002	2003	2004	2005	2006	2007	2008
Total	.	.	.	1 834.1 [3]	2 074.6 [4]	2 053.5	1 981.3	2 133.6	2 269.0	2 294.4
A	.	.	.	19.0 [3]	28.0 [4]	28.4	32.7	27.3	34.1	25.2
B	.	.	.	8.0 [3]	13.0 [4]	4.1	7.5	8.0	6.3	4.3
C	.	.	.	5.1 [3]	3.1 [4]	15.4	13.5	16.9	18.9	19.2
D	.	.	.	372.8 [3]	345.7 [4]	420.3	382.7	418.3	476.6	462.3
E	.	.	.	7.3 [3]	6.3 [4]	5.2	6.5	7.8	8.1	6.5
F	.	.	.	183.1 [3]	237.4 [4]	227.9	173.8	230.2	241.9	239.2
G	.	.	.	348.0 [3]	421.7 [4]	349.7	391.4	373.9	363.7	359.8
H	.	.	.	84.2 [3]	89.9 [4]	68.8	87.8	82.5	79.9	82.3
I	.	.	.	252.4 [3]	299.0 [4]	277.3	280.6	325.6	340.8	389.0
J	.	.	.	19.2 [3]	19.0 [4]	17.4	24.5	28.0	23.3	36.4
K	.	.	.	166.4 [3]	191.9 [4]	192.8	141.4	185.4	195.6	190.8
L	.	.	.	100.3 [3]	105.4 [4]	103.1	107.4	108.9	148.2	127.2
M	.	.	.	52.8 [3]	57.0 [4]	72.1	72.4	76.3	86.1	85.5
N	.	.	.	34.0 [3]	35.7 [4]	42.8	37.4	27.0	41.9	53.2
O	.	.	.	174.2 [3]	200.0 [4]	204.0	205.2	199.2	187.8	199.5
P	.	.	.	7.4 [3]	21.4 [4]	21.7	16.6	17.7	15.9	13.8
Q	.	.	.	- [3]	- [4]	2.5	-	0.7	-	-
X	.	.	.	-	- [4]	-	-	-	-	-

Women - Femmes - Mujeres
ISIC 3 - CITI 3 - CIIU 3

	1999	2000	2001	2002	2003	2004	2005	2006	2007	2008
Total	.	.	.	1 504.7 [3]	1 628.4 [4]	1 598.5	1 547.7	1 717.6	1 894.7	1 951.8
A	.	.	.	7.7 [3]	10.4 [4]	9.7	4.7	11.4	7.7	8.6
B	.	.	.	- [3]	1.5 [4]	-	-	-	0.3	-
C	.	.	.	- [3]	- [4]	1.3	2.6	1.9	3.4	2.0
D	.	.	.	147.7 [3]	157.9 [4]	188.0	192.3	209.8	251.5	263.0
E	.	.	.	1.8 [3]	2.2 [4]	-	4.9	1.8	0.9	2.0
F	.	.	.	8.8 [3]	13.9 [4]	2.6	7.0	10.4	4.0	12.5
G	.	.	.	456.7 [3]	479.3 [4]	505.7	437.1	517.5	537.7	572.2
H	.	.	.	174.5 [3]	203.7 [4]	203.8	168.9	193.9	191.7	218.0
I	.	.	.	38.6 [3]	45.3 [4]	32.7	39.0	38.8	63.3	60.7
J	.	.	.	15.7 [3]	18.6 [4]	15.1	24.2	19.5	16.8	25.7
K	.	.	.	82.9 [3]	120.1 [4]	62.3	70.4	84.6	110.7	98.8
L	.	.	.	55.5 [3]	43.6 [4]	36.1	45.1	67.0	57.4	40.2
M	.	.	.	136.4 [3]	147.4 [4]	151.0	162.1	130.0	164.2	173.4
N	.	.	.	62.3 [3]	54.0 [4]	73.8	58.3	69.4	89.2	92.4
O	.	.	.	94.6 [3]	82.4 [4]	79.6	109.6	87.3	121.4	122.1
P	.	.	.	221.4 [3]	247.1 [4]	236.5	221.3	274.3	273.2	257.7
Q	.	.	.	- [3]	1.2 [4]	0.3	-	-	1.2	2.2
X	.	.	.	- [3]	- [4]	-	-	-	-	-

Explanatory notes: see p. 77.

Notes explicatives: voir p. 80.

Notas explicativas: véase p. 83.

[1] Persons aged 14 years and over. [2] Metropolitan Lima. [3] Fourth quarter. [4] May-Dec.

[1] Personnes âgées de 14 ans et plus. [2] Lima métropolitaine. [3] Quatrième trimestre. [4] Mai-déc.

[1] Personas de 14 años y más. [2] Lima metropolitana. [3] Cuarto trimestre. [4] Mayo-dic.

EMPLOYMENT   EMPLOI   EMPLEO

Total employment, by economic activity — **Emploi total, par activité économique** — **Empleo total, por actividad económica**

Thousands — Milliers — Millares

Perú (BA) [1][2] — Total employment - Emploi total - Empleo total

Total - Total - Total
ISIC 3 - CITI 3 - CIIU 3

	1999	2000	2001	2002	2003	2004	2005	2006	2007	2008
Total	7 211.2	7 128.4	7 619.9	7 578.2 [3]	8 165.7 [4]	8 238.1	8 216.0	8 694.0	9 197.8	9 445.5
A	355.0	456.4	620.7	733.7 [3]	870.1 [4]	831.6	838.5	857.3	698.5	710.7
B	65.3	25.8	47.1	55.1 [3]	57.0 [4]	50.0	50.1	42.0	58.7	59.0
C	31.3	52.5	45.9	58.0 [3]	59.5 [4]	84.6	77.1	94.2	97.2	98.8
D	897.6	963.5	956.4	983.6 [3]	939.6 [4]	1 067.5	1 053.1	1 135.7	1 292.2	1 316.6
E	41.3	28.1	20.4	28.4 [3]	24.1 [4]	19.5	30.2	26.3	21.1	35.8
F	378.2	299.5	341.3	367.2 [3]	438.5 [4]	406.2	368.5	431.6	469.8	512.0
G	2 077.0	2 060.5	2 124.5	1 794.6 [3]	1 954.1 [4]	1 944.7	1 956.5	2 035.2	2 087.6	2 101.4
H	470.6	431.9	593.8	545.0 [3]	648.3 [4]	608.6	609.4	631.1	680.5	730.2
I	618.2	639.0	641.0	605.5 [3]	660.7 [4]	646.4	663.8	750.7	840.5	907.0
J	76.3	66.6	47.9	51.4 [3]	54.0 [4]	52.5	64.1	74.5	69.5	92.3
K	407.5	413.4	342.6	392.4 [3]	443.2 [4]	420.4	374.4	426.8	483.0	486.4
L	349.0	346.7	298.1	346.2 [3]	326.9 [4]	317.7	359.1	396.5	437.6	423.2
M	551.5	479.7	552.1	507.9 [3]	529.1 [4]	553.8	547.7	545.7	650.3	641.5
N	165.1	169.7	213.5	183.6 [3]	180.1 [4]	217.5	187.3	201.1	248.4	270.5
O	372.9	368.2	406.2	542.2 [3]	533.9 [4]	561.0	622.4	568.7	587.1	634.5
P	353.8	326.8	366.3	383.4 [3]	445.3 [4]	453.2	413.8	476.0	474.3	423.4
Q	-	-	-	- [3]	1.4 [4]	2.7	-	0.7	1.5	2.2
X	-	-	-	- [3]	- [4]	0.3		-	-	-

Men - Hommes - Hombres
ISIC 3 - CITI 3 - CIIU 3

	1999	2000	2001	2002	2003	2004	2005	2006	2007	2008
Total	3 980.4	4 067.6	4 232.6	4 234.2 [3]	4 537.0 [4]	4 615.7	4 562.8	4 821.9	5 015.0	5 142.8
A	250.9	339.3	414.9	484.6 [3]	595.5 [4]	555.1	547.3	567.1	468.2	473.7
B	63.1	24.4	46.8	53.5 [3]	52.5 [4]	49.4	49.9	41.3	58.0	57.2
C	28.3	48.7	43.4	54.8 [3]	56.5 [4]	78.0	71.5	89.0	88.8	91.7
D	555.7	631.1	625.5	650.7 [3]	620.0 [4]	710.1	670.6	730.5	800.6	805.6
E	35.1	24.4	17.3	25.5 [3]	20.2 [4]	17.5	23.3	21.4	19.0	29.8
F	370.0	287.4	333.9	357.0 [3]	421.2 [4]	403.0	358.5	420.0	459.9	494.7
G	956.6	952.5	998.0	713.7 [3]	785.3 [4]	744.6	807.4	795.2	791.9	751.4
H	111.0	109.7	155.4	151.5 [3]	158.0 [4]	140.6	163.7	155.3	174.1	172.7
I	568.9	591.0	601.2	551.5 [3]	597.5 [4]	591.5	594.1	670.1	738.0	797.4
J	42.6	42.0	33.5	30.4 [3]	28.8 [4]	27.9	34.6	43.2	41.1	51.6
K	270.4	283.7	233.6	272.2 [3]	289.4 [4]	319.3	261.8	305.8	316.6	331.2
L	258.2	255.3	212.1	243.2 [3]	239.4 [4]	236.8	264.4	276.0	316.1	311.7
M	225.3	213.2	227.5	205.6 [3]	198.8 [4]	229.2	210.6	227.3	258.7	248.8
N	63.4	57.1	75.5	65.9 [3]	76.2 [4]	86.1	69.9	67.4	86.4	101.0
O	169.8	196.4	189.0	358.5 [3]	370.5 [4]	393.6	408.8	382.4	370.5	402.3
P	11.3	11.3	23.1	15.6 [3]	27.0 [4]	29.9	26.3	29.1	26.4	21.9
Q	-	-	-	- [3]	0.2 [4]	2.5	-	0.7	0.4	-
X	-	-	-	- [3]	- [4]	0.3		-	-	-

Women - Femmes - Mujeres
ISIC 3 - CITI 3 - CIIU 3

	1999	2000	2001	2002	2003	2004	2005	2006	2007	2008
Total	3 230.8	3 060.7	3 387.3	3 344.0 [3]	3 628.8 [4]	3 622.4	3 653.2	3 872.1	4 182.8	4 302.7
A	104.1	117.0	205.8	249.1 [3]	274.6 [4]	276.5	291.2	290.2	230.3	237.0
B	2.2	1.4	0.3	1.5 [3]	4.5 [4]	0.5	0.2	0.7	0.7	1.7
C	3.0	3.8	2.5	3.2 [3]	3.0 [4]	6.6	5.6	5.1	8.4	7.1
D	341.9	332.4	330.9	332.9 [3]	319.6 [4]	357.4	382.5	405.2	491.6	511.0
E	6.3	3.7	3.1	2.9 [3]	3.8 [4]	1.9	7.0	4.9	2.0	6.0
F	8.2	12.1	7.4	10.2 [3]	17.3 [4]	3.1	10.0	11.6	9.9	17.3
G	1 120.4	1 108.0	1 126.5	1 080.9 [3]	1 168.8 [4]	1 200.0	1 149.1	1 240.0	1 295.7	1 350.0
H	359.6	322.2	438.5	393.5 [3]	490.2 [4]	467.9	445.7	475.7	506.4	557.4
I	49.3	48.0	39.9	53.9 [3]	63.2 [4]	54.9	69.7	80.6	102.4	109.6
J	33.7	24.6	14.4	21.0 [3]	25.2 [4]	24.6	29.5	31.3	28.3	40.8
K	137.1	129.7	109.1	120.2 [3]	153.9 [4]	101.0	112.6	121.0	166.4	155.2
L	90.7	91.4	86.0	103.0 [3]	87.5 [4]	80.9	94.7	120.4	121.5	111.5
M	326.2	266.5	324.6	302.3 [3]	330.3 [4]	324.6	337.0	318.4	391.6	392.7
N	101.7	112.6	138.1	117.8 [3]	103.8 [4]	131.4	117.4	133.7	162.0	169.5
O	203.2	171.8	217.2	183.7 [3]	163.4 [4]	167.4	213.6	186.4	216.6	232.2
P	342.4	315.5	343.1	367.9 [3]	418.3 [4]	423.3	387.5	446.9	447.9	401.5
Q	-	-	-	- [3]	1.2 [4]	0.3	-	-	1.2	2.2
X	-	-	-	- [3]	- [4]			-	-	-

Puerto Rico (BA) [5][6] — Total employment - Emploi total - Empleo total

Total - Total - Total
ISIC 2 - CITI 2 - CIIU 2

	1999	2000	2001	2002	2003	2004	2005	2006	2007	2008
Total	1 142	1 162	1 134	1 170	1 201	1 226	1 250	1 253	1 241	1 209
1	25	22	23	23	24	26	26	18	14	18
2	1	1	2	2	1	1	1	1	-	1
3	156	162	145	134	136	135	136	136	133	126
4	13	14	15	14	13	14	16	16	15	16
5	84	82	84	84	85	88	85	91	90	76
6 [7]	230	244	235	246	253	258	270	263	256	251
7	44	41	44	43	42	43	43	38	39	39
8	42	41	40	41	42	44	45	46	42	44
9 [8]	549	556	548	585	604	618	630	644	652	638

Explanatory notes: see p. 77.

[1] Persons aged 14 years and over. [2] Urban areas. [3] Fourth quarter. [4] May-Dec. [5] Persons aged 16 years and over. [6] Civilian labour force employed. [7] Excl. hotels. [8] Incl. hotels.

Notes explicatives: voir p. 80.

[1] Personnes âgées de 14 ans et plus. [2] Régions urbaines. [3] Quatrième trimestre. [4] Mai-déc. [5] Personnes âgées de 16 ans et plus. [6] Main-d'oeuvre civile occupée. [7] Non compris les hôtels. [8] Y compris les hôtels.

Notas explicativas: véase p. 83.

[1] Personas de 14 años y más. [2] Areas urbanas. [3] Cuarto trimestre. [4] Mayo-dic. [5] Personas de 16 años y más. [6] Fuerza de trabajo civil ocupada. [7] Excl. hoteles. [8] Incl. hoteles.

Total employment, by economic activity   Emploi total, par activité économique   Empleo total, por actividad económica

	Thousands			Milliers				Millares		
	1999	2000	2001	2002	2003	2004	2005	2006	2007	2008

Puerto Rico (BA) [1] [2]   Total employment - Emploi total - Empleo total

Men - Hommes - Hombres
ISIC 2 - CITI 2 - CIIU 2

	1999	2000	2001	2002	2003	2004	2005	2006	2007	2008
Total	665	670	652	665	676	690	697	695	677	659
1	23	21	22	22	23	24	23	16	13	15
2	1	1	2	1	1	1	1	1	-	1
3	93	95	85	81	83	85	84	81	81	79
4	11	11	12	11	10	11	12	13	13	13
5	80	78	79	80	83	83	80	86	85	72
6 [3]	137	144	133	136	141	142	147	146	139	138
7	34	31	34	32	32	33	33	28	29	31
8	17	16	16	17	16	16	18	19	15	17
9 [4]	269	272	268	285	290	295	301	304	302	294

Women - Femmes - Mujeres
ISIC 2 - CITI 2 - CIIU 2

	1999	2000	2001	2002	2003	2004	2005	2006	2007	2008
Total	477	492	482	502	525	537	553	558	564	550
1	1	1	1	1	1	1	2	2	2	3
2	-	-	-	1	1	-	-	-	-	-
3	62	66	60	53	54	50	52	54	51	47
4	3	2	3	3	2	3	4	3	2	3
5	4	4	4	4	6	6	5	6	5	4
6 [3]	92	100	102	110	111	116	122	117	117	113
7	10	10	10	11	10	10	10	9	10	9
8	25	25	24	25	26	28	28	27	27	27
9 [4]	279	283	279	299	314	322	330	340	350	344

Saint Lucia (BA) [5]   Total employment - Emploi total - Empleo total

Total - Total - Total
ISIC 3 - CITI 3 - CIIU 3

	1999	2000	2001	2002	2003	2004	2005	2006	2007	2008
Total	59.850	63.470	.	58.525	63.868	62.265	.	.	.	.
A	12.335	12.350	.	6.685	7.690	8.490	.	.	.	.
B	0.645	0.845	.	0.450	0.595	0.753	.	.	.	.
D	5.570	6.200	.	4.455	4.608	4.668	.	.	.	.
E	0.560	0.685	.	0.615	0.560	0.428	.	.	.	.
F	5.365	5.995	.	4.825	4.978	4.928	.	.	.	.
G	10.545	11.345	.	8.600	10.408	9.778	.	.	.	.
H	5.710	6.585	.	6.165	6.755	6.760	.	.	.	.
I	4.235	4.095	.	3.185	4.165	3.325	.	.	.	.
J	1.140	0.985	.	0.865	1.243	1.153	.	.	.	.
K	1.525	1.305	.	1.600	2.135	2.535	.	.	.	.
L	7.770	7.530	.	6.900	7.310	8.180	.	.	.	.
M	0.750	1.140	.	1.880	2.070	1.058	.	.	.	.
N	0.440	0.600	.	0.280	0.593	0.385	.	.	.	.
O	1.490	1.505	.	1.380	1.640	1.953	.	.	.	.
P	1.715	1.455	.	1.980	2.145	1.850	.	.	.	.
X	0.055	0.850	.	8.660	6.975	6.025	.	.	.	.

Men - Hommes - Hombres
ISIC 3 - CITI 3 - CIIU 3

	1999	2000	2001	2002	2003	2004	2005	2006	2007	2008
Total	31.830	35.030	.	32.105	36.475	34.838	.	.	.	.
A	7.785	8.315	.	4.415	5.385	5.888	.	.	.	.
B	0.645	0.825	.	0.420	0.563	0.660	.	.	.	.
D	2.295	2.560	.	1.950	2.343	2.288	.	.	.	.
E	0.435	0.560	.	0.505	0.473	0.368	.	.	.	.
F	4.985	5.570	.	4.560	4.735	4.758	.	.	.	.
G	4.245	4.300	.	3.430	4.705	4.375	.	.	.	.
H	2.515	3.040	.	2.895	3.328	3.023	.	.	.	.
I	3.325	3.305	.	2.380	3.070	2.488	.	.	.	.
J	0.340	0.315	.	0.285	0.615	0.430	.	.	.	.
K	0.750	0.810	.	0.905	1.105	1.470	.	.	.	.
L	3.285	3.190	.	3.210	3.570	3.715	.	.	.	.
M	0.140	0.355	.	0.460	0.620	0.205	.	.	.	.
N	0.095	0.240	.	0.055	0.083	0.050	.	.	.	.
O	0.575	0.680	.	0.865	0.843	1.063	.	.	.	.
P	0.300	0.385	.	0.500	0.528	0.195	.	.	.	.
X	0.025	0.580	.	5.270	4.513	3.865	.	.	.	.

Explanatory notes: see p. 77.

[1] Persons aged 16 years and over. [2] Civilian labour force employed. [3] Excl. hotels. [4] Incl. hotels. [5] Persons aged 15 years and over.

Notes explicatives: voir p. 80.

[1] Personnes âgées de 16 ans et plus. [2] Main-d'oeuvre civile occupée. [3] Non compris les hôtels. [4] Y compris les hôtels. [5] Personnes âgées de 15 ans et plus.

Notas explicativas: véase p. 83.

[1] Personas de 16 años y más. [2] Fuerza de trabajo civil ocupada. [3] Excl. hoteles. [4] Incl. hoteles. [5] Personas de 15 años y más.

2B EMPLOYMENT — EMPLOI — EMPLEO

Total employment, by economic activity — Emploi total, par activité économique — Empleo total, por actividad económica

Thousands — Milliers — Millares

Saint Lucia (BA) [1]
Total employment - Emploi total - Empleo total

Women - Femmes - Mujeres
ISIC 3 - CITI 3 - CIIU 3

	1999	2000	2001	2002	2003	2004	2005	2006	2007	2008
Total	28.020	28.440	.	26.420	27.393	27.428	.	.	.	.
A	4.460	4.035	.	2.270	2.305	2.603				
B	-	0.020	.	0.030	0.033	0.093				
D	3.275	3.640	.	2.505	2.265	2.380				
E	0.125	0.125	.	0.110	0.088	0.060				
F	0.380	0.425	.	0.265	0.243	0.170				
G	6.300	7.045	.	5.170	5.703	5.403				
H	3.195	3.545	.	3.270	3.428	3.738				
I	0.910	0.790	.	0.805	1.095	0.838				
J	0.800	0.670	.	0.580	0.628	0.723				
K	0.775	0.495	.	0.695	1.030	1.065				
L	4.485	4.340	.	3.690	3.740	4.465				
M	0.610	0.785	.	1.420	1.450	0.853				
N	0.345	0.360	.	0.225	0.510	0.335				
O	0.915	0.825	.	0.515	0.798	0.890				
P	1.415	1.070	.	1.480	1.618	1.655				
X	0.030	0.270	.	3.390	2.463	2.160				

Trinidad and Tobago (BA) [1]
Total employment - Emploi total - Empleo total

Total - Total - Total
ISIC 2 - CITI 2 - CIIU 2

	1999	2000	2001	2002	2003	2004	2005	2006	2007	2008
Total	489.4	503.1	514.1	525.1	534.1	562.2	574.0	586.2	587.8	597.6
1	39.7	36.3	40.3	36.1	31.4	26.0	24.8	25.8	22.4	22.9
2	15.6	16.5	16.6	18.0	17.0 [2]	20.1 [2]	20.4 [2]	20.4 [2]	22.8 [2]	21.1 [2]
3	53.0	54.9	52.7	55.8	55.0	58.7	55.6	55.5	54.1	55.1
4	6.2	6.9	7.5	6.6	7.4 [3]	7.3 [3]	6.9 [3]	7.7 [3]	7.2 [3]	7.9 [3]
5	60.8	62.8	71.2	68.9	72.6	83.8	94.8	96.7	103.0	108.5
6	88.8	95.2	89.9	94.6	99.0	101.2	103.5	106.6	108.3	108.2
7	35.7	39.2	38.9	41.9	41.5	41.6	41.8	42.7	41.5	41.2
8	37.6	39.2	41.0	43.8	45.0	46.3	45.0	48.1	49.6	52.5
9	151.5	151.4	154.6	158.1	163.2	175.3	178.5	181.1	178.6	179.5
0	0.4	0.5	1.5	1.2	1.9	1.8	2.5	1.6	0.3	0.7

Men - Hommes - Hombres
ISIC 2 - CITI 2 - CIIU 2

	1999	2000	2001	2002	2003	2004	2005	2006	2007	2008
Total	310.1	316.9	326.0	329.0	330.6	341.9	343.6	348.5	354.2	353.5
1	34.6	30.9	34.4	32.1	27.3	21.6	20.9	21.1	18.2	18.4
2	13.2	13.9	14.5	15.1	14.4 [2]	16.7 [2]	16.8 [2]	16.0 [2]	18.6 [2]	16.6 [2]
3	37.3	39.0	38.0	40.0	39.2	41.8	38.7	37.8	39.2	40.3
4	5.3	5.6	6.4	5.7	5.8 [3]	5.8 [3]	5.5 [3]	6.4 [3]	5.6 [3]	6.1 [3]
5	56.6	57.8	65.4	60.9	66.1	72.6	80.2	82.8	88.7	91.9
6	39.5	43.8	39.9	43.3	43.8	44.8	44.4	46.0	45.6	43.7
7	29.5	31.8	31.2	33.6	33.5	32.6	33.5	33.2	32.9	33.7
8	18.6	20.4	21.2	21.9	22.2	22.5	21.8	22.2	23.9	23.9
9	75.2	73.2	74.4	75.5	77.2	82.6	80.1	82.0	81.4	78.4
0	0.2	0.3	0.8	0.9	1.1	1.0	1.5	1.0	0.1	0.5

Women - Femmes - Mujeres
ISIC 2 - CITI 2 - CIIU 2

	1999	2000	2001	2002	2003	2004	2005	2006	2007	2008
Total	179.3	186.2	188.1	196.1	203.5	220.3	230.4	237.7	233.6	245.9
1	5.1	5.4	5.9	4.0	4.1	4.4	3.9	4.7	4.2	4.5
2	2.4	2.6	2.1	2.9	2.6 [2]	3.4 [2]	3.6 [2]	4.4 [2]	4.2 [2]	4.5 [2]
3	15.7	15.9	14.7	15.8	15.8	16.9	16.9	17.7	14.9	14.8
4	0.9	1.3	1.1	0.9	1.6 [3]	1.5 [3]	1.4 [3]	1.3 [3]	1.6 [3]	1.8 [3]
5	4.2	5.0	5.8	8.0	6.5	11.2	14.6	13.9	14.3	16.6
6	49.3	51.4	50.0	51.3	55.2	56.4	59.1	60.6	62.7	64.5
7	6.2	7.4	7.7	8.3	8.0	9.0	8.3	9.5	8.6	7.5
8	19.0	18.8	19.8	21.9	22.8	23.8	23.2	25.9	25.7	28.6
9	76.3	78.2	80.2	82.6	86.0	92.7	98.4	99.1	97.2	101.1
0	0.2	0.2	0.7	0.3	0.8	0.8	1.0	0.6	0.2	-

Explanatory notes: see p. 77.

[1] Persons aged 15 years and over. [2] Incl. petroleum and gas extraction. [3] Excl. gas.

Notes explicatives: voir p. 80.

[1] Personnes âgées de 15 ans et plus. [2] Y compris l'extraction du pétrole et du gaz. [3] Non compris le gaz.

Notas explicativas: véase p. 83.

[1] Personas de 15 años y más. [2] Incl. extracción de petróleo y gas. [3] Excl. gas.

Total employment, by economic activity
Emploi total, par activité économique
Empleo total, por actividad económica

	Thousands					Milliers				Millares	
	1999	2000	2001	2002	2003	2004	2005	2006	2007	2008	

Turks and Caicos Islands (BA) [1]   Total employment - Emploi total - Empleo total

Total - Total - Total
ISIC 3 - CITI 3 - CIIU 3

	1999	2000	2001	2002	2003	2004	2005	2006	2007	2008
Total	.	.	10.180	11.473	14.051	15.161	17.442	18.195	19.587	.
A	.	.	0.084	0.083	0.085	0.087	0.092	0.152	0.111	.
B	.	.	0.153	0.108	0.125	0.153	0.155	0.178	0.126	.
C	.	.	0.017	0.051	0.053	0.055	0.056	0.016	0.016	.
D	.	.	0.224	0.165	0.165	0.190	0.202	0.150	0.246	.
E	.	.	0.163	0.205	0.220	0.217	0.269	0.199	0.192	.
F	.	.	1.374	1.398	1.867	2.082	2.402	3.151	4.306	.
G	.	.	0.657	0.812	1.047	1.284	1.298	1.547	1.729	.
H	.	.	2.368	2.341	2.530	2.552	2.935	3.723	4.065	.
I	.	.	0.470	0.570	0.594	0.630	0.650	0.717	0.846	.
J	.	.	0.303	0.475	0.411	0.455	0.496	0.470	0.515	.
K	.	.	0.559	1.027	1.272	1.325	1.607	2.027	2.384	.
L	.	.	1.215	1.640	1.997	2.261	2.310	2.757	2.298	.
M-N	.	.	0.681	0.416	0.415	0.459	0.496	0.806	0.771	.
O	.	.	1.007	0.676	0.983	0.944	0.971	0.953	1.190	.
P	.	.		0.608	0.925	1.386	1.608	0.909	0.376	.
X	.	.	0.905	0.898	1.362	1.081	1.895	0.440	0.416	.

United States (BA) [2][3]   Total employment - Emploi total - Empleo total

Total - Total - Total
ISIC 2 - CITI 2 - CIIU 2 / ISIC 3 - CITI 3 - CIIU 3

	1999	2000	2001	2002	2003	2004	2005	2006	2007	2008	
Total	133 488	135 208	135 073	136 485	137 736	139 252	141 730	144 427	146 047	145 362	Total
1	3 416	3 457	3 277	3 479	2 275	2 232	2 197	2 206	2 095	2 168	A-B
2	565	521	567	516	525	539	624	687	736	819	C
3	20 070	19 940	18 970	18 147	16 902	16 484	16 253	16 377	16 302	15 904	D
4 [4]	1 468	1 447	1 408	1 468	1 193	1 168	1 176	1 186	1 193	1 225	E
5	8 987	9 433	9 581	9 669	10 138	10 768	11 197	11 749	11 856	10 974	F
6 [5]	27 572	27 832	27 672	28 096	20 706	20 869	21 404	21 328	20 937	20 585	G
7	8 086	8 294	8 330	8 212	9 021	9 131	9 306	9 474	9 582	9 795	H
8	16 054	16 515	16 669	16 679	5 758	5 844	6 184	6 269	6 457	6 501	I
9 [6]	47 271	47 770	48 599	50 218	6 834	6 940	7 035	7 254	7 306	7 279	J
					16 793	17 137	17 461	18 105	18 802	18 489	K
					6 243	6 365	6 530	6 524	6 746	6 763	L
					11 826	12 058	12 264	12 522	12 828	13 169	M
					16 434	16 661	16 910	17 416	17 834	18 233	N
					13 089	13 056	13 187	13 332	13 371	13 458	O-X

Men - Hommes - Hombres
ISIC 2 - CITI 2 - CIIU 2 / ISIC 3 - CITI 3 - CIIU 3

	1999	2000	2001	2002	2003	2004	2005	2006	2007	2008	
Total	71 446	72 293	72 080	72 903	73 322	74 524	75 973	77 502	78 254	77 486	Total
1	2 539	2 552	2 377	2 585	1 695	1 687	1 654	1 663	1 604	1 650	A-B
2	495	450	484	453	452	483	545	598	635	714	C
3	13 647	13 458	12 937	12 571	11 734	11 485	11 370	11 543	11 416	11 249	D
4 [4]	1 145	1 146	1 102	1 143	913	892	926	926	936	987	E
5	8 101	8 520	8 647	8 772	9 164	9 727	10 118	10 618	10 738	9 905	F
6 [5]	14 448	14 705	14 661	14 971	11 434	11 580	11 896	11 802	11 524	11 327	G
7	5 670	5 800	5 796	5 768	4 232	4 323	4 348	4 452	4 525	4 592	H
8	7 871	8 039	8 150	8 225	4 335	4 449	4 707	4 722	4 836	4 954	I
9 [6]	17 530	17 625	17 925	18 416	2 773	2 791	2 920	3 035	3 030	3 056	J
					9 454	9 673	9 804	10 184	10 613	10 524	K
					3 343	3 458	3 558	3 563	3 720	3 707	L
					3 608	3 752	3 804	3 892	3 962	3 994	M
					3 383	3 470	3 500	3 632	3 794	3 805	N
					6 809	6 752	6 823	6 873	6 922	7 022	O-X

Women - Femmes - Mujeres
ISIC 2 - CITI 2 - CIIU 2 / ISIC 3 - CITI 3 - CIIU 3

	1999	2000	2001	2002	2003	2004	2005	2006	2007	2008	
Total	62 042	62 915	62 992	63 582	64 404	64 728	65 757	66 925	67 792	67 876	Total
1	877	905	900	894	580	546	544	543	490	518	A-B
2	69	71	83	63	73	55	80	89	101	105	C
3	6 423	6 482	6 033	5 576	5 168	4 998	4 882	4 834	4 885	4 655	D
4 [4]	324	301	306	325	280	276	250	259	257	239	E
5	886	913	934	897	975	1 041	1 079	1 131	1 119	1 069	F
6 [5]	13 124	13 127	13 011	13 125	9 272	9 289	9 508	9 526	9 414	9 258	G
7	2 416	2 494	2 534	2 444	4 788	4 807	4 958	5 023	5 057	5 203	H
8	8 182	8 477	8 519	8 454	1 422	1 395	1 477	1 547	1 621	1 547	I
9 [6]	29 740	30 144	30 674	31 802	4 061	4 149	4 115	4 219	4 276	4 223	J
					7 339	7 463	7 657	7 920	8 190	7 965	K
					2 899	2 908	2 971	2 961	3 026	3 056	L
					8 218	8 306	8 459	8 630	8 866	9 174	M
					13 050	13 191	13 410	13 784	14 040	14 429	N
					6 279	6 304	6 365	6 459	6 449	6 436	O-X

Explanatory notes: see p. 77.

[1] Persons aged 15 years and over. [2] Excl. armed forces. [3] Persons aged 16 years and over. [4] Incl. sanitary services. [5] Excl. hotels. [6] Incl. hotels; excl. sanitary services.

Notes explicatives: voir p. 80.

[1] Personnes âgées de 15 ans et plus. [2] Non compris les forces armées. [3] Personnes âgées de 16 ans et plus. [4] Y compris les services sanitaires. [5] Non compris les hôtels. [6] Y compris les hôtels; non compris les services sanitaires.

Notas explicativas: véase p. 83.

[1] Personas de 15 años y más. [2] Excl. las fuerzas armadas. [3] Personas de 16 años y más. [4] Incl. los servicios de saneamiento. [5] Excl. hoteles. [6] Incl. los hoteles; excl. los servicios de saneamiento.

2B

EMPLOYMENT	EMPLOI	EMPLEO
Total employment, by economic activity	Emploi total, par activité économique	Empleo total, por actividad económica
Thousands	Milliers	Millares

	1999	2000	2001	2002	2003	2004	2005	2006	2007	2008	

Uruguay (BA) [1]
Total - Total - Total
ISIC 2 - CITI 2 - CIIU 2 [2]
Total employment - Emploi total - Empleo total
ISIC 3 - CITI 3 - CIIU 3 [3]

	1999	2000	2001	2002	2003	2004	2005	2006[4]	2007	2008	
Total	1 082.1	1 067.6	1 076.2	1 038.3	1 032.0	1 075.6	1 114.5	1 413.5	1 482.1	.	Total
1	41.8	43.3	45.4	43.7	46.9						A-B
2	1.4					53.9	51.7	157.2	163.3		A-C
3	170.5	2.0	1.3	1.2	1.2						C
4	10.2	171.0	167.1	154.2	151.1	159.7	169.1	209.6	219.9		D-E
5	90.5	90.3	87.9	77.4	69.6	70.9	74.6	90.6	102.1		F
6	214.3	239.4	240.8	228.9	225.4	238.4	255.2	308.2	319.2		G-H
7	66.2	61.8	66.8	62.4	61.1	62.2	61.5	75.8	83.9		I
8	71.9	87.2	97.4	96.5	91.0	92.4	104.0	101.7	114.4		J-K
9	415.4	82.6	84.8	86.7	90.7	91.2	86.2	104.5	94.4		L
0	-	63.8	57.7	62.7	62.0	66.1	67.7	78.4	84.2		M
		70.9	73.1	76.5	76.7	81.5	81.1	93.7	97.2		N
		53.8	56.8	52.9	56.1	62.7	64.3	69.2	75.2		O.Q
		101.3	99.7	97.1	102.3	96.6	99.0	122.8	128.2		P
		0.3	-	-	0.3	-	-	1.9	1.9		X

Men - Hommes - Hombres
ISIC 2 - CITI 2 - CIIU 2 [2] — ISIC 3 - CITI 3 - CIIU 3 [3]

	1999	2000	2001	2002	2003	2004	2005	2006[4]	2007	2008	
Total	623.7	613.4	617.7	597.9	589.7	617.3	620.1	822.4	852.9	.	Total
1	36.2	38.1	37.7	38.0	39.3						A-B
2	1.4					45.8	44.3	126.7	132.9		A-C
3	112.2	1.9	1.2	1.1	1.1						C
4	7.2	112.1	107.5	102.2	98.9	103.9	107.2	138.0	143.5		D-E
5	88.7	88.4	85.9	75.8	68.3	69.9	73.2	88.5	99.3		F
6	120.6	145.6	145.7	141.6	140.9	148.3	152.2	184.3	183.5		G-H
7	54.1	52.3	56.2	53.1	51.9	51.6	49.1	61.5	68.5		I
8	40.1	47.7	59.7	56.6	54.2	56.8	64.0	61.1	67.4		J-K
9	163.2	56.2	57.6	59.7	61.5	62.5	56.4	70.9	62.5		L
0	-	13.2	13.6	13.7	14.3	15.6	14.4	18.9	19.8		M
		19.2	17.9	20.2	18.9	22.0	19.6	24.8	25.2		N
		28.5	28.9	28.6	31.1	34.0	32.3	35.5	38.7		O.Q
		9.9	6.1	7.3	9.3	6.9	7.4	11.2	11.6		P
		0.2	-	-	0.3	-	-	1.1	-		X

Women - Femmes - Mujeres
ISIC 2 - CITI 2 - CIIU 2 [2] — ISIC 3 - CITI 3 - CIIU 3 [3]

	1999	2000	2001	2002	2003	2004	2005	2006[4]	2007	2008	
Total	458.4	454.2	458.5	440.4	442.3	460.6	494.4	591.0	629.0	.	Total
1	5.7	5.2	7.7	5.7	7.5						A-B
2	-					8.5	7.4	30.5	30.4		A-C
3	58.5	0.1	0.1	0.2	0.2						C
4	3.0	58.9	59.6	52.0	52.2	56.3	62.0	71.6	76.4		D-E
5	2.2	1.9	2.0	1.6	1.4	1.7	1.5	2.1	2.9		F
6	93.7	93.7	95.1	87.3	84.6	90.9	103.0	123.9	135.8		G-H
7	12.3	9.5	10.6	9.3	9.4	11.0	12.4	14.3	15.4		I
8	31.7	39.4	37.7	39.9	36.9	35.9	40.0	40.6	47.0		J-K
9	251.3	26.4	27.5	27.1	29.4	29.2	29.7	33.6	31.8		L
0	-	50.6	43.7	48.5	47.1	50.1	53.3	59.5	64.4		M
		51.8	54.6	55.8	57.1	59.2	61.5	68.9	72.0		N
		25.3	27.7	24.3	25.0	28.8	32.0	33.7	36.0		O.Q
		91.4	92.4	88.7	91.6	89.0	91.6	111.6	116.6		P
		0.1	-	-			-		0.8	-		X

Venezuela, Rep. Bolivariana de (BA) [5][6][7]
Total - Total - Total
ISIC 2 - CITI 2 - CIIU 2
Total employment - Emploi total - Empleo total

	1999	2000	2001	2002	2003	2004	2005	2006	2007	2008
Total	8 741.6	8 960.9	9 685.6	9 786.2	9 993.8	10 417.6	10 734.0	11 116.9	11 491.9	11 863.1
1	890.1	950.2	934.1	973.2	1 072.2	1 078.4	1 039.1	1 016.0	1 001.9	1 005.9
2	57.1	53.4	52.7	46.3	54.9	66.2	71.3	77.9	102.7	106.8
3	1 202.1	1 191.1	1 222.4	1 149.1	1 160.7	1 175.3	1 245.5	1 350.9	1 418.4	1 416.4
4	59.1	57.8	57.4	52.1	53.3	52.2	56.9	50.4	51.5	54.7
5	665.2	740.7	805.1	771.5	706.8	793.7	857.6	1 057.6	1 109.7	1 153.7
6	2 266.8	2 311.7	2 542.3	2 623.2	2 563.1	2 518.2	2 619.6	2 620.0	2 703.8	2 808.9
7	604.5	608.0	676.9	715.6	748.9	850.4	870.3	913.6	994.4	1 042.5
8	474.8	440.4	479.6	474.7	472.9	495.7	516.9	551.0	589.6	614.0
9	2 514.4	2 597.7	2 904.6	2 954.8	3 125.6	3 242.7	3 364.8	3 452.6	3 494.8	3 633.8
0	7.5	9.8	10.7	25.7	35.5	144.7	92.0	27.0	25.2	26.3

Explanatory notes: see p. 77.

[1] Persons aged 14 years and over. [2] Urban areas. [3] Excl. conscripts. [4] Prior to 2006: urban areas. [5] Excl. armed forces. [6] Persons aged 15 years and over. [7] Second semester.

Notes explicatives: voir p. 80.

[1] Personnes âgées de 14 ans et plus. [2] Régions urbaines. [3] Non compris les conscrits. [4] Avant 2006: régions urbaines. [5] Non compris les forces armées. [6] Personnes âgées de 15 ans et plus. [7] Second semestre.

Notas explicativas: véase p. 83.

[1] Personas de 14 años y más. [2] Areas urbanas. [3] Excl. los conscriptos. [4] Antes de 2006: areas urbanas. [5] Excl. las fuerzas armadas. [6] Personas de 15 años y más. [7] Segundo semestre.

Total employment, by economic activity   Emploi total, par activité économique   Empleo total, por actividad económica

Thousands   Milliers   Millares

	1999	2000	2001	2002	2003	2004	2005	2006	2007	2008
Venezuela, Rep. Bolivariana de (BA) [1][2][3]				Total employment - Emploi total - Empleo total						
Men - Hommes - Hombres										
ISIC 2 - CITI 2 - CIIU 2										
Total	5 610.3	5 722.8	5 995.7	6 029.7	6 140.7	6 403.4	6 620.8	6 894.0	7 073.0	7 264.4
1	837.4	896.7	871.0	901.6	984.6	993.9	956.2	939.4	924.0	920.1
2	52.3	47.4	47.0	38.0	50.4	55.8	59.7	66.9	86.2	91.2
3	834.0	826.3	823.7	762.2	767.7	785.4	843.6	936.6	966.2	985.4
4	49.0	48.9	46.8	39.8	41.1	39.7	44.0	39.5	39.2	42.8
5	642.6	710.5	777.6	742.8	678.4	761.6	824.1	1 009.0	1 059.2	1 099.9
6	1 235.9	1 224.2	1 265.9	1 316.8	1 276.9	1 230.6	1 306.7	1 289.8	1 308.2	1 340.2
7	556.1	555.6	622.2	657.5	690.3	760.8	767.2	819.5	898.4	943.1
8	289.6	276.3	300.8	298.3	302.5	318.9	337.2	355.6	366.4	386.2
9	1 108.4	1 130.8	1 236.3	1 256.9	1 327.7	1 365.8	1 423.0	1 421.5	1 409.0	1 440.1
0	5.0	6.2	4.3	15.8	21.1	91.0	59.2	16.3	16.3	15.5
Women - Femmes - Mujeres										
ISIC 2 - CITI 2 - CIIU 2										
Total	3 131.3	3 238.1	3 689.9	3 756.5	3 853.1	4 014.2	4 113.1	4 223.0	4 418.9	4 598.6
1	52.7	53.4	63.1	71.6	87.6	84.4	83.0	76.7	77.9	85.8
2	4.8	6.1	5.6	8.3	4.5	10.5	11.5	11.0	16.5	15.6
3	368.1	364.8	398.6	386.9	393.0	389.9	401.9	414.3	452.2	431.0
4	10.1	8.9	10.7	12.3	12.2	12.5	12.9	10.9	12.3	11.9
5	22.6	30.2	27.5	28.8	28.4	32.1	33.5	48.7	50.5	53.9
6	1 031.0	1 087.5	1 276.3	1 306.3	1 286.2	1 287.7	1 312.9	1 330.2	1 395.5	1 468.8
7	48.4	52.5	54.6	58.1	58.6	89.7	103.1	94.1	96.0	99.4
8	185.2	164.1	178.8	176.3	170.4	176.8	179.7	195.4	223.2	227.8
9	1 406.0	1 466.9	1 668.3	1 697.9	1 797.8	1 876.9	1 941.9	2 031.1	2 085.9	2 193.7
0	2.5	3.6	6.3	9.9	14.4	53.8	32.8	10.7	8.8	10.7

ASIA-ASIE-ASIA

	1999	2000	2001	2002	2003	2004	2005	2006	2007	2008
Armenia (BA) [4][5]				Total employment - Emploi total - Empleo total						
Total - Total - Total										
ISIC 3 - CITI 3 - CIIU 3										
Total	.	.	.	.	.	.	.	.	1 188.5	.
A	.	.	.	.	.	.	.	.	433.8	.
B	.	.	.	.	.	.	.	.	0.4	.
C	.	.	.	.	.	.	.	.	17.1	.
D	.	.	.	.	.	.	.	.	81.5	.
E	.	.	.	.	.	.	.	.	35.4	.
F	.	.	.	.	.	.	.	.	91.4	.
G	.	.	.	.	.	.	.	.	116.3	.
H	.	.	.	.	.	.	.	.	11.0	.
I	.	.	.	.	.	.	.	.	72.2	.
J	.	.	.	.	.	.	.	.	14.0	.
K	.	.	.	.	.	.	.	.	17.3	.
L	.	.	.	.	.	.	.	.	70.5	.
M	.	.	.	.	.	.	.	.	110.6	.
N	.	.	.	.	.	.	.	.	57.1	.
O	.	.	.	.	.	.	.	.	52.0	.
P	.	.	.	.	.	.	.	.	4.3	.
Q	.	.	.	.	.	.	.	.	3.6	.
Men - Hommes - Hombres										
ISIC 3 - CITI 3 - CIIU 3										
Total	.	.	.	.	.	.	.	.	654.6	.
A	.	.	.	.	.	.	.	.	199.3	.
B	.	.	.	.	.	.	.	.	0.3	.
C	.	.	.	.	.	.	.	.	14.2	.
D	.	.	.	.	.	.	.	.	51.2	.
E	.	.	.	.	.	.	.	.	29.3	.
F	.	.	.	.	.	.	.	.	89.3	.
G	.	.	.	.	.	.	.	.	70.7	.
H	.	.	.	.	.	.	.	.	5.6	.
I	.	.	.	.	.	.	.	.	60.7	.
J	.	.	.	.	.	.	.	.	7.6	.
K	.	.	.	.	.	.	.	.	9.6	.
L	.	.	.	.	.	.	.	.	52.4	.
M	.	.	.	.	.	.	.	.	18.8	.
N	.	.	.	.	.	.	.	.	10.8	.
O	.	.	.	.	.	.	.	.	32.0	.
P	.	.	.	.	.	.	.	.	0.5	.
Q	.	.	.	.	.	.	.	.	2.4	.

Explanatory notes: see p. 77.

[1] Excl. armed forces. [2] Persons aged 15 years and over. [3] Second semester. [4] Incl. armed forces, Excl. conscripts. [5] Persons aged 16 years and over.

Notes explicatives: voir p. 80.

[1] Non compris les forces armées. [2] Personnes âgées de 15 ans et plus. [3] Second semestre. [4] Y compris les forces armées, Excl. conscrits [5] Personnes âgées de 16 ans et plus.

Notas explicativas: véase p. 83.

[1] Excl. las fuerzas armadas. [2] Personas de 15 años y más. [3] Segundo semestre. [4] Incl. las fuerzas armadas, excl. los conscriptos. [5] Personas de 16 años y más.

EMPLOYMENT EMPLOI EMPLEO

Total employment, by economic activity Total employment, Emploi total, par activité économique Empleo total, por actividad económica

	Thousands			Milliers				Millares		
	1999	2000	2001	2002	2003	2004	2005	2006	2007	2008

Armenia (BA) [1][2] Total employment - Emploi total - Empleo total

Women - Femmes - Mujeres
ISIC 3 - CITI 3 - CIIU 3

	1999	2000	2001	2002	2003	2004	2005	2006	2007	2008
Total									533.9	
A									234.5	
B									0.1	
C									2.9	
D									30.3	
E									6.1	
F									2.1	
G									45.7	
H									5.5	
I									11.5	
J									6.4	
K									7.7	
L									18.0	
M									91.8	
N									46.4	
O									20.0	
P									3.7	
Q									1.3	

Azerbaijan (BA) [3][4] Total employment - Emploi total - Empleo total

Total - Total - Total
ISIC 3 - CITI 3 - CIIU 3

	1999	2000	2001	2002	2003	2004	2005	2006	2007	2008
Total					3 377.8			3 985.9	4 014.0	4 056.0
A					1 283.4			1 564.9	1 543.0	1 601.4
B					7.0			11.4	4.4	4.5
C					36.7			60.7	44.1	45.3
D					164.3			147.6	194.0	195.5
E					45.9			52.3	40.0	44.6
F					188.7			231.8	228.7	206.6
G					580.8			745.9	659.5	657.4
H					32.7			48.5	27.1	23.4
I					147.0			154.5	203.5	167.0
J					21.1			53.9	17.8	35.1
K					41.6			19.9	129.7	194.8
L					96.6			140.2	275.5	249.5
M					317.4			352.1	334.3	311.3
N					137.6			166.2	180.7	180.5
O					242.7			158.7	131.1	138.6
P					28.8			68.0	-	-
Q					5.5			9.3	0.7	0.5

Men - Hommes - Hombres
ISIC 3 - CITI 3 - CIIU 3

	1999	2000	2001	2002	2003	2004	2005	2006	2007	2008
Total					1 975.6			2 105.7	2 020.5	2 048.3
A					698.9			752.9	708.7	785.0
B					6.0			8.8	1.7	3.6
C					32.4			54.7	38.9	35.2
D					109.3			98.4	141.7	114.6
E					36.6			46.8	34.0	32.5
F					178.9			217.4	216.8	187.4
G					380.2			312.9	186.8	206.7
H					20.5			32.8	21.4	11.7
I					124.6			138.1	178.4	143.7
J					13.1			30.3	9.4	10.5
K					32.2			15.2	54.4	95.4
L					78.8			101.4	167.7	198.3
M					108.2			122.3	120.4	96.6
N					37.0			47.7	51.5	52.1
O					104.8			87.5	88.1	74.5
P					9.5			31.1	-	-
Q					4.6			7.5	0.7	0.5

Women - Femmes - Mujeres
ISIC 3 - CITI 3 - CIIU 3

	1999	2000	2001	2002	2003	2004	2005	2006	2007	2008
Total					1 402.2			1 880.2	1 993.5	2 007.7
A					584.5			811.9	834.3	816.4
B					1.0			2.6	2.7	0.9
C					4.3			6.0	5.2	10.1
D					55.0			49.2	52.3	80.9
E					9.3			5.6	6.1	12.1
F					9.8			14.4	11.9	19.2
G					200.6			433.1	472.7	450.7
H					12.2			15.7	5.7	11.7
I					22.4			16.4	25.1	23.3
J					8.0			23.6	8.4	24.6
K					9.4			4.7	75.3	99.4
L					17.8			38.9	107.9	51.2
M					209.2			229.8	213.9	214.7
N					100.6			118.4	129.2	128.4
O					137.9			71.2	43.0	64.1
P					19.3			36.9	-	-
Q					0.9			1.8	-	-

Explanatory notes: see p. 77.

[1] Incl. armed forces, Excl. conscripts. [2] Persons aged 16 years and over. [3] Persons aged 15 years and over. [4] Excl. armed forces and conscripts.

Notes explicatives: voir p. 80.

[1] Y compris les forces armées, Excl. conscrits [2] Personnes âgées de 16 ans et plus. [3] Personnes âgées de 15 ans et plus. [4] Non compris les forces armées et les conscrits.

Notas explicativas: véase p. 83.

[1] Incl. las fuerzas armadas, excl. los conscriptos. [2] Personas de 16 años y más. [3] Personas de 15 años y más. [4] Excl. las fuerzas armadas y los conscriptos.

EMPLOYMENT · EMPLOI · EMPLEO

Total employment, by economic activity
Emploi total, par activité économique
Empleo total, por actividad económica

	Thousands / Milliers / Millares									
	1999	2000	2001	2002	2003	2004	2005	2006	2007	2008

Azerbaijan (E) [1] — Total employment - Emploi total - Empleo total

Total - Total - Total
ISIC 3 - CITI 3 - CIIU 3

	1999	2000	2001	2002	2003	2004	2005	2006	2007	2008
Total	3 702.8	3 704.5	3 715.0	3 726.5	3 747.0	3 809.1	3 850.2	3 973.0	4 014.1	4 056.0
A	1 566.3	1 517.2	1 482.0	1 495.0	1 497.0	1 502.7	1 510.0	1 548.0	1 550.7	1 553.1
B	0.5	2.0	2.3	2.5	2.8	3.3	3.8	4.3	4.3	4.3
C	39.6	39.6	42.1	42.2	42.3	41.9	42.2	45.0	45.0	45.0
D	180.6	169.3	163.9	169.5	169.9	181.2	188.7	195.0	198.4	198.6
E	38.8	40.5	41.0	39.9	39.8	39.8	39.7	41.0	44.8	45.5
F	154.7	153.6	155.0	178.0	180.0	190.6	194.4	222.8	225.6	226.1
G	576.4	626.1	659.5	611.9	618.3	630.7	638.8	650.4	652.3	654.2
H	9.8	9.8	11.0	11.3	11.8	12.4	14.2	22.0	22.8	23.3
I	168.4	167.0	167.5	169.8	178.5	190.5	191.5	201.8	206.8	208.5
J	15.2	13.5	13.0	13.2	13.0	13.1	13.2	13.4	16.3	19.0
K	98.7	98.0	97.0	97.2	97.5	100.0	100.6	106.7	120.3	139.4
L	260.2	257.7	267.3	265.3	265.0	269.7	270.5	271.2	273.2	274.2
M	299.6	317.9	318.0	329.9	330.0	330.8	335.3	339.4	339.4	345.7
N	168.2	168.9	170.0	173.6	173.8	174.6	177.2	180.5	180.5	183.1
O	125.5	123.2	125.0	126.7	126.8	127.3	129.5	131.7	133.1	135.4
Q	0.3	0.2	0.4	0.5	0.5	0.5	0.6	0.6	0.6	0.6

Men - Hommes - Hombres
ISIC 3 - CITI 3 - CIIU 3

	1999	2000	2001	2002	2003	2004	2005	2006	2007	2008
Total	1 936.6	1 937.5	1 945.0	1 948.0	1 959.7	1 995.8	2 017.4	2 054.1	2 028.5	2 048.3
A	725.6	703.0	725.1	795.0	799.8	814.3	827.0	845.5	798.9	750.9
B	0.5	2.0	2.3	2.3	2.4	2.0	2.1	2.4	1.6	3.4
C	29.7	29.7	31.9	33.6	33.5	33.9	34.2	35.1	35.1	34.8
D	81.2	76.5	77.3	74.2	74.6	75.8	76.3	77.6	80.2	107.4
E	29.3	29.4	28.6	28.5	29.4	29.9	30.1	26.7	26.7	37.3
F	135.3	134.1	136.1	160.1	160.8	163.7	165.4	192.0	194.5	192.4
G	296.2	318.9	297.5	232.6	233.4	237.5	238.4	237.7	238.8	212.1
H	6.4	6.4	6.7	6.9	7.8	8.0	8.1	11.1	11.8	11.6
I	127.4	127.5	126.0	128.1	129.3	131.7	132.2	141.6	145.2	145.1
J	8.3	8.1	8.3	8.6	8.1	8.0	8.1	5.9	6.9	10.7
K	58.2	58.0	58.7	58.7	58.8	59.9	60.5	64.1	72.3	96.6
L	163.5	162.4	168.4	170.1	170.5	173.6	175.5	175.7	177.0	205.2
M	125.4	132.4	125.7	100.9	102.0	103.8	104.0	90.5	90.4	113.2
N	73.2	73.6	73.9	68.3	68.6	71.4	72.3	63.8	63.8	52.5
O	76.2	75.3	78.2	79.7	80.3	81.8	82.7	83.9	84.8	74.6
Q	0.2	0.2	0.3	0.4	0.4	0.5	0.5	0.5	0.5	0.5

Women - Femmes - Mujeres
ISIC 3 - CITI 3 - CIIU 3

	1999	2000	2001	2002	2003	2004	2005	2006	2007	2008
Total	1 766.2	1 767.0	1 770.0	1 778.5	1 787.3	1 813.3	1 832.8	1 918.9	1 985.6	2 007.7
A	840.7	814.2	756.9	700.0	697.2	688.4	683.0	702.5	751.8	802.2
B	-	-	-	0.2	0.4	1.3	1.7	1.9	2.7	0.9
C	9.9	9.9	10.2	8.6	8.8	8.0	8.0	9.9	9.9	10.2
D	99.4	92.8	86.6	95.3	95.3	105.4	112.4	117.4	118.2	91.2
E	9.5	11.1	12.4	11.4	10.4	9.9	9.6	14.3	18.1	8.2
F	19.4	19.5	18.9	17.9	19.2	26.9	29.0	30.8	31.1	33.7
G	280.2	307.2	362.0	379.3	384.9	393.2	400.4	412.7	413.5	442.1
H	3.4	3.4	4.3	4.4	4.0	4.4	6.1	10.9	11.0	11.7
I	41.0	39.5	41.5	41.7	49.2	58.8	59.3	60.2	61.6	63.4
J	6.9	5.4	4.7	4.6	4.9	5.1	5.1	7.5	9.4	8.3
K	40.5	40.0	38.3	38.5	38.7	40.1	40.1	42.6	48.0	42.8
L	96.7	95.3	98.9	95.2	94.5	96.1	95.0	95.5	96.2	69.0
M	174.2	185.5	192.3	229.0	228.0	227.0	231.3	248.9	249.0	232.5
N	95.0	95.3	96.1	105.3	105.2	103.2	104.9	116.7	116.7	130.6
O	49.3	47.9	46.8	47.0	46.5	45.5	46.8	47.8	48.3	60.8
Q	0.1	-	0.1	0.1	0.1	-	0.1	0.1	0.1	0.1

China (E) [2][3] — Total employment - Emploi total - Empleo total

Total - Total - Total
ISIC 3 - CITI 3 - CIIU 3

	1999	2000	2001	2002	2003	2004	2005	2006	2007	2008
Total	.	.	.	.	109 697	110 989	114 040	117 132	120 244	.
A-B	.	.	.	.	4 845	4 661	4 463	4 352	4 263	.
C	.	.	.	.	4 883	5 007	5 092	5 297	5 350	.
D	.	.	.	.	29 805	30 508	32 109	33 516	34 654	.
E	.	.	.	.	2 976	3 006	2 999	3 025	3 034	.
F	.	.	.	.	8 337	8 410	9 266	9 887	10 508	.
G	.	.	.	.	6 281	5 867	5 440	5 157	5 069	.
H	.	.	.	.	1 721	1 771	1 812	1 839	1 858	.
I	.	.	.	.	6 365	6 318	6 139	6 127	6 231	.
J	.	.	.	.	3 533	3 560	3 593	3 674	3 897	.
K	.	.	.	.	5 274	5 499	5 927	6 261	6 571	.
L	.	.	.	.	11 710	11 990	12 408	12 656	12 912	.
M	.	.	.	.	14 428	14 668	14 832	15 044	15 209	.
N	.	.	.	.	4 858	4 947	5 089	5 254	5 428	.
O	.	.	.	.	1 278	1 234	1 225	1 224	1 250	.
X	.	.	.	.	3 421	3 540	3 644	3 818	4 011	.

Explanatory notes: see p. 77.

[1] Persons aged 15 years and over. [2] State-owned units, urban collective-owned units and other ownership units. [3] Dec. of each year.

Notes explicatives: voir p. 80.

[1] Personnes âgées de 15 ans et plus. [2] Unités d'Etat, unités collectives urbaines et autres. [3] Déc. de chaque année.

Notas explicativas: véase p. 83.

[1] Personas de 15 años y más. [2] Unidades estatales, unidades colectivas y otras. [3] Dic. de cada año.

	EMPLOYMENT	EMPLOI	EMPLEO

Total employment, by economic activity — **Emploi total, par activité économique** — **Empleo total, por actividad económica**

Thousands — Milliers — Millares

	1999	2000	2001	2002	2003	2004	2005	2006	2007	2008

China (E) [1] [2] — Total employment - Emploi total - Empleo total

Men - Hommes - Hombres
ISIC 3 - CITI 3 - CIIU 3

	1999	2000	2001	2002	2003	2004	2005	2006	2007	2008
Total					68 136	68 716	70 794	72 675	74 841	
A-B					3 084	2 938	2 806	2 717	2 690	
C					3 686	3 836	3 962	4 147	4 253	
D					16 878	17 210	18 134	18 876	19 704	
E					2 049	2 075	2 086	2 112	2 127	
F					7 053	7 117	7 924	8 506	9 084	
G					3 478	3 265	3 017	2 854	2 781	
H					771	793	823	844	850	
I					4 540	4 542	4 429	4 480	4 538	
J					1 888	1 855	1 873	1 888	1 968	
K					3 536	3 691	3 988	4 224	4 434	
L					8 629	8 794	9 039	9 170	9 352	
M					7 700	7 701	7 700	7 706	7 732	
N					2 013	2 025	2 080	2 125	2 187	
O					759	731	724	717	729	
X					2 090	2 140	2 206	2 579	2 413	

Women - Femmes - Mujeres
ISIC 3 - CITI 3 - CIIU 3

	1999	2000	2001	2002	2003	2004	2005	2006	2007	2008
Total					41 561	42 273	43 246	44 457	45 403	
A-B					1 761	1 723	1 657	1 635	1 573	
C					1 197	1 171	1 130	1 150	1 097	
D					12 927	13 298	13 975	14 640	14 950	
E					927	931	913	913	907	
F					1 284	1 293	1 342	1 381	1 424	
G					2 803	2 602	2 423	2 303	2 288	
H					950	978	989	995	1 008	
I					1 825	1 776	1 710	1 647	1 693	
J					1 645	1 705	1 720	1 786	1 929	
K					1 738	1 808	1 939	2 037	2 137	
L					3 081	3 196	3 369	3 486	3 560	
M					6 728	6 967	7 132	7 338	7 477	
N					2 845	2 922	3 009	3 129	3 241	
O					519	503	501	507	521	
X					1 331	1 400	1 438	1 239	1 598	

Georgia (BA) [3] [4] — Total employment - Emploi total - Empleo total

Total - Total - Total
ISIC 3 - CITI 3 - CIIU 3

	1999	2000	2001	2002	2003	2004	2005	2006	2007	2008
Total	1 732.6	1 839.3	1 877.7	1 839.2	1 814.5	1 783.3	1 744.6	1 747.3	1 704.3	
A	903.2	957.5	989.9	988.4	994.9	962.0	947.8	966.4	910.5	
B	1.2	0.8	0.6	0.6	0.7	0.4	-	-	-	
C	6.1	6.6	7.3	5.2	2.8	3.9	5.8	3.4	4.7	
D	111.5	109.3	102.4	85.3	88.8	90.8	89.8	81.5	82.7	
E	21.0	30.6	29.2	26.6	19.8	20.7	23.4	18.4	18.2	
F	24.9	33.7	35.3	34.1	40.1	42.1	43.1	54.8	71.2	
G	153.7	183.8	181.5	215.4	198.5	196.9	188.2	168.1	168.8	
H	15.4	15.8	16.0	15.1	16.6	18.7	16.3	16.9	18.0	
I	68.5	75.6	83.1	78.3	76.9	74.3	69.3	77.8	71.7	
J	10.9	9.5	10.2	7.7	9.8	12.8	13.3	14.3	17.3	
K	40.3	39.7	38.7	20.4	32.3	28.4	25.9	26.9	34.7	
L	106.4	111.3	105.6	108.5	91.4	86.8	81.8	78.5	64.3	
M	138.5	120.1	138.7	129.7	135.6	134.1	130.9	132.2	124.2	
N	77.9	89.6	85.3	63.4	49.0	54.8	58.0	52.2	59.9	
O	42.5	47.6	46.5	52.0	45.2	42.7	38.2	41.9	43.9	
P	6.9	3.4	4.1	8.2	7.8	8.4	9.2	11.7	11.1	
Q	1.9	2.0	2.0	0.3	3.5	4.4	3.3	2.3	2.9	
X	1.8	2.4	1.3	-	0.8	1.4	0.3	-	-	

Men - Hommes - Hombres
ISIC 3 - CITI 3 - CIIU 3

	1999	2000	2001	2002	2003	2004	2005	2006	2007	2008
Total	884.8	946.9	966.7	954.1	957.5	926.5	915.2	920.5	888.1	
A	444.7	444.3	509.2	499.0	508.3	478.2	473.5	491.9	448.5	
B	1.1	0.8	0.5	0.5	0.5	0.4	-	-	-	
C	5.0	5.7	5.6	4.1	2.3	3.7	5.2	2.5	4.3	
D	76.0	80.7	68.2	62.2	57.8	60.6	60.1	54.8	60.6	
E	17.1	26.9	25.0	20.9	15.7	17.1	18.1	14.8	14.7	
F	23.5	30.6	21.5	33.0	39.7	41.3	42.4	53.7	66.5	
G	87.6	92.0	113.1	115.0	112.4	108.7	107.9	86.6	88.4	
H	9.0	7.7	4.5	5.2	6.8	7.6	7.6	4.8	7.0	
I	52.8	62.4	68.2	63.5	65.4	61.6	57.9	70.3	65.7	
J	4.8	3.2	3.1	2.6	4.8	5.0	7.2	8.4	8.0	
K	22.3	30.4	14.6	10.1	19.0	15.8	15.8	16.4	21.6	
L	73.1	86.9	74.0	75.8	63.5	60.6	56.1	55.4	47.6	
M	25.8	18.6	26.3	24.2	27.5	26.6	29.6	23.4	21.2	
N	15.0	25.2	12.2	11.6	8.0	12.6	12.0	12.8	9.3	
O	21.2	27.8	19.4	25.1	22.2	22.0	18.1	22.1	22.2	
P	3.7	2.1	0.1	1.1	1.0	0.7	0.6	1.6	1.4	
Q	1.3	1.6	1.0	0.2	2.4	3.1	2.9	0.9	1.1	
X	0.8	0.1	0.2	-	0.2	0.8	-	-	-	

Explanatory notes: see p. 77.

Notes explicatives: voir p. 80.

Notas explicativas: véase p. 83.

[1] State-owned units, urban collective-owned units and other ownership units. [2] Dec. of each year. [3] Excl. armed forces. [4] Persons aged 15 years and over.

[1] Unités d'Etat, unités collectives urbaines et autres. [2] Déc. de chaque année. [3] Non compris les forces armées. [4] Personnes âgées de 15 ans et plus.

[1] Unidades estatales, unidades colectivas y otras. [2] Dic. de cada año. [3] Excl. las fuerzas armadas. [4] Personas de 15 años y más.

Total employment, by economic activity   **Emploi total, par activité économique**   **Empleo total, por actividad económica**

Thousands   Milliers   Millares

	1999	2000	2001	2002	2003	2004	2005	2006	2007	2008
Georgia (BA) [1] [2]				Total employment - Emploi total - Empleo total						
Women - Femmes - Mujeres										
ISIC 3 - CITI 3 - CIIU 3										
Total	847.8	892.4	911.0	885.1	857.0	856.8	829.4	826.8	816.2	.
A	458.5	513.2	480.7	489.4	486.6	483.7	474.3	474.5	462.1	.
B	0.1	-	0.1	0.1	0.2	-	-	-	-	.
C	1.1	0.9	1.7	1.1	0.5	0.2	0.6	0.9	0.4	.
D	35.5	28.6	34.2	23.1	31.0	30.1	29.7	26.7	22.1	.
E	3.9	3.7	4.2	5.7	4.1	3.6	5.3	3.7	3.5	.
F	1.4	3.1	13.8	1.1	0.4	0.7	0.7	1.2	4.6	.
G	66.1	91.8	68.4	100.4	86.1	88.2	80.3	81.5	80.5	.
H	6.4	8.1	11.5	9.9	9.8	11.1	8.7	12.1	11.0	.
I	15.7	13.2	14.9	14.8	11.5	12.7	11.3	7.5	6.0	.
J	6.1	6.3	7.1	5.1	5.0	7.8	6.1	5.9	9.3	.
K	18.0	9.3	24.1	10.3	13.3	12.6	10.1	10.5	13.1	.
L	33.3	24.4	31.6	32.7	27.9	26.1	25.7	23.1	16.7	.
M	112.7	101.5	112.4	105.5	108.1	107.4	101.2	108.8	103.0	.
N	62.9	64.4	73.1	51.8	41.0	42.1	46.0	39.4	50.6	.
O	21.4	19.8	27.1	26.9	23.0	20.7	20.1	19.8	21.7	.
P	3.2	1.3	4.0	7.1	6.8	7.7	8.6	10.1	9.8	.
Q	0.6	0.4	1.0	0.1	1.1	1.3	0.4	1.4	1.8	.
X	1.0	2.4	1.1	-	0.6	0.6	0.3	-	-	.
Hong Kong, China (BA) [2] [3]				Total employment - Emploi total - Empleo total						
Total - Total - Total										
ISIC 2 - CITI 2 - CIIU 2										
Total	3 112.1	3 207.3	3 252.9	3 218.4	3 190.6	3 273.5	3 336.6	3 400.8	3 483.8	3 518.8
1	9.2	9.3	7.1	9.1	7.0	8.5	8.7	8.2	6.4	8.3
2	-	-	-	-	0.6	-	-	-	-	-
3	353.9	333.7	325.0	287.8	268.8	232.1	224.3	216.9	202.4	191.2
4	17.0	16.6	15.8	15.8	16.1	14.6	15.0	14.6	15.2	14.1
5	286.8	301.7	288.7	284.1	260.8	263.1	263.7	269.2	274.7	268.6
6	935.1	981.7	981.0	978.2	983.7	1 061.9	1 093.8	1 104.8	1 143.8	1 145.5
7	339.4	356.6	352.9	343.1	343.5	355.1	357.3	369.2	372.2	377.9
8	437.7	452.7	482.0	474.9	468.4	480.2	503.3	525.7	548.0	580.0
9	732.9	754.7	800.1	825.0	841.7	857.8	870.2	892.1	921.1	933.1
Men - Hommes - Hombres										
ISIC 2 - CITI 2 - CIIU 2										
Total	1 816.5	1 854.5	1 845.7	1 794.0	1 764.3	1 800.8	1 822.6	1 840.4	1 869.0	1 870.0
1	6.5	6.3	5.0	6.1	4.6	5.8	6.0	5.2	4.0	5.7
2	-	-	-	-	-	-	-	-	-	-
3	222.3	213.3	208.9	181.4	175.0	147.2	146.8	140.0	130.3	127.2
4	15.1	14.7	13.5	12.9	13.6	12.4	12.5	12.3	12.6	11.7
5	267.9	282.7	268.2	262.6	240.7	243.2	244.7	250.0	254.3	248.0
6	493.9	503.5	499.4	492.2	498.4	534.8	546.3	545.9	561.0	554.7
7	272.4	284.0	279.7	270.5	267.6	280.1	278.1	285.3	286.9	290.3
8	262.2	270.6	283.5	283.7	278.0	284.2	298.0	307.9	319.0	334.8
9	275.9	279.0	287.2	284.3	286.0	292.7	289.8	293.8	301.0	297.4
Women - Femmes - Mujeres										
ISIC 2 - CITI 2 - CIIU 2										
Total	1 295.6	1 352.8	1 407.3	1 424.4	1 426.3	1 472.7	1 514.0	1 560.4	1 614.8	1 648.8
1	2.7	3.0	2.1	3.0	2.4	2.7	2.7	3.0	2.4	2.6
2	-	-	-	-	-	-	-	-	-	-
3	131.5	120.4	116.1	106.3	93.8	84.9	77.5	76.9	72.1	63.9
4	1.9	1.8	2.3	2.8	2.5	2.2	2.5	2.4	2.7	2.5
5	18.9	19.1	20.5	21.5	20.1	19.9	19.0	19.3	20.4	20.6
6	441.3	478.1	481.6	486.0	485.3	527.1	547.5	558.9	582.8	590.8
7	67.0	72.6	73.2	72.6	75.9	75.0	79.2	83.8	85.4	87.5
8	175.5	182.0	198.5	191.2	190.4	196.0	205.3	217.8	229.0	245.2
9	457.0	475.7	512.8	540.8	555.7	565.0	580.4	598.3	620.1	635.7

Explanatory notes: see p. 77.

[1] Excl. armed forces. [2] Persons aged 15 years and over. [3] Excl. marine, military and institutional populations.

Notes explicatives: voir p. 80.

[1] Non compris les forces armées. [2] Personnes âgées de 15 ans et plus. [3] Non compris le personnel militaire, de la marine et la population institutionnelle.

Notas explicativas: véase p. 83.

[1] Excl. las fuerzas armadas. [2] Personas de 15 años y más. [3] Excl. el personal militar y de la marina, y la población institucional.

2B

EMPLOYMENT	EMPLOI	EMPLEO
Total employment, by economic activity	**Emploi total, par activité économique**	**Empleo total, por actividad económica**
Thousands	Milliers	Millares

Indonesia (BA) [1][2]
Total employment - Emploi total - Empleo total

Total - Total - Total
ISIC 2 - CITI 2 - CIIU 2 — ISIC 3 - CITI 3 - CIIU 3

ISIC2	1999	2000	2001	2002	2003	2004	2005	2006	2007	2008	ISIC3
Total	89 838	89 838	90 807	91 647	92 811	93 722	93 958 [3]	95 457	99 930	102 553	Total
1	40 677	39 012	38 151	39 134	41 470	38 927	39 766 [3]	38 604	39 371	39 556	A
2	452	1 665	1 593	1 500	1 572	1 681	1 544 [3]	1 532	1 836	1 775	B
3	11 642	452	950	632	733	1 035	904 [3]	924	995	1 071	C
4	71	11 642	12 086	12 110	11 496	11 070	11 953 [3]	11 890	12 369	12 549	D
5	3 497	71	141	178	152	228	195 [3]	228	175	201	E
6	18 489	3 497	3 838	4 274	4 055	4 540	4 565 [3]	4 697	5 253	5 439	F
7	4 554	15 225	16 901	17 315	16 787	18 458	16 748 [3]	17 383	16 531	17 153	G
8	883	3 264	568	480	462	661	1 161 [3]	1 832	4 023	4 069	H
9	9 570	4 554	4 448	4 673	4 940	5 481	5 653 [3]	5 662	5 959	6 180	I
0	4	469	466	499	408	486	556 [3]	678	740	691	J
		413	662	493	899	639	586 [3]	668	660	769	K
		2 841	2 736	2 779	2 638	2 683	2 587 [3]	2 837	2 679	2 521	L
		2 413	2 566	2 501	2 362	2 660	2 872 [3]	3 179	3 460	3 286	M
		438	586	446	434	572	651 [3]	701	683	744	N
		1 817	715	783	932	828	1 450 [3]	2 172	3 246	4 213	O
		2 065	4 393	3 849	3 466	3 769	2 703 [3]	2 416	1 885	2 229	P
		0	1	0	1	0	4 [3]	11	4	8	Q
		0	7	3	5	4	61 [3]	42	63	98	X

Men - Hommes - Hombres
ISIC 2 - CITI 2 - CIIU 2 — ISIC 3 - CITI 3 - CIIU 3

ISIC2	1999	2000	2001	2002	2003	2004	2005	2006	2007	2008	ISIC3
Total	55 439	55 439	57 131	58 583	59 500	60 582	61 439 [3]	61 977	63 148	63 899	Total
1	24 600	23 105	23 262	24 210	25 726	24 229	25 457 [3]	24 972	24 290	24 294	A
2	370	1 495	1 487	1 411	1 480	1 590	1 434 [3]	1 397	1 693	1 620	B
3	6 723	370	785	548	639	869	765 [3]	818	874	938	C
4	65	6 723	6 954	7 117	6 688	6 660	7 034 [3]	7 005	7 119	7 129	D
5	3 357	65	126	160	140	208	179 [3]	203	154	184	E
6	9 685	3 357	3 725	4 153	3 917	4 429	4 466 [3]	4 574	5 120	5 311	F
7	4 364	8 383	8 664	9 139	8 875	9 854	9 121 [3]	9 416	8 508	8 716	G
8	627	1 302	327	297	267	377	591 [3]	914	1 865	1 798	H
9	5 644	4 364	4 279	4 508	4 766	5 286	5 480 [3]	5 372	5 587	5 466	I
0	4	314	342	346	279	347	379 [3]	447	472	454	J
		313	509	385	665	497	457 [3]	506	523	574	K
		2 233	2 181	2 175	2 098	2 105	2 086 [3]	2 275	2 138	2 000	L
		1 307	1 295	1 270	1 184	1 368	1 435 [3]	1 512	1 620	1 490	M
		186	249	190	179	239	274 [3]	290	273	303	N
		1 118	534	604	715	656	1 175 [3]	1 511	2 406	3 021	O
		805	2 408	2 067	1 876	1 866	1 066 [3]	723	460	525	P
		0	0	0	0	0	2 [3]	9	2	7	Q
		0	4	2	5	2	39 [3]	31	44	70	X

Women - Femmes - Mujeres
ISIC 2 - CITI 2 - CIIU 2 — ISIC 3 - CITI 3 - CIIU 3

ISIC2	1999	2000	2001	2002	2003	2004	2005	2006	2007	2008	ISIC3
Total	34 399	34 399	33 676	33 064	33 311	33 141	32 519 [3]	33 480	36 782	38 653	Total
1	16 076	15 907	14 889	14 923	15 745	14 698	14 309 [3]	13 632	15 081	15 262	A
2	82	170	105	88	92	91	110 [3]	135	142	156	B
3	4 919	82	166	84	94	166	139 [3]	106	120	132	C
4	6	4 919	5 133	4 993	4 808	4 410	4 919 [3]	4 884	5 249	5 421	D
5	141	6	15	18	12	20	15 [3]	25	21	17	E
6	8 804	141	112	121	138	111	100 [3]	123	133	128	F
7	190	6 842	8 237	8 176	7 912	8 605	7 627 [3]	7 967	8 024	8 437	G
8	255	1 962	241	183	195	284	570 [3]	918	2 159	2 271	H
9	3 926	190	169	164	173	195	173 [3]	290	372	714	I
0	0	155	123	153	128	139	177 [3]	231	267	237	J
		100	153	108	234	143	129 [3]	162	137	194	K
		608	555	604	540	578	501 [3]	562	541	522	L
		1 106	1 271	1 231	1 178	1 291	1 437 [3]	1 667	1 840	1 797	M
		253	337	256	255	333	377 [3]	411	411	441	N
		699	181	179	217	172	275 [3]	660	840	1 191	O
		1 260	1 985	1 782	1 590	1 903	1 638 [3]	1 692	1 424	1 704	P
		-	1	0	1	0	2 [3]	3	2	1	Q
		-	3	1	0	2	22 [3]	11	19	28	X

Explanatory notes: see p. 77.
[1] Persons aged 15 years and over. [2] Aug. of each year. [3] Nov.

Notes explicatives: voir p. 80.
[1] Personnes âgées de 15 ans et plus. [2] Août de chaque année. [3] Nov.

Notas explicativas: véase p. 83.
[1] Personas de 15 años y más. [2] Agosto de cada año. [3] Nov.

Total employment, by economic activity

Emploi total, par activité économique

Empleo total, por actividad económica

	Thousands			Milliers			Millares			
	1999	2000	2001	2002	2003	2004	2005	2006	2007	2008

Iran, Islamic Rep. of (BA) [1]   Total employment - Emploi total - Empleo total

Total - Total - Total
ISIC 3 - CITI 3 - CIIU 3

Total	.	.	.	.	.	.	20 619	20 841	21 092	.
A	.	.	.	.	.	.	5 031	4 745	4 730	.
B	.	.	.	.	.	.	69	82	79	.
C	.	.	.	.	.	.	127	139	128	.
D	.	.	.	.	.	.	3 789	3 908	3 834	.
E	.	.	.	.	.	.	198	191	196	.
F	.	.	.	.	.	.	2 143	2 367	2 601	.
G	.	.	.	.	.	.	2 959	3 031	3 017	.
H	.	.	.	.	.	.	182	187	193	.
I	.	.	.	.	.	.	1 817	1 910	1 976	.
J	.	.	.	.	.	.	260	278	282	.
K	.	.	.	.	.	.	418	424	438	.
L	.	.	.	.	.	.	1 317	1 323	1 353	.
M	.	.	.	.	.	.	1 369	1 325	1 321	.
N	.	.	.	.	.	.	464	453	461	.
O	.	.	.	.	.	.	433	435	442	.
P	.	.	.	.	.	.	28	29	28	.
Q	.	.	.	.	.	.	0	1	1	.
X	.	.	.	.	.	.	4	5	4	.

Men - Hommes - Hombres
ISIC 3 - CITI 3 - CIIU 3

Total	.	.	.	.	.	.	16 657	16 872	17 230	.
A	.	.	.	.	.	.	3 702	3 520	3 454	.
B	.	.	.	.	.	.	68	82	78	.
C	.	.	.	.	.	.	120	131	124	.
D	.	.	.	.	.	.	2 700	2 688	2 745	.
E	.	.	.	.	.	.	189	181	188	.
F	.	.	.	.	.	.	2 125	2 345	2 578	.
G	.	.	.	.	.	.	2 780	2 863	2 850	.
H	.	.	.	.	.	.	170	177	180	.
I	.	.	.	.	.	.	1 778	1 867	1 938	.
J	.	.	.	.	.	.	224	235	244	.
K	.	.	.	.	.	.	353	358	368	.
L	.	.	.	.	.	.	1 208	1 212	1 249	.
M	.	.	.	.	.	.	687	668	665	.
N	.	.	.	.	.	.	253	240	259	.
O	.	.	.	.	.	.	281	281	291	.
P	.	.	.	.	.	.	7	11	7	.
Q	.	.	.	.	.	.	0	1	1	.
X	.	.	.	.	.	.	3	4	3	.

Women - Femmes - Mujeres
ISIC 3 - CITI 3 - CIIU 3

Total	.	.	.	.	.	.	3 962	3 970	3 862	.
A	.	.	.	.	.	.	1 329	1 225	1 276	.
B	.	.	.	.	.	.	1	0	2	.
C	.	.	.	.	.	.	7	9	4	.
D	.	.	.	.	.	.	1 089	1 219	1 089	.
E	.	.	.	.	.	.	9	10	8	.
F	.	.	.	.	.	.	18	22	23	.
G	.	.	.	.	.	.	178	168	167	.
H	.	.	.	.	.	.	12	10	13	.
I	.	.	.	.	.	.	39	43	38	.
J	.	.	.	.	.	.	36	42	38	.
K	.	.	.	.	.	.	65	65	70	.
L	.	.	.	.	.	.	109	111	104	.
M	.	.	.	.	.	.	682	657	656	.
N	.	.	.	.	.	.	211	213	202	.
O	.	.	.	.	.	.	152	154	150	.
P	.	.	.	.	.	.	21	18	21	.
Q	.	.	.	.	.	.	0	1	0	.
X	.	.	.	.	.	.	1	1	0	.

Explanatory notes: see p. 77.

Notes explicatives: voir p. 80.

Notas explicativas: véase p. 83.

[1] Persons aged 10 years and over.

[1] Personnes âgées de 10 ans et plus.

[1] Personas de 10 años y más.

EMPLOYMENT EMPLOI EMPLEO

Total employment, by economic activity
Emploi total, par activité économique
Empleo total, por actividad económica

Thousands — Milliers — Millares

	1999	2000	2001	2002	2003[3]	2004	2005	2006	2007	2008
Israel (BA) [1][2]					**Total employment - Emploi total - Empleo total**					
Total - Total - Total										
ISIC 3 - CITI 3 - CIIU 3										
Total	2 136.6	2 221.2	2 264.9	2 284.3	2 330.2	2 400.8	2 493.6	2 573.6	2 682.0	2 776.7
A	47.6	46.3	44.4	43.5	41.9	48.0	49.2	43.9	42.2	46.5
B	2.0	-	-	-	-	-	-	-	-	-
C	6.1	5.1	3.3	3.5	3.3	2.9	3.9	4.3	4.1	5.0
D	377.1	385.3	381.3	366.1	366.7	375.2	380.8	390.0	409.0	421.0
E	19.3	19.3	18.8	18.9	18.3	19.3	21.3	18.1	16.8	19.9
F	120.2	116.4	117.0	118.7	129.8	128.7	127.1	134.4	150.2	150.7
G	281.6	295.6	299.1	311.8	315.8	324.7	337.2	336.7	358.2	377.9
H	90.2	101.8	95.9	92.9	93.5	103.4	115.1	122.1	122.1	129.9
I	135.5	144.9	149.9	146.9	150.0	154.0	162.6	171.5	171.2	174.5
J	73.7	73.1	75.2	76.2	78.0	79.1	82.1	87.4	95.0	99.2
K	224.7	258.8	277.8	275.3	301.3	320.1	335.3	354.4	375.3	388.9
L	116.3	119.8	129.1	134.3	120.3	111.5	116.0	115.6	120.3	130.6
M	267.9	272.4	279.5	287.5	295.0	303.5	314.1	325.9	344.4	349.3
N	211.9	213.6	225.0	233.6	250.2	255.2	265.6	263.7	267.0	274.6
O	99.1	106.3	107.2	110.3	111.4	109.5	116.8	128.2	124.2	130.3
P	40.1	34.7	34.9	34.9	33.4	38.5	40.5	45.8	49.0	46.2
Q	-	-	-	2.1	-	-	2.0	-	-	-
X	21.4	24.7	24.2	26.7	18.0	24.2	23.4	28.5	30.6	29.0
Men - Hommes - Hombres										
ISIC 3 - CITI 3 - CIIU 3										
Total	1 176.1	1 211.7	1 236.1	1 238.0	1 257.6	1 300.3	1 339.9	1 383.6	1 441.9	1 489.1
A	37.1	37.7	38.2	36.3	33.4	38.8	40.2	36.7	35.2	37.9
B	-	-	-	-	-	-	-	-	-	-
C	5.5	4.6	2.8	2.8	2.8	2.7	3.5	3.8	3.8	4.7
D	270.8	277.3	275.5	264.0	265.2	269.3	274.8	283.6	292.2	299.7
E	15.9	16.0	15.2	15.3	15.1	15.4	16.8	15.2	13.2	15.7
F	111.8	107.9	108.1	109.7	119.3	117.9	117.3	125.7	141.1	139.5
G	169.3	175.5	176.4	181.3	185.8	195.6	197.0	194.9	210.8	219.2
H	51.1	57.3	57.4	52.7	53.5	59.1	69.5	72.3	72.7	75.2
I	100.2	102.8	108.1	106.1	108.7	109.0	115.9	121.8	120.1	121.9
J	31.9	30.5	30.5	33.3	31.9	30.4	34.3	35.1	37.5	39.0
K	127.5	147.2	155.6	159.7	173.0	190.4	196.4	208.3	216.2	227.4
L	65.6	66.9	73.5	75.0	67.3	62.6	64.6	63.9	67.5	71.1
M	64.2	61.3	65.3	68.5	70.5	70.9	70.1	74.4	80.5	81.2
N	52.2	51.1	54.9	54.1	58.8	60.5	59.1	60.5	62.4	62.5
O	50.2	52.5	54.4	54.9	53.8	55.5	60.9	63.4	63.3	69.6
P	5.0	4.1	2.6	3.3	3.5	2.7	2.4	4.3	4.2	4.0
Q	-	-	-	-	-	-	-	-	-	-
X	15.0	16.8	16.3	18.5	12.8	17.1	15.0	17.0	19.6	18.1
Women - Femmes - Mujeres										
ISIC 3 - CITI 3 - CIIU 3										
Total	960.5	1 009.5	1 028.8	1 046.4	1 072.6	1 100.5	1 153.7	1 190.0	1 240.1	1 287.6
A	10.5	8.6	6.3	7.2	8.5	9.2	9.1	7.2	7.0	8.5
B	-	-	-	-	-	-	-	-	-	-
C	0.5	0.5	0.5	0.8	0.5	0.3	0.4	0.4	0.3	0.3
D	106.3	108.0	105.9	102.2	101.5	106.0	106.0	106.4	116.8	121.3
E	3.3	3.3	3.6	3.5	3.2	3.9	4.5	3.0	3.6	4.2
F	8.5	8.5	9.0	9.0	10.6	10.8	9.8	8.7	9.0	11.2
G	112.3	120.1	122.7	130.6	130.1	129.1	140.2	141.8	147.4	158.7
H	39.1	44.4	38.5	40.2	40.0	44.3	45.6	49.8	49.4	54.7
I	35.2	42.1	41.8	40.8	41.3	45.1	46.7	49.7	51.1	52.5
J	41.8	42.7	44.7	42.9	46.1	48.7	47.8	52.3	57.6	60.2
K	97.3	111.5	122.2	115.5	128.3	129.7	138.9	146.1	159.1	161.5
L	50.7	53.0	55.5	59.3	53.0	48.9	51.3	51.8	52.8	59.5
M	203.7	211.1	214.2	219.0	224.5	232.5	244.0	251.5	263.9	268.2
N	159.7	162.5	170.1	179.6	191.5	194.7	206.5	203.2	204.6	212.1
O	49.0	53.9	52.8	55.3	57.6	54.0	55.9	64.8	60.9	60.7
P	35.1	30.6	32.3	31.6	29.9	35.7	38.0	41.5	44.8	42.2
Q	-	-	-	-	-	-	-	-	-	-
X	6.4	8.0	8.0	8.2	5.2	7.1	8.4	11.5	11.0	10.9

Explanatory notes: see p. 77.

[1] Excl. armed forces. [2] Persons aged 15 years and over. [3] Methodology revised; data not strictly comparable.

Notes explicatives: voir p. 80.

[1] Non compris les forces armées. [2] Personnes âgées de 15 ans et plus. [3] Méthodologie révisée; les données ne sont pas strictement comparables.

Notas explicativas: véase p. 83.

[1] Excl. las fuerzas armadas. [2] Personas de 15 años y más. [3] Metodología revisada; los datos no son estrictamente comparables.

Total employment, by economic activity
Emploi total, par activité économique
Empleo total, por actividad económica

Thousands — Milliers — Millares

Japan (BA) [1]

Total employment - Emploi total - Empleo total

Total - Total - Total
ISIC 2 - CITI 2 - CIIU 2   ISIC 3 - CITI 3 - CIIU 3

ISIC2	1999	2000	2001	2002	2003	2004	2005	2006	2007	2008	ISIC3
Total	64 620	64 460	64 120	63 300	63 160	63 290	63 560	63 820	64 120	63 850	Total
1	3 350	3 260	3 130	2 960	2 660	2 640	2 590	2 500	2 510	2 450	A
2	60	50	50	50	270	220	230	220	210	230	B
3	13 450	13 210	12 840	12 220	50	40	30	30	40	30	C
4	380	340	340	340	12 070	11 770	11 690	11 910	11 980	11 740	D
5	6 570	6 530	6 320	6 180	320	310	350	360	330	320	E
6 [2]	14 830	14 740	14 730	14 380	6 040	5 840	5 680	5 590	5 520	5 370	F
7	4 060	4 140	4 070	4 010	11 980	11 900	11 860	11 800	11 780	11 690	G
8	5 990	6 160	6 290	6 400	3 500	3 470	3 430	3 370	3 420	3 340	H
9 [3]	15 520	15 640	15 910	16 220	3 980	3 950	3 850	3 960	3 970	3 910	I
0	410	390	440	560	1 610	1 590	1 570	1 550	1 550	1 640	J
					6 460	6 840	7 290	7 410	7 610	7 710	K
					2 270	2 330	2 290	2 220	2 260	2 230	L [4]
					2 790	2 840	2 860	2 870	2 840	2 880	M
					5 020	5 310	5 530	5 710	5 790	5 980	N
					3 530	3 530	3 550	3 600	3 540	3 570	O
					590	670	740	710	770	740	X

Men - Hommes - Hombres
ISIC 2 - CITI 2 - CIIU 2   ISIC 3 - CITI 3 - CIIU 3

ISIC2	1999	2000	2001	2002	2003	2004	2005	2006	2007	2008	ISIC3
Total	38 310	38 180	37 830	37 360	37 190	37 130	37 230	37 300	37 530	37 290	Total
1	1 850	1 810	1 750	1 680	1 470	1 480	1 460	1 420	1 420	1 400	A
2	50	50	50	40	200	160	170	160	160	170	B
3	8 730	8 600	8 420	8 110	40	30	30	30	30	20	C
4	320	300	300	290	8 040	7 900	7 920	8 070	8 210	8 120	D
5	5 550	5 550	5 360	5 260	270	270	310	320	290	290	E
6 [2]	7 250	7 170	7 160	6 970	5 150	4 980	4 870	4 780	4 710	4 590	F
7	3 310	3 370	3 290	3 250	6 220	6 150	6 090	6 040	6 020	5 990	G
8	3 350	3 460	3 520	3 610	1 420	1 400	1 410	1 360	1 380	1 370	H
9 [3]	7 650	7 630	7 740	7 820	3 250	3 200	3 080	3 180	3 200	3 100	I
0	240	240	270	330	810	780	790	770	760	800	J
					3 960	4 210	4 490	4 560	4 650	4 740	K
					1 790	1 850	1 800	1 750	1 760	1 720	L [4]
					1 320	1 330	1 290	1 300	1 310	1 300	M
					1 160	1 230	1 300	1 350	1 390	1 440	N
					1 740	1 760	1 770	1 800	1 780	1 790	O
					340	390	430	410	440	430	X

Women - Femmes - Mujeres
ISIC 2 - CITI 2 - CIIU 2   ISIC 3 - CITI 3 - CIIU 3

ISIC2	1999	2000	2001	2002	2003	2004	2005	2006	2007	2008	ISIC3
Total	26 320	26 300	26 290	25 940	25 970	26 160	26 330	26 520	26 590	26 560	Total
1	1 510	1 450	1 380	1 270	1 190	1 170	1 130	1 080	1 080	1 050	A
2	10	10	10	10	70	50	60	60	60	60	B
3	4 710	4 610	4 430	4 110	10	10	10	10	10	0	C
4	50	50	40	50	4 040	3 870	3 770	3 830	3 770	3 620	D
5	1 020	980	960	920	50	40	40	40	30	30	E
6 [2]	7 590	7 570	7 570	7 410	890	860	810	820	810	780	F
7	750	780	780	770	5 760	5 750	5 770	5 760	5 760	5 700	G
8	2 630	2 700	2 770	2 780	2 090	2 070	2 020	2 010	2 040	1 980	H
9 [3]	7 890	8 000	8 190	8 400	720	740	750	780	780	800	I
0	170	150	170	230	800	810	790	770	780	840	J
					2 490	2 670	2 800	2 870	2 940	2 970	K
					470	480	490	470	510	510	L [4]
					1 480	1 510	1 570	1 570	1 530	1 590	M
					3 860	4 080	4 240	4 360	4 400	4 540	N
					1 790	1 780	1 780	1 800	1 760	1 780	O
					250	280	310	300	330	310	X

Kazakhstan (BA) [1]

Total employment - Emploi total - Empleo total

Total - Total - Total
ISIC 3 - CITI 3 - CIIU 3

	1999	2000	2001	2002	2003	2004	2005	2006	2007	2008
Total	.	.	6 699	6 709	6 985	7 182	7 261	7 404	7 631	7 857
A	.	.	2 366	2 367	2 447	2 388	2 336	2 318	2 366	2 350
B			13	14	16	18	17	16	17	20
C			167	167	182	186	184	187	194	200
D			514	504	506	520	541	555	570	573
E			150	153	167	164	167	163	163	165
F			264	268	330	381	416	461	518	549
G			1 006	1 007	1 015	1 059	1 039	1 067	1 071	1 150
H			54	57	70	82	87	91	100	103
I			506	504	504	520	529	539	553	589
J			46	50	54	61	67	74	88	96
K			214	203	207	234	292	319	355	378
L			281	280	318	335	330	335	344	353
M			576	589	631	666	690	721	733	754
N			287	293	300	319	328	332	336	347
O			183	186	196	201	203	198	197	205
P			71	67	43	49	36	29	28	24
Q			0	0	0	1	0	0	0	0

Explanatory notes: see p. 77.
[1] Persons aged 15 years and over. [2] Excl. hotels. [3] Incl. hotels. [4] Incl. self-defence forces.

Notes explicatives: voir p. 80.
[1] Personnes âgées de 15 ans et plus. [2] Non compris les hôtels. [3] Y compris les hôtels. [4] Y compris les forces d'autodéfense.

Notas explicativas: véase p. 83.
[1] Personas de 15 años y más. [2] Excl. hoteles. [3] Incl. hoteles. [4] Incl. a las fuerzas de autodefensa.

EMPLOYMENT EMPLOI EMPLEO

Total employment, by economic activity Emploi total, par activité économique Empleo total, por actividad económica

	Thousands				Milliers				Millares	
	1999	2000	2001	2002	2003	2004	2005	2006	2007	2008

Kazakhstan (BA) [1]

Total employment - Emploi total - Empleo total

Men - Hommes - Hombres
ISIC 3 - CITI 3 - CIIU 3

	1999	2000	2001	2002	2003	2004	2005	2006	2007	2008
Total	.	.	3 470	3 486	3 618	3 719	3 764	3 809	3 923	4 018
A	.	.	1 265	1 251	1 303	1 283	1 244	1 238	1 267	1 234
B			11	12	15	16	15	12	14	16
C			125	131	141	146	139	133	143	149
D			334	323	316	331	343	352	361	360
E			107	107	122	110	115	116	111	115
F			214	218	263	303	329	347	384	418
G			397	415	410	422	423	425	426	470
H			14	16	18	22	22	25	28	32
I			370	364	384	390	403	400	417	434
J			15	20	19	24	24	28	36	37
K			129	131	114	120	158	168	178	182
L			172	159	189	192	195	193	193	200
M			147	160	163	179	181	190	193	195
N			55	62	60	65	65	79	80	82
O			90	90	90	94	96	93	87	88
P			26	27	12	20	12	7	6	7
Q			0	0	0	-	0	0	0	0

Women - Femmes - Mujeres
ISIC 3 - CITI 3 - CIIU 3

	1999	2000	2001	2002	2003	2004	2005	2006	2007	2008
Total	.	.	3 229	3 223	3 367	3 463	3 497	3 595	3 708	3 840
A	.	.	1 102	1 116	1 144	1 105	1 092	1 080	1 099	1 116
B			2	1	1	2	3	5	3	4
C			41	36	40	40	45	54	51	51
D			180	181	190	189	197	203	209	213
E			43	46	45	54	53	47	52	50
F			51	50	67	78	87	113	134	131
G			609	592	605	636	615	641	645	681
H			40	41	52	60	66	66	72	71
I			137	140	120	130	126	138	136	155
J			31	31	35	37	42	46	52	59
K			84	72	93	113	134	151	177	197
L			109	122	129	143	135	142	151	152
M			430	429	468	487	508	530	540	559
N			232	231	240	254	263	252	256	265
O			93	96	107	107	107	105	110	118
P			46	40	31	29	24	22	22	18
Q			-	-	0	1	0	0	0	0

Korea, Republic of (BA) [1][2]

Total employment - Emploi total - Empleo total

Total - Total - Total
ISIC 3 - CITI 3 - CIIU 3

	1999	2000	2001	2002	2003	2004	2005	2006	2007	2008
Total	20 281	21 156 [3]	21 572	22 169	22 139	22 557	22 856	23 151	23 433	.
A	2 264	2 162 [3]	2 065	1 999	1 877	1 749	1 747	1 721	1 670	
B	85	81 [3]	83	70	73	76	68	64	56	
C	20	17 [3]	18	18	17	16	17	18	18	
D	4 006	4 293 [3]	4 267	4 241	4 205	4 290	4 234	4 167	4 119	
E	61	64 [3]	58	52	76	72	71	76	86	
F	1 476	1 580 [3]	1 585	1 746	1 816	1 820	1 814	1 835	1 850	
G	3 904	3 833 [3]	3 931	3 991	3 871	3 805	3 748	3 713	3 677	
H	1 820	1 919 [3]	1 943	2 007	1 981	2 057	2 058	2 049	2 049	
I	1 202	1 260 [3]	1 322	1 371	1 333	1 376	1 429	1 470	1 498	
J	723	752 [3]	760	734	751	738	746	786	809	
K	1 202	1 361 [3]	1 530	1 664	1 726	1 914	2 037	2 168	2 350	
L	870	758 [3]	701	702	757	768	791	801	797	
M	1 122	1 191 [3]	1 236	1 335	1 484	1 506	1 568	1 658	1 687	
N	380	428 [3]	484	551	539	594	646	686	745	
O	926	1 251 [3]	1 368	1 456	1 419	1 627	1 727	1 781	1 845	
P	201	186 [3]	206	215	192	125	130	138	161	
Q	18	19 [3]	16	18	22	24	24	20	15	

Men - Hommes - Hombres
ISIC 3 - CITI 3 - CIIU 3

	1999	2000	2001	2002	2003	2004	2005	2006	2007	2008
Total	11 978	12 387 [3]	12 581	12 944	13 031	13 193	13 330	13 444	13 607	.
A	1 189	1 114 [3]	1 071	1 033	976	911	920	905	879	
B	59	57 [3]	61	52	50	48	45	42	35	
C	19	17 [3]	17	16	16	15	16	16	17	
D	2 563	2 758 [3]	2 748	2 723	2 730	2 797	2 821	2 795	2 775	
E	52	53 [3]	44	41	64	59	58	60	67	
F	1 354	1 446 [3]	1 449	1 596	1 668	1 658	1 656	1 668	1 678	
G	2 172	2 059 [3]	2 084	2 126	2 039	2 010	1 994	1 992	1 999	
H	586	615 [3]	622	643	632	636	639	635	633	
I	1 080	1 111 [3]	1 167	1 215	1 167	1 193	1 228	1 272	1 316	
J	351	347 [3]	343	336	366	364	370	382	390	
K	855	942 [3]	1 053	1 134	1 200	1 324	1 361	1 423	1 522	
L	610	535 [3]	496	503	568	554	552	542	543	
M	463	461 [3]	468	490	528	515	522	532	544	
N	120	125 [3]	135	157	154	174	171	181	199	
O	483	727 [3]	803	860	853	914	956	981	994	
P	4	4 [3]	6	3	4	4	4	4	4	
Q	17	18 [3]	13	15	16	18	18	15	12	

Explanatory notes: see p. 77.

[1] Persons aged 15 years and over. [2] Excl. armed forces.
[3] Estimates based on the 2000 Population Census results.

Notes explicatives: voir p. 80.

[1] Personnes âgées de 15 ans et plus. [2] Non compris les forces armées. [3] Estimations basées sur les résultats du Recensement de la population de 2000.

Notas explicativas: véase p. 83.

[1] Personas de 15 años y más. [2] Excl. las fuerzas armadas. [3] Estimaciones basadas en los resultados del Censo de población de 2000.

Total employment, by economic activity	Emploi total, par activité économique	Empleo total, por actividad económica

Thousands			Milliers				Millares		
1999	2000	2001	2002	2003	2004	2005	2006	2007	2008

Korea, Republic of (BA) [1] [2] — Total employment - Emploi total - Empleo total

Women - Femmes - Mujeres
ISIC 3 - CITI 3 - CIIU 3

	1999	2000	2001	2002	2003	2004	2005	2006	2007	2008
Total	8 303	8 769 [3]	8 991	9 225	9 108	9 364	9 526	9 706	9 826	.
A	1 075	1 048 [3]	994	966	901	838	827	816	791	
B	26	25 [3]	22	17	23	28	23	22	21	
C	1	- [3]	1	1	1	1	1	2	1	
D	1 443	1 535 [3]	1 519	1 518	1 475	1 493	1 413	1 372	1 344	
E	9	11 [3]	14	11	12	13	13	16	19	
F	122	134 [3]	136	150	148	162	158	167	172	
G	1 732	1 774 [3]	1 847	1 865	1 832	1 795	1 755	1 721	1 677	
H	1 234	1 304 [3]	1 321	1 364	1 349	1 421	1 419	1 415	1 416	
I	122	150 [3]	156	155	167	183	201	198	182	
J	372	405 [3]	417	397	385	374	376	404	419	
K	347	419 [3]	476	529	527	590	677	745	828	
L	260	223 [3]	205	199	188	213	239	260	254	
M	659	730 [3]	768	844	956	991	1 046	1 125	1 143	
N	261	304 [3]	349	394	385	419	476	505	546	
O	442	524 [3]	565	596	566	713	771	800	851	
P	197	183 [3]	200	212	188	121	126	135	157	
Q	-	1 [3]	2	3	7	7	6	5	3	

Kyrgyzstan (BA) [2] [4] — Total employment - Emploi total - Empleo total

Total - Total - Total
ISIC 3 - CITI 3 - CIIU 3

	1999	2000	2001	2002	2003	2004	2005	2006	2007	2008
Total	.	.	.	1 850.1	1 930.5	1 991.2	2 077.1	2 096.1	2 152.7	.
A-B	.	.	.	908.2	834.7	774.6	799.7	760.2	742.3	.
C-E	.	.	.	161.7	187.7	206.0	211.5	225.3	231.2	.
F	.	.	.	60.2	102.2	144.0	153.7	181.4	205.3	.
G-I	.	.	.	335.5	389.6	438.9	466.2	477.7	508.5	.
J-K	.	.	.	37.7	38.4	47.0	42.3	46.0	55.5	.
L-P	.	.	.	346.7	378.0	380.6	403.7	405.5	409.9	.
Q	.	.	.	0.1	0.8	0.4	0.5	0.5		.

Men - Hommes - Hombres
ISIC 3 - CITI 3 - CIIU 3

	1999	2000	2001	2002	2003	2004	2005	2006	2007	2008
Total	.	.	.	1 051.4	1 083.8	1 140.7	1 195.9	1 214.4	.	.
A	.	.	.	518.0	470.0	445.4	470.2	448.2	.	.
B	.	.	.	1.5	0.3	0.2	0.2	0.1	.	.
C	.	.	.	7.1	11.1	12.1	11.3	11.2	.	.
D	.	.	.	76.3	72.9	79.0	90.5	97.2	.	.
E	.	.	.	23.2	27.3	30.0	27.4	29.3	.	.
F	.	.	.	56.1	94.5	136.1	145.4	174.3	.	.
G	.	.	.	119.2	132.1	144.1	154.1	156.7	.	.
H	.	.	.	11.2	11.3	14.2	17.1	14.9	.	.
I	.	.	.	75.0	82.2	95.8	96.5	100.7	.	.
J	.	.	.	3.9	4.7	3.7	3.7	4.2	.	.
K	.	.	.	18.9	17.6	25.1	18.6	19.7	.	.
L	.	.	.	62.0	70.4	64.2	67.4	64.3	.	.
M	.	.	.	37.7	46.1	44.2	44.6	40.0	.	.
N	.	.	.	19.9	18.3	19.9	20.3	19.8	.	.
O	.	.	.	20.5	18.4	20.4	23.7	24.7	.	.
P	.	.	.	1.0	6.2	6.2	4.9	9.0	.	.
Q	.	.	.	-	0.3	0.1	-	0.0	.	.

Women - Femmes - Mujeres
ISIC 3 - CITI 3 - CIIU 3

	1999	2000	2001	2002	2003	2004	2005	2006	2007	2008
Total	.	.	.	798.7	846.7	850.5	881.2	881.6	.	.
A	.	.	.	388.4	364.1	328.5	328.9	311.8	.	.
B	.	.	.	0.3	0.3	0.5	0.4	0.1	.	.
C	.	.	.	0.7	1.4	1.4	1.1	0.6	.	.
D	.	.	.	48.4	67.2	74.4	73.4	80.7	.	.
E	.	.	.	6.1	7.7	9.1	7.8	6.3	.	.
F	.	.	.	4.2	7.7	7.9	8.3	7.1	.	.
G	.	.	.	100.4	125.7	137.5	147.4	151.7	.	.
H	.	.	.	14.2	22.8	30.2	31.9	34.1	.	.
I	.	.	.	15.5	15.3	17.1	19.2	19.6	.	.
J	.	.	.	3.9	5.3	4.8	4.5	5.4	.	.
K	.	.	.	11.0	10.8	13.4	15.5	16.7	.	.
L	.	.	.	20.2	20.8	27.6	34.9	36.7	.	.
M	.	.	.	106.7	110.3	117.6	117.2	112.9	.	.
N	.	.	.	58.1	62.6	54.0	65.1	67.2	.	.
O	.	.	.	16.3	20.1	21.2	21.2	24.0	.	.
P	.	.	.	4.3	4.0	4.8	3.9	6.3	.	.
Q	.	.	.	0.1	0.5	0.3	0.5	0.5	.	.

Explanatory notes: see p. 77.

[1] Excl. armed forces. [2] Persons aged 15 years and over. [3] Estimates based on the 2000 Population Census results. [4] Nov. of each year.

Notes explicatives: voir p. 80.

[1] Non compris les forces armées. [2] Personnes âgées de 15 ans et plus. [3] Estimations basées sur les résultats du Recensement de la population de 2000. [4] Nov. de chaque année.

Notas explicativas: véase p. 83.

[1] Excl. las fuerzas armadas. [2] Personas de 15 años y más. [3] Estimaciones basadas en los resultados del Censo de población de 2000. [4] Nov. de cada año.

2B EMPLOYMENT — EMPLOI — EMPLEO

Total employment, by economic activity — **Emploi total, par activité économique** — **Empleo total, por actividad económica**

Thousands — Milliers — Millares

	1999	2000	2001	2002	2003	2004	2005	2006	2007	2008

Kyrgyzstan (E) — Total employment - Emploi total - Empleo total

Total - Total - Total
ISIC 3 - CITI 3 - CIIU 3

	1999	2000	2001	2002	2003	2004	2005	2006	2007	2008
Total	1 764.3	1 768.4	1 787.0	1 807.1	1 837.0	1 879.9	1 931.8	.	.	.
A	923.8	938.4	944.5	950.8	951.2	936.2	926.6	.	.	.
B	0.5	0.1	1.2	1.1	1.5	1.5	1.6	.	.	.
C	9.5	8.5	8.4	6.5	5.5	7.5	7.2	.	.	.
D	127.0	113.0	111.5	111.9	113.7	119.8	129.6	.	.	.
E	22.1	20.4	21.4	21.8	22.3	24.2	24.6	.	.	.
F	45.2	43.4	43.6	45.6	54.7	65.4	79.9	.	.	.
G	183.7	188.0	194.3	200.1	205.8	214.3	227.8	.	.	.
H	11.5	13.1	14.5	16.9	20.7	26.5	32.1	.	.	.
I	65.8	63.5	64.5	68.0	72.3	80.3	90.4	.	.	.
J	7.1	7.4	8.2	8.1	9.3	10.1	10.2	.	.	.
K	28.7	29.0	30.3	30.2	30.0	34.4	36.8	.	.	.
L	65.7	65.2	64.2	66.3	69.6	71.7	72.1	.	.	.
M	140.7	144.9	146.0	149.2	151.3	153.4	154.9	.	.	.
N	85.2	84.7	82.0	76.7	72.1	71.8	71.4	.	.	.
O	43.0	44.0	47.0	46.3	47.3	51.8	54.4	.	.	.
P	4.8	4.8	5.4	7.6	9.7	11.0	12.2	.	.	.

Macau, China (BA) [1][2] — Total employment - Emploi total - Empleo total

Total - Total - Total
ISIC 3 - CITI 3 - CIIU 3

	1999	2000	2001	2002	2003	2004	2005	2006	2007	2008
Total	196.1	195.3	205.0	204.9	205.4	219.1	237.5	265.1	300.4	323.0
A	0.1	0.1	-	0.1	0.1	0.2	0.1	0.2	0.1	.
B	0.1	0.3	0.2	0.2	0.5	0.5	0.2	0.3	0.1	.
A-C	.	.	.	.	.	.	.	.	.	0.6
C	-	-	-	0.1	-	.	.	.	.	.
D	42.7	38.0	44.6	42.0	37.7	36.1	35.3	29.5	24.0	24.6
E	1.1	0.8	1.0	1.2	1.3	1.1	1.2	0.9	1.2	0.9
F	16.2	16.2	17.1	15.3	16.4	18.1	22.9	31.1	38.6	38.4
G	30.4	30.1	30.5	31.4	33.2	35.2	35.3	36.4	38.4	39.6
H	21.0	21.1	22.7	23.6	22.4	24.1	24.9	30.0	34.7	41.3
I	14.5	14.6	14.7	13.1	14.4	15.0	14.8	16.8	16.4	16.0
J	5.8	6.9	6.1	6.3	6.3	6.2	6.6	6.9	7.9	7.5
K	9.3	10.5	10.8	11.0	12.0	12.6	14.3	16.3	20.1	23.8
L	16.3	16.4	16.2	17.4	18.1	18.1	18.8	20.3	22.0	20.2
M	8.7	8.0	8.2	10.2	9.8	10.6	10.3	11.3	11.9	11.5
N	5.0	5.2	5.1	4.3	4.7	5.0	5.3	5.4	6.0	6.5
O	19.3	21.5	22.4	23.5	23.9	31.3	40.8	52.5	69.1	78.9
P	5.4	5.3	4.9	4.8	4.3	5.0	6.2	6.9	9.6	13.3
Q	0.1	0.1	0.1	0.1	0.1	0.1	0.2	0.1	0.1	-
X	0.1	0.1	0.3	0.3	0.2	0.1	0.1	0.1	-	0.0

Men - Hommes - Hombres
ISIC 3 - CITI 3 - CIIU 3

	1999	2000	2001	2002	2003	2004	2005	2006	2007	2008
Total	104.2	103.2	108.0	106.4	108.3	115.2	124.3	141.6	160.5	172.3
A	.	-	0.0	0.1	-	0.1	-	0.1	-	.
B	0.1	0.2	0.1	0.1	0.4	0.3	0.2	0.2	0.1	.
A-C	.	.	.	.	.	.	.	.	.	0.3
C	-	0.0	-	0.1	-	.	.	.	.	.
D	13.2	11.9	13.2	12.9	11.8	11.4	11.8	10.5	8.7	11.5
E	0.9	0.7	0.9	1.0	1.0	0.9	1.0	0.8	1.0	0.6
F	15.0	14.7	15.7	14.0	14.8	16.1	20.5	27.8	33.9	33.7
G	16.8	16.9	17.1	17.2	17.4	18.6	18.5	17.8	19.3	19.3
H	10.7	10.2	11.7	11.4	11.8	11.9	11.5	14.6	16.7	20.5
I	10.9	11.0	10.6	9.5	10.6	11.2	11.0	12.0	11.8	11.8
J	2.6	3.3	2.8	2.9	2.6	2.6	2.8	2.9	3.1	2.8
K	6.4	6.9	7.4	7.4	7.7	8.1	9.0	9.9	11.7	14.5
L	11.7	11.8	11.6	12.2	12.5	12.6	12.6	14.0	14.2	13.0
M	2.8	2.5	2.5	3.1	3.1	3.3	3.0	3.7	3.8	3.5
N	1.6	1.7	1.8	1.4	1.5	1.5	1.4	1.4	1.7	2.0
O	11.1	10.9	12.2	12.5	12.8	16.3	20.5	25.6	33.9	38.3
P	0.2	0.4	0.3	0.3	0.2	0.4	0.3	0.3	0.5	0.3
Q	-	-	0.1	-	0.1	-	0.1	-	-	-
X	-	-	0.1	0.2	0.1	-	0.1	-	-	0.0

Explanatory notes: see p. 77.

[1] Persons aged 14 years and over. [2] Excl. armed forces and conscripts.

Notes explicatives: voir p. 80.

[1] Personnes âgées de 14 ans et plus. [2] Non compris les forces armées et les conscrits.

Notas explicativas: véase p. 83.

[1] Personas de 14 años y más. [2] Excl. las fuerzas armadas y los conscriptos.

Total employment, by economic activity
Emploi total, par activité économique
Empleo total, por actividad económica

Thousands — Milliers — Millares

	1999	2000	2001	2002	2003	2004	2005	2006	2007	2008
Macau, China (BA) [1][2]					Total employment - Emploi total - Empleo total					
Women - Femmes - Mujeres										
ISIC 3 - CITI 3 - CIIU 3										
Total	91.9	92.1	96.9	98.5	97.1	103.9	113.2	123.5	139.8	150.7
A	-	-	-	0.1	-	0.1	0.1	0.2	0.1	.
B	-	0.1	0.1	0.1	0.1	0.1	0.1	0.1	-	.
A-C	.	.	.	.	.	.	.	.	.	0.3
C	0.0	-	0.0	0.0	0.0	0.0	0.0	0.0	0.0	.
D	29.5	26.1	31.4	29.1	25.9	24.7	23.5	19.1	15.4	13.1
E	0.2	0.1	0.2	0.2	0.3	0.2	0.2	0.1	0.2	0.2
F	1.3	1.6	1.4	1.3	1.6	2.0	2.5	3.2	4.7	4.7
G	13.6	13.2	13.4	14.2	15.7	16.7	16.8	18.6	19.1	20.3
H	10.2	10.9	10.9	12.2	10.7	12.2	13.4	15.4	18.1	20.8
I	3.6	3.7	4.1	3.6	3.9	3.8	3.8	4.8	4.5	4.2
J	3.1	3.6	3.4	3.5	3.7	3.6	3.8	4.0	4.8	4.7
K	2.9	3.6	3.5	3.6	4.3	4.5	5.3	6.4	8.5	9.3
L	4.5	4.6	4.6	5.1	5.6	5.5	6.2	6.4	7.8	7.2
M	6.0	5.5	5.7	7.0	6.7	7.2	7.4	7.7	8.1	7.9
N	3.4	3.5	3.3	2.9	3.2	3.6	3.9	4.1	4.3	4.4
O	8.2	10.6	10.1	11.0	11.1	15.0	20.2	26.9	35.2	40.6
P	5.2	4.9	4.5	4.5	4.1	4.6	5.9	6.6	9.1	12.9
Q	-	-	0.1	0.1	-	-	0.1	0.1	0.1	-
X	-	-	0.2	0.1	0.1	0.1	-	-	-	0.0
Malaysia (BA) [3][4]					Total employment - Emploi total - Empleo total					
Total - Total - Total										
ISIC 3 - CITI 3 - CIIU 3										
Total	.	.	9 357.0	9 542.6	9 869.7	9 979.5	10 045.4	10 275.4	10 538.1	10 659.6
A	.	.	1 288.2	1 316.8	1 301.2	1 326.5	1 355.2	1 375.3	1 437.3	1 365.6
B	.	.	127.7	107.7	107.0	126.1	115.2	128.2	120.9	122.1
C	.	.	26.7	27.5	29.5	34.7	36.1	42.0	39.4	54.5
D	.	.	2 184.1	2 068.9	2 131.0	2 023.0	1 989.3	2 082.8	1 977.3	1 944.7
E	.	.	57.3	50.6	57.6	57.9	56.6	75.4	60.8	60.5
F	.	.	829.8	905.1	942.5	890.8	904.4	908.9	922.5	998.0
G	.	.	1 458.1	1 497.0	1 592.2	1 607.2	1 620.3	1 650.5	1 712.1	1 729.4
H	.	.	585.1	616.1	644.2	698.2	671.8	721.3	760.7	783.6
I	.	.	468.3	496.8	481.6	532.9	544.7	539.7	538.2	583.4
J	.	.	225.3	240.5	223.4	236.1	247.4	242.3	282.2	276.0
K	.	.	348.6	397.1	404.2	458.5	459.0	508.4	558.1	553.2
L	.	.	664.6	663.6	666.5	684.3	728.5	674.1	716.1	751.1
M	.	.	508.6	508.6	594.3	610.7	607.1	600.1	632.7	656.5
N	.	.	173.3	189.3	217.3	198.2	212.6	223.2	238.9	252.6
O	.	.	190.4	192.5	216.1	231.3	234.9	247.1	266.5	274.2
P	.	.	219.9	262.7	258.0	260.9	260.6	254.6	272.7	253.0
Q	.	.	1.2	2.0	3.2	2.2	1.7	1.2	1.7	1.1
Men - Hommes - Hombres										
ISIC 3 - CITI 3 - CIIU 3										
Total	.	.	6 055.9	6 141.8	6 323.6	6 390.4	6 470.5	6 618.6	6 747.1	6 851.1
A	.	.	895.1	924.9	915.1	952.3	996.6	1 013.9	1 064.5	1 027.5
B	.	.	123.6	104.0	103.1	123.2	110.3	123.2	115.4	117.4
C	.	.	22.9	24.9	26.7	32.4	31.5	35.9	33.7	44.6
D	.	.	1 276.3	1 215.5	1 255.9	1 205.7	1 201.5	1 270.4	1 196.6	1 182.6
E	.	.	49.4	44.5	48.7	50.7	49.0	63.4	52.0	50.1
F	.	.	769.1	839.8	876.5	824.8	832.1	834.4	854.5	914.7
G	.	.	982.8	1 000.4	1 050.0	1 054.8	1 063.5	1 081.0	1 120.2	1 119.5
H	.	.	312.1	317.9	339.5	354.6	349.3	385.5	397.7	403.4
I	.	.	403.0	427.6	410.3	452.2	464.9	449.9	450.2	487.0
J	.	.	119.2	122.6	118.7	118.1	120.3	120.5	142.2	134.2
K	.	.	212.3	239.7	249.4	281.2	284.8	317.8	343.5	342.7
L	.	.	505.7	487.1	491.1	501.6	525.8	486.5	514.6	536.4
M	.	.	201.7	198.5	229.8	224.6	219.6	209.7	221.7	226.1
N	.	.	54.7	63.3	69.3	63.1	69.8	70.6	74.9	76.2
O	.	.	113.6	113.9	120.9	135.6	134.0	135.2	144.9	158.4
P	.	.	13.9	16.2	16.5	13.8	16.1	19.6	19.5	29.4
Q	.	.	0.6	1.1	2.2	1.8	1.3	1.0	1.0	0.9

Explanatory notes: see p. 77.

[1] Persons aged 14 years and over. [2] Excl. armed forces and conscripts. [3] Persons aged 15 to 64 years. [4] Excl. armed forces.

Notes explicatives: voir p. 80.

[1] Personnes âgées de 14 ans et plus. [2] Non compris les forces armées et les conscrits. [3] Personnes âgées de 15 à 64 ans. [4] Non compris les forces armées.

Notas explicativas: véase p. 83.

[1] Personas de 14 años y más. [2] Excl. las fuerzas armadas y los conscriptos. [3] Personas de 15 a 64 años. [4] Excl. las fuerzas armadas.

2B

EMPLOYMENT   **EMPLOI**   **EMPLEO**

Total employment, by economic activity   **Emploi total, par activité économique**   **Empleo total, por actividad económica**

Thousands   Milliers   Millares

	1999	2000	2001	2002	2003	2004	2005	2006	2007	2008
Malaysia (BA) [1] [2]				Total employment - Emploi total - Empleo total						
Women - Femmes - Mujeres										
ISIC 3 - CITI 3 - CIIU 3										
Total	.	.	3 301.1	3 400.8	3 546.1	3 589.1	3 574.8	3 656.8	3 791.0	3 808.5
A	.	.	393.1	391.9	386.1	374.3	358.6	361.4	372.8	338.2
B	.	.	4.1	3.7	3.9	2.9	4.9	5.0	5.4	4.7
C	.	.	3.8	2.6	2.9	2.3	4.5	6.1	5.7	9.8
D	.	.	907.8	853.4	875.1	817.3	787.8	812.4	780.7	762.2
E	.	.	7.9	6.1	9.0	7.2	7.6	12.0	8.8	10.3
F	.	.	60.7	65.3	66.0	65.9	72.3	74.5	68.0	83.4
G	.	.	475.2	496.6	542.2	552.4	556.8	569.6	592.0	609.9
H	.	.	273.0	298.2	304.7	343.6	322.5	335.8	363.0	380.2
I	.	.	65.2	69.2	71.3	80.7	79.7	89.8	88.0	96.3
J	.	.	106.2	117.8	104.7	118.1	127.0	121.8	140.0	141.8
K	.	.	136.7	157.4	154.8	177.3	174.2	190.6	214.7	210.6
L	.	.	158.9	176.5	175.4	182.8	202.8	187.6	201.5	214.7
M	.	.	306.9	310.2	364.5	386.1	387.4	390.4	411.0	430.4
N	.	.	118.6	126.0	148.0	135.1	142.8	152.6	164.0	176.5
O	.	.	76.8	78.6	95.2	95.6	100.9	111.9	121.7	115.8
P	.	.	206.0	246.5	241.6	247.1	244.5	235.0	253.2	223.6
Q	.	.	0.5	0.9	1.0	0.4	0.4	0.2	0.7	0.2
Mongolia (E) [3] [4]				Total employment - Emploi total - Empleo total						
Total - Total - Total										
ISIC 3 - CITI 3 - CIIU 3										
Total	813.6	809.0	832.3	870.8	926.5	950.5	968.3	1 009.9	1 024.1	1 041.7
A-B	402.6	393.5	402.4	391.4	387.5	381.8	386.2	391.4	385.6	377.6
C	19.0	18.6	19.9	23.8	31.9	33.5	39.8	41.9	44.1	46.5
D	58.5	54.6	55.6	55.6	54.9	57.3	45.6	47.0	47.9	47.5
E	21.3	17.8	17.8	19.8	22.7	23.4	28.5	30.0	31.1	30.1
F	27.6	23.4	20.4	25.5	35.1	39.2	48.9	56.3	60.0	66.8
G	83.1	83.9	90.3	104.5	129.7	133.7	141.9	160.6	162.2	169.7
H	16.1	13.3	16.5	20.9	23.3	28.4	29.5	31.0	32.4	34.5
I	34.9	34.1	35.1	38.8	39.5	42.2	42.4	41.2	44.1	46.3
J	7.7	6.8	7.3	9.4	12.6	15.9	16.1	16.8	17.4	19.8
K	5.0	7.2	6.8	10.9	9.3	11.2	9.0	12.0	14.5	12.0
L	31.5	34.7	41.0	43.9	44.8	46.2	46.7	46.9	48.5	50.9
M	43.2	54.4	55.2	59.3	55.3	57.8	58.8	62.0	64.8	66.2
N	34.8	33.5	33.0	34.5	36.8	39.4	39.5	39.3	40.2	42.3
O	25.2	29.0	26.9	27.5	37.0	34.5	26.7	22.9	19.7	19.7
P	3.1	4.2	4.1	5.0	6.1	6.0	8.7	10.6	11.6	11.8
Men - Hommes - Hombres										
ISIC 3 - CITI 3 - CIIU 3										
Total	426.9	416.9	424.6	440.2	468.8	467.1	479.4	491.8	504.2	512.7
A-B	215.8	211.0	212.8	208.8	205.3	200.2	206.3	207.0	204.6	200.6
C	13.8	13.1	14.1	17.0	21.9	23.3	26.1	26.8	29.5	29.9
D	34.3	32.3	30.3	25.2	24.7	26.6	21.9	21.4	21.9	22.7
E	14.3	11.0	12.2	12.1	14.3	14.6	15.9	16.3	18.2	18.2
F	16.3	13.7	12.8	13.7	20.2	22.3	26.5	31.4	34.2	38.2
G	43.6	38.8	39.2	46.1	60.0	53.7	59.3	64.5	65.7	66.9
H	4.8	3.7	6.4	8.7	8.1	10.0	10.3	10.3	10.8	11.9
I	21.8	19.2	22.1	21.0	22.6	24.8	26.0	25.8	28.8	30.2
J	2.8	2.5	2.8	4.2	5.4	6.2	6.3	6.8	7.1	7.9
K	2.7	3.4	2.9	6.2	5.3	5.4	4.3	6.0	6.8	5.8
L	17.7	19.2	23.7	26.7	27.0	26.1	26.1	26.2	27.3	29.0
M	14.5	20.7	19.6	21.8	20.3	20.3	20.4	20.4	20.9	21.6
N	10.6	10.8	9.5	11.6	12.0	13.6	12.6	12.4	12.7	13.9
O	12.3	15.1	13.8	14.6	18.5	16.9	13.7	11.8	10.3	10.0
P	1.6	2.4	2.4	2.5	3.2	3.1	3.7	5.0	5.4	5.9
Women - Femmes - Mujeres										
ISIC 3 - CITI 3 - CIIU 3										
Total	386.7	392.1	407.7	430.6	457.7	483.4	488.9	518.1	519.9	529.0
A-B	186.8	182.5	189.6	182.6	182.2	181.6	179.9	184.4	181.0	177.0
C	5.2	5.5	5.8	6.8	10.0	10.2	13.7	15.1	14.6	16.6
D	24.2	22.3	25.3	30.4	30.2	30.7	23.7	25.6	26.0	24.8
E	7.0	6.8	5.6	7.7	8.4	8.8	12.6	13.7	12.9	11.9
F	11.3	9.7	7.6	11.8	14.9	16.9	22.4	24.9	25.8	28.6
G	39.5	45.1	51.1	58.4	69.7	80.0	82.5	96.1	96.5	102.8
H	11.3	9.6	10.1	12.2	15.2	18.4	19.2	20.7	21.6	22.6
I	13.1	14.9	13.0	17.8	16.9	17.6	16.4	15.4	15.3	16.1
J	4.9	4.3	4.5	5.2	7.2	9.7	9.8	10.0	10.3	11.9
K	2.3	3.8	3.9	4.7	4.0	5.8	4.7	6.0	7.7	6.2
L	13.8	15.5	17.3	17.2	17.8	20.1	20.6	20.7	21.2	21.9
M	28.7	33.7	35.6	37.5	35.0	37.5	38.4	41.6	43.9	44.6
N	24.2	22.7	23.5	22.9	24.8	25.8	26.9	26.9	27.5	28.4
O	12.9	13.9	13.1	12.9	18.5	17.6	13.0	11.1	9.4	9.7
P	1.5	1.8	1.7	2.5	2.9	2.9	5.0	5.6	6.2	5.9

Explanatory notes; see p. 77.

[1] Persons aged 15 to 64 years. [2] Excl. armed forces. [3] Persons aged 16 years and over. [4] Dec. of each year.

Notes explicatives: voir p. 80.

[1] Personnes âgées de 15 à 64 ans. [2] Non compris les forces armées. [3] Personnes âgées de 16 ans et plus. [4] Déc. de chaque année.

Notas explicativas: véase p. 83.

[1] Personas de 15 a 64 años. [2] Excl. las fuerzas armadas. [3] Personas de 16 años y más. [4] Dic. de cada año.

EMPLOYMENT — EMPLOI — EMPLEO

2B

Total employment, by economic activity
Emploi total, par activité économique
Empleo total, por actividad económica

Thousands — Milliers — Millares

Pakistan (BA) [1] [2] [3]

Total employment - Emploi total - Empleo total

Total - Total - Total — ISIC 2 - CITI 2 - CIIU 2

	1999	2000	2001	2002	2003	2004	2005	2006	2007	2008
Total	37 296	36 847	37 481	38 882	39 852	42 009	42 816	46 952	47 651	.
1	17 623	17 841	18 148	16 366	16 774	18 084	18 431	20 364	20 780	.
2	72	25		26	27	28	29	43	52	.
3	3 714	4 230	4 302	5 380	5 514	5 770	5 881	6 499	6 454	.
4	260	259	264	313	321	282	287	308	360	.
5	2 336	2 130	2 167	2 353	2 412	2 449	2 496	2 880	3 127	.
6	5 173	4 976	5 062	5 776	5 920	6 216	6 336	6 886	6 872	.
7	2 045	1 853	1 885	2 295	2 352	2 409	2 455	2 697	2 569	.
8	324	301	306	346	355	444	453	518	544	.
9	5 732	5 231	5 321	6 027	6 177	6 306	6 427	6 739	6 868	.
0	17	1	1	-	-	21	21	18	25	.

Men - Hommes - Hombres — ISIC 2 - CITI 2 - CIIU 2

	1999	2000	2001	2002	2003	2004	2005	2006	2007	2008
Total	32 099	31 688	32 233	33 189	34 017	34 903	35 573	37 808	38 118	.
1	14 011	14 080	14 323	12 687	13 003	13 299	13 554	14 069	13 882	.
2	66	24	23	25	26	26	27	41	51	.
3	3 257	3 797	3 862	4 517	4 630	4 727	4 816	5 170	5 309	.
4	253	255	260	308	316	279	284	306	354	.
5	2 304	2 105	2 141	2 335	2 394	2 431	2 478	2 843	3 075	.
6	5 081	4 844	4 927	5 669	5 810	6 098	6 216	6 694	6 660	.
7	2 014	1 841	1 873	2 273	2 329	2 399	2 445	2 667	2 550	.
8	311	291	296	342	351	439	448	501	531	.
9	4 785	4 450	4 527	5 033	5 158	5 185	5 284	5 498	5 682	.
0	17	1	1	-	-	21	21	18	24	.

Women - Femmes - Mujeres — ISIC 2 - CITI 2 - CIIU 2

	1999	2000	2001	2002	2003	2004	2005	2006	2007	2008
Total	5 197	5 159	5 248	5 693	5 835	7 106	7 243	9 144	9 533	.
1	3 612	3 761	3 825	3 679	3 771	4 785	4 877	6 295	6 898	.
2	6	1	2	1	1	2	2	1	1	.
3	457	433	440	863	884	1 044	1 065	1 329	1 145	.
4	7	4	4	5	5	3	3	2	6	.
5	32	25	26	18	18	18	18	37	52	.
6	92	132	135	107	110	118	120	192	212	.
7	31	12	12	22	23	10	10	30	19	.
8	13	10	10	4	4	5	5	17	13	.
9	947	781	794	994	1 019	1 121	1 143	1 241	1 186	.
0	-	-	-	-	-	-	-	-	1	.

Philippines (BA) [4] [5]

Total employment - Emploi total - Empleo total

Total - Total - Total — ISIC 2 - CITI 2 - CIIU 2 [6] / ISIC 3 - CITI 3 - CIIU 3

ISIC 2	1999	2000	2001	2002	2003	2004	2005	2006	2007	2008	ISIC 3
Total	27 742	27 452	29 156	30 062	30 635	31 613	32 313	32 636	33 560	34 089	Total
1	10 774	10 181	9 716	9 963	9 956	10 013	10 234	10 254	10 342	10 604	A
2	97	108	1 134	1 159	1 264	1 368	1 394	1 428	1 444	1 426	B
3	2 759	2 745	103	113	104	118	123	139	149	158	C
4	140	122	2 906	2 869	2 941	3 061	3 077	3 053	3 059	2 926	D
5	1 519	1 479	119	117	112	120	117	128	135	130	E
6 [7]	4 353	4 484	1 585	1 596	1 683	1 700	1 708	1 677	1 778	1 834	F
7	1 907	1 986	5 255	5 613	5 601	5 872	6 147	6 202	6 354	6 446	G
8	713	711	668	693	750	806	861	887	907	953	H
9 [8]	5 472	5 630	2 118	2 162	2 310	2 427	2 451	2 483	2 599	2 590	I
0	7	6	292	312	303	328	341	344	359	368	J
			516	544	639	690	734	783	885	953	K
			1 382	1 442	1 415	1 491	1 481	1 485	1 551	1 676	L
			920	935	926	938	978	999	1 035	1 071	M
			314	348	371	361	375	359	373	391	N
			906	881	861	835	775	801	849	833	O
			1 218	1 313	1 399	1 487	1 517	1 612	1 740	1 729	P
			4	3	2	2	1	2	2	2	Q

Explanatory notes: see p. 77.

[1] Excl. armed forces. [2] Persons aged 10 years and over. [3] Jan. [4] Persons aged 15 years and over. [5] Excl. regular military living in barracks. [6] Oct. of each year. [7] Excl. restaurants and hotels. [8] Incl. restaurants and hotels.

Notes explicatives: voir p. 80.

[1] Non compris les forces armées. [2] Personnes âgées de 10 ans et plus. [3] Janv. [4] Personnes âgées de 15 ans et plus. [5] Non compris les militaires de carrière vivant dans des casernes. [6] Oct. de chaque année. [7] Non compris les restaurants et hôtels. [8] Y compris les restaurants et hôtels.

Notas explicativas: véase p. 83.

[1] Excl. las fuerzas armadas. [2] Personas de 10 años y más. [3] Enero. [4] Personas de 15 años y más. [5] Excl. los militares profesionales que viven en casernas. [6] Oct. de cada año. [7] Excl. restaurantes y hoteles. [8] Incl. restaurantes y hoteles.

Total employment, by economic activity   **Emploi total, par activité économique**   **Empleo total, por actividad económica**

Thousands — Milliers — Millares

	1999	2000	2001	2002	2003	2004	2005	2006	2007	2008	

Philippines (BA) [1] [2]   Total employment - Emploi total - Empleo total

Men - Hommes - Hombres
ISIC 2 - CITI 2 - CIIU 2 [3]   ISIC 3 - CITI 3 - CIIU 3

	1999	2000	2001	2002	2003	2004	2005	2006	2007	2008	
Total	17 253	17 193	17 923	18 306	18 873	19 646	19 910	20 013	20 542	20 959	Total
1	7 932	7 733	7 024	7 114	7 182	7 316	7 393	7 382	7 437	7 666	A
2	90	99	1 061	1 091	1 175	1 272	1 294	1 327	1 327	1 316	B
3	1 458	1 442	95	100	96	107	109	124	135	146	C
4	117	99	1 558	1 541	1 593	1 692	1 660	1 653	1 684	1 622	D
5	1 497	1 451	99	98	93	99	98	107	112	110	E
6 [4]	1 579	1 597	1 549	1 570	1 649	1 670	1 672	1 648	1 742	1 798	F
7	1 799	1 884	1 985	2 115	2 165	2 306	2 452	2 464	2 526	2 565	G
8	412	406	288	306	332	358	395	402	409	436	H
9 [5]	2 364	2 479	2 016	2 062	2 198	2 307	2 318	2 329	2 428	2 425	I
0	6	5	121	133	133	147	143	148	156	156	J
			330	348	439	478	501	508	578	624	K
			849	893	884	943	934	927	950	1 023	L
			252	231	226	231	236	249	259	269	M
			85	102	91	96	97	99	101	114	N
			426	415	420	418	381	405	434	426	O
			186	187	199	209	228	239	262	262	P
			2	1	1	1	1	1	2	1	Q

Women - Femmes - Mujeres
ISIC 2 - CITI 2 - CIIU 2 [3]   ISIC 3 - CITI 3 - CIIU 3

	1999	2000	2001	2002	2003	2004	2005	2006	2007	2008	
Total	10 489	10 259	11 232	11 756	11 762	11 968	12 403	12 622	13 018	13 129	Total
1	2 843	2 448	2 692	2 850	2 774	2 697	2 842	2 872	2 905	2 937	A
2	8	9	73	67	89	95	100	101	117	110	B
3	1 302	1 303	9	13	8	11	14	14	14	12	C
4	22	23	1 348	1 328	1 348	1 369	1 417	1 400	1 375	1 304	D
5	22	29	20	18	19	21	19	21	23	20	E
6 [4]	2 774	2 887	36	27	35	30	36	29	36	36	F
7	109	102	3 270	3 498	3 436	3 566	3 695	3 738	3 828	3 880	G
8	302	306	380	387	419	449	466	484	498	518	H
9 [5]	3 108	3 151	102	100	113	120	132	154	170	165	I
0	1	1	171	179	171	181	198	196	203	211	J
			186	196	200	212	234	275	307	329	K
			533	549	531	548	548	558	601	653	L
			668	704	700	707	742	750	776	802	M
			229	247	280	266	279	260	272	277	N
			480	466	441	417	394	396	415	407	O
			1 033	1 127	1 200	1 278	1 289	1 374	1 478	1 467	P
			2	2	2	1	1	-	1	-	Q

Philippines (CA) [6]   Total employment - Emploi total - Empleo total

Total - Total - Total
ISIC 3 - CITI 3 - CIIU 3

	1999	2001	2003	2005
Total	2 853.9	2 418.9	2 428.8	2 742.8
A	113.0	96.4	98.4	104.6
B	21.6	17.9	18.9	20.4
C	14.6	11.4	10.8	10.3
D	1 089.8	937.3	986.9	1 025.8
E	61.5	59.7	62.0	65.9
F	138.0	131.2	97.1	92.3
G	410.4	287.6	256.9	318.4
H	140.4	120.4	116.8	159.2
I	192.5	156.4	144.8	153.4
J	124.9	101.4	123.5	132.2
K	253.3	214.4	224.4	325.8
M [7]	189.1	183.0	186.4	206.7
N [8]	55.6	54.3	55.1	73.5
O	49.1	47.4	46.7	54.3

Men - Hommes - Hombres
ISIC 3 - CITI 3 - CIIU 3

	1999	2001	2003	2005
Total	1 683.7	1 413.5	1 393.9	1 552.4
A	93.2	79.4	80.4	83.2
B	20.3	16.8	17.7	18.9
C	13.4	10.5	10.0	9.5
D	562.5	469.1	496.4	513.1
E	50.4	48.6	50.5	53.9
F	129.4	123.1	90.2	82.3
G	225.9	162.0	139.0	178.8
H	83.6	71.2	69.4	96.5
I	148.9	121.3	110.1	115.5
J	52.4	42.3	49.0	52.3
K	187.6	156.8	165.6	216.6
M [7]	68.4	64.6	67.4	75.0
N [8]	16.7	16.7	18.2	22.8
O	31.1	31.2	29.9	34.1

Explanatory notes: see p. 77.

[1] Persons aged 15 years and over. [2] Excl. regular military living in barracks. [3] Oct. of each year. [4] Excl. restaurants and hotels. [5] Incl. restaurants and hotels. [6] Establishments with 20 or more persons employed. [7] Private education only. [8] Excludes public medical, dental and other health services.

Notes explicatives: voir p. 80.

[1] Personnes âgées de 15 ans et plus. [2] Non compris les militaires de carrière vivant dans des casernes. [3] Oct. de chaque année. [4] Non compris les restaurants et hôtels. [5] Y compris les restaurants et hôtels. [6] Etablissements occupant 20 personnes et plus. [7] Education privée seulement. [8] Non compris les services publics médicaux, dentaires et autres services de santé.

Notas explicativas: véase p. 83.

[1] Personas de 15 años y más. [2] Excl. los militares profesionales que viven en casernas. [3] Oct. de cada año. [4] Excl. restaurantes y hoteles. [5] Incl. restaurantes y hoteles. [6] Establecimientos con 20 y más trabajadores. [7] Educación privada solamente. [8] Excl. los servicios públicos médicos, dentales y otros servicios de salud.

Total employment, by economic activity
Emploi total, par activité économique
Empleo total, por actividad económica

	Thousands				Milliers				Millares		
	1999	2000	2001	2002	2003	2004	2005	2006	2007	2008

Philippines (CA) [1]

Total employment - Emploi total - Empleo total

Women - Femmes - Mujeres
ISIC 3 - CITI 3 - CIIU 3

	1999	2000	2001	2002	2003	2004	2005	2006	2007	2008
Total	1 170.1 *	.	1 005.4	.	1 034.9	.	1 190.4	.	.	.
A	19.8		17.1		18.1		21.5			
B	1.3		1.2		1.2		1.5			
C	1.2		1.0		0.8		0.7			
D	527.4		468.2		490.5		512.7			
E	11.1		11.1		11.5		12.0			
F	8.6		8.2		6.9		9.9			
G	184.5		125.6		117.9		139.7			
H	56.8		49.2		47.4		62.7			
I	43.6		35.0		34.6		38.0			
J	72.5		59.1		74.6		79.9			
K	65.7		57.6		58.8		109.3			
M [2]	120.8		118.4		119.0		131.7			
N [3]	38.9		37.6		36.9		50.7			
O	18.0		16.2		16.8		20.2			

Qatar (BA) [4] [5]

Total employment - Emploi total - Empleo total

Total - Total - Total
ISIC 3 - CITI 3 - CIIU 3

	1999	2000	2001	2002	2003	2004	2005	2006	2007	2008
Total	.	.	310.291	.	.	.	.	529.304	827.583	.
A	.	.	5.165	.	.	.	.	12.463	15.854	.
B	.	.	1.909	.	.	.	.	3.247	3.581	.
C	.	.	13.138	.	.	.	.	27.199	43.650	.
D	.	.	41.041	.	.	.	.	62.641	71.893	.
E	.	.	4.951	.	.	.	.	4.678	5.498	.
F	.	.	59.286	.	.	.	.	125.510	307.381	.
G	.	.	35.643	.	.	.	.	69.987	101.608	.
H	.	.	6.969	.	.	.	.	15.010	16.209	.
I	.	.	9.860	.	.	.	.	23.784	35.874	.
J	.	.	3.973	.	.	.	.	6.190	9.024	.
K	.	.	6.159	.	.	.	.	15.919	28.405	.
L	.	.	43.785	.	.	.	.	46.982	52.544	.
M	.	.	15.245	.	.	.	.	22.791	26.164	.
N	.	.	5.920	.	.	.	.	16.691	21.130	.
O	.	.	9.877	.	.	.	.	12.085	12.738	.
P	.	.	45.040	.	.	.	.	62.497	72.780	.
Q	.	.	0.476	.	.	.	.	1.630	1.731	.
X	.	.	1.855 [6]	.	.	.	.	.	1.519	.

Men - Hommes - Hombres
ISIC 3 - CITI 3 - CIIU 3

	1999	2000	2001	2002	2003	2004	2005	2006	2007	2008
Total	.	.	266.371	.	.	.	.	452.599	726.752	.
A	.	.	5.165	.	.	.	.	12.463	15.854	.
B	.	.	1.909	.	.	.	.	3.247	3.581	.
C	.	.	12.180	.	.	.	.	25.886	41.297	.
D	.	.	40.956	.	.	.	.	61.974	70.981	.
E	.	.	4.896	.	.	.	.	4.440	5.099	.
F	.	.	59.030	.	.	.	.	124.740	306.235	.
G	.	.	34.575	.	.	.	.	67.645	98.262	.
H	.	.	6.835	.	.	.	.	13.864	14.141	.
I	.	.	9.106	.	.	.	.	21.028	32.804	.
J	.	.	3.361	.	.	.	.	4.541	6.451	.
K	.	.	6.071	.	.	.	.	15.097	27.277	.
L	.	.	40.304	.	.	.	.	40.630	45.162	.
M	.	.	5.812	.	.	.	.	7.642	9.462	.
N	.	.	3.190	.	.	.	.	8.152	8.191	.
O	.	.	9.314	.	.	.	.	10.045	10.263	.
P	.	.	21.771	.	.	.	.	29.736	28.973	.
Q	.	.	0.356	.	.	.	.	1.469	1.535	.
X	.	.	1.543 [6]	.	.	.	.	.	1.184	.

Explanatory notes: see p. 77.

[1] Establishments with 20 or more persons employed. [2] Private education only. [3] Excludes public medical, dental and other health services. [4] Persons aged 15 years and over. [5] March of each year. [6] Persons temporary absent from work.

Notes explicatives: voir p. 80.

[1] Etablissements occupant 20 personnes et plus. [2] Education privée seulement. [3] Non compris les services publics médicaux, dentaires et autres services de santé. [4] Personnes âgées de 15 ans et plus. [5] Mars de chaque année. [6] Personnes temporairement absentes de leur travail.

Notas explicativas: véase p. 83.

[1] Establecimientos con 20 y más trabajadores. [2] Educación privada solamente. [3] Excl. los servicios públicos médicos, dentales y otros servicios de salud. [4] Personas de 15 años y más. [5] Marzo de cada año. [6] Personas temporalment ausentes de su trabajo.

Total employment,   **Emploi total,**   **Empleo total,**
by economic activity   **par activité économique**   **por actividad económica**

	Thousands				Milliers				Millares	
	1999	2000	2001	2002	2003	2004	2005	2006	2007	2008

Qatar (BA) [1] [2]   Total employment - Emploi total - Empleo total

Women - Femmes - Mujeres
ISIC 3 - CITI 3 - CIIU 3

	1999	2000	2001	2002	2003	2004	2005	2006	2007	2008
Total			43.920					76.705	100.831	
A										
B										
C			0.958					1.313	2.353	
D			0.085					0.667	0.912	
E			0.055					0.238	0.399	
F			0.257					0.770	1.146	
G			1.068					2.342	3.346	
H			0.134					1.146	2.068	
I			0.754					2.756	3.070	
J			0.612					1.649	2.573	
K			0.088					0.822	1.128	
L			3.481					6.352	7.382	
M			9.433					15.149	16.702	
N			2.730					8.539	12.939	
O			0.563					2.040	2.475	
P			23.269					32.761	43.807	
Q			0.119					0.161	0.196	
X			0.313 [3]						0.335	

Saudi Arabia (BA) [1]   Total employment - Emploi total - Empleo total

Total - Total - Total
ISIC 3 - CITI 3 - CIIU 3

	1999	2000	2001	2002	2003	2004	2005	2006	2007	2008
Total	5 592.854	5 713.345	5 808.617	5 913.010				7 522.984 [4]	7 766.350	7 956.832
A-B								299.5 [4]	364.2	382.4
A	339.2	341.5	340.2	263.4						
B	11.0	7.9	9.1	12.2						
C	88.925	101.879	87.909	95.390				102.178 [4]	102.807	107.688
D	441.726	440.651	467.785	448.283				505.107 [4]	565.774	508.844
E	74.970	76.020	77.329	65.648				79.466 [4]	74.381	66.902
F	566.722	515.931	585.342	629.569				836.898 [4]	793.586	745.774
G	846.509	901.485	837.224	861.741				1 210.079 [4]	1 250.270	1 257.941
H	140.512	164.595	154.606	170.349				241.378 [4]	248.697	279.128
I	236.007	242.294	247.887	265.283				291.290 [4]	343.552	361.909
J	49.294	42.530	58.536	49.803				86.571 [4]	83.787	86.003
K	147.027	139.470	144.279	143.248				252.603 [4]	250.247	313.469
L	1 072.793	1 116.194	1 157.546	1 212.865				1 425.995 [4]	1 400.092	1 502.913
M	703.168	712.965	720.065	751.523				907.173 [4]	929.199	932.507
N	229.094	217.644	278.142	223.977				325.494 [4]	335.921	365.459
O	127.398	133.016	101.902	115.415				169.152 [4]	175.877	163.050
P	508.767	550.966	521.391	595.930				781.540 [4]	838.126	876.596
Q	6.342	5.282	6.807	8.365				8.566 [4]	9.850	6.277
X	3.373	3.306	12.477	-				- [4]	-	-

Men - Hommes - Hombres
ISIC 3 - CITI 3 - CIIU 3

	1999	2000	2001	2002	2003	2004	2005	2006	2007	2008
Total	4 800.625	4 943.511	5 027.718	5 115.826				6 461.485 [4]	6 664.014	6 837.240
A-B								295.2 [4]	359.8	381.9
A	331.4	323.7	334.2	258.6						
B	11.0	7.9	9.1	12.2						
C	85.959	98.119	87.103	94.631				102.067 [4]	101.610	107.061
D	431.974	434.023	460.318	439.392				495.687 [4]	557.442	498.491
E	74.084	75.474	77.329	65.648				79.466 [4]	74.381	66.902
F	566.722	515.549	585.005	629.326				835.389 [4]	790.726	743.518
G	843.433	896.394	832.640	856.395				1 200.306 [4]	1 242.461	1 249.601
H	140.512	163.731	154.200	166.812				239.829 [4]	246.024	274.132
I	230.642	242.294	242.116	258.924				289.504 [4]	331.813	359.675
J	47.993	41.520	56.842	48.515				81.450 [4]	79.305	81.448
K	143.753	138.840	144.279	142.364				245.303 [4]	245.826	305.851
L	1 052.976	1 098.667	1 138.956	1 195.225				1 394.803 [4]	1 367.622	1 469.825
M	386.608	399.716	411.145	419.243				490.182 [4]	512.983	534.115
N	161.546	168.637	187.937	172.595				235.218 [4]	248.937	282.037
O	123.253	130.619	100.175	112.451				162.280 [4]	168.188	157.313
P	160.296	201.577	191.744	235.583				306.985 [4]	327.092	319.794
Q	5.338	5.282	5.841	7.977				7.864 [4]	9.850	5.623
X	3.076	1.904	8.778	-				- [4]	-	-

Explanatory notes: see p. 77.   Notes explicatives: voir p. 80.   Notas explicativas: véase p. 83.

[1] Persons aged 15 years and over. [2] March of each year. [3] Persons temporary absent from work. [4] April.

[1] Personnes âgées de 15 ans et plus. [2] Mars de chaque année. [3] Personnes temporairement absentes de leur travail. [4] Avril.

[1] Personas de 15 años y más. [2] Marzo de cada año. [3] Personas temporalment ausentes de su trabajo. [4] Abril.

Total employment, by economic activity   Emploi total, par activité économique   Empleo total, por actividad económica

Thousands   Milliers   Millares

Saudi Arabia (BA) [1] — Total employment - Emploi total - Empleo total

Women - Femmes - Mujeres
ISIC 3 - CITI 3 - CIIU 3

	1999	2000	2001	2002	2003	2004	2005	2006	2007	2008
Total	792.233	769.834	780.899	797.184	.	.	.	1 061.487 [2]	1 102.336	1 119.592
A-B	.	.	.	.	.	.	.	4.3 [2]	4.4	0.5
A	7.8	17.8	6.1	4.9	.	.	.	.	.	.
C	2.966	3.760	0.805	0.759	.	.	.	0.111 [2]	1.197	0.627
D	9.752	6.628	7.464	8.891	.	.	.	9.420 [2]	8.332	10.353
E	0.866	0.546	-	-	.	.	.	- [2]	-	0.000
F	-	0.382	0.339	0.243	.	.	.	1.508 [2]	2.860	2.256
G	3.976	5.091	4.586	5.346	.	.	.	9.771 [2]	7.809	8.340
H	-	0.864	0.405	3.537	.	.	.	1.548 [2]	2.673	4.996
I	5.365	-	5.770	6.359	.	.	.	1.785 [2]	11.739	2.234
J	1.301	1.010	1.695	1.288	.	.	.	5.120 [2]	4.482	4.555
K	3.274	0.630	-	0.884	.	.	.	7.300 [2]	4.421	7.618
L	19.817	17.527	18.589	17.640	.	.	.	31.192 [2]	32.470	33.088
M	316.560	313.249	308.923	332.280	.	.	.	416.989 [2]	416.216	398.392
N	67.548	49.007	90.203	51.382	.	.	.	90.274 [2]	86.984	83.422
O	4.145	2.847	1.727	2.964	.	.	.	6.872 [2]	7.689	5.737
P	348.471	349.389	329.647	360.347	.	.	.	474.556 [2]	511.034	556.802
Q	1.004	.	0.966	0.388	.	.	.	0.702 [2]	-	0.654
X	0.297	1.132	3.701	-	.	.	.	- [2]	.	.

Singapore (BA) [3][4] — Total employment - Emploi total - Empleo total

Total - Total - Total
ISIC 3 - CITI 3 - CIIU 3

ISIC 3	1999	2000	2001	2002	2003	2004	2005	2006	2007	2008	ISIC 4 - CITI 4 - CIIU 4
Total	1 518.3	.	1 582.5 [5]	1 573.7	1 605.4	1 632.1	.	1 796.7	1 803.2	1 852.0	Total
A-C,E,X	13.8	.	14.1 [5]	13.3	13.8	13.7	.	22.5	20.7	22.7	B,D,E,X
D	329.2	.	307.8 [5]	299.0	303.6	298.3	.	301.7	304.5	311.9	C
F	109.0	.	100.0 [5]	96.5	97.7	92.6	.	95.0	100.8	105.5	F
G	238.3	.	253.8 [5]	256.4	253.7	275.4	.	301.1	277.0	269.5	G
H	101.7	.	105.0 [5]	103.5	107.8	107.9	.	174.0	179.9	182.4	H
I	172.2	.	190.1 [5]	183.9	183.5	183.3	.	128.8	123.1	120.0	I
J	86.1	.	89.1 [5]	90.8	88.6	91.9	.	74.8	87.8	87.0	J
K	165.5	.	199.7 [5]	198.0	206.8	216.2	.	106.3	109.7	123.6	K
L,M	179.0	.	189.2 [5]	198.7	216.4	212.2	.	39.9	41.0	43.0	L
N	44.5	.	54.0 [5]	53.2	55.8	61.9	.	99.0	97.2	109.6	M
O-Q	79.0	.	79.7 [5]	80.4	77.7	78.0	.	78.4	85.7	84.9	N
								223.3	220.3	228.5	O-P
								70.8	69.9	74.3	Q
								81.0	85.6	89.1	R-U

Men - Hommes - Hombres
ISIC 3 - CITI 3 - CIIU 3

ISIC 3	1999	2000	2001	2002	2003	2004	2005	2006	2007	2008	ISIC 4 - CITI 4 - CIIU 4
Total	912.1	.	938.4 [5]	937.7	948.7	960.8	.	1 036.5	1 038.4	1 053.6	Total
A-C,E,X	11.3	.	10.8 [5]	10.7	10.4	10.9	.	16.5	16.6	16.9	B,D,E,X
D	196.8	.	191.2 [5]	184.0	188.6	183.9	.	191.3	189.5	199.5	C
F	91.3	.	83.1 [5]	81.6	80.1	77.6	.	77.8	82.1	84.9	F
G	141.7	.	145.9 [5]	146.1	142.6	155.3	.	161.1	146.9	139.6	G
H	51.7	.	50.1 [5]	51.4	53.0	52.3	.	134.8	139.6	137.6	H
I	129.1	.	141.1 [5]	138.8	136.6	135.2	.	61.9	59.6	53.5	I
J	34.4	.	36.6 [5]	36.8	35.4	37.9	.	44.9	52.1	52.1	J
K	92.1	.	107.6 [5]	110.5	116.6	123.4	.	45.4	46.5	52.7	K
L,M	107.5	.	115.4 [5]	119.4	130.1	129.4	.	19.9	22.3	22.4	L
N	11.2	.	12.9 [5]	12.9	13.6	14.1	.	50.5	49.6	56.4	M
O-Q	45.0	.	43.8 [5]	45.4	41.6	40.7	.	45.5	48.6	47.5	N
								129.6	125.3	127.2	O-P
								16.6	17.1	17.1	Q
								40.9	42.6	46.2	R-U

Women - Femmes - Mujeres
ISIC 3 - CITI 3 - CIIU 3

ISIC 3	1999	2000	2001	2002	2003	2004	2005	2006	2007	2008	ISIC 4 - CITI 4 - CIIU 4
Total	606.2	.	644.0 [5]	636.0	656.6	671.3	.	760.2	764.8	798.5	Total
A-C,E,X	2.5	.	3.3 [5]	2.6	3.4	2.8	.	6.0	4.0	5.9	B,D,E,X
D	132.5	.	116.6 [5]	115.1	115.0	114.0	.	110.4	115.1	112.4	C
F	17.7	.	17.0 [5]	14.9	17.6	15.0	.	17.2	18.6	20.6	F
G	96.7	.	107.9 [5]	110.3	111.1	120.1	.	140.0	130.1	130.0	G
H	49.9	.	54.9 [5]	52.1	54.8	55.6	.	39.2	40.3	44.8	H
I	43.1	.	49.0 [5]	45.1	46.9	48.1	.	66.9	63.5	66.4	I
J	51.7	.	52.5 [5]	54.0	53.2	53.9	.	29.9	35.6	34.9	J
K	73.4	.	92.1 [5]	87.5	90.1	92.8	.	61.0	63.2	70.8	K
L,M	71.5	.	73.8 [5]	79.3	86.3	82.8	.	20.0	18.8	20.7	L
N	33.2	.	41.1 [5]	40.3	42.1	47.8	.	48.6	47.6	53.1	M
O-Q	34.0	.	35.9 [5]	35.0	36.1	38.0	.	32.9	37.1	37.4	N
								93.8	95.0	101.3	O-P
								54.2	52.8	57.2	Q
								40.1	43.0	42.8	R-U

Explanatory notes: see p. 77.

[1] Persons aged 15 years and over. [2] April. [3] The data refer to the residents (Singapore citizens and permanent residents) aged 15 years and over. [4] June. [5] Methodology revised; data not strictly comparable.

Notes explicatives: voir p. 80.

[1] Personnes âgées de 15 ans et plus. [2] Avril. [3] Les données se réfèrent aux résidents (citoyens de Singapour et résidents permanents) âgés de 15 ans et plus. [4] Juin. [5] Méthodologie révisée; les données ne sont pas strictement comparables.

Notas explicativas: véase p. 83.

[1] Personas de 15 años y más. [2] Abril. [3] Los datos se refieren a los residentes (ciudadanos de Singapur y residentes permanentes) de 15 años y más. [4] Junio. [5] Metodología revisada; los datos no son estrictamente comparables.

EMPLOYMENT   EMPLOI   EMPLEO

Total employment, by economic activity   Emploi total, par activité économique   Empleo total, por actividad económica

Thousands — Milliers — Millares

	1999	2000	2001	2002	2003	2004	2005	2006	2007	2008
Sri Lanka (BA) [1][2]				— Total employment - Emploi total - Empleo total						
Total - Total - Total										
ISIC 3 - CITI 3 - CIIU 3										
Total	.	.	.	6 519.4	7 012.8 [3]	7 394.0 [4]	7 518.0 [5]	7 105.3	7 041.9	7 174.7
A-B	.	.	.	2 247.6	2 384.4 [3]	2 474.7 [4]	2 306.0 [5]	2 287.3	2 202.1	2 344.4
C.E	.	.	.	386.5	454.8 [3]	470.1 [4]	542.6 [5]	526.9	542.5	533.1
D	.	.	.	1 072.7	1 156.7 [3]	1 307.4 [4]	1 385.4 [5]	1 363.1	1 331.4	1 354.9
G	.	.	.	838.8	867.1 [3]	910.8 [4]	904.0 [5]	955.0	932.0	924.5
H	.	.	.	117.6	121.6 [3]	120.6 [4]	138.9 [5]	129.4	118.5	103.8
I	.	.	.	309.6	363.4 [3]	417.3 [4]	485.0 [5]	430.3	456.8	426.0
J-K	.	.	.	169.0	191.4 [3]	175.6 [4]	233.7 [5]	221.1	215.2	236.0
L	.	.	.	524.7	541.1 [3]	535.1 [4]	512.8 [5]	400.5	433.0	462.6
M	.	.	.	227.8	262.4 [3]	273.6 [4]	297.4 [5]	276.8	259.5	298.8
N	.	.	.	82.3	98.1 [3]	104.0 [4]	129.2 [5]	109.7	115.9	110.9
O.Q	.	.	.	110.4	110.8 [3]	122.4 [4]	133.5 [5]	123.9	104.6	128.8
P	.	.	.	93.3	75.9 [3]	68.8 [4]	53.3 [5]	80.2	87.4	84.1
X	.	.	.	339.3	385.0 [3]	409.7 [4]	395.9 [5]	201.2	242.9	166.7
Men - Hommes - Hombres										
ISIC 3 - CITI 3 - CIIU 3										
Total	.	.	.	4 395.2	4 833.5 [3]	5 049.4 [4]	5 134.8 [5]	4 610.6	4 653.1	4 713.3
A-B	.	.	.	1 397.4	1 529.1 [3]	1 559.3 [4]	1 482.6 [5]	1 342.2	1 322.0	1 438.7
C.E	.	.	.	373.5	436.4 [3]	456.0 [4]	519.2 [5]	507.2	523.5	510.5
D	.	.	.	569.8	624.8 [3]	710.9 [4]	750.0 [5]	683.9	703.1	716.3
G	.	.	.	656.5	681.2 [3]	721.8 [4]	702.0 [5]	717.3	688.7	680.1
H	.	.	.					93.7	85.2	
I	.	.	.					407.6	435.2	
J-K	.	.	.	115.2	138.1 [3]	122.4 [4]	171.3 [5]	156.0	151.8	162.6
L	.	.	.	387.3	405.6 [3]	392.9 [4]	376.9 [5]	294.6	308.1	344.7
M	.	.	.	70.8	98.1 [3]	102.6 [4]	83.6 [5]	86.5	79.1	87.9
N	.	.	.					45.2	49.3	
O.Q	.	.	.					87.1	77.8	
P	.	.	.					16.0	27.0	
X	.	.	.	824.6	920.2 [3]	983.4 [4]	1 049.2 [5]	178.8	209.8	772.5
Women - Femmes - Mujeres										
ISIC 3 - CITI 3 - CIIU 3										
Total	.	.	.	2 124.3	2 179.3 [3]	2 344.6 [4]	2 383.2 [5]	2 494.7	2 388.8	2 511.4
A-B	.	.	.	850.2	855.3 [3]	915.4 [4]	823.4 [5]	945.1	880.1	955.7
C.E	.	.	.	13.0	18.4 [3]	18.0 [4]	23.4 [5]	19.7	19.0	22.6
D	.	.	.	503.0	531.9 [3]	596.4 [4]	635.4 [5]	679.2	628.3	638.6
G	.	.	.	182.3	185.9 [3]	189.0 [4]	202.0 [5]	237.7	243.4	244.4
H	.	.	.					35.6	33.4	
I	.	.	.					22.7	21.6	
J-K	.	.	.	53.8	53.2 [3]	53.3 [4]	62.4 [5]	65.1	63.4	73.4
L	.	.	.	137.4	135.5 [3]	142.1 [4]	135.9 [5]	105.9	124.9	117.9
M	.	.	.	157.0	164.4 [3]	171.0 [4]	213.9 [5]	190.3	180.4	210.9
N	.	.	.					64.4	66.7	
O.Q	.	.	.					36.8	26.8	
P	.	.	.					64.2	60.4	
X	.	.	.	227.7	234.6 [3]	259.4 [4]	286.8 [5]	22.4	33.1	247.9
Syrian Arab Republic (BA) [6]				— Total employment - Emploi total - Empleo total						
Total - Total - Total										
ISIC 3 - CITI 3 - CIIU 3										
Total	.	.	.	.	.	.	.	.	4 946.0	.
A-B	.	.	.	.	.	.	.	.	946.5	.
C	.	.	.	.	.	.	.	.	34.7	.
D	.	.	.	.	.	.	.	.	633.1	.
E	.	.	.	.	.	.	.	.	33.5	.
F	.	.	.	.	.	.	.	.	735.9	.
G	.	.	.	.	.	.	.	.	727.2	.
H	.	.	.	.	.	.	.	.	55.9	.
I	.	.	.	.	.	.	.	.	352.2	.
J	.	.	.	.	.	.	.	.	10.1	.
K	.	.	.	.	.	.	.	.	122.3	.
L	.	.	.	.	.	.	.	.	648.5	.
M	.	.	.	.	.	.	.	.	383.9	.
N	.	.	.	.	.	.	.	.	119.6	.
O-Q	.	.	.	.	.	.	.	.	142.3	.
X	.	.	.	.	.	.	.	.	0.4	.

Explanatory notes: see p. 77.

[1] Persons aged 10 years and over. [2] Excl. Northern and Eastern provinces. [3] Excl. Northern province. [4] Excl. Mullativu and Killinochchi districts. [5] Whole country. [6] Persons aged 15 years and over.

Notes explicatives: voir p. 80.

[1] Personnes âgées de 10 ans et plus. [2] Non compris les provinces du Nord et de l'Est. [3] Non compris la province du Nord. [4] Non compris les provinces de Mullativu et Killinochchi. [5] Ensemble du pays. [6] Personnes âgées de 15 ans et plus.

Notas explicativas: véase p. 83.

[1] Personas de 10 años y más. [2] Excl. las provincias del Norte y del Este. [3] Excl. la provincia del Norte. [4] Excl. las provincias de Mullativu y Killinocchchi. [5] Todo el país. [6] Personas de 15 años y más.

Total employment,
by economic activity

Emploi total,
par activité économique

Empleo total,
por actividad económica

	Thousands			Milliers			Millares		
1999	2000	2001	2002	2003	2004	2005	2006	2007	2008

Syrian Arab Republic (BA) [1] Total employment - Emploi total - Empleo total

Men - Hommes - Hombres
ISIC 3 - CITI 3 - CIIU 3

	1999	2000	2001	2002	2003	2004	2005	2006	2007	2008
Total	.	.	.	.	.	.	.	.	4 316.4	.
A-B	.	.	.	.	.	.	.	.	780.8	.
C	.	.	.	.	.	.	.	.	31.9	.
D	.	.	.	.	.	.	.	.	595.4	.
E	.	.	.	.	.	.	.	.	31.2	.
F	.	.	.	.	.	.	.	.	729.7	.
G	.	.	.	.	.	.	.	.	699.3	.
H	.	.	.	.	.	.	.	.	54.5	.
I	.	.	.	.	.	.	.	.	342.8	.
J	.	.	.	.	.	.	.	.	6.5	.
K	.	.	.	.	.	.	.	.	110.6	.
L	.	.	.	.	.	.	.	.	566.1	.
M	.	.	.	.	.	.	.	.	181.1	.
N	.	.	.	.	.	.	.	.	64.8	.
O-Q	.	.	.	.	.	.	.	.	121.0	.
X	.	.	.	.	.	.	.	.	0.4	.

Women - Femmes - Mujeres
ISIC 3 - CITI 3 - CIIU 3

	1999	2000	2001	2002	2003	2004	2005	2006	2007	2008
Total	.	.	.	.	.	.	.	.	629.6	.
A-B	.	.	.	.	.	.	.	.	165.6	.
C	.	.	.	.	.	.	.	.	2.8	.
D	.	.	.	.	.	.	.	.	37.6	.
E	.	.	.	.	.	.	.	.	2.3	.
F	.	.	.	.	.	.	.	.	6.2	.
G	.	.	.	.	.	.	.	.	27.9	.
H	.	.	.	.	.	.	.	.	1.4	.
I	.	.	.	.	.	.	.	.	9.4	.
J	.	.	.	.	.	.	.	.	3.5	.
K	.	.	.	.	.	.	.	.	11.7	.
L	.	.	.	.	.	.	.	.	82.4	.
M	.	.	.	.	.	.	.	.	202.8	.
N	.	.	.	.	.	.	.	.	54.7	.
O-Q	.	.	.	.	.	.	.	.	21.2	.
X	.	.	.	.	.	.	.	.	-	.

Taiwan, China (BA) [1][2] Total employment - Emploi total - Empleo total

Total - Total - Total
ISIC 3 - CITI 3 - CIIU 3

	1999	2000	2001	2002	2003	2004	2005	2006	2007	2008
Total	.	.	.	.	.	.	9 942	10 111	10 294	10 403
A-B	.	.	.	.	.	.	590	554	543	535
C	.	.	.	.	.	.	7	7	6	6
D	.	.	.	.	.	.	2 732	2 777	2 842	2 886
E	.	.	.	.	.	.	89	88	93	99
F	.	.	.	.	.	.	791	829	846	842
G	.	.	.	.	.	.	1 726	1 759	1 782	1 770
H	.	.	.	.	.	.	634	665	681	687
I [3]	.	.	.	.	.	.	611	626	621	617
J	.	.	.	.	.	.	406	407	404	411
K	.	.	.	.	.	.	513	535	589	622
L	.	.	.	.	.	.	336	334	332	343
M	.	.	.	.	.	.	556	563	588	605
N	.	.	.	.	.	.	323	334	340	355
O	.	.	.	.	.	.	513	524	523	528
X	.	.	.	.	.	.	116	111	101	98

Thailand (BA) [1][2][4] Total employment - Emploi total - Empleo total

Total - Total - Total
ISIC 3 - CITI 3 - CIIU 3

	1999	2000	2001	2002	2003	2004	2005	2006	2007	2008
Total	.	.	.	34 262.9	34 677.1	35 711.6	36 302.4	36 344.6	37 122.2	37 836.6
A	.	.	.	15 311.3	15 146.1	14 719.4	15 007.7	14 887.1	15 081.8	15 641.4
B	.	.	.	488.0	415.4	396.0	440.9	428.2	410.0	425.6
C	.	.	.	36.9	39.6	35.2	40.1	54.6	53.9	55.0
D	.	.	.	5 039.8	5 086.3	5 313.3	5 350.1	5 306.6	5 593.0	5 231.4
E	.	.	.	95.4	105.2	98.7	106.8	99.3	104.9	103.1
F	.	.	.	1 619.5	1 614.1	1 878.1	1 853.0	2 038.9	1 938.7	2 012.1
G	.	.	.	4 739.4	5 057.2	5 451.6	5 297.0	5 401.9	5 525.4	5 634.9
H	.	.	.	1 988.1	2 103.3	2 206.4	2 300.1	2 214.9	2 302.5	2 353.2
I	.	.	.	964.6	987.5	1 067.5	1 075.9	1 052.9	1 026.5	1 090.5
J	.	.	.	263.2	279.3	303.4	339.7	349.7	350.2	396.2
K	.	.	.	498.7	567.4	633.7	651.7	659.3	717.4	717.0
L	.	.	.	956.7	902.8	1 015.0	1 095.6	1 170.1	1 286.9	1 303.3
M	.	.	.	946.7	957.1	1 082.5	1 122.3	1 079.9	1 085.0	1 097.5
N	.	.	.	471.3	518.0	535.1	611.0	602.8	647.2	720.4
O	.	.	.	602.3	621.1	712.7	718.8	710.3	718.0	818.9
P	.	.	.	221.6	254.8	239.0	241.5	221.9	229.1	196.1
Q	.	.	.	4.9	0.9	0.9	2.2	0.4	1.1	1.4
X	.	.	.	14.5	21.0	23.1	47.7	65.8	50.6	38.5

Explanatory notes: see p. 77.

[1] Persons aged 15 years and over. [2] Excl. armed forces. [3] Incl. information service activities. [4] Third quarter.

Notes explicatives: voir p. 80.

[1] Personnes âgées de 15 ans et plus. [2] Non compris les forces armées. [3] Y compris les activités de service d'information. [4] Troisième trimestre.

Notas explicativas: véase p. 83.

[1] Personas de 15 años y más. [2] Excl. las fuerzas armadas. [3] Incl. actividad de servicio de información. [4] Tercer trimestre.

	EMPLOYMENT	EMPLOI	EMPLEO
	Total employment, by economic activity	Emploi total, par activité économique	Empleo total, por actividad económica

	Thousands					Milliers			Millares	
	1999	2000	2001	2002	2003	2004	2005	2006	2007	2008

Thailand (BA) [1] [2] [3] — Total employment - Emploi total - Empleo total

Men - Hommes - Hombres
ISIC 3 - CITI 3 - CIIU 3

	1999	2000	2001	2002	2003	2004	2005	2006	2007	2008
Total	.	.	.	18 872.1	19 081.5	19 698.8	19 470.3	19 638.4	19 976.8	20 405.0
A	.	.	.	8 642.7	8 597.8	8 341.0	8 250.9	8 117.9	8 323.2	8 716.0
B	.	.	.	386.8	336.2	313.9	348.7	337.7	317.9	323.5
C	.	.	.	27.6	30.3	26.1	30.2	42.6	42.4	44.4
D	.	.	.	2 383.5	2 415.8	2 550.2	2 507.3	2 479.6	2 640.2	2 405.4
E	.	.	.	82.5	89.8	87.2	88.9	85.0	89.8	85.0
F	.	.	.	1 383.4	1 383.4	1 594.8	1 578.3	1 716.4	1 619.6	1 702.5
G	.	.	.	2 485.4	2 654.5	2 868.9	2 759.0	2 817.0	2 854.5	2 945.8
H	.	.	.	717.6	757.9	781.7	759.8	777.2	761.3	822.8
I	.	.	.	839.1	849.2	914.7	900.8	887.4	873.2	916.3
J	.	.	.	131.2	141.2	145.7	162.1	147.8	152.4	179.2
K	.	.	.	297.0	332.9	385.9	377.5	371.7	417.1	396.4
L	.	.	.	627.9	602.8	679.4	726.3	784.0	890.6	853.5
M	.	.	.	420.1	426.2	469.0	469.2	454.4	473.6	435.5
N	.	.	.	132.7	144.8	159.8	155.9	143.7	154.9	174.3
O	.	.	.	280.7	269.8	334.7	298.5	307.9	305.5	364.7
P	.	.	.	27.1	37.3	31.0	29.8	34.0	31.9	21.3
Q	.	.	.	0.7	0.3	0.3	0.3	-	0.9	0.4
X	.	.	.	6.1	11.3	14.5	27.0	34.1	27.8	18.1

Women - Femmes - Mujeres
ISIC 3 - CITI 3 - CIIU 3

	1999	2000	2001	2002	2003	2004	2005	2006	2007	2008
Total	.	.	.	15 390.8	15 595.6	16 012.8	16 832.1	16 706.2	17 145.4	17 431.6
A	.	.	.	6 668.6	6 548.3	6 378.4	6 756.9	6 669.2	6 758.6	6 925.5
B	.	.	.	101.2	79.2	82.1	92.2	90.5	92.1	102.2
C	.	.	.	9.3	9.3	9.1	9.9	12.0	11.5	10.7
D	.	.	.	2 656.3	2 670.5	2 763.1	2 842.9	2 827.0	2 952.8	2 826.0
E	.	.	.	12.9	15.4	11.5	18.0	14.3	15.1	18.1
F	.	.	.	236.1	230.7	283.3	274.8	322.5	319.1	309.6
G	.	.	.	2 254.0	2 402.7	2 582.7	2 538.0	2 584.9	2 670.9	2 689.2
H	.	.	.	1 270.5	1 345.4	1 424.7	1 540.3	1 437.7	1 541.2	1 530.4
I	.	.	.	125.5	138.3	152.8	175.0	165.5	153.3	174.2
J	.	.	.	132.0	138.1	157.7	177.6	201.9	197.8	216.9
K	.	.	.	201.7	234.5	247.8	274.2	287.6	300.3	320.6
L	.	.	.	328.8	300.0	335.6	369.4	386.1	396.3	449.0
M	.	.	.	526.6	530.9	613.5	653.2	625.5	611.4	662.0
N	.	.	.	338.6	373.2	375.2	455.2	459.1	492.3	546.1
O	.	.	.	321.6	351.3	378.0	420.3	402.4	412.5	454.3
P	.	.	.	194.5	217.5	208.0	211.7	187.9	197.2	174.8
Q	.	.	.	4.2	0.6	0.6	1.9	0.4	0.2	1.0
X	.	.	.	8.4	9.7	8.6	20.8	31.7	22.8	20.5

United Arab Emirates (BA) [2] [4] — Total employment - Emploi total - Empleo total

Total - Total - Total
ISIC 3 - CITI 3 - CIIU 3

	1999	2000	2001	2002	2003	2004	2005	2006	2007	2008
Total	.	.	.	.	.	.	.	.	.	1 846.150
A	.	.	.	.	.	.	.	.	.	72.460
B	.	.	.	.	.	.	.	.	.	6.000
C	.	.	.	.	.	.	.	.	.	35.928
D	.	.	.	.	.	.	.	.	.	160.456
E	.	.	.	.	.	.	.	.	.	25.199
F	.	.	.	.	.	.	.	.	.	227.856
G	.	.	.	.	.	.	.	.	.	300.364
H	.	.	.	.	.	.	.	.	.	72.459
I	.	.	.	.	.	.	.	.	.	132.586
J	.	.	.	.	.	.	.	.	.	58.727
K	.	.	.	.	.	.	.	.	.	147.894
L	.	.	.	.	.	.	.	.	.	170.300
M	.	.	.	.	.	.	.	.	.	83.943
N	.	.	.	.	.	.	.	.	.	48.573
O	.	.	.	.	.	.	.	.	.	59.268
P	.	.	.	.	.	.	.	.	.	236.545
Q	.	.	.	.	.	.	.	.	.	3.826
X	.	.	.	.	.	.	.	.	.	3.766

Explanatory notes: see p. 77.

[1] Excl. armed forces. [2] Persons aged 15 years and over. [3] Third quarter. [4] February.

Notes explicatives: voir p. 80.

[1] Non compris les forces armées. [2] Personnes âgées de 15 ans et plus. [3] Troisième trimestre. [4] Février.

Notas explicativas: véase p. 83.

[1] Excl. las fuerzas armadas. [2] Personas de 15 años y más. [3] Tercer trimestre. [4] Febrero.

Total employment, by economic activity
Emploi total, par activité économique
Empleo total, por actividad económica

	Thousands			Milliers			Millares			
	1999	2000	2001	2002	2003	2004	2005	2006	2007	2008

United Arab Emirates (BA) [1] [2]   Total employment - Emploi total - Empleo total

Men - Hommes - Hombres
ISIC 3 - CITI 3 - CIIU 3

	1999	2000	2001	2002	2003	2004	2005	2006	2007	2008
Total	.	.	.	.	.	.	.	.	.	1 501.293
A	.	.	.	.	.	.	.	.	.	71.971
B	.	.	.	.	.	.	.	.	.	5.854
C	.	.	.	.	.	.	.	.	.	33.235
D	.	.	.	.	.	.	.	.	.	149.107
E	.	.	.	.	.	.	.	.	.	23.484
F	.	.	.	.	.	.	.	.	.	219.194
G	.	.	.	.	.	.	.	.	.	278.296
H	.	.	.	.	.	.	.	.	.	63.854
I	.	.	.	.	.	.	.	.	.	118.986
J	.	.	.	.	.	.	.	.	.	41.279
K	.	.	.	.	.	.	.	.	.	132.768
L	.	.	.	.	.	.	.	.	.	154.181
M	.	.	.	.	.	.	.	.	.	38.231
N	.	.	.	.	.	.	.	.	.	24.253
O	.	.	.	.	.	.	.	.	.	50.176
P	.	.	.	.	.	.	.	.	.	90.470
Q	.	.	.	.	.	.	.	.	.	2.881
X	.	.	.	.	.	.	.	.	.	3.073

Women - Femmes - Mujeres
ISIC 3 - CITI 3 - CIIU 3

	1999	2000	2001	2002	2003	2004	2005	2006	2007	2008
Total	.	.	.	.	.	.	.	.	.	344.857
A	.	.	.	.	.	.	.	.	.	0.489
B	.	.	.	.	.	.	.	.	.	0.146
C	.	.	.	.	.	.	.	.	.	2.693
D	.	.	.	.	.	.	.	.	.	11.349
E	.	.	.	.	.	.	.	.	.	1.715
F	.	.	.	.	.	.	.	.	.	8.662
G	.	.	.	.	.	.	.	.	.	22.068
H	.	.	.	.	.	.	.	.	.	8.605
I	.	.	.	.	.	.	.	.	.	13.600
J	.	.	.	.	.	.	.	.	.	17.448
K	.	.	.	.	.	.	.	.	.	15.126
L	.	.	.	.	.	.	.	.	.	16.119
M	.	.	.	.	.	.	.	.	.	45.712
N	.	.	.	.	.	.	.	.	.	24.320
O	.	.	.	.	.	.	.	.	.	9.092
P	.	.	.	.	.	.	.	.	.	146.075
Q	.	.	.	.	.	.	.	.	.	0.945
X	.	.	.	.	.	.	.	.	.	0.693

Viet Nam (BA) [2] [3]   Total employment - Emploi total - Empleo total

Total - Total - Total
ISIC 3 - CITI 3 - CIIU 3

	1999	2000	2001	2002	2003	2004	2005	2006	2007	2008
Total	38 119.9	38 367.6	39 000.3	40 162.3	41 175.7	42 315.6	.	.	.	.
A	23 900.8	24 307.7	23 861.0	23 645.4	23 236.7	23 068.6	.	.	.	.
B	867.7	729.3	1 096.9	1 271.9	1 334.4	1 429.2	.	.	.	.
C	149.1	191.9	270.4	244.4	322.1	294.9	.	.	.	.
D	3 443.7	3 535.7	3 789.0	4 050.9	4 511.5	4 949.8	.	.	.	.
E	85.0	77.1	102.8	118.0	128.1	141.8	.	.	.	.
F	897.3	966.6	1 254.3	1 490.9	1 796.4	1 956.6	.	.	.	.
G	4 262.6	4 116.3	3 990.6	4 306.5	4 507.4	4 696.0	.	.	.	.
H	601.0	506.1	494.3	521.1	643.2	595.0	.	.	.	.
I	1 140.1	1 125.6	1 168.0	1 267.3	1 297.4	1 292.9	.	.	.	.
J	107.3	105.4	117.2	130.0	148.5	159.0	.	.	.	.
K	83.9	106.4	131.8	184.4	218.5	219.2	.	.	.	.
L	530.7	594.8	538.8	590.0	620.1	698.9	.	.	.	.
M	993.1	917.6	967.3	1 058.5	1 098.0	1 185.0	.	.	.	.
N	285.9	268.6	271.9	278.9	306.1	328.0	.	.	.	.
O	671.3	723.9	797.6	812.0	788.8	1 056.4	.	.	.	.
P	96.4	91.9	146.9	190.2	217.0	241.1	.	.	.	.
Q	3.8	2.6	1.5	2.0	1.4	3.3	.	.	.	.

Explanatory notes: see p. 77.   Notes explicatives: voir p. 80.   Notas explicativas: véase p. 83.

[1] February. [2] Persons aged 15 years and over. [3] July of each year.   [1] Février. [2] Personnes âgées de 15 ans et plus. [3] Juillet de chaque année.   [1] Febrero. [2] Personas de 15 años y más. [3] Julio de cada año.

Total employment, by economic activity — **Emploi total, par activité économique** — **Empleo total, por actividad económica**

	Thousands				Milliers				Millares	
	1999	2000	2001	2002	2003	2004	2005	2006	2007	2008

Viet Nam (BA) [1] [2] — Total employment - Emploi total - Empleo total

Men - Hommes - Hombres
ISIC 3 - CITI 3 - CIIU 3

	1999	2000	2001	2002	2003	2004	2005	2006	2007	2008
Total	19 028.5	19 292.1	19 743.7	20 355.6	20 959.2	21 649.3	.	.	.	.
A	11 589.4	11 791.0	11 608.2	11 460.7	11 072.5	11 041.3	.	.	.	.
B	680.6	600.2	836.1	948.6	1 023.1	1 059.3	.	.	.	.
C	107.3	132.9	166.6	156.5	194.7	182.7	.	.	.	.
D	1 708.9	1 765.8	1 888.3	1 972.1	2 203.6	2 429.1	.	.	.	.
E	67.4	64.3	81.1	97.8	103.9	117.6	.	.	.	.
F	807.2	876.5	1 131.1	1 357.3	1 631.8	1 774.1	.	.	.	.
G	1 524.3	1 484.4	1 417.8	1 521.5	1 673.1	1 778.0	.	.	.	.
H	177.0	145.7	139.0	145.3	195.3	176.1	.	.	.	.
I	1 019.2	1 016.5	1 030.1	1 117.4	1 150.5	1 128.2	.	.	.	.
J	52.2	48.5	57.9	59.0	74.0	80.8	.	.	.	.
K	53.5	68.0	82.5	113.8	144.4	142.6	.	.	.	.
L	398.3	451.7	398.9	432.4	457.5	516.0	.	.	.	.
M	286.0	270.8	289.1	318.7	335.1	359.6	.	.	.	.
N	122.7	114.0	115.0	115.6	135.1	140.1	.	.	.	.
O	396.7	424.8	448.8	468.7	480.2	624.6	.	.	.	.
P	35.2	36.2	52.7	69.2	84.1	97.4	.	.	.	.
Q	2.7	0.8	0.5	0.9	0.4	1.8	.	.	.	.

Women - Femmes - Mujeres
ISIC 3 - CITI 3 - CIIU 3

	1999	2000	2001	2002	2003	2004	2005	2006	2007	2008
Total	19 091.4	19 075.5	19 256.5	19 806.7	20 216.5	20 666.3	.	.	.	.
A	12 311.4	12 516.6	12 252.8	12 184.7	12 164.2	12 027.3	.	.	.	.
B	187.1	129.1	260.8	323.3	311.3	369.9	.	.	.	.
C	41.9	59.0	103.8	87.8	127.4	112.2	.	.	.	.
D	1 734.8	1 769.9	1 900.6	2 078.8	2 308.0	2 520.8	.	.	.	.
E	17.6	12.8	21.7	20.3	24.3	24.1	.	.	.	.
F	90.1	90.1	123.1	133.6	164.7	182.5	.	.	.	.
G	2 738.3	2 631.9	2 572.8	2 785.0	2 834.2	2 918.0	.	.	.	.
H	424.1	360.4	355.3	375.7	447.9	418.9	.	.	.	.
I	120.9	109.2	138.0	149.9	146.8	164.7	.	.	.	.
J	55.1	56.9	59.3	71.0	74.5	78.2	.	.	.	.
K	30.4	38.4	49.3	70.6	74.2	76.6	.	.	.	.
L	132.4	143.1	139.9	157.6	162.6	182.8	.	.	.	.
M	707.1	646.8	678.2	739.9	762.9	825.4	.	.	.	.
N	163.2	154.7	156.9	163.3	171.0	187.9	.	.	.	.
O	274.6	299.1	348.7	343.3	308.6	431.8	.	.	.	.
P	61.2	55.7	94.2	121.0	132.9	143.7	.	.	.	.
Q	1.2	1.8	1.0	1.1	1.0	1.4	.	.	.	.

West Bank and Gaza Strip (BA) [1] — Total employment - Emploi total - Empleo total

Total - Total - Total
ISIC 3 - CITI 3 - CIIU 3

	1999	2000	2001	2002	2003	2004	2005	2006	2007	2008
Total	588.000	597.440	504.661 [3]	476.661	564.571	578.439	632.939	666.375	665.620	647.022
A	74.031	81.520	58.759 [3]	70.376	88.191	91.768	91.774	106.113	102.205	85.755
B	0.272	0.345	0.276 [3]	0.331	0.299	0.310	0.536	0.911	1.516	0.692
C	2.282	1.688	1.357 [3]	1.639	1.344	1.717	1.377	2.237	1.542	1.462
D	89.333	83.960	69.056 [3]	59.798	69.400	71.535	80.874	80.543	81.964	
E	1.377	1.372	1.259 [3]	1.005	1.069	2.067	2.366	2.500	2.230	2.780
F	130.561	118.243	73.169 [3]	52.029	74.082	67.436	81.644	73.905	72.722	70.688
G	85.087	90.980	89.408 [3]	86.760	104.120	102.340	110.110	114.662	116.408	111.537
H	14.964	13.677	10.206 [3]	8.789	9.374	10.508	12.813	13.492	13.407	19.599
I	27.843	29.698	28.287 [3]	26.457	32.659	31.252	36.134	38.242	37.404	32.046
J	4.847	5.142	5.024 [3]	4.446	3.847	4.492	3.513	4.503	4.214	4.916
K	7.013	7.090	7.615 [3]	7.967	9.004	9.413	10.492	11.217	11.380	
L	65.380	71.487	70.316 [3]	66.533	67.982	78.038	92.977	98.922	99.584	101.723
M	48.355	54.086	53.149 [3]	51.418	58.238	60.850	60.743	67.704	68.034	71.114
N	18.308	19.303	19.314 [3]	20.076	22.147	23.711	22.804	24.400	24.525	27.265
O	15.387	15.981	13.124 [3]	13.185	16.086	15.390	17.462	19.426	20.594	19.189
P	0.366	0.418	0.617 [3]	0.339	0.418	0.276	0.133	0.348	0.182	0.483
Q	2.592	2.451	3.596 [3]	4.801	6.101	7.325	7.186	7.221	7.411	6.449
X	-	-	0.252 [3]	0.712	0.212	0.012	-	0.030		91.324

Explanatory notes: see p. 77.

Notes explicatives: voir p. 80.

Notas explicativas: véase p. 83.

[1] Persons aged 15 years and over. [2] July of each year. [3] Prior to 2001: persons aged 10 years and over.

[1] Personnes âgées de 15 ans et plus. [2] Juillet de chaque année. [3] Avant 2001: personnes agées de 10 ans et plus.

[1] Personas de 15 años y más. [2] Julio de cada año. [3] Antes de 2001: personas de 10 años y más.

Total employment, by economic activity
Emploi total, par activité économique
Empleo total, por actividad económica

Thousands   Milliers   Millares

	1999	2000	2001	2002	2003	2004	2005	2006	2007	2008
West Bank and Gaza Strip (BA) [1]				*Total employment - Emploi total - Empleo total*						
Men - Hommes - Hombres										
ISIC 3 - CITI 3 - CIIU 3										
Total	502.000	504.220	427.889 [2]	398.778	467.371	473.755	527.806	546.000	538.019	525.696
A	46.583	49.244	38.797 [2]	47.074	55.446	56.448	57.603	64.877	56.556	52.378
B	0.272	0.345	0.276 [2]	0.331	0.299	0.310	0.536	0.911	1.516	0.692
C	2.259	1.666	1.357 [2]	1.639	1.344	1.717	1.377	2.237	1.542	1.446
D	78.227	73.795	61.781 [2]	53.520	62.041	63.114	72.359	70.301	69.937	.
E	1.377	1.372	1.155 [2]	0.885	0.957	2.026	2.282	2.376	2.230	2.710
F	129.892	117.947	72.550 [2]	51.856	73.972	67.262	81.374	73.672	72.414	70.135
G	79.230	84.486	83.443 [2]	81.307	96.449	94.941	101.611	106.180	107.081	103.404
H	14.436	12.928	9.708 [2]	8.701	9.101	10.352	12.602	13.103	12.868	18.748
I	27.032	28.999	27.971 [2]	26.167	32.141	30.570	35.500	37.161	36.856	31.264
J	3.880	3.747	3.345 [2]	3.343	3.078	3.411	2.747	3.320	3.239	3.828
K	5.816	5.754	5.991 [2]	6.771	7.312	7.289	8.735	8.872	9.569	.
L	60.235	66.511	65.561 [2]	61.220	62.596	71.978	87.563	92.685	92.619	94.362
M	26.124	30.178	28.828 [2]	27.449	30.554	31.561	30.853	34.172	34.410	32.607
N	11.347	12.293	12.853 [2]	12.815	14.441	15.161	13.683	15.082	15.880	16.656
O	13.130	13.100	11.017 [2]	11.338	12.455	12.031	13.761	15.595	16.143	14.317
P	0.193	0.118	0.062 [2]	0.080	0.118	0.052	0.021	0.166	0.037	0.273
Q	1.969	1.738	2.991 [2]	3.711	4.918	5.520	5.200	5.259	5.122	4.634
X	-	-	0.203 [2]	0.569	0.176	0.012	-	0.030	-	78.242
Women - Femmes - Mujeres										
ISIC 3 - CITI 3 - CIIU 3										
Total	86.000	93.220	76.897 [2]	77.883	97.200	104.683	105.132	120.375	127.602	121.326
A	27.448	32.276	19.963 [2]	23.302	32.745	35.319	34.171	41.235	45.945	33.377
B	-	-	- [2]	-	-	-	-	-	-	-
C	0.024	0.022	- [2]	-	-	-	-	-	-	0.016
D	11.106	10.165	7.275 [2]	6.278	7.386	8.420	8.514	10.242	12.027	.
E	-	-	0.105 [2]	0.121	0.112	0.041	0.084	0.124	-	0.070
F	0.670	0.296	0.619 [2]	0.173	0.110	0.174	0.271	0.233	0.308	0.553
G	5.857	6.495	5.965 [2]	5.453	7.671	7.399	8.499	8.482	9.327	8.133
H	0.528	0.749	0.498 [2]	0.087	0.272	0.156	0.211	0.389	0.539	0.851
I	0.812	0.700	0.316 [2]	0.290	0.518	0.681	0.635	1.081	0.548	0.782
J	0.967	1.394	1.680 [2]	1.103	0.770	1.081	0.767	1.183	0.976	1.088
K	1.197	1.336	1.623 [2]	1.196	1.693	2.124	1.758	2.344	1.811	.
L	5.146	4.976	4.755 [2]	5.312	5.386	6.060	5.414	6.237	6.965	7.362
M	22.232	23.908	24.321 [2]	23.968	27.681	29.289	29.890	33.532	33.624	38.506
N	6.961	7.010	6.461 [2]	7.261	7.705	8.550	9.121	9.317	8.645	10.609
O	2.257	2.881	2.107 [2]	1.847	3.631	3.359	3.701	3.831	4.450	4.872
P	0.174	0.300	0.555 [2]	0.259	0.300	0.224	0.112	0.182	0.145	0.210
Q	0.623	0.713	0.605 [2]	1.089	1.183	1.805	1.985	1.962	2.289	1.815
X	-	-	0.050 [2]	0.143	0.037	-	-	-	-	13.082

EUROPE-EUROPE-EUROPA

	1999	2000	2001	2002	2003	2004	2005	2006	2007	2008
Albania (E)				*Total employment - Emploi total - Empleo total*						
Total - Total - Total										
ISIC 3 - CITI 3 - CIIU 3										
Total	1 065	1 068	1 063	920	926	931	932	935	.	.
A-B	768	767	767	531	538	545	545	542	.	.
C	16	9	8	7	6	6	6	5	.	.
D	53	34	32	47	46	56	56	58	.	.
E	13	15	16	16	15	13	12	10	.	.
F	11	13	13	56	57	52	52	53	.	.
G	29	49	46	67	68	64	64	68	.	.
H	14	19	9	16	16	17	15	16	.	.
I	32	26	24	32	32	20	19	19	.	.
J-L,O-Q	55	66	71	71	72	81	90	90	.	.
M	48	47	51	49	49	48	47	48	.	.
N	26	23	26	26	27	27	24	25	.	.

Explanatory notes: see p. 77.

[1] Persons aged 15 years and over. [2] Prior to 2001: persons aged 10 years and over.

Notes explicatives: voir p. 80.

[1] Personnes âgées de 15 ans et plus. [2] Avant 2001: personnes agées de 10 ans et plus.

Notas explicativas: véase p. 83.

[1] Personas de 15 años y más. [2] Antes de 2001: personas de 10 años y más.

EMPLOYMENT — EMPLOI — EMPLEO

Total employment, by economic activity — Emploi total, par activité économique — Empleo total, por actividad económica

Thousands — Milliers — Millares

Austria (BA) [1][2] — Total employment - Emploi total - Empleo total

Total - Total - Total — ISIC 3 - CITI 3 - CIIU 3

	1999	2000	2001	2002	2003	2004	2005	2006	2007	2008
Total	3 762.3	3 776.5	3 799.6	3 835.7	3 798.4	3 744.0 [3]	3 824.4	3 928.3	4 027.9	4 090.0
A	230.3	217.7	215.1	214.6	210.1	187.3 [3]	210.3	216.7	230.7	227.3
B	0.3	0.3	0.1	0.7	0.8	1.2 [3]	0.1	0.2	0.6	0.9
C	11.2	9.6	9.5	8.3	6.1	8.6 [3]	8.6	9.8	8.8	10.6
D	763.3	763.9	746.3	747.1	734.3	695.5 [3]	699.9	741.5	730.5	694.8
E	31.2	29.9	31.5	35.2	34.8	28.1 [3]	31.2	31.3	30.1	25.6
F	336.4	339.3	339.5	338.0	338.6	304.0 [3]	313.6	323.7	329.1	332.0
G	592.8	593.7	602.7	601.2	594.6	592.8 [3]	593.5	610.8	645.6	663.8
H	212.2	214.0	207.8	217.7	217.7	227.0 [3]	244.2	242.6	258.6	251.1
I	254.4	245.6	254.9	251.8	238.2	238.3 [3]	241.3	241.8	243.2	244.9
J	141.8	138.5	132.4	132.8	131.8	140.2 [3]	143.5	133.1	135.1	142.5
K	240.6	269.4	293.2	303.4	308.1	327.2 [3]	334.0	350.7	363.3	398.4
L	247.7	253.0	258.3	248.4	237.2	254.1 [3]	238.6	253.0	275.4	278.3
M	220.2	225.5	224.5	230.1	230.7	210.1 [3]	221.9	222.2	211.6	229.5
N	301.3	299.9	310.6	327.3	327.7	325.8 [3]	349.6	347.8	347.3	364.9
O	161.6	159.4	156.0	162.2	169.4	187.2 [3]	175.4	186.9	202.9	206.6
P	12.3	11.8	12.6	13.4	13.6	8.5 [3]	9.6	10.0	8.8	11.7
Q	4.8	5.0	4.6	3.5	4.6	8.1 [3]	8.2	6.1	6.3	7.2

Men - Hommes - Hombres — ISIC 3 - CITI 3 - CIIU 3

	1999	2000	2001	2002	2003	2004	2005	2006	2007	2008
Total	2 139.7	2 145.6	2 142.5	2 139.0	2 101.8	2 061.5 [3]	2 095.2	2 147.5	2 208.5	2 222.1
A	119.8	118.1	113.8	113.8	111.8	98.9 [3]	114.2	116.1	123.5	123.2
B	0.2	0.1	0.1	0.4	0.7	- [3]	0.1	0.2	0.3	0.6
C	9.9	8.7	8.6	7.5	5.3	7.6 [3]	7.4	8.4	7.5	8.4
D	564.4	566.3	553.9	558.3	546.0	513.3 [3]	520.2	546.5	543.1	515.8
E	27.4	25.3	26.9	30.6	30.5	23.8 [3]	25.5	25.6	24.2	20.9
F	310.2	313.5	308.8	309.1	311.8	268.9 [3]	277.0	287.1	288.8	286.6
G	269.5	270.7	269.5	265.0	257.9	276.4 [3]	267.7	273.3	305.1	309.2
H	76.4	76.2	74.9	80.2	75.8	83.4 [3]	90.8	85.8	92.5	89.5
I	197.1	185.2	193.8	190.2	179.5	181.0 [3]	179.3	182.4	176.5	185.2
J	71.8	71.4	66.3	65.3	63.8	68.1 [3]	71.1	67.5	68.9	71.3
K	114.2	132.1	144.5	147.1	156.6	162.7 [3]	167.4	178.9	187.0	211.7
L	157.4	160.3	163.9	155.4	146.6	146.6 [3]	136.8	144.4	155.3	156.1
M	71.1	70.8	70.9	67.4	64.3	64.5 [3]	67.7	66.8	60.4	67.8
N	74.6	75.0	74.7	76.0	75.0	76.1 [3]	88.4	80.2	81.6	82.8
O	72.6	69.5	69.6	71.0	73.9	84.7 [3]	77.1	80.6	89.8	90.2
P	0.4	0.2	0.8	0.2	0.4	1.0 [3]	0.4	0.4	0.5	0.5
Q	2.7	2.3	1.7	1.6	1.9	4.5 [3]	4.2	3.4	3.5	2.5

Women - Femmes - Mujeres — ISIC 3 - CITI 3 - CIIU 3

	1999	2000	2001	2002	2003	2004	2005	2006	2007	2008
Total	1 622.7	1 631.0	1 657.1	1 696.7	1 696.6	1 682.5 [3]	1 728.1	1 780.7	1 819.4	1 867.9
A	110.5	99.6	101.4	100.8	98.3	88.5 [3]	96.1	100.5	107.2	104.1
B	0.1	0.2	0.1	0.3	0.1	- [3]	0.0	0.0	0.3	0.3
C	1.3	0.9	0.9	0.8	0.8	1.0 [3]	1.2	1.4	1.3	2.3
D	198.9	197.6	192.4	188.8	188.3	182.3 [3]	179.8	195.0	187.4	179.1
E	3.8	4.7	4.6	4.7	4.4	4.3 [3]	5.8	5.7	6.0	4.7
F	26.2	25.8	30.7	28.9	26.8	35.1 [3]	36.6	36.6	40.2	45.5
G	323.3	323.0	333.2	336.2	336.7	316.4 [3]	325.9	337.5	340.5	354.6
H	135.8	137.8	132.9	137.6	141.9	143.6 [3]	153.4	156.8	166.2	161.6
I	57.2	60.5	61.0	61.6	58.7	57.3 [3]	62.0	59.4	66.7	59.7
J	70.0	67.1	66.1	67.5	68.0	72.1 [3]	72.4	65.6	66.1	71.2
K	126.3	137.2	148.7	156.3	151.5	164.5 [3]	166.7	171.8	176.3	186.7
L	90.3	92.7	94.4	93.0	90.6	107.5 [3]	101.9	108.6	120.1	122.2
M	149.2	154.8	153.6	162.7	166.4	145.7 [3]	154.3	155.4	151.3	161.7
N	226.7	224.9	235.9	251.3	252.8	249.7 [3]	261.3	267.6	265.7	282.0
O	89.0	89.9	86.4	91.2	95.5	102.6 [3]	98.4	106.3	113.1	116.4
P	11.9	11.6	11.8	13.2	13.2	8.2 [3]	9.2	9.6	8.2	11.2
Q	2.1	2.7	2.9	1.9	2.6	3.6 [3]	4.0	2.7	2.9	4.6

Explanatory notes: see p. 77.

[1] Excl. conscripts on compulsory military service. [2] Persons aged 15 years and over. [3] Prior to 2004: incl. conscripts.

Notes explicatives: voir p. 80.

[1] Non compris conscrits ceux du contingent. [2] Personnes âgées de 15 ans et plus. [3] Avant 2004: y compris les conscrits.

Notas explicativas: véase p. 83.

[1] Excl. los conscriptos del servicio obligatorio. [2] Personas de 15 años y más. [3] Antes de 2004: incl. los conscriptos.

Total employment, by economic activity — Emploi total, par activité économique — Empleo total, por actividad económica

Thousands — Milliers — Millares

	1999	2000	2001	2002	2003	2004	2005	2006	2007	2008

Belgique (BA) [1] [2] — Total employment - Emploi total - Empleo total

Total - Total - Total
ISIC 3 - CITI 3 - CIIU 3

	1999	2000	2001	2002	2003	2004	2005	2006	2007	2008
Total	4 006.9 [3]	4 092.2	4 051.2	4 069.8	4 070.4	4 139.2	4 235.3	4 262.8	4 380.3	4 445.9
A-B	79.5 [3]	72.4								
A			65.4	68.7	71.4	81.4	85.5	82.9	80.2	79.4
B			0.8	0.6	0.6	0.6	0.0	0.4	1.1	1.0
C	10.2 [3]	7.8	6.7	6.8	5.8	6.8	9.3	9.4	9.1	6.2
D	750.9 [3]	772.5	756.2	737.2	714.3	718.5	727.3	715.2	724.6	727.5
E	33.5 [3]	34.6	30.9	30.5	32.1	32.3	32.3	35.1	34.3	40.4
F	272.7 [3]	261.2	260.2	260.1	259.1	272.6	277.0	292.9	302.1	321.8
G	589.3 [3]	572.4	554.4	582.9	560.3	565.3	568.0	559.4	589.0	571.0
H	136.1 [3]	132.8	129.5	139.0	132.9	132.0	143.8	140.1	150.8	141.9
I	296.1 [3]	317.7	325.5	313.4	311.7	313.3	313.5	320.0	316.1	331.8
J			161.3	156.9	154.5	152.3	162.0	155.6	162.6	175.7
J-K	465.4 [3]	512.5								
K			358.4	369.7	382.4	378.7	368.8	404.4	414.0	417.9
L			392.5	395.1	397.1	419.4	419.8	422.1	431.7	436.9
L-O	1 331.9 [3]	1 371.3								
M			348.4	339.1	351.0	371.3	389.5	375.6	378.5	375.6
N			470.2	494.1	518.6	508.6	516.8	528.9	534.7	564.1
O			160.1	153.8	160.4	159.5	170.0	172.0	185.1	181.8
P			11.4	10.6	9.6	13.3	20.8	23.7	33.9	42.1
P-Q	41.2 [3]	37.1								
Q			19.1	11.2	8.7	13.3	31.3	24.8	32.7	30.7

Men - Hommes - Hombres
ISIC 3 - CITI 3 - CIIU 3

	1999	2000	2001	2002	2003	2004	2005	2006	2007	2008
Total	2 321.4 [3]	2 367.6	2 346.3	2 339.2	2 317.0	2 354.3	2 386.8	2 391.0	2 443.7	2 460.7
A-B	54.9 [3]	53.2								
A			47.2	48.2	50.2	57.3	57.8	59.0	55.3	59.1
B			0.8	0.5	0.4	0.6	-	0.4	0.6	0.9
C	8.1 [3]	7.0	6.0	6.4	5.4	6.1	7.8	8.0	7.0	5.1
D	578.6 [3]	588.9	576.5	557.5	535.8	545.7	548.5	543.5	545.8	554.9
E	29.0 [3]	30.0	25.6	25.8	25.9	26.3	25.8	28.1	25.2	31.5
F	252.4 [3]	243.6	243.5	242.4	241.7	252.8	253.8	271.5	278.2	295.0
G	310.1 [3]	297.2	290.6	305.8	296.4	301.5	295.8	293.6	308.7	294.8
H	67.5 [3]	64.6	66.0	69.6	66.3	66.9	74.0	71.7	76.4	72.4
I	231.4 [3]	250.0	252.0	248.8	248.4	245.7	236.8	243.0	242.7	254.5
J			87.3	84.4	85.2	80.2	88.3	82.4	88.1	90.5
J-K	259.5 [3]	297.6								
K			207.2	217.4	221.8	217.2	214.8	227.5	229.5	227.4
L			226.7	218.1	220.7	230.2	236.5	225.0	232.1	234.1
L-O	514.7 [3]	522.0								
M			107.6	109.0	115.9	121.1	128.3	120.1	116.2	112.7
N			118.2	126.3	123.1	116.5	120.0	122.4	129.0	126.2
O			80.0	71.4	73.5	76.9	79.0	78.1	87.9	82.5
P			2.3	2.4	1.6	2.1	4.0	2.8	3.2	3.5
P-Q	15.2 [3]	13.6								
Q			8.9	5.2	4.7	7.3	16.5	14.0	17.7	15.6

Women - Femmes - Mujeres
ISIC 3 - CITI 3 - CIIU 3

	1999	2000	2001	2002	2003	2004	2005	2006	2007	2008
Total	1 685.5 [3]	1 724.5	1 704.9	1 730.7	1 753.4	1 784.9	1 848.5	1 871.5	1 936.6	1 985.2
A-B	24.6 [3]	19.2								
A			18.2	20.5	21.2	24.2	27.0	24.0	24.9	20.4
B			-	0.2	0.2	-	-	-	0.4	0.1
C	2.1 [3]	0.7	0.7	0.4	0.4	0.7	1.5	1.4	2.1	1.1
D	172.4 [3]	183.7	179.7	179.7	178.5	172.8	178.5	171.7	178.8	172.6
E	4.5 [3]	4.6	5.3	4.6	6.2	6.0	6.8	7.0	9.1	8.9
F	20.4 [3]	17.7	16.8	17.8	17.5	19.8	23.0	21.4	23.8	26.8
G	279.2 [3]	275.2	263.8	277.1	263.9	263.8	272.3	265.9	280.3	276.2
H	68.6 [3]	68.2	63.6	69.4	66.6	65.2	70.0	68.3	74.4	69.6
I	64.7 [3]	67.6	73.6	64.7	63.3	67.6	76.5	76.9	73.4	77.3
J			74.0	72.6	69.3	72.1	73.5	73.2	74.5	85.2
J-K	205.9 [3]	214.9								
K			151.3	152.3	160.6	161.5	154.0	176.9	184.5	190.5
L			165.8	177.0	176.3	189.2	183.0	197.1	199.5	202.8
L-O	817.1 [3]	849.3								
M			240.9	230.1	235.1	250.2	261.0	255.4	262.3	262.9
N			352.0	367.8	395.6	392.1	397.0	406.5	405.7	437.9
O			80.1	82.4	86.9	82.6	91.0	94.0	97.2	99.4
P			9.1	8.2	7.9	11.2	18.0	20.9	30.7	38.5
P-Q	26.0 [3]	23.6								
Q			10.2	6.0	3.9	6.0	15.0	10.8	15.0	15.2

Explanatory notes: see p. 77.   Notes explicatives: voir p. 80.   Notas explicativas: véase p. 83.

[1] Incl. professional army. [2] Persons aged 15 years and over. [3] Prior to 1999: April of each year.

[1] Y compris les militaires de carrière. [2] Personnes âgées de 15 ans et plus. [3] Avant 1999: avril de chaque année.

[1] Incl. los militares profesionales. [2] Personas de 15 años y más. [3] Antes de 1999: abril de cada año.

Total employment, by economic activity / **Emploi total, par activité économique** / **Empleo total, por actividad económica**

Thousands / Milliers / Millares

Bulgaria (BA) [1] [2]

Total employment - Emploi total - Empleo total

Total - Total - Total

ISIC 3 - CITI 3 - CIIU 3	1999	2000	2001	2002	2003	2004	2005	2006	2007	2008	ISIC 4 - CITI 4 - CIIU 4
Total	.	.	.	.	2 834.0	2 922.2	2 980.0	3 110.0	3 252.6	3 360.7	Total
A-B	.	.	.	.	285.9	282.1	265.4	252.2	245.4	251.2	A
C	.	.	.	.	41.5	38.9	36.9	38.2	35.5	35.0	B
D	.	.	.	.	676.6	697.2	728.7	745.1	766.5	769.7	C
E	.	.	.	.	60.0	62.5	64.0	58.9	60.4	42.1	D
F	.	.	.	.	151.4	169.7	190.6	230.0	292.3	37.0	E
G	.	.	.	.	423.5	435.6	447.1	494.0	519.2	340.3	F
H	.	.	.	.	128.4	140.6	150.2	156.4	163.0	530.0	G
I	.	.	.	.	214.8	211.6	213.9	220.3	220.0	189.5	H
J	.	.	.	.	30.8	34.4	37.8	39.1	43.7	168.8	I
K	.	.	.	.	115.6	132.2	141.6	147.1	163.2	71.2	J
L	.	.	.	.	230.2	220.8	214.1	225.0	238.9	57.0	K
M	.	.	.	.	210.7	210.4	207.2	214.9	217.5	14.1	L
N	.	.	.	.	155.3	157.0	159.6	163.8	161.7	83.9	M
O-Q	.	.	.	.	107.6	127.2	120.8	125.1	125.3	73.9	N
X	.	.	.	.	1.7	1.7	2.1	-	-	235.3	O
										205.6	P
										158.1	Q
										43.8	R
										54.1	S-U
										-	X

Men - Hommes - Hombres

ISIC 3 - CITI 3 - CIIU 3	1999	2000	2001	2002	2003	2004	2005	2006	2007	2008	ISIC 4 - CITI 4 - CIIU 4
Total	.	.	.	.	1 500.0	1 550.7	1 591.4	1 652.8	1 731.5	1 792.9	Total
A-B	.	.	.	.	184.5	181.1	170.6	162.7	159.1	160.0	A
C	.	.	.	.	33.8	32.1	31.2	31.2	28.7	28.2	B
D	.	.	.	.	331.9	343.9	364.8	375.6	377.0	380.4	C
E	.	.	.	.	46.6	47.8	47.9	44.2	47.2	31.9	D
F	.	.	.	.	136.5	153.7	175.3	212.2	267.9	26.0	E
G	.	.	.	.	213.1	216.3	219.7	239.3	246.4	307.8	F
H	.	.	.	.	49.1	55.6	59.1	58.6	57.8	246.9	G
I	.	.	.	.	156.4	155.5	157.8	163.6	165.1	144.7	H
J	.	.	.	.	10.8	11.0	14.3	12.7	12.5	60.5	I
K	.	.	.	.	64.8	74.9	80.2	83.7	95.3	39.9	J
L	.	.	.	.	139.8	135.5	130.8	131.4	142.2	18.7	K
M	.	.	.	.	47.1	46.5	43.2	44.8	41.2	5.9	L
N	.	.	.	.	36.5	36.2	36.2	36.0	36.7	34.0	M
O-Q	.	.	.	.	48.0	59.3	58.9	56.7	54.4	53.7	N
X	.	.	.	.	1.0	1.0	1.3	-	-	141.5	O
										38.5	P
										32.0	Q
										21.2	R
										21.1	S-U
										-	X

Women - Femmes - Mujeres

ISIC 3 - CITI 3 - CIIU 3	1999	2000	2001	2002	2003	2004	2005	2006	2007	2008	ISIC 4 - CITI 4 - CIIU 4
Total	.	.	.	.	1 334.0	1 371.5	1 388.7	1 457.2	1 521.1	1 567.8	Total
A-B	.	.	.	.	101.3	101.0	94.8	89.4	86.3	91.2	A
C	.	.	.	.	7.7	6.8	5.6	7.0	6.8	6.8	B
D	.	.	.	.	344.7	353.3	363.9	369.4	389.5	389.2	C
E	.	.	.	.	13.4	14.7	16.1	14.7	13.3	10.3	D
F	.	.	.	.	14.9	16.0	15.2	17.8	24.4	11.0	E
G	.	.	.	.	210.5	219.3	227.4	254.7	272.7	32.6	F
H	.	.	.	.	79.3	85.0	91.1	97.8	105.3	283.1	G
I	.	.	.	.	58.4	56.1	56.1	56.7	54.9	44.9	H
J	.	.	.	.	19.9	23.4	23.5	26.4	31.2	108.3	I
K	.	.	.	.	50.8	57.4	61.4	63.4	67.8	31.3	J
L	.	.	.	.	90.4	85.3	83.3	93.7	96.7	38.3	K
M	.	.	.	.	163.5	163.9	164.0	170.1	176.3	8.2	L
N	.	.	.	.	118.8	120.8	123.4	127.7	125.0	49.9	M
O-Q	.	.	.	.	59.6	67.9	61.9	68.4	70.9	20.2	N
X	.	.	.	.	0.7	0.7	0.8	-	-	93.8	O
										167.1	P
										126.1	Q
										22.5	R
										33.1	S-U
										-	X

Explanatory notes: see p. 77.

[1] Persons aged 15 years and over. [2] Excl. conscripts.

Notes explicatives: voir p. 80.

[1] Personnes âgées de 15 ans et plus. [2] Non compris les conscrits.

Notas explicativas: véase p. 83.

[1] Personas de 15 años y más. [2] Excl. los conscriptos.

Total employment, by economic activity

Emploi total, par activité économique

Empleo total, por actividad económica

Thousands   Milliers   Millares

Croatia (BA) [1] [2]

Total employment - Emploi total - Empleo total

	1999	2000	2001	2002	2003	2004	2005	2006	2007	2008
Total - Total - Total										
ISIC 3 - CITI 3 - CIIU 3										
Total	1 491.6	1 553.0	1 469.5	1 527.2	1 536.4	1 562.7	1 572.9	1 586.4	1 614.4	1 635.6
A	243.5	220.2	224.5	227.1	254.0	251.5	267.4	222.2	206.0	216.4
B	3.9	5.0	3.9	5.7	4.6	5.0	4.6	3.6	. [3]	5.3 [4]
C	8.8	7.2	9.1	9.0	10.4	8.9	9.1	7.3	10.5 [4]	8.8 [4]
D	325.0	310.9	305.6	312.5	293.0	301.0	284.0	302.0	312.2	316.1
E	26.2	29.7	29.1	26.8	28.1	28.7	28.8	22.7	28.6 [4]	28.6 [4]
F	97.1	99.9	96.6	105.0	125.1	127.4	128.2	133.2	142.4	145.0
G	197.2	219.8	211.3	212.9	212.7	215.8	219.4	233.9	230.0	245.7
H	74.0	79.7	77.0	86.0	84.5	86.2	83.5	89.8	95.3	89.1
I	101.1	108.1	103.2	106.1	101.4	103.3	103.1	104.2	114.8	108.8
J	34.6	37.2	28.5	35.4	32.4	30.5	28.4	38.8	36.4 [4]	34.4 [4]
K	56.6	68.2	59.8	61.2	64.0	63.2	75.6	81.2	83.8	82.7
L	105.4	123.7	105.5	110.5	96.5	101.9	100.4	98.7	93.7	94.0
M	80.8	88.0	76.4	87.5	83.0	90.5	87.4	92.1	88.9	91.5
N	89.1	91.3	82.8	83.0	87.5	87.4	84.6	84.8	90.6	92.3
O	44.9	58.2	48.9	51.1	52.9	57.1	62.3	65.5	71.1	69.9
P	3.4	3.4	3.9	6.1	4.4	3.3	4.6	4.2	5.1 [4]	5.4 [4]
Q	-	-	-	1.0	-	-	-	-	. [3]	. [3]
Men - Hommes - Hombres										
ISIC 3 - CITI 3 - CIIU 3										
Total	802.2	848.7	818.9	842.5	850.5	866.4	867.0	868.1	897.3	905.1
A	125.2	113.2	125.2	124.6	133.7	130.4	134.7	115.5	104.0	108.1
B	3.6	4.5	3.8	5.3	4.1	4.1	3.9	3.0	3.4	4.5 [4]
C	7.6	6.7	7.5	8.2	8.7	8.3	8.3	5.9	9.4 [4]	8.1 [4]
D	188.5	188.9	183.3	190.9	181.3	189.3	174.6	192.7	198.7	199.9
E	20.8	23.7	23.5	21.5	22.0	21.9	22.2	16.6	21.7 [4]	23.1 [4]
F	87.5	88.5	87.2	95.1	115.4	116.9	117.2	121.9	131.4	133.0
G	90.2	107.3	101.8	102.4	104.2	101.4	105.4	107.9	106.0	120.6
H	34.3	40.1	35.8	39.8	37.2	39.5	38.1	39.7	46.2	42.0
I	79.1	80.6	80.3	81.4	79.2	82.5	81.9	81.9	89.8	87.3
J	9.6	11.5	7.0	9.4	9.4	9.2	9.8	11.1	11.6 [4]	11.9 [4]
K	29.9	33.3	30.8	33.2	32.6	36.7	41.7	44.7	43.6	41.6
L	62.3	74.4	67.0	66.9	57.8	57.3	58.1	53.8	52.8	49.8
M	18.7	24.1	19.8	19.6	18.4	23.1	20.5	21.4	23.2 [4]	22.2 [4]
N	19.3	21.2	18.2	16.8	18.0	18.6	19.7	18.7	20.5 [4]	18.5 [4]
O	25.9	28.4	25.8	25.7	25.7	25.7	30.0	31.6	34.0 [4]	33.0 [4]
P	0.3	2.3	0.7	1.4	1.6	0.2	0.3	0.5	. [3]	. [3]
Q	-	-	-	0.3	-	-	-	-	. [3]	. [3]
Women - Femmes - Mujeres										
ISIC 3 - CITI 3 - CIIU 3										
Total	689.5	704.3	650.6	684.7	685.9	696.4	705.9	718.3	717.1	730.5
A	118.3	107.0	99.3	102.5	120.4	121.1	132.7	106.7	102.0	108.3
B	0.3	0.5	0.1	0.4	0.5	0.9	0.7	0.6	. [3]	. [3]
C	1.2	0.5	1.6	0.8	1.7	0.5	0.8	1.4	- [3]	.
D	136.5	122.0	122.3	121.7	111.7	111.5	109.4	109.3	113.6	116.2
E	5.4	6.0	5.6	5.3	6.1	6.9	6.6	6.1	6.9 [4]	5.5 [4]
F	9.6	11.4	9.4	9.9	9.7	10.5	11.0	11.2	11.0 [4]	12.0 [4]
G	107.0	112.5	109.5	110.4	108.5	114.4	114.1	126.0	124.0	125.0
H	39.7	39.6	41.2	46.2	47.4	46.7	45.4	50.1	49.0	47.1
I	22.0	27.5	22.9	24.8	22.1	20.8	21.2	22.3	25.0 [4]	21.5 [4]
J	25.0	25.7	21.5	28.0	23.0	21.3	18.6	27.7	24.7 [4]	22.4 [4]
K	26.7	34.9	29.0	28.0	31.4	26.5	33.9	36.4	40.2	41.1 [4]
L	43.1	49.3	38.5	43.7	38.7	44.6	42.3	44.9	40.9	44.3
M	62.1	63.9	56.6	67.9	64.7	67.5	67.0	70.7	65.7	69.3
N	69.6	70.1	64.6	66.2	69.5	68.7	64.9	66.1	70.1	73.8
O	19.0	29.8	23.1	25.4	27.2	31.4	32.4	33.9	37.1 [4]	36.9 [4]
P	3.1	1.5	3.2	4.7	2.8	3.1	4.3	3.7	4.7 [4]	4.4 [4]
Q	-	-	-	0.7	-	-	-	-	. [3]	. [3]

Explanatory notes: see p. 77.

[1] Incl. armed forces, Excl. conscripts. [2] Persons aged 15 years and over. [3] Not indicated due to lack of statistical reliability. [4] Estimate not sufficiently reliable.

Notes explicatives: voir p. 80.

[1] Y compris les forces armées, Excl. conscrits [2] Personnes âgées de 15 ans et plus. [3] Non indiqué en raison du manque de fiabilité statistique. [4] Estimation pas suffisamment fiable.

Notas explicativas: véase p. 83.

[1] Incl. las fuerzas armadas, excl. los conscriptos. [2] Personas de 15 años y más. [3] No se indica por la falta de confiabilidad estadística. [4] Estimación no suficientemente fiable.

EMPLOYMENT

EMPLOI

EMPLEO

**Total employment,
by economic activity**

**Emploi total,
par activité économique**

**Empleo total,
por actividad económica**

	Thousands					Milliers			Millares	
	1999	2000	2001	2002	2003	2004	2005	2006	2007	2008

Cyprus (BA) [1] [2] [3]   Total employment - Emploi total - Empleo total

Total - Total - Total
ISIC 3 - CITI 3 - CIIU 3

	1999	2000	2001	2002	2003	2004	2005	2006	2007	2008
Total	279.2	288.6	309.5	315.3	327.1	338.0	348.0	357.3	377.9	382.9
A	11.7	14.7	14.4	16.0	16.7	15.9	16.0	14.6	15.9	15.9
B	1.0	0.4	0.6	0.5	0.3	0.4	0.5	0.6	0.7	0.6
C	0.4	0.7	0.5	0.5	0.5	0.5	0.8	0.7	0.5	0.5
D	36.6	35.9	39.5	38.5	35.9	37.6	40.0	37.3	37.2	37.5
E	2.3	2.7	3.1	3.0	3.6	3.6	2.7	2.9	2.7	3.1
F	27.0	27.8	30.3	31.1	34.9	39.4	40.2	40.0	44.7	44.9
G	50.2	51.1	56.7	59.3	59.2	61.3	60.3	63.2	68.0	69.5
H	27.0	26.8	28.4	28.0	28.8	30.0	27.1	23.9	23.9	25.7
I	18.9	16.3	18.4	16.2	17.3	18.2	18.5	20.2	22.4	21.2
J	13.8	15.6	19.5	18.2	16.4	15.8	18.1	18.9	18.8	19.6
K	15.8	16.2	16.6	18.0	22.4	22.5	24.6	26.7	31.4	32.7
L	21.4	24.7	24.2	23.8	24.4	23.5	26.3	29.9	31.2	30.2
M	14.9	15.7	19.3	20.2	21.4	21.5	22.6	24.8	26.4	27.1
N	10.8	10.4	12.4	12.8	14.4	15.1	14.9	14.2	16.9	16.2
O	12.1	12.6	14.8	15.9	17.2	16.9	18.2	21.6	18.8	18.4
P	3.7	5.1	8.3	10.2	10.9	13.7	14.2	14.8	15.7	16.9
Q	2.4	2.3	2.5	2.9	2.4	2.2	3.0	2.9	2.8	2.6
X	9.2	9.4	-	-	0.5	-	-	-	-	-

Men - Hommes - Hombres
ISIC 3 - CITI 3 - CIIU 3

	1999	2000	2001	2002	2003	2004	2005	2006	2007	2008
Total	172.9	176.1	176.2	176.8	181.6	190.8	197.3	200.4	209.5	212.2
A	7.3	9.4	9.1	10.1	10.9	10.5	10.8	10.1	12.0	11.3
B	1.0	0.4	0.6	0.5	0.3	0.4	0.5	0.6	0.6	0.5
C	0.3	0.7	0.5	0.5	0.4	0.5	0.7	0.7	0.5	0.4
D	23.6	23.3	25.3	24.2	22.4	24.4	27.2	25.1	25.4	25.1
E	1.8	2.2	2.5	2.6	3.2	3.0	2.2	2.5	2.4	2.6
F	25.7	26.1	28.4	29.0	32.4	37.3	37.7	36.6	40.7	41.6
G	30.3	31.3	32.1	33.7	32.7	34.5	34.2	37.4	37.9	38.7
H	13.2	13.9	13.9	13.4	12.9	13.3	12.3	11.0	10.6	12.5
I	13.6	11.2	12.1	10.7	11.0	12.4	12.6	13.2	13.4	13.4
J	6.7	7.2	8.4	7.8	6.8	6.8	9.2	9.3	8.7	8.5
K	7.0	7.5	8.3	8.3	11.4	11.6	11.6	11.9	14.4	14.6
L	15.1	17.0	15.9	14.9	15.3	15.9	17.9	20.1	19.6	18.4
M	5.1	4.6	5.3	6.4	6.8	6.4	5.6	6.1	7.5	7.4
N	4.0	3.2	4.0	3.9	4.1	4.2	4.2	4.0	4.9	5.5
O	7.2	7.1	8.1	8.5	9.3	7.9	8.5	9.6	8.8	9.2
P	0.1	0.1	0.1	0.1	0.1	0.3	0.4	0.4	0.2	0.3
Q	1.7	1.6	1.6	2.0	1.5	1.5	1.9	2.0	2.1	2.1
X	9.2	9.4	-	-	-	-	-	-		

Women - Femmes - Mujeres
ISIC 3 - CITI 3 - CIIU 3

	1999	2000	2001	2002	2003	2004	2005	2006	2007	2008
Total	106.3	112.5	133.3	138.6	145.5	147.2	150.7	156.9	168.5	170.6
A	4.4	5.4	5.3	5.9	5.7	5.4	5.3	4.6	3.9	4.6
B	-	-	-	-	-	-	-	0.0	0.2	0.1
C	0.1	-	-	-	0.1	-	0.1	0.0	0.0	0.1
D	13.1	12.7	14.2	14.3	13.5	13.2	12.8	12.2	11.8	12.4
E	0.5	0.5	0.6	0.4	0.4	0.6	0.5	0.4	0.4	0.5
F	1.4	1.7	1.9	2.1	2.5	2.0	2.5	3.4	4.0	3.3
G	19.9	19.9	24.6	25.6	27.0	26.8	26.0	25.8	30.1	30.8
H	13.8	13.0	14.5	14.6	15.9	16.7	14.9	12.9	13.3	13.3
I	5.3	5.1	6.3	5.5	6.3	5.8	5.9	7.0	9.0	7.8
J	7.1	8.4	11.0	10.4	9.7	9.0	9.0	9.6	10.0	11.1
K	8.6	8.7	8.3	9.7	11.1	10.9	13.0	14.8	17.0	18.2
L	6.3	7.7	8.3	8.9	9.1	7.6	8.4	9.8	11.6	11.8
M	9.8	11.2	14.0	13.8	14.5	15.1	17.1	18.7	18.9	19.7
N	6.8	7.2	8.4	8.9	10.2	10.9	10.7	10.2	12.0	10.8
O	4.9	5.4	6.7	7.5	7.9	9.0	9.7	12.0	10.0	9.1
P	3.6	5.0	8.3	10.1	10.8	13.4	13.8	14.4	15.5	16.7
Q	0.7	0.7	0.8	0.8	0.8	0.7	1.1	1.0	0.7	0.6
X										

Explanatory notes: see p. 77.

[1] Incl. armed forces, Excl. conscripts. [2] Government-controlled area. [3] Persons aged 15 years and over.

Notes explicatives: voir p. 80.

[1] Y compris les forces armées, Excl. conscrits [2] Région sous contrôle gouvernemental. [3] Personnes âgées de 15 ans et plus.

Notas explicativas: véase p. 83.

[1] Incl. las fuerzas armadas, excl. los conscriptos. [2] Area controlada por el gobierno. [3] Personas de 15 años y más.

	Total employment, by economic activity	Emploi total, par activité économique	Empleo total, por actividad económica
	Thousands	Milliers	Millares

	1999	2000	2001	2002	2003	2004	2005	2006	2007	2008

Czech Republic (BA) [1] Total employment - Emploi total - Empleo total

Total - Total - Total
ISIC 3 - CITI 3 - CIIU 3

	1999	2000	2001	2002	2003	2004	2005	2006	2007	2008
Total	4 764	4 732	4 728	4 765	4 733	4 707	4 764	4 828	4 922	5 002
A-B	247	241	225	228	213	202	189	182	.	.
A	.	.	.	.	.	.	.	.	173	163
B	.	.	.	.	.	.	.	.	3	3
C	77	70	67	61	53	59	49	55	54	56
D	1 308	1 282	1 310	1 318	1 294	1 274	1 296	1 362	1 406	1 433
E	84	77	87	84	77	76	77	77	73	78
F	443	439	428	425	439	436	459	436	447	462
G	641	613	605	620	628	631	615	614	613	633
H	157	156	159	171	171	175	182	187	181	177
I	371	373	363	368	359	364	360	361	364	375
J	99	100	101	95	96	94	97	92	102	115
K	257	266	256	269	285	282	288	321	353	370
L	336	343	339	326	332	323	333	326	326	327
M	287	299	300	309	288	279	297	288	290	282
N	277	291	304	304	307	324	328	330	338	328
O	176	176	178	179	185	184	190	193	194	199
P	2	2	1	3	3	3	3	3	3	3
Q	2	2	1	1	1	1	1	1	1	-
X	1	2	3	4	1	1	2	1	1	-

Men - Hommes - Hombres
ISIC 3 - CITI 3 - CIIU 3

	1999	2000	2001	2002	2003	2004	2005	2006	2007	2008
Total	2 694	2 676	2 674	2 700	2 686	2 663	2 706	2 742	2 806	2 863
A-B	168	164	158	157	147	140	131	123	.	.
A	.	.	.	.	.	.	.	.	120	113
B	.	.	.	.	.	.	.	.	3	2
C	68	60	54	52	47	52	44	48	48	48
D	790	781	806	816	798	786	813	856	896	921
E	66	60	65	63	61	61	60	60	58	61
F	408	402	386	388	405	402	420	403	410	422
G	299	285	277	289	302	308	292	286	289	301
H	67	66	70	76	76	82	84	85	79	81
I	255	256	251	258	248	246	250	259	263	269
J	33	34	42	39	34	33	38	34	38	44
K	142	147	147	147	156	159	163	185	200	205
L	198	206	200	186	193	180	179	170	165	170
M	66	70	74	77	69	64	71	73	72	69
N	52	59	63	64	64	62	68	65	67	63
O	81	83	79	83	83	88	93	93	96	95
P	-	-	-	-	1	-	1	1	1	1
Q	1	1	-	1	-	-	-	1	1	-
X	1	1	2	3	1	1	1	-	1	-

Women - Femmes - Mujeres
ISIC 3 - CITI 3 - CIIU 3

	1999	2000	2001	2002	2003	2004	2005	2006	2007	2008
Total	2 070	2 056	2 054	2 065	2 047	2 044	2 059	2 086	2 116	2 139
A-B	79	76	68	71	66	62	58	58	.	.
A	.	.	.	.	.	.	.	.	53	50
B	.	.	.	.	.	.	.	.	-	1
C	9	10	13	9	7	7	6	7	6	7
D	517	501	504	502	496	488	484	506	509	512
E	18	17	22	21	16	15	17	17	15	17
F	35	37	41	37	33	34	39	33	37	40
G	342	328	328	331	326	323	323	327	324	333
H	90	90	89	94	95	93	97	102	102	96
I	116	117	112	110	110	118	110	102	101	106
J	66	66	60	56	62	61	59	58	64	71
K	114	119	109	122	129	122	126	136	153	165
L	139	137	139	140	139	143	155	155	161	157
M	220	229	226	232	219	215	226	215	218	213
N	225	232	241	240	242	262	260	265	271	265
O	95	93	99	96	102	97	97	100	99	104
P	2	2	1	3	4	3	3	3	2	2
Q	1	1	1	-	1	1	1	1	-	-
X	-	1	1	1	1	-	1	1	-	-

Explanatory notes: see p. 77.   Notes explicatives: voir p. 80.   Notas explicativas: véase p. 83.

[1] Persons aged 15 years and over.   [1] Personnes âgées de 15 ans et plus.   [1] Personas de 15 años y más.

EMPLOYMENT EMPLOI EMPLEO

Total employment, by economic activity / Emploi total, par activité économique / Empleo total, por actividad económica

	1999	2000	2001	2002	2003	2004	2005	2006	2007	2008
		Thousands				Milliers			Millares	

Denmark (BA) [1][2]

Total employment - Emploi total - Empleo total

Total - Total - Total
ISIC 3 - CITI 3 - CIIU 3

	1999	2000	2001	2002	2003	2004	2005	2006	2007	2008
Total	.	2 722.1	2 725.1	2 715.3	2 692.5	2 720.1	2 732.8	2 786.6	2 778.6	2 827.4
A	.	86.7	84.9	80.4	77.0	81.2	80.4	79.4	79.7	73.8
B	.	3.2	4.0	5.2	4.6	3.4	-	-	-	-
C	.	2.6	2.6	4.5	5.7	4.3	-	5.6	5.2	3.6
D	.	509.9	488.4	459.2	440.9	434.5	442.3	427.6	432.9	426.0
E	.	14.6	13.5	14.9	14.4	15.9	15.2	16.6	16.5	17.6
F	.	184.2	181.6	181.2	180.0	184.5	192.5	201.2	192.9	193.0
G	.	376.6	379.0	390.0	395.8	406.3	400.8	409.1	412.1	430.5
H	.	66.5	63.4	67.5	66.4	68.9	69.7	76.7	81.1	82.0
I	.	176.2	182.9	185.5	188.3	185.5	175.3	176.1	173.1	158.9
J	.	85.1	84.3	85.6	81.8	81.3	88.9	93.0	85.9	86.9
K	.	249.4	257.4	252.4	248.8	248.0	253.4	275.9	268.4	292.2
L	.	160.3	161.7	161.0	157.8	163.8	166.7	168.2	164.2	177.6
M	.	197.1	202.4	208.6	208.5	213.0	216.1	211.1	215.2	210.6
N	.	474.6	483.0	481.8	477.7	480.6	474.8	486.9	499.9	516.2
O	.	122.2	128.3	128.3	136.0	140.5	141.6	150.7	145.7	148.8
P	.	4.2	1.5	2.7	1.8	3.2	-	-	3.9	-
Q	.	1.3	0.7	1.1	2.3	1.6	-	-	1.9	-
X	.	7.4	5.6	5.4	4.6	3.9	3.7	-	-	3.7

Men - Hommes - Hombres
ISIC 3 - CITI 3 - CIIU 3

	1999	2000	2001	2002	2003	2004	2005	2006	2007	2008
Total	.	1 458.1	1 456.3	1 449.3	1 447.8	1 451.6	1 456.1	1 482.3	1 476.1	1 497.3
A	.	64.2	64.5	60.4	59.1	61.8	60.3	60.9	60.1	58.3
B	.	3.1	4.0	5.2	4.6	3.3	-	-	-	-
C	.	2.6	2.6	3.8	4.9	4.0	-	4.8	3.9	-
D	.	347.5	335.2	313.5	307.8	302.7	305.6	296.1	295.4	288.5
E	.	12.3	10.4	12.0	12.1	12.8	11.5	12.6	12.4	12.9
F	.	169.3	167.1	165.8	165.3	168.7	174.3	185.3	174.4	176.0
G	.	212.9	218.5	223.5	224.9	233.5	230.0	230.1	235.6	243.9
H	.	27.6	27.2	29.6	29.9	28.7	29.8	33.4	37.7	38.6
I	.	126.3	128.4	133.1	134.4	127.7	125.6	124.1	123.2	114.9
J	.	43.3	41.1	45.4	41.2	42.1	41.6	44.9	43.0	43.5
K	.	152.5	149.4	146.3	147.1	146.5	148.0	159.3	158.6	178.4
L	.	82.3	81.0	79.8	80.9	83.4	81.8	86.4	83.4	88.5
M	.	86.4	85.5	85.1	83.2	85.1	89.5	87.7	88.2	88.4
N	.	69.9	76.2	77.9	79.9	80.6	81.2	75.1	88.2	87.8
O	.	52.5	61.4	64.9	68.6	68.4	68.2	77.1	71.5	70.6
P	.	0.5	0.3	0.1	0.3	0.1	-	-	0.3	-
Q	.	0.6	0.5	-	1.0	0.5	-	-	-	-
X	.	4.4	3.1	2.8	2.9	1.8	-	-	-	-

Women - Femmes - Mujeres
ISIC 3 - CITI 3 - CIIU 3

	1999	2000	2001	2002	2003	2004	2005	2006	2007	2008
Total	.	1 263.9	1 268.9	1 265.9	1 244.6	1 268.5	1 276.6	1 304.3	1 302.6	1 330.1
A	.	22.6	20.4	19.9	18.0	19.3	20.2	18.5	19.5	15.5
B	.	0.1	-	-	-	0.2	-	-	-	-
C	.	-	0.0	0.6	0.8	0.3	-	0.8	1.3	-
D	.	162.5	153.2	145.7	133.1	131.8	136.8	131.5	137.5	137.6
E	.	2.3	3.0	2.9	2.3	3.2	3.7	3.9	4.1	4.7
F	.	14.9	14.5	15.4	14.7	15.8	18.2	15.9	18.6	17.0
G	.	163.7	160.4	166.5	171.2	172.8	170.8	179.0	176.5	186.6
H	.	38.9	36.1	37.9	36.5	40.2	39.9	43.3	43.4	43.4
I	.	49.9	54.5	52.4	54.0	57.8	49.8	52.0	49.9	44.0
J	.	41.8	43.3	40.2	40.6	39.2	47.3	48.1	43.0	43.4
K	.	97.0	108.0	106.1	101.6	101.6	105.4	116.6	109.8	113.9
L	.	78.0	80.8	81.1	76.9	80.3	85.0	81.8	80.8	89.1
M	.	110.6	116.9	123.5	125.3	127.9	126.7	123.3	127.0	122.2
N	.	404.7	406.8	403.9	397.8	399.9	393.6	411.9	411.6	428.3
O	.	69.6	66.9	63.4	67.4	72.0	73.4	73.6	74.2	78.3
P	.	3.6	1.2	2.6	1.5	3.1	-	-	3.6	-
Q	.	0.8	0.2	1.1	1.3	1.1	-	-	1.9	-
X	.	2.9	2.5	2.6	1.6	2.1	-	-	-	-

Explanatory notes: see p. 77.

[1] Included armed forces and conscripts. [2] Persons aged 15 to 66 years.

Notes explicatives: voir p. 80.

[1] Y compris les forces armées et les conscrits. [2] Personnes âgées de 15 à 66 ans.

Notas explicativas: véase p. 83.

[1] Incluye las fuezas armadas y los conscriptos. [2] Personas de 15 a 66 años.

EMPLOYMENT — EMPLOI — EMPLEO

Total employment, by economic activity
Emploi total, par activité économique
Empleo total, por actividad económica

Thousands — Milliers — Millares

	1999	2000	2001	2002	2003	2004	2005	2006	2007	2008
España (BA) [1][2]					Total employment - Emploi total - Empleo total					
Total - Total - Total										
ISIC 3 - CITI 3 - CIIU 3										
Total	14 689.8	15 505.9	16 146.3	16 630.3	17 295.9	17 970.8	18 973.2 [3]	19 747.7	20 356.0	20 257.6
A	989.5	964.5	981.8	940.7	942.9	937.6	940.6 [3]	893.0	873.3	831.3
B	59.2	64.1	63.4	54.7	48.1	51.4	60.1 [3]	51.3	52.2	47.8
C	67.1	65.9	64.1	65.2	63.6	59.6	60.4 [3]	66.4	60.1	53.0
D	2 800.3	2 918.4	3 014.8	3 035.1	3 034.6	3 047.6	3 113.0 [3]	3 106.9	3 089.8	3 059.8
E	90.6	98.1	97.8	90.4	99.6	103.7	106.6 [3]	118.8	111.9	112.7
F	1 572.2	1 722.7	1 876.2	1 980.2	2 101.6	2 253.2	2 357.2 [3]	2 542.9	2 697.3	2 404.2
G	2 399.8	2 512.0	2 565.3	2 577.1	2 698.8	2 817.5	2 886.8 [3]	2 983.5	3 128.6	3 239.1
H	923.2	1 003.6	1 023.5	1 102.1	1 136.9	1 200.5	1 291.1 [3]	1 402.7	1 450.5	1 452.6
I	868.0	929.9	975.9	1 008.3	1 050.7	1 067.2	1 117.2 [3]	1 158.2	1 177.1	1 182.0
J	384.6	411.6	392.9	399.9	397.6	401.0	457.3 [3]	472.5	500.0	506.9
K	1 016.3	1 135.5	1 251.7	1 327.5	1 418.6	1 545.5	1 678.4 [3]	1 857.4	2 017.1	2 073.7
L	936.3	974.9	1 002.3	1 035.4	1 089.9	1 125.5	1 196.7 [3]	1 221.6	1 238.4	1 277.3
M	835.5	841.4	891.4	946.8	957.4	1 009.9	1 090.5 [3]	1 108.8	1 112.3	1 132.6
N	781.3	830.4	852.4	919.0	998.1	1 029.4	1 134.6 [3]	1 180.8	1 229.2	1 277.1
O	552.4	603.9	628.9	658.3	710.5	728.0	793.7 [3]	815.3	846.2	852.7
P	411.9	427.0	460.9	487.2	542.6	591.4	682.8 [3]	760.6	770.0	752.6
Q	1.6	1.8	3.5	2.3	1.5	1.7	6.1 [3]	7.0	2.1	2.3
Men - Hommes - Hombres										
ISIC 3 - CITI 3 - CIIU 3										
Total	9 433.8	9 821.1	10 150.5	10 365.0	10 652.9	10 934.3	11 388.8 [3]	11 742.6	11 987.3	11 720.7
A	732.1	705.9	720.6	692.0	683.9	684.9	686.3 [3]	638.8	632.6	610.8
B	52.3	55.2	54.9	46.5	40.7	43.7	44.9 [3]	42.5	42.5	39.8
C	60.4	61.1	59.4	61.4	58.7	53.4	53.4 [3]	60.6	53.6	48.4
D	2 156.5	2 193.1	2 260.1	2 264.7	2 284.2	2 282.8	2 327.8 [3]	2 343.2	2 298.4	2 275.3
E	78.7	84.0	83.3	73.5	83.3	84.2	85.7 [3]	97.2	89.5	89.1
F	1 507.5	1 640.3	1 789.1	1 879.5	1 990.5	2 134.3	2 230.1 [3]	2 408.5	2 544.7	2 253.6
G	1 351.7	1 402.5	1 404.3	1 420.1	1 460.1	1 493.0	1 523.4 [3]	1 538.6	1 594.6	1 653.7
H	503.9	542.9	535.7	556.5	563.3	591.0	605.2 [3]	639.6	652.4	640.5
I	705.4	747.9	777.2	798.6	832.6	834.5	864.6 [3]	892.1	907.2	906.4
J	257.3	262.5	240.4	240.9	252.1	244.4	249.9 [3]	254.0	266.9	276.9
K	551.8	594.6	644.9	682.5	721.3	776.8	847.4 [3]	936.9	1 007.9	1 021.0
L	589.2	604.6	641.2	664.0	680.7	685.6	736.7 [3]	730.9	744.2	755.7
M	315.2	327.5	336.7	350.8	344.3	350.7	384.1 [3]	387.6	388.0	404.7
N	244.4	244.8	235.2	242.3	259.6	263.8	297.1 [3]	298.2	288.7	295.6
O	277.3	301.9	316.7	339.3	344.9	352.7	387.1 [3]	401.1	411.5	394.8
P	49.2	48.2	48.2	51.4	52.0	54.6	61.9 [3]	69.5	63.3	53.0
Q	0.9	1.5	2.7	0.7	0.6	0.7	3.1 [3]	3.2	1.1	1.4
Women - Femmes - Mujeres										
ISIC 3 - CITI 3 - CIIU 3										
Total	5 256.0	5 684.8	5 995.7	6 265.3	6 643.1	7 036.5	7 584.4 [3]	8 005.1	8 368.8	8 536.9
A	257.5	258.7	261.2	248.7	258.9	252.7	254.3 [3]	254.2	240.7	220.4
B	6.9	8.9	8.5	8.2	7.4	7.6	15.2 [3]	8.8	9.6	8.0
C	6.7	4.9	4.7	3.8	4.9	6.2	6.9 [3]	5.8	6.5	4.6
D	643.8	725.3	754.8	770.4	753.4	764.8	785.2 [3]	763.7	791.5	784.5
E	11.8	14.0	14.5	16.9	16.3	19.5	20.9 [3]	21.6	22.4	23.6
F	64.7	82.4	87.2	100.6	111.2	118.9	127.1 [3]	134.4	152.6	150.6
G	1 048.1	1 109.5	1 161.0	1 157.0	1 238.7	1 324.5	1 363.5 [3]	1 444.9	1 533.9	1 585.4
H	419.3	461.1	487.8	545.6	573.5	609.5	685.9 [3]	763.1	798.2	812.1
I	162.6	182.0	198.7	209.6	218.1	229.7	252.6 [3]	266.0	269.9	275.5
J	127.3	149.1	152.5	158.9	145.5	156.6	207.4 [3]	218.5	233.1	230.0
K	464.5	540.9	606.8	645.0	697.3	768.7	831.0 [3]	920.5	1 009.2	1 052.8
L	347.0	370.4	361.1	371.3	409.2	439.9	460.1 [3]	490.7	494.1	521.7
M	520.3	513.8	554.7	596.0	613.1	659.2	706.4 [3]	721.2	724.3	727.8
N	536.9	585.7	617.3	676.6	738.5	765.6	837.5 [3]	882.6	940.5	981.5
O	275.2	299.0	311.5	319.0	365.6	375.4	406.6 [3]	414.3	434.7	457.9
P	362.7	378.9	412.7	435.8	490.6	536.8	620.9 [3]	691.1	706.7	699.6
Q	0.7	0.3	0.8	1.7	0.9	1.0	3.0 [3]	3.8	1.0	0.9
Estonia (BA) [4][5]					Total employment - Emploi total - Empleo total					
Total - Total - Total										
ISIC 3 - CITI 3 - CIIU 3										
Total	579.3	572.5	577.7	585.5	594.3	595.5	607.4	646.3	655.3	656.5
A	43.9	38.3	37.3	38.8	34.4	31.4	29.4	29.9	28.8	24.4
B	3.1	2.9	2.7	1.9	2.3	3.6	2.8	2.2	2.1	1.1
C	7.9	7.2	5.8	5.7	5.7	8.0	5.9	5.2	5.5	6.0
D	122.8	129.2	134.1	128.2	134.1	140.9	139.5	136.4	134.8	138.5
E	16.5	14.7	11.4	10.5	10.2	12.0	12.5	12.4	9.5	8.9
F	38.9	39.7	39.3	38.9	42.9	46.8	48.7	62.8	80.9	79.9
G	81.8	79.3	83.6	86.3	80.8	80.0	80.6	88.7	88.1	93.5
H	13.0	19.9	17.4	17.9	17.4	16.2	22.1	22.3	22.8	24.2
I	59.4	56.9	53.7	54.5	56.2	51.5	54.6	61.5	58.4	55.7
J	8.6	7.7	7.2	7.9	7.6	7.9	6.9	7.3	9.4	10.4
K	37.4	40.0	38.2	44.3	44.4	39.4	46.4	48.1	49.5	51.9
L	34.7	34.1	34.8	33.2	34.5	36.9	37.2	39.0	39.2	38.4
M	50.3	44.6	51.0	55.6	56.9	54.5	54.9	58.5	54.5	59.6
N	31.3	28.5	30.9	31.6	36.4	37.5	35.0	37.5	36.4	31.6
O	29.7	29.6	30.4	30.1	30.4	28.8	31.1	34.3	35.6	32.4

Explanatory notes: see p. 77.

[1] Excl. compulsory military service. [2] Persons aged 16 years and over. [3] Methodology revised; data not strictly comparable. [4] Persons aged 15 to 74 years. [5] Excl. conscripts.

Notes explicatives: voir p. 80.

[1] Non compris les militaires du contingent. [2] Personnes âgées de 16 ans et plus. [3] Méthodologie révisée; les données ne sont pas strictement comparables. [4] Personnes âgées de 15 à 74 ans. [5] Non compris les conscrits.

Notas explicativas: véase p. 83.

[1] Excl. a los militares en servicio obligatorio. [2] Personas de 16 años y más. [3] Metodología revisada; los datos no son estrictamente comparables. [4] Personas de 15 a 74 años. [5] Excl. los conscriptos.

2B

EMPLOYMENT	EMPLOI	EMPLEO
Total employment, by economic activity	**Emploi total, par activité économique**	**Empleo total, por actividad económica**
Thousands	Milliers	Millares

	1999	2000	2001	2002	2003	2004	2005	2006	2007	2008

Estonia (BA) [1] [2] — Total employment - Emploi total - Empleo total

Men - Hommes - Hombres
ISIC 3 - CITI 3 - CIIU 3

	1999	2000	2001	2002	2003	2004	2005	2006	2007	2008
Total	294.2	291.1	293.9	297.5	302.5	299.1	300.5	322.9	330.0	330.9
A	27.3	25.4	26.5	26.8	23.3	21.1	19.0	19.7	19.4	16.9
B	2.9	2.8	2.5	1.7	2.2	3.1	2.5	2.0	1.6	0.8
C	6.6	5.7	4.4	5.0	5.0	6.5	5.4	4.7	4.9	5.3
D	66.2	71.4	74.8	72.2	73.6	75.1	73.2	74.2	72.7	74.6
E	11.1	10.6	9.1	8.6	8.0	8.5	9.4	10.2	8.2	6.9
F	35.2	35.9	36.3	35.7	39.9	42.1	44.2	58.1	73.4	72.6
G	34.5	34.2	34.2	35.8	32.7	33.4	33.0	35.5	35.9	38.7
H	2.7	4.4	3.1	4.5	3.6	4.3	4.7	4.2	4.0	5.1
I	42.6	39.0	37.3	36.1	36.7	35.3	38.7	42.1	39.1	38.1
J	3.2	3.4	2.6	2.4	2.6	2.2	1.2	1.7	2.5	3.2
K	20.8	20.5	19.9	25.5	27.4	22.6	27.3	26.4	25.8	27.1
L	16.9	16.3	18.2	17.0	19.0	18.4	17.5	18.8	18.0	17.1
M	9.5	7.5	9.6	10.8	10.7	10.4	9.1	9.8	8.8	12.0
N	4.2	3.3	5.0	5.1	5.6	5.6	4.9	4.8	4.4	3.0
O	10.6	11.0	10.5	10.3	12.1	10.7	10.3	10.8	11.3	9.5

Women - Femmes - Mujeres
ISIC 3 - CITI 3 - CIIU 3

	1999	2000	2001	2002	2003	2004	2005	2006	2007	2008
Total	285.1	281.4	283.8	288.1	291.8	296.4	306.9	323.3	325.4	325.6
A	16.6	12.9	10.8	11.9	11.1	10.3	10.4	10.2	9.4	7.6
B	0.2	0.1	0.2	0.2	0.1	0.5	0.3	0.2	0.5	0.3
C	1.3	1.5	1.4	0.7	0.7	1.5	0.5	0.5	0.6	0.7
D	56.6	57.8	59.3	56.0	60.6	65.8	66.2	62.2	62.1	63.9
E	5.5	4.1	2.3	2.0	2.2	3.5	3.1	2.2	1.3	2.0
F	3.7	3.8	2.9	3.2	3.0	4.7	4.5	4.7	7.5	7.3
G	47.4	45.1	49.4	50.5	48.1	46.7	47.7	53.1	52.2	54.8
H	10.3	15.5	14.3	13.4	13.8	11.9	17.3	18.2	18.8	19.1
I	16.8	17.9	16.4	18.4	19.5	16.2	15.8	19.5	19.3	17.7
J	5.3	4.3	4.5	5.5	5.0	5.7	5.7	5.6	6.9	7.2
K	16.6	19.5	18.4	18.8	17.0	16.9	19.2	21.7	23.7	24.8
L	17.7	17.8	16.7	16.2	15.5	18.5	19.6	20.2	21.2	21.3
M	40.8	37.1	41.4	44.8	46.1	44.1	45.8	48.6	45.6	47.6
N	27.1	25.2	25.9	26.4	30.8	32.0	30.2	32.7	32.0	28.7
O	19.1	18.6	19.8	19.8	18.3	18.2	20.7	23.5	24.3	22.8

Finland (BA) [1] [3] — Total employment - Emploi total - Empleo total

Total - Total - Total
ISIC 3 - CITI 3 - CIIU 3

	1999	2000	2001	2002	2003	2004	2005	2006	2007	2008
Total	2 317	2 356	2 388	2 393	2 385	2 387	2 421	2 466	2 512	2 553
A	142	140	133	125	119	115	114	113	111	113
B	2	2	2	2	1	2	2	1	2	1
C	5	4	3	5	5	5	6	5	5	5
D	460	467	472	466	444	435	436	443	445	438
E	22	22	22	21	20	19	19	17	16	17
F	149	149	145	148	151	148	158	162	174	184
G	279	278	278	282	287	293	301	303	311	314
H	77	76	80	82	76	75	77	78	84	89
I	168	172	174	169	173	171	172	181	175	174
J	45	49	50	47	49	49	47	47	50	52
K	221	238	251	261	264	266	275	289	308	315
L	138	134	133	137	138	138	130	137	137	139
M	155	163	164	162	166	171	169	170	166	162
N	321	326	343	346	346	352	366	371	373	384
O	121	123	127	129	132	133	136	137	141	144
P	5	4	4	3	5	7	8	7	7	8
Q	1	1	1	1	-	1	1	1	1	1
X	6	7	7	7	8	7	5	4	6	13

Men - Hommes - Hombres
ISIC 3 - CITI 3 - CIIU 3

	1999	2000	2001	2002	2003	2004	2005	2006	2007	2008
Total	1 227	1 248	1 261	1 249	1 247	1 250	1 263	1 288	1 310	1 337
A	97	97	91	84	81	81	81	80	80	81
B	2	2	2	1	1	1	1	1	1	1
C	4	3	3	5	5	5	5	5	4	4
D	321	329	331	328	317	309	310	317	323	321
E	18	17	17	16	15	15	14	13	12	13
F	138	139	136	137	140	138	147	152	162	171
G	143	144	144	143	146	150	153	155	156	163
H	24	22	23	23	20	20	22	21	23	23
I	121	125	128	122	128	127	127	131	126	125
J	14	15	16	14	13	15	15	16	17	17
K	125	138	144	148	148	151	151	161	172	180
L	79	74	74	75	76	76	72	76	73	73
M	53	54	54	54	56	56	58	56	56	54
N	38	37	39	40	41	44	44	44	42	41
O	47	48	54	53	53	55	58	55	55	57
P	1	-	1	-	1	2	4	3	3	4
Q	-	-	-	-	-	1	1	-	-	-
X	4	4	4	4	5	5	2	2	3	7

Explanatory notes: see p. 77.
Notes explicatives: voir p. 80.
Notas explicativas: véase p. 83.

[1] Persons aged 15 to 74 years. [2] Excl. conscripts. [3] Included armed forces and conscripts.

[1] Personnes âgées de 15 à 74 ans. [2] Non compris les conscrits. [3] Y compris les forces armées et les conscrits.

[1] Personas de 15 a 74 años. [2] Excl. los conscriptos. [3] Incluye las fuezas armadas y los conscriptos.

Total employment, by economic activity — Emploi total, par activité économique — Empleo total, por actividad económica

Thousands — Milliers — Millares

Finland (BA) [1][2]

Total employment - Emploi total - Empleo total

Women - Femmes - Mujeres
ISIC 3 - CITI 3 - CIIU 3

	1999	2000	2001	2002	2003	2004	2005	2006	2007	2008
Total	1 090	1 108	1 127	1 144	1 138	1 137	1 158	1 178	1 202	1 217
A	46	43	42	41	38	33	33	33	31	32
B	-	-	1	1	-	1	1	-	1	1
C	1	1	-	-	-	-	1	-	1	-
D	140	138	141	138	127	126	127	125	122	116
E	4	5	5	5	5	4	5	4	4	4
F	11	10	9	11	11	11	11	10	11	13
G	135	134	133	138	141	143	147	149	154	151
H	52	54	57	59	56	54	55	57	62	66
I	48	46	46	47	45	45	45	50	48	49
J	32	34	34	33	36	35	32	31	34	34
K	97	100	108	114	115	115	124	127	136	135
L	59	60	59	61	62	62	59	61	64	66
M	102	110	110	109	111	115	111	114	110	109
N	283	289	303	306	305	308	322	328	331	343
O	74	75	72	76	78	79	78	82	87	87
P	4	4	3	3	4	3	4	4	4	4
Q	-	-	-	-	-	-	-	1	-	-
X	3	3	3	3	4	3	3	2	2	6

France (BA) [3]

Total employment - Emploi total - Empleo total

Total - Total - Total
ISIC 3 - CITI 3 - CIIU 3 / ISIC 4 - CITI 4 - CIIU 4

	1999	2000	2001	2002	2003	2004	2005	2006	2007	2008	
Total	.	.	.	.	24 695.8	24 800.3	24 978.0	25 133.5	25 565.2	25 913.2	Total
A					1 013.6	937.4	887.8	913.5	861.5	693.4	A
B					19.1	17.0	17.9	18.0	14.4	21.6	B
C					35.0	32.6	42.1	29.0	24.3	3 644.6	C
D					4 119.3	4 062.7	4 014.5	3 984.8	3 949.8	148.7	D
E					228.6	224.7	218.6	245.8	200.4	170.7	E
F					1 624.8	1 624.2	1 640.4	1 705.4	1 755.1	1 866.9	F
G					3 291.8	3 344.6	3 334.8	3 352.8	3 538.8	3 280.3	G
H					804.5	834.8	851.1	911.1	878.8	1 407.7	H
I					1 566.6	1 590.1	1 585.4	1 518.9	1 602.9	863.1	I
J					740.6	685.4	753.2	807.4	826.0	661.1	J
K					2 452.3	2 502.6	2 546.8	2 662.6	2 666.0	814.7	K
L					2 255.9	2 300.2	2 347.7	2 407.2	2 563.3	355.2	L
M					1 707.5	1 709.1	1 744.1	1 776.7	1 735.9	1 244.5	M
N					2 823.8	2 925.5	2 970.2	3 066.4	3 143.4	903.7	N
O					1 010.9	1 060.8	1 112.6	1 102.9	1 156.9	2 616.2	O
P					650.0	645.3	605.0	580.7	592.4	1 764.5	P
Q					14.0	14.9	15.5	18.4	18.9	3 132.6	Q
X					337.5	288.3	290.5	31.8	36.4	334.9	R
										687.5	S
										586.9	T
										17.6	U
										696.7	X

Men - Hommes - Hombres
ISIC 3 - CITI 3 - CIIU 3 / ISIC 4 - CITI 4 - CIIU 4

	1999	2000	2001	2002	2003	2004	2005	2006	2007	2008	
Total	.	.	.	.	13 302.9	13 315.7	13 350.0	13 381.5	13 521.9	13 670.2	Total
A					704.6	627.8	621.2	655.5	605.0	472.4	A
B					15.8	14.4	16.7	15.1	13.0	17.5	B
C					26.9	28.7	36.0	25.4	19.2	2 597.6	C
D					2 905.4	2 832.7	2 818.9	2 825.2	2 768.8	114.7	D
E					178.9	186.1	174.9	193.1	156.2	140.1	E
F					1 467.2	1 474.9	1 483.8	1 545.5	1 599.6	1 676.9	F
G					1 755.6	1 784.6	1 763.9	1 809.6	1 920.2	1 705.3	G
H					418.8	443.1	451.7	463.2	434.0	1 016.0	H
I					1 077.6	1 100.6	1 081.6	1 070.0	1 134.9	452.9	I
J					336.2	306.2	331.2	333.4	337.7	448.8	J
K					1 349.7	1 392.1	1 427.1	1 468.7	1 446.6	337.7	K
L					1 115.4	1 192.0	1 203.8	1 193.2	1 236.0	164.5	L
M					575.7	577.6	588.4	562.9	555.1	648.0	M
N					641.9	652.3	636.0	622.2	665.1	495.8	N
O					449.1	448.5	487.7	488.7	502.0	1 256.7	O
P					138.0	127.5	103.4	85.4	98.9	570.3	P
Q					6.9	6.7	6.8	7.8	8.4	647.0	Q
X					139.3	120.0	117.0	16.6	21.4	189.1	R
										230.2	S
										106.2	T
										7.4	U
										374.9	X

Explanatory notes: see p. 77.

[1] Included armed forces and conscripts. [2] Persons aged 15 to 74 years. [3] Persons aged 15 years and over.

Notes explicatives: voir p. 80.

[1] Y compris les forces armées et les conscrits. [2] Personnes âgées de 15 à 74 ans. [3] Personnes âgées de 15 ans et plus.

Notas explicativas: véase p. 83.

[1] Incluye las fuezas armadas y los conscriptos. [2] Personas de 15 a 74 años. [3] Personas de 15 años y más.

EMPLOYMENT — EMPLOI — EMPLEO

Total employment, by economic activity
Emploi total, par activité économique
Empleo total, por actividad económica

	Thousands — Milliers — Millares									
	1999	2000	2001	2002	2003	2004	2005	2006	2007	2008

France (BA) [1]
Women - Femmes - Mujeres
ISIC 3 - CITI 3 - CIIU 3   ISIC 4 - CITI 4 - CIIU 4

Total employment - Emploi total - Empleo total

	2003	2004	2005	2006	2007	2008	
Total	11 392.9	11 484.7	11 628.0	11 752.0	12 043.3	12 243.0	Total
A	309.1	309.6	266.6	258.0	256.5	221.0	A
B	3.2	2.5	1.1	3.0	1.4	4.1	B
C	8.1	3.9	6.1	3.6	5.2	1 047.1	C
D	1 213.9	1 230.1	1 195.6	1 159.6	1 181.0	34.0	D
E	49.7	38.6	43.7	52.8	44.3	30.6	E
F	157.6	149.3	156.6	159.9	155.4	190.0	F
G	1 536.2	1 560.0	1 570.8	1 543.3	1 618.7	1 575.0	G
H	385.7	391.7	399.4	447.9	444.8	391.7	H
I	489.0	489.5	503.8	448.8	468.0	410.2	I
J	404.4	379.2	422.0	474.0	488.3	212.3	J
K	1 102.6	1 110.6	1 119.7	1 194.0	1 219.4	477.1	K
L	1 140.5	1 108.2	1 143.9	1 214.0	1 327.3	190.7	L
M	1 131.8	1 131.5	1 155.7	1 213.8	1 180.7	596.5	M
N	2 182.0	2 273.2	2 334.3	2 444.1	2 478.3	407.9	N
O	561.8	612.3	624.9	614.2	654.9	1 359.5	O
P	512.0	517.8	501.6	495.3	493.6	1 194.2	P
Q	7.2	8.2	8.7	10.5	10.5	2 485.5	Q
X	198.2	168.3	173.5	15.3	15.0	145.7	R
						457.3	S
						480.7	T
						10.1	U
						321.8	X

Germany (BA) [1]

Total employment - Emploi total - Empleo total

Total - Total - Total
ISIC 3 - CITI 3 - CIIU 3

	1999	2000	2001	2002	2003	2004	2005	2006	2007	2008
Total	36 402	36 604 [2]	36 816	36 536 [3]	36 172 [2]	35 659 [4]	36 566 [5]	37 322	38 163	38 734
A	1 020	982 [2]	937	917 [3]	890 [2]	827 [4]	861 [5]	837	854	866
B	6	6 [2]	5	6 [3]	5 [2]	5 [4]	7 [5]	6	5	6
C	161	152 [2]	139	136 [3]	128 [2]	120 [4]	123 [5]	116	107	109
D	8 532	8 542 [2]	8 609	8 483 [3]	8 243 [2]	8 135 [4]	8 032 [5]	8 157	8 395	8 516
E	311	290 [2]	282	287 [3]	287 [2]	296 [4]	315 [5]	316	334	346
F	3 146	3 118 [2]	2 904	2 750 [3]	2 607 [2]	2 435 [4]	2 400 [5]	2 446	2 527	2 521
G	5 208	5 190 [2]	5 248	5 085 [3]	5 069 [2]	5 010 [4]	5 257 [5]	5 281	5 308	5 290
H	1 188	1 219 [2]	1 228	1 240 [3]	1 227 [2]	1 206 [4]	1 295 [5]	1 381	1 428	1 459
I	1 953	2 008 [2]	2 055	2 030 [3]	2 001 [2]	1 971 [4]	1 949 [5]	2 060	2 148	2 147
J	1 291	1 333 [2]	1 346	1 343 [3]	1 351 [2]	1 296 [4]	1 307 [5]	1 306	1 303	1 301
K	2 738	2 923 [2]	3 005	3 120 [3]	3 221 [2]	3 276 [4]	3 522 [5]	3 735	3 909	4 172
L	3 178	3 103 [2]	3 065	2 986 [3]	2 973 [2]	2 896 [4]	2 879 [5]	2 901	2 916	2 836
M	1 948	1 928 [2]	1 996	2 021 [3]	2 033 [2]	2 033 [4]	2 100 [5]	2 174	2 237	2 290
N	3 665	3 696 [2]	3 797	3 926 [3]	4 030 [2]	4 063 [4]	4 150 [5]	4 264	4 398	4 515
O	1 879	1 944 [2]	2 028	2 038 [3]	1 943 [2]	1 911 [4]	2 153 [5]	2 125	2 058	2 112
P	141	137 [2]	142	137 [3]	138 [2]	152 [4]	179 [5]	187	206	216
Q	37	33 [2]	30	31 [3]	28 [2]	26 [4]	34 [5]	29	29	33

Men - Hommes - Hombres
ISIC 3 - CITI 3 - CIIU 3

	1999	2000	2001	2002	2003	2004	2005	2006	2007	2008
Total	20 659	20 680 [2]	20 629	20 336 [3]	19 996 [2]	19 681 [4]	20 135 [5]	20 462	20 890	21 188
A	653	635 [2]	604	597 [3]	588 [2]	554 [4]	578 [5]	567	576	585
B	5	4 [2]	4	4 [3]	4 [2]	3 [4]	5 [5]	5	4	5
C	148	139 [2]	127	123 [3]	115 [2]	109 [4]	111 [5]	106	97	95
D	6 115	6 128 [2]	6 170	6 104 [3]	5 919 [2]	5 851 [4]	5 785 [5]	5 843	6 029	6 137
E	249	235 [2]	221	224 [3]	227 [2]	233 [4]	246 [5]	242	255	267
F	2 746	2 729 [2]	2 522	2 391 [3]	2 273 [2]	2 119 [4]	2 090 [5]	2 138	2 223	2 216
G	2 442	2 393 [2]	2 416	2 327 [3]	2 327 [2]	2 338 [4]	2 528 [5]	2 531	2 520	2 512
H	492	507 [2]	519	532 [3]	518 [2]	518 [4]	554 [5]	584	592	615
I	1 396	1 426 [2]	1 465	1 438 [3]	1 419 [2]	1 411 [4]	1 405 [5]	1 469	1 552	1 553
J	639	648 [2]	651	646 [3]	666 [2]	643 [4]	657 [5]	657	642	642
K	1 422	1 530 [2]	1 573	1 634 [3]	1 692 [2]	1 730 [4]	1 869 [5]	1 975	2 052	2 222
L	1 859	1 804 [2]	1 771	1 705 [3]	1 701 [2]	1 642 [4]	1 622 [5]	1 627	1 621	1 538
M	697	669 [2]	698	687 [3]	679 [2]	675 [4]	688 [5]	706	736	748
N	927	939 [2]	956	990 [3]	1 001 [2]	1 009 [4]	1 015 [5]	1 052	1 076	1 108
O	839	868 [2]	905	906 [3]	845 [2]	820 [4]	947 [5]	933	883	910
P	8	7 [2]	7	9 [3]	8 [2]	8 [4]	13 [5]	11	14	15
Q	22	19 [2]	20	19 [3]	17 [2]	18 [4]	21 [5]	16	18	19

Explanatory notes: see p. 77.

[1] Persons aged 15 years and over. [2] May. [3] Prior to 2002: April of each year. [4] March. [5] Methodology revised; data not strictly comparable.

Notes explicatives: voir p. 80.

[1] Personnes âgées de 15 ans et plus. [2] Mai. [3] Avant 2002: avril de chaque année. [4] Mars. [5] Méthodologie révisée; les données ne sont pas strictement comparables.

Notas explicativas: véase p. 83.

[1] Personas de 15 años y más. [2] Mayo. [3] Antes del 2002: abril de cada año. [4] Marzo. [5] Metodología revisada; los datos no son estrictamente comparables.

Total employment, by economic activity
Emploi total, par activité économique
Empleo total, por actividad económica

Thousands — Milliers — Millares

	1999	2000	2001	2002	2003	2004	2005	2006	2007	2008
Germany (BA) [1]				Total employment - Emploi total - Empleo total						
Women - Femmes - Mujeres										
ISIC 3 - CITI 3 - CIIU 3										
Total	15 743	15 924 [2]	16 187	16 200 [3]	16 176 [2]	15 978 [4]	16 432 [5]	16 860	17 272	17 546
A	367	347 [2]	333	321 [3]	302 [2]	272 [4]	283 [5]	270	278	281
B	1	2 [2]	1	2 [3]	1 [2]	2 [4]	2 [5]	1	1	1
C	13	13 [2]	12	12 [3]	13 [2]	11 [4]	12 [5]	11	11	14
D	2 417	2 414 [2]	2 439	2 379 [3]	2 324 [2]	2 284 [4]	2 247 [5]	2 314	2 365	2 379
E	62	55 [2]	61	64 [3]	60 [2]	63 [4]	69 [5]	74	79	79
F	400	389 [2]	382	359 [3]	334 [2]	316 [4]	310 [5]	308	304	305
G	2 766	2 797 [2]	2 832	2 758 [3]	2 742 [2]	2 673 [4]	2 729 [5]	2 750	2 788	2 778
H	696	712 [2]	709	708 [3]	709 [2]	688 [4]	742 [5]	796	836	844
I	557	582 [2]	590	592 [3]	582 [2]	560 [4]	544 [5]	591	596	593
J	652	685 [2]	695	696 [3]	686 [2]	654 [4]	649 [5]	650	661	659
K	1 316	1 393 [2]	1 432	1 487 [3]	1 529 [2]	1 546 [4]	1 653 [5]	1 760	1 857	1 949
L	1 319	1 299 [2]	1 294	1 281 [3]	1 272 [2]	1 254 [4]	1 257 [5]	1 274	1 295	1 298
M	1 251	1 259 [2]	1 298	1 333 [3]	1 354 [2]	1 358 [4]	1 412 [5]	1 468	1 501	1 542
N	2 738	2 757 [2]	2 841	2 936 [3]	3 029 [2]	3 055 [4]	3 135 [5]	3 213	3 322	3 407
O	1 040	1 076 [2]	1 123	1 132 [3]	1 098 [2]	1 091 [4]	1 206 [5]	1 192	1 175	1 202
P	133	130 [2]	135	129 [3]	130 [2]	144 [4]	166 [5]	176	192	201
Q	15	14 [2]	10	11 [3]	11 [2]	8 [4]	13 [5]	13	12	14
Gibraltar (DA) [6]				Total employment - Emploi total - Empleo total						
Total - Total - Total										
ISIC 3 - CITI 3 - CIIU 3										
Total	12.9	13.4	13.9	14.3	15.4	16.0	16.9	18.5	19.7	.
D	0.4	0.5	0.4	0.4	0.5	0.5	0.4	0.5	0.4	.
E	0.2	0.2	0.2	0.2	0.3	0.3	0.3	0.3	0.3	.
F	1.4	1.4	1.6	1.6	1.7	1.8	1.9	2.1	2.5	.
G	2.5	2.4	2.5	2.5	2.7	2.7	2.7	2.7	2.8	.
H	0.7	0.8	0.8	0.9	0.9	1.0	1.0	1.1	1.1	.
I	0.7	0.8	0.8	0.9	0.9	0.9	1.0	1.0	1.1	.
J	1.1	1.1	1.2	1.2	1.2	1.3	1.4	1.7	1.9	.
K	1.3	1.3	1.4	1.4	1.7	1.8	1.8	2.1	2.5	.
L	2.1	2.2	2.2	2.2	2.2	2.2	2.2	2.2	2.3	.
M	0.7	0.7	0.7	0.7	0.7	0.7	0.8	0.8	0.9	.
N	0.9	1.0	1.0	1.0	1.1	1.2	1.4	1.4	1.6	.
O	0.9	1.1	0.9	1.0	1.4	1.7	2.0	2.5	2.5	.

Greece (BA) [1] [7] [8]   Total employment - Emploi total - Empleo total

Total - Total - Total
ISIC 3 - CITI 3 - CIIU 3   ISIC 4 - CITI 4 - CIIU 4

	1999	2000	2001	2002	2003	2004	2005	2006	2007	2008	
Total	4 040.4	4 097.9	4 103.2	4 190.2	4 286.6	4 330.5	4 382.1	4 452.8	4 520.0	4 582.5	Total
A	691.6	700.9	649.2	633.9	642.6	533.5	530.4	523.0	507.3	518.7	A
B	12.6	11.9	12.1	14.3	12.9	12.1	14.2	13.1	15.1	18.0	B
C	20.8	18.6	19.7	21.0	12.6	14.7	17.7	18.2	18.1	538.8	C
D	577.0	571.5	580.3	579.2	565.0	569.7	560.3	563.2	558.9	36.1	D
E	42.5	40.1	37.0	35.9	42.4	39.1	37.7	40.9	40.0	30.0	E
F	287.6	295.9	308.0	318.5	345.9	350.1	367.3	358.5	394.4	399.3	F
G	687.9	702.1	703.2	722.9	737.5	748.5	782.1	789.3	800.6	832.6	G
H	267.9	272.8	277.2	293.9	297.9	279.6	304.2	300.9	317.9	215.4	H
I	248.4	254.5	258.9	250.7	263.1	272.4	267.7	281.7	267.6	325.5	I
J	93.3	108.0	110.0	98.3	110.1	112.4	113.1	115.8	112.7	73.9	J
K	198.9	197.2	218.6	244.6	244.9	283.0	289.4	284.1	294.8	121.0	K
L	281.1	301.3	303.1	311.1	324.3	356.0	343.6	380.9	390.9	9.2	L
M	249.7	249.8	262.1	266.9	285.9	318.2	312.2	331.1	328.4	221.6	M
N	187.0	188.2	183.5	189.3	188.1	219.0	220.2	227.8	240.9	77.8	N
O	143.4	132.1	131.0	155.4	156.1	155.1	153.6	150.4	162.4	381.9	O
P	49.7	52.6	49.1	53.3	57.0	65.8	67.6	73.4	68.5	323.7	P
Q	1.0	0.3	-	0.8	0.3	1.4	0.6	0.6	1.4	231.1	Q
										59.0	R
										94.0	S
										73.4	T
										1.7	U
										-	X

Explanatory notes: see p. 77.

[1] Persons aged 15 years and over. [2] May. [3] Prior to 2002: April of each year. [4] March. [5] Methodology revised; data not strictly comparable. [6] Oct. of each year. [7] Excl. conscripts. [8] Second quarter of each year.

Notes explicatives: voir p. 80.

[1] Personnes âgées de 15 ans et plus. [2] Mai. [3] Avant 2002: avril de chaque année. [4] Mars. [5] Méthodologie révisée; les données ne sont pas strictement comparables. [6] Oct. de chaque année. [7] Non compris les conscrits. [8] Deuxième trimestre de chaque année.

Notas explicativas: véase p. 83.

[1] Personas de 15 años y más. [2] Mayo. [3] Antes del 2002: abril de cada año. [4] Marzo. [5] Metodología revisada; los datos no son estrictamente comparables. [6] Oct. de cada año. [7] Excl. los conscriptos. [8] Segundo trimestre de cada año.

EMPLOYMENT — EMPLOI — EMPLEO

Total employment, by economic activity
Emploi total, par activité économique
Empleo total, por actividad económica

Thousands — Milliers — Millares

Greece (BA) [1] [2] [3]

Total employment - Emploi total - Empleo total

Men - Hommes - Hombres

ISIC 3 - CITI 3 - CIIU 3 (1999–2007); ISIC 4 - CITI 4 - CIIU 4 (2008)

ISIC 3	1999	2000	2001	2002	2003	2004	2005	2006	2007	2008	ISIC 4
Total	2 554.1	2 577.7	2 582.2	2 622.5	2 666.1	2 680.2	2 705.8	2 725.7	2 762.0	2 788.8	Total
A	398.5	403.8	381.3	365.0	370.7	302.0	299.1	295.6	289.0	305.6	A
B	11.6	10.4	11.2	13.0	11.1	10.5	12.6	11.6	13.0	15.8	B
C	19.6	17.5	18.6	19.9	12.0	14.0	16.7	16.9	16.9	396.3	C
D	404.9	401.0	414.2	415.0	402.5	412.1	407.6	411.1	404.5	27.2	D
E	35.5	31.8	31.8	31.0	35.5	30.6	30.9	33.8	31.6	24.6	E
F	283.0	290.5	302.6	313.0	336.3	343.2	360.7	350.7	386.7	390.9	F
G	428.5[1]	440.8	429.6	440.3	445.7	447.8	466.1	460.4	463.4	477.3	G
H	158.5	157.7	151.6	161.8	162.3	149.3	167.6	168.8	173.7	182.0	H
I	209.3	212.1	217.5	210.5	222.0	220.2	219.5	227.2	215.3	176.1	I
J	48.7	56.7	57.5	51.0	53.8	56.7	56.9	61.2	57.1	48.4	J
K	111.9	109.1	118.5	132.4	131.6	155.5	153.3	147.3	162.7	58.9	K
L	187.9	204.6	203.7	208.2	219.3	244.3	232.3	251.6	249.1	5.4	L
M	101.6	97.8	103.3	100.3	101.7	124.9	122.5	126.7	123.1	121.8	M
N	68.0	65.8	64.0	69.4	73.4	82.4	78.5	79.8	86.5	39.9	N
O	83.2	74.8	74.4	87.6	84.7	82.0	78.5	79.6	83.5	241.1	O
P	2.7	3.0	2.4	4.0	3.0	4.4	2.6	3.3	4.5	118.2	P
Q	0.7	0.3	-	0.3	0.3	0.4	0.6	0.1	1.3	78.4	Q
										36.8	R
										40.0	S
										2.8	T
										1.4	U
										-	X

Women - Femmes - Mujeres

ISIC 3 - CITI 3 - CIIU 3 (1999–2007); ISIC 4 - CITI 4 - CIIU 4 (2008)

ISIC 3	1999	2000	2001	2002	2003	2004	2005	2006	2007	2008	ISIC 4
Total	1 486.2	1 520.2	1 521.0	1 567.7	1 620.5	1 650.3	1 676.2	1 727.1	1 758.0	1 793.7	Total
A	293.1	297.1	268.0	269.0	271.9	231.5	231.3	227.4	218.3	213.1	A
B	1.0	1.6	0.9	1.3	1.8	1.6	1.6	1.4	2.1	2.2	B
C	1.2	1.1	1.1	1.1	0.6	0.7	1.1	1.3	1.3	142.5	C
D	172.0	170.6	166.0	164.2	162.5	157.6	152.7	152.1	154.4	8.9	D
E	7.0	8.3	5.3	5.0	6.8	8.5	6.8	7.0	8.5	5.4	E
F	4.6	5.4	5.4	5.5	9.6	6.9	6.6	7.9	7.7	8.4	F
G	259.4	261.3	273.6	282.6	291.8	300.7	316.0	328.8	337.3	355.3	G
H	109.4	115.0	125.6	132.2	135.6	130.3	136.6	132.1	144.2	33.4	H
I	39.1	42.4	41.5	40.2	41.0	52.2	48.3	54.5	52.3	149.4	I
J	44.6	51.3	52.5	47.2	56.3	55.7	56.1	54.5	55.6	25.5	J
K	87.0	88.1	100.2	112.3	113.3	127.5	136.1	136.8	132.1	62.2	K
L	93.2	96.7	99.4	102.9	105.1	111.7	111.4	129.3	141.8	3.8	L
M	148.1	152.0	158.7	166.6	184.2	193.3	189.8	204.4	205.4	99.7	M
N	119.0	122.5	119.5	119.9	114.7	136.6	141.7	148.0	154.3	38.0	N
O	60.2	57.3	56.7	67.9	71.4	73.1	75.1	70.9	78.9	140.8	O
P	47.0	49.6	46.7	49.3	53.9	61.4	65.0	70.1	64.1	205.5	P
Q	0.3	-	-	0.5	0.1	1.0	-	0.5	0.1	152.6	Q
										22.3	R
										53.9	S
										70.6	T
										0.4	U
										-	X

Hungary (BA) [2] [4]

Total employment - Emploi total - Empleo total

Total - Total - Total

ISIC 3 - CITI 3 - CIIU 3

	1999	2000	2001	2002	2003	2004	2005	2006	2007	2008
Total	3 811.5	3 849.1	3 859.5	3 870.6[5]	3 921.9	3 900.4	3 901.5	3 930.1	3 926.2	3 879.4
A-B	270.4	251.7	239.4	240.9[5]	215.2	204.9	194.0	190.8	182.9	174.1
C	24.4	19.2	13.0	14.8[5]	12.8	14.2	14.9	15.0	14.6	9.0
D	928.9	931.3	955.8	959.9[5]	925.5	893.9	869.4	865.2	872.0	870.8
E	89.8	80.1	79.5	74.2[5]	68.2	63.7	64.6	67.6	64.2	57.4
F	253.0	267.8	272.7	271.0[5]	299.4	308.7	315.1	321.6	330.5	309.5
G	517.5	540.9	548.4	552.0[5]	553.1	545.7	585.9	582.0	591.5	585.0
H	133.2	133.3	143.0	137.3[5]	139.4	148.8	154.3	157.2	156.1	157.2
I	308.3	311.8	310.9	309.7[5]	303.2	296.1	285.4	301.3	301.7	287.4
J	80.9	83.7	78.9	75.3[5]	72.8	80.1	80.3	80.3	83.8	94.7
K	183.9	204.6	219.6	232.8[5]	265.9	272.5	275.8	282.8	282.9	306.6
L	301.9	299.0	289.6	282.1[5]	295.4	298.8	297.9	299.2	285.3	288.6
M	306.9	317.8	309.8	318.0[5]	329.0	333.0	323.4	322.9	316.3	310.7
N	239.2	241.7	234.9	240.8[5]	267.2	269.4	262.7	269.5	260.4	249.1
O	169.8	162.7	160.3	158.5[5]	172.5	168.4	174.4	172.4	180.3	176.9
P	2.0	1.9	2.5	2.2[5]	1.1	1.5	2.1	1.7	2.5	1.9
Q	1.4	1.6	1.2	1.1[5]	1.2	0.7	1.3	0.6	1.2	0.5

Explanatory notes: see p. 77.

[1] Persons aged 15 years and over. [2] Excl. conscripts. [3] Second quarter of each year. [4] Persons aged 15 to 74 years. [5] Estimates based on the 2001 Population Census results.

Notes explicatives: voir p. 80.

[1] Personnes âgées de 15 ans et plus. [2] Non compris les conscrits. [3] Deuxième trimestre de chaque année. [4] Personnes âgées de 15 à 74 ans. [5] Estimations basées sur les résultats du Recensement de la population de 2001.

Notas explicativas: véase p. 83.

[1] Personas de 15 años y más. [2] Excl. los conscriptos. [3] Segundo trimestre de cada año. [4] Personas de 15 a 74 años. [5] Estimaciones basadas en los resultados del Censo de población de 2001.

EMPLOYMENT   EMPLOI   EMPLEO   **2B**

Total employment, by economic activity   Emploi total, par activité économique   Empleo total, por actividad económica

Thousands   Milliers   Millares

	1999	2000	2001	2002	2003	2004	2005	2006	2007	2008
Hungary (BA) [1][2]				Total employment - Emploi total - Empleo total						
Men - Hommes - Hombres										
ISIC 3 - CITI 3 - CIIU 3										
Total	2 103.1	2 122.4	2 130.6	2 112.5 [3]	2 126.5	2 117.3	2 116.1	2 137.4	2 143.0	2 110.8
A-B	204.5	190.3	179.3	176.9 [3]	166.6	158.0	145.4	142.2	140.8	132.1
C	19.4	15.4	11.4	13.4 [3]	11.0	11.3	12.6	13.0	12.7	8.2
D	551.7	542.6	557.5	564.3 [3]	547.3	536.1	530.7	530.7	533.3	537.7
E	65.4	60.5	60.3	55.6 [3]	50.2	46.2	47.9	48.7	48.0	44.0
F	232.6	247.0	251.2	250.3 [3]	275.1	284.3	293.9	300.0	307.3	284.7
G	241.6	262.8	269.4	263.8 [3]	267.6	266.2	267.2	269.6	277.0	279.7
H	63.9	63.3	72.9	62.5 [3]	59.7	62.6	70.8	69.3	67.7	69.6
I	222.8	225.8	225.4	227.3 [3]	219.5	215.5	212.5	218.9	224.0	209.9
J	26.6	28.2	24.3	23.2 [3]	22.6	25.7	26.6	27.8	26.9	30.4
K	102.2	111.0	121.6	128.4 [3]	143.6	149.2	152.8	157.7	153.0	168.2
L	160.8	164.9	157.0	147.8 [3]	151.5	151.0	146.3	151.0	139.0	141.9
M	71.9	70.5	69.7	69.4 [3]	71.4	72.0	72.7	72.2	72.4	68.1
N	56.5	59.7	55.0	56.6 [3]	62.5	61.3	58.4	60.0	57.0	55.9
O	81.9	78.7	74.7	72.4 [3]	77.1	77.2	76.9	75.5	82.5	79.8
P	0.6	0.5	0.5	0.3 [3]	0.1	0.2	0.3	0.2	0.5	0.4
Q	0.7	1.2	0.4	0.3 [3]	0.7	0.5	1.1	0.6	0.9	0.2
Women - Femmes - Mujeres										
ISIC 3 - CITI 3 - CIIU 3										
Total	1 708.4	1 726.7	1 728.9	1 758.1 [3]	1 795.4	1 783.1	1 785.4	1 792.7	1 783.2	1 768.6
A-B	65.9	61.4	60.1	64.0 [3]	48.6	46.9	48.6	48.6	42.1	42.0
C	5.0	3.8	1.6	1.4 [3]	1.8	2.9	2.3	2.0	1.9	0.8
D	377.2	388.7	398.3	395.6 [3]	378.2	357.8	338.7	334.5	338.7	333.1
E	24.4	19.6	19.2	18.6 [3]	18.0	17.5	16.7	18.9	16.2	13.4
F	20.4	20.8	21.5	20.7 [3]	24.3	24.4	21.2	21.6	23.2	24.8
G	275.9	278.1	279.0	288.3 [3]	285.5	279.5	318.7	312.4	314.5	305.3
H	69.3	70.0	70.1	74.8 [3]	79.7	86.2	83.5	87.9	88.4	87.6
I	85.5	86.0	85.5	82.4 [3]	83.7	80.6	72.9	82.4	77.7	77.5
J	54.3	55.5	54.6	52.1 [3]	50.2	54.5	53.7	52.5	56.9	64.3
K	81.7	93.6	98.0	104.4 [3]	122.3	123.3	123.0	125.1	129.9	138.4
L	141.1	134.1	132.6	134.3 [3]	143.9	147.8	151.6	148.2	146.3	146.7
M	235.0	247.3	240.1	248.6 [3]	257.6	261.0	250.7	250.7	243.9	242.6
N	182.7	182.0	179.9	184.1 [3]	204.7	208.1	204.3	209.5	203.4	193.2
O	87.9	84.1	85.6	86.1 [3]	95.4	91.2	97.5	96.9	97.8	97.1
P	1.4	1.4	2.0	1.9 [3]	1.0	1.3	1.8	1.5	2.0	1.5
Q	0.7	0.4	0.8	0.8 [3]	0.5	0.2	0.2	-	0.3	0.3
Iceland (BA) [4][5]				Total employment - Emploi total - Empleo total						
Total - Total - Total										
ISIC 3 - CITI 3 - CIIU 3										
Total	153.3	156.4	159.0	156.7	156.9	156.1	161.3	169.6	177.2	178.6
A	6.5	6.9	6.4	6.0	5.7	5.4	5.5	6.4	6.0	4.4
B	7.2	6.1	6.0	5.3	5.1	4.6	5.0	4.3	4.5	4.2
C	0.3	0.2	0.3	0.3	0.2	0.2	0.1	0.1	0.1	0.1
D	23.3	23.9	22.9	22.2	21.5	21.7	21.0	20.0	19.3	20.3
E	1.2	1.3	1.5	1.5	1.6	1.6	1.5	1.5	1.7	1.8
F	10.6	10.5	11.4	12.2	10.8	11.5	12.4	14.7	15.7	17.5
G	21.2	21.9	23.2	21.4	20.6	19.9	22.5	23.6	25.5	23.1
H	5.9	6.4	6.3	5.5	5.5	5.3	5.4	6.1	6.2	6.4
I	11.6	10.6	10.1	9.7	9.7	10.8	11.7	12.0	11.2	11.5
J	5.7	6.6	6.5	6.1	6.2	6.9	6.6	7.3	8.7	9.0
K	11.1	13.0	13.5	13.3	14.3	14.5	15.0	15.1	17.2	16.3
L	7.6	7.0	6.2	7.8	8.2	7.6	7.4	10.1	9.0	9.6
M	9.1	9.8	11.7	12.7	12.2	12.1	11.9	12.5	13.5	14.6
N	21.3	20.6	22.1	21.6	24.8	23.0	24.5	24.6	26.0	27.1
O	9.8	10.5	9.6	10.1	9.8	10.5	10.1	10.9	12.1	12.5
P	-	-	-	-	-	-	-	-	-	-
Q	0.7	0.8	0.9	0.8	0.5	0.3	0.4	0.4	0.5	0.1
X	0.1	0.2	0.4	0.3	0.1	0.3	0.2	-	0.3	0.1

Explanatory notes: see p. 77.

[1] Persons aged 15 to 74 years. [2] Excl. conscripts. [3] Estimates based on the 2001 Population Census results. [4] Persons aged 16 to 74 years. [5] Excl. armed forces and conscripts.

Notes explicatives: voir p. 80.

[1] Personnes âgées de 15 à 74 ans. [2] Non compris les conscrits. [3] Estimations basées sur les résultats du Recensement de la population de 2001. [4] Personnes âgées de 16 à 74 ans. [5] Non compris les forces armées et les conscrits.

Notas explicativas: véase p. 83.

[1] Personas de 15 a 74 años. [2] Excl. los conscriptos. [3] Estimaciones basadas en los resultados del Censo de población de 2001. [4] Personas de 16 a 74 años. [5] Excl. las fuerzas armadas y los conscriptos.

Total employment, by economic activity	Emploi total, par activité économique	Empleo total, por actividad económica
Thousands	Milliers	Millares

	1999	2000	2001	2002	2003	2004	2005	2006	2007	2008

Iceland (BA) [1] [2] — Total employment - Emploi total - Empleo total

Men - Hommes - Hombres
ISIC 3 - CITI 3 - CIIU 3

	1999	2000	2001	2002	2003	2004	2005	2006	2007	2008
Total	82.2	83.6	85.0	83.0	82.4	82.5	85.7	92.0	96.6	97.1
A	4.2	4.5	4.3	4.0	3.8	3.5	3.6	4.5	4.2	2.9
B	6.3	5.3	5.5	4.8	4.7	4.2	4.6	4.0	4.3	3.9
C	0.3	0.2	0.2	0.2	0.2	0.2	0.1	0.1	0.1	0.1
D	15.6	16.6	15.9	15.1	14.5	14.6	14.1	14.0	13.4	14.4
E	1.0	1.0	1.1	1.0	1.3	1.4	1.2	1.1	1.3	1.4
F	10.1	10.1	10.9	11.6	10.4	11.0	11.5	13.9	15.2	16.4
G	11.3	11.5	12.6	11.2	11.4	11.4	13.1	13.6	14.4	13.2
H	2.3	3.1	2.8	2.6	2.3	2.2	2.5	3.1	2.5	2.8
I	7.2	6.2	6.0	6.1	6.2	7.1	7.6	7.8	7.4	7.8
J	2.5	2.6	2.1	2.1	1.9	2.1	2.1	2.7	3.6	3.8
K	6.7	7.9	8.4	7.6	8.8	8.4	9.0	9.6	11.4	10.5
L	4.2	3.8	3.2	4.1	4.0	3.4	3.6	4.8	4.5	4.7
M	2.8	2.7	3.4	3.6	4.0	4.0	3.6	4.0	4.6	4.8
N	3.1	2.7	3.0	3.4	3.5	3.6	3.6	3.2	3.9	4.2
O	4.1	4.5	4.6	4.8	4.9	4.9	5.0	5.2	5.5	6.1
P	-	-	-	-	-	-	-	-	-	-
Q	0.5	0.6	0.7	0.5	0.4	0.3	0.2	0.3	0.3	0.0
X	0.1	0.1	0.2	0.2	-	0.1	0.2	-	0.2	0.1

Women - Femmes - Mujeres
ISIC 3 - CITI 3 - CIIU 3

	1999	2000	2001	2002	2003	2004	2005	2006	2007	2008
Total	71.2	72.8	74.0	73.8	74.6	73.6	75.6	77.5	80.7	81.5
A	2.4	2.4	2.1	2.1	1.9	1.8	1.9	1.8	1.8	1.5
B	0.9	0.8	0.5	0.5	0.4	0.4	0.4	0.3	0.2	0.4
C	-	-	0.1	0.1	-	-	-	-	-	-
D	7.7	7.3	7.0	7.1	7.0	7.1	6.9	6.1	5.7	5.9
E	0.1	0.3	0.3	0.5	0.3	0.2	0.3	0.3	0.4	0.4
F	0.5	0.4	0.5	0.6	0.4	0.6	0.8	0.8	0.6	1.1
G	9.9	10.4	10.6	10.2	9.2	8.5	9.4	10.0	11.1	10.0
H	3.6	3.4	3.4	2.8	3.2	3.1	2.9	2.9	3.7	3.5
I	4.4	4.3	4.1	3.6	3.5	3.7	4.1	4.1	3.8	3.7
J	3.2	4.0	4.4	4.0	4.3	4.8	4.6	4.7	5.1	5.2
K	4.4	5.1	5.1	5.7	5.5	6.0	6.0	5.4	5.8	5.8
L	3.4	3.2	3.0	3.6	4.1	4.2	3.8	5.2	4.5	4.8
M	6.3	7.1	8.3	9.0	8.2	8.1	8.3	8.5	8.9	9.8
N	18.3	17.9	19.1	18.2	21.3	19.3	20.9	21.4	22.1	23.0
O	5.8	5.9	5.0	5.3	4.9	5.5	5.1	5.7	6.6	6.4
P	-	-	-	-	-	-	-	-	-	-
Q	0.1	0.2	0.2	0.3	0.2	0.1	0.2	0.1	0.3	0.1
X	0.1	0.1	0.2	0.1	-	0.1	-	-	0.1	0.1

Ireland (BA) [3] [4] — Total employment - Emploi total - Empleo total

Total - Total - Total
ISIC 3 - CITI 3 - CIIU 3

	1999	2000	2001	2002	2003	2004	2005	2006	2007	2008
Total	1 591.1	1 670.7	1 716.5	1 760.6	1 790.1	1 834.6	1 931.6	2 021.1	2 101.6	2 108.5
A	132.8	127.9	117.0	119.5	113.3	113.6	111.6	110.8	111.3	119.2
B	3.1	3.0	3.1	4.0	2.6	2.8	2.0	2.5	2.4	2.1
C	5.7	6.3	7.3	8.0	6.7	6.9	9.0	10.8	10.8	10.5
D	291.4	292.2	297.9	284.5	286.9	280.4	273.2	269.0	270.8	262.5
E	11.8	11.5	11.9	12.0	12.6	13.5	13.0	10.9	13.6	13.4
F	142.1	166.3	180.2	181.1	189.8	204.7	243.0	265.2	281.8	255.0
G	223.3	235.8	247.8	245.6	249.5	258.9	266.5	283.4	294.5	310.7
H	102.6	109.0	104.8	106.0	117.3	111.1	115.3	122.8	132.3	128.6
I	95.0	100.8	110.4	111.0	111.2	112.4	117.6	119.9	122.2	119.2
J	61.2	68.5	68.6	70.1	72.6	81.7	83.6	83.9	91.1	94.0
K	134.6	143.6	149.7	159.1	154.1	154.3	172.1	182.2	194.8	202.4
L	74.4	77.8	80.4	89.5	91.2	88.4	96.4	102.3	101.6	103.0
M	100.5	102.3	102.7	110.9	115.6	117.8	122.7	134.1	139.7	142.0
N	119.9	132.4	142.6	159.6	171.1	178.0	188.7	202.6	213.2	223.9
O	74.0	73.8	76.3	82.9	79.1	93.4	94.9	99.7	103.2	101.2
P	8.4	7.4	7.3	6.5	8.9	6.8	7.6	8.3	9.7	10.1
Q	0.6	0.7	0.6	0.5	0.8	0.4	0.8	1.2	1.2	0.7
X	8.7	11.5	8.1	10.0	7.0	8.7	13.5	11.6	7.6	10.1

Explanatory notes: see p. 77.

[1] Persons aged 16 to 74 years. [2] Excl. armed forces and conscripts. [3] Persons aged 15 years and over. [4] Second quarter of each year.

Notes explicatives: voir p. 80.

[1] Personnes âgées de 16 à 74 ans. [2] Non compris les forces armées et les conscrits. [3] Personnes âgées de 15 ans et plus. [4] Deuxième trimestre de chaque année.

Notas explicativas: véase p. 83.

[1] Personas de 16 a 74 años. [2] Excl. las fuerzas armadas y los conscriptos. [3] Personas de 15 años y más. [4] Segundo trimestre de cada año.

**Total employment,
by economic activity**

**Emploi total,
par activité économique**

**Empleo total,
por actividad económica**

	Thousands			Milliers				Millares		
	1999	2000	2001	2002	2003	2004	2005	2006	2007	2008

Ireland (BA) [1][2] — Total employment - Emploi total - Empleo total

Men - Hommes - Hombres
ISIC 3 - CITI 3 - CIIU 3

	1999	2000	2001	2002	2003	2004	2005	2006	2007	2008
Total	947.3	989.9	1 013.9	1 026.2	1 039.3	1 065.0	1 113.3	1 166.7	1 201.5	1 186.9
A	117.7	113.5	104.4	107.0	99.8	102.4	100.1	100.2	99.7	104.8
B	2.7	2.9	2.8	3.7	2.3	2.6	2.0	2.3	2.1	1.8
C	5.3	5.9	6.7	7.5	6.3	6.3	8.1	9.9	9.8	9.6
D	200.4	198.0	205.9	197.3	200.4	192.3	188.9	187.6	190.9	185.6
E	10.0	9.1	9.7	9.9	10.8	10.7	10.1	8.7	11.0	11.1
F	135.9	159.2	172.0	172.1	180.4	194.4	230.9	251.9	267.9	241.0
G	118.2	125.7	130.7	125.4	126.6	130.8	133.3	143.7	150.5	157.1
H	41.8	44.0	43.1	45.9	50.2	51.5	48.1	53.4	55.4	53.9
I	72.0	75.5	80.9	82.0	84.5	86.5	90.6	91.2	95.2	91.9
J	26.3	29.4	29.4	29.1	30.9	34.8	35.7	35.2	36.9	38.9
K	72.9	77.7	81.1	85.9	85.4	86.0	93.5	100.8	102.4	109.1
L	45.1	45.8	45.4	48.5	50.7	48.4	48.0	50.1	49.3	51.6
M	32.6	33.4	32.3	34.2	34.7	33.5	35.8	38.5	37.2	38.1
N	24.9	27.2	27.4	32.0	34.4	34.4	34.3	35.7	38.7	38.3
O	35.9	35.8	37.3	39.6	36.8	43.4	44.0	48.6	47.9	47.2
P	0.9	0.6	0.9	0.6	0.8	0.9	0.8	0.6	0.7	0.6
Q	0.3	0.3	0.2	0.3	0.5	0.2	0.3	0.5	0.5	0.4
X	4.4	5.9	3.7	5.2	3.8	5.3	8.9	8.1	5.3	5.7

Women - Femmes - Mujeres
ISIC 3 - CITI 3 - CIIU 3

	1999	2000	2001	2002	2003	2004	2005	2006	2007	2008
Total	643.9	680.8	702.5	734.4	750.9	769.6	818.4	854.5	900.1	921.6
A	15.1	14.4	12.6	12.5	13.5	11.2	11.5	10.6	11.7	14.5
B	0.4	0.2	0.3	0.2	0.3	0.2	0.1	0.2	0.3	0.2
C	0.4	0.4	0.6	0.5	0.3	0.6	0.9	0.9	1.0	0.9
D	91.0	94.1	92.0	87.2	86.5	88.1	84.3	81.4	79.9	76.9
E	1.8	2.3	2.2	2.0	1.8	2.8	3.0	2.2	2.6	2.3
F	6.1	7.2	8.2	9.0	9.4	10.3	12.1	13.3	13.8	13.9
G	105.1	110.1	117.1	120.3	122.8	128.1	133.2	139.7	144.0	153.5
H	60.8	65.0	61.6	60.1	67.1	59.6	67.2	69.4	76.9	74.7
I	23.9	25.2	29.5	29.0	26.7	25.8	27.0	28.8	26.9	27.2
J	34.8	39.1	39.2	41.0	41.7	46.9	47.9	48.7	54.2	55.0
K	61.8	65.9	68.6	73.2	68.7	68.3	78.7	81.4	92.4	93.3
L	29.3	32.0	35.0	41.0	40.5	40.1	48.4	52.2	52.3	51.4
M	67.9	68.9	70.4	76.7	80.9	84.3	86.8	95.6	102.5	103.9
N	95.1	105.2	115.1	127.6	136.7	143.6	154.3	166.9	174.5	185.6
O	38.1	38.0	38.9	43.3	42.3	50.0	50.9	51.1	55.2	54.0
P	7.6	6.8	6.4	5.8	8.0	5.8	6.8	7.8	9.0	9.6
Q	0.3	0.3	0.4	0.2	0.3	0.2	0.5	0.8	0.6	0.3
X	4.3	5.6	4.4	4.8	3.2	3.4	4.6	3.6	2.3	4.4

Italy (BA) [1] — Total employment - Emploi total - Empleo total

Total - Total - Total
ISIC 3 - CITI 3 - CIIU 3

	1999	2000	2001	2002	2003	2004	2005	2006	2007	2008
Total	20 864	21 225	21 634	21 922	22 133	22 404 [3]	22 563	22 988	23 222	23 405
A	1 089	1 071	1 084	1 057	1 038	956 [3]	914	948	888	860
B	45	49	42	39	37	34 [3]	33	34	35	35
C	70	64	64	63	59	38 [3]	40	42	39	36
D	4 928	4 918	4 907	4 962	4 990	4 846 [3]	4 825	4 826	4 870	4 805
E	176	167	162	159	161	152 [3]	163	159	139	144
F	1 575	1 618	1 707	1 748	1 809	1 833 [3]	1 913	1 900	1 955	1 970
G	3 308	3 377	3 416	3 456	3 530	3 434 [3]	3 416	3 522	3 541	3 540
H	739	814	880	907	953	1 035 [3]	1 060	1 114	1 154	1 179
I	1 133	1 190	1 180	1 167	1 162	1 241 [3]	1 239	1 224	1 257	1 294
J	671	662	659	663	665	640 [3]	640	675	664	653
K	1 336	1 478	1 550	1 675	1 728	2 326 [3]	2 376	2 434	2 542	2 618
L	1 943	1 942	1 987	1 982	1 934	1 452 [3]	1 440	1 443	1 418	1 436
M	1 445	1 467	1 520	1 531	1 532	1 602 [3]	1 541	1 597	1 606	1 584
N	1 289	1 288	1 321	1 329	1 331	1 505 [3]	1 549	1 570	1 575	1 659
O	898	905	939	970	985	1 041 [3]	1 093	1 164	1 167	1 136
P	201	196	193	198	202	250 [3]	303	324	349	419
Q	17	20	20	16	17	20 [3]	17	12	22	36
X	.	.	.		.		.	.	.	.

Explanatory notes: see p. 77.

[1] Persons aged 15 years and over. [2] Second quarter of each year. [3] Methodology revised; data not strictly comparable.

Notes explicatives: voir p. 80.

[1] Personnes âgées de 15 ans et plus. [2] Deuxième trimestre de chaque année. [3] Méthodologie révisée; les données ne sont pas strictement comparables.

Notas explicativas: véase p. 83.

[1] Personas de 15 años y más. [2] Segundo trimestre de cada año. [3] Metodología revisada; los datos no son estrictamente comparables.

2B

EMPLOYMENT	EMPLOI	EMPLEO
Total employment, by economic activity	Emploi total, par activité économique	Empleo total, por actividad económica
Thousands	Milliers	Millares

	1999	2000	2001	2002	2003	2004	2005	2006	2007	2008

Italy (BA) [1]

Total employment - Emploi total - Empleo total

Men - Hommes - Hombres
ISIC 3 - CITI 3 - CIIU 3

	1999	2000	2001	2002	2003	2004	2005	2006	2007	2008
Total	13 330	13 461	13 574	13 685	13 769	13 622 [2]	13 738	13 939	14 057	14 064
A	737	723	724	710	710	652 [2]	628	649	611	594
B	42	46	40	36	34	31 [2]	31	31	32	32
C	61	55	51	51	51	34 [2]	36	36	34	31
D	3 442	3 417	3 399	3 453	3 475	3 408 [2]	3 418	3 438	3 493	3 443
E	156	146	141	139	138	129 [2]	141	134	115	115
F	1 481	1 516	1 603	1 634	1 694	1 726 [2]	1 806	1 803	1 852	1 860
G	2 066	2 110	2 108	2 119	2 136	2 031 [2]	2 061	2 117	2 087	2 114
H	400	434	463	480	500	521 [2]	533	567	591	586
I	910	954	938	919	908	972 [2]	960	939	965	996
J	434	419	405	410	413	379 [2]	379	404	395	384
K	774	854	880	942	973	1 275 [2]	1 299	1 331	1 421	1 450
L	1 343	1 327	1 327	1 316	1 281	989 [2]	967	971	949	948
M	416	421	430	424	410	421 [2]	394	400	407	400
N	547	518	526	516	502	515 [2]	529	528	512	515
O	469	467	485	490	494	492 [2]	504	544	542	523
P	43	46	42	37	39	34 [2]	41	41	39	49
Q	11	11	10	9	10	12 [2]	11	7	12	22
X										

Women - Femmes - Mujeres
ISIC 3 - CITI 3 - CIIU 3

	1999	2000	2001	2002	2003	2004	2005	2006	2007	2008
Total	7 533	7 764	8 060	8 236	8 365	8 783 [2]	8 825	9 049	9 165	9 341
A	352	348	360	347	328	304 [2]	286	299	278	266
B	3	3	3	2	3	4 [2]	2	3	3	3
C	10	9	13	12	8	4 [2]	4	6	5	5
D	1 487	1 501	1 508	1 509	1 515	1 437 [2]	1 407	1 387	1 377	1 362
E	20	21	21	20	22	22 [2]	22	24	25	29
F	94	102	104	113	115	107 [2]	107	98	103	110
G	1 242	1 267	1 308	1 336	1 395	1 402 [2]	1 355	1 405	1 454	1 426
H	339	380	417	427	453	514 [2]	526	547	562	593
I	223	236	242	248	255	269 [2]	279	286	291	298
J	236	243	254	254	251	261 [2]	261	271	269	269
K	562	624	669	733	755	1 051 [2]	1 077	1 103	1 122	1 168
L	600	615	660	666	654	463 [2]	472	472	468	488
M	1 029	1 046	1 090	1 107	1 122	1 181 [2]	1 147	1 197	1 198	1 183
N	742	770	795	812	829	990 [2]	1 021	1 042	1 063	1 144
O	428	438	453	480	490	549 [2]	589	620	626	613
P	158	150	151	162	163	216 [2]	263	283	310	370
Q	6	9	10	7	7	8 [2]	6	5	10	14
X										

Jersey (E) [3]

Total employment - Emploi total - Empleo total

Total - Total - Total
ISIC 3 - CITI 3 - CIIU 3

	1999	2000	2001	2002	2003	2004	2005	2006	2007	2008
Total	.	49.8	50.1	50.3	49.6	49.6	50.3	51.6	53.0	53.5
A-B	.	1.7	1.6	1.6	1.6	1.5	1.5	1.5	1.6	1.5
C,F	.	4.5	4.9	4.9	4.5	4.7	4.9	5.1	5.1	5.3
D	.	2.3	2.3	2.2	2.0	1.8	1.7	1.6	1.5	1.4
E	.	0.6	0.6	0.6	0.5	0.5	0.5	0.5	0.5	0.5
G	.	8.0	8.0	7.9	8.1	8.5	8.6	8.7	8.6	8.4
H	.	4.7	4.4	4.4	4.4	4.2	4.3	4.3	4.6	4.6
I	.	2.7	2.6	2.6	2.5	2.5	2.5	2.6	2.7	2.7
J	.	11.9	12.3	12.4	11.9	11.7	11.9	12.4	13.1	13.4
K	.	3.2	3.0	3.2	3.3	3.2	3.4	3.5	3.7	4.0
L	.	6.0	6.1	6.3	6.4	6.5	6.4	6.6	6.6	6.7
M-O	.	4.3	4.3	4.4	4.5	4.5	4.6	4.8	4.9	5.1

Jersey (FD) [3]

Total employment - Emploi total - Empleo total

Total - Total - Total
ISIC 3 - CITI 3 - CIIU 3

	1999	2000	2001	2002	2003	2004	2005	2006	2007	2008
Total	42.3	42.5	42.6	42.5	41.6	41.3	41.9	42.9	44.1	.
A-B	1.6	1.6	1.5	1.6	1.5	1.4	1.4	1.4	1.5	.
C,F	4.3	4.3	4.6	4.6	4.2	4.3	4.5	4.7	4.7	.
D	2.3	2.3	2.2	2.1	1.9	1.7	1.6	1.5	1.4	.
E	0.6	0.6	0.6	0.6	0.5	0.5	0.5	0.5	0.5	.
G	8.0	7.8	7.8	7.6	7.8	8.2	8.3	8.3	8.2	.
H	4.7	4.7	4.4	4.4	4.4	4.2	4.3	4.4	4.5	.
I	2.6	2.6	2.6	2.5	2.4	2.4	2.4	2.4	2.5	.
J	11.4	11.8	12.2	12.2	11.7	11.6	11.7	12.5	13.0	.
K	2.7	2.9	2.8	3.0	3.0	2.9	3.0	2.7	3.0	.
L-O	4.0	4.0	4.1	4.1	4.2	4.2	4.2	4.4	4.5	.

Explanatory notes: see p. 77.

[1] Persons aged 15 years and over. [2] Methodology revised; data not strictly comparable. [3] December.

Notes explicatives: voir p. 80.

[1] Personnes âgées de 15 ans et plus. [2] Méthodologie révisée; les données ne sont pas strictement comparables. [3] Décembre.

Notas explicativas: véase p. 83.

[1] Personas de 15 años y más. [2] Metodología revisada; los datos no son estrictamente comparables. [3] Diciembre.

Total employment, by economic activity
Emploi total, par activité économique
Empleo total, por actividad económica

	Thousands			Milliers				Millares		
	1999	2000	2001	2002	2003	2004	2005	2006	2007	2008

Latvia (BA) [1][2] Total employment - Emploi total - Empleo total

Total - Total - Total
ISIC 3 - CITI 3 - CIIU 3

	1999	2000	2001	2002	2003	2004	2005	2006	2007	2008
Total	968.5	941.1	962.1	989.0 [3]	1 006.9	1 017.7	1 035.9	1 087.6	1 119.0	1 124.1
A	156.4	133.9	142.7	146.9 [3]	135.0	132.5	122.3	117.8	107.5	87.3
B	4.3	2.1	2.4	5.5 [3]	3.5	2.3	2.9	2.4	2.8	1.8
C	-	-	-	3.4 [3]	2.5	2.2	-	3.8	6.6	2.8
D	170.3	170.2	165.6	167.2 [3]	173.6	163.5	154.1	169.6	164.8	171.0
E	21.6	21.0	19.3	22.5 [3]	21.5	25.5	23.1	22.3	20.7	21.3
F	57.9	56.1	67.9	60.3 [3]	74.4	86.8	90.5	103.9	125.6	125.5
G	141.8	145.3	150.8	147.7 [3]	152.6	151.2	157.7	170.2	184.6	186.6
H	20.7	22.1	22.2	24.4 [3]	24.7	25.6	27.6	29.2	31.2	30.4
I	81.6	78.8	78.2	86.2 [3]	94.5	95.9	94.6	100.8	104.0	105.8
J	11.5	12.4	13.7	12.7 [3]	15.7	18.3	20.1	25.1	22.0	19.6
K	40.7	44.8	40.8	38.5 [3]	41.9	40.2	49.2	60.7	74.0	78.1
L	74.2	70.9	67.5	67.8 [3]	67.4	73.1	81.8	88.2	83.9	86.6
M	87.0	86.7	88.3	87.6 [3]	78.6	82.8	90.5	87.8	81.8	90.4
N	52.3	48.0	49.9	60.4 [3]	59.0	54.4	57.9	51.0	50.1	54.7
O	44.2	44.4	49.1	53.3 [3]	56.7	59.8	57.6	49.5	53.7	57.4
P	2.7	2.5	-	4.5 [3]	5.0	3.3	3.7	4.2	3.3	4.4
Q	-	-	-	-	-	-	-	-	-	-
X	-	-	-	-	-	-	-	-	-	-

Men - Hommes - Hombres
ISIC 3 - CITI 3 - CIIU 3

	1999	2000	2001	2002	2003	2004	2005	2006	2007	2008
Total	502.9	479.7	486.4	504.6 [3]	516.6	521.8	534.1	559.2	573.5	571.5
A	89.7	77.5	87.7	92.4 [3]	86.3	83.3	81.5	76.1	67.7	56.4
B	-	-	-	-	-	-	-	-	-	-
C	-	-	-	-	-	-	-	-	-	-
D	100.4	97.3	88.9	96.7 [3]	99.3	89.9	88.0	94.5	93.7	95.5
E	15.5	15.0	15.8	17.9 [3]	16.6	18.3	16.4	16.8	16.1	17.2
F	51.6	51.0	62.1	53.8 [3]	65.6	77.2	82.2	97.8	115.4	113.8
G	64.9	60.6	61.2	59.5 [3]	57.8	56.6	59.8	64.0	70.3	70.1
H	4.9	5.6	5.1	4.1 [3]	4.9	7.5	7.3	4.9	5.6	5.4
I	55.5	55.2	54.1	58.9 [3]	65.5	68.7	66.0	70.2	71.7	73.7
J	3.8	4.7	4.8	5.0 [3]	6.1	8.4	7.6	7.2	5.8	5.0
K	21.4	23.5	22.0	21.8 [3]	25.1	21.3	24.9	31.4	36.3	41.6
L	41.1	39.6	38.0	36.5 [3]	35.3	39.8	44.7	46.0	39.2	41.6
M	18.8	18.5	16.0	18.7 [3]	15.0	14.2	17.3	15.9	14.4	18.2
N	9.9	6.7	8.0	9.7 [3]	8.0	7.3	8.8	7.1	7.3	8.1
O	20.0	20.6	18.7	21.7 [3]	24.6	25.0	25.3	20.3	20.3	18.6
P	-	-	-	-	-	-	-	-	-	-
Q	-	-	-	-	-	-	-	-	-	-
X	-	-	-	-	-	-	-	-	-	-

Women - Femmes - Mujeres
ISIC 3 - CITI 3 - CIIU 3

	1999	2000	2001	2002	2003	2004	2005	2006	2007	2008
Total	465.6	461.4	475.7	484.3 [3]	490.2	495.9	501.8	528.5	545.5	552.6
A	66.8	56.4	55.1	54.5 [3]	48.7	49.2	40.8	41.7	39.8	30.9
B	-	-	-	-	-	-	-	-	-	-
C	-	-	-	-	-	-	-	-	-	-
D	69.9	72.9	76.7	70.4 [3]	74.3	73.6	66.1	75.0	71.0	75.5
E	6.1	6.1	3.4	4.6 [3]	4.9	7.2	6.7	5.5	4.6	4.1
F	6.3	5.1	5.8	6.5 [3]	8.8	9.6	8.3	6.1	10.3	11.7
G	77.0	84.7	89.6	88.2 [3]	94.8	94.7	97.9	106.2	114.3	116.5
H	15.8	16.5	17.1	20.4 [3]	19.7	18.1	20.4	24.3	25.6	25.0
I	26.2	23.5	24.1	27.3 [3]	29.0	27.2	28.5	30.6	32.3	32.1
J	7.8	7.6	8.9	7.7 [3]	9.6	10.0	12.5	17.9	16.2	14.7
K	19.3	21.3	18.9	16.7 [3]	16.9	18.9	24.3	29.3	37.8	36.5
L	33.1	31.4	29.5	31.3 [3]	32.0	33.3	37.1	42.2	44.7	45.0
M	68.2	68.2	72.3	69.0 [3]	63.7	68.7	73.2	71.9	67.4	72.2
N	42.4	41.3	41.8	50.8 [3]	51.1	47.1	49.1	43.8	42.8	46.6
O	24.2	23.7	30.4	31.5 [3]	32.3	34.8	32.3	29.2	33.4	38.8
P	-	-	-	-	-	-	-	-	-	-
Q	-	-	-	-	-	-	-	-	-	-
X	-	-	-	-	-	-	-	-	-	-

Explanatory notes: see p. 77.

[1] Persons aged 15 to 74 years. [2] Excl. conscripts. [3] Prior to 2002: persons aged 15 years and over.

Notes explicatives: voir p. 80.

[1] Personnes âgées de 15 à 74 ans. [2] Non compris les conscrits. [3] Avant 2002: personnes agées de 15 ans et plus.

Notas explicativas: véase p. 83.

[1] Personas de 15 a 74 años. [2] Excl. los conscriptos. [3] Antes de 2002: personas de 15 años y más.

**Total employment,
by economic activity**

**Emploi total,
par activité économique**

**Empleo total,
por actividad económica**

	Thousands				Milliers				Millares	
	1999	2000	2001	2002	2003	2004	2005	2006	2007	2008

Lithuania (BA) [1] [2]

Total employment - Emploi total - Empleo total

Total - Total - Total
ISIC 3 - CITI 3 - CIIU 3

	1999	2000	2001	2002	2003	2004	2005	2006	2007	2008
Total	1 456.5	1 397.8	1 351.8	1 405.9	1 438.0	1 436.3	1 473.9	1 499.0	1 534.2	1 520.0
A	278.8	258.1	231.3	249.8	255.5	225.6	204.2	183.9	156.9	116.6
B	2.6	3.5	2.6	0.8	1.5	1.9	2.8	2.7	2.6	4.1
C	3.2	3.1	2.8	4.3	5.1	4.3	3.3	4.3	5.3	4.0
D	265.7	254.0	243.2	260.6	264.6	254.9	266.5	264.6	267.9	266.0
E	37.4	33.7	35.1	28.4	27.8	29.5	26.5	27.1	26.2	27.6
F	91.7	83.7	84.8	93.2	107.1	116.2	132.5	148.7	170.9	165.7
G	205.2	200.4	205.7	211.2	214.7	228.0	233.3	254.6	262.4	274.9
H	27.8	27.1	25.8	28.0	29.4	32.7	33.1	39.0	33.5	38.9
I	92.2	90.5	86.0	87.4	92.2	93.9	93.9	98.9	111.4	104.5
J	15.2	14.5	10.9	14.0	16.8	15.0	16.3	16.6	22.3	20.3
K	41.2	43.2	41.1	54.9	53.5	55.8	62.3	78.3	75.4	101.3
L	77.7	73.7	71.9	81.3	74.9	77.9	81.7	75.7	83.5	83.3
M	151.9	161.0	155.0	138.9	134.8	141.0	148.0	131.5	144.3	148.5
N	102.3	96.5	99.6	94.6	98.9	98.4	98.6	105.7	100.7	95.7
O	60.0	53.6	51.9	53.8	54.6	55.8	63.7	63.7	67.1	64.8
P	3.1	1.4	4.2	4.8	6.7	5.0	7.1	3.6	3.9	3.7
Q	0.5	-	-	0.1	-	0.2	0.2	0.1	-	0.2

Men - Hommes - Hombres
ISIC 3 - CITI 3 - CIIU 3

	1999	2000	2001	2002	2003	2004	2005	2006	2007	2008
Total	729.2	686.5	664.5	707.8	726.2	733.8	750.9	755.8	777.7	768.7
A	166.3	151.2	142.8	150.9	152.4	131.6	122.6	108.1	97.6	73.2
B	2.3	2.9	2.5	0.8	1.4	1.8	2.2	2.5	2.5	3.4
C	1.8	1.5	2.2	3.0	3.9	3.2	2.3	3.9	4.4	3.5
D	131.1	128.9	115.5	129.9	129.8	129.7	134.6	137.9	138.4	144.3
E	27.3	23.2	28.9	24.0	20.5	23.1	20.8	19.1	19.4	21.0
F	83.6	76.6	77.5	84.1	96.2	106.2	120.5	139.0	158.5	149.7
G	102.2	90.4	100.6	103.7	103.0	112.1	111.1	115.9	117.2	124.6
H	5.6	7.3	5.9	6.3	5.5	6.4	7.1	7.6	6.3	5.6
I	64.0	62.7	59.9	63.4	69.8	70.2	68.5	69.6	80.1	75.3
J	5.0	6.2	5.3	5.5	5.9	4.6	4.4	5.5	6.8	5.4
K	21.2	23.0	21.1	26.8	26.8	30.5	34.2	43.2	37.8	52.3
L	45.1	40.4	39.3	40.9	45.1	45.3	45.1	38.4	43.0	42.5
M	32.7	34.6	31.8	29.7	27.9	30.7	35.3	25.6	26.1	31.6
N	16.2	13.6	12.3	14.1	14.2	15.9	17.2	16.6	14.6	12.0
O	24.2	23.9	16.4	22.4	21.1	19.5	21.6	21.7	22.4	23.1
P	0.6	0.1	2.5	2.4	2.7	3.0	3.0	1.1	2.3	1.1
Q	-	-	-	-	-	0.1	0.2	0.1	-	0.1

Women - Femmes - Mujeres
ISIC 3 - CITI 3 - CIIU 3

	1999	2000	2001	2002	2003	2004	2005	2006	2007	2008
Total	727.4	711.3	687.3	698.1	711.8	702.5	723.0	743.2	756.5	751.4
A	112.5	106.9	88.4	98.9	103.1	94.0	81.6	75.7	59.3	43.5
B	0.3	0.6	0.1	-	0.1	0.2	0.6	0.2	0.1	0.7
C	1.4	1.6	0.6	1.4	1.2	1.2	0.9	0.4	0.9	0.6
D	134.6	125.0	127.7	130.6	134.7	125.2	131.8	126.7	129.5	121.7
E	10.0	10.6	6.2	4.4	7.3	6.4	5.7	7.9	6.8	6.6
F	8.1	7.1	7.2	9.0	10.9	9.9	12.0	9.7	12.4	16.0
G	103.0	109.9	105.1	107.4	111.8	116.0	122.2	138.7	145.2	150.3
H	22.3	19.8	19.9	21.8	23.9	26.3	26.0	31.5	27.2	33.3
I	28.2	27.7	26.1	24.0	22.4	23.7	25.4	29.3	31.3	29.2
J	10.2	8.3	5.6	8.5	10.9	10.4	11.9	11.1	15.5	14.8
K	20.0	20.2	20.0	28.1	26.7	25.4	28.1	35.1	37.5	49.0
L	32.5	33.3	32.6	40.4	29.8	32.6	36.6	37.2	40.5	40.8
M	119.2	126.4	123.2	109.2	106.9	110.3	112.7	106.0	118.2	116.9
N	86.1	82.9	87.3	80.5	84.6	82.5	81.3	89.1	86.1	83.7
O	35.8	29.7	35.5	31.4	33.5	36.3	42.1	42.1	44.7	41.7
P	2.6	1.3	1.7	2.3	4.0	2.1	4.1	2.4	1.5	2.7
Q	0.5	-	-	0.1	-	0.1	-	-	-	0.1

Luxembourg (E)

Total employment - Emploi total - Empleo total

Total - Total - Total
ISIC 3 - CITI 3 - CIIU 3

	1999	2000	2001	2002	2003	2004	2005	2006	2007	2008
Total	249.9	263.8	278.4	286.5	291.8	298.5	307.3	319.1	333.2	348.7
A-B	4.0	4.0	3.9	3.9	3.9	3.9	3.9	4.6	5.0	5.0
C	0.3	0.3	0.3	0.3	0.3	0.3	0.3	0.3		
C-E									35.7	37.7
D	32.9	33.1	33.6	33.4	32.6	32.5	32.6	33.7		
E	1.5	1.5	1.5	1.6	1.6	1.7	1.8	1.6		
F	25.4	25.9	27.2	28.1	28.7	29.2	30.3	33.6	35.3	38.4
G	37.2	38.0	39.4	40.5	41.1	41.7	42.8	43.1		
G-I									85.2	89.6
H	12.4	12.7	13.0	13.3	13.6	13.9	14.2	15.0		
I	18.5	19.9	21.4	22.0	22.5	22.5	22.9	24.5		
J	27.0	29.5	32.6	33.1	32.7	32.9	33.8	36.4	38.4	41.3
K	36.1	41.0	44.5	46.6	48.1	50.5	52.0	53.6	54.9	59.5
L	13.2	13.8	14.1	14.8	15.5	16.2	16.7	17.1		
L-P									74.0	77.1
M	11.4	12.1	12.7	13.2	13.6	13.9	14.4	14.9		
N	15.6	16.6	18.0	19.2	20.5	21.6	22.8	24.5		
O	8.9	9.4	9.7	9.8	10.0	10.2	10.6	11.6		
P	5.6	5.9	6.3	6.7	7.1	7.5	8.2	4.6		

Explanatory notes: see p. 77.   Notes explicatives: voir p. 80.   Notas explicativas: véase p. 83.

[1] Persons aged 15 years and over. [2] Excl. conscripts.   [1] Personnes âgées de 15 ans et plus. [2] Non compris les conscrits.   [1] Personas de 15 años y más. [2] Excl. los conscriptos.

Total employment, by economic activity — Emploi total, par activité économique — Empleo total, por actividad económica

	Thousands			Milliers				Millares		
	1999	2000	2001	2002	2003	2004	2005	2006	2007	2008

Macedonia, The Former Yugoslav Rep. of (BA) [1] — Total employment - Emploi total - Empleo total

Total - Total - Total
ISIC 3 - CITI 3 - CIIU 3

	1999	2000	2001	2002	2003	2004	2005	2006	2007	2008
Total	.	.	.	561.341	545.108	522.995 [2]	545.253	570.404	590.234	609.015
A	.	.	.	133.581	119.951	87.608 [2]	106.179	114.485	107.433	119.498
B				0.712	0.181	0.442 [2]	0.354	0.292	0.284	0.251
C				6.937	2.498	2.813 [2]	3.554	3.861	5.093	6.680
D				132.405	131.307	116.300 [2]	119.953	123.066	126.193	128.953
E				14.769	15.176	15.784 [2]	17.035	15.955	15.636	15.516
F				32.806	35.874	36.493 [2]	35.326	43.203	38.006	39.381
G				64.265	62.507	74.218 [2]	74.690	73.015	82.971	86.553
H				11.230	12.766	12.672 [2]	13.558	19.034	17.486	19.117
I				32.595	30.642	30.785 [2]	32.720	30.000	35.461	37.726
J				8.422	7.093	7.703 [2]	6.303	7.081	9.041	7.739
K				11.953	10.811	13.529 [2]	14.804	15.376	15.909	16.298
L				32.956	34.744	39.700 [2]	38.301	39.343	41.409	42.227
M				33.700	32.027	33.635 [2]	31.652	33.394	34.367	33.615
N				26.226	30.233	29.914 [2]	31.320	32.584	32.947	32.906
O				17.521	17.760	19.654 [2]	18.175	18.290	24.714	21.008
P				0.319	-	0.156 [2]	0.414	0.464	1.415	0.733
Q				0.945	1.537	1.589 [2]	0.916	0.962	1.869	0.814

Men - Hommes - Hombres
ISIC 3 - CITI 3 - CIIU 3

	1999	2000	2001	2002	2003	2004	2005	2006	2007	2008
Total	.	.	.	342.779	327.283	320.640 [2]	332.179	351.974	358.835	373.483
A	.	.	.	79.669	71.608	57.353 [2]	65.390	70.125	67.444	72.976
B				0.652	0.181	0.363 [2]	0.283	0.255	0.284	0.130
C				6.471	2.118	2.537 [2]	3.320	3.554	4.837	6.290
D				73.142	70.298	62.230 [2]	62.155	64.650	65.180	67.895
E				12.732	13.118	13.644 [2]	14.605	13.699	13.205	13.136
F				29.923	32.469	32.490 [2]	32.100	40.267	35.344	37.466
G				39.427	36.145	43.104 [2]	43.618	45.023	48.341	51.343
H				7.279	8.475	8.819 [2]	9.099	12.947	11.801	12.744
I				26.248	25.461	26.027 [2]	28.238	25.576	29.567	31.436
J				3.336	2.489	2.914 [2]	2.234	3.321	4.535	3.098
K				7.080	6.349	7.724 [2]	9.009	7.455	8.332	9.620
L				24.079	24.130	28.002 [2]	27.357	27.616	29.424	30.606
M				13.636	13.187	13.741 [2]	13.615	14.653	13.239	14.150
N				7.703	8.100	7.949 [2]	8.548	9.780	9.593	8.593
O				11.087	12.465	13.044 [2]	12.222	12.651	16.067	13.138
P				-	-	- [2]	0.027	0.133	0.859	0.272
Q				0.317	0.692	0.701 [2]	0.360	0.268	0.782	0.590

Women - Femmes - Mujeres
ISIC 3 - CITI 3 - CIIU 3

	1999	2000	2001	2002	2003	2004	2005	2006	2007	2008
Total	.	.	.	218.562	217.825	202.355 [2]	213.074	218.431	231.399	235.532
A	.	.	.	53.912	48.343	30.256 [2]	40.790	44.360	39.989	46.521
B				0.061	-	0.078 [2]	0.071	0.037	-	0.121
C				0.466	0.380	0.276 [2]	0.234	0.307	0.256	0.390
D				59.263	61.009	54.070 [2]	57.798	58.416	61.013	61.058
E				2.037	2.058	2.140 [2]	2.430	2.256	2.431	2.380
F				2.882	3.405	4.004 [2]	3.226	2.936	2.662	1.915
G				24.838	26.362	31.113 [2]	31.072	27.992	34.630	35.210
H				3.951	4.291	3.853 [2]	4.459	6.086	5.685	6.373
I				6.347	5.182	4.759 [2]	4.482	4.425	5.894	6.290
J				5.086	4.604	4.789 [2]	4.070	3.761	4.506	4.641
K				4.873	4.462	5.806 [2]	5.795	7.920	7.577	6.677
L				8.877	10.614	11.698 [2]	10.943	11.727	11.985	11.621
M				20.064	18.840	19.894 [2]	18.037	18.741	21.128	19.466
N				18.523	22.133	21.966 [2]	22.771	22.804	23.354	24.313
O				6.434	5.295	6.611 [2]	5.953	5.640	8.647	7.870
P				0.319	-	0.156 [2]	0.387	0.330	0.556	0.461
Q				0.628	0.845	0.888 [2]	0.556	0.693	1.087	0.224

Malta (BA) [1] — Total employment - Emploi total - Empleo total

Total - Total - Total
ISIC 3 - CITI 3 - CIIU 3

	1999	2000	2001	2002	2003	2004	2005	2006	2007	2008
Total	.	145.2	145.6	148.4	147.0	148.6	148.5	152.5	155.5	161.0
A	.	2.2	2.4	2.6	2.5	2.6	2.3	2.2	2.5	2.8
B	.	0.3	0.8	-	-	0.5	0.7	-	-	0.4
C	.	0.8	0.5	-	-	0.7	-	0.7	-	0.6
D	.	33.7	31.4	28.3	28.1	29.1	28.8	26.5	25.7	24.3
E	.	3.3	3.1	3.7	4.1	3.2	2.8	3.4	3.1	3.7
F	.	10.1	11.3	12.1	11.2	10.7	12.3	12.2	11.5	12.4
G	.	20.6	20.7	20.8	22.2	22.2	21.3	23.8	24.6	25.0
H	.	10.6	12.4	13.1	11.8	12.3	12.3	11.6	12.9	13.3
I	.	11.2	13.0	12.8	11.3	11.3	11.5	11.5	12.0	13.0
J	.	5.3	5.4	5.8	5.3	4.4	5.8	6.4	6.4	6.1
K	.	6.0	5.8	7.3	7.3	7.9	8.0	9.1	11.5	11.5
L	.	12.5	10.9	12.5	13.2	14.1	12.5	14.4	13.9	14.3
M	.	11.8	11.0	11.8	10.8	12.6	11.5	12.3	12.7	13.5
N	.	10.4	10.7	10.7	10.5	11.1	11.8	11.6	11.2	12.2
O	.	5.9	5.4	5.6	6.4	5.5	6.3	6.0	6.4	7.5
P	.	0.4	0.5	-	-	-	-	-	-	0.1
Q	.	0.2	0.3	-	-	-	-	-	-	0.3

Explanatory notes: see p. 77.
[1] Persons aged 15 years and over. [2] Prior to 2004: April of each year.

Notes explicatives: voir p. 80.
[1] Personnes âgées de 15 ans et plus. [2] Avant 2004: Avril de chaque année.

Notas explicativas: véase p. 83.
[1] Personas de 15 años y más. [2] Antes de 2004: Abril de cada año.

2B

EMPLOYMENT	EMPLOI	EMPLEO
Total employment, by economic activity	Emploi total, par activité économique	Empleo total, por actividad económica
Thousands	Milliers	Millares

	1999	2000	2001	2002	2003	2004	2005	2006	2007	2008

Malta (BA) [1]

Total employment - Emploi total - Empleo total

Men - Hommes - Hombres
ISIC 3 - CITI 3 - CIIU 3

	1999	2000	2001	2002	2003	2004	2005	2006	2007	2008
Total	.	101.4	103.6	102.1	101.2	103.8	102.8	104.4	104.4	107.5
A	.	2.2	2.2	2.4	2.3	2.4	2.3	2.1	2.3	2.6
B	.	0.3	0.7	-	-	-	0.5	-	-	0.4
C	.	0.8	0.5	-	-	0.7	-	0.7	-	0.6
D	.	24.1	23.0	19.0	20.6	21.7	21.3	19.8	19.4	19.2
E	.	3.1	3.0	3.3	3.8	2.9	2.5	3.1	2.8	3.5
F	.	9.7	11.1	11.6	10.8	10.4	12.0	12.0	11.1	12.0
G	.	13.6	14.1	15.0	14.3	16.5	14.3	16.2	16.5	16.9
H	.	6.7	8.6	9.0	7.4	7.8	7.8	8.0	8.2	7.9
I	.	10.1	11.0	10.0	8.7	8.8	9.0	8.9	9.4	9.8
J	.	2.9	2.7	2.9	2.7	2.6	3.0	3.5	3.0	2.8
K	.	4.1	3.9	5.4	5.2	5.5	5.5	6.2	7.1	7.5
L	.	9.5	8.5	9.3	9.9	10.5	10.0	10.1	10.0	9.6
M	.	5.6	4.5	4.6	4.1	4.5	4.3	4.4	4.7	4.7
N	.	4.6	6.0	5.1	5.1	5.5	5.0	5.3	5.1	5.4
O	.	3.9	3.6	3.5	4.8	3.4	3.3	3.5	3.7	4.4
P	.	0.1	0.1	-	-	-	-	-	-	0.0
Q	.	0.1	0.1	-	-	-	-	-	-	0.2

Women - Femmes - Mujeres
ISIC 3 - CITI 3 - CIIU 3

	1999	2000	2001	2002	2003	2004	2005	2006	2007	2008
Total	.	43.8	42.0	46.3	45.8	44.8	46.0	48.1	51.1	53.5
A	.	0.1	0.2	0.2	0.2	0.3	-	0.1	0.2	0.2
B	.	-	0.0	-	-	-	0.3	-	-	0.0
C	.	-	-	-	-	0.0	-	0.0	-	0.0
D	.	9.6	8.4	9.3	7.5	7.4	7.3	6.7	6.2	5.1
E	.	0.3	0.1	0.4	0.3	0.3	0.3	0.2	0.2	0.2
F	.	0.4	0.2	0.5	0.4	0.3	0.3	0.2	0.4	0.5
G	.	7.0	6.5	5.8	7.8	5.7	6.5	7.7	8.1	8.1
H	.	3.9	3.9	4.1	4.4	4.5	4.5	3.5	4.7	5.3
I	.	1.1	2.0	2.8	2.6	2.4	2.5	2.6	2.6	3.2
J	.	2.4	2.8	2.9	2.6	1.8	3.0	3.0	3.4	3.2
K	.	1.8	1.9	1.9	2.1	2.4	2.0	2.9	4.3	4.0
L	.	2.9	2.4	3.2	3.3	3.6	2.8	4.3	3.8	4.7
M	.	6.2	6.5	7.1	6.8	8.0	7.0	7.9	8.0	8.8
N	.	5.8	4.7	5.6	5.4	5.6	6.3	6.2	6.1	6.8
O	.	2.0	1.8	2.1	1.7	2.1	3.3	2.5	2.7	3.1
P	.	0.3	0.4	-	-	-	-	-	-	0.1
Q	.	0.1	0.1	-	-	-	-	-	-	0.1

Moldova, Republic of (BA) [1]

Total employment - Emploi total - Empleo total

Total - Total - Total
ISIC 3 - CITI 3 - CIIU 3

	1999	2000	2001	2002	2003	2004	2005	2006	2007	2008
Total	1 494.4	1 514.6	1 499.0	1 505.1	1 356.5	1 316.0	1 318.7	1 257.3	1 247.2	1 251.0
A	730.0	769.0	763.4	745.2	581.6	531.9	534.0	421.6	407.8	387.4
B	1.0	1.4	1.4	1.9	1.6	1.0	1.5	0.8	0.8	1.2
C	3.0	1.7	2.0	2.6	1.4	0.8	1.8	3.4	3.7	3.8
D	135.0	135.8	136.8	142.3	136.7	135.4	131.8	134.5	128.5	136.2
E	22.0	28.5	26.4	26.5	26.4	25.6	25.8	23.5	25.9	23.3
F	44.0	44.4	43.2	46.0	53.2	52.0	51.6	67.3	75.7	82.8
G	135.0	147.3	144.5	155.1	158.2	159.6	159.9	174.1	176.4	187.6
H	15.0	18.0	19.3	19.7	17.5	19.1	23.0	21.8	21.5	21.2
I	70.0	63.9	64.3	61.7	67.6	73.4	71.0	65.3	68.7	70.8
J	10.0	8.1	9.2	9.2	10.5	13.6	13.4	15.0	15.5	17.0
K	35.0	19.5	19.5	20.2	25.8	28.9	28.7	31.0	28.9	30.4
L	49.0	64.5	65.8	65.8	65.6	64.1	61.5	71.9	66.3	68.1
M	137.0	101.5	100.9	105.3	109.5	107.9	108.2	120.4	116.8	112.0
N	80.0	74.2	70.7	72.2	68.9	68.7	69.4	64.3	67.4	68.1
O	29.0	28.2	28.2	27.7	26.9	30.3	32.1	36.5	37.1	35.7
P	-	8.6	3.1	3.5	4.4	3.3	3.3	4.7	5.3	4.5
Q	-	-	0.1	0.1	0.5	0.4	0.5	1.1	0.9	0.9
X										

Men - Hommes - Hombres
ISIC 3 - CITI 3 - CIIU 3

	1999	2000	2001	2002	2003	2004	2005	2006	2007	2008
Total	.	747.4	736.5	730.9	661.3	631.5	629.7	628.6	621.5	628.8
A	.	387.3	379.8	368.6	291.8	257.6	257.6	220.8	219.7	210.7
B	.	1.3	1.4	1.9	1.4	1.0	1.4	0.8	0.8	1.2
C	.	1.6	1.6	1.9	1.1	0.7	1.5	3.2	3.2	3.3
D	.	70.0	70.8	71.9	67.6	68.4	65.3	69.1	65.4	67.9
E	.	22.8	21.2	21.1	20.0	19.1	19.5	17.5	19.2	17.4
F	.	37.6	37.0	39.2	46.0	46.1	45.4	60.9	68.6	73.3
G	.	65.3	63.9	67.8	67.2	66.3	69.0	77.2	75.5	81.7
H	.	4.2	4.2	4.6	4.4	4.0	4.9	6.0	5.3	5.4
I	.	48.0	48.8	46.1	52.7	56.9	52.4	47.0	49.0	53.1
J	.	3.4	3.2	3.1	4.2	4.5	4.3	5.2	5.1	6.1
K	.	10.7	11.1	12.8	15.8	16.0	16.4	19.8	17.7	17.5
L	.	42.8	42.9	42.4	41.7	40.2	39.0	43.3	37.6	38.8
M	.	21.7	22.2	23.6	23.8	22.7	22.7	26.3	23.7	21.6
N	.	14.2	14.9	14.5	13.1	14.9	14.2	13.3	13.1	14.9
O	.	13.1	12.2	10.4	9.5	12.1	14.7	17.0	16.5	15.0
P	.	3.3	1.4	0.9	0.7	0.9	0.8	0.7	0.8	0.6
Q	.	-	0.1	0.1	0.1	0.1	0.4	0.4	0.4	0.4
X										

Explanatory notes: see p. 77.	Notes explicatives: voir p. 80.	Notas explicativas: véase p. 83.
[1] Persons aged 15 years and over.	[1] Personnes âgées de 15 ans et plus.	[1] Personas de 15 años y más.

Total employment, by economic activity
Emploi total, par activité économique
Empleo total, por actividad económica

Thousands — Milliers — Millares

	1999	2000	2001	2002	2003	2004	2005	2006	2007	2008
Moldova, Republic of (BA) [1]										

Women - Femmes - Mujeres
ISIC 3 - CITI 3 - CIIU 3

Total employment - Emploi total - Empleo total

	1999	2000	2001	2002	2003	2004	2005	2006	2007	2008
Total	.	767.2	762.5	774.2	695.2	684.6	689.0	628.7	625.7	622.3
A	.	381.7	383.6	376.6	289.8	274.3	277.3	200.8	188.1	176.7
B	.	0.1	-	-	0.2	-	0.1	0.0	0.0	0.0
C	.	0.2	0.3	0.7	0.3	0.1	0.3	0.2	0.5	0.5
D	.	65.8	66.0	70.4	69.1	67.0	66.5	65.3	63.1	68.4
E	.	5.7	5.2	5.5	6.4	6.5	6.3	6.0	6.7	6.0
F	.	6.7	6.3	6.8	7.2	5.9	6.2	6.4	7.1	9.5
G	.	82.0	80.6	87.3	91.0	93.3	90.9	96.9	100.8	105.9
H	.	13.8	15.1	15.1	13.1	15.1	18.1	15.9	16.2	15.8
I	.	15.8	15.5	15.6	15.1	16.5	18.6	18.2	19.7	17.7
J	.	4.6	6.0	6.2	6.2	9.1	9.1	9.9	10.4	10.9
K	.	8.8	8.5	7.4	10.0	12.9	12.2	11.2	11.2	12.9
L	.	21.7	22.9	23.4	23.9	23.9	22.6	28.6	28.6	29.4
M	.	79.8	78.7	81.6	85.7	85.2	85.6	94.1	93.2	90.4
N	.	60.0	55.9	57.7	55.7	53.8	55.2	51.0	54.3	53.2
O	.	15.1	16.1	17.3	17.4	18.2	17.4	19.5	20.6	20.7
P	.	5.3	1.7	2.6	3.7	2.4	2.5	4.0	4.5	3.9
Q	.	-	-	-	0.4	0.3	0.1	0.7	0.5	0.5
X	.	.	.	.			.			

Montenegro (BA) [2][3]

Total employment - Emploi total - Empleo total

Total - Total - Total
ISIC 3 - CITI 3 - CIIU 3

	1999	2000	2001	2002	2003	2004	2005	2006	2007	2008
Total	.	.	.	.	.	.	178.8	.	.	.
A	.	.	.	.	.	.	15.2	.	.	.
B	.	.	.	.	.	.	0.2	.	.	.
C	.	.	.	.	.	.	1.7	.	.	.
D	.	.	.	.	.	.	21.9	.	.	.
E	.	.	.	.	.	.	5.6	.	.	.
F	.	.	.	.	.	.	5.2	.	.	.
G	.	.	.	.	.	.	29.9	.	.	.
H	.	.	.	.	.	.	11.0	.	.	.
I	.	.	.	.	.	.	14.6	.	.	.
J	.	.	.	.	.	.	2.2	.	.	.
K	.	.	.	.	.	.	4.5	.	.	.
L	.	.	.	.	.	.	22.8	.	.	.
M	.	.	.	.	.	.	13.5	.	.	.
N	.	.	.	.	.	.	12.2	.	.	.
O	.	.	.	.	.	.	17.8	.	.	.
P	.	.	.	.	.	.	-	.	.	.
Q	.	.	.	.	.	.	0.4	.	.	.

Men - Hommes - Hombres
ISIC 3 - CITI 3 - CIIU 3

	1999	2000	2001	2002	2003	2004	2005	2006	2007	2008
Total	.	.	.	.	.	.	105.6	.	.	.
A	.	.	.	.	.	.	8.8	.	.	.
B	.	.	.	.	.	.	0.2	.	.	.
C	.	.	.	.	.	.	0.8	.	.	.
D	.	.	.	.	.	.	17.0	.	.	.
E	.	.	.	.	.	.	4.6	.	.	.
F	.	.	.	.	.	.	5.2	.	.	.
G	.	.	.	.	.	.	13.7	.	.	.
H	.	.	.	.	.	.	7.0	.	.	.
I	.	.	.	.	.	.	11.4	.	.	.
J	.	.	.	.	.	.	1.0	.	.	.
K	.	.	.	.	.	.	2.9	.	.	.
L	.	.	.	.	.	.	14.4	.	.	.
M	.	.	.	.	.	.	4.4	.	.	.
N	.	.	.	.	.	.	4.0	.	.	.
O	.	.	.	.	.	.	9.8	.	.	.
P	.	.	.	.	.	.	-	.	.	.
Q	.	.	.	.	.	.	0.4	.	.	.

Women - Femmes - Mujeres
ISIC 3 - CITI 3 - CIIU 3

	1999	2000	2001	2002	2003	2004	2005	2006	2007	2008
Total	.	.	.	.	.	.	73.2	.	.	.
A	.	.	.	.	.	.	6.5	.	.	.
B	.	.	.	.	.	.	0.0	.	.	.
C	.	.	.	.	.	.	0.9	.	.	.
D	.	.	.	.	.	.	4.8	.	.	.
E	.	.	.	.	.	.	1.0	.	.	.
F	.	.	.	.	.	.	0.0	.	.	.
G	.	.	.	.	.	.	16.2	.	.	.
H	.	.	.	.	.	.	4.0	.	.	.
I	.	.	.	.	.	.	3.2	.	.	.
J	.	.	.	.	.	.	1.2	.	.	.
K	.	.	.	.	.	.	1.6	.	.	.
L	.	.	.	.	.	.	8.4	.	.	.
M	.	.	.	.	.	.	9.1	.	.	.
N	.	.	.	.	.	.	8.3	.	.	.
O	.	.	.	.	.	.	8.0	.	.	.
P	.	.	.	.	.	.	-	.	.	.
Q	.	.	.	.	.	.	0.0	.	.	.

Explanatory notes: see p. 77.
[1] Persons aged 15 years and over. [2] Persons aged 15 to 64 years. [3] Oct. of each year.

Notes explicatives: voir p. 80.
[1] Personnes âgées de 15 ans et plus. [2] Personnes âgées de 15 à 64 ans. [3] Oct. de chaque année.

Notas explicativas: véase p. 83.
[1] Personas de 15 años y más. [2] Personas de 15 a 64 años. [3] Oct. de cada año.

EMPLOYMENT	EMPLOI	EMPLEO
Total employment, by economic activity	Emploi total, par activité économique	Empleo total, por actividad económica
Thousands	Milliers	Millares

	1999	2000	2001	2002	2003	2004	2005	2006	2007	2008

Netherlands (BA) [1]   Total employment - Emploi total - Empleo total

Total - Total - Total
ISIC 3 - CITI 3 - CIIU 3

	1999	2000	2001	2002	2003	2004	2005	2006	2007	2008
Total	7 613	7 798	7 953	8 018	7 991	7 928	7 958	8 108	8 310	8 457
A-B	233	250	246	253	257	258	273	269	252	228
C	10	12	10	9	8	7	7	7	11	11
D	1 105	1 096	1 073	1 042	1 031	1 032	1 033	1 024	1 003	973
E	36	35	36	38	35	36	43	43	41	40
F	465	472	501	495	476	479	488	499	500	509
G	1 184	1 252	1 235	1 256	1 253	1 182	1 153	1 200	1 211	1 186
H	274	274	280	301	299	309	319	334	352	337
I	446	469	478	458	463	483	489	500	506	512
J	275	274	285	272	259	261	258	264	258	245
K	880	937	926	961	994	948	945	974	1 045	1 099
L	511	489	531	542	528	519	529	529	541	541
M	472	465	452	495	509	494	508	522	534	549
N	1 003	1 052	1 100	1 161	1 197	1 183	1 204	1 249	1 310	1 353
O	307	355	346	359	375	338	316	333	381	389
P	18	3	3	5	5	4	4	5	5	6
Q	2	2	3		2					
X	393	359	447	369	299	393	390	359	360	479

Men - Hommes - Hombres
ISIC 3 - CITI 3 - CIIU 3

	1999	2000	2001	2002	2003	2004	2005	2006	2007	2008
Total	4 382	4 459	4 522	4 526	4 480	4 432	4 421	4 475	4 548	4 594
A-B	166	175	168	177	184	185	192	191	179	160
C	8	11	9	7	7	7	6	5	9	9
D	859	853	835	805	799	799	803	796	774	736
E	30	27	29	30	29	29	32	32	30	29
F	431	431	461	454	437	442	445	455	457	463
G	651	691	678	686	677	616	603	638	646	620
H	129	131	133	145	137	144	150	158	167	159
I	325	348	353	338	339	359	364	369	372	376
J	149	155	161	153	144	148	143	141	137	133
K	531	570	563	580	603	574	571	591	632	669
L	348	320	343	347	334	332	333	327	328	326
M	213	204	197	211	216	202	204	205	210	215
N	213	221	223	223	224	223	226	226	230	238
O	145	162	150	167	174	153	140	148	171	168
P										
Q			2							
X	182	160	219	200	174	217	208	194	205	293

Women - Femmes - Mujeres
ISIC 3 - CITI 3 - CIIU 3

	1999	2000	2001	2002	2003	2004	2005	2006	2007	2008
Total	3 231	3 339	3 431	3 492	3 511	3 495	3 537	3 633	3 763	3 863
A-B	67	75	78	77	73	73	80	78	74	69
C	2	2			2		2	2	2	
D	246	244	239	237	231	232	230	227	229	237
E	7	8	7	8	7	7	10	11	11	11
F	34	41	40	41	40	37	43	45	43	46
G	533	561	557	570	576	566	550	562	565	566
H	145	144	147	157	162	165	169	176	185	178
I	121	121	126	120	124	124	125	131	134	136
J	126	119	125	119	115	113	115	124	121	112
K	349	367	363	380	391	374	374	383	413	430
L	162	169	188	196	194	186	196	201	213	215
M	259	261	255	283	293	292	303	316	323	334
N	789	831	877	938	972	960	978	1 023	1 080	1 115
O	162	193	196	192	201	185	176	185	210	221
P	18	3	3	4	4	3	4	5	5	5
Q										
X	211	199	228	169	126	176	182	165	155	186

Norway (BA) [2]   Total employment - Emploi total - Empleo total

Total - Total - Total
ISIC 3 - CITI 3 - CIIU 3

	1999	2000	2001	2002	2003	2004	2005	2006	2007	2008
Total	2 259	2 269	2 278	2 286	2 269	2 276	2 289	2 362 [3]	2 443	2 524
A	84	77	72	69	67	63	60	63 [3]	56	56
B	18	16	17	17	16	16	15	14 [3]	13	14
C	32	33	36	35	32	33	35	35 [3]	39	42
D	300	290	286	289	278	264	265	272 [3]	277	286
E	18	20	18	14	17	16	16	16 [3]	17	18
F	146	147	152	157	159	160	159	167 [3]	180	183
G	338	346	330	332	337	345	350	353 [3]	358	362
H	72	73	67	68	70	70	71	68 [3]	67	68
I	170	168	169	161	149	149	152	157 [3]	158	156
J	53	50	49	51	47	48	51	54 [3]	55	55
K	200	206	224	221	225	223	231	252 [3]	269	290
L	153	157	151	145	149	144	138	143 [3]	154	162
M	179	184	190	188	186	195	190	193 [3]	215	220
N	397	403	417	440	440	449	458	471 [3]	476	502
O	90	90	94	92	92	96	95	98 [3]	105	107
P	5	4	2	3	2	2	2	3 [3]	3	2
X	2	3	3	3	2	1	1	1 [3]	1	1

Explanatory notes: see p. 77.

[1] Persons aged 15 years and over. [2] Persons aged 15 to 74 years. [3] Prior to 2006: persons aged 16 to 74 years.

Notes explicatives: voir p. 80.

[1] Personnes âgées de 15 ans et plus. [2] Personnes âgées de 15 à 74 ans. [3] Avant 2006: personnes âgées de 16 à 74 ans.

Notas explicativas: véase p. 83.

[1] Personas de 15 años y más. [2] Personas de 15 a 74 años. [3] Antes de 2006: personas de 16 a 74 años.

Total employment, by economic activity
Emploi total, par activité économique
Empleo total, por actividad económica

	Thousands			Milliers				Millares		
	1999	2000	2001	2002	2003	2004	2005	2006	2007	2008

Norway (BA) [1] — Total employment - Emploi total - Empleo total

Men - Hommes - Hombres
ISIC 3 - CITI 3 - CIIU 3

	1999	2000	2001	2002	2003	2004	2005	2006	2007	2008
Total	1 209	1 212	1 214	1 210	1 198	1 201	1 211	1 251 [2]	1 289	1 332
A	60	55	52	50	48	46	45	48 [2]	42	41
B	16	14	15	15	15	15	13	12 [2]	12	13
C	26	27	29	30	27	27	29	28 [2]	31	33
D	222	214	211	214	206	195	198	205 [2]	210	213
E	15	16	14	12	14	12	13	13 [2]	13	14
F	134	135	140	144	146	149	149	156 [2]	167	172
G	187	189	174	174	177	181	184	184 [2]	187	190
H	23	26	24	24	25	28	27	25 [2]	23	23
I	120	117	118	116	109	109	113	117 [2]	117	117
J	26	24	26	26	24	25	26	28 [2]	29	29
K	121	126	139	137	138	140	146	157 [2]	169	187
L	89	90	85	78	83	80	77	79 [2]	81	85
M	61	65	70	68	66	68	65	67 [2]	77	77
N	66	68	71	77	76	80	83	86 [2]	84	86
O	39	41	42	43	43	43	41	44 [2]	47	51
P	-	-	-	1	-	-	-	1 [2]	-	-
X	1	2	2	2	1	1	1	1 [2]	1	1

Women - Femmes - Mujeres
ISIC 3 - CITI 3 - CIIU 3

	1999	2000	2001	2002	2003	2004	2005	2006	2007	2008
Total	1 050	1 057	1 064	1 076	1 071	1 074	1 078	1 111 [2]	1 154	1 192
A	25	22	20	19	19	17	16	15 [2]	14	15
B	2	2	2	2	1	1	1	1 [2]	1	1
C	6	6	7	6	6	6	7	6 [2]	8	9
D	77	76	74	75	71	68	67	67 [2]	67	73
E	3	4	3	3	3	4	3	3 [2]	4	5
F	12	12	12	13	13	11	10	12 [2]	13	11
G	151	157	156	159	160	164	166	169 [2]	170	172
H	49	47	43	45	45	42	44	43 [2]	45	45
I	50	51	51	45	40	40	39	40 [2]	40	39
J	28	25	23	25	23	23	24	26 [2]	26	26
K	79	80	84	84	86	83	84	95 [2]	101	103
L	63	67	66	67	66	64	62	65 [2]	73	78
M	118	119	120	120	120	127	125	127 [2]	138	143
N	330	335	346	363	364	369	375	385 [2]	392	416
O	51	48	52	49	49	53	54	54 [2]	58	56
P	5	4	2	2	2	2	2	3 [2]	3	1
X	1	1	1	1	1	1	-	- [2]	1	1

Poland (BA) [3][4] — Total employment - Emploi total - Empleo total

Total - Total - Total
ISIC 3 - CITI 3 - CIIU 3 …… ISIC 4 - CITI 4 - CIIU 4

	1999	2000	2001	2002	2003	2004	2005	2006	2007	2008	
Total	14 757 [5]	14 526	14 207	13 782	13 617	13 795	14 116	14 594	15 241	15 800	Total
A	2 657 [5]	2 715	2 711	2 652	2 497	2 472	2 439	2 294	2 239	2 206	A
B	10 [5]	11	9	12	11	12	13	10	8	234	B
C	315 [5]	293	274	258	247	227	225	237	248	3 228	C
D	3 049 [5]	2 901	2 830	2 575	2 592	2 740	2 831	2 988	3 162	174	D
E	246 [5]	263	269	263	250	222	228	223	218	166	E
F	1 012 [5]	1 024	958	851	803	789	843	925	1 054	1 234	F
G	2 095 [5]	2 043	2 007	1 955	1 962	1 997	2 020	2 060	2 264	2 326	G
H	222 [5]	241	253	252	229	236	247	272	291	897	H
I	895 [5]	893	852	832	823	832	862	942	973	307	I
J	387 [5]	380	340	314	281	271	294	329	363	295	J
K	506 [5]	531	627	675	694	799	822	836	953	340	K
L	772 [5]	764	749	801	853	865	892	917	937	143	L
M	1 029 [5]	1 013	955	933	1 078	1 060	1 103	1 140	1 128	411	M
N	1 028 [5]	938	903	940	838	824	820	871	871	363	N
O	527 [5]	507	459	455	449	436	459	534	511	984	O
P	5 [5]	8	11	11	8	15	12	11	16	1 184	P
Q										857	Q
X	- [5]	.	.	-	-	-	5	.	-	197	R
										225	S
										19	T
										8	X

Explanatory notes: see p. 77.

[1] Persons aged 15 to 74 years. [2] Prior to 2006: persons aged 16 to 74 years. [3] Persons aged 15 years and over. [4] Excl. regular military living in barracks and conscripts. [5] First and fourth quarters.

Notes explicatives: voir p. 80.

[1] Personnes âgées de 15 à 74 ans. [2] Avant 2006: personnes âgées de 16 à 74 ans. [3] Personnes âgées de 15 ans et plus. [4] Non compris les militaires de carrière vivant dans des casernes et les conscrits. [5] Premier et quatrième trimestres.

Notas explicativas: véase p. 83.

[1] Personas de 15 a 74 años. [2] Antes de 2006: personas de 16 a 74 años. [3] Personas de 15 años y más. [4] Excl. los militares profesionales que viven en casernas y los conscriptos. [5] Primero y cuarto trimestres.

EMPLOYMENT   EMPLOI   EMPLEO

Total employment, by economic activity   **Emploi total, par activité économique**   **Empleo total, por actividad económica**

Thousands — Milliers — Millares

Poland (BA) [1][2]

Total employment - Emploi total - Empleo total

Men - Hommes - Hombres
ISIC 3 - CITI 3 - CIIU 3   ISIC 4 - CITI 4 - CIIU 4

Code	1999	2000	2001	2002	2003	2004	2005	2006	2007	2008	Code
Total	8 132[3]	8 004	7 797	7 529	7 432	7 566	7 809	8 081	8 403	8 718	Total
A	1 496[3]	1 521	1 491	1 483	1 413	1 400	1 391	1 316	1 270	1 226	A
B	9[3]	10	7	8	9	10	11	9	6	206	B
C	277[3]	250	236	228	219	199	201	212	215	2 129	C
D	1 900[3]	1 847	1 815	1 661	1 670	1 795	1 882	1 989	2 084	139	D
E	195[3]	210	210	204	202	179	181	172	170	130	E
F	918[3]	936	888	779	736	735	784	864	991	1 164	F
G	997[3]	969	939	925	936	950	961	963	1 038	1 059	G
H	72[3]	75	83	77	72	81	87	87	89	710	H
I	663[3]	669	631	616	612	621	658	735	760	97	I
J	132[3]	120	103	102	84	84	94	96	113	192	J
K	290[3]	303	370	401	417	468	485	472	532	115	K
L	436[3]	416	398	415	433	436	451	457	469	59	L
M	276[3]	258	237	222	232	238	251	260	256	198	M
N	193[3]	166	150	167	170	160	158	171	168	204	N
O	277[3]	254	237	238	226	205	213	274	239	495	O
P	-[3]	1	1	2	1	-	1	2	-	263	P
Q	.	.	.	.	.	.	.	.	.	156	Q
X	.	.	.	.	.	.	.	.	.	85	R
										88	S
										-	T
											X

Women - Femmes - Mujeres
ISIC 3 - CITI 3 - CIIU 3   ISIC 4 - CITI 4 - CIIU 4

Code	1999	2000	2001	2002	2003	2004	2005	2006	2007	2008	Code
Total	6 624[3]	6 522	6 410	6 253	6 185	6 230	6 307	6 513	6 838	7 082	Total
A	1 161[3]	1 195	1 220	1 169	1 085	1 072	1 048	977	969	980	A
B	1[3]	1	1	4	2	2	2	1	1	28	B
C	38[3]	43	38	29	28	28	25	26	33	1 099	C
D	1 149[3]	1 054	1 015	914	923	945	949	1 000	1 078	35	D
E	51[3]	53	59	59	48	43	47	51	48	35	E
F	94[3]	89	70	73	67	54	59	61	63	71	F
G	1 098[3]	1 074	1 068	1 030	1 026	1 047	1 059	1 097	1 226	1 267	G
H	150[3]	165	170	175	157	155	161	185	202	187	H
I	232[3]	225	220	216	211	211	205	207	213	210	I
J	255[3]	260	237	212	197	187	200	232	250	103	J
K	216[3]	228	257	274	276	331	337	365	422	225	K
L	336[3]	348	351	386	420	429	442	460	469	85	L
M	753[3]	755	718	711	846	822	852	880	872	213	M
N	835[3]	773	753	774	668	664	662	700	703	160	N
O	250[3]	253	222	217	223	231	246	260	272	490	O
P	5[3]	7	10	9	7	15	11	9	16	921	P
X	.	.	.	.	.	.	.	.	.	701	Q
										112	R
										137	S
										19	T
										-	X

Portugal (BA) [1]

Total - Total - Total

Total employment - Emploi total - Empleo total

ISIC 3 - CITI 3 - CIIU 3   ISIC 4 - CITI 4 - CIIU 4

Code	1999	2000	2001	2002	2003	2004	2005	2006	2007	2008	Code
Total	4 921.6	5 032.9	5 121.7	5 145.6	5 127.7	5 127.5	5 122.6	5 159.5	5 169.7	5 197.8	Total
A	600.9	615.2	631.9	616.0	623.6	596.7	587.5	587.7	584.3	581.2	A
B	21.0	20.1	20.7	20.9	18.5	21.4	18.7	16.2	17.1	17.9	B
C	13.3	16.4	16.2	17.4	14.3	14.5	19.1	17.6	19.3	894.0	C
D	1 104.5	1 093.8	1 095.8	1 052.1	1 018.8	1 002.2	968.6	980.5	954.0	23.2	D
E	33.8	29.7	38.0	39.8	36.1	31.2	24.9	26.1	33.7	34.8	E
F	537.5	593.8	578.8	618.4	583.6	548.0	554.1	553.0	570.8	555.1	F
G	716.0	742.9	771.5	774.3	774.7	782.0	773.0	751.2	750.2	766.1	G
H	253.8	258.7	259.7	267.5	259.5	265.4	275.8	280.0	288.8	177.7	H
I	175.0	186.9	202.6	204.7	213.7	214.5	220.8	239.6	223.7	319.4	I
J	89.2	91.8	91.0	84.1	87.0	96.6	95.2	90.1	95.7	93.2	J
K	209.9	213.7	232.9	242.7	262.1	292.2	283.7	294.5	325.4	96.3	K
L	316.7	330.0	334.7	341.0	339.1	336.3	347.5	354.3	327.0	27.1	L
M	290.6	282.2	294.7	291.4	286.6	306.6	314.9	318.7	306.7	174.8	M
N	238.1	250.6	258.6	255.7	294.1	313.0	326.8	329.8	340.2	134.8	N
O	170.9	156.7	149.4	162.6	156.0	157.2	158.6	164.9	162.4	341.8	O
P	146.1	147.9	143.6	155.7	158.1	147.3	150.9	152.4	167.5	344.3	P
Q[4]	-	-	-	-	-	2.2	2.6	2.9	2.8	302.9	Q
										46.0	R
										89.4	S
										175.5	T
										2.1[4]	U

Explanatory notes: see p. 77.

[1] Persons aged 15 years and over. [2] Excl. regular military living in barracks and conscripts. [3] First and fourth quarters. [4] Data not reliable; coefficient of variation greater than 20%.

Notes explicatives: voir p. 80.

[1] Personnes âgées de 15 ans et plus. [2] Non compris les militaires de carrière vivant dans des casernes et les conscrits. [3] Premier et quatrième trimestres. [4] Données non fiables; coefficient de variation supérieur à 20%.

Notas explicativas: véase p. 83.

[1] Personas de 15 años y más. [2] Excl. los militares profesionales que viven en casernas y los conscriptos. [3] Primero y cuarto trimestres. [4] Datos no fiables; coeficiente de variación superior a 20%.

Total employment, by economic activity — Emploi total, par activité économique — Empleo total, por actividad económica

	Thousands			Milliers				Millares		
	1999	2000	2001	2002	2003	2004	2005	2006	2007	2008

Portugal (BA) [1] — Total employment - Emploi total - Empleo total

Men - Hommes - Hombres
ISIC 3 - CITI 3 - CIIU 3 / ISIC 4 - CITI 4 - CIIU 4

	1999	2000	2001	2002	2003	2004	2005	2006	2007	2008	
Total	2 720.5	2 777.2	2 819.2	2 824.7	2 796.8	2 788.8	2 765.4	2 789.7	2 789.3	2 797.1	Total
A	287.5	295.9	305.4	299.3	311.4	302.1	285.4	295.5	294.7	296.7	A
B	20.5	19.1	19.2	19.8	17.4	18.8	16.5	14.9	15.8	16.5	B
C	12.5	15.5	15.2	16.2	12.8	13.3	17.9	16.2	18.1	525.8	C
D	615.8	605.7	609.1	586.5	574.1	574.7	561.5	565.5	551.4	18.7	D
E	30.7	26.1	32.6	34.0	30.6	26.3	20.4	21.0	26.3	28.1	E
F	517.6	570.2	554.9	591.7	557.3	521.9	528.7	527.9	545.5	531.0	F
G	422.1	418.9	438.2	443.0	437.6	437.6	435.0	419.7	416.2	426.2	G
H	105.7	102.3	103.5	104.6	101.7	106.3	108.7	108.1	118.8	147.6	H
I	136.6	148.8	158.6	163.4	168.7	164.8	163.9	178.8	175.0	128.0	I
J	57.3	56.7	56.4	45.9	52.8	60.8	55.3	52.4	51.3	58.3	J
K	103.6	108.0	121.6	122.8	126.3	153.0	150.5	159.6	157.0	52.6	K
L	209.5	213.1	216.5	219.2	215.6	207.1	214.9	219.2	204.4	14.7	L
M	73.8	66.6	69.0	62.1	67.3	75.2	75.4	77.4	76.4	81.2	M
N	47.9	52.0	52.6	45.3	46.9	52.7	60.0	59.7	61.2	64.3	N
O	74.6	75.1	64.2	67.6	70.5	71.2	68.2	70.1	73.2	220.8	O
P	1.8	1.9	1.4	2.2	2.6	2.1	1.7	2.2	2.4	80.5	P
Q [2]	-	-	-	-	-	1.2	1.3	1.5	1.5	50.4	Q
										27.2	R
										25.1	S
										2.0 [2]	T
										1.3 [2]	U

Women - Femmes - Mujeres
ISIC 3 - CITI 3 - CIIU 3 / ISIC 4 - CITI 4 - CIIU 4

	1999	2000	2001	2002	2003	2004	2005	2006	2007	2008	
Total	2 201.1	2 255.7	2 302.0	2 320.9	2 330.9	2 338.6	2 357.2	2 369.8	2 380.4	2 400.7	Total
A	313.3	319.3	326.5	316.7	312.2	294.6	302.2	292.2	289.7	284.5	A
B [2]	0.5	1.0	1.5	1.1	1.1	2.6	2.2	1.3	1.3	1.5 [2]	B
C [2]	0.8	0.9	1.0	1.2	1.5	1.3	1.2	1.4	1.2	368.2	C
D	488.6	488.1	486.6	465.6	444.7	427.5	407.1	414.9	402.6	4.5	D
E	3.1	3.6	5.3	5.9	5.5	4.9	4.4	5.1	7.4	6.7	E
F	19.8	23.6	23.9	26.7	26.3	26.2	25.3	25.1	25.3	24.1	F
G	293.8	324.0	333.3	331.3	337.2	344.4	337.9	331.6	334.0	339.9	G
H	148.2	156.4	156.2	163.0	157.8	159.2	167.1	171.9	170.0	30.1	H
I	38.4	38.1	44.0	41.2	45.0	49.7	56.8	60.8	48.7	191.4	I
J	31.9	35.2	34.6	38.2	34.1	35.9	39.9	37.7	44.4	34.9	J
K	106.3	105.7	111.3	120.0	135.8	139.2	133.2	134.9	168.4	43.7	K
L	107.2	116.8	118.2	121.8	123.5	129.3	132.6	135.1	122.5	12.5	L
M	216.9	215.5	225.7	229.3	219.3	231.4	239.5	241.3	230.3	93.5	M
N	190.2	198.6	206.0	210.4	245.3	260.3	266.9	270.1	279.0	70.5	N
O	96.3	81.6	85.2	94.9	85.4	86.0	90.3	94.8	89.2	121.0	O
P	144.3	146.0	142.2	153.5	155.5	145.2	149.2	150.2	165.1	263.8	P
Q [2]	-	-	-	-	-	1.0	1.3	1.4	1.3	252.6	Q
										18.8	R
										64.2	S
										173.4	T
										0.9 [2]	U

Roumanie (BA) [1] — Total employment - Emploi total - Empleo total

Total - Total - Total
ISIC 3 - CITI 3 - CIIU 3

	1999	2000	2001	2002	2003	2004	2005	2006	2007	2008
Total	10 775.6	10 763.7	10 696.9	9 234.1 [3]	9 222.5	9 157.6	9 146.6	9 313.3	9 353.3	9 369.1
A	4 491.6	4 598.7	4 523.0	3 356.7 [3]	3 285.7	2 892.8	2 939.3	2 840.3	2 756.7	2 689.9
B	7.6	7.8	3.7	4.6 [3]	6.5	3.3	-	-	-	-
C	186.3	163.2	149.9	144.2 [3]	138.1	134.4	119.2	119.7	109.2	107.2
D	2 164.8	2 053.7	2 024.7	1 971.6 [3]	1 999.0	2 051.3	1 959.7	1 978.5	1 973.8	1 929.8
E	223.5	195.7	198.9	194.8 [3]	187.0	191.7	190.3	197.5	175.9	161.4
F	397.0	403.4	430.0	412.7 [3]	425.9	478.5	506.6	557.6	678.6	746.4
G	926.2	928.3	951.8	859.2 [3]	861.3	943.3	967.7	1 049.3	1 151.4	1 178.2
H	123.8	122.8	130.9	111.9 [3]	119.3	147.8	150.7	143.0	136.6	154.2
I	499.7	511.2	519.4	457.7 [3]	461.3	454.0	450.0	491.8	488.7	508.5
J	87.0	92.5	75.9	75.4 [3]	82.9	86.1	85.5	92.0	97.2	110.4
K	141.1	132.3	124.1	135.1 [3]	149.8	231.5	231.7	281.6	282.0	298.3
L	532.6	563.1	581.4	548.8 [3]	529.8	538.1	520.1	507.5	468.4	476.1
M	423.1	415.0	409.2	410.7 [3]	406.0	402.7	412.7	410.6	400.2	396.9
N	340.4	345.7	350.5	350.3 [3]	350.2	361.6	353.5	378.3	375.4	396.0
O-Q	230.2	229.5	222.8	199.5 [3]	218.8	239.6	255.5	262.5	253.9	211.5

Explanatory notes: see p. 77.

[1] Persons aged 15 years and over. [2] Data not reliable; coefficient of variation greater than 20%. [3] Estimates based on the 2002 Population Census results.

Notes explicatives: voir p. 80.

[1] Personnes âgées de 15 ans et plus. [2] Données non fiables; coefficient de variation supérieur à 20%. [3] Estimations basées sur les résultats du Recensement de la population de 2002.

Notas explicativas: véase p. 83.

[1] Personas de 15 años y más. [2] Datos no fiables; coeficiente de variación superior a 20%. [3] Estimaciones basadas en los resultados del Censo de población de 2002.

2B

Total employment, by economic activity — **Emploi total, par activité économique** — **Empleo total, por actividad económica**

	Thousands				Milliers				Millares	
	1999	2000	2001	2002	2003	2004	2005	2006	2007	2008

Roumanie (BA) [1] — Total employment - Emploi total - Empleo total

Men - Hommes - Hombres
ISIC 3 - CITI 3 - CIIU 3

	1999	2000	2001	2002	2003	2004	2005	2006	2007	2008
Total	5 799.0	5 772.1	5 719.3	5 031.5 [2]	5 056.7	4 980.0	5 011.2	5 074.0	5 116.3	5 157.4
A	2 249.8	2 325.6	2 280.6	1 737.2 [2]	1 731.2	1 543.1	1 572.9	1 508.7	1 443.9	1 408.8
B	6.5	6.9	2.9	4.5 [2]	5.9	2.3	-	-	-	-
C	158.7	141.8	131.3	125.8 [2]	120.1	114.9	101.3	101.2	95.1	93.1
D	1 198.5	1 118.4	1 066.2	1 049.1 [2]	1 061.5	1 072.4	1 044.6	1 028.8	1 052.5	1 045.4
E	178.4	151.3	150.6	150.8 [2]	148.2	147.6	145.9	148.6	134.9	127.4
F	348.0	352.5	378.2	371.6 [2]	382.8	430.8	459.5	501.6	610.1	676.1
G	412.8	407.1	423.3	392.8 [2]	404.5	430.1	444.3	483.1	530.9	542.0
H	42.1	47.0	45.5	37.6 [2]	48.2	49.3	52.2	52.6	46.6	53.6
I	369.3	388.8	397.3	345.5 [2]	350.4	339.4	341.9	376.6	380.1	396.1
J	25.0	27.9	24.3	26.3 [2]	28.7	29.0	30.2	29.2	29.0	34.8
K	74.7	74.5	77.1	79.6 [2]	92.4	140.6	139.2	172.3	175.9	179.7
L	411.5	422.0	426.5	396.4 [2]	368.1	370.0	349.9	335.5	299.6	298.1
M	129.0	117.7	116.4	118.6 [2]	115.0	107.4	110.4	107.0	102.6	100.4
N	72.1	65.6	73.1	82.1 [2]	75.5	77.5	80.8	86.7	84.2	92.4
O-Q	122.0	124.3	125.4	113.0 [2]	123.2	124.7	135.0	139.6	126.5	105.7

Women - Femmes - Mujeres
ISIC 3 - CITI 3 - CIIU 3

	1999	2000	2001	2002	2003	2004	2005	2006	2007	2008
Total	4 976.5	4 991.5	4 977.5	4 202.6 [2]	4 165.7	4 177.5	4 135.4	4 239.3	4 237.0	4 211.7
A	2 241.7	2 273.0	2 242.4	1 619.5 [2]	1 554.5	1 349.7	1 366.5	1 331.7	1 312.8	1 281.1
B	-	-	-	- [2]	-	-	-	-	-	-
C	27.5	21.4	18.6	18.3 [2]	18.0	19.4	17.9	18.5	14.2	14.1
D	966.2	935.3	958.5	922.5 [2]	937.5	978.8	915.1	949.4	921.3	884.4
E	45.0	44.4	48.3	43.9 [2]	38.7	44.1	44.4	49.0	41.0	34.0
F	49.0	50.8	51.7	41.1 [2]	43.0	47.6	47.1	56.0	68.4	70.3
G	513.4	521.1	528.5	466.4 [2]	456.7	513.2	523.4	566.3	620.5	636.2
H	81.7	75.7	85.3	74.3 [2]	71.1	98.4	98.6	90.4	90.0	100.6
I	130.4	122.4	122.0	112.1 [2]	110.8	114.5	108.0	115.2	108.5	112.4
J	62.0	64.6	51.5	49.1 [2]	54.1	57.1	55.3	62.8	68.2	75.6
K	66.3	57.7	46.9	55.5 [2]	57.3	90.8	92.5	109.2	106.2	118.6
L	121.1	141.0	154.9	152.3 [2]	161.6	168.0	170.2	172.0	168.8	178.0
M	294.1	297.3	292.8	292.1 [2]	290.9	295.2	302.4	303.6	297.6	296.5
N	268.3	280.1	277.4	268.2 [2]	274.6	284.0	272.8	291.6	291.3	303.6
O-Q	108.2	105.1	97.4	86.4 [2]	95.6	114.8	120.5	123.0	127.4	105.8

Russian Federation (BA) [3] — Total employment - Emploi total - Empleo total

Total - Total - Total
ISIC 3 - CITI 3 - CIIU 3

	1999	2000	2001	2002	2003	2004	2005	2006	2007	2008
Total	62 945	65 070	65 123	66 659	66 432	67 275	68 169	68 855	70 570	70 965
A	9 296	9 243	7 637	7 399	7 035	6 627	6 769	6 691	6 155	5 994
B	150	188	207	158	195	205	166	176	192	141
C	1 179	1 294	1 343	1 209	1 247	1 212	1 236	1 198	1 324	1 350
D	11 528	12 178	12 656	13 067	12 820	12 674	12 534	12 472	12 324	11 663
E	1 555	1 686	1 722	1 789	2 032	2 001	1 959	2 063	2 017	2 116
F	3 462	3 329	3 426	3 623	4 090	4 127	4 575	4 462	4 933	5 413
G	7 304	7 887	8 602	9 241	9 689	10 131	10 383	10 599	11 096	10 774
H	853	924	1 023	1 142	1 265	1 223	1 297	1 392	1 344	1 467
I	5 505	5 484	5 813	5 960	5 972	6 261	6 249	6 211	6 573	6 560
J	833	843	857	868	811	918	962	1 060	1 249	1 316
K	1 839	2 028	2 373	2 743	3 791	4 119	4 039	4 148	4 410	4 448
L	4 612	4 824	4 770	4 618	4 675	4 702	4 815	4 876	4 903	5 409
M	5 885	5 911	5 673	5 929	6 018	6 142	6 204	6 198	6 420	6 442
N	4 338	4 392	4 622	4 594	4 676	4 833	4 701	4 896	5 177	5 243
O	4 561	4 836	4 381	4 303	2 099	2 100	2 247	2 388	2 439	2 580
P	38	21	14	12	11	-	26	21	16	43
Q	7	4	5	2	5	1	4	4	-	5

Men - Hommes - Hombres
ISIC 3 - CITI 3 - CIIU 3

	1999	2000	2001	2002	2003	2004	2005	2006	2007	2008
Total	32 570	33 574	33 504	34 014	33 827	34 181	34 549	34 695	35 650	36 139
A	5 572	5 585	4 732	4 507	4 381	4 056	4 106	4 069	3 764	3 671
B	125	154	164	132	163	168	138	144	157	119
C	897	961	1 030	921	959	938	966	926	1 044	1 053
D	6 504	6 910	7 088	7 321	7 269	7 165	7 129	7 163	7 073	6 844
E	1 110	1 190	1 181	1 265	1 407	1 401	1 361	1 441	1 390	1 497
F	2 641	2 575	2 644	2 799	3 269	3 335	3 708	3 606	4 047	4 500
G	2 977	3 148	3 455	3 685	3 857	4 049	4 057	4 090	4 313	4 141
H	183	177	195	221	267	270	293	292	281	308
I	3 798	3 794	4 032	4 133	4 179	4 412	4 321	4 343	4 593	4 722
J	282	273	257	266	270	290	347	359	417	410
K	981	1 099	1 259	1 497	2 072	2 343	2 265	2 327	2 496	2 511
L	3 103	3 164	3 175	3 045	2 967	2 967	3 023	3 005	3 076	3 275
M	1 195	1 188	1 136	1 165	1 176	1 215	1 243	1 198	1 268	1 225
N	791	806	865	859	883	893	845	943	964	1 041
O	2 383	2 534	2 282	2 192	702	679	739	779	762	808
P	22	12	6	5	2	-	4	4	5	9
Q	6	3	4	1	3	-	3	2	-	4

Explanatory notes: see p. 77.

[1] Persons aged 15 years and over. [2] Estimates based on the 2002 Population Census results. [3] Persons aged 15 to 72 years.

Notes explicatives: voir p. 80.

[1] Personnes âgées de 15 ans et plus. [2] Estimations basées sur les résultats du Recensement de la population de 2002. [3] Personnes âgées de 15 à 72 ans.

Notas explicativas: véase p. 83.

[1] Personas de 15 años y más. [2] Estimaciones basadas en los resultados del Censo de población de 2002. [3] Personas de 15 a 72 años.

Total employment, by economic activity — **Emploi total, par activité économique** — **Empleo total, por actividad económica**

Thousands — Milliers — Millares

	1999	2000	2001	2002	2003	2004	2005	2006	2007	2008
Russian Federation (BA) [1]				Total employment - Emploi total - Empleo total						
Women - Femmes - Mujeres										
ISIC 3 - CITI 3 - CIIU 3										
Total	30 375	31 496	31 619	32 645	32 605	33 094	33 620	34 160	34 920	34 826
A	3 723	3 657	2 905	2 892	2 654	2 572	2 664	2 622	2 391	2 324
B	25	34	43	27	32	37	28	31	34	22
C	282	332	313	287	288	274	270	272	280	296
D	5 024	5 268	5 569	5 747	5 551	5 510	5 406	5 309	5 252	4 819
E	445	496	540	524	625	599	599	622	627	619
F	821	753	782	824	820	792	867	856	886	913
G	4 327	4 739	5 147	5 556	5 832	6 082	6 326	6 509	6 783	6 633
H	670	747	828	921	999	953	1 004	1 100	1 062	1 160
I	1 707	1 690	1 782	1 826	1 793	1 849	1 928	1 868	1 979	1 838
J	551	570	600	602	541	628	615	701	833	906
K	858	929	1 114	1 247	1 719	1 776	1 774	1 820	1 914	1 936
L	1 509	1 660	1 595	1 573	1 709	1 734	1 792	1 871	1 827	2 134
M	4 689	4 723	4 537	4 764	4 842	4 926	4 960	5 000	5 152	5 218
N	3 547	3 586	3 757	3 735	3 793	3 941	3 856	3 953	4 212	4 202
O	2 178	2 301	2 099	2 111	1 396	1 421	1 507	1 609	1 677	1 772
P	16	9	8	7	9	-	22	17	11	34
Q	1	1	1	1	2	1	1	1	-	1
San Marino (E) [2][3]				Total employment - Emploi total - Empleo total						
Total - Total - Total										
ISIC 3 - CITI 3 - CIIU 3										
Total	18.667	.	19.112	19.249	19.340	19.890	20.124	20.695	21.483	21.995
A	0.249	.	0.088	0.084	0.080	0.079	0.093	0.093	0.082	0.076
D	5.934	.	6.256	6.202	6.280	6.397	6.197	6.289	6.422	6.398
F	1.569	.	1.622	1.641	1.680	1.729	1.721	1.746	1.687	1.716
G	2.439	.	2.600	3.025	3.220	3.248	2.980	3.130	3.358	3.513
H	0.620	.	0.648	0.255	-	-	0.167	0.163	0.188	0.218
I	0.394	.	0.457	0.461	0.470	0.489	0.502	0.534	0.560	0.615
J	0.541	.	0.624	0.650	0.680	0.746	0.800	0.860	0.959	1.017
K	1.079	.	-	-	-	-	2.546	2.670	2.926	3.047
L	2.279	.	2.306	2.212	2.120	2.180	2.430	2.410	4.020	4.030
M	0.938	.	0.042	0.036	0.030	0.040	0.636	0.648	0.045	0.042
N	1.029	.	1.100	1.064	1.050	1.054	1.121	1.149	0.174	0.191
O	0.807	.	3.365	3.611	3.700	3.928	0.931	1.003	1.047	1.115
P	0.131	.	-	-	-	-	-	-	-	-
Q	0.001	.	-	-	-	-	-	-	-	-
X	0.657	.	0.004	0.008	-	-	-	-	0.015	0.017
Men - Hommes - Hombres										
ISIC 3 - CITI 3 - CIIU 3										
Total	11.319	.	11.404	11.483	11.480	11.768	11.902	12.219	12.667	12.967
A	0.146	.	0.058	0.058	0.050	0.056	0.067	0.067	0.058	0.054
D	4.218	.	4.483	4.469	4.500	4.573	4.411	4.447	4.616	4.627
F	1.485	.	1.527	1.529	1.550	1.590	1.585	1.612	1.554	1.579
G	1.170	.	1.242	1.469	1.510	1.542	1.566	1.655	1.759	1.852
H	0.276	.	0.274	0.085	-	-	0.045	0.051	0.062	0.085
I	0.276	.	0.306	0.311	0.300	0.314	0.311	0.333	0.347	0.391
J	0.295	.	0.332	0.352	0.370	0.400	0.419	0.461	0.514	0.543
K	0.626	.	-	-	-	-	1.462	1.517	1.680	1.733
L	1.508	.	0.819	0.778	0.750	0.746	1.317	1.308	1.702	1.708
M	0.169	.	0.024	0.007	0.010	0.010	0.123	0.122	0.023	0.024
N	0.292	.	0.320	0.313	0.300	0.326	0.354	0.365	0.045	0.052
O	0.354	.	2.017	2.110	2.120	2.211	0.242	0.281	0.297	0.308
P	0.006	.	-	-	-	-	-	-	-	-
Q	-	-	-	-	-	-	-	-	-	-
X	0.498	.	0.002	0.002	-	-	-	-	0.010	0.011
Women - Femmes - Mujeres										
ISIC 3 - CITI 3 - CIIU 3										
Total	7.348	.	7.708	7.766	7.860	8.122	8.222	8.476	8.816	9.028
A	0.103	.	0.030	0.026	0.020	0.023	0.026	0.026	0.024	0.022
D	1.716	.	1.773	1.733	1.780	1.824	1.786	1.842	1.806	1.771
F	0.084	.	0.095	0.112	0.130	0.139	0.136	0.134	0.133	0.137
G	1.269	.	1.358	1.556	1.710	1.706	1.414	1.475	1.599	1.661
H	0.344	.	0.374	0.170	-	-	0.122	0.112	0.126	0.133
I	0.118	.	0.151	0.150	0.160	0.175	0.191	0.201	0.213	0.224
J	0.246	.	0.292	0.298	0.310	0.346	0.381	0.399	0.445	0.474
K	0.453	.	-	-	-	-	1.084	1.153	1.246	1.314
L	0.771	.	1.487	1.434	1.370	1.434	1.108	1.109	2.318	2.322
M	0.769	.	0.018	0.029	0.030	0.030	0.518	0.519	0.022	0.018
N	0.737	.	0.780	0.751	0.750	0.728	0.767	0.784	0.129	0.139
O	0.453	.	1.348	1.501	1.580	1.717	0.689	0.722	0.750	0.807
P	0.125	.	-	-	-	-	-	-	-	-
Q	0.001	.	-	-	-	-	-	-	-	-
X	0.159	.	0.002	0.006	-	-	-	-	0.005	0.006

Explanatory notes: see p. 77.

[1] Persons aged 15 to 72 years. [2] Persons aged 15 years and over. [3] Dec.

Notes explicatives: voir p. 80.

[1] Personnes âgées de 15 à 72 ans. [2] Personnes âgées de 15 ans et plus. [3] Déc.

Notas explicativas: véase p. 83.

[1] Personas de 15 a 72 años. [2] Personas de 15 años y más. [3] Dic.

	EMPLOYMENT	EMPLOI	EMPLEO
	Total employment, by economic activity	Emploi total, par activité économique	Empleo total, por actividad económica
	Thousands	Milliers	Millares

	1999	2000	2001	2002	2003	2004	2005	2006	2007	2008

Serbia (BA) [1][2]

Total - Total - Total
ISIC 3 - CITI 3 - CIIU 3

Total employment - Emploi total - Empleo total

	1999	2000	2001	2002	2003	2004	2005	2006	2007	2008
Total						2 930.8	2 733.4	2 630.7	2 655.7	2 821.7
A						700.7	635.4	538.6	551.7	707.3
B						3.3	2.1	1.7	0.9	1.5
C						37.6	33.0	31.1	41.3	32.4
D						551.4	497.4	518.6	521.7	484.3
E						47.5	57.0	61.9	58.0	45.0
F						152.3	166.5	159.2	161.3	177.5
G						441.8	406.7	406.9	398.5	418.1
H						80.7	80.0	84.5	72.3	83.9
I						163.6	152.8	151.4	169.8	157.2
J						45.1	43.5	43.0	43.0	56.6
K						82.4	69.8	70.2	88.9	91.8
L						170.9	159.4	143.0	141.9	135.7
M						149.0	143.4	129.5	118.1	122.5
N						166.6	158.6	173.7	166.4	176.3
O						122.2	120.8	110.1	114.1	123.9
P						8.1	5.4	6.9	6.4	6.6
Q						3.9	1.6	0.4	1.5	1.2
X						3.5	-	-	-	-

Men - Hommes - Hombres
ISIC 3 - CITI 3 - CIIU 3

	1999	2000	2001	2002	2003	2004	2005	2006	2007	2008
Total						1 708.9	1 635.0	1 554.7	1 545.8	1 611.3
A						406.1	379.7	332.0	335.2	392.8
B						3.0	1.6	1.7	0.9	1.4
C						34.5	29.8	30.7	31.6	27.6
D						357.5	332.9	343.1	347.0	317.9
E						37.6	46.4	51.0	41.7	38.1
F						133.1	152.6	145.3	144.4	161.0
G						218.3	208.7	209.7	186.5	201.2
H						41.2	36.4	43.4	34.9	44.6
I						132.6	125.6	119.2	135.6	122.7
J						19.1	16.5	17.0	17.4	21.0
K						40.9	38.9	32.9	51.7	47.8
L						111.0	108.9	91.0	80.3	80.8
M						51.1	47.4	33.7	38.3	37.1
N						41.7	37.8	37.9	38.2	39.5
O						73.9	71.2	64.3	61.2	75.4
P						2.1	0.4	1.5	0.4	1.6
Q						2.7	0.4	0.4	0.5	0.8
X						2.5	-	-	-	-

Women - Femmes - Mujeres
ISIC 3 - CITI 3 - CIIU 3

	1999	2000	2001	2002	2003	2004	2005	2006	2007	2008
Total						1 222.0	1 098.4	1 076.0	1 110.0	1 210.4
A						294.6	255.7	206.7	216.5	314.6
B						0.4	0.5	-	-	0.2
C						3.2	3.1	0.4	9.7	4.8
D						193.9	164.6	175.5	174.7	166.4
E						9.9	10.6	10.9	16.2	6.9
F						19.3	13.9	13.9	16.8	16.5
G						223.5	198.0	197.2	212.0	216.9
H						39.5	43.6	41.1	37.4	39.2
I						31.1	27.2	32.2	34.2	34.4
J						26.0	27.0	26.0	25.7	35.6
K						41.5	31.0	37.3	37.2	44.0
L						59.8	50.5	52.0	61.6	54.9
M						97.9	96.1	95.8	79.7	85.4
N						124.9	120.8	135.8	128.2	136.8
O						48.3	49.5	45.7	52.9	48.5
P						6.1	5.0	5.4	6.0	5.0
Q						1.2	1.2	-	1.0	0.3
X						1.1	-	-	-	-

Explanatory notes: see p. 77.

[1] Persons aged 15 years and over. [2] Oct.

Notes explicatives: voir p. 80.

[1] Personnes âgées de 15 ans et plus. [2] Oct.

Notas explicativas: véase p. 83.

[1] Personas de 15 años y más. [2] Oct.

Total employment, by economic activity — Emploi total, par activité économique — Empleo total, por actividad económica

	Thousands / Milliers / Millares									
	1999	2000	2001	2002	2003	2004	2005	2006	2007	2008
Slovakia (BA) [1][2][3]				Total employment - Emploi total - Empleo total						
Total - Total - Total ISIC 3 - CITI 3 - CIIU 3										
Total	2 132.1	2 101.7	2 123.7	2 127.0	2 164.6	2 170.4	2 216.2	2 301.4	2 357.3	2 433.8
A-B	157.2	139.8	130.6	131.4	125.3	109.8	105.1	100.8	99.3	98.0
C	29.9	24.8	22.2	21.4	18.7	14.5	14.7	16.0	16.4	14.2
D	547.5	540.4	553.6	573.5	570.0	582.5	591.9	608.6	634.2	647.6
E	52.9	50.1	53.1	46.1	45.4	44.3	42.6	41.9	40.3	42.1
F	189.7	167.7	169.5	176.0	194.9	205.3	209.8	226.1	237.1	256.7
G	260.4	259.6	255.7	271.5	270.0	260.2	269.5	290.6	300.0	298.9
H	64.8	65.3	71.6	68.5	79.5	84.3	90.3	101.8	102.0	107.6
I	166.0	167.1	162.1	154.4	149.4	140.7	147.2	156.2	165.3	177.7
J	36.7	37.1	38.3	39.8	43.6	45.8	48.1	51.8	47.6	55.2
K	80.0	90.8	104.3	103.3	108.7	120.4	129.2	131.6	145.7	157.9
L	150.4	158.3	157.8	149.7	159.7	151.6	154.6	161.8	159.8	167.1
M	166.7	161.6	168.9	162.8	158.9	161.0	163.7	166.8	163.4	163.8
N	155.0	147.9	143.6	141.5	152.9	154.4	150.0	154.5	154.7	154.1
O	72.9	86.6	87.0	79.1	77.0	83.9	88.4	85.3	82.1	86.4
P	1.9	3.9	4.7	7.9	8.0	7.3	7.4	5.8	8.2	5.7
Q	0.2	0.4	0.5	0.4	0.9	0.4	0.2	0.2	0.8	0.7
X	-	0.4	0.5	0.2	1.9	4.1	3.8	1.9	0.5	0.3
Men - Hommes - Hombres ISIC 3 - CITI 3 - CIIU 3										
Total	1 163.7	1 137.3	1 145.8	1 156.8	1 177.1	1 193.7	1 233.0	1 291.1	1 321.6	1 363.7
A-B	111.8	101.3	94.0	92.0	90.6	82.4	79.2	76.7	76.0	74.5
C	25.9	21.7	19.4	19.9	17.3	13.3	13.4	15.3	15.5	12.8
D	325.8	320.3	329.5	339.9	340.0	352.1	366.2	380.5	403.3	412.3
E	43.6	41.2	44.0	38.5	37.0	34.8	34.6	33.9	33.4	35.2
F	171.7	153.9	155.8	163.9	180.8	191.4	196.9	213.1	224.2	242.6
G	103.1	106.6	109.4	118.7	113.9	112.3	119.7	129.4	129.3	124.8
H	23.9	25.3	28.6	26.8	34.3	31.6	32.0	35.5	37.5	43.1
I	116.5	115.8	111.8	109.3	107.1	103.1	106.1	116.9	123.3	130.0
J	10.6	11.7	10.2	13.2	13.4	15.1	16.6	19.4	17.1	17.5
K	48.6	55.1	62.2	61.4	64.6	70.4	78.7	75.7	83.5	83.6
L	80.5	76.9	77.5	71.1	78.0	78.9	77.6	82.5	79.0	82.0
M	35.0	35.0	34.5	35.8	30.3	34.9	38.6	40.7	34.4	35.0
N	28.7	26.3	25.4	27.7	31.5	28.3	27.7	29.9	27.6	28.2
O	38.0	45.5	42.8	38.6	36.5	41.7	43.4	41.0	37.0	41.9
P	0.1	0.2	0.1	0.2	0.4	0.8	0.5	0.2	0.1	0.2
Q	0.1	0.1	0.3	0.1	0.4	0.2	0.2	0.1	0.2	0.2
X	-	0.3	0.5	0.2	1.1	2.8	2.1	0.7	0.4	0.1
Women - Femmes - Mujeres ISIC 3 - CITI 3 - CIIU 3										
Total	968.4	964.4	977.9	970.2	987.5	976.7	983.1	1 010.3	1 035.6	1 070.0
A-B	45.4	38.4	36.5	39.4	34.7	27.5	25.9	24.2	23.3	23.5
C	3.9	3.1	2.8	1.5	1.5	1.1	1.4	0.8	0.9	1.4
D	221.7	220.1	224.1	233.7	230.0	230.5	225.7	228.2	230.9	235.4
E	9.3	8.8	9.2	7.7	8.4	9.6	8.1	8.0	6.9	6.9
F	18.0	13.8	13.7	12.2	14.2	14.0	12.9	13.0	12.9	14.1
G	157.3	153.0	146.3	152.8	156.1	147.9	149.8	161.2	170.7	174.1
H	41.0	39.9	43.0	41.7	45.2	52.7	58.3	66.3	64.5	64.6
I	49.5	51.4	50.3	45.1	42.3	37.5	41.2	39.3	42.0	47.7
J	26.1	25.4	28.2	26.6	30.2	30.8	31.5	32.5	30.5	37.7
K	31.5	35.7	42.1	41.9	44.1	50.0	50.6	55.9	62.3	74.3
L	69.9	81.5	80.2	78.7	81.7	72.8	77.0	79.3	80.9	85.2
M	131.8	126.6	134.4	126.9	128.5	126.1	125.1	126.1	129.0	128.8
N	126.3	121.5	118.3	113.8	121.3	126.1	122.4	124.6	127.2	125.9
O	34.9	41.1	44.2	40.5	40.5	42.2	44.9	44.4	45.1	44.5
P	1.9	3.7	4.6	7.7	7.6	6.5	7.0	5.6	8.1	5.6
Q	0.1	0.3	0.2	0.3	0.5	0.2	0.1	0.1	0.6	0.5
X	-	0.1	0.1	-	0.9	1.3	1.7	1.2	0.1	0.2

Explanatory notes: see p. 77.

[1] Persons aged 15 years and over. [2] Excl. conscripts. [3] Excl. persons on child-care leave.

Notes explicatives: voir p. 80.

[1] Personnes âgées de 15 ans et plus. [2] Non compris les conscrits. [3] Non compris les personnes en congé parental.

Notas explicativas: véase p. 83.

[1] Personas de 15 años y más. [2] Excl. los conscriptos. [3] Excl. las personas con licencia parental.

EMPLOYMENT — EMPLOI — EMPLEO

Total employment, by economic activity — Emploi total, par activité économique — Empleo total, por actividad económica

Thousands — Milliers — Millares

Slovenia (BA) [1][2]

Total employment - Emploi total - Empleo total

Total - Total - Total

ISIC 3	1999	2000	2001	2002	2003	2004	2005	2006	2007	2008	ISIC 4
Total	892	894	914	922	896	946	947	969	994	990	Total
A	96	85	90	89	75	91	83	93	101	89	A
C	6	7	5	4	6	6	5	6	4	3	B
D	278	269	277	287	264	270	278	266	266	260	C
E	8	10	11	11	9	10	10	10	9	11	D
F	45	48	55	54	52	54	59	57	61	7	E
G	109	119	113	120	118	120	111	122	119	70	F
H	34	34	34	36	36	38	41	38	37	117	G
I	54	60	57	55	59	56	53	54	60	53	H
J	21	22	24	22	22	22	23	21	23	41	I
K	49	43	45	45	53	58	62	65	66	28	J
L	49	53	48	50	50	56	59	59	59	23	K
M	60	57	62	61	62	65	68	75	78	3	L
N	45	46	47	51	47	48	51	61	57	40	M
O	36	34	33	33	37	40	37	39	44	22	N
P	-	-	1	-	-	-	-	1	1	53	O
X	3	6	10	6	6	10	5	3	10	74	P
										57	Q
										16	R
										14	S
										5	X

Men - Hommes - Hombres

ISIC 3	1999	2000	2001	2002	2003	2004	2005	2006	2007	2008	ISIC 4
Total	482	481	497	500	488	511	512	521	542	540	Total
A	51	45	50	48	41	49	44	51	54	49	A
C	6	6	5	3	5	5	5	5	3	3	B
D	169	160	166	173	165	168	174	168	170	168	C
E	6	8	10	9	7	9	8	8	7	9	D
F	41	43	49	49	47	50	55	53	56	5	E
G	53	57	57	57	55	56	51	58	57	63	F
H	14	14	13	14	15	15	16	12	13	54	G
I	42	46	43	42	47	44	40	39	47	44	H
J	5	7	8	8	7	7	9	8	7	16	I
K	25	25	25	25	29	31	34	38	37	19	J
L	25	26	23	25	23	27	30	29	32	7	K
M	14	12	15	14	15	16	16	18	16	1	L
N	9	9	10	12	9	8	8	12	12	19	M
O	17	17	17	16	18	21	18	19	23	10	N
P	-	-	-	-	-	-	-	-	-	28	O
X	2	4	6	3	3	6	4	2	5	16	P
										12	Q
										9	R
										4	S
										2	X

Women - Femmes - Mujeres

ISIC 3	1999	2000	2001	2002	2003	2004	2005	2006	2007	2008	ISIC 4
Total	410	413	417	423	409	434	435	448	451	450	Total
A	45	40	40	41	34	42	39	41	47	40	A
C	-	1	-	1	1	1	-	1	1	-	B
D	109	109	112	114	99	103	104	97	96	92	C
E	1	2	1	1	1	1	2	2	2	2	D
F	4	5	6	5	5	5	4	5	5	2	E
G	56	62	57	62	63	64	60	63	61	7	F
H	19	20	22	23	21	23	25	26	24	63	G
I	11	14	14	13	12	13	13	15	13	9	H
J	15	15	15	14	15	15	14	13	15	25	I
K	24	18	20	20	24	27	28	28	28	9	J
L	24	26	25	25	26	29	29	30	26	16	K
M	46	45	47	47	47	49	53	57	62	2	L
N	36	37	36	39	38	40	43	48	45	21	M
O	19	17	17	17	20	19	19	20	20	12	N
P	-	-	-	-	-	-	-	1	1	25	O
X	1	2	4	3	3	4	1	2	5	58	P
										45	Q
										7	R
										10	S
										3	X

Explanatory notes: see p. 77.

[1] Persons aged 15 years and over. [2] Second quarter of each year.

Notes explicatives: voir p. 80.

[1] Personnes âgées de 15 ans et plus. [2] Deuxième trimestre de chaque année.

Notas explicativas: véase p. 83.

[1] Personas de 15 años y más. [2] Segundo trimestre de cada año.

Total employment, by economic activity	Emploi total, par activité économique	Empleo total, por actividad económica
Thousands	Milliers	Millares

	1999	2000	2001	2002	2003	2004	2005	2006	2007	2008
Suisse (BA) [1][2][3]				*Total employment - Emploi total - Empleo total*						
Total - Total - Total										
ISIC 3 - CITI 3 - CIIU 3										
Total	3 862	3 879	3 938	3 965	3 963	3 959	3 974	4 051	4 122	4 229
A-B	191	181	171	168	167	153	154	153	164	171
C-E	679	692	710	694	659	642	643	653	668	680
F	263	267	260	251	248	253	261	277	276	266
G	610	591	599	606	577	577	565	560	552	564
H	112	118	135	145	145	151	148	160	154	155
I	238	223	231	234	242	226	226	216	218	222
J	196	197	206	217	230	223	218	231	238	244
K	399	390	405	412	448	460	454	466	505	517
L,Q	214	219	207	216	217	215	221	224	216	219
M	251	269	298	280	290	301	313	325	326	343
N	429	445	453	450	463	476	482	485	515	540
O-P	275	277	257	272	270	275	282	294	284	300
X	6 [4]	10 [4]	6 [4]	20	7	9	5	7	7	8
Men - Hommes - Hombres										
ISIC 3 - CITI 3 - CIIU 3										
Total	2 157	2 172	2 190	2 175	2 177	2 173	2 172	2 214	2 259	2 289
A-B	126	115	112	109	109	102	103	104	112	117
C-E	501	515	527	509	481	463	467	473	495	494
F	226	234	226	220	218	225	234	246	244	235
G	315	312	302	296	288	287	269	273	269	278
H	39	44	48	56	61	63	61	65	65	64
I	156	149	152	160	167	159	157	149	155	159
J	116	115	123	123	131	132	129	137	139	142
K	247	239	248	253	271	286	287	291	313	315
L,Q	120	122	126	129	129	127	127	131	120	122
M	99	105	119	108	113	111	117	121	121	131
N	115	114	115	105	111	113	112	108	118	118
O-P	92	103	90	98	95	102	106	112	105	111
X	4 [4]	6 [4]	. [5]	10	3 [4]	4 [4]	3 [4]	3 [4]	4 [4]	4 [4]
Women - Femmes - Mujeres										
ISIC 3 - CITI 3 - CIIU 3										
Total	1 705	1 707	1 748	1 790	1 786	1 786	1 802	1 837	1 863	1 940
A-B	65	66	59	59	58	51	51	50	52	54
C-E	177	178	184	185	178	179	176	180	173	185
F	37	33	34	31	29	28	27	30	32	31
G	295	279	298	310	289	290	297	287	283	287
H	73	74	86	89	85	88	87	95	89	91
I	82	75	79	75	75	67	70	68	62	63
J	80	81	83	94	100	91	90	94	99	102
K	151	151	156	159	177	174	166	175	192	202
L,Q	94	97	81	87	88	88	94	93	97	97
M	152	164	179	172	177	190	196	204	205	212
N	313	331	338	345	352	363	370	377	397	423
O-P	183	174	167	175	175	173	176	182	178	189
X	. [5]	4	4	10	4	4	3	4	4	4
Suisse (E) [6]				*Total employment - Emploi total - Empleo total*						
Total - Total - Total										
ISIC 3 - CITI 3 - CIIU 3										
Total	4 038	4 080	4 146	4 171	4 156	4 169	4 201	4 304	4 413	4 495
A-B	193	184	175	173	169	159	160	162	172	178
C	5	5	5	5	5	5	5	5	5	5
D	706	721	729	707	671	666	671	690	704	711
E	26	26	25	24	25	25	25	25	26	25
F	286	295	299	296	288	289	294	303	310	307
G	648	632	635	642	648	652	648	652	666	671
H	253	250	249	246	241	242	241	244	249	257
I	263	270	274	271	270	272	270	274	277	280
J	200	200	214	222	219	218	215	219	229	231
K	408	429	461	478	484	489	495	520	541	565
L	154	159	161	163	169	173	178	185	192	189
M	246	247	253	264	274	272	274	280	284	289
N	418	429	435	446	462	471	486	497	506	523
O	171	172	174	173	176	180	186	195	199	203
P	61	60	57	60	55	56	53	53	52	61

Explanatory notes: see p. 77.

[1] Excluding armed forces and seasonal/border workers. [2] Persons aged 15 years and over. [3] Second quarter of each year. [4] Relative statistical reliability. [5] Not indicated due to lack of statistical reliability. [6] Civilian labour force employed.

Notes explicatives: voir p. 80.

[1] Non compris les forces armées et les travailleurs saisonniers et frontaliers. [2] Personnes âgées de 15 ans et plus. [3] Deuxième trimestre de chaque année. [4] Fiabilité statistique relative. [5] Non indiqué en raison du manque de fiabilité statistique. [6] Main-d'oeuvre civile occupée.

Notas explicativas: véase p. 83.

[1] Excluidas las fuerzas armadas y excl. a los trabajadores temporales y fronterizos. [2] Personas de 15 años y más. [3] Segundo trimestre de cada año. [4] Confiabilidad estadística relativa. [5] No se indica por la falta de confiabilidad estadística. [6] Fuerza de trabajo civil ocupada.

EMPLOYMENT / EMPLOI / EMPLEO

Total employment, by economic activity — Emploi total, par activité économique — Empleo total, por actividad económica

Thousands — Milliers — Millares

Suisse (E) [1]

Total employment - Emploi total - Empleo total

Men - Hommes - Hombres
ISIC 3 - CITI 3 - CIIU 3

	1999	2000	2001	2002	2003	2004	2005	2006	2007	2008
Total	2 280	2 301	2 328	2 321	2 307	2 315	2 331	2 385	2 447	2 472
A-B	127	119	115	113	111	106	108	111	118	123
C	5	5	5	4	4	4	4	4	4	4
D	512	526	530	512	484	480	486	500	513	513
E	23	22	21	21	20	21	21	21	22	21
F	254	263	265	262	256	257	263	269	277	273
G	322	313	315	315	319	321	320	321	328	332
H	109	108	106	106	108	107	103	104	106	111
I	181	182	183	182	183	186	185	189	191	192
J	116	115	121	125	124	125	124	127	133	135
K	245	257	277	281	285	289	294	306	315	329
L	96	99	97	97	100	102	103	107	109	105
M	103	101	106	110	115	115	113	114	116	115
N	102	103	102	104	109	112	114	117	118	120
O	78	78	78	78	80	83	85	89	89	91
P	8	10	7	10	8	7	9	7	7	9

Women - Femmes - Mujeres
ISIC 3 - CITI 3 - CIIU 3

	1999	2000	2001	2002	2003	2004	2005	2006	2007	2008
Total	1 759	1 779	1 818	1 850	1 848	1 854	1 870	1 919	1 966	2 023
A-B	65	65	59	60	58	52	52	52	54	55
C	1	1	-	-	-	1	1	1	1	1
D	193	195	199	195	187	186	185	190	191	199
E	4	3	4	4	4	4	4	4	4	4
F	33	32	34	34	32	32	32	33	33	34
G	326	319	320	327	328	331	328	331	338	339
H	144	142	143	140	134	135	138	141	143	146
I	82	88	91	89	87	86	85	85	86	88
J	84	85	93	97	95	93	91	92	96	97
K	162	172	184	197	199	200	201	215	226	236
L	58	61	64	66	69	71	75	77	83	84
M	143	146	147	154	159	157	161	166	168	174
N	316	325	333	342	354	359	372	379	388	403
O	93	95	97	95	96	97	101	106	110	111
P	53	49	50	50	47	49	45	46	45	52

Sweden (BA) [2][3]

Total employment - Emploi total - Empleo total

Total - Total - Total
ISIC 3 - CITI 3 - CIIU 3 / ISIC 4 - CITI 4 - CIIU 4

ISIC 3	1999	2000	2001	2002	2003	2004	2005[4]	2006	2007	2008	ISIC 4
Total	4 068	4 159	4 239	4 244	4 234	4 213	4 263	4 341	4 541	4 593	Total
A	101	95	93	88	87	89	84	84	99	97	A
B	2	3	3	3	2	1	2	2	3	9	B
C	9	9	7	7	7	6	7	8	9	621	C
D	757	757	742	714	689	679	652	653	658	22	D
E	31	30	27	25	27	27	27	25	25	18	E
F	225	225	232	235	239	242	253	270	290	306	F
G	512	520	520	515	527	529	535	536	557	559	G
H	114	116	118	113	119	124	117	128	143	237	H
I	275	279	283	284	275	265	269	274	281	148	I
J	85	87	89	90	90	87	81	84	89	182	J
K	446	499	549	564	548	545	582	603	664	94	K
L.Q	208	223	232	241	243	246	238	249	260	66	L
M	315	329	343	348	471	472	472	480	491	335	M
N	776	770	778	792	687	683	707	701	724	208	N
O-P	207	211	215	217	219	214	228	233	240	261	O
X	3	6	8	6	4	3	10	9	8	106	P
										111	Q
										1	R
										1	S
										489	T
										714	U
										8	X

Explanatory notes: see p. 77.

[1] Civilian labour force employed. [2] Incl. professional army; excl. compulsory military service. [3] Persons aged 15 to 74 years; prior to 2007: 16 to 64 years. [4] Methodology revised; data not strictly comparable.

Notes explicatives: voir p. 80.

[1] Main-d'oeuvre civile occupée. [2] Y compris les militaires de carrière; non compris les militaires du contingent. [3] Personnes âgées de 15 à 74 ans; avant 2007: 16 à 64 ans. [4] Méthodologie révisée; les données ne sont pas strictement comparables.

Notas explicativas: véase p. 83.

[1] Fuerza de trabajo civil ocupada. [2] Incl. los militares profesionales; excl. los militares en servicio obligatorio. [3] Personas de 15 a 74 años; antes de 2007: 16 a 64 años. [4] Metodología revisada; los datos no son estrictamente comparables.

EMPLOYMENT — EMPLOI — EMPLEO 2B

Total employment, by economic activity — Emploi total, par activité économique — Empleo total, por actividad económica

Thousands — Milliers — Millares

Sweden (BA) [1][2] — Total employment - Emploi total - Empleo total

Men - Hommes - Hombres

ISIC 3 - CITI 3 - CIIU 3 · ISIC 4 - CITI 4 - CIIU 4

ISIC 3	1999	2000	2001	2002	2003	2004	2005	2006	2007	2008	ISIC 4
Total	2 121	2 167	2 203	2 197	2 191	2 186	2 225 [3]	2 273	2 390	2 422	Total
A	76	73	70	67	68	70	65 [3]	66	79	79	A
B	2	3	3	3	2	1	2 [3]	2	3	8	B
C	8	8	6	6	6	5	6 [3]	7	8	476	C
D	558	557	545	528	514	506	489 [3]	488	491	17	D
E	23	21	20	19	20	19	19 [3]	18	18	15	E
F	206	208	214	217	221	224	236 [3]	251	268	282	F
G	289	290	292	287	298	304	306 [3]	306	317	315	G
H	49	51	52	51	52	56	54 [3]	58	66	179	H
I	197	200	200	200	197	191	199 [3]	203	207	65	I
J	37	38	39	39	39	38	35 [3]	37	43	127	J
K	271	303	339	344	331	327	357 [3]	370	407	45	K
L,Q	104	111	111	113	116	115	110 [3]	113	122	43	L
M	104	107	110	111	118	119	119 [3]	122	125	199	M
N	103	100	101	105	107	110	119 [3]	122	123	112	N
O-P	92	93	97	102	99	98	105 [3]	105	108	117	O
X	2	4	5	4	3	2	5 [3]	5	5	53	P
										43	Q
										-	R
										1	S
										124	T
										119	U
										4	X

Women - Femmes - Mujeres

ISIC 3 - CITI 3 - CIIU 3 · ISIC 4 - CITI 4 - CIIU 4

ISIC 3	1999	2000	2001	2002	2003	2004	2005	2006	2007	2008	ISIC 4
Total	1 946	1 992	2 036	2 047	2 043	2 027	2 038 [3]	2 067	2 150	2 171	Total
A	26	23	23	21	19	19	19 [3]	18	20	19	A
B	-	-	-	1	1	1	1 [3]	1	1	1	B
C	1	1	1	1	1	1	1 [3]	1	1	145	C
D	198	200	197	186	175	173	163 [3]	165	166	5	D
E	8	8	8	7	7	7	8 [3]	7	7	3	E
F	19	18	18	18	18	18	17 [3]	19	22	24	F
G	223	230	229	228	229	225	229 [3]	230	240	245	G
H	65	66	66	62	67	69	63 [3]	69	77	58	H
I	78	79	84	84	78	75	70 [3]	71	74	83	I
J	48	48	50	51	51	49	46 [3]	47	45	55	J
K	175	195	210	220	217	218	225 [3]	233	258	49	K
L,Q	104	112	121	129	127	131	128 [3]	136	138	23	L
M	212	222	233	237	354	353	353 [3]	359	366	136	M
N	673	670	677	687	579	572	588 [3]	579	601	96	N
O-P	114	118	117	116	120	116	123 [3]	128	132	143	O
X	1	2	2	2	1	1	4 [3]	4	3	54	P
										68	Q
										1	R
										-	S
										364	T
										596	U
										3	X

Turkey (BA) [4][5] — Total employment - Emploi total - Empleo total

Total - Total - Total · ISIC 3 - CITI 3 - CIIU 3

	1999	2000	2001	2002	2003	2004	2005	2006	2007	2008
Total	.	21 581	21 524	21 354	21 147	21 791	22 046	22 330	20 738	21 194
A-B	.	.	.	.	.	.	6 493	6 088	4 867	5 016
A	.	7 745	8 053	7 438	7 152	7 373	.	.	.	.
B	.	24	35	19	13	27	.	.	.	.
C	.	82	98	120	83	104	120	128	128	115
D	.	3 638	3 582	3 731	3 664	3 801	4 084	4 186	4 089	4 235
E	.	91	95	103	100	83	80	93	97	92
F	.	1 364	1 110	958	965	1 029	1 173	1 267	1 231	1 241
G	.	3 041	2 942	3 154	3 205	3 307	3 611	3 729	3 569	3 575
H	.	776	796	826	847	872	949	1 001	989	998
I	.	1 068	1 034	1 004	1 022	1 100	1 133	1 163	1 136	1 089
J	.	281	258	238	229	237	238	238	248	260
K	.	428	439	460	509	549	638	772	807	910
L	.	1 174	1 158	1 151	1 177	1 252	1 217	1 225	1 260	1 265
M	.	750	798	850	867	818	906	907	868	921
N	.	479	462	506	522	469	530	591	560	594
O	.	498	513	620	618	583	.	.	.	.
O-Q	.	.	.	.	.	.	874	942	889	883
P	.	138	149	174	174	182	.	.	.	.
Q	.	4	4	1	2	4	.	.	.	.

Explanatory notes: see p. 77.

[1] Incl. professional army; excl. compulsory military service. [2] Persons aged 15 to 74 years; prior to 2007: 16 to 64 years. [3] Methodology revised; data not strictly comparable. [4] Excl. armed forces. [5] Persons aged 15 years and over.

Notes explicatives: voir p. 80.

[1] Y compris les militaires de carrière; non compris les militaires du contingent. [2] Personnes âgées de 15 à 74 ans; avant 2007: 16 à 64 ans. [3] Méthodologie révisée; les données ne sont pas strictement comparables. [4] Non compris les forces armées. [5] Personnes âgées de 15 ans et plus.

Notas explicativas: véase p. 83.

[1] Incl. los militares profesionales; excl. los militares en servicio obligatorio. [2] Personas de 15 a 74 años; antes de 2007: 16 a 64 años. [3] Metodología revisada; los datos no son estrictamente comparables. [4] Excl. las fuerzas armadas. [5] Personas de 15 años y más.

EMPLOYMENT   EMPLOI   EMPLEO

Total employment, by economic activity   Emploi total, par activité économique   Empleo total, por actividad económica

Thousands   Milliers   Millares

	1999	2000	2001	2002	2003	2004	2005	2006	2007	2008
Turkey (BA) [1][2]				Total employment - Emploi total - Empleo total						
Men - Hommes - Hombres										
ISIC 3 - CITI 3 - CIIU 3										
Total		15 780	15 555	15 232	15 256	16 023	16 346	16 520	15 382	15 598
A-B							3 550	3 272	2 578	2 663
A		4 238	4 275	3 765	3 706	4 075				
B		23	34	19	12	26				
C		77	95	115	80	103	117	126	126	112
D		2 918	2 888	2 923	2 910	3 022	3 262	3 358	3 268	3 406
E		85	88	99	93	77	74	87	93	85
F		1 331	1 089	935	936	1 004	1 145	1 231	1 195	1 199
G		2 717	2 622	2 787	2 806	2 895	3 130	3 167	3 001	2 975
H		712	729	747	773	782	847	885	851	850
I		999	972	942	959	1 038	1 062	1 086	1 055	1 002
J		172	168	158	151	153	157	154	152	153
K		316	335	347	394	416	485	581	607	691
L		1 010	1 020	1 009	1 022	1 122	1 084	1 077	1 083	1 089
M		453	497	535	544	512	557	537	488	503
N		247	238	253	267	237	256	287	261	256
O		419	442	535	536	496				
O-Q							621	673	623	615
P		59	60	63	64	62				
Q		3	3	1	1	3				
Women - Femmes - Mujeres										
ISIC 3 - CITI 3 - CIIU 3										
Total		5 801	5 969	6 122	5 891	5 768	5 700	5 810	5 356	5 595
A-B							2 943	2 816	2 288	2 354
A		3 507	3 779	3 673	3 447	3 298				
B		1	1	1	1	1				
C		4	3	5	3	2	3	2	2	3
D		720	693	808	753	779	822	828	821	828
E		6	7	4	6	5	5	6	4	7
F		33	21	23	29	25	28	36	35	42
G		324	320	368	399	413	481	563	568	600
H		64	67	79	75	90	102	115	138	148
I		68	62	62	63	62	71	77	81	87
J		109	90	80	78	84	82	84	96	107
K		112	104	113	115	132	154	192	200	219
L		164	137	142	155	129	132	148	177	176
M		297	300	315	323	306	350	370	380	418
N		233	224	253	255	232	275	304	299	338
O		78	71	85	81	87				
O-Q							253	269	266	269
P		79	90	111	110	120				
Q		1	1	-	1	2				
Ukraine (BA) [3]				Total employment - Emploi total - Empleo total						
Total - Total - Total										
ISIC 3 - CITI 3 - CIIU 3										
Total		19 971.5	20 091.2	20 163.3	20 295.7	20 680.0	20 730.4	20 904.7	20 972.3	
A-B		4 164.9	4 144.6	4 105.7	3 998.3	4 005.5	3 649.1	3 484.5	3 322.1	
C-E		4 390.3	4 220.4	4 123.2	4 077.1	4 072.4	4 036.9	3 973.0	3 871.4	
F		865.4	838.9	833.5	907.5	941.5	987.1	1 030.2	1 043.4	
G-H		3 422.2	3 657.1	3 752.4	3 971.2	4 175.2	4 406.9	4 564.4	4 744.4	
I		1 325.9	1 353.5	1 361.4	1 374.9	1 400.5	1 428.8	1 451.9	1 465.8	
J		171.9	178.0	190.3	216.1	247.9	286.0	344.4	394.9	
K		834.3	848.2	914.8	919.9	966.6	1 041.9	1 134.7	1 150.4	
L		1 146.2	1 174.6	1 170.6	1 050.2	1 028.9	1 033.7	1 036.4	1 067.5	
M		1 621.3	1 630.3	1 637.2	1 648.7	1 668.2	1 690.5	1 693.7	1 702.4	
N		1 361.8	1 359.8	1 366.5	1 348.9	1 356.6	1 356.7	1 359.0	1 369.9	
O-Q		667.3	685.8	707.7	782.9	816.7	812.8	832.5	840.1	

Explanatory notes: see p. 77.

[1] Excl. armed forces. [2] Persons aged 15 years and over. [3] Persons aged 15-70 years.

Notes explicatives: voir p. 80.

[1] Non compris les forces armées. [2] Personnes âgées de 15 ans et plus. [3] Personnes âgées de 15 à 70 ans.

Notas explicativas: véase p. 83.

[1] Excl. las fuerzas armadas. [2] Personas de 15 años y más. [3] Personas de 15 á 70 años.

Total employment, by economic activity / Emploi total, par activité économique / Empleo total, por actividad económica

	Thousands / Milliers / Millares									
	1999	2000	2001	2002	2003	2004	2005	2006	2007	2008

United Kingdom (BA) [1] [2] — Total employment - Emploi total - Empleo total

Total - Total - Total
ISIC 3 - CITI 3 - CIIU 3

	1999	2000	2001	2002	2003	2004	2005	2006	2007	2008
Total	27 023	27 399	27 643	27 852	28 132	28 365	28 665	28 926	29 100	29 475
A	408	408	376	365	340	354	376	356	388	418
B	16	13	14	19	12	13	10	18	10	15
C	99	105	110	109	103	91	106	110	133	127
D	4 755	4 619	4 460	4 296	4 124	3 817	3 804	3 755	3 745	3 547
E	181	199	195	218	179	182	175	174	213	199
F	1 878	1 952	1 995	1 984	2 115	2 207	2 266	2 332	2 387	2 380
G	4 191	4 216	4 159	4 197	4 360	4 398	4 355	4 237	4 160	4 316
H	1 166	1 158	1 181	1 280	1 206	1 248	1 249	1 270	1 299	1 283
I	1 780	1 861	1 964	1 954	1 954	1 904	1 973	1 940	1 956	1 963
J	1 140	1 188	1 211	1 262	1 245	1 202	1 206	1 253	1 263	1 279
K	2 953	3 040	3 136	3 167	3 125	3 218	3 287	3 328	3 484	3 602
L	1 622	1 691	1 834	1 865	1 920	1 950	1 995	2 045	2 038	2 092
M	2 169	2 204	2 212	2 318	2 428	2 558	2 601	2 673	2 645	2 686
N	2 991	2 993	3 112	3 108	3 226	3 414	3 483	3 582	3 462	3 641
O	1 445	1 519	1 466	1 516	1 593	1 576	1 584	1 632	1 681	1 675
P	140	135	120	121	137	152	121	125	120	138
Q	16	23	18	16	15	11	8	21	11	13
X	73	74	79	58	50	71	65	75	105	102

Men - Hommes - Hombres
ISIC 3 - CITI 3 - CIIU 3

	1999	2000	2001	2002	2003	2004	2005	2006	2007	2008
Total	14 692	14 859	14 961	15 033	15 256	15 327	15 468	15 578	15 747	15 904
A	312	310	287	279	263	276	278	274	289	304
B	14	13	12	16	12	12	9	18	9	13
C	84	91	99	95	93	81	92	86	105	101
D	3 454	3 381	3 286	3 182	3 072	2 851	2 843	2 803	2 808	2 638
E	130	143	144	163	134	133	128	127	153	146
F	1 706	1 758	1 794	1 793	1 913	1 987	2 035	2 075	2 160	2 148
G	2 084	2 068	2 056	2 083	2 185	2 216	2 193	2 135	2 143	2 192
H	460	468	487	538	521	553	560	567	581	596
I	1 323	1 377	1 464	1 461	1 478	1 457	1 491	1 477	1 481	1 499
J	537	562	574	613	609	584	602	631	649	664
K	1 710	1 768	1 834	1 841	1 828	1 909	1 937	1 967	2 014	2 102
L	878	917	940	932	985	995	993	1 008	1 005	1 070
M	632	614	601	650	675	710	707	753	724	720
N	584	558	602	590	633	698	744	738	695	786
O	683	732	682	716	768	754	762	806	818	803
P	39	40	37	40	46	58	48	56	51	53
Q	10	16	11	8	9	7	5	11	6	8
X	51	44	52	35	32	45	40	47	57	61

Women - Femmes - Mujeres
ISIC 3 - CITI 3 - CIIU 3

	1999	2000	2001	2002	2003	2004	2005	2006	2007	2008
Total	12 331	12 540	12 681	12 819	12 876	13 038	13 198	13 348	13 353	13 572
A	96	98	89	87	77	78	98	82	100	114
B	1	-	2	2	-	-	1	-	-	2
C	15	14	11	14	10	10	14	23	28	27
D	1 300	1 238	1 173	1 114	1 053	966	960	952	937	909
E	51	56	51	55	45	49	47	46	60	53
F	173	194	202	191	202	220	231	257	228	233
G	2 108	2 148	2 103	2 114	2 175	2 182	2 162	2 102	2 017	2 124
H	706	689	693	742	685	695	689	703	717	688
I	457	484	500	493	476	447	483	463	475	464
J	603	627	637	649	636	619	604	623	614	615
K	1 243	1 272	1 303	1 326	1 297	1 309	1 351	1 362	1 470	1 500
L	744	774	894	933	935	955	1 002	1 036	1 033	1 022
M	1 537	1 591	1 611	1 668	1 753	1 848	1 894	1 920	1 921	1 966
N	2 407	2 435	2 511	2 519	2 593	2 716	2 739	2 844	2 767	2 855
O	762	787	784	800	825	822	822	826	863	871
P	101	95	83	81	91	94	73	69	69	84
Q	6	7	7	8	5	4	4	10	4	5
X	21	31	27	23	18	25	26	28	48	42

Explanatory notes: see p. 77.   Notes explicatives: voir p. 80.   Notas explicativas: véase p. 83.

[1] Persons aged 16 years and over. [2] Second quarter.   [1] Personnes âgées de 16 ans et plus. [2] Deuxième trimestre.   [1] Personas de 16 años y más. [2] Segundo trimestre.

Total employment,
by economic activity

Emploi total,
par activité économique

Empleo total,
por actividad económica

	Thousands				Milliers				Millares	
	1999	2000	2001	2002	2003	2004	2005	2006	2007	2008

OCEANIA-OCÉANIE-OCEANIA

Australia (BA) [1][2]   Total employment - Emploi total - Empleo total

Total - Total - Total
ISIC 3 - CITI 3 - CIIU 3

	1999	2000	2001	2002	2003	2004	2005	2006	2007	2008
Total	8 720.2	8 951.3	9 081.4	9 245.8	9 464.9	9 623.3	9 968.6	10 218.3	10 512.3	10 740.5
A	418.6	425.6	420.4	387.9	348.3	343.3	342.1	340.2	339.7	343.5
B	14.4	17.9	17.9	17.6	17.7	13.8	13.1	10.1	11.4	11.2
C	70.1	67.4	69.5	71.6	77.1	87.1	105.7	116.7	119.0	133.0
D	1 066.3	1 124.5	1 090.7	1 110.8	1 092.2	1 097.2	1 083.8	1 074.3	1 092.2	1 102.1
E	64.3	64.6	69.5	67.2	75.6	74.3	81.8	85.3	86.2	98.5
F	657.4	689.6	674.0	699.4	753.1	799.1	854.9	914.4	946.3	987.0
G	1 827.5	1 758.7	1 615.5	1 664.4	1 721.4	1 713.3	1 765.4	1 785.3	1 823.4	1 847.1
H	418.2	455.1	628.7	639.7	650.1	663.2	691.7	667.0	704.4	708.3
I	568.6	588.1	586.4	561.7	592.0	608.8	633.8	641.2	678.6	695.6
J	314.0	332.7	349.9	343.2	348.5	348.7	374.9	387.1	407.1	401.5
K	983.7	1 061.8	1 062.8	1 091.2	1 141.6	1 142.4	1 213.3	1 279.6	1 291.8	1 326.3
L	451.3	457.2	510.3	550.9	582.8	596.4	612.2	626.0	641.6	644.5
M	614.1	612.8	663.6	673.7	702.9	712.5	719.5	741.7	771.0	807.5
N	817.0	849.8	903.8	933.6	933.0	981.2	1 015.8	1 078.1	1 097.6	1 129.6
O	424.4	435.8	413.6	426.7	425.5	439.3	460.1	470.7	500.1	502.5
P	9.7	6.5	4.7	6.0	3.2	2.6	0.4	0.5	1.8	2.1
Q	0.8	1.4	.	.	.	.	.	.	.	.
X	-	1.7	.	.	.	.	.	.	.	.

Men - Hommes - Hombres
ISIC 3 - CITI 3 - CIIU 3

	1999	2000	2001	2002	2003	2004	2005	2006	2007	2008
Total	4 917.6	5 006.0	5 036.4	5 131.0	5 225.6	5 331.0	5 488.0	5 605.6	5 769.9	5 879.2
A	286.9	292.1	283.7	265.7	240.7	231.5	235.2	233.2	233.1	237.0
B	12.1	14.6	15.0	14.7	15.1	11.1	10.4	7.8	9.5	9.5
C	64.0	60.0	61.8	63.7	68.8	76.5	93.2	101.4	103.7	113.0
D	779.6	818.0	793.8	811.9	785.9	797.9	787.6	779.7	793.4	806.6
E	53.0	53.5	54.7	52.2	60.3	61.4	65.1	66.3	68.4	75.7
F	575.1	602.3	586.8	608.9	657.2	702.1	743.2	803.3	833.5	870.2
G	992.0	934.4	888.1	912.7	937.7	936.1	948.9	962.2	980.2	991.3
H	187.7	203.3	274.7	280.6	283.5	298.0	304.2	282.6	308.9	312.7
I	413.4	433.1	433.9	421.7	434.6	443.8	463.5	468.7	496.5	512.6
J	142.0	146.5	152.0	158.1	157.0	160.5	167.7	181.2	197.3	188.0
K	551.8	590.6	572.5	596.7	620.6	629.1	659.2	693.3	703.2	717.7
L	266.6	269.0	292.4	317.4	324.0	323.9	335.8	342.2	345.0	337.7
M	201.8	196.6	219.1	214.0	231.6	234.6	234.8	233.3	252.2	249.8
N	184.2	182.7	200.4	205.9	203.4	214.0	221.4	234.8	227.0	234.6
O	205.6	206.4	206.3	206.0	204.8	210.2	217.7	215.7	217.6	222.3
P	1.4	1.6	1.2	0.9	0.3	0.4	0.2	0.1	0.4	0.3
Q	0.5	0.5	.	.	.	.	.	.	.	.
X	-	1.0	.	.	.	.	.	.	.	.

Women - Femmes - Mujeres
ISIC 3 - CITI 3 - CIIU 3

	1999	2000	2001	2002	2003	2004	2005	2006	2007	2008
Total	3 802.6	3 945.3	4 045.0	4 114.8	4 239.4	4 292.3	4 480.6	4 612.8	4 742.4	4 861.3
A	131.6	133.5	136.7	122.3	107.6	111.8	107.0	107.0	106.7	106.6
B	2.3	3.3	3.0	2.9	2.6	2.7	2.6	2.3	1.9	1.7
C	6.2	7.4	7.7	7.9	8.3	10.6	12.4	15.3	15.4	20.0
D	286.6	306.6	296.9	298.9	306.4	299.3	296.2	294.6	298.8	295.4
E	11.3	11.1	14.8	15.0	15.3	12.9	16.7	19.1	17.9	22.8
F	82.4	87.3	87.2	90.5	95.9	97.1	111.7	111.1	112.8	116.8
G	835.4	824.3	727.4	751.7	783.6	777.2	816.5	823.2	843.2	855.8
H	230.5	251.9	354.0	359.1	366.6	365.1	387.5	384.4	395.4	395.7
I	155.2	155.0	152.5	140.1	157.4	165.0	170.3	172.5	182.1	183.0
J	171.9	186.2	197.9	185.1	191.5	188.2	207.2	205.9	209.8	213.5
K	431.9	471.2	490.4	494.6	521.0	513.3	554.2	586.3	588.6	608.6
L	184.8	188.1	217.8	233.6	258.8	272.6	276.5	283.8	296.6	306.9
M	412.3	416.3	444.5	459.7	471.3	477.9	484.8	508.4	518.8	557.7
N	632.8	667.1	703.4	727.8	729.6	767.2	794.4	843.3	870.6	895.0
O	218.8	229.4	207.3	220.7	220.7	229.1	242.4	255.0	282.5	280.2
P	8.3	4.9	3.6	5.1	2.8	2.2	0.3	0.5	1.4	1.8
Q	0.3	0.9	.	.	.	.	.	.	.	.
X	-	0.7	.	.	.	.	.	.	.	.

Explanatory notes: see p. 77. Notes explicatives: voir p. 80. Notas explicativas: véase p. 83.

[1] Excl. armed forces. [2] Persons aged 15 years and over. [1] Non compris les forces armées. [2] Personnes âgées de 15 ans et plus. [1] Excl. las fuerzas armadas. [2] Personas de 15 años y más.

Total employment, by economic activity / Emploi total, par activité économique / Empleo total, por actividad económica

Thousands — Milliers — Millares

	1999	2000	2001	2002	2003	2004	2005	2006	2007	2008
New Zealand (BA) [1][2]					Total employment - Emploi total - Empleo total					
Total - Total - Total										
ISIC 3 - CITI 3 - CIIU 3										
Total	1 750.3	1 779.0	1 823.4	1 876.8	1 955.6 [3]	2 024.1	2 084.6	2 134.7	2 174.5	2 188.2
A	160.1	150.1	161.5	161.3	155.7 [3]	149.9	145.8	150.6	153.5	149.4
B	4.1	4.1	3.9	3.6	4.0 [3]	3.3	2.8	1.8	2.4	2.6
C	3.4	3.8	3.5	3.7	3.4 [3]	4.0	4.1	4.8	5.2	4.0
D	279.2	281.5	289.1	290.8	284.9 [3]	295.2	287.0	280.6	279.2	278.0
E	8.9	8.5	10.1	9.8	8.8 [3]	9.6	8.4	8.3	8.8	12.0
F	109.3	118.4	112.1	120.7	140.7 [3]	153.0	162.8	185.1	185.3	179.2
G	301.2	311.1	314.1	316.8	350.0 [3]	356.8	361.5	368.4	377.7	387.1
H	86.7	92.9	94.5	106.9	96.0 [3]	94.2	99.7	97.1	108.2	101.0
I	110.4	110.9	112.4	113.3	113.7 [3]	120.6	120.5	118.7	118.1	123.1
J	53.8	55.4	52.2	53.7	54.7 [3]	59.9	65.2	70.2	70.8	68.1
K	175.7	175.5	180.7	190.2	198.8 [3]	216.6	233.9	246.3	248.7	254.0
L	98.5	91.3	93.4	84.5	114.5 [3]	116.0	128.7	136.6	138.1	132.7
M	125.4	129.7	137.3	146.7	155.6 [3]	162.8	165.8	166.0	169.6	175.4
N	141.1	142.4	158.0	172.8	177.6 [3]	181.1	188.7	196.2	203.5	207.8
O	80.1	86.2	88.7	92.2	91.3 [3]	94.7	102.2	92.4	91.1	99.9
P	8.0	8.6	7.3	6.6	2.6 [3]	2.6	2.6	3.3	3.7	2.2
Q	0.7	0.9	0.9	1.0	.	.	.	.	.	.
X	3.8	7.9	4.0	2.2	3.3 [3]	3.9	5.2	8.2	10.7	11.8
Men - Hommes - Hombres										
ISIC 3 - CITI 3 - CIIU 3										
Total	956.6	972.7	993.9	1 025.1	1 056.8 [3]	1 095.6	1 120.1	1 146.3	1 165.0	1 164.9
A	107.5	103.4	112.6	113.6	107.5 [3]	102.0	98.3	100.4	103.7	100.1
B	3.6	3.6	3.1	2.9	3.5 [3]	2.8	2.1	1.3	1.9	2.1
C	3.1	3.3	3.0	3.1	2.8 [3]	3.7	3.6	4.1	4.4	3.6
D	195.8	197.1	205.7	210.2	203.1 [3]	208.7	206.3	203.4	201.6	194.7
E	7.1	6.3	7.1	7.3	6.6 [3]	7.4	5.9	6.0	7.0	9.7
F	97.9	107.1	100.7	106.1	125.5 [3]	136.3	144.6	162.5	164.4	158.9
G	169.4	171.6	170.6	173.3	186.6 [3]	194.3	193.5	196.0	197.8	201.6
H	33.2	35.7	37.0	43.2	35.6 [3]	33.3	35.7	33.1	39.9	40.3
I	75.1	77.4	78.6	77.8	79.5 [3]	84.2	83.8	80.8	84.6	86.7
J	23.1	23.6	19.9	22.6	23.5 [3]	24.9	28.1	32.6	32.7	29.7
K	94.4	94.4	100.4	104.9	109.0 [3]	120.9	129.4	133.6	129.9	134.0
L	48.2	46.0	44.3	42.0	56.7 [3]	56.2	63.8	63.8	67.2	63.4
M	34.3	34.8	38.9	44.0	45.5 [3]	45.7	47.8	49.4	50.3	48.1
N	25.8	25.2	28.6	29.5	28.8 [3]	32.9	31.1	33.8	32.1	36.6
O	35.2	37.8	40.4	42.4	40.4 [3]	40.3	42.9	40.6	40.9	48.0
P	0.8	0.9	0.6	0.5	- [3]	-	-	-	-	-
Q	0.4	0.5	0.3	0.6	- [3]	-	-	-	-	-
X	1.8	4.1	2.1	1.4	1.9 [3]	1.9	2.8	4.5	6.3	7.3
Women - Femmes - Mujeres										
ISIC 3 - CITI 3 - CIIU 3										
Total	793.7	806.3	829.5	851.7	898.8 [3]	928.5	964.6	988.4	1 009.5	1 023.2
A	52.5	46.6	48.8	47.7	48.2 [3]	47.9	47.5	50.3	49.7	49.3
B	0.5	0.5	0.8	0.7	- [3]	-	-	-	-	-
C	0.3	0.5	0.5	0.7	- [3]	-	-	-	-	-
D	83.4	84.4	83.4	80.5	81.8 [3]	86.6	80.6	77.2	77.6	83.3
E	1.8	2.3	3.0	2.5	2.2 [3]	2.2	2.5	2.3	1.8	2.3
F	11.4	11.2	11.4	14.7	15.2 [3]	16.6	18.1	22.6	20.9	20.2
G	131.9	139.4	143.5	143.5	163.3 [3]	162.4	168.0	172.4	179.9	185.6
H	53.4	57.2	57.4	63.7	60.3 [3]	61.0	64.0	64.0	68.3	60.7
I	35.4	33.5	33.8	35.6	34.2 [3]	36.4	36.7	37.9	33.4	36.4
J	30.7	31.8	32.3	31.1	31.2 [3]	35.1	37.1	37.6	38.1	38.4
K	81.3	81.1	80.2	85.4	89.9 [3]	95.7	104.6	112.7	118.8	120.0
L	50.3	45.3	49.1	42.5	57.9 [3]	59.8	64.8	72.8	70.9	69.2
M	91.1	94.9	98.5	102.7	110.1 [3]	117.1	118.0	116.6	119.3	127.2
N	115.2	117.2	129.4	143.3	148.8 [3]	148.1	157.6	162.3	171.4	171.2
O	44.9	48.5	48.3	49.8	50.9 [3]	54.4	59.3	51.8	50.2	51.9
P	7.2	7.7	6.6	6.1	2.3 [3]	2.4	2.4	2.9	3.4	2.1
Q	0.2	0.4	0.6	0.4	- [3]	-	-	-	-	-
X	2.0	3.7	2.0	0.8	1.5 [3]	2.0	2.3	3.7	4.4	4.5

Explanatory notes: see p. 77.

[1] Excl. armed forces. [2] Persons aged 15 years and over. [3] Methodology revised; data not strictly comparable.

Notes explicatives: voir p. 80.

[1] Non compris les forces armées. [2] Personnes âgées de 15 ans et plus. [3] Méthodologie révisée; les données ne sont pas strictement comparables.

Notas explicativas: véase p. 83.

[1] Excl. las fuerzas armadas. [2] Personas de 15 años y más. [3] Metodología revisada; los datos no son estrictamente comparables.

Total employment, by occupation — Emploi total, par profession — Empleo total, por ocupación

Thousands — Milliers — Millares

AFRICA-AFRIQUE-AFRICA

Botswana (BA) [1][2]

Total employment - Emploi total - Empleo total

Total - Total - Total
ISCO-88 - CITP-88 - CIUO-88

	1999	2000	2001	2002	2003	2004	2005	2006	2007	2008
Total	.	483.4	.	.	462.4	.	.	539.2	.	.
1	.	14.7	.	.	12.8	.	.	30.2	.	.
2	.	24.1	.	.	23.5	.	.	27.1	.	.
3	.	31.5	.	.	33.0	.	.	34.9	.	.
4	.	31.5	.	.	33.5	.	.	39.9	.	.
5	.	69.5	.	.	55.7	.	.	90.6	.	.
6	.	58.5	.	.	59.8	.	.	136.6	.	.
7	.	92.2	.	.	70.3	.	.	50.5	.	.
8	.	29.7	.	.	27.1	.	.	26.8	.	.
9	.	115.0	.	.	144.1	.	.	102.5	.	.
X	.	16.0	.	.	2.5	.	.	-	.	.

Men - Hommes - Hombres
ISCO-88 - CITP-88 - CIUO-88

	1999	2000	2001	2002	2003	2004	2005	2006	2007	2008
Total	.	269.4	.	.	245.4	.	.	281.8	.	.
1	.	9.5	.	.	8.6	.	.	21.0	.	.
2	.	14.3	.	.	13.8	.	.	14.7	.	.
3	.	12.1	.	.	13.8	.	.	13.0	.	.
4	.	10.2	.	.	7.7	.	.	12.1	.	.
5	.	30.0	.	.	22.3	.	.	31.6	.	.
6	.	28.5	.	.	39.5	.	.	78.9	.	.
7	.	67.9	.	.	43.3	.	.	33.6	.	.
8	.	26.4	.	.	25.4	.	.	24.0	.	.
9	.	60.2	.	.	68.7	.	.	52.8	.	.
X	.	10.3	.	.	2.5	.	.		.	.

Women - Femmes - Mujeres
ISCO-88 - CITP-88 - CIUO-88

	1999	2000	2001	2002	2003	2004	2005	2006	2007	2008
Total	.	214.0	.	.	217.0	.	.	257.4	.	.
1	.	5.2	.	.	4.2	.	.	9.2	.	.
2	.	9.8	.	.	9.7	.	.	12.4	.	.
3	.	19.3	.	.	19.2	.	.	21.9	.	.
4	.	21.3	.	.	25.9	.	.	27.8	.	.
5	.	39.6	.	.	33.4	.	.	59.0	.	.
6	.	30.1	.	.	20.3	.	.	57.7	.	.
7	.	24.3	.	.	27.0	.	.	16.9	.	.
8	.	3.3	.	.	1.7	.	.	2.8	.	.
9	.	55.4	.	.	75.4	.	.	49.7	.	.
X	.	5.8	.	.	-	.	.	-	.	.

Egypt (BA) [1][3][4]

Total employment - Emploi total - Empleo total

Total - Total - Total
ISCO-88 - CITP-88 - CIUO-88

	1999	2000	2001	2002	2003	2004	2005	2006	2007	2008
Total	16 750.2	17 203.3	17 556.7	17 856.2	18 118.6	18 717.4	19 341.7	20 443.6	21 723.8	.
1	1 661.1	1 672.1	1 794.2	1 998.5	2 009.5	1 976.8	1 723.3	1 593.9	1 780.3	
2	2 211.6	2 516.5	2 558.9	2 687.5	2 713.3	2 532.5	2 604.6	2 688.2	2 822.1	
3	1 359.5	1 404.4	1 633.4	1 648.4	1 630.0	1 714.1	1 700.3	1 790.9	1 971.9	
4	1 041.1	989.3	984.4	1 068.4	1 007.1	914.9	728.6	694.4	677.4	
5	1 720.2	1 675.8	1 777.2	1 778.4	1 702.1	1 711.9	1 888.2	2 053.6	2 074.6	
6	4 629.4	4 973.1	4 842.8	4 723.7	5 237.2	5 815.0	5 824.0	6 217.5	6 723.2	
7	2 501.6	2 432.5	2 418.9	2 399.6	2 246.8	2 305.5	2 758.4	3 104.7	3 335.1	
8	1 189.4	1 099.2	1 157.5	1 151.0	1 154.5	1 223.7	1 413.1	1 523.1	1 547.9	
9	435.2	440.4	389.1	400.5	418.1	523.0	677.8	742.9	765.2	
X	0.9	-	-	-	-	-	23.4	34.4	25.6	.

Men - Hommes - Hombres
ISCO-88 - CITP-88 - CIUO-88

	1999	2000	2001	2002	2003	2004	2005	2006	2007	2008
Total	13 611.0	13 958.5	14 361.1	14 550.7	14 651.7	14 936.4	15 592.6	16 559.4	17 089.5	.
1	1 491.9	1 503.0	1 626.7	1 818.6	1 838.1	1 818.7	1 543.7	1 421.2	1 583.0	
2	1 561.0	1 766.3	1 822.8	1 861.5	1 898.4	1 777.9	1 802.6	1 824.3	1 868.3	
3	909.3	998.0	1 097.7	1 112.3	1 134.0	1 200.2	1 164.2	1 210.8	1 296.1	
4	704.3	679.2	669.7	698.3	691.6	650.8	528.9	478.7	477.8	
5	1 460.7	1 502.9	1 527.6	1 532.0	1 520.1	1 542.6	1 726.5	1 871.0	1 857.6	
6	3 640.6	3 708.4	3 861.8	3 826.5	3 902.4	4 070.9	4 099.4	4 557.4	4 591.9	
7	2 333.4	2 334.4	2 272.3	2 235.2	2 164.0	2 213.6	2 700.4	3 030.4	3 219.4	
8	1 105.8	1 060.7	1 116.6	1 097.2	1 115.6	1 181.0	1 367.3	1 457.4	1 481.7	
9	403.0	405.6	365.7	369.0	387.5	480.7	638.4	680.8	693.4	
X	0.9	-	-	-	-	-	21.2	27.4	20.3	.

Explanatory notes: see p. 77.

[1] Excl. armed forces. [2] Persons aged 12 years and over. [3] Persons aged 15 to 64 years. [4] May and Nov.

Notes explicatives: voir p. 80.

[1] Non compris les forces armées. [2] Personnes âgées de 12 ans et plus. [3] Personnes âgées de 15 à 64 ans. [4] Mai et nov.

Notas explicativas: véase p. 83.

[1] Excl. las fuerzas armadas. [2] Personas de 12 años y más. [3] Personas de 15 a 64 años. [4] Mayo y nov.

EMPLOYMENT — EMPLOI — EMPLEO

Total employment, by occupation — Emploi total, par profession — Empleo total, por ocupación

	Thousands					Milliers				Millares
	1999	2000	2001	2002	2003	2004	2005	2006	2007	2008

Egypt (BA) [1] [2] [3] — Total employment - Emploi total - Empleo total

Women - Femmes - Mujeres
ISCO-88 - CITP-88 - CIUO-88

Total	3 139.2	3 244.8	3 195.6	3 305.5	3 466.9	3 781.0	3 749.1	3 884.2	4 634.3	.
1	169.2	169.1	167.5	179.9	171.4	158.1	179.6	172.7	197.8	.
2	650.6	750.2	736.1	826.0	814.9	754.6	802.0	863.9	953.8	.
3	450.2	406.4	535.7	536.1	496.0	513.9	536.1	580.1	675.8	.
4	336.8	310.1	314.7	370.1	315.5	264.1	199.7	215.7	199.6	.
5	259.5	172.9	249.6	246.4	182.0	169.3	161.7	182.6	217.0	.
6	988.8	1 264.7	981.0	897.2	1 334.8	1 744.1	1 724.6	1 660.1	2 131.3	.
7	168.2	98.1	146.6	164.4	82.8	91.9	58.0	74.3	115.7	.
8	83.6	38.5	40.9	53.8	38.9	42.7	45.8	65.7	66.2	.
9	32.2	34.8	23.4	31.5	30.6	42.3	39.4	62.1	71.8	.
X	-	-	-	-	-	-	2.2	7.0	5.3	.

Madagascar (B) [4] [5] — Total employment - Emploi total - Empleo total

Total - Total - Total
ISCO-88 - CITP-88 - CIUO-88

Total	.	.	.	.	.	.	9 570.4	.	.	.
1							21.2			
2							146.5			
3							57.8			
4							70.7			
5							442.6			
6							7 575.4			
7							491.5			
8							98.8			
9							628.3			
0							37.7			

Men - Hommes - Hombres
ISCO-88 - CITP-88 - CIUO-88

Total	.	.	.	.	.	.	4 841.8	.	.	.
1							16.5			
2							74.9			
3							41.2			
4							40.6			
5							165.3			
6							3 803.6			
7							275.6			
8							79.7			
9							315.1			
0							29.3			

Women - Femmes - Mujeres
ISCO-88 - CITP-88 - CIUO-88

Total	.	.	.	.	.	.	4 728.6	.	.	.
1							4.7			
2							71.6			
3							16.6			
4							30.1			
5							277.3			
6							3 771.8			
7							215.9			
8							19.1			
9							313.2			
0							8.4			

Maroc (BA) [6] — Total employment - Emploi total - Empleo total

Total - Total - Total
ISCO-88 - CITP-88 - CIUO-88

Total	.	.	.	.	.	9 821.9	9 913.3	9 927.7	10 056.2	10 189.3
1						73.0	79.1	109.7	93.4	94.5
2						114.2	114.3	159.0	153.9	167.6
3						354.1	351.8	440.7	428.1	429.3
4						770.3	780.5	839.4	889.2	900.0
5						739.0	747.6	700.8	717.6	741.2
6						4 451.7	4 461.9	4 236.1	4 165.8	4 101.1
7						1 592.3	1 614.5	1 589.2	1 613.5	1 764.1
8						288.2	298.6	326.5	330.4	361.8
9						1 436.2	1 464.2	1 522.6	1 660.7	1 625.5
X						2.9	1.0	3.7	3.7	4.1

Explanatory notes: see p. 77.

[1] Persons aged 15 to 64 years. [2] Excl. armed forces. [3] May and Nov. [4] Persons aged 6 years and over. [5] Excl. armed forces and conscripts. [6] Persons aged 15 years and over.

Notes explicatives: voir p. 80.

[1] Personnes âgées de 15 à 64 ans. [2] Non compris les forces armées. [3] Mai et nov. [4] Personnes âgées de 6 ans et plus. [5] Non compris les forces armées et les conscrits. [6] Personnes âgées de 15 ans et plus.

Notas explicativas: véase p. 83.

[1] Personas de 15 a 64 años. [2] Excl. las fuerzas armadas. [3] Mayo y nov. [4] Personas de 6 años y más. [5] Excl. las fuerzas armadas y los conscriptos. [6] Personas de 15 años y más.

Total employment, by occupation
Emploi total, par profession
Empleo total, por ocupación

	Thousands			Milliers				Millares		
	1999	2000	2001	2002	2003	2004	2005	2006	2007	2008
Maroc (BA) [1]					**Total employment - Emploi total - Empleo total**					
Men - Hommes - Hombres										
ISCO-88 - CITP-88 - CIUO-88										
Total	.	.	.	.	.	7 155.0	7 240.7	7 233.3	7 323.7	7 453.5
1	.	.	.	.	.	65.1	69.3	96.7	82.1	82.4
2	.	.	.	.	.	80.5	83.3	117.1	111.9	116.7
3	.	.	.	.	.	223.6	217.3	272.9	266.7	267.4
4	.	.	.	.	.	565.9	587.3	634.9	662.7	683.0
5	.	.	.	.	.	704.7	712.7	665.2	677.1	697.3
6	.	.	.	.	.	2 849.1	2 827.6	2 591.0	2 531.6	2 487.5
7	.	.	.	.	.	1 248.0	1 290.9	1 294.2	1 313.6	1 442.4
8	.	.	.	.	.	280.6	285.5	316.4	319.7	350.2
9	.	.	.	.	.	1 135.1	1 165.7	1 241.5	1 355.4	1 323.3
X	.	.	.	.	.	2.4	0.8	3.4	2.9	3.3
Women - Femmes - Mujeres										
ISCO-88 - CITP-88 - CIUO-88										
Total	.	.	.	.	.	2 666.9	2 672.6	2 694.4	2 732.6	2 735.8
1	.	.	.	.	.	7.9	9.8	13.0	11.3	12.1
2	.	.	.	.	.	33.6	31.0	41.9	42.0	50.9
3	.	.	.	.	.	130.5	134.4	167.7	161.4	161.9
4	.	.	.	.	.	204.4	192.9	204.5	226.5	217.1
5	.	.	.	.	.	34.3	34.9	35.6	40.5	43.9
6	.	.	.	.	.	1 602.5	1 634.3	1 645.1	1 634.2	1 613.5
7	.	.	.	.	.	344.3	323.6	295.0	299.9	321.7
8	.	.	.	.	.	7.6	13.1	10.2	10.7	11.6
9	.	.	.	.	.	301.2	298.5	281.1	305.3	302.2
X	.	.	.	.	.	0.6	0.1	0.4	0.8	0.9
Mauritius (BA) [2] [3]					**Total employment - Emploi total - Empleo total**					
Total - Total - Total										
ISCO-88 - CITP-88 - CIUO-88										
Total	.	.	.	.	.	487.0	490.4	499.1 |	502.1 [4]	519.0
1	.	.	.	.	.	15.7	13.8	14.4 |	14.8 [4]	14.7
2	.	.	.	.	.	16.0	16.5	18.0 |	17.7 [4]	18.1
3	.	.	.	.	.	44.3	45.1	45.4 |	45.6 [4]	49.2
4	.	.	.	.	.	44.2	43.5	45.0 |	46.0 [4]	49.8
5	.	.	.	.	.	81.5	90.8	93.0 |	93.4 [4]	96.9
6	.	.	.	.	.	19.6	20.0	20.1 |	18.5 [4]	22.1
7	.	.	.	.	.	94.5	93.1	93.4 |	96.6 [4]	98.1
8	.	.	.	.	.	66.0	65.6	63.6 |	64.7 [4]	64.7
9	.	.	.	.	.	104.0	101.4	104.9 |	101.8 [4]	103.3
X	.	.	.	.	.	1.2	0.6	1.3 |	3.0 [4]	2.1
Men - Hommes - Hombres										
ISCO-88 - CITP-88 - CIUO-88										
Total	.	.	.	.	.	327.9	329.1	332.5 |	335.0 [4]	341.0
1	.	.	.	.	.	12.5	10.4	12.2 |	11.8 [4]	11.3
2	.	.	.	.	.	10.3	10.5	11.8 |	11.5 [4]	11.5
3	.	.	.	.	.	25.3	24.7	24.7 |	23.3 [4]	25.6
4	.	.	.	.	.	18.2	17.4	18.1 |	18.8 [4]	19.9
5	.	.	.	.	.	54.1	60.4	59.3 |	58.1 [4]	59.3
6	.	.	.	.	.	16.1	15.5	16.0 |	14.5 [4]	16.8
7	.	.	.	.	.	82.2	80.2	80.6 |	84.1 [4]	85.1
8	.	.	.	.	.	43.7	45.0	43.5 |	47.5 [4]	47.3
9	.	.	.	.	.	64.4	64.5	65.3 |	63.2 [4]	62.7
X	.	.	.	.	.	1.1	0.5	1.0 |	2.2 [4]	1.5
Women - Femmes - Mujeres										
ISCO-88 - CITP-88 - CIUO-88										
Total	.	.	.	.	.	159.1	161.3	166.6 |	167.1 [4]	178.0
1	.	.	.	.	.	3.2	3.4	2.2 |	3.0 [4]	3.4
2	.	.	.	.	.	5.7	6.0	6.2 |	6.2 [4]	6.6
3	.	.	.	.	.	19.0	20.4	20.7 |	22.3 [4]	23.6
4	.	.	.	.	.	26.0	26.1	26.9 |	27.2 [4]	29.9
5	.	.	.	.	.	27.4	30.4	33.7 |	35.3 [4]	37.6
6	.	.	.	.	.	3.5	4.5	4.1 |	4.0 [4]	5.3
7	.	.	.	.	.	12.3	12.9	12.8 |	12.5 [4]	13.0
8	.	.	.	.	.	22.3	20.6	20.1 |	17.2 [4]	17.4
9	.	.	.	.	.	39.6	36.9	39.6 |	38.6 [4]	40.6
X	.	.	.	.	.	0.1	0.1	0.3 |	0.8 [4]	0.6

Explanatory notes: see p. 77.

[1] Persons aged 15 years and over. [2] Excl. armed forces. [3] Persons aged 16 years and over. [4] Prior to 2007: persons aged 15 years and over.

Notes explicatives: voir p. 80.

[1] Personnes âgées de 15 ans et plus. [2] Non compris les forces armées. [3] Personnes âgées de 16 ans et plus. [4] Avant 2006: personnes âgées de 15 ans et plus.

Notas explicativas: véase p. 83.

[1] Personas de 15 años y más. [2] Excl. las fuerzas armadas. [3] Personas de 16 años y más. [4] Antes de 2006: personas de 15 años y más.

	EMPLOYMENT		EMPLOI			EMPLEO

	Total employment, by occupation		Emploi total, par profession			Empleo total, por ocupación

	Thousands				Milliers				Millares	
1999	2000	2001	2002	2003	2004	2005	2006	2007	2008	

Namibia (BA) [1]

Total employment - Emploi total - Empleo total

Total - Total - Total
ISCO-88 - CITP-88 - CIUO-88

	1999	2000	2001	2002	2003	2004	2005	2006	2007	2008
Total		431.849				385.329				
1		7.897				10.754				
2		35.008				34.258				
3		24.357				20.154				
4		26.054				25.565				
5		59.073				52.671				
6		106.580				52.285				
7		61.063				56.203				
8		17.450				17.452				
9		86.378				112.216				
0		5.121				3.262				
X		2.868				0.509				

Men - Hommes - Hombres
ISCO-88 - CITP-88 - CIUO-88

	1999	2000	2001	2002	2003	2004	2005	2006	2007	2008
Total		226.828				216.651				
1		5.513				6.885				
2		15.097				15.214				
3		11.366				10.690				
4		7.997				6.978				
5		22.756				25.014				
6		53.783				28.565				
7		45.184				42.494				
8		16.722				16.323				
9		42.513				61.428				
0		4.344				2.654				
X		1.553				0.406				

Women - Femmes - Mujeres
ISCO-88 - CITP-88 - CIUO-88

	1999	2000	2001	2002	2003	2004	2005	2006	2007	2008
Total		205.021				168.678				
1		2.384				3.869				
2		19.911				19.044				
3		12.991				9.464				
4		18.057				18.587				
5		36.316				27.657				
6		52.797				23.720				
7		15.879				13.709				
8		0.727				1.129				
9		43.865				50.788				
0		0.777				0.608				
X		1.315				0.103				

South Africa (BA) [2] [3]

Total employment - Emploi total - Empleo total

Total - Total - Total
ISCO-88 - CITP-88 - CIUO-88

	1999	2000	2001	2002	2003	2004	2005	2006	2007	2008
Total		12 238	11 181	11 296	11 424	11 643	12 301	12 800	13 234	13 713
1		574	664	731	822	910	857	873	884	1 021
2		587	486	502	544	458	589	601	853	752
3		1 133	1 176	1 207	1 159	1 149	1 196	1 231	1 252	1 473
4		1 056	1 091	1 110	1 156	1 169	1 188	1 246	1 206	1 456
5		1 470	1 429	1 244	1 361	1 453	1 607	1 638	1 595	1 766
6		1 203	521	706	341	329	302	432	342	107
7		1 587	1 529	1 460	1 454	1 538	1 744	1 921	1 822	1 915
8		1 218	1 127	1 156	1 145	1 113	1 127	1 118	1 262	1 179
9		3 351	3 134	3 140	3 425	3 500	3 670	3 727	3 980	4 044
X		59	24	42	17	23	21	14	38	1

Men - Hommes - Hombres
ISCO-88 - CITP-88 - CIUO-88

	1999	2000	2001	2002	2003	2004	2005	2006	2007	2008
Total									7 554	7 672
1									585	715
2									405	402
3									544	657
4									385	454
5									918	920
6									193	78
7									1 527	1 628
8									1 065	1 005
9									1 910	1 811
X									21	1

Explanatory notes: see p. 77.

[1] Persons aged 15 to 69 years. [2] Persons aged 15 to 64 years. [3] Prior to 2008: persons aged 15 years and over; September of each year.

Notes explicatives: voir p. 80.

[1] Personnes âgées de 15 à 69 ans. [2] Personnes âgées de 15 à 64 ans. [3] Avant 2008: personnes agées de 15 ans et plus; septembre de chaque année.

Notas explicativas: véase p. 83.

[1] Personas de 15 a 69 años. [2] Personas de 15 a 64 años. [3] Antes de 2008: personas de 15 años y más; Septiembre de cada año.

Total employment, by occupation — Emploi total, par profession — Empleo total, por ocupación

Thousands — Milliers — Millares

	1999	2000	2001	2002	2003	2004	2005	2006	2007	2008

South Africa (BA) [1] [2] Total employment - Emploi total - Empleo total

Women - Femmes - Mujeres
ISCO-88 - CITP-88 - CIUO-88

	1999	2000	2001	2002	2003	2004	2005	2006	2007	2008
Total	.	.	.	.	.	.	.	.	5 668	6 041
1	.	.	.	.	.	.	.	.	298	306
2	.	.	.	.	.	.	.	.	445	350
3	.	.	.	.	.	.	.	.	708	815
4	.	.	.	.	.	.	.	.	815	1 002
5	.	.	.	.	.	.	.	.	677	846
6	.	.	.	.	.	.	.	.	149	29
7	.	.	.	.	.	.	.	.	295	286
8	.	.	.	.	.	.	.	.	196	174
9	.	.	.	.	.	.	.	.	2 069	2 233
X	.	.	.	.	.	.	.	.	17	-

Tanzania, United Republic of (BA) [3] Total employment - Emploi total - Empleo total

Total - Total - Total
ISCO-88 - CITP-88 - CIUO-88

	1999	2000	2001	2002	2003	2004	2005	2006	2007	2008
Total	.	.	.	.	.	.	.	17 944.6	.	.
1	.	.	.	.	.	.	.	31.2	.	.
2	.	.	.	.	.	.	.	111.5	.	.
3	.	.	.	.	.	.	.	318.0	.	.
4	.	.	.	.	.	.	.	72.4	.	.
5	.	.	.	.	.	.	.	1 789.3	.	.
6	.	.	.	.	.	.	.	13 110.2	.	.
7	.	.	.	.	.	.	.	874.5	.	.
8	.	.	.	.	.	.	.	236.2	.	.
9	.	.	.	.	.	.	.	1 401.1	.	.

Men - Hommes - Hombres
ISCO-88 - CITP-88 - CIUO-88

	1999	2000	2001	2002	2003	2004	2005	2006	2007	2008
Total	.	.	.	.	.	.	.	8 779.8	.	.
1	.	.	.	.	.	.	.	26.0	.	.
2	.	.	.	.	.	.	.	72.6	.	.
3	.	.	.	.	.	.	.	193.5	.	.
4	.	.	.	.	.	.	.	35.7	.	.
5	.	.	.	.	.	.	.	935.3	.	.
6	.	.	.	.	.	.	.	6 055.3	.	.
7	.	.	.	.	.	.	.	673.6	.	.
8	.	.	.	.	.	.	.	205.7	.	.
9	.	.	.	.	.	.	.	582.1	.	.

Women - Femmes - Mujeres
ISCO-88 - CITP-88 - CIUO-88

	1999	2000	2001	2002	2003	2004	2005	2006	2007	2008
Total	.	.	.	.	.	.	.	9 164.7	.	.
1	.	.	.	.	.	.	.	5.1	.	.
2	.	.	.	.	.	.	.	39.0	.	.
3	.	.	.	.	.	.	.	124.5	.	.
4	.	.	.	.	.	.	.	36.7	.	.
5	.	.	.	.	.	.	.	854.1	.	.
6	.	.	.	.	.	.	.	7 054.9	.	.
7	.	.	.	.	.	.	.	201.0	.	.
8	.	.	.	.	.	.	.	30.5	.	.
9	.	.	.	.	.	.	.	819.0	.	.

AMERICA-AMÉRIQUE-AMERICA

Argentina (BA) [4] [5] [6] Total employment - Emploi total - Empleo total

Total - Total - Total
ISCO-88 - CITP-88 - CIUO-88

	1999	2000	2001	2002	2003	2004	2005	2006	2007	2008
Total	8 285.2	8 261.7	8 143.4	8 016.1	8 956.2 [7]	9 415.0	9 638.7	10 040.5 [8]	.	.
1	509.6	550.5	507.8	420.4	27.3 [7]	33.7	32.3	19.0 [8]	.	.
2	495.2	469.9	481.0	496.0	531.6 [7]	437.9	388.8	399.9 [8]	.	.
3	1 309.4	1 275.9	1 272.5	1 286.7	1 322.5 [7]	1 272.8	1 373.1	1 359.5 [8]	.	.
4	742.4	761.7	765.3	714.6	818.4 [7]	937.1	1 002.4	1 154.9 [8]	.	.
5	1 360.6	1 339.1	1 349.0	1 367.3	1 990.2 [7]	1 923.5	1 800.7	1 946.4 [8]	.	.
6	97.2	96.3	105.3	140.7	55.1 [7]	54.9	34.2	28.8 [8]	.	.
7	1 257.1	1 216.6	1 118.1	1 101.3	1 278.1 [7]	1 395.6	1 386.7	1 465.1 [8]	.	.
8	668.0	648.7	661.0	603.9	637.3 [7]	827.8	851.2	859.9 [8]	.	.
9	1 775.6	1 810.8	1 811.3	1 804.6	1 746.4 [7]	1 811.9	1 915.9	1 945.7 [8]	.	.
0	22.2	22.5	28.0	25.2	26.1 [7]	28.5	66.7	77.9 [8]	.	.
X	47.8	69.7	44.2	55.4	523.1 [7]	691.4	786.7	783.4 [8]	.	.

Explanatory notes: see p. 77.

[1] Persons aged 15 to 64 years. [2] Prior to 2008: persons aged 15 years and over; September of each year. [3] Persons aged 15 years and over. [4] Persons aged 10 years and over. [5] 31 Urban agglomerations. [6] Second semester. [7] Methodology revised; data not strictly comparable; Prior to 2003: May and October. [8] Prior to 2006: 28 urban agglomerations.

Notes explicatives: voir p. 80.

[1] Personnes âgées de 15 à 64 ans. [2] Avant 2008: personnes agées de 15 ans et plus; septembre de chaque année. [3] Personnes âgées de 15 ans et plus. [4] Personnes âgées de 10 ans et plus. [5] 31 agglomérations urbaines. [6] Second semestre. [7] Méthodologie révisée; les données ne sont pas strictement comparables; Avant 2003: mai et octobre. [8] Avant 2006: 28 agglomérations urbaines.

Notas explicativas: véase p. 83.

[1] Personas de 15 a 64 años. [2] Antes de 2008: personas de 15 años y más; Septiembre de cada año. [3] Personas de 15 años y más. [4] Personas de 10 años y más. [5] 31 aglomerados úrbanos. [6] Segundo semestre. [7] Metodología revisada; los datos no son estrictamente comparables; antes de 2003: mayo y octubre. [8] Antes de 2006: 28 aglomerados úrbanos

EMPLOYMENT   EMPLOI   EMPLEO

Total employment, by occupation   Emploi total, par profession   Empleo total, por ocupación

Thousands / Milliers / Millares

Argentina (BA) [1][2][3] — Total employment - Emploi total - Empleo total

Men - Hommes - Hombres
ISCO-88 - CITP-88 - CIUO-88

	1999	2000	2001	2002	2003[4]	2004	2005	2006[5]	2007	2008
Total	4 971.4	4 942.0	4 832.4	4 653.6	5 150.9	5 446.9	5 557.3	5 786.7	.	.
1	373.3	399.7	369.9	312.1	19.4	21.7	21.7	14.6		
2	274.9	257.7	252.3	261.6	270.3	224.3	189.7	188.8		
3	620.2	599.5	599.2	581.2	617.8	590.0	642.5	617.6		
4	318.4	327.9	338.2	311.5	362.8	418.0	435.9	510.9		
5	726.2	732.7	715.2	724.1	1 099.3	959.9	898.4	1 027.1		
6	84.1	84.1	95.7	116.1	34.9	32.4	24.1	24.0		
7	1 107.0	1 071.0	977.3	905.1	1 052.7	1 180.0	1 194.7	1 279.8		
8	624.2	611.0	622.5	564.1	533.1	690.1	709.3	699.7		
9	791.8	797.3	814.3	822.1	774.9	826.6	873.6	847.5		
0	21.5	21.4	26.0	23.5	25.7	27.4	39.7	56.8		
X	29.8	39.7	21.9	32.2	359.9	476.6	527.8	519.9		

Women - Femmes - Mujeres
ISCO-88 - CITP-88 - CIUO-88

	1999	2000	2001	2002	2003[4]	2004	2005	2006[5]	2007	2008
Total	3 313.8	3 319.8	3 310.9	3 362.5	3 805.3	3 968.0	4 081.4	4 253.8	.	.
1	136.3	150.8	138.0	108.3	7.9	12.0	10.6	4.4		
2	220.3	212.2	228.7	234.4	261.3	213.6	199.1	211.1		
3	689.2	676.4	673.3	705.5	704.6	682.8	730.8	742.0		
4	424.0	433.7	427.1	403.2	455.6	519.1	566.4	643.9		
5	634.4	606.4	633.7	643.2	890.9	963.6	902.3	919.3		
6	13.0	12.2	9.5	24.6	20.2	22.4	10.1	4.9		
7	150.2	145.6	140.8	196.1	225.5	215.5	192.0	185.4		
8	43.8	37.7	38.5	39.8	104.1	137.7	141.9	160.2		
9	983.7	1 013.4	997.0	982.5	971.5	985.3	1 042.2	1 098.2		
0	0.7	1.2	2.1	1.7	0.3	1.1	27.0	21.1		
X	18.0	30.0	22.3	23.2	163.2	214.8	258.9	263.5		

Aruba (BA) [6][7] — Total employment - Emploi total - Empleo total

Total - Total - Total
ISCO-88 - CITP-88 - CIUO-88

	1999	2000	2001	2002	2003	2004	2005	2006	2007	2008
Total	.	.	.	.	.	.	.	.	51.605	.
1									5.595	
2									3.307	
3									5.961	
4									8.918	
5									9.751	
6									0.349	
7									6.827	
8									2.258	
9									8.550	
0									0.089	
X									-	

Men - Hommes - Hombres
ISCO-88 - CITP-88 - CIUO-88

	2007
Total	27.210
1	3.343
2	1.675
3	3.374
4	2.763
5	3.743
6	0.251
7	6.191
8	2.158
9	3.622
0	0.089
X	-

Women - Femmes - Mujeres
ISCO-88 - CITP-88 - CIUO-88

	2007
Total	24.396
1	2.252
2	1.631
3	2.586
4	6.155
5	6.008
6	0.098
7	0.636
8	0.100
9	4.928
0	
X	-

Explanatory notes: see p. 77.

[1] Persons aged 10 years and over. [2] 31 Urban agglomerations. [3] Second semester. [4] Methodology revised; data not strictly comparable; Prior to 2003: May and October. [5] Prior to 2006: 28 urban agglomerations. [6] Persons aged 15 years and over. [7] Oct.

Notes explicatives: voir p. 80.

[1] Personnes âgées de 10 ans et plus. [2] 31 agglomérations urbaines. [3] Second semestre. [4] Méthodologie révisée; les données ne sont pas strictement comparables; Avant 2003: mai et octobre. [5] Avant 2006: 28 agglomérations urbaines. [6] Personnes âgées de 15 ans et plus. [7] Oct.

Notas explicativas: véase p. 83.

[1] Personas de 10 años y más. [2] 31 aglomerados úrbanos. [3] Segundo semestre. [4] Metodología revisada; los datos no son estrictamente comparables; antes de 2003: mayo y octubre. [5] Antes de 2006: 28 aglomerados úrbanos [6] Personas de 15 años y más. [7] Oct.

<table>
<tr><td colspan="3">Total employment,
by occupation</td><td colspan="3">Emploi total,
par profession</td><td colspan="3">Empleo total,
por ocupación</td></tr>
</table>

	Thousands				Milliers				Millares		
	1999	2000	2001	2002	2003	2004	2005	2006	2007	2008	

Bahamas (BA) [1] [2] [3]   Total employment - Emploi total - Empleo total

Total - Total - Total
ISCO-88 - CITP-88 - CIUO-88

	1999	2000	2001	2002	2003	2004	2005	2006	2007	2008
Total	145.35	.	153.31	152.69	154.97	158.34	160.53	166.51 [4]	171.49	.
1	9.32	.	14.16	14.98	12.86	12.61	12.77	14.57 [4]	16.69	.
2-3	24.32	.	29.86	28.32	26.25	29.59	25.99	30.65 [4]	33.20	.
4	21.87	.	20.27	21.38	20.25	20.30	22.11	22.17 [4]	21.49	.
5	28.16	.	28.68	30.26	33.59	33.54	33.87	35.19 [4]	33.27	.
6	5.46	.	4.26	5.12	2.97	4.03	3.12	3.69 [4]	3.48	.
7-8	28.84	.	30.16	27.86	28.77	29.13	32.18	33.82 [4]	34.39	.
9	26.32	.	25.30	23.85	29.61	28.87	29.79	25.75 [4]	28.11	.
X	1.08	.	0.64	0.94	0.69	0.30	0.71	0.68 [4]	0.88	.

Men - Hommes - Hombres
ISCO-88 - CITP-88 - CIUO-88

	1999	2000	2001	2002	2003	2004	2005	2006	2007	2008
Total	77.25	.	79.08	78.41	79.14	81.78	82.79	85.97 [4]	89.61	.
1	6.15	.	8.51	8.92	7.67	7.12	6.90	8.54 [4]	9.47	.
2-3	10.75	.	11.81	11.04	10.19	11.87	10.36	11.67 [4]	12.18	.
4	4.06	.	2.86	3.70	3.17	2.57	3.60	3.77 [4]	3.49	.
5	10.71	.	11.66	12.03	12.70	12.47	12.56	13.14 [4]	14.41	.
6	5.25	.	4.04	4.61	2.77	3.84	3.03	3.47 [4]	3.42	.
7-8	26.07	.	27.13	25.67	26.07	26.62	28.96	30.52 [4]	30.98	.
9	13.52	.	12.90	11.92	16.09	17.01	17.03	14.49 [4]	15.21	.
X	0.76	.	0.18	0.54	0.49	0.21	0.34	0.38 [4]	0.47	.

Women - Femmes - Mujeres
ISCO-88 - CITP-88 - CIUO-88

	1999	2000	2001	2002	2003	2004	2005	2006	2007	2008
Total	68.11	.	74.23	74.28	75.83	76.56	77.74	80.54 [4]	81.89	.
1	3.17	.	5.66	6.06	5.19	5.40	5.85	6.03 [4]	7.22	.
2-3	13.58	.	18.05	17.28	16.06	17.72	15.63	18.99 [4]	21.02	.
4	17.81	.	17.41	17.68	17.08	17.73	18.51	18.40 [4]	18.01	.
5	17.45	.	17.02	18.24	20.89	21.08	21.31	22.05 [4]	18.86	.
6	0.21	.	0.22	0.51	0.20	0.19	0.09	0.22 [4]	0.06	.
7-8	2.78	.	3.03	2.20	2.70	2.51	3.26	3.30 [4]	3.41	.
9	12.80	.	12.40	11.93	13.52	11.86	12.77	11.26 [4]	12.91	.
X	0.32	.	0.46	0.40	0.20	0.10	0.37	0.30 [4]	0.41	.

Bermuda (CA) [5] [6]   All persons engaged - Effectif occupé - Efectivo ocupado

Total - Total - Total
ISCO-68 - CITP-68 - CIUO-68

	1999	2000	2001	2002	2003	2004	2005	2006	2007	2008
Total	37.849	38.017	37.597	37.815	37.686	38.363	38.947	39.686	39.851	.
0/1	7.032	7.046	7.178	7.415	7.501	7.801	7.877	8.262	8.487	.
2	4.763	4.852	5.084	5.220	5.325	5.442	5.631	5.942	6.113	.
3	7.843	8.107	7.540	7.449	7.251	7.246	7.290	7.376	7.438	.
4	2.771	2.848	2.637	2.585	2.482	2.456	2.315	2.311	2.340	.
5	7.809	7.485	7.380	7.359	7.177	7.178	7.417	7.183	7.089	.
6	0.907	0.902	0.903	0.931	0.929	0.927	0.949	0.961	0.952	.
7/8/9	6.724	6.777	6.875	6.856	7.021	7.313	7.468	7.651	7.432	.

Men - Hommes - Hombres
ISCO-68 - CITP-68 - CIUO-68

	1999	2000	2001	2002	2003	2004	2005	2006	2007	2008
Total	19.197	19.310	19.301	19.411	19.520	19.937	20.257	20.730	20.727	.
0/1	3.101	3.144	3.208	3.290	3.349	3.466	3.498	3.656	3.713	.
2	2.795	2.838	2.962	2.987	3.022	3.058	3.141	3.351	3.469	.
3	1.252	1.333	1.160	1.123	1.119	1.122	1.128	1.179	1.233	.
4	1.034	1.071	1.004	0.978	0.937	0.907	0.872	0.892	0.894	.
5	3.966	3.838	3.809	3.850	3.775	3.827	3.860	3.696	3.688	.
6	0.851	0.852	0.851	0.884	0.889	0.888	0.904	0.921	0.911	.
7/8/9	6.198	6.234	6.307	6.299	6.429	6.669	6.854	7.035	6.819	.

Women - Femmes - Mujeres
ISCO-68 - CITP-68 - CIUO-68

	1999	2000	2001	2002	2003	2004	2005	2006	2007	2008
Total	18.652	18.707	18.296	18.404	18.166	18.426	18.690	18.956	19.124	.
0/1	3.931	3.902	3.970	4.125	4.152	4.335	4.379	4.606	4.774	.
2	1.968	2.014	2.122	2.233	2.303	2.384	2.490	2.591	2.644	.
3	6.591	6.774	6.380	6.326	6.132	6.124	6.162	6.197	6.205	.
4	1.737	1.777	1.633	1.607	1.545	1.549	1.443	1.419	1.446	.
5	3.843	3.647	3.571	3.509	3.402	3.351	3.557	3.487	3.401	.
6	0.056	0.050	0.052	0.047	0.040	0.039	0.045	0.040	0.041	.
7/8/9	0.526	0.543	0.568	0.557	0.592	0.644	0.614	0.616	0.613	.

Explanatory notes: see p. 77.

[1] Excl. armed forces. [2] Persons aged 15 years and over. [3] April of each year. [4] May. [5] Excl. unpaid family workers. [6] Aug. of each year.

Notes explicatives: voir p. 80.

[1] Non compris les forces armées. [2] Personnes âgées de 15 ans et plus. [3] Avril de chaque année. [4] Mai. [5] Non compris les travailleurs familiaux non rémunérés. [6] Août de chaque année.

Notas explicativas: véase p. 83.

[1] Excl. las fuerzas armadas. [2] Personas de 15 años y más. [3] Abril de cada año. [4] Mayo. [5] Excl. los trabajadores familiares no remunerados. [6] Agosto de cada año.

EMPLOYMENT — EMPLOI — EMPLEO

Total employment, by occupation — Emploi total, par profession — Empleo total, por ocupación

Thousands — Milliers — Millares

Bolivia (BA) [1][2] — Total employment - Emploi total - Empleo total

Total - Total - Total
ISCO-88 - CITP-88 - CIUO-88

	1999	2000	2001	2002	2003	2004	2005	2006	2007	2008
Total	3 637.9	3 637.0	3 884.3	3 824.9	.	4 194.8	4 257.2	4 550.3	4 672.4	.
1	66.7	46.9	35.8	54.2	.	50.4	63.3	77.1	87.1	.
2	149.0	107.1	196.7	179.3	.	163.0	220.9	284.7	312.5	.
3	186.3	241.4	150.1	145.6	.	194.4	233.2	241.9	269.5	.
4	115.3	116.7	131.8	96.3	.	103.1	132.3	143.6	160.7	.
5	580.6	576.3	610.8	579.3	.	735.0	647.5	693.5	693.9	.
6	1 404.5	1 347.8	1 182.2	1 537.1	.	1 405.2	1 575.9	1 753.8	1 587.5	.
7	668.3	626.0	589.0	644.2	.	825.6	708.7	705.6	758.7	.
8	169.5	178.0	198.6	185.8	.	213.5	256.1	235.3	287.6	.
9	290.4	390.2	786.3	400.5	.	501.5	415.1	413.0	508.9	.
0	7.3	6.5	3.0	-	.	3.2	4.2	1.7	6.0	.

Men - Hommes - Hombres
ISCO-88 - CITP-88 - CIUO-88

	1999	2000	2001	2002	2003	2004	2005	2006	2007	2008
Total	2 000.5	2 032.2	2 128.4	2 160.2	.	2 283.0	2 356.0	2 505.6	2 577.0	.
1	47.9	28.8	29.5	43.6	.	35.0	43.1	55.8	61.9	.
2	80.9	66.9	100.1	90.3	.	79.8	128.5	142.2	169.5	.
3	126.6	143.1	105.5	98.6	.	133.5	139.0	157.1	177.0	.
4	52.1	50.6	52.4	44.7	.	44.9	49.5	52.5	74.7	.
5	151.6	168.3	172.6	163.4	.	208.3	190.8	212.8	220.6	.
6	752.0	765.6	716.0	892.6	.	751.1	837.8	950.3	802.8	.
7	505.6	496.0	449.0	466.9	.	622.8	538.7	530.4	591.5	.
8	168.6	175.2	195.8	182.2	.	206.2	252.9	232.4	285.1	.
9	107.9	131.3	304.4	175.3	.	198.3	171.7	170.4	188.0	.
0	7.3	6.5	3.0	2.6	.	3.2	4.2	1.7	6.0	.

Women - Femmes - Mujeres
ISCO-88 - CITP-88 - CIUO-88

	1999	2000	2001	2002	2003	2004	2005	2006	2007	2008
Total	1 637.4	1 604.9	1 755.8	1 664.8	.	1 911.7	1 901.1	2 044.7	2 095.4	.
1	18.8	18.1	6.3	10.6	.	15.5	20.2	21.4	25.2	.
2	68.2	40.2	96.6	89.0	.	83.2	92.4	142.5	143.0	.
3	59.7	98.3	44.5	47.0	.	60.9	94.1	84.8	92.5	.
4	63.2	66.1	79.4	51.6	.	58.2	82.8	91.1	86.0	.
5	429.0	408.1	438.3	415.9	.	526.7	456.7	480.7	473.3	.
6	652.6	582.3	466.2	644.5	.	654.1	738.1	803.5	784.7	.
7	162.7	130.0	140.1	177.3	.	202.7	170.0	175.2	167.2	.
8	0.9	2.8	2.8	3.7	.	7.2	3.2	2.8	2.5	.
9	182.5	259.0	481.8	225.2	.	303.2	243.5	242.6	321.0	.
0	-		-			-	-	-		.

Brasil (BA) [1][3] — Total employment - Emploi total - Empleo total

Total - Total - Total
ISCO-88 - CITP-88 - CIUO-88

	1999	2000	2001	2002	2003	2004	2005	2006	2007	2008
Total	.	.	.	78 959	80 163	84 596	87 189	89 318	90 786	.
1	.	.	.	4 047	3 993	4 075	4 459	4 741	4 482	.
2	.	.	.	4 684	4 962	5 102	5 201	5 846	6 061	.
3	.	.	.	5 703	5 685	5 957	6 447	6 572	6 987	.
4	.	.	.	6 115	6 422	6 885	6 848	7 228	7 469	.
5	.	.	.	23 101	23 641	25 024	12 326	12 992	13 579	.
6	.	.	.	16 124	16 467	17 607	17 397	16 848	16 185	.
7	.	.	.	15 072	15 014	15 721	10 302	10 201	10 827	.
8	.	.	.	1 718	1 694	1 828	8 076	8 380	8 491	.
9	.	.	.	1 625	1 588	1 687	15 474	15 839	16 073	.
0	.	.	.	628	659	654	631	665	596	.
X	.	.	.	140	39	55	25	6	36	.

Men - Hommes - Hombres
ISCO-88 - CITP-88 - CIUO-88

	1999	2000	2001	2002	2003	2004	2005	2006	2007	2008
Total	.	.	.	46 334	46 935	49 242	50 494	51 400	52 363	.
1	.	.	.	2 728	2 641	2 694	2 879	3 073	2 865	.
2	.	.	.	1 986	2 039	2 076	2 116	2 408	2 507	.
3	.	.	.	2 982	3 000	3 197	3 390	3 489	3 723	.
4	.	.	.	2 559	2 729	2 843	2 843	2 958	3 087	.
5	.	.	.	9 218	9 448	9 831	5 375	5 579	5 765	.
6	.	.	.	10 768	11 139	11 956	11 560	11 178	10 890	.
7	.	.	.	12 556	12 487	13 023	8 911	8 921	9 488	.
8	.	.	.	1 263	1 238	1 308	5 909	6 106	6 248	.
9	.	.	.	1 603	1 561	1 660	6 897	7 053	7 198	.
0	.	.	.	606	634	622	600	631	567	.
X	.	.	.	66	21	31	12	3	24	.

Explanatory notes: see p. 77.

[1] Persons aged 10 years and over. [2] Excl. conscripts. [3] Sep. of each year. [4] Prior to 2003: Excl. rural population of Rondõnia, Acre, Amazonas, Roraima, Pará and Amapá.

Notes explicatives: voir p. 80.

[1] Personnes âgées de 10 ans et plus. [2] Non compris les conscrits. [3] Sept. de chaque année. [4] Avant 2003: Non compris la population rurale de Rondõnia, Acre, Amazonas, Roraima, Pará et Amapá.

Notas explicativas: véase p. 83.

[1] Personas de 10 años y más. [2] Excl. los conscriptos. [3] Sept. de cada año. [4] Antes de 2003: Excl. la población rural de Rondonia, Acre, Amazonas, Roraima, Pará y Amapá.

Total employment, by occupation — **Emploi total, par profession** — **Empleo total, por ocupación**

Thousands — Milliers — Millares

	1999	2000	2001	2002	2003	2004	2005	2006	2007	2008
Brasil (BA) [1][2]				Total employment - Emploi total - Empleo total						
Women - Femmes - Mujeres										
ISCO-88 - CITP-88 - CIUO-88										
Total	.	.	.	32 625	33 228 [3]	35 354	36 696	37 918	38 423	.
1				1 319	1 352 [3]	1 381	1 580	1 668	1 617	
2				2 698	2 923 [3]	3 026	3 085	3 438	3 554	
3				2 721	2 686 [3]	2 760	3 057	3 083	3 264	
4				3 556	3 694 [3]	4 042	4 005	4 270	4 381	
5				13 884	14 194 [3]	15 193	6 952	7 414	7 815	
6				5 357	5 328 [3]	5 651	5 837	5 670	5 295	
7				2 516	2 527 [3]	2 698	1 391	1 280	1 338	
8				455	456 [3]	520	2 167	2 274	2 243	
9				22	27 [3]	27	8 578	8 785	8 875	
0				23	25 [3]	32	31	34	29	
X				74	18 [3]	24	13	3	12	
Canada (BA) [4][5][6]				Total employment - Emploi total - Empleo total						
Total - Total - Total										
ISCO-88 - CITP-88 - CIUO-88										
Total	14 406.7	14 758.6	14 946.7	15 307.9	15 665.1	15 949.7	16 169.7	16 484.3	16 866.4	17 125.8
1	1 389.6	1 439.9	1 360.3	1 373.3	1 394.2	1 466.3	1 482.1	1 534.5	1 533.2	1 597.0
2	2 304.0	2 335.8	2 416.6	2 472.6	2 461.2	2 513.6	2 736.7	2 821.4	2 930.8	3 008.5
3	1 961.5	2 054.4	2 126.4	2 178.4	2 279.9	2 287.7	2 394.6	2 478.5	2 562.8	2 653.4
4	1 981.3	2 035.8	2 114.2	2 110.9	2 170.1	2 246.4	2 227.9	2 267.7	2 278.5	2 288.7
5	2 049.4	2 088.6	2 172.3	2 247.2	2 296.3	2 338.6	2 285.0	2 335.7	2 458.1	2 482.3
6	454.8	430.7	387.1	381.1	395.6	386.7	392.2	393.0	386.0	361.7
7	1 513.2	1 518.7	1 546.2	1 629.6	1 658.9	1 679.8	1 663.5	1 657.9	1 717.8	1 801.2
8	1 548.3	1 625.7	1 607.3	1 654.4	1 690.8	1 682.8	1 612.2	1 591.3	1 572.7	1 529.8
9	1 182.3	1 206.5	1 191.6	1 232.9	1 285.6	1 317.3	1 346.9	1 376.5	1 395.9	1 374.1
0	4.7	4.5	6.0	6.1	6.4	4.1	5.9	4.4	3.7	2.3
Men - Hommes - Hombres										
ISCO-88 - CITP-88 - CIUO-88										
Total	7 797.2	7 970.0	8 035.2	8 181.5	8 344.3	8 479.6	8 594.7	8 727.1	8 888.9	9 021.3
1	900.8	929.1	884.9	905.6	896.2	931.4	950.1	978.3	967.1	1 022.2
2	1 126.9	1 132.7	1 159.1	1 187.2	1 168.4	1 190.2	1 289.2	1 353.1	1 400.6	1 426.2
3	826.3	875.0	901.6	879.1	930.2	927.0	978.5	983.2	1 000.3	1 032.2
4	427.2	442.8	457.9	480.1	488.6	509.6	500.7	529.7	529.8	542.3
5	748.2	761.3	822.5	820.6	831.6	860.4	839.8	849.2	901.9	905.5
6	343.7	329.9	300.1	291.4	303.8	296.0	297.8	295.4	290.4	278.9
7	1 388.1	1 396.5	1 422.9	1 478.1	1 502.2	1 517.8	1 516.0	1 520.0	1 574.5	1 643.0
8	1 226.5	1 285.4	1 282.7	1 313.7	1 344.3	1 347.2	1 303.5	1 293.4	1 276.0	1 252.5
9	793.8	802.7	787.0	807.3	858.1	883.4	898.7	904.8	925.8	898.1
0	3.7	3.2	4.6	5.2	5.2	3.1	4.2	3.6	3.5	1.8
Women - Femmes - Mujeres										
ISCO-88 - CITP-88 - CIUO-88										
Total	6 609.6	6 788.6	6 911.5	7 126.4	7 320.7	7 470.1	7 575.0	7 757.2	7 977.5	8 104.5
1	488.9	510.8	475.4	467.7	497.9	535.0	532.0	556.2	566.1	574.8
2	1 177.1	1 203.2	1 257.6	1 285.4	1 292.8	1 323.4	1 447.5	1 468.3	1 530.2	1 582.3
3	1 135.2	1 179.3	1 224.8	1 299.3	1 349.6	1 360.7	1 416.0	1 495.3	1 562.4	1 621.2
4	1 554.1	1 593.1	1 656.3	1 630.8	1 681.5	1 736.8	1 727.2	1 738.0	1 748.7	1 746.4
5	1 301.2	1 327.3	1 349.8	1 426.7	1 464.8	1 478.2	1 445.2	1 486.5	1 556.1	1 576.8
6	111.1	100.8	87.0	89.6	91.7	90.6	94.3	97.5	95.6	82.8
7	125.0	122.1	123.3	151.5	156.7	162.0	147.5	137.9	143.3	158.1
8	321.7	342.1	326.0	342.6	349.8	341.9	308.6	297.9	296.7	277.3
9	388.5	403.9	404.6	425.5	427.5	433.9	448.2	471.7	470.1	476.0
0	1.0	1.3	1.4	0.9	1.2	1.0	1.7	0.8	0.2	0.5
Cayman Islands (BA) [4][7][8]				Total employment - Emploi total - Empleo total						
Total - Total - Total										
ISCO-88 - CITP-88 - CIUO-88										
Total	.	.	25.862	27.354	.	22.420 [9]	.	35.016 [9]	35.081	37.450
1			1.755	1.871	.	3.318 [9]	.	4.240 [9]	4.605	3.905
2-3			7.650	8.366	.	5.019 [9]	.	8.363 [9]	8.839	9.936
4			3.545	3.569	.	3.634 [9]	.	2.908 [9]	4.647	4.499
5			4.130	4.564	.	2.889 [9]	.	6.754 [9]	4.452	6.115
6			0.455	0.547	.	0.475 [9]	.	0.692 [9]	0.711	0.867
7			3.340	3.192	.	2.504 [9]	.	4.198 [9]	5.057	5.133
8			0.680	0.866	.	0.864 [9]	.	2.524 [9]	1.568	1.511
9			4.305	4.369	.	3.712 [9]	.	5.337 [9]	4.625	5.115
X			0.002	0.010	.	- [9]	.	- [9]	0.576	0.370

Explanatory notes: see p. 77.

[1] Persons aged 10 years and over. [2] Sep. of each year. [3] Prior to 2003: Excl. rural population of Rondõnia,Acre, Amazonas, Roraima, Pará and Amapá. [4] Persons aged 15 years and over. [5] Excl. residents of the Territories and indigenous persons living on reserves. [6] Excl. full-time members of the armed forces. [7] Excl. armed forces and conscripts. [8] Oct. [9] April.

Notes explicatives: voir p. 80.

[1] Personnes âgées de 10 ans et plus. [2] Sept. de chaque année. [3] Avant 2003: Non compris la population rurale de Rondõnia, Acre, Amazonas, Roraima, Pará et Amapá. [4] Personnes âgées de 15 ans et plus. [5] Non compris les habitants des "Territoires" et les populations indigènes vivant dans les réserves. [6] Non compris les membres à temps complet des forces armées. [7] Non compris les forces armées et les conscrits. [8] Oct. [9] Avril.

Notas explicativas: véase p. 83.

[1] Personas de 10 años y más. [2] Sept. de cada año. [3] Antes de 2003: Excl. la población rural de Rondonia, Acre, Amazonas, Roraima, Pará y Amapá. [4] Personas de 15 años y más. [5] Excl. a los habitantes de los "Territorios" y a las poblaciones indígenas que viven en reservas. [6] Excl. los miembros a tiempo completo de las fuerzas armadas. [7] Excl. las fuerzas armadas y los conscriptos. [8] Oct. [9] Abril.

EMPLOYMENT — EMPLOI — EMPLEO

Total employment, by occupation — Emploi total, par profession — Empleo total, por ocupación

Thousands — Milliers — Millares

	1999	2000	2001	2002	2003	2004	2005	2006	2007	2008
Cayman Islands (BA) [1][2][3]					Total employment - Emploi total - Empleo total					
Men - Hommes - Hombres										
ISCO-88 - CITP-88 - CIUO-88										
Total	.	.	.	.	10.358 [4]	.	.	.	18.305	19.355
1	.	.	.	.	1.613 [4]	.	.	.	2.484	2.173
2-3	.	.	.	.	2.267 [4]	.	.	.	4.286	4.458
4	.	.	.	.	0.545 [4]	.	.	.	1.023	0.792
5	.	.	.	.	1.201 [4]	.	.	.	1.979	2.765
6	.	.	.	.	0.475 [4]	.	.	.	0.692	0.811
7	.	.	.	.	2.310 [4]	.	.	.	4.802	4.864
8	.	.	.	.	0.731 [4]	.	.	.	1.402	1.332
9	.	.	.	.	1.216 [4]	.	.	.	1.379	1.952
X	.	.	.	.	- [4]	.	.	.	0.259	0.208
Women - Femmes - Mujeres										
ISCO-88 - CITP-88 - CIUO-88										
Total	.	.	.	.	12.062 [4]	.	.	.	16.776	18.094
1	.	.	.	.	1.705 [4]	.	.	.	2.120	1.732
2-3	.	.	.	.	2.752 [4]	.	.	.	4.553	5.477
4	.	.	.	.	3.089 [4]	.	.	.	3.624	3.707
5	.	.	.	.	1.688 [4]	.	.	.	2.474	3.350
6	.	.	.	.	- [4]	.	.	.	0.019	0.056
7	.	.	.	.	0.194 [4]	.	.	.	0.256	0.269
8	.	.	.	.	0.138 [4]	.	.	.	0.166	0.179
9	.	.	.	.	2.496 [4]	.	.	.	3.246	3.162
X	.	.	.	.	- [4]	.	.	.	0.317	0.162
Colombia (BA) [5][6][7]					Total employment - Emploi total - Empleo total					
Total - Total - Total										
ISCO-88 - CITP-88 - CIUO-88										
Total	.	.	15 813.5	15 844.3	16 650.1	16 704.0	17 154.9	16 701.6	17 076.5	17 425.7
1	.	.	1 338.0	1 441.3	1 512.1	1 517.5	1 600.1	1 520.5	1 663.0	1 710.3
2	.	.	265.2	326.4	317.7	380.2	410.3	288.5	393.9	460.5
4	.	.	1 132.5	1 195.0	1 204.4	1 252.2	1 267.2	1 163.3	1 560.7	1 589.4
5	.	.	5 844.4	5 790.6	6 196.4	6 003.1	6 065.0	5 561.1	5 958.8	6 132.4
6	.	.	3 288.2	3 056.7	3 226.7	3 234.1	3 582.6	2 828.9	2 955.1	2 914.1
7	.	.	3 717.3	3 782.3	3 890.3	4 030.1	3 905.5	3 752.1	4 409.7	4 465.9
X	.	.	228.0	252.0	302.5	286.8	324.1	1 587.3	135.2	153.1
Men - Hommes - Hombres										
ISCO-88 - CITP-88 - CIUO-88										
Total	.	.	9 658.1	9 689.2	10 106.6	10 196.8	10 491.3	10 202.0	10 399.9	10 611.0
1	.	.	669.9	743.8	776.8	772.4	833.9	784.5	902.5	921.3
2	.	.	170.5	211.9	207.9	246.8	263.7	195.1	231.5	277.8
4	.	.	509.1	488.5	554.0	595.2	582.0	570.1	661.1	670.8
5	.	.	2 263.1	2 250.6	2 376.3	2 300.8	2 280.3	2 153.1	2 306.8	2 353.2
6	.	.	2 949.1	2 744.1	2 822.4	2 856.4	3 116.2	2 504.2	2 608.3	2 578.0
7	.	.	2 890.8	3 029.1	3 091.2	3 179.5	3 120.0	2 968.0	3 568.5	3 683.5
X	.	.	205.6	221.3	278.0	245.7	295.1	1 027.1	121.3	126.5
Women - Femmes - Mujeres										
ISCO-88 - CITP-88 - CIUO-88										
Total	.	.	6 155.4	6 155.1	6 543.5	6 507.2	6 663.6	6 499.6	6 676.5	6 814.7
1	.	.	668.1	697.5	735.3	745.0	766.2	736.0	760.5	789.0
2	.	.	94.7	114.5	109.8	133.4	146.7	93.4	162.5	182.7
4	.	.	623.4	706.5	650.4	657.0	685.2	593.2	899.6	918.6
5	.	.	3 581.3	3 540.0	3 820.1	3 702.3	3 784.7	3 408.0	3 652.0	3 779.2
6	.	.	339.1	312.7	404.3	377.7	466.4	324.6	346.8	336.2
7	.	.	826.5	753.2	799.1	850.6	785.5	784.1	841.3	782.5
X	.	.	22.4	30.7	24.5	41.1	28.9	560.2	13.9	26.6
Costa Rica (BA) [8][9]					Total employment - Emploi total - Empleo total					
Total - Total - Total										
ISCO-88 - CITP-88 - CIUO-88										
Total	1 300.1	1 318.6	1 552.9	1 586.5	1 640.4	1 653.9	1 776.7	1 829.9	1 925.7	1 957.7
1	70.4	74.7	37.1	36.3	40.4	44.8	50.4	49.6	65.2	65.8
2	87.0	91.9	146.8	151.1	164.5	165.7	177.6	190.8	190.6	209.3
3	56.5	63.5	180.6	180.4	193.7	190.7	204.1	211.4	228.4	261.9
4	54.0	48.1	111.5	113.0	122.2	126.9	133.1	138.9	162.4	162.7
5	419.3	410.9	239.9	257.4	262.2	258.2	284.4	286.1	282.4	302.0
6	74.0	66.9	77.5	76.4	75.2	80.8	77.9	72.4	81.2	78.3
7	253.1	248.9	182.8	190.8	189.5	197.3	207.6	220.5	219.6	222.3
8	239.8	263.5	148.1	142.4	139.1	144.4	154.6	160.0	169.3	172.0
9	42.3	43.9	423.3	432.2	449.0	442.9	483.6	497.5	521.3	477.8
X	3.8	6.3	5.2	6.6	4.7	2.2	3.6	2.7	5.2	5.7

Explanatory notes: see p. 77. — Notes explicatives: voir p. 80. — Notas explicativas: véase p. 83.

[1] Persons aged 15 years and over. [2] Excl. armed forces and conscripts. [3] Oct. [4] April. [5] From 2001, figures revised on the basis of the 2005 census results. [6] Excl. armed forces. [7] Persons aged 10 years and over. [8] Persons aged 12 years and over. [9] July of each year.

[1] Personnes âgées de 15 ans et plus. [2] Non compris les forces armées et les conscrits. [3] Oct. [4] Avril. [5] A partir de 2001, données révisées sur la base des résultats du recensement de 2005. [6] Non compris les forces armées. [7] Personnes âgées de 10 ans et plus. [8] Personnes âgées de 12 ans et plus. [9] Juillet de chaque année.

[1] Personas de 15 años y más. [2] Excl. las fuerzas armadas y los conscriptos. [3] Oct. [4] Abril. [5] A partir de 2001, datos revisados de acuerdo con los resultados del censo de 2005. [6] Excl. las fuerzas armadas. [7] Personas de 10 años y más. [8] Personas de 12 años y más. [9] Julio de cada año.

| Total employment, by occupation | | | | Emploi total, par profession | | | | Empleo total, por ocupación | | |

Thousands — Milliers — Millares

	1999	2000	2001	2002	2003	2004	2005	2006	2007	2008
Costa Rica (BA) [1] [2]						Total employment - Emploi total - Empleo total				
Men - Hommes - Hombres										
ISCO-88 - CITP-88 - CIUO-88										
Total	879.6	902.5	1 013.0	1 037.5	1 069.0	1 093.6	1 153.9	1 172.6	1 222.6	1 229.5
1	49.4	50.1	27.7	26.8	28.6	33.0	37.8	34.7	47.6	45.8
2	42.1	44.4	68.5	73.7	77.5	80.8	84.3	94.4	89.9	98.6
3	33.9	39.1	128.2	126.0	135.7	133.5	143.7	140.3	150.0	167.7
4	16.2	14.4	47.0	50.3	54.1	52.6	58.5	59.2	69.7	71.9
5	214.4	215.1	118.8	130.7	129.1	133.4	133.4	133.2	129.5	141.3
6	71.4	64.4	74.4	72.0	70.8	76.2	73.0	68.9	73.4	73.1
7	201.0	201.9	152.0	157.9	161.4	167.4	174.6	189.9	189.9	193.7
8	227.5	246.1	117.4	118.2	116.5	124.5	135.9	140.2	146.5	145.3
9	21.3	21.9	274.6	277.0	291.3	290.7	310.0	309.4	322.2	287.6
X	2.5	5.1	4.3	4.9	4.0	1.5	2.5	2.5	4.0	4.7
Women - Femmes - Mujeres										
ISCO-88 - CITP-88 - CIUO-88										
Total	420.5	416.1	539.9	549.0	571.4	560.3	622.8	657.3	703.1	728.2
1	21.1	24.6	9.4	9.5	11.7	11.7	12.5	14.8	17.6	20.0
2	44.9	47.5	78.4	77.4	87.0	85.0	93.2	96.5	100.7	110.7
3	22.6	24.4	52.4	54.4	58.0	57.2	60.4	71.1	78.5	94.2
4	37.8	33.7	64.5	62.7	68.0	74.4	74.6	79.6	92.8	90.8
5	204.8	195.8	121.1	126.7	133.1	124.8	150.9	153.0	152.9	160.7
6	2.6	2.5	3.0	4.3	4.5	4.6	4.8	3.5	7.8	5.2
7	52.2	47.1	30.8	32.9	28.2	30.0	33.0	30.6	29.7	28.6
8	12.3	17.4	30.7	24.3	22.6	19.9	18.6	19.8	22.8	26.7
9	21.0	22.0	148.7	155.2	157.7	152.3	173.5	188.1	199.1	190.2
X	1.3	1.2	0.9	1.6	0.7	0.7	1.1	0.3	1.2	9.6
Cuba (BA) [3] [4]						Total employment - Emploi total - Empleo total				
Total - Total - Total										
ISCO-68 - CITP-68 - CIUO-68										
Total	4 359.4	4 379.3	4 505.1	4 558.2	4 607.0	4 641.7	4 722.5	4 754.6	4 867.7	4 948.2 [5]
0/1	899.6	924.0	964.1	997.4	1 013.5	1 081.7	1 203.4	1 284.2	1 403.5	1 401.8 [5]
2	336.1	346.0	342.4	340.1	368.6	345.3	393.2	366.2	386.7	381.0 [5]
3	181.2	175.2	166.7	168.0	138.2	148.3	255.1	263.3	248.7	257.9 [5]
4-5	750.1	735.7	761.4	802.9	829.3	881.9	1 107.9	1 068.2	1 108.1	1 138.2 [5]
6-7/8/9	2 192.4	2 198.4	2 270.5	2 249.8	2 257.4	2 184.5	1 762.9	1 772.7	1 720.7	1 769.3 [5]
Men - Hommes - Hombres										
ISCO-68 - CITP-68 - CIUO-68										
Total	2 814.5	2 819.8	2 906.3	2 926.8	2 945.8	2 955.7	2 998.5	2 985.8	3 016.0	3 073.0 [5]
0/1	344.5	354.7	340.0	376.2	365.6	407.0	483.4	513.9	562.6	565.9 [5]
2	237.1	243.1	241.1	231.1	252.3	229.4	275.6	258.2	266.4	265.0 [5]
3	36.2	34.8	23.3	33.2	21.9	32.1	92.1	99.2	96.4	102.6 [5]
4-5	393.3	375.5	380.7	427.1	447.3	487.5	662.6	635.9	657.9	665.2 [5]
6-7/8/9	1 803.4	1 811.7	1 921.2	1 859.2	1 858.7	1 799.7	1 484.8	1 478.6	1 432.7	1 474.3 [5]
Women - Femmes - Mujeres										
ISCO-68 - CITP-68 - CIUO-68										
Total	1 544.9	1 559.5	1 598.8	1 631.4	1 661.2	1 686.0	1 724.0	1 768.8	1 851.7	1 875.2 [5]
0/1	555.1	569.3	624.1	621.2	647.9	674.7	720.0	770.3	840.9	835.9 [5]
2	99.0	102.9	101.3	109.0	116.3	115.9	117.6	108.0	120.3	116.0 [5]
3	145.0	140.4	143.4	134.8	116.3	116.2	163.0	164.1	152.3	155.3 [5]
4-5	356.8	360.2	380.7	375.8	382.0	394.4	445.3	432.3	450.2	473.0 [5]
6-7/8/9	389.0	386.7	349.3	390.6	398.7	384.8	278.1	294.1	288.0	295.0 [5]
Chile (BA) [3] [6]						Total employment - Emploi total - Empleo total				
Total - Total - Total										
ISCO-68 - CITP-68 - CIUO-68										
Total	5 404.5	5 381.5	5 479.4	5 531.3	5 675.1	5 862.9	5 905.0	6 411.0 [7]	6 566.1	6 740.4
0/1	558.3	537.8	556.1	581.9	608.4	633.8	646.6	735.1 [7]	738.0	773.0
2	199.3	195.9	204.0	187.5	188.0	211.4	217.2	242.7 [7]	265.3	264.2
3	768.7	773.3	769.3	786.2	812.4	881.0	928.4	966.2 [7]	992.0	1 027.2
4	670.9	655.7	662.7	701.5	706.2	720.6	696.2	806.2 [7]	812.0	851.8
5	717.2	729.5	766.7	751.6	808.3	819.9	803.0	895.5 [7]	933.7	990.1
6	799.3	791.9	756.0	766.4	790.9	800.4	796.4	822.0 [7]	810.0	799.6
7/8/9	1 645.3	1 655.0	1 719.4	1 710.3	1 709.2	1 752.9	1 767.1	1 888.7 [7]	1 961.1	1 975.5
X	45.5	42.4	45.3	46.0	51.6	43.0	50.2	54.6 [7]	54.1	58.7
Men - Hommes - Hombres										
ISCO-68 - CITP-68 - CIUO-68										
Total	3 603.6	3 600.5	3 663.7	3 697.0	3 749.7	3 816.1	3 840.2	4 130.2 [7]	4 188.4	4 239.4
0/1	268.5	260.0	277.0	277.0	291.7	303.7	313.1	364.5 [7]	368.3	382.7
2	155.0	145.5	155.0	148.5	143.4	160.7	162.3	185.0 [7]	203.7	199.7
3	398.9	396.6	381.8	407.2	415.2	467.2	478.2	491.0 [7]	490.1	485.1
4	339.9	338.0	343.4	366.4	358.2	340.9	338.9	377.0 [7]	362.9	394.8
5	231.7	243.2	276.0	265.3	286.1	288.7	280.7	312.2 [7]	318.2	330.2
6	719.5	712.0	678.2	683.6	702.2	693.0	681.8	693.0 [7]	681.3	669.7
7/8/9	1 446.7	1 464.7	1 507.8	1 506.4	1 504.7	1 520.1	1 539.0	1 655.4 [7]	1 714.1	1 726.6
X	43.5	40.6	44.4	42.5	48.3	41.9	46.3	52.2 [7]	49.8	50.3

Explanatory notes: see p. 77.

[1] Persons aged 12 years and over. [2] July of each year. [3] Persons aged 15 years and over. [4] Dec. [5] February - April [6] Fourth quarter of each year. [7] Methodology revised; data not strictly comparable.

Notes explicatives: voir p. 80.

[1] Personnes âgées de 12 ans et plus. [2] Juillet de chaque année. [3] Personnes âgées de 15 ans et plus. [4] Déc. [5] Février - Avril [6] Quatrième trimestre de chaque année. [7] Méthodologie révisée; les données ne sont pas strictement comparables.

Notas explicativas: véase p. 83.

[1] Personas de 12 años y más. [2] Julio de cada año. [3] Personas de 15 años y más. [4] Dic. [5] Febrero - Abril [6] Cuarto trimestre de cada año. [7] Metodología revisada; los datos no son estrictamente comparables.

	EMPLOYMENT			EMPLOI				EMPLEO	
	Total employment, by occupation			**Emploi total, par profession**				**Empleo total, por ocupación**	
	Thousands			Milliers				Millares	
	1999	2000	2001	2002	2003	2004	2005	2006	2007	2008

Chile (BA) [1] [2] — Total employment - Emploi total - Empleo total

Women - Femmes - Mujeres
ISCO-68 - CITP-68 - CIUO-68

	1999	2000	2001	2002	2003	2004	2005	2006	2007	2008
Total	1 800.9	1 781.0	1 815.8	1 834.3	1 925.4	2 046.8	2 064.8	2 280.8 [3]	2 377.7	2 501.0
0/1	289.8	277.9	279.1	304.8	316.7	330.1	333.5	370.6 [3]	369.7	390.4
2	44.3	50.4	49.0	39.0	44.7	50.7	55.0	57.7 [3]	61.6	64.5
3	369.8	376.8	387.5	378.9	397.3	413.8	450.3	475.2 [3]	501.9	542.1
4	331.0	317.7	319.3	335.1	347.9	379.7	357.3	429.2 [3]	449.0	457.0
5	485.5	486.2	490.7	486.3	522.2	531.1	522.3	583.3 [3]	615.6	659.9
6	79.8	79.9	77.8	82.7	88.7	107.4	114.6	129.0 [3]	128.7	129.9
7/8/9	198.6	190.3	211.6	203.9	204.6	232.9	228.0	233.3 [3]	247.0	248.9
X	2.0	1.8	0.9	3.6	3.3	1.2	3.9	2.5 [3]	4.3	8.4

República Dominicana (BA) [4] — Total employment - Emploi total - Empleo total

Total - Total - Total
ISCO-88 - CITP-88 - CIUO-88

	1999	2000	2001	2002	2003	2004	2005	2006	2007	2008
Total	2 979.5	3 041.1	3 001.7	3 105.5	3 093.0	3 212.8	3 279.1	3 469.9	3 550.9	.
1	77.3	86.3	97.7	93.6	91.9	90.2	98.6	109.9	107.4	
2	175.4	179.8	161.7	182.2	192.2	205.5	202.4	230.9	223.7	
3	140.4	189.2	192.5	196.3	224.0	216.7	223.2	226.7	230.6	
4	196.9	196.9	218.4	212.0	230.5	207.5	222.0	219.2	236.5	
5 [5]	572.2	574.1	580.9	596.4	585.9	567.3	604.1	650.4	691.0	
6	388.6	308.9	309.1	342.8	306.6	337.6	330.2	360.0	365.7	
7	445.2	481.3	468.6	440.6	462.4	502.8	536.5	553.0	536.8	
8	403.5	380.6	376.3	378.6	382.3	398.4	376.2	373.3	392.4	
9	630.1	603.1	644.5	641.8	641.7	659.6	658.5	720.4	736.8	
0						27.2	27.6	26.0	30.0	

Men - Hommes - Hombres
ISCO-88 - CITP-88 - CIUO-88

	1999	2000	2001	2002	2003	2004	2005	2006	2007	2008
Total	2 069.9	2 027.9	2 010.7	2 055.2	2 053.1	2 148.4	2 175.4	2 272.0	2 336.8	.
1	51.1	60.0	67.5	65.1	63.5	60.6	66.6	64.1	74.5	
2	97.8	92.5	78.5	92.3	89.7	100.1	87.4	102.4	99.0	
3	71.8	93.4	93.4	101.6	115.0	110.4	120.3	123.5	123.8	
4	71.8	75.9	78.3	76.1	76.1	72.0	77.3	74.0	76.6	
5 [5]	291.2	309.2	298.6	289.4	292.2	275.4	289.3	301.4	331.0	
6	323.2	295.9	298.5	330.4	297.3	326.2	312.0	344.5	347.9	
7	386.0	419.4	419.3	393.3	419.7	457.3	483.7	499.9	488.8	
8	326.3	276.5	300.6	306.4	306.3	321.7	306.6	316.9	334.4	
9	450.8	405.1	376.0	401.8	402.0	402.2	407.7	424.0	434.3	
0						22.6	24.3	21.4	26.5	

Women - Femmes - Mujeres
ISCO-88 - CITP-88 - CIUO-88

	1999	2000	2001	2002	2003	2004	2005	2006	2007	2008
Total	909.6	1 013.2	991.1	1 050.3	1 039.9	1 064.4	1 103.7	1 197.9	1 214.1	.
1	26.2	26.4	30.2	28.6	28.5	29.6	32.0	45.9	32.9	
2	77.5	87.3	83.2	90.7	102.5	105.4	114.9	128.6	124.7	
3	68.6	95.9	99.1	94.7	109.0	106.3	102.9	103.2	106.8	
4	125.2	142.5	133.7	154.5	138.5	135.5	144.6	145.3	159.9	
5 [5]	281.0	264.9	282.3	307.0	293.7	291.9	314.8	349.0	360.0	
6	15.4	15.4	13.0	10.6	12.5	11.4	18.1	15.5	17.8	
7	59.2	61.9	49.3	47.4	42.7	45.5	52.8	53.1	48.0	
8	77.2	104.1	75.7	72.2	46.0	76.7	69.6	56.5	58.0	
9	179.3	217.2	277.1	242.7	239.7	257.4	250.8	296.4	302.5	
0						4.7	3.3	4.6	3.5	

Ecuador (BA) [4] [6] [7] — Total employment - Emploi total - Empleo total

Total - Total - Total
ISCO-88 - CITP-88 - CIUO-88

	1999	2000	2001	2002	2003	2004	2005	2006	2007	2008
Total	3 226.1	3 376.1	3 673.2 [8]	3 459.4	3 531.2	3 858.5	3 891.9	4 031.6	.	
1	89.0	92.9	97.9 [8]	95.0	90.0	136.6	132.1	121.9		
2	285.5	298.4	324.2 [8]	310.6	277.2	318.2	323.3	339.2		
3	196.8	197.1	230.9 [8]	214.4	300.1	294.5	307.7	268.0		
4	219.4	227.0	231.5 [8]	211.7	203.7	203.4	215.5	280.6		
5	790.0	810.3	858.2 [8]	825.6	833.9	958.4	994.9	1 012.9		
6	144.1	107.1	98.8 [8]	138.2	114.3	169.1	120.4	131.7		
7	604.0	638.4	596.9 [8]	597.6	570.7	618.7	552.2	603.6		
8	255.2	256.1	247.3 [8]	260.3	270.1	300.0	289.6	281.9		
9	630.7	730.7	972.1 [8]	786.9	853.3	847.4	941.0	975.2		
0	11.5	18.0	15.5 [8]	18.3	17.7	12.3	15.0	16.7		

Explanatory notes: see p. 77.

[1] Persons aged 15 years and over. [2] Fourth quarter of each year. [3] Methodology revised; data not strictly comparable. [4] Persons aged 10 years and over. [5] Incl. the armed forces. [6] Urban areas. [7] Nov. of each year. [8] July.

Notes explicatives: voir p. 80.

[1] Personnes âgées de 15 ans et plus. [2] Quatrième trimestre de chaque année. [3] Méthodologie révisée; les données ne sont pas strictement comparables. [4] Personnes âgées de 10 ans et plus. [5] Y compris les forces armées. [6] Régions urbaines. [7] Nov. de chaque année. [8] Juillet.

Notas explicativas: véase p. 83.

[1] Personas de 15 años y más. [2] Cuarto trimestre de cada año. [3] Metodología revisada; los datos no son estrictamente comparables. [4] Personas de 10 años y más. [5] Incl. las fuerzas armadas. [6] Areas urbanas. [7] Nov. de cada año. [8] Julio.

Total employment, by occupation
Emploi total, par profession
Empleo total, por ocupación

	Thousands			Milliers				Millares		
	1999	2000	2001	2002	2003	2004	2005	2006	2007	2008

Ecuador (BA) [1] [2] [3]

Total employment - Emploi total - Empleo total

Men - Hommes - Hombres
ISCO-88 - CITP-88 - CIUO-88

Total	1 978.3	2 078.2	2 211.7 [4]	2 131.7	.	2 288.5	2 327.8	2 416.5	.	.
1	.	65.7	73.1 [4]	71.2	.	90.9	86.3	88.1	.	.
2	.	158.9	168.8 [4]	167.1	.	163.4	165.9	167.3	.	.
3	.	106.2	139.9 [4]	128.0	.	151.8	162.2	140.2	.	.
4	.	83.9	89.4 [4]	85.3	.	81.2	88.3	118.5	.	.
5	.	394.1	380.1 [4]	390.2	.	427.0	457.0	474.2	.	.
6	.	89.3	81.8 [4]	102.7	.	120.7	91.0	106.2	.	.
7	.	521.6	469.6 [4]	470.5	.	483.4	444.6	488.8	.	.
8	.	239.3	232.3 [4]	248.0	.	282.8	275.7	260.1	.	.
9	.	401.6	561.1 [4]	450.5	.	476.6	541.8	556.5	.	.
0	.	17.8	15.5 [4]	18.1	.	10.7	15.0	16.7	.	.

Women - Femmes - Mujeres
ISCO-88 - CITP-88 - CIUO-88

Total	1 247.8	1 297.9	1 461.6 [4]	1 327.7	.	1 570.1	1 564.0	1 615.1	.	.
1	.	27.2	24.7 [4]	23.8	.	45.8	45.7	33.8	.	.
2	.	139.6	155.5 [4]	143.5	.	154.8	157.4	172.0	.	.
3	.	90.9	90.9 [4]	86.4	.	142.7	145.5	127.8	.	.
4	.	143.2	142.1 [4]	126.5	.	122.2	127.3	162.1	.	.
5	.	416.2	478.2 [4]	435.4	.	531.4	537.9	538.8	.	.
6	.	17.9	17.0 [4]	35.5	.	48.5	29.4	25.5	.	.
7	.	116.8	127.3 [4]	127.1	.	135.3	107.7	114.8	.	.
8	.	16.9	14.9 [4]	12.3	.	17.2	13.9	21.8	.	.
9	.	329.1	411.0 [4]	336.4	.	370.8	399.2	418.6	.	.
0	.	0.2	- [4]	0.8	.	1.6	-	-	.	.

El Salvador (BA) [1] [5]

Total employment - Emploi total - Empleo total

Total - Total - Total
ISCO-88 - CITP-88 - CIUO-88

Total	2 182.5	2 198.9	2 275.2	2 219.6	2 280.7	2 253.6	2 283.6	2 337.1	2 419.2	.
1	41.9	31.7	28.9	23.0	29.7	24.6	35.9	38.4	37.5	.
2	61.5	80.1	68.1	67.7	69.2	63.7	64.7	73.9	80.6	.
3	160.3	157.9	169.4	184.2	185.8	176.0	194.7	178.4	184.1	.
4	113.5	111.2	126.3	114.5	111.2	115.8	106.0	109.4	127.1	.
5	339.5	344.3	380.0	389.7	416.0	405.7	434.5	445.3	459.7	.
6	207.2	213.9	200.8	196.6	171.3	158.5	181.3	152.3	175.3	.
7	333.1	339.7	355.1	351.8	366.8	367.7	363.9	366.7	412.0	.
8	183.6	190.4	178.3	177.2	193.2	195.1	167.5	180.5	179.3	.
9	736.3	723.4	763.0	710.3	732.2	741.0	730.2	787.2	757.7	.
X	5.8	6.3	5.3	4.4	5.3	5.5	4.7	5.0	5.9	.

Men - Hommes - Hombres
ISCO-88 - CITP-88 - CIUO-88

Total	1 294.5	1 301.2	1 354.3	1 292.0	1 328.2	1 332.7	1 330.6	1 342.0	1 401.8	.
1	27.9	23.5	21.5	17.1	20.2	16.5	26.1	27.3	28.3	.
2	35.8	42.9	39.4	36.5	42.5	38.1	34.7	38.9	46.1	.
3	82.8	90.2	93.7	99.7	101.2	93.9	97.2	92.6	96.6	.
4	42.8	40.4	50.4	39.7	44.1	48.3	42.2	41.6	49.1	.
5	107.0	107.3	126.3	121.6	130.1	133.0	145.3	139.0	153.6	.
6	195.7	203.1	190.2	190.2	161.2	149.0	171.0	143.8	164.1	.
7	209.0	211.1	216.3	210.4	236.2	224.2	221.5	229.7	247.0	.
8	119.8	123.7	117.9	112.9	120.9	133.8	113.1	125.1	124.4	.
9	467.9	452.7	493.2	459.5	466.4	490.2	475.0	499.0	486.8	.
X	5.8	6.3	5.3	4.4	5.3	5.5	4.6	5.0	5.9	.

Women - Femmes - Mujeres
ISCO-88 - CITP-88 - CIUO-88

Total	888.1	897.8	920.9	927.6	952.5	920.9	952.9	995.1	1 017.3	.
1	14.0	8.3	7.3	5.9	9.5	8.1	9.8	11.1	9.3	.
2	25.8	37.2	28.8	31.2	26.6	25.6	30.1	35.0	34.5	.
3	77.4	67.8	75.7	84.5	84.5	82.1	97.5	85.9	87.6	.
4	70.7	70.8	75.8	74.8	67.0	67.4	63.8	67.8	78.1	.
5	232.5	237.0	253.7	268.1	285.9	272.7	289.2	306.3	306.1	.
6	11.4	10.7	10.6	6.4	10.1	9.4	10.3	8.5	11.1	.
7	124.1	128.5	138.8	141.4	130.6	143.4	142.5	137.0	165.0	.
8	63.8	66.7	60.4	64.3	72.3	61.4	54.4	55.4	54.8	.
9	268.4	270.7	269.8	250.8	265.8	250.8	255.2	288.2	270.9	.
X	-	-	-	-	-	-	0.2	-	-	.

Jamaica (BA) [6]

Total employment - Emploi total - Empleo total

Total - Total - Total
ISCO-88 - CITP-88 - CIUO-88

Total	936.8	935.6	942.3	1 025.9	1 056.5	1 058.7	1 091.7	1 129.5	1 170.2	1 167.8
1-3	148.7	150.3	151.8	189.4	199.3	181.4	205.4	214.8	224.5	234.9
4	78.9	84.2	80.1	81.5	93.8	87.2	93.0	96.7	105.0	105.4
5	146.9	153.4	160.8	168.4	166.4	188.4	191.0	206.5	209.6	220.6
6	177.7	176.4	175.2	190.8	200.6	183.2	186.3	193.5	199.6	216.0
7	157.5	156.9	153.9	165.4	159.7	172.1	170.5	178.7	182.6	161.2
8	61.7	55.0	59.5	65.0	64.3	72.3	71.4	67.2	70.0	71.4
9	165.4	158.6	160.5	164.6	172.1	174.1	173.3	171.6	177.8	157.4
X	-	0.8	0.5	0.8	0.9	0.0	0.8	0.5	1.1	0.9

Explanatory notes: see p. 77.

[1] Persons aged 10 years and over. [2] Urban areas. [3] Nov. of each year. [4] July. [5] Dec. [6] Persons aged 14 years and over.

Notes explicatives: voir p. 80.

[1] Personnes âgées de 10 ans et plus. [2] Régions urbaines. [3] Nov. de chaque année. [4] Juillet. [5] Déc. [6] Personnes âgées de 14 ans et plus.

Notas explicativas: véase p. 83.

[1] Personas de 10 años y más. [2] Areas urbanas. [3] Nov. de cada año. [4] Julio. [5] Dic. [6] Personas de 14 años y más.

EMPLOYMENT	EMPLOI	EMPLEO
Total employment, by occupation	**Emploi total, par profession**	**Empleo total, por ocupación**
Thousands	Milliers	Millares

	1999	2000	2001	2002	2003	2004	2005	2006	2007	2008

Jamaica (BA) [1]

Total employment - Emploi total - Empleo total

Men - Hommes - Hombres
ISCO-88 - CITP-88 - CIUO-88

	1999	2000	2001	2002	2003	2004	2005	2006	2007	2008
Total	.	552.5	556.6	596.3	615.3	613.9	629.3	649.8	670.4	658.3
1-3	.	63.6	68.3	79.7	83.4	73.3	83.3	87.8	92.1	95.7
4	.	21.9	16.8	17.9	24.1	21.2	24.1	21.7	27.4	24.1
5	.	62.2	63.4	65.6	67.1	67.9	69.0	75.9	78.5	82.2
6	.	146.9	144.8	156.1	168.3	150.1	152.1	160.7	163.9	172.2
7	.	136.6	133.4	147.3	141.2	151.5	151.8	157.4	160.8	145.4
8	.	46.7	52.1	57.0	56.7	65.2	65.0	62.0	63.8	65.5
9	.	74.3	77.3	72.5	74.5	84.7	83.5	84.3	83.0	72.8
X	.	0.3	0.1	0.2	0.3	0.0	0.5	0.0	0.9	0.4

Women - Femmes - Mujeres
ISCO-88 - CITP-88 - CIUO-88

	1999	2000	2001	2002	2003	2004	2005	2006	2007	2008
Total	.	383.1	385.7	429.6	441.2	444.8	462.4	479.7	499.8	509.5
1-3	.	86.7	83.5	109.7	115.9	108.1	122.1	127.0	132.4	139.2
4	.	62.3	63.3	63.6	69.7	66.0	68.9	75.0	77.6	81.3
5	.	91.2	97.4	102.8	99.3	120.5	122.0	130.6	131.1	138.4
6	.	29.5	30.4	34.7	32.3	33.1	34.2	32.8	35.7	43.8
7	.	20.3	20.5	18.1	18.5	20.6	18.7	21.3	21.8	15.8
8	.	8.3	7.4	8.0	7.6	7.1	6.4	5.2	6.2	5.9
9	.	84.3	83.2	92.1	97.6	89.4	89.8	87.3	94.8	84.6
X	.	0.5	0.4	0.6	0.6	0.0	0.3	0.5	0.2	0.5

México (BA) [1][2]

Total employment - Emploi total - Empleo total

Total - Total - Total
ISCO-88 - CITP-88 - CIUO-88

	1999	2000	2001	2002	2003	2004	2005	2006	2007	2008
Total	37 279.9	38 044.5	38 065.8	38 939.7	39 221.5	40 561.0	40 791.8	42 197.8	42 906.7	43 866.7
1	713.4	893.5	876.3	836.9	787.9	813.9	916.2	898.7	914.7	862.5
2	2 045.7	2 258.0	2 371.2	2 447.9	2 567.9	2 668.6	2 577.4	2 803.5	2 972.3	2 961.1
3	3 294.0	3 577.7	3 533.4	3 550.7	3 580.1	3 877.6	4 084.7	4 154.5	4 076.3	4 266.2
4	2 374.5	2 467.1	2 495.4	2 468.4	2 510.8	2 678.2	2 532.7	2 830.8	2 972.1	3 058.2
5	5 721.0	5 937.3	6 041.0	6 400.6	6 515.9	6 782.7	7 382.2	7 537.4	7 789.8	8 090.1
6	7 459.7	6 526.8	6 485.5	6 634.4	6 202.3	6 274.2	5 943.1	5 802.6	5 644.0	5 634.2
7	5 808.7	6 106.1	6 057.1	5 908.8	6 037.4	6 270.0	6 179.2	6 605.5	6 738.8	6 958.7
8	3 466.0	3 640.4	3 589.4	3 553.0	3 513.5	3 615.4	3 689.3	3 806.8	3 646.2	3 647.4
9	6 306.5	6 568.7	6 550.4	7 075.4	7 432.4	7 510.4	7 428.5	7 684.4	8 091.3	8 305.0
0	75.2	58.8	60.2	55.2	60.7	61.0	53.4	69.9	60.6	82.8
X	15.2	10.1	6.0	8.2	12.6	9.2	5.1	3.6	0.4	0.6

Men - Hommes - Hombres
ISCO-88 - CITP-88 - CIUO-88

	1999	2000	2001	2002	2003	2004	2005	2006	2007	2008
Total	24 805.7	25 014.1	25 055.1	25 422.8	25 713.5	26 138.0	25 853.1	26 597.9	26 840.6	27 401.7
1	550.7	682.6	655.3	639.0	600.8	613.4	656.0	653.2	630.6	597.5
2	1 175.8	1 296.4	1 351.5	1 394.2	1 489.1	1 499.8	1 469.7	1 565.6	1 632.2	1 640.5
3	2 023.8	2 124.5	2 159.0	2 100.3	2 133.2	2 304.9	2 415.6	2 496.0	2 483.2	2 598.7
4	937.2	982.2	978.0	968.7	1 020.1	1 069.5	984.6	1 101.2	1 162.8	1 194.9
5	2 836.1	2 917.0	2 943.2	3 073.1	3 173.4	3 142.7	3 387.1	3 437.8	3 617.8	3 705.4
6	6 400.1	5 662.7	5 743.5	5 830.6	5 543.3	5 505.4	5 244.8	5 109.2	4 980.3	5 008.3
7	4 482.0	4 699.2	4 648.7	4 506.9	4 612.8	4 840.7	4 661.7	5 094.5	5 133.6	5 217.9
8	2 736.3	2 834.9	2 799.7	2 819.0	2 795.1	2 888.7	2 947.4	2 996.4	2 955.6	2 976.6
9	3 575.5	3 747.2	3 710.9	4 030.6	4 274.9	4 204.8	4 028.7	4 073.0	4 185.1	4 378.7
0	74.9	58.8	60.0	54.5	60.3	60.9	53.4	68.9	59.0	82.6
X	13.4	8.6	5.3	5.9	10.6	7.2	4.1	2.1	0.4	0.6

Women - Femmes - Mujeres
ISCO-88 - CITP-88 - CIUO-88

	1999	2000	2001	2002	2003	2004	2005	2006	2007	2008
Total	12 474.2	13 030.4	13 010.6	13 516.8	13 508.0	14 423.0	14 938.7	15 599.9	16 066.0	16 465.0
1	162.7	210.9	221.0	197.9	187.0	200.4	260.2	245.5	284.1	265.0
2	870.0	961.6	1 019.7	1 053.7	1 078.8	1 168.8	1 107.7	1 237.9	1 340.0	1 320.6
3	1 270.1	1 453.2	1 374.3	1 450.4	1 446.9	1 572.7	1 669.1	1 658.5	1 593.1	1 667.5
4	1 437.3	1 484.9	1 517.4	1 499.7	1 490.7	1 608.7	1 548.1	1 729.6	1 809.4	1 863.2
5	2 884.9	3 020.4	3 097.7	3 327.5	3 342.6	3 640.0	3 995.1	4 099.6	4 172.0	4 384.7
6	1 059.6	864.1	742.0	803.9	659.0	768.8	698.3	693.5	663.7	625.9
7	1 326.7	1 406.9	1 408.4	1 401.9	1 424.7	1 429.3	1 517.6	1 511.0	1 605.2	1 740.7
8	729.7	805.5	789.7	734.0	718.4	726.7	741.9	810.4	690.6	670.8
9	2 731.0	2 821.5	2 839.5	3 044.9	3 157.4	3 305.6	3 399.8	3 611.4	3 906.2	3 926.3
0	0.3	0.0	0.2	0.7	0.5	0.1	0.0	1.0	1.6	0.2
X	1.8	1.6	0.7	2.3	1.9	2.0	0.9	1.5	0.0	0.0

Explanatory notes: see p. 77.

[1] Persons aged 14 years and over. [2] Second quarter of each year.

Notes explicatives: voir p. 80.

[1] Personnes âgées de 14 ans et plus. [2] Deuxième trimestre de chaque année.

Notas explicativas: véase p. 83.

[1] Personas de 14 años y más. [2] Segundo trimestre de cada año.

Total employment, by occupation — Emploi total, par profession — Empleo total, por ocupación

Thousands — Milliers — Millares

	1999	2000	2001	2002	2003	2004	2005	2006	2007	2008
Netherlands Antilles (BA) [1][2][3]				Total employment - Emploi total - Empleo total						
Total - Total - Total ISCO-88 - CITP-88 - CIUO-88										
Total	.	50.1	47.7	49.1	52.1	51.5	51.3	52.1	53.8	.
1	.	5.0	4.7	4.9	5.3	5.7	6.2	6.6	7.0	.
2	.	4.8	4.4	4.3	4.5	4.7	4.8	4.8	4.9	.
3	.	7.6	7.3	7.3	7.6	7.6	7.7	7.8	8.1	.
4	.	8.5	8.1	7.8	7.9	8.0	8.2	8.6	8.7	.
5	.	8.2	7.5	7.7	8.2	8.4	8.2	8.3	8.4	.
6	.	0.6	0.3	0.3	0.5	0.3	0.2	0.3	0.4	.
7	.	5.8	5.7	5.9	6.0	5.6	5.6	5.9	6.1	.
8	.	2.5	2.5	2.6	2.7	2.4	2.3	2.5	2.6	.
9	.	6.5	6.8	7.7	8.9	8.5	7.8	7.0	6.9	.
0	.	0.5	0.4	0.6	0.6	0.4	0.3	0.3	0.4	.
Men - Hommes - Hombres ISCO-88 - CITP-88 - CIUO-88										
Total	.	25.7	24.5	25.2	26.6	24.7	25.3	26.0	26.5	.
1	.	3.4	3.2	3.4	3.6	3.8	4.2	4.4	4.6	.
2	.	2.3	2.1	2.0	2.2	2.1	2.2	2.1	2.0	.
3	.	4.0	3.9	3.9	4.0	3.6	3.6	3.5	3.6	.
4	.	1.9	1.8	1.7	1.8	1.7	1.7	1.9	1.9	.
5	.	3.3	2.9	2.8	3.0	3.1	3.3	3.3	3.3	.
6	.	0.4	0.3	0.3	0.4	0.2	0.3	0.3	0.3	.
7	.	5.5	5.4	5.5	5.5	5.0	5.2	5.5	5.6	.
8	.	2.1	2.2	2.4	2.4	2.0	1.9	2.1	2.2	.
9	.	2.4	2.5	2.8	3.2	2.9	2.8	2.6	2.5	.
0	.	0.3	0.3	0.4	0.5	0.3	0.3	0.3	0.3	.
Women - Femmes - Mujeres ISCO-88 - CITP-88 - CIUO-88										
Total	.	24.4	23.1	23.8	25.5	25.7	26.0	26.0	27.3	.
1	.	1.6	1.5	1.5	1.8	1.8	2.1	2.2	2.4	.
2	.	2.5	2.3	2.2	2.3	2.5	2.6	2.8	2.9	.
3	.	3.7	3.4	3.5	3.6	3.8	4.1	4.3	4.5	.
4	.	6.5	6.3	6.0	6.1	6.2	6.6	6.7	6.8	.
5	.	4.9	4.7	4.9	5.2	5.2	4.9	4.9	5.1	.
6	.	0.2	0.0	0.0	0.1	0.1	0.1	-	0.1	.
7	.	0.3	0.3	0.4	0.5	0.5	0.5	0.4	0.5	.
8	.	0.4	0.3	0.2	0.4	0.3	0.4	0.3	0.5	.
9	.	4.1	4.3	4.9	5.4	5.2	4.7	4.4	4.4	.
0	.	0.0	-	-	-	-	-	-	-	.
Nicaragua (BA) [4]				Total employment - Emploi total - Empleo total						
Total - Total - Total ISCO-88 - CITP-88 - CIUO-88										
Total	.	.	.	.	1 917.0	1 973.1	2 080.9	2 089.8	.	.
1	.	.	.	.	44.2	44.9	49.9	53.4	.	.
2	.	.	.	.	72.3	69.5	68.0	72.1	.	.
3	.	.	.	.	155.9	171.7	176.6	184.3	.	.
4	.	.	.	.	42.2	41.6	43.3	46.7	.	.
5	.	.	.	.	423.5	411.6	458.7	455.8	.	.
6	.	.	.	.	228.5	231.2	225.9	244.3	.	.
7	.	.	.	.	238.8	232.9	265.0	247.5	.	.
8	.	.	.	.	103.5	120.0	127.9	130.5	.	.
9	.	.	.	.	604.2	645.5	662.4	651.8	.	.
0	.	.	.	.	3.3	3.8	2.9	2.8	.	.
X	.	.	.	.	0.3	0.5	0.0	0.6	.	.
Men - Hommes - Hombres ISCO-88 - CITP-88 - CIUO-88										
Total	.	.	.	.	1 178.5	1 239.3	1 296.6	1 303.5	.	.
1	.	.	.	.	26.5	27.6	29.8	31.5	.	.
2	.	.	.	.	40.7	37.7	36.4	39.9	.	.
3	.	.	.	.	68.4	79.4	85.0	84.9	.	.
4	.	.	.	.	14.9	16.4	17.9	18.4	.	.
5	.	.	.	.	147.4	154.7	167.4	164.8	.	.
6	.	.	.	.	207.8	217.9	213.8	227.6	.	.
7	.	.	.	.	174.9	171.5	190.0	181.7	.	.
8	.	.	.	.	87.3	96.5	105.4	105.2	.	.
9	.	.	.	.	406.9	434.0	447.9	447.1	.	.
0	.	.	.	.	3.3	3.4	2.8	2.3	.	.
X	.	.	.	.	0.1	0.2	0.0	0.0	.	.

Explanatory notes: see p. 77.

[1] Persons aged 15 years and over. [2] Curaçao. [3] Oct. of each year. [4] Persons aged 10 years and over.

Notes explicatives: voir p. 80.

[1] Personnes âgées de 15 ans et plus. [2] Curaçao. [3] Oct. de chaque année. [4] Personnes âgées de 10 ans et plus.

Notas explicativas: véase p. 83.

[1] Personas de 15 años y más. [2] Curaçao. [3] Oct. de cada año. [4] Personas de 10 años y más.

EMPLOYMENT   EMPLOI   EMPLEO

Total employment, by occupation **Emploi total, par profession** **Empleo total, por ocupación**

Thousands — Milliers — Millares

	1999	2000	2001	2002	2003	2004	2005	2006	2007	2008

Nicaragua (BA) [1]

Women - Femmes - Mujeres
ISCO-88 - CITP-88 - CIUO-88

Total employment - Emploi total - Empleo total

	1999	2000	2001	2002	2003	2004	2005	2006	2007	2008
Total					738.4	733.8	784.3	786.3		
1					17.8	17.3	20.1	21.9		
2					31.6	31.7	31.7	32.2		
3					87.4	92.3	91.6	99.3		
4					27.3	25.2	25.4	28.2		
5					276.0	256.9	291.3	291.0		
6					20.7	13.4	12.1	16.7		
7					64.0	61.3	75.0	65.8		
8					16.2	23.5	22.5	25.3		
9					197.3	211.4	214.5	204.6		
0					0.2	0.4	0.1	0.5		
X					0.0	0.3	0.0	0.6		

Panamá (BA) [2]

Total - Total - Total

ISCO-68 - CITP-68 - CIUO-68 [3]   (1999)   ISCO-88 - CITP-88 - CIUO-88 [3]   (2007–2008)

Total employment - Emploi total - Empleo total

ISCO-68	1999	2000	2001	2002	2003	2004	2005	2006	2007	2008	ISCO-88
Total	961.4		984.2	1 049.5	1 080.5	1 134.7	1 188.3	1 210.7	1 264.0	1 333.8	Total
0/1	121.4		30.2	31.1	30.7	34.4	33.6	35.4	37.2	41.6	1
2	60.5		93.2	98.6	105.3	104.8	108.5	107.8	117.7	126.3	2
3	100.1		45.8	50.7	55.0	53.2	57.1	52.8	61.7	67.7	3
4	113.7		117.1	119.0	117.0	127.5	130.3	139.3	141.6	152.9	4
5	161.5		144.8	171.8	170.0	180.9	208.4	196.7	210.4	215.2	5
6	163.2		173.6	178.8	186.0	178.4	182.9	191.1	183.2	181.4	6
7/8/9	240.3		122.8	129.6	134.9	151.2	155.5	168.1	180.7	192.6	7
X	0.2		75.8	78.3	79.3	86.6	87.5	80.7	84.6	96.7	8
			180.9	191.5	202.4	217.8	224.4	238.9	246.7	259.5	9
			0.1	0.2	-	-	-	-	-	-	X

Men - Hommes - Hombres

ISCO-68 - CITP-68 - CIUO-68 [3]   (1999)   ISCO-88 - CITP-88 - CIUO-88 [3]   (2007–2008)

ISCO-68	1999	2000	2001	2002	2003	2004	2005	2006	2007	2008	ISCO-88
Total	638.0		659.2	687.6	703.3	734.3	755.7	777.5	799.1	837.0	Total
0/1	65.3		18.0	19.4	18.5	20.8	19.3	19.4	21.0	21.5	1
2	40.8		41.1	42.8	45.0	45.1	47.0	47.8	50.7	53.0	2
3	24.8		29.1	32.9	35.8	32.2	33.9	33.5	35.9	38.1	3
4	58.9		38.4	37.7	34.4	38.1	40.0	45.7	43.9	49.5	4
5	73.0		83.9	98.1	96.7	101.6	113.8	104.3	107.6	111.2	5
6	157.6		165.5	168.7	173.0	167.4	165.4	172.3	168.4	163.8	6
7/8/9	215.5		110.2	112.3	118.3	129.6	133.1	145.1	154.6	166.4	7
X	0.1		72.7	74.0	75.1	82.5	84.0	77.8	81.6	92.6	8
			100.3	101.5	106.5	116.9	119.1	131.6	135.4	141.0	9
			0.1	0.2	-	-	-	-	-	-	X

Women - Femmes - Mujeres

ISCO-68 - CITP-68 - CIUO-68 [3]   (1999)   ISCO-88 - CITP-88 - CIUO-88 [3]   (2007–2008)

ISCO-68	1999	2000	2001	2002	2003	2004	2005	2006	2007	2008	ISCO-88
Total	323.4		325.1	362.0	377.2	400.4	432.6	433.2	464.9	496.8	Total
0/1	56.2		12.2	11.7	12.1	13.6	14.4	15.9	16.2	20.0	1
2	19.7		52.2	55.8	60.3	59.7	61.5	60.0	67.1	73.3	2
3	75.8		16.7	17.7	19.1	21.0	23.2	19.3	25.7	29.6	3
4	54.8		78.8	81.3	82.5	89.4	90.3	93.6	97.8	103.4	4
5	88.5		60.8	73.7	73.4	79.2	94.6	92.4	102.9	104.0	5
6	5.6		8.1	10.1	13.0	11.0	17.5	18.9	14.8	17.6	6
7/8/9	22.8		12.6	17.3	16.6	21.6	22.4	23.0	26.1	26.2	7
X	0.1		3.1	4.3	4.2	4.0	3.5	2.9	3.0	4.1	8
			80.6	90.0	95.4	100.8	105.3	107.2	111.3	118.5	9
			-	-	-	-	-	-	-	-	X

Paraguay (BA) [4] [5]

Total - Total - Total
ISCO-88 - CITP-88 - CIUO-88

Total employment - Emploi total - Empleo total

	1999	2000	2001	2002	2003	2004	2005	2006	2007	2008
Total									2 716.4	2 810.5
1									91.1	93.6
2									131.4	164.8
3									115.2	135.3
4									147.6	147.0
5									425.6	432.6
6									739.8	677.0
7									423.0	433.0
8									109.8	129.0
9									523.7	591.3
0									9.2	6.6
X									-	0.2

Explanatory notes: see p. 77.
[1] Persons aged 10 years and over. [2] Persons aged 15 years and over. [3] Aug. of each year. [4] Persons aged 10 years and over. [5] Fourth quarter.

Notes explicatives: voir p. 80.
[1] Persónnes âgées de 10 ans et plus. [2] Personnes âgées de 15 ans et plus. [3] Août de chaque année. [4] Personnes âgées de 10 ans et plus. [5] Quatrième trimestre.

Notas explicativas: véase p. 83.
[1] Personas de 10 años y más. [2] Personas de 15 años y más. [3] Agosto de cada año. [4] Personas de 10 años y más. [5] Cuarto trimestre.

EMPLOYMENT — EMPLOI — EMPLEO

Total employment, by occupation — Emploi total, par profession — Empleo total, por ocupación

Thousands — Milliers — Millares

	1999	2000	2001	2002	2003	2004	2005	2006	2007	2008
Paraguay (BA) [1][2]				Total employment - Emploi total - Empleo total						
Men - Hommes - Hombres ISCO-88 - CITP-88 - CIUO-88										
Total	.	.	.	.	.	.	.	.	1 653.6	1 726.4
1	.	.	.	.	.	.	.	.	59.6	61.7
2	.	.	.	.	.	.	.	.	54.1	62.1
3	.	.	.	.	.	.	.	.	68.6	86.7
4	.	.	.	.	.	.	.	.	69.1	78.8
5	.	.	.	.	.	.	.	.	174.3	182.3
6	.	.	.	.	.	.	.	.	496.5	476.1
7	.	.	.	.	.	.	.	.	351.7	352.9
8	.	.	.	.	.	.	.	.	105.6	122.9
9	.	.	.	.	.	.	.	.	265.3	296.1
0	.	.	.	.	.	.	.	.	8.8	6.6
X	.	.	.	.	.	.	.	.	-	-
Women - Femmes - Mujeres ISCO-88 - CITP-88 - CIUO-88										
Total	.	.	.	.	.	.	.	.	1 062.8	1 084.1
1	.	.	.	.	.	.	.	.	31.6	31.9
2	.	.	.	.	.	.	.	.	77.2	102.7
3	.	.	.	.	.	.	.	.	46.7	48.6
4	.	.	.	.	.	.	.	.	78.3	68.2
5	.	.	.	.	.	.	.	.	251.2	250.3
6	.	.	.	.	.	.	.	.	243.3	200.9
7	.	.	.	.	.	.	.	.	71.3	80.1
8	.	.	.	.	.	.	.	.	4.1	6.1
9	.	.	.	.	.	.	.	.	258.4	295.2
0	.	.	.	.	.	.	.	.	0.4	-
X	.	.	.	.	.	.	.	.	-	0.2
Perú (BA) [3][4]				Total employment - Emploi total - Empleo total						
Total - Total - Total ISCO-88 - CITP-88 - CIUO-88										
Total	.	.	.	3 338.9 [2]	3 703.0 [5]	3 652.5	3 529.0	3 851.2	4 163.7	4 246.3
1	.	.	.	20.5 [2]	33.5 [5]	17.1	24.7	20.6	16.3	33.9
2	.	.	.	366.1 [2]	395.5 [5]	347.5	334.6	330.2	390.0	401.3
3	.	.	.	324.2 [2]	436.8 [5]	388.0	376.8	411.4	503.6	474.4
4	.	.	.	228.0 [2]	264.0 [5]	265.8	258.6	287.2	315.9	384.0
5	.	.	.	551.2 [2]	656.0 [5]	564.0	557.4	618.0	645.6	679.1
6	.	.	.	12.2 [2]	20.0 [5]	16.1	14.1	20.0	21.7	17.0
7	.	.	.	372.4 [2]	366.8 [5]	387.8	425.1	446.8	519.8	484.4
8	.	.	.	369.2 [2]	369.6 [5]	401.5	353.1	423.5	412.1	490.8
9	.	.	.	1 031.5 [2]	1 113.0 [5]	1 206.6	1 129.6	1 235.2	1 262.7	1 220.9
0	.	.	.	63.7 [2]	47.7 [5]	58.1	55.1	58.2	76.0	60.5
Men - Hommes - Hombres ISCO-88 - CITP-88 - CIUO-88										
Total	.	.	.	1 834.1 [2]	2 074.6 [5]	2 053.5	1 981.3	2 133.6	2 269.0	2 294.4
1	.	.	.	16.2 [2]	24.7 [5]	15.7	18.1	14.7	11.8	32.0
2	.	.	.	174.3 [2]	191.5 [5]	174.6	151.2	159.2	173.5	177.9
3	.	.	.	194.1 [2]	273.1 [5]	247.7	244.0	272.1	299.1	282.1
4	.	.	.	89.8 [2]	112.2 [5]	123.3	107.1	126.3	145.5	177.0
5	.	.	.	221.4 [2]	252.8 [5]	193.0	198.2	221.2	221.6	217.0
6	.	.	.	10.4 [2]	13.6 [5]	15.1	11.2	15.6	18.8	12.3
7	.	.	.	296.8 [2]	285.2 [5]	295.3	303.5	317.5	380.9	343.6
8	.	.	.	350.6 [2]	350.6 [5]	366.3	331.8	405.3	379.7	456.7
9	.	.	.	430.2 [2]	527.7 [5]	572.3	565.9	550.4	565.4	542.1
0	.	.	.	50.4 [2]	43.3 [5]	50.7	50.4	51.1	72.6	53.9
Women - Femmes - Mujeres ISCO-88 - CITP-88 - CIUO-88										
Total	.	.	.	1 504.7 [2]	1 628.4 [5]	1 598.5	1 547.7	1 717.6	1 894.7	1 951.8
1	.	.	.	4.4 [2]	8.7 [5]	1.4	6.6	5.8	4.5	1.9
2	.	.	.	191.8 [2]	204.0 [5]	172.9	183.4	171.0	216.5	223.4
3	.	.	.	130.1 [2]	163.7 [5]	140.4	132.8	139.3	204.5	192.3
4	.	.	.	138.1 [2]	151.9 [5]	142.5	151.5	160.9	170.4	207.0
5	.	.	.	329.8 [2]	403.2 [5]	371.0	359.3	396.8	424.0	462.1
6	.	.	.	1.8 [2]	6.5 [5]	1.0	2.8	4.4	2.9	4.7
7	.	.	.	75.5 [2]	81.7 [5]	92.5	121.5	129.4	138.8	140.8
8	.	.	.	18.6 [2]	18.9 [5]	35.2	21.3	18.2	32.4	34.2
9	.	.	.	601.3 [2]	585.3 [5]	634.2	563.7	684.7	697.3	678.8
0	.	.	.	13.3 [2]	4.4 [5]	7.4	4.7	7.1	3.4	6.6

Explanatory notes: see p. 77.

[1] Persons aged 10 years and over. [2] Fourth quarter. [3] Persons aged 14 years and over. [4] Metropolitan Lima. [5] May-Dec.

Notes explicatives: voir p. 80.

[1] Personnes âgées de 10 ans et plus. [2] Quatrième trimestre. [3] Personnes âgées de 14 ans et plus. [4] Lima métropolitaine. [5] Mai-déc.

Notas explicativas: véase p. 83.

[1] Personas de 10 años y más. [2] Cuarto trimestre. [3] Personas de 14 años y más. [4] Lima metropolitana. [5] Mayo-dic.

2C

EMPLOYMENT	EMPLOI	EMPLEO
Total employment, by occupation	**Emploi total, par profession**	**Empleo total, por ocupación**
Thousands	Milliers	Millares

	1999	2000	2001	2002	2003	2004	2005	2006	2007	2008

Perú (BA) [1][2]

Total employment - Emploi total - Empleo total

Total - Total - Total
ISCO-88 - CITP-88 - CIUO-88

	1999	2000	2001	2002	2003	2004	2005	2006	2007	2008
Total	7 211.2	7 128.4	7 619.9	7 578.2 [3]	8 165.7 [4]	8 238.6	8 216.0	8 694.0	9 197.8	9 445.5
1	79.5	32.4	48.7	44.3 [3]	46.4 [4]	40.8	53.3	39.5	42.1	63.3
2	730.3	621.5	688.0	742.6 [3]	769.1 [4]	720.9	687.0	720.8	830.8	852.4
3	613.2	714.4	689.7	574.0 [3]	696.9 [4]	647.6	648.0	733.8	860.8	836.0
4	473.9	373.1	337.9	380.6 [3]	443.7 [4]	461.8	467.9	502.2	540.9	649.2
5	1 328.7	1 378.9	1 260.1	1 320.2 [3]	1 450.9 [4]	1 329.8	1 401.6	1 477.9	1 543.2	1 602.6
6	225.5	225.5	323.5	363.2 [3]	402.3 [4]	392.1	412.6	410.1	390.0	404.9
7	776.4	888.9	819.0	833.4 [3]	790.5 [4]	844.7	889.7	924.3	1 028.1	1 057.1
8	719.1	701.5	729.5	724.9 [3]	740.8 [4]	757.5	717.3	833.8	875.8	993.5
9	2 152.7	2 096.5	2 631.4	2 489.2 [3]	2 735.3 [4]	2 949.3	2 843.9	2 955.5	2 972.2	2 891.6
0	111.9	95.5	92.2	105.9 [3]	89.9 [4]	94.0	94.9	96.3	114.0	94.8

Men - Hommes - Hombres
ISCO-88 - CITP-88 - CIUO-88

	1999	2000	2001	2002	2003	2004	2005	2006	2007	2008
Total	3 980.4	4 067.6	4 232.6	4 234.2 [3]	4 537.0 [4]	4 616.2	4 562.8	4 821.9	5 015.0	5 142.8
1	61.0	23.3	35.6	33.1 [3]	33.7 [4]	30.7	39.4	28.4	29.6	51.0
2	367.7	326.8	322.9	367.0 [3]	373.1 [4]	368.7	314.8	343.0	368.2	393.0
3	418.3	484.0	443.8	364.9 [3]	448.2 [4]	423.2	422.9	498.5	541.1	525.5
4	211.4	182.7	136.3	164.5 [3]	198.1 [4]	220.8	214.5	232.0	252.0	310.5
5	495.8	489.5	444.4	470.9 [3]	479.4 [4]	403.6	442.6	463.4	483.4	484.0
6	190.8	181.3	262.0	269.0 [3]	303.3 [4]	300.3	305.8	299.2	294.3	300.2
7	548.8	636.8	591.9	616.4 [3]	589.6 [4]	632.0	638.2	649.4	713.7	721.0
8	662.4	663.1	705.5	689.1 [3]	712.7 [4]	712.5	683.5	801.4	827.2	940.0
9	917.1	992.1	1 206.1	1 169.6 [3]	1 314.5 [4]	1 438.7	1 412.8	1 417.8	1 395.4	1 330.3
0	107.0	88.2	84.2	89.6 [3]	84.5 [4]	85.8	88.4	88.6	110.3	87.1

Women - Femmes - Mujeres
ISCO-88 - CITP-88 - CIUO-88

	1999	2000	2001	2002	2003	2004	2005	2006	2007	2008
Total	3 230.8	3 060.7	3 387.3	3 344.0 [3]	3 628.8 [4]	3 622.4	3 653.2	3 872.1	4 182.8	4 302.7
1	18.5	9.1	13.2	11.2 [3]	12.8 [4]	10.2	13.9	11.1	12.5	12.3
2	362.6	294.7	365.1	375.6 [3]	396.0 [4]	352.3	372.1	377.7	462.7	459.4
3	194.9	230.4	245.9	209.1 [3]	248.7 [4]	224.4	225.2	235.3	319.7	310.5
4	262.5	190.6	201.6	216.1 [3]	245.6 [4]	241.0	253.4	270.1	289.0	338.6
5	832.9	889.4	815.7	849.3 [3]	971.5 [4]	926.2	959.0	1 014.4	1 059.8	1 118.6
6	34.7	44.2	61.5	94.2 [3]	99.0 [4]	91.8	106.7	110.8	95.7	104.7
7	227.6	252.1	227.0	217.0 [3]	200.9 [4]	212.7	251.5	274.9	314.4	336.1
8	56.6	38.4	24.0	35.8 [3]	28.1 [4]	45.0	33.8	32.4	48.6	53.4
9	1 235.6	1 104.5	1 425.3	1 319.6 [3]	1 420.8 [4]	1 510.6	1 431.0	1 537.6	1 576.8	1 561.3
0	4.9	7.4	8.0	16.2 [3]	5.4 [4]	8.3	6.5	7.6	3.6	7.7

Puerto Rico (BA) [5][6]

Total employment - Emploi total - Empleo total

Total - Total - Total
ISCO-88 - CITP-88 - CIUO-88

	1999	2000	2001	2002	2003	2004	2005	2006	2007	2008
Total	1 142	1 162	1 134	1 170	1 201	1 226	1 250	1 253	1 241	1 209
1	136	146	131	135	146	149	150	153	151	137
2	170	168	170	182	184	187	197	208	209	203
3	42	39	38	41	44	43	43	47	48	46
4	183	191	183	189	198	202	203	204	202	196
5 [7]	259	258	266	276	284	286	295	293	298	296
6	36	34	34	36	35	39	42	35	30	30
7	118	121	115	122	121	124	116	116	108	103
8	150	155	149	142	136	139	147	142	136	135
9 [8]	48	50	48	47	53	57	57	54	59	62

Men - Hommes - Hombres
ISCO-88 - CITP-88 - CIUO-88

	1999	2000	2001	2002	2003	2004	2005	2006	2007	2008
Total	665	670	652	665	676	690	697	695	677	659
1	86	90	80	80	86	87	88	91	90	78
2	67	65	66	72	71	72	73	74	71	67
3	18	16	16	18	19	17	19	21	21	19
4	39	43	43	43	46	44	40	45	44	45
5 [7]	154	152	153	154	156	153	164	166	166	167
6	35	32	33	34	33	37	39	33	28	27
7	116	119	113	119	118	122	113	113	105	101
8	105	106	104	102	98	103	108	103	101	100
9 [8]	44	46	44	43	47	51	51	49	52	55

Women - Femmes - Mujeres
ISCO-88 - CITP-88 - CIUO-88

	1999	2000	2001	2002	2003	2004	2005	2006	2007	2008
Total	477	492	482	505	525	537	553	558	564	550
1	51	54	51	55	60	62	62	62	62	59
2	104	102	104	110	113	114	124	134	138	136
3	24	23	23	24	24	25	25	26	28	27
4	143	149	139	145	152	157	161	160	158	152
5 [7]	104	107	113	122	128	132	131	127	132	129
6	1	2	1	2	2	2	2	2	2	3
7	2	2	2	3	3	2	2	3	3	3
8	44	50	45	39	38	36	39	39	36	34
9 [8]	4	5	4	4	6	6	6	5	7	7

Explanatory notes: see p. 77.

[1] Persons aged 14 years and over. [2] Urban areas. [3] Fourth quarter. [4] May-Dec. [5] Persons aged 16 years and over. [6] Civilian labour force employed. [7] Incl. sales and services elementary occupations. [8] Excl. sales and services elementary occupations.

Notes explicatives: voir p. 80.

[1] Personnes âgées de 14 ans et plus. [2] Régions urbaines. [3] Quatrième trimestre. [4] Mai-déc. [5] Personnes âgées de 16 ans et plus. [6] Main-d'oeuvre civile occupée. [7] Y compris les employés non qualifiés des services et de la vente. [8] Non compris les employés non qualifiés des services et de la vente.

Notas explicativas: véase p. 83.

[1] Personas de 14 años y más. [2] Áreas urbanas. [3] Cuarto trimestre. [4] Mayo-dic. [5] Personas de 16 años y más. [6] Fuerza de trabajo civil ocupada. [7] Incl. los trabajadores no calificados de ventas y servicios. [8] Excl. los trabajadores no calificados de ventas y servicios.

EMPLOYMENT — EMPLOI — EMPLEO

Total employment,
by occupation

Emploi total,
par profession

Empleo total,
por ocupación

	Thousands			Milliers				Millares		
	1999	2000	2001	2002	2003	2004	2005	2006	2007	2008

Saint Lucia (BA) [1]   Total employment - Emploi total - Empleo total

Total - Total - Total
ISCO-88 - CITP-88 - CIUO-88

	1999	2000	2001	2002	2003	2004	2005	2006	2007	2008
Total	59.850	63.470	.	58.525	63.867	62.265	.	.	.	.
1	4.145	5.070	.	3.065	4.632	3.895	.	.	.	.
2	3.910	4.355	.	4.525	4.860	5.405	.	.	.	.
3	2.725	3.290	.	2.660	3.280	2.582	.	.	.	.
4	5.150	5.455	.	3.735	4.340	4.380	.	.	.	.
5	10.640	10.020	.	8.045	8.607	7.980	.	.	.	.
6	10.075	10.575	.	5.645	7.437	8.450	.	.	.	.
7	8.725	9.685	.	8.700	9.642	7.502	.	.	.	.
8	4.235	4.035	.	3.905	3.570	3.042	.	.	.	.
9	8.880	9.940	.	7.650	8.167	8.385	.	.	.	.
X	1.365	1.045	.	10.595	9.330	10.642	.	.	.	.

Men - Hommes - Hombres
ISCO-88 - CITP-88 - CIUO-88

	1999	2000	2001	2002	2003	2004	2005	2006	2007	2008
Total	31.830	35.030	.	32.105	36.475	34.837	.	.	.	.
1	1.775	2.260	.	1.380	1.880	1.857	.	.	.	.
2	1.405	1.940	.	1.690	1.977	2.057	.	.	.	.
3	1.270	1.685	.	1.400	1.605	1.450	.	.	.	.
4	1.135	1.205	.	0.775	1.082	0.827	.	.	.	.
5	3.825	4.080	.	3.670	4.107	4.012	.	.	.	.
6	7.020	7.485	.	3.960	5.042	5.880	.	.	.	.
7	7.025	7.735	.	7.190	7.952	6.445	.	.	.	.
8	3.220	3.125	.	2.730	2.782	2.305	.	.	.	.
9	4.315	4.765	.	3.845	4.720	3.945	.	.	.	.
X	0.840	0.750	.	5.465	5.325	6.058	.	.	.	.

Women - Femmes - Mujeres
ISCO-88 - CITP-88 - CIUO-88

	1999	2000	2001	2002	2003	2004	2005	2006	2007	2008
Total	28.020	28.440	.	26.420	27.392	27.427	.	.	.	.
1	2.370	2.810	.	1.685	2.752	2.037	.	.	.	.
2	2.505	2.415	.	2.835	2.882	3.347	.	.	.	.
3	1.455	1.605	.	1.260	1.675	1.132	.	.	.	.
4	4.015	4.250	.	2.960	3.257	3.552	.	.	.	.
5	6.815	5.940	.	4.375	4.500	3.967	.	.	.	.
6	3.055	3.090	.	1.685	2.395	2.570	.	.	.	.
7	1.700	1.950	.	1.510	1.690	1.057	.	.	.	.
8	1.015	0.910	.	1.175	0.787	0.737	.	.	.	.
9	4.565	5.175	.	3.805	3.447	4.440	.	.	.	.
X	0.525	0.295	.	5.130	4.005	4.585	.	.	.	.

Trinidad and Tobago (BA) [1]   Total employment - Emploi total - Empleo total

Total - Total - Total
ISCO-88 - CITP-88 - CIUO-88

	1999	2000	2001	2002	2003	2004	2005	2006	2007	2008
Total	489.4	503.1	514.1	525.1	534.1	562.2	574.0	.	.	.
1	33.2	36.2	38.9	40.2	39.4	43.0	46.0	.	.	.
2	16.1	14.6	16.7	17.4	17.1	19.0	19.1	.	.	.
3	52.8	53.0	56.6	64.9	61.1	63.6	65.5	.	.	.
4	52.8	54.9	56.9	60.9	63.1	70.0	71.7	.	.	.
5,0	70.0	75.9	73.0	70.4	79.4	80.8	82.5	.	.	.
6	16.5	16.2	18.8	15.8	15.2	14.0	14.8	.	.	.
7	84.6	87.2	89.0	89.8	89.4	93.6	90.5	.	.	.
8	46.9	49.5	47.9	48.8	49.7	51.6	51.5	.	.	.
9	116.5	115.3	114.8	115.7	117.7	124.7	130.1	.	.	.
X	0.3	0.2	1.4	1.0	1.8	1.9	2.1	.	.	.

Men - Hommes - Hombres
ISCO-88 - CITP-88 - CIUO-88

	1999	2000	2001	2002	2003	2004	2005	2006	2007	2008
Total	310.1	316.9	326.0	329.0	330.6	341.9	343.6	.	.	.
1	19.3	22.0	23.4	25.0	23.9	25.4	26.0	.	.	.
2	9.1	8.2	9.4	9.8	8.7	10.0	10.2	.	.	.
3	23.6	24.5	26.7	28.4	28.4	29.2	29.3	.	.	.
4	13.2	13.4	14.9	15.8	15.7	17.7	17.0	.	.	.
5,0	34.9	35.8	33.7	33.7	38.3	37.8	36.0	.	.	.
6	14.4	14.1	16.3	14.4	13.8	12.2	13.1	.	.	.
7	74.4	76.6	78.7	79.4	79.8	84.2	80.6	.	.	.
8	41.8	44.0	43.5	44.2	44.6	46.4	47.1	.	.	.
9	79.3	78.1	78.6	77.5	76.3	77.8	82.6	.	.	.
X	0.2	0.2	0.8	0.7	1.1	1.3	1.5	.	.	.

Women - Femmes - Mujeres
ISCO-88 - CITP-88 - CIUO-88

	1999	2000	2001	2002	2003	2004	2005	2006	2007	2008
Total	179.3	186.2	188.1	196.1	203.5	220.3	230.4	.	.	.
1	13.9	14.2	15.5	15.2	15.5	17.6	20.0	.	.	.
2	7.0	6.4	7.3	7.6	8.4	9.0	8.9	.	.	.
3	29.2	28.5	29.9	36.5	32.7	34.4	36.2	.	.	.
4	39.6	41.5	42.0	45.1	47.4	52.3	54.7	.	.	.
5,0	35.1	40.1	39.3	36.7	41.1	43.0	46.5	.	.	.
6	2.1	2.1	2.5	1.4	1.4	1.8	1.7	.	.	.
7	10.2	10.6	10.3	10.4	9.6	9.4	9.9	.	.	.
8	5.1	5.5	4.4	4.6	5.1	5.2	4.4	.	.	.
9	37.2	37.2	36.2	38.2	41.4	46.9	47.5	.	.	.
X	0.1	-	0.6	0.3	0.7	0.6	0.6	.	.	.

Explanatory notes: see p. 77.

[1] Persons aged 15 years and over.

Notes explicatives: voir p. 80.

[1] Personnes âgées de 15 ans et plus.

Notas explicativas: véase p. 83.

[1] Personas de 15 años y más.

EMPLOYMENT — EMPLOI — EMPLEO

Total employment, by occupation — **Emploi total, par profession** — **Empleo total, por ocupación**

Thousands — Milliers — Millares

Turks and Caicos Islands (BA) [1]

Total - Total - Total
ISCO-88 - CITP-88 - CIUO-88

Total employment - Emploi total - Empleo total

	1999	2000	2001	2002	2003	2004	2005	2006	2007	2008
Total	.	.	10.180	11.473	14.051	15.161	17.442	18.195	19.587	.
1	.	.	1.195	0.705	0.739	0.786	0.847	1.042	1.174	.
2	.	.	0.809	0.890	0.918	1.018	1.084	1.329	1.345	.
3	.	.	0.966	0.722	0.772	0.833	0.909	1.056	1.149	.
4	.	.	0.761	0.799	0.867	1.049	1.170	1.282	1.400	.
5	.	.	1.683	1.688	1.900	1.967	2.297	2.393	2.587	.
6	.	.	0.199	0.237	0.272	0.306	0.319	0.428	0.435	.
7	.	.	1.287	1.005	1.165	1.226	1.416	1.329	1.710	.
8	.	.	0.304	0.290	0.351	0.353	0.419	0.231	0.274	.
9	.	.	2.125	3.163	4.133	4.802	5.891	5.188	5.443	.
X	.	.	0.851	1.974	2.934	2.821	3.090	3.917	4.070	.

United States (BA) [2] [3]

Total - Total - Total
ISCO-68 - CITP-68 - CIUO-68 / ISCO-88 - CITP-88 - CIUO-88 (2008)

Total employment - Emploi total - Empleo total

ISCO-68	1999	2000	2001	2002	2003	2004	2005	2006	2007	2008	ISCO-88
Total	133 488	135 208	135 073	136 485	137 736	139 252	141 729	144 426	146 047	145 362	Total
0/1	25 238	25 498	26 053	26 430	19 934	20 235	20 450	21 233	21 577	22 059	1
2	19 584	19 774	20 338	20 561	27 995	28 297	28 795	29 187	30 210	30 702	2-3
3	18 448	18 717	18 503	18 184	19 536	19 481	19 529	19 500	19 513	19 249	4
4	16 118	16 340	16 044	16 254	38 046	38 703	39 566	40 452	40 835	40 746	5
5	17 915	18 278	18 359	19 219	1 050	991	976	961	960	988	6
6	3 426	3 399	3 245	3 480	31 175	31 544	32 413	33 093	32 951	31 619	7-8
7/8/9	32 760	33 201	32 531	32 357							

Men - Hommes - Hombres
ISCO-68 - CITP-68 - CIUO-68 / ISCO-88 - CITP-88 - CIUO-88

ISCO-68	1999	2000	2001	2002	2003	2004	2005	2006	2007	2008	ISCO-88
Total	71 446	72 293	72 080	72 903	73 322	74 524	75 973	77 502	78 254	77 486	Total
0/1	11 796	11 846	12 073	11 990	11 534	11 718	11 761	12 347	12 375	12 647	1
2	10 744	10 814	10 990	11 115	12 201	12 418	12 588	12 581	13 218	13 301	2-3
3	3 936	3 939	3 950	3 914	4 714	4 700	4 829	4 797	4 840	4 845	4
4	8 049	8 231	8 120	8 285	17 597	17 931	18 244	18 637	18 761	18 692	5
5	7 093	7 245	7 263	7 701	819	786	756	750	759	780	6
6	2 749	2 698	2 570	2 765	26 466	26 971	27 796	28 392	28 302	27 221	7-8
7/8/9	27 079	27 520	27 114	27 134							

Women - Femmes - Mujeres
ISCO-68 - CITP-68 - CIUO-68 / ISCO-88 - CITP-88 - CIUO-88

ISCO-68	1999	2000	2001	2002	2003	2004	2005	2006	2007	2008	ISCO-88
Total	62 042	62 915	62 992	63 582	64 404	64 728	65 757	66 925	67 792	67 876	Total
0/1	13 442	13 652	13 980	14 440	8 400	8 517	8 689	8 886	9 203	9 412	1
2	8 840	8 960	9 348	9 446	15 794	15 879	16 207	16 606	16 992	17 401	2-3
3	14 512	14 778	14 553	14 270	14 823	14 781	14 700	14 703	14 673	14 404	4
4	8 069	8 110	7 924	7 969	20 449	20 772	21 323	21 816	22 075	22 053	5
5	10 822	11 034	11 096	11 518	231	204	220	212	201	208	6
6	676	701	675	715	4 708	4 573	4 617	4 703	4 647	4 398	7-8
7/8/9	5 681	5 682	5 416	5 223							

Uruguay (BA) [4] [5]

Total - Total - Total
ISCO-88 - CITP-88 - CIUO-88

Total employment - Emploi total - Empleo total

	1999	2000	2001	2002	2003	2004	2005	2006	2007	2008
Total	.	1 067.6	1 076.2	1 038.3	1 032.0	.	1 114.5	1 413.5 [6]	1 482.1	.
1	.	65.9	68.8	67.5	64.0	.	69.7	75.9 [6]	87.4	.
2	.	101.1	97.5	102.0	103.9	.	115.8	129.0 [6]	139.1	.
3	.	68.4	68.4	62.2	64.8	.	72.0	83.0 [6]	90.6	.
4	.	139.4	143.3	141.7	131.6	.	146.8	171.7 [6]	180.7	.
5	.	169.4	171.0	158.1	162.4	.	176.0	210.3 [6]	204.1	.
6	.	30.8	31.2	34.0	34.9	.	36.9	85.6 [6]	82.2	.
7	.	184.6	182.2	177.1	173.5	.	184.0	221.3 [6]	216.4	.
8	.	79.7	74.4	72.4	65.1	.	70.0	96.7 [6]	105.8	.
9	.	214.1	225.8	211.6	219.1	.	232.9	326.9 [6]	363.9	.
0	.	14.2	13.5	11.7	12.8	.	10.4	11.1 [6]	11.9	.
X	.	-	-	-	-	.	-	1.9 [6]	-	.

Men - Hommes - Hombres
ISCO-88 - CITP-88 - CIUO-88

	1999	2000	2001	2002	2003	2004	2005	2006	2007	2008
Total	.	613.4	617.7	597.9	589.7	.	620.1	822.4 [6]	852.9	.
1	.	42.0	43.3	42.5	41.5	.	42.1	45.9 [6]	52.1	.
2	.	35.8	36.9	38.6	38.9	.	42.7	48.3 [6]	51.1	.
3	.	41.9	42.9	35.5	39.7	.	43.2	50.5 [6]	56.5	.
4	.	56.1	58.4	57.1	52.4	.	57.2	69.3 [6]	71.3	.
5	.	68.4	68.0	66.5	68.2	.	65.7	80.9 [6]	70.4	.
6	.	28.0	28.0	30.8	31.0	.	33.3	73.8 [6]	70.1	.
7	.	158.0	156.1	151.3	144.6	.	152.9	186.8 [6]	180.6	.
8	.	70.8	66.3	65.9	57.8	.	61.6	84.3 [6]	92.5	.
9	.	99.7	105.7	98.5	103.5	.	111.7	170.6 [6]	196.7	.
0	.	12.7	12.0	11.2	12.3	.	9.7	10.8 [6]	11.6	.
X	.	-	-	-	-	.	-	1.2 [6]	-	.

Explanatory notes: see p. 77.

[1] Persons aged 15 years and over. [2] Excl. armed forces. [3] Persons aged 16 years and over. [4] Persons aged 14 years and over. [5] Excl. conscripts. [6] Prior to 2006: urban areas.

Notes explicatives: voir p. 80.

[1] Personnes âgées de 15 ans et plus. [2] Non compris les forces armées. [3] Personnes âgées de 16 ans et plus. [4] Personnes âgées de 14 ans et plus. [5] Non compris les conscrits. [6] Avant 2006: régions urbaines.

Notas explicativas: véase p. 83.

[1] Personas de 15 años y más. [2] Excl. las fuerzas armadas. [3] Personas de 16 años y más. [4] Personas de 14 años y más. [5] Excl. los conscriptos. [6] Antes de 2006: areas urbanas.

Total employment, by occupation / Emploi total, par profession / Empleo total, por ocupación

	Thousands / Milliers / Millares									
	1999	2000	2001	2002	2003	2004	2005	2006	2007	2008

Uruguay (BA) [1] [2] — Total employment - Emploi total - Empleo total

Women - Femmes - Mujeres
ISCO-88 - CITP-88 - CIUO-88

	1999	2000	2001	2002	2003	2004	2005	2006	2007	2008
Total	.	454.2	458.5	440.4	442.3	.	494.4	591.0 [3]	629.1	.
1	.	23.9	25.5	25.0	22.5	.	27.6	30.0 [3]	35.2	.
2	.	65.2	60.5	63.4	65.0	.	73.1	80.7 [3]	88.0	.
3	.	26.6	25.4	26.7	25.1	.	28.8	32.5 [3]	34.0	.
4	.	83.3	84.9	84.6	79.2	.	89.6	102.4 [3]	109.4	.
5	.	101.0	103.0	91.5	94.2	.	110.3	129.4 [3]	133.7	.
6	.	2.8	3.2	3.1	4.0	.	3.6	11.8 [3]	12.1	.
7	.	26.6	26.1	25.8	28.9	.	31.1	34.5 [3]	35.8	.
8	.	8.9	8.2	6.6	7.3	.	8.4	12.3 [3]	13.4	.
9	.	114.4	120.2	113.2	115.5	.	121.3	156.3 [3]	167.2	.
0	.	1.5	1.5	0.5	0.6	.	0.7	0.3 [3]	0.3	.
X	.	-	-	-	-	.	-	0.8 [3]	-	.

Venezuela, Rep. Bolivariana de (BA) [4] [5] [6] — Total employment - Emploi total - Empleo total

Total - Total - Total
ISCO-68 - CITP-68 - CIUO-68

	1999	2000	2001	2002	2003	2004	2005	2006	2007	2008
Total	8 741.6	8 960.9	9 685.6	9 786.2	9 993.8	10 417.6	10 734.0	11 116.9	11 491.9	11 863.1
0/1	985.3	989.6	1 038.7	1 050.4	1 099.8	1 196.4	1 221.7	1 383.2	1 432.0	1 520.1
2	310.6	280.6	341.3	232.2	275.3	353.6	602.0	419.9	439.8	440.7
3	713.6	706.3	774.9	721.8	681.0	674.9	736.8	771.3	827.0	871.4
4	1 725.8	1 743.8	1 911.2	2 027.5	2 065.8	2 117.8	2 022.8	2 060.8	2 079.9	2 123.4
5	1 492.7	1 569.8	1 785.8	1 898.5	1 945.8	2 027.3	1 994.6	2 103.3	2 177.2	2 269.8
6	907.2	970.7	951.5	1 005.2	1 095.7	1 091.2	1 059.1	1 006.7	988.7	990.6
7/8/9	2 580.0	2 663.9	2 842.6	2 801.3	2 761.3	2 897.9	2 985.8	3 269.7	3 466.0	3 554.5
X	26.6	36.2	39.5	49.4	69.1	58.4	111.1	102.2	81.2	92.5

Men - Hommes - Hombres
ISCO-68 - CITP-68 - CIUO-68

	1999	2000	2001	2002	2003	2004	2005	2006	2007	2008
Total	5 610.3	5 722.8	5 995.7	6 029.7	6 140.7	6 403.4	6 620.8	6 894.0	7 073.0	7 264.4
0/1	398.6	383.3	398.5	402.8	415.4	442.2	447.8	519.9	518.6	540.1
2	223.1	197.2	243.8	169.4	196.1	249.6	415.0	292.8	300.0	305.5
3	257.2	268.3	278.2	256.0	244.5	225.4	256.1	258.0	278.4	290.9
4	910.2	890.1	906.1	973.1	989.9	1 024.8	983.3	992.2	996.2	1 004.6
5	649.7	659.1	727.1	775.0	787.1	835.7	830.6	869.9	881.7	920.8
6	863.9	928.7	897.0	941.4	1 019.1	1 021.3	970.3	941.1	923.3	921.8
7/8/9	2 281.5	2 363.3	2 509.7	2 471.7	2 434.4	2 556.9	2 638.6	2 938.9	3 105.1	3 208.7
X	26.0	32.9	35.3	40.1	54.1	47.5	79.1	81.1	69.8	72.0

Women - Femmes - Mujeres
ISCO-68 - CITP-68 - CIUO-68

	1999	2000	2001	2002	2003	2004	2005	2006	2007	2008
Total	3 131.3	3 238.1	3 689.9	3 756.5	3 853.1	4 014.2	4 113.1	4 223.0	4 418.9	4 598.6
0/1	586.6	606.3	640.2	647.6	684.4	754.2	773.9	863.2	913.4	979.9
2	87.4	83.4	97.5	62.7	79.2	104.1	186.9	127.0	139.8	135.2
3	456.3	438.0	496.7	465.8	436.4	449.5	480.7	513.3	548.7	580.5
4	815.5	853.7	1 005.1	1 054.4	1 075.9	1 093.0	1 039.5	1 068.6	1 083.8	1 118.8
5	843.1	910.8	1 058.7	1 123.4	1 158.7	1 191.7	1 164.0	1 233.3	1 295.5	1 349.0
6	43.3	42.1	54.5	63.7	76.6	69.9	88.8	65.6	65.4	68.8
7/8/9	298.5	300.6	332.9	329.5	326.9	341.0	347.2	330.8	360.9	345.8
X	0.6	3.3	4.2	9.3	15.0	10.8	32.1	21.1	11.4	20.5

ASIA-ASIE-ASIA

Azerbaijan (BA) [5] [7] — Total employment - Emploi total - Empleo total

Total - Total - Total
ISCO-88 - CITP-88 - CIUO-88

	1999	2000	2001	2002	2003	2004	2005	2006	2007	2008
Total	.	.	.	.	3 377.8	.	.	3 985.9	4 014.0	4 056.0
1	.	.	.	.	74.7	.	.	54.8	52.0	47.7
2	.	.	.	.	525.3	.	.	665.0	667.1	614.4
3	.	.	.	.	142.3	.	.	158.2	216.3	159.8
4	.	.	.	.	63.4	.	.	69.3	89.1	239.0
5	.	.	.	.	445.8	.	.	366.5	284.9	229.7
6	.	.	.	.	947.7	.	.	751.5	756.7	807.9
7	.	.	.	.	279.8	.	.	310.1	300.3	372.3
8	.	.	.	.	137.6	.	.	231.7	215.8	217.9
9	.	.	.	.	761.2	.	.	1 363.4	1 425.2	1 362.0
0	.	.	.	.	-	.	.	15.4	6.7	5.3

Explanatory notes: see p. 77.

[1] Persons aged 14 years and over. [2] Excl. conscripts. [3] Prior to 2006: urban areas. [4] Excl. armed forces. [5] Persons aged 15 years and over. [6] Second semester. [7] Excl. armed forces and conscripts.

Notes explicatives: voir p. 80.

[1] Personnes âgées de 14 ans et plus. [2] Non compris les conscrits. [3] Avant 2006: régions urbaines. [4] Non compris les forces armées. [5] Personnes âgées de 15 ans et plus. [6] Second semestre. [7] Non compris les forces armées et les conscrits.

Notas explicativas: véase p. 83.

[1] Personas de 14 años y más. [2] Excl. los conscriptos. [3] Antes de 2006: areas urbanas. [4] Excl. las fuerzas armadas. [5] Personas de 15 años y más. [6] Segundo semestre. [7] Excl. las fuerzas armadas y los conscriptos.

2C	EMPLOYMENT	EMPLOI	EMPLEO

Total employment, by occupation / Emploi total, par profession / Empleo total, por ocupación

	1999	2000	2001	2002	2003	2004	2005	2006	2007	2008

Azerbaijan (BA) [1] [2] — Total employment - Emploi total - Empleo total

Men - Hommes - Hombres — ISCO-88 - CITP-88 - CIUO-88

	1999	2000	2001	2002	2003	2004	2005	2006	2007	2008
Total	.	.	.	.	1 975.6	.	.	2 105.7	2 020.5	2 048.3
1	.	.	.	.	63.4	.	.	46.0	49.3	44.3
2	.	.	.	.	239.0	.	.	322.4	305.4	280.9
3	.	.	.	.	63.7	.	.	81.7	113.0	75.6
4	.	.	.	.	24.4	.	.	31.2	50.1	141.4
5	.	.	.	.	249.5	.	.	237.6	200.7	150.9
6	.	.	.	.	522.4	.	.	427.3	502.9	550.8
7	.	.	.	.	255.8	.	.	272.3	271.3	236.1
8	.	.	.	.	125.5	.	.	169.4	188.0	178.0
9	.	.	.	.	431.9	.	.	507.0	333.1	385.0
0	.	.	.	.	-	.	.	10.6	6.7	5.3

Women - Femmes - Mujeres — ISCO-88 - CITP-88 - CIUO-88

	1999	2000	2001	2002	2003	2004	2005	2006	2007	2008
Total	.	.	.	.	1 402.2	.	.	1 880.2	1 993.5	2 007.7
1	.	.	.	.	11.3	.	.	8.7	2.7	3.4
2	.	.	.	.	286.3	.	.	342.6	361.7	333.5
3	.	.	.	.	78.6	.	.	76.5	103.2	84.2
4	.	.	.	.	39.0	.	.	38.1	39.0	97.6
5	.	.	.	.	196.3	.	.	128.9	84.2	78.8
6	.	.	.	.	425.3	.	.	324.2	253.8	257.1
7	.	.	.	.	24.0	.	.	37.8	29.0	136.2
8	.	.	.	.	12.1	.	.	62.3	27.8	39.9
9	.	.	.	.	329.3	.	.	856.4	1 092.1	977.0
0	.	.	.	.	-	.	.	4.8	-	-

Bahrain (FA) [3] [4] — All persons engaged - Effectif occupé - Efectivo ocupado

Total - Total - Total — ISCO-68 - CITP-68 - CIUO-68

	1999	2000	2001	2002	2003	2004	2005	2006	2007	2008
Total	147.7	149.4	157.4	164.7	189.9	211.1	246.5	297.4	332.2	431.2
0/1	17.9	18.1	18.5	19.6	21.7	22.8	25.1	28.6	32.3	41.7
2	4.6	4.6	4.8	5.0	5.4	5.7	6.3	7.6	8.9	24.9
3	14.4	14.4	14.8	15.4	17.0	18.3	19.7	21.3	22.5	22.8
4	7.1	7.1	7.5	8.0	8.7	9.5	11.0	14.6	16.8	21.6
5	16.8	8.2	18.0	19.2	21.8	24.3	29.7	37.0	41.8	2.4
6	0.8	0.9	0.9	0.9	1.0	1.0	1.2	1.7	2.1	265.4
7/8/9	69.7	61.6	73.9	74.7	83.2	90.2	104.6	119.4	134.2	50.5
X	16.4	17.3	19.0	21.9	31.2	39.3	48.8	67.2	74.1	1.8
AF		17.2								

Men - Hommes - Hombres — ISCO-68 - CITP-68 - CIUO-68

	1999	2000	2001	2002	2003	2004	2005	2006	2007	2008
Total	129.7	131.0	136.8	143.9	165.8	186.9	219.6	267.0	300.5	390.1
0/1	14.4	14.5	14.9	15.8	17.3	18.3	20.2	23.0	26.2	34.1
2	4.2	4.2	4.4	4.6	4.9	5.1	5.6	6.7	7.7	19.3
3	8.8	8.9	9.0	9.2	9.8	10.5	11.1	11.9	12.4	11.8
4	6.0	6.0	6.2	6.6	7.0	7.7	8.9	12.0	13.9	17.9
5	14.8	8.0	15.7	16.8	19.1	21.2	25.5	31.7	35.6	2.4
6	0.8	0.8	0.8	0.9	1.0	1.0	1.1	1.7	2.1	260.2
7/8/9	65.0	56.9	67.6	68.8	76.4	84.6	99.1	114.5	129.9	43.0
X	15.7	15.2	18.2	21.2	30.5	38.6	47.9	65.6	72.7	1.4
AF		16.5								

Women - Femmes - Mujeres — ISCO-68 - CITP-68 - CIUO-68

	1999	2000	2001	2002	2003	2004	2005	2006	2007	2008
Total	18.0	18.4	20.6	20.8	24.2	24.2	26.9	30.4	31.7	41.1
0/1	3.5	3.6	3.6	3.8	4.4	4.5	4.9	5.6	6.2	7.6
2	0.4	0.4	0.4	0.5	0.5	0.6	0.7	0.9	1.1	5.6
3	5.6	5.6	5.8	6.2	7.2	7.8	8.6	9.4	10.0	11.0
4	1.1	1.1	1.3	1.4	1.7	1.8	2.1	2.6	2.9	3.7
5	2.0	0.2	2.3	2.4	2.8	3.1	4.2	5.3	6.1	0.0
6	0.2	0.0	0.0	0.0	0.0	0.0	0.0	0.0	0.0	5.1
7/8/9	4.7	4.6	6.3	5.8	6.8	5.6	5.5	4.9	4.2	7.6
X	0.7	2.2	0.8	0.7	0.7	0.7	0.9	1.6	1.5	0.4
AF		0.7								

Explanatory notes: see p. 77. — Notes explicatives: voir p. 80. — Notas explicativas: véase p. 83.

[1] Persons aged 15 years and over. [2] Excl. armed forces and conscripts. [3] Data refer to Paid Employment. [4] Private sector.

[1] Personnes âgées de 15 ans et plus. [2] Non compris les forces armées et les conscrits. [3] Les données se rapportent au emploi rémunéré [4] Secteur privé.

[1] Personas de 15 años y más. [2] Excl. las fuerzas armadas y los conscriptos. [3] Los datos se refieren a el empleo remunerado [4] Sector privado.

218 ILO YEARBOOK OF LABOUR STATISTICS 2009   ANNUAIRE DES STATISTIQUES DU TRAVAIL DU BIT 2009   ANUARIO DE ESTADISTICAS DEL TRABAJO DEL OIT 2009

EMPLOYMENT

Total employment, by occupation

EMPLOI

Emploi total, par profession

EMPLEO

Empleo total, por ocupación

2C

	Thousands			Milliers				Millares		
	1999	2000	2001	2002	2003	2004	2005	2006	2007	2008

Georgia (BA) [1] [2] — Total employment - Emploi total - Empleo total

Total - Total - Total
ISCO-88 - CITP-88 - CIUO-88

	1999	2000	2001	2002	2003	2004	2005	2006	2007	2008
Total	1 732.6	1 839.3	1 877.7	1 839.2	1 814.5	1 783.3	1 744.6	1 747.3	1 704.3	.
1	84.4	90.1	94.7	76.7	64.9	68.1	59.4	52.9	60.6	.
2	220.0	233.6	240.9	209.2	214.9	204.1	195.4	199.2	218.5	.
3	126.2	134.3	138.3	117.3	111.0	114.3	109.7	110.9	100.1	.
4	31.2	33.1	30.1	25.6	19.8	21.6	20.2	19.5	16.1	.
5	156.1	165.5	174.6	198.4	186.1	190.3	183.2	165.8	162.8	.
6	786.2	812.2	828.0	978.6	968.1	938.4	926.7	944.6	891.2	.
7	71.0	75.4	86.3	87.1	102.7	94.8	94.8	101.2	104.2	.
8	60.6	85.5	80.7	60.6	63.0	67.9	61.5	69.2	60.6	.
9	166.9	176.5	170.2	84.2	76.2	78.4	85.5	84.1	89.8	.
0	6.2	7.3	7.5	-	-	-	6.8	-	-	.
X	23.7	25.8	26.3	1.5	7.8	5.4	1.4	-	-	.

Men - Hommes - Hombres
ISCO-88 - CITP-88 - CIUO-88

	1999	2000	2001	2002	2003	2004	2005	2006	2007	2008
Total	884.2	946.9	966.7	954.1	957.5	926.5	915.2	920.4	888.1	.
1	57.5	71.0	72.5	55.6	46.5	50.7	43.8	35.5	40.1	.
2	79.6	94.6	96.6	73.7	79.1	68.7	74.8	76.7	80.6	.
3	46.1	52.1	54.1	44.3	42.5	49.5	42.4	42.6	40.9	.
4	6.2	4.8	4.8	10.0	6.8	6.3	5.7	6.8	5.9	.
5	85.1	92.8	94.7	93.8	95.6	90.8	88.6	70.7	73.8	.
6	381.4	388.4	395.5	488.1	484.8	458.7	455.4	472.9	431.7	.
7	55.5	65.3	66.7	74.0	84.3	80.7	81.9	89.1	92.9	.
8	55.2	71.9	73.5	57.1	59.3	65.1	60.5	67.8	59.4	.
9	93.0	76.7	78.3	56.3	55.2	53.2	54.8	58.4	63.2	.
0	5.6	4.8	4.8	-	-	-	6.7	-	-	.
X	19.0	24.6	25.2	1.2	3.4	3.3	0.7	-	-	.

Women - Femmes - Mujeres
ISCO-88 - CITP-88 - CIUO-88

	1999	2000	2001	2002	2003	2004	2005	2006	2007	2008
Total	847.8	892.4	911.0	885.1	857.0	856.9	829.4	826.8	816.2	.
1	26.9	17.1	22.2	21.1	18.4	17.4	15.6	17.2	20.6	.
2	140.4	141.1	144.3	135.5	135.8	135.4	120.6	122.5	137.9	.
3	80.1	83.6	84.2	73.0	68.5	65.1	67.4	68.3	59.2	.
4	25.0	29.4	25.3	15.6	13.0	15.4	14.5	12.8	10.7	.
5	71.0	72.1	79.9	104.6	90.5	99.6	94.6	95.1	88.9	.
6	404.9	426.2	432.5	490.5	483.3	479.7	471.3	471.8	459.7	.
7	15.5	7.9	19.6	13.1	18.4	14.1	12.9	12.0	11.3	.
8	5.4	11.3	7.2	3.5	3.7	2.8	1.0	1.4	1.2	.
9	74.0	101.0	91.9	27.9	21.0	25.2	30.7	25.7	26.7	.
0	0.6	2.4	2.7	0.3	4.4	2.0	0.1	-	-	.
X	3.9	0.2	1.2	-	-	2.1	0.7	-	-	.

Hong Kong, China (BA) [2] [3] — Total employment - Emploi total - Empleo total

Total - Total - Total
ISCO-88 - CITP-88 - CIUO-88

	1999	2000	2001	2002	2003	2004	2005	2006	2007	2008
Total	3 112.1	3 207.3	3 252.9	3 218.4	3 190.6	3 273.5	3 336.6	3 400.8	3 483.8	3 518.8
1	242.6	233.3	278.6	300.3	271.0	280.3	312.3	341.8	351.3	347.9
2	168.5	182.7	198.1	196.0	203.0	210.5	229.3	233.8	240.8	250.0
3	525.2	549.8	573.1	573.1	583.8	610.4	618.2	656.3	672.4	667.2
4	568.1	588.0	559.6	535.7	527.8	543.0	544.7	530.5	545.5	552.3
5	440.6	461.5	474.3	468.6	481.3	513.5	524.9	514.6	536.6	557.9
6	8.5	8.9	6.7	8.7	6.9	8.0	7.7	7.0	5.2	5.5
7	327.8	332.7	306.9	288.2	270.5	266.8	265.9	258.9	261.7	260.3
8	259.5	263.4	249.7	237.1	233.2	233.9	224.9	223.0	217.8	216.4
9	571.3	586.9	605.9	610.6	613.0	607.2	608.7	635.0	652.5	661.3

Men - Hommes - Hombres
ISCO-88 - CITP-88 - CIUO-88

	1999	2000	2001	2002	2003	2004	2005	2006	2007	2008
Total	1 816.5	1 854.5	1 845.7	1 794.0	1 764.3	1 800.8	1 822.6	1 840.4	1 869.0	1 870.0
1	189.4	176.8	206.9	223.7	200.2	204.8	227.7	241.5	246.7	245.3
2	113.2	123.7	133.4	128.0	132.9	135.9	151.9	149.1	152.6	155.5
3	315.2	330.5	340.6	335.0	344.2	354.7	355.1	365.0	379.1	369.0
4	158.0	162.0	151.7	138.1	132.8	145.2	144.4	142.0	147.3	147.1
5	249.2	256.4	254.1	243.9	250.3	256.9	255.9	251.3	253.9	261.2
6	6.4	6.2	4.8	6.0	4.7	5.7	5.3	4.6	3.5	4.0
7	315.8	323.0	297.1	276.7	260.1	255.2	256.0	249.9	251.6	250.9
8	218.6	226.6	215.2	207.0	204.5	207.2	201.4	201.4	197.1	200.1
9	250.6	249.4	241.9	235.7	234.6	235.2	224.9	235.7	237.3	236.9

Women - Femmes - Mujeres
ISCO-88 - CITP-88 - CIUO-88

	1999	2000	2001	2002	2003	2004	2005	2006	2007	2008
Total	1 295.6	1 352.8	1 407.3	1 424.4	1 426.3	1 472.7	1 514.0	1 560.4	1 614.8	1 648.8
1	53.2	56.5	71.7	76.6	70.8	75.5	84.6	100.3	104.6	102.6
2	55.3	59.0	64.8	68.1	70.1	74.7	77.4	84.7	88.2	94.5
3	210.0	219.3	232.5	238.2	239.6	255.7	263.0	291.3	293.2	298.2
4	410.0	426.0	407.9	397.6	395.0	397.8	400.3	388.5	398.2	405.2
5	191.4	205.1	220.2	224.8	231.0	256.6	269.0	263.3	282.8	296.8
6	2.1	2.7	1.9	2.7	2.3	2.3	2.5	2.4	1.7	1.4
7	12.0	9.8	9.8	11.5	10.4	11.6	9.9	9.0	10.1	9.4
8	40.9	36.9	34.5	30.1	28.8	26.6	23.5	21.6	20.7	16.3
9	320.7	337.6	364.0	374.9	378.4	371.9	383.8	399.3	415.2	424.4

Explanatory notes: see p. 77.

[1] Excl. armed forces. [2] Persons aged 15 years and over. [3] Excl. marine, military and institutional populations.

Notes explicatives: voir p. 80.

[1] Non compris les forces armées. [2] Personnes âgées de 15 ans et plus. [3] Non compris le personnel militaire, de la marine et la population institutionnelle.

Notas explicativas: véase p. 83.

[1] Excl. las fuerzas armadas. [2] Personas de 15 años y más. [3] Excl. el personal militar y de la marina, y la población institucional.

EMPLOYMENT — EMPLOI — EMPLEO

Total employment, by occupation
Emploi total, par profession
Empleo total, por ocupación

	Thousands								Millares	
						Milliers				
	1999	2000	2001	2002	2003	2004	2005	2006	2007	2008

Indonesia (BA) [1][2] Total employment - Emploi total - Empleo total

Total - Total - Total
ISCO-68 - CITP-68 - CIUO-68 / ISCO-88 - CITP-88 - CIUO-88

	1999	2000	2001	2002	2003	2004	2005	2006	2007	2008	
Total	88 817	.	90 807	91 647	92 811	93 722	93 958 [3]	95 457	99 930	102 553	Total
0/1	3 725		3 208	3 061	2 793	3 131	3 450 [3]	3 890	2 160	1 715	1
2	253		235	202	170	176	232 [3]	391	3 676	3 920	2
3	4 354		4 259	4 388	4 349	4 376	4 117 [3]	4 585	1 712	1 962	3
4	16 821		16 062	16 511	16 106	17 174	15 826 [3]	16 895	3 616	3 763	4
5	4 108		4 419	3 975	4 066	4 888	5 045 [3]	5 526	18 153	18 505	5
6	38 203		39 597	40 329	42 914	40 410	41 012 [3]	39 777	34 350	35 534	6
7/8/9	21 353		22 632	22 801	22 008	23 247	23 855 [3]	23 902	11 931	11 921	7
X			395	379	406	320	421 [3]	490	6 380	6 712	8
									17 461	18 041	9
									492	481	0

Men - Hommes - Hombres
ISCO-68 - CITP-68 - CIUO-68 / ISCO-88 - CITP-88 - CIUO-88

	1999	2000	2001	2002	2003	2004	2005	2006	2007	2008	
Total	54 909	.	57 131	58 583	59 500	60 582	61 439 [3]	61 977	63 148	63 899	Total
0/1	2 045		1 694	1 554	1 418	1 592	1 738 [3]	1 913	1 735	1 336	1
2	213		195	171	146	156	204 [3]	306	1 759	1 844	2
3	3 039		2 886	3 009	3 011	3 002	2 786 [3]	2 977	1 189	1 399	3
4	8 071		8 013	8 391	8 240	8 725	8 214 [3]	8 778	2 175	2 193	4
5	2 149		2 317	2 274	2 344	2 776	2 772 [3]	2 836	9 139	8 719	5
6	23 623		24 623	25 370	27 104	25 650	26 649 [3]	26 085	21 334	22 048	6
7/8/9	15 768		17 022	17 450	16 859	18 372	18 670 [3]	18 609	7 796	7 892	7
X			382	365	377	308	407 [3]	473	5 691	5 880	8
									11 862	12 126	9
									469	462	0

Women - Femmes - Mujeres
ISCO-68 - CITP-68 - CIUO-68 / ISCO-88 - CITP-88 - CIUO-88

	1999	2000	2001	2002	2003	2004	2005	2006	2007	2008	
Total	33 908	.	33 676	33 064	33 311	33 141	32 519 [3]	33 480	36 782	38 653	Total
0/1	1 679		1 515	1 507	1 374	1 539	1 712 [3]	1 977	426	379	1
2	40		41	31	24	20	28 [3]	85	1 917	2 076	2
3	1 315		1 373	1 379	1 338	1 374	1 331 [3]	1 608	523	563	3
4	8 750		8 049	8 121	7 865	8 449	7 613 [3]	8 117	1 441	1 569	4
5	1 959		2 102	1 702	1 722	2 112	2 274 [3]	2 690	9 014	9 786	5
6	14 581		14 974	14 959	15 810	14 760	14 363 [3]	13 692	13 016	13 485	6
7/8/9	5 585		5 610	5 351	5 149	4 875	5 185 [3]	5 293	4 135	4 029	7
X			12	14	28	11	13 [3]	17	689	832	8
									5 599	5 914	9
									23	19	0

Iran, Islamic Rep. of (BA) [4] Total employment - Emploi total - Empleo total

Total - Total - Total
ISCO-88 - CITP-88 - CIUO-88

	1999	2000	2001	2002	2003	2004	2005	2006	2007	2008
Total	.	.	.	.	.	.	20 619	20 841	21 092	.
1							637	609	593	
2							1 690	1 628	1 657	
3							978	969	978	
4							914	1 003	1 009	
5							2 579	2 636	2 689	
6							4 064	3 967	3 995	
7							4 118	4 305	4 165	
8							2 202	2 284	2 382	
9							2 962	2 968	3 133	
X							475	472	491	

Men - Hommes - Hombres
ISCO-88 - CITP-88 - CIUO-88

	1999	2000	2001	2002	2003	2004	2005	2006	2007	2008
Total	.	.	.	.	.	.	16 657	16 872	17 230	.
1							534	520	514	
2							957	905	934	
3							806	788	812	
4							674	746	765	
5							2 290	2 359	2 400	
6							3 039	2 950	2 917	
7							3 127	3 182	3 192	
8							2 180	2 260	2 358	
9							2 581	2 694	2 852	
X							469	468	486	

Women - Femmes - Mujeres
ISCO-88 - CITP-88 - CIUO-88

	1999	2000	2001	2002	2003	2004	2005	2006	2007	2008
Total	.	.	.	.	.	.	3 962	3 970	3 862	.
1							103	89	79	
2							733	723	723	
3							172	181	166	
4							240	257	244	
5							289	277	289	
6							1 025	1 017	1 078	
7							991	1 123	973	
8							23	25	25	
9							381	274	281	
X							5	4	5	

Explanatory notes: see p. 77. Notes explicatives: voir p. 80. Notas explicativas: véase p. 83.

[1] Persons aged 15 years and over. [2] Aug. of each year. [3] Nov. [4] Persons aged 10 years and over.

[1] Personnes âgées de 15 ans et plus. [2] Août de chaque année. [3] Nov. [4] Personnes âgées de 10 ans et plus.

[1] Personas de 15 años y más. [2] Agosto de cada año. [3] Nov. [4] Personas de 10 años y más.

EMPLOYMENT — EMPLOI — EMPLEO

Total employment, by occupation — Emploi total, par profession — Empleo total, por ocupación

	Thousands / Milliers / Millares									
	1999	2000	2001	2002	2003	2004	2005	2006	2007	2008

Israel (BA) [1][2] — Total employment - Emploi total - Empleo total

Total - Total - Total
ISCO-88 - CITP-88 - CIUO-88

	1999	2000	2001	2002	2003	2004	2005	2006	2007	2008
Total	2 136.6	2 221.2	2 264.9	2 284.4	2 330.2	2 400.8	2 493.7	2 573.6	2 682.0	2 776.7
1	150.3	176.1	177.2	183.0	182.0	166.8	164.0	180.0	201.3	216.7
2	303.2	309.6	327.6	338.7	354.4	368.9	389.8	402.6	423.3	439.7
3	341.7	373.8	385.2	393.4	400.3	406.8	432.2	464.3	484.4	489.4
4	344.5	356.3	365.9	364.4	358.5	371.7	381.8	384.7	402.8	418.0
5	314.1	321.5	332.0	338.0	360.0	386.5	407.6	406.6	424.8	451.3
6	38.8	35.8	34.6	33.3	32.5	35.1	35.8	32.1	31.6	34.5
7	248.3	247.0	238.4	233.8	241.4	246.1	244.9	252.0	266.7	262.7
8	197.0	193.4	197.4	190.6	195.6	202.0	205.2	215.6	217.4	234.4
9	175.7	179.0	182.2	182.7	184.2	193.5	206.0	205.9	199.6	199.6
X	23.1	28.7	24.5	26.6	21.3	23.4	26.3	29.8	30.1	30.3

Men - Hommes - Hombres
ISCO-88 - CITP-88 - CIUO-88

	1999	2000	2001	2002	2003	2004	2005	2006	2007	2008
Total	1 176.2	1 211.7	1 236.1	1 238.0	1 257.6	1 300.3	1 339.9	1 383.6	1 441.9	1 489.1
1	111.3	128.2	129.1	133.8	128.2	119.0	118.8	125.8	141.4	147.1
2	151.5	150.9	161.9	167.5	177.6	184.5	191.7	195.3	207.6	223.8
3	155.9	170.3	175.3	178.3	182.4	188.3	201.6	218.9	223.9	221.6
4	91.2	90.8	93.0	93.9	89.5	96.1	97.5	97.1	105.6	107.0
5	126.2	125.4	133.8	130.6	138.7	157.3	161.4	156.4	167.8	176.6
6	33.2	31.7	31.5	30.2	28.0	30.4	31.9	29.1	28.3	30.6
7	232.5	231.5	223.4	220.7	229.3	232.2	230.7	238.1	253.2	249.6
8	159.7	160.8	165.4	161.9	163.3	166.0	170.7	180.7	181.0	195.6
9	97.8	101.1	104.4	101.9	104.1	109.2	117.1	121.9	111.9	115.6
X	16.9	21.2	18.3	19.3	16.4	17.4	18.5	20.3	21.0	21.7

Women - Femmes - Mujeres
ISCO-88 - CITP-88 - CIUO-88

	1999	2000	2001	2002	2003	2004	2005	2006	2007	2008
Total	960.5	1 009.5	1 028.8	1 046.4	1 072.6	1 100.5	1 153.7	1 190.0	1 240.1	1 287.6
1	38.9	47.9	48.1	49.2	53.8	47.8	45.3	54.2	59.8	69.6
2	151.7	158.7	165.6	171.1	176.8	184.5	198.1	207.3	215.8	215.9
3	185.8	203.5	209.9	215.1	217.9	218.5	230.6	245.3	260.5	267.8
4	253.3	265.5	272.9	270.4	269.0	275.7	284.4	287.6	297.2	311.0
5	187.9	196.2	198.2	207.3	221.3	229.2	246.2	250.3	257.0	274.7
6	5.6	4.2	3.1	3.1	4.5	4.7	3.9	3.0	3.3	3.9
7	15.8	15.5	15.0	13.2	12.0	13.9	14.2	13.8	13.5	13.1
8	37.3	32.6	31.9	28.7	32.3	36.0	34.5	34.9	36.4	38.9
9	77.9	77.9	77.8	80.8	80.2	84.3	88.9	84.1	87.6	84.1
X	6.2	7.5	6.3	7.4	4.9	6.0	7.8	9.4	9.1	8.6

Japan (BA) [2] — Total employment - Emploi total - Empleo total

Total - Total - Total
ISCO-68 - CITP-68 - CIUO-68

	1999	2000	2001	2002	2003	2004	2005	2006	2007	2008
Total	64 620	64 460	64 120	63 300	63 160	63 290	63 560	63 820	64 120	63 850
0/1	8 460	8 560	8 730	8 900	9 060	9 200	9 370	9 380	9 380	9 500
2	2 150	2 060	2 020	1 870	1 850	1 890	1 890	1 850	1 730	1 720
3	12 730	12 850	12 490	12 280	12 300	12 440	12 470	12 600	12 620	12 920
4	9 210	9 110	9 680	9 340	9 170	9 010	8 920	8 810	8 880	8 700
5 [3]	6 680	6 770	6 930	7 170	7 290	7 480	7 570	7 720	7 870	7 890
6	3 320	3 210	3 090	2 910	2 890	2 840	2 790	2 690	2 690	2 640
7/8/9 [4]	21 700	21 520	20 760	20 320	20 040	19 790	19 860	20 110	20 250	19 790
X	390	370	420	520	550	630	690	660	700	690

Men - Hommes - Hombres
ISCO-68 - CITP-68 - CIUO-68

	1999	2000	2001	2002	2003	2004	2005	2006	2007	2008
Total	38 310	38 180	37 830	37 360	37 190	37 130	37 230	37 300	37 530	37 290
0/1	4 740	4 750	4 800	4 850	4 910	4 960	5 060	5 000	5 050	5 070
2	1 950	1 860	1 830	1 680	1 670	1 700	1 710	1 660	1 560	1 560
3	5 010	5 090	4 870	4 750	4 810	4 870	4 860	4 900	4 890	5 030
4	5 740	5 700	6 000	5 840	5 760	5 630	5 510	5 440	5 510	5 420
5 [3]	2 920	2 990	3 060	3 170	3 200	3 270	3 300	3 370	3 400	3 430
6	1 860	1 820	1 760	1 690	1 690	1 660	1 650	1 610	1 610	1 580
7/8/9 [4]	15 860	15 730	15 240	15 080	14 830	14 670	14 740	14 940	15 100	14 780
X	240	230	270	310	320	370	410	390	410	410

Women - Femmes - Mujeres
ISCO-68 - CITP-68 - CIUO-68

	1999	2000	2001	2002	2003	2004	2005	2006	2007	2008
Total	26 320	26 300	26 290	25 940	25 970	26 160	26 330	26 520	26 590	26 560
0/1	3 720	3 810	3 930	4 050	4 150	4 250	4 310	4 380	4 330	4 430
2	200	190	180	180	180	190	190	190	160	160
3	7 720	7 770	7 620	7 530	7 500	7 580	7 610	7 700	7 730	7 890
4	3 470	3 410	3 680	3 500	3 410	3 390	3 410	3 370	3 370	3 280
5 [3]	3 760	3 790	3 860	4 010	4 090	4 210	4 270	4 360	4 470	4 450
6	1 460	1 390	1 340	1 220	1 210	1 180	1 140	1 080	1 090	1 050
7/8/9 [4]	5 840	5 790	5 520	5 240	5 210	5 130	5 120	5 180	5 150	5 010
X	150	140	160	210	230	250	280	270	290	280

Explanatory notes: see p. 77.

[1] Excl. armed forces. [2] Persons aged 15 years and over. [3] Incl. self-defence forces. Excl. cleaners. [4] Incl. cleaners.

Notes explicatives: voir p. 80.

[1] Non compris les forces armées. [2] Personnes âgées de 15 ans et plus. [3] Y compris les forces d'autodéfense. Non compris les netoyeurs. [4] Y compris les nettoyeurs.

Notas explicativas: véase p. 83.

[1] Excl. las fuerzas armadas. [2] Personas de 15 años y más. [3] Incl. a las fuerzas de autodefensa. Excl. los limpiadores. [4] Incl. los limpiadores.

EMPLOYMENT   EMPLOI   EMPLEO

Total employment, by occupation   **Emploi total, par profession**   **Empleo total, por ocupación**

Thousands   Milliers   Millares

	1999	2000	2001	2002	2003	2004	2005	2006	2007	2008
Kazakhstan (BA) [1]				Total employment - Emploi total - Empleo total						
Total - Total - Total										
ISCO-88 - CITP-88 - CIUO-88										
Total	.	.	6 699	6 709	6 985	7 182	7 261	7 404	7 631	7 857
1	.	.	288	305	345	374	390	438	492	506
2	.	.	673	714	769	829	861	924	982	1 006
3	.	.	499	499	555	576	626	643	678	714
4	.	.	113	128	136	171	163	169	172	170
5	.	.	780	827	921	995	959	1 007	991	1 077
6	.	.	1 248	1 274	1 274	1 277	1 264	1 075	1 124	1 281
7	.	.	700	670	679	700	706	690	752	739
8	.	.	478	565	595	622	644	650	653	713
9	.	.	1 901	1 702	1 685	1 605	1 616	1 780	1 757	1 625
X	.	.	20	24	27	34				
Men - Hommes - Hombres										
ISCO-88 - CITP-88 - CIUO-88										
Total	.	.	3 470	3 486	3 618	3 719	3 764	3 809	3 923	4 018
1	.	.	194	202	227	232	252	281	311	312
2	.	.	215	233	254	266	278	303	317	323
3	.	.	177	176	201	204	220	234	249	247
4	.	.	22	30	30	42	39	38	39	46
5	.	.	283	290	319	335	335	349	321	360
6	.	.	646	653	671	695	671	568	602	657
7	.	.	550	528	532	550	546	529	579	570
8	.	.	426	509	533	563	587	578	581	636
9	.	.	944	849	833	805	811	908	899	848
X	.	.	14	17	20	26				
Women - Femmes - Mujeres										
ISCO-88 - CITP-88 - CIUO-88										
Total	.	.	3 229	3 223	3 367	3 463	3 497	3 595	3 708	3 840
1	.	.	95	103	118	142	139	157	181	194
2	.	.	458	481	514	562	583	621	665	683
3	.	.	323	323	355	372	406	409	428	468
4	.	.	90	99	106	129	124	132	133	123
5	.	.	497	537	602	660	624	658	670	717
6	.	.	602	621	603	581	593	507	522	624
7	.	.	149	142	147	149	160	160	172	169
8	.	.	52	56	62	59	57	72	72	77
9	.	.	958	853	852	800	805	872	857	777
X	.	.	6	7	7	8				
Korea, Republic of (BA) [1][2]				Total employment - Emploi total - Empleo total						
Total - Total - Total										
ISCO-88 - CITP-88 - CIUO-88										
Total	20 281	21 156 [3]	21 572	22 169	22 139	22 557	22 856	23 151	23 433	23 577
1	480	465 [3]	524	570	597	576	574	571	556	542
2	1 061	1 403 [3]	1 498	1 577	1 702	1 731	1 839	1 948	2 032	2 208
3	2 322	2 074 [3]	2 079	2 115	2 140	2 324	2 363	2 478	2 609	2 540
4	2 219	2 512 [3]	2 671	2 822	3 188	3 269	3 284	3 309	3 503	
5	4 819	5 501 [3]	5 656	5 795	5 570	5 643	5 625	5 585	5 567	5 534
6	2 217	2 115 [3]	2 035	1 964	1 834	1 700	1 708	1 676	1 624	1 575
7	2 600	2 688 [3]	2 638	2 697	2 407	2 455	2 436	2 455	2 423	2 358
8	2 116	2 292 [3]	2 332	2 373	2 387	2 490	2 563	2 579	2 588	2 564
9	2 446	2 107 [3]	2 138	2 255	2 329	2 449	2 479	2 576	2 725	2 754
Men - Hommes - Hombres										
ISCO-88 - CITP-88 - CIUO-88										
Total	11 978	12 387 [3]	12 581	12 944	13 031	13 193	13 330	13 444	13 607	13 703
1	458	442 [3]	493	538	562	536	529	524	507	489
2	711	787 [3]	867	908	925	945	979	1 029	1 095	1 208
3	1 618	1 487 [3]	1 451	1 445	1 412	1 568	1 599	1 621	1 694	1 595
4	1 102	1 227 [3]	1 290	1 347	1 676	1 607	1 615	1 599	1 586	1 736
5	1 907	2 137 [3]	2 165	2 218	2 184	2 145	2 107	2 091	2 082	2 124
6	1 201	1 131 [3]	1 100	1 057	1 005	936	943	922	889	884
7	1 955	2 065 [3]	2 048	2 157	1 972	2 031	2 048	2 080	2 056	1 998
8	1 834	1 987 [3]	2 024	2 071	2 082	2 145	2 214	2 244	2 265	2 239
9	1 191	1 124 [3]	1 144	1 203	1 213	1 281	1 297	1 335	1 433	1 432
Women - Femmes - Mujeres										
ISCO-88 - CITP-88 - CIUO-88										
Total	8 303	8 769 [3]	8 991	9 225	9 108	9 364	9 526	9 706	9 826	9 874
1	22	23 [3]	31	32	35	40	45	47	49	52
2	350	615 [3]	632	669	777	786	860	920	936	999
3	705	587 [3]	627	670	729	756	764	857	915	945
4	1 116	1 285 [3]	1 382	1 476	1 496	1 581	1 654	1 685	1 723	1 768
5	2 912	3 364 [3]	3 491	3 578	3 387	3 498	3 518	3 494	3 485	3 411
6	1 017	984 [3]	935	907	828	764	765	754	735	691
7	645	623 [3]	590	540	435	424	388	375	367	360
8	282	305 [3]	308	302	305	345	349	335	322	326
9	1 255	983 [3]	994	1 051	1 116	1 168	1 183	1 241	1 292	1 322

Explanatory notes: see p. 77.

[1] Persons aged 15 years and over. [2] Excl. armed forces. [3] Estimates based on the 2000 Population Census results.

Notes explicatives: voir p. 80.

[1] Personnes âgées de 15 ans et plus. [2] Non compris les forces armées. [3] Estimations basées sur les résultats du Recensement de la population de 2000.

Notas explicativas: véase p. 83.

[1] Personas de 15 años y más. [2] Excl. las fuerzas armadas. [3] Estimaciones basadas en los resultados del Censo de población de 2000.

Total employment, by occupation

Emploi total, par profession

Empleo total, por ocupación

	Thousands			Milliers				Millares		
	1999	2000	2001	2002	2003	2004	2005	2006	2007	2008

Kyrgyzstan (BA) [1] [2]

Total employment - Emploi total - Empleo total

Total - Total - Total
ISCO-88 - CITP-88 - CIUO-88

	1999	2000	2001	2002	2003	2004	2005	2006	2007	2008
Total	.	.	.	1 850.1	1 930.5	1 991.2	2 077.1	2 096.1	.	.
1	.	.	.	73.3	16.7	24.7	39.6	49.2	.	.
2	.	.	.	147.5	179.5	196.0	206.0	197.2	.	.
3	.	.	.	121.5	143.7	141.8	142.8	137.4	.	.
4	.	.	.	28.2	48.2	49.0	47.9	45.8	.	.
5	.	.	.	258.6	285.8	308.1	322.7	342.7	.	.
6	.	.	.	806.3	759.3	721.1	762.8	718.0	.	.
7	.	.	.	131.0	222.9	265.5	281.0	319.9	.	.
8	.	.	.	107.1	113.1	128.8	136.8	135.2	.	.
9	.	.	.	176.6	161.3	156.4	137.6	150.7	.	.

Men - Hommes - Hombres
ISCO-88 - CITP-88 - CIUO-88

	1999	2000	2001	2002	2003	2004	2005	2006	2007	2008
Total	.	.	.	1 051.4	1 083.8	1 140.7	1 195.9	1 214.4	.	.
1	.	.	.	53.0	12.3	18.4	27.7	31.9	.	.
2	.	.	.	57.3	75.3	82.4	85.0	74.8	.	.
3	.	.	.	40.3	64.3	62.7	54.5	50.7	.	.
4	.	.	.	6.5	13.2	12.2	11.5	11.7	.	.
5	.	.	.	119.6	127.2	133.9	144.8	147.6	.	.
6	.	.	.	465.1	430.2	417.8	448.0	424.9	.	.
7	.	.	.	108.9	172.5	209.8	224.3	260.3	.	.
8	.	.	.	98.8	105.0	120.8	130.2	130.8	.	.
9	.	.	.	101.8	83.7	82.5	70.0	81.8	.	.

Women - Femmes - Mujeres
ISCO-88 - CITP-88 - CIUO-88

	1999	2000	2001	2002	2003	2004	2005	2006	2007	2008
Total	.	.	.	798.7	846.7	850.5	881.2	881.6	.	.
1	.	.	.	20.3	4.3	6.2	11.9	17.3	.	.
2	.	.	.	90.2	104.2	113.6	121.0	122.4	.	.
3	.	.	.	81.1	79.5	79.0	88.3	86.7	.	.
4	.	.	.	21.7	35.0	36.8	36.4	34.1	.	.
5	.	.	.	139.0	158.6	174.2	177.8	195.1	.	.
6	.	.	.	341.2	329.0	303.2	314.9	293.1	.	.
7	.	.	.	22.1	50.4	55.6	56.7	59.6	.	.
8	.	.	.	8.2	8.0	8.0	6.6	4.4	.	.
9	.	.	.	74.8	77.6	73.9	67.6	68.9	.	.

Liban (B) [1]

Total employment - Emploi total - Empleo total

Total - Total - Total
ISCO-88 - CITP-88 - CIUO-88

	1999	2000	2001	2002	2003	2004	2005	2006	2007	2008
Total	.	.	.	.	.	1 108.1	.	.	1 118.4	.
1	.	.	.	.	.	118.6	.	.	132.8	.
2	.	.	.	.	.	106.3	.	.	115.4	.
3	.	.	.	.	.	81.9	.	.	108.1	.
4	.	.	.	.	.	98.2	.	.	84.3	.
5	.	.	.	.	.	116.4	.	.	132.0	.
6	.	.	.	.	.	51.5	.	.	52.5	.
7	.	.	.	.	.	213.1	.	.	188.2	.
8	.	.	.	.	.	100.8	.	.	93.7	.
9	.	.	.	.	.	171.9	.	.	126.7	.
0	.	.	.	.	.	49.2	.	.	84.2	.
X	.	.	.	.	.	0.2	.	.	0.6	.

Men - Hommes - Hombres
ISCO-88 - CITP-88 - CIUO-88

	1999	2000	2001	2002	2003	2004	2005	2006	2007	2008
Total	.	.	.	.	.	850.1	.	.	842.4	.
1	.	.	.	.	.	105.4	.	.	121.6	.
2	.	.	.	.	.	57.4	.	.	60.2	.
3	.	.	.	.	.	44.3	.	.	55.4	.
4	.	.	.	.	.	58.3	.	.	44.5	.
5	.	.	.	.	.	77.0	.	.	92.9	.
6	.	.	.	.	.	47.9	.	.	44.8	.
7	.	.	.	.	.	199.3	.	.	173.8	.
8	.	.	.	.	.	98.5	.	.	91.3	.
9	.	.	.	.	.	113.9	.	.	73.5	.
0	.	.	.	.	.	48.1	.	.	83.9	.
X	.	.	.	.	.	0.1	.	.	0.4	.

Women - Femmes - Mujeres
ISCO-88 - CITP-88 - CIUO-88

	1999	2000	2001	2002	2003	2004	2005	2006	2007	2008
Total	.	.	.	.	.	258.1	.	.	276.0	.
1	.	.	.	.	.	13.2	.	.	11.2	.
2	.	.	.	.	.	48.9	.	.	55.2	.
3	.	.	.	.	.	37.7	.	.	52.6	.
4	.	.	.	.	.	39.9	.	.	39.8	.
5	.	.	.	.	.	39.4	.	.	39.0	.
6	.	.	.	.	.	3.6	.	.	7.7	.
7	.	.	.	.	.	13.8	.	.	14.4	.
8	.	.	.	.	.	2.3	.	.	2.4	.
9	.	.	.	.	.	58.0	.	.	53.1	.
0	.	.	.	.	.	1.1	.	.	0.3	.
X	.	.	.	.	.	0.1	.	.	0.2	.

Explanatory notes: see p. 77.

Notes explicatives: voir p. 80.

Notas explicativas: véase p. 83.

[1] Persons aged 15 years and over. [2] Nov. of each year.   [1] Personnes âgées de 15 ans et plus. [2] Nov. de chaque année.   [1] Personas de 15 años y más. [2] Nov. de cada año.

2C

EMPLOYMENT	EMPLOI	EMPLEO
Total employment, by occupation	Emploi total, par profession	Empleo total, por ocupación
Thousands	Milliers	Millares

	1999	2000	2001	2002	2003	2004	2005	2006	2007	2008

Macau, China (BA) [1][2] — Total employment - Emploi total - Empleo total

Total - Total - Total
ISCO-88 - CITP-88 - CIUO-88

	1999	2000	2001	2002	2003	2004	2005	2006	2007	2008
Total	196.1	195.3	205.0	204.9	205.4	219.1	237.5	265.1	300.4	323.0
1	11.9	12.0	10.7	12.2	12.2	13.5	15.8	17.0	14.6	14.5
2	5.9	6.1	6.2	6.9	7.8	7.8	7.5	9.4	10.3	11.7
3	17.2	16.8	17.4	18.9	19.3	20.4	21.4	23.5	28.2	26.3
4	35.5	37.4	37.3	36.2	39.0	44.7	51.1	60.8	79.4	79.9
5	39.2	39.4	40.7	43.4	40.8	45.3	48.5	54.8	60.7	72.8
6	1.2	1.3	1.3	1.3	1.9	1.9	1.2	1.4	0.9	1.6
7	24.5	24.0	25.1	23.0	22.7	23.0	24.8	27.9	31.8	32.7
8	28.8	24.9	30.0	27.7	25.3	25.8	26.7	25.3	21.9	23.1
9	32.0	33.3	36.3	35.3	36.4	36.8	40.4	44.9	52.5	60.4
X	0.0	0.0	0.0	0.0	0.0	0.0	0.0	0.0	0.0	0.0

Men - Hommes - Hombres
ISCO-88 - CITP-88 - CIUO-88

	1999	2000	2001	2002	2003	2004	2005	2006	2007	2008
Total	104.2	103.2	108.0	106.4	108.3	115.2	124.3	141.6	160.5	172.3
1	9.7	9.7	8.5	9.4	9.5	10.6	11.8	12.8	10.9	10.6
2	3.4	3.5	3.6	4.0	4.5	4.4	4.2	5.4	6.0	7.3
3	8.8	9.1	9.3	10.1	10.1	10.3	10.6	12.0	15.1	13.1
4	13.2	12.7	14.1	12.6	13.3	15.2	19.1	23.3	30.5	30.8
5	22.5	21.9	22.6	24.4	22.5	25.0	25.8	28.2	32.6	38.8
6	1.2	1.0	1.1	1.0	1.6	1.5	1.0	1.1	0.7	1.2
7	20.3	19.9	20.5	18.5	18.8	19.8	21.4	25.9	30.4	31.2
8	10.7	10.7	11.2	10.3	10.6	11.5	12.6	14.1	13.8	15.4
9	14.3	14.8	17.4	16.0	17.5	16.9	17.8	18.8	20.6	23.8
X	0.0	0.0	0.0	0.0	0.0	0.0	0.0	0.0	0.0	0.0

Women - Femmes - Mujeres
ISCO-88 - CITP-88 - CIUO-88

	1999	2000	2001	2002	2003	2004	2005	2006	2007	2008
Total	91.9	92.1	96.9	98.5	97.1	103.9	113.2	123.5	139.8	150.7
1	2.2	2.3	2.2	2.8	2.7	2.9	4.2	4.2	3.8	3.9
2	2.4	2.6	2.6	2.9	3.2	3.4	3.3	4.0	4.3	4.4
3	8.4	7.8	8.2	8.8	9.2	10.2	10.8	11.5	13.1	13.2
4	22.3	24.6	23.3	23.5	25.8	29.6	32.0	37.5	49.0	49.1
5	16.7	17.6	18.1	19.0	18.4	20.3	22.7	26.6	28.1	33.9
6	0.1	0.3	0.2	0.3	0.3	0.4	0.2	0.4	0.2	0.3
7	4.2	4.1	4.7	4.5	3.8	3.2	3.4	2.0	1.4	1.5
8	18.0	14.2	18.9	17.5	14.8	14.2	14.1	11.2	8.1	7.7
9	17.7	18.5	18.9	19.3	18.9	19.9	22.6	26.2	31.9	36.6
X	0.0	0.0	0.0	0.0	0.0	0.0	0.0	0.0	0.0	0.0

Malaysia (BA) [3][4] — Total employment - Emploi total - Empleo total

Total - Total - Total
ISCO-68 - CITP-68 - CIUO-68 .... ISCO-88 - CITP-88 - CIUO-88

	1999	2000		2001	2002	2003	2004	2005	2006	2007	2008	
Total	8 837.8	9 321.7	|	9 357.0	9 542.6	9 869.7	9 979.5	10 045.4	10 275.4	10 538.1	10 659.6	Total
0/1	937.0	985.1	|	695.0	786.3	793.5	859.3	777.4	829.6	770.4	748.8	1
2	348.3	371.3	|	457.2	483.5	530.3	561.3	555.1	565.9	596.8	613.7	2
3	985.6	990.0	|	1 126.1	1 194.6	1 219.9	1 211.6	1 266.8	1 307.5	1 400.5	1 496.4	3
4	991.7	1 050.8	|	890.6	890.3	937.9	931.2	992.3	968.3	1 029.5	1 053.4	4
5	1 052.8	1 149.9	|	1 291.1	1 307.7	1 399.4	1 479.7	1 483.7	1 597.1	1 705.6	1 776.1	5
6	1 633.1	1 713.3	|	1 265.3	1 260.8	1 249.8	1 292.8	1 268.6	1 335.9	1 355.3	1 271.3	6
7/8/9	2 889.3	3 061.3	|	1 160.2	1 168.1	1 235.6	1 165.2	1 145.5	1 154.8	1 133.2	1 153.8	7
			|	1 476.6	1 373.0	1 420.7	1 409.9	1 427.5	1 408.0	1 347.4	1 344.1	8
			|	994.9	1 078.2	1 082.7	1 068.5	1 128.3	1 108.4	1 199.3	1 202.0	9

Men - Hommes - Hombres
ISCO-68 - CITP-68 - CIUO-68 .... ISCO-88 - CITP-88 - CIUO-88

	1999	2000		2001	2002	2003	2004	2005	2006	2007	2008	
Total	5 851.2	6 086.2	|	6 055.9	6 141.8	6 323.6	6 390.4	6 470.5	6 618.6	6 747.1	6 851.1	Total
0/1	528.3	545.4	|	543.5	604.6	609.4	647.6	579.4	635.7	593.1	567.4	1
2	273.5	296.4	|	272.7	277.6	303.0	319.4	315.9	314.9	326.5	334.3	2
3	422.0	418.5	|	714.6	755.1	749.8	743.1	784.4	797.7	852.8	899.2	3
4	627.3	654.9	|	317.3	303.6	311.8	301.3	314.1	289.7	320.3	320.4	4
5	556.2	580.9	|	733.7	727.3	781.1	819.3	833.0	888.5	952.0	1 012.0	5
6	1 231.8	1 263.2	|	889.5	890.2	881.4	940.6	936.3	993.4	1 002.6	958.2	6
7/8/9	2 212.0	2 326.9	|	977.7	977.3	1 036.9	981.0	985.3	1 002.0	973.7	996.9	7
			|	990.7	949.4	990.1	1 000.3	1 023.2	1 004.4	966.1	985.0	8
			|	616.3	656.6	660.0	637.8	699.1	692.3	760.0	777.7	9

Women - Femmes - Mujeres
ISCO-68 - CITP-68 - CIUO-68 .... ISCO-88 - CITP-88 - CIUO-88

	1999	2000		2001	2002	2003	2004	2005	2006	2007	2008	
Total	2 986.6	3 235.5	|	3 301.1	3 400.8	3 546.1	3 589.1	3 574.8	3 656.8	3 791.0	3 808.5	Total
0/1	408.6	439.6	|	151.5	181.7	184.1	211.7	198.0	193.8	177.3	181.4	1
2	74.8	75.0	|	184.5	205.9	227.2	241.9	239.3	251.0	270.3	279.4	2
3	563.6	571.5	|	411.5	439.5	470.1	468.6	482.5	509.8	547.8	597.2	3
4	364.5	395.9	|	573.3	586.7	626.1	629.9	678.2	678.6	709.2	733.0	4
5	496.5	569.1	|	557.5	580.4	618.2	660.4	650.8	708.6	753.5	764.1	5
6	401.3	450.0	|	375.8	370.7	368.4	352.2	332.3	342.5	352.7	313.0	6
7/8/9	677.3	734.4	|	182.5	190.8	198.7	184.1	160.2	152.7	159.5	156.9	7
			|	485.9	423.6	430.6	409.6	404.4	403.6	381.4	359.2	8
			|	378.6	421.6	422.7	430.7	429.2	416.1	439.3	424.3	9

Explanatory notes: see p. 77.

[1] Persons aged 14 years and over. [2] Excl. armed forces and conscripts. [3] Persons aged 15 to 64 years. [4] Excl. armed forces.

Notes explicatives: voir p. 80.

[1] Personnes âgées de 14 ans et plus. [2] Non compris les forces armées et les conscrits. [3] Personnes âgées de 15 à 64 ans. [4] Non compris les forces armées.

Notas explicativas: véase p. 83.

[1] Personas de 14 años y más. [2] Excl. las fuerzas armadas y los conscriptos. [3] Personas de 15 a 64 años. [4] Excl. las fuerzas armadas.

Total employment, by occupation
Emploi total, par profession
Empleo total, por ocupación

	Thousands				Milliers				Millares	
	1999	2000	2001	2002	2003	2004	2005	2006	2007	2008

Mongolia (E) [1] [2]

Total employment - Emploi total - Empleo total

Total - Total - Total
ISCO-88 - CITP-88 - CIUO-88

	1999	2000	2001	2002	2003	2004	2005	2006	2007	2008
Total	.	.	.	.	.	.	968.3	1 009.9	1 024.1	1 041.7
1	.	.	.	.	.	.	40.8	41.7	43.1	43.5
2	.	.	.	.	.	.	101.6	104.0	113.2	119.4
3	.	.	.	.	.	.	46.4	46.7	45.1	47.6
4	.	.	.	.	.	.	23.4	24.9	24.4	24.4
5	.	.	.	.	.	.	143.0	164.1	174.3	177.2
6	.	.	.	.	.	.	287.3	294.9	302.6	300.8
7	.	.	.	.	.	.	78.8	79.8	74.2	79.1
8	.	.	.	.	.	.	32.1	30.0	32.2	34.6
9	.	.	.	.	.	.	215.0	224.0	214.9	215.1

Men - Hommes - Hombres
ISCO-88 - CITP-88 - CIUO-88

	1999	2000	2001	2002	2003	2004	2005	2006	2007	2008
Total	.	.	.	.	.	.	479.4	491.8	504.2	512.8
1	.	.	.	.	.	.	20.5	21.3	22.4	22.9
2	.	.	.	.	.	.	42.1	41.0	46.9	50.2
3	.	.	.	.	.	.	26.7	26.4	25.9	25.7
4	.	.	.	.	.	.	9.3	10.3	9.8	9.9
5	.	.	.	.	.	.	56.4	66.3	71.4	71.5
6	.	.	.	.	.	.	152.7	154.8	160.1	161.0
7	.	.	.	.	.	.	41.3	42.0	40.6	46.1
8	.	.	.	.	.	.	22.1	19.9	21.2	23.1
9	.	.	.	.	.	.	108.2	109.8	105.9	102.4

Women - Femmes - Mujeres
ISCO-88 - CITP-88 - CIUO-88

	1999	2000	2001	2002	2003	2004	2005	2006	2007	2008
Total	.	.	.	.	.	.	489.0	518.1	519.9	529.0
1	.	.	.	.	.	.	20.3	20.4	20.7	20.6
2	.	.	.	.	.	.	59.5	63.0	66.3	69.2
3	.	.	.	.	.	.	19.7	20.3	19.3	21.9
4	.	.	.	.	.	.	14.1	14.6	14.5	14.6
5	.	.	.	.	.	.	86.6	97.8	102.9	105.7
6	.	.	.	.	.	.	134.6	140.0	142.5	139.8
7	.	.	.	.	.	.	37.4	37.7	33.6	33.0
8	.	.	.	.	.	.	10.0	10.2	11.0	11.6
9	.	.	.	.	.	.	106.8	114.2	109.1	112.7

Pakistan (BA) [3] [4] [5]

Total employment - Emploi total - Empleo total

Total - Total - Total
ISCO-88 - CITP-88 - CIUO-88

	1999	2000	2001	2002	2003	2004	2005	2006	2007	2008
Total	.	.	37 481	38 882	39 852	42 009	42 816	46 952	47 651	.
1	.	.	4 121	4 494	4 606	4 821	4 914	5 627	5 865	.
2	.	.	829	807	827	833	849	782	783	.
3	.	.	1 563	1 841	1 887	2 051	2 090	2 389	2 377	.
4	.	.	583	666	683	688	701	674	684	.
5	.	.	1 715	2 205	2 260	2 166	2 208	2 520	2 658	.
6	.	.	15 004	13 488	13 824	14 670	14 952	16 581	17 328	.
7	.	.	5 640	6 301	6 458	6 670	6 798	7 398	7 290	.
8	.	.	1 229	1 524	1 562	1 575	1 605	1 951	1 945	.
9	.	.	6 797	7 556	7 745	8 535	8 699	9 026	8 721	.
X	.	.	-	-	-	-	-	3	-	.

Men - Hommes - Hombres
ISCO-88 - CITP-88 - CIUO-88

	1999	2000	2001	2002	2003	2004	2005	2006	2007	2008
Total	.	.	32 233	33 189	34 017	34 903	35 573	37 808	38 118	.
1	.	.	4 000	4 388	4 497	4 720	4 811	5 437	5 662	.
2	.	.	706	665	681	700	713	675	687	.
3	.	.	1 230	1 301	1 334	1 431	1 458	1 676	1 689	.
4	.	.	570	647	664	671	684	644	662	.
5	.	.	1 692	2 133	2 186	2 114	2 155	2 441	2 582	.
6	.	.	12 043	10 966	11 239	11 232	11 448	11 637	11 790	.
7	.	.	5 135	5 450	5 586	5 654	5 762	6 063	6 116	.
8	.	.	1 218	1 512	1 550	1 565	1 595	1 928	1 931	.
9	.	.	5 639	6 127	6 280	6 816	6 947	7 305	6 999	.
X	.	.	-	-	-	-	-	2	-	.

Women - Femmes - Mujeres
ISCO-88 - CITP-88 - CIUO-88

	1999	2000	2001	2002	2003	2004	2005	2006	2007	2008
Total	.	.	5 248	5 693	5 835	7 106	7 243	9 144	9 533	.
1	.	.	121	106	109	101	103	189	203	.
2	.	.	123	142	146	133	136	108	96	.
3	.	.	333	540	553	620	632	713	688	.
4	.	.	13	19	19	17	17	29	22	.
5	.	.	23	72	74	52	53	80	76	.
6	.	.	2 961	2 522	2 585	3 438	3 504	4 944	5 538	.
7	.	.	505	851	872	1 016	1 036	1 335	1 174	.
8	.	.	11	12	12	10	10	23	14	.
9	.	.	1 158	1 429	1 465	1 719	1 752	1 721	1 722	.
X	.	.	-	-	-	-	-	1		.

Explanatory notes: see p. 77.

[1] Persons aged 16 years and over. [2] Dec. of each year. [3] Excl. armed forces. [4] Persons aged 10 years and over. [5] Jan.

Notes explicatives: voir p. 80.

[1] Personnes âgées de 16 ans et plus. [2] Déc. de chaque année. [3] Non compris les forces armées. [4] Personnes âgées de 10 ans et plus. [5] Janv.

Notas explicativas: véase p. 83.

[1] Personas de 16 años y más. [2] Dic. de cada año. [3] Excl. las fuerzas armadas. [4] Personas de 10 años y más. [5] Enero.

EMPLOYMENT	EMPLOI	EMPLEO
Total employment, by occupation	Emploi total, par profession	Empleo total, por ocupación
Thousands	Milliers	Millares

	1999	2000	2001	2002	2003	2004	2005	2006	2007	2008	

Philippines (BA) [1] [2]

Total - Total - Total
ISCO-68 - CITP-68 - CIUO-68 [3]

Total employment - Emploi total - Empleo total

ISCO-88 - CITP-88 - CIUO-88

	1999	2000	2001	2002	2003	2004	2005	2006	2007	2008	
Total	27 742	27 452	29 156	30 062	30 635	31 613	32 313	32 636	33 560	34 089	Total
0/1	1 666	1 664	2 921	3 217	3 398	3 775	3 784	3 811	3 958	4 327	1
2	599	613	1 323	1 385	1 349	1 353	1 395	1 404	1 454	1 526	2
3	1 260	1 307	748	819	882	883	858	880	908	876	3
4	4 135	4 230	1 317	1 332	1 356	1 352	1 454	1 505	1 652	1 715	4
5 [4]	2 936	2 967	2 582	2 658	2 715	2 888	3 005	3 121	3 248	3 394	5
6	10 672	10 072	6 353	6 240	6 220	5 921	6 161	6 127	6 069	5 999	6
7/8/9	6 440	6 560	3 075	2 993	2 932	2 866	2 887	2 803	2 811	2 730	7
X	34	38	2 283	2 197	2 348	2 429	2 446	2 495	2 573	2 354	8
			8 420	9 097	9 303	10 005	10 176	10 343	10 749	11 021	9
			135	124	133	143	146	147	138	147	X

Men - Hommes - Hombres
ISCO-68 - CITP-68 - CIUO-68 [3]

ISCO-88 - CITP-88 - CIUO-88

	1999	2000	2001	2002	2003	2004	2005	2006	2007	2008	
Total	17 253	17 193	17 923	18 306	18 873	19 646	19 910	20 013	20 542	20 959	Total
0/1	610	603	1 198	1 358	1 444	1 613	1 613	1 605	1 677	1 955	1
2	397	397	422	442	428	428	443	439	447	479	2
3	522	547	381	407	434	442	413	432	443	431	3
4	1 383	1 383	433	447	459	475	508	539	609	621	4
5 [4]	1 243	1 264	1 205	1 262	1 324	1 453	1 499	1 524	1 583	1 678	5
6	7 846	7 651	5 274	5 207	5 225	5 099	5 293	5 195	5 139	5 143	6
7/8/9	5 229	5 326	2 205	2 166	2 145	2 128	2 148	2 099	2 121	2 133	7
X	24	24	2 097	2 027	2 162	2 219	2 228	2 265	2 332	2 129	8
			4 594	4 878	5 134	5 664	5 637	5 786	6 072	6 262	9
			115	110	120	126	128	130	120	128	X

Women - Femmes - Mujeres
ISCO-68 - CITP-68 - CIUO-68 [3]

ISCO-88 - CITP-88 - CIUO-88

	1999	2000	2001	2002	2003	2004	2005	2006	2007	2008	
Total	10 489	10 259	11 232	11 756	11 762	11 968	12 403	12 622	13 018	13 129	Total
0/1	1 055	1 062	1 722	1 859	1 954	2 162	2 171	2 206	2 281	2 372	1
2	202	216	901	944	921	925	953	966	1 007	1 047	2
3	739	760	367	412	449	442	445	448	465	444	3
4	2 753	2 848	884	885	898	878	946	965	1 043	1 095	4
5 [4]	1 693	1 704	1 377	1 396	1 391	1 435	1 507	1 597	1 665	1 716	5
6	2 827	2 422	1 079	1 033	995	822	868	932	930	856	6
7/8/9	1 211	1 235	870	826	787	738	740	704	690	597	7
X	11	15	186	170	186	210	219	230	241	225	8
			3 826	4 219	4 169	4 341	4 539	4 557	4 677	4 759	9
			20	14	13	18	18	18	19	19	X

Qatar (BA) [1] [5]

Total - Total - Total
ISCO-88 - CITP-88 - CIUO-88

Total employment - Emploi total - Empleo total

	1999	2000	2001	2002	2003	2004	2005	2006	2007	2008	
Total	.	.	310.291	.	.	.	.	529.304	827.583	.	
1	.	.	6.821	.	.	.	.	16.349	24.619	.	
2	.	.	33.835	.	.	.	.	72.053	109.008	.	
3	.	.	20.063	.	.	.	.	39.092	66.646	.	
4	.	.	35.243	.	.	.	.	40.585	73.654	.	
5	.	.	28.759	.	.	.	.	48.528	73.891	.	
6	.	.	3.457	.	.	.	.	5.231	6.943	.	
7	.	.	71.459	.	.	.	.	127.953	211.051	.	
8	.	.	39.689	.	.	.	.	63.597	88.815	.	
9	.	.	68.824	.	.	.	.	115.916	171.437	.	
X	.	.	2.715 [6]	.	.	.	.	-	1.519	.	

Men - Hommes - Hombres
ISCO-88 - CITP-88 - CIUO-88

	1999	2000	2001	2002	2003	2004	2005	2006	2007	2008	
Total	.	.	266.371	.	.	.	.	452.599	726.752	.	
1	.	.	6.500	.	.	.	.	15.158	22.937	.	
2	.	.	23.514	.	.	.	.	51.984	85.682	.	
3	.	.	17.846	.	.	.	.	31.623	55.698	.	
4	.	.	30.072	.	.	.	.	31.389	60.857	.	
5	.	.	26.032	.	.	.	.	42.370	66.457	.	
6	.	.	3.457	.	.	.	.	5.231	6.943	.	
7	.	.	71.271	.	.	.	.	127.780	210.686	.	
8	.	.	39.689	.	.	.	.	63.569	88.225	.	
9	.	.	46.162	.	.	.	.	83.495	128.083	.	
X	.	.	1.829 [6]	.	.	.	.	-	-	.	

Explanatory notes: see p. 77.

[1] Persons aged 15 years and over. [2] Excl. regular military living in barracks. [3] Oct. of each year. [4] Incl. members of the armed forces living in private households. [5] March of each year. [6] Incl. persons temporarily absent from work.

Notes explicatives: voir p. 80.

[1] Personnes âgées de 15 ans et plus. [2] Non compris les militaires de carrière vivant dans des casernes. [3] Oct. de chaque année. [4] Y compris les membres des forces armées vivant en ménages privés. [5] Mars de chaque année. [6] Y compris les salaries temporairement absents de leur travail.

Notas explicativas: véase p. 83.

[1] Personas de 15 años y más. [2] Excl. los militares profesionales que viven en casernas. [3] Oct. de cada año. [4] Incl. miembros de las fuerzas armadas viviendo en hogares privados. [5] Marzo de cada año. [6] Incl. las personas temporalmente ausentes de su trabajo.

Total employment, by occupation — **Emploi total, par profession** — **Empleo total, por ocupación**

Thousands — Milliers — Millares

Qatar (BA) [1][2] — Total employment - Emploi total - Empleo total

Women - Femmes - Mujeres
ISCO-88 - CITP-88 - CIUO-88

	1999	2000	2001	2002	2003	2004	2005	2006	2007	2008
Total	.	.	43.920	.	.	.	.	76.705	100.831	.
1	.	.	0.321	.	.	.	.	1.191	1.682	.
2	.	.	10.321	.	.	.	.	20.069	23.326	.
3	.	.	2.218	.	.	.	.	7.469	10.948	.
4	.	.	5.171	.	.	.	.	9.196	12.797	.
5	.	.	2.727	.	.	.	.	6.158	7.434	.
6	.	.	-	.	.	.	.	-	-	.
7	.	.	0.188	.	.	.	.	0.173	0.365	.
8	.	.	-	.	.	.	.	0.028	0.590	.
9	.	.	22.662	.	.	.	.	32.421	43.354	.
X	.	.	0.312 [3]	.	.	.	.	-	0.335	.

Saudi Arabia (BA) [1] — Total employment - Emploi total - Empleo total

Total - Total - Total
ISCO-68 - CITP-68 - CIUO-68   ISCO-88 - CITP-88 - CIUO-88

	1999	2000	2001	2002	2003	2004	2005	2006	2007	2008	
Total	5 592.854	5 713.345	5 808.617	5 913.008	.	.	.	7 522.992 [4]	7 766.347	7 956.832	Total
0/1	1 093.498	1 105.221	1 199.327	1 099.484	.	.	.	270.722 [4]	335.550	336.255	1
2	92.878	122.644	133.334	220.211	.	.	.	589.718 [4]	613.942	664.926	2
3	526.941	528.311	602.984	501.298	.	.	.	846.173 [4]	884.370	869.451	3
4	494.901	573.194	512.437	532.841	.	.	.	547.149 [4]	578.278	608.312	4
5 [5]	1 538.859	1 522.350	1 485.613	1 799.398	.	.	.	698.228 [4]	713.794	768.848	5
6	350.060	368.727	352.139	291.608	.	.	.	2 406.704 [4]	2 407.490	2 559.603	6
7/8/9	1 492.524	1 490.484	1 519.416	1 468.168	.	.	.	318.203 [4]	393.076	363.035	7
X	3.193	2.214	3.365	-	.	.	.	183.443 [4]	203.626	188.526	8
								1 662.552 [4]	1 636.221	1 597.876	9

Men - Hommes - Hombres
ISCO-68 - CITP-68 - CIUO-68   ISCO-88 - CITP-88 - CIUO-88

	1999	2000	2001	2002	2003	2004	2005	2006	2007	2008	
Total	4 800.625	4 943.511	5 027.718	5 115.827	.	.	.	6 461.497 [4]	6 664.019	6 837.240	Total
0/1	731.611	763.019	829.804	760.014	.	.	.	246.500 [4]	302.055	307.954	1
2	91.884	122.174	132.170	199.864	.	.	.	458.399 [4]	499.217	541.517	2
3	505.089	506.507	574.587	475.618	.	.	.	535.847 [4]	569.447	577.390	3
4	490.311	567.581	506.039	528.111	.	.	.	497.767 [4]	527.095	553.991	4
5 [5]	1 154.626	1 149.626	1 125.215	1 405.149	.	.	.	689.697 [4]	706.221	761.222	5
6	342.269	350.575	346.918	286.127	.	.	.	1 888.421 [4]	1 845.526	1 959.708	6
7/8/9	1 481.935	1 483.047	1 511.114	1 460.944	.	.	.	313.426 [4]	388.647	362.517	7
X	2.896	0.988	1.876	-	.	.	.	175.245 [4]	199.320	181.314	8
								1 656.195 [4]	1 626.491	1 591.627	9

Women - Femmes - Mujeres
ISCO-68 - CITP-68 - CIUO-68   ISCO-88 - CITP-88 - CIUO-88

	1999	2000	2001	2002	2003	2004	2005	2006	2007	2008	
Total	792.233	769.834	780.899	797.181	.	.	.	1 061.495 [4]	1 102.328	1 119.592	Total
0/1	361.887	342.202	369.523	339.470	.	.	.	24.222 [4]	33.495	28.301	1
2	0.994	0.470	1.164	20.347	.	.	.	131.319 [4]	114.725	123.409	2
3	21.852	21.804	28.397	25.680	.	.	.	310.326 [4]	314.923	292.061	3
4	4.590	5.613	6.398	4.730	.	.	.	49.482 [4]	51.183	54.321	4
5 [5]	384.233	372.924	360.398	394.249	.	.	.	8.531 [4]	7.573	7.626	5
6	7.791	18.152	5.221	5.481	.	.	.	518.283 [4]	561.964	599.895	6
7/8/9	10.589	7.437	8.302	7.224	.	.	.	4.777 [4]	4.429	0.518	7
X	0.297	1.226	1.489	-	.	.	.	8.198 [4]	4.306	7.212	8
								6.357 [4]	9.730	6.249	9

Singapore (BA) [6][7] — Total employment - Emploi total - Empleo total

Total - Total - Total
ISCO-88 - CITP-88 - CIUO-88

	1999	2000	2001	2002	2003	2004	2005	2006	2007	2008
Total	1 518.3	.	1 582.5 [8]	1 573.7	1 605.4	1 632.1	.	1 796.7 [8]	1 803.2	1 852.0
1	191.3	.	224.0 [8]	224.6	230.0	229.8	.	268.9 [8]	263.4	284.7
2	170.0	.	195.9 [8]	193.3	210.6	211.0	.	256.2 [8]	270.7	288.3
3	276.3	.	281.2 [8]	284.5	288.7	309.4	.	319.8 [8]	342.4	371.9
4	223.2	.	231.5 [8]	228.5	231.5	233.5	.	251.6 [8]	247.5	249.7
5	213.3	.	191.2 [8]	189.2	185.4	190.7	.	215.7 [8]	209.5	208.2
6	1.7	.	1.7 [8]	1.5	1.4	1.1	.	1.4 [8]	1.2	1.0
7	116.0	.	101.5 [8]	104.2	97.2	96.0	.	95.0 [8]	94.2	89.5
8	185.1	.	176.7 [8]	171.4	166.8	165.4	.	173.3 [8]	167.0	156.4
9	87.1	.	115.6 [8]	116.1	125.2	125.2	.	149.3 [8]	145.3	140.0
0-X	54.3	.	63.3 [8]	60.4	68.4	70.0	.	65.5 [8]	61.8	62.5

Explanatory notes: see p. 77.
[1] Persons aged 15 years and over. [2] March of each year. [3] Incl. persons temporarily absent from work. [4] April. [5] Incl. the armed forces. [6] The data refer to the residents (Singapore citizens and permanent residents) aged 15 years and over. [7] June. [8] Methodology revised; data not strictly comparable.

Notes explicatives: voir p. 80.
[1] Personnes âgées de 15 ans et plus. [2] Mars de chaque année. [3] Y compris les salaries temporairement absents de leur travail. [4] Avril. [5] Y compris les forces armées. [6] Les données se réfèrent aux résidents (citoyens de Singapour et résidents permanents) âgés de 15 ans et plus. [7] Juin. [8] Méthodologie révisée; les données ne sont pas strictement comparables.

Notas explicativas: véase p. 83.
[1] Personas de 15 años y más. [2] Marzo de cada año. [3] Incl. las personas temporalmente ausentes de su trabajo. [4] Abril. [5] Incl. las fuerzas armadas. [6] Los datos se refieren a los residentes (ciudadanos de Singapur y residentes permanentes) de 15 años y más. [7] Junio. [8] Metodología revisada; los datos no son estrictamente comparables.

2C

EMPLOYMENT	EMPLOI	EMPLEO
Total employment, by occupation	Emploi total, par profession	Empleo total, por ocupación
Thousands	Milliers	Millares

	1999	2000	2001	2002	2003	2004	2005	2006	2007	2008

Singapore (BA) [1][2]
Total employment - Emploi total - Empleo total

Men - Hommes - Hombres
ISCO-88 - CITP-88 - CIUO-88

	1999	2000	2001	2002	2003	2004	2005	2006	2007	2008
Total	912.1	.	938.4 [3]	937.7	948.7	960.8	.	1 036.5 [3]	1 038.4	1 053.6
1	149.6	.	168.4 [3]	166.4	170.1	166.1	.	185.6 [3]	182.9	195.1
2	103.4	.	115.6 [3]	115.4	126.4	129.6	.	154.7 [3]	159.2	172.0
3	155.7	.	153.5 [3]	153.5	150.4	166.0	.	170.0 [3]	176.6	190.0
4	46.6	.	50.9 [3]	50.6	51.7	48.9	.	55.5 [3]	55.6	57.5
5	120.0	.	104.3 [3]	107.8	104.2	104.0	.	110.8 [3]	114.5	106.9
6	1.6	.	1.3 [3]	1.4	1.1	0.9	.	1.2 [3]	1.1	1.0
7	105.5	.	93.4 [3]	95.3	88.9	88.1	.	86.3 [3]	84.6	80.0
8	127.8	.	130.4 [3]	127.4	123.4	123.5	.	133.6 [3]	132.3	126.1
9	49.0	.	58.7 [3]	60.3	65.6	65.3	.	74.3 [3]	71.0	63.8
0-X	52.8	.	61.9 [3]	59.4	67.0	68.4	.	64.6 [3]	60.5	61.2

Women - Femmes - Mujeres
ISCO-88 - CITP-88 - CIUO-88

	1999	2000	2001	2002	2003	2004	2005	2006	2007	2008
Total	606.2	.	644.0 [3]	636.0	656.6	671.3	.	760.2 [3]	764.8	798.5
1	41.7	.	55.6 [3]	58.2	60.0	63.7	.	83.3 [3]	80.5	89.5
2	66.6	.	80.3 [3]	77.9	84.3	81.5	.	101.5 [3]	111.6	116.3
3	120.6	.	127.7 [3]	131.0	138.3	143.4	.	149.8 [3]	165.8	181.8
4	176.6	.	180.6 [3]	177.9	179.9	184.6	.	196.1 [3]	191.9	192.2
5	93.3	.	86.9 [3]	81.4	81.3	86.7	.	104.9 [3]	95.0	101.3
6	0.1	.	0.4 [3]	0.1	0.2	0.2	.	0.2 [3]	0.2	-
7	10.5	.	8.1 [3]	8.9	8.3	7.9	.	8.7 [3]	9.6	9.5
8	57.3	.	46.3 [3]	44.0	43.4	41.8	.	39.7 [3]	34.7	30.3
9	38.0	.	56.9 [3]	55.8	59.6	59.8	.	75.0 [3]	74.3	76.2
0-X	1.5	.	1.3 [3]	0.9	1.4	1.6	.	0.9 [3]	1.3	1.2

Sri Lanka (BA) [4][5]
Total employment - Emploi total - Empleo total

Total - Total - Total
ISCO-88 - CITP-88 - CIUO-88

	1999	2000	2001	2002	2003	2004	2005	2006	2007	2008
Total	.	.	.	6 519.4	7 012.8 [6]	7 394.0 [7]	7 518.0 [8]	7 105.3	7 041.9	7 174.7
1	.	.	.	492.5	416.8 [6]	520.2 [7]	636.4 [8]	655.2	617.8	598.5
2	.	.	.	352.2	367.7 [6]	404.4 [7]	471.2 [8]	376.5	366.7	416.0
3	.	.	.	316.8	341.6 [6]	366.5 [7]	403.9 [8]	362.3	381.6	398.5
4	.	.	.	283.7	303.8 [6]	322.7 [7]	300.3 [8]	276.6	283.7	299.3
5	.	.	.	510.1	628.7 [6]	671.5 [7]	574.4 [8]	513.2	508.5	546.1
6	.	.	.	1 579.0	1 634.3 [6]	1 513.6 [7]	1 561.9 [8]	1 590.1	1 503.7	1 603.7
7	.	.	.	935.5	1 084.4 [6]	1 124.7 [7]	1 216.2 [8]	1 214.2	1 201.6	1 165.1
8	.	.	.	373.6	419.5 [6]	460.6 [7]	531.4 [8]	501.6	563.9	526.9
9	.	.	.	1 608.5	1 735.3 [6]	1 951.1 [7]	1 760.3 [8]	1 577.0	1 574.1	1 576.3
X	.	.	.	67.4	80.5 [6]	58.8 [7]	61.9 [8]	38.7	40.3	44.3

Men - Hommes - Hombres
ISCO-88 - CITP-88 - CIUO-88

	1999	2000	2001	2002	2003	2004	2005	2006	2007	2008
Total	.	.	.	4 395.2	4 833.5 [6]	5 049.4 [7]	5 134.8 [8]	4 610.6	4 653.1	4 663.3
1	.	.	.	385.4	331.8 [6]	417.2 [7]	493.9 [8]	520.8	470.8	454.5
2	.	.	.	146.7	161.4 [6]	174.5 [7]	187.0 [8]	146.3	147.8	154.4
3	.	.	.	215.5	236.3 [6]	250.9 [7]	266.9 [8]	238.8	258.1	275.9
4	.	.	.	151.5	167.6 [6]	175.0 [7]	159.6 [8]	143.6	138.4	161.3
5	.	.	.	379.7	464.6 [6]	498.5 [7]	418.6 [8]	314.2	319.0	339.8
6	.	.	.	1 024.2	1 109.2 [6]	1 004.9 [7]	1 013.9 [8]	966.3	925.9	975.5
7	.	.	.	596.5	711.7 [6]	726.6 [7]	801.4 [8]	743.7	779.1	731.4
8	.	.	.	335.6	368.5 [6]	426.5 [7]	484.4 [8]	444.7	504.6	478.8
9	.	.	.	1 097.4	1 205.4 [6]	1 319.3 [7]	1 249.2 [8]	1 055.8	1 070.9	1 050.2
X	.	.	.	62.6	77.0 [6]	56.0 [7]	59.9 [8]	38.7	40.3	41.4

Women - Femmes - Mujeres
ISCO-88 - CITP-88 - CIUO-88

	1999	2000	2001	2002	2003	2004	2005	2006	2007	2008
Total	.	.	.	2 124.3	2 179.3 [6]	2 341.9 [7]	2 383.2 [8]	2 494.7	2 388.8	2 510.7
1	.	.	.	107.1	85.0 [6]	102.9 [7]	142.5 [8]	134.4	147.0	143.2
2	.	.	.	205.6	206.3 [6]	229.9 [7]	284.2 [8]	230.1	218.8	261.5
3	.	.	.	101.2	105.4 [6]	115.6 [7]	137.0 [8]	123.5	123.5	122.6
4	.	.	.	132.2	136.2 [6]	147.7 [7]	140.8 [8]	133.0	145.3	138.1
5	.	.	.	130.5	164.1 [6]	173.0 [7]	155.8 [8]	199.0	189.5	206.3
6	.	.	.	554.8	525.1 [6]	508.7 [7]	548.0 [8]	623.8	577.7	628.2
7	.	.	.	339.0	372.7 [6]	398.1 [7]	414.8 [8]	470.4	422.5	433.7
8	.	.	.	38.0	51.1 [6]	34.1 [7]	47.1 [8]	56.9	59.3	48.1
9	.	.	.	511.1	530.0 [6]	631.8 [7]	511.2 [8]	521.2	503.2	526.0
X	.	.	.	4.8	3.4 [6]	2.7 [7]	1.9 [8]	-	-	2.9

Explanatory notes: see p. 77.

[1] The data refer to the residents (Singapore citizens and permanent residents) aged 15 years and over. [2] June. [3] Methodology revised; data not strictly comparable. [4] Persons aged 10 years and over. [5] Excl. Northern and Eastern provinces. [6] Excl. Northern province. [7] Excl. Mullativu and Killinochchi districts. [8] Whole country.

Notes explicatives: voir p. 80.

[1] Les données se réfèrent aux résidents (citoyens de Singapour et résidents permanents) âgés de 15 ans et plus. [2] Juin. [3] Méthodologie révisée; les données ne sont pas strictement comparables. [4] Personnes âgées de 10 ans et plus. [5] Non compris les provinces du Nord et de l'Est. [6] Non compris la province du Nord. [7] Non compris les provinces de Mullativu et Killinochchi. [8] Ensemble du pays.

Notas explicativas: véase p. 83.

[1] Los datos se refieren a los residentes (ciudadanos de Singapur y residentes permanentes) de 15 años y más. [2] Junio. [3] Metodología revisada; los datos no son estrictamente comparables. [4] Personas de 10 años y más. [5] Excl. las provincias del Norte y del Este. [6] Excl. la provincia del Norte. [7] Excl. las provincias de Mullativu y Killinocchchi. [8] Todo el país.

Total employment, by occupation	Emploi total, par profession	Empleo total, por ocupación
Thousands	Milliers	Millares

	1999	2000	2001	2002	2003	2004	2005	2006	2007	2008

Syrian Arab Republic (BA) [1]   Total employment - Emploi total - Empleo total

Total - Total - Total
ISCO-88 - CITP-88 - CIUO-88

	1999	2000	2001	2002	2003	2004	2005	2006	2007	2008
Total	.	.	.	.	.	.	.	.	4 946.0	.
1	.	.	.	.	.	.	.	.	70.6	.
2	.	.	.	.	.	.	.	.	273.1	.
3	.	.	.	.	.	.	.	.	423.8	.
4	.	.	.	.	.	.	.	.	433.1	.
5	.	.	.	.	.	.	.	.	560.9	.
6	.	.	.	.	.	.	.	.	321.7	.
7	.	.	.	.	.	.	.	.	939.9	.
8	.	.	.	.	.	.	.	.	463.0	.
9	.	.	.	.	.	.	.	.	1 459.5	.
X	.	.	.	.	.	.	.	.	0.2	.

Men - Hommes - Hombres
ISCO-88 - CITP-88 - CIUO-88

	1999	2000	2001	2002	2003	2004	2005	2006	2007	2008
Total	.	.	.	.	.	.	.	.	4 316.4	.
1	.	.	.	.	.	.	.	.	63.4	.
2	.	.	.	.	.	.	.	.	194.0	.
3	.	.	.	.	.	.	.	.	215.0	.
4	.	.	.	.	.	.	.	.	352.3	.
5	.	.	.	.	.	.	.	.	541.3	.
6	.	.	.	.	.	.	.	.	295.0	.
7	.	.	.	.	.	.	.	.	775.4	.
8	.	.	.	.	.	.	.	.	430.4	.
9	.	.	.	.	.	.	.	.	1 449.2	.
X	.	.	.	.	.	.	.	.	0.1	.

Women - Femmes - Mujeres
ISCO-88 - CITP-88 - CIUO-88

	1999	2000	2001	2002	2003	2004	2005	2006	2007	2008
Total	.	.	.	.	.	.	.	.	629.6	.
1	.	.	.	.	.	.	.	.	7.2	.
2	.	.	.	.	.	.	.	.	79.1	.
3	.	.	.	.	.	.	.	.	208.9	.
4	.	.	.	.	.	.	.	.	80.7	.
5	.	.	.	.	.	.	.	.	19.6	.
6	.	.	.	.	.	.	.	.	26.7	.
7	.	.	.	.	.	.	.	.	164.5	.
8	.	.	.	.	.	.	.	.	32.5	.
9	.	.	.	.	.	.	.	.	10.2	.
X	.	.	.	.	.	.	.	.	0.1	.

Taiwan, China (BA) [1][2]   Total employment - Emploi total - Empleo total

Total - Total - Total
ISCO-88 - CITP-88 - CIUO-88

	1999	2000	2001	2002	2003	2004	2005	2006	2007	2008
Total	9 385	9 491	9 383	9 454	9 573	9 786	9 942	10 111	10 294	10 403
1	414	412	406	424	427	447	449	452	462	461
2	601	610	615	649	678	726	795	831	866	913
3	1 571	1 591	1 615	1 662	1 716	1 774	1 834	1 929	2 020	2 134
4	995	1 027	1 025	1 041	1 062	1 106	1 132	1 138	1 133	1 124
5	1 667	1 712	1 745	1 791	1 817	1 849	1 866	1 926	1 964	1 938
6	764	726	695	699	683	629	578	541	531	519
8,9	3 373	3 413	3 281	3 188	3 191	3 256	3 289	3 293	3 319	3 314

Thailand (BA) [1][2][3]   Total employment - Emploi total - Empleo total

Total - Total - Total
ISCO-88 - CITP-88 - CIUO-88

	1999	2000	2001	2002	2003	2004	2005	2006	2007	2008
Total	.	.	33 484	34 263	34 677	35 712	36 302	36 344	37 124	37 839
1	.	.	2 193	2 334	2 361	2 374	2 382	2 400	2 480	999
2	.	.	1 267	1 178	1 205	1 342	1 472	1 504	1 478	1 532
3	.	.	1 183	1 165	1 252	1 346	1 466	1 520	1 569	1 543
4	.	.	1 119	1 123	1 178	1 251	1 351	1 277	1 361	1 428
5	.	.	4 214	4 244	4 474	4 854	4 868	4 921	5 186	6 200
6	.	.	14 092	14 598	14 299	13 666	13 893	13 894	14 219	14 866
7	.	.	3 360	3 611	3 700	3 907	3 772	3 762	3 856	4 212
8	.	.	2 530	2 552	2 609	2 914	2 911	2 896	2 966	2 875
9	.	.	3 511	3 444	3 586	4 035	4 147	4 111	3 956	4 150
X	.	.	15	14	14	22	40	59	53	33

Men - Hommes - Hombres
ISCO-88 - CITP-88 - CIUO-88

	1999	2000	2001	2002	2003	2004	2005	2006	2007	2008
Total	.	.	18 471	18 872	19 082	19 699	19 470	19 638	19 977	20 405
1	.	.	1 634	1 743	1 741	1 720	1 695	1 699	1 743	762
2	.	.	536	530	545	591	626	622	638	633
3	.	.	618	583	628	685	715	733	782	733
4	.	.	414	400	404	449	469	434	438	490
5	.	.	1 513	1 500	1 599	1 762	1 696	1 784	1 856	2 437
6	.	.	8 011	8 229	8 109	7 726	7 627	7 686	7 860	8 333
7	.	.	2 175	2 338	2 425	2 627	2 516	2 559	2 598	2 929
8	.	.	1 736	1 759	1 806	2 003	2 019	1 985	2 048	1 984
9	.	.	1 828	1 785	1 817	2 123	2 090	2 102	1 983	2 088
X	.	.	8	6	9	13	19	34	31	17

Explanatory notes: see p. 77.

[1] Persons aged 15 years and over. [2] Excl. armed forces. [3] Third quarter.

Notes explicatives: voir p. 80.

[1] Personnes âgées de 15 ans et plus. [2] Non compris les forces armées. [3] Troisième trimestre.

Notas explicativas: véase p. 83.

[1] Personas de 15 años y más. [2] Excl. las fuerzas armadas. [3] Tercer trimestre.

Total employment,
by occupation

Emploi total,
par profession

Empleo total,
por ocupación

	Thousands				Milliers				Millares	
	1999	2000	2001	2002	2003	2004	2005	2006	2007	2008

Thailand (BA) [1] [2] [3]

Total employment - Emploi total - Empleo total

Women - Femmes - Mujeres
ISCO-88 - CITP-88 - CIUO-88

	1999	2000	2001	2002	2003	2004	2005	2006	2007	2008
Total	.	.	15 013	15 391	15 596	16 013	16 832	16 706	17 147	17 432
1	.	.	560	591	620	654	687	701	737	237
2	.	.	732	648	660	751	847	882	840	899
3	.	.	564	582	624	662	751	787	787	811
4	.	.	705	723	774	802	883	843	923	938
5	.	.	2 702	2 744	2 876	3 092	3 172	3 137	3 360	3 763
6	.	.	6 082	6 368	6 190	5 939	6 266	6 208	6 359	6 533
7	.	.	1 185	1 273	1 275	1 280	1 257	1 203	1 258	1 283
8	.	.	794	794	802	912	892	911	918	890
9	.	.	1 683	1 659	1 770	1 912	2 058	2 009	1 973	2 063
X	.	.	7	8	5	9	21	25	22	17

United Arab Emirates (BA) [2] [4]

Total employment - Emploi total - Empleo total

Total - Total - Total
ISCO-88 - CITP-88 - CIUO-88

	1999	2000	2001	2002	2003	2004	2005	2006	2007	2008
Total	.	.	.	.	.	.	.	.	.	1 846.229
1										137.841
2										261.173
3										267.301
4										114.249
5										447.870
6										40.403
7										187.533
8										162.467
9										176.447
0										45.810
X										5.135

Men - Hommes - Hombres
ISCO-88 - CITP-88 - CIUO-88

	1999	2000	2001	2002	2003	2004	2005	2006	2007	2008
Total	.	.	.	.	.	.	.	.	.	1 501.291
1										124.132
2										202.084
3										211.042
4										71.058
5										283.857
6										40.136
7										186.484
8										161.356
9										173.256
0										43.932
X										3.954

Women - Femmes - Mujeres
ISCO-88 - CITP-88 - CIUO-88

	1999	2000	2001	2002	2003	2004	2005	2006	2007	2008
Total	.	.	.	.	.	.	.	.	.	344.938
1										13.709
2										59.089
3										56.259
4										43.191
5										164.013
6										0.267
7										1.049
8										1.111
9										3.191
0										1.878
X										1.181

Viet Nam (BA) [2] [5]

Total employment - Emploi total - Empleo total

Total - Total - Total
ISCO-88 - CITP-88 - CIUO-88

	1999	2000	2001	2002	2003	2004	2005	2006	2007	2008
Total	38 119.9	38 367.6	39 000.3	40 162.3	41 175.7	42 315.6	.	.	.	.
1	180.2	212.9	174.0	201.0	209.5	312.6				
2	892.6	909.3	1 111.1	1 179.1	1 323.2	1 475.1				
3	1 144.5	1 114.5	1 053.1	1 137.6	1 221.6	1 346.9				
4	358.7	360.4	334.7	413.4	406.4	420.6				
5	2 360.6	3 196.8	3 257.1	3 581.9	3 661.7	3 610.2				
6	1 773.3	2 724.3	4 455.7	4 275.2	3 467.1	2 659.6				
7	3 590.6	3 692.5	4 084.0	4 414.0	4 886.7	5 238.0				
8	1 090.6	1 183.1	1 272.3	1 350.3	1 478.0	1 436.1				
9	26 521.8	24 519.9	22 821.1	23 330.1	24 261.6	25 816.5				
X	207.0	453.8	437.1	279.7	260.0	-				

Explanatory notes: see p. 77.

[1] Excl. armed forces. [2] Persons aged 15 years and over. [3] Third quarter. [4] February. [5] July of each year.

Notes explicatives: voir p. 80.

[1] Non compris les forces armées. [2] Personnes âgées de 15 ans et plus. [3] Troisième trimestre. [4] Février. [5] Juillet de chaque année.

Notas explicativas: véase p. 83.

[1] Excl. las fuerzas armadas. [2] Personas de 15 años y más. [3] Tercer trimestre. [4] Febrero. [5] Julio de cada año.

Total employment, by occupation / Emploi total, par profession / Empleo total, por ocupación

	Thousands			Milliers				Millares		
	1999	2000	2001	2002	2003	2004	2005	2006	2007	2008

Viet Nam (BA) [1] [2] — Total employment - Emploi total - Empleo total

Men - Hommes - Hombres
ISCO-88 - CITP-88 - CIUO-88

Total	19 028.5	19 292.1	19 743.7	20 355.6	20 959.2	21 649.3	.	.	.	.
1	146.6	177.2	140.9	162.3	167.9	243.3	.	.	.	.
2	462.0	454.5	546.2	590.4	680.0	771.8	.	.	.	.
3	491.5	494.1	485.0	502.6	550.1	605.8	.	.	.	.
4	182.1	193.1	157.6	210.0	190.3	209.5	.	.	.	.
5	825.1	1 013.5	1 023.2	1 121.0	1 213.3	1 250.9	.	.	.	.
6	1 055.9	1 609.6	2 567.4	2 479.4	2 026.6	1 620.1	.	.	.	.
7	2 229.1	2 287.3	2 593.5	2 774.2	3 130.6	3 277.8	.	.	.	.
8	852.9	953.0	1 007.6	1 098.6	1 177.6	1 221.2	.	.	.	.
9	12 692.1	11 919.9	11 046.1	11 311.8	11 712.7	12 449.0	.	.	.	.
X	91.2	189.9	176.3	105.2	110.2	-	.	.	.	.

Women - Femmes - Mujeres
ISCO-88 - CITP-88 - CIUO-88

Total	19 091.4	19 075.5	19 256.5	19 806.7	20 216.5	20 666.3	.	.	.	.
1	33.6	35.7	33.2	38.7	41.6	69.3	.	.	.	.
2	430.5	454.8	565.0	588.7	643.1	703.3	.	.	.	.
3	653.0	620.5	568.1	635.0	671.6	741.1	.	.	.	.
4	176.7	167.4	177.1	203.4	216.1	211.1	.	.	.	.
5	1 535.5	2 183.3	2 233.9	2 460.8	2 448.4	2 359.3	.	.	.	.
6	717.4	1 114.7	1 888.3	1 795.7	1 440.5	1 039.5	.	.	.	.
7	1 361.5	1 405.2	1 490.5	1 639.8	1 756.1	1 960.2	.	.	.	.
8	237.7	230.1	264.7	251.7	300.4	214.9	.	.	.	.
9	13 829.8	12 599.9	11 775.0	12 018.3	12 548.9	13 367.5	.	.	.	.
X	115.8	263.9	260.8	174.5	149.8	-	.	.	.	.

West Bank and Gaza Strip (BA) [1] — Total employment - Emploi total - Empleo total

Total - Total - Total
ISCO-88 - CITP-88 - CIUO-88

Total	588.000	597.440	504.786 [3]	476.661	564.571	578.439	632.939	666.375	665.620	647.023
1	23.345	17.720	19.203 [3]	21.425	22.847	22.254	22.453	22.418	25.777	26.605
2	45.379	52.232	53.320 [3]	53.818	63.093	70.820	73.642	75.191	79.131	82.718
3	45.857	46.878	47.205 [3]	43.799	46.059	50.716	57.485	58.264	55.592	53.428
4	17.896	19.994	17.693 [3]	15.770	15.828	14.528	14.143	16.796	14.889	15.279
5	97.145	102.753	94.265 [3]	89.970	105.708	105.665	119.503	133.240	136.404	140.682
6	59.747	67.543	50.754 [3]	60.233	76.471	82.359	78.307	90.557	90.053	71.712
7	133.722	131.363	96.018 [3]	83.262	105.277	98.634	110.888	107.375	106.863	100.744
8	47.724	48.895	46.207 [3]	40.473	48.979	50.900	58.475	62.425	63.775	52.788
9	117.138	109.378	79.900 [3]	67.212	80.051	82.486	97.980	100.077	93.066	102.595
X	0.048	0.683	0.222 [3]	0.700	0.258	0.077	0.062	0.030	0.070	0.471

Men - Hommes - Hombres
ISCO-88 - CITP-88 - CIUO-88

Total	502.000	504.220	427.889 [3]	398.778	467.371	473.755	527.806	546.000	538.090	525.696
1	20.996	15.449	17.068 [3]	19.322	20.052	19.836	19.688	19.704	23.091	23.976
2	32.674	37.001	36.513 [3]	36.078	41.510	44.032	46.318	47.320	49.140	48.684
3	29.751	31.223	32.255 [3]	29.591	30.872	35.429	41.734	40.303	39.218	34.877
4	10.986	12.248	11.410 [3]	10.079	10.465	9.736	9.975	10.555	9.974	9.674
5	90.142	94.940	87.403 [3]	83.906	96.584	96.707	109.714	122.491	123.704	128.425
6	33.046	36.422	31.371 [3]	37.893	44.365	47.699	44.755	50.088	44.696	39.271
7	124.622	123.649	90.857 [3]	78.353	100.037	93.977	106.763	101.406	100.134	93.736
8	47.022	48.262	45.216 [3]	39.788	47.317	48.409	55.551	58.994	59.518	49.483
9	112.730	104.458	75.593 [3]	63.211	75.966	77.853	93.255	95.108	88.473	97.182
X	0.032	0.569	0.203 [3]	0.557	0.202	0.077	0.055	0.030	0.070	0.390

Women - Femmes - Mujeres
ISCO-88 - CITP-88 - CIUO-88

Total	86.000	93.220	76.897 [3]	77.883	97.200	104.683	105.132	120.375	127.602	121.326
1	2.349	2.271	2.136 [3]	2.103	2.795	2.418	2.765	2.714	2.686	2.629
2	12.705	15.231	16.806 [3]	17.739	21.582	26.787	27.325	27.871	29.991	34.034
3	16.106	15.655	14.950 [3]	14.207	15.187	15.287	15.751	17.961	16.374	18.551
4	6.910	7.745	6.283 [3]	5.691	5.363	4.792	4.168	6.241	4.914	5.605
5	7.004	7.813	6.862 [3]	6.064	9.123	8.958	9.789	10.749	12.700	12.258
6	26.701	31.121	19.383 [3]	22.341	32.106	34.660	33.552	40.469	45.357	32.442
7	9.101	7.714	5.161 [3]	4.909	5.240	4.657	4.125	5.970	6.729	7.009
8	0.701	0.634	0.991 [3]	0.684	1.663	2.491	2.924	3.431	4.257	3.305
9	4.408	4.921	4.307 [3]	4.002	4.084	4.633	4.726	4.969	4.594	5.413
X	0.016	0.115	0.019 [3]	0.143	0.056	-	0.007	-	-	0.081

Explanatory notes: see p. 77.

[1] Persons aged 15 years and over. [2] July of each year. [3] Prior to 2001: persons aged 10 years and over.

Notes explicatives: voir p. 80.

[1] Personnes âgées de 15 ans et plus. [2] Juillet de chaque année. [3] Avant 2001: personnes agées de 10 ans et plus.

Notas explicativas: véase p. 83.

[1] Personas de 15 años y más. [2] Julio de cada año. [3] Antes de 2001: personas de 10 años y más.

	EMPLOYMENT	EMPLOI	EMPLEO
	Total employment, by occupation	**Emploi total, par profession**	**Empleo total, por ocupación**
	Thousands	Milliers	Millares

	1999	2000	2001	2002	2003	2004	2005	2006	2007	2008

EUROPE-EUROPE-EUROPA

Austria (BA) [1] [2]   Total employment - Emploi total - Empleo total

Total - Total - Total
ISCO-88 - CITP-88 - CIUO-88

	1999	2000	2001	2002	2003	2004	2005	2006	2007	2008
Total	3 762.3	3 776.5	3 799.6	3 835.7	3 798.4	3 744.0 [3]	3 823.5	3 928.3	4 027.9	4 090.0
1	276.5	276.9	293.8	274.2	283.7	243.3 [3]	286.2	279.4	286.7	281.6
2	359.9	362.0	379.6	385.6	379.4	348.7 [3]	372.9	388.5	399.0	407.0
3	501.9	530.7	541.9	567.5	566.0	811.4 [3]	796.5	809.5	796.5	814.0
4	523.0	524.0	511.5	518.3	525.7	493.9 [3]	478.0	493.8	512.1	545.9
5	528.0	541.4	547.6	576.6	564.6	542.2 [3]	500.7	516.1	554.5	570.1
6	212.2	199.1	195.5	198.6	192.8	174.2 [3]	200.2	206.9	211.2	213.9
7	651.0	665.3	649.9	634.9	603.5	517.0 [3]	526.4	549.3	552.4	547.0
8	322.1	312.0	298.9	299.3	291.1	232.4 [3]	251.3	257.9	250.4	242.7
9	355.8	329.6	346.4	346.6	356.0	369.1 [3]	401.7	416.5	453.6	454.6
0	31.8	35.6	34.4	34.2	35.6	11.6 [3]	10.6	10.4	11.5	13.0

Men - Hommes - Hombres
ISCO-88 - CITP-88 - CIUO-88

	1999	2000	2001	2002	2003	2004	2005	2006	2007	2008
Total	2 139.7	2 145.6	2 142.5	2 139.0	2 101.8	2 061.5 [3]	2 095.4	2 147.5	2 208.5	2 222.1
1	205.1	198.8	207.7	194.8	206.5	176.1 [3]	208.3	199.6	210.1	201.9
2	183.2	180.2	187.7	189.4	181.0	197.0 [3]	203.2	216.3	219.9	222.2
3	260.1	278.9	287.9	302.7	297.0	427.6 [3]	395.0	405.2	404.0	429.6
4	180.2	171.3	161.0	157.7	163.7	143.8 [3]	143.4	148.7	158.9	160.1
5	174.4	186.1	186.5	187.0	178.9	176.2 [3]	145.4	153.2	160.7	156.8
6	109.2	106.3	101.3	103.8	101.1	87.8 [3]	104.4	106.8	111.3	112.6
7	587.8	606.5	596.1	583.6	552.8	477.4 [3]	487.0	506.6	512.7	507.4
8	268.4	257.1	242.9	245.4	239.7	204.0 [3]	219.6	222.6	216.7	214.6
9	139.5	124.9	137.1	140.6	145.5	160.1 [3]	178.2	178.4	203.1	204.6
0	31.8	35.6	34.4	34.2	35.5	11.4 [3]	10.6	10.2	11.2	12.3

Women - Femmes - Mujeres
ISCO-88 - CITP-88 - CIUO-88

	1999	2000	2001	2002	2003	2004	2005	2006	2007	2008
Total	1 622.7	1 631.0	1 657.1	1 696.7	1 696.6	1 682.5 [3]	1 728.1	1 780.7	1 819.4	1 867.9
1	71.4	78.1	86.2	79.4	77.2	67.2 [3]	77.9	79.8	76.6	79.7
2	176.8	181.8	191.9	196.2	198.3	151.7 [3]	169.7	172.2	179.1	184.8
3	241.8	251.8	254.1	264.8	268.9	383.8 [3]	401.5	404.3	392.5	384.4
4	342.8	352.7	350.5	360.6	362.1	350.1 [3]	334.5	345.0	353.2	385.8
5	353.5	355.3	361.1	389.6	385.7	366.0 [3]	355.2	362.9	393.7	413.4
6	103.0	92.8	94.3	94.9	91.7	86.4 [3]	95.8	100.1	99.9	101.3
7	63.3	58.8	53.8	51.3	50.8	39.6 [3]	39.3	42.7	39.7	39.6
8	53.8	54.8	56.0	53.9	51.4	28.4 [3]	31.7	35.3	33.7	28.1
9	216.4	204.7	209.3	206.0	210.5	209.0 [3]	223.5	238.1	250.5	250.0
0	-	-	-	-	0.1	0.2 [3]	-	0.3	0.3	0.7

Belgique (BA) [2] [4]   Total employment - Emploi total - Empleo total

Total - Total - Total
ISCO-88 - CITP-88 - CIUO-88

	1999	2000	2001	2002	2003	2004	2005	2006	2007	2008
Total	.	.	4 051.2	4 069.8	4 070.5	4 139.0	4 235.3	4 264.0	4 380.3	4 445.9
1			454.4	450.2	454.3	473.1	486.5	487.6	498.6	486.7
2			766.6	787.6	796.2	833.3	877.5	898.7	919.9	939.5
3			445.0	447.1	465.3	473.8	505.8	505.1	524.7	504.4
4			658.2	671.1	648.0	642.9	671.3	639.0	626.5	675.0
5			424.0	432.7	439.8	442.2	455.5	460.3	488.4	518.1
6			67.7	73.4	73.5	85.2	91.0	86.8	81.7	82.3
7			466.5	458.9	423.9	433.1	429.5	427.3	441.0	463.6
8			280.1	326.6	338.3	325.0	320.5	318.1	341.8	334.2
9			438.7	377.7	383.9	385.4	355.8	394.9	425.1	408.6
0			41.9	35.0	36.7	36.1	32.8	33.0	32.6	33.5
X	.	.	8.2	9.4	10.5	9.0	9.5	13.0	-	0.1

Men - Hommes - Hombres
ISCO-88 - CITP-88 - CIUO-88

	1999	2000	2001	2002	2003	2004	2005	2006	2007	2008
Total	.	.	2 346.3	2 339.2	2 317.0	2 354.0	2 386.8	2 391.6	2 443.7	2 460.7
1			309.2	313.0	311.9	331.4	331.8	334.1	329.9	327.7
2			355.1	363.8	359.2	376.5	402.3	404.1	406.3	410.4
3			285.7	275.2	294.2	298.3	309.0	311.1	331.7	325.6
4			259.1	263.8	247.1	235.9	249.0	228.8	220.9	245.2
5			143.5	148.3	141.3	146.5	155.3	152.9	164.7	163.6
6			50.6	53.1	53.3	61.9	65.8	63.9	60.5	63.5
7			432.0	422.7	393.1	402.4	398.0	397.0	405.0	432.7
8			235.0	275.7	281.6	275.6	267.8	271.3	290.4	279.1
9			232.4	186.2	195.5	187.1	172.3	190.0	204.4	182.8
0			39.1	31.9	34.2	34.4	30.3	31.1	29.9	30.0
X	.	.	4.5	5.4	5.6	4.3	5.3	7.4	-	-

Explanatory notes: see p. 77.

[1] Excl. conscripts on compulsory military service. [2] Persons aged 15 years and over. [3] Prior to 2004: incl. conscripts. [4] Incl. professional army.

Notes explicatives: voir p. 80.

[1] Non compris conscrits ceux du contingent. [2] Personnes âgées de 15 ans et plus. [3] Avant 2004: y compris les conscrits. [4] Y compris les militaires de carrière.

Notas explicativas: véase p. 83.

[1] Excl. los conscriptos del servicio obligatorio. [2] Personas de 15 años y más. [3] Antes de 2004: incl. los conscriptos. [4] Incl. los militares profesionales.

Total employment, by occupation — Emploi total, par profession — Empleo total, por ocupación

Thousands — Milliers — Millares

	1999	2000	2001	2002	2003	2004	2005	2006	2007	2008
Belgique (BA) [1] [2]					Total employment - Emploi total - Empleo total					
Women - Femmes - Mujeres										
ISCO-88 - CITP-88 - CIUO-88										
Total	.	.	1 704.9	1 730.7	1 753.4	1 785.0	1 848.5	1 872.4	1 936.6	1 985.2
1	.	.	145.2	137.2	142.4	141.8	154.8	153.6	168.8	159.0
2	.	.	411.5	423.9	436.9	456.8	475.0	494.6	513.6	529.1
3	.	.	159.2	171.9	171.1	175.5	196.3	194.1	193.0	178.8
4	.	.	399.1	407.3	400.9	407.0	422.3	410.2	405.6	429.8
5	.	.	280.5	284.3	298.5	295.7	300.0	307.4	323.7	354.4
6	.	.	17.1	20.2	20.3	23.3	25.5	22.8	21.2	18.7
7	.	.	34.5	36.1	30.8	30.6	31.5	30.3	36.0	30.9
8	.	.	45.1	51.0	56.7	49.4	52.8	46.9	51.4	55.0
9	.	.	206.3	191.5	188.4	198.3	183.8	204.9	220.7	225.8
0	.	.	2.9	3.1	2.5	1.7	3.5	2.0	2.7	3.5
X	.	.	3.7	4.0	4.9	4.8	4.3	5.6	-	0.1
Bulgaria (BA) [2] [3]					Total employment - Emploi total - Empleo total					
Total - Total - Total										
ISCO-88 - CITP-88 - CIUO-88										
Total	.	.	.	.	2 834.0	2 922.2	2 980.0	3 110.0	3 252.6	3 360.7
1	.	.	.	.	218.4	207.8	195.1	200.6	214.7	220.8
2	.	.	.	.	335.6	336.6	347.5	380.1	400.0	414.8
3	.	.	.	.	343.3	339.1	342.0	287.5	310.8	325.3
4	.	.	.	.	191.5	186.8	191.9	222.1	225.1	241.9
5	.	.	.	.	389.5	420.0	444.9	510.0	526.7	532.9
6	.	.	.	.	188.9	187.4	168.3	165.4	156.1	155.0
7	.	.	.	.	397.2	406.3	429.5	472.5	512.6	535.2
8	.	.	.	.	414.2	434.3	467.7	459.0	462.1	470.3
9	.	.	.	.	338.2	372.6	360.5	382.9	414.7	434.7
X	.	.	.	.	17.2	31.2	32.6	29.8	29.7	29.9
Men - Hommes - Hombres										
ISCO-88 - CITP-88 - CIUO-88										
Total	.	.	.	.	1 500.0	1 550.7	1 591.4	1 652.8	1 731.5	1 792.9
1	.	.	.	.	151.7	139.5	128.7	137.2	147.3	149.5
2	.	.	.	.	114.3	118.6	121.1	124.7	136.3	139.2
3	.	.	.	.	156.1	147.9	152.7	131.2	139.3	151.1
4	.	.	.	.	54.0	52.4	55.9	56.9	56.3	57.5
5	.	.	.	.	136.6	146.2	154.0	199.8	203.8	208.0
6	.	.	.	.	110.1	109.4	95.6	96.6	89.2	87.6
7	.	.	.	.	281.5	296.8	319.6	344.5	378.4	397.4
8	.	.	.	.	285.8	294.2	320.0	316.5	320.0	329.4
9	.	.	.	.	194.0	216.4	214.3	218.7	233.9	246.4
X	.	.	.	.	15.9	29.2	29.7	26.9	27.0	26.6
Women - Femmes - Mujeres										
ISCO-88 - CITP-88 - CIUO-88										
Total	.	.	.	.	1 334.0	1 371.5	1 388.7	1 457.2	1 521.1	1 567.8
1	.	.	.	.	66.6	68.3	66.5	63.4	67.4	71.3
2	.	.	.	.	221.3	218.0	226.4	255.4	263.7	275.6
3	.	.	.	.	187.2	191.3	189.5	156.3	171.5	174.2
4	.	.	.	.	137.5	134.4	136.0	165.2	168.8	184.4
5	.	.	.	.	252.9	273.8	290.9	310.2	322.9	324.8
6	.	.	.	.	78.8	78.0	72.7	68.8	66.9	67.4
7	.	.	.	.	115.7	109.5	109.9	128.1	134.2	137.8
8	.	.	.	.	128.3	140.2	147.6	142.6	142.1	140.9
9	.	.	.	.	144.1	156.2	146.2	164.2	180.9	188.2
X	.	.	.	.	1.6	2.0	2.9	2.9	2.7	3.3
Croatia (BA) [2] [3]					Total employment - Emploi total - Empleo total					
Total - Total - Total										
ISCO-88 - CITP-88 - CIUO-88										
Total	1 491.6	1 553.0	1 469.5	1 527.2	1 536.4	1 562.7	1 572.9	1 586.4	1 614.4	1 635.6
1	100.6	104.2	82.7	85.7	83.9	76.2	86.4	83.5	81.6	86.4
2	124.0	143.9	122.7	124.2	141.1	143.7	146.5	151.2	149.8	161.1
3	228.7	236.8	211.9	228.8	212.7	214.6	226.2	233.6	235.2	244.6
4	177.9	195.3	166.6	182.0	170.8	171.4	169.8	176.6	196.2	193.1
5	177.9	208.6	216.1	219.3	212.2	226.0	216.9	238.4	237.1	234.9
6	211.4	187.7	199.6	200.7	222.8	221.3	238.2	195.0	183.8	192.4
7	176.1	191.3	194.6	191.7	197.6	201.3	190.1	205.0	225.6	220.1
8	143.7	143.8	142.6	157.3	157.7	162.2	167.2	170.0	167.8	167.5
9	133.0	118.4	109.0	115.8	121.7	134.0	119.5	120.4	125.9	126.5
0	16.6	22.0	20.3	21.6	14.4	11.4	11.8	11.1	11.4 [4]	8.6 [4]
X	1.8	1.0	-	-	-	-	-	-	. [5]	. [5]

Explanatory notes: see p. 77.

[1] Incl. professional army. [2] Persons aged 15 years and over. [3] Incl. armed forces, Excl. conscripts. [4] Estimate not sufficiently reliable. [5] Not indicated due to lack of statistical reliability.

Notes explicatives: voir p. 80.

[1] Y compris les militaires de carrière. [2] Personnes âgées de 15 ans et plus. [3] Y compris les forces armées, Excl. conscrits [4] Estimation pas suffisamment fiable. [5] Non indiqué en raison du manque de fiabilité statistique.

Notas explicativas: véase p. 83.

[1] Incl. los militares profesionales. [2] Personas de 15 años y más. [3] Incl. las fuerzas armadas, excl. los conscriptos. [4] Estimación no suficientemente fiable. [5] No se indica por la falta de confiabilidad estadística.

2C

	EMPLOYMENT	EMPLOI	EMPLEO
	Total employment, by occupation	Emploi total, par profession	Empleo total, por ocupación
	Thousands	Milliers	Millares

	1999	2000	2001	2002	2003	2004	2005	2006	2007	2008
Croatia (BA) [1] [2]				Total employment - Emploi total - Empleo total						
Men - Hommes - Hombres										
ISCO-88 - CITP-88 - CIUO-88										
Total	802.2	848.7	818.9	842.5	850.5	866.4	867.0	868.1	897.3	905.1
1	74.2	78.6	62.4	63.1	62.1	58.6	65.6	62.1	64.6	63.5
2	61.3	64.3	59.1	56.5	63.6	63.1	66.4	64.2	67.4	71.6
3	109.0	113.1	107.4	115.0	106.0	110.2	120.5	124.0	122.3	126.9
4	51.9	57.8	54.5	50.1	50.7	55.2	47.0	46.1	58.0	60.0
5	71.6	93.6	86.1	92.3	86.0	90.1	90.6	94.5	93.6	94.8
6	105.1	92.6	108.8	106.3	109.6	109.5	112.6	95.3	88.2	91.2
7	146.5	169.2	166.4	171.3	181.1	184.9	175.9	189.1	208.4	202.3
8	105.2	107.8	106.5	115.4	116.6	118.1	120.2	125.9	128.6	126.6
9	60.0	49.3	46.1	51.1	60.1	65.3	56.7	55.6	55.0	59.6
0	15.9	21.5	19.8	21.1	13.5	10.9	11.0	10.2	11.3 [3]	8.2 [3]
X	1.5	0.9	-	-	-	-	-	-	. [4]	. [4]
Women - Femmes - Mujeres										
ISCO-88 - CITP-88 - CIUO-88										
Total	689.5	704.3	650.6	684.7	685.9	696.4	706.0	718.3	717.1	730.5
1	26.4	25.7	20.4	22.1	21.7	17.6	20.8	21.4	17.0 [3]	22.9 [3]
2	62.8	79.7	63.6	67.7	77.5	80.6	80.2	87.0	82.4	89.5
3	119.7	123.7	104.5	113.9	106.7	104.4	105.8	109.7	112.9	117.7
4	126.0	137.5	112.1	131.9	120.2	116.2	122.8	130.4	138.2	133.1
5	106.4	115.0	130.0	127.0	126.2	135.9	126.3	143.9	143.5	140.1
6	106.3	95.0	90.9	94.5	113.2	111.8	125.5	99.7	95.6	101.2
7	29.6	22.1	28.2	20.3	16.5	16.5	14.2	16.0	17.2 [3]	17.8 [3]
8	38.5	36.0	36.2	41.9	41.2	44.0	47.0	44.1	39.2	40.9
9	73.0	69.2	63.0	64.7	61.6	68.7	62.8	64.8	70.9	66.9
0	0.7	0.5	0.5	0.5	0.9	0.6	0.8	0.9	- [4]	0.4
X	0.2	0.1	-	-	-	-	-	-	. [4]	. [4]
Cyprus (BA) [1] [2] [5]				Total employment - Emploi total - Empleo total						
Total - Total - Total										
ISCO-88 - CITP-88 - CIUO-88										
Total	279.2	288.6	309.5	315.3	327.1	338.0	348.0	357.3	377.9	382.9
1	7.4	8.3	9.8	7.8	8.5	8.1	9.3	11.6	13.4	16.2
2	30.8	35.1	41.2	41.7	43.3	42.7	45.3	48.6	57.5	56.5
3	31.4	30.8	36.0	39.5	43.2	43.2	44.0	44.6	44.4	47.6
4	34.9	38.7	42.5	42.8	42.2	44.8	48.3	51.4	56.0	50.7
5	48.7	48.8	52.2	52.5	55.8	57.3	55.7	56.2	61.0	63.1
6	10.2	10.2	9.8	10.4	10.9	10.3	11.0	9.9	10.9	11.5
7	46.1	42.8	45.0	45.9	47.1	52.2	54.2	51.7	53.7	54.3
8	21.5	22.6	21.2	20.7	19.2	18.7	19.8	20.5	20.6	20.5
9	36.5	38.3	48.7	50.3	53.3	57.2	57.0	59.1	56.3	57.3
0	2.6	3.7	3.3	3.7	3.6	3.6	3.6	3.7	4.2	5.0
X	9.2	9.4	-	-	-	-	-	-	-	-
Men - Hommes - Hombres										
ISCO-88 - CITP-88 - CIUO-88										
Total	172.9	176.1	176.2	176.8	181.6	190.8	197.3	200.4	209.5	212.2
1	6.3	7.1	7.9	6.5	7.0	6.9	7.9	9.8	11.4	13.6
2	17.1	19.2	21.4	20.5	21.9	21.6	22.3	22.7	27.9	27.1
3	19.8	19.1	21.0	22.8	24.1	25.9	27.1	27.9	25.0	26.3
4	8.5	9.8	10.5	10.9	10.1	11.3	11.7	12.3	13.6	11.7
5	26.4	26.3	26.0	25.4	25.6	26.1	25.6	26.0	26.7	28.5
6	7.9	7.8	7.7	8.7	9.7	8.9	8.7	7.6	8.9	9.0
7	43.6	40.4	42.5	43.5	44.7	50.1	51.9	49.4	51.6	51.9
8	17.8	18.9	17.6	16.9	16.3	16.2	17.4	18.6	18.5	18.3
9	14.0	14.9	18.7	18.6	19.3	20.8	21.7	22.8	22.3	21.7
0	2.2	3.3	2.8	3.1	3.0	3.3	3.3	3.2	3.6	4.2
X	9.2	9.4	-	-	-	-	-	-	-	-
Women - Femmes - Mujeres										
ISCO-88 - CITP-88 - CIUO-88										
Total	106.3	112.5	133.3	138.6	145.5	147.2	150.7	156.9	168.5	170.6
1	1.1	1.2	1.9	1.4	1.5	1.2	1.4	1.9	2.1	2.6
2	13.7	15.9	19.8	21.2	21.4	21.1	23.0	25.9	29.6	29.4
3	11.5	11.7	15.0	16.8	19.1	17.3	16.9	16.7	19.4	21.3
4	26.3	28.9	31.9	32.0	32.1	33.6	36.6	39.1	42.3	39.0
5	22.3	22.5	26.2	27.1	30.2	31.2	30.1	30.2	34.4	34.7
6	2.2	2.5	2.1	1.7	1.2	1.5	2.3	2.3	2.0	2.5
7	2.5	2.4	2.5	2.4	2.5	2.1	2.3	2.3	2.1	2.5
8	3.7	3.7	3.6	3.8	3.0	2.6	2.4	1.9	2.1	2.2
9	22.5	23.5	29.9	31.7	34.0	36.3	35.3	36.3	34.0	35.7
0	0.3	0.4	0.5	0.6	0.6	0.3	0.3	0.4	0.6	0.8
X										

Explanatory notes: see p. 77.

[1] Incl. armed forces, Excl. conscripts. [2] Persons aged 15 years and over. [3] Estimate not sufficiently reliable. [4] Not indicated due to lack of statistical reliability. [5] Government-controlled area.

Notes explicatives: voir p. 80.

[1] Y compris les forces armées, Excl. conscrits [2] Personnes âgées de 15 ans et plus. [3] Estimation pas suffisamment fiable. [4] Non indiqué en raison du manque de fiabilité statistique. [5] Région sous contrôle gouvernemental.

Notas explicativas: véase p. 83.

[1] Incl. las fuerzas armadas, excl. los conscriptos. [2] Personas de 15 años y más. [3] Estimación no suficientemente fiable. [4] No se indica por la falta de confiabilidad estadística. [5] Area controlada por el gobierno.

Total employment, by occupation — Emploi total, par profession — Empleo total, por ocupación

Thousands — Milliers — Millares

	1999	2000	2001	2002	2003	2004	2005	2006	2007	2008
Czech Republic (BA) [1]				Total employment - Emploi total - Empleo total						
Total - Total - Total										
ISCO-88 - CITP-88 - CIUO-88										
Total	4 764	4 732	4 728	4 765	4 733	4 707	4 764	4 828	4 922	5 002
1	313	291	301	304	286	292	294	318	328	334
2	478	505	506	487	485	499	516	519	544	557
3	878	883	897	912	952	974	1 039	1 056	1 099	1 135
4	368	365	381	407	380	373	358	339	344	353
5	577	568	579	597	594	578	575	584	578	579
6	98	96	91	91	88	82	76	74	73	68
7	994	966	937	935	926	905	888	879	915	935
8	609	607	618	629	625	631	655	690	682	677
9	392	393	372	366	361	348	345	351	345	349
0	55	56	43	35	36	23	15	17	14	16
X	1	3	2	3	1	2	2	1	1	1
Men - Hommes - Hombres										
ISCO-88 - CITP-88 - CIUO-88										
Total	2 694	2 676	2 674	2 700	2 686	2 663	2 706	2 742	2 806	2 863
1	236	218	222	225	209	211	207	226	234	240
2	225	241	240	237	242	243	257	259	264	267
3	403	405	422	438	450	464	487	487	516	532
4	74	75	79	92	80	73	82	84	84	91
5	193	194	205	206	209	206	204	197	192	198
6	55	57	53	53	54	49	48	44	46	42
7	836	815	793	801	797	792	778	773	805	828
8	463	453	462	471	466	464	488	515	506	503
9	154	160	153	142	143	137	140	141	146	147
0	54	55	42	34	35	21	13	15	13	15
X	1	2	1	2	1	2	1	-	1	-
Women - Femmes - Mujeres										
ISCO-88 - CITP-88 - CIUO-88										
Total	2 070	2 056	2 054	2 065	2 047	2 044	2 059	2 086	2 116	2 139
1	77	72	80	79	77	81	87	92	94	94
2	253	264	266	250	243	256	258	261	280	290
3	475	478	475	475	502	510	553	570	583	603
4	294	290	302	314	300	300	275	254	260	262
5	383	373	373	391	385	372	371	387	386	381
6	43	39	38	38	34	33	28	30	27	26
7	158	150	143	134	129	113	110	106	110	107
8	146	154	156	157	159	167	168	175	176	174
9	238	233	219	225	218	211	205	209	199	201
0	1	1	1	1	1	2	2	2	1	1
X	-	1	1	1	-	-	1	1	-	-
Denmark (BA) [2][3]				Total employment - Emploi total - Empleo total						
Total - Total - Total										
ISCO-88 - CITP-88 - CIUO-88										
Total	.	2 722.1	2 725.1	2 715.3	2 692.5	2 720.1	2 732.8	2 786.6	2 778.6	2 827.4
1	.	193.8	187.6	193.1	207.6	195.6	197.1	208.6	214.4	168.4
2	.	379.2	391.7	384.9	395.4	403.4	424.9	433.2	408.2	454.0
3	.	532.4	546.7	557.2	560.9	567.6	575.5	593.7	594.2	654.1
4	.	301.8	297.6	275.8	261.2	268.0	269.5	266.8	254.6	258.9
5	.	411.6	414.9	411.3	413.3	416.9	412.8	432.7	458.2	466.6
6	.	58.8	57.7	60.7	61.8	64.1	62.6	61.0	59.9	56.5
7	.	312.0	308.0	313.3	305.4	302.8	296.0	306.6	290.6	291.5
8	.	182.1	184.7	180.7	181.2	183.1	176.4	172.1	183.3	169.6
9	.	320.2	313.0	315.2	287.8	297.5	298.5	294.8	303.1	291.3
0	.	16.1	15.2	17.0	14.1	17.5	17.6	15.3	11.5	15.2
X	.	14.0	7.9	6.0	3.7	3.5	-	-	0.9	-
Men - Hommes - Hombres										
ISCO-88 - CITP-88 - CIUO-88										
Total	.	1 458.1	1 456.3	1 449.3	1 447.8	1 451.6	1 456.1	1 482.3	1 476.1	1 497.3
1	.	149.3	148.0	149.8	153.2	146.2	148.7	157.1	154.6	128.3
2	.	227.4	230.3	222.9	231.2	229.7	241.8	245.0	230.8	259.7
3	.	233.8	233.2	235.9	237.6	235.3	230.4	235.2	254.1	270.3
4	.	81.4	77.2	69.4	69.2	67.2	73.1	73.5	65.0	73.8
5	.	88.7	92.7	95.6	100.8	104.1	102.9	109.0	120.1	120.4
6	.	49.9	49.5	51.4	52.8	53.2	50.1	48.8	48.6	47.2
7	.	295.3	291.0	295.8	289.0	290.1	281.1	290.1	271.5	276.6
8	.	136.0	143.4	141.2	140.4	142.1	139.9	139.0	147.2	135.6
9	.	170.7	170.9	166.8	157.6	165.5	169.8	168.8	173.1	170.3
0	.	15.1	14.2	16.5	13.5	16.3	17.2	15.0	10.8	14.2
X	.	10.6	5.9	3.9	2.4	1.9	-	-	0.3	-

Explanatory notes: see p. 77.

[1] Persons aged 15 years and over. [2] Included armed forces and conscripts. [3] Persons aged 15 to 66 years.

Notes explicatives: voir p. 80.

[1] Personnes âgées de 15 ans et plus. [2] Y compris les forces armées et les conscrits. [3] Personnes âgées de 15 à 66 ans.

Notas explicativas: véase p. 83.

[1] Personas de 15 años y más. [2] Incluye las fuezas armadas y los conscriptos. [3] Personas de 15 a 66 años.

2C

<table>
<tr><td>EMPLOYMENT</td><td>EMPLOI</td><td>EMPLEO</td></tr>
<tr><td>Total employment,
by occupation</td><td>Emploi total,
par profession</td><td>Empleo total,
por ocupación</td></tr>
<tr><td>Thousands</td><td>Milliers</td><td>Millares</td></tr>
</table>

Denmark (BA) [1][2] — Total employment - Emploi total - Empleo total

Women - Femmes - Mujeres
ISCO-88 - CITP-88 - CIUO-88

	1999	2000	2001	2002	2003	2004	2005	2006	2007	2008
Total	.	1 263.9	1 268.9	1 265.9	1 244.6	1 268.5	1 276.6	1 304.3	1 302.6	1 330.1
1		44.5	39.6	43.3	54.4	49.4	48.4	51.5	59.8	40.0
2		151.7	161.5	162.0	164.1	173.7	183.1	188.2	177.4	194.3
3		298.6	313.6	321.3	323.3	332.3	345.0	358.5	340.1	383.8
4		220.5	220.4	206.4	192.0	200.8	196.3	193.3	189.5	185.2
5		322.9	322.2	315.7	312.5	312.8	309.9	323.7	338.1	346.2
6		8.9	8.2	9.3	9.0	11.0	12.5	12.2	11.3	9.3
7		16.7	17.0	17.6	16.4	12.7	14.8	16.6	19.1	14.9
8		46.1	41.3	39.5	40.8	41.0	36.6	33.0	36.1	34.0
9		149.5	142.1	148.4	130.2	132.0	128.7	126.0	130.0	121.1
0		1.0	1.0	0.5	0.7	1.2	0.4	0.3	0.7	1.1
X		3.5	2.0	2.0	1.3	1.6	-	-	0.5	-

España (BA) [3][4] — Total employment - Emploi total - Empleo total

Total - Total - Total
ISCO-88 - CITP-88 - CIUO-88

	1999	2000	2001	2002	2003	2004	2005	2006	2007	2008
Total	14 689.8	15 505.9	16 146.3	16 630.3	17 295.9	17 970.8	18 973.3 [5]	19 747.7	20 356.0	20 257.6
1	1 192.5	1 216.2	1 250.5	1 247.7	1 281.7	1 326.5	1 313.0 [5]	1 438.1	1 511.3	1 558.1
2	1 692.9	1 797.8	1 928.7	2 017.7	2 119.8	2 274.8	2 363.6 [5]	2 408.7	2 516.6	2 572.6
3	1 323.4	1 491.6	1 631.8	1 693.6	1 778.9	1 889.5	2 157.6 [5]	2 263.6	2 421.6	2 441.6
4	1 429.6	1 526.1	1 541.3	1 542.9	1 610.0	1 600.9	1 768.8 [5]	1 849.6	1 886.2	1 852.2
5	2 064.9	2 200.6	2 285.7	2 418.4	2 514.7	2 635.6	2 891.9 [5]	3 085.8	3 138.9	3 277.5
6	713.9	693.7	661.0	631.1	625.7	615.8	573.6 [5]	538.9	503.8	490.1
7	2 519.1	2 655.4	2 811.4	2 896.0	2 974.3	3 068.1	3 222.7 [5]	3 285.4	3 357.5	3 174.9
8	1 553.8	1 618.4	1 635.5	1 647.1	1 674.3	1 729.7	1 766.0 [5]	1 819.1	1 881.5	1 875.5
9	2 129.9	2 224.9	2 310.5	2 455.1	2 628.2	2 742.4	2 826.1 [5]	2 971.0	3 050.5	2 919.0
0	69.7	81.2	89.8	90.7	88.3	87.5	89.9 [5]	87.6	88.3	96.2

Men - Hommes - Hombres
ISCO-88 - CITP-88 - CIUO-88

	1999	2000	2001	2002	2003	2004	2005	2006	2007	2008
Total	9 433.8	9 821.1	10 150.5	10 365.0	10 652.9	10 934.3	11 388.8 [5]	11 742.6	11 987.3	11 720.7
1	830.2	836.6	850.7	862.7	896.4	901.0	892.8 [5]	982.0	1 027.1	1 055.3
2	880.1	925.4	983.9	1 020.3	1 051.1	1 133.2	1 150.4 [5]	1 159.5	1 189.1	1 197.3
3	830.2	902.8	965.8	975.3	1 019.4	1 060.9	1 196.8 [5]	1 258.1	1 343.3	1 330.8
4	581.4	608.4	607.6	604.6	599.4	562.5	633.6 [5]	648.2	653.4	625.0
5	890.7	937.9	939.4	980.0	976.6	1 000.1	1 098.0 [5]	1 154.7	1 139.1	1 171.3
6	544.3	522.4	506.2	480.5	472.5	478.9	451.7 [5]	421.6	392.2	386.0
7	2 332.6	2 459.7	2 615.4	2 703.3	2 781.2	2 855.0	2 981.8 [5]	3 057.1	3 150.0	2 987.4
8	1 320.0	1 373.7	1 388.8	1 410.8	1 451.2	1 502.9	1 540.3 [5]	1 592.5	1 630.5	1 622.7
9	1 156.6	1 178.2	1 209.9	1 244.3	1 324.2	1 364.2	1 362.2 [5]	1 390.2	1 382.8	1 257.4
0	67.7	76.0	82.9	83.2	80.8	75.5	81.3 [5]	78.7	79.6	87.5

Women - Femmes - Mujeres
ISCO-88 - CITP-88 - CIUO-88

	1999	2000	2001	2002	2003	2004	2005	2006	2007	2008
Total	5 256.0	5 684.8	5 995.7	6 265.3	6 643.1	7 036.5	7 584.5 [5]	8 005.1	8 368.8	8 536.9
1	362.3	379.6	399.8	385.0	385.4	425.6	420.2 [5]	456.1	484.1	502.8
2	812.8	872.4	944.8	997.5	1 068.7	1 141.5	1 213.2 [5]	1 249.2	1 327.5	1 375.3
3	493.1	588.9	666.0	718.3	759.4	828.7	960.8 [5]	1 005.6	1 078.3	1 110.9
4	848.2	917.6	933.6	938.3	1 010.6	1 038.3	1 135.3 [5]	1 201.4	1 232.7	1 227.2
5	1 174.2	1 262.7	1 346.4	1 438.4	1 538.1	1 635.5	1 793.9 [5]	1 931.0	1 999.9	2 106.2
6	169.6	171.3	154.8	150.6	153.1	136.9	121.9 [5]	117.3	111.6	104.0
7	186.5	195.7	196.0	192.7	193.1	213.1	240.9 [5]	228.3	207.4	187.5
8	233.9	244.7	246.8	236.3	223.1	226.8	225.7 [5]	226.6	250.9	252.8
9	973.4	1 046.6	1 100.6	1 200.8	1 304.0	1 378.2	1 463.9 [5]	1 580.8	1 667.7	1 661.6
0	2.1	5.2	6.9	7.5	7.5	11.9	8.6 [5]	8.8	8.7	8.7

Estonia (BA) [6][7] — Total employment - Emploi total - Empleo total

Total - Total - Total
ISCO-88 - CITP-88 - CIUO-88

	1999	2000	2001	2002	2003	2004	2005	2006	2007	2008
Total	579.3	572.5	577.7	585.5	594.3	595.5	607.4	646.3	655.3	656.5
1	75.0	72.4	68.8	69.6	69.8	73.6	76.9	83.0	83.1	79.5
2	72.3	75.7	73.8	84.0	82.6	78.9	85.9	94.8	95.2	90.3
3	77.1	80.3	78.4	74.8	71.7	78.5	80.7	79.1	83.3	84.9
4	27.4	27.0	29.2	30.2	30.2	25.9	29.4	32.8	31.5	35.0
5	64.4	62.1	67.3	67.3	76.3	71.6	73.5	81.2	77.8	83.3
6	23.1	21.3	18.3	19.2	15.0	15.4	14.4	11.7	12.4	12.0
7	95.9	90.7	90.2	88.7	93.6	94.1	92.7	100.4	110.2	110.6
8	79.6	79.0	81.0	81.4	83.0	83.2	84.1	94.0	90.5	93.5
9	62.5	62.5	68.1	67.5	68.4	71.4	65.9	65.1	67.8	64.3
X	2.0	1.5	2.6	2.8	3.7	2.9	3.9	4.2	3.5	3.1

Explanatory notes: see p. 77.

[1] Included armed forces and conscripts. [2] Persons aged 15 to 66 years. [3] Excl. compulsory military service. [4] Persons aged 16 years and over. [5] Methodology revised; data not strictly comparable. [6] Persons aged 15 to 74 years. [7] Excl. conscripts.

Notes explicatives: voir p. 80.

[1] Y compris les forces armées et les conscrits. [2] Personnes âgées de 15 à 66 ans. [3] Non compris les militaires du contingent. [4] Personnes âgées de 16 ans et plus. [5] Méthodologie révisée; les données ne sont pas strictement comparables. [6] Personnes âgées de 15 à 74 ans. [7] Non compris les conscrits.

Notas explicativas: véase p. 83.

[1] Incluye las fuezas armadas y los conscriptos. [2] Personas de 15 a 66 años. [3] Excl. a los militares en servicio obligatorio. [4] Personas de 16 años y más. [5] Metodología revisada; los datos no son estrictamente comparables. [6] Personas de 15 a 74 años. [7] Excl. los conscriptos.

Total employment, by occupation
Emploi total, par profession
Empleo total, por ocupación

	Thousands			Milliers				Millares		
	1999	2000	2001	2002	2003	2004	2005	2006	2007	2008

Estonia (BA) [1][2]   Total employment - Emploi total - Empleo total

Men - Hommes - Hombres
ISCO-88 - CITP-88 - CIUO-88

	1999	2000	2001	2002	2003	2004	2005	2006	2007	2008
Total	294.2	291.1	293.9	297.5	302.5	299.1	300.5	322.9	330.0	330.9
1	48.3	45.6	44.4	43.8	45.4	47.5	48.5	54.9	54.9	50.7
2	23.7	22.3	22.3	28.7	29.9	27.9	28.2	30.0	28.8	28.8
3	24.8	28.1	23.9	21.4	17.6	23.8	22.3	25.1	27.4	26.8
4	6.3	6.4	8.4	10.3	9.3	6.0	9.6	8.7	7.1	9.0
5	13.6	15.3	13.5	13.8	20.0	16.4	16.7	15.6	14.2	18.4
6	12.8	12.7	11.7	13.0	9.4	9.2	8.4	6.8	7.5	7.2
7	76.6	75.4	79.2	77.7	80.7	78.8	78.7	88.2	97.8	100.9
8	60.4	58.9	58.7	58.5	58.5	59.0	59.5	63.7	62.6	61.7
9	25.8	25.3	29.3	27.5	28.4	27.7	25.1	26.4	26.5	25.0
X	1.9	1.1	2.5	2.8	3.3	2.8	3.5	3.5	3.2	2.4

Women - Femmes - Mujeres
ISCO-88 - CITP-88 - CIUO-88

	1999	2000	2001	2002	2003	2004	2005	2006	2007	2008
Total	285.1	281.4	283.8	288.1	291.8	296.4	306.9	323.3	325.4	325.6
1	26.7	26.8	24.4	25.7	24.4	26.0	28.4	28.1	28.2	28.8
2	48.6	53.4	51.5	55.4	52.7	50.9	57.7	64.9	66.4	61.5
3	52.2	52.2	54.5	53.3	54.1	54.7	58.4	54.0	55.9	58.1
4	21.1	20.6	20.7	20.0	20.9	19.9	19.8	24.1	24.3	26.0
5	50.7	46.8	53.9	53.5	56.3	55.3	56.8	65.6	63.7	64.9
6	10.2	8.6	6.6	6.2	5.6	6.2	6.0	4.9	4.9	4.8
7	19.3	15.3	11.1	11.0	12.9	15.3	14.1	12.2	12.3	9.7
8	19.3	20.1	22.3	22.9	24.6	24.2	24.6	30.3	27.9	31.8
9	36.7	37.2	38.8	40.0	40.0	43.7	40.8	38.7	41.3	39.3
X	0.3	0.4	0.1	-	0.3	0.1	0.3	0.5	0.5	0.7

Finland (BA) [1][3]   Total employment - Emploi total - Empleo total

Total - Total - Total
ISCO-88 - CITP-88 - CIUO-88

	1999	2000	2001	2002	2003	2004	2005	2006	2007	2008
Total	.	2 356	2 388	2 393	2 385	2 387	2 421	2 466	2 512	2 553
1	.	193	187	200	214	230	237	240	249	253
2	.	370	381	390	401	404	407	429	449	457
3	.	396	407	391	380	388	405	404	401	408
4	.	193	192	193	185	169	164	171	169	168
5	.	349	360	365	364	370	383	384	390	399
6	.	130	125	120	115	109	109	105	105	106
7	.	294	297	298	293	283	289	299	306	309
8	.	206	209	203	203	207	203	202	207	213
9	.	190	196	198	199	194	195	200	203	201
0	.	31	30	29	29	31	29	32	30	31
X	.	4	5	5	2	1	-	-	4	7

Men - Hommes - Hombres
ISCO-88 - CITP-88 - CIUO-88

	1999	2000	2001	2002	2003	2004	2005	2006	2007	2008
Total	.	1 248	1 261	1 249	1 247	1 250	1 263	1 288	1 310	1 337
1	.	142	137	145	155	165	166	169	178	179
2	.	188	191	199	205	206	203	214	224	226
3	.	183	189	175	162	159	165	164	157	161
4	.	34	35	36	35	32	33	35	34	34
5	.	75	77	74	77	80	80	78	76	79
6	.	87	82	77	75	73	73	70	72	71
7	.	268	270	271	267	255	262	272	280	287
8	.	162	168	161	165	171	168	167	170	178
9	.	75	80	81	77	79	84	87	87	87
0	.	31	29	29	28	30	29	32	29	30
X	.	3	3	2	1	1	-	-	2	4

Women - Femmes - Mujeres
ISCO-88 - CITP-88 - CIUO-88

	1999	2000	2001	2002	2003	2004	2005	2006	2007	2008
Total	.	1 108	1 127	1 144	1 138	1 137	1 158	1 178	1 202	1 217
1	.	50	50	55	59	65	70	71	71	75
2	.	182	190	192	195	198	204	215	225	231
3	.	212	219	215	218	229	239	240	244	247
4	.	158	156	157	150	137	131	136	134	134
5	.	275	283	291	288	290	304	306	314	319
6	.	43	43	43	40	36	36	35	34	35
7	.	26	26	27	26	28	27	27	26	22
8	.	44	42	42	39	36	34	35	37	35
9	.	115	116	118	122	116	111	113	116	114
0	.	1	1	1	1	1	-	-	1	1
X	.	2	2	2	1	-	-	-	1	3

Explanatory notes: see p. 77.

[1] Persons aged 15 to 74 years. [2] Excl. conscripts. [3] Included armed forces and conscripts.

Notes explicatives: voir p. 80.

[1] Personnes âgées de 15 à 74 ans. [2] Non compris les conscrits. [3] Y compris les forces armées et les conscrits.

Notas explicativas: véase p. 83.

[1] Personas de 15 a 74 años. [2] Excl. los conscriptos. [3] Incluye las fuezas armadas y los conscriptos.

EMPLOYMENT — EMPLOI — EMPLEO

Total employment, by occupation
Emploi total, par profession
Empleo total, por ocupación

	1999	2000	2001	2002	2003	2004	2005	2006	2007	2008
	Thousands				Milliers				Millares	

France (BA) [1]   Total employment - Emploi total - Empleo total

Total - Total - Total
ISCO-88 - CITP-88 - CIUO-88

	1999	2000	2001	2002	2003	2004	2005	2006	2007	2008
Total					24 695.8	24 800.3	24 978.0	25 133.5	25 565.2	25 913.2
1					1 950.9	1 998.9	2 039.4	2 055.8	2 152.5	2 204.6
2					3 212.0	3 231.6	3 359.4	3 408.3	3 435.4	3 473.5
3					4 263.9	4 411.4	4 432.8	4 465.5	4 596.6	4 886.2
4					3 241.1	3 108.8	3 077.6	3 037.3	3 098.6	3 115.5
5					3 003.2	3 039.9	3 132.9	3 203.9	3 265.1	3 233.9
6					1 078.6	1 029.2	979.4	984.5	938.2	849.1
7					2 980.9	2 988.0	2 961.3	2 992.4	2 970.7	3 041.7
8					2 361.7	2 322.0	2 300.8	2 265.9	2 315.6	2 279.7
9					2 267.7	2 327.9	2 346.1	2 388.7	2 442.4	2 505.3
0					285.2	319.2	323.7	302.7	322.7	295.7
X					50.6	·23.4	24.7	28.5	27.4	28.0

Men - Hommes - Hombres
ISCO-88 - CITP-88 - CIUO-88

	1999	2000	2001	2002	2003	2004	2005	2006	2007	2008
Total					13 302.9	13 315.7	13 350.0	13 381.5	13 521.9	13 670.2
1					1 268.7	1 260.6	1 277.2	1 275.3	1 336.7	1 355.6
2					1 807.6	1 833.2	1 876.4	1 911.2	1 936.0	1 884.6
3					2 133.3	2 176.4	2 177.8	2 161.7	2 203.3	2 367.4
4					778.3	746.9	745.3	730.6	722.0	759.7
5					823.3	822.1	839.9	863.1	876.2	869.0
6					779.1	726.8	720.5	732.1	687.1	629.6
7					2 729.4	2 722.4	2 716.7	2 747.4	2 730.5	2 794.0
8					1 892.2	1 843.7	1 826.2	1 806.6	1 855.9	1 853.0
9					797.0	863.7	856.9	861.0	869.9	869.2
0					259.7	297.8	290.5	268.1	278.6	263.8
X					34.3	22.1	22.8	24.5	25.7	24.2

Women - Femmes - Mujeres
ISCO-88 - CITP-88 - CIUO-88

	1999	2000	2001	2002	2003	2004	2005	2006	2007	2008
Total					11 392.9	11 484.7	11 628.0	11 752.0	12 043.3	12 243.0
1					682.2	738.2	762.1	780.5	815.8	849.0
2					1 404.4	1 398.4	1 483.0	1 497.0	1 499.4	1 588.9
3					2 130.7	2 235.1	2 255.1	2 303.9	2 393.3	2 518.9
4					2 462.8	2 361.9	2 332.3	2 306.7	2 376.6	2 355.7
5					2 179.9	2 217.8	2 293.0	2 340.8	2 388.9	2 364.9
6					299.5	302.4	258.9	252.4	251.1	219.4
7					251.4	265.6	244.6	245.0	240.3	247.7
8					469.5	478.2	474.6	459.3	459.7	426.7
9					1 470.8	1 464.2	1 489.2	1 527.8	1 572.4	1 636.1
0					25.4	21.4	33.3	34.6	44.1	31.8
X					16.3	1.4	2.0	4.1	1.7	3.8

Germany (BA) [1]   Total employment - Emploi total - Empleo total

Total - Total - Total
ISCO-88 - CITP-88 - CIUO-88

	1999	2000	2001	2002	2003	2004	2005	2006	2007	2008
Total	36 402	36 604 [2]	36 816	36 536 [3]	36 172 [2]	35 659 [4]	36 566 [5]	37 322	38 163	38 734
1	2 083	2 067 [2]	2 124	2 457 [3]	2 411 [2]	2 433 [4]	2 496 [5]	2 551	2 658	2 764
2	4 586	4 583 [2]	4 685	4 882 [3]	4 944 [2]	5 024 [4]	5 274 [5]	5 357	5 449	5 571
3	7 166	7 433 [2]	7 518	7 356 [3]	7 354 [2]	7 308 [4]	7 488 [5]	7 649	7 720	7 900
4	4 602	4 658 [2]	4 646	4 463 [3]	4 444 [2]	4 297 [4]	4 335 [5]	4 433	4 510	4 544
5	4 214	4 227 [2]	4 297	4 288 [3]	4 306 [2]	4 264 [4]	4 419 [5]	4 581	4 677	4 729
6	784	765 [2]	759	715 [3]	706 [2]	668 [4]	686 [5]	689	713	709
7	6 456	6 337 [2]	6 230	6 010 [3]	5 756 [2]	5 521 [4]	5 575 [5]	5 604	5 730	5 753
8	2 696	2 705 [2]	2 690	2 641 [3]	2 559 [2]	2 558 [4]	2 609 [5]	2 596	2 747	2 748
9	2 926	2 983 [2]	2 962	2 896 [3]	2 882 [2]	2 863 [4]	2 890 [5]	3 090	3 227	3 312
0	355	340 [2]	326	300 [3]	318 [2]	291 [4]	269 [5]	247	243	222
X	534	506 [2]	579	529 [3]	493 [2]	432 [4]	525 [5]	525	488	481

Men - Hommes - Hombres
ISCO-88 - CITP-88 - CIUO-88

	1999	2000	2001	2002	2003	2004	2005	2006	2007	2008
Total	20 659	20 680 [2]	20 629	20 336 [3]	19 996 [2]	19 681 [4]	20 135 [5]	20 462	20 890	21 188
1	1 535	1 510 [2]	1 552	1 609 [3]	1 544 [2]	1 576 [4]	1 565 [5]	1 589	1 651	1 719
2	2 890	2 888 [2]	2 936	3 047 [3]	3 075 [2]	3 094 [4]	3 216 [5]	3 242	3 285	3 340
3	3 020	3 150 [2]	3 155	3 145 [3]	3 129 [2]	3 088 [4]	3 229 [5]	3 273	3 254	3 351
4	1 452	1 505 [2]	1 484	1 397 [3]	1 414 [2]	1 378 [4]	1 401 [5]	1 427	1 464	1 484
5	1 100	1 105 [2]	1 118	1 126 [3]	1 119 [2]	1 111 [4]	1 150 [5]	1 197	1 188	1 214
6	530	525 [2]	510	492 [3]	481 [2]	464 [4]	472 [5]	473	491	491
7	5 833	5 732 [2]	5 644	5 419 [3]	5 192 [2]	4 986 [4]	5 042 [5]	5 080	5 185	5 201
8	2 276	2 277 [2]	2 275	2 225 [3]	2 164 [2]	2 146 [4]	2 194 [5]	2 187	2 324	2 327
9	1 351	1 355 [2]	1 288	1 284 [3]	1 287 [2]	1 302 [4]	1 306 [5]	1 438	1 524	1 582
0	352	334 [2]	323	294 [3]	311 [2]	283 [4]	260 [5]	235	232	211
X	320	299 [2]	344	298 [3]	280 [2]	252 [4]	303 [5]	320	293	269

Explanatory notes: see p. 77.

[1] Persons aged 15 years and over. [2] May. [3] Prior to 2002: April of each year. [4] March. [5] Methodology revised; data not strictly comparable.

Notes explicatives: voir p. 80.

[1] Personnes âgées de 15 ans et plus. [2] Mai. [3] Avant 2002: avril de chaque année. [4] Mars. [5] Méthodologie révisée; les données ne sont pas strictement comparables.

Notas explicativas: véase p. 83.

[1] Personas de 15 años y más. [2] Mayo. [3] Antes del 2002: abril de cada año. [4] Marzo. [5] Metodología revisada; los datos no son estrictamente comparables.

Total employment, by occupation / Emploi total, par profession / Empleo total, por ocupación

Thousands / Milliers / Millares

	1999	2000	2001	2002	2003	2004	2005	2006	2007	2008

Germany (BA) [1] — Total employment - Emploi total - Empleo total

Women - Femmes - Mujeres
ISCO-88 - CITP-88 - CIUO-88

	1999	2000	2001	2002	2003	2004	2005	2006	2007	2008
Total	15 743	15 924 [2]	16 187	16 200 [3]	16 176 [2]	15 978 [4]	16 432 [5]	16 860	17 272	17 546
1	548	557 [2]	572	847 [3]	866 [2]	857 [4]	932 [5]	962	1 008	1 045
2	1 696	1 695 [2]	1 749	1 835 [3]	1 869 [2]	1 931 [4]	2 059 [5]	2 115	2 164	2 231
3	4 146	4 283 [2]	4 363	4 211 [3]	4 225 [2]	4 220 [4]	4 259 [5]	4 376	4 466	4 549
4	3 150	3 153 [2]	3 162	3 066 [3]	3 030 [2]	2 918 [4]	2 935 [5]	3 006	3 046	3 061
5	3 114	3 122 [2]	3 179	3 162 [3]	3 186 [2]	3 153 [4]	3 269 [5]	3 384	3 490	3 515
6	254	240 [2]	249	224 [3]	226 [2]	204 [4]	215 [5]	216	222	218
7	623	605 [2]	586	591 [3]	564 [2]	535 [4]	533 [5]	524	545	551
8	420	428 [2]	415	415 [3]	395 [2]	411 [4]	416 [5]	409	424	421
9	1 575	1 628 [2]	1 674	1 612 [3]	1 595 [2]	1 561 [4]	1 584 [5]	1 651	1 703	1 731
0	3	6 [2]	3	6 [3]	7 [2]	8 [4]	9 [5]	12	10	11
X	214	207 [2]	235	231 [3]	213 [2]	180 [4]	222 [5]	205	195	212

Greece (BA) [1][6][7] — Total employment - Emploi total - Empleo total

Total - Total - Total
ISCO-88 - CITP-88 - CIUO-88

	1999	2000	2001	2002	2003	2004	2005	2006	2007	2008
Total	4 040.4	4 097.9	4 103.2	4 190.2	4 286.6	4 330.5	4 382.1	4 452.8	4 520.0	4 582.5
1	405.4	407.9	387.3	424.2	396.8	451.9	451.3	459.7	468.4	481.5
2	485.1	480.8	500.7	522.4	538.4	609.0	608.3	633.9	644.4	665.0
3	261.7	273.8	268.3	295.8	322.5	332.3	342.1	375.2	392.8	388.2
4	422.1	459.8	478.8	449.5	452.3	490.2	498.7	519.6	510.3	532.6
5	535.2	530.2	544.8	561.8	602.5	593.2	611.4	602.5	632.4	661.6
6	691.8	699.3	650.7	638.3	640.3	522.5	525.4	516.3	505.3	495.6
7	665.3	656.5	667.4	668.4	691.1	664.9	676.0	653.0	687.9	662.3
8	305.4	314.6	308.6	312.6	311.0	329.2	323.8	341.1	329.2	330.1
9	229.5	233.9	256.7	275.5	292.3	276.8	284.2	295.9	290.2	309.1
X	38.9	41.1	39.9	41.6	39.3	60.6	60.9	55.7	59.0	56.5

Men - Hommes - Hombres
ISCO-88 - CITP-88 - CIUO-88

	1999	2000	2001	2002	2003	2004	2005	2006	2007	2008
Total	2 554.1	2 577.7	2 582.2	2 622.5	2 666.1	2 680.2	2 705.8	2 725.7	2 762.0	2 788.8
1	309.1	305.4	291.7	318.2	293.1	334.7	335.0	337.7	338.8	345.1
2	261.4	255.1	266.5	271.9	272.5	319.9	317.1	328.4	332.3	339.2
3	140.5	143.9	140.2	156.4	166.8	171.4	170.7	187.0	200.8	196.9
4	181.0	197.2	202.0	188.4	190.5	199.0	211.0	208.5	199.2	212.5
5	263.2	263.6	266.4	272.0	293.5	274.6	286.7	279.2	287.4	297.6
6	403.5	405.3	385.7	372.9	372.8	299.2	299.9	294.1	291.9	290.7
7	573.0	569.5	584.2	594.1	616.7	604.9	614.3	591.5	629.5	613.2
8	279.0	285.5	281.7	282.9	283.0	296.3	291.0	312.3	301.6	301.1
9	108.3	113.9	126.5	128.5	141.1	124.8	125.1	137.3	127.6	141.4
X	35.2	38.1	37.4	37.2	36.2	55.4	55.0	49.8	52.6	51.2

Women - Femmes - Mujeres
ISCO-88 - CITP-88 - CIUO-88

	1999	2000	2001	2002	2003	2004	2005	2006	2007	2008
Total	1 486.2	1 520.2	1 521.0	1 567.7	1 620.5	1 650.3	1 676.2	1 727.1	1 758.0	1 793.7
1	96.4	102.5	95.6	106.0	103.8	117.2	116.2	122.1	129.6	136.4
2	223.7	225.7	234.2	250.5	265.9	289.1	291.2	305.5	312.1	325.9
3	121.2	129.8	128.1	139.5	155.8	160.9	171.4	188.2	192.0	191.3
4	241.2	262.6	276.8	261.1	261.8	291.2	287.7	311.0	311.2	320.2
5	272.0	266.6	278.4	289.9	309.0	318.6	324.7	323.3	345.0	364.0
6	288.3	294.0	265.0	265.4	267.6	223.3	225.5	222.1	213.3	204.9
7	92.2	87.0	83.2	74.2	74.4	60.0	61.8	61.5	58.5	49.1
8	26.4	29.1	26.9	29.8	28.1	32.9	32.8	28.8	27.6	29.0
9	121.2	120.0	130.3	147.0	151.2	152.0	159.1	158.6	162.6	167.7
X	3.7	3.0	2.5	4.4	3.1	5.2	5.9	6.0	6.5	5.3

Hungary (BA) [6][8] — Total employment - Emploi total - Empleo total

Total - Total - Total
ISCO-88 - CITP-88 - CIUO-88

	1999	2000	2001	2002	2003	2004	2005	2006	2007	2008
Total	3 811.5	3 849.1	3 859.5	3 870.6 [9]	3 921.9	3 900.4	3 901.5	3 930.1	3 926.2	3 879.4
1	247.5	265.4	260.3	261.7 [9]	271.2	292.2	307.4	295.1	283.1	291.6
2	434.6	450.0	453.9	454.5 [9]	497.0	521.7	501.7	521.1	530.2	541.3
3	507.2	509.5	465.2	544.7 [9]	565.1	556.9	566.6	578.1	566.6	589.5
4	257.3	261.3	358.2	246.8 [9]	243.9	239.0	240.1	251.1	256.1	236.2
5	586.4	585.1	538.1	600.6 [9]	609.9	603.0	622.8	629.7	639.0	618.5
6	139.4	133.6	133.0	134.8 [9]	120.7	116.9	108.1	110.9	102.4	96.3
7	849.4	841.4	803.4	820.7 [9]	798.6	767.3	754.4	752.4	755.2	713.9
8	424.9	440.4	485.2	480.8 [9]	474.6	462.7	458.0	458.8	475.4	468.6
9	302.3	297.6	305.6	284.8 [9]	296.2	296.3	296.9	289.2	282.1	289.2
0	61.6	64.8	56.6	41.2 [9]	44.7	44.4	45.5	43.3	36.1	34.3

Explanatory notes: see p. 77. / Notes explicatives: voir p. 80. / Notas explicativas: véase p. 83.

[1] Persons aged 15 years and over. [2] May. [3] Prior to 2002: April of each year. [4] March. [5] Methodology revised; data not strictly comparable. [6] Excl. conscripts. [7] Second quarter of each year. [8] Persons aged 15 to 74 years. [9] Estimates based on the 2001 Population Census results.

[1] Personnes âgées de 15 ans et plus. [2] Mai. [3] Avant 2002: avril de chaque année. [4] Mars. [5] Méthodologie révisée; les données ne sont pas strictement comparables. [6] Non compris les conscrits. [7] Deuxième trimestre de chaque année. [8] Personnes âgées de 15 à 74 ans. [9] Estimations basées sur les résultats du Recensement de la population de 2001.

[1] Personas de 15 años y más. [2] Mayo. [3] Antes del 2002: abril de cada año. [4] Marzo. [5] Metodología revisada; los datos no son estrictamente comparables. [6] Excl. los conscriptos. [7] Segundo trimestre de cada año. [8] Personas de 15 a 74 años. [9] Estimaciones basadas en los resultados del Censo de población de 2001.

2C

EMPLOYMENT	EMPLOI	EMPLEO
Total employment, by occupation	Emploi total, par profession	Empleo total, por ocupación
Thousands	Milliers	Millares

	1999	2000	2001	2002	2003	2004	2005	2006	2007	2008

Hungary (BA) [1] [2]   Total employment - Emploi total - Empleo total

Men - Hommes - Hombres
ISCO-88 - CITP-88 - CIUO-88

	1999	2000	2001	2002	2003	2004	2005	2006	2007	2008
Total	2 103.1	2 122.4	2 130.6	2 112.5 [3]	2 126.5	2 117.3	2 116.1	2 137.4	2 143.0	2 110.8
1	162.4	175.5	170.8	170.4 [3]	178.1	193.1	200.3	185.4	183.4	185.5
2	182.0	188.1	192.4	194.6 [3]	215.7	224.8	213.1	225.3	232.4	238.1
3	179.7	181.7	166.9	189.6 [3]	193.9	193.2	196.0	205.9	202.1	209.9
4	19.0	20.5	79.6	18.9 [3]	16.1	17.2	16.7	15.5	20.3	20.3
5	261.6	261.0	221.4	265.8 [3]	263.2	257.7	269.9	279.7	277.9	269.3
6	102.4	97.1	95.4	95.3 [3]	90.0	86.8	79.1	81.3	74.8	69.9
7	685.7	678.9	665.9	682.8 [3]	668.7	649.3	643.8	649.4	650.3	623.3
8	320.5	321.6	345.5	339.3 [3]	336.9	328.8	331.7	335.0	347.7	338.8
9	134.4	139.3	141.3	122.3 [3]	125.3	129.6	129.2	125.0	123.9	127.4
0	55.0	58.7	51.4	33.5 [3]	38.6	36.8	36.3	34.9	30.2	28.3

Women - Femmes - Mujeres
ISCO-88 - CITP-88 - CIUO-88

	1999	2000	2001	2002	2003	2004	2005	2006	2007	2008
Total	1 708.4	1 726.7	1 728.9	1 758.1 [3]	1 795.4	1 783.1	1 785.4	1 792.7	1 783.2	1 768.6
1	85.1	89.9	89.5	91.3 [3]	93.1	99.1	107.1	109.7	99.7	106.1
2	252.6	261.9	261.5	259.9 [3]	281.3	296.9	288.6	295.8	297.8	303.2
3	327.5	327.8	298.3	355.1 [3]	371.2	363.7	370.6	372.6	364.5	379.6
4	238.3	240.8	278.6	227.9 [3]	227.8	221.8	223.4	235.6	235.8	215.9
5	324.8	324.1	316.7	334.8 [3]	346.7	345.3	352.9	350.0	361.1	349.2
6	37.0	36.5	37.6	39.5 [3]	30.7	30.1	29.0	29.6	27.6	26.4
7	163.7	162.5	137.5	137.9 [3]	129.9	118.0	110.6	103.0	104.9	90.6
8	104.4	118.8	139.7	141.5 [3]	137.7	133.9	126.3	123.8	127.7	129.8
9	167.9	158.3	164.3	162.5 [3]	170.9	166.7	167.7	164.2	158.2	161.8
0	6.6	6.1	5.2	7.7 [3]	6.1	7.6	9.2	8.4	5.9	6.0

Iceland (BA) [4] [5]   Total employment - Emploi total - Empleo total

Total - Total - Total
ISCO-88 - CITP-88 - CIUO-88

	1999	2000	2001	2002	2003	2004	2005	2006	2007	2008
Total	153.9	156.4	159.0	156.7	156.9	156.1	161.3	169.4	177.3	178.6
1	10.3	9.9	12.4	12.7	10.6	11.9	12.1	14.3	16.7	17.2
2	21.5	21.3	23.3	25.1	27.0	24.7	28.0	29.5	31.1	35.6
3	19.7	22.0	22.5	21.8	21.6	25.2	25.7	26.1	28.5	29.4
4	13.9	13.9	13.2	12.6	13.5	11.5	12.4	12.8	12.0	10.6
5	31.9	32.2	32.0	30.8	31.7	30.0	32.2	33.7	36.6	35.3
6	10.2	10.3	9.4	9.0	8.0	7.3	8.1	8.2	7.2	6.6
7	24.4	24.2	24.2	22.5	22.1	21.4	20.9	22.4	21.4	22.2
8	9.5	10.6	10.2	9.8	8.2	9.8	9.5	9.7	9.9	9.3
9	12.0	11.8	11.8	12.3	14.0	13.9	12.3	12.7	14.1	12.4
X	-	0.1	0.2	0.2	0.3	0.4	0.1	-	-	-

Men - Hommes - Hombres
ISCO-88 - CITP-88 - CIUO-88

	1999	2000	2001	2002	2003	2004	2005	2006	2007	2008
Total	82.2	83.6	85.0	83.0	82.4	82.5	85.7	91.9	96.6	97.7
1	7.4	7.2	8.6	8.9	7.0	8.3	8.8	10.1	11.7	11.5
2	11.3	10.6	11.0	11.3	12.6	11.6	13.2	14.1	15.2	17.3
3	8.4	9.7	9.6	9.5	9.5	10.9	11.1	10.3	11.1	11.2
4	2.5	2.5	2.1	1.6	1.8	1.4	1.9	2.5	1.8	2.2
5	9.9	9.7	10.1	10.8	11.1	9.9	11.0	12.4	13.9	14.0
6	7.8	8.0	7.4	7.1	6.3	5.7	6.3	6.6	5.9	5.3
7	20.1	20.2	21.1	19.4	19.2	18.8	18.5	20.0	19.2	20.4
8	8.5	9.6	9.2	8.7	7.8	8.9	8.7	9.0	9.4	8.6
9	6.2	5.9	5.9	5.5	6.8	6.8	6.2	6.9	8.4	6.6
X	-	0.1	0.1	0.2	0.2	0.2	-	-	-	-

Women - Femmes - Mujeres
ISCO-88 - CITP-88 - CIUO-88

	1999	2000	2001	2002	2003	2004	2005	2006	2007	2008
Total	71.2	72.8	74.0	73.8	74.6	73.6	75.6	77.5	80.7	81.5
1	2.9	2.7	3.8	3.7	3.5	3.6	3.3	4.2	5.0	5.7
2	10.2	10.7	12.3	13.7	14.4	13.1	14.9	15.4	15.8	18.3
3	11.3	12.3	12.9	12.3	12.1	14.3	14.6	15.8	17.4	18.2
4	11.4	11.4	11.1	11.0	11.7	10.1	10.5	10.2	10.2	8.4
5	21.9	22.5	21.9	20.0	20.5	20.0	21.2	21.3	22.6	21.4
6	2.3	2.4	2.0	1.9	1.7	1.6	1.8	1.6	1.3	1.4
7	4.3	4.0	3.1	3.1	3.0	2.7	2.4	2.5	2.1	1.8
8	1.1	1.0	1.0	1.1	0.4	0.9	0.8	0.7	0.6	0.7
9	5.8	5.9	5.9	6.8	7.2	7.1	6.0	5.8	5.7	5.8
X	-	-	0.1	0.1	0.1	0.1	0.1	-	-	-

Explanatory notes: see p. 77.   Notes explicatives: voir p. 80.   Notas explicativas: véase p. 83.

[1] Persons aged 15 to 74 years. [2] Excl. conscripts. [3] Estimates based on the 2001 Population Census results. [4] Persons aged 16 to 74 years. [5] Excl. armed forces and conscripts.

[1] Personnes âgées de 15 à 74 ans. [2] Non compris les conscrits. [3] Estimations basées sur les résultats du Recensement de la population de 2001. [4] Personnes âgées de 16 à 74 ans. [5] Non compris les forces armées et les conscrits.

[1] Personas de 15 a 74 años. [2] Excl. los conscriptos. [3] Estimaciones basadas en los resultados del Censo de población de 2001. [4] Personas de 16 a 74 años. [5] Excl. las fuerzas armadas y los conscriptos.

Total employment, by occupation — Emploi total, par profession — Empleo total, por ocupación

	Thousands			Milliers				Millares		
	1999	2000	2001	2002	2003	2004	2005	2006	2007	2008

Ireland (BA) [1][2] — Total employment - Emploi total - Empleo total

Total - Total - Total
ISCO-88 - CITP-88 - CIUO-88

	1999	2000	2001	2002	2003	2004	2005	2006	2007	2008
Total	1 591.1	1 670.7	1 716.5	1 760.6	1 790.1	1 834.6	1 931.6	2 021.1	2 101.6	2 108.5
1	173.5	289.2	293.9	304.1	302.2	321.2	303.2	298.0	310.4	324.0
2	240.3	253.5	263.3	288.6	302.3	317.7	325.4	342.9	353.1	359.5
3	102.7	90.3	93.9	99.0	110.4	115.2	119.3	121.7	130.7	135.0
4	213.7	217.2	224.4	234.6	229.0	230.6	245.8	256.9	265.1	266.0
5	224.4	262.2	269.4	272.3	287.3	284.3	312.9	345.8	367.8	383.2
6	121.9	14.9	15.5	14.7	13.4	12.5	13.1	15.7	14.7	15.5
7	213.5	224.9	230.5	222.3	239.1	243.7	274.2	290.3	303.0	278.0
8	156.8	164.0	175.5	168.0	157.2	143.8	152.7	152.3	155.9	155.6
9	136.6	147.0	142.3	149.7	141.9	158.3	178.3	190.9	194.4	184.7
0	7.7	7.6	7.2	7.3	7.3	7.1	6.6	6.6	6.4	6.6
X	-	-	0.5	-	-	-	-	-	-	-

Men - Hommes - Hombres
ISCO-88 - CITP-88 - CIUO-88

	1999	2000	2001	2002	2003	2004	2005	2006	2007	2008
Total	947.3	989.9	1 013.9	1 026.2	1 039.3	1 065.0	1 113.3	1 166.7	1 201.5	1 186.9
1	115.0	212.4	212.0	221.1	215.5	228.9	210.6	206.3	213.6	220.6
2	112.9	122.2	127.2	133.8	143.1	144.3	147.6	156.3	159.6	160.8
3	60.1	53.2	54.5	54.0	61.6	66.1	64.7	65.2	67.1	69.7
4	57.0	56.4	58.6	60.6	58.1	59.4	65.2	68.6	71.0	66.7
5	78.1	92.4	96.7	95.9	97.8	97.0	102.6	115.4	120.7	128.3
6	112.1	13.8	14.2	13.6	11.8	11.4	11.9	14.5	13.4	13.8
7	197.9	211.0	217.0	211.0	226.7	231.5	262.9	279.1	290.9	267.7
8	118.4	124.3	135.7	133.3	126.4	119.5	126.8	129.1	133.6	135.6
9	88.4	97.0	90.9	95.9	91.3	100.3	114.7	126.0	125.5	117.5
0	7.4	7.4	7.0	6.9	6.9	6.7	6.3	6.2	6.1	6.0
X	-	-	0.2	-	-	-	-	-	-	-

Women - Femmes - Mujeres
ISCO-88 - CITP-88 - CIUO-88

	1999	2000	2001	2002	2003	2004	2005	2006	2007	2008
Total	643.9	680.8	702.5	734.4	750.9	769.6	818.4	854.5	900.1	921.6
1	58.6	76.6	81.9	83.0	86.7	92.3	92.6	91.7	96.8	103.3
2	127.4	131.3	136.1	154.8	159.2	173.5	177.8	186.6	193.6	198.8
3	42.6	37.1	39.4	45.0	48.7	49.1	54.6	56.4	63.6	65.3
4	156.7	160.8	165.8	174.1	171.0	171.2	180.6	188.2	194.1	199.4
5	146.3	169.8	172.8	176.4	189.4	187.4	210.4	230.4	247.1	254.9
6	9.7	1.2	1.3	1.0	1.6	1.1	1.3	1.2	1.3	1.7
7	15.6	13.9	13.4	11.2	12.4	12.3	11.3	11.2	12.1	10.3
8	38.5	39.7	39.8	34.7	30.7	24.2	25.8	23.3	22.3	20.0
9	48.2	50.0	51.3	53.8	50.6	58.0	63.6	64.9	68.9	67.2
0	0.3	0.2	0.3	0.4	0.4	0.5	0.3	0.5	0.3	0.6
X	-	-	0.4	-	-	-	-	-	-	-

Italy (BA) [1] — Total employment - Emploi total - Empleo total

Total - Total - Total
ISCO-88 - CITP-88 - CIUO-88

	1999	2000	2001	2002	2003	2004	2005	2006	2007	2008
Total	20 864	21 225	21 634	21 922	22 133	22 404 [3]	22 563	22 988	23 222	23 405
1	680	691	685	723	751	2 035 [3]	2 005	1 977	1 923	1 913
2	2 108	2 109	2 199	2 257	2 250	2 254 [3]	2 224	2 215	2 317	2 425
3	3 217	3 458	3 611	3 733	3 841	4 401 [3]	4 425	4 927	5 104	4 942
4	2 877	2 903	2 978	2 981	2 948	2 643 [3]	2 698	2 564	2 513	2 694
5	3 243	3 348	3 434	3 478	3 602	2 335 [3]	2 357	2 564	2 685	2 660
6	706	687	669	636	636	579 [3]	545	508	470	509
7	3 796	3 757	3 801	3 849	3 819	3 691 [3]	3 757	3 773	3 792	3 836
8	1 971	2 023	1 983	1 990	2 036	2 068 [3]	2 093	2 056	2 058	1 975
9	1 848	1 847	1 882	1 907	1 877	2 140 [3]	2 203	2 154	2 108	2 206
0	371	351	334	309	312	258 [3]	256	250	252	245
X	45	51	57	58	61	. [3]	.	.	.	.

Men - Hommes - Hombres
ISCO-88 - CITP-88 - CIUO-88

	1999	2000	2001	2002	2003	2004	2005	2006	2007	2008
Total	13 330	13 461	13 574	13 685	13 769	13 622 [3]	13 738	13 939	14 057	14 064
1	552	562	554	571	594	1 370 [3]	1 356	1 328	1 279	1 277
2	971	976	1 006	1 022	1 000	1 235 [3]	1 219	1 210	1 270	1 323
3	2 046	2 164	2 236	2 280	2 327	2 340 [3]	2 353	2 592	2 678	2 572
4	1 315	1 316	1 334	1 338	1 297	1 071 [3]	1 068	1 048	1 019	1 069
5	1 682	1 730	1 748	1 763	1 802	978 [3]	987	1 092	1 142	1 126
6	505	489	475	459	465	429 [3]	407	386	358	387
7	3 225	3 179	3 228	3 278	3 268	3 169 [3]	3 256	3 221	3 243	3 310
8	1 565	1 597	1 566	1 583	1 632	1 656 [3]	1 683	1 677	1 688	1 613
9	1 075	1 075	1 068	1 053	1 043	1 120 [3]	1 155	1 140	1 134	1 148
0	371	351	334	309	312	253 [3]	253	246	246	239
X	24	24	26	28	29	. [3]	.	.	.	.

Explanatory notes: see p. 77.

[1] Persons aged 15 years and over. [2] Second quarter of each year. [3] Methodology revised; data not strictly comparable.

Notes explicatives: voir p. 80.

[1] Personnes âgées de 15 ans et plus. [2] Deuxième trimestre de chaque année. [3] Méthodologie révisée; les données ne sont pas strictement comparables.

Notas explicativas: véase p. 83.

[1] Personas de 15 años y más. [2] Segundo trimestre de cada año. [3] Metodología revisada; los datos no son estrictamente comparables.

2C

EMPLOYMENT	EMPLOI	EMPLEO
Total employment, by occupation	Emploi total, par profession	Empleo total, por ocupación
Thousands	Milliers	Millares

	1999	2000	2001	2002	2003	2004	2005	2006	2007	2008

Italy (BA) [1] — Total employment - Emploi total - Empleo total

Women - Femmes - Mujeres
ISCO-88 - CITP-88 - CIUO-88

	1999	2000	2001	2002	2003	2004	2005	2006	2007	2008
Total	7 533	7 764	8 060	8 236	8 365	8 783 [2]	8 825	9 049	9 165	9 341
1	128	130	132	152	158	666 [2]	649	649	644	636
2	1 137	1 133	1 193	1 236	1 250	1 019 [2]	1 005	1 005	1 047	1 102
3	1 171	1 293	1 375	1 453	1 513	2 061 [2]	2 072	2 335	2 426	2 370
4	1 561	1 587	1 645	1 642	1 651	1 572 [2]	1 630	1 516	1 495	1 625
5	1 560	1 619	1 686	1 715	1 800	1 357 [2]	1 370	1 472	1 543	1 535
6	202	198	194	176	171	150 [2]	138	123	111	122
7	573	577	573	571	552	522 [2]	501	552	549	525
8	407	427	417	407	404	412 [2]	410	378	370	362
9	773	772	814	854	834	1 020 [2]	1 048	1 014	975	1 058
0	-	-	-	-	-	5 [2]	3	4	6	6
X	21	27	31	31	32	. [2]	.	.	.	.

Latvia (BA) [3][4] — Total employment - Emploi total - Empleo total

Total - Total - Total
ISCO-88 - CITP-88 - CIUO-88

	1999	2000	2001	2002	2003	2004	2005	2006	2007	2008
Total	968.5	941.1	962.1	989.0 [5]	1 006.9	1 017.7	1 035.9	1 087.6	1 119.0	1 124.1
1	84.6	97.4	98.6	93.8 [5]	89.9	104.8	101.4	95.6	94.0	100.8
2	106.9	106.4	111.8	113.3 [5]	110.9	119.4	120.5	140.5	151.7	164.5
3	124.6	121.8	117.2	131.1 [5]	125.7	118.1	134.5	151.8	181.4	186.5
4	47.2	42.4	48.4	46.9 [5]	55.9	60.8	61.3	60.1	53.2	52.1
5	131.4	128.2	131.0	130.9 [5]	138.1	136.8	147.9	138.6	140.9	138.7
6	97.5	82.4	86.6	83.0 [5]	84.3	76.5	63.5	70.0	56.5	46.0
7	137.0	132.6	135.5	146.1 [5]	149.7	158.6	166.2	185.8	189.9	169.5
8	107.0	100.1	104.2	108.0 [5]	111.6	114.1	112.2	113.0	111.2	111.1
9	131.4	128.4	127.1	134.9 [5]	139.6	127.1	126.7	129.1	137.1	150.9
X	-	-	-	-	-	-	-	-	-	-

Men - Hommes - Hombres
ISCO-88 - CITP-88 - CIUO-88

	1999	2000	2001	2002	2003	2004	2005	2006	2007	2008
Total	502.9	479.7	486.4	504.6 [5]	516.6	521.8	534.1	559.2	573.5	571.5
1	51.3	60.9	61.4	59.4 [5]	54.0	60.8	58.9	56.1	55.3	59.1
2	34.8	31.5	28.8	37.5 [5]	39.8	43.0	40.3	44.3	50.8	57.1
3	45.5	45.2	43.8	46.5 [5]	45.0	41.8	48.6	62.3	63.5	57.4
4	7.9	7.4	9.1	7.2 [5]	9.4	12.6	14.2	10.0	12.0	8.1
5	35.7	35.5	33.5	36.0 [5]	33.3	32.8	38.0	31.5	34.2	40.1
6	51.8	42.1	46.6	43.0 [5]	46.5	39.8	35.7	38.6	31.2	28.5
7	109.5	103.8	109.2	116.6 [5]	119.5	129.0	138.2	150.2	156.3	139.3
8	92.6	84.4	84.7	88.3 [5]	93.0	93.3	92.3	96.0	96.0	97.2
9	73.1	67.8	67.9	69.8 [5]	75.1	67.3	66.1	67.9	72.1	81.5
X	-	-	-	-	-	-	-	-	-	-

Women - Femmes - Mujeres
ISCO-88 - CITP-88 - CIUO-88

	1999	2000	2001	2002	2003	2004	2005	2006	2007	2008
Total	465.6	461.4	475.7	484.3 [5]	490.2	495.9	501.8	528.5	545.5	552.6
1	33.3	36.5	37.2	34.4 [5]	35.9	44.1	42.5	39.5	38.8	41.7
2	72.1	74.8	83.0	75.9 [5]	71.0	76.4	80.1	96.2	101.0	107.4
3	79.1	76.6	73.3	84.6 [5]	80.7	76.3	85.9	89.5	117.8	129.1
4	39.4	35.0	39.3	39.7 [5]	46.5	48.2	47.1	50.2	41.2	44.0
5	95.7	92.8	97.5	95.0 [5]	104.8	104.0	110.0	107.1	106.7	98.6
6	45.6	40.3	40.2	40.0 [5]	37.8	36.7	27.8	31.4	25.3	17.5
7	27.5	28.9	26.3	29.6 [5]	30.1	29.6	28.0	35.6	33.5	30.2
8	14.4	15.7	19.5	19.7 [5]	18.6	20.8	19.9	17.1	15.2	13.9
9	58.3	60.6	59.2	65.1 [5]	64.6	59.8	60.5	61.3	64.9	69.4
X	-	-	-	-	-	-	-	-	-	-

Lithuania (BA) [1][4] — Total employment - Emploi total - Empleo total

Total - Total - Total
ISCO-88 - CITP-88 - CIUO-88

	1999	2000	2001	2002	2003	2004	2005	2006	2007	2008
Total	1 456.5	1 397.8	1 351.8	1 405.9	1 438.0	1 436.3	1 473.9	1 499.0	1 534.2	1 520.0
1	137.6	115.8	99.1	105.9	107.6	109.0	117.1	129.2	148.1	158.9
2	204.3	202.6	208.1	205.5	220.4	237.8	256.0	253.5	279.1	274.2
3	110.9	111.2	121.0	140.0	129.2	126.2	128.3	132.5	133.9	169.6
4	68.7	67.9	58.5	55.4	52.1	54.3	60.7	56.7	67.6	68.8
5	170.7	174.2	173.4	166.8	172.1	167.1	169.8	188.2	188.4	183.3
6	218.9	214.6	202.2	210.2	211.7	187.6	166.9	137.0	110.7	79.0
7	247.8	235.5	233.3	243.6	254.6	260.4	273.4	290.5	290.2	288.3
8	138.9	130.8	135.2	137.7	132.2	134.2	137.9	146.2	151.8	155.6
9	155.2	143.1	117.3	137.6	155.0	154.7	158.9	160.6	160.0	139.1
0	3.5	2.2	3.7	3.2	3.1	5.0	4.9	4.6	4.3	3.3

Explanatory notes: see p. 77.

[1] Persons aged 15 years and over. [2] Methodology revised; data not strictly comparable. [3] Persons aged 15 to 74 years. [4] Excl. conscripts. [5] Prior to 2002: persons aged 15 years and over.

Notes explicatives: voir p. 80.

[1] Personnes âgées de 15 ans et plus. [2] Méthodologie révisée; les données ne sont pas strictement comparables. [3] Personnes âgées de 15 à 74 ans. [4] Non compris les conscrits. [5] Avant 2002: personnes âgées de 15 ans et plus.

Notas explicativas: véase p. 83.

[1] Personas de 15 años y más. [2] Metodología revisada; los datos no son estrictamente comparables. [3] Personas de 15 a 74 años. [4] Excl. los conscriptos. [5] Antes de 2002: personas de 15 años y más.

Total employment, by occupation
Emploi total, par profession
Empleo total, por ocupación

	Thousands			Milliers				Millares		
	1999	2000	2001	2002	2003	2004	2005	2006	2007	2008

Lithuania (BA) [1] [2] — Total employment - Emploi total - Empleo total

Men - Hommes - Hombres
ISCO-88 - CITP-88 - CIUO-88

	1999	2000	2001	2002	2003	2004	2005	2006	2007	2008
Total	729.2	686.5	664.5	707.8	726.2	733.8	750.9	755.8	777.7	768.7
1	85.2	66.1	51.8	59.8	65.9	63.1	66.8	77.0	91.4	95.0
2	59.2	55.7	59.8	61.3	69.8	80.2	87.5	82.5	88.8	88.1
3	34.0	36.8	39.3	41.5	36.3	35.7	38.1	31.3	36.1	57.1
4	12.2	12.3	9.0	12.1	10.4	10.6	14.6	11.6	15.8	13.8
5	50.5	54.7	50.6	52.6	54.2	53.5	48.9	48.5	47.4	49.3
6	118.6	119.3	121.5	121.3	121.1	105.9	95.6	72.9	64.1	45.9
7	171.4	166.2	161.5	172.5	177.8	185.1	196.9	215.5	219.5	220.7
8	121.5	110.5	114.9	117.3	111.7	117.2	119.8	127.4	131.7	134.7
9	73.7	62.9	52.7	66.1	76.2	77.8	77.6	84.5	78.7	61.0
0	2.7	2.1	3.4	3.2	3.1	4.8	4.8	4.6	4.1	3.2

Women - Femmes - Mujeres
ISCO-88 - CITP-88 - CIUO-88

	1999	2000	2001	2002	2003	2004	2005	2006	2007	2008
Total	727.4	711.3	687.3	698.1	711.8	702.5	723.0	743.2	756.5	751.4
1	52.4	49.7	47.3	46.1	41.7	45.9	50.2	52.1	56.8	63.9
2	145.2	147.0	148.3	144.2	150.7	157.6	168.4	171.0	190.3	186.1
3	76.8	74.3	81.7	98.5	92.9	90.5	90.2	101.2	97.8	112.5
4	56.4	55.6	49.5	43.3	41.7	43.8	46.1	45.1	51.9	55.1
5	120.2	119.5	122.8	114.1	117.9	113.6	120.9	139.7	141.0	134.1
6	100.3	95.3	80.7	88.9	90.6	81.7	71.3	64.1	46.6	33.1
7	76.4	69.4	71.8	71.1	76.8	75.3	76.5	75.1	70.7	67.6
8	17.4	20.3	20.2	20.3	20.7	17.0	18.1	18.7	20.0	20.9
9	81.5	80.2	64.6	71.5	78.8	76.8	81.3	76.1	81.3	78.1
0	0.8	0.1	0.3	-	-	0.2	0.1	-	0.3	0.1

Macedonia, The Former Yugoslav Rep. of (BA) [1] — Total employment - Emploi total - Empleo total

Total - Total - Total
ISCO-88 - CITP-88 - CIUO-88

	1999	2000	2001	2002	2003	2004	2005	2006	2007	2008
Total	.	.	.	561.341	545.108	522.995 [3]	545.253	570.404	590.234	609.015
1	.	.	.	25.233	26.097	32.518 [3]	32.568	33.814	34.225	39.762
2	.	.	.	56.220	58.078	55.283 [3]	52.332	52.423	58.720	54.493
3	.	.	.	58.320	60.276	68.398 [3]	68.847	67.756	63.424	61.179
4	.	.	.	35.471	38.298	34.502 [3]	32.801	35.510	40.629	41.517
5	.	.	.	65.355	66.297	70.941 [3]	72.683	78.670	83.634	85.598
6	.	.	.	109.120	41.571	13.630 [3]	11.778	7.319	7.670	7.286
7	.	.	.	106.954	87.265	69.681 [3]	65.185	74.598	80.113	73.606
8	.	.	.	49.945	51.242	65.512 [3]	85.225	74.589	76.334	84.630
9	.	.	.	50.300	111.499	107.365 [3]	119.231	140.198	138.739	153.365
0	.	.	.	4.423	4.485	5.166 [3]	4.603	5.528	6.748	7.579

Men - Hommes - Hombres
ISCO-88 - CITP-88 - CIUO-88

	1999	2000	2001	2002	2003	2004	2005	2006	2007	2008
Total	.	.	.	342.779	327.283	320.640 [3]	332.179	351.974	358.835	373.483
1	.	.	.	20.430	19.094	23.404 [3]	23.281	24.627	24.195	28.415
2	.	.	.	27.421	27.774	25.358 [3]	24.034	24.652	27.685	25.743
3	.	.	.	28.286	29.997	32.774 [3]	34.692	34.428	30.210	30.460
4	.	.	.	16.571	19.212	17.631 [3]	16.824	18.771	20.525	20.974
5	.	.	.	40.025	38.882	41.804 [3]	42.470	48.603	50.398	51.059
6	.	.	.	61.351	25.310	9.646 [3]	8.588	5.705	5.919	5.295
7	.	.	.	70.990	56.040	53.937 [3]	57.052	66.301	65.673	64.098
8	.	.	.	43.345	41.113	41.121 [3]	47.841	41.210	44.494	47.754
9	.	.	.	30.383	65.376	69.888 [3]	72.827	82.358	83.292	92.256
0	.	.	.	4.278	4.485	5.076 [3]	4.571	5.319	6.445	7.428

Women - Femmes - Mujeres
ISCO-88 - CITP-88 - CIUO-88

	1999	2000	2001	2002	2003	2004	2005	2006	2007	2008
Total	.	.	.	218.562	217.825	202.355 [3]	213.074	218.431	231.399	235.532
1	.	.	.	4.803	7.004	9.115 [3]	9.286	9.187	10.030	11.347
2	.	.	.	28.799	30.305	29.925 [3]	28.299	27.771	31.035	28.750
3	.	.	.	30.034	30.279	35.624 [3]	34.692	33.328	33.214	30.719
4	.	.	.	18.900	19.085	16.870 [3]	15.978	16.740	20.104	20.543
5	.	.	.	25.331	27.414	29.136 [3]	30.213	30.067	33.236	34.538
6	.	.	.	47.769	16.261	3.983 [3]	3.190	1.613	1.750	1.992
7	.	.	.	35.964	31.225	15.744 [3]	8.134	8.297	14.440	9.508
8	.	.	.	6.899	10.129	24.391 [3]	37.384	33.379	31.840	36.876
9	.	.	.	19.917	46.123	37.477 [3]	46.403	57.840	55.448	61.109
0	.	.	.	0.146	-	0.090 [3]	0.032	0.209	0.303	0.152

Explanatory notes: see p. 77.

[1] Persons aged 15 years and over. [2] Excl. conscripts. [3] Prior to 2004: April of each year.

Notes explicatives: voir p. 80.

[1] Personnes âgées de 15 ans et plus. [2] Non compris les conscrits. [3] Avant 2004: Avril de chaque année.

Notas explicativas: véase p. 83.

[1] Personas de 15 años y más. [2] Excl. los conscriptos. [3] Antes de 2004: Abril de cada año.

	EMPLOYMENT	EMPLOI	EMPLEO
	Total employment, by occupation	Emploi total, par profession	Empleo total, por ocupación
	Thousands	Milliers	Millares

	1999	2000	2001	2002	2003	2004	2005	2006	2007	2008
Malta (BA) [1]					Total employment - Emploi total - Empleo total					
Total - Total - Total										
ISCO-88 - CITP-88 - CIUO-88										
Total	.	.	145.6	148.4	147.0	148.6	148.5	152.5	155.5	161.0
1	.	.	12.2	13.8	13.8	13.4	12.8	13.5	12.1	12.5
2	.	.	12.6	14.1	14.8	15.8	16.3	17.3	18.0	20.4
3	.	.	19.7	20.6	20.7	20.8	21.5	23.9	23.5	24.9
4	.	.	17.9	17.1	17.1	16.8	17.5	18.2	18.9	19.1
5	.	.	19.2	21.0	22.9	22.7	22.3	24.2	25.0	25.7
6	.	.	2.4	2.7	2.5	2.6	2.3	2.3	2.2	2.7
7	.	.	19.7	20.3	19.6	20.8	20.5	19.9	20.6	20.9
8	.	.	18.6	17.9	15.8	15.7	15.5	13.3	13.7	12.8
9	.	.	21.7	20.8	18.6	18.3	18.3	18.2	19.7	20.1
0	.	.	1.6	-	1.4	1.8	2.0	1.8	1.7	1.7
Men - Hommes - Hombres										
ISCO-88 - CITP-88 - CIUO-88										
Total	.	.	103.6	102.1	101.2	103.8	102.8	104.4	104.4	107.5
1	.	.	10.2	11.5	11.2	11.3	10.5	11.0	9.9	10.3
2	.	.	7.2	7.5	8.0	9.2	9.5	9.6	9.5	11.0
3	.	.	13.9	13.2	13.7	13.3	14.0	14.8	15.1	15.6
4	.	.	7.7	7.5	7.5	7.2	7.3	8.0	7.5	7.7
5	.	.	12.2	13.4	12.5	13.3	12.8	14.3	14.2	14.3
6	.	.	2.2	2.6	2.4	2.4	2.3	2.2	2.1	2.6
7	.	.	19.5	19.7	18.9	20.3	20.5	19.4	19.9	20.4
8	.	.	12.5	11.1	11.2	11.0	10.8	9.0	9.7	9.6
9	.	.	16.6	15.6	14.3	14.0	13.5	14.2	14.8	14.3
0	.	.	1.6	-	1.4	1.8	2.0	1.8	1.7	1.7
Women - Femmes - Mujeres										
ISCO-88 - CITP-88 - CIUO-88										
Total	.	.	42.0	46.3	45.9	44.8	46.0	48.1	51.1	53.5
1	.	.	2.0	2.3	2.5	2.1	2.5	2.5	2.2	2.2
2	.	.	5.4	6.6	6.8	6.6	7.0	7.7	8.5	9.4
3	.	.	5.7	7.5	7.0	7.5	7.3	9.1	8.5	9.3
4	.	.	10.2	9.6	9.6	9.5	10.0	10.3	11.4	11.4
5	.	.	7.0	7.6	10.4	9.3	9.8	9.8	10.8	11.5
6	.	.	0.1	0.1	0.1	0.2	-	-	0.1	0.1
7	.	.	0.2	0.6	0.7	0.6	-	-	0.6	0.6
8	.	.	6.1	6.8	4.5	4.7	4.3	4.2	4.0	3.2
9	.	.	5.1	5.2	4.3	4.3	4.3	4.0	4.9	5.8
0	.	.	-	-	-	0.0	-	-	0.0	0.0
Moldova, Republic of (BA) [1]					Total employment - Emploi total - Empleo total					
Total - Total - Total										
ISCO-88 - CITP-88 - CIUO-88										
Total	1 494.4	1 514.6	1 499.0	1 505.1	1 356.5	1 316.0	1 318.7	1 257.3	1 247.2	1 251.0
1	54.5	50.6	54.8	60.4	64.3	67.7	74.9	88.6	82.6	85.6
2	130.1	132.5	132.1	140.0	146.9	155.6	151.8	171.8	161.3	169.4
3	113.9	114.1	105.9	101.3	98.1	94.7	96.4	97.7	97.4	97.5
4	26.4	25.8	26.6	27.1	25.3	25.7	26.8	25.7	22.5	23.4
5	124.7	130.3	137.3	152.2	153.5	151.2	147.8	158.7	163.6	161.9
6	613.7	624.2	544.8	519.2	405.5	406.5	382.6	225.1	185.0	164.5
7	125.4	112.5	114.1	119.1	117.3	116.4	114.8	119.6	123.8	131.9
8	119.7	115.8	104.0	99.2	98.7	98.5	92.5	87.8	92.3	94.8
9	172.7	197.8	268.6	277.8	237.3	190.5	222.3	274.7	311.6	314.3
0	13.3	11.0	10.8	8.9	9.6	9.3	8.8	7.7	7.1	7.8
Men - Hommes - Hombres										
ISCO-88 - CITP-88 - CIUO-88										
Total	739.1	747.4	736.5	730.9	661.3	631.5	629.7	628.6	621.5	628.8
1	34.6	33.8	34.3	36.1	39.0	41.3	45.8	54.2	49.5	53.1
2	50.4	48.9	49.7	55.5	54.6	58.9	56.3	65.1	57.4	62.0
3	31.1	32.6	31.7	30.3	29.9	26.6	29.2	30.9	25.5	27.5
4	3.6	4.9	4.9	4.6	3.9	4.3	4.0	4.6	4.0	2.9
5	37.7	42.2	42.0	42.2	44.5	41.4	40.5	45.8	42.3	40.9
6	276.6	280.3	249.0	237.2	183.9	177.8	169.6	106.7	92.6	84.5
7	83.8	73.7	74.9	80.1	77.6	76.8	77.5	85.7	90.6	96.6
8	112.2	108.9	97.6	92.7	93.0	93.6	86.9	81.9	85.8	86.8
9	96.1	111.0	142.0	143.5	125.5	101.7	111.0	145.9	167.0	167.2
0	13.1	10.9	10.4	8.7	9.4	9.3	8.8	7.6	7.0	7.3
Women - Femmes - Mujeres										
ISCO-88 - CITP-88 - CIUO-88										
Total	755.3	767.2	762.5	774.2	695.2	684.6	689.0	628.7	625.7	622.3
1	19.9	16.8	20.5	24.3	25.4	26.4	29.1	34.5	33.2	32.5
2	79.7	83.6	82.5	84.4	92.3	96.7	95.5	106.7	103.9	107.4
3	82.9	81.5	74.1	71.0	68.2	68.2	67.2	66.8	71.9	69.9
4	22.7	20.8	21.7	22.5	21.4	21.4	22.8	21.0	18.5	20.4
5	87.0	88.1	95.2	110.0	109.0	109.8	107.3	112.9	121.3	121.0
6	337.2	343.9	295.8	282.0	221.6	228.7	212.9	118.4	92.4	80.0
7	41.6	38.8	39.3	39.0	39.7	39.7	37.2	33.8	33.2	35.3
8	7.4	6.9	6.4	6.5	5.6	4.9	5.7	5.8	6.5	8.0
9	76.6	86.8	126.7	134.3	111.8	88.7	111.3	128.7	144.7	147.1
0	0.2	0.2	0.3	0.3	0.2	-	0.0	0.1	0.1	0.6

Explanatory notes: see p. 77.   Notes explicatives: voir p. 80.   Notas explicativas: véase p. 83.

[1] Persons aged 15 years and over.   [1] Personnes âgées de 15 ans et plus.   [1] Personas de 15 años y más.

Total employment, by occupation

Emploi total, par profession

Empleo total, por ocupación

	Thousands			Milliers				Millares		
	1999	2000	2001	2002	2003	2004	2005	2006	2007	2008

Montenegro (BA) [1][2]   Total employment - Emploi total - Empleo total

Total - Total - Total
ISCO-88 - CITP-88 - CIUO-88

	1999	2000	2001	2002	2003	2004	2005	2006	2007	2008
Total	.	.	.	.	.	.	178.8	.	.	.
1	.	.	.	.	.	.	12.9	.	.	.
2	.	.	.	.	.	.	16.4	.	.	.
3	.	.	.	.	.	.	35.0	.	.	.
4	.	.	.	.	.	.	16.4	.	.	.
5	.	.	.	.	.	.	32.7	.	.	.
6	.	.	.	.	.	.	14.2	.	.	.
7	.	.	.	.	.	.	19.5	.	.	.
8	.	.	.	.	.	.	14.8	.	.	.
9	.	.	.	.	.	.	14.7	.	.	.
0	.	.	.	.	.	.	2.3	.	.	.

Men - Hommes - Hombres
ISCO-88 - CITP-88 - CIUO-88

	1999	2000	2001	2002	2003	2004	2005	2006	2007	2008
Total	.	.	.	.	.	.	105.6	.	.	.
1	.	.	.	.	.	.	10.3	.	.	.
2	.	.	.	.	.	.	8.1	.	.	.
3	.	.	.	.	.	.	12.6	.	.	.
4	.	.	.	.	.	.	9.3	.	.	.
5	.	.	.	.	.	.	13.7	.	.	.
6	.	.	.	.	.	.	8.1	.	.	.
7	.	.	.	.	.	.	18.8	.	.	.
8	.	.	.	.	.	.	14.7	.	.	.
9	.	.	.	.	.	.	7.9	.	.	.
0	.	.	.	.	.	.	2.1	.	.	.

Women - Femmes - Mujeres
ISCO-88 - CITP-88 - CIUO-88

	1999	2000	2001	2002	2003	2004	2005	2006	2007	2008
Total	.	.	.	.	.	.	73.2	.	.	.
1	.	.	.	.	.	.	2.5	.	.	.
2	.	.	.	.	.	.	8.3	.	.	.
3	.	.	.	.	.	.	22.3	.	.	.
4	.	.	.	.	.	.	7.1	.	.	.
5	.	.	.	.	.	.	19.0	.	.	.
6	.	.	.	.	.	.	6.1	.	.	.
7	.	.	.	.	.	.	0.7	.	.	.
8	.	.	.	.	.	.	0.2	.	.	.
9	.	.	.	.	.	.	6.8	.	.	.
0	.	.	.	.	.	.	0.2	.	.	.

Netherlands (BA) [3]   Total employment - Emploi total - Empleo total

Total - Total - Total
ISCO-88 - CITP-88 - CIUO-88

	1999	2000	2001	2002	2003	2004	2005	2006	2007	2008
Total	.	7 798	7 953	8 018	7 991	7 928	7 958	8 108	8 310	8 457
1	.	1 017	1 011	1 001	1 009	840	785	847	879	888
2	.	1 313	1 270	1 351	1 383	1 425	1 438	1 472	1 528	1 591
3	.	1 325	1 378	1 417	1 423	1 432	1 426	1 409	1 462	1 513
4	.	923	992	970	941	964	1 001	993	1 009	1 027
5	.	954	984	1 022	1 018	1 085	1 110	1 137	1 171	1 191
6	.	139	125	124	128	125	126	123	121	113
7	.	747	782	781	741	736	757	749	740	743
8	.	484	475	483	475	481	471	474	475	476
9	.	633	671	712	727	714	737	772	786	774
0	.	37	37	36	33	34	35	36	36	37
X	.	226	228	121	113	90	71	96	103	104

Men - Hommes - Hombres
ISCO-88 - CITP-88 - CIUO-88

	1999	2000	2001	2002	2003	2004	2005	2006	2007	2008
Total	.	4 459	4 522	4 526	4 480	4 432	4 421	4 475	4 548	4 594
1	.	748	755	747	747	626	587	623	637	644
2	.	765	742	767	779	785	782	786	824	851
3	.	653	671	668	658	693	694	659	674	708
4	.	297	320	297	286	309	315	310	309	311
5	.	292	294	309	306	323	336	354	364	353
6	.	98	88	89	94	94	92	89	88	82
7	.	708	738	736	699	701	720	711	706	709
8	.	430	417	426	422	429	421	426	427	426
9	.	324	340	373	385	379	392	419	415	411
0	.	33	35	32	30	31	32	34	33	33
X	.	111	123	80	74	62	49	65	70	67

Explanatory notes: see p. 77.

[1] Persons aged 15 to 64 years. [2] Oct. of each year. [3] Persons aged 15 years and over.

Notes explicatives: voir p. 80.

[1] Personnes âgées de 15 à 64 ans. [2] Oct. de chaque année. [3] Personnes âgées de 15 ans et plus.

Notas explicativas: véase p. 83.

[1] Personas de 15 a 64 años. [2] Oct. de cada año. [3] Personas de 15 años y más.

	EMPLOYMENT				EMPLOI			EMPLEO		
	Total employment, by occupation				**Emploi total, par profession**			**Empleo total, por ocupación**		
	Thousands				Milliers			Millares		
	1999	2000	2001	2002	2003	2004	2005	2006	2007	2008

Netherlands (BA) [1] — Total employment - Emploi total - Empleo total

Women - Femmes - Mujeres
ISCO-88 - CITP-88 - CIUO-88

	1999	2000	2001	2002	2003	2004	2005	2006	2007	2008
Total	.	3 339	3 431	3 492	3 511	3 495	3 537	3 633	3 763	3 863
1	.	270	256	253	262	214	198	224	242	244
2	.	548	529	584	604	641	656	686	704	740
3	.	672	707	749	766	739	732	750	788	805
4	.	626	672	673	655	655	686	683	700	716
5	.	662	690	713	712	762	774	782	807	838
6	.	41	37	35	34	32	34	34	33	31
7	.	39	44	45	42	35	38	38	34	33
8	.	55	58	57	52	52	50	48	47	50
9	.	309	331	339	342	335	345	353	371	363
0	.	3	2	3	3	3	3	2	3	4
X	.	115	104	41	39	28	22	32	33	37

Norway (BA) [2] — Total employment - Emploi total - Empleo total

Total - Total - Total
ISCO-88 - CITP-88 - CIUO-88

	1999	2000	2001	2002	2003	2004	2005	2006	2007	2008
Total	2 259	2 269	2 278	2 286	2 269	2 276	2 289	2 362 [3]	2 443	2 524
1	173	182	162	174	170	163	151	146 [3]	141	150
2	228	238	262	255	251	267	269	262 [3]	277	300
3	486	497	523	523	524	530	550	573 [3]	616	647
4	219	202	192	183	177	171	164	166 [3]	169	173
5	458	477	486	500	506	522	539	577 [3]	591	602
6	92	83	79	77	74	69	65	65 [3]	61	60
7	261	255	250	251	250	253	255	267 [3]	275	277
8	182	180	178	177	175	166	170	170 [3]	178	185
9	132	128	122	123	119	114	111	119 [3]	117	111
0	29	26	24	21	23	21	17	18 [3]	19	19

Men - Hommes - Hombres
ISCO-88 - CITP-88 - CIUO-88

	1999	2000	2001	2002	2003	2004	2005	2006	2007	2008
Total	1 209	1 212	1 214	1 210	1 198	1 201	1 211	1 251 [3]	1 289	1 332
1	129	136	120	125	119	115	105	97 [3]	96	103
2	135	139	155	147	144	150	150	148 [3]	153	162
3	232	235	252	249	245	247	257	267 [3]	285	298
4	58	58	59	59	59	58	57	60 [3]	64	63
5	130	136	132	134	139	147	156	175 [3]	182	185
6	68	61	60	58	57	54	51	52 [3]	48	48
7	239	234	230	233	232	236	238	249 [3]	255	259
8	154	150	147	146	147	140	144	143 [3]	150	155
9	37	37	37	38	36	36	38	43 [3]	41	42
0	27	24	21	20	20	18	16	17 [3]	16	18

Women - Femmes - Mujeres
ISCO-88 - CITP-88 - CIUO-88

	1999	2000	2001	2002	2003	2004	2005	2006	2007	2008
Total	1 050	1 057	1 064	1 076	1 071	1 074	1 078	1 111 [3]	1 154	1 192
1	44	46	42	49	51	48	46	48 [3]	44	47
2	94	98	107	108	106	117	118	113 [3]	124	138
3	254	262	271	275	279	283	293	307 [3]	331	349
4	162	144	133	125	118	113	107	106 [3]	105	110
5	327	341	355	365	367	375	383	402 [3]	409	417
6	23	22	19	18	18	15	14	13 [3]	13	12
7	21	22	20	19	18	17	17	17 [3]	20	18
8	29	29	31	30	28	26	26	27 [3]	28	29
9	94	91	84	85	83	78	73	76 [3]	77	69
0	2	2	2	2	3	2	2	2 [3]	2	1

Poland (BA) [1][4] — Total employment - Emploi total - Empleo total

Total - Total - Total
ISCO-88 - CITP-88 - CIUO-88

	1999	2000	2001	2002	2003	2004	2005	2006	2007	2008
Total	14 757 [5]	14 526	14 207	13 782	13 617	13 795	14 116	14 594	15 241	15 800
1	909 [5]	891	840	799	820	855	863	925	970	993
2	1 555 [5]	1 550	1 552	1 546	1 635	1 762	2 135	2 241	2 337	2 401
3	1 884 [5]	1 831	1 752	1 743	1 769	1 757	1 546	1 607	1 701	1 787
4	1 141 [5]	1 103	1 088	1 072	961	951	977	1 042	1 114	1 104
5	1 538 [5]	1 557	1 553	1 581	1 591	1 593	1 585	1 667	1 783	1 847
6	2 462 [5]	2 540	2 557	2 482	2 318	2 283	2 241	2 093	2 033	2 014
7	2 704 [5]	2 557	2 438	2 212	2 151	2 177	2 250	2 351	2 498	2 676
8	1 353 [5]	1 308	1 249	1 210	1 262	1 307	1 370	1 486	1 563	1 669
9	1 133 [5]	1 125	1 112	1 066	1 034	1 024	1 065	1 110	1 180	1 235
0	76 [5]	65	65	70	74	81	81	67	57	68
X	- [5]	-	-	-	-	-	-	5	5	8

Explanatory notes: see p. 77.

[1] Persons aged 15 years and over. [2] Persons aged 15 to 74 years. [3] Prior to 2006: persons aged 16 to 74 years. [4] Excl. regular military living in barracks and conscripts. [5] First and fourth quarters.

Notes explicatives: voir p. 80.

[1] Personnes âgées de 15 ans et plus. [2] Personnes âgées de 15 à 74 ans. [3] Avant 2006: personnes âgées de 16 à 74 ans. [4] Non compris les militaires de carrière vivant dans des casernes et les conscrits. [5] Premier et quatrième trimestres.

Notas explicativas: véase p. 83.

[1] Personas de 15 años y más. [2] Personas de 15 a 74 años. [3] Antes de 2006: personas de 16 a 74 años. [4] Excl. los militares profesionales que viven en casernas y los conscriptos. [5] Primero y cuarto trimestres.

Total employment, by occupation — Emploi total, par profession — Empleo total, por ocupación

	Thousands / Milliers / Millares									
	1999	2000	2001	2002	2003	2004	2005	2006	2007	2008

Poland (BA) [1][2] — Total employment - Emploi total - Empleo total

Men - Hommes - Hombres
ISCO-88 - CITP-88 - CIUO-88

	1999	2000	2001	2002	2003	2004	2005	2006	2007	2008
Total	8 132 [3]	8 004	7 797	7 529	7 432	7 566	7 809	8 081	8 403	8 718
1	604 [3]	601	569	530	542	567	580	598	619	634
2	586 [3]	588	599	604	641	700	756	794	837	857
3	761 [3]	730	718	704	682	666	680	719	790	807
4	304 [3]	303	295	283	275	299	317	342	386	374
5	533 [3]	547	547	586	588	581	559	581	604	620
6	1 351 [3]	1 396	1 379	1 359	1 287	1 273	1 257	1 172	1 124	1 090
7	2 217 [3]	2 107	2 018	1 845	1 785	1 808	1 888	1 985	2 113	2 287
8	1 191 [3]	1 154	1 103	1 067	1 094	1 127	1 192	1 303	1 348	1 423
9	510 [3]	514	505	480	463	464	501	518	522	553
0	75 [3]	65	65	70	74	80	80	66	56	67
X	- [3]	-	-	-	-	-	-	-	-	5

Women - Femmes - Mujeres
ISCO-88 - CITP-88 - CIUO-88

	1999	2000	2001	2002	2003	2004	2005	2006	2007	2008
Total	6 624 [3]	6 522	6 410	6 253	6 185	6 230	6 307	6 513	6 838	7 082
1	305 [3]	290	271	269	278	288	283	327	351	359
2	969 [3]	962	953	942	994	1 063	1 379	1 447	1 500	1 544
3	1 123 [3]	1 101	1 034	1 039	1 087	1 091	866	888	911	980
4	837 [3]	800	793	789	686	652	661	700	729	729
5	1 005 [3]	1 010	1 006	995	1 003	1 012	1 026	1 086	1 179	1 227
6	1 111 [3]	1 144	1 178	1 123	1 031	1 011	985	922	908	924
7	487 [3]	450	421	368	366	370	362	367	385	389
8	162 [3]	154	147	143	168	180	178	183	215	246
9	623 [3]	611	607	586	570	561	564	592	658	682
0	1 [3]	-	-	1	-	1	-	-	-	-
X	- [3]	-	-	-	-	-	-	-	-	-

Portugal (BA) [1] — Total employment - Emploi total - Empleo total

Total - Total - Total
ISCO-88 - CITP-88 - CIUO-88

	1999	2000	2001	2002	2003	2004	2005	2006	2007	2008
Total	4 921.6	5 032.9	5 121.7	5 145.6	5 127.7	5 127.5	5 122.6	5 159.5	5 169.7	5 197.8
1	360.7	339.7	348.5	375.9	427.6	458.8	468.5	397.2	344.5	321.7
2	332.3	335.5	362.8	350.5	371.5	434.5	438.7	448.5	442.6	464.6
3	363.8	379.8	379.1	378.8	386.4	423.2	439.6	452.7	453.0	480.5
4	455.7	492.8	494.9	491.6	506.3	516.2	506.7	492.9	479.7	482.0
5	666.5	655.0	690.9	701.4	678.8	676.5	695.7	742.8	767.1	789.8
6	543.4	559.8	590.4	578.3	586.5	561.7	560.0	559.2	562.2	565.7
7	1 095.4	1 092.5	1 103.4	1 089.2	1 037.2	966.8	955.8	1 014.9	1 020.8	1 006.3
8	406.4	435.2	424.4	441.3	439.2	419.8	409.3	410.9	402.8	390.3
9	649.5	698.1	681.8	700.6	650.3	629.6	619.7	610.5	662.1	665.9
0	47.2	44.6	45.5	38.1	44.1	40.4	28.5	29.8	35.0	31.1

Men - Hommes - Hombres
ISCO-88 - CITP-88 - CIUO-88

	1999	2000	2001	2002	2003	2004	2005	2006	2007	2008
Total	2 720.5	2 777.2	2 819.7	2 824.7	2 796.8	2 788.8	2 765.4	2 789.7	2 789.3	2 797.1
1	248.5	231.4	239.9	264.8	291.3	308.2	309.5	266.8	235.9	221.4
2	155.7	150.9	155.1	143.7	144.4	182.9	187.3	192.2	193.0	205.2
3	197.5	209.7	213.7	211.2	222.5	246.5	248.5	247.5	248.3	250.5
4	177.5	192.7	191.7	186.5	192.6	185.1	186.8	191.1	179.5	187.3
5	244.9	233.4	248.0	238.1	214.7	216.8	224.3	235.2	243.2	256.0
6	273.2	280.4	295.3	292.5	298.6	287.1	276.6	284.0	287.8	287.3
7	818.0	832.0	839.4	846.6	808.6	758.4	749.7	800.0	805.3	810.5
8	311.9	338.1	334.3	339.5	342.0	331.9	336.0	333.5	334.8	329.6
9	247.7	265.7	258.9	265.7	240.7	234.8	220.3	212.2	231.7	221.0
0	45.3	43.0	43.4	36.2	41.4	37.3	26.4	27.0	29.9	28.3

Women - Femmes - Mujeres
ISCO-88 - CITP-88 - CIUO-88

	1999	2000	2001	2002	2003	2004	2005	2006	2007	2008
Total	2 201.1	2 255.7	2 302.0	2 320.9	2 330.9	2 338.6	2 357.2	2 369.8	2 380.4	2 400.7
1	112.1	108.3	108.6	111.0	136.3	150.6	159.0	130.4	108.6	100.3
2	176.6	184.6	207.7	206.8	227.1	251.6	251.4	256.4	249.6	259.5
3	166.3	170.1	165.3	167.6	164.0	176.7	191.1	205.2	204.7	230.0
4	278.2	300.1	302.3	305.0	313.7	331.0	319.9	301.9	300.2	294.7
5	421.6	421.6	442.9	463.3	464.0	459.7	471.4	507.6	523.9	533.7
6	270.2	279.4	295.1	285.8	287.7	274.7	283.5	275.2	274.4	278.4
7	277.4	260.5	264.0	242.6	228.6	208.5	206.0	214.8	215.5	195.8
8	94.5	97.1	90.1	101.9	97.2	87.9	73.4	77.4	68.0	60.7
9	401.8	432.4	422.9	434.9	409.5	394.8	399.4	398.3	430.4	444.9
0	1.9	1.6	2.1	1.9	2.7	3.1	2.2	2.7	5.1	2.7

Explanatory notes: see p. 77.

[1] Persons aged 15 years and over. [2] Excl. regular military living in barracks and conscripts. [3] First and fourth quarters.

Notes explicatives: voir p. 80.

[1] Personnes âgées de 15 ans et plus. [2] Non compris les militaires de carrière vivant dans des casernes et les conscrits. [3] Premier et quatrième trimestres.

Notas explicativas: véase p. 83.

[1] Personas de 15 años y más. [2] Excl. los militares profesionales que viven en casernas y los conscriptos. [3] Primero y cuarto trimestres.

EMPLOYMENT — EMPLOI — EMPLEO

Total employment, by occupation — Emploi total, par profession — Empleo total, por ocupación

Thousands — Milliers — Millares

Roumanie (BA) [1]

Total - Total - Total
ISCO-88 - CITP-88 - CIUO-88

Total employment - Emploi total - Empleo total

	1999	2000	2001	2002	2003	2004	2005	2006	2007	2008
Total	10 775.6	10 763.7	10 696.9	9 234.1 [2]	9 222.5	9 157.6	9 146.6	9 313.3	9 353.3	9 369.1
1	240.0	233.4	232.5	238.0 [2]	225.2	259.8	265.5	269.1	252.6	232.7
2	663.9	687.6	684.9	662.9 [2]	688.4	768.5	793.5	863.8	876.2	950.2
3	882.9	873.5	888.7	849.4 [2]	835.8	828.4	830.0	860.0	857.4	859.6
4	422.5	418.1	400.1	376.9 [2]	372.4	406.9	392.4	391.2	410.8	450.2
5	721.2	730.9	768.2	728.2 [2]	745.2	840.6	852.7	914.8	946.0	944.7
6	4 151.8	4 272.7	4 091.2	3 035.9 [2]	3 004.0	2 450.4	2 462.6	2 319.5	2 343.5	2 224.4
7	1 906.5	1 772.7	1 719.4	1 653.5 [2]	1 641.6	1 624.7	1 522.5	1 537.5	1 523.8	1 528.0
8.0.X	1 121.1	1 097.7	1 089.1	1 022.1 [2]	1 035.9	1 076.1	1 069.8	1 120.4	1 089.6	1 124.0
9	665.4	676.7	822.5	666.7 [2]	673.6	901.8	957.4	1 037.0	1 053.4	1 055.3

Men - Hommes - Hombres
ISCO-88 - CITP-88 - CIUO-88

	1999	2000	2001	2002	2003	2004	2005	2006	2007	2008
Total	5 799.0	5 772.1	5 719.3	5 031.5 [2]	5 056.7	4 980.0	5 011.2	5 074.0	5 116.3	5 157.4
1	176.8	172.7	165.9	164.9 [2]	154.9	183.8	188.0	188.0	181.5	164.3
2	335.0	346.1	339.0	339.3 [2]	351.4	379.0	382.3	414.1	427.8	460.2
3	339.9	325.6	336.3	319.3 [2]	305.9	306.4	314.2	321.6	332.5	329.4
4	111.3	114.4	113.7	108.6 [2]	111.4	112.1	110.4	113.9	115.3	133.7
5	197.3	204.4	228.5	228.7 [2]	244.2	277.4	284.1	321.4	335.0	324.2
6	1 981.9	2 070.8	1 985.8	1 516.0 [2]	1 530.1	1 259.4	1 271.0	1 196.1	1 184.7	1 119.4
7	1 367.5	1 254.6	1 208.8	1 169.2 [2]	1 193.3	1 164.5	1 115.6	1 129.4	1 142.3	1 179.4
8.0.X	898.6	882.1	856.7	790.4 [2]	771.2	788.4	793.8	808.0	787.2	826.1
9	390.3	401.2	484.3	394.5 [2]	393.8	508.6	551.8	581.2	610.0	620.7

Women - Femmes - Mujeres
ISCO-88 - CITP-88 - CIUO-88

	1999	2000	2001	2002	2003	2004	2005	2006	2007	2008
Total	4 976.5	4 991.5	4 977.5	4 202.6 [2]	4 165.7	4 177.5	4 135.4	4 239.3	4 237.0	4 211.7
1	63.1	60.7	66.6	73.0 [2]	70.2	75.9	77.5	81.1	71.1	68.4
2	328.9	341.5	345.9	323.6 [2]	336.9	389.4	411.2	449.7	448.4	490.0
3	542.9	547.9	552.3	530.0 [2]	529.9	522.0	515.8	538.4	524.8	530.2
4	311.1	303.7	286.4	268.2 [2]	260.9	294.7	282.0	277.3	295.5	316.5
5	523.9	526.4	539.6	499.5 [2]	501.0	563.2	568.7	593.3	611.0	620.5
6	2 169.8	2 201.8	2 105.3	1 519.9 [2]	1 473.9	1 190.9	1 191.7	1 123.4	1 158.9	1 105.0
7	538.9	518.1	510.6	484.3 [2]	448.2	460.1	406.9	408.1	381.5	348.6
8.0.X	222.5	215.6	232.3	231.7 [2]	264.6	287.6	276.0	312.4	302.4	297.9
9	275.0	275.5	338.2	272.1 [2]	279.7	393.2	405.6	455.8	443.4	434.6

Russian Federation (BA) [3]

Total - Total - Total
ISCO-88 - CITP-88 - CIUO-88

Total employment - Emploi total - Empleo total

	1999	2000	2001	2002	2003	2004	2005	2006	2007	2008
Total	62 945	65 070	65 123	66 659	66 432	67 275	68 169	68 855	70 570	70 965
1	2 771	2 852	2 795	2 913	4 433	4 531	4 750	4 602	4 868	4 952
2	9 429	10 129	10 518	10 669	10 840	11 218	11 519	11 875	12 693	13 124
3	9 633	9 889	10 155	10 462	9 778	9 839	9 673	10 102	10 532	10 799
4	1 984	2 191	2 208	2 245	2 021	2 058	2 110	2 148	2 101	2 082
5	7 160	7 710	8 159	8 607	8 892	9 157	9 504	9 583	9 868	9 814
6	4 271	4 071	2 539	3 457	3 075	3 124	3 309	3 393	3 147	2 884
7	10 128	10 635	11 598	11 159	10 896	10 795	10 901	10 624	10 666	10 505
8	8 662	8 801	9 009	9 147	8 711	8 841	8 739	8 601	8 650	8 851
9	8 907	8 791	8 142	8 000	7 785	7 712	7 660	7 926	8 045	7 955

Men - Hommes - Hombres
ISCO-88 - CITP-88 - CIUO-88

	1999	2000	2001	2002	2003	2004	2005	2006	2007	2008
Total	32 570	33 574	33 504	34 014	33 827	34 181	34 549	34 695	35 650	36 139
1	1 758	1 836	1 772	1 822	2 717	2 806	2 898	2 814	2 985	3 115
2	3 716	4 046	4 117	4 128	4 165	4 291	4 401	4 585	4 923	5 027
3	2 988	3 044	3 201	3 258	3 152	3 202	3 084	3 260	3 441	3 530
4	211	245	270	262	202	196	205	212	208	212
5	2 449	2 640	2 752	2 829	2 676	2 744	2 810	2 775	2 875	2 857
6	1 925	1 856	1 257	1 648	1 478	1 466	1 544	1 663	1 543	1 388
7	7 611	7 975	8 309	8 248	8 146	8 087	8 265	8 055	8 135	8 202
8	7 581	7 652	7 833	7 942	7 543	7 686	7 604	7 458	7 559	7 798
9	4 331	4 278	3 995	3 877	3 748	3 703	3 736	3 872	3 981	4 010

Women - Femmes - Mujeres
ISCO-88 - CITP-88 - CIUO-88

	1999	2000	2001	2002	2003	2004	2005	2006	2007	2008
Total	30 375	31 496	31 619	32 645	32 605	33 094	33 620	34 160	34 920	34 826
1	1 013	1 016	1 024	1 091	1 715	1 725	1 853	1 788	1 883	1 836
2	5 713	6 083	6 401	6 540	6 675	6 927	7 118	7 291	7 771	8 097
3	6 645	6 844	6 955	7 204	6 626	6 637	6 589	6 842	7 091	7 269
4	1 774	1 946	1 938	1 983	1 819	1 862	1 905	1 936	1 893	1 869
5	4 710	5 070	5 407	5 778	6 216	6 413	6 693	6 808	6 993	6 956
6	2 346	2 215	1 282	1 809	1 598	1 659	1 765	1 730	1 604	1 497
7	2 517	2 661	3 289	2 911	2 750	2 708	2 637	2 569	2 531	2 304
8	1 081	1 149	1 177	1 205	1 168	1 155	1 135	1 143	1 091	1 053
9	4 576	4 513	4 147	4 123	4 037	4 009	3 924	4 053	4 064	3 946

Explanatory notes: see p. 77.

[1] Persons aged 15 years and over. [2] Estimates based on the 2002 Population Census results. [3] Persons aged 15 to 72 years.

Notes explicatives: voir p. 80.

[1] Personnes âgées de 15 ans et plus. [2] Estimations basées sur les résultats du Recensement de la population de 2002. [3] Personnes âgées de 15 à 72 ans.

Notas explicativas: véase p. 83.

[1] Personas de 15 años y más. [2] Estimaciones basadas en los resultados del Censo de población de 2002. [3] Personas de 15 a 72 años.

Total employment, by occupation
Emploi total, par profession
Empleo total, por ocupación

Thousands — Milliers — Millares

	1999	2000	2001	2002	2003	2004	2005	2006	2007	2008
San Marino (E) [1][2]				Total employment - Emploi total - Empleo total						
Total - Total - Total										
ISCO-88 - CITP-88 - CIUO-88										
Total	18.667	.	.	.	.	.	.	.	21.483	21.995
1	0.438	.	.	.	.	.	.	.	0.332	0.360
2	1.309	.	.	.	.	.	.	.	1.950	2.030
3	3.521	.	.	.	.	.	.	.	4.440	4.617
4	2.065	.	.	.	.	.	.	.	2.910	3.070
5	1.846	.	.	.	.	.	.	.	0.120	0.125
6	0.090	.	.	.	.	.	.	.	-	-
7	3.545	.	.	.	.	.	.	.	3.951	3.950
8	1.237	.	.	.	.	.	.	.	2.979	3.028
9	1.379	.	.	.	.	.	.	.	2.654	2.738
X	3.237	.	.	.	.	.	.	.	2.147	2.077
Men - Hommes - Hombres										
ISCO-88 - CITP-88 - CIUO-88										
Total	11.319	.	.	.	.	.	.	.	12.667	12.967
1	0.359	.	.	.	.	.	.	.	0.269	0.296
2	0.666	.	.	.	.	.	.	.	1.090	1.112
3	1.722	.	.	.	.	.	.	.	2.007	2.123
4	0.879	.	.	.	.	.	.	.	1.120	1.229
5	0.702	.	.	.	.	.	.	.	0.112	0.118
6	0.089	.	.	.	.	.	.	.	-	-
7	3.152	.	.	.	.	.	.	.	3.365	3.366
8	0.921	.	.	.	.	.	.	.	1.933	1.964
9	0.591	.	.	.	.	.	.	.	1.289	1.306
X	2.238	.	.	.	.	.	.	.	1.482	1.453
Women - Femmes - Mujeres										
ISCO-88 - CITP-88 - CIUO-88										
Total	7.348	.	.	.	.	.	.	.	8.816	9.028
1	0.079	.	.	.	.	.	.	.	0.063	0.064
2	0.643	.	.	.	.	.	.	.	0.860	0.918
3	1.799	.	.	.	.	.	.	.	2.433	2.494
4	1.186	.	.	.	.	.	.	.	1.790	1.841
5	1.144	.	.	.	.	.	.	.	0.008	0.007
6	0.001	.	.	.	.	.	.	.	-	-
7	0.393	.	.	.	.	.	.	.	0.586	0.584
8	0.316	.	.	.	.	.	.	.	1.046	1.064
9	0.788	.	.	.	.	.	.	.	1.365	1.432
X	0.999	.	.	.	.	.	.	.	0.665	0.624
Serbia (BA) [1][3]				Total employment - Emploi total - Empleo total						
Total - Total - Total										
ISCO-88 - CITP-88 - CIUO-88										
Total	.	.	.	.		2 930.8	2 733.4	2 630.7	2 655.7	2 821.7
1	.	.	.	.		105.1	101.3	87.2	93.9	149.9
2	.	.	.	.		263.2	250.8	265.1	264.5	289.0
3	.	.	.	.		459.2	401.4	422.0	412.6	371.6
4	.	.	.	.		175.9	159.6	139.1	150.9	166.6
5	.	.	.	.		429.4	378.4	368.9	384.4	374.4
6	.	.	.	.		617.4	538.9	449.0	463.7	626.0
7	.	.	.	.		398.0	389.1	388.4	361.8	389.2
8	.	.	.	.		233.1	214.9	209.4	226.9	200.9
9	.	.	.	.		230.1	278.8	288.5	285.8	246.4
0	.	.	.	.		19.4	20.1	13.0	11.0	7.7
Men - Hommes - Hombres										
ISCO-88 - CITP-88 - CIUO-88										
Total	.	.	.	.		1 708.9	1 635.0	1 554.7	1 545.8	1 611.3
1	.	.	.	.		77.9	76.2	65.5	60.7	95.6
2	.	.	.	.		130.2	129.6	125.2	130.1	128.0
3	.	.	.	.		193.0	168.9	173.8	176.1	162.3
4	.	.	.	.		93.9	84.1	68.7	75.9	73.9
5	.	.	.	.		188.8	164.4	169.7	156.4	158.5
6	.	.	.	.		352.7	315.2	272.6	282.7	341.9
7	.	.	.	.		333.3	326.5	326.7	301.1	331.3
8	.	.	.	.		206.5	194.2	185.4	203.1	183.6
9	.	.	.	.		113.6	155.6	154.1	148.6	128.5
0	.	.	.	.		19.1	20.1	13.0	11.0	7.7
Women - Femmes - Mujeres										
ISCO-88 - CITP-88 - CIUO-88										
Total	.	.	.	.		1 222.0	1 098.4	1 076.0	1 110.0	1 210.4
1	.	.	.	.		27.2	25.1	21.7	33.2	54.3
2	.	.	.	.		133.1	121.2	140.0	134.4	161.1
3	.	.	.	.		266.2	232.5	248.2	236.6	209.3
4	.	.	.	.		81.9	75.5	70.4	75.0	92.7
5	.	.	.	.		240.6	214.0	199.2	228.0	215.9
6	.	.	.	.		264.7	223.7	176.4	181.0	284.1
7	.	.	.	.		64.7	62.7	61.7	60.8	57.8
8	.	.	.	.		26.7	20.7	24.0	23.8	17.3
9	.	.	.	.		116.6	123.2	134.4	137.2	118.0
0	.	.	.	.		0.4	-	-	-	-

Explanatory notes: see p. 77.   Notes explicatives: voir p. 80.   Notas explicativas: véase p. 83.

[1] Persons aged 15 years and over. [2] Dec. [3] Oct.   [1] Personnes âgées de 15 ans et plus. [2] Déc. [3] Oct.   [1] Personas de 15 años y más. [2] Dic. [3] Oct.

EMPLOYMENT — EMPLOI — EMPLEO

Total employment, by occupation — Emploi total, par profession — Empleo total, por ocupación

Thousands — Milliers — Millares

	1999	2000	2001	2002	2003	2004	2005	2006	2007	2008
Slovakia (BA) [1][2][3]				Total employment - Emploi total - Empleo total						
Total - Total - Total										
ISCO-88 - CITP-88 - CIUO-88										
Total	2 132.1	2 101.7	2 123.7	2 127.0	2 164.6	2 170.4	2 216.2	2 301.4	2 357.3	2 433.8
1	123.8	132.0	118.1	107.3	127.0	137.8	138.2	131.8	128.5	134.0
2	222.4	215.0	217.3	213.4	213.8	230.6	252.1	251.9	246.9	249.7
3	371.5	371.4	398.0	397.5	407.1	391.3	402.4	431.1	443.1	457.3
4	157.1	151.8	142.3	139.8	137.3	137.7	140.5	141.2	150.0	147.3
5	274.3	275.3	287.2	296.1	310.9	307.4	317.6	323.4	332.5	348.3
6	31.4	27.5	23.1	26.4	26.8	26.5	25.3	25.9	23.1	24.7
7	437.7	422.6	411.8	407.3	395.1	418.4	409.2	421.9	434.4	438.9
8	299.5	285.2	292.7	310.2	313.7	298.5	306.9	337.8	359.3	371.4
9	214.2	220.7	228.2	222.5	222.5	208.8	209.7	223.0	227.6	249.4
0			5.0	6.5	10.5	13.5	14.3	13.6	12.1	12.9
X	0.3	0.2	-	-	-	-	-	-	-	-
Men - Hommes - Hombres										
ISCO-88 - CITP-88 - CIUO-88										
Total	1 163.7	1 137.3	1 145.8	1 156.8	1 177.1	1 193.7	1 233.0	1 291.1	1 321.6	1 363.7
1	83.8	91.5	82.0	73.6	83.0	93.2	95.7	95.0	88.7	94.2
2	87.4	81.4	80.8	78.9	81.0	90.1	106.5	106.5	103.0	104.7
3	148.3	144.2	156.9	159.1	158.9	155.1	167.5	179.3	184.8	183.4
4	34.8	34.5	36.0	40.3	40.8	41.1	40.7	43.2	48.1	44.2
5	85.3	92.3	94.7	92.9	105.2	101.4	101.0	100.7	99.4	108.0
6	17.0	14.1	12.4	14.2	15.9	18.4	17.9	18.5	17.0	15.9
7	356.6	340.6	340.3	341.1	328.4	347.7	350.2	363.0	374.0	380.0
8	242.7	227.8	228.4	236.7	240.9	226.8	232.3	258.6	279.7	290.5
9	107.7	110.8	109.6	113.7	113.7	109.3	110.2	114.7	115.3	131.0
0			4.8	6.4	9.5	10.7	11.3	11.7	11.6	12.1
X	0.2	0.2	-	-	-	-	-	-	-	-
Women - Femmes - Mujeres										
ISCO-88 - CITP-88 - CIUO-88										
Total	968.4	964.4	977.9	970.2	987.5	976.7	983.1	1 010.3	1 035.6	1 070.0
1	40.0	40.6	36.1	33.6	44.0	44.6	42.5	36.8	39.7	39.8
2	135.0	133.6	136.5	134.6	132.8	140.5	145.6	145.4	144.0	145.0
3	223.2	227.3	241.1	238.4	248.2	236.2	234.9	251.8	258.2	273.8
4	122.3	117.3	106.4	99.6	96.5	96.6	99.8	98.0	101.8	103.2
5	189.0	183.0	192.5	203.2	205.8	206.0	216.7	222.7	233.1	240.4
6	14.3	13.4	10.7	12.3	10.9	8.1	7.4	7.4	6.1	8.8
7	81.1	82.0	71.6	66.2	66.7	70.8	59.1	58.9	60.4	59.0
8	56.8	57.4	64.3	73.5	72.8	71.7	74.6	79.3	79.6	80.9
9	106.6	109.8	118.7	108.8	108.9	99.5	99.6	108.4	112.4	118.4
0			0.1	0.1	1.0	2.8	3.0	1.9	0.5	0.8
X	0.1		-	-	-	-	-	-	-	-
Slovenia (BA) [1][4]				Total employment - Emploi total - Empleo total						
Total - Total - Total										
ISCO-88 - CITP-88 - CIUO-88										
Total	892	894	914	922	896	946	947	969	994	990
1	54	64	65	59	54	58	66	61	58	65
2	96	95	103	109	118	128	136	147	147	149
3	123	124	128	138	144	148	154	166	160	162
4	99	99	90	96	92	84	77	78	84	87
5	107	108	106	112	103	106	109	118	115	128
6	88	74	81	79	67	80	68	71	75	46
7	98	98	112	116	120	123	112	108	108	120
8	178	170	165	153	144	150	155	141	157	150
9	41	48	47	46	43	51	60	68	71	71
0	3	2	3	5	4	4	5	5	5	6
X	4	13	15	9	9	13	6	6	14	7
Men - Hommes - Hombres										
ISCO-88 - CITP-88 - CIUO-88										
Total	482	481	497	500	488	511	512	521	542	540
1	37	44	44	42	36	39	44	41	38	42
2	39	36	41	46	47	51	54	61	60	59
3	68	63	64	64	68	67	72	78	75	79
4	29	31	30	33	31	29	27	28	34	31
5	39	40	39	40	37	39	39	44	42	40
6	46	40	44	42	36	44	37	40	42	34
7	92	92	103	106	111	113	103	98	100	110
8	113	106	101	96	93	97	103	95	108	101
9	12	18	18	20	20	21	25	28	30	35
0	3	2	2	4	4	4	4	4	5	6
X	3	8	9	5	6	8	5	4	8	3

Explanatory notes: see p. 77.

[1] Persons aged 15 years and over. [2] Excl. conscripts. [3] Excl. persons on child-care leave. [4] Second quarter of each year.

Notes explicatives: voir p. 80.

[1] Personnes âgées de 15 ans et plus. [2] Non compris les conscrits. [3] Non compris les personnes en congé parental. [4] Deuxième trimestre de chaque année.

Notas explicativas: véase p. 83.

[1] Personas de 15 años y más. [2] Excl. los conscriptos. [3] Excl. las personas con licencia parental. [4] Segundo trimestre de cada año.

Total employment, by occupation — Emploi total, par profession — Empleo total, por ocupación

Thousands — Milliers — Millares

	1999	2000	2001	2002	2003	2004	2005	2006	2007	2008
Slovenia (BA) [1] [2]				Total employment - Emploi total - Empleo total						
Women - Femmes - Mujeres										
ISCO-88 - CITP-88 - CIUO-88										
Total	410	413	417	423	409	434	435	448	451	450
1	17	19	20	17	18	20	22	20	20	23
2	58	58	61	63	71	77	82	86	87	90
3	55	61	63	74	75	81	82	88	86	83
4	70	68	61	63	61	56	50	49	50	56
5	69	67	67	72	66	67	71	74	72	88
6	42	34	37	37	30	36	32	30	33	12
7	6	6	9	10	10	10	9	11	8	9
8	65	64	64	57	51	53	51	46	49	49
9	28	30	29	26	23	30	35	40	41	36
0	-	-	1	1	-	-	-	1	-	-
X	1	5	6	4	4	5	1	2	6	4
Suisse (BA) [1] [2] [3]				Total employment - Emploi total - Empleo total						
Total - Total - Total										
ISCO-88 - CITP-88 - CIUO-88										
Total	3 862	3 879	3 938	3 965	3 963	3 959	3 974	4 051	4 122	4 229
1	225	232	219	241	249	249	248	257	264	280
2	588	609	643	636	665	679	702	728	743	792
3	791	826	801	791	807	812	818	847	877	921
4	544	527	544	544	535	515	522	489	474	462
5	499	477	502	546	526	535	534	543	540	559
6	196	182	174	177	171	159	161	162	171	173
7	595	602	596	597	581	582	571	594	611	596
8	195	183	194	195	186	184	185	188	190	188
9	205	218	231	217	222	215	212	218	229	236
X	24	23	35	21	22	30	20	25	24	24
Men - Hommes - Hombres										
ISCO-88 - CITP-88 - CIUO-88										
Total	2 157	2 172	2 190	2 175	2 177	2 173	2 172	2 214	2 259	2 289
1	177	177	164	174	178	182	178	179	184	195
2	408	409	433	427	439	441	460	479	481	504
3	382	394	379	361	367	366	370	379	386	394
4	160	154	157	166	161	157	152	144	138	139
5	135	137	148	160	163	171	170	172	171	176
6	134	123	114	115	113	105	108	109	119	120
7	518	531	519	514	501	497	492	502	526	513
8	160	151	162	163	156	157	153	151	157	150
9	71	79	91	84	86	79	79	83	87	82
X	12	15	23	11	14	18	11	15	12	14
Women - Femmes - Mujeres										
ISCO-88 - CITP-88 - CIUO-88										
Total	1 705	1 707	1 748	1 790	1 786	1 786	1 802	1 837	1 863	1 940
1	48	54	56	67	70	67	70	79	80	84
2	179	201	210	209	225	238	243	249	262	288
3	409	431	422	430	440	447	448	468	491	527
4	385	372	387	377	374	357	370	344	336	323
5	365	340	354	386	363	364	364	371	370	382
6	61	59	59	62	58	54	54	52	52	53
7	77	71	77	84	80	84	79	93	85	82
8	35	32	32	32	30	28	32	36	33	37
9	133	139	140	132	136	135	133	136	142	153
X	12	8	12	11	9	13	9	10	11	10
Sweden (BA) [4] [5]				Total employment - Emploi total - Empleo total						
Total - Total - Total										
ISCO-88 - CITP-88 - CIUO-88										
Total	4 068	4 159	4 239	4 244	4 234	4 213	4 263 [6]	4 341	4 541	4 593
1	191	192	197	203	209	223	204 [6]	220	236	235
2	647	689	738	770	770	780	828 [6]	839	881	901
3	810	844	841	828	835	841	831 [6]	846	889	906
4	436	436	436	431	410	403	390 [6]	387	401	398
5	747	762	791	801	814	800	811 [6]	834	866	872
6	98	90	89	87	88	89	85 [6]	85	92	92
7	455	452	466	468	468	444	454 [6]	464	482	491
8	455	462	449	436	425	430	431 [6]	434	446	450
9	212	211	209	197	196	188	214 [6]	217	230	233
0	12	11	10	9	10	10	11 [6]	10	10	9
X	5	9	14	13	9	6	4 [6]	5	7	7

Explanatory notes: see p. 77.

[1] Persons aged 15 years and over. [2] Second quarter of each year. [3] Excluding armed forces and seasonal/border workers. [4] Incl. professional army; excl. compulsory military service. [5] Persons aged 15 to 74 years; prior to 2007: 16 to 64 years. [6] Methodology revised; data not strictly comparable.

Notes explicatives: voir p. 80.

[1] Personnes âgées de 15 ans et plus. [2] Deuxième trimestre de chaque année. [3] Non compris les forces armées et les travailleurs saisonniers et frontaliers. [4] Y compris les militaires de carrière; non compris les militaires du contingent. [5] Personnes âgées de 15 à 74 ans; avant 2007: 16 à 64 ans. [6] Méthodologie révisée; les données ne sont pas strictement comparables.

Notas explicativas: véase p. 83.

[1] Personas de 15 años y más. [2] Segundo trimestre de cada año. [3] Excluidas las fuerzas armadas y excl. a los trabajadores temporales y fronterizos. [4] Incl. los militares profesionales; excl. los militares en servicio obligatorio. [5] Personas de 15 a 74 años; antes de 2007: 16 a 64 años. [6] Metodología revisada; los datos no son estrictamente comparables.

ILO YEARBOOK OF LABOUR STATISTICS 2009 — ANNUAIRE DES STATISTIQUES DU TRAVAIL DU BIT 2009 — ANUARIO DE ESTADISTICAS DEL TRABAJO DEL OIT 2009

251

2C

EMPLOYMENT	EMPLOI	EMPLEO
Total employment, by occupation	Emploi total, par profession	Empleo total, por ocupación
Thousands	Milliers	Millares

	1999	2000	2001	2002	2003	2004	2005	2006	2007	2008

Sweden (BA) [1][2] — Total employment - Emploi total - Empleo total

Men - Hommes - Hombres
ISCO-88 - CITP-88 - CIUO-88

	1999	2000	2001	2002	2003	2004	2005	2006	2007	2008
Total	2 121	2 167	2 203	2 197	2 191	2 186	2 225 [3]	2 273	2 390	2 422
1	136	135	137	141	146	152	144 [3]	149	162	160
2	319	337	367	383	376	377	407 [3]	413	435	445
3	428	449	444	422	415	418	402 [3]	410	439	448
4	122	123	123	123	119	115	111 [3]	119	128	124
5	160	160	170	180	194	197	201 [3]	213	217	220
6	73	69	67	65	65	68	64 [3]	64	72	71
7	427	424	436	440	439	416	430 [3]	438	453	464
8	371	378	368	357	351	360	366 [3]	369	378	383
9	71	73	71	68	68	68	87 [3]	85	92	92
0	12	11	10	9	10	9	11 [3]	9	10	9
X	3	6	10	9	6	4	3 [3]	3	5	5

Women - Femmes - Mujeres
ISCO-88 - CITP-88 - CIUO-88

	1999	2000	2001	2002	2003	2004	2005	2006	2007	2008
Total	1 946	1 992	2 036	2 047	2 043	2 027	2 038 [3]	2 067	2 150	2 171
1	55	56	60	62	63	70	61 [3]	71	75	76
2	328	351	371	387	394	402	421 [3]	426	446	455
3	383	396	397	406	420	423	430 [3]	435	450	458
4	314	313	313	308	291	287	279 [3]	268	273	274
5	586	601	621	621	620	603	610 [3]	621	648	651
6	25	21	22	22	23	21	21 [3]	21	20	21
7	29	28	30	28	28	28	24 [3]	26	29	27
8	84	84	81	79	74	70	64 [3]	65	69	67
9	141	138	137	129	127	120	127 [3]	132	138	141
0	-	-	1	1	1	1	- [3]	2	-	1
X	2	3	4	4	3	2	1 [3]	2	3	2

Turkey (BA) [4][5] — Total employment - Emploi total - Empleo total

Total - Total - Total
ISCO-88 - CITP-88 - CIUO-88

	1999	2000	2001	2002	2003	2004	2005	2006	2007	2008
Total	.	.	21 524	21 354	21 147	21 791	22 046	22 330	20 738	21 194
1	.	.	1 731	1 755	1 846	1 859	2 162	2 026	1 835	1 860
2	.	.	1 237	1 324	1 383	1 317	1 405	1 470	1 333	1 322
3	.	.	1 052	1 037	1 062	1 064	1 215	1 323	1 401	1 506
4	.	.	952	1 140	1 196	1 115	1 188	1 323	1 324	1 406
5	.	.	1 928	2 172	2 179	2 195	2 270	2 538	2 566	2 553
6	.	.	7 774	6 784	6 755	6 450	5 674	5 112	4 068	4 121
7	.	.	3 299	3 079	2 944	3 011	3 194	3 179	3 042	3 023
8	.	.	1 716	1 765	1 801	2 107	2 253	2 336	2 314	2 282
9	.	.	1 836	2 299	1 982	2 674	2 685	3 023	2 855	3 120

Men - Hommes - Hombres
ISCO-88 - CITP-88 - CIUO-88

	1999	2000	2001	2002	2003	2004	2005	2006	2007	2008
Total	.	.	15 555	15 232	15 256	16 023	16 346	16 520	15 382	15 598
1	.	.	1 594	1 636	1 732	1 737	2 012	1 869	1 678	1 677
2	.	.	827	882	940	892	934	959	818	799
3	.	.	736	737	762	755	850	915	988	1 035
4	.	.	623	715	718	695	740	823	767	822
5	.	.	1 667	1 830	1 827	1 842	1 864	2 055	2 042	2 005
6	.	.	4 113	3 501	3 486	3 676	3 170	2 854	2 281	2 331
7	.	.	2 910	2 661	2 597	2 661	2 844	2 845	2 758	2 736
8	.	.	1 597	1 627	1 640	1 918	2 034	2 112	2 084	2 075
9	.	.	1 491	1 643	1 555	1 847	1 897	2 088	1 966	2 118

Women - Femmes - Mujeres
ISCO-88 - CITP-88 - CIUO-88

	1999	2000	2001	2002	2003	2004	2005	2006	2007	2008
Total	.	.	5 969	6 122	5 891	5 768	5 700	5 810	5 356	5 594
1	.	.	138	119	114	122	150	157	157	183
2	.	.	410	442	443	425	471	511	515	522
3	.	.	316	299	300	309	365	409	413	471
4	.	.	330	425	478	420	447	500	557	584
5	.	.	261	342	352	353	405	483	524	548
6	.	.	3 661	3 283	3 269	2 774	2 504	2 258	1 787	1 790
7	.	.	389	418	347	350	351	334	284	287
8	.	.	119	138	161	188	220	224	230	207
9	.	.	345	656	427	827	788	935	889	1 002

Explanatory notes: see p. 77.

[1] Incl. professional army; excl. compulsory military service. [2] Persons aged 15 to 74 years; prior to 2007: 16 to 64 years. [3] Methodology revised; data not strictly comparable. [4] Excl. armed forces. [5] Persons aged 15 years and over.

Notes explicatives: voir p. 80.

[1] Y compris les militaires de carrière; non compris les militaires du contingent. [2] Personnes âgées de 15 à 74 ans; avant 2007: 16 à 64 ans. [3] Méthodologie révisée; les données ne sont pas strictement comparables. [4] Non compris les forces armées. [5] Personnes âgées de 15 ans et plus.

Notas explicativas: véase p. 83.

[1] Incl. los militares profesionales; excl. los militares en servicio obligatorio. [2] Personas de 15 a 74 años; antes de 2007: 16 a 64 años. [3] Metodología revisada; los datos no son estrictamente comparables. [4] Excl. las fuerzas armadas. [5] Personas de 15 años y más.

Total employment, by occupation — Emploi total, par profession — Empleo total, por ocupación

Thousands — Milliers — Millares

	1999	2000	2001	2002	2003	2004	2005	2006	2007	2008
Ukraine (BA) [1]				Total employment - Emploi total - Empleo total						
Total - Total - Total										
ISCO-88 - CITP-88 - CIUO-88										
Total	19 947.8	20 175.0	19 971.5	20 091.2	20 163.3	20 295.7	20 680.0	20 730.4	20 904.7	20 972.3
1	1 421.9	1 464.5	1 497.9	1 460.9	1 429.3	1 423.7	1 470.3	1 505.9	1 589.8	1 580.7
2	2 606.3	2 593.4	2 599.3	2 542.5	2 664.3	2 594.6	2 484.7	2 522.5	2 634.3	2 723.7
3	3 103.4	3 001.8	2 876.3	2 734.4	2 767.5	2 549.1	2 530.4	2 488.7	2 390.7	2 422.3
4	823.4	837.1	813.1	890.0	835.1	769.5	755.0	758.7	759.7	727.3
5	2 151.8	2 244.7	2 406.8	2 526.9	2 646.1	2 654.9	2 700.0	2 728.7	2 846.8	2 952.9
6	646.0	620.0	513.1	467.0	429.9	375.4	361.1	310.3	270.4	234.8
7	2 625.7	2 663.7	2 619.3	2 683.0	2 679.5	2 524.6	2 527.4	2 498.0	2 624.3	2 822.0
8	3 145.7	3 112.2	2 952.3	2 954.0	2 855.7	2 697.4	2 705.0	2 649.9	2 624.3	2 642.0
9	3 423.6	3 637.6	3 693.4	3 832.5	3 855.9	4 706.5	5 146.1	5 267.7	5 164.4	4 866.6
Men - Hommes - Hombres										
ISCO-88 - CITP-88 - CIUO-88										
Total	10 043.7	10 318.1	10 176.7	10 189.9	10 199.7	10 288.8	10 604.5	10 675.6	10 764.8	10 849.7
1	872.4	926.5	937.4	899.0	863.3	809.6	908.6	928.7	963.4	970.4
2	871.5	900.0	931.3	915.0	967.7	1 043.1	858.3	861.3	951.7	994.7
3	1 176.7	1 149.0	1 052.7	976.8	998.0	1 032.8	932.0	929.7	844.9	860.2
4	100.5	92.3	91.3	149.4	120.9	203.8	133.4	136.0	129.3	112.7
5	590.8	641.3	712.6	745.2	799.4	1 004.9	847.0	848.2	897.7	936.4
6	234.1	230.2	199.5	198.7	179.0	190.2	196.2	172.3	155.2	142.7
7	2 117.5	2 196.3	2 199.3	2 243.3	2 251.5	1 796.4	2 136.2	2 131.6	2 251.4	2 432.9
8	2 488.9	2 486.8	2 305.7	2 272.8	2 220.6	1 845.4	2 109.3	2 062.1	2 066.8	2 076.5
9	1 591.3	1 695.7	1 746.9	1 789.7	1 799.3	2 362.6	2 483.5	2 607.7	2 504.4	2 323.2
Women - Femmes - Mujeres										
ISCO-88 - CITP-88 - CIUO-88										
Total	9 904.1	9 856.9	9 794.8	9 901.3	9 963.6	10 006.9	10 075.5	10 054.8	10 139.9	10 122.6
1	549.5	538.0	560.5	561.9	566.0	614.1	561.7	577.2	626.4	610.3
2	1 734.8	1 693.4	1 668.0	1 627.5	1 696.6	1 551.5	1 626.4	1 661.2	1 682.6	1 729.0
3	1 926.7	1 852.8	1 823.6	1 757.6	1 769.5	1 516.3	1 598.4	1 559.0	1 545.8	1 562.1
4	722.9	744.8	721.8	740.6	714.2	565.7	621.6	622.7	630.4	614.6
5	1 561.0	1 603.4	1 694.2	1 781.7	1 846.7	1 650.0	1 853.0	1 882.5	1 949.1	2 016.5
6	411.9	389.8	313.6	268.3	250.9	185.2	164.9	138.0	115.2	92.1
7	508.2	467.4	420.0	439.7	428.0	728.2	391.2	366.4	372.9	389.1
8	656.8	625.4	646.6	681.2	635.1	852.0	595.7	587.8	557.5	565.5
9	1 832.3	1 941.9	1 946.5	2 042.8	2 056.6	2 343.9	2 662.6	2 660.0	2 660.0	2 543.4
United Kingdom (BA) [2] [3]				Total employment - Emploi total - Empleo total						
Total - Total - Total										
ISCO-88 - CITP-88 - CIUO-88										
Total	.	.	27 643	27 852	28 132	28 365	28 665	28 926	29 100	29 475
1	.	.	3 765	3 932	4 065	4 135	4 194	4 331	4 356	4 558
2	.	.	3 265	3 230	3 389	3 531	3 594	3 754	3 769	3 767
3	.	.	3 673	3 811	3 782	3 820	3 918	4 051	4 056	4 212
4	.	.	3 741	3 664	3 632	3 544	3 549	3 477	3 434	3 329
5	.	.	4 171	4 208	4 325	4 427	4 482	4 494	4 515	4 659
6,9	.	.	3 391	3 399	3 330	3 322	3 307	3 306	3 305	3 403
7	.	.	3 247	3 271	3 230	3 238	3 232	3 136	3 277	3 208
8	.	.	2 335	2 292	2 200	2 122	2 167	2 176	2 167	2 080
0	.	.	.	.	131	168	162	140	135	167
X	.	.	55	46	47	60	62	63	86	92
Men - Hommes - Hombres										
ISCO-88 - CITP-88 - CIUO-88										
Total	.	.	14 961	15 033	15 256	15 327	15 468	15 578	15 747	15 904
1	.	.	2 598	2 674	2 756	2 769	2 765	2 837	2 876	2 981
2	.	.	1 941	1 879	1 998	2 059	2 088	2 149	2 156	2 148
3	.	.	1 953	2 025	1 961	1 937	1 970	1 985	1 973	2 041
4	.	.	763	766	739	720	697	760	739	697
5	.	.	964	979	999	1 042	1 089	1 068	1 095	1 143
6,9	.	.	1 811	1 777	1 812	1 824	1 820	1 821	1 838	1 907
7	.	.	2 968	2 990	2 977	2 984	2 982	2 896	3 021	2 959
8	.	.	1 925	1 913	1 867	1 817	1 890	1 906	1 886	1 827
0	.	.	.	.	115	140	131	119	114	142
X	.	.	37	29	31	36	35	38	49	58
Women - Femmes - Mujeres										
ISCO-88 - CITP-88 - CIUO-88										
Total	.	.	12 681	12 819	12 876	13 038	13 198	13 348	13 353	13 572
1	.	.	1 167	1 257	1 309	1 366	1 429	1 494	1 480	1 577
2	.	.	1 324	1 351	1 391	1 473	1 505	1 605	1 613	1 619
3	.	.	1 720	1 786	1 821	1 883	1 947	2 066	2 083	2 171
4	.	.	2 978	2 898	2 893	2 825	2 852	2 717	2 695	2 632
5	.	.	3 207	3 229	3 327	3 385	3 392	3 425	3 420	3 516
6,9	.	.	1 580	1 622	1 517	1 498	1 487	1 485	1 467	1 496
7	.	.	278	280	253	254	249	240	256	249
8	.	.	410	379	333	305	278	270	281	253
0	.	.	.	.	16	28	31	21	21	25
X	.	.	18	17	16	23	27	25	37	34

Explanatory notes: see p. 77.   Notes explicatives: voir p. 80.   Notas explicativas: véase p. 83.

[1] Persons aged 15-70 years. [2] Persons aged 16 years and over. [3] Second quarter.

[1] Personnes âgées de 15 à 70 ans. [2] Personnes âgées de 16 ans et plus. [3] Deuxième trimestre.

[1] Personas de 15 á 70 años. [2] Personas de 16 años y más. [3] Segundo trimestre.

EMPLOYMENT   EMPLOI   EMPLEO

**Total employment,
by occupation**   **Emploi total,
par profession**   **Empleo total,
por ocupación**

Thousands   Milliers   Millares

	1999	2000	2001	2002	2003	2004	2005	2006	2007	2008
OCEANIA-OCÉANIE-OCEANIA										
Australia (BA) [1][2]				Total employment - Emploi total - Empleo total						
Total - Total - Total										
ISCO-88 - CITP-88 - CIUO-88										
Total	8 720.2	8 951.3	9 081.4	9 245.8	9 464.9	9 623.3	9 968.6	10 218.3	10 512.3	10 740.5
1	1 010.3	1 030.8	897.0	910.5	949.3	1 005.4	1 072.3	1 120.3	1 164.8	1 189.3
2	1 515.3	1 565.6	1 541.5	1 587.7	1 624.0	1 675.8	1 723.1	1 807.1	1 858.4	1 946.2
3	1 088.9	1 153.9	1 132.6	1 138.8	1 191.9	1 225.1	1 336.4	1 392.1	1 435.2	1 468.7
4	1 194.2	1 210.2	1 319.2	1 332.3	1 359.4	1 301.9	1 335.4	1 360.4	1 398.7	1 420.2
5	1 189.5	1 228.1	1 381.7	1 406.8	1 459.1	1 488.7	1 555.8	1 548.1	1 595.6	1 615.3
6	254.1	274.7	325.1	320.7	290.8	293.4	302.0	308.1	313.5	310.8
7	1 095.9	1 118.6	1 064.4	1 096.2	1 150.1	1 164.3	1 186.2	1 226.7	1 255.1	1 290.2
8	742.4	731.1	636.6	637.4	637.5	660.5	636.6	637.9	669.6	679.3
9	620.6	626.7	783.4	815.4	802.9	808.2	820.8	817.8	821.4	820.6
X	9.0	11.6	.	.	.	.	.	.	.	.
Men - Hommes - Hombres										
ISCO-88 - CITP-88 - CIUO-88										
Total	4 917.6	5 006.0	5 036.4	5 131.0	5 225.6	5 331.0	5 488.0	5 605.6	5 769.9	5 879.2
1	694.1	691.5	608.7	615.3	635.7	662.7	696.5	726.9	753.1	752.6
2	767.0	778.3	771.4	795.5	802.5	812.4	838.0	869.8	891.0	921.7
3	447.9	470.9	530.4	524.4	548.3	566.8	596.2	606.6	620.7	659.6
4	372.1	375.4	317.2	327.8	339.5	326.2	347.1	362.9	382.3	379.7
5	404.5	416.7	524.3	535.1	548.8	559.0	592.3	562.9	574.1	590.6
6	197.2	207.4	246.7	243.9	224.1	226.7	230.2	238.3	239.9	241.7
7	1 021.2	1 047.5	1 011.8	1 043.6	1 091.5	1 108.5	1 126.8	1 173.4	1 204.5	1 233.0
8	660.2	652.3	555.1	549.8	548.6	577.5	553.6	558.5	588.8	588.8
9	351.0	360.3	470.7	495.6	486.6	491.1	507.4	506.3	515.5	511.5
X	2.4	5.7	.	.	.	.	.	.	.	.
Women - Femmes - Mujeres										
ISCO-88 - CITP-88 - CIUO-88										
Total	3 802.6	3 945.3	4 045.0	4 114.8	4 239.4	4 292.3	4 480.6	4 612.8	4 742.4	4 861.3
1	316.3	339.4	288.2	295.3	313.5	342.6	375.8	393.5	411.7	436.7
2	748.2	787.3	770.1	792.2	821.6	863.5	885.1	937.2	967.4	1 024.4
3	641.0	683.0	602.2	614.4	643.6	658.3	740.2	785.5	814.5	809.1
4	822.2	834.8	1 001.9	1 004.4	1 019.8	975.7	988.3	997.5	1 016.3	1 040.4
5	785.0	811.5	857.5	871.7	910.3	929.7	963.5	985.2	1 021.5	1 024.7
6	56.8	67.2	78.4	76.7	66.6	66.7	71.8	69.8	73.7	69.1
7	74.7	71.1	52.5	52.7	58.7	55.7	59.4	53.3	50.6	57.1
8	82.3	78.8	81.5	87.6	88.9	83.0	83.0	79.4	80.8	90.5
9	269.6	266.4	312.7	319.9	316.3	317.1	313.4	311.5	305.9	309.1
X	6.6	5.9	.	.	.	.	.	.	.	.
New Zealand (BA) [1][2][3]				Total employment - Emploi total - Empleo total						
Total - Total - Total										
ISCO-88 - CITP-88 - CIUO-88										
Total	1 766.3	1 800.0	1 845.8	1 906.2	1 955.6	2 024.1	2 084.6	2 134.7	2 174.5	2 188.2
1	216.4	232.6	244.5	240.3	242.6	243.5	254.8	269.8	283.2	299.1
2	225.0	232.7	250.7	273.5	286.4	292.0	318.5	342.4	357.3	367.8
3	217.3	218.0	230.0	216.1	215.0	230.2	246.4	258.6	257.4	272.3
4	223.6	214.0	213.3	241.3	245.4	253.8	257.0	267.2	265.7	263.8
5	262.3	278.1	279.3	290.9	315.3	325.3	324.2	308.3	328.7	324.8
6	161.7	156.5	162.8	162.4	162.2	159.2	153.0	152.2	150.7	147.0
7	166.5	171.5	169.2	179.5	184.6	189.2	201.6	214.4	223.1	203.8
8	151.6	164.8	166.9	176.5	171.0	184.6	195.0	187.8	181.8	177.6
9	134.0	123.9	121.8	123.4	130.5	143.6	130.8	125.4	120.1	122.3
0	7.9	7.8	7.3	2.3	2.6	2.7	3.5	8.5	6.4	9.7
X	-	-	.	.	.	.	.	-	-	-
Men - Hommes - Hombres										
ISCO-88 - CITP-88 - CIUO-88										
Total	963.1	981.6	1 001.7	1 035.5	1 056.8	1 095.6	1 120.1	1 146.3	1 165.0	1 164.9
1	135.2	143.8	150.2	147.5	154.2	155.1	161.8	162.1	170.0	179.6
2	99.1	99.0	112.6	130.1	133.4	138.1	147.7	159.2	164.1	162.1
3	112.4	107.3	109.0	102.1	103.4	108.6	116.4	123.2	114.3	122.9
4	48.4	49.8	45.2	54.0	53.1	53.3	52.1	56.0	59.4	57.5
5	93.0	98.1	99.3	99.4	101.9	105.8	102.5	100.3	110.0	116.9
6	111.5	109.2	115.1	115.8	115.9	111.7	105.7	105.2	107.7	102.7
7	153.7	158.3	157.0	167.8	172.7	179.2	190.2	203.4	213.1	194.6
8	120.8	131.6	131.3	141.9	138.1	150.3	160.4	155.7	150.4	149.2
9	83.3	80.1	75.9	75.8	82.6	92.3	81.6	76.3	72.7	74.1
0	5.8	4.3	6.1	1.1	1.4	1.1	1.6	4.9	3.4	5.5
X	-	-	.	.	.	.	.	-	-	-

Explanatory notes: see p. 77.

[1] Excl. armed forces. [2] Persons aged 15 years and over. [3] Methodology revised; data not strictly comparable.

Notes explicatives: voir p. 80.

[1] Non compris les forces armées. [2] Personnes âgées de 15 ans et plus. [3] Méthodologie révisée; les données ne sont pas strictement comparables.

Notas explicativas: véase p. 83.

[1] Excl. las fuerzas armadas. [2] Personas de 15 años y más. [3] Metodología revisada; los datos no son estrictamente comparables.

**Total employment,
by occupation**

**Emploi total,
par profession**

**Empleo total,
por ocupación**

	Thousands			Milliers				Millares		
	1999	2000	2001	2002	2003	2004	2005	2006	2007	2008

New Zealand (BA) [1] [2] [3]   **Total employment - Emploi total - Empleo total**

Women - Femmes - Mujeres
ISCO-88 - CITP-88 - CIUO-88

	1999	2000	2001	2002	2003	2004	2005	2006	2007	2008
Total	803.3	818.4	844.1	870.6	898.8	928.5	964.6	988.4	1 009.5	1 023.2
1	81.2	88.8	94.3	92.8	88.4	88.4	93.0	107.6	113.2	119.5
2	125.8	133.7	138.1	143.5	153.1	153.9	170.8	183.2	193.3	205.7
3	105.0	110.7	121.0	114.0	111.6	121.6	129.9	135.4	143.1	149.4
4	175.2	164.2	168.1	187.4	192.4	200.5	205.0	211.2	206.3	206.3
5	169.3	180.0	180.0	191.4	213.4	219.5	221.7	207.9	218.7	207.9
6	50.2	47.3	47.8	46.6	46.2	47.6	47.3	47.0	43.0	44.3
7	12.8	13.2	12.3	11.7	11.9	10.0	11.4	11.1	10.0	9.2
8	30.8	33.3	35.6	34.6	32.9	34.3	34.6	32.2	31.4	28.5
9	50.8	43.8	45.9	47.5	47.9	51.3	49.1	49.1	47.4	48.2
0	2.2 [3]	3.4	1.2	1.1	1.1	1.6	1.8	3.7	3.0	4.2
X	-	-	-	-	-	-	-	-	-	-

Explanatory notes: see p. 77.

[1] Excl. armed forces. [2] Persons aged 15 years and over. [3] Methodology revised; data not strictly comparable.

Notes explicatives: voir p. 80.

[1] Non compris les forces armées. [2] Personnes âgées de 15 ans et plus. [3] Méthodologie révisée; les données ne sont pas strictement comparables.

Notas explicativas: véase p. 83.

[1] Excl. las fuerzas armadas. [2] Personas de 15 años y más. [3] Metodología revisada; los datos no son estrictamente comparables.

EMPLOYMENT — EMPLOI — EMPLEO

Total employment, by status in employment — Thousands
Emploi total, par situation dans la profession — Milliers
Empleo total, por situación en el empleo — Millares

AFRICA-AFRIQUE-AFRICA

	1999	2000	2001	2002	2003	2004	2005	2006	2007	2008
Botswana (BA) [1][2]				Total employment - Emploi total - Empleo total						
Total - Total - Total										
ICSE-93 - CISP-93 - CISE-93										
Total	.	483.4	.	.	462.4	.	.	539.2	.	.
1	.	337.2	.	.	338.6	.	.	326.1	.	.
2	.	.	.	.	.	.	.	20.1	.	.
2,3	.	63.6	.	.	56.3	.	.	.	.	.
3	.	.	.	.	.	.	.	46.3	.	.
5	.	82.7	.	.	10.4	.	.	17.1	.	.
6	.	.	.	.	57.1	.	.	184.4	.	.
Men - Hommes - Hombres										
ICSE-93 - CISP-93 - CISE-93										
Total	.	269.4	.	.	245.4	.	.	281.8	.	.
1	.	191.8	.	.	182.5	.	.	175.3	.	.
2	.	.	.	.	.	.	.	13.6	.	.
2,3	.	32.1	.	.	19.9	.	.	.	.	.
3	.	.	.	.	.	.	.	13.4	.	.
5	.	45.5	.	.	5.5	.	.	6.0	.	.
6	.	.	.	.	37.5	.	.	73.4	.	.
Women - Femmes - Mujeres										
ICSE-93 - CISP-93 - CISE-93										
Total	.	214.0	.	.	217.0	.	.	257.4	.	.
1	.	145.3	.	.	156.1	.	.	150.8	.	.
2	.	.	.	.	.	.	.	6.5	.	.
2,3	.	31.5	.	.	36.5	.	.	.	.	.
3	.	.	.	.	.	.	.	32.9	.	.
5	.	37.1	.	.	4.8	.	.	11.2	.	.
6	.	.	.	.	19.6	.	.	56.1	.	.
Egypt (BA) [1][3][4]				Total employment - Emploi total - Empleo total						
Total - Total - Total										
ICSE-93 - CISP-93 - CISE-93										
Total	16 750.2	17 203.3	17 556.7	17 856.2	18 118.6	18 717.4	19 341.7	20 444.0	21 723.8	.
1	10 237.5	10 311.9	10 797.9	10 747.3	10 485.7	10 572.8	11 605.1	12 635.0	12 715.1	.
2	2 677.5	2 945.7	3 139.3	3 115.6	3 235.3	3 237.1	2 844.0	2 736.1	3 068.2	.
3	1 931.7	1 963.6	1 987.3	2 129.5	2 191.7	2 292.9	2 382.8	2 388.1	2 884.6	.
5	1 903.4	1 982.0	1 632.1	1 863.8	2 205.9	2 614.6	2 509.9	2 684.2	3 055.9	.
Men - Hommes - Hombres										
ICSE-93 - CISP-93 - CISE-93										
Total	13 611.0	13 958.5	14 361.1	14 550.7	14 651.7	14 936.4	15 592.7	16 559.0	17 089.5	.
1	8 217.1	8 455.4	8 728.7	8 502.0	8 526.8	8 709.0	9 698.9	10 550.0	10 496.7	.
2	2 492.1	2 799.6	2 933.5	2 926.8	3 084.6	3 059.7	2 702.7	2 626.5	2 909.7	.
3	1 688.6	1 565.5	1 610.8	1 903.2	1 727.3	1 768.7	1 861.7	1 965.8	2 200.1	.
5	1 213.1	1 137.9	1 088.1	1 218.7	1 313.1	1 399.0	1 329.4	1 417.0	1 483.1	.
Women - Femmes - Mujeres										
ICSE-93 - CISP-93 - CISE-93										
Total	3 139.2	3 244.8	3 195.6	3 305.5	3 466.9	3 781.0	3 749.1	3 884.2	4 634.3	.
1	2 020.4	1 856.5	2 069.2	2 245.3	1 958.9	1 863.8	1 906.2	2 085.1	2 218.4	.
2	185.4	146.1	205.8	188.8	150.7	177.4	141.3	109.6	158.5	.
3	243.1	398.1	376.5	226.3	464.4	524.2	521.1	422.3	684.5	.
5	690.3	844.1	544.0	645.1	892.8	1 215.6	1 180.5	1 267.2	1 572.8	.
Madagascar (B) [5][6]				Total employment - Emploi total - Empleo total						
Total - Total - Total										
ICSE-93 - CISP-93 - CISE-93										
Total	.	.	.	.	8 098.5	.	9 570.4	.	.	.
1	.	.	.	.	1 214.2	.	1 285.8	.	.	.
2	.	.	.	.	170.6	.	.	.	.	.
3	.	.	.	.	3 368.2	.	3 268.2	.	.	.
5	.	.	.	.	3 286.7	.	5 004.8	.	.	.
6	.	.	.	.	58.9	.	11.5	.	.	.
Men - Hommes - Hombres										
ICSE-93 - CISP-93 - CISE-93										
Total	.	.	.	.	4 135.7	.	4 841.8	.	.	.
1	.	.	.	.	738.2	.	775.1	.	.	.
2	.	.	.	.	102.3	.	.	.	.	.
3	.	.	.	.	2 032.8	.	2 506.4	.	.	.
5	.	.	.	.	1 229.1	.	1 553.9	.	.	.
6	.	.	.	.	33.4	.	6.4	.	.	.

Explanatory notes: see p. 77.

[1] Excl. armed forces. [2] Persons aged 12 years and over. [3] Persons aged 15 to 64 years. [4] May and Nov. [5] Persons aged 6 years and over. [6] Excl. armed forces and conscripts.

Notes explicatives: voir p. 80.

[1] Non compris les forces armées. [2] Personnes âgées de 12 ans et plus. [3] Personnes âgées de 15 à 64 ans. [4] Mai et nov. [5] Personnes âgées de 6 ans et plus. [6] Non compris les forces armées et les conscrits.

Notas explicativas: véase p. 83.

[1] Excl. las fuerzas armadas. [2] Personas de 12 años y más. [3] Personas de 15 a 64 años. [4] Mayo y nov. [5] Personas de 6 años y más. [6] Excl. las fuerzas armadas y los conscriptos.

	EMPLOYMENT	EMPLOI	EMPLEO

Total employment, by status in employment — Thousands
Emploi total, par situation dans la profession — Milliers
Empleo total, por situación en el empleo — Millares

	1999	2000	2001	2002	2003	2004	2005	2006	2007	2008
Madagascar (B) [1] [2]					Total employment - Emploi total - Empleo total					
Women - Femmes - Mujeres										
ICSE-93 - CISP-93 - CISE-93										
Total					3 962.8		4 728.6			
1					476.0		510.7			
2					68.2					
3					1 335.4		761.8			
5					2 057.7		3 451.0			
6					25.4		5.1			
Mali (BA) [3]					Total employment - Emploi total - Empleo total					
Total - Total - Total										
ICSE-93 - CISP-93 - CISE-93										
Total						2 370.8				
1						322.8				
2,3						1 692.0				
5 [4]						355.3				
Men - Hommes - Hombres										
ICSE-93 - CISP-93 - CISE-93										
Total						1 388.3				
1						211.0				
2,3						922.0				
5 [4]						255.2				
Women - Femmes - Mujeres										
ICSE-93 - CISP-93 - CISE-93										
Total						982.5				
1						111.8				
2,3						770.0				
5 [4]						100.1				
Maroc (BA) [3]					Total employment - Emploi total - Empleo total					
Total - Total - Total										
ICSE-93 - CISP-93 - CISE-93										
Total				9 487.5 [5]	9 602.8	9 821.9	9 913.3	9 927.7	10 056.2	10 189.3
1				3 604.6 [5]	3 654.6	3 649.2	3 705.2	4 286.2	4 510.1	4 468.0
2				222.9 [5]	242.4	224.2	246.1	252.0	233.2	257.9
3				2 479.4 [5]	2 509.7	2 559.0	2 582.7	2 427.5	2 507.6	2 842.1
4				216.8 [5]	238.6	237.0	232.3	227.3	167.7	160.8
5				2 832.2 [5]	2 853.3	3 145.6	3 138.9	2 721.8	2 626.6	2 450.2
6				131.6 [5]	104.2	6.9	8.2	12.9	11.1	10.2
Men - Hommes - Hombres										
ICSE-93 - CISP-93 - CISE-93										
Total				7 100.6 [5]	7 074.8	7 155.0	7 240.7	7 233.3	7 323.7	7 453.5
1				2 807.9 [5]	2 805.4	2 812.4	2 859.5	3 387.6	3 577.5	3 538.6
2				210.0 [5]	230.9	212.6	229.7	236.4	217.5	237.3
3				2 190.1 [5]	2 204.3	2 258.2	2 284.2	2 164.6	2 161.1	2 403.2
4				200.1 [5]	216.1	218.0	212.2	207.3	150.4	147.5
5				1 579.8 [5]	1 526.7	1 649.5	1 650.4	1 230.8	1 210.5	1 120.7
6				112.6 [5]	91.4	4.3	4.7	6.7	6.8	6.3
Women - Femmes - Mujeres										
ICSE-93 - CISP-93 - CISE-93										
Total				2 387.0 [5]	2 528.0	2 666.9	2 672.6	2 694.4	2 732.6	2 735.8
1				796.6 [5]	849.1	836.8	845.7	898.6	932.6	929.5
2				13.0 [5]	11.5	11.6	16.5	15.6	15.7	20.6
3				289.3 [5]	305.5	300.8	298.4	262.9	346.5	438.9
4				16.7 [5]	22.5	19.0	20.1	20.0	17.3	13.3
5				1 252.4 [5]	1 326.6	1 496.2	1 488.4	1 491.0	1 416.1	1 329.5
6				19.1 [5]	12.8	2.6	3.5	6.1	4.3	3.9
Mauritius (BA) [6] [7]					Total employment - Emploi total - Empleo total					
Total - Total - Total										
ICSE-93 - CISP-93 - CISE-93										
Total						487.0	490.4	499.1	502.1 [8]	519.0
1						389.8	394.4	401.4	397.7 [8]	415.1
2						14.7	12.8	14.5	16.1 [8]	16.9
3						71.3	71.4	70.6	73.6 [8]	73.9
4							0.7	1.0	0.8 [8]	0.3
5						10.0	10.5	10.3	10.9 [8]	10.7
6						1.2	1.3	1.3	3.0 [8]	2.1

Explanatory notes: see p. 77.

[1] Persons aged 6 years and over. [2] Excl. armed forces and conscripts. [3] Persons aged 15 years and over. [4] Incl. apprentices. [5] Persons aged 7 years and over. [6] Excl. armed forces. [7] Persons aged 16 years and over. [8] Prior to 2007: persons aged 15 years and over.

Notes explicatives: voir p. 80.

[1] Personnes âgées de 6 ans et plus. [2] Non compris les forces armées et les conscrits. [3] Personnes âgées de 15 ans et plus. [4] Y compris les apprentis. [5] Personnes âgées de 7 ans et plus. [6] Non compris les forces armées. [7] Personnes âgées de 16 ans et plus. [8] Avant 2006: personnes âgées de 15 ans et plus.

Notas explicativas: véase p. 83.

[1] Personas de 6 años y más. [2] Excl. las fuerzas armadas y los conscriptos. [3] Personas de 15 años y más. [4] Incl. los aprendices. [5] Personas de 7 años y más. [6] Excl. las fuerzas armadas. [7] Personas de 16 años y más. [8] Antes de 2006: personas de 15 años y más.

Total employment, by status in employment
Thousands

Emploi total, par situation dans la profession
Milliers

Empleo total, por situación en el empleo
Millares

	1999	2000	2001	2002	2003	2004	2005	2006	2007	2008
Mauritius (BA) [1][2]					Total employment - Emploi total - Empleo total					
Men - Hommes - Hombres										
ICSE-93 - CISP-93 - CISE-93										
Total	.	.	.	.	.	327.9	329.1	332.5	335.0 [3]	341.0
1						254.8 [4]	258.7	261.6	258.6 [3]	266.0
2						13.1	11.2	12.4	13.8 [3]	14.9
3						56.4	55.3	54.6	56.8 [3]	55.4
4							0.5	0.6	0.5 [3]	0.3
5						2.5	2.9	2.3	3.1 [3]	2.9
6						1.1	1.0	1.0	2.2 [3]	1.5
Women - Femmes - Mujeres										
ICSE-93 - CISP-93 - CISE-93										
Total	.	.	.	.	.	159.1	161.3	166.6	167.1 [3]	178.0
1						135.0 [4]	135.7	139.8	139.1 [3]	149.1
2						1.6	1.6	2.1	2.3 [3]	2.0
3						14.9	16.1	16.0	16.8 [3]	18.5
4							0.2	0.4	0.3 [3]	-
5						7.5	7.6	8.0	7.8 [3]	7.8
6						0.1	0.3	0.3	0.8 [3]	0.6
Namibia (BA) [5]					Total employment - Emploi total - Empleo total					
Total - Total - Total										
ICSE-93 - CISP-93 - CISE-93										
Total	.	431.849	.	.	.	385.329	.	.	.	.
1	.	268.604	.	.	.	280.329	.	.	.	.
2	.	35.326	.	.	.	21.686	.	.	.	.
3	.	105.102	.	.	.	64.404	.	.	.	.
5	.	14.343	.	.	.	16.867	.	.	.	.
6	.	8.474	.	.	.	1.696	.	.	.	.
Men - Hommes - Hombres										
ICSE-93 - CISP-93 - CISE-93										
Total	.	226.828	.	.	.	216.651	.	.	.	.
1	.	153.565	.	.	.	164.563	.	.	.	.
2	.	23.118	.	.	.	14.372	.	.	.	.
3	.	39.314	.	.	.	29.774	.	.	.	.
5	.	5.868	.	.	.	7.005	.	.	.	.
6	.	4.963	.	.	.	0.937	.	.	.	.
Women - Femmes - Mujeres										
ICSE-93 - CISP-93 - CISE-93										
Total	.	205.021	.	.	.	168.678	.	.	.	.
1	.	115.039	.	.	.	116.113	.	.	.	.
2	.	12.208	.	.	.	7.314	.	.	.	.
3	.	65.788	.	.	.	37.630	.	.	.	.
5	.	8.475	.	.	.	9.862	.	.	.	.
6	.	3.511	.	.	.	0.759	.	.	.	.
South Africa (BA) [6][7]					Total employment - Emploi total - Empleo total					
Total - Total - Total										
ICSE-93 - CISP-93 - CISE-93										
Total	.	.	.	.	.	.	.	.	13 234	13 713
1	.	.	.	.	.	.	.	.	10 902	11 573
2	.	.	.	.	.	.	.	.	1 946	753
3	.	.	.	.	.	.	.	.	300	1 267
5	.	.	.	.	.	.	.	.	53	120
6	.	.	.	.	.	.	.	.	33	-
Men - Hommes - Hombres										
ICSE-93 - CISP-93 - CISE-93										
Total	.	.	.	.	.	.	.	.	7 554	7 672
1	.	.	.	.	.	.	.	.	6 311	6 486
2	.	.	.	.	.	.	.	.	1 061	573
3	.	.	.	.	.	.	.	.	144	579
5	.	.	.	.	.	.	.	.	20	34
6	.	.	.	.	.	.	.	.	18	-
Women - Femmes - Mujeres										
ICSE-93 - CISP-93 - CISE-93										
Total	.	.	.	.	.	.	.	.	5 668	6 041
1	.	.	.	.	.	.	.	.	4 580	5 088
2	.	.	.	.	.	.	.	.	884	180
3	.	.	.	.	.	.	.	.	156	687
5	.	.	.	.	.	.	.	.	33	86
6	.	.	.	.	.	.	.	.	14	-

Explanatory notes: see p. 77.

[1] Excl. armed forces. [2] Persons aged 16 years and over. [3] Prior to 2007: persons aged 15 years and over. [4] Incl. apprentices. [5] Persons aged 15 to 69 years. [6] Persons aged 15 to 64 years. [7] Prior to 2008: persons aged 15 years and over; September of each year.

Notes explicatives: voir p. 80.

[1] Non compris les forces armées. [2] Personnes âgées de 16 ans et plus. [3] Avant 2006: personnes âgées de 15 ans et plus. [4] Y compris les apprentis. [5] Personnes âgées de 15 à 69 ans. [6] Personnes âgées de 15 à 64 ans. [7] Avant 2008: personnes âgées de 15 ans et plus; septembre de chaque année.

Notas explicativas: véase p. 83.

[1] Excl. las fuerzas armadas. [2] Personas de 16 años y más. [3] Antes de 2006: personas de 15 años y más. [4] Incl. los aprendices. [5] Personas de 15 a 69 años. [6] Personas de 15 a 64 años. [7] Antes de 2008: personas de 15 años y más; Septiembre de cada año.

Total employment,
by status
in employment
Thousands

Emploi total,
par situation
dans la profession
Milliers

Empleo total,
por situación
en el empleo
Millares

	1999	2000	2001	2002	2003	2004	2005	2006	2007	2008

Tunisie (BA) [1]   Total employment - Emploi total - Empleo total

Total - Total - Total
ICSE-93 - CISP-93 - CISE-93

	1999	2000	2001	2002	2003	2004	2005	2006	2007	2008
Total	2 635.0	2 704.9	2 788.8	2 852.0	2 951.2	.	.	.	.	.
1	1 801.4	1 842.6	1 885.1	1 929.6	1 896.5	.	.	.	.	.
2,3	615.2	638.8	682.4	717.1	791.9	.	.	.	.	.
5	206.7	200.1	219.5	202.7	257.4	.	.	.	.	.
6	11.7	23.4	1.8	2.6	5.4	.	.	.	.	.

AMERICA-AMÉRIQUE-AMERICA

Argentina (BA) [2] [3] [4]   Total employment - Emploi total - Empleo total

Total - Total - Total
ICSE-93 - CISP-93 - CISE-93

	1999	2000	2001	2002	2003	2004	2005	2006	2007	2008
Total	8 285.2	8 261.7	8 143.4	8 016.1 |	8 956.2 [5]	9 415.0	9 638.7 |	10 040.5 [6]	.	.
1	6 000.0	5 975.9	5 845.6	5 743.3 |	6 590.1 [5]	6 977.6	7 182.0 |	7 608.3 [6]	.	.
2	372.3	395.6	359.8	302.6 |	337.6 [5]	388.5	396.0 |	414.3 [6]	.	.
3	1 798.7	1 789.5	1 845.9	1 879.1 |	1 869.1 [5]	1 921.4	1 943.1 |	1 905.9 [6]	.	.
5	112.2	95.3	88.9	89.3 |	148.4 [5]	127.5	117.6 |	112.0 [6]	.	.
6	1.9	5.4	3.2	1.8 |	9.9 [5]	.	- |	- [6]	.	.

Men - Hommes - Hombres
ICSE-93 - CISP-93 - CISE-93

	1999	2000	2001	2002	2003	2004	2005	2006	2007	2008
Total	4 971.4	4 942.0	4 832.4	4 653.6 |	5 150.9 [5]	5 446.9	5 557.3 |	5 786.7 [6]	.	.
1	3 485.8	3 439.6	3 325.0	3 118.5 |	3 600.7 [5]	3 857.5	3 956.1 |	4 197.2 [6]	.	.
2	290.0	297.7	278.8	237.9 |	253.3 [5]	295.2	297.9 |	307.3 [6]	.	.
3	1 150.4	1 167.3	1 197.2	1 259.7 |	1 233.5 [5]	1 253.9	1 264.5 |	1 239.5 [6]	.	.
5	44.6	33.9	30.0	36.4 |	56.6 [5]	40.4	38.8 |	42.7 [6]	.	.
6	0.6	3.4	1.4	1.1 |	6.3 [5]	.	- |	- [6]	.	.

Women - Femmes - Mujeres
ICSE-93 - CISP-93 - CISE-93

	1999	2000	2001	2002	2003	2004	2005	2006	2007	2008
Total	3 313.8	3 319.8	3 310.9	3 362.5 |	3 805.3 [5]	3 968.0	4 081.4 |	4 253.8 [6]	.	.
1	2 514.2	2 536.3	2 520.6	2 624.8 |	2 989.3 [5]	3 120.1	3 225.9 |	3 411.0 [6]	.	.
2	82.3	97.9	81.1	64.6 |	84.3 [5]	93.3	98.1 |	107.1 [6]	.	.
3	648.1	622.2	648.7	619.4 |	635.6 [5]	667.6	678.6 |	666.4 [6]	.	.
5	67.6	61.4	58.8	52.9 |	91.7 [5]	87.0	78.8 |	69.3 [6]	.	.
6	1.2	2.0	1.8	0.7 |	3.5 [5]	.	- |	- [6]	.	.

Aruba (BA) [1] [7]   Total employment - Emploi total - Empleo total

Total - Total - Total
ICSE-93 - CISP-93 - CISE-93

	1999	2000	2001	2002	2003	2004	2005	2006	2007	2008
Total	.	.	.	.	.	.	.	.	51.606	.
1	.	.	.	.	.	.	.	.	46.710	.
2	.	.	.	.	.	.	.	.	2.319	.
3	.	.	.	.	.	.	.	.	2.149	.
5	.	.	.	.	.	.	.	.	0.125	.
6	.	.	.	.	.	.	.	.	0.181	.

Men - Hommes - Hombres
ICSE-93 - CISP-93 - CISE-93

	1999	2000	2001	2002	2003	2004	2005	2006	2007	2008
Total	.	.	.	.	.	.	.	.	27.210	.
1	.	.	.	.	.	.	.	.	23.820	.
2	.	.	.	.	.	.	.	.	1.706	.
3	.	.	.	.	.	.	.	.	1.433	.
5	.	.	.	.	.	.	.	.	0.026	.
6	.	.	.	.	.	.	.	.	0.129	.

Women - Femmes - Mujeres
ICSE-93 - CISP-93 - CISE-93

	1999	2000	2001	2002	2003	2004	2005	2006	2007	2008
Total	.	.	.	.	.	.	.	.	24.396	.
1	.	.	.	.	.	.	.	.	22.890	.
2	.	.	.	.	.	.	.	.	0.613	.
3	.	.	.	.	.	.	.	.	0.716	.
5	.	.	.	.	.	.	.	.	0.099	.
6	.	.	.	.	.	.	.	.	0.052	.

Bolivia (BA) [2] [8]   Total employment - Emploi total - Empleo total

Total - Total - Total
ICSE-93 - CISP-93 - CISE-93

	1999	2000	2001	2002	2003	2004	2005	2006	2007	2008
Total	3 637.9	3 637.0	3 884.3	3 824.9	.	4 194.8	4 257.2	4 550.3	4 672.4	.
1	1 051.3	1 056.0	1 144.8	1 117.5	.	1 361.6	1 341.0	1 446.3	1 586.3	.
2	107.0	70.7	85.7	170.2	.	200.3	224.6	201.2	252.5	.
3	1 463.2	1 453.0	1 387.7	1 399.0	.	1 495.7	1 472.0	1 563.8	1 558.9	.
4	11.4	12.2	15.4	9.9	.	27.2	34.7	11.1	10.9	.
5	936.5	888.0	1 132.2	1 039.1	.	989.2	1 080.4	1 211.0	1 106.7	.
6	68.6	93.5	118.5	89.3	.	120.9	104.5	117.0	157.0	.

Explanatory notes: see p. 77.

[1] Persons aged 15 years and over. [2] Persons aged 10 years and over. [3] 31 Urban agglomerations. [4] Second semester. [5] Methodology revised; data not strictly comparable; Prior to 2003: May and October. [6] Prior to 2006: 28 urban agglomerations. [7] Oct. [8] Excl. conscripts.

Notes explicatives: voir p. 80.

[1] Personnes âgées de 15 ans et plus. [2] Personnes âgées de 10 ans et plus. [3] 31 agglomérations urbaines. [4] Second semestre. [5] Méthodologie révisée; les données ne sont pas strictement comparables; Avant 2003: mai et octobre. [6] Avant 2006: 28 agglomérations urbaines. [7] Oct. [8] Non compris les conscrits.

Notas explicativas: véase p. 83.

[1] Personas de 15 años y más. [2] Personas de 10 años y más. [3] 31 aglomerados úrbanos. [4] Segundo semestre. [5] Metodología revisada; los datos no son estrictamente comparables; antes de 2003: mayo y octubre. [6] Antes de 2006: 28 aglomerados úrbanos [7] Oct. [8] Excl. los conscriptos.

Total employment, by status in employment
Thousands

Emploi total, par situation dans la profession
Milliers

Empleo total, por situación en el empleo
Millares

	1999	2000	2001	2002	2003	2004	2005	2006	2007	2008
Bolivia (BA) [1] [2]				Total employment - Emploi total - Empleo total						
Men - Hommes - Hombres										
ICSE-93 - CISP-93 - CISE-93										
Total	2 000.5	2 032.2	2 128.4	2 160.2	.	2 283.0	2 356.0	2 505.6	2 577.0	.
1	739.8	733.6	801.6	781.2	.	975.5	942.6	963.6	1 109.9	.
2	84.1	54.9	60.9	136.1	.	163.1	169.8	158.7	184.9	.
3	838.5	930.7	820.9	837.1	.	773.8	830.7	943.4	878.6	.
4	11.4	12.2	14.7	9.6	.	26.1	30.2	11.1	10.1	.
5	323.2	298.7	425.7	393.0	.	341.7	380.3	420.5	386.6	.
6	3.4	2.0	4.6	3.1	.	2.9	2.4	8.2	6.8	.
Women - Femmes - Mujeres										
ICSE-93 - CISP-93 - CISE-93										
Total	1 637.4	1 604.9	1 755.8	1 664.8	.	1 911.7	1 901.1	2 044.7	2 095.4	.
1	311.5	321.0	343.1	336.2	.	386.1	398.3	482.7	476.4	.
2	22.9	16.0	24.8	34.0	.	37.1	54.8	42.5	67.5	.
3	624.6	585.8	566.8	561.8	.	721.9	641.3	620.3	680.3	.
4	-	-	0.7	0.4	.	1.1	4.5	-	0.8	.
5	613.3	589.0	706.5	646.1	.	647.5	700.1	790.4	720.1	.
6	65.2	91.5	114.0	86.2	.	118.0	102.1	108.7	150.2	.
Brasil (BA) [1] [3]				Total employment - Emploi total - Empleo total						
Total - Total - Total										
ICSE-93 - CISP-93 - CISE-93										
Total	.	.	76 098	78 959 ǀ	80 163 [4]	84 596	87 189	89 318	90 786	.
1	.	.	47 234	48 955 ǀ	49 756 [4]	53 172	54 709	56 838	58 815	.
2	.	.	3 211	3 352 ǀ	3 363 [4]	3 688	3 977	3 411		.
3	.	.	20 025	20 844 ǀ	21 379 [4]	22 062	18 853	18 924	19 213	.
5	.	.	5 625	5 805 ǀ	5 665 [4]	5 883	5 920	5 402	5 311	.
6	.	.	3	3 ǀ	- [4]	-	4 021	4 177	4 036	.
Men - Hommes - Hombres										
ICSE-93 - CISP-93 - CISE-93										
Total	.	.	45 127	46 334 ǀ	46 935 [4]	49 242	50 494	51 400	52 363	.
1	.	.	27 123	27 943 ǀ	28 208 [4]	30 012	30 934	31 811	32 980	.
2	.	.	2 459	2 482 ǀ	2 528 [4]	2 582	2 717	2 926	2 508	.
3	.	.	12 963	13 286 ǀ	13 635 [4]	13 975	12 895	12 816	12 962	.
5	.	.	2 579	2 621 ǀ	2 564 [4]	2 673	2 606	2 339	2 342	.
6	.	.	2	2 ǀ	- [4]	-	1 341	1 508	1 572	.
Women - Femmes - Mujeres										
ICSE-93 - CISP-93 - CISE-93										
Total	.	.	30 972	32 625 ǀ	33 228 [4]	35 354	36 696	37 918	38 423	.
1	.	.	20 110	21 012 ǀ	21 548 [4]	23 161	23 774	25 027	25 835	.
2	.	.	752	870 ǀ	835 [4]	897	971	1 051	904	.
3	.	.	7 062	7 558 ǀ	7 744 [4]	8 087	5 958	6 108	6 251	.
5	.	.	3 046	3 184 ǀ	3 101 [4]	3 210	3 313	3 063	2 969	.
6	.	.	1	0 ǀ	- [4]	-	2 679	2 669	2 464	.
Canada (BA) [5] [6] [7]				Total employment - Emploi total - Empleo total						
Total - Total - Total										
ICSE-93 - CISP-93 - CISE-93										
Total	14 389.8	14 758.6	14 946.7	15 307.9	15 665.1	15 949.7	16 169.7	16 484.3	16 866.4	17 125.8
1	11 937.6	12 373.6	12 668.6	12 988.8	13 265.2	13 497.9	13 658.2	13 986.3	14 251.4	14 496.2
2,3	2 407.1	2 343.1	2 245.6	2 286.6	2 366.1	2 422.3	2 486.0	2 469.7	2 589.7	2 604.3
5	44.8	41.9	32.5	32.5	33.8	29.6	25.6	28.3	25.3	25.3
Men - Hommes - Hombres										
ICSE-93 - CISP-93 - CISE-93										
Total	7 793.6	7 970.0	8 035.2	8 181.5	8 344.3	8 479.6	8 594.7	8 727.1	8 888.9	9 021.3
1	6 201.1	6 425.2	6 531.0	6 649.4	6 774.7	6 867.1	6 949.1	7 105.7	7 185.8	7 301.6
2,3	1 577.3	1 531.6	1 493.8	1 491.2	1 557.3	1 602.3	1 635.6	1 611.1	1 695.5	1 709.7
5	15.2	13.1	10.4	10.9	12.2	10.2	10.0	10.3	7.7	10.0
Women - Femmes - Mujeres										
ICSE-93 - CISP-93 - CISE-93										
Total	6 596.3	6 788.6	6 911.5	7 126.4	7 320.7	7 470.1	7 575.0	7 757.2	7 977.5	8 104.5
1	5 736.5	5 948.4	6 137.7	6 309.4	6 490.5	6 630.8	6 709.1	6 880.6	7 065.6	7 194.6
2,3	829.8	811.4	751.9	795.4	808.6	820.0	850.3	858.6	894.3	894.6
5	30.0	28.8	22.1	21.6	21.5	19.4	15.7	18.0	17.6	15.3

Explanatory notes: see p. 77.

[1] Persons aged 10 years and over. [2] Excl. conscripts. [3] Sep. of each year. [4] Prior to 2003: Excl. rural population of Rondônia, Acre, Amazonas, Roraima, Pará and Amapá. [5] Persons aged 15 years and over. [6] Excl. residents of the Territories and indigenous persons living on reserves. [7] Excl. full-time members of the armed forces.

Notes explicatives: voir p. 80.

[1] Personnes âgées de 10 ans et plus. [2] Non compris les conscrits. [3] Sept. de chaque année. [4] Avant 2003: Non compris la population rurale de Rondônia, Acre, Amazonas, Roraima, Pará et Amapá. [5] Personnes âgées de 15 ans et plus. [6] Non compris les habitants des "Territoires" et les populations indigènes vivant dans les réserves. [7] Non compris les membres à temps complet des forces armées.

Notas explicativas: véase p. 83.

[1] Personas de 10 años y más. [2] Excl. los conscriptos. [3] Sept. de cada año. [4] Antes de 2003: Excl. la población rural de Rondonia, Acre, Amazonas, Roraima, Pará y Amapá. [5] Personas de 15 años y más. [6] Excl. a los habitantes de los "Territorios" y a las poblaciones indígenas que viven en reservas. [7] Excl. los miembros a tiempo completo de las fuerzas armadas.

EMPLOYMENT — EMPLOI — EMPLEO

Total employment, by status in employment — Thousands
Emploi total, par situation dans la profession — Milliers
Empleo total, por situación en el empleo — Millares

Cayman Islands (BA) [1][2][3]

Total employment - Emploi total - Empleo total

Total - Total - Total
ICSE-93 - CISP-93 - CISE-93

	1999	2000	2001	2002	2003	2004	2005	2006	2007	2008
Total	.	.	.	.	.	.	.	35.016 +	35.081	37.450
1								31.433 +	32.227	33.933
2								3.583 +	1.309	1.951
3								- +	1.363	1.295
6								- +	0.181	0.251

Men - Hommes - Hombres
ICSE-93 - CISP-93 - CISE-93

	1999	2000	2001	2002	2003	2004	2005	2006	2007	2008
Total								18.408 +	18.305	19.355
1								15.913 +	16.343	16.810
2								2.495 +	0.870	1.463
3								- +	1.008	0.941
6								- +	0.100	0.141

Women - Femmes - Mujeres
ICSE-93 - CISP-93 - CISE-93

	1999	2000	2001	2002	2003	2004	2005	2006	2007	2008
Total								16.608 +	16.776	18.094
1								15.520 +	15.884	17.123
2								1.088 +	0.439	0.488
3								- +	0.355	0.353
6								- +	0.081	0.110

Colombia (BA) [5][6][7]

Total employment - Emploi total - Empleo total

Total - Total - Total
ICSE-93 - CISP-93 - CISE-93

	1999	2000	2001	2002	2003	2004	2005	2006	2007	2008
Total	.	.	15 813.5	15 844.3	16 650.1	16 704.0	17 154.9	16 701.6	17 076.5	17 425.7
1			7 798.5	7 953.5	8 181.8	8 166.8	8 824.2	9 524.1	9 351.3	8 520.4
2			681.4	723.5	728.1	844.8	890.4	480.0	761.6	807.1
3			6 388.9	6 308.4	6 626.1	6 761.2	6 512.6	6 188.0	6 180.4	7 373.5
5			907.1	814.7	1 070.4	895.4	882.1	471.8	747.1	720.1
6			37.5	44.2	44.3	35.7	45.6	37.7	36.2	4.6

Men - Hommes - Hombres
ICSE-93 - CISP-93 - CISE-93

	1999	2000	2001	2002	2003	2004	2005	2006	2007	2008
Total			9 658.1	9 689.2	10 106.6	10 196.8	10 491.3	10 202.0	10 399.9	10 611.1
1			4 620.6	4 640.0	4 879.9	4 790.3	5 321.8	5 431.1	5 582.3	5 020.0
2			542.0	542.0	555.0	653.3	688.3	360.1	562.5	628.0
3			4 003.5	4 145.6	4 181.7	4 376.3	4 097.2	4 173.0	3 893.9	4 669.7
5			462.5	330.0	466.2	356.7	354.0	216.0	335.1	289.3
6			29.5	31.6	23.8	20.3	29.9	22.3	26.1	4.0

Women - Femmes - Mujeres
ICSE-93 - CISP-93 - CISE-93

	1999	2000	2001	2002	2003	2004	2005	2006	2007	2008
Total			6 155.4	6 155.1	6 543.5	6 507.2	6 663.6	6 499.6	6 676.5	6 814.7
1			3 177.9	3 313.5	3 301.2	3 376.5	3 502.4	4 093.0	3 768.9	3 500.4
2			139.4	181.5	173.1	191.6	202.1	119.9	199.1	179.1
3			2 385.4	2 162.8	2 444.4	2 384.9	2 415.4	2 015.0	2 286.5	2 703.8
5			444.6	484.7	604.3	538.7	528.1	255.8	411.9	430.9
6			8.1	12.6	20.6	15.5	15.6	15.4	10.1	0.5

Costa Rica (BA) [8][9]

Total employment - Emploi total - Empleo total

Total - Total - Total
ICSE-93 - CISP-93 - CISE-93

	1999	2000	2001	2002	2003	2004	2005	2006	2007	2008
Total	1 300.1	1 318.6	1 552.9	1 586.5	1 640.4	1 653.9	1 776.9	1 829.9	1 925.7	1 957.7
1	922.6	933.1	1 068.9	1 083.6	1 139.6	1 137.3	1 268.9	1 293.7	1 406.6	1 426.6
2	105.3	75.3	123.4	125.3	140.8	134.2	132.5	140.9	139.2	146.7
3	233.7	276.5	315.6	328.4	316.7	343.1	334.9	354.4	344.8	354.0
5	38.6	33.8	45.0	49.2	43.3	39.3	40.7	40.9	35.1	30.4

Men - Hommes - Hombres
ICSE-93 - CISP-93 - CISE-93

	1999	2000	2001	2002	2003	2004	2005	2006	2007	2008
Total	879.6	902.5	1 013.0	.	1 069.0	1 093.6	1 153.9	1 172.6	1 222.6	1 229.5
1	608.6	614.3	683.9	.	733.4	741.6	813.2	809.0	871.4	877.5
2	86.6	63.3	96.8	.	112.8	109.6	105.9	110.1	111.0	115.5
3	163.5	205.0	206.5	.	200.1	222.9	215.6	233.7	224.5	225.2
5	20.8	19.9	25.8	.	22.7	19.5	19.1	19.9	15.7	11.3

Women - Femmes - Mujeres
ICSE-93 - CISP-93 - CISE-93

	1999	2000	2001	2002	2003	2004	2005	2006	2007	2008
Total	420.5	416.1	539.9	.	571.4	560.3	623.0	657.3	703.1	728.2
1	314.0	318.8	385.0	.	406.2	395.8	455.7	484.7	535.2	549.1
2	18.7	11.9	26.6	.	28.1	24.6	26.5	30.8	28.2	31.2
3	70.1	71.5	109.1	.	116.6	120.2	119.3	120.8	120.2	128.8
5	17.7	13.9	19.2	.	20.6	19.8	21.5	21.1	19.4	19.1

Explanatory notes: see p. 77.

[1] Persons aged 15 years and over. [2] Excl. armed forces and conscripts. [3] Oct. [4] April. [5] From 2001, figures revised on the basis of the 2005 census results. [6] Excl. armed forces. [7] Persons aged 10 years and over. [8] Persons aged 12 years and over. [9] July of each year.

Notes explicatives: voir p. 80.

[1] Personnes âgées de 15 ans et plus. [2] Non compris les forces armées et les conscrits. [3] Oct. [4] Avril. [5] A partir de 2001, données révisées sur la base des résultats du recensement de 2005. [6] Non compris les forces armées. [7] Personnes âgées de 10 ans et plus. [8] Personnes âgées de 12 ans et plus. [9] Juillet de chaque année.

Notas explicativas: véase p. 83.

[1] Personas de 15 años y más. [2] Excl. las fuerzas armadas y los conscriptos. [3] Oct. [4] Abril. [5] A partir de 2001, datos revisados de acuerdocon los resultados del censo de 2005. [6] Excl. las fuerzas armadas. [7] Personas de 10 años y más. [8] Personas de 12 años y más. [9] Julio de cada año.

Total employment, by status in employment / Emploi total, par situation dans la profession / Empleo total, por situación en el empleo

Thousands — Milliers — Millares

	1999	2000	2001	2002	2003	2004	2005	2006	2007	2008
Cuba (BA) [1][2]				Total employment - Emploi total - Empleo total						
Total - Total - Total										
ICSE-93 - CISP-93 - CISE-93										
Total	4 359.4	4 379.3	4 505.1	4 558.2	4 607.0	4 641.7	4 722.5	4 754.6	4 867.7	4 948.2 [3]
1	3 552.3	3 548.3	3 609.8	3 655.5	3 673.9	3 702.7	3 795.5	3 898.4	4 045.9	4 120.9 [3]
3	482.2	507.6	576.9	585.9	640.3	658.9	655.7	599.2	579.7	593.5 [3]
4	324.9	323.4	318.5	316.9	292.7	280.1	271.3	257.0	242.1	233.8 [3]
Men - Hommes - Hombres										
ICSE-93 - CISP-93 - CISE-93										
Total	2 814.5	2 819.8	2 906.3	2 926.8	2 945.8	2 955.7	2 998.5	2 985.8	3 016.0	3 073.0 [3]
1	2 141.9	2 121.7	2 148.1	2 159.4	2 157.8	2 158.9	2 212.7	2 271.4	2 314.3	2 370.2 [3]
3	405.3	432.7	496.9	509.8	549.4	566.7	563.0	516.3	501.3	509.7 [3]
4	267.3	265.3	261.3	257.5	238.6	230.1	222.8	198.1	200.4	193.1 [3]
Women - Femmes - Mujeres										
ICSE-93 - CISP-93 - CISE-93										
Total	1 544.9	1 559.5	1 598.8	1 631.4	1 661.2	1 686.0	1 724.0	1 768.0	1 851.7	1 875.2 [3]
1	1 410.3	1 426.5	1 461.6	1 496.1	1 516.1	1 543.8	1 582.8	1 627.0	1 731.6	1 750.7 [3]
3	77.0	74.9	80.0	76.0	90.9	92.2	92.7	82.9	78.4	83.8 [3]
4	57.6	58.1	57.2	59.3	54.1	50.0	48.5	58.9	41.7	40.7 [3]
Chile (BA) [1][4]				Total employment - Emploi total - Empleo total						
Total - Total - Total										
ICSE-93 - CISP-93 - CISE-93										
Total	5 404.5	5 381.5	5 479.4	5 531.3	5 675.1	5 862.9	5 905.0	6 411.0	6 566.1	6 740.4
1	3 740.1	3 736.0	3 759.3	3 787.3	3 872.6	3 996.1	4 142.8	4 556.8	4 736.1	4 903.9
2	178.4	162.1	166.3	157.9	165.1	181.9	169.5	187.8	200.6	194.2
3	1 359.9	1 358.0	1 444.0	1 469.8	1 522.9	1 556.1	1 472.9	1 544.4	1 522.6	1 531.8
5	126.1	125.4	109.9	116.2	114.5	128.8	119.9	122.1	106.9	110.5
Men - Hommes - Hombres										
ICSE-93 - CISP-93 - CISE-93										
Total	3 603.6	3 600.5	3 663.7	3 697.0	3 749.7	3 816.1	3 840.2	4 131.1	4 188.4	4 239.4
1	2 403.4	2 402.8	2 427.7	2 444.3	2 463.6	2 524.7	2 603.1	2 874.9	2 967.1	3 044.6
2	144.4	125.5	131.7	129.6	131.4	142.8	134.8	148.6	160.2	148.2
3	995.9	1 014.8	1 057.6	1 070.8	1 104.0	1 089.4	1 049.3	1 052.8	1 021.4	1 002.4
5	60.1	57.4	46.7	52.3	50.8	59.2	53.1	54.7	39.7	44.3
Women - Femmes - Mujeres										
ICSE-93 - CISP-93 - CISE-93										
Total	1 800.9	1 781.0	1 815.8	1 834.3	1 925.4	2 046.8	2 064.8	2 282.8	2 377.7	2 501.0
1	1 336.8	1 333.2	1 331.6	1 343.1	1 409.1	1 471.4	1 539.7	1 681.9	1 769.0	1 859.3
2	34.0	36.6	34.6	28.3	33.7	39.2	34.7	39.2	40.4	46.0
3	364.1	343.2	386.4	399.1	418.9	466.7	423.6	491.5	501.2	529.4
5	66.0	68.0	63.2	63.9	63.7	69.6	66.8	68.5	67.2	66.3
República Dominicana (BA) [5]				Total employment - Emploi total - Empleo total						
Total - Total - Total										
ICSE-93 - CISP-93 - CISE-93										
Total	2 979.5	3 041.1	3 001.7	3 105.5	3 093.0	3 212.8	3 279.1	3 469.9	3 550.9	.
1	1 549.3	1 713.5	1 646.7	1 674.0	1 674.7	1 769.8	1 728.0	1 841.9	1 903.5	.
2	101.5	92.6	105.9	100.5	99.6	157.6	151.3	132.2	141.7	.
3	1 263.6	1 168.5	1 196.6	1 282.1	1 265.9	1 221.7	1 284.8	1 379.6	1 397.1	.
5	65.0	66.5	52.4	48.9	52.8	63.7	115.1	116.2	108.5	.
Men - Hommes - Hombres										
ICSE-93 - CISP-93 - CISE-93										
Total	2 069.9	2 027.9	2 010.7	2 055.7	2 053.1	2 148.4	2 175.4	2 272.0	2 336.8	.
1	957.1	1 007.2	975.4	967.5	953.0	1 026.4	994.9	1 033.0	1 086.4	.
2	75.7	74.0	83.4	78.8	80.9	125.2	119.6	97.6	110.9	.
3	997.5	905.5	923.7	980.0	987.0	956.6	1 000.8	1 069.5	1 072.5	.
5	39.6	41.2	28.1	28.9	32.2	40.2	60.2	71.9	66.9	.
Women - Femmes - Mujeres										
ICSE-93 - CISP-93 - CISE-93										
Total	909.6	1 013.2	991.1	1 050.3	1 039.9	1 064.4	1 103.7	1 197.9	1 214.1	.
1	592.2	706.3	671.3	706.5	721.7	743.4	733.1	808.8	817.1	.
2	25.8	18.6	22.6	21.8	18.6	32.4	31.7	34.6	30.8	.
3	266.2	263.1	272.9	302.1	278.9	265.1	284.0	310.2	324.5	.
5	25.4	25.3	24.3	19.9	20.6	23.5	54.9	44.3	41.6	.

Explanatory notes: see p. 77.

[1] Persons aged 15 years and over. [2] Dec. [3] February - April [4] Fourth quarter of each year. [5] Persons aged 10 years and over.

Notes explicatives: voir p. 80.

[1] Personnes âgées de 15 ans et plus. [2] Déc. [3] Février - Avril [4] Quatrième trimestre de chaque année. [5] Personnes âgées de 10 ans et plus.

Notas explicativas: véase p. 83.

[1] Personas de 15 años y más. [2] Dic. [3] Febrero - Abril [4] Cuarto trimestre de cada año. [5] Personas de 10 años y más.

EMPLOYMENT — EMPLOI — EMPLEO

	Total employment, by status in employment (Thousands)	Emploi total, par situation dans la profession (Milliers)	Empleo total, por situación en el empleo (Millares)

	1999	2000	2001	2002	2003	2004	2005	2006	2007	2008
Ecuador (BA) [1][2][3]				Total employment - Emploi total - Empleo total						
Total - Total - Total ICSE-93 - CISP-93 - CISE-93										
Total	3 226.1	3 376.1	3 673.2 [4]	3 459.4	3 531.2	3 858.5	3 891.9	4 031.6		
1	1 914.3	2 007.5	2 182.3 [4]	2 019.4	2 165.0	2 244.9	2 340.6	2 405.7		
2	273.7	155.9	214.5 [4]	238.2	183.6	266.6	247.8	261.4		
3	854.8	1 010.5	1 029.5 [4]	1 022.8	1 028.7	1 090.6	1 085.8	1 079.8		
5	183.2	202.2	247.0 [4]	178.9	154.0	256.5	217.6	284.7		
6	-	-	- [4]	-	-	-	-	-		
Men - Hommes - Hombres ICSE-93 - CISP-93 - CISE-93										
Total	1 978.3	2 078.2	2 211.7 [4]	2 131.7	.	2 288.5	2 327.8	2 416.5		
1	1 203.6	1 258.2	1 379.1 [4]	1 288.6	.	1 424.1	1 451.1	1 525.9		
2	213.7	123.5	163.5 [4]	178.9	.	190.4	178.9	188.2		
3	501.5	627.9	570.9 [4]	599.9	.	589.9	627.7	596.6		
5	59.5	68.6	98.1 [4]	64.3	.	84.1	70.1	105.8		
6	-	-	- [4]	-	.	-	-	-		
Women - Femmes - Mujeres ICSE-93 - CISP-93 - CISE-93										
Total	1 247.8	1 297.9	1 461.6 [4]	1 327.7	.	1 570.1	1 564.0	1 615.1		
1	710.7	749.3	803.1 [4]	730.9	.	820.8	889.6	879.8		
2	60.0	32.4	51.0 [4]	59.3	.	76.1	68.9	73.2		
3	353.4	382.6	458.6 [4]	422.9	.	500.7	458.2	483.2		
5	123.7	133.6	148.8 [4]	114.7	.	172.4	147.4	178.9		
6	-	-	- [4]	-	.	-	-	-		
El Salvador (BA) [1][5]				Total employment - Emploi total - Empleo total						
Total - Total - Total ICSE-93 - CISP-93 - CISE-93										
Total	2 182.5	2 198.9	2 275.2	2 219.6	2 280.7	2 253.6	2 283.6	2 337.1	2 419.2	
1	1 313.4	1 145.8	1 177.3	1 131.8	1 219.6	1 236.4	1 188.7	1 278.2	1 303.9	
2	95.9	118.4	103.6	102.2	105.8	96.5	99.6	100.7	104.7	
3	578.8	647.8	625.6	669.5	638.8	630.9	661.0	614.0	658.7	
4	9.5	8.2	3.4	0.9	1.2	1.8	0.6	0.4	0.3	
5	182.9	173.7	246.3	202.8	198.2	173.2	224.8	216.2	228.0	
6	2.1	105.0	119.0	112.5	117.0	114.9	108.8	127.6	123.5	
Men - Hommes - Hombres ICSE-93 - CISP-93 - CISE-93										
Total	1 294.5	1 301.2	1 354.3	1 292.0	1 328.2	1 332.7	1 330.6	1 342.0	1 401.8	
1	831.7	776.0	808.7	753.1	817.0	856.0	803.0	854.9	874.7	
2	73.4	90.4	77.1	78.4	79.9	71.1	72.0	73.2	72.7	
3	272.5	304.8	297.5	311.6	295.7	284.3	309.4	274.3	301.4	
4	8.6	8.1	3.3	0.8	1.1	1.6	0.6	0.4	0.3	
5	106.8	107.5	148.3	123.0	112.2	102.1	126.8	117.6	126.6	
6	1.4	14.5	19.3	25.1	22.2	17.6	18.9	21.7	26.0	
Women - Femmes - Mujeres ICSE-93 - CISP-93 - CISE-93										
Total	888.1	897.8	920.9	927.6	952.5	920.9	952.9	995.1	1 017.3	
1	481.7	369.8	368.6	378.7	402.6	380.4	385.8	423.3	429.2	
2	22.4	28.0	26.5	23.7	25.9	25.4	27.6	27.5	32.0	
3	306.3	343.0	328.0	357.9	343.1	346.5	351.6	339.7	357.2	
4	0.9	0.2	0.1	0.1	0.1	0.1	-	0.0	-	
5	76.1	66.2	98.0	79.8	86.0	71.1	98.0	98.6	101.4	
6	0.7	90.6	99.7	87.4	94.8	97.3	89.9	105.9	97.5	
Honduras (BA) [1][6]				Total employment - Emploi total - Empleo total						
Total - Total - Total ICSE-93 - CISP-93 - CISE-93										
Total	2 299.0 [7]	.	2 284.4	2 348.0	2 421.8	2 434.2	2 541.8	2 721.8	2 836.1	
1	1 075.8 [7]	.	1 117.9	1 093.5	1 114.6	1 172.3	1 269.5	1 288.4	1 348.6	
2	79.9 [7]	.	76.4	64.7	77.0	89.0	60.0	73.6	66.0	
3	832.9 [7]	.	808.0	900.4	946.7	875.9	934.4	1 048.6	1 089.0	
5	298.8 [7]	.	282.1	289.4	283.6	297.1	277.5	310.8	332.5	
Men - Hommes - Hombres ICSE-93 - CISP-93 - CISE-93										
Total	1 472.1 [7]	.	1 533.4	1 591.0	1 607.0	1 633.9	1 735.1	1 786.9	1 848.7	
1	708.1 [7]	.	739.5	733.2	750.0	771.9	845.3	850.5	894.0	
2	64.0 [7]	.	57.8	47.5	58.8	70.4	46.0	53.7	48.8	
3	510.7 [7]	.	539.1	604.3	596.5	567.7	632.8	673.4	682.5	
5	180.3 [7]	.	196.9	206.9	201.6	224.0	210.8	209.0	223.2	

Explanatory notes: see p. 77.

[1] Persons aged 10 years and over. [2] Urban areas. [3] Nov. of each year. [4] July. [5] Dec. [6] Excl. armed forces. [7] March.

Notes explicatives: voir p. 80.

[1] Personnes âgées de 10 ans et plus. [2] Régions urbaines. [3] Nov. de chaque année. [4] Juillet. [5] Déc. [6] Non compris les forces armées. [7] Mars.

Notas explicativas: véase p. 83.

[1] Personas de 10 años y más. [2] Areas urbanas. [3] Nov. de cada año. [4] Julio. [5] Dic. [6] Excl. las fuerzas armadas. [7] Marzo.

	Total employment, by status in employment Thousands			Emploi total, par situation dans la profession Milliers				Empleo total, por situación en el empleo Millares		
	1999	2000	2001	2002	2003	2004	2005	2006	2007	2008

Honduras (BA) [1] [2]   Total employment - Emploi total - Empleo total

Women - Femmes - Mujeres
ICSE-93 - CISP-93 - CISE-93

Total	826.9 [3]	.	751.0	757.0	814.8	800.3	806.6	934.9	987.4	.
1	367.4 [3]	.	378.3	360.3	364.6	400.3	424.2	438.0	454.6	.
2	15.9 [3]	.	18.6	17.2	18.2	18.6	14.1	18.8	17.2	.
3	322.2 [3]	.	268.9	296.1	350.2	308.2	301.6	375.2	406.4	.
5	118.5 [3]	.	85.2	83.4	81.9	73.1	66.7	101.8	109.3	.

Jamaica (BA) [4]   Total employment - Emploi total - Empleo total

Total - Total - Total
ICSE-93 - CISP-93 - CISE-93

Total	936.8	935.6	942.3	1 025.9	1 056.5	1 058.7	1 091.7	1 129.5	1 170.2	1 167.8
1	551.6	551.8	560.0	629.0	644.0	647.2	676.7	691.7	738.9	703.3
2	25.7	25.0	25.9	25.5	29.1	27.3	33.9	35.0	37.4	36.4
3	334.1	335.7	332.1	352.8	364.3	368.2	363.0	386.2	376.3	412.6
5	20.3	18.8	19.7	14.7	14.0	13.7	13.9	13.6	14.3	13.5
6	5.1	4.3	4.6	3.9	5.1	2.3	4.2	3.0	3.3	2.0

Men - Hommes - Hombres
ICSE-93 - CISP-93 - CISE-93

Total	551.9	552.5	556.6	596.3	615.3	613.9	629.3	649.8	670.4	658.3
1	302.5	303.4	308.3	338.1	346.1	354.5	368.1	374.6	396.9	364.0
2	19.0	18.8	21.1	17.2	20.5	19.7	25.5	25.0	26.7	25.6
3	219.3	221.0	217.9	235.0	241.3	234.9	230.8	246.1	242.0	265.1
5	8.7	7.2	6.4	3.9	4.2	3.1	2.4	3.2	3.5	2.7
6	2.4	2.1	2.9	2.1	3.2	1.7	2.5	0.9	1.3	0.9

Women - Femmes - Mujeres
ICSE-93 - CISP-93 - CISE-93

Total	384.9	383.1	385.7	429.6	441.2	444.8	462.4	479.7	499.8	509.5
1	249.1	248.4	251.7	290.9	297.9	292.7	308.6	317.1	342.0	339.3
2	6.7	6.2	4.8	8.3	8.6	7.6	8.4	10.0	10.7	10.8
3	114.8	114.7	114.2	117.8	123.0	133.3	132.2	140.1	134.3	147.5
5	11.6	11.6	13.3	10.8	9.8	10.6	11.5	10.4	10.8	10.8
6	2.7	2.2	1.7	1.8	1.9	0.6	1.7	2.1	2.0	1.1

México (BA) [4] [5]   Total employment - Emploi total - Empleo total

Total - Total - Total
ICSE-93 - CISP-93 - CISE-93

Total	37 279.9	38 044.5	38 065.8	38 939.7	39 221.5	40 561.0	40 791.8	42 197.8	42 906.7	43 866.7
1	23 003.4	24 294.9	24 144.2	24 521.1	24 782.8	25 664.9	26 230.3	27 592.0	28 104.0	28 905.4
2	1 543.1	1 649.3	1 713.9	1 700.5	1 600.1	1 746.7	1 908.5	2 057.3	2 161.9	2 169.1
3	9 098.2	8 918.0	9 140.3	9 430.5	9 737.1	9 956.3	9 615.2	9 606.1	9 704.3	9 867.5
5	3 622.8	3 171.1	3 056.9	3 276.3	3 085.6	3 178.9	3 037.8	2 942.4	2 936.4	2 924.7
6	12.4	11.3	10.5	11.1	16.0	14.2	0.0	0.0	0.0	0.0

Men - Hommes - Hombres
ICSE-93 - CISP-93 - CISE-93

Total	24 805.7	25 014.1	25 055.1	25 422.8	25 713.5	26 138.0	25 853.1	26 597.9	26 840.6	27 401.7
1	15 274.0	15 876.8	15 781.1	15 977.6	16 255.8	16 622.8	16 589.6	17 412.4	17 638.2	18 179.4
2	1 308.7	1 392.2	1 469.9	1 444.0	1 368.2	1 469.8	1 603.1	1 693.7	1 753.2	1 766.3
3	6 383.6	6 202.0	6 292.1	6 398.6	6 532.0	6 536.3	6 249.4	6 168.3	6 127.1	6 133.2
5	1 828.3	1 533.2	1 502.4	1 593.7	1 542.8	1 495.8	1 411.0	1 323.5	1 322.2	1 322.7
6	11.2	9.8	9.7	9.0	14.8	13.3	0.0	0.0	0.0	0.0

Women - Femmes - Mujeres
ICSE-93 - CISP-93 - CISE-93

Total	12 474.2	13 030.4	13 010.6	13 516.8	13 508.0	14 423.0	14 938.7	15 599.9	16 066.0	16 465.0
1	7 729.3	8 418.1	8 363.1	8 543.6	8 527.0	9 042.2	9 640.7	10 179.7	10 465.8	10 726.0
2	234.4	257.0	243.9	256.5	231.9	276.8	305.4	363.5	408.8	402.7
3	2 714.7	2 716.0	2 848.2	3 031.9	3 205.1	3 420.0	3 365.8	3 437.8	3 577.2	3 734.4
5	1 794.5	1 637.9	1 554.5	1 682.7	1 542.8	1 683.1	1 626.9	1 618.9	1 614.3	1 602.0
6	1.2	1.5	0.9	2.2	1.2	0.9	0.0	0.0	0.0	0.0

Netherlands Antilles (BA) [6] [7] [8]   Total employment - Emploi total - Empleo total

Total - Total - Total
ICSE-93 - CISP-93 - CISE-93

Total	.	52.2	.	49.1 [9]	52.1	51.5	51.3	52.1	53.8	.
1	.	45.8	.	37.7 [9]	39.2	38.7	39.1	40.2	41.3	.
2	.	1.7	.	4.8 [9]	5.2	5.3	5.7	6.6	6.2	.
3	.	3.0	.	5.7 [9]	6.9	6.9	5.9	4.7	5.9	.
5	.	0.3	.	0.2 [9]	0.3	0.3	0.2	0.3	0.1	.
6	.	1.4	.	0.6 [9]	0.6	0.3	0.5	0.2	0.2	.

Explanatory notes: see p. 77.

[1] Excl. armed forces. [2] Persons aged 10 years and over. [3] March. [4] Persons aged 14 years and over. [5] Second quarter of each year. [6] Persons aged 15 years and over. [7] Curaçao. [8] Oct. of each year. [9] Methodology revised; data not strictly comparable.

Notes explicatives: voir p. 80.

[1] Non compris les forces armées. [2] Personnes âgées de 10 ans et plus. [3] Mars. [4] Personnes âgées de 14 ans et plus. [5] Deuxième trimestre de chaque année. [6] Personnes âgées de 15 ans et plus. [7] Curaçao. [8] Oct. de chaque année. [9] Méthodologie révisée; les données ne sont pas strictement comparables.

Notas explicativas: véase p. 83.

[1] Excl. las fuerzas armadas. [2] Personas de 10 años y más. [3] Marzo. [4] Personas de 14 años y más. [5] Segundo trimestre de cada año. [6] Personas de 15 años y más. [7] Curaçao. [8] Oct. de cada año. [9] Metodología revisada; los datos no son estrictamente comparables.

EMPLOYMENT — EMPLOI — EMPLEO

Total employment, by status in employment (Thousands) — **Emploi total, par situation dans la profession** (Milliers) — **Empleo total, por situación en el empleo** (Millares)

	1999	2000	2001	2002	2003	2004	2005	2006	2007	2008
Nicaragua (BA)[1]					Total employment - Emploi total - Empleo total					
Total - Total - Total										
ICSE-93 - CISP-93 - CISE-93										
Total	.	.	.	.	1 917.0	1 973.1	2 080.9	2 089.8	.	.
1					904.2	961.8	1 033.1	1 054.8		
2					83.2	82.9	98.7	88.8		
3					666.5	668.6	663.3	708.3		
4						5.0	5.8	2.6		
5					263.0 [2]	254.8	279.8	230.6		
6								4.7		
Men - Hommes - Hombres										
ICSE-93 - CISP-93 - CISE-93										
Total	.	.	.	.	1 178.5	1 239.3	1 296.6	1 303.5	.	.
1					547.0	590.8	637.0	648.1		
2					65.6	67.4	78.8	69.4		
3					391.5	399.1	388.9	422.4		
4						3.5	3.4	1.8		
5					174.6 [2]	178.6	188.3	159.1		
6								2.7		
Women - Femmes - Mujeres										
ICSE-93 - CISP-93 - CISE-93										
Total	.	.	.	.	738.4	733.8	784.3	786.3	.	.
1					357.3	371.0	396.2	406.8		
2					17.6	15.5	19.9	19.4		
3					275.1	269.5	274.4	285.9		
4						1.6	2.4	0.8		
5					88.4 [2]	76.3	91.5	71.5		
6								2.0		
Panamá (BA)[3][4]					Total employment - Emploi total - Empleo total					
Total - Total - Total										
ICSE-93 - CISP-93 - CISE-93										
Total	961.4	940.1	984.2	1 049.5	1 080.5	1 134.7	1 188.3	1 210.7	1 264.0	1 333.8
1	642.1	627.0	654.6	685.6	701.4	747.2	771.8	801.7	873.3	925.8
2	28.1	26.4	26.2	32.4	33.0	38.6	38.3	39.8	40.6	45.3
3	266.2	262.5	270.0	299.8	309.5	313.5	333.0	325.3	312.9	319.5
4	-	-	-	-	-	0.5	0.4	0.1	0.1	0.1
5	25.0	24.2	33.3	31.8	36.6	34.9	44.8	43.9	37.1	43.1
Men - Hommes - Hombres										
ICSE-93 - CISP-93 - CISE-93										
Total	638.0	625.0	659.2	687.6	703.3	734.3	755.7	777.5	799.1	837.0
1	393.1	377.0	396.7	413.2	418.7	447.5	460.6	487.9	526.5	562.4
2	22.5	21.5	21.7	26.1	26.7	32.5	30.9	31.6	32.0	34.4
3	204.2	208.0	218.1	228.1	236.2	233.6	243.1	235.9	221.9	219.3
4	-	-	-	-	-	0.3	0.3	-	0.1	-
5	18.2	18.5	22.7	20.2	21.6	20.4	20.9	22.1	18.6	20.9
Women - Femmes - Mujeres										
ICSE-93 - CISP-93 - CISE-93										
Total	323.4	315.1	325.1	362.0	377.2	400.4	432.6	433.2	464.9	496.8
1	249.0	250.0	257.9	272.4	282.6	299.7	311.3	313.8	346.8	363.4
2	5.5	4.9	4.5	6.3	6.3	6.1	7.4	8.2	8.5	10.9
3	62.1	54.5	52.0	71.7	73.3	80.0	90.0	89.3	91.0	100.3
4	-	-	-	-	-	0.2	0.1	-	-	-
5	6.7	5.6	10.7	11.6	15.0	14.5	23.9	21.8	18.5	22.1
Paraguay (BA)[5][6]					Total employment - Emploi total - Empleo total					
Total - Total - Total										
ICSE-93 - CISP-93 - CISE-93										
Total	.	.	.	.	.	.	.	.	2 716.4	2 810.5
1									1 307.4	1 417.5
2									138.1	140.5
3									997.2	951.2
5									273.1	298.3
6									0.6	3.0
Men - Hommes - Hombres										
ICSE-93 - CISP-93 - CISE-93										
Total	.	.	.	.	.	.	.	.	1 653.6	1 726.4
1									809.9	884.5
2									108.2	116.0
3									556.7	545.6
5									178.6	179.4
6									0.2	0.9

Explanatory notes: see p. 77.

[1] Persons aged 10 years and over. [2] Incl. members of producers' cooperatives. [3] Persons aged 15 years and over. [4] Aug. of each year. [5] Persons aged 10 years and over. [6] Fourth quarter.

Notes explicatives: voir p. 80.

[1] Personnes âgées de 10 ans et plus. [2] Y compris les membres de coopératives de producteurs. [3] Personnes âgées de 15 ans et plus. [4] Août de chaque année. [5] Personnes âgées de 10 ans et plus. [6] Quatrième trimestre.

Notas explicativas: véase p. 83.

[1] Personas de 10 años y más. [2] Incl. los miembros de cooperativas de productores. [3] Personas de 15 años y más. [4] Agosto de cada año. [5] Personas de 10 años y más. [6] Cuarto trimestre.

EMPLOYMENT — EMPLOI — EMPLEO · 2D

Total employment, by status in employment — Thousands
Emploi total, par situation dans la profession — Milliers
Empleo total, por situación en el empleo — Millares

	1999	2000	2001	2002	2003	2004	2005	2006	2007	2008
Paraguay (BA) [1][2]				Total employment - Emploi total - Empleo total						
Women - Femmes - Mujeres ICSE-93 - CISP-93 - CISE-93										
Total	.	.	.	.	.	.	.	.	1 062.8	1 084.1
1	.	.	.	.	.	.	.	.	497.5	533.0
2	.	.	.	.	.	.	.	.	29.9	24.5
3	.	.	.	.	.	.	.	.	440.5	405.6
5	.	.	.	.	.	.	.	.	94.5	118.9
6	.	.	.	.	.	.	.	.	0.4	2.1
Perú (BA) [3][4]				Total employment - Emploi total - Empleo total						
Total - Total - Total ICSE-93 - CISP-93 - CISE-93										
Total	.	.	.	3 338.9 [2]	3 703.0 [5]	3 652.5	3 529.0	3 851.2	4 163.7	4 246.7
1	.	.	.	2 098.8 [2]	2 212.0 [5]	2 198.9	2 140.0	2 409.0	2 625.3	2 704.0
2	.	.	.	138.0 [2]	195.6 [5]	189.0	216.8	175.9	234.0	226.1
3	.	.	.	927.0 [2]	1 092.5 [5]	1 033.6	1 025.1	1 079.1	1 119.0	1 155.4
5	.	.	.	169.4 [2]	201.2 [5]	228.0	147.1	181.7	180.2	159.7
6	.	.	.	5.7 [2]	1.6 [5]	3.1	-	5.4	5.2	1.5
Men - Hommes - Hombres ICSE-93 - CISP-93 - CISE-93										
Total	.	.	.	1 834.1 [2]	2 074.6 [5]	2 054.0	1 981.3	2 133.6	2 269.0	2 294.8
1	.	.	.	1 181.3 [2]	1 261.4 [5]	1 278.5	1 242.4	1 382.5	1 494.0	1 501.5
2	.	.	.	109.4 [2]	145.7 [5]	148.7	153.7	115.8	165.8	166.6
3	.	.	.	485.1 [2]	589.5 [5]	535.6	529.8	564.4	539.0	559.7
5	.	.	.	55.7 [2]	77.3 [5]	89.2	55.5	69.1	67.3	67.0
6	.	.	.	2.7 [2]	0.6 [5]	1.9	-	1.7	3.0	-
Women - Femmes - Mujeres ICSE-93 - CISP-93 - CISE-93										
Total	.	.	.	1 504.7 [2]	1 628.4 [5]	1 598.5	1 547.7	1 717.6	1 894.7	1 951.8
1	.	.	.	917.6 [2]	950.6 [5]	920.3	897.6	1 026.5	1 131.4	1 202.4
2	.	.	.	28.5 [2]	49.9 [5]	40.3	63.1	60.2	68.2	59.5
3	.	.	.	442.0 [2]	503.0 [5]	498.0	495.3	514.7	580.0	595.6
5	.	.	.	113.6 [2]	123.9 [5]	138.7	91.7	112.6	112.9	92.7
6	.	.	.	3.0 [2]	1.0 [5]	1.2	-	3.7	2.2	1.5
Perú (BA) [3][6]				Total employment - Emploi total - Empleo total						
Total - Total - Total ICSE-93 - CISP-93 - CISE-93										
Total	7 211.2	7 128.4	7 619.9	7 578.2	8 165.7	8 238.6	8 216.0	8 694.0	9 197.8	9 445.9
1	3 298.2	3 091.6	3 329.9	4 107.1	4 181.4	4 254.0	4 260.9	4 698.9	4 960.6	5 144.3
2	444.2	400.7	443.2	378.3	429.9	454.7	499.1	472.6	566.7	530.1
3	2 570.1	2 586.1	2 837.2	2 476.2	2 819.6	2 723.3	2 744.1	2 795.6	2 994.2	3 134.7
5	503.1	527.4	589.4	596.5	707.8	779.0	684.4	701.7	648.4	606.5
6	395.7	522.6	420.2	20.2	27.0	27.6	27.6	25.2	27.9	30.3
Men - Hommes - Hombres ICSE-93 - CISP-93 - CISE-93										
Total	3 980.4	4 067.6	4 232.6	4 234.2	4 537.0	4 616.2	4 562.8	4 821.9	5 015.0	5 143.2
1	2 144.9	2 094.6	2 204.0	2 473.5	2 500.4	2 579.4	2 571.9	2 831.8	2 918.1	3 022.0
2	348.6	312.9	342.1	290.6	323.6	348.0	356.7	335.4	409.5	385.6
3	1 295.2	1 323.6	1 443.1	1 241.1	1 433.0	1 368.0	1 365.8	1 380.9	1 438.5	1 491.7
5	159.2	200.2	198.4	218.9	264.1	308.9	257.1	262.1	235.7	231.9
6	33.1	136.5	45.0	10.1	15.9	11.8	11.4	11.7	13.2	12.1
Women - Femmes - Mujeres ICSE-93 - CISP-93 - CISE-93										
Total	3 230.8	3 060.7	3 387.3	3 344.0	3 628.8	3 622.4	3 653.2	3 872.1	4 182.8	4 302.7
1	1 153.7	997.0	1 125.8	1 633.6	1 681.0	1 674.6	1 689.0	1 867.1	2 042.5	2 122.3
2	95.6	87.8	101.1	87.7	106.4	106.7	142.4	137.2	157.2	144.5
3	1 274.9	1 262.5	1 394.2	1 235.1	1 386.6	1 355.2	1 378.3	1 414.7	1 555.7	1 643.0
5	343.9	327.3	390.9	377.6	443.7	470.1	427.3	439.6	412.6	374.6
6	362.6	386.2	375.2	10.0	11.1	15.7	16.1	13.5	14.7	18.2
Puerto Rico (BA) [7][8]				Total employment - Emploi total - Empleo total						
Total - Total - Total ICSE-93 - CISP-93 - CISE-93										
Total	1 142	1 162	1 134	1 170	1 201	1 226	1 250	1 253	1 241	1 209
1	975	994	976	996	1 028	1 048	1 068	1 063	1 050	1 031
2,3	161	162	153	167	165	172	176	188	189	177
5	6	6	5	7	6	6	6	-	2	-

Explanatory notes: see p. 77.

[1] Persons aged 10 years and over. [2] Fourth quarter. [3] Persons aged 14 years and over. [4] Metropolitan Lima. [5] May-Dec. [6] Urban areas. [7] Persons aged 16 years and over. [8] Civilian labour force employed.

Notes explicatives: voir p. 80.

[1] Personnes âgées de 10 ans et plus. [2] Quatrième trimestre. [3] Personnes âgées de 14 ans et plus. [4] Lima métropolitaine. [5] Mai-déc. [6] Régions urbaines. [7] Personnes âgées de 16 ans et plus. [8] Main-d'oeuvre civile occupée.

Notas explicativas: véase p. 83.

[1] Personas de 10 años y más. [2] Cuarto trimestre. [3] Personas de 14 años y más. [4] Lima metropolitana. [5] Mayo-dic. [6] Areas urbanas. [7] Personas de 16 años y más. [8] Fuerza de trabajo civil ocupada.

| | Total employment, by status in employment
Thousands | | | Emploi total, par situation dans la profession
Milliers | | | Empleo total, por situación en el empleo
Millares | | |

	1999	2000	2001	2002	2003	2004	2005	2006	2007	2008
Puerto Rico (BA) [1][2]					Total employment - Emploi total - Empleo total					
Men - Hommes - Hombres										
ICSE-93 - CISP-93 - CISE-93										
Total	665	670	652	665	676	690	697	695	677	659
1	534	538	530	533	543	555	559	553	538	525
2,3	131	131	121	132	130	134	137	141	139	134
5	-	1	1	1	1	1	1	-	-	-
Women - Femmes - Mujeres										
ICSE-93 - CISP-93 - CISE-93										
Total	478	492	482	505	525	537	553	558	564	550
1	442	456	448	463	485	493	509	510	512	506
2,3	30	31	31	35	34	38	38	47	50	43
5	6	5	5	6	6	5	5	-	-	-
Trinidad and Tobago (BA) [3]					Total employment - Emploi total - Empleo total					
Total - Total - Total										
ICSE-93 - CISP-93 - CISE-93										
Total	489.4	503.1	514.1	525.1	534.1	562.3	574.0	.	.	.
1	373.9	386.0	392.6	405.7	416.9	442.1	453.7	.	.	.
2	20.1	23.7	26.9	25.9	25.0	25.0	25.3	.	.	.
3	81.6	81.8	84.7	83.1	82.9	84.4	84.8	.	.	.
5	8.8	7.2	5.5	5.3	5.1	5.0	5.0	.	.	.
6	4.9	4.4	4.4	4.9	4.2	5.7	5.2	.	.	.
Men - Hommes - Hombres										
ICSE-93 - CISP-93 - CISE-93										
Total	310.1	316.9	326.0	329.0	330.6	342.0	343.5	.	.	.
1	231.6	236.8	242.1	244.2	248.9	257.1	262.4	.	.	.
2	15.9	18.9	20.9	20.9	20.1	19.7	18.9	.	.	.
3	56.4	56.0	58.4	58.9	57.5	60.3	58.5	.	.	.
5	2.6	1.8	1.4	1.5	1.1	1.1	1.0	.	.	.
6	3.5	3.4	3.2	3.4	3.0	3.7	2.7	.	.	.
Women - Femmes - Mujeres										
ICSE-93 - CISP-93 - CISE-93										
Total	179.3	186.2	188.1	196.1	203.5	220.3	230.4	.	.	.
1	142.3	149.2	150.5	161.5	168.0	185.0	191.3	.	.	.
2	4.2	4.8	6.0	5.0	4.9	5.3	6.4	.	.	.
3	25.2	25.8	26.3	24.2	25.4	24.1	26.3	.	.	.
5	6.2	5.4	4.1	3.8	4.0	3.9	4.0	.	.	.
6	1.4	1.0	1.2	1.5	1.2	2.0	2.5	.	.	.
Turks and Caicos Islands (BA) [3]					Total employment - Emploi total - Empleo total					
Total - Total - Total										
ICSE-93 - CISP-93 - CISE-93										
Total	.	.	.	.	14.051	15.161	17.442	18.195	19.587	.
1	.	.	.	.	12.594	13.695	16.042	17.218	18.610	.
2,3	.	.	.	.	1.457	1.466	1.400	0.977	0.977	.
Men - Hommes - Hombres										
ICSE-93 - CISP-93 - CISE-93										
Total	.	.	.	.	8.439	8.957	10.349	10.936	12.214	.
1	.	.	.	.	7.429	7.922	9.369	10.244	11.522	.
2,3	.	.	.	.	1.010	1.035	0.980	0.692	0.692	.
Women - Femmes - Mujeres										
ICSE-93 - CISP-93 - CISE-93										
Total	.	.	.	.	5.612	6.204	7.093	7.259	7.373	.
1	.	.	.	.	5.165	5.773	6.673	6.974	7.088	.
2,3	.	.	.	.	0.447	0.431	0.420	0.285	0.285	.
United States (BA) [1][4]					Total employment - Emploi total - Empleo total					
Total - Total - Total										
ICSE-93 - CISP-93 - CISE-93										
Total	133 488	135 208	135 073	136 485	137 736	139 252	141 730	144 427	146 047	145 362
1	123 267	125 162	125 119	126 603	127 314	128 705	131 143	133 736	135 502	135 161
2,3	10 087	9 907	9 827	9 756	10 295	10 431	10 464	10 586	10 413	10 079
5	135	139	128	126	126	117	123	105	131	121
Men - Hommes - Hombres										
ICSE-93 - CISP-93 - CISE-93										
Total	71 446	72 293	72 080	72 903	73 332	74 525	75 973	77 502	78 254	77 486
1	65 074	66 086	65 950	66 789	66 862	67 921	69 294	70 800	71 670	71 069
2,3	6 328	6 154	6 086	6 068	6 430	6 562	6 632	6 668	6 544	6 373
5	45	53	44	47	41	42	47	34	41	45

Explanatory notes: see p. 77.

[1] Persons aged 16 years and over. [2] Civilian labour force employed. [3] Persons aged 15 years and over. [4] Excl. armed forces.

Notes explicatives: voir p. 80.

[1] Personnes âgées de 16 ans et plus. [2] Main-d'oeuvre civile occupée. [3] Personnes âgées de 15 ans et plus. [4] Non compris les forces armées.

Notas explicativas: véase p. 83.

[1] Personas de 16 años y más. [2] Fuerza de trabajo civil ocupada. [3] Personas de 15 años y más. [4] Excl. las fuerzas armadas.

**Total employment,
by status
in employment**
Thousands

**Emploi total,
par situation
dans la profession**
Milliers

**Empleo total,
por situación
en el empleo**
Millares

	1999	2000	2001	2002	2003	2004	2005	2006	2007	2008
United States (BA) [1][2]				Total employment - Emploi total - Empleo total						
Women - Femmes - Mujeres										
ICSE-93 - CISP-93 - CISE-93										
Total	62 042	62 915	62 993	63 582	64 404	64 728	65 757	66 925	67 792	67 876
1	58 193	59 076	59 169	59 814	60 452	60 783	61 849	62 936	63 832	64 092
2,3	3 759	3 753	3 741	3 688	3 866	3 869	3 832	3 919	3 869	3 707
5	90	86	84	79	86	75	76	71	90	77
Uruguay (BA) [3][4]				Total employment - Emploi total - Empleo total						
Total - Total - Total										
ICSE-93 - CISP-93 - CISE-93										
Total	.	1 067.6	1 076.2	1 038.3	1 032.0	.	1 114.5	1 413.5 [5]	1 482.1	.
1	.	777.8	766.1	706.2	724.3	.	795.2	988.6 [5]	1 035.7	.
2	.	39.5	42.5	46.8	35.5	.	43.9	67.8 [5]	71.1	.
3	.	232.8	252.7	274.0	258.3	.	260.6	326.6 [5]	345.3	.
5	.	15.6	14.9	11.3	14.0	.	14.8	28.5 [5]	26.4	.
6	.	1.9	-	.	.	.	-	2.0 [5]	3.1	.
Men - Hommes - Hombres										
ICSE-93 - CISP-93 - CISE-93										
Total	.	613.4	617.7	597.9	589.7	.	620.1	822.4 [5]	852.9	.
1	.	426.3	418.6	392.4	386.5	.	419.3	556.1 [5]	577.4	.
2	.	29.6	32.6	29.5	27.3	.	32.7	51.2 [5]	53.4	.
3	.	151.9	162.8	170.8	170.8	.	164.0	206.5 [5]	213.7	.
5	.	5.1	3.7	5.2	5.2	.	4.1	8.2 [5]	7.7	.
6	.	0.5	-	.	.	.	-	- [5]	0.8	.
Women - Femmes - Mujeres										
ICSE-93 - CISP-93 - CISE-93										
Total	.	454.2	458.5	440.4	442.3	.	494.4	591.0 [5]	629.0	.
1	.	351.5	347.5	313.7	337.8	.	375.9	432.5 [5]	457.2	.
2	.	10.0	9.9	17.3	8.2	.	11.2	16.6 [5]	18.5	.
3	.	80.9	89.9	103.2	87.5	.	96.6	120.1 [5]	132.4	.
5	.	10.6	11.1	6.1	8.9	.	10.7	20.3 [5]	18.7	.
6	.	1.4	-	.	.	.	-	1.6 [5]	2.3	.
Venezuela, Rep. Bolivariana de (BA) [1][6][7]				Total employment - Emploi total - Empleo total						
Total - Total - Total										
ICSE-93 - CISP-93 - CISE-93										
Total	.	.	.	.	.	.	.	.	11 491.9	.
1	.	.	.	.	.	.	.	.	6 814.7	.
2	.	.	.	.	.	.	.	.	479.2	.
3	.	.	.	.	.	.	.	.	3 315.7	.
4	.	.	.	.	.	.	.	.	769.7	.
5	.	.	.	.	.	.	.	.	112.7	.
6	.	.	.	.	.	.	.	.	-	.
Men - Hommes - Hombres										
ICSE-93 - CISP-93 - CISE-93										
Total	.	.	.	.	.	.	.	.	7 073.0	.
1	.	.	.	.	.	.	.	.	4 134.8	.
2	.	.	.	.	.	.	.	.	395.4	.
3	.	.	.	.	.	.	.	.	1 934.3	.
4	.	.	.	.	.	.	.	.	566.8	.
5	.	.	.	.	.	.	.	.	41.7	.
6	.	.	.	.	.	.	.	.	-	.
Women - Femmes - Mujeres										
ICSE-93 - CISP-93 - CISE-93										
Total	.	.	.	.	.	.	.	.	4 418.9	.
1	.	.	.	.	.	.	.	.	2 679.9	.
2	.	.	.	.	.	.	.	.	83.8	.
3	.	.	.	.	.	.	.	.	1 381.4	.
4	.	.	.	.	.	.	.	.	202.8	.
5	.	.	.	.	.	.	.	.	71.0	.
6	.	.	.	.	.	.	.	.	-	.

Explanatory notes: see p. 77.

[1] Excl. armed forces. [2] Persons aged 16 years and over. [3] Persons aged 14 years and over. [4] Excl. conscripts. [5] Prior to 2006: urban areas. [6] Persons aged 15 years and over. [7] Second semester.

Notes explicatives: voir p. 80.

[1] Non compris les forces armées. [2] Personnes âgées de 16 ans et plus. [3] Personnes âgées de 14 ans et plus. [4] Non compris les conscrits. [5] Avant 2006: régions urbaines. [6] Personnes âgées de 15 ans et plus. [7] Second semestre.

Notas explicativas: véase p. 83.

[1] Excl. las fuerzas armadas. [2] Personas de 16 años y más. [3] Personas de 14 años y más. [4] Excl. los conscriptos. [5] Antes de 2006: areas urbanas. [6] Personas de 15 años y más. [7] Segundo semestre.

EMPLOYMENT — EMPLOI — EMPLEO

Total employment, by status in employment — Thousands	Emploi total, par situation dans la profession — Milliers	Empleo total, por situación en el empleo — Millares							
1999	2000	2001	2002	2003	2004	2005	2006	2007	2008

ASIA-ASIE-ASIA

Armenia (BA) [1] [2]

Total employment - Emploi total - Empleo total

Total - Total - Total
ICSE-93 - CISP-93 - CISE-93

	1999	2000	2001	2002	2003	2004	2005	2006	2007	2008
Total	.	.	.	.	.	.	.	.	1 188.5	.
1									690.0	
2									6.3	
3									423.5	
4									66.5	
5									0.7	
6									1.4	

Men - Hommes - Hombres
ICSE-93 - CISP-93 - CISE-93

	1999	2000	2001	2002	2003	2004	2005	2006	2007	2008
Total									654.6	
1									406.5	
2									5.7	
3									219.8	
4									21.0	
5									0.7	
6									0.9	

Women - Femmes - Mujeres
ICSE-93 - CISP-93 - CISE-93

	1999	2000	2001	2002	2003	2004	2005	2006	2007	2008
Total									533.9	
1									283.4	
2									0.6	
3									203.7	
4									45.5	
5									0.0	
6									0.5	

Azerbaijan (BA) [3] [4]

Total employment - Emploi total - Empleo total

Total - Total - Total
ICSE-93 - CISP-93 - CISE-93

	1999	2000	2001	2002	2003	2004	2005	2006	2007	2008
Total	.	.	.	.	3 377.8	.	.	3 985.9	4 014.0	4 056.0
1					1 848.2			1 635.3	1 677.2	1 719.3
2					239.4			87.2	202.7	119.7
3					636.5			2 252.9	2 134.1	2 217.0
4					26.3			10.5	-	-
5					627.4			-	-	-

Men - Hommes - Hombres
ICSE-93 - CISP-93 - CISE-93

	1999	2000	2001	2002	2003	2004	2005	2006	2007	2008
Total					1 975.6			2 105.7	2 020.5	2 048.3
1					1 111.1			999.2	1 025.2	977.2
2					140.3			71.5	176.3	101.2
3					397.6			1 029.0	819.0	969.9
4					15.7			6.1	-	-
5					310.9			-	-	-

Women - Femmes - Mujeres
ICSE-93 - CISP-93 - CISE-93

	1999	2000	2001	2002	2003	2004	2005	2006	2007	2008
Total					1 402.2			1 880.2	1 993.5	2 007.7
1					737.1			636.1	652.1	742.1
2					99.1			15.7	26.3	18.5
3					238.9			1 223.9	1 315.1	1 247.1
4					10.6			4.4	-	-
5					316.5			-	-	-

Georgia (BA) [3] [5]

Total employment - Emploi total - Empleo total

Total - Total - Total
ICSE-93 - CISP-93 - CISE-93

	1999	2000	2001	2002	2003	2004	2005	2006	2007	2008
Total	1 732.6	1 839.3	1 877.6	1 839.2	1 814.5	1 783.3	1 744.6	1 747.3	1 704.3	1 601.9
1	731.4	684.3	654.6	650.9	618.5	600.9	600.3	603.9	625.4	572.4
2	19.9	27.6	28.7	28.3	21.3	19.4	18.6	13.3	19.4	16.8
3	423.0	558.8	578.4	633.1	651.0	663.8	623.6	626.4	575.8	561.0
4	9.2	11.8	10.4	2.8	-	-	-	-	-	-
5	530.7	542.2	590.5	520.1	522.4	496.9	497.1	501.9	483.6	450.6
6	18.4	14.6	15.1	4.0	1.2	2.3	4.9	1.8	0.1	1.1

Men - Hommes - Hombres
ICSE-93 - CISP-93 - CISE-93

	1999	2000	2001	2002	2003	2004	2005	2006	2007	2008
Total	884.8	946.9	966.7	954.1	957.5	926.5	915.2			855.6
1	378.4	354.8	336.0	333.0	323.6	304.4	314.1			313.1
2	17.1	24.3	25.3	23.5	16.8	16.0	15.1			11.7
3	282.8	335.0	364.7	400.8	426.0	430.0	409.4			361.8
4	6.1	9.4	7.7	2.3	-	-	-			-
5	190.2	215.0	224.3	191.5	190.3	174.4	174.1			168.0
6	10.3	8.4	8.7	3.0	0.8	1.8	2.5			1.0

[1] Incl. armed forces, Excl. conscripts. [2] Persons aged 16 years and over. [3] Persons aged 15 years and over. [4] Excl. armed forces and conscripts. [5] Excl. armed forces.

[1] Y compris les forces armées, Excl. conscrits [2] Personnes âgées de 16 ans et plus. [3] Personnes âgées de 15 ans et plus. [4] Non compris les forces armées et les conscrits. [5] Non compris les forces armées.

[1] Incl. las fuerzas armadas, excl. los conscriptos. [2] Personas de 16 años y más. [3] Personas de 15 años y más. [4] Excl. las fuerzas armadas y los conscriptos. [5] Excl. las fuerzas armadas.

**Total employment,
by status
in employment**
Thousands

**Emploi total,
par situation
dans la profession**
Milliers

**Empleo total,
por situación
en el empleo**
Millares

	1999	2000	2001	2002	2003	2004	2005	2006	2007	2008
Georgia (BA) [1] [2]				Total employment - Emploi total - Empleo total						
Women - Femmes - Mujeres										
ICSE-93 - CISP-93 - CISE-93										
Total	847.8	892.4	911.0	885.1	857.0	856.9	829.4	.	.	746.3
1	353.0	329.5	318.6	317.9	294.9	296.5	286.2	.	.	259.2
2	2.9	3.3	3.4	4.8	4.6	3.5	3.5	.	.	5.2
3	140.2	223.8	213.7	232.2	225.1	233.9	214.2	.	.	199.2
4	3.1	2.4	2.7	0.5	-	-	-	.	.	-
5	340.4	327.2	366.2	328.6	332.1	322.5	323.1	.	.	282.6
6	8.2	6.2	6.4	1.0	0.4	0.5	2.4	.	.	0.1
Hong Kong, China (BA) [2] [3]				Total employment - Emploi total - Empleo total						
Total - Total - Total										
ICSE-93 - CISP-93 - CISE-93										
Total	3 112.1	3 207.3	3 252.9	3 218.4	3 190.6	3 273.5	3 336.6	3 400.8	3 483.8	3 518.8
1	2 774.8	2 869.9	2 865.2	2 804.2	2 786.6	2 864.9	2 928.5	2 985.5	3 090.3	3 125.8
2	159.7	156.0	165.5	162.4	159.1	156.2	151.1	150.8	143.8	132.3
3	156.4	162.6	202.8	230.7	222.6	228.3	232.6	243.5	230.1	241.7
5	21.3	18.7	19.4	21.1	22.2	24.2	24.3	21.0	19.7	19.0
Men - Hommes - Hombres										
ICSE-93 - CISP-93 - CISE-93										
Total	1 816.5	1 854.5	1 845.7	1 794.0	1 764.3	1 800.8	1 822.6	1 840.4	1 869.0	1 870.0
1	1 549.3	1 585.1	1 539.0	1 471.9	1 456.6	1 495.4	1 515.9	1 527.5	1 574.0	1 579.4
2	136.4	133.6	138.0	133.9	130.9	128.0	123.5	122.1	115.7	105.2
3	128.5	133.5	166.1	185.6	173.9	174.2	179.5	188.0	177.4	182.6
5	2.2	2.2	2.5	2.7	2.9	3.3	3.7	2.8	2.0	2.7
Women - Femmes - Mujeres										
ICSE-93 - CISP-93 - CISE-93										
Total	1 295.6	1 352.8	1 407.3	1 424.4	1 426.3	1 472.7	1 514.0	1 560.4	1 614.8	1 648.8
1	1 225.4	1 284.7	1 326.2	1 332.3	1 330.0	1 369.4	1 412.6	1 458.0	1 516.3	1 546.4
2	23.3	22.4	27.5	28.5	28.3	28.2	27.7	28.7	28.1	27.0
3	27.9	29.1	36.7	45.1	48.8	54.1	53.1	55.5	52.7	59.0
5	19.0	16.5	16.9	18.4	19.3	20.9	20.7	18.2	17.7	16.4
Indonesia (BA) [2]				Total employment - Emploi total - Empleo total						
Total - Total - Total										
ICSE-93 - CISP-93 - CISE-93										
Total	.	.	90 807	91 647	92 811	93 722	93 958 [4]	95 457 [5]	99 930 [5]	102 553 [5]
1	.	.	30 212	29 563	28 757	29 909	31 563 [4]	32 363 [5]	33 960 [5]	33 476 [5]
2	.	.	2 789	2 786	2 673	2 966	2 849 [4]	2 850 [5]	2 884 [5]	3 015 [5]
3	.	.	40 220	43 212	42 511	43 555	42 609 [4]	44 070 [5]	45 808 [5]	48 686 [5]
5	.	.	17 587	16 085	18 870	17 292	16 938 [4]	16 174 [5]	17 279 [5]	17 375 [5]
Men - Hommes - Hombres										
ICSE-93 - CISP-93 - CISE-93										
Total	.	.	57 131	58 583	59 500	60 582	61 439 [4]	61 977 [5]	63 148 [5]	.
1	.	.	20 344	20 035	19 565	20 471	21 349 [4]	21 659 [5]	22 679 [5]	.
2	.	.	2 426	2 430	2 328	2 602	2 461 [4]	2 466 [5]	2 375 [5]	.
3	.	.	29 761	32 007	32 571	32 970	32 891 [4]	33 090 [5]	33 161 [5]	.
5	.	.	4 601	4 112	5 036	4 538	4 738 [4]	4 762 [5]	4 933 [5]	.
Women - Femmes - Mujeres										
ICSE-93 - CISP-93 - CISE-93										
Total	.	.	33 676	33 064	33 311	33 141	32 519 [4]	33 480 [5]	36 782 [5]	.
1	.	.	9 868	9 529	9 192	9 439	10 214 [4]	10 704 [5]	11 281 [5]	.
2	.	.	363	357	345	364	388 [4]	384 [5]	509 [5]	.
3	.	.	10 459	11 205	9 940	10 585	9 717 [4]	10 980 [5]	12 646 [5]	.
5	.	.	12 986	11 974	13 835	12 754	12 200 [4]	11 411 [5]	12 346 [5]	.
Iran, Islamic Rep. of (BA) [6]				Total employment - Emploi total - Empleo total						
Total - Total - Total										
ICSE-93 - CISP-93 - CISE-93										
Total	.	.	.	.	.	.	20 619	20 841	21 092	.
1	.	.	.	.	.	.	6 257	6 714	6 825	.
2	.	.	.	.	.	.	1 233	1 163	1 145	.
3	.	.	.	.	.	.	3 945	3 856	3 899	.
5	.	.	.	.	.	.	6 439	6 778	6 935	.
6	.	.	.	.	.	.	2 625	2 216	2 186	.
Men - Hommes - Hombres										
ICSE-93 - CISP-93 - CISE-93										
Total	.	.	.	.	.	.	16 657	16 872	17 230	.
1	.	.	.	.	.	.	5 483	5 761	5 922	.
2	.	.	.	.	.	.	1 185	1 125	1 109	.
3	.	.	.	.	.	.	3 043	2 972	3 036	.
5	.	.	.	.	.	.	5 674	5 976	6 167	.
6	.	.	.	.	.	.	1 184	960	925	.

Explanatory notes: see p. 77.

Notes explicatives: voir p. 80.

Notas explicativas: véase p. 83.

[1] Excl. armed forces. [2] Persons aged 15 years and over. [3] Excl. marine, military and institutional populations. [4] Nov. [5] Aug. [6] Persons aged 10 years and over.

[1] Non compris les forces armées. [2] Personnes âgées de 15 ans et plus. [3] Non compris le personnel militaire, de la marine et la population institutionnelle. [4] Nov. [5] Août. [6] Personnes âgées de 10 ans et plus.

[1] Excl. las fuerzas armadas. [2] Personas de 15 años y más. [3] Excl. el personal militar y de la marina, y la población institucional. [4] Nov. [5] Agosto. [6] Personas de 10 años y más.

2D · EMPLOYMENT · EMPLOI · EMPLEO

Total employment, by status in employment — Thousands
Emploi total, par situation dans la profession — Milliers
Empleo total, por situación en el empleo — Millares

	1999	2000	2001	2002	2003	2004	2005	2006	2007	2008
Iran, Islamic Rep. of (BA) [1]					Total employment - Emploi total - Empleo total					
Women - Femmes - Mujeres										
ICSE-93 - CISP-93 - CISE-93										
Total	.	.	.	.	.	.	3 962	3 970	3 862	.
1	.	.	.	.	.	.	773	953	904	.
2	.	.	.	.	.	.	48	38	36	.
3	.	.	.	.	.	.	901	884	863	.
5	.	.	.	.	.	.	765	802	768	.
6	.	.	.	.	.	.	1 441	1 256	1 261	.
Israel (BA) [2][3]					Total employment - Emploi total - Empleo total					
Total - Total - Total										
ICSE-93 - CISP-93 - CISE-93										
Total	2 136.7	2 221.2	2 264.9	2 284.4	2 330.2	2 400.8	2 493.6	2 573.6	2 682.0	2 776.7
1	1 815.0	1 906.1	1 959.1	1 976.1	2 008.4	2 084.5	2 166.5	2 235.1	2 341.7	2 424.8
2	96.1	100.2	101.9	101.7	105.9	104.4	107.8	106.0	112.3	123.9
3	151.5	148.2	144.6	150.1	160.1	163.1	178.5	195.3	192.2	195.5
4	64.1	56.8	48.5	47.3	45.4	40.3	32.2	29.8	30.0	26.7
5	10.1	10.1	10.7	9.2	10.3	8.6	8.7	7.2	5.7	5.8
Men - Hommes - Hombres										
ICSE-93 - CISP-93 - CISE-93										
Total	1 176.2	1 211.7	1 236.1	1 238.0	1 257.6	1 300.3	1 339.9	1 383.6	1 441.9	1 489.1
1	948.6	990.3	1 018.1	1 020.2	1 030.4	1 076.7	1 107.4	1 147.3	1 203.5	1 240.2
2	81.6	86.0	88.3	86.7	88.9	85.2	90.4	88.5	91.5	101.7
3	110.0	103.0	101.4	104.4	111.2	114.0	122.9	129.5	129.5	131.8
4	33.8	30.2	25.4	24.5	24.0	22.1	16.8	16.6	16.3	14.0
5	2.2	2.3	2.9	2.2	3.0	2.3	2.4	1.6	1.0	1.4
Women - Femmes - Mujeres										
ICSE-93 - CISP-93 - CISE-93										
Total	960.5	1 009.5	1 028.6	1 046.4	1 072.6	1 100.5	1 153.7	1 190.0	1 240.1	1 287.6
1	866.4	915.8	941.0	955.9	978.0	1 007.8	1 059.1	1 087.8	1 138.2	1 184.6
2	14.5	14.2	13.6	15.0	17.0	19.2	17.4	17.5	20.8	22.2
3	41.5	45.2	43.2	45.7	48.9	49.1	55.6	65.8	62.7	63.7
4	30.3	26.6	23.1	22.8	21.4	18.2	15.4	13.2	13.7	12.6
5	7.9	7.8	7.8	7.0	7.3	6.3	6.3	5.6	4.7	4.4
Japan (BA) [3]					Total employment - Emploi total - Empleo total					
Total - Total - Total										
ICSE-93 - CISP-93 - CISE-93										
Total	64 620	64 460	64 120	63 300	63 160	63 290	63 560	63 820	64 120	63 850
1	53 310	53 560	53 690	53 310	53 350	53 550	53 930	54 720	55 230	55 240
2	1 840	1 820	1 760	1 700	1 650	1 640	1 640	1 650	1 640	1 610
3	5 700	5 500	5 170	4 990	4 950	4 920	4 870	4 680	4 580	4 450
5	3 560	3 400	3 250	3 050	2 960	2 900	2 820	2 470	2 360	2 240
6	210	190	250	250	250	270	310	300	300	310
Men - Hommes - Hombres										
ICSE-93 - CISP-93 - CISE-93										
Total	38 310	38 180	37 830	37 360	37 190	37 130	37 230	37 300	37 530	37 290
1	32 150	32 160	32 010	31 700	31 580	31 520	31 640	31 940	32 260	32 120
2	1 490	1 490	1 430	1 390	1 350	1 340	1 340	1 360	1 360	1 340
3	3 890	3 780	3 630	3 560	3 540	3 520	3 500	3 370	3 320	3 240
5	660	630	600	580	580	580	560	450	420	410
6	130	110	160	140	140	160	190	180	170	180
Women - Femmes - Mujeres										
ICSE-93 - CISP-93 - CISE-93										
Total	26 320	26 300	26 290	25 940	25 970	26 160	26 330	26 520	26 590	26 560
1	21 160	21 400	21 680	21 610	21 770	22 030	22 290	22 770	22 970	23 120
2	350	330	330	310	300	300	290	290	290	270
3	1 810	1 720	1 550	1 440	1 420	1 400	1 370	1 310	1 260	1 210
5	2 910	2 780	2 650	2 470	2 380	2 320	2 260	2 020	1 940	1 820
6	90	70	100	110	110	110	130	120	130	130
Kazakhstan (BA) [3]					Total employment - Emploi total - Empleo total					
Total - Total - Total										
ICSE-93 - CISP-93 - CISE-93										
Total	.	.	6 699	6 709	6 985	7 182	7 261	7 404	7 631	7 857
1	.	.	3 863	4 030	4 230	4 470	4 641	4 777	4 974	5 199
2	.	.	59	59	65	82	90	109	123	122
3	.	.	2 610	2 487	2 548	2 487	2 427	2 403	2 428	2 449
4	.	.	2 610	2 487	2 548	2 487	2 427	2 403	2 428	2 449
5	.	.	70	68	68	84	71	84	76	61

Explanatory notes: see p. 77.

[1] Persons aged 10 years and over. [2] Excl. armed forces. [3] Persons aged 15 years and over.

Notes explicatives: voir p. 80.

[1] Personnes âgées de 10 ans et plus. [2] Non compris les forces armées. [3] Personnes âgées de 15 ans et plus.

Notas explicativas: véase p. 83.

[1] Personas de 10 años y más. [2] Excl. las fuerzas armadas. [3] Personas de 15 años y más.

Total employment, by status in employment
Thousands

Emploi total, par situation dans la profession
Milliers

Empleo total, por situación en el empleo
Millares

	1999	2000	2001	2002	2003	2004	2005	2006	2007	2008
Kazakhstan (BA) [1]					Total employment - Emploi total - Empleo total					
Men - Hommes - Hombres										
ICSE-93 - CISP-93 - CISE-93										
Total	.	.	3 470	3 486	3 618	3 719	3 764	3 809	3 923	4 018
1	.	.	2 117	2 217	2 288	2 384	2 481	2 501	2 590	2 711
2	.	.	43	45	49	60	69	75	82	79
3	.	.	1 215	1 155	1 200	1 199	1 152	1 168	1 198	1 182
4	.	.	65	45	53	37	23	21	18	20
5	.	.	30	25	29	38	39	44	35	26
Women - Femmes - Mujeres										
ICSE-93 - CISP-93 - CISE-93										
Total	.	.	3 229	3 223	3 367	3 463	3 497	3 595	3 708	3 840
1	.	.	1 746	1 814	1 942	2 086	2 160	2 276	2 383	2 489
2	.	.	16	15	16	22	21	34	41	43
3	.	.	1 394	1 333	1 348	1 288	1 275	1 235	1 230	1 267
4	.	.	32	19	22	21	10	10	13	7
5	.	.	40	43	39	46	31	41	41	35
Korea, Republic of (BA) [1] [2]					Total employment - Emploi total - Empleo total					
Total - Total - Total										
ICSE-93 - CISP-93 - CISE-93										
Total	20 281 |	21 156 [3]	21 572	22 169	22 139	22 557	22 856	23 151	23 433	23 577
1	12 522 |	13 360 [3]	13 659	14 181	14 402	14 894	15 185	15 551	15 970	16 206
2	. |	1 458 [3]	1 554	1 617	1 629	1 679	1 664	1 632	1 562	1 527
2,3	5 841									
3	. |	4 407 [3]	4 497	4 574	4 413	4 431	4 508	4 503	4 487	4 443
5	1 918 |	1 931 [3]	1 863	1 797	1 694	1 553	1 499	1 466	1 413	1 401
Men - Hommes - Hombres										
ICSE-93 - CISP-93 - CISE-93										
Total	11 978 |	12 387 [3]	12 581	12 944	13 031	13 193	13 330	13 444	13 607	13 703
1	7 570 |	7 963 [3]	8 050	8 325	8 432	8 657	8 794	8 979	9 214	9 338
2	. |	1 195 [3]	1 258	1 312	1 339	1 358	1 328	1 298	1 214	1 180
2,3	4 177									
3	. |	2 986 [3]	3 040	3 092	3 085	3 011	3 038	3 009	3 014	3 015
5	230 |	243 [3]	234	215	175	167	170	160	165	170
Women - Femmes - Mujeres										
ICSE-93 - CISP-93 - CISE-93										
Total	8 303 |	8 769 [3]	8 991	9 225	9 108	9 364	9 526	9 706	9 826	9 874
1	4 952 |	5 397 [3]	5 609	5 857	5 970	6 237	6 391	6 573	6 756	6 868
2	. |	263 [3]	296	304	290	321	336	335	348	347
2,3	1 663									
3	. |	1 421 [3]	1 457	1 482	1 328	1 420	1 470	1 494	1 473	1 428
5	1 688 |	1 688 [3]	1 629	1 582	1 519	1 386	1 329	1 306	1 249	1 230
Kyrgyzstan (BA) [1] [4]					Total employment - Emploi total - Empleo total					
Total - Total - Total										
ICSE-93 - CISP-93 - CISE-93										
Total	.	.	.	1 850.1	1 930.5	1 991.2	2 077.1	2 096.1	.	.
1	.	.	.	790.5	901.7	966.1	1 013.7	1 065.6	.	.
2	.	.	.	29.5	26.3	20.7	28.2	23.6	.	.
3	.	.	.	757.3	732.0	697.7	700.4	714.1	.	.
4	.	.	.	77.3	18.3	11.9	28.8	16.3	.	.
5	.	.	.	195.5	252.1	294.8	306.0	276.4	.	.
Men - Hommes - Hombres										
ICSE-93 - CISP-93 - CISE-93										
Total	.	.	.	1 051.4	1 083.8	1 140.7	1 195.9	1 214.5	.	.
1	.	.	.	438.6	508.9	551.7	574.4	609.3	.	.
2	.	.	.	21.3	18.2	13.8	21.8	18.0	.	.
3	.	.	.	479.5	442.8	457.4	461.6	469.4	.	.
4	.	.	.	43.3	11.5	8.1	17.0	11.3	.	.
5	.	.	.	68.8	102.3	109.6	121.1	106.5	.	.
Women - Femmes - Mujeres										
ICSE-93 - CISP-93 - CISE-93										
Total	.	.	.	798.7	846.7	850.5	881.2	881.6	.	.
1	.	.	.	351.9	392.8	414.4	439.4	456.2	.	.
2	.	.	.	8.2	8.2	6.9	6.3	5.7	.	.
3	.	.	.	277.8	289.1	240.3	238.8	244.9	.	.
4	.	.	.	34.1	6.8	3.7	11.7	5.0	.	.
5	.	.	.	126.8	149.8	185.2	184.9	169.9	.	.

Explanatory notes: see p. 77.

[1] Persons aged 15 years and over. [2] Excl. armed forces. [3] Estimates based on the 2000 Population Census results. [4] Nov. of each year.

Notes explicatives: voir p. 80.

[1] Personnes âgées de 15 ans et plus. [2] Non compris les forces armées. [3] Estimations basées sur les résultats du Recensement de la population de 2000. [4] Nov. de chaque année.

Notas explicativas: véase p. 83.

[1] Personas de 15 años y más. [2] Excl. las fuerzas armadas. [3] Estimaciones basadas en los resultados del Censo de población de 2000. [4] Nov. de cada año.

Total employment, by status in employment — Thousands
Emploi total, par situation dans la profession — Milliers
Empleo total, por situación en el empleo — Millares

Liban (B) [1]

Total employment - Emploi total - Empleo total

Total - Total - Total — ICSE-93 - CISP-93 - CISE-93

	1999	2000	2001	2002	2003	2004	2005	2006	2007	2008
Total						1 108.1			1 118.4	
1						687.7			694.4	
2						56.8			106.8	
3						316.1			260.8	
5						36.1			49.6	
6						11.4			6.8	

Men - Hommes - Hombres — ICSE-93 - CISP-93 - CISE-93

	1999	2000	2001	2002	2003	2004	2005	2006	2007	2008
Total						850.1			842.4	
1						472.2			469.3	
2						54.1			102.0	
3						289.9			233.3	
5						25.7			33.3	
6						8.1			4.5	

Women - Femmes - Mujeres — ICSE-93 - CISP-93 - CISE-93

	1999	2000	2001	2002	2003	2004	2005	2006	2007	2008
Total						258.1			276.0	
1						215.5			225.1	
2						2.7			4.8	
3						26.2			27.5	
5						10.4			16.3	
6						3.3			2.3	

Macau, China (BA) [2] [3]

Total employment - Emploi total - Empleo total

Total - Total - Total — ICSE-93 - CISP-93 - CISE-93

	1999	2000	2001	2002	2003	2004	2005	2006	2007	2008
Total	196.1	195.3	205.0	204.9	205.4	219.1	237.5	265.1	300.4	323.0
1	174.8	172.2	183.0	183.4	183.1	193.7	212.9	240.4	274.4	298.9
2	7.0	6.6	6.0	7.2	6.8	7.8	9.3	10.0	10.4	9.0
3	11.1	13.5	13.1	11.5	12.2	13.7	12.4	12.2	13.4	12.6
5	3.2	2.9	2.9	2.8	3.3	4.0	2.9	2.5	2.1	2.4

Men - Hommes - Hombres — ICSE-93 - CISP-93 - CISE-93

	1999	2000	2001	2002	2003	2004	2005	2006	2007	2008
Total	104.2	103.2	108.0	106.4	108.3	115.2	124.3	141.6	160.5	172.3
1	89.2	87.5	93.2	91.3	92.8	97.7	107.1	124.7	142.1	155.3
2	6.1	5.8	5.0	6.0	5.8	6.6	7.6	7.9	8.3	7.0
3	8.6	9.6	9.6	8.8	9.2	10.7	9.4	8.7	9.9	9.6
5	0.3	0.2	0.2	0.3	0.5	0.3	0.2	0.2	0.2	0.3

Women - Femmes - Mujeres — ICSE-93 - CISP-93 - CISE-93

	1999	2000	2001	2002	2003	2004	2005	2006	2007	2008
Total	91.9	92.1	96.9	98.5	97.1	103.9	113.2	123.5	139.8	150.7
1	85.6	84.7	89.8	92.1	90.3	96.0	105.8	115.8	132.3	143.5
2	0.9	0.8	1.0	1.2	1.1	1.2	1.7	2.0	2.1	2.0
3	2.5	3.9	3.5	2.7	3.0	3.0	3.0	3.5	3.5	3.0
5	3.0	2.7	2.7	2.5	2.7	3.6	2.6	2.2	1.9	2.1

Malaysia (BA) [4] [5]

Total employment - Emploi total - Empleo total

Total - Total - Total — ICSE-93 - CISP-93 - CISE-93

	1999	2000	2001	2002	2003	2004	2005	2006	2007	2008
Total	8 837.8	9 269.2	9 357.0	9 542.6	9 869.7	9 979.5	10 045.4	10 275.8	10 538.1	10 659.6
1	6 602.5	6 882.6	7 056.2	7 320.2	7 523.8	7 445.0	7 583.4	7 632.9	7 824.0	7 951.1
2	202.2	275.8	306.8	288.6	333.0	354.7	337.0	396.9	362.5	371.4
3	1 489.1	1 586.0	1 514.9	1 479.8	1 536.3	1 678.1	1 671.7	1 733.4	1 831.5	1 851.1
5	543.9	524.8	478.5	453.9	476.3	501.7	453.2	512.2	520.1	486.0

Men - Hommes - Hombres — ICSE-93 - CISP-93 - CISE-93

	1999	2000	2001	2002	2003	2004	2005	2006	2007	2008
Total	5 851.2	5 973.5	6 055.9	6 141.8	6 323.6	6 390.4	6 470.5	6 618.6	6 747.1	6 851.1
1	4 347.5	4 363.6	4 519.9	4 692.6	4 776.2	4 690.6	4 778.1	4 775.9	4 893.4	4 947.0
2	178.3	248.3	271.4	252.7	290.9	308.0	287.4	341.0	311.6	318.9
3	1 132.3	1 202.9	1 124.6	1 070.0	1 119.9	1 236.4	1 256.3	1 319.2	1 356.9	1 406.7
5	193.0	158.7	139.7	126.3	136.6	155.4	148.7	182.4	185.2	178.5

Women - Femmes - Mujeres — ICSE-93 - CISP-93 - CISE-93

	1999	2000	2001	2002	2003	2004	2005	2006	2007	2008
Total	2 986.5	3 295.7	3 301.1	3 400.8	3 546.1	3 589.1	3 574.8	3 656.8	3 791.0	3 808.5
1	2 255.0	2 519.0	2 536.2	2 627.6	2 747.7	2 754.5	2 805.3	2 856.9	2 930.7	3 004.1
2	23.9	27.6	35.4	35.8	42.0	46.8	49.6	55.9	50.9	52.5
3	356.8	383.1	390.3	409.8	416.5	441.7	415.4	414.2	474.6	444.4
5	350.9	366.1	338.8	327.6	339.7	346.2	304.5	329.8	334.9	307.5

Explanatory notes: see p. 77.

[1] Persons aged 15 years and over. [2] Persons aged 14 years and over. [3] Excl. armed forces and conscripts. [4] Persons aged 15 to 64 years. [5] Excl. armed forces.

Notes explicatives: voir p. 80.

[1] Personnes âgées de 15 ans et plus. [2] Personnes âgées de 14 ans et plus. [3] Non compris les forces armées et les conscrits. [4] Personnes âgées de 15 à 64 ans. [5] Non compris les forces armées.

Notas explicativas: véase p. 83.

[1] Personas de 15 años y más. [2] Personas de 14 años y más. [3] Excl. las fuerzas armadas y los conscriptos. [4] Personas de 15 a 64 años. [5] Excl. las fuerzas armadas.

Total employment, by status in employment
Thousands

Emploi total, par situation dans la profession
Milliers

Empleo total, por situación en el empleo
Millares

	1999	2000	2001	2002	2003	2004	2005	2006	2007	2008
Pakistan (BA) [1][2][3]				Total employment - Emploi total - Empleo total						
Total - Total - Total										
ICSE-93 - CISP-93 - CISE-93										
Total	37 296	36 847	37 481	38 882	39 852	42 009	42 816	46 952	47 651	.
1	13 146	13 109	13 334	15 495	15 882	15 915	16 221	17 490	17 829	.
2	318	289	294	319	327	370	377	414	391	.
3	15 489	15 562	15 830	14 971	15 344	15 574	15 873	16 411	16 449	.
5	8 343	7 887	8 023	8 097	8 299	10 150	10 345	12 637	12 982	.
Men - Hommes - Hombres										
ICSE-93 - CISP-93 - CISE-93										
Total	32 099	31 688	32 233	33 189	34 017	34 903	35 573	37 808	38 118	.
1	11 851	11 401	11 597	13 382	13 716	13 697	13 960	15 142	15 483	.
2	314	283	288	302	310	364	371	403	379	.
3	14 881	14 703	14 956	14 076	14 427	14 444	14 721	15 041	15 175	.
5	5 053	5 301	5 392	5 429	5 564	6 398	6 521	7 221	7 081	.
Women - Femmes - Mujeres										
ICSE-93 - CISP-93 - CISE-93										
Total	5 197	5 159	5 248	5 693	5 835	7 106	7 243	9 144	9 533	.
1	1 295	1 708	1 737	2 113	2 166	2 218	2 261	2 348	2 346	.
2	4	6	6	17	17	6	6	11	12	.
3	608	859	874	895	917	1 130	1 152	1 370	1 274	.
5	3 290	2 586	2 631	2 668	2 735	3 752	3 824	5 416	5 901	.
Philippines (BA) [4][5]				Total employment - Emploi total - Empleo total						
Total - Total - Total										
ICSE-93 - CISP-93 - CISE-93										
Total	27 742	27 452	29 156	30 062	30 635	31 613	32 313	32 636	33 560	34 089
1	13 761	13 925	14 438	14 653	15 354	16 472	16 316	16 673	17 508	17 846
2	1 341	1 315	1 552	1 662	1 605	1 604	1 520	1 425	1 430	1 426
3	8 864	8 869	9 375	9 737	9 912	10 011	10 584	10 525	10 570	10 654
5	3 775	3 344	3 792	4 009	3 765	3 527	3 893	4 012	4 052	4 161
Men - Hommes - Hombres										
ICSE-93 - CISP-93 - CISE-93										
Total	17 253	17 193	17 923	18 306	18 873	19 646	19 910	20 013	20 542	20 959
1	8 645	8 717	8 978	9 022	9 554	10 368	10 130	10 316	10 827	11 093
2	1 054	1 053	1 238	1 338	1 287	1 291	1 203	1 114	1 100	1 107
3	5 799	5 805	5 907	6 091	6 296	6 391	6 854	6 766	6 784	6 877
5	1 756	1 618	1 800	1 854	1 736	1 597	1 723	1 818	1 832	1 882
Women - Femmes - Mujeres										
ICSE-93 - CISP-93 - CISE-93										
Total	10 489	10 259	11 232	11 756	11 762	11 968	12 403	12 622	13 018	13 129
1	5 116	5 208	5 459	5 631	5 800	6 105	6 187	6 357	6 682	6 754
2	288	262	313	324	318	313	316	311	330	320
3	3 066	3 063	3 468	3 646	3 616	3 620	3 730	3 759	3 787	3 777
5	2 019	1 726	1 992	2 155	2 029	1 931	2 170	2 195	2 219	2 279
Singapore (BA) [6][7]				Total employment - Emploi total - Empleo total						
Total - Total - Total										
ICSE-93 - CISP-93 - CISE-93										
Total	1 518.3	.	1 582.5 [8]	1 573.7	1 605.4	1 632.1	.	1 796.7 [8]	1 803.2	1 852.0
1	1 281.5	.	1 339.3 [8]	1 335.4	1 365.5	1 378.2	.	1 525.5 [8]	1 525.9	1 572.8
2	92.4	.	81.8 [8]	81.9	83.9	88.4	.	91.4 [8]	92.0	94.4
3	127.0	.	145.2 [8]	142.9	142.8	152.8	.	167.9 [8]	171.0	172.9
5	17.5	.	16.2 [8]	13.6	13.1	12.8	.	12.0 [8]	14.3	12.0
Men - Hommes - Hombres										
ICSE-93 - CISP-93 - CISE-93										
Total	912.1	.	938.4 [8]	937.7	948.7	960.8	.	1 036.5 [8]	1 038.4	1 053.6
1	733.0	.	756.1 [8]	759.0	771.1	771.6	.	842.1 [8]	838.1	853.5
2	76.9	.	68.1 [8]	66.0	67.4	70.7	.	69.3 [8]	70.8	71.5
3	97.9	.	111.0 [8]	109.4	107.0	115.1	.	121.3 [8]	124.8	125.0
5	4.4	.	3.3 [8]	3.3	3.2	3.3	.	3.7 [8]	4.6	3.5
Women - Femmes - Mujeres										
ICSE-93 - CISP-93 - CISE-93										
Total	606.2	.	644.0 [8]	636.0	656.6	671.3	.	760.2 [8]	764.8	798.5
1	548.5	.	583.3 [8]	576.4	594.3	606.6	.	683.3 [8]	687.8	719.2
2	15.5	.	13.7 [8]	15.9	16.6	17.7	.	22.1 [8]	21.2	22.9
3	29.1	.	34.2 [8]	33.5	35.8	37.6	.	46.5 [8]	46.2	47.9
5	13.2	.	12.9 [8]	10.3	9.9	9.4	.	8.3 [8]	9.7	8.5

Explanatory notes: see p. 77.

[1] Excl. armed forces. [2] Persons aged 10 years and over. [3] Jan. [4] Persons aged 15 years and over. [5] Excl. regular military living in barracks. [6] The data refer to the residents (Singapore citizens and permanent residents) aged 15 years and over. [7] June. [8] Methodology revised; data not strictly comparable.

Notes explicatives: voir p. 80.

[1] Non compris les forces armées. [2] Personnes âgées de 10 ans et plus. [3] Janv. [4] Personnes âgées de 15 ans et plus. [5] Non compris les militaires de carrière vivant dans des casernes. [6] Les données se réfèrent aux résidents (citoyens de Singapour et résidents permanents) âgés de 15 ans et plus. [7] Juin. [8] Méthodologie révisée; les données ne sont pas strictement comparables.

Notas explicativas: véase p. 83.

[1] Excl. las fuerzas armadas. [2] Personas de 10 años y más. [3] Enero. [4] Personas de 15 años y más. [5] Excl. los militares profesionales que viven en casernas. [6] Los datos se refieren a los residentes (ciudadanos de Singapur y residentes permanentes) de 15 años y más. [7] Junio. [8] Metodología revisada; los datos no son estrictamente comparables.

EMPLOYMENT   EMPLOI   EMPLEO

	Total employment, by status in employment	Emploi total, par situation dans la profession	Empleo total, por situación en el empleo
	Thousands	Milliers	Millares

	1999	2000	2001	2002	2003	2004	2005	2006	2007	2008
Sri Lanka (BA) [1][2]				Total employment - Emploi total - Empleo total						
Total - Total - Total										
ICSE-93 - CISP-93 - CISE-93										
Total	6 082.7	6 310.1	6 235.6	6 519.4	7 012.8 [3]	7 394.0 [4]	7 518.0 [5]	7 105.3	7 041.9	7 174.7
1	3 495.0	3 548.8	3 655.4	3 774.5	4 059.6 [3]	4 394.9 [4]	4 457.6 [5]	3 949.8	3 976.6	4 017.8
2	122.6	148.0	141.7	179.7	183.9 [3]	218.0 [4]	232.0 [5]	221.5	200.4	213.4
3	1 720.7	1 789.4	1 780.8	1 865.5	2 073.3 [3]	2 089.6 [4]	2 230.3 [5]	2 189.6	2 140.1	2 170.3
5	744.3	823.9	657.6	699.7	696.0 [3]	691.5 [4]	598.1 [5]	744.5	724.7	773.1
Men - Hommes - Hombres										
ICSE-93 - CISP-93 - CISE-93										
Total	4 107.5	4 241.5	4 248.9	4 395.2	4 833.5 [3]	5 049.4 [4]	5 134.8 [5]	4 610.6	4 653.1	4 663.3
1	2 367.2	2 400.7	2 462.3	2 525.4	2 773.9 [3]	2 974.1 [4]	3 070.6 [5]	2 583.3	2 660.6	2 646.4
2	110.8	131.5	131.7	162.7	164.3 [3]	196.9 [4]	210.5 [5]	200.6	183.5	194.7
3	1 375.0	1 433.6	1 421.1	1 495.9	1 663.6 [3]	1 651.2 [4]	1 689.3 [5]	1 622.8	1 603.0	1 612.3
5	254.5	275.7	233.8	211.2	231.8 [3]	227.2 [4]	164.3 [5]	203.9	205.9	211.0
Women - Femmes - Mujeres										
ICSE-93 - CISP-93 - CISE-93										
Total	1 975.2	2 068.7	1 986.7	2 124.3	2 179.3 [3]	2 344.6 [4]	2 383.2 [5]	2 494.7	2 388.8	2 511.4
1	1 127.8	1 148.1	1 193.1	1 249.1	1 285.8 [3]	1 420.8 [4]	1 387.0 [5]	1 366.4	1 316.0	1 374.4
2	11.9	16.5	10.0	17.0	19.6 [3]	21.1 [4]	21.4 [5]	20.9	16.9	17.6
3	345.7	355.8	359.7	369.6	409.7 [3]	438.4 [4]	541.0 [5]	566.8	537.1	556.9
5	489.8	548.2	423.9	488.6	464.2 [3]	464.2 [4]	433.3 [5]	540.6	518.0	562.6
Syrian Arab Republic (BA) [6]				Total employment - Emploi total - Empleo total						
Total - Total - Total										
ICSE-93 - CISP-93 - CISE-93										
Total	.	.	4 730	.	.	.	.	.	4 946	.
1	.	.	2 329	.	.	.	.	.	2 658	.
2	.	.	394	.	.	.	.	.	420	.
3	.	.	1 228	.	.	.	.	.	1 428	.
5	.	.	779	.	.	.	.	.	440	.
Men - Hommes - Hombres										
ICSE-93 - CISP-93 - CISE-93										
Total	.	.	3 926	.	.	.	.	.	4 316	.
1	.	.	1 954	.	.	.	.	.	2 224	.
2	.	.	383	.	.	.	.	.	408	.
3	.	.	1 165	.	.	.	.	.	1 365	.
5	.	.	424	.	.	.	.	.	319	.
Women - Femmes - Mujeres										
ICSE-93 - CISP-93 - CISE-93										
Total	.	.	804	.	.	.	.	.	630	.
1	.	.	375	.	.	.	.	.	434	.
2	.	.	11	.	.	.	.	.	13	.
3	.	.	63	.	.	.	.	.	63	.
5	.	.	355	.	.	.	.	.	120	.
Taiwan, China (BA) [6][7]				Total employment - Emploi total - Empleo total						
Total - Total - Total										
ICSE-93 - CISP-93 - CISE-93										
Total	9 385	9 491	9 383	9 454	9 573	9 786	9 942	10 111	10 294	10 403
1	6 624	6 746	6 727	6 771	6 898	7 131	7 336	7 542	7 735	7 902
2	511	513	492	492	496	510	503	517	523	
2,3										1 882
3	1 523	1 523	1 483	1 496	1 484	1 458	1 438	1 406	1 396	
5	726	710	681	695	695	686	666	647	641	619
Thailand (BA) [6][7][8]				Total employment - Emploi total - Empleo total						
Total - Total - Total										
ICSE-93 - CISP-93 - CISE-93										
Total	32 087.1	33 001.0	33 483.7 [9]	34 262.6	34 677.1	35 711.6	36 302.4	36 344.5	37 122.0	37 836.6
1	12 276.3	13 069.7	13 539.3 [9]	13 711.8	14 058.5	15 643.0	15 847.0	15 869.6	16 175.0	16 341.2
2	933.6	1 100.9	956.2 [9]	1 092.1	1 134.6	1 090.9	1 129.6	1 092.3	1 101.3	984.9
3	10 175.8	9 940.9	10 700.8 [9]	10 681.9	10 919.0	11 013.9	11 447.6	11 527.0	11 866.5	12 044.9
4	-	-	18.9 [9]	16.5	32.3	50.1	51.3	34.5	51.6	45.5
5	8 701.1	8 888.8	8 268.6 [9]	8 760.3	8 531.9	7 913.7	7 826.9	7 821.1	7 927.6	8 420.1
6	-	-	- [9]	-	0.8	0.2	-	-		

Explanatory notes: see p. 77.

[1] Persons aged 10 years and over. [2] Excl. Northern and Eastern provinces. [3] Excl. Northern province. [4] Excl. Mullativu and Killinochchi districts. [5] Whole country. [6] Persons aged 15 years and over. [7] Excl. armed forces. [8] Third quarter. [9] Prior to 2001: persons aged 13 years and over

Notes explicatives: voir p. 80.

[1] Personnes âgées de 10 ans et plus. [2] Non compris les provinces du Nord et de l'Est. [3] Non compris la province du Nord. [4] Non compris les provinces de Mullativu et Killinochchi. [5] Ensemble du pays. [6] Personnes âgées de 15 ans et plus. [7] Non compris les forces armées. [8] Troisième trimestre. [9] Avant 2001: personnes agées de 13 ans et pl us.

Notas explicativas: véase p. 83.

[1] Personas de 10 años y más. [2] Excl. las provincias del Norte y del Este. [3] Excl. la provincia del Norte. [4] Excl. las provincias de Mullativu y Killinocchchi. [5] Todo el país. [6] Personas de 15 años y más. [7] Excl. las fuerzas armadas. [8] Tercer trimestre. [9] Antes de 2001: personas de 13 años y más.

Total employment, by status in employment
Thousands

Emploi total, par situation dans la profession
Milliers

Empleo total, por situación en el empleo
Millares

	1999	2000	2001	2002	2003	2004	2005	2006	2007	2008
Thailand (BA) [1][2][3]				Total employment - Emploi total - Empleo total						
Men - Hommes - Hombres										
ICSE-93 - CISP-93 - CISE-93										
Total	17 721.1	18 164.9	18 471.1 [4]	18 872.2	19 081.5	19 698.8	19 470.3	19 638.2	19 976.7	20 405.0
1	6 885.5	7 309.7	7 542.9 [4]	7 657.9	7 795.5	8 766.6	8 656.0	8 708.5	8 900.3	8 920.4
2	765.7	845.2	757.0 [4]	877.4	910.6	847.4	874.0	827.4	840.1	756.7
3	7 151.2	7 026.1	7 289.9 [4]	7 330.1	7 317.9	7 173.0	7 280.3	7 365.3	7 408.2	7 717.2
4	-	-	3.2 [4]	3.2	11.2	24.4	24.5	11.4	21.4	15.7
5	2 918.2	2 983.5	2 878.1 [4]	3 003.6	3 046.0	2 887.4	2 635.5	2 725.6	2 806.7	2 995.0
6	-	-	- [4]	-	-	0.3	-	-	-	-
Women - Femmes - Mujeres										
ICSE-93 - CISP-93 - CISE-93										
Total	14 365.7	14 836.1	15 012.7 [4]	15 390.4	15 595.6	16 012.8	16 832.1	16 706.3	17 145.3	17 431.6
1	5 390.3	5 760.0	5 996.4 [4]	6 053.9	6 263.0	6 876.2	7 191.0	7 161.1	7 274.7	7 420.8
2	167.8	255.7	199.2 [4]	214.7	224.0	243.4	255.6	264.9	261.2	228.2
3	3 024.5	2 914.8	3 410.9 [4]	3 351.8	3 601.1	3 841.0	4 167.3	4 161.7	4 458.3	4 327.7
4	-	-	15.7 [4]	13.3	21.1	25.7	26.8	23.1	30.2	29.8
5	5 782.8	5 905.3	5 390.5 [4]	5 756.7	5 485.9	5 026.3	5 191.4	5 095.5	5 120.9	5 425.1
6	-	-	- [4]	-	0.5	0.2	-	-	-	-
United Arab Emirates (BA) [2][5]				Total employment - Emploi total - Empleo total						
Total - Total - Total										
ICSE-93 - CISP-93 - CISE-93										
Total	.	.	.	.	.	.	.	.	.	1 846.229
1	.	.	.	.	.	.	.	.	.	1 768.975
2	.	.	.	.	.	.	.	.	.	55.902
3	.	.	.	.	.	.	.	.	.	21.326
5	.	.	.	.	.	.	.	.	.	0.026
Men - Hommes - Hombres										
ICSE-93 - CISP-93 - CISE-93										
Total	.	.	.	.	.	.	.	.	.	1 501.291
1	.	.	.	.	.	.	.	.	.	1 427.547
2	.	.	.	.	.	.	.	.	.	53.411
3	.	.	.	.	.	.	.	.	.	20.333
5	.	.	.	.	.	.	.	.	.	-
Women - Femmes - Mujeres										
ICSE-93 - CISP-93 - CISE-93										
Total	.	.	.	.	.	.	.	.	.	344.938
1	.	.	.	.	.	.	.	.	.	341.428
2	.	.	.	.	.	.	.	.	.	2.491
3	.	.	.	.	.	.	.	.	.	0.993
5	.	.	.	.	.	.	.	.	.	0.026
Viet Nam (BA) [2][6]				Total employment - Emploi total - Empleo total						
Total - Total - Total										
ICSE-93 - CISP-93 - CISE-93										
Total	38 119.9	38 367.6	39 000.3	40 162.3	41 175.7	42 315.6	.	.	.	.
1	6 946.3	7 071.3	8 074.5	8 200.2	9 005.1	10 818.7	.	.	.	.
2	45.4	79.5	118.3	155.2	142.4	215.3	.	.	.	.
3	16 242.2	16 505.8	15 733.5	16 243.8	16 931.2	17 437.4	.	.	.	.
5	14 615.0	14 212.0	14 509.7	15 219.8	14 770.7	13 842.9	.	.	.	.
6	271.0	499.1	564.3	343.4	326.3	1.3	.	.	.	.
Men - Hommes - Hombres										
ICSE-93 - CISP-93 - CISE-93										
Total	19 028.5	19 292.1	19 743.7	20 355.6	20 959.2	21 649.3	.	.	.	.
1	4 035.8	4 189.9	4 787.6	4 852.6	5 394.5	6 447.0	.	.	.	.
2	31.0	51.1	61.2	101.3	95.0	152.7	.	.	.	.
3	10 553.1	10 751.0	10 326.7	10 454.0	10 723.1	10 967.7	.	.	.	.
5	4 277.0	4 090.8	4 315.8	4 802.6	4 593.3	4 081.2	.	.	.	.
6	131.6	209.3	252.5	145.2	153.2	0.7	.	.	.	.
Women - Femmes - Mujeres										
ICSE-93 - CISP-93 - CISE-93										
Total	19 091.4	19 075.5	19 256.5	19 806.7	20 216.5	20 666.3	.	.	.	.
1	2 910.5	2 881.4	3 286.9	3 347.6	3 610.5	4 371.7	.	.	.	.
2	14.4	28.3	57.1	53.8	47.4	62.6	.	.	.	.
3	5 689.1	5 754.9	5 406.8	5 789.9	6 208.1	6 469.7	.	.	.	.
5	10 338.0	10 121.2	10 193.9	10 417.2	10 177.4	9 761.7	.	.	.	.
6	139.4	289.7	311.8	198.2	173.1	0.7	.	.	.	.

Explanatory notes: see p. 77.

[1] Excl. armed forces. [2] Persons aged 15 years and over. [3] Third quarter. [4] Prior to 2001: persons aged 13 years and over. [5] February. [6] July of each year.

Notes explicatives: voir p. 80.

[1] Non compris les forces armées. [2] Personnes âgées de 15 ans et plus. [3] Troisième trimestre. [4] Avant 2001: personnes agées de 13 ans et pl us. [5] Février. [6] Juillet de chaque année.

Notas explicativas: véase p. 83.

[1] Excl. las fuerzas armadas. [2] Personas de 15 años y más. [3] Tercer trimestre. [4] Antes de 2001: personas de 13 años y más. [5] Febrero. [6] Julio de cada año.

	EMPLOYMENT	EMPLOI	EMPLEO
	Total employment, by status in employment Thousands	**Emploi total, par situation dans la profession** Milliers	**Empleo total, por situación en el empleo** Millares

	1999	2000	2001	2002	2003	2004	2005	2006	2007	2008

West Bank and Gaza Strip (BA) [1]   Total employment - Emploi total - Empleo total

Total - Total - Total
ICSE-93 - CISP-93 - CISE-93

Total	588.000	597.440	504.786 [2]	476.661	564.571	578.439	632.939	666.375	665.620	647.022
1	398.742	395.484	313.330 [2]	282.044	322.960	336.792	376.176	395.129	397.915	422.607
2	32.400	27.376	23.920 [2]	17.678	20.125	24.089	27.426	30.639	26.975	27.474
3	110.446	117.225	121.313 [2]	127.514	156.841	153.256	165.263	166.707	160.705	134.135
5	46.412	57.355	46.222 [2]	48.991	64.457	64.302	64.073	73.900	80.025	62.661
6	-	-	- [2]	0.435	0.188	-	-	-	-	0.146

Men - Hommes - Hombres
ICSE-93 - CISP-93 - CISE-93

Total	502.000	504.220	427.889 [2]	398.778	467.371	473.755	527.806	546.000	538.019	525.696
1	349.894	343.374	263.964 [2]	234.438	269.604	277.389	316.802	328.933	331.360	348.497
2	31.626	26.724	23.267 [2]	17.337	19.434	23.418	26.565	29.708	26.198	26.557
3	97.890	107.903	115.005 [2]	120.210	145.370	142.390	152.774	151.379	144.425	119.545
5	22.590	26.219	25.653 [2]	26.396	32.796	30.557	31.666	35.979	36.036	30.986
6	-	-	- [2]	0.396	0.166	-	-	-	-	0.111

Women - Femmes - Mujeres
ICSE-93 - CISP-93 - CISE-93

Total	86.000	93.220	76.897 [2]	77.883	97.200	104.683	105.132	120.375	127.602	121.326
1	48.848	52.110	49.366 [2]	47.606	53.356	59.403	59.374	66.196	66.555	74.110
2	0.774	0.653	0.654 [2]	0.341	0.691	0.670	0.862	0.931	0.777	0.916
3	12.556	9.322	6.308 [2]	7.304	11.472	10.866	12.489	15.328	16.280	14.590
5	23.822	31.135	20.569 [2]	22.594	31.661	33.744	32.407	37.921	43.989	31.674
6	-	-	- [2]	0.038	0.021	-	-	-	-	0.035

EUROPE-EUROPE-EUROPA

Austria (BA) [1][3]   Total employment - Emploi total - Empleo total

Total - Total - Total
ICSE-93 - CISP-93 - CISE-93

Total	3 762.3	3 776.5	3 799.6	3 835.7	3 798.4	3 744.0 [4]	3 823.5	3 928.3	4 027.9	4 090.0
1	3 263.2	3 286.3	3 301.2	3 338.1	3 318.2	3 266.5 [4]	3 316.1	3 396.7	3 450.2	3 528.0
2	204.1	203.5	210.0	218.3	212.3	170.7 [4]	181.3	196.2	207.6	195.5
3	194.0	190.4	195.8	192.9	189.1	268.4 [4]	271.7	277.1	273.8	270.7
5	101.0	96.3	92.6	86.5	78.8	38.4 [4]	54.4	58.2	96.3	95.8

Men - Hommes - Hombres
ICSE-93 - CISP-93 - CISE-93

Total	2 139.7	2 145.6	2 142.5	2 139.0	2 101.8	2 061.5 [4]	2 095.4	2 147.5	2 208.5	2 222.1
1	1 845.5	1 853.7	1 845.2	1 840.6	1 813.2	1 757.5 [4]	1 776.1	1 818.0	1 853.9	1 874.1
2	147.2	144.7	148.4	156.4	150.9	130.2 [4]	139.0	145.1	154.7	143.8
3	114.8	115.7	118.5	113.1	110.1	161.7 [4]	159.0	162.9	156.8	159.1
5	32.2	31.5	30.5	28.8	27.5	12.1 [4]	21.3	21.5	43.1	45.1

Women - Femmes - Mujeres
ICSE-93 - CISP-93 - CISE-93

Total	1 622.7	1 631.0	1 657.1	1 696.7	1 696.6	1 682.5 [4]	1 728.1	1 780.7	1 819.4	1 867.9
1	1 417.7	1 432.7	1 456.1	1 497.5	1 505.0	1 509.0 [4]	1 540.0	1 578.7	1 596.2	1 653.9
2	57.0	58.8	61.6	61.8	61.4	40.5 [4]	42.3	51.1	52.9	51.6
3	79.2	74.7	77.3	79.8	79.0	106.7 [4]	112.7	114.2	117.1	111.7
5	68.9	64.8	62.2	57.6	51.2	26.3 [4]	33.1	36.7	53.1	50.7

Belgique (BA) [1][5]   Total employment - Emploi total - Empleo total

Total - Total - Total
ICSE-93 - CISP-93 - CISE-93

Total	.	.	.	.	.	.	4 235.3	4 262.9	4 380.3	4 445.9
1	.	.	.	.	.	.	3 590.3	3 620.3	3 730.9	3 813.5
2	.	.	.	.	.	.	197.0	199.3	197.5	186.9
3	.	.	.	.	.	.	376.0	377.9	395.3	391.7
5	.	.	.	.	.	.	72.3	65.4	56.6	53.9

Men - Hommes - Hombres
ICSE-93 - CISP-93 - CISE-93

Total	.	.	.	.	.	.	2 386.8	2 391.1	2 443.7	2 460.7
1	.	.	.	.	.	.	1 968.8	1 969.5	2 017.8	2 042.1
2	.	.	.	.	.	.	154.3	154.1	153.3	145.4
3	.	.	.	.	.	.	254.5	257.2	263.9	262.7
5	.	.	.	.	.	.	9.3	10.3	8.6	10.5

Women - Femmes - Mujeres
ICSE-93 - CISP-93 - CISE-93

Total	.	.	.	.	.	.	1 848.5	1 871.8	1 936.6	1 985.2
1	.	.	.	.	.	.	1 621.5	1 650.8	1 713.1	1 771.4
2	.	.	.	.	.	.	42.5	45.2	44.1	41.4
3	.	.	.	.	.	.	121.3	120.7	131.4	128.9
5	.	.	.	.	.	.	62.8	55.1	48.0	43.4

Explanatory notes: see p. 77.

[1] Persons aged 15 years and over. [2] Prior to 2001: persons aged 10 years and over. [3] Excl. conscripts on compulsory military service. [4] Prior to 2004: incl. conscripts. [5] Incl. professional army.

Notes explicatives: voir p. 80.

[1] Personnes âgées de 15 ans et plus. [2] Avant 2001: personnes âgées de 10 ans et plus. [3] Non compris conscrits ceux du contingent. [4] Avant 2004: y compris les conscrits. [5] Y compris les militaires de carrière.

Notas explicativas: véase p. 83.

[1] Personas de 15 años y más. [2] Antes de 2001: personas de 10 años y más. [3] Excl. los conscriptos del servicio obligatorio. [4] Antes de 2004: incl. los conscriptos. [5] Incl. los militares profesionales.

Total employment, by status in employment Thousands			Emploi total, par situation dans la profession Milliers				Empleo total, por situación en el empleo Millares		
1999	2000	2001	2002	2003	2004	2005	2006	2007	2008

Bosnia and Herzegovina (BA) [1]

Total employment - Emploi total - Empleo total

Total - Total - Total
ICSE-93 - CISP-93 - CISE-93

	1999	2000	2001	2002	2003	2004	2005	2006	2007	2008
Total	.	.	.	.	.	.	.	811	850	890
1	.	.	.	.	.	.	.	588	620	645
2,3	.	.	.	.	.	.	.	176	192	197
5	.	.	.	.	.	.	.	47 [2]	37 [2]	48

Men - Hommes - Hombres
ICSE-93 - CISP-93 - CISE-93

Total	.	.	.	.	.	.	.	528	557	573
1	.	.	.	.	.	.	.	381	405	416
2,3	.	.	.	.	.	.	.	132	141	143
5	.	.	.	.	.	.	.	16 [2]	11 [2]	15 [2]

Women - Femmes - Mujeres
ICSE-93 - CISP-93 - CISE-93

Total	.	.	.	.	.	.	.	283	292	317
1	.	.	.	.	.	.	.	207	215	230
2,3	.	.	.	.	.	.	.	45	52	54
5	.	.	.	.	.	.	.	31 [2]	26 [2]	33

Bulgaria (BA) [1] [3]

Total employment - Emploi total - Empleo total

Total - Total - Total
ICSE-93 - CISP-93 - CISE-93

	1999	2000	2001	2002	2003	2004	2005	2006	2007	2008
Total	.	.	.	.	2 834.0	2 922.2	2 980.0	3 110.0	3 252.6	3 360.7
1	.	.	.	.	2 399.6	2 478.7	2 555.7	2 701.5	2 848.9	2 943.8
2	.	.	.	.	99.6	111.0	114.5	122.7	131.8	122.9
3-4	.	.	.	.	271.7	270.6	257.5	246.1	234.0	259.9
5	.	.	.	.	54.5	54.6	45.5	39.8	37.9	34.0
6	.	.	.	.	8.7	7.4	6.8	-	-	-

Men - Hommes - Hombres
ICSE-93 - CISP-93 - CISE-93

Total	.	.	.	.	1 500.0	1 550.7	1 591.4	1 652.8	1 731.5	1 792.9
1	.	.	.	.	1 222.6	1 267.0	1 322.6	1 390.8	1 470.8	1 529.9
2	.	.	.	.	74.5	82.3	82.8	90.4	96.1	87.3
3-4	.	.	.	.	178.2	178.0	167.0	158.5	151.8	165.3
5	.	.	.	.	19.6	18.9	14.5	13.1	12.9	10.4
6	.	.	.	.	5.1	4.4	4.5	-	-	-

Women - Femmes - Mujeres
ICSE-93 - CISP-93 - CISE-93

Total	.	.	.	.	1 334.0	1 371.5	1 388.7	1 457.2	1 521.1	1 567.8
1	.	.	.	.	1 176.9	1 211.7	1 233.1	1 310.7	1 378.2	1 413.9
2	.	.	.	.	25.0	28.6	31.7	32.2	35.7	35.6
3-4	.	.	.	.	93.5	92.6	90.6	87.6	82.2	94.6
5	.	.	.	.	35.0	35.6	31.0	26.6	25.0	23.6
6	.	.	.	.	3.6	3.0	2.3	-	-	-

Croatia (BA) [1] [4]

Total employment - Emploi total - Empleo total

Total - Total - Total
ICSE-93 - CISP-93 - CISE-93

	1999	2000	2001	2002	2003	2004	2005	2006	2007	2008
Total	1 491.6	1 553.0	1 469.5	1 527.2	1 536.4	1 562.7	1 572.9	1 586.4	1 614.4	1 635.6
1	1 121.0	1 182.4	1 113.1	1 166.8	1 164.2	1 195.4	1 181.4	1 221.8	1 266.2	1 282.4
2	75.9	79.3	74.1	76.9	74.5	80.8	79.0	80.4	87.0	87.3
3	210.2	214.9	212.1	213.1	239.1	244.5	274.7	248.8	224.7	230.2
5	84.4	76.4	70.2	70.5	58.6	42.1	37.8	35.4	36.6	35.6

Men - Hommes - Hombres
ICSE-93 - CISP-93 - CISE-93

Total	802.2	848.7	818.9	842.5	850.5	866.4	867.0	868.1	897.3	905.1
1	592.4	633.2	598.2	626.9	635.9	655.9	647.1	656.2	693.7	700.4
2	53.2	56.7	57.6	54.0	55.7	58.1	58.9	57.5	65.8	64.7
3	134.0	140.6	143.4	142.5	143.7	140.9	151.5	144.9	127.8	131.1
5	22.6	18.4	19.7	19.2	15.1	11.5	9.5	9.5	9.9 [2]	8.8 [2]

Women - Femmes - Mujeres
ICSE-93 - CISP-93 - CISE-93

Total	689.2	704.3	650.6	684.7	685.9	696.4	706.0	718.3	717.1	730.5
1	528.6	549.3	514.9	540.0	528.2	539.4	534.3	565.6	572.5	582.0
2	22.7	22.7	16.5	22.9	18.8	22.7	20.1	22.9	21.2 [2]	22.6 [2]
3	76.3	74.4	68.8	70.6	95.4	103.6	123.2	103.9	96.9	99.1
5	61.8	58.0	50.5	51.4	43.5	30.6	28.3	25.9	26.7 [2]	26.8 [2]

Explanatory notes: see p. 77.

[1] Persons aged 15 years and over. [2] Estimate not sufficiently reliable. [3] Excl. conscripts. [4] Incl. armed forces, Excl. conscripts.

Notes explicatives: voir p. 80.

[1] Personnes âgées de 15 ans et plus. [2] Estimation pas suffisamment fiable. [3] Non compris les conscrits. [4] Y compris les forces armées, Excl. conscrits

Notas explicativas: véase p. 83.

[1] Personas de 15 años y más. [2] Estimación no suficientemente fiable. [3] Excl. los conscriptos. [4] Incl. las fuerzas armadas, excl. los conscriptos.

EMPLOYMENT — EMPLOI — EMPLEO

Total employment, by status in employment — Thousands
Emploi total, par situation dans la profession — Milliers
Empleo total, por situación en el empleo — Millares

Cyprus (BA) [1,2,3]

Total employment - Emploi total - Empleo total

Total - Total - Total
ICSE-93 - CISP-93 - CISE-93

	1999	2000	2001	2002	2003	2004	2005	2006	2007	2008
Total	279.2	288.6	309.5	315.3	327.1	338.0	348.0	357.3	377.9	382.9
1	205.9	210.7	236.3	242.7	249.6	258.5	267.2	280.5	301.1	306.5
2	13.7	17.6	20.1	17.8	18.7	23.2	25.7	22.7	23.0	21.2
3	44.5	42.1	42.9	44.7	47.3	45.8	45.5	46.3	47.4	48.0
5	5.9	8.7	10.2	10.1	11.4	10.5	9.6	7.8	6.5	7.1
6	9.2	9.4	-	-	-	-	-	-	-	-

Men - Hommes - Hombres
ICSE-93 - CISP-93 - CISE-93

	1999	2000	2001	2002	2003	2004	2005	2006	2007	2008
Total	172.9	176.1	176.2	176.8	181.6	190.8	197.3	200.4	209.5	212.2
1	116.4	117.0	124.2	126.1	127.0	134.6	140.7	146.9	154.8	157.8
2	12.5	15.8	17.7	16.0	17.0	20.6	22.6	20.0	20.0	19.0
3	34.1	32.8	32.3	33.0	35.7	33.6	31.6	31.3	32.8	33.4
5	0.8	1.1	2.0	1.6	2.0	2.0	2.4	2.2	1.9	2.0
6	9.2	9.4	-	-	-	-	-	-	-	-

Women - Femmes - Mujeres
ICSE-93 - CISP-93 - CISE-93

	1999	2000	2001	2002	2003	2004	2005	2006	2007	2008
Total	106.3	112.5	133.3	138.6	145.5	147.2	150.7	156.9	168.5	170.6
1	89.5	93.7	112.0	116.6	122.7	123.9	126.5	133.6	146.3	148.7
2	1.2	1.9	2.4	1.8	1.7	2.6	3.1	2.7	3.0	2.3
3	10.4	9.3	10.6	11.7	11.6	12.1	13.9	15.0	14.6	14.6
5	5.1	7.6	8.2	8.5	9.5	8.5	7.2	5.6	4.6	5.1
6	-	-	-	-	-	-	-	-	-	-

Czech Republic (BA) [3]

Total employment - Emploi total - Empleo total

Total - Total - Total
ICSE-93 - CISP-93 - CISE-93

	1999	2000	2001	2002	2003	2004	2005	2006	2007	2008
Total	4 764	4 732	4 728	4 765	4 733	4 707	4 764	4 828	4 922	5 002
1	4 024	3 972	3 970	3 966	3 894	3 890	3 980	4 032	4 111	4 184
2	196	196	186	193	197	188	177	196	184	179
3	464	486	500	541	581	573	551	551	582	596
4	55	51	44	36	28	24	21	16	14	12
5	25	27	28	29	33	31	35	32	30	31
6	-	-	1	1	-	-	-	1	1	-

Men - Hommes - Hombres
ICSE-93 - CISP-93 - CISE-93

	1999	2000	2001	2002	2003	2004	2005	2006	2007	2008
Total	2 694	2 676	2 674	2 700	2 686	2 663	2 706	2 742	2 806	2 863
1	2 173	2 143	2 140	2 134	2 092	2 079	2 141	2 177	2 223	2 276
2	151	151	144	149	153	146	136	150	145	138
3	329	343	354	389	416	415	404	397	421	432
4	36	32	30	24	17	15	15	12	9	8
5	5	6	6	4	8	8	9	6	7	10
6	-	-	-	-	-	-	-	1	1	-

Women - Femmes - Mujeres
ICSE-93 - CISP-93 - CISE-93

	1999	2000	2001	2002	2003	2004	2005	2006	2007	2008
Total	2 070	2 056	2 054	2 065	2 047	2 044	2 059	2 086	2 116	2 139
1	1 851	1 828	1 830	1 833	1 801	1 812	1 838	1 855	1 888	1 908
2	45	45	43	44	44	42	41	46	39	40
3	135	143	145	152	166	158	147	154	161	165
4	19	19	14	12	11	9	6	4	5	4
5	20	21	22	25	25	23	26	26	23	22
6										

Denmark (BA) [4,5]

Total employment - Emploi total - Empleo total

Total - Total - Total
ICSE-93 - CISP-93 - CISE-93

	1999	2000	2001	2002	2003	2004	2005	2006	2007	2008
Total	.	2 722.025	2 725.134	2 715.277	2 692.460	2 720.109	2 732.758	2 786.593	2 778.649	2 827.429
1	.	2 487.097	2 484.587	2 471.911	2 456.567	2 485.193	2 498.702	2 541.195	2 533.335	2 581.513
2,3	.	210.396	218.891	222.473	217.191	212.995	214.359	227.574	228.949	233.275
5	.	24.557	21.655	20.892	18.701	21.820	19.697	17.825	16.365	12.640
6		-	-	-	-	0.099	-	-	-	-

Men - Hommes - Hombres
ICSE-93 - CISP-93 - CISE-93

	1999	2000	2001	2002	2003	2004	2005	2006	2007	2008
Total	.	1 458.131	1 456.252	1 449.333	1 447.840	1 451.626	1 456.120	1 482.282	1 476.051	1 497.344
1	.	1 291.527	1 277.853	1 271.422	1 278.453	1 282.199	1 289.664	1 311.186	1 300.796	1 319.902
2,3	.	163.806	175.112	174.078	165.316	166.453	163.401	168.065	171.388	174.608
5	.	2.798	3.287	3.833	4.071	2.975	3.056	3.031	3.866	2.633
6										

Explanatory notes: see p. 77.
[1] Incl. armed forces, Excl. conscripts. [2] Government-controlled area. [3] Persons aged 15 years and over. [4] Included armed forces and conscripts. [5] Persons aged 15 to 66 years.

Notes explicatives: voir p. 80.
[1] Y compris les forces armées, Excl. conscrits [2] Région sous contrôle gouvernemental. [3] Personnes âgées de 15 ans et plus. [4] Y compris les forces armées et les conscrits. [5] Personnes âgées de 15 à 66 ans.

Notas explicativas: véase p. 83.
[1] Incl. las fuerzas armadas, excl. los conscriptos. [2] Area controlada por el gobierno. [3] Personas de 15 años y más. [4] Incluye las fuezas armadas y los conscriptos. [5] Personas de 15 a 66 años.

Total employment, by status in employment Thousands			Emploi total, par situation dans la profession Milliers			Empleo total, por situación en el empleo Millares			
1999	2000	2001	2002	2003	2004	2005	2006	2007	2008

Denmark (BA) [1] [2] — Total employment - Emploi total - Empleo total

Women - Femmes - Mujeres
ICSE-93 - CISP-93 - CISE-93

	1999	2000	2001	2002	2003	2004	2005	2006	2007	2008
Total	.	1 263.919	1 268.882	1 265.943	1 244.620	1 268.483	1 276.638	1 304.311	1 302.598	1 330.085
1	.	1 195.569	1 206.734	1 200.490	1 178.115	1 202.995	1 209.038	1 230.008	1 232.539	1 261.611
2,3	.	46.590	43.780	48.394	51.876	46.543	50.959	59.510	57.561	58.667
5	.	21.760	18.368	17.060	14.629	18.846	16.641	14.793	12.498	9.806
6	.	-	-	-	-	-	-	-	-	-

España (BA) [3] [4] — Total employment - Emploi total - Empleo total

Total - Total - Total
ICSE-93 - CISP-93 - CISE-93

	1999	2000	2001	2002	2003	2004	2005	2006	2007	2008
Total	14 689.8	15 505.9	16 146.3	16 630.3	17 295.9	17 970.8	18 973.2 [5]	19 747.7	20 356.0	20 257.6
1	11 560.9	12 378.1	12 949.4	13 471.9	14 127.4	14 720.8	15 502.1 [5]	16 208.1	16 760.1	16 681.2
2	794.9	799.9	849.1	876.7	926.5	967.9	980.1 [5]	1 080.8	1 117.9	1 165.4
3	1 873.6	1 896.0	1 932.4	1 886.7	1 852.3	1 918.6	2 075.7 [5]	2 084.7	2 167.4	2 125.1
4	96.2	91.5	93.2	90.1	94.8	86.5	82.9 [5]	92.2	79.5	65.5
5	344.6	324.4	302.7	283.1	274.1	258.8	306.8 [5]	264.5	221.9	208.1
6	19.6	16.0	19.5	21.8	20.8	18.3	25.8 [5]	17.4	9.3	12.3

Men - Hommes - Hombres
ICSE-93 - CISP-93 - CISE-93

	1999	2000	2001	2002	2003	2004	2005	2006	2007	2008
Total	9 433.8	9 821.1	10 150.5	10 365.0	10 652.9	10 934.3	11 388.8 [5]	11 742.6	11 987.3	11 720.7
1	7 244.6	7 643.9	7 931.7	8 160.0	8 454.0	8 695.4	9 025.5 [5]	9 313.9	9 521.8	9 279.4
2	634.5	636.1	662.3	682.5	728.5	747.2	742.9 [5]	813.2	842.6	867.7
3	1 345.2	1 352.9	1 375.9	1 348.5	1 294.4	1 331.7	1 420.2 [5]	1 434.4	1 472.5	1 434.2
4	66.5	62.3	63.9	60.5	63.9	58.3	57.4 [5]	61.9	56.0	43.0
5	130.5	115.7	103.8	102.7	98.9	92.3	127.6 [5]	108.6	88.1	88.0
6	12.5	10.2	12.8	11.0	13.1	9.4	15.2 [5]	10.6	6.2	8.4

Women - Femmes - Mujeres
ICSE-93 - CISP-93 - CISE-93

	1999	2000	2001	2002	2003	2004	2005	2006	2007	2008
Total	5 256.0	5 684.8	5 995.7	6 265.3	6 643.1	7 036.5	7 584.4 [5]	8 005.1	8 368.8	8 536.9
1	4 316.2	4 734.2	5 017.7	5 311.9	5 673.4	6 025.4	6 476.5 [5]	6 894.3	7 238.3	7 401.8
2	160.4	163.8	186.8	194.2	198.0	220.7	237.2 [5]	267.5	275.3	297.8
3	528.4	543.1	556.5	538.2	557.9	587.0	655.5 [5]	650.3	694.9	690.9
4	29.8	29.1	29.3	29.7	30.9	28.2	25.6 [5]	30.2	23.5	22.5
5	214.2	208.7	198.9	180.4	175.3	166.5	179.2 [5]	155.9	133.7	120.1
6	7.1	5.8	6.6	10.9	7.7	8.8	10.6 [5]	6.8	3.1	3.9

Estonia (BA) [6] [7] — Total employment - Emploi total - Empleo total

Total - Total - Total
ICSE-93 - CISP-93 - CISE-93

	1999	2000	2001	2002	2003	2004	2005	2006	2007	2008
Total	579.3	572.5	577.7	585.5	594.3	595.5	607.4	646.3	655.3	656.5
1	529.5	520.7	529.8	538.2	541.4	538.0	558.2	594.7	596.8	605.9
2	19.2	17.8	15.4	16.1	16.9	18.3	16.2	16.8	20.7	21.3
3	26.0	29.9	27.6	28.0	33.7	36.0	31.5	33.8	36.5	28.3
5	4.6	4.1	4.9	3.2	2.3	3.2	1.5	1.0	1.4	0.9

Men - Hommes - Hombres
ICSE-93 - CISP-93 - CISE-93

	1999	2000	2001	2002	2003	2004	2005	2006	2007	2008
Total	294.2	291.1	293.9	297.5	302.5	299.1	300.5	322.9	330.0	330.9
1	261.7	257.5	261.6	265.6	266.8	260.3	266.9	286.6	288.9	296.2
2	14.0	12.9	10.5	11.0	11.9	13.8	12.3	13.2	15.8	16.4
3	16.7	19.1	19.5	19.2	22.8	23.3	20.5	22.7	24.9	18.1
5	1.8	1.7	2.4	1.6	1.0	1.6	0.8	-	-	-

Women - Femmes - Mujeres
ICSE-93 - CISP-93 - CISE-93

	1999	2000	2001	2002	2003	2004	2005	2006	2007	2008
Total	285.1	281.4	283.8	288.1	291.8	296.4	306.9	323.3	325.4	325.6
1	267.8	263.3	268.2	272.6	274.6	278.0	291.3	308.1	307.9	309.7
2	5.2	4.9	4.9	5.1	4.9	4.5	3.9	3.6	4.9	4.9
3	9.4	10.8	8.1	8.8	10.9	12.7	11.0	11.1	11.6	10.3
5	2.8	2.4	2.6	1.6	1.3	1.6	0.7	-	-	-

Finland (BA) [1] [6] — Total employment - Emploi total - Empleo total

Total - Total - Total
ICSE-93 - CISP-93 - CISE-93

	1999	2000	2001	2002	2003	2004	2005	2006	2007	2008
Total	2 317	2 356	2 388	2 393	2 385	2 387	2 421	2 466	2 512	2 553
1	1 975	2 016	2 060	2 068	2 061	2 064	2 098	2 129	2 178	2 207
2	305	304	294	292	294	290	290	301	300	311
5	16	15	13	12	10	11	13	13	14	13
6	21	21	21	21	20	22	20	23	20	23

Explanatory notes: see p. 77.

[1] Included armed forces and conscripts. [2] Persons aged 15 to 66 years. [3] Excl. compulsory military service. [4] Persons aged 16 years and over. [5] Methodology revised; data not strictly comparable. [6] Persons aged 15 to 74 years. [7] Excl. conscripts.

Notes explicatives: voir p. 80.

[1] Y compris les forces armées et les conscrits. [2] Personnes âgées de 15 à 66 ans. [3] Non compris les militaires du contingent. [4] Personnes âgées de 16 ans et plus. [5] Méthodologie révisée; les données ne sont pas strictement comparables. [6] Personnes âgées de 15 à 74 ans. [7] Non compris les conscrits.

Notas explicativas: véase p. 83.

[1] Incluye las fuezas armadas y los conscriptos. [2] Personas de 15 a 66 años. [3] Excl. a los militares en servicio obligatorio. [4] Personas de 16 años y más. [5] Metodología revisada; los datos no son estrictamente comparables. [6] Personas de 15 a 74 años. [7] Excl. los conscriptos.

2D EMPLOYMENT — EMPLOI — EMPLEO

Total employment, by status in employment — Thousands
Emploi total, par situation dans la profession — Milliers
Empleo total, por situación en el empleo — Millares

	1999	2000	2001	2002	2003	2004	2005	2006	2007	2008
Finland (BA) [1][2]				Total employment - Emploi total - Empleo total						
Men - Hommes - Hombres ICSE-93 - CISP-93 - CISE-93										
Total	1 227	1 248	1 261	1 249	1 247	1 250	1 263	1 288	1 310	1 337
1	989	1 011	1 033	1 025	1 024	1 025	1 038	1 051	1 075	1 095
2	208	209	200	197	199	197	197	207	206	212
5	9	8	8	7	5	6	8	7	8	8
6	21	20	21	20	19	21	20	23	20	22
Women - Femmes - Mujeres ICSE-93 - CISP-93 - CISE-93										
Total	1 090	1 108	1 127	1 144	1 138	1 137	1 158	1 178	1 202	1 217
1	986	1 006	1 027	1 043	1 037	1 039	1 060	1 078	1 103	1 112
2	99	95	95	96	95	93	93	94	94	99
5	7	7	5	5	5	4	5	6	5	5
6	-	1	-	1	1	1	-	-	-	1
France (BA) [3]				Total employment - Emploi total - Empleo total						
Total - Total - Total ICSE-93 - CISP-93 - CISE-93										
Total	.	.	.	.	24 695.8	24 800.3	24 978.0	25 133.5	25 565.2	25 913.2
1	.	.	.	.	21 865.2	22 100.0	22 238.2	22 292.0	22 769.9	23 187.9
2	.	.	.	.	1 080.3	1 071.7	1 095.5	1 115.0	1 121.4	1 180.7
3	.	.	.	.	1 444.5	1 353.0	1 393.6	1 489.2	1 502.1	1 384.5
4	.	.	.	.	3.0	5.2	4.2	4.8	2.1	2.2
5	.	.	.	.	302.7	270.4	246.5	232.4	169.7	157.9
Men - Hommes - Hombres ICSE-93 - CISP-93 - CISE-93										
Total	.	.	.	.	13 302.9	13 315.7	13 350.0	13 381.5	13 521.9	13 670.2
1	.	.	.	.	11 394.4	11 486.0	11 482.5	11 448.5	11 612.1	11 839.7
2	.	.	.	.	832.0	819.1	848.8	867.6	846.0	870.2
3	.	.	.	.	995.0	932.5	952.0	997.9	1 018.0	919.0
4	.	.	.	.	2.9	4.7	4.0	3.8	1.2	0.4
5	.	.	.	.	78.7	73.3	62.7	63.7	44.6	40.9
Women - Femmes - Mujeres ICSE-93 - CISP-93 - CISE-93										
Total	.	.	.	.	11 392.9	11 484.7	11 628.0	11 752.0	12 043.3	12 243.0
1	.	.	.	.	10 470.8	10 614.0	10 755.8	10 843.5	11 157.8	11 348.2
2	.	.	.	.	248.3	252.6	246.7	247.4	275.5	310.6
3	.	.	.	.	449.6	420.5	441.6	491.3	484.1	465.5
4	.	.	.	.	0.2	0.5	0.2	1.0	0.9	1.8
5	.	.	.	.	224.0	197.1	183.8	168.7	125.1	117.0
Germany (BA) [3]				Total employment - Emploi total - Empleo total						
Total - Total - Total ICSE-93 - CISP-93 - CISE-93										
Total	36 402	36 604 [4]	36 816	36 536 [5]	36 172 [4]	35 659 [6]	36 566 [7]	37 322	38 163	38 734
1	32 497	32 638 [4]	32 743	32 467 [5]	32 043 [4]	31 405 [6]	32 066 [7]	32 808	33 607	34 241
2	1 786	1 801 [4]	1 821	1 858 [5]	1 784 [4]	3 852 [6]	4 080 [7]	4 132	4 160	4 143
3	1 809	1 842 [4]	1 811	1 797 [5]	1 960 [4]					
5	310	323 [4]	441	414 [5]	385 [4]	402 [6]	421 [7]	382	396	349
Men - Hommes - Hombres ICSE-93 - CISP-93 - CISE-93										
Total	20 659	20 680 [4]	20 629	20 336 [5]	19 996 [4]	19 681 [6]	20 135 [7]	20 462	20 890	21 188
1	17 980	17 969 [4]	17 910	17 614 [5]	17 225 [4]	16 846 [6]	17 181 [7]	17 506	17 927	18 245
2	1 197	1 391 [4]	1 226	1 247 [5]	1 374 [4]	2 740 [6]	2 852 [7]	2 868	2 873	2 858
3	1 406	1 240 [4]	1 393	1 382 [5]	1 304 [4]					
5	76	80 [4]	100	93 [5]	93 [4]	95 [6]	102 [7]	89	90	85
Women - Femmes - Mujeres ICSE-93 - CISP-93 - CISE-93										
Total	15 743	15 924 [4]	16 187	16 200 [5]	16 176 [4]	15 978 [6]	16 432 [7]	16 860	17 272	17 546
1	14 517	14 669 [4]	14 833	14 853 [5]	14 818 [4]	14 559 [6]	14 885 [7]	15 303	15 680	15 996
2	589	410 [4]	595	611 [5]	410 [4]	1 112 [6]	1 228 [7]	1 264	1 287	1 285
3	403	602 [4]	418	415 [5]	656 [4]					
5	234	243 [4]	341	321 [5]	292 [4]	307 [6]	318 [7]	293	305	264

Explanatory notes: see p. 77.

[1] Included armed forces and conscripts. [2] Persons aged 15 to 74 years. [3] Persons aged 15 years and over. [4] May. [5] Prior to 2002: April of each year. [6] March. [7] Methodology revised; data not strictly comparable.

Notes explicatives: voir p. 80.

[1] Y compris les forces armées et les conscrits. [2] Personnes âgées de 15 à 74 ans. [3] Personnes âgées de 15 ans et plus. [4] Mai. [5] Avant 2002: avril de chaque année. [6] Mars. [7] Méthodologie révisée; les données ne sont pas strictement comparables.

Notas explicativas: véase p. 83.

[1] Incluye las fuezas armadas y los conscriptos. [2] Personas de 15 a 74 años. [3] Personas de 15 años y más. [4] Mayo. [5] Antes del 2002: abril de cada año. [6] Marzo. [7] Metodología revisada; los datos no son estrictamente comparables.

Total employment, by status in employment
Thousands

Emploi total, par situation dans la profession
Milliers

Empleo total, por situación en el empleo
Millares

	1999	2000	2001	2002	2003	2004	2005	2006	2007	2008
Greece (BA) [1,2,3]				Total employment - Emploi total - Empleo total						
Total - Total - Total										
ICSE-93 - CISP-93 - CISE-93										
Total	4 040.4	4 097.9	4 103.2	4 190.2	4 286.6	4 330.5	4 382.1	4 452.8	4 520.0	4 582.5
1	2 337.4	2 378.7	2 466.3	2 545.3	2 616.0	2 746.2	2 784.9	2 834.1	2 896.4	2 974.8
2	305.8	326.7	336.3	315.1	310.2	346.8	352.2	364.6	369.7	381.2
3	991.6	998.4	954.3	996.5	1 018.5	962.5	967.5	962.8	963.4	957.6
5	405.6	394.1	346.3	333.3	341.9	274.9	277.5	291.2	290.4	268.9
Men - Hommes - Hombres										
ICSE-93 - CISP-93 - CISE-93										
Total	2 554.1	2 577.7	2 582.2	2 622.5	2 666.1	2 680.2	2 705.8	2 725.7	2 762.0	2 788.8
1	1 435.2	1 450.7	1 493.9	1 536.7	1 571.5	1 624.8	1 645.9	1 661.0	1 685.3	1 736.0
2	258.2	268.2	278.2	262.8	255.8	285.0	284.5	293.5	297.5	304.1
3	729.5	726.1	690.7	710.2	720.7	684.5	686.2	669.0	676.4	654.1
5	131.2	132.6	119.5	112.7	118.1	86.0	89.3	102.2	102.5	94.6
Women - Femmes - Mujeres										
ICSE-93 - CISP-93 - CISE-93										
Total	1 486.2	1 520.2	1 521.0	1 567.7	1 620.5	1 650.3	1 676.2	1 727.1	1 758.0	1 793.7
1	902.2	928.0	972.5	1 008.6	1 044.5	1 121.4	1 139.0	1 173.1	1 211.0	1 238.8
2	47.6	58.5	58.1	52.3	54.4	61.9	67.7	71.1	72.3	77.1
3	262.1	272.2	263.6	286.3	297.8	278.0	281.3	293.8	287.0	303.6
5	274.4	261.5	226.8	220.6	223.9	188.9	188.2	189.1	187.9	174.3
Hungary (BA) [2,4]				Total employment - Emploi total - Empleo total						
Total - Total - Total										
ICSE-93 - CISP-93 - CISE-93										
Total	3 811.5	3 849.1	3 859.5	3 870.6 [5]	3 921.9	3 900.4	3 901.5	3 930.1	3 926.2	3 879.4
1	3 201.3	3 255.5	3 296.3	3 337.2 [5]	3 399.2	3 347.8	3 367.3	3 431.4	3 439.7	3 405.0
2	114.8	196.0	206.9	203.8 [5]	202.5	228.8	229.4	214.1	205.5	199.2
3	404.7	314.4	284.3	283.2 [5]	290.6	298.3	281.7	259.8	258.9	259.0
4	42.5	37.1	30.7	22.5 [5]	8.6	8.1	5.8	4.8	4.4	2.4
5	28.2	26.1	26.3	23.9 [5]	21.0	17.4	17.3	20.0	17.7	13.8
6	20.0	20.0	15.0	- [5]	-	-	-	-	-	-
Men - Hommes - Hombres										
ICSE-93 - CISP-93 - CISE-93										
Total	2 103.1	2 122.4	2 130.6	2 112.5 [5]	2 126.5	2 117.3	2 116.1	2 137.4	2 143.0	2 110.8
1	1 682.6	1 708.8	1 743.0	1 753.8 [5]	1 768.1	1 745.0	1 756.3	1 801.0	1 820.1	1 788.6
2	82.1	144.2	152.3	147.9 [5]	148.8	163.7	165.4	155.5	148.7	146.1
3	278.0	214.6	190.3	189.2 [5]	196.0	198.4	184.8	171.9	165.7	168.4
4	30.2	26.1	20.8	14.5 [5]	5.8	5.4	3.6	3.2	3.0	1.9
5	10.2	8.7	9.2	7.1 [5]	7.8	5.1	5.4	5.8	5.5	5.8
6	20.0	20.0	15.0	- [5]	-	-	-	-	-	-
Women - Femmes - Mujeres										
ICSE-93 - CISP-93 - CISE-93										
Total	1 708.4	1 726.7	1 728.9	1 758.1 [5]	1 795.4	1 783.1	1 785.4	1 792.7	1 783.2	1 768.6
1	1 518.7	1 546.7	1 553.3	1 583.4 [5]	1 631.1	1 602.8	1 610.4	1 630.4	1 619.6	1 616.4
2	32.7	51.8	54.6	55.9 [5]	53.7	65.0	64.0	58.6	56.8	53.1
3	126.7	99.8	94.0	94.0 [5]	94.6	100.2	96.9	87.9	93.2	90.6
4	12.3	11.0	9.9	8.0 [5]	2.8	2.7	2.2	1.6	1.4	0.5
5	18.0	17.4	17.1	16.8 [5]	13.2	12.3	11.9	14.2	12.2	8.0
6	0.0	0.0	0.0	- [5]	-	-	-	-	-	-
Iceland (BA) [6,7]				Total employment - Emploi total - Empleo total						
Total - Total - Total										
ICSE-93 - CISP-93 - CISE-93										
Total	153.3	156.4	159.0	156.7	156.9	156.1	161.3	169.4	177.3	178.6
1	126.2	128.3	132.2	130.7	134.6	133.5	137.8	144.0	152.5	155.8
2	10.2	11.5	9.8	9.5	7.8	7.7	8.5	8.6	8.6	8.1
3	16.5	15.9	16.5	16.1	13.7	13.8	14.0	15.8	15.4	14.2
5	0.4	0.6	0.5	0.4	0.1	-	0.1	0.2	0.1	0.0
6	.	.	.	.	0.7	1.1	0.9	0.8	0.6	0.4
Men - Hommes - Hombres										
ICSE-93 - CISP-93 - CISE-93										
Total	82.2	83.6	85.0	83.0	82.4	82.5	85.7	91.9	96.6	97.1
1	62.7	63.5	65.5	63.4	66.2	66.3	68.2	72.7	78.3	80.5
2	7.8	8.6	7.6	7.6	5.9	5.7	6.4	6.7	6.4	6.2
3	11.4	11.3	11.6	11.7	9.8	9.8	10.7	12.0	11.6	10.2
5	0.3	0.2	0.3	0.2	-	-	0.1	0.2	0.1	0.0
6	.	.	.	.	0.5	0.7	0.3	0.3	0.2	0.1

Explanatory notes: see p. 77.
[1] Persons aged 15 years and over. [2] Excl. conscripts. [3] Second quarter of each year. [4] Persons aged 15 to 74 years. [5] Estimates based on the 2001 Population Census results. [6] Persons aged 16 to 74 years. [7] Excl. armed forces and conscripts.

Notes explicatives: voir p. 80.
[1] Personnes âgées de 15 ans et plus. [2] Non compris les conscrits. [3] Deuxième trimestre de chaque année. [4] Personnes âgées de 15 à 74 ans. [5] Estimations basées sur les résultats du Recensement de la population de 2001. [6] Personnes âgées de 16 à 74 ans. [7] Non compris les forces armées et les conscrits.

Notas explicativas: véase p. 83.
[1] Personas de 15 años y más. [2] Excl. los conscriptos. [3] Segundo trimestre de cada año. [4] Personas de 15 a 74 años. [5] Estimaciones basadas en los resultados del Censo de población de 2001. [6] Personas de 16 a 74 años. [7] Excl. las fuerzas armadas y los conscriptos.

EMPLOYMENT — EMPLOI — EMPLEO

Total employment, by status in employment — Thousands
Emploi total, par situation dans la profession — Milliers
Empleo total, por situación en el empleo — Millares

	1999	2000	2001	2002	2003	2004	2005	2006	2007	2008
Iceland (BA) [1][2]					Total employment - Emploi total - Empleo total					
Women - Femmes - Mujeres										
ICSE-93 - CISP-93 - CISE-93										
Total	71.2	72.8	74.0	73.8	74.6	73.6	75.6	77.5	80.7	81.5
1	63.5	64.8	66.8	67.3	68.4	67.2	69.6	71.4	74.2	75.3
2	2.5	3.0	2.1	1.9	2.0	2.0	2.1	1.9	2.2	1.9
3	5.1	4.6	4.9	4.3	3.9	4.0	3.4	3.9	3.8	4.0
5	0.2	0.4	0.2	0.2	0.1	-	0.1	-	-	0.0
6	.	.	.	.	0.2	0.4	0.4	0.3	0.4	0.2
Ireland (BA) [3][4]					Total employment - Emploi total - Empleo total					
Total - Total - Total										
ICSE-93 - CISP-93 - CISE-93										
Total	1 591.1	1 670.7	1 716.5	1 760.6	1 790.1	1 834.6	1 931.6	2 021.1	2 101.6	2 108.5
1	1 287.6	1 355.6	1 406.4	1 443.3	1 473.8	1 505.6	1 597.8	1 692.9	1 749.2	1 745.5
2	92.7	98.3	101.1	103.3	103.3	106.2	109.9	109.7	122.7	119.0
3	190.4	195.2	190.8	198.2	195.4	209.3	210.4	207.2	216.6	229.2
5	20.4	21.6	18.2	15.8	17.7	13.5	13.6	11.4	13.1	14.8
6	-	-	-	-	-	-	-	-	-	-
Men - Hommes - Hombres										
ICSE-93 - CISP-93 - CISE-93										
Total	947.3	989.9	1 013.9	1 026.2	1 039.3	1 065.0	1 113.3	1 166.7	1 201.5	1 186.9
1	702.3	735.8	760.1	765.4	781.8	796.8	840.3	895.6	913.0	892.7
2	75.2	80.1	82.4	85.2	85.2	85.6	90.2	91.5	100.1	98.1
3	160.8	165.2	163.6	168.3	164.9	176.3	176.5	175.6	183.3	189.4
5	9.0	8.8	7.9	7.2	7.4	6.3	6.4	4.0	5.2	6.7
6	-	-	-	-	-	-	-	-	-	-
Women - Femmes - Mujeres										
ICSE-93 - CISP-93 - CISE-93										
Total	643.9	680.8	702.5	734.4	750.9	769.6	818.4	854.5	900.1	921.6
1	585.3	619.8	646.3	677.9	692.0	708.8	757.5	797.3	836.2	852.8
2	17.6	18.2	18.7	18.1	18.1	20.6	19.7	18.2	22.6	20.9
3	29.6	30.0	27.2	29.9	30.5	33.0	33.9	31.6	33.3	39.8
5	11.4	12.8	10.3	8.6	10.2	7.2	7.2	7.4	8.0	8.2
6	-	-	-	-	-	-	-	-	-	-
Italy (BA) [3]					Total employment - Emploi total - Empleo total					
Total - Total - Total										
ICSE-93 - CISP-93 - CISE-93										
Total	20 864	21 225	21 634	21 922	22 133	22 404 [5]	22 563	22 988	23 222	23 405
1	14 995	15 276	15 636	15 942	16 125	16 117 [5]	16 534	16 915	17 167	17 446
2	2 466	3 041	2 598	2 636	2 694	402 [5]	383	346	317	285
3	2 350	1 796	2 263	2 249	2 217	4 761 [5]	4 725	4 767	4 778	4 771
4	255	273	240	203	196	60 [5]	43	39	48	35
5	798	838	898	892	901	566 [5]	421	425	421	403
6	.	.	.	.	.	497 [5]	457	497	490	465
Men - Hommes - Hombres										
ICSE-93 - CISP-93 - CISE-93										
Total	13 330	13 461	13 574	13 685	13 769	13 622 [5]	13 738	13 939	14 057	14 064
1	9 165	9 223	9 317	9 449	9 523	9 285 [5]	9 526	9 717	9 834	9 908
2	1 889	2 320	1 982	2 009	2 052	320 [5]	310	279	254	226
3	1 763	1 359	1 708	1 692	1 656	3 530 [5]	3 515	3 532	3 543	3 532
4	166	181	155	127	124	37 [5]	26	23	29	25
5	347	379	412	409	414	241 [5]	171	177	181	170
6	.	.	.	.	.	208 [5]	190	212	217	203
Women - Femmes - Mujeres										
ICSE-93 - CISP-93 - CISE-93										
Total	7 533	7 764	8 060	8 236	8 365	8 783 [5]	8 825	9 049	9 165	9 341
1	5 830	6 053	6 319	6 493	6 603	6 832 [5]	7 008	7 198	7 333	7 537
2	577	721	615	627	642	82 [5]	73	67	63	59
3	587	437	555	557	562	1 231 [5]	1 210	1 235	1 236	1 239
4	89	92	84	76	72	23 [5]	17	16	19	10
5	451	460	486	483	486	325 [5]	250	248	241	233
6	.	.	.	.	.	289 [5]	267	285	273	262
Latvia (BA) [6][7]					Total employment - Emploi total - Empleo total					
Total - Total - Total										
ICSE-93 - CISP-93 - CISE-93										
Total	968.5	941.1	962.1	989.0 [8]	1 006.9	1 017.7	1 035.9	1 087.6	1 119.0	1 124.1
1	810.2	800.3	817.0	852.6 [8]	876.0	885.9	915.3	961.5	1 000.1	1 011.2
2	35.8	39.5	40.3	31.8 [8]	32.2	34.6	35.9	37.3	36.0	36.6
3	70.4	63.7	58.7	61.7 [8]	61.4	62.9	60.8	72.4	65.3	61.8
5	49.7	36.4	44.4	42.8 [8]	37.3	34.3	23.9	16.3	17.6	14.5
6	.	.	-	.	.	.	.	.	.	.

Explanatory notes: see p. 77.

[1] Persons aged 16 to 74 years. [2] Excl. armed forces and conscripts. [3] Persons aged 15 years and over. [4] Second quarter of each year. [5] Methodology revised; data not strictly comparable. [6] Persons aged 15 to 74 years. [7] Excl. conscripts. [8] Prior to 2002: persons aged 15 years and over.

Notes explicatives: voir p. 80.

[1] Personnes âgées de 16 à 74 ans. [2] Non compris les forces armées et les conscrits. [3] Personnes âgées de 15 ans et plus. [4] Deuxième trimestre de chaque année. [5] Méthodologie révisée; les données ne sont pas strictement comparables. [6] Personnes âgées de 15 à 74 ans. [7] Non compris les conscrits. [8] Avant 2002: personnes agées de 15 ans et plus.

Notas explicativas: véase p. 83.

[1] Personas de 16 a 74 años. [2] Excl. las fuerzas armadas y los conscriptos. [3] Personas de 15 años y más. [4] Segundo trimestre de cada año. [5] Metodología revisada; los datos no son estrictamente comparables. [6] Personas de 15 a 74 años. [7] Excl. los conscriptos. [8] Antes de 2002: personas de 15 años y más.

Total employment, by status in employment
Thousands

Emploi total, par situation dans la profession
Milliers

Empleo total, por situación en el empleo
Millares

	1999	2000	2001	2002	2003	2004	2005	2006	2007	2008
Latvia (BA) [1][2]				Total employment - Emploi total - Empleo total						
Men - Hommes - Hombres										
ICSE-93 - CISP-93 - CISE-93										
Total	502.9	479.7	486.4 |	504.6 [3]	516.6	521.8	534.1	559.2	573.5	571.5
1	415.5	400.8	402.2 |	425.6 [3]	439.6	448.6	461.9	484.6	499.5	498.7
2	24.5	28.0	29.4 |	24.3 [3]	23.0	22.5	24.2	23.3	25.4	27.0
3	38.5	33.5	32.2 |	33.5 [3]	35.8	35.4	34.4	42.4	39.9	37.6
5	23.0	16.6	21.5 |	21.3 [3]	18.2	15.3	13.6	8.7	8.7	8.2
6	-	- |	-							-
Women - Femmes - Mujeres										
ICSE-93 - CISP-93 - CISE-93										
Total	465.6	461.4	475.7 |	484.3 [3]	490.2	495.9	501.8	528.5	545.5	552.6
1	394.7	399.5	414.9 |	427.1 [3]	436.4	437.2	453.5	476.9	500.5	512.5
2	11.2	11.5	10.9 |	7.5 [3]	9.2	12.1	11.6	14.0	10.6	9.5
3	31.9	30.2	26.5 |	28.2 [3]	25.6	27.5	26.4	29.9	25.4	24.2
5	26.7	19.8	22.9 |	21.6 [3]	19.0	19.1	10.3	7.6	8.9	6.4
6	-	- |	-						-	-
Lithuania (BA) [2][4]				Total employment - Emploi total - Empleo total						
Total - Total - Total										
ICSE-93 - CISP-93 - CISE-93										
Total	1 456.5	1 397.8	1 351.8	1 405.9	1 438.0	1 436.3	1 473.9	1 499.0	1 534.2	1 520.0
1	1 164.4	1 116.0	1 090.9	1 124.0	1 144.8	1 169.6	1 224.1	1 263.7	1 324.4	1 345.0
2,3	229.2	228.2	218.0	233.3	242.8	216.7	206.3	199.8	183.2	152.9
5	58.0	48.2	42.9	48.6	50.4	49.9	43.5	35.5	26.7	22.1
6	4.9	5.7	-	-	-	-	-	-	-	-
Men - Hommes - Hombres										
ICSE-93 - CISP-93 - CISE-93										
Total	729.2	686.5	664.5	707.8	726.2	733.8	750.9	755.8	777.7	768.7
1	560.0	528.1	509.1	543.9	554.8	580.8	606.7	622.7	651.1	659.8
2,3	141.4	138.2	136.8	144.0	151.2	133.8	128.6	123.1	117.9	101.5
5	25.6	17.9	18.6	19.9	20.2	19.1	15.5	10.0	8.7	7.4
6	2.2	2.6	-	-	-	-	-	-	-	-
Women - Femmes - Mujeres										
ICSE-93 - CISP-93 - CISE-93										
Total	727.4	711.3	687.3	698.1	711.8	702.5	723.0	743.2	756.5	751.4
1	604.3	587.9	581.8	580.0	589.9	588.8	617.3	641.0	673.3	685.2
2,3	87.8	90.0	81.2	89.2	91.6	82.9	77.7	76.6	65.2	51.5
5	32.4	30.3	24.3	28.8	30.3	30.8	28.0	25.5	18.0	14.7
6	2.9	3.0	-	-	-	-	-	-	-	-
Macedonia, The Former Yugoslav Rep. of (BA) [4]				Total employment - Emploi total - Empleo total						
Total - Total - Total										
ICSE-93 - CISP-93 - CISE-93										
Total	545.222	549.846	599.308	561.341	545.108	522.995 [5]	545.253	570.404	590.234	609.015
1	405.991	408.698	419.843	396.680	396.501	394.345 [5]	391.651	403.564	426.662	437.475
2	43.431	23.675	38.206	38.369	41.433	30.798 [5]	31.276	33.853	32.655	30.084
3	39.713	57.684	55.020	57.594	44.814	53.252 [5]	65.487	70.789	71.245	78.824
5	56.087	59.789	86.239	68.698	62.361	44.600 [5]	56.840	62.199	59.672	62.632
Men - Hommes - Hombres										
ICSE-93 - CISP-93 - CISE-93										
Total	337.994	339.550	357.266	342.779	327.283	320.640 [5]	332.179	351.979	358.835	373.483
1	244.974	249.448	250.930	240.347	234.975	231.478 [5]	229.996	240.956	248.649	261.113
2	37.230	19.804	29.289	29.598	32.773	23.836 [5]	25.140	26.903	24.972	22.879
3	33.303	45.199	43.503	46.109	36.575	44.929 [5]	55.714	59.082	60.034	65.847
5	22.487	25.099	33.545	26.725	22.960	20.396 [5]	21.330	25.033	25.181	23.645
Women - Femmes - Mujeres										
ICSE-93 - CISP-93 - CISE-93										
Total	207.229	210.297	242.042	218.562	217.825	202.355 [5]	213.074	218.431	231.399	235.532
1	161.017	159.250	168.914	156.333	161.526	162.867 [5]	161.654	162.608	178.013	176.362
2	6.201	3.871	8.917	8.771	8.660	6.961 [5]	6.136	6.950	7.683	7.205
3	6.410	12.486	11.518	11.485	8.238	8.323 [5]	9.773	11.706	11.212	12.977
5	33.600	34.690	52.694	41.974	39.401	24.204 [5]	35.510	37.166	34.491	38.988
Malta (BA) [4]				Total employment - Emploi total - Empleo total						
Total - Total - Total										
ICSE-93 - CISP-93 - CISE-93										
Total	.	.	145.6	148.4	147.9	148.6	148.5	152.5	155.5	161.0
1	.	.	124.3	127.6	125.9	127.6	128.0	131.7	134.0	139.5
2	.	.	5.6	6.1	6.8	6.9	6.8	6.7	7.1	6.9
3	.	.	15.2	14.6	14.2	14.0	13.5	14.1	14.3	14.5
5	.	.	.	.	.	.	.	.	.	0.0

Explanatory notes: see p. 77.

[1] Persons aged 15 to 74 years. [2] Excl. conscripts. [3] Prior to 2002: persons aged 15 years and over. [4] Persons aged 15 years and over. [5] Prior to 2004: April of each year.

Notes explicatives: voir p. 80.

[1] Personnes âgées de 15 à 74 ans. [2] Non compris les conscrits. [3] Avant 2002: personnes âgées de 15 ans et plus. [4] Personnes âgées de 15 ans et plus. [5] Avant 2004: Avril de chaque année.

Notas explicativas: véase p. 83.

[1] Personas de 15 a 74 años. [2] Excl. los conscriptos. [3] Antes de 2002: personas de 15 años y más. [4] Personas de 15 años y más. [5] Antes de 2004: Abril de cada año.

2D — EMPLOYMENT — EMPLOI — EMPLEO

Total employment, by status in employment — Thousands
Emploi total, par situation dans la profession — Milliers
Empleo total, por situación en el empleo — Millares

	1999	2000	2001	2002	2003	2004	2005	2006	2007	2008
Malta (BA) [1] — Total employment - Emploi total - Empleo total										
Men - Hommes - Hombres — ICSE-93 - CISP-93 - CISE-93										
Total	.	.	103.6	102.1	101.2	103.8	102.8	104.4	104.4	107.5
1	.	.	85.9	83.9	83.8	85.6	85.0	86.3	86.5	89.3
2	.	.	4.7	5.4	6.0	6.0	5.8	6.0	6.3	6.2
3	.	.	12.8	12.8	11.4	12.1	11.5	12.0	11.5	11.9
5	.	.	.	.	.	.	.	.	.	0.0
Women - Femmes - Mujeres — ICSE-93 - CISP-93 - CISE-93										
Total	.	.	42.0	46.3	45.9	44.8	46.0	48.1	51.1	53.5
1	.	.	38.3	43.7	42.1	41.9	43.3	45.3	47.5	50.1
2	.	.	0.8	0.8	0.8	0.8	1.0	0.7	0.8	0.7
3	.	.	2.4	1.8	2.9	1.9	3.0	2.0	2.8	2.6
5	.	.	.	.	.	.	.	.	.	0.0
Moldova, Republic of (BA) [1] — Total employment - Emploi total - Empleo total										
Total - Total - Total — ICSE-93 - CISP-93 - CISE-93										
Total	1 494.4	1 514.6	1 499.0	1 505.1	1 356.5	1 316.0	1 318.7	1 257.3	1 247.2	1 251.0
1	998.2	950.9	899.2	891.8	868.2	840.9	830.6	842.7	831.7	850.3
2	8.3	8.0	7.4	11.4	7.7	8.4	8.7	12.2	11.2	12.0
3	375.0	443.5	466.2	486.8	447.5	453.0	464.7	364.9	375.2	358.9
4	13.6	3.6	9.9	1.1	0.8	0.2	-	0.6	0.1	-
5	99.3	108.6	116.3	114.1	32.4	13.5	14.6	36.8	29.0	29.8
Men - Hommes - Hombres — ICSE-93 - CISP-93 - CISE-93										
Total	739.1	747.4	736.5	730.9	661.3	631.5	629.7	628.6	621.5	628.8
1	501.4	476.1	449.3	435.6	416.0	398.9	389.1	410.1	395.8	408.4
2	6.9	6.6	5.4	7.8	5.1	5.2	6.8	8.9	6.9	8.3
3	184.2	221.4	240.8	252.2	231.0	223.8	228.8	199.1	210.9	203.9
4	7.4	2.5	6.1	0.6	0.5	0.2	-	0.6	0.1	-
5	39.1	40.9	34.9	34.7	8.7	3.4	5.0	9.9	7.9	8.2
Women - Femmes - Mujeres — ICSE-93 - CISP-93 - CISE-93										
Total	755.3	767.2	762.5	774.2	695.2	684.6	689.0	628.7	625.7	622.3
1	496.8	474.8	449.9	456.2	452.2	442.0	441.5	432.6	435.9	441.9
2	1.4	1.3	1.9	3.7	2.6	3.2	2.0	3.3	4.4	3.7
3	190.8	222.2	225.4	234.6	216.5	229.2	235.9	165.8	164.3	155.1
4	6.1	1.1	3.8	0.5	0.3	-	-	0.1	-	-
5	60.2	67.8	81.4	79.3	23.6	10.1	9.6	26.9	21.1	21.6
Montenegro (BA) [2][3] — Total employment - Emploi total - Empleo total										
Total - Total - Total — ICSE-93 - CISP-93 - CISE-93										
Total							178.8			
1							143.9			
2.3							31.0			
5							3.9			
Men - Hommes - Hombres — ICSE-93 - CISP-93 - CISE-93										
Total							105.6			
1							81.4			
2.3							22.3			
5							2.0			
Women - Femmes - Mujeres — ICSE-93 - CISP-93 - CISE-93										
Total							73.2			
1							62.5			
2.3							8.7			
5							1.9			
Netherlands (BA) [1] — Total employment - Emploi total - Empleo total										
Total - Total - Total — ICSE-93 - CISP-93 - CISE-93										
Total	7 613	7 798	7 953	8 018	7 991	7 928	7 958	8 108	8 310	8 457
1.4	6 763	6 863	6 969	7 004	6 959	6 866	6 868	6 992	7 172	7 311
2.3	789	876	926	962	983	1 015	1 041	1 068	1 090	1 107
5	61	59	58	51	50	46	50	48	48	38

Explanatory notes: see p. 77.

[1] Persons aged 15 years and over. [2] Persons aged 15 to 64 years. [3] Oct. of each year.

Notes explicatives: voir p. 80.

[1] Personnes âgées de 15 ans et plus. [2] Personnes âgées de 15 à 64 ans. [3] Oct. de chaque année.

Notas explicativas: véase p. 83.

[1] Personas de 15 años y más. [2] Personas de 15 a 64 años. [3] Oct. de cada año.

Total employment, by status in employment Thousands			Emploi total, par situation dans la profession Milliers				Empleo total, por situación en el empleo Millares		
1999	2000	2001	2002	2003	2004	2005	2006	2007	2008

Netherlands (BA) [1]

Total employment - Emploi total - Empleo total

Men - Hommes - Hombres
ICSE-93 - CISP-93 - CISE-93

	1999	2000	2001	2002	2003	2004	2005	2006	2007	2008
Total	4 382	4 459	4 522	4 526	4 480	4 432	4 421	4 475	4 548	4 594
1,4	3 835	3 864	3 895	3 872	3 801	3 748	3 713	3 748	3 802	3 844
2,3	537	581	616	644	670	675	698	718	735	741
5	10	13	11	10	9	9	10	9	11	8

Women - Femmes - Mujeres
ICSE-93 - CISP-93 - CISE-93

	1999	2000	2001	2002	2003	2004	2005	2006	2007	2008
Total	3 231	3 339	3 431	3 492	3 511	3 495	3 537	3 633	3 763	3 863
1,4	2 928	2 998	3 074	3 131	3 158	3 118	3 155	3 244	3 370	3 467
2,3	252	295	310	319	313	340	342	350	355	366
5	51	46	47	42	40	37	40	39	37	30

Norway (BA) [2]

Total employment - Emploi total - Empleo total

Total - Total - Total
ICSE-93 - CISP-93 - CISE-93

	1999	2000	2001	2002	2003	2004	2005	2006	2007	2008
Total	2 259	2 269	2 278	2 286	2 269	2 276	2 289	2 362 [3]	2 443	2 524
1	2 083	2 099	2 108	2 118	2 098	2 105	2 105	2 162 [3]	2 248	2 328
2	.	.	.	.	.	.	.	48	52	52
2,3	166	158	154	154	158	161	163	. [3]	.	.
3	.	.	.	.	.	.	.	143	136	137
5	9	8	8	7	7	7	6	8 [3]	6	7
6	1	4	8	6	5	3	3	2 [3]	-	-

Men - Hommes - Hombres
ICSE-93 - CISP-93 - CISE-93

	1999	2000	2001	2002	2003	2004	2005	2006	2007	2008
Total	1 209	1 212	1 214	1 210	1 198	1 201	1 211	1 251 [3]	1 289	1 332
1	1 086	1 095	1 098	1 091	1 076	1 078	1 088	1 104 [3]	1 148	1 189
2	.	.	.	.	.	.	.	35	37	37
2,3	119	113	109	113	116	118	119	. [3]	.	.
3	.	.	.	.	.	.	.	106	101	102
5	3	3	3	3	3	4	3	3 [3]	3	3
6	1	1	4	3	3	2	1	1 [3]	-	-

Women - Femmes - Mujeres
ICSE-93 - CISP-93 - CISE-93

	1999	2000	2001	2002	2003	2004	2005	2006	2007	2008
Total	1 050	1 057	1 064	1 076	1 071	1 074	1 078	1 111 [3]	1 154	1 192
1	997	1 004	1 010	1 027	1 022	1 027	1 028	1 057 [3]	1 100	1 139
2	.	.	.	.	.	.	.	13	15	14
2,3	46	46	45	40	42	43	45	. [3]	.	.
3	.	.	.	.	.	.	.	36	35	35
5	6	5	5	5	4	3	3	5 [3]	4	4
6	1	2	4	4	3	1	2	- [3]	-	-

Poland (BA) [1][4]

Total employment - Emploi total - Empleo total

Total - Total - Total
ICSE-93 - CISP-93 - CISE-93

	1999	2000	2001	2002	2003	2004	2005	2006	2007	2008
Total	14 757 [5]	14 526	14 207	13 782	13 617	13 795	14 116	14 594	15 241	15 800
1	10 782 [5]	10 546	10 226	9 904	9 904	10 107	10 481	11 028	11 666	12 179
2	580 [5]	569	540	520	517	550	558	588	616	642
3-4	2 758 [5]	2 686	2 695	2 606	2 451	2 376	2 336	2 315	2 317	2 329
5	636 [5]	724	745	752	745	762	742	662	643	651

Men - Hommes - Hombres
ICSE-93 - CISP-93 - CISE-93

	1999	2000	2001	2002	2003	2004	2005	2006	2007	2008
Total	8 132 [5]	8 004	7 797	7 529	7 432	7 565	7 809	8 081	8 403	8 718
1	5 757 [5]	5 642	5 465	5 241	5 220	5 376	5 630	5 933	6 258	6 541
2	394 [5]	390	379	366	363	382	384	408	427	448
3-4	1 729 [5]	1 680	1 641	1 603	1 549	1 499	1 497	1 485	1 484	1 493
5	252 [5]	292	312	320	300	308	298	255	235	236

Women - Femmes - Mujeres
ICSE-93 - CISP-93 - CISE-93

	1999	2000	2001	2002	2003	2004	2005	2006	2007	2008
Total	6 624 [5]	6 522	6 409	6 253	6 185	6 230	6 307	6 513	6 838	7 082
1	5 025 [5]	4 904	4 761	4 663	4 684	4 731	4 850	5 096	5 408	5 637
2	186 [5]	179	161	155	154	168	174	180	189	194
3-4	1 029 [5]	1 006	1 054	1 003	902	877	839	830	833	836
5	384 [5]	433	433	433	445	454	443	407	408	415

Explanatory notes: see p. 77.

[1] Persons aged 15 years and over. [2] Persons aged 15 to 74 years. [3] Prior to 2006: persons aged 16 to 74 years. [4] Excl. regular military living in barracks and conscripts. [5] First and fourth quarters.

Notes explicatives: voir p. 80.

[1] Personnes âgées de 15 ans et plus. [2] Personnes âgées de 15 à 74 ans. [3] Avant 2006: personnes âgées de 16 à 74 ans. [4] Non compris les militaires de carrière vivant dans des casernes et les conscrits. [5] Premier et quatrième trimestres.

Notas explicativas: véase p. 83.

[1] Personas de 15 años y más. [2] Personas de 15 a 74 años. [3] Antes de 2006: personas de 16 a 74 años. [4] Excl. los militares profesionales que viven en casernas y los conscriptos. [5] Primero y cuarto trimestres.

	Total employment, by status in employment Thousands			Emploi total, par situation dans la profession Milliers			Empleo total, por situación en el empleo Millares			
	1999	2000	2001	2002	2003	2004	2005	2006	2007	2008

Portugal (BA) [1] — Total employment - Emploi total - Empleo total

Total - Total - Total
ICSE-93 - CISP-93 - CISE-93

	1999	2000	2001	2002	2003	2004	2005	2006	2007	2008
Total	4 921.6	5 032.9	5 121.7	5 145.6	5 127.7	5 127.5	5 122.6	5 159.5	5 169.7	5 197.8
1	3 563.4	3 661.6	3 720.9	3 756.2	3 745.8	3 786.9	3 813.8	3 898.1	3 902.2	3 949.7
2	297.7	299.6	314.9	316.6	325.0	328.6	300.2	280.1	286.7	287.2
3	912.2	879.5	943.1	954.2	952.5	910.1	903.8	891.4	900.1	910.4
5	104.4	119.1	104.8	94.9	81.0	76.6	74.6	62.1	55.1	47.6
6	44.0	73.0	38.1	23.8	23.3	25.3	30.2	27.9	25.6	2.9

Men - Hommes - Hombres
ICSE-93 - CISP-93 - CISE-93

Total	2 720.5	2 777.2	2 819.7	2 824.7	2 796.8	2 788.8	2 765.4	2 789.7	2 789.3	2 797.1
1	1 948.0	1 999.2	2 012.6	2 025.0	2 003.8	2 010.7	2 020.6	2 072.9	2 061.1	2 086.9
2	223.9	224.0	240.6	238.9	239.9	241.8	223.3	204.3	205.1	207.6
3	487.7	484.4	519.1	520.5	511.4	496.9	481.2	478.8	490.9	481.5
5	40.2	40.3	30.4	28.3	28.4	26.1	26.0	20.4	20.0	19.4
6	20.6	29.3	17.1	12.0	13.3	13.4	14.3	13.2	12.2	1.7

Women - Femmes - Mujeres
ICSE-93 - CISP-93 - CISE-93

Total	2 201.1	2 255.7	2 302.0	2 320.9	2 330.9	2 338.6	2 357.2	2 369.8	2 380.4	2 400.7
1	1 615.3	1 662.4	1 708.3	1 731.2	1 742.0	1 776.2	1 793.1	1 825.1	1 841.1	1 862.8
2	73.8	75.6	74.3	77.6	85.1	86.8	77.0	75.7	81.6	79.6
3	424.4	395.2	424.0	433.7	441.2	413.2	422.6	412.6	409.1	428.9
5	64.1	78.8	74.3	66.6	52.6	50.5	48.6	41.7	35.1	28.2
6	23.5	43.7	21.0	11.8	10.0	12.0	15.9	14.7	13.4	1.2

Roumanie (BA) [1] — Total employment - Emploi total - Empleo total

Total - Total - Total
ICSE-93 - CISP-93 - CISE-93

Total	10 775.6	10 763.7	10 696.9	9 234.1 [2]	9 222.5	9 157.6	9 146.6	9 313.3	9 353.3	9 369.1
1	6 228.4	6 037.0	5 963.3	5 696.8 [2]	5 760.2	6 035.9	5 920.7	6 167.1	6 197.2	6 316.9
2	110.8	119.5	132.3	136.5 [2]	122.2	155.1	154.3	149.3	136.7	124.7
3	2 381.5	2 488.5	2 529.5	1 985.3 [2]	1 954.1	1 683.3	1 795.1	1 768.1	1 840.0	1 818.2
4	36.3	41.2	27.7	23.8 [2]	17.2	12.5	9.7	-	-	-
5	2 018.4	2 077.4	2 043.8	1 391.5 [2]	1 368.6	1 270.7	1 266.8	1 222.1	1 175.3	1 105.9

Men - Hommes - Hombres
ICSE-93 - CISP-93 - CISE-93

Total	5 799.0	5 772.1	5 719.3	5 031.5 [2]	5 056.7	4 980.0	5 011.2	5 074.0	5 116.3	5 157.4
1	3 514.5	3 358.4	3 294.9	3 169.2 [2]	3 197.2	3 274.4	3 225.3	3 324.1	3 376.4	3 467.8
2	84.8	92.2	95.1	100.6 [2]	91.8	113.3	116.7	112.3	107.5	96.1
3	1 601.2	1 683.7	1 719.5	1 339.3 [2]	1 362.7	1 197.7	1 274.5	1 255.9	1 297.3	1 283.1
4	21.3	25.3	15.4	12.7 [2]	11.3	9.0	-	-	-	-
5	577.0	612.3	594.2	409.5 [2]	393.4	385.4	388.5	377.7	331.7	308.0

Women - Femmes - Mujeres
ICSE-93 - CISP-93 - CISE-93

Total	4 976.5	4 991.5	4 977.5	4 202.6 [2]	4 165.7	4 177.5	4 135.4	4 239.3	4 237.0	4 211.7
1	2 713.8	2 678.6	2 668.4	2 527.6 [2]	2 562.9	2 761.4	2 695.4	2 843.0	2 820.8	2 849.1
2	26.0	27.2	37.1	35.8 [2]	30.3	41.7	37.6	36.9	29.2	28.6
3	780.2	804.7	810.0	646.0 [2]	591.3	485.5	520.6	512.2	542.7	535.1
4	14.9	15.8	12.2	11.0 [2]	5.9	3.4	-	-	-	-
5	1 441.4	1 465.0	1 449.5	981.9 [2]	975.1	885.2	878.2	844.5	843.6	797.9

Russian Federation (BA) [3] — Total employment - Emploi total - Empleo total

Total - Total - Total
ICSE-93 - CISP-93 - CISE-93

Total	62 945	65 070	65 123	66 659	66 432	67 275	68 169	68 855	70 570	70 965
1	56 115	58 512	59 853	61 477	61 522	62 189	62 871	63 648	65 384	65 774
2	545	599	871	869	765	873	874	838	980	1 057
3	5 031	4 951	3 894	3 913	3 760	3 901	4 169	4 099	4 033	3 941
4	1 145	923	467	346	313	253	182	214	93	104
5	109	85	38	55	73	59	73	56	80	88

Men - Hommes - Hombres
ICSE-93 - CISP-93 - CISE-93

Total	32 570	33 574	33 504	34 014	33 827	34 181	34 549	34 695	35 650	36 139
1	28 976	30 058	30 674	31 259	31 108	31 381	31 695	31 849	32 801	33 271
2	369	427	557	531	499	563	526	531	598	667
3	2 449	2 440	1 951	1 972	1 975	2 042	2 167	2 146	2 143	2 079
4	712	597	302	220	205	161	118	135	64	69
5	64	51	21	32	40	35	43	33	43	53

Explanatory notes: see p. 77.   Notes explicatives: voir p. 80.   Notas explicativas: véase p. 83.

[1] Persons aged 15 years and over. [2] Estimates based on the 2002 Population Census results. [3] Persons aged 15 to 72 years.

[1] Personnes âgées de 15 ans et plus. [2] Estimations basées sur les résultats du Recensement de la population de 2002. [3] Personnes âgées de 15 à 72 ans.

[1] Personas de 15 años y más. [2] Estimaciones basadas en los resultados del Censo de población de 2002. [3] Personas de 15 a 72 años.

Total employment, by status in employment
Thousands

Emploi total, par situation dans la profession
Milliers

Empleo total, por situación en el empleo
Millares

	1999	2000	2001	2002	2003	2004	2005	2006	2007	2008
Russian Federation (BA) [1]				Total employment - Emploi total - Empleo total						
Women - Femmes - Mujeres										
ICSE-93 - CISP-93 - CISE-93										
Total	30 375	31 496	31 619	32 645	32 605	33 094	33 620	34 160	34 920	34 826
1	27 139	28 454	29 179	30 218	30 414	30 808	31 177	31 799	32 583	32 503
2	177	172	315	337	266	310	348	307	382	390
3	2 582	2 511	1 942	1 941	1 785	1 859	2 002	1 952	1 890	1 862
4	432	326	165	125	108	93	64	79	29	35
5	45	33	18	23	32	24	30	23	37	36
San Marino (E) [2][3]				Total employment - Emploi total - Empleo total						
Total - Total - Total										
ICSE-93 - CISP-93 - CISE-93										
Total	18.667	.	19.112	19.249	19.350	19.890	20.125	20.695	21.483	21.995
1	15.430	.	16.884	16.992	17.120	17.690	17.946	18.614	19.427	19.965
2-4	2.548	.	2.228	2.257	2.230	2.200	2.179	2.081	2.056	2.030
5	0.032	.	-	-	-	-	-	-	-	-
6	0.657	.	-	-	-	-	-	-	-	-
Men - Hommes - Hombres										
ICSE-93 - CISP-93 - CISE-93										
Total	11.319	.	11.404	11.559	11.480	11.770	11.903	12.219	12.667	12.967
1	9.081	.	9.883	9.991	9.940	10.226	10.392	10.791	11.241	11.550
2-4	1.730	.	1.521	1.568	1.540	1.542	1.511	1.428	1.426	1.417
5	0.010	.	-	-	-	-	-	-	-	-
6	0.498	.	-	-	-	-	-	-	-	-
Women - Femmes - Mujeres										
ICSE-93 - CISP-93 - CISE-93										
Total	7.348	.	7.708	7.690	7.860	8.120	8.222	8.476	8.816	9.028
1	6.349	.	7.001	7.001	7.170	7.460	7.554	7.823	8.186	8.415
2-4	0.818	.	0.707	0.689	0.680	0.662	0.668	0.653	0.630	0.613
5	0.022	.	-	-	-	-	-	-	-	-
6	0.159	.	-	-	-	-	-	-	-	-
Serbia (BA) [2][4]				Total employment - Emploi total - Empleo total						
Total - Total - Total										
ICSE-93 - CISP-93 - CISE-93										
Total	.	.	.	.	.	2 930.8	2 733.4	2 630.7	2 655.7	2 821.7
1	.	.	.	.	.	2 059.4	1 950.2	1 920.8	1 940.8	1 867.2
2	.	.	.	.	.	145.3	115.6	118.3	111.1	125.7
3	.	.	.	.	.	514.2	447.9	411.0	423.7	574.5
5	.	.	.	.	.	212.0	219.8	180.6	180.1	254.3
Men - Hommes - Hombres										
ICSE-93 - CISP-93 - CISE-93										
Total	.	.	.	.	.	1 708.9	1 635.0	1 554.7	1 545.8	1 611.3
1	.	.	.	.	.	1 155.3	1 138.6	1 085.7	1 088.4	1 044.8
2	.	.	.	.	.	109.7	88.1	92.3	78.6	89.6
3	.	.	.	.	.	386.5	341.0	321.2	331.2	411.3
5	.	.	.	.	.	57.4	67.3	55.5	47.5	65.6
Women - Femmes - Mujeres										
ICSE-93 - CISP-93 - CISE-93										
Total	.	.	.	.	.	1 222.0	1 098.4	1 076.0	1 110.0	1 210.4
1	.	.	.	.	.	904.2	811.6	835.2	852.4	822.4
2	.	.	.	.	.	35.5	27.5	25.9	32.5	36.1
3	.	.	.	.	.	127.7	106.9	89.8	92.5	163.2
5	.	.	.	.	.	154.6	152.5	125.2	132.6	188.7
Slovakia (BA) [2][5][6]				Total employment - Emploi total - Empleo total						
Total - Total - Total										
ICSE-93 - CISP-93 - CISE-93										
Total	2 132.1	2 101.7	2 123.7	2 127.0	2 164.6	2 170.4	2 216.2	2 301.4	2 357.3	2 433.8
1,4	1 965.0	1 931.0	1 943.4	1 940.9	1 947.6	1 904.2	1 929.1	2 002.6	2 043.6	2 094.2
2	49.8	52.0	56.3	51.8	60.0	71.7	71.5	71.3	73.5	77.9
3	111.6	112.4	118.9	129.4	148.1	185.1	206.3	216.7	227.9	254.3
5	3.1	3.0	2.7	2.0	2.9	3.1	1.5	1.1	2.2	3.0
6	2.6	3.3	2.3	2.7	5.9	6.0	7.8	9.2	9.6	4.3
Men - Hommes - Hombres										
ICSE-93 - CISP-93 - CISE-93										
Total	1 163.7	1 137.3	1 145.8	1 156.8	1 177.1	1 193.7	1 233.0	1 291.1	1 321.6	1 363.7
1,4	1 042.0	1 014.0	1 015.1	1 019.1	1 023.2	1 000.9	1 020.5	1 073.5	1 091.4	1 111.6
2	37.2	37.3	39.9	39.6	44.5	54.1	53.5	52.5	53.2	59.7
3	83.4	84.8	89.3	97.3	107.5	136.3	157.3	162.2	173.9	190.5
5	0.8	1.0	1.2	0.5	0.6	0.8	0.5	0.5	0.9	1.2
6	0.3	0.4	0.4	0.3	1.1	1.3	1.3	2.0	1.9	0.7

Explanatory notes: see p. 77.

[1] Persons aged 15 to 72 years. [2] Persons aged 15 years and over. [3] Dec. [4] Oct. [5] Excl. conscripts. [6] Excl. persons on child-care leave.

Notes explicatives: voir p. 80.

[1] Personnes âgées de 15 à 72 ans. [2] Personnes âgées de 15 ans et plus. [3] Déc. [4] Oct. [5] Non compris les conscrits. [6] Non compris les personnes en congé parental.

Notas explicativas: véase p. 83.

[1] Personas de 15 a 72 años. [2] Personas de 15 años y más. [3] Dic. [4] Oct. [5] Excl. los conscriptos. [6] Excl. las personas con licencia parental.

EMPLOYMENT / EMPLOI / EMPLEO

	EMPLOYMENT	EMPLOI	EMPLEO
	Total employment, by status in employment	Emploi total, par situation dans la profession	Empleo total, por situación en el empleo
	Thousands	Milliers	Millares

	1999	2000	2001	2002	2003	2004	2005	2006	2007	2008

Slovakia (BA) [1] [2] [3]

Total employment - Emploi total - Empleo total

Women - Femmes - Mujeres
ICSE-93 - CISP-93 - CISE-93

	1999	2000	2001	2002	2003	2004	2005	2006	2007	2008
Total	968.4	964.4	977.9	970.2	987.5	976.7	983.1	1 010.3	1 035.6	1 070.0
1,4	923.0	917.0	928.3	921.8	924.5	903.3	908.6	929.2	952.2	982.6
2	12.6	14.8	16.5	12.2	15.5	17.6	18.0	18.9	20.4	18.2
3	28.2	27.6	29.6	32.1	40.5	48.7	49.0	54.5	54.1	63.7
5	2.3	2.1	1.6	1.5	2.3	2.3	1.1	0.6	1.4	1.9
6	2.3	2.9	1.9	2.5	4.8	4.7	6.5	7.2	7.0	3.6

Slovenia (BA) [1] [4]

Total employment - Emploi total - Empleo total

Total - Total - Total
ICSE-93 - CISP-93 - CISE-93

	1999	2000	2001	2002	2003	2004	2005	2006	2007	2008
Total	892	894	914	922	896	946	947	969	994	990
1	728	750	758	773	771	798	808	810	831	847
2	33	33	34	32	29	33	32	35	33	30
3	80	67	74	75	59	63	63	76	81	70
5	52	43	48	42	38	52	44	49	48	44

Men - Hommes - Hombres
ICSE-93 - CISP-93 - CISE-93

	1999	2000	2001	2002	2003	2004	2005	2006	2007	2008
Total	482	481	497	500	488	511	512	521	542	540
1	381	391	399	404	407	420	427	424	443	449
2	23	25	25	25	21	25	23	24	25	23
3	57	48	54	54	45	44	47	56	56	50
5	21	16	19	16	15	22	16	17	17	18

Women - Femmes - Mujeres
ICSE-93 - CISP-93 - CISE-93

	1999	2000	2001	2002	2003	2004	2005	2006	2007	2008
Total	410	413	417	423	409	434	435	448	451	450
1	347	359	359	368	364	378	381	386	387	397
2	9	8	9	8	7	7	9	10	7	7
3	23	19	20	21	14	19	16	20	25	20
5	30	27	29	26	23	30	28	32	32	26

Suisse (BA) [1] [4] [5]

Total employment - Emploi total - Empleo total

Total - Total - Total
ICSE-93 - CISP-93 - CISE-93

	1999	2000	2001	2002	2003	2004	2005	2006	2007	2008
Total	3 862	3 879	3 938	3 965	3 963	3 959	3 974	4 051	4 122	4 229
1	3 168	3 180	3 262	3 293	3 269	3 317	3 338	3 406	3 456	3 557
2	269	278	267	259	263	254	255	254	248	261
3	316	324	307	311	337	308	301	302	320	327
5	109	97	102	102	93	81	81	90	97	83

Men - Hommes - Hombres
ICSE-93 - CISP-93 - CISE-93

	1999	2000	2001	2002	2003	2004	2005	2006	2007	2008
Total	2 157	2 172	2 190	2 175	2 177	2 173	2 172	2 214	2 259	2 289
1	1 726	1 733	1 765	1 758	1 746	1 765	1 777	1 817	1 853	1 874
2	209	213	202	194	200	196	196	196	186	198
3	183	190	181	182	193	181	170	170	182	184
5	39	36	42	41	38	31	29	30	38	33

Women - Femmes - Mujeres
ICSE-93 - CISP-93 - CISE-93

	1999	2000	2001	2002	2003	2004	2005	2006	2007	2008
Total	1 705	1 707	1 748	1 790	1 786	1 786	1 802	1 837	1 863	1 940
1	1 442	1 447	1 497	1 535	1 523	1 551	1 561	1 589	1 603	1 683
2	60	65	64	65	64	58	59	57	62	64
3	134	134	127	129	144	127	131	131	138	143
5	69	61	60	61	55	50	52	59	59	50

Sweden (BA) [6] [7]

Total employment - Emploi total - Empleo total

Total - Total - Total
ICSE-93 - CISP-93 - CISE-93

	1999	2000	2001	2002	2003	2004	2005	2006	2007	2008
Total	4 068	4 159	4 239	4 244	4 234	4 213	4 263 [8]	4 341	4 541	4 593
1	3 636	3 731	3 815	3 827	3 826	3 796	3 844 [8]	3 908	4 060	4 115
2	419	415	410	404	397	405	410 [8]	425	468	466
5	14	13	14	13	11	11	9 [8]	8	13	12

Men - Hommes - Hombres
ICSE-93 - CISP-93 - CISE-93

	1999	2000	2001	2002	2003	2004	2005	2006	2007	2008
Total	2 121	2 167	2 203	2 197	2 191	2 186	2 225 [8]	2 273	2 390	2 422
1	1 807	1 853	1 892	1 889	1 887	1 874	1 913 [8]	1 951	2 034	2 072
2	309	308	304	302	298	307	307 [8]	318	349	344
5	5	6	6	6	6	6	5 [8]	5	7	6

Explanatory notes: see p. 77.

[1] Persons aged 15 years and over. [2] Excl. conscripts. [3] Excl. persons on child-care leave. [4] Second quarter of each year. [5] Excluding armed forces and seasonal/border workers. [6] Incl. professional army; excl. compulsory military service. [7] Persons aged 15 to 74 years; prior to 2007: 16 to 64 years. [8] Methodology revised; data not strictly comparable.

Notes explicatives: voir p. 80.

[1] Personnes âgées de 15 ans et plus. [2] Non compris les conscrits. [3] Non compris les personnes en congé parental. [4] Deuxième trimestre de chaque année. [5] Non compris les forces armées et les travailleurs saisonniers et frontaliers. [6] Y compris les militaires de carrière; non compris les militaires du contingent. [7] Personnes âgées de 15 à 74 ans; avant 2007: 16 à 64 ans. [8] Méthodologie révisée; les données ne sont pas strictement comparables.

Notas explicativas: véase p. 83.

[1] Personas de 15 años y más. [2] Excl. los conscriptos. [3] Excl. las personas con licencia parental. [4] Segundo trimestre de cada año. [5] Excluidas las fuerzas armadas y excl. a los trabajadores temporales y fronterizos. [6] Incl. los militares profesionales; excl. los militares en servicio obligatorio. [7] Personas de 15 a 74 años; antes de 2007: 16 a 64 años. [8] Metodología revisada; los datos no son estrictamente comparables.

EMPLOYMENT · EMPLOI · EMPLEO **2D**

Total employment, by status in employment — Thousands
Emploi total, par situation dans la profession — Milliers
Empleo total, por situación en el empleo — Millares

	1999	2000	2001	2002	2003	2004	2005	2006	2007	2008

Sweden (BA) [1] [2] — Total employment - Emploi total - Empleo total

Women - Femmes - Mujeres
ICSE-93 - CISP-93 - CISE-93

	1999	2000	2001	2002	2003	2004	2005	2006	2007	2008
Total	1 946	1 992	2 036	2 047	2 043	2 027	2 038 [3]	2 067	2 150	2 171
1	1 828	1 878	1 923	1 939	1 939	1 922	1 931 [3]	1 956	2 025	2 043
2	109	106	106	102	99	99	103 [3]	107	119	123
5	9	7	8	6	5	6	4 [3]	4	6	6

Turkey (BA) [4] [5] — Total employment - Emploi total - Empleo total

Total - Total - Total
ICSE-93 - CISP-93 - CISE-93

	1999	2000	2001	2002	2003	2004	2005	2006	2007	2008
Total	21 414	21 581 [6]	21 524	21 354	21 147	21 791	22 046	22 330	20 738	21 194
1	9 487	10 488 [6]	10 156	10 625	10 707	11 079	11 949	12 617	12 535	12 937
2	1 093	1 109 [6]	1 139	1 186	1 052	1 020	1 132	1 201	1 189	1 249
3	5 151	5 325 [6]	5 365	5 089	5 250	5 388	5 438	5 246	4 386	4 324
5	5 683	4 659 [6]	4 865	4 455	4 138	4 303	3 527	3 266	2 628	2 684

Men - Hommes - Hombres
ICSE-93 - CISP-93 - CISE-93

	1999	2000	2001	2002	2003	2004	2005	2006	2007	2008
Total	15 258	15 780 [6]	15 555	15 232	15 256	16 023	16 346	16 520	15 382	15 598
1	7 685	8 441 [6]	8 173	8 361	8 462	8 814	9 451	9 903	9 726	9 962
2	1 055	1 066 [6]	1 100	1 125	1 010	971	1 081	1 132	1 114	1 172
3	4 604	4 638 [6]	4 596	4 326	4 533	4 805	4 664	4 485	3 769	3 707
5	1 914	1 635 [6]	1 686	1 421	1 250	1 433	1 150	999	773	757

Women - Femmes - Mujeres
ICSE-93 - CISP-93 - CISE-93

	1999	2000	2001	2002	2003	2004	2005	2006	2007	2008
Total	6 158	5 801 [6]	5 969	6 122	5 891	5 768	5 700	5 810	5 356	5 595
1	1 804	2 047 [6]	1 983	2 264	2 246	2 265	2 498	2 714	2 809	2 975
2	38	43 [6]	40	61	42	49	51	69	75	77
3	547	687 [6]	769	763	716	583	774	761	617	616
5	3 769	3 024 [6]	3 179	3 034	2 888	2 870	2 377	2 267	1 855	1 927

Ukraine (BA) [7] — Total employment - Emploi total - Empleo total

Total - Total - Total
ICSE-93 - CISP-93 - CISE-93

	1999	2000	2001	2002	2003	2004	2005	2006	2007	2008
Total	19 947.8	20 175.0	19 971.5	20 091.2	20 163.3	20 295.7	20 680.0	20 730.4	20 904.7	20 972.3
1	18 196.5	18 145.3	17 790.8	17 649.0	17 642.7	16 959.9	16 912.6	16 791.7	16 868.2	17 197.8
2,3	1 558.0	1 806.4	1 922.4	2 067.3	2 204.8	3 222.7	3 664.1	3 852.5	3 957.9	3 701.9
5	193.3	223.3	258.3	374.9	315.8	113.1	103.3	86.2	78.6	72.6

Men - Hommes - Hombres
ICSE-93 - CISP-93 - CISE-93

	1999	2000	2001	2002	2003	2004	2005	2006	2007	2008
Total	10 043.7	10 318.1	10 176.7	10 189.9	10 199.7	10 288.8	10 604.5	10 675.6	10 764.8	10 849.7
1	9 194.3	9 348.7	9 086.8	8 990.6	8 939.9	8 578.0	8 789.8	8 748.4	8 807.3	9 025.1
2,3	781.0	890.7	1 002.8	1 050.8	1 146.6	1 654.2	1 757.3	1 874.9	1 910.4	1 786.6
5	68.4	78.7	87.1	148.5	113.2	56.6	57.4	52.3	47.1	38.0

Women - Femmes - Mujeres
ICSE-93 - CISP-93 - CISE-93

	1999	2000	2001	2002	2003	2004	2005	2006	2007	2008
Total	9 904.1	9 856.9	9 794.8	9 901.3	9 963.6	10 006.9	10 075.5	10 054.8	10 139.9	10 122.6
1	9 002.2	8 796.6	8 704.0	8 658.4	8 702.8	8 381.9	8 122.8	8 043.3	8 060.9	8 172.7
2,3	777.0	915.7	919.6	1 016.5	1 058.2	1 568.5	1 906.8	1 977.6	2 047.5	1 915.3
5	124.9	144.6	171.2	226.4	202.6	56.5	45.9	33.9	31.5	34.6

United Kingdom (BA) [8] [9] — Total employment - Emploi total - Empleo total

Total - Total - Total
ICSE-93 - CISP-93 - CISE-93

	1999	2000	2001	2002	2003	2004	2005	2006	2007	2008
Total	27 023	27 399	27 643	27 852	28 132	28 365	28 665	28 926	29 100	29 475
1	23 614	24 048	24 284	24 437	24 509	24 620	24 976	25 156	25 237	25 553
2,3	3 311	3 241	3 266	3 320	3 537	3 650	3 592	3 680	3 763	3 813
5	98	110	93	95	86	95	98	90	100	110

Men - Hommes - Hombres
ICSE-93 - CISP-93 - CISE-93

	1999	2000	2001	2002	2003	2004	2005	2006	2007	2008
Total	14 692	14 859	14 961	15 033	15 256	15 327	15 468	15 578	15 747	15 904
1	12 233	12 478	12 538	12 578	12 642	12 614	12 796	12 872	12 971	13 095
2,3	2 426	2 345	2 391	2 425	2 583	2 674	2 635	2 670	2 740	2 769
5	33	36	32	30	31	40	36	36	36	39

Explanatory notes: see p. 77.

[1] Incl. professional army; excl. compulsory military service. [2] Persons aged 15 to 74 years; prior to 2007: 16 to 64 years. [3] Methodology revised; data not strictly comparable. [4] Excl. armed forces. [5] Persons aged 15 years and over. [6] Estimates based on the 2000 Population Census results. Prior to 2000: persons aged 12 years and over. [7] Persons aged 15-70 years. [8] Persons aged 16 years and over. [9] Second quarter.

Notes explicatives: voir p. 80.

[1] Y compris les militaires de carrière; non compris les militaires du contingent. [2] Personnes âgées de 15 à 74 ans; avant 2007: 16 à 64 ans. [3] Méthodologie révisée; les données ne sont pas strictement comparables. [4] Non compris les forces armées. [5] Personnes âgées de 15 ans et plus. [6] Estimations basées sur les résultats du Recensement de la population de 2000. Avant 2000: personnes âgées de 12 ans et plus. [7] Personnes âgées de 15 à 70 ans. [8] Personnes âgées de 16 ans et plus. [9] Deuxième trimestre.

Notas explicativas: véase p. 83.

[1] Incl. los militares profesionales; excl. los militares en servicio obligatorio. [2] Personas de 15 a 74 años; antes de 2007: 16 a 64 años. [3] Metodología revisada; los datos no son estrictamente comparables. [4] Excl. las fuerzas armadas. [5] Personas de 15 años y más. [6] Estimaciones basadas en los resultados del Censo de población de 2000. Antes de 2000: personas de 12 años y más. [7] Personas de 15 á 70 años. [8] Personas de 16 años y más. [9] Segundo trimestre.

	EMPLOYMENT				**EMPLOI**				**EMPLEO**	
	Total employment, by status in employment Thousands				Emploi total, par situation dans la profession Milliers				Empleo total, por situación en el empleo Millares	
	1999	2000	2001	2002	2003	2004	2005	2006	2007	2008

United Kingdom (BA) [1] [2]   Total employment - Emploi total - Empleo total

Women - Femmes - Mujeres
ICSE-93 - CISP-93 - CISE-93

Total	12 331	12 540	12 681	12 819	12 876	13 038	13 198	13 348	13 353	13 572
1	11 380	11 570	11 746	11 859	11 867	12 006	12 180	12 284	12 267	12 457
2,3	885	895	875	895	954	976	957	1 010	1 023	1 043
5	65	75	61	65	55	56	62	54	63	71

OCEANIA-OCÉANIE-OCEANIA

Australia (BA) [3] [4]   Total employment - Emploi total - Empleo total

Total - Total - Total
ICSE-93 - CISP-93 - CISE-93

Total	8 720.2	8 951.3	9 081.4	9 245.8	9 464.9	9 623.3	9 968.6	10 218.3	10 512.3	10 740.5
1	7 456.7	7 690.5	7 832.7	7 964.7	8 195.7	8 354.5	8 678.2	8 943.5	9 251.8	9 472.1
2	349.1	329.8	323.3	313.5	307.0	305.3	310.8	302.6	284.2	299.1
3	843.5	858.8	884.8	925.8	925.2	927.0	947.1	940.6	947.5	944.3
5	70.9	72.1	40.7	41.7	37.0	36.5	32.5	31.6	28.9	25.0

Men - Hommes - Hombres
ICSE-93 - CISP-93 - CISE-93

Total	4 917.6	5 006.0	5 036.4	5 131.0	5 225.6	5 331.0	5 488.0	5 605.6	5 769.9	5 879.2
1	4 076.2	4 168.5	4 201.2	4 278.9	4 379.6	4 484.7	4 635.7	4 760.6	4 935.1	5 047.9
2	236.3	219.9	211.6	207.3	204.4	201.6	206.3	196.0	186.8	197.1
3	578.2	588.3	605.6	627.5	626.8	629.9	633.2	636.5	636.0	623.8
5	26.9	29.3	18.0	17.3	14.7	14.8	12.9	12.5	12.1	10.3

Women - Femmes - Mujeres
ICSE-93 - CISP-93 - CISE-93

Total	3 802.6	3 945.3	4 045.0	4 114.8	4 239.4	4 292.3	4 480.6	4 612.8	4 742.4	4 861.3
1	3 380.6	3 522.0	3 631.5	3 685.8	3 816.1	3 869.8	4 042.5	4 182.9	4 316.7	4 424.1
2	112.8	109.9	111.7	106.2	102.7	103.7	104.5	106.7	97.4	102.0
3	265.3	270.5	279.1	298.4	298.4	297.1	313.9	304.1	311.6	320.4
5	43.9	42.9	22.7	24.4	22.3	21.7	19.6	19.1	16.7	14.7

New Zealand (BA) [3] [4]   Total employment - Emploi total - Empleo total

Total - Total - Total
ICSE-93 - CISP-93 - CISE-93

Total	1 766.3	1 800.0	1 845.8	1 906.2	1 955.6	2 024.1	2 084.6	2 134.7	2 174.5	2 188.2
1	1 395.6	1 425.2	1 482.2	1 540.1	1 579.7	1 637.9	1 702.1	1 759.7	1 800.3	1 811.2
2	130.2	126.7	131.6	131.5	138.0	140.5	134.0	114.5	114.4	110.5
3	224.1	228.1	215.9	219.5	224.2	233.4	234.6	239.1	233.3	243.3
5	16.4	15.2	16.0	14.9	13.3	11.6	13.1	19.5	24.1	21.0
6	-	4.9	-	-	-	-	-	1.9	2.3	2.2

Men - Hommes - Hombres
ICSE-93 - CISP-93 - CISE-93

Total	963.1	981.6	1 001.7	1 035.5	1 056.8	1 095.6	1 120.1	1 146.3	1 165.0	1 164.9
1	711.5	727.8	755.1	784.2	798.4	834.5	865.5	894.9	918.9	916.8
2	91.2	89.8	92.2	93.6	98.9	99.3	93.0	81.3	82.2	78.6
3	154.4	156.4	148.4	151.9	154.3	157.8	156.8	162.1	153.7	160.2
5	6.0	4.9	5.8	5.8	5.0	3.7	4.4	7.0	8.8	8.2
6	-	2.8	-	-	-	-	-	-	1.4	1.2

Women - Femmes - Mujeres
ICSE-93 - CISP-93 - CISE-93

Total	803.3	818.4	844.1	870.6	898.8	928.5	964.6	988.4	1 009.5	1 023.2
1	684.1	697.4	727.1	755.9	781.3	803.4	836.6	864.8	881.4	894.4
2	39.0	36.9	39.4	37.9	39.1	41.2	41.0	33.2	32.2	31.9
3	69.7	71.7	67.4	67.6	70.0	75.6	77.8	77.0	79.6	83.1
5	10.4	10.3	10.2	9.1	8.3	7.9	8.7	12.5	15.4	12.8
6	-	2.1	-	-	-	-	-	-	-	-

Explanatory notes: see p. 77.

[1] Persons aged 16 years and over. [2] Second quarter. [3] Excl. armed forces. [4] Persons aged 15 years and over.

Notes explicatives: voir p. 80.

[1] Personnes âgées de 16 ans et plus. [2] Deuxième trimestre. [3] Non compris les forces armées. [4] Personnes âgées de 15 ans et plus.

Notas explicativas: véase p. 83.

[1] Personas de 16 años y más. [2] Segundo trimestre. [3] Excl. las fuerzas armadas. [4] Personas de 15 años y más.

Paid employment, by economic activity
Emploi rémunéré, par activité économique
Empleo remunerado, por actividad económica

Thousands — Milliers — Millares

AFRICA-AFRIQUE-AFRICA

Botswana (BA) [1] — Employees - Salariés - Asalariados

Total - Total - Total
ISIC 3 - CITI 3 - CIIU 3

	1999	2000	2001	2002	2003	2004	2005	2006	2007	2008
Total	.	337.2	371.3	.	351.1	.	.	326.1	.	.
A-B	.	20.4	30.9	.	32.7	.	.	27.3	.	.
C	.	11.2	13.0	.	13.4	.	.	14.2	.	.
D	.	33.2	28.5	.	33.2	.	.	22.9	.	.
E	.	2.2	3.7	.	4.4	.	.	4.1	.	.
F	.	34.0	49.8	.	40.4	.	.	21.6	.	.
G	.	39.1	40.1	.	38.8	.	.	36.7	.	.
H	.	8.2	11.1	.	11.1	.	.	9.5	.	.
I	.	11.4	13.0	.	11.1	.	.	12.1	.	.
J	.	4.3	5.4	.	4.7	.	.	7.8	.	.
K	.	15.0	22.0	.	13.7	.	.	21.4	.	.
L	.	72.3	70.0	.	67.2	.	.	60.2	.	.
M	.	42.5	37.5	.	38.6	.	.	42.8	.	.
N	.	11.9	13.8	.	13.5	.	.	12.9	.	.
O	.	9.5	7.8	.	6.6	.	.	6.7	.	.
P	.	20.0	22.2	.	21.5	.	.	25.2	.	.
Q	.	0.3	0.7	.	0.2	.	.	0.9	.	.
X	.	1.7	2.0	.	0.0	.	.	.	.	.

Botswana (DA) [2] [3] — Employees - Salariés - Asalariados

Total - Total - Total
ISIC 3 - CITI 3 - CIIU 3

	1999	2000	2001	2002	2003	2004	2005	2006	2007	2008
Total	257.1	265.3	270.6	278.9	285.4	297.4	288.8	298.8	302.0	.
A-B	5.4	5.8	6.3	6.0	6.3	5.8	5.6	5.6	5.5	.
C	8.3	7.9	7.0	7.5	8.0	9.3	9.4	11.5	11.7	.
D	28.0	29.8	29.7	29.8	30.2	34.7	32.4	34.5	35.2	.
E	2.7	2.9	2.8	3.1	2.8	2.6	2.4	2.9	2.8	.
F	27.5	27.3	28.6	28.9	29.8	27.5	24.4	22.8	21.8	.
G	34.2	37.0	40.4	41.0	42.1	41.7	41.4	43.0	44.1	.
H	10.3	10.6	11.6	12.8	13.2	11.6	14.6	15.1	15.0	.
I	9.8	9.9	10.1	10.1	10.3	12.3	12.6	12.7	12.6	.
J	4.8	5.0	5.6	5.7	5.8	4.4	5.2	6.6	6.8	.
K	12.4	13.3	12.5	12.6	13.3	16.6	16.6	16.9	17.9	.
L	104.0	105.1	104.4	109.4	110.9	118.4	111.4	113.0	114.4	.
M	5.6	6.2	6.6	6.8	7.1	8.3	7.9	8.8	8.8	.
N	2.0	2.0	2.3	2.3	2.6	1.9	2.0	2.2	2.2	.
O	2.2	2.3	2.9	3.0	3.2	2.4	3.2	3.1	3.2	.

Men - Hommes - Hombres
ISIC 3 - CITI 3 - CIIU 3

	1999	2000	2001	2002	2003	2004	2005	2006	2007	2008
Total	.	.	160.2	162.3	169.9	180.1	166.3	168.7	171.3	.
A-B	.	.	4.5	4.4	4.8	3.7	3.6	3.3	3.5	.
C	.	.	6.5	6.8	7.1	8.4	8.2	10.0	10.2	.
D	.	.	14.2	13.5	13.9	17.4	15.9	17.1	17.7	.
E	.	.	2.3	2.6	2.3	2.1	2.0	2.3	2.3	.
F	.	.	25.0	25.3	26.6	23.5	21.2	19.3	18.8	.
G	.	.	22.1	22.9	24.2	23.1	23.1	22.8	23.2	.
H	.	.	4.3	5.0	4.7	4.3	5.4	4.6	5.8	.
I	.	.	7.0	7.1	7.2	9.2	9.5	9.0	8.8	.
J	.	.	2.2	2.1	2.2	1.6	1.8	2.7	2.6	.
K	.	.	8.6	8.9	10.0	12.0	10.9	12.3	12.6	.
L	.	.	58.0	57.9	61.0	69.2	58.8	59.1	59.6	.
M	.	.	3.3	3.4	3.6	4.0	3.8	4.2	3.9	.
N	.	.	0.6	0.5	0.7	0.6	0.6	0.6	0.6	.
O	.	.	1.5	1.4	1.6	1.0	1.3	1.3	1.6	.

Women - Femmes - Mujeres
ISIC 3 - CITI 3 - CIIU 3

	1999	2000	2001	2002	2003	2004	2005	2006	2007	2008
Total	.	.	110.4	117.4	115.5	117.3	122.5	130.1	130.6	.
A-B	.	.	1.8	1.6	1.5	2.1	2.0	2.3	2.0	.
C	.	.	0.4	0.7	0.9	1.0	1.2	1.5	1.6	.
D	.	.	15.5	16.3	16.2	17.3	16.5	17.4	17.5	.
E	.	.	0.5	0.5	0.5	0.5	0.4	0.6	0.5	.
F	.	.	3.6	3.6	3.1	3.9	3.2	3.5	3.0	.
G	.	.	18.3	18.1	17.9	18.5	18.3	20.1	20.9	.
H	.	.	7.4	7.8	8.6	7.3	9.1	10.5	9.2	.
I	.	.	3.0	3.0	3.0	3.1	3.1	3.7	3.8	.
J	.	.	3.4	3.6	3.6	2.8	3.4	4.0	4.2	.
K	.	.	3.2	3.7	3.3	4.5	5.7	4.6	5.3	.
L	.	.	46.3	51.5	49.9	49.2	52.6	53.8	54.8	.
M	.	.	3.2	3.3	3.5	4.3	4.1	4.6	4.9	.
N	.	.	1.7	1.8	1.9	1.3	1.4	1.6	1.5	.
O	.	.	1.3	1.6	1.7	1.4	1.8	1.8	1.5	.

Explanatory notes: see p. 77.

[1] Persons aged 12 years and over. [2] Excl. armed forces. [3] Sep. of each year.

Notes explicatives: voir p. 80.

[1] Personnes âgées de 12 ans et plus. [2] Non compris les forces armées. [3] Sept. de chaque année.

Notas explicativas: véase p. 83.

[1] Personas de 12 años y más. [2] Excl. las fuerzas armadas. [3] Sept. de cada año.

EMPLOYMENT — EMPLOI — EMPLEO

Paid employment, by economic activity — Emploi rémunéré, par activité économique — Empleo remunerado, por actividad económica

	Thousands — Milliers — Millares									
	1999	2000	2001	2002	2003	2004	2005	2006	2007	2008
Egypt (BA) [1][2][3]				Employees - Salariés - Asalariados						
Total - Total - Total										
ISIC 3 - CITI 3 - CIIU 3										
Total	10 237.5	10 311.9	10 797.9	10 747.3	10 485.7	10 572.8	11 605.1	12 635.0	12 715.1	
A	1 065.6	1 023.0	1 219.3	981.2	972.3	987.1	1 203.8	1 507.1	1 377.7	
B	12.0	26.7	42.0	31.6	23.3	27.8	43.6	60.4	44.3	
C	42.2	35.4	55.4	38.0	30.2	30.6	27.7	51.8	33.3	
D	1 756.9	1 617.6	1 684.7	1 623.0	1 500.6	1 622.8	1 793.4	1 929.7	1 842.1	
E	202.4	205.0	201.5	238.4	225.0	216.2	244.5	249.1	266.1	
F	1 012.9	1 033.7	1 040.5	1 006.3	1 004.6	1 057.0	1 221.5	1 367.6	1 470.5	
G	703.1	649.1	644.9	689.3	610.3	696.5	806.4	883.2	878.3	
H	197.9	170.6	229.5	218.3	171.6	218.1	269.3	321.4	276.1	
I	704.7	785.4	789.8	749.4	742.2	777.4	933.4	965.8	1 025.5	
J	183.8	184.8	196.1	218.0	198.7	194.8	169.0	174.5	193.4	
K	157.4	177.7	183.2	165.9	177.3	182.8	230.7	261.7	246.9	
L	1 625.7	1 820.9	1 873.4	1 934.6	2 011.0	1 917.0	1 845.3	1 898.7	1 961.5	
M	1 758.7	1 783.0	1 796.4	1 949.0	1 959.7	1 832.5	1 900.2	1 961.2	2 066.5	
N	515.3	507.9	532.7	575.7	523.8	479.8	486.1	526.5	539.3	
O	262.6	245.8	254.6	277.8	302.2	300.3	356.0	401.9	423.9	
P	35.5	43.4	50.6	49.3	31.3	30.6	48.0	39.5	47.3	
Q	-	-	-	-	-	-	2.7	2.5	1.0	
X	0.9	1.9	3.4	1.4	1.4	1.5	23.5	32.7	21.4	
Men - Hommes - Hombres										
ISIC 3 - CITI 3 - CIIU 3										
Total	8 217.1	8 455.4	8 728.7	8 502.0	8 526.8	8 709.0	9 698.8	10 550.0	10 496.7	
A	959.2	929.1	1 121.9	921.0	901.9	917.2	1 133.0	1 424.4	1 306.6	
B	11.4	26.7	42.0	31.2	22.8	27.5	43.6	60.0	44.3	
C	41.2	34.2	54.5	35.5	28.7	30.1	26.2	48.0	32.8	
D	1 493.3	1 480.5	1 436.8	1 370.6	1 372.7	1 495.6	1 665.6	1 778.9	1 712.2	
E	184.3	188.0	187.1	216.7	205.2	200.8	226.3	227.9	241.7	
F	994.2	1 009.0	1 017.5	974.4	979.5	1 037.2	1 208.4	1 353.8	1 454.0	
G	579.1	580.6	557.0	569.1	537.4	608.3	733.1	801.6	776.6	
H	161.3	165.2	180.5	171.7	164.3	208.2	264.0	309.7	270.3	
I	664.5	726.5	732.9	683.7	693.3	724.5	888.6	912.5	973.3	
J	142.2	141.2	149.6	159.3	150.8	147.9	128.8	133.2	973.9	
K	129.5	139.4	151.2	126.4	140.2	146.2	186.6	214.4	143.9	
L	1 287.0	1 439.9	1 483.5	1 513.7	1 567.1	1 512.3	1 442.7	1 473.1	199.5	
M	1 057.6	1 058.3	1 090.7	1 167.4	1 184.9	1 107.9	1 127.7	1 133.7	1 509.2	
N	243.1	276.3	271.3	286.2	275.2	241.1	231.4	246.3	1 158.3	
O	242.0	222.5	219.0	240.4	275.0	276.4	330.1	370.7	239.8	
P	26.3	36.9	31.0	33.3	26.7	26.4	39.6	30.4	34.2	
Q	-	-	-	-	-	-	1.9	2.1	0.5	
X	0.9	1.1	2.3	1.4	1.1	1.4	21.2	29.5	19.5	
Women - Femmes - Mujeres										
ISIC 3 - CITI 3 - CIIU 3										
Total	2 020.4	1 856.5	2 069.2	2 245.3	1 958.9	1 863.8	1 906.3	2 085.1	2 218.4	
A	106.4	93.9	97.4	60.2	70.4	69.9	70.8	82.7	71.1	
B	0.6	-	-	0.4	0.5	0.3	-	0.4	-	
C	1.0	1.2	0.9	2.5	1.5	0.5	1.5	3.8	0.5	
D	263.6	137.1	247.9	252.4	127.9	127.2	127.8	150.8	129.9	
E	18.1	17.0	14.4	21.7	19.8	15.4	18.2	21.2	24.4	
F	18.7	24.7	23.0	31.9	25.1	19.8	13.1	13.8	16.5	
G	124.0	68.5	87.9	120.2	72.9	88.2	73.3	81.6	101.7	
H	36.6	5.4	49.0	46.6	7.3	9.9	5.3	11.7	5.8	
I	40.2	58.9	56.9	65.7	49.1	52.9	44.8	53.3	51.6	
J	41.6	43.6	46.5	58.7	47.9	46.9	40.2	41.3	49.5	
K	27.9	38.3	32.0	39.5	37.1	36.6	44.1	47.3	47.4	
L	338.7	381.0	389.9	420.9	443.9	404.7	402.6	425.6	452.3	
M	701.1	724.7	705.7	781.6	774.8	724.6	772.5	827.5	908.2	
N	272.2	231.6	261.4	289.5	248.6	238.7	254.7	280.2	299.9	
O	20.6	23.3	35.6	37.4	27.2	23.9	25.9	31.2	44.1	
P	9.2	6.5	19.6	16.0	4.6	4.2	8.4	9.1	13.1	
Q	-	-	-	-	-	-	0.8	0.4	0.5	
X	-	0.8	1.1	-	0.3	0.1	2.3	3.2	1.9	
Madagascar (B) [4]				Employees - Salariés - Asalariados						
Total - Total - Total										
ISIC 3 - CITI 3 - CIIU 3										
Total							1 285.8			
A							300.8			
B							7.4			
C							11.1			
D							222.9			
E							18.1			
F							10.4			
G							56.1			
H							27.6			
I							73.7			
J							4.1			
K										
L							195.4			
M							42.3			
N							8.1			
O							307.9			

Explanatory notes: see p. 77. Notes explicatives: voir p. 80. Notas explicativas: véase p. 83.

[1] Persons aged 15 to 64 years. [2] Excl. armed forces. [3] May and Nov. [4] Persons aged 6 years and over.

[1] Personnes âgées de 15 à 64 ans. [2] Non compris les forces armées. [3] Mai et nov. [4] Personnes âgées de 6 ans et plus.

[1] Personas de 15 a 64 años. [2] Excl. las fuerzas armadas. [3] Mayo y nov. [4] Personas de 6 años y más.

Paid employment, by economic activity / Emploi rémunéré, par activité économique / Empleo remunerado, por actividad económica

	Thousands			Milliers				Millares		
	1999	2000	2001	2002	2003	2004	2005	2006	2007	2008

Madagascar (B) [1] — Employees - Salariés - Asalariados

Men - Hommes - Hombres
ISIC 3 - CITI 3 - CIIU 3

	1999	2000	2001	2002	2003	2004	2005	2006	2007	2008
Total	.	.	.	.	.	.	775.1	.	.	.
A	.	.	.	.	.	.	159.2	.	.	.
B	.	.	.	.	.	.	6.5	.	.	.
C	.	.	.	.	.	.	6.1	.	.	.
D	.	.	.	.	.	.	171.1	.	.	.
E	.	.	.	.	.	.	12.6	.	.	.
F	.	.	.	.	.	.	9.9	.	.	.
G	.	.	.	.	.	.	29.8	.	.	.
H	.	.	.	.	.	.	14.4	.	.	.
I	.	.	.	.	.	.	68.5	.	.	.
J	.	.	.	.	.	.	2.7	.	.	.
K	.	.	.	.	.	.		.	.	.
L	.	.	.	.	.	.	129.5	.	.	.
M	.	.	.	.	.	.	17.2	.	.	.
N	.	.	.	.	.	.	3.7	.	.	.
O	.	.	.	.	.	.	143.8	.	.	.

Women - Femmes - Mujeres
ISIC 3 - CITI 3 - CIIU 3

	1999	2000	2001	2002	2003	2004	2005	2006	2007	2008
Total	.	.	.	.	.	.	510.7	.	.	.
A	.	.	.	.	.	.	141.6	.	.	.
B	.	.	.	.	.	.	0.9	.	.	.
C	.	.	.	.	.	.	5.0	.	.	.
D	.	.	.	.	.	.	51.8	.	.	.
E	.	.	.	.	.	.	5.5	.	.	.
F	.	.	.	.	.	.	0.5	.	.	.
G	.	.	.	.	.	.	26.3	.	.	.
H	.	.	.	.	.	.	13.2	.	.	.
I	.	.	.	.	.	.	5.1	.	.	.
J	.	.	.	.	.	.	1.4	.	.	.
K	.	.	.	.	.	.		.	.	.
L	.	.	.	.	.	.	65.9	.	.	.
M	.	.	.	.	.	.	25.0	.	.	.
N	.	.	.	.	.	.	4.3	.	.	.
O	.	.	.	.	.	.	164.2	.	.	.

Mauritius (DA) [2] — Employees - Salariés - Asalariados

Total - Total - Total
ISIC 3 - CITI 3 - CIIU 3

	1999	2000	2001	2002	2003	2004	2005	2006	2007	2008
Total	297.670	296.787	301.085	294.641	298.537	295.417	290.516	293.896	299.361	304.395
A-B	34.294	32.663	31.253	25.258	23.394	23.111	22.044	21.636	21.684	18.512
C	0.225	0.193	0.192	0.170	0.214	0.217	0.182	0.180	0.140	0.140
D	115.558	114.987	116.960	111.017	108.907	101.715	92.620	91.021	92.261	91.978
E	3.102	3.006	2.955	3.041	2.992	2.932	2.980	2.988	2.999	3.081
F	13.605	13.528	13.287	13.027	14.621	15.333	12.524	12.925	13.629	13.477
G	16.394	16.459	16.477	16.909	17.691	18.157	18.091	18.113	18.835	19.624
H	13.003	14.117	15.870	16.755	17.815	18.476	21.035	21.341	22.026	24.346
I	16.359	16.010	16.540	17.398	17.752	17.801	18.050	18.333	18.513	19.051
J	6.624	6.693	7.037	6.975	7.347	7.494	8.401	9.009	9.293	10.608
K	8.316	9.776	9.823	10.351	11.061	12.394	14.295	15.145	17.196	19.071
L	34.763	34.888	35.664	37.780	38.823	38.738	39.547	40.298	39.582	39.849
M	17.859	17.826	18.295	18.914	20.635	21.331	22.202	24.045	24.040	24.347
N	11.410	11.257	11.002	10.986	11.608	12.127	12.604	12.670	12.984	13.344
O	6.158	5.384	5.749	6.079	5.700	5.591	5.941	6.192	6.179	6.877

Men - Hommes - Hombres
ISIC 3 - CITI 3 - CIIU 3

	1999	2000	2001	2002	2003	2004	2005	2006	2007	2008
Total	188.104	186.713	187.905	186.628	188.477	189.377	187.768	188.989	192.438	195.197
A-B	25.840	24.559	23.426	19.972	19.106	19.080	18.244	18.052	18.047	15.393
C	0.110	0.097	0.092	0.085	0.109	0.115	0.088	0.090	0.075	0.076
D	49.958	49.558	50.151	49.191	47.415	46.484	44.427	43.626	45.004	46.203
E	2.936	2.843	2.790	2.868	2.833	2.780	2.830	2.824	2.821	2.894
F	13.201	13.073	12.812	12.500	14.094	14.780	11.943	12.345	13.070	12.863
G	11.681	11.706	11.726	12.063	12.425	12.710	12.414	12.395	12.860	13.205
H	10.454	11.333	12.644	13.336	13.940	14.505	16.258	16.298	16.746	18.042
I	13.846	13.430	13.692	14.569	14.667	14.609	14.793	14.927	15.049	15.495
J	4.075	4.048	4.238	4.160	4.276	4.302	4.648	4.910	5.031	5.517
K	6.447	7.175	7.248	7.170	7.724	8.184	9.290	9.839	10.884	12.051
L	28.388	28.257	28.462	29.880	30.560	30.371	30.823	31.130	30.251	30.591
M	10.422	10.330	10.178	10.251	10.869	10.836	10.997	11.432	11.337	11.185
N	5.966	5.949	5.848	5.777	6.069	6.262	6.456	6.494	6.619	6.605
O	4.780	4.355	4.598	5.806	4.390	4.359	4.557	4.627	4.644	5.077

Explanatory notes: see p. 77.

[1] Persons aged 6 years and over. [2] Establishments with 10 or more persons employed.

Notes explicatives: voir p. 80.

[1] Personnes âgées de 6 ans et plus. [2] Etablissements occupant 10 personnes et plus.

Notas explicativas: véase p. 83.

[1] Personas de 6 años y más. [2] Establecimientos con 10 y más trabajadores.

EMPLOYMENT — EMPLOI — EMPLEO

Paid employment, by economic activity
Emploi rémunéré, par activité économique
Empleo remunerado, por actividad económica

Thousands — Milliers — Millares

Mauritius (DA) [1]
Employees - Salariés - Asalariados

Women - Femmes - Mujeres
ISIC 3 - CITI 3 - CIIU 3

	1999	2000	2001	2002	2003	2004	2005	2006	2007	2008
Total	109.566	110.074	113.180	108.013	110.060	106.040	102.748	104.907	106.923	109.198
A-B	8.454	8.104	7.827	5.286	4.288	4.031	3.800	3.584	3.637	3.119
C	0.115	0.096	0.100	0.085	0.105	0.102	0.094	0.090	0.065	0.064
D	65.600	65.429	66.809	61.826	61.492	55.321	48.193	47.395	47.257	45.775
E	0.166	0.163	0.165	0.173	0.159	0.152	0.150	0.164	0.178	0.187
F	0.404	0.455	0.456	0.508	0.504	0.553	0.581	0.580	0.559	0.614
G	4.713	4.753	4.751	4.846	5.266	5.447	5.677	5.718	5.975	6.419
H	2.549	2.784	3.226	3.419	4.875	3.971	4.777	5.043	5.280	6.304
I	2.513	2.580	2.848	2.829	3.085	3.192	3.257	3.406	3.464	3.556
J	2.549	2.645	2.799	2.815	3.071	3.192	3.753	4.099	4.262	5.091
K	1.869	2.601	2.575	3.181	3.337	4.210	5.005	5.306	6.312	7.020
L	6.375	6.631	7.202	7.900	8.263	8.367	8.724	9.168	9.331	9.258
M	7.437	7.496	8.117	8.663	9.766	10.495	11.205	12.613	12.703	13.252
N	5.444	5.308	5.154	5.209	5.539	5.865	6.148	6.176	6.365	6.739
O	1.378	1.029	1.151	1.273	1.310	1.232	1.384	1.565	1.535	1.800

Réunion (E)
Employees - Salariés - Asalariados

Total - Total - Total
ISIC 3 - CITI 3 - CIIU 3

	1999	2000	2001	2002	2003	2004	2005	2006	2007	2008
Total	159.4	167.5	175.0	180.6	183.4	184.6	189.6	197.8	206.6	.
A-B	2.9	3.1	3.2	3.1	3.0	3.2	3.2	3.2	3.3	.
D	11.0	11.3	11.5	11.3	11.7	11.9	12.1	12.3	12.6	.
E	1.3	1.5	1.8	1.7	1.6	1.7	1.8	1.8	1.8	.
F	9.1	9.7	10.3	10.5	11.4	12.6	14.5	17.0	18.7	.
G	21.2	22.4	23.4	24.5	25.1	25.6	26.3	26.8	27.1	.
H	3.5	3.7	3.9	4.2	4.4	4.6	4.9	4.7	5.1	.
I	7.3	7.9	8.5	8.8	9.0	9.5	9.8	10.1	10.9	.
J	3.1	3.4	3.5	3.5	3.5	3.7	3.7	3.7	4.0	.
K	10.5	11.5	12.5	12.9	13.7	14.4	15.1	15.9	18.8	.
L	38.2	40.2	40.8	41.8	43.0	40.6	40.1	41.1	41.9	.
M	22.9	23.3	23.8	24.8	23.9	23.7	24.1	24.9	23.5	.
N	14.4	14.9	15.9	16.7	16.3	16.0	16.4	17.4	18.3	.
O	7.2	7.8	7.8	8.1	7.4	7.6	7.7	8.8	9.5	.
P	6.647	6.985	8.168	8.835	9.420	9.769	9.954	10.580	11.270	.

Seychelles (FA)
Employees - Salariés - Asalariados

Total - Total - Total
ISIC 2 - CITI 2 - CIIU 2   (right: ISIC 3 - CITI 3 - CIIU 3)

ISIC 2	1999	2000	2001	2002	2003	2004	2005	2006	2007	2008	ISIC 3
Total [2]	31.01	32.13	33.11	34.02	33.111	32.779	34.545	37.625	39.572	.	Total
1	2.16	2.13	2.14	2.12	0.697	0.611	0.695	0.719	0.642	.	A
3	3.67	3.81	3.75	3.66	0.383	0.433	0.440	0.470	0.404	.	B
4	0.88	0.97	1.02	1.03	0.018	0.018	0.018	0.015	0.018	.	C
5 [3]	2.79	2.54	2.54	2.78	4.398	4.213	4.324	4.465	4.455	.	D
6	6.57	6.99	7.34	7.41	1.050	1.052	1.068	1.089	1.085	.	E
7	3.33	3.52	3.63	3.69	2.037	2.123	2.668	3.702	4.255	.	F
8	1.61	1.81	1.89	1.90	2.494	2.482	2.591	2.756	2.851	.	G
9	5.99	6.11	6.56	7.29	4.692	4.543	4.923	5.222	5.728	.	H
0 [4]	4.26	4.25	4.23	4.14	2.953	3.094	3.269	3.366	3.917	.	I
					0.605	0.633	0.677	0.731	0.781	.	J
					1.676	1.413	1.472	1.639	1.897	.	K
					5.452	5.705	5.795	5.995	6.095	.	L
					2.794	2.609	2.600	2.591	2.643	.	M
					1.765	1.716	1.628	1.643	1.705	.	N
					2.097	2.134	2.377	3.223	3.094	.	O

South Africa (DA) [5]
Employees - Salariés - Asalariados

Total - Total - Total
ISIC 2 - CITI 2 - CIIU 2

	1999	2000	2001	2002	2003	2004	2005	2006	2007	2008
Total	4 886.032	4 739.895	4 659.748	4 646.015	6 335.652 [6]	6 491.613	7 077.915	8 059.366	8 288.418	.
2	441.459	412.752	404.963	409.677	419.942 [6]	457.295	443.790	458.506	496.894	.
3	1 314.488	1 306.795	1 259.672	1 261.309	1 237.015 [6]	1 265.357	1 182.057	1 331.332	1 323.498	.
4	43.167	39.743	39.235	38.663	42.565 [6]	43.932	43.698	51.502	53.640	.
5	232.174	222.999	224.906	213.528	295.597 [6]	272.692	431.841	455.772	472.571	.
6	872.300	865.977	884.877	885.193	1 263.937 [6]	1 276.554	1 373.337	1 663.744	1 729.862	.
7	243.180	221.522	207.723	199.843	206.111 [6]	206.134	320.398	352.495	358.939	.
8	204.665	196.699	192.649	186.092	1 131.230 [6]	1 171.799	1 478.211	1 744.558	1 824.609	.
9	1 534.583	1 473.403	1 445.723	1 451.710	1 739.255 [6]	1 797.850	1 804.583	2 001.457	2 028.405	.

Explanatory notes: see p. 77.

[1] Establishments with 10 or more persons employed. [2] Excl. domestic workers (private households), self-employed and family workers. [3] Incl. mining and quarrying. [4] Inc. public administration. [5] Second quarter of each year. [6] Methodology revised; data not strictly comparable.

Notes explicatives: voir p. 80.

[1] Etablissements occupant 10 personnes et plus. [2] Non compris le personnel domestique (ménages privés), les travailleurs indépendants et les travailleurs familiaux. [3] Y compris les industries extractives. [4] Y compris l'administration publique. [5] Deuxième trimestre de chaque année. [6] Méthodologie révisée; les données ne sont pas strictement comparables.

Notas explicativas: véase p. 83.

[1] Establecimientos con 10 y más trabajadores. [2] Excl. el personal doméstico (hogares privados), los trabajadores independientes y los trabajadores familiares. [3] Incl. las minas y canteras. [4] Incl. la administración pública. [5] Segundo trimestre de cada año. [6] Metodología revisada; los datos no son estrictamente comparables.

Paid employment, by economic activity
Emploi rémunéré, par activité économique
Empleo remunerado, por actividad económica

	Thousands			Milliers				Millares		
	1999	2000	2001	2002	2003	2004	2005	2006	2007	2008

Tanzania, United Republic of (BA) [1]   Employees - Salariés - Asalariados

Total - Total - Total
ISIC 3 - CITI 3 - CIIU 3

	1999	2000	2001	2002	2003	2004	2005	2006	2007	2008
Total	.	.	.	.	.	.	.	2 091.0	.	.
A-B	.	.	.	.	.	.	.	564.2	.	.
C	.	.	.	.	.	.	.	25.7	.	.
D	.	.	.	.	.	.	.	152.4	.	.
E	.	.	.	.	.	.	.	15.1	.	.
F	.	.	.	.	.	.	.	103.7	.	.
G	.	.	.	.	.	.	.	194.0	.	.
H	.	.	.	.	.	.	.	91.6	.	.
I	.	.	.	.	.	.	.	183.0	.	.
J	.	.	.	.	.	.	.	16.4	.	.
K	.	.	.	.	.	.	.	63.4	.	.
L	.	.	.	.	.	.	.	179.3	.	.
M	.	.	.	.	.	.	.	217.0	.	.
N	.	.	.	.	.	.	.	86.3	.	.
O	.	.	.	.	.	.	.	65.3	.	.
P	.	.	.	.	.	.	.	133.5	.	.

Men - Hommes - Hombres
ISIC 3 - CITI 3 - CIIU 3

	1999	2000	2001	2002	2003	2004	2005	2006	2007	2008
Total	.	.	.	.	.	.	.	1 486.5	.	.
A-B	.	.	.	.	.	.	.	424.7	.	.
C	.	.	.	.	.	.	.	23.4	.	.
D	.	.	.	.	.	.	.	115.4	.	.
E	.	.	.	.	.	.	.	11.6	.	.
F	.	.	.	.	.	.	.	98.5	.	.
G	.	.	.	.	.	.	.	152.9	.	.
H	.	.	.	.	.	.	.	36.6	.	.
I	.	.	.	.	.	.	.	170.9	.	.
J	.	.	.	.	.	.	.	10.7	.	.
K	.	.	.	.	.	.	.	53.3	.	.
L	.	.	.	.	.	.	.	153.2	.	.
M	.	.	.	.	.	.	.	120.8	.	.
N	.	.	.	.	.	.	.	35.4	.	.
O	.	.	.	.	.	.	.	50.0	.	.
P	.	.	.	.	.	.	.	28.9	.	.

Women - Femmes - Mujeres
ISIC 3 - CITI 3 - CIIU 3

	1999	2000	2001	2002	2003	2004	2005	2006	2007	2008
Total	.	.	.	.	.	.	.	604.5	.	.
A-B	.	.	.	.	.	.	.	139.5	.	.
C	.	.	.	.	.	.	.	2.3	.	.
D	.	.	.	.	.	.	.	37.1	.	.
E	.	.	.	.	.	.	.	3.5	.	.
F	.	.	.	.	.	.	.	5.2	.	.
G	.	.	.	.	.	.	.	41.1	.	.
H	.	.	.	.	.	.	.	55.0	.	.
I	.	.	.	.	.	.	.	12.0	.	.
J	.	.	.	.	.	.	.	5.7	.	.
K	.	.	.	.	.	.	.	10.1	.	.
L	.	.	.	.	.	.	.	26.1	.	.
M	.	.	.	.	.	.	.	96.2	.	.
N	.	.	.	.	.	.	.	50.8	.	.
O	.	.	.	.	.	.	.	15.3	.	.
P	.	.	.	.	.	.	.	104.6	.	.

Zambia (FD)   Employees - Salariés - Asalariados

Total - Total - Total
ISIC 2 - CITI 2 - CIIU 2

	1999	2000	2001	2002	2003	2004	2005	2006	2007	2008
Total	477.51	476.35	475.32	429.41	416.80	416.23	436.07	.	.	.
1	60.00	59.38	59.25	43.82	64.10	65.14	65.50	.	.	.
2	38.52	35.04	34.97	37.25	48.60	46.08	32.10	.	.	.
3	46.00	47.78	47.68	67.75	39.39	45.34	40.15	.	.	.
4	5.30	5.05	5.04	7.32	10.83	12.35	6.31	.	.	.
5	12.90	13.83	13.80	2.41	3.47	5.79	7.95	.	.	.
6	51.10	52.34	52.22	50.81	53.45	44.46	67.25	.	.	.
7	45.00	46.72	46.62	21.57	26.73	26.51	20.68	.	.	.
8	34.68	31.48	31.42	52.73	28.56	31.88	22.31	.	.	.
9	184.01	184.73	184.33	145.76	141.70	138.69	173.99	.	.	.

Explanatory notes: see p. 77.   Notes explicatives: voir p. 80.   Notas explicativas: véase p. 83.

[1] Persons aged 15 years and over.   [1] Personnes âgées de 15 ans et plus.   [1] Personas de 15 años y más.

Paid employment, by economic activity — Emploi rémunéré, par activité économique — Empleo remunerado, por actividad económica

	Thousands				Milliers			Millares		
	1999	2000	2001	2002	2003	2004	2005	2006	2007	2008

AMERICA-AMÉRIQUE-AMERICA

Argentina (BA) [1] [2] [3] — Employees - Salariés - Asalariados

Total - Total - Total
ISIC 3 - CITI 3 - CIIU 3

	1999	2000	2001	2002	2003	2004	2005	2006	2007	2008
Total	6 000.0	5 975.9	5 845.6	5 743.3	6 590.1 [4]	6 977.6	7 182.0	7 608.3 [5]		
A	32.2	27.8	34.3	45.7	79.7 [4]	74.3	70.9	46.7 [5]		
B	2.6	4.9	5.2	5.5	4.9 [4]	10.5	6.4	8.3 [5]		
C	14.2	13.9	18.9	19.5	27.6 [4]	32.4	29.8	38.9 [5]		
D	939.3	892.0	848.6	764.6	872.3 [4]	1 002.0	1 043.0	1 106.5 [5]		
E	49.5	47.2	51.7	41.9	45.7 [4]	43.2	47.9	43.5 [5]		
F	372.3	333.2	266.6	186.8	335.8 [4]	401.6	474.7	548.2 [5]		
G	883.2	912.6	885.1	785.6	954.8 [4]	1 035.9	1 020.5	1 114.5 [5]		
H	167.2	189.2	206.2	177.2	197.4 [4]	244.1	236.1	283.0 [5]		
I	538.5	525.9	501.4	453.7	455.2 [4]	523.8	510.8	516.6 [5]		
J	192.2	196.7	185.9	176.5	137.5 [4]	128.2	151.4	176.7 [5]		
K	399.9	370.2	362.1	342.3	404.7 [4]	417.6	471.0	505.6 [5]		
L	638.7	631.8	657.9	776.1	788.1 [4]	772.9	728.4	768.7 [5]		
M	554.7	578.1	599.0	675.9	692.6 [4]	660.8	677.1	743.1 [5]		
N	390.1	389.6	354.6	396.7	559.4 [4]	553.5	538.4	488.9 [5]		
O	332.2	335.9	351.2	419.9	340.9 [4]	389.8	442.7	405.8 [5]		
P	472.9	500.0	494.7	456.3	646.7 [4]	661.5	702.2	789.3 [5]		
Q	2.0	2.5	1.4	2.7	4.3 [4]	-	3.5	2.2 [5]		
X	18.3	24.5	21.0	16.3	42.3 [4]	25.5	27.4	21.8 [5]		

Men - Hommes - Hombres
ISIC 3 - CITI 3 - CIIU 3

	1999	2000	2001	2002	2003	2004	2005	2006	2007	2008
Total	3 485.8	3 439.6	3 325.0	3 118.5	3 600.7 [4]	3 857.5	3 956.1	4 197.2 [5]		
A	28.3	24.0	28.9	33.2	48.9 [4]	46.1	48.0	35.7 [5]		
B	2.6	4.9	5.2	5.2	4.0 [4]	7.6	5.4	7.5 [5]		
C	12.1	13.3	18.0	16.7	24.9 [4]	29.8	22.7	33.3 [5]		
D	699.0	670.3	629.9	575.1	646.5 [4]	732.0	759.5	807.6 [5]		
E	43.1	39.4	40.5	34.2	33.4 [4]	33.1	43.0	37.5 [5]		
F	358.5	316.9	257.2	179.7	322.3 [4]	392.0	458.4	521.3 [5]		
G	585.7	583.3	573.8	505.7	638.5 [4]	680.0	678.5	728.4 [5]		
H	95.8	109.2	125.6	106.4	125.7 [4]	132.7	128.4	162.8 [5]		
I	459.2	455.1	433.1	385.0	390.6 [4]	448.5	427.1	443.0 [5]		
J	111.9	120.1	105.7	100.4	84.1 [4]	79.8	84.1	86.4 [5]		
K	227.4	224.2	212.3	194.5	259.1 [4]	254.0	277.3	310.8 [5]		
L	398.2	388.5	400.0	455.2	484.1 [4]	466.2	429.4	444.4 [5]		
M	108.8	130.0	137.0	155.3	142.4 [4]	143.3	164.0	170.5 [5]		
N	113.7	115.3	112.2	108.6	156.6 [4]	162.3	140.8	127.8 [5]		
O	217.5	215.8	223.0	243.9	190.1 [4]	218.4	249.3	249.3 [5]		
P	12.6	12.9	16.1	13.5	18.4 [4]	16.7	24.6	17.0 [5]		
Q	0.1	1.2	0.2	0.1	2.0 [4]	-	2.1	2.0 [5]		
X	11.3	15.3	6.3	5.7	29.2 [4]	14.9	13.3	11.9 [5]		

Women - Femmes - Mujeres
ISIC 3 - CITI 3 - CIIU 3

	1999	2000	2001	2002	2003	2004	2005	2006	2007	2008
Total	2 514.2	2 536.3	2 520.6	2 624.8	2 989.3 [4]	3 120.1	3 225.9	3 411.0 [5]		
A	3.9	3.9	5.4	12.5	30.9 [4]	28.2	22.9	11.0 [5]		
B	-	0.0	-	0.3	0.9 [4]	2.9	1.0	0.8 [5]		
C	2.1	0.6	0.9	2.7	2.7 [4]	2.6	7.1	5.6 [5]		
D	240.3	221.7	218.7	189.5	225.8 [4]	270.1	283.4	298.9 [5]		
E	6.5	7.7	11.2	7.7	12.3 [4]	10.1	5.0	5.9 [5]		
F	13.8	16.3	9.4	7.1	13.5 [4]	9.6	16.3	27.0 [5]		
G	297.6	329.3	311.2	279.9	316.3 [4]	355.9	341.9	386.0 [5]		
H	71.4	80.0	80.6	70.8	71.7 [4]	111.3	107.6	120.2 [5]		
I	79.3	70.8	68.3	68.7	64.7 [4]	75.3	83.7	73.5 [5]		
J	80.3	76.6	80.2	76.2	53.4 [4]	48.4	67.3	90.3 [5]		
K	172.5	146.0	149.8	147.8	145.7 [4]	163.6	193.7	194.8 [5]		
L	240.5	243.2	257.9	320.9	303.9 [4]	306.7	299.0	324.3 [5]		
M	445.8	448.1	462.0	520.7	550.2 [4]	517.5	513.1	572.6 [5]		
N	276.4	274.3	242.4	288.1	402.8 [4]	391.1	397.6	361.0 [5]		
O	114.7	120.1	128.2	176.0	150.8 [4]	171.5	193.3	156.5 [5]		
P	460.3	487.1	478.6	442.7	628.4 [4]	644.8	677.6	772.4 [5]		
Q	1.9	1.3	1.2	2.6	2.4 [4]	-	1.4	0.2 [5]		
X	7.0	9.3	14.8	10.6	13.0 [4]	10.6	14.1	9.9 [5]		

Explanatory notes: see p. 77.

[1] Persons aged 10 years and over. [2] 31 Urban agglomerations. [3] Second semester. [4] Methodology revised; data not strictly comparable; Prior to 2003: May and October. [5] Prior to 2006: 28 urban agglomerations.

Notes explicatives: voir p. 80.

[1] Personnes âgées de 10 ans et plus. [2] 31 agglomérations urbaines. [3] Second semestre. [4] Méthodologie révisée; les données ne sont pas strictement comparables; Avant 2003: mai et octobre. [5] Avant 2006: 28 agglomérations urbaines.

Notas explicativas: véase p. 83.

[1] Personas de 10 años y más. [2] 31 aglomerados úrbanos. [3] Segundo semestre. [4] Metodología revisada; los datos no son estrictamente comparables; antes de 2003: mayo y octubre. [5] Antes de 2006: 28 aglomerados úrbanos

Paid employment, by economic activity	Emploi rémunéré, par activité économique	Empleo remunerado, por actividad económica
Thousands	Milliers	Millares

	1999	2000	2001	2002	2003	2004	2005	2006	2007	2008
Aruba (BA) [1] [2]					Employees - Salariés - Asalariados					

Total - Total - Total
ISIC 3 - CITI 3 - CIIU 3

	1999	2000	2001	2002	2003	2004	2005	2006	2007	2008
Total	.	.	.	.	.	.	.	.	46.709	.
A	.	.	.	.	.	.	.	.	0.239	.
B	.	.	.	.	.	.	.	.	-	.
C	.	.	.	.	.	.	.	.	0.017	.
D	.	.	.	.	.	.	.	.	2.720	.
E	.	.	.	.	.	.	.	.	0.699	.
F	.	.	.	.	.	.	.	.	5.396	.
G	.	.	.	.	.	.	.	.	6.435	.
H	.	.	.	.	.	.	.	.	8.369	.
I	.	.	.	.	.	.	.	.	2.401	.
J	.	.	.	.	.	.	.	.	1.869	.
K	.	.	.	.	.	.	.	.	6.274	.
L	.	.	.	.	.	.	.	.	3.983	.
M	.	.	.	.	.	.	.	.	1.566	.
N	.	.	.	.	.	.	.	.	2.868	.
O	.	.	.	.	.	.	.	.	2.664	.
P	.	.	.	.	.	.	.	.	1.119	.
Q	.	.	.	.	.	.	.	.	0.033	.
X	.	.	.	.	.	.	.	.	0.056	.

Men - Hommes - Hombres
ISIC 3 - CITI 3 - CIIU 3

	1999	2000	2001	2002	2003	2004	2005	2006	2007	2008
Total	.	.	.	.	.	.	.	.	23.819	.
A	.	.	.	.	.	.	.	.	0.144	.
B	.	.	.	.	.	.	.	.	-	.
C	.	.	.	.	.	.	.	.	0.017	.
D	.	.	.	.	.	.	.	.	2.228	.
E	.	.	.	.	.	.	.	.	0.646	.
F	.	.	.	.	.	.	.	.	4.635	.
G	.	.	.	.	.	.	.	.	2.646	.
H	.	.	.	.	.	.	.	.	3.347	.
I	.	.	.	.	.	.	.	.	1.603	.
J	.	.	.	.	.	.	.	.	0.480	.
K	.	.	.	.	.	.	.	.	3.078	.
L	.	.	.	.	.	.	.	.	2.059	.
M	.	.	.	.	.	.	.	.	0.632	.
N	.	.	.	.	.	.	.	.	0.777	.
O	.	.	.	.	.	.	.	.	1.468	.
P	.	.	.	.	.	.	.	.	0.028	.
Q	.	.	.	.	.	.	.	.	-	.
X	.	.	.	.	.	.	.	.	0.031	.

Women - Femmes - Mujeres
ISIC 3 - CITI 3 - CIIU 3

	1999	2000	2001	2002	2003	2004	2005	2006	2007	2008
Total	.	.	.	.	.	.	.	.	22.890	.
A	.	.	.	.	.	.	.	.	0.096	.
B	.	.	.	.	.	.	.	.	-	.
C	.	.	.	.	.	.	.	.	-	.
D	.	.	.	.	.	.	.	.	0.492	.
E	.	.	.	.	.	.	.	.	0.053	.
F	.	.	.	.	.	.	.	.	0.761	.
G	.	.	.	.	.	.	.	.	3.789	.
H	.	.	.	.	.	.	.	.	5.023	.
I	.	.	.	.	.	.	.	.	0.798	.
J	.	.	.	.	.	.	.	.	1.389	.
K	.	.	.	.	.	.	.	.	3.196	.
L	.	.	.	.	.	.	.	.	1.924	.
M	.	.	.	.	.	.	.	.	0.934	.
N	.	.	.	.	.	.	.	.	2.091	.
O	.	.	.	.	.	.	.	.	1.195	.
P	.	.	.	.	.	.	.	.	1.092	.
Q	.	.	.	.	.	.	.	.	0.033	.
X	.	.	.	.	.	.	.	.	0.024	.

Explanatory notes: see p. 77.   Notes explicatives: voir p. 80.   Notas explicativas: véase p. 83.

[1] Persons aged 15 years and over. [2] Oct.   [1] Personnes âgées de 15 ans et plus. [2] Oct.   [1] Personas de 15 años y más. [2] Oct.

Paid employment, by economic activity

Emploi rémunéré, par activité économique

Empleo remunerado, por actividad económica

	Thousands				Milliers				Millares	
	1999	2000	2001	2002	2003	2004	2005	2006	2007	2008

Bermuda (CA) [1] [2]   All persons engaged - Effectif occupé - Efectivo ocupado

Total - Total - Total
ISIC 3 - CITI 3 - CIIU 3

	1999	2000	2001	2002	2003	2004	2005	2006	2007	2008
Total	37.849	38.017	37.597	37.815	37.686	38.363	38.947	39.686	39.851	.
A	0.415	0.426	0.466	0.500	0.497	0.521	0.527	0.569	0.583	.
B	0.146	0.133	0.143	0.144	0.137	0.124	0.116	0.118	0.109	.
C	0.005	0.005	0.004	0.004	0.004	0.006	0.006	0.005	0.005	.
D	1.208	1.235	1.171	1.107	1.063	1.012	1.003	0.965	0.935	.
E	0.466	0.449	0.425	0.412	0.405	0.405	0.390	0.372	0.394	.
F	2.508	2.638	2.794	2.917	2.959	3.230	3.494	3.653	3.544	.
G	5.287	5.174	5.010	5.056	5.015	4.910	4.692	4.775	4.754	.
H	5.657	5.280	5.088	4.913	4.760	4.888	5.069	4.901	4.810	.
I	2.868	2.958	2.983	2.859	2.861	2.903	2.782	2.829	2.756	.
J	2.907	2.984	2.891	2.882	2.821	2.737	2.859	2.902	2.952	.
K	3.811	4.201	4.306	4.363	4.263	4.229	4.406	4.609	4.801	.
L	4.054	4.191	3.834	3.896	3.982	4.104	4.056	4.069	4.113	.
M	0.783	0.749	0.745	0.795	0.828	0.805	0.835	0.884	0.903	.
N	2.107	2.071	2.103	2.178	2.088	2.201	2.287	2.337	2.348	.
O	1.716	1.597	1.635	1.572	1.577	1.570	1.528	1.504	1.471	.
P	0.656	0.645	0.634	0.608	0.617	0.616	0.657	0.678	0.657	.
Q	3.255	3.281	3.365	3.609	3.809	4.102	4.240	4.516	4.716	.

Men - Hommes - Hombres
ISIC 3 - CITI 3 - CIIU 3

	1999	2000	2001	2002	2003	2004	2005	2006	2007	2008
Total	19.197	19.310	19.301	19.411	19.520	19.937	20.257	20.730	20.727	.
A	0.370	0.387	0.421	0.450	0.454	0.476	0.480	0.520	0.522	.
B	0.142	0.130	0.136	0.139	0.130	0.115	0.106	0.111	0.103	.
C	0.005	0.005	0.004	0.004	0.004	0.006	0.006	0.005	0.005	.
D	0.852	0.857	0.808	0.751	0.732	0.706	0.695	0.684	0.657	.
E	0.381	0.367	0.341	0.330	0.326	0.324	0.311	0.295	0.315	.
F	2.352	2.480	2.637	2.737	2.787	3.048	3.295	3.453	3.337	.
G	2.540	2.552	2.505	2.542	2.529	2.443	2.411	2.485	2.476	.
H	3.082	2.970	2.844	2.785	2.732	2.760	2.873	2.821	2.768	.
I	1.885	1.932	1.938	1.868	1.911	1.932	1.855	1.869	1.799	.
J	0.871	0.897	0.836	0.841	0.839	0.810	0.844	0.844	0.873	.
K	1.764	1.905	2.018	2.023	1.985	1.998	2.082	2.213	2.311	.
L	2.005	2.014	1.888	1.912	1.946	2.003	1.974	1.972	2.020	.
M	0.204	0.187	0.182	0.188	0.203	0.197	0.201	0.211	0.205	.
N	0.469	0.448	0.461	0.486	0.460	0.511	0.496	0.515	0.527	.
O	0.714	0.631	0.680	0.641	0.692	0.695	0.668	0.667	0.640	.
P	0.135	0.134	0.136	0.122	0.123	0.120	0.115	0.102	0.109	.
Q	1.426	1.414	1.466	1.592	1.667	1.793	1.845	1.963	2.060	.

Women - Femmes - Mujeres
ISIC 3 - CITI 3 - CIIU 3

	1999	2000	2001	2002	2003	2004	2005	2006	2007	2008
Total	18.652	18.707	18.296	18.404	18.166	18.426	18.690	18.956	19.124	.
A	0.045	0.039	0.045	0.050	0.043	0.045	0.047	0.049	0.061	.
B	0.004	0.003	0.007	0.005	0.007	0.009	0.010	0.007	0.006	.
C	.	.	.	.	.	.	.	.	.	.
D	0.356	0.378	0.363	0.356	0.331	0.306	0.308	0.281	0.278	.
E	0.085	0.082	0.084	0.082	0.079	0.081	0.079	0.077	0.079	.
F	0.156	0.158	0.157	0.180	0.172	0.182	0.199	0.200	0.207	.
G	2.747	2.622	2.505	2.514	2.486	2.467	2.281	2.290	2.278	.
H	2.575	2.310	2.244	2.128	2.028	2.128	2.196	2.080	2.042	.
I	0.983	1.026	1.045	0.991	0.950	0.971	0.927	0.960	0.957	.
J	2.036	2.087	2.055	2.041	1.982	1.927	2.015	2.058	2.079	.
K	2.049	2.296	2.288	2.340	2.278	2.231	2.324	2.396	2.490	.
L	2.047	2.177	1.946	1.984	2.036	2.101	2.082	2.097	2.093	.
M	0.579	0.562	0.563	0.607	0.625	0.608	0.634	0.673	0.698	.
N	1.638	1.623	1.642	1.692	1.628	1.690	1.791	1.822	1.821	.
O	1.002	0.966	0.955	0.931	0.885	0.875	0.860	0.837	0.831	.
P	0.521	0.511	0.498	0.486	0.494	0.496	0.542	0.576	0.548	.
Q	1.829	1.867	1.899	2.017	2.142	2.309	2.395	2.553	2.656	.

Explanatory notes: see p. 77.

[1] Excl. unpaid family workers. [2] Aug. of each year.

Notes explicatives: voir p. 80.

[1] Non compris les travailleurs familiaux non rémunérés. [2] Août de chaque année.

Notas explicativas: véase p. 83.

[1] Excl. los trabajadores familiares no remunerados. [2] Agosto de cada año.

Paid employment, by economic activity
Emploi rémunéré, par activité économique
Empleo remunerado, por actividad económica

Thousands — Milliers — Millares

	1999	2000	2001	2002	2003	2004	2005	2006	2007	2008

Brasil (BA) [1] [2] — Employees - Salariés - Asalariados

Total - Total - Total
ISIC 3 - CITI 3 - CIIU 3

	1999	2000	2001	2002	2003	2004	2005	2006	2007	2008
Total	.	.	.	48 955	49 756 [3]	53 172	54 709	56 838	58 815	.
A	.	.	.	4 390	4 509 [3]	4 825	4 845	4 716	4 694	.
B	.	.	.	76	69 [3]	67	67	57	52	.
C	.	.	.	202	236 [3]	269	245	302	333	.
D	.	.	.	7 909	8 011 [3]	8 862	8 991	9 239	9 902	.
E	.	.	.	307	328 [3]	351	358	392	359	.
F	.	.	.	2 741	2 460 [3]	2 690	2 766	2 951	3 025	.
G	.	.	.	7 301	7 723 [3]	8 046	8 772	9 007	9 506	.
H	.	.	.	1 519	1 533 [3]	1 635	1 766	1 901	1 968	.
I	.	.	.	2 381	2 428 [3]	2 560	2 646	2 715	2 922	.
J	.	.	.	916	956 [3]	927	930	991	1 085	.
K	.	.	.	3 141	3 265 [3]	3 499	3 698	3 974	4 148	.
L	.	.	.	3 862	3 982 [3]	4 196	4 256	4 439	4 492	.
M	.	.	.	4 041	4 114 [3]	4 336	4 409	4 587	4 781	.
N	.	.	.	2 275	2 357 [3]	2 379	2 490	2 637	2 809	.
O	.	.	.	1 736	1 605 [3]	2 013	1 777	2 130	1 942	.
P	.	.	.	6 110	6 155 [3]	6 472	6 666	6 782	6 732	.
Q	.	.	.	5	4 [3]	4	7	4	3	.
X	.	.	.	42	24 [3]	41	17	16	63	.

Men - Hommes - Hombres
ISIC 3 - CITI 3 - CIIU 3

	1999	2000	2001	2002	2003	2004	2005	2006	2007	2008
Total	.	.	.	27 943	28 208 [3]	30 012	30 934	31 811	32 980	.
A	.	.	.	3 907	4 023 [3]	4 260	4 336	4 179	4 156	.
B	.	.	.	75	68 [3]	66	64	56	51	.
C	.	.	.	186	217 [3]	250	227	277	300	.
D	.	.	.	5 641	5 672 [3]	6 270	6 357	6 532	7 040	.
E	.	.	.	256	270 [3]	298	299	322	295	.
F	.	.	.	2 642	2 380 [3]	2 595	2 662	2 819	2 899	.
G	.	.	.	4 737	5 028 [3]	5 083	5 620	5 683	5 951	.
H	.	.	.	742	751 [3]	788	834	877	910	.
I	.	.	.	2 039	2 070 [3]	2 168	2 189	2 255	2 407	.
J	.	.	.	477	489 [3]	469	444	482	536	.
K	.	.	.	2 019	2 071 [3]	2 195	2 382	2 488	2 573	.
L	.	.	.	2 500	2 516 [3]	2 632	2 628	2 763	2 773	.
M	.	.	.	839	860 [3]	927	960	968	1 048	.
N	.	.	.	493	527 [3]	533	541	586	596	.
O	.	.	.	921	848 [3]	1 014	925	1 052	983	.
P	.	.	.	433	403 [3]	432	453	460	418	.
Q	.	.	.	3	2 [3]	2	3	1	2	.
X	.	.	.	31	14 [3]	29	12	12	40	.

Women - Femmes - Mujeres
ISIC 3 - CITI 3 - CIIU 3

	1999	2000	2001	2002	2003	2004	2005	2006	2007	2008
Total	.	.	.	21 012	21 548 [3]	23 161	23 774	25 027	25 835	.
A	.	.	.	483	486 [3]	564	509	537	538	.
B	.	.	.	1	1 [3]	1	3	1	0	.
C	.	.	.	15	19 [3]	19	18	25	33	.
D	.	.	.	2 268	2 339 [3]	2 592	2 635	2 707	2 862	.
E	.	.	.	51	58 [3]	53	60	70	64	.
F	.	.	.	99	79 [3]	95	104	131	127	.
G	.	.	.	2 564	2 695 [3]	2 962	3 152	3 324	3 554	.
H	.	.	.	778	782 [3]	847	932	1 023	1 058	.
I	.	.	.	342	358 [3]	392	457	460	515	.
J	.	.	.	439	466 [3]	459	486	509	548	.
K	.	.	.	1 121	1 194 [3]	1 304	1 316	1 486	1 575	.
L	.	.	.	1 362	1 466 [3]	1 564	1 628	1 676	1 719	.
M	.	.	.	3 202	3 253 [3]	3 409	3 450	3 619	3 732	.
N	.	.	.	1 783	1 830 [3]	1 846	1 949	2 052	2 214	.
O	.	.	.	815	757 [3]	999	852	1 078	959	.
P	.	.	.	5 677	5 752 [3]	6 040	6 214	6 322	6 313	.
Q	.	.	.	2	2 [3]	2	4	2	1	.
X	.	.	.	10	10 [3]	12	5	5	22	.

Explanatory notes: see p. 77.

[1] Employees of 10 years and over. [2] Sep. of each year. [3] Prior to 2003: Excl. rural population of Rondõnia, Acre, Amazonas, Roraima, Pará and Amapá.

Notes explicatives: voir p. 80.

[1] Salariés de 10 ans et plus. [2] Sept. de chaque année. [3] Avant 2003: Non compris la population rurale de Rondõnia, Acre, Amazonas, Roraima, Pará et Amapá.

Notas explicativas: véase p. 83.

[1] Asalariados de 10 años y más. [2] Sept. de cada año. [3] Antes de 2003: Excl. la población rural de Rondonia, Acre, Amazonas, Roraima, Pará y Amapá.

EMPLOYMENT   EMPLOI   EMPLEO

Paid employment, by economic activity   Emploi rémunéré, par activité économique   Empleo remunerado, por actividad económica

Thousands   Milliers   Millares

	1999	2000	2001	2002	2003	2004	2005	2006	2007	2008
Canada (BA) [1][2][3]					Employees - Salariés - Asalariados					
Total - Total - Total										
ISIC 3 - CITI 3 - CIIU 3										
Total	11 974.0	12 391.0	12 670.0	12 996.0	13 271.0	13 494.0	13 658.0	13 986.3	14 251.4	14 496.2
A	188.1	188.9	173.1	172.3	174.7	168.8	179.7	181.3	169.0	160.2
B	12.6	14.6	13.0	12.5	13.4	13.9	13.0	14.2	13.3	12.1
C	144.9	150.1	166.4	159.8	162.5	170.7	190.1	217.9	233.2	243.1
D	2 106.2	2 163.2	2 130.4	2 197.1	2 192.8	2 203.1	2 109.9	2 096.2	2 010.5	1 934.1
E	111.5	113.7	122.0	130.7	130.3	132.8	124.8	121.8	137.9	151.6
F	493.7	529.2	558.9	588.9	622.3	637.7	694.3	737.0	780.5	859.9
G	2 066.5	2 142.2	2 219.3	2 260.8	2 319.1	2 360.3	2 427.6	2 492.3	2 539.9	2 561.5
H	819.3	843.4	852.9	893.1	910.4	921.3	911.8	925.5	970.4	983.4
I	935.5	963.0	998.3	971.7	972.6	996.0	997.8	905.4	958.8	980.9
J	562.8	557.0	583.3	590.1	585.5	617.6	640.4	675.9	686.7	714.6
K	1 113.0	1 178.6	1 239.0	1 260.0	1 303.5	1 324.0	1 373.0	1 441.9	1 493.3	1 506.3
L	756.9	762.3	776.8	790.7	818.1	827.9	830.5	834.1	862.0	923.6
M	913.3	927.8	934.2	961.2	979.2	990.9	1 050.7	1 108.8	1 129.9	1 140.9
N	1 205.5	1 304.4	1 359.1	1 423.8	1 477.5	1 521.3	1 521.4	1 570.2	1 620.9	1 669.7
O	478.4	503.9	512.8	545.3	569.1	579.9	559.1	629.0	652.4	651.4
P	27.5	28.7	26.6	28.5	32.3	30.5	31.1	31.5	33.3	45.1
Q	1.9	2.7	2.4	2.3	1.8	-	2.5	3.3	2.5	2.0
Men - Hommes - Hombres										
ISIC 3 - CITI 3 - CIIU 3										
Total	6 201.1	6 425.2	6 531.0	6 679.4	6 774.7	6 867.1	6 949.1	7 105.7	7 185.8	7 301.6
A	134.4	135.7	124.1	121.5	126.8	118.7	123.7	124.9	115.9	109.3
B	10.0	11.0	10.3	10.6	11.5	11.0	11.0	12.0	10.7	9.6
C	122.7	124.2	139.0	132.6	134.9	141.9	159.3	174.7	187.9	196.9
D	1 506.2	1 558.3	1 532.3	1 560.8	1 552.4	1 571.0	1 506.0	1 478.6	1 423.0	1 366.4
E	84.2	88.0	91.0	98.3	101.9	97.3	93.0	92.3	98.8	115.6
F	437.3	464.5	495.8	527.7	551.3	558.3	618.1	647.8	678.0	749.8
G	1 089.0	1 124.6	1 163.8	1 177.3	1 211.2	1 234.5	1 246.0	1 285.3	1 296.8	1 306.2
H	311.7	328.7	331.0	337.1	354.0	352.3	349.3	354.1	378.4	381.2
I	633.7	647.5	656.6	654.2	639.0	647.4	658.6	625.3	650.0	661.7
J	172.7	177.4	186.4	199.5	188.4	199.3	205.3	228.2	224.4	253.9
K	563.2	602.8	631.9	653.0	657.4	679.0	710.1	753.9	794.4	802.0
L	406.5	403.9	412.9	419.3	422.2	426.2	425.8	426.1	429.6	453.2
M	328.8	327.4	322.9	327.5	348.8	338.0	359.8	393.0	391.5	386.2
N	194.2	217.4	218.2	224.1	228.0	246.2	240.5	239.4	248.4	259.7
O	205.1	211.6	212.5	232.6	243.6	243.6	239.2	265.4	280.3	271.3
P	1.1	1.5	1.5	1.8	2.1	1.3	2.7	2.4	1.5	1.8
Q	0.3	0.8	0.8	-	1.8	-	0.8	2.3	-	-
Women - Femmes - Mujeres										
ISIC 3 - CITI 3 - CIIU 3										
Total	5 736.5	5 948.4	6 137.7	6 309.4	6 490.5	6 630.8	6 709.1	6 880.6	7 065.6	7 194.6
A	53.7	53.2	48.9	50.9	47.9	50.1	56.0	56.4	53.1	50.8
B	2.6	3.5	2.7	1.9	1.9	2.8	2.0	2.3	2.6	2.4
C	22.1	25.9	27.4	27.2	27.6	28.7	30.9	43.2	45.3	46.2
D	600.0	605.0	598.2	636.4	640.5	632.1	603.9	617.6	587.5	567.7
E	27.4	25.7	31.0	32.4	28.5	35.5	31.8	29.4	39.1	36.1
F	56.4	64.7	63.2	61.2	71.1	79.4	76.2	89.2	102.5	110.1
G	977.4	1 017.6	1 055.5	1 083.5	1 107.9	1 125.8	1 181.7	1 207.1	1 243.0	1 255.3
H	507.6	514.8	521.9	556.0	556.4	569.0	562.6	571.3	592.0	602.3
I	301.8	315.6	341.7	317.5	333.6	348.5	339.3	280.1	308.8	319.2
J	390.1	379.7	396.9	390.6	397.0	418.3	435.2	447.7	462.3	460.7
K	549.7	575.8	607.2	606.9	646.0	645.0	662.9	688.0	698.9	704.3
L	350.5	358.3	363.9	371.3	395.9	401.7	404.8	408.0	432.4	470.5
M	584.6	600.4	611.3	633.7	630.4	652.8	690.9	715.8	738.4	754.7
N	1 011.3	1 087.0	1 140.9	1 199.7	1 249.5	1 275.1	1 281.0	1 330.9	1 372.4	1 410.0
O	273.3	292.3	300.3	312.7	325.5	336.3	320.0	363.6	372.2	380.1
P	26.4	27.2	25.2	26.6	30.2	29.2	28.4	29.1	31.7	43.4
Q	1.6	1.9	1.6	-	-	-	1.7	1.0	-	-
Canada (DA)					Employees - Salariés - Asalariados					
Total - Total - Total										
ISIC 3 - CITI 3 - CIIU 3										
Total	12 055.8	12 460.9	12 881.1	13 093.3	13 372.8	13 595.7	13 877.3	14 252.6	14 572.2	14 817.7
A [4]	77.9	78.3	75.4	74.1	66.1	63.5	61.2	58.0	54.4	47.6
C	132.4	136.3	138.8	141.1	148.5	153.6	162.5	181.0	192.2	202.2
D	2 006.1	2 099.7	2 040.7	1 991.6	1 969.6	1 928.6	1 897.6	1 878.1	1 818.9	1 735.9
E	108.2	110.5	107.2	107.5	108.7	117.1	116.1	119.0	122.8	120.1
F	511.0	540.6	580.4	610.4	634.0	662.8	694.4	736.6	785.8	829.6
G	2 238.1	2 308.4	2 392.8	2 465.4	2 549.1	2 576.1	2 610.8	2 673.2	2 763.1	2 819.5
H	867.8	906.3	945.0	966.1	972.3	970.0	977.2	1 008.6	1 046.5	1 078.6
I	771.3	786.3	771.1	771.6	781.1	805.3	825.4	850.7	872.8	873.7
J	609.8	618.1	649.0	659.4	658.6	668.4	687.8	717.5	756.2	781.2
K	1 249.2	1 359.4	1 435.9	1 475.4	1 511.7	1 559.2	1 623.7	1 713.4	1 766.8	1 811.2
L	705.0	713.0	837.6	839.7	888.2	897.7	921.3	945.4	961.0	1 007.8
M	930.2	935.4	979.3	1 011.3	1 020.7	1 041.1	1 059.0	1 082.9	1 109.7	1 135.5
N	1 219.9	1 239.3	1 295.0	1 326.5	1 368.5	1 378.5	1 403.4	1 447.1	1 484.6	1 528.0
O	547.0	578.1	568.8	587.9	597.9	605.2	609.0	624.4	642.3	654.8

Explanatory notes: see p. 77.

[1] Persons aged 15 years and over. [2] Excl. residents of the Territories and indigenous persons living on reserves. [3] Excl. full-time members of the armed forces. [4] Excl. agriculture, fishing and hunting.

Notes explicatives: voir p. 80.

[1] Personnes âgées de 15 ans et plus. [2] Non compris les habitants des "Territoires" et les populations indigènes vivant dans les réserves. [3] Non compris les membres à temps complet des forces armées. [4] Non compris l'agriculture, la pêche et la chasse.

Notas explicativas: véase p. 83.

[1] Personas de 15 años y más. [2] Excl. a los habitantes de los "Territorios" y a las poblaciones indígenas que viven en reservas. [3] Excl. los miembros a tiempo completo de las fuerzas armadas. [4] Excl. agricultura, pesca y caza.

Paid employment, by economic activity   **Emploi rémunéré, par activité économique**   **Empleo remunerado, por actividad económica**

Thousands — Milliers — Millares

	1999	2000	2001	2002	2003	2004	2005	2006	2007	2008
Colombia (BA) [1][2][3]				Employees - Salariés - Asalariados						
Total - Total - Total										
ISIC 3 - CITI 3 - CIIU 3										
Total	.	.	7 024.8	7 953.5	8 181.1	8 166.8	8 824.2	8 914.6	9 351.3	8 520.4
A	.	.	2 412.1	1 287.4	1 377.9	1 183.1	1 560.6	1 495.1	1 553.5	1 254.3
C	.	.	564.6	135.1	97.4	107.4	76.5	72.1	75.9	114.7
D	.	.	40.7	1 143.6	1 220.3	1 267.3	1 344.0	1 241.3	1 415.7	1 298.7
E	.	.	1 208.3	63.7	57.7	64.8	79.3	61.1	80.8	75.5
F	.	.	83.4	389.1	391.6	356.9	403.5	418.9	488.1	390.6
G	.	.	289.4	1 428.3	1 449.1	1 498.0	1 633.1	1 498.2	1 784.9	1 676.0
I	.	.	1 461.6	421.4	436.4	504.3	480.5	479.2	588.8	530.9
J	.	.	454.8	171.3	179.9	189.4	195.3	184.8	199.0	189.0
K	.	.	175.7	318.5	369.0	377.0	413.3	451.5	536.0	556.3
O	.	.	332.7	2 590.2	2 599.1	2 615.3	2 637.7	2 333.2	2 625.8	2 427.1
X	.	.	1.4	5.1	2.8	3.2	0.4	679.4	2.7	7.3
Men - Hommes - Hombres										
ISIC 3 - CITI 3 - CIIU 3										
Total	.	.	3 891.3	4 640.0	4 879.9	4 790.3	5 321.8	5 461.7	5 582.3	5 020.0
A	.	.	498.5	1 168.1	1 254.8	1 072.4	1 391.5	941.8	1 374.9	1 094.9
C	.	.	34.7	117.4	88.8	106.0	70.8	55.0	71.8	108.4
D	.	.	778.1	715.4	780.3	775.6	831.6	538.0	912.0	846.5
E	.	.	60.7	53.6	47.2	53.7	61.1	29.5	68.5	61.5
F	.	.	272.4	363.1	375.7	336.1	384.6	272.1	463.5	370.1
G	.	.	830.9	835.5	848.9	865.6	922.6	584.0	982.3	883.9
I	.	.	353.5	332.6	351.2	385.8	372.6	256.3	439.0	393.0
J	.	.	81.9	78.4	82.2	93.0	91.8	64.2	90.1	92.3
K	.	.	203.8	191.5	216.1	227.9	268.3	197.1	316.3	350.3
O	.	.	776.7	780.5	834.5	871.7	926.5	570.2	861.7	814.3
X	.	.	-	3.9	0.3	2.5	0.3	1 953.5	2.2	4.8
Women - Femmes - Mujeres										
ISIC 3 - CITI 3 - CIIU 3										
Total	.	.	3 133.5	3 313.5	3 301.2	3 376.5	3 502.4	3 452.9	3 768.9	3 500.4
A	.	.	66.1	119.2	123.1	110.7	169.0	101.2	178.6	159.4
C	.	.	6.0	17.7	8.6	1.5	5.7	6.3	4.1	6.3
D	.	.	430.2	428.2	440.0	491.7	512.4	271.9	503.8	452.2
E	.	.	22.6	10.1	10.5	11.1	18.2	10.8	12.3	14.0
F	.	.	17.1	26.1	15.9	20.7	18.8	20.8	24.7	20.6
G	.	.	630.7	592.8	600.2	632.5	710.5	454.1	802.5	792.1
I	.	.	101.3	88.8	85.2	118.4	107.9	89.3	149.7	137.9
J	.	.	93.8	92.8	97.7	96.4	103.5	55.1	108.9	96.7
K	.	.	128.9	126.9	152.9	149.2	145.1	101.3	219.7	205.9
O	.	.	1 635.4	1 809.7	1 764.6	1 743.6	1 711.2	1 087.7	1 764.1	1 612.9
X	.	.	1.4	1.2	2.5	0.7	0.0	1 254.4	0.6	2.4
Costa Rica (BA) [4][5]				Employees - Salariés - Asalariados						
Total - Total - Total										
ISIC 3 - CITI 3 - CIIU 3										
Total	.	933.2	1 068.9	.	1 139.6	1 137.3	1 268.9	1 293.7	1 406.6	1 426.6
A	.	157.4	135.5	.	144.8	138.3	161.0	149.2	157.6	153.9
B	.	3.8	4.5	.	4.6	4.2	5.4	4.9	6.4	4.3
C	.	2.0	1.4	.	1.6	2.5	3.3	4.2	2.2	1.6
D	.	145.4	168.4	.	167.2	172.5	183.2	180.0	192.3	182.4
E	.	10.8	19.4	.	21.8	23.4	20.5	21.9	21.1	27.8
F	.	54.5	70.1	.	71.7	64.7	79.0	79.1	110.4	103.9
G	.	123.1	160.6	.	181.0	185.2	191.7	207.2	216.5	223.1
H	.	48.4	58.1	.	63.8	63.3	73.4	74.4	82.7	77.5
I	.	51.9	54.3	.	56.5	60.6	69.6	73.7	80.1	97.4
J	.	23.6	28.6	.	34.1	35.5	34.6	37.2	48.5	51.7
K	.	3.6	51.3	.	58.2	65.9	70.5	73.2	84.4	93.0
L	.	.	73.3	.	76.3	78.5	81.4	86.4	88.7	93.8
L,O	.	118.6	.	.	.	.	.	.	.	.
M	.	72.3	83.2	.	93.4	90.6	100.3	103.0	106.1	109.2
N	.	47.4	50.0	.	43.9	45.9	56.3	55.9	59.6	58.9
O	.	.	34.8	.	39.1	32.9	38.0	41.2	42.7	46.5
P	.	62.8	68.3	.	73.0	65.3	92.5	95.3	100.6	91.7
Q	.	1.4	2.2	.	2.4	3.9	2.0	2.6	1.1	2.7
X	.	6.0	5.0	.	6.2	4.2	6.4	4.2	5.6	7.3

Explanatory notes: see p. 77.

[1] Excl. armed forces. [2] Persons aged 10 years and over. [3] Third quarter. [4] Persons aged 12 years and over. [5] July of each year.

Notes explicatives: voir p. 80.

[1] Non compris les forces armées. [2] Personnes âgées de 10 ans et plus. [3] Troisième trimestre. [4] Personnes âgées de 12 ans et plus. [5] Juillet de chaque année.

Notas explicativas: véase p. 83.

[1] Excl. las fuerzas armadas. [2] Personas de 10 años y más. [3] Tercer trimestre. [4] Personas de 12 años y más. [5] Julio de cada año.

EMPLOYMENT — EMPLOI — EMPLEO

Paid employment, by economic activity — **Emploi rémunéré, par activité économique** — **Empleo remunerado, por actividad económica**

Thousands — Milliers — Millares

Costa Rica (BA) [1][2] — Employees - Salariés - Asalariados

Men - Hommes - Hombres — ISIC 3 - CITI 3 - CIIU 3

	1999	2000	2001	2002	2003	2004	2005	2006	2007	2008
Total	.	614.3	683.9	.	733.4	741.6	813.2	809.0	871.4	877.5
A	.	142.2	122.8	.	130.2	126.0	142.8	128.9	133.0	131.4
B	.	3.7	4.3	.	4.5	3.7	5.0	4.8	5.9	4.2
C	.	1.8	1.2	.	1.4	1.9	2.5	3.6	1.9	1.2
D	.	100.1	115.1	.	119.5	129.8	137.7	130.9	137.5	126.7
E	.	9.2	15.6	.	17.8	19.7	17.8	17.5	16.7	21.7
F	.	52.6	66.7	.	70.9	62.9	76.8	77.5	106.3	100.1
G	.	78.3	110.1	.	125.0	124.5	128.5	139.6	143.4	148.7
H	.	23.5	29.5	.	29.8	31.1	33.7	33.6	34.3	33.9
I	.	44.0	45.6	.	46.6	50.7	57.9	61.7	65.2	77.3
J	.	14.9	17.8	.	20.3	23.4	21.6	22.4	25.1	24.9
K	.	1.9	34.0	.	40.7	45.8	48.7	48.4	57.2	56.4
L	.		46.4	.	47.5	47.6	53.2	55.8	54.6	58.6
L.O	.	89.5		.						
M	.	22.8	24.7	.	26.9	25.5	28.7	28.8	32.4	29.9
N	.	21.1	18.6	.	15.4	17.6	22.1	20.5	21.0	20.7
O	.		21.3	.	25.4	19.6	23.1	23.8	23.6	30.0
P	.	3.3	5.4	.	5.9	6.1	7.2	8.0	9.5	5.5
Q	.	1.2	1.5	.	1.7	2.2	0.6	0.9	0.8	1.2
X	.	4.0	3.3	.	4.1	3.4	5.4	2.4	3.1	5.0

Women - Femmes - Mujeres — ISIC 3 - CITI 3 - CIIU 3

	1999	2000	2001	2002	2003	2004	2005	2006	2007	2008
Total	.	318.8	385.0	.	406.2	395.8	455.7	484.7	535.2	549.1
A	.	15.2	12.8	.	14.7	12.3	18.3	20.3	24.6	22.5
B	.	0.1	0.1	.	0.1	0.5	0.4	0.1	0.5	0.1
C	.	0.2	0.2	.	0.2	0.7	0.8	0.6	0.3	0.4
D	.	45.3	53.3	.	47.8	42.7	45.5	49.1	54.7	55.7
E	.	1.5	3.8	.	4.1	3.7	2.7	4.5	4.4	6.1
F	.	1.9	3.5	.	0.8	1.7	2.2	1.6	4.1	3.8
G	.	44.8	50.5	.	56.0	60.6	63.2	67.7	73.0	74.4
H	.	24.9	28.6	.	34.0	32.2	39.7	40.8	48.4	43.6
I	.	7.9	8.6	.	9.9	9.9	11.6	12.0	14.9	20.1
J	.	8.7	10.8	.	13.8	12.1	12.9	14.9	23.4	26.8
K	.	1.7	17.3	.	17.5	20.0	21.8	24.8	27.2	36.6
L	.		26.9	.	28.8	30.9	28.2	30.5	34.1	35.2
L.O	.	29.2		.						
M	.	49.5	58.4	.	66.5	65.0	71.6	74.2	73.7	79.4
N	.	26.2	31.4	.	28.5	28.3	34.2	35.4	38.6	38.2
O	.		13.5	.	13.7	13.3	14.9	17.4	19.1	16.5
P	.	59.5	63.0	.	67.1	59.2	85.2	87.4	91.1	86.2
Q	.	0.2	0.6	.	0.6	1.7	1.5	1.7	0.4	1.5
X	.	2.0	1.7	.	2.2	0.8	1.0	1.8	2.6	2.3

Cuba (BA) [3][4] — Employees - Salariés - Asalariados

Total - Total - Total — ISIC 2 - CITI 2 - CIIU 2

	1999	2000	2001	2002	2003	2004	2005	2006	2007	2008
Total	3 552.3	3 548.3	3 609.8	3 655.5	3 673.9	3 702.7	3 795.5	3 898.4	4 045.9	4 120.9 [5]
1	606.0	555.4	333.0	248.2	246.1	248.6	233.7	240.0	249.1	253.7 [5]
2	42.6	42.8	18.1	18.3	18.1	27.6	26.2	26.9	27.9	28.4 [5]
3	411.7	415.7	583.1	592.6	599.0	562.1	554.7	569.8	591.4	602.4 [5]
4	85.0	85.4	63.5	64.3	65.0	62.6	67.4	69.2	71.8	73.1 [5]
5	276.0	276.2	230.4	234.6	236.1	234.3	240.9	247.4	256.8	261.6 [5]
6	461.1	462.3	608.8	617.1	619.2	595.2	599.8	616.1	639.4	651.2 [5]
7	224.5	209.6	223.8	221.3	226.8	236.3	238.9	245.4	254.7	259.4 [5]
8	144.8	149.3	142.1	147.5	149.2	98.1	99.3	102.0	105.9	107.9 [5]
9	1 300.5	1 351.5	1 406.9	1 511.7	1 514.5	1 637.8	1 734.5	1 781.6	1 848.9	1 883.2 [5]

Men - Hommes - Hombres — ISIC 2 - CITI 2 - CIIU 2

	1999	2000	2001	2002	2003	2004	2005	2006	2007	2008
Total	2 141.9	2 121.7	2 148.1	2 159.4	2 157.8	2 158.9	2 212.7	2 271.4	2 314.3	2 370.2 [5]
1	470.4	424.1	273.9	194.2	198.5	176.4	168.9	173.4	178.2	182.0 [5]
2	35.7	35.9	14.9	15.0	14.9	22.2	21.6	22.2	22.9	23.3 [5]
3	275.8	278.3	392.3	396.7	399.4	387.9	388.1	398.5	409.1	418.1 [5]
4	63.9	64.1	47.0	47.4	47.8	47.6	50.4	51.7	53.2	54.3 [5]
5	228.7	228.7	193.7	197.1	198.0	196.7	204.4	209.8	216.8	221.2 [5]
6	250.4	251.3	350.6	358.7	354.4	352.3	352.1	361.4	368.3	377.1 [5]
7	164.2	149.6	161.2	160.4	162.8	174.4	176.8	181.5	186.7	190.6 [5]
8	81.9	83.4	78.1	80.3	80.6	45.2	47.9	49.2	49.7	51.1 [5]
9	570.9	606.4	636.5	709.6	701.5	756.3	802.5	823.7	829.4	852.5 [5]

Explanatory notes: see p. 77.

[1] Persons aged 12 years and over. [2] July of each year. [3] Persons aged 15 years and over. [4] Dec. [5] February - April

Notes explicatives: voir p. 80.

[1] Personnes âgées de 12 ans et plus. [2] Juillet de chaque année. [3] Personnes âgées de 15 ans et plus. [4] Déc. [5] Février - Avril

Notas explicativas: véase p. 83.

[1] Personas de 12 años y más. [2] Julio de cada año. [3] Personas de 15 años y más. [4] Dic. [5] Febrero - Abril

Paid employment, by economic activity
Emploi rémunéré, par activité économique
Empleo remunerado, por actividad económica

Thousands — Milliers — Millares

Cuba (BA) [1][2]

Employees - Salariés - Asalariados

Women - Femmes - Mujeres
ISIC 2 - CITI 2 - CIIU 2

	1999	2000	2001	2002	2003	2004	2005	2006	2007	2008
Total	1 410.3	1 426.5	1 461.6	1 496.1	1 516.1	1 543.8	1 582.8	1 627.0	1 731.6	1 750.7 [3]
1	135.5	131.3	59.0	53.9	47.6	72.3	64.8	66.6	70.9	71.7 [3]
2	6.9	6.9	3.2	3.2	3.2	5.4	4.6	4.7	5.0	5.1 [3]
3	135.9	137.4	190.8	195.9	199.7	174.2	166.6	171.3	182.3	184.3 [3]
4	21.1	21.3	16.6	16.9	17.2	15.0	17.0	17.5	18.6	18.8 [3]
5	47.4	47.5	36.7	37.5	38.1	37.6	36.5	37.6	40.0	40.4 [3]
6	210.7	211.0	258.2	258.4	264.8	242.9	247.7	254.7	271.1	274.1 [3]
7	60.4	60.0	62.7	60.9	64.0	62.0	62.1	63.9	68.0	68.8 [3]
8	62.9	65.9	64.1	67.3	68.6	52.9	51.4	52.8	56.2	56.8 [3]
9	729.6	745.1	770.4	802.1	813.0	881.5	932.1	957.9	1 019.5	1 030.7 [3]

Chile (BA) [1][4]

Employees - Salariés - Asalariados

Total - Total - Total
ISIC 2 - CITI 2 - CIIU 2

	1999	2000	2001	2002	2003	2004	2005	2006	2007	2008
Total	.	.	.	.	.	.	.	4 271.5	4 460.8	4 632.2
1	.	.	.	.	.	.	.	476.4	490.3	485.3
2	.	.	.	.	.	.	.	80.7	86.0	93.0
3	.	.	.	.	.	.	.	650.1	661.6	661.2
4	.	.	.	.	.	.	.	37.2	39.0	37.3
5	.	.	.	.	.	.	.	416.3	431.5	459.4
6	.	.	.	.	.	.	.	717.9	753.0	792.1
7	.	.	.	.	.	.	.	357.5	380.9	406.2
8	.	.	.	.	.	.	.	450.6	508.3	513.5
9	.	.	.	.	.	.	.	1 084.8	1 110.2	1 184.2

Men - Hommes - Hombres
ISIC 2 - CITI 2 - CIIU 2

	1999	2000	2001	2002	2003	2004	2005	2006	2007	2008
Total	.	.	.	.	.	.	.	2 865.3	2 959.8	3 039.0
1	.	.	.	.	.	.	.	393.9	399.8	393.2
2	.	.	.	.	.	.	.	75.0	82.4	88.9
3	.	.	.	.	.	.	.	505.7	510.5	504.3
4	.	.	.	.	.	.	.	32.0	33.4	29.5
5	.	.	.	.	.	.	.	394.6	408.1	434.5
6	.	.	.	.	.	.	.	382.8	397.6	403.7
7	.	.	.	.	.	.	.	291.6	309.5	328.7
8	.	.	.	.	.	.	.	271.6	301.6	298.0
9	.	.	.	.	.	.	.	518.0	516.8	558.4

Women - Femmes - Mujeres
ISIC 2 - CITI 2 - CIIU 2

	1999	2000	2001	2002	2003	2004	2005	2006	2007	2008
Total	.	.	.	.	.	.	.	1 406.2	1 501.0	1 593.2
1	.	.	.	.	.	.	.	82.5	90.5	92.1
2	.	.	.	.	.	.	.	5.8	3.6	4.2
3	.	.	.	.	.	.	.	144.3	151.1	157.0
4	.	.	.	.	.	.	.	5.1	5.6	7.8
5	.	.	.	.	.	.	.	21.7	23.3	24.9
6	.	.	.	.	.	.	.	335.1	355.4	388.5
7	.	.	.	.	.	.	.	65.8	71.3	77.5
8	.	.	.	.	.	.	.	179.1	206.7	215.5
9	.	.	.	.	.	.	.	566.8	593.4	625.9

República Dominicana (BA) [5][6]

Employees - Salariés - Asalariados

Total - Total - Total
ISIC 3 - CITI 3 - CIIU 3

	1999	2000	2001	2002	2003	2004	2005	2006	2007	2008
Total	.	.	.	.	.	3 149.9	3 164.6	3 353.7	3 442.8	.
A	.	.	.	.	.	452.4	443.2	457.3	462.1	.
B	.	.	.	.	.	7.1	11.3	11.6	12.8	.
C	.	.	.	.	.	5.0	6.0	3.5	6.1	.
D	.	.	.	.	.	487.2	470.5	482.5	490.4	.
E	.	.	.	.	.	26.7	26.2	26.6	30.8	.
F	.	.	.	.	.	211.7	213.1	239.4	246.4	.
G	.	.	.	.	.	626.7	647.7	679.6	684.6	.
H	.	.	.	.	.	173.8	182.9	200.6	211.8	.
I	.	.	.	.	.	231.7	237.7	247.1	256.8	.
J	.	.	.	.	.	55.7	61.9	66.1	73.5	.
K	.	.	.	.	.	95.5	96.7	86.7	92.4	.
L	.	.	.	.	.	140.8	147.5	149.1	152.6	.
M	.	.	.	.	.	145.4	150.2	152.3	169.3	.
N	.	.	.	.	.	100.8	104.0	102.8	96.1	.
O	.	.	.	.	.	231.4	212.2	267.1	260.8	.
P	.	.	.	.	.	156.6	151.6	180.6	194.6	.
Q	.	.	.	.	.	1.3	2.0	0.9	1.7	.

Explanatory notes: see p. 77.

[1] Persons aged 15 years and over. [2] Dec. [3] February - April [4] Fourth quarter of each year. [5] Persons aged 10 years and over. [6] Total employment, excl. unpaid family workers.

Notes explicatives: voir p. 80.

[1] Personnes âgées de 15 ans et plus. [2] Déc. [3] Février - Avril [4] Quatrième trimestre de chaque année. [5] Personnes âgées de 10 ans et plus. [6] Emploi total, non compris les travailleurs familiaux non rémunérés.

Notas explicativas: véase p. 83.

[1] Personas de 15 años y más. [2] Dic. [3] Febrero - Abril [4] Cuarto trimestre de cada año. [5] Personas de 10 años y más. [6] Empleo total, excl. a trabajadores familiares no remunerados.

EMPLOYMENT	EMPLOI	EMPLEO
Paid employment, **by economic activity**	**Emploi rémunéré,** **par activité économique**	**Empleo remunerado,** **por actividad económica**
Thousands	Milliers	Millares

	1999	2000	2001	2002	2003	2004	2005	2006	2007	2008

República Dominicana (BA) [1] [2] — Employees - Salariés - Asalariados

Men - Hommes - Hombres
ISIC 3 - CITI 3 - CIIU 3

	1999	2000	2001	2002	2003	2004	2005	2006	2007	2008
Total	.	.	.	.	.	2 108.5	2 115.7	2 200.1	2 270.1	.
A						433.1	416.0	436.6	440.6	
B						7.1	11.3	11.6	12.5	
C						4.7	5.8	3.1	5.8	
D						340.4	327.2	327.8	342.9	
E						20.1	17.2	21.2	22.1	
F						204.2	206.7	234.2	239.0	
G						418.8	434.2	458.4	465.6	
H						87.2	84.7	96.9	100.3	
I						204.9	215.5	229.2	233.7	
J						28.9	34.1	31.8	33.1	
K						65.2	65.9	60.6	61.8	
L						94.9	103.6	95.0	105.8	
M						43.9	44.0	42.1	55.1	
N						28.5	29.2	27.1	28.2	
O						108.5	100.3	109.6	103.7	
P						17.3	18.9	15.0	19.5	
Q						0.8	0.9	-	0.4	

Women - Femmes - Mujeres
ISIC 3 - CITI 3 - CIIU 3

	1999	2000	2001	2002	2003	2004	2005	2006	2007	2008
Total	.	.	.	.	.	1 041.4	1 048.9	1 153.6	1 172.8	.
A						19.3	27.2	20.7	21.5	
B						-	-	-	0.3	
C						0.3	0.2	0.5	0.3	
D						146.8	143.3	154.7	147.5	
E						6.6	9.0	5.5	8.7	
F						7.5	6.3	5.2	7.4	
G						207.8	213.5	221.3	219.0	
H						86.6	98.2	103.6	111.5	
I						26.8	22.2	17.9	23.1	
J						26.8	27.8	34.3	40.5	
K						30.3	30.7	26.0	30.5	
L						45.9	43.9	54.1	46.8	
M						101.4	106.2	110.2	114.3	
N						72.3	74.8	75.7	67.9	
O						122.9	111.9	157.5	157.1	
P						139.3	132.7	165.6	175.1	
Q						0.5	1.0	0.9	1.3	

Ecuador (BA) [1] [3] [4] — Employees - Salariés - Asalariados

Total - Total - Total
ISIC 3 - CITI 3 - CIIU 3

	1999	2000	2001	2002	2003	2004	2005	2006	2007	2008
Total	.	.	.	2 019.4	2 165.0	2 244.9	2 340.6	2 405.7	.	.
A				164.3	179.5	186.6	173.2	168.9		
B				23.9	33.2	24.8	37.4	38.9		
C				18.1	19.2	14.7	8.9	13.7		
D				279.3	300.3	322.3	312.5	338.3		
E				14.0	17.0	22.9	18.6	19.2		
F				156.0	165.3	176.9	183.2	218.1		
G				333.6	365.3	374.8	399.3	404.6		
H				63.1	63.7	74.4	77.7	91.4		
I				117.0	140.6	141.5	163.4	169.7		
J				44.5	48.6	48.2	49.3	45.7		
K				106.3	102.8	121.4	127.1	127.2		
L				146.1	180.1	172.3	168.2	170.3		
M				230.3	224.6	250.9	247.2	267.8		
N				100.6	96.8	107.5	112.2	92.8		
O				64.5	63.4	53.9	60.0	70.4		
P				157.3	163.4	150.4	201.7	167.7		
Q				0.4	1.0	1.4	0.7	0.9		

Men - Hommes - Hombres
ISIC 3 - CITI 3 - CIIU 3

	1999	2000	2001	2002	2003	2004	2005	2006	2007	2008
Total	.	.	.	1 288.6	.	1 424.1	1 451.1	1 525.9	.	.
A				137.3		165.1	151.3	145.7		
B				18.6		22.2	26.0	33.1		
C				16.4		13.4	8.8	12.2		
D				208.1		227.7	226.0	239.5		
E				12.3		17.3	15.3	15.6		
F				145.9		169.7	175.6	209.5		
G				219.2		247.9	258.7	269.1		
H				31.4		33.2	33.1	41.0		
I				97.5		117.8	133.0	138.1		
J				22.9		25.5	24.3	24.1		
K				83.4		88.4	91.3	92.7		
L				109.5		123.9	125.6	126.4		
M				99.5		96.1	88.6	96.3		
N				33.6		33.0	36.1	32.5		
O				38.7		34.7	36.0	40.4		
P				14.0		7.0	20.9	9.7		
Q				0.4		1.2	0.4	-		

Explanatory notes: see p. 77.

[1] Persons aged 10 years and over. [2] Total employment, excl. unpaid family workers. [3] Urban areas. [4] Nov. of each year.

Notes explicatives: voir p. 80.

[1] Personnes âgées de 10 ans et plus. [2] Emploi total, non compris les travailleurs familiaux non rémunérés. [3] Régions urbaines. [4] Nov. de chaque année.

Notas explicativas: véase p. 83.

[1] Personas de 10 años y más. [2] Empleo total, excl. a trabajadores familiares no remunerados. [3] Areas urbanas. [4] Nov. de cada año.

Paid employment, by economic activity
Emploi rémunéré, par activité économique
Empleo remunerado, por actividad económica

Thousands · Milliers · Millares

	1999	2000	2001	2002	2003	2004	2005	2006	2007	2008
Ecuador (BA) [1][2][3]				**Employees - Salariés - Asalariados**						
Women - Femmes - Mujeres										
ISIC 3 - CITI 3 - CIIU 3										
Total	.	.	.	730.9	.	820.8	889.6	879.8	.	.
A	.	.	.	27.0	.	21.5	21.9	23.2	.	.
B	.	.	.	5.4	.	2.6	11.4	5.8	.	.
C	.	.	.	1.7	.	1.3	0.1	1.5	.	.
D	.	.	.	71.2	.	94.6	86.5	98.8	.	.
E	.	.	.	1.6	.	5.6	3.4	3.6	.	.
F	.	.	.	10.1	.	7.2	7.6	8.5	.	.
G	.	.	.	114.4	.	126.8	140.6	135.5	.	.
H	.	.	.	31.7	.	41.2	44.6	50.4	.	.
I	.	.	.	19.5	.	23.8	30.5	31.6	.	.
J	.	.	.	21.6	.	22.7	24.9	21.7	.	.
K	.	.	.	23.0	.	33.0	35.8	34.5	.	.
L	.	.	.	36.7	.	48.4	42.6	43.9	.	.
M	.	.	.	130.8	.	154.8	158.6	171.5	.	.
N	.	.	.	67.1	.	74.5	76.1	60.3	.	.
O	.	.	.	25.8	.	19.2	24.1	30.0	.	.
P	.	.	.	143.3	.	143.4	180.8	158.0	.	.
Q	.	.	.	-	.	0.2	0.3	0.9	.	.
El Salvador (BA) [1][4][5]				**Employees - Salariés - Asalariados**						
Total - Total - Total										
ISIC 3 - CITI 3 - CIIU 3										
Total	1 999.6	2 025.2	2 028.6	2 016.8	2 082.4	2 080.5	2 058.7	2 120.9	2 191.1	.
A	386.0	373.6	361.0	321.5	302.0	340.2	350.7	335.4	322.7	.
B	14.3	14.2	10.9	13.6	23.2	14.5	10.6	11.7	12.2	.
C	1.7	1.4	2.6	3.2	2.0	1.6	2.2	2.0	3.6	.
D	379.3	382.1	365.4	375.5	378.6	353.0	340.1	339.0	370.9	.
E	8.1	8.3	10.1	9.8	5.7	9.2	6.4	9.0	10.2	.
F	123.9	111.1	122.6	123.7	146.0	144.0	128.4	156.3	147.2	.
G-H	489.2	524.1	538.4	559.3	579.1	592.1	579.3	609.5	632.3	.
I	94.7	102.3	104.1	94.3	101.6	110.9	104.7	104.0	102.2	.
J-K	80.5	82.5	91.9	89.4	97.9	90.5	107.2	99.4	113.1	.
L	108.6	117.2	90.4	92.5	93.9	87.8	88.4	92.1	98.7	.
M	71.6	66.1	81.6	86.9	76.6	77.6	85.7	81.7	90.0	.
N-O	133.6	146.1	141.1	142.6	168.2	152.6	157.0	163.8	176.6	.
P	106.8	95.1	106.7	94.9	106.4	105.9	98.1	117.0	111.0	.
Q	-	1.1	1.4	-	1.1	0.7	-	-	-	.
X	1.2	-	-	9.6	-	-	-	-	0.4	.
Men - Hommes - Hombres										
ISIC 3 - CITI 3 - CIIU 3										
Total	1 187.6	1 193.7	1 205.9	1 169.0	1 215.9	1 230.7	1 203.9	1 224.5	1 275.2	.
A	351.5	346.5	339.1	307.2	278.9	316.8	319.9	302.2	298.8	.
B	13.3	13.5	10.0	12.8	21.5	12.9	10.1	10.7	10.8	.
C	1.7	1.4	2.6	3.2	1.9	1.5	2.2	2.0	3.6	.
D	190.5	185.0	189.2	180.7	191.1	176.5	170.6	177.1	191.6	.
E	7.7	8.0	9.8	8.5	4.9	8.0	5.5	7.8	9.2	.
F	119.5	109.6	119.6	119.1	143.0	139.8	126.1	151.4	143.6	.
G-H	201.4	218.2	221.3	223.3	238.0	248.7	244.9	246.5	261.7	.
I	87.5	94.5	92.4	86.0	91.5	99.3	94.0	96.1	93.7	.
J-K	49.9	56.6	58.2	57.6	65.9	66.7	73.5	63.8	76.1	.
L	79.0	81.8	65.7	66.1	68.1	65.4	62.4	67.0	73.2	.
M	25.3	24.4	29.6	33.6	29.1	26.9	27.3	28.9	34.0	.
N-O	49.5	47.0	58.5	53.3	69.2	58.2	57.8	59.8	65.0	.
P	10.1	6.3	8.8	8.8	12.1	9.4	9.6	11.2	13.5	.
Q	.	0.9	1.2	-	0.7	0.6	-	-	-	.
X	0.5	-	-	8.8	-	-	-	-	0.4	.
Women - Femmes - Mujeres										
ISIC 3 - CITI 3 - CIIU 3										
Total	812.0	831.6	822.7	847.9	866.5	849.8	854.9	896.5	915.9	.
A	34.6	27.2	21.9	14.3	23.1	23.4	30.8	33.2	23.9	.
B	1.0	0.7	1.0	0.8	1.7	1.6	0.5	1.0	1.4	.
C	-	-	-	0.1	0.1	0.1	0.0	-	-	.
D	188.8	197.1	176.3	194.7	187.6	176.4	169.5	162.0	179.3	.
E	0.4	0.3	0.3	1.4	0.7	1.2	0.9	1.2	1.0	.
F	4.4	1.5	2.9	4.6	3.0	4.2	2.3	4.9	3.6	.
G-H	287.8	305.9	317.1	336.0	341.1	343.4	334.3	363.0	370.7	.
I	7.2	7.8	11.8	8.3	10.1	11.6	10.7	7.9	8.5	.
J-K	30.6	25.9	33.7	31.9	32.0	23.8	33.7	35.6	36.9	.
L	29.5	35.4	24.8	26.4	25.8	22.4	26.0	25.2	25.5	.
M	46.2	41.7	52.0	53.3	47.5	50.7	58.4	52.8	56.0	.
N-O	84.1	99.1	82.6	89.3	99.0	94.4	99.2	104.0	111.7	.
P	96.7	88.7	97.9	86.1	94.3	96.5	88.5	105.8	97.5	.
Q	-	0.2	0.3	-	0.4	0.1	-	-	-	.
X	0.7	-	-	0.8	-	-	-	-	0.0	.

Explanatory notes: see p. 77.

[1] Persons aged 10 years and over. [2] Urban areas. [3] Nov. of each year. [4] Total employment, excl. unpaid family workers. [5] Dec.

Notes explicatives: voir p. 80.

[1] Personnes âgées de 10 ans et plus. [2] Régions urbaines. [3] Nov. de chaque année. [4] Emploi total, non compris les travailleurs familiaux non rémunérés. [5] Déc.

Notas explicativas: véase p. 83.

[1] Personas de 10 años y más. [2] Areas urbanas. [3] Nov. de cada año. [4] Empleo total, excl. a trabajadores familiares no remunerados. [5] Dic.

ILO YEARBOOK OF LABOUR STATISTICS 2009 · *ANNUAIRE DES STATISTIQUES DU TRAVAIL DU BIT 2009* · *ANUARIO DE ESTADISTICAS DEL TRABAJO DEL OIT 2009*

307

EMPLOYMENT	EMPLOI	EMPLEO
Paid employment, by economic activity	Emploi rémunéré, par activité économique	Empleo remunerado, por actividad económica
Thousands	Milliers	Millares

	1999	2000	2001	2002	2003	2004	2005	2006	2007	2008

Guyane française (E) [1]

Employees - Salariés - Asalariados

Total - Total - Total
ISIC 3 - CITI 3 - CIIU 3

	1999	2000	2001	2002	2003	2004	2005	2006	2007	2008
Total	37.333	39.452	41.360	42.711	43.712	43.429	43.540	45.097	46.997	
A-B							0.974			
D							2.705			
E							0.643			
F							2.698			
G							3.920			
H							1.029			
I							2.308			
J							0.527			
K							4.062			
L							9.827			
M							6.728			
N							4.484			
O							1.908			
P							1.461			

Honduras (BA) [2] [3] [4]

Employees - Salariés - Asalariados

Total - Total - Total
ISIC 2 - CITI 2 - CIIU 2

	2005
Total	1 266.1
1	319.7
2	4.8
3	242.5
4	10.2
5	89.8
6	197.3
7	48.5
8	64.2
9	289.0

Men - Hommes - Hombres
ISIC 2 - CITI 2 - CIIU 2

	2005
Total	842.3
1	289.1
2	4.3
3	149.4
4	8.8
5	88.1
6	124.3
7	40.1
8	39.3
9	98.9

Women - Femmes - Mujeres
ISIC 2 - CITI 2 - CIIU 2

	2005
Total	423.8
1	30.7
2	0.5
3	93.1
4	1.4
5	1.7
6	73.0
7	8.4
8	24.9
9	190.1

Martinique (E) [1]

Employees - Salariés - Asalariados

Total - Total - Total
ISIC 3 - CITI 3 - CIIU 3

	2005
Total	113.1
A-B	5.9
D	7.8
E	1.2
F	6.0
G	15.0
H	4.7
I	5.9
J	2.3
K	8.7
L	19.5
M	13.9
N	12.3
O	4.6
P	5.4

Explanatory notes: see p. 77.

[1] Persons aged 15 years and over. [2] Excl. armed forces. [3] Persons aged 10 years and over. [4] March of each year.

Notes explicatives: voir p. 80.

[1] Personnes âgées de 15 ans et plus. [2] Non compris les forces armées. [3] Personnes âgées de 10 ans et plus. [4] Mars de chaque année.

Notas explicativas: véase p. 83.

[1] Personas de 15 años y más. [2] Excl. las fuerzas armadas. [3] Personas de 10 años y más. [4] Marzo de cada año.

Paid employment, by economic activity
Emploi rémunéré, par activité économique
Empleo remunerado, por actividad económica

	Thousands			Milliers				Millares		
	1999	2000	2001	2002	2003	2004	2005	2006	2007	2008

México (BA) [1] [2]

Employees - Salariés - Asalariados

Total - Total - Total
ISIC 3 - CITI 3 - CIIU 3

	1999	2000	2001	2002	2003	2004	2005	2006	2007	2008
Total	23 003.4	24 294.9	24 144.2	24 521.1	24 782.8	25 664.9	26 230.3	27 592.0	28 104.0	28 905.4
A	2 307.9	2 258.5	2 161.5	2 202.3	2 054.4	2 057.7	2 034.3	2 187.1	2 001.5	2 087.2
B	57.4	61.5	52.4	38.6	49.6	47.7	52.0	51.3	37.4	39.4
C	113.1	144.9	122.1	138.3	133.9	155.9	176.7	154.8	177.3	174.9
D	5 460.6	5 749.1	5 600.9	5 297.0	5 177.6	5 472.0	5 229.8	5 337.6	5 449.3	5 509.4
E	188.1	186.3	193.6	193.9	212.2	231.2	183.5	184.7	219.7	205.2
F	1 450.6	1 719.8	1 668.1	1 753.1	1 935.7	1 899.1	2 187.7	2 415.6	2 580.1	2 597.9
G	3 792.1	4 027.0	4 165.0	4 324.4	4 344.0	4 587.8	4 451.9	4 628.8	4 622.0	4 759.4
H	931.1	1 005.9	1 092.1	1 098.1	1 139.4	1 248.0	1 358.6	1 427.6	1 481.8	1 606.6
I	1 318.6	1 303.1	1 357.9	1 388.6	1 399.4	1 412.7	1 386.0	1 496.8	1 503.5	1 580.9
J	292.4	289.8	275.6	280.6	276.1	275.1	295.8	350.4	389.9	391.0
K	713.0	814.3	825.3	818.6	904.2	975.0	1 247.7	1 360.4	1 411.6	1 565.3
L	1 691.6	1 741.1	1 682.3	1 789.4	1 817.2	1 793.7	1 909.4	2 018.0	2 029.0	2 157.6
M	1 656.4	1 847.8	1 941.1	1 969.2	1 993.8	2 120.7	2 120.6	2 169.3	2 248.3	2 245.3
N	856.0	921.2	895.3	942.2	952.8	1 008.3	959.8	974.6	1 016.5	1 030.7
O	805.1	784.3	730.9	818.2	861.1	915.3	722.2	794.1	790.9	809.2
P	1 231.1	1 302.4	1 257.9	1 336.2	1 410.4	1 317.1	1 693.5	1 755.8	1 858.3	1 851.8
Q	0.0	1.7	0.7	0.0	0.0	2.8	2.3	2.8	6.3	3.8
X	138.3	136.5	121.4	132.4	121.0	144.8	218.6	282.1	280.7	290.0

Men - Hommes - Hombres
ISIC 3 - CITI 3 - CIIU 3

	1999	2000	2001	2002	2003	2004	2005	2006	2007	2008
Total	15 274.0	15 876.8	15 781.1	15 977.6	16 255.8	16 622.8	16 589.6	17 412.4	17 638.2	18 179.4
A	2 089.2	2 038.3	1 972.9	2 022.6	1 899.0	1 855.8	1 846.3	1 965.0	1 807.0	1 903.5
B	55.6	58.5	48.7	34.8	44.8	45.9	45.4	47.5	34.9	36.1
C	102.6	126.9	109.8	117.7	119.8	139.0	153.1	138.9	157.2	154.1
D	3 719.4	3 814.1	3 713.6	3 506.6	3 491.5	3 673.1	3 439.9	3 503.9	3 577.8	3 660.7
E	164.1	155.6	163.5	163.8	179.0	192.7	155.6	149.3	182.2	173.5
F	1 413.8	1 658.7	1 608.2	1 690.3	1 886.9	1 822.5	2 094.2	2 324.7	2 479.2	2 487.0
G	2 611.6	2 739.7	2 830.2	2 938.6	2 955.5	3 056.9	2 943.7	3 074.3	2 982.0	3 098.6
H	513.9	529.4	569.2	563.1	581.1	633.0	676.7	691.2	737.8	770.5
I	1 152.8	1 155.5	1 180.2	1 227.0	1 259.4	1 263.2	1 235.5	1 317.5	1 324.3	1 384.0
J	172.9	148.8	167.6	162.2	151.2	155.7	152.5	183.1	206.5	199.0
K	429.6	492.8	513.2	493.0	558.6	614.6	742.7	801.1	851.9	896.0
L	1 164.2	1 169.6	1 140.5	1 206.9	1 237.2	1 194.8	1 243.5	1 325.8	1 311.7	1 380.9
M	701.1	759.9	797.0	790.6	809.9	876.5	822.2	825.9	887.8	884.4
N	277.0	283.9	284.8	300.4	303.8	288.8	290.1	274.3	282.8	309.1
O	471.6	499.3	440.6	504.5	504.0	559.5	440.4	454.0	480.0	484.6
P	121.2	140.7	140.7	148.9	179.4	135.0	154.5	142.7	144.6	151.2
Q	0.0	0.4	0.6	0.0	0.0	0.8	1.0	0.9	3.1	3.5
X	113.3	104.7	99.8	106.6	94.5	114.9	152.4	192.3	187.4	202.7

Women - Femmes - Mujeres
ISIC 3 - CITI 3 - CIIU 3

	1999	2000	2001	2002	2003	2004	2005	2006	2007	2008
Total	7 729.3	8 418.1	8 363.1	8 543.6	8 527.0	9 042.2	9 640.7	10 179.7	10 465.8	10 726.0
A	218.7	220.2	188.6	179.7	155.4	201.9	188.0	222.1	194.5	183.6
B	1.8	3.0	3.7	3.9	4.8	1.8	6.6	3.8	2.5	3.3
C	10.4	18.0	12.4	20.6	14.1	16.9	23.6	15.9	20.1	20.8
D	1 741.2	1 935.0	1 887.2	1 790.4	1 686.1	1 798.9	1 789.9	1 833.6	1 871.5	1 848.7
E	24.0	30.6	30.1	30.1	33.2	38.5	27.9	35.4	37.5	31.6
F	36.9	61.1	59.9	62.8	48.8	76.6	93.5	91.0	101.0	110.9
G	1 180.5	1 287.3	1 334.7	1 385.8	1 388.5	1 531.0	1 508.3	1 554.5	1 640.0	1 660.8
H	417.3	476.5	522.9	535.0	558.3	615.0	681.9	736.4	744.0	836.1
I	165.8	147.6	177.7	161.7	140.1	149.5	150.5	179.3	179.2	196.9
J	119.5	141.0	107.9	118.4	124.9	119.3	143.3	167.3	183.4	192.0
K	283.4	321.4	312.2	325.6	345.6	360.4	505.0	559.4	559.8	669.3
L	527.4	571.5	541.8	582.5	580.0	599.0	665.9	692.2	717.3	776.6
M	955.3	1 087.9	1 144.1	1 178.6	1 183.9	1 244.2	1 298.4	1 343.4	1 360.5	1 360.9
N	579.0	637.2	610.5	641.8	648.9	719.4	669.7	700.3	733.7	721.6
O	333.5	285.0	290.4	313.7	357.1	355.8	281.8	340.1	310.8	324.5
P	1 109.9	1 161.7	1 117.1	1 187.3	1 231.0	1 182.1	1 539.0	1 613.2	1 713.7	1 700.6
Q	0.0	1.3	0.1	0.0	0.0	2.0	1.2	1.9	3.2	0.3
X	25.0	31.8	21.6	25.8	26.5	30.0	66.2	89.8	93.2	87.3

Explanatory notes: see p. 77.

[1] Persons aged 14 years and over. [2] Second quarter of each year.

Notes explicatives: voir p. 80.

[1] Personnes âgées de 14 ans et plus. [2] Deuxième trimestre de chaque année.

Notas explicativas: véase p. 83.

[1] Personas de 14 años y más. [2] Segundo trimestre de cada año.

EMPLOYMENT   EMPLOI   EMPLEO

Paid employment, by economic activity   Emploi rémunéré, par activité économique   Empleo remunerado, por actividad económica

Thousands — Milliers — Millares

	1999	2000	2001	2002	2003	2004	2005	2006	2007	2008
Panamá (BA) [1][2]										
Total - Total - Total										
ISIC 3 - CITI 3 - CIIU 3				*Employees - Salariés - Asalariados*						
Total	642.1	627.0	654.6	685.6	701.4	747.2	771.8	801.7	873.3	925.8
A	54.4	47.8	57.0	60.0	61.1	61.3	59.3	67.4	70.6	68.3
B	2.9	2.6	3.9	3.5	3.3	3.0	2.0	3.1	4.0	2.8
C	0.7	0.7	1.4	1.4	0.9	0.6	0.8	1.9	3.6	3.2
D	68.0	61.5	61.7	66.4	65.4	65.7	68.1	70.2	72.0	73.6
E	7.0	6.4	9.6	8.6	8.8	8.4	7.7	8.5	8.1	6.9
F	45.3	40.7	42.2	45.3	50.0	64.2	63.6	73.7	90.3	105.7
G	113.1	113.1	112.6	116.6	117.5	124.6	135.0	138.5	148.6	163.9
H	29.3	26.5	30.4	33.1	34.7	40.1	45.6	39.9	46.0	48.4
I	39.7	37.4	42.6	42.3	44.0	43.8	47.1	50.0	53.0	57.0
J	23.6	25.3	21.6	21.3	19.7	23.5	22.8	24.9	27.3	27.2
K	32.0	30.5	28.4	32.0	33.3	39.0	46.5	49.9	53.8	57.2
L	68.1	70.3	69.4	69.6	73.8	73.7	69.4	70.3	79.6	78.7
M	49.8	54.9	56.7	59.9	61.8	65.5	63.8	61.6	64.2	73.0
N	30.2	31.1	35.3	37.1	36.3	37.9	40.5	40.1	43.3	46.7
O	24.5	24.1	25.4	26.4	25.7	25.8	29.0	28.9	32.3	34.9
P	51.2	53.2	55.9	61.9	64.0	69.4	70.0	74.9	76.1	77.4
Q	2.4	0.9	0.5	0.2	1.0	0.7	0.6	0.8	0.7	0.9
Men - Hommes - Hombres										
ISIC 3 - CITI 3 - CIIU 3										
Total	393.1	377.0	396.7	413.2	418.7	447.5	460.6	487.9	526.5	562.4
A	52.5	45.9	54.9	58.3	58.9	59.9	56.6	64.7	68.2	65.7
B	2.8	2.3	3.5	3.2	3.2	2.6	2.0	3.0	3.8	2.8
C	0.6	0.7	1.3	1.4	0.8	0.6	0.8	1.7	3.4	2.8
D	51.3	48.5	48.1	51.7	51.7	50.7	53.5	55.9	54.9	55.9
E	5.8	5.2	7.4	7.2	7.6	7.5	6.5	6.7	5.8	4.8
F	42.9	38.5	39.7	42.6	47.4	62.5	60.5	70.4	86.3	102.3
G	71.8	70.9	71.8	73.6	71.9	78.8	83.2	88.8	89.0	99.2
H	15.0	14.7	15.2	16.2	18.5	20.9	21.9	18.0	21.8	23.0
I	29.6	26.9	32.9	32.5	34.5	32.3	36.9	38.3	42.2	47.3
J	9.8	10.8	8.7	8.6	7.4	8.3	8.8	10.4	10.7	10.5
K	20.3	19.1	19.5	21.2	20.3	22.2	29.4	32.4	31.7	33.0
L	41.1	41.8	41.7	41.9	43.0	42.8	40.3	41.8	46.4	46.0
M	17.2	18.5	17.9	18.3	18.5	21.6	21.1	19.9	21.8	24.8
N	11.4	10.6	13.7	13.4	14.0	14.2	14.2	14.6	15.4	16.0
O	13.4	14.6	14.4	15.4	13.4	14.3	15.7	16.1	16.2	19.3
P	5.7	7.6	5.7	7.5	7.0	8.0	9.0	7.6	8.5	8.6
Q	1.6	0.5	0.2	0.2	0.5	0.7	0.1	0.6	0.4	0.3
Women - Femmes - Mujeres										
ISIC 3 - CITI 3 - CIIU 3										
Total	249.0	250.0	257.9	272.4	282.6	299.7	311.3	313.8	346.8	363.4
A	1.8	1.9	2.1	1.7	2.2	1.7	2.7	2.8	2.4	2.6
B	0.1	0.3	0.5	0.2	0.1	0.4	0.0	0.2	0.2	-
C	0.0	0.0	0.1	0.0	0.0	-	0.0	0.2	0.2	0.4
D	16.7	13.1	13.6	14.7	13.8	15.0	14.6	14.3	17.1	17.7
E	1.1	1.2	2.3	1.5	1.2	0.9	1.3	1.8	2.3	2.0
F	2.4	2.2	2.5	2.7	2.6	1.7	3.1	3.4	4.0	3.3
G	41.3	42.2	40.8	43.0	45.5	45.9	51.9	49.7	59.6	64.7
H	14.3	11.8	15.1	17.0	16.2	19.1	23.7	21.9	24.2	25.4
I	10.1	10.4	9.7	9.8	9.5	11.5	10.2	11.7	10.8	9.7
J	13.8	14.5	12.8	12.7	12.3	15.3	14.0	14.6	16.6	16.6
K	11.7	11.4	8.8	10.8	13.0	16.8	17.1	17.5	22.1	24.2
L	27.0	28.6	27.7	27.6	30.8	30.9	29.0	28.5	33.2	32.7
M	32.6	36.5	38.8	41.6	43.3	43.8	42.7	41.7	42.4	48.2
N	18.8	20.5	21.6	23.7	22.2	23.7	26.2	25.6	27.8	30.7
O	11.0	9.5	11.0	11.0	12.3	11.5	13.4	12.8	16.1	15.6
P	45.4	45.6	50.2	54.4	56.9	61.3	61.0	67.3	67.7	68.8
Q	0.8	0.3	0.2	0.0	0.5	0.1	0.4	0.2	0.3	0.6
Paraguay (BA) [3][4]										
Total - Total - Total				*Employees - Salariés - Asalariados*						
ISIC 3 - CITI 3 - CIIU 3										
Total	.	.	.	.	.	.	.	.	1 307.4	1 417.5
A-B	.	.	.	.	.	.	.	.	86.1	96.0
C	.	.	.	.	.	.	.	.	6.0	5.2
D	.	.	.	.	.	.	.	.	201.6	217.1
E	.	.	.	.	.	.	.	.	8.8	10.6
F	.	.	.	.	.	.	.	.	98.0	114.5
G-H	.	.	.	.	.	.	.	.	254.4	281.5
I	.	.	.	.	.	.	.	.	81.5	81.7
J-K	.	.	.	.	.	.	.	.	75.1	86.9
L-Q	.	.	.	.	.	.	.	.	495.7	523.9
X	.	.	.	.	.	.	.	.	0.2	-

Explanatory notes: see p. 77.
[1] Persons aged 15 years and over. [2] Aug. of each year. [3] Persons aged 10 years and over. [4] Fourth quarter.

Notes explicatives: voir p. 80.
[1] Personnes âgées de 15 ans et plus. [2] Août de chaque année. [3] Personnes âgées de 10 ans et plus. [4] Quatrième trimestre.

Notas explicativas: véase p. 83.
[1] Personas de 15 años y más. [2] Agosto de cada año. [3] Personas de 10 años y más. [4] Cuarto trimestre.

Paid employment, by economic activity	Emploi rémunéré, par activité économique	Empleo remunerado, por actividad económica

	Thousands			Milliers				Millares		
	1999	2000	2001	2002	2003	2004	2005	2006	2007	2008

Paraguay (BA) [1][2] — Employees - Salariés - Asalariados

Men - Hommes - Hombres
ISIC 3 - CITI 3 - CIIU 3

	1999	2000	2001	2002	2003	2004	2005	2006	2007	2008
Total	.	.	.	.	.	.	.	.	809.9	884.5
A-B	.	.	.	.	.	.	.	.	80.6	84.7
C	.	.	.	.	.	.	.	.	6.0	5.1
D	.	.	.	.	.	.	.	.	163.7	178.2
E	.	.	.	.	.	.	.	.	8.0	8.6
F	.	.	.	.	.	.	.	.	97.0	114.0
G-H	.	.	.	.	.	.	.	.	179.8	193.9
I	.	.	.	.	.	.	.	.	68.6	71.6
J-K	.	.	.	.	.	.	.	.	46.1	59.8
L-Q	.	.	.	.	.	.	.	.	159.9	168.6
X	.	.	.	.	.	.	.	.	0.2	-

Women - Femmes - Mujeres
ISIC 3 - CITI 3 - CIIU 3

	1999	2000	2001	2002	2003	2004	2005	2006	2007	2008
Total	.	.	.	.	.	.	.	.	497.5	533.0
A-B	.	.	.	.	.	.	.	.	5.9	11.3
C	.	.	.	.	.	.	.	.	-	0.2
D	.	.	.	.	.	.	.	.	37.9	38.9
E	.	.	.	.	.	.	.	.	0.8	2.0
F	.	.	.	.	.	.	.	.	1.0	0.6
G-H	.	.	.	.	.	.	.	.	74.5	87.5
I	.	.	.	.	.	.	.	.	12.9	10.2
J-K	.	.	.	.	.	.	.	.	29.1	27.1
L-Q	.	.	.	.	.	.	.	.	335.8	355.3
X	.	.	.	.	.	.	.	.	-	-

Perú (BA) [3][4] — Employees - Salariés - Asalariados

Total - Total - Total
ISIC 3 - CITI 3 - CIIU 3

	1999	2000	2001	2002	2003	2004	2005	2006	2007	2008
Total	.	.	.	1 870.0 [2]	1 956.4 [5]	1 951.9	1 905.3	2 122.3	2 348.1	2 437.4
A	.	.	.	17.5 [2]	23.4 [5]	17.2	21.5	18.2	21.5	16.3
B	.	.	.	6.3 [2]	6.2 [5]	1.5	4.4	4.7	3.7	3.6
C	.	.	.	5.1 [2]	3.1 [5]	16.7	16.1	18.8	21.7	21.3
D	.	.	.	382.6 [2]	339.8 [5]	420.7	409.1	440.2	536.4	538.8
E	.	.	.	9.1 [2]	8.5 [5]	4.6	11.4	9.5	9.0	7.9
F	.	.	.	124.5 [2]	167.1 [5]	144.5	104.1	162.5	155.6	184.7
G	.	.	.	286.0 [2]	289.9 [5]	300.8	264.3	324.2	338.7	356.1
H	.	.	.	107.2 [2]	105.7 [5]	98.6	113.9	110.5	104.0	127.7
I	.	.	.	171.1 [2]	188.9 [5]	147.0	159.9	189.4	189.7	202.9
J	.	.	.	34.5 [2]	36.9 [5]	30.4	46.8	46.2	37.3	58.0
K	.	.	.	187.3 [2]	207.6 [5]	159.6	144.8	196.6	215.6	218.6
L	.	.	.	155.8 [2]	149.0 [5]	139.2	152.5	176.0	205.7	167.4
M	.	.	.	172.2 [2]	171.0 [5]	213.8	217.8	184.9	224.9	241.6
N	.	.	.	82.5 [2]	83.5 [5]	104.5	87.5	85.2	112.0	127.8
O	.	.	.	128.4 [2]	173.6 [5]	150.3	151.2	154.6	170.5	162.6
P	.	.	.	- [2]	1.0 [5]	-	-	-	0.8	-
Q	.	.	.	- [2]	1.2 [5]	2.7	-	0.7	1.2	2.2
X	.	.	.	- [2]	- [5]	-	-	-	-	-

Men - Hommes - Hombres
ISIC 3 - CITI 3 - CIIU 3

	1999	2000	2001	2002	2003	2004	2005	2006	2007	2008
Total	.	.	.	1 173.9 [2]	1 241.0 [5]	1 257.8	1 226.3	1 366.2	1 478.3	1 488.4
A	.	.	.	12.5 [2]	20.7 [5]	16.3	20.8	16.2	17.4	13.1
B	.	.	.	6.3 [2]	5.5 [5]	1.5	4.4	4.7	3.4	3.6
C	.	.	.	5.1 [2]	3.1 [5]	15.4	13.5	16.9	18.2	19.2
D	.	.	.	284.0 [2]	241.1 [5]	305.9	290.1	314.8	367.9	363.0
E	.	.	.	7.3 [2]	6.3 [5]	4.6	6.5	7.8	8.1	6.5
F	.	.	.	117.8 [2]	153.9 [5]	141.9	97.1	152.1	153.3	172.2
G	.	.	.	153.4 [2]	164.6 [5]	162.9	172.6	181.9	190.9	171.5
H	.	.	.	52.2 [2]	52.0 [5]	34.3	54.6	48.5	45.6	48.2
I	.	.	.	138.0 [2]	145.2 [5]	119.5	132.6	159.0	146.0	157.4
J	.	.	.	19.2 [2]	19.0 [5]	16.1	23.0	27.1	21.5	33.2
K	.	.	.	120.8 [2]	116.7 [5]	120.7	90.9	131.0	138.3	143.9
L	.	.	.	100.3 [2]	105.4 [5]	103.1	107.4	108.9	148.2	127.2
M	.	.	.	46.3 [2]	50.5 [5]	65.5	65.8	67.1	75.0	80.5
N	.	.	.	23.5 [2]	31.9 [5]	38.5	33.7	22.2	35.7	40.2
O	.	.	.	87.4 [2]	124.2 [5]	109.2	113.3	107.2	108.8	108.7
P	.	.	.	- [2]	1.0 [5]	-	-	-	-	-
Q	.	.	.	- [2]	- [5]	2.5	-	0.7	-	-
X	.	.	.	- [2]	- [5]	-	-	-	-	-

Explanatory notes: see p. 77.

[1] Persons aged 10 years and over. [2] Fourth quarter. [3] Persons aged 14 years and over. [4] Metropolitan Lima. [5] May-Dec.

Notes explicatives: voir p. 80.

[1] Personnes âgées de 10 ans et plus. [2] Quatrième trimestre. [3] Personnes âgées de 14 ans et plus. [4] Lima métropolitaine. [5] Mai-déc.

Notas explicativas: véase p. 83.

[1] Personas de 10 años y más. [2] Cuarto trimestre. [3] Personas de 14 años y más. [4] Lima metropolitana. [5] Mayo-dic.

EMPLOYMENT | EMPLOI | EMPLEO

Paid employment, by economic activity | Emploi rémunéré, par activité économique | Empleo remunerado, por actividad económica

	Thousands			Milliers				Millares		
	1999	2000	2001	2002	2003	2004	2005	2006	2007	2008

Perú (BA) [1][2] — Employees - Salariés - Asalariados

Women - Femmes - Mujeres
ISIC 3 - CITI 3 - CIIU 3

	1999	2000	2001	2002	2003	2004	2005	2006	2007	2008
Total	.	.	.	696.2 [3]	715.4 [4]	694.1	679.0	756.1	869.8	949.0
A				5.0 [3]	2.7 [4]	0.9	0.7	2.0	4.1	3.2
B				- [3]	0.7 [4]	-	-	-	0.3	-
C				- [3]	- [4]	1.3	2.6	1.9	3.4	2.0
D				98.7 [3]	98.7 [4]	114.8	119.0	125.5	168.4	175.7
E				1.8 [3]	2.2 [4]	-	4.9	1.8	0.9	1.3
F				6.7 [3]	13.3 [4]	2.6	7.0	10.4	2.2	12.5
G				132.7 [3]	125.3 [4]	137.9	91.6	142.3	147.8	184.6
H				55.0 [3]	53.7 [4]	64.3	59.3	62.0	58.4	79.5
I				33.1 [3]	43.7 [4]	27.5	27.3	30.4	43.7	45.5
J				15.3 [3]	18.0 [4]	14.2	23.8	19.1	15.8	24.8
K				66.5 [3]	91.0 [4]	38.9	53.9	65.6	77.3	74.7
L				55.5 [3]	43.6 [4]	36.1	45.1	67.0	57.4	40.2
M				125.9 [3]	120.5 [4]	148.2	152.0	117.8	149.9	161.1
N				59.1 [3]	51.6 [4]	66.0	53.8	63.1	76.3	87.6
O				41.0 [3]	49.4 [4]	41.1	37.9	47.4	61.7	53.9
P				- [3]	- [4]	-	-	-	0.8	-
Q				- [3]	1.2 [4]	0.3	-	-	1.2	2.2
X				- [3]	- [4]	-	-	-	-	-

Perú (BA) [1][5] — Employees - Salariés - Asalariados

Total - Total - Total
ISIC 3 - CITI 3 - CIIU 3

	1999	2000	2001	2002	2003	2004	2005	2006	2007	2008
Total	3 298.2	3 091.6	3 329.9	3 723.7 [3]	3 776.7 [4]	3 837.1	3 853.4	4 235.4	4 516.2	4 730.0
A	130.4	163.0	206.2	233.6 [3]	317.1 [4]	264.6	273.4	300.7	222.9	220.9
B	28.3	13.0	18.8	40.4 [3]	30.8 [4]	31.7	29.0	27.3	31.5	31.9
C	28.2	50.7	41.3	50.2 [3]	56.9 [4]	77.6	74.0	88.3	87.2	92.1
D	501.8	534.6	548.8	604.3 [3]	540.9 [4]	635.4	639.6	676.4	799.4	819.1
E	40.5	26.4	18.7	23.6 [3]	21.3 [4]	18.4	29.2	24.5	20.8	31.7
F	242.8	180.5	211.8	241.6 [3]	285.6 [4]	247.6	227.7	285.7	307.5	365.8
G	505.0	485.9	521.9	509.1 [3]	488.5 [4]	512.8	488.2	569.0	586.3	599.5
H	141.2	109.4	177.1	179.3 [3]	184.4 [4]	167.0	197.1	200.4	213.4	256.6
I	274.4	273.1	269.1	301.2 [3]	288.1 [4]	259.5	271.1	322.6	322.4	336.6
J	69.3	58.1	43.5	49.2 [3]	52.3 [4]	47.8	61.2	72.1	64.3	85.2
K	259.1	229.0	191.7	275.8 [3]	284.5 [4]	259.8	253.1	305.5	320.3	343.9
L	339.2	303.1	290.6	345.9 [3]	326.0 [4]	317.7	359.1	396.5	437.6	423.0
M	499.0	411.8	487.7	473.5 [3]	462.4 [4]	532.6	513.1	504.4	602.8	599.4
N	122.9	120.1	167.5	155.9 [3]	153.0 [4]	189.1	163.2	175.6	214.1	232.7
O	115.6	132.9	133.4	240.3 [3]	282.3 [4]	271.4	274.2	285.8	283.4	289.4
P	-	-	-	- [3]	1.3 [4]	1.0	0.2	-	0.8	-
Q	0.6	-	1.9	- [3]	1.4 [4]	2.7	-	0.7	1.5	2.2
X	-	-	-	- [3]	- [4]	0.3	-	-	-	-

Men - Hommes - Hombres
ISIC 3 - CITI 3 - CIIU 3

	1999	2000	2001	2002	2003	2004	2005	2006	2007	2008
Total	2 144.5	2 094.6	2 204.0	2 458.0 [3]	2 474.9 [4]	2 551.6	2 546.6	2 805.1	2 892.4	3 000.9
A	90.5	136.7	155.0	176.6 [3]	251.2 [4]	210.0	211.6	233.6	168.5	171.1
B	28.3	12.1	18.5	38.9 [3]	29.7 [4]	31.5	28.8	27.1	31.2	30.9
C	26.5	47.3	39.7	48.6 [3]	54.7 [4]	74.4	69.2	85.8	80.7	87.1
D	318.2	383.0	401.3	449.5 [3]	390.7 [4]	467.3	451.6	490.9	552.9	568.4
E	34.3	23.2	15.7	20.9 [3]	17.9 [4]	16.6	22.7	20.8	18.9	26.9
F	238.8	171.9	204.4	233.6 [3]	269.9 [4]	244.7	218.3	274.1	299.7	348.8
G	347.3	312.2	333.6	284.4 [3]	271.2 [4]	283.2	304.5	323.6	325.0	304.9
H	57.6	35.0	78.6	76.1 [3]	77.2 [4]	58.7	85.2	77.6	85.8	89.5
I	240.4	239.8	241.9	256.4 [3]	230.0 [4]	217.5	227.1	266.8	255.3	263.0
J	36.9	35.3	30.0	28.8 [3]	28.3 [4]	24.9	32.3	41.5	37.8	46.0
K	172.4	154.1	125.1	188.2 [3]	174.2 [4]	199.5	171.5	217.3	214.2	230.5
L	250.5	228.0	208.9	242.9 [3]	239.4 [4]	236.8	264.4	276.0	316.1	311.4
M	201.9	182.3	207.4	189.4 [3]	178.3 [4]	216.5	194.8	209.3	240.5	233.1
N	36.8	37.1	54.7	49.1 [3]	60.5 [4]	71.5	59.1	54.8	71.7	78.2
O	64.1	96.7	87.2	174.4 [3]	200.4 [4]	195.0	205.6	205.0	193.9	210.8
P	-	-	-	- [3]	1.2 [4]	0.8	-	-	-	-
Q	-	-	1.9	- [3]	0.2 [4]	2.5	-	0.7	0.4	-
X	-	-	-	- [3]	- [4]	0.3	-	-	-	-

Explanatory notes: see p. 77.

[1] Persons aged 14 years and over. [2] Metropolitan Lima. [3] Fourth quarter. [4] May-Dec. [5] Urban areas.

Notes explicatives: voir p. 80.

[1] Personnes âgées de 14 ans et plus. [2] Lima métropolitaine. [3] Quatrième trimestre. [4] Mai-déc. [5] Régions urbaines.

Notas explicativas: véase p. 83.

[1] Personas de 14 años y más. [2] Lima metropolitana. [3] Cuarto trimestre. [4] Mayo-dic. [5] Areas urbanas.

Paid employment, by economic activity
Emploi rémunéré, par activité économique
Empleo remunerado, por actividad económica

	Thousands			Milliers				Millares		
	1999	2000	2001	2002	2003	2004	2005	2006	2007	2008

Perú (BA) [1][2] — Employees - Salariés - Asalariados

Women - Femmes - Mujeres
ISIC 3 - CITI 3 - CIIU 3

	1999	2000	2001	2002	2003	2004	2005	2006	2007	2008
Total	1 153.7	997.0	1 125.8	1 265.7 [3]	1 301.8 [4]	1 285.5	1 306.8	1 430.3	1 623.7	1 729.1
A	39.8	26.2	51.1	56.9 [3]	65.8 [4]	54.6	61.8	67.1	54.4	49.8
B	-	0.9	0.3	1.5 [3]	1.1 [4]	0.2	0.2	0.2	0.3	1.0
C	1.7	3.5	1.6	1.5 [3]	2.2 [4]	3.2	4.8	2.5	6.6	5.0
D	183.6	151.7	147.5	154.8 [3]	150.2 [4]	168.1	188.0	185.5	246.4	250.7
E	6.3	3.2	3.0	2.7 [3]	3.3 [4]	1.8	6.5	3.7	1.9	4.8
F	4.1	8.7	7.4	7.9 [3]	15.8 [4]	2.9	9.4	11.6	7.8	16.9
G	157.7	173.7	188.2	224.7 [3]	217.4 [4]	229.7	183.7	245.4	261.2	294.6
H	83.6	74.4	98.5	103.2 [3]	107.2 [4]	108.3	111.9	122.8	127.6	167.0
I	33.9	33.2	27.1	44.8 [3]	58.1 [4]	42.1	44.0	55.8	67.1	73.6
J	32.4	22.8	13.4	20.3 [3]	24.0 [4]	22.9	28.9	30.6	26.5	39.1
K	86.7	74.9	66.6	87.6 [3]	110.3 [4]	60.3	81.6	88.2	106.2	113.4
L	88.7	75.1	81.7	103.0 [3]	86.6 [4]	80.9	94.7	120.4	121.5	111.5
M	297.1	229.5	280.2	284.1 [3]	284.1 [4]	316.1	318.4	295.1	362.3	366.4
N	86.1	83.0	112.8	106.7 [3]	92.5 [4]	117.6	104.1	120.7	142.4	154.4
O	51.6	36.2	46.2	65.9 [3]	81.9 [4]	76.4	68.7	80.8	89.5	78.5
P	-	-	-	- [3]	0.2 [4]	0.3	0.2	-	0.8	-
Q	0.6	-	-	- [3]	1.2 [4]	0.3	-	-	1.2	2.2
X	-	-	-	- [3]	- [4]				-	-

Turks and Caicos Islands (BA) [5] — Employees - Salariés - Asalariados

Total - Total - Total
ISIC 3 - CITI 3 - CIIU 3

	1999	2000	2001	2002	2003	2004	2005	2006	2007	2008
Total	.	.	.	.	12.594	13.695	16.042	17.218	18.610	.
A	.	.	.	.	0.076	0.080	0.084	0.148	0.108	.
B	.	.	.	.	0.044	0.048	0.052	0.088	0.025	.
C	.	.	.	.	0.053	0.055	0.056	0.016	0.016	.
D	.	.	.	.	0.155	0.180	0.190	0.140	0.236	.
E	.	.	.	.	0.220	0.217	0.269	0.199	0.192	.
F	.	.	.	.	1.696	1.911	2.244	3.053	4.213	.
G	.	.	.	.	0.994	1.234	1.252	1.521	1.558	.
H	.	.	.	.	2.488	2.513	2.896	3.691	4.028	.
I	.	.	.	.	0.574	0.610	0.628	0.705	0.810	.
J	.	.	.	.	0.407	0.451	0.491	0.465	0.511	.
K	.	.	.	.	1.138	1.191	1.483	1.959	2.261	.
L	.	.	.	.	1.996	2.260	2.309	2.234	2.298	.
M	.	.	.	.	-	-	-	0.554	0.553	.
M-N	.	.	.	.	0.380	0.426	0.464	-	-	.
N	.	.	.	.	-	-	-	0.228	0.202	.
O	.	.	.	.	0.923	0.881	0.906	0.913	1.145	.
P	.	.	.	.	0.925	1.386	1.608	0.909	0.376	.
X	.	.	.	.	0.525	0.252	1.110	0.395	0.078	.

Men - Hommes - Hombres
ISIC 3 - CITI 3 - CIIU 3

	1999	2000	2001	2002	2003	2004	2005	2006	2007	2008
Total	.	.	.	.	.	.	.	10.244	11.522	.
A	.	.	.	.	.	.	.	0.129	0.094	.
B	.	.	.	.	.	.	.	0.072	0.023	.
C	.	.	.	.	.	.	.	0.013	0.013	.
D	.	.	.	.	.	.	.	0.065	0.103	.
E	.	.	.	.	.	.	.	0.173	0.155	.
F	.	.	.	.	.	.	.	2.882	3.954	.
G	.	.	.	.	.	.	.	0.829	0.847	.
H	.	.	.	.	.	.	.	1.937	2.080	.
I	.	.	.	.	.	.	.	0.459	0.538	.
J	.	.	.	.	.	.	.	0.152	0.170	.
K	.	.	.	.	.	.	.	1.191	1.476	.
L	.	.	.	.	.	.	.	1.137	1.154	.
M	.	.	.	.	.	.	.	0.134	0.139	.
N	.	.	.	.	.	.	.	0.065	0.051	.
O	.	.	.	.	.	.	.	0.472	0.586	.
P	.	.	.	.	.	.	.	0.236	0.089	.
X	.	.	.	.	.	.	.	0.298	0.050	.

Explanatory notes: see p. 77.

[1] Persons aged 14 years and over. [2] Urban areas. [3] Fourth quarter. [4] May-Dec. [5] Persons aged 15 years and over.

Notes explicatives: voir p. 80.

[1] Personnes âgées de 14 ans et plus. [2] Régions urbaines. [3] Quatrième trimestre. [4] Mai-déc. [5] Personnes âgées de 15 ans et plus.

Notas explicativas: véase p. 83.

[1] Personas de 14 años y más. [2] Areas urbanas. [3] Cuarto trimestre. [4] Mayo-dic. [5] Personas de 15 años y más.

**Paid employment,
by economic activity**

**Emploi rémunéré,
par activité économique**

**Empleo remunerado,
por actividad económica**

	Thousands				Milliers				Millares	
	1999	2000	2001	2002	2003	2004	2005	2006	2007	2008

Turks and Caicos Islands (BA) [1]   Employees - Salariés - Asalariados

Women - Femmes - Mujeres
ISIC 3 - CITI 3 - CIIU 3

	1999	2000	2001	2002	2003	2004	2005	2006	2007	2008
Total	.	.	.	.	.	.	.	6.974	7.088	.
A	.	.	.	.	.	.	.	0.019	0.014	.
B	.	.	.	.	.	.	.	0.016	0.002	.
C	.	.	.	.	.	.	.	0.003	0.003	.
D	.	.	.	.	.	.	.	0.075	0.133	.
E	.	.	.	.	.	.	.	0.026	0.037	.
F	.	.	.	.	.	.	.	0.171	0.259	.
G	.	.	.	.	.	.	.	0.692	0.711	.
H	.	.	.	.	.	.	.	1.754	1.948	.
I	.	.	.	.	.	.	.	0.246	0.272	.
J	.	.	.	.	.	.	.	0.313	0.341	.
K	.	.	.	.	.	.	.	0.768	0.785	.
L	.	.	.	.	.	.	.	1.097	1.144	.
M	.	.	.	.	.	.	.	0.420	0.414	.
N	.	.	.	.	.	.	.	0.163	0.151	.
O	.	.	.	.	.	.	.	0.441	0.559	.
P	.	.	.	.	.	.	.	0.673	0.287	.
X	.	.	.	.	.	.	.	0.097	0.028	.

United States (DA) [2]   Employees - Salariés - Asalariados

Total - Total - Total
ISIC 3 - CITI 3 - CIIU 3

	1999	2000	2001	2002	2003	2004	2005	2006	2007	2008
Total	128 912.2	131 706.0	131 752.5	130 270.6	129 929.6	131 367.4	133 637.8	136 021.6	137 537.9	137 009.0
C	517.4	520.2	532.5	512.2	502.7	523.0	562.2	619.7	663.8	717.0
D	18 357.3	18 329.0	17 491.9	16 250.4	15 459.2	15 245.9	15 150.4	15 078.7	14 801.9	14 333.3
E [3]	608.5	601.3	599.4	596.2	577.0	563.8	554.0	548.5	553.4	559.5
F	6 545.0	6 787.0	6 826.0	6 716.0	6 735.0	6 976.0	7 336.0	7 691.0	7 630.0	7 215.0
G	22 033.6	22 406.8	22 219.5	21 876.3	21 713.0	21 905.5	22 235.7	22 462.8	22 746.5	22 504.9
H	9 833.7	10 073.5	10 211.3	10 203.2	10 359.8	10 643.2	10 923.0	11 181.1	11 457.4	11 489.3
I	6 460.8	6 686.6	6 668.9	6 346.9	6 160.8	6 145.8	6 206.4	6 286.9	6 340.6	6 273.9
J	5 665.5	5 676.4	5 769.6	5 813.7	5 919.5	5 945.5	6 019.5	6 155.5	6 131.9	6 015.8
K	18 064.9	18 837.9	18 662.7	18 119.3	18 114.7	18 529.0	19 123.5	19 766.1	20 139.1	19 933.2
L	10 313.7	10 585.8	10 652.8	10 773.4	10 810.0	10 835.6	10 913.8	10 998.8	11 144.6	11 317.9
M	11 424.0	11 714.9	12 102.8	12 540.0	12 659.2	12 765.8	12 951.8	13 106.4	13 245.7	13 471.2
N	12 477.1	12 718.0	13 134.0	13 555.7	13 892.6	14 190.2	14 536.3	14 925.3	15 380.2	15 818.5
O [4]	6 689.5	6 879.2	6 980.8	7 044.2	7 094.1	7 163.7	7 191.3	7 269.7	7 375.4	7 440.8

Men - Hommes - Hombres
ISIC 3 - CITI 3 - CIIU 3

	1999	2000	2001	2002	2003	2004	2005	2006	2007	2008
Total	67 110.3	68 490.7	68 076.1	66 917.3	66 699.3	67 635.4	68 926.9	70 503.2	70 739.4	69 820.6
C	429.5	436.4	449.9	433.5	429.6	450.4	490.5	544.6	577.5	620.5
D	12 456.5	12 449.9	11 945.1	11 201.9	10 721.3	10 619.4	10 591.3	10 592.6	10 377.4	10 061.2
E [3]	457.0	450.4	448.8	446.2	430.2	417.6	410.7	402.5	403.2	408.7
F	5 727.0	5 941.0	5 994.0	5 889.0	5 913.0	6 135.0	6 446.0	6 747.0	6 683.0	6 292.0
G	12 491.2	12 705.1	12 617.2	12 509.9	12 477.8	12 610.7	12 779.4	12 879.2	12 954.3	12 727.6
H	4 681.1	4 806.7	4 828.2	4 789.6	4 850.3	4 964.8	5 081.7	5 189.3	5 339.3	5 354.9
I	4 358.5	4 464.4	4 453.4	4 289.5	4 206.0	4 251.8	4 319.1	4 464.1	4 507.0	4 469.0
J	1 939.2	1 932.1	1 954.7	1 978.1	2 032.3	2 074.9	2 131.5	2 206.8	2 230.6	2 200.6
K	9 664.1	10 095.4	10 000.1	9 741.6	9 795.2	10 086.4	10 422.1	10 782.8	10 956.7	10 853.0
L	5 394.3	5 507.9	5 569.9	5 615.0	5 640.8	5 665.5	5 728.1	5 763.9	5 819.6	5 898.6
M	3 886.1	3 974.0	4 025.6	4 132.5	4 205.8	4 259.9	4 360.8	4 690.3	4 535.9	4 450.8
N	2 520.4	2 550.0	2 594.1	2 661.2	2 722.4	2 782.2	2 841.0	2 918.9	2 988.6	3 086.7
O [4]	3 154.7	3 245.6	3 259.2	3 280.4	3 318.1	3 357.4	3 364.6	3 362.6	3 411.7	3 446.3

Women - Femmes - Mujeres
ISIC 3 - CITI 3 - CIIU 3

	1999	2000	2001	2002	2003	2004	2005	2006	2007	2008
Total	61 801.9	63 215.3	63 676.4	63 353.3	63 230.3	63 732.0	64 710.9	65 518.4	66 798.5	67 188.4
C	87.9	83.8	82.6	78.7	73.1	72.6	71.7	75.1	86.3	96.5
D	5 900.8	5 879.1	5 546.8	5 048.5	4 737.9	4 626.5	4 559.1	4 486.1	4 424.5	4 272.1
E [3]	151.5	150.9	150.6	150.0	146.8	146.2	143.3	146.0	150.2	150.8
F	818.0	846.0	832.0	827.0	822.0	841.0	890.0	944.0	947.0	923.0
G	9 542.4	9 701.7	9 602.3	9 366.4	9 235.2	9 294.8	9 456.3	9 583.6	9 792.2	9 777.3
H	5 152.6	5 266.8	5 383.1	5 413.6	5 509.5	5 678.4	5 841.3	5 991.8	6 118.1	6 134.4
I	2 102.3	2 222.2	2 215.5	2 057.4	1 954.8	1 894.0	1 887.3	1 822.8	1 833.6	1 804.9
J	3 726.3	3 744.3	3 814.9	3 835.6	3 887.2	3 870.6	3 888.0	3 948.7	3 901.3	3 815.2
K	8 400.8	8 742.5	8 662.6	8 377.7	8 319.5	8 442.6	8 701.4	8 983.3	9 182.4	9 080.2
L	4 919.4	5 077.9	5 082.9	5 158.4	5 169.5	5 170.1	5 185.7	5 234.9	5 325.0	5 419.3
M	7 537.9	7 740.9	8 077.2	8 407.5	8 453.4	8 505.9	8 591.0	8 416.1	8 709.8	9 020.4
N	9 956.7	10 168.0	10 539.9	10 894.5	11 170.2	11 408.0	11 695.3	12 006.4	12 391.6	12 731.8
O [4]	3 534.8	3 633.6	3 721.6	3 763.8	3 776.0	3 806.3	3 826.7	3 907.1	3 963.7	3 994.5

Explanatory notes: see p. 77.

[1] Persons aged 15 years and over. [2] Due to rounding, total may not equal sum of components. [3] Incl. sewage and refuse disposal, sanitation and similar activities. [4] Excl. sewage and refuse disposal, sanitation and similar activities.

Notes explicatives: voir p. 80.

[1] Personnes âgées de 15 ans et plus. [2] En raison des arrondis, le total peut différer de la somme des composantes. [3] Y compris l'assainissement et l'enlèvement des ordures; voirie et acticvités similaires. [4] Non compris l'assainissement et l'enlèvement des ordures; voirie et activités similaires.

Notas explicativas: véase p. 83.

[1] Personas de 15 años y más. [2] Debido a redondeos, el total puedee diferir de la suma de sus componentes. [3] Incl. la eliminación de desperdicios y aguas residuales, saneamiento y actividades similares. [4] Excl. la eliminación de desperdicios y aguas residuales, saneamiento y actividades similares.

Paid employment, by economic activity
Emploi rémunéré, par activité économique
Empleo remunerado, por actividad económica

Thousands — Milliers — Millares

	1999	2000	2001	2002	2003	2004	2005	2006	2007	2008
Uruguay (BA) [1][2]				*Employees - Salariés - Asalariados*						
Total - Total - Total										
ISIC 3 - CITI 3 - CIIU 3										
Total	.	777.8	766.1	706.2	.	.	795.2	988.6 [3]	1 034.5	.
A-B	.	25.3	28.1	25.6	.	.	.	. [3]	.	.
A-C	.	.	.	.	.	.	32.0	89.1 [3]	93.4	.
C	.	1.6	1.0	0.7	.	.	.	. [3]	.	.
D-E	.	125.8	118.3	104.6	.	.	115.3	152.3 [3]	156.6	.
F	.	47.6	41.0	31.9	.	.	38.5	45.3 [3]	58.7	.
G-H	.	137.0	138.1	119.2	.	.	136.7	170.7 [3]	181.3	.
I	.	48.1	50.5	47.1	.	.	46.8	59.0 [3]	64.8	.
J-K	.	58.9	62.2	57.5	.	.	62.1	58.0 [3]	64.2	.
L	.	82.5	85.3	85.0	.	.	89.3	104.0 [3]	94.2	.
M	.	58.1	51.6	53.7	.	.	60.5	71.6 [3]	76.8	.
N	.	60.9	62.0	63.3	.	.	71.9	80.5 [3]	81.1	.
O,Q	.	35.1	35.0	31.2	.	.	37.3	44.5 [3]	47.8	.
P	.	94.9	93.1	86.2	.	.	105.0	112.3 [3]	115.6	.
X	.	0.2	-	-	.	.	-	1.3 [3]	-	.
Men - Hommes - Hombres										
ISIC 3 - CITI 3 - CIIU 3										
Total	.	426.3	418.6	392.4	.	.	419.3	556.1 [3]	577.4	.
A-B	.	22.9	24.1	23.3	.	.	.	. [3]	.	.
A-C	.	.	.	.	.	.	28.3	76.5 [3]	80.6	.
C	.	1.6	0.9	0.7	.	.	.	. [3]	.	.
D-E	.	87.1	81.7	75.9	.	.	80.9	107.7 [3]	110.5	.
F	.	46.1	39.6	30.7	.	.	37.4	43.9 [3]	56.8	.
G-H	.	83.2	84.0	75.3	.	.	85.5	104.1 [3]	105.4	.
I	.	39.9	41.9	39.5	.	.	37.6	46.9 [3]	51.8	.
J-K	.	30.4	35.5	31.3	.	.	34.3	31.4 [3]	32.9	.
L	.	56.2	57.8	59.7	.	.	56.6	70.9 [3]	62.6	.
M	.	12.3	12.3	12.2	.	.	12.9	17.4 [3]	17.9	.
N	.	15.7	14.9	17.5	.	.	16.2	20.7 [3]	20.7	.
O,Q	.	22.3	20.2	19.6	.	.	22.7	25.6 [3]	27.7	.
P	.	6.9	5.6	6.7	.	.	7.0	10.2 [3]	10.4	.
X	.	0.1	-	-	.	.	-	0.7 [3]	-	.
Women - Femmes - Mujeres										
ISIC 3 - CITI 3 - CIIU 3										
Total	.	351.5	347.5	313.7	.	.	375.9	432.5 [3]	457.2	.
A-B	.	2.4	4.0	2.3	.	.	.	. [3]	.	.
A-C	.	.	.	.	.	.	3.7	12.6 [3]	12.8	.
C	.	0.1	0.1	.	.	.	.	. [3]	.	.
D-E	.	38.8	36.6	28.7	.	.	34.4	44.6 [3]	46.1	.
F	.	1.5	1.4	1.2	.	.	1.0	1.4 [3]	1.9	.
G-H	.	53.9	54.1	43.9	.	.	51.1	66.6 [3]	75.9	.
I	.	8.2	8.7	7.6	.	.	9.2	12.1 [3]	13.0	.
J-K	.	28.5	26.7	26.3	.	.	27.9	26.5 [3]	31.2	.
L	.	26.3	27.5	25.3	.	.	32.7	33.1 [3]	31.7	.
M	.	45.8	39.3	41.5	.	.	47.6	54.2 [3]	58.9	.
N	.	45.2	47.1	45.8	.	.	55.7	59.7 [3]	60.4	.
O,Q	.	12.8	14.8	11.6	.	.	14.6	18.9 [3]	20.1	.
P	.	87.9	87.4	79.4	.	.	98.0	102.1 [3]	105.1	.
X	.	0.1	-	-	.	.	-	0.6 [3]	.	.
Virgin Islands (British) (DA)				*Employees - Salariés - Asalariados*						
Total - Total - Total										
ISIC 3 - CITI 3 - CIIU 3										
Total	12.774	13.637	14.290	14.440	14.815	15.518	16.232	.	.	.
A	0.040	0.033	0.047	0.053	0.055	0.067	0.078	.	.	.
B	0.016	0.021	0.020	0.021	0.013	0.020	0.014	.	.	.
C	0.030	0.026	0.046	0.040	0.040	0.033	0.037	.	.	.
D	0.308	0.309	0.333	0.337	0.350	0.380	0.404	.	.	.
E	0.106	0.155	0.140	0.122	0.129	0.130	0.145	.	.	.
F	1.030	1.105	1.174	1.171	1.202	1.288	1.260	.	.	.
G	1.215	1.242	1.368	1.406	1.414	1.530	1.624	.	.	.
H	2.345	2.497	2.520	2.440	2.486	2.505	2.573	.	.	.
I	0.330	0.360	0.392	0.391	0.412	0.456	0.454	.	.	.
J	0.577	0.636	0.665	0.688	0.712	0.742	0.797	.	.	.
K	0.978	0.975	1.059	1.077	1.121	1.223	1.307	.	.	.
L	3.839	4.469	4.532	4.652	4.770	4.864	5.142	.	.	.
M	0.897	0.847	0.931	0.957	0.981	1.095	1.119	.	.	.
N	0.093	0.113	0.118	0.127	0.124	0.122	0.141	.	.	.
O	0.561	0.536	0.597	0.584	0.617	0.650	0.724	.	.	.
P	0.337	0.313	0.347	0.367	0.384	0.404	0.404	.	.	.
Q	-	-	-	-	-	-	-	.	.	.
X	0.072	-	0.001	0.007	0.005	0.009	0.009	.	.	.

Explanatory notes: see p. 77.

[1] Persons aged 14 years and over. [2] Excl. conscripts. [3] Prior to 2006: urban areas.

Notes explicatives: voir p. 80.

[1] Personnes âgées de 14 ans et plus. [2] Non compris les conscrits. [3] Avant 2006: régions urbaines.

Notas explicativas: véase p. 83.

[1] Personas de 14 años y más. [2] Excl. los conscriptos. [3] Antes de 2006: areas urbanas.

EMPLOYMENT / EMPLOI / EMPLEO

Paid employment,
by economic activity

Emploi rémunéré,
par activité économique

Empleo remunerado,
por actividad económica

	1999	2000	2001	2002	2003	2004	2005	2006	2007	2008
	Thousands				Milliers				Millares	

ASIA-ASIE-ASIA

Armenia (BA) [1] [2]

Total - Total - Total
ISIC 3 - CITI 3 - CIIU 3

Employees - Salariés - Asalariados

	2007
Total	690.0
A	21.1
B	0.4
C	16.9
D	74.4
E	35.3
F	79.9
G	71.0
H	10.5
I	64.5
J	13.7
K	15.8
L	70.5
M	108.6
N	56.0
O	44.2
P	3.7
Q	3.5

Men - Hommes - Hombres
ISIC 3 - CITI 3 - CIIU 3

	2007
Total	406.5
A	14.4
B	0.3
C	14.0
D	45.3
E	29.2
F	77.9
G	40.4
H	5.1
I	53.1
J	7.5
K	8.4
L	52.4
M	18.8
N	10.3
O	26.6
P	0.5
Q	2.4

Women - Femmes - Mujeres
ISIC 3 - CITI 3 - CIIU 3

	2007
Total	283.4
A	6.7
B	0.1
C	2.9
D	29.1
E	6.1
F	2.0
G	30.7
H	5.5
I	11.4
J	6.2
K	7.3
L	18.0
M	89.8
N	45.7
O	17.6
P	3.2
Q	1.2

Explanatory notes: see p. 77.

[1] Incl. armed forces, Excl. conscripts. [2] Persons aged 16 years and over.

Notes explicatives: voir p. 80.

[1] Y compris les forces armées, Excl. conscrits [2] Personnes âgées de 16 ans et plus.

Notas explicativas: véase p. 83.

[1] Incl. las fuerzas armadas, excl. los conscriptos. [2] Personas de 16 años y más.

Paid employment, by economic activity — Emploi rémunéré, par activité économique — Empleo remunerado, por actividad económica

	Thousands			Milliers				Millares		
	1999	2000	2001	2002	2003	2004	2005	2006	2007	2008

Azerbaijan (BA) [1][2] — Employees - Salariés - Asalariados

Total - Total - Total
ISIC 3 - CITI 3 - CIIU 3

	1999	2000	2001	2002	2003	2004	2005	2006	2007	2008
Total	.	.	.	.	1 848.2	.	.	1 690.0	1 376.0	1 719.3
A	.	.	.	.	151.5	.	.	63.5	150.8	152.1
B	.	.	.	.	6.5	.	.	5.2	1.3	0.7
C	.	.	.	.	36.1	.	.	60.1	41.8	44.8
D	.	.	.	.	153.1	.	.	137.3	176.0	154.3
E	.	.	.	.	45.1	.	.	51.3	34.8	43.9
F	.	.	.	.	181.1	.	.	208.4	134.9	181.8
G	.	.	.	.	281.2	.	.	159.3	55.8	282.4
H	.	.	.	.	27.3	.	.	38.4	14.5	16.7
I	.	.	.	.	120.7	.	.	110.8	73.1	102.0
J	.	.	.	.	21.0	.	.	53.3	8.3	35.1
K	.	.	.	.	39.1	.	.	18.0	22.0	65.8
L	.	.	.	.	96.3	.	.	139.1	204.5	64.8
M	.	.	.	.	316.7	.	.	351.1	279.2	310.0
N	.	.	.	.	136.3	.	.	161.5	133.8	180.5
O	.	.	.	.	221.2	.	.	100.4	44.5	83.9
P	.	.	.	.	9.5	.	.	23.4	-	-
Q	.	.	.	.	5.5	.	.	8.9	0.7	0.5

Men - Hommes - Hombres
ISIC 3 - CITI 3 - CIIU 3

	1999	2000	2001	2002	2003	2004	2005	2006	2007	2008
Total	.	.	.	.	1 111.1	.	.	1 046.7	833.9	970.7
A	.	.	.	.	98.0	.	.	47.4	88.6	132.6
B	.	.	.	.	5.5	.	.	3.5	0.7	0.7
C	.	.	.	.	31.9	.	.	54.1	36.6	34.7
D	.	.	.	.	101.1	.	.	90.0	127.0	98.0
E	.	.	.	.	35.9	.	.	45.7	29.2	31.8
F	.	.	.	.	171.8	.	.	195.3	124.7	162.2
G	.	.	.	.	188.9	.	.	110.2	37.5	97.4
H	.	.	.	.	15.7	.	.	24.3	8.9	8.1
I	.	.	.	.	99.7	.	.	95.4	63.2	81.4
J	.	.	.	.	13.0	.	.	29.9	6.5	10.5
K	.	.	.	.	29.8	.	.	13.7	16.9	54.5
L	.	.	.	.	78.5	.	.	101.0	130.7	51.6
M	.	.	.	.	107.8	.	.	122.1	100.9	95.7
N	.	.	.	.	36.3	.	.	44.5	37.1	52.1
O	.	.	.	.	88.1	.	.	51.5	24.7	58.9
P	.	.	.	.	4.5	.	.	10.7	-	-
Q	.	.	.	.	4.6	.	.	7.3	0.7	0.5

Women - Femmes - Mujeres
ISIC 3 - CITI 3 - CIIU 3

	1999	2000	2001	2002	2003	2004	2005	2006	2007	2008
Total	.	.	.	.	737.1	.	.	643.4	542.1	748.6
A	.	.	.	.	53.5	.	.	16.1	62.2	19.5
B	.	.	.	.	1.0	.	.	1.8	0.7	-
C	.	.	.	.	4.2	.	.	6.0	5.2	10.1
D	.	.	.	.	52.0	.	.	47.3	49.0	56.3
E	.	.	.	.	9.2	.	.	5.6	5.6	12.1
F	.	.	.	.	9.3	.	.	13.1	10.2	19.6
G	.	.	.	.	92.3	.	.	49.0	18.3	185.0
H	.	.	.	.	11.6	.	.	14.1	5.7	8.6
I	.	.	.	.	21.0	.	.	15.5	9.8	20.6
J	.	.	.	.	8.0	.	.	23.4	1.7	24.6
K	.	.	.	.	9.3	.	.	4.3	5.2	11.3
L	.	.	.	.	17.8	.	.	38.1	73.8	13.2
M	.	.	.	.	208.9	.	.	229.0	178.3	214.3
N	.	.	.	.	100.0	.	.	117.1	96.8	128.4
O	.	.	.	.	133.1	.	.	48.8	19.8	25.0
P	.	.	.	.	5.0	.	.	12.7	-	-
Q	.	.	.	.	0.9	.	.	1.6	-	-

Azerbaijan (DA) [1] — Employees - Salariés - Asalariados

Total - Total - Total
ISIC 3 - CITI 3 - CIIU 3

	1999	2000	2001	2002	2003	2004	2005	2006	2007	2008
Total	1 390.7	1 217.8	1 205.0	1 201.5	1 226.6	1 263.9	1 300.4	1 337.5	1 376.0	1 410.3
A	203.2	88.0	51.2	43.0	42.7	35.8	44.9	46.4	45.0	44.2
B	0.3	2.0	1.0	0.6	0.5	0.6	0.8	0.8	0.8	1.0
C	38.0	39.6	41.3	35.2	39.2	39.7	40.8	41.3	41.2	39.8
D	170.4	143.2	138.3	107.6	96.6	96.8	108.1	111.0	110.8	106.9
E	38.4	40.5	39.6	36.1	37.2	35.9	37.6	40.8	44.6	45.2
F	97.4	71.7	72.0	70.5	55.3	59.2	60.5	65.4	69.0	78.8
G	76.9	76.3	94.6	167.7	236.1	246.6	251.8	259.8	268.5	268.1
H	8.1	8.3	5.7	5.5	6.4	8.0	13.4	12.5	14.9	16.2
I	107.2	98.0	107.2	92.7	80.6	85.5	88.4	90.1	90.3	95.9
J	13.8	13.5	7.1	7.0	8.6	9.7	11.5	13.4	16.2	18.7
K	98.5	75.2	50.8	45.3	50.0	56.0	57.1	58.0	66.7	73.0
L	59.9	44.9	50.0	50.2	48.3	50.6	49.5	50.9	51.9	52.8
M	285.1	317.9	315.6	327.7	319.6	330.0	326.7	332.3	338.9	344.2
N	111.6	123.9	144.6	135.5	127.8	130.2	131.9	135.3	136.3	138.9
O	81.6	74.8	86.0	76.9	77.7	79.3	77.4	79.5	80.9	86.6
Q	0.3	.	.	.	.	.	.	.	.	.

Explanatory notes: see p. 77.

[1] Persons aged 15 years and over. [2] Excl. armed forces and conscripts.

Notes explicatives: voir p. 80.

[1] Personnes âgées de 15 ans et plus. [2] Non compris les forces armées et les conscrits.

Notas explicativas: véase p. 83.

[1] Personas de 15 años y más. [2] Excl. las fuerzas armadas y los conscriptos.

2E

EMPLOYMENT	EMPLOI	EMPLEO
Paid employment, by economic activity	Emploi rémunéré, par activité économique	Empleo remunerado, por actividad económica
Thousands	Milliers	Millares

	1999	2000	2001	2002	2003	2004	2005	2006	2007	2008

Azerbaijan (DA) [1]   Employees - Salariés - Asalariados

Men - Hommes - Hombres
ISIC 3 - CITI 3 - CIIU 3

	1999	2000	2001	2002	2003	2004	2005	2006	2007	2008
Total	767.0	661.7	653.4	652.7	671.6	704.1	708.7	733.5	774.2	806.4
A	143.1	68.8	41.2	34.4	34.3	27.8	36.8	37.6	36.3	35.1
B	0.3	1.8	0.8	0.5	0.4	0.5	0.7	0.6	0.6	0.8
C	29.2	30.6	31.4	27.3	31.4	32.1	33.7	35.3	35.3	34.3
D	98.3	93.1	87.1	69.8	64.2	64.4	74.6	79.1	78.0	77.3
E	29.1	31.6	30.9	28.7	30.1	29.1	30.2	32.7	36.1	37.1
F	86.4	64.1	65.4	64.2	50.3	54.4	55.9	59.6	63.3	72.9
G	57.4	56.5	75.0	126.6	164.7	172.3	161.9	171.0	182.4	184.8
H	5.1	5.4	3.6	3.4	4.2	6.2	8.8	8.1	10.1	11.4
I	80.6	74.5	81.3	71.2	61.7	64.6	67.1	67.8	68.1	71.9
J	7.7	7.9	5.6	4.7	5.5	6.2	7.3	8.6	10.7	12.1
K	51.0	38.6	28.3	24.3	28.5	35.7	34.3	34.5	42.6	46.3
L	27.5	28.9	34.9	34.7	34.4	35.6	34.1	36.3	37.5	37.8
M	91.6	99.2	96.1	100.0	98.4	107.9	98.9	95.9	102.8	113.0
N	25.6	30.6	35.9	32.7	30.1	32.4	31.5	32.1	35.7	32.4
O	33.9	30.1	35.9	30.2	33.4	34.9	32.9	34.3	34.7	39.2
Q	0.2									

Women - Femmes - Mujeres
ISIC 3 - CITI 3 - CIIU 3

	1999	2000	2001	2002	2003	2004	2005	2006	2007	2008
Total	623.7	556.1	551.6	548.8	555.0	559.8	591.7	604.0	601.8	603.9
A	60.1	19.2	10.0	8.6	8.4	8.0	8.0	8.8	8.7	9.1
B	0.0	0.2	0.2	0.1	0.1	0.1	0.1	0.2	0.2	0.2
C	8.8	9.0	9.9	7.9	7.8	7.7	7.1	6.0	5.9	5.5
D	72.1	50.1	51.2	37.8	32.4	32.4	33.5	31.9	32.8	29.6
E	9.3	8.9	8.7	7.4	7.1	6.8	7.5	8.1	8.5	8.1
F	11.0	7.6	6.6	6.3	5.0	4.8	4.6	5.8	5.7	5.9
G	19.5	19.8	19.6	41.1	71.4	74.3	89.9	88.8	86.1	83.3
H	3.0	2.9	2.1	2.1	2.2	1.8	4.6	4.4	4.8	4.8
I	26.6	23.5	25.9	21.5	18.9	20.9	21.3	22.3	22.2	24.0
J	6.1	5.6	1.5	2.3	3.1	3.5	4.2	4.8	5.6	6.6
K	47.5	36.6	22.5	21.0	21.5	20.3	22.8	23.5	24.0	26.7
L	32.4	16.0	15.1	15.5	13.9	14.9	15.4	14.6	14.4	15.0
M	193.5	218.7	219.5	227.7	221.2	222.1	227.8	236.4	236.1	231.2
N	86.0	93.3	108.7	102.8	97.7	97.8	100.4	103.2	100.6	106.5
O	47.7	44.7	50.1	46.7	44.3	44.4	44.5	45.2	46.2	47.4
Q	0.1									

Bahrain (FA) [2]   All persons engaged - Effectif occupé - Efectivo ocupado

Total - Total - Total
ISIC 2 - CITI 2 - CIIU 2 [3]   ISIC 3 - CITI 3 - CIIU 3 [4]

	1999	2000	2001	2002	2003	2004	2005	2006	2007		ISIC 3	
Total	147.744	149.413	157.396	164.700	189.932	211.109	246.478	297.404	332.616	|	431.190	Total
1	1.224	1.268	1.366	1.432	1.448	1.484	2.093	3.737	4.484	|	2.034	A
2	0.285	0.313	0.293	0.282	-	-	0.005	0.008	0.012	|	4.175	B
3	35.893	36.301	40.445	42.198	51.320	51.984	56.565	61.942	64.128	|	2.107	C
4	3.530	3.488	3.426	3.445	1.456	1.487	1.493	1.313	1.372	|	75.641	D
5	40.370	40.721	42.196	43.550	53.937	64.609	77.916	89.407	101.983	|	0.581	E
6	28.072	28.729	30.331	33.513	38.734	44.328	54.558	72.795	81.010	|	128.750	F
7	10.264	10.338	10.342	10.201	10.263	10.917	12.095	13.009	13.818	|	106.171	G
8	8.653	8.822	9.016	9.190	9.735	10.510	12.018	14.618	16.846	|	28.249	H
9	17.266	17.283	17.835	18.521	22.878	25.584	29.495	40.298	48.654	|	18.103	I
0	2.187	2.150	2.146	2.368	0.161	0.206	0.240	0.277	0.309	|	14.910	J
										|	32.517	K
										|	0.023	L
										|	5.336	M
										|	1.052	N
										|	9.102	O
										|	0.244	P
										|	0.891	Q
										|	1.304	X

Men - Hommes - Hombres
ISIC 2 - CITI 2 - CIIU 2 [3]   ISIC 3 - CITI 3 - CIIU 3 [4]

	1999	2000	2001	2002	2003	2004	2005	2006	2007		ISIC 3	
Total	129.698	130.968	136.782	143.862	165.780	186.948	219.599	267.045	300.461	|	390.122	Total
1	1.175	1.223	1.322	1.393	1.404	1.446	2.046	3.685	4.431	|	1.933	A
2	0.270	0.285	0.231	0.226	-	-	0.005	0.008	0.010	|	4.166	B
3	30.121	30.362	32.928	35.052	43.016	44.930	49.728	55.435	58.442	|	2.044	C
4	3.361	3.325	3.263	3.266	1.387	1.416	1.405	1.245	1.301	|	70.068	D
5	38.887	39.213	40.504	41.638	51.763	62.080	74.886	86.126	98.723	|	0.548	E
6	25.154	25.688	26.938	29.546	33.722	38.934	48.350	65.236	72.621	|	124.448	F
7	8.029	8.053	8.130	8.140	8.416	8.981	9.699	10.559	11.087	|	97.287	G
8	6.633	6.787	6.918	7.126	7.550	8.205	9.419	11.416	13.205	|	24.292	H
9	14.118	14.100	14.604	15.297	18.397	20.805	23.896	33.158	40.445	|	14.829	I
0	1.950	1.932	1.944	2.178	0.125	0.148	0.165	0.177	0.196	|	10.827	J
										|	27.916	K
										|	0.020	L
										|	2.229	M
										|	0.531	N
										|	6.983	O
										|	0.229	P
										|	0.746	Q
										|	1.026	X

Explanatory notes: see p. 77.

[1] Persons aged 15 years and over. [2] Private sector. [3] Establishments with 10 or more persons employed. [4] Persons aged 18 years and over.

Notes explicatives: voir p. 80.

[1] Personnes âgées de 15 ans et plus. [2] Secteur privé. [3] Etablissements occupant 10 personnes et plus. [4] Personnes âgées de 18 ans et plus.

Notas explicativas: véase p. 83.

[1] Personas de 15 años y más. [2] Sector privado. [3] Establecimientos con 10 y más trabajadores. [4] Personas de 18 años y más.

Paid employment, by economic activity

Emploi rémunéré, par activité économique

Empleo remunerado, por actividad económica

	Thousands			Milliers				Millares		
	1999	2000	2001	2002	2003	2004	2005	2006	2007	2008

Bahrain (FA) [1]

Women - Femmes - Mujeres

ISIC 2 - CITI 2 - CIIU 2 [2]

All persons engaged - Effectif occupé - Efectivo ocupado

ISIC 3 - CITI 3 - CIIU 3 [3]

	1999	2000	2001	2002	2003	2004	2005	2006	2007	2008	
Total	18.046	18.445	20.614	20.838	24.152	24.161	26.879	30.359	32.155	41.068	Total
1	0.049	0.045	0.044	0.039	0.044	0.038	0.047	0.052	0.053	0.101	A
2	0.015	0.028	0.062	0.056	-	-	-	-	0.002	0.009	B
3	5.772	5.939	7.517	7.146	8.304	7.054	6.837	6.507	5.686	0.063	C
4	0.169	0.163	0.163	0.179	0.069	0.071	0.088	0.068	0.071	5.573	D
5	1.483	1.508	1.692	1.912	2.174	2.529	3.030	3.281	3.326	0.033	E
6	2.918	3.041	3.393	3.967	5.012	5.394	6.208	7.559	8.389	4.302	F
7	2.235	2.285	2.212	2.061	1.847	1.936	2.396	2.450	2.731	8.884	G
8	2.020	2.035	2.098	2.064	2.185	2.302	2.599	3.202	3.641	3.957	H
9	3.148	3.183	3.231	3.224	4.481	4.779	5.599	7.140	8.209	3.274	I
0	0.237	0.218	0.202	0.190	0.036	0.058	0.075	0.100	0.113	4.083	J
										4.601	K
										0.003	L
										3.107	M
										0.521	N
										2.119	O
										0.015	P
										0.145	Q
										0.278	X

China (DA) [4] [5]

Total - Total - Total

ISIC 3 - CITI 3 - CIIU 3

Employees - Salariés - Asalariados

	1999	2000	2001	2002	2003	2004	2005	2006	2007	2008
Total	117 730	112 590	107 920	105 580	104 920	105 759	108 503	111 606	114 270	115 154
A-B	5 190	4 940	4 580	4 300	4 597	4 381	4 142	4 021	3 855	3 624
C [6]	6 500	5 810	5 440	5 370	4 810	4 912	4 976	5 181	5 238	5 256
D	34 960	32 400	30 100	29 070	28 989	29 600	30 965	32 503	33 584	33 293
E	2 830	2 820	2 840	2 850	2 923	2 940	2 937	2 964	2 977	2 968
F	7 780	7 440	7 330	7 560	7 735	7 777	8 543	9 098	9 616	9 712
G-H [7]	11 100	9 770	8 400	7 330	7 514	7 135	6 748	6 555	6 509	6 652
I [8]	7 820	6 590	6 290	6 130	6 097	5 984	5 792	5 787	5 835	5 826
J	3 000	2 940	2 920	2 870	2 862	2 869	2 950	2 999	3 111	3 264
K [9]	900	930	970	1 070	4 822	5 041	5 442	5 751	6 519	6 443
L	10 880	10 910	10 880	10 560	11 463	11 702	12 135	12 354	12 601	12 919
M [10]	14 800	15 000	15 120	15 170	14 017	14 245	14 447	14 663	14 836	14 908
N	4 730	4 760	4 810	4 800	4 717	4 768	4 914	5 058	5 215	5 362
O	-	-	-	-	1 220	1 177	1 170	1 166	1 186	1 191
X	19 340	18 070	16 650	8 500	3 154	3 227	3 343	3 506	3 688	3 736

Georgia (BA) [11] [12]

Total - Total - Total

ISIC 3 - CITI 3 - CIIU 3

Employees - Salariés - Asalariados

	1999	2000	2001	2002	2003	2004	2005	2006	2007	2008
Total	731.5	.	.	650.9	618.5	600.9	600.5	603.8	625.4	.
A	34.4	.	.	17.8	24.6	20.7	19.4	21.8	22.2	.
B	0.4	.	.	0.5	0.4	0.1	-	-	-	.
C	5.3	.	.	4.7	2.0	3.4	5.3	3.2	4.6	.
D	96.0	.	.	65.2	67.7	65.3	64.7	61.6	63.0	.
E	20.5	.	.	26.6	19.0	20.4	23.0	18.2	17.1	.
F	20.9	.	.	23.4	23.5	23.4	25.2	33.9	53.9	.
G	74.3	.	.	70.9	67.3	63.1	59.7	62.0	73.7	.
H	13.2	.	.	13.0	10.6	13.2	12.8	15.2	14.4	.
I	55.4	.	.	56.4	49.4	42.4	46.5	46.1	40.4	.
J	10.5	.	.	7.6	9.4	12.2	12.9	13.2	16.7	.
K	36.1	.	.	18.8	29.7	26.4	24.9	26.0	33.3	.
L	105.4	.	.	108.3	90.8	85.5	80.5	78.3	62.7	.
M	135.9	.	.	128.4	134.0	132.6	129.2	131.5	120.6	.
N	76.8	.	.	61.3	46.1	50.5	55.4	49.5	57.3	.
O	39.0	.	.	43.6	38.3	33.1	31.1	34.1	36.6	.
P	4.9	.	.	4.1	2.3	4.0	6.7	6.9	6.6	.
Q	1.8	.	.	0.3	3.3	4.3	3.2	2.3	2.8	.
X	0.7	.	.	-	-	0.4	0.2	-	-	.

Explanatory notes: see p. 77.

[1] Private sector. [2] Establishments with 10 or more persons employed. [3] Persons aged 18 years and over. [4] State-owned units, urban collective-owned units and other ownership units. [5] Dec. of each year. [6] Excl. quarrying. [7] Incl. catering. [8] Excl. communications, incl. post. [9] Excl. business services. [10] Incl. cultural, art, radio and television activities. [11] Excl. armed forces. [12] Persons aged 15 years and over.

Notes explicatives: voir p. 80.

[1] Secteur privé. [2] Etablissements occupant 10 personnes et plus. [3] Personnes âgées de 18 ans et plus. [4] Unités d'Etat, unités collectives urbaines et autres. [5] Déc. de chaque année. [6] Non compris les carrières. [7] Y compris la restauration. [8] Non compris les communications, y compris la poste. [9] Non compris les services aux entreprises. [10] Y compris les activités culturelles, artistiques, radiophoniques et télévisuelles. [11] Non compris les forces armées. [12] Personnes âgées de 15 ans et plus.

Notas explicativas: véase p. 83.

[1] Sector privado. [2] Establecimientos con 10 y más trabajadores. [3] Personas de 18 años y más. [4] Unidades estatales, unidades colectivas y otras. [5] Dic. de cada año. [6] Excl. las canteras. [7] Incl. la restauración. [8] Excl. las comunicaciones, incl. el correo. [9] Excl. servicios para las empresas. [10] Incl. actividades culturales, artísticas, radiofónicas y televisuales. [11] Excl. las fuerzas armadas. [12] Personas de 15 años y más.

EMPLOYMENT   EMPLOI   EMPLEO

Paid employment, by economic activity
Emploi rémunéré, par activité économique
Empleo remunerado, por actividad económica

	Thousands				Milliers				Millares	
	1999	2000	2001	2002	2003	2004	2005	2006	2007	2008

Georgia (BA) [1] [2]   Employees - Salariés - Asalariados

Men - Hommes - Hombres
ISIC 3 - CITI 3 - CIIU 3

	1999	2000	2001	2002	2003	2004	2005	2006	2007	2008
Total	378.4	.	.	333.0	323.6	304.4	314.1	.	.	.
A	24.2	.	.	13.6	19.9	16.5	15.3	.	.	.
B	0.4	.	.	0.3	0.3	0.1	-	.	.	.
C	4.4	.	.	3.8	1.8	3.3	4.7	.	.	.
D	64.8	.	.	47.7	42.8	43.1	44.1	.	.	.
E	16.6	.	.	20.9	15.2	16.9	17.6	.	.	.
F	19.5	.	.	22.3	23.1	23.0	24.5	.	.	.
G	41.4	.	.	37.9	38.8	32.7	32.5	.	.	.
H	7.1	.	.	3.9	3.3	4.2	5.3	.	.	.
I	40.3	.	.	42.0	38.5	30.2	35.4	.	.	.
J	4.6	.	.	2.5	4.4	4.6	6.9	.	.	.
K	19.4	.	.	8.9	16.8	14.3	15.4	.	.	.
L	72.6	.	.	75.8	63.0	59.6	55.6	.	.	.
M	25.4	.	.	24.0	27.0	25.7	29.2	.	.	.
N	14.7	.	.	10.6	7.4	10.8	10.3	.	.	.
O	18.9	.	.	18.2	18.7	16.0	14.1	.	.	.
P	2.6	.	.	0.4	0.1	0.1	0.3	.	.	.
Q	1.2	.	.	0.2	2.5	3.0	2.8	.	.	.
X	0.4	.	.	-	-	0.3	-	.	.	.

Women - Femmes - Mujeres
ISIC 3 - CITI 3 - CIIU 3

	1999	2000	2001	2002	2003	2004	2005	2006	2007	2008
Total	353.0	.	.	317.9	294.8	296.5	286.4	.	.	.
A	10.2	.	.	4.2	4.7	4.2	4.1	.	.	.
B	0.1	.	.	0.2	0.1	-	-	.	.	.
C	0.9	.	.	0.9	0.2	0.1	0.6	.	.	.
D	31.2	.	.	17.5	24.9	22.2	20.6	.	.	.
E	3.9	.	.	5.7	3.8	3.5	5.3	.	.	.
F	1.3	.	.	1.1	0.4	0.5	0.6	.	.	.
G	32.9	.	.	33.0	28.5	30.3	27.2	.	.	.
H	6.1	.	.	9.1	7.3	8.9	7.4	.	.	.
I	15.0	.	.	14.4	10.9	12.2	11.1	.	.	.
J	5.9	.	.	5.1	5.0	7.6	6.0	.	.	.
K	16.7	.	.	9.9	12.9	12.1	9.5	.	.	.
L	32.8	.	.	32.5	27.8	26.0	24.9	.	.	.
M	110.6	.	.	104.4	107.0	106.9	100.1	.	.	.
N	62.1	.	.	50.7	38.7	39.6	45.1	.	.	.
O	20.1	.	.	25.4	19.6	17.1	17.0	.	.	.
P	2.3	.	.	3.7	2.2	4.0	6.4	.	.	.
Q	0.6	.	.	0.1	0.8	1.3	0.4	.	.	.
X	0.2	.	.	-	-	0.1	0.2	.	.	.

Hong Kong, China (DA)   All persons engaged - Effectif occupé - Efectivo ocupado

Total - Total - Total
ISIC 2 - CITI 2 - CIIU 2

	1999	2000	2001	2002	2003	2004	2005	2006	2007	2008
Total	2 438.54	2 475.70	2 460.01	2 431.59	2 398.38	2 460.47	2 504.19	2 533.01 [3]	2 586.07	2 630.39
2	0.35	0.15	0.18	0.12	0.18	0.13	0.13	0.13 [3]	0.11	0.10
3	244.72	226.21	202.98	184.50	168.35	165.27	167.37	160.50 [3]	157.00	151.62
4 [4]	8.61	8.20	8.10	8.41	8.34	8.13	8.00	7.98 [3]	7.91	7.79
5 [5]	71.79	83.92	76.60	66.39	68.31	61.25	54.46	52.87 [3]	50.19	49.42
6 [6]	1 002.26	1 009.09	996.97	982.96	973.86	1 003.47	1 023.74	1 038.05 [3]	1 055.57	1 062.99
7 [7]	172.00	176.95	181.70	175.69	174.31	181.27	183.75	185.29 [3]	189.43	194.99
8 [8]	415.33	434.11	433.87	441.31	423.83	447.45	464.43	479.09 [3]	505.44	527.92
9 [9]	336.49	354.54	385.05	402.57	416.51	435.15	446.80	454.76 [3]	466.63	481.59
0 [10]	187.00	182.53	174.55	169.65	164.70	158.36	155.52	154.35 [3]	153.80	153.97

Men - Hommes - Hombres
ISIC 2 - CITI 2 - CIIU 2

	1999	2000	2001	2002	2003	2004	2005	2006	2007	2008
Total	1 363.40	1 367.80	1 341.83	1 314.69	1 276.38	1 296.53	1 308.04	1 320.25 [3]	1 338.39	1 350.87
2	0.33	0.14	0.17	0.11	0.18	0.13	0.12	0.12 [3]	0.11	0.10
3	140.19	128.99	116.49	106.81	97.26	92.86	94.40	91.89 [3]	90.21	88.45
4 [4]	7.53	7.08	7.04	7.19	7.10	6.96	6.82	6.78 [3]	6.70	6.61
5 [5]	67.69	78.90	71.18	61.88	63.50	56.35	49.59	48.89 [3]	46.58	45.78
6 [6]	536.78	530.17	517.01	505.78	491.70	499.36	508.51	512.97 [3]	517.50	515.23
7 [7]	113.14	116.72	119.90	114.40	112.14	114.57	115.85	117.86 [3]	119.40	122.14
8 [8]	238.48	247.46	248.42	255.25	242.69	255.58	265.93	271.74 [3]	285.87	296.09
9 [9]	134.05	136.65	145.56	150.51	152.80	165.56	163.62	167.65 [3]	170.28	175.09
0 [10]	125.22	121.70	116.05	112.76	109.02	105.17	103.20	102.36 [3]	101.74	101.39

Explanatory notes: see p. 77.

[1] Excl. armed forces. [2] Persons aged 15 years and over. [3] Prior to 2006: Dec. of each year. [4] Excl. water. [5] Manual workers at construction sites only. [6] Hawkers and retail pitches are excluded. [7] Taxis, public light buses, goods vehicles, barges, lighters and stevedoring services are excluded. [8] Excl. self-employed insurance with no business registration. [9] Public admin., religious org., indep. artists, domestic helpers, miscellaneous recreational and personal services are excluded. [10] Civil servants. Incl. water.

Notes explicatives: voir p. 80.

[1] Non compris les forces armées. [2] Personnes âgées de 15 ans et plus. [3] Avant 2006: Dec. de chaque année. [4] Non compris l'eau. [5] Seulement travailleurs manuels sur les chantiers. [6] Les colporteurs et vendeurs au détail sont exclus. [7] Les taxis, les autobus publiques, les véhicules de marchandises, les chalends, les allumeurs et les services d'arrimage sont exclus. [8] Non compris les travailleurs indépendants des assurances qui ne sont pas inscrits au registre du commerce. [9] L'admin. publique, les org. religieux, les artistes indép., les aides ménagères, les centres de loisirs et pers. divers sont exclus. [10] Fonctionnaires. Y compris l'eau.

Notas explicativas: véase p. 83.

[1] Excl. las fuerzas armadas. [2] Personas de 15 años y más. [3] Antes de 2006: Dec de cada año. [4] Excl. el agua. [5] Unicamente trabajadores manuales de la construcción. [6] Excluyen a los vendedores ambulantes y los vendedores al detalle. [7] Los taxis, autobuses públicos pequeños, bienes vehículos, barcazas, y servicios de trasbordo son excluidos. [8] Excl. los trabajadores independientes de los seguros que no estan registrados en el registro del comercio. [9] La admin. pública, org. religiosas, artistas ind. ayudantes domésticos, y servicios mixtos vacacionales son excluidos. [10] Funcionarios. Incl. el agua.

Paid employment, by economic activity

Emploi rémunéré, par activité économique

Empleo remunerado, por actividad económica

	Thousands / Milliers / Millares									
	1999	2000	2001	2002	2003	2004	2005	2006	2007	2008

Hong Kong, China (DA) — All persons engaged - Effectif occupé - Efectivo ocupado

Women - Femmes - Mujeres
ISIC 2 - CITI 2 - CIIU 2

	1999	2000	2001	2002	2003	2004	2005	2006	2007	2008
Total	1 075.14	1 107.90	1 118.18	1 116.90	1 122.00	1 163.94	1 196.16	1 212.76 ı	1 247.68	1 279.53
2	0.02	0.01	0.01	0.01	0.01	0.01	0.01	0.01 ı	-	-
3	104.53	97.21	86.49	77.69	71.09	72.41	72.97	68.62 ı	66.79	63.17
4 [2]	1.08	1.13	1.05	1.21	1.24	1.17	1.18	1.20 ı	1.21	1.18
5 [3]	4.10	5.03	5.42	4.52	4.81	4.89	4.87	3.98 ı	3.60	3.64
6 [4]	465.49	478.92	479.96	477.17	482.17	504.11	515.23	525.08 ı	538.07	547.76
7 [5]	58.85	60.23	61.80	61.29	62.17	66.70	67.90	67.43 ı	70.03	72.85
8 [6]	176.85	186.65	185.46	186.05	181.15	191.87	198.50	207.35 ı	219.57	231.83
9 [7]	202.44	217.89	239.49	252.06	263.70	269.60	283.18	287.11 ı	296.35	306.50
0 [8]	61.78	60.83	58.50	56.89	55.68	55.68	53.19	52.32	51.98 ı	52.06	52.58

India (DA) [9] [10] [11] — Employees - Salariés - Asalariados

Total - Total - Total
ISIC 2 - CITI 2 - CIIU 2

	1999	2000	2001	2002	2003	2004	2005	2006	2007	2008
Total	28 113	27 960	27 789	27 206	27 000	26 443	26 458	.	.	.
1	1 387	1 418	1 435	1 339	1 401	1 410	1 479	.	.	.
2	1 013	1 005	953	928	913	1 095	1 093	.	.	.
3	6 747	6 615	6 443	6 217	6 004	5 678	5 619	.	.	.
4	1 003	987	987	965	963	922	910	.	.	.
5	1 178	1 148	1 138	1 082	992	977	960	.	.	.
6	486	493	502	492	542	532	559	.	.	.
7	3 152	3 146	3 118	3 085	3 018	2 896	2 837	.	.	.
8	1 652	1 653	1 650	1 621	1 803	1 866	1 931	.	.	.
9	11 494	11 493	11 564	11 477	11 364	11 068	11 072	.	.	.

Men - Hommes - Hombres
ISIC 2 - CITI 2 - CIIU 2

	1999	2000	2001	2002	2003	2004	2005	2006	2007	2008
Total	23 284	23 037	22 840	22 271	22 032	21 509	21 442	.	.	.
1	915	908	922	876	934	951	995	.	.	.
2	944	939	889	866	852	1 022	1 015	.	.	.
3	5 713	5 582	5 413	5 201	4 994	4 729	4 780	.	.	.
4	959	942	941	918	916	870	857	.	.	.
5	1 109	1 080	1 070	1 014	928	911	893	.	.	.
6	442	447	455	444	498	486	510	.	.	.
7	2 974	2 969	2 935	2 899	2 829	2 707	2 645	.	.	.
8	1 418	1 418	1 405	1 365	1 528	1 579	1 628	.	.	.
9	8 808	8 750	8 809	8 688	8 553	8 256	8 220	.	.	.

Women - Femmes - Mujeres
ISIC 2 - CITI 2 - CIIU 2

	1999	2000	2001	2002	2003	2004	2005	2006	2007	2008
Total	4 829	4 923	4 949	4 935	4 968	4 934	5 016	.	.	.
1	472	510	513	463	466	459	484	.	.	.
2	69	66	64	62	61	73	77	.	.	.
3	1 034	1 033	1 030	1 016	1 010	949	939	.	.	.
4	44	45	46	47	48	52	53	.	.	.
5	69	68	67	68	64	66	67	.	.	.
6	44	46	47	48	44	46	50	.	.	.
7	178	177	183	186	189	189	192	.	.	.
8	234	235	245	256	274	287	302	.	.	.
9	2 686	2 743	2 755	2 789	2 812	2 812	2 852	.	.	.

Explanatory notes: see p. 77.

[1] Prior to 2006: Dec. of each year. [2] Excl. water. [3] Manual workers at construction sites only. [4] Hawkers and retail pitches are excluded. [5] Taxis, public light buses, goods vehicles, barges, lighters and stevedoring services are excluded [6] Excl. self-employed insurance with no business registration. [7] Public admin., religious org., indep. artists, domestic helpers, miscellaneous recreational and personal services are excluded. [8] Civil servants. Incl. water. [9] Public sector and establishments of non-agricultural private sector with 10 or more persons employed. [10] Incl. working proprietors. [11] March of each year.

Notes explicatives: voir p. 80.

[1] Avant 2006: Dec. de chaque année. [2] Non compris l'eau. [3] Seulement travailleurs manuels sur les chantiers. [4] Les colporteurs et vendeurs au détail sont exclus. [5] Les taxis, les autobus publiques, les véhicules de marchandises, les chalends, les allumeurs et les services d'arrimage sont exclus. [6] Non compris les travailleurs indépendants des assurances qui ne sont pas inscrits au registre du commerce. [7] L'admin. publique, les org. religieux, les artistes indép., les aides ménagères, les centres de loisirs et pers. divers sont exclus. [8] Fonctionnaires. Y compris l'eau. [9] Secteur public et établissements du secteur privé non agricole occupant 10 personnes et plus. [10] Y compris les propriétaires-exploitants. [11] Mars de chaque année.

Notas explicativas: véase p. 83.

[1] Antes de 2006: Dec de cada año. [2] Excl. el agua. [3] Unicamente trabajadores manuales de la construcción. [4] Excluyen a los vendedores ambulantes y los vendedores al detalle. [5] Los taxis, autobuses públicos pequeños, bienes vehículos, barcazas, y servicios de trasbordo son excluidos. [6] Excl. los trabajadores independientes de los seguros que no estan registrados en el registro del comercio. [7] La admin. pública, org. religiosas, artistas ind. ayudantes domésticos, y servicios mixtos vacacionales son excluidos. [8] Funcionarios. Incl. el agua. [9] Sector público y establecimientos del sector no agrícola con 10 y más trabajadores. [10] Incl. los empresarios propietarios. [11] Marzo de cada año.

EMPLOYMENT — EMPLOI — EMPLEO

Paid employment, by economic activity — Emploi rémunéré, par activité économique — Empleo remunerado, por actividad económica

Thousands — Milliers — Millares

Indonesia (BA) [1] [2]　　Wage earners - Ouvriers - Obreros

Total - Total - Total
ISIC 2 - CITI 2 - CIIU 2 　　　 ISIC 3 - CITI 3 - CIIU 3

	1999	2000	2001	2002	2003	2004	2005	2006	2007	2008	
Total	88 817	89 838	32 651	33 123	32 043	33 642	35 888	36 981	38 419	39 468	Total
1	38 378	40 677	6 445	6 842	6 732	6 560	7 713	7 864	7 778	8 033	A
2	726	452	514	341	443	546	535	510	514	570	B
3	11 516	11 642	7 995	7 941	7 558	7 389	8 422	7 647	647	656	C
4	188	71	112	165	136	201	168	202	7 839	7 708	D
5	3 415	3 497	3 037	3 451	3 326	3 758	3 892	3 927	155	165	E
6	17 529	18 489	3 173	3 427	3 162	3 797	3 854	4 262	4 488	4 546	F
7	4 206	4 554	1 700	1 683	1 626	1 956	1 878	2 024	3 355	3 689	G
8	634	883	1 020	922	1 212	1 014	959	1 153	889	928	H
9	12 225	9 574	8 654	8 349	7 847	8 419	8 456	9 386	2 166	2 107	I
0	.	.	0	2	1	1	12	6	722	670	J
									472	490	K
									2 661	2 517	L
									3 361	3 205	M
									542	605	N
									1 451	1 629	O
									1 362	1 908	P
									4	8	Q
									14	34	X

Men - Hommes - Hombres
ISIC 2 - CITI 2 - CIIU 2 　　　 ISIC 3 - CITI 3 - CIIU 3

	1999	2000	2001	2002	2003	2004	2005	2006	2007	2008	
Total	54 909	55 439	22 401	23 030	22 352	23 700	24 984	25 528	26 393	26 660	Total
1	23 764	24 600	4 253	4 558	4 517	4 476	5 338	5 532	5 085	5 269	A
2	621	370	453	325	417	503	498	478	485	534	B
3	6 481	6 723	5 011	5 053	4 820	4 836	5 270	4 876	597	604	C
4	178	65	99	147	124	181	154	182	4 848	4 657	D
5	3 295	3 357	2 955	3 356	3 221	3 674	3 812	3 829	135	151	E
6	8 456	9 685	2 069	2 311	2 064	2 511	2 513	2 737	4 373	4 442	F
7	4 083	4 364	1 581	1 560	1 520	1 828	1 769	1 845	2 134	2 345	G
8	445	627	758	676	872	755	698	804	534	530	H
9	7 585	5 648	5 221	5 042	4 797	4 933	4 921	5 242	1 974	1 916	I
0	.	.	0	1	1	1	10	3	461	443	J
									378	381	K
									2 120	1 997	L
									1 562	1 446	M
									203	236	N
									1 168	1 298	O
									322	375	P
									2	7	Q
									11	27	X

Women - Femmes - Mujeres
ISIC 2 - CITI 2 - CIIU 2 　　　 ISIC 3 - CITI 3 - CIIU 3

	1999	2000	2001	2002	2003	2004	2005	2006	2007	2008	
Total	33 908	34 399	10 250	10 094	9 691	9 943	10 904	11 453	12 026	12 807	Total
1	14 614	16 076	2 192	2 285	2 215	2 083	2 374	2 332	2 692	2 765	A
2	105	82	61	16	27	43	38	32	29	36	B
3	5 035	4 919	2 984	2 889	2 738	2 553	3 152	2 771	50	51	C
4	10	6	13	18	12	20	13	20	2 991	3 050	D
5	120	141	82	95	104	84	80	97	20	14	E
6	9 073	8 804	1 104	1 116	1 098	1 286	1 341	1 526	115	104	F
7	124	190	118	123	107	128	108	179	1 221	1 344	G
8	189	255	262	245	339	260	261	349	355	398	H
9	4 639	3 926	3 434	3 308	3 050	3 486	3 535	4 143	192	190	I
0	.	.	0	1	0	0	2	3	261	227	J
									94	109	K
									541	520	L
									1 799	1 758	M
									339	369	N
									283	331	O
									1 040	1 534	P
									1	1	Q
									3	7	X

Explanatory notes: see p. 77.　　Notes explicatives: voir p. 80.　　Notas explicativas: véase p. 83.

[1] Persons aged 15 years and over. [2] Aug. of each year.　　[1] Personnes âgées de 15 ans et plus. [2] Août de chaque année.　　[1] Personas de 15 años y más. [2] Agosto de cada año.

Paid employment, by economic activity
Emploi rémunéré, par activité économique
Empleo remunerado, por actividad económica

	Thousands			Milliers				Millares		
	1999	2000	2001	2002	2003	2004	2005	2006	2007	2008

Israel (BA) [1] [2] — **Employees - Salariés - Asalariados**

Total - Total - Total
ISIC 3 - CITI 3 - CIIU 3

	1999	2000	2001	2002	2003	2004	2005	2006	2007	2008
Total	1 815.0	1 906.1	1 959.2	1 976.1	2 008.5 [3]	2 084.5	2 166.5	2 235.1	2 341.6	2 424.8
A-B	24.4	21.4	22.0	23.2	21.9	27.0	30.3	26.2	28.4	.
A	23.6	21.1	21.8	22.7	21.3 [3]	26.4	29.7	25.4	27.9	27.9
B	.	.	.	.	.	.	.	.	.	.
C	5.9	5.1	3.3	3.5	3.1 [3]	2.9	3.9	4.3	4.0	5.0
C-D	343.7	356.5	355.8	342.4	343.2	356.3	361.5	369.1	391.7	.
D	331.4	345.5	345.1	331.6	333.2 [3]	345.8	350.7	357.3	379.7	391.3
E	19.2	19.1	18.5	18.7	18.1 [3]	19.2	21.0	18.1	16.6	19.9
F	95.1	94.4	93.7	94.9	104.9 [3]	104.7	102.4	106.9	122.5	119.4
G	215.6	231.8	238.2	249.5	249.0 [3]	258.8	271.6	271.3	292.7	313.2
H	77.2	87.1	79.9	78.6	79.1 [3]	90.0	101.7	108.7	107.6	114.3
I	107.8	117.6	122.2	119.3	122.8 [3]	128.0	133.6	140.9	143.8	148.8
J	67.6	67.7	68.7	69.5	69.4 [3]	73.2	75.3	80.4	87.0	92.4
K	180.4	211.8	230.0	222.5	243.6 [3]	259.9	271.2	290.2	307.3	318.5
L	115.2	118.8	128.5	133.7	119.7 [3]	111.1	115.7	115.3	119.9	127.5
M	252.5	258.2	266.7	274.3	281.6 [3]	288.8	300.0	312.8	327.8	333.1
N	191.0	191.9	204.6	214.0	228.1 [3]	233.3	241.6	237.9	243.0	246.7
O	73.1	79.4	81.9	84.7	83.9 [3]	80.7	84.9	94.0	86.2	93.3
P	36.6	31.8	32.0	31.8	31.5 [3]	36.8	38.4	41.8	45.3	44.1
Q	-	-	-	2.0	- [3]	-	-	-	-	-
X	20.1	23.3	22.4	24.6	16.7 [3]	22.5	22.4	27.0	28.6	26.8

Men - Hommes - Hombres
ISIC 3 - CITI 3 - CIIU 3

	1999	2000	2001	2002	2003	2004	2005	2006	2007	2008
Total	948.6	990.3	1 018.2	1 020.2	1 030.4 [3]	1 076.7	1 107.4	1 147.3	1 203.5	1 240.2
A-B	17.6	16.3	18.6	18.8	16.2	20.7	23.4	21.7	23.0	.
A	16.9	15.9	18.4	18.5	15.7 [3]	20.1	22.8	20.8	22.4	22.1
B	.	.	.	.	.	.	.	.	.	.
C	5.4	4.6	2.8	2.7	2.6 [3]	2.7	3.5	3.8	3.7	4.7
C-D	246.9	254.8	255.8	245.8	248.5	255.5	259.2	267.1	278.2	.
D	237.0	246.0	247.9	237.2	240.6 [3]	247.4	251.5	258.5	269.4	276.6
E	15.8	15.8	14.9	15.1	15.0 [3]	15.4	16.6	15.2	13.0	15.7
F	87.1	86.2	84.9	86.3	94.7 [3]	94.5	93.0	98.8	114.0	108.5
G	120.3	128.1	131.7	135.9	135.8 [3]	145.8	146.9	145.5	162.4	171.3
H	42.7	47.5	46.3	42.9	44.1 [3]	50.4	59.9	63.0	61.6	63.0
I	74.2	76.4	81.8	80.2	83.1 [3]	84.0	88.6	93.2	94.1	97.9
J	26.8	25.8	25.0	27.8	24.8 [3]	25.6	28.9	29.5	30.8	32.9
K	95.3	114.8	121.7	122.1	133.1 [3]	147.0	150.5	164.8	170.3	176.4
L	64.9	66.0	73.1	74.7	66.9 [3]	62.5	64.5	63.7	67.3	69.5
M	60.1	57.9	61.4	64.9	66.3 [3]	66.2	65.8	69.6	74.8	75.8
N	44.4	44.1	48.0	46.6	50.3 [3]	52.5	50.4	50.5	53.3	53.6
O	38.3	41.0	42.5	43.9	41.3 [3]	42.6	46.4	48.2	43.9	50.1
P	3.7	3.3	2.2	2.8	3.1 [3]	2.5	2.3	4.0	3.7	3.8
Q	-	-	-	-	- [3]	-	-	-	-	-
X	13.8	15.7	14.7	16.9	11.7 [3]	15.8	14.1	15.9	17.8	16.3

Women - Femmes - Mujeres
ISIC 3 - CITI 3 - CIIU 3

	1999	2000	2001	2002	2003	2004	2005	2006	2007	2008
Total	866.4	915.8	941.0	955.9	978.0 [3]	1 007.8	1 059.1	1 087.8	1 138.1	1 184.6
A-B	6.8	5.1	3.4	4.4	5.7	6.3	6.9	4.5	5.4	.
A	6.7	5.1	3.4	4.3	5.7 [3]	6.3	6.9	4.5	5.4	5.8
C	-	-	-	-	-	-	-	-	-	-
C-D	96.8	101.7	100.6	96.6	94.7	100.8	102.3	102.0	113.5	.
D	94.4	99.5	97.2	94.4	92.7 [3]	98.4	99.2	98.8	110.3	114.7
E	3.3	3.3	3.6	3.5	3.2 [3]	3.8	4.4	3.0	3.6	4.2
F	8.0	8.2	8.8	8.6	10.1 [3]	10.2	9.4	8.1	8.5	10.9
G	95.3	103.7	106.5	113.6	113.2 [3]	113.1	124.7	125.8	130.3	141.9
H	34.5	39.5	33.6	35.8	35.1 [3]	39.6	41.8	45.7	46.0	51.3
I	33.6	41.2	40.4	39.1	39.7 [3]	44.0	45.0	47.7	49.7	50.9
J	40.7	41.9	43.7	41.6	44.6 [3]	47.6	46.4	50.9	56.2	59.5
K	85.1	96.9	108.3	100.4	110.6 [3]	112.8	120.7	125.5	137.1	142.2
L	50.3	52.8	55.4	58.9	52.8 [3]	48.6	51.2	51.6	52.6	58.0
M	192.4	200.2	205.2	209.3	215.3 [3]	222.5	234.2	243.2	253.0	257.3
N	146.6	147.8	156.6	167.4	177.9 [3]	180.8	191.1	187.4	189.7	193.1
O	34.8	38.4	39.5	40.8	42.6 [3]	38.1	38.5	45.8	42.3	43.2
P	32.9	28.4	29.8	29.0	28.4 [3]	34.2	36.1	37.8	41.7	40.2
Q	-	-	-	-	- [3]	-	-	-	-	-
X	6.3	7.6	7.7	7.7	5.0 [3]	6.7	8.4	11.2	10.8	10.5

Explanatory notes: see p. 77.

[1] Excl. armed forces. [2] Persons aged 15 years and over. [3] Methodology revised; data not strictly comparable.

Notes explicatives: voir p. 80.

[1] Non compris les forces armées. [2] Personnes âgées de 15 ans et plus. [3] Méthodologie révisée; les données ne sont pas strictement comparables.

Notas explicativas: véase p. 83.

[1] Excl. las fuerzas armadas. [2] Personas de 15 años y más. [3] Metodología revisada; los datos no son estrictamente comparables.

EMPLOYMENT — EMPLOI — EMPLEO

Paid employment, by economic activity
Emploi rémunéré, par activité économique
Empleo remunerado, por actividad económica

Thousands — Milliers — Millares

Israel (FA) [1] — Wage earners - Ouvriers - Obreros
Total - Total - Total
ISIC 3 - CITI 3 - CIIU 3

	1999	2000	2001	2002	2003	2004	2005	2006	2007	2008
Total	2 309.5	2 389.3	2 422.3	2 429.8	2 424.5	2 462.9	2 482.7 [2]	2 596.0	2 720.2	2 810.9
A-B	73.4	71.4	68.5	71.6	73.0	67.5	47.4 [2]	49.2	50.5	50.0
C	.	.	.	.	.	.	3.8	3.8	3.7	3.6
C-D	347.1	352.6	346.7	336.2	330.7	327.4				
D	.	.	.	.	.	.	325.8 [2]	334.5	349.7	357.9
E	18.0	17.8	17.7	17.8	17.8	17.6	17.8 [2]	17.4	17.1	16.5
F	153.0	145.2	145.9	143.1	137.4	134.6	122.4 [2]	128.3	134.4	132.5
G	279.2	290.6	303.4	311.3	308.0	322.5	340.0 [2]	357.9	379.7	396.2
H	101.9	106.2	104.3	100.6	105.5	116.6	123.7 [2]	133.1	147.3	151.1
I	117.2	126.8	133.0	132.0	130.7	131.9	139.7 [2]	145.9	154.1	161.9
J	71.5	71.8	72.6	73.2	73.3	73.4	75.2 [2]	79.9	84.7	89.2
K	378.4	417.5	428.6	417.1	415.6	432.4	448.1 [2]	474.5	498.1	517.2
L	129.9	129.2	102.5	104.7	105.8	107.1	107.2 [2]	108.5	108.1	110.6
M	289.4	295.6	318.5	323.2	321.7	326.4	332.2 [2]	345.1	361.6	374.0
N	230.4	242.5	258.5	272.5	274.4	273.6	264.7 [2]	272.7	281.1	291.7
O	109.4	113.0	122.2	126.3	130.6	131.8	134.3 [2]	144.8	149.6	158.0
X	10.6	9.0	.							

Japan (BA) [3] — Employees - Salariés - Asalariados
Total - Total - Total
ISIC 2 - CITI 2 - CIIU 2 / ISIC 3 - CITI 3 - CIIU 3

	1999	2000	2001	2002	2003	2004	2005	2006	2007	2008	
Total	53 310	53 560	53 690	53 310	53 350	53 550	53 930	54 720	55 230	55 240	Total
1	400	420	470	480	390	360	360	420	450	460	A
2	60	50	50	50	90	70	70	70	70	80	B
3	12 230	12 050	11 850	11 310	50	40	30	30	40	30	C
4	380	340	340	330	11 190	10 920	10 850	11 100	11 220	11 050	D
5	5 440	5 390	5 200	5 040	320	310	350	360	330	320	E
6 [4]	11 960	11 970	12 030	11 860	4 930	4 760	4 580	4 530	4 490	4 370	F
7	3 850	3 930	3 870	3 820	10 240	10 190	10 240	10 290	10 320	10 270	G
8	5 440	5 630	5 760	5 890	2 630	2 610	2 600	2 570	2 660	2 640	H
9 [5]	13 360	13 580	13 900	14 200	3 770	3 760	3 650	3 770	3 780	3 730	I
0	200	200	220	330	1 540	1 520	1 510	1 490	1 490	1 590	J
					5 520	5 910	6 310	6 500	6 660	6 770	K
					2 270	2 330	2 290	2 220	2 260	2 230	L [6]
					2 510	2 540	2 590	2 600	2 590	2 630	M
					4 690	4 980	5 150	5 360	5 470	5 650	N
					2 860	2 860	2 880	3 010	2 930	2 970	O
					360	400	450	420	480	450	X

Men - Hommes - Hombres
ISIC 2 - CITI 2 - CIIU 2 / ISIC 3 - CITI 3 - CIIU 3

	1999	2000	2001	2002	2003	2004	2005	2006	2007	2008	
Total	32 150	32 160	32 010	31 700	31 580	31 520	31 640	31 940	32 260	32 120	Total
1	240	250	280	290	210	200	210	230	240	250	A
2	50	40	40	40	70	60	60	60	60	60	B
3	8 160	8 030	7 930	7 650	40	30	30	30	30	20	C
4	320	300	300	290	7 580	7 450	7 480	7 640	7 800	7 740	D
5	4 580	4 570	4 400	4 280	270	270	310	320	290	290	E
6 [4]	5 890	5 850	5 850	5 740	4 180	4 040	3 910	3 850	3 800	3 700	F
7	3 120	3 180	3 110	3 070	5 280	5 240	5 200	5 190	5 200	5 180	G
8	3 080	3 190	3 240	3 340	1 040	1 030	1 050	1 020	1 050	1 040	H
9 [5]	6 580	6 620	6 730	6 800	3 070	3 030	2 930	3 010	3 040	2 950	I
0	120	120	130	200	760	730	740	730	730	760	J
					3 390	3 590	3 870	3 950	4 030	4 120	K
					1 790	1 850	1 800	1 750	1 760	1 720	L [6]
					1 250	1 240	1 220	1 230	1 250	1 240	M
					960	1 030	1 070	1 140	1 180	1 230	N
					1 480	1 490	1 500	1 560	1 540	1 540	O
					200	230	250	230	280	260	X

Women - Femmes - Mujeres
ISIC 2 - CITI 2 - CIIU 2 / ISIC 3 - CITI 3 - CIIU 3

	1999	2000	2001	2002	2003	2004	2005	2006	2007	2008	
Total	21 160	21 400	21 680	21 610	21 770	22 030	22 290	22 770	22 970	23 120	Total
1	160	170	190	180	170	160	160	190	210	210	A
2	10	10	10	10	20	10	10	20	20	20	B
3	4 070	4 020	3 920	3 660	10	10	10	10	10	0	C
4	50	50	40	50	3 610	3 470	3 370	3 460	3 420	3 320	D
5	860	820	800	770	50	40	40	40	30	30	E
6 [4]	6 060	6 110	6 180	6 120	750	720	670	680	690	670	F
7	720	750	750	750	4 950	4 950	5 040	5 120	5 120	5 080	G
8	2 370	2 430	2 530	2 550	1 580	1 580	1 540	1 560	1 610	1 600	H
9 [5]	6 780	6 960	7 180	7 400	700	710	730	750	760	780	I
0	80	80	90	140	780	790	770	760	770	820	J
					2 150	2 320	2 450	2 530	2 620	2 650	K
					470	480	490	470	510	510	L [6]
					1 270	1 300	1 370	1 370	1 340	1 390	M
					3 730	3 950	4 080	4 230	4 290	4 420	N
					1 380	1 370	1 380	1 420	1 390	1 450	O
					160	170	200	180	210	190	X

Explanatory notes: see p. 77.
[1] Incl. those working in Israel from West Bank and Gaza Strip. [2] Methodology revised; data not strictly comparable. [3] Persons aged 15 years and over. [4] Excl. hotels. [5] Incl. hotels. [6] Incl. self-defence forces.

Notes explicatives: voir p. 80.
[1] Y compris ceux travaillant en Israël et provenant de la rive ouest et la bande de Gaza. [2] Méthodologie révisée; les données ne sont pas strictement comparables. [3] Personnes âgées de 15 ans et plus. [4] Non compris les hôtels. [5] Y compris les hôtels. [6] Y compris les forces d'autodéfense.

Notas explicativas: véase p. 83.
[1] Incl. a los que trabajan en Israel y provienen de la Ribera Occidental y la Faja de Gaza. [2] Metodología revisada; los datos no son estrictamente comparables. [3] Personas de 15 años y más. [4] Excl. hoteles. [5] Incl. hoteles. [6] Incl. a las fuerzas de autodefensa.

EMPLOYMENT   EMPLOI   EMPLEO

**Paid employment,
by economic activity**   **Emploi rémunéré,
par activité économique**   **Empleo remunerado,
por actividad económica**

Thousands   Milliers   Millares

	1999	2000	2001	2002	2003	2004	2005	2006	2007	2008
Kazakhstan (BA) [1]				*Employees - Salariés - Asalariados*						
Total - Total - Total										
ISIC 3 - CITI 3 - CIIU 3										
Total	.	.	3 863	4 030	4 230	4 470	4 641	4 777	4 974	5 199
A	.	.	554	561	577	606	605	611	647	677
B	.	.	7	7	6	8	7	8	8	9
C	.	.	167	167	182	186	184	187	194	200
D	.	.	491	481	483	496	519	532	545	546
E	.	.	149	153	167	164	167	163	163	165
F	.	.	221	233	290	333	353	390	429	452
G	.	.	352	421	422	457	477	488	502	567
H	.	.	45	51	64	72	74	78	82	87
I	.	.	370	399	397	396	403	401	414	438
J	.	.	46	50	54	61	67	74	88	96
K	.	.	198	191	185	220	277	301	332	346
L	.	.	281	280	318	335	330	335	344	353
M	.	.	572	581	626	657	684	714	729	750
N	.	.	276	287	295	311	322	325	328	341
O	.	.	130	147	154	154	157	157	156	161
P	.	.	7	19	11	15	15	14	13	14
Q	.	.	0	0	0	1	0	0	0	0
Men - Hommes - Hombres										
ISIC 3 - CITI 3 - CIIU 3										
Total	.	.	2 117	2 217	2 288	2 384	2 481	2 501	2 590	2 711
A	.	.	409	414	412	426	425	413	430	449
B	.	.	5	6	5	7	5	5	5	6
C	.	.	125	131	141	146	139	133	143	149
D	.	.	323	312	305	319	332	341	348	349
E	.	.	107	107	122	110	115	116	111	115
F	.	.	182	191	229	264	278	295	315	342
G	.	.	135	174	169	176	190	188	194	228
H	.	.	11	14	16	18	17	18 734	21	26
I	.	.	250	270	283	273	285	274	290	298
J	.	.	15	20	19	24	24	28	36	37
K	.	.	121	126	102	113	150	157	164	167
L	.	.	172	159	189	192	195	193	193	200
M	.	.	145	158	162	176	180	187	191	194
N	.	.	51	59	59	63	63	76	76	79
O	.	.	64	70	70	72	77	72	69	69
P	.	.	2	7	4	5	6	5	4	3
Q	.	.	0	0	0	0	0	0	0	0
Women - Femmes - Mujeres										
ISIC 3 - CITI 3 - CIIU 3										
Total	.	.	1 746	1 814	1 942	2 086	2 160	2 276	2 383	2 489
A	.	.	145	147	165	179	180	199	216	228
B	.	.	1	1	1	1	2	3	3	3
C	.	.	41	36	40	40	45	54	51	51
D	.	.	168	170	178	177	187	191	197	197
E	.	.	43	46	45	54	53	47	52	50
F	.	.	38	43	60	69	76	95	115	110
G	.	.	218	247	253	282	287	300	308	338
H	.	.	34	37	49	53	57	59	61	61
I	.	.	120	129	114	123	118	127	124	140
J	.	.	31	31	35	37	42	46	52	59
K	.	.	77	65	83	108	126	144	167	179
L	.	.	109	122	129	143	135	142	151	152
M	.	.	427	423	464	481	504	527	537	556
N	.	.	225	229	236	248	259	249	253	262
O	.	.	66	78	84	82	81	85	87	92
P	.	.	5	12	7	10	9	9	9	10
Q	.	.	0	0	0	1	0	0	0	0
Korea, Republic of (BA) [1][2]				*Employees - Salariés - Asalariados*						
Total - Total - Total										
ISIC 3 - CITI 3 - CIIU 3										
Total	12 522	13 360 [3]	13 659	14 181	14 402	14 894	15 185	15 551	15 970	.
A	152	145 [3]	128	124	136	143	141	145	151	.
B	37	33 [3]	35	28	26	28	21	19	23	.
C	19	15 [3]	16	15	13	15	16	17	18	.
D	3 304	3 564 [3]	3 535	3 521	3 553	3 655	3 603	3 544	3 520	.
E	61	64 [3]	58	52	75	70	70	74	85	.
F	1 163	1 228 [3]	1 211	1 333	1 354	1 367	1 347	1 363	1 423	.
G	1 699	1 755 [3]	1 812	1 896	1 873	1 893	1 900	1 911	1 968	.
H	882	992 [3]	1 032	1 074	1 023	1 084	1 114	1 123	1 133	.
I	847	879 [3]	900	891	844	851	889	928	901	.
J	678	699 [3]	700	674	712	690	698	733	758	.
K	918	1 072 [3]	1 212	1 322	1 386	1 555	1 663	1 802	1 979	.
L	869	758 [3]	701	702	756	766	791	801	797	.
M	893	944 [3]	977	1 089	1 198	1 217	1 269	1 328	1 339	.
N	319	371 [3]	428	485	495	551	594	626	683	.
O	494	670 [3]	741	803	798	874	921	985	1 024	.
P	172	151 [3]	157	156	139	111	127	133	156	.
Q	17	19 [3]	16	18	22	24	24	20	15	.

Explanatory notes: see p. 77.

[1] Persons aged 15 years and over. [2] Excl. armed forces. [3] Estimates based on the 2000 Population Census results.

Notes explicatives: voir p. 80.

[1] Personnes âgées de 15 ans et plus. [2] Non compris les forces armées. [3] Estimations basées sur les résultats du Recensement de la population de 2000.

Notas explicativas: véase p. 83.

[1] Personas de 15 años y más. [2] Excl. las fuerzas armadas. [3] Estimaciones basadas en los resultados del Censo de población de 2000.

EMPLOYMENT	EMPLOI	EMPLEO
Paid employment, by economic activity	**Emploi rémunéré, par activité économique**	**Empleo remunerado, por actividad económica**
Thousands	Milliers	Millares

	1999	2000	2001	2002	2003	2004	2005	2006	2007	2008

Korea, Republic of (BA) [1] [2]   Employees - Salariés - Asalariados

Men - Hommes - Hombres
ISIC 3 - CITI 3 - CIIU 3

	1999	2000	2001	2002	2003	2004	2005	2006	2007	2008
Total	7 570	7 963 [3]	8 050	8 325	8 432	8 657	8 794	8 978	9 214	.
A	53	45 [3]	38	38	39	43	44	44	52	.
B	30	26 [3]	29	23	17	16	13	12	12	.
C	18	15 [3]	15	14	13	14	15	15	16	.
D	2 098	2 280 [3]	2 278	2 246	2 281	2 354	2 378	2 358	2 354	.
E	52	53 [3]	44	41	64	58	57	59	66	.
F	1 059	1 122 [3]	1 104	1 216	1 236	1 232	1 218	1 224	1 277	.
G	937	923 [3]	915	958	891	915	928	955	996	.
H	239	272 [3]	283	301	264	272	282	280	286	.
I	738	746 [3]	764	757	695	687	708	754	745	.
J	319	313 [3]	308	300	338	335	342	355	359	.
K	641	725 [3]	812	875	938	1 048	1 084	1 147	1 245	.
L	609	534 [3]	496	502	568	553	552	542	543	.
M	393	388 [3]	384	414	448	432	444	453	459	.
N	79	86 [3]	97	114	123	145	141	147	162	.
O	286	414 [3]	466	507	498	532	567	616	626	.
P	3	3 [3]	4	2	3	3	4	2	4	.
Q	17	18 [3]	13	15	16	18	18	15	12	.

Women - Femmes - Mujeres
ISIC 3 - CITI 3 - CIIU 3

	1999	2000	2001	2002	2003	2004	2005	2006	2007	2008
Total	4 952	5 397 [3]	5 609	5 857	5 970	6 237	6 391	6 573	6 756	.
A	99	101 [3]	90	87	97	100	97	100	99	.
B	8	7 [3]	6	5	9	12	8	7	10	.
C	1	- [3]	1	1	1	1	1	2	1	.
D	1 206	1 284 [3]	1 257	1 274	1 272	1 301	1 225	1 186	1 165	.
E	9	11 [3]	14	11	11	12	12	15	19	.
F	103	106 [3]	108	117	118	135	129	139	146	.
G	762	832 [3]	897	938	982	978	972	955	972	.
H	643	720 [3]	749	773	759	812	832	844	847	.
I	109	134 [3]	136	134	148	165	181	174	156	.
J	359	386 [3]	392	373	374	354	356	378	399	.
K	277	347 [3]	400	446	448	507	579	655	733	.
L	260	223 [3]	205	199	188	213	239	260	254	.
M	500	557 [3]	593	674	750	784	824	875	879	.
N	240	285 [3]	331	370	372	406	453	479	521	.
O	208	256 [3]	274	297	299	342	354	369	397	.
P	168	148 [3]	153	154	136	108	123	130	153	.
Q	-	1 [3]	2	3	7	7	6	5	3	.

Kyrgyzstan (BA) [2] [4]   Employees - Salariés - Asalariados

Total - Total - Total
ISIC 3 - CITI 3 - CIIU 3

	1999	2000	2001	2002	2003	2004	2005	2006	2007	2008
Total	.	.	.	.	.	.	.	1 065.6	.	.
A	.	.	.	.	.	.	.	38.5	.	.
B	.	.	.	.	.	.	.	0.2	.	.
C	.	.	.	.	.	.	.	11.6	.	.
D	.	.	.	.	.	.	.	155.3	.	.
E	.	.	.	.	.	.	.	34.6	.	.
F	.	.	.	.	.	.	.	165.8	.	.
G	.	.	.	.	.	.	.	114.3	.	.
H	.	.	.	.	.	.	.	44.1	.	.
I	.	.	.	.	.	.	.	64.9	.	.
J	.	.	.	.	.	.	.	9.5	.	.
K	.	.	.	.	.	.	.	34.3	.	.
L	.	.	.	.	.	.	.	101.0	.	.
M	.	.	.	.	.	.	.	152.3	.	.
N	.	.	.	.	.	.	.	85.4	.	.
O	.	.	.	.	.	.	.	37.8	.	.
P	.	.	.	.	.	.	.	15.3	.	.
Q	.	.	.	.	.	.	.	0.5	.	.

Men - Hommes - Hombres
ISIC 3 - CITI 3 - CIIU 3

	1999	2000	2001	2002	2003	2004	2005	2006	2007	2008
Total	.	.	.	.	.	.	.	609.3	.	.
A	.	.	.	.	.	.	.	30.7	.	.
B	.	.	.	.	.	.	.	0.1	.	.
C	.	.	.	.	.	.	.	11.0	.	.
D	.	.	.	.	.	.	.	85.9	.	.
E	.	.	.	.	.	.	.	28.8	.	.
F	.	.	.	.	.	.	.	158.9	.	.
G	.	.	.	.	.	.	.	63.7	.	.
H	.	.	.	.	.	.	.	13.2	.	.
I	.	.	.	.	.	.	.	45.4	.	.
J	.	.	.	.	.	.	.	4.2	.	.
K	.	.	.	.	.	.	.	18.4	.	.
L	.	.	.	.	.	.	.	64.3	.	.
M	.	.	.	.	.	.	.	39.5	.	.
N	.	.	.	.	.	.	.	18.8	.	.
O	.	.	.	.	.	.	.	17.2	.	.
P	.	.	.	.	.	.	.	9.0	.	.
Q	.	.	.	.	.	.	.	0.5	.	.

Explanatory notes: see p. 77.

[1] Excl. armed forces. [2] Persons aged 15 years and over. [3] Estimates based on the 2000 Population Census results. [4] Nov. of each year.

Notes explicatives: voir p. 80.

[1] Non compris les forces armées. [2] Personnes âgées de 15 ans et plus. [3] Estimations basées sur les résultats du Recensement de la population de 2000. [4] Nov. de chaque année.

Notas explicativas: véase p. 83.

[1] Excl. las fuerzas armadas. [2] Personas de 15 años y más. [3] Estimaciones basadas en los resultados del Censo de población de 2000. [4] Nov. de cada año.

Paid employment, by economic activity
Emploi rémunéré, par activité économique
Empleo remunerado, por actividad económica

Thousands — Milliers — Millares

	1999	2000	2001	2002	2003	2004	2005	2006	2007	2008
Kyrgyzstan (BA) [1] [2]				**Employees - Salariés - Asalariados**						
Women - Femmes - Mujeres										
ISIC 3 - CITI 3 - CIIU 3										
Total	.	.	.	.	.	.	.	456.2	.	.
A	.	.	.	.	.	.	.	7.8	.	.
B	.	.	.	.	.	.	.	0.1	.	.
C	.	.	.	.	.	.	.	0.6	.	.
D	.	.	.	.	.	.	.	69.4	.	.
E	.	.	.	.	.	.	.	5.8	.	.
F	.	.	.	.	.	.	.	6.9	.	.
G	.	.	.	.	.	.	.	50.6	.	.
H	.	.	.	.	.	.	.	30.8	.	.
I	.	.	.	.	.	.	.	19.5	.	.
J	.	.	.	.	.	.	.	5.4	.	.
K	.	.	.	.	.	.	.	15.9	.	.
L	.	.	.	.	.	.	.	36.7	.	.
M	.	.	.	.	.	.	.	112.8	.	.
N	.	.	.	.	.	.	.	66.5	.	.
O	.	.	.	.	.	.	.	20.6	.	.
P	.	.	.	.	.	.	.	6.3	.	.
Q	.	.	.	.	.	.	.	0.5	.	.
Kyrgyzstan (E)				**Employees - Salariés - Asalariados**						
Total - Total - Total										
ISIC 3 - CITI 3 - CIIU 3										
Total	649.4	623.2	594.9	571.3	560.4	554.6	550.0	533.4	559.7	.
A	72.7	59.5	45.9	40.4	38.5	35.6	30.5	27.7	22.1	.
B	0.4	0.1	0.8	0.1	0.3	0.1	0.1	0.1	0.1	.
C	6.7	6.3	5.4	5.5	4.9	6.0	5.9	5.7	5.7	.
D	105.5	93.6	89.2	83.4	79.4	74.4	72.0	68.3	67.8	.
E	21.7	20.3	21.1	21.7	22.3	23.8	24.3	24.6	25.2	.
F	34.9	33.5	30.7	27.7	26.1	25.4	24.0	21.7	23.4	.
G	32.0	32.9	29.0	26.1	24.1	20.6	20.8	22.5	23.2	.
H	5.1	5.6	5.2	4.5	4.7	3.5	3.6	4.4	4.1	.
I	51.5	48.0	45.4	43.3	39.6	36.5	35.2	34.2	33.2	.
J	6.7	6.6	6.2	5.8	6.3	6.5	6.6	8.1	12.2	.
K	28.1	27.8	27.4	26.3	25.6	27.7	28.4	29.0	34.1	.
L	38.0	39.0	39.2	42.6	44.6	48.1	49.7	51.8	50.8	.
M	139.8	144.1	144.2	146.2	148.7	150.1	152.7	139.9	153.9	.
N	83.5	82.7	80.0	73.6	68.7	67.5	66.6	65.6	66.2	.
O	22.7	23.2	25.3	24.1	26.4	28.9	29.7	29.8	37.7	.
P	0.1	.	.	.	.	.	.	.	.	.
Men - Hommes - Hombres										
ISIC 3 - CITI 3 - CIIU 3										
Total	355.1	348.7	333.8	322.8	303.3	288.9	272.7	260.9	280.8	.
A	53.1	42.9	34.7	30.3	28.1	26.4	22.8	19.0	16.3	.
B	0.4	0.1	0.7	0.1	0.3	0.0	0.1	0.0	0.1	.
C	5.4	5.5	4.7	4.8	4.3	5.1	4.9	4.9	4.8	.
D	63.4	58.3	57.5	53.3	51.2	48.7	44.8	42.4	42.4	.
E	16.3	15.6	18.2	16.8	17.3	18.0	18.0	18.4	18.8	.
F	29.5	28.6	25.9	23.5	22.4	21.8	20.3	18.0	19.3	.
G	20.2	20.8	19.0	16.9	15.1	12.6	12.7	13.4	13.1	.
H	2.7	2.9	3.0	2.3	2.8	1.8	1.6	2.1	1.8	.
I	38.5	36.2	33.8	31.8	28.4	24.5	23.2	21.6	20.9	.
J	3.1	3.4	3.4	2.8	3.2	3.0	3.2	3.7	6.6	.
K	17.0	18.1	17.9	17.8	16.0	16.9	17.2	17.3	21.7	.
L	25.6	27.1	27.2	29.0	30.0	31.5	31.7	31.8	31.7	.
M	46.2	51.8	49.4	55.5	51.7	46.9	43.0	40.6	42.5	.
N	22.1	24.6	24.3	24.6	19.5	18.5	14.9	14.7	14.7	.
O	11.6	12.9	14.1	13.2	13.0	13.1	14.2	13.6	26.0	.
P	0.1	.	.	.	.	.	.	.	.	.
Women - Femmes - Mujeres										
ISIC 3 - CITI 3 - CIIU 3										
Total	294.3	274.5	261.1	248.5	257.1	265.7	277.3	272.5	278.9	.
A	19.6	16.6	11.2	10.1	10.3	9.2	7.7	8.7	5.8	.
B	0.0	0.0	0.1	0.0	0.0	0.0	0.0	0.0	0.0	.
C	1.3	0.8	0.7	0.7	0.6	0.9	1.0	0.8	1.0	.
D	42.1	35.4	31.7	30.1	28.3	25.6	27.2	25.9	25.4	.
E	5.4	4.7	2.8	4.9	5.1	5.8	6.3	6.3	6.3	.
F	5.4	4.8	4.9	4.2	3.7	3.6	3.7	3.7	4.1	.
G	11.8	12.0	10.0	9.2	9.1	7.9	8.0	9.8	10.1	.
H	2.3	2.7	2.2	2.2	1.9	1.7	2.0	2.3	2.2	.
I	13.0	11.8	11.6	11.5	11.1	12.0	12.1	12.6	12.3	.
J	3.6	3.2	2.8	3.0	3.1	3.5	3.4	4.3	5.6	.
K	11.1	9.7	9.4	8.4	9.6	10.9	11.2	11.7	12.4	.
L	12.4	12.0	12.1	13.5	14.6	16.6	17.9	20.0	19.1	.
M	93.6	92.3	94.7	90.7	97.0	103.2	109.7	99.3	111.4	.
N	61.4	58.1	55.7	49.0	49.2	49.0	51.7	50.9	51.5	.
O	11.2	10.4	11.2	11.0	13.4	15.8	15.5	16.2	11.7	.
P	0.0	.	.	.	.	.	.	.	.	.

Explanatory notes: see p. 77.   Notes explicatives: voir p. 80.   Notas explicativas: véase p. 83.

[1] Persons aged 15 years and over. [2] Nov. of each year.   [1] Personnes âgées de 15 ans et plus. [2] Nov. de chaque année.   [1] Personas de 15 años y más. [2] Nov. de cada año.

2E

EMPLOYMENT	EMPLOI	EMPLEO
Paid employment, **by economic activity**	**Emploi rémunéré,** **par activité économique**	**Empleo remunerado,** **por actividad económica**

	Thousands				Milliers				Millares	
	1999	2000	2001	2002	2003	2004	2005	2006	2007	2008

Macau, China (BA) [1][2]   Employees - Salariés - Asalariados

Total - Total - Total
ISIC 3 - CITI 3 - CIIU 3

	1999	2000	2001	2002	2003	2004	2005	2006	2007	2008
Total	174.8	172.2	183.0	183.4	183.1	193.7	212.9	240.4	274.4	298.9
A	0.0	-	-	-	-	0.1	0.1	0.2	0.1	.
B	0.1	0.1	-	-	0.2	0.2	0.1	0.1	-	.
A-C	.			.		.	.	.	.	0.3
C	-	-	-	0.1		.	.	.	.	.
D	40.7	36.3	42.8	39.9	35.8	34.0	33.4	27.6	22.3	22.8
E	1.1	0.8	1.0	1.2	1.3	1.1	1.2	0.9	1.2	0.9
F	15.0	14.4	15.9	13.8	15.2	16.6	21.1	29.0	36.6	35.8
G	19.5	19.6	19.0	20.6	21.5	22.4	23.6	25.1	26.1	29.2
H	19.0	19.2	21.0	21.9	21.0	21.9	23.0	28.1	33.2	39.5
I	12.8	12.3	12.5	10.9	11.7	12.1	12.2	14.1	13.1	13.1
J	5.7	6.7	5.8	6.1	5.9	5.7	6.1	6.7	7.6	7.3
K	7.9	9.5	10.0	9.9	11.1	11.4	12.5	14.1	17.8	21.7
L	16.3	16.4	16.2	17.4	18.1	18.1	18.8	20.3	22.0	20.2
M	8.2	7.2	7.8	10.0	9.7	10.5	10.1	11.1	11.6	11.3
N	4.4	4.5	4.6	3.9	4.0	4.3	4.8	4.7	5.5	6.0
O	18.7	20.8	21.5	22.7	23.2	30.1	39.4	51.3	67.7	77.6
P	5.3	4.4	4.5	4.8	4.3	5.0	6.2	6.9	9.6	13.2
Q	0.1	0.1	0.1	0.1	0.1	0.1	0.2	0.1	0.1	.
X	0.0	0.0	0.2	-	0.0	-	-	-	-	0.0

Men - Hommes - Hombres
ISIC 3 - CITI 3 - CIIU 3

	1999	2000	2001	2002	2003	2004	2005	2006	2007	2008
Total	89.2	87.5	93.2	91.3	92.8	97.7	107.1	124.7	142.1	155.3
A	0.0	0.0	0.0	0.0	0.0	0.0	0.0	0.0	0.0	.
B	0.1	0.1	-	-	0.1	0.1	0.1	0.1	0.0	.
A-C	.			.	.	.	.	.	.	0.1
C	0.0	-	-	0.1	.	.	.	.	.	.
D	11.5	10.6	11.8	11.2	10.3	9.8	10.3	8.9	7.4	10.2
E	0.9	0.7	0.9	1.0	1.0	0.9	1.0	0.8	1.0	0.6
F	13.8	13.0	14.6	12.8	13.6	14.8	18.8	25.9	32.0	31.3
G	9.7	9.9	9.9	10.4	10.0	10.6	11.2	10.9	11.6	12.9
H	9.5	9.0	10.8	10.3	10.9	10.7	10.3	13.5	15.7	19.4
I	9.2	8.7	8.4	7.5	8.0	8.5	8.4	9.5	8.8	9.1
J	2.6	3.2	2.6	2.7	2.5	2.4	2.6	2.8	2.9	2.7
K	5.3	6.3	6.8	6.7	7.1	7.2	7.9	8.7	10.1	13.1
L	11.7	11.8	11.6	12.2	12.5	12.6	12.6	14.0	14.2	13.0
M	2.6	2.2	2.3	3.0	3.1	3.3	2.9	3.6	3.6	3.5
N	1.2	1.3	1.5	1.1	1.1	1.0	1.1	0.9	1.3	1.7
O	10.7	10.4	11.7	11.9	12.4	15.4	19.6	24.7	33.0	37.4
P	0.2	0.4	0.3	0.3	0.2	0.4	0.3	0.3	0.5	0.3
Q	-	-	0.1	-	0.1	-	0.1	-	-	.
X	0.0	0.0	-	-	0.0	0.0	-	0.0	-	0.0

Women - Femmes - Mujeres
ISIC 3 - CITI 3 - CIIU 3

	1999	2000	2001	2002	2003	2004	2005	2006	2007	2008
Total	85.6	84.7	89.8	92.1	90.3	96.0	105.8	115.8	132.3	143.5
A	0.0	-	-	-	-	0.1	0.1	0.2	0.1	.
B	-	-	-	0.0	-	-	-	0.0	-	.
A-C	.			.	.	.	.	.	.	0.2
C	0.0	-	0.0	0.0	0.0	0.0	0.0	0.0	0.0	.
D	29.2	25.7	31.0	28.7	25.5	24.2	23.1	18.7	14.9	12.6
E	0.2	0.1	0.2	0.2	0.3	0.2	0.2	0.1	0.2	0.2
F	1.2	1.4	1.4	1.1	1.5	1.8	2.4	3.0	4.6	4.5
G	9.8	9.6	9.1	10.2	11.5	11.9	12.4	14.2	14.5	16.3
H	9.5	10.1	10.3	11.6	10.1	11.3	12.7	14.6	17.5	20.2
I	3.6	3.6	4.1	3.5	3.7	3.6	3.8	4.6	4.2	4.0
J	3.1	3.5	3.2	3.4	3.5	3.3	3.5	3.9	4.7	4.6
K	2.6	3.3	3.2	3.3	4.0	4.2	4.6	5.4	7.6	8.6
L	4.5	4.6	4.6	5.1	5.6	5.5	6.2	6.4	7.8	7.2
M	5.6	5.0	5.5	7.0	6.6	7.2	7.3	7.6	8.0	7.9
N	3.2	3.3	3.1	2.7	2.9	3.3	3.8	3.8	4.2	4.3
O	8.0	10.4	9.8	10.8	10.8	14.7	19.8	26.6	34.7	40.2
P	5.1	4.0	4.2	4.5	4.1	4.6	5.9	6.6	9.1	12.9
Q	-	-	0.1	0.1	-	-	0.1	0.1	0.1	.
X	-	-	0.1	-	-	-	-	-	-	0.0

Macau, China (DA) [3]   Employees - Salariés - Asalariados

Total - Total - Total
ISIC 3 - CITI 3 - CIIU 3

	1999	2000	2001	2002	2003	2004	2005	2006	2007	2008
D	.	41.9	41.2	36.8	36.0	36.2	31.6	31.3	28.0	23.9
E	.	1.1	1.0	1.0	1.1	1.0	1.0	1.0	1.1	1.1
G	.	12.5	13.8	14.4	15.7	18.1	20.0	21.3	24.1	26.0
H	.	16.6	17.0	16.9	17.4	19.3	21.2	27.0	42.6	49.5
I [4]	.	7.9	8.2	8.1	8.1	8.7	6.7	7.1	7.3	7.8
J	.	4.2	4.2	4.1	4.0	4.2	4.4	4.7	5.1	5.6
K	.	.	.	.	.	.	.	3.5	3.7	3.9
O [5]	.	.	.	.	.	21.3	26.1	36.4	44.7	43.8

Explanatory notes: see p. 77.

[1] Persons aged 14 years and over. [2] Excl. armed forces and conscripts. [3] Third quarter of each year. [4] Excluding travel agencies. [5] Including Gaming industry.

Notes explicatives: voir p. 80.

[1] Personnes âgées de 14 ans et plus. [2] Non compris les forces armées et les conscrits. [3] Troisième trimestre de chaque année. [4] Non compris les agences de voyages. [5] Inclus les industries du jeux.

Notas explicativas: véase p. 83.

[1] Personas de 14 años y más. [2] Excl. las fuerzas armadas y los conscriptos. [3] Tercer trimestre de cada año. [4] Excl. Las agencias de viajes. [5] Incl. las industrias de juegos de azar.

Paid employment, by economic activity — Emploi rémunéré, par activité économique — Empleo remunerado, por actividad económica

	Thousands — Milliers — Millares									
	1999	2000	2001	2002	2003	2004	2005	2006	2007	2008

Macau, China (DA) [1] — Employees - Salariés - Asalariados

Men - Hommes - Hombres
ISIC 3 - CITI 3 - CIIU 3

	1999	2000	2001	2002	2003	2004	2005	2006	2007	2008
D	.	10.3	10.3	8.8	8.9	8.8	8.0	8.6	8.3	7.6
E	.	0.9	0.8	0.8	0.8	0.8	0.8	0.8	0.8	0.8
G	.	6.0	6.6	7.0	7.9	8.4	9.0	10.1	11.3	11.5
H	.	7.9	8.0	7.9	8.0	9.1	9.8	11.9	20.1	23.9
I [2]	.	4.6	4.9	4.9	4.9	5.3	4.4	4.7	4.8	5.2
J	.	1.8	1.8	1.8	1.7	1.7	1.8	2.0	2.1	2.2
K	.	.	.	.	.	.	.	2.8	3.1	3.2
O [3]	.	.	.	.	.	11.2	13.4	18.0	21.7	20.9

Women - Femmes - Mujeres
ISIC 3 - CITI 3 - CIIU 3

	1999	2000	2001	2002	2003	2004	2005	2006	2007	2008
D	.	31.7	30.9	27.9	27.0	27.5	23.6	22.7	19.7	16.3
E	.	0.2	0.2	0.2	0.2	0.2	0.2	0.2	0.2	0.2
G	.	6.5	7.2	7.5	8.0	9.7	11.0	11.2	12.8	14.5
H	.	8.7	9.0	9.0	9.4	10.2	11.4	15.0	22.4	26.6
I [2]	.	3.2	3.3	3.2	3.2	3.3	2.2	2.4	2.6	2.7
J	.	2.4	2.4	2.3	2.3	2.4	2.6	2.8	3.1	3.4
K	.	.	.	.	.	.	.	0.7	0.6	0.7
O [3]	.	.	.	.	.	10.1	12.7	18.5	23.1	23.0

Malaysia (BA) [4] [5] — Employees - Salariés - Asalariados

Total - Total - Total
ISIC 3 - CITI 3 - CIIU 3

	1999	2000	2001	2002	2003	2004	2005	2006	2007	2008
Total	.	.	7 056.2	7 320.2	7 523.8	7 445.0	7 583.4	7 632.8	7 824.0	7 951.1
A	.	.	484.1	529.2	514.5	496.3	544.1	495.0	565.0	544.3
B	.	.	37.1	33.2	33.1	32.5	30.9	33.8	28.6	29.7
C	.	.	25.6	26.8	28.2	34.3	34.5	40.9	37.9	52.8
D	.	.	2 019.1	1 902.6	1 955.0	1 840.2	1 819.2	1 903.2	1 789.8	1 745.9
E	.	.	56.8	49.9	56.7	57.5	56.2	75.2	60.2	60.2
F	.	.	665.3	763.6	762.3	694.6	692.6	681.1	688.8	751.0
G	.	.	913.5	978.8	1 035.9	1 014.6	1 054.2	1 064.9	1 103.1	1 118.3
H	.	.	335.1	365.7	377.0	387.9	386.6	416.4	435.3	460.4
I	.	.	371.7	406.5	389.3	431.9	434.8	425.4	436.0	459.9
J	.	.	210.2	224.7	207.1	222.2	234.1	219.3	262.0	250.4
K	.	.	304.9	349.1	353.2	397.3	403.0	435.1	484.7	482.6
L	.	.	658.3	657.3	660.4	676.9	720.9	669.5	709.7	741.6
M	.	.	495.2	492.1	575.8	592.5	588.4	583.3	614.6	637.8
N	.	.	154.9	170.9	194.6	176.9	193.0	206.0	218.8	235.0
O	.	.	150.5	155.7	171.8	185.6	186.8	186.5	202.0	209.4
P	.	.	172.7	212.2	205.8	201.8	202.6	195.9	185.9	170.5
Q	.	.	1.2	2.0	3.2	2.2	1.7	1.2	1.7	1.1

Men - Hommes - Hombres
ISIC 3 - CITI 3 - CIIU 3

	1999	2000	2001	2002	2003	2004	2005	2006	2007	2008
Total	.	.	4 520.0	4 692.6	4 776.1	4 690.6	4 778.1	4 775.9	4 893.4	4 947.0
A	.	.	381.1	423.8	408.7	392.7	436.1	391.5	452.5	435.5
B	.	.	35.6	32.6	32.0	31.9	29.9	31.9	27.5	28.6
C	.	.	22.0	24.2	25.3	32.0	30.3	35.3	32.2	43.5
D	.	.	1 200.4	1 146.6	1 181.3	1 122.0	1 122.6	1 181.6	1 109.6	1 078.9
E	.	.	48.9	43.8	47.8	50.3	48.6	63.3	51.4	49.9
F	.	.	606.5	701.3	699.5	633.1	624.3	611.6	625.9	674.6
G	.	.	606.3	644.9	667.0	652.2	667.0	664.9	692.3	685.4
H	.	.	179.4	188.4	198.7	192.1	197.0	226.8	228.7	233.8
I	.	.	310.7	340.9	321.2	355.4	360.9	343.7	355.4	373.2
J	.	.	107.9	112.5	106.2	108.0	111.0	104.7	127.5	116.3
K	.	.	179.1	200.7	208.9	231.6	239.9	258.2	286.2	284.5
L	.	.	499.9	482.6	485.9	496.8	520.3	483.1	509.6	528.5
M	.	.	196.4	191.6	222.3	216.9	214.1	203.4	213.5	218.0
N	.	.	48.1	57.1	62.1	55.7	60.6	63.1	65.6	67.9
O	.	.	89.0	89.3	96.3	109.0	104.0	100.7	105.3	116.3
P	.	.	8.3	11.2	10.5	9.1	10.1	11.1	9.4	11.2
Q	.	.	0.6	1.1	2.2	1.8	1.3	1.0	1.0	0.9

Explanatory notes: see p. 77.

[1] Third quarter of each year. [2] Excluding travel agencies. [3] Including Gaming industry. [4] Persons aged 15 to 64 years. [5] Excl. armed forces.

Notes explicatives: voir p. 80.

[1] Troisième trimestre de chaque année. [2] Non compris les agences de voyages. [3] Inclus les industries du jeux. [4] Personnes âgées de 15 à 64 ans. [5] Non compris les forces armées.

Notas explicativas: véase p. 83.

[1] Tercer trimestre de cada año. [2] Excl. Las agencias de viajes. [3] Incl. las industrias de juegos de azar. [4] Personas de 15 a 64 años. [5] Excl. las fuerzas armadas.

	EMPLOYMENT			EMPLOI			EMPLEO		
	Paid employment, **by economic activity**			**Emploi rémunéré,** **par activité économique**			**Empleo remunerado,** **por actividad económica**		
	Thousands				Milliers			Millares		
1999	2000	2001	2002	2003	2004	2005	2006	2007	2008

Malaysia (BA) [1] [2]   **Employees - Salariés - Asalariados**

Women - Femmes - Mujeres
ISIC 3 - CITI 3 - CIIU 3

	1999	2000	2001	2002	2003	2004	2005	2006	2007	2008
Total	.	.	2 536.2	2 627.6	2 747.7	2 754.5	2 805.3	2 856.9	2 930.7	3 004.1
A	.	.	103.0	105.4	105.8	103.6	108.0	103.5	112.5	108.9
B	.	.	1.5	0.6	1.1	0.6	1.0	1.9	1.1	1.2
C	.	.	3.6	2.6	2.9	2.2	4.1	5.6	5.7	9.3
D	.	.	818.8	755.9	773.7	718.2	696.5	721.6	680.2	667.0
E	.	.	7.9	6.1	8.9	7.2	7.6	12.0	8.8	10.3
F	.	.	58.8	62.3	62.8	61.6	68.3	69.5	62.9	76.4
G	.	.	307.2	333.9	368.8	362.4	387.2	400.0	410.8	432.9
H	.	.	155.7	177.3	178.3	195.8	189.6	189.6	206.6	226.5
I	.	.	61.1	65.7	68.1	76.4	73.9	81.7	80.7	86.7
J	.	.	102.3	112.2	100.9	114.1	123.1	114.6	134.4	134.0
K	.	.	125.9	148.4	144.3	165.7	163.0	176.9	198.5	198.1
L	.	.	158.4	174.7	174.5	180.0	200.7	186.4	200.1	213.1
M	.	.	298.9	300.5	353.4	375.7	374.3	379.9	401.2	419.7
N	.	.	106.8	113.8	132.5	121.2	132.4	142.9	153.3	167.1
O	.	.	61.6	66.4	75.5	76.6	82.8	85.8	96.7	93.2
P	.	.	164.4	201.0	195.3	192.7	192.5	184.8	176.5	159.3
Q	.	.	0.5	0.9	1.0	0.4	0.4	0.2	0.7	0.2

Pakistan (BA) [2] [3] [4]   **Employees - Salariés - Asalariados**

Total - Total - Total
ISIC 2 - CITI 2 - CIIU 2

	1999	2000	2001	2002	2003	2004	2005	2006	2007	2008
Total	.	.	.	.	.	.	.	17 490	.	.
1	.	.	.	.	.	.	.	1 854	.	.
2	.	.	.	.	.	.	.	40	.	.
3	.	.	.	.	.	.	.	4 331	.	.
4	.	.	.	.	.	.	.	306	.	.
5	.	.	.	.	.	.	.	2 643	.	.
6	.	.	.	.	.	.	.	1 430	.	.
7	.	.	.	.	.	.	.	1 627	.	.
8	.	.	.	.	.	.	.	293	.	.
9	.	.	.	.	.	.	.	4 946	.	.
0	.	.	.	.	.	.	.	18	.	.

Men - Hommes - Hombres
ISIC 2 - CITI 2 - CIIU 2

	1999	2000	2001	2002	2003	2004	2005	2006	2007	2008
Total	.	.	.	.	.	.	.	15 142	.	.
1	.	.	.	.	.	.	.	1 246	.	.
2	.	.	.	.	.	.	.	39	.	.
3	.	.	.	.	.	.	.	3 715	.	.
4	.	.	.	.	.	.	.	304	.	.
5	.	.	.	.	.	.	.	2 611	.	.
6	.	.	.	.	.	.	.	1 400	.	.
7	.	.	.	.	.	.	.	1 605	.	.
8	.	.	.	.	.	.	.	280	.	.
9	.	.	.	.	.	.	.	3 924	.	.
0	.	.	.	.	.	.	.	18	.	.

Women - Femmes - Mujeres
ISIC 2 - CITI 2 - CIIU 2

	1999	2000	2001	2002	2003	2004	2005	2006	2007	2008
Total	.	.	.	.	.	.	.	2 348	.	.
1	.	.	.	.	.	.	.	609	.	.
2	.	.	.	.	.	.	.	1	.	.
3	.	.	.	.	.	.	.	617	.	.
4	.	.	.	.	.	.	.	2	.	.
5	.	.	.	.	.	.	.	32	.	.
6	.	.	.	.	.	.	.	30	.	.
7	.	.	.	.	.	.	.	22	.	.
8	.	.	.	.	.	.	.	14	.	.
9	.	.	.	.	.	.	.	1 022	.	.
0	.	.	.	.	.	.	.	-	.	.

Explanatory notes: see p. 77.

[1] Persons aged 15 to 64 years. [2] Excl. armed forces. [3] Persons aged 10 years and over. [4] July.

Notes explicatives: voir p. 80.

[1] Personnes âgées de 15 à 64 ans. [2] Non compris les forces armées. [3] Personnes âgées de 10 ans et plus. [4] Juillet.

Notas explicativas: véase p. 83.

[1] Personas de 15 a 64 años. [2] Excl. las fuerzas armadas. [3] Personas de 10 años y más. [4] Julio.

Paid employment, by economic activity
Emploi rémunéré, par activité économique
Empleo remunerado, por actividad económica

Thousands — Milliers — Millares

Philippines (BA) [1] [2] — Employees - Salariés - Asalariados

Total - Total - Total
ISIC 2 - CITI 2 - CIIU 2 [3] / ISIC 3 - CITI 3 - CIIU 3

	1999	2000	2001	2002	2003	2004	2005	2006	2007	2008	
Total	13 761	13 925	14 438	14 653	15 354	16 472	16 316	16 673	17 508	17 846	Total
1	2 492	2 482	2 239	2 239	2 349	2 593	2 395	2 510	2 649	2 739	A
2	69	81	302	287	313	340	323	338	343	368	B
3	2 018	1 988	79	80	69	70	67	79	92	98	C
4	132	114	2 072	2 040	2 141	2 278	2 277	2 252	2 284	2 169	D
5	1 381	1 338	116	113	109	117	115	124	130	125	E
6 [4]	1 228	1 285	1 446	1 460	1 526	1 569	1 566	1 561	1 665	1 711	F
7	1 136	1 160	1 531	1 587	1 668	1 858	1 912	1 948	2 021	2 077	G
8	621	627	422	457	505	548	594	616	641	664	H
9 [5]	4 682	4 846	1 202	1 173	1 306	1 450	1 369	1 366	1 438	1 430	I
0	5	5	272	288	288	312	324	324	337	347	J
			398	428	517	572	599	643	722	784	K
			1 378	1 439	1 412	1 490	1 478	1 484	1 551	1 676	L
			908	924	917	929	970	990	1 023	1 061	M
			267	284	313	315	324	311	327	344	N
			607	556	540	558	496	518	545	524	O
			1 198	1 299	1 382	1 473	1 506	1 609	1 740	1 729	P
			4	3	2	1	1	2	2	2	Q

Men - Hommes - Hombres
ISIC 2 - CITI 2 - CIIU 2 [3] / ISIC 3 - CITI 3 - CIIU 3

	1999	2000	2001	2002	2003	2004	2005	2006	2007	2008	
Total	8 645	8 717	8 978	9 022	9 554	10 368	10 130	10 316	10 827	11 093	Total
1	1 929	1 956	1 692	1 691	1 796	2 011	1 851	1 963	2 062	2 144	A
2	66	76	291	281	302	329	313	327	332	356	B
3	1 158	1 132	73	73	64	65	65	75	85	93	C
4	112	95	1 215	1 186	1 253	1 350	1 323	1 313	1 345	1 292	D
5	1 360	1 313	96	95	91	97	98	104	108	107	E
6 [4]	645	649	1 415	1 437	1 496	1 543	1 536	1 535	1 635	1 680	F
7	1 053	1 078	851	878	943	1 040	1 084	1 091	1 138	1 167	G
8	353	354	214	228	252	276	305	316	324	339	H
9 [5]	1 966	2 063	1 124	1 099	1 219	1 353	1 263	1 241	1 297	1 294	I
0	5	4	112	123	127	139	137	140	147	148	J
			258	278	358	399	412	423	480	518	K
			846	891	882	942	932	926	950	1 023	L
			247	228	223	228	233	247	255	266	M
			71	79	71	80	81	83	87	98	N
			292	271	281	310	274	292	319	306	O
			180	184	196	206	226	238	262	262	P
			3	1	1	1	1	1	2	1	Q

Women - Femmes - Mujeres
ISIC 2 - CITI 2 - CIIU 2 [3] / ISIC 3 - CITI 3 - CIIU 3

	1999	2000	2001	2002	2003	2004	2005	2006	2007	2008	
Total	5 116	5 208	5 459	5 631	5 800	6 105	6 187	6 357	6 682	6 754	Total
1	563	527	546	549	553	582	544	547	587	594	A
2	3	5	11	6	11	12	11	11	11	11	B
3	861	856	5	7	5	4	3	4	7	5	C
4	20	20	857	854	889	928	954	939	939	877	D
5	21	25	19	18	18	21	18	20	22	18	E
6 [4]	583	636	30	23	31	26	30	26	30	31	F
7	83	83	680	708	725	819	828	858	884	910	G
8	268	272	207	229	252	273	289	300	317	325	H
9 [5]	2 716	2 783	77	74	87	96	107	126	141	136	I
0	-	1	160	165	161	173	187	184	189	200	J
			141	151	159	173	187	219	242	266	K
			533	548	530	548	547	558	601	653	L
			660	696	694	701	737	744	768	795	M
			197	205	242	236	243	228	241	246	N
			314	285	259	248	223	226	227	218	O
			1 019	1 114	1 187	1 268	1 280	1 371	1 478	1 467	P
			2	2	2	1	1	-	1	-	Q

Philippines (CA) [6] — Employees - Salariés - Asalariados

Total - Total - Total
ISIC 3 - CITI 3 - CIIU 3

	1999	2000	2001	2002	2003	2004	2005	2006	2007	2008
Total	2 823.1	.	2 401.3	.	2 413.7	.	2 727.2	.	.	.
A	111.4	.	95.2	.	96.7	.	104.3	.	.	.
B	21.1	.	17.6	.	18.6	.	20.1	.	.	.
C	14.4	.	11.3	.	10.8	.	10.1	.	.	.
D	1 084.2	.	932.5	.	983.9	.	1 022.1	.	.	.
E	61.2	.	59.7	.	62.0	.	65.9	.	.	.
F	137.1	.	130.7	.	96.5	.	91.9	.	.	.
G	401.0	.	285.5	.	254.5	.	316.4	.	.	.
H	138.8	.	119.1	.	115.7	.	157.2	.	.	.
I	189.7	.	153.6	.	143.8	.	152.6	.	.	.
J	122.8	.	100.2	.	123.1	.	131.7	.	.	.
K	251.8	.	213.9	.	223.4	.	324.8	.	.	.
M [7]	186.7	.	182.2	.	184.9	.	204.6	.	.	.
N [8]	54.8	.	53.6	.	54.3	.	72.5	.	.	.
O	48.0	.	46.2	.	45.5	.	52.9	.	.	.

Explanatory notes: see p. 77.

[1] Persons aged 15 years and over. [2] Excl. regular military living in barracks. [3] Oct. of each year. [4] Excl. restaurants and hotels. [5] Incl. restaurants and hotels. [6] Establishments with 20 or more persons employed. [7] Private education only. [8] Excludes public medical, dental and other health services.

Notes explicatives: voir p. 80.

[1] Personnes âgées de 15 ans et plus. [2] Non compris les militaires de carrière vivant dans des casernes. [3] Oct. de chaque année. [4] Non compris les restaurants et hôtels. [5] Y compris les restaurants et hôtels. [6] Etablissements occupant 20 personnes et plus. [7] Education privée seulement. [8] Non compris les services publics médicaux, dentaires et autres services de santé.

Notas explicativas: véase p. 83.

[1] Personas de 15 años y más. [2] Excl. los militares profesionales que viven en casernas. [3] Oct. de cada año. [4] Excl. restaurantes y hoteles. [5] Incl. restaurantes y hoteles. [6] Establecimientos con 20 y más trabajadores. [7] Educación privada solamente. [8] Excl. los servicios públicos médicos, dentales y otros servicios de salud.

EMPLOYMENT	EMPLOI	EMPLEO
Paid employment, by economic activity	**Emploi rémunéré, par activité économique**	**Empleo remunerado, por actividad económica**
Thousands	Milliers	Millares

	1999	2000	2001	2002	2003	2004	2005	2006	2007	2008
Philippines (CA) [1]					**Employees - Salariés - Asalariados**					
Men - Hommes - Hombres										
ISIC 3 - CITI 3 - CIIU 3										
Total	1 665.3	.	1 402.7	.	1 384.9	.	1 543.8	.	.	.
A	91.8	.	78.4	.	79.0	.	83.0	.	.	.
B	19.9	.	16.6	.	17.5	.	18.7	.	.	.
C	13.2	.	10.4	.	10.0	.	9.4	.	.	.
D	559.4	.	466.7	.	494.7	.	511.0	.	.	.
E	50.2	.	48.6	.	50.5	.	53.9	.	.	.
F	128.8	.	122.7	.	89.9	.	82.1	.	.	.
G	221.0	.	160.8	.	137.7	.	177.6	.	.	.
H	82.7	.	70.4	.	68.9	.	95.5	.	.	.
I	146.5	.	118.8	.	109.4	.	114.9	.	.	.
J	51.2	.	41.9	.	48.8	.	52.1	.	.	.
K	186.7	.	156.4	.	164.9	.	216.0	.	.	.
M [2]	67.3	.	64.2	.	66.7	.	74.2	.	.	.
N [3]	16.4	.	16.4	.	18.0	.	22.4	.	.	.
O	30.3	.	30.3	.	29.0	.	33.1	.	.	.
Women - Femmes - Mujeres										
ISIC 3 - CITI 3 - CIIU 3										
Total	1 157.8	.	998.6	.	1 028.8	.	1 183.4	.	.	.
A	19.6	.	16.8	.	17.7	.	21.4	.	.	.
B	1.2	.	1.0	.	1.1	.	1.5	.	.	.
C	1.1	.	0.9	.	0.7	.	0.7	.	.	.
D	524.9	.	465.7	.	489.2	.	511.1	.	.	.
E	11.0	.	11.1	.	11.5	.	12.0	.	.	.
F	8.3	.	8.0	.	6.7	.	9.8	.	.	.
G	180.1	.	124.7	.	116.8	.	138.8	.	.	.
H	56.1	.	48.8	.	46.7	.	61.7	.	.	.
I	43.2	.	34.8	.	34.5	.	37.7	.	.	.
J	71.6	.	58.3	.	74.3	.	79.5	.	.	.
K	65.1	.	57.5	.	58.5	.	108.7	.	.	.
M [2]	119.5	.	118.0	.	118.1	.	130.5	.	.	.
N [3]	38.4	.	37.1	.	36.3	.	50.1	.	.	.
O	17.7	.	15.9	.	16.5	.	19.8	.	.	.
Qatar (BA) [4]					**Employees - Salariés - Asalariados**					
Total - Total - Total										
ISIC 3 - CITI 3 - CIIU 3										
Total	.	.	.	.	.	.	.	527.1	821.9	.
A	.	.	.	.	.	.	.	12.5	15.9	.
B	.	.	.	.	.	.	.	3.2	3.6	.
C	.	.	.	.	.	.	.	27.3	43.8	.
D	.	.	.	.	.	.	.	62.3	71.5	.
E	.	.	.	.	.	.	.	4.8	5.5	.
F	.	.	.	.	.	.	.	124.8	306.1	.
G	.	.	.	.	.	.	.	68.4	99.5	.
H	.	.	.	.	.	.	.	14.8	16.0	.
I	.	.	.	.	.	.	.	23.5	35.8	.
J	.	.	.	.	.	.	.	6.2	9.0	.
K	.	.	.	.	.	.	.	15.6	27.8	.
L	.	.	.	.	.	.	.	47.6	52.9	.
M	.	.	.	.	.	.	.	23.2	26.3	.
N	.	.	.	.	.	.	.	16.7	21.0	.
O	.	.	.	.	.	.	.	12.1	12.8	.
P	.	.	.	.	.	.	.	62.5	72.8	.
Q	.	.	.	.	.	.	.	1.6	1.7	.
Men - Hommes - Hombres										
ISIC 3 - CITI 3 - CIIU 3										
Total	.	.	.	.	.	.	.	450.0	721.2	.
A	.	.	.	.	.	.	.	12.5	15.9	.
B	.	.	.	.	.	.	.	3.2	3.6	.
C	.	.	.	.	.	.	.	26.0	41.5	.
D	.	.	.	.	.	.	.	61.7	70.6	.
E	.	.	.	.	.	.	.	4.5	5.1	.
F	.	.	.	.	.	.	.	124.0	304.9	.
G	.	.	.	.	.	.	.	66.1	96.1	.
H	.	.	.	.	.	.	.	13.6	13.9	.
I	.	.	.	.	.	.	.	20.7	32.7	.
J	.	.	.	.	.	.	.	4.5	6.4	.
K	.	.	.	.	.	.	.	14.7	26.7	.
L	.	.	.	.	.	.	.	41.3	45.4	.
M	.	.	.	.	.	.	.	7.7	9.5	.
N	.	.	.	.	.	.	.	8.1	8.1	.
O	.	.	.	.	.	.	.	10.1	10.3	.
P	.	.	.	.	.	.	.	29.7	29.0	.
Q	.	.	.	.	.	.	.	1.5	1.5	.

Explanatory notes: see p. 77.

[1] Establishments with 20 or more persons employed. [2] Private education only. [3] Excludes public medical, dental and other health services. [4] Persons aged 15 years and over.

Notes explicatives: voir p. 80.

[1] Etablissements occupant 20 personnes et plus. [2] Education privée seulement. [3] Non compris les services publics médicaux, dentaires et autres services de santé. [4] Personnes âgées de 15 ans et plus.

Notas explicativas: véase p. 83.

[1] Establecimientos con 20 y más trabajadores. [2] Educación privada solamente. [3] Excl. los servicios públicos médicos, dentales y otros servicios de salud. [4] Personas de 15 años y más.

EMPLOYMENT — EMPLOI — EMPLEO   2E

Paid employment, by economic activity
Emploi rémunéré, par activité économique
Empleo remunerado, por actividad económica

	Thousands — Milliers — Millares									
	1999	2000	2001	2002	2003	2004	2005	2006	2007	2008

Qatar (BA) [1]
Employees - Salariés - Asalariados

Women - Femmes - Mujeres
ISIC 3 - CITI 3 - CIIU 3

	1999	2000	2001	2002	2003	2004	2005	2006	2007	2008
Total	.	.	.	.	.	.	.	77.1	100.7	.
C	.	.	.	.	.	.	.	1.3	2.4	.
D	.	.	.	.	.	.	.	0.7	0.9	.
E	.	.	.	.	.	.	.	0.2	0.4	.
F	.	.	.	.	.	.	.	0.8	1.2	.
G	.	.	.	.	.	.	.	2.3	3.4	.
H	.	.	.	.	.	.	.	1.1	2.1	.
I	.	.	.	.	.	.	.	2.8	3.1	.
J	.	.	.	.	.	.	.	1.6	2.6	.
K	.	.	.	.	.	.	.	0.8	1.2	.
L	.	.	.	.	.	.	.	6.4	7.4	.
M	.	.	.	.	.	.	.	15.5	16.8	.
N	.	.	.	.	.	.	.	8.6	12.9	.
O	.	.	.	.	.	.	.	2.0	2.5	.
P	.	.	.	.	.	.	.	32.8	43.8	.
Q	.	.	.	.	.	.	.	0.2	0.2	.

Singapore (BA) [2][3]
Employees - Salariés - Asalariados

Total - Total - Total
ISIC 3 - CITI 3 - CIIU 3 / ISIC 4 - CITI 4 - CIIU 4

ISIC3	1999	2000	2001	2002	2003	2004	2005	2006	2007	2008	ISIC4
Total	1 281.5	.	1 339.3 [4]	1 335.4	1 365.5	1 378.2	.	1 525.5	1 525.9	1 572.8	Total
A-C,E,X	12.0	.	12.6 [4]	11.9	12.7	12.8	.	20.9	19.0	21.7	B,D,E,X
D	309.2	.	291.1 [4]	281.7	285.8	279.7	.	284.5	287.0	293.1	C
F	84.6	.	76.7 [4]	73.7	74.8	70.2	.	74.7	79.9	82.7	F
G	173.1	.	192.5 [4]	197.4	195.9	212.4	.	241.8	219.9	214.1	G
H	74.9	.	78.9 [4]	77.9	82.8	83.8	.	125.2	128.1	134.7	H
I	133.1	.	147.9 [4]	140.2	141.9	138.2	.	102.0	97.8	96.5	I
J	78.0	.	78.9 [4]	80.2	77.6	79.2	.	68.7	80.5	79.0	J
K	143.2	.	171.9 [4]	171.7	176.5	184.0	.	90.5	94.2	105.9	K
L,M	170.9	.	180.3 [4]	189.0	204.8	200.9	.	30.1	28.1	30.2	L
N	41.2	.	49.4 [4]	49.1	52.1	57.6	.	82.4	80.7	92.3	M
O-Q	61.2	.	59.1 [4]	62.7	60.6	59.4	.	71.8	78.6	77.3	N
								208.3	207.4	212.3	O-P
								66.0	64.1	69.4	Q
								58.6	60.6	63.6	R-U

Men - Hommes - Hombres
ISIC 3 - CITI 3 - CIIU 3 / ISIC 4 - CITI 4 - CIIU 4

ISIC3	1999	2000	2001	2002	2003	2004	2005	2006	2007	2008	ISIC4
Total	733.0	.	756.1 [4]	759.0	771.1	771.6	.	842.1	838.1	853.5	Total
A-C,E,X	9.7	.	9.4 [4]	9.5	9.4	10.1	.	15.1	15.2	15.9	B,D,E,X
D	181.3	.	177.6 [4]	170.1	174.3	168.8	.	178.4	175.8	185.2	C
F	68.1	.	61.3 [4]	60.1	59.0	56.6	.	59.0	63.0	64.3	F
G	92.4	.	98.7 [4]	101.6	99.8	109.3	.	117.6	105.6	100.0	G
H	35.7	.	35.5 [4]	36.7	38.4	38.1	.	87.5	90.0	92.3	H
I	91.8	.	100.3 [4]	96.7	96.1	92.0	.	46.7	44.8	40.1	I
J	29.2	.	30.3 [4]	29.9	28.5	29.2	.	39.9	46.2	45.7	J
K	75.7	.	88.1 [4]	91.6	95.6	99.7	.	35.0	36.5	40.9	K
L,M	105.6	.	112.2 [4]	117.0	126.5	125.8	.	14.1	14.3	14.7	L
N	9.0	.	10.0 [4]	10.3	11.2	11.5	.	38.6	38.2	44.0	M
O-Q	34.6	.	32.7 [4]	35.6	32.4	30.5	.	41.1	43.5	42.1	N
								124.6	121.3	122.0	O-P
								14.3	13.5	13.7	Q
								30.1	30.2	32.6	R-U

Women - Femmes - Mujeres
ISIC 3 - CITI 3 - CIIU 3 / ISIC 4 - CITI 4 - CIIU 4

ISIC3	1999	2000	2001	2002	2003	2004	2005	2006	2007	2008	ISIC4
Total	548.5	.	583.3	576.4	594.3	606.6	.	683.3	687.8	719.2	Total
A-C,E,X	2.3	.	3.1	2.4	3.3	2.7	.	5.8	3.8	5.7	B,D,E,X
D	127.9	.	113.6	111.7	111.5	110.8	.	106.1	111.1	108.0	C
F	16.5	.	15.4	13.6	15.8	13.6	.	15.7	16.9	18.4	F
G	80.7	.	93.8	95.8	96.1	103.1	.	124.2	114.4	114.1	G
H	39.2	.	43.4	41.2	44.4	45.7	.	37.6	38.1	42.4	H
I	41.4	.	47.7	43.5	45.7	46.2	.	55.3	53.0	56.3	I
J	48.9	.	48.6	50.2	49.1	50.0	.	28.8	34.3	33.3	J
K	67.5	.	83.8	80.1	80.8	84.3	.	55.4	57.6	65.1	K
L,M	65.3	.	68.0	72.0	78.4	75.2	.	16.0	13.8	15.5	L
N	32.2	.	39.4	38.8	41.0	46.1	.	43.7	42.5	48.3	M
O-Q	26.6	.	26.4	27.1	28.2	28.9	.	30.7	35.1	35.2	N
								83.7	86.1	90.3	O-P
								51.7	50.6	55.7	Q
								28.5	30.5	31.0	R-U

Explanatory notes: see p. 77.

[1] Persons aged 15 years and over. [2] The data refer to the residents (Singapore citizens and permanent residents) aged 15 years and over. [3] June. [4] Methodology revised; data not strictly comparable.

Notes explicatives: voir p. 80.

[1] Personnes âgées de 15 ans et plus. [2] Les données se réfèrent aux résidents (citoyens de Singapour et résidents permanents) âgés de 15 ans et plus. [3] Juin. [4] Méthodologie révisée; les données ne sont pas strictement comparables.

Notas explicativas: véase p. 83.

[1] Personas de 15 años y más. [2] Los datos se refieren a los residentes (ciudadanos de Singapur y residentes permanentes) de 15 años y más. [3] Junio. [4] Metodología revisada; los datos no son estrictamente comparables.

EMPLOYMENT	EMPLOI	EMPLEO
Paid employment, by economic activity	**Emploi rémunéré, par activité économique**	**Empleo remunerado, por actividad económica**
Thousands	Milliers	Millares

	1999	2000	2001	2002	2003	2004	2005	2006	2007	2008
Sri Lanka (BA) [1][2]										
Total - Total - Total										
ISIC 3 - CITI 3 - CIIU 3										
Total				3 775.1	3 819.4	4 004.4	4 036.2	3 949.8	3 976.6	
A-B				687.8	664.8	821.3	698.8	693.7	689.1	
C.E [3]				323.5	287.3	287.3	407.4	439.9	434.4	
D				782.3	796.4	872.0	888.4	904.0	863.7	
G				282.5	265.4	282.2	315.2	327.2	326.6	
H				75.2	69.5	71.5	77.8	70.4	71.9	
I				202.6	229.3	233.9	263.3	247.6	260.0	
J-K				142.5	149.1	139.8	178.4	181.6	181.6	
L				519.3	501.1	473.6	458.8	397.5	432.3	
M				203.7	227.4	210.4	223.7	244.8	230.4	
N				71.0	79.4	82.7	106.8	101.3	103.4	
O.Q				67.1	53.5	59.2	58.0	68.1	62.7	
P				90.4	74.3	66.8	47.9	79.7	86.7	
X				327.2	422.1	403.6	311.6	194.0	233.8	
Men - Hommes - Hombres										
ISIC 3 - CITI 3 - CIIU 3										
Total				2 526.1	2 569.4	2 650.0	2 689.0	2 583.3	2 660.6	
A-B				394.3	361.4	454.4	417.1	375.9	391.5	
C.E [3]				312.4	280.5	279.9	386.2	422.7	418.2	
D				406.9	420.2	461.1	477.8	471.0	470.7	
G				234.9	219.6	235.9	258.7	262.4	265.9	
H				64.1	63.4	62.9	62.4	59.6	59.9	
I				188.9	210.9	215.2	247.6	229.0	243.2	
J-K				90.4	101.5	94.1	129.4	122.6	122.7	
L				382.7	374.5	345.5	336.5	293.2	307.4	
M				61.4	84.3	73.1	62.6	74.7	70.8	
N				25.8	32.3	26.3	43.5	40.5	40.2	
O.Q				55.1	42.9	41.6	39.8	49.0	47.9	
P				27.5	22.8	19.9	6.1	15.7	26.8	
X				281.7	355.1	340.3	221.4	167.0	195.4	
Women - Femmes - Mujeres										
ISIC 3 - CITI 3 - CIIU 3										
Total				1 249.1	1 250.0	1 354.4	1 347.2	1 366.4	1 316.0	
A-B				293.5	303.4	366.9	281.7	317.8	297.6	
C.E [3]				11.0	6.8	7.4	21.2	17.2	16.2	
D				375.4	376.1	410.9	410.6	433.0	393.0	
G				47.6	45.8	46.3	56.5	64.8	60.7	
H				11.1	6.0	8.6	15.4	10.8	11.9	
I				13.7	18.5	18.7	15.8	18.6	16.8	
J-K				52.1	47.6	45.8	49.0	59.0	58.9	
L				136.5	126.6	128.0	122.3	104.2	124.9	
M				142.3	143.0	137.3	161.1	170.1	159.5	
N				45.2	47.1	56.4	63.4	60.7	63.2	
O.Q				12.0	10.6	17.7	18.2	19.2	14.8	
P				62.9	51.5	47.0	41.9	64.0	59.8	
X				42.9	67.0	63.4	90.2	27.0	38.4	
Sri Lanka (DA) [4][5]										
Total - Total - Total										
ISIC 3 - CITI 3 - CIIU 3										
Total	866.3	1 030.2	1 006.6	821.6	917.1	823.4	896.4	787.1	916.1	
A-B	315.4	294.4	243.7	233.5	247.0	241.2	240.2	220.1	189.1	
C	3.5	3.3	3.4	2.8	4.1	2.5	3.9	4.6	4.7	
D	264.7	402.3	405.7	250.8	329.4	259.9	298.8	243.9	392.4	
E	18.8	17.0	19.5	15.8	16.8	14.4	17.6	16.3	18.9	
F	10.7	15.4	20.9	15.0	16.5	16.5	23.2	23.8	19.5	
G-H	69.5	72.6	82.8	68.4	70.6	73.1	84.6	74.1	83.2	
I	67.2	75.4	76.8	86.1	71.8	74.0	71.0	53.9	52.5	
J-K	63.3	60.2	66.9	69.2	66.5	57.6	62.2	56.7	63.7	
N-O	53.2	89.6	86.9	80.0	94.9	84.2	94.9	93.7	92.1	
Men - Hommes - Hombres										
ISIC 3 - CITI 3 - CIIU 3										
Total	472.1	534.8	531.7	483.2	489.4	462.3	508.7	442.6	483.7	
A-B	148.0	137.2	115.2	114.6	119.4	114.8	113.9	102.6	86.2	
C	3.1	3.0	2.9	2.4	1.9	2.1	3.4	3.8	3.8	
D	103.0	140.2	147.0	111.1	121.8	103.4	130.0	105.9	155.1	
E	17.3	15.6	17.5	14.7	15.1	13.3	16.1	14.8	17.0	
F	9.7	12.8	16.7	11.6	13.4	14.5	20.5	19.9	17.0	
G-H	49.0	52.0	57.1	47.8	49.6	50.4	55.1	49.7	57.3	
I	63.0	69.3	70.7	79.7	65.1	68.5	64.3	47.9	46.2	
J-K	42.2	42.1	45.6	47.6	44.7	38.8	41.2	37.8	40.5	
N-O	36.8	62.6	59.0	53.8	57.9	56.5	64.2	60.2	60.6	

Explanatory notes: see p. 77.

[1] Persons aged 10 years and over. [2] Excl. Northern and Eastern provinces. [3] Incl. construction. [4] Establishments with 5 or more persons employed. [5] June of each year.

Notes explicatives: voir p. 80.

[1] Personnes âgées de 10 ans et plus. [2] Non compris les provinces du Nord et de l'Est. [3] Y compris la construction. [4] Etablissements occupant 5 personnes et plus. [5] Juin de chaque année.

Notas explicativas: véase p. 83.

[1] Personas de 10 años y más. [2] Excl. las provincias del Norte y del Este. [3] Incl. construcción. [4] Establecimientos con 5 y más trabajadores. [5] Junio de cada año.

Paid employment, by economic activity   Emploi rémunéré, par activité économique   Empleo remunerado, por actividad económica

Thousands   Milliers   Millares

	1999	2000	2001	2002	2003	2004	2005	2006	2007	2008
Sri Lanka (DA) [1][2]				**Employees - Salariés - Asalariados**						
Women - Femmes - Mujeres										
ISIC 3 - CITI 3 - CIIU 3										
Total	394.2	495.5	474.8	338.4	428.2	361.1	387.7	344.5	432.2	.
A-B	167.3	157.2	128.5	118.9	127.6	126.4	126.3	117.5	102.9	.
C	0.3	0.4	0.5	0.4	1.9	0.4	0.5	0.8	0.8	.
D	161.9	262.1	258.7	139.8	207.6	156.5	168.8	138.0	237.3	.
E	1.4	1.4	2.0	1.2	1.7	1.1	1.5	1.5	1.9	.
F	1.0	2.5	4.2	3.4	3.1	2.0	2.7	3.9	2.4	.
G-H	20.5	20.7	25.7	20.7	20.9	22.8	29.5	24.4	25.9	.
I	4.2	6.1	6.1	6.5	6.7	5.5	6.7	6.0	6.3	.
J-K	21.1	18.1	21.3	21.5	21.8	18.8	21.1	18.9	23.3	.
N-O	16.5	27.0	27.9	26.2	37.0	27.6	30.6	33.5	31.4	.
Syrian Arab Republic (BA) [3]				**Employees - Salariés - Asalariados**						
Total - Total - Total										
ISIC 3 - CITI 3 - CIIU 3										
Total	.	.	.	.	.	.	.	.	2 658.1	.
A-B	.	.	.	.	.	.	.	.	143.4	.
C	.	.	.	.	.	.	.	.	26.6	.
D	.	.	.	.	.	.	.	.	407.1	.
E	.	.	.	.	.	.	.	.	32.2	.
F	.	.	.	.	.	.	.	.	412.7	.
G	.	.	.	.	.	.	.	.	185.7	.
H	.	.	.	.	.	.	.	.	38.7	.
I	.	.	.	.	.	.	.	.	163.4	.
J	.	.	.	.	.	.	.	.	9.8	.
K	.	.	.	.	.	.	.	.	41.2	.
L	.	.	.	.	.	.	.	.	643.3	.
M	.	.	.	.	.	.	.	.	379.6	.
N	.	.	.	.	.	.	.	.	89.8	.
O-Q	.	.	.	.	.	.	.	.	84.6	.
X	.	.	.	.	.	.	.	.	0.3	.
Men - Hommes - Hombres										
ISIC 3 - CITI 3 - CIIU 3										
Total	.	.	.	.	.	.	.	.	2 224.1	.
A-B	.	.	.	.	.	.	.	.	118.8	.
C	.	.	.	.	.	.	.	.	24.4	.
D	.	.	.	.	.	.	.	.	379.8	.
E	.	.	.	.	.	.	.	.	29.9	.
F	.	.	.	.	.	.	.	.	408.8	.
G	.	.	.	.	.	.	.	.	176.1	.
H	.	.	.	.	.	.	.	.	37.5	.
I	.	.	.	.	.	.	.	.	154.8	.
J	.	.	.	.	.	.	.	.	6.3	.
K	.	.	.	.	.	.	.	.	33.3	.
L	.	.	.	.	.	.	.	.	561.1	.
M	.	.	.	.	.	.	.	.	178.3	.
N	.	.	.	.	.	.	.	.	41.5	.
O-Q	.	.	.	.	.	.	.	.	73.2	.
X	.	.	.	.	.	.	.	.	0.3	.
Women - Femmes - Mujeres										
ISIC 3 - CITI 3 - CIIU 3										
Total	.	.	.	.	.	.	.	.	434.0	.
A-B	.	.	.	.	.	.	.	.	24.6	.
C	.	.	.	.	.	.	.	.	2.2	.
D	.	.	.	.	.	.	.	.	27.3	.
E	.	.	.	.	.	.	.	.	2.3	.
F	.	.	.	.	.	.	.	.	3.9	.
G	.	.	.	.	.	.	.	.	9.6	.
H	.	.	.	.	.	.	.	.	1.1	.
I	.	.	.	.	.	.	.	.	8.6	.
J	.	.	.	.	.	.	.	.	3.5	.
K	.	.	.	.	.	.	.	.	7.9	.
L	.	.	.	.	.	.	.	.	82.2	.
M	.	.	.	.	.	.	.	.	201.3	.
N	.	.	.	.	.	.	.	.	48.2	.
O-Q	.	.	.	.	.	.	.	.	11.4	.
X	.	.	.	.	.	.	.	.	-	.

Explanatory notes: see p. 77.

[1] Establishments with 5 or more persons employed. [2] June of each year. [3] Persons aged 15 years and over.

Notes explicatives: voir p. 80.

[1] Etablissements occupant 5 personnes et plus. [2] Juin de chaque année. [3] Personnes âgées de 15 ans et plus.

Notas explicativas: véase p. 83.

[1] Establecimientos con 5 y más trabajadores. [2] Junio de cada año. [3] Personas de 15 años y más.

	EMPLOYMENT	EMPLOI	EMPLEO
	Paid employment, by economic activity	**Emploi rémunéré, par activité économique**	**Empleo remunerado, por actividad económica**
	Thousands	Milliers	Millares

	1999	2000	2001	2002	2003	2004	2005	2006	2007	2008	

Taiwan, China (DA) — Employees - Salariés - Asalariados

Total - Total - Total
ISIC 2 - CITI 2 - CIIU 2 — ISIC 3 - CITI 3 - CIIU 3

	1999	2000	2001	2002	2003	2004	2005	2006	2007	2008	
Total	5 770.818	5 811.462	5 680.136	5 598.463	5 665.225	5 832.909	5 939.235	6 037.923			Total
2	10.863	9.841	8.701	7.934	7.347	6.855	6.284	5.946			C
3	2 417.019	2 466.847	2 355.995	2 307.029	2 345.600	2 420.106	2 429.902	2 457.691			D
4	36.114	36.323	35.974	35.174	35.138	34.286	33.768	33.716			E
5	484.211	462.544	446.748	389.738	378.914	379.144	389.761	396.526			F
6	1 387.156	1 396.068	1 427.564	1 366.092	1 378.750	1 410.790	1 452.097	1 479.000			G
7	332.363	330.359	330.093	143.993	141.520	151.555	157.242	163.423			H
8	673.028	681.626	662.788	326.410	322.004	323.327	321.299	320.601			I
9	430.064	427.854	412.273	341.514	347.947	359.532	370.172	368.905			J
				69.422	69.213	73.354	77.785	82.380			K
				171.826	181.372	196.024	208.983	218.681			M
				184.336	189.660	197.581	204.025	210.689			N
				84.905	82.942	82.364	81.563	81.496			O
				170.090	184.818	197.991	206.354	218.869			X

United Arab Emirates (BA) [1][2] — Employees - Salariés - Asalariados

Total - Total - Total
ISIC 3 - CITI 3 - CIIU 3

	1999	2000	2001	2002	2003	2004	2005	2006	2007	2008
Total										1 768.897
A										71.768
B										5.699
C										35.663
D										150.162
E										24.919
F										217.347
G										274.774
H										70.453
I										124.854
J										57.965
K										137.054
L										169.874
M										83.517
N										47.794
O										53.402
P										236.390
Q										3.826
X										3.436

Men - Hommes - Hombres
ISIC 3 - CITI 3 - CIIU 3

	2008
Total	1 427.549
A	71.279
B	5.553
C	32.970
D	139.173
E	23.204
F	208.740
G	253.433
H	62.046
I	111.254
J	40.517
K	122.591
L	153.779
M	37.945
N	23.726
O	45.247
P	90.394
Q	2.881
X	2.817

Women - Femmes - Mujeres
ISIC 3 - CITI 3 - CIIU 3

	2008
Total	341.348
A	0.489
B	0.146
C	2.693
D	10.989
E	1.715
F	8.607
G	21.341
H	8.407
I	13.600
J	17.448
K	14.463
L	16.095
M	45.572
N	24.068
O	8.155
P	145.996
Q	0.945
X	0.619

Explanatory notes: see p. 77.   Notes explicatives: voir p. 80.   Notas explicativas: véase p. 83.

[1] February. [2] Persons aged 15 years and over.   [1] Février. [2] Personnes âgées de 15 ans et plus.   [1] Febrero. [2] Personas de 15 años y más.

Paid employment, by economic activity

Emploi rémunéré, par activité économique

Empleo remunerado, por actividad económica

	Thousands			Milliers				Millares		
	1999	2000	2001	2002	2003	2004	2005	2006	2007	2008

West Bank and Gaza Strip (BA) [1]   Employees - Salariés - Asalariados

Total - Total - Total
ISIC 3 - CITI 3 - CIIU 3

	1999	2000	2001	2002	2003	2004	2005	2006	2007	2008
Total	398.742	395.484	313.330 [2]	282.044	322.960	336.792	376.176	395.129	397.915	422.607
A	17.908	16.483	8.514 [2]	10.244	11.850	10.264	13.930	16.047	13.353	13.598
B	0.008	-	- [2]	0.040	0.042	0.014	0.089	-	0.187	-
C	1.836	1.128	0.985 [2]	0.989	1.055	1.284	0.999	1.353	1.092	1.168
D	65.265	59.971	45.171 [2]	37.933	42.676	45.096	51.092	50.396	49.867	-
E	1.364	1.334	1.223 [2]	1.005	1.036	1.889	2.171	2.351	2.178	2.544
F	107.365	96.717	52.728 [2]	38.010	53.457	46.090	54.851	50.002	53.562	57.386
G	29.037	30.553	25.989 [2]	21.706	26.343	28.903	32.207	34.259	35.620	37.333
H	12.126	10.519	7.170 [2]	5.422	6.005	6.985	8.305	8.960	9.860	16.750
I	11.744	12.111	9.592 [2]	7.231	9.363	9.778	11.977	13.302	12.325	13.303
J	3.688	4.430	4.019 [2]	3.875	3.622	3.994	2.940	3.998	3.811	-
K	4.752	5.550	4.223 [2]	5.031	4.991	5.237	6.102	7.134	5.798	8.751
L	65.022	70.985	70.229 [2]	66.339	67.876	77.931	92.776	98.741	99.416	101.599
M	47.563	52.719	51.878 [2]	50.188	56.466	59.197	58.773	66.217	65.939	69.303
N	16.870	17.595	17.618 [2]	18.301	19.969	21.920	20.775	22.268	22.453	25.661
O	11.347	12.128	9.686 [2]	10.468	11.630	10.751	11.974	12.694	14.874	14.479
P	0.252	0.358	0.569 [2]	0.286	0.342	0.133	0.030	0.157	0.170	-
Q	2.557	2.439	3.596 [2]	4.801	6.101	7.325	7.186	7.221	7.411	6.449
X	0.040	0.466	0.137 [2]	0.175	0.045	-	-	0.030	-	54.283

Men - Hommes - Hombres
ISIC 3 - CITI 3 - CIIU 3

	1999	2000	2001	2002	2003	2004	2005	2006	2007	2008
Total	349.894	343.374	263.964 [2]	234.438	269.604	277.389	316.802	328.933	331.360	348.497
A	17.148	15.914	7.901 [2]	9.351	11.274	9.718	13.176	15.172	12.704	13.001
B	0.008	-	- [2]	0.040	0.042	0.014	0.089	-	0.187	-
C	1.813	1.107	0.985 [2]	0.989	1.055	1.284	0.999	1.353	1.092	1.151
D	58.116	52.696	39.577 [2]	33.527	37.902	39.703	45.846	44.888	42.643	-
E	1.364	1.334	1.118 [2]	0.885	0.924	1.847	2.087	2.227	2.178	2.474
F	106.816	96.445	52.158 [2]	37.837	53.466	45.948	54.593	49.796	53.313	56.990
G	27.672	28.811	24.418 [2]	20.653	24.829	26.620	29.885	31.531	33.290	34.934
H	11.733	9.964	6.895 [2]	5.361	5.901	6.888	8.204	8.842	9.564	16.092
I	11.016	11.455	9.292 [2]	6.984	8.941	9.132	11.380	12.253	11.896	12.555
J	2.795	3.096	2.438 [2]	2.772	2.861	2.913	2.174	2.852	2.905	-
K	3.594	3.843	2.875 [2]	4.059	3.566	3.421	4.626	5.047	4.490	6.735
L	59.876	66.045	65.504 [2]	61.027	62.490	71.871	87.363	92.504	92.451	94.238
M	25.702	29.465	28.100 [2]	26.684	29.793	30.686	29.736	33.332	33.107	31.804
N	10.310	10.858	11.424 [2]	11.249	12.631	13.716	12.072	13.489	14.406	15.435
O	9.842	10.121	8.130 [2]	9.140	8.901	8.070	9.373	10.255	11.975	11.215
P	0.121	0.105	0.062 [2]	0.027	0.088	0.037	-	0.103	0.036	-
Q	1.937	1.732	2.991 [2]	3.711	4.918	5.520	5.200	5.259	5.122	4.634
X	0.032	0.385	0.096 [2]	0.140	0.021	-	-	0.030	-	47.239

Women - Femmes - Mujeres
ISIC 3 - CITI 3 - CIIU 3

	1999	2000	2001	2002	2003	2004	2005	2006	2007	2008
Total	48.848	52.110	49.366 [2]	47.606	53.356	59.403	59.374	66.196	66.555	74.110
A	0.760	0.569	0.613 [2]	0.893	0.575	0.546	0.754	0.874	0.649	0.597
B	-	-	- [2]	-	-	-	-	-	-	-
C	0.023	0.022	- [2]	-	-	-	-	-	-	0.016
D	7.148	7.275	5.594 [2]	4.406	4.774	5.393	5.245	5.509	7.224	-
E	-	-	0.105 [2]	0.121	0.112	0.041	0.084	0.124	-	0.070
F	0.549	0.272	0.570 [2]	0.173	0.081	0.142	0.258	0.206	0.248	0.395
G	1.364	1.742	1.571 [2]	1.053	1.514	2.283	2.322	2.728	2.330	2.399
H	0.393	0.555	0.275 [2]	0.061	0.104	0.097	0.101	0.118	0.295	0.658
I	0.728	0.656	0.301 [2]	0.247	0.422	0.646	0.597	1.049	0.429	0.748
J	0.892	1.334	1.581 [2]	1.103	0.761	1.081	0.767	1.145	0.906	-
K	1.158	1.708	1.348 [2]	0.972	1.424	1.817	1.476	2.087	1.308	2.016
L	5.146	4.939	4.726 [2]	5.312	5.386	6.060	5.414	6.237	6.965	7.362
M	21.861	23.253	23.778 [2]	23.503	26.674	28.512	29.037	32.885	32.832	37.499
N	6.560	6.737	6.194 [2]	7.052	7.338	8.203	8.703	8.779	8.047	10.226
O	1.505	2.006	1.556 [2]	1.328	2.728	2.681	2.600	2.439	2.899	3.264
P	0.131	0.253	0.507 [2]	0.259	0.254	0.096	0.030	0.054	0.134	-
Q	0.620	0.707	0.605 [2]	1.089	1.183	1.805	1.985	1.962	2.289	1.815
X	0.009	0.081	0.042 [2]	0.035	0.024	-	-	-	-	7.045

EUROPE-EUROPE-EUROPA

Albania (CA)   Employees - Salariés - Asalariados

Total - Total - Total
ISIC 3 - CITI 3 - CIIU 3

	1999	2000	2001	2002	2003	2004	2005	2006	2007	2008
Total	105.922	101.168	97.897	102.706	104.018	111.580	120.419	.	.	.
B	0.257	0.126	0.221	0.112	0.135	0.214	0.195	.	.	.
C	9.667	8.495	6.053	6.081	5.808	5.615	5.652	.	.	.
D	30.814	32.328	30.674	34.774	37.030	38.161	37.613	.	.	.
E	15.776	15.286	17.251	14.943	13.392	13.045	13.775	.	.	.
F	11.484	10.182	10.566	11.328	12.924	15.244	19.828	.	.	.
G	9.900	8.487	8.083	9.025	9.733	12.544	15.014	.	.	.
H,J-Q	12.160	12.027	10.648	13.382	12.496	14.846	16.516	.	.	.
I	15.864	14.237	14.401	13.061	12.600	11.911	11.826	.	.	.

Explanatory notes: see p. 77.	Notes explicatives: voir p. 80.	Notas explicativas: véase p. 83.
[1] Persons aged 15 years and over. [2] Prior to 2001: persons aged 10 years and over.	[1] Personnes âgées de 15 ans et plus. [2] Avant 2001: personnes agées de 10 ans et plus.	[1] Personas de 15 años y más. [2] Antes de 2001: personas de 10 años y más.

| Paid employment, by economic activity | Emploi rémunéré, par activité économique | Empleo remunerado, por actividad económica |

Thousands				Milliers			Millares		
1999	2000	2001	2002	2003	2004	2005	2006	2007	2008

Andorre (FA)

Employees - Salariés - Asalariados

Total - Total - Total
ISIC 3 - CITI 3 - CIIU 3

	1999	2000	2001	2002	2003	2004	2005	2006	2007	2008
Total	32.587	34.494	36.193	37.515	39.374 [1]	41.087	42.416	43.380	43.240	.
A	0.172	0.161	0.143	0.132	0.134 [1]	0.139	0.138	0.145	0.147	.
D	1.372	1.367	1.368	1.388	1.573 [1]	1.629	1.710	1.758	1.730	.
E	0.133	0.130	0.141	0.132	0.156 [1]	0.156	0.160	0.160	0.159	.
F	4.917	5.247	5.451	5.645	5.862 [1]	6.282	6.747	6.908	6.682	.
G	9.283	9.820	10.117	10.375	11.087 [1]	11.261	11.404	11.454	11.316	.
H	4.701	4.876	5.144	5.370	5.393 [1]	5.606	5.648	5.670	5.523	.
I	1.038	1.105	1.160	1.215	1.496 [1]	1.277	1.271	1.295	1.300	.
J	1.356	1.439	1.546	1.538	1.455 [1]	1.446	1.510	1.559	1.609	.
K	2.215	2.460	2.864	3.105	3.334 [1]	3.613	3.757	4.147	4.215	.
L	2.957	3.118	3.267	3.453	3.620 [1]	3.831	4.030	4.332	4.452	.
M	0.441	0.484	0.520	0.555	0.565 [1]	0.592	0.610	0.632	0.670	.
N	0.769	0.853	0.931	0.980	1.182 [1]	1.232	1.302	1.374	1.431	.
O	1.709	1.843	1.898	1.962	1.946 [1]	2.295	2.352	2.450	2.441	.
P	1.102	1.141	1.136	1.148	1.101 [1]	1.206	1.245	1.262	1.334	.
Q	0.007	0.008	0.009	0.009	0.007 [1]	0.008	0.009	0.009	0.010	.
X	0.416	0.441	0.498	0.508	0.463 [1]	0.514	0.523	0.225	0.217	.

Men - Hommes - Hombres
ISIC 3 - CITI 3 - CIIU 3

	1999	2000	2001	2002	2003	2004	2005	2006	2007	2008
Total	.	.	.	.	21.420	22.304	22.989	23.385	23.088	.
A	.	.	.	.	0.081	0.088	0.086	0.088	0.093	.
D	.	.	.	.	1.050	1.073	1.130	1.162	1.140	.
E	.	.	.	.	0.121	0.121	0.124	0.124	0.122	.
F	.	.	.	.	5.392	5.764	6.170	6.321	6.099	.
G	.	.	.	.	5.414	5.513	5.538	5.530	5.468	.
H	.	.	.	.	2.558	2.614	2.597	2.578	2.519	.
I	.	.	.	.	1.018	0.848	0.844	0.851	0.852	.
J	.	.	.	.	0.866	0.836	0.856	0.874	0.865	.
K	.	.	.	.	1.671	1.803	1.892	2.055	2.085	.
L	.	.	.	.	1.699	1.791	1.867	2.009	2.049	.
M	.	.	.	.	0.150	0.151	0.151	0.156	0.161	.
N	.	.	.	.	0.241	0.254	0.270	0.281	0.300	.
O	.	.	.	.	0.961	1.201	1.201	1.224	1.186	.
P	.	.	.	.	0.090	0.138	0.155	0.096	0.116	.
Q	.	.	.	.	0.003	0.004	0.004	0.004	0.004	.
X	.	.	.	.	0.105	0.106	0.104	0.033	0.028	.

Women - Femmes - Mujeres
ISIC 3 - CITI 3 - CIIU 3

	1999	2000	2001	2002	2003	2004	2005	2006	2007	2008
Total	.	.	.	.	17.951	18.781	19.427	19.996	20.147	.
A	.	.	.	.	0.052	0.051	0.052	0.057	0.054	.
D	.	.	.	.	0.523	0.557	0.580	0.596	0.590	.
E	.	.	.	.	0.035	0.035	0.036	0.036	0.037	.
F	.	.	.	.	0.469	0.519	0.577	0.588	0.583	.
G	.	.	.	.	5.673	5.747	5.866	5.925	5.848	.
H	.	.	.	.	2.835	2.992	3.051	3.092	3.005	.
I	.	.	.	.	0.478	0.428	0.428	0.444	0.447	.
J	.	.	.	.	0.589	0.609	0.654	0.685	0.744	.
K	.	.	.	.	1.664	1.810	1.865	2.092	2.130	.
L	.	.	.	.	1.921	2.040	2.164	2.323	2.403	.
M	.	.	.	.	0.414	0.441	0.458	0.476	0.509	.
N	.	.	.	.	0.941	0.978	1.033	1.093	1.130	.
O	.	.	.	.	0.985	1.093	1.151	1.226	1.254	.
P	.	.	.	.	1.011	1.068	1.090	1.166	1.218	.
Q	.	.	.	.	0.004	0.004	0.006	0.005	0.005	.
X	.	.	.	.	0.357	0.408	0.416	0.192	0.189	.

Austria (BA) [2] [3]

Employees - Salariés - Asalariados

Total - Total - Total
ISIC 3 - CITI 3 - CIIU 3

	1999	2000	2001	2002	2003	2004	2005	2006	2007	2008
Total	.	.	3 301.2	3 338.1	3 318.2	3 266.5 [4]	3 317.1	3 396.7	3 450.2	3 528.0
A	.	.	36.4	41.7	45.8	36.1 [4]	32.8	37.0	38.2	36.2
B	.	.	-	0.1	0.3	1.1 [4]	-	0.2	0.2	0.5
C	.	.	9.2	8.1	6.1	8.3 [4]	8.6	9.4	8.5	10.4
D	.	.	709.8	711.8	698.3	656.3 [4]	667.6	701.2	688.7	659.6
E	.	.	31.3	35.0	34.5	27.8 [4]	31.0	31.1	29.5	25.1
F	.	.	314.2	315.1	314.8	276.3 [4]	283.4	295.4	297.9	302.7
G	.	.	528.6	531.2	528.6	533.9 [4]	531.5	544.2	576.0	594.5
H	.	.	163.5	170.5	172.6	186.2 [4]	198.4	194.2	202.1	199.7
I	.	.	238.3	234.7	225.5	224.6 [4]	226.6	222.6	227.2	228.9
J	.	.	126.4	127.6	128.2	132.2 [4]	134.4	125.7	129.0	135.1
K	.	.	238.3	243.3	245.2	260.2 [4]	268.0	275.9	283.5	318.6
L	.	.	258.3	248.4	237.2	252.4 [4]	238.6	253.0	275.4	278.3
M	.	.	218.1	222.7	225.1	204.2 [4]	215.5	216.4	203.4	220.8
N	.	.	285.6	300.1	301.5	300.3 [4]	322.3	319.1	313.2	334.1
O	.	.	126.0	131.1	136.4	150.3 [4]	141.3	155.7	163.3	165.4
P	.	.	12.6	13.3	13.6	8.2 [4]	8.9	9.6	7.5	11.0
Q	.	.	4.6	3.5	4.5	8.1 [4]	8.2	6.1	6.3	7.2

Explanatory notes: see p. 77.

[1] Prior to 2003: January. [2] Excl. conscripts on compulsory military service. [3] Persons aged 15 years and over. [4] Prior to 2004: incl. conscripts.

Notes explicatives: voir p. 80.

[1] Avant 2003: janvier. [2] Non compris conscrits ceux du contingent. [3] Personnes âgées de 15 ans et plus. [4] Avant 2004: y compris les conscrits.

Notas explicativas: véase p. 83.

[1] Antes de 2003: enero. [2] Excl. los conscriptos del servicio obligatorio. [3] Personas de 15 años y más. [4] Antes de 2004: incl. los conscriptos.

Paid employment,
by economic activity

Emploi rémunéré,
par activité économique

Empleo remunerado,
por actividad económica

	Thousands				Milliers				Millares		
	1999	2000	2001	2002	2003	2004	2005	2006	2007	2008

Austria (BA) [1] [2]   **Employees - Salariés - Asalariados**

Men - Hommes - Hombres
ISIC 3 - CITI 3 - CIIU 3

	1999	2000	2001	2002	2003	2004	2005	2006	2007	2008
Total	.	.	1 845.2	1 840.6	1 813.2	1 757.5 [3]	1 775.7	1 818.0	1 853.9	1 874.1
A	.	.	22.7	25.6	29.3	21.0 [3]	21.2	23.4	22.4	22.7
B	.	.	-	-	0.3	0.2 [3]	-	0.2	0.2	0.4
C	.	.	8.4	7.3	5.3	7.4 [3]	7.3	8.0	7.3	8.1
D	.	.	524.8	529.2	515.9	479.9 [3]	493.2	515.6	510.2	485.4
E	.	.	26.7	30.3	30.1	23.6 [3]	25.2	25.4	23.6	20.4
F	.	.	286.9	288.3	290.6	243.1 [3]	249.5	260.0	259.7	260.2
G	.	.	224.4	222.6	215.3	236.9 [3]	225.6	228.6	258.4	261.8
H	.	.	53.4	56.4	53.5	60.6 [3]	66.5	62.4	62.4	63.8
I	.	.	181.6	177.6	170.1	169.3 [3]	166.7	166.7	163.9	170.0
J	.	.	62.2	61.4	60.8	61.6 [3]	63.7	61.4	63.3	65.0
K	.	.	103.2	104.0	111.2	113.6 [3]	118.2	123.1	129.6	152.3
L	.	.	163.9	155.4	146.6	145.6 [3]	136.7	144.4	155.3	156.1
M	.	.	68.1	63.6	62.1	62.1 [3]	65.4	64.3	57.3	65.4
N	.	.	62.5	62.1	62.5	63.2 [3]	74.2	65.6	66.0	70.1
O	.	.	54.1	54.9	57.1	64.1 [3]	57.7	65.0	70.3	69.5
P	.	.	0.8	0.2	0.4	0.3 [3]	0.4	0.4	0.5	0.4
Q	.	.	1.7	1.6	1.9	4.4 [3]	4.2	3.4	3.5	2.5

Women - Femmes - Mujeres
ISIC 3 - CITI 3 - CIIU 3

	1999	2000	2001	2002	2003	2004	2005	2006	2007	2008
Total	.	.	1 456.1	1 497.5	1 505.0	1 509.0 [3]	1 541.1	1 578.6	1 596.2	1 653.9
A	.	.	13.7	16.1	16.5	15.1 [3]	11.6	13.6	15.8	13.5
B	.	.	-	0.1	-	0.9 [3]	-	-	-	0.1
C	.	.	0.8	0.7	0.8	0.9 [3]	1.3	1.4	1.1	2.2
D	.	.	185.0	182.7	182.4	176.3 [3]	174.3	185.6	178.5	174.2
E	.	.	4.6	4.7	4.4	4.3 [3]	5.7	5.7	5.9	4.7
F	.	.	27.2	26.8	24.2	33.2 [3]	33.9	35.4	38.2	42.5
G	.	.	304.2	308.6	313.3	297.0 [3]	305.9	315.5	317.7	332.6
H	.	.	110.2	114.1	119.1	125.6 [3]	131.9	131.9	139.7	135.9
I	.	.	56.7	57.1	55.3	55.4 [3]	59.9	55.9	63.4	58.9
J	.	.	64.2	66.2	67.4	70.6 [3]	70.7	64.3	65.7	70.1
K	.	.	135.2	139.3	134.0	146.6 [3]	149.8	152.7	154.0	166.4
L	.	.	94.4	93.0	90.6	106.8 [3]	101.9	108.6	120.1	122.2
M	.	.	150.0	159.1	162.9	142.2 [3]	150.1	152.0	146.1	155.4
N	.	.	223.1	238.0	239.0	237.1 [3]	248.1	253.5	247.1	264.0
O	.	.	72.0	76.2	79.3	86.3 [3]	83.5	90.7	93.0	95.9
P	.	.	11.8	13.1	13.2	7.9 [3]	8.5	9.2	7.0	10.6
Q	.	.	2.9	1.9	2.6	3.6 [3]	4.0	2.7	2.9	4.6

Austria (DA) [2] [4]   **Employees - Salariés - Asalariados**

Total - Total - Total
ISIC 3 - CITI 3 - CIIU 3

	1999	2000	2001	2002	2003	2004	2005	2006	2007	2008
D	526.998	530.918	531.380	520.494	522.185	526.493	526.095	550.542	.	.
E	30.022	28.800	27.785	27.596	27.401	27.366	27.857	27.634	.	.
F	174.197	171.904	162.786	159.167	164.314	162.291	160.584	183.420	.	.

Men - Hommes - Hombres
ISIC 3 - CITI 3 - CIIU 3

	1999	2000	2001	2002	2003	2004	2005	2006	2007	2008
D	388.737	389.326	390.384	384.950	387.728	391.299	393.170	411.789	.	.
E	25.845	24.692	23.639	23.473	23.351	23.234	23.623	23.311	.	.
F	157.873	155.081	146.344	143.271	147.255	145.192	143.611	163.553	.	.

Women - Femmes - Mujeres
ISIC 3 - CITI 3 - CIIU 3

	1999	2000	2001	2002	2003	2004	2005	2006	2007	2008
D	138.261	141.592	140.996	135.544	134.457	135.194	132.925	138.753	.	.
E	4.177	4.108	4.146	4.123	4.050	4.132	4.234	4.323	.	.
F	16.324	16.823	16.442	15.896	17.059	17.099	16.973	19.867	.	.

Explanatory notes: see p. 77.

[1] Excl. conscripts on compulsory military service. [2] Persons aged 15 years and over. [3] Prior to 2004: incl. conscripts. [4] 31st Dec. of each year.

Notes explicatives: voir p. 80.

[1] Non compris conscrits ceux du contingent. [2] Personnes âgées de 15 ans et plus. [3] Avant 2004: y compris les conscrits. [4] 31 déc. de chaque année.

Notas explicativas: véase p. 83.

[1] Excl. los conscriptos del servicio obligatorio. [2] Personas de 15 años y más. [3] Antes de 2004: incl. los conscriptos. [4] 31 dic. de cada año.

EMPLOYMENT   EMPLOI   EMPLEO

Paid employment, by economic activity   **Emploi rémunéré, par activité économique**   **Empleo remunerado, por actividad económica**

	Thousands				Milliers				Millares	
	1999	2000	2001	2002	2003	2004	2005	2006	2007	2008
Belgique (BA) [1][2]					Employees - Salariés - Asalariados					
Total - Total - Total										
ISIC 3 - CITI 3 - CIIU 3										
Total	.	.	3 441.1	3 443.3	3 460.6	3 521.0	3 590.4	3 619.9	3 730.9	3 813.5
A	.	.	15.7	19.2	20.8	22.7	20.7	19.4	21.8	23.5
B	.	.	0.4	0.5	0.5	0.6	0.5	0.3	0.5	0.7
C	.	.	6.2	6.5	5.4	6.7	8.5	9.2	8.4	6.0
D	.	.	712.2	697.2	672.3	677.2	681.5	667.2	676.5	682.6
E	.	.	30.6	30.3	31.9	32.1	32.1	34.3	33.5	39.7
F	.	.	197.0	200.3	198.8	204.0	211.5	224.7	227.9	242.8
G	.	.	388.4	405.4	407.9	405.1	414.9	417.2	438.4	431.1
H	.	.	76.8	82.3	80.8	80.6	88.4	85.9	93.8	96.9
I	.	.	309.3	296.5	295.2	296.4	295.1	298.0	297.3	314.4
J	.	.	146.2	139.9	137.6	136.0	144.2	140.6	147.2	156.7
K	.	.	268.8	279.8	286.0	289.3	269.2	298.3	314.5	315.3
L	.	.	391.4	394.0	395.9	417.0	417.5	420.3	429.9	434.7
M	.	.	345.6	335.8	348.2	367.9	383.4	371.4	374.4	370.5
N	.	.	399.9	419.0	444.7	441.1	443.7	457.2	461.2	490.6
O	.	.	122.3	115.5	116.9	118.2	127.6	128.4	140.2	136.7
P	.	.	11.0	10.2	9.2	13.0	20.5	23.1	33.2	41.1
Q	.	.	19.1	11.1	8.6	13.2	31.0	24.4	32.3	30.2
Men - Hommes - Hombres										
ISIC 3 - CITI 3 - CIIU 3										
Total	.	.	1 948.5	1 935.8	1 929.0	1 950.4	1 968.5	1 969.4	2 017.8	2 042.1
A	.	.	11.6	14.8	15.2	17.4	14.6	15.0	16.3	19.5
B	.	.	0.4	0.4	0.4	0.6	0.5	0.3	0.3	0.6
C	.	.	5.5	6.1	5.0	5.9	6.9	7.8	6.5	5.0
D	.	.	542.5	527.1	504.0	514.3	513.5	506.6	508.9	519.6
E	.	.	25.3	25.8	25.7	26.2	25.4	27.4	24.5	30.9
F	.	.	185.6	187.4	186.7	190.3	194.0	210.1	209.6	222.0
G	.	.	192.7	201.1	206.1	202.6	204.1	205.9	216.8	209.1
H	.	.	37.3	38.7	39.5	38.7	43.1	41.5	45.0	45.6
I	.	.	238.8	235.2	234.6	231.5	222.2	225.4	227.6	240.6
J	.	.	76.2	71.7	71.3	68.6	74.9	70.8	76.1	75.9
K	.	.	141.8	151.1	154.6	152.1	142.8	152.7	156.2	154.2
L	.	.	226.1	217.1	220.1	228.5	235.2	224.1	231.1	233.1
M	.	.	106.3	107.5	114.8	119.9	125.9	118.0	114.2	110.7
N	.	.	84.6	90.4	88.8	85.7	85.2	87.7	95.7	93.4
O	.	.	63.0	54.3	56.2	58.9	61.2	60.0	68.6	63.5
P	.	.	2.1	2.1	1.4	2.1	2.7	2.5	2.9	3.1
Q	.	.	8.9	5.1	4.7	7.2	16.3	13.7	17.5	15.3
Women - Femmes - Mujeres										
ISIC 3 - CITI 3 - CIIU 3										
Total	.	.	1 492.5	1 507.5	1 531.6	1 570.6	1 621.9	1 650.5	1 713.1	1 771.4
A	.	.	4.2	4.4	5.6	5.2	6.1	4.4	5.5	4.0
B	.	.	-	0.1	0.2	-	0.1	-	0.2	0.1
C	.	.	0.7	0.4	0.4	0.7	1.6	1.4	1.9	1.1
D	.	.	169.7	170.1	168.3	162.9	168.0	160.7	167.7	163.0
E	.	.	5.3	4.5	6.2	6.0	6.7	6.9	9.0	8.7
F	.	.	11.4	12.8	12.1	13.7	17.5	14.6	18.3	20.8
G	.	.	195.7	204.2	201.7	202.5	210.8	211.3	221.6	222.0
H	.	.	39.5	43.6	41.2	41.9	45.3	44.4	48.9	51.3
I	.	.	70.5	61.3	60.6	65.0	72.8	72.6	69.7	73.8
J	.	.	70.0	68.2	66.4	67.4	69.3	69.8	71.1	80.8
K	.	.	127.0	128.6	131.4	137.2	126.4	145.6	158.2	161.0
L	.	.	165.3	176.8	175.8	188.5	182.3	196.2	198.8	201.6
M	.	.	239.2	228.3	233.4	248.0	257.6	253.4	260.1	259.8
N	.	.	315.4	328.6	355.9	355.5	358.5	369.5	365.5	397.2
O	.	.	59.3	61.2	60.7	59.4	66.5	68.4	71.6	73.2
P	.	.	8.9	8.1	7.8	10.8	17.8	20.6	30.3	38.0
Q	.	.	10.2	6.0	3.9	6.0	14.7	10.7	14.8	14.9

Explanatory notes: see p. 77.   Notes explicatives: voir p. 80.   Notas explicativas: véase p. 83.

[1] Incl. professional army. [2] Persons aged 15 years and over.   [1] Y compris les militaires de carrière. [2] Personnes âgées de 15 ans et plus.   [1] Incl. los militares profesionales. [2] Personas de 15 años y más.

Paid employment, by economic activity

Emploi rémunéré, par activité économique

Empleo remunerado, por actividad económica

	Thousands			Milliers			Millares				
	1999	2000	2001	2002	2003	2004	2005	2006	2007	2008	

Bulgaria (DA) — Employees - Salariés - Asalariados

Total - Total - Total
ISIC 3 - CITI 3 - CIIU 3   ISIC 4 - CITI 4 - CIIU 4 [1][2]

	1999	2000	2001	2002	2003	2004	2005	2006	2007	2008	
Total	1 994.3	1 900.9	1 899.9	1 927.7	2 079.9	2 152.3	2 177.3	2 267.7	2 380.3	2 415.2	Total
A	101.4	89.3	79.5	78.1	74.4	71.4	67.8	63.6	60.8	60.1	A
B	0.4	0.3	0.4	0.4	0.5	0.6	29.1	29.4	29.1	27.9	B
C	48.3	40.3	36.9	33.8	32.8	30.7	598.1	615.7	627.2	608.2	C
D	615.8	562.4	562.3	573.9	597.9	606.8	38.1	36.8	34.6	33.7	D
E	58.3	59.3	59.2	59.1	58.7	58.3	37.5	35.5	35.9	33.8	E
F	105.7	98.0	97.1	95.3	108.1	119.6	142.6	167.4	205.3	198.4	F
G	186.3	210.5	222.7	239.1	282.5	301.6	310.0	334.5	365.8	427.2	G
H	45.0	49.9	55.7	58.2	75.1	79.5	129.4	133.7	141.3	138.1	H
I	171.0	164.3	163.4	162.2	159.7	163.0	83.2	91.2	99.4	108.2	I
J	29.9	27.9	27.5	27.7	29.1	30.9	53.6	55.5	57.0	56.1	J
K	78.1	89.2	100.1	105.1	113.7	124.6	33.9	38.4	45.8	50.6	K
L	89.3	89.8	95.8	96.9	111.7	118.7	13.1	16.2	18.9	18.3	L
M	228.7	215.4	202.4	198.2	193.9	193.5	57.2	58.0	66.7	69.6	M
N	162.1	140.7	132.5	132.1	132.4	133.7	86.0	87.0	91.3	88.7	N
O	74.0	63.1	64.7	67.8	109.3	119.4	131.1	136.7	135.1	131.6	O
P							193.4	190.8	185.3	178.8	P
Q							123.2	125.2	125.0	126.9	Q
R							24.7	26.6	27.8	28.4	R
S							25.5	25.7	27.9	30.7	S

Men - Hommes - Hombres
ISIC 3 - CITI 3 - CIIU 3   ISIC 4 - CITI 4 - CIIU 4 [1][2]

	1999	2000	2001	2002	2003	2004	2005	2006	2007	2008	
Total	971.7	916.7	909.2	920.5	991.9	1 031.7	1 055.2	1 114.6	1 186.1	.	Total
A	70.5	61.8	54.4	53.5	50.6	48.2	46.5	43.3	41.1	.	A
B	0.3	0.3	0.3	0.4	0.4	0.5	23.7	23.8	23.6	.	B
C	37.9	32.2	29.7	27.2	26.3	24.8	285.0	297.8	306.9	.	C
D	305.9	273.7	267.7	270.7	279.7	286.2	26.8	26.8	25.9	.	D
E	42.4	42.8	43.3	43.4	43.1	42.9	24.6	23.8	23.7	.	E
F	87.9	80.5	79.9	79.1	91.2	102.1	123.3	145.6	178.9	.	F
G	85.5	94.7	99.7	107.7	126.6	135.4	140.3	153.2	169.0	.	G
H	17.1	18.3	19.5	20.4	25.8	26.8	91.3	94.4	99.7	.	H
I	115.4	109.6	109.1	107.0	105.2	107.8	28.2	30.2	33.4	.	I
J	10.1	9.6	9.4	9.5	9.7	10.1	28.7	29.8	31.3	.	J
K	44.9	52.1	58.4	62.8	67.4	74.9	11.1	12.0	13.9	.	K
L	37.6	36.0	38.9	39.0	45.3	48.1	6.3	7.7	8.9	.	L
M	51.0	47.8	43.5	42.0	41.2	40.7	28.0	27.6	30.0	.	M
N	32.1	28.4	26.2	26.1	26.6	27.3	55.8	58.0	61.7	.	N
O	33.1	28.9	29.3	31.9	52.7	55.9	51.0	54.1	52.1	.	O
P							40.2	40.3	38.6	.	P
Q							24.0	25.0	25.0	.	Q
R							11.2	12.2	12.9	.	R
S							9.3	9.0	9.6	.	S

Women - Femmes - Mujeres
ISIC 3 - CITI 3 - CIIU 3   ISIC 4 - CITI 4 - CIIU 4 [1][2]

	1999	2000	2001	2002	2003	2004	2005	2006	2007	2008	
Total	1 022.6	984.2	990.6	1 007.2	1 088.1	1 120.6	1 122.0	1 153.2	1 194.1	.	Total
A	30.9	27.4	24.7	24.7	23.8	23.2	21.3	20.2	19.7	.	A
B	0.1	0.1	0.1	0.1	0.1	0.2	5.4	5.6	5.5	.	B
C	10.4	8.1	7.2	6.5	6.4	5.9	313.1	317.9	320.3	.	C
D	309.9	288.6	294.5	303.2	318.2	320.6	11.3	10.0	8.7	.	D
E	15.9	16.5	16.0	16.8	15.7	15.4	12.9	11.7	12.2	.	E
F	17.8	17.6	17.1	16.2	16.9	17.5	19.3	21.8	26.4	.	F
G	100.8	116.0	123.1	131.4	155.9	166.2	169.7	181.4	196.9	.	G
H	27.9	31.6	36.2	37.8	49.3	52.7	38.1	39.3	41.6	.	H
I	55.6	54.7	54.3	55.2	54.5	55.2	55.0	61.1	66.0	.	I
J	19.8	18.3	18.1	18.2	19.4	20.8	24.9	25.7	25.7	.	J
K	33.2	37.1	41.7	42.3	46.3	49.7	22.8	26.4	31.9	.	K
L	51.7	53.8	57.0	57.8	66.4	70.6	6.8	8.5	10.0	.	L
M	177.7	167.6	158.9	156.2	152.7	152.8	29.3	30.4	36.8	.	M
N	130.0	112.3	106.4	106.0	105.9	106.4	30.2	29.0	29.6	.	N
O	40.9	34.5	35.4	35.8	56.6	63.4	80.1	82.6	83.1	.	O
P							153.1	150.5	146.7	.	P
Q							99.2	100.2	100.0	.	Q
R							13.5	14.4	14.9	.	R
S							16.2	16.7	18.3	.	S

Explanatory notes: see p. 77.   Notes explicatives: voir p. 80.   Notas explicativas: véase p. 83.

[1] Persons aged 15 years and over. [2] Excl. conscripts.   [1] Personnes âgées de 15 ans et plus. [2] Non compris les conscrits.   [1] Personas de 15 años y más. [2] Excl. los conscriptos.

Paid employment, by economic activity — Emploi rémunéré, par activité économique — Empleo remunerado, por actividad económica

Thousands — Milliers — Millares

Croatia (BA) [1] [2]   Employees - Salariés - Asalariados

Total - Total - Total — ISIC 3 - CITI 3 - CIIU 3

	1999	2000	2001	2002	2003	2004	2005	2006	2007	2008
Total	1 121.0	1 182.4	1 113.1	1 166.8	1 164.2	1 195.3	1 181.4	1 221.8	1 266.2	1 282.4
A	28.1	29.8	27.2	28.7	33.4	30.6	30.4	28.1	26.7 [3]	31.0 [3]
B	3.8	3.3	1.2	2.7	2.2	2.7	2.4	2.4	2.4	. [4]
C	8.2	6.8	8.8	8.8	10.3	8.5	9.1	7.2	10.3 [3]	8.8 [3]
D	302.8	284.7	284.0	290.9	271.8	283.2	266.6	279.5	288.0	292.8
E	26.0	29.4	29.1	26.8	28.1	28.9	28.7	22.5	28.6 [3]	28.6 [3]
F	79.0	79.6	74.6	82.8	104.3	107.6	103.3	105.9	116.6	115.4
G	151.3	166.1	164.5	166.6	173.9	180.0	181.7	193.7	188.8	201.6
H	56.4	60.6	59.2	66.3	65.2	68.4	67.1	70.6	77.0	74.3
I	87.2	97.0	89.7	96.1	88.2	87.7	92.1	91.5	102.9	98.7
J	33.3	35.8	27.4	33.8	31.3	29.7	27.3	36.2	36.1 [3]	33.9 [3]
K	41.4	50.0	46.0	45.9	49.4	46.4	54.9	61.5	64.4	64.6
L	105.3	123.2	104.5	109.9	96.3	101.8	100.1	98.4	93.2	93.4
M	78.6	86.8	74.8	86.4	82.0	89.5	85.8	90.5	86.4	89.5
N	83.6	82.6	77.9	77.7	81.5	81.6	78.8	79.2	84.8	86.0
O	35.9	44.5	38.3	41.1	43.1	45.9	49.9	51.4	58.4	58.2
P	-	2.2	1.0	-	-	-	1.8	3.2 [3]	1.0 [3]	. [4]

Men - Hommes - Hombres — ISIC 3 - CITI 3 - CIIU 3

	1999	2000	2001	2002	2003	2004	2005	2006	2007	2008
Total	592.4	633.2	598.2	626.9	635.9	655.9	647.1	656.2	693.7	700.4
A	20.3	21.2	19.1	21.8	26.0	23.2	23.5	21.3	20.0 [3]	22.3 [3]
B	2.1	2.8	1.1	2.3	1.8	2.2	1.8	1.9	. [4]	. [4]
C	7.1	6.3	7.3	8.0	8.6	8.0	8.3	5.8	9.3 [3]	8.1 [3]
D	174.3	169.0	166.1	174.3	164.8	176.5	160.9	174.7	178.7	180.8
E	20.7	23.5	23.5	21.5	22.0	21.9	22.1	16.4	21.7 [3]	23.1 [3]
F	70.6	69.3	67.1	73.8	95.6	97.5	92.9	95.7	106.4	104.8
G	60.7	71.8	69.8	73.0	77.6	76.2	80.4	81.0	77.6	90.4
H	23.7	28.2	25.5	28.2	26.6	28.7	27.3	29.3	34.1 [3]	31.5 [3]
I	66.1	70.7	67.5	71.3	67.0	69.4	71.7	70.9	79.1	77.7
J	9.2	10.4	6.3	8.4	9.0	8.7	9.0	9.4	11.6 [3]	11.6 [3]
K	20.2	22.2	22.5	22.9	23.6	25.8	29.1	33.6	32.4 [3]	31.0 [3]
L	62.3	74.0	66.5	66.6	57.8	57.3	57.8	53.7	52.6	49.9
M	17.9	23.4	18.9	18.9	17.7	22.3	19.7	19.9	22.3 [3]	21.1 [3]
N	16.3	18.3	16.4	14.8	15.3	16.6	17.7	16.9	17.3 [3]	16.2 [3]
O	20.8	21.4	20.1	21.0	21.4	21.3	24.4	24.9	29.1 [3]	29.3 [3]
P	-	0.7	-	-	-	-	0.5	0.8 [3]	0.5 [3]	. [4]

Women - Femmes - Mujeres — ISIC 3 - CITI 3 - CIIU 3

	1999	2000	2001	2002	2003	2004	2005	2006	2007	2008
Total	528.6	549.3	514.9	540.0	528.2	539.4	534.3	565.6	572.4	582.0
A	7.8	8.6	8.2	7.0	7.5	7.4	6.9	6.8	6.7 [3]	8.7 [3]
B	1.7	0.5	0.1	0.4	0.4	0.5	0.6	0.5	2.0	. [4]
C	1.1	0.5	1.1	0.8	1.8	0.5	0.8	1.4	1.0	. [4]
D	128.5	115.7	117.9	116.6	107.0	106.7	105.8	104.7	109.3	112.0
E	5.3	6.0	5.6	5.3	6.1	6.1	6.6	6.1	6.9 [3]	5.5 [3]
F	8.5	10.4	9.0	9.0	8.8	10.2	10.3	10.2	10.2 [3]	10.6 [3]
G	90.5	94.3	94.7	93.6	96.3	103.8	101.3	112.6	111.2	111.2
H	32.8	32.4	33.7	38.1	38.7	39.7	39.9	41.3	42.9	42.8
I	21.1	26.3	22.2	24.5	21.2	19.7	20.4	20.6	23.8 [3]	21.0 [3]
J	24.1	25.4	21.2	25.4	22.3	20.9	18.3	26.8	24.5 [3]	22.3 [3]
K	21.1	27.8	23.5	22.9	25.8	20.6	25.9	27.9	32.0 [3]	33.6 [3]
L	42.9	49.3	38.0	43.3	38.6	44.5	42.3	44.7	40.6	43.5
M	60.8	63.5	55.9	67.5	64.3	67.1	66.2	70.6	64.1	68.4
N	67.4	64.3	61.4	62.9	66.2	65.0	61.1	62.3	67.5	69.8
O	15.1	23.1	18.3	20.1	21.6	24.5	25.5	26.5	29.3 [3]	28.9 [3]
P	-	1.2	-	-	-	-	1.8	2.4 [3]	0.5 [3]	. [4]

Croatia (DA)   Employees - Salariés - Asalariados

Total - Total - Total — ISIC 3 - CITI 3 - CIIU 3

	1999	2000	2001	2002	2003	2004	2005	2006	2007	2008
Total	1 172.0	1 170.5	1 183.6	1 197.6	1 235.4	1 258.9	1 274.3	1 324.8	1 377.9	1 416.9
A	32.0	31.3	31.0	30.2	30.4	28.9	28.5	28.5	29.3	30.4
B	2.0	2.1	2.2	2.5	2.7	2.7	2.8	2.8	3.0	3.1
C	8.4	8.2	7.7	6.9	8.0	8.2	8.4	8.7	8.7	9.1
D	285.2	277.9	275.9	273.6	276.6	276.7	274.3	279.6	289.2	290.3
E	27.1	27.4	27.6	27.1	26.8	27.1	23.7	27.2	26.9	26.8
F	85.9	79.3	80.8	88.7	98.1	104.3	109.0	118.4	125.5	133.0
G	177.6	178.3	185.5	193.1	205.9	216.7	220.3	231.5	245.2	252.1
H	61.0	62.9	64.0	64.6	65.6	67.5	67.8	73.3	76.2	78.7
I	86.1	86.7	87.2	86.8	88.2	87.9	87.5	89.7	90.4	91.0
J	28.6	29.8	29.3	29.8	30.7	31.0	32.2	34.1	35.7	37.5
K	56.2	58.2	61.1	63.1	67.7	75.2	79.2	87.9	98.1	105.3
L	120.8	122.3	121.3	118.2	116.2	107.2	105.1	105.1	104.8	106.6
M	80.1	82.5	83.7	85.3	86.8	89.3	91.8	94.5	97.4	100.8
N	77.4	76.5	76.6	76.7	78.0	79.3	80.8	82.6	85.1	87.9
O	33.8	35.4	36.6	39.0	42.0	45.2	47.3	49.6	52.0	55.1
P	7.3	9.4	10.9	10.0	9.8	9.9	10.3	9.7	8.8	8.0
X	2.5	2.3	2.2	2.0	1.9	1.9	1.6	1.5	1.4	1.2

Explanatory notes: see p. 77.   Notes explicatives: voir p. 80.   Notas explicativas: véase p. 83.

[1] Incl. armed forces, Excl. conscripts. [2] Persons aged 15 years and over. [3] Estimate not sufficiently reliable. [4] Not indicated due to lack of statistical reliability.

[1] Y compris les forces armées, Excl. conscrits [2] Personnes âgées de 15 ans et plus. [3] Estimation pas suffisamment fiable. [4] Non indiqué en raison du manque de fiabilité statistique.

[1] Incl. las fuerzas armadas, excl. los conscriptos. [2] Personas de 15 años y más. [3] Estimación no suficientemente fiable. [4] No se indica por la falta de confiabilidad estadística.

Paid employment, by economic activity
Emploi rémunéré, par activité économique
Empleo remunerado, por actividad económica

	Thousands			Milliers				Millares		
	1999	2000	2001	2002	2003	2004	2005	2006	2007	2008

Croatia (DA) — Employees - Salariés - Asalariados

Men - Hommes - Hombres
ISIC 3 - CITI 3 - CIIU 3

	1999	2000	2001	2002	2003	2004	2005	2006	2007	2008
Total	628.1	625.0	633.6	646.5	670.5	683.4	688.7	716.9	745.2	765.9
A	23.4	22.9	22.7	22.1	22.2	21.0	20.7	20.4	20.7	21.2
B	1.6	1.8	1.8	2.0	2.1	2.1	2.2	2.2	2.4	2.5
C	7.2	7.0	6.6	5.9	6.9	7.0	7.1	7.4	7.3	7.7
D	166.0	162.5	162.8	164.6	167.7	168.8	168.4	173.0	179.3	180.5
E	21.7	21.9	22.1	21.7	21.4	21.7	21.8	21.7	21.4	21.3
F	74.4	68.4	70.0	77.6	86.1	91.3	95.4	103.8	110.5	117.3
G	81.4	83.1	87.9	92.3	99.3	104.4	105.1	109.7	116.1	119.2
H	24.4	25.3	26.1	26.3	27.2	27.9	27.8	30.4	31.6	32.7
I	61.8	62.4	62.3	62.2	63.2	62.9	62.2	63.8	64.4	64.8
J	7.5	8.0	8.1	8.4	8.7	8.8	9.2	9.9	10.4	11.1
K	31.4	32.6	34.2	35.2	37.6	41.8	43.9	48.7	54.1	57.9
L	71.6	72.3	71.2	69.1	67.5	63.4	61.0	60.2	59.2	59.7
M	20.8	21.3	21.6	22.1	22.1	22.4	22.8	23.2	23.8	24.4
N	16.0	15.9	16.1	16.0	16.5	16.6	17.0	17.2	17.8	18.5
O	16.9	17.6	18.0	19.0	20.1	21.6	22.6	23.8	24.7	25.9
P	0.6	0.7	0.8	0.8	0.7	0.6	0.6	0.6	0.5	0.5
X	1.4	1.3	1.3	1.2	1.2	1.1	1.0	0.9	0.9	0.7

Women - Femmes - Mujeres
ISIC 3 - CITI 3 - CIIU 3

	1999	2000	2001	2002	2003	2004	2005	2006	2007	2008
Total	543.9	545.5	550.0	551.1	564.9	575.5	585.5	607.9	632.6	651.1
A	8.6	8.4	8.3	8.1	8.2	7.9	7.8	8.1	8.6	9.2
B	0.4	0.3	0.4	0.5	0.6	0.6	0.6	0.6	0.6	0.6
C	1.2	1.2	1.1	1.0	1.1	1.2	1.3	1.3	1.4	1.4
D	119.2	115.4	113.1	109.0	108.9	107.9	105.9	106.7	109.9	109.8
E	5.4	5.5	5.5	5.4	5.4	5.4	5.5	5.5	5.5	5.5
F	11.5	10.9	10.8	11.1	12.0	13.0	13.6	14.7	15.0	15.7
G	96.2	95.2	97.6	100.8	106.6	112.3	115.2	121.8	129.2	133.0
H	36.6	37.6	37.9	38.3	38.4	39.6	40.0	42.9	44.5	46.0
I	24.3	24.3	24.9	24.6	25.0	25.0	25.3	25.8	26.0	26.2
J	21.1	21.8	21.2	21.4	22.0	22.2	23.0	24.2	25.3	26.4
K	24.8	25.6	26.9	27.9	30.1	33.4	35.3	39.2	44.0	47.4
L	49.2	50.0	50.1	49.1	48.7	43.8	44.0	44.8	45.6	46.9
M	59.3	61.2	62.1	63.2	64.7	66.9	69.0	71.3	73.6	76.4
N	61.4	60.6	60.5	60.7	61.5	62.7	63.8	65.4	67.3	69.4
O	16.9	17.8	18.6	20.0	21.9	23.6	24.8	25.8	27.4	29.2
P	6.7	8.7	10.1	9.2	9.1	9.3	9.7	9.1	8.3	7.5
X	1.1	1.0	0.9	0.8	0.7	0.7	0.6	0.6	0.6	0.5

Cyprus (BA) [1] [2] [3] — Employees - Salariés - Asalariados

Total - Total - Total
ISIC 3 - CITI 3 - CIIU 3

	1999	2000	2001	2002	2003	2004	2005	2006	2007	2008
Total	205.9	210.7	236.3	242.7	249.6	258.5	267.2	280.5	301.1	306.5
A	2.6	3.6	3.6	3.8	3.5	3.4	3.9	4.6	4.6	3.4
B	0.2	0.1	0.1	-	-	-	-	0.2	0.4	0.2
C	0.3	0.7	0.5	0.4	0.4	0.4	0.7	0.6	0.5	0.5
D	29.5	27.3	31.2	30.8	28.5	29.3	30.9	29.7	29.8	30.7
E	2.3	2.7	3.1	3.0	3.6	3.6	2.7	2.9	2.7	3.1
F	20.3	20.1	22.4	23.9	26.8	29.7	29.0	29.6	33.4	33.1
G	33.6	35.0	37.2	40.1	38.7	40.9	42.9	44.8	49.9	55.0
H	21.7	21.0	22.3	22.0	22.4	23.5	20.7	18.6	19.4	20.8
I	14.9	13.5	15.2	13.7	14.9	15.2	14.7	16.8	18.6	17.1
J	12.5	14.0	17.6	16.3	15.0	14.2	16.3	17.7	17.8	18.5
K	9.6	9.7	11.9	13.6	16.4	16.2	16.4	18.2	24.0	24.8
L	21.4	24.6	24.2	23.8	24.4	23.4	26.3	29.9	31.2	30.2
M	13.9	14.6	17.4	18.4	19.5	19.4	20.3	22.2	23.9	24.9
N	9.1	8.5	9.8	9.9	11.5	12.5	12.6	12.6	14.0	12.9
O	7.9	8.0	10.0	10.8	11.3	11.5	12.7	14.5	12.4	11.8
P	3.6	5.0	7.3	9.4	10.4	13.1	14.2	14.6	15.7	16.8
Q	2.4	2.3	2.5	2.9	2.4	2.2	3.0	2.9	2.8	2.6

Men - Hommes - Hombres
ISIC 3 - CITI 3 - CIIU 3

	1999	2000	2001	2002	2003	2004	2005	2006	2007	2008
Total	116.4	117.0	124.2	126.1	127.0	134.6	140.7	146.9	154.8	157.8
A	1.3	2.3	2.3	2.6	2.4	2.7	3.2	3.7	3.7	2.3
B	0.2	0.1	0.1	-	0.7	-	-	0.2	0.2	0.2
C	0.3	0.7	0.5	0.4	0.4	0.4	0.6	0.6	0.5	0.4
D	17.8	16.4	18.6	18.3	16.6	17.4	19.7	18.9	19.3	19.5
E	1.8	2.2	2.5	2.6	3.2	3.0	2.2	2.5	2.4	2.6
F	19.1	18.5	20.5	21.9	24.3	27.8	26.8	26.3	29.4	29.9
G	18.1	19.3	18.8	19.2	17.5	19.4	21.8	23.9	25.1	28.1
H	9.9	10.2	9.9	9.7	8.8	9.3	8.4	7.8	7.7	9.5
I	10.0	8.6	9.2	8.3	8.7	9.7	9.3	10.1	9.9	9.7
J	5.8	6.2	7.1	6.4	5.8	5.6	7.7	8.3	8.2	7.9
K	3.1	3.1	4.3	5.0	6.5	6.8	6.1	6.7	9.7	9.9
L	15.1	16.9	15.9	14.9	15.3	15.9	17.9	20.1	19.6	18.4
M	4.9	4.3	4.6	5.9	6.0	5.9	5.2	5.5	6.9	6.9
N	2.7	1.8	2.6	2.5	2.2	2.6	2.9	3.1	3.5	3.5
O	4.6	4.9	5.6	6.4	7.0	6.3	6.5	6.9	6.5	6.6
P	0.1	0.1	0.1	0.1	0.1	0.3	0.4	0.3	0.2	0.2
Q	1.7	1.6	1.6	2.0	1.5	1.5	1.9	2.0	2.1	2.1

Explanatory notes: see p. 77.

[1] Incl. armed forces, Excl. conscripts. [2] Government-controlled area. [3] Persons aged 15 years and over.

Notes explicatives: voir p. 80.

[1] Y compris les forces armées, Excl. conscrits [2] Région sous contrôle gouvernemental. [3] Personnes âgées de 15 ans et plus.

Notas explicativas: véase p. 83.

[1] Incl. las fuerzas armadas, excl. los conscriptos. [2] Area controlada por el gobierno. [3] Personas de 15 años y más.

EMPLOYMENT   EMPLOI   EMPLEO

Paid employment, by economic activity
Emploi rémunéré, par activité économique
Empleo remunerado, por actividad económica

	Thousands				Milliers			Millares		
	1999	2000	2001	2002	2003	2004	2005	2006	2007	2008

Cyprus (BA) [1] [2] [3] — Employees - Salariés - Asalariados

Women - Femmes - Mujeres
ISIC 3 - CITI 3 - CIIU 3

	1999	2000	2001	2002	2003	2004	2005	2006	2007	2008
Total	89.5	93.7	112.0	116.6	122.7	123.9	126.5	133.6	146.3	148.7
A	1.3	1.4	1.3	1.2	1.1	0.7	0.7	0.9	0.9	1.1
B	-	-	-	-	-	-	-	0.0	0.2	-
C	0.1	-	-	-	0.1	-	0.1	0.0	0.0	0.1
D	11.7	10.8	12.5	12.5	11.9	12.0	11.2	10.8	10.5	11.2
E	0.5	0.5	0.6	0.4	0.4	0.6	0.5	0.4	0.4	0.5
F	1.2	1.6	1.9	2.1	2.5	1.8	2.2	3.3	3.9	3.2
G	15.5	15.8	18.4	20.9	20.9	21.5	21.1	21.0	24.8	26.9
H	11.8	10.8	12.4	12.2	13.3	14.2	12.3	10.8	11.7	11.4
I	4.9	4.9	6.0	5.4	6.2	5.5	5.4	6.7	8.7	7.4
J	6.7	7.8	10.5	9.9	9.2	8.6	8.6	9.4	9.6	10.6
K	6.5	6.6	7.6	8.6	9.8	9.4	10.3	11.5	14.3	14.9
L	6.3	7.7	8.3	8.8	9.0	7.5	8.4	9.8	11.6	11.8
M	9.1	10.4	12.8	12.6	13.5	13.5	15.1	16.7	17.1	17.9
N	6.4	6.7	7.1	7.4	9.3	9.9	9.6	9.6	10.5	9.3
O	3.3	3.1	4.4	4.3	4.2	5.2	6.2	7.6	6.0	5.2
P	3.5	4.9	7.3	9.3	10.3	12.8	13.7	14.3	15.5	16.6
Q	0.7	0.7	0.8	0.8	0.8	0.7	1.1	1.0	0.7	0.6

Czech Republic (BA) [3] — Employees - Salariés - Asalariados

Total - Total - Total
ISIC 3 - CITI 3 - CIIU 3

	1999	2000	2001	2002	2003	2004	2005	2006	2007	2008
Total	4 024	3 972	3 970	3 966	3 894	3 890	3 980	4 032	4 111	4 184
A-B	160	157	149	158	146	141	135	132		
A	.	.	.	.	.	.	.	.	127	117
B	.	.	.	.	.	.	.	.	3	2
C	76	69	67	60	52	58	48	53	53	54
D	1 212	1 192	1 213	1 216	1 189	1 175	1 197	1 254	1 295	1 324
E	78	74	85	79	71	72	73	73	69	73
F	312	301	283	273	272	269	291	279	279	286
G	459	433	438	441	446	450	459	467	464	478
H	127	122	125	131	132	136	144	149	147	143
I	331	330	322	325	314	319	315	310	319	333
J	89	87	83	77	78	74	77	71	77	92
K	172	174	167	171	178	180	187	205	226	243
L	334	340	336	321	327	318	328	320	322	323
M	280	292	292	300	278	269	287	278	280	270
N	255	267	279	280	278	294	298	299	312	304
O	133	128	129	128	128	132	137	137	135	140
P	2	2	1	3	3	3	3	3	2	1
Q	1	2	1	1	1	1	1	1	1	-
X	-	2	2	2	1	-	1	1	-	-

Men - Hommes - Hombres
ISIC 3 - CITI 3 - CIIU 3

	1999	2000	2001	2002	2003	2004	2005	2006	2007	2008
Total	2 173	2 143	2 140	2 134	2 092	2 079	2 141	2 177	2 223	2 276
A-B	104	103	100	104	98	94	89	85		
A	.	.	.	.	.	.	.	.	83	77
B	.	.	.	.	.	.	.	.	2	2
C	67	59	53	51	45	51	42	46	47	47
D	718	715	734	738	717	709	734	771	807	830
E	61	57	63	59	56	57	56	57	54	57
F	282	270	248	241	244	241	256	250	250	254
G	183	171	171	174	180	187	189	192	191	197
H	48	45	49	53	53	59	61	61	58	59
I	220	218	215	220	209	208	212	216	224	232
J	27	27	30	28	25	24	28	24	26	33
K	95	96	94	90	94	96	105	115	123	132
L	196	204	197	183	190	176	175	167	162	167
M	63	67	70	72	66	60	66	68	69	65
N	43	48	53	55	54	51	55	51	57	55
O	65	63	60	62	61	66	73	73	71	69
P	-	-	-	-	-	-	1	1	-	-
Q	1	1	1	1	-	-	-	1	1	-
X	-	1	1	2	-	-	1	-	-	-

Explanatory notes: see p. 77.

Notes explicatives: voir p. 80.

Notas explicativas: véase p. 83.

[1] Incl. armed forces, Excl. conscripts. [2] Government-controlled area. [3] Persons aged 15 years and over.

[1] Y compris les forces armées, Excl. conscrits [2] Région sous contrôle gouvernemental. [3] Personnes âgées de 15 ans et plus.

[1] Incl. las fuerzas armadas, excl. los conscriptos. [2] Area controlada por el gobierno. [3] Personas de 15 años y más.

Paid employment, by economic activity / **Emploi rémunéré, par activité économique** / **Empleo remunerado, por actividad económica**

Thousands — Milliers — Millares

	1999	2000	2001	2002	2003	2004	2005	2006	2007	2008
Czech Republic (BA) [1]					Employees - Salariés - Asalariados					
Women - Femmes - Mujeres										
ISIC 3 - CITI 3 - CIIU 3										
Total	1 851	1 828	1 830	1 833	1 801	1 812	1 838	1 855	1 888	1 908
A-B	56	54	49	54	48	47	46	47	.	.
A	.	.	.	.	.	.	.	.	44	40
B	.	.	.	.	.	.	.	.	.	.
C	9	10	13	9	7	7	6	7	6	7
D	495	477	479	478	472	466	463	483	489	494
E	18	17	22	20	16	15	17	17	14	17
F	31	30	35	32	28	28	35	29	30	32
G	276	262	267	267	265	263	270	275	273	282
H	79	77	75	78	79	77	83	88	89	83
I	111	112	107	105	105	111	103	94	96	100
J	62	60	53	49	53	50	50	47	51	59
K	77	78	72	81	84	84	82	90	104	112
L	138	136	138	138	137	141	153	154	160	156
M	218	226	222	227	212	209	221	210	212	206
N	212	218	225	225	225	243	243	247	255	249
O	68	65	69	66	67	66	64	64	64	71
P	2	2	1	3	3	3	2	2	2	1
Q	1	1	-	-	1	1	-	-	-	-
X	-	1	1	1	1	-	-	1	-	-
Czech Republic (DA)					Employees - Salariés - Asalariados					
Total - Total - Total										
ISIC 3 - CITI 3 - CIIU 3										
Total	4 099	4 059	4 080	4 049	4 021	4 006	4 049	4 096	4 138	.
A	198	181	172	169	161	149	145	139	131	.
B	2	2	2	2	2	2	2	1	1	.
C	64	58	57	53	49	47	46	44	41	.
D	1 254	1 243	1 265	1 229	1 196	1 203	1 206	1 226	1 230	.
E	77	73	70	71	66	64	60	56	55	.
F	298	283	269	258	254	256	262	262	267	.
G	486	476	485	496	490	489	506	517	537	.
H	125	116	119	117	121	122	126	124	120	.
I	309	312	313	311	314	309	302	304	301	.
J	76	72	71	70	66	67	65	66	68	.
K	274	297	304	312	319	323	344	367	398	.
L	284	289	295	296	300	296	293	297	293	.
M	295	291	288	288	299	290	292	293	295	.
N	242	243	246	254	259	258	268	268	266	.
O	115	123	124	123	125	131	132	132	135	.
Men - Hommes - Hombres										
ISIC 3 - CITI 3 - CIIU 3										
Total	2 208	2 210	2 211	2 185	2 171	2 193	2 207	2 249	2 270	.
A	129	120	114	112	106	98	97	101	95	.
B	2	2	2	2	2	2	2	1	1	.
C	54	50	49	46	42	40	39	38	35	.
D	743	746	759	740	728	741	744	765	767	.
E	57	54	52	53	49	48	46	42	41	.
F	264	250	238	228	225	228	231	230	235	.
G	212	215	218	222	222	222	235	237	246	.
H	50	48	49	48	48	52	49	51	49	.
I	201	207	208	206	209	209	207	210	208	.
J	25	23	24	23	22	24	23	23	24	.
K	143	162	166	170	177	189	192	205	223	.
L	152	149	148	150	155	152	150	151	150	.
M	73	76	74	74	74	74	75	75	76	.
N	45	47	48	50	50	50	52	53	52	.
O	58	61	62	61	62	64	65	67	68	.
Women - Femmes - Mujeres										
ISIC 3 - CITI 3 - CIIU 3										
Total	1 891	1 849	1 869	1 864	1 850	1 813	1 842	1 847	1 868	.
A	69	61	58	57	55	51	48	38	36	.
B	.	.	.	.	.	.	.	-	-	.
C	10	8	8	7	7	7	7	6	6	.
D	511	497	506	489	468	462	462	461	463	.
E	20	19	18	18	17	16	14	14	14	.
F	34	33	31	30	29	28	31	32	32	.
G	274	261	267	274	268	267	271	280	291	.
H	75	68	70	69	73	70	77	73	71	.
I	108	105	105	105	105	100	95	94	93	.
J	51	49	47	47	44	43	42	43	44	.
K	131	135	138	142	142	134	152	162	175	.
L	132	140	147	146	145	144	143	146	143	.
M	222	215	214	214	225	216	217	218	219	.
N	197	196	198	204	209	208	216	215	214	.
O	57	62	62	62	63	67	67	65	67	.

Explanatory notes: see p. 77.
[1] Persons aged 15 years and over.

Notes explicatives: voir p. 80.
[1] Personnes âgées de 15 ans et plus.

Notas explicativas: véase p. 83.
[1] Personas de 15 años y más.

EMPLOYMENT — EMPLOI — EMPLEO

Paid employment, by economic activity
Emploi rémunéré, par activité économique
Empleo remunerado, por actividad económica

	1999	2000	2001	2002	2003	2004	2005	2006	2007	2008
			Thousands			Milliers			Millares	

Denmark (BA) [1] [2] — Employees - Salariés - Asalariados

Total - Total - Total
ISIC 3 - CITI 3 - CIIU 3

	1999	2000	2001	2002	2003	2004	2005	2006	2007	2008
Total	.	2 487.097	2 484.587	2 471.911	2 456.567	2 485.193	2 495.178	2 541.195	2 533.335	2 581.513
A	.	39.810	39.552	39.692	36.277	39.625	41.739	43.158	39.194	39.054
B	.	2.576	2.176	2.434	2.350	2.146	-	-	-	-
C	.	2.611	2.310	4.457	5.225	3.932	-	5.640	3.850	-
D	.	488.407	467.214	440.844	422.415	418.926	424.139	410.702	417.102	409.265
E	.	14.627	13.457	14.943	14.408	15.909	15.226	16.566	16.377	17.564
F	.	156.821	150.954	149.388	153.856	154.994	159.266	164.405	156.447	154.559
G	.	333.454	335.205	340.441	346.990	357.807	360.545	364.134	371.378	390.685
H	.	58.226	56.492	59.238	57.917	61.392	61.901	67.421	71.186	72.526
I	.	163.780	171.250	172.702	176.952	172.923	163.762	165.920	161.333	147.687
J	.	83.859	83.229	84.345	80.761	79.858	87.848	91.453	84.642	85.710
K	.	209.728	214.408	208.928	204.598	208.525	212.904	228.186	222.951	241.855
L	.	160.209	161.307	160.514	157.568	163.427	166.115	167.787	164.025	177.451
M	.	194.482	199.891	205.965	205.909	209.950	212.983	208.610	210.263	207.309
N	.	459.074	466.881	465.296	461.635	461.720	452.726	466.656	478.346	495.948
O	.	107.435	113.303	113.773	121.540	125.636	126.436	133.790	127.615	130.603
P	.	4.156	1.517	2.672	1.646	3.197	-	-	3.705	
Q	.	1.221	0.565	1.118	2.334	1.579	-	-	-	-
X	.	6.620	5.175	5.163	4.187	3.648	3.524	-	4.921	-

Men - Hommes - Hombres
ISIC 3 - CITI 3 - CIIU 3

	1999	2000	2001	2002	2003	2004	2005	2006	2007	2008
Total	.	1 291.527	1 277.853	1 271.422	1 278.453	1 282.199	1 287.514	1 311.186	1 300.796	1 319.902
A	.	29.746	28.923	29.286	26.765	28.911	30.175	32.589	27.762	30.679
B	.	2.576	2.176	2.434	2.331	1.995	-	-	-	-
C	.	2.611	2.287	3.811	4.421	3.607	-	4.814	1.900	-
D	.	332.250	319.702	299.718	293.846	290.669	291.776	283.957	283.854	276.400
E	.	12.299	10.432	12.034	12.106	12.759	11.527	12.630	12.308	12.902
F	.	145.245	139.719	136.670	142.151	141.952	143.508	150.397	140.979	140.355
G	.	183.936	187.414	188.759	193.246	199.846	201.291	201.020	208.437	216.298
H	.	22.957	22.790	24.506	23.661	24.216	25.574	26.734	31.128	31.977
I	.	115.304	117.921	121.572	124.079	116.755	115.985	115.670	112.800	105.357
J	.	42.213	39.940	44.388	40.151	40.832	40.662	43.576	41.715	42.384
K	.	120.827	115.667	113.926	114.206	116.718	117.629	125.542	125.509	140.634
L	.	82.218	80.870	79.388	80.767	83.227	81.142	86.262	83.314	88.420
M	.	84.847	83.936	83.453	81.693	82.720	86.996	86.548	85.192	87.036
N	.	62.572	68.640	70.972	72.659	73.414	72.517	68.597	78.840	79.459
O	.	47.036	54.075	57.623	62.330	62.270	63.180	69.984	63.025	62.452
P	.	0.517	0.269	0.097	0.295	0.127	-	-	2.533	-
Q	.	0.449	0.361	-	1.046	0.476				
X	.	3.923	2.732	2.784	2.699	1.706	-	-	1.500	-

Women - Femmes - Mujeres
ISIC 3 - CITI 3 - CIIU 3

	1999	2000	2001	2002	2003	2004	2005	2006	2007	2008
Total	.	1 195.569	1 206.734	1 200.490	1 178.115	1 202.995	1 207.664	1 230.008	1 232.539	1 261.611
A	.	10.064	10.629	10.406	9.512	10.715	11.564	10.568	11.432	8.375
B	.	-	-	-	-	0.151	-	-	-	-
C	.	-	0.023	0.646	0.803	0.250	-	0.826	1.950	-
D	.	156.157	147.513	141.127	128.659	128.257	132.363	126.745	133.247	132.866
E	.	2.328	3.025	2.908	2.303	3.150	3.699	3.935	4.068	4.662
F	.	11.576	11.235	12.718	11.705	13.042	15.757	14.008	15.468	14.204
G	.	149.518	147.791	151.682	153.744	157.960	159.254	163.114	162.941	174.387
H	.	35.269	33.702	34.732	34.256	37.176	36.327	40.688	40.057	40.548
I	.	48.476	53.330	51.130	52.873	56.168	47.776	50.249	48.533	42.330
J	.	41.646	43.289	39.957	40.610	39.027	47.186	47.876	42.927	43.326
K	.	88.900	98.741	95.002	90.392	91.806	95.275	102.644	97.442	101.220
L	.	77.991	80.437	81.126	76.801	80.200	84.973	81.525	80.711	89.031
M	.	109.635	115.956	122.512	124.217	127.230	125.987	122.062	125.071	120.273
N	.	396.502	398.241	394.324	388.976	388.305	380.209	398.059	399.506	416.489
O	.	60.399	58.928	56.150	59.210	63.366	63.256	63.806	64.590	68.151
P	.	3.639	1.248	2.574	1.350	3.070	-	-	1.172	-
Q	.	0.772	0.204	1.118	1.288	1.103	-	-	-	-
X	.	2.697	2.443	2.378	1.488	1.942	-	-	3.421	-

Explanatory notes: see p. 77.

[1] Included armed forces and conscripts. [2] Persons aged 15 to 66 years.

Notes explicatives: voir p. 80.

[1] Y compris les forces armées et les conscrits. [2] Personnes âgées de 15 à 66 ans.

Notas explicativas: véase p. 83.

[1] Incluye las fuezas armadas y los conscriptos. [2] Personas de 15 a 66 años.

Paid employment, by economic activity
Emploi rémunéré, par activité économique
Empleo remunerado, por actividad económica

	Thousands			Milliers			Millares		
	1999	2000	2001	2002	2003	2004	2005	2006	2007	2008

España (BA) [1] [2]   Employees - Salariés - Asalariados

Total - Total - Total
ISIC 3 - CITI 3 - CIIU 3

	1999	2000	2001	2002	2003	2004	2005	2006	2007	2008
Total	11 560.9	12 378.1	12 949.4	13 471.9	14 127.4	14 720.8	15 502.0 [3]	16 208.1	16 760.1	16 681.2
A	392.6	393.0	427.0	414.9	436.9	452.8	459.2 [3]	450.2	460.3	445.8
B	36.7	39.6	39.5	32.7	27.4	29.5	31.1 [3]	33.3	34.1	27.4
C	63.4	63.5	61.7	61.6	60.0	55.8	57.2 [3]	63.3	55.9	48.7
D	2 460.0	2 577.9	2 661.9	2 687.7	2 680.4	2 708.8	2 719.6 [3]	2 716.2	2 711.8	2 682.6
E	89.4	96.1	95.3	89.1	97.8	101.4	104.1 [3]	116.0	108.6	110.9
F	1 245.1	1 370.3	1 502.3	1 590.4	1 709.6	1 818.3	1 877.4 [3]	2 028.9	2 167.0	1 893.0
G	1 571.6	1 708.8	1 735.9	1 804.7	1 924.1	2 002.9	2 066.9 [3]	2 153.4	2 282.7	2 357.2
H	600.9	686.2	710.2	792.2	817.9	874.4	971.7 [3]	1 074.6	1 104.7	1 102.0
I	653.4	728.9	774.3	785.9	831.1	857.4	884.2 [3]	926.4	953.2	968.2
J	353.3	385.2	366.6	370.7	365.7	365.1	410.0 [3]	430.1	444.7	453.9
K	798.7	881.8	976.1	1 037.5	1 127.6	1 224.9	1 329.0 [3]	1 452.2	1 577.7	1 627.0
L	936.6	974.9	1 002.3	1 035.4	1 089.9	1 125.5	1 196.7 [3]	1 221.6	1 238.4	1 277.3
M	801.0	807.3	850.5	901.9	915.5	967.4	1 043.2 [3]	1 053.6	1 055.7	1 075.3
N	730.1	773.0	799.6	865.1	940.3	967.0	1 053.6 [3]	1 094.8	1 149.5	1 197.4
O	416.5	464.6	485.1	514.9	560.5	578.0	613.9 [3]	629.8	645.0	661.7
P	411.9	427.0	460.9	487.2	542.6	591.4	682.8 [3]	760.6	770.0	752.6
Q	-	-	-	-	0.1	0.1	1.5 [3]	3.2	0.8	0.2

Men - Hommes - Hombres
ISIC 3 - CITI 3 - CIIU 3

	1999	2000	2001	2002	2003	2004	2005	2006	2007	2008
Total	7 244.6	7 643.9	7 931.7	8 160.0	8 454.0	8 695.4	9 025.5 [3]	9 313.9	9 521.8	9 279.4
A	302.8	303.8	324.9	316.3	326.7	336.5	335.0 [3]	323.2	334.6	326.6
B	34.9	36.9	37.2	29.7	25.5	28.5	26.4 [3]	28.8	30.5	25.5
C	57.6	59.0	57.5	58.2	55.7	50.3	51.2 [3]	57.6	49.9	44.4
D	1 890.3	1 929.7	1 984.5	1 994.0	2 006.8	2 023.0	2 029.8 [3]	2 043.1	2 008.7	1 981.3
E	77.6	82.1	81.4	72.4	81.8	82.4	83.5 [3]	94.8	87.1	87.4
F	1 191.3	1 300.1	1 429.2	1 508.2	1 616.7	1 720.7	1 784.7 [3]	1 925.5	2 046.1	1 773.3
G	870.3	938.0	921.8	959.5	1 001.4	1 027.0	1 059.2 [3]	1 061.9	1 102.7	1 138.0
H	310.1	351.7	352.7	377.5	374.7	399.5	423.7 [3]	453.9	451.6	445.6
I	504.7	559.6	590.5	591.9	629.5	642.0	656.8 [3]	686.6	710.3	717.6
J	235.1	244.7	224.7	223.6	228.1	218.5	220.8 [3]	227.8	231.8	242.2
K	393.7	410.5	454.0	485.7	529.9	567.1	619.5 [3]	662.4	713.0	722.9
L	589.2	604.6	641.2	664.0	680.7	685.6	736.7 [3]	730.9	744.2	755.7
M	300.8	313.2	317.0	331.5	328.6	331.6	362.6 [3]	363.9	362.9	381.3
N	217.0	215.4	211.2	217.8	232.4	234.8	260.7 [3]	260.5	256.7	263.1
O	220.1	246.5	255.8	278.2	283.4	293.4	311.8 [3]	321.8	327.7	321.4
P	49.2	48.2	48.2	51.4	52.0	54.6	61.9 [3]	69.5	63.3	53.0
Q	-	-	-	-	0.1	0.1	1.2 [3]	1.6	0.7	-

Women - Femmes - Mujeres
ISIC 3 - CITI 3 - CIIU 3

	1999	2000	2001	2002	2003	2004	2005	2006	2007	2008
Total	4 316.2	4 734.2	5 017.7	5 311.9	5 673.4	6 025.4	6 476.5 [3]	6 894.3	7 238.3	7 401.8
A	89.8	89.1	102.1	98.6	110.1	116.3	124.2 [3]	127.0	125.8	119.2
B	1.8	2.7	2.3	3.1	1.9	1.0	4.7 [3]	4.5	3.5	1.9
C	5.8	4.5	4.3	3.4	4.3	5.6	6.0 [3]	5.7	6.0	4.2
D	569.6	648.2	677.5	693.8	673.6	685.8	689.8 [3]	673.0	703.1	701.3
E	11.8	14.0	14.0	16.7	16.0	19.0	20.6 [3]	21.2	21.5	23.5
F	53.9	70.2	73.1	82.2	92.9	97.6	92.7 [3]	103.5	121.0	119.7
G	701.2	770.8	814.2	845.2	922.7	976.0	1 007.7 [3]	1 091.5	1 180.0	1 219.1
H	290.8	334.4	357.5	414.7	443.3	474.9	548.1 [3]	620.7	653.1	656.3
I	148.7	169.3	183.8	194.0	201.5	215.4	224.4 [3]	239.8	243.0	250.7
J	118.2	140.5	141.9	147.0	137.6	146.6	189.2 [3]	202.3	212.9	211.7
K	405.0	471.3	522.1	551.7	597.8	657.9	709.5 [3]	789.8	864.8	904.0
L	347.0	370.4	361.1	371.3	409.2	439.9	460.1 [3]	490.7	494.1	521.7
M	500.2	494.1	533.5	570.3	586.9	635.8	680.6 [3]	689.7	692.8	694.0
N	513.2	557.7	588.4	647.4	707.8	732.3	792.9 [3]	834.2	892.7	934.3
O	196.5	218.1	229.3	236.7	277.1	284.6	302.1 [3]	308.0	317.2	340.3
P	362.7	378.9	412.7	435.8	490.6	536.8	620.9 [3]	691.1	706.7	699.6
Q	-	-	-	-	-	-	0.3 [3]	1.6	0.1	0.2

Estonia (BA) [4] [5]   Employees - Salariés - Asalariados

Total - Total - Total
ISIC 3 - CITI 3 - CIIU 3

	1999	2000	2001	2002	2003	2004	2005	2006	2007	2008
Total	529.5	520.7	529.8	538.2	541.4	538.0	558.2	594.7	596.8	605.9
A	30.0	25.6	22.9	22.9	21.3	18.6	19.8	22.1	19.0	16.3
B	2.1	2.0	1.7	1.4	1.6	2.0	1.2	1.4	1.3	0.7
C	7.9	7.2	5.8	5.7	5.7	7.8	5.8	5.2	5.5	6.0
D	118.6	124.8	130.6	123.1	129.1	134.3	132.9	131.4	129.0	134.7
E	16.5	14.7	11.4	10.5	10.2	11.9	12.3	12.2	9.4	8.4
F	35.3	35.7	34.9	35.5	36.7	40.0	42.3	53.5	68.9	72.3
G	70.7	66.1	72.7	75.9	70.0	69.4	71.6	78.5	78.0	84.2
H	11.7	18.7	15.9	16.6	16.3	15.1	21.0	21.5	21.8	23.0
I	55.0	52.3	50.3	51.2	51.7	47.4	51.2	57.6	53.8	50.8
J	8.5	7.7	6.9	7.8	7.2	7.5	6.8	7.0	8.9	10.1
K	32.2	34.5	33.7	40.7	38.6	33.4	41.4	41.7	42.9	44.6
L	34.7	34.1	34.8	33.2	34.4	36.9	37.1	38.9	39.2	38.4
M	49.7	44.3	50.6	55.3	56.4	54.2	54.7	57.9	53.9	58.4
N	30.6	27.7	30.4	31.0	35.5	35.1	33.4	36.2	35.6	30.9
O	26.0	25.4	27.1	27.5	26.9	24.4	26.9	29.5	29.9	27.0

Explanatory notes: see p. 77.

[1] Excl. compulsory military service. [2] Persons aged 16 years and over. [3] Methodology revised; data not strictly comparable. [4] Persons aged 15 to 74 years. [5] Excl. conscripts.

Notes explicatives: voir p. 80.

[1] Non compris les militaires du contingent. [2] Personnes âgées de 16 ans et plus. [3] Méthodologie révisée; les données ne sont pas strictement comparables. [4] Personnes âgées de 15 à 74 ans. [5] Non compris les conscrits.

Notas explicativas: véase p. 83.

[1] Excl. a los militares en servicio obligatorio. [2] Personas de 16 años y más. [3] Metodología revisada; los datos no son estrictamente comparables. [4] Personas de 15 a 74 años. [5] Excl. los conscriptos.

EMPLOYMENT — EMPLOI — EMPLEO

Paid employment, by economic activity — Emploi rémunéré, par activité économique — Empleo remunerado, por actividad económica

Thousands — Milliers — Millares

Estonia (BA) [1] [2] — Employees - Salariés - Asalariados

Men - Hommes - Hombres
ISIC 3 - CITI 3 - CIIU 3

	1999	2000	2001	2002	2003	2004	2005	2006	2007	2008
Total	261.7	257.5	261.6	265.6	266.8	260.3	266.9	286.6	288.9	296.2
A	18.9	17.2	16.0	15.2	14.0	11.6	11.7	14.0	12.8	11.6
B	2.0	1.8	1.5	1.1	1.5	1.5	0.9	-	-	
C	6.6	5.7	4.4	5.0	5.0	6.3	5.2	4.7	4.9	5.3
D	62.9	68.2	72.3	68.6	70.2	71.0	68.9	70.8	69.0	71.7
E	11.0	10.6	9.1	8.6	7.9	8.4	9.2	10.0	8.1	6.6
F	31.8	32.0	32.0	32.3	33.8	35.9	38.5	49.1	61.6	65.2
G	28.0	26.7	27.7	29.3	27.1	27.2	27.0	28.9	29.1	32.5
H	2.1	3.8	2.8	4.2	3.1	3.9	4.3	3.8	3.3	4.3
I	38.4	34.7	34.3	33.3	32.5	31.4	35.5	38.3	34.8	33.4
J	3.2	3.4	2.4	2.3	2.6	2.1	1.1	1.6	2.3	3.0
K	17.1	17.1	17.6	23.5	23.3	18.1	23.7	21.8	21.7	22.3
L	16.9	16.3	18.2	17.0	18.9	18.4	17.5	18.8	18.0	17.1
M	9.2	7.5	9.5	10.8	10.7	10.3	8.9	9.2	8.6	11.5
N	4.1	3.3	5.0	4.9	5.5	4.7	4.6	4.4	4.0	2.7
O	9.5	9.2	9.0	9.7	10.8	9.4	9.8	10.0	9.9	8.5

Women - Femmes - Mujeres
ISIC 3 - CITI 3 - CIIU 3

	1999	2000	2001	2002	2003	2004	2005	2006	2007	2008
Total	267.8	263.3	268.2	272.6	274.6	277.7	291.3	308.1	307.9	309.7
A	11.1	8.4	6.8	7.7	7.3	7.0	8.2	8.1	6.2	4.7
B	0.1	0.2	0.2	0.3	0.1	0.5	0.3	-	-	
C	1.3	1.5	1.4	0.7	0.7	1.5	0.6	0.5	0.6	0.7
D	55.7	56.6	58.3	54.4	58.9	63.3	64.0	60.7	60.0	63.1
E	5.5	4.1	2.3	2.0	2.2	3.5	3.1	2.2	1.3	1.8
F	3.5	3.8	2.9	3.2	2.9	4.1	3.7	4.3	7.3	7.1
G	42.8	39.4	45.0	46.6	42.9	42.1	44.6	49.6	48.9	51.7
H	9.6	14.9	13.1	12.4	13.2	11.2	16.7	17.7	18.5	18.6
I	16.6	17.6	16.1	17.9	19.2	15.9	15.7	19.3	18.9	17.4
J	5.3	4.3	4.5	5.5	4.6	5.4	5.7	5.4	6.6	7.1
K	15.1	17.4	16.1	17.1	15.3	15.2	17.7	20.0	21.2	22.4
L	17.7	17.8	16.7	16.2	15.5	18.5	19.6	20.2	21.2	21.3
M	40.4	36.8	41.1	44.5	45.7	44.0	45.7	48.6	45.3	46.9
N	26.4	24.4	25.5	26.1	30.0	30.4	28.7	31.8	31.6	28.2
O	16.5	16.1	18.1	17.9	16.1	15.0	17.0	19.4	20.0	18.6

Finland (BA) [1] [3] — Employees - Salariés - Asalariados

Total - Total - Total
ISIC 3 - CITI 3 - CIIU 3

	1999	2000	2001	2002	2003	2004	2005	2006	2007	2008
Total	1 975	2 016	2 060	2 068	2 061	2 064	2 098	2 129	2 178	2 207
A	39	39	37	34	32	34	35	33	32	34
B	1	1	1	1	-	-	1	1	1	1
C	4	3	2	4	4	4	5	5	4	4
D	431	437	444	436	418	411	412	417	420	412
E	22	22	22	21	20	19	18	17	16	17
F	120	120	118	118	118	117	122	123	135	142
G	232	233	234	240	244	249	258	258	268	274
H	66	65	68	71	66	65	66	67	73	79
I	145	148	154	148	151	147	150	160	153	153
J	45	48	49	45	49	48	45	44	48	49
K	186	201	216	226	228	231	239	248	263	268
L	116	114	112	117	118	117	110	115	117	116
M	153	162	163	161	164	169	167	167	164	159
N	310	315	330	333	331	336	351	357	358	366
O	95	97	100	103	105	105	106	108	112	113
P	4	4	3	3	5	6	7	7	7	8
Q	1	1	1	1	-	1	1	-	1	1
X	5	6	6	6	7	9	5	2	5	12

Men - Hommes - Hombres
ISIC 3 - CITI 3 - CIIU 3

	1999	2000	2001	2002	2003	2004	2005	2006	2007	2008
Total	989	1 011	1 033	1 025	1 024	1 025	1 038	1 051	1 075	1 095
A	26	27	25	22	22	23	24	23	23	24
B	1	1	1	-	-	-	1	1	1	
C	3	3	2	3	4	4	4	4	4	4
D	299	307	310	305	298	291	292	299	305	303
E	18	17	17	16	15	14	14	13	12	13
F	112	112	110	109	109	109	114	115	125	132
G	113	113	116	115	117	122	126	124	129	136
H	18	17	18	18	15	16	16	16	17	18
I	100	104	109	104	107	105	107	113	108	106
J	13	14	15	13	13	14	13	13	15	15
K	100	111	119	125	124	126	127	133	140	148
L	58	54	53	56	56	55	52	54	53	51
M	52	53	54	53	55	55	57	55	55	52
N	35	34	36	37	37	39	40	40	38	36
O	38	40	45	45	45	45	46	44	45	46
P	-	-	-	-	1	3	3	3	3	4
Q	-	-	-	-	-	-	1			
X	3	4	3	3	4	4	2	1	3	6

Explanatory notes: see p. 77.

[1] Persons aged 15 to 74 years. [2] Excl. conscripts. [3] Included armed forces and conscripts.

Notes explicatives: voir p. 80.

[1] Personnes âgées de 15 à 74 ans. [2] Non compris les conscrits. [3] Y compris les forces armées et les conscrits.

Notas explicativas: véase p. 83.

[1] Personas de 15 a 74 años. [2] Excl. los conscriptos. [3] Incluye las fuezas armadas y los conscriptos.

Paid employment,
by economic activity

Emploi rémunéré,
par activité économique

Empleo remunerado,
por actividad económica

	Thousands				Milliers				Millares	
	1999	2000	2001	2002	2003	2004	2005	2006	2007	2008

Finland (BA) [1][2]   Employees - Salariés - Asalariados

Women - Femmes - Mujeres
ISIC 3 - CITI 3 - CIIU 3

	1999	2000	2001	2002	2003	2004	2005	2006	2007	2008
Total	986	1 006	1 027	1 043	1 037	1 039	1 060	1 078	1 103	1 112
A	13	12	12	12	10	10	11	10	9	10
B	-	-	-	-	-	-	-	-	-	-
C	1	1	-	1	-	-	1	1	-	-
D	131	130	133	131	120	120	120	118	116	109
E	4	6	5	5	5	4	4	4	4	4
F	9	9	8	9	9	8	9	8	10	11
G	119	119	118	125	127	127	132	134	139	137
H	47	48	50	53	51	49	50	51	56	61
I	45	44	44	45	43	43	43	47	45	46
J	32	34	34	33	36	34	32	31	33	34
K	87	90	97	101	103	105	112	115	123	120
L	59	60	59	61	62	62	58	61	64	65
M	101	108	109	108	109	114	110	112	109	107
N	275	281	295	296	294	296	311	317	320	329
O	57	57	55	58	60	60	61	64	67	67
P	4	4	3	4	4	3	4	4	4	4
Q	-	-	-	-	-	-	-	-	-	-
X	2	1	3	3	4	3	3	2	2	6

France (BA) [3]   Employees - Salariés - Asalariados

Total - Total - Total
ISIC 3 - CITI 3 - CIIU 3   ISIC 4 - CITI 4 - CIIU 4

	1999	2000	2001	2002	2003	2004	2005	2006	2007	2008	
Total	.	.	.	.	21 865.2	22 100.0	22 238.2	22 292.0	22 769.9	23 187.9	Total
A	.	.	.	.	296.3	300.1	275.3	280.9	314.7	234.5	A
B	.	.	.	.	10.8	10.2	10.3	10.6	10.7	21.4	B
C	.	.	.	.	32.7	32.1	41.4	27.0	23.7	3 455.6	C
D	.	.	.	.	3 892.9	3 845.1	3 791.0	3 767.4	3 730.9	148.5	D
E	.	.	.	.	228.6	224.5	218.2	244.9	199.8	167.2	E
F	.	.	.	.	1 274.7	1 294.5	1 308.6	1 345.9	1 412.1	1 522.7	F
G	.	.	.	.	2 782.9	2 849.6	2 841.2	2 869.3	3 016.5	2 842.5	G
H	.	.	.	.	632.1	648.2	647.9	725.6	716.7	1 336.9	H
I	.	.	.	.	1 503.3	1 526.9	1 519.4	1 452.2	1 526.8	675.5	I
J	.	.	.	.	722.5	669.0	730.6	772.7	795.9	610.3	J
K	.	.	.	.	2 170.7	2 229.8	2 251.6	2 309.1	2 316.8	785.5	K
L	.	.	.	.	2 255.0	2 298.7	2 345.8	2 405.8	2 562.8	305.0	L
M	.	.	.	.	1 684.2	1 679.5	1 723.9	1 755.3	1 708.4	1 042.4	M
N	.	.	.	.	2 526.4	2 657.5	2 702.3	2 775.5	2 830.0	818.2	N
O	.	.	.	.	857.3	892.4	924.0	919.8	958.4	2 615.5	O
P	.	.	.	.	648.0	641.9	602.9	580.7	591.7	1 730.5	P
Q	.	.	.	.	14.0	14.9	15.5	18.4	18.3	2 841.9	Q
X	.	.	.	.	333.1	284.9	288.3	31.1	35.6	264.4	R
										550.6	S
										586.2	T
										17.3	U
										615.4	X

Men - Hommes - Hombres
ISIC 3 - CITI 3 - CIIU 3   ISIC 4 - CITI 4 - CIIU 4

	1999	2000	2001	2002	2003	2004	2005	2006	2007	2008	
Total	.	.	.	.	11 394.4	11 486.0	11 482.5	11 448.5	11 612.1	11 839.7	Total
A	.	.	.	.	212.9	202.8	194.0	206.1	217.2	156.6	A
B	.	.	.	.	10.1	9.0	9.9	9.0	9.8	17.2	B
C	.	.	.	.	24.9	28.3	35.5	23.9	18.7	2 452.5	C
D	.	.	.	.	2 741.7	2 669.6	2 656.5	2 668.1	2 599.4	114.5	D
E	.	.	.	.	178.9	185.8	174.6	192.1	155.5	136.7	E
F	.	.	.	.	1 152.9	1 169.7	1 174.5	1 217.2	1 285.0	1 362.5	F
G	.	.	.	.	1 434.6	1 475.1	1 451.0	1 495.3	1 585.0	1 439.6	G
H	.	.	.	.	315.1	332.4	332.7	359.7	340.2	953.2	H
I	.	.	.	.	1 024.7	1 049.1	1 027.3	1 012.5	1 066.2	335.8	I
J	.	.	.	.	325.7	291.7	312.6	310.0	316.4	406.5	J
K	.	.	.	.	1 140.7	1 178.9	1 209.4	1 217.6	1 199.9	313.8	K
L	.	.	.	.	1 115.1	1 191.7	1 202.4	1 192.4	1 235.6	130.4	L
M	.	.	.	.	560.7	559.5	579.5	551.9	538.5	509.9	M
N	.	.	.	.	493.3	520.7	503.0	475.6	504.9	429.3	N
O	.	.	.	.	382.9	372.4	394.6	407.8	411.6	1 256.7	O
P	.	.	.	.	137.0	125.4	102.4	85.4	98.9	548.8	P
Q	.	.	.	.	6.9	6.7	6.8	7.8	8.4	511.9	Q
X	.	.	.	.	136.3	117.1	115.8	16.1	20.8	147.0	R
										181.8	S
										106.2	T
										7.4	U
										321.3	X

Explanatory notes: see p. 77.

[1] Included armed forces and conscripts. [2] Persons aged 15 to 74 years. [3] Persons aged 15 years and over.

Notes explicatives: voir p. 80.

[1] Y compris les forces armées et les conscrits. [2] Personnes âgées de 15 à 74 ans. [3] Personnes âgées de 15 ans et plus.

Notas explicativas: véase p. 83.

[1] Incluye las fuezas armadas y los conscriptos. [2] Personas de 15 a 74 años. [3] Personas de 15 años y más.

EMPLOYMENT — EMPLOI — EMPLEO

Paid employment, by economic activity — Emploi rémunéré, par activité économique — Empleo remunerado, por actividad económica

Thousands — Milliers — Millares

	1999	2000	2001	2002	2003	2004	2005	2006	2007	2008	

France (BA) [1]

Employees - Salariés - Asalariados

Women - Femmes - Mujeres
ISIC 3 - CITI 3 - CIIU 3 .... ISIC 4 - CITI 4 - CIIU 4

ISIC 3	2003	2004	2005	2006	2007	2008	ISIC 4
Total	10 470.8	10 614.0	10 755.8	10 843.5	11 157.8	11 348.2	Total
A	83.4	97.3	81.4	74.8	97.5	77.9	A
B	0.7	1.2	0.4	1.6	1.0	4.1	B
C	7.8	3.8	5.9	3.1	5.0	1 003.1	C
D	1 151.2	1 175.5	1 134.5	1 099.3	1 131.4	34.0	D
E	49.7	38.6	43.7	52.8	44.3	30.5	E
F	121.8	125.0	134.1	128.6	127.1	160.2	F
G	1 348.3	1 374.4	1 390.2	1 374.0	1 431.5	1 403.0	G
H	316.9	315.8	315.2	365.9	376.5	383.8	H
I	478.6	477.8	492.1	439.7	460.6	339.7	I
J	396.8	377.3	418.0	462.6	479.5	203.8	J
K	1 030.0	1 050.9	1 042.2	1 091.4	1 116.9	471.7	K
L	1 139.9	1 107.1	1 143.3	1 213.5	1 327.2	174.6	L
M	1 123.4	1 120.0	1 144.4	1 203.4	1 169.9	532.5	M
N	2 033.1	2 136.8	2 199.3	2 299.9	2 325.1	388.8	N
O	474.5	520.0	529.4	512.0	546.8	1 358.8	O
P	510.9	516.6	500.5	495.3	492.9	1 181.6	P
Q	7.2	8.2	8.7	10.5	9.9	2 330.0	Q
X	196.8	167.8	172.5	15.0	14.8	117.4	R
						368.8	S
						480.0	T
						9.9	U
						294.1	X

Germany (BA) [1]

Employees - Salariés - Asalariados

Total - Total - Total
ISIC 3 - CITI 3 - CIIU 3

	1999	2000 [2]	2001	2002 [3]	2003 [2]	2004 [4]	2005 [5]	2006	2007	2008
Total	32 497	32 638	32 743	32 467	32 043	31 405	32 066	32 808	33 607	33 486
A	545	506	456	451	444	403	435	440	444	443
B	-	4	4	4	-	4	5	-	-	-
C	159	149	138	135	126	118	119	114	105	105
D	8 132	8 141	8 194	8 080	7 839	7 723	7 613	7 742	7 996	8 017
E	308	287	279	284	284	293	310	309	328	339
F	2 748	2 711	2 481	2 330	2 184	2 012	1 940	1 981	2 047	2 032
G	4 480	4 472	4 503	4 377	4 354	4 270	4 492	4 540	4 574	4 458
H	906	936	946	948	946	933	1 014	1 105	1 145	1 102
I	1 798	1 852	1 901	1 880	1 853	1 825	1 794	1 898	1 984	1 956
J	1 161	1 197	1 214	1 209	1 208	1 149	1 149	1 143	1 149	1 145
K	2 158	2 321	2 395	2 471	2 532	2 522	2 731	2 891	3 047	3 218
L	3 178	3 103	3 065	2 985	2 971	2 896	2 879	2 901	2 916	2 822
M	1 866	1 844	1 907	1 928	1 938	1 932	1 974	2 041	2 094	2 055
N	3 348	3 370	3 458	3 583	3 656	3 664	3 733	3 846	3 969	4 024
O	1 535	1 585	1 641	1 644	1 549	1 495	1 685	1 657	1 594	1 560
P	134	127	131	127	128	140	159	167	185	173
Q	37	33	30	31	28	26	33	29	29	32

Men - Hommes - Hombres
ISIC 3 - CITI 3 - CIIU 3

	1999	2000 [2]	2001	2002 [3]	2003 [2]	2004 [4]	2005 [5]	2006	2007	2008
Total	17 980	17 969	17 910	17 614	17 225	16 846	17 181	17 506	17 927	17 901
A	342	327	302	298	299	275	299	302	305	308
B	-	3	3	3	-	3	-	-	-	-
C	147	137	126	122	113	107	108	104	95	92
D	5 796	5 801	5 844	5 786	5 605	5 531	5 464	5 529	5 733	5 778
E	247	232	219	221	224	230	241	236	250	260
F	2 382	2 355	2 153	2 018	1 892	1 742	1 676	1 720	1 792	1 777
G	1 967	1 928	1 939	1 873	1 859	1 849	2 032	2 044	2 033	1 997
H	333	348	361	367	357	361	391	427	429	425
I	1 270	1 301	1 343	1 319	1 299	1 294	1 284	1 343	1 424	1 411
J	533	538	543	541	552	524	531	528	523	521
K	991	1 089	1 130	1 158	1 188	1 190	1 309	1 390	1 453	1 567
L	1 859	1 804	1 771	1 704	1 700	1 642	1 622	1 627	1 620	1 531
M	657	627	652	643	636	630	635	647	678	646
N	767	774	792	826	824	819	832	867	894	904
O	658	680	705	709	652	625	723	713	667	652
P	7	6	7	7	7	6	9	8	11	10
Q	22	19	20	19	17	18	20	16	17	19

Explanatory notes: see p. 77.

[1] Persons aged 15 years and over. [2] May. [3] Prior to 2002: April of each year. [4] March. [5] Methodology revised; data not strictly comparable.

Notes explicatives: voir p. 80.

[1] Personnes âgées de 15 ans et plus. [2] Mai. [3] Avant 2002: avril de chaque année. [4] Mars. [5] Méthodologie révisée; les données ne sont pas strictement comparables.

Notas explicativas: véase p. 83.

[1] Personas de 15 años y más. [2] Mayo. [3] Antes del 2002: abril de cada año. [4] Marzo. [5] Metodología revisada; los datos no son estrictamente comparables.

Paid employment, by economic activity	Emploi rémunéré, par activité économique	Empleo remunerado, por actividad económica
Thousands	Milliers	Millares

	1999	2000	2001	2002	2003	2004	2005	2006	2007	2008
Germany (BA) [1]					Employees - Salariés - Asalariados					
Women - Femmes - Mujeres										
ISIC 3 - CITI 3 - CIIU 3										
Total	14 517	14 669 [2]	14 833	14 853 [3]	14 818 [2]	14 559 [4]	14 885 [5]	15 303	15 680	15 585
A	203	179 [2]	154	153 [3]	145 [2]	128 [4]	136 [5]	137	138	135
B	-	1 [2]	1	1 [3]	- [2]	1 [4]	5 [5]	-	-	-
C	12	12 [2]	12	12 [3]	12 [2]	11 [4]	12 [5]	10	10	13
D	2 336	2 340 [2]	2 350	2 294 [3]	2 234 [2]	2 193 [4]	2 149 [5]	2 212	2 262	2 239
E	61	55 [2]	60	63 [3]	60 [2]	63 [4]	69 [5]	73	78	78
F	366	356 [2]	328	312 [3]	292 [2]	270 [4]	264 [5]	261	255	256
G	2 513	2 544 [2]	2 564	2 504 [3]	2 495 [2]	2 421 [4]	2 459 [5]	2 496	2 541	2 460
H	573	588 [2]	585	581 [3]	590 [2]	573 [4]	623 [5]	679	716	677
I	528	551 [2]	558	562 [3]	554 [2]	531 [4]	510 [5]	555	560	545
J	628	659 [2]	671	668 [3]	656 [2]	625 [4]	619 [5]	614	626	625
K	1 167	1 232 [2]	1 265	1 313 [3]	1 344 [2]	1 332 [4]	1 422 [5]	1 501	1 594	1 651
L	1 319	1 299 [2]	1 294	1 281 [3]	1 271 [2]	1 254 [4]	1 257 [5]	1 274	1 295	1 291
M	1 209	1 217 [2]	1 255	1 285 [3]	1 302 [2]	1 302 [4]	1 338 [5]	1 394	1 416	1 409
N	2 581	2 596 [2]	2 666	2 758 [3]	2 833 [2]	2 845 [4]	2 900 [5]	2 979	3 075	3 120
O	877	905 [2]	936	935 [3]	897 [2]	870 [4]	962 [5]	944	927	908
P	127	121 [2]	124	120 [3]	121 [2]	134 [4]	150 [5]	158	174	163
Q	15	14 [2]	10	11 [3]	11 [2]	8 [4]	13 [5]	13	12	14
Gibraltar (DA) [6] [7]					Employees - Salariés - Asalariados					
Total - Total - Total										
ISIC 2 - CITI 2 - CIIU 2										
Total	12.9	13.4	13.9	14.3	15.4	16.0	16.9	18.5	.	.
3	0.4	0.5	0.4	0.4	0.5	0.5	0.4	0.5	.	.
4	0.2	0.2	0.2	0.2	0.3	0.3	0.3	0.3	.	.
5	1.4	1.4	1.6	1.6	1.7	1.8	1.9	2.1	.	.
6	3.2	3.1	3.4	3.5	3.6	3.7	3.7	3.8	.	.
7	0.7	0.8	0.8	0.9	0.9	0.9	1.0	1.0	.	.
8	1.6	1.7	1.8	1.9	2.0	2.2	2.3	3.8	.	.
9	5.3	5.7	5.6	5.7	6.4	6.7	7.3	7.0	.	.
Men - Hommes - Hombres										
ISIC 2 - CITI 2 - CIIU 2										
Total	7.9	8.1	8.4	8.5	9.0	9.4	9.8	.	.	.
3	0.3	0.4	0.4	0.3	0.4	0.4	0.4	.	.	.
4	0.2	0.2	0.2	0.2	0.2	0.3	0.3	.	.	.
5	1.3	1.3	1.5	1.5	1.6	1.7	1.7	.	.	.
6	1.8	1.7	1.8	1.9	2.0	2.0	2.0	.	.	.
7	0.5	0.6	0.6	0.7	0.7	0.7	0.7	.	.	.
8	0.6	0.7	0.7	0.7	0.8	0.9	0.9	.	.	.
9	3.0	3.1	3.1	3.2	3.3	3.5	3.8	.	.	.
Women - Femmes - Mujeres										
ISIC 2 - CITI 2 - CIIU 2										
Total	5.1	5.3	5.6	5.7	6.4	6.6	7.1	.	.	.
3	0.1	0.1	0.1	0.1	0.1	0.1	0.1	.	.	.
4	0.0	0.0	0.0	0.0	0.0	0.0	0.0	.	.	.
5	0.1	0.1	0.1	0.1	0.1	0.1	0.1	.	.	.
6	1.4	1.4	1.5	1.6	1.7	1.7	1.7	.	.	.
7	0.2	0.2	0.2	0.2	0.3	0.3	0.3	.	.	.
8	1.0	1.0	1.1	1.1	1.2	1.3	1.4	.	.	.
9	2.3	2.5	2.5	2.6	3.1	3.2	3.5	.	.	.

Explanatory notes: see p. 77.

[1] Persons aged 15 years and over. [2] May. [3] Prior to 2002: April of each year. [4] March. [5] Methodology revised; data not strictly comparable. [6] Non-agricultural activities. [7] Oct. of each year.

Notes explicatives: voir p. 80.

[1] Personnes âgées de 15 ans et plus. [2] Mai. [3] Avant 2002: avril de chaque année. [4] Mars. [5] Méthodologie révisée; les données ne sont pas strictement comparables. [6] Activités non agricoles. [7] Oct. de chaque année.

Notas explicativas: véase p. 83.

[1] Personas de 15 años y más. [2] Mayo. [3] Antes del 2002: abril de cada año. [4] Marzo. [5] Metodología revisada; los datos no son estrictamente comparables. [6] Actividades no agrícolas. [7] Oct. de cada año.

EMPLOYMENT	EMPLOI	EMPLEO
Paid employment, by economic activity	**Emploi rémunéré, par activité économique**	**Empleo remunerado, por actividad económica**
Thousands	Milliers	Millares

Greece (BA) [1][2][3] — Employees - Salariés - Asalariados

Total - Total - Total

ISIC 3 - CITI 3 - CIIU 3	1999	2000	2001	2002	2003	2004	2005	2006	2007	2008	ISIC 4 - CITI 4 - CIIU 4
Total	2 337.4	2 378.7	2 466.3	2 545.3	2 616.0	2 746.2	2 784.9	2 834.1	2 896.4	2 974.8	Total
A	27.2	24.8	25.2	30.1	31.9	36.9	34.1	33.7	29.4	40.2	A
B	3.5	3.1	2.6	3.3	3.4	2.8	2.8	2.7	5.0	16.4	B
C	19.2	17.6	18.1	19.9	11.9	13.2	16.8	17.0	16.5	400.6	C
D	408.3	409.0	426.4	429.5	412.8	418.5	413.0	409.1	408.1	35.2	D
E	42.2	40.1	37.0	35.9	41.8	38.9	37.7	40.9	40.0	28.9	E
F	187.4	189.1	201.0	212.8	232.7	235.5	244.3	239.7	263.6	281.7	F
G	322.9	335.2	344.9	361.7	367.8	369.3	406.6	412.5	419.6	439.3	G
H	144.4	146.3	165.3	170.6	170.5	162.0	177.7	169.9	184.3	154.3	H
I	178.7	185.6	187.5	184.0	197.9	204.4	199.5	203.5	193.1	191.2	I
J	86.4	97.9	98.8	89.3	99.3	100.7	101.9	103.2	100.3	66.8	J
K	102.3	100.5	120.4	131.5	135.2	160.5	160.2	152.3	165.8	108.6	K
L	279.9	299.9	301.9	309.1	322.5	354.3	342.2	380.6	390.9	1.5	L
M	226.6	224.1	238.5	247.2	262.6	292.7	285.8	300.7	302.0	102.7	M
N	163.1	161.9	155.6	157.0	160.2	182.5	186.8	191.7	198.7	64.3	N
O	98.0	95.9	97.9	112.3	112.1	110.5	110.9	108.7	114.1	381.9	O
P	46.2	47.5	45.2	50.1	53.0	62.3	64.1	67.2	63.6	298.5	P
Q	1.0	0.3	0.0	0.8	0.3	1.4	0.6	0.6	1.4	196.4	Q
R										43.4	R
S										53.0	S
T										68.1	T
U										1.7	U
X										-	X

Men - Hommes - Hombres

ISIC 3 - CITI 3 - CIIU 3	1999	2000	2001	2002	2003	2004	2005	2006	2007	2008	ISIC 4 - CITI 4 - CIIU 4
Total	1 435.2	1 450.7	1 493.9	1 536.7	1 571.5	1 624.8	1 645.9	1 661.0	1 685.3	1 736.0	Total
A	19.3	17.0	18.2	22.8	24.3	24.3	23.3	24.7	21.3	30.8	A
B	3.2	2.4	2.3	2.9	2.5	2.2	2.4	2.4	4.0	14.7	B
C	18.1	16.6	17.0	18.8	11.3	12.5	15.8	15.9	15.6	290.2	C
D	279.3	281.2	297.2	296.9	286.9	291.5	292.2	293.8	288.4	26.3	D
E	35.2	31.8	31.8	31.0	34.9	30.4	30.9	33.8	31.6	23.8	E
F	184.3	185.8	197.1	208.3	224.9	230.9	240.6	234.5	258.8	276.2	F
G	185.2	194.3	190.5	199.3	201.7	194.7	212.3	211.6	212.6	223.5	G
H	81.4	81.1	83.4	88.4	86.8	79.2	89.7	87.3	93.3	125.2	H
I	142.6	147.0	148.4	146.7	159.5	157.0	157.3	155.1	145.5	95.6	I
J	44.5	50.6	50.0	44.4	47.0	49.9	50.2	52.0	48.5	42.7	J
K	47.4	43.9	54.1	58.6	60.5	71.2	71.0	63.8	75.7	50.8	K
L	187.5	204.1	202.7	206.9	218.4	243.7	231.0	251.4	249.1	0.7	L
M	90.4	85.1	92.5	91.1	91.4	112.5	110.4	112.0	110.8	44.4	M
N	52.9	49.7	48.3	51.1	55.6	59.5	56.8	59.3	62.5	30.1	N
O	60.7	57.5	58.2	65.7	63.3	60.8	58.9	60.6	63.2	241.1	O
P	2.5	2.4	2.0	3.6	2.3	4.0	2.4	2.9	3.3	107.9	P
Q	0.7	0.3	0.0	0.3	0.2	0.4	0.6	0.1	1.3	60.3	Q
R										26.1	R
S										21.7	S
T										2.7	T
U										1.4	U
X										-	X

Women - Femmes - Mujeres

ISIC 3 - CITI 3 - CIIU 3	1999	2000	2001	2002	2003	2004	2005	2006	2007	2008	ISIC 4 - CITI 4 - CIIU 4
Total	902.2	928.0	972.5	1 008.6	1 044.5	1 121.4	1 139.0	1 173.1	1 211.0	1 238.8	Total
A	8.0	7.7	6.9	7.3	7.6	12.6	10.8	8.9	8.1	9.4	A
B	0.3	0.7	0.3	0.4	1.0	0.6	0.3	0.3	1.0	1.7	B
C	1.1	1.0	1.0	1.0	0.6	0.7	1.1	1.1	0.9	110.5	C
D	129.0	127.8	129.2	132.7	125.9	127.0	120.8	115.3	119.7	8.9	D
E	6.9	8.3	5.3	5.0	6.8	8.4	6.8	7.0	8.5	5.0	E
F	3.1	3.3	3.9	4.5	7.8	4.6	3.7	5.2	4.8	5.4	F
G	137.7	140.9	154.4	162.4	166.1	174.6	194.3	200.9	207.0	215.8	G
H	63.0	65.2	81.9	82.3	83.7	82.8	88.0	82.7	91.1	29.2	H
I	36.1	38.7	39.1	37.3	38.4	47.4	42.2	48.4	47.7	95.6	I
J	41.9	47.3	48.8	44.9	52.3	50.8	51.7	51.3	51.8	24.2	J
K	54.9	56.6	66.3	72.9	74.7	89.3	89.3	88.6	90.2	57.8	K
L	92.4	95.8	99.2	102.2	104.1	110.6	111.1	129.3	141.8	0.8	L
M	136.2	139.0	146.0	156.1	171.2	180.2	175.4	188.8	191.2	58.3	M
N	110.3	112.2	107.3	105.9	104.7	123.0	129.9	132.4	136.1	34.2	N
O	37.4	38.4	39.6	46.6	48.8	49.6	52.0	48.2	50.9	140.8	O
P	43.7	45.1	43.2	46.5	50.7	58.3	61.7	64.3	60.3	190.7	P
Q	0.3	0.0	0.0	0.5	0.1	1.0	0.0	0.5	0.1	136.1	Q
R										17.3	R
S										31.4	S
T										65.4	T
U										0.4	U
X										-	X

Explanatory notes: see p. 77.

[1] Persons aged 15 years and over. [2] Excl. conscripts. [3] Second quarter of each year.

Notes explicatives: voir p. 80.

[1] Personnes âgées de 15 ans et plus. [2] Non compris les conscrits. [3] Deuxième trimestre de chaque année.

Notas explicativas: véase p. 83.

[1] Personas de 15 años y más. [2] Excl. los conscriptos. [3] Segundo trimestre de cada año.

**Paid employment,
by economic activity**

**Emploi rémunéré,
par activité économique**

**Empleo remunerado,
por actividad económica**

	Thousands					Milliers			Millares	
	1999	2000	2001	2002	2003	2004	2005	2006	2007	2008

Hungary (DA) — Employees - Salariés - Asalariados

Total - Total - Total
ISIC 3 - CITI 3 - CIIU 3

	1999	2000	2001	2002	2003	2004	2005	2006	2007	2008
Total	2 678.7	2 703.2	2 698.1	2 739.2	2 754.8	2 764.6	2 737.0	3 307.5	3 329.0	2 762.6
A	142.1	129.9	118.2	111.7	105.6	99.9	96.0	107.9	103.1	85.6
B	1.6	1.5	1.4	1.3	1.2	1.2	1.1	1.4	1.3	1.2
C	8.6	6.6	6.3	6.0	.	5.2	4.8	5.4	5.1	4.7
D	743.0	753.2	752.8	746.3	734.4	715.2	688.8	753.0	750.1	696.3
E	78.2	72.7	66.5	62.9	61.3	59.3	57.2	54.4	49.0	46.5
F	107.3	112.4	117.0	118.8	125.0	129.6	129.3	199.2	200.1	125.4
G	267.4	283.2	292.2	305.8	314.5	323.5	326.8	494.7	515.7	365.1
H	74.0	77.4	77.0	80.1	80.3	80.8	79.1	120.9	123.8	88.6
I	226.4	227.7	224.5	228.9	224.5	224.5	216.5	245.3	245.1	211.5
J	57.1	54.0	51.5	52.8	53.0	52.7	56.7	56.7	63.8	70.4
K	135.1	150.0	158.4	166.3	175.8	194.2	209.7	358.5	389.2	252.8
L	304.4	300.6	302.9	311.0	320.2	318.1	317.0	312.6	267.3	262.9
M	248.6	248.2	247.9	251.7	252.7	255.7	254.5	260.1	278.7	266.9
N	209.8	209.6	207.6	218.2	222.8	225.1	218.6	232.7	233.2	201.5
O	75.0	76.2	73.9	77.4	77.6	79.6	80.9	104.9	103.6	83.2

Iceland (BA) [2] — Employees - Salariés - Asalariados

Total - Total - Total
ISIC 3 - CITI 3 - CIIU 3

	1999	2000	2001	2002	2003	2004	2005	2006	2007	2008
Total	126.2	128.3	132.2	130.7	134.7	133.8	138.1	144.2	152.7	156.3
A	0.9	1.4	1.2	1.4	1.9	1.6	1.4	1.7	2.0	1.4
B	6.2	5.0	4.9	4.2	4.3	4.0	4.2	3.6	3.8	3.4
C	0.3	0.2	0.3	0.3	0.2	0.2	0.1	0.1	0.1	0.1
D	20.5	21.3	21.0	20.0	19.3	19.9	19.4	18.2	17.4	18.3
E	1.2	1.3	1.5	1.5	1.6	1.6	1.5	1.4	1.7	1.8
F	6.1	6.3	6.4	7.3	7.0	7.7	8.3	9.8	10.8	12.3
G	17.8	18.3	19.4	18.3	18.1	17.0	18.9	20.5	22.7	21.1
H	5.1	5.3	5.4	4.7	4.7	4.7	4.8	5.0	5.6	5.9
I	9.8	9.2	8.4	7.9	8.6	9.5	10.5	10.3	9.6	9.9
J	5.5	6.2	6.3	5.9	6.0	6.8	6.4	7.1	8.4	8.8
K	8.1	9.7	10.8	10.0	11.0	11.2	11.9	11.7	13.4	13.3
L	7.4	6.8	6.1	7.7	8.2	7.6	7.4	10.1	8.8	9.5
M	9.1	9.7	11.3	12.4	12.0	11.8	11.7	12.4	13.3	14.3
N	20.1	19.0	20.3	20.1	23.2	21.8	23.4	23.2	24.6	26.0
O	7.4	7.6	7.7	7.9	8.1	8.0	7.9	8.7	9.7	9.9
P	-	-	-	-	-	-	-	-	-	-
Q	0.7	0.8	0.9	0.8	0.5	0.3	0.4	0.4	0.5	0.1
X	0.1	0.1	0.3	0.3	-	0.2	0.1	-	0.2	0.1

Men - Hommes - Hombres
ISIC 3 - CITI 3 - CIIU 3

	1999	2000	2001	2002	2003	2004	2005	2006	2007	2008
Total	62.7	63.5	65.5	63.4	66.2	66.4	68.3	72.7	78.3	80.5
A	0.6	0.7	0.7	0.8	1.1	0.9	0.9	1.2	1.3	0.8
B	5.6	4.4	4.6	3.8	3.9	3.6	3.9	3.4	3.6	3.1
C	0.3	0.2	0.2	0.2	0.2	0.2	0.1	0.1	0.1	0.1
D	13.6	14.6	14.4	13.4	12.8	13.1	12.8	12.5	12.0	12.9
E	1.0	1.0	1.1	1.0	1.3	1.4	1.2	1.1	1.3	1.4
F	5.8	6.0	6.1	6.9	6.7	7.2	7.5	9.1	10.4	11.4
G	9.0	9.0	10.1	9.2	9.6	9.4	10.4	11.3	12.6	12.0
H	1.8	2.3	2.4	2.1	1.8	1.9	2.1	2.4	2.2	2.5
I	5.6	4.9	4.6	4.6	5.3	6.0	6.5	6.2	5.9	6.4
J	2.3	2.3	1.8	1.9	1.7	2.0	1.9	2.4	3.3	3.6
K	4.3	5.2	6.1	5.1	6.4	6.2	6.7	7.0	8.5	8.6
L	4.1	3.7	3.1	4.0	4.0	3.4	3.6	4.8	4.5	4.7
M	2.8	2.6	3.2	3.4	3.9	3.9	3.5	3.8	4.4	4.6
N	2.5	2.2	2.4	3.0	2.9	3.0	3.0	2.8	3.5	3.7
O	2.9	3.4	3.8	3.4	4.2	3.9	3.9	4.2	4.4	4.7
P	-	-	-	-	-	-	-	-	-	-
Q	0.5	0.6	0.7	0.5	0.4	0.3	0.2	0.3	0.3	0.0
X	-	-	0.1	0.2	-	0.1	0.1	-	0.2	0.1

Women - Femmes - Mujeres
ISIC 3 - CITI 3 - CIIU 3

	1999	2000	2001	2002	2003	2004	2005	2006	2007	2008
Total	63.5	64.8	66.8	67.3	68.5	67.4	69.8	71.5	74.4	75.8
A	0.3	0.6	0.6	0.6	0.8	0.7	0.5	0.5	0.7	0.6
B	0.6	0.6	0.3	0.4	0.3	0.3	0.2	0.3	0.2	0.3
C	-	-	0.1	0.1	-	-	-	-	-	-
D	6.9	6.7	6.6	6.6	6.5	6.8	6.6	5.7	5.4	5.4
E	0.1	0.3	0.3	0.5	0.3	0.2	0.3	0.3	0.4	0.4
F	0.4	0.3	0.3	0.5	0.3	0.5	0.7	0.8	0.4	1.0
G	8.8	9.3	9.4	9.1	8.4	7.7	8.5	9.2	10.1	9.2
H	3.2	3.0	3.0	2.5	2.9	2.8	2.7	2.6	3.5	3.3
I	4.2	4.2	3.9	3.3	3.3	3.5	4.0	4.1	3.7	3.5
J	3.2	3.9	4.4	4.0	4.3	4.8	4.5	4.7	5.1	5.2
K	3.7	4.5	4.6	5.0	4.6	5.1	5.1	4.7	4.9	4.8
L	3.3	3.1	3.0	3.6	4.1	4.2	3.8	5.2	4.4	4.8
M	6.3	7.1	8.1	9.0	8.1	7.9	8.2	8.5	8.9	9.7
N	17.6	16.7	17.8	17.2	20.3	18.7	20.4	20.4	21.1	22.3
O	4.5	4.2	3.9	4.5	3.9	4.1	4.0	4.5	5.3	5.2
P	-	-	-	-	-	-	-	-	-	-
Q	0.1	0.2	0.2	0.3	0.2	0.1	0.2	0.1	0.3	0.1
X	0.1	0.1	0.1	0.1	-	0.1	-	-	0.1	0.1

Explanatory notes: see p. 77.

Notes explicatives: voir p. 80.

Notas explicativas: véase p. 83.

[1] Prior to 2006: establishments with 5 or more persons employed. [2] Persons aged 16 to 74 years.

[1] Avant 2006: établissements occupant 5 personnes et plus. [2] Personnes âgées de 16 à 74 ans.

[1] Antes de 2006: establecimientos con 5 y más trabajadores. [2] Personas de 16 a 74 años.

EMPLOYMENT   EMPLOI   EMPLEO

**Paid employment,
by economic activity**   **Emploi rémunéré,
par activité économique**   **Empleo remunerado,
por actividad económica**

	1999	2000	2001	2002	2003	2004	2005	2006	2007	2008
		Thousands				Milliers			Millares	

Ireland (BA) [1][2]   Employees - Salariés - Asalariados

Total - Total - Total
ISIC 3 - CITI 3 - CIIU 3

	1999	2000	2001	2002	2003	2004	2005	2006	2007	2008
Total	1 287.6	1 355.6	1 406.4	1 443.3	1 473.8	1 505.6	1 597.8	1 692.9	1 749.2	1 745.5
A	24.7	22.8	21.0	22.4	20.9	20.9	20.8	22.8	23.8	23.5
B	2.2	1.8	1.8	2.1	1.3	1.2	1.2	1.2	1.4	0.8
C	5.4	5.8	6.8	7.5	6.3	6.4	8.4	9.7	9.8	9.3
D	269.0	270.0	276.9	261.0	262.8	258.0	252.3	247.1	246.6	237.3
E	11.5	11.3	11.5	11.7	12.2	12.9	12.7	10.4	12.8	12.7
F	105.1	121.1	131.8	130.6	135.4	148.7	183.5	200.5	208.5	180.8
G	182.6	194.8	205.4	204.9	209.3	215.9	225.3	246.7	254.4	272.1
H	84.6	91.1	88.5	90.1	101.8	95.4	99.6	107.2	116.5	113.4
I	78.9	83.7	91.6	89.4	89.9	90.1	92.7	95.6	96.5	92.9
J	58.4	65.8	65.4	66.5	69.4	78.2	79.1	80.0	87.1	90.2
K	107.7	115.4	120.8	130.0	124.9	122.9	136.5	149.7	156.9	162.1
L	74.2	77.5	80.0	89.0	91.0	88.2	96.1	101.7	101.0	102.5
M	96.5	97.8	98.4	106.6	111.2	112.7	117.8	128.6	134.6	136.1
N	111.9	122.8	133.5	150.9	161.9	166.8	177.2	191.1	201.1	213.9
O	58.9	56.8	58.5	65.3	61.3	73.6	75.2	82.4	81.9	79.0
P	7.4	5.9	6.1	5.6	7.1	5.4	6.5	7.1	8.2	8.6
Q	0.5	0.7	0.6	0.5	0.8	0.4	0.7	1.2	1.2	0.7
X	8.1	10.6	7.6	9.1	6.3	7.5	12.2	9.8	7.1	9.5

Men - Hommes - Hombres
ISIC 3 - CITI 3 - CIIU 3

	1999	2000	2001	2002	2003	2004	2005	2006	2007	2008
Total	702.3	735.8	760.1	765.4	781.8	796.8	840.3	895.6	913.0	892.7
A	20.9	19.2	17.8	18.6	17.1	17.0	15.9	18.2	18.7	17.9
B	1.9	1.7	1.6	1.8	1.0	1.2	1.1	1.1	1.1	0.6
C	5.1	5.5	6.3	7.0	6.0	5.8	7.5	8.8	8.9	8.4
D	182.1	179.4	187.9	177.5	180.3	173.4	171.2	169.1	170.7	164.7
E	9.7	8.9	9.4	9.7	10.4	10.2	9.7	8.3	10.3	10.5
F	100.3	115.3	124.6	122.6	127.7	139.8	173.3	188.8	196.2	168.6
G	87.3	95.3	98.8	95.1	95.6	98.9	102.2	116.0	120.0	127.7
H	31.9	33.9	34.6	37.2	41.7	42.2	39.2	44.0	46.5	45.8
I	56.9	60.5	64.0	62.9	65.4	66.4	68.1	69.3	71.8	68.6
J	24.0	27.3	26.6	26.1	28.1	31.9	32.1	32.0	33.5	36.1
K	52.3	56.6	59.0	63.8	63.3	62.5	67.3	75.8	74.7	79.6
L	45.0	45.6	45.2	48.3	50.6	48.3	47.7	49.8	49.0	51.2
M	31.6	32.0	30.5	32.8	33.3	31.7	34.4	36.8	36.1	36.4
N	21.1	22.8	23.1	28.3	30.0	29.7	29.2	31.1	33.8	34.2
O	27.4	25.8	26.8	28.2	26.6	32.3	32.5	39.1	35.7	36.1
P	0.7	0.5	0.5	0.4	0.7	0.8	0.6	0.5	0.6	0.3
Q	0.2	0.3	0.2	0.3	0.5	0.2	0.3	0.5	0.5	0.4
X	3.8	5.3	3.2	4.7	3.4	4.4	8.0	6.5	4.9	5.3

Women - Femmes - Mujeres
ISIC 3 - CITI 3 - CIIU 3

	1999	2000	2001	2002	2003	2004	2005	2006	2007	2008
Total	585.3	619.8	646.3	677.9	692.0	708.8	757.5	797.3	836.2	852.8
A	3.8	3.6	3.2	3.8	3.9	3.9	5.0	4.6	5.1	5.6
B	0.4	0.2	0.2	0.2	0.3	0.3	0.1	0.2	0.3	0.2
C	0.3	0.2	0.6	0.5	0.3	0.6	0.9	0.8	1.0	0.8
D	86.9	90.6	89.0	83.5	82.5	84.6	81.1	78.0	75.9	72.7
E	1.8	2.3	2.1	2.0	1.8	2.8	3.0	2.1	2.4	2.2
F	4.8	5.8	7.2	7.9	7.7	8.9	10.2	11.7	12.2	12.2
G	95.3	99.5	106.6	109.8	113.7	117.1	123.1	130.6	134.4	144.5
H	52.7	57.2	53.9	53.0	60.1	53.2	60.4	63.2	69.9	67.6
I	22.0	23.2	27.6	26.6	24.6	23.7	24.6	26.4	24.7	24.3
J	34.4	38.6	38.8	40.5	41.3	46.3	47.0	48.1	53.5	54.1
K	55.4	58.9	61.8	66.1	61.6	60.4	69.3	74.0	82.2	82.4
L	29.2	31.9	34.8	40.7	40.4	40.0	48.3	51.9	52.0	51.2
M	64.9	65.8	67.9	73.7	77.9	81.0	83.4	91.8	98.5	99.7
N	90.7	100.0	110.4	122.6	131.9	137.1	147.9	160.1	167.3	179.7
O	31.5	30.9	31.7	37.1	34.7	41.2	42.7	43.3	46.2	42.9
P	6.7	5.4	5.6	5.2	6.4	4.6	5.9	6.6	7.6	8.2
Q	0.3	0.3	0.4	0.2	0.3	0.2	0.4	0.8	0.6	0.3
X	4.2	5.3	4.3	4.4	2.9	3.1	4.1	3.2	2.3	4.2

Explanatory notes: see p. 77.   Notes explicatives: voir p. 80.   Notas explicativas: véase p. 83.

[1] Persons aged 15 years and over. [2] Second quarter of each year.   [1] Personnes âgées de 15 ans et plus. [2] Deuxième trimestre de chaque année.   [1] Personas de 15 años y más. [2] Segundo trimestre de cada año.

Paid employment, by economic activity
Emploi rémunéré, par activité économique
Empleo remunerado, por actividad económica

	Thousands			Milliers				Millares		
	1999	2000	2001	2002	2003	2004	2005	2006	2007	2008

Italy (BA) [1] — Employees - Salariés - Asalariados

Total - Total - Total
ISIC 3 - CITI 3 - CIIU 3

	1999	2000	2001	2002	2003	2004	2005	2006	2007	2008
Total	14 995	15 276	15 636	15 942	16 125	16 117 [2]	16 534	16 915	17 167	17 446
A	428	431	445	444	434	400 [2]	419	459	428	410
B	21	20	19	18	19	16 [2]	17	17	14	15
C	64	56	56	55	52	32 [2]	36	38	36	32
D	4 075	4 060	4 061	4 103	4 126	4 067 [2]	4 086	4 075	4 114	4 078
E	166	159	154	152	152	145 [2]	156	154	135	139
F	948	984	1 040	1 084	1 135	1 106 [2]	1 186	1 189	1 229	1 250
G	1 498	1 593	1 635	1 723	1 788	1 789 [2]	1 880	1 997	2 042	2 093
H	407	459	506	517	542	635 [2]	673	722	757	786
I	938	979	975	969	962	1 032 [2]	1 040	1 015	1 051	1 084
J	574	561	557	567	571	520 [2]	531	562	556	543
K	725	801	871	953	999	1 291 [2]	1 329	1 365	1 448	1 517
L	1 927	1 923	1 962	1 957	1 909	1 430 [2]	1 420	1 416	1 390	1 411
M	1 401	1 424	1 474	1 482	1 486	1 511 [2]	1 465	1 516	1 522	1 505
N	1 101	1 098	1 128	1 143	1 151	1 255 [2]	1 305	1 335	1 347	1 417
O	537	548	573	601	615	619 [2]	671	720	728	711
P	168	163	160	159	170	250 [2]	303	324	349	419
Q	16	18	18	15	16	19 [2]	17	11	21	35

Men - Hommes - Hombres
ISIC 3 - CITI 3 - CIIU 3

	1999	2000	2001	2002	2003	2004	2005	2006	2007	2008
Total	9 165	9 223	9 317	9 449	9 523	9 285 [2]	9 526	9 717	9 834	9 908
A	283	285	291	284	288	267 [2]	277	303	290	280
B	19	18	18	17	17	15 [2]	16	15	14	14
C	56	48	45	44	44	29 [2]	32	32	32	29
D	2 793	2 768	2 767	2 807	2 827	2 820 [2]	2 851	2 864	2 910	2 886
E	147	139	135	133	132	124 [2]	136	131	111	112
F	889	917	968	1 006	1 056	1 030 [2]	1 106	1 115	1 149	1 164
G	857	898	905	944	962	936 [2]	1 016	1 090	1 085	1 129
H	211	233	247	255	269	294 [2]	304	331	360	362
I	735	764	758	746	734	793 [2]	786	760	789	825
J	362	346	330	337	342	289 [2]	298	323	316	299
K	334	366	389	429	455	586 [2]	595	618	668	694
L	1 333	1 315	1 311	1 300	1 265	978 [2]	957	958	938	937
M	397	402	410	401	389	388 [2]	367	370	376	375
N	428	396	407	406	400	392 [2]	409	411	398	399
O	276	279	290	298	298	298 [2]	324	349	348	335
P	37	39	36	32	35	34 [2]	41	41	39	49
Q	10	10	9	9	9	12 [2]	10	7	12	22

Women - Femmes - Mujeres
ISIC 3 - CITI 3 - CIIU 3

	1999	2000	2001	2002	2003	2004	2005	2006	2007	2008
Total	5 830	6 053	6 319	6 493	6 603	6 832 [2]	7 008	7 198	7 333	7 537
A	145	146	153	160	145	133 [2]	142	155	138	129
B	2	2	1	1	2	1 [2]	1	2	1	1
C	8	8	11	10	8	3 [2]	4	6	5	3
D	1 282	1 292	1 293	1 296	1 298	1 247 [2]	1 235	1 211	1 204	1 193
E	19	20	19	19	20	21 [2]	20	23	24	27
F	59	67	73	78	80	76 [2]	80	74	80	86
G	641	695	730	779	826	853 [2]	864	907	957	965
H	197	226	258	262	273	341 [2]	369	391	398	425
I	203	215	218	223	228	239 [2]	253	256	262	260
J	212	215	227	230	228	232 [2]	233	238	240	244
K	392	435	482	524	544	705 [2]	734	747	780	823
L	594	608	651	657	644	451 [2]	463	458	452	474
M	1 004	1 022	1 065	1 081	1 097	1 123 [2]	1 098	1 146	1 146	1 131
N	673	701	721	737	751	863 [2]	896	924	949	1 017
O	262	269	283	303	317	322 [2]	347	371	380	377
P	131	124	123	127	135	216 [2]	263	283	310	370
Q	6	8	9	7	6	7 [2]	6	5	9	13

Latvia (BA) [3] [4] — Employees - Salariés - Asalariados

Total - Total - Total
ISIC 3 - CITI 3 - CIIU 3

	1999	2000	2001	2002	2003	2004	2005	2006	2007	2008
Total	810.2	800.3	817.0	852.6 [5]	876.0	885.9	915.3	961.5	1 000.1	1 011.2
A	47.6	44.3	53.2	59.1 [5]	58.2	59.2	60.6	54.8	52.3	41.2
B	3.5	-	-	5.2 [5]	3.0	1.9	2.5	2.0	2.7	1.7
C	-	-	-	3.2 [5]	2.4	2.2	-	3.8	6.2	2.6
D	163.6	163.2	157.6	159.9 [5]	166.7	156.2	146.4	161.6	156.0	161.3
E	21.2	21.0	18.9	22.3 [5]	21.3	25.5	23.0	22.1	20.6	20.7
F	53.4	50.0	59.3	55.7 [5]	67.4	78.1	83.5	94.7	114.6	111.8
G	121.8	127.2	131.7	130.8 [5]	136.8	136.1	143.3	155.3	166.7	170.1
H	19.4	21.2	21.2	24.1 [5]	23.1	23.1	25.7	28.8	30.1	29.1
I	79.1	75.7	74.9	82.6 [5]	89.6	92.6	89.6	93.0	99.7	102.6
J	10.9	12.1	13.4	12.5 [5]	15.5	18.0	19.6	24.7	21.5	19.4
K	36.7	39.3	36.8	34.0 [5]	37.1	34.9	44.2	54.8	66.5	70.4
L	73.6	69.9	67.1	67.3 [5]	67.1	72.6	81.2	87.3	82.9	86.2
M	86.5	86.5	87.7	87.2 [5]	78.2	82.3	89.7	86.8	80.8	89.5
N	51.3	45.9	47.3	58.0 [5]	57.0	52.0	54.0	47.2	47.2	50.4
O	39.2	38.5	42.2	47.3 [5]	48.7	49.5	47.6	42.2	47.8	51.9
P	-	-	-	3.4	3.9	1.7	2.3	-	1.9	1.9

Explanatory notes: see p. 77.

[1] Persons aged 15 years and over. [2] Methodology revised; data not strictly comparable. [3] Persons aged 15 to 74 years. [4] Excl. conscripts. [5] Prior to 2002: persons aged 15 years and over.

Notes explicatives: voir p. 80.

[1] Personnes âgées de 15 ans et plus. [2] Méthodologie révisée; les données ne sont pas strictement comparables. [3] Personnes âgées de 15 à 74 ans. [4] Non compris les conscrits. [5] Avant 2002: personnes agées de 15 ans et plus.

Notas explicativas: véase p. 83.

[1] Personas de 15 años y más. [2] Metodología revisada; los datos no son estrictamente comparables. [3] Personas de 15 a 74 años. [4] Excl. los conscriptos. [5] Antes de 2002: personas de 15 años y más.

EMPLOYMENT	EMPLOI	EMPLEO
Paid employment, by economic activity	**Emploi rémunéré, par activité économique**	**Empleo remunerado, por actividad económica**

	Thousands				Milliers				Millares	
	1999	2000	2001	2002	2003	2004	2005	2006	2007	2008

Latvia (BA) [1,2] — Employees - Salariés - Asalariados

Men - Hommes - Hombres
ISIC 3 - CITI 3 - CIIU 3

	1999	2000	2001	2002	2003	2004	2005	2006	2007	2008
Total	415.5	400.8	402.2	425.6 [3]	439.6	448.6	461.9	484.6	499.5	498.7
A	34.7	31.3	38.9	45.3 [3]	44.2	45.2	46.4	41.4	36.9	28.0
B	-	-	-	-	-	-	-	-	-	-
C	-	-	-	-	-	-	-	-	-	-
D	95.4	91.7	83.4	91.7 [3]	94.3	84.6	82.9	89.2	87.2	88.5
E	15.1	14.9	15.4	17.7 [3]	16.4	18.3	16.4	16.8	16.0	16.6
F	47.3	45.2	54.1	49.6 [3]	59.0	68.9	75.5	88.8	104.6	100.5
G	54.1	49.0	49.6	48.0 [3]	48.4	49.2	51.1	55.8	59.2	59.6
H	4.5	5.1	4.5	3.8 [3]	4.4	6.5	6.3	4.8	5.3	4.6
I	53.1	52.4	50.9	55.4 [3]	61.3	65.7	61.3	63.9	68.0	71.3
J	3.5	4.7	4.6	4.8 [3]	6.0	8.2	7.2	7.1	5.7	4.8
K	18.3	21.2	20.0	18.9 [3]	21.7	18.0	21.8	26.9	30.5	36.4
L	40.6	39.0	37.9	36.4 [3]	35.3	39.8	44.6	45.5	38.9	41.5
M	18.4	18.3	15.8	18.5 [3]	14.8	14.2	17.1	15.6	13.7	17.7
N	9.4	6.2	7.5	9.3 [3]	7.6	6.9	7.9	6.4	7.1	7.4
O	16.8	18.3	16.0	18.8 [3]	20.8	19.6	19.9	16.5	17.3	16.7
P	-	-	-	-	-	-	-	-	-	-

Women - Femmes - Mujeres
ISIC 3 - CITI 3 - CIIU 3

	1999	2000	2001	2002	2003	2004	2005	2006	2007	2008
Total	394.7	399.5	414.9	427.1 [3]	436.4	437.2	453.5	476.9	500.5	512.5
A	12.9	13.0	14.3	13.9 [3]	14.0	14.1	14.2	13.4	15.4	13.2
B	-	-	-	-	-	-	-	-	-	-
C	-	-	-	-	-	-	-	-	-	-
D	68.2	71.5	74.2	68.2 [3]	72.4	71.6	63.5	72.4	68.9	72.7
E	6.0	6.1	3.5	4.6 [3]	4.9	7.2	6.6	5.3	4.6	4.0
F	6.1	4.8	5.2	6.1 [3]	8.3	9.2	8.1	5.9	10.0	11.3
G	67.7	78.2	82.1	82.9 [3]	88.5	86.9	92.2	99.5	107.5	110.5
H	14.9	16.1	16.7	20.3 [3]	18.7	16.5	19.3	24.0	24.8	24.6
I	26.0	23.3	24.0	27.2 [3]	28.3	26.8	28.2	29.1	31.7	31.3
J	7.4	7.4	8.8	7.7 [3]	9.5	9.8	12.4	17.6	15.8	14.6
K	18.5	18.1	16.9	15.1 [3]	15.4	16.9	22.4	27.9	36.0	34.0
L	33.0	30.9	29.2	30.9 [3]	31.8	32.8	36.6	41.9	44.0	44.7
M	68.1	68.0	71.9	68.7 [3]	63.4	68.2	72.5	71.2	67.2	71.8
N	41.9	39.7	39.8	48.7 [3]	49.4	45.1	46.1	40.8	40.1	43.0
O	22.5	20.2	26.2	28.5 [3]	27.9	29.9	27.7	25.7	30.6	35.1
P	-	-	-	-	-	-	-	-	-	-

Latvia (DA) [4] — Employees - Salariés - Asalariados

Total - Total - Total
ISIC 3 - CITI 3 - CIIU 3

	1999	2000	2001	2002	2003	2004	2005	2006	2007	2008
Total	783.9	782.2	800.1	802.0	827.4	868.3	885.8	925.4	1 005.5	1 001.1
A	28.0	19.8	19.9	18.4	18.9	19.3	19.2	19.8	20.6	19.7
B	2.0	1.9	1.8	1.6	1.5	1.7	1.5	1.8	1.5	1.5
C	1.5	1.8	1.6	1.5	1.8	1.9	2.1	2.1	2.3	2.4
D	150.1	148.9	154.8	153.8	157.0	162.5	157.7	159.8	159.9	150.9
E	20.2	19.5	17.7	16.9	16.6	17.2	16.7	15.7	14.4	14.4
F	39.6	38.4	40.6	41.7	44.4	48.9	53.7	63.6	83.9	88.2
G	126.2	133.0	144.7	145.6	149.4	163.1	170.9	178.1	193.7	189.1
H	13.9	15.9	17.6	16.3	19.6	22.0	24.3	28.7	32.1	32.7
I	72.4	70.8	70.6	70.7	73.5	74.1	76.5	81.4	87.5	85.1
J	14.5	14.9	16.0	17.3	16.9	17.3	18.3	19.6	21.4	23.1
K	48.9	53.3	53.0	54.9	59.9	69.9	71.4	78.2	99.8	100.1
L	67.4	67.9	69.4	69.9	70.0	71.9	74.6	74.6	76.5	76.9
M	100.9	99.2	97.5	97.4	100.9	99.7	100.3	99.7	102.5	102.6
N	57.1	56.5	54.5	53.7	54.1	53.2	53.1	53.1	55.3	58.2
O	41.1	40.2	40.6	42.2	42.9	45.8	45.6	49.1	54.1	56.3

Men - Hommes - Hombres
ISIC 3 - CITI 3 - CIIU 3

	1999	2000	2001	2002	2003	2004	2005	2006	2007	2008
Total	377.1	371.1	383.7	379.5	390.5	410.6	416.6	440.6	486.1	477.3
A	18.5	12.8	12.5	11.7	12.0	12.3	12.2	12.8	13.1	12.5
B	1.7	1.7	1.5	1.4	1.3	1.5	1.2	1.4	1.2	1.2
C	1.2	1.5	1.3	1.2	1.5	1.5	1.6	1.7	1.8	1.9
D	83.6	83.5	86.6	85.2	88.0	90.8	88.3	90.1	89.3	85.1
E	14.8	14.3	12.9	12.3	12.1	12.3	12.0	11.2	10.3	10.2
F	32.6	32.0	33.7	34.3	36.8	40.7	44.8	53.4	71.0	73.5
G	52.3	54.8	63.3	61.5	61.9	69.3	73.4	74.4	83.7	80.1
H	4.0	3.8	5.5	4.4	5.5	6.1	6.4	7.4	9.6	8.7
I	45.6	44.0	44.7	43.9	46.1	46.3	48.1	53.8	56.8	55.3
J	5.4	5.5	6.2	6.5	6.4	5.9	6.3	6.7	7.0	7.2
K	26.8	29.0	28.9	29.7	31.7	36.9	36.2	41.2	53.2	52.6
L	37.5	37.6	37.5	37.7	37.5	37.4	37.6	36.9	37.2	36.5
M	23.8	22.4	21.9	21.7	22.3	22.0	21.4	21.2	21.4	20.9
N	11.3	11.0	10.4	10.5	10.2	10.0	9.6	9.8	9.8	10.1
O	18.2	17.3	16.9	17.6	17.4	17.5	17.4	18.3	21.1	21.9

Explanatory notes: see p. 77.

[1] Persons aged 15 to 74 years. [2] Excl. conscripts. [3] Prior to 2002: persons aged 15 years and over. [4] First quarter of each year.

Notes explicatives: voir p. 80.

[1] Personnes âgées de 15 à 74 ans. [2] Non compris les conscrits. [3] Avant 2002: personnes agées de 15 ans et plus. [4] Premier trimestre de chaque année.

Notas explicativas: véase p. 83.

[1] Personas de 15 a 74 años. [2] Excl. los conscriptos. [3] Antes de 2002: personas de 15 años y más. [4] Primer trimestre de cada año.

**Paid employment,
by economic activity**

**Emploi rémunéré,
par activité économique**

**Empleo remunerado,
por actividad económica**

	Thousands			Milliers				Millares		
	1999	2000	2001	2002	2003	2004	2005	2006	2007	2008

Latvia (DA) [1] — Employees - Salariés - Asalariados

Women - Femmes - Mujeres
ISIC 3 - CITI 3 - CIIU 3

	1999	2000	2001	2002	2003	2004	2005	2006	2007	2008
Total	406.9	411.1	416.4	422.4	436.9	457.8	469.2	484.8	519.4	523.9
A	9.6	7.0	7.4	6.8	6.9	7.0	7.0	7.0	7.5	7.1
B	0.3	0.2	0.3	0.2	0.2	0.2	0.3	0.4	0.3	0.3
C	0.3	0.3	0.3	0.3	0.3	0.4	0.5	0.4	0.5	0.5
D	66.5	65.4	68.1	68.6	69.0	71.7	69.4	69.7	70.6	65.8
E	5.4	5.2	4.8	4.6	4.5	4.9	4.7	4.4	4.1	4.2
F	7.0	6.5	6.9	7.4	7.6	8.1	8.9	10.1	13.0	14.7
G	74.0	78.2	81.4	84.1	87.6	93.7	97.4	103.7	110.0	109.0
H	9.9	12.1	12.1	11.8	14.1	15.9	17.9	21.3	22.4	23.9
I	26.8	26.8	25.9	26.8	27.4	27.7	28.4	27.6	30.7	29.8
J	9.1	9.4	9.8	10.8	10.5	11.3	12.0	12.8	14.4	15.8
K	22.0	24.2	24.1	25.2	28.2	33.0	35.2	37.0	46.6	47.5
L	29.9	30.3	31.9	32.2	32.6	34.5	37.0	37.7	39.4	40.4
M	77.1	76.8	75.6	75.7	78.6	77.7	78.8	78.5	81.1	81.7
N	45.9	45.5	44.1	43.2	43.9	43.2	43.5	43.2	45.4	48.0
O	22.9	23.0	23.7	24.6	25.5	28.3	28.2	30.8	33.0	34.4

Lithuania (BA) [2] [3] — Employees - Salariés - Asalariados

Total - Total - Total
ISIC 3 - CITI 3 - CIIU 3

	1999	2000	2001	2002	2003	2004	2005	2006	2007	2008
Total	1 164.4	1 116.0	1 090.9	1 124.0	1 144.8	1 169.6	1 224.1	1 263.7	1 324.4	1 345.0
A	76.8	60.1	48.6	54.9	53.2	48.0	50.4	56.1	54.8	50.4
B	1.8	2.6	2.4	0.8	1.5	1.9	2.8	2.7	2.4	3.9
C	3.0	3.1	2.8	4.3	4.9	4.1	3.2	4.3	5.3	3.9
D	256.4	243.4	234.6	251.7	253.9	245.9	255.3	254.7	255.3	248.6
E	37.4	33.7	35.1	28.4	27.7	29.5	26.5	26.9	26.0	27.5
F	82.2	77.7	80.9	87.7	99.8	109.0	120.0	131.2	150.0	142.2
G	156.4	156.3	159.3	164.3	167.5	182.5	192.2	208.0	222.7	238.6
H	26.5	25.8	24.6	24.9	27.2	30.6	31.0	36.5	30.8	35.8
I	88.8	86.1	82.8	82.9	87.3	88.1	89.3	94.5	107.2	99.7
J	14.7	14.5	10.5	13.9	16.7	14.7	15.7	15.4	21.7	19.8
K	37.2	39.2	35.8	49.1	46.9	49.6	53.4	68.2	64.7	91.4
L	76.7	73.4	71.8	81.0	74.6	77.8	81.7	75.7	83.5	83.2
M	150.4	159.6	154.7	138.1	134.3	140.7	147.4	131.0	143.5	147.7
N	98.2	94.2	97.8	92.3	95.9	96.1	95.6	101.5	96.8	93.9
O	55.1	45.3	45.5	45.1	46.8	46.5	52.8	54.1	56.9	55.3
P	2.2	1.2	3.9	4.5	6.7	4.6	6.5	2.8	2.9	2.9
Q	0.5	-	-	0.1	-	0.2	0.2	0.1	-	0.2

Men - Hommes - Hombres
ISIC 3 - CITI 3 - CIIU 3

	1999	2000	2001	2002	2003	2004	2005	2006	2007	2008
Total	560.0	528.1	509.1	543.9	554.8	580.8	606.7	622.7	651.1	659.8
A	53.2	40.1	31.9	38.2	37.5	32.5	37.4	41.3	40.3	35.4
B	1.8	2.3	2.4	0.8	1.4	1.8	2.2	2.5	2.3	3.2
C	1.8	1.5	2.2	3.0	3.8	2.9	2.3	3.9	4.4	3.4
D	124.8	121.4	108.9	124.4	122.2	124.2	127.1	130.9	129.9	131.4
E	27.3	23.2	28.9	24.0	20.4	23.1	20.8	19.0	19.1	20.9
F	75.0	70.7	73.8	78.8	89.1	99.3	108.5	122.1	138.3	126.9
G	72.0	67.1	74.8	75.5	74.0	83.6	86.5	89.3	94.6	103.8
H	4.8	6.8	5.6	4.8	4.7	5.5	5.6	5.6	4.7	4.3
I	61.2	59.3	56.9	59.4	65.3	65.2	64.8	65.8	76.3	71.5
J	4.7	6.2	5.2	5.5	5.9	4.5	4.3	5.0	6.4	5.3
K	19.4	21.1	18.7	23.6	22.3	26.4	28.8	37.2	31.6	45.9
L	44.2	40.1	39.2	40.7	45.1	45.3	45.1	38.4	43.0	42.5
M	32.4	34.2	31.5	29.3	27.5	30.5	34.9	25.5	26.1	31.3
N	14.7	12.7	11.2	13.3	13.2	14.7	16.1	15.8	12.6	11.6
O	22.4	21.6	15.4	20.4	19.7	18.5	19.5	19.5	19.7	21.6
P	0.5	-	2.5	2.4	2.7	2.8	2.8	0.9	1.7	0.8
Q	-	-	-	-	-	0.1	0.2	0.1	-	0.1

Women - Femmes - Mujeres
ISIC 3 - CITI 3 - CIIU 3

	1999	2000	2001	2002	2003	2004	2005	2006	2007	2008
Total	604.3	587.9	581.8	580.0	589.9	588.8	617.3	641.0	673.3	685.2
A	23.6	19.9	16.6	16.7	15.6	15.5	13.0	14.9	14.6	15.0
B	0.1	0.3	-	-	0.1	0.2	0.6	0.2	0.1	0.6
C	1.3	1.6	0.6	1.4	1.1	1.2	0.9	0.4	0.9	0.6
D	131.6	122.1	125.6	127.3	131.6	121.7	128.2	123.8	125.4	117.3
E	10.0	10.6	6.2	4.4	7.3	6.4	5.7	7.9	6.8	6.6
F	7.2	7.0	7.1	8.9	10.7	9.6	11.5	9.1	11.7	15.3
G	84.4	89.2	84.4	88.8	93.5	98.9	105.8	118.7	128.1	134.8
H	21.6	19.0	19.0	20.1	22.5	25.1	25.4	30.9	26.1	31.5
I	27.6	26.8	25.9	23.5	22.0	23.0	24.6	28.7	30.8	28.2
J	10.0	8.3	5.3	8.4	10.8	10.2	11.4	10.4	15.3	14.5
K	17.9	18.1	17.1	25.5	24.5	23.1	24.7	30.9	33.1	45.5
L	32.5	33.3	32.6	40.3	29.5	32.5	36.6	37.1	40.5	40.7
M	118.0	125.4	123.2	108.9	106.8	110.2	112.5	105.5	117.4	116.4
N	83.5	81.5	86.6	79.0	82.8	81.4	79.5	85.7	84.2	82.3
O	32.7	23.7	30.1	24.7	27.1	27.9	33.3	34.6	37.2	33.7
P	1.7	1.2	1.4	2.2	4.0	1.8	3.7	2.0	1.1	2.1
Q	0.5	-	-	0.1	-	0.1	-	-	-	0.1

Explanatory notes: see p. 77.

Notes explicatives: voir p. 80.

Notas explicativas: véase p. 83.

[1] First quarter of each year. [2] Persons aged 15 years and over. [3] Excl. conscripts.

[1] Premier trimestre de chaque année. [2] Personnes âgées de 15 ans et plus. [3] Non compris les conscrits.

[1] Primer trimestre de cada año. [2] Personas de 15 años y más. [3] Excl. los conscriptos.

EMPLOYMENT

Paid employment, by economic activity

EMPLOI

Emploi rémunéré, par activité économique

EMPLEO

Empleo remunerado, por actividad económica

	Thousands				Milliers				Millares	
	1999	2000	2001	2002	2003	2004	2005	2006	2007	2008
Lithuania (DA)					Employees - Salariés - Asalariados					
Total - Total - Total										
ISIC 3 - CITI 3 - CIIU 3										
Total	1 106.9	1 072.3	1 051.4	1 071.4	1 149.3 [1]	1 159.7	1 195.8	1 240.3	1 291.8	.
A	56.3	43.2	37.1	34.5	33.1 [1]	31.6	32.7	32.9	32.4	.
B	1.1	1.1	1.1	1.4	1.4 [1]	2.1	1.9	1.9	1.8	.
C	3.4	3.1	2.7	2.8	2.9 [1]	3.2	3.4	3.4	3.3	.
D	240.3	236.4	233.1	240.2	246.4 [1]	244.5	246.1	243.9	240.1	.
E	38.7	35.9	31.7	30.9	29.9 [1]	28.1	27.0	25.5	24.7	.
F	76.5	66.0	64.2	69.3	78.3 [1]	81.6	89.4	100.7	115.4	.
G	155.2	157.6	158.7	165.2	182.2 [1]	191.8	206.2	218.0	231.6	.
H	20.6	20.4	21.2	22.2	25.1 [1]	26.5	29.3	32.5	36.2	.
I	85.7	83.7	81.3	82.3	85.8 [1]	84.3	88.9	94.5	100.5	.
J	15.9	15.2	15.0	16.1	17.5 [1]	17.3	17.7	17.3	19.2	.
K	49.5	48.1	49.4	52.6	62.7 [1]	68.0	73.4	83.9	95.1	.
L	68.4	71.4	71.3	72.5	76.5 [1]	77.0	78.9	81.4	83.7	.
M	147.8	146.7	145.1	144.2	162.1 [1]	166.4	160.6	160.1	159.7	.
N	98.8	96.6	94.5	92.4	96.1 [1]	93.3	93.7	94.6	95.9	.
O	48.9	46.9	45.0	44.8	49.5 [1]	44.1	46.8	49.7	52.3	.
Men - Hommes - Hombres										
ISIC 3 - CITI 3 - CIIU 3										
Total	543.5	512.0	505.3	515.3	544.2 [1]	548.5	568.4	589.7	613.1	.
A	38.4	29.7	25.5	23.6	21.7 [1]	20.6	21.1	21.0	20.2	.
B	0.8	0.9	0.9	1.1	1.1 [1]	1.8	1.5	1.5	1.5	.
C	2.6	2.5	2.2	2.3	2.4 [1]	2.7	2.8	2.8	2.8	.
D	124.9	119.4	119.3	123.0	121.5 [1]	122.1	124.0	123.4	121.5	.
E	29.3	27.0	24.0	23.4	22.6 [1]	21.1	20.2	18.9	18.1	.
F	66.0	57.2	55.3	60.8	68.1 [1]	71.1	77.8	87.7	100.0	.
G	75.0	69.5	76.3	80.8	84.7 [1]	89.5	94.7	98.8	103.8	.
H	5.7	6.2	6.0	6.5	5.9 [1]	6.2	6.7	6.9	7.3	.
I	58.9	55.7	52.8	55.1	57.8 [1]	57.3	60.8	64.8	68.6	.
J	6.0	5.6	5.4	5.6	5.6 [1]	5.3	5.2	4.8	5.0	.
K	25.0	24.7	26.1	26.1	30.4 [1]	33.3	36.1	40.7	45.7	.
L	39.9	41.0	38.8	37.9	42.7 [1]	42.1	43.3	43.9	43.5	.
M	32.9	34.9	33.8	31.0	41.3 [1]	40.1	38.1	37.8	37.0	.
N	15.1	15.4	15.9	15.5	16.1 [1]	15.8	15.6	15.6	15.7	.
O	22.8	22.3	23.0	22.4	22.3 [1]	19.5	20.4	21.2	22.2	.
Women - Femmes - Mujeres										
ISIC 3 - CITI 3 - CIIU 3										
Total	563.4	560.2	546.0	556.1	605.1 [1]	611.2	627.4	650.6	678.7	.
A	17.9	13.4	11.7	10.9	11.5 [1]	11.0	11.6	11.9	12.2	.
B	0.2	0.2	0.2	0.3	0.3 [1]	0.3	0.3	0.4	0.3	.
C	0.7	0.6	0.6	0.5	0.5 [1]	0.5	0.6	0.6	0.6	.
D	115.3	117.0	113.7	117.2	124.9 [1]	122.4	122.1	120.5	118.6	.
E	9.4	8.9	7.7	7.5	7.3 [1]	6.9	6.8	6.6	6.6	.
F	10.5	8.8	8.9	8.5	10.3 [1]	10.5	11.6	13.0	15.3	.
G	80.2	88.1	82.4	84.4	97.5 [1]	102.3	111.6	119.3	127.9	.
H	14.9	14.2	15.2	15.7	19.1 [1]	20.3	22.6	25.6	28.9	.
I	26.8	28.0	28.5	27.2	28.0 [1]	27.0	28.1	29.7	31.9	.
J	9.9	9.6	9.6	10.5	11.8 [1]	12.0	12.5	12.5	14.1	.
K	24.6	23.4	23.3	26.5	32.3 [1]	34.7	37.3	43.2	49.3	.
L	28.4	30.4	32.4	34.6	33.8 [1]	34.9	35.6	37.4	40.2	.
M	114.8	111.8	111.3	113.2	120.7 [1]	126.3	122.5	122.3	122.6	.
N	83.7	81.2	78.7	76.9	79.9 [1]	77.5	78.0	79.0	80.1	.
O	26.1	24.6	22.0	22.4	27.2 [1]	24.6	26.4	28.5	30.1	.
Luxembourg (E)					Employees - Salariés - Asalariados					
Total - Total - Total										
ISIC 3 - CITI 3 - CIIU 3										
Total	230.8	244.4	258.9	266.7	271.9	278.5	287.3	299.1	313.2	328.2
A-B	1.0	1.0	1.0	1.0	1.1	1.1	1.1	1.3	1.8	1.8
C	0.3	0.3	0.3	0.3	0.3	0.3	0.3	0.3	.	.
C-E	.	.	.	.	.	.	.	.	35.2	37.2
D	32.4	32.6	33.1	32.8	32.0	32.0	32.1	33.2	.	.
E	1.5	1.5	1.5	1.6	1.6	1.6	1.6	1.6	.	.
F	24.3	24.9	26.1	27.0	27.4	28.0	29.3	32.4	35.6	37.2
G	32.3	32.9	34.3	35.2	35.6	36.3	37.5	39.2	.	.
G-I	.	.	.	.	.	.	.	.	79.7	82.5
H	9.8	10.0	10.3	10.6	10.7	11.0	11.4	12.5	.	.
I	17.9	19.2	20.8	21.4	21.8	21.8	22.2	24.0	.	.
J	27.0	29.5	32.6	33.2	32.7	32.8	34.1	36.5	.	.
J-K	.	.	.	.	.	.	.	.	92.8	95.8
K	32.2	37.0	40.5	42.6	44.8	46.8	47.7	49.0	.	.
L	13.2	13.8	13.8	14.1	15.4	16.2	16.7	17.1	.	.
L-P	.	.	.	.	.	.	.	.	70.4	73.8
M	11.3	12.0	12.6	13.1	13.5	13.9	14.3	14.7	.	.
N	14.5	15.4	16.8	18.0	19.2	20.3	21.5	22.8	.	.
O	7.8	8.2	8.5	8.6	8.7	9.0	9.4	10.0	.	.
P	5.6	5.9	6.3	6.7	7.0	7.5	8.2	4.6	.	.

Explanatory notes: see p. 77.

[1] Methodology revised; data not strictly comparable.

Notes explicatives: voir p. 80.

[1] Méthodologie révisée; les données ne sont pas strictement comparables.

Notas explicativas: véase p. 83.

[1] Metodología revisada; los datos no son estrictamente comparables.

Paid employment, by economic activity
Emploi rémunéré, par activité économique
Empleo remunerado, por actividad económica

	Thousands			Milliers				Millares		
	1999	2000	2001	2002	2003	2004	2005	2006	2007	2008

Macedonia, The Former Yugoslav Rep. of (BA) [1]

Employees - Salariés - Asalariados

Total - Total - Total
ISIC 3 - CITI 3 - CIIU 3

	1999	2000	2001	2002	2003	2004	2005	2006	2007	2008
Total	.	.	.	.	.	.	391.651	403.564	426.662	437.475
A	.	.	.	.	.	.	13.776	12.106	12.388	15.914
B	.	.	.	.	.	.	0.354	0.218	0.209	0.105
C	.	.	.	.	.	.	3.554	3.835	5.027	6.473
D	.	.	.	.	.	.	111.452	114.193	116.820	119.691
E	.	.	.	.	.	.	17.035	15.955	15.636	15.516
F	.	.	.	.	.	.	27.349	33.605	28.826	31.578
G	.	.	.	.	.	.	47.524	47.257	54.372	57.871
H	.	.	.	.	.	.	10.711	14.580	14.512	14.608
I	.	.	.	.	.	.	25.930	23.289	28.086	29.494
J	.	.	.	.	.	.	6.263	7.023	8.821	7.435
K	.	.	.	.	.	.	11.700	11.553	11.788	13.195
L	.	.	.	.	.	.	38.301	39.343	41.409	42.227
M	.	.	.	.	.	.	31.150	32.666	33.873	33.233
N	.	.	.	.	.	.	30.371	31.052	30.701	30.549
O	.	.	.	.	.	.	15.169	15.760	21.711	18.265
P	.	.	.	.	.	.	0.097	0.168	0.613	0.506
Q	.	.	.	.	.	.	0.916	0.962	1.869	0.814

Men - Hommes - Hombres
ISIC 3 - CITI 3 - CIIU 3

	1999	2000	2001	2002	2003	2004	2005	2006	2007	2008
Total	.	.	.	.	.	.	.	.	248.649	261.113
A	.	.	.	.	.	.	.	.	10.069	12.879
B	.	.	.	.	.	.	.	.	0.209	0.014
C	.	.	.	.	.	.	.	.	4.772	6.083
D	.	.	.	.	.	.	.	.	57.847	60.232
E	.	.	.	.	.	.	.	.	13.205	13.136
F	.	.	.	.	.	.	.	.	26.394	29.754
G	.	.	.	.	.	.	.	.	27.891	30.561
H	.	.	.	.	.	.	.	.	9.256	9.505
I	.	.	.	.	.	.	.	.	22.574	23.920
J	.	.	.	.	.	.	.	.	4.316	2.868
K	.	.	.	.	.	.	.	.	5.973	7.706
L	.	.	.	.	.	.	.	.	29.424	30.606
M	.	.	.	.	.	.	.	.	13.177	13.991
N	.	.	.	.	.	.	.	.	8.448	7.486
O	.	.	.	.	.	.	.	.	14.068	11.677
P	.	.	.	.	.	.	.	.	0.244	0.104
Q	.	.	.	.	.	.	.	.	0.782	0.590

Women - Femmes - Mujeres
ISIC 3 - CITI 3 - CIIU 3

	1999	2000	2001	2002	2003	2004	2005	2006	2007	2008
Total	.	.	.	.	.	.	.	.	178.013	176.362
A	.	.	.	.	.	.	.	.	2.318	3.035
B	.	.	.	.	.	.	.	.	0.000	0.091
C	.	.	.	.	.	.	.	.	0.256	0.390
D	.	.	.	.	.	.	.	.	58.973	59.459
E	.	.	.	.	.	.	.	.	2.431	2.380
F	.	.	.	.	.	.	.	.	2.432	1.824
G	.	.	.	.	.	.	.	.	26.481	27.310
H	.	.	.	.	.	.	.	.	5.256	5.103
I	.	.	.	.	.	.	.	.	5.511	5.574
J	.	.	.	.	.	.	.	.	4.506	4.567
K	.	.	.	.	.	.	.	.	5.816	5.489
L	.	.	.	.	.	.	.	.	11.986	11.621
M	.	.	.	.	.	.	.	.	20.696	19.242
N	.	.	.	.	.	.	.	.	22.253	23.063
O	.	.	.	.	.	.	.	.	7.643	6.587
P	.	.	.	.	.	.	.	.	0.369	0.402
Q	.	.	.	.	.	.	.	.	1.087	0.224

Macedonia, The Former Yugoslav Rep. of (DA)

Employees - Salariés - Asalariados

Total - Total - Total
ISIC 2 - CITI 2 - CIIU 2   ISIC 3 - CITI 3 - CIIU 3 [2]

	1999	2000	2001	2002	2003	2004	2005	2006	2007	2008	
Total	316	312	298	280	267	411 [3]	411	418	434	435	Total
1	18	16	14	12	11	15 [3]	12	12	13	13	A
2	8	7	0	0	0	0 [3]	0	0	0	0	B
3	104	99	7	5	2	2 [3]	2	3	3	3	C
4	10	10	101	91	89	114 [3]	110	109	113	108	D
5	25	26	14	15	15	14 [3]	13	14	14	14	E
6	23	23	25	24	22	31 [3]	29	28	26	25	F
7	19	21	22	20	12	67 [3]	72	73	77	76	G
8	9	10	6	4	4	12 [3]	13	13	13	13	H
9	88	88	19	18	18	26 [3]	28	27	30	27	I
0	12	12	6	6	6	7 [3]	6	6	7	8	J
			6	6	6	13 [3]	15	18	22	24	K
			13	13	15	36 [3]	37	39	39	41	L
			27	27	29	30 [3]	31	32	32	34	M
			29	29	29	31 [3]	30	33	32	33	N
			9	8	9	13 [3]	13	13	14	15	O

Explanatory notes: see p. 77.

[1] Persons aged 15 years and over. [2] March and Sep. of each year. [3] Prior to 2004: April of each year.

Notes explicatives: voir p. 80.

[1] Personnes âgées de 15 ans et plus. [2] Mars et sept. de chaque année. [3] Avant 2004: Avril de chaque année.

Notas explicativas: véase p. 83.

[1] Personas de 15 años y más. [2] Marzo y sept. de cada año. [3] Antes de 2004: Abril de cada año.

EMPLOYMENT EMPLOI EMPLEO

Paid employment, by economic activity Emploi rémunéré, par activité économique Empleo remunerado, por actividad económica

Thousands Milliers Millares

Macedonia, The Former Yugoslav Rep. of (DA)

Employees - Salariés - Asalariados

Men - Hommes - Hombres
ISIC 2 - CITI 2 - CIIU 2 .... ISIC 3 - CITI 3 - CIIU 3 [1]
(2004 column: footnote [2])

ISIC 2	1999	2000	2001	2002	2003	2004 [2]	2005	2006	2007	2008	ISIC 3
Total	189	185	176	164	152	236	238	242	250	254	Total
1	14	12	11	9	9	11	9	9	9	10	A
2	7	6	0	0	0	2	2	0	0	0	B
3	59	54	6	4	2	2	2	2	2	3	C
4	9	9	57	51	48	60	57	56	57	55	D
5	22	23	12	13	13	12	11	11	11	12	E
6	13	13	22	21	20	26	25	23	22	21	F
7	15	17	13	11	6	33	39	41	42	44	G
8	4	5	3	2	2	7	8	7	8	8	H
9	36	36	15	14	14	20	21	21	23	22	I
0	10	10	2	2	3	3	2	2	3	3	J
			3	3	2	7	8	10	13	15	K
			6	6	7	25	26	27	27	29	L
			12	12	12	13	13	14	14	14	M
			8	7	7	9	9	10	9	10	N
			6	5	6	8	8	8	10	9	O

Women - Femmes - Mujeres
ISIC 2 - CITI 2 - CIIU 2 .... ISIC 3 - CITI 3 - CIIU 3 [1]
(2004 column: footnote [2])

ISIC 2	1999	2000	2001	2002	2003	2004 [2]	2005	2006	2007	2008	ISIC 3
Total	127	127	122	116	115	175	173	176	184	180	Total
1	4	4	3	3	2	4	3	3	3	3	A
2	1	1	0	0	0	0	0	0	0	0	B
3	45	45	1	1	-	0	0	0	0	0	C
4	1	1	44	40	41	54	53	53	56	52	D
5	3	3	2	2	2	2	2	2	2	2	E
6	10	10	3	3	2	5	4	4	4	4	F
7	4	4	9	9	6	34	33	32	34	31	G
8	5	5	3	2	2	5	5	6	5	5	H
9	52	52	4	4	4	6	7	6	7	6	I
0	2	2	4	4	3	4	4	4	5	5	J
			3	3	3	6	7	8	9	10	K
			7	7	8	11	11	12	12	12	L
			15	15	17	17	18	18	19	20	M
			21	22	21	22	21	23	23	23	N
			3	3	3	5	5	5	5	6	O

Malta (BA) [3]

Employees - Salariés - Asalariados

Total - Total - Total
ISIC 3 - CITI 3 - CIIU 3

	1999	2000	2001	2002	2003	2004	2005	2006	2007	2008
Total	.	126.278	124.273	127.648	125.932	127.581	128.700	131.646	134.048	160.979
A	.	1.276	1.175	-	-	1.456	1.398	1.043	1.213	2.770
B	.	0.075	0.432	-	-	-	-	-	-	0.373
C	.	0.597	0.377	-	-	-	0.671	-	-	0.585
D	.	31.013	28.766	26.163	26.447	26.583	26.090	24.466	23.612	24.311
E	.	3.166	2.941	3.748	4.116	3.210	2.811	3.362	3.058	3.684
F	.	7.418	8.530	8.987	8.205	7.931	9.150	8.791	7.740	12.441
G	.	15.159	13.102	13.522	14.628	15.203	14.680	16.252	17.564	25.044
H	.	9.843	10.759	11.575	10.952	11.015	11.220	10.555	11.838	13.260
I	.	9.943	11.591	11.340	10.244	9.747	10.220	10.258	10.325	13.029
J	.	5.105	5.235	5.699	5.319	4.629	5.929	6.241	6.288	6.052
K	.	4.416	4.661	5.358	4.897	5.946	6.450	7.139	8.992	11.531
L	.	12.278	10.913	12.415	13.051	13.873	12.460	14.263	13.798	14.265
M	.	11.320	10.833	11.636	10.706	12.514	11.030	12.157	12.569	13.476
N	.	9.776	10.290	10.195	10.067	10.726	10.980	11.142	10.864	12.233
O	.	4.664	3.961	4.541	4.563	4.093	5.061	4.947	5.213	7.532
P	.	0.062	0.442	-	-	-	-	-	-	0.137
Q	.	0.167	0.265	-	-	-	-	-	-	0.256

Men - Hommes - Hombres
ISIC 3 - CITI 3 - CIIU 3

	1999	2000	2001	2002	2003	2004	2005	2006	2007	2008
Total	.	85.323	85.925	83.925	83.806	85.641	85.600	86.327	86.547	107.467
A	.	1.276	1.060	-	-	1.297	1.348	0.953	1.125	2.568
B	.	0.075	0.432	-	-	-	-	-	-	0.363
C	.	0.597	0.377	-	-	-	0.653	-	-	0.571
D	.	21.581	20.383	16.952	19.093	19.319	18.990	17.838	17.467	19.190
E	.	2.910	2.820	3.321	3.818	2.927	2.627	3.141	2.847	3.491
F	.	7.016	8.320	8.486	7.896	7.714	8.831	8.542	7.400	11.962
G	.	9.107	8.291	8.745	8.212	10.451	9.110	9.743	10.796	16.938
H	.	6.007	7.167	7.584	6.802	6.802	7.049	7.197	7.258	7.912
I	.	8.880	9.882	8.735	7.812	7.450	7.941	7.764	7.944	9.816
J	.	2.813	2.504	2.833	2.670	2.670	2.887	3.298	2.888	2.833
K	.	2.640	2.950	3.831	3.457	3.726	4.286	4.566	5.188	7.525
L	.	9.355	8.483	9.212	9.711	10.301	9.657	10.000	9.953	9.569
M	.	5.325	4.480	4.563	4.023	4.496	4.185	4.274	4.616	4.715
N	.	4.367	5.747	4.637	4.769	5.288	4.759	4.957	4.960	5.444
O	.	3.196	2.780	2.938	3.556	2.666	2.806	3.203	3.335	4.391
P	.	0.062	0.116	-	-	-	-	-	-	0.000
Q	.	0.166	0.133	-	-	-	-	-	-	0.179

Explanatory notes: see p. 77. Notes explicatives: voir p. 80. Notas explicativas: véase p. 83.

[1] March and Sep. of each year. [2] Prior to 2004: April of each year. [3] Persons aged 15 years and over. [1] Mars et sept. de chaque année. [2] Avant 2004: Avril de chaque année. [3] Personnes âgées de 15 ans et plus. [1] Marzo y sept. de cada año. [2] Antes de 2004: Abril de cada año. [3] Personas de 15 años y más.

**Paid employment,
by economic activity**

**Emploi rémunéré,
par activité économique**

**Empleo remunerado,
por actividad económica**

	Thousands				Milliers				Millares	
	1999	2000	2001	2002	2003	2004	2005	2006	2007	2008

Malta (BA) [1] — Employees - Salariés - Asalariados

Women - Femmes - Mujeres
ISIC 3 - CITI 3 - CIIU 3

	1999	2000	2001	2002	2003	2004	2005	2006	2007	2008
Total	.	40.901	38.348	43.723	42.126	41.940	43.080	45.319	47.501	53.512
A	.	0.000	0.115	-	-	0.159	0.050	0.090	0.088	0.202
B	.	0.000	0.000	-	-	-	-	-	-	0.010
C	.	0.000	0.000	-	-	-	0.018	-	-	0.014
D	.	9.432	8.383	9.211	7.354	7.264	7.096	6.628	6.145	5.121
E	.	0.255	0.121	0.427	0.298	0.283	0.184	0.221	0.211	0.193
F	.	0.402	0.210	0.501	0.309	0.217	0.319	0.249	0.340	0.479
G	.	6.052	4.811	4.777	6.416	4.752	5.573	6.509	6.768	8.106
H	.	3.835	3.592	3.991	4.150	4.213	4.169	3.358	4.580	5.348
I	.	1.063	1.709	2.605	2.432	2.297	2.277	2.494	2.381	3.213
J	.	2.292	2.731	2.866	2.649	1.807	3.042	2.943	3.400	3.219
K	.	1.776	1.711	1.527	1.440	2.220	2.164	2.573	3.804	4.006
L	.	2.923	2.430	3.203	3.340	3.572	2.799	4.263	3.845	4.696
M	.	5.994	6.353	7.073	6.683	8.018	6.840	7.883	7.953	8.761
N	.	5.409	4.543	5.558	5.298	5.438	6.220	6.285	5.904	6.789
O	.	1.468	1.181	1.603	1.007	1.427	2.255	1.744	1.878	3.141
P	.	-	0.326	-	-	-	-	-	-	0.137
Q	.	-	0.132	-	-	-	-	-	-	0.077

Moldova, Republic of (BA) [1] — Employees - Salariés - Asalariados

Total - Total - Total
ISIC 3 - CITI 3 - CIIU 3

	1999	2000	2001	2002	2003	2004	2005	2006	2007	2008
Total	998.2	950.9	899.2	891.8	868.2	840.9	830.6	842.7	831.7	850.3
A	323.0	286.0	246.8	218.7	187.9	151.5	133.4	101.8	90.2	83.3
B	0.9	1.0	1.2	1.5	1.3	0.8	1.3	0.6	0.6	1.0
C	1.9	1.6	1.9	2.5	1.3	0.8	1.8	3.3	3.7	3.8
D	128.4	130.1	130.1	134.7	128.7	128.6	126.3	128.8	122.8	129.4
E	28.4	28.4	26.0	26.5	26.4	25.6	25.8	23.3	25.8	23.3
F	40.3	33.8	30.8	30.1	31.5	30.8	30.9	41.9	45.7	51.5
G	86.5	101.8	98.6	107.8	109.6	112.3	116.1	126.9	130.2	144.2
H	15.9	16.9	18.2	18.5	16.8	18.3	22.0	20.4	20.8	20.1
I	65.7	59.0	57.3	55.0	57.7	62.4	63.0	58.4	62.1	62.8
J	8.4	8.1	9.2	9.2	10.5	13.6	13.4	15.0	15.5	17.0
K	16.6	18.8	19.0	18.7	23.4	26.1	26.6	27.8	25.4	28.7
L	65.3	64.4	65.4	65.8	65.6	64.1	61.5	71.9	66.3	68.1
M	109.9	101.4	99.5	105.0	109.4	107.6	107.8	120.4	116.7	111.9
N	77.4	73.7	69.6	71.6	68.6	67.6	68.5	63.1	66.4	67.3
O	29.0	24.8	24.2	25.1	24.4	27.2	28.5	33.3	33.3	32.6
P	0.7	1.2	1.1	1.0	4.4	3.3	3.3	4.7	5.3	4.5
Q	-	-	0.1	0.1	0.5	0.4	0.5	1.1	0.9	0.9

Men - Hommes - Hombres
ISIC 3 - CITI 3 - CIIU 3

	1999	2000	2001	2002	2003	2004	2005	2006	2007	2008
Total	501.4	476.1	449.3	435.6	416.0	398.9	389.1	410.1	395.8	408.4
A	183.2	161.7	139.9	123.2	106.4	85.6	74.3	65.1	58.6	55.6
B	0.9	0.9	1.2	1.5	1.2	0.8	1.2	0.6	0.5	1.0
C	1.7	1.4	1.6	1.8	1.1	0.7	1.5	3.1	3.2	3.3
D	63.9	67.1	67.2	67.5	63.0	64.1	61.7	65.0	61.7	63.5
E	21.5	22.7	20.8	21.0	20.0	19.1	19.5	17.4	19.1	17.3
F	33.4	28.0	26.1	25.0	25.9	26.3	26.7	37.2	40.3	44.5
G	37.2	44.6	43.8	47.3	44.9	44.8	47.1	54.7	55.0	61.1
H	3.5	3.3	3.7	3.9	4.2	3.9	4.5	5.1	5.0	5.0
I	49.0	43.2	42.0	40.0	43.0	45.9	44.4	40.5	42.6	45.1
J	3.6	3.4	3.2	3.1	4.2	4.5	4.3	5.1	5.1	6.1
K	9.6	10.0	10.6	11.8	14.5	14.6	14.8	17.8	15.5	16.4
L	42.4	42.6	42.7	42.4	41.7	40.2	39.0	43.3	37.6	38.8
M	23.4	21.7	21.9	23.6	23.8	22.7	22.7	26.3	23.5	21.5
N	15.4	13.9	14.4	14.1	12.9	14.0	13.3	12.6	12.5	14.6
O	12.2	10.8	9.6	9.1	8.4	10.8	13.1	15.2	14.3	13.6
P	0.5	0.7	0.6	0.3	0.7	0.9	0.8	0.7	0.8	0.6
Q	-	-	0.1	0.1	0.1	0.1	0.4	0.4	0.4	0.4

Women - Femmes - Mujeres
ISIC 3 - CITI 3 - CIIU 3

	1999	2000	2001	2002	2003	2004	2005	2006	2007	2008
Total	496.8	474.8	449.9	456.2	452.2	442.0	441.5	432.6	435.9	441.9
A	139.9	124.3	106.9	95.5	81.5	65.9	59.1	36.8	31.6	27.7
B	-	0.1	-	-	0.2	-	0.1	0.0	0.0	0.0
C	0.2	0.2	0.3	0.7	0.3	0.1	0.3	0.2	0.5	0.5
D	64.5	63.0	62.9	67.2	65.7	64.5	64.6	63.8	61.1	66.0
E	6.9	5.7	5.2	5.5	6.4	6.5	6.3	6.0	6.7	6.0
F	6.8	5.8	4.7	5.1	5.6	4.5	4.2	4.8	5.4	7.0
G	49.4	57.2	54.9	60.5	64.8	67.5	69.0	72.2	75.3	83.1
H	12.4	13.5	14.5	14.6	12.7	14.4	17.5	15.3	15.8	15.0
I	16.7	15.8	15.3	15.0	14.7	16.5	18.5	17.9	19.5	17.7
J	4.8	4.6	6.0	6.2	6.2	9.1	9.1	9.9	10.4	10.9
K	7.0	8.8	8.3	6.9	9.0	11.5	11.8	10.0	9.9	12.3
L	22.9	21.7	22.7	23.4	23.9	23.9	22.6	28.6	28.6	29.4
M	86.4	79.7	77.6	81.4	85.6	84.9	85.1	94.1	93.2	90.4
N	62.0	59.7	55.2	57.5	55.7	53.6	55.1	50.5	53.9	52.7
O	16.7	14.0	14.6	16.0	16.0	16.5	15.4	18.0	19.0	19.0
P	0.2	0.6	0.5	0.7	3.7	2.4	2.5	4.0	4.5	3.9
Q	-	-	-	-	0.4	0.3	0.1	0.7	0.5	0.5

Explanatory notes: see p. 77.
[1] Persons aged 15 years and over.

Notes explicatives: voir p. 80.
[1] Personnes âgées de 15 ans et plus.

Notas explicativas: véase p. 83.
[1] Personas de 15 años y más.

EMPLOYMENT EMPLOI EMPLEO

Paid employment, by economic activity
Emploi rémunéré, par activité économique
Empleo remunerado, por actividad económica

Thousands Milliers Millares

	1999	2000	2001	2002	2003	2004	2005	2006	2007	2008
Moldova, Republic of (CA) [1]					Employees - Salariés - Asalariados					
Total - Total - Total										
ISIC 3 - CITI 3 - CIIU 3										
Total	932	810	780	776	779	776	779	775	750	746
A	271	193	177	167	152	135	124	105	88	79
B	1	1	1	1	1	1	1	1	1	1
C	3	3	2	2	2	2	3	3	3	3
D	128	118	117	117	118	123	123	122	116	111
E	22	20	21	20	20	18	18	18	18	18
F	34	28	25	24	24	24	27	31	32	33
G	73	70	67	69	75	81	86	91	94	100
H	10	9	8	9	10	11	11	13	13	14
I	57	54	53	53	55	57	58	58	57	58
J	10	9	9	10	10	11	12	12	14	15
K	35	34	34	36	38	39	41	44	45	47
L	49	50	51	53	58	58	58	58	57	56
M	136	128	123	124	126	126	126	126	122	121
N	80	70	69	68	65	64	64	64	62	62
O	23	23	23	23	25	26	27	29	28	28
Netherlands (BA) [2]					Employees - Salariés - Asalariados					
Total - Total - Total										
ISIC 3 - CITI 3 - CIIU 3										
Total	6 763	6 863	6 969	7 004	6 959	6 866	6 868	6 992	7 172	7 311
A-B	106	120	112	115	124	127	136	136	124	112
C	10	12	10	9	8	7	7	7	11	11
D	1 058	1 043	1 023	995	973	970	968	957	942	915
E	36	35	36	38	35	35	41	42	40	39
F	397	404	413	403	384	385	384	391	387	389
G	1 048	1 096	1 081	1 097	1 094	1 027	991	1 026	1 045	1 038
H	232	224	229	247	254	263	269	279	298	290
I	422	440	448	434	439	455	456	463	468	473
J	263	263	273	260	244	247	244	251	246	233
K	759	791	775	785	804	752	753	774	820	862
L	508	486	526	535	523	514	524	524	536	537
M	458	449	432	470	485	475	485	499	508	520
N	941	976	1 016	1 086	1 127	1 106	1 117	1 160	1 212	1 249
O	226	265	251	262	272	239	224	239	269	269
P	17	2	2	3	3	2	3	3	4	4
Q	2	2	3	.	2	.	.	.	.	.
X	281	254	340	264	189	260	266	242	262	369
Men - Hommes - Hombres										
ISIC 3 - CITI 3 - CIIU 3										
Total	3 835	3 864	3 895	3 872	3 801	3 748	3 713	3 748	3 802	3 844
A-B	71	83	75	80	87	90	93	96	87	77
C	8	10	9	7	7	7	6	5	9	9
D	826	815	799	771	756	755	755	746	727	690
E	30	27	29	30	29	28	31	32	29	29
F	370	372	384	373	354	357	351	357	354	352
G	561	589	577	579	573	521	499	523	534	522
H	103	103	104	112	111	118	120	125	134	131
I	307	326	328	319	319	336	338	340	342	344
J	141	146	151	143	132	137	132	131	128	124
K	442	458	449	453	464	431	429	444	467	497
L	347	318	340	342	331	330	330	325	325	324
M	207	197	189	201	205	193	192	193	197	200
N	187	185	186	193	197	192	190	193	196	200
O	108	124	110	123	127	109	98	107	122	118
P	0	0	.	.	.	.	.	.	.	.
Q	-	-	2	.	.	.	.	.	.	.
X	126	110	164	143	108	143	146	133	152	228
Women - Femmes - Mujeres										
ISIC 3 - CITI 3 - CIIU 3										
Total	2 928	2 998	3 074	3 131	3 158	3 118	3 155	3 244	3 370	3 467
A-B	35	38	37	34	37	37	42	41	37	35
C	2	2	.	.	2	.	2	2	2	.
D	232	228	224	224	217	215	213	210	215	225
E	7	8	7	8	7	7	10	10	11	11
F	27	33	29	31	30	28	33	34	33	37
G	487	507	504	517	521	507	491	502	511	517
H	129	121	125	134	142	145	149	154	164	160
I	115	115	120	115	120	119	118	124	126	129
J	122	117	122	116	112	110	112	120	118	110
K	317	333	326	333	340	321	324	330	353	365
L	161	168	186	193	193	184	194	200	211	213
M	252	252	243	269	280	282	292	306	312	320
N	754	790	830	893	930	914	927	967	1 017	1 049
O	118	140	141	139	145	130	126	132	147	151
P	17	2	2	2	2	2	2	3	3	4
Q	.	.	.	.	.	.	.	.	.	.
X	156	143	176	121	81	117	120	109	110	141

Explanatory notes: see p. 77. Notes explicatives: voir p. 80. Notas explicativas: véase p. 83.

[1] Enterprises with 20 or more employees. [2] Persons aged 15 years and over. [1] Entreprises occupant 20 salariés et plus. [2] Personnes âgées de 15 ans et plus. [1] Empresas con 20 y más asalariados. [2] Personas de 15 años y más.

Paid employment, by economic activity
Emploi rémunéré, par activité économique
Empleo remunerado, por actividad económica

Thousands — Milliers — Millares

	1999	2000	2001	2002	2003	2004	2005	2006	2007	2008
Norway (BA) [1]					Employees - Salariés - Asalariados					
Total - Total - Total										
ISIC 3 - CITI 3 - CIIU 3										
Total	2 083	2 099	2 108	2 118	2 098	2 105	2 116	2 162 [2]	2 248	2 328
A	24	23	22	20	20	19	18	19 [2]	17	17
B	14	11	13	13	13	13	12	10 [2]	9	10
C	31	33	36	35	32	33	35	35 [2]	39	41
D	293	284	277	281	268	255	256	262 [2]	268	277
E	18	20	18	14	17	16	16	16 [2]	17	18
F	128	128	132	133	135	137	137	139 [2]	153	155
G	319	327	311	315	319	325	332	332 [2]	335	341
H	69	68	63	64	66	66	67	64 [2]	63	64
I	157	156	156	149	139	139	139	143 [2]	145	143
J	53	49	49	50	47	47	50	54 [2]	54	54
K	180	188	206	203	203	201	206	218 [2]	236	256
L	153	157	151	145	149	144	138	143 [2]	154	162
M	178	183	189	186	184	194	188	191 [2]	212	217
N	386	389	402	426	426	432	439	451 [2]	456	482
O	77	77	80	79	79	81	79	81 [2]	86	88
P	2	2	2	1	1	1	1	2 [2]	3	2
X	2	-	2	2	1	1	1	1 [2]	1	1
Men - Hommes - Hombres										
ISIC 3 - CITI 3 - CIIU 3										
Total	1 086	1 095	1 098	1 091	1 076	1 078	1 088	1 104 [2]	1 148	1 189
A	17	17	17	15	13	13	13	14 [2]	12	11
B	12	10	11	11	11	12	11	9 [2]	8	9
C	26	27	29	30	26	27	29	28 [2]	31	33
D	218	210	206	208	199	189	191	197 [2]	203	206
E	15	16	14	12	14	12	13	13 [2]	13	14
F	116	116	120	121	122	127	127	128 [2]	141	144
G	175	177	162	163	165	168	173	170 [2]	173	178
H	22	24	22	22	23	26	25	22 [2]	21	21
I	109	107	107	106	101	101	102	105 [2]	106	106
J	25	24	26	26	23	24	26	27 [2]	28	28
K	106	113	126	122	121	122	128	131 [2]	143	160
L	89	90	85	78	82	80	77	78 [2]	81	85
M	60	64	69	67	65	68	65	65 [2]	75	74
N	61	62	65	71	71	73	75	78 [2]	75	77
O	34	37	38	38	38	36	34	36 [2]	38	42
P	-	-	-	-	-	-	-	- [2]	-	-
X	1	-	1	1	1	-	1	1 [2]	1	1
Women - Femmes - Mujeres										
ISIC 3 - CITI 3 - CIIU 3										
Total	997	1 004	1 010	1 027	1 022	1 027	1 028	1 057 [2]	1 100	1 136
A	7	6	6	5	7	6	5	5 [2]	6	6
B	2	2	2	2	1	1	1	1 [2]	1	-
C	6	6	7	6	6	6	7	6 [2]	8	9
D	75	74	72	73	69	66	66	65 [2]	65	70
E	3	4	3	3	3	4	3	3 [2]	4	5
F	12	11	12	13	13	11	10	11 [2]	12	11
G	143	156	149	152	154	157	159	162 [2]	162	163
H	48	44	41	42	43	40	42	41 [2]	42	43
I	49	50	49	43	39	38	37	39 [2]	39	37
J	28	25	23	25	23	23	24	26 [2]	26	26
K	73	76	80	81	82	79	78	86 [2]	94	96
L	63	67	66	67	66	64	62	65 [2]	73	78
M	118	118	120	119	118	126	124	126 [2]	137	142
N	325	327	338	355	355	359	364	373 [2]	381	405
O	43	40	41	41	42	45	45	45 [2]	48	46
P	2	2	1	1	1	1	1	2 [2]	3	1
X	1	-	1	1	1	1	0	0 [2]	1	-

Explanatory notes: see p. 77.

[1] Persons aged 15 to 74 years. [2] Prior to 2006: persons aged 16 to 74 years.

Notes explicatives: voir p. 80.

[1] Personnes âgées de 15 à 74 ans. [2] Avant 2006: personnes âgées de 16 à 74 ans.

Notas explicativas: véase p. 83.

[1] Personas de 15 a 74 años. [2] Antes de 2006: personas de 16 a 74 años.

2E

EMPLOYMENT	EMPLOI	EMPLEO
Paid employment, by economic activity	Emploi rémunéré, par activité économique	Empleo remunerado, por actividad económica
Thousands	Milliers	Millares

Poland (BA) [1][2] — Employees - Salariés - Asalariados

Total - Total - Total — ISIC 3 - CITI 3 - CIIU 3 / ISIC 4 - CITI 4 - CIIU 4

	1999	2000	2001	2002	2003	2004	2005	2006	2007	2008	
Total	10 782 [3]	10 546	10 226	9 904	9 904	10 107	10 481	11 028	11 666	12 177	Total
A	249 [3]	218	196	199	201	206	209	211	223	215	A
B	8 [3]	11	7	9	8	10	9	6	-	234	B
C	315 [3]	292	273	257	246	226	224	235	245	3 036	C
D	2 820 [3]	2 684	2 632	2 398	2 404	2 533	2 625	2 765	2 952	174	D
E	245 [3]	261	267	261	249	220	227	221	216	156	E
F	821 [3]	839	761	671	634	634	679	738	840	988	F
G	1 431 [3]	1 425	1 403	1 365	1 398	1 452	1 502	1 541	1 722	1 783	G
H	167 [3]	194	208	209	187	193	209	232	255	750	H
I	731 [3]	746	711	695	689	702	722	793	830	265	I
J	342 [3]	341	308	277	244	234	260	299	328	245	J
K	424 [3]	444	522	555	566	642	673	680	759	300	K
L	770 [3]	759	749	801	853	865	892	916	936	129	L
M	1 017 [3]	999	943	922	1 065	1 044	1 087	1 121	1 109	274	M
N	1 000 [3]	903	857	892	780	772	765	808	806	332	N
O	438 [3]	425	376	380	370	360	380	448	422	984	O
P	3 [3]	7	11	11	8	15	12	10	14	1 157	P
Q	- [3]	-	-	-	-	-	-	-	-	804	Q
X	- [3]	-	-	-	-	-	5	-	-	175	R
										153	S
										18	T
										8	X

Men - Hommes - Hombres — ISIC 3 - CITI 3 - CIIU 3 / ISIC 4 - CITI 4 - CIIU 4

	1999	2000	2001	2002	2003	2004	2005	2006	2007	2008	
Total	5 757 [3]	5 642	5 465	5 241	5 220	5 376	5 630	5 933	6 258	6 541	Total
A	187 [3]	156	146	149	146	148	156	159	165	156	A
B	7 [3]	9	6	6	6	9	8	6	-	206	B
C	277 [3]	249	236	228	218	198	201	210	214	1 983	C
D	1 732 [3]	1 691	1 665	1 525	1 534	1 648	1 726	1 814	1 928	139	D
E	194 [3]	208	208	203	201	178	180	170	168	122	E
F	740 [3]	761	704	611	575	587	628	690	790	928	F
G	608 [3]	615	596	587	607	630	652	662	726	749	G
H	45 [3]	50	60	58	52	59	65	68	74	579	H
I	512 [3]	532	500	488	488	503	531	601	635	77	I
J	104 [3]	100	89	84	65	67	78	83	97	152	J
K	238 [3]	246	300	318	333	368	388	376	406	93	K
L	435 [3]	413	398	414	433	436	451	456	468	49	L
M	269 [3]	250	231	216	225	229	242	249	245	115	M
N	181 [3]	151	134	150	145	141	140	147	144	184	N
O	228 [3]	211	192	201	190	172	181	237	195	495	O
P	- [3]	1	1	2	1	1	-	-	-	251	P
Q	- [3]	-	-	-	-	-	-	-	-	138	Q
X	- [3]	-	-	-	-	-	-	-	-	68	R
										55	S
										-	T
										-	X

Women - Femmes - Mujeres — ISIC 3 - CITI 3 - CIIU 3 / ISIC 4 - CITI 4 - CIIU 4

	1999	2000	2001	2002	2003	2004	2005	2006	2007	2008	
Total	5 025 [3]	4 904	4 761	4 663	4 684	4 731	4 850	5 096	5 408	5 637	Total
A	62 [3]	61	50	51	55	58	53	53	59	59	A
B	1 [3]	1	1	3	2	-	-	-	-	28	B
C	38 [3]	43	38	29	28	28	24	25	31	1 053	C
D	1 088 [3]	992	967	873	869	885	899	950	1 025	35	D
E	51 [3]	53	59	58	48	42	47	51	48	34	E
F	81 [3]	78	57	60	59	46	51	48	50	61	F
G	823 [3]	810	807	777	791	822	850	879	996	1 034	G
H	122 [3]	144	147	151	136	134	144	164	181	171	H
I	219 [3]	214	211	207	201	198	191	192	195	189	I
J	238 [3]	242	219	193	179	167	183	217	231	94	J
K	186 [3]	198	222	237	233	274	284	304	353	207	K
L	335 [3]	346	351	386	420	429	442	459	469	81	L
M	748 [3]	750	713	706	840	815	845	872	864	159	M
N	819 [3]	752	723	742	635	631	625	661	663	147	N
O	210 [3]	214	185	179	180	187	199	211	227	490	O
P	3 [3]	6	10	9	7	12	11	8	14	906	P
Q	- [3]	-	-	-	-	-	-	-	-	666	Q
X	- [3]	-	-	-	-	-	-	-	-	107	R
										97	S
										17	T
										-	X

Explanatory notes: see p. 77.
[1] Persons aged 15 years and over. [2] Excl. regular military living in barracks and conscripts. [3] First and fourth quarters.

Notes explicatives: voir p. 80.
[1] Personnes âgées de 15 ans et plus. [2] Non compris les militaires de carrière vivant dans des casernes et les conscrits. [3] Premier et quatrième trimestres.

Notas explicativas: véase p. 83.
[1] Personas de 15 años y más. [2] Excl. los militares profesionales que viven en casernas y los conscriptos. [3] Primero y cuarto trimestres.

Paid employment, by economic activity   **Emploi rémunéré, par activité économique**   **Empleo remunerado, por actividad económica**

	Thousands			Milliers				Millares			
	1999	2000	2001	2002	2003	2004	2005	2006	2007	2008	

Poland (DA)   **Employees - Salariés - Asalariados**

Total - Total - Total
ISIC 3 - CITI 3 - CIIU 3

	1999	2000	2001	2002	2003	2004	2005	2006	2007	2008
Total	9 637.1	9 354.1	9 050.2	8 759.5	8 661.7	8 640.2	8 786.7	8 930.7	9 272.0	.
A	220.6	211.2	199.5	189.7	159.6	154.0	153.2	152.1	152.6	.
B	8.3	8.6	6.0	4.9	4.4	3.9	3.6	3.4	3.3	.
C	271.4	239.7	221.4	211.0	200.0	193.4	186.8	183.0	179.5	.
D	2 611.4	2 467.1	2 358.6	2 220.8	2 206.3	2 243.9	2 259.4	2 310.6	2 426.1	.
E	255.6	248.2	240.6	238.7	232.8	225.8	219.2	215.6	213.4	.
F	710.4	661.9	627.8	545.5	496.4	453.1	483.6	502.1	549.1	.
G	1 318.4	1 325.0	1 295.6	1 291.1	1 308.0	1 295.4	1 360.7	1 392.0	1 465.5	.
H	142.8	144.5	145.0	136.3	134.8	141.6	147.3	149.4	159.2	.
I	686.3	654.9	630.4	601.9	586.3	583.0	577.7	585.2	613.4	.
J	287.3	251.8	240.9	237.0	226.3	226.7	243.0	250.2	258.5	.
K	583.0	614.2	637.3	671.3	699.5	700.6	695.8	718.9	760.5	.
L	419.0	470.9	514.4	507.9	531.1	538.3	552.3	560.5	574.9	.
M	894.5	899.6	876.5	867.1	960.8	979.7	1 004.9	1 003.2	1 002.9	.
N	941.2	869.8	804.1	776.4	653.6	636.2	634.0	634.1	641.0	.
O	286.9	286.7	252.1	260.0	261.8	264.6	265.2	270.4	272.7	.

Portugal (BA) [1]   **Employees - Salariés - Asalariados**

Total - Total - Total
ISIC 3 - CITI 3 - CIIU 3   ISIC 4 - CITI 4 - CIIU 4

	1999	2000	2001	2002	2003	2004	2005	2006	2007		2008	
Total	3 563.4	3 661.6	3 720.9	3 756.2	3 745.8	3 786.9	3 813.8	3 898.1	3 902.2	|	3 949.7	Total
A	81.4	78.7	86.6	85.6	85.6	87.3	86.1	86.7	88.0	|	88.9	A
B	14.4	14.0	14.7	13.2	12.4	12.3	11.9	11.4	9.9	|	17.0	B
C	12.6	15.5	15.3	16.1	13.3	12.8	18.0	16.4	18.4	|	805.7	C
D	964.8	960.7	956.0	918.3	883.9	872.0	853.4	867.1	841.6	|	22.6	D
E	29.4	28.0	36.5	39.0	34.8	29.7	24.5	25.4	31.5	|	33.6	E
F	396.7	445.1	429.0	462.3	437.0	404.4	417.5	428.5	439.3	|	424.7	F
G	431.9	464.6	482.2	494.9	503.6	526.7	519.5	529.7	534.5	|	556.4	G
H	174.8	174.2	175.8	177.6	168.9	173.8	185.7	195.0	199.5	|	152.1	H
I	152.7	166.1	181.3	179.0	186.4	189.7	196.1	215.2	199.2	|	223.5	I
J	82.3	85.4	85.6	79.2	80.9	89.3	88.3	82.8	89.1	|	82.8	J
K	156.4	160.9	173.9	186.4	197.3	217.8	216.2	225.4	254.8	|	90.0	K
L	313.4	326.7	332.8	338.5	336.5	335.0	345.0	351.2	324.0	|	18.7	L
M	284.8	277.0	288.2	283.2	279.3	299.1	305.5	308.2	298.2	|	119.0	M
N	227.4	239.7	245.0	244.3	281.1	297.1	310.9	312.4	319.1	|	121.7	N
O	122.9	113.9	110.3	117.4	114.0	119.6	117.3	122.4	119.3	|	340.0	O
P	113.0	108.6	106.0	119.7	128.9	118.2	115.5	117.4	133.2	|	336.7	P
Q [2]	-	-	-	-	-	2.2	2.4	2.8	2.5	|	286.4	Q
R										|	36.8	R
S										|	54.7	S
T										|	136.3	T
U										|	2.1 [2]	U

Men - Hommes - Hombres
ISIC 3 - CITI 3 - CIIU 3   ISIC 4 - CITI 4 - CIIU 4

	1999	2000	2001	2002	2003	2004	2005	2006	2007		2008	
Total	1 948.0	1 999.2	2 012.6	2 025.0	2 003.8	2 010.7	2 020.6	2 072.9	2 061.1	|	2 086.9	Total
A	50.6	48.5	51.2	52.8	54.7	58.6	53.0	59.2	59.8	|	61.3	A
B	14.1	13.4	13.9	12.6	11.6	11.4	11.1	10.7	9.7	|	15.7	B
C	11.8	15.0	14.4	14.9	11.8	11.9	16.8	15.1	17.3	|	463.6	C
D	525.7	518.0	514.2	493.7	482.4	488.4	486.6	486.7	473.8	|	18.1	D
E	26.5	24.4	31.2	33.2	29.3	24.9	20.1	20.5	24.8	|	27.2	E
F	380.4	424.7	409.4	441.7	416.9	384.4	397.4	409.1	419.4	|	407.1	F
G	255.7	256.7	261.2	275.5	280.9	288.2	285.7	287.6	286.5	|	298.6	G
H	62.0	59.1	62.0	57.7	57.8	59.0	60.3	63.9	70.9	|	124.0	H
I	116.8	130.0	139.7	141.2	144.2	142.4	140.9	157.4	152.6	|	78.2	I
J	53.4	52.8	52.8	42.9	48.6	55.4	49.7	46.7	46.4	|	50.0	J
K	67.4	72.4	83.2	85.2	83.4	102.7	104.8	115.2	112.4	|	48.6	K
L	206.7	210.7	215.4	218.3	213.6	206.4	212.7	217.5	202.6	|	8.4	L
M	71.8	64.9	66.7	59.8	64.5	71.8	71.4	72.8	71.9	|	46.6	M
N	43.8	48.9	46.4	42.1	45.4	46.7	53.3	51.5	53.4	|	56.2	N
O	57.1	56.9	49.1	50.4	54.9	55.7	54.3	55.9	56.2	|	220.0	O
P [2]	1.5	1.6	0.8	1.8	2.3	1.5	1.2	1.6	1.9	|	76.9	P
Q [2]	-	-	-	-	-	1.2	1.3	1.5	1.5	|	46.1	Q
R										|	20.9	R
S										|	16.2	S
T										|	1.9 [2]	T
U										|	1.3 [2]	U

Explanatory notes: see p. 77.
[1] Persons aged 15 years and over. [2] Data not reliable; coefficient of variation greater than 20%.

Notes explicatives: voir p. 80.
[1] Personnes âgées de 15 ans et plus. [2] Données non fiables; coefficient de variation supérieur à 20%.

Notas explicativas: véase p. 83.
[1] Personas de 15 años y más. [2] Datos no fiables; coeficiente de variación superior a 20%.

EMPLOYMENT — EMPLOI — EMPLEO

Paid employment, by economic activity
Emploi rémunéré, par activité économique
Empleo remunerado, por actividad económica

Thousands — Milliers — Millares

Portugal (BA) [1] — Employees - Salariés - Asalariados

Women - Femmes - Mujeres
ISIC 3 - CITI 3 - CIIU 3 | ISIC 4 - CITI 4 - CIIU 4

	1999	2000	2001	2002	2003	2004	2005	2006	2007	2008	
Total	1 615.3	1 662.4	1 708.3	1 731.2	1 742.0	1 776.2	1 793.1	1 825.1	1 841.1	1 862.8	Total
A	30.8	30.1	35.5	32.8	30.9	28.7	33.1	27.5	28.3	27.6	A
B [2]	0.3	0.6	0.8	0.6	0.8	0.9	0.9	0.7	0.3	1.3 [2]	B
C [2]	0.8	0.5	0.9	1.2	1.5	0.9	1.2	1.3	1.1	342.0	C
D	439.2	442.7	441.9	424.7	401.5	383.6	366.8	380.3	367.8	4.5	D
E	2.9	3.6	5.3	5.8	5.5	4.8	4.4	4.9	6.7	6.4	E
F	16.3	20.4	19.6	20.5	20.2	20.0	20.1	19.4	19.9	17.5	F
G	176.2	207.9	221.0	219.5	222.7	238.5	233.7	242.1	248.0	257.8	G
H	112.8	115.1	113.8	119.9	111.1	114.8	125.4	131.1	128.7	28.1	H
I	36.0	36.1	41.6	37.8	42.2	47.3	55.1	57.9	46.6	145.3	I
J	29.0	32.6	32.9	36.4	32.3	33.9	38.7	36.1	42.7	32.8	J
K	89.0	88.5	90.7	101.2	113.8	115.0	111.4	110.2	142.4	41.5	K
L	106.8	116.1	117.3	120.1	122.9	128.6	132.3	133.7	121.3	10.3	L
M	213.0	212.1	221.6	223.4	214.7	227.3	234.2	235.4	226.3	72.4	M
N	183.6	190.8	198.6	202.2	235.7	250.4	257.5	260.9	265.7	65.5	N
O	65.8	57.1	61.2	67.0	59.1	64.0	63.0	66.5	63.0	120.0	O
P	111.5	107.0	105.2	117.9	126.6	116.7	114.3	115.5	131.3	259.9	P
Q [2]	-	-	-	-	-	1.0	1.1	1.3	1.0	240.3	Q
R										15.9	R
S										38.5	S
T										134.4	T
U										0.9 [2]	U

Roumanie (BA) [1] — Employees - Salariés - Asalariados

Total - Total - Total
ISIC 3 - CITI 3 - CIIU 3

	1999	2000	2001	2002	2003	2004	2005	2006	2007	2008
Total	6 228.4	6 037.0	5 963.3	5 696.8 [3]	5 760.2	6 035.9	5 920.7	6 167.1	6 197.2	6 316.9
A	326.9	288.6	238.6	196.5 [3]	182.4	190.5	175.5	178.8	142.5	149.1
B	6.4	6.4	2.4	4.5 [3]	6.0	2.2	-	-	-	-
C	186.3	163.0	149.3	143.1 [3]	138.0	133.2	118.4	119.0	107.8	106.7
D	2 096.5	1 986.4	1 962.9	1 907.5 [3]	1 931.3	1 994.0	1 902.1	1 925.4	1 924.0	1 879.1
E	222.9	194.8	198.7	193.9 [3]	186.5	191.3	189.8	197.2	175.8	161.4
F	355.2	355.1	363.4	359.8 [3]	374.6	396.8	406.5	440.3	527.9	579.6
G	757.2	756.5	771.4	710.1 [3]	726.9	780.9	795.8	878.3	951.9	1 008.3
H	114.6	113.8	119.0	102.3 [3]	107.4	135.5	139.8	133.5	128.2	145.2
I	471.5	468.5	473.7	416.6 [3]	421.2	422.2	416.3	454.7	452.3	469.0
J	86.8	91.5	73.5	73.5 [3]	81.7	84.7	84.5	90.6	95.5	108.3
K	134.5	124.7	114.6	125.5 [3]	138.3	212.3	214.1	253.7	261.5	277.9
L	530.2	559.1	577.8	544.3 [3]	527.9	537.4	520.1	507.4	468.4	476.1
M	422.3	414.6	407.8	408.0 [3]	404.7	400.8	410.7	409.2	398.8	394.4
N	335.9	337.7	340.4	342.1 [3]	341.6	352.6	345.2	367.8	363.4	384.2
O-Q	180.6	175.7	169.1	168.5 [3]	191.1	200.8	199.5	209.2	196.1	174.5

Men - Hommes - Hombres
ISIC 3 - CITI 3 - CIIU 3

	1999	2000	2001	2002	2003	2004	2005	2006	2007	2008
Total	3 514.5	3 358.4	3 294.9	3 169.2 [3]	3 197.2	3 274.4	3 225.3	3 324.1	3 376.4	3 467.8
A	251.7	221.6	185.9	153.2 [3]	141.9	148.3	137.4	128.5	111.3	123.8
B	5.3	5.5	-	4.4 [3]	5.4	-	-	-	-	-
C	158.8	141.6	130.8	125.2 [3]	120.0	114.3	100.6	100.5	93.9	92.6
D	1 145.7	1 068.0	1 019.5	1 000.6 [3]	1 007.8	1 027.1	997.2	986.4	1 010.7	1 001.8
E	178.0	150.5	150.4	149.9 [3]	147.7	147.3	145.4	148.3	134.8	127.4
F	307.6	305.4	314.1	320.6 [3]	332.5	351.6	361.4	386.3	461.4	511.8
G	296.6	291.3	307.5	294.8 [3]	315.2	324.8	328.3	366.9	401.4	424.0
H	35.3	40.8	36.8	31.2 [3]	41.1	41.8	44.4	45.5	40.5	47.5
I	341.4	346.7	352.7	306.8 [3]	310.8	309.1	310.0	341.8	344.7	357.9
J	25.0	27.7	23.5	25.7 [3]	28.0	28.4	29.6	28.7	28.3	33.6
K	70.3	69.5	70.0	73.9 [3]	85.8	129.4	128.5	154.9	163.2	168.5
L	410.5	419.2	424.5	394.0 [3]	367.5	369.6	349.9	335.4	299.6	298.1
M	128.4	117.4	115.3	116.3 [3]	113.7	105.8	108.8	106.1	101.9	99.0
N	70.5	62.0	70.0	78.8 [3]	71.5	72.5	76.3	81.5	79.1	88.0
O-Q	88.9	90.5	91.6	93.1 [3]	107.6	102.1	105.5	112.1	103.3	91.0

Women - Femmes - Mujeres
ISIC 3 - CITI 3 - CIIU 3

	1999	2000	2001	2002	2003	2004	2005	2006	2007	2008
Total	2 713.8	2 678.6	2 668.4	2 527.6 [3]	2 562.9	2 761.4	2 695.4	2 843.0	2 820.8	2 849.1
A	75.1	67.0	52.7	43.2 [3]	40.4	42.1	38.1	50.3	31.2	25.3
B	-	-	-	- [3]	-	-	-	-	-	-
C	27.5	21.4	18.5	17.9 [3]	18.0	18.9	17.8	18.5	13.9	14.1
D	950.8	918.3	943.3	906.8 [3]	923.5	966.9	904.8	939.0	913.3	877.3
E	44.8	44.2	48.3	43.9 [3]	38.7	44.0	44.4	48.9	41.0	34.0
F	47.6	49.7	49.3	39.1 [3]	42.1	45.2	45.1	54.0	66.5	67.8
G	460.6	465.2	463.9	415.3 [3]	411.7	456.0	467.4	511.4	550.5	584.3
H	79.2	72.9	82.1	71.1 [3]	66.2	93.6	95.4	88.0	87.7	97.7
I	130.0	121.8	120.9	109.8 [3]	110.4	113.1	106.3	112.9	107.6	111.1
J	61.7	63.8	50.0	47.8 [3]	53.6	56.2	54.9	61.9	67.2	74.7
K	64.1	55.2	44.5	51.5 [3]	52.4	82.8	85.6	98.8	98.3	109.4
L	119.7	139.8	153.3	150.3 [3]	160.4	167.8	170.2	172.0	168.8	178.0
M	293.9	297.1	292.5	291.7 [3]	290.9	294.9	302.0	303.2	296.9	295.4
N	265.4	275.7	270.3	263.2 [3]	270.1	280.0	268.9	286.3	284.3	296.2
O-Q	91.7	85.1	77.5	75.4 [3]	83.5	98.6	94.0	97.2	92.8	83.5

Explanatory notes: see p. 77.

[1] Persons aged 15 years and over. [2] Data not reliable; coefficient of variation greater than 20%. [3] Estimates based on the 2002 Population Census results.

Notes explicatives: voir p. 80.

[1] Personnes âgées de 15 ans et plus. [2] Données non fiables; coefficient de variation supérieur à 20%. [3] Estimations basées sur les résultats du Recensement de la population de 2002.

Notas explicativas: véase p. 83.

[1] Personas de 15 años y más. [2] Datos no fiables; coeficiente de variación superior a 20%. [3] Estimaciones basadas en los resultados del Censo de población de 2002.

Paid employment, by economic activity
Emploi rémunéré, par activité économique
Empleo remunerado, por actividad económica

Thousands — Milliers — Millares

	1999	2000	2001	2002	2003	2004	2005	2006	2007	2008
Roumanie (DA)					Employees - Salariés - Asalariados					
Total - Total - Total										
ISIC 3 - CITI 3 - CIIU 3										
Total	4 760.5	4 623.0	4 619.0	4 567.8	4 590.9	4 468.8	4 558.9	4 667.3	4 885.3	.
A	240.1	196.0	188.5	158.6	151.7	143.4	143.9	133.6	125.5	.
B	3.6	2.8	2.3	2.5	2.7	2.4	2.8	2.7	2.2	.
C	154.2	140.6	140.9	136.2	127.9	117.6	114.3	94.5	84.5	.
D	1 659.9	1 559.7	1 590.0	1 593.4	1 581.5	1 491.6	1 424.8	1 408.8	1 402.9	.
E	177.2	172.8	169.9	161.1	138.9	132.2	133.0	128.3	127.6	.
F	308.8	316.2	309.0	300.6	325.4	322.5	347.7	352.1	405.6	.
G	578.8	568.2	583.8	561.9	587.5	597.5	677.1	739.2	798.5	.
H	91.2	83.8	68.1	76.1	81.3	88.8	89.7	93.3	106.8	.
I	373.2	369.9	358.7	348.5	343.5	318.6	319.6	327.2	336.0	.
J	68.9	71.3	64.2	66.0	68.3	68.1	76.9	85.0	96.7	.
K	166.6	176.9	185.4	210.7	220.3	228.9	240.2	286.0	324.6	.
L	140.8	147.9	143.3	147.1	152.3	154.5	166.7	175.1	198.0	.
M	415.5	407.2	402.4	390.2	389.4	381.3	380.7	382.6	394.0	.
N	283.2	305.0	304.0	312.7	312.9	306.2	321.1	328.3	343.2	.
O-Q	98.5	104.7	108.5	102.2	107.3	115.2	120.4	130.6	139.2	.
Men - Hommes - Hombres										
ISIC 3 - CITI 3 - CIIU 3										
Total	.	.	.	.	2 455.6	2 350.3	2 412.6	2 461.2	2 627.9	.
A	.	.	.	.	115.2	101.6	108.0	100.0	93.9	.
B	.	.	.	.	2.3	2.1	2.4	2.2	1.9	.
C	.	.	.	.	109.6	100.5	97.2	80.1	71.9	.
D	.	.	.	.	804.5	754.7	723.0	717.6	733.8	.
E	.	.	.	.	103.0	97.9	99.4	95.8	96.0	.
F	.	.	.	.	283.6	282.3	300.9	303.8	354.0	.
G	.	.	.	.	279.3	272.0	323.0	349.3	398.9	.
H	.	.	.	.	29.3	30.5	31.0	34.7	40.1	.
I	.	.	.	.	246.6	228.0	229.0	232.1	241.0	.
J	.	.	.	.	23.3	22.0	24.2	26.8	30.3	.
K	.	.	.	.	145.5	150.8	153.7	183.1	207.4	.
L	.	.	.	.	62.9	63.8	70.0	73.9	88.1	.
M	.	.	.	.	119.7	118.6	119.5	121.8	122.6	.
N	.	.	.	.	73.6	64.5	66.8	71.1	74.0	.
O-Q	.	.	.	.	57.2	61.0	64.5	68.9	74.0	.
Women - Femmes - Mujeres										
ISIC 3 - CITI 3 - CIIU 3										
Total	.	.	.	.	2 135.3	2 118.5	2 146.3	2 206.1	2 257.4	.
A	.	.	.	.	36.5	41.8	35.9	33.6	31.5	.
B	.	.	.	.	0.4	0.3	0.4	0.5	0.3	.
C	.	.	.	.	18.3	17.1	17.1	14.4	12.7	.
D	.	.	.	.	777.0	736.9	701.8	691.2	669.1	.
E	.	.	.	.	35.9	34.3	33.6	32.5	31.6	.
F	.	.	.	.	41.8	40.2	46.8	48.3	51.7	.
G	.	.	.	.	308.2	325.5	354.1	389.9	399.6	.
H	.	.	.	.	52.0	58.3	58.7	58.6	66.6	.
I	.	.	.	.	96.9	90.6	90.6	95.1	95.0	.
J	.	.	.	.	45.0	46.1	52.7	58.2	66.4	.
K	.	.	.	.	74.8	78.1	86.5	102.9	117.2	.
L	.	.	.	.	89.4	90.7	96.7	101.2	109.9	.
M	.	.	.	.	269.7	262.7	261.2	260.8	271.4	.
N	.	.	.	.	239.3	241.7	254.3	257.2	269.2	.
O-Q	.	.	.	.	50.1	54.2	55.9	61.7	65.2	.
Russian Federation (BA) [1]					Employees - Salariés - Asalariados					
Total - Total - Total										
ISIC 3 - CITI 3 - CIIU 3										
Total	56 115	58 512	59 853	61 477	61 522	62 189	62 871	63 625	65 384	65 774
A	5 441	5 428	5 130	4 949	4 753	4 245	4 151	3 971	3 645	3 786
B	143	177	180	130	164	169	136	141	160	119
C	1 153	1 276	1 338	1 206	1 243	1 208	1 233	1 193	1 318	1 348
D	11 235	11 934	12 445	12 855	12 536	12 448	12 277	12 233	12 089	11 358
E	1 535	1 668	1 715	1 784	2 026	1 995	1 954	2 061	2 010	2 108
F	3 337	3 245	3 354	3 535	3 910	3 947	4 373	4 245	4 690	5 112
G	5 687	6 300	6 841	7 516	8 119	8 520	8 814	9 200	9 624	9 239
H	825	895	983	1 103	1 223	1 182	1 253	1 359	1 303	1 424
I	5 259	5 270	5 571	5 689	5 716	5 939	5 950	5 936	6 224	6 158
J	810	833	852	865	802	914	960	1 053	1 244	1 311
K	1 730	1 939	2 301	2 671	3 695	4 015	3 939	4 038	4 297	4 301
L	4 563	4 806	4 760	4 609	4 675	4 702	4 815	4 875	4 903	5 409
M	5 794	5 843	5 637	5 902	5 993	6 114	6 180	6 175	6 401	6 423
N	4 272	4 350	4 593	4 569	4 649	4 798	4 673	4 865	5 143	5 207
O	4 288	4 525	4 133	4 081	2 001	1 993	2 132	2 254	2 317	2 421
P	38	21	14	12	11	-	26	21	16	43
Q	7	4	5	2	5	1	4	4	-	5

Explanatory notes: see p. 77.   Notes explicatives: voir p. 80.   Notas explicativas: véase p. 83.

[1] Persons aged 15 to 72 years.   [1] Personnes âgées de 15 à 72 ans.   [1] Personas de 15 a 72 años.

	EMPLOYMENT			EMPLOI			EMPLEO		
	Paid employment, by economic activity			**Emploi rémunéré, par activité économique**			**Empleo remunerado, por actividad económica**		
	Thousands			Milliers			Millares		
1999	2000	2001	2002	2003	2004	2005	2006	2007	2008

Russian Federation (BA) [1] — Employees - Salariés - Asalariados

Men - Hommes - Hombres
ISIC 3 - CITI 3 - CIIU 3

	1999	2000	2001	2002	2003	2004	2005	2006	2007	2008
Total	28 976	30 058	30 674	31 259	31 108	31 381	31 695	31 838	32 801	33 271
A	3 682	3 676	3 482	3 291	3 215	2 864	2 821	2 699	2 504	2 597
B	119	145	140	105	133	135	110	114	130	97
C	880	948	1 026	918	955	934	964	922	1 040	1 052
D	6 355	6 783	6 973	7 207	7 127	7 039	6 998	7 034	6 935	6 669
E	1 096	1 176	1 176	1 261	1 403	1 396	1 356	1 439	1 383	1 492
F	2 538	2 502	2 577	2 724	3 108	3 173	3 524	3 418	3 831	4 230
G	2 124	2 296	2 573	2 841	3 034	3 236	3 265	3 383	3 604	3 384
H	171	162	179	207	248	250	274	275	264	290
I	3 577	3 600	3 805	3 880	3 937	4 102	4 039	4 081	4 267	4 340
J	266	270	254	264	264	287	345	354	412	408
K	909	1 039	1 211	1 450	2 006	2 271	2 199	2 259	2 421	2 418
L	3 072	3 147	3 166	3 039	2 967	2 967	3 023	3 005	3 076	3 275
M	1 173	1 170	1 127	1 159	1 169	1 210	1 241	1 195	1 263	1 220
N	776	794	852	849	871	872	829	926	951	1 024
O	2 211	2 335	2 124	2 057	666	646	701	730	714	761
P	22	12	6	5	2	-	4	4	5	9
Q	6	3	4	1	3	-	3	2	-	4

Women - Femmes - Mujeres
ISIC 3 - CITI 3 - CIIU 3

	1999	2000	2001	2002	2003	2004	2005	2006	2007	2008
Total	27 139	28 454	29 179	30 218	30 414	30 808	31 177	31 787	32 583	32 503
A	1 759	1 752	1 648	1 658	1 539	1 381	1 330	1 272	1 142	1 189
B	24	32	40	24	31	34	26	28	31	22
C	272	328	313	287	288	274	269	271	278	296
D	4 881	5 151	5 472	5 648	5 409	5 409	5 272	5 199	5 155	4 690
E	439	492	539	524	624	599	597	622	627	616
F	799	743	777	811	801	774	849	828	859	883
G	3 563	4 003	4 268	4 675	5 085	5 284	5 549	5 817	6 020	5 855
H	654	733	805	896	974	932	980	1 085	1 038	1 134
I	1 682	1 671	1 766	1 809	1 779	1 837	1 911	1 856	1 957	1 818
J	544	563	598	601	538	626	615	699	830	903
K	821	899	1 089	1 221	1 688	1 744	1 740	1 779	1 876	1 883
L	1 492	1 658	1 594	1 570	1 709	1 734	1 792	1 871	1 827	2 134
M	4 621	4 673	4 510	4 743	4 824	4 905	4 940	4 980	5 138	5 203
N	3 495	3 556	3 741	3 720	3 778	3 926	3 844	3 939	4 191	4 183
O	2 077	2 190	2 010	2 024	1 335	1 347	1 431	1 525	1 603	1 661
P	16	9	8	7	9	-	22	17	11	34
Q	1	1	1	1	2	1	1	1	-	1

Russian Federation (DA) [1] — Employees - Salariés - Asalariados

Total - Total - Total
ISIC 3 - CITI 3 - CIIU 3

	1999	2000	2001	2002	2003	2004	2005	2006	2007	2008
Total	51 157.9	51 238.2	50 613.2	50 615.4	49 881.8	49 130.0	48 197.2	48 096.4	48 943.7	49 362.9
A	5 338.2	5 071.7	4 688.4	4 377.6	3 875.7	3 453.9	3 249.1	2 828.5	2 524.0	2 287.2
B	125.8	124.7	116.5	92.3	86.2	80.0	98.2	96.0	89.7	83.6
C	1 059.5	1 081.6	1 178.6	1 125.4	1 064.7	1 031.8	985.6	975.7	974.5	975.8
D	11 301.3	11 272.3	10 987.0	10 798.9	10 302.9	9 919.8	9 511.6	9 240.5	9 258.9	9 126.2
E	1 850.8	1 873.9	1 901.8	1 870.2	1 856.1	1 859.0	1 861.1	1 869.2	1 845.3	1 818.4
F	3 024.3	2 941.2	2 841.9	2 807.4	2 765.8	2 865.4	2 816.2	2 923.9	3 163.3	3 295.7
G	4 109.5	4 072.3	4 131.6	4 401.2	4 525.4	4 532.1	4 470.8	4 706.8	5 259.3	5 689.0
H	791.0	793.0	819.7	860.4	838.2	800.3	677.8	680.9	792.1	795.4
I	4 421.6	4 459.4	4 377.3	4 264.4	4 227.2	4 181.9	4 193.1	4 198.5	4 166.5	4 132.0
J	621.2	626.5	654.7	673.2	733.8	783.2	795.5	895.7	977.0	1 057.5
K	3 897.1	4 013.1	4 202.4	4 415.6	4 359.9	4 270.2	4 241.6	4 290.8	4 319.8	4 444.8
L	2 987.7	3 055.7	3 037.8	3 079.2	3 168.8	3 379.8	3 294.5	3 404.8	3 542.5	3 648.3
M	5 914.5	5 850.4	5 809.7	5 844.7	5 923.5	5 931.2	5 833.9	5 770.6	5 767.7	5 714.5
N	4 301.5	4 307.4	4 239.6	4 308.8	4 322.9	4 329.7	4 357.3	4 386.6	4 450.9	4 459.5
O	1 613.6	1 694.6	1 620.7	1 695.5	1 718.0	1 711.3	1 810.2	1 828.3	1 811.3	1 834.3
Q	.	0.3	0.4	0.6	0.5	0.5	0.7	0.6	0.7	0.7

San Marino (E) [2][3] — Employees - Salariés - Asalariados

Total - Total - Total
ISIC 3 - CITI 3 - CIIU 3

	1999	2000	2001	2002	2003	2004	2005	2006	2007	2008
Total	15.430	.	16.884	16.992	17.128	17.686	17.945	18.614	19.427	19.965
A	0.027	.	0.024	0.026	0.026	0.024	0.035	0.038	0.031	0.029
D	5.610	.	5.974	5.931	6.026	6.132	5.998	6.103	6.239	6.219
F	1.275	.	1.345	1.340	1.380	1.436	1.439	1.487	1.436	1.470
G	1.720	.	1.976	2.291	2.450	2.559	2.187	2.400	2.671	2.843
H	0.421	.	0.483	0.229	-	-	0.150	0.149	0.173	0.206
I	0.301	.	0.362	0.365	0.387	0.405	0.426	0.465	0.493	0.553
J	0.529	.	0.611	0.641	0.674	0.739	0.788	0.849	0.949	1.008
K	0.586	.	-	-	-	-	1.994	2.106	2.335	2.444
L	2.279	.	2.306	2.212	2.124	2.180	2.430	2.410	4.020	4.030
M	0.938	.	0.036	0.036	0.037	0.040	0.632	0.645	0.041	0.038
N	1.029	.	1.100	1.064	1.054	1.054	1.079	1.103	0.126	0.141
O	0.583	.	2.663	2.849	2.916	3.117	0.787	0.859	0.907	0.976
P	0.131	.	-	-	-	-	-	-	-	-
Q	0.001	.	-	-	-	-	-	-	-	-
X	.	.	0.004	0.008	-	0.003	-	-	0.006	0.008

Explanatory notes: see p. 77.

[1] Persons aged 15 to 72 years. [2] Persons aged 15 years and over. [3] Dec.

Notes explicatives: voir p. 80.

[1] Personnes âgées de 15 à 72 ans. [2] Personnes âgées de 15 ans et plus. [3] Déc.

Notas explicativas: véase p. 83.

[1] Personas de 15 a 72 años. [2] Personas de 15 años y más. [3] Dic.

Paid employment, by economic activity
Emploi rémunéré, par activité économique
Empleo remunerado, por actividad económica

Thousands   Milliers   Millares

	1999	2000	2001	2002	2003	2004	2005	2006	2007	2008
San Marino (E) [1][2]				Employees - Salariés - Asalariados						
Men - Hommes - Hombres										
ISIC 3 - CITI 3 - CIIU 3										
Total	9.081	.	9.883	9.915	9.941	10.226	10.391	10.791	11.241	11.550
A	0.023	.	0.018	0.021	0.021	0.021	0.030	0.033	0.026	0.024
D	3.957	.	4.250	4.240	2.283	4.646	4.245	4.295	4.465	4.477
F	1.198	.	1.258	1.236	1.260	1.308	1.314	1.361	1.306	1.337
G	0.834	.	0.964	1.110	1.155	1.200	1.112	1.239	1.367	1.467
H	0.165	.	0.177	0.069	-	-	0.034	0.043	0.052	0.077
I	0.186	.	0.215	0.219	0.227	0.237	0.240	0.269	0.285	0.334
J	0.287	.	0.324	0.345	0.364	0.395	0.411	0.453	0.506	0.536
K	0.219	.	-	-	-	-	1.040	1.096	1.237	1.280
L	1.508	.	0.819	0.778	0.751	0.746	1.317	1.308	1.702	1.708
M	0.169	.	0.019	0.007	0.009	0.010	0.119	0.119	0.020	0.021
N	0.292	.	0.320	0.313	0.299	0.326	0.333	0.342	0.021	0.026
O	0.237	.	1.517	1.575	1.572	1.637	0.196	0.233	0.249	0.257
P	0.006	.	-	-	-	-	-	-	-	-
Q	.	.	.	.	.	.	.	.	.	.
X	.	.	0.002	0.002	.	.	.	.	0.005	0.006
Women - Femmes - Mujeres										
ISIC 3 - CITI 3 - CIIU 3										
Total	6.349	.	7.001	7.077	7.177	7.460	7.554	7.823	8.186	8.415
A	0.004	.	0.006	0.005	0.005	0.003	0.005	0.005	0.005	0.005
D	1.653	.	1.724	1.691	1.743	1.786	1.753	1.808	1.774	1.742
F	0.077	.	0.087	0.104	0.120	0.128	0.125	0.126	0.130	0.133
G	0.886	.	1.012	1.181	1.340	1.359	1.075	1.161	1.304	1.376
H	0.256	.	0.306	0.160	-	-	0.116	0.106	0.121	0.129
I	0.115	.	0.147	0.146	0.160	0.168	0.186	0.196	0.208	0.219
J	0.242	.	0.287	0.296	0.310	0.344	0.377	0.396	0.443	0.472
K	0.367	.	-	-	-	-	0.954	1.010	1.098	1.164
L	0.771	.	1.487	1.434	1.373	1.434	1.113	1.102	2.318	2.322
M	0.769	.	0.017	0.029	0.028	0.030	0.513	0.526	0.021	0.017
N	0.737	.	0.751	0.780	0.755	0.728	0.746	0.761	0.105	0.115
O	0.346	.	1.146	1.274	1.343	1.480	0.591	0.626	0.658	0.719
P	0.125	.	-	-	-	-	-	-	-	-
Q	0.001	.	-	-	-	-	-	-	-	-
X	.	.	0.002	0.006	-	-	-	-	0.001	0.002
Slovakia (BA) [3][4][5]				Employees - Salariés - Asalariados						
Total - Total - Total										
ISIC 3 - CITI 3 - CIIU 3										
Total	1 965.0	1 931.0	1 943.4	1 940.9	1 947.6	1 904.2	1 929.0	2 002.6	2 043.6	2 094.2
A-B	148.3	132.0	121.6	122.3	116.9	95.7	91.0	85.5	83.8	80.0
C	29.8	24.7	22.0	21.1	18.6	14.1	14.5	16.0	16.1	13.9
D	522.0	515.9	528.7	549.2	539.0	546.8	556.5	573.9	597.4	609.9
E	51.0	48.5	51.1	44.8	44.6	42.9	40.0	40.2	37.8	40.2
F	159.5	135.9	131.5	134.6	146.5	144.4	141.2	152.6	151.2	157.0
G	212.3	212.7	209.6	223.3	222.1	207.7	211.0	232.0	240.6	243.5
H	57.5	56.4	62.1	61.0	69.9	72.4	79.2	88.0	89.6	94.1
I	157.4	155.0	151.9	144.5	136.5	128.1	131.8	140.0	148.2	158.8
J	35.4	35.1	36.1	35.7	37.6	37.8	38.0	38.6	36.7	43.9
K	63.7	74.3	82.7	81.7	84.1	85.6	94.5	97.3	107.4	113.7
L	149.3	157.3	157.3	149.0	158.7	150.8	154.4	161.7	159.7	167.1
M	166.2	160.6	168.1	162.1	157.8	158.7	162.1	164.4	161.3	161.2
N	148.9	142.3	138.3	135.8	145.3	146.1	141.2	144.2	146.2	142.0
O	62.2	77.3	77.8	69.1	63.2	65.2	67.7	65.8	64.9	66.1
P	1.5	2.5	3.7	6.5	4.7	4.5	2.7	1.0	1.9	2.2
Q	0.2	0.4	0.5	0.4	0.8	0.4	0.2	0.2	0.8	0.7
X	-	0.4	0.5	0.2	1.5	3.4	3.3	1.4	0.2	0.2
Men - Hommes - Hombres										
ISIC 3 - CITI 3 - CIIU 3										
Total	1 042.0	1 014.0	1 015.1	1 019.1	1 023.2	1 000.9	1 020.5	1 073.5	1 091.4	1 111.6
A-B	104.4	94.5	86.4	83.7	83.0	70.4	66.4	62.1	61.1	58.9
C	25.9	21.6	19.2	19.7	17.1	13.0	13.1	15.2	15.2	12.5
D	305.2	300.5	309.9	320.5	314.9	323.3	336.7	351.4	372.2	380.3
E	41.7	39.7	41.9	37.1	36.2	33.3	32.2	32.3	31.0	33.3
F	142.5	123.5	119.0	123.7	134.2	132.1	129.6	140.5	139.4	144.6
G	73.9	77.7	79.3	85.2	84.8	79.5	78.4	90.0	91.0	87.7
H	19.6	19.5	22.5	22.3	28.4	24.6	26.1	26.9	30.2	33.2
I	108.4	104.2	101.9	100.0	95.1	91.4	92.6	102.8	108.1	112.9
J	9.6	10.6	8.9	11.3	10.9	11.2	11.3	12.9	12.0	13.7
K	38.6	45.5	49.7	48.7	51.0	49.4	58.2	56.8	63.4	60.2
L	79.5	76.1	77.2	70.7	77.3	78.0	77.6	82.5	79.0	82.0
M	34.5	34.2	33.9	35.7	29.8	33.9	37.7	39.4	33.4	33.6
N	27.0	24.6	24.1	25.5	28.3	24.7	24.4	26.1	24.0	23.1
O	31.4	41.5	40.3	34.8	30.8	33.5	34.4	34.3	31.4	35.5
P	-	0.1	0.1	0.2	0.2	0.2	0.2	-	-	0.0
Q	0.1	0.1	0.3	0.1	0.4	0.2	0.2	0.1	0.2	0.2
X	-	0.3	0.5	0.2	1.0	2.4	1.7	0.4	0.1	-

Explanatory notes: see p. 77.

[1] Persons aged 15 years and over. [2] Dec. [3] Employees and members of producers' cooperatives aged 15 years and over. [4] Excl. conscripts. [5] Excl. persons on child-care leave.

Notes explicatives: voir p. 80.

[1] Personnes âgées de 15 ans et plus. [2] Déc. [3] Salariés et membres de coopératives de producteurs âgés de 15 ans et plus. [4] Non compris les conscrits. [5] Non compris les personnes en congé parental.

Notas explicativas: véase p. 83.

[1] Personas de 15 años y más. [2] Dic. [3] Asalariados y miembros de cooperativas de productores de 15 años y más. [4] Excl. los conscriptos. [5] Excl. las personas con licencia parental.

	EMPLOYMENT				EMPLOI				EMPLEO	

Paid employment, by economic activity — **Emploi rémunéré, par activité économique** — **Empleo remunerado, por actividad económica**

	Thousands				Milliers				Millares	
	1999	2000	2001	2002	2003	2004	2005	2006	2007	2008

Slovakia (BA) [1] [2] [3] — Employees - Salariés - Asalariados

Women - Femmes - Mujeres
ISIC 3 - CITI 3 - CIIU 3

	1999	2000	2001	2002	2003	2004	2005	2006	2007	2008
Total	923.0	917.0	928.3	921.8	924.5	903.3	908.5	929.2	952.2	982.6
A-B	43.9	37.5	35.2	38.6	33.8	25.3	24.6	23.4	22.7	21.0
C	3.9	3.1	2.8	1.5	1.5	1.1	1.4	0.8	0.9	1.4
D	216.8	215.4	218.7	228.7	224.1	223.5	219.9	222.5	225.2	229.6
E	9.3	8.8	9.2	7.7	8.4	9.6	7.8	7.9	6.9	6.9
F	17.0	12.4	12.5	10.9	12.3	12.3	11.6	12.2	11.9	12.5
G	138.4	134.9	130.3	138.1	137.3	128.2	132.6	141.9	149.6	155.8
H	37.9	36.8	39.6	38.6	41.5	47.8	53.2	61.1	59.4	60.9
I	49.0	50.8	50.0	44.5	41.3	36.7	39.2	37.2	40.1	45.9
J	25.9	24.6	27.2	24.4	26.8	26.6	26.7	25.7	24.7	30.3
K	25.1	28.8	33.1	33.1	33.1	36.2	36.2	40.5	44.0	53.5
L	69.8	81.3	80.1	78.4	81.3	72.8	76.8	79.2	80.8	85.2
M	131.7	126.4	134.1	126.4	128.1	124.8	124.5	125.1	127.9	127.6
N	121.9	117.7	114.2	110.3	117.1	121.5	116.8	118.1	122.2	118.9
O	30.9	35.8	37.6	34.3	32.4	31.7	33.3	31.5	33.5	30.6
P	1.5	2.4	3.6	6.2	4.5	4.3	2.5	1.0	1.9	2.2
Q	0.1	0.3	0.2	0.3	0.4	0.2	0.1	0.1	0.6	0.5
X	-	0.1	0.1	-	0.5	1.0	1.6	1.0	0.1	0.2

Slovakia (DA) [4] [5] — Employees - Salariés - Asalariados

Total - Total - Total
ISIC 3 - CITI 3 - CIIU 3

	1999	2000	2001	2002	2003	2004	2005	2006	2007	2008
Total	1 321	1 339	1 277	1 273	1 220	1 213	1 229	1 276	1 295	1 300
A	97	90	82	75	62	56	53	49	46	44
B	-	-	-	-	-	-	-	-	-	-
C	16	14	13	11	10	9	9	8	9	8
D	375	379	373	376	360	358	364	372	378	371
E	48	46	35	46	43	41	39	36	35	33
F	61	54	47	45	44	43	46	45	46	50
G	73	74	77	84	84	88	92	94	99	111
H	11	11	11	12	11	11	12	11	13	11
I	121	115	112	109	104	101	98	98	101	103
J	35	35	34	31	31	31	32	32	33	34
K	61	58	59	57	53	61	69	72	78	79
L	79	80	81	84	88	95	102	148	145	147
M	181	177	176	177	178	168	165	164	160	160
N	117	120	117	115	108	105	101	100	106	105
O	46	86	60	51	44	46	47	47	46	44

Men - Hommes - Hombres
ISIC 3 - CITI 3 - CIIU 3

	1999	2000	2001	2002	2003	2004	2005	2006	2007	2008
Total	667	678	634	630	600	596	609	645	653	654
A	68	64	59	54	45	40	38	35	33	32
B	-	-	-	-	-	-	-	-	-	-
C	13	12	11	10	9	8	8	7	8	7
D	218	219	217	217	210	208	212	217	220	217
E	37	36	27	36	34	32	31	28	27	25
F	53	47	41	39	38	37	40	39	40	43
G	31	30	31	34	34	36	38	38	40	46
H	4	4	4	5	4	4	4	4	5	4
I	79	75	73	71	68	66	64	65	67	69
J	11	11	10	9	9	9	10	10	10	10
K	36	34	35	34	32	37	41	42	47	46
L	27	28	28	30	33	35	39	77	75	75
M	42	41	41	40	41	39	39	39	36	36
N	22	23	22	22	20	20	20	19	20	21
O	26	54	35	29	23	25	25	25	25	23

Women - Femmes - Mujeres
ISIC 3 - CITI 3 - CIIU 3

	1999	2000	2001	2002	2003	2004	2005	2006	2007	2008
Total	652	661	643	643	620	617	620	631	642	646
A	29	26	23	21	17	16	15	14	13	12
B	-	-	-	-	-	-	-	-	-	-
C	2	2	2	1	1	1	1	1	1	1
D	157	160	156	159	150	150	152	155	158	154
E	10	10	8	10	9	9	8	8	8	8
F	8	7	6	6	6	6	6	6	6	7
G	42	44	46	50	50	52	54	56	59	65
H	7	7	7	7	7	7	8	7	8	7
I	42	40	39	38	36	35	34	33	34	34
J	24	24	24	22	22	22	22	22	23	24
K	25	24	24	23	21	24	28	30	31	33
L	52	52	53	54	55	60	63	71	70	72
M	139	136	135	137	137	129	126	125	124	124
N	95	97	95	93	88	85	81	81	86	84
O	20	32	25	22	21	21	22	22	21	21

Explanatory notes: see p. 77.

[1] Employees and members of producers' cooperatives aged 15 years and over. [2] Excl. conscripts. [3] Excl. persons on child-care leave. [4] Excl. enterprises with less than 20 employees. [5] 31st Dec. of each year.

Notes explicatives: voir p. 80.

[1] Salariés et membres de coopératives de producteurs âgés de 15 ans et plus. [2] Non compris les conscrits. [3] Non compris les personnes en congé parental. [4] Non compris les entreprises occupant moins de 20 salariés. [5] 31 déc. de chaque année.

Notas explicativas: véase p. 83.

[1] Asalariados y miembros de cooperativas de productores de 15 años y más. [2] Excl. los conscriptos. [3] Excl. las personas con licencia parental. [4] Excl. las empresas con menos de 20 asalariados. [5] 31 dic. de cada año.

Paid employment, by economic activity
Emploi rémunéré, par activité économique
Empleo remunerado, por actividad económica

Thousands — Milliers — Millares

Slovenia (BA) [1] [2]   Employees - Salariés - Asalariados

Total - Total - Total
ISIC 3 - CITI 3 - CIIU 3   ISIC 4 - CITI 4 - CIIU 4

ISIC 3	1999	2000	2001	2002	2003	2004	2005	2006	2007	2008	ISIC 4
Total	728	750	758	773	771	798	808	810	831	847	Total
A	8	10	9	11	11	14	12	11	12	11	A
C	6	7	5	4	5	6	5	6	4	3	B
D	260	253	260	269	252	254	261	248	251	249	C
E	8	10	11	11	9	10	10	10	9	10	D
F	37	40	45	44	44	45	49	47	48	7	E
G	94	106	99	105	108	106	99	107	107	58	F
H	28	29	29	31	31	33	36	34	32	107	G
I	43	52	50	47	52	49	47	47	52	47	H
J	20	21	24	22	22	21	22	21	23	37	I
K	38	33	34	37	43	47	51	52	55	26	J
L	49	53	48	50	50	56	59	58	59	23	K
M	59	57	62	60	62	64	68	74	77	2	L
N	44	46	45	50	46	47	50	58	53	31	M
O	30	29	29	27	32	35	34	34	38	21	N
P	-	-	1	-	-	-	-	1	-	53	O
X	3	5	8	6	5	10	5	3	9	75	P
										56	Q
										15	R
										10	S
										1	T
										-	U
										5	X

Men - Hommes - Hombres
ISIC 3 - CITI 3 - CIIU 3   ISIC 4 - CITI 4 - CIIU 4

ISIC 3	1999	2000	2001	2002	2003	2004	2005	2006	2007	2008	ISIC 4
Total	381	391	399	404	407	420	427	424	443	449	Total
A	6	6	7	8	7	8	7	8	8	8	A
C	6	6	5	3	5	5	5	5	3	3	B
D	155	148	152	159	155	156	161	154	159	158	C
E	6	8	10	9	7	9	8	8	7	9	D
F	34	35	40	39	39	40	46	43	44	5	E
G	43	48	46	46	47	46	43	48	48	51	F
H	12	12	10	10	11	12	13	11	11	47	G
I	33	38	37	35	40	37	34	34	40	37	H
J	5	7	9	8	7	7	8	8	7	13	I
K	18	17	18	19	23	25	27	29	31	17	J
L	25	26	23	25	23	27	30	29	32	7	K
M	13	12	15	14	15	16	15	17	15	1	L
N	8	9	9	11	9	7	8	12	11	14	M
O	14	14	15	14	16	19	17	17	22	10	N
P	-	-	-	-	-	-	-	-	-	28	O
X	2	3	5	3	3	6	4	1	4	16	P
										12	Q
										8	R
										3	S
										-	T
										-	U
										2	X

Women - Femmes - Mujeres
ISIC 3 - CITI 3 - CIIU 3   ISIC 4 - CITI 4 - CIIU 4

ISIC 3	1999	2000	2001	2002	2003	2004	2005	2006	2007	2008	ISIC 4
Total	347	359	359	368	364	378	381	386	387	397	Total
A	2	4	2	3	4	5	4	3	4	3	A
C	-	1	1	-	-	-	-	1	1	-	B
D	105	105	108	110	97	98	100	93	92	91	C
E	1	2	1	1	2	1	2	2	2	2	D
F	4	5	6	5	5	4	3	4	4	2	E
G	51	58	52	58	61	60	56	59	59	7	F
H	17	17	19	21	19	21	23	23	21	61	G
I	11	13	13	12	12	12	12	14	12	9	H
J	15	15	15	14	15	15	14	13	15	23	I
K	20	15	16	18	20	23	24	23	24	8	J
L	24	26	25	25	26	29	29	29	26	16	K
M	45	45	47	46	47	49	52	57	62	2	L
N	36	37	36	38	37	39	41	46	43	17	M
O	16	14	14	13	16	16	16	16	17	12	N
P	-	-	-	-	-	-	-	1	-	25	O
X	-	1	3	3	2	4	-	2	5	58	P
										44	Q
										7	R
										7	S
										-	T
										-	U
										3	X

Explanatory notes: see p. 77.

[1] Persons aged 15 years and over. [2] Second quarter of each year.

Notes explicatives: voir p. 80.

[1] Personnes âgées de 15 ans et plus. [2] Deuxième trimestre de chaque année.

Notas explicativas: véase p. 83.

[1] Personas de 15 años y más. [2] Segundo trimestre de cada año.

EMPLOYMENT | EMPLOI | EMPLEO

Paid employment, by economic activity | **Emploi rémunéré, par activité économique** | **Empleo remunerado, por actividad económica**

Thousands — Milliers — Millares

	1999	2000	2001	2002	2003	2004	2005	2006	2007	2008
Slovenia (DA)				All persons engaged - Effectif occupé - Efectivo ocupado						
Total - Total - Total										
ISIC 3 - CITI 3 - CIIU 3										
Total	758.474	768.172	779.041	783.449	777.247	782.206	.	.	.	.
A	45.439	43.069	41.658	42.972	35.896	37.080	.	.	.	.
B	0.247	0.210	0.201	0.198	0.196	0.192	.	.	.	.
C	7.010	5.746	5.444	5.092	4.809	4.346	.	.	.	.
D	234.057	233.967	236.066	238.412	234.590	232.437	.	.	.	.
E	11.638	11.379	11.286	11.541	11.235	11.107	.	.	.	.
F	55.099	57.351	56.834	57.056	57.424	57.877	.	.	.	.
G	94.184	97.357	99.211	100.537	100.559	100.773	.	.	.	.
H	28.066	28.899	29.041	29.120	28.864	29.019	.	.	.	.
I	47.069	47.558	48.492	49.497	49.317	48.178	.	.	.	.
J	18.624	19.294	19.850	20.320	19.981	20.419	.	.	.	.
K	44.621	45.995	48.813	52.696	54.956	57.304	.	.	.	.
L	42.781	44.149	45.812	46.853	48.955	50.255	.	.	.	.
M	52.161	53.053	54.107	55.095	55.750	56.959	.	.	.	.
N	52.421	54.165	55.656	47.150	47.182	48.536	.	.	.	.
O	24.345	25.215	25.714	26.218	27.033	27.269	.	.	.	.
P	-	-	-	-	0.499	0.456	.	.	.	.
Suisse (BA) [1][2][3]				Employees - Salariés - Asalariados						
Total - Total - Total										
ISIC 3 - CITI 3 - CIIU 3										
Total	2 983	2 983	3 068	3 086	3 071	3 121	3 138	3 195	3 240	3 345
A-B	31	26	29	26	28	27	29	27	29	37
C-E	573	582	590	570	530	533	535	547	566	575
F	177	175	170	170	165	175	173	185	187	180
G	441	436	447	447	426	436	431	424	420	422
H	88	91	110	115	114	122	116	128	122	124
I	216	204	209	214	216	204	210	197	197	204
J	183	180	193	200	209	205	202	216	223	228
K	265	258	279	285	318	325	324	329	352	367
L,Q	208	209	201	208	210	209	212	214	208	210
M	228	243	271	254	266	275	286	300	296	317
N	361	367	372	375	378	395	402	406	423	454
O-P	208	206	195	209	207	209	213	218	211	223
X	4 [4]	7 [4]	. [5]	12	4 [4]	6	3 [4]	4 [4]	5 [4]	4 [4]
Men - Hommes - Hombres										
ISIC 3 - CITI 3 - CIIU 3										
Total	1 621	1 625	1 656	1 639	1 637	1 656	1 666	1 699	1 728	1 750
A-B	25	21	23	19	19	19	20	18	20	27
C-E	423	432	437	414	386	384	390	400	418	413
F	155	156	150	154	149	156	156	166	169	163
G	218	220	214	210	204	204	196	197	195	192
H	29	30	36	42	45	49	48	52	51	50
I	142	136	137	145	150	144	146	136	140	147
J	106	104	114	113	118	121	119	128	129	130
K	151	146	161	158	179	189	192	193	203	208
L,Q	117	119	124	125	126	124	124	127	117	118
M	92	96	108	96	103	100	105	111	107	120
N	91	89	86	80	83	86	88	88	94	97
O-P	70	73	64	75	73	77	81	82	80	83
X	. [5]	. [5]	. [5]	7	1 [4]	3 [4]	. [5]	2 [4]	2 [4]	. [5]
Women - Femmes - Mujeres										
ISIC 3 - CITI 3 - CIIU 3										
Total	1 362	1 358	1 412	1 447	1 435	1 465	1 472	1 496	1 512	1 595
A-B	6	6	6	7	8	8	8	9	9	10
C-E	150	151	152	157	145	150	145	147	148	162
F	22	18	20	16	17	18	17	19	18	18
G	224	217	233	237	222	232	235	227	225	229
H	59	61	74	73	68	73	70	76	72	74
I	74	68	72	69	66	60	64	61	57	57
J	77	76	79	87	91	84	83	89	94	98
K	114	112	118	126	139	137	132	135	149	159
L,Q	90	90	77	82	85	84	89	87	91	92
M	137	147	164	158	164	175	181	190	189	197
N	270	277	286	295	295	308	315	318	329	357
O-P	139	133	131	134	134	132	132	137	131	140
X	. [5]	3 [4]	. [5]	6	3 [4]	3 [4]	2 [4]	2 [4]	2 [4]	2 [4]

Explanatory notes: see p. 77.

[1] Persons aged 15 years and over. [2] Excl. apprentices. [3] Second quarter of each year. [4] Relative statistical reliability. [5] Not indicated due to lack of statistical reliability.

Notes explicatives: voir p. 80.

[1] Personnes âgées de 15 ans et plus. [2] Non compris les apprentis. [3] Deuxième trimestre de chaque année. [4] Fiabilité statistique relative. [5] Non indiqué en raison du manque de fiabilité statistique.

Notas explicativas: véase p. 83.

[1] Personas de 15 años y más. [2] Excl. los aprendices. [3] Segundo trimestre de cada año. [4] Confiabilidad estadística relativa. [5] No se indica por la falta de confiabilidad estadística.

Paid employment, by economic activity
Emploi rémunéré, par activité économique
Empleo remunerado, por actividad económica

Thousands — Milliers — Millares

Sweden (BA) [1][2] — Employees - Salariés - Asalariados

Total - Total - Total

ISIC 3 - CITI 3 - CIIU 3	1999	2000	2001	2002	2003	2004	2005	2006	2007	2008	ISIC 4 - CITI 4 - CIIU 4
Total	3 636	3 731	3 815	3 827	3 826	3 796	3 844 [3]	3 908	4 060	4 115	Total
A-B	35	37	37	35	33	35	37 [3]	37	38	34	A
C	8	9	7	7	7	6	7 [3]	8	8	9	B
D	720	721	704	676	653	641	616 [3]	614	618	585	C
E	31	30	27	25	27	27	26 [3]	25	25	22	D
F	179	181	188	190	192	194	201 [3]	215	233	18	E
G	427	434	439	439	451	450	459 [3]	458	474	247	F
H	93	97	97	92	98	104	96 [3]	105	118	484	G
I	247	254	256	258	252	244	245 [3]	250	256	216	H
J	83	84	87	88	89	86	79 [3]	82	86	124	I
K	364	411	460	474	459	452	488 [3]	510	556	160	J
L,Q	208	222	231	241	243	246	238 [3]	248	260	91	K
M	312	326	339	344	467	467	466 [3]	475	484	56	L
N	762	755	763	778	674	670	693 [3]	687	706	262	M
O-P	162	166	172	177	178	172	185 [3]	186	190	192	N
X	3	6	7	5	3	3	9 [3]	7	7	260	O
										85	P
										85	Q
										1	R
										1	S
										480	T
										698	U
										7	X

Men - Hommes - Hombres

ISIC 3 - CITI 3 - CIIU 3	1999	2000	2001	2002	2003	2004	2005	2006	2007	2008	ISIC 4 - CITI 4 - CIIU 4
Total	1 807	1 853	1 892	1 889	1 887	1 874	1 913 [3]	1 951	2 034	2 072	Total
A-B	26	28	28	27	25	27	27 [3]	27	29	26	A
C	8	8	6	6	6	5	6 [3]	7	7	8	B
D	530	528	515	497	484	475	460 [3]	457	460	446	C
E	23	21	20	19	20	20	19 [3]	18	18	17	D
F	162	164	172	173	176	177	186 [3]	198	212	15	E
G	228	228	234	233	242	243	248 [3]	248	257	226	F
H	35	37	38	37	38	41	40 [3]	43	48	263	G
I	172	177	175	175	176	172	177 [3]	181	184	159	H
J	35	36	37	38	38	38	33 [3]	35	41	48	I
K	209	237	271	277	266	257	288 [3]	300	325	107	J
L,Q	104	111	111	113	116	115	110 [3]	113	122	43	K
M	102	108	108	109	115	117	116 [3]	118	121	35	L
N	96	96	94	100	102	105	113 [3]	116	117	149	M
O-P	75	77	81	84	81	81	86 [3]	86	87	101	N
X	2	3	5	4	2	2	4 [3]	4	4	117	O
										39	P
										37	Q
										-	R
										1	S
										120	T
										114	U
										4	X

Women - Femmes - Mujeres

ISIC 3 - CITI 3 - CIIU 3	1999	2000	2001	2002	2003	2004	2005	2006	2007	2008	ISIC 4 - CITI 4 - CIIU 4
Total	1 828	1 878	1 923	1 939	1 939	1 922	1 931 [3]	1 956	2 025	2 043	Total
A-B	10	9	9	8	8	7	10 [3]	9	9	8	A
C	1	1	1	1	1	1	1 [3]	1	1	1	B
D	191	193	189	179	169	166	156 [3]	157	158	139	C
E	8	8	8	7	7	7	8 [3]	7	7	5	D
F	17	16	16	17	17	17	15 [3]	17	20	3	E
G	198	206	206	206	209	207	211 [3]	210	218	21	F
H	58	60	59	55	60	62	56 [3]	62	70	221	G
I	75	77	82	82	76	72	68 [3]	69	72	56	H
J	48	48	50	51	51	49	45 [3]	47	45	76	I
K	155	174	189	197	194	196	200 [3]	210	231	53	J
L,Q	104	112	121	129	127	131	128 [3]	136	138	48	K
M	210	221	231	235	352	350	350 [3]	357	363	21	L
N	666	662	669	678	571	565	580 [3]	571	589	113	M
O-P	87	89	91	93	97	91	98 [3]	100	102	91	N
X	1	2	2	2	1	1	4 [3]	3	3	143	O
										45	P
										48	Q
										1	R
										360	S
										584	T
										3	U
										3	X

Explanatory notes: see p. 77.

[1] Incl. professional army; excl. compulsory military service. [2] Persons aged 15 to 74 years; prior to 2007: 16 to 64 years. [3] Methodology revised; data not strictly comparable.

Notes explicatives: voir p. 80.

[1] Y compris les militaires de carrière; non compris les militaires du contingent. [2] Personnes âgées de 15 à 74 ans; avant 2007: 16 à 64 ans. [3] Méthodologie révisée; les données ne sont pas strictement comparables.

Notas explicativas: véase p. 83.

[1] Incl. los militares profesionales; excl. los militares en servicio obligatorio. [2] Personas de 15 a 74 años; antes de 2007: 16 a 64 años. [3] Metodología revisada; los datos no son estrictamente comparables.

EMPLOYMENT   EMPLOI   EMPLEO

Paid employment, by economic activity   **Emploi rémunéré, par activité économique**   **Empleo remunerado, por actividad económica**

Thousands — Milliers — Millares

Turkey (BA) [1] — Employees - Salariés - Asalariados

Total - Total - Total
ISIC 3 - CITI 3 - CIIU 3

	1999	2000	2001	2002	2003	2004	2005	2006	2007	2008
Total	.	10 487	10 155	10 624	10 707	11 079	11 949	12 617	12 534	12 937
A-B	.	.	.	.	.	.	521	530	403	433
A	.	419	345	387	383	489	.	.	.	.
B	.	10	11	8	6	9	.	.	.	.
C	.	76	94	112	81	100	116	123	122	110
D	.	2 845	2 846	3 034	3 026	3 121	3 368	3 480	3 470	3 614
E	.	90	95	103	99	83	80	93	97	92
F	.	1 176	921	758	775	831	899	991	988	1 002
G	.	1 349	1 288	1 397	1 421	1 503	1 682	1 834	1 882	1 907
H	.	481	504	549	549	580	652	682	679	716
I	.	648	618	630	643	679	707	712	722	709
J	.	268	248	224	216	225	226	219	231	243
K	.	274	293	311	340	385	457	586	625	721
L	.	1 173	1 157	1 151	1 177	1 248	1 217	1 225	1 260	1 265
M	.	742	791	846	861	807	896	897	858	911
N	.	454	439	482	498	444	507	571	537	566
O	.	348	360	466	464	400	.	.	.	.
O-Q	.	.	.	.	.	.	622	673	660	648
P	.	130	142	165	168	170	.	.	.	.
Q	.	4	3	1	2	4	.	.	.	.

Men - Hommes - Hombres
ISIC 3 - CITI 3 - CIIU 3

	1999	2000	2001	2002	2003	2004	2005	2006	2007	2008
Total	.	8 442	8 172	8 360	8 462	8 814	9 451	9 903	9 727	9 963
A-B	.	.	.	.	.	.	340	347	256	264
A	.	301	227	232	262	328	.	.	.	.
B	.	9	10	8	6	9	.	.	.	.
C	.	72	91	108	78	98	113	121	120	107
D	.	2 295	2 298	2 354	2 368	2 463	2 696	2 788	2 757	2 902
E	.	84	88	99	93	77	74	87	93	85
F	.	1 147	902	737	748	809	874	958	956	963
G	.	1 132	1 077	1 152	1 167	1 237	1 376	1 473	1 489	1 502
H	.	439	453	489	492	512	573	595	574	599
I	.	585	559	571	585	621	640	639	645	627
J	.	161	159	146	141	143	146	137	138	138
K	.	184	206	220	246	274	329	422	453	527
L	.	1 010	1 020	1 009	1 022	1 119	1 084	1 077	1 083	1 089
M	.	446	493	532	539	504	548	530	481	496
N	.	228	222	238	252	219	238	273	244	237
O	.	289	306	402	401	339	.	.	.	.
O-Q	.	.	.	.	.	.	418	456	438	427
P	.	57	58	62	62	59	.	.	.	.
Q	.	3	3	1	1	2	.	.	.	.

Women - Femmes - Mujeres
ISIC 3 - CITI 3 - CIIU 3

	1999	2000	2001	2002	2003	2004	2005	2006	2007	2008
Total	.	2 045	1 983	2 264	2 246	2 265	2 498	2 714	2 807	2 973
A-B	.	.	.	.	.	.	181	183	147	169
A	.	118	118	155	121	161	.	.	.	.
B	.	1	1	-	-	-	.	.	.	.
C	.	4	3	4	3	2	3	2	2	3
D	.	550	548	680	658	658	672	692	713	712
E	.	6	7	4	6	5	5	6	4	7
F	.	29	19	21	27	23	25	33	32	39
G	.	217	211	245	254	266	306	361	393	405
H	.	42	51	60	57	68	80	88	105	117
I	.	63	59	59	58	58	67	72	77	82
J	.	107	89	78	75	82	80	82	93	104
K	.	90	86	91	94	111	128	164	172	194
L	.	163	137	142	155	129	132	148	177	176
M	.	296	298	314	322	303	347	367	377	415
N	.	226	217	244	246	225	269	299	293	329
O	.	59	54	64	63	61	.	.	.	.
O-Q	.	.	.	.	.	.	204	217	222	221
P	.	73	84	103	106	111	.	.	.	.
Q	.	1	-	-	1	2	.	.	.	.

Turkey (FA) [2] — Wage earners - Ouvriers - Obreros

Total - Total - Total
ISIC 2 - CITI 2 - CIIU 2

	1999	2000	2001	2002	2003	2004	2005	2006	2007	2008
Total	5 005.4	5 254.1	4 886.9	5 223.3	5 615.2	6 181.3	6 918.6	7 818.6	8 505.4	.
1	67.1	65.5	65.6	65.8	67.0	69.5	73.9	79.8	85.6	.
2	85.3	98.4	82.0	84.5	83.1	86.4	97.2	107.8	109.1	.
3	1 920.2	2 002.4	1 801.8	2 005.1	2 226.2	2 412.2	2 541.1	2 732.1	2 895.8	.
4	197.0	202.9	206.3	203.0	204.7	206.9	209.1	192.2	193.3	.
5	761.5	780.4	681.9	713.6	685.9	752.1	933.5	1 185.7	1 248.0	.
6	608.7	638.2	607.6	631.5	703.5	795.8	896.2	1 014.1	1 141.8	.
7	333.2	359.3	337.5	356.6	383.1	438.8	506.0	573.2	626.1	.
8	89.6	95.0	86.7	81.1	85.5	92.1	101.9	115.9	129.9	.
9	942.9	1 012.1	1 017.4	1 081.9	1 176.3	1 327.3	1 559.8	1 817.9	2 075.8	.

Explanatory notes: see p. 77.   Notes explicatives: voir p. 80.   Notas explicativas: véase p. 83.

[1] Persons aged 15 years and over. [2] Sep. of each year.   [1] Personnes âgées de 15 ans et plus. [2] Sept. de chaque année.   [1] Personas de 15 años y más. [2] Sept. de cada año.

Paid employment, by economic activity   **Emploi rémunéré, par activité économique**   **Empleo remunerado, por actividad económica**

Thousands   Milliers   Millares

	1999	2000	2001	2002	2003	2004	2005	2006	2007	2008
Turkey (FA) [1]				*Wage earners - Ouvriers - Obreros*						
Men - Hommes - Hombres										
ISIC 2 - CITI 2 - CIIU 2										
Total	4 040.2	4 226.8	3 914.1	4 176.6	4 448.5	4 927.1	5 486.5	6 191.3	6 603.5	.
1	58.1	56.4	57.0	57.2	58.5	61.6	64.2	68.7	72.4	.
2	84.0	89.8	80.4	83.1	81.4	84.6	95.3	105.7	106.8	.
3	1 526.2	1 601.8	1 416.8	1 548.7	1 744.9	1 917.8	2 028.0	2 190.4	2 312.8	.
4	182.8	177.2	194.8	187.5	189.0	192.1	191.3	177.3	176.0	.
5	734.9	663.0	649.3	690.7	655.9	720.3	896.8	1 138.8	1 189.5	.
6	454.2	493.4	453.4	480.7	522.5	592.0	661.5	740.4	819.8	.
7	293.1	293.6	293.3	314.5	334.7	384.5	443.1	501.4	545.9	.
8	53.6	71.5	52.4	53.4	50.8	56.6	58.3	65.7	73.1	.
9	653.1	780.1	716.6	760.7	810.9	917.5	1 047.9	1 202.8	1 307.1	.
Women - Femmes - Mujeres										
ISIC 2 - CITI 2 - CIIU 2										
Total	965.2	1 027.3	972.7	1 046.7	1 166.7	1 254.2	1 432.1	1 627.3	1 901.9	.
1	8.9	9.2	8.7	8.6	8.5	7.9	9.7	11.1	13.2	.
2	1.3	8.6	1.6	1.4	1.7	1.7	1.9	2.1	2.3	.
3	394.0	400.7	385.0	456.4	481.3	494.4	513.1	541.7	582.9	.
4	14.2	25.6	11.5	15.5	15.7	14.8	17.8	14.9	17.4	.
5	26.5	117.3	32.6	22.9	30.0	31.9	36.7	46.9	58.5	.
6	154.5	144.8	154.2	150.8	181.0	203.8	234.6	273.7	322.0	.
7	40.1	65.7	44.2	42.2	48.5	54.3	62.9	71.7	80.2	.
8	36.0	23.5	34.3	27.8	34.7	35.5	43.6	50.1	56.8	.
9	289.7	232.0	300.8	321.2	365.3	409.8	511.9	615.1	768.7	.
Ukraine (DA)				*Employees - Salariés - Asalariados*						
Total - Total - Total										
ISIC 3 - CITI 3 - CIIU 3										
Total	14 479	13 678	12 931	12 235	11 712	11 316	11 388	11 433	11 413	11 389
A	2 799	2 551	2 206	1 877	1 536	1 274	1 137	1 004	868	783
B	33	31	28	26	23	19	16	15	12	11
C	612	615	581	550	531	529	518	513	501	480
D	3 137	2 917	2 704	2 500	2 356	2 351	2 371	2 329	2 268	2 192
E	534	529	526	528	529	528	527	520	518	516
F	679	590	526	453	431	441	460	477	500	497
G	701	630	600	571	563	590	677	781	874	947
H	128	100	91	87	81	78	82	85	88	94
I	1 161	1 110	1 048	1 014	994	981	992	991	977	974
J	151	146	151	156	169	189	216	246	298	339
K	652	596	594	569	560	545	564	599	615	631
L	590	610	631	667	702	551	570	590	599	627
M	1 574	1 551	1 565	1 576	1 584	1 598	1 610	1 632	1 641	1 642
N	1 322	1 304	1 291	1 283	1 281	1 273	1 271	1 270	1 274	1 267
O	407	398	390	379	370	371	377	381	383	389
Men - Hommes - Hombres										
ISIC 3 - CITI 3 - CIIU 3										
Total	.	.	.	5 936	5 641	5 340	5 372	5 398	5 358	5 335
A	.	.	.	1 200	991	827	745	662	573	519
B	.	.	.	20	18	16	13	12	10	9
C	.	.	.	398	384	384	378	375	368	356
D	.	.	.	1 371	1 306	1 315	1 339	1 324	1 297	1 263
E	.	.	.	331	334	332	330	324	322	319
F	.	.	.	345	332	341	362	379	400	400
G	.	.	.	248	255	276	328	387	435	472
H	.	.	.	21	20	20	22	23	25	27
I	.	.	.	595	582	572	579	581	573	575
J	.	.	.	49	53	60	68	76	92	107
K	.	.	.	282	280	269	281	303	314	324
L	.	.	.	314	333	177	185	196	198	208
M	.	.	.	388	389	388	378	386	383	382
N	.	.	.	232	228	226	222	225	221	224
O	.	.	.	142	138	138	142	145	147	150
Women - Femmes - Mujeres										
ISIC 3 - CITI 3 - CIIU 3										
Total	.	.	.	6 299	6 070	5 976	6 016	6 035	6 055	6 054
A	.	.	.	677	545	447	392	342	295	264
B	.	.	.	5	5	4	3	3	2	2
C	.	.	.	152	147	146	140	138	133	124
D	.	.	.	1 129	1 050	1 036	1 032	1 005	971	929
E	.	.	.	197	196	196	197	196	196	197
F	.	.	.	108	99	100	98	98	100	97
G	.	.	.	323	307	314	349	394	439	475
H	.	.	.	66	61	58	60	62	63	67
I	.	.	.	419	413	408	413	410	404	399
J	.	.	.	107	116	129	148	170	206	232
K	.	.	.	287	281	276	283	296	301	307
L	.	.	.	353	370	374	385	394	401	419
M	.	.	.	1 188	1 196	1 209	1 232	1 246	1 258	1 260
N	.	.	.	1 051	1 053	1 047	1 049	1 045	1 050	1 043
O	.	.	.	237	233	232	235	236	236	239

Explanatory notes: see p. 77.   Notes explicatives: voir p. 80.   Notas explicativas: véase p. 83.

[1] Sep. of each year.   [1] Sept. de chaque année.   [1] Sept. de cada año.

Paid employment, by economic activity   **Emploi rémunéré, par activité économique**   **Empleo remunerado, por actividad económica**

Thousands   Milliers   Millares

United Kingdom (BA) [1] [2] — Wage earners and working proprietors - Ouvriers et propriétaires-exploitants - Obreros y empresarios propietarios

	1999	2000	2001	2002	2003	2004	2005	2006	2007	2008
Total - Total - Total ISIC 3 - CITI 3 - CIIU 3										
Total	26 925	27 289	27 550	27 757	28 046	28 270	28 568	28 836	29 000	29 365
A	393	389	363	350	329	344	359	346	369	401
B	15	13	14	18	12	13	10	18	10	15
C	99	105	110	109	103	91	106	110	133	127
D	4 741	4 609	4 453	4 288	4 116	3 809	3 796	3 745	3 738	3 540
E	181	199	195	218	179	182	175	174	213	199
F	1 866	1 937	1 982	1 971	2 102	2 195	2 253	2 319	2 374	2 368
G	4 172	4 189	4 135	4 171	4 344	4 380	4 338	4 219	4 142	4 290
H	1 157	1 153	1 176	1 272	1 201	1 237	1 244	1 263	1 292	1 279
I	1 777	1 853	1 961	1 950	1 952	1 900	1 968	1 938	1 951	1 961
J	1 139	1 188	1 211	1 261	1 243	1 201	1 206	1 252	1 262	1 278
K	2 937	3 026	3 123	3 156	3 111	3 201	3 275	3 314	3 471	3 584
L	1 622	1 691	1 834	1 865	1 919	1 949	1 995	2 045	2 037	2 090
M	2 168	2 201	2 210	2 318	2 427	2 556	2 598	2 669	2 641	2 684
N	2 989	2 989	3 109	3 106	3 223	3 412	3 477	3 578	3 454	3 635
O	1 439	1 514	1 458	1 510	1 585	1 569	1 574	1 628	1 677	1 665
P	139	135	119	120	137	151	121	123	119	136
Q	16	23	18	16	15	11	8	21	11	13
X	73	74	79	58	50	71	65	75	105	99
Men - Hommes - Hombres ISIC 3 - CITI 3 - CIIU 3										
Total	14 659	14 823	14 929	15 002	15 225	15 287	15 431	15 542	15 711	15 865
A	307	304	283	273	261	275	272	269	278	297
B	14	13	12	16	12	12	9	18	9	13
C	84	91	99	95	93	81	92	86	105	101
D	3 449	3 377	3 283	3 180	3 068	2 847	2 841	2 799	2 806	2 635
E	130	143	144	163	134	133	128	127	153	146
F	1 703	1 755	1 792	1 791	1 911	1 984	2 031	2 072	2 158	2 146
G	2 078	2 060	2 047	2 074	2 180	2 207	2 186	2 128	2 137	2 183
H	456	467	485	533	519	549	557	564	578	594
I	1 323	1 376	1 463	1 461	1 477	1 455	1 490	1 477	1 480	1 498
J	536	562	574	613	608	583	602	630	648	663
K	1 705	1 762	1 829	1 838	1 821	1 900	1 932	1 960	2 010	2 096
L	878	917	940	932	985	995	993	1 008	1 005	1 070
M	632	612	600	650	674	709	705	750	722	719
N	583	558	600	588	632	698	744	737	692	784
O	681	728	679	713	764	751	757	804	817	800
P	39	40	36	40	46	57	48	56	51	52
Q	10	16	11	8	9	7	5	11	6	8
X	51	44	52	35	32	45	40	47	57	59
Women - Femmes - Mujeres ISIC 3 - CITI 3 - CIIU 3										
Total	12 266	12 466	12 621	12 754	12 821	12 983	13 136	13 294	13 290	13 501
A	86	86	80	77	68	69	87	76	91	104
B	1	-	2	2	-	-	1	-	-	2
C	15	14	11	14	10	10	13	23	28	27
D	1 293	1 232	1 170	1 108	1 048	962	956	946	932	905
E	51	56	51	55	45	49	47	46	60	53
F	164	182	190	180	192	211	222	247	217	222
G	2 094	2 130	2 088	2 097	2 164	2 173	2 151	2 091	2 005	2 107
H	701	685	691	739	682	688	687	699	714	684
I	454	478	498	490	474	445	479	461	472	463
J	603	626	637	648	635	618	604	623	613	615
K	1 232	1 264	1 294	1 318	1 290	1 300	1 343	1 354	1 462	1 489
L	744	774	894	933	935	955	1 002	1 036	1 032	1 020
M	1 537	1 589	1 610	1 668	1 752	1 847	1 893	1 919	1 919	1 965
N	2 406	2 431	2 508	2 518	2 590	2 714	2 733	2 841	2 763	2 851
O	758	785	779	797	821	818	817	824	860	866
P	100	95	83	80	91	94	73	68	69	84
Q	6	7	7	8	5	4	4	10	4	5
X	21	31	27	23	18	25	26	28	48	40

Explanatory notes: see p. 77.   Notes explicatives: voir p. 80.   Notas explicativas: véase p. 83.

[1] Persons aged 16 years and over. [2] Second quarter.   [1] Personnes âgées de 16 ans et plus. [2] Deuxième trimestre.   [1] Personas de 16 años y más. [2] Segundo trimestre.

Paid employment, by economic activity
Emploi rémunéré, par activité économique
Empleo remunerado, por actividad económica

Thousands — Milliers — Millares

	1999	2000	2001	2002	2003	2004	2005	2006	2007	2008

OCEANIA-OCÉANIE-OCEANIA

Australia (BA) [1] [2]   Employees - Salariés - Asalariados

Total - Total - Total
ISIC 3 - CITI 3 - CIIU 3

	1999	2000	2001	2002	2003	2004	2005	2006	2007	2008
Total	7 456.7	7 690.5	7 832.7	7 964.7	8 195.7	8 354.5	8 678.2	8 943.5	9 251.8	9 472.1
A	182.1	194.5	203.3	180.6	177.0	171.4	171.6	168.8	166.5	167.9
B	9.3	8.9	10.5	10.8	10.0	9.5	9.6	5.9	8.1	6.7
C	68.5	66.6	67.8	69.4	75.0	84.6	103.8	115.1	117.2	132.0
D	985.6	1 038.7	1 007.6	1 024.4	1 014.0	1 018.4	1 005.7	999.2	1 021.8	1 029.6
E	64.1	64.3	68.6	66.8	75.0	73.4	80.1	82.7	84.7	97.7
F	433.7	453.8	437.7	452.2	491.9	536.4	579.8	629.7	677.2	703.0
G	1 585.1	1 547.3	1 433.2	1 477.2	1 531.5	1 527.3	1 592.1	1 612.8	1 644.1	1 668.1
H	377.6	409.2	560.4	568.0	583.1	596.7	627.3	609.6	645.8	655.9
I	482.3	503.6	497.4	481.1	506.3	527.0	548.1	563.5	595.8	616.1
J	301.8	318.4	333.8	326.0	333.9	329.8	356.1	368.1	388.7	382.0
K	826.0	900.8	886.4	902.9	942.8	947.5	1 007.7	1 067.7	1 077.0	1 123.5
L	449.4	454.0	497.8	538.0	568.2	582.6	597.6	617.2	636.1	639.6
M	590.0	590.4	640.3	649.4	672.6	680.8	688.5	709.1	736.8	769.2
N	769.2	798.9	848.0	876.8	872.5	916.9	947.8	1 016.1	1 037.8	1 063.0
O	323.0	332.6	335.6	335.5	338.8	349.9	362.0	377.5	412.4	415.6
P	8.1	5.7	4.5	5.4	3.0	2.3	0.4	0.5	1.8	2.1
Q	0.8	1.5	.	.	.	.	.	.	.	.
X	-	1.3	.	.	.	.	.	.	.	.

Men - Hommes - Hombres
ISIC 3 - CITI 3 - CIIU 3

	1999	2000	2001	2002	2003	2004	2005	2006	2007	2008
Total	4 076.2	4 168.5	4 201.2	4 278.9	4 379.6	4 484.7	4 635.7	4 760.6	4 935.1	5 047.9
A	129.7	140.0	144.0	129.7	127.5	119.0	126.0	121.1	117.0	121.8
B	7.9	7.6	9.2	9.0	8.2	8.0	7.7	4.7	6.9	6.2
C	62.7	59.3	60.5	61.7	66.8	74.4	91.5	99.9	102.1	112.1
D	727.8	760.3	737.6	753.6	734.4	743.3	734.2	729.9	746.2	757.2
E	52.9	53.3	54.1	51.9	59.8	60.5	63.7	64.4	67.0	75.1
F	384.0	397.5	383.7	393.3	429.0	468.7	503.1	552.5	591.4	617.7
G	842.3	811.2	773.1	799.0	822.5	818.4	842.6	857.2	868.8	881.3
H	165.7	179.8	239.8	242.4	249.8	263.9	270.2	253.1	279.8	285.9
I	346.4	365.3	360.4	356.5	366.0	376.7	392.9	404.6	429.1	448.2
J	133.2	136.2	140.3	145.2	146.7	146.4	154.2	168.1	183.8	173.1
K	448.6	488.5	462.4	481.7	498.3	511.9	539.1	565.0	576.2	601.7
L	264.8	266.6	285.6	309.9	315.6	315.9	327.5	337.0	341.1	334.2
M	192.5	188.4	209.6	205.2	217.5	221.8	221.2	220.5	237.6	234.7
N	164.1	162.2	176.1	183.0	180.0	190.0	197.1	210.1	206.2	211.9
O	152.2	149.6	163.7	156.1	157.1	165.3	164.5	172.4	181.6	186.5
P	1.0	1.4	1.2	0.7	0.3	0.4	0.2	0.1	0.4	0.3
Q	0.5	0.5	.	.	.	.	.	.	.	.
X	-	0.8	.	.	.	.	.	.	.	.

Women - Femmes - Mujeres
ISIC 3 - CITI 3 - CIIU 3

	1999	2000	2001	2002	2003	2004	2005	2006	2007	2008
Total	3 380.6	3 522.0	3 631.5	3 685.8	3 816.1	3 869.8	4 042.5	4 182.9	4 316.7	4 424.1
A	52.5	54.4	59.3	51.0	49.5	52.3	45.6	47.7	49.6	46.1
B	1.4	1.3	1.3	1.9	1.8	1.5	1.9	1.2	1.2	0.5
C	5.9	7.3	7.3	7.7	8.2	10.2	12.3	15.2	15.1	19.9
D	257.8	278.4	270.0	270.8	279.6	275.0	271.5	269.3	275.6	272.3
E	11.2	11.0	14.5	14.9	15.1	12.9	16.5	18.3	17.7	22.7
F	49.7	56.3	54.0	58.9	62.8	67.7	76.7	77.2	85.8	85.3
G	742.8	736.1	660.1	678.2	709.0	708.9	749.4	755.6	775.3	786.8
H	212.0	229.5	320.6	325.6	333.3	332.8	357.1	356.5	365.9	370.0
I	136.0	138.3	137.0	124.6	140.3	150.3	155.2	158.9	166.7	167.9
J	168.6	182.2	193.5	180.7	187.2	183.4	201.9	200.0	205.0	209.0
K	377.4	412.3	424.0	421.3	444.5	435.6	468.6	502.7	500.9	521.8
L	184.6	187.4	212.2	228.2	252.6	266.8	270.1	280.2	295.1	305.4
M	397.5	402.0	430.7	444.1	455.1	459.0	467.3	488.6	499.2	534.5
N	605.1	636.8	671.9	693.8	692.6	726.9	750.7	806.0	831.6	851.1
O	170.8	183.0	171.9	179.4	181.7	184.5	197.5	205.0	230.8	229.1
P	7.1	4.3	3.3	4.7	2.7	1.9	0.3	0.5	1.4	1.8
Q	0.3	0.9	.	.	.	.	.	.	.	.
X	-	0.5	.	.	.	.	.	.	.	.

Guam (DA) [3] [4]   Employees - Salariés - Asalariados

Total - Total - Total
ISIC 2 - CITI 2 - CIIU 2

	1999	2000	2001	2002	2003	2004	2005	2006	2007	2008
Total	.	.	.	.	.	.	.	43.2	.	.
1	.	.	.	.	.	.	.	0.3	.	.
3	.	.	.	.	.	.	.	1.6	.	.
5	.	.	.	.	.	.	.	4.1	.	.
6	.	.	.	.	.	.	.	14.1	.	.
7	.	.	.	.	.	.	.	5.0	.	.
8	.	.	.	.	.	.	.	2.4	.	.
9	.	.	.	.	.	.	.	15.8	.	.

Explanatory notes: see p. 77.
[1] Excl. armed forces. [2] Persons aged 15 years and over. [3] Private sector. [4] Dec. of each year.

Notes explicatives: voir p. 80.
[1] Non compris les forces armées. [2] Personnes âgées de 15 ans et plus. [3] Secteur privé. [4] Déc. de chaque année.

Notas explicativas: véase p. 83.
[1] Excl. las fuerzas armadas. [2] Personas de 15 años y más. [3] Sector privado. [4] Dic. de cada año.

2E

EMPLOYMENT	EMPLOI	EMPLEO
Paid employment, by economic activity	Emploi rémunéré, par activité économique	Empleo remunerado, por actividad económica

	Thousands				Milliers				Millares	
	1999	2000	2001	2002	2003	2004	2005	2006	2007	2008

Guam (DA) [1][2] — Employees - Salariés - Asalariados

Men - Hommes - Hombres
ISIC 2 - CITI 2 - CIIU 2

	1999	2000	2001	2002	2003	2004	2005	2006	2007	2008
Total	.	.	.	.	.	.	.	24.8	.	.
1	.	.	.	.	.	.	.	0.2	.	.
3	.	.	.	.	.	.	.	1.3	.	.
5	.	.	.	.	.	.	.	3.8	.	.
6	.	.	.	.	.	.	.	7.2	.	.
7	.	.	.	.	.	.	.	3.0	.	.
8	.	.	.	.	.	.	.	0.7	.	.
9	.	.	.	.	.	.	.	8.5	.	.

Women - Femmes - Mujeres
ISIC 2 - CITI 2 - CIIU 2

	1999	2000	2001	2002	2003	2004	2005	2006	2007	2008
Total	.	.	.	.	.	.	.	18.4	.	.
1	.	.	.	.	.	.	.	0.0	.	.
3	.	.	.	.	.	.	.	0.4	.	.
5	.	.	.	.	.	.	.	0.3	.	.
6	.	.	.	.	.	.	.	6.8	.	.
7	.	.	.	.	.	.	.	2.0	.	.
8	.	.	.	.	.	.	.	1.7	.	.
9	.	.	.	.	.	.	.	7.3	.	.

New Zealand (BA) [3][4] — Employees - Salariés - Asalariados

Total - Total - Total
ISIC 3 - CITI 3 - CIIU 3

	1999	2000	2001	2002	2003	2004	2005	2006	2007	2008
Total	1 380.0	1 405.7	1 461.0	1 513.9	1 579.7 [5]	1 637.9	1 702.1	1 759.7	1 800.3	1 811.2
A	66.3	61.9	71.9	77.7	76.5 [5]	74.8	71.6	77.8	84.0	80.2
B	2.1	1.8	2.0	2.0	2.3 [5]	1.7	1.1	1.2	1.4	1.5
C	3.1	3.4	3.0	3.4	2.9 [5]	3.8	3.9	4.7	4.8	3.7
D	242.6	246.4	255.7	257.3	253.7 [5]	261.8	254.2	250.9	249.9	249.2
E	8.6	8.3	9.7	9.3	8.6 [5]	9.3	8.3	8.1	8.6	11.6
F	61.2	68.6	66.7	73.0	87.8 [5]	97.4	105.7	123.7	126.3	122.1
G	248.4	259.1	264.6	266.1	294.5 [5]	299.8	305.4	315.5	324.6	338.9
H	71.6	74.3	76.6	87.6	81.9 [5]	82.2	89.0	84.9	94.2	85.5
I	92.9	92.4	94.4	95.9	95.4 [5]	103.2	105.4	102.2	101.8	107.6
J	48.0	49.4	46.9	48.1	48.9 [5]	54.3	59.8	64.7	64.6	62.7
K	118.7	116.8	125.3	129.9	134.3 [5]	146.5	164.1	178.0	179.2	177.8
L	95.8	88.8	91.0	83.3	111.0 [5]	114.0	126.7	132.9	133.4	128.9
M	120.1	124.4	131.2	141.6	150.8 [5]	155.8	158.8	159.2	162.9	168.8
N	129.3	131.5	144.6	160.2	163.8 [5]	166.1	175.1	182.5	187.6	191.4
O	61.5	66.2	68.2	71.3	63.0 [5]	62.3	66.9	64.6	65.8	70.0
P	6.3	6.5	5.4	5.0	2.2 [5]	2.3	2.2	2.6	3.2	1.8
Q	0.6	0.9	0.9	1.0	.	.	.	.	.	.
X	2.9	4.9	3.0	1.3	2.0 [5]	2.7	3.6	6.2	7.8	9.3

Men - Hommes - Hombres
ISIC 3 - CITI 3 - CIIU 3

	1999	2000	2001	2002	2003	2004	2005	2006	2007	2008
Total	704.9	719.6	747.7	775.6	798.4 [5]	834.5	865.5	894.9	918.9	916.8
A	46.1	44.8	52.7	56.3	54.7 [5]	51.9	50.5	54.5	59.2	55.0
B	1.7	1.5	1.6	1.6	2.0 [5]	1.6	-	-	1.1	1.1
C	2.8	3.0	2.6	2.6	2.5 [5]	3.5	3.4	3.9	4.1	3.3
D	170.5	172.2	181.1	185.6	180.6 [5]	186.2	182.3	181.3	180.8	174.1
E	6.9	6.0	6.8	7.0	6.4 [5]	7.1	5.9	5.8	6.9	9.3
F	54.1	61.6	59.1	63.1	77.7 [5]	85.6	94.2	109.4	112.8	108.6
G	135.2	138.2	138.8	141.3	150.8 [5]	157.3	157.2	160.9	163.7	171.1
H	25.6	26.6	28.4	33.3	29.3 [5]	27.7	30.7	27.0	32.9	33.2
I	60.8	63.0	64.2	63.4	64.4 [5]	70.0	71.6	67.8	72.1	73.5
J	18.7	19.1	16.0	18.0	18.8 [5]	20.3	24.0	28.5	28.1	25.3
K	55.3	55.1	62.1	62.5	64.4 [5]	72.5	82.3	88.4	86.1	87.5
L	46.9	44.8	42.9	41.5	54.7 [5]	55.0	62.7	61.5	64.4	61.3
M	32.6	32.8	36.4	41.9	43.5 [5]	43.6	45.7	47.1	48.3	46.3
N	20.1	20.7	23.0	23.7	23.0 [5]	26.7	26.6	28.6	26.8	30.6
O	25.2	26.8	30.0	31.8	24.3 [5]	24.2	25.6	25.9	26.7	30.8
P	0.5	0.6	0.2	0.4	- [5]	.	.	-	.	.
Q	0.4	0.5	0.3	0.6	. [5]	.	.	.	.	.
X	1.4	2.3	1.4	0.8	1.0 [5]	1.3	1.8	3.3	4.7	5.6

Explanatory notes: see p. 77.

[1] Private sector. [2] Dec. of each year. [3] Excl. armed forces. [4] Persons aged 15 years and over. [5] Methodology revised; data not strictly comparable.

Notes explicatives: voir p. 80.

[1] Secteur privé. [2] Déc. de chaque année. [3] Non compris les forces armées. [4] Personnes âgées de 15 ans et plus. [5] Méthodologie révisée; les données ne sont pas strictement comparables.

Notas explicativas: véase p. 83.

[1] Sector privado. [2] Dic. de cada año. [3] Excl. las fuerzas armadas. [4] Personas de 15 años y más. [5] Metodología revisada; los datos no son estrictamente comparables.

**Paid employment,
by economic activity**

**Emploi rémunéré,
par activité économique**

**Empleo remunerado,
por actividad económica**

	Thousands				Milliers				Millares		
	1999	2000	2001	2002	2003	2004	2005	2006	2007	2008	

New Zealand (BA) [1] [2]   **Employees - Salariés - Asalariados**

Women - Femmes - Mujeres
ISIC 3 - CITI 3 - CIIU 3

	1999	2000	2001	2002	2003	2004	2005	2006	2007	2008
Total	675.1	686.1	713.3	738.3	781.3 [3]	803.4	836.6	864.8	881.4	894.4
A	20.2	17.2	19.2	21.5	21.8 [3]	22.9	21.1	23.3	24.8	25.3
B	0.4	0.3	0.4	0.3	- [3]	-	-	-	-	-
C	0.3	0.4	0.4	0.6	- [3]	-	-	-	-	-
D	72.1	74.2	74.5	71.7	73.0 [3]	75.7	71.9	69.7	69.1	75.2
E	1.8	2.3	2.9	2.4	2.2 [3]	2.2	2.4	2.2	1.7	2.3
F	7.1	6.9	7.4	9.8	10.1 [3]	11.8	11.6	14.3	13.5	13.5
G	113.2	120.9	125.8	124.8	143.6 [3]	142.4	148.3	154.6	161.0	167.8
H	46.0	47.7	48.2	54.3	52.7 [3]	54.5	58.2	58.0	61.2	52.3
I	32.1	29.4	30.2	32.5	31.0 [3]	33.3	33.8	34.4	29.7	34.1
J	29.2	30.3	30.9	30.1	30.1 [3]	34.1	35.8	36.2	36.5	37.4
K	63.4	61.6	63.3	67.4	70.0 [3]	74.0	81.8	89.7	93.2	90.4
L	49.0	44.1	48.1	41.8	56.2 [3]	59.0	64.0	71.3	69.0	67.6
M	87.5	91.6	94.8	99.7	107.4 [3]	112.2	113.1	112.1	114.6	122.4
N	109.2	110.9	121.6	136.4	140.8 [3]	139.4	148.6	153.9	160.8	160.7
O	36.3	39.4	38.2	39.4	38.7 [3]	38.2	41.3	38.7	39.0	39.3
P	5.7	5.9	5.2	4.6	1.9 [3]	2.1	2.0	2.4	3.0	1.8
Q	0.2	0.4	0.6	0.4	. [3]	.	.	.	.	.
X	1.5	2.6	1.6	0.6	- [3]	1.4	1.9	2.8	3.1	3.7

Explanatory notes: see p. 77.

[1] Excl. armed forces. [2] Persons aged 15 years and over. [3] Methodology revised; data not strictly comparable.

Notes explicatives: voir p. 80.

[1] Non compris les forces armées. [2] Personnes âgées de 15 ans et plus. [3] Méthodologie révisée; les données ne sont pas strictement comparables.

Notas explicativas: véase p. 83.

[1] Excl. las fuerzas armadas. [2] Personas de 15 años y más. [3] Metodología revisada; los datos no son estrictamente comparables.

EMPLOYMENT — EMPLOI — EMPLEO

Paid employment in manufacturing — Thousands

Emploi rémunéré dans les industries manufacturières — Milliers

Empleo remunerado en las industrias manufactureras — Millares

AFRICA-AFRIQUE-AFRICA

Botswana (DA) [1][2]

Employees - Salariés - Asalariados

Total - Total - Total
ISIC 3 - CITI 3 - CIIU 3

	1999	2000	2001	2002	2003	2004	2005	2006	2007	2008
Total	36.6	29.8	29.8	30.3	30.2	35.1	32.4	34.5	35.2	.
15	10.5	6.1	7.0	6.5	6.8	7.0	7.4	10.5	7.8	.
16	0.0	-	-	-	-	-	-	-	-	.
17	4.5	2.7	2.6	2.4	2.8	3.3	2.7	1.9	3.0	.
18	6.9	7.6	6.8	9.4	8.3	8.5	7.3	4.4	4.9	.
19	1.0	0.4	0.5	0.8	0.6	0.5	0.6	0.6	0.6	.
20	0.5	0.6	0.5	0.5	0.7	0.5	0.5	0.5	0.4	.
21	1.0	0.6	0.3	0.3	0.4	0.3	0.3	0.4	0.3	.
22	0.4	1.6	1.3	0.5	1.1	1.9	1.6	1.2	1.3	.
24	0.3	0.8	1.1	1.0	0.7	0.7	0.7	1.2	1.0	.
25	0.9	0.6	1.1	1.1	0.9	0.7	1.2	0.5	0.5	.
26	2.8	2.1	2.6	2.2	2.2	2.9	2.7	2.5	2.0	.
27	0.9	0.4	0.4	0.3	0.3	0.1	0.1	0.1	0.1	.
28	0.7	1.8	2.6	2.8	3.0	5.1	3.1	2.9	4.3	.
29	0.5	0.2	-	0.3	0.3	0.7	1.0	0.8	1.1	.
30	0.2	-	-	-	-	-	-	0.2	0.5	.
31	0.5	-	-	0.3	0.1	-	0.1	-	-	.
32	-	-	-	0.1	-	-	-	-	-	.
33	1.5	-	-	-	-	0.1	0.3	0.1	0.3	.
34	2.0	0.2	-	0.1	0.2	0.3	0.3	0.1	0.2	.
35	-	0.1	-	-	-	-	-	-	-	.
36	1.4	4.0	2.8	1.8	1.7	2.5	2.6	6.7	7.0	.
37	-	-	-	-	-	-	-	-	-	.

Men - Hommes - Hombres
ISIC 3 - CITI 3 - CIIU 3

	1999	2000	2001	2002	2003	2004	2005	2006	2007	2008
Total	18.9	13.8	14.3	14.0	13.9	17.4	15.9	17.1	17.7	.
15	7.2	4.2	4.4	4.2	4.5	2.3	5.0	6.8	5.0	.
17	0.8	1.1	0.9	0.9	0.9	2.1	0.9	0.8	1.5	.
18	1.5	1.0	1.0	1.9	1.1	7.1	1.0	0.8	0.7	.
19	0.6	0.1	0.1	0.1	0.1	0.5	0.1	0.1	0.1	.
20	0.4	0.5	0.4	0.4	0.5	0.1	0.4	0.3	0.3	.
21	0.8	0.4	0.1	0.1	0.2	0.2	0.1	0.2	0.2	.
22	0.1	0.8	0.5	0.2	0.6	1.1	0.8	0.5	0.5	.
24	0.1	0.5	0.8	0.7	0.5	0.2	0.5	0.8	0.6	.
25	0.4	0.4	0.7	0.8	0.5	0.3	0.8	0.2	0.2	.
26	2.1	1.5	2.0	1.4	1.6	0.9	1.8	1.7	1.5	.
27	0.7	0.4	0.4	0.3	0.3	0.0	0.1	0.1	0.1	.
28	0.6	1.6	1.8	1.9	2.1	1.1	2.2	2.4	3.2	.
29	0.5	0.2	-	0.2	0.2	0.2	0.6	0.6	0.7	.
30	0.1	-	-	-	-	-	-	0.1	0.2	.
31	0.3	-	-	0.1	-	-	0.1	-	-	.
32	-	-	-	-	-	-	-	-	-	.
33	0.4	-	-	-	-	0.1	0.1	0.1	0.2	.
34	1.6	0.2	-	0.1	0.2	-	0.3	0.1	0.2	.
35	-	-	-	-	-	-	-	-	-	.
36	0.7	1.1	1.1	0.6	0.6	1.4	1.1	1.5	2.6	.
37	0.1	-	-	-	-	-	-	-	-	.

Women - Femmes - Mujeres
ISIC 3 - CITI 3 - CIIU 3

	1999	2000	2001	2002	2003	2004	2005	2006	2007	2008
Total	17.7	16.1	15.5	16.3	16.2	17.6	16.5	17.4	17.5	.
15	3.3	1.9	2.6	2.3	2.3	4.7	2.4	3.7	2.8	.
16	0.0	-	-	-	-	-	-	-	-	.
17	3.7	1.6	1.7	1.5	1.9	1.3	1.8	1.1	1.5	.
18	5.5	6.6	5.9	7.6	7.2	1.4	6.4	3.6	4.2	.
19	0.3	0.3	0.5	0.6	0.5	0.1	0.5	0.5	0.5	.
20	0.1	0.1	0.1	0.1	0.2	0.4	0.1	0.2	0.1	.
21	0.2	0.3	0.1	0.1	0.2	0.2	0.2	0.2	0.2	.
22	0.3	0.8	0.8	0.3	0.6	0.9	0.8	0.7	0.8	.
24	0.3	0.3	0.2	0.3	0.2	0.5	0.2	0.4	0.4	.
25	0.5	0.2	0.4	0.2	0.4	0.4	0.4	0.2	0.2	.
26	0.7	0.7	0.6	0.8	0.6	2.0	0.9	0.8	0.6	.
27	0.3	-	-	-	-	0.1	-	-	-	.
28	-	0.2	0.8	0.9	0.9	4.1	0.9	0.5	1.1	.
29	-	-	-	0.1	0.1	0.4	0.4	0.2	0.4	.
30	0.1	-	-	-	-	-	-	0.1	0.3	.
31	0.2	-	-	0.2	-	-	-	-	-	.
32	-	-	-	0.1	-	-	-	-	-	.
33	1.1	-	-	-	-	0.1	0.1	0.1	0.1	.
34	0.4	-	-	-	-	0.3	-	-	-	.
35	-	-	-	-	-	-	-	-	-	.
36	0.7	2.9	1.7	1.1	1.2	1.0	1.5	5.2	4.4	.
37	-	-	-	-	-	-	-	-	-	.

Explanatory notes: see p. 77.
[1] Excl. armed forces. [2] Sep. of each year.

Notes explicatives: voir p. 80.
[1] Non compris les forces armées. [2] Sept. de chaque année.

Notas explicativas: véase p. 83.
[1] Excl. las fuerzas armadas. [2] Sept. de cada año.

	Paid employment in manufacturing Thousands				Emploi rémunéré dans les industries manufacturières Milliers			Empleo remunerado en las industrias manufactureras Millares		
	1999	2000	2001	2002	2003	2004	2005	2006	2007	2008

Mauritius (DA) [1] [2]   Employees - Salariés - Asalariados

Total - Total - Total
ISIC 3 - CITI 3 - CIIU 3

	1999	2000	2001	2002	2003	2004	2005	2006	2007	2008
Total	115.558	114.987	116.960	111.017	108.907	101.715	92.620	91.021	92.261	91.978
15-16	12.683	12.306	12.690	12.672	11.920	12.466	12.421	13.718	13.754	13.522
17	7.158	9.210	8.180	7.995	7.784	8.282	8.054	6.813	6.926	6.778
18	75.699	72.810	75.766	69.982	68.344	59.691	52.659	49.501	50.881	50.561
19	1.424	1.334	1.197	1.163	1.243	1.248	1.209	1.112	0.962	1.022
20	0.630	0.632	0.606	0.551	0.512	0.530	0.527	0.538	0.599	0.613
21	0.680	0.726	0.717	0.744	0.776	0.780	0.773	0.716	0.624	0.672
22	2.225	2.375	2.349	2.423	2.567	2.684	2.857	2.771	2.717	2.812
23-24	2.070	2.170	2.141	2.148	2.185	2.301	2.099	2.233	2.275	2.200
25	1.485	1.538	1.662	1.640	1.744	1.799	1.764	1.746	1.700	1.516
26	1.246	1.313	1.218	1.539	1.577	1.520	1.434	1.528	1.478	1.742
27	0.424	0.433	0.405	0.374	0.406	0.402	0.376	0.361	0.353	0.305
28	1.601	1.790	1.794	1.793	1.836	1.873	2.273	2.177	2.335	2.424
29-30	0.525	0.471	0.442	0.430	0.538	0.533	0.535	0.592	0.598	0.495
31	0.506	0.464	0.516	0.507	0.501	0.478	0.604	0.552	0.541	0.661
32	0.080	0.120	0.115	0.200	0.177	0.167	0.160	0.131	0.126	0.116
33	1.873	2.026	1.999	1.700	1.641	1.729	1.591	1.691	1.706	1.832
34-35	0.510	0.476	0.310	0.268	0.294	0.314	0.433	0.489	0.460	0.465
36-37	4.639	4.793	4.853	4.888	4.862	4.918	4.851	4.352	4.226	4.242

Men - Hommes - Hombres
ISIC 3 - CITI 3 - CIIU 3

	1999	2000	2001	2002	2003	2004	2005	2006	2007	2008
Total	49.958	49.558	50.151	49.191	47.415	46.484	44.427	43.626	45.004	46.203
15-16	10.262	9.774	9.815	9.723	8.899	8.978	8.897	9.146	9.201	8.873
17	4.793	5.655	5.348	5.046	4.908	5.094	5.666	4.212	4.243	4.216
18	21.769	20.531	21.690	21.006	20.020	18.487	17.871	16.496	17.937	19.244
19	0.529	0.511	0.412	0.470	0.444	0.419	0.435	0.398	0.337	0.360
20	0.460	0.456	0.433	0.368	0.342	0.356	0.343	0.348	0.411	0.369
21	0.480	0.522	0.550	0.579	0.592	0.609	0.598	0.566	0.455	0.499
22	1.570	1.682	1.653	1.698	1.748	1.847	1.902	1.855	1.813	1.869
23-24	1.684	1.753	1.696	1.716	1.766	1.868	1.671	1.756	1.741	1.714
25	1.058	1.089	1.206	1.207	1.239	1.305	1.270	1.265	1.220	1.134
26	1.192	1.168	1.095	1.387	1.432	1.385	1.294	1.372	1.336	1.611
27	0.407	0.404	0.386	0.356	0.389	0.383	0.357	0.335	0.327	0.279
28	1.365	1.577	1.566	1.548	1.554	1.594	1.975	1.880	2.029	2.104
29-30	0.488	0.430	0.402	0.386	0.485	0.476	0.482	0.592	0.513	0.473
30										0.4
31	0.355	0.296	0.369	0.324	0.342	0.339	0.410	0.384	0.368	0.066
32	0.051	0.092	0.089	0.131	0.124	0.105	0.097	0.080	0.068	0.068
33	0.727	0.795	0.771	0.648	0.694	0.738	0.641	0.658	0.660	
34-35	0.484	0.455	0.296	0.254	0.271	0.293	0.410	0.463	0.444	0.450
36-37	2.284	2.368	2.374	2.344	2.166	2.208	2.108	1.902	1.901	1.878

Women - Femmes - Mujeres
ISIC 3 - CITI 3 - CIIU 3

	1999	2000	2001	2002	2003	2004	2005	2006	2007	2008
Total	65.600	65.429	66.809	61.826	61.492	55.231	48.193	47.395	47.257	45.775
15-16	2.421	2.532	2.875	2.949	3.021	3.488	3.524	4.572	4.553	4.649
17	2.365	3.555	2.832	2.949	2.876	3.188	2.388	2.601	2.683	2.562
18	53.930	52.279	54.076	48.976	48.324	41.204	34.788	33.005	32.944	31.317
19	0.895	0.823	0.785	0.693	0.799	0.829	0.774	0.714	0.625	0.662
20	0.170	0.176	0.173	0.183	0.170	0.174	0.184	0.190	0.188	0.244
21	0.200	0.204	0.167	0.165	0.184	0.171	0.175	0.150	0.169	0.173
22	0.655	0.693	0.696	0.725	0.819	0.837	0.955	0.916	0.904	0.943
23-24	0.386	0.417	0.445	0.432	0.419	0.433	0.428	0.477	0.534	0.486
25	0.427	0.449	0.456	0.433	0.505	0.494	0.494	0.481	0.480	0.382
26	0.154	0.145	0.123	0.152	0.145	0.135	0.140	0.156	0.142	0.131
27	0.017	0.029	0.019	0.018	0.017	0.019	0.019	0.026	0.026	0.026
28	0.236	0.213	0.228	0.245	0.282	0.279	0.298	0.297	0.306	0.320
29-30	0.037	0.041	0.040	0.044	0.053	0.057	0.053	0.082	0.085	0.009
31	0.151	0.168	0.147	0.183	0.159	0.139	0.194	0.168	0.173	0.279
32	0.029	0.028	0.026	0.069	0.053	0.062	0.063	0.051	0.058	0.050
33	1.146	1.231	1.228	1.052	0.947	0.991	0.950	1.033	1.046	1.150
34-35	0.026	0.021	0.014	0.014	0.023	0.021	0.023	0.026	0.016	0.015
36-37	2.355	2.425	2.479	2.544	2.696	2.710	2.743	2.450	2.325	2.301

Explanatory notes: see p. 77.   Notes explicatives: voir p. 80.   Notas explicativas: véase p. 83.

[1] Establishments with 10 or more persons employed. [2] March of each year.   [1] Etablissements occupant 10 personnes et plus. [2] Mars de chaque année.   [1] Establecimientos con 10 y más trabajadores. [2] Marzo de cada año.

Paid employment in manufacturing
Thousands

Emploi rémunéré dans les industries manufacturières
Milliers

Empleo remunerado en las industrias manufactureras
Millares

AMERICA-AMÉRIQUE-AMERICA

Argentina (BA) [1][2][3] Employees - Salariés - Asalariados

Total - Total - Total
ISIC 3 - CITI 3 - CIIU 3

	1999	2000	2001	2002	2003	2004	2005	2006	2007	2008
Total	939.3	892.0	848.6	764.6	872.3 [4]	1 002.0	1 043.0	1 106.5 [5]	.	.
15	179.1	191.0	195.6	197.8	197.6 [4]	213.8	213.5	199.5 [5]	.	.
16	3.5	1.8	2.3	2.0	2.1 [4]	3.8	4.1	2.2 [5]	.	.
17	35.6	43.6	32.7	41.0	30.2 [4]	41.0	51.6	53.9 [5]	.	.
18	85.0	68.6	60.0	55.4	86.3 [4]	100.0	113.9	123.9 [5]	.	.
19	41.7	36.6	39.9	31.5	43.5 [4]	50.3	53.6	52.7 [5]	.	.
20	17.0	13.4	12.4	11.5	34.9 [4]	27.3	25.7	32.1 [5]	.	.
21	18.9	21.7	24.0	16.0	15.0 [4]	18.9	16.2	25.1 [5]	.	.
22	59.4	59.5	66.3	49.8	49.3 [4]	57.6	41.1	59.1 [5]	.	.
23	11.1	5.9	4.4	6.7	1.8 [4]	8.8	6.6	9.7 [5]	.	.
24	91.6	87.3	92.5	83.0	98.2 [4]	95.2	88.0	97.0 [5]	.	.
25	49.9	51.5	43.1	42.2	32.2 [4]	45.5	48.3	43.2 [5]	.	.
26	30.3	30.4	27.4	21.4	25.6 [4]	36.1	33.2	31.6 [5]	.	.
27	18.5	21.3	18.3	14.1	14.3 [4]	17.1	14.2	20.6 [5]	.	.
28	78.8	67.4	69.4	62.4	74.2 [4]	79.2	117.6	90.9 [5]	.	.
29	63.4	50.0	38.7	38.1	36.5 [4]	52.4	48.0	68.0 [5]	.	.
30	3.6	3.6	4.7	2.2	0.6 [4]	4.1	1.2	2.1 [5]	.	.
31	18.5	17.3	17.2	7.9	15.9 [4]	15.7	24.4	28.3 [5]	.	.
32	8.5	6.8	3.9	6.9	4.8 [4]	1.6	4.2	6.1 [5]	.	.
33	6.3	10.9	6.6	3.8	15.0 [4]	14.2	5.6	9.0 [5]	.	.
34	64.3	51.4	51.2	34.4	35.5 [4]	40.9	48.5	66.1 [5]	.	.
35	8.4	5.1	5.9	4.1	12.0 [4]	16.5	22.0	13.9 [5]	.	.
36	43.1	42.9	30.5	30.2	46.6 [4]	62.9	63.0	73.0 [5]	.	.
37	2.8	3.9	1.7	2.2	1.3 [4]	0.4	0.5	0.3 [5]	.	.

Men - Hommes - Hombres
ISIC 3 - CITI 3 - CIIU 3

	1999	2000	2001	2002	2003	2004	2005	2006	2007	2008
Total	699.0	670.3	629.9	575.1	646.5 [4]	732.0	759.5	807.6 [5]	.	.
15	135.9	144.2	147.3	155.9	152.5 [4]	164.1	166.6	152.8 [5]	.	.
16	2.9	1.7	1.7	1.3	2.1 [4]	3.6	2.6	1.5 [5]	.	.
17	22.7	30.5	25.1	28.0	19.5 [4]	25.6	32.3	35.6 [5]	.	.
18	23.1	21.9	25.7	22.6	23.1 [4]	32.8	36.2	43.0 [5]	.	.
19	28.5	26.0	29.4	23.9	26.2 [4]	37.3	40.4	30.9 [5]	.	.
20	16.0	12.9	10.9	10.6	33.8 [4]	26.3	24.4	28.5 [5]	.	.
21	16.5	15.1	17.1	13.4	13.8 [4]	9.6	11.6	18.0 [5]	.	.
22	43.7	42.4	44.0	34.7	35.0 [4]	44.8	30.2	37.5 [5]	.	.
23	10.5	5.4	3.9	6.2	1.8 [4]	6.5	6.0	9.0 [5]	.	.
24	53.0	49.6	53.5	47.5	75.0 [4]	54.3	53.0	61.7 [5]	.	.
25	39.8	43.2	34.8	33.4	26.8 [4]	40.8	40.5	35.6 [5]	.	.
26	27.9	28.2	23.1	18.8	19.6 [4]	32.8	31.3	30.3 [5]	.	.
27	18.0	21.1	16.1	12.4	13.0 [4]	15.1	13.2	19.4 [5]	.	.
28	71.1	61.2	60.8	52.7	67.3 [4]	71.5	106.6	79.9 [5]	.	.
29	51.9	44.2	32.5	35.0	30.2 [4]	44.9	40.7	62.1 [5]	.	.
30	1.3	2.5	3.6	1.2	0.6 [4]	4.0	1.2	1.3 [5]	.	.
31	16.9	16.4	15.1	5.1	12.5 [4]	13.4	20.1	22.8 [5]	.	.
32	5.1	5.3	2.7	6.1	3.8 [4]	1.1	1.8	4.7 [5]	.	.
33	5.3	4.4	4.4	3.3	10.4 [4]	9.9	2.8	7.8 [5]	.	.
34	58.9	48.9	46.0	31.8	33.3 [4]	38.6	45.1	59.0 [5]	.	.
35	8.0	4.8	5.5	4.1	9.8 [4]	12.1	16.9	13.8 [5]	.	.
36	39.2	37.1	24.8	25.1	36.1 [4]	43.6	37.2	54.0 [5]	.	.
37	2.8	3.2	1.6	1.9	1.3 [4]	0.4	0.5	0.2 [5]	.	.

Women - Femmes - Mujeres
ISIC 3 - CITI 3 - CIIU 3

	1999	2000	2001	2002	2003	2004	2005	2006	2007	2008
Total	240.3	221.7	218.7	189.5	225.8 [4]	270.1	283.4	299.2 [5]	.	.
15	43.2	46.8	48.3	41.9	45.1 [4]	49.7	46.8	46.8 [5]	.	.
16	0.6	0.1	0.6	0.6	0.0 [4]	0.1	1.5	0.7 [5]	.	.
17	12.8	13.1	7.6	12.9	10.8 [4]	15.4	19.4	18.3 [5]	.	.
18	61.9	46.7	34.3	32.7	63.2 [4]	67.2	77.7	80.9 [5]	.	.
19	13.1	10.6	10.4	7.6	17.3 [4]	12.9	13.2	21.8 [5]	.	.
20	1.0	0.5	1.5	0.9	1.0 [4]	1.0	1.2	3.6 [5]	.	.
21	2.4	6.6	6.9	2.5	1.2 [4]	9.2	4.5	7.1 [5]	.	.
22	15.8	17.6	22.2	15.1	14.3 [4]	12.8	10.9	21.6 [5]	.	.
23	0.6	0.4	0.5	0.6	0.0 [4]	2.3	0.6	0.7 [5]	.	.
24	38.7	37.7	39.0	35.5	23.2 [4]	40.9	35.0	35.3 [5]	.	.
25	10.1	8.4	8.4	8.8	5.4 [4]	4.7	7.8	7.6 [5]	.	.
26	2.3	2.2	4.2	2.7	6.1 [4]	3.3	1.8	1.4 [5]	.	.
27	0.5	0.2	2.1	1.7	1.3 [4]	2.1	1.0	1.2 [5]	.	.
28	7.7	6.2	8.6	9.8	6.9 [4]	7.7	11.1	11.0 [5]	.	.
29	11.5	5.7	6.2	3.1	6.3 [4]	7.5	7.4	5.9 [5]	.	.
30	2.2	1.0	1.1	1.0	- [4]	0.1	-	0.8 [5]	.	.
31	1.6	0.9	2.1	2.8	3.4 [4]	2.3	4.3	5.6 [5]	.	.
32	3.5	1.5	1.2	0.8	1.0 [4]	0.5	2.4	1.4 [5]	.	.
33	1.0	6.5	2.2	0.5	4.6 [4]	4.3	2.7	1.2 [5]	.	.
34	5.4	2.5	5.1	2.5	2.2 [4]	2.3	3.4	7.1 [5]	.	.
35	0.4	0.3	0.4	0.1	2.2 [4]	4.4	5.0	0.1 [5]	.	.
36	3.9	5.9	5.7	5.1	10.5 [4]	19.3	25.8	19.0 [5]	.	.
37	-	0.7	0.1	0.3	0.0 [4]	0.0	0.0	0.1 [5]	.	.

Explanatory notes: see p. 77.

[1] Persons aged 10 years and over. [2] 31 Urban agglomerations. [3] Second semester. [4] Methodology revised; data not strictly comparable; Prior to 2003: May and October. [5] Prior to 2006: 28 urban agglomerations.

Notes explicatives: voir p. 80.

[1] Personnes âgées de 10 ans et plus. [2] 31 agglomérations urbaines. [3] Second semestre. [4] Méthodologie révisée; les données ne sont pas strictement comparables; Avant 2003: mai et octobre. [5] Avant 2006: 28 agglomérations urbaines.

Notas explicativas: véase p. 83.

[1] Personas de 10 años y más. [2] 31 aglomerados úrbanos. [3] Segundo semestre. [4] Metodología revisada; los datos no son estrictamente comparables; antes de 2003: mayo y octubre. [5] Antes de 2006: 28 aglomerados úrbanos

EMPLOYMENT EMPLOI EMPLEO

Paid employment in manufacturing — Thousands
Emploi rémunéré dans les industries manufacturières — Milliers
Empleo remunerado en las industrias manufactureras — Millares

	1999	2000	2001	2002	2003	2004	2005	2006	2007	2008
Aruba (BA) [1][2]				Employees - Salariés - Asalariados						
Total - Total - Total										
ISIC 3 - CITI 3 - CIIU 3										
Total									2.720	
15									0.466	
18									0.026	
20									0.125	
22									0.204	
23									0.875	
24									0.095	
26									0.103	
27									0.028	
28									0.683	
35									0.063	
37									0.052	
Men - Hommes - Hombres										
ISIC 3 - CITI 3 - CIIU 3										
Total									2.229	
15									0.367	
20									0.125	
22									0.140	
23									0.823	
24									0.044	
26									0.070	
27									0.028	
28									0.543	
35									0.063	
37									0.026	
Women - Femmes - Mujeres										
ISIC 3 - CITI 3 - CIIU 3										
Total									0.493	
15									0.099	
18									0.026	
22									0.065	
23									0.052	
24									0.052	
26									0.033	
28									0.140	
37									0.026	
Bermuda (CA) [3][4]				All persons engaged - Effectif occupé - Efectivo ocupado						
Total - Total - Total										
ISIC 3 - CITI 3 - CIIU 3										
Total	1.208	1.235	1.171	1.107	1.063	1.012	1.003	0.965	0.935	
15	0.343	0.353	0.309	0.245	0.233	0.208	0.209	0.210	0.202	
17	0.010	0.012	0.017	0.014	0.013	0.018	0.019	0.019	0.014	
18	0.014	0.015	0.017	0.017	0.017	0.015	0.014	0.012	0.011	
20	0.030	0.028	0.029	0.031	0.033	0.037	0.035	0.035	0.026	
22	0.390	0.396	0.380	0.376	0.370	0.355	0.352	0.321	0.324	
24	0.030	0.033	0.040	0.042	0.031	0.028	0.023	0.020	0.020	
25	0.003	0.001	0.001	0.004	0.005	0.005	0.007	0.007	0.008	
26	0.126	0.134	0.127	0.135	0.126	0.122	0.121	0.118	0.113	
28	0.044	0.045	0.045	0.045	0.041	0.047	0.048	0.048	0.050	
29	0.003	0.003	0.003	0.003	0.002	0.003	0.003	0.001	-	
31	0.004	0.005	0.005	0.004	0.004	0.004	-	0.006	0.010	
35	0.074	0.071	0.064	0.048	0.067	0.057	0.059	0.062	0.061	
36	0.137	0.139	0.134	0.123	0.121	0.111	0.113	0.106	0.096	
Men - Hommes - Hombres										
ISIC 3 - CITI 3 - CIIU 3										
Total	0.852	0.857	0.808	0.751	0.732	0.706	0.695	0.684	0.657	
15	0.266	0.269	0.243	0.188	0.182	0.163	0.165	0.169	0.165	
17	0.080	0.080	0.010	0.006	0.004	0.009	0.011	0.012	0.006	
18	0.008	0.008	0.006	0.007	0.008	0.008	0.007	0.007	0.006	
20	0.030	0.026	0.027	0.029	0.031	0.034	0.032	0.031	0.023	
22	0.210	0.213	0.199	0.196	0.195	0.196	0.188	0.177	0.175	
24	0.023	0.023	0.024	0.024	0.022	0.022	0.018	0.015	0.015	
25	0.003	0.001	0.001	0.003	0.004	0.007	0.006	0.006	0.007	
26	0.101	0.108	0.101	0.107	0.103	0.098	0.096	0.093	0.088	
28	0.040	0.041	0.041	0.040	0.036	0.042	0.043	0.042	0.043	
29	0.002	0.002	0.002	0.002	0.001	0.002	0.002	0.001	-	
31	0.004	0.004	0.004	0.003	0.003	0.003	-	0.005	0.008	
35	0.068	0.064	0.059	0.062	0.062	0.048	0.052	0.056	0.055	
36	0.092	0.093	0.091	0.084	0.081	0.074	0.075	0.070	0.066	

Explanatory notes: see p. 77.

[1] Persons aged 15 years and over. [2] Oct. [3] Excl. unpaid family workers. [4] Aug. of each year.

Notes explicatives: voir p. 80.

[1] Personnes âgées de 15 ans et plus. [2] Oct. [3] Non compris les travailleurs familiaux non rémunérés. [4] Août de chaque année.

Notas explicativas: véase p. 83.

[1] Personas de 15 años y más. [2] Oct. [3] Excl. los trabajadores familiares no remunerados. [4] Agosto de cada año.

Paid employment in manufacturing	Emploi rémunéré dans les industries manufacturières	Empleo remunerado en las industrias manufactureras
Thousands	Milliers	Millares

	1999	2000	2001	2002	2003	2004	2005	2006	2007	2008

Bermuda (CA) [1] [2]

All persons engaged - Effectif occupé - Efectivo ocupado

Women - Femmes - Mujeres
ISIC 3 - CITI 3 - CIIU 3

	1999	2000	2001	2002	2003	2004	2005	2006	2007	2008
Total	0.356	0.378	0.363	0.356	0.331	0.306	0.308	0.281	0.278	.
15	0.077	0.084	0.066	0.057	0.051	0.045	0.044	0.041	0.037	.
17	0.002	0.004	0.007	0.008	0.009	0.009	0.008	0.007	0.008	.
18	0.009	0.004	0.011	0.010	0.009	0.007	0.007	0.005	0.005	.
20	-	0.002	0.002	0.002	0.002	0.003	0.003	0.004	0.003	.
22	0.180	0.183	0.181	0.180	0.175	0.159	0.164	0.144	0.149	.
24	0.007	0.010	0.016	0.016	0.009	0.006	0.005	0.005	0.005	.
25	-	-	-	0.001	0.001	0.002	0.001	0.001	0.001	.
26	0.023	0.026	0.026	0.029	0.023	0.024	0.025	0.025	0.025	.
28	0.004	0.004	0.004	0.005	0.005	0.005	0.005	0.006	0.007	.
29	0.001	0.001	0.001	0.001	0.001	0.001	0.001	-	-	.
31	-	0.001	0.001	0.001	0.001	0.001	-	0.001	0.002	.
35	0.006	0.007	0.005	0.006	0.005	0.009	0.007	0.006	0.006	.
36	0.045	0.046	0.043	0.039	0.040	0.037	0.038	0.036	0.030	.

Brasil (BA) [3] [4]

Employees - Salariés - Asalariados

Total - Total - Total
ISIC 3 - CITI 3 - CIIU 3

	1999	2000	2001	2002	2003	2004	2005	2006	2007	2008
Total	.	.	.	7 909	8 011 [5]	8 862	8 991	9 239	9 902	.
15	.	.	.	1 273	1 204 [5]	1 366	1 410	1 479	1 541	.
16	.	.	.	18	18 [5]	17	16	13	16	.
17	.	.	.	468	350 [5]	366	397	410	447	.
18	.	.	.	684	737 [5]	839	868	875	911	.
19	.	.	.	614	685 [5]	735	708	745	786	.
20	.	.	.	434	402 [5]	452	426	439	406	.
21	.	.	.	157	172 [5]	182	168	190	220	.
22	.	.	.	300	308 [5]	318	327	334	330	.
23	.	.	.	113	107 [5]	125	116	111	183	.
24	.	.	.	506	619 [5]	685	619	678	788	.
25	.	.	.	257	279 [5]	300	347	339	359	.
26	.	.	.	532	475 [5]	514	543	534	528	.
27	.	.	.	254	284 [5]	289	312	344	356	.
28	.	.	.	523	502 [5]	570	525	608	747	.
29	.	.	.	444	514 [5]	582	598	560	648	.
30	.	.	.	28	33 [5]	31	45	30	42	.
31	.	.	.	103	110 [5]	164	170	140	122	.
32	.	.	.	97	90 [5]	121	112	114	137	.
33	.	.	.	81	85 [5]	93	96	109	88	.
34	.	.	.	377	408 [5]	441	484	479	507	.
35	.	.	.	79	83 [5]	103	98	120	109	.
36	.	.	.	542	506 [5]	520	544	528	561	.
37	.	.	.	26	41 [5]	50	63	61	69	.

Men - Hommes - Hombres
ISIC 3 - CITI 3 - CIIU 3

	1999	2000	2001	2002	2003	2004	2005	2006	2007	2008
Total	.	.	.	5 641	5 672 [5]	6 270	6 357	6 532	7 040	.
15	.	.	.	912	869 [5]	955	991	1 048	1 098	.
16	.	.	.	12	12 [5]	11	10	6	10	.
17	.	.	.	253	198 [5]	216	213	228	252	.
18	.	.	.	151	166 [5]	190	209	209	228	.
19	.	.	.	321	355 [5]	391	377	388	414	.
20	.	.	.	386	353 [5]	386	373	370	346	.
21	.	.	.	122	133 [5]	137	130	139	162	.
22	.	.	.	204	202 [5]	221	229	234	225	.
23	.	.	.	98	97 [5]	110	103	100	164	.
24	.	.	.	370	448 [5]	484	437	495	565	.
25	.	.	.	199	217 [5]	228	270	254	281	.
26	.	.	.	460	414 [5]	456	489	473	464	.
27	.	.	.	235	254 [5]	263	288	308	328	.
28	.	.	.	463	462 [5]	504	472	542	659	.
29	.	.	.	382	450 [5]	507	511	470	565	.
30	.	.	.	17	23 [5]	23	25	20	25	.
31	.	.	.	81	86 [5]	130	128	112	96	.
32	.	.	.	69	56 [5]	75	68	80	93	.
33	.	.	.	53	58 [5]	62	62	78	59	.
34	.	.	.	328	344 [5]	385	413	414	434	.
35	.	.	.	71	73 [5]	89	87	110	96	.
36	.	.	.	438	376 [5]	404	426	411	427	.
37	.	.	.	17	27 [5]	44	46	43	49	.

Explanatory notes: see p. 77.

[1] Excl. unpaid family workers. [2] Aug. of each year. [3] Employees of 10 years and over. [4] Sep. of each year. [5] Prior to 2003: Excl. rural population of Rondônia, Acre, Amazonas, Roraima, Pará and Amapá.

Notes explicatives: voir p. 80.

[1] Non compris les travailleurs familiaux non rémunérés. [2] Août de chaque année. [3] Salariés de 10 ans et plus. [4] Sept. de chaque année. [5] Avant 2003: Non compris la population rurale de Rondônia, Acre, Amazonas, Roraima, Pará et Amapá.

Notas explicativas: véase p. 83.

[1] Excl. los trabajadores familiares no remunerados. [2] Agosto de cada año. [3] Asalariados de 10 años y más. [4] Sept. de cada año. [5] Antes de 2003: Excl. la población rural de Rondonia, Acre, Amazonas, Roraima, Pará y Amapá.

EMPLOYMENT

EMPLOI

EMPLEO

Paid employment in manufacturing
Thousands

Emploi rémunéré dans les industries manufacturières
Milliers

Empleo remunerado en las industrias manufactureras
Millares

	1999	2000	2001	2002	2003	2004	2005	2006	2007	2008
Brasil (BA) [1][2]					**Employees - Salariés - Asalariados**					
Women - Femmes - Mujeres										
ISIC 3 - CITI 3 - CIIU 3										
Total				2 268	2 339 [3]	2 592	2 635	2 707	2 862	.
15				361	335 [3]	411	420	431	444	
16				6	6 [3]	6	5	7	7	
17				214	152 [3]	150	184	183	195	
18				533	571 [3]	649	659	666	683	
19				294	330 [3]	344	330	356	372	
20				48	49 [3]	65	53	69	60	.
21				35	40 [3]	45	38	50	58	
22				95	107 [3]	97	98	100	105	
23				15	10 [3]	15	13	11	19	
24				136	171 [3]	201	182	183	224	
25				57	62 [3]	72	77	85	78	
26				72	61 [3]	58	54	61	64	
27				19	30 [3]	26	24	36	28	
28				60	40 [3]	67	54	66	88	
29				62	64 [3]	75	87	90	82	.
30				11	11 [3]	8	20	10	16	.
31				22	24 [3]	35	42	28	26	
32				29	34 [3]	46	44	34	43	
33				28	27 [3]	31	35	31	29	
34				49	64 [3]	55	71	66	72	.
35				8	10 [3]	13	11	10	13	
36				104	130 [3]	117	117	117	134	
37				9	14 [3]	7	17	17	20	
Canada (BA) [4][5][6]					**Employees - Salariés - Asalariados**					
Total - Total - Total										
ISIC 3 - CITI 3 - CIIU 3										
Total	2 096.1	2 159.3	2 129.9	2 192.7	2 185.3	2 198.5	2 109.9	2 025.8	1 943.8	1 869.4
15	253.0	252.5	255.2	279.3	285.9	297.3	291.8	276.7	280.6	283.6
16	5.8	5.2	4.3	3.1	6.3	4.0	3.1	2.1	2.9	1.6
17	58.0	54.1	49.8	52.5	47.7	47.6	42.2	33.5	33.6	23.5
18	95.3	83.1	90.9	79.9	81.0	71.3	54.6	56.8	48.4	37.9
19	10.5	9.1	11.2	7.9	5.4	6.5	8.0	5.2	6.4	7.5
20	143.4	155.1	153.1	166.2	178.3	178.7	161.6	157.0	138.4	121.3
21	116.1	115.3	108.3	106.0	107.8	103.6	100.4	93.2	86.4	90.5
22	96.9	86.5	85.6	92.7	102.9	102.9	89.5	83.9	81.2	88.7
23	16.5	19.1	16.7	16.5	16.2	17.6	18.1	16.4	18.6	19.1
24	110.3	116.3	116.7	122.0	119.5	116.1	113.7	102.5	106.8	107.6
25	122.8	125.6	116.6	127.3	130.2	134.9	139.3	127.3	116.7	99.5
26	53.5	52.7	54.1	48.8	48.6	59.6	58.7	57.9	52.1	55.6
27	104.0	107.1	97.2	99.2	95.6	91.5	89.9	89.5	77.3	76.9
28	147.1	160.5	161.7	163.0	158.0	163.5	176.0	170.3	166.2	163.9
29	107.7	117.5	125.4	123.3	127.8	134.1	125.9	118.2	116.6	107.4
30	33.7	34.6	37.6	31.0	25.7	20.6	20.0	16.4	21.5	17.5
31	91.6	97.4	97.4	94.1	93.4	82.9	78.3	82.0	80.0	77.4
32	38.2	53.5	43.7	37.1	32.7	29.7	29.3	36.1	35.2	35.7
33	36.8	34.8	38.4	46.5	38.3	36.7	39.9	39.5	40.4	42.4
34	222.9	233.8	220.4	240.3	238.7	236.8	229.4	223.7	199.7	186.1
35	81.5	80.3	82.0	85.6	76.6	77.8	75.2	76.5	74.9	81.5
36	95.2	100.6	99.2	106.7	108.1	116.3	101.2	99.4	95.1	90.7
37	55.3	64.5	64.4	63.5	60.6	68.6	63.6	61.7	64.9	53.2
Men - Hommes - Hombres										
ISIC 3 - CITI 3 - CIIU 3										
Total	1 499.9	1 556.5	1 531.9	1 558.2	1 547.7	1 569.1	1 506.0	1 447.0	1 389.6	1 336.3
15	159.7	162.8	164.2	177.3	177.9	184.3	178.0	164.6	168.3	174.2
16	3.9	3.6	2.8	2.1	4.4	2.7	1.9	1.6	0.9	-
17	29.2	28.8	26.2	26.1	23.2	25.4	20.2	16.5	14.2	10.5
18	20.0	16.4	20.8	21.2	22.4	20.2	13.2	16.0	12.2	8.7
19	4.9	4.9	4.4	2.6	1.9	3.8	4.2	2.2	1.9	3.0
20	125.8	136.3	131.3	141.8	151.3	150.9	137.4	133.0	116.9	101.3
21	98.8	95.5	91.6	87.5	88.5	85.9	82.9	77.9	70.5	74.0
22	61.3	58.3	53.1	57.5	64.7	64.3	58.2	52.7	50.8	55.0
23	14.2	15.4	13.8	13.0	13.4	14.3	15.1	14.3	15.8	14.7
24	68.1	76.7	72.0	72.1	69.4	66.5	62.1	60.4	65.7	60.3
25	83.4	85.8	81.3	87.8	88.0	94.2	93.9	87.7	79.5	69.7
26	45.7	45.6	43.7	40.1	39.8	47.2	49.2	45.4	43.1	46.5
27	93.8	96.2	85.9	87.1	84.0	82.8	79.4	81.0	66.8	68.2
28	123.7	130.5	139.3	139.1	130.0	136.1	145.2	140.3	140.6	134.1
29	90.0	95.4	106.9	96.2	104.2	112.9	106.3	100.3	98.9	90.1
30	20.7	22.8	26.5	20.4	15.5	13.5	12.3	11.4	15.0	13.0
31	59.8	61.9	60.9	61.1	59.0	53.0	53.6	53.2	52.8	50.0
32	25.0	35.0	30.8	24.5	21.6	20.8	21.4	24.8	25.6	25.9
33	22.6	21.4	23.5	26.4	25.0	21.9	25.6	20.5	24.7	25.1
34	174.8	179.4	168.4	182.4	181.8	180.1	172.8	172.2	157.2	145.2
35	66.8	67.4	69.2	71.1	63.9	64.9	61.2	59.8	61.2	68.6
36	75.0	76.6	76.6	82.5	80.1	83.3	71.6	69.6	69.0	66.2
37	32.6	39.7	38.6	38.3	37.8	40.1	40.4	41.6	38.2	30.8

Explanatory notes: see p. 77.

[1] Employees of 10 years and over. [2] Sep. of each year. [3] Prior to 2003: Excl. rural population of Rondônia, Acre, Amazonas, Roraima, Pará and Amapá. [4] Persons aged 15 years and over. [5] Excl. residents of the Territories and indigenous persons living on reserves. [6] Excl. full-time members of the armed forces.

Notes explicatives: voir p. 80.

[1] Salariés de 10 ans et plus. [2] Sept. de chaque année. [3] Avant 2003: Non compris la population rurale de Rondônia, Acre, Amazonas, Roraima, Pará et Amapá. [4] Personnes âgées de 15 ans et plus. [5] Non compris les habitants des "Territoires" et les populations indigènes vivant dans les réserves. [6] Non compris les membres à temps complet des forces armées.

Notas explicativas: véase p. 83.

[1] Asalariados de 10 años y más. [2] Sept. de cada año. [3] Antes de 2003: Excl. la población rural de Rondonia, Acre, Amazonas, Roraima, Pará y Amapá. [4] Personas de 15 años y más. [5] Excl. a los habitantes de los "Territorios" y a las poblaciones indígenas que viven en reservas. [6] Excl. los miembros a tiempo completo de las fuerzas armadas.

Paid employment in manufacturing
Thousands

Emploi rémunéré dans les industries manufacturières
Milliers

Empleo remunerado en las industrias manufactureras
Millares

	1999	2000	2001	2002	2003	2004	2005	2006	2007	2008

Canada (BA) [1] [2] [3] — Employees - Salariés - Asalariados

Women - Femmes - Mujeres
ISIC 3 - CITI 3 - CIIU 3

	1999	2000	2001	2002	2003	2004	2005	2006	2007	2008
Total	596.2	602.8	598.0	634.5	637.6	629.3	603.9	578.8	554.2	533.1
15	93.3	89.7	90.9	102.1	108.1	113.0	113.8	112.1	112.3	109.4
16	1.9	1.5	1.5	1.0	1.9	1.3	1.2	0.5	2.0	-
17	28.8	25.2	23.5	26.5	24.5	22.2	21.9	17.0	19.5	13.0
18	75.3	66.7	70.1	58.7	58.6	51.1	41.5	40.8	36.2	29.3
19	5.5	4.2	6.8	5.2	3.5	2.7	3.8	3.0	4.5	4.5
20	17.6	18.8	21.8	24.4	27.0	27.8	24.3	23.9	21.6	20.0
21	17.3	19.8	16.8	18.5	19.3	17.7	17.5	15.3	15.9	16.5
22	35.6	28.2	32.5	35.3	38.1	38.6	31.3	31.2	30.4	33.8
23	2.3	3.7	2.9	3.5	2.8	3.3	3.0	2.1	2.8	4.4
24	42.2	39.7	44.7	49.9	50.0	49.6	51.5	42.1	41.1	47.4
25	39.4	39.9	35.3	39.5	42.2	40.7	45.4	39.6	37.2	29.8
26	7.8	7.1	10.4	8.7	8.8	12.5	9.5	12.5	9.0	9.2
27	10.2	10.9	11.3	12.1	11.7	8.7	10.5	8.4	10.6	8.8
28	23.3	30.0	22.4	23.9	28.0	27.3	30.8	30.0	25.6	29.8
29	17.6	22.1	18.6	27.1	23.5	21.2	19.6	17.9	17.7	17.3
30	12.9	11.8	11.2	10.6	10.3	7.1	7.7	5.0	6.5	4.5
31	31.8	35.6	36.5	33.0	34.4	29.8	24.7	28.8	27.2	27.4
32	13.3	18.5	12.9	12.6	11.1	8.8	8.0	11.3	9.7	9.8
33	14.2	13.5	14.9	20.1	13.3	14.8	14.3	19.0	15.7	17.3
34	48.1	54.4	51.9	57.9	56.9	56.8	56.6	51.5	42.5	40.9
35	14.7	13.0	12.8	14.6	12.7	12.9	14.1	16.7	13.7	12.9
36	20.2	24.0	22.6	24.2	27.9	32.9	29.6	29.9	26.0	24.5
37	22.7	24.8	25.7	25.2	22.8	28.6	23.2	20.1	26.7	22.4

Canada (DA) — Employees - Salariés - Asalariados

Total - Total - Total
ISIC 3 - CITI 3 - CIIU 3

	1999	2000	2001	2002	2003	2004	2005	2006	2007	2008
Total	2 006.1	2 099.7	2 040.7	1 991.6	1 969.6	1 928.6	1 897.6	1 878.1	1 818.9	1 735.9
15	253.0	263.0	262.1	263.4	262.2	263.3	256.4	257.5	252.9	250.5
16	5.0	5.1	4.7	4.6	4.7	4.1	3.8	4.0	3.1	2.5
17	64.8	66.7	57.5	54.9	52.0	46.8	41.5	37.0	32.9	26.4
18	74.6	77.7	71.1	64.2	60.5	54.6	45.4	40.1	35.3	29.6
19	11.2	12.2	9.5	8.5	7.5	6.6	5.8	5.0	4.5	3.8
20	134.2	141.9	135.8	134.2	133.8	137.2	135.3	130.2	122.9	110.3
21	103.1	110.1	103.7	96.0	97.0	93.7	87.7	83.8	79.4	73.5
22	142.0	148.5	145.6	141.8	140.5	132.3	131.8	130.6	132.1	132.5
23	15.5	15.9	15.3	15.4	15.7	15.3	15.8	16.3	16.7	17.9
24	91.4	95.5	93.4	92.2	92.8	92.8	93.0	90.8	89.0	88.5
25	117.7	123.5	125.2	126.1	125.8	127.4	125.8	124.8	118.3	107.5
26	53.3	56.4	53.7	51.4	51.3	51.4	51.3	53.7	52.8	52.7
27	100.5	104.3	91.2	90.3	85.4	79.7	78.7	80.7	78.8	69.1
28	173.1	183.2	184.3	181.1	180.6	176.4	176.1	179.7	175.1	171.1
29	132.5	136.4	134.9	137.3	137.2	136.0	140.4	144.5	139.7	138.1
30	13.9	14.7	14.7	11.4	10.5	9.4	8.3	8.3	8.2	8.4
31	80.5	87.7	81.4	77.4	75.0	72.6	69.9	66.5	66.0	63.8
32	28.1	29.5	32.2	28.3	25.8	25.9	26.7	28.4	27.1	29.5
33	43.2	43.9	42.4	39.9	40.5	39.9	40.1	42.0	42.7	42.2
34	167.6	172.0	170.7	166.3	166.1	165.4	164.6	158.3	152.6	137.5
35	67.9	72.2	72.1	67.3	65.1	63.9	64.8	64.5	63.0	61.9
36	88.7	94.4	98.6	98.6	98.6	93.1	94.2	90.7	85.8	79.8
37	44.2	44.9	40.7	40.8	40.9	40.8	40.1	40.7	40.2	38.5

Colombia (DA) [4] — Employees - Salariés - Asalariados

Total - Total - Total
ISIC 3 - CITI 3 - CIIU 3

	1999	2000	2001	2002	2003	2004	2005	2006	2007	2008
Total	.	449.9	436.3	430.4	428.0	428.1	588.3	.	.	.
15	.	109.1	102.6	98.2	95.2	92.2	128.1	.	.	.
16	.	1.0	1.0	1.1	1.1	1.2	1.3	.	.	.
17	.	39.3	37.5	36.4	36.0	34.7	50.4	.	.	.
18	.	60.6	60.7	61.3	61.3	60.7	82.4	.	.	.
19	.	14.6	13.5	12.4	12.3	13.1	18.8	.	.	.
20	.	3.8	3.7	3.7	3.7	3.9	4.8	.	.	.
21	.	17.4	17.2	17.1	16.7	17.0	20.1	.	.	.
22	.	21.5	19.8	20.0	20.0	20.3	25.1	.	.	.
23	.	4.6	4.0	3.8	3.7	3.6	3.5	.	.	.
24	.	38.9	41.6	39.9	39.7	40.7	55.9	.	.	.
25	.	27.1	27.2	28.3	29.8	30.0	42.6	.	.	.
26	.	23.3	22.3	22.0	21.7	22.5	30.3	.	.	.
27	.	10.1	9.8	10.2	9.7	10.7	15.5	.	.	.
28	.	16.8	16.2	15.8	16.2	16.1	23.5	.	.	.
29	.	16.5	15.4	14.7	15.5	16.1	23.1	.	.	.
31	.	10.2	10.2	10.3	9.5	9.6	13.6	.	.	.
32	.	2.2	1.7	1.7	1.7	1.7	1.2	.	.	.
33	.	2.1	2.3	2.3	2.3	2.3	3.1	.	.	.
34	.	8.0	8.7	8.9	8.7	9.8	14.1	.	.	.
35	.	3.6	3.6	3.3	3.0	2.9	4.0	.	.	.
36	.	19.3	17.3	19.1	19.6	19.0	27.0	.	.	.

Explanatory notes: see p. 77.

[1] Persons aged 15 years and over. [2] Excl. residents of the Territories and indigenous persons living on reserves. [3] Excl. full-time members of the armed forces. [4] Establishments with 10 or more persons employed.

Notes explicatives: voir p. 80.

[1] Personnes âgées de 15 ans et plus. [2] Non compris les habitants des "Territoires" et les populations indigènes vivant dans les réserves. [3] Non compris les membres à temps complet des forces armées. [4] Etablissements occupant 10 personnes et plus.

Notas explicativas: véase p. 83.

[1] Personas de 15 años y más. [2] Excl. a los habitantes de los "Territorios" y a las poblaciones indígenas que viven en reservas. [3] Excl. los miembros a tiempo completo de las fuerzas armadas. [4] Establecimientos con 10 y más trabajadores.

EMPLOYMENT	EMPLOI	EMPLEO
Paid employment in manufacturing	Emploi rémunéré dans les industries manufacturières	Empleo remunerado en las industrias manufactureras
Thousands	Milliers	Millares

	1999	2000	2001	2002	2003	2004	2005	2006	2007	2008

Colombia (DA) [1] — Employees - Salariés - Asalariados

Men - Hommes - Hombres
ISIC 3 - CITI 3 - CIIU 3

	1999	2000	2001	2002	2003	2004	2005	2006	2007	2008
Total	.	284.6	275.0	270.3	268.4	268.5	367.2	.	.	.
15	.	77.0	72.1	69.2	66.8	64.8	87.6	.	.	.
16	.	0.7	0.8	0.8	0.9	0.9	1.1	.	.	.
17	.	26.2	25.0	24.2	23.8	22.4	32.3	.	.	.
18	.	11.9	12.4	11.8	12.8	13.0	19.0	.	.	.
19	.	7.2	6.8	6.2	6.1	6.5	9.6	.	.	.
20	.	3.2	3.1	3.2	3.2	3.3	4.0	.	.	.
21	.	13.1	13.0	13.0	12.7	12.5	15.1	.	.	.
22	.	13.2	12.0	12.0	11.8	11.9	14.3	.	.	.
23	.	4.1	3.6	3.5	3.3	3.0	2.9	.	.	.
24	.	22.5	24.3	22.8	22.7	22.9	30.7	.	.	.
25	.	18.2	18.3	19.1	19.8	20.0	27.8	.	.	.
26	.	20.2	19.5	19.3	19.1	19.7	26.8	.	.	.
27	.	8.8	8.7	9.0	8.6	9.5	14.0	.	.	.
28	.	13.3	12.6	12.6	13.0	12.7	18.8	.	.	.
29	.	13.7	12.7	12.1	12.9	13.4	18.6	.	.	.
31	.	6.4	6.3	6.3	6.1	6.3	8.7	.	.	.
32	.	1.3	0.9	0.9	0.9	1.0	0.8	.	.	.
33	.	1.0	1.1	1.1	1.1	1.1	1.5	.	.	.
34	.	6.9	7.6	7.6	7.4	8.3	12.2	.	.	.
35	.	3.0	3.0	2.8	2.4	2.3	3.2	.	.	.
36	.	12.7	11.2	12.9	13.2	12.7	18.2	.	.	.

Women - Femmes - Mujeres
ISIC 3 - CITI 3 - CIIU 3

	1999	2000	2001	2002	2003	2004	2005	2006	2007	2008
Total	.	165.3	161.2	160.1	159.5	159.6	221.1	.	.	.
15	.	32.1	30.5	29.0	28.8	27.3	40.5	.	.	.
16	.	0.2	0.2	0.2	0.2	0.3	0.2	.	.	.
17	.	13.1	12.5	12.3	12.2	12.3	18.0	.	.	.
18	.	48.7	48.3	49.5	48.6	47.7	63.4	.	.	.
19	.	7.5	6.7	6.2	6.2	6.6	9.2	.	.	.
20	.	0.6	0.6	0.5	0.5	0.6	0.8	.	.	.
21	.	4.3	4.2	4.1	4.0	4.4	5.0	.	.	.
22	.	8.3	7.8	8.0	8.3	8.4	10.8	.	.	.
23	.	0.4	0.4	0.3	0.4	0.6	0.6	.	.	.
24	.	16.4	17.3	17.1	17.1	17.9	25.3	.	.	.
25	.	9.0	8.9	9.3	9.9	10.0	14.8	.	.	.
26	.	3.0	2.8	2.7	2.7	2.8	3.5	.	.	.
27	.	1.2	1.1	1.2	1.2	1.2	1.5	.	.	.
28	.	3.5	3.6	3.2	3.2	3.4	4.7	.	.	.
29	.	2.9	2.7	2.5	2.7	2.7	4.5	.	.	.
31	.	3.8	3.9	4.0	3.4	3.3	4.9	.	.	.
32	.	0.9	0.8	0.8	0.8	0.7	0.4	.	.	.
33	.	1.1	1.1	1.1	1.2	1.2	1.6	.	.	.
34	.	1.1	1.2	1.3	1.3	1.4	1.9	.	.	.
35	.	0.6	0.6	0.5	0.5	0.6	0.8	.	.	.
36	.	6.6	6.0	6.2	6.5	6.3	8.8	.	.	.

Costa Rica (BA) [2] [3] — Employees - Salariés - Asalariados

Total - Total - Total
ISIC 3 - CITI 3 - CIIU 3

	1999	2000	2001	2002	2003	2004	2005	2006	2007	2008
Total	.	145.4	168.4	.	167.2	172.5	183.2	180.0	192.3	182.4
15	.	37.8	48.9	.	51.5	54.0	57.1	54.8	63.3	60.4
16	.	-	0.1	.	0.1	0.4	0.2	-	0.4	0.2
17	.	6.4	4.1	.	6.1	4.7	3.1	4.5	3.9	3.2
18	.	25.2	31.0	.	18.9	15.5	16.6	15.7	17.8	15.9
19	.	2.7	2.8	.	2.3	2.1	2.0	0.9	1.1	1.5
20	.	4.9	4.5	.	6.5	6.4	6.2	6.9	5.1	4.5
21	.	3.1	4.7	.	4.6	4.3	4.3	4.8	5.0	7.4
22	.	6.2	6.2	.	6.9	8.6	7.7	8.3	7.9	7.1
23	.	1.8	-	.	-	-	0.2		0.4	0.2
24	.	9.5	8.3	.	10.8	11.1	15.7	12.0	12.1	12.7
25	.	8.5	7.4	.	7.8	7.8	10.6	12.0	15.5	11.0
26	.	4.3	6.5	.	5.4	6.6	7.1	6.6	5.7	5.9
27	.	0.1	1.4	.	0.9	1.7	1.4	1.3	0.9	0.9
28	.	8.3	9.5	.	10.2	9.5	9.6	8.9	11.2	10.1
29	.	1.3	6.0	.	2.7	5.6	4.1	4.3	4.6	3.1
30	.	4.8	0.6	.	0.3	0.5	1.3	-	1.5	0.5
31	.	1.1	2.2	.	3.4	3.2	3.2	3.3	2.2	3.0
32	.	5.6	3.1	.	3.9	5.4	8.2	8.8	6.2	7.8
33	.	0.8	6.5	.	9.4	6.7	6.7	10.1	9.6	11.3
34	.	0.6	1.1	.	1.3	1.4	0.4	0.9	1.1	0.4
35	.	1.0	2.0	.	1.0	1.3	1.9	1.9	1.3	1.4
36	.	10.1	11.4	.	12.1	14.6	15.1	12.9	15.0	13.3
37	.	0.3	1.0	.	1.2	1.0	0.5	1.1	0.4	0.6

Explanatory notes: see p. 77.

[1] Establishments with 10 or more persons employed. [2] Persons aged 12 years and over. [3] July of each year.

Notes explicatives: voir p. 80.

[1] Etablissements occupant 10 personnes et plus. [2] Personnes âgées de 12 ans et plus. [3] Juillet de chaque année.

Notas explicativas: véase p. 83.

[1] Establecimientos con 10 y más trabajadores. [2] Personas de 12 años y más. [3] Julio de cada año.

Paid employment in manufacturing — Emploi rémunéré dans les industries manufacturières — Empleo remunerado en las industrias manufactureras

Thousands — Milliers — Millares

	1999	2000	2001	2002	2003	2004	2005	2006	2007	2008
Costa Rica (BA) [1][2]					Employees - Salariés - Asalariados					
Men - Hommes - Hombres										
ISIC 3 - CITI 3 - CIIU 3										
Total	.	100.1	115.1	.	119.5	129.8	137.7	130.9	137.5	126.7
15	.	28.6	35.4	.	38.1	40.9	43.1	40.5	43.7	39.9
16	.	-	0.1	.	0.1	0.4	0.2	-	0.2	0.2
17	.	3.3	1.7	.	4.2	3.0	2.1	2.4	2.1	1.4
18	.	10.2	12.9	.	7.6	5.5	8.1	5.9	4.7	4.9
19	.	2.0	2.1	.	2.0	1.4	1.9	0.9	0.5	1.1
20	.	4.6	4.1	.	6.1	6.3	6.1	6.2	4.8	4.4
21	.	2.6	4.0	.	3.1	3.4	3.7	4.0	3.5	5.2
22	.	4.4	5.3	.	4.5	6.3	5.2	6.3	5.2	4.2
23	.	1.5	-	.	-	-	-	-	0.3	0.2
24	.	5.4	5.3	.	7.7	8.5	12.0	9.0	10.0	8.6
25	.	6.2	5.7	.	6.4	6.7	9.1	9.5	13.9	10.2
26	.	3.6	5.8	.	5.1	5.9	6.0	6.0	5.1	5.3
27	.	0.1	1.2	.	0.7	1.5	1.4	1.3	0.9	0.7
28	.	7.3	8.3	.	8.5	8.2	8.9	8.2	10.4	8.9
29	.	1.3	4.7	.	1.9	4.7	2.9	2.5	4.1	2.7
30	.	2.9	0.3	.	0.3	0.3	0.2	-	1.0	0.2
31	.	0.8	1.7	.	2.1	2.8	2.3	2.1	1.4	2.3
32	.	3.8	1.2	.	2.6	3.9	4.6	6.5	4.2	6.0
33	.	0.5	2.5	.	4.8	3.9	3.8	4.5	5.3	6.3
34	.	0.6	0.8	.	0.8	0.4	0.2	0.9	1.1	0.2
35	.	1.0	1.6	.	1.0	1.3	1.9	1.8	1.3	1.3
36	.	9.2	9.7	.	10.6	13.6	13.5	11.8	13.5	12.4
37	.	0.3	0.8	.	1.2	1.0	0.5	0.9	0.4	0.2
Women - Femmes - Mujeres										
ISIC 3 - CITI 3 - CIIU 3										
Total	.	45.3	53.3	.	47.8	42.7	45.5	49.1	54.7	55.7
15	.	9.2	13.5	.	13.4	13.2	14.0	14.3	19.6	20.5
16	.	-	0.1	.	-	-	-	-	0.2	-
17	.	3.1	2.3	.	1.9	1.7	1.0	2.1	1.8	1.8
18	.	16.1	18.2	.	11.3	10.0	8.6	9.9	13.1	11.1
19	.	0.7	0.7	.	0.3	0.6	0.1	0.1	0.6	0.4
20	.	0.3	0.4	.	0.4	0.2	0.1	0.7	0.3	0.1
21	.	0.5	0.7	.	1.4	0.9	0.6	0.7	1.5	2.1
22	.	1.8	0.9	.	2.4	2.3	2.4	2.1	2.8	2.9
23	.	0.3	-	.	-	-	0.2	-	0.1	-
24	.	4.1	3.0	.	3.1	2.5	3.7	3.0	2.0	4.2
25	.	2.2	1.8	.	1.4	1.2	1.5	2.5	1.5	0.8
26	.	0.7	0.8	.	0.3	0.7	1.2	0.6	0.6	0.5
27	.	-	0.2	.	0.2	0.2	-	-	-	0.2
28	.	1.0	0.3	.	1.7	1.3	0.7	0.7	0.8	1.2
29	.	-	1.3	.	0.9	0.9	1.2	1.8	0.5	0.5
30	.	1.9	0.3	.	-	0.2	1.1	-	0.5	0.4
31	.	0.3	0.5	.	1.3	0.3	0.9	1.2	0.7	0.7
32	.	1.7	2.0	.	1.3	1.5	3.6	2.3	2.0	1.8
33	.	0.3	4.0	.	4.6	2.8	2.9	5.6	4.4	5.0
34	.	-	0.3	.	0.5	1.0	0.1	-	0.1	0.2
35	.	-	0.4	.	-	-	-	0.2	-	0.2
36	.	0.9	1.6	.	1.5	1.1	1.6	1.2	1.5	0.9
37	.	-	0.2	.	-	-	-	0.2	-	0.4
República Dominicana (BA) [3][4]					Employees - Salariés - Asalariados					
Total - Total - Total										
ISIC 3 - CITI 3 - CIIU 3										
Total	.	.	.	.	.	488.0	472.5	482.5	491.4	.
15						96.2	95.8	92.5	98.9	
16						15.0	17.0	20.8	20.5	
17						8.4	8.9	16.7	18.2	
18						146.6	125.6	110.5	110.1	
19						10.8	9.0	8.9	9.5	
20						7.4	8.3	9.4	8.5	
21						7.6	5.8	8.6	9.1	
22						14.1	13.6	17.5	18.9	
23						0.5	0.4	1.9	0.9	
24						21.9	19.2	22.6	23.6	
25						9.0	10.9	8.3	9.6	
26						18.8	19.7	26.0	18.0	
27						2.3	2.4	1.9	2.4	
28						32.4	38.9	44.8	36.8	
29						2.7	3.2	2.3	3.6	
30						0.8	-	-	0.6	
31						11.4	8.3	7.5	13.3	
32						2.8	5.1	2.8	6.3	
33						8.5	6.7	8.7	8.6	
34						2.0	5.5	1.8	2.2	
35						0.5	2.7	0.8	2.7	
36						68.3	65.5	68.2	69.1	

Explanatory notes: see p. 77.

[1] Persons aged 12 years and over. [2] July of each year. [3] Persons aged 10 years and over. [4] Total employment, excl. unpaid family workers.

Notes explicatives: voir p. 80.

[1] Personnes âgées de 12 ans et plus. [2] Juillet de chaque année. [3] Personnes âgées de 10 ans et plus. [4] Emploi total, non compris les travailleurs familiaux non rémunérés.

Notas explicativas: véase p. 83.

[1] Personas de 12 años y más. [2] Julio de cada año. [3] Personas de 10 años y más. [4] Empleo total, excl. a trabajadores familiares no remunerados.

	EMPLOYMENT			EMPLOI			EMPLEO		
	Paid employment in manufacturing Thousands			**Emploi rémunéré dans les industries manufacturières** Milliers			**Empleo remunerado en las industrias manufactureras** Millares		

	1999	2000	2001	2002	2003	2004	2005	2006	2007	2008
República Dominicana (BA) [1] [2]					Employees - Salariés - Asalariados					
Men - Hommes - Hombres										
ISIC 3 - CITI 3 - CIIU 3										
Total	.	.	.	.	.	340.2	327.3	327.8	343.6	.
15						78.9	74.0	74.0	80.3	
16						6.8	7.1	7.2	8.9	
17						3.1	3.8	9.9	8.0	
18						67.0	57.5	47.5	52.2	
19						8.1	6.1	5.7	7.6	
20						7.1	7.2	8.0	7.3	
21						6.3	3.9	6.0	5.1	
22						10.7	10.3	10.4	14.6	
23						0.5	0.2	1.9	0.9	
24						15.4	15.0	15.9	13.0	
25						6.1	9.2	5.6	6.5	
26						15.8	17.1	21.4	15.4	
27						2.3	2.4	1.9	2.4	
28						31.5	36.9	42.7	34.9	
29						2.0	2.7	2.3	3.4	
30						0.6	-	-	0.6	
31						8.0	7.1	5.7	10.6	
32						1.7	2.8	1.4	4.1	
33						4.4	2.5	3.0	3.8	
34						1.1	1.2	0.3	0.9	
35						0.1	1.8	0.8	2.3	
36						62.8	58.3	56.3	60.8	
Women - Femmes - Mujeres										
ISIC 3 - CITI 3 - CIIU 3										
Total	.	.	.	.	.	147.8	145.3	154.7	147.8	.
15						17.2	21.8	18.5	18.6	
16						8.2	9.8	13.5	11.6	
17						5.3	5.1	6.9	10.2	
18						79.7	68.1	63.0	57.9	
19						2.7	2.9	3.2	2.0	
20						0.3	1.1	1.5	1.2	
21						1.4	1.9	2.6	4.0	
22						3.5	3.3	7.1	4.4	
23						-	0.2	-	-	
24						6.5	4.2	6.7	10.7	
25						2.8	1.7	2.7	3.1	
26						3.0	2.5	4.6	2.6	
27						-	-	-	-	
28						1.0	2.0	2.1	1.8	
29						0.7	0.6	-	0.2	
30						0.2	-	-	-	
31						3.3	1.2	1.8	2.7	
32						1.1	2.3	1.4	2.2	
33						4.2	4.3	5.6	4.8	
34						0.9	4.3	1.5	1.4	
35						0.4	1.0	-	0.4	
36						5.5	7.2	11.9	8.4	
Ecuador (BA) [1] [3] [4]					Employees - Salariés - Asalariados					
Total - Total - Total										
ISIC 3 - CITI 3 - CIIU 3										
Total	.	.	.	279.3	300.3	322.3	312.5	338.3	.	.
15				75.1	81.3	97.5	73.7	107.8		
16				1.7	2.2	1.3	2.0	0.1		
17				15.4	20.3	18.5	13.5	17.5		
18				31.0	33.9	31.1	36.9	36.8		
19				10.5	9.4	10.4	12.2	10.5		
20				12.6	10.5	6.1	7.7	8.1		
21				7.0	7.6	9.1	8.3	11.8		
22				13.6	11.2	15.0	18.8	15.2		
23				2.3	1.3	1.0	4.0	1.5		
24				10.0	15.0	18.4	23.2	15.3		
25				7.2	9.9	14.4	11.6	12.1		
26				10.9	18.6	16.3	19.9	14.5		
27				1.4	7.5	5.1	4.8	8.0		
28				25.2	22.2	26.3	23.3	24.4		
29				5.5	6.3	5.6	3.3	7.2		
31				0.5	3.2	2.6	1.5	2.7		
32				5.3	1.4	-	1.5	-		
33				0.9	1.0	1.5	0.9	0.6		
34				0.7	4.9	4.1	3.4	5.7		
35				9.0	3.2	3.0	2.5	0.8		
36				32.8	28.4	33.7	37.8	36.9		
37				0.8	1.2	1.4	1.7	1.0		

Explanatory notes: see p. 77.

[1] Persons aged 10 years and over. [2] Total employment, excl. unpaid family workers. [3] Urban areas. [4] Nov. of each year.

Notes explicatives: voir p. 80.

[1] Personnes âgées de 10 ans et plus. [2] Emploi total, non compris les travailleurs familiaux non rémunérés. [3] Régions urbaines. [4] Nov. de chaque année.

Notas explicativas: véase p. 83.

[1] Personas de 10 años y más. [2] Empleo total, excl. a trabajadores familiares no remunerados. [3] Areas urbanas. [4] Nov. de cada año.

EMPLOYMENT — EMPLOI — EMPLEO

Paid employment in manufacturing
Thousands

Emploi rémunéré dans les industries manufacturières
Milliers

Empleo remunerado en las industrias manufactureras
Millares

	1999	2000	2001	2002	2003	2004	2005	2006	2007	2008
Ecuador (BA) [1][2][3] — Employees - Salariés - Asalariados										
Men - Hommes - Hombres ISIC 3 - CITI 3 - CIIU 3										
Total	.	.	.	208.1	.	227.7	226.0	239.5	.	.
15	.	.	.	56.3	.	67.2	53.3	73.1	.	.
16	.	.	.	1.7	.	0.6	1.4	0.1	.	.
17	.	.	.	11.0	.	11.4	10.2	10.7	.	.
18	.	.	.	8.8	.	8.3	10.7	10.7	.	.
19	.	.	.	7.8	.	8.4	7.4	6.5	.	.
20	.	.	.	11.0	.	4.9	7.2	6.8	.	.
21	.	.	.	5.6	.	5.1	6.8	9.0	.	.
22	.	.	.	9.5	.	10.0	13.6	9.8	.	.
23	.	.	.	2.2	.	1.0	3.6	1.3	.	.
24	.	.	.	6.5	.	10.8	17.7	10.9	.	.
25	.	.	.	6.8	.	11.6	8.2	10.1	.	.
26	.	.	.	8.7	.	13.8	15.9	11.8	.	.
27	.	.	.	1.4	.	5.1	3.9	6.0	.	.
28	.	.	.	24.0	.	25.6	22.7	23.4	.	.
29	.	.	.	4.8	.	5.3	3.1	5.5	.	.
31	.	.	.	3.7	.	2.0	1.4	2.7	.	.
32	.	.	.	0.4	.	-	1.0	-	.	.
33	.	.	.	0.3	.	0.1	0.4	0.6	.	.
34	.	.	.	7.9	.	4.1	2.6	5.6	.	.
35	.	.	.	0.8	.	2.9	2.5	0.8	.	.
36	.	.	.	28.5	.	28.3	31.1	33.0	.	.
37	.	.	.	-	.	1.4	1.2	1.0	.	.
Women - Femmes - Mujeres ISIC 3 - CITI 3 - CIIU 3										
Total	.	.	.	71.2	.	94.6	86.5	98.8	.	.
15	.	.	.	18.8	.	30.3	20.5	34.6	.	.
16	.	.	.	-	.	0.7	0.6	-	.	.
17	.	.	.	4.5	.	7.1	3.3	6.8	.	.
18	.	.	.	22.2	.	22.8	26.2	26.0	.	.
19	.	.	.	2.8	.	2.1	4.8	4.0	.	.
20	.	.	.	1.6	.	1.2	0.4	1.3	.	.
21	.	.	.	1.4	.	3.9	1.5	2.8	.	.
22	.	.	.	4.1	.	5.0	5.2	5.3	.	.
23	.	.	.	0.1	.	-	0.5	0.2	.	.
24	.	.	.	3.5	.	7.6	5.5	4.3	.	.
25	.	.	.	0.4	.	2.8	3.4	2.0	.	.
26	.	.	.	2.2	.	2.5	3.9	2.7	.	.
27	.	.	.	-	.	-	0.9	2.0	.	.
28	.	.	.	1.2	.	0.7	0.6	1.0	.	.
29	.	.	.	0.7	.	0.3	0.2	1.7	.	.
31	.	.	.	1.5	.	0.6	0.1	-	.	.
32	.	.	.	0.5	.	-	0.5	-	.	.
33	.	.	.	0.4	.	1.4	0.5	-	.	.
34	.	.	.	1.2	.	-	0.8	0.1	.	.
35	.	.	.	8.2	.	0.1	-	-	.	.
36	.	.	.	4.3	.	5.4	6.7	3.9	.	.
37	.	.	.	-	.	-	0.5	.	.	.
El Salvador (BA) [1][4][5] — Employees - Salariés - Asalariados										
Total - Total - Total ISIC 3 - CITI 3 - CIIU 3										
Total	409.3	410.4	400.5	399.3	405.2	353.0	340.1	339.0	370.9	.
15	10.9	8.9	11.6	6.9	6.3	8.4	8.5	6.2	8.4	.
16	0.8	1.2	0.8	0.8	0.7	0.6	0.1	0.3	0.5	.
17	5.2	5.2	9.7	7.3	4.3	4.5	4.8	6.0	5.4	.
18	122.8	131.3	115.8	129.5	142.8	123.3	105.4	103.6	107.1	.
19	15.0	11.4	12.9	12.5	8.6	9.3	9.4	10.3	8.1	.
20	9.6	8.1	6.2	7.4	9.4	5.1	4.1	4.8	5.9	.
21	4.0	4.4	3.2	4.0	4.8	5.2	4.1	3.1	4.0	.
22	6.1	6.7	5.2	7.7	5.7	4.4	4.7	4.1	6.5	.
23	-	-	-	-	-	-	-	0.2	-	.
24	13.4	12.5	14.0	16.1	13.0	15.6	14.7	11.7	13.1	.
25	7.2	7.6	5.2	4.6	7.4	4.3	5.2	6.1	5.4	.
26	16.6	17.0	13.0	13.6	12.6	12.3	8.8	9.6	9.2	.
27	0.6	0.5	1.4	1.1	0.9	0.7	1.0	0.2	0.1	.
28	4.0	3.6	4.2	2.3	3.7	1.7	7.4	2.9	5.5	.
29	0.2	0.9	0.6	0.2	0.2	-	0.1	0.1	0.3	.
30	-	-	-	-	-	0.1	-	-	0.1	.
31	-	-	0.3	-	-	0.3	0.1	0.1	0.5	.
32	0.5	0.1	0.1	-	-	-	-	-	-	.
33	0.2	0.3	0.1	0.7	1.0	0.1	0.7	0.4	1.1	.
34	0.1	-	-	-	0.3	-	-	-	-	.
35	7.3	6.0	8.2	4.7	4.8	6.2	6.8	7.1	6.3	.
36	20.6	20.1	17.8	17.3	22.5	17.5	17.5	19.4	24.7	.
37	164.3	164.6	170.2	162.6	156.1	133.2	136.4	142.9	158.8	.

Explanatory notes: see p. 77.

[1] Persons aged 10 years and over. [2] Urban areas. [3] Nov. of each year. [4] Total employment, excl. unpaid family workers. [5] Dec.

Notes explicatives: voir p. 80.

[1] Personnes âgées de 10 ans et plus. [2] Régions urbaines. [3] Nov. de chaque année. [4] Emploi total, non compris les travailleurs familiaux non rémunérés. [5] Déc.

Notas explicativas: véase p. 83.

[1] Personas de 10 años y más. [2] Areas urbanas. [3] Nov. de cada año. [4] Empleo total, excl. a trabajadores familiares no remunerados. [5] Dic.

	EMPLOYMENT			EMPLOI			EMPLEO		
	Paid employment in manufacturing Thousands			**Emploi rémunéré dans les industries manufacturières** Milliers			**Empleo remunerado en las industrias manufactureras** Millares		
	1999	2000	2001	2002	2003	2004	2005	2006	2007	2008

El Salvador (BA) [1][2][3]

Employees - Salariés - Asalariados

Men - Hommes - Hombres
ISIC 3 - CITI 3 - CIIU 3

	1999	2000	2001	2002	2003	2004	2005	2006	2007	2008
Total	198.6	193.9	200.2	187.1	200.7	176.5	170.6	177.1	191.6	.
15	9.5	7.2	10.7	5.9	5.2	5.6	7.2	5.6	7.3	.
16	0.4	0.6	0.3	0.4	0.6	0.1	-	0.2	0.1	.
17	3.6	3.5	6.2	5.4	3.0	3.7	4.2	4.7	4.1	.
18	29.2	32.1	30.6	32.3	41.6	36.3	25.4	29.1	31.3	.
19	10.7	9.6	9.9	10.5	7.0	6.3	8.4	7.6	6.0	.
20	4.8	3.9	3.5	3.1	5.1	2.2	2.1	1.9	3.3	.
21	2.9	2.4	2.4	2.5	2.6	3.2	3.0	2.0	3.4	.
22	3.5	3.6	3.5	4.6	4.7	3.3	3.5	3.3	5.5	.
23	-	-	-	-	-	-	-	0.2		.
24	8.1	7.3	9.0	7.8	8.0	10.1	7.5	6.6	6.8	.
25	4.9	4.4	3.4	3.2	4.8	3.6	4.5	5.0	4.4	.
26	15.5	16.2	12.0	12.9	10.5	10.2	7.1	8.0	8.3	.
27	0.6	0.4	0.7	1.1	0.7	0.7	1.0	0.2	0.1	.
28	3.8	3.0	3.3	2.3	3.5	1.7	6.2	2.4	4.9	.
29	0.2	0.9	0.6	0.2	0.2	-	0.1	0.1	0.2	.
30	-	-	-	-	-	0.1	-	-	0.1	.
31			0.3	-	-	0.3	0.1	0.1	0.1	.
32	0.5	0.1	0.1	-	-	-	-	-	-	.
33	0.2	0.3	0.1	0.7	0.5	0.1	0.6	0.4	0.7	.
34	0.1	-	-	-	-	-	-	-	-	.
35	4.3	3.6	4.8	2.1	2.1	2.3	3.9	3.4	3.2	.
36	19.4	19.4	17.3	16.7	22.0	16.8	16.6	18.4	21.9	.
37	76.5	75.5	81.6	75.3	78.6	69.8	68.9	77.7	79.8	.

Women - Femmes - Mujeres
ISIC 3 - CITI 3 - CIIU 3

	1999	2000	2001	2002	2003	2004	2005	2006	2007	2008
Total	210.7	216.5	200.4	212.2	204.5	176.4	169.5	162.0	179.3	.
15	1.4	1.7	0.9	1.0	1.1	2.8	1.3	0.6	1.1	.
16	0.4	0.5	0.6	0.4	0.2	0.5	0.1	0.1	0.4	.
17	1.6	1.7	3.5	1.9	1.3	0.7	0.6	1.3	1.3	.
18	93.7	99.2	85.2	97.2	101.3	86.9	80.0	74.4	75.8	.
19	4.2	1.8	3.0	2.0	1.6	3.0	1.0	2.7	2.1	.
20	4.8	4.2	2.7	4.3	4.2	2.9	2.0	2.9	2.6	.
21	1.1	2.0	0.8	1.5	2.2	2.0	1.1	1.0	0.7	.
22	2.7	3.1	1.8	3.1	0.9	1.1	1.2	0.7	0.9	.
23	-	-	-	-	-	-	-	-		.
24	5.3	5.3	5.1	8.3	5.0	5.6	7.2	5.1	6.3	.
25	2.4	3.2	1.7	1.4	2.6	0.7	0.7	1.1	1.0	.
26	1.0	0.8	1.0	0.7	2.1	2.1	1.7	1.6	0.9	.
27	-	0.1	0.7	-	0.1	-	-	-		.
28	0.2	0.5	0.9	0.1	0.2	-	1.2	0.5	0.5	.
29	-	-	-	-	-	-	-	-	0.1	.
30	-	-	-	-	-	-	-	-		.
31	-	-	-	-	-	-	-	-	0.4	.
32	-	-	-	-	-	-	0.0	-		.
33	0.1	-	-	-	0.5	-	0.1	-	0.3	.
34	-	-	-	-	-	-	-	-		.
35	2.9	2.4	3.4	2.6	2.7	3.9	2.9	3.8	3.1	.
36	1.2	0.7	0.5	0.6	0.6	0.7	0.9	0.9	2.8	.
37	87.8	89.2	88.6	87.3	77.5	63.4	67.5	65.3	79.0	.

México (BA) [4][5]

Employees - Salariés - Asalariados

Total - Total - Total
ISIC 3 - CITI 3 - CIIU 3

	1999	2000	2001	2002	2003	2004	2005	2006	2007	2008
Total	5 460.6	5 749.1	5 600.9	5 297.0	5 177.6	5 472.0	5 229.8	5 337.6	5 449.3	5 509.4
15	968.8	1 026.3	1 065.4	1 032.8	1 056.2	1 114.5	1 041.6	1 065.4	1 161.4	1 151.1
16	0.0	0.0	0.0	0.0	0.0	0.0	0.0	0.0	0.0	0.0
17	255.0	266.5	314.5	279.4	265.8	266.4	121.3	132.1	116.8	116.0
18	704.1	752.2	673.6	626.1	648.1	679.6	84.3	93.0	81.9	67.6
19	283.8	303.7	270.3	247.5	193.0	232.1	902.8	836.3	795.7	839.4
20	127.5	145.0	124.2	100.1	103.0	111.1	86.3	84.9	75.7	81.3
21	104.6	94.9	96.7	104.9	98.9	91.8	99.8	124.5	138.5	140.0
22	219.8	206.8	202.3	188.9	179.5	210.9	184.2	212.0	208.2	200.8
23	60.8	68.5	99.3	79.0	67.4	78.2	53.6	60.7	60.8	60.9
24	310.8	251.0	253.0	242.6	215.1	252.4	248.7	226.8	239.1	267.5
25	245.4	242.4	226.8	239.3	241.6	279.4	190.3	242.0	257.1	258.5
26	299.0	306.9	283.1	282.6	256.8	270.3	255.4	250.3	275.4	272.1
27	107.1	100.6	87.3	80.0	79.8	91.5	143.2	108.0	113.8	101.3
28	338.5	369.2	334.2	327.3	345.0	321.8	347.3	352.6	391.8	367.8
29	62.4	90.6	109.8	88.5	77.3	82.7	61.4	101.4	78.5	88.2
30	253.8	283.7	299.8	228.7	232.6	224.0	227.3	223.1	229.3	185.7
31	249.8	251.5	239.0	214.9	203.2	238.0	235.8	235.6	206.2	227.6
32	0.0	0.0	0.0	0.0	0.0	0.0	0.0	0.0	0.0	0.0
33	41.5	55.4	58.9	64.7	53.9	41.6	154.6	161.4	171.0	192.5
34	499.8	600.9	533.4	529.3	513.0	518.5	520.2	566.8	559.7	573.9
35	0.0	0.0	0.0	0.0	0.0	0.0	0.0	0.0	0.0	0.0
36	327.9	330.9	328.2	337.7	344.6	365.6	271.6	260.6	288.5	317.3
37	0.2	2.1	1.2	3.0	2.8	1.5	0.0	0.0	0.0	0.0

Explanatory notes: see p. 77.

[1] Persons aged 10 years and over. [2] Total employment, excl. unpaid family workers. [3] Dec. [4] Persons aged 14 years and over. [5] Second quarter of each year.

Notes explicatives: voir p. 80.

[1] Personnes âgées de 10 ans et plus. [2] Emploi total, non compris les travailleurs familiaux non rémunérés. [3] Déc. [4] Personnes âgées de 14 ans et plus. [5] Deuxième trimestre de chaque année.

Notas explicativas: véase p. 83.

[1] Personas de 10 años y más. [2] Empleo total, excl. a trabajadores familiares no remunerados. [3] Dic. [4] Personas de 14 años y más. [5] Segundo trimestre de cada año.

Paid employment in manufacturing
Thousands

Emploi rémunéré dans les industries manufacturières
Milliers

Empleo remunerado en las industrias manufactureras
Millares

	1999	2000	2001	2002	2003	2004	2005	2006	2007	2008
México (BA) [1] [2]				Employees - Salariés - Asalariados						
Men - Hommes - Hombres										
ISIC 3 - CITI 3 - CIIU 3										
Total	3 719.4	3 814.1	3 713.6	3 506.6	3 491.5	3 673.1	3 439.9	3 503.9	3 577.8	3 660.7
15	686.6	727.7	756.5	715.9	745.3	776.7	718.9	726.3	779.9	774.9
16	0.0	0.0	0.0	0.0	0.0	0.0	0.0	0.0	0.0	0.0
17	173.3	177.7	204.9	175.1	162.7	154.8	90.6	93.3	83.4	86.5
18	238.5	263.0	218.1	203.7	239.2	261.0	37.2	37.5	42.2	31.1
19	192.7	192.2	171.5	165.2	134.7	155.5	410.3	373.4	358.9	395.1
20	110.1	125.5	111.3	84.1	96.6	99.9	78.7	74.4	67.1	71.0
21	73.9	70.4	67.9	74.5	71.4	70.5	78.6	91.2	97.1	92.3
22	170.9	145.5	139.1	131.3	127.4	142.2	133.6	151.0	138.4	141.1
23	52.0	53.2	83.8	67.5	55.8	61.0	45.5	55.0	52.2	51.5
24	189.2	152.5	159.8	144.9	131.3	159.9	143.1	142.1	161.0	177.0
25	171.8	154.1	154.9	146.6	153.6	174.6	113.9	149.6	149.9	159.8
26	260.5	255.9	239.1	242.1	224.5	243.2	219.9	216.9	240.7	223.1
27	93.3	93.0	77.4	74.2	70.7	81.2	126.3	90.2	91.3	85.5
28	314.9	327.0	301.6	285.2	304.6	285.9	292.8	315.9	344.0	325.6
29	48.3	74.0	89.4	71.1	60.7	65.4	42.4	76.6	59.1	67.3
30	118.9	140.4	146.5	126.7	121.9	112.1	107.6	109.0	115.9	102.0
31	172.1	146.2	151.8	132.5	128.8	155.0	136.5	141.7	117.8	119.6
32	0.0	0.0	0.0	0.0	0.0	0.0	0.0	0.0	0.0	0.0
33	27.6	33.0	30.3	34.2	26.7	16.9	73.3	79.3	86.0	102.0
34	345.7	419.3	360.5	363.3	352.0	348.2	345.9	362.4	347.4	379.9
35	0.0	0.0	0.0	0.0	0.0	0.0	0.0	0.0	0.0	0.0
36	279.0	261.6	248.2	266.8	280.9	307.9	244.7	218.3	245.7	275.4
37	0.1	1.9	1.2	1.6	2.7	1.2	0.0	0.0	0.0	0.0
Women - Femmes - Mujeres										
ISIC 3 - CITI 3 - CIIU 3										
Total	1 741.2	1 935.0	1 887.2	1 790.4	1 686.1	1 798.9	1 789.9	1 833.6	1 871.5	1 848.7
15	282.2	298.6	308.9	316.9	311.0	337.7	322.7	339.1	381.5	376.2
16	0.0	0.0	0.0	0.0	0.0	0.0	0.0	0.0	0.0	0.0
17	81.7	88.8	109.6	104.3	103.0	111.6	30.7	38.9	33.4	29.5
18	465.6	489.2	455.5	422.4	408.9	418.7	47.1	55.5	39.7	36.5
19	91.1	111.5	98.9	82.3	58.3	76.6	492.9	462.9	436.8	444.3
20	17.3	19.5	12.9	16.0	6.4	11.2	7.7	10.6	8.6	10.4
21	30.7	24.5	28.8	30.4	27.5	21.2	21.2	33.3	41.4	47.7
22	48.9	61.3	63.2	57.5	52.1	68.7	50.6	61.0	69.8	59.7
23	8.8	15.3	15.5	11.5	11.6	17.2	8.0	5.7	8.6	9.3
24	121.6	98.4	93.2	97.7	83.8	92.5	105.6	84.7	78.0	90.5
25	73.6	88.3	72.0	92.6	87.9	104.8	76.4	92.4	107.2	98.6
26	38.5	51.0	44.0	40.4	32.4	27.1	35.5	33.4	34.7	49.0
27	13.8	7.6	9.9	5.8	9.0	10.4	16.9	17.9	22.5	15.8
28	23.7	42.2	32.6	42.0	40.5	35.8	54.5	36.8	47.9	42.1
29	14.0	16.6	20.4	17.5	16.7	17.3	19.0	24.8	19.4	21.0
30	134.9	143.3	153.3	102.0	110.7	111.9	119.6	114.1	113.3	83.6
31	77.7	105.4	87.2	82.4	74.4	83.0	99.3	93.9	88.5	108.1
32	0.0	0.0	0.0	0.0	0.0	0.0	0.0	0.0	0.0	0.0
33	13.9	22.4	28.6	30.4	27.2	24.8	81.3	82.1	85.0	90.6
34	154.1	181.6	172.9	166.0	161.1	170.3	174.3	204.4	212.2	194.1
35	0.0	0.0	0.0	0.0	0.0	0.0	0.0	0.0	0.0	0.0
36	48.9	69.3	80.0	70.9	63.7	57.7	26.9	42.4	42.8	41.9
37	0.2	0.3	0.0	1.4	0.0	0.3	0.0	0.0	0.0	0.0
Perú (BA) [1] [3]				Employees - Salariés - Asalariados						
Total - Total - Total										
ISIC 3 - CITI 3 - CIIU 3										
Total	.	.	.	382.6 [4]	339.8 [5]	420.7	409.1	440.2	536.4	538.8
15	.	.	.	57.0 [4]	49.9 [5]	53.7	49.6	49.7	73.5	69.8
16	.	.	.	0.7 [4]	- [5]	1.6	-	1.0	-	-
17	.	.	.	30.6 [4]	29.6 [5]	42.8	57.8	60.5	52.6	52.8
18	.	.	.	68.1 [4]	68.7 [5]	80.7	82.4	68.6	130.8	152.8
19	.	.	.	15.3 [4]	15.5 [5]	21.7	11.0	11.4	27.8	19.6
20	.	.	.	2.8 [4]	1.2 [5]	1.1	2.2	1.7	1.9	1.3
21	.	.	.	7.4 [4]	9.2 [5]	10.9	5.5	10.4	6.1	7.4
22	.	.	.	24.8 [4]	20.0 [5]	36.2	26.1	33.2	36.0	32.4
23	.	.	.	- [4]	7.5 [5]	2.3	0.7	-	-	0.7
24	.	.	.	28.1 [4]	13.5 [5]	24.6	13.4	34.3	31.1	24.6
25	.	.	.	20.1 [4]	21.0 [5]	21.7	19.0	24.0	15.8	16.7
26	.	.	.	19.2 [4]	5.1 [5]	9.0	10.8	13.6	14.4	16.0
27	.	.	.	3.6 [4]	3.6 [5]	9.5	5.7	6.5	6.3	6.7
28	.	.	.	30.8 [4]	14.7 [5]	43.6	38.7	33.9	34.8	38.0
29	.	.	.	10.0 [4]	7.1 [5]	10.4	16.4	23.2	30.4	24.2
30	.	.	.	2.3 [4]	4.2 [5]	5.9	5.1	1.4	0.0	3.7
31	.	.	.	1.4 [4]	8.6 [5]	2.4	2.3	5.0	9.3	6.8
32	.	.	.	- [4]	- [5]	-	-	-	-	-
33	.	.	.	0.7 [4]	1.3 [5]	0.0	2.4	2.7	3.5	4.0
34	.	.	.	5.7 [4]	3.1 [5]	1.3	2.9	3.1	5.8	5.6
35	.	.	.	2.0 [4]	3.2 [5]	2.6	5.1	3.9	3.3	5.8
36	.	.	.	52.0 [4]	52.7 [5]	38.8	52.0	52.1	53.0	49.9

Explanatory notes: see p. 77.

[1] Persons aged 14 years and over. [2] Second quarter of each year. [3] Metropolitan Lima. [4] Fourth quarter. [5] May-Dec.

Notes explicatives: voir p. 80.

[1] Personnes âgées de 14 ans et plus. [2] Deuxième trimestre de chaque année. [3] Lima métropolitaine. [4] Quatrième trimestre. [5] Mai-déc.

Notas explicativas: véase p. 83.

[1] Personas de 14 años y más. [2] Segundo trimestre de cada año. [3] Lima metropolitana. [4] Cuarto trimestre. [5] Mayo-dic.

EMPLOYMENT EMPLOI EMPLEO

Paid employment in manufacturing		Emploi rémunéré dans les industries manufacturières		Empleo remunerado en las industrias manufactureras	
Thousands		Milliers		Millares	

Perú (BA) [1] [2] — Employees - Salariés - Asalariados

Men - Hommes - Hombres
ISIC 3 - CITI 3 - CIIU 3

	1999	2000	2001	2002	2003	2004	2005	2006	2007	2008
Total				284.0	241.1	305.9	290.1	314.8	367.9	363.0
15				42.2	32.0	38.8	40.6	28.9	53.6	48.9
16				0.7	-	1.6	-	1.0	-	-
17				24.1	22.2	28.0	28.2	31.8	33.7	35.6
18				29.2	26.3	37.7	39.3	36.1	66.4	75.4
19				12.9	12.4	15.9	7.9	9.8	23.9	16.7
20				2.0	1.2	1.1	2.2	1.7	1.9	1.3
21				6.6	9.2	9.6	3.1	8.1	3.3	4.9
22				20.8	17.4	24.5	19.8	28.0	16.4	10.6
23				-	7.5	2.3	0.7	-		0.7
24				18.1	10.4	16.1	12.7	26.0	19.1	17.5
25				17.1	19.1	21.7	16.6	19.1	13.4	13.6
26				14.7	5.1	8.0	9.2	12.2	11.8	13.3
27				3.6	3.6	9.5	5.1	6.5	6.3	6.2
28				28.2	13.9	41.5	34.5	28.0	31.1	36.4
29				10.0	5.1	9.3	14.0	22.6	26.9	21.1
30				2.3	3.4	5.9	5.1	1.4	0.0	3.7
31				1.4	5.3	2.4	2.3	5.0	7.6	6.1
32				-	-	-	-	-		
33				0.7	1.3	-	2.4	2.7	1.5	3.0
34				5.7	3.1	-	2.9	2.6	5.8	4.3
35				1.7	3.2	2.6	3.9	3.4	3.3	5.8
36				42.0	39.3	29.6	39.5	40.0	42.1	37.9

Women - Femmes - Mujeres
ISIC 3 - CITI 3 - CIIU 3

	1999	2000	2001	2002	2003	2004	2005	2006	2007	2008
Total				98.7	98.7	114.8	119.0	125.5	168.4	175.7
15				14.8	17.9	15.0	9.0	20.8	19.8	20.9
16				-	-	-	-	-		
17				6.5	7.4	14.8	29.7	28.8	18.9	17.2
18				39.0	42.4	43.0	43.1	32.5	64.4	77.4
19				2.3	3.1	5.8	3.1	1.6	3.9	2.9
20				0.8	-					
21				0.7	-	1.3	2.4	2.4	2.8	2.4
22				4.0	2.5	11.7	6.2	5.2	19.7	21.8
23				-	-	-				
24				10.0	3.1	8.5	0.7	8.3	12.0	7.0
25				3.1	1.9	-	2.3	4.9	2.4	3.1
26				4.5	-	1.1	1.6	1.4	2.5	2.7
27				-	-	-	0.5	-		0.5
28				2.6	0.8	2.2	4.2	5.9	3.7	1.6
29				-	2.0	1.0	2.4	0.6	3.5	3.1
30				-	0.8	-	-			
31				-	3.3	-	-		1.8	0.7
32				-	-	-				
33				-	-	-	-		2.0	1.0
34				-	-	1.3	-	0.5	-	1.3
35				0.3	-	-	1.2	0.5	-	
36				10.0	13.4	9.1	12.5	12.1	11.0	12.0

Perú (BA) [1] [5] — Employees - Salariés - Asalariados

Total - Total - Total
ISIC 3 - CITI 3 - CIIU 3

	1999	2000	2001	2002	2003	2004	2005	2006	2007	2008
Total	501.8	534.6	548.8	604.3	540.9	635.4	639.6	676.4	799.4	819.1
15	120.6	134.3	143.7	156.3	135.4	141.3	142.1	151.0	185.8	188.4
16	-	0.6	0.1	0.7	-	1.6	-	1.0	0.1	0.1
17	41.5	54.0	57.0	45.0	40.1	53.4	71.4	78.9	70.4	70.1
18	64.8	75.9	88.9	84.8	82.0	96.3	104.9	84.0	155.0	178.7
19	21.6	31.5	26.1	29.7	28.2	45.9	30.8	28.2	39.0	36.4
20	4.0	17.8	11.1	12.4	6.9	9.3	12.2	13.4	16.5	16.8
21	17.2	15.6	3.7	8.8	10.4	12.2	6.1	11.2	7.0	9.0
22	56.0	25.2	18.1	29.7	27.1	42.0	31.8	40.6	44.8	38.3
23	1.2	-	2.0	-	7.7	3.0	0.7	-	1.1	1.2
24	18.2	17.4	31.1	31.0	15.1	28.0	18.2	36.5	34.1	28.2
25	43.9	10.7	19.4	21.1	21.4	25.7	20.1	27.6	17.9	18.7
26	11.8	10.8	30.6	29.9	19.0	21.4	22.5	20.8	22.2	27.8
27	3.1	7.7	3.9	11.6	4.6	12.3	12.7	10.0	10.8	11.1
28	23.3	47.8	35.4	43.4	34.8	55.7	48.1	46.4	51.6	55.6
29	2.2	12.8	4.5	11.0	9.3	12.2	19.5	30.4	35.7	28.6
30	-	-	-	3.7	5.1	5.9	6.8	3.8	2.4	6.4
31	1.1	7.9	2.0	2.3	8.6	2.4	2.9	5.5	10.9	7.9
32	1.4	-	0.9	-	0.5	-	-	-		
33	2.8	0.5	3.0	0.7	1.3	-	2.7	2.9	3.9	4.0
34	1.5	2.1	7.0	5.7	4.1	2.4	3.0	4.1	7.1	6.3
35	4.3	3.7	3.4	4.5	7.2	4.9	8.2	7.6	7.8	12.8
36	59.6	57.9	57.6	72.1	72.1	59.6	74.9	72.6	75.1	72.7
37	-	0.2	-	-	-	-	-	-		

Explanatory notes: see p. 77.

[1] Persons aged 14 years and over. [2] Metropolitan Lima. [3] Fourth quarter. [4] May-Dec. [5] Urban areas.

Notes explicatives: voir p. 80.

[1] Personnes âgées de 14 ans et plus. [2] Lima métropolitaine. [3] Quatrième trimestre. [4] Mai-déc. [5] Régions urbaines.

Notas explicativas: véase p. 83.

[1] Personas de 14 años y más. [2] Lima metropolitana. [3] Cuarto trimestre. [4] Mayo-dic. [5] Areas urbanas.

EMPLOYMENT · EMPLOI · EMPLEO 2F

Paid employment in manufacturing
Emploi rémunéré dans les industries manufacturières
Empleo remunerado en las industrias manufactureras

Thousands · Milliers · Millares

	1999	2000	2001	2002	2003	2004	2005	2006	2007	2008
Perú (BA) [1][2]					Employees - Salariés - Asalariados					
Men - Hommes - Hombres										
ISIC 3 - CITI 3 - CIIU 3										
Total	318.2	383.0	401.3	449.5 [3]	390.7 [4]	467.3	451.6	490.9	552.9	568.4
15	84.2	100.4	105.7	114.3 [3]	93.0 [4]	99.0	103.9	102.0	123.8	131.5
16	-	0.2	0.1	0.7 [3]	- [4]	1.6	-	1.0	-	-
17	20.1	31.3	44.6	32.4 [3]	28.3 [4]	33.6	35.3	40.7	43.5	46.0
18	19.8	30.4	38.6	38.4 [3]	30.8 [4]	44.2	46.9	42.8	75.6	84.9
19	15.7	27.5	18.8	23.6 [3]	20.4 [4]	36.5	22.1	22.7	32.6	29.0
20	3.7	16.3	9.9	10.1 [3]	6.6 [4]	8.4	11.3	13.4	15.1	15.9
21	12.7	8.5	1.1	7.8 [3]	10.4 [4]	10.9	3.7	8.8	3.7	6.2
22	27.8	21.0	14.6	24.6 [3]	23.1 [4]	28.6	24.5	32.1	22.7	14.0
23	1.2	-	1.0	- [3]	7.7 [4]	3.0	0.7	-	1.0	1.2
24	9.0	5.7	21.2	19.9 [3]	11.6 [4]	17.8	15.6	27.9	21.2	20.2
25	30.4	8.4	15.8	18.0 [3]	19.5 [4]	25.7	17.5	22.7	15.5	15.0
26	11.8	8.9	27.8	24.5 [3]	18.4 [4]	18.9	19.0	18.6	17.6	24.2
27	3.1	7.5	3.7	10.4 [3]	4.2 [4]	12.3	11.7	10.0	10.1	10.2
28	21.0	44.4	35.4	40.8 [3]	33.2 [4]	53.5	43.9	40.5	47.2	52.8
29	1.9	12.4	4.5	10.5 [3]	7.3 [4]	10.9	16.9	29.7	32.2	25.1
30	-	-	-	3.6 [3]	3.8 [4]	5.9	6.8	2.4	2.4	6.4
31	-	7.9	1.0	2.3 [3]	5.3 [4]	2.4	2.9	5.5	9.1	7.2
32	1.4	-	0.9	- [3]	0.5 [4]	-	-	-	-	-
33	2.8	0.5	3.0	0.7 [3]	1.3 [4]	-	2.7	2.7	1.9	3.0
34	-	2.1	7.0	5.7 [3]	4.1 [4]	1.1	2.9	3.3	7.1	5.0
35	4.3	3.7	3.4	4.2 [3]	7.2 [4]	4.6	6.5	7.0	7.8	12.7
36	46.0	45.6	44.0	57.0 [3]	54.1 [4]	48.4	56.7	57.2	62.9	57.9
37	-	0.2	-	- [3]	- [4]	-	-	-	-	-
Women - Femmes - Mujeres										
ISIC 3 - CITI 3 - CIIU 3										
Total	183.6	151.7	147.5	154.8 [3]	150.2 [4]	168.1	188.0	185.5	246.4	250.7
15	36.4	34.0	38.0	42.1 [3]	42.4 [4]	42.3	38.1	49.1	61.9	56.9
16	-	0.4	-	- [3]	- [4]	-	-	-	0.1	0.1
17	21.4	22.7	12.4	12.6 [3]	11.8 [4]	19.7	36.1	38.2	26.9	24.1
18	45.0	45.5	50.3	46.4 [3]	51.3 [4]	52.1	58.0	41.3	79.4	93.8
19	6.0	4.0	7.3	6.1 [3]	7.8 [4]	9.5	8.7	5.4	6.4	7.4
20	0.4	1.5	1.2	2.3 [3]	0.3 [4]	0.8	0.9	-	1.5	0.9
21	4.6	7.1	2.6	1.0 [3]	- [4]	1.3	2.4	2.4	3.3	2.8
22	28.2	4.2	3.6	5.1 [3]	4.0 [4]	13.4	7.3	8.5	22.1	24.3
23	-	-	1.0	- [3]	- [4]	-	-	-	0.2	-
24	9.3	11.7	9.9	11.1 [3]	3.5 [4]	10.2	2.6	8.6	12.9	8.0
25	13.4	2.3	3.6	3.1 [3]	1.9 [4]	-	2.6	4.9	2.4	3.7
26	-	1.9	2.8	5.3 [3]	0.6 [4]	2.5	3.5	2.2	4.7	3.6
27	-	0.2	0.2	1.2 [3]	0.4 [4]	-	1.0	-	0.6	0.9
28	2.3	3.5	-	2.6 [3]	1.6 [4]	2.2	4.2	5.9	4.5	2.8
29	0.4	0.3	-	0.6 [3]	2.0 [4]	1.3	2.6	0.7	3.5	3.5
30	-	-	-	0.1 [3]	1.3 [4]	-	-	1.4	-	-
31	1.1	-	0.9	- [3]	3.3 [4]	-	-	-	1.8	0.7
32	-	-	-	- [3]	- [4]	-	-	-	-	-
33	-	-	-	- [3]	- [4]	-	-	0.2	2.0	1.0
34	1.5	-	-	- [3]	- [4]	1.3	0.2	0.8	-	1.3
35	-	-	-	0.3 [3]	- [4]	0.3	1.7	0.7	-	0.1
36	13.6	12.4	13.7	15.0 [3]	18.0 [4]	11.2	18.2	15.4	12.3	14.8
37	-	-	-	-	-	-	-	-	-	-
United States (DA) [5]					Employees - Salariés - Asalariados					
Total - Total - Total										
ISIC 3 - CITI 3 - CIIU 3										
Total	18 465.6	18 438.6	17 591.5	16 345.7	15 552.3	15 343.5	15 250.4	15 185.2	14 914.3	14 446.6
15	1 723.0	1 727.9	1 728.3	1 699.6	1 686.2	1 659.5	1 644.1	1 650.1	1 660.2	1 661.8
16	35.0	32.2	31.8	33.5	30.9	28.9	25.4	23.5	22.1	22.0
17	629.5	607.8	549.9	495.1	449.0	420.1	394.0	361.7	327.4	298.5
18	540.5	483.5	415.2	350.0	303.9	278.0	250.5	232.4	214.6	198.4
19	74.9	68.8	58.0	50.2	44.5	41.8	39.6	36.8	33.8	33.6
20	620.3	613.0	574.1	554.9	537.6	549.6	559.2	558.8	515.3	459.6
21	615.6	604.7	577.6	546.6	516.2	495.5	484.2	470.5	458.2	445.8
22	1 910.4	1 936.2	1 880.1	1 752.9	1 678.1	1 639.8	1 615.2	1 599.6	1 582.9	1 531.3
23	127.8	123.2	121.1	118.1	114.3	111.7	112.1	113.2	114.5	117.1
24	982.5	980.4	959.0	927.5	906.1	887.0	872.1	865.9	860.9	849.8
25	947.0	950.9	896.2	846.8	814.3	804.7	802.3	785.5	757.2	734.2
26	540.8	554.2	544.5	516.0	494.2	505.5	505.3	509.6	500.5	468.1
27	625.0	621.8	570.9	509.4	477.4	466.8	466.0	464.0	455.8	443.3
28	1 728.4	1 752.6	1 676.4	1 548.5	1 478.9	1 497.1	1 522.0	1 553.1	1 562.8	1 528.3
29	1 430.0	1 415.6	1 329.4	1 200.1	1 126.2	1 120.3	1 139.7	1 153.8	1 155.1	1 152.3
30	457.1	449.0	428.9	379.9	342.4	324.6	316.0	305.1	294.2	288.1
31	479.3	485.2	455.4	398.3	366.6	355.4	348.4	353.2	353.4	352.9
32	911.6	967.0	918.2	745.5	647.4	629.6	625.8	625.5	605.3	588.4
33	799.9	792.6	789.7	759.8	734.5	733.2	740.9	747.5	749.1	751.3
34	1 312.6	1 313.6	1 212.8	1 151.2	1 125.4	1 112.8	1 096.7	1 070.0	994.3	877.0
35	776.0	743.5	726.3	678.8	649.7	653.9	675.6	698.9	717.6	729.5
36	1 090.0	1 105.6	1 048.5	987.2	934.9	930.4	915.5	900.8	866.9	802.1
37	108.3	109.6	99.6	95.3	93.1	97.6	100.0	106.5	112.4	113.3

Explanatory notes: see p. 77.

[1] Persons aged 14 years and over. [2] Urban areas. [3] Fourth quarter. [4] May-Dec. [5] Due to rounding, total may not equal sum of components.

Notes explicatives: voir p. 80.

[1] Personnes âgées de 14 ans et plus. [2] Régions urbaines. [3] Quatrième trimestre. [4] Mai-déc. [5] En raison des arrondis, le total peut différer de la somme des composantes.

Notas explicativas: véase p. 83.

[1] Personas de 14 años y más. [2] Areas urbanas. [3] Cuarto trimestre. [4] Mayo-dic. [5] Debido a redondeos, el total puedee diferir de la suma de sus componentes.

2F

EMPLOYMENT	EMPLOI	EMPLEO
Paid employment in manufacturing	Emploi rémunéré dans les industries manufacturières	Empleo remunerado en las industrias manufactureras
Thousands	Milliers	Millares

	1999	2000	2001	2002	2003	2004	2005	2006	2007	2008

United States (DA) [1] — Employees - Salariés - Asalariados

Men - Hommes - Hombres
ISIC 3 - CITI 3 - CIIU 3

	1999	2000	2001	2002	2003	2004	2005	2006	2007	2008
Total	12 543.2	12 538.1	12 026.0	11 280.8	10 797.5	10 698.6	10 673.5	10 678.3	10 469.6	10 153.9
15	1 117.6	1 119.7	1 127.8	1 115.7	1 105.0	1 081.3	1 065.7	1 071.8	1 074.1	1 089.5
16	22.1	20.1	19.9	20.7	19.7	18.9	16.5	15.9	15.1	15.7
17	336.2	324.5	294.7	265.2	243.2	223.9	208.6	195.0	170.5	156.5
18	142.2	131.2	114.7	100.9	91.1	86.1	76.3	73.0	70.0	63.9
19	38.5	35.3	30.3	26.8	24.7	23.2	21.6	21.1	17.8	17.7
20	509.7	503.1	472.5	461.0	449.4	461.8	469.0	465.2	431.4	387.6
21	468.0	457.5	437.3	416.6	394.1	379.2	370.5	355.4	342.7	333.0
22	1 057.6	1 081.0	1 055.2	986.6	955.4	943.4	923.9	900.2	898.9	875.0
23	103.9	100.6	99.5	99.0	94.3	93.0	94.0	99.2	99.8	98.2
24	672.8	668.5	650.6	628.7	614.5	595.9	587.1	592.6	585.9	575.6
25	631.6	633.4	603.5	571.2	550.6	547.1	550.3	541.2	515.9	504.1
26	435.1	448.9	445.1	426.5	410.6	421.9	420.4	420.2	409.2	382.5
27	541.1	536.6	491.6	438.9	410.6	400.6	398.9	393.6	386.1	379.8
28	1 363.8	1 382.7	1 325.4	1 232.6	1 180.8	1 196.7	1 223.0	1 260.5	1 263.8	1 230.4
29	1 125.9	1 113.1	1 045.6	944.7	888.9	882.2	899.7	920.2	922.9	921.4
30	305.7	302.5	290.4	261.9	239.1	227.6	222.2	214.3	206.3	200.8
31	292.9	298.6	283.5	249.3	231.3	226.2	225.0	238.3	238.0	233.0
32	528.0	560.7	540.8	454.8	401.9	400.6	399.1	400.7	384.1	376.5
33	468.2	464.0	465.0	450.0	438.9	437.2	448.6	455.3	453.4	454.6
34	971.4	963.4	890.9	853.4	831.4	824.7	814.0	785.3	724.0	632.0
35	618.1	588.1	577.0	543.6	524.6	529.0	544.0	567.8	581.1	591.9
36	706.2	716.5	684.1	653.4	620.4	619.7	612.7	606.4	586.1	542.2
37	86.7	88.2	80.9	78.9	76.2	79.2	82.2	85.7	92.2	92.7

Women - Femmes - Mujeres
ISIC 3 - CITI 3 - CIIU 3

	1999	2000	2001	2002	2003	2004	2005	2006	2007	2008
Total	5 922.4	5 900.5	5 565.5	5 064.9	4 754.8	4 644.9	4 576.9	4 506.9	4 444.7	4 292.7
15	605.4	608.2	600.5	583.9	581.2	578.2	578.4	578.3	586.1	572.3
16	12.9	12.1	11.9	12.8	11.2	10.0	8.9	7.6	7.0	6.3
17	293.3	283.3	255.2	229.9	205.8	196.2	185.4	166.7	156.9	142.0
18	398.3	352.3	300.5	249.1	212.8	191.9	174.2	159.4	144.6	134.5
19	36.4	33.5	27.7	23.4	19.8	18.6	18.0	15.7	16.0	15.9
20	110.6	109.9	101.6	93.9	88.2	87.8	90.2	93.6	83.9	72.0
21	147.6	147.2	140.3	130.0	122.1	116.3	113.7	115.1	115.5	112.8
22	852.8	855.2	824.9	766.3	722.7	696.4	691.3	699.4	684.0	656.3
23	23.9	22.6	21.6	19.1	20.0	18.7	18.1	14.0	14.7	18.9
24	309.7	311.9	308.4	298.8	291.6	291.1	285.0	273.3	275.0	274.2
25	315.4	317.5	292.7	275.6	263.7	257.6	252.0	244.3	241.3	230.1
26	105.7	105.3	99.4	89.5	83.6	83.6	84.9	89.4	91.3	85.6
27	83.9	85.2	79.3	70.5	66.8	66.2	67.1	70.4	69.7	63.5
28	364.6	369.9	351.0	315.9	298.1	300.4	299.0	292.6	299.0	297.9
29	304.1	302.5	283.8	255.4	237.3	238.1	240.0	233.6	232.2	230.9
30	151.4	146.5	138.5	118.0	103.3	97.0	93.8	90.8	87.9	87.3
31	186.4	186.6	171.9	149.0	135.3	129.2	123.4	114.9	115.4	119.9
32	383.6	406.3	377.4	290.7	245.5	229.0	226.7	224.8	221.2	211.9
33	331.7	328.6	324.7	309.8	295.6	296.0	292.3	292.2	295.7	296.7
34	341.2	350.2	321.9	297.8	294.0	288.1	282.7	284.7	270.3	245.0
35	157.9	155.4	149.3	135.2	125.1	124.9	131.6	131.1	136.5	137.6
36	383.8	389.1	364.4	333.8	314.5	310.7	302.8	294.4	280.8	259.9
37	21.6	21.4	18.7	16.4	16.9	18.4	17.8	20.8	20.2	20.6

Explanatory notes: see p. 77.

[1] Due to rounding, total may not equal sum of components.

Notes explicatives: voir p. 80.

[1] En raison des arrondis, le total peut différer de la somme des composantes.

Notas explicativas: véase p. 83.

[1] Debido a redondeos, el total puedee diferir de la suma de sus componentes.

	Paid employment in manufacturing Thousands			Emploi rémunéré dans les industries manufacturières Milliers				Empleo remunerado en las industrias manufactureras Millares		
	1999	2000	2001	2002	2003	2004	2005	2006	2007	2008

ASIA-ASIE-ASIA

Azerbaijan (DA) [1]   Employees - Salariés - Asalariados

Total - Total - Total
ISIC 3 - CITI 3 - CIIU 3

	1999	2000	2001	2002	2003	2004	2005	2006	2007	2008
Total [2]	170.8	165.4	152.1	141.0	133.9	134.9	139.3	140.8	144.6	144.8
15	16.4	17.7	16.8	14.7	12.3	15.5	17.3	18.6	18.2	19.9
16	1.1	1.4	1.2	1.3	1.1	1.1	1.2	1.1	0.9	0.9
17	17.8	20.3	17.8	13.6	10.8	10.8	10.9	11.1	9.9	8.7
18	4.3	4.3	4.1	3.1	2.4	2.1	2.1	2.0	1.5	1.3
19	1.3	1.7	1.8	1.7	1.5	1.1	1.0	0.9	0.8	0.7
20	1.5	1.6	1.3	1.5	1.0	1.5	1.2	1.5	1.0	1.0
21	0.3	0.2	0.2	0.2	0.2	0.2	0.3	0.3	0.4	0.5
22	3.1	2.1	2.1	2.3	2.0	2.3	2.2	2.3	2.4	2.4
23	6.7	6.7	6.2	6.3	6.4	6.8	6.7	6.5	6.4	6.3
24	15.3	13.6	15.6	12.5	11.5	11.4	11.0	10.9	10.5	9.9
25	3.1	5.2	2.1	1.8	1.3	1.6	1.8	1.9	3.0	3.2
26	18.2	9.8	6.4	6.3	5.3	6.0	6.6	6.7	8.6	9.1
27	7.0	6.8	6.7	8.9	9.0	9.4	9.7	9.8	9.6	9.9
28	3.0	3.0	2.5	2.5	3.2	3.7	3.7	3.9	4.5	4.6
29	19.3	16.6	13.6	12.8	11.2	9.7	9.4	8.7	9.0	8.1
30	0.7	0.6	0.6	0.5	0.4	0.4	0.3	0.3	0.3	0.3
31	4.5	4.4	3.7	3.0	2.2	1.7	1.8	1.8	1.8	1.7
32	1.8	1.5	1.3	0.8	0.9	0.8	0.9	0.9	0.7	0.8
33	3.0	2.8	2.5	2.3	2.0	1.6	1.5	1.4	1.3	1.3
34	0.1	0.7	0.1	0.1	0.1	0.5	0.3	0.6	0.9	0.9
35	5.7	8.2	7.2	7.3	8.1	8.4	8.8	8.9	9.0	9.1
36	2.7	2.2	2.4	2.3	1.9	3.0	2.9	3.0	2.8	3.8
37	0.3	0.3	0.3	0.3	0.5	0.4	0.2	0.3	0.2	0.3
X	33.6	39.1	54.3	64.7	75.5	70.8	69.0	67.4	67.1	66.1

Men - Hommes - Hombres
ISIC 3 - CITI 3 - CIIU 3

	1999	2000	2001	2002	2003	2004	2005	2006	2007	2008
Total [2]	110.7	111.7	96.9	96.9	93.5	94.9	101.3	104.6	108.4	112.9
15	10.8	12.0	11.6	10.6	8.6	11.3	12.4	12.6	12.0	14.1
16	0.8	1.1	0.9	1.0	1.0	0.9	0.9	0.9	0.8	0.7
17	7.4	9.7	7.6	6.4	3.8	3.7	5.0	5.5	4.4	5.6
18	1.1	2.0	1.6	1.2	0.7	0.7	0.7	0.8	0.3	0.4
19	0.6	0.9	0.7	0.6	0.3	0.5	0.5	0.5	0.5	0.4
20	1.4	1.3	1.0	1.1	0.7	1.3	1.0	1.3	0.8	0.8
21	0.2	0.2	0.1	0.1	0.1	0.1	0.2	0.2	0.3	0.3
22	1.9	1.2	1.3	1.5	1.2	1.4	1.5	1.6	1.4	1.4
23	4.6	3.8	3.6	3.7	4.9	4.2	4.1	4.1	4.0	4.0
24	9.5	8.1	9.6	7.7	7.1	7.1	6.7	6.9	6.5	6.1
25	1.9	3.4	1.5	1.3	0.9	1.3	1.5	1.6	2.3	2.6
26	16.2	7.2	5.2	4.3	3.6	4.7	5.2	5.5	7.2	7.9
27	3.7	4.5	4.5	6.1	6.7	7.0	7.8	7.8	8.0	8.2
28	2.2	2.3	2.0	2.0	2.5	2.8	2.9	3.2	3.8	3.9
29	13.8	12.2	9.5	9.1	8.0	6.9	7.0	6.4	6.8	6.6
30	0.4	0.3	0.3	0.3	0.2	0.4	0.3	0.2	0.2	0.2
31	3.2	2.9	2.4	2.0	1.4	1.2	1.2	1.3	1.4	1.3
32	0.9	1.1	0.6	0.4	0.5	0.4	0.5	0.6	0.5	0.7
33	2.0	1.7	1.6	1.5	1.4	1.1	1.1	1.1	0.9	1.0
34	0.1	0.7	0.1	0.1	0.1	0.4	0.3	0.5	0.8	0.8
35	4.9	6.9	6.2	6.4	7.0	7.3	7.7	7.8	7.8	8.0
36	2.1	1.8	1.7	1.9	1.6	2.6	2.5	2.5	2.3	3.2
37	0.2	0.2	0.3	0.2	0.4	0.3	0.2	0.3	0.1	0.2
X	20.8	25.2	36.8	41.2	48.0	43.1	39.5	37.5	37.6	32.3

Women - Femmes - Mujeres
ISIC 3 - CITI 3 - CIIU 3

	1999	2000	2001	2002	2003	2004	2005	2006	2007	2008
Total [2]	60.1	53.7	55.2	44.1	40.4	40.0	38.0	36.2	36.2	31.9
15	5.6	5.7	5.2	4.1	3.8	4.2	4.9	5.9	6.2	5.8
16	0.3	0.3	0.3	0.3	0.1	0.2	0.3	0.2	0.1	0.2
17	10.4	10.5	10.2	7.2	7.0	7.1	5.9	5.6	5.5	3.1
18	3.2	2.4	2.6	2.0	1.7	1.4	1.4	1.3	1.2	0.9
19	0.7	0.8	1.1	1.1	1.1	0.6	0.5	0.5	0.3	0.3
20	0.1	0.3	0.3	0.4	0.2	0.2	0.2	0.2	0.2	0.2
21	0.1	0.1	0.1	0.1	0.1	0.1	0.1	0.1	0.1	0.2
22	1.2	0.8	0.8	0.9	0.9	0.9	0.7	0.7	1.0	1.0
23	2.1	2.9	2.6	2.6	1.5	2.6	2.6	2.4	2.4	2.3
24	5.8	5.4	6.0	4.8	4.4	4.3	4.3	4.0	4.0	3.8
25	1.2	1.8	0.7	0.5	0.3	0.3	0.3	0.3	0.7	0.6
26	2.0	2.6	1.3	2.1	1.7	1.3	1.4	1.2	1.4	1.2
27	3.3	2.4	2.2	2.8	2.4	2.4	1.9	2.0	1.6	1.7
28	0.8	0.7	0.5	0.4	0.8	0.9	0.8	0.7	0.7	0.7
29	5.5	4.4	4.1	3.7	3.1	2.8	2.4	2.3	2.2	1.5
30	0.3	0.3	0.3	0.3	0.2	-	-	-	0.1	0.1
31	1.3	1.5	1.3	0.9	0.8	0.5	0.6	0.5	0.4	0.4
32	0.9	0.4	0.7	0.3	0.4	0.4	0.4	0.3	0.2	0.2
33	1.0	1.1	0.9	0.8	0.6	0.5	0.4	0.3	0.4	0.3
34	0.0	0.0	-	-	-	0.1	-	0.1	0.1	0.1
35	0.8	1.2	0.9	1.0	1.1	1.1	1.1	1.1	1.2	1.1
36	0.6	0.4	0.6	0.4	0.4	0.4	0.4	0.5	0.5	0.6
37	0.1	0.1	-	0.1	0.1	0.1		-	0.1	0.1
X	12.8	14.0	17.4	23.3	27.4	27.7	29.5	29.9	29.5	33.7

Explanatory notes: see p. 77.

[1] Persons aged 15 years and over. [2] Incl. mining and quarrying.

Notes explicatives: voir p. 80.

[1] Personnes âgées de 15 ans et plus. [2] Y compris les industries extractives.

Notas explicativas: véase p. 83.

[1] Personas de 15 años y más. [2] Incl. las minas y canteras.

2F

EMPLOYMENT	EMPLOI	EMPLEO
Paid employment in manufacturing	Emploi rémunéré dans les industries manufacturières	Empleo remunerado en las industrias manufactureras
Thousands	Milliers	Millares

Hong Kong, China (DA) — All persons engaged - Effectif occupé - Efectivo ocupado

Total - Total - Total
ISIC 2 - CITI 2 - CIIU 2

	1999	2000	2001	2002	2003	2004	2005	2006	2007	2008
Total	244.72	226.21	202.98	184.50	168.35	165.27	167.37	160.50 ¹	157.00	151.62
311-312	18.36	18.98	19.40	18.90	19.41	19.43	21.51	21.69 ¹	22.84	22.57
313	3.13	3.05	3.31	3.20	3.17	3.28	3.47	3.45 ¹	3.63	3.59
314	0.63	0.43	0.44	0.47	0.50	0.53	0.52	0.50 ¹	0.44	0.45
321	30.84	27.49	26.62	25.42	20.32	20.01	20.16	19.02 ¹	18.11	16.00
322	40.32	36.33	29.60	23.29	22.48	22.48	21.81	19.35 ¹	16.62	13.97
323	0.49	0.43	0.32	0.24	0.19	0.15	0.13	0.14 ¹	0.14	0.16
324	0.20	0.18	0.19	0.14	0.11	0.09	0.07	0.06 ¹	0.04	0.03
331	0.73	0.54	0.48	0.45	0.44	0.39	0.31	0.29 ¹	0.27	0.31
332	1.28	0.66	0.51	0.42	0.37	0.30	0.43	0.40 ¹	0.52	0.42
341	3.99	3.75	2.79	2.82	2.38	2.17	2.06	1.85 ¹	1.79	1.72
342	44.36	43.85	44.05	39.98	37.95	36.83	37.41	37.52 ¹	37.72	36.77
351-352	5.47	5.03	4.79	4.71	5.13	5.54	5.49	5.29 ¹	5.45	5.50
353-354	0.10	0.10	0.05	0.08	0.09	0.12	0.12	0.12 ¹	0.18	0.12
355	0.37	0.49	0.40	0.44	0.35	0.27	0.32	0.30 ¹	0.28	0.29
356	8.41	7.11	5.65	4.72	3.80	3.25	3.66	3.03 ¹	2.92	2.96
36	3.01	2.21	1.75	1.82	1.48	1.20	1.28	1.12 ¹	0.97	0.95
37	1.39	1.24	1.14	1.36	1.32	1.13	1.21	1.24 ¹	1.16	1.29
381	13.02	11.19	8.91	7.91	6.10	5.59	5.43	5.63 ¹	5.37	5.28
382-383	41.41	38.65	29.88	26.90	23.86	22.32	20.86	18.90 ¹	17.89	18.27
384	9.68	8.86	9.01	8.53	8.57	8.76	9.75	9.64 ¹	10.19	10.19
385	5.70	4.11	3.61	2.66	2.35	2.29	2.41	2.29 ¹	2.07	2.14
390	11.85	11.54	10.10	10.04	7.96	9.14	8.96	8.67 ¹	8.42	8.44

Men - Hommes - Hombres
ISIC 2 - CITI 2 - CIIU 2

	1999	2000	2001	2002	2003	2004	2005	2006	2007	2008
Total	140.19	128.99	116.49	106.81	97.26	92.86	94.40	91.89 ¹	90.21	88.45
311-312	11.43	11.66	11.46	10.87	11.41	11.20	12.02	11.99 ¹	12.45	12.23
313	2.64	2.25	2.66	2.47	2.42	2.48	2.57	2.57 ¹	2.59	.
314	0.45	0.33	0.35	0.36	0.37	0.39	0.38	0.36 ¹	0.30	.
321	15.31	13.72	13.24	11.94	9.84	9.68	9.25	8.85 ¹	8.03	.
322	10.41	9.13	7.28	5.90	4.95	4.53	4.42	4.36 ¹	3.91	.
323	0.29	0.21	0.20	0.14	0.11	0.11	0.09	- ¹	-	.
324	0.14	0.12	0.13	0.10	0.07	0.06	0.05	- ¹	-	.
331	0.59	0.43	0.35	0.39	0.36	0.30	0.26	- ¹	-	.
332	1.05	0.55	0.44	0.34	0.31	0.25	0.34	- ¹	-	.
341	2.88	2.84	2.05	2.13	1.65	1.50	1.47	1.30 ¹	1.21	1.16
342	29.60	29.29	28.52	25.79	24.54	23.09	23.49	23.61 ¹	23.32	22.68
351-352	3.04	2.72	2.65	2.56	2.98	3.12	2.99	2.86 ¹	2.80	2.82
353-354	0.10	0.10	0.05	0.08	0.08	0.11	0.11	- ¹	-	.
355	0.28	0.34	0.30	0.29	0.24	0.21	0.24	- ¹	-	.
356	5.58	4.71	3.83	3.13	2.41	2.02	2.26	1.94 ¹	1.90	1.84
36	2.48	1.84	1.50	1.48	1.17	0.98	1.09	- ¹	-	.
37	1.11	1.07	0.97	1.13	1.09	0.93	1.02	0.99 ¹	0.94	1.08
381	9.76	8.59	6.74	6.19	4.72	4.36	4.19	4.20 ¹	4.01	3.80
382-383	24.16	22.33	18.10	16.55	14.93	13.62	13.47			
382-383,385								13.58 ¹	13.16	13.48
384	8.52	7.89	7.67	7.52	7.54	7.28	8.11	8.00 ¹	8.59	8.86
390	7.86	7.17	6.38	6.24	5.04	5.50	5.48	5.31 ¹	5.05	4.99

Women - Femmes - Mujeres
ISIC 2 - CITI 2 - CIIU 2

	1999	2000	2001	2002	2003	2004	2005	2006	2007	2008
Total	104.53	97.21	86.49	77.69	71.09	72.41	72.97	68.62 ¹	66.79	63.17
311-312	6.93	7.32	7.94	8.03	8.00	8.24	9.48	9.70 ¹	10.39	10.35
313	0.49	0.80	0.65	0.73	0.75	0.80	0.90	0.89 ¹	1.04	0.94
314	0.18	0.10	0.09	0.11	0.13	0.14	0.15	0.14 ¹	0.14	0.14
321	15.53	13.77	13.38	13.47	10.48	10.32	10.91	10.17 ¹	10.08	8.78
322	29.92	27.21	22.33	17.39	17.53	17.95	17.39	14.99 ¹	12.71	10.46
323	0.19	0.22	0.12	0.10	0.08	0.04	0.04	- ¹	-	-
324	0.06	0.05	0.05	0.05	0.05	0.03	0.02	- ¹	-	-
331	0.14	0.11	0.13	0.06	0.09	0.09	0.05	- ¹	-	-
332	0.23	0.11	0.07	0.08	0.06	0.04	0.09	- ¹	-	-
341	1.12	0.91	0.73	0.69	0.73	0.66	0.59	0.54 ¹	0.58	0.58
342	14.76	14.56	15.53	14.19	13.41	13.74	13.92	13.91 ¹	14.40	14.09
351-352	2.43	2.31	2.14	2.15	2.15	2.42	2.50	2.43 ¹	2.66	2.68
353-354	-	-	-	-	0.01	0.01	0.01	- ¹	-	-
355	0.09	0.15	0.10	0.15	0.11	0.06	0.08	- ¹	-	-
356	2.83	2.40	1.82	1.59	1.39	1.23	1.40	1.09 ¹	1.02	1.12
36	0.53	0.37	0.25	0.33	0.31	0.21	0.19	- ¹	-	-
37	0.28	0.17	0.17	0.23	0.23	0.19	0.18	0.25 ¹	0.21	0.22
381	3.26	2.60	2.17	1.72	1.38	1.23	1.24	1.43 ¹	1.37	1.48
382-383	17.25	16.32	11.78	10.36	8.93	8.69	7.40		-	-
382-383,385								7.61 ¹	6.80	6.93
384	1.17	0.97	1.34	1.01	1.02	1.48	1.64	1.64 ¹	1.60	1.52
385	3.16	2.39	1.99	1.45	1.33	1.19	1.32	- ¹	-	-
390	3.99	4.37	3.72	3.81	2.92	3.64	3.47	3.36 ¹	3.37	3.45

Explanatory notes: see p. 77.
¹ Prior to 2006: Dec. of each year.

Notes explicatives: voir p. 80.
¹ Avant 2006: Dec. de chaque année.

Notas explicativas: véase p. 83.
¹ Antes de 2006: Dec de cada año.

Paid employment in manufacturing
Thousands

Emploi rémunéré dans les industries manufacturières
Milliers

Empleo remunerado en las industrias manufactureras
Millares

	1999	2000	2001	2002	2003	2004	2005	2006	2007	2008
Indonesia (BA) [1][2]					Wage earners - Ouvriers - Obreros					
Total - Total - Total										
ISIC 3 - CITI 3 - CIIU 3										
Total	.	.	.	.	.	.	.	.	7 839.0	7 708.0
15	.	.	.	.	.	.	.	.	1 413	1 325
16	.	.	.	.	.	.	.	.	431	407
17	.	.	.	.	.	.	.	.	856	909
18	.	.	.	.	.	.	.	.	877	950
19	.	.	.	.	.	.	.	.	300	302
20	.	.	.	.	.	.	.	.	756	645
21	.	.	.	.	.	.	.	.	179	183
22	.	.	.	.	.	.	.	.	217	215
23	.	.	.	.	.	.	.	.	19	23
24	.	.	.	.	.	.	.	.	277	256
25	.	.	.	.	.	.	.	.	335	337
26	.	.	.	.	.	.	.	.	518	549
27	.	.	.	.	.	.	.	.	88	102
28	.	.	.	.	.	.	.	.	244	235
29	.	.	.	.	.	.	.	.	91	90
30	.	.	.	.	.	.	.	.	7	12
31	.	.	.	.	.	.	.	.	66	72
32	.	.	.	.	.	.	.	.	165	159
33	.	.	.	.	.	.	.	.	13	9
34	.	.	.	.	.	.	.	.	68	75
35	.	.	.	.	.	.	.	.	114	147
36	.	.	.	.	.	.	.	.	788	691
37	.	.	.	.	.	.	.	.	20	14
Men - Hommes - Hombres										
ISIC 3 - CITI 3 - CIIU 3										
Total	.	.	.	.	.	.	.	.	4 848	4 657
15	.	.	.	.	.	.	.	.	871	807
16	.	.	.	.	.	.	.	.	105	100
17	.	.	.	.	.	.	.	.	428	415
18	.	.	.	.	.	.	.	.	322	328
19	.	.	.	.	.	.	.	.	161	167
20	.	.	.	.	.	.	.	.	581	509
21	.	.	.	.	.	.	.	.	120	129
22	.	.	.	.	.	.	.	.	165	159
23	.	.	.	.	.	.	.	.	17	22
24	.	.	.	.	.	.	.	.	187	170
25	.	.	.	.	.	.	.	.	220	229
26	.	.	.	.	.	.	.	.	410	425
27	.	.	.	.	.	.	.	.	82	94
28	.	.	.	.	.	.	.	.	214	201
29	.	.	.	.	.	.	.	.	72	66
30	.	.	.	.	.	.	.	.	3	4
31	.	.	.	.	.	.	.	.	41	47
32	.	.	.	.	.	.	.	.	69	57
33	.	.	.	.	.	.	.	.	7	6
34	.	.	.	.	.	.	.	.	63	67
35	.	.	.	.	.	.	.	.	104	136
36	.	.	.	.	.	.	.	.	594	509
37	.	.	.	.	.	.	.	.	12	11
Women - Femmes - Mujeres										
ISIC 3 - CITI 3 - CIIU 3										
Total	.	.	.	.	.	.	.	.	2 991	3 050
15	.	.	.	.	.	.	.	.	541	518
16	.	.	.	.	.	.	.	.	326	307
17	.	.	.	.	.	.	.	.	428	494
18	.	.	.	.	.	.	.	.	554	622
19	.	.	.	.	.	.	.	.	139	135
20	.	.	.	.	.	.	.	.	175	135
21	.	.	.	.	.	.	.	.	59	55
22	.	.	.	.	.	.	.	.	52	56
23	.	.	.	.	.	.	.	.	2	2
24	.	.	.	.	.	.	.	.	90	86
25	.	.	.	.	.	.	.	.	114	108
26	.	.	.	.	.	.	.	.	108	125
27	.	.	.	.	.	.	.	.	6	8
28	.	.	.	.	.	.	.	.	30	34
29	.	.	.	.	.	.	.	.	19	24
30	.	.	.	.	.	.	.	.	3	8
31	.	.	.	.	.	.	.	.	24	25
32	.	.	.	.	.	.	.	.	96	102
33	.	.	.	.	.	.	.	.	6	3
34	.	.	.	.	.	.	.	.	6	8
35	.	.	.	.	.	.	.	.	10	12
36	.	.	.	.	.	.	.	.	194	182
37	.	.	.	.	.	.	.	.	8	4

Explanatory notes: see p. 77.

Notes explicatives: voir p. 80.

Notas explicativas: véase p. 83.

[1] Persons aged 15 years and over. [2] Aug. of each year.

[1] Personnes âgées de 15 ans et plus. [2] Août de chaque année.

[1] Personas de 15 años y más. [2] Agosto de cada año.

2F   EMPLOYMENT · EMPLOI · EMPLEO

	Paid employment in manufacturing — Thousands				Emploi rémunéré dans les industries manufacturières — Milliers			Empleo remunerado en las industrias manufactureras — Millares		
	1999	2000	2001	2002	2003	2004	2005	2006	2007	2008

Israel (BA) [1][2] — Employees - Salariés - Asalariados

Total - Total - Total
ISIC 3 - CITI 3 - CIIU 3

	1999	2000	2001	2002	2003	2004	2005	2006	2007	2008
Total	331.4	345.5	345.1	331.6	333.2 [3]	345.8	350.7	357.3	379.7	391.3
15	40.5	43.0	46.3	48.3	46.6 [3]	50.3	45.3	42.6	45.3	48.7
16										
17	15.8	12.6	12.1	9.8	9.6 [3]	11.4	10.7	9.9	8.7	7.5
18	14.1	13.7	12.3	10.3	10.3 [3]	8.8	8.5	8.0	9.2	8.4
19	2.4	2.4	-	-	-	-	-	-	-	-
20	5.7	4.8	3.2	3.7	3.6 [3]	4.9	5.0	4.6	4.6	4.7
21	6.6	5.8	6.2	6.1	6.2 [3]	6.0	6.8	7.0	7.9	7.3
22	22.8	21.8	18.7	20.2	22.0 [3]	22.1	23.5	22.0	23.1	21.8
23	2.1	2.6	3.1	2.7	2.0 [3]	2.9	2.4	-	2.0	2.0
24	23.3	23.9	25.8	25.3	25.1 [3]	25.4	26.7	29.8	28.9	32.5
25	12.9	13.5	16.8	18.2	17.4 [3]	18.0	15.3	20.3	21.5	22.3
26	11.3	11.3	12.8	11.0	9.8 [3]	9.8	10.1	12.2	10.6	12.6
27	4.6	4.0	3.9	2.6	3.8 [3]	4.3	3.3	3.8	3.3	3.2
28	37.8	38.8	36.8	35.6	37.6 [3]	39.6	41.3	39.9	44.4	47.0
29	19.3	23.5	19.0	18.4	19.7 [3]	17.4	19.2	17.1	20.7	21.0
30	4.9	5.5	6.9	4.8	2.4 [3]	3.1	3.2	4.8	4.0	4.4
31	10.0	9.8	9.5	9.4	10.0 [3]	8.4	8.6	9.7	9.5	9.5
32	30.6	39.1	36.7	34.3	36.4 [3]	40.6	41.0	42.4	44.2	43.4
33	22.3	23.6	25.1	26.6	25.0 [3]	26.0	30.6	30.0	32.0	36.0
34	3.7	3.1	4.0	3.3	2.4 [3]	2.6	4.0	3.8	4.3	3.9
35	15.7	15.9	16.1	15.3	16.7 [3]	16.9	17.9	19.8	23.4	23.9
36	23.4	24.6	25.8	21.7	22.8 [3]	23.8	23.1	23.9	28.4	27.6
X	-	2.3	2.2	-	- [3]	-	2.1	2.7	2.0	-

Men - Hommes - Hombres
ISIC 3 - CITI 3 - CIIU 3

	1999	2000	2001	2002	2003	2004	2005	2006	2007	2008
Total	237.0	246.0	247.9	237.2	240.6 [3]	247.4	251.5	258.5	269.4	276.6
15	28.0	31.6	31.9	32.1	31.6 [3]	34.8	31.0	30.0	31.9	34.9
16										
17	7.6	6.6	6.8	4.8	4.8 [3]	5.2	5.5	4.8	4.7	3.9
18	3.5	3.2	3.2	3.9	3.3 [3]	2.7	2.2	3.0	3.6	2.2
19	-	-	-	-	-	-	-	-	-	-
20	5.2	4.4	2.9	3.1	3.2 [3]	4.5	4.5	4.1	4.0	4.1
21	5.2	4.3	4.5	4.2	4.2 [3]	4.8	4.9	5.1	5.2	5.3
22	13.1	11.4	10.9	13.5	13.9 [3]	12.9	13.9	12.8	13.0	12.4
23	-	2.2	2.6	2.1	- [3]	2.6	-	-	-	-
24	15.2	15.8	16.6	15.8	15.1 [3]	15.6	16.6	18.2	17.5	19.7
25	9.5	10.7	13.1	14.6	13.3 [3]	13.7	12.0	15.3	15.7	16.5
26	9.5	9.9	11.5	9.9	9.2 [3]	8.9	8.9	10.5	9.2	10.5
27	4.2	3.4	3.4	2.2	3.3 [3]	3.8	3.0	3.1	2.9	2.8
28	33.7	32.2	31.4	30.0	33.2 [3]	33.4	35.5	34.2	36.7	39.2
29	15.3	18.8	16.4	15.4	15.7 [3]	13.7	15.7	14.6	17.2	16.5
30	3.3	4.1	4.5	3.6	- [3]	2.4	2.5	3.4	3.1	3.3
31	8.1	7.2	7.3	7.4	7.4 [3]	6.4	6.4	7.1	6.6	6.6
32	19.7	24.1	23.3	22.3	23.7 [3]	26.3	26.9	28.0	28.0	26.4
33	16.1	17.3	17.7	17.7	18.4 [3]	18.7	21.1	21.1	21.7	24.1
34	3.0	2.3	3.3	2.6	2.1 [3]	2.0	3.3	3.3	3.2	3.1
35	13.3	13.8	13.0	13.0	13.8 [3]	14.3	15.6	16.7	19.9	20.3
36	19.1	19.5	20.2	16.1	18.1 [3]	18.2	16.9	18.5	20.8	20.4
X	-	-	-	-	- [3]	-	-	2.0	-	-

Women - Femmes - Mujeres
ISIC 3 - CITI 3 - CIIU 3

	1999	2000	2001	2002	2003	2004	2005	2006	2007	2008
Total	94.4	99.5	97.2	94.4	92.7 [3]	98.4	99.2	98.8	110.3	114.7
15	12.6	11.4	14.4	16.2	15.0 [3]	15.5	14.3	12.7	13.4	13.8
16										
17	8.3	6.0	5.3	5.1	4.8 [3]	6.2	5.3	5.1	4.0	3.6
18	10.6	10.5	9.1	6.3	7.0 [3]	6.1	6.3	4.9	5.6	6.2
19	-	-	-	-	- [3]	-	-	-	-	-
20	-	-	-	-	- [3]	-	-	-	-	-
21	-	-	-	-	2.0 [3]	-	-	-	2.7	2.0
22	9.7	10.4	7.8	6.6	8.1 [3]	9.1	9.6	9.2	10.1	9.4
23	-	-	-	-	- [3]	-	-	-	-	-
24	8.2	8.1	9.2	9.5	10.0 [3]	9.8	10.0	11.6	11.4	12.8
25	3.3	2.8	3.7	3.7	4.1 [3]	4.3	3.3	5.0	5.7	5.8
26	-	-	-	-	- [3]	-	-	-	-	2.1
27	-	-	-	-	- [3]	-	-	-	-	-
28	4.1	6.6	5.4	5.6	4.4 [3]	6.2	5.9	5.6	7.7	7.8
29	4.0	4.7	2.6	3.1	4.0 [3]	3.7	3.5	2.5	3.6	4.5
30	-	-	2.3	-	- [3]	-	-	-	-	-
31	-	2.6	2.2	2.0	2.6 [3]	2.3	2.2	2.6	2.9	2.9
32	10.9	15.0	13.5	12.0	12.8 [3]	14.3	14.1	14.4	16.2	17.0
33	6.2	6.3	7.3	8.8	6.7 [3]	7.3	9.5	9.0	10.3	11.9
34	-	-	-	-	- [3]	-	-	-	-	-
35	2.3	2.1	3.2	2.3	3.0 [3]	2.5	2.3	3.0	3.5	3.6
36	4.3	5.1	5.6	5.7	4.7 [3]	5.6	6.2	5.4	7.6	7.2
X	-	-	-	-	- [3]	-	-	-	-	-

Explanatory notes: see p. 77.

[1] Excl. armed forces. [2] Persons aged 15 years and over. [3] Methodology revised; data not strictly comparable.

Notes explicatives: voir p. 80.

[1] Non compris les forces armées. [2] Personnes âgées de 15 ans et plus. [3] Méthodologie révisée; les données ne sont pas strictement comparables.

Notas explicativas: véase p. 83.

[1] Excl. las fuerzas armadas. [2] Personas de 15 años y más. [3] Metodología revisada; los datos no son estrictamente comparables.

EMPLOYMENT / EMPLOI / EMPLEO

Paid employment in manufacturing
Thousands

Emploi rémunéré dans les industries manufacturières
Milliers

Empleo remunerado en las industrias manufactureras
Millares

	1999	2000	2001	2002	2003	2004	2005	2006	2007	2008

Israel (FA) [1] — Wage earners - Ouvriers - Obreros

Total - Total - Total
ISIC 3 - CITI 3 - CIIU 3

	1999	2000	2001	2002	2003	2004	2005	2006	2007	2008
Total	.	.	.	.	.	.	325.8	334.5	349.7	357.9
15	.	.	.	.	.	.	53.1	51.8	53.3	55.0
17	.	.	.	.	.	.	12.4	11.7	10.7	9.1
18	.	.	.	.	.	.	6.5	6.2	6.1	6.0
19	.	.	.	.	.	.	1.6	1.6	1.9	1.6
20	.	.	.	.	.	.	3.4	4.0	4.2	4.3
21	.	.	.	.	.	.	9.2	9.5	9.8	10.5
22	.	.	.	.	.	.	22.7	23.6	23.6	23.6
23	.	.	.	.	.	.	1.6	1.6	1.6	1.7
24	.	.	.	.	.	.	24.8	25.4	26.8	28.4
25	.	.	.	.	.	.	15.8	17.3	18.8	19.8
26	.	.	.	.	.	.	9.1	9.3	10.0	9.6
27	.	.	.	.	.	.	5.3	4.9	5.5	5.9
28	.	.	.	.	.	.	36.7	37.6	40.6	40.7
29	.	.	.	.	.	.	15.7	15.8	17.3	17.9
30	.	.	.	.	.	.	-	-	-	
31	.	.	.	.	.	.	6.9	7.6	8.0	8.2
32	.	.	.	.	.	.	30.8	33.4	34.4	36.2
33	.	.	.	.	.	.	30.9	31.4	33.0	33.4
34	.	.	.	.	.	.	16.2	17.8	18.4	20.7
36	.	.	.	.	.	.	22.6	23.3	25.0	24.6

Japan (BA) [2] — Employees - Salariés - Asalariados

Total - Total - Total
ISIC 3 - CITI 3 - CIIU 3

	1999	2000	2001	2002	2003	2004	2005	2006	2007	2008
Total	.	.	.	.	11 190	10 920	10 850	11 100	11 220	11 050
15-16	.	.	.	.	1 480	1 470	1 410	1 460	1 500	1 420
17	.	.	.	.	190	180	180	170	170	160
18 [3]	.	.	.	.	430	390	370	360	340	320
19 [4]	.	.	.	.	50	40	40	50	50	50
20 [5]	.	.	.	.	170	170	150	150	150	140
21	.	.	.	.	280	270	260	260	270	250
22	.	.	.	.	800	760	750	790	800	760
23 [6]	.	.	.	.	30	40	30	30	30	40
24	.	.	.	.	620	590	590	620	580	580
25	.	.	.	.	560	590	590	620	630	630
26	.	.	.	.	400	380	370	370	360	370
27 [7]	.	.	.	.	400	410	380	420	440	420
28	.	.	.	.	1 040	1 000	990	1 010	1 050	1 040
29	.	.	.	.	1 050	1 030	1 090	1 130	1 160	1 230
30,32	.	.	.	.	920	920	950	1 010	1 010	1 000
31	.	.	.	.	980	970	940	800	780	770
33	.	.	.	.	330	320	290	300	300	280
34-35	.	.	.	.	970	940	1 020	1 100	1 150	1 150
36 [8]	.	.	.	.	490	460	450	450	450	450

Men - Hommes - Hombres
ISIC 3 - CITI 3 - CIIU 3

	1999	2000	2001	2002	2003	2004	2005	2006	2007	2008
Total	.	.	.	.	7 580	7 450	7 480	7 640	7 800	7 740
15-16	.	.	.	.	690	700	670	690	710	690
17	.	.	.	.	110	110	100	100	100	100
18 [3]	.	.	.	.	110	100	100	100	100	90
19 [4]	.	.	.	.	30	20	20	30	20	30
20 [5]	.	.	.	.	130	130	120	110	110	110
21	.	.	.	.	190	190	180	180	190	180
22	.	.	.	.	540	510	510	530	540	520
23 [6]	.	.	.	.	30	30	20	20	20	30
24	.	.	.	.	460	440	440	460	440	440
25	.	.	.	.	380	390	400	410	420	420
26	.	.	.	.	320	290	290	290	290	290
27 [7]	.	.	.	.	350	360	310	360	390	370
28	.	.	.	.	790	770	750	770	800	790
29	.	.	.	.	860	840	900	920	940	1 000
30,32	.	.	.	.	620	610	640	690	690	690
31	.	.	.	.	660	680	670	560	550	530
33	.	.	.	.	210	210	200	190	190	180
34-35	.	.	.	.	800	770	860	930	990	980
36 [8]	.	.	.	.	330	300	280	300	300	300

	EMPLOYMENT	EMPLOI	EMPLEO
	Paid employment in manufacturing	Emploi rémunéré dans les industries manufacturières	Empleo remunerado en las industrias manufactureras
	Thousands	Milliers	Millares

	1999	2000	2001	2002	2003	2004	2005	2006	2007	2008

Japan (BA) [1] — Employees - Salariés - Asalariados

Women - Femmes - Mujeres
ISIC 3 - CITI 3 - CIIU 3

	1999	2000	2001	2002	2003	2004	2005	2006	2007	2008
Total	.	.	.	.	3 610	3 470	3 370	3 460	3 420	3 320
15-16	.	.	.	.	800	780	750	760	780	730
17	.	.	.	.	80	80	80	70	70	60
18 [2]	.	.	.	.	310	290	270	270	240	230
19 [3]	.	.	.	.	20	20	20	20	20	20
20 [4]	.	.	.	.	40	40	40	30	40	30
21	.	.	.	.	80	80	70	80	80	70
22	.	.	.	.	260	240	240	260	260	250
23 [5]	.	.	.	.	-	10	0	0	0	0
24	.	.	.	.	160	150	150	150	140	140
25	.	.	.	.	190	200	190	210	210	210
26	.	.	.	.	80	80	80	80	80	80
27 [6]	.	.	.	.	50	50	50	70	50	50
28	.	.	.	.	250	240	240	240	250	240
29	.	.	.	.	190	190	200	210	220	230
30,32	.	.	.	.	310	300	290	320	310	300
31	.	.	.	.	320	290	270	250	230	240
33	.	.	.	.	120	110	100	100	110	100
34-35	.	.	.	.	170	160	160	170	160	170
36 [7]	.	.	.	.	170	170	160	150	160	160

Kyrgyzstan (E) — Employees - Salariés - Asalariados

Total - Total - Total
ISIC 3 - CITI 3 - CIIU 3

	1999	2000	2001	2002	2003	2004	2005	2006	2007	2008
Total	.	.	.	83.4	79.4	74.4	72.0	68.3	67.7	.
15	.	.	.	17.3	17.3	16.8	16.3	15.6	16.0	.
16	.	.	.	2.3	1.9	1.7	1.3	1.2	1.0	.
17	.	.	.	11.9	11.2	10.3	9.5	8.7	7.2	.
18	.	.	.	4.6	4.2	3.5	2.2	2.0	2.0	.
19	.	.	.	0.9	0.6	0.4	0.4	0.5	0.5	.
20	.	.	.	1.0	1.0	0.5	0.9	0.6	0.6	.
21	.	.	.	0.6	0.6	0.6	0.6	0.7	0.7	.
22	.	.	.	3.5	3.7	3.6	3.4	3.3	3.4	.
23	.	.	.	0.5	1.1	1.1	1.2	1.2	1.1	.
24	.	.	.	2.9	2.7	2.5	2.6	2.6	2.8	.
25	.	.	.	1.6	1.2	1.4	1.7	1.6	1.8	.
26	.	.	.	9.0	8.9	8.9	9.5	9.3	10.2	.
27	.	.	.	4.7	4.4	4.4	4.5	4.8	4.9	.
28	.	.	.	2.5	2.6	3.4	3.4	3.1	3.0	.
29	.	.	.	6.9	6.2	5.1	5.1	4.5	4.0	.
30	.	.	.	0.5	0.3	0.2	0.1	0.1	0.1	.
31	.	.	.	6.9	6.0	6.1	5.8	5.3	5.2	.
32	.	.	.	1.0	0.9	0.8	0.7	0.3	0.4	.
33	.	.	.	1.8	1.7	0.4	0.3	0.3	0.2	.
34	.	.	.	1.0	0.9	0.7	0.7	0.7	0.5	.
35	.	.	.	0.1	0.1	0.0	0.0	0.0	0.1	.
36	.	.	.	1.7	1.9	1.9	1.9	1.9	1.9	.
37	.	.	.	0.1	0.1	0.0	0.1	0.1	0.1	.

Men - Hommes - Hombres
ISIC 3 - CITI 3 - CIIU 3

	1999	2000	2001	2002	2003	2004	2005	2006	2007	2008
Total	.	.	.	53.3	51.2	48.7	44.8	42.4	42.3	.
15	.	.	.	11.3	10.8	11.1	9.6	9.3	9.5	.
16	.	.	.	1.6	1.3	1.2	1.0	0.9	0.7	.
17	.	.	.	6.0	6.0	5.6	4.7	4.3	4.0	.
18	.	.	.	1.2	1.2	1.0	0.4	0.5	0.4	.
19	.	.	.	0.5	0.4	0.2	0.2	0.3	0.4	.
20	.	.	.	0.9	0.8	0.4	0.7	0.5	0.5	.
21	.	.	.	0.4	0.4	0.4	0.4	0.5	0.5	.
22	.	.	.	2.0	2.0	1.8	1.7	1.6	1.5	.
23	.	.	.	0.4	0.8	0.7	0.7	0.7	0.7	.
24	.	.	.	2.2	2.1	1.9	1.8	1.7	1.7	.
25	.	.	.	1.0	0.7	0.9	1.0	0.9	1.1	.
26	.	.	.	6.9	7.2	6.8	7.1	6.9	7.7	.
27	.	.	.	3.8	3.6	3.6	3.7	4.0	4.0	.
28	.	.	.	1.8	2.0	2.8	2.4	2.2	2.0	.
29	.	.	.	5.3	4.4	3.8	3.6	3.0	2.7	.
30	.	.	.	0.3	0.3	0.1	0.1	0.1	0.1	.
31	.	.	.	3.8	3.6	3.8	3.4	3.1	3.0	.
32	.	.	.	0.6	0.6	0.4	0.4	0.2	0.2	.
33	.	.	.	1.1	1.0	0.3	0.2	0.2	0.1	.
34	.	.	.	0.7	0.6	0.7	0.4	0.4	0.3	.
35	.	.	.	0.1	0.1	0.0	0.0	0.0	0.1	.
36	.	.	.	1.2	1.3	1.2	1.2	1.1	1.2	.
37	.	.	.	0.1	0.1	0.0	0.1	0.1	0.1	.

Explanatory notes: see p. 77.

[1] Persons aged 15 years and over. [2] Excl. dressing and dyeing of fur. [3] Incl. dressing and dying of fur. [4] Excl. articles of straw. [5] Excl. nuclear fuel. [6] Incl. nuclear fuel. [7] Incl. articles of straw.

Notes explicatives: voir p. 80.

[1] Personnes âgées de 15 ans et plus. [2] Non compris la préparation et teinture des fourrures. [3] Y compris la préparation et teinture des fourrures. [4] Non compris les articles de vannerie. [5] Non compris les combustibles nucléaires. [6] Y compris les combustibles nucléaires. [7] Y compris les articles de vannerie.

Notas explicativas: véase p. 83.

[1] Personas de 15 años y más. [2] Excl. el adobo y teñida de pieles. [3] Incl. el adobo y teñida de pieles. [4] Excl. los artículos de paja. [5] Excl. el combustible nuclear. [6] Incl. el combustible nuclear. [7] Incl. los artículos de paja.

Paid employment in manufacturing
Thousands

Emploi rémunéré dans les industries manufacturières
Milliers

Empleo remunerado en las industrias manufactureras
Millares

	1999	2000	2001	2002	2003	2004	2005	2006	2007	2008
Kyrgyzstan (E)				Employees - Salariés - Asalariados						
Women - Femmes - Mujeres										
ISIC 3 - CITI 3 - CIIU 3										
Total	.	.	.	30.1	28.3	25.6	27.2	25.9	25.4	.
15	.	.	.	6.1	6.5	5.7	6.7	6.4	6.5	.
16	.	.	.	0.7	0.6	0.5	0.3	0.3	0.3	.
17	.	.	.	6.0	5.2	4.7	4.8	4.4	3.2	.
18	.	.	.	3.5	3.0	2.5	1.8	1.5	1.6	.
19	.	.	.	0.4	0.2	0.2	0.2	0.2	0.1	.
20	.	.	.	0.1	0.1	0.1	0.1	0.1	0.1	.
21	.	.	.	0.1	0.2	0.2	0.2	0.2	0.2	.
22	.	.	.	1.4	1.7	1.7	1.8	1.7	1.9	.
23	.	.	.	0.1	0.3	0.4	0.4	0.4	0.4	.
24	.	.	.	0.7	0.7	0.7	0.8	0.8	1.1	.
25	.	.	.	0.6	0.5	0.6	0.6	0.7	0.7	.
26	.	.	.	2.1	1.7	2.1	2.3	2.4	2.6	.
27	.	.	.	1.0	0.8	0.8	0.8	0.8	0.9	.
28	.	.	.	0.7	0.6	0.6	0.9	0.9	0.9	.
29	.	.	.	1.6	1.9	1.3	1.5	1.4	1.3	.
30	.	.	.	0.2	0.0	0.1	0.0	0.0	0.0	.
31	.	.	.	3.0	2.4	2.3	2.4	2.2	2.3	.
32	.	.	.	0.4	0.3	0.3	0.3	0.1	0.1	.
33	.	.	.	0.6	0.6	0.1	0.1	0.1	0.1	.
34	.	.	.	0.3	0.3	0.1	0.3	0.3	0.2	.
35	.	.	.	0.0	0.0	0.0	0.0	0.0	0.0	.
36	.	.	.	0.5	0.6	0.7	0.7	0.8	0.7	.
37	.	.	.	0.0	0.0	0.0	0.0	0.0	0.0	.
Macau, China (BA) [1] [2]				Employees - Salariés - Asalariados						
Total - Total - Total										
ISIC 3 - CITI 3 - CIIU 3										
Total	40.7	36.3	42.8	39.9	35.8	34.0	33.4	27.6	22.3	22.8
17	4.4	4.1	4.8	4.3	3.6	3.5	2.7	2.4	2.3	2.6
18	28.0	24.5	30.3	27.8	25.0	23.4	24.1	19.3	14.5	14.3
Men - Hommes - Hombres										
ISIC 3 - CITI 3 - CIIU 3										
Total	11.5	10.6	11.8	11.2	10.3	9.8	10.3	8.9	7.4	10.2
17	1.2	1.3	1.1	1.3	1.2	1.0	0.9	0.8	0.8	1.4
18	5.0	4.5	5.8	4.8	4.9	3.9	4.9	4.1	3.2	4.5
Women - Femmes - Mujeres										
ISIC 3 - CITI 3 - CIIU 3										
Total	29.2	25.7	31.0	28.7	25.5	24.2	23.1	18.7	14.9	12.6
17	3.1	2.8	3.6	3.1	2.5	2.5	1.9	1.6	1.5	1.1
18	23.0	20.0	24.5	22.9	20.1	19.5	19.1	15.3	11.3	9.8
Malaysia (BA) [3] [4]				Employees - Salariés - Asalariados						
Total - Total - Total										
ISIC 3 - CITI 3 - CIIU 3										
Total	.	.	2 019.1	1 902.6	1 955.0	1 840.2	1 819.2	1 903.2	1 789.8	1 944.6
15	.	.	191.1	178.7	197.9	202.9	206.1	215.7	190.6	243.1
16	.	.	5.6	6.3	4.6	6.6	5.1	3.6	2.8	5.3
17	.	.	37.1	39.3	44.5	38.5	35.1	32.2	27.8	29.7
18	.	.	106.1	87.5	96.0	83.9	75.6	71.1	61.7	122.1
19	.	.	14.2	12.8	11.4	13.2	13.1	11.6	12.0	11.9
20	.	.	177.6	158.3	179.0	168.2	155.3	167.5	153.6	147.1
21	.	.	37.8	46.2	43.4	48.8	46.5	47.3	36.8	45.1
22	.	.	52.5	55.4	57.3	60.5	53.9	55.5	57.1	59.9
23	.	.	16.6	13.0	23.1	20.9	21.6	27.4	28.1	23.8
24	.	.	53.2	57.1	61.0	58.3	61.7	63.3	62.0	64.3
25	.	.	167.5	151.1	156.8	154.2	161.2	144.5	137.6	144.4
26	.	.	71.5	65.2	70.6	68.1	69.1	64.9	59.5	58.3
27	.	.	62.9	63.0	65.1	54.5	60.4	62.8	70.1	71.3
28	.	.	91.9	87.8	104.3	85.7	91.1	107.7	105.1	97.2
29	.	.	49.5	51.6	58.1	60.0	71.1	83.9	83.1	86.7
30	.	.	80.7	79.1	76.5	73.2	64.0	68.5	71.9	59.7
31	.	.	58.6	63.0	55.6	52.1	52.3	63.3	55.6	52.6
32	.	.	485.3	410.5	404.2	356.6	356.8	362.0	345.7	353.6
33	.	.	24.7	27.7	20.4	22.0	15.5	21.7	21.7	26.1
34	.	.	63.4	75.8	65.1	65.4	62.2	81.4	57.5	71.8
35	.	.	33.7	34.8	36.5	27.5	32.3	35.0	38.1	47.2
36	.	.	134.9	134.5	121.2	115.8	105.6	106.7	107.0	114.7
37	.	.	2.5	3.7	2.7	3.3	3.8	5.4	4.4	8.7

Explanatory notes: see p. 77.

[1] Persons aged 14 years and over. [2] Excl. armed forces and conscripts. [3] Persons aged 15 to 64 years. [4] Excl. armed forces.

Notes explicatives: voir p. 80.

[1] Personnes âgées de 14 ans et plus. [2] Non compris les forces armées et les conscrits. [3] Personnes âgées de 15 à 64 ans. [4] Non compris les forces armées.

Notas explicativas: véase p. 83.

[1] Personas de 14 años y más. [2] Excl. las fuerzas armadas y los conscriptos. [3] Personas de 15 a 64 años. [4] Excl. las fuerzas armadas.

	EMPLOYMENT	EMPLOI	EMPLEO

	Paid employment in manufacturing	Emploi rémunéré dans les industries manufacturières	Empleo remunerado en las industrias manufactureras
	Thousands	Milliers	Millares

	1999	2000	2001	2002	2003	2004	2005	2006	2007	2008
Malaysia (BA) [1][2]				Employees - Salariés - Asalariados						
Men - Hommes - Hombres										
ISIC 3 - CITI 3 - CIIU 3										
Total			1 200.4	1 146.6	1 181.3	1 122.0	1 122.6	1 181.6	1 109.6	1 182.5
15			129.3	121.4	126.7	141.6	146.0	146.2	131.2	151.6
16			2.9	4.3	3.2	4.8	3.1	2.4	1.5	3.3
17			21.7	22.3	25.9	23.7	18.2	17.3	15.5	14.8
18			31.1	27.1	27.3	24.4	19.6	20.7	14.1	26.4
19			8.5	6.7	6.0	7.8	5.6	6.5	6.7	6.2
20			129.3	113.9	130.7	123.4	117.0	127.4	113.7	113.7
21			26.5	28.0	30.6	34.9	32.1	31.1	23.2	29.4
22			31.8	33.3	31.4	37.5	32.1	32.6	34.7	35.6
23			13.3	9.3	17.5	17.3	17.9	19.8	21.5	18.5
24			38.2	38.9	42.2	36.9	41.8	43.4	42.0	43.7
25			89.1	84.5	91.4	91.3	98.0	88.7	76.0	79.3
26			57.6	53.6	56.1	53.2	51.1	52.0	46.9	46.7
27			53.5	54.7	53.2	45.9	51.2	55.7	59.6	59.9
28			77.3	75.6	87.1	70.0	79.1	86.8	88.5	79.7
29			39.2	37.6	43.8	47.8	50.1	61.3	63.6	66.1
30			33.7	34.3	36.0	29.6	27.8	33.9	35.8	27.1
31			28.7	35.0	29.5	22.1	22.8	32.9	30.2	28.7
32			197.3	167.7	164.2	141.4	152.1	146.9	141.2	153.8
33			10.6	11.0	10.2	9.2	8.0	9.8	10.0	12.0
34			52.7	58.4	50.6	49.6	46.3	60.8	42.6	53.6
35			28.4	30.1	30.9	23.4	26.8	29.4	33.1	40.6
36			98.1	96.0	84.6	82.9	73.2	71.6	74.1	84.6
37			1.6	3.0	2.1	3.2	2.9	4.3	4.0	7.2
Women - Femmes - Mujeres										
ISIC 3 - CITI 3 - CIIU 3										
Total			818.8	755.9	773.7	718.2	696.5	721.6	680.2	762.1
15			61.8	57.4	71.2	61.3	60.1	69.5	59.4	91.6
16			2.7	2.0	1.4	1.8	2.0	1.2	1.3	2.0
17			15.4	17.0	18.6	14.8	16.9	14.8	12.3	14.9
18			75.0	60.4	68.6	59.5	56.0	50.4	47.6	95.7
19			5.8	6.1	5.3	5.4	7.5	5.1	5.3	5.7
20			48.4	44.4	48.3	44.7	38.3	40.1	40.0	33.4
21			11.3	18.2	12.9	13.9	14.4	16.2	13.7	15.7
22			20.7	22.1	25.8	23.0	21.8	22.9	22.4	24.3
23			3.3	3.8	5.6	3.6	3.7	7.6	6.5	5.4
24			14.9	18.2	18.8	21.4	19.9	19.8	20.0	20.6
25			78.4	66.6	65.4	62.9	63.2	55.9	61.5	65.1
26			13.9	11.6	14.4	14.9	18.0	12.9	12.6	11.6
27			9.4	8.3	11.9	8.6	9.2	7.2	10.5	11.3
28			14.6	12.2	17.2	15.7	12.0	20.9	16.6	17.5
29			10.4	14.0	14.4	12.2	21.0	22.6	19.4	20.6
30			47.0	44.8	40.5	43.6	36.2	34.6	36.2	32.6
31			30.0	28.1	26.1	30.0	29.5	30.5	25.4	23.9
32			288.0	242.8	240.0	215.2	204.7	215.0	204.5	199.8
33			14.1	16.7	10.2	12.8	7.5	11.9	11.7	14.2
34			10.7	17.5	14.5	15.8	15.9	20.6	14.9	18.2
35			5.3	4.8	5.6	4.1	5.5	5.7	5.0	6.6
36			36.8	38.5	36.6	33.0	32.3	35.1	33.0	30.0
37			0.9	0.6	0.5	0.1	0.9	1.1	0.4	1.4
Philippines (BA) [3][4]				Employees - Salariés - Asalariados						
Total - Total - Total										
ISIC 3 - CITI 3 - CIIU 3										
Total			2 072	2 040	2 141	2 278	2 277	2 252	2 284	2 169
15			485	480	483	531	544	559	560	558
16			15	16	12	12	9	9	8	10
17			132	113	117	114	105	96	91	77
18			277	310	357	348	358	321	315	268
19			58	57	53	67	55	55	47	56
20			105	106	115	148	148	144	146	121
21			39	43	42	44	51	44	48	46
22			65	64	66	69	68	69	72	61
23			8	6	6	5	5	4	6	3
24			79	68	73	70	74	81	78	73
25			63	54	56	67	65	59	60	61
26			65	62	73	81	78	76	78	72
27			51	47	47	45	42	42	44	41
28			96	96	101	114	107	99	97	104
29			69	75	63	62	57	53	60	54
30			12	16	16	16	10	15	15	13
31			57	54	56	45	49	50	48	45
32			168	161	183	223	253	256	297	292
33			30	28	20	20	16	16	18	15
34			29	28	30	37	29	29	27	29
35			24	21	19	24	21	22	26	38
36			144	135	147	131	129	150	140	128
37			1	1	3	4	2	2	3	2

Explanatory notes: see p. 77.

[1] Persons aged 15 to 64 years. [2] Excl. armed forces. [3] Persons aged 15 years and over. [4] Excl. regular military living in barracks.

Notes explicatives: voir p. 80.

[1] Personnes âgées de 15 à 64 ans. [2] Non compris les forces armées. [3] Personnes âgées de 15 ans et plus. [4] Non compris les militaires de carrière vivant dans des casernes.

Notas explicativas: véase p. 83.

[1] Personas de 15 a 64 años. [2] Excl. las fuerzas armadas. [3] Personas de 15 años y más. [4] Excl. los militares profesionales que viven en casernas.

EMPLOYMENT   EMPLOI   EMPLEO   2F

Paid employment in manufacturing
Thousands

Emploi rémunéré dans les industries manufacturières
Milliers

Empleo remunerado en las industrias manufactureras
Millares

	1999	2000	2001	2002	2003	2004	2005	2006	2007	2008
Philippines (BA) [1][2]				Employees - Salariés - Asalariados						
Men - Hommes - Hombres										
ISIC 3 - CITI 3 - CIIU 3										
Total	.	.	1 215	1 186	1 253	1 350	1 323	1 313	1 345	1 292
15	.	.	343	345	346	383	387	395	393	390
16	.	.	8	9	7	7	6	6	6	6
17	.	.	48	46	49	43	40	38	34	29
18	.	.	56	69	84	89	89	78	81	69
19	.	.	29	28	26	34	30	30	26	27
20	.	.	77	80	86	106	102	97	102	85
21	.	.	25	28	27	26	33	27	30	28
22	.	.	46	48	46	47	46	46	50	39
23	.	.	8	5	5	4	4	3	4	2
24	.	.	55	44	45	46	48	52	51	49
25	.	.	41	35	39	49	46	41	40	44
26	.	.	55	53	60	67	66	64	67	62
27	.	.	46	41	42	40	37	39	41	36
28	.	.	89	87	95	106	101	94	92	98
29	.	.	51	54	51	50	47	44	50	45
30	.	.	5	4	6	5	4	8	9	6
31	.	.	25	22	25	21	22	25	25	24
32	.	.	51	46	60	71	80	76	98	96
33	.	.	12	10	7	7	6	5	5	6
34	.	.	24	22	26	29	23	21	21	22
35	.	.	21	19	17	22	18	19	23	34
36	.	.	99	90	104	91	88	103	96	94
37	.	.	1	1	2	3	1	1	1	2
Women - Femmes - Mujeres										
ISIC 3 - CITI 3 - CIIU 3										
Total	.	.	857	854	889	928	954	939	939	877
15	.	.	141	135	137	148	157	164	167	167
16	.	.	7	7	5	5	4	3	2	3
17	.	.	84	66	69	71	65	58	57	48
18	.	.	221	241	273	259	269	243	233	199
19	.	.	30	29	28	33	25	25	22	29
20	.	.	27	26	29	42	47	48	43	36
21	.	.	14	15	15	18	19	16	18	19
22	.	.	20	16	20	22	22	23	22	22
23	.	.	1	1	1	1	1	1	1	1
24	.	.	24	24	28	24	26	29	27	23
25	.	.	21	19	17	18	20	18	20	17
26	.	.	11	9	13	14	12	12	11	10
27	.	.	5	6	6	5	5	4	3	5
28	.	.	8	9	7	8	6	6	6	6
29	.	.	18	21	12	12	10	9	11	10
30	.	.	7	12	10	11	6	7	7	7
31	.	.	32	32	31	24	28	25	23	21
32	.	.	117	114	124	152	174	181	200	196
33	.	.	18	18	13	13	11	11	13	9
34	.	.	5	6	5	8	6	7	5	6
35	.	.	2	2	2	2	3	3	4	4
36	.	.	45	45	43	40	41	46	44	35
37	.	.	-	-	1	1	1	1	1	1
Philippines (CA) [3]				Employees - Salariés - Asalariados						
Total - Total - Total										
ISIC 3 - CITI 3 - CIIU 3										
Total	1 084.2	.	932.5	.	983.9	.	1 022.1	.	.	.
15	200.6	.	168.1	.	154.0	.	164.3	.	.	.
16	10.9	.	10.5	.	9.6	.	9.6	.	.	.
17	54.2	.	49.1	.	39.6	.	35.2	.	.	.
18	143.8	.	134.8	.	142.8	.	158.6	.	.	.
19	30.5	.	22.0	.	19.5	.	20.6	.	.	.
20	19.8	.	17.6	.	20.9	.	20.4	.	.	.
21	24.0	.	18.0	.	20.8	.	21.3	.	.	.
22	23.3	.	20.4	.	20.0	.	20.3	.	.	.
23	1.4	.	1.2	.	1.1	.	1.5	.	.	.
24	46.6	.	45.2	.	44.1	.	49.9	.	.	.
25	42.3	.	37.3	.	50.4	.	43.1	.	.	.
26	49.8	.	27.3	.	29.6	.	26.6	.	.	.
27	35.5	.	27.2	.	27.8	.	25.0	.	.	.
28	36.7	.	28.5	.	35.3	.	32.5	.	.	.
29	32.6	.	22.7	.	29.9	.	25.1	.	.	.
30	34.6	.	30.3	.	37.0	.	58.2	.	.	.
31	49.3	.	42.5	.	52.2	.	56.7	.	.	.
32	126.4	.	136.4	.	149.4	.	145.4	.	.	.
33	40.7	.	23.4	.	26.3	.	19.4	.	.	.
34	19.7	.	15.0	.	20.2	.	23.4	.	.	.
35	9.9	.	7.7	.	10.8	.	11.1	.	.	.
36	51.2	.	46.5	.	40.7	.	53.2	.	.	.
37	0.4	.	0.7	.	2.1	.	1.1	.	.	.

Explanatory notes: see p. 77.

[1] Persons aged 15 years and over. [2] Excl. regular military living in barracks. [3] Establishments with 20 or more persons employed.

Notes explicatives: voir p. 80.

[1] Personnes âgées de 15 ans et plus. [2] Non compris les militaires de carrière vivant dans des casernes. [3] Etablissements occupant 20 personnes et plus.

Notas explicativas: véase p. 83.

[1] Personas de 15 años y más. [2] Excl. los militares profesionales que viven en casernas. [3] Establecimientos con 20 y más trabajadores.

Paid employment in manufacturing	Emploi rémunéré dans les industries manufacturières	Empleo remunerado en las industrias manufactureras
Thousands	Milliers	Millares

	1999	2000	2001	2002	2003	2004	2005	2006	2007	2008

Philippines (CA) [1]   Employees - Salariés - Asalariados

Men - Hommes - Hombres
ISIC 3 - CITI 3 - CIIU 3

	1999	2000	2001	2002	2003	2004	2005	2006	2007	2008
Total	559.4	.	466.7	.	494.7	.	511.0	.	.	.
15	136.5	.	114.7	.	104.0	.	110.1	.	.	.
16	5.9	.	5.5	.	5.4	.	6.1	.	.	.
17	24.9	.	21.1	.	18.0	.	18.3	.	.	.
18	31.1	.	28.7	.	37.9	.	38.3	.	.	.
19	11.7	.	9.1	.	9.0	.	9.7	.	.	.
20	15.6	.	14.0	.	16.8	.	15.5	.	.	.
21	16.5	.	12.3	.	14.5	.	15.8	.	.	.
22	14.9	.	12.9	.	12.7	.	12.6	.	.	.
23	1.2	.	0.9	.	0.9	.	1.2	.	.	.
24	32.6	.	31.3	.	30.0	.	33.0	.	.	.
25	28.6	.	23.9	.	31.8	.	26.8	.	.	.
26	31.9	.	21.7	.	22.3	.	20.6	.	.	.
27	28.3	.	22.7	.	22.9	.	20.8	.	.	.
28	26.9	.	20.8	.	25.0	.	23.0	.	.	.
29	23.8	.	14.9	.	17.5	.	15.5	.	.	.
30	11.3	.	7.1	.	10.4	.	15.6	.	.	.
31	18.9	.	15.9	.	18.9	.	23.0	.	.	.
32	32.6	.	35.7	.	42.2	.	40.8	.	.	.
33	10.9	.	6.1	.	7.0	.	6.1	.	.	.
34	16.0	.	11.7	.	13.3	.	15.0	.	.	.
35	8.1	.	6.6	.	9.1	.	9.3	.	.	.
36	30.9	.	28.9	.	23.6	.	33.4	.	.	.
37	0.3	.	0.4	.	1.4	.	0.7	.	.	.

Women - Femmes - Mujeres
ISIC 3 - CITI 3 - CIIU 3

	1999	2000	2001	2002	2003	2004	2005	2006	2007	2008
Total	524.9	.	465.7	.	489.2	.	511.1	.	.	.
15	64.1	.	53.4	.	49.9	.	54.2	.	.	.
16	5.0	.	5.0	.	4.2	.	3.4	.	.	.
17	29.4	.	28.0	.	21.6	.	16.9	.	.	.
18	112.7	.	106.1	.	104.9	.	120.2	.	.	.
19	18.8	.	12.9	.	10.5	.	10.9	.	.	.
20	4.2	.	3.6	.	4.1	.	4.9	.	.	.
21	7.4	.	5.7	.	6.3	.	5.5	.	.	.
22	8.4	.	7.5	.	7.3	.	7.6	.	.	.
23	0.2	.	0.2	.	0.2	.	0.4	.	.	.
24	14.0	.	13.9	.	14.1	.	16.9	.	.	.
25	13.7	.	13.4	.	18.6	.	16.3	.	.	.
26	17.9	.	5.6	.	7.3	.	6.0	.	.	.
27	7.2	.	4.5	.	4.9	.	4.2	.	.	.
28	9.8	.	7.8	.	10.3	.	9.5	.	.	.
29	8.8	.	7.9	.	12.4	.	9.6	.	.	.
30	23.3	.	23.2	.	26.5	.	42.6	.	.	.
31	30.4	.	26.7	.	33.3	.	33.7	.	.	.
32	93.8	.	100.7	.	107.1	.	104.5	.	.	.
33	29.8	.	17.3	.	19.3	.	13.3	.	.	.
34	3.7	.	3.4	.	6.9	.	8.3	.	.	.
35	1.8	.	1.1	.	1.7	.	1.9	.	.	.
36	20.3	.	17.5	.	17.2	.	19.8	.	.	.
37	0.2	.	0.2	.	0.7	.	0.4	.	.	.

Sri Lanka (DA) [2] [3]   Employees - Salariés - Asalariados

Total - Total - Total
ISIC 2 - CITI 2 - CIIU 2

	1999	2000	2001	2002	2003	2004	2005	2006	2007	2008
Total	264.12	399.68	405.49	250.77	334.91	260.61	.	243.38	389.59	
311-312	23.26	35.11	24.83	25.95	29.22	27.32	.	24.54	28.45	
313	2.55	2.95	2.57	1.97	3.08	2.36	.	2.83	3.62	
314	3.38	4.39	3.72	0.40	0.45	0.47	.	1.47	2.21	
321	38.83	32.14	52.46	18.08	28.18	19.92	.	14.38	44.71	
322	121.15	213.14	207.72	127.74	189.53	132.63	.	131.72	215.72	
323	2.78	7.33	3.39	2.49	3.05	3.14	.	2.86	5.73	
324	6.14	7.38	3.68	0.96	1.00	1.66	.	2.47	3.36	
331	1.93	3.42	7.90	3.73	3.48	3.59	.	3.13	3.05	
332	2.76	3.44	0.94	4.27	4.12	3.38	.	3.52	3.76	
341	2.76	5.23	5.66	3.02	2.81	2.93	.	1.78	2.34	
342	6.58	3.40	3.67	2.82	3.25	3.48	.	4.75	9.54	
351	3.92	6.66	10.15	4.98	7.94	5.78	.	5.10	6.89	
352-354	5.60	5.48	5.93	5.09	4.87	5.94	.	4.33	4.07	
355	10.45	14.26	14.69	12.98	10.14	10.36	.	10.09	15.01	
356	0.68	1.38	4.78	1.47	1.14	0.97	.	0.88	1.42	
361	3.50	4.19	2.25	3.98	4.89	5.20	.	4.37	4.31	
362	1.63	0.55	2.34	0.57	0.59	0.14	.	0.31	0.14	
369	5.60	6.43	6.61	4.01	4.65	3.80	.	3.85	4.82	
371	1.55	2.58	2.56	1.91	2.50	1.78	.	2.21	1.83	
372	0.14	0.32	0.42	1.22	0.73	0.72	.	0.33	0.65	
381	1.90	2.36	3.40	1.22	1.06	1.82	.	0.79	1.96	
382	1.09	4.96	5.18	4.49	2.77	3.87	.	2.30	2.44	
383	5.98	14.00	11.40	5.83	8.78	9.26	.	5.92	8.52	
384	2.49	5.43	7.59	10.02	9.07	6.82	.	6.15	5.25	
385	0.22	0.26	0.18	0.19	0.30	0.10	.	0.14	1.71	
390	7.22	12.89	11.47	1.38	1.84	2.59	.	3.16	7.98	

Explanatory notes: see p. 77.

[1] Establishments with 20 or more persons employed. [2] Establishments with 5 or more persons employed. [3] June of each year.

Notes explicatives: voir p. 80.

[1] Etablissements occupant 20 personnes et plus. [2] Etablissements occupant 5 personnes et plus. [3] Juin de chaque année.

Notas explicativas: véase p. 83.

[1] Establecimientos con 20 y más trabajadores. [2] Establecimientos con 5 y más trabajadores. [3] Junio de cada año.

Paid employment in manufacturing
Thousands

Emploi rémunéré dans les industries manufacturières
Milliers

Empleo remunerado en las industrias manufactureras
Millares

Sri Lanka (DA) [1] [2]   Employees - Salariés - Asalariados

	1999	2000	2001	2002	2003	2004	2005	2006	2007	2008
Men - Hommes - Hombres										
ISIC 2 - CITI 2 - CIIU 2										
Total	102.44	140.09	146.86	111.05	122.41	103.94	.	105.68	154.53	.
311-312	14.40	21.23	14.73	15.11	16.08	16.23	.	16.18	18.90	.
313	2.16	2.52	2.30	1.67	2.36	2.06	.	2.40	3.18	.
314	0.88	1.10	0.81	0.38	0.37	0.39	.	0.66	0.41	.
321	13.02	11.49	18.26	8.43	10.90	7.82	.	6.60	21.13	.
322	22.54	37.78	42.46	28.48	38.33	26.03	.	32.54	50.65	.
323	1.48	2.33	1.80	1.87	1.87	1.43	.	2.13	2.79	.
324	2.06	2.64	1.35	0.34	0.30	0.56	.	0.95	1.26	.
331	1.47	2.86	6.08	3.02	2.87	3.01	.	2.41	2.00	.
332	2.45	2.96	0.80	3.28	3.31	2.64	.	2.81	3.08	.
341	2.51	4.46	4.27	2.61	2.27	1.95	.	1.40	1.93	.
342	5.88	2.84	3.08	2.39	2.76	2.92	.	3.97	7.85	.
351	2.90	4.60	5.37	3.78	5.33	3.86	.	3.69	4.60	.
352-354	3.12	3.79	4.29	3.92	2.84	3.72	.	2.75	2.94	.
355	8.35	9.60	10.46	9.25	6.68	6.77	.	6.13	9.30	.
356	0.22	0.67	1.49	0.86	0.58	0.84	.	0.81	0.72	.
361	2.24	2.59	1.30	2.68	2.93	3.59	.	3.17	2.24	.
362	1.21	0.51	1.53	0.51	0.56	0.01	.	0.30	0.10	.
369	4.54	5.55	4.78	3.52	3.63	2.99	.	3.20	4.05	.
371	1.43	2.33	2.38	1.55	2.04	1.45	.	1.97	1.46	.
372	0.13	0.29	0.38	1.04	0.66	0.56	.	0.31	0.57	.
381	1.55	2.15	2.40	1.05	0.93	1.61	.	0.66	1.66	.
382	1.01	4.19	3.91	3.96	2.56	2.59	.	2.00	1.89	.
383	2.06	2.91	2.85	1.19	1.87	1.99	.	2.04	2.79	.
384	2.40	4.97	6.86	9.48	8.52	6.31	.	5.24	4.98	.
385	0.21	0.20	0.12	0.13	0.18	0.57	.	0.09	1.01	.
390	2.58	3.53	2.81	0.52	1.06	1.24	.	1.27	3.04	.
Women - Femmes - Mujeres										
ISIC 2 - CITI 2 - CIIU 2										
Total	161.58	261.29	258.62	139.79	212.50	156.68	.	137.81	235.11	.
311-312	9.22	14.38	10.09	10.84	13.13	11.09	.	8.36	9.55	.
313	0.37	0.43	0.27	0.31	0.72	0.30	.	0.43	0.44	.
314	2.50	3.28	2.91	0.02	0.09	0.08	.	0.81	1.81	.
321	25.81	20.64	34.20	9.65	17.27	12.10	.	7.78	23.58	.
322	98.61	175.36	165.26	99.26	151.20	106.59	.	99.17	165.07	.
323	1.30	5.00	1.59	0.62	1.19	1.71	.	0.74	2.94	.
324	4.08	4.74	2.33	0.62	0.70	1.11	.	1.52	2.10	.
331	0.45	0.55	1.82	0.71	0.61	0.58	.	0.72	1.05	.
332	0.31	0.48	0.14	0.99	0.81	0.74	.	0.71	0.68	.
341	0.25	0.77	1.39	0.42	0.55	0.98	.	0.38	0.42	.
342	0.70	0.55	0.59	0.43	0.49	0.57	.	0.78	1.69	.
351	1.02	2.05	4.78	1.20	2.65	1.92	.	1.40	2.29	.
352-354	2.48	1.69	1.64	1.17	2.02	2.22	.	1.69	1.13	.
355	2.09	4.66	4.23	3.73	3.46	3.59	.	3.96	5.71	.
356	0.45	0.71	3.29	0.62	0.56	0.14	.	0.07	0.70	.
361	1.26	1.60	0.95	1.80	1.96	1.84	.	1.19	2.07	.
362	0.41	0.04	0.82	0.07	0.04	-	.	0.02	0.04	.
369	1.06	0.88	1.83	0.48	1.02	0.81	.	0.65	0.77	.
371	0.11	0.24	0.19	0.36	0.43	0.33	.	0.24	0.37	.
372	0.01	0.03	0.04	0.18	0.07	0.16	.	0.03	0.09	.
381	0.35	0.21	1.00	0.18	0.13	0.21	.	0.13	0.30	.
382	0.08	0.76	1.27	0.54	0.21	0.27	.	0.30	0.55	.
383	3.91	11.08	8.55	4.64	6.91	7.27	.	3.88	5.73	.
384	0.08	0.46	0.73	0.54	0.55	0.51	.	0.91	0.38	.
385	0.03	0.06	0.05	0.06	0.12	0.43	.	0.05	0.71	.
390	4.64	10.64	8.66	0.86	0.78	1.35	.	1.89	4.94	.

Explanatory notes: see p. 77.

[1] Establishments with 5 or more persons employed. [2] June of each year.

Notes explicatives: voir p. 80.

[1] Etablissements occupant 5 personnes et plus. [2] Juin de chaque année.

Notas explicativas: véase p. 83.

[1] Establecimientos con 5 y más trabajadores. [2] Junio de cada año.

2F | EMPLOYMENT | EMPLOI | EMPLEO

Paid employment in manufacturing	Emploi rémunéré dans les industries manufacturières	Empleo remunerado en las industrias manufactureras
Thousands	Milliers	Millares

	1999	2000	2001	2002	2003	2004	2005	2006	2007	2008

West Bank and Gaza Strip (BA) [1]   Employees - Salariés - Asalariados

Total - Total - Total
ISIC 3 - CITI 3 - CIIU 3

	1999	2000	2001	2002	2003	2004	2005	2006	2007	2008
Total	65.265	59.971	45.171 [2]	37.933	42.676	45.096	51.092	50.396	49.867	49.276
15	10.786	9.877	8.408 [2]	7.190	6.937	8.064	10.263	10.097	8.207	9.899
16	0.055	0.243	0.283 [2]	0.238	0.085	0.134	0.120	0.272	0.492	0.484
17	1.642	1.266	0.958 [2]	0.765	0.870	1.111	1.476	1.393	1.358	1.183
18	16.026	14.813	11.550 [2]	9.072	9.486	9.788	8.872	7.740	9.916	9.264
19	2.902	2.065	1.624 [2]	1.127	1.955	1.841	1.726	1.703	0.860	1.397
20	1.689	1.540	0.990 [2]	1.008	0.977	1.517	0.851	0.806	0.674	0.942
21	0.605	0.468	0.600 [2]	0.589	0.664	0.596	0.412	0.628	0.367	0.395
22	2.028	2.466	1.949 [2]	1.499	1.383	1.806	2.250	2.397	2.639	2.071
23	-	0.148	0.025 [2]	0.043	0.103	0.020	0.059	0.027	-	0.022
24	1.421	1.687	1.689 [2]	1.005	1.420	0.886	0.729	1.375	1.957	-
25	1.681	1.166	1.086 [2]	0.981	1.066	0.726	0.938	1.126	1.184	1.325
26	11.593	10.661	6.438 [2]	5.887	6.969	7.766	10.332	9.763	8.978	9.481
27	0.498	0.607	0.461 [2]	0.388	0.462	0.352	0.555	0.580	0.769	0.593
28	6.786	6.992	4.403 [2]	4.445	4.164	4.515	6.044	4.870	5.383	5.724
29	0.826	0.579	0.438 [2]	0.419	0.617	0.587	0.653	0.860	0.671	0.487
30	-	0.032	0.029 [2]	-	-	-	0.037	0.019	0.034	-
31	0.296	0.331	0.173 [2]	0.179	0.176	0.167	0.147	0.230	0.237	0.177
32	0.075	0.057	0.062 [2]	-	0.032	-	-	-	-	-
33	0.106	0.047	0.153 [2]	-	0.177	0.135	0.096	0.109	0.071	0.020
34	0.039	0.196	0.055 [2]	0.030	0.043	0.054	0.100	0.013	0.117	0.023
35	0.024	0.024	- [2]	-	-	0.041	-	-	-	0.000
36	6.185	4.707	3.797 [2]	3.068	5.026	4.818	5.122	6.142	5.583	5.471
37	-	-	- [2]	-	0.063	0.140	0.309	0.248	0.369	0.318

Men - Hommes - Hombres
ISIC 3 - CITI 3 - CIIU 3

	1999	2000	2001	2002	2003	2004	2005	2006	2007	2008
Total	58.116	52.696	39.577 [2]	33.527	37.902	39.703	45.846	44.888	42.643	43.496
15	10.290	9.340	8.153 [2]	6.903	6.665	7.716	9.775	9.817	7.966	9.660
16	0.055	0.149	0.226 [2]	0.238	0.085	0.134	0.120	0.272	0.442	0.461
17	1.292	1.001	0.883 [2]	0.672	0.686	0.944	1.364	1.268	1.284	0.986
18	10.622	9.233	6.761 [2]	5.775	5.928	5.736	5.113	3.645	4.118	4.325
19	2.735	2.022	1.609 [2]	0.989	1.864	1.603	1.632	1.656	0.797	1.397
20	1.655	1.504	0.990 [2]	1.008	0.977	1.517	0.851	0.806	0.661	0.911
21	0.497	0.404	0.600 [2]	0.589	0.566	0.523	0.412	0.628	0.329	0.395
22	1.965	2.330	1.916 [2]	1.499	1.326	1.710	2.136	2.219	2.503	1.997
23	-	0.148	0.025 [2]	0.043	0.103	0.020	-	0.027	-	0.022
24	1.196	1.400	1.494 [2]	0.679	1.084	0.665	0.440	0.788	1.239	-
25	1.667	1.166	1.074 [2]	0.858	1.066	0.714	0.938	1.126	1.184	1.325
26	11.450	10.507	6.396 [2]	5.845	6.913	7.766	10.246	9.727	8.954	9.443
27	0.498	0.607	0.439 [2]	0.388	0.462	0.352	0.555	0.580	0.769	0.527
28	6.777	6.936	4.403 [2]	4.445	4.107	4.515	6.014	4.846	5.369	5.615
29	0.826	0.579	0.438 [2]	0.388	0.617	0.553	0.574	0.819	0.671	0.487
30	-	0.032	- [2]	-	-	-	0.037	0.019	0.034	-
31	0.296	0.331	0.173 [2]	0.179	0.176	0.125	0.147	0.197	0.237	0.177
32	0.075	0.057	0.062 [2]	-	0.032	0.031	-	-	-	-
33	0.078	0.047	0.135 [2]	-	0.177	0.135	0.096	0.109	0.071	0.020
34	0.039	0.196	0.055 [2]	0.030	0.043	0.054	0.100	0.013	0.117	0.023
35	0.024	0.024	- [2]	-	-	-	-	-	-	-
36	6.079	4.684	3.744 [2]	3.000	4.960	4.751	4.986	6.080	5.528	5.407
37	-	-	- [2]	-	0.063	0.140	0.309	0.248	0.369	0.318

Women - Femmes - Mujeres
ISIC 3 - CITI 3 - CIIU 3

	1999	2000	2001	2002	2003	2004	2005	2006	2007	2008
Total	7.148	7.275	5.594 [2]	4.406	4.774	5.393	5.245	5.509	7.224	5.781
15	0.496	0.537	0.255 [2]	0.287	0.273	0.348	0.487	0.280	0.242	0.239
16	-	0.094	0.057 [2]	-	-	-	-	-	0.050	0.023
17	0.350	0.265	0.074 [2]	0.092	0.184	0.167	0.112	0.125	0.073	0.198
18	5.405	5.581	4.789 [2]	3.298	3.557	4.053	3.759	4.096	5.798	4.939
19	0.167	0.043	0.015 [2]	0.138	0.090	0.238	0.094	0.048	0.063	-
20	0.033	0.037	- [2]	-	-	-	-	-	0.013	0.031
21	0.108	0.063	- [2]	-	0.098	0.073	-	-	0.038	0.000
22	0.063	0.136	0.034 [2]	-	0.057	0.096	0.113	0.179	0.136	0.073
23	-	-	- [2]	-	-	-	0.059	-	-	-
24	0.225	0.287	0.195 [2]	0.327	0.336	0.221	0.289	0.586	0.718	-
25	0.014	-	0.012 [2]	0.123	-	0.013	-	-	-	-
26	0.143	0.153	0.042 [2]	0.042	0.056	-	0.086	0.036	0.025	0.038
27	-	-	0.022 [2]	-	-	-	-	-	-	0.066
28	0.009	0.057	- [2]	-	0.057	-	0.030	0.024	0.014	0.109
29	-	-	- [2]	0.031	-	0.034	0.078	0.041	-	-
30	-	-	0.029 [2]	-	-	-	-	-	-	-
31	-	-	- [2]	-	-	0.043	-	0.033	-	-
32	-	-	- [2]	-	-	-	-	-	-	-
33	0.028	-	0.018 [2]	-	-	-	-	-	-	-
34	-	-	- [2]	-	-	-	-	-	-	-
35	-	-	- [2]	-	-	0.041	-	-	-	-
36	0.106	0.023	0.053 [2]	0.068	0.066	0.067	0.137	0.062	0.055	0.064
37	-	-	- [2]	-	-	-	-	-	-	-

Explanatory notes: see p. 77.

[1] Persons aged 15 years and over. [2] Prior to 2001: persons aged 10 years and over.

Notes explicatives: voir p. 80.

[1] Personnes âgées de 15 ans et plus. [2] Avant 2001: personnes agées de 10 ans et plus.

Notas explicativas: véase p. 83.

[1] Personas de 15 años y más. [2] Antes de 2001: personas de 10 años y más.

			Paid employment in manufacturing Thousands	**Emploi rémunéré dans les industries manufacturières** Milliers			**Empleo remunerado en las industrias manufactureras** Millares		
1999	2000	2001	2002	2003	2004	2005	2006	2007	2008

EUROPE-EUROPE-EUROPA

Andorre (FA) — Employees - Salariés - Asalariados

Total - Total - Total
ISIC 3 - CITI 3 - CIIU 3

	1999	2000	2001	2002	2003	2004	2005	2006	2007	2008
Total	.	.	.	.	1.573	1.629	1.710	1.758	1.730	.
15					0.222	0.224	0.244	0.257	0.231	
16					0.306	0.314	0.296	0.286	0.265	
17					0.066	0.058	0.060	0.061	0.061	
18					0.005	0.004	0.002	0.001	0.001	
20					0.337	0.323	0.318	0.307	0.290	
22					0.250	0.269	0.281	0.298	0.286	
24					0.061	0.065	0.072	0.074	0.087	
25					0.008	0.005	0.001	0.001	0.001	
26					0.065	0.065	0.070	0.067	0.065	
27					0.002	0.002	0.003	0.004	0.003	
28					0.070	0.116	0.124	0.142	0.160	
29					0.111	0.107	0.122	0.124	0.138	
31					0.001	0.001	0.001	0.009	0.010	
32					0.001	0.001	0.001	0.001	0.001	
33					0.017	0.019	0.052	0.067	0.072	
35					0.001	0.001	0.001	-	-	
36					0.045	0.049	0.050	0.045	0.046	
37					0.005	0.006	0.012	0.014	0.014	

Austria (BA) [1][2] — Employees - Salariés - Asalariados

Total - Total - Total
ISIC 3 - CITI 3 - CIIU 3

	1999	2000	2001	2002	2003	2004	2005	2006	2007	2008
Total	.	.	.	711.8	698.3	656.3 [3]	667.6	701.2	688.7	659.6
15				62.7	69.8	70.9 [3]	66.6	69.4	74.6	70.0
16				1.2	2.1	- [3]	1.5	0.5	1.1	1.0
17				20.2	19.9	15.0 [3]	12.2	14.1	16.0	13.1
18				11.5	13.7	10.2 [3]	7.8	7.7	6.6	8.0
19				7.0	6.8	4.0 [3]	3.7	3.1	4.8	5.1
20				27.0	29.7	38.5 [3]	36.5	36.5	38.7	45.5
21				16.4	19.6	17.7 [3]	21.1	17.8	18.6	17.1
22				38.1	36.4	33.1 [3]	35.2	32.6	33.7	31.1
23				3.3	4.6	3.7 [3]	5.1	4.4	2.4	3.3
24				43.4	42.9	41.5 [3]	41.8	39.7	34.7	31.5
25				24.8	22.5	18.7 [3]	19.8	23.4	26.3	26.0
26				30.7	28.2	27.4 [3]	27.4	32.5	36.0	30.4
27				36.3	34.7	19.6 [3]	24.5	25.6	26.3	22.8
28				125.0	125.4	121.5 [3]	123.4	123.7	109.4	118.6
29				76.7	69.3	76.4 [3]	76.6	88.9	93.2	85.8
30				7.0	5.5	5.1 [3]	4.8	3.9	3.5	2.4
31				14.5	12.9	17.7 [3]	16.6	24.2	23.9	25.7
32				23.5	24.3	19.0 [3]	19.9	24.6	28.2	20.0
33				35.5	29.4	21.0 [3]	20.7	20.3	20.1	20.8
34				29.8	29.2	36.0 [3]	37.4	44.4	35.2	30.2
35				11.9	11.7	16.3 [3]	14.6	17.2	19.4	11.6
36				65.5	59.4	41.4 [3]	49.9	45.1	33.8	38.0
37				0.8	0.3	- [3]	0.8	1.7	2.1	1.7

Men - Hommes - Hombres
ISIC 3 - CITI 3 - CIIU 3

	1999	2000	2001	2002	2003	2004	2005	2006	2007	2008
Total	.	.	.	529.2	515.9	479.9 [3]	493.2	515.6	510.2	485.4
15				40.5	46.7	41.8 [3]	39.4	39.6	42.7	39.6
16				0.9	1.4	- [3]	1.1	0.3	0.4	0.7
17				9.1	9.0	6.9 [3]	7.3	7.9	8.2	6.6
18				2.8	2.9	1.6 [3]	1.3	1.6	1.3	1.1
19				3.5	2.8	- [3]	1.9	1.3	2.0	2.5
20				21.8	24.2	31.2 [3]	28.6	28.7	30.9	37.9
21				13.1	15.6	14.6 [3]	15.4	13.7	14.3	13.0
22				21.5	21.7	19.3 [3]	18.5	17.3	19.2	16.8
23				2.9	3.8	3.5 [3]	3.4	3.2	2.2	2.7
24				27.9	27.4	25.5 [3]	27.7	25.1	23.0	20.6
25				17.4	15.7	14.5 [3]	14.0	16.5	18.6	19.4
26				23.2	21.3	21.3 [3]	20.9	25.6	28.1	22.9
27				31.8	31.3	17.1 [3]	21.8	22.0	23.1	19.3
28				101.4	100.7	98.1 [3]	99.6	100.1	91.6	100.0
29				66.7	60.3	65.8 [3]	66.5	74.2	76.3	70.7
30				6.0	4.6	3.4 [3]	3.2	2.7	2.5	1.5
31				9.6	8.6	12.5 [3]	12.0	18.6	19.0	19.2
32				18.3	19.4	12.8 [3]	14.4	18.7	20.2	15.0
33				22.5	16.3	11.5 [3]	14.7	12.3	12.8	11.6
34				24.5	23.1	29.0 [3]	28.4	36.9	29.3	25.1
35				10.9	10.8	15.3 [3]	13.2	15.6	16.4	8.4
36				52.1	48.3	31.3 [3]	39.3	32.3	26.5	29.5
37				0.8	0.1	- [3]	0.6	1.2	1.6	1.2

Explanatory notes: see p. 77.

[1] Excl. conscripts on compulsory military service. [2] Persons aged 15 years and over. [3] Prior to 2004: incl. conscripts.

Notes explicatives: voir p. 80.

[1] Non compris conscrits ceux du contingent. [2] Personnes âgées de 15 ans et plus. [3] Avant 2004: y compris les conscrits.

Notas explicativas: véase p. 83.

[1] Excl. los conscriptos del servicio obligatorio. [2] Personas de 15 años y más. [3] Antes de 2004: incl. los conscriptos.

	EMPLOYMENT		EMPLOI		EMPLEO				
	Paid employment in manufacturing Thousands			Emploi rémunéré dans les industries manufacturières Milliers			Empleo remunerado en las industrias manufactureras Millares		
	1999	2000	2001	2002	2003	2004	2005	2006	2007	2008

Austria (BA) [1][2] — Employees - Salariés - Asalariados

Women - Femmes - Mujeres
ISIC 3 - CITI 3 - CIIU 3

	1999	2000	2001	2002	2003	2004	2005	2006	2007	2008
Total	.	.	.	182.7	182.4	176.3 [3]	174.3	185.6	178.5	174.2
15	.	.	.	22.2	23.2	29.1 [3]	27.2	29.8	31.9	30.4
16	.	.	.	0.2	0.7	- [3]	0.4	0.2	0.7	0.3
17	.	.	.	11.1	10.8	8.1 [3]	4.8	6.2	7.8	6.4
18	.	.	.	8.7	10.8	8.6 [3]	6.5	6.1	5.4	7.0
19	.	.	.	3.6	4.1	- [3]	1.8	1.8	2.7	2.6
20	.	.	.	5.2	5.5	7.2 [3]	7.9	7.8	7.8	7.6
21	.	.	.	3.3	4.0	3.1 [3]	5.7	4.1	4.3	4.1
22	.	.	.	16.7	14.6	13.8 [3]	16.7	15.2	14.5	14.4
23	.	.	.	0.4	0.8	0.2 [3]	1.7	1.1	0.2	0.5
24	.	.	.	15.5	15.5	16.0 [3]	14.0	14.5	11.7	10.9
25	.	.	.	7.4	6.8	4.2 [3]	5.8	6.9	7.7	6.5
26	.	.	.	7.6	6.9	6.1 [3]	6.5	6.9	7.9	7.5
27	.	.	.	4.5	3.4	2.5 [3]	2.8	3.5	3.2	3.4
28	.	.	.	23.7	24.7	23.4 [3]	23.8	23.6	17.8	18.7
29	.	.	.	10.0	9.0	10.6 [3]	10.0	14.7	16.9	15.1
30	.	.	.	1.0	0.9	1.7 [3]	1.6	1.2	1.1	0.9
31	.	.	.	4.8	4.3	5.2 [3]	4.6	5.6	4.9	6.4
32	.	.	.	5.2	5.0	6.2 [3]	5.5	5.9	7.9	5.0
33	.	.	.	13.0	13.1	9.5 [3]	5.9	8.0	7.3	9.2
34	.	.	.	5.3	6.2	7.0 [3]	9.0	7.4	5.9	5.1
35	.	.	.	1.1	0.9	1.0 [3]	1.4	1.6	3.0	3.2
36	.	.	.	12.4	11.1	10.1 [3]	10.6	12.8	7.3	8.5
37	.	.	.	-	0.1	- [3]	0.2	0.5	0.6	0.5

Austria (DA) [2][4] — Employees - Salariés - Asalariados

Total - Total - Total
ISIC 3 - CITI 3 - CIIU 3

	1999	2000	2001	2002	2003	2004	2005	2006	2007	2008
Total	527.00	530.92	531.38	520.49	522.19	526.49	526.10	550.54	.	.
15	60.63	60.49	60.53	60.40	60.79	61.22	60.81	62.73	.	.
16	1.07	1.06	1.07	1.13	1.16	1.12	1.04	0.98	.	.
17	17.73	17.55	16.47	15.62	14.80	14.48	12.61	12.23	.	.
18	10.08	9.29	8.58	7.88	7.04	6.23	6.09	5.66	.	.
19	5.94	5.75	5.85	5.51	4.72	4.54	3.91	3.58	.	.
20	29.21	27.38	26.22	26.12	26.66	27.54	27.87	30.08	.	.
21	17.08	17.02	17.13	17.17	17.41	17.54	17.36	17.27	.	.
22	20.80	20.75	21.67	20.60	20.86	20.56	19.91	20.95	.	.
23	2.40	2.30	2.21	2.24	2.31	1.70	1.68	1.62	.	.
24	23.39	22.32	23.00	23.65	23.73	24.01	23.87	26.21	.	.
25	24.78	26.15	26.65	24.56	24.58	24.95	24.54	25.63	.	.
26	30.21	31.04	30.64	30.61	30.57	30.70	30.10	31.24	.	.
27	31.17	31.84	31.49	31.58	31.67	32.31	32.78	33.79	.	.
28	53.73	55.20	55.43	54.26	56.90	57.66	57.17	62.47	.	.
29	65.02	66.36	68.20	70.62	68.87	70.13	70.97	76.37	.	.
30	0.69	0.74	0.81	0.86	0.99	0.95	1.06	0.89	.	.
31	26.53	27.19	25.91	26.11	24.89	25.03	25.23	26.34	.	.
32	27.72	28.46	27.62	24.05	23.38	23.95	23.05	24.53	.	.
33	10.26	10.91	11.69	11.73	12.11	12.21	12.46	13.16	.	.
34	27.32	27.89	29.49	27.67	30.78	32.45	32.18	32.17	.	.
35	4.69	4.95	5.49	5.93	6.45	6.51	10.92	10.56	.	.
36	35.94	35.71	34.66	31.62	30.92	31.03	29.73	31.22	.	.
37	0.61	0.57	0.57	0.59	0.65	0.70	0.77	0.86	.	.

Men - Hommes - Hombres
ISIC 3 - CITI 3 - CIIU 3

	1999	2000	2001	2002	2003	2004	2005	2006	2007	2008
Total	388.74	389.33	390.38	384.95	387.73	391.30	393.17	411.79	.	.
15	35.20	34.41	33.97	34.22	34.19	34.15	33.93	34.90	.	.
16	0.71	0.70	0.72	0.80	0.80	0.78	0.72	0.70	.	.
17	9.47	9.16	8.74	8.33	8.00	7.18	6.62	6.38	.	.
18	1.73	1.58	1.51	1.36	1.19	1.04	1.01	0.91	.	.
19	2.29	2.23	2.26	2.27	2.07	2.02	1.73	1.60	.	.
20	24.62	22.88	21.87	21.82	22.11	22.80	23.17	24.85	.	.
21	14.11	14.03	14.11	14.14	14.26	14.36	14.29	14.22	.	.
22	13.51	13.49	13.97	13.37	13.44	13.13	12.72	13.23	.	.
23	1.96	1.87	1.79	1.81	1.87	1.46	1.43	1.37	.	.
24	16.45	15.49	15.87	16.31	16.33	16.48	16.27	17.46	.	.
25	18.20	19.02	19.46	17.90	18.04	18.31	18.10	18.81	.	.
26	24.45	24.64	24.16	24.14	24.10	24.07	23.46	24.36	.	.
27	27.54	28.13	27.95	28.13	28.21	28.82	29.26	30.17	.	.
28	43.84	44.78	44.94	44.19	46.38	47.14	46.76	51.24	.	.
29	55.24	56.48	58.16	60.31	59.32	60.37	61.05	65.84	.	.
30	0.47	0.48	0.51	0.56	0.60	0.58	0.67	0.57	.	.
31	18.26	18.49	17.92	18.31	17.38	17.32	17.56	18.42	.	.
32	19.90	20.30	19.86	17.42	17.19	17.85	17.30	18.46	.	.
33	6.40	6.67	7.18	7.30	7.54	7.76	7.98	8.34	.	.
34	23.72	24.10	25.31	23.81	26.07	27.27	27.03	27.10	.	.
35	4.11	4.28	4.72	5.08	5.54	5.55	9.82	9.43	.	.
36	26.05	25.62	24.94	22.87	22.57	22.26	21.63	22.72	.	.
37	0.53	0.50	0.50	0.51	0.56	0.60	0.67	0.74	.	.

Explanatory notes: see p. 77.

[1] Excl. conscripts on compulsory military service. [2] Persons aged 15 years and over. [3] Prior to 2004: incl. conscripts. [4] 31st Dec. of each year.

Notes explicatives: voir p. 80.

[1] Non compris conscrits ceux du contingent. [2] Personnes âgées de 15 ans et plus. [3] Avant 2004: y compris les conscrits. [4] 31 déc. de chaque année.

Notas explicativas: véase p. 83.

[1] Excl. los conscriptos del servicio obligatorio. [2] Personas de 15 años y más. [3] Antes de 2004: incl. los conscriptos. [4] 31 dic. de cada año.

Paid employment in manufacturing
Thousands

Emploi rémunéré dans les industries manufacturières
Milliers

Empleo remunerado en las industrias manufactureras
Millares

	1999	2000	2001	2002	2003	2004	2005	2006	2007	2008

Austria (DA) [1][2]   Employees - Salariés - Asalariados

Women - Femmes - Mujeres
ISIC 3 - CITI 3 - CIIU 3

	1999	2000	2001	2002	2003	2004	2005	2006	2007	2008
Total	138.26	141.59	141.00	135.54	134.46	135.19	132.93	138.75	.	.
15	25.44	26.08	26.56	26.18	26.60	27.07	26.87	27.83	.	.
16	0.36	0.36	0.35	0.34	0.36	0.34	0.31	0.28	.	.
17	8.26	8.39	7.73	7.29	6.80	6.30	6.00	5.85	.	.
18	8.35	7.72	7.07	6.53	5.84	5.19	5.08	4.75	.	.
19	3.66	3.52	3.58	3.24	2.65	2.52	2.18	1.99	.	.
20	4.59	4.51	4.35	4.30	4.55	4.74	4.70	5.23	.	.
21	2.97	2.99	3.03	3.03	3.15	3.18	3.07	3.05	.	.
22	7.29	7.26	7.70	7.23	7.42	7.43	7.19	7.72	.	.
23	0.44	0.43	0.43	0.43	0.44	0.25	0.25	0.25	.	.
24	6.93	6.84	7.14	7.34	7.40	7.53	7.60	8.75	.	.
25	6.58	7.13	7.19	6.67	6.54	6.64	6.45	6.81	.	.
26	5.76	6.41	6.49	6.47	6.47	6.63	6.64	6.88	.	.
27	3.63	3.71	3.54	3.45	3.46	3.49	3.52	3.62	.	.
28	9.89	10.42	10.49	10.07	10.52	10.52	10.41	11.23	.	.
29	9.78	9.88	10.05	10.31	9.56	9.76	9.92	10.53	.	.
30	0.22	0.26	0.31	0.30	0.39	0.37	0.39	0.33	.	.
31	8.27	8.71	8.00	7.80	7.51	7.71	7.67	7.92	.	.
32	7.83	8.16	7.76	6.63	6.19	6.10	5.75	6.08	.	.
33	3.86	4.24	4.51	4.43	4.57	4.44	4.48	4.82	.	.
34	3.60	3.79	4.18	3.86	4.71	5.17	5.15	5.07	.	.
35	0.59	0.67	0.77	0.85	0.91	0.96	1.09	1.14	.	.
36	9.89	10.09	9.72	8.75	8.35	8.76	8.10	8.50	.	.
37	0.08	0.07	0.07	0.08	0.09	0.10	0.10	0.13	.	.

Belgique (BA) [1][3]   Employees - Salariés - Asalariados

Total - Total - Total
ISIC 3 - CITI 3 - CIIU 3

	1999	2000	2001	2002	2003	2004	2005	2006	2007	2008
Total	.	.	712.2	697.2	672.3	677.2	681.5	667.2	676.5	682.6
15	.	.	91.9	93.1	92.2	94.8	96.5	95.6	90.6	92.5
16	.	.	3.7	2.5	2.1	3.5	1.4	1.9	2.4	2.1
17	.	.	43.7	41.6	35.0	36.9	33.2	33.0	33.1	29.1
18	.	.	11.4	8.9	12.2	9.2	6.7	8.6	7.2	4.5
19	.	.	2.0	2.7	1.4	1.2	1.9	1.5	2.1	2.0
20	.	.	19.7	21.2	18.5	22.0	19.9	20.3	20.0	19.1
21	.	.	15.8	17.4	17.0	14.2	14.9	15.0	16.0	14.6
22	.	.	42.8	37.8	33.3	35.3	35.1	34.4	34.3	36.7
23	.	.	4.1	6.8	7.1	10.2	9.7	9.6	8.8	10.4
24	.	.	82.7	87.2	90.5	92.1	92.2	92.0	96.6	100.9
25	.	.	28.4	29.5	26.5	27.8	25.0	25.9	23.8	27.5
26	.	.	38.3	35.5	33.9	35.3	34.2	30.3	34.1	35.8
27	.	.	47.7	47.7	51.3	43.9	40.8	44.7	45.0	43.3
28	.	.	59.7	59.1	60.5	59.4	66.4	60.1	62.6	69.4
29	.	.	52.9	48.1	42.4	46.0	52.6	49.0	49.6	49.7
30	.	.	8.0	4.0	3.1	4.2	4.2	2.5	5.4	4.9
31	.	.	30.1	24.9	25.0	21.4	24.8	21.7	20.4	19.9
32	.	.	18.7	21.6	16.1	17.4	16.4	13.6	15.5	15.7
33	.	.	9.2	8.6	8.8	8.1	8.4	9.6	11.1	10.7
34	.	.	53.5	51.7	47.9	51.2	52.0	54.1	56.4	56.1
35	.	.	16.9	16.0	20.4	17.5	18.2	18.1	12.9	13.2
36	.	.	26.6	27.0	19.7	19.5	22.3	20.1	23.6	21.0
37	.	.	4.4	4.5	7.5	6.2	4.7	5.7	5.1	3.4

Men - Hommes - Hombres
ISIC 3 - CITI 3 - CIIU 3

	1999	2000	2001	2002	2003	2004	2005	2006	2007	2008
Total	.	.	542.5	527.1	504.0	514.3	513.5	506.6	508.9	519.6
15	.	.	63.3	64.3	56.7	65.2	62.0	64.8	57.5	62.0
16	.	.	1.7	0.9	1.3	2.0	0.4	1.0	0.7	0.9
17	.	.	26.6	22.9	20.3	21.2	17.4	19.4	19.3	17.3
18	.	.	1.9	1.3	2.4	2.1	1.2	2.3	1.2	0.8
19	.	.	1.1	1.4	0.7	0.5	0.8	0.9	1.6	0.8
20	.	.	17.3	19.2	16.5	19.6	18.2	18.9	18.3	17.5
21	.	.	12.2	13.0	12.1	11.2	11.5	11.0	11.8	11.7
22	.	.	26.8	24.1	21.5	23.9	23.2	21.1	21.9	23.7
23	.	.	3.1	5.4	5.4	8.8	8.2	7.5	7.3	8.3
24	.	.	59.0	59.1	62.8	61.4	63.9	63.6	67.2	69.7
25	.	.	23.0	23.1	21.7	23.0	20.1	21.4	18.7	22.5
26	.	.	33.6	31.4	30.2	30.5	30.3	26.5	30.7	31.1
27	.	.	44.5	43.6	46.7	40.9	37.3	41.0	39.7	38.4
28	.	.	51.7	52.0	52.9	50.8	56.3	51.5	54.3	58.8
29	.	.	45.4	41.5	36.6	39.4	44.1	41.8	42.1	44.0
30	.	.	5.8	2.7	1.8	3.2	2.8	2.0	3.9	3.7
31	.	.	22.3	18.2	17.6	15.2	17.4	15.4	14.4	14.8
32	.	.	12.5	14.4	10.9	11.9	11.6	9.3	10.2	10.8
33	.	.	6.3	5.2	6.2	5.4	5.3	5.6	7.0	6.1
34	.	.	46.5	44.6	41.2	41.9	43.9	45.7	48.7	47.8
35	.	.	14.9	14.3	18.4	15.6	16.7	15.9	11.6	10.7
36	.	.	19.7	21.2	13.9	15.4	16.2	15.9	16.5	15.7
37	.	.	3.2	3.4	6.3	5.3	4.1	4.1	4.2	2.7

Explanatory notes: see p. 77.
[1] Persons aged 15 years and over. [2] 31st Dec. of each year. [3] Incl. professional army.

Notes explicatives: voir p. 80.
[1] Personnes âgées de 15 ans et plus. [2] 31 déc. de chaque année. [3] Y compris les militaires de carrière.

Notas explicativas: véase p. 83.
[1] Personas de 15 años y más. [2] 31 dic. de cada año. [3] Incl. los militares profesionales.

EMPLOYMENT — EMPLOI — EMPLEO

Paid employment in manufacturing — Thousands
Emploi rémunéré dans les industries manufacturières — Milliers
Empleo remunerado en las industrias manufactureras — Millares

Belgique (BA) [1] [2] — Employees - Salariés - Asalariados

Women - Femmes - Mujeres — ISIC 3 - CITI 3 - CIIU 3

	1999	2000	2001	2002	2003	2004	2005	2006	2007	2008
Total	.	.	169.7	170.1	168.3	162.9	168.0	160.7	167.7	163.0
15			28.7	28.9	35.5	29.6	34.4	30.8	33.0	30.5
16			2.0	1.6	0.8	1.4	1.0	0.8	1.7	1.3
17			17.1	18.7	14.7	15.7	15.3	13.6	13.8	11.8
18			9.5	7.7	9.8	7.1	5.5	6.3	6.0	3.7
19			1.0	1.3	0.7	0.6	1.1	0.7	0.5	1.2
20			2.4	2.0	2.0	2.4	1.8	1.4	1.7	1.6
21			3.6	4.4	5.0	3.0	3.3	4.0	4.3	2.8
22			16.0	13.7	11.8	11.4	11.9	13.3	12.3	13.0
23			1.0	1.4	1.7	1.4	1.5	2.1	1.4	2.1
24			23.7	28.1	27.7	30.6	28.3	28.4	29.3	31.2
25			5.4	6.3	4.8	4.8	4.9	4.5	5.1	5.0
26			4.6	4.2	3.7	4.9	4.0	3.8	3.4	4.7
27			3.2	4.1	4.6	3.0	3.5	3.7	5.3	4.9
28			8.0	7.1	7.6	8.7	10.1	8.6	8.3	10.6
29			7.5	6.6	5.7	6.6	8.4	7.2	7.5	5.7
30			2.2	1.2	1.3	1.0	1.5	0.5	1.5	1.2
31			7.7	6.6	7.4	6.2	7.4	6.3	6.0	5.1
32			6.2	7.1	5.3	5.5	4.7	4.4	5.3	5.0
33			2.8	3.4	2.6	2.7	3.1	3.9	4.1	4.7
34			7.1	7.1	6.7	9.3	8.1	8.3	7.7	8.3
35			2.0	1.7	2.0	1.8	1.5	2.2	1.3	2.5
36			6.9	5.9	5.7	4.2	6.0	4.3	7.1	5.3
37			1.2	1.1	1.2	0.9	0.7	1.6	1.0	0.8

Bulgaria (DA) — Employees - Salariés - Asalariados

Total - Total - Total — ISIC 3 - CITI 3 - CIIU 3 / ISIC 4 - CITI 4 - CIIU 4 [2] [3]

	1999	2000	2001	2002	2003	2004	2005	2006	2007	2008	ISIC 4
Total	615.8	562.3	562.3	573.9	598.0	606.8	598.1	615.7	627.2	608.2	Total
15	90.6	84.9	83.1	85.1	93.2	94.9	81.3	85.1	87.2	90.6	10
16	11.6	10.3	10.8	11.4	10.3	8.5	17.2	17.4	17.2	16.5	11
17	34.3	31.0	32.8	34.1	34.4	34.7	7.3	6.2	4.8	4.2	12
18	95.5	102.5	117.5	127.1	138.7	144.5	19.9	19.4	19.6	18.6	13
19	19.9	19.0	20.4	19.7	20.3	19.3	148.6	147.0	142.6	133.4	14
20	14.0	13.1	13.6	14.1	15.8	17.1	18.8	19.9	19.6	17.9	15
21	13.4	11.9	10.2	12.2	12.2	11.9	17.9	17.9	18.2	18.4	16
22	10.8	10.8	11.5	12.2	12.7	14.0	12.9	12.1	11.8	12.1	17
23	11.7	10.4	10.3	9.2	-	-	5.2	5.1	6.3	5.9	18
24	39.4	32.5	31.6	27.6	25.4	23.9	16.1	16.6	16.1	16.2	20
25	18.0	16.1	15.6	16.2	18.4	17.9	8.1	8.2	8.0	7.5	21
26	29.3	24.4	22.6	21.7	21.8	22.9	19.4	22.4	24.8	22.9	22
27	49.3	31.5	27.6	23.8	23.2	22.0	25.8	27.9	29.7	30.3	23
28	23.3	23.2	22.4	26.7	30.7	32.2	22.2	22.6	22.2	20.5	24
29	80.3	75.1	69.2	68.6	65.0	63.5	44.4	47.2	51.1	47.6	25
30	3.8	3.3	2.9	1.6	1.5	1.8	11.4	12.5	11.6	10.8	26
31	20.3	17.7	16.7	18.8	18.2	18.2	17.1	18.2	19.9	19.2	27
32	5.9	5.8	6.3	5.4	5.7	5.8	40.3	43.2	43.5	41.9	28
33	7.1	6.4	5.7	5.6	5.2	5.6	4.9	5.8	8.2	10.4	29
34	4.0	3.5	3.4	3.1	2.8	2.7	5.0	5.6	7.0	7.0	30
35	14.0	9.5	9.7	9.4	9.6	10.2	22.7	24.5	26.6	25.4	31
36	19.2	19.2	18.8	20.0	24.2	27.6	18.7	18.7	19.2	19.6	33
37	0.1	0.3	0.3	0.4	-	-					

Men - Hommes - Hombres — ISIC 3 - CITI 3 - CIIU 3 / ISIC 4 - CITI 4 - CIIU 4 [2] [3]

	1999	2000	2001	2002	2003	2004	2005	2006	2007	2008	ISIC 4
Total	305.9	273.6	267.7	270.7	279.7	286.2	285.0	297.8	306.9	.	Total
15	47.5	44.7	42.9	44.4	47.6	48.3	38.8	40.4	41.0	.	10
16	5.3	4.9	5.0	5.1	4.6	4.4	10.3	10.3	10.2	.	11
17	11.2	9.9	10.0	10.4	10.4	11.0	3.7	3.2	2.5	.	12
18	10.6	11.7	13.6	14.5	15.8	17.3	7.4	7.1	7.0	.	13
19	4.6	4.4	4.7	4.5	4.6	4.5	18.0	17.9	16.9	.	14
20	9.3	8.8	9.3	9.9	11.4	12.4	4.4	4.2	3.9	.	15
21	6.7	6.2	5.3	6.5	6.4	6.2	12.9	13.0	13.2	.	16
22	4.8	4.9	5.3	5.7	5.8	6.4	6.7	6.4	6.1	.	17
23	7.8	7.0	7.0	6.4	-	-	2.9	2.7	3.5	.	18
24	21.0	17.6	16.1	14.6	13.5	12.6	9.2	9.6	9.3	.	20
25	9.0	8.3	8.3	8.8	10.4	10.9	3.5	3.5	3.4	.	21
26	19.4	16.2	15.2	15.3	15.5	16.5	11.7	13.9	15.2	.	22
27	33.0	22.5	20.4	17.8	17.4	16.7	19.0	20.8	22.2	.	23
28	15.5	16.3	15.9	19.3	22.7	24.0	17.1	17.4	17.0	.	24
29	55.7	51.3	49.0	48.2	46.6	45.9	30.8	33.3	36.2	.	25
30	1.9	1.7	1.6	0.9	0.8	0.9	5.7	6.2	5.7	.	26
31	11.3	9.9	9.3	10.4	9.9	9.8	10.2	10.7	11.9	.	27
32	2.8	2.8	3.2	2.6	2.8	3.0	30.1	32.5	32.8	.	28
33	3.7	3.2	2.9	3.0	2.7	3.0	2.4	2.6	3.6	.	29
34	3.0	2.7	2.7	2.4	2.2	2.1	4.0	4.5	5.6	.	30
35	10.4	7.3	7.7	7.5	7.7	8.3	15.1	16.5	18.0	.	31
36	11.3	11.4	11.3	12.2	15.0	15.0	14.4	14.8	15.5	.	33
37	0.1	0.2	0.2	0.3	-	-					

Explanatory notes: see p. 77.
Notes explicatives: voir p. 80.
Notas explicativas: véase p. 83.

[1] Incl. professional army. [2] Persons aged 15 years and over. [3] Excl. conscripts.
[1] Y compris les militaires de carrière. [2] Personnes âgées de 15 ans et plus. [3] Non compris les conscrits.
[1] Incl. los militares profesionales. [2] Personas de 15 años y más. [3] Excl. los conscriptos.

EMPLOYMENT — EMPLOI — EMPLEO

Paid employment in manufacturing — Thousands
Emploi rémunéré dans les industries manufacturières — Milliers
Empleo remunerado en las industrias manufactureras — Millares

Bulgaria (DA)

Employees - Salariés - Asalariados

Women - Femmes - Mujeres
ISIC 3 - CITI 3 - CIIU 3   ISIC 4 - CITI 4 - CIIU 4 [1][2]

ISIC 3	1999	2000	2001	2002	2003	2004		2005	2006	2007	2008	ISIC 4
Total	309.9	288.7	294.5	303.2	318.2	320.6	|	313.1	317.9	320.3	.	Total
15	43.1	40.2	40.1	40.7	45.6	46.6	|	42.5	44.7	46.2	.	10
16	6.3	5.4	5.8	6.3	5.6	4.1	|	6.9	7.1	7.1	.	11
17	23.1	21.1	22.0	23.6	24.0	23.8	|	3.6	3.0	2.3	.	12
18	84.9	90.8	104.0	112.7	123.0	127.2	|	12.5	12.3	12.6	.	13
19	15.3	14.6	15.7	15.2	15.7	14.9	|	130.6	129.1	125.7	.	14
20	4.7	4.3	4.3	4.2	4.5	4.7	|	14.4	15.7	15.7	.	15
21	6.7	5.8	4.9	5.8	5.7	5.7	|	5.0	4.9	5.0	.	16
22	6.0	5.9	6.2	6.5	6.9	7.6	|	6.1	5.7	5.8	.	17
23	3.9	3.4	3.3	2.8	-	-	|	2.3	2.4	2.9	.	18
24	18.4	15.0	14.7	13.0	12.0	11.4	|	6.9	7.0	6.8	.	20
25	9.0	7.8	7.4	7.4	8.1	7.1	|	4.6	4.7	4.6	.	21
26	9.9	8.2	7.4	6.3	6.3	6.3	|	7.7	8.5	9.6	.	22
27	16.3	9.0	7.2	6.0	5.8	5.3	|	6.9	7.1	7.5	.	23
28	7.8	7.0	6.5	7.4	8.0	8.2	|	5.2	5.2	5.2	.	24
29	24.6	23.9	20.2	20.4	18.5	17.6	|	13.6	13.9	15.0	.	25
30	1.9	1.6	1.3	0.7	0.7	0.9	|	5.7	6.3	6.0	.	26
31	9.0	7.8	7.4	8.4	8.3	8.3	|	6.9	7.4	8.0	.	27
32	3.1	3.0	3.1	2.7	3.0	2.7	|	10.2	10.7	10.7	.	28
33	3.4	3.2	2.8	2.6	2.4	2.7	|	2.5	3.2	4.6	.	29
34	1.0	0.9	0.7	0.7	0.6	0.6	|	1.0	1.1	1.4	.	30
35	3.6	2.2	2.0	1.9	1.9	1.9	|	7.6	8.0	8.6	.	31
36	7.9	7.8	7.5	7.8	9.2	10.8	|	4.3	4.0	3.8	.	33
37	0.0	0.1	0.1	0.1	-	-	|					

Croatia (DA)

Employees - Salariés - Asalariados

Total - Total - Total
ISIC 3 - CITI 3 - CIIU 3

ISIC 3	1999	2000	2001	2002	2003	2004	2005	2006	2007	2008
Total	285.2	277.9	275.9	273.6	276.6	276.7	274.3	279.6	289.2	290.3
15	49.4	49.6	51.7	52.4	54.0	53.7	52.6	54.0	54.9	55.0
16	1.5	1.3	1.3	1.1	1.1	1.3	1.2	1.0	0.9	0.8
17	12.6	12.3	10.8	10.4	9.9	9.3	8.8	8.9	9.1	8.6
18	33.1	31.8	31.5	29.8	29.1	28.6	27.1	25.1	23.5	22.3
19	12.2	11.9	10.8	9.8	9.0	8.2	7.8	7.8	8.6	9.0
20	14.3	13.6	15.6	15.0	15.2	15.5	15.4	15.8	16.7	16.6
21	6.1	6.0	5.9	5.7	5.8	5.4	5.1	5.1	4.9	4.6
22	12.7	12.3	12.2	12.0	12.0	13.6	13.7	14.0	15.0	15.2
23	4.5	4.5	4.5	4.3	4.2	4.0	4.0	3.8	3.7	3.6
24	16.6	16.0	14.7	13.8	13.4	12.1	11.7	12.1	12.3	13.1
25	9.1	8.2	8.2	8.1	8.3	8.4	8.4	8.7	9.2	9.8
26	14.8	14.7	14.3	14.5	15.1	15.5	15.6	15.8	16.2	15.7
27	8.7	8.3	7.7	8.3	7.7	7.3	7.2	7.2	7.0	7.0
28	20.8	20.4	21.4	22.7	25.1	25.9	26.4	28.7	31.8	33.2
29	14.5	12.7	11.8	11.2	11.9	12.2	12.8	13.5	14.5	14.6
30	1.5	1.3	1.5	1.7	1.9	2.0	2.0	2.2	2.2	2.3
31	11.2	11.4	11.5	10.9	10.8	11.6	11.3	11.7	11.4	10.9
32	4.3	4.9	3.3	3.2	3.2	3.6	4.2	4.5	5.3	4.5
33	2.4	2.3	1.8	2.0	2.0	2.1	2.3	2.3	2.4	2.6
34	2.8	2.6	3.0	2.9	3.1	3.0	3.0	3.1	3.7	3.7
35	17.4	17.2	18.1	19.2	18.9	19.1	19.5	19.4	18.8	20.4
36	13.6	13.5	13.2	13.4	12.8	12.9	12.9	13.2	14.1	14.3
37	1.1	1.1	1.1	1.2	1.3	1.4	1.5	1.7	2.1	2.5

Men - Hommes - Hombres
ISIC 3 - CITI 3 - CIIU 3

ISIC 3	1999	2000	2001	2002	2003	2004	2005	2006	2007	2008
Total	166.0	162.5	162.8	164.6	167.7	168.8	168.4	173.0	179.3	180.5
15	28.3	28.5	29.7	29.9	30.6	30.3	29.3	29.7	29.9	29.3
16	0.8	0.7	0.7	0.6	0.6	0.7	0.7	0.6	0.6	0.5
17	4.1	3.9	3.3	3.3	2.9	2.7	2.4	2.3	2.3	2.1
18	4.2	4.0	4.0	3.8	3.8	3.7	3.6	3.2	2.9	2.9
19	3.4	3.3	2.4	2.3	2.1	1.8	1.7	1.6	1.6	1.8
20	9.6	9.2	11.3	11.0	11.2	11.5	11.3	11.6	12.2	12.0
21	3.8	3.9	3.8	3.8	3.9	3.5	3.4	3.4	3.3	3.1
22	6.7	6.6	6.5	6.4	6.7	7.1	7.0	7.2	7.7	7.8
23	3.4	3.3	3.4	3.1	3.0	2.8	2.7	2.6	2.5	2.4
24	10.0	9.6	8.8	8.1	7.8	7.2	7.0	7.3	7.3	7.8
25	5.8	5.3	5.4	5.6	5.8	5.8	5.9	6.2	6.5	6.9
26	11.5	11.5	11.1	11.5	11.9	12.4	12.4	12.5	12.8	12.4
27	7.3	7.0	6.5	6.8	6.3	6.0	5.9	5.9	5.8	5.8
28	16.9	16.7	18.0	19.3	21.6	22.3	22.7	24.8	27.7	28.9
29	11.8	10.5	9.8	9.4	10.1	10.3	10.8	11.4	12.2	12.3
30	1.0	0.9	1.0	1.2	1.4	1.4	1.5	1.6	1.7	1.8
31	6.8	7.0	7.1	6.9	6.9	7.6	7.6	7.9	7.6	7.3
32	2.3	2.7	2.0	1.9	1.9	2.0	2.3	2.4	2.7	2.5
33	1.6	1.5	1.0	1.1	1.0	1.1	1.2	1.2	1.3	1.3
34	2.0	1.9	1.8	1.8	2.1	2.0	2.0	2.1	2.5	2.5
35	15.4	15.2	16.1	17.2	17.0	17.2	17.6	17.5	17.8	18.2
36	8.5	8.4	8.3	8.6	8.1	8.3	8.3	8.6	9.0	9.1
37	0.8	0.9	0.9	1.0	1.0	1.1	1.2	1.3	1.5	1.8

Explanatory notes: see p. 77.
[1] Persons aged 15 years and over. [2] Excl. conscripts.

Notes explicatives: voir p. 80.
[1] Personnes âgées de 15 ans et plus. [2] Non compris les conscrits.

Notas explicativas: véase p. 83.
[1] Personas de 15 años y más. [2] Excl. los conscriptos.

EMPLOYMENT	EMPLOI	EMPLEO
Paid employment in manufacturing	Emploi rémunéré dans les industries manufacturières	Empleo remunerado en las industrias manufactureras
Thousands	Milliers	Millares

	1999	2000	2001	2002	2003	2004	2005	2006	2007	2008
Croatia (DA)					Employees - Salariés - Asalariados					
Women - Femmes - Mujeres										
ISIC 3 - CITI 3 - CIIU 3										
Total	119.2	115.4	113.1	109.0	108.9	107.9	105.9	106.7	109.9	109.8
15	21.1	21.1	22.0	22.5	23.4	23.4	23.3	24.4	25.0	25.7
16	0.7	0.6	0.6	0.5	0.5	0.6	0.5	0.4	0.3	0.3
17	8.5	8.4	7.5	7.1	7.0	6.6	6.4	6.6	6.8	6.5
18	28.9	27.8	27.5	26.0	25.3	24.9	23.5	21.9	20.6	19.4
19	8.8	8.6	8.4	7.5	6.9	6.4	6.1	6.2	7.0	7.2
20	4.7	4.4	4.3	4.0	4.0	4.0	4.1	4.2	4.5	4.6
21	2.3	2.1	2.1	1.9	1.9	1.9	1.7	1.7	1.6	1.5
22	6.0	5.7	5.7	5.6	6.1	6.5	6.7	6.8	7.3	7.4
23	1.1	1.2	1.2	1.2	1.2	1.2	1.3	1.2	1.2	1.2
24	6.6	6.4	5.9	5.7	5.6	4.9	4.6	4.8	5.0	5.3
25	3.3	2.9	2.8	2.5	2.5	2.6	2.5	2.5	2.7	2.9
26	3.3	3.2	3.2	3.0	3.2	3.1	3.2	3.3	3.3	3.3
27	1.4	1.3	1.2	1.5	1.4	1.3	1.3	1.2	1.2	1.2
28	3.9	3.7	3.4	3.4	3.5	3.6	3.6	3.9	4.1	4.3
29	2.7	2.2	2.0	1.8	1.8	1.9	2.0	2.2	2.3	2.3
30	0.5	0.4	0.5	0.5	0.5	0.6	0.6	0.6	0.6	0.5
31	4.4	4.4	4.4	4.0	3.9	4.0	3.7	3.7	3.8	3.6
32	2.0	2.2	1.3	1.3	1.3	1.6	1.8	2.1	2.6	2.0
33	0.8	0.8	0.8	0.9	1.0	1.0	1.0	1.1	1.2	1.3
34	0.8	0.7	1.2	1.1	1.0	1.0	1.0	1.0	1.2	1.2
35	2.0	2.0	2.0	2.0	1.9	1.9	1.9	1.9	2.0	2.2
36	5.1	5.1	4.9	4.8	4.7	4.6	4.6	4.6	5.1	5.2
37	0.3	0.2	0.2	0.2	0.3	0.3	0.3	0.4	0.6	0.7
Cyprus (BA) [1] [2] [3]					Employees - Salariés - Asalariados					
Total - Total - Total										
ISIC 3 - CITI 3 - CIIU 3										
Total	29.5	27.3	31.2	30.8	28.5	29.3	30.9	29.7	29.8	37.5
15	8.3	7.9	9.8	8.9	8.8	10.5	10.8	10.5	10.9	12.1
16	0.2	0.7	0.5	0.6	0.5	0.3	0.1	0.0	0.1	0.1
17	0.9	0.7	0.3	0.5	0.3	0.2	0.3	0.4	0.3	0.6
18	2.7	3.2	3.2	2.4	1.5	1.3	1.2	0.8	0.9	1.1
19	1.4	1.0	1.0	0.9	0.6	0.5	0.5	0.5	0.3	0.1
20	1.6	1.5	1.5	1.3	1.2	1.6	2.0	1.8	2.0	3.6
21	0.8	0.4	0.3	0.4	0.7	0.8	0.5	0.3	0.4	0.3
22	1.6	1.3	1.8	2.7	2.3	2.1	2.4	2.1	1.9	2.7
23	0.1	0.2	0.2	0.3	0.5	0.4	0.1	-	0.0	-
24	1.0	1.4	1.4	1.7	2.0	2.2	2.2	1.8	1.7	2.1
25	1.3	1.1	1.3	1.1	0.9	0.8	1.3	1.1	1.5	1.3
26	2.5	2.2	2.3	2.2	1.9	2.2	3.2	3.4	3.3	3.2
27	-	0.2	0.3	0.1	0.3	0.2	0.2	0.1	0.0	-
28	2.4	1.9	2.2	3.6	3.0	2.5	2.7	2.8	3.1	5.2
29	0.3	0.5	0.3	0.4	0.6	0.6	0.9	0.7	0.4	0.2
30	-	-	0.1	-	-	-	-	-	-	-
31	0.5	0.3	0.3	0.3	0.4	0.8	0.1	0.2	0.1	0.4
32	-	-	-	-	-	-	-	0.0	0.1	-
33	0.2	0.2	0.1	0.1	0.4	0.2	0.1	0.3	0.2	0.2
34	0.3	0.3	0.3	0.3	-	-	0.0	-	0.1	0.2
35	0.2	-	-	0.1	-	0.2	0.2	0.1	0.1	0.2
36	3.3	2.9	3.5	2.8	2.7	2.4	2.3	2.9	2.5	3.7
37	-	-	-	0.1	0.1	0.1	-	0.0	0.1	0.0
Men - Hommes - Hombres										
ISIC 3 - CITI 3 - CIIU 3										
Total	17.8	16.4	18.6	18.3	16.6	17.4	19.7	18.9	19.3	25.1
15	5.0	5.1	5.8	5.5	5.1	6.0	6.1	5.7	5.6	6.4
16	0.2	0.2	0.2	0.3	0.1	0.1	-	0.0	-	-
17	0.3	0.2	0.1	0.3	0.1	0.1	0.2	0.2	0.1	0.3
18	0.3	0.6	0.4	0.3	-	0.0	0.1	0.1	0.0	0.2
19	0.4	0.3	0.6	0.7	0.3	0.2	0.3	0.3	0.2	0.1
20	1.6	1.5	1.4	1.3	1.1	1.5	1.8	1.5	1.7	3.2
21	0.6	0.2	0.1	-	0.2	0.2	0.2	0.2	0.3	0.2
22	0.8	0.6	1.0	1.1	1.2	1.2	1.4	0.9	0.9	1.5
23	0.1	0.2	0.1	0.2	0.4	0.3	0.1	-	0.0	-
24	0.4	0.6	0.8	0.7	0.6	0.6	1.0	0.8	0.8	1.5
25	0.8	0.7	1.0	0.7	0.6	0.6	0.9	0.6	1.1	1.0
26	1.7	1.8	1.6	1.6	1.4	1.6	2.6	2.7	2.7	2.7
27	-	0.2	0.2	0.1	0.3	0.2	0.2	0.1	0.0	-
28	2.1	1.6	1.8	2.9	2.4	2.1	2.4	2.5	2.7	4.5
29	0.3	0.4	0.2	0.2	0.4	0.4	0.6	0.6	0.4	0.2
30	-	-	0.1	-	-	-	-	-	-	-
31	0.2	0.1	0.1	0.2	0.3	0.2	0.1	0.1	0.0	0.3
32	-	-	-	-	-	-	-	0.0	0.1	-
33	0.1	0.1	-	0.1	0.3	0.1	0.1	0.2	0.2	0.2
34	0.1	0.1	0.2	0.1	-	-	-	-	0.1	0.1
35	0.2	-	-	0.1	-	0.2	-	0.2	0.1	0.1
36	2.5	2.1	2.7	1.8	1.6	1.7	1.6	2.3	2.0	2.9
37	-	-	-	0.1	0.1	0.1	-	0.0	0.1	0.0

Explanatory notes: see p. 77.

[1] Incl. armed forces, Excl. conscripts. [2] Government-controlled area. [3] Persons aged 15 years and over.

Notes explicatives: voir p. 80.

[1] Y compris les forces armées, Excl. conscrits [2] Région sous contrôle gouvernemental. [3] Personnes âgées de 15 ans et plus.

Notas explicativas: véase p. 83.

[1] Incl. las fuerzas armadas, excl. los conscriptos. [2] Area controlada por el gobierno. [3] Personas de 15 años y más.

Paid employment in manufacturing — Thousands

Emploi rémunéré dans les industries manufacturières — Milliers

Empleo remunerado en las industrias manufactureras — Millares

	1999	2000	2001	2002	2003	2004	2005	2006	2007	2008
Cyprus (BA) [1][2][3]				Employees - Salariés - Asalariados						
Women - Femmes - Mujeres										
ISIC 3 - CITI 3 - CIIU 3										
Total	11.7	10.8	12.5	12.5	11.9	12.0	11.2	10.8	10.5	12.4
15	3.3	2.8	4.0	3.3	3.7	4.5	4.7	4.8	5.2	5.9
16	-	0.1	0.3	0.3	0.4	0.2	0.1	0.0	0.1	0.1
17	0.6	0.5	0.2	0.2	0.1	0.1	0.1	0.2	0.2	0.3
18	2.3	2.6	2.8	2.1	1.5	1.3	1.1	0.6	0.8	1.0
19	1.0	0.7	0.4	0.3	0.3	0.3	0.2	0.2	0.1	0.0
20	0.1	-	0.1	0.1	0.1	0.1	0.2	0.3	0.2	0.4
21	0.2	0.2	0.3	0.4	0.5	0.6	0.3	0.2	0.1	0.1
22	0.7	0.7	1.0	1.6	1.1	0.8	1.0	1.2	1.0	1.3
23	-	-	0.1	0.1	0.1	0.1	0.0	-	-	-
24	0.6	0.8	0.6	1.1	1.4	1.5	1.2	1.0	0.9	0.7
25	0.5	0.4	0.5	0.4	0.3	0.2	0.4	0.5	0.4	0.2
26	0.8	0.4	0.7	0.5	0.5	0.7	0.6	0.8	0.6	0.6
27	-	-	0.1	-	-	0.0	-	-	-	-
28	0.3	0.3	0.4	0.7	0.6	0.4	0.3	0.3	0.3	0.7
29	0.1	0.1	0.1	0.2	0.2	0.2	0.2	0.1	-	-
30	.	.	.	.	.	.	.	.	.	.
31	0.2	0.2	0.2	0.1	0.1	0.0	0.0	0.1	0.0	0.1
32	.	.	.	.	.	.	.	.	.	.
33	0.1	0.1	0.1	.	0.1	0.1	0.0	0.1	0.1	0.0
34	0.2	0.1	0.1	0.2	-	-	0.0	-	0.0	0.1
35	.	.	.	.	.	.	.	.	.	0.1
36	0.7	0.8	0.8	1.0	1.1	0.7	0.7	0.6	0.5	0.8
37	.	.	.	.	.	.	.	.	.	-
Czech Republic (BA) [3]				Employees - Salariés - Asalariados						
Total - Total - Total										
ISIC 3 - CITI 3 - CIIU 3										
Total	1 212	1 192	1 213	1 216	1 189	1 175	1 197	1 254	1 295	1 324
15	133	123	128	132	130	126	119	120	115	113
16	2	1	1	2	1	1	1	1	1	1
17	74	79	76	72	66	63	62	57	53	47
18	47	41	37	36	36	25	23	26	25	22
19	24	25	18	15	13	11	9	9	9	7
20	52	52	48	55	52	49	47	48	50	47
21	26	25	21	26	24	23	26	25	24	21
22	31	30	33	33	33	33	32	37	40	38
23	6	7	7	7	3	3	5	5	4	3
24	48	48	46	46	44	48	45	47	47	50
25	49	52	61	66	70	71	71	71	81	81
26	75	79	75	71	75	65	68	65	65	71
27	91	85	85	81	74	74	68	71	67	73
28	123	126	133	143	149	147	161	172	179	180
29	159	139	137	132	129	122	129	130	128	150
30	5	7	10	10	9	9	12	17	22	20
31	63	63	66	68	64	64	73	76	89	98
32	32	34	38	36	35	35	33	41	41	42
33	16	16	21	15	12	15	21	20	24	23
34	62	74	70	79	85	99	102	128	141	151
35	21	20	22	19	20	19	19	23	20	22
36	68	62	73	64	60	66	65	59	63	58
37	6	6	7	7	5	7	6	5	8	8
Men - Hommes - Hombres										
ISIC 3 - CITI 3 - CIIU 3										
Total	718	715	734	738	717	709	734	771	807	830
15	65	60	64	62	64	62	58	60	55	53
16	1	1	1	2	1	1	1	1	1	1
17	21	22	26	23	18	17	18	18	18	16
18	5	4	4	3	3	2	2	3	2	2
19	8	6	4	5	3	3	3	2	3	2
20	41	40	36	42	41	38	36	38	41	36
21	14	15	11	15	13	13	15	14	13	11
22	15	16	16	16	16	16	15	20	22	21
23	5	6	6	5	3	2	4	4	3	2
24	28	27	28	27	28	27	24	24	26	28
25	30	29	34	39	43	45	45	43	50	49
26	46	47	48	46	45	36	40	40	43	47
27	71	68	69	63	58	60	55	58	57	61
28	94	96	103	113	117	111	123	131	138	138
29	118	105	104	102	95	92	99	103	100	113
30	3	5	7	6	6	5	8	11	14	13
31	33	33	35	34	33	33	40	38	47	49
32	14	15	16	16	15	14	15	19	19	20
33	8	8	9	7	6	7	9	9	12	11
34	41	53	48	52	56	67	67	80	88	97
35	16	17	17	15	15	15	16	20	16	18
36	38	38	44	38	35	37	38	34	34	32
37	4	5	5	5	3	5	4	5	6	7

Explanatory notes: see p. 77.

[1] Incl. armed forces, Excl. conscripts. [2] Government-controlled area. [3] Persons aged 15 years and over.

Notes explicatives: voir p. 80.

[1] Y compris les forces armées, Excl. conscrits [2] Région sous contrôle gouvernemental. [3] Personnes âgées de 15 ans et plus.

Notas explicativas: véase p. 83.

[1] Incl. las fuerzas armadas, excl. los conscriptos. [2] Area controlada por el gobierno. [3] Personas de 15 años y más.

2F

EMPLOYMENT	EMPLOI	EMPLEO
Paid employment in manufacturing	Emploi rémunéré dans les industries manufacturières	Empleo remunerado en las industrias manufactureras
Thousands	Milliers	Millares

	1999	2000	2001	2002	2003	2004	2005	2006	2007	2008
Czech Republic (BA) [1]				Employees - Salariés - Asalariados						
Women - Femmes - Mujeres										
ISIC 3 - CITI 3 - CIIU 3										
Total	495	477	479	478	472	466	463	483	489	494
15	68	62	64	70	66	65	61	60	60	59
16	1	-	-	1	-	-	-	-	-	0
17	53	57	50	50	47	46	44	39	35	32
18	43	37	34	33	33	24	21	23	23	20
19	16	18	14	11	10	7	6	7	7	5
20	12	12	12	13	11	11	11	11	9	10
21	12	10	10	11	11	10	11	12	11	10
22	16	14	17	17	18	16	16	18	18	17
23	2	2	2	2	1	1	1	1	1	1
24	19	20	19	19	16	21	21	24	21	23
25	19	23	27	26	27	26	27	28	31	31
26	30	31	28	25	30	29	27	25	22	24
27	20	17	17	18	16	14	12	13	10	12
28	30	30	29	30	33	36	38	41	41	42
29	41	34	34	30	34	30	31	27	28	36
30	1	2	3	4	3	4	4	6	8	6
31	30	30	30	34	31	31	33	38	42	48
32	18	20	22	20	20	21	18	22	22	22
33	8	8	11	8	6	7	12	11	13	12
34	21	21	22	27	29	32	36	48	53	54
35	6	4	5	4	5	4	4	4	3	4
36	30	24	30	25	25	29	27	26	29	25
37	1	1	1	2	1	2	1	1	1	1
Czech Republic (DA) [2] [3]				Employees - Salariés - Asalariados						
Total - Total - Total										
ISIC 3 - CITI 3 - CIIU 3										
Total	804.0	796.0	812.0	790.0	782.0	779.0	787.0	797.0	811.0	
15	97.0	88.0	90.0	88.0	88.0	85.0	82.0	79.0	76.0	
17	54.0	50.0	51.0	46.0	43.0	39.0	36.0	34.0	30.0	
18	34.0	33.0	32.0	29.0	25.0	22.0	19.0	17.0	15.0	
19	18.0	16.0	14.0	11.0	9.0	8.0	7.0	7.0	6.0	
20	28.0	25.0	24.0	23.0	23.0	22.0	22.0	22.0	21.0	
21	14.0	14.0	13.0	14.0	14.0	13.0	14.0	13.0	13.0	
22	12.0	13.0	13.0	12.0	12.0	13.0	13.0	13.0	14.0	
23	3.0	3.0	3.0	2.0	2.0	2.0	2.0	2.0	2.0	
24	26.0	25.0	24.0	24.0	25.0	23.0	24.0	23.0	23.0	
25	33.0	36.0	40.0	43.0	47.0	50.0	52.0	57.0	60.0	
26	53.0	56.0	59.0	58.0	55.0	52.0	51.0	50.0	49.0	
27	62.0	55.0	53.0	48.0	46.0	45.0	44.0	43.0	44.0	
28	80.0	77.0	77.0	75.0	73.0	77.0	81.0	83.0	88.0	
29	95.0	90.0	90.0	90.0	92.0	91.0	95.0	101.0	106.0	
30	1.0	2.0	4.0	4.0	5.0	6.0	5.0	6.0	4.0	
31	51.0	56.0	62.0	62.0	64.0	67.0	71.0	70.0	72.0	
32	17.0	22.0	22.0	18.0	18.0	19.0	17.0	18.0	23.0	
33	12.0	14.0	15.0	14.0	14.0	15.0	16.0	18.0	16.0	
34	46.0	56.0	62.0	66.0	68.0	73.0	79.0	86.0	93.0	
35	16.0	14.0	15.0	15.0	13.0	12.0	13.0	13.0	14.0	
36	47.0	45.0	47.0	45.0	42.0	41.0	40.0	39.0	39.0	
Men - Hommes - Hombres										
ISIC 3 - CITI 3 - CIIU 3										
Total	477.0	470.0	480.0	468.0	467.0	468.0	477.0	487.0	502.0	
15	49.0	44.0	45.0	43.0	44.0	42.0	40.0	38.0	36.0	
17	17.0	16.0	16.0	14.0	13.0	13.0	11.0	11.0	11.0	
18	3.0	3.0	3.0	3.0	2.0	2.0	1.0	1.0	1.0	
19	5.0	3.0	3.0	2.0	2.0	2.0	2.0	2.0	1.0	
20	20.0	18.0	18.0	17.0	17.0	16.0	16.0	16.0	15.0	
21	8.0	7.0	7.0	9.0	8.0	8.0	8.0	8.0	8.0	
22	6.0	7.0	6.0	6.0	6.0	7.0	7.0	7.0	8.0	
23	2.0	2.0	2.0	2.0	2.0	1.0	2.0	2.0	2.0	
24	17.0	16.0	16.0	15.0	16.0	13.0	14.0	13.0	13.0	
25	19.0	21.0	24.0	25.0	28.0	29.0	30.0	33.0	35.0	
26	35.0	40.0	40.0	38.0	36.0	36.0	35.0	34.0	34.0	
27	51.0	45.0	45.0	40.0	39.0	38.0	38.0	37.0	38.0	
28	61.0	59.0	60.0	59.0	57.0	60.0	64.0	65.0	69.0	
29	76.0	73.0	72.0	73.0	75.0	75.0	77.0	82.0	85.0	
30	-	1.0	2.0	2.0	2.0	2.0	2.0	2.0	2.0	
31	25.0	27.0	29.0	28.0	28.0	29.0	32.0	32.0	34.0	
32	7.0	8.0	8.0	7.0	7.0	7.0	6.0	6.0	9.0	
33	6.0	7.0	6.0	6.0	6.0	6.0	6.0	8.0	7.0	
34	31.0	37.0	40.0	41.0	44.0	47.0	51.0	57.0	60.0	
35	13.0	11.0	12.0	12.0	11.0	10.0	11.0	11.0	11.0	
36	22.0	22.0	24.0	23.0	21.0	22.0	21.0	20.0	21.0	

Explanatory notes: see p. 77.

[1] Persons aged 15 years and over. [2] Wage earners. [3] Enterprises with 20 or more employees.

Notes explicatives: voir p. 80.

[1] Personnes âgées de 15 ans et plus. [2] Ouvriers. [3] Entreprises occupant 20 salariés et plus.

Notas explicativas: véase p. 83.

[1] Personas de 15 años y más. [2] Obreros. [3] Empresas con 20 y más asalariados.

EMPLOYMENT — EMPLOI — EMPLEO

Paid employment in manufacturing / Emploi rémunéré dans les industries manufacturières / Empleo remunerado en las industrias manufactureras

Thousands — Milliers — Millares

	1999	2000	2001	2002	2003	2004	2005	2006	2007	2008
Czech Republic (DA) [1][2]				Employees - Salariés - Asalariados						
Women - Femmes - Mujeres										
ISIC 3 - CITI 3 - CIIU 3										
Total	327.0	326.0	332.0	322.0	315.0	311.0	310.0	310.0	309.0	.
15	48.0	44.0	45.0	45.0	44.0	43.0	42.0	41.0	40.0	.
17	37.0	34.0	35.0	32.0	30.0	26.0	25.0	23.0	19.0	.
18	31.0	30.0	29.0	26.0	23.0	20.0	18.0	16.0	14.0	.
19	13.0	13.0	10.0	9.0	7.0	6.0	5.0	5.0	5.0	.
20	8.0	7.0	6.0	6.0	6.0	6.0	6.0	6.0	6.0	.
21	6.0	6.0	6.0	5.0	6.0	5.0	6.0	5.0	5.0	.
22	6.0	6.0	7.0	6.0	6.0	6.0	6.0	6.0	6.0	.
23	1.0	1.0	1.0	-	-	1.0	-	-	-	.
24	9.0	8.0	8.0	9.0	9.0	10.0	10.0	10.0	10.0	.
25	14.0	15.0	16.0	18.0	19.0	21.0	22.0	24.0	25.0	.
26	18.0	19.0	19.0	20.0	19.0	16.0	16.0	16.0	15.0	.
27	11.0	10.0	8.0	8.0	7.0	7.0	6.0	6.0	6.0	.
28	19.0	18.0	17.0	16.0	16.0	17.0	17.0	18.0	19.0	.
29	19.0	17.0	18.0	17.0	17.0	16.0	18.0	19.0	21.0	.
30	1.0	1.0	3.0	2.0	3.0	4.0	3.0	4.0	2.0	.
31	26.0	32.0	33.0	34.0	36.0	38.0	39.0	38.0	38.0	.
32	10.0	13.0	14.0	11.0	11.0	12.0	11.0	12.0	14.0	.
33	6.0	7.0	9.0	8.0	8.0	9.0	10.0	10.0	9.0	.
34	15.0	19.0	22.0	25.0	24.0	26.0	28.0	29.0	33.0	.
35	3.0	3.0	3.0	3.0	2.0	2.0	2.0	2.0	3.0	.
36	25.0	23.0	23.0	22.0	21.0	19.0	19.0	19.0	18.0	.
Czech Republic (DA) [1][2]				Wage earners - Ouvriers - Obreros						
Total - Total - Total										
ISIC 3 - CITI 3 - CIIU 3										
Total	804	796	812	790	782	779	783	795	.	.
15	97	88	90	88	88	85	82	79	.	.
17	54	50	51	46	43	39	36	34	.	.
18	34	33	32	29	25	22	19	17	.	.
19	18	16	14	11	9	8	7	7	.	.
20	28	25	24	23	23	22	22	22	.	.
21	14	14	13	14	14	13	14	14	.	.
22	12	13	13	12	12	13	13	13	.	.
23	3	3	3	2	2	2	2	2	.	.
24	26	25	24	24	25	23	24	23	.	.
25	33	36	40	43	47	50	52	56	.	.
26	53	56	59	58	55	52	51	50	.	.
27	62	55	53	48	46	45	44	43	.	.
28	80	77	77	75	73	77	81	85	.	.
29	95	90	90	90	92	91	95	98	.	.
30	1	2	4	4	5	6	5	6	.	.
31	51	56	62	62	64	67	71	71	.	.
32	17	22	22	18	18	19	17	18	.	.
33	12	14	15	14	14	15	16	17	.	.
34	46	56	62	66	68	73	79	84	.	.
35	16	14	15	15	13	12	13	13	.	.
36	47	45	47	45	42	41	40	40	.	.
37	-	-	-	-	-	-	-	-	.	.
Men - Hommes - Hombres										
ISIC 3 - CITI 3 - CIIU 3										
Total	477	470	480	468	467	468	474	486	.	.
15	49	44	45	43	44	42	40	38	.	.
17	17	16	16	14	13	13	11	11	.	.
18	3	3	3	3	2	2	1	1	.	.
19	5	3	3	2	2	2	2	2	.	.
20	20	18	18	17	17	16	16	16	.	.
21	8	7	7	9	8	8	8	8	.	.
22	6	7	6	6	6	7	7	7	.	.
23	2	2	2	2	2	1	2	2	.	.
24	17	16	16	15	16	13	14	14	.	.
25	19	21	24	25	28	29	30	33	.	.
26	35	40	40	38	36	36	35	34	.	.
27	51	45	45	40	39	38	38	37	.	.
28	61	59	60	59	57	60	64	66	.	.
29	76	73	72	73	75	75	77	80	.	.
30	-	1	2	2	2	2	2	2	.	.
31	25	27	29	28	28	29	32	33	.	.
32	7	8	8	7	7	7	6	6	.	.
33	6	7	6	6	6	6	6	7	.	.
34	31	37	40	41	44	47	51	55	.	.
35	13	11	12	12	11	10	11	11	.	.
36	22	22	24	23	21	22	21	21	.	.
37	-	-	-	-	-	-	-	-	.	.

Explanatory notes: see p. 77. Notes explicatives: voir p. 80. Notas explicativas: véase p. 83.

[1] Wage earners. [2] Enterprises with 20 or more employees. [1] Ouvriers. [2] Entreprises occupant 20 salariés et plus. [1] Obreros. [2] Empresas con 20 y más asalariados.

EMPLOYMENT	EMPLOI	EMPLEO
Paid employment in manufacturing	**Emploi rémunéré dans les industries manufacturières**	**Empleo remunerado en las industrias manufactureras**
Thousands	Milliers	Millares

Czech Republic (DA) [1][2] — **Wage earners - Ouvriers - Obreros**

Women - Femmes - Mujeres
ISIC 3 - CITI 3 - CIIU 3

	1999	2000	2001	2002	2003	2004	2005	2006	2007	2008
Total	327	326	332	322	315	311	310	309	.	.
15	48	44	45	45	44	43	42	41	.	.
17	37	34	35	32	30	26	25	23	.	.
18	31	30	29	26	23	20	18	16	.	.
19	13	13	10	9	7	6	5	5	.	.
20	8	7	6	6	6	6	6	6	.	.
21	6	6	6	5	6	5	6	6	.	.
22	6	6	7	6	6	6	6	6	.	.
23	1	1	1	-	-	1	-	-	.	.
24	9	8	8	9	9	10	10	9	.	.
25	14	15	16	18	19	21	22	23	.	.
26	18	19	19	20	19	16	16	16	.	.
27	11	10	8	8	7	7	6	6	.	.
28	19	18	17	16	16	17	17	19	.	.
29	19	17	18	17	17	16	18	18	.	.
30	1	1	3	2	3	4	3	4	.	.
31	26	32	33	34	36	38	39	38	.	.
32	10	13	14	11	11	12	11	12	.	.
33	6	7	9	8	8	9	10	10	.	.
34	15	19	22	25	24	26	28	29	.	.
35	3	3	3	3	2	2	2	2	.	.
36	25	23	23	22	21	19	19	19	.	.
37	-	-	-	-	-	-	-	-	.	.

Denmark (BA) [3][4] — **Employees - Salariés - Asalariados**

Total - Total - Total
ISIC 3 - CITI 3 - CIIU 3

	1999	2000	2001	2002	2003	2004	2005	2006	2007	2008
Total	.	488.4	467.2	440.8	422.4	418.9	424.1	410.7	417.1	409.3
15	.	87.0	85.8	82.9	78.0	77.0	79.1	75.2	75.8	70.1
16	.	1.5	2.5	2.2	1.7	1.0	-	-	-	-
17	.	9.1	8.1	7.4	5.0	5.9	5.5	5.0	5.6	7.3
18	.	6.7	6.9	4.9	4.9	4.3	3.9	3.0	3.0	4.2
19	.	1.4	1.4	1.3	1.5	1.3	1.7	1.5	2.0	
20	.	17.8	13.4	11.3	11.5	15.4	12.9	12.2	14.9	12.2
21	.	6.7	7.4	7.2	6.8	7.1	8.0	6.1	6.0	6.3
22	.	44.7	39.5	32.5	33.3	31.7	34.9	32.9	29.6	29.6
23	.	0.5	0.6	0.8	0.6	0.2	-	-	-	
24	.	27.9	32.5	34.6	34.5	36.3	34.9	37.3	35.2	37.3
25	.	22.8	19.0	19.1	17.6	19.1	17.5	16.8	18.1	18.2
26	.	22.4	20.5	18.3	20.9	16.3	14.6	15.1	19.9	20.2
27	.	6.4	7.6	7.1	7.6	5.3	6.1	5.5	7.6	8.6
28	.	49.2	42.5	41.7	47.2	43.8	43.5	42.9	43.7	43.7
29	.	73.9	73.1	65.3	63.8	63.9	69.1	63.4	60.6	63.3
30	.	2.4	2.1	2.0	1.4	1.3	1.0	1.3	1.8	
31	.	26.6	24.1	25.3	23.2	22.7	20.0	24.9	25.4	24.7
32	.	12.5	12.5	11.3	10.3	9.9	7.9	7.3	9.5	6.8
33	.	12.6	12.4	14.7	14.5	15.4	14.5	13.3	18.1	15.7
34	.	7.0	8.0	6.3	5.2	6.0	7.1	5.8	6.0	5.1
35	.	9.2	12.6	10.8	8.8	8.7	8.7	11.3	8.6	7.8
36	.	34.9	33.5	31.3	23.6	25.0	29.5	28.2	23.6	23.3
37	.	5.4	1.3	2.5	0.5	1.4	-	-	-	

Men - Hommes - Hombres
ISIC 3 - CITI 3 - CIIU 3

	1999	2000	2001	2002	2003	2004	2005	2006	2007	2008
Total	.	332.3	319.7	299.7	293.8	290.7	291.8	284.0	283.9	276.4
15	.	52.5	49.5	47.2	48.0	46.7	47.8	46.5	44.5	40.3
16	.	1.2	1.8	1.7	1.0	0.7	-	-	-	
17	.	4.5	4.0	3.8	2.5	3.0	2.5	2.0	2.0	3.7
18	.	1.3	1.7	1.0	1.8	1.5	2.0	2.0	1.9	
19	.	0.5	0.7	0.7	1.1	0.3	1.2	0.9	1.4	
20	.	14.0	11.4	9.2	9.5	13.1	9.2	9.4	11.3	9.4
21	.	4.6	5.5	5.4	5.4	4.8	5.4	4.8	4.1	4.2
22	.	29.6	23.7	18.4	18.1	18.9	21.6	19.0	17.9	17.5
23	.	0.5	0.5	0.8	0.6	0.2	-	-	-	
24	.	14.8	17.3	19.1	21.2	20.1	18.7	19.4	19.0	20.3
25	.	14.1	11.9	12.8	11.3	12.4	12.5	11.7	11.8	11.4
26	.	17.5	17.1	15.5	17.6	13.3	11.8	12.1	16.0	16.6
27	.	4.8	6.3	6.2	6.2	3.8	5.0	4.6	5.3	6.1
28	.	40.8	35.5	35.8	39.8	36.9	35.7	34.5	35.3	36.5
29	.	57.2	57.3	50.7	51.4	52.8	55.3	51.6	48.4	49.8
30	.	2.0	1.2	1.4	1.2	0.8	0.5	0.7	1.0	
31	.	17.0	15.3	15.9	15.9	16.0	14.9	18.3	16.9	16.8
32	.	7.4	7.8	7.5	6.1	7.0	4.6	4.3	6.1	4.2
33	.	6.2	8.5	9.2	7.8	7.7	8.0	7.4	10.9	9.6
34	.	5.5	6.2	4.8	4.1	5.2	5.2	4.3	5.1	4.4
35	.	8.0	11.5	9.9	7.4	7.3	7.0	9.7	7.7	6.8
36	.	23.7	23.7	21.3	15.7	16.9	20.9	19.6	15.6	14.9
37	.	4.3	1.3	1.6	0.5	1.3	-	-	-	

Explanatory notes: see p. 77.

[1] Wage earners. [2] Enterprises with 20 or more employees. [3] Included armed forces and conscripts. [4] Persons aged 15 to 66 years.

Notes explicatives: voir p. 80.

[1] Ouvriers. [2] Entreprises occupant 20 salariés et plus. [3] Y compris les forces armées et les conscrits. [4] Personnes âgées de 15 à 66 ans.

Notas explicativas: véase p. 83.

[1] Obreros. [2] Empresas con 20 y más asalariados. [3] Incluye las fuezas armadas y los conscriptos. [4] Personas de 15 a 66 años.

EMPLOYMENT — EMPLOI — EMPLEO — 2F

Paid employment in manufacturing — *Thousands*

Emploi rémunéré dans les industries manufacturières — *Milliers*

Empleo remunerado en las industrias manufactureras — *Millares*

	1999	2000	2001	2002	2003	2004	2005	2006	2007	2008
Denmark (BA) [1] [2]				Employees - Salariés - Asalariados						
Women - Femmes - Mujeres										
ISIC 3 - CITI 3 - CIIU 3										
Total	.	156.2	147.5	141.1	128.6	128.3	132.4	126.7	133.2	132.9
15	.	34.5	36.3	35.7	30.0	30.3	31.2	28.7	31.3	29.9
16	.	0.2	0.6	0.5	0.7	0.3	-	-	-	.
17	.	4.5	4.1	3.6	2.6	3.0	3.0	3.0	3.6	3.6
18	.	5.4	5.2	3.9	3.2	2.8	1.9	1.0	1.1	.
19	.	0.9	0.7	0.6	0.4	1.0	0.5	0.6	0.6	.
20	.	3.8	2.1	2.1	2.0	2.3	3.7	2.8	3.6	2.8
21	.	2.1	1.9	1.8	1.4	2.3	2.6	1.3	1.9	2.1
22	.	15.1	15.8	14.1	15.2	12.8	13.3	13.9	11.7	12.1
23	.	-	0.1	-	-	-	-	-	-	-
24	.	13.1	15.2	15.5	13.3	16.2	16.3	17.9	16.2	16.9
25	.	8.7	7.1	6.3	6.3	6.7	5.1	5.1	6.3	6.7
26	.	4.9	3.3	2.7	3.3	3.0	2.7	3.0	3.9	3.6
27	.	1.6	1.3	1.0	1.4	1.5	1.1	0.9	2.3	2.5
28	.	8.4	6.9	5.9	7.4	6.9	7.8	8.3	8.4	7.2
29	.	16.7	15.8	14.6	12.4	11.1	13.7	11.8	12.1	13.6
30	.	0.4	0.9	0.6	0.3	0.5	0.5	0.6	0.8	.
31	.	9.5	8.8	9.4	7.3	6.7	5.1	6.6	8.4	8.0
32	.	5.0	4.7	3.8	4.2	2.9	3.4	3.0	3.4	2.6
33	.	6.4	4.0	5.6	6.7	7.7	6.5	5.9	7.2	6.1
34	.	1.5	1.8	1.6	1.1	0.8	1.9	1.6	0.9	0.7
35	.	1.2	1.1	0.9	1.4	1.4	1.7	1.6	0.9	1.0
36	.	11.2	9.8	10.0	8.0	8.2	8.7	8.6	8.1	8.5
37	.	1.0	0.0	0.9	0.0	0.1	-	-	-	-
España (BA) [3] [4]				Employees - Salariés - Asalariados						
Total - Total - Total										
ISIC 3 - CITI 3 - CIIU 3										
Total	2 460.0	2 577.9	2 661.9	2 687.7	2 680.4	2 708.8	2 719.6 [5]	2 716.1	2 711.8	2 682.6
15	337.6	357.0	369.9	373.2	387.5	395.0	413.4 [5]	424.2	423.3	439.4
16	10.7	10.7	7.5	7.0	6.7	7.6	8.4 [5]	11.3	7.9	6.2
17	99.3	103.1	100.7	98.4	79.7	83.3	103.1 [5]	97.9	78.5	72.4
18	125.5	123.3	125.1	116.0	111.3	111.2	94.6 [5]	77.4	74.8	70.0
19	81.1	74.7	76.5	84.1	80.7	69.8	62.9 [5]	55.5	53.8	45.0
20	79.3	87.9	93.7	94.5	91.2	90.1	101.2 [5]	95.3	82.2	83.6
21	47.9	49.7	46.9	44.7	45.0	49.6	45.9 [5]	43.9	38.8	42.7
22	140.1	142.6	157.2	166.0	155.4	172.9	162.6 [5]	157.1	157.7	149.2
23	13.5	13.0	13.5	12.5	12.5	17.3	18.3 [5]	15.3	17.5	17.9
24	153.1	156.3	168.1	175.1	167.9	154.2	166.4 [5]	179.9	194.7	192.9
25	89.0	97.9	98.0	105.0	115.9	112.5	110.0 [5]	98.4	100.7	101.3
26	155.1	165.6	178.5	188.8	186.2	182.5	186.5 [5]	191.5	199.3	196.8
27	105.4	111.5	117.9	115.9	124.8	120.6	120.2 [5]	120.2	115.1	109.2
28	244.8	257.0	256.0	267.5	259.4	284.9	291.4 [5]	307.8	303.2	307.1
29	174.7	176.9	196.7	203.8	194.3	186.6	212.7 [5]	208.4	224.9	223.7
30	24.3	24.2	18.8	15.8	15.0	16.3	18.9 [5]	18.2	9.4	9.0
31	83.0	82.8	86.2	83.1	72.8	76.2	75.4 [5]	86.4	81.4	83.5
32	33.8	45.1	41.2	34.6	43.3	35.8	35.1 [5]	33.8	41.8	33.2
33	22.7	20.0	26.4	21.4	19.3	31.1	28.6 [5]	30.2	28.5	27.5
34	201.3	226.7	233.5	231.2	240.4	244.4	209.8 [5]	217.2	219.5	218.8
35	65.3	62.2	65.5	69.3	66.7	73.5	72.0 [5]	71.6	74.0	76.3
36	163.9	178.3	168.8	166.1	188.4	175.6	166.9 [5]	157.3	167.2	164.5
37	8.6	11.5	14.2	13.6	16.0	17.7	15.3 [5]	16.6	17.7	12.6
Men - Hommes - Hombres										
ISIC 3 - CITI 3 - CIIU 3										
Total	1 890.3	1 929.7	1 984.5	1 994.0	2 006.8	2 023.0	2 029.8 [5]	2 043.1	2 008.7	1 981.3
15	229.6	241.0	249.3	249.3	256.0	260.7	265.8 [5]	268.1	258.8	267.1
16	5.6	5.3	4.6	4.3	3.6	4.6	5.4 [5]	8.0	4.2	2.4
17	59.3	56.9	57.0	56.7	42.2	49.8	62.4 [5]	55.6	41.6	38.6
18	27.8	25.9	24.9	20.1	28.0	26.0	20.0 [5]	18.0	18.2	15.7
19	45.6	41.6	42.9	44.1	41.9	36.8	36.7 [5]	31.6	29.1	25.5
20	70.5	77.1	80.6	81.9	80.2	77.0	88.7 [5]	82.6	71.4	74.0
21	41.0	38.9	39.1	36.0	35.2	39.1	36.4 [5]	31.7	29.6	35.7
22	103.7	96.4	103.7	109.5	104.8	113.0	103.6 [5]	101.4	105.9	93.1
23	12.0	11.5	11.1	10.1	11.1	15.4	15.1 [5]	13.2	14.3	14.6
24	107.9	105.3	114.2	119.0	112.4	95.8	112.7 [5]	121.3	127.2	124.5
25	69.1	72.3	74.4	80.0	90.1	89.5	86.1 [5]	79.8	77.0	77.0
26	133.6	143.0	153.7	164.2	161.5	157.6	157.5 [5]	165.2	170.4	165.6
27	95.4	105.1	112.5	107.9	115.2	112.0	111.9 [5]	110.9	105.1	100.6
28	222.6	228.0	227.5	240.7	226.8	247.3	255.0 [5]	273.0	262.6	263.4
29	154.9	155.4	166.6	172.8	170.8	162.9	182.3 [5]	179.5	192.9	191.0
30	18.9	15.7	12.4	10.3	9.4	9.0	13.0 [5]	14.6	5.9	7.1
31	63.3	59.3	59.4	59.2	56.6	58.0	58.8 [5]	65.5	59.6	64.1
32	25.4	29.4	28.7	24.3	30.5	25.4	25.1 [5]	24.6	29.1	23.6
33	17.1	14.2	17.0	16.6	13.3	18.6	18.3 [5]	18.7	18.4	16.8
34	181.0	198.5	199.7	186.2	197.7	201.0	167.5 [5]	178.0	176.6	172.9
35	60.6	56.2	59.1	61.4	59.4	67.2	64.2 [5]	63.3	63.5	66.1
36	137.2	143.0	134.3	128.8	148.9	142.5	132.7 [5]	124.3	134.0	131.4
37	8.1	9.9	11.8	10.5	11.2	13.5	10.6 [5]	13.1	13.4	10.4

Explanatory notes: see p. 77.

[1] Included armed forces and conscripts. [2] Persons aged 15 to 66 years. [3] Excl. compulsory military service. [4] Persons aged 16 years and over. [5] Methodology revised; data not strictly comparable.

Notes explicatives: voir p. 80.

[1] Y compris les forces armées et les conscrits. [2] Personnes âgées de 15 à 66 ans. [3] Non compris les militaires du contingent. [4] Personnes âgées de 16 ans et plus. [5] Méthodologie révisée; les données ne sont pas strictement comparables.

Notas explicativas: véase p. 83.

[1] Incluye las fuezas armadas y los conscriptos. [2] Personas de 15 a 66 años. [3] Excl. a los militares en servicio obligatorio. [4] Personas de 16 años y más. [5] Metodología revisada; los datos no son estrictamente comparables.

2F

EMPLOYMENT	EMPLOI	EMPLEO
Paid employment in manufacturing	**Emploi rémunéré dans les industries manufacturières**	**Empleo remunerado en las industrias manufactureras**
Thousands	Milliers	Millares

	1999	2000	2001	2002	2003	2004	2005	2006	2007	2008

España (BA) [1][2]

Employees - Salariés - Asalariados

Women - Femmes - Mujeres
ISIC 3 - CITI 3 - CIIU 3

	1999	2000	2001	2002	2003	2004	2005	2006	2007	2008
Total	569.6	648.2	677.5	693.8	673.6	685.8 |	689.8 [3]	673.0	703.1	701.3
15	107.9	116.0	120.7	123.9	131.5	134.3 |	147.6 [3]	156.0	164.5	172.3
16	5.1	5.4	2.9	2.7	3.1	3.0 |	3.0 [3]	3.2	3.7	3.7
17	40.0	46.2	43.7	41.7	37.5	33.5 |	40.7 [3]	42.2	37.0	33.7
18	97.7	97.4	100.2	95.9	83.2	85.2 |	74.6 [3]	59.3	56.6	54.3
19	35.5	33.1	33.5	39.9	38.8	33.0 |	26.2 [3]	23.9	24.7	19.5
20	8.8	10.8	13.1	12.6	11.1	13.1 |	12.4 [3]	12.6	10.9	9.6
21	6.9	10.8	7.8	8.7	9.8	10.4 |	9.5 [3]	12.1	9.2	7.0
22	36.4	46.3	53.5	56.5	50.7	59.8 |	59.0 [3]	55.6	51.8	56.1
23	1.4	1.4	2.4	2.5	1.5	1.9 |	3.2 [3]	2.1	3.2	3.2
24	45.2	51.0	54.0	56.1	55.5	58.4 |	53.6 [3]	58.5	67.5	68.4
25	20.0	25.6	23.6	25.0	25.8	23.0 |	23.9 [3]	18.5	23.7	24.2
26	21.5	22.6	24.7	24.6	24.7	24.9 |	29.0 [3]	26.3	28.8	31.2
27	10.0	6.5	5.5	8.1	9.6	8.5 |	8.3 [3]	9.2	10.0	8.6
28	22.1	29.0	28.4	26.8	32.5	37.6 |	36.4 [3]	34.7	40.6	43.7
29	19.8	21.5	30.1	31.1	23.5	23.7 |	30.3 [3]	28.8	32.1	32.7
30	5.4	8.5	6.4	5.5	5.6	7.3 |	5.9 [3]	3.6	3.4	1.9
31	19.8	23.5	26.9	23.9	16.2	18.2 |	16.7 [3]	20.9	21.8	19.4
32	8.4	15.7	12.5	10.2	12.8	10.5 |	10.0 [3]	9.1	12.8	9.7
33	5.7	5.8	9.4	4.8	6.0	12.5 |	10.4 [3]	11.4	10.1	10.6
34	20.4	28.2	33.8	45.0	42.7	43.4 |	42.3 [3]	39.1	42.9	45.8
35	4.7	5.9	6.4	7.9	7.2	6.3 |	7.8 [3]	8.3	10.5	10.3
36	26.7	35.3	35.5	37.2	39.6	33.1 |	34.2 [3]	33.0	33.2	33.1
37	0.5	1.6	2.4	3.1	4.8	4.2 |	4.6 [3]	3.4	4.3	2.2

Estonia (BA) [4]

Employees - Salariés - Asalariados

Total - Total - Total
ISIC 3 - CITI 3 - CIIU 3

	1999	2000	2001	2002	2003	2004	2005	2006	2007	2008
Total	125.7 [5]	133.0	130.6	123.1	129.1	134.1	132.9	131.4	129.0	134.7
15	23.6 [5]	23.0	19.7	20.0	21.5	21.1	19.8	15.7	14.9	19.7
17	7.7 [5]	9.5	9.9	8.1	9.5	10.1	7.7	9.1	9.8	8.3
18	14.2 [5]	15.3	14.4	14.9	11.8	10.2	12.9	12.7	11.5	11.0
19	3.2 [5]	2.4	2.6	2.9	2.0	2.9	3.1	2.0	1.2	1.6
20	19.1 [5]	20.8	18.1	19.0	21.0	21.6	20.2	20.4	18.7	15.2
21	- [5]	2.2	2.0	2.4	1.5	1.4	1.5	2.0	1.7	2.4
22	2.9 [5]	3.1	4.6	4.1	3.2	4.9	7.7	5.8	4.9	6.7
23	1.1 [5]	1.5	1.9	1.0	-	1.4	-	-	-	-
24	3.3 [5]	2.1	2.7	1.8	1.5	2.1	3.2	2.7	2.5	3.5
25	3.1 [5]	2.5	1.9	1.2	2.4	3.6	2.9	4.7	5.4	5.6
26	4.9 [5]	5.4	5.3	5.3	4.7	3.9	5.0	5.4	6.2	5.6
28	7.0 [5]	7.7	14.1	13.8	14.2	13.1	14.9	16.0	16.5	14.9
29	4.3 [5]	5.5	4.6	3.8	2.7	3.4	3.4	3.8	4.3	4.7
31	2.9 [5]	2.6	5.4	5.4	4.3	4.6	9.4	4.4	4.8	9.4
32	4.9 [5]	6.5	4.5	3.1	4.0	5.5	5.3	4.8	4.9	6.5
33	- [5]	-	-	-	-	1.5	1.3	1.2	1.5	1.9
34	- [5]	-	-	-	-	5.1	-	2.7	3.5	1.9
35	5.2 [5]	5.1	4.9	4.3	4.3	4.8	3.8	3.6	3.5	4.3
36	12.4 [5]	12.3	10.7	9.3	14.4	12.9	10.8	12.8	12.4	9.9

Men - Hommes - Hombres
ISIC 3 - CITI 3 - CIIU 3

	1999	2000	2001	2002	2003	2004	2005	2006	2007	2008
Total	67.3 [5]	73.4	72.3	68.6	70.2	71.0	68.9	70.8	69.0	71.7
15	9.8 [5]	9.5	9.2	10.3	8.7	7.3	7.0	5.5	5.3	8.6
17	2.6 [5]	3.6	3.1	3.0	1.9	1.5	1.2	1.6	2.2	2.2
18	1.4 [5]	1.4	0.7	0.7	0.7	0.6	0.4	1.4	0.9	0.6
19	- [5]	-	-	-	-	1.9	0.6	0.4	0.2	0.1
20	14.6 [5]	16.9	14.6	13.9	15.1	14.8	15.3	15.3	13.2	10.5
21	- [5]	-	-	-	-	1.0	1.5	-	-	1.7
22	- [5]	-	-	-	-	2.0	3.3	2.6	1.3	2.6
23	- [5]	-	-	-	-	1.0	-	-	-	-
24	- [5]	-	-	-	' -	0.6	1.6	1.5	1.5	2.2
25	2.0 [5]	1.8	1.5	-	-	1.9	1.8	2.6	2.6	3.3
26	3.4 [5]	4.1	4.5	4.7	4.1	3.5	4.0	4.0	5.1	4.7
28	6.1 [5]	6.9	11.2	11.3	12.3	11.6	12.7	13.8	14.8	13.1
29	3.4 [5]	3.7	3.6	2.4	1.9	2.8	2.9	3.1	3.8	4.1
31	- [5]	1.8	3.3	2.7	2.0	2.0	3.2	2.0	1.8	4.4
32	- [5]	1.8	1.5	0.8	1.1	2.3	1.8	1.9	1.8	2.1
33	- [5]	-	-	-	-	1.5	1.3	-	-	0.3
34	- [5]	-	-	-	-	2.3	-	1.4	1.6	-
35	4.4 [5]	4.6	4.3	3.7	3.7	4.4	3.4	3.1	3.3	3.8
36	8.0 [5]	7.8	6.7	6.5	9.3	8.0	6.9	8.0	7.1	6.2

Explanatory notes: see p. 77.

[1] Excl. compulsory military service. [2] Persons aged 16 years and over. [3] Methodology revised; data not strictly comparable. [4] Persons aged 15 to 74 years. [5] Second quarter.

Notes explicatives: voir p. 80.

[1] Non compris les militaires du contingent. [2] Personnes âgées de 16 ans et plus. [3] Méthodologie révisée; les données ne sont pas strictement comparables. [4] Personnes âgées de 15 à 74 ans. [5] Deuxième trimestre.

Notas explicativas: véase p. 83.

[1] Excl. a los militares en servicio obligatorio. [2] Personas de 16 años y más. [3] Metodología revisada; los datos no son estrictamente comparables. [4] Personas de 15 a 74 años. [5] Segundo trimestre.

Paid employment in manufacturing
Thousands

Emploi rémunéré dans les industries manufacturières
Milliers

Empleo remunerado en las industrias manufactureras
Millares

	1999	2000	2001	2002	2003	2004	2005	2006	2007	2008

Estonia (BA) [1] — Employees - Salariés - Asalariados

Women - Femmes - Mujeres
ISIC 3 - CITI 3 - CIIU 3

	1999	2000	2001	2002	2003	2004	2005	2006	2007	2008
Total	58.4[2]	59.5	58.3	54.4	58.9	63.3	64.0	60.7	60.0	63.1
15	13.8[2]	13.5	10.6	9.7	12.8	13.8	12.8	10.2	9.7	11.1
17	5.2[2]	5.9	6.8	5.0	7.6	8.6	6.5	7.5	7.6	6.1
18	12.8[2]	13.9	13.7	14.2	11.1	9.6	12.5	11.3	10.6	10.4
19	-[2]	-	-	-	-	1.0	2.5	1.6	1.0	1.5
20	4.5[2]	3.8	3.4	5.1	5.9	6.8	4.9	5.1	5.5	4.7
21	-[2]	-	-	-	-	0.4	-	-	-	0.7
22	-[2]	-	-	-	-	2.9	4.4	3.2	3.6	4.1
23	-[2]	-	-	-	-	0.4	-	-	-	-
24	-[2]	-	-	-	-	1.5	1.6	1.2	1.0	1.3
25	1.1[2]	0.7	0.4	-	-	1.7	1.1	2.1	2.8	2.3
26	1.5[2]	1.3	0.8	0.6	0.6	0.4	1.0	1.4	1.1	0.9
28	0.9[2]	0.8	2.9	2.5	1.9	1.5	2.2	2.2	1.7	1.7
29	0.9[2]	1.8	1.0	1.4	0.8	0.6	0.5	0.7	0.5	0.6
31	-[2]	0.8	2.1	2.7	2.3	2.6	6.2	2.5	3.0	5.0
32	-[2]	4.7	3.0	2.3	2.9	3.2	3.5	2.9	3.1	4.4
33	-	-	-	-	-	-	-	-	-	1.6
34	-[2]	-	-	-	-	2.8	-	1.3	1.9	-
35	0.8[2]	0.5	0.6	0.6	0.6	0.4	0.4	0.5	0.2	0.5
36	4.4[2]	4.5	4.1	2.7	5.1	4.9	3.9	4.9	5.2	3.7

Finland (BA) [1][3] — Employees - Salariés - Asalariados

Total - Total - Total
ISIC 3 - CITI 3 - CIIU 3

	1999	2000	2001	2002	2003	2004	2005	2006	2007	2008
Total	431	437	444	436	418	411	414	417	421	412
15	43	44	42	41	42	42	39	36	37	36
17	7	7	7	7	5	6	5	4	4	5
18	6	5	6	5	5	5	5	5	3	3
19	3	3	3	2	2	2	3	2	2	2
20	28	30	30	28	28	27	30	30	30	27
21	40	37	37	39	36	34	36	34	31	27
22	34	33	34	34	32	33	32	34	31	30
23	4	4	3	3	3	3	3	3	3	2
24	20	20	20	19	18	18	17	18	18	18
25	17	19	19	19	18	20	20	16	17	17
26	16	16	16	16	17	16	15	17	18	15
27	17	18	19	18	15	16	18	17	15	17
28	37	41	41	38	41	40	40	42	45	45
29	61	61	61	62	60	57	53	57	64	65
30	2	1	1	1	1	1	1	1	3	1
31	19	17	18	18	16	16	17	16	17	20
32	33	36	40	37	34	33	36	36	33	31
33	11	9	11	11	9	12	13	14	14	12
34	7	8	8	8	8	7	7	7	6	7
35	12	13	13	13	12	10	11	14	16	15
36	14	15	16	16	16	14	12	13	13	13
37	-	-	-	1	1	1	1	1	2	2

Men - Hommes - Hombres
ISIC 3 - CITI 3 - CIIU 3

	1999	2000	2001	2002	2003	2004	2005	2006	2007	2008
Total	299	307	310	305	298	291	292	299	305	303
15	19	21	21	22	23	22	19	19	20	18
17	3	3	3	3	2	3	2	2	2	3
18	1	1	1	-	1	-	1	1	-	-
19	1	1	1	1	1	1	1	-	-	1
20	23	24	24	23	22	21	24	24	25	23
21	30	27	26	28	28	28	28	26	23	21
22	18	18	17	17	16	17	17	16	17	16
23	3	3	3	2	3	2	2	2	2	1
24	12	12	12	10	11	12	11	12	11	10
25	11	12	13	13	12	14	14	11	11	11
26	13	13	13	13	13	13	12	14	14	13
27	14	15	15	15	13	14	15	14	12	15
28	31	35	34	33	36	33	32	35	38	40
29	53	54	53	52	51	47	45	48	54	55
30	1	1	1	1	1	-	-	1	2	1
31	12	11	12	12	11	11	12	12	13	15
32	20	23	25	23	21	22	25	24	22	22
33	7	5	7	7	6	7	9	10	9	8
34	6	6	7	7	6	6	6	6	5	6
35	11	12	12	12	11	9	10	12	14	14
36	10	10	11	10	10	9	8	9	8	9
37	-	-	-	1	-	1	1	1	2	1

Explanatory notes: see p. 77.

[1] Persons aged 15 to 74 years. [2] Second quarter. [3] Included armed forces and conscripts.

Notes explicatives: voir p. 80.

[1] Personnes âgées de 15 à 74 ans. [2] Deuxième trimestre. [3] Y compris les forces armées et les conscrits.

Notas explicativas: véase p. 83.

[1] Personas de 15 a 74 años. [2] Segundo trimestre. [3] Incluye las fuezas armadas y los conscriptos.

EMPLOYMENT — EMPLOI — EMPLEO

Paid employment in manufacturing — Emploi rémunéré dans les industries manufacturières — Empleo remunerado en las industrias manufactureras

Thousands — Milliers — Millares

	1999	2000	2001	2002	2003	2004	2005	2006	2007	2008
Finland (BA) [1][2]					Employees - Salariés - Asalariados					
Women - Femmes - Mujeres										
ISIC 3 - CITI 3 - CIIU 3										
Total	131	130	133	131	120	120	120	118	116	109
15	24	23	21	20	19	20	20	18	18	18
17	5	5	4	4	3	3	3	2	2	2
18	6	5	5	5	4	5	4	4	3	3
19	1	2	2	2	1	1	2	2	2	1
20	5	6	6	5	6	6	6	5	5	4
21	10	10	10	11	8	6	8	8	8	6
22	16	15	16	18	16	16	15	17	14	14
23	1	1	1	1	-	1	1	1	1	1
24	8	8	8	8	7	7	6	6	7	7
25	6	7	6	6	6	6	6	5	6	6
26	4	3	3	3	4	3	3	4	4	3
27	4	3	3	3	2	2	3	3	3	2
28	5	7	7	5	5	7	8	7	7	5
29	8	7	9	10	9	9	8	9	10	10
30	1	-	1	-	-	-	-	-	1	-
31	6	5	5	6	5	5	5	4	4	5
32	13	14	15	14	13	11	11	11	10	9
33	4	3	4	3	3	4	4	4	5	5
34	1	1	1	1	1	1	1	1	1	1
35	1	1	1	1	1	2	1	2	1	2
36	5	4	5	5	6	5	4	4	5	4
37	-	-	-	1	-	-	-	-	-	-
Finland (DA)					Employees - Salariés - Asalariados					
Total - Total - Total										
ISIC 3 - CITI 3 - CIIU 3										
Total	414.30	425.10	427.71	418.74	414.99	404.51	401.40	395.87	395.74	396.38
15	40.86	39.38	38.79	38.50	39.49 ³	37.69 ³	36.71 ³	35.28 ³	37.79 ³	34.58 ³
16	0.39	0.39	0.41	0.40						
17	6.13	5.78	5.56	5.59	5.40	5.46	5.31	4.86	4.76	4.34
18	6.63	6.18	5.97	5.41	5.40	4.81	4.47	3.77	3.42	3.21
19	2.82	2.66	2.51	2.37	2.42	2.19	2.04	1.91	1.98	1.86
20	27.87	28.49	27.95	27.30	27.49	27.54	27.04	26.63	26.53	25.47
21	37.20	37.40	37.38	36.59	35.99	34.43	31.40	29.59	26.99	27.92
22	30.40	31.05	30.35	29.53	29.55	28.93	28.11	27.13	26.86	26.57
23	2.95	3.36	3.39	3.12	2.75	2.89	2.32	2.41	2.50	2.53
24	18.32	18.42	18.71	18.50	18.67	18.30	17.70	17.43	17.60	17.91
25	17.29	18.25	17.62	17.67	16.27	16.36	16.13	15.42	14.99	15.58
26	14.65	15.36	15.24	15.10	15.15	15.33	15.41	15.63	15.94	15.09
27	16.95	16.89	16.67	16.28	15.54	15.36	16.30	16.23	15.52	15.78
28	34.76	37.69	40.16	40.12	42.35	41.65	42.98	43.04	45.34	47.00
29	55.84	57.72	59.68	59.17	59.56	57.98	60.04	61.86	61.91	66.61
30	2.09	0.93	0.52	0.39	0.36	0.37	0.27	0.32	0.33	0.35
31	16.04	16.66	16.98	16.11	14.87	14.63	14.84	15.30	15.84	17.48
32	34.24	37.29	38.27	35.47	34.49	34.65	35.36	34.41	34.92	31.60
33	11.51	11.66	11.92	12.89	11.57	10.97	10.87	10.86	10.92	11.00
34	7.16	7.32	7.34	7.40	7.40	6.66	6.84	7.06	7.34	7.65
35	14.90	16.14	16.48	15.96	14.95	13.33	12.80	13.11	13.35	13.04
36	15.00	15.42	15.33	14.53	14.77	14.42	13.76	12.76	13.08	12.53
37	0.33	0.66	0.49	0.46	0.57	0.57	0.68	0.87	0.85	1.31

France (BA) [4] — Employees - Salariés - Asalariados
Total - Total - Total
ISIC 3 - CITI 3 - CIIU 3 — ISIC 4 - CITI 4 - CIIU 4

	1999	2000	2001	2002	2003	2004	2005	2006	2007	2008	
Total	.	.	.	.	3 892.9	3 845.1	3 791.0	3 767.4	3 730.9 |	3 455.6	Total
15					577.7	603.8	613.9	552.5	581.2 |	530.1	10
16					7.3	3.2	1.3	2.1	2.4 |	38.9	11
17					99.7	85.2	76.8	70.8	58.9 |	2.4	12
18					58.0	58.5	54.1	49.2	47.7 |	49.4	13
19					32.5	32.5	35.4	30.1	30.9 |	66.2	14
20					86.6	87.7	75.1	80.8	81.0 |	24.3	15
21					89.4	94.7	84.8	71.7	85.5 |	86.0	16
22					202.2	206.2	200.2	211.8	192.8 |	81.2	17
23					28.9	26.1	23.6	29.1	34.0 |	106.4	18
24					312.7	332.1	308.6	276.9	276.6 |	19.7	19
25					243.2	231.0	230.7	228.8	223.3 |	179.6	20
26					164.8	150.1	134.6	138.5	139.4 |	101.0	21
27					126.6	120.5	119.1	133.1	121.6 |	222.6	22
28					438.5	436.6	427.5	468.7	427.5 |	112.9	23
29					316.3	326.4	320.3	317.8	310.0 |	118.1	24
30					27.0	18.5	15.8	31.1	26.9 |	318.8	25
31					141.8	134.1	148.2	150.3	151.3 |	196.4	26
32					124.8	133.6	129.1	100.8	97.1 |	148.5	27
33					150.2	135.5	145.7	168.2	181.0 |	238.5	28
34					330.3	329.0	330.6	317.0	337.9 |	341.2	29
35					155.8	140.6	138.1	160.4	173.4 |	156.0	30
36					146.4	131.6	145.0	145.7	118.4 |	57.2	31
37					32.4	27.7	32.4	31.9	32.2 |	81.8	32
									|	178.4	33

Explanatory notes: see p. 77.   Notes explicatives: voir p. 80.   Notas explicativas: véase p. 83.

[1] Included armed forces and conscripts. [2] Persons aged 15 to 74 years. [3] Incl. group 16. [4] Persons aged 15 years and over.

[1] Y compris les forces armées et les conscrits. [2] Personnes âgées de 15 à 74 ans. [3] Y compris la classe 16. [4] Personnes âgées de 15 ans et plus.

[1] Incluye las fuezas armadas y los conscriptos. [2] Personas de 15 a 74 años. [3] Incl. la agrupación 16. [4] Personas de 15 años y más.

Paid employment in manufacturing
Thousands

Emploi rémunéré dans les industries manufacturières
Milliers

Empleo remunerado en las industrias manufactureras
Millares

	1999	2000	2001	2002	2003	2004	2005	2006	2007	2008	

France (BA) [1]   Employees - Salariés - Asalariados

Men - Hommes - Hombres
ISIC 3 - CITI 3 - CIIU 3   ISIC 4 - CITI 4 - CIIU 4

	1999	2000	2001	2002	2003	2004	2005	2006	2007	2008	
Total	.	.	.	.	2 741.7	2 669.6	2 656.5	2 668.1	2 599.4 ǀ	2 452.5	Total
15	.	.	.	.	354.7	368.5	370.5	339.5	334.9 ǀ	303.6	10
16	.	.	.	.	5.4	2.0	0.1	1.0	1.2 ǀ	29.0	11
17	.	.	.	.	51.3	46.0	38.6	39.3	28.8 ǀ	1.8	12
18	.	.	.	.	14.8	14.2	12.6	11.4	9.8 ǀ	30.6	13
19	.	.	.	.	9.8	10.6	13.3	11.6	13.5 ǀ	17.4	14
20	.	.	.	.	73.1	74.5	64.4	66.0	63.6 ǀ	10.9	15
21	.	.	.	.	66.0	66.0	60.3	49.8	57.8 ǀ	75.4	16
22	.	.	.	.	121.0	104.7	108.5	122.4	104.7 ǀ	59.0	17
23	.	.	.	.	23.6	21.4	20.8	25.0	29.3 ǀ	64.0	18
24	.	.	.	.	185.7	188.7	177.8	161.4	147.3 ǀ	14.9	19
25	.	.	.	.	172.4	162.8	163.1	160.2	158.1 ǀ	114.0	20
26	.	.	.	.	136.6	117.8	104.2	109.5	108.9 ǀ	44.4	21
27	.	.	.	.	112.2	110.6	108.4	116.7	104.7 ǀ	156.6	22
28	.	.	.	.	346.4	348.6	356.1	394.7	353.9 ǀ	91.0	23
29	.	.	.	.	256.7	265.8	267.8	261.5	260.1 ǀ	104.5	24
30	.	.	.	.	14.6	11.2	10.4	21.9	22.1 ǀ	255.7	25
31	.	.	.	.	100.7	81.1	93.9	102.7	99.9 ǀ	139.4	26
32	.	.	.	.	82.6	85.6	82.6	61.5	59.4 ǀ	98.8	27
33	.	.	.	.	102.6	94.0	99.0	112.3	120.1 ǀ	202.0	28
34	.	.	.	.	273.5	275.5	274.0	259.4	278.1 ǀ	286.0	29
35	.	.	.	.	122.3	112.2	111.7	125.2	147.0 ǀ	125.0	30
36	.	.	.	.	90.0	87.2	91.4	91.4	76.4 ǀ	42.2	31
37	.	.	.	.	25.7	20.6	26.9	23.9	19.9 ǀ	38.3	32
									ǀ	147.8	33

Women - Femmes - Mujeres
ISIC 3 - CITI 3 - CIIU 3   ISIC 4 - CITI 4 - CIIU 4

	1999	2000	2001	2002	2003	2004	2005	2006	2007	2008	
Total	.	.	.	.	1 151.2	1 175.5	1 134.5	1 099.3	1 131.4 ǀ	1 003.1	Total
15	.	.	.	.	223.1	235.3	243.4	213.0	246.3 ǀ	226.5	10
16	.	.	.	.	1.9	1.2	1.2	1.1	1.2 ǀ	9.8	11
17	.	.	.	.	48.3	39.2	38.2	31.5	30.1 ǀ	0.6	12
18	.	.	.	.	43.3	44.3	41.4	37.8	37.9 ǀ	18.8	13
19	.	.	.	.	22.7	21.9	22.1	18.5	17.4 ǀ	48.8	14
20	.	.	.	.	13.5	13.1	10.7	14.8	17.4 ǀ	13.5	15
21	.	.	.	.	23.3	28.7	24.4	21.8	27.7 ǀ	10.6	16
22	.	.	.	.	81.2	101.5	91.7	89.5	88.1 ǀ	22.2	17
23	.	.	.	.	5.3	4.7	2.8	4.1	4.7 ǀ	42.4	18
24	.	.	.	.	127.0	143.4	130.8	115.6	129.3 ǀ	4.8	19
25	.	.	.	.	70.8	68.3	67.5	68.6	65.2 ǀ	65.6	20
26	.	.	.	.	28.2	32.3	30.4	29.0	30.4 ǀ	56.6	21
27	.	.	.	.	14.4	9.9	10.7	16.4	16.8 ǀ	66.0	22
28	.	.	.	.	92.1	88.0	71.3	74.0	73.6 ǀ	21.9	23
29	.	.	.	.	59.6	60.5	52.5	56.3	49.8 ǀ	13.6	24
30	.	.	.	.	12.3	7.3	5.4	9.2	4.9 ǀ	63.0	25
31	.	.	.	.	41.1	53.0	54.3	47.7	51.4 ǀ	57.0	26
32	.	.	.	.	42.2	48.1	46.5	39.4	37.7 ǀ	49.7	27
33	.	.	.	.	47.6	41.5	46.8	55.9	60.9 ǀ	36.5	28
34	.	.	.	.	56.8	53.5	56.6	57.6	59.8 ǀ	55.2	29
35	.	.	.	.	33.5	28.4	26.5	35.2	26.4 ǀ	31.0	30
36	.	.	.	.	56.4	44.5	53.6	54.3	42.0 ǀ	15.0	31
37	.	.	.	.	6.7	7.1	5.4	8.1	12.4 ǀ	43.5	32
									ǀ	30.5	33

Germany (BA) [1]   Employees - Salariés - Asalariados

Total - Total - Total
ISIC 3 - CITI 3 - CIIU 3

	1999	2000	2001	2002	2003	2004	2005	2006	2007	2008
Total	8 132	8 141 [2]	8 194	8 080 [3]	7 839 [2]	7 723 [4]ǀ	7 613 [5]	7 741	7 995	8 017
15	814	776 [2]	792	783 [3]	770 [2]	757 [4]ǀ	809 [5]	837	865	858
16	12	13 [2]	14	14 [3]	15 [2]	12 [4]ǀ	14 [5]	13	14	14
17	184	168 [2]	154	146 [3]	134 [2]	122 [4]ǀ	122 [5]	120	118	112
18	114	117 [2]	118	105 [3]	102 [2]	91 [4]ǀ	69 [5]	73	74	63
19	35	34 [2]	37	32 [3]	30 [2]	29 [4]ǀ	28 [5]	25	24	23
20	213	216 [2]	191	189 [3]	155 [2]	148 [4]ǀ	148 [5]	130	130	130
21	148	153 [2]	148	146 [3]	148 [2]	151 [4]ǀ	144 [5]	143	145	142
22	489	491 [2]	494	483 [3]	466 [2]	459 [4]ǀ	470 [5]	477	506	461
23	20	25 [2]	23	23 [3]	22 [2]	24 [4]ǀ	21 [5]	27	30	29
24	668	655 [2]	640	657 [3]	636 [2]	611 [4]ǀ	553 [5]	558	563	558
25	314	335 [2]	338	336 [3]	318 [2]	319 [4]ǀ	325 [5]	312	341	354
26	260	252 [2]	246	225 [3]	219 [2]	209 [4]ǀ	197 [5]	191	204	193
27	443	317 [2]	297	291 [3]	268 [2]	245 [4]ǀ	251 [5]	256	270	296
28	883	936 [2]	1 001	993 [3]	1 013 [2]	1 009 [4]ǀ	972 [5]	951	990	1 013
29	1 146	1 188 [2]	1 189	1 173 [3]	1 075 [2]	1 091 [4]ǀ	1 056 [5]	1 068	1 100	1 128
30	113	103 [2]	105	101 [3]	79 [2]	67 [4]ǀ	61 [5]	68	63	61
31	413	422 [2]	396	386 [3]	367 [2]	361 [4]ǀ	309 [5]	333	342	331
32	226	268 [2]	290	272 [3]	267 [2]	250 [4]ǀ	246 [5]	254	267	256
33	241	262 [2]	269	275 [3]	293 [2]	288 [4]ǀ	284 [5]	308	318	331
34	846	867 [2]	897	926 [3]	948 [2]	1 000 [4]ǀ	1 014 [5]	1 053	1 089	1 122
35	159	182 [2]	174	185 [3]	167 [2]	167 [4]ǀ	195 [5]	205	202	205
36	355	327 [2]	348	306 [3]	314 [2]	282 [4]ǀ	293 [5]	301	298	293
37	36	34 [2]	33	33 [3]	32 [2]	31 [4]ǀ	33 [5]	38	42	44

Explanatory notes: see p. 77.

[1] Persons aged 15 years and over. [2] May. [3] Prior to 2002: April of each year. [4] March. [5] Methodology revised; data not strictly comparable.

Notes explicatives: voir p. 80.

[1] Personnes âgées de 15 ans et plus. [2] Mai. [3] Avant 2002: avril de chaque année. [4] Mars. [5] Méthodologie révisée; les données ne sont pas strictement comparables.

Notas explicativas: véase p. 83.

[1] Personas de 15 años y más. [2] Mayo. [3] Antes del 2002: abril de cada año. [4] Marzo. [5] Metodología revisada; los datos no son estrictamente comparables.

EMPLOYMENT   EMPLOI   EMPLEO

Paid employment in manufacturing
Thousands

Emploi rémunéré dans les industries manufacturières
Milliers

Empleo remunerado en las industrias manufactureras
Millares

Germany (BA) [1]

Employees - Salariés - Asalariados

Men - Hommes - Hombres
ISIC 3 - CITI 3 - CIIU 3

	1999	2000	2001	2002	2003	2004	2005	2006	2007	2008
Total	5 796	5 801 [2]	5 844	5 786 [3]	5 605 [2]	5 527 [4]	5 464 [5]	5 529	5 735	5 778
15	397	383 [2]	384	386 [3]	373 [2]	372 [4]	381 [5]	396	415	413
16	8	9 [2]	9	9 [3]	10 [2]	7 [4]	8 [5]	8	10	8
17	84	77 [2]	76	72 [3]	63 [2]	59 [4]	57 [5]	59	59	57
18	31	31 [2]	31	28 [3]	27 [2]	26 [4]	22 [5]	20	20	16
19	16	15 [2]	17	15 [3]	14 [2]	14 [4]	12 [5]	11	12	11
20	174	174 [2]	156	155 [3]	128 [2]	118 [4]	120 [5]	106	107	106
21	108	112 [2]	105	107 [3]	108 [2]	109 [4]	107 [5]	104	105	100
22	271	269 [2]	263	262 [3]	262 [2]	252 [4]	255 [5]	260	274	246
23	16	18 [2]	17	17 [3]	17 [2]	19 [4]	18 [5]	22	23	24
24	467	462 [2]	441	455 [3]	430 [2]	404 [4]	376 [5]	368	370	374
25	225	235 [2]	239	241 [3]	225 [2]	226 [4]	227 [5]	218	242	252
26	194	188 [2]	190	170 [3]	167 [2]	158 [4]	143 [5]	137	152	142
27	374	269 [2]	256	247 [3]	229 [2]	212 [4]	219 [5]	224	237	260
28	712	755 [2]	807	801 [3]	816 [2]	820 [4]	789 [5]	768	809	834
29	942	979 [2]	986	971 [3]	884 [2]	895 [4]	876 [5]	883	911	927
30	80	77 [2]	79	75 [3]	60 [2]	49 [4]	47 [5]	48	45	44
31	287	289 [2]	274	270 [3]	265 [2]	258 [4]	226 [5]	242	247	236
32	152	181 [2]	195	186 [3]	182 [2]	173 [4]	171 [5]	173	182	176
33	142	153 [2]	161	168 [3]	177 [2]	169 [4]	171 [5]	189	198	206
34	700	712 [2]	739	754 [3]	780 [2]	820 [4]	842 [5]	875	897	927
35	139	159 [2]	149	159 [3]	143 [2]	142 [4]	167 [5]	178	177	176
36	249	229 [2]	245	213 [3]	223 [2]	201 [4]	203 [5]	208	210	208
37	28	25 [2]	25	25 [3]	24 [2]	24 [4]	26 [5]	32	33	35

Women - Femmes - Mujeres
ISIC 3 - CITI 3 - CIIU 3

	1999	2000	2001	2002	2003	2004	2005	2006	2007	2008
Total	2 336	2 340 [2]	2 350	2 294 [3]	2 234 [2]	2 191 [4]	2 149 [5]	2 213	2 261	2 239
15	417	393 [2]	408	397 [3]	396 [2]	385 [4]	427 [5]	442	450	445
16	4	4 [2]	5	5 [3]	5 [2]	5 [4]	5 [5]	5	4	6
17	100	91 [2]	78	74 [3]	72 [2]	63 [4]	65 [5]	61	59	55
18	83	86 [2]	87	77 [3]	75 [2]	64 [4]	47 [5]	53	54	47
19	19	19 [2]	20	17 [3]	16 [2]	15 [4]	16 [5]	14	13	12
20	39	42 [2]	35	34 [3]	27 [2]	30 [4]	27 [5]	24	23	24
21	40	41 [2]	43	39 [3]	41 [2]	42 [4]	37 [5]	39	40	42
22	218	222 [2]	231	221 [3]	204 [2]	207 [4]	215 [5]	217	231	215
23	4	7 [2]	6	6 [3]	5 [2]	5 [4]	4 [5]	5	7	6
24	201	193 [2]	199	202 [3]	206 [2]	206 [4]	177 [5]	190	192	184
25	89	100 [2]	99	95 [3]	93 [2]	93 [4]	98 [5]	94	99	101
26	66	64 [2]	56	55 [3]	52 [2]	51 [4]	54 [5]	54	52	51
27	69	48 [2]	41	44 [3]	39 [2]	33 [4]	32 [5]	31	33	36
28	171	181 [2]	194	192 [3]	197 [2]	189 [4]	183 [5]	183	182	179
29	204	209 [2]	203	202 [3]	191 [2]	196 [4]	180 [5]	185	189	201
30	33	26 [2]	26	26 [3]	20 [2]	18 [4]	14 [5]	20	18	17
31	126	133 [2]	122	116 [3]	102 [2]	103 [4]	82 [5]	91	96	95
32	74	87 [2]	95	86 [3]	85 [2]	77 [4]	75 [5]	81	85	79
33	99	109 [2]	108	107 [3]	117 [2]	118 [4]	113 [5]	119	120	125
34	146	155 [2]	158	172 [3]	168 [2]	180 [4]	172 [5]	178	192	196
35	20	23 [2]	25	26 [3]	24 [2]	24 [4]	28 [5]	27	25	29
36	106	98 [2]	103	93 [3]	91 [2]	81 [4]	90 [5]	93	88	85
37	8	9 [2]	8	8 [3]	8 [2]	7 [4]	7 [5]	7	9	9

Greece (BA) [1][6][7]

Employees - Salariés - Asalariados

Total - Total - Total
ISIC 3 - CITI 3 - CIIU 3   ISIC 4 - CITI 4 - CIIU 4

	1999	2000	2001	2002	2003	2004	2005	2006	2007	2008	
Total	408.3	409.0	426.4	429.5	412.8	418.5	413.0	409.1	408.1	400.6	Total
15	79.3	85.2	92.0	95.0	84.5	85.7	92.5	88.2	87.6	77.4	10
16	7.8	8.3	6.8	6.0	6.9	6.4	8.9	5.1	5.0	9.4	11
17	22.5	21.1	19.1	19.5	20.4	18.5	15.6	13.3	15.0	3.3	12
18	50.2	49.9	51.2	47.5	49.1	38.6	34.2	32.7	28.5	16.6	13
19	8.7	6.5	8.4	6.7	5.1	6.4	6.7	6.5	4.5	29.7	14
20	15.2	15.0	14.0	14.7	13.2	17.4	19.1	16.8	15.0	4.0	15
21	9.2	8.0	6.3	8.3	6.2	6.5	6.7	9.1	8.4	15.7	16
22	30.5	27.4	29.6	29.6	29.1	33.1	27.4	30.3	38.3	7.6	17
23	8.7	7.9	8.2	8.4	7.7	8.9	9.0	8.1	5.9	32.4	18
24	22.7	23.2	22.0	23.5	18.6	27.1	27.2	28.3	31.3	5.7	19
25	11.9	11.2	13.7	13.8	14.2	16.6	12.6	14.5	11.7	14.9	20
26	24.7	26.0	26.3	26.6	24.7	26.1	26.2	25.0	24.2	15.2	21
27	13.6	11.7	11.8	13.0	16.9	11.4	13.8	13.9	14.0	12.7	22
28	28.9	32.7	37.4	37.4	35.4	36.1	35.7	38.0	35.5	28.7	23
29	18.4	18.6	21.0	19.5	19.4	23.6	20.1	20.0	21.4	18.2	24
30	0.4	0.6	1.3	0.9	1.0	0.8	0.6	0.3	0.2	35.7	25
31	8.3	7.6	6.7	9.2	7.2	8.0	6.7	8.7	9.5	5.0	26
32	2.8	3.0	2.6	3.1	3.1	3.0	3.1	3.8	3.0	11.3	27
33	2.8	3.4	2.8	4.0	4.2	1.8	2.7	3.4	6.0	8.6	28
34	1.9	3.2	3.3	2.5	3.5	1.5	2.4	2.0	1.7	2.4	29
35	14.8	12.4	15.5	15.7	15.8	16.2	15.3	18.8	17.6	11.9	30
36	24.8	25.9	26.2	24.5	26.3	24.6	25.5	21.3	22.5	20.2	31
37	0.2	0.2	0.2	0.3	0.2	0.3	0.8	0.9	1.1	6.6	32
										7.4	33

Explanatory notes: see p. 77.

[1] Persons aged 15 years and over. [2] May. [3] Prior to 2002: April of each year. [4] March. [5] Methodology revised; data not strictly comparable. [6] Excl. conscripts. [7] Second quarter of each year.

Notes explicatives: voir p. 80.

[1] Personnes âgées de 15 ans et plus. [2] Mai. [3] Avant 2002: avril de chaque année. [4] Mars. [5] Méthodologie révisée; les données ne sont pas strictement comparables. [6] Non compris les conscrits. [7] Deuxième trimestre de chaque année.

Notas explicativas: véase p. 83.

[1] Personas de 15 años y más. [2] Mayo. [3] Antes del 2002: abril de cada año. [4] Marzo. [5] Metodología revisada; los datos no son estrictamente comparables. [6] Excl. los conscriptos. [7] Segundo trimestre de cada año.

Paid employment in manufacturing — *Thousands*

Emploi rémunéré dans les industries manufacturières — *Milliers*

Empleo remunerado en las industrias manufactureras — *Millares*

Greece (BA) [1][2][3] — Employees - Salariés - Asalariados

Men - Hommes - Hombres
ISIC 3 - CITI 3 - CIIU 3 ⋯ ISIC 4 - CITI 4 - CIIU 4

ISIC 3	1999	2000	2001	2002	2003	2004	2005	2006	2007	2008	ISIC 4
Total	279.3	281.2	297.2	296.9	286.9	291.5	292.2	293.8	288.4	290.2	Total
15	52.7	57.0	61.9	61.7	53.6	55.2	55.8	57.3	53.1	46.6	10
16	4.5	4.0	3.5	3.3	3.5	4.0	6.0	2.4	2.3	6.9	11
17	13.8	13.0	10.9	11.7	11.9	11.0	8.7	8.7	10.4	2.2	12
18	10.0	11.4	12.4	11.6	13.4	11.5	11.1	10.0	7.0	9.4	13
19	5.1	3.0	3.9	3.1	2.5	3.1	3.0	3.5	2.3	13.6	14
20	13.9	13.7	13.2	14.0	11.7	16.4	17.2	15.6	14.2	2.3	15
21	7.6	6.9	4.9	6.2	4.9	4.8	5.7	6.2	5.8	14.5	16
22	17.3	15.7	18.7	17.8	17.9	18.8	19.2	19.6	23.9	5.7	17
23	7.4	7.1	7.2	7.0	6.3	6.9	7.9	6.9	4.6	19.5	18
24	15.4	14.6	14.4	14.8	12.4	16.6	17.4	18.3	19.2	5.1	19
25	8.8	8.8	10.5	9.5	10.1	10.4	8.5	11.6	9.8	11.0	20
26	22.7	23.0	23.1	23.9	22.8	22.2	22.9	22.3	22.3	8.3	21
27	12.5	10.4	10.5	11.6	14.8	10.2	13.1	13.0	12.8	9.5	22
28	26.6	31.0	33.9	34.0	33.2	31.7	32.1	32.7	30.3	25.9	23
29	16.1	15.9	19.0	16.8	16.8	20.9	17.3	16.9	19.0	17.4	24
30	0.3	0.4	1.0	0.9	1.0	0.8	0.4	0.3	0.2	30.7	25
31	7.2	5.9	5.2	7.2	5.8	6.5	5.7	6.5	7.0	3.9	26
32	1.9	1.9	2.1	2.4	2.1	2.7	2.7	3.0	2.4	9.3	27
33	1.5	2.1	1.4	2.9	2.7	1.2	1.3	1.9	4.2	7.6	28
34	1.4	2.3	2.9	1.9	2.7	1.5	2.3	1.8	1.4	2.2	29
35	13.8	11.7	14.6	14.8	15.7	15.3	13.5	17.5	16.0	10.5	30
36	18.8	21.1	22.2	19.4	21.2	19.5	19.5	16.6	19.3	16.9	31
37	0.1	0.1	0.1	0.2	0.0	0.3	0.8	0.9	1.0	4.2	32
										7.2	33

Women - Femmes - Mujeres
ISIC 3 - CITI 3 - CIIU 3 ⋯ ISIC 4 - CITI 4 - CIIU 4

ISIC 3	1999	2000	2001	2002	2003	2004	2005	2006	2007	2008	ISIC 4
Total	129.0	127.8	129.2	132.7	125.9	127.0	120.8	115.3	119.7	110.5	Total
15	26.6	28.2	30.1	33.2	31.0	30.5	36.7	30.9	34.5	30.8	10
16	3.3	4.3	3.4	2.7	3.4	2.4	3.0	2.7	2.7	2.5	11
17	8.8	8.1	8.2	7.8	8.4	7.5	6.9	4.6	4.6	1.1	12
18	40.2	38.4	38.8	35.9	35.8	27.1	23.2	22.7	21.5	7.2	13
19	3.6	3.4	4.5	3.6	2.6	3.3	3.8	2.9	2.2	16.1	14
20	1.3	1.3	0.8	0.6	1.4	1.0	1.9	1.2	0.9	1.7	15
21	1.6	1.2	1.4	2.0	1.3	1.6	1.0	3.0	2.6	1.2	16
22	13.2	11.8	10.9	11.8	11.2	14.2	8.2	10.7	14.3	1.9	17
23	1.4	0.9	1.0	1.4	1.4	2.0	1.0	1.2	1.3	12.9	18
24	7.3	8.5	7.6	8.7	6.2	10.6	9.8	10.0	12.1	0.6	19
25	3.1	2.4	3.3	4.2	4.1	6.1	4.1	2.8	1.9	3.9	20
26	2.0	3.0	3.2	2.7	1.9	3.9	3.3	2.7	1.8	6.9	21
27	1.1	1.4	1.3	1.4	2.2	1.2	0.7	0.9	1.2	3.3	22
28	2.2	1.7	3.5	3.4	2.2	4.4	3.6	5.3	5.3	2.8	23
29	2.3	2.7	2.3	2.7	2.6	2.7	2.7	3.1	2.5	0.8	24
30	0.1	0.1	0.3	0.0	0.0	0.0	0.2	0.0	0.0	5.0	25
31	1.1	1.7	1.5	2.0	1.3	1.4	1.0	2.2	2.5	1.2	26
32	1.0	1.1	0.5	0.7	1.1	0.4	0.4	0.7	0.6	2.0	27
33	1.2	1.3	1.5	1.1	1.4	0.7	1.4	1.5	1.8	1.1	28
34	0.4	0.9	0.4	0.6	0.8	0.0	0.1	0.2	0.2	0.2	29
35	1.0	0.7	0.9	0.9	0.2	0.9	1.8	1.3	1.6	1.4	30
36	6.0	4.7	4.0	5.1	5.1	5.1	6.0	4.7	3.3	3.3	31
37	0.1	0.1	0.1	0.1	0.2	0.0	0.0	0.0	0.1	2.3	32
										0.2	33

Hungary (DA) — Employees - Salariés - Asalariados

Total - Total - Total
ISIC 3 - CITI 3 - CIIU 3

ISIC 3	1999	2000	2001	2002	2003	2004	2005	2006	2007	2008
Total	743.0	753.2	752.8	746.3	734.4	715.2	688.8	753.0 [4]	750.1	696.3
15	127.5	120.7	118.1	124.1	125.6	114.6	109.3	113.0 [4]	109.8	100.3
16	2.0	2.1	2.1	2.1	2.1	1.7	1.6	0.9 [4]	1.0	1.0
17	34.3	33.3	30.5	28.5	26.9	26.9	23.7	22.5 [4]	19.3	16.7
18	73.0	68.3	66.4	60.3	52.4	46.1	36.7	35.9 [4]	32.5	25.7
19	24.4	22.5	22.4	21.2	17.5	13.6	12.8	16.3 [4]	14.1	12.6
20	20.5	22.5	22.2	21.3	22.6	21.5	19.7	24.4 [4]	23.0	16.2
21	10.0	10.1	9.8	11.1	14.5	17.9	16.2	17.0 [4]	13.6	12.6
22	22.1	24.2	24.5	27.3	28.0	23.7	24.0	31.2 [4]	33.4	24.6
23	14.7	13.0	11.5	9.8	8.2	7.0	6.7	6.4 [4]	6.4	6.5
24	37.2	35.4	34.2	33.0	32.9	32.2	30.8	31.3 [4]	30.7	30.2
25	30.2	31.5	32.9	35.9	34.5	36.0	36.4	40.4 [4]	44.2	44.2
26	31.3	30.5	29.1	27.8	27.4	26.5	25.2	27.4 [4]	28.3	27.8
27	20.8	20.8	20.3	19.9	20.1	18.7	19.3	18.9 [4]	19.4	22.0
28	53.9	54.4	58.2	54.1	55.6	55.4	54.6	69.9 [4]	70.2	63.3
29	57.6	57.3	59.1	60.2	59.2	59.1	59.2	64.9 [4]	67.6	62.1
30	11.4	11.2	13.1	13.8	12.2	7.6	7.8	8.8 [4]	10.7	9.5
31	61.2	73.6	72.2	70.4	65.1	67.5	65.2	68.3 [4]	66.6	63.3
32	29.6	39.6	40.6	37.3	41.4	51.7	50.2	48.4 [4]	46.1	45.7
33	13.7	14.0	14.5	15.6	14.5	14.5	14.1	17.9 [4]	18.0	15.2
34	32.1	33.2	36.1	35.8	38.3	39.9	41.8	51.0 [4]	55.7	56.7
35	7.7	7.2	7.3	9.0	9.0	8.4	8.1	7.8 [4]	8.7	12.0
36	26.3	26.3	26.1	26.4	25.4	23.6	23.9	28.3 [4]	29.2	26.6
37	1.3	1.5	1.6	1.4	1.0	1.1	1.5	2.0 [4]	1.6	1.5

Explanatory notes: see p. 77.

[1] Persons aged 15 years and over. [2] Excl. conscripts. [3] Second quarter of each year. [4] Prior to 2006: establishments with 5 or more persons employed.

Notes explicatives: voir p. 80.

[1] Personnes âgées de 15 ans et plus. [2] Non compris les conscrits. [3] Deuxième trimestre de chaque année. [4] Avant 2006: établissements occupant 5 personnes et plus.

Notas explicativas: véase p. 83.

[1] Personas de 15 años y más. [2] Excl. los conscriptos. [3] Segundo trimestre de cada año. [4] Antes de 2006: establecimientos con 5 y más trabajadores.

2F

EMPLOYMENT	EMPLOI	EMPLEO
Paid employment in manufacturing	**Emploi rémunéré dans les industries manufacturières**	**Empleo remunerado en las industrias manufactureras**
Thousands	Milliers	Millares

	1999	2000	2001	2002	2003	2004	2005	2006	2007	2008

Iceland (BA) [1] — Employees - Salariés - Asalariados

Total - Total - Total
ISIC 3 - CITI 3 - CIIU 3

	1999	2000	2001	2002	2003	2004	2005	2006	2007	2008
Total	20.5	21.3	21.0	20.0	19.3	19.9	19.4	18.2	17.4	18.3
15	10.0	10.3	10.5	10.4	9.3	9.3	9.0	7.7	6.6	7.0
17	0.5	0.4	0.6	0.4	0.5	0.4	0.3	0.3	0.2	0.4
18	0.7	0.4	0.4	0.2	0.3	0.2	0.2	0.1	0.2	-
19	-	-	-	0.1	0.1	-	-	-	-	-
20	0.5	0.6	0.4	0.3	0.6	0.7	0.6	0.6	0.8	0.3
21	0.1	0.2	0.3	0.3	0.2	0.2	0.1	-	0.1	0.0
22	2.8	3.1	2.5	1.8	2.1	2.0	2.0	2.0	1.7	2.2
24	0.8	0.7	0.6	0.8	0.7	0.8	0.9	0.7	0.9	1.2
25	0.5	0.8	0.6	0.5	0.5	0.3	0.4	0.3	0.2	0.2
26	0.8	0.7	0.8	1.1	0.4	0.8	0.8	1.0	1.0	1.4
27	0.9	1.1	0.9	1.0	0.9	1.1	1.0	1.3	1.7	2.1
28	1.1	0.9	1.0	1.0	0.9	1.5	1.7	1.5	1.3	1.1
29	0.6	0.9	0.6	0.6	0.9	0.9	1.0	0.9	1.0	1.0
30	-	-	-	-	-	-	-	-	-	-
31	-	0.1	0.1	0.1	0.2	0.1	0.2	0.1	0.2	0.1
32					-	-	-	0.1	0.0	0.1
33	0.1	0.2	0.2	0.4	0.6	0.5	0.4	0.4	0.5	0.5
34	-	-	0.1	-	0.1	0.1	0.1	-	0.2	-
35	0.6	0.4	0.7	0.5	0.7	0.6	0.4	0.3	0.3	0.3
36	0.6	0.7	0.6	0.4	0.2	0.3	0.3	0.5	0.6	0.5
37	0.1	-	0.1	0.1	-	-	0.1	0.1	0.0	

Men - Hommes - Hombres
ISIC 3 - CITI 3 - CIIU 3

	1999	2000	2001	2002	2003	2004	2005	2006	2007	2008
Total	13.6	14.6	14.4	13.4	12.8	13.1	12.8	12.5	12.0	12.9
15	5.8	5.9	5.8	5.8	5.1	4.8	5.0	4.7	3.8	4.3
17	0.3	0.3	0.3	0.2	0.4	0.3	0.2	0.2	0.1	0.2
18	0.2	0.2	0.2	0.1	0.1	0.1	0.1	0.1	0.0	-
19	-	-	-	-	-	-	-	-	0.0	-
20	0.4	0.5	0.3	0.3	0.6	0.6	0.5	0.5	0.6	0.3
21	0.1	0.2	0.3	0.2	0.2	0.1	0.1	-	0.1	0.0
22	1.7	2.0	1.8	1.3	1.2	1.2	1.2	1.1	1.0	1.3
24	0.5	0.5	0.3	0.4	0.4	0.3	0.3	0.3	0.4	0.5
25	0.3	0.7	0.5	0.4	0.5	0.2	0.3	0.2	0.1	0.2
26	0.7	0.6	0.8	1.0	0.3	0.7	0.7	0.9	0.8	1.2
27	0.7	0.9	0.8	0.7	0.8	1.1	0.9	1.1	1.4	1.6
28	1.0	0.8	0.9	1.0	0.9	1.4	1.6	1.4	1.2	1.0
29	0.6	0.8	0.6	0.6	0.8	0.8	0.8	0.8	0.9	0.9
30	-	-	-	-	-	-	-	-	-	-
31	-	0.1	0.1	0.1	0.2	0.1	0.1	0.1	0.2	0.1
32					-	-	-	0.1	0.0	0.1
33	0.1	0.1	0.1	0.3	0.4	0.2	0.2	0.2	0.3	0.4
34	-	-	0.1	-	0.1	0.1	0.1	-	0.2	-
35	0.6	0.4	0.7	0.5	0.7	0.6	0.3	0.2	0.3	0.2
36	0.6	0.7	0.6	0.3	0.2	0.3	0.3	0.4	0.4	0.4
37	0.1	-	0.1	0.1	-	-	0.1	0.1	0.0	-

Women - Femmes - Mujeres
ISIC 3 - CITI 3 - CIIU 3

	1999	2000	2001	2002	2003	2004	2005	2006	2007	2008
Total	6.9	6.7	6.6	6.6	6.5	6.8	6.6	5.7	5.4	5.4
15	4.2	4.4	4.7	4.7	4.2	4.4	4.0	3.0	2.8	2.7
17	0.2	0.2	0.2	0.1	0.2	0.2	-	0.1	0.0	0.1
18	0.5	0.2	0.2	0.2	0.2	0.1	0.2	0.1	0.1	-
19	-	-	-	0.1	-	-	-	-	-	-
20	0.1	0.1	0.1	-	-	0.1	0.1	0.1	0.1	0.0
21	-	-	0.1	0.1	-	-	-	-	-	-
22	1.1	1.1	0.7	0.6	0.9	0.8	0.8	0.9	0.7	0.9
24	0.3	0.2	0.3	0.4	0.3	0.4	0.6	0.5	0.5	0.6
25	0.2	0.1	0.1	0.1	-	0.1	-	-	0.0	0.0
26	0.1	0.1	-	0.1	0.1	0.1	0.1	0.1	0.2	0.2
27	0.2	0.2	0.1	0.2	0.1	-	0.1	0.2	0.3	0.5
28	0.1	0.1	0.1	-	0.1	0.1	0.1	0.1	0.1	0.1
29	0.1	0.1	-	0.1	0.1	0.1	0.2	0.1	0.1	0.1
30	-	-	-	-	-	-	-	-	-	-
31	-	-	-	-	-	-	-	0.1	-	-
32	-	-	-	-	-	-	-	-	-	-
33	-	-	-	0.1	0.2	0.3	0.2	0.2	0.2	0.1
34	-	-	-	-	-	-	-	-	-	-
35	-	-	0.1	-	-	-	0.1	0.1	0.0	0.1
36	0.1	-	0.1	-	-	-	-	0.1	0.1	0.1
37	-	-	-	-	-	-	-	-	-	-

Explanatory notes: see p. 77.
[1] Persons aged 16 to 74 years.

Notes explicatives: voir p. 80.
[1] Personnes âgées de 16 à 74 ans.

Notas explicativas: véase p. 83.
[1] Personas de 16 a 74 años.

Paid employment in manufacturing — Thousands
Emploi rémunéré dans les industries manufacturières — Milliers
Empleo remunerado en las industrias manufactureras — Millares

	1999	2000	2001	2002	2003	2004	2005	2006	2007	2008

Ireland (BA) [1][2]   Employees - Salariés - Asalariados

Total - Total - Total — ISIC 3 - CITI 3 - CIIU 3

	1999	2000	2001	2002	2003	2004	2005	2006	2007	2008
Total	269.0	270.0	276.9	261.0	262.8	258.0	252.3	247.1	246.6	237.3
15	50.7	50.9	50.2	49.3	51.3	51.8	52.1	54.1	49.9	47.6
16	0.6	0.5	0.8	1.0	0.9	0.7	0.4	0.3	0.4	0.4
17	8.3	7.5	7.1	6.7	6.7	3.8	3.0	3.5	3.1	3.2
18	8.0	6.0	4.3	3.7	3.6	3.0	3.4	4.1	4.3	3.8
19	1.4	1.1	0.6	0.7	0.6	0.8	0.3	0.3	0.1	-
20	6.6	7.5	6.6	6.3	5.7	6.5	7.5	5.7	6.1	6.2
21	4.0	3.7	3.2	3.8	4.4	3.4	2.7	2.2	2.2	1.4
22	16.5	17.2	19.7	17.5	17.2	17.0	14.9	14.2	15.6	16.0
23	0.2	0.1	0.3	0.4	0.5	1.4	0.9	0.4	0.4	0.4
24	26.1	25.1	28.4	31.8	30.3	34.4	32.7	33.1	31.3	32.3
25	9.8	10.8	9.9	8.7	8.9	7.2	8.4	7.0	7.4	7.8
26	12.4	12.7	12.2	13.6	14.6	12.5	12.0	12.6	12.9	9.7
27	3.6	2.7	2.7	3.0	1.7	5.1	6.2	4.1	3.4	3.9
28	20.4	23.0	24.1	18.5	23.6	15.8	14.8	15.8	21.9	20.1
29	16.4	13.9	13.4	13.5	13.0	9.5	9.5	10.1	10.8	10.1
30	15.7	20.2	21.9	21.9	17.1	19.6	20.0	18.9	16.4	16.2
31	7.8	7.2	8.5	6.9	6.2	10.6	9.3	5.5	4.1	3.7
32	19.4	19.8	22.6	15.7	13.3	7.8	10.5	12.8	12.2	13.1
33	15.6	16.2	15.9	16.2	20.0	21.3	20.7	20.8	22.7	22.8
34	4.8	4.0	4.4	3.8	3.1	5.8	4.5	4.2	3.3	2.9
35	5.6	5.9	5.8	4.3	4.4	4.6	3.7	3.6	3.3	3.9
36	14.9	13.3	13.4	12.4	13.8	14.5	13.9	11.6	11.8	9.7
37	0.5	0.7	0.8	1.3	1.9	1.0	1.0	2.3	2.8	2.0

Men - Hommes - Hombres — ISIC 3 - CITI 3 - CIIU 3

	1999	2000	2001	2002	2003	2004	2005	2006	2007	2008
Total	182.1	179.4	187.9	177.5	180.3	173.4	171.2	169.1	170.7	164.7
15	36.7	33.6	36.0	35.4	37.4	35.1	35.4	38.3	33.3	32.9
16	0.4	0.3	0.5	0.6	0.5	0.6	0.3	0.3	0.3	0.3
17	4.7	3.7	3.8	4.1	4.0	1.7	1.6	2.2	1.5	1.8
18	2.1	1.6	1.0	1.3	1.1	1.0	0.9	1.3	1.6	1.1
19	0.8	0.6	0.3	0.3	0.4	0.4	0.2	0.1	0.0	-
20	5.8	6.5	5.6	5.5	4.9	5.7	6.7	5.2	5.6	5.3
21	2.9	2.6	2.3	2.7	2.9	2.6	1.7	1.6	1.7	1.1
22	10.5	11.5	12.7	10.5	10.9	10.6	9.4	9.0	10.0	9.6
23	0.2	0.1	0.3	0.4	0.5	0.9	0.8	0.3	0.4	0.3
24	15.1	15.4	17.2	19.2	19.8	21.1	19.0	19.0	18.6	19.9
25	7.2	7.7	7.6	6.0	6.7	5.0	6.6	5.3	6.0	6.6
26	10.3	10.5	10.3	11.3	11.3	9.3	9.9	10.5	11.0	8.5
27	3.2	2.6	2.4	2.7	1.4	4.1	5.5	3.7	3.2	3.6
28	18.3	19.9	20.6	16.5	20.3	13.9	12.6	13.6	18.6	16.8
29	13.5	10.9	10.8	10.1	10.5	7.9	7.8	8.0	9.0	8.9
30	8.7	11.8	13.8	13.9	9.9	12.9	13.3	12.0	11.6	10.9
31	4.3	4.1	4.9	4.2	4.0	6.9	6.2	3.8	2.8	2.7
32	11.2	11.7	13.6	9.3	7.9	5.2	7.6	8.7	8.3	8.1
33	6.5	6.5	7.0	7.5	9.2	9.7	9.8	10.0	11.0	11.8
34	3.2	2.6	3.0	2.6	2.1	4.2	2.8	2.5	1.9	1.8
35	5.2	5.4	4.5	3.3	3.8	3.8	3.2	3.2	3.0	3.4
36	11.0	9.2	9.1	8.9	9.5	10.5	9.4	9.0	9.4	7.9
37	0.3	0.5	0.6	1.1	1.4	0.7	0.8	1.6	2.0	1.5

Women - Femmes - Mujeres — ISIC 3 - CITI 3 - CIIU 3

	1999	2000	2001	2002	2003	2004	2005	2006	2007	2008
Total	86.9	90.6	89.0	83.5	82.5	84.6	81.1	78.0	75.9	72.7
15	14.0	17.2	14.2	14.0	13.9	16.7	16.7	15.8	16.6	14.7
16	0.2	0.2	0.3	0.3	0.4	0.1	0.1	0.0	0.1	0.1
17	3.6	3.7	3.3	2.6	2.7	2.1	1.4	1.3	1.6	1.4
18	5.8	4.4	3.3	2.4	2.6	2.1	2.6	2.8	2.7	2.7
19	0.5	0.5	0.2	0.3	0.2	0.4	0.2	0.2	0.1	-
20	0.8	1.0	1.1	0.8	0.8	0.8	0.8	0.5	0.5	1.0
21	1.1	1.2	0.9	1.1	1.5	0.7	1.1	0.6	0.5	0.3
22	6.1	5.7	6.9	7.0	6.4	6.4	5.5	5.1	5.6	6.4
23	-	-	-	0.0	0.0	0.5	0.1	0.1	0.0	0.1
24	10.9	9.7	11.1	12.6	10.5	13.3	13.7	14.1	12.8	12.4
25	2.6	3.1	2.3	2.7	2.2	2.2	1.8	1.7	1.3	1.2
26	2.1	2.2	1.9	2.4	3.3	3.2	2.1	2.1	1.9	1.2
27	0.3	0.1	0.3	0.3	0.3	1.0	0.7	0.4	0.2	0.3
28	2.1	3.1	3.5	1.9	3.3	1.9	2.1	2.2	3.3	3.4
29	2.9	3.0	2.7	3.4	2.5	1.7	1.7	2.2	1.9	1.3
30	6.9	8.3	8.1	8.0	7.2	6.7	6.7	6.9	4.8	5.3
31	3.5	3.1	3.7	2.6	2.2	3.7	3.1	1.7	1.3	1.0
32	8.1	8.2	9.1	6.4	5.5	2.6	2.9	4.2	3.9	5.0
33	9.0	9.7	8.9	8.7	10.8	11.5	10.8	10.8	11.7	11.0
34	1.5	1.4	1.4	1.3	1.0	1.6	1.8	1.7	1.5	1.1
35	0.4	0.5	1.3	1.0	0.6	0.9	0.6	0.3	0.3	0.6
36	3.9	4.1	4.3	3.6	4.3	4.1	4.5	2.6	2.4	1.8
37	0.2	0.2	0.2	0.2	0.5	0.2	0.2	0.7	0.8	0.5

Explanatory notes: see p. 77.
[1] Persons aged 15 years and over. [2] Second quarter of each year.

Notes explicatives: voir p. 80.
[1] Personnes âgées de 15 ans et plus. [2] Deuxième trimestre de chaque année.

Notas explicativas: véase p. 83.
[1] Personas de 15 años y más. [2] Segundo trimestre de cada año.

	EMPLOYMENT	EMPLOI	EMPLEO
	Paid employment in manufacturing Thousands	**Emploi rémunéré dans les industries manufacturières** Milliers	**Empleo remunerado en las industrias manufactureras** Millares

Italy (BA) [1]

Employees - Salariés - Asalariados

Total - Total - Total
ISIC 3 - CITI 3 - CIIU 3

	1999	2000	2001	2002	2003	2004	2005	2006	2007	2008
Total	4 075	4 060	4 061	4 103	4 126	4 067 [2]	4 086	4 075	4 114	4 078
15	289	282	268	292	304	332 [2]	328	329	331	316
16	9	9	9	7	5	4 [2]	4	4	2	2
17	334	352	344	335	323	237 [2]	217	207	199	201
18	209	206	206	198	188	206 [2]	196	177	180	187
19	172	168	165	152	151	125 [2]	114	100	100	113
20	114	119	119	114	113	113 [2]	110	112	103	119
21	92	95	92	90	87	90 [2]	80	78	77	90
22	139	138	140	143	143	135 [2]	134	137	133	139
23	31	29	30	33	30	31 [2]	29	30	29	27
24	243	231	223	212	215	211 [2]	222	215	217	215
25	192	182	186	194	190	210 [2]	207	195	190	180
26	162	164	171	196	201	215 [2]	225	201	216	221
27	132	130	141	154	147	190 [2]	208	200	210	202
28	540	513	532	523	525	434 [2]	429	460	479	477
29	565	582	584	600	629	570 [2]	592	607	597	559
30	42	44	43	40	40	21 [2]	23	25	18	18
31	175	176	173	167	171	174 [2]	176	179	178	177
32	68	63	65	67	70	83 [2]	94	103	103	96
33	67	70	79	81	81	88 [2]	100	117	130	128
34	184	182	173	176	176	228 [2]	216	210	223	219
35	85	83	81	89	83	106 [2]	108	124	139	135
36	224	232	227	228	239	254 [2]	258	251	244	242
37	9	11	11	12	13	11 [2]	14	15	15	16

Men - Hommes - Hombres
ISIC 3 - CITI 3 - CIIU 3

	1999	2000	2001	2002	2003	2004	2005	2006	2007	2008
Total	2 793	2 768	2 767	2 807	2 827	2 820 [2]	2 851	2 864	2 910	2 886
15	196	190	182	190	195	213 [2]	207	212	210	201
16	6	6	5	4	3	2 [2]	3	3	2	1
17	138	143	138	135	129	106 [2]	100	100	93	85
18	37	38	38	37	37	36 [2]	38	32	33	38
19	83	79	81	78	77	62 [2]	54	48	51	56
20	91	92	93	96	96	94 [2]	93	90	82	99
21	69	71	70	68	66	68 [2]	58	55	57	68
22	97	96	94	91	92	89 [2]	91	87	82	87
23	29	26	26	28	27	28 [2]	26	25	27	25
24	177	167	161	152	154	145 [2]	153	145	149	150
25	131	126	129	133	124	149 [2]	147	142	140	127
26	119	122	125	143	147	166 [2]	176	159	170	175
27	115	113	122	132	128	171 [2]	186	178	187	183
28	431	414	428	421	422	347 [2]	347	376	401	395
29	455	465	470	487	505	459 [2]	473	477	479	452
30	31	32	30	28	28	13 [2]	15	17	12	13
31	122	120	118	116	118	121 [2]	128	127	119	121
32	43	40	43	44	48	51 [2]	61	74	71	68
33	38	41	43	48	47	55 [2]	59	67	76	78
34	152	145	139	145	143	179 [2]	169	168	180	177
35	75	72	69	75	71	92 [2]	92	108	120	117
36	151	161	155	147	159	165 [2]	165	162	159	159
37	8	9	9	10	11	8 [2]	10	12	12	12

Women - Femmes - Mujeres
ISIC 3 - CITI 3 - CIIU 3

	1999	2000	2001	2002	2003	2004	2005	2006	2007	2008
Total	1 282	1 292	1 293	1 296	1 298	1 247 [2]	1 235	1 211	1 204	1 193
15	93	92	86	102	109	120 [2]	121	118	120	116
16	3	3	4	3	2	2 [2]	2	1	1	1
17	197	209	206	201	194	131 [2]	118	107	107	116
18	171	167	168	160	151	170 [2]	158	145	147	148
19	89	89	84	75	75	63 [2]	60	52	49	57
20	22	27	26	18	18	19 [2]	17	22	21	20
21	23	24	22	22	21	22 [2]	22	23	20	22
22	43	42	46	52	50	47 [2]	43	50	51	52
23	3	3	3	5	3	3 [2]	3	4	2	2
24	66	64	63	59	61	65 [2]	69	69	68	65
25	61	56	57	61	66	61 [2]	60	53	50	53
26	43	42	46	53	54	49 [2]	49	42	46	47
27	17	18	20	23	19	19 [2]	21	22	24	19
28	109	99	104	102	103	86 [2]	82	84	79	81
29	110	117	114	113	123	111 [2]	119	129	118	107
30	11	12	13	12	12	8 [2]	8	8	7	5
31	53	56	55	50	53	53 [2]	48	52	58	56
32	25	23	22	23	22	32 [2]	33	29	31	27
33	29	29	36	33	34	33 [2]	41	50	54	51
34	32	37	34	31	32	50 [2]	47	42	44	42
35	10	11	11	14	12	14 [2]	17	16	19	19
36	73	71	72	81	80	88 [2]	93	89	85	83
37	1	2	1	3	3	3 [2]	3	4	3	4

Explanatory notes: see p. 77.

[1] Persons aged 15 years and over. [2] Methodology revised; data not strictly comparable.

Notes explicatives: voir p. 80.

[1] Personnes âgées de 15 ans et plus. [2] Méthodologie révisée; les données ne sont pas strictement comparables.

Notas explicativas: véase p. 83.

[1] Personas de 15 años y más. [2] Metodología revisada; los datos no son estrictamente comparables.

	Paid employment in manufacturing			Emploi rémunéré dans les industries manufacturières			Empleo remunerado en las industrias manufactureras		
	Thousands			Milliers			Millares		
	1999	2000	2001	2002	2003	2004	2005	2006	2007	2008

Latvia (DA) [1]   **Employees - Salariés - Asalariados**

Total - Total - Total
ISIC 3 - CITI 3 - CIIU 3

	1999	2000	2001	2002	2003	2004	2005	2006	2007	2008
Total	150.1	148.9	154.8	153.8	157.0	162.5	157.7	159.8	159.9	150.9
15	35.1	36.6	37.5	35.3	34.7	35.3	34.6	34.6	33.8	31.3
16	-	-	-	-	-	-	-	-	-	-
17	10.3	10.5	10.7	10.3	10.0	9.8	7.9	7.2	7.3	6.4
18	13.3	13.1	14.1	15.0	14.3	14.0	12.7	12.7	12.4	10.8
19	2.2	2.4	0.9	0.8	0.6	0.7	0.7	0.6	0.5	-
20	26.5	29.8	32.6	30.9	33.3	33.6	30.7	32.0	30.3	27.4
21	1.3	1.4	1.7	1.6	1.6	1.6	1.6	1.5	1.6	1.6
22	9.3	9.5	8.5	8.8	9.0	10.0	10.3	8.6	9.3	9.3
23	-	-	-	-	-	-	-	-	-	-
24	6.5	3.4	4.5	4.6	4.5	4.6	3.9	4.3	4.5	4.3
25	1.7	2.0	2.4	2.6	2.8	3.8	4.1	4.0	4.8	4.7
26	4.5	4.3	3.8	3.8	4.1	4.0	5.0	5.7	7.0	7.1
27	2.8	3.0	3.2	3.2	3.4	3.4	3.5	3.4	3.6	3.6
28	5.7	6.2	6.9	7.0	7.3	8.3	8.1	10.3	9.8	11.3
29	7.4	6.9	6.6	6.7	6.8	7.1	7.6	7.5	7.0	6.0
30	-	-	-	-	-	-	-	-	-	-
31	3.4	2.7	3.0	2.8	3.0	3.3	3.2	3.5	3.9	4.0
32	2.3	1.4	1.2	1.3	1.2	1.3	1.2	1.0	1.0	1.0
33	1.1	1.3	1.3	1.3	1.3	1.7	1.7	1.7	1.9	1.6
34	0.7	0.5	0.7	0.6	0.7	0.8	0.9	1.0	1.2	1.3
35	7.3	5.5	5.2	5.6	5.8	6.1	5.9	5.8	5.3	6.7
36	7.4	8.3	8.9	10.6	11.8	12.1	13.1	13.2	13.5	10.9
37	0.6	0.7	0.5	-	-	-	0.5	0.5	0.8	0.7

Men - Hommes - Hombres
ISIC 3 - CITI 3 - CIIU 3

	1999	2000	2001	2002	2003	2004	2005	2006	2007	2008
Total	83.6	83.5	86.6	85.2	88.0	90.8	88.3	90.1	89.3	85.1
15	16.2	16.1	16.8	15.2	15.2	14.9	14.7	14.3	13.9	13.2
16	-	-	-	-	-	-	-	-	-	-
17	3.3	3.4	3.5	3.2	3.2	3.1	2.5	2.2	2.1	1.8
18	1.6	1.5	1.8	1.6	1.5	1.3	1.2	1.7	1.5	1.3
19	0.8	0.5	-	-	-	-	-	-	-	-
20	21.9	24.1	26.1	24.7	26.2	26.4	23.7	24.4	22.6	20.2
21	0.8	0.8	1.0	0.9	1.0	1.0	0.9	0.9	0.9	0.9
22	4.0	4.4	3.8	3.8	3.7	4.1	4.1	3.8	4.2	3.8
23	-	-	-	-	-	-	-	-	-	-
24	2.8	1.7	2.3	2.3	2.1	2.2	1.8	1.9	1.9	1.9
25	1.1	1.4	1.5	1.8	1.9	2.7	2.9	2.6	3.2	3.3
26	2.8	2.9	2.5	2.6	2.8	2.9	3.5	4.0	5.2	5.2
27	2.2	2.4	2.5	2.5	2.7	2.8	2.8	2.7	2.8	2.8
28	4.4	4.8	5.4	5.6	5.8	6.5	6.3	7.7	7.6	9.0
29	5.5	5.1	4.8	4.9	4.7	5.0	5.4	5.4	4.8	4.2
30	-	-	-	-	-	-	-	-	-	-
31	2.0	1.6	1.7	1.6	1.7	1.8	1.8	1.9	2.1	2.2
32	1.3	0.8	0.6	0.8	0.7	0.8	0.7	0.6	0.6	0.6
33	0.8	0.9	0.8	0.9	0.8	1.1	1.0	1.0	1.2	0.9
34	0.6	0.4	0.6	0.5	0.6	0.7	0.8	0.8	1.0	1.0
35	5.7	4.3	4.2	4.5	4.6	4.8	4.8	4.6	4.1	5.2
36	4.9	5.5	5.6	7.0	7.8	7.8	8.6	8.4	8.5	6.8
37	0.5	0.6	-	-	-	-	-	-	0.6	0.5

Women - Femmes - Mujeres
ISIC 3 - CITI 3 - CIIU 3

	1999	2000	2001	2002	2003	2004	2005	2006	2007	2008
Total	66.5	65.4	68.1	68.6	69.0	71.7	69.4	69.7	70.6	65.8
15	18.9	20.5	20.7	20.1	19.5	20.4	19.9	20.3	20.0	18.1
16	-	-	-	-	-	-	-	-	-	-
17	7.0	7.0	7.2	7.2	6.8	6.7	5.5	4.9	5.1	4.6
18	11.7	11.6	12.4	13.4	12.8	12.7	11.5	11.0	10.9	9.5
19	1.4	0.9	0.6	0.5	0.4	0.4	-	-	-	-
20	4.6	5.7	6.5	6.2	7.0	7.3	7.0	7.7	7.7	7.2
21	0.6	0.6	0.7	0.7	0.7	0.6	0.7	0.6	0.7	0.7
22	5.4	5.1	4.7	5.0	5.3	5.9	6.2	4.8	5.2	5.5
23	-	-	-	-	-	-	-	-	-	-
24	3.7	1.7	2.2	2.3	2.3	2.4	2.2	2.4	2.5	2.4
25	0.6	0.6	0.8	0.8	0.9	1.1	1.2	1.4	1.6	1.4
26	1.7	1.4	1.3	1.2	1.3	1.1	1.6	1.7	1.8	1.9
27	0.6	0.7	0.7	0.7	0.7	0.7	0.7	0.7	0.8	0.8
28	1.3	1.4	1.5	1.4	1.6	1.8	1.8	2.6	2.2	2.2
29	1.8	1.8	1.8	1.9	2.1	2.0	2.2	2.1	2.2	1.8
30	-	-	-	-	-	-	-	-	-	-
31	1.4	1.0	1.3	1.2	1.2	1.5	1.4	1.6	1.8	1.8
32	1.0	0.6	0.5	0.6	0.5	0.5	0.5	-	-	0.5
33	-	-	-	0.5	0.5	0.6	0.7	0.7	0.7	0.7
35	1.6	1.1	1.0	1.1	1.1	1.3	1.2	1.2	1.1	1.5
36	2.5	2.8	3.4	3.5	4.0	4.2	4.6	4.8	5.0	4.1
37	-	-		-	-	-	-	-	-	-

Explanatory notes: see p. 77.   Notes explicatives: voir p. 80.   Notas explicativas: véase p. 83.

[1] First quarter of each year.   [1] Premier trimestre de chaque année.   [1] Primer trimestre de cada año.

2F EMPLOYMENT — EMPLOI — EMPLEO

Paid employment in manufacturing — **Emploi rémunéré dans les industries manufacturières** — **Empleo remunerado en las industrias manufactureras**

Thousands — Milliers — Millares

Lithuania (DA)
Employees - Salariés - Asalariados
Total - Total - Total
ISIC 3 - CITI 3 - CIIU 3

	1999	2000	2001	2002	2003	2004	2005	2006	2007	2008
Total	240.259	236.442	233.081	240.181	246.383 [1]	244.543	246.076	243.919	240.148	.
15	56.750	56.094	51.223	50.354	49.067 [1]	49.595	51.226	49.605	48.313	
16	0.432	0.473	0.475	0.486	0.483 [1]	0.518	0.528	0.561	0.484	
17	24.160	21.657	21.020	19.473	18.881 [1]	17.643	16.945	16.537	14.869	
18	32.791	35.328	36.951	40.207	39.452 [1]	36.349	32.680	29.986	26.089	
19	4.691	3.287	2.726	2.812	2.509 [1]	2.199	1.917	1.617	1.512	
20	19.728	20.488	22.600	25.748	27.932 [1]	26.893	26.892	27.586	27.562	
21	3.578	3.891	3.685	2.149	1.914 [1]	1.997	2.008	2.117	2.724	
22	10.586	10.067	9.729	9.788	10.495 [1]	9.958	10.304	10.322	10.980	
23	3.807	3.805	3.509	3.635	3.634 [1]	3.565	3.457	3.415	3.515	
24	7.133	6.388	5.872	5.341	5.538 [1]	5.159	5.306	5.631	5.834	
25	5.148	5.434	5.839	6.648	7.210 [1]	7.338	8.181	8.807	9.258	
26	11.574	10.584	10.284	9.687	9.708 [1]	9.736	10.300	10.905	11.334	
27	1.622	1.349	1.343	1.387	0.994 [1]	0.900	0.926	0.903	1.272	
28	8.706	8.930	9.225	10.184	11.936 [1]	13.199	14.673	16.198	16.880	
29	13.369	11.553	10.700	10.665	10.219 [1]	10.421	9.478	10.121	10.348	
30	0.286	0.247	0.293	0.304	0.224 [1]	0.406	0.283	0.282	0.814	
31	3.653	3.995	4.711	4.694	6.331 [1]	6.857	6.329	5.918	5.784	
32	8.151	8.420	7.878	8.163	8.361 [1]	9.359	8.282	4.617	2.610	
33	2.621	3.326	3.440	3.669	3.751 [1]	3.357	3.815	3.662	3.805	
34	1.763	0.437	0.303	0.381	0.421 [1]	0.423	1.038	1.079	1.282	
35	6.929	6.221	6.069	6.316	6.549 [1]	6.112	6.472	6.625	7.018	
36	11.747	13.092	13.809	16.817	19.394 [1]	21.081	23.536	26.031	26.040	
37	1.034	1.376	1.397	1.273	1.380 [1]	1.477	1.502	1.394	1.821	

Luxembourg (E)
Employees - Salariés - Asalariados
Total - Total - Total
ISIC 3 - CITI 3 - CIIU 3

	1999	2000	2001	2002	2003	2004	2005	2006	2007	2008
Total	32.4	32.6	33.1	32.9	32.2	32.0	32.1	33.2	34.6	.
15-16	4.1	4.1	4.2	4.2	4.1	4.1	4.1	4.4	4.5	
17-18	0.9	0.7	0.8	0.9	0.8	0.8	0.8	1.4	1.4	
19	0.0	0.0	0.0	0.0	0.0	0.0	0.0	0.0	0.0	
20,36,37	1.2	1.2	1.3	1.4	1.0	1.0	1.0	1.1	1.2	
21-22	2.4	2.6	2.7	2.9	2.8	2.8	2.9	2.9	2.8	
23	0.0	0.0	0.0	0.0	0.0	0.0	0.0	0.0	0.0	
24	1.4	1.5	1.5	1.4	1.4	1.4	1.3	1.1	0.8	
25	4.6	4.1	4.0	3.8	3.8	4.1	4.1	4.1	4.4	
26	2.9	2.9	2.9	2.8	2.8	2.6	2.5	2.7	2.8	
27	6.4	6.2	6.1	5.9	5.8	5.5	5.5	4.9	5.3	
28	4.1	4.6	4.8	4.6	4.5	4.5	4.5	4.7	5.2	
29	2.3	2.4	2.5	2.4	2.5	2.6	2.7	2.8	3.0	
30-33	2.0	2.1	2.1	2.1	2.2	2.2	2.4	2.6	2.8	
34-35	0.3	0.3	0.3	0.3	0.3	0.4	0.4	0.5	0.6	

Macedonia, The Former Yugoslav Rep. of (DA) [2]
Employees - Salariés - Asalariados
Total - Total - Total
ISIC 2 - CITI 2 - CIIU 2 / ISIC 3 - CITI 3 - CIIU 3

ISIC 2	1999	2000	2001	2002	2003	2004	2005	2006	2007	2008	ISIC 3
Total	105	99	101	91	89	114 [3]	110	109	.	.	Total
311-312	9	9	12	11	11	13 [3]	13	12			15
313	2	2	5	5	5	4 [3]	3	3			16
314	6	6	7	6	6	8 [3]	6	5			17
321	9	6	23	20	22	32 [3]	35	35			18
322	23	24	4	4	4	4 [3]	4	5			19
323	2	4	1	1	1	3 [3]	3	3			20
324	5	5	1	1	1	2 [3]	1	2			21
331	-	-	3	3	2	4 [3]	4	3			22
332	2	2	1	1	1	1 [3]	1	1			23
341	1	1	6	5	2	3 [3]	3	3			24
342	2	2	2	2	4	6 [3]	5	5			25
351	5	4	6	6	5	4 [3]	5	4			26
352	3	3	7	5	6	6 [3]	6	6			27
353	1	1	7	7	6	9 [3]	8	8			28
36	7	6	2	2	2	2 [3]	2	2			29
371	5	6	.	.	.	1 [3]	1	1			30
372	4	3	5	3	2	3 [3]	3	3			31
381	7	7	.	.	.	0 [3]	0	0			32
382	1	1	.	.	.	0 [3]	0	0			33
383	7	5	3	3	3	3 [3]	2	2			34
384	4	4	2	2	2	2 [3]	2	2			35
390	-	-	2	2	2	4 [3]	4	4			36
			.	.	.	0 [3]	0	0			37

Explanatory notes: see p. 77. — Notes explicatives: voir p. 80. — Notas explicativas: véase p. 83.

[1] Methodology revised; data not strictly comparable. [2] March and Sep. of each year. [3] Prior to 2004: April of each year.

[1] Méthodologie révisée; les données ne sont pas strictement comparables. [2] Mars et sept. de chaque année. [3] Avant 2004: Avril de chaque année.

[1] Metodología revisada; los datos no son estrictamente comparables. [2] Marzo y sept. de cada año. [3] Antes de 2004: Abril de cada año.

Paid employment in manufacturing — Thousands
Emploi rémunéré dans les industries manufacturières — Milliers
Empleo remunerado en las industrias manufactureras — Millares

	1999	2000	2001	2002	2003	2004	2005	2006	2007	2008

Macedonia, The Former Yugoslav Rep. of (DA) [1] — Employees - Salariés - Asalariados

Men - Hommes - Hombres
ISIC 2 - CITI 2 - CIIU 2   (right: ISIC 3 - CITI 3 - CIIU 3)

ISIC 2	1999	2000	2001	2002	2003	2004	2005	2006	2007	2008	ISIC 3
Total	58	54	57	51	48	60[2]	57	56	.	.	Total
311-312	6	6	8	7	7	8[2]	8	8	.	.	15
313	1	1	3	3	3	2[2]	2	2	.	.	16
314	4	4	2	2	2	3[2]	2	2	.	.	17
321	4	2	4	3	2	5[2]	5	5	.	.	18
322	4	3	1	1	1	1[2]	1	1	.	.	19
323	1	1	1	1	1	3[2]	2	2	.	.	20
324	1	2	1	1	1	1[2]	1	1	.	.	21
331	-	-	2	2	1	2[2]	2	1	.	.	22
332	1	1	1	1	1	1[2]	1	1	.	.	23
341	1	1	4	3	1	2[2]	2	2	.	.	24
342	1	1	2	2	3	4[2]	3	3	.	.	25
351	4	3	5	5	4	3[2]	3	3	.	.	26
352	1	1	6	4	5	6[2]	6	6	.	.	27
353	1	1	6	6	6	7[2]	7	7	.	.	28
36	6	6	2	2	2	2[2]	2	2	.	.	29
371	4	5	.	.	.	0[2]	0	1	.	.	30
372	3	2	4	2	1	2[2]	2	2	.	.	31
381	6	6	.	.	.	0[2]	0	0	.	.	32
382	1	1	.	.	.	0[2]	0	0	.	.	33
383	5	4	2	2	2	2[2]	2	2	.	.	34
384	3	3	-	2	2	2[2]	2	2	.	.	35
390	-	-	1	1	1	3[2]	3	3	.	.	36
			.	.	.	0[2]	0	0	.	.	37

Women - Femmes - Mujeres
ISIC 2 - CITI 2 - CIIU 2   (right: ISIC 3 - CITI 3 - CIIU 3)

ISIC 2	1999	2000	2001	2002	2003	2004	2005	2006	2007	2008	ISIC 3
Total	47	45	44	40	40	54[2]	53	53	.	.	Total
311-312	3	3	4	4	4	5[2]	5	4	.	.	15
313	1	1	2	2	2	2[2]	1	1	.	.	16
314	2	2	5	4	4	5[2]	4	3	.	.	17
321	5	4	19	17	20	27[2]	30	30	.	.	18
322	19	21	3	3	3	3[2]	3	4	.	.	19
323	1	1	0	0	0	0[2]	1	1	.	.	20
324	4	3	0	0	0	1[2]	0	1	.	.	21
332	1	1	1	1	1	2[2]	2	2	.	.	22
341	1	-	0	0	0	0[2]	0	0	.	.	23
342	1	1	2	2	1	1[2]	1	1	.	.	24
351	2	1	-	-	1	2[2]	2	2	.	.	25
352	1	2	1	1	1	1[2]	1	0	.	.	26
36	1	-	1	1	1	0[2]	0	1	.	.	27
371	1	1	1	1	1	2[2]	1	1	.	.	28
372	1	1	0	0	0	0[2]	0	0	.	.	29
381	-	1	.	.	.	0[2]	0	0	.	.	30
383	2	1	1	1	1	1[2]	1	1	.	.	31
384	1	1	.	.	.	0[2]	0	0	.	.	32
			.	.	.	0[2]	0	0	.	.	33
			1	1	1	1[2]	0	0	.	.	34
			0	0	0	0[2]	0	0	.	.	35
			1	1	1	1[2]	1	1	.	.	36
			.	.	.	0[2]	0	0	.	.	37

Malta (BA) [3] — Employees - Salariés - Asalariados

Total - Total - Total
ISIC 3 - CITI 3 - CIIU 3

ISIC 3	1999	2000	2001	2002	2003	2004	2005	2006	2007	2008
Total	.	31.010	28.770	28.160	26.450	26.580	26.090	24.466	23.612	.
15	.	3.943	5.129	3.347	4.343	4.117	4.858	4.355	4.455	.
16	.	0.171	0.261	-	-	-	-	-	-	.
17	.	2.083	0.839	-	-	-	-	-	-	.
18	.	1.855	3.036	3.841	2.309	2.184	-	1.396	0.988	.
19	.	0.932	0.397	-	-	-	-	-	-	.
20	.	0.412	-	-	-	-	-	-	-	.
21	.	0.465	0.356	-	-	-	-	-	-	.
22	.	1.723	1.921	1.671	2.126	2.165	1.832	1.591	1.727	.
23	.	0.233	0.142	-	-	-	-	1.016	-	.
24	.	1.292	1.049	-	-	1.377	1.356	-	1.204	.
25	.	2.104	2.061	2.036	-	1.413	1.707	1.532	1.500	.
26	.	0.879	0.674	-	-	0.892	0.833	0.972	1.399	.
27	.	0.531	0.383	-	-	-	-	-	-	.
28	.	0.851	0.752	-	-	1.116	1.754	1.052	0.947	.
29	.	0.369	0.466	-	-	-	-	0.467	-	.
30	.	0.449	-	-	-	-	-	1.144	-	.
31	.	1.819	0.751	-	-	0.737	0.805	-	1.321	.
32	.	2.516	3.425	3.007	4.464	3.533	3.613	3.619	3.277	.
33	.	0.833	0.466	-	-	1.337	1.103	1.086	0.917	.
34	.	0.245	0.057	-	-	-	-	-	-	.
35	.	4.186	3.857	3.224	2.931	2.642	2.628	2.287	2.452	.
36	.	3.007	2.744	2.518	3.286	3.051	3.543	2.733	2.093	.
37	.	0.116	-	-	-	-	-	-	-	.

Explanatory notes: see p. 77.

[1] March and Sep. of each year. [2] Prior to 2004: April of each year. [3] Persons aged 15 years and over.

Notes explicatives: voir p. 80.

[1] Mars et sept. de chaque année. [2] Avant 2004: Avril de chaque année. [3] Personnes âgées de 15 ans et plus.

Notas explicativas: véase p. 83.

[1] Marzo y sept. de cada año. [2] Antes de 2004: Abril de cada año. [3] Personas de 15 años y más.

2F

EMPLOYMENT	EMPLOI	EMPLEO
Paid employment in manufacturing	**Emploi rémunéré dans les industries manufacturières**	**Empleo remunerado en las industrias manufactureras**
Thousands	Milliers	Millares

	1999	2000	2001	2002	2003	2004	2005	2006	2007	2008
Malta (BA) [1]				**Employees - Salariés - Asalariados**						
Men - Hommes - Hombres										
ISIC 3 - CITI 3 - CIIU 3										
Total	.	21.580	20.380	16.950	19.090	19.320	18.990	17.838	17.467	.
15	.	3.097	4.134	2.746	3.110	3.284	4.131	3.564	3.566	.
16	.	0.114	0.199	-	-	-	-	-	-	
17	.	0.750	0.536	-	-	-	-	-	-	
18	.	0.177	0.890	1.054	-	0.882	1.290	0.234	0.283	.
19	.	0.460	0.000	-	-	-	-	-	-	
20	.	0.347	-							
21	.	0.396	0.283	-	-	-	-	-	-	
22	.	1.337	1.338	-	-	1.532	1.068	1.112	1.352	
23	.	0.233	0.142	-	-	-	-	-	-	
24	.	0.893	0.756	-	-	1.180	0.987	0.622	0.867	
25	.	1.463	1.750	-	-	1.070	1.020	1.085	0.849	
26	.	0.818	0.611	-	-	0.800	0.833	0.859	1.288	
27	.	0.531	0.383	-	-	-	-	-	-	
28	.	0.722	0.611	-	-	0.997	1.479	0.990	0.909	
29	.	0.312	0.326	-	-	-	-	-	-	
30	.	0.201	-							
31	.	1.300	0.510	-	-	-	-	0.815	0.974	
32	.	1.071	1.496	-	2.413	2.024	2.552	2.117	1.732	
33	.	0.289	0.262	-	-	0.591	0.351	0.494	0.417	
34	.	0.125	0.057	-	-	-	-	-	-	
35	.	4.186	3.725	3.224	2.794	2.574	2.554	2.172	2.439	
36	.	2.643	2.374	2.054	2.323	2.631	3.186	2.359	1.794	
37	.	0.116	-							
Women - Femmes - Mujeres										
ISIC 3 - CITI 3 - CIIU 3										
Total	.	9.432	8.383	9.211	7.354	7.264	7.096	6.628	6.145	.
15	.	0.847	0.995	0.601	1.233	0.833	0.727	0.791	0.889	
16	.	0.057	0.062	-	-	-	-	-	-	
17	.	1.332	0.303	-	-	-	-	-	-	
18	.	1.677	2.146	2.787	-	1.302	1.042	1.162	0.705	
19	.	0.472	0.397	-	-	-	-	-	-	
20	.	0.065	-							
21	.	0.069	0.073	-	-	-	-	-	-	
22	.	0.386	0.583	-	-	0.633	0.764	0.479	0.375	
23	.	0.000	0.000	-	-	-	-	-	-	
24	.	0.398	0.293	-	-	0.197	0.369	-	0.337	
25	.	0.641	0.311	-	-	0.343	0.687	0.447	0.651	
26	.	0.060	0.063	-	-	0.092	0.000	0.113	0.111	
27	.	-	-							
28	.	0.129	0.141	-	-	0.119	0.275	0.062	0.038	
29	.	0.057	0.140	-	-	-	-	-	-	
30	.	0.249	-							
31	.	0.518	0.241	-	-	-	-	-	0.347	
32	.	1.445	1.929	-	2.051	1.509	1.061	1.502	1.545	
33	.	0.544	0.204	-	-	0.746	0.752	0.592	0.500	
34	.	0.120	0.000	-	-	-	-	-	-	
35	.	0.000	0.132	0.000	0.137	0.068	0.074	0.115	0.013	
36	.	0.364	0.370	0.464	0.963	0.420	0.357	0.374	0.299	
37	.	-	-							
Moldova, Republic of (CA) [2]				**Employees - Salariés - Asalariados**						
Total - Total - Total										
ISIC 3 - CITI 3 - CIIU 3										
Total	111.1	98.1	105.1	103.6	103.6	107.5	106.1	104.2	97.2	93.4
15	46.1	40.4	43.4	43.6	44.2	46.2	45.7	43.3	38.4	36.2
16	2.4	2.4	2.8	2.6	2.2	2.1	2.1	1.8	1.5	1.3
17	7.5	7.2	10.3	8.1	5.9	6.1	4.7	3.8	3.4	3.2
18	9.5	9.4	9.9	12.6	14.3	15.9	16.9	19.0	19.1	17.6
19	3.9	3.4	3.7	4.0	3.6	3.7	3.7	4.0	4.0	4.5
20	1.4	1.5	1.6	1.5	1.6	1.7	1.7	1.5	1.2	1.1
21	1.1	1.0	1.1	1.1	1.2	1.4	1.7	1.6	1.6	1.3
22	2.1	2.0	2.2	2.1	2.0	2.2	2.2	2.3	1.8	1.9
23								0.1		0.1
24	1.0	0.9	1.4	1.3	1.4	1.3	1.4	1.5	1.3	1.4
25	0.9	0.6	0.7	0.8	1.6	1.6	1.5	1.6	1.8	2.0
26	8.4	7.3	7.2	6.8	6.7	6.9	6.9	6.9	6.7	6.1
27	0.3	0.3	0.2	0.2	0.2	0.3	0.2	0.2	0.2	0.2
28	2.3	1.8	1.9	2.1	2.5	2.4	2.3	2.3	2.5	2.6
29	13.1	10.5	9.8	9.1	8.5	7.7	7.0	6.0	5.4	4.8
30	0.5	0.3	0.4	0.2	0.4	0.5	0.5	0.5	0.4	0.4
31	1.8	1.6	1.5	1.2	1.0	1.1	1.2	1.2	1.4	2.4
32	2.4	2.0	1.8	1.4	1.2	0.9	0.6	0.5	0.4	0.4
33	4.0	3.5	3.2	2.7	2.6	2.5	2.4	2.2	2.0	1.9
34	-	-	-	0.1	0.1	0.0	0.0	0.0	0.0	0.0
35	0.1	0.2	0.1	0.1	0.1	0.1	0.2	0.2	0.1	0.1
36	2.2	1.7	0.1	1.8	2.0	2.5	2.9	3.4	3.6	3.5
37	0.1	0.1	1.8	0.2	0.3	0.4	0.3	0.3	0.4	0.4

Explanatory notes: see p. 77.

[1] Persons aged 15 years and over. [2] Enterprises with 20 or more employees.

Notes explicatives: voir p. 80.

[1] Personnes âgées de 15 ans et plus. [2] Entreprises occupant 20 salariés et plus.

Notas explicativas: véase p. 83.

[1] Personas de 15 años y más. [2] Empresas con 20 y más asalariados.

EMPLOYMENT — EMPLOI — EMPLEO

Paid employment in manufacturing — Thousands

Emploi rémunéré dans les industries manufacturières — Milliers

Empleo remunerado en las industrias manufactureras — Millares

Netherlands (BA) [1]

Employees - Salariés - Asalariados

Total - Total - Total
ISIC 3 - CITI 3 - CIIU 3

	1999	2000	2001	2002	2003	2004	2005	2006	2007	2008
Total	1 058	1 043	1 023	995	973	970	968	957	942	915
15	164	150	156	150	149	143	137	141	145	137
16	7	6	5	5	7	5	5	4	4	3
17	23	18	19	18	16	12	9	10	11	10
18	8	7	6	6	6	4	2	2	4	3
19	4	3	2	2	2	.	.	.	2	.
20	18	23	20	18	19	17	14	14	18	19
21	30	27	22	25	22	25	24	23	22	22
22	113	107	119	120	109	110	117	108	94	93
23	8	7	5	6	6	6	9	10	10	11
24	86	87	78	73	74	78	83	82	79	74
25	44	34	35	34	36	38	40	41	38	33
26	32	36	33	31	31	27	29	28	29	28
27	28	32	31	28	23	22	22	25	27	24
28	97	106	101	96	101	103	110	108	110	103
29	90	98	90	87	91	70	57	58	71	80
30	11	9	11	9	8	7	6	6	8	7
31	24	20	18	18	17	13	11	11	12	13
32	46	40	47	43	37	31	28	26	26	27
33	24	23	25	25	21	18	18	18	22	24
34	32	30	28	28	25	22	20	19	19	21
35	26	30	29	29	30	29	27	27	30	28
36	140	148	140	140	142	186	200	193	161	148
37	2	3	2	3	2	3	2	2	3	3

Men - Hommes - Hombres
ISIC 3 - CITI 3 - CIIU 3

	1999	2000	2001	2002	2003	2004	2005	2006	2007	2008
Total	826	815	799	771	756	755	755	746	727	690
15	108	100	102	100	97	95	92	97	97	88
16	6	5	4	4	6	4	4	3	3	3
17	16	12	13	12	10	9	6	6	7	7
18	2	3	2	2	2	.	.	.	.	.
19	2	.	.	.	.	.	.	.	.	.
20	16	21	18	16	17	14	12	13	16	17
21	24	22	19	20	18	21	19	18	19	18
22	75	70	78	79	74	71	77	72	62	58
23	7	6	5	6	5	6	7	8	8	9
24	67	70	61	57	57	61	64	63	59	55
25	34	26	28	27	29	31	33	33	28	25
26	28	32	30	28	28	24	25	26	25	25
27	27	29	28	26	22	20	21	22	25	22
28	86	95	90	85	92	91	97	96	97	91
29	79	86	81	77	80	61	50	50	63	70
30	8	7	8	7	7	6	5	5	6	5
31	20	16	15	16	13	11	9	9	10	11
32	37	31	36	33	29	24	22	22	20	19
33	17	17	19	18	17	14	13	13	15	16
34	29	27	24	25	22	20	19	18	17	19
35	23	28	27	26	27	25	24	24	26	24
36	110	107	106	102	101	140	152	146	118	106
37	2	2	2	3	2	3	.	.	2	2

Women - Femmes - Mujeres
ISIC 3 - CITI 3 - CIIU 3

	1999	2000	2001	2002	2003	2004	2005	2006	2007	2008
Total	232	228	224	224	217	215	213	210	215	225
15	56	50	53	50	52	48	45	44	48	49
16	2	.	.	.	.	.	.	.	.	.
17	7	5	6	6	6	3	3	4	4	3
18	6	5	4	4	4	3	2	2	2	.
19	2	.	.	.	.	.	.	.	.	.
20	2	2	2	2	2	2	.	.	2	2
21	6	5	3	4	4	4	4	5	3	4
22	38	37	42	41	35	39	40	35	33	35
23	.	.	.	.	.	.	.	2	2	2
24	19	17	16	16	17	17	18	19	20	20
25	10	9	7	7	6	7	7	7	9	9
26	3	4	4	4	3	3	3	3	3	4
27	.	3	3	2	.	2	.	2	2	2
28	11	10	11	11	9	11	12	12	13	12
29	10	11	10	10	11	9	7	8	8	10
30	3	2	3	2	.	.	.	.	2	2
31	4	4	3	2	3	2	2	2	2	3
32	10	9	10	10	9	6	6	5	7	8
33	7	6	6	7	5	4	5	5	6	8
34	3	3	3	3	3	2	2	2	2	2
35	4	2	2	3	3	3	2	3	4	4
36	29	41	34	38	41	46	48	48	43	42
37	.	.	.	.	.	.	.	.	.	.

Explanatory notes: see p. 77.
[1] Persons aged 15 years and over.

Notes explicatives: voir p. 80.
[1] Personnes âgées de 15 ans et plus.

Notas explicativas: véase p. 83.
[1] Personas de 15 años y más.

2F

	EMPLOYMENT			EMPLOI			EMPLEO		

Paid employment in manufacturing — Thousands
Emploi rémunéré dans les industries manufacturières — Milliers
Empleo remunerado en las industrias manufactureras — Millares

Norway (BA) [1] — Employees - Salariés - Asalariados

Total - Total - Total
ISIC 3 - CITI 3 - CIIU 3

	1999	2000	2001	2002	2003	2004	2005	2006	2007	2008
Total	293	284	277	281	268	255	256	262 [2]	268	277
15	53	52	48	51	53	50	48	47 [2]	47	51
16	1	1	1	1	-	-	-	- [2]	-	-
17	4	5	6	4	3	2	3	4 [2]	4	3
18	2	1	1	1	1	2	2	2 [2]	1	1
19	1	-	-	-	-	-	-	- [2]	-	-
20	14	16	16	16	15	16	16	14 [2]	16	16
21	10	10	12	9	8	8	8	6 [2]	5	5
22	35	33	32	31	31	31	32	28 [2]	30	31
23	3	2	1	1	-	1	1	1 [2]	1	1
24	16	16	16	16	16	17	17	15 [2]	15	15
25	7	7	6	6	6	5	5	6 [2]	6	5
26	11	11	10	9	8	8	9	11 [2]	12	11
27	16	16	16	14	15	14	13	12 [2]	12	13
28	19	18	18	19	18	19	18	21 [2]	21	21
29	23	23	22	26	23	20	20	26 [2]	26	26
30	1	1	1	-	-	-	1	1 [2]	1	-
31	12	10	8	9	10	7	8	9 [2]	7	7
32	6	5	6	6	6	6	4	4 [2]	5	7
33	6	8	7	7	7	6	7	6 [2]	7	10
34	6	5	4	5	5	4	4	4 [2]	4	4
35	34	31	31	33	31	30	31	35 [2]	36	37
36	12	13	14	15	10	10	9	9 [2]	10	9
37	1	1	1	1	1	1	1	1 [2]	1	2

Men - Hommes - Hombres
ISIC 3 - CITI 3 - CIIU 3

	1999	2000	2001	2002	2003	2004	2005	2006	2007	2008
Total	218	210	206	208	199	189	191	197 [2]	203	206
15	32	31	29	32	32	29	31	32 [2]	30	30
16	-	-	-	1	-	-	-	- [2]	-	-
17	2	3	3	2	2	1	1	2 [2]	2	2
18	1	-	-	-	-	1	1	- [2]	-	-
19	-	-	-	-	-	-	-	- [2]	-	-
20	11	13	13	13	12	13	13	12 [2]	13	13
21	8	8	10	7	6	6	6	4 [2]	4	4
22	21	20	21	20	18	19	18	16 [2]	19	18
23	2	2	1	1	-	1	1	1 [2]	1	1
24	12	11	11	11	12	13	13	11 [2]	11	11
25	5	5	6	5	5	4	4	5 [2]	5	4
26	10	9	8	7	6	6	6	8 [2]	10	10
27	14	14	14	13	13	11	11	10 [2]	10	12
28	16	16	16	17	16	16	16	18 [2]	19	19
29	19	20	20	22	20	17	19	23 [2]	23	23
30	-	-	-	-	-	-	1	1 [2]	1	-
31	11	8	5	6	8	5	6	7 [2]	6	6
32	3	3	4	4	5	5	3	2 [2]	3	4
33	4	5	5	6	5	4	4	4 [2]	4	6
34	6	5	4	4	4	3	3	3 [2]	4	3
35	30	28	28	28	27	27	28	32 [2]	32	32
36	7	7	7	7	6	6	5	5 [2]	6	6
37	1	1	1	1	1	1	1	1 [2]	1	1

Women - Femmes - Mujeres
ISIC 3 - CITI 3 - CIIU 3

	1999	2000	2001	2002	2003	2004	2005	2006	2007	2008
Total	75	74	72	73	69	66	66	65 [2]	65	70
15	21	21	19	19	22	21	17	15 [2]	16	20
16	1	-	-	-	-	-	-	- [2]	-	-
17	2	3	3	3	1	1	2	3 [2]	2	2
18	1	1	1	1	1	1	1	1 [2]	1	1
19	-	-	-	-	-	-	-	- [2]	-	-
20	2	3	3	3	3	3	3	2 [2]	3	3
21	2	2	3	2	2	2	2	1 [2]	1	1
22	14	13	11	12	12	12	13	12 [2]	11	13
23	1	-	-	-	-	-	-	- [2]	-	-
24	4	5	5	5	4	4	5	4 [2]	4	4
25	1	1	1	1	1	1	1	1 [2]	1	1
26	2	2	2	2	2	2	3	3 [2]	2	1
27	3	3	2	2	2	3	2	2 [2]	1	1
28	3	2	2	3	3	3	2	3 [2]	2	2
29	4	3	2	3	3	2	2	3 [2]	3	3
30	-	1	-	-	-	-	-	- [2]	-	-
31	2	2	3	3	2	1	1	2 [2]	1	2
32	3	2	2	2	1	1	1	2 [2]	2	2
33	2	2	2	2	2	2	2	2 [2]	3	3
34	-	-	-	1	1	1	-	1 [2]	1	1
35	4	3	3	5	4	3	3	4 [2]	4	5
36	5	6	7	7	4	4	4	4 [2]	4	3
37	-	-	-	-	-	-	-	- [2]	-	-

Explanatory notes: see p. 77.

[1] Persons aged 15 to 74 years. [2] Prior to 2006: persons aged 16 to 74 years.

Notes explicatives: voir p. 80.

[1] Personnes âgées de 15 à 74 ans. [2] Avant 2006: personnes âgées de 16 à 74 ans.

Notas explicativas: véase p. 83.

[1] Personas de 15 a 74 años. [2] Antes de 2006: personas de 16 a 74 años.

Paid employment in manufacturing
Emploi rémunéré dans les industries manufacturières
Empleo remunerado en las industrias manufactureras

Thousands — Milliers — Millares

	1999	2000	2001	2002	2003	2004	2005	2006	2007	2008
Poland (DA)				Employees - Salariés - Asalariados						
Total - Total - Total										
ISIC 3 - CITI 3 - CIIU 3										
Total	2 611.4	2 467.1	2 358.6	2 220.8	2 206.3	2 243.9	2 259.4	2 316.5	.	.
15	488.3	457.4	443.6	430.7	427.7	422.9	417.6	417.8	.	.
16	10.3	9.4	8.3	7.5	6.3	6.4	6.3	6.6	.	.
17	108.4	97.1	88.3	79.7	79.7	80.5	77.2	75.3	.	.
18	225.0	210.5	193.7	173.4	162.3	153.5	148.0	139.8	.	.
19	52.7	47.0	43.1	39.7	37.7	34.7	32.2	30.2	.	.
20	120.1	121.4	119.2	110.2	107.6	115.3	111.7	115.8	.	.
21	39.9	39.6	37.4	35.9	36.3	39.1	39.7	40.7	.	.
22	81.3	81.1	85.6	77.4	80.8	78.7	78.5	80.2	.	.
23	21.5	22.9	19.4	18.5	17.2	16.1	15.6	15.0	.	.
24	121.5	112.3	105.5	100.0	98.6	99.9	99.9	102.2	.	.
25	110.3	109.7	113.7	112.2	116.8	123.0	129.2	138.3	.	.
26	158.7	156.6	146.0	134.8	125.6	127.5	125.8	125.4	.	.
27	121.4	98.1	83.0	74.6	68.5	66.5	66.3	69.1	.	.
28	180.1	179.3	179.5	180.2	190.0	199.9	215.6	235.2	.	.
29	240.9	218.0	202.5	184.1	175.8	174.8	179.9	184.8	.	.
30	5.0	5.0	5.7	4.7	4.7	4.1	5.4	5.1	.	.
31	94.0	89.3	88.8	83.1	87.3	84.9	88.8	96.3	.	.
32	34.7	32.8	31.5	27.3	23.8	27.0	27.6	31.7	.	.
33	39.5	37.4	37.7	40.8	39.4	39.2	38.9	38.8	.	.
34	100.1	96.5	86.1	80.0	84.0	98.2	105.2	113.2	.	.
35	85.2	79.3	79.5	70.2	68.4	67.5	67.9	67.5	.	.
36	165.1	159.5	153.2	147.7	159.2	175.5	172.5	177.0	.	.
37	7.4	6.9	7.3	8.1	8.6	8.7	9.9	10.5	.	.

Portugal (BA) [1] — Employees - Salariés - Asalariados
Total - Total - Total
ISIC 3 - CITI 3 - CIIU 3 .... ISIC 4 - CITI 4 - CIIU 4

ISIC 3	1999	2000	2001	2002	2003	2004	2005	2006	2007		2008	ISIC 4
Total	964.8	960.7	956.0	918.3	883.9	872.0	853.4	867.1	841.6	|	805.7	Total
15	99.5	106.0	98.9	102.8	99.8	93.3	95.3	98.6	101.2	|	91.1	10
16 [2]	-	-	-	-	-	1.0	1.3	1.1	1.1	|	11.2	11
17	101.6	102.1	106.2	105.7	110.1	108.4	104.1	99.9	98.9	|	1.7 [2]	12
18	158.2	155.9	150.3	143.8	129.8	109.5	104.3	106.2	93.8	|	62.0	13
19	69.7	67.4	64.9	56.2	58.1	54.1	46.6	48.0	52.3	|	118.7	14
20	62.0	54.6	58.4	56.4	43.7	54.6	59.9	57.3	56.8	|	44.4	15
21	14.4	14.6	13.2	12.7	12.4	15.8	14.5	12.0	11.9	|	46.4	16
22	37.4	41.4	34.5	38.1	35.0	30.1	32.4	34.4	29.6	|	15.4	17
23 [2]	-	5.2	6.5	-	-	3.0	4.5	3.5	2.7	|	21.2	18
24	35.8	28.9	26.1	28.4	27.3	29.3	25.7	28.2	31.2	|	2.7 [2]	19
25	20.5	20.8	20.5	17.6	20.1	24.0	26.4	21.7	19.2	|	13.1	20
26	63.6	67.3	69.9	73.4	64.2	55.6	59.3	63.1	61.4	|	16.3	21
27	14.7	12.3	9.7	9.6	11.2	10.1	10.6	13.6	13.2	|	23.0	22
28	86.1	78.7	81.9	71.3	69.7	79.3	78.1	84.9	79.1	|	55.7	23
29	33.5	38.9	36.5	37.4	45.5	47.0	39.8	41.4	44.3	|	10.9	24
30 [2]	-	-	-	-	-	1.3	2.3	2.1	1.6	|	93.1	25
31	26.4	31.5	34.7	30.5	25.2	24.7	20.0	18.9	18.4	|	16.4	26
32	15.2	15.4	18.1	14.2	10.1	15.3	13.1	13.2	11.8	|	17.5	27
33	4.7	6.8	6.2	3.9	3.5	4.9	5.7	5.3	6.8	|	24.4	28
34	37.7	32.8	31.1	32.0	33.0	36.4	35.7	34.5	35.6	|	47.6	29
35	13.4	14.2	14.4	11.3	12.4	13.7	14.2	15.2	13.2	|	13.7	30
36	63.3	61.8	70.0	68.3	67.2	57.9	58.4	61.8	53.4	|	43.4	31
37 [2]	-	-	-	-	-	2.7	1.1	2.2	4.0	|	8.5	32
										|	7.1	33

Men - Hommes - Hombres
ISIC 3 - CITI 3 - CIIU 3 .... ISIC 4 - CITI 4 - CIIU 4

ISIC 3	1999	2000	2001	2002	2003	2004	2005	2006	2007		2008	ISIC 4
Total	525.7	518.0	514.2	493.7	482.4	488.4	486.6	486.7	473.8	|	463.6	Total
15	51.6	55.9	53.0	60.7	58.0	48.3	52.2	49.1	49.2	|	40.0	10
16 [2]	-	-	-	-	-	-	0.8	1.0	0.9	|	7.5	11
17	44.9	42.9	46.9	41.8	45.2	47.5	42.3	45.7	40.4	|	1.4 [2]	12
18	19.0	17.2	18.6	15.2	14.0	13.2	9.9	8.4	9.2	|	32.7	13
19	27.6	25.4	22.9	17.9	22.3	21.8	19.7	17.7	17.9	|	13.3	14
20	48.1	41.3	44.1	43.1	34.3	41.9	46.7	44.6	41.4	|	17.9	15
21	9.7	10.5	10.1	9.9	9.2	10.6	10.3	8.4	7.4	|	32.9	16
22	24.8	26.0	23.2	26.6	23.2	18.6	19.6	20.5	18.4	|	12.0	17
23 [2]	-	-	-	-	-	2.3	3.7	2.6	2.0	|	14.7	18
24	21.9	15.6	14.1	15.0	16.4	16.3	14.8	17.2	18.0	|	2.0 [2]	19
25	13.9	12.9	13.5	12.2	13.1	16.5	18.6	14.8	13.2	|	8.4	20
26	41.7	48.4	51.0	49.4	41.0	38.2	42.1	41.5	43.4	|	5.8	21
27	12.2	10.9	8.3	7.8	8.0	8.6	8.4	11.8	12.1	|	16.0	22
28	71.6	67.4	69.7	59.9	57.0	66.5	64.5	68.0	65.7	|	40.5	23
29	25.2	29.2	26.1	29.7	35.2	36.6	33.1	33.0	35.8	|	9.8	24
30 [2]	-	-	-	-	-	1.7	1.1	1.1	1.3	|	82.2	25
31	12.6	15.2	15.1	14.6	14.6	11.2	8.4	9.7	11.4	|	8.6	26
32	7.4	7.8	6.2	5.4	5.0	7.3	6.6	6.5	5.5	|	12.2	27
33 [2]	-	-	-	-	-	2.3	3.1	3.6	4.6	|	22.3	28
34	23.7	22.3	20.7	20.1	23.0	26.3	24.8	23.8	24.5	|	30.9	29
35	12.9	13.4	11.6	9.7	11.5	11.9	12.1	13.1	10.9	|	12.1	30
36	48.3	46.3	48.9	49.3	45.9	39.2	42.6	43.0	37.4	|	29.5	31
37 [2]	-	-	-	-	-	1.6	0.6	1.6	3.1	|	3.8 [2]	32
										|	7.1	33

Explanatory notes: see p. 77.

[1] Persons aged 15 years and over. [2] Data not reliable; coefficient of variation greater than 20%.

Notes explicatives: voir p. 80.

[1] Personnes âgées de 15 ans et plus. [2] Données non fiables; coefficient de variation supérieur à 20%.

Notas explicativas: véase p. 83.

[1] Personas de 15 años y más. [2] Datos no fiables; coeficiente de variación superior a 20%.

2F

EMPLOYMENT	EMPLOI	EMPLEO
Paid employment in manufacturing	**Emploi rémunéré dans les industries manufacturières**	**Empleo remunerado en las industrias manufactureras**
Thousands	Milliers	Millares

	1999	2000	2001	2002	2003	2004	2005	2006	2007	2008	

Portugal (BA) [1]
Employees - Salariés - Asalariados

Women - Femmes - Mujeres
ISIC 3 - CITI 3 - CIIU 3 .... ISIC 4 - CITI 4 - CIIU 4

ISIC3	1999	2000	2001	2002	2003	2004	2005	2006	2007	2008	ISIC4
Total	439.2	442.7	441.9	424.7	401.5	383.6	366.8	380.3	367.8	342.0	Total
15	47.9	50.1	45.8	42.1	41.7	45.0	43.1	49.5	52.0	51.1	10
16 [2]	-	-	-	-	-	-	0.5	0.1	0.2	3.7 [2]	11
17	56.8	59.2	59.4	63.9	64.9	60.9	61.9	54.2	58.5	0.2 [2]	12
18	139.2	138.7	131.7	128.6	115.8	96.3	94.4	97.8	84.6	29.3	13
19	42.1	41.9	42.1	38.4	35.8	32.4	26.9	30.3	34.3	105.4	14
20	13.8	13.3	14.3	13.3	9.4	12.7	13.2	12.7	15.4	26.5	15
21	4.7	4.1	3.1	2.8	3.2	5.2	4.2	3.6	4.5	13.5	16
22	12.6	15.3	11.3	11.5	11.8	11.5	12.8	13.9	11.3	3.4 [2]	17
23 [2]	-	-	-	-	-	-	0.9	0.9	0.7	6.6	18
24	13.9	13.2	12.0	13.3	10.9	12.9	11.0	11.0	13.2	0.7 [2]	19
25	6.6	7.9	7.0	5.4	6.9	7.5	7.8	6.9	6.1	4.7	20
26	21.9	18.8	18.8	24.0	23.2	17.4	17.2	21.6	18.0	10.4	21
27	2.5	1.4	1.4	1.8	3.2	1.4	2.2	1.8	1.1	7.1	22
28	14.5	11.2	12.2	11.4	12.7	12.8	13.7	16.9	13.5	15.2	23
29	8.3	9.8	10.4	7.6	10.3	10.4	6.7	8.4	8.5	1.2 [2]	24
30 [2]	-	-	-	-	-	-	0.6	1.0	0.3	11.0	25
31	13.8	16.3	19.6	15.8	10.7	13.5	11.6	9.1	6.9	7.8	26
32	7.7	7.6	11.9	8.8	5.1	8.0	6.5	6.7	6.2	5.3	27
33 [2]	-	-	-	-	-	2.6	2.5	1.7	2.2	2.1 [2]	28
34	14.0	10.4	10.6	11.9	10.1	10.1	10.9	10.7	11.1	16.7	29
35	0.5	0.8	2.8	1.6	0.9	1.8	2.1	2.1	2.3	1.6 [2]	30
36	14.9	15.5	21.0	19.0	21.3	18.7	15.8	18.7	16.0	13.9	31
37 [2]	-	-	-	-	-	1.1	0.4	0.6	0.9	4.7	32
										0.1 [2]	33

Roumanie (DA)
Employees - Salariés - Asalariados

Total - Total - Total
ISIC 3 - CITI 3 - CIIU 3

ISIC3	1999	2000	2001	2002	2003	2004	2005	2006	2007	2008
Total	1 659.9	1 559.7	1 590.0	1 593.4	1 581.5	1 491.6	1 424.8	1 408.8	1 402.9	.
15	186.6	169.1	160.5	163.3	161.5	160.8	165.6	174.6	181.5	.
16	4.4	4.3	5.3	4.2	3.6	2.5	2.3	2.2	2.0	.
17	104.7	94.3	98.2	91.4	84.4	77.8	67.0	65.0	57.9	.
18	239.6	260.9	290.1	302.3	303.0	280.8	259.1	246.6	215.4	.
19	76.4	85.3	97.6	101.1	101.9	100.0	92.8	94.1	87.3	.
20	75.8	70.3	69.6	75.4	78.2	74.9	72.6	72.7	72.4	.
21	17.9	17.1	16.5	16.9	16.3	15.1	12.0	11.5	14.0	.
22	26.3	19.8	21.7	26.1	27.7	29.0	27.7	29.5	34.1	.
23	23.8	21.8	21.6	17.6	15.2	14.7	13.8	12.4	11.6	.
24	83.1	72.9	68.9	63.8	58.3	51.5	48.9	45.8	46.5	.
25	35.0	33.2	32.4	34.8	37.1	36.8	37.3	38.5	44.4	.
26	91.6	85.1	84.0	77.1	72.4	63.3	60.0	54.4	56.4	.
27	107.5	95.3	94.6	85.2	75.9	62.9	56.6	54.9	50.0	.
28	86.9	68.3	72.8	78.0	86.3	86.0	85.6	89.3	97.0	.
29	182.4	150.4	144.2	139.0	138.4	118.2	104.0	96.5	91.2	.
30	1.7	1.5	1.9	2.5	3.0	3.0	2.8	3.5	3.4	.
31	49.8	51.2	54.1	56.2	58.6	64.5	73.6	77.5	87.1	.
32	9.9	11.0	10.9	10.6	9.8	8.6	7.6	8.0	10.8	.
33	11.7	14.0	12.8	14.8	15.1	13.7	13.6	13.5	14.9	.
34	79.3	70.6	66.8	64.7	56.5	55.9	55.8	56.3	58.8	.
35	67.0	60.5	59.0	62.1	62.7	57.7	57.5	56.4	57.6	.
36	101.8	95.3	98.7	99.3	106.1	102.9	98.8	96.1	96.6	.
37	5.7	7.5	7.8	8.0	9.5	11.0	9.8	9.9	12.0	.

Men - Hommes - Hombres
ISIC 3 - CITI 3 - CIIU 3

ISIC3	1999	2000	2001	2002	2003	2004	2005	2006	2007	2008
Total	.	.	.	.	804.5	757.7	723.0	717.6	733.8	.
15					81.9	81.4	82.9	87.8	92.6	.
16					2.0	1.5	1.4	1.4	1.4	.
17					19.6	17.8	15.3	15.8	13.6	.
18					43.2	35.9	36.0	35.3	29.1	.
19					25.3	25.3	23.7	22.1	21.8	.
20					57.8	56.3	54.3	53.5	53.9	.
21					9.9	9.2	7.3	6.8	8.1	.
22					13.7	15.4	13.3	14.8	18.2	.
23					10.1	9.9	9.3	8.3	8.0	.
24					34.8	31.4	29.5	26.9	28.1	.
25					21.8	21.8	22.7	23.2	28.1	.
26					46.3	41.0	40.5	37.4	39.7	.
27					60.2	50.4	45.0	44.3	40.3	.
28					68.9	68.9	68.2	72.0	78.1	.
29					103.0	88.5	78.4	73.1	69.3	.
30					1.7	2.1	2.0	2.5	2.0	.
31					28.4	29.4	32.1	33.2	36.6	.
32					4.7	4.1	3.3	3.6	4.9	.
33					9.4	8.1	8.3	7.9	9.3	.
34					35.0	35.1	34.8	34.7	34.7	.
35					51.3	48.0	47.5	47.5	48.4	.
36					67.6	64.3	59.5	57.9	57.9	.
37					7.9	8.9	7.7	7.6	9.7	.

Explanatory notes: see p. 77.

[1] Persons aged 15 years and over. [2] Data not reliable; coefficient of variation greater than 20%.

Notes explicatives: voir p. 80.

[1] Personnes âgées de 15 ans et plus. [2] Données non fiables; coefficient de variation supérieur à 20%.

Notas explicativas: véase p. 83.

[1] Personas de 15 años y más. [2] Datos no fiables; coeficiente de variación superior a 20%.

Paid employment in manufacturing — *Emploi rémunéré dans les industries manufacturières* — *Empleo remunerado en las industrias manufactureras*

Thousands / Milliers / Millares

	1999	2000	2001	2002	2003	2004	2005	2006	2007	2008
Roumanie (DA)					Employees - Salariés - Asalariados					
Women - Femmes - Mujeres										
ISIC 3 - CITI 3 - CIIU 3										
Total	.	.	.	.	777.0	736.9	701.8	691.2	669.1	.
15	.	.	.	.	79.6	79.4	82.7	86.8	88.8	.
16	.	.	.	.	1.6	1.0	0.9	0.8	0.6	.
17	.	.	.	.	64.8	60.0	51.7	49.2	44.3	.
18	.	.	.	.	259.8	244.9	223.1	211.3	186.3	.
19	.	.	.	.	76.6	74.7	69.1	72.0	65.5	.
20	.	.	.	.	20.4	18.6	18.3	19.2	18.5	.
21	.	.	.	.	6.4	5.9	4.7	4.7	6.0	.
22	.	.	.	.	14.0	13.6	14.4	14.7	15.9	.
23	.	.	.	.	5.1	4.8	4.5	4.1	3.6	.
24	.	.	.	.	23.5	20.1	19.4	18.9	18.4	.
25	.	.	.	.	15.3	15.0	14.6	15.2	16.3	.
26	.	.	.	.	26.1	22.3	19.5	17.0	16.8	.
27	.	.	.	.	15.7	12.5	11.6	10.3	9.8	.
28	.	.	.	.	17.4	17.1	17.4	17.3	18.9	.
29	.	.	.	.	35.4	29.7	25.6	23.4	21.9	.
30	.	.	.	.	1.3	0.9	0.8	1.0	1.3	.
31	.	.	.	.	30.2	35.1	41.5	44.3	50.4	.
32	.	.	.	.	5.1	4.5	4.3	4.4	5.9	.
33	.	.	.	.	5.7	5.6	5.3	5.6	5.6	.
34	.	.	.	.	21.5	20.8	21.0	21.6	24.1	.
35	.	.	.	.	11.4	9.7	10.0	8.9	9.2	.
36	.	.	.	.	38.5	38.6	39.3	38.2	38.7	.
37	.	.	.	.	1.6	2.1	2.1	2.3	2.3	.
Russian Federation (BA) [1]					Employees - Salariés - Asalariados					
Total - Total - Total										
ISIC 3 - CITI 3 - CIIU 3										
Total	11 604	12 335	12 844	13 185	12 536	12 448	12 278	12 233	12 089	11 358
15-16	1 737	1 975	2 042	2 125	2 078	2 008	2 009	2 073	1 924	1 972
17-18	871	906	1 005	1 035	998	953	983	910	862	780
19	142	145	157	156	125	123	129	113	102	105
20	388	419	468	523	546	539	554	573	578	680
21-22	389	361	414	457	429	481	464	458	508	483
23	180	197	194	205	199	184	149	189	180	154
24	708	787	733	776	755	678	695	663	616	530
25	241	272	328	323	255	281	327	320	335	311
26	600	716	735	769	738	731	736	717	721	780
27-28	1 312	1 413	1 340	1 329	1 406	1 354	1 334	1 366	1 426	1 347
29	2 193	1 940	2 076	2 144	1 745	1 746	1 666	1 549	1 553	1 372
30-33	1 025	1 130	1 171	1 183	1 234	1 235	1 149	1 120	1 084	920
34-35	1 320	1 546	1 563	1 576	1 509	1 569	1 518	1 619	1 594	1 393
36-37	498	528	618	584	519	566	564	563	606	532
Men - Hommes - Hombres										
ISIC 3 - CITI 3 - CIIU 3										
Total	6 612	7 065	7 262	7 448	7 127	7 039	6 998	7 034	6 935	6 669
15-16	852	970	971	1 017	1 008	913	946	971	851	889
17-18	235	228	223	231	193	176	199	157	144	147
19	69	58	68	67	46	50	54	36	40	48
20	267	312	360	379	406	410	408	442	442	528
21-22	190	182	194	225	214	234	213	213	237	234
23	120	138	134	135	130	128	100	125	118	103
24	416	424	397	422	397	386	381	356	343	283
25	129	154	193	185	160	175	184	195	210	198
26	382	466	490	494	495	463	484	483	480	542
27-28	871	935	888	912	954	921	924	951	975	928
29	1 327	1 250	1 303	1 354	1 128	1 129	1 055	1 017	1 009	932
30-33	575	632	630	634	685	672	668	651	632	573
34-35	847	966	997	1 003	937	975	999	1 034	1 017	907
36-37	332	350	414	390	374	407	384	403	436	356
Women - Femmes - Mujeres										
ISIC 3 - CITI 3 - CIIU 3										
Total	4 992	5 270	5 582	5 737	5 409	5 409	5 279	5 199	5 155	4 690
15-16	884	1 005	1 071	1 107	1 070	1 095	1 064	1 102	1 074	1 083
17-18	637	678	782	804	805	777	784	753	718	633
19	73	87	89	89	78	73	75	77	61	57
20	121	107	109	144	140	129	146	132	136	152
21-22	199	178	220	232	215	247	251	245	270	250
23	59	59	60	70	69	56	49	64	62	51
24	293	363	336	354	358	292	314	307	273	247
25	111	118	135	138	94	106	144	125	125	113
26	218	250	245	275	242	269	253	234	241	237
27-28	441	478	452	416	452	433	410	415	451	419
29	866	690	773	789	617	617	610	532	544	440
30-33	450	498	542	548	550	563	481	468	452	347
34-35	473.0	579.0	566.0	573.0	572.0	594.0	519.0	585.0	577.0	486.0
36-37	167	180	202	198	147	158	180	160	170	176

Explanatory notes: see p. 77.
[1] Persons aged 15 to 72 years.

Notes explicatives: voir p. 80.
[1] Personnes âgées de 15 à 72 ans.

Notas explicativas: véase p. 83.
[1] Personas de 15 a 72 años.

EMPLOYMENT	EMPLOI	EMPLEO
Paid employment in manufacturing	**Emploi rémunéré dans les industries manufacturières**	**Empleo remunerado en las industrias manufactureras**
Thousands	Milliers	Millares

	1999	2000	2001	2002	2003	2004	2005	2006	2007	2008

Russian Federation (DA) [1] — Employees - Salariés - Asalariados

Total - Total - Total
ISIC 3 - CITI 3 - CIIU 3

	1999	2000	2001	2002	2003	2004	2005	2006	2007	2008
Total	.	.	.	10 798.9	10 302.9	9 919.8	9 511.6	9 240.5	9 258.9	9 126.2
15	.	.	.	1 582.3	1 566.6	1 522.6	1 431.9	1 421.8	1 443.7	1 398.4
16				22.6	21.2	19.1	15.2	14.1	12.8	12.5
17				398.9	338.9	295.6	249.1	221.4	198.6	171.6
18				297.5	272.1	260.7	246.2	241.1	232.1	220.4
19				105.5	93.9	81.0	69.5	67.3	79.1	72.9
20				408.9	390.2	381.5	357.6	335.8	340.5	326.9
21				163.4	154.8	142.4	131.1	130.6	131.5	124.4
22				216.8	221.3	227.7	262.0	269.9	267.4	275.3
23				201.6	202.1	137.9	136.1	134.1	131.2	120.5
24				649.5	623.9	550.3	563.0	550.4	511.9	488.2
25				236.5	229.1	239.4	256.8	270.5	285.2	294.8
26				753.6	708.6	675.3	649.1	643.5	675.0	597.8
27				827.6	812.9	781.9	748.7	668.7	627.5	603.8
28				439.2	427.1	426.6	470.9	503.0	526.2	526.2
29				1 993.9	1 802.9	1 387.4	1 205.0	1 152.6	1 108.6	1 088.8
30				23.1	25.8	22.6	18.6	20.0	22.8	23.6
31				334.5	340.4	339.2	382.5	369.4	407.3	408.4
32				290.9	266.2	240.6	198.4	194.5	186.3	184.9
33				304.3	298.5	302.9	287.4	284.9	289.4	295.2
34				577.8	549.8	511.4	506.9	475.0	481.5	480.4
35				693.4	687.9	695.5	694.6	669.4	666.4	675.9
36				203.1	205.6	205.3	233.3	233.4	251.6	268.2
37				73.9	63.1	67.6	64.6	63.6	67.6	63.1
X				-	-	405.3	333.1	305.5	382.3	467.1

San Marino (E) [2][3] — Employees - Salariés - Asalariados

Total - Total - Total
ISIC 3 - CITI 3 - CIIU 3

	1999	2000	2001	2002	2003	2004	2005	2006	2007	2008
Total	5.610		5.974	5.931	6.026	6.132	5.998	6.103	6.239	6.219
15	0.198		0.225	0.247	0.228	0.261	0.327	0.336	0.251	0.272
17	0.034		0.044	0.045	0.042	0.039	0.053	0.040	0.041	0.041
18	0.322		0.317	0.303	0.307	0.304	0.254	0.304	0.272	0.283
19	0.194		0.204	0.190	0.180	0.179	0.136	0.108	0.059	0.062
20	0.181		0.229	0.217	0.214	0.220	0.245	0.244	0.231	0.231
21	0.096		0.084	0.085	0.083	0.092	0.090	0.091	0.090	0.095
22	0.219		0.243	0.238	0.228	0.216	0.200	0.199	0.197	0.209
24	0.617		0.656	0.647	0.700	0.734	0.582	0.585	0.695	0.711
25	0.347		0.420	0.426	0.433	0.047	0.432	0.433	0.415	0.408
26	0.295		0.304	0.302	0.293	0.391	0.278	0.284	0.269	0.249
27	-		-	-	-	-	0.018	0.016	0.017	0.025
28	0.890		0.808	0.884			0.975	0.986	1.012	1.003
28-31					2.425	0.275				
29	0.659		1.438	1.330			0.769	0.780	0.845	0.828
30	0.033		0.023	0.003			0.155	0.156	0.037	0.032
31	0.614		0.121	0.110			0.431	0.448	0.627	0.611
32	0.079		0.050	0.055	0.063	0.059	0.001	0.001	0.061	0.059
33	0.026		0.028	0.065	-	-	0.058	0.085	0.082	0.090
34	0.142		0.133	0.127	0.105	0.129	0.052	0.058	0.052	0.054
35							0.079	0.033	0.036	0.024
36	0.509		0.647	0.657	0.715		0.863	0.916	0.950	0.932
37	0.155		-	-	-		-			

Men - Hommes - Hombres
ISIC 3 - CITI 3 - CIIU 3

	1999	2000	2001	2002	2003	2004	2005	2006	2007	2008
Total	3.952		4.250	4.240			4.245	4.295	4.465	4.477
15	0.122		0.138	0.153			0.166	0.158	0.134	0.143
17	0.012		0.016	0.016			0.019	0.017	0.017	0.019
18	0.112		0.108	0.121			0.094	0.130	0.120	0.124
19	0.093		0.107	0.106			0.083	0.062	0.032	0.036
20	0.139		0.179	0.176			0.199	0.194	0.186	0.183
21	0.080		0.070	0.071			0.078	0.079	0.080	0.084
22	0.152		0.165	0.148			0.122	0.123	0.126	0.133
24	0.302		0.303	0.300			0.289	0.286	0.328	0.334
25	0.279		0.337	0.345			0.359	0.362	0.355	0.349
26	0.214		0.221	0.220			0.206	0.210	0.199	0.183
27	-		-	-			0.013	0.012	0.012	0.017
28	0.698		0.665	0.714			0.758	0.761	0.787	0.785
29	0.565		1.151	1.074			0.672	0.680	0.731	0.730
30	0.026		0.017	0.002			0.136	0.135	0.021	0.016
31	0.449		0.099	0.091			0.303	0.317	0.485	0.470
32	0.074		0.037	0.039			-	-	0.058	0.056
33	0.018		0.020	0.054			0.037	0.057	0.051	0.056
34	0.123		0.115	0.107			0.046	0.051	0.047	0.049
35							0.057	0.022	0.025	0.018
36	0.396		0.502	0.503			0.608	0.639	0.671	0.692
37	0.103		-	-						

Explanatory notes: see p. 77.

[1] Persons aged 15 to 72 years. [2] Persons aged 15 years and over. [3] Dec.

Notes explicatives: voir p. 80.

[1] Personnes âgées de 15 à 72 ans. [2] Personnes âgées de 15 ans et plus. [3] Déc.

Notas explicativas: véase p. 83.

[1] Personas de 15 a 72 años. [2] Personas de 15 años y más. [3] Dic.

Paid employment in manufacturing / Emploi rémunéré dans les industries manufacturières / Empleo remunerado en las industrias manufactureras

Thousands — Milliers — Millares

	1999	2000	2001	2002	2003	2004	2005	2006	2007	2008
San Marino (E) [1][2]				*Employees - Salariés - Asalariados*						
Women - Femmes - Mujeres										
ISIC 3 - CITI 3 - CIIU 3										
Total	1.653	.	1.724	1.691	.	.	1.753	1.808	1.774	1.742
15	0.076	.	0.087	0.094	.	.	0.161	0.178	0.117	0.129
17	0.022	.	0.028	0.029	.	.	0.034	0.023	0.024	0.022
18	0.210	.	0.209	0.182	.	.	0.160	0.174	0.152	0.159
19	0.101	.	0.097	0.084	.	.	0.053	0.046	0.027	0.026
20	0.042	.	0.050	0.041	.	.	0.046	0.050	0.045	0.048
21	0.016	.	0.014	0.014	.	.	0.012	0.012	0.010	0.011
22	0.067	.	0.078	0.090	.	.	0.078	0.076	0.071	0.076
24	0.315	.	0.353	0.347	.	.	0.293	0.299	0.367	0.377
25	0.068	.	0.083	0.081	.	.	0.073	0.071	0.060	0.059
26	0.081	.	0.083	0.082	.	.	0.072	0.074	0.070	0.066
27	-	.	-	-	.	.	0.005	0.004	0.005	0.008
28	0.192	.	0.143	0.170	.	.	0.217	0.225	0.225	0.218
29	0.094	.	0.287	0.256	.	.	0.097	0.100	0.114	0.098
30	0.007	.	0.006	0.001	.	.	0.019	0.021	0.016	0.016
31	0.165	.	0.022	0.019	.	.	0.128	0.131	0.142	0.141
32	0.005	.	0.013	0.016	.	.	0.001	0.001	0.003	0.003
33	0.008	.	0.008	0.011	.	.	0.021	0.028	0.031	0.034
34	0.019	.	0.018	0.020	.	.	0.006	0.007	0.005	0.005
35	.	.	.	.	.	.	0.022	0.011	0.011	0.006
36	0.113	.	0.145	0.154	.	.	0.255	0.277	0.279	0.240
37	0.052	.	-	-	.	.	-	-	-	-
Slovakia (BA) [3][4][5]				*Employees - Salariés - Asalariados*						
Total - Total - Total										
ISIC 3 - CITI 3 - CIIU 3										
Total	522.0	515.9	528.7	549.2	539.0	546.8	556.5	573.9	597.4	609.9
15	68.9	64.0	65.5	64.7	53.8	56.4	58.0	56.4	56.2	54.8
16	0.9	1.4	0.8	0.8	0.6	0.5	1.0	0.3	0.1	0.2
17	23.7	23.8	23.2	22.5	26.2	20.9	14.6	13.7	15.2	13.7
18	46.3	43.5	46.4	49.0	48.0	46.9	38.0	37.5	35.3	31.8
19	19.4	21.2	20.8	21.7	19.7	19.8	20.2	18.9	17.4	14.9
20	31.2	30.6	27.2	29.1	26.0	24.0	25.1	31.2	29.3	23.3
21	12.9	14.4	14.2	12.3	11.5	10.3	8.7	7.9	7.5	9.6
22	12.8	13.0	12.8	11.4	11.3	11.7	12.4	13.6	13.2	12.4
23	5.0	5.8	7.1	3.5	3.0	4.7	3.9	4.5	3.0	3.7
24	24.7	25.4	24.3	23.9	25.0	26.5	22.9	20.8	19.4	20.8
25	20.6	20.3	22.1	19.6	22.0	23.4	23.3	29.0	35.5	37.8
26	22.8	25.4	27.3	25.9	23.8	22.7	24.6	21.5	20.0	23.9
27	45.4	37.7	41.2	40.5	36.1	31.3	34.6	31.3	35.5	37.2
28	53.9	52.7	55.3	56.8	57.9	58.9	65.2	66.5	71.1	69.9
29	42.5	41.3	41.8	40.9	38.3	39.8	45.0	52.3	52.7	52.6
30	1.5	1.5	1.9	3.0	2.9	2.8	5.2	6.5	4.9	4.3
31	23.7	22.8	23.9	34.2	38.2	40.0	46.7	46.3	52.4	55.4
32	13.5	15.8	16.3	20.3	21.1	27.8	29.1	29.1	30.5	31.5
33	5.0	3.3	3.9	5.7	3.5	4.6	3.6	3.8	4.8	4.4
34	17.4	23.0	24.3	27.6	31.0	34.8	40.1	45.2	52.9	66.9
35	11.9	9.2	9.6	14.5	12.9	10.6	10.2	11.2	10.1	9.4
36	17.1	18.3	16.9	20.5	25.0	27.0	21.6	24.7	27.3	29.1
37	1.0	1.9	2.0	1.2	1.3	1.7	2.2	1.7	2.9	2.4
Men - Hommes - Hombres										
ISIC 3 - CITI 3 - CIIU 3										
Total	305.2	300.5	309.9	320.5	314.9	323.3	336.7	351.4	372.2	380.3
15	36.5	36.2	35.9	36.8	26.9	29.3	28.8	30.3	30.6	26.2
16	0.6	0.5	0.3	0.4	0.4	0.3	0.2	0.1	0.1	0.2
17	6.3	4.8	5.6	5.6	6.5	6.5	4.7	4.1	5.5	4.1
18	4.2	3.2	4.3	3.6	3.4	3.7	3.9	4.1	3.5	2.4
19	5.7	5.7	5.3	4.5	5.6	4.8	5.0	4.7	5.3	3.4
20	24.6	24.7	22.0	23.4	21.3	20.0	20.4	25.0	22.4	18.2
21	8.0	8.5	7.3	6.9	6.8	6.3	6.0	5.9	5.1	6.7
22	5.2	6.1	6.2	6.6	5.6	6.3	6.7	4.9	7.3	8.2
23	4.1	4.5	5.4	3.3	2.1	3.6	3.1	3.4	2.4	2.8
24	16.5	15.2	16.2	16.3	17.7	18.8	14.6	12.5	13.8	14.8
25	12.9	13.9	15.3	14.6	13.8	16.0	14.9	19.7	22.4	23.7
26	15.4	16.6	18.5	17.4	18.4	14.3	15.0	13.9	14.4	17.4
27	36.7	30.4	32.6	30.9	28.2	26.1	29.1	26.6	28.6	31.8
28	41.5	41.6	44.1	45.2	47.1	49.9	55.2	57.6	60.8	59.4
29	30.2	30.7	32.3	33.3	32.1	32.2	36.7	41.1	40.6	40.9
30	0.8	0.7	1.3	1.5	1.2	1.5	2.8	3.5	2.7	2.9
31	13.3	11.3	11.0	15.5	15.9	16.6	22.1	23.3	27.6	26.4
32	6.5	7.2	6.2	7.0	9.1	11.4	11.8	10.5	10.7	12.9
33	3.3	2.1	1.6	3.0	1.8	2.7	1.9	1.8	3.5	2.7
34	11.4	17.4	18.4	19.1	23.0	25.3	28.2	29.4	35.7	47.5
35	10.0	7.2	7.6	11.7	10.4	8.9	8.9	9.7	8.6	8.4
36	11.3	11.2	10.7	12.9	16.5	17.9	14.4	17.8	18.5	17.5
37	0.7	1.4	1.9	1.2	1.3	1.5	2.1	1.4	2.2	2.0

Explanatory notes: see p. 77.

[1] Persons aged 15 years and over. [2] Dec. [3] Employees and members of producers' cooperatives aged 15 years and over. [4] Excl. conscripts. [5] Excl. persons on child-care leave.

Notes explicatives: voir p. 80.

[1] Personnes âgées de 15 ans et plus. [2] Déc. [3] Salariés et membres de coopératives de producteurs âgés de 15 ans et plus. [4] Non compris les conscrits. [5] Non compris les personnes en congé parental.

Notas explicativas: véase p. 83.

[1] Personas de 15 años y más. [2] Dic. [3] Asalariados y miembros de cooperativas de productores de 15 años y más. [4] Excl. los conscriptos. [5] Excl. las personas con licencia parental.

Paid employment in manufacturing
Thousands

Emploi rémunéré dans les industries manufacturières
Milliers

Empleo remunerado en las industrias manufactureras
Millares

	1999	2000	2001	2002	2003	2004	2005	2006	2007	2008
Slovakia (BA) [1] [2] [3]					Employees - Salariés - Asalariados					
Women - Femmes - Mujeres										
ISIC 3 - CITI 3 - CIIU 3										
Total	216.8	215.4	218.7	228.7	224.1	223.5	219.8	222.5	225.2	229.6
15	32.4	27.9	29.7	27.9	26.8	27.1	29.1	26.1	25.6	28.6
16	0.4	1.0	0.5	0.5	0.2	0.2	0.8	0.2	-	-
17	17.3	19.0	17.6	16.9	19.7	14.4	9.9	9.6	9.7	9.6
18	42.1	40.2	42.2	45.4	44.7	43.3	34.1	33.4	31.8	29.4
19	13.8	15.6	15.5	17.2	14.2	15.0	15.1	14.2	12.2	11.5
20	6.7	5.9	5.2	5.8	4.7	4.1	4.7	6.2	6.8	5.1
21	4.9	6.0	6.9	5.4	4.8	4.1	2.7	2.0	2.4	2.9
22	7.6	6.9	6.6	4.8	5.8	5.4	5.8	8.7	5.9	4.2
23	0.9	1.3	1.7	0.2	1.0	1.2	0.8	1.1	0.7	0.9
24	8.2	10.2	8.1	7.6	7.3	7.8	8.3	8.3	5.6	6.0
25	7.7	6.4	6.8	5.0	8.3	7.4	8.5	9.3	13.1	14.1
26	7.4	8.8	8.8	8.5	5.5	8.4	9.6	7.6	5.6	6.5
27	8.7	7.3	8.7	9.6	7.8	5.2	5.5	4.7	7.0	5.4
28	12.5	11.2	11.1	11.6	10.8	9.0	10.0	8.9	10.3	10.5
29	12.3	10.7	9.5	7.5	6.2	7.6	8.2	11.2	12.1	11.7
30	0.8	0.8	0.7	1.5	1.6	1.4	2.4	3.0	2.3	1.3
31	10.5	11.5	12.9	18.7	22.3	23.5	24.6	23.0	24.8	29.0
32	7.1	8.6	10.1	13.3	12.0	16.4	17.2	18.6	19.9	18.6
33	1.7	1.2	2.3	2.7	1.8	1.9	1.6	2.0	1.4	1.8
34	6.1	5.6	5.9	8.5	8.0	9.5	12.0	15.8	17.2	19.4
35	1.9	2.0	2.0	2.8	2.4	1.6	1.3	1.4	1.5	1.0
36	5.9	7.2	6.1	7.6	8.6	9.1	7.2	6.8	8.8	11.6
37	0.3	0.5	0.1	-		0.1	0.2	0.3	0.7	0.4
Slovakia (DA) [4] [5]					Employees - Salariés - Asalariados					
Total - Total - Total										
ISIC 3 - CITI 3 - CIIU 3										
Total	375.07	379.29	373.25	376.00	359.99	358.32	364.46	371.93	377.98	371.30
15	46.71	43.93	42.08	42.13	38.77	35.69	35.52	34.38	32.52	33.41
16	0.55	0.41	0.38	0.36	0.34	0.23	0.22	0.14	-	-
17	16.72	16.03	18.42	18.59	16.16	14.58	13.71	13.10	12.34	9.76
18	28.77	28.91	27.92	27.50	22.13	24.27	22.70	21.43	16.81	14.65
19	14.75	16.27	14.17	15.39	15.30	13.80	13.78	13.64	12.44	11.28
20	10.97	10.80	9.98	10.17	8.29	8.65	9.38	9.17	8.78	7.48
21	9.98	10.18	9.34	8.91	7.86	7.25	7.19	7.08	7.06	7.25
22	7.90	7.92	7.71	6.99	7.10	7.32	7.53	6.92	7.20	6.64
23	4.72	4.60	4.84	4.35	3.90	3.72	3.40	2.59	2.69	2.61
24	20.27	19.45	18.58	16.37	13.68	11.93	11.51	11.68	11.37	11.93
25	12.27	12.92	13.26	14.40	15.73	15.42	17.35	18.79	21.48	23.66
26	22.75	21.60	21.84	21.58	20.30	20.13	19.87	18.61	18.90	17.47
27	25.13	29.98	30.74	31.34	27.61	27.57	26.64	26.88	26.87	25.44
28	22.62	24.57	26.07	23.32	24.30	24.85	28.22	27.78	28.76	31.79
29	53.70	49.48	43.34	41.94	39.73	40.78	39.52	43.13	44.20	43.77
30	1.31	1.43	1.48	1.04	2.11	3.24	3.21	1.17	0.92	1.67
31	24.46	28.81	30.61	35.61	37.08	41.28	43.32	43.19	46.19	42.50
32	8.55	10.55	8.78	8.92	9.30	8.85	10.52	12.99	16.23	16.49
33	5.38	5.21	4.99	5.89	5.81	5.42	5.57	6.64	5.25	6.11
34	14.54	14.25	15.89	18.80	22.81	21.57	22.90	30.30	33.93	34.04
35	9.67	9.43	9.35	8.70	7.91	7.76	7.28	6.93	7.36	7.64
36	12.08	12.09	13.12	13.27	13.29	13.43	14.25	14.49	15.66	14.74
37	1.27	0.47	0.36	0.43	0.48	0.58	0.87	0.90	1.02	0.97
Men - Hommes - Hombres										
ISIC 3 - CITI 3 - CIIU 3										
Total	217.67	219.76	217.44	217.34	210.96	208.11	212.53	216.54	219.91	217.25
15	23.58	22.47	21.65	21.57	19.89	18.41	18.27	17.39	16.07	16.74
16	0.30	0.27	0.25	0.23	0.23	0.14	0.14	0.10	-	-
17	4.40	4.06	4.31	4.23	3.73	3.24	2.96	2.74	2.60	2.14
18	3.38	3.44	3.20	3.20	2.38	2.74	2.43	2.34	1.75	1.32
19	3.80	3.97	3.28	3.88	3.87	3.32	3.51	3.47	3.17	2.67
20	8.00	7.87	7.31	7.42	5.95	6.15	6.79	6.65	6.33	5.26
21	6.75	6.76	6.28	5.94	5.30	4.84	4.76	4.70	4.79	4.81
22	3.69	3.74	3.72	3.40	3.52	3.53	3.69	3.36	3.47	3.23
23	3.37	3.31	3.42	3.18	2.95	2.79	2.56	1.94	1.96	1.87
24	12.70	12.01	11.60	10.24	8.65	7.42	7.14	7.28	7.11	7.51
25	7.98	8.68	9.02	9.47	10.01	10.05	10.79	11.26	12.15	13.17
26	16.44	15.43	15.63	15.42	14.46	14.42	14.17	13.28	14.08	13.02
27	19.93	23.64	24.28	24.89	22.15	22.13	21.45	21.78	21.46	20.33
28	17.66	19.28	20.82	18.34	19.38	19.78	22.53	22.05	22.69	24.22
29	39.91	37.38	33.63	32.49	31.17	32.00	30.88	33.20	33.66	33.43
30	0.58	0.70	0.74	0.45	1.02	1.39	1.31	0.50	0.36	0.66
31	10.71	12.31	12.88	15.32	16.52	17.68	18.64	18.13	18.30	17.48
32	3.57	4.74	3.82	3.68	3.50	3.35	4.08	5.02	6.21	6.44
33	3.20	3.01	2.80	3.32	3.13	3.13	3.21	3.36	2.96	3.11
34	12.12	11.86	13.11	15.42	18.46	16.87	18.06	23.24	24.82	24.70
35	7.67	7.59	7.64	7.06	6.55	6.39	5.93	5.64	6.00	6.20
36	6.98	6.84	7.73	7.82	7.71	7.83	8.45	8.34	9.09	8.09
37	0.95	0.40	0.32	0.37	0.43	0.51	0.78	0.77	0.88	0.85

Explanatory notes: see p. 77.

[1] Employees and members of producers' cooperatives aged 15 years and over. [2] Excl. conscripts. [3] Excl. persons on child-care leave. [4] Before 1997: excl. enterprises with less than 25 employees; beginning 1997: excl. enterprises with less than 20 employees. [5] 31st Dec. of each year.

Notes explicatives: voir p. 80.

[1] Salariés et membres de coopératives de producteurs âgés de 15 ans et plus. [2] Non compris les conscrits. [3] Non compris les personnes en congé parental. [4] Avant 1997: non compris les entreprises occupant moins de 25 salariés; à partir de 1997 non compris celles de moins de 20 salariés. [5] 31 déc. de chaque année.

Notas explicativas: véase p. 83.

[1] Asalariados y miembros de cooperativas de productores de 15 años y más. [2] Excl. los conscriptos. [3] Excl. las personas con licencia parental. [4] Antes de 1997: excl. las empresas con menos de 25 asalariados; a partir de 1997: excl. las empresas con menos de 20 asalariados. [5] 31 dic. de cada año.

Paid employment in manufacturing	Emploi rémunéré dans les industries manufacturières	Empleo remunerado en las industrias manufactureras	
Thousands	Milliers	Millares	

	1999	2000	2001	2002	2003	2004	2005	2006	2007	2008

Slovakia (DA) [1] [2] — Employees - Salariés - Asalariados

Women - Femmes - Mujeres
ISIC 3 - CITI 3 - CIIU 3

	1999	2000	2001	2002	2003	2004	2005	2006	2007	2008
Total	157.40	159.53	155.81	158.66	149.03	150.21	151.93	155.39	158.07	154.05
15	23.13	21.46	20.43	20.56	18.88	17.28	17.25	16.99	16.45	16.67
16	0.25	0.14	0.13	0.13	0.11	0.09	0.08	0.04	-	-
17	12.32	11.97	14.11	14.36	12.43	11.34	10.75	10.36	9.74	7.62
18	25.39	25.47	24.72	24.30	19.75	21.53	20.27	19.09	15.06	13.33
19	10.95	12.30	10.89	11.51	11.43	10.48	10.27	10.17	9.27	8.61
20	2.97	2.93	2.67	2.75	2.34	2.50	2.59	2.52	2.45	2.22
21	3.23	3.42	3.06	2.97	2.56	2.41	2.43	2.38	2.27	2.44
22	4.21	4.18	3.99	3.59	3.58	3.79	3.84	3.56	3.73	3.41
23	1.35	1.29	1.42	1.17	0.95	0.93	0.84	0.65	0.73	0.74
24	7.57	7.44	6.98	6.13	5.03	4.51	4.37	4.40	4.26	4.42
25	4.29	4.24	4.24	4.93	5.72	5.37	6.56	7.53	9.33	10.49
26	6.31	6.17	6.21	6.16	5.84	5.71	5.70	5.33	4.82	4.45
27	5.20	6.34	6.46	6.45	5.46	5.44	5.19	5.10	5.41	5.11
28	4.96	5.29	5.25	4.98	4.92	5.07	5.69	5.73	6.07	7.57
29	13.79	12.10	9.71	9.45	8.56	8.78	8.64	9.93	10.54	10.34
30	0.73	0.73	0.74	0.59	1.09	1.85	1.90	0.67	0.56	1.01
31	13.75	16.50	17.73	20.29	20.56	23.60	24.68	25.06	27.89	25.02
32	4.98	5.81	4.96	5.24	5.80	5.50	6.44	7.97	10.02	10.05
33	2.18	2.20	2.19	2.57	2.68	2.29	2.36	3.28	2.29	3.00
34	2.42	2.39	2.78	3.38	4.35	4.70	4.84	7.06	9.11	9.34
35	2.00	1.84	1.71	1.64	1.36	1.37	1.35	1.29	1.36	1.44
36	5.10	5.25	5.39	5.45	5.58	5.60	5.80	6.15	6.57	6.65
37	0.32	0.07	0.04	0.06	0.05	0.07	0.09	0.13	0.14	0.12

Slovenia (BA) [3] [4] — Employees - Salariés - Asalariados

Total - Total - Total
ISIC 3 - CITI 3 - CIIU 3 .... ISIC 4 - CITI 4 - CIIU 4

	1999	2000	2001	2002	2003	2004	2005	2006	2007	2008	
Total	260	253	260	269	252	254	261	248	251	249	Total
15	24	24	24	25	24	20	22	22	22	20	10
16	1	1	-	-	-	-	-	-	-	2	11
17	17	18	13	14	13	14	12	11	13	-	12
18	21	18	22	20	14	15	14	11	12	7	13
19	8	8	9	9	7	5	4	4	4	9	14
20	14	17	15	12	14	12	11	12	13	5	15
21	7	6	7	7	6	8	9	9	5	11	16
22	11	13	11	9	9	11	10	9	11	6	17
23	-	-	-	-	-	-	-	-	-	5	18
24	12	14	15	16	15	16	19	17	15	-	19
25	10	9	11	13	12	14	13	12	16	12	20
26	11	10	10	9	11	11	12	11	11	7	21
27	8	7	8	10	9	9	11	9	10	15	22
28	33	28	32	36	35	35	32	37	35	12	23
29	21	17	22	23	26	27	28	24	25	9	24
30	-	-	-	-	-	-	-	-	-	35	25
31	22	25	22	24	20	17	18	17	16	9	26
32	4	4	5	5	4	5	6	5	6	25	27
33	4	4	2	2	3	5	5	5	5	20	28
34	8	9	8	10	8	6	10	10	15	17	29
35	2	3	3	3	2	2	3	2	2	4	30
36	22	19	19	20	19	19	20	18	13	11	31
37	1	1	1	1	1	1	2	1	1	5	32
										3	33

Men - Hommes - Hombres
ISIC 3 - CITI 3 - CIIU 3 .... ISIC 4 - CITI 4 - CIIU 4

	1999	2000	2001	2002	2003	2004	2005	2006	2007	2008	
Total	155	148	152	159	155	156	161	154	159	158	Total
15	15	14	15	14	14	11	12	11	12	10	10
16	-	-	-	-	-	-	-	-	-	1	11
17	5	4	3	4	5	4	3	3	5	-	12
18	3	3	3	3	3	2	3	2	1	2	13
19	3	3	3	3	2	2	2	1	2	2	14
20	11	12	11	8	11	10	9	9	9	2	15
21	4	3	4	5	4	5	6	6	3	8	16
22	6	7	7	5	6	6	4	5	7	4	17
23	-	-	-	-	-	-	-	-	-	3	18
24	7	8	8	9	8	9	10	8	9	-	19
25	7	5	7	8	8	9	8	8	10	8	20
26	7	7	7	7	7	8	7	8	7	4	21
27	7	6	7	8	8	7	9	7	10	11	22
28	25	22	25	29	27	28	27	29	28	8	23
29	16	12	14	16	19	20	21	19	19	8	24
30	-	-	-	-	-	-	-	-	-	27	25
31	11	13	11	11	10	8	9	9	9	5	26
32	2	3	2	3	3	3	4	3	4	12	27
33	2	1	1	1	1	3	2	2	2	16	28
34	6	6	7	8	5	4	7	7	11	12	29
35	2	2	2	2	1	2	2	2	2	3	30
36	15	13	11	12	12	13	14	12	9	8	31
37	1	1	1	1	1	-	1	1	1	2	32
										2	33

Explanatory notes: see p. 77.

[1] Before 1997: excl. enterprises with less than 25 employees; beginning 1997: excl. enterprises with less than 20 employees. [2] 31st Dec. of each year. [3] Persons aged 15 years and over. [4] Second quarter of each year.

Notes explicatives: voir p. 80.

[1] Avant 1997: non compris les entreprises occupant moins de 25 salariés; à partir de 1997 non compris celles de moins de 20 salariés. [2] 31 déc. de chaque année. [3] Personnes âgées de 15 ans et plus. [4] Deuxième trimestre de chaque année.

Notas explicativas: véase p. 83.

[1] Antes de 1997: excl. las empresas con menos de 25 asalariados; a partir de 1997: excl. las empresas con menos de 20 asalariados. [2] 31 dic. de cada año. [3] Personas de 15 años y más. [4] Segundo trimestre de cada año.

EMPLOYMENT — EMPLOI — EMPLEO

Paid employment in manufacturing — **Emploi rémunéré dans les industries manufacturières** — **Empleo remunerado en las industrias manufactureras**

Thousands — Milliers — Millares

Slovenia (BA) [1] [2]

Women - Femmes - Mujeres

Employees - Salariés - Asalariados

ISIC 3 - CITI 3 - CIIU 3	1999	2000	2001	2002	2003	2004	2005	2006	2007	2008	ISIC 4 - CITI 4 - CIIU 4
Total	105	105	108	110	97	98	100	93	92	91	Total
15	9	10	9	11	11	9	10	10	9	10	10
16	-	1	-	-	-	-	-	-	-	1	11
17	12	14	9	9	8	11	9	8	8	-	12
18	18	15	18	16	11	13	11	10	10	5	13
19	5	5	6	6	4	3	2	3	2	8	14
20	4	5	4	4	3	2	3	3	4	3	15
21	3	3	3	2	3	3	3	3	2	3	16
22	5	6	4	4	3	5	6	4	5	2	17
23	-	-	-	-	-	-	-	-	-	2	18
24	5	6	7	7	7	7	8	9	6	-	19
25	3	4	5	4	4	5	5	4	6	4	20
26	5	4	3	3	3	4	5	4	4	4	21
27	1	1	1	2	1	1	2	2	1	4	22
28	8	5	7	7	7	7	5	8	7	4	23
29	5	4	7	7	7	7	7	6	6	2	24
30	-	-	-	-	-	-	-	-	-	7	25
31	11	11	12	13	9	8	9	7	8	3	26
32	1	2	3	2	2	2	2	2	2	13	27
33	2	1	1	1	2	2	3	3	3	4	28
34	2	3	2	2	3	2	2	3	4	5	29
35	-	1	1	1	1	-	1	-	-	-	30
36	7	6	7	8	7	6	7	6	4	3	31
37	-	-	-	-	-	-	-	-	-	3	32
										-	33

Sweden (BA) [3] [4]

Total - Total - Total

Employees - Salariés - Asalariados

ISIC 3 - CITI 3 - CIIU 3	1999	2000	2001	2002	2003	2004	2005	2006	2007	2008	ISIC 4 - CITI 4 - CIIU 4
Total	720	721	704	676	656	641	616[5]	614	618	585	Total
15-16	68	67	65	63	61	60	55[5]	55	53	48	10
17-19	12	12	11	10	12	12	8[5]	8	9	3	11
20	34	35	35	33	32	33	34[5]	33	35	1	12
21	43	40	40	40	36	35	37[5]	36	35	6	13
22	56	55	50	47	43	41	44[5]	45	43	1	14
23-24	39	38	39	39	42	43	41[5]	40	39	1	15
25	26	27	26	23	25	23	22[5]	22	22	34	16
26	17	16	18	18	16	14	16[5]	17	15	34	17
27	32	33	31	32	33	34	35[5]	34	35	14	18
28	77	78	77	76	72	66	70[5]	70	72	2	19
29	98	92	87	87	90	88	81[5]	88	92	20	20
30-33	97	101	98	85	70	69	66[5]	60	60	9	21
34-35	92	99	100	96	96	98	85[5]	83	85	22	22
36-37	27	28	28	26	26	25	23[5]	24	23	16	23
										33	24
										73	25
										24	26
										26	27
										79	28
										74	29
										16	30
										17	31
										12	32
										17	33

Explanatory notes: see p. 77.

[1] Persons aged 15 years and over. [2] Second quarter of each year. [3] Incl. professional army; excl. compulsory military service. [4] Persons aged 15 to 74 years; prior to 2007: 16 to 64 years. [5] Methodology revised; data not strictly comparable.

Notes explicatives: voir p. 80.

[1] Personnes âgées de 15 ans et plus. [2] Deuxième trimestre de chaque année. [3] Y compris les militaires de carrière; non compris les militaires du contingent. [4] Personnes âgées de 15 à 74 ans; avant 2007: 16 à 64 ans. [5] Méthodologie révisée; les données ne sont pas strictement comparables.

Notas explicativas: véase p. 83.

[1] Personas de 15 años y más. [2] Segundo trimestre de cada año. [3] Incl. los militares profesionales; excl. los militares en servicio obligatorio. [4] Personas de 15 a 74 años; antes de 2007: 16 a 64 años. [5] Metodología revisada; los datos no son estrictamente comparables.

Paid employment in manufacturing — Thousands

Emploi rémunéré dans les industries manufacturières — Milliers

Empleo remunerado en las industrias manufactureras — Millares

Sweden (BA) [1][2] — Employees - Salariés - Asalariados

Men - Hommes - Hombres
ISIC 3 - CITI 3 - CIIU 3   ISIC 4 - CITI 4 - CIIU 4

Age	1999	2000	2001	2002	2003	2004	2005	2006	2007	2008	Age
Total	530	528	515	497	484	475	460 [3]	457	460	446	Total
15-16	46	43	40	41	39	37	36 [3]	35	33	30	10
17-19	6	6	6	6	6	6	4 [3]	5	5	2	11
20	29	29	29	27	27	28	28 [3]	27	28	-	12
21	34	31	30	31	28	28	30 [3]	28	27	3	13
22	33	33	30	26	25	25	25 [3]	25	24	1	14
23-24	25	24	24	23	25	25	23 [3]	24	25	1	15
25	18	18	17	16	17	16	15 [3]	15	16	29	16
26	13	13	14	14	13	11	13 [3]	13	12	27	17
27	27	27	24	26	28	28	30 [3]	28	28	10	18
28	61	63	63	64	60	55	58 [3]	59	61	2	19
29	81	74	72	72	75	73	68 [3]	72	75	15	20
30-33	64	65	63	56	48	48	47 [3]	42	41	5	21
34-35	75	82	81	77	76	78	67 [3]	66	67	16	22
36-37	18	20	20	20	17	17	16 [3]	17	17	13	23
										28	24
										61	25
										16	26
										19	27
										64	28
										57	29
										13	30
										12	31
										6	32
										15	33

Women - Femmes - Mujeres
ISIC 3 - CITI 3 - CIIU 3   ISIC 4 - CITI 4 - CIIU 4

Age	1999	2000	2001	2002	2003	2004	2005	2006	2007	2008	Age
Total	191	193	189	179	169	166	156 [3]	157	158	139	Total
15-16	23	24	25	23	22	23	20 [3]	19	19	17	10
17-19	6	6	5	4	5	6	4 [3]	4	4	1	11
20	5	6	6	6	6	5	5 [3]	6	7	-	12
21	10	10	10	9	8	7	7 [3]	7	8	3	13
22	23	22	21	21	18	16	19 [3]	20	19	1	14
23-24	14	14	15	16	17	18	18 [3]	16	15	5	16
25	8	9	8	8	8	6	7 [3]	7	6	8	17
26	4	4	3	3	3	2	3 [3]	4	3	4	18
27	5	6	6	6	5	6	5 [3]	6	6	-	19
28	17	15	14	13	12	11	12 [3]	11	11	6	20
29	17	18	16	16	15	15	13 [3]	16	17	4	21
30-33	33	36	35	30	22	21	19 [3]	18	19	6	22
34-35	17	17	20	19	19	21	17 [3]	17	18	2	23
36-37	9	7	7	6	8	8	7 [3]	6	6	5	24
										13	25
										8	26
										7	27
										15	28
										17	29
										3	30
										5	31
										5	32
										2	33

Turkey (BA) [4] — Employees - Salariés - Asalariados

Total - Total - Total
ISIC 3 - CITI 3 - CIIU 3

Age	1999	2000	2001	2002	2003	2004	2005	2006	2007	2008
Total	.	2 845	2 846	3 034	3 026	3 121	3 366	3 478	3 469	3 615
15	.	371	377	351	335	371	409	415	413	438
16	.	28	32	35	25	26	23	18	16	16
17	.	475	496	585	553	455	432	470	407	408
18	.	492	471	502	520	598	643	630	642	619
19	.	98	87	109	99	103	102	105	101	95
20	.	84	80	81	81	87	82	89	80	72
21	.	23	26	31	35	37	42	45	41	43
22	.	65	56	57	57	75	82	84	84	90
23	.	15	26	21	16	10	18	17	11	13
24	.	110	110	133	134	173	184	187	167	163
25	.	74	86	94	105	119	131	150	151	157
26	.	168	168	179	160	156	188	212	215	236
27	.	83	83	92	106	116	122	127	149	171
28	.	153	147	142	168	156	173	167	189	224
29	.	130	144	151	153	164	180	180	193	228
30	.	-	-	-	-	-	-	-	4	4
31	.	49	49	48	58	56	67	68	72	74
32	.	27	21	20	20	19	24	21	25	23
33	.	15	13	17	16	20	26	25	20	25
34	.	138	142	166	178	161	182	187	190	210
35	.	27	33	36	42	33	36	44	47	74
36	.	220	196	179	163	179	217	235	247	227
37	.	-	-	-	-	-	-	-	5.0	5.0
X	.	-	-	-	-	-	-	-	5	-

Explanatory notes: see p. 77.

[1] Incl. professional army; excl. compulsory military service. [2] Persons aged 15 to 74 years; prior to 2007: 16 to 64 years. [3] Methodology revised; data not strictly comparable. [4] Persons aged 15 years and over.

Notes explicatives: voir p. 80.

[1] Y compris les militaires de carrière; non compris les militaires du contingent. [2] Personnes âgées de 15 à 74 ans; avant 2007: 16 à 64 ans. [3] Méthodologie révisée; les données ne sont pas strictement comparables. [4] Personnes âgées de 15 ans et plus.

Notas explicativas: véase p. 83.

[1] Incl. los militares profesionales; excl. los militares en servicio obligatorio. [2] Personas de 15 a 74 años; antes de 2007: 16 a 64 años. [3] Metodología revisada; los datos no son estrictamente comparables. [4] Personas de 15 años y más.

	EMPLOYMENT	EMPLOI	EMPLEO

Paid employment in manufacturing — Thousands
Emploi rémunéré dans les industries manufacturières — Milliers
Empleo remunerado en las industrias manufactureras — Millares

Turkey (BA) [1]
Employees - Salariés - Asalariados

Men - Hommes - Hombres
ISIC 3 - CITI 3 - CIIU 3

	1999	2000	2001	2002	2003	2004	2005	2006	2007	2008
Total	.	2 295	2 298	2 354	2 368	2 463	2 694	2 786	2 755	2 904
15	.	319	329	297	291	316	342	352	338	361
16	.	23	25	24	19	20	19	15	13	13
17	.	346	343	363	346	267	276	302	260	268
18	.	270	261	258	273	350	373	361	360	351
19	.	89	83	98	90	92	91	96	91	84
20	.	79	75	76	78	83	77	85	75	68
21	.	21	23	26	29	32	37	40	36	36
22	.	53	47	48	48	65	73	71	70	72
23	.	13	24	20	15	8	17	15	10	12
24	.	87	90	106	107	137	147	148	130	127
25	.	65	75	85	97	109	120	136	135	143
26	.	152	153	165	147	145	174	197	199	213
27	.	78	80	89	102	112	116	121	139	164
28	.	146	137	136	158	147	164	156	172	207
29	.	119	130	139	136	150	164	168	176	207
30	.	-	-	-	-	-	-	-	3	3
31	.	38	42	39	50	49	57	57	60	64
32	.	19	17	14	16	15	19	16	19	18
33	.	11	11	13	11	15	20	21	16	17
34	.	126	130	151	161	150	170	172	176	191
35	.	25	33	34	40	32	34	41	46	71
36	.	212	187	168	149	166	202	215	226	209
37	.	-	-	-	-	-	-	-	5	5
X	.	-	-	-	-	-	-	-	5	-

Women - Femmes - Mujeres
ISIC 3 - CITI 3 - CIIU 3

	1999	2000	2001	2002	2003	2004	2005	2006	2007	2008
Total	.	550	548	680	658	658	670	693	714	711
15	.	52	48	54	43	55	67	63	75	77
16	.	6	7	11	4	6	4	2	3	3
17	.	129	154	222	207	188	156	168	147	140
18	.	222	210	244	246	248	269	269	282	268
19	.	8	5	11	9	11	11	9	10	11
20	.	4	4	5	3	4	5	4	5	4
21	.	2	3	5	6	6	4	5	5	7
22	.	12	10	9	9	10	9	13	14	18
23	.	1	1	1	2	2	2	2	1	1
24	.	23	20	27	26	36	37	39	37	36
25	.	9	10	9	8	11	11	14	16	14
26	.	16	15	14	13	11	14	16	16	23
27	.	5	3	3	4	4	6	6	10	7
28	.	7	10	7	10	9	9	11	17	17
29	.	11	13	12	17	15	15	12	17	21
30	.	-	-	-	-	-	-	-	1	1
31	.	11	6	10	8	7	10	12	12	10
32	.	7	5	6	4	4	4	5	6	5
33	.	3	2	4	5	5	6	4	4	8
34	.	12	12	15	17	12	12	15	14	19
35	.	2	1	2	2	1	2	3	1	3
36	.	7	9	11	14	14	15	20	21	18
X	.	-	-	-	-	-	-	-	-	-

Ukraine (DA)
Employees - Salariés - Asalariados

Total - Total - Total
ISIC 2 - CITI 2 - CIIU 2   ISIC 3 - CITI 3 - CIIU 3

ISIC 2	1999	2000	2001	2002	2003	2004	2005	2006	2007	2008	ISIC 3
Total	2 898 I	2 916	2 704	2 500	2 356	2 351	2 371	2 329	2 268	2 192	Total
311-312	494 I	512	479	459	440	447	460	460	450	432	15
313	68 I	6	6	5	5	5	5	5	4	4	16
314	6 I	95	79	58	45	41	40	35	30	28	17
321	97 I	126	119	103	90	87	86	77	70	61	18
322	107 I	40	33	25	22	22	21	21	20	19	19
323	11 I	41	36	34	33	34	37	38	40	40	20
324	33 I	24	24	22	22	22	24	23	24	25	21
331	33 I	38	38	36	36	39	42	45	47	47	22
332	56 I	54	55	57	58	59	59	54	52	50	23
341	21 I	159	153	151	140	135	134	130	124	119	24
342	22 I	42	40	39	39	43	48	54	57	55	25
351	117 I	203	184	161	150	150	154	151	152	149	26
352	38 I	362	365	358	350	354	358	356	341	329	27
353	17 I	72	62	60	59	61	67	74	79	78	28
354	41 I	497	462	415	378	361	352	334	310	293	29
355	27 I	11	7	7	5	5	4	4	5	5	30
356	14 I	136	121	111	96	99	99	101	100	102	31
361	21 I	79	61	42	36	30	26	24	23	21	32
362	35 I	55	50	45	46	45	45	43	40	37	33
369	182 I	61	58	53	51	56	56	50	55	57	34
371	288 I	223	199	195	196	196	191	184	177	172	35
372	41 I	66	55	45	42	42	45	50	52	55	36
381	295 I	17	19	19	17	18	18	16	16	14	37
382	341 I										
383	126 I										
384	206 I										
385	63 I										
390	52 I										

Explanatory notes: see p. 77.   Notes explicatives: voir p. 80.   Notas explicativas: véase p. 83.

[1] Persons aged 15 years and over.   [1] Personnes âgées de 15 ans et plus.   [1] Personas de 15 años y más.

444   *ILO YEARBOOK OF LABOUR STATISTICS 2009*   *ANNUAIRE DES STATISTIQUES DU TRAVAIL DU BIT 2009*   *ANUARIO DE ESTADISTICAS DEL TRABAJO DEL OIT 2009*

Paid employment in manufacturing
Thousands

Emploi rémunéré dans les industries manufacturières
Milliers

Empleo remunerado en las industrias manufactureras
Millares

	1999	2000	2001	2002	2003	2004	2005	2006	2007	2008
Ukraine (DA)				Employees - Salariés - Asalariados						
Men - Hommes - Hombres										
ISIC 3 - CITI 3 - CIIU 3										
Total	.	.	.	1 371	1 306	1 315	1 339	1 324	1 297	1 263
15	.	.	.	222	212	216	222	224	218	212
16	.	.	.	3	3	3	3	3	3	3
17	.	.	.	16	14	13	13	12	10	10
18	.	.	.	16	14	13	12	11	10	9
19	.	.	.	8	7	8	7	7	7	6
20	.	.	.	24	23	25	26	27	28	28
21	.	.	.	13	13	14	15	15	15	16
22	.	.	.	16	15	17	19	20	21	21
23	.	.	.	37	38	38	39	35	34	32
24	.	.	.	81	75	72	73	71	68	65
25	.	.	.	23	23	25	29	33	35	34
26	.	.	.	95	89	91	95	95	98	98
27	.	.	.	227	223	227	231	230	222	214
28	.	.	.	38	37	39	44	50	53	53
29	.	.	.	256	234	226	223	214	200	191
30	.	.	.	4	3	3	2	2	3	3
31	.	.	.	59	52	54	54	55	55	55
32	.	.	.	20	18	15	13	13	12	11
33	.	.	.	24	25	24	24	23	21	20
34	.	.	.	33	32	36	36	32	35	36
35	.	.	.	116	118	118	117	110	105	102
36	.	.	.	26	25	25	28	30	32	33
37	.	.	.	14	13	13	14	12	12	11
Women - Femmes - Mujeres										
ISIC 3 - CITI 3 - CIIU 3										
Total	.	.	.	1 129	1 050	1 036	1 032	1 005	971	929
15	.	.	.	237	228	231	238	236	232	220
16	.	.	.	2	2	2	2	2	1	1
17	.	.	.	42	31	29	27	23	20	18
18	.	.	.	87	76	74	74	66	60	52
19	.	.	.	17	14	14	14	14	13	13
20	.	.	.	10	9	10	11	11	12	12
21	.	.	.	9	9	8	9	8	9	9
22	.	.	.	20	20	22	23	25	26	26
23	.	.	.	20	21	20	20	19	18	18
24	.	.	.	70	65	62	61	59	56	54
25	.	.	.	16	16	18	19	21	22	21
26	.	.	.	66	60	59	59	56	54	51
27	.	.	.	131	127	127	127	126	119	115
28	.	.	.	22	22	22	23	24	26	25
29	.	.	.	159	144	135	129	120	110	102
30	.	.	.	3	3	2	2	2	2	2
31	.	.	.	52	44	46	45	46	45	47
32	.	.	.	22	19	15	13	11	11	10
33	.	.	.	21	22	21	21	20	19	17
34	.	.	.	20	19	20	20	18	20	21
35	.	.	.	79	78	78	74	74	72	70
36	.	.	.	19	17	17	17	20	20	22
37	.	.	.	5	4	4	4	4	4	3
United Kingdom (BA) [1][2]				Wage earners and working proprietors - Ouvriers et propriétaires-exploitants - Obreros y empresarios propietarios						
Total - Total - Total										
ISIC 3 - CITI 3 - CIIU 3										
Total	4 741	4 609	4 453	4 288	4 116	3 809	3 796	3 745	3 738	3 540
15	482	480	417	433	429	410	391	408	426	397
16	9	7	5	8	8	7	7	7	3	8
17	171	151	142	139	109	114	94	98	102	84
18	153	114	98	86	78	70	62	51	48	51
19	30	26	24	17	22	16	15	16	15	11
20	85	86	84	98	74	86	95	84	84	85
21	109	114	99	103	103	93	92	99	84	77
22	421	429	414	374	424	375	374	366	340	356
23	42	44	59	58	50	52	49	55	66	49
24	333	313	302	322	296	286	272	261	255	242
25	264	253	241	235	232	206	211	199	205	185
26	169	161	140	131	153	143	128	130	122	106
27	132	137	135	128	118	105	106	111	113	114
28	410	385	399	389	366	342	351	339	360	375
29	466	440	444	427	384	358	398	354	374	367
30	131	132	127	104	97	88	96	82	69	62
31	211	209	226	207	200	174	166	186	164	147
32	161	157	149	123	107	92	94	83	79	63
33	133	127	140	133	141	122	118	127	123	124
34	335	326	308	280	286	258	247	264	266	231
35	254	268	249	254	235	206	219	232	242	238
36	232	245	243	237	202	199	202	187	190	159
37	7	4	9	4	4	8	8	8	11	7

Explanatory notes: see p. 77.

[1] Persons aged 16 years and over. [2] Second quarter.

Notes explicatives: voir p. 80.

[1] Personnes âgées de 16 ans et plus. [2] Deuxième trimestre.

Notas explicativas: véase p. 83.

[1] Personas de 16 años y más. [2] Segundo trimestre.

2F EMPLOYMENT · EMPLOI · EMPLEO

Paid employment in manufacturing · **Emploi rémunéré dans les industries manufacturières** · **Empleo remunerado en las industrias manufactureras**

Thousands · Milliers · Millares

United Kingdom (BA) [1] [2]

Wage earners and working proprietors - Ouvriers et propriétaires-exploitants - Obreros y empresarios propietarios

Men - Hommes - Hombres
ISIC 3 - CITI 3 - CIIU 3

	1999	2000	2001	2002	2003	2004	2005	2006	2007	2008
Total	3 449	3 377	3 283	3 180	3 068	2 847	2 841	2 799	2 806	2 635
15	321	315	268	279	289	272	263	276	293	256
16	5	6	4	4	3	4	5	5	1	5
17	88	80	78	68	59	61	51	54	55	45
18	45	33	32	30	27	26	23	21	16	24
19	17	15	16	9	9	9	7	11	8	4
20	73	74	74	81	65	72	86	72	74	75
21	80	83	70	78	73	69	73	74	69	61
22	262	264	258	242	263	236	226	212	217	210
23	31	36	49	49	42	41	36	43	47	41
24	226	211	200	216	197	186	177	174	170	154
25	195	193	194	189	190	165	163	159	161	151
26	128	124	107	104	114	111	105	105	96	83
27	115	120	120	113	107	97	93	95	102	99
28	338	324	342	331	303	293	304	293	301	320
29	385	358	351	336	315	285	310	282	299	288
30	95	94	90	78	78	65	72	61	53	48
31	154	160	167	153	150	135	125	142	125	104
32	112	100	98	86	78	63	63	57	56	48
33	92	89	101	93	100	91	80	89	82	91
34	279	277	261	243	247	223	216	233	230	194
35	230	239	218	221	209	180	196	203	203	206
36	170	180	177	175	147	155	160	132	136	122
37	6	3	7	3	4	6	5	7	10	5

Women - Femmes - Mujeres
ISIC 3 - CITI 3 - CIIU 3

	1999	2000	2001	2002	2003	2004	2005	2006	2007	2008
Total	1 293	1 232	1 170	1 108	1 048	962	956	946	932	905
15	162	165	149	154	140	138	128	131	132	141
16	4	-	1	3	5	3	2	2	1	3
17	83	71	64	71	50	53	43	44	47	39
18	108	82	66	56	51	44	39	30	32	27
19	13	11	8	8	13	8	7	5	6	8
20	12	12	10	17	9	13	10	12	10	10
21	30	31	29	25	29	23	19	25	15	16
22	159	165	156	132	160	139	148	153	123	146
23	11	7	10	10	8	11	13	13	19	8
24	107	103	102	106	99	100	94	87	84	88
25	69	59	47	46	42	41	48	40	43	35
26	41	37	33	27	39	32	23	25	26	22
27	17	18	15	15	11	7	13	16	12	15
28	72	61	57	58	64	49	48	46	59	55
29	81	82	93	91	69	74	88	72	74	79
30	36	39	36	26	19	23	24	21	15	13
31	57	50	59	54	50	38	41	44	39	43
32	49	57	51	37	28	28	32	26	22	15
33	41	38	39	40	40	31	38	37	41	33
34	55	48	47	37	39	35	32	31	36	37
35	24	30	31	33	26	26	23	29	38	32
36	62	64	65	62	55	43	41	55	54	37
37	-	1	2	-	-	1	3	-	1	1

Explanatory notes: see p. 77.
[1] Persons aged 16 years and over. [2] Second quarter.

Notes explicatives: voir p. 80.
[1] Personnes âgées de 16 ans et plus. [2] Deuxième trimestre.

Notas explicativas: véase p. 83.
[1] Personas de 16 años y más. [2] Segundo trimestre.

Paid employment in manufacturing
Thousands

Emploi rémunéré dans les industries manufacturières
Milliers

Empleo remunerado en las industrias manufactureras
Millares

	1999	2000	2001	2002	2003	2004	2005	2006	2007	2008

OCEANIA-OCÉANIE-OCEANIA

Australia (BA) [1] [2]   Employees - Salariés - Asalariados

Total - Total - Total
ISIC 3 - CITI 3 - CIIU 3

	1999	2000	2001	2002	2003	2004	2005	2006	2007	2008
Total	985.6	1 038.7	1 007.6	1 024.4	1 014.0	1 018.4	1 005.7	999.2	1 021.8	1 029.6
15	164.1	166.3	209.8	222.6	218.2	261.3	281.1	254.4	281.9	293.6
16	1.6	1.6	2.6	2.0	2.0	1.3	1.7	2.0	1.9	1.0
17	30.0	29.8	26.0	25.8	24.8	17.5	17.3	15.4	18.5	11.3
18	33.6	33.0	36.0	34.5	29.4	31.2	25.0	25.8	23.3	21.7
19	9.3	9.8	3.4	3.2	3.3	1.3	1.7	1.5	1.3	1.9
20	38.5	44.6	40.2	46.2	53.9	48.5	45.2	42.7	45.6	45.0
21	21.3	19.7	28.8	24.9	23.3	23.3	22.2	25.7	21.4	19.8
22	102.7	112.3	96.4	96.4	98.2	99.1	99.3	97.2	102.5	97.8
23	5.6	9.4	11.2	11.1	8.0	8.8	9.4	8.3	6.5	7.8
24	57.1	53.7	47.9	50.0	46.8	41.6	39.3	38.1	41.8	45.3
25	38.8	40.3	46.4	47.1	46.3	45.3	40.0	39.7	43.8	41.4
26	43.3	39.8	38.7	37.9	40.7	34.9	32.0	35.4	35.5	38.3
27	55.5	73.0	63.3	63.0	66.9	63.9	78.1	82.0	78.1	86.7
28	105.9	98.3	81.9	84.5	85.9	72.4	62.4	73.1	66.0	64.7
29	60.1	56.8	59.1	62.9	54.7	58.9	51.8	57.3	55.3	58.9
30	-	-	24.0	20.5	20.5	18.4	21.4	20.1	22.1	19.0
31	36.0	38.2	21.1	20.5	16.8	16.6	15.4	14.6	16.6	15.5
32	19.0	23.7	.	.	.	.	.	.	.	.
33	9.2	11.0	11.3	12.3	11.9	12.4	9.7	14.3	14.6	16.1
34	57.7	62.3	66.3	68.7	73.4	71.1	72.1	73.1	66.5	59.0
35	29.8	30.5	29.6	29.0	29.9	30.8	29.4	28.2	34.2	34.0
36	66.5	64.0	63.4	61.3	59.1	59.9	51.1	50.3	44.5	50.8
X	-	20.8	.	.	.	.	.	.	.	.

Men - Hommes - Hombres
ISIC 3 - CITI 3 - CIIU 3

	1999	2000	2001	2002	2003	2004	2005	2006	2007	2008
Total	727.8	760.3	737.6	753.6	734.4	743.3	734.2	729.9	746.2	757.2
15	113.7	110.1	139.6	147.0	141.1	176.0	186.8	165.8	180.4	192.6
16	0.9	1.1	1.4	1.5	1.3	1.0	1.1	1.4	1.1	1.0
17	17.6	14.1	14.4	13.5	12.3	7.5	8.7	7.7	10.4	5.5
18	9.2	10.2	12.3	11.6	9.2	9.9	8.4	8.2	9.0	6.7
19	5.1	5.2	3.2	2.8	2.4	0.9	1.2	0.6	0.9	0.9
20	32.3	38.7	35.4	40.1	47.1	44.0	39.1	36.8	40.0	37.7
21	17.1	16.6	21.5	18.7	16.7	17.2	16.6	19.6	16.2	16.2
22	59.6	66.1	51.3	58.0	55.5	58.1	56.7	54.9	59.0	55.5
23	4.6	8.1	9.7	9.6	5.7	7.2	7.6	6.7	5.7	6.5
24	37.8	32.2	30.6	30.6	29.5	27.1	24.3	23.8	24.1	26.3
25	28.5	29.5	33.6	35.3	33.6	31.9	28.7	28.8	33.1	31.3
26	36.7	34.8	33.1	32.3	34.6	29.3	27.9	29.1	30.2	34.3
27	50.7	65.9	57.8	57.8	60.7	56.6	69.3	74.0	69.9	77.2
28	88.0	81.4	70.5	71.8	71.2	62.6	53.4	61.3	56.6	56.9
29	50.8	50.2	49.9	51.7	44.9	49.3	43.3	48.8	47.2	49.9
30	-	-	16.7	14.4	13.7	12.3	14.4	15.4	17.4	13.3
31	26.9	27.9	16.6	15.0	12.9	12.6	12.0	11.2	12.9	13.1
32	12.6	16.5	.	.	.	.	.	.	.	.
33	6.4	5.8	7.5	8.2	8.4	8.3	5.9	8.1	8.6	9.3
34	48.4	52.2	56.8	58.7	59.7	57.9	60.9	63.0	56.2	51.0
35	27.8	27.7	27.4	26.9	27.2	27.5	26.9	25.4	31.1	31.2
36	53.3	51.3	48.6	48.2	46.8	46.1	41.0	39.5	36.5	40.8
X	-	14.8	.	.	.	.	.	.	.	.

Women - Femmes - Mujeres
ISIC 3 - CITI 3 - CIIU 3

	1999	2000	2001	2002	2003	2004	2005	2006	2007	2008
Total	257.8	278.4	270.0	270.8	279.6	275.0	271.5	269.3	275.6	272.3
15	50.4	56.2	70.2	75.6	77.2	85.3	94.3	88.6	101.5	101.1
16	0.6	0.4	1.2	0.6	0.7	0.3	0.5	0.6	0.9	.
17	12.4	15.7	11.6	12.3	12.6	10.0	8.6	7.7	8.1	5.8
18	24.4	22.8	23.8	23.0	20.2	21.3	16.6	17.6	14.3	15.0
19	4.3	4.7	0.3	0.4	0.9	0.4	0.5	0.9	0.4	1.0
20	6.2	5.9	4.8	6.0	6.8	4.5	6.1	5.9	5.6	7.3
21	4.2	3.2	7.3	6.3	6.6	6.0	5.7	6.1	5.2	3.6
22	43.2	46.2	45.1	38.4	42.7	41.0	42.6	42.3	43.5	42.3
23	1.0	1.3	1.5	1.5	2.3	1.6	1.9	1.6	0.8	1.3
24	19.3	21.5	17.3	19.3	17.4	14.5	15.0	14.3	17.7	19.0
25	10.3	10.8	12.7	11.8	12.7	13.4	11.3	10.9	10.8	10.1
26	6.6	5.0	5.7	5.6	6.1	5.6	4.1	6.3	5.4	4.0
27	4.8	7.1	5.5	5.2	6.3	7.3	8.8	8.0	8.2	9.5
28	17.9	16.9	11.5	12.7	14.7	9.7	9.0	11.7	9.4	7.8
29	9.3	6.5	9.2	11.2	9.8	9.5	8.4	8.5	8.0	9.0
30	-	-	7.4	6.1	6.7	6.2	7.1	4.8	4.6	5.7
31	9.2	10.3	4.5	5.4	3.8	4.0	3.4	3.4	3.7	2.4
32	6.5	7.2	.	.	.	.	.	.	.	.
33	2.9	5.2	3.8	4.1	3.5	4.1	3.8	6.2	6.0	6.7
34	9.4	10.1	9.5	10.0	13.7	13.2	11.3	10.2	10.3	8.0
35	2.0	2.8	2.2	2.1	2.7	3.3	2.5	2.9	3.1	2.8
36	13.2	12.7	14.9	13.2	12.2	13.8	10.1	10.8	8.1	9.9
X	-	6.0	.	.	.	.	.	.	.	.

Explanatory notes: see p. 77.   Notes explicatives: voir p. 80.   Notas explicativas: véase p. 83.

[1] Excl. armed forces. [2] Persons aged 15 years and over.   [1] Non compris les forces armées. [2] Personnes âgées de 15 ans et plus.   [1] Excl. las fuerzas armadas. [2] Personas de 15 años y más.

2F EMPLOYMENT — EMPLOI — EMPLEO

Paid employment in manufacturing (Thousands)
Emploi rémunéré dans les industries manufacturières (Milliers)
Empleo remunerado en las industrias manufactureras (Millares)

New Zealand (BA) [1][2] Employees - Salariés - Asalariados

Total - Total - Total
ISIC 3 - CITI 3 - CIIU 3

	1999	2000	2001	2002	2003	2004	2005	2006	2007	2008
Total	242.6	246.4	255.7	257.3	253.7[3]	261.8	254.2	250.9	249.9	249.2
15-16	62.8	66.0	67.4	72.3	70.2[3]	72.1	71.5	71.3	67.7	65.5
17	7.9	8.0	7.8	9.0						
17-19					19.4	18.5	20.3	18.8	16.6	15.1
18	8.9	9.6	9.2	9.0						
19	3.7	4.1	4.0	2.9						
20	16.6	18.1	18.1	18.3						
20-21					25.9	25.7	24.8	23.6	25.6	25.6
21	11.0	8.9	8.7	9.5						
22	21.3	21.6	23.9	23.0	23.8[3]	26.9	24.9	20.9	22.4	21.3
23	1.1	1.1	0.8	0.7						
23-25					21.2	24.3	21.7	20.5	23.0	22.7
24	10.1	10.0	10.7	10.7						
25	9.9	10.7	11.6	10.7						
26	7.0	5.7	7.1	6.9	4.7[3]	5.4	7.0	7.7	7.7	7.5
27	7.8	7.9	10.7	10.6						
27-28					31.4	31.3	28.3	29.1	29.4	31.3
28	24.7	29.0	28.7	26.9						
29	16.0	10.9	12.1	13.2						
29-35					44.3	43.4	43.4	46.0	44.2	46.7
31	13.5	14.5	13.5	11.1						
33	1.0	1.2	1.2	1.2						
34-35	6.4	7.2	8.3	9.5						
36	12.9	11.9	12.0	11.9	12.8[3]	14.2	12.5	13.0	13.2	13.4

Men - Hommes - Hombres
ISIC 3 - CITI 3 - CIIU 3

	1999	2000	2001	2002	2003	2004	2005	2006	2007	2008
Total	170.5	172.2	181.1	185.6	180.6[3]	186.2	182.3	181.3	180.8	174.1
15-16	41.3	43.1	45.7	48.4	49.0[3]	47.4	46.5	48.5	44.7	40.8
17	4.7	4.6	3.7	5.3						
17-19					8.4	7.6	8.6	8.5	8.0	6.7
18	1.7	1.6	1.4	2.0						
19	2.5	2.5	2.8	2.3						
20	13.8	15.9	15.7	15.8						
20-21					21.4	21.6	21.1	19.8	22.3	21.4
21	8.0	6.6	6.1	7.4						
22	12.3	11.6	13.2	12.9	12.6[3]	14.6	12.8	10.9	12.7	11.4
23	0.9	1.0	0.7	0.6						
23-25					15.0	18.2	16.0	15.1	15.8	15.2
24	7.0	6.5	6.2	6.2						
25	7.9	8.2	8.7	8.3						
26	5.8	4.7	5.8	5.8	3.9[3]	4.8	6.4	6.8	6.2	5.7
27	6.4	6.8	9.9	9.6						
27-28					25.7	26.2	25.5	25.2	25.7	26.0
28	19.5	24.1	24.6	23.2						
29	13.7	9.2	10.2	11.5						
29-35					35.1	34.8	35.8	37.0	36.6	37.5
31	9.7	9.5	9.5	8.3						
33	0.6	0.8	0.7	0.7						
34-35	5.6	6.4	7.5	8.4						
36	9.1	9.0	8.7	8.8	9.5[3]	11.0	9.7	9.5	8.8	9.3

Women - Femmes - Mujeres
ISIC 3 - CITI 3 - CIIU 3

	1999	2000	2001	2002	2003	2004	2005	2006	2007	2008
Total	72.1	74.2	74.5	71.7	73.0[3]	75.7	71.9	69.7	69.1	75.2
15-16	21.5	22.9	21.7	23.9	21.2[3]	24.7	25.0	22.9	23.1	24.7
17	3.3	3.4	4.0	3.7						
17-19					11.0	10.9	11.7	10.3	8.6	8.4
18	7.1	8.0	7.8	7.0						
19	1.2	1.6	1.2	0.6						
20	2.8	2.2	2.3	2.5						
20-21					4.4	4.1	3.7	3.8	3.3	4.2
21	3.0	2.4	2.6	2.2						
22	9.0	10.0	10.7	10.0	11.3[3]	12.2	12.0	10.0	9.6	9.9
23	0.2	0.1	0.1	0.1						
23-25					6.2	6.2	5.7	5.4	7.2	7.6
24	3.1	3.4	4.5	4.4						
25	2.0	2.5	2.9	2.4						
26	1.2	1.0	1.3	1.1	-[3]	-	-	-	1.5	1.8
27	1.4	1.1	0.8	0.9						
27-28					5.7	5.0	2.8	3.8	3.8	5.3
28	5.2	4.9	4.1	3.6						
29	2.3	1.7	1.9	1.7						
29-35					9.2	8.6	7.6	9.0	7.6	9.2
31	3.8	5.0	4.0	2.8						
33	0.4	0.4	0.5	0.5						
34-35	0.8	0.8	0.8	1.1						
36	3.7	2.9	3.3	3.0	3.3[3]	3.2	2.8	3.5	4.4	4.1

Explanatory notes: see p. 77.

[1] Excl. armed forces. [2] Persons aged 15 years and over. [3] Methodology revised; data not strictly comparable.

Notes explicatives: voir p. 80.

[1] Non compris les forces armées. [2] Personnes âgées de 15 ans et plus. [3] Méthodologie révisée; les données ne sont pas strictement comparables.

Notas explicativas: véase p. 83.

[1] Excl. las fuerzas armadas. [2] Personas de 15 años y más. [3] Metodología revisada; los datos no son estrictamente comparables.

Unemployment

Chômage

Desempleo

Unemployment

Unemployment is defined as follows in the Resolution concerning statistics of the economically active population, employment, unemployment and underemployment, adopted by the Thirteenth International Conference of Labour Statisticians (Geneva, 1982):

(1) The "unemployed" comprise all persons above a specified age who during the reference period were:

(a) "without work", i.e. were not in paid employment or self-employment, as defined in paragraph 9;

(b) "currently available for work", i.e. were available for paid employment or self-employment during the reference period; and

(c) "seeking work", i.e. had taken specific steps in a specified reference period to seek paid employment or self-employment. The specific steps may include registration at a public or private employment exchange; application to employers; checking at worksites, farms, factory gates, market or other assembly places; placing or answering newspaper advertisements; seeking assistance of friends or relatives; looking for land, building, machinery or equipment to establish own enterprise; arranging for financial resources; applying for permits and licences, etc.

(2) In situations where the conventional means of seeking work are of limited relevance, where the labour market is largely unorganized or of limited scope, where labour absorption is, at the time, inadequate, or where the labour force is largely self-employed, the standard definition of unemployment given in subparagraph (1) above may be applied by relaxing the criterion of seeking work.

(3) In the application of the criterion of current availability for work, especially in situations covered by subparagraph (2) above, appropriate tests should be developed to suit national circumstances. Such tests may be based on notions such as present desire for work and previous work experience, willingness to take up work for wage or salary on locally prevailing terms, or readiness to undertake self-employment activity given the necessary resources and facilities.

(4) Notwithstanding the criterion of seeking work embodied in the standard definition of unemployment, persons without work and currently available for work who had made arrangements to take up paid employment or undertake self-employment activity at a date subsequent to the reference period should be considered as unemployed.

(5) Persons temporarily absent from their jobs with no formal job attachment who were currently available for work and seeking work should also be regarded as unemployed in accordance with the standard definition of unemployment. Countries may, however, depending on national circumstances and policies, prefer to relax the seeking work criterion in the case of persons temporarily laid off. In such cases, persons temporarily laid off who were not seeking work but classified as unemployed should be identified as a separate subcategory.

(6) Students, homemakers and others mainly engaged in non-economic activities during the reference period who satisfy the criteria laid down in subparagraphs (1) and (2) above should be regarded as unemployed on the same basis as other categories of unemployed identified separately, where possible.

National definitions of unemployment may differ from the recommended international standard definition. The national definitions used may vary from one country to another as regards inter alia age limits, reference periods, criteria for seeking work, treatment of persons temporarily laid off and of persons seeking work for the first time.

Differences between countries with regard to the treatment of unemployed persons with respect to classification by status in employment are particularly pronounced. In general, unemployed persons with previous job experience, classified according to their last job, are included with *employees*, but in some cases they and unemployed persons seeking their first job form the most important part of the group *persons not classifiable by status*.

The classification according to industry (main economic activity carried out where work is performed) is fundamentally different from that according to *occupation* (main type of duties performed). In the former, all persons working in a given establishment are classified under the same industry irrespective of their particular occupations. The latter, on the other hand, brings together individuals working in similar types of work, irrespective of where the work is performed. As indicated in the tables, most countries have supplied data on the basis of the *International Standard Industrial Classification of all Economic Activities, ISIC Rev.2, ISIC Rev.3 or ISIC Rev.4* and the *International Standard Classification of Occupations, ISCO-68* or *ISCO-88* (see Appendix).

Even when using international classification schemes (economic activity and occupation), national practices may also diverge concerning the classification of the unemployed with previous job experience, who are often included in the residual category of the international classification scheme, i.e. under *activities not adequately defined* (ISIC) or *workers not classifiable by occupation* (ISCO).

Intercountry comparisons are further hampered by the variety of types of source used to obtain information on unemployment and the differences in the scope and coverage of such sources.[1]

In general, four main sources of unemployment statistics may be distinguished. These sources are identified in the tables by codes in parentheses to the right of the country name. These codes (BA), (E), (FA), (FB) are described below:

Source (BA). *Labour force sample surveys*. These sample surveys generally yield comprehensive statistics on unemployment since, in particular, they include groups of persons who are often not covered in unemployment statistics obtained by other methods, particularly persons seeking work for the first time and persons subing work without the assistance of public employment offices. Generally the definition of unemployment used for this type of statistics follows more closely the international recommendations and such statistics are more comparable internationally than those obtained from other sources. The percentages of unemployment are also generally more reliable since they are calculated by relating the estimated number of persons unemployed to the estimate of the total number of employed and unemployed persons (the labour force) derived from the same survey.

Source (E). *Official estimates*. These statistics are official estimates provided by national authorities and are usually based on combined information drawn from one or more of the other sources described here. However, as the data in tables 3A to 3E attest to, the prevalence of this source is decreasing due to the increasing existence of labour force surveys in countries throughout the world.

Source (FA). *Social insurance statistics*. The statistics from this source are drawn from the records of compulsory unemployment insurance schemes which, where they exist, as a rule have a broad industrial coverage related to wage earners and salaried employees or to wage earners only. Unemployment rates are computed by comparing the number of recipients of insurance benefits to the total number of insured persons covered by the schemes. However, the extent to which the numbers and percentages of unemployed reported are representative of the general level of unemployment in the countries with this type of source is difficult if not impossible to ascertain.

Source (FB). *Employment office statistics*. These statistics generally refer to the number of persons looking for work who are entered on the registers at the end of each month. In addition to persons without a job, they may include persons on strike, or temporarily ill and unable to work and persons engaged on unemployment relief projects. In principle, these statistics do not include persons who are already in employment, which is identified in the tables as *registered unemployment*. However, some applicants are persons already in employment who are seeking a change of job or extra work who are also registered at employment offices. The coverage of these series is therefore identified in the tables as *work applicants*.

The value of the statistics from this source varies widely. In cases where the employment offices function in close connection with unemployment insurance, registration being a qualifying condition for the receipt of unemployment benefits, they are comparable in reliability to compulsory unemployment insurance statistics (source FA). Similarly, where employment offices operate in close connection with large unemployment relief schemes, they may also provide reasonably satisfactory figures during the currency of the schemes. However, where registration is entirely voluntary, and especially where the employment offices function only in the more populous, urban areas of a country or are not widely patronised by employees seeking work or by employers seeking workers, the data are generally very incomplete and do not give a reliable indication of the true extent of unemployment. The scope of the figures is determined partly by the manner in which the system of exchanges is organized and the advantages which registration brings, and partly by the extent to which workers are accustomed to register. In many cases persons engaged in agriculture and living in less populous areas are scarcely represented in the statistics, if at all. The scope of employment office statistics is therefore most difficult to ascertain, and in very few cases can satisfactory percentages of unemployment be calculated. In general, these statistics are not comparable from country to country. However, within a country, if there are no changes in legislation, administrative regulations and the like, fluctuations may reflect changes in the prevalence of registered unemployment over time.

Table 3A

Unemployment: General level

As far as possible, the statistics in this summary table are presented both in absolute numbers and in percentages. Unless otherwise indicated, the data are generally annual averages of monthly, quarterly or semi-annual data. The numbers indicate the size of the problem and the percentages (*unemployment rates*) illustrate the relative severity of unemployment. These rates are calculated by relating the number of persons in the given group who are unemployed during the reference period (usually a particular day or a given week) to the total of employed and unemployed persons in the group at the same date (see: labour force surveys). The percentages for series from other sources should be interpreted with due regard to the representativeness (see: social insurance and employment office statistics described above).

Table 3B

Unemployment, by age group

This table shows the age composition of the unemployed. Data by age group are presented according to five-year age groups as far as possible, with the mini- mum and maximum ages indicated. Countries vary in their national classifications, however, some using age based on year of birth or age rounded to nearest year, while others use age at last birthday. In comparing the unemployment totals shown in this table to those shown in other tables of Chapter 3, due regard should be given not only to differences in sources but also to reference periods. Often statistics by age are only collected at a fixed calendar period or on a specific date of the year and are not therefore annual averages of monthly, quarterly or semi-annual data.

Table 3C

Unemployment, by level of education

This table presents unemployment series, in absolute numbers, by sex and level of education, according to the *International Standard Classification of Education*, ISCED-76 or the revised version ISCED-97, or to both versions side by side, in cases where the revised version of this international classification has been adopted during the 10-year time series covered in the *Yearbook*.

In principle, the data should refer to the highest level of education completed, although many countries' national classifications use criteria which differ from the recommended international practice (e.g. registration, attendance, diploma obtained).

Other factors of incomparability arise from differences in national educational programmes as concerns entrance requirements, normal duration of schooling, requirement of full or part-time attendance, actual programme content and competency or diploma acquired at each level of education.

It should also be noted that level of education and the workers' ability to become employed (*employability*) are not automatically connected. How well the bridge from the educational system over to the world of work functions varies among countries. Many workers may not be specifically trained for the duties they carry out. Imbalances between the training possibilities available to workers and the national labour market's capacity to absorb them may also exist. The impact of continuous and on-the-job training which are not officially awarded any diploma is another factor difficult to measure.

When relating the data presented in this table with the data on economically active population by level of education (Chapter 1, Table 1B), due note must be taken of differences in source, scope, coverage and reference periods.

Table 3D

Unemployment, by economic activity

This table provides absolute figures on the previous work experience of the unemployed by economic activity according to the *International Standard Industrial Classification of all Economic Activities*, ISIC Rev.2, ISIC Rev.3 or to the latest revision ISIC Rev.4, or to two out of three versions side by side, in cases where the latest revision of this international classification has been introduced during the 10-year time series covered in the *Yearbook*. For the coding of classification categories in this and the following tables, see the explanatory text following Table 3E below.

Table 3E

Unemployment, by occupation

This table presents absolute figures on the previous work experience of the unemployed by occupation according to the *International Standard Classification of Occupations*, ISCO-68 or ISCO-88, or to both versions side by side, in cases where the later revision of this international classification has been introduced during the 10-year time series covered in the *Yearbook*.

In conformity with the international recommendations, unemployed persons with previous work experience are classified by industry or occupation in the two above tables on the basis of their last activity (under numerical codes according to the relevant category of the classification scheme presented). Unemployed persons without previous work experience are shown separately (under code UB) as far as possible, in order to distinguish them from unemployed persons with previous work experience classified under activities not adequately defined in ISIC or workers not classifiable by occupation in ISCO (under code *X*).

All of the data presented in Chapter 3 should in principle be annual averages and relate to the whole country. Nonetheless many exceptions exist. Further information concerning divergences in scope or coverage of the series is contained in the tables themselves and their footnotes.

Note

[1] For information on the differences in scope, definitions and methods of calculation, etc., used for the various national series, see ILO: *Statistical Sources and Methods* (Technical guide to series published in the *Bulletin* and *Year Book* of Labour Statistics), Vol. 3: "Economically Active Population, Employment, Unemployment and Hours of Work (Household Surveys)", second edition (Geneva, 1990); Vol. 4: "Employment, Unemployment, Wages and Hours of Work (Administrative Records and Related Sources)" (Geneva, 1989).

Chômage

Le chômage est défini de la manière suivante dans la Résolution concernant les statistiques de la population active, de l'emploi, du chômage et du sous-emploi adoptée par la treizième Conférence internationale des statisticiens du travail (Genève, 1982):

1) Les «chômeurs» comprennent toutes les personnes ayant dépassé un âge spécifié qui au cours de la période de référence, étaient:

a) «sans travail», c'est-à-dire qui n'étaient pourvues ni d'un emploi salarié ni d'un emploi non salarié, comme défini au paragraphe 9;

b) «disponibles pour travailler» dans un emploi salarié ou non salarié durant la période de référence;

c) «à la recherche d'un travail», c'est-à-dire qui avaient pris des dispositions spécifiques au cours d'une période récente spécifiée pour chercher un emploi salarié ou un emploi non salarié. Ces dispositions spécifiques peuvent inclure: l'inscription à un bureau de placement public ou privé; la candidature auprès d'employeurs; les démarches sur les lieux de travail, dans les fermes ou à la porte des usines, sur les marchés ou dans les autres endroits où sont traditionnellement recrutés les travail- leurs; l'insertion ou la réponse à des annonces dans les journaux; les recherches par relations personnelles; la recherche de terrain, d'immeubles, de machines ou d'équipement pour créer une entreprise personnelle; les démarches pour obtenir des ressources financières, des permis et licences, etc.

2) Dans les situations où les moyens conventionnels de recherche de travail sont peu appropriés, où le marché du travail est largement inorganisé ou d'une portée limitée, où l'absorption de l'offre de travail est, au moment considéré, insuffisante, où la proportion standard de main-d'œuvre non salariée est importante, la définition standard du chômage donnée au sous-paragraphe 1) ci-dessus peut être appliquée en renonçant au critère de la recherche de travail.

3) Pour appliquer le critère de la disponibilité pour le travail, spécialement dans les situations couvertes par le sous-paragraphe 2) ci-dessus, des méthodes appropriées devraient être mises au point pour tenir compte des circonstances nationales. De telles méthodes pourraient être fondées sur des notions comme l'actuelle envie de travailler et le fait d'avoir déjà travaillé, la volonté de prendre un emploi salarié sur la base des conditions locales ou le désir d'entreprendre une activité indépendante si les ressources et les facilités nécessaires sont accordées.

4) En dépit du critère de recherche de travail incorporé dans la définition standard du chômage, les personnes sans travail et disponibles pour travailler, qui ont pris des dispositions pour prendre un emploi salarié ou pour entreprendre une activité indépendante à une date ultérieure à la période de référence, devraient être considérées comme chômeurs.

5) Les personnes temporairement absentes de leur travail sans lien formel avec leur emploi, qui étaient disponibles pour travailler et à la recherche d'un travail, devraient être considérées comme chômeurs conformément à la définition standard du chômage. Les pays peuvent, cependant, en fonction des situations et politiques nationales, préférer renoncer au critère de la recherche d'un travail dans le cas des personnes temporairement mises à pied. Dans de tels cas, les personnes temporaire- ment mises à pied qui n'étaient pas à la recherche d'un travail mais qui étaient néanmoins classées comme chômeurs devraient être identifiées et former une sous-catégorie à part.

6) Les étudiants, les personnes s'occupant du foyer et les autres personnes principalement engagées dans les activités non économiques durant la période de référence et qui satisfont aux critères exposés aux sous-paragraphes 1) et 2) ci-dessus devraient être considérés comme chômeurs au même titre que les autres catégories de chômeurs et être identifiés séparément lorsque cela est possible.

Dans un certain nombre de cas, les définitions nationales du chômage peuvent s'écarter de la définition internationale type recommandée. Les définitions nationales peuvent varier d'un pays à un autre en ce qui concerne les limites d'âge, les périodes de référence, les critères retenus en matière de recherche d'emploi, le traitement des données concernant les personnes mises à pied temporairement et celles en quête d'emploi pour la première fois.

Selon les pays, les différences sont particulièrement marquées en ce qui concerne le traitement des chômeurs selon leur situation dans la dernière profession exercée. En général, les chômeurs ayant déjà travaillé, classifiés selon leur dernier emploi, sont inclus dans le groupe des salariés; mais, dans quelques cas, ceux-ci et les chômeurs à la recherche d'un premier emploi constituent la majeure partie du groupe des *travailleurs inclassables d'après la situation dans la profession*.

La classification selon l'*industrie* (activité économique principale exercée) est fondamentalement différente de celle selon la *profession* (principales tâches accomplies).

Dans la première, toutes les personnes travaillant dans un établissement donné sont classées dans la même industrie quelles que soient leurs professions. Par contre, dans la seconde, sont regroupées dans une même catégorie toutes les personnes accomplissant le même genre de travail quel que soit le lieu où ce travail est effectué. La plupart des pays ont transmis les données sur la base de la *Classification internationale type, par industrie, de toutes les branches d'activités économiques* CITI Rév. 2, CITI Rév. 3 ou CITI Rév. 4 et la *Classification internationale type des professions* CITP-68 ou CITP-88 (voir annexe).

En dépit de l'utilisation des classifications internationales (activités économiques et profession), les pratiques nationales peuvent également être différentes quant à la classification des personnes n'ayant jamais travaillé; très souvent, celles-ci sont incluses dans la catégorie résiduelle de ces classifications, à savoir activités mal désignées (CITI) ou travailleurs ne pouvant être classés selon la profession (CITP).

Les comparaisons de pays à pays sont, de plus, affectées par la variété des sources utilisées pour rassembler les informations sur le chômage ainsi que par les différences dans le champ d'application et la portée propres à ces sources [1].

On distingue, en général, quatre sources principales de statistiques, identifiées dans les tableaux de ce chapitre par des codes, entre parenthèses à la droite du nom du pays. Ces codes, définis ci-dessous, sont les suivants: (BA), (E), (FA) et (FB).

Source (BA). *Enquêtes par sondage* sur la main-d'œuvre. Ces enquêtes par sondage sur la main-d'œuvre fournissent généralement les statistiques les plus complètes sur le chômage, car elles permettent en particulier de couvrir des groupes (tels que les personnes en quête d'emploi pour la première fois ou les personnes enquête d'emploi sans avoir recours aux services d'un bureau de placement) qui, souvent, ne sont pas compris dans les statistiques du chômage obtenues par d'autres méthodes. En général, la définition du chômage adoptée pour ce type de statistiques suit plus fidèlement les recommandations internationales et de telles statistiques sont plus comparables sur le plan international que celles obtenues d'autres sources. De même, les pourcentages de chômage sont généralement plus fiables du fait qu'ils sont calculés en rapportant le nombre évalué de personnes occupées et de personnes en chômage dérivé des mêmes enquêtes.

Source (E). *Evaluations officielles*. Ces statistiques sont des évaluations officielles fournies par les autorités nationales et sont généralement basées sur une combinaison d'informations tirées d'une ou plusieurs sources mentionnées dans ce texte. Toutefois, comme cela apparaît dans les tableaux 3A à 3E, leur rôle a tendance à décroître du fait, corrélativement, de l'accroissement du nombre d'enquêtes sur la main-d'œuvre réalisées dans le monde.

Source (FA). *Statistiques d'assurances sociales*. Les statistiques de cette source sont tirées de régimes d'assurance chômage obligatoire qui ont ordinairement une large portée industrielle et couvrent, en général, l'ensemble des ouvriers et des employés ou les ouvriers seulement. Les taux de chômage sont calculés en divisant le nombre de bénéficiaires d'allocations de chômage par le nombre total de travailleurs assurés couverts par les régimes. Toutefois il est difficile, sinon impossible, de déterminer jusqu'à quel point de telles statistiques indiquent le niveau général du chômage dans un pays donné.

Source (FB). *Statistiques des bureaux de placement*. Ces statistiques donnent généralement le nombre de demandeurs d'emploi figurant sur les registres à la fin de chaque mois. Elles peuvent comprendre, outre les personnes sans travail, des personnes en grève ou dans l'incapacité temporaire de travailler par suite de maladie et des personnes occupées à des travaux entrepris pour secourir les chômeurs. En principe, lorsque les personnes déjà pourvues d'un emploi en sont exclues, ces statistiques sont présentées sous la rubrique *chômage enregistré*. Cependant, si la série comprend également les personnes pourvues d'un emploi mais désireuses d'en changer ou d'effectuer, en plus d'autres travaux, et inscrites dans les bureaux de placement, cette série est présentée sous la rubrique *demandeurs d'emploi*.

La qualité de ces statistiques est très variable. Lorsque les bureaux de placement fonctionnent en rapport étroit avec une assurance chômage, l'inscription étant une des conditions mises à l'octroi des indemnités, les données sont aussi fiables que celles des statistiques d'assurance chômage obligatoire (source FA). Quand les bureaux sont en étroite relation avec des régimes d'assistance publique d'une large portée, les chiffres relevés peuvent également fournir des données satisfaisantes durant l'existence de tels régimes. Toutefois, lorsque les inscriptions sont purement volontaires et surtout lorsque les bureaux de placement ne fonctionnent que dans les régions à forte densité de population ou ne sont pas utilisés largement par les salariés en quête de travail ou par les employeurs qui cherchent des travailleurs, les statistiques sont en général très incomplètes et ne fournissent pas une indication sûre du niveau du chômage. La portée des données dépend donc, d'une part, de l'organisation du réseau des bureaux et, d'autre part, de l'habitude qu'ont les travailleurs de s'y inscrire et de l'intérêt qu'ils ont à le faire. Dans bien des cas, les personnes occupées dans l'agriculture et habitant des régions à population moins dense sont à peine couvertes par les statistiques, quand elles le sont.

La portée des statistiques des bureaux de placement est de ce fait très difficile à préciser et il est très rare que les données permettent de calculer des pourcentages de chômage satisfaisants. En général, ces statistiques ne seront donc pas comparables d'un pays à un autre. Cependant, s'il n'y a pas de changements dans la législation ou dans les réglementations administratives et similaires, leurs fluctuations au sein d'un même pays peuvent indiquer les variations dans l'étendue du chômage dans le temps.

Tableau 3A

Chômage: niveau général

Dans la mesure du possible, les statistiques sont présentées en chiffres absolus et en *pourcentages*. Sauf indication contraire figurant en notes de bas de page, les données sont généralement des moyennes annuelles de données mensuelles, trimestrielles ou semestrielles. Le nombre de chômeurs indique l'étendue du problème et les *taux de chômage* font ressortir la gravité relative du chômage. Ces taux sont calculés en rapportant le nombre de travailleurs d'un certain groupe qui se trouvaient en chômage pendant la période de référence (en général, un jour donné ou une semaine donnée) au nombre total des personnes occupées et des chômeurs dans ce groupe à la même date (voir: enquêtes par sondage sur la main-d'œuvre). Les taux de chômage dérivés d'autres sources doivent être interprétés avec une attention particulière quant à leur degré de représentativité (voir: statistiques d'assurances sociales et des bureaux de placement décrites ci-dessus).

Tableau 3B

Chômage, par groupe d'âge

Ce tableau présente la composition du chômage, d'après l'âge et le sexe. Les données sont présentées, autant que possible, selon des groupes d'âge de cinq ans, avec indication des limites d'âge inférieures et supérieures. Cependant, pour définir les groupes d'âge, certains pays retiendront l'âge en fonction de l'année de naissance ou arrondi à l'année la plus immédiate, alors que pour d'autres il s'agira de l'âge au dernier anniversaire. En comparant les totaux du chômage présentés dans ce tableau de ce chapitre, il faut bien prendre en considération non seulement les différences concernant les sources mais également les dates de référence. Les statistiques du tableau 3B se rapportent souvent à une période déterminée ou à une date en cours de l'année et non pas à des moyennes annuelles ou à des données mensuelles, trimestrielles ou semestrielles.

Tableau 3C

Chômage, par niveau d'instruction

Ce tableau fournit les données, en nombres absolus, sur le chômage par sexe et niveau d'instruction, selon la *Classification internationale type de l'éducation*, qu'il s'agisse de la CITE-76 ou de la version révisée CITE-97, ou selon l'une et l'autre versions dans tous les cas où la CITE-97 a été introduite au cours de la période décennale couverte par l'*Annuaire*.

En principe, les données devraient se référer au niveau

d'instruction le plus élevé complété, bien que beaucoup de pays appliquent des classifications basées sur des critères différents des recommandations internationales (par exemple, inscription, obligation scolaire, diplôme obtenu).

D'autres facteurs de non-comparabilité sont les différences entre programmes nationaux d'instruction quant aux conditions d'entrée, à la durée de la scolarité, à l'organisation à plein temps ou à temps partiel, au contenu réel des programmes et aux diplômes ou qualifications obtenus à chaque niveau d'instruction.

Il convient aussi de noter que le lien entre *niveau d'instruction* et *employabilité* n'est pas automatique: l'articulation entre le système d'enseignement et le monde du travail est très différente d'un pays à l'autre. De nombreuses personnes exercent une profession pour laquelle elles n'ont pas été formées a priori. Il n'y a pas forcément adéquation entre les possibilités de formation et les capacités d'absorption du marché national du travail. L'influence de la formation continue non officiellement sanctionnée par des titres n'est pas facilement mesurable.

Si l'on veut rapprocher les données de ce tableau de celles sur la population active par niveau d'instruction (chapitre 1, tableau 1B), il faut veiller à la similitude des sources, champs d'application et périodes de référence.

Tableau 3D

Chômage, par activité économique

Ce tableau présente, par industrie, le nombre de chômeurs ayant déjà travaillé, répartis selon la *Classification internationale type, par industrie, de toutes les branches d'activité économique*, qu'il s'agisse de la CITI Rév.2, de la CITI Rév.3, ou de la dernière révision CITI Rév.4, ou selon deux des trois versions dans tous les cas où la révision postérieure de cette classification a été introduite au cours de la période décennale couverte par l'*Annuaire*. Pour ce qui est de la codification des différentes catégories de ce tableau et des tableaux suivants, voir le texte suivant la présentation du tableau 3E ci- dessus.

Tableau 3E

Chômage, par profession

Ce tableau présente, par profession, le nombre de chômeurs ayant déjà travaillé, répartis selon la *Classification internationale type des professions*, qu'il s'agisse de la CITP-68 ou de la CITP-88, ou selon l'une et l'autre versions dans tous les cas où la révision ultérieure de cette classification internationales a été introduite au cours de la période décennale couverte par l'*Annuaire*.

En conformité avec les recommandations internationales, dans les tableaux qui précèdent, les personnes en chômage ayant précédemment travaillé sont classées par industrie ou par profession sur la base de leur dernier emploi (en utilisant les *codes numériques spécifiques* des classifications pertinentes). Les personnes n'ayant jamais travaillé sont présentées séparément (code UB), dans la mesure du possible, afin de les distinguer des personnes ayant précédemment travaillé mais classées sous *activités mal désignées CITI* ou sous *travailleurs ne pouvant être classés selon la profession CITP* (code X).

En principe malgré les nombreuses exceptions, les données correspondent aux moyennes annuelles et se rapportent à l'ensemble du pays. Des informations complémentaires concernant les divergences quant au champ d'application de ces séries sont indiquées dans les tableaux ou sous forme de notes de bas de page.

Note

¹ Pour des renseignements sur les différences de portée, définitions et méthodes de calcul, etc., utilisées pour les diverses séries nationales, voir BIT: *Sources et méthodes statistiques* (Guide technique des séries publiées dans le *Bulletin* et l'*Annuaire des statistiques du travail*), vol. 3: «Population active, emploi, chômage et durée du travail (enquêtes auprès des ménages)», deuxième édition (Genève, 1991); vol. 4: «Emploi, chômage, salaires et durée du travail (documents administratifs et sources assimilées)», (Genève, 1989). Les volumes 3 et 4 sont disponibles sous forme brochée uniquement en anglais, mais une édition française non brochée peut être obtenue sur demande auprès du Département de statistique.

Desempleo

En la Resolución sobre estadísticas de la población económicamente activa, del empleo, del desempleo y del subempleo, adoptada por la decimotercera Conferencia Internacional de Estadísticos del Trabajo (Ginebra, 1982), figura la siguiente definición del desempleo:

1) «Personas desempleadas» son todas aquellas personas que tengan más de cierta edad especificada y que durante el período de referencia se hallen:

a) «sin empleo», es decir, que no tengan un empleo asalariado o un empleo independiente, tal como se les define en el párrafo 9;

b) «corrientemente disponibles para trabajar», es decir, disponibles para trabajar en empleo asalariado o en empleo independiente durante el período de referencia; y

c) «en busca de empleo», es decir, que habían tomado medidas concretas para buscar un empleo asalariado o un empleo independiente en un período reciente especificado. Las medidas concretas pueden incluir el registro en oficinas de colocación públicas o privadas, diligencias en los lugares de trabajo, explotaciones agrícolas, fábricas, mercados u otros lugares de concurrencia, avisos en los periódicos o respuestas a las ofertas que aparecen en ellos, solicitud de ayuda a amigos y familiares, búsqueda de terrenos, edificios, maquinaria o equipos para establecer su propia empresa, gestiones para conseguir recursos financieros, solicitudes para obtener permisos y licencias, etc.

2) En situaciones en que los medios convencionales de búsqueda de empleo son insuficientes, en que el mercado laboral está bastante desorganizado o es de alcance limitado, en que la absorción de la mano de obra es, en el momento considerado, inadecuada, o en que la fuerza de trabajo está compuesta principalmente por personas con empleo independiente, la definición estándar de desempleo dada en el subpárrafo 1) anterior puede aplicarse suprimiendo el criterio de búsqueda de empleo.

3) Al aplicarse el criterio de disponibilidad actual para trabajar, especialmente en las situaciones descritas en el subpárrafo 2) anterior, deberían considerarse métodos apropiados a fin de tener en cuenta las circunstancias nacionales. Estos métodos podrían basarse en nociones tales como el deseo actual de trabajar y que haya trabajado ya, la voluntad de aceptar un empleo remunerado con sueldo o salario en las condiciones prevalecientes en la localidad y la disposición para emprender una actividad independiente, de contar con los recursos financieros y las facilidades indispensables.

4) Aunque la definición estándar de desempleo implica el criterio de búsqueda de trabajo, las personas sin empleo y corrientemente disponibles para trabajar, que hayan tomado medidas para empezar a trabajar en un empleo asalariado o en un empleo independiente, en una fecha subsiguiente al período de referencia, deberían ser consideradas como desempleadas.

5) Se debería considerar como desempleadas a las personas ausentes temporalmente de su trabajo y sin un vínculo formal a su empleo, que se hallen actualmente disponibles para trabajar y buscando empleo, de conformidad con la definición estándar de desempleo. Sin embargo, y dependiendo de las circunstancias y políticas nacionales, los países podrían preferir suprimir el criterio de búsqueda de empleo en el caso de personas suspendidas de su trabajo. En tales casos, las personas suspendidas de su trabajo que no estaban en busca de empleo, pero se incluían en la categoría de desempleadas, deberían ser identificadas como una subcategoría aparte.

6) Los estudiantes, trabajadores del hogar y otras personas dedicadas a actividades no económicas durante el período de referencia, que satisfagan los criterios establecidos en los subpárrafos 1) y 2) anteriores, deberían considerarse como personas desempleadas y, si fuese posible, clasificarse aparte.

Las definiciones nacionales de desempleo pueden diferir de la definición internacional estándar recomendada. Entre otros aspectos, las definiciones nacionales pueden variar de un país a otro respecto de los límites de edad, los períodos de referencia, los criterios para determinar que una persona está buscando trabajo, el tratamiento de las personas temporalmente suspendidas y de las que buscan empleo por primera vez.

La forma de considerar las personas desempleadas con respecto a la clasificación por situación en el empleo también presenta marcadas diferencias según los países. Por lo general, los desempleados con una experiencia de trabajo anterior se clasifican según su último empleo y se incluyen entre los *asalariados*, pero en ciertos casos, al igual que buscan un primer empleo, forman la parte más importante del grupo de *personas no clasificables por su situación en el empleo*.

La clasificación por industria (principal actividad económica que se desarrolla en el lugar de trabajo) difiere fundamentalmente de la que se refiere a la clase principal de tareas que se llevan a cabo (ocupación). En la antigua presentación, todas las personas que trabajaban en el mismo establecimiento se clasificaban en la misma industria, con independencia de sus ocupaciones. En la actual, por el contrario, se reúnen los individuos que desempeñan el mismo tipo de trabajo, con independencia del lugar en que lo realizan. Como lo demuestran los cuadros, la mayoría de los países ha comunicado datos en base a la Clasificación Internacional Industrial Uniforme de Todas las Actividades Económicas, CIIU Rev.2, CIIU Rev.3 o CIIU Rev. 4 y la Clasificación Internacional Uniforme de Ocupaciones, CIUO-68 o la CIUO-88 (véase apéndice).

Aún utilizando los sistemas internacionales de clasificación (de actividad económica y ocupación), las prácticas nacionales también pueden diferir en cuanto a la clasificación de los desempleados con experiencia de trabajo anterior, a menudo incluidos en la categoría residual de los sistemas internacionales, es decir *las actividades no definidas con precisión* de la CIIU o *los trabajadores no clasificables por ocupación* de la CIUO.

La comparación entre países también se ve obstaculizada por la diversidad de fuentes utilizadas para obtener información sobre el desempleo y por las diferencias de ámbito y alcance de dichas fuentes[1].

En general, se pueden distinguir cuatro fuentes principales de las estadísticas de desempleo, que se señalan en los cuadros mediante los códigos (BA), (E), (FA) y (FB), colocados entre paréntesis a continuación del nombre del país, que se describen a continuación:

Fuente (BA). *Encuesta de la fuerza de trabajo.* Estas encuestas proporcionan generalmente estadísticas más completas sobre el desempleo pues incluyen, en particular, grupos de personas a menudo no abarcadas por las elaboradas a partir de otros métodos de recolección de datos, especialmente las personas que buscan un primer empleo o las personas buscando trabajo sin la ayuda de una oficina de colocación. Habitualmente la definición de desempleo se ajusta bastante a las recomendaciones internacionales y las estadísticas poseen un grado de comparabilidad internacional mayor que las obtenidas de otras fuentes. También son más fiables los porcentajes de desempleo pues se calculan relacionando el número estimado de personas desempleadas con el total estimado de empleados y desempleados (la fuerza de trabajo) derivados de las mismas encuestas.

Fuente (E). *Estimaciones oficiales*. Estas estadísticas son estimaciones comunicadas por autoridades oficiales nacionales que habitualmente se combinan con informaciones de una o más de las otras fuentes que aquí se describen. No obstante, como lo demuestran los cuadros 3A y 3E, la importancia de esta fuente disminuye a medida que en todos los países aumentan las encuestas de la fuerza de trabajo.

Fuente (FA). *Registros de seguros*. Las estadísticas de esta fuente se elaboran a partir de datos obtenidos de los registros de los regímenes obligatorios de seguro de paro que, donde funcionan, suelen tener un vasto alcance de obreros y empleados, o sólo de obreros, del sector industrial. Las tasas de desempleo se calculan cotejando el número de quienes perciben las prestaciones del seguro con el número total de asegurados. Sin embargo, no es posible determinar en qué medida las cifras y los porcentajes de desempleo así obtenidos representan el nivel general del desempleo de los países donde se puede recurrir a esta fuente.

Fuente (FB). *Registros de oficina de colocación*. Estas estadísticas se refieren por lo general al número de personas que buscan trabajo que figuran en los registros al final de cada mes. Además de las personas sin trabajo, también pueden incluir las que están en huelga, enfermas e incapacitadas temporalmente para trabajar y las que participan en programas de ayuda a los desempleados. En principio no comprenden las personas que ya tienen un empleo cuyo alcance se señala en los cuadros de *desempleo registrado*. Sin embargo, algunos solicitantes son personas con empleo que buscan otro adicional o un cambio de empleo que también se inscriben en las oficinas de colocación. En consecuencia el alcance de estas series se señala en los cuadros como *solicitantes de empleo*.

El valor de las estadísticas de esta fuente es muy variable. En ciertos casos, cuando las oficinas de colocación funcionan en estrecha colaboración con el seguro de paro y la inscripción en las primeras es condición para recibir las prestaciones del segundo, su fiabilidad es semejante a las estadísticas de los seguros obligatorios de la fuente (FA). En forma similar, cuando las oficinas de colocación funcionan en estrecha colaboración con otros grandes sistemas o programas de ayuda a los desempleados las cifras que de ellas pueden obtenerse son también relativamente satisfactorias durante el desarrollo de dichos programas o sistemas. Por el contrario, si el registro es totalmente voluntario, y especialmente cuando las oficinas sólo funcionan en las zonas urbanas más pobladas de un país, o no son respaldadas ampliamente por las personas que buscan empleo o los empleadores que buscan personal, los datos suelen ser muy incompletos y no constituyen una indicación fiable de la amplitud real del desempleo. El alcance de las cifras se determina en parte por la forma en que se organiza el sistema de colocación y por las ventajas que la inscripción trae consigo, y en parte por la medida en que los trabajadores están habituados a inscribirse. En muchos casos las personas que trabajan en la agricultura y viven en regiones poco pobladas resultan, en el mejor de los casos, poco representadas en las estadísticas. El alcance de las estadísticas de las oficinas de colocación es, pues, más difícil de determinar y sólo en un número muy reducido de casos permiten obtener porcentajes de desempleo satisfactorios. En términos generales, estas estadísticas no son comparables entre países pero, dentro de un mismo país, si no se modifican las leyes ni los reglamentos administrativos u otras disposiciones similares, sus fluctuaciones pueden reflejar como cambia la extensión del desempleo registrado con el correr del tiempo.

Cuadro 3A

Desempleo: nivel general

En la medida de lo posible, las estadísticas de este cuadro resumido se presentan tanto en cifras absolutas como en *porcentajes*. Salvo se indique lo contrario, los datos suelen ser medias anuales de datos mensuales, trimestrales o semestrales. Los números indican el tamaño del problema y los *porcentajes (tasas de desempleo)* su relativa gravedad. Estas tasas se calculan relacionando el número de personas de un grupo dado que estaban desempleadas durante el período de referencia (generalmente un determinado día o semana) con el total de personas empleadas y desempleadas en las mismas fechas (véase la encuesta de la fuerza de trabajo). Los porcentajes de las series con otras fuentes deben interpretarse tomando debidamente en cuenta la representatividad (véanse las descripciones anteriores de las estadísticas de registros de seguros y de oficinas de colocación).

Cuadro 3B

Desempleo, por grupo de edad

Este cuadro muestra la composición del desempleo por edad. En la medida de lo posible, los datos se presentan por grupos de edad de cinco años cada uno, con indicación de las edades mínima y máxima. En los distintos países las clasificaciones varían pues en algunos la edad se cuenta a partir del año de nacimiento o redondeada a dicho año, mientras que en otros en relación con la fecha del último cumpleaños. Comparando los totales del desempleo de este cuadro con los de otros de este capítulo, cabe considerar debidamente no solo las diferentes fuentes sino también los distintos períodos de referencia. A menudo las estadísticas por edad sólo se reúnen en un período determinado o en una fecha específica del año civil y, por lo tanto, no son medias anuales de datos mensuales, trimestrales o semestrales.

Cuadro 3C

Desempleo, por nivel de educación

Este cuadro presenta series de desempleo, en cifras absolutas, desglosadas por sexo y por nivel de educación según la *Clasificación Internacional Normalizada de la Educación*, CINE-76 o la versión revisada CINE-97, o según ambas, lado a lado, si la segunda de ellas ha sido adoptada durante el período de diez años de las series del *Anuario*.

En principio, los datos deberían referirse al nivel de educación más elevado que se haya completado, pero las clasificaciones de muchos países siguen criterios distintos de los recomendados por la práctica internacional (por ejemplo, inscripción, asistencia, diploma alcanzado).

Otros factores que impiden la comparabilidad surgen de las diferencias entre los programas nacionales de educación en cuanto a los requisitos de ingreso, duración normal de la escolarización, asistencia total o parcial a los cursos, contenido de los programas en vigor y calificaciones o diploma adquiridos en cada nivel de educación.

También cabe señalar que el *nivel de educación* y la capacidad de los trabajadores para ser empleados («*empleabilidad*») no se relacionan automáticamente. La forma de salvar la brecha entre el sistema de educación y el mundo del trabajo varía según los países. Muchos trabajadores pueden no haber recibido una formación específica para las tareas que realizan. También pueden darse desequilibrios entre las posibilidades de formación de los trabajadores y la capacidad del mercado para absorberlos. La repercusión de la formación continua y de la adquirida en los lugares de trabajo, no coronadas por ningún diploma o certificado de estudios oficial, es otro factor difícil de medir.

Al relacionar los datos de este cuadro con los de la población económicamente activa por nivel de educación (capítulo 1, cuadro 1B) cabe tener en cuenta las diferencias en materia de fuentes, ámbito, alcance y períodos de referencia.

Cuadro 3D

Desempleo, por actividad económica

Este cuadro presenta cifras absolutas sobre la experiencia anterior de trabajo de los desempleados, por actividad económica según la *Clasificación Internacional Industrial Uniforme de Todas las Actividades Económicas* CIIU Rev.2, CIIU Rev. 3 o su última revisión CIIU Rev.4, o según dos de las tres versiones, lado a lado, si la última de ellas se ha introducido durante el período de diez años de las series del *Anuario*. Para la codificación de las categorías de clasificación de este cuadro y de los siguientes, véase la explicación que sigue al cuadro 3E abajo.

Cuadro 3E

Desempleo, por ocupación

Este cuadro presenta cifras absolutas sobre los desempleados con experiencia anterior de trabajo, por ocupación según la *Clasificación Internacional Industrial Uniforme de Ocupaciones* (CIUO) de 1968 o su revisión posterior de 1988, o según ambas, lado a lado, si la revisión posterior de esta clasificación internacional ha sido introducida en el curso del período de diez años que abarcan las series del *Anuario*.

De conformidad con las recomendaciones internacionales, las personas desempleadas con experiencia de trabajo anterior de los dos cuadros anteriores se clasifican por industria y ocupación en función del último empleo y con los *códigos numéricos* que corresponden a la categoría pertinente del correspondiente sistema de clasificación. Por otra parte, siempre que es posible se muestran por separado, bajo el código (UB), los desempleados sin experiencia de trabajo anterior con la finalidad de distinguirlos de los desempleados con experiencia de trabajo anterior clasificados en actividades no definidas adecuadamente por ocupación de la CIUO (véase código X).

Todos los datos figuran, en principio, como medias anuales y se refieren a todo el país, aun cuando las excepciones son numerosas. En los propios cuadros, y sus notas de pie de página, figuran más amplias informaciones sobre los diferentes ámbitos y alcances de las series.

Nota

[1] Para informaciones sobre las diferencias de alcance, definiciones, métodos de cálculo, etc., de las series nacionales, véase OIT: *Fuentes y Métodos: Estadísticas del Trabajo* (anteriormente *Fuentes y Métodos Estadísticos*), vol.3: «Población económicamente activa, empleo, desempleo y horas de trabajo (encuestas de hogares)», segunda edición (Ginebra, 1990), y vol.4: «Empleo, desempleo, salarios y horas de trabajo (registros administrativos y fuentes conexas)» (Ginebra, 1989).

	Thousands			Milliers				Millares		
	1999	2000	2001	2002	2003	2004	2005	2006	2007	2008

AFRICA-AFRIQUE-AFRICA

Algérie (BA) [1] — Total unemployment - Chômage total - Desempleo total

	1999	2000	2001	2002	2003	2004	2005	2006	2007	2008
Total	.	2 427.7	2 339.4	2 247.3	2 078.0	1 671.5	1 474.5	1 240.8	1 374.6	.
M-H	.	2 132.7	1 934.9	.	1 759.9	1 370.4	1 221.0	988.3	1 072.0	.
W-F-M	.	295.0	404.5	.	318.3	301.1	253.5	252.6	302.7	.
Total %	.	.	27.3	25.9	23.7	17.7	15.3	12.3	13.8	.
M-H %	.	.	26.6	.	23.4	17.5	14.9	11.8	12.9	.
W-F-M %	.	.	31.4	.	25.4	18.1	17.5	14.4	18.4	.

Botswana (BA) [2] — Total unemployment - Chômage total - Desempleo total

	1999	2000	2001	2002	2003	2004	2005	2006	2007	2008
Total	.	90.728	.	.	144.460	.	.	114.442	.	.
M-H	.	46.273	.	.	66.880	.	.	50.876	.	.
W-F-M	.	44.455	.	.	77.580	.	.	63.546	.	.
Total %	.	15.8	.	.	23.8	.	.	17.6	.	.
M-H %	.	14.7	.	.	21.4	.	.	15.3	.	.
W-F-M %	.	17.2	.	.	26.3	.	.	19.9	.	.

Egypt (BA) [3][4] — Total unemployment - Chômage total - Desempleo total

	1999	2000	2001	2002	2003	2004	2005	2006	2007	2008
Total	1 480.5	1 698.0	1 783.0	2 020.6	2 240.7	2 153.9	2 450.0	2 434.5	2 135.1	.
M-H	726.2	743.5	851.8	983.2	1 186.7	942.6	1 194.5	1 207.7	1 077.6	.
W-F-M	754.3	954.5	931.2	1 037.4	1 054.0	1 211.3	1 255.5	1 226.8	1 057.5	.
Total %	8.1	9.0	9.2	10.2	11.0	10.3	11.2	10.6	8.9	.
M-H %	5.1	5.1	5.6	6.3	7.5	5.9	7.1	6.8	5.9	.
W-F-M %	19.4	22.7	22.6	23.9	23.3	25.1	24.3	24.0	18.6	.

Ethiopia (BA) [5][6] — Total unemployment - Chômage total - Desempleo total

	1999	2000	2001	2002	2003	2004	2005	2006	2007	2008
Total	.	.	.	.	.	845.9 [7]	849.2 [8]	767.1 [9]	.	.
M-H	.	.	.	.	.	304.5 [7]	292.7 [8]	273.1 [9]	.	.
W-F-M	.	.	.	.	.	541.4 [7]	601.5 [8]	493.9 [9]	.	.
Total %	.	.	.	.	.	22.9 [7]	.	16.7 [9]	.	.
M-H %	.	.	.	.	.	15.8 [7]	.	11.5 [9]	.	.
W-F-M %	.	.	.	.	.	30.6 [7]	.	22.1 [9]	.	.

Madagascar (B) [10] — Total unemployment - Chômage total - Desempleo total

	1999	2000	2001	2002	2003	2004	2005	2006	2007	2008
Total	.	.	.	.	383.0 [11]	.	274.3	.	.	.
M-H	.	.	.	.	149.8 [11]	.	100.4	.	.	.
W-F-M	.	.	.	.	233.2 [11]	.	173.8	.	.	.
Total %	.	.	.	.	4.5	.	2.8	.	.	.
M-H %	.	.	.	.	3.5	.	2.0	.	.	.
W-F-M %	.	.	.	.	5.6	.	3.6	.	.	.

Mali (BA) [1] — Total unemployment - Chômage total - Desempleo total

	1999	2000	2001	2002	2003	2004	2005	2006	2007	2008
Total	.	.	.	.	227.5	.	.	.	.	.
M-H	.	.	.	.	107.0	.	.	.	.	.
W-F-M	.	.	.	.	120.5	.	.	.	.	.
Total %	.	.	.	.	8.8	.	.	.	.	.
M-H %	.	.	.	.	7.2	.	.	.	.	.
W-F-M %	.	.	.	.	10.9	.	.	.	.	.

Maroc (BA) [1] — Total unemployment - Chômage total - Desempleo total

	1999	2000	2001	2002	2003	2004	2005	2006	2007	2008
Total	1 432.2	1 394.3	1 275.0	1 202.7	1 299.0	1 192.5	1 226.4	1 062.5	1 092.1	1 077.8
M-H	1 044.8	1 035.5	952.0	878.4	922.4	851.2	877.6	774.1	794.5	781.2
W-F-M	387.9	358.7	323.0	324.3	376.6	341.4	348.8	288.4	297.6	296.7
Total %	13.9	13.6	12.5	11.6	11.9	10.8	11.0	9.7	9.6	9.4
M-H %	14.2	13.8	12.5	11.6	11.5	10.6	10.8	9.7	9.6	9.4
W-F-M %	13.3	13.0	12.5	12.5	13.0	11.4	11.5	9.7	9.5	9.5

Mauritius (BA) [12] — Total unemployment - Chômage total - Desempleo total

	1999	2000	2001	2002	2003	2004	2005	2006	2007	2008
Total	.	.	.	.	.	45.1	52.1	50.1	46.8 [13]	40.4
M-H	.	.	.	.	.	20.3	20.2	19.5	18.6 [13]	14.6
W-F-M	.	.	.	.	.	24.8	31.8	30.6	28.2 [13]	25.8
Total %	.	.	.	.	.	8.5	9.6	9.1	8.5 [13]	7.2
M-H %	.	.	.	.	.	5.8	5.8	5.5	5.3 [13]	4.1
W-F-M %	.	.	.	.	.	13.5	16.5	15.5	14.4 [13]	12.7

Mauritius (FB) [1][14] — Registered unemployment - Chômage enregistré - Desempleo registrado

	1999	2000	2001	2002	2003	2004	2005	2006	2007	2008
Total	12.130	18.024	21.576	21.976	23.373	21.950	33.614	.	36.100	20.600
M-H	5.328	8.567	10.477	10.116	10.069	10.512	15.365	.	17.900	7.100
W-F-M	6.802	9.457	11.099	11.860	13.304	11.438	18.249	.	18.200	13.400
Total %	.	.	.	.	.	.	.	.	.	7.1
M-H %	.	.	.	.	.	.	.	.	.	4.1
W-F-M %	.	.	.	.	.	.	.	.	.	12.7

Explanatory notes: see p. 451.

[1] Persons aged 15 years and over. [2] Persons aged 12 years and over. [3] Persons aged 15 to 64 years. [4] May and Nov. [5] Persons aged 10 years and over. [6] Urban areas. [7] April. [8] March. [9] July. [10] Persons aged 6 years and over. [11] Totals include persons still attending school (incl. full-time tertiary students). [12] Persons aged 16 years and over. [13] Prior to 2007: persons aged 15 years and over. [14] Excl. Rodrigues.

Notes explicatives: voir p. 454.

[1] Personnes âgées de 15 ans et plus. [2] Personnes âgées de 12 ans et plus. [3] Personnes âgées de 15 à 64 ans. [4] Mai et nov. [5] Personnes âgées de 10 ans et plus. [6] Régions urbaines. [7] Avril. [8] Mars. [9] Juillet. [10] Personnes âgées de 6 ans et plus. [11] Les totaux incluent les personnes encore en cours d'études (y compris les étudiants à plein temps de l'enseignement supérieur). [12] Personnes âgées de 16 ans et plus. [13] Avant 2006: personnes âgées de 15 ans et plus. [14] Non compris Rodrigues.

Notas explicativas: véase p. 457.

[1] Personas de 15 años y más. [2] Personas de 12 años y más. [3] Personas de 15 a 64 años. [4] Mayo y nov. [5] Personas de 10 años y más. [6] Areas urbanas. [7] Abril. [8] Marzo. [9] Julio. [10] Personas de 6 años y más. [11] Los totales incluyen a las personas que siguen estudiando (incl. los estudiantes a tiempo completo de la enseñanza superior). [12] Personas de 16 años y más. [13] Antes de 2006: personas de 15 años y más. [14] Excl. Rodríguez.

	UNEMPLOYMENT	CHÔMAGE	DESEMPLEO
	General level	Niveau général	Nivel general

	Thousands			Milliers					Millares	
	1999	2000	2001	2002	2003	2004	2005	2006	2007	2008
Réunion (BA) [1][2]				**Total unemployment - Chômage total - Desempleo total**						
Total	101.574	103.788	83.265	80.945	90.141	96.180	88.940	86.744	75.852	78.040
M-H	54.708	54.388	44.456	41.936	48.877	52.320	45.709	46.828	39.857	39.356
W-F-M	46.866	49.400	38.809	39.009	41.264	43.860	43.231	39.916	35.995	38.684
Total %	37.7	36.5	29.7	28.3	30.8	32.2	29.5	27.5	24.2	24.5
M-H %	36.3	34.4	28.0	26.0	29.5	30.7	26.6	26.5	22.9	22.8
W-F-M %	39.5	39.1	32.1	31.1	32.5	34.1	33.3	28.8	25.9	26.5
Sao Tomé-et-Principe (E) [1]				**Total unemployment - Chômage total - Desempleo total**						
Total	.	6.321	8.212	9.516	8.968	8.254	8.738	8.869	.	.
M-H	.	3.500	3.062	3.745	3.252	3.390	3.362	3.437		
W-F-M	.	2.827	5.150	5.771	5.716	4.865	5.375	5.432		
Sénégal (B) [1]				**Total unemployment - Chômage total - Desempleo total**						
Total	.	.	.	.	.	.	.	351.370	.	.
M-H	.	.	.	.	.	.	.	176.810		
W-F-M	.	.	.	.	.	.	.	174.519		
Total %	.	.	.	.	.	.	.	11.100		
M-H %	.	.	.	.	.	.	.	7.900		
W-F-M %	.	.	.	.	.	.	.	13.600		
South Africa (BA) [3][4]				**Total unemployment - Chômage total - Desempleo total**						
Total	.	4 162	4 655	4 936	4 434	4 135	4 487	4 391	3 945 |	4 075
M-H	.	1 983	2 236	2 316	2 166	2 029	2 057	1 967	1 883 |	1 917
W-F-M	.	2 179	2 420	2 619	2 268	2 103	2 428	2 424	2 059 |	2 158
Total %	.	25.4	29.4	30.4	28.0	26.2	26.7	25.5	23.0 |	22.9
M-H %	.	22.2	25.8	25.9	24.7	23.1	22.6	21.2	20.0 |	20.0
W-F-M %	.	29.2	33.8	35.9	32.0	30.2	31.7	30.7	26.7 |	26.3
Saint Helena (FB) [1]				**Registered unemployment - Chômage enregistré - Desempleo registrado**						
Total	0.381	0.273	0.265	.	0.245	0.177	0.123	0.110	0.076	.
M-H	0.251	0.175	0.175	.	0.168	0.123	0.079	0.067	0.048	.
W-F-M	0.130	0.098	0.090	.	0.077	0.054	0.044	0.043	0.028	.
Sudan (E) [5]				**Total unemployment - Chômage total - Desempleo total**						
Total	.	.	.	.	.	.	.	.	2 300	.
Tanzania, United Republic of (BA) [5]				**Total unemployment - Chômage total - Desempleo total**						
Total	.	.	.	.	.	.	.	892.2	.	.
M-H	.	.	.	.	.	.	.	281.7		
W-F-M	.	.	.	.	.	.	.	610.5		
Total %	.	.	.	.	.	.	.	4.3		
M-H %	.	.	.	.	.	.	.	2.8		
W-F-M %	.	.	.	.	.	.	.	5.8		
Tunisie (BA) [1][6]				**Total unemployment - Chômage total - Desempleo total**						
Total	472.5	475.1	469.2	485.5	473.4	473.9	486.4	.	.	.
M-H	345.1	347.4	341.4	351.6	334.7	322.7	328.8	.		
W-F-M	127.5	127.7	127.8	133.9	138.6	151.2	157.6	.		
Total %	16.0	15.7	15.1	15.3	14.5	14.2	14.2	.		
M-H %	15.6	15.3	14.5	14.9	13.9	13.2	13.1	.		
W-F-M %	17.2	16.9	16.2	16.3	16.2	17.1	17.3	.		
Tunisie (FB) [6][7]				**Work applicants - Demandeurs d'emploi - Solicitantes**						
Total	.	76.96	71.92	73.52	77.87	.	.	.	.	.
M-H	.	42.71	40.46	40.47	41.65	.				
W-F-M	.	34.25	31.46	33.05	36.22	.				

AMERICA-AMÉRIQUE-AMERICA

	1999	2000	2001	2002	2003	2004	2005	2006	2007	2008
Argentina (BA) [5][8][9]				**Total unemployment - Chômage total - Desempleo total**						
Total	1 359.6	1 460.9	1 709.8	1 955.8 |	1 633.0 [10]	1 361.6	1 141.5 |	1 049.2 [11]	936.0 [12]	898.0 [12]
M-H	764.9	809.9	1 021.9	1 175.2 |	824.8 [10]	687.6	561.7 |	488.9 [11]	.	.
W-F-M	594.7	651.0	688.4	780.6 |	808.2 [10]	673.9	579.8 |	560.3 [11]	.	.
Total %	14.1	15.0	17.4	19.6 |	15.4 [10]	12.6	10.6 |	9.5 [11]	.	.
M-H %	13.3	14.1	17.4	20.2 |	13.8 [10]	11.2	9.2 |	7.8 [11]	.	.
W-F-M %	15.2	16.4	17.2	18.8 |	17.5 [10]	14.5	12.4 |	11.7 [11]	.	.
Aruba (BA) [1][13]				**Total unemployment - Chômage total - Desempleo total**						
Total	.	.	.	.	.	.	.	.	3.123	.
M-H	.	.	.	.	.	.	.	.	1.420	.
W-F-M	.	.	.	.	.	.	.	.	1.704	.
Total %	.	.	.	.	.	.	.	.	5.700	.
M-H %	.	.	.	.	.	.	.	.	5.000	.
W-F-M %	.	.	.	.	.	.	.	.	6.500	.

Explanatory notes: see p. 451.

[1] Persons aged 15 years and over. [2] Second quarter of each year. [3] Persons aged 15 to 64 years. [4] Prior to 2008: persons aged 15 years and over; September of each year. [5] Persons aged 10 years and over. [6] 1999-2003: figures revised on the basis of the 2004 census results. [7] Persons aged 18 years and over. [8] 31 Urban agglomerations. [9] Second semester. [10] Methodology revised; data not strictly comparable; Prior to 2003: May and October. [11] Prior to 2006: 28 urban agglomerations. [12] Second quarter. [13] Oct.

Notes explicatives: voir p. 454.

[1] Personnes âgées de 15 ans et plus. [2] Deuxième trimestre de chaque année. [3] Personnes âgées de 15 à 64 ans. [4] Avant 2008: personnes agées de 15 ans et plus; septembre de chaque année. [5] Personnes âgées de 10 ans et plus. [6] 1999-2003: données révisées sur la base des résultats du Recensement de 2004. [7] Personnes âgées de 18 ans et plus. [8] 31 agglomérations urbaines. [9] Second semestre. [10] Méthodologie révisée; les données ne sont pas strictement comparables; Avant 2003: mai et octobre. [11] Avant 2006: 28 agglomérations urbaines. [12] Deuxième trimestre. [13] Oct.

Notas explicativas: véase p. 457.

[1] Personas de 15 años y más. [2] Segundo trimestre de cada año. [3] Personas de 15 a 64 años. [4] Antes de 2008: personas de 15 años y más; Septiembre de cada año. [5] Personas de 10 años y más. [6] 1999-2003: datos revisados de acuerdo con los resultados del Censo de 2004. [7] Personas de 18 años y más. [8] 31 aglomerados úrbanos. [9] Segundo semestre. [10] Metodología revisada; los datos no son estrictamente comparables; antes de 2003: mayo y octubre. [11] Antes de 2006: 28 aglomerados úrbanos. [12] Segundo trimestre. [13] Oct.

UNEMPLOYMENT CHÔMAGE DESEMPLEO 3A

General level Niveau général Nivel general

	Thousands			Milliers				Millares		
	1999	2000	2001	2002	2003	2004	2005	2006	2007	2008
Bahamas (BA) [1] [2]				Total unemployment - Chômage total - Desempleo total						
Total	12.29	.	11.33	15.28	18.83	17.99	18.18	13.83 [3]	14.62	.
M-H	4.96	.	5.72	7.56	8.78	8.50	8.38	6.38 [3]	6.45	.
W-F-M	7.34	.	5.61	7.72	10.05	9.50	9.80	7.46 [3]	8.17	.
Total %	7.8	.	6.9	9.1	10.8	10.2	10.2	7.6 [3]	7.9	.
M-H %	6.0	.	6.7	8.8	10.0	9.4	9.2	6.9 [3]	6.7	.
W-F-M %	9.7	.	7.0	9.4	11.7	11.0	11.2	8.4 [3]	9.1	.
Barbados (BA) [1]				Total unemployment - Chômage total - Desempleo total						
Total	14.4	13.3	14.3	14.8	16.0	14.3	13.3	12.5	10.7	11.6
M-H	5.6	5.5	6.0	6.4	7.1	6.7	5.5	5.6	4.8	5.0
W-F-M	8.8	7.9	8.3	8.4	8.9	7.5	7.8	6.8	5.9	6.6
Total %	10.5	9.4	9.9	10.3	11.0	9.8	9.1	8.7	7.4	8.1
M-H %	7.7	7.5	8.0	8.2	9.6	9.0	7.3	7.6	6.4	6.8
W-F-M %	13.3	11.5	11.9	12.4	12.6	10.6	10.9	9.7	8.5	9.4
Belize (BA) [2] [4]				Total unemployment - Chômage total - Desempleo total						
Total	11.5	.	8.6	9.5	.	.	12.2	10.6	10.4	10.2 [3]
M-H	5.3	.	3.6	4.7	.	.	5.2	4.5	4.5	.
W-F-M	6.1	.	5.0	4.7	.	.	7.0	6.1	5.9	.
Total %	12.8	.	9.1	10.0	.	.	11.0	9.4	8.5	8.2 [3]
M-H %	9.0	.	5.8	7.5	.	.	7.4	6.2	5.8	.
W-F-M %	20.3	.	15.4	15.3	.	.	17.2	15.0	13.1	.
Bolivia (BA) [5] [6]				Total unemployment - Chômage total - Desempleo total						
Total	156.66	168.62	200.25	201.62	.	155.04	215.97	219.04	.	.
M-H	74.37	77.43	93.90	92.05	.	68.58	99.48	107.16	.	.
W-F-M	82.29	91.19	106.35	109.58	.	86.47	116.50	111.88	.	.
Total %	7.2	7.5	8.5	8.7	.	6.2	8.1	8.0	.	.
M-H %	6.2	6.2	7.5	7.3	.	5.0	6.8	7.1	.	.
W-F-M %	8.5	9.0	9.7	10.3	.	7.5	9.9	9.1	.	.
Bolivia (BA) [6] [7]				Total unemployment - Chômage total - Desempleo total						
Total	164.47	183.16	214.90	221.60	.	182.39	245.20	243.53	255.01	.
M-H	76.89	83.29	99.38	97.36	.	84.22	112.14	119.06	122.39	.
W-F-M	87.57	99.87	115.52	124.24	.	98.17	133.06	124.48	132.61	.
Total %	4.3	4.8	5.2	5.5	.	4.2	5.4	5.1	5.2	.
M-H %	3.7	3.9	4.5	4.3	.	3.6	4.5	4.5	4.5	.
W-F-M %	5.1	5.9	6.2	6.9	.	4.9	6.5	5.7	6.0	.
Brasil (BA) [6] [8]				Total unemployment - Chômage total - Desempleo total						
Total	7 639.1	.	7 853.4	7 958.5 ∣	8 640.0 [9]	8 263.8	8 953.0	8 210.0	8 059.6	.
M-H	3 667.9	.	3 674.9	3 685.1 ∣	3 972.8 [9]	3 590.7	3 859.0	3 510.0	3 390.9	.
W-F-M	3 971.2	.	4 178.5	4 273.3 ∣	4 667.1 [9]	4 673.1	5 094.0	4 700.0	4 668.7	.
Total %	9.6	.	9.4	9.2 ∣	9.7 [9]	8.9	9.3	8.4	8.2	.
M-H %	7.9	.	7.5	7.4 ∣	7.8 [9]	6.8	7.1	6.4	6.1	.
W-F-M %	12.1	.	11.9	11.6 ∣	12.3 [9]	11.7	12.2	11.0	10.8	.
Canada (BA) [1] [10]				Total unemployment - Chômage total - Desempleo total						
Total	1 181.6	1 082.8	1 163.6	1 268.9	1 286.2	1 235.3	1 172.8	1 108.4	1 079.4	1 119.3
M-H	660.4	595.3	655.1	721.7	719.6	685.4	649.0	608.3	603.9	632.6
W-F-M	521.2	487.5	508.5	547.2	566.6	549.9	523.8	500.1	475.5	486.6
Total %	7.6	6.8	7.2	7.7	7.6	7.2	6.8	6.3	6.0	6.1
M-H %	7.8	6.9	7.5	8.1	7.9	7.5	7.0	6.5	6.4	6.6
W-F-M %	7.3	6.7	6.9	7.1	7.2	6.9	6.5	6.1	5.6	5.7
Cayman Islands (BA) [1] [11]				Total unemployment - Chômage total - Desempleo total						
Total	.	.	2.110	1.551	1.079	1.311 [12]	1.303	0.943 [12]	1.395	1.549
M-H	.	.	.	.	.	.	.	0.462 [12]	0.662	0.773
W-F-M	.	.	.	.	.	.	.	0.481 [12]	0.733	0.777
Total %	.	.	7.5	5.4	3.6	4.3 [12]	3.5	2.6 [12]	3.8	4.0
M-H %	.	.	.	.	.	.	.	.	3.5	3.8
W-F-M %	.	.	.	.	.	.	.	.	4.2	4.1
Colombia (BA) [6] [13] [14]				Total unemployment - Chômage total - Desempleo total						
Total	.	.	2 708.8	2 848.6	2 797.3	2 462.0	2 260.6	2 424.8	2 097.1	2 245.7
M-H	.	.	1 257.6	1 341.3	1 264.8	1 132.1	1 019.4	1 093.9	996.4	1 033.0
W-F-M	.	.	1 451.2	1 507.3	1 532.5	1 329.9	1 241.2	1 330.9	1 092.8	1 212.7
Total %	.	.	14.6	15.2	14.4	12.8	11.6	12.7	10.9	11.4
M-H %	.	.	11.5	12.2	11.1	9.9	8.8	9.7	8.7	8.9
W-F-M %	.	.	19.1	19.7	18.9	16.9	15.7	17.0	14.1	15.1

Explanatory notes: see p. 451.

[1] Persons aged 15 years and over. [2] April of each year. [3] May. [4] Persons aged 14 years and over. [5] Urban areas, Nov. [6] Persons aged 10 years and over. [7] Nov. [8] Sep. of each year. [9] Prior to 2003: Excl. rural population of Rondônia, Acre, Amazonas, Roraima, Pará and Amapá. [10] Excl. residents of the Territories and indigenous persons living on reserves. [11] Oct. [12] April. [13] From 2001, figures revised on the basis of the 2005 census results. [14] Third quarter.

Notes explicatives: voir p. 454.

[1] Personnes âgées de 15 ans et plus. [2] Avril de chaque année. [3] Mai. [4] Personnes âgées de 14 ans et plus. [5] Régions urbaines, nov. [6] Personnes âgées de 10 ans et plus. [7] Nov. [8] Sept. de chaque année. [9] Avant 2003: Non compris la population rurale de Rondônia, Acre, Amazonas, Roraima, Pará et Amapá. [10] Non compris les habitants des "Territoires" et les populations indigènes vivant dans les réserves. [11] Oct. [12] Avril. [13] A partir de 2001, données révisées sur la base des résultats du recensement de 2005. [14] Troisième trimestre.

Notas explicativas: véase p. 457.

[1] Personas de 15 años y más. [2] Abril de cada año. [3] Mayo. [4] Personas de 14 años y más. [5] Areas urbanas, nov. [6] Personas de 10 años y más. [7] Nov. [8] Sept. de cada año. [9] Antes de 2003: Excl. la población rural de Rondonia, Acre, Amazonas, Roraima, Pará y Amapá. [10] Excl. a los habitantes de los "Territorios" y a las poblaciones indígenas que viven en reservas. [11] Oct. [12] Abril. [13] A partir de 2001, datos revisados de acuerdocon los resultados del censo de 2005. [14] Tercer trimestre.

3A

<table>
<tr><td></td><td colspan="3">UNEMPLOYMENT</td><td colspan="4">CHÔMAGE</td><td colspan="3">DESEMPLEO</td></tr>
<tr><td></td><td colspan="3">General level</td><td colspan="4">Niveau général</td><td colspan="3">Nivel general</td></tr>
</table>

<table>
<tr><td></td><td colspan="3">Thousands</td><td colspan="4">Milliers</td><td colspan="3">Millares</td></tr>
<tr><td></td><td>1999</td><td>2000</td><td>2001</td><td>2002</td><td>2003</td><td>2004</td><td>2005</td><td>2006</td><td>2007</td><td>2008</td></tr>
<tr><td colspan="11">Costa Rica (BA) [1][2]</td></tr>
<tr><td colspan="11">Total unemployment - Chômage total - Desempleo total</td></tr>
<tr><td>Total</td><td>83.3</td><td>71.9</td><td>100.4</td><td>108.5</td><td>117.2</td><td>114.9</td><td>126.2</td><td>116.0</td><td>92.8</td><td>101.9</td></tr>
<tr><td>M-H</td><td>45.6</td><td>41.2</td><td>55.8</td><td>61.6</td><td>66.0</td><td>62.5</td><td>60.2</td><td>53.8</td><td>41.3</td><td>53.5</td></tr>
<tr><td>W-F-M</td><td>37.7</td><td>30.8</td><td>44.6</td><td>46.9</td><td>51.2</td><td>52.4</td><td>66.0</td><td>62.3</td><td>51.5</td><td>48.4</td></tr>
<tr><td>Total %</td><td>6.0</td><td>5.2</td><td>6.1</td><td>6.4</td><td>6.7</td><td>6.5</td><td>6.6</td><td>6.0</td><td>4.6</td><td>4.9</td></tr>
<tr><td>M-H %</td><td>4.9</td><td>4.4</td><td>5.2</td><td>5.6</td><td>5.8</td><td>5.4</td><td>5.0</td><td>4.4</td><td>3.3</td><td>4.2</td></tr>
<tr><td>W-F-M %</td><td>8.2</td><td>6.9</td><td>7.6</td><td>7.9</td><td>8.2</td><td>8.5</td><td>9.6</td><td>8.7</td><td>6.8</td><td>6.2</td></tr>
<tr><td colspan="11">Cuba (BA) [3][4]</td></tr>
<tr><td colspan="11">Total unemployment - Chômage total - Desempleo total</td></tr>
<tr><td>Total</td><td>290.9</td><td>252.3</td><td>191.6</td><td>156.1</td><td>109.7</td><td>87.7</td><td>93.9</td><td>92.7</td><td>88.6</td><td>79.7 [5]</td></tr>
<tr><td>M-H</td><td>126.1</td><td>111.8</td><td>93.8</td><td>76.9</td><td>51.3</td><td>49.7</td><td>55.0</td><td>52.6</td><td>53.3</td><td>42.0 [5]</td></tr>
<tr><td>W-F-M</td><td>164.8</td><td>140.5</td><td>97.8</td><td>79.2</td><td>58.4</td><td>38.0</td><td>38.9</td><td>40.1</td><td>35.3</td><td>37.7 [5]</td></tr>
<tr><td>Total %</td><td>6.3</td><td>5.4</td><td>4.1</td><td>3.3</td><td>2.3</td><td>1.9</td><td>1.9</td><td>1.9</td><td>1.8</td><td>1.6 [5]</td></tr>
<tr><td>M-H %</td><td>4.3</td><td>3.8</td><td>3.1</td><td>2.6</td><td>1.7</td><td>1.7</td><td>1.8</td><td>1.7</td><td>1.7</td><td>1.3 [5]</td></tr>
<tr><td>W-F-M %</td><td>9.6</td><td>8.3</td><td>5.8</td><td>4.6</td><td>3.4</td><td>2.2</td><td>2.2</td><td>2.2</td><td>1.9</td><td>2.0 [5]</td></tr>
<tr><td colspan="11">Chile (BA) [6][7]</td></tr>
<tr><td colspan="11">Total unemployment - Chômage total - Desempleo total</td></tr>
<tr><td>Total</td><td>529.1</td><td>489.4</td><td>469.4</td><td>468.7</td><td>453.1</td><td>494.7</td><td>440.4 |</td><td>409.9 [8]</td><td>510.7</td><td>544.7</td></tr>
<tr><td>M-H</td><td>322.9</td><td>312.5</td><td>302.6</td><td>298.5</td><td>279.2</td><td>280.8</td><td>248.2 |</td><td>239.3 [8]</td><td>280.1</td><td>306.7</td></tr>
<tr><td>W-F-M</td><td>206.2</td><td>176.9</td><td>166.9</td><td>170.2</td><td>173.9</td><td>213.9</td><td>192.2 |</td><td>170.6 [8]</td><td>230.6</td><td>238.0</td></tr>
<tr><td>Total %</td><td>8.9</td><td>8.3</td><td>7.9</td><td>7.8</td><td>7.4</td><td>7.8</td><td>6.9 |</td><td>6.0 [8]</td><td>7.2</td><td>7.5</td></tr>
<tr><td>M-H %</td><td>8.2</td><td>8.0</td><td>7.6</td><td>7.5</td><td>6.9</td><td>6.9</td><td>6.1 |</td><td>5.5 [8]</td><td>6.3</td><td>6.7</td></tr>
<tr><td>W-F-M %</td><td>10.3</td><td>9.0</td><td>8.4</td><td>8.5</td><td>8.3</td><td>9.5</td><td>8.5 |</td><td>7.0 [8]</td><td>8.8</td><td>8.7</td></tr>
<tr><td colspan="11">República Dominicana (BA) [9]</td></tr>
<tr><td colspan="11">Total unemployment - Chômage total - Desempleo total</td></tr>
<tr><td>Total</td><td>477.9</td><td>491.4</td><td>556.3</td><td>596.3</td><td>619.7</td><td>723.7</td><td>715.8</td><td>661.4</td><td>654.0</td><td>602.5</td></tr>
<tr><td>M-H</td><td>175.8</td><td>174.7</td><td>208.0</td><td>215.5</td><td>243.0</td><td>252.5</td><td>269.6</td><td>233.5</td><td>240.7</td><td>218.3</td></tr>
<tr><td>W-F-M</td><td>302.1</td><td>316.8</td><td>348.2</td><td>380.8</td><td>376.8</td><td>471.2</td><td>446.3</td><td>428.0</td><td>413.3</td><td>384.2</td></tr>
<tr><td>Total %</td><td>13.8</td><td>13.9</td><td>15.6</td><td>16.1</td><td>16.7</td><td>18.4</td><td>17.9</td><td>16.0</td><td>15.6</td><td>14.2</td></tr>
<tr><td>M-H %</td><td>7.8</td><td>7.9</td><td>9.4</td><td>9.5</td><td>10.6</td><td>10.5</td><td>11.0</td><td>9.3</td><td>9.3</td><td>8.5</td></tr>
<tr><td>W-F-M %</td><td>24.9</td><td>23.8</td><td>26.0</td><td>26.6</td><td>26.6</td><td>30.7</td><td>28.8</td><td>26.3</td><td>25.4</td><td>22.8</td></tr>
<tr><td colspan="11">Ecuador (BA) [9][10][11]</td></tr>
<tr><td colspan="11">Total unemployment - Chômage total - Desempleo total</td></tr>
<tr><td>Total</td><td>543.5</td><td>333.1</td><td>450.9 [12]</td><td>352.9</td><td>461.1</td><td>362.1</td><td>333.6</td><td>341.8</td><td>260.4 [4]</td><td>320.4 [4]</td></tr>
<tr><td>M-H</td><td>239.5</td><td>138.3</td><td>169.0 [12]</td><td>136.2</td><td>215.0</td><td>160.7</td><td>143.3</td><td>143.4</td><td>123.2 [4]</td><td>142.1 [4]</td></tr>
<tr><td>W-F-M</td><td>304.0</td><td>194.8</td><td>282.0 [12]</td><td>216.7</td><td>246.1</td><td>201.4</td><td>190.3</td><td>198.4</td><td>137.2 [4]</td><td>178.3 [4]</td></tr>
<tr><td>Total %</td><td>14.4</td><td>9.0</td><td>11.0 [12]</td><td>9.3</td><td>11.5</td><td>8.6</td><td>7.9</td><td>7.8</td><td>6.1 [4]</td><td>7.3 [4]</td></tr>
<tr><td>M-H %</td><td>10.8</td><td>6.2</td><td>7.1 [12]</td><td>6.0</td><td>9.1</td><td>6.6</td><td>5.8</td><td>5.6</td><td>4.9 [4]</td><td>5.6 [4]</td></tr>
<tr><td>W-F-M %</td><td>19.6</td><td>13.1</td><td>16.2 [12]</td><td>14.0</td><td>15.0</td><td>11.4</td><td>10.8</td><td>10.9</td><td>7.6 [4]</td><td>9.6 [4]</td></tr>
<tr><td colspan="11">El Salvador (BA) [4][9]</td></tr>
<tr><td colspan="11">Total unemployment - Chômage total - Desempleo total</td></tr>
<tr><td>Total</td><td>163.3</td><td>164.4</td><td>170.3</td><td>147.4</td><td>169.4</td><td>164.0</td><td>177.6</td><td>164.2</td><td>166.6</td><td></td></tr>
<tr><td>M-H</td><td>120.2</td><td>129.5</td><td>119.6</td><td>113.7</td><td>134.5</td><td>127.3</td><td>129.6</td><td>123.9</td><td>126.6</td><td></td></tr>
<tr><td>W-F-M</td><td>54.2</td><td>34.9</td><td>50.7</td><td>33.7</td><td>34.9</td><td>36.7</td><td>48.1</td><td>40.4</td><td>40.0</td><td></td></tr>
<tr><td>Total %</td><td>7.3</td><td>7.0</td><td>7.0</td><td>6.2</td><td>6.9</td><td>6.8</td><td>7.2</td><td>6.6</td><td>6.4</td><td></td></tr>
<tr><td>M-H %</td><td>8.4</td><td>9.1</td><td>8.1</td><td>8.1</td><td>9.2</td><td>8.7</td><td>8.9</td><td>8.5</td><td>8.3</td><td></td></tr>
<tr><td>W-F-M %</td><td>4.6</td><td>3.6</td><td>5.2</td><td>3.5</td><td>3.5</td><td>3.8</td><td>4.8</td><td>3.9</td><td>3.8</td><td></td></tr>
<tr><td colspan="11">Greenland (E) [6][13]</td></tr>
<tr><td colspan="11">Total unemployment - Chômage total - Desempleo total</td></tr>
<tr><td>Total</td><td>2.312</td><td>2.839</td><td>2.495</td><td>2.328</td><td>2.746</td><td>2.822</td><td>2.530</td><td>2.317</td><td></td><td></td></tr>
<tr><td>M-H</td><td>1.389</td><td>1.584</td><td>1.514</td><td>1.325</td><td>1.630</td><td>1.663</td><td>1.463</td><td>1.417</td><td></td><td></td></tr>
<tr><td>W-F-M</td><td>0.923</td><td>1.255</td><td>0.981</td><td>1.003</td><td>1.116</td><td>1.159</td><td>1.067</td><td>0.900</td><td></td><td></td></tr>
<tr><td>Total %</td><td>9.0</td><td>11.0</td><td>9.5</td><td>8.8</td><td>10.3</td><td>10.4</td><td>9.3</td><td></td><td></td><td></td></tr>
<tr><td>M-H %</td><td>10.6</td><td>12.0</td><td>11.3</td><td>9.8</td><td>11.9</td><td>12.0</td><td>10.4</td><td></td><td></td><td></td></tr>
<tr><td>W-F-M %</td><td>7.4</td><td>10.0</td><td>7.7</td><td>7.8</td><td>8.6</td><td>8.8</td><td>8.0</td><td></td><td></td><td></td></tr>
<tr><td colspan="11">Guadeloupe (BA) [6][14]</td></tr>
<tr><td colspan="11">Total unemployment - Chômage total - Desempleo total</td></tr>
<tr><td>Total</td><td>55.0</td><td>49.4</td><td>43.7</td><td>41.5</td><td>44.0</td><td>40.3</td><td>42.0</td><td>46.2</td><td>38.0</td><td></td></tr>
<tr><td>M-H</td><td>22.3</td><td>21.7</td><td>19.1</td><td>19.0</td><td>20.9</td><td>17.5</td><td>18.1</td><td>20.8</td><td>15.9</td><td></td></tr>
<tr><td>W-F-M</td><td>32.7</td><td>27.7</td><td>24.6</td><td>22.5</td><td>23.1</td><td>22.8</td><td>23.9</td><td>25.4</td><td>22.1</td><td></td></tr>
<tr><td>Total %</td><td>29.8</td><td>25.7</td><td>27.6</td><td>25.7</td><td>26.9</td><td>24.7</td><td>26.0</td><td>27.3</td><td>22.7</td><td></td></tr>
<tr><td>M-H %</td><td>23.2</td><td>21.2</td><td>23.4</td><td>22.6</td><td>24.6</td><td>21.0</td><td>22.0</td><td>24.2</td><td>19.2</td><td></td></tr>
<tr><td>W-F-M %</td><td>37.1</td><td>30.8</td><td>32.0</td><td>29.1</td><td>29.4</td><td>28.5</td><td>30.1</td><td>30.5</td><td>26.1</td><td></td></tr>
<tr><td colspan="11">Guatemala (BA) [9]</td></tr>
<tr><td colspan="11">Total unemployment - Chômage total - Desempleo total</td></tr>
<tr><td>Total</td><td>79.8</td><td>64.9</td><td>62.2</td><td>154.3</td><td>172.2</td><td>156.2</td><td>. |</td><td>100.1 [8]</td><td></td><td></td></tr>
<tr><td>M-H</td><td>59.2</td><td>40.3</td><td>34.4</td><td>77.1</td><td>79.4</td><td>91.7</td><td>. |</td><td>50.6 [8]</td><td></td><td></td></tr>
<tr><td>W-F-M</td><td>20.6</td><td>24.6</td><td>27.8</td><td>77.2</td><td>92.8</td><td>64.5</td><td>. |</td><td>49.5 [8]</td><td></td><td></td></tr>
<tr><td>Total %</td><td>1.9</td><td>1.4</td><td>1.3</td><td>3.1</td><td>3.4</td><td>3.1</td><td>. |</td><td>1.8 [8]</td><td></td><td></td></tr>
<tr><td>M-H %</td><td>2.2</td><td>1.4</td><td>1.3</td><td>2.5</td><td>2.5</td><td>2.8</td><td>. |</td><td>1.5 [8]</td><td></td><td></td></tr>
<tr><td>W-F-M %</td><td>1.4</td><td>1.5</td><td>1.4</td><td>4.3</td><td>4.9</td><td>3.7</td><td>. |</td><td>2.4 [8]</td><td></td><td></td></tr>
</table>

Explanatory notes: see p. 451.

[1] Persons aged 12 years and over. [2] July of each year. [3] Men aged 17 to 60 years; women aged 17 to 55 years. [4] Dec. [5] February - April [6] Persons aged 15 years and over. [7] Fourth quarter of each year. [8] Methodology revised; data not strictly comparable. [9] Persons aged 10 years and over. [10] Urban areas. [11] Nov. of each year. [12] July. [13] Jan. of each year. [14] June of each year.

Notes explicatives: voir p. 454.

[1] Personnes âgées de 12 ans et plus. [2] Juillet de chaque année. [3] Hommes âgés de 17 à 60 ans; femmes âgées de 17 à 55 ans. [4] Déc. [5] Février - Avril [6] Personnes âgées de 15 ans et plus. [7] Quatrième trimestre de chaque année. [8] Méthodologie révisée; les données ne sont pas strictement comparables. [9] Personnes âgées de 10 ans et plus. [10] Régions urbaines. [11] Nov. de chaque année. [12] Juillet. [13] Jan. de chaque année. [14] Juin de chaque année.

Notas explicativas: véase p. 457.

[1] Personas de 12 años y más. [2] Julio de cada año. [3] Hombres de 17 a 60 años; mujeres de 17 a 55 años. [4] Dic. [5] Febrero - Abril [6] Personas de 15 años y más. [7] Cuarto trimestre de cada año. [8] Metodología revisada; los datos no son estrictamente comparables. [9] Personas de 10 años y más. [10] Areas urbanas. [11] Nov. de cada año. [12] Julio. [13] Ene. de cada año. [14] Junio de cada año.

UNEMPLOYMENT CHÔMAGE DESEMPLEO

General level — Niveau général — Nivel general

	Thousands / Milliers / Millares									
	1999	2000	2001	2002	2003	2004	2005	2006	2007	2008
Guyane française (BA) [1][2]				Total unemployment - Chômage total - Desempleo total						
Total	15.5	15.2	15.0	13.5	14.1	15.2	15.9	18.4	12.8	.
M-H	7.8	7.3	7.4	6.4	6.6	7.3	7.9	8.2	5.9	.
W-F-M	7.7	7.9	7.6	7.1	7.5	8.0	8.0	10.3	6.9	.
Total %	26.6	25.8	26.3	23.4	24.5	26.3	26.5	29.1	.	.
M-H %	22.8	21.2	23.0	19.8	20.5	22.6	23.8	23.9	.	.
W-F-M %	32.1	32.2	30.5	27.8	29.6	30.8	29.7	35.3	.	.
Honduras (BA) [3]				Total unemployment - Chômage total - Desempleo total						
Total	89.3 [4]	.	93.0	93.7	130.3	153.2	107.8	87.4	85.3	.
M-H	56.7 [4]	.	58.9	56.8	74.9	81.1	55.2	46.8	55.9	.
W-F-M	32.6 [4]	.	34.1	37.0	55.5	72.2	52.6	40.7	29.5	.
Total %	3.7 [4]	.	3.9	3.8	5.1	5.9	4.1	3.1	2.9	.
M-H %	3.7 [4]	.	3.7	3.4	4.4	4.7	3.1	2.5	2.9	.
W-F-M %	3.8 [4]	.	4.3	4.7	6.4	8.3	6.1	4.2	2.9	.
Jamaica (BA) [5]				Total unemployment - Chômage total - Desempleo total						
Total	175.2	171.8	165.4 [6]	171.8	128.9	136.8	133.3	119.6	119.4	134.6
M-H	61.4	62.5	63.4 [6]	65.7	47.6	54.0	50.0	48.0	37.8	52.8
W-F-M	113.8	109.2	102.1 [6]	106.1	81.3	82.8	83.3	71.6	81.6	81.8
Total %	15.7	15.5	15.0 [6]	14.3	10.9	11.4	10.9	9.6	9.3	10.3
M-H %	10.0	10.2	10.3 [6]	9.9	7.2	8.1	7.4	6.9	5.3	7.4
W-F-M %	22.4	22.3	21.0 [6]	19.8	15.6	15.7	15.3	13.0	14.0	13.8
Martinique (BA) [1][2]				Total unemployment - Chômage total - Desempleo total						
Total	46.9	44.1	39.8	32.3 [7]	31.4	32.6	27.2	36.9	34.5	34.7
M-H	20.9	18.9	16.3	13.9 [7]	13.9	14.4	12.1	17.4	16.3	14.6
W-F-M	26.0	25.2	23.6	18.4 [7]	17.5	18.3	15.1	19.5	18.2	20.1
Total %	28.1	26.3	24.7	20.6 [7]	20.0	20.7	17.8	22.9	21.1	21.5
M-H %	24.5	22.1	20.1	17.8 [7]	17.8	18.5	15.9	21.7	20.7	19.0
W-F-M %	32.0	30.8	29.3	23.4 [7]	22.1	22.9	19.8	24.2	21.6	23.8
México (BA) [5][8]				Total unemployment - Chômage total - Desempleo total						
Total	954.2	998.9	996.1	1 145.6	1 195.6	1 539.8	1 482.5	1 377.7	1 505.2	1 593.3
M-H	494.4	559.7	550.6	656.5	687.0	828.7	917.8	811.5	885.6	927.4
W-F-M	459.8	439.2	445.5	489.0	508.7	711.0	564.7	566.2	619.6	665.9
Total %	2.5	2.6	2.6	2.9	3.0	3.7	3.5	3.2	3.4	3.5
M-H %	2.0	2.2	2.2	2.5	2.6	3.1	3.4	3.0	3.2	3.3
W-F-M %	3.6	3.3	3.3	3.5	3.6	4.7	3.6	3.5	3.7	3.9
Netherlands Antilles (BA) [1][9][10]				Total unemployment - Chômage total - Desempleo total						
Total	.	8.531	.	9.056	9.274	9.861	11.392	8.931	7.659	6.486
M-H	.	3.721	.	4.120	4.002	4.498	5.227	3.323	3.044	2.483
W-F-M	.	4.810	.	4.936	5.272	5.362	6.165	5.608	4.615	4.002
Total %	.	14.2	.	15.6	15.1	16.1	18.2	14.6	12.4	10.3
M-H %	.	12.0	.	14.0	13.1	15.1	17.1	11.3	10.2	8.1
W-F-M %	.	16.2	.	17.1	17.1	17.0	19.2	17.7	14.4	12.4
Nicaragua (BA) [3]				Total unemployment - Chômage total - Desempleo total						
Total	.	.	.	.	160.5	138.0	122.5	114.5	106.9	.
M-H	.	.	.	.	97.1	74.2	73.4	74.1	65.9	.
W-F-M	.	.	.	.	63.4	63.8	49.1	40.3	41.0	.
Total %	.	.	.	.	7.7	6.5	5.6	5.2	4.9	.
M-H %	.	.	.	.	7.6	5.7	5.4	5.4	4.8	.
W-F-M %	.	.	.	.	7.9	8.0	5.9	4.9	5.0	.
Panamá (BA) [1][11]				Total unemployment - Chômage total - Desempleo total						
Total	128.0	147.0	169.7	172.4	170.4	159.9	136.8	121.4	92.0	82.9
M-H	62.1	77.7	92.0	86.5	82.9	76.3	66.7	60.2	44.5	40.2
W-F-M	65.9	69.3	77.8	85.9	87.3	83.6	70.2	61.1	47.5	42.7
Total %	11.8	13.5	14.7	14.1	13.6	12.4	10.3	9.1	6.8	5.8
M-H %	8.9	11.1	12.2	11.2	10.5	9.4	8.1	7.2	5.3	4.6
W-F-M %	16.9	.	19.3	19.2	18.8	17.3	14.0	12.4	9.3	7.8
Paraguay (BA) [3][12]				Total unemployment - Chômage total - Desempleo total						
Total	.	198.7 [13]	.	272.6	206.0	.	.	.	161.2	170.6
M-H	.	108.5 [13]	.	141.9	105.6	.	.	.	74.6	83.9
W-F-M	.	89.9 [13]	.	130.9	100.4	.	.	.	86.6	86.7
Total %	.	7.6 [13]	.	10.8	8.1	.	.	.	5.6	5.7
M-H %	.	6.8 [13]	.	9.0	6.7	.	.	.	4.3	4.6
W-F-M %	.	8.9 [13]	.	13.6	10.1	.	.	.	7.5	7.4

Explanatory notes: see p. 451.

[1] Persons aged 15 years and over. [2] June of each year. [3] Persons aged 10 years and over. [4] March. [5] Persons aged 14 years and over. [6] First and second quarters. [7] Methodology revised; data not strictly comparable. [8] Second quarter of each year. [9] Curaçao. [10] Oct. of each year. [11] Aug. of each year. [12] Fourth quarter. [13] Year beginning in September of year indicated.

Notes explicatives: voir p. 454.

[1] Personnes âgées de 15 ans et plus. [2] Juin de chaque année. [3] Personnes âgées de 10 ans et plus. [4] Mars. [5] Personnes âgées de 14 ans et plus. [6] Premier et deuxième trimestres. [7] Méthodologie révisée; les données ne sont pas strictement comparables. [8] Deuxième trimestre de chaque année. [9] Curaçao. [10] Oct. de chaque année. [11] Août de chaque année. [12] Quatrième trimestre. [13] Année commençant en septembre de l'année indiquée.

Notas explicativas: véase p. 457.

[1] Personas de 15 años y más. [2] Junio de cada año. [3] Personas de 10 años y más. [4] Marzo. [5] Personas de 14 años y más. [6] Primero y secondo trimestres. [7] Metodología revisada; los datos no son estrictamente comparables. [8] Segundo trimestre de cada año. [9] Curaçao. [10] Oct. de cada año. [11] Agosto de cada año. [12] Cuarto trimestre. [13] Año que comienza en septiembre del año indicado.

UNEMPLOYMENT	CHÔMAGE	DESEMPLEO
General level	Niveau général	Nivel general

	Thousands				Milliers				Millares	
	1999	2000	2001	2002	2003	2004	2005	2006	2007	2008
Perú (BA) [1] [2]				**Total unemployment - Chômage total - Desempleo total**						
Total	.	.	.	359.4 [3]	316.0 [4]	339.5	333.4	297.6	300.1	308.0
M-H	.	.	.	194.0 [3]	182.5 [4]	159.4	155.4	136.3	139.1	131.3
W-F-M	.	.	.	165.4 [3]	133.6 [4]	180.1	178.0	161.3	161.0	176.6
Total %	.	.	.	7.7 [3]	7.2 [4]	7.4	7.5	7.2	6.7	6.8
M-H %	.	.	.	7.5 [3]	7.3 [4]	6.6	7.1	6.0	5.8	5.4
W-F-M %	.	.	.	7.8 [3]	7.0 [4]	8.3	8.1	8.6	7.8	8.3
Puerto Rico (BA) [5] [6]				**Total unemployment - Chômage total - Desempleo total**						
Total	152	131	145	163	164	145	160	156	152	158
M-H	101	90	97	101	99	92	97	90	93	97
W-F-M	51	42	48	62	65	53	63	66	59	60
Total %	11.8	10.1	11.4	12.3	12.0	10.6	11.3	11.1	10.9	11.5
M-H %	13.2	11.8	13.0	13.2	12.8	11.8	12.2	11.5	12.1	12.9
W-F-M %	9.6	7.7	9.1	10.9	10.9	9.0	10.2	10.5	9.5	9.9
Saint Lucia (BA) [7]				**Total unemployment - Chômage total - Desempleo total**						
Total	13.220	12.535	.	14.990	18.205	16.527	.	.	.	.
M-H	6.065	5.070	.	6.710	7.557	7.382	.	.	.	.
W-F-M	7.155	7.465	.	8.280	10.647	9.145	.	.	.	.
Total %	18.1	16.4	.	20.4	22.3	21.0	.	.	.	.
M-H %	16.0	12.6	.	17.3	17.3	17.5	.	.	.	.
W-F-M %	20.3	20.7	.	23.8	28.0	25.0	.	.	.	.
Trinidad and Tobago (BA) [7]				**Total unemployment - Chômage total - Desempleo total**						
Total	74.0	69.6	62.4	61.1	62.4	51.1	49.7	39.0	34.5	29.0
M-H	37.9	36.1	30.7	27.9	29.8	23.4	21.3	16.4	14.4	12.9
W-F-M	36.1	33.5	31.7	33.2	32.6	27.7	28.4	22.6	20.1	16.1
Total %	13.1	12.2	10.8	10.4	10.5	8.3	8.0	6.2	5.5	4.6
M-H %	10.9	10.2	8.6	7.8	8.3	6.4	5.8	4.5	3.9	3.5
W-F-M %	16.8	15.2	14.4	14.5	13.8	11.2	11.0	8.7	7.9	6.2
Turks and Caicos Islands (BA) [7]				**Total unemployment - Chômage total - Desempleo total**						
Total	.	.	.	.	3.714	4.179	4.938	6.373	6.774	.
W-F-M %	.	.	.	.	7.8	9.9	8.0	7.4	5.4	.
Turks and Caicos Islands (E) [7]				**Total unemployment - Chômage total - Desempleo total**						
Total	.	.	1.1	0.8	1.2	1.7	1.5	.	.	.
United States (BA) [6]				**Total unemployment - Chômage total - Desempleo total**						
Total	5 880	5 655	6 742	8 378	8 774	8 149	7 591	7 001	7 078	8 924
M-H	3 066	2 954	3 663	4 597	4 906	4 456	4 059	3 753	3 882	5 033
W-F-M	2 814	2 701	3 079	3 781	3 868	3 694	3 531	3 247	3 196	3 891
Total %	4.2	4.0	4.8	5.8	6.0	5.5	5.1	4.6	4.6	5.8
M-H %	4.1	3.9	4.8	5.9	6.3	5.6	5.1	4.6	4.7	6.1
W-F-M %	4.3	4.1	4.7	5.6	5.7	5.4	5.1	4.6	4.5	5.4
Uruguay (BA) [1]				**Total unemployment - Chômage total - Desempleo total**						
Total	137.7	167.7	193.2	211.3	208.5	.	154.9 |	167.0 [8]	149.3	.
M-H	59.4	74.7	80.4	93.3	92.2	.	65.4 |	70.0 [8]	60.0	.
W-F-M	78.3	93.0	112.8	118.0	116.2	.	89.5 |	96.9 [8]	89.3	.
Total %	11.3	13.6	15.3	17.0	16.9	.	12.2 |	10.6 [8]	9.2	.
M-H %	8.7	10.9	11.5	13.5	13.5	.	9.5 |	7.8 [8]	6.6	.
W-F-M %	14.6	17.0	19.7	21.2	20.8	.	15.3 |	14.1 [8]	12.4	.
Venezuela, Rep. Bolivariana de (BA) [7] [9]				**Total unemployment - Chômage total - Desempleo total**						
Total	1 483.4	1 365.8	1 419.2	1 887.7	2 014.9	1 687.7	1 374.3	1 143.7	928.2	872.9
M-H	882.3	821.2	788.1	1 017.1	1 034.2	900.9	762.4	618.9	536.7	506.3
W-F-M	601.1	544.6	631.1	870.6	980.7	786.8	611.9	524.8	391.5	366.6
Total %	14.5	13.2	12.8	16.2	16.8	13.9	11.4	9.3	7.5	6.9
M-H %	13.6	12.5	11.6	14.4	14.4	12.3	10.3	8.2	7.1	6.5
W-F-M %	16.1	14.4	14.6	18.8	20.3	16.4	13.0	11.1	8.1	7.4

ASIA-ASIE-ASIA

	1999	2000	2001	2002	2003	2004	2005	2006	2007	2008
Armenia (BA) [6]				**Total unemployment - Chômage total - Desempleo total**						
Total	.	.	.	.	.	.	.	.	470.9	.
M-H	.	.	.	.	.	.	.	.	183.7	.
W-F-M	.	.	.	.	.	.	.	.	287.2	.
Total %	.	.	.	.	.	.	.	.	28.4	.
M-H %	.	.	.	.	.	.	.	.	21.9	.
W-F-M %	.	.	.	.	.	.	.	.	35.0	.
Armenia (FB) [10] [11]				**Registered unemployment - Chômage enregistré - Desempleo registrado**						
Total	175.0	153.9	138.4	127.3	118.6	108.6	89.0	84.6	75.1	74.7
M-H	62.3	54.4	47.1	85.7	37.0	32.3	26.0	23.9	19.9	18.3
W-F-M	112.7	99.5	91.3	41.6	81.6	76.3	63.0	60.7	55.2	56.4

Explanatory notes: see p. 451.

[1] Persons aged 14 years and over. [2] Metropolitan Lima. [3] Fourth quarter. [4] May-Dec. [5] Excl. persons temporarily laid off. [6] Persons aged 16 years and over. [7] Persons aged 15 years and over. [8] Prior to 2006: urban areas. [9] Second semester. [10] Persons aged 16 to 63 years. [11] Dec. of each year.

Notes explicatives: voir p. 454.

[1] Personnes âgées de 14 ans et plus. [2] Lima métropolitaine. [3] Quatrième trimestre. [4] Mai-déc. [5] Non compris les personnes temporairement mises à pied. [6] Personnes âgées de 16 ans et plus. [7] Personnes âgées de 15 ans et plus. [8] Avant 2006: régions urbaines. [9] Second semestre. [10] Personnes âgées de 16 à 63 ans. [11] Déc. de chaque année.

Notas explicativas: véase p. 457.

[1] Personas de 14 años y más. [2] Lima metropolitana. [3] Cuarto trimestre. [4] Mayo-dic. [5] Excl. las personas temporalmente despedidas. [6] Personas de 16 años y más. [7] Personas de 15 años y más. [8] Antes de 2006: areas urbanas. [9] Segundo semestre. [10] Personas de 16 a 63 años de edad. [11] Dic. de cada año.

General level   Niveau général   Nivel general

	Thousands — Milliers — Millares									
	1999	2000	2001	2002	2003	2004	2005	2006	2007	2008
Azerbaijan (BA) [1]	*Total unemployment - Chômage total - Desempleo total*									
Total	.	.	.	.	404.7	.	.	291.2	281.1	261.4
M-H	.	.	.	.	210.5	.	.	157.0	169.9	156.9
W-F-M	.	.	.	.	194.2	.	.	134.2	111.2	104.5
Total %	.	.	.	.	10.7	.	.	6.8	6.5	6.1
M-H %	.	.	.	.	9.6	.	.	6.9	7.8	7.1
W-F-M %	.	.	.	.	12.2	.	.	6.7	5.3	4.9
Azerbaijan (FB) [1][2]	*Registered unemployment - Chômage enregistré - Desempleo registrado*									
Total	45.2	43.7	48.4	51.0	54.4	55.9	56.3	53.9	50.7	44.5
M-H	19.6	19.3	21.8	23.1	25.3	26.7	27.3	26.3	25.3	23.6
W-F-M	25.6	24.5	26.6	27.9	29.1	29.3	29.1	27.5	25.3	20.9
Total %	1.2	1.2	1.3	1.3	1.3	1.3	1.4	1.3	1.2	1.0
M-H %	1.0	1.0	1.1	1.2	1.2	1.2	1.2	1.2	1.2	1.1
W-F-M %	1.4	1.4	1.5	1.5	1.5	1.5	1.5	1.3	1.2	1.0
Bahrain (FB) [3][4]	*Work applicants - Demandeurs d'emploi - Solicitantes*									
Total	3.754	6.160	.	8.735	11.778	6.293	6.441	6.805	9.536 ǀ	5.311 [5]
M-H	2.639	4.183	.	4.377	6.034	3.077	2.898	1.525	1.240 ǀ	0.783 [5]
W-F-M	1.115	1.977	.	4.358	5.744	3.216	3.543	5.280	8.296 ǀ	4.528 [5]
Bangladesh (BA) [3][6]	*Total unemployment - Chômage total - Desempleo total*									
Total	.	1 750	.	.	2 002	.	2 104	.	.	.
M-H	.	1 083	.	.	1 500	.	1 256	.	.	.
W-F-M	.	666	.	.	502	.	854	.	.	.
Total %	.	3.3	.	.	4.3	.	4.3	.	.	.
M-H %	.	3.2	.	.	4.2	.	3.4	.	.	.
W-F-M %	.	3.3	.	.	4.9	.	7.0	.	.	.
China (E) [2][3][7]	*Total unemployment - Chômage total - Desempleo total*									
Total	5 750	5 950	6 810	7 700	8 000	8 270	8 390	8 470	8 300	8 860
Total %	3.1	3.1	3.6	4.0	4.3	4.2	4.2	4.1	4.0	4.2
Georgia (BA) [3]	*Total unemployment - Chômage total - Desempleo total*									
Total	277.5	212.2	235.6	265.0	235.9	257.6	279.3	274.5	261.0	.
M-H	160.1	116.7	126.9	155.5	124.2	143.2	159.2	165.4	143.7	.
W-F-M	117.4	95.5	108.7	109.5	111.7	114.4	120.1	109.1	117.3	.
Total %	13.8	10.8	11.0	12.3	11.5	12.6	13.8	13.6	13.3	.
M-H %	15.3	11.1	11.6	13.7	11.5	13.4	14.8	15.2	13.9	.
W-F-M %	12.2	10.5	10.7	10.7	11.5	11.8	12.6	11.7	12.6	.
Hong Kong, China (BA) [3][8]	*Total unemployment - Chômage total - Desempleo total*									
Total	207.5	166.9	174.3	254.2	275.2	239.2	197.6	171.1	145.7	130.1
M-H	140.6	109.6	117.8	164.0	180.0	151.8	127.5	110.2	89.2	79.4
W-F-M	66.9	57.3	56.5	90.1	95.3	87.4	70.1	60.8	56.5	50.7
Total %	6.2	4.9	5.1	7.3	7.9	6.8	5.6	4.8	4.0	3.6
M-H %	7.2	5.6	6.0	8.4	9.3	7.8	6.5	5.7	4.6	4.1
W-F-M %	4.9	4.1	3.9	6.0	6.3	5.6	4.4	3.8	3.4	3.0
India (FB) [2][9]	*Work applicants - Demandeurs d'emploi - Solicitantes*									
Total	40 371	41 344	41 996	41 171	41 389	40 458	39 348	41 466	39 974	39 112
M-H	30 438	30 887	31 111	30 521	30 636	29 746	28 742	29 685	27 972	26 785
W-F-M	9 933	10 457	10 885	10 650	10 752	10 712	10 606	11 781	12 002	12 327
Indonesia (BA) [3][10]	*Total unemployment - Chômage total - Desempleo total*									
Total	6 030.3	5 813.2	8 005.0	9 132.1	9 939.3	10 251.4	11 899.3 [11]	10 932.0	10 011.1	9 394.5
M-H	3 524.2	3 340.7	4 032.4	4 727.8	5 100.1	5 345.7	6 292.4 [11]	5 772.6	5 571.9	5 245.1
W-F-M	2 506.1	2 472.6	3 972.6	4 404.3	4 839.2	4 905.7	5 606.8 [11]	5 159.4	4 439.2	4 149.5
Total %	6.4	6.1	8.1	9.1	9.7	9.9	11.2 [11]	10.3	9.1	8.4
M-H %	6.0	5.7	6.6	7.5	7.9	8.1	9.3 [11]	8.5	8.1	7.6
W-F-M %	6.9	6.7	10.6	11.8	12.7	12.9	14.7 [11]	13.4	10.8	9.7
Iran, Islamic Rep. of (BA) [12]	*Total unemployment - Chômage total - Desempleo total*									
Total	.	.	.	.	.	.	2 675	2 643	2 486	2 392
M-H	.	.	.	.	.	.	1 856	1 878	1 764	1 715
W-F-M	.	.	.	.	.	.	819	765	722	677
Total %	.	.	.	.	.	.	11.5	11.3	10.5	10.4
M-H %	.	.	.	.	.	.	10.0	10.0	9.3	9.1
W-F-M %	.	.	.	.	.	.	17.0	16.2	15.8	16.7
Iraq (BA) [3]	*Total unemployment - Chômage total - Desempleo total*									
Total %	.	.	.	.	28.1	26.8	.	.	.	.
M-H %	.	.	.	.	30.2	29.4	.	.	.	.
W-F-M %	.	.	.	.	16.0	15.0	.	.	.	.

Explanatory notes: see p. 451.

[1] Men aged 15 to 61 years; women aged 15 to 56 years. [2] Dec. of each year. [3] Persons aged 15 years and over. [4] Jan. [5] Persons aged 18 years and over. [6] Year ending in June of the year indicated. [7] Urban areas. [8] Excl. marine, military and institutional populations. [9] Persons aged 14 years and over. [10] Aug. of each year. [11] Nov. [12] Persons aged 10 years and over.

Notes explicatives: voir p. 454.

[1] Hommes âgés de 15 à 61 ans; femmes âgées de 15 à 56 ans. [2] Déc. de chaque année. [3] Personnes âgées de 15 ans et plus. [4] Janv. [5] Personnes âgées de 18 ans et plus. [6] Année se terminant en juin de l'année indiquée. [7] Régions urbaines. [8] Non compris le personnel militaire, de la marine et la population institutionnelle. [9] Personnes âgées de 14 ans et plus. [10] Août de chaque année. [11] Nov. [12] Personnes âgées de 10 ans et plus.

Notas explicativas: véase p. 457.

[1] Hombres de 15 a 61 años; mujeres de 15 a 56 años. [2] Dic. de cada año. [3] Personas de 15 años y más. [4] Enero. [5] Personas de 18 años y más. [6] Año que se termina en junio del año indicado. [7] Areas urbanas. [8] Excl. el personal militar y de la marina, y la población institucional. [9] Personas de 14 años y más. [10] Agosto de cada año. [11] Nov. [12] Personas de 10 años y más.

	Thousands			Milliers					Millares	
	1999	2000	2001	2002	2003	2004	2005	2006	2007	2008
Israel (BA) [1]				Total unemployment - Chômage total - Desempleo total						
Total	208.5	213.8	233.9	262.4	279.9	277.7	246.4	236.1	211.8	180.4
M-H	108.8	111.7	120.9	138.4	142.8	136.5	124.9	118.5	104.8	90.8
W-F-M	99.7	102.1	113.0	124.0	137.1	141.2	121.5	117.6	107.0	89.6
Total %	8.9	8.8	9.4	10.3	10.7	10.4	9.0	8.4	7.3	6.1
M-H %	8.5	8.4	8.9	10.1	10.2	9.5	8.5	7.9	6.8	5.7
W-F-M %	9.4	9.2	9.9	10.6	11.3	11.4	9.5	9.0	7.9	6.5
Japan (BA) [1]				Total unemployment - Chômage total - Desempleo total						
Total	3 170	3 190	3 400	3 590 [2]	3 500	3 130	2 940	2 750	2 570	2 650
M-H	1 940	1 960	2 090	2 190 [2]	2 150	1 920	1 780	1 680	1 540	1 590
W-F-M	1 230	1 230	1 310	1 400 [2]	1 350	1 210	1 160	1 070	1 030	1 060
Total %	4.7	4.7	5.0	5.4 [2]	5.3	4.7	4.4	4.1	3.9	4.0
M-H %	4.8	4.9	5.2	5.5 [2]	5.5	4.9	4.6	4.3	3.9	4.1
W-F-M %	4.5	4.5	4.7	5.1 [2]	4.9	4.4	4.2	3.9	3.7	3.8
Kazakhstan (BA) [1]				Total unemployment - Chômage total - Desempleo total						
Total	.	.	780.3	690.7	672.1	658.8	640.7	625.4	597.2	557.8
M-H	.	.	338.0	283.8	281.4	281.1	270.6	262.5	244.5	226.5
W-F-M	.	.	442.3	406.9	390.7	377.7	370.2	362.8	352.6	331.4
Total %	.	.	10.4	9.3	8.8	8.4	8.1	7.8	7.3	6.6
M-H %	.	.	8.9	7.5	7.2	7.0	6.7	6.4	5.9	5.3
W-F-M %	.	.	12.0	11.2	10.4	9.8	9.6	9.2	8.7	7.9
Kazakhstan (FB) [3]				Registered unemployment - Chômage enregistré - Desempleo registrado						
Total	251.4	231.4	216.1	193.7	142.8	117.7	94.0	75.2	54.7	48.4
M-H	101.9	99.0	97.9	79.8	55.7	43.7	33.4	20.7	16.2	15.6
W-F-M	149.5	132.4	118.3	113.9	87.2	74.0	60.6	51.4	38.5	32.8
Total %	3.9	3.7	2.8	2.6	1.8	1.5	1.2	0.9	0.7	0.6
M-H %			2.6	2.1	1.4	1.1	0.8	0.5	0.4	0.4
W-F-M %			3.2	3.1	2.3	1.9	1.6	1.3	0.9	0.8
Korea, Republic of (BA) [1]				Total unemployment - Chômage total - Desempleo total						
Total	1 353	979 [4]	899	752	818	860	887	827	783	769
M-H	911	647 [4]	591	491	508	534	553	533	517	505
W-F-M	442	332 [4]	308	261	310	326	334	294	266	265
Total %	6.3	4.4 [4]	4.0	3.3	3.6	3.7	3.7	3.5	3.2	3.2
M-H %	7.1	5.0 [4]	4.5	3.7	3.8	3.9	4.0	3.8	3.7	3.6
W-F-M %	5.1	3.6 [4]	3.3	2.8	3.3	3.4	3.4	2.9	2.8	2.6
Kuwait (FD) [5]				Registered unemployment - Chômage enregistré - Desempleo registrado						
Total	8.921	9.305	9.464	15.074	18.061	23.205	25.698	24.921	.	.
M-H	7.264	7.467	7.584	9.448	10.129	11.601	12.836	11.874	.	.
W-F-M	1.657	1.838	1.880	5.626	7.932	11.604	12.862	13.047	.	.
Total %	0.7	0.8	0.8	1.1	1.3	1.4	1.5	1.3	.	.
M-H %	0.8	0.8	0.8	1.0	1.0	0.9	1.0	0.8	.	.
W-F-M %	0.6	0.7	0.6	1.7	2.2	2.9	3.1	2.9	.	.
Kyrgyzstan (BA) [1] [6]				Total unemployment - Chômage total - Desempleo total						
Total	.	.	.	265.5	212.3	185.7	183.5	188.9	191.1	.
M-H	.	.	.	132.6	113.1	98.8	95.7	101.5	102.5	.
W-F-M	.	.	.	132.9	99.2	86.9	87.8	87.5	88.6	.
Total %	.	.	.	12.5	9.9	8.5	8.1	8.3	8.2	.
M-H %	.	.	.	11.2	9.4	8.0	7.4	7.7	7.6	.
W-F-M %	.	.	.	14.3	10.5	9.3	9.1	9.0	9.0	.
Kyrgyzstan (FB) [1]				Registered unemployment - Chômage enregistré - Desempleo registrado						
Total	54.7	58.3	60.5	60.2	57.4	58.2	68.0	73.4	71.3	.
M-H	24.2	27.1	28.0	27.6	26.5	26.8	32.2	37.9	35.8	.
W-F-M	30.6	31.2	32.5	32.6	30.9	31.4	35.8	35.5	35.5	.
Liban (B) [1]				Total unemployment - Chômage total - Desempleo total						
Total	.	.	.	.	.	94.442	.	.	110.395	.
M-H	.	.	.	.	.	67.324	.	.	79.258	.
W-F-M	.	.	.	.	.	27.118	.	.	31.137	.
Total %	.	.	.	.	.	7.9	.	.	9.0	.
M-H %	.	.	.	.	.	7.3	.	.	8.6	.
W-F-M %	.	.	.	.	.	9.5	.	.	10.1	.
Macau, China (BA) [7]				Total unemployment - Chômage total - Desempleo total						
Total	13.2	14.2	14.0	13.7	13.1	11.2	10.3	10.4	9.5	10.1
M-H	9.1	9.8	9.5	9.1	8.3	6.8	5.8	5.6	5.6	5.7
W-F-M	4.2	4.4	4.5	4.6	4.8	4.4	4.5	4.8	3.9	4.3
Total %	6.3	6.8	6.4	6.3	6.0	4.9	4.1	3.8	3.1	3.0
M-H %	8.0	8.6	8.1	7.9	7.1	5.6	4.4	3.8	3.4	3.2
W-F-M %	4.4	4.6	4.4	4.5	4.7	4.0	3.8	3.8	2.7	2.8

Explanatory notes: see p. 451.

[1] Persons aged 15 years and over. [2] Prior to 2002: Special Labour Force Survey, february of each year. [3] 31st Dec. of each year. [4] Estimates based on the 2000 Population Census results. [5] June of each year. [6] Nov. of each year. [7] Persons aged 14 years and over.

Notes explicatives: voir p. 454.

[1] Personnes âgées de 15 ans et plus. [2] Avant 2002: Enquête spécial sur la main-d'oeuvre, février de chaque année. [3] 31 déc. de chaque année. [4] Estimations basées sur les résultats du Recensement de la population de 2000. [5] Juin de chaque année. [6] Nov. de chaque année. [7] Personnes âgées de 14 ans et plus.

Notas explicativas: véase p. 457.

[1] Personas de 15 años y más. [2] Antes de 2002: encuesta especial sobre la fuerza de trabajo, febrero de cada año. [3] 31 dic. de cada año. [4] Estimaciones basadas en los resultados del Censo de población de 2000. [5] Junio de cada año. [6] Nov. de cada año. [7] Personas de 14 años y más.

General level	Niveau général	Nivel general

	Thousands			Milliers				Millares		
	1999	2000	2001	2002	2003	2004	2005	2006	2007	2008
Malaysia (BA) [1]				Total unemployment - Chômage total - Desempleo total						
Total	313.7	286.9	342.4	343.5	369.8	366.6	368.1	353.6	351.4	368.5
M-H	212.3	182.7	212.3	210.5	235.8	224.7	230.4	224.9	216.4	223.5
W-F-M	101.4	104.2	130.1	133.1	134.0	142.0	137.7	128.7	135.0	145.0
Total %	3.4	3.0	3.5	3.5	3.6	3.5	3.5	3.3	3.2	3.3
M-H %	3.5	3.0	3.4	3.3	3.6	3.4	3.4	3.3	3.1	3.2
W-F-M %	3.3	3.1	3.8	3.8	3.6	3.8	3.7	3.4	3.4	3.7
Mongolia (E) [2][3]				Registered unemployment - Chômage enregistré - Desempleo registrado						
Total	39.8	38.6	40.3	30.9	33.3	35.6	32.9	32.9	29.9	29.8
M-H	18.1	17.8	18.5	14.1	15.3	15.9	14.6	14.2	12.9	17.6
W-F-M	21.6	20.7	21.9	16.8	18.1	19.6	18.3	18.7	17.0	12.2
Total %	4.7	4.6	4.6	3.5	3.5	3.6	3.3	3.2	2.8	2.8
M-H %	4.1	4.1	4.2	3.4	3.2	3.3	3.0	2.8	2.5	2.3
W-F-M %	5.3	5.0	5.1	3.8	3.8	3.9	3.6	3.5	3.2	3.2
Myanmar (FB) [4]				Registered unemployment - Chômage enregistré - Desempleo registrado						
Total	425.3	382.1	398.4	435.7	326.5	291.3	189.7	183.4	118.7	137.8
Pakistan (BA) [5][6]				Total unemployment - Chômage total - Desempleo total						
Total	2 334	3 127	3 181	3 506	3 594	3 499	3 566	3 103	2 680	.
M-H	1 419	2 046	2 082	2 381	2 441	2 461	2 508	2 166	1 807	.
W-F-M	915	1 081	1 099	1 125	1 153	1 038	1 058	937	873	.
Total %	5.9	7.8	7.8	8.3	8.3	7.7	7.7	6.2	5.3	.
M-H %	4.2	6.1	6.1	6.7	6.7	6.6	6.6	5.4	4.5	.
W-F-M %	15.0	17.3	17.3	16.5	16.5	12.8	12.8	6.2	8.4	.
Pakistan (FB) [7]				Work applicants - Demandeurs d'emploi - Solicitantes						
Total	217	469	477	493	505	576	587	420	.	.
M-H	190	421	428	442	453	477	486	360	.	.
W-F-M	27	48	49	51	52	99	101	60	.	.
Philippines (BA) [8]				Total unemployment - Chômage total - Desempleo total						
Total	3 017	3 459	3 653	3 874	3 936	4 249 |	2 748 [9]	2 829	2 653	2 716
M-H	1 852	2 113	2 174	2 295	2 343	2 558 |	1 685 [9]	1 798	1 675	1 714
W-F-M	1 165	1 346	1 478	1 579	1 592	1 692 |	1 062 [9]	1 031	978	1 002
Total %	9.8	11.2	11.1	11.4	11.4	11.8 |	7.8 [9]	8.0	7.3	7.4
M-H %	9.7	10.9	10.8	11.1	11.0	11.5 |	7.8 [9]	8.2	7.5	7.6
W-F-M %	10.0	11.6	11.6	11.8	11.9	12.4 |	7.8 [9]	7.6	7.0	7.1
Qatar (BA) [8][10]				Total unemployment - Chômage total - Desempleo total						
Total	.	.	12.615	.	.	.	.	.	4.303	.
M-H	.	.	6.137	.	.	.	.	.	1.569	.
W-F-M	.	.	6.478	.	.	.	.	.	2.734	.
Total %	.	.	3.9	.	.	.	.	.		
M-H %	.	.	2.3	.	.	.	.	.		
W-F-M %	.	.	12.6	.	.	.	.	.		
Saudi Arabia (BA) [8]				Total unemployment - Chômage total - Desempleo total						
Total	254.054	273.641	281.187	326.646	.	.	.	501.898 [11]	463.315	418.062
M-H	183.780	194.330	202.550	224.986	.	.	.	319.059 [11]	295.474	250.402
W-F-M	70.274	79.311	78.582	103.660	.	.	.	182.839 [11]	167.841	167.660
Total %	4.3	4.6	4.6	5.2	.	.	.	6.3 [11]	5.6	5.0
M-H %	3.7	3.8	3.9	4.2	.	.	.	4.7 [11]	4.2	3.5
W-F-M %	8.1	9.3	9.1	11.5	.	.	.	14.7 [11]	13.2	13.0
Singapore (BA) [12][13]				Total unemployment - Chômage total - Desempleo total						
Total	77.5	.	61.9	94.2	101.0	101.3	.	84.2	74.8	76.2
M-H	44.3	.	35.7	55.3	57.6	56.8	.	44.7	40.0	39.6
W-F-M	33.3	.	26.2	39.0	43.4	44.5	.	39.5	34.8	36.6
Total %	4.9	.	3.8	5.6	5.9	5.8	.	4.5	4.0	4.0
M-H %	4.6	.	3.7	5.6	5.7	5.6	.	4.1	3.7	3.6
W-F-M %	5.2	.	3.9	5.8	6.2	6.2	.	4.9	4.3	4.4
Singapore (FB) [14]				Registered unemployment - Chômage enregistré - Desempleo registrado						
Total	5.9	4.2	6.4	11.6	13.9 |	49.6 [15]	43.8 |	22.2 [15]	16.7	13.4
M-H	3.2	2.3	3.2	5.6	6.8 |	25.3 [15]	22.0 |	11.2 [15]	8.3	6.5
W-F-M	2.7	1.8	3.2	6.0	7.1 |	24.3 [15]	21.8 |	11.0 [15]	8.4	6.9

Explanatory notes: see p. 451.

[1] Persons aged 15 to 64 years. [2] Persons aged 16 years and over. [3] Dec. of each year. [4] Persons aged 18 years and over. [5] Persons aged 10 years and over. [6] Jan. [7] Persons aged 18 to 60 years. [8] Persons aged 15 years and over. [9] Definitions revised; data not strictly comparable. [10] March. [11] April. [12] The data refer to the residents (Singapore citizens and permanent residents) aged 15 years and over. [13] June. [14] Persons aged 14 years and over. [15] Methodology revised; data not strictly comparable.

Notes explicatives: voir p. 454.

[1] Personnes âgées de 15 à 64 ans. [2] Personnes âgées de 16 ans et plus. [3] Déc. de chaque année. [4] Personnes âgées de 18 ans et plus. [5] Personnes âgées de 10 ans et plus. [6] Janv. [7] Personnes âgées de 18 à 60 ans. [8] Personnes âgées de 15 ans et plus. [9] Définitions révisées; les données ne sont pas strictement comparables. [10] Mars. [11] Avril. [12] Les données se réfèrent aux résidents (citoyens de Singapour et résidents permanents) âgés de 15 ans et plus. [13] Juin. [14] Personnes âgées de 14 ans et plus. [15] Méthodologie révisée; les données ne sont pas strictement comparables.

Notas explicativas: véase p. 457.

[1] Personas de 15 a 64 años. [2] Personas de 16 años y más. [3] Dic. de cada año. [4] Personas de 18 años y más. [5] Personas de 10 años y más. [6] Enero. [7] Personas de 18 a 60 años. [8] Personas de 15 años y más. [9] Definiciones revisadas; los datos no son estrictamente comparables. [10] Marzo. [11] Abril. [12] Los datos se refieren a los residentes (ciudadanos de Singapur y residentes permanentes) de 15 años y más. [13] Junio. [14] Personas de 14 años y más. [15] Metodología revisada; los datos no son estrictamente comparables.

Thousands   Milliers   Millares

	1999	2000	2001	2002	2003	2004	2005	2006	2007	2008
Sri Lanka (BA) [1][2]				Total unemployment - Chômage total - Desempleo total						
Total	590.8	517.2	537.2	626.0	641.0 [3]	667.3 [4]	623.4 [5]	493.4	447.0	394.0
M-H	295.2	260.1	280.1	310.4	310.7 [3]	323.5 [4]	301.6 [5]	226.7	209.7	175.2
W-F-M	295.6	257.0	257.1	315.5	330.2 [3]	343.9 [4]	321.7 [5]	266.8	237.3	218.8
Total %	8.9	7.6	7.9	8.8	8.4 [3]	8.3 [4]	7.7 [5]	6.5	6.0	5.2
M-H %	6.7	5.8	6.2	6.6	6.0 [3]	6.0 [4]	5.5 [5]	4.7	4.3	3.6
W-F-M %	13.0	11.0	11.5	12.9	13.2 [3]	12.8 [4]	11.9 [5]	9.7	9.0	8.0
Syrian Arab Republic (BA) [6][7]				Total unemployment - Chômage total - Desempleo total						
Total	.	.	613.4	637.8 [8]	512.9 [9]	.	.	.	454.8	
M-H	.	.	348.4	355.8 [8]	311.6 [9]	.	.	.	237.3	
W-F-M	.	.	265.0	282.0 [8]	201.3 [9]	.	.	.	217.5	
Total %	.	.	11.2	11.7 [8]	10.3 [9]	.	.	.	8.4	
M-H %	.	.	8.0	8.3 [8]	7.6 [9]	.	.	.	5.2	
W-F-M %	.	.	23.9	24.1 [8]	20.9 [9]	.	.	.	25.7	
Taiwan, China (BA) [6]				Total unemployment - Chômage total - Desempleo total						
Total	283	293	450	515	503	454	428	411	419	450
M-H	188	197	302	348	326	288	259	245	248	271
W-F-M	95	96	148	167	177	166	169	166	171	179
Total %	2.9	3.0	4.6	5.2	5.0	4.4	4.1	3.9	3.9	4.1
M-H %	3.2	3.4	5.2	5.9	5.5	4.8	4.3	4.1	4.1	4.4
W-F-M %	2.5	2.4	3.7	4.1	4.3	3.9	3.9	3.7	3.7	3.8
Tajikistan (FB) [6]				Registered unemployment - Chômage enregistré - Desempleo registrado						
Total	49.7	43.2	42.9	46.7	42.9	38.8	43.8	46.5	51.7	.
M-H	23.4	20.4	20.2	21.0	19.7	16.9	19.8	21.2	23.4	.
W-F-M	26.3	22.8	22.7	25.7	23.2	21.9	23.8	25.3	28.3	.
Total %	3.0	2.7	2.3	2.5	2.4	2.0	2.0	2.2	2.5	.
Thailand (BA) [6][10]				Total unemployment - Chômage total - Desempleo total						
Total	985.7	812.6	896.3 [11]	616.3	543.7	548.9	495.8	449.9	442.2	450.9
M-H	546.4	454.5	511.2 [11]	372.1	314.7	324.2	289.9	259.7	258.1	268.1
W-F-M	439.3	358.0	385.1 [11]	244.2	229.0	224.7	206.0	190.2	184.1	182.8
Total %	3.0	2.4	2.6 [11]	1.8	1.5	1.5	1.4	1.2	1.2	1.2
M-H %	3.0	2.4	2.7 [11]	2.0	1.6	1.6	1.5	1.3	1.3	1.3
W-F-M %	3.0	2.3	2.5 [11]	1.6	1.4	1.4	1.2	1.1	1.1	1.0
United Arab Emirates (BA) [6][12]				Total unemployment - Chômage total - Desempleo total						
Total	.	.	.	.	.	.	.	.	.	77.108
M-H	.	.	.	.	.	.	.	.	.	30.254
W-F-M	.	.	.	.	.	.	.	.	.	46.854
Total %	.	.	.	.	.	.	.	.	.	4.009
M-H %	.	.	.	.	.	.	.	.	.	1.975
W-F-M %	.	.	.	.	.	.	.	.	.	11.958
Uzbekistan (FB) [6]				Work applicants - Demandeurs d'emploi - Solicitantes						
Total	.	35.4	37.5	35.0	32.0	34.9	27.7	.	.	.
Total %	.	0.4	0.4	.	.	0.4	0.3	.	.	.
Viet Nam (BA) [6][13]				Total unemployment - Chômage total - Desempleo total						
Total	908.9	885.7	1 107.4	871.0	949.0	926.4	.	.	.	.
M-H	438.6	468.0	457.9	398.0	402.4	409.8	.	.	.	.
W-F-M	470.3	417.7	649.6	473.0	546.6	516.6	.	.	.	.
Total %	2.3	2.3	2.8	2.1	2.3	2.1	.	.	.	.
M-H %	2.3	2.4	2.3	1.9	1.9	1.9	.	.	.	.
W-F-M %	2.1	2.1	3.3	2.3	2.6	2.4	.	.	.	.
West Bank and Gaza Strip (BA) [1]				Total unemployment - Chômage total - Desempleo total						
Total	79.000	98.836	170.544 [14]	217.532	194.321	212.157	194.458	206.150	183.689	227.990
M-H	66.101	85.399	158.016 [14]	201.518	172.224	185.786	164.569	175.153	153.676	190.126
W-F-M	12.899	13.437	12.528 [14]	16.014	22.097	26.371	30.088	30.997	30.013	37.866
Total %	11.8	14.1	25.2 [14]	31.2	25.4	26.7	23.3	23.2	21.3	25.7
M-H %	11.6	14.4	26.9 [14]	33.5	26.7	28.0	23.6	23.9	21.8	26.2
W-F-M %	13.0	12.3	14.0 [14]	17.0	18.4	20.0	22.1	20.1	18.7	23.5

EUROPE-EUROPE-EUROPA

	1999	2000	2001	2002	2003	2004	2005	2006	2007	2008
Albania (FB) [6][15]				Registered unemployment - Chômage enregistré - Desempleo registrado						
Total	240	215	181	172	163	157	153	150	.	.
M-H	130	113	96	91	86	82	79	77	.	.
W-F-M	110	102	85	81	77	75	74	73	.	.
Total %	18.4	16.8	16.4	15.8	15.0	14.4	14.1	13.8	.	.
M-H %	16.4	14.9	14.2	13.6	12.9	12.4	12.1	11.8	.	.
W-F-M %	21.4	19.3	19.9	19.1	18.2	17.5	17.2	16.8	.	.

Explanatory notes: see p. 451.

[1] Persons aged 10 years and over. [2] Excl. Northern and Eastern provinces. [3] Excl. Northern province. [4] Excl. Mullativu and Killinochchi districts. [5] Whole country. [6] Persons aged 15 years and over. [7] Sep. of each year. [8] Prior to 2001: persons aged 10 years and over. [9] Methodology revised; data not strictly comparable. [10] Third quarter. [11] Prior to 2001: persons aged 13 years and over [12] February. [13] July of each year. [14] Prior to 2001: persons aged 15 years and over. [15] Dec. of each year.

Notes explicatives: voir p. 454.

[1] Personnes âgées de 10 ans et plus. [2] Non compris les provinces du Nord et de l'Est. [3] Non compris la province du Nord. [4] Non compris les provinces de Mullativu et Killinochchi. [5] Ensemble du pays. [6] Personnes âgées de 15 ans et plus. [7] Sept. de chaque année. [8] Avant 2001: personnes agées de 10 ans et plus. [9] Méthodologie révisée; les données ne sont pas strictement comparables. [10] Troisième trimestre. [11] Avant 2001: personnes agées de 13 ans et pl us. [12] Février. [13] Juillet de chaque année. [14] Avant 2001: personnes agées de 15 ans et plus. [15] Déc. de chaque année.

Notas explicativas: véase p. 457.

[1] Personas de 10 años y más. [2] Excl. las provincias del Norte y del Este. [3] Excl. la provincia del Norte. [4] Excl. las provincias de Mullativu y Killinocchchi. [5] Todo el país. [6] Personas de 15 años y más. [7] Sept. de cada año. [8] Antes de 2001: personas de 10 años y más. [9] Metodología revisada; los datos no son estrictamente comparables. [10] Tercer trimestre. [11] Antes de 2001: personas de 13 años y más. [12] Febrero. [13] Julio de cada año. [14] Antes de 2001: personas de 15 años y más. [15] Dic. de cada año.

	Thousands			Milliers				Millares		
	1999	2000	2001	2002	2003	2004	2005	2006	2007	2008
Austria (BA) [1]				Total unemployment - Chômage total - Desempleo total						
Total	146.7	138.8	142.5	161.0	168.8 [2]	194.6 [3]	207.7	195.6	185.6	162.3
M-H	81.7	73.8	77.0	91.7	94.7 [2]	98.0 [3]	107.8	97.1	89.7	81.8
W-F-M	65.0	65.0	65.5	69.3	74.3 [2]	96.6 [3]	100.0	98.5	95.8	80.5
Total %	3.8	3.6	3.6	4.0	4.3 [2]	4.9 [3]	5.2	4.7	4.4	3.8
M-H %	3.7	3.3	3.5	4.1	4.3 [2]	4.5 [3]	4.9	4.3	3.9	3.6
W-F-M %	3.9	3.8	3.8	3.9	4.2 [2]	5.4 [3]	5.5	5.2	5.0	4.1
Austria (FB) [1]				Registered unemployment - Chômage enregistré - Desempleo registrado						
Total	221.7	194.3	203.9	232.4	240.1	243.9	252.7	239.2	222.2	212.3
M-H	121.5	107.5	115.3	134.4	139.7	140.2	144.2	135.8	124.3	118.8
W-F-M	100.2	86.8	88.6	98.0	100.4	103.6	108.4	103.4	97.9	93.4
Total %	6.7	5.8	6.1	6.9	7.0	7.1	7.3	6.8	6.2	5.8
M-H %	6.5	5.8	6.2	7.2	7.5	7.5	7.7	7.1	6.5	6.1
W-F-M %	6.9	5.9	5.9	6.4	6.5	6.6	6.8	6.4	6.0	5.6
Belarus (FB) [4] [5]				Registered unemployment - Chômage enregistré - Desempleo registrado						
Total	95.4	95.8	102.9	130.5	136.1	83.0	67.9	52.0	44.1	37.3
M-H	34.2	37.6	40.9	47.8	46.1	25.5	21.1	17.7	15.2	14.7
W-F-M	61.2	58.2	62.0	82.7	90.0	57.5	46.8	34.3	28.9	22.6
Total %	2.1	2.1	2.3	3.0	3.1	1.9	1.5	1.2	1.0	0.8
M-H %	1.6	1.7	1.9	2.3	1.2	1.2	1.0	0.8	0.7	0.7
W-F-M %	2.6	2.4	2.6	3.5	3.9	2.4	2.0	1.5	1.2	0.9
Belgique (BA) [1]				Total unemployment - Chômage total - Desempleo total						
Total	375.2 [6]	308.5	286.4	332.1	364.3	380.3	390.3	383.2	353.0	333.7
M-H	179.4 [6]	144.6	147.9	168.1	193.0	191.4	196.0	191.0	174.4	170.4
W-F-M	195.8 [6]	163.9	138.4	164.0	171.3	188.9	194.3	192.2	178.6	163.2
Total %	8.6 [6]	7.0	6.6	7.5	8.2	8.5	8.5	8.3	7.5	7.0
M-H %	7.2 [6]	5.8	6.0	6.7	7.7	7.6	7.7	7.5	6.7	6.5
W-F-M %	10.4 [6]	8.7	7.5	8.7	8.9	9.6	9.6	9.4	8.5	7.6
Bosnia and Herzegovina (BA) [1]				Total unemployment - Chômage total - Desempleo total						
Total	.	.	.	.	.	.	.	366	347	272
M-H	.	.	.	.	.	.	.	215	203	156
W-F-M	.	.	.	.	.	.	.	151	144	116
Total %	.	.	.	.	.	.	.	31.1	29.0	23.4
M-H %	.	.	.	.	.	.	.	28.9	26.7	21.4
W-F-M %	.	.	.	.	.	.	.	34.9	32.9	26.8
Bulgaria (BA) [7]				Total unemployment - Chômage total - Desempleo total						
Total	486.7 [8]	559.0 [8]	661.1 [8]	599.2 [8]	449.1	399.8	334.2	305.7	240.2	199.7
M-H	258.6 [8]	306.3 [8]	363.2 [8]	328.7 [8]	246.1	221.6	182.5	156.4	120.7	103.9
W-F-M	228.1 [8]	252.6 [8]	297.8 [8]	270.4 [8]	203.0	178.2	151.6	149.3	119.5	95.8
Total %	14.1 [8]	16.3 [8]	19.4 [8]	17.6 [8]	13.7	12.0	10.1	9.0	6.9	5.6
M-H %	14.0 [8]	16.7 [8]	20.2 [8]	18.3 [8]	14.1	12.5	10.3	8.6	6.5	5.5
W-F-M %	14.1 [8]	15.9 [8]	18.4 [8]	16.9 [8]	13.2	11.5	9.8	9.3	7.3	5.8
Bulgaria (FB) [5] [9]				Registered unemployment - Chômage enregistré - Desempleo registrado						
Total	610.6	682.8	662.3	602.5	500.7	450.6	397.3	337.8	255.9	232.3
M-H	284.5	323.4	321.1	281.1	227.1	201.6	171.8	140.0	100.0	86.7
W-F-M	326.1	359.4	341.2	321.5	273.6	249.0	225.5	197.8	156.0	145.6
Total %	16.0	17.9	17.3	16.3	13.5	12.2	10.7	9.1	6.9	6.3
Croatia (BA) [1]				Total unemployment - Chômage total - Desempleo total						
Total	234.0	297.2	276.2	265.8	255.7	249.7	229.1	198.7	171.0	149.2
M-H	117.4	149.8	134.8	129.7	127.7	120.0	114.4	94.4	81.6	67.9
W-F-M	116.6	147.4	141.4	136.0	128.1	129.7	114.7	104.2	89.4	81.3
Total %	13.5	16.1	15.8	14.8	14.3	13.8	12.7	11.1	9.6	8.4
M-H %	12.8	15.0	14.2	13.4	13.1	12.0	11.7	9.8	8.3	7.0
W-F-M %	14.5	17.3	17.9	16.6	15.7	15.7	14.0	12.7	11.1	10.0
Croatia (FB) [10]				Registered unemployment - Chômage enregistré - Desempleo registrado						
Total	322	358	380	390	330	310	309	292	264	237
M-H	153	169	177	177	140	129	128	117	102	90
W-F-M	169	189	203	213	190	181	181	175	162	147
Total %	19.1	21.1	22.0	22.3	19.2	18.0	17.9	16.6	14.8	.
M-H %	17.2	19.0	19.5	19.3	15.5	14.3	14.1	12.6	11.0	.
W-F-M %	21.2	23.4	24.7	25.6	23.2	22.2	22.0	20.9	19.1	.
Cyprus (BA) [1] [11]				Total unemployment - Chômage total - Desempleo total						
Total	16.9	14.5	12.8	10.8	14.1	16.7	19.5	17.0	15.4	14.5
M-H	7.7	5.5	4.8	4.7	7.1	7.0	9.0	8.0	7.3	7.0
W-F-M	9.1	8.9	8.1	6.0	7.0	9.7	10.4	9.0	8.1	7.6
Total %	5.7	4.9	4.0	3.3	4.1	4.7	5.3	4.5	3.9	3.7
M-H %	4.3	3.2	2.6	2.6	3.8	3.5	4.4	3.9	3.4	3.2
W-F-M %	7.9	7.4	5.7	4.2	4.6	6.2	6.5	5.4	4.6	4.2

Explanatory notes: see p. 451.

[1] Persons aged 15 years and over. [2] Prior to 2003: May and November of each year. [3] Methodology revised; data not strictly comparable. [4] Men aged 16 to 59 years; women aged 16 to 54 years. [5] Dec. of each year. [6] Prior to 1999: April of each year. [7] Persons aged 15 to 74 years. [8] June. [9] Men aged 16 to 60 years; women aged 16 to 55 years. After 1999, age limits vary according to the year. [10] 31st Dec. of each year. [11] Government-controlled area.

Notes explicatives: voir p. 454.

[1] Personnes âgées de 15 ans et plus. [2] Avant 2003: mai et novembre de chaque année. [3] Méthodologie révisée; les données ne sont pas strictement comparables. [4] Hommes âgés de 16 à 59 ans; femmes âgées de 16 à 54 ans. [5] Déc. de chaque année. [6] Avant 1999: avril de chaque année. [7] Personnes âgées de 15 à 74 ans. [8] Juin. [9] Hommes âgés de 16 à 60 ans; femmes âgées de 16 à 55 ans. Après 1999, les limites d'âge varient selon l'année. [10] 31 déc. de chaque année. [11] Région sous contrôle gouvernemental.

Notas explicativas: véase p. 457.

[1] Personas de 15 años y más. [2] Antes de 2003: mayo y noviembre de cada año. [3] Metodología revisada; los datos no son estrictamente comparables. [4] Hombres de 16 a 59 años; mujeres de 16 a 54 años. [5] Dic. de cada año. [6] Antes de 1999: abril de cada año. [7] Personas de 15 a 74 años. [8] Junio. [9] Hombres de 16 a 60 años; mujeres de 16 a 55 años. Después de 1999, los límites de edad varían según el año. [10] 31 dic. de cada año. [11] Area controlada por el gobierno.

3A

UNEMPLOYMENT	CHÔMAGE	DESEMPLEO
General level	Niveau général	Nivel general

	Thousands				Milliers				Millares	
	1999	2000	2001	2002	2003	2004	2005	2006	2007	2008

Cyprus (FB) [1] [2] — Registered unemployment - Chômage enregistré - Desempleo registrado

	1999	2000	2001	2002	2003	2004	2005	2006	2007	2008
Total	11.375	10.934	9.546	10.561	11.961	12.650	13.153	12.824	12.017	11.541
M-H	5.580	5.266	4.535	4.692	5.113	5.415	5.819	5.737	5.210	4.929
W-F-M	5.795	5.668	5.011	5.869	6.848	7.235	7.334	7.087	6.808	6.612
Total %	3.6	3.4	2.9	3.2	3.5	3.6	3.7			
M-H %	2.9	2.7	2.3	2.3	2.5	2.6	2.9			
W-F-M %	4.8	4.4	3.8	4.3	5.0	5.1	4.7			

Czech Republic (BA) [2] — Total unemployment - Chômage total - Desempleo total

	1999	2000	2001	2002	2003	2004	2005	2006	2007	2008
Total	454	455	418	374	399	426	410	371	276	230
M-H	211	212	193	169	175	201	187	169	124	103
W-F-M	243	243	225	205	224	225	223	202	153	127
Total %	8.7	8.8	8.1	7.3	7.8	8.3	7.9	7.1	5.3	4.4
M-H %	7.3	7.3	6.8	5.9	6.1	7.0	6.5	5.8	4.2	3.5
W-F-M %	10.5	10.6	9.9	9.0	9.9	9.9	9.8	8.8	6.7	5.6

Czech Republic (FB) [3] — Registered unemployment - Chômage enregistré - Desempleo registrado

	1999	2000	2001	2002	2003	2004	2005	2006	2007	2008
Total	488	457	462	514	542	542	510	449	355	352
M-H	240	227	230	257	270	266	244	210	164	168
W-F-M	248	230	232	257	272	276	266	239	191	184
Total %	9.4	8.8	8.9	9.8	10.3	9.5	8.9	7.7	6.0	6.0
M-H %	8.2	7.8	7.9	8.7	9.2	8.3	7.6	6.4	4.9	5.0
W-F-M %	10.8	10.0	10.1	11.2	11.8	10.9	10.5	9.3	7.4	7.2

Denmark (BA) [4] — Total unemployment - Chômage total - Desempleo total

	1999	2000	2001	2002	2003	2004	2005	2006	2007	2008
Total	158.000	131.074	137.000	134.026	157.559	162.559	143.296	117.896	114.539	98.380
M-H	71.000	61.246	66.000	66.021	75.740	79.867	69.433	53.421	55.079	47.077
W-F-M	87.000	69.828	71.000	68.005	81.825	82.686	73.863	64.475	59.460	51.303
Total %	5.5	4.6	4.8	4.7	5.5	5.6	5.0	4.1	4.0	3.4
M-H %	4.8	4.0	4.4	4.4	5.0	5.2	4.6	3.5	3.6	3.0
W-F-M %	6.5	5.2	5.3	5.1	6.2	6.1	5.5	4.7	4.4	3.7

Denmark (FB) [5] — Registered unemployment - Chômage enregistré - Desempleo registrado

	1999	2000	2001	2002	2003	2004	2005	2006	2007	2008
Total	.	.	130.578 [6]	132.971	159.112	160.403	140.162	108.422 [7]	77.168	51.721 [6]
M-H	.	.	61.074 [6]	64.388	78.594	77.621	65.591	48.281 [7]	33.774	25.795 [6]
W-F-M	.	.	69.504 [6]	68.583	80.519	82.782	74.572	60.142 [7]	43.394	25.925 [6]
Total %	.	.	4.7 [6]	4.8	5.8	5.8	5.1	3.9 [7]	2.8	1.8 [6]
M-H %	.	.	4.1 [6]	4.4	5.4	5.4	4.5	3.3 [7]	2.3	1.8 [6]
W-F-M %	.	.	5.2 [6]	5.2	6.1	6.3	5.7	4.5 [7]	3.2	1.9 [6]

España (BA) [8] — Total unemployment - Chômage total - Desempleo total

	1999	2000	2001	2002	2003	2004	2005	2006	2007	2008
Total	2 722.2	2 496.4	1 904.4 [9]	2 155.3	2 242.2	2 213.6	1 912.5	1 837.1	1 833.9	2 590.6
M-H	1 158.3	1 037.4	828.1 [9]	929.3	976.4	970.8	862.9	791.5	815.2	1 311.0
W-F-M	1 563.9	1 458.9	1 076.3 [9]	1 226.0	1 265.8	1 242.8	1 049.6 [9]	1 045.6	1 018.7	1 279.6
Total %	15.6	13.9	10.6 [9]	11.5	11.5	11.0	9.2 [9]	8.5	8.3	11.3
M-H %	10.9	9.6	7.5 [9]	8.2	8.4	8.2	7.0 [9]	6.3	6.4	10.1
W-F-M %	22.9	20.4	15.2 [9]	16.4	16.0	15.0	12.2 [9]	11.6	10.9	13.0

España (FB) [10] — Registered unemployment - Chômage enregistré - Desempleo registrado

	1999	2000	2001	2002	2003	2004	2005	2006	2007	2008
Total	2 085.2	1 963.5	1 930.2 [9]	2 049.6	2 096.9	2 113.7	2 069.9 [9]	2 039.4	2 039.0	2 539.9
M-H	871.3	789.7	771.5 [9]	836.7	851.1	854.3	818.0 [9]	788.2	791.8	1 146.9
W-F-M	1 213.9	1 173.8	1 158.7 [9]	1 212.9	1 245.8	1 259.4	1 251.8 [9]	1 251.2	1 247.2	1 393.0
Total %	12.0	10.9	10.7 [9]	10.9	10.7	10.5	9.9 [9]	9.4	9.2	11.1
M-H %	8.2	7.3	7.0 [9]	7.4	7.3	7.2	6.7 [9]	6.3	6.2	8.8
W-F-M %	17.8	16.4	16.4 [9]	16.2	15.8	15.2	14.5 [9]	13.8	13.3	14.2

Estonia (BA) [11] — Total unemployment - Chômage total - Desempleo total

	1999	2000	2001	2002	2003	2004	2005	2006	2007	2008
Total	80.5	89.9 [12]	83.1	67.2	66.2	63.6	52.2	40.5	32.0	38.4
M-H	45.7	49.5 [12]	43.7	36.1	34.2	34.7	28.9	21.3	18.9	20.2
W-F-M	34.8	40.5 [12]	39.3	31.0	32.0	28.9	23.3	19.2	13.1	18.1
Total %	12.2	13.6 [12]	12.6	10.3	10.0	9.7	7.9	5.9	4.7	5.5
M-H %	13.4	14.5 [12]	12.9	10.8	10.2	10.4	8.8	6.2	5.4	5.8
W-F-M %	10.9	12.6 [12]	12.2	9.7	9.9	8.9	7.1	5.6	3.9	5.3

Finland (BA) [11] — Total unemployment - Chômage total - Desempleo total

	1999	2000	2001	2002	2003	2004	2005	2006	2007	2008
Total	261	253	238	237	235	229	220	204	183	172 [9]
M-H	130	122	117	123	124	118	111	101	90	85 [9]
W-F-M	131	131	121	114	111	111	109	103	93	87 [9]
Total %	10.1	9.7	9.1	9.1	9.0	8.8	8.3	7.7	6.8	6.4 [9]
M-H %	9.6	8.9	8.6	9.1	9.2	8.7	8.1	7.4	6.4	6.1 [9]
W-F-M %	10.7	10.6	9.7	9.1	8.9	8.9	8.6	8.1	7.2	6.7 [9]

Explanatory notes: see p. 451.

[1] Government-controlled area. [2] Persons aged 15 years and over. [3] Dec. of each year. [4] Persons aged 15 to 66 years. [5] Persons aged 16 to 66 years. [6] Methodology revised. [7] Beginning 1 July 2006, Persons aged 16 to 64. [8] Persons aged 16 to 74 years. [9] Methodology revised; data not strictly comparable. [10] Persons aged 16 to 64 years. [11] Persons aged 15 to 74 years. [12] Prior to 2000: second quarter of each year.

Notes explicatives: voir p. 454.

[1] Région sous contrôle gouvernemental. [2] Personnes âgées de 15 ans et plus. [3] Déc. de chaque année. [4] Personnes âgées de 15 à 66 ans. [5] Personnes âgées de 16 à 66 ans. [6] Méthodologie révisée. [7] A partir 1 juillet 2006, personnes âgées de 16 à 64 ans. [8] Personnes âgées de 16 à 74 ans. [9] Méthodologie révisée; les données ne sont pas strictement comparables. [10] Personnes âgées de 16 à 64 ans. [11] Personnes âgées de 15 à 74 ans. [12] Avant 2000: deuxième trimestre de chaque année.

Notas explicativas: véase p. 457.

[1] Area controlada por el gobierno. [2] Personas de 15 años y más. [3] Dic. de cada año. [4] Personas de 15 a 66 años. [5] Personas de 16 a 66 años. [6] Metodología revisada. [7] Desde el 1 de julio 2006, personas de 16 a 644 años. [8] Personas de 16 a 74 años. [9] Metodología revisada; los datos no son estrictamente comparables. [10] Personas de 16 a 64 años. [11] Personas de 15 a 74 años. [12] Antes de 2000: segundo trimestre de cada año.

	Thousands			Milliers				Millares		
	1999	2000	2001	2002	2003	2004	2005	2006	2007	2008

Finland (FB) [1] [2] [3] Registered unemployment - Chômage enregistré - Desempleo registrado

Total	337	321	302	294	288	288	275	250	217	204
M-H	169	162	153	154	153	152	144	129	111	108
W-F-M	168	159	149	140	135	136	131	120	106	96

France (BA) [2] Total unemployment - Chômage total - Desempleo total

Total	2 630 [4]	2 265	2 075	2 137	2 295 [5]	2 408	2 429	2 435	2 222	2 070
M-H	1 245 [4]	1 037	938	1 024	1 097 [5]	1 153	1 163	1 175	1 092	1 018
W-F-M	1 385 [4]	1 228	1 137	1 113	1 198 [5]	1 255	1 266	1 260	1 130	1 053
Total %	10.0 [4]	8.5	7.8	7.9	8.5 [5]	8.9	8.9	8.8	8.0	7.4
M-H %	8.8 [4]	7.3	6.5	7.1	7.6 [5]	8.0	8.0	8.1	7.5	6.9
W-F-M %	11.5 [4]	10.1	9.2	8.9	9.5 [5]	9.8	9.8	9.7	8.6	7.9

France (E) [2] Total unemployment - Chômage total - Desempleo total

Total	2 647	2 281	2 088	2 151	2 321	2 434	2 452	2 455	2 236	.
M-H	1 255	1 047	948	1 038	1 119	1 177	1 188	1 201	1 110	.
W-F-M	1 392	1 233	1 140	1 113	1 202	1 258	1 264	1 254	1 126	.
Total %	10.1	8.6	7.9	8.0	8.6	9.0	9.0	8.9	8.2	.
M-H %	8.8	7.3	6.6	7.2	7.7	8.1	8.1	8.2	7.6	.
W-F-M %	11.7	10.2	9.4	9.0	9.6	10.0	9.9	9.7	8.7	.

France (FB) [6] Registered unemployment - Chômage enregistré - Desempleo registrado

Total	2 825.6	2 446.7	2 479.8	2 589.3	2 718.2	2 702.8	2 563.5	2 260.5	2 015.0	.
M-H	1 276.2	1 085.3	1 150.6	1 246.0	1 324.9	1 314.6	1 239.6	1 099.2	979.0	.
W-F-M	1 549.4	1 361.4	1 329.2	1 343.3	1 393.3	1 388.2	1 323.9	1 161.3	1 037.0	.

Germany (BA) [2] Total unemployment - Chômage total - Desempleo total

Total	3 503	3 127 [7]	3 150	3 486 [8]	4 023 [7]	4 388 [9]|	4 583 [10]	4 279	3 608	3 141
M-H	1 905	1 691 [7]	1 754	1 982 [8]	2 316 [7]	2 551 [9]|	2 574 [10]	2 358	1 944	1 690
W-F-M	1 598	1 436 [7]	1 396	1 504 [8]	1 707 [7]	1 836 [9]|	2 009 [10]	1 921	1 664	1 451
Total %	8.8	7.9 [7]	7.9	8.7 [8]	10.0 [7]	11.0 [9]|	11.1 [10]	10.3	8.6	7.5
M-H %	8.4	7.6 [7]	7.8	8.9 [8]	10.4 [7]	11.5 [9]|	11.3 [10]	10.3	8.5	7.4
W-F-M %	9.2	8.3 [7]	7.9	8.5 [8]	9.5 [7]	10.3 [9]|	10.9 [10]	10.2	8.8	7.6

Germany (FB) [11] [12] Registered unemployment - Chômage enregistré - Desempleo registrado

Total	4 101	3 890	3 853	4 061	4 377		4 381 [10]	4 861	4 487	3 776	3 268
M-H	2 161	2 053	2 064	2 240	2 446		2 449 [10]	2 606	2 338	1 900	1 668
W-F-M	1 940	1 836	1 789	1 821	1 931		1 932 [10]	2 255	2 149	1 873	1 600
Total %	11.7	10.7	10.4	10.8	11.6		11.7 [10]	13.0	12.0	10.1	8.7
M-H %	11.3	10.5	10.4	11.3	12.4		12.5 [10]	13.4	12.0	9.8	8.6
W-F-M %	12.2	10.9	10.2	10.3	10.8		10.8 [10]	12.7	12.0	10.4	8.9

Gibraltar (FB) [13] Registered unemployment - Chômage enregistré - Desempleo registrado

Total	0.4	0.4	0.4	0.5	0.5	0.4	0.5	0.5	0.5	0.5
M-H	0.3	0.3	0.2	0.3	0.3	0.3	0.3	0.3	0.3	0.3
W-F-M	0.1	0.1	0.2	0.2	0.2	0.2	0.2	0.2	0.2	0.2

Greece (BA) [2] [14] Total unemployment - Chômage total - Desempleo total

Total	543.3	519.3	478.4	462.1	441.8	492.7	466.7	427.4	398.0	357.1
M-H	212.8	207.2	191.4	180.5	170.8	181.7	166.8	160.9	144.0	136.6
W-F-M	330.5	312.1	287.0	281.6	271.0	311.0	299.9	266.5	254.0	220.5
Total %	11.9	11.2	10.4	9.9	9.3	10.2	9.6	8.8	8.1	7.2
M-H %	7.7	7.4	6.9	6.4	6.0	6.3	5.8	5.6	5.0	4.6
W-F-M %	18.2	17.0	15.9	15.2	14.3	15.9	15.2	13.4	12.6	10.9

Hungary (BA) [15] Total unemployment - Chômage total - Desempleo total

Total	284.7	262.5	232.9	238.8 [16]	244.5	252.9	303.9	316.8	311.9	329.2
M-H	170.7	159.5	142.7	138.0 [16]	138.5	136.8	159.1	164.6	164.2	174.3
W-F-M	114.0	103.0	90.2	100.8 [16]	106.0	116.1	144.8	152.2	147.7	154.9
Total %	7.0	6.4	5.7	5.8 [16]	5.7	6.1	7.2	7.5	7.4	7.8
M-H %	7.5	7.0	6.3	6.1 [16]	6.1	6.1	7.0	7.2	7.1	7.6
W-F-M %	6.3	5.6	5.0	5.4 [16]	5.3	6.1	7.5	7.8	7.6	8.1

Hungary (FB) [17] Registered unemployment - Chômage enregistré - Desempleo registrado

Total	404.5	372.4	342.8	344.9	359.9	400.6	410.6	403.4	445.0	477.4
M-H	220.1	202.2	188.7	186.8	189.4	209.6	213.7	210.1	232.7	250.9
W-F-M	184.4	170.2	154.1	158.1	170.5	191.0	197.0	193.3	212.3	226.5
Total %	9.6	.	.	.	8.4	.	.	.	.	.
M-H %	.	.	.	.	7.9	.	.	.	.	.
W-F-M %	.	.	.	.	8.9	.	.	.	.	.

Explanatory notes: see p. 451.

[1] Excl. persons temporarily laid off. [2] Persons aged 15 years and over. [3] Beginning 1980: excl. elderly unemployment pensioners no longer seeking work. [4] Jan. [5] Prior to 2003: March of each year. [6] Persons aged 16 years and over. [7] May. [8] Prior to 2002: April of each year. [9] March. [10] Methodology revised; data not strictly comparable. [11] 1997-2007: Due to methodology revised, total may not equal sum of components. [12] Persons aged 15 to 64 years. [13] Persons aged 15 to 65 years. [14] Second quarter of each year. [15] Persons aged 15 to 74 years. [16] Estimates based on the 2001 Population Census results. [17] Dec. of each year.

Notes explicatives: voir p. 454.

[1] Non compris les personnes temporairement mises à pied. [2] Personnes âgées de 15 ans et plus. [3] A partir de 1980: non compris les chômeurs indemnisés âgés ne recherchant plus de travail. [4] Janv. [5] Avant 2003: mars de chaque année. [6] Personnes âgées de 16 ans et plus. [7] Mai. [8] Avant 2002: avril de chaque année. [9] Mars. [10] Méthodologie révisée; les données ne sont pas strictement comparables. [11] 1997-2007: En raison des changements méthodologiques, le total peut différer de la somme des composantes. [12] Personnes âgées de 15 à 64 ans. [13] Personnes âgées de 15 à 65 ans. [14] Deuxième trimestre de chaque année. [15] Personnes âgées de 15 à 74 ans. [16] Estimations basées sur les résultats du Recensement de la population de 2001. [17] Déc. de chaque année.

Notas explicativas: véase p. 457.

[1] Excl. las personas temporalmente despedidas. [2] Personas de 15 años y más. [3] A partir de 1980: excl. los desocupados subsidiados de mayor edad que ya no buscan trabajo. [4] Enero. [5] Antes de 2003: marzo de cada año. [6] Personas de 16 años y más. [7] Mayo. [8] Antes del 2002: abril de cada año. [9] Marzo. [10] Metodología revisada; los datos no son estrictamente comparables. [11] 1997-2007: Debido a cambios en la metodología, el total puede diferir de la suma de sus componentes. [12] Personas de 15 a 64 años. [13] Personas de 15 a 65 años. [15] Personas de 15 a 74 años. [16] Estimaciones basadas en los resultados del Censo de población de 2001. [17] Dic. de cada año.

UNEMPLOYMENT CHÔMAGE DESEMPLEO

General level Niveau général Nivel general

	Thousands				Milliers				Millares	
	1999	2000	2001	2002	2003	2004	2005	2006	2007	2008
Iceland (BA) [1]				Total unemployment - Chômage total - Desempleo total						
Total	3.1	3.7	3.7	5.3	5.4	4.9	4.3	5.0	4.2	5.5
M-H	1.2	1.5	1.8	3.1	3.1	2.7	2.3	2.6	2.3	3.3
W-F-M	1.9	2.2	1.9	2.2	2.4	2.2	2.0	2.4	1.9	2.2
Total %	2.0	2.3	2.3	3.3	3.4	3.1	2.6	2.9	2.3	3.0
M-H %	1.5	1.8	2.0	3.6	3.6	2.9	2.6	2.7	2.3	3.3
W-F-M %	2.6	2.9	2.5	2.9	3.1	2.9	2.6	3.1	2.3	2.6
Ireland (BA) [2][3]				Total unemployment - Chômage total - Desempleo total						
Total	96.9	74.9	65.4	77.1	82.6	84.6	86.5	92.6	100.3	115.5
M-H	59.4	44.9	39.8	48.8	51.9	54.6	53.7	55.9	60.0	78.0
W-F-M	37.5	30.0	25.6	28.4	30.6	30.0	32.9	36.7	40.3	37.5
Total %	5.7	4.3	3.7	4.2	4.4	4.4	4.2	4.6	4.6	5.2
M-H %	5.9	4.3	3.8	4.5	4.8	4.9	4.6	4.5	4.8	6.2
W-F-M %	5.5	4.2	3.5	3.7	3.9	3.8	3.8	4.0	4.3	3.9
Ireland (FB) [4]				Registered unemployment - Chômage enregistré - Desempleo registrado						
Total	193.2	155.4	142.3	162.5	172.4	166.0	153.3		.	.
M-H	111.6	88.7	83.0	96.3	100.2	96.1	91.0			
W-F-M	81.6	66.7	59.3	66.2	72.2	70.0	62.3			
Total %	5.5	4.1	3.9	4.4	4.6	4.4	4.2			
Isle of Man (FB)				Registered unemployment - Chômage enregistré - Desempleo registrado						
Total	0.277	0.213	0.186	0.211	0.299	0.392	0.562	0.571	0.594	0.599
M-H	0.203	0.150	0.131	0.142	0.208	0.281	0.400	0.387	0.378	0.415
W-F-M	0.074	0.063	0.055	0.069	0.091	0.111	0.162	0.184	0.215	0.184
Total %	0.8	0.6	0.5	0.5	0.8	1.0	1.4	1.4	1.4	1.4
M-H %	1.0	0.8	0.6	0.7	1.0	1.3	1.8	1.7	1.7	1.8
W-F-M %	0.5	0.4	0.3	0.4	0.5	0.6	0.9	1.0	1.1	1.0
Italy (BA) [2]				Total unemployment - Chômage total - Desempleo total						
Total	2 669	2 495	2 267	2 163	2 096	1 960 [5]	1 889	1 673	1 506	1 692
M-H	1 266	1 179	1 066	1 016	996	925 [5]	902	801	722	820
W-F-M	1 404	1 316	1 201	1 147	1 100	1 036 [5]	986	873	784	872
Total %	11.4	10.5	9.5	9.0	8.7	8.0 [5]	7.7	6.8	6.1	6.7
M-H %	8.8	8.1	7.3	6.9	6.7	6.4 [5]	6.2	5.4	4.9	5.5
W-F-M %	15.7	14.5	13.0	12.2	11.6	10.5 [5]	10.1	8.8	7.9	8.5
Jersey (FB) [6]				Registered unemployment - Chômage enregistré - Desempleo registrado						
Total	0.2	0.2	0.2	0.2	0.7	0.5	0.4	0.4	0.3	0.7
Total %	.	.	.	.					0.6	2.3
Kosovo (Serbia) (BA) [7]				Total unemployment - Chômage total - Desempleo total						
Total %	.	.	57.0	55.0	49.7	39.7	41.4	44.9	46.3	
M-H %	.	.	52.0	45.2	40.3	31.5	32.9	34.6	38.5	
W-F-M %	.	.	70.0	74.5	71.9	60.7	60.5	61.6	55.2	
Latvia (BA) [8]				Total unemployment - Chômage total - Desempleo total						
Total	161.4	158.7	144.7	134.5 [9]	119.2	118.6	99.1	79.9	72.1	91.6
M-H	88.7	87.0	81.9	74.9 [9]	61.7	61.7	52.8	43.7	39.4	50.3
W-F-M	72.7	71.7	62.7	59.6 [9]	57.5	56.9	46.2	36.2	32.7	41.4
Total %	14.3	14.4	13.1	12.0 [9]	10.6	10.4	8.7	6.8	6.0	7.5
M-H %	15.0	15.4	14.4	12.9 [9]	10.7	10.6	9.0	7.2	6.4	8.1
W-F-M %	13.5	13.5	11.7	11.0 [9]	10.5	10.3	8.4	6.4	5.7	7.0
Latvia (FB) [10][11]				Registered unemployment - Chômage enregistré - Desempleo registrado						
Total	109.5	93.3	91.6	89.7	90.6	90.8	78.5	68.9	52.3	.
M-H	46.7	39.5	39.1	37.0	37.6	37.3	31.5	27.0	20.1	.
W-F-M	62.8	53.8	52.6	52.7	53.0	53.5	47.0	42.0	32.2	.
Total %	9.1	7.8	7.7	8.5	8.6	8.5	7.4	6.5	4.9	.
Liechtenstein (E)				Total unemployment - Chômage total - Desempleo total						
Total	0.299	0.290	0.354	0.413	0.651	0.725			.	.
Lithuania (BA) [2][12]				Total unemployment - Chômage total - Desempleo total						
Total	249.0	273.7	284.0	224.4	203.9	184.4	132.9	89.3	69.0	94.3
M-H	140.5	158.5	165.6	121.1	105.4	90.6	67.1	46.7	34.6	49.5
W-F-M	108.5	115.2	118.4	103.3	98.4	93.8	65.8	42.6	34.3	44.8
Total %	14.6	16.4	17.4	13.8	12.4	11.4	8.3	5.6	4.3	5.8
M-H %	16.2	18.8	19.9	14.6	12.7	11.0	8.2	5.8	4.3	6.0
W-F-M %	13.0	13.9	14.7	12.9	12.2	11.8	8.3	5.4	4.3	5.6

Explanatory notes: see p. 451.

[1] Persons aged 16 to 74 years. [2] Persons aged 15 years and over. [3] Second quarter of each year. [4] Persons aged 16 years and over. [5] Methodology revised; data not strictly comparable. [6] December. [7] Persons aged 15 to 64 years. [8] Persons aged 15 to 74 years. [9] Prior to 2002: persons aged 15 years and over. [10] Age limits vary according to the year. [11] 31st Dec. of each year. [12] Incl. the unemployed whose last job was 8 years ago or over.

Notes explicatives: voir p. 454.

[1] Personnes âgées de 16 à 74 ans. [2] Personnes âgées de 15 ans et plus. [3] Deuxième trimestre de chaque année. [4] Personnes âgées de 16 ans et plus. [5] Méthodologie révisée; les données ne sont pas strictement comparables. [6] Décembre. [7] Personnes âgées de 15 à 64 ans. [8] Personnes âgées de 15 à 74 ans. [9] Avant 2002: personnes agées de 15 ans et plus. [10] Les limites d'âge varient selon l'année. [11] 31 déc. de chaque année. [12] Y compris les chômeurs dont le dernier emploi date de 8 ans ou plus.

Notas explicativas: véase p. 457.

[1] Personas de 16 a 74 años. [2] Personas de 15 años y más. [3] Segundo trimestre de cada año. [4] Personas de 16 años y más. [5] Metodología revisada; los datos no son estrictamente comparables. [6] Diciembre. [7] Personas de 15 a 64 años. [8] Personas de 15 a 74 años. [9] Antes de 2002: personas de 15 años y más. [10] Los límites de edad varían según el año. [11] 31 dic. de cada año. [12] Incl. los desempleados cuyo último trabajo fue hace 8 años o más.

	Thousands			Milliers				Millares		
	1999	2000	2001	2002	2003	2004	2005	2006	2007	2008
Lithuania (FB) [1][2]	Registered unemployment - Chômage enregistré - Desempleo registrado									
Total	177.4	225.9	224.0	191.2	158.8	126.4	87.2	79.3	69.7	95.0
M-H	94.6	123.1	117.7	95.1	73.7	53.8	33.9	29.9	27.4	49.0
W-F-M	82.8	102.8	106.3	96.1	85.1	72.6	53.3	49.4	42.3	46.0
Total %	10.0	12.6	12.9	10.9	9.8	7.8	5.4	5.0	4.3	5.9
M-H %	10.6	13.5	13.5	10.8	9.0	6.5	4.1	3.7	3.4	6.0
W-F-M %	9.3	11.6	12.2	11.0	10.5	9.1	6.8	6.3	5.3	5.8
Luxembourg (BA) [3]	Total unemployment - Chômage total - Desempleo total									
Total	.	.	.	.	.	.	.	9.7	8.9	10.4
M-H	.	.	.	.	.	.	.	4.0	4.3	4.9
W-F-M	.	.	.	.	.	.	.	5.7	4.6	5.5
Total %	.	.	.	.	.	.	.	.	.	4.8
M-H %	.	.	.	.	.	.	.	.	.	4.0
W-F-M %	.	.	.	.	.	.	.	.	.	5.8
Luxembourg (FB) [1]	Registered unemployment - Chômage enregistré - Desempleo registrado									
Total	5.4	5.0	4.9	5.8	7.6	8.7	9.8	9.5	9.6	9.9
M-H	2.8	2.6	2.6	3.2	4.1	4.7	5.4	5.0	4.9	5.2
W-F-M	2.5	2.3	2.3	2.7	3.5	4.0	4.4	4.5	4.7	4.7
Total %	2.9	2.7	2.7	3.0	3.8	4.2	4.7	4.6	4.5	.
M-H %	.	.	.	.	.	.	.	4.3	.	.
W-F-M %	.	.	.	.	.	.	.	5.0	.	.
Macedonia, The Former Yugoslav Rep. of (BA) [3]	Total unemployment - Chômage total - Desempleo total									
Total	.	.	263.196	263.483	315.868	309.286 [4]	323.934	321.274	316.905	310.409
M-H	.	.	149.372	159.144	191.850	186.223 [4]	191.096	191.856	189.306	188.222
W-F-M	.	.	113.825	104.339	124.018	123.063 [4]	132.838	129.418	127.599	122.187
Total %	.	.	30.5	31.9	36.7	37.2 [4]	37.3	36.0	34.9	33.8
M-H %	.	.	29.5	31.7	37.0	36.7 [4]	36.5	35.3	34.5	33.5
W-F-M %	.	.	32.0	32.3	36.3	37.8 [4]	38.4	37.2	35.5	34.2
Macedonia, The Former Yugoslav Rep. of (FB) [3]	Work applicants - Demandeurs d'emploi - Solicitantes									
Total	.	366	360	374	390	391	360	367	357	343
M-H	.	.	.	.	222	225	208	214	209	198
W-F-M	.	.	.	.	168	166	152	153	148	145
Malta (BA) [3]	Total unemployment - Chômage total - Desempleo total									
Total	.	10.305	10.052	11.017	12.098	11.518	11.745	11.925	10.729	10.389
M-H	.	7.333	6.841	7.217	7.778	7.080	7.279	7.242	6.474	6.442
W-F-M	.	2.972	3.212	3.800	4.320	4.438	4.466	4.683	4.255	3.947
Total %	.	6.7	6.4	7.0	7.6	7.2	7.3	7.3	6.5	6.1
M-H %	.	6.8	6.2	6.6	7.1	6.4	6.6	6.5	5.8	5.7
W-F-M %	.	6.4	7.0	7.7	8.7	9.0	8.9	8.9	7.7	6.9
Malta (FB) [5][6]	Registered unemployment - Chômage enregistré - Desempleo registrado									
Total	7.695	6.583	6.753	6.774	8.175 [7]	8.103	7.379	7.161	6.172	.
M-H	6.611	5.665	5.646	5.602	6.606 [7]	6.511	5.715	5.544	4.684	.
W-F-M	1.084	0.918	1.107	1.172	1.569 [7]	1.592	1.664	1.617	1.488	.
Total %	5.3	4.5	4.7	4.7	5.7 [7]	5.4	5.1	5.0	4.1	.
M-H %	6.3	5.4	5.4	5.4	6.4 [7]	6.1	5.6	5.5	4.5	.
W-F-M %	2.6	2.2	2.7	2.9	3.8 [7]	3.8	3.9	3.9	3.2	.
Moldova, Republic of (BA) [3]	Total unemployment - Chômage total - Desempleo total									
Total	187.2	140.1	117.7	110.0	117.1	116.5	103.7	99.9	66.7	51.7
M-H	113.6	80.6	70.1	64.4	69.9	70.1	59.8	61.7	41.5	30.0
W-F-M	73.6	59.5	47.6	45.4	47.2	46.4	43.9	38.2	25.2	21.8
Total %	11.1	8.5	7.3	6.8	7.9	8.1	7.3	7.4	5.1	4.0
M-H %	13.3	9.7	8.7	8.1	9.6	10.0	8.7	8.9	6.3	4.6
W-F-M %	8.9	7.2	5.9	5.5	6.4	6.3	6.0	5.7	3.9	3.4
Moldova, Republic of (FB) [6]	Registered unemployment - Chômage enregistré - Desempleo registrado									
Total	34.9	28.9	27.6	24.0	19.7	21.0	21.7	20.4	18.9	17.8
M-H	13.3	11.9	13.6	11.7	10.3	11.7	11.3	9.6	8.3	7.3
W-F-M	21.6	17.0	14.0	12.3	9.4	9.3	10.4	10.8	10.6	10.5
Total %	2.1	2.3	2.2	2.1	2.0	2.0	2.0	1.9	1.9	1.6
Netherlands (BA) [8]	Total unemployment - Chômage total - Desempleo total									
Total	279	246	204	252	332	411	425	354	300	257
M-H	128	111	93	126	178	219	220	174	143	128
W-F-M	151	135	111	125	153	192	205	180	157	128
Total %	3.6	3.1	2.5	3.1	4.0	5.0	5.1	4.2	3.5	3.0
M-H %	2.9	2.4	2.0	2.7	3.9	4.8	4.8	3.8	3.1	2.8
W-F-M %	4.5	3.9	3.1	3.5	4.2	5.2	5.5	4.7	4.0	3.2

Explanatory notes: see p. 451.

[1] Persons aged 16 to 64 years. [2] 31st Dec. of each year. [3] Persons aged 15 years and over. [4] Prior to 2004: April of each year. [5] Persons aged 16 to 61 years. [6] Dec. of each year. [7] Methodology revised; data not strictly comparable. [8] Persons aged 15 to 64 years.

Notes explicatives: voir p. 454.

[1] Personnes âgées de 16 à 64 ans. [2] 31 déc. de chaque année. [3] Personnes âgées de 15 ans et plus. [4] Avant 2004: Avril de chaque année. [5] Personnes âgées de 16 à 61 ans. [6] Déc. de chaque année. [7] Méthodologie révisée; les données ne sont pas strictement comparables. [8] Personnes âgées de 15 à 64 ans.

Notas explicativas: véase p. 457.

[1] Personas de 16 a 64 años. [2] 31 dic. de cada año. [3] Personas de 15 años y más. [4] Antes de 2004: Abril de cada año. [5] Personas de 16 a 61 años de edad. [6] Dic. de cada año. [7] Metodología revisada; los datos no son estrictamente comparables. [8] Personas de 15 a 64 años.

	Thousands					Milliers				Millares
	1999	2000	2001	2002	2003	2004	2005	2006	2007	2008
Netherlands (FB) [1]			Registered unemployment - Chômage enregistré - Desempleo registrado							
Total	220	188	146	170	255	319	311	260	182	145
M-H	114	98	77	91	144	179	164	133	93	77
W-F-M	105	90	69	79	111	141	146	127	89	68
Total %	3	3	2	2	4	4	4	4	2	2
M-H %	3	2	2	2	3	4	4	3	2	2
W-F-M %	4	3	2	3	4	5	5	4	3	2
Norway (BA) [2]			Total unemployment - Chômage total - Desempleo total							
Total	75	81	84	92	107	106	111	84 [3]	63	67
M-H	42	46	46	52	62	62	61	45 [3]	34	38
W-F-M	33	35	38	40	45	45	49	39 [3]	29	30
Total %	3.2	3.4	3.6	3.9	4.5	4.5	4.6	3.4 [3]	2.5	2.6
M-H %	3.4	3.6	3.7	4.1	4.9	4.9	4.8	3.5 [3]	2.6	2.8
W-F-M %	3.0	3.2	3.4	3.6	4.0	4.0	4.4	3.4 [3]	2.5	2.4
Norway (FB) [2]			Registered unemployment - Chômage enregistré - Desempleo registrado							
Total	60	63	63	75	93	92	83	63 [3]	46	43
M-H	34	36	36	43	54	52	46	33 [3]	24	24
W-F-M	26	26	27	33	39	39	38	30 [3]	22	19
Total %	2.6	2.7	2.7	3.2	3.9	3.9	3.5	2.6 [3]	1.9	1.7
M-H %	.	.	.	.	4.3	4.1	3.6	2.6 [3]	1.9	1.8
W-F-M %	.	.	.	.	3.5	3.5	3.4	2.7 [3]	1.9	1.6
Poland (BA) [2]			Total unemployment - Chômage total - Desempleo total							
Total	2 391 [4]	2 785	3 170 [5]	3 431	3 329	3 230	3 045	2 344	1 619	1 211
M-H	1 147 [4]	1 344	1 583 [5]	1 779	1 741	1 681	1 553	1 202	831	599
W-F-M	1 244 [4]	1 440	1 587 [5]	1 652	1 588	1 550	1 493	1 140	788	612
Total %	13.9 [4]	16.1	18.2 [5]	19.9	19.6	19.0	17.7	13.8	9.6	7.1
M-H %	12.4 [4]	14.4	16.9 [5]	19.1	19.0	18.2	16.6	13.0	9.0	6.4
W-F-M %	15.8 [4]	18.1	19.8 [5]	20.9	20.4	19.9	19.1	14.9	10.3	8.0
Poland (FB) [6][7]			Registered unemployment - Chômage enregistré - Desempleo registrado							
Total	2 349.8	2 702.6	3 115.1	3 217.0 [8]	3 175.7	2 999.6	2 773.0	2 309.4	1 746.6	1 473.8
M-H	1 042.5	1 211.0	1 473.0	1 571.2 [8]	1 541.0	1 431.1	1 286.6	1 003.7	729.3	640.4
W-F-M	1 307.3	1 491.6	1 642.1	1 645.8 [8]	1 634.7	1 568.5	1 486.4	1 305.7	1 017.3	833.4
Total %	13.1	15.1	17.5	20.0 [8]	20.0	19.1	17.6	14.9	11.4	9.5
Portugal (BA) [9]			Total unemployment - Chômage total - Desempleo total							
Total	225.8	205.5	213.5	270.5	342.3	365.0	422.3	427.8	448.6	427.1
M-H	108.9	89.3	91.6	121.4	160.9	172.9	198.1	194.8	196.8	194.3
W-F-M	116.9	116.2	122.0	149.1	181.4	192.2	224.1	233.1	251.1	232.7
Total %	4.4	3.9	4.0	5.0	6.3	6.7	7.6	7.7	8.0	7.6
M-H %	3.9	3.1	3.2	4.1	5.5	5.8	6.7	6.5	6.6	6.5
W-F-M %	5.0	4.9	5.0	6.0	7.2	7.6	8.7	9.0	9.6	8.8
Portugal (FB) [9]			Registered unemployment - Chômage enregistré - Desempleo registrado							
Total	356.8	327.4	324.7	344.6	427.3	461.0	477.2	456.1	410.3	
M-H	144.9	128.7	127.0	139.6	182.3	199.5	206.0	194.4	167.1	
W-F-M	211.9	198.8	197.7	205.3	245.0	261.5	271.6	264.1	243.1	
Roumanie (BA) [9]			Total unemployment - Chômage total - Desempleo total							
Total	789.9	821.2	749.9	845.2 [10]	691.7	799.5	704.5	728.4	641.0	575.5
M-H	462.5	481.6	436.0	494.0 [10]	408.0	490.7	420.3	452.4	398.7	369.2
W-F-M	327.3	339.5	313.9	351.1 [10]	283.7	308.7	284.1	276.0	242.3	206.3
Total %	6.8	7.1	6.6	8.4 [10]	7.0	8.0	7.2	7.3	6.4	5.8
M-H %	7.4	7.7	7.1	8.9 [10]	7.5	9.0	7.7	8.2	7.3	6.7
W-F-M %	6.2	6.4	5.9	7.7 [10]	6.4	6.9	6.4	6.1	5.4	4.7
Roumanie (FB) [9][11]			Registered unemployment - Chômage enregistré - Desempleo registrado							
Total	1 130.3	1 007.1	826.9	760.6	658.9	557.9	523.0	460.5	367.8	403.4
M-H	600.2	535.5	445.8	421.1	372.6	323.3	303.8	269.0	201.2	216.2
W-F-M	530.1	471.6	381.1	339.5	286.3	234.6	219.2	191.5	166.6	187.2
Total %	11.8	10.5	8.8	8.4	7.4	6.3	5.9	5.2	4.0	4.4
M-H %	12.1	10.7	9.2	8.9	7.8	7.0	6.4	5.7	4.2	4.5
W-F-M %	11.6	10.1	8.4	7.8	6.8	5.6	5.2	4.6	3.9	4.4
Russian Federation (BA) [12]			Total unemployment - Chômage total - Desempleo total							
Total	9 436	7 700	6 424	5 698	5 959	5 675	5 263	5 312	4 588	4 791
M-H	4 939	4 057	3 450	3 014	3 121	2 975	2 725	2 811	2 453	2 542
W-F-M	4 497	3 643	2 974	2 685	2 838	2 699	2 538	2 501	2 136	2 250
Total %	12.6	9.8	8.9	7.9	8.0	7.8	7.2	7.2	6.1	6.3
M-H %	12.8	10.2	9.3	7.9	8.3	7.6	7.3	7.5	6.4	6.6
W-F-M %	12.3	9.4	8.5	7.9	7.8	8.0	7.0	6.8	5.8	6.1

Explanatory notes: see p. 451.

[1] Persons aged 16 to 64 years. [2] Persons aged 15 to 74 years. [3] Prior to 2006: persons aged 16 to 74 years. [4] First and fourth quarters. [5] Prior to 2001: persons aged 15 years and over. [6] Men aged 18 to 64 years; women aged 18 to 59 years (with the exception of juvenile graduates). [7] 31st Dec. of each year. [8] Methodology revised; data not strictly comparable. [9] Persons aged 15 years and over. [10] Estimates based on the 2002 Population Census results. [11] Dec. of each year. [12] Persons aged 15 to 72 years.

Notes explicatives: voir p. 454.

[1] Personnes âgées de 16 à 64 ans. [2] Personnes âgées de 15 à 74 ans. [3] Avant 2006: personnes âgées de 16 à 74 ans. [4] Premier et quatrième trimestres. [5] Avant 2001: personnes agées de 15 ans et plus. [6] Hommes âgés de 18 à 64 ans; femmes âgées de 18 à 59 ans (à l'exception des jeunes diplômés). [7] 31 déc. de chaque année. [8] Méthodologie révisée; les données ne sont pas strictement comparables. [9] Personnes âgées de 15 ans et plus. [10] Estimations basées sur les résultats du Recensement de la population de 2002. [11] Déc. de chaque année. [12] Personnes âgées de 15 à 72 ans.

Notas explicativas: véase p. 457.

[1] Personas de 16 a 64 años. [2] Personas de 15 a 74 años. [3] Antes de 2006: personas de 16 a 74 años. [4] Primero y cuarto trimestres. [5] Antes de 2001: personas de 15 años y más. [6] Hombres de 18 a 64 años; mujeres de 18 a 59 años (salvo los jovenes diplomados universitarios). [7] 31 dic. de cada año. [8] Metodología revisada; los datos no son estrictamente comparables. [9] Personas de 15 años y más. [10] Estimaciones basadas en los resultados del Censo de población de 2002. [11] Dic. de cada año. [12] Personas de 15 a 72 años.

	Thousands / Milliers / Millares									
	1999	2000	2001	2002	2003	2004	2005	2006	2007	2008
Russian Federation (FB) [1]	Registered unemployment - Chômage enregistré - Desempleo registrado									
Total	1 263	1 037	1 123	1 500	1 639	1 920	1 830	1 742	1 553	1 522
M-H	383	322	360	487	533	647	630	610	570	604
W-F-M	880	715	763	1 013	1 106	1 273	1 200	1 132	983	918
Total %	.	1.4	1.6	2.1	2.3	2.6	2.5	2.3	2.1	2.0
San Marino (E) [2][3]	Registered unemployment - Chômage enregistré - Desempleo registrado									
Total	0.423	0.428	0.514	0.710	0.628	0.577	0.671	0.595	0.573	0.713
M-H	0.121	0.127	0.164	0.184	0.174	0.133	0.180	0.144	0.153	0.197
W-F-M	0.302	0.301	0.350	0.526	0.454	0.444	0.491	0.451	0.420	0.516
Total %	3.0	2.8	2.6	3.6	3.1	2.8	2.1	1.6	.	.
M-H %	1.6	1.7	1.4	1.6	1.5	1.1	1.7	1.2	.	.
W-F-M %	4.6	4.1	4.3	6.3	5.5	5.2	2.6	2.0	.	.
Serbia (BA) [2][4]	Total unemployment - Chômage total - Desempleo total									
Total	.	.	.	.	.	665.4	719.9	693.0	585.5	445.4
M-H	.	.	.	.	.	303.2	329.8	339.8	289.8	217.5
W-F-M	.	.	.	.	.	362.2	390.1	353.2	295.7	227.9
Total %	.	.	.	.	.	18.5	20.8	20.9	18.1	13.6
M-H %	.	.	.	.	.	15.1	16.8	17.9	15.1	11.9
W-F-M %	.	.	.	.	.	22.9	26.2	24.7	21.0	15.8
Slovakia (BA) [2][5]	Total unemployment - Chômage total - Desempleo total									
Total	416.8	485.2	508.0	486.9	459.2	481.0	427.5	353.4	291.9	257.5
M-H	226.6	265.5	282.5	263.9	246.5	250.0	223.6	179.5	143.5	124.6
W-F-M	190.2	219.7	225.5	223.0	212.7	231.0	203.8	173.9	148.4	132.8
Total %	16.2	18.6	19.2	18.5	17.4	18.1	16.2	13.3	11.0	9.6
M-H %	16.0	18.6	19.5	18.4	17.2	17.3	15.3	12.0	9.8	8.4
W-F-M %	16.4	18.6	18.8	18.7	17.7	19.1	17.2	14.7	12.5	11.1
Slovakia (FB) [2]	Registered unemployment - Chômage enregistré - Desempleo registrado									
Total	485.2	517.9	520.6	513.2	443.4	409.0	340.4	299.2	250.9	230.4
M-H	265.8	283.7	284.7	280.8	240.0	211.0	167.9	143.6	118.3	107.0
W-F-M	219.4	234.2	235.9	232.4	203.4	198.0	172.5	155.6	132.6	123.4
Total %	17.3	18.2	18.3	17.8	15.2	14.3	11.6	10.4	8.4	7.7
M-H %	17.9	18.8	18.9	19.0	15.3	13.7	10.8	9.2	7.3	6.5
W-F-M %	16.6	17.6	17.5	16.5	15.0	14.9	12.7	11.8	9.9	9.1
Slovenia (BA) [2][6]	Total unemployment - Chômage total - Desempleo total									
Total	71	69	57	58	63	61	58	61	48	43
M-H	37	36	29	30	32	31	30	28	20	20
W-F-M	34	33	28	28	31	30	28	33	28	23
Total %	7.4	7.2	5.9	5.9	6.6	6.1	5.8	5.9	4.6	4.2
M-H %	7.2	7.0	5.6	5.7	6.1	5.7	5.5	5.1	3.6	3.5
W-F-M %	7.6	7.4	6.3	6.3	7.1	6.4	6.1	6.8	5.8	4.9
Slovenia (FB) [2][7]	Registered unemployment - Chômage enregistré - Desempleo registrado									
Total	118.95	106.60	101.86	102.63	97.67	93.07	91.88	79.97	71.34	.
M-H	58.75	52.51	50.16	50.11	46.08	43.80	42.42	38.83	32.19	.
W-F-M	60.20	54.09	51.69	52.13	51.60	49.27	49.43	47.00	39.14	.
Total %	13.6	12.2	11.6	11.6	11.2	10.6	10.1	9.4	7.7	.
M-H %	12.4	11.1	10.4	10.4	9.7	9.1	.	7.7	6.3	.
W-F-M %	15.0	13.5	12.9	13.1	13.0	12.4	.	11.5	9.6	.
Suisse (BA) [2][6]	Total unemployment - Chômage total - Desempleo total									
Total	122	106	101	119	170	179	185	169	156	147
M-H	59	51	38	62	86	89	88	78	68	66
W-F-M	62	55	63	57	84	89	97	91	88	80
Total %	3.1	2.7	2.5	2.9	4.1	4.3	4.4	4.0	3.6	3.4
M-H %	2.7	2.3	1.7	2.8	3.8	3.9	3.9	3.4	2.9	2.8
W-F-M %	3.5	3.1	3.5	3.1	4.5	4.8	5.1	4.7	4.5	4.0
Suisse (FB) [2]	Registered unemployment - Chômage enregistré - Desempleo registrado									
Total	98.6	72.0	67.2	100.5	145.7	153.1	148.5	131.5	109.2	101.7
M-H	52.6	37.8	35.4	55.9	81.7	83.6	78.8	68.1	56.3	53.5
W-F-M	46.0	34.2	31.8	44.6	64.0	69.5	69.7	63.4	52.9	48.3
Total %	2.7 |	1.8 [8]	1.7	2.5	3.7	3.9	3.8	3.3	2.8	2.6
M-H %	2.4 |	1.7 [8]	1.6	2.5	3.7	3.8	3.6	3.1	2.6	2.4
W-F-M %	3.3 |	2.0 [8]	1.8	2.6	3.7	4.0	4.0	3.6	3.0	2.8
Sweden (BA) [9]	Total unemployment - Chômage total - Desempleo total									
Total	241	203	175	176	217	246 |	270 [10]	246	298	305
M-H	133	114	99	101	123	137 |	148 [10]	131	149	152
W-F-M	107	89	76	76	94	109 |	123 [10]	114	148	152
Total %	5.6	4.7	4.0	4.0	4.9	5.5 |	6.0 [10]	5.4	6.1	6.2
M-H %	5.9	5.0	4.3	4.4	5.3	5.9 |	6.2 [10]	5.5	5.9	5.9
W-F-M %	5.2	4.3	3.6	3.6	4.4	5.1 |	5.7 [10]	5.2	6.5	6.6

Explanatory notes: see p. 451.

[1] Dec. of each year. [2] Persons aged 15 years and over. [3] Dec. [4] Oct. [5] Excl. persons on child-care leave. [6] Second quarter of each year. [7] 31st Dec. of each year. [8] Beginning 2000: rates calculated on basis of 2000 Census. [9] Persons aged 15 to 74 years; prior to 2007: 16 to 64 years. [10] Methodology revised; data not strictly comparable.

Notes explicatives: voir p. 454.

[1] Déc. de chaque année. [2] Personnes âgées de 15 ans et plus. [3] Déc. [4] Oct. [5] Non compris les personnes en congé parental. [6] Deuxième trimestre de chaque année. [7] 31 déc. de chaque année. [8] A partir de 2000: taux calculés sur la base du Recensement de 2000. [9] Personnes âgées de 15 à 74 ans; avant 2007: 16 à 64 ans. [10] Méthodologie révisée; les données ne sont pas strictement comparables.

Notas explicativas: véase p. 457.

[1] Dic. de cada año. [2] Personas de 15 años y más. [3] Dic. [4] Oct. [5] Excl. las personas con licencia parental. [6] Segundo trimestre de cada año. [7] 31 dic. de cada año. [8] A partir de 2000: tasas calculadas en base al Censo de 2000. [9] Personas de 15 a 74 años; antes de 2007: 16 a 64 años. [10] Metodología revisada; los datos no son estrictamente comparables.

3A — UNEMPLOYMENT / CHÔMAGE / DESEMPLEO

General level / Niveau général / Nivel general

Thousands / Milliers / Millares

	1999	2000	2001	2002	2003	2004	2005	2006	2007	2008
Sweden (FB) [1]	Registered unemployment - Chômage enregistré - Desempleo registrado									
Total	276.680	231.240	193.009	185.838	223.023	239.201	241.434	210.891	169.516	150.384
M-H	151.690	126.940	107.188	105.418	127.430	135.090	132.000	114.169	90.268	80.903
W-F-M	124.990	104.305	85.820	80.420	95.593	104.111	109.435	96.722	79.248	69.481
Total %	6.4	5.3	4.4	4.2	4.9	5.5	5.3	4.6	3.5	2.5
M-H %	6.7	5.6	4.7	4.6	5.3	5.9		4.7	3.6	2.7
W-F-M %	6.1	5.0	4.1	3.8	4.4	5.1		4.4	3.5	2.4
Turkey (BA) [1]	Total unemployment - Chômage total - Desempleo total									
Total	1 774	1 497	1 967	2 464	2 493	2 498	2 519	2 446	2 376	2 611
M-H	1 275	1 111	1 485	1 826	1 830	1 878	1 867	1 777	1 716	1 877
W-F-M	499	387	482	638	663	620	652	670	660	734
Total %	7.7	6.5	8.4	10.3	10.5	10.3	10.3	9.9	10.3	11.0
M-H %	7.7	6.6	8.7	10.7	10.7	10.5	10.3	9.7	10.0	10.7
W-F-M %	7.5	6.3	7.5	9.4	10.1	9.7	10.3	10.3	11.0	11.6
Turkey (FB) [2][3]	Registered unemployment - Chômage enregistré - Desempleo registrado									
Total	487.5	730.5	718.7	464.3	587.4	811.9	881.3	1 061.9	696.5	987.8
M-H	413.8	591.9	582.9	379.8	469.4	611.3	656.2	782.7	520.1	724.3
W-F-M	73.7	138.6	135.8	84.5	118.0	200.6	225.0	279.2	176.4	263.5
Ukraine (BA) [4]	Total unemployment - Chômage total - Desempleo total									
Total	2 614.3	2 655.8	2 455.0	2 140.7	2 008.0	1 906.7	1 600.8	1 515.0	1 417.6	1 425.1
M-H	1 346.5	1 357.4	1 263.0	1 106.5	1 055.7	1 001.6	862.5	804.1	770.7	768.9
W-F-M	1 267.8	1 298.4	1 192.0	1 034.2	952.3	905.1	738.3	710.9	646.9	656.2
Total %	11.6	11.6	10.9	9.6	9.1	8.6	7.2	6.8	6.4	6.4
M-H %	11.8	11.6	11.0	9.8	9.4	8.9	7.5	7.0	6.7	6.6
W-F-M %	11.3	11.6	10.8	9.5	8.7	8.3	6.8	6.6	6.0	6.1
Ukraine (FB) [5][6]	Registered unemployment - Chômage enregistré - Desempleo registrado									
Total	1 174.5	1 155.2	1 008.1	1 034.2	988.9	981.8	881.5	759.5	642.3	844.9
M-H	444.9	424.8	362.5	369.2	361.3	361.9	345.9	300.4	256.5	379.7
W-F-M	729.6	730.4	645.6	665.0	627.6	619.9	535.6	459.1	385.8	465.2
Total %	5.5	5.5	4.8	5.0	4.8	4.8	4.3	3.7	3.1	4.1
M-H %	4.0	3.8	3.3	3.4	3.4	3.4	3.2	2.7	2.3	3.4
W-F-M %	7.3	7.2	6.4	6.7	6.3	6.3	5.6	4.8	4.0	4.9
United Kingdom (BA) [7][8]	Total unemployment - Chômage total - Desempleo total									
Total	1 710	1 559	1 423	1 472	1 420	1 394	1 397	1 649	1 621	1 643
M-H	1 047	942	861	892	867	824	817	959	930	969
W-F-M	663	617	562	580	553	570	580	690	691	674
Total %	6.0	5.4	4.9	5.0	4.8	4.7	4.6	5.4	5.3	5.3
M-H %	6.7	6.0	5.4	5.6	5.4	5.1	5.0	5.8	5.6	5.7
W-F-M %	5.1	4.7	4.2	4.3	4.1	4.2	4.2	4.9	4.9	4.7
United Kingdom (FA) [9][10]	Total unemployment - Chômage total - Desempleo total									
Total	1 263.1	1 102.3	983.0	958.8	945.9	866.1	874.4	956.7	873.0	
M-H	963.5	839.6	746.8	723.8	707.6	643.0				
W-F-M	299.5	262.6	236.2	235.0	238.5	223.2				
Total %	4.3	3.8	3.3	3.2	3.1	2.8	2.8	3.0	2.7	
M-H %	6.0	5.2	4.6	4.4	4.3	3.8				
W-F-M %	2.3	2.0	1.7	1.7	1.7	1.6				

OCEANIA-OCÉANIE-OCEANIA

	1999	2000	2001	2002	2003	2004	2005	2006	2007	2008
Australia (BA) [1][11]	Total unemployment - Chômage total - Desempleo total									
Total	654.9	607.5	663.5	631.2	596.0	554.7	529.0	517.7	487.5	470.9
M-H	379.5	347.7	381.8	360.9	324.9	299.4	283.1	277.5	245.7	236.9
W-F-M	275.4	259.8	281.7	270.3	271.1	255.4	245.9	240.1	241.7	234.0
Total %	7.0	6.4	6.8	6.4	5.9	5.5	5.0	4.8	4.4	4.2
M-H %	7.2	6.5	7.1	6.6	5.9	5.3	4.9	4.7	4.1	3.9
W-F-M %	6.8	6.2	6.5	6.2	6.0	5.6	5.2	4.9	4.8	4.6
New Zealand (BA) [1]	Total unemployment - Chômage total - Desempleo total									
Total	133.7 [12]	117.7	106.3	106.4	97.8	84.9	82.5	85.4	82.8	95.0
M-H	76.0 [12]	65.7	58.1	56.2	49.3	40.7	40.9	42.3	41.0	49.8
W-F-M	57.7 [12]	52.0	48.2	50.2	48.5	44.2	41.6	43.1	41.7	45.2
Total %	7.0 [12]	6.1	5.4	5.3	4.8	4.0	3.8	3.8	3.7	4.2
M-H %	7.3 [12]	6.3	5.5	5.1	4.5	3.6	3.5	3.6	3.4	4.1
W-F-M %	6.7 [12]	6.0	5.4	5.5	5.1	4.5	4.1	4.2	4.0	4.2
Nouvelle-Calédonie (FB) [7]	Registered unemployment - Chômage enregistré - Desempleo registrado									
Total	8.849	9.439	9.860	10.511	10.187	9.632	8.725	7.049	6.572	
M-H	3.926	4.229	4.439	4.779	4.594					
W-F-M	4.887	5.209	5.421	5.732	5.593					

Explanatory notes: see p. 451.

[1] Persons aged 15 years and over. [2] Persons aged 14 years and over. [3] Dec. of each year. [4] Persons aged 15-70 years. [5] Men aged 16 to 59 years; women aged 16 to 54 years. [6] 31st Dec. of each year. [7] Persons aged 16 years and over. [8] Second quarter. [9] Excl. persons temporarily laid off. [10] Claimants at unemployment benefits offices. [11] Excl. armed forces. [12] Methodology revised; data not strictly comparable.

Notes explicatives: voir p. 454.

[1] Personnes âgées de 15 ans et plus. [2] Personnes âgées de 14 ans et plus. [3] Déc. de chaque année. [4] Personnes âgées de 15 à 70 ans. [5] Hommes âgés de 16 à 59 ans; femmes âgées de 16 à 54 ans. [6] 31 déc. de chaque année. [7] Personnes âgées de 16 ans et plus. [8] Deuxième trimestre. [9] Non compris les personnes temporairement mises à pied. [10] Demandeurs auprès des bureaux de prestations de chômage. [11] Non compris les forces armées. [12] Méthodologie révisée; les données ne sont pas strictement comparables.

Notas explicativas: véase p. 457.

[1] Personas de 15 años y más. [2] Personas de 14 años y más. [3] Dic. de cada año. [4] Personas de 15 á 70 años. [5] Hombres de 16 a 59 años; mujeres de 16 a 54 años. [6] 31 dic. de cada año. [7] Personas de 16 años y más. [8] Segundo trimestre. [9] Excl. las personas temporalmente despedidas. [10] Solicitantes en las oficinas de subsidios de desempleo. [11] Excl. las fuerzas armadas. [12] Metodología revisada; los datos no son estrictamente comparables.

By age group — Par groupe d'âge — Por grupo de edad

	Thousands			Milliers			Millares		
	1999	2000	2001	2002	2003	2004	2005	2006	2007	2008

AFRICA-AFRIQUE-AFRICA

Algérie (BA) [1][2] — Total unemployment - Chômage total - Desempleo total

Total - Total - Total

	1999	2000	2001	2002	2003	2004	2005	2006	2007	2008
Total	.	.	2 339.4	.	2 078.3	1 671.5	1 474.5	1 240.8	.	.
15-19	.	.	393.4	.	329.1	256.9	209.0	166.4	.	.
20-24	.	.	688.0	.	666.9	505.4	490.1	370.0	.	.
25-29	.	.	579.0	.	509.3	462.6	406.2	333.5	.	.
30-34	.	.	280.9	.	245.6	206.4	179.9	170.4	.	.
35-39	.	.	155.9	.	133.5	104.3	85.7	91.1	.	.
40-44	.	.	93.9	.	75.1	58.3	43.8	48.9	.	.
45-49	.	.	72.7	.	62.5	41.6	32.2	28.4	.	.
50-54	.	.	58.2	.	40.3	24.6	19.8	25.5	.	.
55+	.	.	17.5	.	16.0	11.4	7.9	6.6	.	.

Botswana (BA) [3] — Total unemployment - Chômage total - Desempleo total

Total - Total - Total

	1999	2000	2001	2002	2003	2004	2005	2006	2007	2008
Total	.	90.728	.	.	144.460	.	.	114.422	.	.
12-14	.	-	.	.	0.225	.	.	0.218	.	.
15-19	.	0.874	.	.	22.750	.	.	10.749	.	.
20-24	.	18.032	.	.	56.141	.	.	36.784	.	.
25-29	.	37.432	.	.	29.502	.	.	24.836	.	.
30-34	.	15.453	.	.	15.359	.	.	13.308	.	.
35-39	.	8.175	.	.	8.767	.	.	9.670	.	.
40-44	.	4.921	.	.	5.449	.	.	7.023	.	.
45-49	.	2.724	.	.	3.166	.	.	5.194	.	.
50-54	.	1.679	.	.	1.684	.	.	3.341	.	.
55-59	.	0.978	.	.	0.738	.	.	1.517	.	.
60+	.	0.460	.	.	0.679	.	.	1.782	.	.

Men - Hommes - Hombres

	1999	2000	2001	2002	2003	2004	2005	2006	2007	2008
Total	.	46.273	.	.	66.880	.	.	50.876	.	.
12-14	.	-	.	.	0.071	.	.	0.046	.	.
15-19	.	0.487	.	.	9.844	.	.	5.225	.	.
20-24	.	8.909	.	.	26.808	.	.	16.220	.	.
25-29	.	17.775	.	.	11.755	.	.	10.836	.	.
30-34	.	8.611	.	.	7.294	.	.	4.750	.	.
35-39	.	4.176	.	.	4.379	.	.	4.099	.	.
40-44	.	2.777	.	.	3.376	.	.	2.963	.	.
45-49	.	1.603	.	.	1.524	.	.	2.489	.	.
50-54	.	1.013	.	.	1.176	.	.	2.120	.	.
55-59	.	0.559	.	.	0.361	.	.	0.909	.	.
60+	.	0.373	.	.	0.292	.	.	1.219	.	.

Women - Femmes - Mujeres

	1999	2000	2001	2002	2003	2004	2005	2006	2007	2008
Total	.	44.455	.	.	77.580	.	.	63.546	.	.
12-14	.	-	.	.	0.154	.	.	0.172	.	.
15-19	.	0.387	.	.	12.906	.	.	5.524	.	.
20-24	.	9.123	.	.	29.333	.	.	20.564	.	.
25-29	.	19.657	.	.	17.747	.	.	14.000	.	.
30-34	.	6.842	.	.	8.065	.	.	8.558	.	.
35-39	.	3.999	.	.	4.388	.	.	5.571	.	.
40-44	.	2.144	.	.	2.073	.	.	4.059	.	.
45-49	.	1.121	.	.	1.642	.	.	2.705	.	.
50-54	.	0.666	.	.	0.509	.	.	1.220	.	.
55-59	.	0.419	.	.	0.377	.	.	0.607	.	.
60+	.	0.087	.	.	0.387	.	.	0.563	.	.

Egypt (BA) [4][5] — Total unemployment - Chômage total - Desempleo total

Total - Total - Total

	1999	2000	2001	2002	2003	2004	2005	2006	2007	2008
Total	1 480.5	1 698.0	1 783.0	2 020.6	2 240.7	2 153.9	2 450.0	2 434.5	2 135.2	.
15-19	310.9	363.0	355.6	379.2	441.7	512.0	592.5	505.7	329.3	.
20-24	569.4	731.5	719.2	773.5	1 035.2	1 009.1	1 170.0	1 126.9	1 013.4	.
25-29	434.6	438.5	498.1	610.8	537.6	460.0	502.1	556.8	551.0	.
30-39	151.2	155.9	195.2	243.9	212.0	162.0	166.1	213.7	213.1	.
40-49	8.9	6.2	11.0	10.1	10.7	9.0	16.4	25.5	27.1	.
50-59	5.5	2.9	3.9	3.1	3.5	1.8	3.0	6.0	1.2	.
60-64	-	-	-	-	-	-	-	-	-	.

Men - Hommes - Hombres

	1999	2000	2001	2002	2003	2004	2005	2006	2007	2008
Total	726.2	743.5	851.8	983.2	1 186.7	942.6	1 194.5	1 207.7	1 077.7	.
15-19	140.6	159.4	174.4	203.9	265.4	222.2	296.3	246.7	164.3	.
20-24	286.8	320.4	370.0	427.3	597.3	449.3	574.3	575.8	534.2	.
25-29	225.2	198.4	233.2	278.7	261.4	219.0	247.2	274.9	286.2	.
30-39	61.6	58.0	64.6	65.0	54.2	44.7	60.5	84.7	76.2	.
40-49	7.6	5.1	7.4	6.6	6.3	5.9	13.2	19.9	15.6	.
50-59	4.5	2.2	2.2	1.7	2.1	1.5	3.0	5.8	1.2	.
60-64	-	-	-	-	-	-	-	-	-	.

Explanatory notes: see p. 451.

[1] Persons aged 15 years and over. [2] Sep. of each year. [3] Persons aged 12 years and over. [4] Persons aged 15 to 64 years. [5] May and Nov.

Notes explicatives: voir p. 454.

[1] Personnes âgées de 15 ans et plus. [2] Sept. de chaque année. [3] Personnes âgées de 12 ans et plus. [4] Personnes âgées de 15 à 64 ans. [5] Mai et nov.

Notas explicativas: véase p. 457.

[1] Personas de 15 años y más. [2] Sept. de cada año. [3] Personas de 12 años y más. [4] Personas de 15 a 64 años. [5] Mayo y nov.

3B

UNEMPLOYMENT	CHÔMAGE	DESEMPLEO
By age group	Par groupe d'âge	Por grupo de edad

	Thousands				Milliers				Millares	
	1999	2000	2001	2002	2003	2004	2005	2006	2007	2008

Egypt (BA) [1] [2] — Total unemployment - Chômage total - Desempleo total

Women - Femmes - Mujeres

	1999	2000	2001	2002	2003	2004	2005	2006	2007	2008
Total	754.3	954.5	931.2	1 037.4	1 054.0	1 211.3	1 255.5	1 226.8	1 057.5	
15-19	170.3	203.6	181.2	175.3	176.3	289.8	296.2	259.0	165.0	
20-24	282.6	411.1	349.2	346.2	437.9	559.8	595.7	551.1	479.2	
25-29	209.4	240.1	264.9	332.1	276.2	241.0	254.9	281.9	264.8	
30-39	89.6	97.9	130.6	178.9	157.8	117.3	105.6	129.0	136.9	
40-49	1.3	1.1	3.6	3.5	4.4	3.1	3.2	5.6	11.5	
50-59	1.0	0.7	1.7	1.4	1.4	0.3	-	0.2	-	
60-64	-									

Ethiopia (BA) [3] [4] — Total unemployment - Chômage total - Desempleo total

Total - Total - Total

	2004	2006
Total	845.9 [5]	767.1 [6]
10-14	10.3 [5]	10.8 [6]
15-19	152.0 [5]	132.1 [6]
20-24	249.3 [5]	221.3 [6]
25-29	175.7 [5]	155.5 [6]
30-34	76.4 [5]	74.2 [6]
35-39	66.8 [5]	51.7 [6]
40-44	34.0 [5]	35.8 [6]
45-49	27.8 [5]	30.4 [6]
50-54	17.9 [5]	13.8 [6]
55-59	15.3 [5]	18.0 [6]
60-64	12.0 [5]	8.5 [6]
65+	8.5 [5]	14.4 [6]

Men - Hommes - Hombres

	2004	2006
Total	304.5 [5]	273.1 [6]
10-14	5.3 [5]	4.3 [6]
15-19	54.3 [5]	46.2 [6]
20-24	90.6 [5]	80.3 [6]
25-29	56.8 [5]	52.3 [6]
30-34	21.0 [5]	24.3 [6]
35-39	19.4 [5]	13.0 [6]
40-44	10.5 [5]	9.3 [6]
45-49	9.8 [5]	9.6 [6]
50-54	11.3 [5]	5.5 [6]
55-59	9.7 [5]	10.0 [6]
60-64	9.0 [5]	5.4 [6]
65+	6.9 [5]	12.4 [6]

Women - Femmes - Mujeres

	2004	2006
Total	541.4 [5]	493.9 [6]
10-14	5.0 [5]	6.5 [6]
15-19	97.7 [5]	85.9 [6]
20-24	158.7 [5]	141.0 [6]
25-29	118.9 [5]	103.1 [6]
30-34	55.4 [5]	49.8 [6]
35-39	47.4 [5]	38.6 [6]
40-44	23.5 [5]	26.5 [6]
45-49	18.0 [5]	20.7 [6]
50-54	6.6 [5]	8.3 [6]
55-59	5.6 [5]	7.9 [6]
60-64	3.0 [5]	3.1 [6]
65+	1.6 [5]	2.0 [6]

Madagascar (B) [7] — Total unemployment - Chômage total - Desempleo total

Total - Total - Total

	2003	2005
Total	383.0 [8]	274.3
6-9	-	24.6
10-14	3.7	17.9
15-19	67.1	20.3
20-24	77.2	35.5
25-29	57.6	37.4
30-34	36.8	12.4
35-39	46.6	9.4
40-44	20.5	8.4
45-49	16.6	10.6
50-54	11.8	27.5
55-59	6.4	29.3
60-64	15.0	32.8
65-69	2.2	2.3
70-74	5.8	2.0
75+	15.6	3.9

Explanatory notes: see p. 451.

[1] Persons aged 15 to 64 years. [2] May and Nov. [3] Persons aged 10 years and over. [4] Urban areas. [5] April. [6] July. [7] Persons aged 6 years and over. [8] Totals include persons still attending school (incl. full-time tertiary students).

Notes explicatives: voir p. 454.

[1] Personnes âgées de 15 à 64 ans. [2] Mai et nov. [3] Personnes âgées de 10 ans et plus. [4] Régions urbaines. [5] Avril. [6] Juillet. [7] Personnes âgées de 6 ans et plus. [8] Les totaux incluent les personnes encore en cours d'études (y compris les étudiants à plein temps de l'enseignement supérieur).

Notas explicativas: véase p. 457.

[1] Personas de 15 a 64 años. [2] Mayo y nov. [3] Personas de 10 años y más. [4] Areas urbanas. [5] Abril. [6] Julio. [7] Personas de 6 años y más. [8] Los totales incluyen a las personas que siguen estudiando (incl. los estudiantes a tiempo completo de la enseñanza superior).

By age group   Par groupe d'âge   Por grupo de edad

Thousands   Milliers   Millares

Madagascar (B) [1]

Total unemployment - Chômage total - Desempleo total

Men - Hommes - Hombres

	1999	2000	2001	2002	2003	2004	2005	2006	2007	2008
Total	.	.	.	.	149.8 [2]	.	100.4	.	.	.
6-9	.	.	.	.	-	.	10.9	.	.	.
10-14	.	.	.	.	3.5	.	11.8	.	.	.
15-19	.	.	.	.	27.9	.	10.1	.	.	.
20-24	.	.	.	.	39.9	.	10.7	.	.	.
25-29	.	.	.	.	26.1	.	19.4	.	.	.
30-34	.	.	.	.	13.0	.	3.4	.	.	.
35-39	.	.	.	.	12.8	.	2.8	.	.	.
40-44	.	.	.	.	4.6	.	1.6	.	.	.
45-49	.	.	.	.	5.6	.	2.0	.	.	.
50-54	.	.	.	.	2.3	.	4.3	.	.	.
55-59	.	.	.	.	1.3	.	6.8	.	.	.
60-64	.	.	.	.	5.5	.	14.2	.	.	.
65-69	.	.	.	.	0.5	.	0.1	.	.	.
70-74	.	.	.	.	0.5	.	1.3	.	.	.
75+	.	.	.	.	6.4	.	1.1	.	.	.

Women - Femmes - Mujeres

	1999	2000	2001	2002	2003	2004	2005	2006	2007	2008
Total	.	.	.	.	233.2 [2]	.	173.8	.	.	.
6-9	.	.	.	.	-	.	13.7	.	.	.
10-14	.	.	.	.	0.2	.	6.1	.	.	.
15-19	.	.	.	.	39.3	.	10.2	.	.	.
20-24	.	.	.	.	37.3	.	24.8	.	.	.
25-29	.	.	.	.	31.5	.	18.1	.	.	.
30-34	.	.	.	.	23.8	.	9.0	.	.	.
35-39	.	.	.	.	33.8	.	6.6	.	.	.
40-44	.	.	.	.	15.9	.	6.8	.	.	.
45-49	.	.	.	.	11.0	.	8.6	.	.	.
50-54	.	.	.	.	9.5	.	23.2	.	.	.
55-59	.	.	.	.	5.1	.	22.5	.	.	.
60-64	.	.	.	.	9.5	.	18.6	.	.	.
65-69	.	.	.	.	1.7	.	2.2	.	.	.
70-74	.	.	.	.	5.3	.	0.7	.	.	.
75+	.	.	.	.	9.2	.	2.8	.	.	.

Maroc (BA) [3]

Total unemployment - Chômage total - Desempleo total

Total - Total - Total

	1999	2000	2001	2002	2003	2004	2005	2006	2007	2008
Total	1 432.2	1 394.3	1 275.0	1 202.7	1 299.0	1 192.5	1 226.4	1 062.5	1 092.1	1 077.8
15-24	590.4	554.0	498.7	461.7	466.0	425.4	420.9	414.9	428.6	449.4
25-34	612.7	615.0	575.3	548.0	599.4	546.2	560.8	433.4	458.2	436.2
35-44	165.2	165.2	148.2	143.0	169.3	164.1	188.4	146.7	144.2	129.3
45-59	58.8	55.6	49.8	47.6	60.1	53.6	52.5	64.3	57.5	58.2
60+	5.6	4.5	3.1	2.3	4.3	3.2	3.8	3.1	3.7	4.7

Men - Hommes - Hombres

	1999	2000	2001	2002	2003	2004	2005	2006	2007	2008
Total	1 044.8	1 035.5	952.0	878.4	922.4	851.2	877.6	744.1	794.5	781.2
15-24	442.2	428.3	389.9	351.2	346.8	313.1	316.8	314.5	321.7	341.0
25-34	422.8	430.2	406.6	379.8	400.0	369.6	376.7	300.0	320.6	301.4
35-44	125.2	125.4	111.9	104.6	120.8	119.9	135.8	103.1	101.1	87.0
45-59	49.3	47.8	41.2	40.8	51.1	45.7	44.7	54.3	48.2	47.2
60+	5.2	4.0	2.5	1.9	3.8	2.9	3.5	2.3	3.0	4.5

Women - Femmes - Mujeres

	1999	2000	2001	2002	2003	2004	2005	2006	2007	2008
Total	387.9	358.7	323.0	324.3	376.6	341.4	348.8	288.4	297.6	296.7
15-24	148.2	125.7	108.7	110.5	119.2	112.3	104.1	100.5	106.9	108.3
25-34	189.9	184.8	168.7	168.2	199.5	176.5	184.1	133.5	137.6	134.8
35-44	40.0	39.8	36.3	38.4	48.5	44.3	52.6	43.7	43.1	42.3
45-59	9.5	7.8	8.6	6.8	8.9	8.0	7.8	10.0	9.3	11.0
60+	0.4	0.6	0.6	0.4	0.5	0.3	0.2	0.8	0.7	0.2

Mauritius (BA) [4]

Total unemployment - Chômage total - Desempleo total

Total - Total - Total

	1999	2000	2001	2002	2003	2004	2005	2006	2007	2008
Total	.	.	.	.	.	45.1	52.1	50.1 |	46.8 [5]	40.4
15-19	.	.	.	.	.	7.2	7.8	6.5	.	.
16-19	.	.	.	.	.	.	.	.	7.4	5.0
20-24	.	.	.	.	.	15.6	14.5	13.1 |	12.0 [5]	9.2
25-29	.	.	.	.	.	6.6	9.3	9.4 |	8.4 [5]	7.3
30-34	.	.	.	.	.	4.0	5.9	7.0 |	6.2 [5]	6.4
35-39	.	.	.	.	.	4.3	5.2	5.4 |	4.2 [5]	4.0
40-44	.	.	.	.	.	3.3	4.6	3.7 |	3.3 [5]	2.9
45-49	.	.	.	.	.	2.1	2.1	2.6 |	2.5 [5]	2.2
50-54	.	.	.	.	.	1.0	1.6	1.1 |	1.4 [5]	1.6
55-59	.	.	.	.	.	0.6	0.8	0.9 |	0.8 [5]	1.3
60-64	.	.	.	.	.	0.1	0.2	0.3 |	0.6 [5]	0.5
65-69	.	.	.	.	.	0.2	0.1	0.1 |	0.0 [5]	0.0
70+	.	.	.	.	.	0.2	0.1	0.1 |	0.0 [5]	0.0

Explanatory notes: see p. 451.

[1] Persons aged 6 years and over. [2] Totals include persons still attending school (incl. full-time tertiary students). [3] Persons aged 15 years and over. [4] Persons aged 16 years and over. [5] Prior to 2007: persons aged 15 years and over.

Notes explicatives: voir p. 454.

[1] Personnes âgées de 6 ans et plus. [2] Les totaux incluent les personnes encore en cours d'études (y compris les étudiants à plein temps de l'enseignement supérieur). [3] Personnes âgées de 15 ans et plus. [4] Personnes âgées de 16 ans et plus. [5] Avant 2006: personnes âgées de 15 ans et plus.

Notas explicativas: véase p. 457.

[1] Personas de 6 años y más. [2] Los totales incluyen a las personas que siguen estudiando (incl. los estudiantes a tiempo completo de la enseñanza superior). [3] Personas de 15 años y más. [4] Personas de 16 años y más. [5] Antes de 2006: personas de 15 años y más.

3B

UNEMPLOYMENT	CHÔMAGE	DESEMPLEO
By age group	Par groupe d'âge	Por grupo de edad

	Thousands					Milliers			Millares	
	1999	2000	2001	2002	2003	2004	2005	2006	2007	2008

Mauritius (BA) [1]

Total unemployment - Chômage total - Desempleo total

Men - Hommes - Hombres

	1999	2000	2001	2002	2003	2004	2005	2006	2007	2008
Total	.	.	.	.	.	20.3	20.3	19.5 |	18.6 [2]	14.6
15-19	.	.	.	.	.	4.0	4.2	3.4		
16-19	.	.	.	.	.	.	.		4.1	2.5
20-24	.	.	.	.	.	8.1	6.6	5.8 |	5.3 [2]	4.2
25-29	.	.	.	.	.	3.1	4.0	3.5 |	3.2 [2]	2.7
30-34	.	.	.	.	.	1.3	1.0	2.2 |	1.5 [2]	1.4
35-39	.	.	.	.	.	1.5	1.3	1.4 |	1.3 [2]	0.5
40-44	.	.	.	.	.	1.0	1.2	1.2 |	0.8 [2]	0.7
45-49	.	.	.	.	.	0.6	0.7	0.9 |	0.9 [2]	0.8
50-54	.	.	.	.	.	0.2	0.8	0.5 |	0.6 [2]	1.0
55-59	.	.	.	.	.	0.2	0.3	0.3 |	0.5 [2]	0.5
60-64	.	.	.	.	.	0.1	0.1	0.2 |	0.4 [2]	0.3
65-69	.	.	.	.	.	0.1	0.1	0.1 |	0.0 [2]	0.0
70+	.	.	.	.	.	0.1	0.1	0.1 |	0.0 [2]	0.0

Women - Femmes - Mujeres

	1999	2000	2001	2002	2003	2004	2005	2006	2007	2008
Total	.	.	.	.	.	24.8	31.8	30.6 |	28.2 [2]	25.8
15-19	.	.	.	.	.	3.2	3.6	3.1		
16-19	.	.	.	.	.	.	.		3.3	2.5
20-24	.	.	.	.	.	7.5	7.9	7.3 |	6.7 [2]	5.0
25-29	.	.	.	.	.	3.5	5.3	5.9 |	5.2 [2]	4.6
30-34	.	.	.	.	.	2.7	4.9	4.8 |	4.7 [2]	5.0
35-39	.	.	.	.	.	2.8	3.9	4.0 |	2.9 [2]	3.5
40-44	.	.	.	.	.	2.3	3.4	2.5 |	2.5 [2]	2.2
45-49	.	.	.	.	.	1.5	1.4	1.7 |	1.6 [2]	1.4
50-54	.	.	.	.	.	0.3	0.8	0.6 |	0.8 [2]	0.6
55-59	.	.	.	.	.	0.4	0.5	0.6 |	0.3 [2]	0.8
60-64	.	.	.	.	.	-	0.1	0.1 |	0.2 [2]	0.2
65-69	.	.	.	.	.	0.1	0.0	0.0 |	0.0 [2]	0.0
70+	.	.	.	.	.	0.1	0.0	0.0 |	0.0 [2]	0.0

Mauritius (FB) [3] [4]

Registered unemployment - Chômage enregistré - Desempleo registrado

Total - Total - Total

	1999	2000	2001	2002	2003	2004	2005	2006	2007	2008
Total	12.130	18.024	21.576	21.976	23.373	21.950	33.614	.	.	20.611
15-17	0.205									
16-19		0.293	2.767		2.761	2.742	3.243	.	.	2.030
18-24	5.118									
20-24		7.804	6.306		6.628	6.812	8.307	.	.	4.152
25-29	1.814	2.783	3.488		3.949	4.029	6.383	.	.	3.425
30-34						3.087	5.454	.	.	3.571
30-54		7.144	8.968		9.983					
30+	4.993									
35-39						2.760	5.200	.	.	3.100
40-44						1.740	3.599	.	.	2.746
45-49						0.532	1.042	.	.	1.153
50-54						0.190	0.293	.	.	0.305
55-60	-		0.317		0.052	0.058	0.093	.	.	0.129

Men - Hommes - Hombres

	1999	2000	2001	2002	2003	2004	2005	2006	2007	2008
Total	5.328	8.567	10.477	10.116	10.069	10.512	15.365	.	.	7.135
15-17	0.125									
16-19		0.170	1.456		1.322	1.353	1.661	.	.	0.962
18-24	2.624									
20-24		4.194	3.394		3.266	3.402	4.132	.	.	1.837
25-29	0.734	1.251	1.638		1.581	1.860	2.896	.	.	1.134
30-34						1.279	2.149	.	.	0.939
30-54		2.952	3.959		3.864					
30+	1.845									
35-39						1.230	2.133	.	.	0.779
40-44						0.910	1.643	.	.	0.855
45-49						0.312	0.528	.	.	0.420
50-54						0.122	0.166	.	.	0.137
55-60		-	0.300		0.036	0.044	0.057	.	.	0.072

Women - Femmes - Mujeres

	1999	2000	2001	2002	2003	2004	2005	2006	2007	2008
Total	6.802	9.457	11.099	11.860	13.304	11.438	18.249	.	.	13.476
15-17	0.080									
16-19		0.123	1.311		1.439	1.389	1.582	.	.	1.068
18-24	2.494									
20-24		3.610	2.912		3.362	3.410	4.175	.	.	2.315
25-29	1.080	1.532	1.850		2.368	2.169	3.487	.	.	2.291
30-34						1.808	3.306	.	.	2.632
30-54		4.192	5.009		6.119					
30+	3.148									
35-39						1.530	3.068	.	.	2.321
40-44						0.830	1.955	.	.	1.891
45-49						0.220	0.514	.	.	0.733
50-54						0.068	0.127	.	.	0.168
55-60			0.017		0.016	0.014	0.035	.	.	0.057

Explanatory notes: see p. 451.

[1] Persons aged 16 years and over. [2] Prior to 2007: persons aged 15 years and over. [3] Persons aged 15 years and over. [4] Excl. Rodrigues.

Notes explicatives: voir p. 454.

[1] Personnes âgées de 16 ans et plus. [2] Avant 2006: personnes âgées de 15 ans et plus. [3] Personnes âgées de 15 ans et plus. [4] Non compris Rodriguez.

Notas explicativas: véase p. 457.

[1] Personas de 16 años y más. [2] Antes de 2006: personas de 15 años y más. [3] Personas de 15 años y más. [4] Excl. Rodríguez.

By age group · Par groupe d'âge · Por grupo de edad

	Thousands · Milliers · Millares									
	1999	2000	2001	2002	2003	2004	2005	2006	2007	2008

Réunion (BA) [1][2] — Total unemployment - Chômage total - Desempleo total

Total - Total - Total

	1999	2000	2001	2002	2003	2004	2005	2006	2007	2008
Total	101.574	103.788	83.265	80.945	90.141	96.180	88.940	86.744	75.852	78.040
15-24	21.988	24.411	20.117	18.880	21.135	23.990	23.018	22.791	19.159	20.852
25-29	19.511	16.578	.	.	.	.	.	.	.	.
25-49	.	.	56.706	56.582	61.507	64.729	58.491	55.998	49.472	47.853
30-34	18.054	17.950	.	.	.	.	.	.	.	.
35-39	15.934	15.222	.	.	.	.	.	.	.	.
40-44	11.312	12.484	.	.	.	.	.	.	.	.
45-49	7.162	8.796	.	.	.	.	.	.	.	.
50-54	5.296	4.933	.	.	.	.	.	.	.	.
50+	.	.	6.442	5.483	7.499	7.461	7.431	7.955	7.221	9.335
55+	2.317	3.414	.	.	.	.	.	.	.	.

Men - Hommes - Hombres

	1999	2000	2001	2002	2003	2004	2005	2006	2007	2008
Total	54.708	54.388	44.456	41.936	48.877	52.320	45.709	46.828	39.857	39.356
15-24	11.758	13.055	11.454	9.660	11.505	13.466	12.497	13.084	11.462	11.036
25-29	10.306	8.324	.	.	.	.	.	.	.	.
25-49	.	.	29.970	29.326	33.308	34.492	29.297	29.039	24.325	24.401
30-34	9.666	9.901	.	.	.	.	.	.	.	.
35-39	8.467	7.332	.	.	.	.	.	.	.	.
40-44	6.415	6.367	.	.	.	.	.	.	.	.
45-49	3.931	4.878	.	.	.	.	.	.	.	.
50-54	2.925	2.684	.	.	.	.	.	.	.	.
50+	.	.	3.032	2.950	4.064	4.362	3.915	4.705	4.070	4.919
55+	1.240	1.847	.	.	.	.	.	.	.	.

Women - Femmes - Mujeres

	1999	2000	2001	2002	2003	2004	2005	2006	2007	2008
Total	46.866	49.400	38.809	39.009	41.264	43.860	43.231	39.916	35.995	38.684
15-24	10.230	11.356	8.663	9.220	9.630	10.524	10.521	9.707	7.697	9.816
25-29	9.205	8.254	.	.	.	.	.	.	.	.
25-49	.	.	26.736	27.256	28.199	30.237	29.194	26.959	25.147	24.452
30-34	8.388	8.049	.	.	.	.	.	.	.	.
35-39	7.467	7.890	.	.	.	.	.	.	.	.
40-44	4.897	6.117	.	.	.	.	.	.	.	.
45-49	3.231	3.918	.	.	.	.	.	.	.	.
50-54	2.371	2.249	.	.	.	.	.	.	.	.
50+	.	.	3.410	2.533	3.435	3.099	3.516	3.250	3.151	4.416
55+	1.077	1.567	.	.	.	.	.	.	.	.

South Africa (BA) [3][4] — Total unemployment - Chômage total - Desempleo total

Total - Total - Total

	1999	2000	2001	2002	2003	2004	2005	2006	2007	2008
Total	.	4 167	4 671	4 947	4 441	4 144	4 501	4 397	3 945	4 075
15-19	.	253	284	290	274	261	315	271	276	250
20-24	.	1 118	1 224	1 339	1 249	1 122	1 186	1 201	1 081	1 125
25-29	.	1 040	1 222	1 228	1 069	981	1 119	1 012	955	978
30-34	.	625	690	724	684	692	689	726	620	670
35-39	.	412	439	476	424	391	423	445	373	435
40-44	.	313	347	366	301	304	298	298	233	249
45-49	.	207	214	274	228	183	232	225	223	175
50-54	.	113	126	132	112	123	124	127	104	112
55-59	.	60	85	82	75	59	75	69	61	61
60-64	.	20	25	24	16	18	21	17	17	21
65-69	.	4	4	3	4	2	8	4	3	.
70-74	.	2	3	4	-	1	2	-	-	.
75+	.	1	2	2	3	1	4	-	-	.
?	.	1	6	3	2	5	3	2	-	-

Men - Hommes - Hombres

	1999	2000	2001	2002	2003	2004	2005	2006	2007	2008
Total	.	1 987	2 247	2 323	2 170	2 034	2 061	1 969	1 883	1 917
15-19	.	129	143	134	141	126	170	128	163	122
20-24	.	549	593	654	629	538	549	570	526	562
25-29	.	481	576	558	503	482	501	441	435	441
30-34	.	267	300	297	301	339	285	293	281	291
35-39	.	182	210	206	186	171	187	195	170	172
40-44	.	157	177	175	147	149	135	118	100	113
45-49	.	106	97	147	123	101	98	98	97	90
50-54	.	63	70	72	65	71	62	62	58	68
55-59	.	36	51	53	54	33	50	49	38	39
60-64	.	12	18	18	14	17	17	13	14	19
65-69	.	3	3	2	3	2	4	2	1	.
70-74	.	1	2	2	-	-	-	-	-	.
75+	.	1	2	1	1	-	2	-	-	.
?	.	-	5	2	2	5	-	-	-	-

Explanatory notes: see p. 451.

[1] Persons aged 15 years and over. [2] Second quarter of each year. [3] Persons aged 15 to 64 years. [4] Prior to 2008: persons aged 15 years and over; September of each year.

Notes explicatives: voir p. 454.

[1] Personnes âgées de 15 ans et plus. [2] Deuxième trimestre de chaque année. [3] Personnes âgées de 15 à 64 ans. [4] Avant 2008: personnes agées de 15 ans et plus; septembre de chaque année.

Notas explicativas: véase p. 457.

[1] Personas de 15 años y más. [2] Segundo trimestre de cada año. [3] Personas de 15 a 64 años. [4] Antes de 2008: personas de 15 años y más; Septiembre de cada año.

UNEMPLOYMENT
CHÔMAGE
DESEMPLEO

By age group
Par groupe d'âge
Por grupo de edad

	Thousands			Milliers				Millares		
	1999	2000	2001	2002	2003	2004	2005	2006	2007	2008

South Africa (BA) [1] [2] — Total unemployment - Chômage total - Desempleo total

Women - Femmes - Mujeres

	1999	2000	2001	2002	2003	2004	2005	2006	2007	2008
Total	.	2 180	2 423	2 623	2 271	2 106	2 438	2 428	2 059	2 158
15-19	.	123	141	156	132	133	145	143	113	127
20-24	.	569	631	685	620	585	635	632	554	563
25-29	.	560	646	670	566	497	618	571	520	537
30-34	.	358	390	426	383	352	405	434	338	379
35-39	.	229	229	270	238	220	236	250	203	263
40-44	.	156	169	190	154	155	164	179	133	135
45-49	.	101	117	126	105	82	133	127	125	84
50-54	.	50	55	61	48	52	62	64	46	44
55-59	.	24	34	29	21	26	25	20	22	23
60-64	.	7	7	5	2	1	4	4	3	2
65-69	.	1	1	1	1	-	4	2	2	
70-74	.	1	1	2	-	1	2	-	-	
75+	.	-	-	1	2	1	2	-	-	
?	.	1	1	1	-	-	3	2	-	

Tanzania, United Republic of (BA) [3] — Total unemployment - Chômage total - Desempleo total

Total - Total - Total

	1999	2000	2001	2002	2003	2004	2005	2006	2007	2008
Total	.	.	.	.	.	.	.	892.2	.	.
10-14	.	.	.	.	.	.	.	15.2	.	.
15-19	.	.	.	.	.	.	.	211.3	.	.
20-24	.	.	.	.	.	.	.	256.2	.	.
25-29	.	.	.	.	.	.	.	145.5	.	.
30-34	.	.	.	.	.	.	.	79.7	.	.
35-39	.	.	.	.	.	.	.	62.9	.	.
40-44	.	.	.	.	.	.	.	30.5	.	.
45-49	.	.	.	.	.	.	.	27.7	.	.
50-54	.	.	.	.	.	.	.	20.2	.	.
55-59	.	.	.	.	.	.	.	11.6	.	.
60-64	.	.	.	.	.	.	.	10.3	.	.
65-69	.	.	.	.	.	.	.	7.3	.	.
70+	.	.	.	.	.	.	.	13.8	.	.

Men - Hommes - Hombres

	1999	2000	2001	2002	2003	2004	2005	2006	2007	2008
Total	.	.	.	.	.	.	.	281.7	.	.
10-14	.	.	.	.	.	.	.	7.4	.	.
15-19	.	.	.	.	.	.	.	87.2	.	.
20-24	.	.	.	.	.	.	.	94.4	.	.
25-29	.	.	.	.	.	.	.	31.6	.	.
30-34	.	.	.	.	.	.	.	18.0	.	.
35-39	.	.	.	.	.	.	.	13.6	.	.
40-44	.	.	.	.	.	.	.	7.5	.	.
45-49	.	.	.	.	.	.	.	2.4	.	.
50-54	.	.	.	.	.	.	.	6.0	.	.
55-59	.	.	.	.	.	.	.	3.4	.	.
60-64	.	.	.	.	.	.	.	3.2	.	.
65-69	.	.	.	.	.	.	.	3.3	.	.
70+	.	.	.	.	.	.	.	3.9	.	.

Women - Femmes - Mujeres

	1999	2000	2001	2002	2003	2004	2005	2006	2007	2008
Total	.	.	.	.	.	.	.	610.5	.	.
10-14	.	.	.	.	.	.	.	7.8	.	.
15-19	.	.	.	.	.	.	.	124.2	.	.
20-24	.	.	.	.	.	.	.	161.8	.	.
25-29	.	.	.	.	.	.	.	113.9	.	.
30-34	.	.	.	.	.	.	.	61.7	.	.
35-39	.	.	.	.	.	.	.	49.3	.	.
40-44	.	.	.	.	.	.	.	23.0	.	.
45-49	.	.	.	.	.	.	.	25.3	.	.
50-54	.	.	.	.	.	.	.	14.2	.	.
55-59	.	.	.	.	.	.	.	8.2	.	.
60-64	.	.	.	.	.	.	.	7.1	.	.
65-69	.	.	.	.	.	.	.	4.1	.	.
70+	.	.	.	.	.	.	.	9.9	.	.

Tunisie (BA) [4] [5] — Total unemployment - Chômage total - Desempleo total

Total - Total - Total

	1999	2000	2001	2002	2003	2004	2005	2006	2007	2008
Total	472.5	475.1	469.2	485.5	473.4	473.9	486.4	.	.	.
15-19	92.4	82.6	74.6	72.6	70.2	72.2	67.7	.	.	.
20-24	135.8	130.8	128.2	135.7	136.0	121.4	138.2	.	.	.
25-29	101.9	108.7	113.4	111.0	113.8	109.1	132.0	.	.	.
30-34	52.5	62.8	57.4	56.3	54.5	60.0	64.4	.	.	.
35-39	32.8	33.8	31.1	31.8	29.6	37.8	32.0	.	.	.
40-44	22.0	19.6	23.6	21.5	20.0	27.7	22.0	.	.	.
45-54	22.5	23.2	25.6	28.3	26.2	31.9	23.3	.	.	.
55+	12.7	13.6	15.3	28.4	23.0	13.7	6.7	.	.	.

Explanatory notes: see p. 451.

[1] Persons aged 15 to 64 years. [2] Prior to 2008: persons aged 15 years and over; September of each year. [3] Persons aged 10 years and over. [4] Persons aged 15 years and over. [5] 1999-2003: figures revised on the basis of the 2004 census results.

Notes explicatives: voir p. 454.

[1] Personnes âgées de 15 à 64 ans. [2] Avant 2008: personnes agées de 15 ans et plus; septembre de chaque année. [3] Personnes âgées de 10 ans et plus. [4] Personnes âgées de 15 ans et plus. [5] 1999-2003: données révisées sur la base des résultats du Recensement de 2004.

Notas explicativas: véase p. 457.

[1] Personas de 15 a 64 años. [2] Antes de 2008: personas de 15 años y más; Septiembre de cada año. [3] Personas de 10 años y más. [4] Personas de 15 años y más. [5] 1999-2003: datos revisados de acuerdo con los resultados del Censo de 2004.

By age group — Par groupe d'âge — Por grupo de edad

	Thousands			Milliers				Millares		
	1999	2000	2001	2002	2003	2004	2005	2006	2007	2008

Tunisie (BA) [1] [2] — Total unemployment - Chômage total - Desempleo total

Men - Hommes - Hombres

	1999	2000	2001	2002	2003	2004	2005	2006	2007	2008
Total	345.1	347.4	341.4	351.6	334.7	322.7	328.8	.	.	.
15-19	64.2	59.1	53.1	53.7	52.1	50.3	49.2	.	.	.
20-24	94.9	95.0	89.7	94.9	95.8	81.2	92.1	.	.	.
25-29	71.7	76.1	78.5	73.6	76.7	69.1	81.4	.	.	.
30-34	38.9	44.9	42.1	39.2	36.3	38.7	40.3	.	.	.
35-39	26.3	25.0	23.9	23.0	20.5	25.3	22.2	.	.	.
40-44	18.0	14.4	19.4	17.4	15.0	20.2	17.2	.	.	.
45-54	19.1	20.0	22.5	24.0	20.1	25.5	20.2	.	.	.
55+	11.5	12.8	12.1	25.8	18.2	12.3	6.2	.	.	.

Women - Femmes - Mujeres

	1999	2000	2001	2002	2003	2004	2005	2006	2007	2008
Total	127.5	127.7	127.8	133.9	138.6	151.2	157.6	.	.	.
15-19	28.2	23.5	21.5	18.9	18.1	21.9	18.5	.	.	.
20-24	41.0	35.8	38.4	40.9	40.2	40.2	46.1	.	.	.
25-29	30.2	32.6	34.9	37.3	37.1	40.0	50.6	.	.	.
30-34	13.6	17.8	15.3	17.0	18.1	21.3	24.0	.	.	.
35-39	6.5	8.8	7.2	8.8	9.1	12.5	9.8	.	.	.
40-44	4.0	5.2	4.3	4.2	5.0	7.6	4.8	.	.	.
45-54	2.9	3.2	3.1	4.3	6.1	6.4	3.2	.	.	.
55+	1.2	0.8	3.1	2.6	4.7	1.4	0.5	.	.	.

AMERICA-AMÉRIQUE-AMERICA

Argentina (BA) [3] [4] [5] — Total unemployment - Chômage total - Desempleo total

Total - Total - Total

	1999	2000	2001	2002	2003	2004	2005	2006	2007	2008
Total	1 359.6	1 460.9	1 709.8	1 955.8	1 633.0 [6]	1 361.6	1 141.5	1 049.2 [7]	.	.
0-14	5.0	2.5	3.4	2.2	.	.	.	.	.	.
10-14	.	.	.	.	7.2 [6]	5.1	3.6	4.5 [7]	.	.
15-19	183.9	184.9	188.7	189.7	239.2 [6]	188.8	173.9	180.2 [7]	.	.
20-24	307.6	338.8	378.8	448.3	403.2 [6]	353.4	276.2	279.6 [7]	.	.
25-29	169.1	206.2	254.6	271.0	230.3 [6]	190.5	177.1	138.7 [7]	.	.
30-34	125.5	127.9	154.7	178.4	139.3 [6]	132.1	106.5	95.7 [7]	.	.
35-39	107.5	119.6	139.6	170.3	95.3 [6]	84.3	64.2	68.7 [7]	.	.
40-44	113.0	122.0	134.5	182.4	112.9 [6]	90.6	70.5	57.1 [7]	.	.
45-49	96.2	107.3	131.4	140.7	96.6 [6]	76.4	66.1	59.3 [7]	.	.
50-54	86.9	92.5	135.1	137.4	94.6 [6]	90.5	69.9	53.5 [7]	.	.
55-59	67.9	68.8	82.0	120.2	91.7 [6]	58.3	54.6	49.6 [7]	.	.
60-64	58.2	51.4	68.8	75.5	67.7 [6]	55.9	41.9	37.9 [7]	.	.
65-69	26.3	24.8	24.1	27.5	28.7 [6]	23.0	24.6	19.5 [7]	.	.
70-74	6.9	10.8	11.6	8.6	16.8 [6]	9.8	9.5	2.5 [7]	.	.
75+	5.5	2.9	2.3	3.0	9.5 [6]	2.9	2.9	2.4 [7]	.	.

Men - Hommes - Hombres

	1999	2000	2001	2002	2003	2004	2005	2006	2007	2008
Total	764.8	809.5	1 021.3	1 175.2	824.8 [6]	687.6	561.7	488.9 [7]	.	.
0-14	3.6	1.9	2.6	1.5	.	.	.	.	.	.
10-14	.	.	.	.	5.0 [6]	4.4	2.6	3.7 [7]	.	.
15-19	102.8	97.7	109.1	120.9	128.7 [6]	100.1	94.9	82.5 [7]	.	.
20-24	171.4	180.9	214.6	238.4	193.5 [6]	185.7	144.1	131.3 [7]	.	.
25-29	93.1	111.7	140.1	146.9	100.1 [6]	84.9	75.1	62.7 [7]	.	.
30-34	62.2	67.4	91.9	110.0	66.6 [6]	63.6	44.8	39.5 [7]	.	.
35-39	56.4	54.2	83.4	97.9	38.9 [6]	33.3	22.5	23.2 [7]	.	.
40-44	53.9	58.6	75.5	98.6	56.2 [6]	41.9	33.9	19.3 [7]	.	.
45-49	51.6	64.2	74.1	91.0	46.6 [6]	38.4	25.2	28.6 [7]	.	.
50-54	56.5	61.3	90.9	95.6	51.5 [6]	40.8	35.2	26.8 [7]	.	.
55-59	42.5	43.6	56.6	84.7	48.9 [6]	33.3	33.9	31.4 [7]	.	.
60-64	42.2	39.9	53.5	56.6	52.0 [6]	36.2	24.2	21.0 [7]	.	.
65-69	20.0	18.3	17.7	23.3	18.0 [6]	15.7	16.5	15.0 [7]	.	.
70-74	5.2	8.0	9.9	6.6	14.3 [6]	7.7	7.1	2.0 [7]	.	.
75+	3.6	1.5	1.4	2.2	4.5 [6]	1.6	1.6	1.9 [7]	.	.

Women - Femmes - Mujeres

	1999	2000	2001	2002	2003	2004	2005	2006	2007	2008
Total	594.7	651.0	688.4	780.6	808.2 [6]	673.9	579.8	560.3 [7]	.	.
0-14	1.4	0.6	0.8	0.7	.	.	.	.	.	.
10-14	.	.	.	.	2.2 [6]	0.7	0.9	0.7 [7]	.	.
15-19	81.1	87.1	79.6	68.9	110.5 [6]	88.7	79.0	97.8 [7]	.	.
20-24	136.2	157.9	164.2	209.9	209.7 [6]	167.7	132.1	148.3 [7]	.	.
25-29	76.0	94.4	114.5	124.1	130.2 [6]	105.6	102.1	76.0 [7]	.	.
30-34	63.3	60.5	62.8	68.4	72.7 [6]	68.5	61.7	56.2 [7]	.	.
35-39	51.1	65.4	56.2	72.3	56.4 [6]	51.0	41.7	45.5 [7]	.	.
40-44	59.1	63.4	59.0	83.8	56.7 [6]	48.7	36.6	37.8 [7]	.	.
45-49	44.6	43.1	57.2	49.6	50.0 [6]	38.0	40.9	30.6 [7]	.	.
50-54	30.5	31.1	44.2	41.4	43.1 [6]	49.7	34.7	26.7 [7]	.	.
55-59	25.5	25.2	25.3	35.5	42.8 [6]	25.0	20.7	18.3 [7]	.	.
60-64	16.0	11.5	15.3	18.9	15.8 [6]	19.7	17.7	16.9 [7]	.	.
65-69	6.3	6.5	6.5	4.2	10.8 [6]	7.4	8.1	4.5 [7]	.	.
70-74	1.7	2.7	1.7	2.0	2.4 [6]	2.1	2.4	0.5 [7]	.	.
75+	2.0	1.5	0.9	0.9	5.0 [6]	1.2	1.4	0.4 [7]	.	.

Explanatory notes: see p. 451.

[1] Persons aged 15 years and over. [2] 1999-2003: figures revised on the basis of the 2004 census results. [3] Persons aged 10 years and over. [4] 31 Urban agglomerations. [5] Second semester. [6] Methodology revised; data not strictly comparable; Prior to 2003: May and October. [7] Prior to 2006: 28 urban agglomerations.

Notes explicatives: voir p. 454.

[1] Personnes âgées de 15 ans et plus. [2] 1999-2003: données révisées sur la base des résultats du Recensement de 2004. [3] Personnes âgées de 10 ans et plus. [4] 31 agglomérations urbaines. [5] Second semestre. [6] Méthodologie révisée; les données ne sont pas strictement comparables; Avant 2003: mai et octobre. [7] Avant 2006: 28 agglomérations urbaines.

Notas explicativas: véase p. 457.

[1] Personas de 15 años y más. [2] 1999-2003: datos revisados de acuerdo con los resultados del Censo de 2004. [3] Personas de 10 años y más. [4] 31 aglomerados úrbanos. [5] Segundo semestre. [6] Metodología revisada; los datos no son estrictamente comparables; antes de 2003: mayo y octubre. [7] Antes de 2006: 28 aglomerados úrbanos

UNEMPLOYMENT   CHÔMAGE   DESEMPLEO

By age group   Par groupe d'âge   Por grupo de edad

Thousands   Milliers   Millares

Aruba (BA) [1] [2]

Total unemployment - Chômage total - Desempleo total

Total - Total - Total

	1999	2000	2001	2002	2003	2004	2005	2006	2007	2008
Total	.	.	.	.	.	.	.	.	3.123	.
15-19	.	.	.	.	.	.	.	.	0.643	.
20-24	.	.	.	.	.	.	.	.	0.735	.
25-29	.	.	.	.	.	.	.	.	0.239	.
30-34	.	.	.	.	.	.	.	.	0.167	.
35-39	.	.	.	.	.	.	.	.	0.321	.
40-44	.	.	.	.	.	.	.	.	0.251	.
45-49	.	.	.	.	.	.	.	.	0.316	.
50-54	.	.	.	.	.	.	.	.	0.225	.
55-59	.	.	.	.	.	.	.	.	0.155	.
60-64	.	.	.	.	.	.	.	.	0.036	.
65-69	.	.	.	.	.	.	.	.	0.018	.
70-74	.	.	.	.	.	.	.	.	0.017	.

Men - Hommes - Hombres

	1999	2000	2001	2002	2003	2004	2005	2006	2007	2008
Total	.	.	.	.	.	.	.	.	1.419	.
15-19	.	.	.	.	.	.	.	.	0.417	.
20-24	.	.	.	.	.	.	.	.	0.362	.
25-29	.	.	.	.	.	.	.	.	0.036	.
30-34	.	.	.	.	.	.	.	.	0.067	.
35-39	.	.	.	.	.	.	.	.	0.031	.
40-44	.	.	.	.	.	.	.	.	0.096	.
45-49	.	.	.	.	.	.	.	.	0.105	.
50-54	.	.	.	.	.	.	.	.	0.158	.
55-59	.	.	.	.	.	.	.	.	0.130	.
60-64	.	.	.	.	.	.	.	.	0.017	.
65-69	.	.	.	.	.	.	.	.	-	.
70-74	.	.	.	.	.	.	.	.	-	.

Women - Femmes - Mujeres

	1999	2000	2001	2002	2003	2004	2005	2006	2007	2008
Total	.	.	.	.	.	.	.	.	1.704	.
15-19	.	.	.	.	.	.	.	.	0.226	.
20-24	.	.	.	.	.	.	.	.	0.373	.
25-29	.	.	.	.	.	.	.	.	0.203	.
30-34	.	.	.	.	.	.	.	.	0.100	.
35-39	.	.	.	.	.	.	.	.	0.290	.
40-44	.	.	.	.	.	.	.	.	0.155	.
45-49	.	.	.	.	.	.	.	.	0.211	.
50-54	.	.	.	.	.	.	.	.	0.067	.
55-59	.	.	.	.	.	.	.	.	0.025	.
60-64	.	.	.	.	.	.	.	.	0.019	.
65-69	.	.	.	.	.	.	.	.	0.018	.
70-74	.	.	.	.	.	.	.	.	0.017	.

Bahamas (BA) [1] [3]

Total unemployment - Chômage total - Desempleo total

Total - Total - Total

	1999	2000	2001	2002	2003	2004	2005	2006	2007	2008
Total	12.29	.	11.33	15.28	18.83	17.99	18.18	13.83 [4]	14.62	.
15-19	2.30	.	1.69	2.18	3.13	3.00	2.56	2.23 [4]	2.61	.
20-24	2.40	.	2.87	3.52	4.56	4.15	3.64	2.52 [4]	3.40	.
25-34	3.81	.	3.17	4.56	5.12	5.08	5.01	3.81 [4]	3.33	.
35-44	1.73	.	1.83	2.69	3.43	2.90	3.49	2.98 [4]	2.80	.
45-54	0.95	.	1.19	1.32	1.55	2.17	2.07	1.50 [4]	1.67	.
55-64	0.49	.	0.54	0.82	0.78	0.50	1.17	0.68 [4]	0.79	.
65+	0.08	.	0.04	0.13	0.13	0.21	0.15	- [4]	-	.
?	0.55	.	0.07	0.09	0.16	0.03	0.12	0.12 [4]	0.04	.

Men - Hommes - Hombres

	1999	2000	2001	2002	2003	2004	2005	2006	2007	2008
Total	4.96	.	5.72	7.56	8.78	8.50	8.38	6.38 [4]	6.45	.
15-19	0.94	.	1.02	1.08	1.38	1.33	1.07	1.16 [4]	1.09	.
20-24	0.78	.	1.54	1.52	2.04	1.90	1.76	1.13 [4]	1.85	.
25-34	1.53	.	1.26	2.33	2.38	2.55	2.24	1.39 [4]	1.38	.
35-44	0.42	.	0.77	1.00	1.46	1.46	1.53	1.42 [4]	1.21	.
45-54	0.51	.	0.70	0.93	0.86	0.79	0.85	0.68 [4]	0.52	.
55-64	0.31	.	0.39	0.50	0.54	0.30	0.81	0.49 [4]	0.37	.
65+	0.48	.	0.04	0.21	0.09	0.18	0.12	- [4]	-	.
?	-	.	-	-	-	-	0.03	0.12 [4]	0.04	.

Women - Femmes - Mujeres

	1999	2000	2001	2002	2003	2004	2005	2006	2007	2008
Total	7.34	.	5.61	7.72	10.05	9.50	9.80	7.46 [4]	8.17	.
15-19	1.36	.	0.67	1.10	1.76	1.67	1.49	1.07 [4]	1.52	.
20-24	1.62	.	1.34	2.01	2.52	2.25	1.88	1.39 [4]	1.55	.
25-34	2.28	.	1.91	2.23	2.74	2.53	2.77	2.43 [4]	1.96	.
35-44	1.31	.	1.06	1.69	1.97	1.45	1.96	1.56 [4]	1.56	.
45-54	0.45	.	0.49	0.39	0.69	1.38	1.22	0.83 [4]	1.15	.
55-64	0.18	.	0.15	0.32	0.24	0.20	0.37	0.19 [4]	0.42	.
65+	0.15	.	-	-	0.15	0.03	0.03	- [4]	-	.
?	-	.	-	-	-	-	0.09	- [4]	-	.

Explanatory notes: see p. 451.   Notes explicatives: voir p. 454.   Notas explicativas: véase p. 457.

[1] Persons aged 15 years and over. [2] Oct. [3] April of each year. [4] May.

[1] Personnes âgées de 15 ans et plus. [2] Oct. [3] Avril de chaque année. [4] Mai.

[1] Personas de 15 años y más. [2] Oct. [3] Abril de cada año. [4] Mayo.

UNEMPLOYMENT — CHÔMAGE — DESEMPLEO — 3B

By age group — Par groupe d'âge — Por grupo de edad

	Thousands / Milliers / Millares									
	1999	2000	2001	2002	2003	2004	2005	2006	2007	2008

Brasil (BA) [1][2] — Total unemployment - Chômage total - Desempleo total

Total - Total - Total

Age	1999	2000	2001	2002	2003	2004	2005	2006	2007	2008
Total	7 639	.	7 853	7 958	8 640 [3]	8 264	8 953	8 210	8 060	.
10-14	285	.	208	234	186 [3]	181	203	185	206	.
15-19	1 993	.	1 899	1 936	1 988 [3]	2 008	2 280	1 970	1 849	.
20-24	1 639	.	1 813	1 902	2 103 [3]	2 014	2 162	1 969	1 795	.
25-29	1 006	.	1 106	1 080	1 204 [3]	1 158	1 288	1 245	1 250	.
30-34	.	.	808	777	888 [3]	823	833	816	833	.
30-39	1 438	.	.	.	.	.	.	.	.	.
35-39	.	.	663	640	698 [3]	659	675	605	654	.
40-44	.	.	488	517	568 [3]	522	530	499	525	.
40-49	803	.	.	.	.	.	.	.	.	.
45-49	.	.	354	359	420 [3]	393	409	386	411	.
50-54	.	.	238	255	278 [3]	253	276	248	264	.
50-59	354	.	.	.	.	.	.	.	.	.
55-59	.	.	150	126	161 [3]	138	152	157	150	.
60-64	.	.	80	80	83 [3]	82	81	82	78	.
60+	117	.	.	.	.	.	.	.	.	.
65-69	.	.	27	36	37 [3]	22	41	27	23	.
70-74	.	.	12	10	14 [3]	7	13	15	16	.
75+	.	.	5	5	10 [3]	4	7	5	6	.
?	4	.	1	-	1 [3]	-	2	.	.	.

Men - Hommes - Hombres

Age	1999	2000	2001	2002	2003	2004	2005	2006	2007	2008
Total	3 668	.	3 675	3 685	3 973 [3]	3 591	3 859	3 510	3 391	.
10-14	167	.	125	138	109 [3]	103	115	102	122	.
15-19	1 027	.	949	963	961 [3]	942	1 115	910	865	.
20-24	745	.	822	841	929 [3]	877	900	835	749	.
25-29	424	.	455	450	491 [3]	438	508	473	449	.
30-34	.	.	322	298	342 [3]	289	287	296	293	.
30-39	615	.	.	.	.	.	.	.	.	.
35-39	.	.	289	263	293 [3]	255	243	210	220	.
40-44	.	.	211	225	275 [3]	206	197	188	201	.
40-49	374	.	.	.	.	.	.	.	.	.
45-49	.	.	181	173	215 [3]	183	178	175	176	.
50-54	.	.	140	157	147 [3]	135	129	134	139	.
50-59	222	.	.	.	.	.	.	.	.	.
55-59	.	.	93	82	103 [3]	82	89	95	90	.
60-64	.	.	58	57	63 [3]	57	50	60	52	.
60+	91	.	.	.	.	.	.	.	.	.
65-69	.	.	19	27	26 [3]	18	30	18	20	.
70-74	.	.	9	6	8 [3]	6	10	11	11	.
75+	.	.	4	5	7 [3]	3	5	4	3	.
?	3	.	1	-	1 [3]	-	1	.	.	.

Women - Femmes - Mujeres

Age	1999	2000	2001	2002	2003	2004	2005	2006	2007	2008
Total	3 971	.	4 178	4 273	4 667 [3]	4 673	5 094	4 700	4 669	.
10-14	118	.	83	96	77 [3]	79	88	84	84	.
15-19	967	.	950	972	1 027 [3]	1 067	1 165	1 060	984	.
20-24	894	.	991	1 061	1 174 [3]	1 137	1 262	1 134	1 046	.
25-29	582	.	651	630	713 [3]	721	779	771	800	.
30-34	.	.	486	480	546 [3]	533	546	520	540	.
30-39	823	.	.	.	.	.	.	.	.	.
35-39	.	.	375	377	404 [3]	405	432	395	434	.
40-44	.	.	277	292	292 [3]	317	333	311	324	.
40-49	429	.	.	.	.	.	.	.	.	.
45-49	.	.	174	186	205 [3]	210	231	211	236	.
50-54	.	.	97	97	131 [3]	118	147	114	125	.
50-59	132	.	.	.	.	.	.	.	.	.
55-59	.	.	57	45	58 [3]	56	62	63	59	.
60-64	.	.	23	23	20 [3]	25	31	22	26	.
60+	26	.	.	.	.	.	.	.	.	.
65-69	.	.	9	10	11 [3]	4	11	9	3	.
70-74	.	.	3	3	5 [3]	2	4	4	5	.
75+	.	.	2	-	4 [3]	1	2	1	2	.
?	1	.	0	-	- [3]	-	1	.	.	.

Canada (BA) [4][5] — Total unemployment - Chômage total - Desempleo total

Total - Total - Total

Age	1999	2000	2001	2002	2003	2004	2005	2006	2007	2008
Total	1 181.6	1 082.8	1 163.6	1 268.9	1 286.2	1 235.3	1 172.8	1 108.4	1 079.4	1 119.3
15-19	186.1	174.4	181.5	204.0	205.7	204.2	184.3	180.8	174.8	187.9
20-24	172.4	157.5	162.2	174.1	180.0	175.8	165.9	152.9	150.9	154.5
25-29	129.8	119.3	129.4	140.3	134.8	140.5	126.6	114.5	120.5	115.1
30-34	135.9	114.1	117.8	133.7	129.8	114.2	110.7	106.3	95.4	100.3
35-39	142.1	126.9	139.9	148.0	140.8	129.7	120.4	111.2	102.4	100.0
40-44	139.8	125.6	142.1	145.5	149.9	143.2	130.0	121.1	115.7	113.2
45-49	103.5	98.5	106.3	118.2	119.7	113.7	119.7	107.0	103.8	109.1
50-54	86.7	83.5	91.4	96.1	102.4	91.0	96.1	89.3	89.3	98.5
55-59	55.4	52.9	58.8	69.3	76.6	77.4	70.4	72.8	73.9	78.3
60-64	23.9	24.5	26.9	31.9	36.8	36.1	37.9	37.9	39.7	50.3
65+	6.0	5.7	7.3	7.8	9.6	9.4	10.9	14.7	13.0	12.1

Explanatory notes: see p. 451.

[1] Persons aged 10 years and over. [2] Sep. of each year. [3] Prior to 2003: Excl. rural population of Rondõnia,Acre, Amazonas, Roraima, Pará and Amapá. [4] Persons aged 15 years and over. [5] Excl. residents of the Territories and indigenous persons living on reserves.

Notes explicatives: voir p. 454.

[1] Personnes âgées de 10 ans et plus. [2] Sept. de chaque année. [3] Avant 2003: Non compris la population rurale de Rondõnia, Acre, Amazonas, Roraima, Pará et Amapá. [4] Personnes âgées de 15 ans et plus. [5] Non compris les habitants des "Territoires" et les populations indigènes vivant dans les réserves.

Notas explicativas: véase p. 457.

[1] Personas de 10 años y más. [2] Sept. de cada año. [3] Antes de 2003: Excl. la población rural de Rondonia, Acre, Amazonas, Roraima, Pará y Amapá. [4] Personas de 15 años y más. [5] Excl. a los habitantes de los "Territorios" y a las poblaciones indígenas que viven en reservas.

3B

UNEMPLOYMENT	CHÔMAGE	DESEMPLEO
By age group	Par groupe d'âge	Por grupo de edad
Thousands	Milliers	Millares

	1999	2000	2001	2002	2003	2004	2005	2006	2007	2008
Canada (BA) [1][2]				Total unemployment - Chômage total - Desempleo total						
Men - Hommes - Hombres										
Total	660.4	595.3	655.1	721.7	719.6	685.4	649.0	608.3	603.9	632.6
15-19	103.4	95.7	103.5	118.3	115.4	110.7	99.6	99.6	96.9	103.3
20-24	101.5	93.8	98.5	103.5	108.8	108.3	104.9	88.6	86.6	95.2
25-29	71.7	64.8	75.9	84.4	77.6	83.9	70.4	64.8	74.2	65.7
30-34	76.6	61.7	65.0	76.2	69.6	60.0	60.4	56.4	54.1	57.2
35-39	72.5	67.7	73.1	79.1	74.8	67.9	62.5	57.8	52.7	52.2
40-44	76.8	66.2	77.0	74.4	75.9	72.7	68.4	63.9	61.0	62.4
45-49	54.3	51.6	56.0	65.2	64.6	60.9	60.8	55.1	55.1	59.6
50-54	48.3	44.8	50.3	53.6	55.8	48.4	53.7	49.3	50.5	55.5
55-59	34.9	30.1	34.2	41.0	45.6	44.5	38.7	41.0	41.3	42.5
60-64	15.9	15.2	17.2	21.0	24.7	21.9	22.9	21.9	22.8	31.6
65+	4.6	3.8	4.4	5.1	6.7	6.2	6.7	10.0	8.7	7.4
Women - Femmes - Mujeres										
Total	521.2	487.5	508.5	547.2	566.6	549.9	523.8	500.1	475.5	486.6
15-19	82.7	78.7	78.0	85.7	90.3	93.5	84.7	81.2	77.9	84.7
20-24	70.9	63.7	63.6	70.6	71.2	67.5	61.0	64.3	64.3	59.4
25-29	58.1	54.5	53.5	56.0	57.2	56.6	56.2	49.6	46.3	49.4
30-34	59.3	52.4	52.8	57.5	60.2	54.2	50.3	49.9	41.3	43.0
35-39	69.5	59.3	66.9	68.9	66.0	61.7	57.8	53.4	49.7	47.8
40-44	63.0	59.4	65.1	71.1	74.0	70.5	61.6	57.2	54.7	50.8
45-49	49.2	46.9	50.3	53.0	55.1	52.8	58.9	51.9	48.7	49.5
50-54	38.4	38.7	41.0	42.5	46.6	42.6	42.4	40.0	38.8	42.9
55-59	20.6	22.8	24.6	28.3	31.0	32.9	31.7	31.8	32.6	35.8
60-64	8.0	9.3	9.6	10.9	12.1	14.3	15.0	16.0	16.9	18.7
65+	1.4	1.9	2.9	2.7	2.8	3.2	4.1	4.6	4.3	4.7
Cayman Islands (BA) [1][3]				Total unemployment - Chômage total - Desempleo total						
Total - Total - Total										
Total	.	.	.	.	.	.	.	0.943 [4]	1.395	1.549
15-19	.	.	.	.	.	.	.	0.115 [4]	0.152	0.282
20-24	.	.	.	.	.	.	.	0.204 [4]	0.175	0.136
25-34	.	.	.	.	.	.	.	0.119 [4]	0.353	0.360
35-44	.	.	.	.	.	.	.	0.198 [4]	0.339	0.307
45-54	.	.	.	.	.	.	.	0.181 [4]	0.213	0.282
55-64	.	.	.	.	.	.	.	0.107 [4]	0.115	0.091
65+	.	.	.	.	.	.	.	0.019 [4]	0.048	0.091
Men - Hommes - Hombres										
Total	.	.	.	.	.	.	.	0.462 [4]	0.662	0.773
15-19	.	.	.	.	.	.	.	0.077 [4]	0.068	0.142
20-24	.	.	.	.	.	.	.	0.125 [4]	0.071	0.068
25-34	.	.	.	.	.	.	.	0.069 [4]	0.168	0.225
35-44	.	.	.	.	.	.	.	0.052 [4]	0.154	0.119
45-54	.	.	.	.	.	.	.	0.102 [4]	0.071	0.108
55-64	.	.	.	.	.	.	.	0.037 [4]	0.082	0.032
65+	.	.	.	.	.	.	.	- [4]	0.048	0.079
Women - Femmes - Mujeres										
Total	.	.	.	.	.	.	.	0.481 [4]	0.733	0.777
15-19	.	.	.	.	.	.	.	0.038 [4]	0.083	0.140
20-24	.	.	.	.	.	.	.	0.079 [4]	0.104	0.068
25-34	.	.	.	.	.	.	.	0.050 [4]	0.185	0.135
35-44	.	.	.	.	.	.	.	0.146 [4]	0.186	0.189
45-54	.	.	.	.	.	.	.	0.079 [4]	0.143	0.175
55-64	.	.	.	.	.	.	.	0.070 [4]	0.033	0.059
65+	.	.	.	.	.	.	.	- [4]	-	0.012
Colombia (BA) [5][6][7]				Total unemployment - Chômage total - Desempleo total						
Total - Total - Total										
Total	.	.	2 708.8	2 848.6	2 797.3	2 462.0	2 260.6	2 424.8	2 089.2	2 245.7
10-11	.	.	2.8	1.4	1.9	2.7	1.0	0.3	0.1	0.2
12-17	.	.	206.6	210.3	220.4	187.0	155.2	164.2	120.1	134.1
18-24	.	.	954.8	982.9	951.6	889.8	837.1	818.1	686.1	771.8
25-55	.	.	1 439.0	1 518.2	1 494.4	1 274.3	1 159.8	1 320.8	1 176.1	1 229.9
56+	.	.	105.6	135.9	129.0	108.2	107.5	121.4	106.5	109.6
Men - Hommes - Hombres										
Total	.	.	1 257.6	1 341.3	1 264.8	1 132.1	1 019.4	1 093.9	996.4	1 033.0
10-11	.	.	1.8	1.4	1.9	0.0	0.4	0.3	0.1	0.1
12-17	.	.	109.6	113.0	117.1	100.4	84.8	93.2	64.6	74.7
18-24	.	.	415.7	435.7	406.8	399.9	375.9	363.9	310.8	350.5
25-55	.	.	640.4	693.1	652.6	556.5	477.3	556.4	541.7	523.3
56+	.	.	90.0	98.2	86.4	74.9	80.9	80.2	79.1	84.3

Explanatory notes: see p. 451.

[1] Persons aged 15 years and over. [2] Excl. residents of the Territories and indigenous persons living on reserves. [3] Oct. [4] April. [5] From 2001, figures revised on the basis of the 2005 census results. [6] Persons aged 10 years and over. [7] Third quarter.

Notes explicatives: voir p. 454.

[1] Personnes âgées de 15 ans et plus. [2] Non compris les habitants des "Territoires" et les populations indigènes vivant dans les réserves. [3] Oct. [4] Avril. [5] A partir de 2001, données révisées sur la base des résultats du recensement de 2005. [6] Personnes âgées de 10 ans et plus. [7] Troisième trimestre.

Notas explicativas: véase p. 457.

[1] Personas de 15 años y más. [2] Excl. a los habitantes de los "Territorios" y a las poblaciones indígenas que viven en reservas. [3] Oct. [4] Abril. [5] A partir de 2001, datos revisados de acuerdocon los resultados del censo de 2005. [6] Personas de 10 años y más. [7] Tercer trimestre.

By age group   Par groupe d'âge   Por grupo de edad

	Thousands / Milliers / Millares									
	1999	2000	2001	2002	2003	2004	2005	2006	2007	2008
Colombia (BA) [1][2][3]				Total unemployment - Chômage total - Desempleo total						
Women - Femmes - Mujeres										
Total	.	.	1 451.2	1 507.3	1 532.5	1 329.9	1 241.2	1 330.9	1 092.8	1 212.7
10-11	.	.	1.0	0.0	0.0	2.2	0.6	0.0	0.0	0.0
12-17	.	.	97.0	97.3	103.3	86.6	70.4	71.0	55.5	59.4
18-24	.	.	539.0	547.1	544.8	489.9	461.2	454.3	375.6	421.3
25-55	.	.	798.6	825.2	841.8	717.8	682.5	764.4	634.4	706.6
56+	.	.	15.6	37.7	42.6	33.3	26.6	41.2	27.4	25.3
Costa Rica (BA) [4][5]				Total unemployment - Chômage total - Desempleo total						
Total - Total - Total										
Total	83.3	71.9	100.4	.	117.2	114.9	126.2	116.0	92.8	101.9
12-14	3.5	1.6	1.7	.	1.3	1.8	0.8	1.9	1.4	0.7
15-19	22.8	20.9	27.1	.	34.1	26.6	32.7	30.1	25.3	23.6
20-24	19.6	17.0	26.7	.	27.5	29.9	30.3	30.3	24.5	25.2
25-29	11.5	8.1	10.4	.	15.1	14.4	14.4	13.1	12.4	16.2
30-34	.	.	8.6	.	8.3	7.7	8.7	9.9	7.5	9.8
30-39	14.3	12.8								
35-39	.	.	8.5	.	9.0	8.7	12.2	5.8	4.6	5.8
40-44	.	.	7.1	.	6.7	9.9	9.3	8.1	4.8	7.3
40-49	7.7	6.8								
45-49	.	.	4.6	.	6.0	6.0	6.3	7.3	4.8	4.8
50-54	.	.	2.5	.	3.9	4.0	5.2	3.6	4.2	3.3
50-59	2.8	3.5								
55-59	.	.	1.8	.	2.4	3.7	2.0	2.1	2.0	2.5
60-64	.	.	0.9	.	2.0	1.4	2.0	2.0	1.2	1.7
60-69	0.9	1.1								
65-69	.	.	0.4	.	0.5	0.8	1.1	1.1	0.1	0.7
70-74	.	.	0.1	.	0.4	-	0.5	0.5	0.1	0.3
70+	0.2	0.1								
75+	.	.	0.2	.	-	0.1	0.1	0.2	0.1	-
?	.	.	.	.	.	0.1	.	.	.	0.2
Men - Hommes - Hombres										
Total	45.6	41.2	55.8	.	66.0	62.5	60.2	53.8	41.3	53.5
12-14	2.3	1.0	1.2	.	0.8	0.8	0.4	1.3	1.2	0.7
15-19	13.4	11.3	16.7	.	19.1	15.8	16.7	15.4	13.7	13.6
20-24	9.9	9.5	14.3	.	16.2	16.3	13.3	13.4	10.0	13.1
25-29	6.2	4.4	4.8	.	7.8	7.2	5.9	4.2	4.6	7.3
30-34	.	.	3.4	.	4.0	3.0	3.2	3.6	2.3	3.9
30-39	6.8	7.0								
35-39	.	.	4.8	.	3.7	4.2	4.1	1.4	1.9	2.4
40-44	.	.	3.3	.	4.4	3.8	5.7	3.2	2.1	4.0
40-49	4.6	4.5								
45-49	.	.	2.9	.	3.3	4.3	3.1	4.4	1.5	2.8
50-54	.	.	1.5	.	2.4	2.4	3.2	2.6	1.7	1.0
50-59	1.5	2.4								
55-59	.	.	1.5	.	1.7	2.5	1.5	1.3	1.4	2.3
60-64	.	.	0.9	.	1.7	1.2	1.2	1.4	0.7	1.4
60-69	0.7	0.9								
65-69	.	.	0.2	.	0.3	0.8	1.1	1.1	0.1	0.7
70-74	.	.	0.1	.	-	0.5	0.4	0.4	0.1	0.3
70+	0.2	0.1								
75+	.	.	0.2	.	-	0.1	0.1	-	-	-
?	.	.	.	.	.	0.1	.	.	.	0.2
Women - Femmes - Mujeres										
Total	37.7	30.8	44.6	.	51.2	52.4	66.0	62.3	51.5	48.4
12-14	1.2	0.6	0.5	.	0.5	0.9	0.5	0.5	0.2	.
15-19	9.5	9.5	10.4	.	15.0	10.8	16.1	14.7	11.6	10.0
20-24	9.6	7.5	12.4	.	11.3	13.6	17.0	16.9	14.5	12.1
25-29	5.3	3.7	5.5	.	7.3	7.1	8.5	8.9	7.8	8.9
30-34	.	.	5.2	.	4.3	4.7	5.6	6.3	5.2	5.9
30-39	7.5	5.8								
35-39	.	.	3.7	.	5.2	4.5	8.1	4.4	2.7	3.4
40-44	.	.	3.8	.	2.2	6.1	3.6	4.9	2.7	3.3
40-49	3.1	2.3								
45-49	.	.	1.6	.	2.7	1.7	3.3	2.9	3.2	2.0
50-54	.	.	0.9	.	1.6	1.6	2.0	1.0	2.5	2.3
50-59	1.3	1.1								
55-59	.	.	0.4	.	0.6	1.2	0.5	0.9	0.5	0.2
60-64	.	.	-	.	0.3	0.1	0.8	0.6	0.4	0.3
60-69	0.2	0.1								
65-69	.	.	0.2	.	.	.	.	.	.	.
70-74	.	.	.	.	.	.	.	0.1	.	.
70+	-	.								
75+	.	.	-	.	-	-	-	-	0.2	-
?	.	.	.	.	.	.	.	.	0.1	-

Explanatory notes: see p. 451.   Notes explicatives: voir p. 454.   Notas explicativas: véase p. 457.

[1] From 2001, figures revised on the basis of the 2005 census results. [2] Persons aged 10 years and over. [3] Third quarter. [4] Persons aged 12 years and over. [5] July of each year.

[1] A partir de 2001, données révisées sur la base des résultats du recensement de 2005. [2] Personnes âgées de 10 ans et plus. [3] Troisième trimestre. [4] Personnes âgées de 12 ans et plus. [5] Juillet de chaque année.

[1] A partir de 2001, datos revisados de acuerdo con los resultados del censo de 2005. [2] Personas de 10 años y más. [3] Tercer trimestre. [4] Personas de 12 años y más. [5] Julio de cada año.

UNEMPLOYMENT   CHÔMAGE   DESEMPLEO

By age group   Par groupe d'âge   Por grupo de edad

	Thousands / Milliers / Millares									
	1999	2000	2001	2002	2003	2004	2005	2006	2007	2008
Cuba (BA) [1][2]			Total unemployment - Chômage total - Desempleo total							
Total - Total - Total										
Total	290.9	252.3	191.6	156.1	109.7	87.7	93.9	92.7	88.6	79.6 [3]
17-19	27.2	22.8	17.6	14.0	10.0	6.1	6.8	5.1	6.8	5.8 [3]
20-29	142.8	119.0	84.1	59.9	42.1	31.8	30.0	29.0	30.1	27.4 [3]
30-39	94.7	73.4	59.7	53.6	36.9	30.5	34.4	32.9	27.8	24.4 [3]
40-59	26.2	37.0	30.2	28.6	20.6	19.3	22.7	25.7	23.9	22.0 [3]
Men - Hommes - Hombres										
Total	126.1	111.8	93.8	76.9	51.3	49.7	55.0	52.6	53.3	42.0 [3]
17-19	14.3	10.1	9.4	8.3	5.6	3.5	3.8	3.3	4.4	2.8 [3]
20-29	69.8	55.6	40.2	28.4	21.6	18.8	18.8	17.1	19.0	15.2 [3]
30-39	39.0	28.4	27.2	24.7	14.7	15.7	18.2	16.6	15.4	11.1 [3]
40-59	3.0	17.6	17.0	15.5	9.3	11.8	14.2	15.6	14.5	12.9 [3]
Women - Femmes - Mujeres										
Total	164.8	140.5	97.8	79.2	58.4	38.0	38.9	40.1	35.3	37.6 [3]
17-19	12.9	12.7	8.2	5.7	4.4	2.7	3.0	1.8	2.4	3.0 [3]
20-29	73.0	63.4	43.8	31.5	20.5	13.1	11.2	11.9	11.1	12.2 [3]
30-39	55.7	45.0	32.5	28.9	22.2	14.8	16.2	16.3	12.4	13.3 [3]
40-59	23.2	19.5	13.3	13.1	11.3	7.5	8.5	10.1	9.4	9.1 [3]
Chile (BA) [4][5]			Total unemployment - Chômage total - Desempleo total							
Total - Total - Total										
Total	529.1	489.4	469.4	468.7	453.1	494.7	440.4 |	409.9 [6]	510.7	544.7
15-19	50.6	41.7	42.3	44.8	40.2	34.1	42.6 |	36.7 [6]	56.4	59.4
20-24	124.9	116.9	106.6	113.2	109.1	121.1	99.3 |	93.1 [6]	123.9	126.0
25-29	90.6	87.9	87.4	81.3	81.8	80.5	80.0 |	72.2 [6]	84.7	92.1
30-34	70.6	69.0	58.3	57.2	54.2	65.6	48.2 |	54.8 [6]	55.0	55.6
35-39	55.6	47.0	52.3	50.2	49.5	54.0	41.5 |	41.4 [6]	47.5	49.5
40-44	48.9	39.4	42.7	43.2	38.3	46.8	48.3 |	36.1 [6]	42.7	47.2
45-49	29.9	29.0	30.2	30.6	34.7	36.1	33.3 |	29.5 [6]	32.5	44.0
50-54	28.3	25.5	21.8	22.5	20.1	26.4	20.2 |	20.9 [6]	32.9	31.9
55-59	17.2	18.7	15.9	15.6	14.6	15.6	16.4 |	12.9 [6]	21.9	22.5
60-64	10.0	11.4	9.0	6.6	6.7	11.7	7.9 |	8.7 [6]	9.0	10.5
65-69	2.5	2.3	2.5	3.3	2.9	2.3	2.1 |	2.4 [6]	3.7	3.6
70+	0.1	0.6	0.6	0.4	0.9	0.5	0.7 |	1.3 [6]	0.1	2.4
Men - Hommes - Hombres										
Total	322.9	312.5	302.6	298.5	279.2	280.8	248.2 |	239.3 [6]	280.1	306.4
15-19	29.2	22.8	27.4	26.1	23.3	20.6	25.3 |	23.5 [6]	31.0	35.2
20-24	76.7	68.5	61.4	71.9	62.5	69.8	53.0 |	52.1 [6]	66.4	75.2
25-29	53.5	54.2	52.8	50.2	49.1	42.6	44.6 |	40.3 [6]	44.1	50.4
30-34	44.0	45.5	36.0	35.1	34.6	35.5	26.1 |	31.1 [6]	26.8	31.0
35-39	30.0	30.0	33.2	29.8	28.6	28.0	21.2 |	22.7 [6]	26.1	26.3
40-44	26.2	26.3	30.8	26.9	24.1	27.0	27.1 |	18.7 [6]	24.7	21.8
45-49	18.1	17.7	20.5	19.1	21.8	19.8	19.0 |	17.2 [6]	16.8	20.5
50-54	21.1	17.8	16.5	18.6	15.2	14.5	11.1 |	13.2 [6]	19.1	18.6
55-59	13.8	15.9	13.1	11.4	10.7	11.0	11.0 |	10.4 [6]	13.7	16.7
60-64	8.0	11.0	8.1	5.9	6.0	9.9	7.2 |	7.2 [6]	7.9	7.4
65-69	2.4	2.3	2.3	3.1	2.4	1.6	1.9 |	2.1 [6]	3.1	2.3
70+	0.1	0.6	0.5	0.4	0.9	0.5	0.7 |	0.8 [6]	-	1.0
Women - Femmes - Mujeres										
Total	206.2	176.9	166.9	170.2	173.9	213.9	192.2 |	170.6 [6]	230.6	237.9
15-19	21.4	18.9	14.9	18.6	16.9	13.6	17.3 |	13.2 [6]	25.3	24.1
20-24	48.3	48.4	45.1	41.3	46.6	51.2	46.3 |	41.0 [6]	57.4	50.8
25-29	37.0	33.7	34.6	31.1	32.7	38.0	35.4 |	31.9 [6]	40.5	41.7
30-34	26.5	23.6	22.4	22.2	19.6	30.2	22.0 |	23.7 [6]	28.1	24.6
35-39	25.6	17.1	19.1	20.4	20.9	26.0	20.3 |	18.7 [6]	21.4	23.1
40-44	22.7	13.1	11.9	16.3	14.2	19.8	21.2 |	17.4 [6]	17.9	25.4
45-49	11.8	11.4	9.7	11.5	12.9	16.3	14.3 |	12.3 [6]	15.6	23.5
50-54	7.2	7.7	5.3	3.9	4.9	11.9	9.1 |	7.7 [6]	13.7	13.2
55-59	3.5	2.7	2.8	4.2	3.9	4.5	5.4 |	2.5 [6]	8.2	5.7
60-64	2.0	0.4	0.8	0.6	0.7	1.8	0.7 |	1.5 [6]	1.1	3.1
65-69	0.0	0.1	0.2	0.1	0.5	0.7	0.2 |	0.3 [6]	0.5	1.2
70+	-	-	0.1	0.1	-	0.1	- |	0.5 [6]	0.1	1.5
República Dominicana (BA) [7]			Total unemployment - Chômage total - Desempleo total							
Total - Total - Total										
Total	.	491.4	556.3	596.3	619.7	723.7	715.8	661.4	654.0	.
10-14	.	7.0	4.0	5.9	4.7	13.0	9.2	1.3	3.7	.
15-19	.	83.6	85.7	96.4	104.8	144.6	129.3	107.9	116.6	.
20-24	.	126.5	139.1	157.8	154.5	157.2	167.0	177.9	172.1	.
25-29	.	77.7	85.7	96.5	100.6	105.2	117.6	105.0	103.0	.
30-34	.	55.7	68.6	78.8	79.3	86.5	93.1	88.0	76.8	.
35-39	.	42.3	59.5	61.1	60.5	70.7	72.7	66.1	63.1	.
40-44	.	35.5	46.7	38.5	49.8	54.2	56.4	50.3	49.5	.
45-49	.	22.9	33.0	28.8	25.4	38.7	33.8	33.2	31.1	.
50-54	.	22.6	16.5	17.0	18.5	26.5	18.0	15.5	21.0	.
55-59	.	8.5	7.8	8.0	10.8	14.2	9.1	10.3	9.5	.
60+	.	9.1	9.7	7.4	10.8	12.8	9.2	5.8	7.6	.

Explanatory notes: see p. 451.

[1] Men aged 17 to 60 years; women aged 17 to 55 years. [2] Dec. [3] February - April [4] Persons aged 15 years and over. [5] Fourth quarter of each year. [6] Methodology revised; data not strictly comparable. [7] Persons aged 10 years and over.

Notes explicatives: voir p. 454.

[1] Hommes âgés de 17 à 60 ans; femmes âgées de 17 à 55 ans. [2] Déc. [3] Février - Avril [4] Personnes âgées de 15 ans et plus. [5] Quatrième trimestre de chaque année. [6] Méthodologie révisée; les données ne sont pas strictement comparables. [7] Personnes âgées de 10 ans et plus.

Notas explicativas: véase p. 457.

[1] Hombres de 17 a 60 años; mujeres de 17 a 55 años. [2] Dic. [3] Febrero - Abril [4] Personas de 15 años y más. [5] Cuarto trimestre de cada año. [6] Metodología revisada; los datos no son estrictamente comparables. [7] Personas de 10 años y más.

	Thousands			Milliers				Millares		
	1999	2000	2001	2002	2003	2004	2005	2006	2007	2008
República Dominicana (BA) [1]				**Total unemployment - Chômage total - Desempleo total**						
Men - Hommes - Hombres										
Total	.	174.7	208.0	215.5	243.0	252.5	269.6	233.5	240.7	.
10-14	.	4.3	2.9	2.9	3.1	7.4	4.7	0.8	2.7	.
15-19	.	37.9	38.5	41.7	50.5	66.6	61.6	45.1	56.1	.
20-24	.	43.4	51.7	63.8	66.7	59.8	74.1	71.7	67.5	.
25-29	.	18.0	26.6	27.0	35.1	29.4	37.4	33.5	33.5	.
30-34	.	17.5	21.3	19.6	20.8	20.4	23.3	26.9	22.0	.
35-39	.	11.1	18.8	16.5	15.0	17.6	18.2	16.2	15.5	.
40-44	.	12.5	15.6	13.3	15.5	12.4	15.8	14.8	13.2	.
45-49	.	8.8	10.8	9.6	10.6	12.5	10.0	10.2	11.3	.
50-54	.	8.1	9.1	10.4	10.2	10.8	11.6	8.7	9.4	.
55-59	.	4.7	4.8	4.7	6.4	6.7	5.4	3.2	4.8	.
60+	.	8.3	8.0	6.0	9.0	9.0	7.2	2.5	4.6	.
Women - Femmes - Mujeres										
Total	.	316.8	348.2	380.8	376.8	471.2	446.3	428.0	413.3	.
10-14	.	2.7	1.1	3.0	1.6	5.6	4.4	0.6	1.0	.
15-19	.	45.7	47.2	54.7	54.3	78.1	67.6	62.8	60.5	.
20-24	.	83.1	87.4	94.0	87.9	97.4	92.9	106.2	104.6	.
25-29	.	59.7	59.1	69.5	65.4	75.8	80.1	71.5	69.5	.
30-34	.	38.2	47.4	59.2	58.5	66.1	69.8	61.2	54.8	.
35-39	.	31.1	40.7	44.5	45.5	53.2	54.4	50.0	47.7	.
40-44	.	23.0	31.3	25.2	34.3	41.7	41.1	35.5	36.3	.
45-49	.	14.1	22.2	19.2	14.8	26.1	23.8	23.0	19.9	.
50-54	.	14.5	7.4	6.6	8.3	15.8	6.4	6.8	11.6	.
55-59	.	3.8	3.0	3.3	4.3	7.5	3.6	7.1	4.6	.
60+	.	0.8	1.7	1.4	1.8	3.8	2.0	3.3	3.0	.
Ecuador (BA) [1][2][3]				**Total unemployment - Chômage total - Desempleo total**						
Total - Total - Total										
Total	543.5	333.1	450.9 [4]	352.9	461.1	362.1	333.6	341.8	.	.
10-14	19.8	11.1	22.8 [4]	14.8	12.6	8.2	12.0	12.5	.	.
15-19	100.5	57.1	85.4 [4]	56.8	85.1	72.1	58.4	69.1	.	.
20-24	133.7	93.4	115.0 [4]	85.3	108.1	83.7	75.7	79.1	.	.
25-29	82.5	44.6	52.1 [4]	52.1	61.7	50.4	57.0	46.7	.	.
30-34	54.3	29.9	42.0 [4]	36.1	52.5	32.3	28.9	30.0	.	.
35-39	44.5	23.0	43.1 [4]	30.4	35.5	26.7	31.8	23.0	.	.
40-44	32.4	22.9	20.6 [4]	24.2	29.4	28.2	24.5	21.4	.	.
45-49	23.7	20.4	26.5 [4]	16.2	22.6	14.7	17.4	20.4	.	.
50-54	18.4	12.9	22.9 [4]	12.3	14.9	14.7	14.0	16.3	.	.
55-59	10.3	8.4	7.2 [4]	9.4	16.4	13.0	4.0	10.4	.	.
60-64	9.1	3.5	5.8 [4]	7.1	9.0	9.0	3.5	5.4	.	.
65-69	8.8	4.1	5.2 [4]	2.1	5.9	3.4	2.7	3.6	.	.
70+	5.3	1.9	2.4 [4]	6.1	7.4	5.7	3.5	3.9	.	.
Men - Hommes - Hombres										
Total	239.5	138.2	169.0 [4]	136.2	215.0	160.7	143.3	143.4	.	.
10-14	13.4	3.7	16.0 [4]	8.0	8.6	4.8	7.5	10.1	.	.
15-19	48.2	28.0	39.1 [4]	24.9	49.0	36.3	31.0	36.6	.	.
20-24	55.9	44.2	44.4 [4]	34.1	52.2	37.5	33.0	30.7	.	.
25-29	27.1	12.9	16.8 [4]	14.8	25.1	15.2	20.3	13.9	.	.
30-34	18.9	8.6	11.3 [4]	10.8	16.8	13.9	9.0	11.3	.	.
35-39	14.5	6.2	7.7 [4]	8.1	10.1	5.8	9.7	7.6	.	.
40-44	11.9	6.9	4.7 [4]	8.1	10.3	12.0	9.9	4.0	.	.
45-49	11.4	8.1	8.2 [4]	6.0	8.9	6.5	7.2	8.0	.	.
50-54	12.3	6.8	10.5 [4]	6.5	7.1	9.5	6.0	7.0	.	.
55-59	6.7	6.5	2.8 [4]	4.2	9.3	6.5	2.4	6.4	.	.
60-64	7.1	2.3	2.7 [4]	3.9	6.9	5.3	2.2	1.5	.	.
65-69	7.3	2.2	2.7 [4]	2.1	4.5	2.4	1.8	2.8	.	.
70+	4.7	1.9	1.9 [4]	4.6	6.2	5.1	3.2	3.4	.	.
Women - Femmes - Mujeres										
Total	304.0	194.8	282.0 [4]	216.7	246.1	201.4	190.3	198.4	.	.
10-14	6.6	7.4	6.8 [4]	6.8	4.0	3.5	4.5	2.4	.	.
15-19	52.3	29.0	46.3 [4]	32.0	36.1	35.8	27.4	32.5	.	.
20-24	77.8	49.2	70.5 [4]	51.2	55.9	46.2	42.7	48.4	.	.
25-29	55.4	31.7	35.3 [4]	37.3	36.5	35.1	36.7	32.9	.	.
30-34	35.4	21.3	30.6 [4]	25.2	35.7	18.5	19.9	18.7	.	.
35-39	30.0	16.8	35.4 [4]	22.2	25.4	20.9	22.2	15.5	.	.
40-44	20.5	16.0	15.9 [4]	16.1	19.1	16.2	14.6	17.3	.	.
45-49	12.4	12.3	18.3 [4]	10.2	13.7	8.2	10.2	12.3	.	.
50-54	6.1	6.0	12.3 [4]	5.8	7.9	5.2	8.0	9.3	.	.
55-59	3.6	1.9	4.4 [4]	5.2	7.0	6.5	1.6	4.0	.	.
60-64	1.9	1.2	3.1 [4]	3.1	2.1	3.7	1.3	3.9	.	.
65-69	1.4	1.9	2.5 [4]	-	1.4	1.0	0.9	0.8	.	.
70+	0.6	0.1	0.6 [4]	1.5	1.3	0.6	0.3	0.5	.	.

Explanatory notes: see p. 451.

[1] Persons aged 10 years and over. [2] Urban areas. [3] Nov. of each year. [4] July.

Notes explicatives: voir p. 454.

[1] Personnes âgées de 10 ans et plus. [2] Régions urbaines. [3] Nov. de chaque année. [4] Juillet.

Notas explicativas: véase p. 457.

[1] Personas de 10 años y más. [2] Areas urbanas. [3] Nov. de cada año. [4] Julio.

3B

UNEMPLOYMENT	CHÔMAGE	DESEMPLEO
By age group	Par groupe d'âge	Por grupo de edad

	Thousands					Milliers				Millares	
	1999	2000	2001	2002	2003	2004	2005	2006	2007	2008

El Salvador (BA) [1][2] — Total unemployment - Chômage total - Desempleo total

Total - Total - Total

	1999	2000	2001	2002	2003	2004	2005	2006	2007	2008
Total	163.3	164.4	170.3	147.4	169.4	164.0	177.6	164.2	166.6	.
10-15	7.8	6.7	5.8	4.4	3.9	3.6	6.8	6.9	6.5	.
16-19	32.3	30.7	26.9	21.7	26.3	27.0	30.8	30.7	30.7	.
20-24	43.8	44.8	40.3	40.8	40.3	37.4	47.3	38.2	31.5	.
25-29	22.2	19.2	21.7	21.3	23.0	22.9	28.8	20.8	23.3	.
30-34	14.5	16.4	15.0	13.7	17.3	17.8	13.9	16.6	18.4	.
35-39	12.4	11.5	11.3	12.5	13.2	13.2	14.9	10.3	9.8	.
40-44	8.9	9.2	14.1	8.3	9.4	10.6	7.7	8.3	9.2	.
45-49	6.8	6.5	7.0	7.3	9.1	7.3	9.0	6.5	9.6	.
50-54	5.9	7.0	7.9	6.5	7.8	7.2	5.6	8.2	6.6	.
55-59	3.5	4.8	6.4	4.3	4.8	3.6	5.0	6.1	7.2	.
60-64	2.9	3.5	5.0	3.3	6.8	4.7	4.8	3.6	5.8	.
65-69	1.1	2.3	4.6	1.5	3.2	4.9	1.9	3.3	2.5	.
70+	1.2	1.7	4.3	1.8	4.3	3.9	1.1	4.9	5.6	.

Men - Hommes - Hombres

	1999	2000	2001	2002	2003	2004	2005	2006	2007	2008
Total	120.2	129.5	119.6	113.7	134.5	127.3	129.6	123.9	126.6	.
10-15	6.7	5.9	4.6	3.9	3.3	3.5	5.0	5.7	5.1	.
16-19	25.5	25.2	20.7	16.8	19.9	21.6	24.1	22.1	24.9	.
20-24	29.5	33.3	27.4	29.5	30.5	24.5	28.7	26.0	22.2	.
25-29	13.7	13.0	14.0	13.8	17.1	16.3	19.2	13.5	15.2	.
30-34	9.9	11.8	10.2	10.5	12.6	13.7	10.4	13.1	13.6	.
35-39	9.0	8.5	6.0	10.3	9.8	9.4	11.4	7.1	6.1	.
40-44	6.8	7.1	9.8	6.2	7.5	9.2	6.2	6.8	6.2	.
45-49	5.5	6.0	5.6	6.5	8.6	6.2	8.1	5.2	7.6	.
50-54	5.4	6.6	6.1	6.1	7.1	6.9	4.3	6.9	6.1	.
55-59	3.3	4.7	4.6	4.0	4.5	3.5	4.7	5.8	6.6	.
60-64	2.7	3.5	3.5	3.0	6.4	4.5	4.4	3.5	5.3	.
65-69	1.0	2.3	3.4	1.3	3.1	4.4	1.9	3.3	2.4	.
70+	1.2	1.6	3.5	1.8	4.1	3.8	1.1	4.8	5.3	.

Women - Femmes - Mujeres

	1999	2000	2001	2002	2003	2004	2005	2006	2007	2008
Total	43.2	34.9	50.7	33.7	34.9	36.7	48.1	40.4	40.0	.
10-15	1.1	0.8	1.2	0.5	0.7	0.1	1.8	1.1	1.4	.
16-19	6.8	5.5	6.2	4.9	6.3	5.5	6.7	8.7	5.8	.
20-24	14.3	11.6	12.8	11.4	9.7	12.9	18.6	12.1	9.3	.
25-29	8.5	6.2	7.7	7.5	5.9	6.6	9.6	7.2	8.1	.
30-34	4.6	4.5	4.8	3.3	4.7	4.1	3.5	3.5	4.8	.
35-39	3.4	3.0	5.3	2.2	3.4	3.8	3.5	3.2	3.7	.
40-44	2.1	2.1	4.3	2.1	1.8	1.4	1.6	1.5	3.0	.
45-49	1.3	0.5	1.4	0.8	0.6	1.0	0.9	1.3	2.0	.
50-54	0.4	0.4	1.8	0.3	0.7	0.3	1.3	1.3	0.5	.
55-59	0.2	0.2	1.8	0.3	0.3	0.1	0.3	0.3	0.5	.
60-64	0.2	-	1.5	0.2	0.4	0.2	0.3	0.1	0.6	.
65-69	0.1	0.0	1.2	0.2	0.1	0.5	-	-	0.1	.
70+	-	0.1	0.8	-	0.3	0.1	-	0.1	0.3	.

Guadeloupe (BA) [3][4] — Total unemployment - Chômage total - Desempleo total

Total - Total - Total

	1999	2000	2001	2002	2003	2004	2005	2006	2007	2008
Total	.	49.4	43.7	41.5	44.0	40.3	42.0	46.2	.	.
15-24	.	10.3	6.3	6.9	5.9	6.2	6.3	7.6	.	.
25-49	.	35.5	34.4	31.1	34.1	30.3	32.2	33.8	.	.
50+	.	3.6	3.0	3.5	4.0	3.8	3.5	4.7	.	.

Men - Hommes - Hombres

	1999	2000	2001	2002	2003	2004	2005	2006	2007	2008
Total	.	21.7	19.1	19.0	20.9	17.5	18.1	20.8	.	.
15-24	.	4.9	3.2	3.6	3.2	3.2	3.5	4.2	.	.
25-49	.	15.0	14.7	13.6	15.4	12.4	13.1	14.4	.	.
50+	.	1.8	1.2	1.9	2.2	1.9	1.5	2.2	.	.

Women - Femmes - Mujeres

	1999	2000	2001	2002	2003	2004	2005	2006	2007	2008
Total	.	27.7	24.6	22.5	23.1	22.8	23.9	25.4	.	.
15-24	.	5.4	3.2	3.4	2.7	3.0	2.8	3.4	.	.
25-49	.	20.5	19.7	17.5	18.7	17.9	19.1	19.5	.	.
50+	.	1.8	1.7	1.6	1.8	1.9	2.1	2.5	.	.

Guyane française (BA) [3][4] — Total unemployment - Chômage total - Desempleo total

Total - Total - Total

	1999	2000	2001	2002	2003	2004	2005	2006	2007	2008
Total	.	15.2	15.0	13.5	14.1	15.2	15.9	18.4	12.8	.
15-24	.	3.3	2.6	2.4	2.5	2.6	2.9	3.2	2.3	.
25-49	.	10.3	10.8	9.5	9.9	10.8	11.0	12.9	9.1	.
50+	.	1.6	1.5	1.5	1.7	1.9	1.9	2.4	1.4	.

Men - Hommes - Hombres

	1999	2000	2001	2002	2003	2004	2005	2006	2007	2008
Total	.	7.3	7.4	6.4	6.6	7.3	7.9	8.2	5.9	.
15-24	.	1.7	1.5	1.3	1.1	1.4	1.6	1.5	1.1	.
25-49	.	4.7	5.0	4.3	4.5	4.8	5.0	5.4	4.0	.
50+	.	1.0	0.9	0.9	0.9	1.1	1.3	1.3	0.8	.

Women - Femmes - Mujeres

	1999	2000	2001	2002	2003	2004	2005	2006	2007	2008
Total	.	7.9	7.6	7.1	7.5	8.0	8.0	10.3	6.9	.
15-24	.	1.6	1.1	1.1	1.4	1.2	1.4	1.6	1.2	.
25-49	.	5.6	5.8	5.3	5.4	6.0	5.9	7.6	5.1	.
50+	.	0.6	0.7	0.7	0.8	0.7	0.7	1.1	0.6	.

Explanatory notes: see p. 451.   Notes explicatives: voir p. 454.   Notas explicativas: véase p. 457.

[1] Persons aged 10 years and over. [2] Dec. [3] Persons aged 15 years and over. [4] June of each year.

[1] Personnes âgées de 10 ans et plus. [2] Déc. [3] Personnes âgées de 15 ans et plus. [4] Juin de chaque année.

[1] Personas de 10 años y más. [2] Dic. [3] Personas de 15 años y más. [4] Junio de cada año.

	Thousands			Milliers				Millares		
	1999	2000	2001	2002	2003	2004	2005	2006	2007	2008

Honduras (BA) [1] [2] — Total unemployment - Chômage total - Desempleo total

Total - Total - Total

Total	89.3	.	.	.	.	153.2 [3]	107.8	.	.	.
10-14	2.8	.	.	.	.	4.1 [3]	1.8	.	.	.
15-19	28.4	.	.	.	.			.	.	.
15-24	.	.	.	.	.	77.8 [3]	53.2	.	.	.
20-24	23.9	.	.	.	.			.	.	.
25-29	9.9	.	.	.	.	25.0 [3]	20.1	.	.	.
30-44	16.2	.	.	.	.	28.7 [3]	23.9	.	.	.
45-59	5.6	.	.	.	.	14.3 [3]	7.1	.	.	.
60+	2.5	.	.	.	.	3.5 [3]	1.6	.	.	.

Men - Hommes - Hombres

Total	56.7	.	.	.	.	81.0 [3]	55.2	.	.	.
10-14	2.1	.	.	.	.	2.4 [3]	1.2	.	.	.
15-19	21.7	.	.	.	.			.	.	.
15-24	.	.	.	.	.	40.3 [3]	27.7	.	.	.
20-24	11.7	.	.	.	.			.	.	.
25-29	4.9	.	.	.	.	11.2 [3]	8.2	.	.	.
30-44	12.0	.	.	.	.	13.8 [3]	11.4	.	.	.
45-59	4.2	.	.	.	.	10.7 [3]	5.2	.	.	.
60+	2.2	.	.	.	.	2.7 [3]	1.6	.	.	.

Women - Femmes - Mujeres

Total	32.6	.	.	.	.	72.2 [3]	52.6	.	.	.
10-14	0.7	.	.	.	.	1.7 [3]	0.6	.	.	.
15-19	6.7	.	.	.	.			.	.	.
15-24	.	.	.	.	.	37.5 [3]	25.6	.	.	.
20-24	12.2	.	.	.	.			.	.	.
25-29	4.9	.	.	.	.	13.8 [3]	11.9	.	.	.
30-44	6.5	.	.	.	.	14.9 [3]	12.6	.	.	.
45-59	1.4	.	.	.	.	3.5 [3]	1.9	.	.	.
60+	0.3	.	.	.	.	0.8 [3]	0.0	.	.	.

Jamaica (BA) [4] — Total unemployment - Chômage total - Desempleo total

Total - Total - Total

Total	175.0	171.8	165.4 [5]	171.8	128.9	136.8	133.3	119.6	119.4	134.6
14-19	31.0	29.9	30.7 [5]	27.3	19.3	19.1	16.7	12.0	14.8	18.3
20-24	61.1	54.5	53.5 [5]	45.3	32.3	39.6	37.7	34.0	31.2	31.8
25-34	52.6	50.6	48.4 [5]	47.9	39.5	37.9	41.0	33.2	37.8	39.4
35-44	18.2	21.8	17.5 [5]	28.6	21.9	25.6	24.3	22.2	22.6	25.1
45-54	6.8	8.8	8.2 [5]	14.7	9.5	9.9	9.5	11.3	9.9	13.7
55-64	3.6	4.4	4.9 [5]	5.5	4.4	3.4	3.4	5.8	2.2	4.7
65+	1.7	1.8	2.4 [5]	2.5	2.0	1.3	1.4	1.1	0.9	1.6

Men - Hommes - Hombres

Total	61.4	62.5	63.4 [5]	65.7	47.6	54.0	50.0	48.0	37.8	52.5
14-19	14.6	15.2	14.0 [5]	12.1	9.4	8.7	7.7	6.6	5.7	9.1
20-24	21.0	19.9	21.7 [5]	18.7	14.0	17.7	15.3	13.6	10.2	12.5
25-34	14.4	13.6	14.9 [5]	14.8	11.5	12.4	13.5	11.0	10.8	12.6
35-44	5.5	6.7	5.0 [5]	8.9	6.0	8.4	7.0	7.8	6.0	9.4
45-54	2.9	3.2	3.3 [5]	6.1	3.3	4.3	3.7	4.2	3.3	5.1
55-64	2.1	2.8	2.9 [5]	3.4	2.4	1.7	1.6	4.3	1.5	3.2
65+	0.9	1.1	1.7 [5]	1.7	1.0	0.8	1.2	0.5	0.3	0.9

Women - Femmes - Mujeres

Total	113.8	109.2	102.1 [5]	106.1	81.3	82.8	83.0	71.6	81.6	81.8
14-19	16.4	14.7	16.7 [5]	15.2	9.9	10.4	9.0	5.4	9.1	9.2
20-24	40.1	34.5	31.8 [5]	26.6	18.3	21.9	21.7	20.4	21.0	19.3
25-34	38.2	37.0	33.6 [5]	33.1	28.0	25.5	27.5	22.2	27.0	26.8
35-44	12.7	15.1	12.5 [5]	19.7	15.9	17.2	17.3	14.4	16.6	15.7
45-54	3.9	5.6	4.9 [5]	8.6	6.2	5.6	5.8	7.1	6.6	8.6
55-64	1.5	1.6	2.0 [5]	2.1	2.0	1.7	1.8	1.5	0.7	1.5
65+	0.8	0.7	0.7 [5]	0.8	1.0	0.5	0.2	0.6	0.6	0.7

Martinique (BA) [6] [7] — Total unemployment - Chômage total - Desempleo total

Total - Total - Total

Total	.	44.1	39.8 |	32.3 [8]	31.4	32.7	27.2	36.9	34.5	34.7
15-19	.			1.0	1.3	1.4	0.9	1.7	1.7	1.4
15-24	.	6.4	5.9 |	. [8]						
20-24	.			4.9	3.8	4.3	4.1	6.3	4.1	5.2
25-29	.			6.0	4.8	4.8	4.0	5.3	4.1	3.5
25-49	.	34.7	30.7 |	. [8]						
30-34	.			5.7	5.6	5.1	4.8	5.2	5.1	4.6
35-39	.			6.1	5.7	5.4	4.5	5.6	5.2	5.0
40-44	.			3.8	4.5	5.6	4.2	4.5	5.5	6.1
45-49	.			2.8	3.2	3.0	2.5	4.1	4.5	4.5
50-54	.			1.9	2.5	3.0	2.2	4.2	4.2	4.4
50+	.	3.1	3.3 |	. [8]						
55-59	.			0.3	0.8	0.9	0.7	1.5	1.5	1.4
60-64	.			0.2	0.1	0.1	0.0	0.0	0.0	0.3
65+	.			0.0	0.0	0.0	0.0	0.0	0.0	0.0

Explanatory notes: see p. 451.

[1] Persons aged 10 years and over. [2] March of each year. [3] May. [4] Persons aged 14 years and over. [5] First and second quarters. [6] Persons aged 15 years and over. [7] June of each year. [8] Methodology revised; data not strictly comparable.

Notes explicatives: voir p. 454.

[1] Personnes âgées de 10 ans et plus. [2] Mars de chaque année. [3] Mai. [4] Personnes âgées de 14 ans et plus. [5] Premier et deuxième trimestres. [6] Personnes âgées de 15 ans et plus. [7] Juin de chaque année. [8] Méthodologie révisée; les données ne sont pas strictement comparables.

Notas explicativas: véase p. 457.

[1] Personas de 10 años y más. [2] Marzo de cada año. [3] Mayo. [4] Personas de 14 años y más. [5] Primero y secondo trimestres. [6] Personas de 15 años y más. [7] Junio de cada año. [8] Metodología revisada; los datos no son estrictamente comparables.

	Thousands			Milliers				Millares		
	1999	2000	2001	2002	2003	2004	2005	2006	2007	2008

Martinique (BA) [1] [2] Total unemployment - Chômage total - Desempleo total

Men - Hommes - Hombres

Total	.	18.9	16.3	13.9 [3]	13.9	14.4	12.1	17.4	16.3	14.6
15-19	.	.	.	0.8	0.6	0.9	0.5	1.0	1.1	0.9
15-24	.	2.9	2.8	. [3]	.	.	.	.	.	.
20-24	.	.	.	2.4	2.1	2.1	2.0	3.0	2.5	2.6
25-29	.	.	.	2.8	2.2	2.3	2.0	2.8	1.9	1.6
25-49	.	14.8	11.8	. [3]	.	.	.	.	.	.
30-34	.	.	.	2.0	2.2	2.1	2.0	2.2	2.3	1.7
35-39	.	.	.	2.4	1.9	2.1	1.7	2.4	2.3	1.9
40-44	.	.	.	1.4	1.8	2.0	1.9	1.7	2.4	2.3
45-49	.	.	.	1.2	1.6	1.4	1.2	1.9	1.7	1.5
50-54	.	.	.	0.9	1.3	1.5	0.9	2.4	2.0	2.1
50+	.	1.2	1.6	. [3]	.	.	.	.	.	.
55-59	.	.	.	0.2	0.5	0.5	0.3	0.9	0.7	0.9
60-64	.	.	.	0.2	0.0	0.0	0.0	0.0	0.0	0.2
65+	.	.	.	0.0	0.0	0.0	0.0	0.0	0.0	0.0

Women - Femmes - Mujeres

Total	.	25.2	23.6	18.4 [3]	17.5	18.3	15.1	19.5	18.2	20.1
15-19	.	.	.	0.2	0.7	0.5	0.4	0.8	0.6	0.5
15-24	.	3.5	3.1	.	.	.	.	.	.	.
20-24	.	.	.	2.6	1.6	2.2	2.1	3.4	1.6	2.6
25-29	.	.	.	3.2	2.6	2.5	2.0	2.5	2.1	1.9
25-49	.	19.8	18.8	.	.	.	.	.	.	.
30-34	.	.	.	3.7	3.4	3.0	2.8	2.9	2.8	3.0
35-39	.	.	.	3.7	3.7	3.3	2.9	3.3	2.9	3.1
40-44	.	.	.	2.4	2.6	3.6	2.3	2.8	3.1	3.8
45-49	.	.	.	1.6	1.6	1.6	1.3	2.2	2.8	3.0
50-54	.	.	.	1.0	1.2	1.5	1.3	1.8	2.2	2.3
50+	.	1.9	1.7	. [3]	.	.	.	.	.	.
55-59	.	.	.	0.1	0.3	0.4	0.3	0.6	0.8	0.5
60-64	.	.	.	0.0	0.0	0.1	0.0	0.0	0.0	0.1
65+	.	.	.	0.0	0.0	0.0	0.0	0.0	0.0	0.0

México (BA) [4] [5] Total unemployment - Chômage total - Desempleo total

Total - Total - Total

Total	954.2	998.9	996.1	1 145.6	1 195.6	1 539.8	1 482.5	1 377.7	1 505.2	1 593.3
14-14	15.8	9.7	14.5	8.4	8.0	11.6	12.0	10.4	9.3	9.4
15-19	191.9	260.3	227.2	252.0	251.4	326.9	264.9	263.5	273.8	284.2
20-24	208.5	244.1	227.4	292.2	305.7	384.6	332.1	306.0	344.3	378.0
25-29	159.7	147.4	160.2	189.0	195.2	265.2	226.0	229.2	264.8	254.7
30-34	108.5	88.8	104.1	107.0	126.5	150.7	170.5	152.4	164.1	173.9
35-39	93.0	82.2	81.2	86.4	92.1	124.0	124.4	106.4	135.3	145.5
40-44	72.2	47.1	54.6	73.9	81.7	92.3	103.9	91.9	100.0	115.5
45-49	35.9	40.3	49.4	52.8	53.7	60.5	75.4	77.0	77.3	74.4
50-54	31.7	30.3	32.0	31.4	35.0	58.7	69.2	62.0	58.2	65.1
55-59	16.3	27.5	24.7	29.1	23.4	33.7	48.0	36.2	38.4	46.8
60-64	10.3	10.5	10.7	15.3	13.0	15.4	24.9	25.2	22.1	25.8
65-69	8.4	5.4	6.1	3.7	6.0	9.0	20.3	10.6	8.6	13.2
70-74	1.0	2.1	1.8	3.0	2.4	3.7	8.2	5.2	4.5	3.7
75+	1.0	2.9	1.9	1.5	1.4	3.6	1.7	1.6	3.7	2.9
?	0.0	0.3	0.2	0.0	0.0	0.0	0.9	0.0	0.7	0.2

Men - Hommes - Hombres

Total	494.4	559.7	550.6	656.5	687.0	828.7	917.8	811.5	885.6	927.4
14-14	8.0	5.6	5.6	5.8	4.3	7.5	7.6	5.4	7.0	6.4
15-19	98.3	148.9	114.9	136.7	144.7	176.7	161.8	145.3	174.9	170.2
20-24	87.3	131.6	112.9	145.7	152.8	181.5	188.2	165.6	185.5	197.2
25-29	82.1	72.0	84.5	98.5	106.1	129.9	131.9	126.1	150.8	138.7
30-34	58.4	39.8	53.3	60.3	71.3	77.2	96.0	93.3	78.4	95.4
35-39	37.0	41.3	53.9	49.6	52.4	59.1	72.3	65.6	71.0	79.3
40-44	39.6	29.8	30.8	51.8	49.8	56.5	65.9	53.9	66.4	67.7
45-49	22.1	27.8	33.2	36.8	39.4	46.0	53.0	49.3	41.1	50.1
50-54	28.8	21.4	23.9	25.1	27.5	45.8	55.3	45.5	41.4	47.3
55-59	15.0	21.4	20.9	26.8	20.1	21.6	38.5	27.7	32.7	36.6
60-64	9.1	9.4	8.1	13.7	12.0	12.7	23.2	18.9	20.2	22.1
65-69	7.4	5.4	5.8	3.0	4.2	7.5	14.3	8.8	7.3	10.1
70-74	1.0	2.1	1.8	1.3	1.4	3.7	7.6	4.4	4.4	3.4
75+	0.1	2.8	0.6	1.5	1.0	3.0	1.4	1.6	3.7	2.6
?	0.0	0.3	0.2	0.0	0.0	0.0	0.9	0.0	0.7	0.2

Explanatory notes: see p. 451.

[1] Persons aged 15 years and over. [2] June of each year. [3] Methodology revised; data not strictly comparable. [4] Persons aged 14 years and over. [5] Second quarter of each year.

Notes explicatives: voir p. 454.

[1] Personnes âgées de 15 ans et plus. [2] Juin de chaque année. [3] Méthodologie révisée; les données ne sont pas strictement comparables. [4] Personnes âgées de 14 ans et plus. [5] Deuxième trimestre de chaque année.

Notas explicativas: véase p. 457.

[1] Personas de 15 años y más. [2] Junio de cada año. [3] Metodología revisada; los datos no son estrictamente comparables. [4] Personas de 14 años y más. [5] Segundo trimestre de cada año.

By age group   Par groupe d'âge   Por grupo de edad

	Thousands			Milliers				Millares		
	1999	2000	2001	2002	2003	2004	2005	2006	2007	2008

México (BA) [1][2] — Total unemployment - Chômage total - Desempleo total

Women - Femmes - Mujeres

	1999	2000	2001	2002	2003	2004	2005	2006	2007	2008
Total	459.8	439.2	445.5	489.0	508.7	711.0	564.7	566.2	619.6	665.9
14-14	7.7	4.1	8.9	2.6	3.7	4.2	4.5	4.9	2.3	3.1
15-19	93.7	111.4	112.3	115.3	106.7	150.3	103.1	118.2	98.9	114.0
20-24	121.2	112.5	114.5	146.5	152.9	203.1	143.9	140.4	158.8	180.8
25-29	77.6	75.4	75.6	90.5	89.2	135.2	94.1	103.1	113.9	115.9
30-34	50.0	49.0	50.8	46.6	55.2	73.5	74.5	59.1	85.7	78.5
35-39	56.0	40.9	27.3	36.8	39.7	64.8	52.1	40.8	64.3	66.1
40-44	32.6	17.2	23.8	22.1	31.9	35.8	38.0	38.0	33.6	47.8
45-49	13.8	12.4	16.2	16.0	14.3	14.5	22.4	27.8	36.2	24.3
50-54	2.9	8.8	8.1	6.2	7.5	12.8	13.9	16.5	16.8	17.8
55-59	1.3	6.2	3.8	2.3	3.3	12.1	9.6	8.4	5.7	10.2
60-64	1.2	1.1	2.6	1.6	1.0	2.7	1.7	6.3	2.0	3.7
65-69	1.0	0.0	0.3	0.8	1.8	1.4	6.0	1.9	1.3	3.1
70-74	0.0	0.0	0.0	1.6	1.0	0.0	0.6	0.8	0.1	0.3
75+	0.8	0.2	1.3	0.0	0.3	0.6	0.3	0.0	0.0	0.3
?	0.0	0.0	0.0	0.0	0.0	0.0	0.0	0.0	0.0	0.0

Netherlands Antilles (BA) [3][4][5] — Total unemployment - Chômage total - Desempleo total

Total - Total - Total

	1999	2000	2001	2002	2003	2004	2005	2006	2007	2008
Total	.	8.531	.	9.057	9.272	9.862	11.393	8.931	7.658	6.486
15-19	.	0.603	.	0.801	0.726	0.735	0.916	0.654	0.361	0.479
20-24	.	0.932	.	1.051	1.269	1.283	1.350	1.257	0.938	0.958
25-29	.	0.987	.	1.056	1.026	1.191	1.385	0.898	1.076	1.008
30-34	.	1.098	.	1.217	1.180	1.333	1.446	1.027	0.962	0.687
35-39	.	1.407	.	1.480	1.375	1.480	1.472	1.348	1.148	1.008
40-44	.	1.305	.	1.285	1.138	1.365	1.623	1.270	0.995	0.945
45-49	.	0.904	.	0.968	1.162	0.880	1.366	1.015	1.042	0.652
50-54	.	0.676	.	0.558	0.728	0.877	0.961	0.706	0.614	0.511
55-59	.	0.619	.	0.261	0.498	0.440	0.589	0.531	0.301	0.320
60-64	.	-	.	0.184	0.096	0.156	0.233	0.104	0.175	0.061
65+	.	-	.	0.196	0.074	0.122	0.052	0.121	0.047	0.018

Men - Hommes - Hombres

	1999	2000	2001	2002	2003	2004	2005	2006	2007	2008
Total	.	3.721	.	4.121	4.002	4.498	5.226	3.324	3.044	2.482
15-19	.	0.347	.	0.430	0.471	0.409	0.519	0.368	0.223	0.263
20-24	.	0.416	.	0.453	0.548	0.597	0.614	0.508	0.478	0.390
25-29	.	0.439	.	0.410	0.525	0.447	0.566	0.351	0.389	0.357
30-34	.	0.497	.	0.559	0.394	0.566	0.778	0.387	0.405	0.254
35-39	.	0.504	.	0.574	0.447	0.653	0.721	0.306	0.353	0.264
40-44	.	0.486	.	0.627	0.498	0.606	0.670	0.388	0.314	0.297
45-49	.	0.408	.	0.445	0.446	0.334	0.589	0.463	0.392	0.273
50-54	.	0.288	.	0.234	0.367	0.553	0.313	0.301	0.242	0.244
55-59	.	0.336	.	0.139	0.250	0.194	0.268	0.170	0.200	0.081
60-64	.	-	.	0.094	0.037	0.056	0.154	0.015	0.033	0.041
65+	.	-	.	0.156	0.019	0.083	0.034	0.067	0.015	0.018

Women - Femmes - Mujeres

	1999	2000	2001	2002	2003	2004	2005	2006	2007	2008
Total	.	4.810	.	4.934	5.272	5.363	6.166	5.610	4.617	4.003
15-19	.	0.256	.	0.371	0.255	0.326	0.397	0.286	0.137	0.216
20-24	.	0.516	.	0.598	0.722	0.686	0.736	0.749	0.461	0.568
25-29	.	0.548	.	0.646	0.501	0.744	0.819	0.548	0.687	0.490
30-34	.	0.601	.	0.658	0.786	0.768	0.669	0.640	0.558	0.433
35-39	.	0.903	.	0.906	0.928	0.827	0.751	1.043	0.796	0.744
40-44	.	0.819	.	0.658	0.640	0.759	0.952	0.883	0.682	0.648
45-49	.	0.496	.	0.522	0.716	0.546	0.777	0.551	0.649	0.379
50-54	.	0.388	.	0.323	0.361	0.324	0.647	0.406	0.372	0.267
55-59	.	0.283	.	0.122	0.248	0.246	0.321	0.361	0.101	0.239
60-64	.	-	.	0.090	0.059	0.099	0.079	0.089	0.142	0.019
65+	.	-	.	0.040	0.056	0.038	0.018	0.054	0.032	0.000

Nicaragua (BA) [6] — Total unemployment - Chômage total - Desempleo total

Total - Total - Total

	1999	2000	2001	2002	2003	2004	2005	2006	2007	2008
Total	.	.	.	.	160.5	138.0	122.5	114.5	.	.
10-14	.	.	.	.	2.9	2.9	4.4	1.3	.	.
15-19	.	.	.	.	27.5	25.9	21.3	19.7	.	.
20-24	.	.	.	.	44.5	40.5	33.7	31.1	.	.
25-29	.	.	.	.	27.4	24.2	20.6	20.8	.	.
30-34	.	.	.	.	15.7	10.9	11.8	11.1	.	.
35-39	.	.	.	.	11.8	12.7	9.1	7.6	.	.
40-44	.	.	.	.	10.7	6.7	6.8	7.7	.	.
45-49	.	.	.	.	7.5	4.6	5.1	5.6	.	.
50-54	.	.	.	.	4.4	4.2	4.1	4.0	.	.
55-59	.	.	.	.	3.8	1.8	2.5	2.9	.	.
60-64	.	.	.	.	2.1	2.1	1.2	0.8	.	.
65-69	.	.	.	.	1.1	0.9	1.7	1.0	.	.
70-74	.	.	.	.	0.7	0.3	0.1	0.5	.	.
75+	.	.	.	.	0.5	0.4	0.2	0.3	.	.

Explanatory notes: see p. 451.   Notes explicatives: voir p. 454.   Notas explicativas: véase p. 457.

[1] Persons aged 14 years and over. [2] Second quarter of each year. [3] Persons aged 15 years and over. [4] Curaçao. [5] Oct. of each year. [6] Persons aged 10 years and over.

[1] Personnes âgées de 14 ans et plus. [2] Deuxième trimestre de chaque année. [3] Personnes âgées de 15 ans et plus. [4] Curaçao. [5] Oct. de chaque année. [6] Personnes âgées de 10 ans et plus.

[1] Personas de 14 años y más. [2] Segundo trimestre de cada año. [3] Personas de 15 años y más. [4] Curaçao. [5] Oct. de cada año. [6] Personas de 10 años y más.

3B UNEMPLOYMENT   CHÔMAGE   DESEMPLEO

By age group   Par groupe d'âge   Por grupo de edad

	Thousands				Milliers				Millares	
	1999	2000	2001	2002	2003	2004	2005	2006	2007	2008
Nicaragua (BA) [1]					Total unemployment - Chômage total - Desempleo total					
Men - Hommes - Hombres										
Total	.	.	.	.	97.1	74.2	73.4	74.1	.	.
10-14	.	.	.	.	2.2	1.9	3.3	1.2	.	.
15-19	.	.	.	.	16.4	14.5	12.4	12.4	.	.
20-24	.	.	.	.	24.8	20.1	19.9	20.2	.	.
25-29	.	.	.	.	14.5	11.0	10.8	11.4	.	.
30-34	.	.	.	.	10.1	5.2	6.3	6.7	.	.
35-39	.	.	.	.	6.4	6.4	4.9	4.8	.	.
40-44	.	.	.	.	6.6	3.4	3.5	5.5	.	.
45-49	.	.	.	.	5.2	3.0	3.9	3.9	.	.
50-54	.	.	.	.	3.8	3.3	3.2	3.0	.	.
55-59	.	.	.	.	3.1	1.5	2.2	2.6	.	.
60-64	.	.	.	.	2.0	2.1	1.2	0.9	.	.
65-69	.	.	.	.	0.9	0.9	1.6	0.9	.	.
70-74	.	.	.	.	0.7	0.3	0.1	0.4	.	.
75+	.	.	.	.	0.3	0.2	0.2	0.3	.	.
Women - Femmes - Mujeres										
Total	.	.	.	.	63.4	63.8	49.1	40.3	.	.
10-14	.	.	.	.	0.7	1.0	1.1	0.1	.	.
15-19	.	.	.	.	11.1	11.4	8.8	7.3	.	.
20-24	.	.	.	.	19.7	20.4	13.8	10.9	.	.
25-29	.	.	.	.	12.8	13.3	9.8	9.4	.	.
30-34	.	.	.	.	5.6	5.6	5.6	4.4	.	.
35-39	.	.	.	.	5.4	6.3	4.2	2.8	.	.
40-44	.	.	.	.	4.0	2.8	3.3	2.3	.	.
45-49	.	.	.	.	2.3	1.7	1.2	1.7	.	.
50-54	.	.	.	.	0.6	0.9	0.8	0.9	.	.
55-59	.	.	.	.	0.7	0.2	0.3	0.3	.	.
60-64	.	.	.	.	0.1	0.0	0.0	0.0	.	.
65-69	.	.	.	.	0.2	0.0	0.1	0.1	.	.
70-74	.	.	.	.	0.0	0.0	0.0	0.1	.	.
75+	.	.	.	.	0.2	0.2	0.0	0.0	.	.
Panamá (BA) [2] [3]					Total unemployment - Chômage total - Desempleo total					
Total - Total - Total										
Total	128.0	.	169.7	172.4	170.4	159.9	136.8	121.4	92.0	82.9
15-19	22.9	.	26.7	26.2	25.1	24.1	20.5	17.9	14.9	15.5
20-24	37.3	.	47.7	48.4	49.2	44.6	37.1	33.2	27.3	24.6
25-29	23.2	.	27.4	30.0	28.4	24.4	22.6	21.8	16.3	14.9
30-39	23.8	.	36.4	38.8	36.9	35.3	27.7	24.0	16.3	15.5
40-49	12.0	.	19.9	17.4	19.9	19.1	17.6	14.9	11.2	7.4
50-59	6.6	.	8.4	8.4	8.1	9.1	8.4	6.4	4.5	3.1
60-69	1.6	.	3.0	2.7	1.9	3.2	2.7	2.3	1.5	1.5
70+	0.6	.	0.2	0.4	0.8	0.1	0.4	0.8	-	0.4
Men - Hommes - Hombres										
Total	62.1	.	92.0	86.5	82.9	76.3	66.7	60.2	44.5	40.2
15-19	13.0	.	17.2	16.3	15.6	14.2	11.8	10.4	9.4	8.9
20-24	17.4	.	24.8	24.8	24.2	23.1	18.4	15.0	12.0	12.4
25-29	9.9	.	12.4	12.4	12.9	9.2	11.5	11.0	6.6	5.9
30-39	9.2	.	17.6	16.2	14.0	13.4	9.4	9.0	6.5	6.1
40-49	5.4	.	10.8	8.1	8.1	7.5	7.6	7.6	5.4	3.4
50-59	5.2	.	6.4	6.4	5.8	6.1	5.5	4.6	3.0	1.5
60-69	1.4	.	2.7	2.0	1.5	2.7	2.2	2.0	1.4	1.4
70+	0.5	.	0.1	0.3	0.7	0.1	0.3	0.6	-	0.4
Women - Femmes - Mujeres										
Total	65.9	.	77.8	85.9	87.4	83.6	70.2	61.1	47.5	42.7
15-19	9.9	.	9.5	9.9	9.5	9.8	8.6	7.6	5.4	6.5
20-24	19.8	.	22.9	23.6	25.0	21.5	18.7	18.2	15.3	12.1
25-29	13.3	.	15.0	17.6	15.5	15.2	11.2	10.8	9.6	9.0
30-39	14.6	.	18.8	22.6	22.8	21.9	18.3	14.9	9.8	9.4
40-49	6.6	.	9.1	9.3	11.8	11.6	10.0	7.4	5.8	4.0
50-59	1.4	.	2.1	2.0	2.3	3.0	2.8	1.8	1.4	1.6
60-69	0.2	.	0.3	0.8	0.4	0.4	0.5	0.3	0.2	0.1
70+	0.1	.	-	0.1	0.1	-	0.1	0.2	-	-
Paraguay (BA) [4] [5]					Total unemployment - Chômage total - Desempleo total					
Total - Total - Total										
Total	.	.	.	.	.	.	.	.	161.2	170.6
10-14	.	.	.	.	.	.	.	.	5.5	12.2
15-19	.	.	.	.	.	.	.	.	42.4	47.3
20-24	.	.	.	.	.	.	.	.	45.1	38.6
25-29	.	.	.	.	.	.	.	.	23.7	19.8
30-34	.	.	.	.	.	.	.	.	10.8	10.8
35-39	.	.	.	.	.	.	.	.	9.8	8.5
40-44	.	.	.	.	.	.	.	.	5.0	6.1
45-49	.	.	.	.	.	.	.	.	5.4	6.8
50-54	.	.	.	.	.	.	.	.	5.2	8.9
55-59	.	.	.	.	.	.	.	.	3.1	4.7
60-64	.	.	.	.	.	.	.	.	1.9	4.3
65+	.	.	.	.	.	.	.	.	3.2	2.5

Explanatory notes: see p. 451.

[1] Persons aged 10 years and over. [2] Persons aged 15 years and over. [3] Aug. of each year. [4] Persons aged 10 years and over. [5] Fourth quarter.

Notes explicatives: voir p. 454.

[1] Personnes âgées de 10 ans et plus. [2] Personnes âgées de 15 ans et plus. [3] Août de chaque année. [4] Personnes âgées de 10 ans et plus. [5] Quatrième trimestre.

Notas explicativas: véase p. 457.

[1] Personas de 10 años y más. [2] Personas de 15 años y más. [3] Agosto de cada año. [4] Personas de 10 años y más. [5] Cuarto trimestre.

By age group — Par groupe d'âge — Por grupo de edad

	Thousands — Milliers — Millares									
	1999	2000	2001	2002	2003	2004	2005	2006	2007	2008
Paraguay (BA) [1][2]				Total unemployment - Chômage total - Desempleo total						
Men - Hommes - Hombres										
Total	.	.	.	.	.	.	.	.	74.6	83.9
10-14	.	.	.	.	.	.	.	.	4.4	9.5
15-19	.	.	.	.	.	.	.	.	18.9	24.0
20-24	.	.	.	.	.	.	.	.	19.8	14.7
25-29	.	.	.	.	.	.	.	.	10.5	5.9
30-34	.	.	.	.	.	.	.	.	4.3	4.0
35-39	.	.	.	.	.	.	.	.	2.6	4.0
40-44	.	.	.	.	.	.	.	.	2.2	3.0
45-49	.	.	.	.	.	.	.	.	1.7	3.7
50-54	.	.	.	.	.	.	.	.	4.6	6.3
55-59	.	.	.	.	.	.	.	.	1.6	3.2
60-64	.	.	.	.	.	.	.	.	1.7	3.1
65+	.	.	.	.	.	.	.	.	2.1	2.5
Women - Femmes - Mujeres										
Total	.	.	.	.	.	.	.	.	86.6	86.7
10-14	.	.	.	.	.	.	.	.	1.1	2.8
15-19	.	.	.	.	.	.	.	.	23.5	23.4
20-24	.	.	.	.	.	.	.	.	25.3	23.9
25-29	.	.	.	.	.	.	.	.	13.2	13.9
30-34	.	.	.	.	.	.	.	.	6.4	6.8
35-39	.	.	.	.	.	.	.	.	7.2	4.6
40-44	.	.	.	.	.	.	.	.	2.8	3.1
45-49	.	.	.	.	.	.	.	.	3.7	3.1
50-54	.	.	.	.	.	.	.	.	0.7	2.6
55-59	.	.	.	.	.	.	.	.	1.5	1.5
60-64	.	.	.	.	.	.	.	.	0.2	1.3
65+	.	.	.	.	.	.	.	.	1.1	-
Perú (BA) [3][4]				Total unemployment - Chômage total - Desempleo total						
Total - Total - Total										
Total	.	.	.	359.4 [2]	316.0 [5]	339.5	333.4	297.6	300.1	308.0
14-14	.	.	.	- [2]	5.4 [5]	9.8	15.4	8.3	13.5	7.3
15-19	.	.	.	44.9 [2]	58.4 [5]	64.0	54.8	73.1	76.5	69.0
20-24	.	.	.	70.4 [2]	69.7 [5]	93.7	85.6	49.4	46.5	65.9
25-29	.	.	.	59.4 [2]	36.9 [5]	38.5	38.1	38.3	46.0	48.5
30-34	.	.	.	38.3 [2]	34.6 [5]	29.6	39.3	27.0	24.3	24.5
35-39	.	.	.	30.2 [2]	19.0 [5]	23.1	15.1	20.5	16.3	21.4
40-44	.	.	.	30.2 [2]	20.0 [5]	27.7	13.8	23.2	13.6	11.9
45-49	.	.	.	24.9 [2]	21.5 [5]	18.6	29.2	14.8	13.6	20.1
50-54	.	.	.	24.7 [2]	17.8 [5]	14.0	15.9	14.6	17.7	10.3
55-59	.	.	.	14.3 [2]	17.4 [5]	10.1	12.7	13.6	13.9	15.4
60-64	.	.	.	13.5 [2]	3.1 [5]	3.5	7.1	7.1	11.5	4.8
65-69	.	.	.	7.3 [2]	8.1 [5]	3.6	2.4	6.4	2.3	4.4
70-74	.	.	.	1.2 [2]	4.0 [5]	1.2	0.9	0.7	2.5	2.3
75+	.	.	.	- [2]	- [5]	2.1	3.2	0.6	1.8	2.4
Men - Hommes - Hombres										
Total	.	.	.	194.0 [2]	182.5 [5]	159.4	155.4	136.3	139.1	131.3
14-14	.	.	.	- [2]	3.0 [5]	5.1	1.6	7.7	8.5	3.0
15-19	.	.	.	26.0 [2]	37.0 [5]	34.2	27.7	38.0	38.6	33.7
20-24	.	.	.	42.8 [2]	46.1 [5]	42.6	40.8	23.4	21.7	28.9
25-29	.	.	.	25.2 [2]	20.5 [5]	19.7	18.3	19.0	23.3	16.7
30-34	.	.	.	18.2 [2]	10.6 [5]	10.9	14.4	7.9	11.1	7.9
35-39	.	.	.	13.4 [2]	13.1 [5]	7.0	5.8	9.0	4.9	6.0
40-44	.	.	.	11.8 [2]	6.1 [5]	11.6	4.4	5.3	3.5	5.6
45-49	.	.	.	13.7 [2]	9.9 [5]	8.0	13.3	3.6	4.2	9.6
50-54	.	.	.	14.4 [2]	8.3 [5]	6.6	10.0	4.5	5.3	1.8
55-59	.	.	.	9.2 [2]	13.3 [5]	6.1	7.1	5.0	4.3	8.1
60-64	.	.	.	11.2 [2]	3.1 [5]	2.9	6.5	5.2	9.6	4.8
65-69	.	.	.	7.0 [2]	7.5 [5]	1.5	1.6	6.4	1.6	2.6
70-74	.	.	.	1.2 [2]	4.0 [5]	1.2	0.9	0.7	0.8	2.3
75+	.	.	.	- [2]	- [5]	2.1	3.2	0.6	1.8	0.4
Women - Femmes - Mujeres										
Total	.	.	.	165.4 [2]	133.6 [5]	180.1	178.0	161.3	161.0	176.6
14-14	.	.	.	- [2]	2.4 [5]	4.7	13.8	0.6	5.0	4.4
15-19	.	.	.	18.9 [2]	21.4 [5]	29.8	27.1	35.0	38.0	35.4
20-24	.	.	.	27.6 [2]	23.7 [5]	51.1	44.8	25.9	24.8	37.0
25-29	.	.	.	34.2 [2]	16.4 [5]	18.8	19.8	19.3	22.7	31.7
30-34	.	.	.	20.1 [2]	24.1 [5]	18.6	25.0	19.1	13.2	16.6
35-39	.	.	.	16.8 [2]	5.9 [5]	16.0	9.3	11.5	11.5	15.4
40-44	.	.	.	18.5 [2]	13.9 [5]	16.2	9.5	17.9	10.1	6.2
45-49	.	.	.	11.2 [2]	11.6 [5]	10.6	15.9	11.2	9.4	10.5
50-54	.	.	.	10.3 [2]	9.5 [5]	7.4	5.9	10.2	12.4	8.5
55-59	.	.	.	5.2 [2]	4.1 [5]	4.0	5.7	8.6	9.6	7.4
60-64	.	.	.	2.3 [2]	- [5]	0.6	0.5	2.0	1.9	-
65-69	.	.	.	0.3 [2]	0.6 [5]	2.2	0.8	-	0.7	1.8
70-74	.	.	.	- [2]	- [5]	-	-	-	1.7	
75+	.	.	.	- [2]	- [5]	-	-	-		2.0

Explanatory notes: see p. 451.

[1] Persons aged 10 years and over. [2] Fourth quarter. [3] Persons aged 14 years and over. [4] Metropolitan Lima. [5] May-Dec.

Notes explicatives: voir p. 454.

[1] Personnes âgées de 10 ans et plus. [2] Quatrième trimestre. [3] Personnes âgées de 14 ans et plus. [4] Lima métropolitaine. [5] Mai-déc.

Notas explicativas: véase p. 457.

[1] Personas de 10 años y más. [2] Cuarto trimestre. [3] Personas de 14 años y más. [4] Lima metropolitana. [5] Mayo-dic.

UNEMPLOYMENT   CHÔMAGE   DESEMPLEO

By age group   Par groupe d'âge   Por grupo de edad

Thousands   Milliers   Millares

	1999	2000	2001	2002	2003	2004	2005	2006	2007	2008
Puerto Rico (BA) [1][2]				Total unemployment - Chômage total - Desempleo total						
Total - Total - Total										
Total	152	132	145	163	164	145	160	156	152	158
16-19	16	12	13	15	15	13	15	11	9	11
20-24	33	29	29	32	34	32	35	31	28	28
25-34	44	38	39	43	45	40	44	41	45	46
35-44	32	29	34	36	37	30	31	34	33	37
45-54	22	17	21	24	23	22	25	26	23	24
55-64	8	6	10	11	9	8	9	11	13	10
65+	1	-	1	1	1	-	1	1	1	1
Men - Hommes - Hombres										
Total	101	90	97	101	99	92	97	90	93	97
16-19	11	8	9	9	9	8	9	8	7	8
20-24	21	20	19	20	21	20	23	18	18	18
25-34	28	25	25	28	26	24	25	22	26	26
35-44	21	20	22	23	22	18	17	19	19	21
45-54	14	12	15	15	15	15	16	14	13	16
55-64	7	6	7	8	7	7	7	7	9	8
65+	1	-	-	1	1	-	-	-	-	-
Women - Femmes - Mujeres										
Total	51	42	48	62	65	53	63	66	59	60
16-19	5	4	4	6	6	4	6	4	2	3
20-24	12	9	10	13	14	12	12	12	10	10
25-34	16	13	15	16	19	16	19	19	19	20
35-44	11	9	12	14	16	12	14	15	14	16
45-54	8	5	6	9	8	7	9	11	10	8
55-64	1	-	3	3	2	1	2	4	4	2
65+	-	-	-	-	-	-	-	-	-	-
Saint Lucia (BA) [3]				Total unemployment - Chômage total - Desempleo total						
Total - Total - Total										
Total	13.220	12.535	.	14.990	18.205	16.527	.	.	.	.
15-19	3.335	3.100	.	2.740	3.030	3.147	.	.	.	.
20-24	3.380	3.100	.	3.180	3.447	3.472	.	.	.	.
25-34	2.795	2.955	.	3.765	4.672	4.395	.	.	.	.
35-44	1.940	2.145	.	2.310	3.340	2.507	.	.	.	.
45-54	0.865	0.715	.	1.385	2.105	1.525	.	.	.	.
55-64	0.545	0.275	.	0.655	0.707	0.820	.	.	.	.
65+	0.360	0.245	.	0.955	0.902	0.660	.	.	.	.
Men - Hommes - Hombres										
Total	6.065	5.070	.	6.710	7.557	7.382	.	.	.	.
15-19	1.580	1.505	.	1.270	1.305	1.720	.	.	.	.
20-24	1.590	1.415	.	1.580	1.412	1.682	.	.	.	.
25-34	1.020	0.935	.	1.365	1.955	1.740	.	.	.	.
35-44	0.745	0.635	.	1.050	1.095	0.802	.	.	.	.
45-54	0.500	0.315	.	0.530	0.887	0.650	.	.	.	.
55-64	0.355	0.125	.	0.320	0.400	0.390	.	.	.	.
65+	0.275	0.140	.	0.595	0.502	0.397	.	.	.	.
Women - Femmes - Mujeres										
Total	7.155	7.465	.	8.280	10.647	9.145	.	.	.	.
15-19	1.755	1.595	.	1.470	1.725	1.427	.	.	.	.
20-24	1.790	1.685	.	1.600	2.035	1.790	.	.	.	.
25-34	1.775	2.020	.	2.400	2.717	2.655	.	.	.	.
35-44	1.195	1.510	.	1.260	2.245	1.705	.	.	.	.
45-54	0.365	0.400	.	0.855	1.217	0.875	.	.	.	.
55-64	0.190	0.150	.	0.335	0.307	0.430	.	.	.	.
65+	0.085	0.105	.	0.360	0.400	0.262	.	.	.	.
Trinidad and Tobago (BA) [3]				Total unemployment - Chômage total - Desempleo total						
Total - Total - Total										
Total	74.0	69.6	62.4	61.1	62.4	51.1	49.7	39.0	34.5	29.0
15-19	13.8	13.0	10.9	10.2	9.9	8.2	7.8	5.1	4.7	3.4
20-24	17.9	17.3	16.8	15.3	16.3	15.3	13.9	11.7	9.3	8.8
25-29	11.4	8.6	9.7	9.1	8.6	6.6	6.4	5.9	5.6	4.3
30-34	7.4	7.7	7.3	6.4	6.4	5.0	4.6	3.5	3.3	2.4
35-39	7.9	6.9	5.6	6.2	5.8	4.5	4.1	2.9	2.2	2.1
40-44	5.6	5.2	4.7	4.7	4.5	4.1	4.2	3.3	2.6	2.3
45-49	4.4	4.3	2.7	4.2	4.7	3.0	3.2	2.7	2.5	2.2
50-54	2.8	3.5	2.5	2.8	3.4	1.9	2.3	2.0	1.8	2.0
55-59	1.7	1.7	1.6	1.3	2.1	1.7	1.8	1.3	1.4	0.7
60-64	0.5	0.7	0.6	0.5	0.6	0.6	1.1	0.7	0.9	0.8
65+	0.5	0.4	0.3	0.2	0.2	0.2	0.2	0.1	0.2	-

Explanatory notes: see p. 451.

[1] Excl. persons temporarily laid off. [2] Persons aged 16 years and over. [3] Persons aged 15 years and over.

Notes explicatives: voir p. 454.

[1] Non compris les personnes temporairement mises à pied. [2] Personnes âgées de 16 ans et plus. [3] Personnes âgées de 15 ans et plus.

Notas explicativas: véase p. 457.

[1] Excl. las personas temporalmente despedidas. [2] Personas de 16 años y más. [3] Personas de 15 años y más.

3B

	Thousands			Milliers			Millares		
	1999	2000	2001	2002	2003	2004	2005	2006	2007	2008

Trinidad and Tobago (BA) [1] — Total unemployment - Chômage total - Desempleo total

Men - Hommes - Hombres

Total	37.9	36.1	30.7	27.9	29.8	23.4	21.3	16.4	14.4	12.9
15-19	7.3	7.2	6.0	5.2	5.1	4.0	3.8	2.3	2.8	1.8
20-24	9.4	9.0	8.4	7.2	8.3	7.4	6.2	5.2	4.1	4.2
25-29	5.6	4.3	4.3	3.6	3.8	3.1	2.7	2.6	2.4	1.9
30-34	3.7	3.2	2.8	2.4	2.9	2.1	1.9	1.5	0.9	0.9
35-39	3.4	3.6	2.9	2.4	2.0	1.4	1.5	1.3	0.6	0.7
40-44	3.3	3.1	2.3	1.8	1.7	1.8	1.6	0.9	1.0	1.0
45-49	1.7	1.6	1.4	2.2	2.2	1.1	1.2	1.1	0.9	0.7
50-54	1.5	1.9	1.2	1.4	2.0	1.2	1.0	0.7	0.6	0.9
55-59	1.1	1.2	1.0	1.0	1.4	0.7	0.7	0.5	0.6	0.4
60-64	0.4	0.6	0.4	0.4	0.4	0.4	0.5	0.4	0.4	0.4
65+	0.4	0.4	0.2	0.1	0.1	0.1	0.1	-	0.1	-

Women - Femmes - Mujeres

Total	36.1	33.5	31.7	33.2	32.6	27.7	28.4	22.6	20.1	16.1
15-19	6.5	5.8	4.9	5.0	4.8	4.2	4.0	2.8	1.9	1.6
20-24	8.5	8.3	8.4	8.1	8.0	7.9	7.7	6.5	5.2	4.6
25-29	5.8	4.3	5.4	5.5	4.8	3.5	3.7	3.3	3.2	2.4
30-34	3.7	4.5	4.5	4.0	3.5	2.9	2.7	2.0	2.4	1.5
35-39	4.5	3.3	2.7	3.8	3.8	3.1	2.6	1.6	1.6	1.4
40-44	2.3	2.1	2.4	2.9	2.8	2.3	2.6	2.4	1.6	1.3
45-49	2.7	2.7	1.3	2.0	2.5	1.9	2.0	1.6	1.6	1.5
50-54	1.3	1.6	1.3	1.4	1.4	0.7	1.3	1.3	1.2	1.1
55-59	0.6	0.5	0.6	0.3	0.7	1.0	1.1	0.8	0.8	0.3
60-64	0.1	0.1	0.2	0.1	0.2	0.2	0.6	0.3	0.5	0.4
65+	0.1	-	0.1	0.1	0.1	0.1	0.1	0.1	0.1	-

United States (BA) [2] — Total unemployment - Chômage total - Desempleo total

Total - Total - Total

Total	5 880	5 655	6 742	8 378	8 774	8 149	7 591	7 001	7 078	8 924
16-19	1 162	1 093	1 187	1 253	1 251	1 208	1 186	1 119	1 101	1 285
20-24	1 042	1 025	1 203	1 430	1 495	1 431	1 335	1 234	1 241	1 545
25-29	681	625	731	978	1 018	955	933	855	883	1 122
30-34	597	542	716	911	941	829	728	666	661	827
35-39	592	583	693	864	908	799	695	628	615	810
40-44	562	558	666	827	907	779	705	651	610	795
45-49	426	420	551	722	756	724	675	615	618	764
50-54	327	330	420	594	601	565	520	478	517	710
55-59	238	217	282	405	457	437	416	395	413	511
60-64	128	131	164	230	257	245	214	200	229	292
65-69	72	72	73	95	112	96	98	89	105	144
70-74	28	39	33	47	43	46	50	43	50	72
75+	23	20	23	21	29	36	36	27	35	48

Men - Hommes - Hombres

Total	3 066	2 954	3 663	4 597	4 906	4 456	4 059	3 753	3 882	5 033
16-19	633	604	660	700	697	664	667	622	623	736
20-24	562	549	680	792	841	811	775	705	721	920
25-29	334	318	385	531	578	535	480	457	498	657
30-34	290	260	346	492	519	446	364	354	358	462
35-39	288	289	362	445	480	430	364	318	311	433
40-44	283	275	360	451	508	409	351	324	323	442
45-49	229	210	287	397	427	388	347	317	318	420
50-54	173	181	243	328	337	296	277	252	273	384
55-59	128	113	162	235	258	240	219	214	219	265
60-64	75	72	103	137	154	133	112	104	129	160
65-69	40	43	43	49	64	54	52	52	59	87
70-74	15	27	19	27	28	28	27	21	29	40
75+	14	13	14	12	16	22	23	14	20	26

Women - Femmes - Mujeres

Total	2 814	2 701	3 079	3 781	3 868	3 694	3 531	3 247	3 196	3 891
16-19	529	489	527	553	554	543	519	496	478	549
20-24	480	476	523	638	654	619	560	530	520	625
25-29	347	307	346	447	440	420	453	398	385	466
30-34	307	282	370	419	423	384	364	313	303	365
35-39	304	294	331	419	428	369	330	310	304	377
40-44	279	283	306	376	399	370	354	327	287	353
45-49	197	210	264	325	329	335	328	298	300	343
50-54	154	149	177	266	263	269	243	226	244	326
55-59	110	104	120	170	199	197	197	181	193	246
60-64	53	59	61	93	103	112	102	97	100	132
65-69	32	29	30	46	47	42	46	37	46	57
70-74	13	12	14	20	15	18	23	22	21	32
75+	9	7	9	9	13	14	12	13	15	22

Explanatory notes: see p. 451.

[1] Persons aged 15 years and over. [2] Persons aged 16 years and over.

Notes explicatives: voir p. 454.

[1] Personnes âgées de 15 ans et plus. [2] Personnes âgées de 16 ans et plus.

Notas explicativas: véase p. 457.

[1] Personas de 15 años y más. [2] Personas de 16 años y más.

3B

UNEMPLOYMENT	CHÔMAGE	DESEMPLEO
By age group	Par groupe d'âge	Por grupo de edad
Thousands	Milliers	Millares

	1999	2000	2001	2002	2003	2004	2005	2006	2007	2008
Uruguay (BA) [1]				Total unemployment - Chômage total - Desempleo total						
Total - Total - Total										
Total	137.7	167.7	193.2	211.3	208.5	.	154.9	167.0 [2]	149.3	.
14-19	31.8	37.4	41.8	38.2	35.6	.	30.0	35.6 [2]	33.6	.
20-24	32.8	40.6	45.1	48.7	47.2	.	34.8	37.8 [2]	32.7	.
25-29	15.4	19.7	24.5	26.4	29.2	.	22.4	21.2 [2]	19.0	.
30-34	11.8	14.3	15.5	20.2	19.3	.	14.7	14.8 [2]	13.9	.
35-39	10.7	12.2	15.9	18.1	16.7	.	12.2	12.3 [2]	11.4	.
40-44	10.0	12.2	12.6	16.7	16.7	.	11.3	11.4 [2]	9.7	.
45-49	8.1	10.4	12.9	14.1	14.8	.	9.8	10.0 [2]	8.5	.
50-54	6.6	8.7	9.1	11.7	11.1	.	8.3	9.0 [2]	7.9	.
55-59	5.2	6.8	7.3	10.0	9.1	.	6.2	6.6 [2]	5.6	.
60-64							3.1	4.6 [2]	3.7	.
60+	1.9	2.3	4.4	2.6	3.1	.	.	.	.	.
65-69							1.3	2.1 [2]	2.0	
70-74							0.4	1.0 [2]	1.0	
75+							0.4	0.5 [2]	0.3	
?	3.4	3.1	4.1	4.6	5.7	.	-	- [2]	-	
Men - Hommes - Hombres										
Total	59.4	74.7	80.4	93.3	92.2	.	65.4	70.0 [2]	60.0	.
14-19	16.9	21.0	22.0	20.3	20.3	.	16.2	19.2 [2]	18.4	.
20-24	14.8	17.8	19.6	22.2	22.6	.	15.8	16.8 [2]	14.2	.
25-29	6.8	8.2	9.2	11.4	12.5	.	8.8	7.4 [2]	6.4	.
30-34	3.7	5.0	6.5	8.1	7.4	.	4.8	4.6 [2]	3.8	.
35-39	2.8	3.4	4.1	5.8	5.7	.	3.9	4.2 [2]	3.1	.
40-44	2.6	4.5	3.1	5.9	5.3	.	3.5	3.2 [2]	2.4	.
45-49	2.7	4.4	4.2	5.7	4.7	.	3.2	3.3 [2]	2.4	.
50-54	3.2	3.4	3.7	4.8	4.6	.	3.5	3.8 [2]	2.6	.
55-59	2.4	3.7	3.3	5.0	4.0	.	3.0	2.9 [2]	3.0	.
60-64							1.4	2.4 [2]	1.8	.
60+	1.4	1.5	2.4	1.3	1.8	.	.	.	.	.
65-69							0.8	1.3 [2]	1.3	
70-74							0.3	0.6 [2]	0.6	
75+							0.2	0.3 [2]	0.2	
?	2.1	1.8	2.3	2.8	3.3	.	-	- [2]	-	
Women - Femmes - Mujeres										
Total	78.3	93.0	112.8	118.0	116.2	.	89.5	96.9 [2]	89.3	.
14-19	14.9	16.4	19.8	17.9	15.3	.	13.8	16.4 [2]	15.2	.
20-24	18.0	22.8	25.5	26.5	24.7	.	18.9	21.0 [2]	18.6	.
25-29	8.6	11.5	15.3	15.1	16.7	.	13.6	13.8 [2]	12.6	.
30-34	8.1	9.3	9.0	12.0	11.9	.	9.9	10.1 [2]	10.1	.
35-39	7.9	8.8	11.8	12.3	11.0	.	8.3	8.1 [2]	8.3	.
40-44	7.4	7.7	9.5	10.7	11.4	.	7.9	8.3 [2]	7.4	.
45-49	5.4	6.0	8.7	8.3	10.1	.	6.5	6.7 [2]	6.1	.
50-54	3.4	5.3	5.4	6.8	6.5	.	4.8	5.2 [2]	5.3	.
55-59	2.8	3.1	4.0	5.0	5.1	.	3.2	3.7 [2]	2.6	.
60-64							1.7	2.2 [2]	1.9	.
60+	0.5	0.8	2.0	1.3	1.3	.	.	.	.	.
65-69							0.5	0.8 [2]	0.7	
70-74							0.1	0.4 [2]	0.4	
75+							0.2	0.3 [2]	0.1	
?	1.3	1.3	1.8	2.1	2.2	.	-	- [2]	-	
Venezuela, Rep. Bolivariana de (BA) [3][4]				Total unemployment - Chômage total - Desempleo total						
Total - Total - Total										
Total	.	.	.	.	.	.	.	1 154.9	941.8	872.9
10-14	.	.	.	.	.	.	.	11.3	13.6	.
15-19	.	.	.	.	.	.	.	142.0	117.9	.
15-24	.	.	.	.	.	.	.	.	.	323.9
20-24	.	.	.	.	.	.	.	267.8	220.8	.
25-29	.	.	.	.	.	.	.	205.7	156.7	.
25-44	.	.	.	.	.	.	.	.	.	402.9
30-34	.	.	.	.	.	.	.	135.1	111.9	.
35-39	.	.	.	.	.	.	.	107.4	85.1	.
40-44	.	.	.	.	.	.	.	88.2	69.4	.
45-49	.	.	.	.	.	.	.	65.1	56.7	.
45-64	.	.	.	.	.	.	.	.	.	129.7
50-54	.	.	.	.	.	.	.	48.0	42.1	.
55-59	.	.	.	.	.	.	.	41.6	31.2	.
60-64	.	.	.	.	.	.	.	21.1	17.8	.
65-69	.	.	.	.	.	.	.	11.1	8.6	.
65+	.	.	.	.	.	.	.	.	.	16.5
70-74	.	.	.	.	.	.	.	5.9	6.2	.
75+	.	.	.	.	.	.	.	4.7	3.9	.

Explanatory notes: see p. 451.

[1] Persons aged 14 years and over. [2] Prior to 2006: urban areas. [3] Persons aged 10 years and over. [4] Second semester.

Notes explicatives: voir p. 454.

[1] Personnes âgées de 14 ans et plus. [2] Avant 2006: régions urbaines. [3] Personnes âgées de 10 ans et plus. [4] Second semestre.

Notas explicativas: véase p. 457.

[1] Personas de 14 años y más. [2] Antes de 2006: areas urbanas. [3] Personas de 10 años y más. [4] Segundo semestre.

	Thousands			Milliers				Millares		
	1999	2000	2001	2002	2003	2004	2005	2006	2007	2008

Venezuela, Rep. Bolivariana de (BA) [1][2]   Total unemployment - Chômage total - Desempleo total

Men - Hommes - Hombres

	1999	2000	2001	2002	2003	2004	2005	2006	2007	2008
Total	.	.	.	.	.	.	.	626.0	545.7	506.3
10-14	.	.	.	.	.	.	.	7.1	9.0	.
15-19	.	.	.	.	.	.	.	80.9	75.0	.
15-24	.	.	.	.	.	.	.	.	.	192.2
20-24	.	.	.	.	.	.	.	142.8	120.7	.
25-29	.	.	.	.	.	.	.	97.0	74.4	.
25-44	.	.	.	.	.	.	.	.	.	212.6
30-34	.	.	.	.	.	.	.	62.9	54.8	.
35-39	.	.	.	.	.	.	.	53.3	48.1	.
40-44	.	.	.	.	.	.	.	46.8	42.9	.
45-49	.	.	.	.	.	.	.	38.6	37.4	.
45-64	.	.	.	.	.	.	.	.	.	89.0
50-54	.	.	.	.	.	.	.	32.5	28.6	.
55-59	.	.	.	.	.	.	.	31.6	24.5	.
60-64	.	.	.	.	.	.	.	16.0	14.5	.
65-69	.	.	.	.	.	.	.	8.7	7.8	.
65+	.	.	.	.	.	.	.	.	.	12.5
70-74	.	.	.	.	.	.	.	4.5	4.4	.
75+	.	.	.	.	.	.	.	3.3	3.6	.

Women - Femmes - Mujeres

	1999	2000	2001	2002	2003	2004	2005	2006	2007	2008
Total	.	.	.	.	.	.	.	529.0	396.1	366.6
10-14	.	.	.	.	.	.	.	4.2	4.6	.
15-19	.	.	.	.	.	.	.	61.1	42.9	.
15-24	.	.	.	.	.	.	.	.	.	131.6
20-24	.	.	.	.	.	.	.	125.0	100.1	.
25-29	.	.	.	.	.	.	.	108.7	82.2	.
25-44	.	.	.	.	.	.	.	.	.	190.3
30-34	.	.	.	.	.	.	.	72.2	57.0	.
35-39	.	.	.	.	.	.	.	54.1	37.1	.
40-44	.	.	.	.	.	.	.	41.4	26.4	.
45-49	.	.	.	.	.	.	.	26.5	19.3	.
45-64	.	.	.	.	.	.	.	.	.	40.7
50-54	.	.	.	.	.	.	.	15.5	13.5	.
55-59	.	.	.	.	.	.	.	10.0	6.7	.
60-64	.	.	.	.	.	.	.	5.1	3.3	.
65-69	.	.	.	.	.	.	.	2.4	0.9	.
65+	.	.	.	.	.	.	.	.	.	4.0
70-74	.	.	.	.	.	.	.	1.4	1.7	.
75+	.	.	.	.	.	.	.	1.4	0.3	.

ASIA-ASIE-ASIA

Armenia (BA) [3]   Total unemployment - Chômage total - Desempleo total

Total - Total - Total

	1999	2000	2001	2002	2003	2004	2005	2006	2007	2008
Total	.	.	.	.	.	.	.	470.9	.	
16-19	.	.	.	.	.	.	.	49.1	.	
20-24	.	.	.	.	.	.	.	104.7	.	
25-29	.	.	.	.	.	.	.	59.4	.	
30-34	.	.	.	.	.	.	.	45.0	.	
35-39	.	.	.	.	.	.	.	29.2	.	
40-44	.	.	.	.	.	.	.	41.3	.	
45-49	.	.	.	.	.	.	.	50.3	.	
50-54	.	.	.	.	.	.	.	41.5	.	
55-59	.	.	.	.	.	.	.	29.0	.	
60-64	.	.	.	.	.	.	.	10.3	.	
65-69	.	.	.	.	.	.	.	8.9	.	
75+	.	.	.	.	.	.	.	2.1	.	

Men - Hommes - Hombres

	1999	2000	2001	2002	2003	2004	2005	2006	2007	2008
Total	.	.	.	.	.	.	.	183.7	.	
16-19	.	.	.	.	.	.	.	19.1	.	
20-24	.	.	.	.	.	.	.	47.8	.	
25-29	.	.	.	.	.	.	.	23.6	.	
30-34	.	.	.	.	.	.	.	17.7	.	
35-39	.	.	.	.	.	.	.	8.3	.	
40-44	.	.	.	.	.	.	.	11.2	.	
45-49	.	.	.	.	.	.	.	15.5	.	
50-54	.	.	.	.	.	.	.	16.2	.	
55-59	.	.	.	.	.	.	.	11.6	.	
60-64	.	.	.	.	.	.	.	5.8	.	
65-69	.	.	.	.	.	.	.	5.5	.	
75+	.	.	.	.	.	.	.	1.4	.	

Explanatory notes: see p. 451.   Notes explicatives: voir p. 454.   Notas explicativas: véase p. 457.

[1] Persons aged 10 years and over. [2] Second semester. [3] Persons aged 16 years and over.

[1] Personnes âgées de 10 ans et plus. [2] Second semestre. [3] Personnes âgées de 16 ans et plus.

[1] Personas de 10 años y más. [2] Segundo semestre. [3] Personas de 16 años y más.

UNEMPLOYMENT	CHÔMAGE	DESEMPLEO
By age group	Par groupe d'âge	Por grupo de edad
Thousands	Milliers	Millares

	1999	2000	2001	2002	2003	2004	2005	2006	2007	2008

Armenia (BA) [1] — Total unemployment - Chômage total - Desempleo total

Women - Femmes - Mujeres

	1999	2000	2001	2002	2003	2004	2005	2006	2007	2008
Total									287.2	
16-19									30.0	
20-24									56.9	
25-29									35.8	
30-34									27.3	
35-39									20.8	
40-44									30.1	
45-49									34.9	
50-54									25.3	
55-59									17.4	
60-64									4.5	
65-69									3.4	
75+									0.7	

Armenia (FB) [2][3] — Registered unemployment - Chômage enregistré - Desempleo registrado

Total - Total - Total

	1999	2000	2001	2002	2003	2004	2005	2006	2007	2008
Total	175.0	153.9	138.4	127.3	118.6	108.6	89.0	84.6	75.1	74.7
16-17	2.3	1.2	0.7	0.5	0.2	0.1	0.1	0.1		
16-19									0.3	0.4
18-21	13.8	11.6	8.8	7.6	6.7	1.7	1.0	2.1		
20-24									5.0	4.1
22-29	38.4	32.8	30.3	27.8	26.5	20.2	12.2	13.2		
25-29									10.2	9.0
30-34									9.8	10.4
30-49	105.0	94.6	85.7	80.2	74.2	73.0	62.7	55.2		
35-44									22.7	23.1
45-54									18.6	19.1
50+	15.5	13.8	12.9	11.2	11.0	13.6	13.0	14.0		
55+									8.5	8.6

Azerbaijan (BA) [4] — Total unemployment - Chômage total - Desempleo total

Total - Total - Total

	1999	2000	2001	2002	2003	2004	2005	2006	2007	2008
Total					404.7			291.2	281.1	261.4
15-19					40.8			35.2	21.8	28.8
20-24					124.8			83.4	69.0	64.3
25-29					71.8			46.9	52.1	29.3
30-34					42.1			26.0	35.5	28.9
35-39					35.0			24.8	34.6	12.9
40-44					33.0			26.7	22.4	31.6
45-49					27.1			24.6	18.2	23.5
50-54					21.8			16.2	18.5	18.0
55-59					5.9			7.1	8.0	22.2
60+					2.4			0.3	0.9	1.9

Men - Hommes - Hombres

	1999	2000	2001	2002	2003	2004	2005	2006	2007	2008
Total					210.5			157.0	169.9	156.9
15-19					16.6			15.8	15.4	23.4
20-24					66.6			44.7	39.3	39.4
25-29					41.0			25.8	26.7	14.2
30-34					23.0			14.0	20.2	14.2
35-39					16.2			13.5	16.0	7.3
40-44					16.4			15.2	16.8	12.7
45-49					12.7			13.2	12.2	10.8
50-54					11.5			9.2	14.4	11.2
55-59					4.2			5.4	8.0	21.8
60+					2.3			0.2	0.9	1.9

Women - Femmes - Mujeres

	1999	2000	2001	2002	2003	2004	2005	2006	2007	2008
Total					194.2			134.2	111.2	104.5
15-19					24.2			19.4	6.4	5.4
20-24					58.2			38.7	29.7	24.9
25-29					30.8			21.1	25.4	15.1
30-34					19.1			12.0	15.3	14.7
35-39					18.8			11.3	18.6	5.6
40-44					16.6			11.5	5.6	18.9
45-49					14.4			11.4	6.0	12.7
50-54					10.3			7.0	4.1	6.8
55-59					1.7			1.7	-	0.4
60+										

Azerbaijan (FB) [3][4] — Registered unemployment - Chômage enregistré - Desempleo registrado

Total - Total - Total

	1999	2000	2001	2002	2003	2004	2005	2006	2007	2008
Total	45.2	43.7	48.4	51.0	54.4	55.9	56.3	53.9	50.6	44.5
15-18	0.5									
15-19		0.3	0.5	0.6	-	0.2	0.2	0.2	0.1	0.2
18-24	10.5									
20-24		8.1	9.0	9.3	10.0	9.7	9.7	9.4	8.9	6.9
25-29	11.2	10.2	11.3	11.8						13.4
25-34					14.6	16.1	16.9	17.6	16.9	
30-34										6.7
30-61	23.0	25.1	27.6	29.3						
35-61					29.8	29.9	29.5	26.7	24.7	17.2

Explanatory notes: see p. 451.

[1] Persons aged 16 years and over. [2] Persons aged 16 to 63 years. [3] Dec. of each year. [4] Men aged 15 to 61 years; women aged 15 to 56 years.

Notes explicatives: voir p. 454.

[1] Personnes âgées de 16 ans et plus. [2] Personnes âgées de 16 à 63 ans. [3] Déc. de chaque année. [4] Hommes âgés de 15 à 61 ans; femmes âgées de 15 à 56 ans.

Notas explicativas: véase p. 457.

[1] Personas de 16 años y más. [2] Personas de 16 a 63 años de edad. [3] Dic. de cada año. [4] Hombres de 15 a 61 años; mujeres de 15 a 56 años.

UNEMPLOYMENT — CHÔMAGE — DESEMPLEO

By age group — Par groupe d'âge — Por grupo de edad

	Thousands			Milliers			Millares			
	1999	2000	2001	2002	2003	2004	2005	2006	2007	2008

Azerbaijan (FB) [1] [2] Registered unemployment - Chômage enregistré - Desempleo registrado

Men - Hommes - Hombres

	1999	2000	2001	2002	2003	2004	2005	2006	2007	2008
Total	19.6	19.2	21.8	23.1	25.3	26.6	27.2	26.3	25.3	23.6
15-18	0.2	.	.	.	.	.	.	.	.	.
15-19	.	0.1	0.2	0.2	-	0.1	0.1	0.1	0.0	0.1
18-24	4.7	.	.	.	.	.	.	.	.	.
20-24	.	3.3	3.7	3.9	4.6	4.4	4.5	4.4	4.3	3.8
25-29	4.3	3.9	4.7	4.8	.	.	.	.	.	7.5
25-34	.	.	.	.	6.4	7.0	7.7	8.6	8.4	.
30-34	.	.	.	.	.	.	.	.	.	2.5
30-61	10.4	11.9	13.2	14.2	.	.	.	.	.	.
35-61	.	.	.	.	14.3	15.1	14.9	13.2	12.6	9.8

Women - Femmes - Mujeres

	1999	2000	2001	2002	2003	2004	2005	2006	2007	2008
Total	25.6	24.5	26.6	27.9	29.1	29.3	29.1	27.6	25.3	20.9
15-18	0.3	.	.	.	.	.	.	.	.	.
15-19	.	0.2	0.3	0.4	-	0.1	0.1	0.1	0.1	0.1
18-24	5.8	.	.	.	.	.	.	.	.	.
20-24	.	4.8	5.3	5.4	5.4	5.3	5.2	5.0	4.6	3.2
25-29	6.9	6.3	6.6	7.0	.	.	.	.	.	5.9
25-34	.	.	.	.	8.2	9.1	9.2	9.0	8.5	.
30-34	.	.	.	.	.	.	.	.	.	4.3
30-61	12.6	13.2	14.4	15.1	.	.	.	.	.	.
35-61	.	.	.	.	15.5	14.8	14.6	13.5	12.1	7.4

Bahrain (FB) [3] [4] Work applicants - Demandeurs d'emploi - Solicitantes

Total - Total - Total

	1999	2000	2001	2002	2003	2004	2005	2006	2007	2008
Total	.	6.160	.	8.735	11.778	6.293	6.441	6.805	9.536	.
15-19	.	0.846	.	1.752	1.000	0.639	0.627	0.202	0.162	.
20-24	.	2.892	.	3.026	4.488	2.435	2.419	2.171	1.931	.
25-29	.	.	.	.	.	.	1.921	2.243	.	.
25-34	.	1.920	.	2.586	4.432	2.323	2.646	.	5.003	.
30-34	.	.	.	.	.	.	0.725	1.087	.	.
35-39	.	.	.	.	.	.	0.380	0.607	.	.
35-49	.	0.434	.	1.244	1.631	0.805	0.675	.	2.277	.
40-44	.	.	.	.	.	.	0.192	0.235	.	.
45-49	.	.	.	.	.	.	0.103	0.103	.	.
50-54	.	.	.	.	.	.	0.046	0.050	.	.
50+	.	0.065	.	0.127	0.227	0.091	.	.	0.163	.
55-59	.	.	.	.	.	.	0.024	0.028	.	.
60-64	.	.	.	.	.	.	0.004	0.001	.	.
?	.	.	.	.	.	.	.	0.078	.	.

Men - Hommes - Hombres

	1999	2000	2001	2002	2003	2004	2005	2006	2007	2008
Total	.	4.183	.	4.377	6.034	3.077	2.898	1.525	1.240	.
15-19	.	0.726	.	1.422	0.826	0.521	0.491	0.110	0.088	.
20-24	.	1.976	.	1.572	2.715	1.419	1.359	0.666	0.474	.
25-29	.	.	.	.	.	.	0.564	0.337	.	.
25-34	.	1.125	.	0.881	1.785	0.808	0.778	.	0.442	.
30-34	.	.	.	.	.	.	0.214	0.140	.	.
35-39	.	.	.	.	.	.	0.108	0.079	.	.
35-49	.	0.293	.	0.400	0.575	0.282	0.217	.	0.165	.
40-44	.	.	.	.	.	.	0.065	0.060	.	.
45-49	.	.	.	.	.	.	0.044	0.031	.	.
50-54	.	.	.	.	.	.	0.030	0.030	.	.
50+	.	0.060	.	0.102	0.133	0.047	.	.	0.071	.
55-59	.	.	.	.	.	.	0.020	0.025	.	.
60-64	.	.	.	.	.	.	0.003	0.001	.	.
?	.	.	.	.	.	.	.	0.046	.	.

Women - Femmes - Mujeres

	1999	2000	2001	2002	2003	2004	2005	2006	2007	2008
Total	.	1.977	.	4.358	5.744	3.216	3.543	5.280	8.296	.
15-19	.	0.120	.	0.330	0.174	0.118	0.136	0.092	0.074	.
20-24	.	0.916	.	1.454	1.773	1.016	1.060	1.505	1.457	.
25-29	.	.	.	.	.	.	1.357	1.906	.	.
25-34	.	0.795	.	1.705	2.647	1.515	1.868	.	4.651	.
30-34	.	.	.	.	.	.	0.511	0.947	.	.
35-39	.	.	.	.	.	.	0.272	0.528	.	.
35-49	.	0.141	.	0.844	1.056	0.523	0.458	.	2.112	.
40-44	.	.	.	.	.	.	0.127	0.175	.	.
45-49	.	.	.	.	.	.	0.059	0.072	.	.
50-54	.	.	.	.	.	.	0.016	0.020	.	.
50+	.	0.005	.	0.025	0.094	0.044	.	.	0.092	.
55-59	.	.	.	.	.	.	0.004	0.003	.	.
60-64	.	.	.	.	.	.	0.001	0.000	.	.
?	.	.	.	.	.	.	.	0.032	.	.

Explanatory notes: see p. 451.

[1] Men aged 15 to 61 years; women aged 15 to 56 years. [2] Dec. of each year. [3] Persons aged 15 years and over. [4] Jan.

Notes explicatives: voir p. 454.

[1] Hommes âgés de 15 à 61 ans; femmes âgées de 15 à 56 ans. [2] Déc. de chaque année. [3] Personnes âgées de 15 ans et plus. [4] Janv.

Notas explicativas: véase p. 457.

[1] Hombres de 15 a 61 años; mujeres de 15 a 56 años. [2] Dic. de cada año. [3] Personas de 15 años y más. [4] Enero.

	Thousands / Milliers / Millares									
	1999	2000	2001	2002	2003	2004	2005	2006	2007	2008

Georgia (BA) [1] — Total unemployment - Chômage total - Desempleo total

Total - Total - Total

	1999	2000	2001	2002	2003	2004	2005	2006	2007	2008
Total	277.5	212.2	235.6	265.0	235.9	257.6	279.3	274.5	261.0	315.8
15-19	11.7	9.1	7.0	9.6	11.1	12.9	13.0	12.5	12.5	13.4
20-24	34.2	31.7	32.9	42.9	40.7	37.3	42.3	46.4	45.2	57.6
25-29	43.1	34.4	44.5	50.3	38.6	42.7	55.0	49.4	43.2	54.6
30-34	35.5	25.7	28.4	29.6	28.1	40.2	38.4	37.2	32.4	41.9
35-39	39.8	29.1	31.0	28.7	26.0	30.1	32.9	33.0	28.0	32.3
40-44	31.8	21.9	30.7	32.2	22.6	26.9	27.8	30.8	27.4	27.3
45-49	26.4	20.9	22.2	24.7	26.9	26.6	27.2	24.8	26.4	28.9
50-54	19.4	15.1	14.3	19.2	19.6	17.3	18.7	19.6	19.0	26.5
55-59	14.8	8.2	10.0	14.0	10.8	12.5	14.5	11.7	17.2	19.6
60-64	15.0	9.8	9.5	8.4	7.7	6.8	5.7	6.2	6.1	9.5
65+	5.7	6.3	5.3	5.4	3.8	4.3	3.9	2.8	3.5	4.2

Men - Hommes - Hombres

	1999	2000	2001	2002	2003	2004	2005	2006	2007	2008
Total	160.1	116.7	126.9	155.5	124.2	143.2	159.2	165.4	143.7	172.4
15-19	6.4	4.9	4.4	6.0	4.2	7.9	8.5	9.0	7.0	9.2
20-24	19.5	19.5	20.3	25.7	20.0	19.6	24.3	26.6	24.4	31.1
25-29	25.3	22.0	23.8	32.3	21.7	25.1	34.5	31.3	23.6	29.5
30-34	18.8	13.9	15.1	16.7	17.7	19.6	20.0	22.1	18.4	24.3
35-39	23.2	14.4	16.3	14.1	13.2	14.2	17.2	18.3	15.7	16.0
40-44	17.5	10.2	12.3	15.7	12.2	16.9	15.8	18.2	14.1	12.8
45-49	14.4	10.6	12.3	15.2	13.3	14.6	14.4	14.8	14.1	15.4
50-54	12.0	6.1	7.1	11.6	10.8	9.0	8.3	10.4	10.1	14.4
55-59	8.5	4.3	4.8	9.1	6.0	8.3	8.5	7.1	9.2	9.6
60-64	10.7	6.1	7.0	5.3	3.4	4.5	4.8	5.6	4.8	7.4
65+	3.8	4.7	3.8	3.8	1.7	3.6	2.7	2.0	2.3	2.9

Women - Femmes - Mujeres

	1999	2000	2001	2002	2003	2004	2005	2006	2007	2008
Total	117.4	95.5	108.7	109.5	111.7	114.4	120.1	109.1	117.3	143.4
15-19	5.3	4.2	2.6	3.6	6.9	5.0	4.4	3.5	5.5	4.2
20-24	14.7	12.2	12.6	17.2	20.7	17.7	18.0	19.8	20.8	26.5
25-29	17.8	12.4	20.7	18.0	16.9	17.6	20.5	18.1	19.6	25.1
30-34	16.7	11.8	13.3	12.9	10.4	20.6	18.4	15.1	14.0	17.6
35-39	16.6	14.7	14.7	14.6	12.8	15.9	15.7	14.7	12.4	16.3
40-44	14.3	11.7	18.4	16.5	10.4	10.0	12.0	12.6	13.4	14.5
45-49	12.0	10.3	9.9	9.5	13.6	12.0	12.8	10.0	12.3	13.6
50-54	7.4	9.0	7.2	7.6	8.8	8.3	10.4	9.2	8.9	12.1
55-59	6.3	3.9	5.2	4.9	4.8	4.3	6.0	4.6	8.0	10.1
60-64	4.3	3.7	2.5	3.1	4.3	2.3	0.9	0.6	1.4	2.1
65+	1.9	1.6	1.5	1.6	2.1	0.7	1.1	0.8	1.2	1.3

Hong Kong, China (BA) [1][2] — Total unemployment - Chômage total - Desempleo total

Total - Total - Total

	1999	2000	2001	2002	2003	2004	2005	2006	2007	2008
Total	207.5	166.9	174.3	254.2	275.2	239.2	197.6	171.1	145.7	130.1
15-19	22.9	18.3	17.0	22.6	21.0	17.7	13.8	13.1	12.5	9.2
20-24	35.6	27.4	29.0	36.6	37.4	30.5	28.6	27.3	22.3	22.1
25-29	26.8	20.6	21.0	28.0	29.6	22.6	19.2	16.6	14.5	14.4
30-34	21.7	16.9	17.7	26.4	28.9	22.4	17.5	15.4	15.3	11.3
35-39	23.0	16.8	19.1	29.8	31.6	25.6	19.1	17.0	12.3	12.1
40-44	24.4	19.6	22.8	34.2	37.6	32.1	25.9	19.3	17.1	14.8
45-49	21.2	18.7	20.7	31.1	36.8	35.1	29.2	25.4	19.1	17.6
50-54	17.9	16.2	16.1	25.4	29.7	28.7	24.0	19.8	17.6	15.9
55-59	9.9	8.9	7.9	14.0	17.5	18.0	15.8	14.0	12.0	10.0
60-64	3.2	3.0	2.6	4.4	4.1	5.3	3.9	2.8	2.8	2.4
65+	0.9	-	0.6	1.4	0.9	1.3	0.6	-	-	-

Men - Hommes - Hombres

	1999	2000	2001	2002	2003	2004	2005	2006	2007	2008
Total	140.6	109.6	117.8	164.0	180.0	151.8	127.5	110.2	89.2	79.4
15-19	13.2	10.1	9.9	13.6	12.3	10.5	8.4	7.9	7.0	5.4
20-24	21.2	15.1	17.0	22.0	23.7	19.3	17.8	16.1	13.1	12.5
25-29	17.6	12.2	13.5	17.9	19.3	14.6	12.1	10.7	9.0	8.3
30-34	13.9	10.2	11.1	15.5	17.4	13.0	10.7	9.6	8.5	6.4
35-39	16.1	10.9	12.7	18.7	18.7	14.9	11.1	10.1	7.1	6.3
40-44	17.2	14.0	15.9	21.7	23.9	18.3	14.7	11.5	10.1	8.8
45-49	15.4	12.8	15.5	20.1	24.2	22.4	19.9	16.6	11.5	10.2
50-54	13.6	13.0	12.6	17.9	21.6	18.9	17.0	14.4	11.7	11.2
55-59	8.6	8.0	6.8	11.4	14.3	14.0	11.8	10.4	8.4	7.7
60-64	2.9	2.7	2.3	3.9	3.6	4.7	3.4	2.6	2.4	2.1
65+	0.8	-	-	1.3	0.9	1.2	0.6	-	-	-

Women - Femmes - Mujeres

	1999	2000	2001	2002	2003	2004	2005	2006	2007	2008
Total	66.9	57.3	56.5	90.1	95.3	87.4	70.1	60.8	56.5	50.7
15-19	9.7	8.2	7.1	9.0	8.7	7.1	5.4	5.2	5.5	3.7
20-24	14.4	12.2	12.0	14.7	13.7	11.2	10.8	11.2	9.2	9.6
25-29	9.1	8.4	7.5	10.1	10.3	8.1	7.1	6.0	5.5	6.1
30-34	7.8	6.7	6.5	10.9	11.5	9.4	6.9	5.8	6.8	4.9
35-39	6.9	5.9	6.4	11.1	12.9	10.7	8.0	7.0	5.2	5.8
40-44	7.2	5.6	6.9	12.5	13.7	13.8	11.2	7.7	7.0	6.0
45-49	5.8	5.9	5.2	10.9	12.6	12.7	9.3	8.8	7.6	7.4
50-54	4.3	3.3	3.5	7.5	8.1	9.8	7.0	5.4	5.8	4.6
55-59	1.3	0.9	1.1	2.6	3.2	4.0	3.9	3.5	3.6	2.3
60-64	-	-	-	0.5	0.5	0.6	0.5	-	-	-
65+	-	-	-	-	-	-	-	-	-	-

Explanatory notes: see p. 451.   Notes explicatives: voir p. 454.   Notas explicativas: véase p. 457.

[1] Persons aged 15 years and over. [2] Excl. marine, military and institutional populations.

[1] Personnes âgées de 15 ans et plus. [2] Non compris le personnel militaire, de la marine et la population institutionnelle.

[1] Personas de 15 años y más. [2] Excl. el personal militar y de la marina, y la población institucional.

UNEMPLOYMENT — CHÔMAGE — DESEMPLEO — 3B

By age group — Par groupe d'âge — Por grupo de edad

	Thousands / Milliers / Millares									
	1999	2000	2001	2002	2003	2004	2005	2006	2007	2008

India (FB) [1][2] — Work applicants - Demandeurs d'emploi - Solicitantes

Total - Total - Total

	1999	2000	2001	2002	2003	2004	2005	2006	2007	2008
Total	40 372	41 344	41 996	41 172	41 388	40 458	39 348	41 466	.	.
14-19	8 282	8 758	8 906	8 848	8 957	8 814	8 960	9 204	.	.
20-29	20 782	20 461	21 044	20 339	20 550	19 948	18 868	19 876	.	.
30-39	9 394	9 849	9 928	9 726	9 660	9 444	9 326	10 099	.	.
40-49	1 601	1 914	1 785	1 859	1 875	1 954	1 961	1 995	.	.
50-59	268	304	276	333	288	265	217	271	.	.
60+	44	57	57	68	60	32	16	20	.	.

Men - Hommes - Hombres

	1999	2000	2001	2002	2003	2004	2005	2006	2007	2008
Total	30 439	30 887	31 111	30 522	30 636	29 746	28 742	29 685	.	.
14-19	6 078	6 370	6 413	6 417	6 465	6 265	6 444	6 454	.	.
20-29	15 861	15 500	15 856	15 386	15 553	14 960	13 977	14 413	.	.
30-39	7 093	7 351	7 337	7 094	7 025	6 937	6 778	7 253	.	.
40-49	1 176	1 405	1 273	1 343	1 352	1 384	1 387	1 370	.	.
50-59	196	219	190	234	199	177	145	180	.	.
60+	35	42	42	48	43	21	11	14	.	.

Women - Femmes - Mujeres

	1999	2000	2001	2002	2003	2004	2005	2006	2007	2008
Total	9 933	10 457	10 885	10 650	10 752	10 712	10 606	11 781	.	.
14-19	2 204	2 388	2 493	2 431	2 492	2 549	2 516	2 750	.	.
20-29	4 921	4 961	5 188	4 953	4 997	4 988	4 891	5 463	.	.
30-39	2 301	2 498	2 591	2 632	2 635	2 507	2 548	2 846	.	.
40-49	425	509	512	516	523	570	574	625	.	.
50-59	72	85	86	99	89	88	72	91	.	.
60+	9	15	15	20	17	11	5	6	.	.

Indonesia (BA) [3][4] — Total unemployment - Chômage total - Desempleo total

Total - Total - Total

	1999	2000	2001	2002	2003	2004	2005	2006	2007	2008
Total	6 030.3	5 813.2	8 005.0	9 132.1	9 939.3	10 251.4	11 899.3 [5]	10 932.0	10 011.1	9 394.5
15-19	1 766.3	1 817.1	2 337.6	2 837.9	2 766.0	3 026.5	3 166.1 [5]	2 955.4	2 423.3	2 305.7
20-24	2 241.7	2 120.2	2 561.1	2 942.2	3 158.8	3 250.5	4 293.5 [5]	3 860.8	3 236.8	2 725.3
25-29	1 108.9	1 024.0	1 183.9	1 306.2	1 359.5	1 393.3	1 758.1 [5]	1 763.3	1 820.6	1 759.4
30-34	436.9	407.3	532.7	595.1	634.5	654.3	800.1 [5]	740.8	1 045.4	1 020.5
35-39	212.5	168.7	309.9	392.5	387.2	379.3	467.6 [5]	403.1	656.9	698.7
40-44	110.0	107.6	235.7	246.1	253.5	270.8	306.1 [5]	334.2	288.9	360.4
45-49	75.4	98.0	200.4	200.3	219.4	203.3	228.2 [5]	205.2	180.8	196.4
50-54	37.5	32.7	165.3	223.9	230.5	220.4	190.7 [5]	202.3	127.4	144.2
55-59	37.1	21.4	121.8	174.2	192.4	183.7	166.8 [5]	170.0	113.0	99.3
60-64	4.0	12.6	144.0	213.6	255.0	223.5	185.6 [5]	146.3	55.9	62.0
65-69	0.0	2.3	106.7	0.0	179.6	147.4	128.9 [5]	114.6	56.7	13.3
70-74	0.0	0.0	47.0	0.0	171.1	145.5	103.3 [5]	35.9	3.3	6.2
75+	0.0	1.3	58.8	0.0	131.7	152.7	104.3 [5]	0.0	2.3	3.1

Men - Hommes - Hombres

	1999	2000	2001	2002	2003	2004	2005	2006	2007	2008
Total	3 524.2	3 340.7	4 032.4	4 727.8	5 100.1	5 345.7	6 292.4 [5]	5 772.6	5 571.9	5 245.1
15-19	941.2	1 003.9	1 199.4	1 462.2	1 448.3	1 580.6	1 644.1 [5]	1 547.9	1 384.8	1 271.0
20-24	1 342.5	1 248.3	1 427.3	1 662.9	1 785.1	1 797.3	2 301.7 [5]	2 140.6	1 893.6	1 548.3
25-29	647.2	593.3	574.9	672.1	696.3	706.7	942.3 [5]	954.7	950.5	983.0
30-34	256.1	225.1	225.3	281.5	286.6	318.9	365.7 [5]	358.0	503.2	563.3
35-39	128.0	95.0	128.9	167.6	145.9	153.4	241.3 [5]	158.6	319.6	364.1
40-44	86.2	57.2	108.1	110.8	123.2	135.8	154.9 [5]	150.2	162.2	203.0
45-49	59.3	72.9	64.9	88.5	91.3	113.3	123.2 [5]	105.3	117.6	117.9
50-54	28.4	23.1	78.9	101.0	98.3	110.1	118.0 [5]	114.2	87.9	92.5
55-59	31.2	12.5	53.3	78.2	85.3	98.0	87.3 [5]	94.3	70.1	65.5
60-64	4.0	9.5	71.5	103.0	123.6	110.3	112.7 [5]	78.7	35.2	36.2
65-69	0.0	0.0	47.8	0.0	91.4	74.1	90.1 [5]	53.6	44.4	0.3
70-74	0.0	0.0	19.2	0.0	73.0	70.7	62.1 [5]	16.5	2.1	0.0
75+	0.0	0.0	33.0	0.0	51.9	76.4	48.9 [5]	0.0	0.8	0.0

Women - Femmes - Mujeres

	1999	2000	2001	2002	2003	2004	2005	2006	2007	2008
Total	2 506.1	2 472.6	3 972.6	4 404.3	4 839.2	4 905.7	5 606.8 [5]	5 159.4	4 439.2	4 149.5
15-19	825.1	813.2	1 138.2	1 375.7	1 317.7	1 445.9	1 522.0 [5]	1 407.5	1 038.5	1 034.7
20-24	899.2	872.0	1 133.8	1 279.3	1 373.7	1 453.2	1 991.7 [5]	1 720.2	1 343.2	1 177.1
25-29	461.7	430.7	609.0	634.1	663.2	686.6	815.7 [5]	808.5	870.1	776.4
30-34	180.8	182.2	307.4	313.6	347.9	335.4	434.3 [5]	382.8	542.2	457.2
35-39	84.5	73.7	181.0	224.9	241.3	225.9	226.4 [5]	244.5	337.3	334.6
40-44	23.8	50.4	127.6	135.4	130.3	135.0	151.2 [5]	184.0	126.7	157.3
45-49	16.1	25.2	135.6	111.8	128.1	90.0	104.9 [5]	100.0	63.2	78.4
50-54	9.0	9.6	86.4	122.9	132.2	110.4	72.7 [5]	88.1	39.5	51.7
55-59	5.9	8.9	68.4	96.0	107.1	85.6	79.4 [5]	75.7	42.9	33.9
60-64	0.0	3.1	72.5	110.6	131.4	113.2	72.9 [5]	67.6	20.7	25.8
65-69	0.0	2.3	58.9	0.0	88.2	73.3	38.8 [5]	61.0	12.3	13.0
70-74	0.0	0.0	27.8	0.0	98.1	74.8	41.2 [5]	19.5	1.2	6.2
75+	0.0	1.3	25.9	0.0	79.8	76.3	55.5 [5]	0.0	1.5	3.1

Explanatory notes: see p. 451.

[1] Persons aged 14 years and over. [2] Dec. of each year. [3] Persons aged 15 years and over. [4] Aug. of each year. [5] Nov.

Notes explicatives: voir p. 454.

[1] Personnes âgées de 14 ans et plus. [2] Déc. de chaque année. [3] Personnes âgées de 15 ans et plus. [4] Août de chaque année. [5] Nov.

Notas explicativas: véase p. 457.

[1] Personas de 14 años y más. [2] Dic. de cada año. [3] Personas de 15 años y más. [4] Agosto de cada año. [5] Nov.

UNEMPLOYMENT — CHÔMAGE — DESEMPLEO

By age group — Par groupe d'âge — Por grupo de edad

	Thousands / Milliers / Millares									
	1999	2000	2001	2002	2003	2004	2005	2006	2007	2008

Iran, Islamic Rep. of (BA) [1]
Total unemployment - Chômage total - Desempleo total

Total - Total - Total

	1999	2000	2001	2002	2003	2004	2005	2006	2007	2008
Total	.	.	.	.	.	.	2 643	2 643	2 486	2 392
10-14	.	.	.	.	.	.	16	13	9	9
15-19	.	.	.	.	.	.	370	330	264	251
20-24	.	.	.	.	.	.	993	981	910	859
25-29	.	.	.	.	.	.	564	603	630	637
30-34	.	.	.	.	.	.	230	235	245	224
35-39	.	.	.	.	.	.	144	154	140	139
40-44	.	.	.	.	.	.	109	107	93	95
45-49	.	.	.	.	.	.	85	88	79	79
50-54	.	.	.	.	.	.	82	74	59	50
55-59	.	.	.	.	.	.	44	30	33	31
60-64	.	.	.	.	.	.	21	18	16	12
65+	.	.	.	.	.	.	17	10	8	6

Men - Hommes - Hombres

	1999	2000	2001	2002	2003	2004	2005	2006	2007	2008
Total	.	.	.	.	.	.	1 856	1 878	1 764	1 715
10-14	.	.	.	.	.	.	13	11	8	8
15-19	.	.	.	.	.	.	261	245	199	191
20-24	.	.	.	.	.	.	651	658	623	587
25-29	.	.	.	.	.	.	358	386	389	409
30-34	.	.	.	.	.	.	158	165	168	156
35-39	.	.	.	.	.	.	101	117	114	111
40-44	.	.	.	.	.	.	87	89	81	85
45-49	.	.	.	.	.	.	75	80	72	72
50-54	.	.	.	.	.	.	74	70	56	48
55-59	.	.	.	.	.	.	41	29	31	29
60-64	.	.	.	.	.	.	19	18	16	11
65+	.	.	.	.	.	.	17	10	8	6

Women - Femmes - Mujeres

	1999	2000	2001	2002	2003	2004	2005	2006	2007	2008
Total	.	.	.	.	.	.	819	765	722	677
10-14	.	.	.	.	.	.	3	2	1	1
15-19	.	.	.	.	.	.	109	85	66	60
20-24	.	.	.	.	.	.	343	323	286	272
25-29	.	.	.	.	.	.	206	216	241	228
30-34	.	.	.	.	.	.	72	70	77	68
35-39	.	.	.	.	.	.	43	37	26	28
40-44	.	.	.	.	.	.	22	18	12	10
45-49	.	.	.	.	.	.	10	8	7	6
50-54	.	.	.	.	.	.	8	4	3	2
55-59	.	.	.	.	.	.	2	2	2	2
60-64	.	.	.	.	.	.	1	0	0	0
65+	.	.	.	.	.	.	0	0	0	0

Israel (BA) [2]
Total unemployment - Chômage total - Desempleo total

Total - Total - Total

	1999	2000	2001	2002	2003	2004	2005	2006	2007	2008
Total	208.5	213.8	233.9	262.4	279.9	277.7	246.4	236.1	211.8	180.4
15-17	5.5	8.9	9.0	7.7	9.7	8.3	7.9	8.4	8.6	4.3
18-24	53.8	53.4	58.7	64.1	67.7	64.6	57.2	59.3	51.3	42.2
25-34	58.1	58.7	65.9	80.1	83.3	76.9	65.6	61.8	58.6	49.0
35-44	41.8	42.4	44.1	47.9	53.3	52.7	51.0	40.4	37.6	35.7
45-54	34.5	34.1	40.7	44.5	46.2	50.0	40.7	41.8	33.6	29.4
55-59	8.5	8.9	8.2	11.5	12.1	15.0	16.6	14.8	12.6	11.4
60-64	4.9	5.4	5.8	4.6	5.5	6.6	5.6	6.9	6.6	6.1
65-69	-	-	-	-	-	2.7	-	2.0	2.0	-
70+	-	-	-	-	-	-	-	-	-	-

Men - Hommes - Hombres

	1999	2000	2001	2002	2003	2004	2005	2006	2007	2008
Total	108.8	111.7	120.9	138.4	142.8	136.5	124.9	118.5	104.8	90.8
15-17	3.1	5.3	5.4	4.4	5.4	4.4	4.7	4.1	4.7	2.6
18-24	25.3	25.3	27.2	30.6	31.3	29.0	25.0	26.6	22.5	18.6
25-34	31.6	30.3	35.7	41.9	43.0	37.7	31.7	30.9	26.9	23.0
35-44	20.4	21.8	21.1	26.3	25.9	25.5	26.4	19.0	19.8	18.4
45-54	17.7	17.2	20.4	22.9	24.4	24.6	21.5	22.9	16.8	16.4
55-59	5.8	5.7	5.3	7.7	7.4	8.3	9.7	8.0	7.5	6.0
60-64	3.9	4.5	4.8	3.3	3.9	4.7	4.5	5.1	4.5	4.0
65-69	-	-	-	-	-	2.3	-	-	-	-
70+	-	-	-	-	-	-	-	-	-	-

Women - Femmes - Mujeres

	1999	2000	2001	2002	2003	2004	2005	2006	2007	2008
Total	99.7	102.1	113.0	124.0	137.1	141.2	121.5	117.6	107.0	89.6
15-17	2.4	3.6	3.6	3.3	4.3	3.9	3.2	4.3	3.9	1.7
18-24	28.5	28.1	31.5	33.5	36.4	35.6	32.2	32.7	28.8	23.6
25-34	26.5	28.4	30.2	38.3	40.3	39.2	33.9	30.9	31.7	25.9
35-44	21.4	20.6	23.0	21.6	27.4	27.2	24.6	21.4	17.8	17.3
45-54	16.8	16.9	20.3	21.6	21.8	25.4	19.2	18.9	16.8	13.0
55-59	2.7	3.2	2.9	3.8	4.7	6.7	6.9	6.8	5.1	5.4
60-64	1.0	0.9	1.0	1.3	1.6	1.9	1.1	1.8	2.1	2.0
65-69	-	-	-	-	-	0.4	-	-	-	-
70+	-	-	-	-	-	-	-	-	-	-

Explanatory notes: see p. 451.   Notes explicatives: voir p. 454.   Notas explicativas: véase p. 457.

[1] Persons aged 10 years and over. [2] Persons aged 15 years and over.   [1] Personnes âgées de 10 ans et plus. [2] Personnes âgées de 15 ans et plus.   [1] Personas de 10 años y más. [2] Personas de 15 años y más.

By age group   Par groupe d'âge   Por grupo de edad

	Thousands			Milliers				Millares		
	1999	2000	2001	2002	2003	2004	2005	2006	2007	2008

Japan (BA) [1]

Total unemployment - Chômage total - Desempleo total

Total - Total - Total

	1999	2000	2001	2002	2003	2004	2005	2006	2007	2008
Total	3 170	3 190	3 400	3 590	3 500	3 130	2 940	2 750	2 570	2 650
15-19	170	160	160	160	140	130	110	100	90	80
20-24	560	540	540	530	540	480	440	400	380	350
25-29	510	510	550	560	540	480	450	420	380	390
30-34	300	330	380	430	420	390	390	360	320	330
35-39	220	220	260	290	310	300	290	270	280	290
40-44	210	200	210	240	240	230	240	210	210	220
45-49	240	240	250	270	240	210	190	190	180	200
50-54	260	300	320	360	310	270	230	220	190	190
55-59	260	260	260	290	310	270	280	290	240	240
60-64	340	350	350	340	340	270	230	200	190	230
65-69	90	90	90	90	100	80	80	80	80	90
70-74	10	20	20	10	20	20	20	20	20	30
75+	0	0	0	0	0	0	0	10	10	0

Men - Hommes - Hombres

	1999	2000	2001	2002	2003	2004	2005	2006	2007	2008
Total	1 940	1 960	2 090	2 190	2 150	1 920	1 780	1 680	1 540	1 590
15-19	110	100	90	100	80	70	60	50	50	50
20-24	310	310	300	310	320	280	260	230	210	190
25-29	270	280	300	310	310	290	260	250	220	230
30-34	160	180	210	230	230	220	200	210	190	190
35-39	120	120	140	160	170	160	160	150	150	160
40-44	120	110	120	140	130	130	130	110	110	120
45-49	140	140	150	160	140	120	110	110	100	110
50-54	160	190	200	230	200	170	140	130	120	120
55-59	180	180	180	210	210	180	200	200	170	170
60-64	280	280	280	270	260	210	180	150	150	170
65-69	80	80	80	80	80	60	60	70	60	70
70-74	10	10	10	10	20	10	20	20	20	20
75+	0	0	0	0	0	0	0	0	10	0

Women - Femmes - Mujeres

	1999	2000	2001	2002	2003	2004	2005	2006	2007	2008
Total	1 230	1 230	1 310	1 400	1 350	1 210	1 160	1 070	1 030	1 060
15-19	60	60	70	60	60	60	50	50	40	30
20-24	250	230	240	220	220	200	180	170	170	160
25-29	240	230	250	250	230	190	190	160	160	160
30-34	140	150	170	200	190	170	190	150	140	150
35-39	100	100	120	130	140	140	130	120	130	130
40-44	90	90	90	100	110	100	100	100	100	100
45-49	100	100	100	110	100	90	80	70	80	90
50-54	100	110	120	130	110	100	90	80	70	70
55-59	80	80	80	80	100	90	80	90	70	80
60-64	60	70	70	70	80	60	50	50	50	50
65-69	10	10	10	10	20	20	10	10	20	20
70-74	0	0	0	0	0	0	0	0	0	10
75+	0	0	0	0	0	0	0	0	0	0

Kazakhstan (BA) [1]

Total unemployment - Chômage total - Desempleo total

Total - Total - Total

	1999	2000	2001	2002	2003	2004	2005	2006	2007	2008
Total	.	.	780.3	690.7	672.1	658.8	640.7	625.4	597.2	557.8
15-19	.	.	99.0	71.9	70.1	73.4	53.3	45.9	36.2	19.1
20-24	.	.	141.4	121.2	118.5	118.2	130.4	123.1	90.6	77.6
25-29	.	.	109.4	94.7	101.9	105.8	103.3	112.3	119.8	112.7
30-34	.	.	89.4	79.6	90.6	88.9	87.1	80.2	90.7	87.2
35-39	.	.	96.2	84.8	78.7	67.3	60.9	57.7	57.3	59.3
40-44	.	.	90.4	86.0	76.7	64.8	59.9	64.1	56.3	43.7
45-49	.	.	69.0	67.2	60.9	61.2	64.4	58.6	60.6	55.8
50-54	.	.	49.0	54.7	48.2	48.3	50.4	46.1	47.3	51.5
55-59	.	.	19.2	20.0	19.1	24.6	26.3	33.3	32.7	37.8
60-64	.	.	14.1	10.2	7.4	6.3	4.8	4.2	5.6	13.2
65+	.	.	3.2	0.4	-	-	.	.	.	.

Men - Hommes - Hombres

	1999	2000	2001	2002	2003	2004	2005	2006	2007	2008
Total	.	.	338.0	283.8	281.4	281.1	270.6	262.5	244.5	226.5
15-19	.	.	50.8	35.3	36.0	37.2	30.3	22.1	22.9	10.8
20-24	.	.	65.1	59.6	55.7	59.2	64.4	54.0	40.0	37.5
25-29	.	.	46.5	36.4	44.5	46.9	41.2	50.6	48.2	48.3
30-34	.	.	32.9	27.2	34.0	30.5	31.8	33.5	34.2	30.8
35-39	.	.	35.6	30.3	28.8	27.6	22.4	21.1	21.5	21.5
40-44	.	.	37.6	31.5	29.7	24.5	20.4	24.4	21.2	16.7
45-49	.	.	29.0	26.1	21.4	24.1	26.2	20.4	20.3	21.1
50-54	.	.	18.8	20.8	17.3	16.0	18.0	20.3	17.0	17.3
55-59	.	.	11.5	9.4	8.6	10.4	12.0	12.6	14.7	14.7
60-64	.	.	8.7	6.9	5.4	4.8	4.2	3.6	4.7	7.7
65+	.	.	1.5	0.3	-	-	.	.	.	.

Explanatory notes: see p. 451.   Notes explicatives: voir p. 454.   Notas explicativas: véase p. 457.

[1] Persons aged 15 years and over.   [1] Personnes âgées de 15 ans et plus.   [1] Personas de 15 años y más.

3B

	Thousands				Milliers				Millares	
	1999	2000	2001	2002	2003	2004	2005	2006	2007	2008

Kazakhstan (BA) [1] — Total unemployment - Chômage total - Desempleo total

Women - Femmes - Mujeres

Total	.	.	442.3	406.9	390.7	377.8	370.2	362.8	352.6	331.4
15-19	.	.	48.2	36.6	34.0	36.2	23.0	23.9	13.3	8.3
20-24	.	.	76.3	61.6	62.7	59.1	66.0	69.2	50.6	40.1
25-29	.	.	62.9	58.3	57.4	58.9	62.1	61.7	71.7	64.4
30-34	.	.	56.5	52.4	56.7	58.4	55.3	46.7	56.6	56.4
35-39	.	.	60.6	54.5	49.9	39.7	38.6	36.6	35.7	37.7
40-44	.	.	52.8	54.5	47.0	40.3	39.6	39.6	35.1	26.9
45-49	.	.	40.0	41.1	39.5	37.2	38.2	38.2	40.4	34.7
50-54	.	.	30.2	33.9	31.0	32.3	32.4	25.7	30.3	34.3
55-59	.	.	7.7	10.6	10.5	14.3	14.3	20.7	18.1	23.1
60-64	.	.	5.4	3.3	2.0	1.4	0.7	0.5	0.8	5.5
65+	.	.	1.7	0.1	-	-	.	.	.	.

Korea, Republic of (BA) [1] — Total unemployment - Chômage total - Desempleo total

Total - Total - Total

Total	1 353 [	979 [2]	899	752	818	860	887	827	783	769
15-19	85 [	66 [2]	60	43	41	42	35	24	22	22
20-24	216 [	183 [2]	173	153	184	189	173	156	126	123
25-29	236 [	181 [2]	179	165	176	181	179	184	180	170
30-34	161 [	123 [2]	106	104	108	108	113	112	107	103
35-39	167 [	109 [2]	98	82	82	88	98	79	90	90
40-44	164 [	106 [2]	101	74	75	77	87	78	76	76
45-49	112 [	84 [2]	70	46	61	70	78	74	59	66
50-54	91 [	54 [2]	53	37	37	41	50	48	53	52
55-59	72 [	43 [2]	33	24	33	38	43	37	34	36
60-64	41 [	23 [2]	20	17	17	18	22	25	26	20
65-69	. [	5 [2]	4	5	5	7	8	8	7	
65+	9 [	.	.	.	.	.	.	.	.	12
70-74	. [	2 [2]	-	2	0	1	2	2	3	.
75+	. [	- [2]	-	-	0	1	0	0	1	.

Men - Hommes - Hombres

Total	911 [	647 [2]	591	491	508	534	553	533	517	
15-19	47 [	34 [2]	30	22	20	20	17	11	10	
20-24	101 [	91 [2]	82	70	81	84	77	69	64	
25-29	180 [	133 [2]	130	126	127	131	121	122	126	
30-34	118 [	91 [2]	78	75	75	75	79	82	75	
35-39	112 [	74 [2]	69	56	52	57	62	54	63	
40-44	107 [	68 [2]	68	50	47	48	55	51	48	
45-49	80 [	61 [2]	50	31	39	42	49	52	41	
50-54	70 [	39 [2]	38	25	26	28	37	34	37	
55-59	56 [	34 [2]	26	20	25	28	31	30	26	
60-64	35 [	17 [2]	16	13	12	13	17	19	19	
65-69	. [	4 [2]	3	4	4	6	7	6	6	
65+	5 [	.	.	.	.	.	.	.	.	
70-74	. [	1 [2]	1	1	0	1	1	2	2	
75+	. [	- [2]	-	-	0	0	0	0	0	

Women - Femmes - Mujeres

Total	442 [	332 [2]	308	261	310	326	334	294	266	
15-19	38 [	32 [2]	30	21	21	22	18	14	11	
20-24	115 [	92 [2]	92	83	103	105	96	87	62	
25-29	56 [	48 [2]	50	39	49	49	58	61	54	
30-34	43 [	32 [2]	28	30	33	32	34	29	33	
35-39	55 [	34 [2]	29	26	30	31	35	25	27	
40-44	57 [	38 [2]	33	24	28	29	32	27	28	
45-49	32 [	23 [2]	20	15	22	28	29	22	18	
50-54	21 [	15 [2]	15	12	11	12	13	14	16	
55-59	16 [	9 [2]	7	4	8	10	12	7	8	
60-64	6 [	6 [2]	4	4	5	5	5	6	7	
65-69	. [	1 [2]	1	1	1	2	1	2	1	
65+	4 [	.	.	.	.	.	.	.	.	
70-74	. [	1 [2]	-	1	0	0	1	0	1	
75+	. [	- [2]	-	-	-	0	0	0	0	

Kyrgyzstan (BA) [1][3] — Total unemployment - Chômage total - Desempleo total

Total - Total - Total

Total	.	.	.	265.5	212.3	185.7	183.5	188.9	.	.
15-19	.	.	.	35.4	25.1	27.9	25.4	26.7	.	.
20-24	.	.	.	60.5	48.9	44.7	47.0	46.1	.	.
25-29	.	.	.	43.6	33.6	32.0	27.5	27.8	.	.
30-34	.	.	.	29.4	26.4	21.2	22.8	23.6	.	.
35-39	.	.	.	29.5	21.2	15.8	15.1	17.2	.	.
40-44	.	.	.	27.4	22.4	15.4	15.0	17.2	.	.
45-49	.	.	.	21.1	18.9	14.6	15.9	15.6	.	.
50-54	.	.	.	11.0	10.6	10.3	11.0	8.4	.	.
55-59	.	.	.	4.2	2.8	2.7	3.0	4.9	.	.
60-64	.	.	.	2.2	1.4	0.9	0.3	1.0	.	.
65+	.	.	.	1.2	1.1	0.2	0.3	0.5	.	.

Explanatory notes: see p. 451.

[1] Persons aged 15 years and over. [2] Estimates based on the 2000 Population Census results. [3] Nov. of each year.

Notes explicatives: voir p. 454.

[1] Personnes âgées de 15 ans et plus. [2] Estimations basées sur les résultats du Recensement de la population de 2000. [3] Nov. de chaque année.

Notas explicativas: véase p. 457.

[1] Personas de 15 años y más. [2] Estimaciones basadas en los resultados del Censo de población de 2000. [3] Nov. de cada año.

UNEMPLOYMENT — CHÔMAGE — DESEMPLEO

3B

By age group — Par groupe d'âge — Por grupo de edad

	Thousands / Milliers / Millares									
	1999	2000	2001	2002	2003	2004	2005	2006	2007	2008

Kyrgyzstan (BA) [1][2] — Total unemployment - Chômage total - Desempleo total

Men - Hommes - Hombres

	1999	2000	2001	2002	2003	2004	2005	2006	2007	2008
Total	.	.	.	132.6	113.1	98.8	95.7	101.4	.	.
15-19	.	.	.	19.5	13.9	13.9	14.5	15.5	.	.
20-24	.	.	.	33.7	27.9	25.0	25.9	26.2	.	.
25-29	.	.	.	22.6	18.7	18.5	15.1	14.5	.	.
30-34	.	.	.	10.9	12.0	10.9	10.4	10.4	.	.
35-39	.	.	.	15.1	9.5	6.5	7.0	8.4	.	.
40-44	.	.	.	11.9	11.9	7.5	6.6	8.8	.	.
45-49	.	.	.	9.3	9.6	7.5	7.2	8.9	.	.
50-54	.	.	.	7.0	6.1	6.5	6.9	4.5	.	.
55-59	.	.	.	1.0	1.8	1.7	1.6	3.3	.	.
60-64	.	.	.	1.4	1.1	0.7	0.2	0.7	.	.
65+	.	.	.	0.4	0.8	0.1	0.3	0.2	.	.

Women - Femmes - Mujeres

	1999	2000	2001	2002	2003	2004	2005	2006	2007	2008
Total	.	.	.	132.9	99.2	86.9	87.8	87.5	.	.
15-19	.	.	.	15.9	11.3	14.0	10.9	11.3	.	.
20-24	.	.	.	26.8	21.0	19.7	21.1	19.9	.	.
25-29	.	.	.	21.0	14.9	13.5	12.4	13.3	.	.
30-34	.	.	.	18.5	14.4	10.3	12.4	13.2	.	.
35-39	.	.	.	14.5	11.7	9.3	8.1	8.8	.	.
40-44	.	.	.	15.6	10.5	7.9	8.4	8.3	.	.
45-49	.	.	.	11.8	9.2	7.1	8.7	6.6	.	.
50-54	.	.	.	4.0	4.5	3.7	4.2	3.9	.	.
55-59	.	.	.	3.2	1.0	0.9	1.4	1.6	.	.
60-64	.	.	.	0.8	0.3	0.3	0.1	0.3	.	.
65+	.	.	.	0.8	0.3	0.1	-	0.3	.	.

Kyrgyzstan (FB) [1] — Registered unemployment - Chômage enregistré - Desempleo registrado

Total - Total - Total

	1999	2000	2001	2002	2003	2004	2005	2006	2007	2008
Total	54.7	58.3	60.5	60.2	57.4	58.2	68.0	73.4	71.3	.
15-19	2.1	5.0	5.5	4.4	4.2	4.1	4.5	4.3	4.1	.
20-24	6.5	10.3	9.5	9.7	8.8	9.8	11.3	13.7	12.9	.
25-29	11.1	8.0	7.5	7.9	7.7	8.4	9.4	10.3	10.9	.
30-34	.	10.3	9.7	9.7	9.8	10.1	11.4	11.4	12.7	.
30-44	19.8	.	.	.	.	.	.	.	.	.
35-39	.	10.4	10.6	10.5	10.6	9.0	9.8	11.2	10.4	.
40-44	.	6.8	8.6	8.9	8.0	7.7	8.8	10.2	8.7	.
45-49	11.7	4.8	5.2	5.7	5.3	5.4	7.5	6.3	6.4	.
50-54	2.7	2.1	3.0	2.5	2.3	2.9	4.3	4.0	3.7	.
55-59	0.8	0.6	0.8	0.8	0.6	0.8	1.0	1.9	1.5	.
60+	-	0.0	0.1	0.1	0.1	0.1	0.1	0.1	0.0	.

Men - Hommes - Hombres

	1999	2000	2001	2002	2003	2004	2005	2006	2007	2008
Total	24.2	27.1	28.0	27.6	26.5	26.8	32.2	37.9	35.8	.
15-19	0.9	2.3	2.7	2.3	2.2	2.1	2.5	2.1	1.9	.
20-24	2.7	4.5	4.3	4.7	4.0	4.6	5.8	7.3	6.5	.
25-29	4.8	3.8	3.4	3.5	3.4	3.7	4.3	5.2	5.6	.
30-34	.	4.8	4.7	4.2	4.0	4.2	5.4	6.1	6.2	.
30-44	8.7	.	.	.	.	.	.	.	.	.
35-39	.	4.9	4.7	4.6	5.4	3.9	4.4	6.3	6.0	.
40-44	.	3.1	3.9	4.0	3.7	3.7	3.9	5.0	4.5	.
45-49	4.8	2.2	2.3	2.4	2.3	2.6	3.5	3.3	3.0	.
50-54	1.4	0.9	1.4	1.3	1.1	1.5	1.9	1.9	1.6	.
55-59	0.8	0.5	0.6	0.4	0.3	0.4	0.3	0.6	0.5	.
60+	-	0.0	0.1	0.1	0.1	0.1	0.1	0.0	0.0	.

Women - Femmes - Mujeres

	1999	2000	2001	2002	2003	2004	2005	2006	2007	2008
Total	30.6	31.2	32.5	32.6	30.9	31.4	35.8	35.5	35.5	.
15-19	1.2	2.7	2.8	2.1	2.0	2.0	2.0	2.3	2.3	.
20-24	3.8	5.8	5.2	5.0	4.8	5.2	5.5	6.4	6.4	.
25-29	6.3	4.2	4.1	4.4	4.4	4.6	5.1	5.1	5.3	.
30-34	.	5.5	5.0	5.5	5.7	5.8	6.0	5.3	6.5	.
30-44	11.0	.	.	.	.	.	.	.	.	.
35-39	.	5.5	5.9	5.9	5.3	5.0	5.4	4.9	4.4	.
40-44	.	3.7	4.8	4.9	4.3	4.0	4.9	5.1	4.2	.
45-49	6.9	2.6	2.9	3.3	3.0	2.8	3.9	3.0	3.4	.
50-54	1.3	1.2	1.6	1.3	1.2	1.4	2.4	2.1	2.1	.
55-59	0.0	0.1	0.2	0.4	0.3	0.4	0.7	1.3	1.0	.
60+	-	-	-	0.0	0.0	-	0.0	0.1	0.0	.

Explanatory notes: see p. 451.
[1] Persons aged 15 years and over. [2] Nov. of each year.

Notes explicatives: voir p. 454.
[1] Personnes âgées de 15 ans et plus. [2] Nov. de chaque année.

Notas explicativas: véase p. 457.
[1] Personas de 15 años y más. [2] Nov. de cada año.

	UNEMPLOYMENT	CHÔMAGE	DESEMPLEO
	By age group	**Par groupe d'âge**	**Por grupo de edad**

	Thousands					Milliers			Millares	
	1999	2000	2001	2002	2003	2004	2005	2006	2007	2008

Liban (B) [1]   **Total unemployment - Chômage total - Desempleo total**

Total - Total - Total

	1999	2000	2001	2002	2003	2004	2005	2006	2007	2008
Total	.	.	.	.	.	94.4	.	.	110.4	.
15-19	.	.	.	.	.	16.6	.	.	15.3	.
20-24	.	.	.	.	.	29.1	.	.	34.4	.
25-29	.	.	.	.	.	15.9	.	.	24.0	.
30-34	.	.	.	.	.	9.3	.	.	11.7	.
35-39	.	.	.	.	.	6.1	.	.	5.1	.
40-44	.	.	.	.	.	5.8	.	.	4.2	.
45-49	.	.	.	.	.	3.3	.	.	3.2	.
50-54	.	.	.	.	.	2.7	.	.	5.3	.
55-59	.	.	.	.	.	1.4	.	.	3.7	.
60-64	.	.	.	.	.	1.8	.	.	1.0	.
65-69	.	.	.	.	.	1.5	.	.	1.4	.
70-74	.	.	.	.	.	0.6	.	.	0.9	.
75+	.	.	.	.	.	0.2	.	.	0.4	.

Men - Hommes - Hombres

	1999	2000	2001	2002	2003	2004	2005	2006	2007	2008
Total	.	.	.	.	.	67.3	.	.	79.3	.
15-19	.	.	.	.	.	13.3	.	.	11.7	.
20-24	.	.	.	.	.	19.9	.	.	24.5	.
25-29	.	.	.	.	.	9.7	.	.	15.6	.
30-34	.	.	.	.	.	6.4	.	.	7.7	.
35-39	.	.	.	.	.	4.3	.	.	3.8	.
40-44	.	.	.	.	.	3.6	.	.	2.6	.
45-49	.	.	.	.	.	2.3	.	.	2.1	.
50-54	.	.	.	.	.	2.5	.	.	5.3	.
55-59	.	.	.	.	.	1.3	.	.	2.5	.
60-64	.	.	.	.	.	1.7	.	.	1.0	.
65-69	.	.	.	.	.	1.5	.	.	1.4	.
70-74	.	.	.	.	.	0.6	.	.	0.9	.
75+	.	.	.	.	.	0.2	.	.	0.4	.

Women - Femmes - Mujeres

	1999	2000	2001	2002	2003	2004	2005	2006	2007	2008
Total	.	.	.	.	.	27.1	.	.	31.1	.
15-19	.	.	.	.	.	3.3	.	.	3.6	.
20-24	.	.	.	.	.	9.2	.	.	9.8	.
25-29	.	.	.	.	.	6.2	.	.	8.4	.
30-34	.	.	.	.	.	3.0	.	.	4.0	.
35-39	.	.	.	.	.	1.8	.	.	1.3	.
40-44	.	.	.	.	.	2.2	.	.	1.7	.
45-49	.	.	.	.	.	1.1	.	.	1.1	.
50-54	.	.	.	.	.	0.2	.	.	0.0	.
55-59	.	.	.	.	.	0.1	.	.	1.2	.
60-64	.	.	.	.	.	0.1	.	.	0.0	.
65-69	.	.	.	.	.	0.0	.	.	0.0	.
70-74	.	.	.	.	.	0.0	.	.	0.0	.
75+	.	.	.	.	.	0.0	.	.	0.0	.

Macau, China (BA) [2]   **Total unemployment - Chômage total - Desempleo total**

Total - Total - Total

	1999	2000	2001	2002	2003	2004	2005	2006	2007	2008
Total	13.2	14.2	14.0	13.7	13.1	11.2	10.3	10.4	9.5	10.1
14-19	1.4	1.1	1.1	1.2	1.1	1.0	1.1	0.9	1.0	1.0
20-24	1.8	1.7	1.6	1.6	1.9	1.8	1.5	1.7	1.7	1.8
25-29	1.3	1.3	1.4	1.2	1.2	1.1	1.0	1.0	0.7	0.8
30-34	1.5	1.6	1.3	1.2	1.1	1.0	0.7	0.7	0.9	0.5
35-39	2.0	2.4	2.1	1.9	1.4	1.2	1.1	1.1	0.8	0.9
40-44	2.4	2.9	2.9	2.6	2.2	1.6	1.4	1.5	1.0	1.2
45-49	1.4	1.8	2.1	2.1	2.3	1.7	1.7	1.5	1.2	1.5
50-54	0.8	1.1	1.0	1.0	1.3	1.1	1.1	1.1	1.2	1.5
55-59	0.4	0.3	0.4	0.6	0.6	0.6	0.6	0.6	0.7	0.6
60-64	0.2	0.1	0.1	0.2	0.1	0.1	0.2	0.2	0.2	0.2
65+	0.1	0.1	-	-	-	0.0	-	-	0.0	0.0

Men - Hommes - Hombres

	1999	2000	2001	2002	2003	2004	2005	2006	2007	2008
Total	9.1	9.8	9.5	9.1	8.3	6.8	5.8	5.6	5.6	5.7
14-19	0.9	0.7	0.7	0.8	0.7	0.7	0.6	0.6	0.7	0.7
20-24	1.1	1.0	1.0	0.9	1.2	1.0	0.9	0.9	1.2	1.0
25-29	0.7	0.8	0.9	0.8	0.8	0.7	0.5	0.6	0.4	0.5
30-34	1.0	0.9	0.8	0.7	0.6	0.6	0.5	0.4	0.4	0.2
35-39	1.3	1.6	1.2	1.1	0.6	0.6	0.4	0.4	0.3	0.3
40-44	1.8	2.2	1.9	1.9	1.4	1.1	0.6	0.6	0.5	0.6
45-49	1.1	1.3	1.7	1.5	1.5	1.0	0.9	0.8	0.7	0.8
50-54	0.7	0.9	0.9	0.7	0.9	0.7	0.7	0.7	0.8	0.9
55-59	0.3	0.2	0.3	0.4	0.5	0.4	0.4	0.4	0.5	0.5
60-64	0.1	0.1	0.1	0.2	0.1	0.1	0.1	0.1	0.2	0.2
65+	0.1	0.1	-	-	-	0.0	-	-	0.0	0.0

Explanatory notes: see p. 451.   Notes explicatives: voir p. 454.   Notas explicativas: véase p. 457.

[1] Persons aged 15 years and over. [2] Persons aged 14 years and over.   [1] Personnes âgées de 15 ans et plus. [2] Personnes âgées de 14 ans et plus.   [1] Personas de 15 años y más. [2] Personas de 14 años y más.

By age group — Par groupe d'âge — Por grupo de edad

	Thousands			Milliers				Millares		
	1999	2000	2001	2002	2003	2004	2005	2006	2007	2008

Macau, China (BA) [1] — Total unemployment - Chômage total - Desempleo total

Women - Femmes - Mujeres

	1999	2000	2001	2002	2003	2004	2005	2006	2007	2008
Total	4.2	4.4	4.5	4.6	4.8	4.4	4.5	4.8	3.9	4.3
14-19	0.5	0.4	0.4	0.4	0.4	0.3	0.4	0.3	0.3	0.3
20-24	0.7	0.7	0.6	0.7	0.7	0.8	0.6	0.8	0.6	0.7
25-29	0.6	0.5	0.5	0.4	0.5	0.5	0.4	0.4	0.4	0.4
30-34	0.5	0.7	0.5	0.5	0.5	0.4	0.2	0.3	0.4	0.3
35-39	0.7	0.8	1.0	0.8	0.7	0.6	0.6	0.7	0.5	0.6
40-44	0.6	0.7	0.9	0.8	0.8	0.5	0.9	0.9	0.5	0.6
45-49	0.3	0.5	0.4	0.6	0.8	0.7	0.8	0.7	0.5	0.6
50-54	0.1	0.2	0.1	0.3	0.3	0.4	0.4	0.5	0.4	0.5
55-59	0.1	0.1	0.1	0.1	0.1	0.2	0.1	0.2	0.3	0.2
60-64	0.1	-	-	-	-	-	0.1	0.1	0.0	-
65+	0.0	-	-	-	0.0	0.0	0.0	0.0	0.0	0.0

Malaysia (BA) [2] — Total unemployment - Chômage total - Desempleo total

Total - Total - Total

	1999	2000	2001	2002	2003	2004	2005	2006	2007	2008
Total	313.7	286.9	342.4	343.5	369.8	366.6	368.1	353.6	351.4	368.5
15-19	99.0	86.0	108.9	100.8	97.8	94.9	92.9	77.2	78.7	85.5
20-24	111.6	100.3	117.3	127.2	142.8	154.5	152.6	151.0	149.2	143.6
25-29	34.0	36.0	39.5	40.6	45.0	46.3	52.2	55.4	56.8	54.7
30-34	18.2	15.0	23.2	18.6	25.7	18.8	21.7	20.2	19.9	21.2
35-39	14.9	16.3	14.1	15.6	14.9	15.8	13.6	15.1	13.0	16.4
40-44	10.8	10.9	12.8	12.1	13.1	11.9	11.8	9.7	10.6	15.1
45-49	11.2	8.3	8.6	10.6	11.6	8.8	11.8	10.8	9.3	12.9
50-54	6.1	6.7	7.9	8.4	9.6	7.6	6.3	7.6	9.2	9.8
55-59	5.9	4.6	5.7	5.9	5.4	3.8	3.0	5.0	2.4	5.9
60-64	2.2	2.8	4.3	3.8	4.0	4.3	2.1	1.4	2.2	3.2

Men - Hommes - Hombres

	1999	2000	2001	2002	2003	2004	2005	2006	2007	2008
Total	212.3	182.7	212.3	210.5	235.8	224.7	230.4	224.9	216.4	223.5
15-19	65.2	51.7	64.1	57.9	59.8	54.3	58.2	47.9	48.2	51.6
20-24	68.2	59.2	67.1	69.9	82.8	87.9	85.0	87.2	83.2	78.5
25-29	22.9	22.5	23.2	26.7	28.4	27.2	32.6	33.8	34.6	31.5
30-34	13.7	10.7	16.7	12.4	18.6	13.7	15.5	14.7	12.9	13.1
35-39	12.4	12.4	10.0	11.6	11.0	11.9	9.4	12.6	10.0	12.2
40-44	8.6	8.1	9.3	9.4	10.8	9.4	10.2	8.6	8.9	10.9
45-49	9.1	6.3	7.2	8.1	8.9	7.2	10.0	9.5	8.4	11.1
50-54	4.9	5.5	6.4	7.4	7.5	6.3	5.4	6.7	7.4	7.9
55-59	5.4	3.7	4.9	4.8	4.8	3.3	2.6	3.3	1.7	4.1
60-64	1.9	2.7	3.4	2.2	3.4	3.5	1.5	0.6	1.1	2.6

Women - Femmes - Mujeres

	1999	2000	2001	2002	2003	2004	2005	2006	2007	2008
Total	101.4	104.2	130.1	133.1	134.0	142.0	137.7	128.7	135.0	145.0
15-19	33.7	34.4	44.8	42.8	38.0	40.6	34.7	29.4	30.5	33.9
20-24	43.4	41.1	50.2	57.3	60.0	66.6	67.7	63.9	66.0	65.2
25-29	11.1	13.5	16.4	13.9	16.6	19.1	19.6	21.6	22.2	23.3
30-34	4.5	4.3	6.5	6.2	7.1	5.1	6.3	5.5	7.0	8.2
35-39	2.5	3.9	4.1	4.0	4.0	3.9	4.2	2.5	3.1	4.2
40-44	2.2	2.8	3.4	2.7	2.3	2.5	1.6	1.1	1.7	4.1
45-49	2.1	2.0	1.4	2.5	2.7	1.6	1.7	1.3	0.9	1.8
50-54	1.2	1.2	1.5	1.0	2.1	1.3	1.0	0.9	1.8	1.9
55-59	0.5	0.9	0.8	1.1	0.6	0.5	0.4	1.6	0.6	1.9
60-64	0.3	0.1	0.9	1.6	0.6	0.8	0.6	0.8	1.2	0.6

Mongolia (E) [3][4] — Registered unemployment - Chômage enregistré - Desempleo registrado

Total - Total - Total

	1999	2000	2001	2002	2003	2004	2005	2006	2007	2008
Total	39.8	38.6	40.3	30.9	33.3	35.6	32.9	32.9	29.9	29.8
16-19	.	.	.	.	.	3.0	2.7	2.6	2.2	2.2
16-24	11.3	10.4	11.4	7.7	8.0	.	.	.	.	.
20-24	.	.	.	.	.	5.3	4.8	4.9	4.9	4.6
25-29	.	.	.	.	.	5.7	5.4	5.4	5.2	5.2
25-34	14.6	14.3	14.2	10.6	11.1	.	.	.	.	.
30-34	.	.	.	.	.	6.3	5.6	5.8	5.1	4.9
35-39	.	.	.	.	.	5.6	5.2	5.0	4.3	4.3
35-44	11.0	11.1	11.7	9.3	10.1	.	.	.	.	.
40-44	.	.	.	.	.	4.9	4.3	4.2	3.5	3.6
45-49	.	.	.	.	.	3.1	3.1	2.9	3.1	3.3
45-59	2.8	2.7	3.1	3.2	4.2	.	.	.	.	.
50-54	.	.	.	.	.	1.2	1.6	1.6	1.3	1.4
55-59	.	.	.	.	.	0.4	0.2	0.5	0.3	0.4
60+	.	.	.	.	.	-	-	-	-	-

Explanatory notes: see p. 451.

[1] Persons aged 14 years and over. [2] Persons aged 15 to 64 years. [3] Persons aged 16 years and over. [4] Dec. of each year.

Notes explicatives: voir p. 454.

[1] Personnes âgées de 14 ans et plus. [2] Personnes âgées de 15 à 64 ans. [3] Personnes âgées de 16 ans et plus. [4] Déc. de chaque année.

Notas explicativas: véase p. 457.

[1] Personas de 14 años y más. [2] Personas de 15 a 64 años. [3] Personas de 16 años y más. [4] Dic. de cada año.

UNEMPLOYMENT — CHÔMAGE — DESEMPLEO

By age group — Par groupe d'âge — Por grupo de edad

	Thousands / Milliers / Millares									
	1999	2000	2001	2002	2003	2004	2005	2006	2007	2008

Mongolia (E) [1][2]   Registered unemployment - Chômage enregistré - Desempleo registrado

Men - Hommes - Hombres

	1999	2000	2001	2002	2003	2004	2005	2006	2007	2008
Total	18.1	17.8	18.5	14.1	15.3	15.9	14.6	14.2	13.0	12.2
16-19	.	.	.	.	.	1.4	1.2	1.1	1.0	1.0
16-24	4.9	4.3	5.1	3.4	3.7	.	.	.	.	.
20-24	.	.	.	.	.	2.2	2.1	2.2	2.2	1.9
25-29	.	.	.	.	.	2.3	2.0	2.0	2.1	2.0
25-34	6.8	7.0	6.3	4.5	4.7	.	.	.	.	.
30-34	.	.	.	.	.	2.6	2.4	2.4	2.1	1.8
35-39	.	.	.	.	.	2.4	2.2	2.1	1.9	1.6
35-44	4.9	5.0	5.2	4.0	4.4	.	.	.	.	.
40-44	.	.	.	.	.	2.1	1.9	1.8	1.3	1.5
45-49	.	.	.	.	.	1.8	1.6	1.4	1.6	1.6
45-59	1.5	1.5	1.8	2.1	2.5	.	.	.	.	.
50-54	.	.	.	.	.	0.7	1.0	0.9	0.7	0.7
55-59	.	.	.	.	.	0.3	0.2	0.3	0.2	0.3
60+	.	.	.	.	.	-	-	-	-	-

Women - Femmes - Mujeres

	1999	2000	2001	2002	2003	2004	2005	2006	2007	2008
Total	21.6	20.7	21.9	16.8	18.1	19.6	18.3	18.8	17.0	17.6
16-19	.	.	.	.	.	1.6	1.5	1.5	1.3	1.2
16-24	6.4	6.1	6.3	4.3	4.4	.	.	.	.	.
20-24	.	.	.	.	.	3.1	2.7	2.7	2.7	2.7
25-29	.	.	.	.	.	3.4	3.3	3.4	3.1	3.2
25-34	7.8	7.3	7.9	6.1	6.4	.	.	.	.	.
30-34	.	.	.	.	.	3.7	3.2	3.4	3.0	3.1
35-39	.	.	.	.	.	3.1	3.0	2.9	2.4	2.7
35-44	6.2	6.1	6.5	5.2	5.6	.	.	.	.	.
40-44	.	.	.	.	.	2.8	2.4	2.4	2.2	2.2
45-49	.	.	.	.	.	1.3	1.5	1.4	1.5	1.7
45-59	1.2	1.2	1.3	1.1	1.7	.	.	.	.	.
50-54	.	.	.	.	.	0.5	0.6	0.7	0.7	0.6
55-59	.	.	.	.	.	0.1	0.1	0.2	0.1	0.2
60+	.	.	.	.	.	-	-	-	-	-

Pakistan (BA) [3][4]   Total unemployment - Chômage total - Desempleo total

Total - Total - Total

	1999	2000	2001	2002	2003	2004	2005	2006	2007	2008
Total	2 334	3 127	3 181	3 506	3 594	3 499	3 566	3 103	2 680	.
10-14	225	405	411	359	368	314	320	241	253	.
15-19	599	747	761	921	944	829	845	704	561	.
20-24	448	610	620	688	705	699	712	545	496	.
25-29	220	299	304	320	328	390	397	286	250	.
30-34	72	128	130	180	185	199	203	140	100	.
35-39	86	99	101	117	120	135	138	120	79	.
40-44	71	85	87	121	124	116	118	118	80	.
45-49	68	104	105	112	115	123	125	114	103	.
50-54	98	110	112	156	160	133	136	174	138	.
55-59	101	116	118	139	142	139	142	184	165	.
60-64	119	147	150	130	133	168	171	185	156	.
65+	227	277	282	263	270	254	259	291	299	.

Men - Hommes - Hombres

	1999	2000	2001	2002	2003	2004	2005	2006	2007	2008
Total	1 419	2 046	2 082	2 381	2 441	2 461	2 508	2 166	1 807	.
10-14	132	272	276	264	271	250	255	191	202	.
15-19	417	547	556	719	737	653	666	564	442	.
20-24	309	445	453	484	496	520	530	408	358	.
25-29	121	204	209	220	225	277	282	205	170	.
30-34	36	69	70	114	117	139	142	95	64	.
35-39	49	58	59	58	59	75	76	66	51	.
40-44	35	45	46	70	72	81	83	71	37	.
45-49	38	64	65	70	72	66	67	67	62	.
50-54	48	54	55	88	90	75	76	102	71	.
55-59	48	53	54	70	72	75	76	106	85	.
60-64	68	69	70	68	70	91	93	96	87	.
65+	118	166	169	156	160	159	162	196	178	.

Women - Femmes - Mujeres

	1999	2000	2001	2002	2003	2004	2005	2006	2007	2008
Total	915	1 081	1 099	1 125	1 153	1 038	1 058	937	873	.
10-14	93	133	135	95	97	64	65	50	51	.
15-19	182	200	205	202	207	176	179	140	119	.
20-24	139	165	167	204	209	179	182	137	138	.
25-29	99	95	95	100	103	113	115	82	80	.
30-34	36	59	60	66	68	60	61	45	36	.
35-39	37	41	42	59	61	61	62	54	28	.
40-44	36	40	41	51	52	35	35	47	43	.
45-49	30	40	40	42	43	57	58	48	41	.
50-54	50	56	57	68	70	58	60	72	67	.
55-59	53	63	64	69	70	64	66	78	80	.
60-64	51	78	80	62	63	77	78	90	69	.
65+	109	111	113	107	110	95	97	95	121	.

Explanatory notes: see p. 451.

Notes explicatives: voir p. 454.

Notas explicativas: véase p. 457.

[1] Persons aged 16 years and over. [2] Dec. of each year. [3] Persons aged 10 years and over. [4] Jan.

[1] Personnes âgées de 16 ans et plus. [2] Déc. de chaque année. [3] Personnes âgées de 10 ans et plus. [4] Janv.

[1] Personas de 16 años y más. [2] Dic. de cada año. [3] Personas de 10 años y más. [4] Enero.

| **By age group** | **Par groupe d'âge** | **Por grupo de edad** |

Thousands			Milliers				Millares		
1999	2000	2001	2002	2003	2004	2005	2006	2007	2008

Philippines (BA) [1]

Total unemployment - Chômage total - Desempleo total

Total - Total - Total

	1999	2000	2001	2002	2003	2004	2005	2006	2007	2008
Total	3 017	3 459	3 653	3 874	3 936	4 249	2 748 [2]	2 829	2 653	2 716
15-24	1 520	1 766	1 819	1 919	1 861	2 009	1 353 [2]	1 415	1 335	1 389
25-34	694	776	816	873	961	1 032	788 [2]	806	763	788
35-44	344	398	407	443	436	464	307 [2]	309	279	264
45-54	222	263	313	329	335	365	196 [2]	199	172	172
55-64	147	161	193	188	221	262	89 [2]	84	85	85
65+	91	95	105	123	122	118	15 [2]	16	19	19

Men - Hommes - Hombres

	1999	2000	2001	2002	2003	2004	2005	2006	2007	2008
Total	1 852	2 113	2 174	2 295	2 343	2 558	1 685 [2]	1 798	1 675	1 714
15-24	878	1 018	1 019	1 081	1 043	1 127	767 [2]	826	777	809
25-34	445	485	502	521	582	633	496 [2]	530	494	509
35-44	218	259	248	276	271	293	204 [2]	215	198	188
45-54	157	185	212	225	226	249	142 [2]	153	130	132
55-64	102	110	130	126	150	184	65 [2]	64	64	65
65+	53	56	63	68	71	73	10 [2]	9	13	13

Women - Femmes - Mujeres

	1999	2000	2001	2002	2003	2004	2005	2006	2007	2008
Total	1 165	1 346	1 478	1 579	1 592	1 692	1 062 [2]	1 031	978	1 002
15-24	642	748	801	838	819	882	585 [2]	588	558	580
25-34	249	291	313	352	378	399	292 [2]	276	270	279
35-44	126	139	158	167	165	172	103 [2]	93	81	76
45-54	66	78	101	105	108	115	54 [2]	47	42	40
55-64	45	52	63	62	71	79	24 [2]	21	21	21
65+	38	39	42	55	51	45	4 [2]	7	7	6

Qatar (BA) [1] [3]

Total unemployment - Chômage total - Desempleo total

Total - Total - Total

	1999	2000	2001	2002	2003	2004	2005	2006	2007	2008
Total	.	.	12.615	.	.	.	.	.	4.303	.
15-19	.	.	1.531	.	.	.	.	.	0.587	.
20-24	.	.	4.174	.	.	.	.	.	1.491	.
25-29	.	.	3.059	.	.	.	.	.	1.157	.
30-34	.	.	1.699	.	.	.	.	.	0.793	.
35-39	.	.	0.863	.	.	.	.	.	0.150	.
40-44	.	.	0.613	.	.	.	.	.	0.043	.
45-49	.	.	0.267	.	.	.	.	.	0.082	.
50-54	.	.	0.285	.	.	.	.	.	-	.
55-59	.	.	0.062	.	.	.	.	.	-	.
60+	.	.	0.063	.	.	.	.	.	-	.

Men - Hommes - Hombres

	1999	2000	2001	2002	2003	2004	2005	2006	2007	2008
Total	.	.	6.137	.	.	.	.	.	1.569	.
15-19	.	.	1.032	.	.	.	.	.	0.248	.
20-24	.	.	2.323	.	.	.	.	.	0.528	.
25-29	.	.	1.281	.	.	.	.	.	0.337	.
30-34	.	.	0.643	.	.	.	.	.	0.386	.
35-39	.	.	0.170	.	.	.	.	.		.
40-44	.	.	0.256	.	.	.	.	.	0.028	.
45-49	.	.	0.143	.	.	.	.	.	0.042	.
50-54	.	.	0.165	.	.	.	.	.	-	.
55-59	.	.	0.062	.	.	.	.	.	-	.
60+	.	.	0.063	.	.	.	.	.	-	.

Women - Femmes - Mujeres

	1999	2000	2001	2002	2003	2004	2005	2006	2007	2008
Total	.	.	6.478	.	.	.	.	.	2.734	.
15-19	.	.	0.499	.	.	.	.	.	0.339	.
20-24	.	.	1.852	.	.	.	.	.	0.963	.
25-29	.	.	1.778	.	.	.	.	.	0.820	.
30-34	.	.	1.056	.	.	.	.	.	0.407	.
35-39	.	.	0.694	.	.	.	.	.	0.150	.
40-44	.	.	0.356	.	.	.	.	.	0.015	.
45-49	.	.	0.124	.	.	.	.	.	0.040	.
50-54	.	.	0.120	.	.	.	.	.	-	.
55-59	.	.	-	.	.	.	.	.	-	.
60+	.	.	-	.	.	.	.	.	-	.

Saudi Arabia (BA) [1]

Total unemployment - Chômage total - Desempleo total

Total - Total - Total

	1999	2000	2001	2002	2003	2004	2005	2006	2007	2008
Total	254.054	273.641	281.147	328.646	.	.	.	501.898 [4]	463.313	418.062
15-19	42.679	41.551	47.488	43.497	.	.	.	49.581 [4]	28.546	20.832
20-24	124.313	123.756	122.344	149.326	.	.	.	241.138 [4]	207.383	195.307
25-29	63.686	63.342	72.425	87.837	.	.	.	157.354 [4]	160.010	148.414
30-34	14.262	21.731	16.863	25.193	.	.	.	34.775 [4]	47.912	38.335
35-39	3.160	8.398	8.672	7.051	.	.	.	10.735 [4]	6.093	7.611
40-44	2.231	5.931	5.149	5.012	.	.	.	4.277 [4]	8.256	4.889
45-49	1.671	2.780	2.035	4.702	.	.	.	2.849 [4]	3.113	2.011
50-54	0.590	1.885	2.139	0.982	.	.	.	0.523 [4]	1.053	0.222
55-59	1.462	1.350	1.787	1.180	.	.	.	0.417 [4]	0.947	0.107
60-64	-	0.865	1.129	0.953	.	.	.	0.249 [4]	-	0.334
65+	-	2.054	1.116	2.913	.	.	.	- [4]	-	-

Explanatory notes: see p. 451.

[1] Persons aged 15 years and over. [2] Definitions revised; data not strictly comparable. [3] March. [4] April.

Notes explicatives: voir p. 454.

[1] Personnes âgées de 15 ans et plus. [2] Définitions révisées; les données ne sont pas strictement comparables. [3] Mars. [4] Avril.

Notas explicativas: véase p. 457.

[1] Personas de 15 años y más. [2] Definiciones revisadas; los datos no son estrictamente comparables. [3] Marzo. [4] Abril.

UNEMPLOYMENT	CHÔMAGE	DESEMPLEO
By age group	Par groupe d'âge	Por grupo de edad

	Thousands				Milliers				Millares	
	1999	2000	2001	2002	2003	2004	2005	2006	2007	2008
Saudi Arabia (BA) [1]				Total unemployment - Chômage total - Desempleo total						
Men - Hommes - Hombres										
Total	183.780	194.330	202.565	224.987				319.059 [2]	295.473	250.402
15-19	37.067	36.362	43.785	39.398				40.726 [2]	26.082	19.171
20-24	89.731	83.103	83.570	96.673				157.194 [2]	137.390	124.223
25-29	40.059	40.716	42.465	51.702				76.792 [2]	86.565	73.735
30-34	10.033	13.220	13.026	15.354				26.342 [2]	27.554	21.051
35-39	2.915	6.781	6.367	6.115				9.786 [2]	5.340	4.961
40-44	1.197	5.215	5.149	5.013				4.277 [2]	7.629	4.587
45-49	1.415	2.780	2.034	4.702				2.753 [2]	2.913	2.011
50-54	0.432	1.885	2.137	0.982				0.523 [2]	1.053	0.222
55-59	0.931	1.349	1.787	1.179				0.417 [2]	0.947	0.107
60-64	-	0.865	1.127	0.954				0.249 [2]	-	0.334
65+	-	2.054	1.116	2.915				- [2]	-	-
Women - Femmes - Mujeres										
Total	70.274	79.311	78.582	103.659				182.839 [2]	167.840	167.660
15-19	5.612	5.189	3.703	4.099				8.855 [2]	2.464	1.661
20-24	34.582	40.653	38.774	52.653				83.944 [2]	69.993	71.084
25-29	23.627	22.626	29.960	36.135				80.562 [2]	73.445	74.679
30-34	4.229	8.511	3.837	9.839				8.433 [2]	20.358	17.284
35-39	0.245	1.617	2.305	0.936				0.949 [2]	0.753	2.650
40-44	1.034	0.716	-	-				- [2]	0.627	0.302
45-49	0.256	-	-	-				0.096 [2]	0.200	-
50-54	0.158	-	-	-				- [2]	-	-
55-59	0.531	-	-	-				- [2]	-	-
60-64	-	-	-	-				- [2]	-	-
65+	-	-	-	-				- [2]	-	-
Singapore (BA) [3] [4]				Total unemployment - Chômage total - Desempleo total						
Total - Total - Total										
Total	77.5		61.9	94.2	101.0	101.3		84.2	74.8	76.2
15-19	3.6		3.8	2.9	2.3	3.3		3.2	3.2	2.7
20-24	13.4		9.7	14.9	14.2	15.2		13.2	12.6	13.9
25-29	10.5		9.2	12.5	14.2	14.5		10.4	10.0	11.3
30-34	9.0		6.5	9.5	13.8	10.1		9.1	7.2	7.6
35-39	9.3		8.1	11.7	13.1	11.1		9.5	7.9	7.0
40-44	10.3		7.7	12.2	13.6	13.9		9.6	7.9	8.5
45-49	9.8		8.0	12.8	12.1	13.1		9.7	8.5	8.3
50-54	5.4		5.1	9.7	10.4	11.1		8.8	7.5	7.2
55-59	3.1		2.4	4.9	5.1	6.1		6.4	6.2	5.5
60-64	1.8		1.0	2.1	1.4	1.9		2.6	2.6	2.6
65+	1.2		0.4	1.1	0.9	1.0		1.7	1.3	1.7
Men - Hommes - Hombres										
Total	44.3		35.7	55.3	57.8	56.8		44.7	40.0	39.6
15-19	0.7		0.7	0.8	0.6	0.8		0.8	1.1	0.5
20-24	5.1		4.0	5.0	4.4	5.3		5.4	5.5	5.6
25-29	5.8		5.3	7.5	7.8	7.7		5.2	5.7	7.1
30-34	5.1		3.8	4.9	7.4	4.5		4.7	3.3	3.0
35-39	5.8		4.8	7.3	8.0	6.5		4.5	3.6	3.1
40-44	6.6		5.1	8.0	8.6	9.0		5.5	3.9	4.0
45-49	6.6		5.4	8.5	7.6	7.9		5.1	5.1	4.7
50-54	4.3		3.7	7.0	7.3	8.1		6.0	4.5	4.5
55-59	2.2		1.9	3.9	4.4	4.5		4.5	4.3	3.9
60-64	1.2		0.7	1.5	1.1	1.8		1.9	2.1	1.7
65+	1.0		0.4	0.8	0.8	0.6		1.2	0.9	1.4
Women - Femmes - Mujeres										
Total	33.3		26.1	39.0	43.4	44.5		39.5	34.8	36.6
15-19	2.9		3.1	2.1	1.7	2.5		2.4	2.1	2.2
20-24	8.4		5.6	9.9	9.8	9.8		7.7	7.1	8.3
25-29	4.7		3.9	5.0	6.4	6.8		5.2	4.3	4.2
30-34	3.9		2.7	4.7	6.4	5.6		4.4	3.9	4.5
35-39	3.5		3.3	4.3	5.1	4.6		5.0	4.3	3.9
40-44	3.7		2.6	4.1	5.1	4.9		4.1	4.0	4.4
45-49	3.2		2.6	4.3	4.5	5.2		4.6	3.5	3.6
50-54	1.1		1.4	2.7	3.1	3.0		2.9	2.9	2.6
55-59	0.9		0.5	1.0	1.0	1.5		2.0	1.9	1.6
60-64	0.7		0.3	0.6	0.3	0.1		0.7	0.5	0.9
65+	0.3		0.1	0.3	0.1	0.3		0.5	0.4	0.4
Sri Lanka (BA) [5] [6]				Total unemployment - Chômage total - Desempleo total						
Total - Total - Total										
Total	590.8	517.2	537.2	626.0	641.0	667.3	623.3	493.4	447.0	394.0
10-14	[7]	[7]	[7]	[7]	[7]	[7]	[7]	[7]	[7]	[7]
15-19	141.2	100.8	113.9	123.9	127.6	120.8	121.6	86.2	69.9	62.5
20-24	239.3	229.6	243.9	294.8	293.6	306.3	279.3	193.5	183.6	151.5
25-29	101.6	95.2	95.6	103.9	110.2	116.1	102.2	106.0	88.0	82.3
30-39	73.9	61.5	55.9	68.9	74.4	78.1	76.0	58.4	58.3	53.9
40+	34.9	30.0	27.4	34.4	35.9	45.4	44.3	48.0	46.5	43.8

Explanatory notes: see p. 451.

[1] Persons aged 15 years and over. [2] April. [3] The data refer to the residents (Singapore citizens and permanent residents) aged 15 years and over. [4] June. [5] Persons aged 10 years and over. [6] Excl. Northern and Eastern provinces. [7] Not indicated due to lack of statistical reliability.

Notes explicatives: voir p. 454.

[1] Personnes âgées de 15 ans et plus. [2] Avril. [3] Les données se réfèrent aux résidents (citoyens de Singapour et résidents permanents) âgés de 15 ans et plus. [4] Juin. [5] Personnes âgées de 10 ans et plus. [6] Non compris les provinces du Nord et de l'Est. [7] Non indiqué en raison du manque de fiabilité statistique.

Notas explicativas: véase p. 457.

[1] Personas de 15 años y más. [2] Abril. [3] Los datos se refieren a los residentes (ciudadanos de Singapur y residentes permanentes) de 15 años y más. [4] Junio. [5] Personas de 10 años y más. [6] Excl. las provincias del Norte y del Este. [7] No se indica por la falta de confiabilidad estadística.

By age group — Par groupe d'âge — Por grupo de edad

	Thousands — Milliers — Millares									
	1999	2000	2001	2002	2003	2004	2005	2006	2007	2008
Sri Lanka (BA) [1][2]				Total unemployment - Chômage total - Desempleo total						
Men - Hommes - Hombres										
Total	295.2	260.1	280.1	310.4	310.7	323.5	301.6	226.7	209.7	175.1
10-14	.[3]	.[3]	.[3]	.[3]	.[3]	.[3]	.[3]	.[3]	.[3]	.[3]
15-19	81.5	62.4	71.2	68.9	70.5	67.3	65.7	47.9	41.8	34.4
20-24	119.9	120.7	129.7	152.4	147.9	146.9	133.6	90.5	85.4	66.0
25-29	42.2	39.5	42.0	41.9	46.0	49.8	45.2	41.5	33.5	31.7
30-39	27.5	23.7	19.9	25.8	25.8	32.7	37.7	18.8	21.3	17.0
40+	24.2	13.8	17.4	21.4	20.5	26.8	19.0	26.9	27.6	26.0
Women - Femmes - Mujeres										
Total	295.6	257.0	257.1	315.5	330.2	343.9	321.7	266.8	237.3	218.9
10-14	.[3]	.[3]	.[3]	.[3]	.[3]	.[3]	.[3]	.[3]	.[3]	.[3]
15-19	59.7	38.8	42.9	55.2	56.8	54.0	55.7	38.3	28.1	27.8
20-24	119.7	108.7	114.4	142.3	145.6	159.5	145.8	103.0	98.2	85.6
25-29	59.1	55.3	53.7	61.5	64.1	66.4	56.6	64.5	54.4	50.5
30-39	46.1	38.0	36.3	43.2	48.5	45.7	38.3	39.7	36.9	37.0
40+	10.9	16.2	9.8	13.3	15.2	18.2	25.1	21.1	18.9	17.9
Syrian Arab Republic (BA) [4]				Total unemployment - Chômage total - Desempleo total						
Total - Total - Total										
Total	.	.	.	637.8[5]	513.0[6]	.	.	.	454.8	.
15-19	.	.	.	255.3[5]	116.0[6]	.	.	.	87.3	.
20-24	.	.	.	243.5[5]	175.8[6]	.	.	.	171.3	.
25-29	.	.	.	81.6[5]	100.9[6]	.	.	.	102.1	.
30-34	.	.	.	27.9[5]	50.7[6]	.	.	.	44.5	.
35-39	.	.	.	13.4[5]	29.3[6]	.	.	.	24.4	.
40-44	.	.	.	4.7[5]	15.1[6]	.	.	.	11.5	.
45-49	.	.	.	2.7[5]	7.4[6]	.	.	.	5.7	.
50-54	.	.	.	2.3[5]	6.2[6]	.	.	.	3.9	.
55-59	.	.	.	2.1[5]	3.7[6]	.	.	.	2.2	.
60-64	.	.	.	2.1[5]	2.6[6]	.	.	.	1.0	.
65-69	.	.	.	.	1.9[6]	.	.	.	.	.
65+	.	.	.	2.3[5]	.	.	.	.	0.9	.
70-74	.	.	.	.	1.6[6]	.	.	.	.	.
75+	.	.	.	.	0.9[6]	.	.	.	.	.
Men - Hommes - Hombres										
Total	.	.	.	355.8[5]	311.6[6]	.	.	.	237.3	.
15-19	.	.	.	145.7[5]	81.6[6]	.	.	.	57.4	.
20-24	.	.	.	146.4[5]	99.7[6]	.	.	.	90.7	.
25-29	.	.	.	38.8[5]	59.3[6]	.	.	.	46.2	.
30-34	.	.	.	10.1[5]	26.4[6]	.	.	.	18.2	.
35-39	.	.	.	4.6[5]	16.8[6]	.	.	.	8.7	.
40-44	.	.	.	1.8[5]	9.7[6]	.	.	.	6.0	.
45-49	.	.	.	1.4[5]	6.1[6]	.	.	.	3.8	.
50-54	.	.	.	1.4[5]	4.7[6]	.	.	.	2.9	.
55-59	.	.	.	1.7[5]	2.4[6]	.	.	.	1.8	.
60-64	.	.	.	1.8[5]	2.0[6]	.	.	.	0.9	.
65-69	.	.	.	.	1.0[6]	.	.	.	.	.
65+	.	.	.	2.2[5]	.	.	.	.	0.7	.
70-74	.	.	.	.	1.4[6]	.	.	.	.	.
75+	.	.	.	.	0.6[6]	.	.	.	.	.
Women - Femmes - Mujeres										
Total	.	.	.	282.0[5]	201.3[6]	.	.	.	217.5	.
15-19	.	.	.	109.6[5]	35.3[6]	.	.	.	29.8	.
20-24	.	.	.	97.1[5]	76.1[6]	.	.	.	80.7	.
25-29	.	.	.	42.8[5]	41.6[6]	.	.	.	55.9	.
30-34	.	.	.	17.8[5]	24.4[6]	.	.	.	26.3	.
35-39	.	.	.	8.8[5]	12.5[6]	.	.	.	15.7	.
40-44	.	.	.	2.9[5]	5.4[6]	.	.	.	5.5	.
45-49	.	.	.	1.3[5]	1.3[6]	.	.	.	1.9	.
50-54	.	.	.	0.9[5]	1.6[6]	.	.	.	1.0	.
55-59	.	.	.	0.4[5]	1.3[6]	.	.	.	0.3	.
60-64	.	.	.	0.3[5]	0.7[6]	.	.	.	0.2	.
65-69	.	.	.	.	0.9[6]	.	.	.	.	.
65+	.	.	.	0.1[5]	.	.	.	.	0.2	.
70-74	.	.	.	.	0.2[6]	.	.	.	.	.
75+	.	.	.	.	0.2[6]	.	.	.	.	.

Explanatory notes: see p. 451.

[1] Persons aged 10 years and over. [2] Excl. Northern and Eastern provinces. [3] Not indicated due to lack of statistical reliability. [4] Persons aged 15 years and over. [5] Prior to 2001: persons aged 10 years and over. [6] Methodology revised; data not strictly comparable.

Notes explicatives: voir p. 454.

[1] Personnes âgées de 10 ans et plus. [2] Non compris les provinces du Nord et de l'Est. [3] Non indiqué en raison du manque de fiabilité statistique. [4] Personnes âgées de 15 ans et plus. [5] Avant 2001: personnes agées de 10 ans et plus. [6] Méthodologie révisée; les données ne sont pas strictement comparables.

Notas explicativas: véase p. 457.

[1] Personas de 10 años y más. [2] Excl. las provincias del Norte y del Este. [3] No se indica por la falta de confiabilidad estadística. [4] Personas de 15 años y más. [5] Antes de 2001: personas de 10 años y más. [6] Metodología revisada; los datos no son estrictamente comparables.

UNEMPLOYMENT

CHÔMAGE

DESEMPLEO

By age group

Par groupe d'âge

Por grupo de edad

	Thousands				Milliers				Millares	
	1999	2000	2001	2002	2003	2004	2005	2006	2007	2008

Taiwan, China (BA) [1]

Total unemployment - Chômage total - Desempleo total

Total - Total - Total

	1999	2000	2001	2002	2003	2004	2005	2006	2007	2008
Total	283	293	450	515	503	454	428	411	419	450
15-19	27	25	34	32	27	23	20	18	17	
15-24	.	.	.	.	.	.	.	.	.	110
20-24	67	69	97	112	104	98	92	86	86	.
25-29	54	54	77	94	93	87	92	97	96	
25-44	.	.	.	.	.	.	.	.	.	251
30-34	36	38	62	69	61	56	53	56	59	.
35-39	31	34	57	59	55	47	43	43	42	.
40-44	26	28	48	58	57	48	42	37	43	.
45-49	21	22	40	47	50	42	39	31	34	
45-64	.	.	.	.	.	.	.	.	.	88
50-54	11	12	23	29	34	34	29	26	25	.
55-59	6	7	10	11	15	13	13	12	12	.
60-64	2	2	4	4	7	6	5	4	3	.
65+	-	-	-	-	-	-	1	-	-	.

Tajikistan (FB) [1]

Registered unemployment - Chômage enregistré - Desempleo registrado

Total - Total - Total

	1999	2000	2001	2002	2003	2004	2005	2006	2007	2008
Total	49.7	43.2	42.9	46.7	42.9	38.8	43.6	46.5	51.7	.
15-17	5.9	5.3	5.3	5.7	4.8	2.4	2.1	2.8	2.1	.
18-24	14.3	11.6	10.4	12.7	11.0	10.5	11.3	10.2	10.0	.
25-29	11.3	11.2	12.5	10.9	13.0	12.0	12.1	9.8	15.3	.
30-34	0.7	1.2	0.4	0.7	0.6	0.6	0.8	2.8	0.6	.
35+	17.5	13.8	14.3	16.7	13.5	13.3	17.3	20.9	23.7	.

Men - Hommes - Hombres

	1999	2000	2001	2002	2003	2004	2005	2006	2007	2008
Total	23.4	20.4	20.2	21.0	19.7	16.9	19.8	21.2	23.4	.
15-17	2.7	2.4	2.2	2.7	2.1	1.1	1.0	1.5	0.9	.
18-24	7.0	5.3	4.7	6.3	4.9	3.7	4.6	4.7	4.3	.
25-29	4.9	5.1	6.0	4.3	5.0	5.4	5.3	3.7	6.5	.
30-34	0.1	0.4	0.2	0.2	0.2	0.2	0.3	1.4	0.2	.
35+	8.8	7.2	7.0	7.5	7.4	6.5	8.6	10.0	11.6	.

Women - Femmes - Mujeres

	1999	2000	2001	2002	2003	2004	2005	2006	2007	2008
Total	26.3	22.8	22.7	25.7	23.2	21.9	23.8	25.3	28.3	.
15-17	3.2	2.9	3.1	3.0	2.7	1.3	1.1	1.3	1.2	.
18-24	7.3	6.3	5.7	6.4	6.1	6.8	6.7	5.5	5.7	.
25-29	6.4	6.1	6.5	6.6	8.0	6.6	6.8	6.1	8.8	.
30-34	0.6	0.8	0.2	0.5	0.4	0.4	0.5	1.4	0.4	.
35+	8.7	6.6	7.3	9.2	6.1	6.8	8.7	10.9	12.1	.

Thailand (BA) [1] [2]

Total unemployment - Chômage total - Desempleo total

Total - Total - Total

	1999	2000	2001	2002	2003	2004	2005	2006	2007	2008
Total	985.7	812.6	896.3 [3]	616.3	543.7	548.9	495.8	449.9	442.3	450.9
13-14	6.1	4.2		.	.	.	.	.	.	.
15-19	180.7	131.0	170.6 [3]	99.1	88.7	99.5	92.3	95.7	73.9	83.3
20-24	295.3	270.3	298.1 [3]	239.6	201.7	165.3	167.7	150.5	159.0	162.5
25-29	163.8	144.4	157.8 [3]	113.2	112.5	107.4	89.0	88.1	67.8	80.8
30-34	102.9	79.6	82.6 [3]	60.0	42.1	66.6	56.6	33.9	40.7	44.9
35-39	77.4	61.4	54.7 [3]	31.5	35.3	44.0	29.9	24.6	28.1	24.6
40-49	96.8	74.6	83.7 [3]	51.5	37.6	44.6	40.4	39.7	43.2	37.2
50-59	54.4	37.4	42.5 [3]	16.1	17.3	15.1	14.5	13.8	22.8	14.8
60+	7.4	8.7	6.3 [3]	5.3	8.5	6.6	5.5	3.6	6.8	3.1

Men - Hommes - Hombres

	1999	2000	2001	2002	2003	2004	2005	2006	2007	2008
Total	546.4	454.5	511.2 [3]	372.1	314.7	324.2	289.9	259.7	258.1	268.1
13-14	2.2	1.9		.	.	.	.	.	.	.
15-19	117.1	82.3	101.1 [3]	64.0	52.7	63.6	52.9	59.7	40.0	50.9
20-24	163.1	154.1	173.9 [3]	153.1	110.2	92.7	99.1	76.3	99.2	97.3
25-29	97.4	77.6	94.4 [3]	67.9	71.4	67.8	51.7	48.5	34.0	45.3
30-34	52.0	41.3	49.1 [3]	35.2	23.9	41.4	35.9	20.0	28.2	30.4
35-39	36.5	36.0	29.5 [3]	13.9	21.2	22.7	17.7	17.3	16.1	12.7
40-49	45.8	36.9	38.1 [3]	27.8	23.8	23.6	21.2	25.7	24.3	20.5
50-59	27.3	19.4	23.5 [3]	7.0	7.4	10.1	7.7	9.6	14.0	9.2
60+	4.5	4.5	1.5 [3]	3.2	4.2	2.4	3.7	2.5	2.3	1.8

Women - Femmes - Mujeres

	1999	2000	2001	2002	2003	2004	2005	2006	2007	2008
Total	438.9	358.0	385.1 [3]	244.2	229.0	224.7	206.0	190.2	184.2	182.8
13-14	3.9	2.3		.	.	.	.	.	.	.
15-19	63.6	48.7	69.5 [3]	35.1	36.0	35.9	39.4	36.0	33.9	32.4
20-24	132.2	116.2	124.2 [3]	86.5	91.5	72.6	68.6	74.1	59.8	65.1
25-29	66.4	66.8	63.4 [3]	45.3	41.1	39.6	37.3	39.6	33.8	35.5
30-34	50.9	38.3	33.5 [3]	24.8	18.2	25.2	20.7	13.9	12.5	14.4
35-39	40.9	25.4	25.2 [3]	17.6	14.1	21.3	12.2	7.2	12.0	11.9
40-49	51.0	37.7	45.6 [3]	23.7	13.8	21.0	19.1	14.0	18.9	16.6
50-59	27.1	18.0	19.0 [3]	9.1	9.9	5.0	6.9	4.2	8.8	5.6
60+	2.9	4.2	4.8 [3]	2.1	4.3	4.2	1.8	1.1	4.5	1.3

Explanatory notes: see p. 451.

[1] Persons aged 15 years and over. [2] Third quarter. [3] Prior to 2001: persons aged 13 years and over

Notes explicatives: voir p. 454.

[1] Personnes âgées de 15 ans et plus. [2] Troisième trimestre. [3] Avant 2001: personnes agées de 13 ans et pl us.

Notas explicativas: véase p. 457.

[1] Personas de 15 años y más. [2] Tercer trimestre. [3] Antes de 2001: personas de 13 años y más.

	Thousands			Milliers				Millares		
	1999	2000	2001	2002	2003	2004	2005	2006	2007	2008

United Arab Emirates (BA) [1][2]   Total unemployment - Chômage total - Desempleo total

Total - Total - Total

	1999	2000	2001	2002	2003	2004	2005	2006	2007	2008
Total	.	.	.	.	.	.	.	.	.	77.107
15-19	.	.	.	.	.	.	.	.	.	7.335
20-24	.	.	.	.	.	.	.	.	.	23.758
25-29	.	.	.	.	.	.	.	.	.	19.040
30-34	.	.	.	.	.	.	.	.	.	11.102
35-39	.	.	.	.	.	.	.	.	.	7.089
40-44	.	.	.	.	.	.	.	.	.	3.457
45-49	.	.	.	.	.	.	.	.	.	2.634
50-54	.	.	.	.	.	.	.	.	.	1.594
55-59	.	.	.	.	.	.	.	.	.	0.742
60-64	.	.	.	.	.	.	.	.	.	0.297
65-69	.	.	.	.	.	.	.	.	.	0.059
70-74	.	.	.	.	.	.	.	.	.	
75+	.	.	.	.	.	.	.	.	.	-

Men - Hommes - Hombres

	1999	2000	2001	2002	2003	2004	2005	2006	2007	2008
Total	.	.	.	.	.	.	.	.	.	30.254
15-19	.	.	.	.	.	.	.	.	.	4.931
20-24	.	.	.	.	.	.	.	.	.	9.176
25-29	.	.	.	.	.	.	.	.	.	5.311
30-34	.	.	.	.	.	.	.	.	.	3.120
35-39	.	.	.	.	.	.	.	.	.	1.538
40-44	.	.	.	.	.	.	.	.	.	2.166
45-49	.	.	.	.	.	.	.	.	.	1.699
50-54	.	.	.	.	.	.	.	.	.	1.274
55-59	.	.	.	.	.	.	.	.	.	0.742
60-64	.	.	.	.	.	.	.	.	.	0.297
65-69	.	.	.	.	.	.	.	.	.	-
70-74	.	.	.	.	.	.	.	.	.	-
75+	.	.	.	.	.	.	.	.	.	-

Women - Femmes - Mujeres

	1999	2000	2001	2002	2003	2004	2005	2006	2007	2008
Total	.	.	.	.	.	.	.	.	.	46.853
15-19	.	.	.	.	.	.	.	.	.	2.404
20-24	.	.	.	.	.	.	.	.	.	14.582
25-29	.	.	.	.	.	.	.	.	.	13.729
30-34	.	.	.	.	.	.	.	.	.	7.982
35-39	.	.	.	.	.	.	.	.	.	5.551
40-44	.	.	.	.	.	.	.	.	.	1.291
45-49	.	.	.	.	.	.	.	.	.	0.935
50-54	.	.	.	.	.	.	.	.	.	0.320
55-59	.	.	.	.	.	.	.	.	.	-
60-64	.	.	.	.	.	.	.	.	.	-
65-69	.	.	.	.	.	.	.	.	.	0.059
70-74	.	.	.	.	.	.	.	.	.	
75+	.	.	.	.	.	.	.	.	.	-

Viet Nam (BA) [2][3]   Total unemployment - Chômage total - Desempleo total

Total - Total - Total

	1999	2000	2001	2002	2003	2004	2005	2006	2007	2008
Total	908.9	885.7	1 107.4	871.0	949.0	926.4	.	.	.	.
15-19	219.4	178.2	270.0	174.7	176.9	152.6	.	.	.	.
20-24	263.1	230.3	275.3	220.9	256.8	275.7	.	.	.	.
25-29	131.0	139.4	166.2	133.2	150.2	146.4	.	.	.	.
30-34	80.5	93.0	116.7	96.8	101.3	100.4	.	.	.	.
35-39	69.9	71.5	90.3	81.1	85.2	81.6	.	.	.	.
40-44	60.7	61.8	67.1	64.2	64.9	68.6	.	.	.	.
45-49	46.1	40.5	53.7	49.0	60.9	55.2	.	.	.	.
50-54	18.8	32.1	34.8	31.6	36.5	28.1	.	.	.	.
55-59	12.2	19.8	19.4	12.4	10.6	13.2	.	.	.	.
60-64	1.4	7.2	8.1	3.2	4.1	2.3	.	.	.	.
65+	5.8	11.9	5.9	3.8	1.5	2.3	.	.	.	.

Men - Hommes - Hombres

	1999	2000	2001	2002	2003	2004	2005	2006	2007	2008
Total	438.6	468.0	457.9	398.0	402.4	409.8	.	.	.	.
15-19	101.1	88.4	100.0	85.5	87.3	78.8	.	.	.	.
20-24	114.2	124.1	115.9	106.0	122.0	135.0	.	.	.	.
25-29	69.5	71.3	80.4	59.9	60.1	61.2	.	.	.	.
30-34	37.0	45.0	44.7	35.9	31.1	31.3	.	.	.	.
35-39	33.0	34.8	37.7	33.2	24.3	23.7	.	.	.	.
40-44	30.8	33.7	28.3	29.0	23.3	29.9	.	.	.	.
45-49	27.8	24.1	21.7	23.1	25.1	25.8	.	.	.	.
50-54	10.7	23.7	16.5	15.4	19.4	14.2	.	.	.	.
55-59	9.2	10.0	8.2	6.7	7.1	7.1	.	.	.	.
60-64	0.2	3.9	2.9	1.3	2.0	1.4	.	.	.	.
65+	5.2	8.9	1.6	2.1	0.7	1.4	.	.	.	.

Explanatory notes: see p. 451.   Notes explicatives: voir p. 454.   Notas explicativas: véase p. 457.

[1] February. [2] Persons aged 15 years and over. [3] July of each year.

[1] Février. [2] Personnes âgées de 15 ans et plus. [3] Juillet de chaque année.

[1] Febrero. [2] Personas de 15 años y más. [3] Julio de cada año.

UNEMPLOYMENT	CHÔMAGE	DESEMPLEO
By age group	Par groupe d'âge	Por grupo de edad

	Thousands							Milliers			Millares	
	1999	2000	2001	2002	2003	2004	2005	2006	2007	2008

Viet Nam (BA) [1] [2] — Total unemployment - Chômage total - Desempleo total

Women - Femmes - Mujeres

	1999	2000	2001	2002	2003	2004	2005	2006	2007	2008
Total	470.3	417.7	649.6	473.0	546.6	516.6	.	.	.	.
15-19	118.4	89.8	170.0	89.2	89.6	73.8	.	.	.	.
20-24	148.9	106.2	159.3	114.9	134.8	140.7	.	.	.	.
25-29	61.5	68.1	85.8	73.4	90.1	85.3	.	.	.	.
30-34	43.5	48.1	72.0	60.9	70.3	69.1	.	.	.	.
35-39	36.9	36.7	52.7	48.0	60.9	57.9	.	.	.	.
40-44	29.9	28.1	38.8	35.2	41.6	38.7	.	.	.	.
45-49	18.4	16.4	32.0	25.9	35.8	29.4	.	.	.	.
50-54	8.0	8.4	18.3	16.2	17.1	13.9	.	.	.	.
55-59	3.0	9.8	11.2	5.8	3.5	6.1	.	.	.	.
60-64	1.2	3.3	5.2	1.9	2.2	0.9	.	.	.	.
65+	0.6	3.0	4.3	1.8	0.8	0.9	.	.	.	.

West Bank and Gaza Strip (BA) [3] — Total unemployment - Chômage total - Desempleo total

Total - Total - Total

	1999	2000	2001	2002	2003	2004	2005	2006	2007	2008
Total	79.000	98.836	170.544 [4]	217.532	194.321	212.157	194.658	206.150	183.689	227.993
10-14			0.466 [4]	0.482	0.478	0.584	0.635	0.579	0.714	0.820
15-19	16.070	19.308	20.177 [4]	20.812	20.753	20.545	19.787	20.270	19.975	24.981
20-24	12.488	16.339	39.594 [4]	47.293	47.213	50.778	47.954	50.539	48.216	58.491
25-29	10.990	13.817	32.124 [4]	40.481	35.564	38.934	37.303	40.270	35.715	45.981
30-34	9.345	11.577	24.455 [4]	33.604	26.615	28.777	24.970	27.235	21.542	28.242
35-39	7.388	9.557	20.347 [4]	28.564	22.759	24.936	21.686	22.427	18.261	22.814
40-44	5.782	7.203	14.385 [4]	18.949	17.490	18.904	16.172	17.495	15.108	18.369
45-49	3.922	5.069	8.767 [4]	12.391	10.647	14.091	12.448	13.064	10.781	13.136
50-54	3.237	3.964	5.486 [4]	7.460	6.845	7.970	7.887	8.402	6.671	7.985
55-59	2.315	3.124	3.242 [4]	4.576	3.820	4.407	3.998	4.530	3.722	4.719
60-64	2.175	2.713	1.065 [4]	2.007	1.559	1.660	1.418	1.055	1.137	1.703
65-69	1.964	2.336	0.343 [4]	0.715	0.347	0.509	0.269	0.249	0.292	0.575
70-74	1.588	1.858	0.053 [4]	0.125	0.092	0.063	0.110	0.035	0.075	0.144
75+	1.737	1.971	0.040 [4]	0.072	0.051	-	0.030	-	0.025	0.033

Men - Hommes - Hombres

	1999	2000	2001	2002	2003	2004	2005	2006	2007	2008
Total	66.101	85.399	158.016 [4]	201.518	172.224	185.786	164.569	175.153	153.676	190.126
10-14			0.466 [4]	0.463	0.457	0.584	0.635	0.564	0.714	0.820
15-19	13.565	17.063	19.847 [4]	20.244	20.420	20.054	19.327	19.906	19.975	24.488
20-24	10.820	14.359	34.329 [4]	40.966	38.229	39.643	36.495	38.292	35.985	42.351
25-29	9.225	12.088	29.087 [4]	36.612	30.343	32.453	27.959	31.452	27.104	34.506
30-34	8.113	10.213	22.654 [4]	31.305	23.407	25.254	21.448	23.452	17.947	23.930
35-39	6.458	8.527	19.310 [4]	27.197	20.855	22.342	18.907	19.405	15.598	20.100
40-44	4.886	6.384	13.770 [4]	18.253	16.183	17.647	14.527	15.803	13.650	17.069
45-49	3.350	4.404	8.552 [4]	11.876	9.984	13.537	11.947	12.237	10.781	12.369
50-54	2.498	3.283	5.294 [4]	7.319	6.572	7.739	7.668	8.187	6.670	7.568
55-59	1.651	2.401	3.215 [4]	4.407	3.751	4.327	3.876	4.398	3.722	4.592
60-64	1.565	2.034	1.065 [4]	1.973	1.533	1.660	1.396	1.055	1.137	1.634
65-69	1.402	1.677	0.334 [4]	0.705	0.347	0.502	0.245	0.249	0.292	0.540
70-74	1.126	1.325	0.053 [4]	0.125	0.092	0.063	0.110	0.035	0.075	0.144
75+	1.442	1.642	0.040 [4]	0.072	0.051	-	0.030	-	0.025	0.016

Women - Femmes - Mujeres

	1999	2000	2001	2002	2003	2004	2005	2006	2007	2008
Total	12.899	13.437	12.528 [4]	16.014	22.097	26.371	30.088	30.997	30.013	37.866
10-14			- [4]	0.019	0.021	-	-	0.015	-	-
15-19	2.505	2.245	0.330 [4]	0.568	0.332	0.491	0.460	0.364	-	0.492
20-24	1.668	1.980	5.265 [4]	6.328	8.984	11.135	11.459	12.247	12.232	16.140
25-29	1.765	1.729	3.037 [4]	3.869	5.310	6.499	9.344	8.818	8.611	11.475
30-34	1.232	1.364	1.801 [4]	2.299	3.208	3.522	3.522	3.664	3.595	4.312
35-39	0.930	1.030	1.037 [4]	1.367	1.903	2.593	2.779	3.022	2.662	2.714
40-44	0.896	0.819	0.615 [4]	0.696	1.307	1.258	1.646	1.692	1.458	1.300
45-49	0.572	0.665	0.214 [4]	0.515	0.662	0.555	0.501	0.827	0.001	0.768
50-54	0.739	0.681	0.192 [4]	0.141	0.273	0.231	0.219	0.215	-	0.417
55-59	0.664	0.723	0.027 [4]	0.169	0.069	0.080	0.112	0.132	-	0.128
60-64	0.610	0.679	- [4]	0.034	0.026	-	0.021	-	-	0.069
65-69	0.562	0.659	0.009 [4]	0.010	-	0.007	0.024	-	-	0.035
70-74	0.462	0.533	- [4]	-	-	-	-	-	-	-
75+	0.295	0.329	- [4]	-	-	-	-	-	-	0.017

EUROPE-EUROPE-EUROPA

Albania (FB) [1] [5] — Registered unemployment - Chômage enregistré - Desempleo registrado

Total - Total - Total

	1999	2000	2001	2002	2003	2004	2005	2006	2007	2008
Total	239.8	215.1	180.5	172.4	163.0	157.0	153.3	149.8	.	.
15-19	30.9	26.7	12.9	13.4	12.6	11.4	11.1	11.3	.	.
20-34	109.3	97.7	84.8	78.4	73.4	66.5	63.9	60.1	.	.
35+	99.6	90.6	82.8	80.6	77.0	79.1	78.3	78.4	.	.

Explanatory notes: see p. 451.

[1] Persons aged 15 years and over. [2] July of each year. [3] Persons aged 10 years and over. [4] Prior to 2001: persons aged 15 years and over. [5] Dec. of each year.

Notes explicatives: voir p. 454.

[1] Personnes âgées de 15 ans et plus. [2] Juillet de chaque année. [3] Personnes âgées de 10 ans et plus. [4] Avant 2001: personnes agées de 15 ans et plus. [5] Déc. de chaque année.

Notas explicativas: véase p. 457.

[1] Personas de 15 años y más. [2] Julio de cada año. [3] Personas de 10 años y más. [4] Antes de 2001: personas de 15 años y más. [5] Dic. de cada año.

	Thousands			Milliers				Millares		
	1999	2000	2001	2002	2003	2004	2005	2006	2007	2008

Austria (BA) [1] — Total unemployment - Chômage total - Desempleo total

Total - Total - Total

	1999	2000	2001	2002	2003	2004	2005	2006	2007	2008
Total	146.7	138.8	142.5	161.0	168.8 [2]	194.6 [3]	207.7	195.6	185.6	162.3
15-19	11.9	11.5	11.9	13.2	13.3 [2]	25.2 [3]	27.0	24.7	24.6	24.1
20-24	14.5	14.8	16.8	18.4	22.6 [2]	28.4 [3]	33.0	28.5	27.6	24.4
25-29	17.4	16.6	16.8	16.5	20.9 [2]	23.4 [3]	25.5	24.6	24.3	21.8
30-34	22.6	20.4	20.5	22.0	20.5 [2]	23.9 [3]	25.6	21.8	19.6	17.1
35-39	17.7	15.0	17.1	19.6	20.5 [2]	26.6 [3]	24.7	25.7	22.7	19.2
40-44	15.6	16.0	17.5	20.8	19.2 [2]	23.6 [3]	25.0	23.1	21.1	16.5
45-49	16.0	12.2	12.5	14.9	17.0 [2]	17.1 [3]	20.3	19.9	19.6	18.9
50-54	17.0	17.5	15.9	19.6	18.4 [2]	15.1 [3]	15.0	14.9	14.9	12.0
55-59	12.8	12.5	11.5	12.8	13.7 [2]	9.5 [3]	9.0	9.9	9.7	7.0
60+	1.1	2.2	2.3	3.1	2.9 [2]	1.8 [3]	2.9	2.4	1.5	1.2

Men - Hommes - Hombres

	1999	2000	2001	2002	2003	2004	2005	2006	2007	2008
Total	81.7	73.8	77.0	91.7	94.7 [2]	98.0 [3]	107.8	97.1	89.7	81.8
15-19	5.4	5.7	6.3	6.9	7.4 [2]	11.9 [3]	14.1	11.7	11.9	11.2
20-24	7.6	8.3	9.6	11.3	13.4 [2]	15.6 [3]	19.2	15.9	14.5	14.0
25-29	8.5	7.4	9.5	9.2	11.6 [2]	11.6 [3]	13.1	13.1	12.0	10.8
30-34	11.2	9.7	10.1	11.4	10.6 [2]	12.3 [3]	11.7	10.6	8.7	8.1
35-39	8.6	7.4	7.7	9.7	10.0 [2]	11.9 [3]	10.9	10.8	8.5	8.4
40-44	9.4	8.5	9.3	12.6	10.6 [2]	11.6 [3]	12.6	9.6	9.8	8.7
45-49	10.2	6.7	6.8	8.1	8.9 [2]	7.6 [3]	10.5	8.5	9.4	10.0
50-54	9.7	9.5	8.2	10.5	10.4 [2]	7.2 [3]	7.7	7.4	8.2	6.3
55-59	10.4	9.0	7.7	9.0	9.3 [2]	6.8 [3]	6.6	7.5	5.6	3.4
60+	0.7	1.6	2.0	2.9	2.5 [2]	1.5 [3]	1.6	1.9	1.1	1.0

Women - Femmes - Mujeres

	1999	2000	2001	2002	2003	2004	2005	2006	2007	2008
Total	65.0	65.0	65.5	69.3	74.3 [2]	96.6 [3]	99.9	98.5	95.8	80.5
15-19	6.5	5.8	5.6	6.4	5.9 [2]	13.3 [3]	12.8	13.0	12.7	13.0
20-24	6.9	6.5	7.2	7.1	9.2 [2]	12.8 [3]	13.8	12.5	13.1	10.4
25-29	8.9	9.2	7.3	7.3	9.2 [2]	11.8 [3]	12.4	11.5	12.3	11.0
30-34	11.4	10.7	10.4	10.6	9.9 [2]	11.6 [3]	13.9	11.2	10.9	9.1
35-39	9.1	7.6	9.4	9.9	10.5 [2]	14.6 [3]	13.8	14.9	14.2	10.7
40-44	6.2	7.5	8.2	8.1	8.7 [2]	11.9 [3]	12.4	13.5	11.3	7.8
45-49	5.8	5.5	5.7	6.8	8.1 [2]	9.5 [3]	9.8	11.4	10.2	9.0
50-54	7.3	8.0	7.7	9.1	8.0 [2]	7.9 [3]	7.3	7.5	6.7	5.7
55-59	2.4	3.5	3.8	3.9	4.4 [2]	2.7 [3]	2.4	2.4	4.1	3.6
60+	0.4	0.6	0.3	0.2	0.4 [2]	0.3 [3]	1.3	0.6	0.4	0.2

Austria (FB) [1] — Registered unemployment - Chômage enregistré - Desempleo registrado

Total - Total - Total

	1999	2000	2001	2002	2003	2004	2005	2006	2007	2008
Total	221.7	194.3	203.9	232.4	240.1	243.9	252.7	239.2	222.2	212.3
15-18	4.2	3.9	4.2	4.6	4.8					
15-19	.	.	.	.	.	9.5	9.9	9.0	8.5	8.5
19-24	27.7	24.0	26.7	32.0	34.6					
20-24	.	.	.	.	.	29.2	31.6	29.1	26.6	25.6
25-29	28.6	23.9	24.6	27.0	27.2	28.4	29.8	28.5	27.1	26.0
30-34	.	.	.	.	.	32.3	32.5	29.8	27.0	24.7
30-39	64.3	55.8	59.8	66.8	67.1					
35-39	.	.	.	.	.	36.6	37.0	34.3	30.8	27.6
40-44	.	.	25.1	29.6	31.5	34.2	35.9	34.5	32.2	29.8
40-49	46.2	43.1	.	.	.					
45-49	.	.	20.5	24.1	25.4	27.5	29.5	29.0	27.1	26.5
50-54	27.5	23.8	23.5	25.1	24.5	22.8	23.6	22.9	22.0	22.1
55-59	21.5	18.1	16.4	19.3	20.5	18.4	18.2	17.9	16.8	16.9
60+	1.5	1.7	2.9	4.0	4.6	4.9	4.7	4.0	4.0	4.6

Men - Hommes - Hombres

	1999	2000	2001	2002	2003	2004	2005	2006	2007	2008
Total	121.5	107.5	115.3	134.4	139.7	140.3	144.2	135.8	124.3	118.8
15-18	1.9	1.9	2.1	2.3	2.3					
15-19	.	.	.	.	.	4.7	4.8	4.3	4.2	4.3
19-24	15.0	13.2	15.1	18.8	20.3					
20-24	.	.	.	.	.	17.2	18.6	17.1	15.3	14.7
25-29	14.2	12.1	13.1	15.1	15.6	16.1	16.8	16.0	15.0	14.3
30-34	.	.	.	.	.	17.3	17.2	15.7	13.9	12.9
30-39	32.7	28.3	31.9	36.7	37.2					
35-39	.	.	.	.	.	20.1	20.0	18.2	15.9	14.1
40-44	.	.	14.3	17.0	18.2	19.4	20.1	19.2	17.4	15.9
40-49	25.7	24.5	.	.	.					
45-49	.	.	11.8	14.1	14.9	15.9	17.0	16.7	15.6	15.1
50-54	13.6	12.0	12.7	14.2	14.1	13.4	13.7	13.1	12.4	12.6
55-59	17.3	14.2	11.8	12.6	13.0	11.6	11.7	11.7	10.9	10.7
60+	1.2	1.4	2.5	3.6	4.2	4.6	4.3	3.7	3.7	4.3

Explanatory notes: see p. 451.

[1] Persons aged 15 years and over. [2] Prior to 2003: May and November of each year. [3] Methodology revised; data not strictly comparable.

Notes explicatives: voir p. 454.

[1] Personnes âgées de 15 ans et plus. [2] Avant 2003: mai et novembre de chaque année. [3] Méthodologie révisée; les données ne sont pas strictement comparables.

Notas explicativas: véase p. 457.

[1] Personas de 15 años y más. [2] Antes de 2003: mayo y noviembre de cada año. [3] Metodología revisada; los datos no son estrictamente comparables.

By age group   Par groupe d'âge   Por grupo de edad

	Thousands / Milliers / Millares									
	1999	2000	2001	2002	2003	2004	2005	2006	2007	2008

Austria (FB) [1]   Registered unemployment - Chômage enregistré - Desempleo registrado

Women - Femmes - Mujeres

	1999	2000	2001	2002	2003	2004	2005	2006	2007	2008
Total	100.2	86.8	88.6	98.0	100.4	103.6	108.4	103.4	97.9	93.4
15-18	2.2	2.0	2.1	2.3	2.5	.	.	.	.	.
15-19	.	.	.	.	.	4.9	5.1	4.6	4.3	4.2
19-24	12.7	10.8	11.6	13.2	14.3	.	.	.	.	.
20-24	.	.	.	.	.	12.0	13.0	12.1	11.3	10.8
25-29	14.5	11.8	11.5	11.9	11.6	12.3	13.0	12.5	12.2	11.7
30-34	.	.	.	.	.	15.0	15.3	14.0	13.1	11.8
30-39	31.7	27.5	27.9	30.0	29.8	.	.	.	.	.
35-39	.	.	.	.	.	16.5	17.1	16.1	14.9	13.5
40-44	.	.	10.9	12.6	13.3	14.8	15.7	15.3	14.8	13.8
40-49	20.5	18.6	.	.	.	.	.	.	.	.
45-49	.	.	8.7	10.0	10.5	11.6	12.4	12.3	11.5	11.4
50-54	13.9	11.8	10.8	10.9	10.4	9.4	9.9	9.8	9.6	9.6
55-59	4.3	3.9	4.6	6.7	7.5	6.8	6.5	6.2	5.9	6.2
60+	0.3	0.4	0.4	0.4	0.4	0.4	0.4	0.3	0.3	0.3

Belarus (FB) [2][3]   Registered unemployment - Chômage enregistré - Desempleo registrado

Total - Total - Total

	1999	2000	2001	2002	2003	2004	2005	2006	2007	2008
Total	95.4	95.8	102.9	130.5	136.1	83.0	67.9	52.0	44.1	37.3
16-19	18.9	21.1	22.0	23.5	20.5	14.3	12.5	6.0	4.0	3.0
20-24	18.7	18.1	19.6	24.4	25.3	14.7	12.5	9.1	7.8	6.9
25-29	12.9	12.4	12.3	15.2	16.6	10.0	8.1	6.6	5.7	5.1
30-34	11.2	10.4	11.2	14.3	15.5	9.0	6.8	5.9	5.1	4.5
35-39	10.9	9.8	11.0	14.1	14.9	8.3	6.4	5.3	4.7	3.9
40-44	9.2	9.4	10.4	14.4	15.6	8.6	6.5	5.5	4.7	3.6
45-49	7.1	7.2	8.1	11.7	13.5	8.3	6.7	5.8	5.1	4.2
50-54	5.2	5.8	6.9	10.7	11.7	8.1	6.8	6.2	5.5	4.8
55+	1.3	1.6	1.4	2.2	2.5	1.7	1.6	1.6	1.5	1.3

Men - Hommes - Hombres

	1999	2000	2001	2002	2003	2004	2005	2006	2007	2008
Total	34.2	37.6	40.9	47.8	46.1	25.5	21.1	17.7	15.2	14.7
16-19	6.2	7.5	7.8	8.3	7.0	5.0	4.7	2.0	1.2	1.0
20-24	7.4	8.0	8.8	9.8	8.7	4.5	3.9	2.7	2.4	2.4
25-29	4.5	5.1	5.0	5.3	5.1	2.8	2.1	2.0	1.7	1.8
30-34	3.7	3.8	4.3	4.8	4.8	2.5	1.8	1.9	1.7	1.8
35-39	3.8	3.5	4.3	5.0	5.0	2.4	1.9	1.8	1.7	1.6
40-44	3.2	3.6	4.0	5.1	5.2	2.5	1.9	1.9	1.7	1.5
45-49	2.5	2.6	2.9	3.9	4.3	2.2	1.7	1.9	1.7	1.7
50-54	1.6	1.9	2.3	4.3	3.5	2.0	1.5	1.9	1.6	1.6
55+	1.3	1.6	1.4	1.3	2.5	1.6	1.6	1.6	1.5	1.3

Women - Femmes - Mujeres

	1999	2000	2001	2002	2003	2004	2005	2006	2007	2008
Total	61.2	58.2	62.0	82.7	90.0	57.5	46.8	34.3	28.9	22.6
16-19	12.7	13.6	14.2	15.2	13.5	9.3	7.8	4.0	2.8	2.0
20-24	11.3	10.1	10.8	14.6	16.6	10.2	8.6	6.4	5.4	4.5
25-29	8.4	7.3	7.3	9.9	11.5	7.2	6.0	4.6	4.0	3.3
30-34	7.5	6.6	6.9	9.5	10.7	6.5	5.0	4.0	3.4	2.7
35-39	7.1	6.3	6.7	9.1	9.9	5.9	4.5	3.5	3.0	2.3
40-44	6.0	5.8	6.4	9.3	10.4	6.1	4.6	3.6	3.0	2.1
45-49	4.6	4.6	5.2	7.8	9.2	6.1	5.0	3.9	3.4	2.5
50-54	3.6	3.9	4.6	7.3	8.2	6.1	5.3	4.3	3.9	3.2
55+	-	-	-	-	-	-	-	-	-	-

Belgique (BA) [1]   Total unemployment - Chômage total - Desempleo total

Total - Total - Total

	1999	2000	2001	2002	2003	2004	2005	2006	2007	2008
Total	375.2[4]	308.5	286.4	332.1	364.3	380.3	391.0	383.2	353.0	333.7
15-19	19.6[4]	17.9	16.0	16.1	18.4	17.5	18.5	17.4	18.2	16.0
20-24	73.8[4]	59.0	59.0	62.8	76.9	76.3	76.3	73.2	63.8	61.9
25-29	63.5[4]	57.0	51.0	54.1	63.7	62.4	61.1	59.7	60.1	54.5
30-34	53.9[4]	42.6	42.4	49.7	51.2	55.9	55.9	50.3	46.4	44.0
35-39	42.9[4]	39.4	37.2	45.4	46.2	49.1	48.5	48.5	42.5	39.4
40-44	45.1[4]	38.1	33.6	37.8	41.5	45.0	42.5	45.0	40.0	37.0
45-49	39.2[4]	27.9	23.7	33.7	34.4	34.8	39.6	36.8	32.2	32.9
50-54	23.5[4]	17.9	15.0	20.3	21.7	25.6	31.2	32.8	30.4	27.2
55-59	12.2[4]	7.0	6.8	10.2	8.0	11.2	13.9	15.8	15.5	16.9
60-64	1.3[4]	1.3	1.5	2.0	1.4	2.5	3.3	3.5	3.5	3.3
65+	0.2	0.3	0.1	0.3	0.7	0.1	0.3	0.2	0.4	0.7

Men - Hommes - Hombres

	1999	2000	2001	2002	2003	2004	2005	2006	2007	2008
Total	179.4[4]	144.6	147.9	168.1	193.0	191.4	196.4	191.0	174.4	170.4
15-19	10.8[4]	9.8	9.6	9.3	11.0	10.7	10.9	9.9	9.9	9.7
20-24	34.9[4]	27.4	30.8	33.2	43.2	37.9	39.5	35.4	30.3	31.2
25-29	32.4[4]	28.8	25.1	28.1	33.9	33.3	32.0	28.9	29.8	26.3
30-34	23.0[4]	15.9	19.9	23.3	25.5	26.4	27.3	24.0	23.9	21.8
35-39	19.9[4]	17.5	18.2	22.6	23.9	23.7	22.5	23.4	20.1	20.2
40-44	20.3[4]	17.7	15.8	16.6	20.6	22.7	20.3	22.1	20.1	19.5
45-49	17.5[4]	11.6	12.9	16.6	16.3	16.7	18.2	19.7	15.8	15.9
50-54	12.6[4]	9.9	9.6	10.6	12.0	12.7	15.9	16.6	14.3	14.9
55-59	6.7[4]	4.5	4.8	6.5	5.3	6.1	7.4	8.7	8.2	8.7
60-64	1.1[4]	1.2	1.3	1.7	1.0	1.3	2.3	2.1	1.6	1.4
65+	0.2[4]	0.3	-	0.1	0.3	0.1	0.2	0.1	0.4	0.6

Explanatory notes: see p. 451.

[1] Persons aged 15 years and over. [2] Men aged 16 to 59 years; women aged 16 to 54 years. [3] Dec. of each year. [4] Prior to 1999: April of each year.

Notes explicatives: voir p. 454.

[1] Personnes âgées de 15 ans et plus. [2] Hommes âgés de 16 à 59 ans; femmes âgées de 16 à 54 ans. [3] Déc. de chaque année. [4] Avant 1999: avril de chaque année.

Notas explicativas: véase p. 457.

[1] Personas de 15 años y más. [2] Hombres de 16 a 59 años; mujeres de 16 a 54 años. [3] Dic. de cada año. [4] Antes de 1999: abril de cada año.

Thousands / Milliers / Millares	1999	2000	2001	2002	2003	2004	2005	2006	2007	2008
Belgique (BA) [1]			*Total unemployment - Chômage total - Desempleo total*							
Women - Femmes - Mujeres										
Total	195.8 [2]	163.9	138.4	164.0	171.3	188.9	194.6	192.2	178.6	163.2
15-19	8.8 [2]	8.1	6.4	6.8	7.4	6.9	7.6	7.5	8.4	6.3
20-24	38.9 [2]	31.6	28.3	29.7	33.8	38.4	36.8	37.8	33.5	30.7
25-29	31.1 [2]	28.2	25.9	26.0	29.8	29.1	29.0	30.8	30.4	28.1
30-34	30.9 [2]	26.7	22.5	26.5	25.7	29.5	28.6	26.3	22.5	22.2
35-39	23.0 [2]	21.9	19.0	22.8	22.2	25.5	25.9	25.1	22.3	19.1
40-44	24.8 [2]	20.4	17.7	21.2	20.9	22.3	22.2	22.8	19.9	17.6
45-49	21.7 [2]	16.3	10.8	17.1	18.1	18.1	21.4	17.1	16.4	17.0
50-54	10.9 [2]	8.0	5.4	9.7	9.8	12.9	15.4	16.2	16.0	12.2
55-59	5.5 [2]	2.5	2.1	3.7	2.7	5.1	6.5	7.1	7.3	8.1
60-64	0.2 [2]	0.1	0.2	0.3	0.4	1.2	1.1	1.4	2.0	1.9
65+	- [2]	-	0.1	0.2	0.5	-	0.1	0.1	-	0.1
Bosnia and Herzegovina (BA) [1]			*Total unemployment - Chômage total - Desempleo total*							
Total - Total - Total										
Total	.	.	.	.	.	.	.	366	347	272
15-24	.	.	.	.	.	.	.	103	95	70
25-49	.	.	.	.	.	.	.	228	210	166
50-64	.	.	.	.	.	.	.	35	41	35
Men - Hommes - Hombres										
Total	.	.	.	.	.	.	.	215	203	156
15-24	.	.	.	.	.	.	.	61	56	42
25-49	.	.	.	.	.	.	.	129	117	88
50-64	.	.	.	.	.	.	.	24	29	25
Women - Femmes - Mujeres										
Total	.	.	.	.	.	.	.	151	144	116
15-24	.	.	.	.	.	.	.	42	38	28
25-49	.	.	.	.	.	.	.	99	93	77
50-64	.	.	.	.	.	.	.	10 [3]	12 [3]	10 [3]
Bulgaria (BA) [4]			*Total unemployment - Chômage total - Desempleo total*							
Total - Total - Total										
Total	486.7 [5]	559.0 [5]	661.1 [5]	599.2 [5]	449.1	399.8	334.2	305.7	240.2	199.7
15-19	29.4 [5]	29.4 [5]	37.0 [5]	30.4 [5]	19.2	20.8	16.3	17.2	12.7	10.3
20-24	87.6 [5]	86.8 [5]	103.8 [5]	89.6 [5]	67.1	58.4	48.9	41.1	31.8	28.0
25-29	64.2 [5]	76.4 [5]	86.8 [5]	85.1 [5]	61.9	51.2	39.9	36.7	26.0	21.5
30-34	56.4 [5]	63.6 [5]	77.0 [5]	73.3 [5]	58.5	50.8	41.0	37.1	26.3	22.9
35-39	57.9 [5]	68.8 [5]	73.3 [5]	66.7 [5]	49.0	44.7	38.6	35.0	31.6	23.7
40-44	60.9 [5]	71.4 [5]	79.2 [5]	70.7 [5]	51.0	46.6	39.6	36.7	26.1	19.7
45-49	63.3 [5]	69.5 [5]	78.0 [5]	68.1 [5]	56.1	50.7	43.0	36.1	31.3	25.1
50-54	44.8 [5]	63.0 [5]	73.9 [5]	67.3 [5]	47.9	40.6	34.7	31.9	23.0	20.8
55-59	18.7 [5]	24.8 [5]	40.4 [5]	37.8 [5]	31.5	29.1	26.3	24.7	22.6	19.8
60-64	2.4 [5]	4.0 [5]	9.0 [5]	8.0 [5]	5.6	6.4	5.5	8.0	7.7	6.7
65-69	0.6 [5]	1.0 [5]	2.8 [5]	2.2 [5]	.	.	.	.	.	.
65-74	.	.	.	.	1.1	0.4	0.5	1.1	1.1	1.3
70-74	0.5 [5]	0.4 [5]	- [5]	- [5]	.	.	.	.	.	.
Men - Hommes - Hombres										
Total	258.6 [5]	306.3 [5]	363.2 [5]	328.7 [5]	246.0	221.6	182.5	156.4	120.7	103.9
15-19	11.6 [5]	14.1 [5]	16.6 [5]	14.9 [5]	10.0	9.3	8.3	7.8	7.4	7.0
20-24	52.5 [5]	57.7 [5]	63.3 [5]	57.1 [5]	42.2	36.6	30.2	23.2	16.4	16.9
25-29	37.6 [5]	44.9 [5]	50.3 [5]	46.8 [5]	35.3	29.3	22.5	19.2	15.0	14.1
30-34	26.4 [5]	34.2 [5]	41.3 [5]	38.0 [5]	31.1	26.4	20.8	18.4	13.5	11.6
35-39	31.5 [5]	34.1 [5]	39.0 [5]	36.7 [5]	27.7	24.7	21.2	17.3	15.4	11.2
40-44	31.9 [5]	35.7 [5]	42.0 [5]	37.6 [5]	25.9	26.3	18.8	18.3	12.5	8.4
45-49	29.4 [5]	34.2 [5]	39.0 [5]	32.8 [5]	27.5	25.9	22.8	17.9	13.3	10.9
50-54	21.7 [5]	28.6 [5]	37.0 [5]	35.3 [5]	23.6	20.7	17.8	15.3	10.3	9.8
55-59	13.8 [5]	19.0 [5]	26.3 [5]	22.4 [5]	17.4	16.7	15.1	12.4	11.0	8.4
60-64	1.4 [5]	2.9 [5]	6.3 [5]	5.8 [5]	4.9	5.6	4.7	5.7	4.9	5.1
65-69	0.6 [5]	0.7 [5]	2.1 [5]	1.3 [5]	.	.	.	.	.	.
65-74	.	.	.	.	0.5	0.2	0.3	0.8	0.9	0.6
70-74	0.4 [5]	0.1 [5]	- [5]	- [5]	.	.	.	.	.	.
Women - Femmes - Mujeres										
Total	228.1 [5]	252.6 [5]	297.8 [5]	270.4 [5]	203.0	178.2	151.6	149.3	119.5	95.8
15-19	17.9 [5]	15.3 [5]	20.4 [5]	15.5 [5]	9.2	11.5	8.0	9.4	5.3	3.4
20-24	35.1 [5]	29.1 [5]	40.5 [5]	32.5 [5]	24.9	21.8	18.7	17.9	15.3	11.1
25-29	26.6 [5]	31.5 [5]	36.5 [5]	38.3 [5]	26.7	21.8	17.3	17.5	11.0	7.4
30-34	30.0 [5]	29.3 [5]	35.7 [5]	35.3 [5]	27.4	24.4	20.2	18.7	12.8	11.3
35-39	26.4 [5]	34.8 [5]	34.3 [5]	30.0 [5]	21.3	20.0	17.4	17.7	16.2	12.5
40-44	29.0 [5]	35.7 [5]	37.2 [5]	33.1 [5]	25.1	20.4	20.8	18.4	13.7	11.3
45-49	34.0 [5]	35.3 [5]	39.0 [5]	35.3 [5]	28.6	24.8	20.1	18.3	18.0	14.2
50-54	23.1 [5]	34.4 [5]	36.9 [5]	32.1 [5]	24.3	20.0	17.0	16.6	12.7	11.0
55-59	4.9 [5]	5.8 [5]	14.2 [5]	15.4 [5]	14.0	12.4	11.2	12.3	11.6	11.4
60-64	1.0 [5]	1.1 [5]	2.7 [5]	2.2 [5]	0.7	0.8	0.8	2.3	2.8	1.6
65-69	- [5]	0.3 [5]	0.7 [5]	0.9 [5]	.	.	.	.	.	.
65-74	.	.	.	.	0.6	0.2	0.2	0.4	0.2	0.6
70-74	0.1 [5]	0.3 [5]	- [5]	- [5]	.	.	.	.	.	.

Explanatory notes: see p. 451.

[1] Persons aged 15 years and over. [2] Prior to 1999: April of each year. [3] Estimate not sufficiently reliable. [4] Persons aged 15 to 74 years. [5] June.

Notes explicatives: voir p. 454.

[1] Personnes âgées de 15 ans et plus. [2] Avant 1999: avril de chaque année. [3] Estimation pas suffisamment fiable. [4] Personnes âgées de 15 à 74 ans. [5] Juin.

Notas explicativas: véase p. 457.

[1] Personas de 15 años y más. [2] Antes de 1999: abril de cada año. [3] Estimación no suficientemente fiable. [4] Personas de 15 a 74 años. [5] Junio.

Thousands   Milliers   Millares

	1999	2000	2001	2002	2003	2004	2005	2006	2007	2008
Bulgaria (FB) [1][2]			Registered unemployment - Chômage enregistré - Desempleo registrado							
Total - Total - Total										
Total	610.5	682.8	662.3	602.6	500.7	450.6	397.3	337.8	255.9	232.3
16-19		26.8	24.2	27.4	21.5	18.2	15.2	10.8	6.5	4.6
16-29	187.8									
20-24		78.7	71.5	68.0	51.9	43.0	36.1	26.7	16.9	14.2
25-29		87.1	84.4	77.4	60.9	53.9	46.0	36.1	23.8	20.6
30-34		87.2	85.6	75.9	60.0	54.2	47.4	38.9	27.0	23.9
30-49	317.4									
35-39		85.4	80.4	68.7	55.9	50.9	45.0	37.7	26.7	23.6
40-44		88.2	84.1	71.8	58.2	52.0	44.8	36.8	26.1	23.7
45-49		91.4	88.6	76.0	63.4	55.8	48.5	41.2	31.2	28.5
50-54		97.0	92.3	81.4	70.2	61.6	53.2	47.9	38.1	34.9
50+	105.4									
55+		41.0	51.2	56.0	58.7	60.9	61.1	61.7	59.6	58.3
Men - Hommes - Hombres										
Total	284.5	323.4	321.1	281.1	227.1	201.6	171.8	140.0	100.0	86.7
16-19		11.5	10.9	12.8	10.2	8.9	7.4	5.0	3.0	2.1
16-29	90.1									
20-24		42.8	39.6	33.6	25.1	20.2	16.2	11.3	6.7	5.4
25-29		41.8	41.4	34.4	26.0	22.7	18.6	14.1	8.5	7.3
30-34		39.6	40.1	33.9	25.8	23.0	19.3	14.8	9.6	8.0
30-49	137.9									
35-39		38.5	37.4	31.7	24.9	22.2	18.9	15.0	10.0	8.5
40-44		38.7	38.2	32.8	25.9	22.9	19.1	15.0	10.0	8.6
45-49		38.6	39.0	33.1	26.9	23.2	19.7	16.2	11.6	10.1
50-54		41.1	40.0	34.5	29.0	25.1	21.1	18.4	13.8	12.3
50+	56.5									
55+		30.9	34.4	34.4	33.2	33.4	31.4	30.2	26.8	24.5
Women - Femmes - Mujeres										
Total	326.0	359.4	341.2	321.5	273.6	249.0	225.5	197.8	156.0	145.6
16-19		15.3	13.3	14.6	11.3	9.3	7.8	5.9	3.5	2.5
16-29	97.7									
20-24		35.9	31.9	34.4	26.8	22.8	19.9	15.3	10.2	8.7
25-29		45.3	43.0	43.0	34.9	31.3	27.3	22.0	15.3	13.3
30-34		47.6	45.5	42.0	34.2	31.2	28.1	24.0	17.4	16.0
30-49	179.5									
35-39		46.9	43.0	37.0	31.0	28.7	26.1	22.7	16.7	15.1
40-44		49.5	45.9	39.0	32.2	29.1	25.7	21.8	16.1	15.1
45-49		52.8	49.6	42.9	36.5	32.6	28.8	25.0	19.6	18.5
50-54		55.9	52.3	46.9	41.1	36.5	32.1	29.5	24.3	22.6
50+	48.9									
55+		10.1	16.8	21.6	25.6	27.5	29.6	31.5	32.8	33.8
Croatia (BA) [3]			Total unemployment - Chômage total - Desempleo total							
Total - Total - Total										
Total	234.0	297.2	276.2	265.8	255.7	249.7	229.1	198.7	171.0	149.2
15-19	31.4	27.3	28.8	26.4	23.2	23.2	20.0	16.2	14.4 [4]	13.8 [4]
20-24	54.2	65.1	66.2	51.2	53.7	46.9	46.9	38.6	29.6 [4]	25.9 [4]
25-29	36.5	53.7	45.1	41.1	35.4	37.7	30.8	26.5	24.2 [4]	19.2 [4]
30-34	22.6	40.0	29.4	31.4	29.0	26.7	20.8	19.8	17.2 [4]	15.0 [4]
35-39	25.7	30.0	28.4	31.3	26.1	28.4	22.8	19.7	17.1 [4]	12.8 [4]
40-44	23.1	28.2	24.7	29.9	29.0	28.4	27.4	23.1	18.2 [4]	16.8 [4]
45-49	20.4	22.5	28.5	25.4	27.1	26.4	23.3	21.1	18.0 [4]	15.6 [4]
50-54	11.4	18.1	17.0	18.4	21.6	21.0	22.5	21.6	18.0 [4]	17.2 [4]
55-59	3.9	8.0	6.0	7.9	8.4	8.5	11.5	9.8	10.0 [4]	10.0 [4]
60+	-	2.1	2.1	2.1	2.1	2.5	3.2	2.3	4.3 [4]	-
?	4.5	2.2								
Men - Hommes - Hombres										
Total	117.4	149.8	134.8	129.7	127.7	120.0	114.4	94.4	81.6	67.9
15-19	14.6	13.9	15.9	14.4	12.3	12.3	10.3	8.5	7.2 [4]	7.6 [4]
20-24	27.0	32.4	33.2	27.8	29.3	23.5	26.1	21.1	15.4 [4]	12.7 [4]
25-29	18.9	28.6	19.4	19.8	16.6	19.2	15.3	12.7	11.4 [4]	7.7 [4]
30-34	10.7	17.9	12.8	11.8	12.8	11.4	8.6	8.4	7.2 [4]	5.5 [4]
35-39	11.3	13.2	12.4	13.5	11.2	10.8	9.0	7.3	6.3 [4]	3.5 [4]
40-44	11.3	13.3	11.1	13.9	13.3	12.8	12.1	8.2	6.9 [4]	6.7 [4]
45-49	9.5	11.5	13.9	11.5	12.6	11.9	11.0	10.3	7.1 [4]	6.3 [4]
50-54	7.5	10.4	10.0	9.5	12.0	10.4	11.0	9.7	9.4 [4]	7.8 [4]
55-59	3.9	5.1	4.5	5.6	5.7	5.9	8.7	6.2	6.4 [4]	6.5 [4]
60+	-	2.1	1.5	2.0	1.8	2.3	2.5	2.0	4.0 [4]	-
?	2.7	1.4								

Explanatory notes: see p. 451.

[1] Men aged 16 to 60 years; women aged 16 to 55 years. After 1999, age limits vary according to the year. [2] Dec. of each year. [3] Persons aged 15 years and over. [4] Estimate not sufficiently reliable.

Notes explicatives: voir p. 454.

[1] Hommes âgés de 16 à 60 ans; femmes âgées de 16 à 55 ans. Après 1999, les limites d'âge varient selon l'année. [2] Déc. de chaque année. [3] Personnes âgées de 15 ans et plus. [4] Estimation pas suffisamment fiable.

Notas explicativas: véase p. 457.

[1] Hombres de 16 a 60 años; mujeres de 16 a 55 años. Después de 1999, los límites de edad varían según el año. [2] Dic. de cada año. [3] Personas de 15 años y más. [4] Estimación no suficientemente fiable.

	Thousands			Milliers				Millares		
	1999	2000	2001	2002	2003	2004	2005	2006	2007	2008

Croatia (BA) [1]   Total unemployment - Chômage total - Desempleo total

Women - Femmes - Mujeres

	1999	2000	2001	2002	2003	2004	2005	2006	2007	2008
Total	116.6	147.4	141.4	136.0	128.1	129.7	114.7	104.2	89.4	81.3
15-19	16.8	13.4	12.9	12.1	10.9	11.0	9.8	7.7	7.2 [2]	6.2 [2]
20-24	27.2	32.6	33.0	23.4	24.4	23.4	20.8	17.5	14.2 [2]	13.2 [2]
25-29	17.6	25.1	25.6	21.3	18.8	18.5	15.5	13.8	12.8 [2]	11.5 [2]
30-34	11.9	22.2	16.6	19.6	16.3	15.3	12.2	11.4	10.0 [2]	9.5 [2]
35-39	14.4	16.8	16.1	17.8	14.9	17.6	13.7	12.4	10.8 [2]	9.3 [2]
40-44	11.9	14.9	13.6	15.9	15.7	15.6	15.3	14.9	11.3 [2]	10.1 [2]
45-49	11.0	11.0	14.6	14.0	14.5	14.5	12.3	10.9	10.9 [2]	8.7 [2]
50-54	4.0	7.7	7.0	8.9	9.5	10.6	11.5	11.9	8.6 [2]	9.4 [2]
55-59	-	2.8	1.4	2.3	2.7	2.7	2.8	3.6	4.6 [2]	3.5 [2]
60+	-	-	0.6	0.1	0.2	0.2	0.7	-	0.3 [2]	-
?	1.9	0.9	.	.	.	.	.	.	.	.

Croatia (FB) [3]   Registered unemployment - Chômage enregistré - Desempleo registrado

Total - Total - Total

	1999	2000	2001	2002	2003	2004	2005	2006	2007	2008
Total	342	378	395	366	318	318	308	293	254	240
15-19	37	36	34	26	20	20	18	18	13	12
20-24	67	73	74	62	49	48	45	41	32	30
25-29	51	55	56	50	41	41	39	37	31	29
30-39	84	90	93	87	72	70	64	59	51	47
40-44	37	42	43	41	37	35	34	31	27	24
45-49	32	39	44	44	40	40	38	34	30	27
50-54	21	28	32	35	36	39	41	41	39	37
55-59	10	11	14	17	18	21	24	25	26	26
60-65	3	4	5	5	5	5	5	6	5	8

Men - Hommes - Hombres

	1999	2000	2001	2002	2003	2004	2005	2006	2007	2008
Total	162	177	180	160	132	133	125	116	97	90
15-19	19	18	17	13	10	9	8	8	6	6
20-24	33	36	36	28	21	21	18	16	12	11
25-29	22	24	23	19	15	15	14	12	10	9
30-39	35	36	36	32	24	23	22	18	15	13
40-44	17	19	19	17	14	13	12	11	9	7
45-49	15	18	19	19	15	16	14	13	11	10
50-54	12	15	16	17	17	17	17	15	14	12
55-59	7	8	10	12	12	14	16	17	16	15
60-65	2	3	4	4	4	4	4	5	4	7

Women - Femmes - Mujeres

	1999	2000	2001	2002	2003	2004	2005	2006	2007	2008
Total	180	201	215	206	186	185	182	178	157	150
15-19	18	18	17	13	10	10	9	9	7	6
20-24	34	37	38	34	28	28	27	25	20	19
25-29	29	31	33	31	26	26	25	25	21	20
30-39	49	54	57	55	48	46	44	40	36	34
40-44	20	23	24	24	23	22	21	20	18	17
45-49	17	21	25	25	25	24	23	22	19	17
50-54	9	13	16	18	19	22	24	26	25	25
55-59	3	3	4	5	6	6	8	9	10	11
60-65	1	1	1	1	1	1	1	1	1	1

Cyprus (BA) [1][4]   Total unemployment - Chômage total - Desempleo total

Total - Total - Total

	1999	2000	2001	2002	2003	2004	2005	2006	2007	2008
Total	.	14.5	12.8	10.8	14.1	16.7	19.5	17.0	15.4	14.5
15-19	.	1.4	0.8	0.6	0.6	0.8	1.0	0.6	0.5	0.5
20-24	.	1.9	2.2	2.1	2.5	3.2	4.5	3.3	3.4	3.0
25-29	.	1.3	0.9	1.4	2.3	2.4	3.4	3.0	2.6	2.7
30-34	.	2.1	1.4	1.2	1.8	1.9	2.1	1.9	1.9	1.8
35-39	.	2.7	1.7	1.2	0.9	2.3	2.0	2.3	1.3	1.4
40-44	.	1.4	1.5	1.5	1.8	1.5	2.0	1.7	1.2	1.4
45-49	.	1.7	1.1	0.5	1.4	1.3	1.6	1.3	1.5	1.1
50-54	.	1.1	1.2	1.1	1.1	1.4	1.4	1.6	1.4	1.0
55-59	.	0.7	0.8	1.1	1.2	1.3	1.0	0.8	1.0	0.9
60-64	.	0.3	1.0	0.1	0.4	0.6	0.4	0.6	0.5	0.7
65+	.	-	0.2	-	0.1	-	-	-	-	-

Men - Hommes - Hombres

	1999	2000	2001	2002	2003	2004	2005	2006	2007	2008
Total	.	5.5	4.7	4.7	7.1	7.0	9.0	8.0	7.3	7.0
15-19	.	0.3	0.2	0.2	0.4	0.4	0.6	0.3	0.3	0.3
20-24	.	0.8	0.9	1.1	1.1	1.4	2.2	1.5	1.8	1.4
25-29	.	0.6	0.2	0.7	1.4	0.9	1.5	1.5	1.2	1.5
30-34	.	1.1	0.7	0.3	0.7	0.6	1.2	0.8	1.2	0.8
35-39	.	0.6	0.5	0.4	0.4	0.6	0.5	0.9	0.4	0.6
40-44	.	0.4	0.4	0.7	0.6	0.6	0.9	0.7	0.4	0.8
45-49	.	0.8	0.3	0.2	0.4	0.6	0.7	0.6	0.6	0.4
50-54	.	0.4	0.6	0.5	0.7	0.6	0.6	0.8	0.6	0.4
55-59	.	0.4	0.3	0.5	1.0	0.8	0.6	0.5	0.5	0.5
60-64	.	0.2	0.6	0.1	0.4	0.4	0.2	0.4	0.4	0.4
65+	.	-	0.2	-	-	0.1	-	-	-	-

Explanatory notes: see p. 451.   Notes explicatives: voir p. 454.   Notas explicativas: véase p. 457.

[1] Persons aged 15 years and over. [2] Estimate not sufficiently reliable. [3] 31st Dec. of each year. [4] Government-controlled area.

[1] Personnes âgées de 15 ans et plus. [2] Estimation pas suffisamment fiable. [3] 31 déc. de chaque année. [4] Région sous contrôle gouvernemental.

[1] Personas de 15 años y más. [2] Estimación no suficientemente fiable. [3] 31 dic. de cada año. [4] Area controlada por el gobierno.

UNEMPLOYMENT	CHÔMAGE	DESEMPLEO
By age group	Par groupe d'âge	Por grupo de edad
Thousands	Milliers	Millares

	1999	2000	2001	2002	2003	2004	2005	2006	2007	2008

Cyprus (BA) [1] [2] — Total unemployment - Chômage total - Desempleo total

Women - Femmes - Mujeres

	1999	2000	2001	2002	2003	2004	2005	2006	2007	2008
Total	.	8.9	8.0	6.0	7.0	9.7	10.4	9.0	8.1	7.6
15-19	.	1.1	0.6	0.4	0.2	0.4	0.4	0.3	0.2	0.3
20-24	.	1.1	1.3	1.0	1.4	1.8	2.4	1.8	1.7	1.6
25-29	.	0.7	0.7	0.7	0.9	1.5	2.0	1.5	1.5	1.2
30-34	.	0.9	0.7	0.9	1.1	1.3	0.9	1.1	0.7	0.9
35-39	.	2.1	1.2	0.8	0.5	1.7	1.4	1.4	0.9	0.8
40-44	.	1.0	1.1	0.8	1.2	0.9	1.1	0.9	0.8	0.7
45-49	.	0.9	0.8	0.3	0.9	0.7	0.9	0.7	0.9	0.7
50-54	.	0.6	0.6	0.6	0.4	0.8	0.8	0.8	0.8	0.7
55-59	.	0.3	0.5	0.6	0.2	0.5	0.3	0.3	0.5	0.4
60-64	.	0.1	0.4	-	0.1	0.2	0.2	0.1	0.1	0.3
65+	.	-	-	-	0.1	-	-	-	-	-

Cyprus (FB) [1] [2] — Registered unemployment - Chômage enregistré - Desempleo registrado

Total - Total - Total

	1999	2000	2001	2002	2003	2004	2005	2006	2007	2008
Total	11.375	10.934	9.546	10.561	11.961	12.650	13.153	12.824	12.017	11.541
15-19	0.711	0.133	0.131	0.138	0.191	0.116	0.096	0.105	0.099	0.105
20-24	1.173	1.067	0.983	1.204	1.435	1.351	1.326	1.294	1.079	0.972
25-29	1.781	1.078	1.033	1.276	1.547	1.686	1.864	1.766	1.693	1.674
30-34	1.127	1.070	0.952	1.186	1.323	1.413				
30-39							2.777	2.710	2.475	2.420
35-39	1.257	1.206	1.026	1.177	1.376	1.383				
40-44	1.331	1.292	1.054	1.234	1.409	1.468				
40-49							2.898	2.821	2.569	2.458
45-49	1.174	1.134	1.006	1.066	1.283	1.398				
50-54	1.212	1.205	0.984	1.009	1.098	1.193				
50-59							2.739	2.788	2.493	2.371
55-59	1.203	1.261	1.175	1.214	1.261	1.337				
60-64	1.382	1.460	1.183	1.039	1.075	1.281	1.420	1.321	1.585	1.505
65+	0.024	0.027	0.020	0.018	0.024	0.024	0.034	0.020	0.025	0.038

Men - Hommes - Hombres

	1999	2000	2001	2002	2003	2004	2005	2006	2007	2008
Total	5.580	5.266	4.535	4.692	5.113	5.415	5.819	5.737	5.209	4.929
15-19	0.053	0.038	0.040	0.037	0.037	0.043	0.035	0.044	0.041	0.048
20-24	0.476	0.517	0.440	0.499	0.584	0.559	0.546	0.560	0.440	0.403
25-29	0.563	0.460	0.440	0.524	0.618	0.651	0.735	0.729	0.660	0.660
30-34	0.511	0.456	0.395	0.477	0.512	0.548				
30-39							1.079	1.034	0.887	0.879
35-39	0.571	0.487	0.411	0.463	0.530	0.540				
40-44	0.609	0.527	0.424	0.447	0.526	0.539				
40-49							1.131	1.107	0.995	0.904
45-49	0.524	0.492	0.430	0.415	0.472	0.517				
50-54	0.590	0.565	0.461	0.446	0.469	0.511				
50-59							1.355	1.416	1.221	1.097
55-59	0.714	0.719	0.683	0.690	0.679	0.700				
60-64	0.952	0.987	0.799	0.686	0.673	0.794	0.918	0.835	0.989	0.915
65+	0.017	0.016	0.013	0.008	0.014	0.013	0.021	0.012	0.017	0.024

Women - Femmes - Mujeres

	1999	2000	2001	2002	2003	2004	2005	2006	2007	2008
Total	5.795	5.668	5.011	5.869	6.848	7.235	7.334	7.087	6.808	6.612
15-19	0.658	0.095	0.091	0.101	0.154	0.073	0.061	0.061	0.058	0.057
20-24	0.697	0.550	0.543	0.705	0.851	0.792	0.780	0.734	0.639	0.569
25-29	1.218	0.618	0.593	0.752	0.929	1.035	1.129	1.037	1.033	1.014
30-34	0.616	0.614	0.557	0.709	0.811	0.865				
30-39							1.698	1.676	1.588	1.541
35-39	0.686	0.719	0.615	0.714	0.846	0.843				
40-44	0.720	0.765	0.630	0.787	0.883	0.929				
40-49							1.767	1.714	1.614	1.554
45-49	0.650	0.642	0.576	0.651	0.811	0.881				
50-54	0.622	0.640	0.523	0.563	0.629	0.682				
50-59							1.384	1.372	1.272	1.274
55-59	0.491	0.542	0.492	0.524	0.582	0.637				
60-64	0.431	0.473	0.384	0.353	0.402	0.487	0.502	0.486	0.596	0.590
65+	0.007	0.011	0.007	0.010	0.010	0.011	0.013	0.008	0.008	0.014

Czech Republic (BA) [2] — Total unemployment - Chômage total - Desempleo total

Total - Total - Total

	1999	2000	2001	2002	2003	2004	2005	2006	2007	2008
Total	454	455	418	374	399	426	410	371	276	230
15-19	47	35	29	24	24	24	25	21	12	12
20-24	87	88	79	70	71	77	63	58	34	30
25-29	62	64	63	56	59	64	59	44	34	26
30-34	56	56	49	42	48	49	51	52	40	36
35-39	43	45	48	42	45	45	42	38	31	26
40-44	46	46	40	34	37	42	41	37	30	21
45-49	49	53	42	41	40	41	42	39	27	26
50-54	41	46	44	43	48	51	52	45	36	26
55-59	15	18	17	16	22	28	29	31	28	24
60-64	5	4	5	4	3	4	4	4	4	4
65+	3	2	3	2	2	1	2	2	1	1

Explanatory notes: see p. 451.

[1] Government-controlled area. [2] Persons aged 15 years and over.

Notes explicatives: voir p. 454.

[1] Région sous contrôle gouvernemental. [2] Personnes âgées de 15 ans et plus.

Notas explicativas: véase p. 457.

[1] Area controlada por el gobierno. [2] Personas de 15 años y más.

Thousands   Milliers   Millares

	1999	2000	2001	2002	2003	2004	2005	2006	2007	2008
Czech Republic (BA) [1]			Total unemployment - Chômage total - Desempleo total							
Men - Hommes - Hombres										
Total	211	212	193	169	175	201	187	169	124	103
15-19	25	17	15	12	12	13	15	13	7	6
20-24	47	51	45	39	39	47	37	30	19	18
25-29	26	27	28	24	28	30	27	22	16	13
30-34	21	21	17	15	15	16	17	20	13	12
35-39	17	19	19	15	15	18	15	14	10	9
40-44	20	19	17	15	14	18	16	14	12	9
45-49	21	22	19	18	17	19	19	16	12	10
50-54	19	21	19	18	20	22	21	18	14	10
55-59	11	12	11	10	12	16	16	18	16	13
60-64	2	2	2	2	2	2	2	3	3	3
65+	1	1	2	1	1	1	1	1	1	-
Women - Femmes - Mujeres										
Total	243	243	225	205	224	225	223	202	153	127
15-19	22	18	14	12	12	11	10	9	5	6
20-24	40	37	34	31	32	30	26	27	14	11
25-29	36	37	35	32	31	34	33	22	18	13
30-34	35	35	32	27	33	33	33	32	27	23
35-39	26	26	29	27	30	27	27	24	22	17
40-44	26	27	23	19	23	24	24	24	17	13
45-49	28	31	23	23	23	22	23	23	15	16
50-54	22	25	25	25	28	29	31	27	22	16
55-59	4	6	6	6	10	12	13	13	12	11
60-64	3	2	3	2	1	2	2	1	1	1
65+	2	1	1	1	1	-	1	1	-	-
Czech Republic (FB) [2]			Registered unemployment - Chômage enregistré - Desempleo registrado							
Total - Total - Total										
Total	488	457	462	514	542	542	510	449	355	352
15-19	24	16	36	38	37	32	27	22	17	18
20-24	120	104	83	92	92	84	69	56	38	42
25-29	64	62	64	70	73	70	62	52	37	38
30-34	54	52	52	56	61	64	63	56	43	42
35-39	48	47	48	52	55	56	53	47	37	37
40-44	50	47	45	47	51	53	52	47	37	36
45-49	56	55	55	59	61	61	55	47	37	36
50-54	53	54	56	64	68	72	71	64	54	49
55-59	18	19	21	33	40	44	51	50	46	45
60+	1	1	2	3	4	6	7	8	9	9
Men - Hommes - Hombres										
Total	240	227	230	257	270	266	244	210	164	168
15-19	13	9	20	22	21	17	14	11	9	9
20-24	69	62	49	55	55	49	38	30	20	23
25-29	29	28	30	34	36	35	31	26	18	20
30-34	21	21	21	22	24	25	25	22	16	17
35-39	21	20	20	22	23	23	21	18	14	14
40-44	23	21	20	21	24	23	22	19	15	15
45-49	25	25	26	27	28	28	24	20	16	16
50-54	23	24	25	28	29	32	31	27	22	21
55-59	15	16	17	23	26	29	32	29	26	25
60+	1	1	2	3	4	5	6	8	8	8
Women - Femmes - Mujeres										
Total	248	230	232	257	272	276	266	239	191	184
15-19	11	7	16	16	16	15	13	11	8	9
20-24	51	42	34	37	37	35	31	26	18	19
25-29	35	34	34	36	37	35	31	26	19	18
30-34	33	31	31	34	37	39	38	34	27	25
35-39	27	27	28	30	32	33	32	29	23	23
40-44	27	26	25	26	27	30	30	28	22	21
45-49	31	30	29	32	33	33	31	27	21	20
50-54	30	30	31	36	39	40	40	37	32	28
55-59	3	3	4	10	14	15	19	21	20	20
60+	-	-	-	-	-	1	1	-	1	1
Denmark (BA) [3]			Total unemployment - Chômage total - Desempleo total							
Total - Total - Total										
Total	.	.	.	134.026	157.559	162.552	143.296	117.896	114.539	98.380
15-19	.	.	.	14.540	18.906	14.788	20.066	22.046	20.970	19.605
20-24	.	.	.	18.406	19.390	20.913	17.389	14.454	15.161	15.705
25-29	.	.	.	18.166	21.551	22.288	16.629	14.906	12.825	9.216
30-34	.	.	.	15.505	18.922	18.914	17.057	10.761	12.914	11.085
35-39	.	.	.	15.803	17.243	16.942	13.774	11.497	11.068	7.983
40-44	.	.	.	14.264	14.097	15.895	14.799	10.741	9.761	9.373
45-49	.	.	.	10.544	13.130	14.500	11.564	7.136	7.978	6.036
50-54	.	.	.	11.531	14.058	13.685	9.943	9.416	7.915	7.464
55-59	.	.	.	13.010	18.071	20.452	19.051	14.417	12.527	9.796
60-64	.	.	.	2.204	2.087	3.743	2.525	2.020	2.420	2.117
65-66	.	.	.	0.054	0.104	0.432	0.500	0.500	1.000	-

Explanatory notes: see p. 451.   Notes explicatives: voir p. 454.   Notas explicativas: véase p. 457.

[1] Persons aged 15 years and over. [2] Dec. of each year. [3] Persons aged 15 to 66 years.

[1] Personnes âgées de 15 ans et plus. [2] Déc. de chaque année. [3] Personnes âgées de 15 à 66 ans.

[1] Personas de 15 años y más. [2] Dic. de cada año. [3] Personas de 15 a 66 años.

	UNEMPLOYMENT		CHÔMAGE			DESEMPLEO			
	By age group		Par groupe d'âge			Por grupo de edad			

	Thousands			Milliers				Millares		
	1999	2000	2001	2002	2003	2004	2005	2006	2007	2008

Denmark (BA) [1] — Total unemployment - Chômage total - Desempleo total

Men - Hommes - Hombres

	1999	2000	2001	2002	2003	2004	2005	2006	2007	2008
Total	.	.	.	66.021	75.734	79.867	69.433	53.421	55.079	47.077
15-19	.	.	.	7.643	9.697	8.860	10.920	12.734	11.898	8.398
20-24	.	.	.	9.474	10.292	11.101	8.477	6.513	7.763	8.046
25-29	.	.	.	8.077	9.065	12.171	8.950	6.217	5.910	4.406
30-34	.	.	.	6.709	8.329	7.937	7.437	3.906	5.261	4.887
35-39	.	.	.	7.690	7.872	6.987	5.960	3.957	5.014	4.429
40-44	.	.	.	7.148	6.542	7.074	6.568	4.198	4.859	4.150
45-49	.	.	.	5.556	6.391	5.589	5.245	3.310	3.308	4.094
50-54	.	.	.	5.694	6.391	6.609	5.179	4.023	3.344	4.019
55-59	.	.	.	6.550	9.123	10.679	8.962	6.811	5.605	4.648
60-64	.	.	.	1.426	1.466	2.646	1.735	1.000	1.735	-
65-66	.	.	.	0.054	0.104	0.214	-	0.500	0.382	-

Women - Femmes - Mujeres

	1999	2000	2001	2002	2003	2004	2005	2006	2007	2008
Total	.	.	.	68.005	81.825	82.686	73.863	64.475	59.460	51.303
15-19	.	.	.	6.897	9.209	5.928	9.146	9.312	9.072	11.208
20-24	.	.	.	8.932	9.097	9.813	8.912	7.941	7.398	7.659
25-29	.	.	.	10.088	12.487	10.117	7.678	8.689	6.915	4.810
30-34	.	.	.	8.796	10.592	10.977	9.620	6.855	7.653	6.197
35-39	.	.	.	8.113	9.371	9.955	7.815	7.540	6.054	3.554
40-44	.	.	.	7.115	7.556	8.822	8.231	6.543	4.902	5.222
45-49	.	.	.	4.987	6.739	8.911	6.319	3.826	4.670	1.942
50-54	.	.	.	5.838	7.667	7.076	4.763	5.392	4.571	3.445
55-59	.	.	.	6.460	8.947	9.773	10.089	7.606	6.922	5.148
60-64	.	.	.	0.778	0.621	1.098	0.790	1.020	0.685	2.117
65-66	.	.	.	-	-	0.218	0.500	-	0.618	-

Denmark (FB) [2] — Registered unemployment - Chômage enregistré - Desempleo registrado

Total - Total - Total

	1999	2000	2001	2002	2003	2004	2005	2006	2007	2008
Total	.	.	130.578 [3]	132.971	159.112	160.403	140.162 |	108.422 [4]	77.168	51.721 [3]
16-24	.	.	10.497	10.670	12.755	12.362	10.166 |	7.947 [4]	5.678	5.074 [3]
25-29	.	.	17.386 [3]	17.938	21.300	20.285	16.410 |	12.223 [4]	9.061	6.536 [3]
30-34	.	.	18.342 [3]	18.953	22.885	23.159	20.163 |	15.455 [4]	11.245	7.503 [3]
35-39	.	.	17.772 [3]	18.377	22.096	22.085	18.825 |	14.200 [4]	10.531	6.988 [3]
40-44	.	.	13.810 [3]	14.177	17.721	18.742	16.793 |	13.549 [4]	9.825	6.723 [3]
45-49	.	.	12.176 [3]	12.303	14.947	15.318	13.470 |	10.306 [4]	7.514	5.313 [3]
50-54	.	.	13.225 [3]	12.248	14.370	14.562	12.717 |	9.674 [4]	6.781	4.715 [3]
55-59	.	.	19.547 [3]	20.560	24.322	24.545	22.526 |	17.283 [4]	10.631	5.672 [3]
60-64	.	.	.	.	.	.	. |	. [4]	5.902	3.196 [3]
60-66	.	.	7.823 [3]	7.745	8.716	9.344	9.092 |	7.787 [4]	.	.

Men - Hommes - Hombres

	1999	2000	2001	2002	2003	2004	2005	2006	2007	2008
Total	.	.	61.074 [3]	64.388	78.594	77.621	65.591 |	48.281 [4]	33.774	25.795 [3]
16-24	.	.	5.373 [3]	5.690	7.021	6.664	5.248 |	3.859 [4]	2.565	2.626 [3]
25-29	.	.	7.813 [3]	8.562	10.517	9.716	7.538 |	5.306 [4]	3.814	3.100 [3]
30-34	.	.	7.734 [3]	8.388	10.387	10.287	8.535 |	6.224 [4]	4.427	3.343 [3]
35-39	.	.	7.785 [3]	8.263	10.100	9.803	8.042 |	5.781 [4]	4.235	3.242 [3]
40-44	.	.	6.494 [3]	6.852	8.592	8.864	7.633 |	5.834 [4]	4.192	3.312 [3]
45-49	.	.	6.009 [3]	6.252	7.671	7.724	6.598 |	4.778 [4]	3.521	2.775 [3]
50-54	.	.	6.398 [3]	6.210	7.538	7.520	6.412 |	4.648 [4]	3.264	2.602 [3]
55-59	.	.	9.078 [3]	9.763	11.688	11.665	10.487 |	7.671 [4]	4.747	3.029 [3]
60-64	.	.	.	.	.	.	. |	. [4]	3.009	1.767 [3]
60-66	.	.	4.391 [3]	4.408	5.080	5.378	5.098 |	4.178 [4]	.	.

Women - Femmes - Mujeres

	1999	2000	2001	2002	2003	2004	2005	2006	2007	2008
Total	.	.	69.504 [3]	68.583	80.519	82.782	74.572 |	60.142 [4]	43.394	25.925 [3]
16-24	.	.	5.125 [3]	4.979	5.734	5.697	4.918 |	4.088 [4]	3.113	2.448 [3]
25-29	.	.	9.573 [3]	9.376	10.783	10.570	8.872 |	6.917 [4]	5.247	3.437 [3]
30-34	.	.	10.608 [3]	10.565	12.497	12.873	11.628 |	9.230 [4]	6.818	4.160 [3]
35-39	.	.	9.987 [3]	10.114	11.996	12.282	10.783 |	8.418 [4]	6.296	3.745 [3]
40-44	.	.	7.316 [3]	7.325	9.129	9.879	9.161 |	7.714 [4]	5.632	3.411 [3]
45-49	.	.	6.167 [3]	6.051	7.276	7.594	6.872 |	5.527 [4]	3.993	2.538 [3]
50-54	.	.	6.827 [3]	6.039	6.832	7.041	6.304 |	5.026 [4]	3.516	2.113 [3]
55-59	.	.	10.469 [3]	10.797	12.634	12.880	12.039 |	9.612 [4]	5.884	2.643 [3]
60-64	.	.	.	.	.	.	.	. [4]	2.894	1.430 [3]
60-66	.	.	3.432 [3]	3.337	3.636	3.966	3.994 |	3.609 [4]	.	.

España (BA) [5] — Total unemployment - Chômage total - Desempleo total

Total - Total - Total

	1999	2000	2001	2002	2003	2004	2005	2006	2007	2008
Total	2 722.2	2 496.4 |	1 904.4 [6]	2 155.3	2 242.2	2 213.6 |	1 912.5 [6]	1 837.1	1 833.9	2 590.6
16-19	213.5	192.8 |	153.1 [6]	151.2	160.4	147.8 |	157.1 [6]	156.9	157.4	211.1
20-24	527.1	464.4 |	361.1 [6]	391.1	390.8	382.5 |	333.4 [6]	286.5	285.3	381.9
25-29	540.4	480.1 |	367.6 [6]	421.5	435.8	407.2 |	349.5 [6]	323.4	287.4	422.8
30-34	402.2	366.2 |	277.4 [6]	312.8	335.3	322.3 |	258.9 [6]	267.4	260.3	377.8
35-39	329.2	302.7 |	221.2 [6]	259.7	281.0	287.4 |	228.4 [6]	221.2	222.0	319.3
40-44	241.3	235.1 |	176.8 [6]	209.9	217.9	226.7 |	193.1 [6]	195.2	197.7	294.6
45-49	177.0	173.1 |	132.6 [6]	156.8	167.4	173.5 |	153.1 [6]	142.9	160.1	229.6
50-54	138.3	126.0 |	103.9 [6]	122.6	121.4	126.7 |	108.3 [6]	116.9	128.9	174.3
55-59	112.5	108.5 |	75.8 [6]	90.0	89.6	91.0 |	86.6 [6]	87.4	89.0	118.2
60-64	39.4	45.0 |	33.1 [6]	38.2	40.5	47.1 |	40.7 [6]	36.9	43.7	57.1
65-69	1.3	2.1 |	1.6 [6]	1.3	1.6	1.3 |	2.8 [6]	2.0	1.7	3.8
70-74	0.2	0.2 |	- [6]	0.2	0.5	0.3 |	0.6 [6]	0.3	0.3	0.2

Explanatory notes: see p. 451.

[1] Persons aged 15 to 66 years. [2] Persons aged 16 to 66 years. [3] Methodology revised. [4] Beginning 1 July 2006, Persons aged 16 to 64. [5] Persons aged 16 to 74 years. [6] Methodology revised; data not strictly comparable.

Notes explicatives: voir p. 454.

[1] Personnes âgées de 15 à 66 ans. [2] Personnes âgées de 16 à 66 ans. [3] Méthodologie révisée. [4] A partir 1 juillet 2006, personnes âgées de 16 à 64 ans. [5] Personnes âgées de 16 à 74 ans. [6] Méthodologie révisée; les données ne sont pas strictement comparables.

Notas explicativas: véase p. 457.

[1] Personas de 15 a 66 años. [2] Personas de 16 a 66 años. [3] Metodología revisada. [4] Desde el 1 de julio 2006, personas de 16 a 644 años. [5] Personas de 16 a 74 años. [6] Metodología revisada; los datos no son estrictamente comparables.

	Thousands			Milliers				Millares		
	1999	2000	2001	2002	2003	2004	2005	2006	2007	2008

España (BA) [1] — Total unemployment - Chômage total - Desempleo total

Men - Hommes - Hombres

	1999	2000	2001	2002	2003	2004	2005	2006	2007	2008
Total	1 158.3	1 037.4	828.1 [2]	929.3	976.4	970.8	862.9 [2]	791.5	815.2	1 311.0
16-19	105.1	93.6	76.5 [2]	80.8	85.9	80.4	80.2 [2]	75.4	78.6	110.8
20-24	217.8	192.5	155.3 [2]	176.1	183.7	176.4	153.9 [2]	130.2	128.9	204.6
25-29	215.9	190.7	154.8 [2]	173.8	178.7	176.1	155.5 [2]	138.2	130.1	224.7
30-34	151.5	131.6	112.4 [2]	124.0	133.4	132.4	111.7 [2]	110.1	110.4	183.1
35-39	119.5	105.7	85.7 [2]	95.9	111.0	113.8	94.6 [2]	88.0	92.2	152.8
40-44	93.9	87.7	67.0 [2]	86.2	85.3	79.6	74.2 [2]	75.5	78.2	133.4
45-49	74.1	68.6	57.1 [2]	58.6	62.5	71.9	62.8 [2]	57.2	67.6	116.9
50-54	75.4	65.6	51.0 [2]	57.3	57.9	59.1	52.5 [2]	46.0	56.9	84.5
55-59	77.9	71.1	46.4 [2]	52.0	50.2	50.8	49.2 [2]	45.9	45.9	64.8
60-64	26.4	30.0	21.5 [2]	23.6	26.9	29.5	26.4 [2]	23.5	25.4	34.0
65-69	0.5	0.6	0.4 [2]	0.8	0.7	0.6	1.5 [2]	1.4	0.9	1.3
70-74	0.2	-	- [2]	0.1	0.2	0.1	0.2 [2]	0.1	0.2	-

Women - Femmes - Mujeres

	1999	2000	2001	2002	2003	2004	2005	2006	2007	2008
Total	1 563.9	1 458.9	1 076.3 [2]	1 226.0	1 265.8	1 242.9	1 049.6 [2]	1 045.6	1 018.7	1 279.6
16-19	108.3	99.2	76.6 [2]	70.4	74.5	67.4	76.9 [2]	81.5	78.8	100.3
20-24	309.3	272.0	205.8 [2]	217.9	207.1	206.1	179.4 [2]	156.2	156.5	177.3
25-29	324.5	289.5	212.8 [2]	247.8	257.1	231.0	194.0 [2]	185.2	157.3	198.1
30-34	250.7	234.7	165.1 [2]	188.7	201.9	189.8	147.3 [2]	157.3	149.9	194.7
35-39	209.6	197.0	135.5 [2]	163.8	170.0	173.6	133.8 [2]	133.2	129.8	166.6
40-44	147.4	147.5	109.8 [2]	123.7	132.6	147.0	118.9 [2]	119.7	119.5	161.3
45-49	102.8	104.5	75.5 [2]	98.2	104.9	101.6	90.2 [2]	85.7	92.5	112.7
50-54	62.9	60.4	53.0 [2]	65.5	63.5	67.6	55.9 [2]	70.9	72.1	89.7
55-59	34.6	37.4	29.4 [2]	38.0	39.4	40.2	37.4 [2]	41.6	43.1	53.4
60-64	13.0	15.1	11.6 [2]	14.5	13.6	17.6	14.2 [2]	13.4	18.3	23.1
65-69	0.8	1.5	1.2 [2]	0.5	0.9	0.7	1.3 [2]	0.6	0.8	2.5
70-74	-	0.2	- [2]	0.1	0.3	0.2	0.4 [2]	0.3	0.2	0.2

España (FB) [3] — Registered unemployment - Chômage enregistré - Desempleo registrado

Total - Total - Total

	1999	2000	2001	2002	2003	2004	2005	2006	2007	2008
Total	2 085.2	1 963.5	1 930.2 [2]	2 049.6	2 096.9	2 113.7	2 069.9 [2]	2 039.4	2 039.0	2 539.9
16-19	92.6	77.6	74.6 [2]	81.4	83.4	78.8	78.4 [2]	77.3	72.2	85.0
20-24	255.7	229.1	219.3 [2]	221.0	219.0	203.4	190.2 [2]	178.2	166.4	219.7
25-29	365.9	334.4	326.9 [2]	341.5	336.4	324.3	298.1 [2]	275.3	259.1	330.6
30-34	336.7	310.7	299.5 [2]	312.9	313.5	310.0	297.4 [2]	288.7	284.5	365.1
35-39	278.9	265.4	258.9 [2]	273.5	280.5	280.8	271.3 [2]	266.5	266.2	338.3
40-44	213.7	208.7	210.7 [2]	224.9	231.4	238.6	234.7 [2]	233.6	236.3	301.1
45-49	162.6	159.3	161.0 [2]	179.2	190.6	202.3	206.1 [2]	209.8	215.2	267.3
50-54	154.3	151.6	151.3 [2]	164.4	168.8	178.5	183.0 [2]	187.9	196.0	239.4
55-59	151.1	150.1	151.4 [2]	167.8	178.5	186.1	188.2 [2]	189.1	199.0	226.0
60+	73.7	76.6	76.5 [2]	83.0	94.7	110.9	122.3 [2]	132.9	144.1	167.5

Men - Hommes - Hombres

	1999	2000	2001	2002	2003	2004	2005	2006	2007	2008
Total	871.3	789.7	771.5 [2]	836.7	851.1	854.3	818.0 [2]	788.2	791.8	1 146.9
16-19	41.7	33.7	34.7 [2]	41.9	44.2	41.7	41.1 [2]	40.2	37.9	49.5
20-24	94.3	79.3	76.3 [2]	87.8	90.7	86.9	83.1 [2]	79.4	76.6	118.9
25-29	135.3	120.9	119.8 [2]	132.7	131.9	128.5	117.1 [2]	109.1	106.0	159.9
30-34	120.1	105.7	101.9 [2]	111.1	110.1	110.1	104.3 [2]	100.4	102.2	161.1
35-39	101.9	92.8	90.2 [2]	98.4	98.5	98.6	93.4 [2]	90.2	91.9	142.8
40-44	81.5	75.4	75.1 [2]	82.0	82.8	85.3	82.2 [2]	80.6	83.1	128.1
45-49	69.2	64.1	62.8 [2]	68.0	70.1	72.8	71.4 [2]	70.4	73.0	109.5
50-54	79.1	73.8	71.0 [2]	71.8	70.2	72.1	69.5 [2]	67.0	67.9	95.8
55-59	98.9	93.4	90.2 [2]	91.9	94.3	92.5	87.1 [2]	80.8	81.0	96.9
60+	49.3	50.6	49.7 [2]	51.1	58.4	66.0	68.7 [2]	70.1	72.3	84.5

Women - Femmes - Mujeres

	1999	2000	2001	2002	2003	2004	2005	2006	2007	2008
Total	1 213.9	1 173.8	1 158.7 [2]	1 212.9	1 245.8	1 259.4	1 251.8 [2]	1 251.2	1 247.2	1 393.0
16-19	51.0	43.9	39.9 [2]	39.5	39.2	37.1	37.2 [2]	37.2	34.3	35.4
20-24	161.5	149.8	143.0 [2]	133.2	128.3	116.5	107.2 [2]	98.9	89.8	100.8
25-29	230.6	213.6	207.2 [2]	208.8	204.5	195.8	181.0 [2]	166.3	153.1	170.7
30-34	216.6	205.0	197.6 [2]	201.8	203.5	199.9	193.1 [2]	188.3	182.4	204.0
35-39	177.0	172.7	168.8 [2]	175.2	182.0	182.2	177.9 [2]	176.3	174.3	195.5
40-44	132.1	133.3	135.6 [2]	142.9	148.6	153.3	152.5 [2]	153.0	153.2	173.0
45-49	93.4	95.3	98.2 [2]	111.2	120.6	129.6	134.8 [2]	139.4	142.2	157.7
50-54	75.2	77.8	80.3 [2]	92.5	98.5	106.4	113.5 [2]	120.9	128.1	143.7
55-59	52.1	56.6	61.3 [2]	75.9	84.2	93.6	101.1 [2]	108.3	118.0	129.1
60+	24.5	26.0	26.9 [2]	31.9	36.4	44.9	53.6 [2]	62.8	71.8	83.0

Estonia (BA) [4] — Total unemployment - Chômage total - Desempleo total

Total - Total - Total

	1999	2000	2001	2002	2003	2004	2005	2006	2007	2008
Total	80.5	89.9 [5]	83.1	67.2	66.2	63.6	52.2	40.5	32.0	38.4
15-19	5.3	6.9 [5]	7.2	3.0	3.6	5.2	3.2	3.5	2.9	3.3
20-24	10.1	12.6 [5]	10.6	9.0	11.7	10.0	8.0	5.5	5.0	6.7
25-29	9.7	10.8 [5]	8.5	8.9	7.6	8.4	6.0	3.5	3.6	4.3
30-34	9.3	9.2 [5]	10.4	7.4	7.4	6.6	4.6	4.5	3.0	3.4
35-39	11.8	12.3 [5]	10.2	8.3	6.0	6.2	4.8	5.0	4.0	4.3
40-44	11.1	11.5 [5]	10.5	7.1	6.8	7.1	8.5	4.8	3.9	2.8
45-49	9.8	9.7 [5]	9.5	7.3	7.1	6.9	6.4	5.5	3.3	4.8
50-54	7.3	9.1 [5]	8.3	9.1	9.8	7.7	5.7	3.9	3.0	4.3
55-74	6.1	7.9 [5]	7.9	7.0	6.2	5.4	4.9	4.3	3.3	4.5

Explanatory notes: see p. 451.

[1] Persons aged 16 to 74 years. [2] Methodology revised; data not strictly comparable. [3] Persons aged 16 years and over. [4] Persons aged 15 to 74 years. [5] Prior to 2000: second quarter of each year.

Notes explicatives: voir p. 454.

[1] Personnes âgées de 16 à 74 ans. [2] Méthodologie révisée; les données ne sont pas strictement comparables. [3] Personnes âgées de 16 ans et plus. [4] Personnes âgées de 15 à 74 ans. [5] Avant 2000: deuxième trimestre de chaque année.

Notas explicativas: véase p. 457.

[1] Personas de 16 a 74 años. [2] Metodología revisada; los datos no son estrictamente comparables. [3] Personas de 16 años y más. [4] Personas de 15 a 74 años. [5] Antes de 2000: segundo trimestre de cada año.

3B

UNEMPLOYMENT	CHÔMAGE	DESEMPLEO
By age group	Par groupe d'âge	Por grupo de edad

	Thousands				Milliers				Millares	
	1999	2000	2001	2002	2003	2004	2005	2006	2007	2008
Estonia (BA) [1]				Total unemployment - Chômage total - Desempleo total						
Men - Hommes - Hombres										
Total	45.7	49.5 [2]	43.7	36.1	34.2	34.7	28.9	21.3	18.9	20.2
15-19	3.2	3.4 [2]	3.3	1.8	2.2	3.1	2.2	2.0	2.1	1.6
20-24	6.1	7.9 [2]	5.7	4.1	5.2	5.9	4.5	2.3	3.5	4.2
25-29	5.2	5.7 [2]	4.3	4.0	4.8	4.7	3.2	2.1	1.5	1.7
30-34	4.9	4.8 [2]	4.7	4.0	3.1	3.4	2.6	2.4	2.3	1.8
35-39	6.9	6.1 [2]	5.8	4.6	3.8	3.6	2.5	2.7	1.6	1.8
40-44	6.6	6.3 [2]	5.4	3.6	2.6	4.6	4.9	2.5	2.0	1.4
45-49	4.7	5.2 [2]	5.1	4.3	4.0	2.9	3.0	2.1	1.5	2.5
50-54	4.2	4.8 [2]	5.4	5.8	4.9	3.6	3.3	2.2	1.6	2.8
55-74	4.0	5.2 [2]	3.9	4.0	3.5	3.0	2.6	3.0	2.9	2.4
Women - Femmes - Mujeres										
Total	34.8	40.5 [2]	39.3	31.0	32.0	28.9	23.3	19.2	13.1	18.1
15-19	2.1	3.5 [2]	3.9	1.2	1.4	2.1	1.0	1.5	0.9	1.7
20-24	4.0	4.7 [2]	4.9	4.9	6.5	4.1	3.5	3.1	1.5	2.5
25-29	4.5	5.1 [2]	4.2	4.9	2.8	3.7	2.8	1.5	2.1	2.5
30-34	4.4	4.4 [2]	5.7	3.4	4.3	3.2	2.0	2.2	0.7	1.6
35-39	4.9	6.1 [2]	4.3	3.7	2.2	2.6	2.3	2.3	2.4	2.4
40-44	4.5	5.2 [2]	5.2	3.5	4.2	2.5	3.6	2.3	1.9	1.4
45-49	5.1	4.5 [2]	4.4	3.0	3.1	4.0	3.4	3.4	1.8	2.3
50-54	3.1	4.3 [2]	2.9	3.3	4.9	4.1	2.4	1.7	1.4	1.5
55-74	2.1	2.7 [2]	4.0	3.0	2.7	2.4	2.3	1.3	0.5	2.2
Finland (BA) [1]				Total unemployment - Chômage total - Desempleo total						
Total - Total - Total										
Total	261	253	238	237	235	229	220	204	183	172
15-19	34	34	31	34	31	29	28	27	28	29
20-24	36	38	35	35	39	36	36	34	29	27
25-29	29	27	24	27	27	26	24	22	20	19
30-34	27	27	26	22	21	19	17	16	15	14
35-39	27	24	22	21	22	22	19	16	15	13
40-44	29	27	24	23	22	23	23	19	17	15
45-49	29	26	24	24	23	25	22	21	16	14
50-54	26	27	26	26	24	22	22	21	18	16
55-59	20	20	23	22	23	23	23	23	22	19
60-64	4	4	4	4	3	4	4	5	6	6
Men - Hommes - Hombres										
Total	130	122	117	123	124	118	111	101	90	85
15-19	16	16	15	15	14	14	13	13	14	14
20-24	19	20	18	19	21	21	20	18	14	15
25-29	14	13	11	14	14	15	12	11	10	10
30-34	13	12	12	11	11	9	9	7	7	6
35-39	12	10	10	11	11	10	10	7	5	6
40-44	14	13	12	12	12	11	12	9	8	6
45-49	16	14	13	13	13	11	11	11	8	6
50-54	13	13	13	14	14	12	10	11	9	8
55-59	11	10	11	11	12	12	12	11	12	10
60-64	2	2	2	2	2	2	2	3	3	3
Women - Femmes - Mujeres										
Total	131	131	121	114	111	111	109	103	93	87
15-19	18	18	16	19	17	15	15	14	14	15
20-24	17	18	17	16	18	15	16	16	15	13
25-29	15	14	13	13	13	11	12	11	9	9
30-34	14	15	14	11	10	10	9	9	8	8
35-39	15	14	12	10	11	12	10	9	9	7
40-44	15	14	12	11	10	12	11	10	9	9
45-49	13	12	11	11	10	13	11	10	8	7
50-54	13	14	13	12	10	10	12	10	9	8
55-59	9	10	12	11	11	11	11	12	10	9
60-64	2	2	2	2	1	2	2	2	3	3
France (BA) [3]				Total unemployment - Chômage total - Desempleo total						
Total - Total - Total										
Total	2 630 [4]	2 265	2 075	2 137	2 295 [5]	2 408	2 429	2 435	2 222	2 070
15-19	102 [4]	91	99	92	96 [5]	110	117	131	123	109
20-24	406 [4]	335	315	356	388 [5]	425	431	451	393	398
25-29	436 [4]	358	314	314	342 [5]	357	357	352	354	316
30-34	390 [4]	318	304	310	320 [5]	322	318	308	270	232
35-39	316 [4]	291	268	253	283 [5]	311	334	298	271	248
40-44	304 [4]	281	243	252	264 [5]	279	264	263	234	217
45-49	278 [4]	243	217	214	230 [5]	219	226	230	206	201
50-54	249 [4]	218	198	220	230 [5]	215	218	214	201	185
55-59	132 [4]	115	104	112	123 [5]	149	142	159	141	129
60+	16 [4]	15	11	14	19 [5]	22	23	29	29	35

Explanatory notes: see p. 451.

[1] Persons aged 15 to 74 years. [2] Prior to 2000: second quarter of each year. [3] Persons aged 15 years and over. [4] Jan. [5] Prior to 2003: March of each year.

Notes explicatives: voir p. 454.

[1] Personnes âgées de 15 à 74 ans. [2] Avant 2000: deuxième trimestre de chaque année. [3] Personnes âgées de 15 ans et plus. [4] Janv. [5] Avant 2003: mars de chaque année.

Notas explicativas: véase p. 457.

[1] Personas de 15 a 74 años. [2] Antes de 2000: segundo trimestre de cada año. [3] Personas de 15 años y más. [4] Enero. [5] Antes de 2003: marzo de cada año.

	Thousands			Milliers				Millares		
	1999	2000	2001	2002	2003	2004	2005	2006	2007	2008

France (BA) [1]   Total unemployment - Chômage total - Desempleo total

Men - Hommes - Hombres

Total	1 245 [2]	1 037	938	1 024	1 097 [3]	1 153	1 163	1 175	1 092	1 018
15-19	59 [2]	50	54	54	55 [3]	62	65	72	66	58
20-24	213 [2]	170	160	189	203 [3]	221	223	232	206	224
25-29	196 [2]	165	142	158	170 [3]	182	184	179	175	152
30-34	183 [2]	147	135	142	146 [3]	136	143	139	126	108
35-39	122 [2]	111	102	102	119 [3]	148	144	127	123	112
40-44	135 [2]	114	94	111	115 [3]	121	115	118	112	94
45-49	128 [2]	107	97	93	104 [3]	94	99	107	99	91
50-54	134 [2]	113	98	109	111 [3]	102	102	103	96	93
55-59	65 [2]	52	49	58	66 [3]	78	78	84	72	65
60+	10 [2]	8	6	7	8 [3]	9	9	15	17	21

Women - Femmes - Mujeres

Total	1 385 [2]	1 228	1 137	1 113	1 198 [3]	1 255	1 266	1 260	1 130	1 053
15-19	43 [2]	42	46	38	41 [3]	48	51	59	57	52
20-24	193 [2]	165	155	167	185 [3]	204	208	219	187	174
25-29	240 [2]	193	172	156	172 [3]	176	173	173	179	163
30-34	208 [2]	171	169	168	175 [3]	185	175	169	145	124
35-39	194 [2]	179	166	151	163 [3]	163	190	171	148	136
40-44	169 [2]	167	148	141	149 [3]	158	149	145	121	124
45-49	150 [2]	136	120	121	126 [3]	124	127	124	108	110
50-54	115 [2]	105	100	112	119 [3]	113	116	111	105	92
55-59	67 [2]	63	56	53	56 [3]	71	64	75	69	64
60+	6 [2]	7	5	7	10 [3]	13	13	14	12	14

France (E) [1]   Total unemployment - Chômage total - Desempleo total

Total - Total - Total

Total	2 647	2 281	2 088	2 151	2 321	2 434	2 452	2 455	2 236	.
15-19	103	93	100	93	98	112	118	134	126	.
20-24	409	338	316	359	394	427	433	449	383	.
25-29	437	357	317	317	347	365	365	360	366	.
30-34	392	322	305	310	321	322	322	313	274	.
35-39	321	294	270	256	287	315	337	299	270	.
40-44	307	282	245	253	267	283	266	265	237	.
45-49	282	245	221	217	234	221	229	231	206	.
50-54	250	220	198	221	229	218	219	217	204	.
55-59	132	115	104	112	123	149	142	159	141	.
60-64	14	15	10	13	16	22	21	25	26	.
65-69	2	-	1	1	3	-	-	3	3	.
70-74	-	-	-	1	-	-	1	-	1	.

Men - Hommes - Hombres

Total	1 255	1 047	948	1 038	1 119	1 177	1 188	1 201	1 110	.
15-19	60	51	54	54	56	64	65	73	68	.
20-24	214	171	161	192	207	224	226	234	203	.
25-29	196	164	144	161	175	187	193	188	185	.
30-34	185	150	136	144	149	138	147	144	129	.
35-39	124	112	103	104	123	151	147	129	124	.
40-44	136	114	96	112	116	124	118	121	114	.
45-49	131	110	100	96	106	94	101	108	98	.
50-54	135	114	98	109	111	104	103	105	99	.
55-59	65	52	49	59	67	80	78	85	73	.
60-64	9	9	6	7	8	10	9	14	16	.
65-69	1	-	-	-	1	-	-	1	1	.
70-74	-	-	1	1	-	-	-	-	1	.

Women - Femmes - Mujeres

Total	1 392	1 233	1 140	1 113	1 202	1 258	1 264	1 254	1 126	.
15-19	43	42	46	38	42	49	52	61	59	.
20-24	194	167	155	167	187	202	207	215	181	.
25-29	241	193	173	156	173	179	172	173	181	.
30-34	207	171	169	166	172	183	176	169	146	.
35-39	197	182	167	153	164	164	190	170	145	.
40-44	171	168	150	142	151	159	148	144	123	.
45-49	151	136	121	122	128	127	128	123	108	.
50-54	115	106	100	112	118	114	116	112	105	.
55-59	67	62	56	53	56	69	63	75	68	.
60-64	5	6	5	6	8	12	12	11	10	.
65-69	1	-	1	1	2	-	-	2	2	.
70-74	-	-	-	-	-	-	1	-	-	.

Explanatory notes: see p. 451.   Notes explicatives: voir p. 454.   Notas explicativas: véase p. 457.

[1] Persons aged 15 years and over. [2] Jan. [3] Prior to 2003: March of each year.   [1] Personnes âgées de 15 ans et plus. [2] Janv. [3] Avant 2003: mars de chaque année.   [1] Personas de 15 años y más. [2] Enero. [3] Antes de 2003: marzo de cada año.

UNEMPLOYMENT — CHÔMAGE — DESEMPLEO

By age group — Par groupe d'âge — Por grupo de edad

	Thousands / Milliers / Millares									
	1999	2000	2001	2002	2003	2004	2005	2006	2007	2008
Germany (BA) [1]				**Total unemployment - Chômage total - Desempleo total**						
Total - Total - Total										
Total	3 503	3 127 [2]	3 150	3 486 [3]	4 023	4 388 [4]	4 583 [5]	4 279	3 608	3 141
15-19	112	111 [2]	106	113 [3]	132 [2]	141 [4]	218 [5]	213	199	166
20-24	281	274 [2]	268	337 [3]	404 [2]	460 [4]	529 [5]	457	388	353
25-29	334	266 [2]	277	306 [3]	370 [2]	425 [4]	479 [5]	466	396	339
30-34	428	364 [2]	352	387 [3]	448 [2]	459 [4]	458 [5]	402	340	307
35-39	437	409 [2]	416	472 [3]	531 [2]	552 [4]	548 [5]	506	404	340
40-44	413	371 [2]	392	458 [3]	530 [2]	593 [4]	628 [5]	563	467	407
45-49	392	366 [2]	380	428 [3]	484 [2]	551 [4]	544 [5]	504	427	380
50-54	354	344 [2]	369	418 [3]	495 [2]	535 [4]	527 [5]	506	407	360
55-59	645	524 [2]	467	414 [3]	451 [2]	469 [4]	476 [5]	494	428	358
60-64	105	96 [2]	118	146 [3]	173 [2]	200 [4]	173 [5]	164	146	125
65+	2	2 [2]	5	7 [3]	7 [2]	3 [4]	- [5]	-	-	5
Men - Hommes - Hombres										
Total	1 905	1 691 [2]	1 754	1 982 [3]	2 316 [2]	2 551 [4]	2 574 [5]	2 358	1 944	1 690
15-19	62	60 [2]	60	62 [3]	79 [2]	81 [4]	120 [5]	119	110	92
20-24	170	167 [2]	170	214 [3]	258 [2]	295 [4]	316 [5]	268	224	200
25-29	197	157 [2]	164	190 [3]	229 [2]	268 [4]	285 [5]	268	222	191
30-34	229	188 [2]	193	222 [3]	263 [2]	268 [4]	262 [5]	233	190	170
35-39	220	210 [2]	220	257 [3]	290 [2]	310 [4]	304 [5]	275	218	182
40-44	208	195 [2]	207	246 [3]	287 [2]	330 [4]	333 [5]	292	239	208
45-49	200	188 [2]	206	236 [3]	267 [2]	307 [4]	296 [5]	270	217	195
50-54	182	173 [2]	193	225 [3]	271 [2]	293 [4]	284 [5]	267	215	188
55-59	354	276 [2]	250	221 [3]	248 [2]	258 [4]	255 [5]	259	216	184
60-64	81	75 [2]	87	103 [3]	123 [2]	139 [4]	117 [5]	105	88	77
65+	2	2 [2]	4	6 [3]	1 [2]	2 [4]	- [5]	-	-	-
Women - Femmes - Mujeres										
Total	1 598	1 436 [2]	1 396	1 504 [3]	1 707 [2]	1 836 [4]	2 009 [5]	1 921	1 664	1 451
15-19	50	51 [2]	46	51 [3]	53 [2]	60 [4]	98 [5]	94	89	74
20-24	111	107 [2]	98	124 [3]	146 [2]	165 [4]	213 [5]	189	163	153
25-29	137	109 [2]	113	116 [3]	141 [2]	156 [4]	194 [5]	198	174	148
30-34	199	176 [2]	159	164 [3]	185 [2]	191 [4]	196 [5]	169	150	137
35-39	217	199 [2]	196	215 [3]	241 [2]	242 [4]	244 [5]	231	186	158
40-44	205	176 [2]	185	212 [3]	242 [2]	263 [4]	295 [5]	272	228	199
45-49	192	178 [2]	174	191 [3]	217 [2]	244 [4]	247 [5]	233	210	186
50-54	172	171 [2]	176	193 [3]	224 [2]	242 [4]	243 [5]	239	192	172
55-59	291	248 [2]	217	192 [3]	203 [2]	210 [4]	221 [5]	235	212	175
60-64	24	21 [2]	31	43 [3]	50 [2]	61 [4]	57 [5]	59	57	48
65+	-	- [2]	1	1 [3]	6 [2]	1 [4]	- [5]	-	-	-
Germany (FB) [6]				**Registered unemployment - Chômage enregistré - Desempleo registrado**						
Total - Total - Total										
Total	4 100	3 890	3 853	4 061	4 377 |	4 381 [5]	4 861	4 487	3 776	3 268
15-19	101	101	101	100	84 |	75 [5]	124	108	83	67
20-24	328	327	343	398	432 |	429 [5]	495	414	322	273
25-29	378	340	340	383	440 |	453 [5]	538	508	432	386
30-34	495	457	453	489	522 |	499 [5]	536	484	404	358
35-39	520	504	519	565	625 |	615 [5]	644	578	480	400
40-44	462	456	478	536	620 |	643 [5]	684	634	540	462
45-49	456	446	456	493	559 |	586 [5]	630	599	527	462
50-54	412	417	449	493	562 |	597 [5]	630	593	512	433
55-59	799	682	557	468	430 |	420 [5]	499	505	433	381
60-64	150	160	157	136	102 |	63 [5]	81	63	42	47
Men - Hommes - Hombres										
Total	2 160	2 053	2 064	2 240	2 446 |	2 449 [5]	2 606	2 338	1 900	1 668
15-19	56	57	57	58	49 |	43 [5]	67	59	45	36
20-24	198	202	215	254	274 |	269 [5]	294	238	179	153
25-29	213	194	200	234	272 |	279 [5]	310	285	234	208
30-34	254	234	238	269	294 |	283 [5]	289	255	205	183
35-39	261	253	266	301	338 |	334 [5]	334	291	233	197
40-44	233	232	248	287	335 |	348 [5]	357	322	264	229
45-49	225	223	234	262	302 |	317 [5]	330	304	258	231
50-54	202	205	225	254	294 |	312 [5]	321	296	248	214
55-59	416	347	280	235	222 |	222 [5]	255	251	211	188
60-64	103	107	101	86	65 |	42 [5]	48	36	24	28
Women - Femmes - Mujeres										
Total	1 940	1 836	1 789	1 821	1 931 |	1 932 [5]	2 255	2 149	1 873	1 600
15-19	46	45	44	43	35 |	32 [5]	56	50	39	31
20-24	130	125	128	144	158 |	161 [5]	201	176	142	120
25-29	165	146	140	148	168 |	174 [5]	228	223	197	178
30-34	241	223	215	219	228 |	216 [5]	247	230	199	175
35-39	259	250	252	264	287 |	281 [5]	310	287	250	203
40-44	229	223	230	250	285 |	294 [5]	327	312	276	233
45-49	231	223	222	231	257 |	270 [5]	300	294	269	231
50-54	210	212	225	239	268 |	284 [5]	308	298	264	218
55-59	383	335	277	233	207 |	198 [5]	244	254	222	192
60-64	47	53	55	50	37 |	21 [5]	34	27	18	20

Explanatory notes: see p. 451.

[1] Persons aged 15 years and over. [2] May. [3] Prior to 2002: April of each year. [4] March. [5] Methodology revised; data not strictly comparable. [6] Persons aged 15 to 64 years.

Notes explicatives: voir p. 454.

[1] Personnes âgées de 15 ans et plus. [2] Mai. [3] Avant 2002: avril de chaque année. [4] Mars. [5] Méthodologie révisée; les données ne sont pas strictement comparables. [6] Personnes âgées de 15 à 64 ans.

Notas explicativas: véase p. 457.

[1] Personas de 15 años y más. [2] Mayo. [3] Antes del 2002: abril de cada año. [4] Marzo. [5] Metodología revisada; los datos no son estrictamente comparables. [6] Personas de 15 a 64 años.

By age group — Par groupe d'âge — Por grupo de edad

	Thousands			Milliers				Millares		
	1999	2000	2001	2002	2003	2004	2005	2006	2007	2008

Greece (BA) [1][2] — Total unemployment - Chômage total - Desempleo total

Total - Total - Total

	1999	2000	2001	2002	2003	2004	2005	2006	2007	2008
Total	543.3	519.3	478.4	462.1	441.8	492.7	466.7	427.4	398.0	357.1
15-19	46.7	41.2	31.0	23.2	20.7	23.9	18.7	18.9	13.6	12.7
20-24	135.7	123.1	114.5	107.2	99.1	102.3	86.8	78.0	66.5	59.1
25-29	115.6	114.9	105.7	107.4	103.4	105.1	98.9	93.9	95.8	84.3
30-34	76.2	80.9	72.7	71.9	66.8	72.0	72.5	65.6	64.0	60.2
35-39	49.1	48.5	46.8	50.3	48.4	62.5	64.2	55.6	49.0	39.9
40-44	41.8	41.0	37.7	34.3	40.4	48.1	44.9	42.2	39.7	37.4
45-49	30.9	29.4	29.5	26.8	24.0	30.2	33.4	30.3	28.6	23.8
50-54	25.6	21.4	20.5	22.0	22.1	26.2	28.3	22.8	21.0	21.4
55-59	13.3	11.7	13.3	14.1	11.1	15.8	13.1	14.9	14.6	12.3
60-64	7.3	6.2	5.7	4.3	4.8	5.4	4.8	4.3	4.0	5.6
65-69	0.8	0.5	0.9	0.7	1.0	0.6	1.1	0.9	0.9	0.6
70-74	0.4	0.2	0.1	-	-	0.4	0.2	-	0.2	-
75+	0.2	0.3	-	-	0.1	0.1	-	-	-	-

Men - Hommes - Hombres

	1999	2000	2001	2002	2003	2004	2005	2006	2007	2008
Total	212.8	207.2	191.4	180.5	170.8	181.7	166.8	160.9	144.0	136.6
15-19	17.7	15.6	13.6	9.9	9.5	10.5	7.9	9.8	5.3	5.4
20-24	53.0	51.5	45.3	42.4	37.3	38.1	32.0	28.6	23.3	24.4
25-29	47.1	45.5	44.2	42.4	44.1	42.1	35.4	37.1	40.2	35.7
30-34	27.8	29.5	26.4	24.6	24.1	24.4	25.3	21.2	21.6	22.0
35-39	15.6	15.6	14.1	18.0	16.1	18.6	20.2	17.3	12.4	10.6
40-44	13.7	14.7	12.7	10.3	10.6	13.3	11.5	14.3	14.1	11.1
45-49	12.6	12.2	11.6	9.8	7.9	10.1	13.1	9.5	8.3	7.4
50-54	11.2	10.7	9.3	11.2	10.1	11.2	9.9	11.2	7.4	8.6
55-59	8.1	7.1	8.6	8.3	6.9	9.3	7.8	8.5	7.7	6.6
60-64	4.8	4.0	4.4	3.0	3.3	3.8	3.2	2.8	2.9	4.3
65-69	0.7	0.5	0.9	0.7	0.9	0.2	0.5	0.5	0.7	0.6
70-74	0.4	0.1	0.1	-	-	0.3	-	-	0.2	-
75+	0.2	0.1	-	-	0.1	-	-	-	-	-

Women - Femmes - Mujeres

	1999	2000	2001	2002	2003	2004	2005	2006	2007	2008
Total	330.5	312.1	287.0	281.6	271.0	311.0	299.9	266.6	254.0	220.5
15-19	29.0	25.6	17.5	13.3	11.3	13.4	10.8	9.0	8.3	7.4
20-24	82.7	71.6	69.2	64.8	61.8	64.8	54.8	49.4	43.3	34.7
25-29	68.5	69.4	61.5	65.0	59.3	63.0	63.5	56.9	55.6	48.6
30-34	48.4	51.4	46.3	47.3	42.6	47.6	47.2	44.4	42.4	38.2
35-39	33.4	32.9	32.7	32.3	32.3	44.0	44.0	38.2	36.6	29.2
40-44	28.1	26.3	25.0	23.9	29.8	34.8	33.3	27.9	25.6	26.3
45-49	18.2	17.2	17.8	17.0	16.1	20.1	20.3	20.8	20.3	16.3
50-54	14.4	10.7	11.2	10.8	11.9	15.1	18.3	11.6	13.6	12.9
55-59	5.2	4.6	4.6	5.8	4.2	6.4	5.2	6.4	6.8	5.7
60-64	2.4	2.2	1.3	1.3	1.5	1.6	1.6	1.5	1.1	1.3
65-69	0.1	-	-	-	0.2	0.4	0.6	0.4	0.3	-
70-74	-	0.1	-	-	-	0.1	0.2	-	-	-
75+	-	0.1	-	-	-	0.1	-	-	-	-

Hungary (BA) [3] — Total unemployment - Chômage total - Desempleo total

Total - Total - Total

	1999	2000	2001	2002	2003	2004	2005	2006	2007	2008
Total	284.7	262.5	232.9	238.8 [4]	244.5	252.9	303.9	316.8	311.9	329.2
15-19	21.4	17.6	12.5	11.7 [4]	11.8	12.0	12.4	12.1	9.8	10.0
20-24	57.3	53.1	43.2	44.8 [4]	43.1	43.9	54.5	52.0	47.8	51.0
25-29	40.6	40.8	42.5	43.2 [4]	43.6	41.6	51.9	53.0	50.3	52.0
30-34	37.5	34.7	30.9	31.7 [4]	33.3	34.5	39.5	43.2	46.0	47.1
35-39	33.9	25.1	24.4	27.2 [4]	29.3	32.1	39.7	41.8	40.8	42.0
40-44	38.6	32.8	25.5	25.9 [4]	26.1	25.7	27.4	32.4	33.6	34.7
45-49	30.8	31.3	25.8	26.2 [4]	28.1	28.6	32.8	32.9	31.2	33.1
50-54	18.7	19.1	19.7	18.4 [4]	19.3	22.4	29.0	32.5	34.4	38.1
55-59	5.4	6.9	7.1	8.7 [4]	8.2	10.2	14.4	14.2	16.6	18.8
60-64	0.4	0.5	1.1	0.7 [4]	1.5	1.4	1.5	2.4	1.2	2.0
65-69	0.1	0.5	0.2	0.2 [4]	0.2	0.5	0.6	0.3	0.2	0.4
70-74	-	0.1	-	0.1 [4]	-	-	0.2	0.0	0.0	0.0

Men - Hommes - Hombres

	1999	2000	2001	2002	2003	2004	2005	2006	2007	2008
Total	170.7	159.5	142.7	138.0 [4]	138.5	136.8	159.1	164.6	164.2	174.3
15-19	12.6	10.3	7.1	6.1 [4]	6.8	8.2	7.9	7.7	6.5	6.6
20-24	36.0	33.8	27.6	26.8 [4]	24.9	25.1	30.3	27.6	26.0	27.3
25-29	25.7	25.5	26.3	26.1 [4]	25.8	22.6	26.3	30.1	28.9	28.5
30-34	21.4	20.0	18.3	18.0 [4]	18.8	18.9	22.1	22.9	23.3	26.2
35-39	21.2	15.4	15.0	15.8 [4]	15.3	16.9	19.6	20.3	19.4	21.6
40-44	20.2	18.6	14.9	13.4 [4]	14.3	12.4	12.8	15.7	15.5	18.4
45-49	17.3	18.5	15.4	14.4 [4]	16.2	14.3	17.1	14.7	15.4	16.2
50-54	11.4	11.0	11.3	10.2 [4]	10.5	11.4	13.3	16.1	18.4	18.2
55-59	4.6	5.7	6.0	6.5 [4]	5.0	6.4	8.8	8.5	9.8	10.4
60-64	0.3	0.4	0.8	0.7 [4]	0.8	0.4	0.8	0.8	0.8	0.8
65-69	-	0.2	-	- [4]	0.1	0.2	0.1	0.2	0.2	0.1
70-74	-	0.1	-	- [4]	-	-	0.0	0.0	0.0	0.0

Explanatory notes: see p. 451.

[1] Persons aged 15 years and over. [2] Second quarter of each year. [3] Persons aged 15 to 74 years. [4] Estimates based on the 2001 Population Census results.

Notes explicatives: voir p. 454.

[1] Personnes âgées de 15 ans et plus. [2] Deuxième trimestre de chaque année. [3] Personnes âgées de 15 à 74 ans. [4] Estimations basées sur les résultats du Recensement de la population de 2001.

Notas explicativas: véase p. 457.

[1] Personas de 15 años y más. [2] Segundo trimestre de cada año. [3] Personas de 15 a 74 años. [4] Estimaciones basadas en los resultados del Censo de población de 2001.

3B

UNEMPLOYMENT	CHÔMAGE	DESEMPLEO
By age group	Par groupe d'âge	Por grupo de edad

	Thousands			Milliers				Millares		
	1999	2000	2001	2002	2003	2004	2005	2006	2007	2008
Hungary (BA) [1]				Total unemployment - Chômage total - Desempleo total						
Women - Femmes - Mujeres										
Total	114.0	103.0	90.2	100.8 [2]	106.0	116.1	144.8	152.2	147.7	154.9
15-19	8.8	7.3	5.4	5.6 [2]	5.0	3.8	4.5	4.4	3.3	3.4
20-24	21.3	19.3	15.6	18.0 [2]	18.2	18.8	24.2	24.4	21.8	23.7
25-29	14.9	15.3	16.2	17.1 [2]	17.8	19.0	25.6	22.9	21.4	23.5
30-34	16.1	14.7	12.6	13.7 [2]	14.5	15.6	17.4	20.3	22.7	20.9
35-39	12.7	9.7	9.4	11.4 [2]	14.0	15.2	20.1	21.5	21.4	20.4
40-44	18.4	14.2	10.6	12.5 [2]	11.8	13.3	14.6	16.7	18.1	16.3
45-49	13.5	12.8	10.4	11.8 [2]	11.9	14.3	15.7	18.2	15.8	16.9
50-54	7.3	8.1	8.4	8.2 [2]	8.8	11.0	15.7	16.4	16.0	19.9
55-59	0.8	1.2	1.1	2.2 [2]	3.2	3.8	5.6	5.7	6.8	8.4
60-64	0.1	0.1	0.3	- [2]	0.7	1.0	0.7	1.6	0.4	1.2
65-69	0.1	0.3	0.2	0.2 [2]	0.1	0.3	0.5	0.1	0.0	0.3
70-74	-	-	-	- [2]	-	-	0.2	0.0	0.0	0.0
Iceland (BA) [3]				Total unemployment - Chômage total - Desempleo total						
Total - Total - Total										
Total	3.1	3.7	3.7	5.3	5.4	4.9	4.3	5.0	4.2	5.5
16-19	0.7	0.9	0.8	1.0	1.1	1.1	1.1	1.7	1.5	1.6
20-24	0.5	0.6	0.6	0.8	1.1	1.0	1.0	0.8	0.8	1.0
25-29	0.5	0.4	0.4	0.5	0.7	0.5	0.4	0.6	0.3	0.5
30-34	0.2	0.3	0.3	0.5	0.8	0.4	0.4	0.5	0.3	0.6
35-39	0.3	0.3	0.4	0.5	0.3	0.3	0.1	0.2	0.3	0.3
40-44	0.1	0.2	0.2	0.5	0.3	0.4	0.4	0.3	0.2	0.2
45-49	0.2	0.2	0.3	0.4	0.3	0.2	0.4	0.3	0.2	0.5
50-54	-	0.2	0.3	0.5	0.3	0.3	0.2	0.3	0.3	0.3
55-59	0.2	0.1	0.2	0.1	0.3	0.4	0.2	0.2	0.1	0.3
60-64	0.1	0.3	0.3	0.2	0.2	0.2	0.2	0.2	0.1	0.2
65-69	0.2	0.1	-	0.2	0.1	0.1	-	0.1	0.1	0.1
70-74	-	-	-	-	-	-	-	-	-	0.0
Men - Hommes - Hombres										
Total	1.2	1.5	1.8	3.1	3.1	2.7	2.3	2.6	2.3	3.3
16-19	0.4	0.6	0.5	0.7	0.7	0.7	0.7	1.0	0.9	0.9
20-24	0.2	0.3	0.3	0.6	0.6	0.5	0.5	0.4	0.4	0.5
25-29	0.1	0.1	0.2	0.3	0.5	0.3	0.2	0.2	0.2	0.4
30-34	-	0.1	0.1	0.2	0.4	0.2	0.2	0.2	0.1	0.4
35-39	0.1	0.1	0.2	0.2	0.1	0.2	0.1	0.1	0.2	0.2
40-44	-	-	0.1	0.2	0.2	0.2	0.1	0.2	0.0	0.1
45-49	0.1	0.1	0.1	0.2	0.2	0.1	0.2	0.2	0.1	0.3
50-54	0.1	0.1	0.1	0.3	0.1	0.2	0.1	0.2	0.2	0.2
55-59	0.1	-	0.1	0.1	0.2	0.2	0.1	0.1	0.1	0.2
60-64	-	0.1	0.2	0.1	0.2	0.1	-	0.1	0.1	0.2
65-69	0.1	-	-	0.1	0.1	0.1	-	-	0.1	0.1
70-74	-	-	-	-	-	-	-	-	-	0.0
Women - Femmes - Mujeres										
Total	1.9	2.2	1.9	2.2	2.4	2.2	2.0	2.4	1.9	2.2
16-19	0.3	0.3	0.3	0.3	0.4	0.4	0.3	0.7	0.6	0.7
20-24	0.3	0.3	0.3	0.2	0.5	0.5	0.5	0.4	0.4	0.4
25-29	0.4	0.3	0.2	0.2	0.3	0.2	0.2	0.4	0.1	0.1
30-34	0.2	0.2	0.2	0.3	0.4	0.2	0.2	0.3	0.1	0.3
35-39	0.2	0.2	0.2	0.3	0.2	0.1	0.1	0.1	0.2	0.1
40-44	0.1	0.2	0.1	0.3	0.1	0.2	0.2	0.1	0.2	0.1
45-49	0.1	0.1	0.2	0.2	0.1	0.1	0.1	0.1	0.1	0.2
50-54	-	0.1	0.2	0.2	0.2	0.1	0.1	0.1	0.1	0.1
55-59	0.1	0.1	0.1	-	0.1	0.1	0.1	0.1	0.0	0.1
60-64	0.1	0.2	0.1	0.1	-	0.1	0.2	0.1	0.1	-
65-69	0.1	0.1	-	0.1	-	-	-	0.1	0.0	0.0
70-74	-	-	-	-	-	-	-	-	-	0.0
Ireland (BA) [4][5]				Total unemployment - Chômage total - Desempleo total						
Total - Total - Total										
Total	96.9	74.9	65.4	77.1	82.6	84.6	86.5	92.8	100.3	115.5
15-19	11.1	10.1	7.9	9.3	9.3	8.6	8.3	9.2	10.7	10.5
20-24	17.2	11.8	12.4	14.8	15.0	16.4	18.2	18.9	18.7	23.1
25-29	12.7	11.3	9.3	12.8	13.4	12.8	11.9	15.4	16.3	20.9
30-34	11.3	8.6	8.9	10.3	11.0	11.6	11.5	12.5	13.3	15.1
35-39	11.1	8.2	6.5	8.2	8.7	8.8	9.1	9.6	10.5	12.6
40-44	10.3	8.2	5.7	6.6	8.0	8.7	8.0	7.8	9.3	10.0
45-49	9.6	7.0	5.1	5.6	6.5	7.0	7.6	7.5	7.5	9.0
50-54	8.3	5.8	5.2	5.1	5.9	5.8	5.7	6.6	7.5	6.9
55-59	4.3	2.7	3.3	3.0	3.2	3.2	4.0	4.2	4.6	5.2
60-64	1.9	1.0	0.9	1.2	1.2	1.5	2.1	1.0	1.5	2.1
65-69	-	0.1	0.1	0.2	0.2	0.2	0.1	0.1	0.4	0.1
70-74	-	-	-	0.0	0.0	0.1	0.0	0.1	0.0	0.0
75+	-	-	-	0.0	0.0	0.0	0.0	0.0	0.0	0.0

Explanatory notes: see p. 451.

[1] Persons aged 15 to 74 years. [2] Estimates based on the 2001 Population Census results. [3] Persons aged 16 to 74 years. [4] Persons aged 15 years and over. [5] Second quarter of each year.

Notes explicatives: voir p. 454.

[1] Personnes âgées de 15 à 74 ans. [2] Estimations basées sur les résultats du Recensement de la population de 2001. [3] Personnes âgées de 16 à 74 ans. [4] Personnes âgées de 15 ans et plus. [5] Deuxième trimestre de chaque année.

Notás explicativas: véase p. 457.

[1] Personas de 15 a 74 años. [2] Estimaciones basadas en los resultados del Censo de población de 2001. [3] Personas de 16 a 74 años. [4] Personas de 15 años y más. [5] Segundo trimestre de cada año.

By age group — Par groupe d'âge — Por grupo de edad

	Thousands			Milliers				Millares		
	1999	2000	2001	2002	2003	2004	2005	2006	2007	2008

Ireland (BA) [1] [2]
Total unemployment - Chômage total - Desempleo total

Men - Hommes - Hombres

	1999	2000	2001	2002	2003	2004	2005	2006	2007	2008
Total	59.4	44.9	39.8	48.8	51.9	54.6	53.7	56.0	60.0	78.0
15-19	6.2	5.7	4.9	5.7	5.7	5.0	4.8	5.3	6.2	7.0
20-24	9.5	5.7	6.9	9.4	9.2	9.7	10.9	11.0	10.8	15.1
25-29	7.7	6.6	5.4	7.9	7.8	8.2	7.6	9.7	9.7	14.1
30-34	6.3	5.2	5.5	6.8	7.1	7.4	7.0	7.1	8.3	10.4
35-39	7.0	5.1	3.7	4.8	6.0	4.9	5.8	5.9	6.5	9.2
40-44	6.5	5.2	3.5	4.0	4.7	6.2	4.9	4.2	5.0	6.1
45-49	6.5	4.6	3.1	3.5	4.2	4.8	4.7	4.6	4.7	6.5
50-54	6.3	4.0	3.8	3.6	4.0	4.5	3.9	4.3	4.6	4.2
55-59	3.0	1.9	2.1	1.9	2.4	2.6	2.6	2.9	2.9	3.8
60-64	1.3	0.8	0.8	1.1	0.8	1.2	1.6	0.7	1.1	1.6
65-69	0.1	-	-	0.1	0.0	0.1	0.0	0.1	0.3	0.1
70-74	-	-	-	0.0	0.0	0.0	0.0	0.1	0.0	0.0
75+	-	-	-	0.0	0.0	0.0	0.0	0.0	0.0	0.0

Women - Femmes - Mujeres

	1999	2000	2001	2002	2003	2004	2005	2006	2007	2008
Total	37.5	30.0	25.6	28.4	30.6	30.0	32.9	36.8	40.3	37.5
15-19	4.9	4.4	3.0	3.6	3.7	3.6	3.5	3.9	4.4	3.5
20-24	7.7	6.1	5.5	5.4	5.8	6.7	7.3	7.8	7.9	8.0
25-29	5.0	4.7	3.9	4.8	5.6	4.5	4.3	5.6	6.7	6.8
30-34	5.0	3.4	3.4	3.5	3.9	4.1	4.6	5.4	5.0	4.7
35-39	4.1	3.1	2.8	3.4	2.7	3.9	3.3	3.7	4.1	3.3
40-44	3.8	3.0	2.2	2.6	3.3	2.6	3.1	3.6	4.2	3.9
45-49	3.1	2.4	2.0	2.2	2.3	2.2	2.9	2.9	2.8	2.5
50-54	2.0	1.8	1.4	1.5	2.0	1.3	1.8	2.3	2.9	2.7
55-59	1.3	0.8	1.2	1.1	0.8	0.6	1.4	1.4	1.7	1.4
60-64	0.6	0.2	0.1	0.1	0.4	0.3	0.6	0.3	0.4	0.5
65-69	-	0.1	0.1	0.1	0.1	0.1	0.1	0.0	0.1	0.0
70-74	0.1	-	-	0.0	0.0	0.0	0.0	0.0	0.0	0.0
75+	-	-	-	0.0	0.0	0.0	0.0	0.0	0.0	0.0

Italy (BA) [1]
Total unemployment - Chômage total - Desempleo total

Total - Total - Total

	1999	2000	2001	2002	2003	2004	2005	2006	2007	2008
Total	2 669	2 495	2 267	2 163	2 096	1 960 [3]	1 889	1 673	1 506	1 692
15-19	222	207	171	155	152	144 [3]	136	112	102	114
20-24	650	592	499	463	448	369 [3]	353	312	278	285
25-29	578	547	494	475	452	393 [3]	372	322	274	286
30-34	421	385	360	341	330	304 [3]	302	269	246	260
35-39	276	268	263	252	250	249 [3]	242	213	194	223
40-44	187	182	175	174	169	177 [3]	179	168	163	201
45-49	134	123	118	118	118	133 [3]	130	123	118	145
50-54	99	95	94	92	88	93 [3]	91	82	69	92
55-59	69	61	56	57	56	64 [3]	56	46	42	59
60-64	26	26	29	27	26	26 [3]	23	20	17	20
65-69	4	3	4	5	6	6 [3]	4	4	2	5
70-74	2	2	1	2	1	1 [3]	1	1	0	1
75+	3	3	3	3	2	. [3]	.	.	.	.

Men - Hommes - Hombres

	1999	2000	2001	2002	2003	2004	2005	2006	2007	2008
Total	1 266	1 179	1 066	1 016	996	925 [3]	902	801	722	820
15-19	114	108	88	77	79	73 [3]	76	64	57	63
20-24	317	285	242	230	227	181 [3]	179	159	147	147
25-29	273	260	230	220	217	186 [3]	176	153	129	138
30-34	185	174	157	148	148	132 [3]	133	123	111	119
35-39	113	107	107	107	104	107 [3]	96	88	81	92
40-44	78	77	73	72	67	71 [3]	77	68	67	89
45-49	63	56	53	52	54	59 [3]	62	57	53	66
50-54	54	49	51	50	45	50 [3]	47	42	35	50
55-59	45	39	36	35	33	41 [3]	35	30	28	38
60-64	21	22	25	21	19	20 [3]	19	13	13	15
65-69	2	1	2	3	3	4 [3]	3	2	1	3
70-74	1	1	-	-	-	0 [3]	0	1	0	1
75+	1	1	1	1	1	. [3]	.	.	.	.

Women - Femmes - Mujeres

	1999	2000	2001	2002	2003	2004	2005	2006	2007	2008
Total	1 404	1 316	1 201	1 147	1 101	1 036 [3]	986	873	784	872
15-19	108	100	83	78	73	71 [3]	60	48	45	51
20-24	333	307	257	232	221	189 [3]	175	153	131	138
25-29	305	287	263	255	235	207 [3]	196	168	146	149
30-34	235	211	203	193	182	172 [3]	169	146	135	140
35-39	163	161	156	146	146	143 [3]	147	126	114	131
40-44	109	105	101	102	102	106 [3]	102	99	96	112
45-49	71	67	65	66	64	74 [3]	68	66	65	79
50-54	45	46	43	42	43	42 [3]	44	40	34	43
55-59	24	22	20	22	23	23 [3]	20	16	14	21
60-64	5	4	4	6	7	6 [3]	5	7	4	5
65-69	2	2	2	2	3	2 [3]	1	2	1	2
70-74	1	1	1	2	1	0 [3]	0	0	0	0
75+	2	2	2	2	1	. [3]	.	.	.	.

Explanatory notes: see p. 451.

[1] Persons aged 15 years and over. [2] Second quarter of each year. [3] Methodology revised; data not strictly comparable.

Notes explicatives: voir p. 454.

[1] Personnes âgées de 15 ans et plus. [2] Deuxième trimestre de chaque année. [3] Méthodologie révisée; les données ne sont pas strictement comparables.

Notas explicativas: véase p. 457.

[1] Personas de 15 años y más. [2] Segundo trimestre de cada año. [3] Metodología revisada; los datos no son estrictamente comparables.

	UNEMPLOYMENT		CHÔMAGE			DESEMPLEO			
	By age group		Par groupe d'âge			Por grupo de edad			
	Thousands			Milliers				Millares	
	1999	2000	2001	2002	2003	2004	2005	2006	2007	2008

Latvia (BA) [1] — Total unemployment - Chômage total - Desempleo total

Total - Total - Total

	1999	2000	2001	2002	2003	2004	2005	2006	2007	2008
Total	161.4	158.7	144.7	134.5 [2]	119.2	118.6	99.1	79.9	72.1	91.6
15-19	10.2	8.4	7.3	9.4 [2]	8.2	8.0	6.6	7.1	5.5	6.5
20-24	24.4	20.4	20.7	18.6 [2]	16.9	16.2	10.9	12.3	11.4	13.3
25-29	18.9	21.2	17.4	15.9 [2]	15.2	16.5	12.6	9.7	9.4	12.0
30-34	19.8	16.9	16.9	14.1 [2]	9.7	12.2	11.6	7.9	7.0	9.5
35-39	22.4	21.5	19.3	15.7 [2]	13.2	11.6	9.4	6.2	8.0	10.4
40-44	18.8	23.0	16.5	20.7 [2]	15.5	13.8	10.1	8.7	7.2	10.0
45-49	19.3	18.2	17.7	11.4 [2]	15.0	12.9	11.4	10.0	8.3	10.7
50-54	15.1	16.3	15.8	14.2 [2]	14.3	14.6	13.2	7.6	7.6	8.9
55-59	7.4	8.4	9.7	8.5 [2]	6.8	8.8	8.3	6.7	5.6	8.8
60-64	2.6	2.8	3.0	3.7 [2]	3.3	2.6	3.0	2.5	-	-
65-69	-	-	-	- [2]	-	-	2.0	1.1	-	-
70-74	-	-	-	-	-	-	-	-	-	-

Men - Hommes - Hombres

	1999	2000	2001	2002	2003	2004	2005	2006	2007	2008
Total	88.7	87.0	81.9	74.9 [2]	61.7	61.7	52.8	43.7	39.4	50.3
15-19	6.4	5.0	4.0	4.9 [2]	4.4	3.9	4.2	3.9	3.5	4.3
20-24	15.2	11.3	12.5	9.4 [2]	9.1	8.7	5.3	5.9	6.8	7.2
25-29	10.0	11.9	11.0	10.0 [2]	8.9	8.7	6.2	5.7	4.8	5.9
30-34	10.1	8.9	9.8	7.0 [2]	4.5	7.4	6.0	4.7	3.5	6.1
35-39	13.0	12.3	10.7	8.6 [2]	6.3	6.6	5.8	3.4	4.7	5.9
40-44	9.6	10.9	8.3	12.1 [2]	8.3	6.8	4.9	5.3	4.2	4.1
45-49	9.7	10.1	9.5	5.8 [2]	7.0	6.3	5.5	4.4	4.5	6.0
50-54	7.9	9.0	7.9	8.5 [2]	7.0	7.4	7.1	4.6	3.6	4.2
55-59	4.4	5.6	6.3	5.1 [2]	3.5	3.5	5.1	3.7	3.0	5.8
60-64	1.1	1.6	1.8	2.3 [2]	2.0	-	1.6	1.5	-	-
65-69	-	-	-	- [2]	-	-	1.1	0.5	-	-
70-74	-	-	-	-	-	-	-	-	-	-

Women - Femmes - Mujeres

	1999	2000	2001	2002	2003	2004	2005	2006	2007	2008
Total	72.7	71.7	62.7	59.6 [2]	57.5	56.9	46.2	36.2	32.7	41.4
15-19	3.9	3.4	3.3	4.5 [2]	3.8	4.1	2.3	3.1	2.0	2.2
20-24	9.2	9.2	8.2	9.2 [2]	7.7	7.6	5.5	6.4	4.6	6.1
25-29	9.0	9.3	6.4	5.8 [2]	6.3	7.8	6.4	4.1	4.6	6.0
30-34	9.7	8.0	7.1	7.1 [2]	5.2	4.8	5.5	3.1	3.5	3.5
35-39	9.4	9.2	8.6	7.1 [2]	6.9	5.1	3.6	2.8	3.4	4.6
40-44	9.2	12.2	8.2	8.6 [2]	7.2	7.0	5.3	3.4	3.0	5.9
45-49	9.6	8.1	8.2	5.6 [2]	7.9	6.6	5.9	5.6	3.8	4.7
50-54	7.2	7.2	7.9	5.8 [2]	7.3	7.2	6.1	3.1	4.0	4.6
55-59	3.0	2.8	3.4	3.4 [2]	3.3	5.3	3.2	3.0	2.6	3.0
60-64	1.5	1.2	1.2	1.4 [2]	1.3	-	1.4	0.9	-	-
65-69	-	-	-	- [2]	-	-	0.8	0.5	-	-
70-74	-	-	-	-	-	-	-	-	-	-

Latvia (FB) [3] [4] — Registered unemployment - Chômage enregistré - Desempleo registrado

Total - Total - Total

	1999	2000	2001	2002	2003	2004	2005	2006	2007	2008
Total	109.5	93.3	91.6	89.7	90.6	90.8	78.5	68.9	52.3	.
15-19	3.0	2.6	2.5	2.1	2.0	1.7	1.8	1.4	0.8	.
20-24	13.2	11.1	10.9	10.4	10.0	9.9	9.3	8.2	5.9	.
25-29	14.0	11.9	11.6	11.0	10.6	10.8	9.2	8.1	6.3	.
30-34									6.1	.
30-49	58.7	48.9	47.7	46.3	46.7	45.9	38.7	33.3		.
35-39									5.9	.
40-44									5.7	.
45-49									6.8	.
50-54	14.0	12.1	11.8	12.0	12.2	12.1	10.0	8.5	6.7	.
55-59	6.5	6.5	6.7	7.3	8.3	9.7	8.7	8.4	6.8	.
60+	-	0.2	0.5	0.6	0.7	0.7	0.8	1.1	1.3	.

Men - Hommes - Hombres

	1999	2000	2001	2002	2003	2004	2005	2006	2007	2008
Total	46.7	39.5	39.1	37.0	37.6	37.3	31.5	27.0	20.1	.
15-19	1.4	1.1	1.0	0.9	0.8	0.7	0.7	0.5	0.3	.
20-24	5.3	4.4	4.4	4.1	4.0	3.7	3.4	3.0	2.0	.
25-29	5.1	4.1	4.0	3.7	3.7	3.8	3.1	2.8	2.2	.
30-34									2.2	.
30-49	23.4	19.7	19.4	18.5	18.8	18.7	15.6	13.0		.
35-39									2.2	.
40-44									2.3	.
45-49									2.8	.
50-54	5.5	5.1	5.1	5.1	5.2	5.2	4.2	3.4	2.7	.
55-59	6.0	5.0	4.5	4.2	4.4	4.5	3.9	3.5	2.7	.
60+	-	0.2	0.5	0.6	0.7	0.7	0.7	0.7	0.7	.

Explanatory notes: see p. 451.

[1] Persons aged 15 to 74 years. [2] Prior to 2002: persons aged 15 years and over. [3] Age limits vary according to the year. [4] 31st Dec. of each year.

Notes explicatives: voir p. 454.

[1] Personnes âgées de 15 à 74 ans. [2] Avant 2002: personnes âgées de 15 ans et plus. [3] Les limites d'âge varient selon l'année. [4] 31 déc. de chaque année.

Notas explicativas: véase p. 457.

[1] Personas de 15 a 74 años. [2] Antes de 2002: personas de 15 años y más. [3] Los límites de edad varían según el año. [4] 31 dic. de cada año.

	Thousands / Milliers / Millares									
	1999	2000	2001	2002	2003	2004	2005	2006	2007	2008

Latvia (FB) [1] [2]   Registered unemployment - Chômage enregistré - Desempleo registrado

Women - Femmes - Mujeres

	1999	2000	2001	2002	2003	2004	2005	2006	2007	2008
Total	62.8	53.8	52.6	52.7	53.0	53.5	47.0	42.0	32.2	.
15-19	1.7	1.5	1.5	1.3	1.2	1.0	1.1	0.9	0.5	.
20-24	7.9	6.8	6.5	6.3	6.0	6.2	5.9	5.3	3.9	.
25-29	9.0	7.8	7.5	7.3	6.9	7.0	6.1	5.3	4.1	.
30-34	.	.	.	.	.	.	.	.	3.9	.
30-49	35.3	29.1	28.2	27.9	27.8	27.2	23.1	20.3		.
35-39									3.6	.
40-44	.	.	.	.	.	.	.	.	3.4	.
45-49	.								4.0	.
50-54	8.5	7.1	6.7	6.9	7.0	6.9	5.8	5.0	4.0	.
55-59	0.5	1.5	2.2	3.1	4.0	5.2	4.8	4.8	4.1	.
60+	-	-	-	-	-	-	0.1	0.4	0.6	.

Lithuania (BA) [3]   Total unemployment - Chômage total - Desempleo total

Total - Total - Total

	1999	2000	2001	2002	2003	2004	2005	2006	2007	2008
Total	249.0	273.7	284.0	224.4	203.9	184.4	132.9	89.3	69.0	94.3
15-19	14.7	13.6	10.6	7.0	9.3	6.1	3.3	2.7	2.5	3.8
20-24	41.9	40.5	39.9	28.8	29.5	24.9	17.4	11.0	9.5	18.2
25-29	33.3	32.9	35.3	27.5	24.0	19.0	12.1	8.7	9.2	11.6
30-34	40.6	43.8	35.8	27.0	23.8	21.0	16.5	11.0	7.5	8.3
35-39	38.9	37.3	41.1	31.9	24.0	23.5	15.5	9.3	9.9	9.9
40-44	30.5	31.0	40.2	32.0	28.6	28.1	18.4	11.2	8.7	10.5
45-49	21.5	29.3	31.8	25.2	21.0	21.4	19.9	11.5	7.0	11.4
50-54	18.0	25.8	27.1	25.8	21.7	20.3	16.9	12.1	7.2	11.0
55-59	8.8	15.7	17.7	15.1	14.0	14.0	10.3	10.1	6.5	6.9
60-64	0.8	2.8	4.2	4.2	6.5	5.2	2.4	1.4	1.0	1.7
65-69	-	0.9	0.3	-	1.4	0.8	0.1	0.4	-	0.6
70-74	.	.	.	.	.	.	.	.	.	0.2
75+	.	.	.	.	.	.	.	.	.	.

Men - Hommes - Hombres

	1999	2000	2001	2002	2003	2004	2005	2006	2007	2008
Total	140.5	158.5	165.6	121.1	105.4	90.6	67.1	46.7	34.6	49.5
15-19	9.5	10.9	7.2	5.0	5.0	3.7	1.9	1.6	1.8	2.0
20-24	25.5	22.7	26.8	15.6	15.3	14.7	10.6	6.3	4.2	10.1
25-29	18.1	20.6	21.0	15.8	15.9	11.2	6.9	5.2	5.2	6.9
30-34	24.6	25.8	19.6	14.6	12.5	10.7	9.3	7.2	4.6	4.6
35-39	22.3	22.3	23.0	15.8	13.4	9.6	6.3	4.5	4.6	5.8
40-44	15.3	15.7	22.3	17.1	13.9	13.3	9.3	5.5	4.3	5.6
45-49	9.7	14.2	16.6	11.6	9.4	9.1	8.2	3.8	3.0	5.3
50-54	7.8	13.0	13.1	12.7	9.4	8.8	7.2	6.0	2.9	4.5
55-59	6.8	10.3	11.9	8.9	5.8	5.3	4.9	5.4	3.3	3.2
60-64	0.8	2.1	3.9	4.1	4.5	4.1	2.2	1.1	0.7	1.0
65-69	-	0.8	0.2	-	0.4	0.2	0.1	0.1	-	0.5
70-74	.	.	.	.	.	.	.	.	.	0.0
75+	.	.	.	.	.	.	.	.	.	.

Women - Femmes - Mujeres

	1999	2000	2001	2002	2003	2004	2005	2006	2007	2008
Total	108.5	115.2	118.4	103.3	98.4	93.8	65.8	42.6	34.3	44.8
15-19	5.3	2.7	3.4	2.1	4.4	2.4	1.3	1.1	0.7	1.8
20-24	16.4	17.9	13.1	13.2	14.3	10.2	6.8	4.7	5.3	8.1
25-29	15.1	12.2	14.3	11.6	8.2	7.8	5.2	3.5	4.0	4.7
30-34	16.0	17.9	16.2	12.4	11.3	10.3	7.2	3.8	2.9	3.7
35-39	16.5	15.0	18.1	16.2	10.7	14.0	9.3	4.7	5.3	4.1
40-44	15.3	15.3	18.0	14.9	14.7	14.8	9.2	5.7	4.3	5.0
45-49	11.8	15.1	15.2	13.6	11.6	12.3	11.7	7.7	4.0	6.1
50-54	10.1	12.8	14.0	13.1	12.3	11.5	9.7	6.1	4.4	6.4
55-59	2.0	5.4	5.9	6.2	8.2	8.7	5.3	4.7	3.2	3.8
60-64	-	0.8	0.3	0.1	1.9	1.2	0.2	0.4	0.3	0.7
65-69	-	0.1	0.1	-	1.0	0.6	.	0.3	-	0.2
70-74	.	.	.	.	.	.	.	.	.	0.2
75+	.	.	.	.	.	.	.	.	.	.

Lithuania (FB) [4] [5]   Registered unemployment - Chômage enregistré - Desempleo registrado

Total - Total - Total

	1999	2000	2001	2002	2003	2004	2005	2006	2007	2008
Total	177.4	225.9	224.0	191.2	158.8	126.4	87.2	79.3	69.7	95.0
16-18	1.8	6.2	4.2	4.4	3.0	1.9	1.1	1.5	1.4	2.2
19-24	29.3	28.2	24.5	17.3	14.2	8.4	4.7	4.9	5.0	9.4
25-29	19.5	23.1	21.2	17.0	13.4	8.8	5.3	5.6	5.6	8.8
30-49	95.7	121.8	121.5	104.4	85.4	67.2	43.5	38.3	33.9	45.8
50-54	18.6	27.5	29.5	28.7	24.7	21.5	15.7	13.0	10.7	13.6
55-59	11.3	17.7	19.3	17.3	16.4	17.5	15.0	14.2	11.5	13.1
60-64	1.2	2.4	3.8	2.1	1.7	1.1	1.9	1.8	1.6	2.1

Men - Hommes - Hombres

	1999	2000	2001	2002	2003	2004	2005	2006	2007	2008
Total	94.6	123.1	117.6	95.1	73.7	53.8	33.9	29.9	27.4	49.0
16-18	1.2	3.9	2.6	2.5	1.7	0.9	0.5	0.7	0.7	1.3
19-24	16.8	16.7	13.8	9.1	7.1	3.9	2.0	1.9	2.1	5.5
25-29	10.3	12.8	11.2	8.5	6.3	3.8	2.1	2.1	2.1	4.8
30-49	48.3	63.7	61.7	50.6	38.6	27.7	16.3	14.1	13.0	23.1
50-54	8.8	12.5	13.0	11.9	9.8	7.9	5.3	4.3	3.8	6.3
55-59	8.0	11.1	11.5	10.4	8.5	8.5	5.8	5.0	4.1	5.9
60-64	1.2	2.4	3.8	2.1	1.7	1.1	1.9	1.8	1.6	2.1

Explanatory notes: see p. 451.

[1] Age limits vary according to the year. [2] 31st Dec. of each year. [3] Persons aged 15 years and over. [4] Persons aged 16 to 64 years. [5] 31st Dec. of each year.

Notes explicatives: voir p. 454.

[1] Les limites d'âge varient selon l'année. [2] 31 déc. de chaque année. [3] Personnes âgées de 15 ans et plus. [4] Personnes âgées de 16 à 64 ans. [5] 31 déc. de chaque année.

Notas explicativas: véase p. 457.

[1] Los límites de edad varían según el año. [2] 31 dic. de cada año. [3] Personas de 15 años y más. [4] Personas de 16 a 64 años. [5] 31 dic. de cada año.

	UNEMPLOYMENT	CHÔMAGE	DESEMPLEO
	By age group	Par groupe d'âge	Por grupo de edad

	Thousands				Milliers				Millares	
	1999	2000	2001	2002	2003	2004	2005	2006	2007	2008

Lithuania (FB) [1][2]   Registered unemployment - Chômage enregistré - Desempleo registrado

Women - Femmes - Mujeres

	1999	2000	2001	2002	2003	2004	2005	2006	2007	2008
Total	82.8	102.8	106.4	96.1	85.1	72.6	53.3	49.4	42.3	46.0
16-18	0.6	2.3	1.6	1.9	1.3	1.0	0.6	0.8	0.7	0.9
19-24	12.5	11.5	10.7	8.2	7.1	4.5	2.7	3.0	2.9	3.9
25-29	9.2	10.3	10.0	8.5	7.1	5.0	3.2	3.5	3.5	4.0
30-49	47.4	58.1	59.8	53.8	46.8	39.5	27.2	24.2	20.9	22.7
50-54	9.8	15.0	16.5	16.8	14.9	13.6	10.4	8.7	6.9	7.3
55-59	3.3	6.6	7.8	6.9	7.9	9.0	9.2	9.2	7.4	7.2
60-64	0.0	0.0	0.0	0.0	0.0	0.0	0.0	0.0	0.0	0.0

Luxembourg (BA) [3]   Total unemployment - Chômage total - Desempleo total

Total - Total - Total

	1999	2000	2001	2002	2003	2004	2005	2006	2007	2008
Total	.	.	.	.	.	.	.	9.7	8.9	10.4
15-19	.	.	.	.	.	.	.	0.8	0.7	0.5
20-24	.	.	.	.	.	.	.	1.5	1.6	2.2
25-29	.	.	.	.	.	.	.	1.7	1.5	2.5
30-34	.	.	.	.	.	.	.	1.2	1.6	0.5
35-39	.	.	.	.	.	.	.	1.5	0.7	1.2
40-44	.	.	.	.	.	.	.	1.0	1.0	1.2
45-49	.	.	.	.	.	.	.	1.1	0.8	1.0
50-54	.	.	.	.	.	.	.	0.7	0.8	0.7
55-59	.	.	.	.	.	.	.	0.2	0.3	0.3
60-64	.	.	.	.	.	.	.	0.0	0.0	0.1
65+	.	.	.	.	.	.	.	0.0	0.0	0.0

Men - Hommes - Hombres

	1999	2000	2001	2002	2003	2004	2005	2006	2007	2008
Total	.	.	.	.	.	.	.	4.0	4.3	4.9
15-19	.	.	.	.	.	.	.	0.4	0.3	0.2
20-24	.	.	.	.	.	.	.	1.0	0.8	0.8
25-29	.	.	.	.	.	.	.	0.7	0.8	1.1
30-34	.	.	.	.	.	.	.	0.5	0.7	0.2
35-39	.	.	.	.	.	.	.	0.4	0.3	0.8
40-44	.	.	.	.	.	.	.	0.4	0.5	0.6
45-49	.	.	.	.	.	.	.	0.4	0.3	0.5
50-54	.	.	.	.	.	.	.	0.2	0.4	0.4
55-59	.	.	.	.	.	.	.	0.0	0.2	0.2
60-64	.	.	.	.	.	.	.	0.0	0.0	0.0
65+	.	.	.	.	.	.	.	0.0	0.0	0.0

Women - Femmes - Mujeres

	1999	2000	2001	2002	2003	2004	2005	2006	2007	2008
Total	.	.	.	.	.	.	.	5.7	4.6	5.5
15-19	.	.	.	.	.	.	.	0.4	0.4	0.3
20-24	.	.	.	.	.	.	.	0.6	0.8	1.4
25-29	.	.	.	.	.	.	.	1.0	0.6	1.4
30-34	.	.	.	.	.	.	.	0.7	0.9	0.3
35-39	.	.	.	.	.	.	.	1.1	0.4	0.4
40-44	.	.	.	.	.	.	.	0.6	0.5	0.7
45-49	.	.	.	.	.	.	.	0.6	0.5	0.5
50-54	.	.	.	.	.	.	.	0.5	0.4	0.4
55-59	.	.	.	.	.	.	.	0.2	0.1	0.1
60-64	.	.	.	.	.	.	.	0.0	0.0	0.1
65+	.	.	.	.	.	.	.	0.0	0.0	0.0

Luxembourg (FB) [1]   Registered unemployment - Chômage enregistré - Desempleo registrado

Total - Total - Total

	1999	2000	2001	2002	2003	2004	2005	2006	2007	2008
Total	5.4	5.0	4.9	5.8	7.6	8.7	9.8	9.5	9.6	9.9
16-25	1.0	0.9	0.9	1.2	1.5	1.7	1.9	1.9	1.8	1.7
26-30	0.7	0.6	0.6	0.8	1.1	1.1	1.3	1.2	1.1	1.1
31-40	1.6	1.5	1.4	1.7	2.2	2.4	2.6	2.4	2.3	2.4
41-50	1.4	1.3	1.3	1.4	1.8	2.1	2.5	2.3	2.4	2.6
51-59	0.6	0.6	0.7	0.7	1.0	1.3	1.6	1.6	1.9	.
51-60	0.6	0.6	0.7	0.7	1.0	1.3	1.6	1.6	1.9	2.0
60+	0.0	0.0	0.0	0.0	0.0	0.0	0.1	0.1	0.1	0.1

Men - Hommes - Hombres

	1999	2000	2001	2002	2003	2004	2005	2006	2007	2008
Total	2.8	2.6	2.6	3.2	4.1	4.7	5.4	5.0	4.9	5.2
16-25	0.5	0.4	0.4	0.6	0.8	0.9	1.0	1.0	1.0	0.9
26-30	0.3	0.3	0.3	0.4	0.5	0.6	0.6	0.6	0.5	0.5
31-40	0.9	0.8	0.7	0.9	1.2	1.3	1.4	1.2	1.1	1.2
41-50	0.7	0.7	0.7	0.8	1.0	1.2	1.4	1.3	1.3	1.4
51-59	0.4	0.4	0.4	0.5	0.6	0.8	1.0	0.9	1.0	.
51-60	0.4	0.4	0.4	0.5	0.6	0.8	1.0	0.9	1.0	1.1
60+	0.0	0.0	0.0	0.0	0.0	0.0	0.0	0.0	0.0	0.1

Women - Femmes - Mujeres

	1999	2000	2001	2002	2003	2004	2005	2006	2007	2008
Total	2.5	2.3	2.3	2.7	3.5	4.0	4.4	4.5	4.7	4.7
16-25	0.5	0.5	0.5	0.6	0.7	0.8	0.8	0.9	1.0	0.8
26-30	0.4	0.3	0.3	0.4	0.5	0.6	0.6	0.6	0.6	0.6
31-40	0.8	0.7	0.7	0.8	1.0	1.1	1.2	1.2	1.2	1.2
41-50	0.6	0.6	0.6	0.6	0.8	0.9	1.1	1.1	1.1	1.2
51-59	0.2	0.2	0.3	0.3	0.4	0.5	0.7	0.7	0.8	.
51-60	0.2	0.2	0.3	0.3	0.4	0.5	0.7	0.7	0.8	0.9
60+	0.0	0.0	0.0	0.0	0.0	0.0	0.0	0.0	0.0	0.0

Explanatory notes: see p. 451.   Notes explicatives: voir p. 454.   Notas explicativas: véase p. 457.

[1] Persons aged 16 to 64 years. [2] 31st Dec. of each year.   [1] Personnes âgées de 16 à 64 ans. [2] 31 déc. de chaque année.   [1] Personas de 16 a 64 años. [2] 31 dic. de cada año. [3] Personas de
[3] Persons aged 15 years and over.   [3] Personnes âgées de 15 ans et plus.   15 años y más.

UNEMPLOYMENT   CHÔMAGE   DESEMPLEO

By age group   Par groupe d'âge   Por grupo de edad

Thousands — Milliers — Millares

Macedonia, The Former Yugoslav Rep. of (BA) [1]

Total unemployment - Chômage total - Desempleo total

	1999	2000	2001	2002	2003	2004	2005	2006	2007	2008
Total - Total - Total										
Total	.	.	263.196	263.483	315.868	309.286 [2]	323.934	321.274	316.905	310.409
15-19	.	.	18.818	16.601	17.103	17.347 [2]	14.833	18.048	18.114	14.695
20-24	.	.	55.178	50.747	59.885	52.548 [2]	52.364	51.555	49.442	50.967
25-29	.	.	51.464	49.164	61.519	55.523 [2]	54.298	52.958	51.311	50.244
30-34	.	.	43.195	40.358	51.693	45.186 [2]	46.522	43.493	45.175	42.845
35-39	.	.	31.071	33.651	39.684	39.251 [2]	39.962	38.244	36.290	35.527
40-44	.	.	24.764	25.720	30.657	33.206 [2]	36.864	35.323	33.987	32.020
45-49	.	.	17.664	21.093	23.730	27.135 [2]	32.089	32.161	29.328	29.064
50-54	.	.	12.846	15.012	18.020	20.607 [2]	25.207	26.541	29.339	27.300
55-59	.	.	5.615	7.411	10.534	14.231 [2]	16.325	16.905	17.534	19.144
60-64	.	.	2.065	3.400	2.831	3.907 [2]	5.229	5.801	6.130	7.913
65-69	.	.	.	.	.	.	0.218	0.225	0.253	.
65+	.	.	0.516	0.326	0.213	0.256 [2]	.	.	.	0.690
70-74	.	.	.	.	.	.	0.024	0.021	-	.
75+	.	.	.	.	.	.	-	-	-	.
Men - Hommes - Hombres										
Total	.	.	149.372	159.144	191.850	186.223 [2]	191.096	191.856	189.306	188.222
15-19	.	.	10.971	9.308	9.372	10.250 [2]	9.207	10.717	12.162	10.312
20-24	.	.	32.279	32.572	35.866	32.108 [2]	31.084	30.593	30.027	29.914
25-29	.	.	28.021	29.615	36.714	31.722 [2]	30.385	30.226	29.668	28.667
30-34	.	.	23.080	23.715	30.675	25.431 [2]	25.625	24.744	24.831	24.476
35-39	.	.	17.397	18.284	23.495	23.037 [2]	21.894	21.404	21.088	21.815
40-44	.	.	13.282	15.048	18.694	19.420 [2]	20.797	20.304	18.545	18.907
45-49	.	.	9.750	12.084	14.662	16.165 [2]	18.832	19.204	16.768	16.761
50-54	.	.	8.131	9.177	11.256	13.216 [2]	16.091	16.785	17.821	16.203
55-59	.	.	4.458	5.986	8.214	10.962 [2]	12.326	12.612	12.952	13.759
60-64	.	.	1.771	3.100	2.762	3.746 [2]	4.643	5.076	5.221	6.896
65-69	.	.	.	.	.	.	0.189	0.169	0.224	.
65+	.	.	0.231	0.255	0.140	0.146 [2]	.	.	.	0.513
70-74	.	.	.	.	.	.	0.024	0.021	-	.
75+	.	.	.	.	.	.	-	-	-	.
Women - Femmes - Mujeres										
Total	.	.	113.825	104.339	124.018	123.063 [2]	132.838	129.418	127.599	122.187
15-19	.	.	7.847	7.293	7.731	7.097 [2]	5.626	7.331	5.953	4.384
20-24	.	.	22.899	18.175	24.019	20.440 [2]	21.280	20.962	19.416	21.054
25-29	.	.	23.443	19.549	24.805	23.801 [2]	23.913	22.732	21.643	21.577
30-34	.	.	20.115	16.643	21.018	19.755 [2]	20.897	18.749	20.345	18.370
35-39	.	.	13.674	15.367	16.189	16.214 [2]	18.068	16.840	15.202	13.712
40-44	.	.	11.482	10.671	11.963	13.786 [2]	16.067	15.019	15.443	13.113
45-49	.	.	7.914	9.009	9.068	10.970 [2]	13.257	12.957	12.560	12.302
50-54	.	.	4.715	5.834	6.764	7.390 [2]	9.117	9.756	11.518	11.096
55-59	.	.	1.157	1.426	2.320	3.270 [2]	3.999	4.292	4.582	5.385
60-64	.	.	0.294	0.300	0.069	0.161 [2]	0.585	0.725	0.909	1.017
65-69	.	.	.	.	.	.	0.029	0.055	0.029	.
65+	.	.	0.285	0.071	0.073	0.110 [2]	.	.	.	0.177
70-74	.	.	.	.	.	.	-	-	-	.
75+	.	.	.	.	.	.	-	-	-	.

Macedonia, The Former Yugoslav Rep. of (FB) [1]

Work applicants - Demandeurs d'emploi - Solicitantes

	1999	2000	2001	2002	2003	2004	2005	2006	2007	2008
Total - Total - Total										
Total	.	.	.	.	390	391	360	367	357	343
15-19	.	.	.	.	14	12	10	10	9	8
20-24	.	.	.	.	58	55	48	48	45	41
25-29	.	.	.	.	61	59	53	53	50	46
30-34	.	.	.	.	55	53	48	48	46	43
35-39	.	.	.	.	50	50	45	45	43	40
40-44	.	.	.	.	44	45	42	43	42	40
45-49	.	.	.	.	39	40	38	39	38	37
50-54	.	.	.	.	33	35	33	36	36	36
55-59	.	.	.	.	26	29	30	31	31	32
60+	.	.	.	.	12	13	14	15	17	20
Men - Hommes - Hombres										
Total	.	.	.	.	222	225	208	214	209	198
15-19	.	.	.	.	7	6	5	5	5	4
20-24	.	.	.	.	30	29	25	25	24	22
25-29	.	.	.	.	32	31	27	28	26	24
30-34	.	.	.	.	30	29	26	27	25	23
35-39	.	.	.	.	28	28	25	26	25	23
40-44	.	.	.	.	25	26	24	25	24	23
45-49	.	.	.	.	22	23	22	23	23	22
50-54	.	.	.	.	19	20	20	22	22	22
55-59	.	.	.	.	18	20	21	21	21	21
60+	.	.	.	.	10	11	12	12	13	16

Explanatory notes: see p. 451.

[1] Persons aged 15 years and over. [2] Prior to 2004: April of each year.

Notes explicatives: voir p. 454.

[1] Personnes âgées de 15 ans et plus. [2] Avant 2004: Avril de chaque année.

Notas explicativas: véase p. 457.

[1] Personas de 15 años y más. [2] Antes de 2004: Abril de cada año.

UNEMPLOYMENT — CHÔMAGE — DESEMPLEO

By age group — Par groupe d'âge — Por grupo de edad

	Thousands — Milliers — Millares									
	1999	2000	2001	2002	2003	2004	2005	2006	2007	2008

Macedonia, The Former Yugoslav Rep. of (FB) [1]
Work applicants - Demandeurs d'emploi - Solicitantes

Women - Femmes - Mujeres

Age	1999	2000	2001	2002	2003	2004	2005	2006	2007	2008
Total	.	.	.	.	168	166	152	153	148	145
15-19	.	.	.	.	7	6	5	5	4	4
20-24	.	.	.	.	28	26	23	22	21	20
25-29	.	.	.	.	29	28	25	25	24	22
30-34	.	.	.	.	25	24	21	22	21	20
35-39	.	.	.	.	22	22	19	19	18	17
40-44	.	.	.	.	19	19	18	18	18	17
45-49	.	.	.	.	17	17	16	16	15	15
50-54	.	.	.	.	13	14	13	14	14	14
55-59	.	.	.	.	8	9	9	10	10	11
60+	.	.	.	.	1	2	2	2	3	4

Malta (BA) [1]
Total unemployment - Chômage total - Desempleo total

Total - Total - Total

Age	1999	2000	2001	2002	2003	2004	2005	2006	2007	2008
Total	.	10.151	10.164	.	11.518	11.745	11.925	10.729	10.389	
15-19	.	3.278	3.243	.	3.137	3.196	2.799	2.530	2.426	
20-24	.	0.698	2.220	.	2.461	2.401	2.521	1.925	1.294	
25-29	.	1.479	0.990	.	1.069	1.076	1.466	1.120	1.152	
30-34	.	0.732	0.646	.	0.752	1.057	0.920	0.959	1.009	
35-39	.	0.613	0.901	.	0.933	0.655	0.668	0.853	0.676	
40-44	.	1.060	0.665	.	1.159	0.753	0.844	1.032	1.156	
45-49	.	1.102	0.709	.	0.983	1.090	1.223	1.075	1.311	
50-54	.	0.793	0.495	.	0.694	1.074	1.159	0.793	0.637	
55-59	.	0.226	0.295	.	.	.	.	.	0.616	
60-64	.	.	.	.	.	.	.	.	0.101	
65-69	.	.	.	.	.	.	.	.	0.011	

Men - Hommes - Hombres

Age	1999	2000	2001	2002	2003	2004	2005	2006	2007	2008
Total	.	7.628	6.626	.	7.080	7.279	7.242	6.474	6.442	
15-19	.	2.166	1.817	.	1.509	1.653	1.739	1.476	1.332	
20-24	.	0.698	1.384	.	1.439	1.404	1.427	1.276	0.945	
25-29	.	1.070	0.714	.	0.717	0.831	0.666	0.796	0.771	
30-34	.	0.477	0.268	.	0.537	0.561	0.575	0.596	0.581	
35-39	.	0.503	0.766	.	0.596	-	0.489	0.377	0.396	
40-44	.	0.771	0.535	.	0.842	-	0.476	0.582	0.726	
45-49	.	0.870	0.414	.	0.535	0.621	0.776	0.490	0.736	
50-54	.	0.733	0.495	.	0.652	0.819	0.854	0.588	0.502	
55-59	.	0.170	0.233	.	-	-	-	-	0.351	
60-64	.	.	.	.	.	.	.	.	0.091	
65-69	.	.	.	.	.	.	.	.	0.011	

Women - Femmes - Mujeres

Age	1999	2000	2001	2002	2003	2004	2005	2006	2007	2008
Total	.	2.523	3.538	.	4.438	4.466	4.683	4.255	3.947	
15-19	.	1.112	1.426	.	1.628	1.543	1.060	1.054	1.094	
20-24	.	-	0.836	.	1.022	0.997	1.094	0.649	0.349	
25-29	.	0.409	0.276	.	0.352	0.245	0.800	0.324	0.381	
30-34	.	0.255	0.378	.	0.215	0.496	0.345	0.363	0.428	
35-39	.	0.110	0.135	.	0.337	-	0.179	0.476	0.280	
40-44	.	0.289	0.130	.	0.317	-	0.368	0.450	0.430	
45-49	.	0.232	0.295	.	0.448	0.469	0.447	0.585	0.575	
50-54	.	0.060	-	.	0.042	0.255	0.305	0.205	0.135	
55-59	.	0.056	0.062	.	-	0.070	-	-	0.265	
60-64	.	.	.	.	.	.	.	.	0.010	
65-69	.	.	.	.	.	.	.	.	0.000	

Malta (FB) [2][3]
Registered unemployment - Chômage enregistré - Desempleo registrado

Total - Total - Total

Age	1999	2000	2001	2002	2003	2004	2005	2006	2007	2008
Total	7.695	6.583	6.753	6.774	8.175 [4]	8.103	7.379	7.161	6.172	.
16-19	1.104	0.943	1.027	0.900	1.058 [4]	1.005	1.008	0.823	0.596	
20-24	1.094	0.867	0.943	1.015	1.362 [4]	1.313	1.229	1.112	0.789	
25-29	0.815	0.740	0.747	0.825	1.033 [4]	1.031	0.948	0.900	0.745	
30-34	0.699				0.818 [4]		0.839			
30-44	.	2.280	2.268	2.264	.	2.498	.	2.146	1.973	
35-39	0.963				0.716 [4]		0.646			
40-44	1.078				0.975 [4]		0.755			
45-49	0.834				0.921 [4]		0.787			
45+	.	1.753	1.768	1.770	.	2.256	.	2.180	2.069	
50-54	0.744				0.741 [4]		0.619			
55-59	0.324				0.499 [4]		0.482			
60-64	-				0.052 [4]		0.066			

Explanatory notes: see p. 451.

[1] Persons aged 15 years and over. [2] Persons aged 16 to 61 years. [3] Dec. of each year. [4] Methodology revised; data not strictly comparable.

Notes explicatives: voir p. 454.

[1] Personnes âgées de 15 ans et plus. [2] Personnes âgées de 16 à 61 ans. [3] Déc. de chaque année. [4] Méthodologie révisée; les données ne sont pas strictement comparables.

Notas explicativas: véase p. 457.

[1] Personas de 15 años y más. [2] Personas de 16 a 61 años de edad. [3] Dic. de cada año. [4] Metodología revisada; los datos no son estrictamente comparables.

	Thousands			Milliers				Millares		
	1999	2000	2001	2002	2003	2004	2005	2006	2007	2008

Malta (FB) [1][2]   Registered unemployment - Chômage enregistré - Desempleo registrado

Men - Hommes - Hombres

	1999	2000	2001	2002	2003	2004	2005	2006	2007	2008
Total	6.611	5.665	5.646	5.602	6.606 [3]	6.511	5.715	5.544	4.684	.
16-19	0.742	0.660	0.653	0.525	0.635 [3]	0.638	0.603	0.490	0.341	.
20-24	0.904	0.724	0.760	0.769	0.982 [3]	0.953	0.852	0.764	0.530	.
25-29	0.714	0.645	0.639	0.712	0.869 [3]	0.833	0.749	0.700	0.549	.
30-34	0.640	.	.	.	0.712 [3]	.	0.692	.	.	.
30-44	.	2.087	2.050	2.036	. [3]	2.145	.	1.741	1.573	.
35-39	0.885	.	.	.	0.623 [3]	.	0.550	.	.	.
40-44	0.986	.	.	.	0.849 [3]	.	0.616	.	.	.
45-49	0.742	.	.	.	0.787 [3]	.	0.642	.	.	.
45+	.	1.549	1.544	1.560	. [3]	1.942	.	1.829	1.691	.
50-54	0.669	.	.	.	0.659 [3]	.	0.533	.	.	.
55-59	0.289	.	.	.	0.438 [3]	.	0.412	.	.	.
60-64	0.040	.	.	.	0.052 [3]	.	0.066	.	.	.

Women - Femmes - Mujeres

	1999	2000	2001	2002	2003	2004	2005	2006	2007	2008
Total	1.084	0.918	1.107	1.172	1.569 [3]	1.592	1.664	1.617	1.488	.
16-19	0.362	0.283	0.374	0.375	0.423 [3]	0.367	0.405	0.333	0.255	.
20-24	0.190	0.143	0.183	0.246	0.380 [3]	0.360	0.377	0.328	0.259	.
25-29	0.101	0.095	0.108	0.113	0.164 [3]	0.198	0.199	0.200	0.196	.
30-34	0.059	.	.	.	0.106 [3]	.	0.147	.	.	.
30-44	.	0.193	0.218	0.228	. [3]	0.353	.	0.405	0.400	.
35-39	0.078	.	.	.	0.093 [3]	.	0.096	.	.	.
40-44	0.092	.	.	.	0.126 [3]	.	0.139	.	.	.
45-49	0.092	.	.	.	0.134 [3]	.	0.145	.	.	.
45+	.	0.204	0.224	0.210	. [3]	0.314	.	0.351	0.378	.
50-54	0.075	.	.	.	0.082 [3]	.	0.086	0.070	.	.
55-59	0.035	.	.	.	0.061 [3]	.	-	.	.	.
60-64	-	.	.	.	- [3]	.	.	.	.	.

Moldova, Republic of (BA) [4]   Total unemployment - Chômage total - Desempleo total

Total - Total - Total

	1999	2000	2001	2002	2003	2004	2005	2006	2007	2008
Total	187.2	140.1	117.7	109.9	117.1	116.5	103.7	99.9	66.7	51.7
15-19	24.4	15.5	16.4	11.6	12.9	12.7	9.7	9.0	6.2	3.6
20-24	35.1	21.5	19.2	20.5	17.6	18.2	18.9	18.3	14.1	12.1
25-29	21.1	17.2	13.6	13.3	13.1	12.9	10.4	13.0	7.5	5.9
30-34	22.3	15.3	12.3	10.5	12.3	12.3	10.8	10.6	7.8	5.8
35-39	25.4	19.0	12.8	11.0	13.0	12.3	10.1	10.8	6.6	5.1
40-44	22.5	20.0	17.9	17.5	19.3	17.4	15.6	11.8	7.1	3.9
45-49	22.6	18.1	13.6	14.6	15.4	15.9	13.2	12.0	7.7	7.6
50-54	7.9	9.3	8.6	6.6	9.4	9.8	9.4	8.8	4.9	3.8
55-59	4.3	2.6	2.7	3.1	3.2	4.4	4.8	4.8	4.2	3.7
60-64	1.2	1.2	0.6	0.8	0.8	0.5	0.8	0.7	0.4	0.4
65+	0.5	0.3	0.1	0.3	0.2	0.7	-	0.3	0.1	0.0

Men - Hommes - Hombres

	1999	2000	2001	2002	2003	2004	2005	2006	2007	2008
Total	113.6	80.6	70.1	64.4	69.9	70.1	59.8	61.7	41.5	30.0
15-19	14.8	8.5	9.8	6.5	6.5	7.0	5.0	5.0	4.3	2.3
20-24	23.1	12.7	12.0	13.0	11.1	11.2	10.5	11.4	7.8	5.7
25-29	13.0	10.1	8.2	7.6	8.1	8.4	6.4	9.1	4.9	3.4
30-34	12.6	9.7	7.5	5.8	7.0	7.5	6.2	6.2	4.6	3.6
35-39	14.8	10.4	7.1	5.9	7.3	7.3	6.0	6.9	4.3	2.9
40-44	12.7	12.0	10.0	9.5	11.5	10.0	7.8	6.8	4.2	2.4
45-49	12.7	9.4	8.2	8.6	9.0	9.8	8.1	7.4	4.5	4.3
50-54	5.5	5.0	4.8	4.2	6.2	5.7	5.8	4.7	3.1	2.0
55-59	3.4	1.9	2.0	2.3	2.5	2.8	3.2	3.4	3.2	2.9
60-64	0.7	0.8	0.5	0.7	0.6	0.4	0.7	0.5	0.4	0.4
65+	0.4	0.2	0.1	0.3	0.2	0.6	-	0.1	0.0	0.0

Women - Femmes - Mujeres

	1999	2000	2001	2002	2003	2004	2005	2006	2007	2008
Total	73.6	59.5	47.6	45.4	47.2	46.4	43.9	38.2	25.2	21.8
15-19	9.6	7.0	6.6	5.1	6.4	5.7	4.6	4.0	1.9	1.2
20-24	12.0	8.8	7.2	7.5	6.5	6.9	8.4	6.9	6.3	6.4
25-29	8.1	7.1	5.4	5.7	5.0	4.5	3.9	3.8	2.6	2.5
30-34	9.7	5.6	4.8	4.7	5.3	4.8	4.6	4.4	3.2	2.2
35-39	10.6	8.6	5.7	5.1	5.7	4.9	4.1	3.9	2.3	2.2
40-44	9.8	8.2	7.9	8.0	7.8	7.4	7.8	5.0	2.9	1.5
45-49	9.9	8.7	5.4	6.0	6.4	6.1	5.1	4.6	3.2	3.2
50-54	2.4	4.3	3.8	2.4	3.2	4.1	3.6	4.1	1.8	1.7
55-59	0.9	0.7	0.7	0.8	0.7	1.6	1.6	1.3	0.9	0.7
60-64	0.5	0.4	0.1	0.1	0.2	0.1	0.1	0.2	0.0	0.0
65+	0.1	0.1	0.0	-	-	0.1	-	0.2	0.1	-

Explanatory notes: see p. 451.

[1] Persons aged 16 to 61 years. [2] Dec. of each year. [3] Methodology revised; data not strictly comparable. [4] Persons aged 15 years and over.

Notes explicatives: voir p. 454.

[1] Personnes âgées de 16 à 61 ans. [2] Déc. de chaque année. [3] Méthodologie révisée; les données ne sont pas strictement comparables. [4] Personnes âgées de 15 ans et plus.

Notas explicativas: véase p. 457.

[1] Personas de 16 a 61 años de edad. [2] Dic. de cada año. [3] Metodología revisada; los datos no son estrictamente comparables. [4] Personas de 15 años y más.

	UNEMPLOYMENT			CHÔMAGE			DESEMPLEO		
	By age group			Par groupe d'âge			Por grupo de edad		

	Thousands				Milliers			Millares		
	1999	2000	2001	2002	2003	2004	2005	2006	2007	2008

Netherlands (BA) [1] — Total unemployment - Chômage total - Desempleo total

Total - Total - Total

	1999	2000	2001	2002	2003	2004	2005	2006	2007	2008
Total	279	246	204	252	332	411	425	354	300	257
15-19	59	51	40	45	53	61	64	56	56	48
20-24	32	30	29	31	41	56	56	39	35	33
25-29	31	29	21	28	37	42	42	33	24	21
30-34	31	25	22	30	42	45	45	31	24	19
35-39	33	29	22	30	43	54	52	40	27	22
40-44	29	25	23	27	35	45	50	41	32	26
45-49	25	23	20	24	29	40	39	37	29	25
50-54	23	20	18	20	28	33	34	33	28	23
55-59	13	10	8	13	19	28	34	32	30	25
60-64	3	3	3	4	5	6	8	11	15	15

Men - Hommes - Hombres

	1999	2000	2001	2002	2003	2004	2005	2006	2007	2008
Total	128	111	93	126	178	219	220	174	143	128
15-19	26	21	19	24	27	29	30	26	26	25
20-24	16	15	14	17	23	32	30	20	17	17
25-29	18	13	10	14	19	23	20	17	10	10
30-34	13	11	9	16	25	23	23	15	11	9
35-39	14	11	9	13	22	29	27	18	11	9
40-44	11	11	9	12	17	22	24	19	12	10
45-49	11	9	7	10	15	21	19	17	13	12
50-54	9	10	9	9	15	18	19	16	13	12
55-59	7	8	5	8	12	19	22	20	18	16
60-64	2	2	2	3	3	5	6	7	10	10

Women - Femmes - Mujeres

	1999	2000	2001	2002	2003	2004	2005	2006	2007	2008
Total	151	135	111	125	153	192	205	180	157	128
15-19	34	30	20	21	26	32	34	30	30	23
20-24	17	15	15	14	18	25	26	19	17	16
25-29	14	15	10	14	18	20	22	16	14	11
30-34	17	14	13	13	17	21	22	16	13	10
35-39	18	18	13	17	21	26	25	22	16	13
40-44	18	14	14	15	18	23	27	22	20	16
45-49	13	14	13	14	14	19	20	19	16	13
50-54	14	11	9	11	13	15	16	17	15	11
55-59	6	3	3	5	6	9	12	12	11	10
60-64	.	.	.	2	.	2	2	3	4	5

Norway (BA) [2] — Total unemployment - Chômage total - Desempleo total

Total - Total - Total

	1999	2000	2001	2002	2003	2004	2005	2006	2007	2008
Total	75	81	84	92	107	106	111	84 [3]	63	67
15-19	.	.	.	.	.	.	.	15 [3]	15	19
16-19	15	18	18	19	17	18	19			
20-24	15	14	15	17	19	18	18	14 [3]	11	10
25-29	12	12	12	12	16	16	14	11 [3]	8	9
30-34	6	8	10	11	14	13	15	11 [3]	6	7
35-39	7	8	9	10	11	12	13	10 [3]	6	5
40-44	6	6	6	8	10	11	11	8 [3]	6	5
45-49	4	4	4	5	6	7	8	5 [3]	4	4
50-54	4	5	4	5	6	5	6	4 [3]	3	4
55-59	2	3	3	3	4	4	4	3 [3]	2	3
60-64	2	1	1	2	2	2	2	2 [3]	2	2
65-69	-	1	1	1	1	-	1	1 [3]	-	-
70-74	2	1	1	2	-	-	-	- [3]	-	-

Men - Hommes - Hombres

	1999	2000	2001	2002	2003	2004	2005	2006	2007	2008
Total	42	46	46	52	62	62	61	45 [3]	34	38
15-19	.	.	.	.	.	.	.	8 [3]	8	10
16-19	8	9	9	10	9	10	10			
20-24	8	7	9	10	11	10	10	7 [3]	6	6
25-29	6	7	7	7	10	10	8	6 [3]	4	5
30-34	4	5	5	6	8	7	8	6 [3]	3	3
35-39	4	5	5	5	5	7	7	5 [3]	3	3
40-44	4	3	3	5	6	7	6	5 [3]	4	3
45-49	3	3	2	3	4	4	4	3 [3]	2	2
50-54	3	3	2	3	5	3	3	2 [3]	2	3
55-59	1	2	2	2	2	2	3	2 [3]	1	1
60-64	1	1	1	1	1	1	2	1 [3]	1	1
65-69	-	1	1	-	1	1	-	- [3]	-	-
70-74	-	-	-	-	-	-	-	- [3]	-	-

Explanatory notes: see p. 451.

[1] Persons aged 15 to 64 years. [2] Persons aged 15 to 74 years. [3] Prior to 2006: persons aged 16 to 74 years.

Notes explicatives: voir p. 454.

[1] Personnes âgées de 15 à 64 ans. [2] Personnes âgées de 15 à 74 ans. [3] Avant 2006: personnes âgées de 16 à 74 ans.

Notas explicativas: véase p. 457.

[1] Personas de 15 a 64 años. [2] Personas de 15 a 74 años. [3] Antes de 2006: personas de 16 a 74 años.

UNEMPLOYMENT	CHÔMAGE	DESEMPLEO
By age group	**Par groupe d'âge**	**Por grupo de edad**

	Thousands			Milliers				Millares		
	1999	2000	2001	2002	2003	2004	2005	2006	2007	2008

Norway (BA) [1] — Total unemployment - Chômage total - Desempleo total

Women - Femmes - Mujeres

	1999	2000	2001	2002	2003	2004	2005	2006	2007	2008
Total	33	35	38	40	45	45	49	39 [2]	29	30
15-19								8 [2]	7	8
16-19	7	9	9	9	8	8	9	.	.	.
20-24	7	7	6	7	8	8	8	7 [2]	5	4
25-29	6	5	5	5	6	6	6	5 [2]	4	4
30-34	2	3	5	5	6	6	7	5 [2]	3	3
35-39	3	3	4	5	6	5	5	5 [2]	3	3
40-44	2	3	3	3	4	4	5	4 [2]	2	2
45-49	1	1	2	2	2	3	3	2 [2]	2	2
50-54	1	2	2	2	1	2	3	2 [2]	1	2
55-59	1	1	1	1	2	2	2	1 [2]	1	1
60-64	1	-	-	1	1	1	-	1 [2]	1	1
65-69	-	-	-	-	-	-	-	- [2]	-	-
70-74	-	-	-	-	-	-	-	- [2]	-	-

Norway (FB) [1] — Registered unemployment - Chômage enregistré - Desempleo registrado

Total - Total - Total

	1999	2000	2001	2002	2003	2004	2005	2006	2007	2008
Total	60	63	63	75	93	92	83	63 [2]	46	43
15-19								2 [2]	2	2
16-19	2	3	3	3	3	3	3	.	.	.
20-24	9	9	9	11	14	14	12	9 [2]	6	6
25-29	10	11	10	13	15	15	13	9 [2]	7	6
30-49	26	28	28	35	44	44	40	30 [2]	22	20
50-59	7	8	8	9	11	11	10	8 [2]	6	5
60+	5	4	4	4	5	5	5	5 [2]	4	3

Men - Hommes - Hombres

	1999	2000	2001	2002	2003	2004	2005	2006	2007	2008
Total	34	36	36	43	54	52	46	33 [2]	24	24
15-19								1 [2]	1	1
16-19	1	2	2	2	2	2	2	.	.	.
20-24	5	6	6	7	9	9	8	5 [2]	4	4
25-29	5	6	6	7	9	8	7	5 [2]	3	3
30-49	14	16	16	19	25	24	21	15 [2]	11	10
50-59	4	5	5	5	7	7	6	4 [2]	3	3
60+	3	2	2	2	3	3	3	2 [2]	2	2

Women - Femmes - Mujeres

	1999	2000	2001	2002	2003	2004	2005	2006	2007	2008
Total	26	26	27	33	39	39	38	30 [2]	22	19
15-19								1 [2]	1	-
16-19	1	1	1	1	1	1	1	.	.	.
20-24	3	3	3	4	5	5	5	4 [2]	3	2
25-29	5	5	5	6	7	7	6	5 [2]	3	3
30-49	12	12	13	16	19	20	19	15 [2]	11	9
50-59	3	3	3	4	4	5	4	4 [2]	3	2
60+	2	2	2	2	2	2	2	2 [2]	2	2

Poland (BA) [1] — Total unemployment - Chômage total - Desempleo total

Total - Total - Total

	1999	2000	2001	2002	2003	2004	2005	2006	2007	2008
Total	2 391 [3]	2 785	3 170 [4]	3 431	3 329	3 230	3 045	2 344	1 619	1 211
15-19	130 [3]	123	129 [4]	109	107	75	55	73	47	40
20-24	546 [3]	650	762 [4]	794	749	714	653	519	356	269
25-29	360 [3]	425	496 [4]	577	565	569	538	386	263	207
30-34	272 [3]	321	348 [4]	401	384	368	362	275	199	145
35-39	266 [3]	302	353 [4]	365	354	306	282	229	140	109
40-44	316 [3]	366	393 [4]	388	368	357	317	241	157	107
45-49	249 [3]	314	363 [4]	390	398	396	381	284	195	121
50-54	140 [3]	173	212 [4]	284	270	299	304	228	164	129
55-59	63 [3]	63	78 [4]	91	105	116	125	90	77	68
60-64	34 [3]	33	27 [4]	23	25	23	21	16	16	12
65-69	.	.						-	-	-
65-74			8	9	5	7	7			
65+	15 [3]	16	.	.	.	.	.	.	.	.
70-74	.	.	.	.	.	.	.			

Men - Hommes - Hombres

	1999	2000	2001	2002	2003	2004	2005	2006	2007	2008
Total	1 147 [3]	1 344	1 583 [4]	1 779	1 741	1 681	1 553	1 202	831	599
15-19	65 [3]	69	72 [4]	63	61	42	31	39	24	18
20-24	265 [3]	327	399 [4]	427	408	382	356	275	184	134
25-29	176 [3]	201	237 [4]	302	307	295	269	195	140	103
30-34	123 [3]	136	162 [4]	201	178	186	184	138	97	70
35-39	118 [3]	140	167 [4]	179	159	141	122	100	60	47
40-44	145 [3]	160	180 [4]	176	182	170	151	115	76	54
45-49	116 [3]	154	177 [4]	195	203	194	174	137	95	52
50-54	73 [3]	92	116 [4]	158	155	173	160	123	87	63
55-59	34 [3]	36	52 [4]	58	67	78	88	67	53	48
60-64	24 [3]	20	15 [4]	15	17	16	14	11	13	9
65-69	.	.						-	-	-
65-74			5	5	4	5	5			
65+	8 [3]	10	.	.	.	.	.	.	.	.
70-74	.	.	.	.	.	.	.			

Explanatory notes: see p. 451.

[1] Persons aged 15 to 74 years. [2] Prior to 2006: persons aged 16 to 74 years. [3] First and fourth quarters. [4] Prior to 2001: persons aged 15 years and over.

Notes explicatives: voir p. 454.

[1] Personnes âgées de 15 à 74 ans. [2] Avant 2006: personnes âgées de 16 à 74 ans. [3] Premier et quatrième trimestres. [4] Avant 2001: personnes agées de 15 ans et plus.

Notas explicativas: véase p. 457.

[1] Personas de 15 a 74 años. [2] Antes de 2006: personas de 16 a 74 años. [3] Primero y cuarto trimestres. [4] Antes de 2001: personas de 15 años y más.

UNEMPLOYMENT / CHÔMAGE / DESEMPLEO

By age group / Par groupe d'âge / Por grupo de edad

	Thousands				Milliers				Millares	
	1999	2000	2001	2002	2003	2004	2005	2006	2007	2008
Poland (BA) [1]					Total unemployment - Chômage total - Desempleo total					
Women - Femmes - Mujeres										
Total	1 244 [2]	1 440	1 587 [3]	1 652	1 588	1 550	1 493	1 142	788	612
15-19	65 [2]	54	57 [3]	46	45	33	24	34	23	22
20-24	281 [2]	323	363 [3]	367	341	332	297	245	171	136
25-29	184 [2]	224	258 [3]	275	257	275	269	191	123	104
30-34	149 [2]	185	186 [3]	201	207	182	178	137	103	75
35-39	148 [2]	162	186 [3]	186	195	165	160	129	81	63
40-44	171 [2]	206	214 [3]	212	186	187	166	127	81	53
45-49	133 [2]	160	187 [3]	195	194	202	207	147	100	69
50-54	67 [2]	81	96 [3]	125	115	126	145	105	77	66
55-59	29 [2]	27	26 [3]	33	39	38	38	22	24	19
60-64	10 [2]	13	12 [3]	8	8	7	7	5	-	3
65-69								-		
65-74			3	4	1	2	2			
65+	7 [2]	6								
70-74										
Poland (FB) [4] [5]					Registered unemployment - Chômage enregistré - Desempleo registrado					
Total - Total - Total										
Total	2 349.8	2 702.6	3 115.1	3 217.0	3 175.7	2 999.6	2 773.0	2 309.4	1 746.6	1 473.8
18-24	729.6	823.5	918.0	895.8	825.4	728.2	626.1	476.7	332.7	304.6
25-34	623.4	713.2	836.7	881.6	889.8	844.7	778.5	641.6	485.2	418.7
35-44	588.0	656.5	724.4	721.2	690.5	628.5	567.0	460.2	336.9	273.9
45-54	367.7	461.9	572.4	639.3	674.4	681.8	660.2	576.8	443.7	347.9
55+	41.1	47.5	63.6	79.1	95.6	116.4	141.2	154.1	148.1	128.7
Men - Hommes - Hombres										
Total	1 042.5	1 211.0	1 473.0	1 571.2	1 541.0	1 431.1	1 286.6	1 003.7	729.2	640.4
18-24	326.9	379.5	443.3	447.7	410.2	350.7	290.3	202.2	132.4	124.3
25-34	240.8	278.6	356.8	391.8	391.9	364.1	321.0	240.4	168.7	157.5
35-44	257.5	285.6	331.8	336.4	317.0	282.8	246.6	184.8	128.1	108.6
45-54	185.5	231.1	293.4	336.6	352.1	349.3	327.3	268.0	196.2	158.1
55+	31.8	36.2	47.7	58.7	69.8	84.2	101.4	108.6	103.7	91.9
Women - Femmes - Mujeres										
Total	1 307.3	1 491.6	1 642.1	1 645.8	1 634.7	1 568.5	1 486.4	1 305.7	1 017.3	833.4
18-24	402.7	444.0	474.7	448.1	415.2	377.5	335.8	274.7	200.2	180.3
25-34	382.6	434.6	479.9	489.8	497.9	480.5	457.6	401.2	316.5	261.2
35-44	330.5	370.9	392.6	384.8	373.5	345.7	320.4	275.4	208.8	165.3
45-54	182.2	230.8	279.0	302.7	322.3	332.6	332.9	308.9	247.5	189.8
55+	9.3	11.3	15.9	20.4	25.8	32.3	39.8	45.5	44.4	36.8
Portugal (BA) [6]					Total unemployment - Chômage total - Desempleo total					
Total - Total - Total										
Total	225.8	205.5	213.5	270.5	342.3	365.0	422.3	427.8	448.6	427.1
15-19	18.4	19.3	22.4	25.4	29.5	27.8	22.4	25.8	23.6	22.0
20-24	43.2	38.8	41.2	52.3	59.9	61.5	68.2	62.6	62.3	61.5
25-29	34.2	30.1	33.4	48.0	60.3	62.5	79.9	78.7	80.2	72.7
30-34	30.3	25.5	23.2	31.9	49.1	44.1	51.6	56.3	63.7	55.4
35-39	25.2	20.9	21.1	29.3	37.8	39.5	47.1	40.7	52.0	48.3
40-44	21.6	19.9	20.9	24.1	31.4	36.5	42.1	48.5	43.3	46.9
45-49	18.6	15.5	16.4	19.6	26.7	30.3	37.8	38.1	39.8	38.7
50-54	16.0	16.4	16.0	17.6	20.5	28.2	32.6	36.2	39.3	36.1
55-59	11.3	11.6	12.0	14.6	19.5	25.4	29.6	28.6	30.5	32.4
60-64	6.3	7.0	6.2	7.3	6.8	8.3	9.7	12.0	13.2	12.7
65-69	-	-	-	-	-	1.0 [7]	0.7 [7]	0.2 [7]	0.6 [7]	0.3 [7]
70-74	-	-	-	-	-	-	-	-	0.1 [7]	0.2 [7]
75+	-	-	-	-	-	-	-	-	-	-
Men - Hommes - Hombres										
Total	108.9	89.3	91.6	121.4	160.9	172.9	198.1	194.8	196.8	194.3
15-19	7.9	6.7	9.8	13.3	15.3	13.7	12.0	15.0	12.6	11.7
20-24	18.7	17.0	17.6	23.4	26.6	30.0	30.9	28.9	26.0	25.3
25-29	15.2	9.9	13.1	18.6	27.9	27.2	34.1	30.3	29.1	27.8
30-34	12.5	9.5	8.8	13.2	20.6	19.2	22.1	23.1	26.6	23.4
35-39	11.8	10.2	8.2	11.5	16.8	15.9	18.9	15.8	22.0	23.7
40-44	8.8	8.7	8.3	9.7	11.9	16.0	18.7	21.3	16.4	20.9
45-49	9.6	6.5	7.6	9.9	13.6	14.5	18.1	16.9	17.3	16.4
50-54	10.1	8.4	6.9	9.1	11.4	15.7	18.9	17.6	20.1	17.7
55-59	8.4	6.8	7.1	8.3	12.2	15.4	18.7	18.0	18.0	19.0
60-64	4.6	5.2	4.2 [7]	4.4 [7]	4.6	4.6	5.3	7.8	8.1	8.2
65-69	-	-	-	-	-	1.0 [7]	0.7 [7]	0.1 [7]	0.5 [7]	0.3 [7]
70-74	-	-	-	-	-	-	-	-	0.1 [7]	0.2 [7]
75+	-	-	-	-	-	-	-	-	-	-

Explanatory notes: see p. 451.

[1] Persons aged 15 to 74 years. [2] First and fourth quarters. [3] Prior to 2001: persons aged 15 years and over. [4] Men aged 18 to 64 years; women aged 18 to 59 years (with the exception of juvenile graduates). [5] 31st Dec. of each year. [6] Persons aged 15 years and over. [7] Data not reliable; coefficient of variation greater than 20%.

Notes explicatives: voir p. 454.

[1] Personnes âgées de 15 à 74 ans. [2] Premier et quatrième trimestres. [3] Avant 2001: personnes âgées de 15 ans et plus. [4] Hommes âgés de 18 à 64 ans; femmes âgées de 18 à 59 ans (à l'exception des jeunes diplômés). [5] 31 déc. de chaque année. [6] Personnes âgées de 15 ans et plus. [7] Données non fiables; coefficient de variation supérieur à 20%.

Notas explicativas: véase p. 457.

[1] Personas de 15 a 74 años. [2] Primero y cuarto trimestres. [3] Antes de 2001: personas de 15 años y más. [4] Hombres de 18 a 64 años; mujeres de 18 a 59 años (salvo los jovenes diplomados universitarios). [5] 31 dic. de cada año. [6] Personas de 15 años y más. [7] Datos no fiables; coeficiente de variación superior a 20%.

	Thousands			Milliers			Millares			
	1999	2000	2001	2002	2003	2004	2005	2006	2007	2008

Portugal (BA) [1] — Total unemployment - Chômage total - Desempleo total

Women - Femmes - Mujeres

	1999	2000	2001	2002	2003	2004	2005	2006	2007	2008
Total	116.9	116.2	122.0	149.1	181.4	192.2	224.1	233.1	251.8	232.7
15-19	10.4	12.7	12.6	12.0	14.2	14.1	10.4	10.8	11.0	10.3
20-24	24.5	21.8	23.6	28.9	33.3	31.5	37.4	33.7	36.3	36.2
25-29	19.0	20.2	20.3	29.4	32.4	35.3	45.8	48.4	51.2	45.0
30-34	17.8	16.0	14.5	18.8	28.5	24.9	29.5	33.2	37.1	32.0
35-39	13.5	10.7	13.0	17.8	21.0	23.6	28.8	24.9	30.0	24.6
40-44	12.8	11.2	12.6	14.4	19.5	20.5	23.4	27.2	27.0	26.0
45-49	9.0	9.0	8.8	9.8	13.0	15.8	19.7	21.3	22.4	22.3
50-54	5.9	8.0	9.1	8.6	9.1	12.4	13.7	18.6	19.2	18.4
55-59	2.9 [2]	4.7	4.9	6.3	7.2	10.1	10.9	10.6	12.4	13.4
60-64	1.7 [2]	1.8 [2]	2.6 [2]	3.1 [2]	3.2 [2]	3.7 [2]	4.4 [2]	4.2 [2]	5.2 [2]	4.5
65-69	-	-	-	-	-	-	0.2 [2]	0.1 [2]	0.1 [2]	-
70-74	-	-	-	-	-	-	-	-	-	-
75+	-	-	-	-	-	-	-	-	-	-

Roumanie (BA) [1] — Total unemployment - Chômage total - Desempleo total

Total - Total - Total

	1999	2000	2001	2002	2003	2004	2005	2006	2007	2008
Total	789.9	821.2	749.9	845.2 [3]	691.7	799.5	704.5	728.4	641.0	575.5
15-19	110.2	99.3	82.6	94.1 [3]	69.0	92.9	65.2	71.2	58.8	56.5
20-24	196.6	192.2	178.7	193.5 [3]	145.9	166.9	145.1	141.7	137.9	120.8
25-29	118.5	118.5	108.0	123.8 [3]	113.8	131.4	117.6	127.7	101.3	84.7
30-34	98.5	117.9	113.5	131.4 [3]	94.5	102.8	88.8	84.5	73.8	69.4
35-39	76.4	77.2	60.9	70.3 [3]	67.4	85.6	88.3	89.7	79.3	72.1
40-44	81.6	93.7	86.5	86.7 [3]	67.5	66.5	58.5	61.7	53.1	50.2
45-49	66.8	70.7	71.9	84.3 [3]	76.9	76.7	71.6	72.7	64.2	48.0
50-54	30.2	39.8	35.5	46.8 [3]	41.4	52.3	47.4	53.4	49.1	47.0
55-59	8.9	10.6	9.7	11.9 [3]	13.3	20.1	19.3	22.5	20.0	23.0
60-64	-	-	-	- [3]	-	-	-	-	-	-
65-69	-	-	-	- [3]	-	-	-	-	-	-
70-74	-	-	-	- [3]	-	-	-	-	-	-
75+	-	-	-	- [3]	-	-	-	-	-	-

Men - Hommes - Hombres

	1999	2000	2001	2002	2003	2004	2005	2006	2007	2008
Total	462.5	481.6	436.0	494.0 [3]	408.0	490.7	420.3	452.4	398.7	369.2
15-19	65.8	62.8	49.2	61.6 [3]	41.7	60.1	40.2	44.5	36.5	36.9
20-24	116.7	116.1	101.6	105.6 [3]	85.5	103.2	90.1	85.0	87.3	71.3
25-29	67.0	71.4	70.9	77.0 [3]	75.5	79.0	69.8	81.4	61.5	55.6
30-34	57.2	62.5	63.0	70.2 [3]	48.9	62.0	51.5	53.0	48.9	43.6
35-39	43.1	42.5	29.1	38.7 [3]	36.3	48.0	47.9	55.7	45.2	44.5
40-44	44.1	50.4	46.4	45.3 [3]	36.5	40.4	33.5	35.9	29.4	29.2
45-49	37.4	37.9	42.2	50.5 [3]	41.3	43.5	42.5	45.2	38.3	31.5
50-54	22.3	28.2	23.3	32.9 [3]	30.5	35.0	27.7	30.2	31.3	33.2
55-59	6.9	8.5	7.6	10.2 [3]	10.3	16.1	15.3	19.4	17.4	19.8
60-64	-	-	-	- [3]	-	-	-	-	-	-
65-69	-	-	-	- [3]	-	-	-	-	-	-
70-74	-	-	-	- [3]	-	-	-	-	-	-
75+	-	-	-	- [3]	-	-	-	-	-	-

Women - Femmes - Mujeres

	1999	2000	2001	2002	2003	2004	2005	2006	2007	2008
Total	327.3	339.5	313.9	351.1 [3]	283.7	308.7	284.1	276.0	242.3	206.3
15-19	44.3	36.5	33.4	32.5 [3]	27.2	32.7	25.0	26.9	22.3	19.6
20-24	79.9	76.0	77.0	87.8 [3]	60.3	63.6	55.0	56.7	50.6	49.5
25-29	51.4	47.1	37.0	46.7 [3]	38.3	52.3	47.8	46.3	39.8	29.1
30-34	41.3	55.3	50.4	61.2 [3]	45.5	40.8	37.2	31.6	24.9	25.8
35-39	33.3	34.7	31.7	31.6 [3]	31.1	37.5	40.5	34.1	34.1	27.6
40-44	37.5	43.3	40.0	41.4 [3]	30.9	26.0	25.0	25.8	23.7	21.0
45-49	29.3	32.8	29.6	33.7 [3]	35.6	33.1	29.1	27.5	25.9	16.5
50-54	7.9	11.5	12.2	13.8 [3]	10.9	17.2	19.7	23.2	17.8	13.8
55-59	-	2.0	2.0	- [3]	3.0	4.0	4.0	3.1	2.6	3.1
60-64	-	-	-	- [3]	-	-	-	-	-	-
65-69	-	-	-	- [3]	-	-	-	-	-	-
70-74	-	-	-	- [3]	-	-	-	-	-	-
75+	-	-	-	- [3]	-	-	-	-	-	-

Roumanie (FB) [1] [4] — Registered unemployment - Chômage enregistré - Desempleo registrado

Total - Total - Total

	1999	2000	2001	2002	2003	2004	2005	2006	2007	2008
Total	.	.	.	.	.	557.9	523.0	460.5	367.8	403.4
16-24	.	.	.	.	.	130.2	106.1	89.4	65.2	71.2
25-29	.	.	.	.	.	58.9	54.1	45.6	33.1	36.6
30-39	.	.	.	.	.	141.8	141.3	128.6	98.4	101.4
40-49	.	.	.	.	.	137.8	128.9	109.5	92.5	101.8
50-54	.	.	.	.	.	67.8	67.5	61.2	51.7	59.2
55+	.	.	.	.	.	21.3	25.0	26.3	26.9	33.2

Men - Hommes - Hombres

	1999	2000	2001	2002	2003	2004	2005	2006	2007	2008
Total	.	.	.	.	.	323.3	303.7	269.0	201.2	216.2
16-24	.	.	.	.	.	73.7	61.6	51.3	35.3	36.8
25-29	.	.	.	.	.	36.7	34.3	29.1	19.0	20.9
30-39	.	.	.	.	.	82.2	80.8	75.6	53.7	53.4
40-49	.	.	.	.	.	75.5	70.1	60.2	47.8	51.9
50-54	.	.	.	.	.	39.4	38.0	33.4	26.4	30.5
55+	.	.	.	.	.	15.8	18.9	19.4	19.0	22.7

Explanatory notes: see p. 451.

[1] Persons aged 15 years and over. [2] Data not reliable; coefficient of variation greater than 20%. [3] Estimates based on the 2002 Population Census results. [4] Dec. of each year.

Notes explicatives: voir p. 454.

[1] Personnes âgées de 15 ans et plus. [2] Données non fiables; coefficient de variation supérieur à 20%. [3] Estimations basées sur les résultats du Recensement de la population de 2002. [4] Déc. de chaque année.

Notas explicativas: véase p. 457.

[1] Personas de 15 años y más. [2] Datos no fiables; coeficiente de variación superior a 20%. [3] Estimaciones basadas en los resultados del Censo de población de 2002. [4] Dic. de cada año.

By age group   **Par groupe d'âge**   **Por grupo de edad**

	Thousands					Milliers			Millares	
	1999	2000	2001	2002	2003	2004	2005	2006	2007	2008

Roumanie (FB) [1] [2]   **Registered unemployment - Chômage enregistré - Desempleo registrado**

Women - Femmes - Mujeres

	1999	2000	2001	2002	2003	2004	2005	2006	2007	2008
Total	.	.	.	.	.	234.6	219.2	191.4	166.6	187.2
16-24	.	.	.	.	.	56.5	44.5	38.1	29.9	34.4
25-29	.	.	.	.	.	22.3	19.8	16.5	14.1	15.8
30-39	.	.	.	.	.	59.6	60.5	53.0	44.7	48.0
40-49	.	.	.	.	.	62.3	58.8	49.2	44.7	49.9
50-54	.	.	.	.	.	28.4	29.6	27.8	25.3	28.7
55+	.	.	.	.	.	5.5	6.0	6.9	7.9	10.4

Russian Federation (BA) [3]   **Total unemployment - Chômage total - Desempleo total**

Total - Total - Total

	1999	2000	2001	2002	2003	2004	2005	2006	2007	2008
Total	9 436	7 700	6 424	5 698	5 959	5 675	5 263	5 312	4 588	4 791
15-19	870	739	580	504	574	553	508	509	431	446
20-24	1 553	1 326	1 127	989	1 100	1 079	981	1 059	956	971
25-29	1 251	966	835	768	778	705	712	701	596	644
30-34	1 090	895	744	645	660	620	610	554	505	510
35-39	1 352	1 046	821	679	652	621	528	538	451	462
40-44	1 150	991	864	762	750	714	611	627	502	463
45-49	1 002	798	679	629	649	607	580	609	518	509
50-54	528	490	460	448	511	471	453	448	390	447
55-59	361	230	161	138	155	171	177	192	172	236
60-64	208	169	118	111	89	87	54	41	40	62
65-72	69	49	34	27	41	48	50	33	27	43

Men - Hommes - Hombres

	1999	2000	2001	2002	2003	2004	2005	2006	2007	2008
Total	4 939	4 057	3 450	3 014	3 121	2 975	2 725	2 811	2 453	2 542
15-19	427	365	292	247	285	276	237	260	236	236
20-24	835	705	607	515	580	573	519	570	522	515
25-29	685	518	473	421	420	381	375	379	320	348
30-34	567	472	395	344	355	328	331	306	266	275
35-39	727	567	451	360	352	325	260	287	236	248
40-44	588	512	455	414	388	380	331	321	264	240
45-49	484	424	362	328	337	304	291	323	263	255
50-54	262	243	237	228	250	233	223	215	203	223
55-59	207	138	98	81	88	98	108	110	105	143
60-64	117	95	62	58	44	50	28	22	21	38
65-72	39	18	18	17	22	27	22	17	16	21

Women - Femmes - Mujeres

	1999	2000	2001	2002	2003	2004	2005	2006	2007	2008
Total	4 497	3 643	2 974	2 685	2 838	2 699	2 538	2 501	2 136	2 250
15-19	443	374	288	257	289	277	271	249	195	210
20-24	718	621	520	474	520	506	461	489	435	456
25-29	566	449	362	347	358	324	337	322	276	296
30-34	523	423	349	301	304	292	280	248	239	236
35-39	625	480	370	319	301	296	268	251	215	214
40-44	562	479	409	347	362	334	280	305	237	223
45-49	518	374	317	301	312	303	288	286	255	253
50-54	266	247	223	220	262	238	230	234	187	224
55-59	154	92	63	57	67	73	69	82	67	92
60-64	91	73	56	53	45	37	26	19	19	24
65-72	31	31	16	10	19	21	27	15	11	22

San Marino (E) [1] [4]   **Registered unemployment - Chômage enregistré - Desempleo registrado**

Total - Total - Total

	1999	2000	2001	2002	2003	2004	2005	2006	2007	2008
Total	0.423	.	0.514	0.710	0.628	0.577	0.671	0.595	0.573	0.713
15-19	0.093	.	0.035	0.047	0.020	0.010	0.032	0.023	0.027	0.041
20-24	0.097	.	0.114	0.138	0.160	0.146	0.097	0.086	0.079	0.106
25-29	0.079	.	0.128	0.138	0.124	0.130	0.172	0.140	0.133	0.132
30-34	0.054	.	0.084	0.129	0.145	0.125	0.094	0.092	0.102	0.113
35-39	0.043	.	0.065	0.088	0.040	0.036	0.099	0.077	0.077	0.094
40-44	0.016	.	0.030	0.055	0.050	0.042	0.073	0.073	0.063	0.097
45-49	0.014	.	0.035	0.055	0.045	0.049	0.042	0.052	0.049	0.054
50-54	0.008	.	0.012	0.033	.	.	0.034	0.034	0.027	0.049
50+					0.044	0.039				
55-59	-	.	0.008	0.020	.	.	0.023	0.011	0.010	0.021
60-64							0.004	0.006	0.005	0.006
60+	-	.	0.002	0.007	.	.				
65-69							0.001	0.001	0.001	-
70-74										-
75+							-	-	-	-

Explanatory notes: see p. 451.   Notes explicatives: voir p. 454.   Notas explicativas: véase p. 457.

[1] Persons aged 15 years and over. [2] Dec. of each year. [3] Persons aged 15 to 72 years. [4] Dec.   [1] Personnes âgées de 15 ans et plus. [2] Déc. de chaque année. [3] Personnes âgées de 15 à 72 ans. [4] Déc.   [1] Personas de 15 años y más. [2] Dic. de cada año. [3] Personas de 15 a 72 años. [4] Dic.

	Thousands				Milliers				Millares	
	1999	2000	2001	2002	2003	2004	2005	2006	2007	2008

San Marino (E) [1][2] — Registered unemployment - Chômage enregistré - Desempleo registrado

Men - Hommes - Hombres

	1999	2000	2001	2002	2003	2004	2005	2006	2007	2008
Total	0.121	.	0.164	0.184	0.174	0.133	0.180	0.144	0.153	0.197
15-19	0.030	.	0.016	0.022	0.012	0.005	0.019	0.018	0.021	0.026
20-24	0.031	.	0.044	0.046	0.054	0.052	0.044	0.021	0.035	0.038
25-29	0.019	.	0.047	0.038	0.031	0.023	0.046	0.031	0.035	0.033
30-34	0.012	.	0.025	0.024	.	0.024	0.021	0.018	0.019	0.019
35-39	0.012	.	0.013	0.020	.	-	0.018	0.016	0.011	0.018
40-44	0.004	.	0.006	0.012	.	0.009	0.013	0.018	0.010	0.022
45-49	0.009	.	0.006	0.007	0.023	0.012	0.007	0.011	0.011	0.013
50-54	0.003	.	0.005	0.005	.	.	0.005	0.007	0.006	0.019
50+	.	.	.	.	0.014	0.008	.	.	.	.
55-59	0.001	.	0.001	0.005	.	.	0.007	0.002	0.004	0.007
60-64	.	.	.	.	.	.	-	0.001	-	0.002
60+	0.001	.	-	0.005	.	.	.	.	.	.
65-69	.	.	.	.	.	.	-	0.001	0.001	-
70-74	.	.	.	.	.	.	.	-	-	-
75+	.	.	.	.	.	.	-	-	-	-

Women - Femmes - Mujeres

	1999	2000	2001	2002	2003	2004	2005	2006	2007	2008
Total	0.302	.	0.350	0.526	0.454	0.444	0.491	0.451	0.420	0.516
15-19	0.063	.	0.019	0.025	0.008	0.005	0.013	0.005	0.006	0.015
20-24	0.066	.	0.070	0.092	0.106	0.094	0.053	0.065	0.044	0.068
25-29	0.060	.	0.081	0.100	0.093	0.107	0.126	0.109	0.098	0.099
30-34	0.042	.	0.059	0.105	.	0.115	0.073	0.074	0.083	0.094
35-39	0.031	.	0.052	0.068	.	0.036	0.081	0.061	0.066	0.076
40-44	0.012	.	0.024	0.043	.	0.033	0.060	0.055	0.053	0.075
45-49	0.005	.	0.029	0.048	0.072	0.037	0.035	0.041	0.038	0.041
50-54	0.005	.	0.007	0.028	.	.	0.029	0.027	0.021	0.030
50+	.	.	.	.	0.030	0.031	.	.	.	.
55-59	-	.	0.007	0.015	.	.	0.016	0.009	0.006	0.014
60-64	.	.	.	.	.	.	0.004	0.005	0.005	0.004
60+	-	.	0.002	0.002	.	.	.	.	.	.
65-69	.	.	.	.	.	.	0.001	-	-	-
70-74	.	.	.	.	.	.	.	-	-	-
75+	.	.	.	.	.	.	-	-	-	-

Serbia (BA) [1][3] — Total unemployment - Chômage total - Desempleo total

Total - Total - Total

	1999	2000	2001	2002	2003	2004	2005	2006	2007	2008
Total	.	.	.	.	.	665.4	719.9	693.0	585.5	445.4
15-19	.	.	.	.	.	48.1	47.5	55.2	34.8	27.4
20-24	.	.	.	.	.	126.4	118.1	114.3	92.9	75.2
25-29	.	.	.	.	.	114.1	128.6	101.3	89.4	78.9
30-34	.	.	.	.	.	78.7	95.6	93.1	77.4	54.7
35-39	.	.	.	.	.	71.1	81.5	72.7	65.8	44.2
40-44	.	.	.	.	.	72.0	80.8	77.6	60.3	42.5
45-49	.	.	.	.	.	61.0	69.9	73.9	62.6	47.5
50-54	.	.	.	.	.	58.4	58.5	69.4	58.8	42.2
55-59	.	.	.	.	.	28.0	30.3	30.0	38.7	27.3
60-64	.	.	.	.	.	6.4	7.9	4.2	3.6	5.0
65-69	.	.	.	.	.	0.7	0.8	1.1	1.3	0.4
70-74	.	.	.	.	.	0.7	0.4	-	-	-
75+	.	.	.	.	.	-	-	-	-	-

Men - Hommes - Hombres

	1999	2000	2001	2002	2003	2004	2005	2006	2007	2008
Total	.	.	.	.	.	303.2	329.8	339.8	289.8	217.5
15-19	.	.	.	.	.	25.8	25.5	33.8	23.0	15.2
20-24	.	.	.	.	.	64.9	64.9	61.0	48.8	38.6
25-29	.	.	.	.	.	48.4	55.6	51.7	45.8	43.8
30-34	.	.	.	.	.	30.6	37.4	38.6	31.7	23.7
35-39	.	.	.	.	.	28.0	27.4	31.7	25.1	18.4
40-44	.	.	.	.	.	25.5	34.2	28.9	26.9	15.2
45-49	.	.	.	.	.	23.8	27.7	37.3	26.8	18.4
50-54	.	.	.	.	.	29.9	27.6	35.1	30.3	21.8
55-59	.	.	.	.	.	20.3	22.0	18.5	27.8	17.4
60-64	.	.	.	.	.	5.2	6.4	2.6	2.8	4.7
65-69	.	.	.	.	.	0.3	0.8	0.8	0.8	0.2
70-74	.	.	.	.	.	0.4	0.4	-	-	-
75+	.	.	.	.	.	-	-	-	-	-

Women - Femmes - Mujeres

	1999	2000	2001	2002	2003	2004	2005	2006	2007	2008
Total	.	.	.	.	.	362.2	390.1	353.2	295.7	227.9
15-19	.	.	.	.	.	22.2	22.0	21.5	11.8	12.2
20-24	.	.	.	.	.	61.5	53.2	53.2	44.1	36.6
25-29	.	.	.	.	.	65.6	72.9	49.6	43.6	35.1
30-34	.	.	.	.	.	48.1	58.3	54.5	45.7	30.9
35-39	.	.	.	.	.	43.2	54.1	41.0	40.7	25.8
40-44	.	.	.	.	.	46.4	46.6	48.7	33.3	27.3
45-49	.	.	.	.	.	37.1	42.2	36.6	35.8	29.1
50-54	.	.	.	.	.	28.5	30.9	34.4	28.5	20.3
55-59	.	.	.	.	.	7.7	8.3	11.6	10.9	9.9
60-64	.	.	.	.	.	1.2	1.5	1.6	0.9	0.3
65-69	.	.	.	.	.	0.4	-	0.4	0.4	0.2
70-74	.	.	.	.	.	0.3	-	-	-	-
75+	.	.	.	.	.	-	-	-	-	-

Explanatory notes: see p. 451.   Notes explicatives: voir p. 454.   Notas explicativas: véase p. 457.

[1] Persons aged 15 years and over. [2] Dec. [3] Oct.   [1] Personnes âgées de 15 ans et plus. [2] Déc. [3] Oct.   [1] Personas de 15 años y más. [2] Dic. [3] Oct.

	UNEMPLOYMENT	CHÔMAGE	DESEMPLEO
	By age group	**Par groupe d'âge**	**Por grupo de edad**

	Thousands				Milliers				Millares	
	1999	2000	2001	2002	2003	2004	2005	2006	2007	2008

Slovakia (BA) [1] [2] — Total unemployment - Chômage total - Desempleo total

Total - Total - Total

	1999	2000	2001	2002	2003	2004	2005	2006	2007	2008
Total	416.8	485.2	508.0	486.9	459.2	481.0	427.5	353.4	291.9	257.5
15-19	61.6	55.9	51.9	39.8	33.0	24.7	21.5	20.5	15.1	11.9
20-24	81.8	97.6	108.1	106.8	90.7	89.4	74.0	59.3	43.9	39.0
25-29	56.5	66.3	70.7	63.8	62.2	68.2	62.1	48.1	42.6	41.3
30-34	52.9	57.1	58.6	54.5	53.5	53.9	51.2	42.8	38.3	34.0
35-39	49.1	60.3	57.4	55.8	53.6	53.9	48.5	40.7	30.0	28.4
40-44	44.3	52.9	54.6	55.4	54.3	53.8	48.4	39.0	36.0	27.8
45-49	36.3	50.3	55.6	50.8	52.0	58.9	51.8	42.1	33.3	28.7
50-54	22.7	30.2	35.8	39.9	41.3	52.5	44.6	40.8	34.5	30.1
55-59	9.8	13.1	13.2	17.8	16.4	22.0	20.6	17.5	15.6	14.7
60-64	1.0	1.0	1.6	1.6	1.8	2.9	3.9	2.5	2.4	1.6
65-69	0.5	0.3	0.5	0.7	0.3	0.3	0.7	0.1	0.2	0.1
70+	0.3	0.7	0.2	0.1	0.1	-	0.1	-	-	0.1

Men - Hommes - Hombres

	1999	2000	2001	2002	2003	2004	2005	2006	2007	2008
Total	226.6	265.5	282.5	263.9	246.5	250.0	223.6	179.5	143.5	124.6
15-19	31.6	27.5	27.4	22.0	18.4	14.1	11.5	12.3	8.1	6.9
20-24	49.3	60.9	66.3	62.3	52.6	52.0	44.1	32.9	25.9	22.2
25-29	31.1	36.9	39.4	33.6	35.6	36.1	32.8	26.8	21.0	21.1
30-34	24.5	26.6	30.8	27.5	23.6	25.2	25.1	18.6	18.4	15.8
35-39	24.2	30.0	30.7	28.8	27.4	26.0	24.7	19.2	13.3	11.9
40-44	24.2	28.4	28.6	31.0	28.1	24.0	21.9	19.1	17.6	11.7
45-49	18.7	25.8	28.6	24.6	24.7	28.3	25.1	18.5	14.2	13.5
50-54	13.8	17.6	18.7	18.4	21.1	25.1	20.7	18.1	13.4	12.3
55-59	8.3	11.0	10.6	14.1	14.0	16.9	15.4	12.4	10.1	8.2
60-64	0.6	0.7	1.0	1.3	1.1	1.9	2.0	1.7	1.5	0.9
65-69	0.3	0.1	0.5	0.3	0.1	0.2	0.3	0.1	0.1	
70+	0.1	0.2	0.2	0.1	-	-	0.1	-	-	0.1

Women - Femmes - Mujeres

	1999	2000	2001	2002	2003	2004	2005	2006	2007	2008
Total	190.2	219.7	225.5	223.0	212.7	231.0	203.8	173.9	148.4	132.8
15-19	30.0	28.4	24.5	17.9	14.6	10.5	10.0	8.2	7.0	5.0
20-24	32.5	36.7	41.8	44.6	38.1	37.5	29.9	26.4	17.9	16.8
25-29	25.4	29.4	31.3	30.2	26.7	32.1	29.3	21.3	21.7	20.1
30-34	28.4	30.5	27.8	26.9	30.0	28.7	26.1	24.2	20.0	18.2
35-39	24.9	30.3	26.7	27.0	26.2	27.9	23.8	21.5	16.7	16.5
40-44	20.1	24.5	26.0	24.4	26.3	29.8	26.5	20.0	18.3	16.0
45-49	17.6	24.5	27.0	26.2	27.4	30.6	26.7	23.7	19.0	15.2
50-54	8.9	12.6	17.1	21.4	20.2	27.5	23.9	22.7	21.1	17.8
55-59	1.5	2.1	2.6	3.8	2.4	5.2	5.3	5.1	5.5	6.5
60-64	0.4	0.3	0.6	0.3	0.7	1.0	1.9	0.9	1.0	0.8
65-69	0.2	0.2	-	0.4	0.2	0.1	0.4	-	0.1	-
70+	0.2	0.5	-	-	-	-	-	-	-	-

Slovakia (FB) [1] [3] — Registered unemployment - Chômage enregistré - Desempleo registrado

Total - Total - Total

	1999	2000	2001	2002	2003	2004	2005	2006	2007	2008
Total	535.2	506.5	533.7	504.1	452.2	383.2	333.8	273.4	239.9	248.5
15-19	71.1	62.1	52.1	38.1	24.6	20.6	18.7	15.1	13.4	6.8
20-24	98.9	98.0	98.6	90.3	73.0	52.1	44.9	34.7	28.7	35.1
25-29	65.8	64.1	69.1	67.0	58.5	47.5	39.6	31.6	27.1	30.5
30-34	59.7	54.3	57.0	55.4	51.2	44.2	39.0	32.7	28.7	29.5
35-39	61.3	55.3	59.1	56.2	51.8	43.5	36.8	29.8	25.8	27.7
40-44	63.5	57.3	60.8	57.4	54.2	47.4	40.7	33.1	28.3	27.2
45-49	61.0	57.2	62.6	61.5	59.6	52.7	45.5	36.9	31.1	30.1
50-54	39.3	42.4	53.1	55.0	55.1	52.1	46.7	39.3	34.8	33.0
55-59	14.0	15.2	20.7	22.4	23.5	21.0	19.9	18.4	19.6	24.6
60+	0.6	0.6	0.6	0.8	0.7	2.1	2.0	1.8	2.4	4.0

Men - Hommes - Hombres

	1999	2000	2001	2002	2003	2004	2005	2006	2007	2008
Total	299.1	275.0	295.0	277.3	247.8	193.1	164.1	130.7	112.8	119.8
15-19	38.8	33.4	29.4	21.3	14.0	11.0	9.9	7.7	6.7	3.8
20-24	60.9	60.2	61.2	55.1	44.3	28.6	23.9	17.7	14.3	18.1
25-29	36.4	34.4	38.6	37.4	32.9	24.7	20.1	15.6	12.9	15.7
30-34	29.8	26.2	28.4	27.7	25.7	20.2	17.3	14.4	12.5	13.8
35-39	31.9	27.4	29.6	28.1	25.4	19.4	16.1	12.9	10.9	12.1
40-44	33.9	29.3	31.4	29.4	27.3	22.0	18.2	14.6	12.1	11.7
45-49	32.3	28.7	31.7	31.2	29.7	24.5	20.6	16.5	13.7	13.4
50-54	22.6	21.9	26.1	26.9	27.2	24.1	20.8	17.3	15.0	14.5
55-59	12.2	13.3	18.3	19.7	20.8	16.7	15.5	12.5	12.5	13.2
60+	0.3	0.2	0.3	0.5	0.5	1.9	1.7	1.5	2.2	3.5

Women - Femmes - Mujeres

	1999	2000	2001	2002	2003	2004	2005	2006	2007	2008
Total	236.1	231.5	238.7	226.8	204.4	190.1	169.7	142.7	127.1	128.7
15-19	32.4	28.7	22.7	16.8	10.6	9.6	8.8	7.4	6.7	3.0
20-24	38.0	37.8	37.4	35.2	28.7	23.5	21.1	17.0	14.4	17.0
25-29	29.3	29.7	30.5	29.6	25.6	22.8	19.4	16.1	14.2	14.8
30-34	29.9	28.1	28.6	27.7	25.5	24.0	21.8	18.3	16.2	15.7
35-39	29.4	27.9	29.5	28.1	26.4	24.1	20.7	16.9	14.9	15.6
40-44	29.6	28.0	29.4	28.0	26.9	25.4	22.5	18.5	16.2	15.5
45-49	28.7	28.5	30.9	30.3	29.9	28.2	24.9	20.3	17.4	16.7
50-54	16.7	20.5	27.0	28.1	27.9	28.0	25.9	22.1	19.8	18.5
55-59	1.8	1.9	2.4	2.7	2.7	4.3	4.4	5.9	7.1	11.4
60+	0.3	0.4	0.3	0.3	0.2	0.2	0.2	0.2	0.2	0.5

Explanatory notes: see p. 451.

Notes explicatives: voir p. 454.

Notas explicativas: véase p. 457.

[1] Persons aged 15 years and over. [2] Excl. persons on child-care leave. [3] 31st Dec. of each year.

[1] Personnes âgées de 15 ans et plus. [2] Non compris les personnes en congé parental. [3] 31 déc. de chaque année.

[1] Personas de 15 años y más. [2] Excl. las personas con licencia parental. [3] 31 dic. de cada año.

By age group — Par groupe d'âge — Por grupo de edad

Thousands — Milliers — Millares

	1999	2000	2001	2002	2003	2004	2005	2006	2007	2008
Slovenia (BA) [1][2]				Total unemployment - Chômage total - Desempleo total						
Total - Total - Total										
Total	71	69	57	58	63	61	58	61	48	43
15-19	6	5	4	3	2	3	2	3	2	2
20-24	17	13	13	13	12	13	11	12	7	8
25-29	10	10	8	9	13	11	10	13	10	8
30-34	8	7	6	8	7	7	5	5	6	5
35-39	7	7	7	5	6	7	9	5	5	4
40-44	6	7	4	5	9	7	7	7	4	4
45-49	10	9	8	9	7	5	6	7	5	5
50-54	5	7	3	5	5	6	5	5	6	4
55-59	2	2	2	1	2	2	2	2	3	3
60-64	-	-	-	-	-	-	-	-	-	1
65-69	-	-	-	-	-	-	-	-	-	-
70-74	-	-	-	-	-	-	-	-	-	-
75+	-	-	-	-	-	-	-	-	-	-
Men - Hommes - Hombres										
Total	37	36	29	30	32	31	30	28	20	20
15-19	3	3	2	2	1	1	1	3	1	1
20-24	8	6	7	7	6	6	5	6	4	4
25-29	6	5	4	3	6	5	4	5	3	3
30-34	4	3	3	4	3	3	2	2	3	2
35-39	4	3	3	3	2	4	3	2	2	2
40-44	3	4	2	3	5	3	4	3	1	2
45-49	5	5	5	5	5	3	3	3	3	2
50-54	3	4	1	3	3	4	4	2	3	2
55-59	2	2	2	1	1	1	2	1	2	2
60-64	-	-	-	-	-	-	-	-	-	-
65-69	-	-	-	-	-	-	-	-	-	-
70-74	-	-	-	-	-	-	-	-	-	-
75+	-	-	-	-	-	-	-	-	-	-
Women - Femmes - Mujeres										
Total	34	33	28	28	31	30	28	33	28	23
15-19	3	2	2	1	1	2	-	1	1	1
20-24	9	7	6	6	6	7	5	7	3	4
25-29	4	5	4	6	7	6	6	8	8	5
30-34	4	4	3	4	4	4	3	3	4	3
35-39	3	4	4	2	4	3	5	3	4	2
40-44	3	3	2	2	4	4	3	4	2	2
45-49	5	4	3	4	2	2	4	3	3	3
50-54	2	3	2	2	2	2	2	3	3	2
55-59	-	-	-	-	1	1	-	1	1	1
60-64	-	-	-	-	-	-	-	-	-	1
65-69	-	-	-	-	-	-	-	-	-	-
70-74	-	-	-	-	-	-	-	-	-	-
75+	-	-	-	-	-	-	-	-	-	-
Slovenia (FB) [1][3]				Registered unemployment - Chômage enregistré - Desempleo registrado						
Total - Total - Total										
Total	.	106.6	101.9	102.6	97.7	93.1	.	.	.	.
15-18	.	0.6	0.5	0.5	0.4	0.3	.	.	.	.
19-25	.	21.7	21.1	21.1	21.8	20.6	.	.	.	.
26-30	.	11.4	11.8	12.8	14.4	14.9	.	.	.	.
31-40	.	17.8	17.0	17.5	18.1	17.4	.	.	.	.
41-44	.	10.8	10.1	10.3	9.7	9.0	.	.	.	.
45-49	.	15.0	13.9	14.3	12.5	11.2	.	.	.	.
50-59	.	28.2	26.3	24.9	19.9	18.8	.	.	.	.
60+	.	1.1	1.2	1.4	1.1	1.0	.	.	.	.
Men - Hommes - Hombres										
Total	.	52.5	50.2	50.1	46.1	43.8	.	.	.	.
15-18	.	0.4	0.3	0.3	0.2	0.2	.	.	.	.
19-25	.	10.2	10.1	9.9	10.2	9.7	.	.	.	.
26-30	.	4.9	5.0	5.2	5.9	6.0	.	.	.	.
31-40	.	7.9	7.4	7.4	7.4	7.0	.	.	.	.
41-44	.	5.2	4.8	4.8	4.4	3.9	.	.	.	.
45-49	.	7.0	6.8	6.9	5.7	5.1	.	.	.	.
50-59	.	15.8	14.6	14.2	11.4	10.8	.	.	.	.
60+	.	1.0	1.1	1.2	1.0	0.9	.	.	.	.
Women - Femmes - Mujeres										
Total	.	54.1	51.7	52.5	51.6	49.3	.	.	.	.
15-18	.	0.2	0.2	0.2	0.2	0.1	.	.	.	.
19-25	.	11.5	11.0	11.2	11.6	10.9	.	.	.	.
26-30	.	6.5	6.7	7.5	8.5	8.8	.	.	.	.
31-40	.	9.9	9.6	10.1	10.7	10.3	.	.	.	.
41-44	.	5.5	5.2	5.5	5.4	5.1	.	.	.	.
45-49	.	8.0	7.1	7.4	6.8	6.2	.	.	.	.
50-59	.	12.4	11.7	10.7	8.5	7.9	.	.	.	.
60+	.	0.1	0.1	0.1	0.1	0.1	.	.	.	.

Explanatory notes: see p. 451. — Notes explicatives: voir p. 454. — Notas explicativas: véase p. 457.

[1] Persons aged 15 years and over. [2] Second quarter of each year. [3] 31st Dec. of each year.
[1] Personnes âgées de 15 ans et plus. [2] Deuxième trimestre de chaque année. [3] 31 déc. de chaque année.
[1] Personas de 15 años y más. [2] Segundo trimestre de cada año. [3] 31 dic. de cada año.

UNEMPLOYMENT	CHÔMAGE	DESEMPLEO
By age group	**Par groupe d'âge**	**Por grupo de edad**

	Thousands			Milliers				Millares		
	1999	2000	2001	2002	2003	2004	2005	2006	2007	2008

Suisse (BA) [1] [2] — Total unemployment - Chômage total - Desempleo total

Total - Total - Total

	1999	2000	2001	2002	2003	2004	2005	2006	2007	2008
Total	122	106	101	119	170	179	185	169	156	147
15-19					17	17	21	19	17	18
15-24	32	27	32	33						
20-24					33	28	30	28	26	25
25-29					27	26	22	19	20	16
25-39	40	36	31	48						
30-34					19	20	21	20	13	12
35-39					19	20	19	19	18	16
40-44					15	17	19	16	15	17
40-54	34	28	27	28						
45-49					14	19	16	15	14	13
50-54					11	14	14	13	12	11
55-59					9	11	13	9	11	9
55-64	13	14	9	11						
60-64					5	8	9	10	9	8
65-69					[3]	[3]	[3]	[3]	[3]	[3]
65+	2	1	1	-						
70-74					[3]	[3]	[3]	[3]	[3]	[3]
75+					[3]	[3]	[3]	[3]	[3]	[3]

Men - Hommes - Hombres

	1999	2000	2001	2002	2003	2004	2005	2006	2007	2008
Total	59	51	38	62	86	89	88	78	68	66
15-19					10	10	9	10	8	8
15-24	16	17	17	22						
20-24					15	14	16	15	13	13
25-29					14	12	10	9	9	8 [4]
25-39	20	15	8	23						
30-34					9	9	9	8	4 [4]	3 [4]
35-39					9	9	7	6	6	6
40-44					6	8	9	6	6	8
40-54	14	10	7	11						
45-49					8	10	7	7	5	5 [4]
50-54					5	7	8	7	6 [4]	6
55-59					5	5	8	4 [4]	4 [4]	4 [4]
55-64	8	9	6	7						
60-64					4	5	5 [4]	5	5 [4]	5 [4]
65-69					[3]	[3]	[3]	[3]	[3]	[3]
65+	1	0	0	-						
70-74					[3]	[3]	[3]	[3]	[3]	[3]
75+					[3]	[3]	[3]	[3]	[3]	[3]

Women - Femmes - Mujeres

	1999	2000	2001	2002	2003	2004	2005	2006	2007	2008
Total	62	55	63	57	84	89	97	91	88	80
15-19					8	7	12	9	8	9
15-24	16	10	15	11						
20-24					17	13	14	12	13	12
25-29					12	14	12	10	11	8
25-39	21	21	22	25						
30-34					10	11	13	11	9	8
35-39					10	11	12	13	12	10
40-44					9	9	10	10	9	9
40-54	20	18	20	17						
45-49					6	9	9	8	8	8
50-54					7	7	6	7	6	5
55-59					4 [4]	6	5 [4]	5 [4]	7	5 [4]
55-64	5	5	3	4						
60-64					2 [4]	2 [4]	4 [4]	4 [4]	4 [4]	3 [4]
65-69					[3]	[3]	[3]	[3]	[3]	[3]
65+	1	1	1	-						
70-74					[3]	[3]	[3]	[3]	[3]	[3]
75+					[3]	[3]	[3]	[3]	[3]	[3]

Suisse (FB) [1] — Registered unemployment - Chômage enregistré - Desempleo registrado

Total - Total - Total

	1999	2000	2001	2002	2003	2004	2005	2006	2007	2008
Total	98.6	72.0	67.2	100.5	145.7	153.1	148.5	131.5	109.2	101.7
15-19	3.5	2.5	2.5	3.9	6.1	7.1	7.3	6.4	5.0	4.3
20-24	11.2	7.6	7.4	12.5	20.0	21.2	20.7	17.4	13.3	12.1
25-29	13.7	9.5	9.0	14.1	20.8	21.2	21.0	17.6	14.6	13.7
30-34	14.9	10.8	10.2	14.9	20.7	20.8	19.4	16.7	13.8	13.1
35-39	13.7	10.3	9.7	14.6	20.4	20.5	18.9	16.2	13.4	12.3
40-44	11.5	8.3	7.9	11.7	17.1	17.9	17.6	15.7	13.4	12.5
45-49	9.3	6.9	6.5	9.5	13.3	14.5	14.3	13.0	11.3	11.1
50-54	8.5	6.2	5.6	7.9	11.1	11.7	11.6	10.7	9.1	8.7
55-59	6.9	5.3	4.7	6.5	9.3	10.2	10.2	9.3	8.0	7.4
60+	5.9	4.5	3.9	5.0	6.8	8.0	8.4	8.3	7.3	6.5

Explanatory notes: see p. 451.

[1] Persons aged 15 years and over. [2] Second quarter of each year. [3] Not indicated due to lack of statistical reliability. [4] Relative statistical reliability.

Notes explicatives: voir p. 454.

[1] Personnes âgées de 15 ans et plus. [2] Deuxième trimestre de chaque année. [3] Non indiqué en raison du manque de fiabilité statistique. [4] Fiabilité statistique relative.

Notas explicativas: véase p. 457.

[1] Personas de 15 años y más. [2] Segundo trimestre de cada año. [3] No se indica por la falta de confiabilidad estadística. [4] Confiabilidad estadística relativa.

UNEMPLOYMENT / CHÔMAGE / DESEMPLEO

By age group / Par groupe d'âge / Por grupo de edad

	Thousands / Milliers / Millares									
	1999	2000	2001	2002	2003	2004	2005	2006	2007	2008

Suisse (FB) [1]

Registered unemployment - Chômage enregistré - Desempleo registrado

Men - Hommes - Hombres

	1999	2000	2001	2002	2003	2004	2005	2006	2007	2008
Total	52.6	37.8	35.4	55.9	81.7	83.6	78.8	68.1	56.3	53.5
15-19	1.7	1.2	1.2	2.0	3.0	3.4	3.5	3.0	2.4	2.2
20-24	5.5	3.5	3.4	6.5	10.7	11.1	10.5	8.6	6.4	6.0
25-29	6.6	4.4	4.3	7.4	11.2	11.1	10.3	8.8	7.2	6.8
30-34	7.3	5.2	4.9	8.0	11.3	11.0	10.0	8.4	6.8	6.6
35-39	7.1	5.2	5.0	8.0	11.3	11.0	9.8	8.3	6.8	6.4
40-44	6.0	4.4	4.2	6.4	9.5	9.7	9.3	8.1	6.9	6.6
45-49	5.0	3.8	3.6	5.4	7.6	8.1	7.7	6.9	6.0	5.9
50-54	4.8	3.5	3.2	4.6	6.4	6.6	6.4	5.8	4.9	4.8
55-59	4.0	3.1	2.8	4.0	5.6	6.0	5.8	5.1	4.4	4.2
60+	4.6	3.5	3.0	3.6	5.0	5.7	5.6	5.3	4.5	4.0

Women - Femmes - Mujeres

	1999	2000	2001	2002	2003	2004	2005	2006	2007	2008
Total	46.0	34.2	31.8	44.6	64.0	69.5	69.7	63.4	52.9	48.3
15-19	1.8	1.3	1.3	1.9	3.1	3.7	3.8	3.4	2.5	2.1
20-24	5.7	4.1	3.9	6.0	9.3	10.1	10.3	8.9	6.9	6.1
25-29	7.1	5.1	4.8	6.7	9.6	10.1	9.8	8.9	7.4	6.9
30-34	7.6	5.6	5.1	6.9	9.5	9.8	9.4	8.4	7.0	6.5
35-39	6.6	5.1	4.8	6.6	9.1	9.5	9.2	7.9	6.6	5.9
40-44	5.1	4.0	3.8	5.2	7.6	8.2	8.3	7.6	6.5	5.9
45-49	4.2	3.1	2.9	4.1	5.7	6.5	6.6	6.2	5.4	5.2
50-54	3.6	2.7	2.4	2.5	4.7	5.1	5.2	4.9	4.2	3.9
55-59	2.9	2.2	1.9	2.5	3.7	4.2	4.4	4.2	3.6	3.3
60+	1.3	1.0	1.0	1.3	1.8	2.3	2.8	3.1	2.8	2.4

Sweden (BA) [2]

Total unemployment - Chômage total - Desempleo total

Total - Total - Total

	1999	2000	2001	2002	2003	2004	2005	2006	2007	2008
Total	241	203	175	176	217	246 |	270 [3]	246	298	305
15-19	.	.	.	.	.	.	.	.	63	70
16-19	11	12	12	13	15	17 |	25 [3]	26	.	.
20-24	34	24	26	29	33	41 |	45 [3]	45	55	58
25-29	31	26	22	23	30	35 |	39 [3]	32	33	32
30-34	31	24	19	19	26	28 |	33 [3]	26	26	25
35-39	27	22	22	20	23	27 |	30 [3]	23	24	23
40-44	25	20	17	17	22	25 |	27 [3]	24	25	22
45-49	22	17	12	14	18	19 |	21 [3]	17	18	21
50-54	20	19	15	13	15	17 |	17 [3]	19	17	18
55-59	21	20	16	16	18	20 |	18 [3]	18	17	17
60-64	17	17	15	14	16	18 |	17 [3]	16	18	16
65-69	.	.	.	.	.	.	.	.	-	-
70-74	.	.	.	.	.	.	.	.	-	-

Men - Hommes - Hombres

	1999	2000	2001	2002	2003	2004	2005	2006	2007	2008
Total	133	114	99	101	123	137 |	148 [3]	131	149	152
15-19	.	.	.	.	.	.	.	.	30	32
16-19	6	6	7	7	7	9 |	13 [3]	13	.	.
20-24	19	14	15	17	20	23 |	26 [3]	25	28	31
25-29	16	14	12	12	16	19 |	20 [3]	17	16	16
30-34	16	12	10	11	14	15 |	16 [3]	13	12	12
35-39	15	12	12	11	13	14 |	15 [3]	11	11	11
40-44	14	11	10	9	13	13 |	14 [3]	12	13	10
45-49	12	10	7	8	10	11 |	12 [3]	9	10	11
50-54	12	12	9	8	10	9 |	9 [3]	11	9	9
55-59	13	12	9	10	11	13 |	11 [3]	10	10	10
60-64	9	10	9	8	9	10 |	11 [3]	10	10	9
65-69	.	.	.	.	.	.	.	.	-	-
70-74	.	.	.	.	.	.	.	.	-	-

Women - Femmes - Mujeres

	1999	2000	2001	2002	2003	2004	2005	2006	2007	2008
Total	107	89	76	76	94	109 |	123 [3]	114	148	152
15-19	.	.	.	.	.	.	.	.	33	38
16-19	5	6	5	6	8	8 |	12 [3]	12	.	.
20-24	15	10	11	12	13	18 |	19 [3]	20	26	27
25-29	15	12	10	11	14	16 |	19 [3]	15	17	16
30-34	15	12	9	8	12	13 |	16 [3]	13	14	14
35-39	12	10	10	9	10	13 |	14 [3]	12	13	11
40-44	11	9	7	8	9	12 |	13 [3]	12	13	13
45-49	10	7	5	6	8	8 |	9 [3]	8	8	10
50-54	8	7	6	5	5	8 |	8 [3]	8	8	8
55-59	8	8	7	6	7	7 |	7 [3]	8	8	8
60-64	8	7	6	6	7	8 |	5 [3]	6	7	7
65-69	.	.	.	.	.	.	.	.	-	-
70-74	.	.	.	.	.	.	.	.	-	-

Explanatory notes: see p. 451.

[1] Persons aged 15 years and over. [2] Persons aged 15 to 74 years; prior to 2007: 16 to 64 years. [3] Methodology revised; data not strictly comparable.

Notes explicatives: voir p. 454.

[1] Personnes âgées de 15 ans et plus. [2] Personnes âgées de 15 à 74 ans; avant 2007: 16 à 64 ans. [3] Méthodologie révisée; les données ne sont pas strictement comparables.

Notas explicativas: véase p. 457.

[1] Personas de 15 años y más. [2] Personas de 15 a 74 años; antes de 2007: 16 a 64 años. [3] Metodología revisada; los datos no son estrictamente comparables.

UNEMPLOYMENT	CHÔMAGE	DESEMPLEO
By age group	**Par groupe d'âge**	**Por grupo de edad**

	Thousands				Milliers				Millares	
	1999	2000	2001	2002	2003	2004	2005	2006	2007	2008

Sweden (FB) [1] — Registered unemployment - Chômage enregistré - Desempleo registrado

Total - Total - Total

	1999	2000	2001	2002	2003	2004	2005	2006	2007	2008
Total	276.680	231.245	193.008	185.838	223.023	239.201	241.434	210.891	169.516	150.384
15-19	7.918	6.257	6.650	6.452	8.133	8.473	9.737	8.429	8.059	8.976
20-24	33.803	25.863	25.825	26.697	34.304	34.320	36.134	30.103	26.333	21.172
25-29	41.376	33.024	28.665	29.914	34.629	37.424	36.944	31.261	21.983	20.198
30-34	40.374	31.361	25.249	25.209	29.922	32.319	31.667	26.702	19.548	18.130
35-39	34.392	28.813	23.624	23.452	28.276	30.215	28.552	24.054	18.426	16.931
40-44	28.169	22.972	18.087	17.728	22.065	24.801	25.354	22.776	18.624	17.068
45-49	24.690	19.841	15.084	14.313	17.734	19.798	19.990	18.005	15.268	14.379
50-54	24.488	19.785	14.390	12.714	15.817	17.387	17.393	15.757	13.274	11.971
55-59	21.780	19.944	15.293	13.096	16.011	17.755	17.909	15.920	13.115	10.972
60-64	19.626	23.339	20.103	16.233	16.098	16.674	17.717	17.827	14.834	10.489
65+	0.065	0.046	0.039	0.029	0.033	0.035	0.038	0.056	0.052	0.098

Men - Hommes - Hombres

	1999	2000	2001	2002	2003	2004	2005	2006	2007	2008
Total	151.690	126.940	107.188	105.418	127.430	135.090	132.000	114.169	90.268	80.903
15-19	4.064	3.189	3.548	3.489	4.346	4.465	5.107	4.397	4.381	5.006
20-24	19.209	14.636	14.911	15.676	20.238	20.033	20.787	17.198	15.079	12.472
25-29	21.514	17.062	15.266	16.550	19.427	20.728	19.925	16.747	11.552	10.801
30-34	20.848	15.917	12.885	13.272	15.925	16.910	15.985	13.400	9.558	9.042
35-39	18.498	15.322	12.523	12.665	15.243	15.998	14.318	11.813	8.694	8.153
40-44	15.740	12.852	10.118	10.101	12.586	13.893	13.445	11.816	9.248	8.441
45-49	14.214	11.422	8.804	8.536	10.484	11.571	11.264	9.986	8.109	7.660
50-54	14.124	11.565	8.486	7.711	9.662	10.500	10.089	9.057	7.491	6.702
55-59	12.636	11.641	8.945	7.984	9.840	10.852	10.554	9.249	7.513	6.380
60-64	10.800	13.305	11.677	9.417	9.653	10.118	10.502	10.473	8.608	6.178
65+	0.040	0.028	0.024	0.018	0.022	0.022	0.024	0.033	0.035	0.068

Women - Femmes - Mujeres

	1999	2000	2001	2002	2003	2004	2005	2006	2007	2008
Total	124.990	104.305	85.820	80.420	95.593	104.111	109.435	96.722	79.248	69.481
15-19	3.854	3.068	3.102	2.963	3.786	4.008	4.630	4.033	3.678	3.970
20-24	14.594	11.227	10.914	11.021	14.066	14.287	15.347	12.905	11.254	8.701
25-29	19.862	15.962	13.399	13.364	15.201	16.696	17.019	14.514	10.431	9.395
30-34	19.526	15.444	12.364	11.938	13.996	15.409	15.682	13.303	9.990	9.088
35-39	15.894	13.491	11.101	10.787	13.033	14.217	14.234	12.241	9.732	8.778
40-44	12.429	10.120	7.969	7.627	9.479	10.908	11.909	10.960	9.376	8.627
45-49	10.476	8.419	6.280	5.777	7.250	8.227	8.726	8.019	7.159	6.720
50-54	10.364	8.220	5.904	5.003	6.154	6.887	7.304	6.700	5.783	5.270
55-59	9.144	8.303	6.348	5.112	6.171	6.904	7.355	6.671	5.602	4.592
60-64	8.826	10.034	8.426	6.816	6.446	6.556	7.216	7.354	6.226	4.310
65+	0.025	0.018	0.015	0.011	0.011	0.013	0.014	0.023	0.017	0.030

Turkey (BA) [1] — Total unemployment - Chômage total - Desempleo total

Total - Total - Total

	1999	2000	2001	2002	2003	2004	2005	2006	2007	2008
Total	1 774	1 497	1 967	2 464	2 493	2 498	2 519	2 446	2 377	2 611
15-19	344	247	317	339	322	288	301	286	325	330
20-24	522	458	546	641	654	656	609	572	547	567
25-29	328	277	371	479	517	558	545	530	479	525
30-34	198	163	229	307	329	341	354	339	303	349
35-39	134	128	190	244	228	234	243	241	237	274
40-44	99	88	125	191	172	171	181	186	187	218
45-49	77	56	100	133	133	121	142	139	150	167
50-54	45	46	51	74	80	79	91	94	87	102
55-59	22	19	25	42	38	30	36	42	42	54
60-64	7	13	9	11	15	14	13	13	16	19
65+	5	3	6	5	5	6	5	4	4	6

Men - Hommes - Hombres

	1999	2000	2001	2002	2003	2004	2005	2006	2007	2008
Total	1 275	1 111	1 485	1 826	1 830	1 878	1 867	1 777	1 716	1 877
15-19	216	170	216	229	218	202	211	194	232	236
20-24	358	319	382	434	438	435	396	362	339	348
25-29	237	204	279	351	380	420	393	383	336	366
30-34	146	124	177	225	241	264	269	241	219	251
35-39	101	100	154	195	176	187	188	182	173	200
40-44	81	74	104	154	141	142	152	151	150	174
45-49	65	49	90	121	113	110	125	122	130	139
50-54	42	37	47	67	71	71	83	87	80	90
55-59	21	18	23	37	35	29	34	39	38	50
60-64	7	12	9	10	13	13	12	12	15	18
65+	4	3	5	4	4	6	4	4	4	5

Women - Femmes - Mujeres

	1999	2000	2001	2002	2003	2004	2005	2006	2007	2008
Total	499	387	482	638	663	620	652	670	660	735
15-19	128	77	101	110	104	86	90	93	93	94
20-24	164	139	164	207	216	222	213	210	208	220
25-29	91	73	92	128	137	138	152	147	143	159
30-34	52	39	52	82	88	77	85	97	84	98
35-39	33	28	36	49	52	47	55	59	64	74
40-44	18	14	21	37	31	29	30	36	37	44
45-49	12	7	10	12	20	12	17	17	20	28
50-54	3	9	4	7	9	8	8	7	7	12
55-59	1	1	2	5	3	1	1	3	3	4
60-64	-	1	-	1	2	1	-	-	1	1
65+	1	-	1	1	1	-	-	-	-	1

Explanatory notes: see p. 451. Notes explicatives: voir p. 454. Notas explicativas: véase p. 457.

[1] Persons aged 15 years and over. [1] Personnes âgées de 15 ans et plus. [1] Personas de 15 años y más.

UNEMPLOYMENT

By age group

CHÔMAGE

Par groupe d'âge

DESEMPLEO

Por grupo de edad

3B

	Thousands			Milliers				Millares		
	1999	2000	2001	2002	2003	2004	2005	2006	2007	2008

Turkey (FB) [1] [2] Registered unemployment - Chômage enregistré - Desempleo registrado

Total - Total - Total

Total	487.5	730.5	718.7	464.2	587.5	812.0	881.2	1 061.9	696.5	987.8
14-14	1.4	-	0.3	0.5	-	-	-	-	-	-
15-19	56.9	103.2	89.2	47.9	16.9	30.4	26.2	29.8	32.3	43.7
20-24	188.9	272.6	267.5	137.6	152.3	195.3	168.8	178.1	156.3	212.5
25-29	122.6	193.2	183.1	128.5	161.4	227.1	231.4	269.1	190.8	262.7
30-34	66.4	92.4	94.3	73.2	109.6	149.7	174.5	213.6	130.4	181.4
35-39	31.0	44.3	46.2	42.8	73.2	97.8	121.0	150.4	86.1	132.3
40-44	12.5	16.9	21.9	21.8	45.9	67.7	91.9	122.9	59.2	86.7
45-64	7.1	7.1	14.4	11.6	27.8	43.5	66.7	96.5	40.8	66.9
65+	0.7	0.7	1.8	0.9	0.4	0.6	0.8	1.5	0.6	1.6

Men - Hommes - Hombres

Total	413.8	591.9	582.9	379.7	469.4	611.4	656.2	782.7	520.1	724.3
14-14	0.8	-	0.1	0.4	-	-	-	-	-	-
15-19	34.5	66.4	56.2	33.2	9.4	16.0	14.2	22.0	19.8	27.1
20-24	166.7	223.8	219.8	110.9	116.5	132.8	113.2	131.2	108.3	143.0
25-29	108.1	163.0	153.9	107.3	130.5	172.4	170.9	198.3	144.7	195.0
30-34	58.7	79.0	80.4	61.7	90.4	119.2	135.0	157.4	101.7	137.8
35-39	27.5	38.4	40.0	37.1	61.1	79.5	95.8	110.9	67.5	103.5
40-44	10.9	14.8	19.2	18.7	38.7	56.4	74.4	90.6	47.5	68.3
45-64	6.0	6.0	11.8	9.8	22.5	34.6	52.1	71.1	30.1	48.7
65+	0.6	0.6	1.6	0.7	0.3	0.5	0.7	1.1	0.4	1.0

Women - Femmes - Mujeres

Total	73.7	138.6	135.8	84.6	118.0	200.6	225.0	279.2	176.4	263.5
14-14	0.6	-	0.2	0.1	-	-	-	-	-	-
15-19	22.4	36.8	33.0	14.2	7.5	14.4	12.1	7.8	12.5	16.6
20-24	22.2	48.8	47.7	26.7	35.9	62.5	55.6	46.8	48.0	69.5
25-29	14.5	30.1	29.2	21.2	30.9	54.7	60.5	70.8	46.1	67.7
30-34	7.7	13.5	14.0	11.5	19.2	30.5	39.5	56.1	28.7	43.6
35-39	3.5	5.9	6.3	5.7	12.1	18.2	25.2	39.6	18.5	28.8
40-44	1.6	2.2	2.7	3.1	7.1	11.3	17.5	32.3	11.7	18.4
45-64	1.1	1.2	2.6	1.9	5.3	8.9	14.6	25.4	10.7	18.2
65+	0.1	0.1	0.2	0.2	0.1	0.1	0.1	0.4	0.2	0.7

Ukraine (BA) [3] Total unemployment - Chômage total - Desempleo total

Total - Total - Total

Total	2 614.3	2 655.8	2 455.0	2 140.7	2 008.0	1 906.7	1 600.8	1 515.0	1 417.6	1 425.1
15-19	228.1	216.5	172.1	154.0	132.7	134.7	135.5	128.5	92.1	102.1
20-24	508.0	489.6	460.4	389.2	338.6	337.2	312.8	305.2	295.7	317.2
25-29	365.3	408.7	335.9	296.0	286.5	260.1	211.8	205.6	194.7	203.2
30-34	335.6	339.4	313.0	269.7	253.4	224.3	187.3	190.7	175.7	151.4
35-39	346.7	350.0	342.8	284.2	254.9	236.2	171.8	146.1	142.3	141.5
40-44	319.5	306.2	313.1	289.7	264.8	256.0	194.3	179.1	150.5	152.3
45-49	257.1	276.4	263.8	235.3	243.1	230.1	201.3	178.5	181.8	196.9
50-54	160.4	192.8	194.0	171.7	171.7	171.9	142.4	135.4	136.0	112.5
55-59	63.8	62.3	49.5	43.5	44.0	49.2	40.2	44.9	48.5	47.7
60-64	24.5	11.9	8.6	6.9	6.0	4.5	2.7	0.8	0.3	0.3
65-70	5.3	2.0	1.8	0.5	1.5	2.5	0.7	0.2	-	-

Men - Hommes - Hombres

Total	1 346.5	1 357.4	1 263.0	1 106.5	1 055.7	1 001.6	862.5	804.1	770.7	768.9
15-19	110.8	109.9	84.2	77.4	65.2	74.2	77.9	68.2	45.9	51.6
20-24	287.3	258.5	255.9	219.9	186.7	188.5	182.5	162.3	175.1	183.9
25-29	200.7	231.8	186.8	155.8	163.7	137.3	115.0	114.6	102.9	113.2
30-34	176.4	168.5	158.9	142.2	135.3	113.7	93.5	93.9	96.3	81.6
35-39	170.6	170.3	174.9	147.2	136.5	121.4	91.6	82.3	82.5	83.5
40-44	149.0	153.3	151.9	138.0	126.0	125.8	100.6	85.2	78.7	75.5
45-49	120.3	125.3	109.6	103.6	115.4	110.2	89.5	84.3	70.8	86.1
50-54	70.0	83.4	90.0	80.1	84.9	89.9	71.9	67.7	70.3	46.4
55-59	45.2	50.4	45.2	38.8	37.5	37.7	38.0	44.6	47.9	46.9
60-64	14.1	5.3	4.7	3.5	4.2	2.1	1.7	0.8	0.3	0.2
65-70	2.1	0.7	0.9	-	0.3	0.8	0.3	0.2	-	-

Women - Femmes - Mujeres

Total	1 267.8	1 298.4	1 192.0	1 034.2	952.3	905.1	738.3	710.9	646.9	656.2
15-19	117.3	106.6	87.9	76.6	67.5	60.5	57.6	60.3	46.2	50.5
20-24	220.7	231.1	204.5	169.3	151.9	148.7	130.3	142.9	120.6	133.3
25-29	164.6	176.9	149.1	140.2	122.8	122.8	96.8	91.0	91.8	90.0
30-34	159.2	170.9	154.1	127.5	118.1	110.6	93.8	96.8	79.4	69.8
35-39	176.1	179.7	167.9	137.0	118.4	114.8	80.2	63.8	59.8	58.0
40-44	170.5	152.9	161.2	151.7	138.8	130.2	93.7	93.9	71.8	76.8
45-49	136.8	151.1	154.2	131.7	127.7	119.9	111.8	94.2	111.0	110.8
50-54	90.4	109.4	104.0	91.6	97.6	82.0	70.5	67.7	65.7	66.1
55-59	18.6	11.9	4.3	4.7	6.5	11.5	2.2	0.3	0.6	0.8
60-64	10.4	6.6	3.9	3.4	1.8	2.4	1.0	-	-	0.1
65-70	3.2	1.3	0.9	0.5	1.2	1.7	0.4	-	-	-

Explanatory notes: see p. 451.

[1] Persons aged 14 years and over. [2] Dec. of each year. [3] Persons aged 15-70 years.

Notes explicatives: voir p. 454.

[1] Personnes âgées de 14 ans et plus. [2] Déc. de chaque année. [3] Personnes âgées de 15 à 70 ans.

Notas explicativas: véase p. 457.

[1] Personas de 14 años y más. [2] Dic. de cada año. [3] Personas de 15 á 70 años.

3B

UNEMPLOYMENT	CHÔMAGE	DESEMPLEO
By age group	Par groupe d'âge	Por grupo de edad

	Thousands						Milliers		Millares	
	1999	2000	2001	2002	2003	2004	2005	2006	2007	2008

Ukraine (FB) [1][2] — Registered unemployment - Chômage enregistré - Desempleo registrado

Total - Total - Total

	1999	2000	2001	2002	2003	2004	2005	2006	2007	2008
Total	.	.	.	.	.	.	881.5	759.5	642.3	844.9
16-19	.	.	.	.	.	.	40.9	27.5	19.0	29.4
20-24	.	.	.	.	.	.	100.6	79.9	62.5	100.7
25-29	.	.	.	.	.	.	103.1	83.9	67.4	96.4
30-34	.	.	.	.	.	.	115.6	97.2	78.7	100.5
35-39	.	.	.	.	.	.	116.0	100.6	84.1	105.5
40-44	.	.	.	.	.	.	121.3	105.1	87.6	107.6
45-49	.	.	.	.	.	.	126.3	115.1	100.0	125.8
50-54	.	.	.	.	.	.	122.6	115.0	106.9	133.2
55-59	.	.	.	.	.	.	35.1	35.2	36.1	45.8

Men - Hommes - Hombres

	1999	2000	2001	2002	2003	2004	2005	2006	2007	2008
Total	.	.	.	.	.	.	345.9	300.4	256.5	379.7
16-19	.	.	.	.	.	.	14.6	9.5	6.4	12.3
20-24	.	.	.	.	.	.	38.7	29.7	22.8	44.1
25-29	.	.	.	.	.	.	38.3	30.8	24.3	41.6
30-34	.	.	.	.	.	.	42.9	36.0	29.1	42.1
35-39	.	.	.	.	.	.	44.3	38.8	32.5	45.3
40-44	.	.	.	.	.	.	44.9	39.4	33.4	45.7
45-49	.	.	.	.	.	.	45.9	42.4	37.1	52.9
50-54	.	.	.	.	.	.	41.2	38.6	34.8	49.9
55-59	.	.	.	.	.	.	35.1	35.2	36.1	45.8

Women - Femmes - Mujeres

	1999	2000	2001	2002	2003	2004	2005	2006	2007	2008
Total	.	.	.	.	.	.	535.6	459.1	385.8	465.2
16-19	.	.	.	.	.	.	26.3	18.0	12.6	17.1
20-24	.	.	.	.	.	.	61.9	50.2	39.7	56.6
25-29	.	.	.	.	.	.	64.8	53.1	43.1	54.8
30-34	.	.	.	.	.	.	72.7	61.2	49.6	58.4
35-39	.	.	.	.	.	.	71.7	61.8	51.6	60.2
40-44	.	.	.	.	.	.	76.4	65.7	54.2	61.9
45-49	.	.	.	.	.	.	80.4	72.7	62.9	72.9
50-54	.	.	.	.	.	.	81.4	76.4	72.1	83.3

United Kingdom (BA) [3][4] — Total unemployment - Chômage total - Desempleo total

Total - Total - Total

	1999	2000	2001	2002	2003	2004	2005	2006	2007	2008
Total	1 710	1 559	1 423	1 472	1 420	1 394	1 397	1 649	1 621	1 643
16-19	293	269	253	265	286	285	298	330	351	331
20-24	264	243	230	236	241	244	269	324	324	345
25-29	213	185	164	177	163	152	151	183	164	177
30-34	211	182	176	160	150	141	128	152	137	148
35-39	175	167	154	167	137	146	131	157	142	148
40-44	137	132	134	122	119	128	120	163	143	142
45-49	132	107	98	103	96	90	98	109	115	119
50-54	124	127	93	104	97	80	86	96	90	98
55-59	98	91	73	83	90	82	76	84	94	84
60-64	53	46	40	42	28	36	31	37	45	38
65-69	9	8	7	12	9	8	8	11	13	9
70-74	-	-	2	-	2	3	1	2	3	3
75+	-	1	-	-	-	-	1	-	-	1

Men - Hommes - Hombres

	1999	2000	2001	2002	2003	2004	2005	2006	2007	2008
Total	1 047	942	861	892	867	824	817	959	930	969
16-19	180	153	148	161	166	164	177	194	205	198
20-24	158	150	139	147	148	138	159	197	193	210
25-29	128	108	99	102	94	95	82	108	91	104
30-34	117	105	103	88	85	87	75	80	70	77
35-39	105	93	80	92	85	73	70	88	74	74
40-44	80	72	75	78	70	74	66	81	74	85
45-49	80	68	60	62	64	45	54	66	62	63
50-54	79	85	61	62	58	50	50	56	49	62
55-59	66	60	52	57	66	58	51	53	65	56
60-64	44	39	35	33	23	30	25	25	35	29
65-69	-	6	6	9	7	6	4	8	10	7
70-74	-	-	1	-	2	3	1	2	2	3
75+	-	1	-	-	-	-	1	-	-	-

Women - Femmes - Mujeres

	1999	2000	2001	2002	2003	2004	2005	2006	2007	2008
Total	663	617	562	580	553	570	580	690	691	674
16-19	113	116	105	105	120	121	121	136	146	133
20-24	105	93	91	88	93	106	110	127	132	135
25-29	84	76	65	75	69	57	69	75	73	73
30-34	94	77	72	72	65	54	53	72	67	70
35-39	70	74	74	76	53	73	60	69	68	74
40-44	57	59	59	43	49	54	54	82	69	57
45-49	52	38	37	41	32	44	43	43	53	56
50-54	45	41	32	42	39	30	37	39	40	36
55-59	32	30	21	26	24	24	25	31	29	29
60-64	9	7	5	9	5	6	5	12	11	9
65-69	1	2	1	3	2	2	3	3	3	2
70-74	-	-	-	-	-	-	-	-	-	-
75+	-	-	-	-	-	-	-	-	-	-

Explanatory notes: see p. 451.

[1] Men aged 16 to 59 years; women aged 16 to 54 years. [2] 31st Dec. of each year. [3] Persons aged 16 years and over. [4] Second quarter.

Notes explicatives: voir p. 454.

[1] Hommes âgés de 16 à 59 ans; femmes âgées de 16 à 54 ans. [2] 31 déc. de chaque année. [3] Personnes âgées de 16 ans et plus. [4] Deuxième trimestre.

Notas explicativas: véase p. 457.

[1] Hombres de 16 a 59 años; mujeres de 16 a 54 años. [2] 31 dic. de cada año. [3] Personas de 16 años y más. [4] Segundo trimestre.

By age group　　Par groupe d'âge　　Por grupo de edad

	Thousands			Milliers				Millares		
	1999	2000	2001	2002	2003	2004	2005	2006	2007	2008

OCEANIA-OCÉANIE-OCEANIA

Australia (BA) [1][2]　　　　Total unemployment - Chômage total - Desempleo total

Total - Total - Total

	1999	2000	2001	2002	2003	2004	2005	2006	2007	2008
Total	654.9	607.5	663.5	631.2	596.0	554.7	529.0	517.7	487.5	470.9
15-19	131.9	125.1	140.5	134.0	125.0	125.6	120.2	119.7	119.9	103.5
20-24	111.6	99.1	110.8	105.3	99.5	91.8	84.5	83.6	76.1	74.3
25-29	79.9	78.3	81.5	78.7	69.4	60.9	60.0	58.1	53.1	52.9
30-34	68.0	62.9	68.8	65.8	60.4	53.0	53.0	50.2	45.7	44.5
35-39	66.1	64.0	65.5	59.0	55.6	51.8	47.1	43.2	41.5	42.5
40-44	62.1	56.0	61.7	54.6	58.1	54.0	48.0	43.9	42.7	44.2
45-49	50.4	44.4	48.8	49.6	48.1	43.8	40.2	38.7	35.3	38.9
50-54	39.6	39.9	42.4	39.7	38.5	30.7	33.4	34.2	33.1	32.4
55-59	31.6	24.8	29.7	30.7	28.9	28.3	26.8	27.4	24.1	20.0
60-64	12.4	11.7	11.6	12.0	10.8	13.2	14.1	15.5	13.4	15.5
65-69	1.2	1.1	1.4	1.1	1.3	1.3	1.7	2.4	2.1	1.9
70+	0.1	0.2	0.8	0.6	0.2	0.3	-	1.0	0.4	0.5

Men - Hommes - Hombres

	1999	2000	2001	2002	2003	2004	2005	2006	2007	2008
Total	379.5	347.7	381.8	360.9	324.9	299.4	283.1	277.5	245.7	236.9
15-19	68.7	67.1	75.3	74.1	66.6	65.5	64.0	63.4	61.8	51.8
20-24	64.6	56.9	64.4	60.9	53.9	51.5	46.2	46.0	41.1	42.9
25-29	50.4	45.4	50.4	44.5	39.3	34.5	33.0	31.3	28.0	27.0
30-34	40.2	36.3	38.4	37.0	31.6	27.7	28.2	25.6	21.0	21.1
35-39	35.6	35.4	35.2	32.6	28.7	24.9	22.3	21.4	20.3	18.7
40-44	33.1	29.1	33.0	28.0	28.7	26.8	22.5	20.5	17.1	19.3
45-49	27.8	26.1	26.8	27.0	26.8	22.4	19.5	18.7	14.3	16.0
50-54	23.7	23.2	25.2	24.3	21.1	17.3	18.9	20.3	17.7	16.3
55-59	22.9	17.6	21.1	21.5	18.6	16.8	17.2	16.3	13.7	13.0
60-64	11.4	9.6	10.4	9.9	8.6	10.6	10.4	11.7	8.9	9.8
65-69	0.9	0.9	1.2	0.7	0.9	1.2	1.1	1.5	1.3	0.8
70+	0.1	0.1	0.5	0.5	0.2	0.1	-	0.8	0.4	0.3

Women - Femmes - Mujeres

	1999	2000	2001	2002	2003	2004	2005	2006	2007	2008
Total	275.4	259.8	281.7	270.3	271.1	255.4	245.9	240.1	241.7	234.0
15-19	63.2	57.9	65.2	60.0	58.4	60.1	56.2	56.3	58.0	51.8
20-24	47.0	42.2	46.4	44.4	45.6	40.3	38.3	37.6	35.0	31.4
25-29	29.5	32.9	31.1	34.2	30.1	26.4	27.0	26.7	25.1	25.9
30-34	27.8	26.6	30.4	28.8	28.9	25.3	24.7	24.6	24.7	23.4
35-39	30.4	28.6	30.3	26.5	26.8	26.9	24.8	21.8	21.2	23.8
40-44	28.9	26.9	28.7	26.6	29.4	27.1	25.6	23.3	25.6	24.9
45-49	22.5	18.3	22.0	22.5	21.3	21.3	20.7	20.0	21.0	22.9
50-54	16.0	16.7	17.2	15.4	17.5	13.4	14.5	13.8	15.4	16.1
55-59	8.6	7.2	8.7	9.2	10.4	11.6	9.6	11.1	10.4	7.0
60-64	1.0	2.1	1.2	2.2	2.2	2.6	3.7	3.8	4.5	5.7
65-69	0.3	0.2	0.2	0.4	0.4	0.1	0.6	0.9	0.8	1.0
70+	-	0.1	0.3	0.1	0.1	0.2	-	0.2	-	0.2

New Zealand (BA) [2]　　　　Total unemployment - Chômage total - Desempleo total

Total - Total - Total

	1999	2000	2001	2002	2003	2004	2005	2006	2007	2008
Total	133.8 [3]	117.8	106.3	106.4	97.8	84.9	82.5	85.4	82.8	95.0
15-19	24.3 [3]	25.3	23.5	24.6	22.5	20.7	21.9	24.0	25.6	27.9
20-24	22.7 [3]	19.3	17.0	16.5	14.8	14.5	14.0	14.6	13.9	16.3
25-29	15.1 [3]	12.8	10.7	12.1	10.7	8.8	9.1	8.4	8.7	10.7
30-34	14.3 [3]	12.1	10.9	10.8	10.9	8.8	6.7	7.3	6.2	7.2
35-39	15.4 [3]	12.1	10.9	10.1	9.4	7.6	7.4	6.7	6.2	6.7
40-44	12.9 [3]	10.9	10.6	9.9	8.8	6.8	6.3	6.6	6.6	7.1
45-49	9.5 [3]	7.9	7.4	6.7	5.2	5.1	5.7	6.4	6.5	6.8
50-54	9.1 [3]	7.4	7.0	7.2	5.6	5.3	5.1	4.2	3.8	4.8
55-59	6.4 [3]	6.1	5.0	4.1	5.8	4.3	3.4	4.0	3.1	3.8
60-64	3.6 [3]	3.3	2.9	3.7	3.5	2.5	2.3	2.2	1.6	2.9
65-69	- [3]	-	-	-	-	-	-	-	-	-
70-74	- [3]	-	-	-	-	-	-	-	-	-
75+	- [3]	-	-	-	-	-	-	-	-	-

Men - Hommes - Hombres

	1999	2000	2001	2002	2003	2004	2005	2006	2007	2008
Total	76.0 [3]	65.7	58.1	56.2	49.3	40.7	40.9	42.3	41.0	49.8
15-19	13.9 [3]	13.9	12.5	12.7	11.9	10.4	10.8	12.0	13.6	15.5
20-24	13.0 [3]	11.5	9.3	9.1	7.6	6.9	7.4	7.5	7.0	8.7
25-29	8.0 [3]	7.2	6.1	6.4	5.5	4.1	4.6	3.8	4.5	5.6
30-34	7.3 [3]	5.9	5.5	5.3	5.3	3.8	2.9	3.9	3.0	3.3
35-39	8.5 [3]	6.1	5.8	5.0	4.0	3.4	3.3	3.1	2.6	3.1
40-44	7.4 [3]	6.1	5.7	5.0	4.4	3.3	2.9	2.4	2.5	3.3
45-49	5.9 [3]	4.3	4.0	3.5	2.2	2.3	2.3	3.3	3.0	2.9
50-54	5.2 [3]	3.9	3.6	3.9	3.0	2.4	3.2	2.6	1.9	2.7
55-59	3.7 [3]	4.2	3.3	2.2	2.5	2.1	1.7	2.2	1.8	2.2
60-64	2.9 [3]	2.4	2.0	2.3	2.6	1.6	1.4	1.1	-	1.9
65-69	- [3]	-	-	-	-	-	-	-	-	-
70-74	- [3]	-	-	-	-	-	-	-	-	-
75+	- [3]	-	-	-	-	-	-	-	-	-

Explanatory notes: see p. 451.

[1] Excl. armed forces. [2] Persons aged 15 years and over. [3] Methodology revised; data not strictly comparable.

Notes explicatives: voir p. 454.

[1] Non compris les forces armées. [2] Personnes âgées de 15 ans et plus. [3] Méthodologie révisée; les données ne sont pas strictement comparables.

Notas explicativas: véase p. 457.

[1] Excl. las fuerzas armadas. [2] Personas de 15 años y más. [3] Metodología revisada; los datos no son estrictamente comparables.

UNEMPLOYMENT

CHÔMAGE

DESEMPLEO

By age group

Par groupe d'âge

Por grupo de edad

	Thousands					Milliers				Millares	
	1999	2000	2001	2002	2003	2004	2005	2006	2007	2008	

New Zealand (BA) [1]   **Total unemployment - Chômage total - Desempleo total**

Women - Femmes - Mujeres

	1999	2000	2001	2002	2003	2004	2005	2006	2007	2008
Total	57.8	52.1	48.3	50.3	48.5	44.2	41.6	43.1	41.7	45.2
15-19	10.5	11.4	11.0	11.9	10.6	10.3	11.1	12.0	12.1	12.4
20-24	9.7	7.8	7.7	7.4	7.2	7.5	6.6	7.1	6.9	7.6
25-29	7.1	5.6	4.6	5.7	5.2	4.6	4.5	4.6	4.2	5.2
30-34	7.0	6.3	5.4	5.5	5.6	5.0	3.8	3.4	3.2	3.8
35-39	7.0	6.0	5.1	5.1	5.4	4.2	4.1	3.6	3.6	3.5
40-44	5.5	4.8	4.9	4.9	4.4	3.5	3.4	4.2	4.1	3.8
45-49	3.6	3.6	3.5	3.1	3.0	2.8	3.3	3.2	3.5	3.9
50-54	3.8	3.6	3.3	3.3	2.6	2.9	1.9	1.6	1.9	2.1
55-59	2.7	1.9	1.7	1.9	3.3	2.3	1.6	1.8	1.3	1.5
60-64	0.7	0.9	0.9	1.5	0.9	0.9	0.9	1.1	-	1.0
65-69	-	-	-	-	-	-	-	-	-	-
70-74	-	-	-	-	-	-	-	-	-	-
75+	-	-	-	-	-	-	-	-	-	-

Explanatory notes: see p. 451.

[1] Persons aged 15 years and over.

Notes explicatives: voir p. 454.

[1] Personnes âgées de 15 ans et plus.

Notas explicativas: véase p. 457.

[1] Personas de 15 años y más.

Thousands   Milliers   Millares

AFRICA-AFRIQUE-AFRICA

Botswana (BA) [1]

Total unemployment - Chômage total - Desempleo total

Total - Total - Total — ISCED-76 - CITE-76 - CINE-76

	1999	2000	2001	2002	2003	2004	2005	2006	2007	2008
Total	.	.	.	.	144.460	.	.	114.042 [2]	.	.
X-0	.	.	.	.	10.504	.	.	11.118	.	.
1	.	.	.	.	32.467	.	.	26.557	.	.
2	.	.	.	.	62.096	.	.	43.571	.	.
3-7	.	.	.	.	39.393	.	.	32.106	.	.
?	.	.	.	.	.	.	.	0.589	.	.

Men - Hommes - Hombres — ISCED-76 - CITE-76 - CINE-76

	1999	2000	2001	2002	2003	2004	2005	2006	2007	2008
Total	.	.	.	.	66.880	.	.	50.832 [2]	.	.
X-0	.	.	.	.	7.804	.	.	6.838	.	.
1	.	.	.	.	16.856	.	.	12.725	.	.
2	.	.	.	.	26.234	.	.	17.816	.	.
3-7	.	.	.	.	15.986	.	.	13.297	.	.
?	.	.	.	.	.	.	.	0.154	.	.

Women - Femmes - Mujeres — ISCED-76 - CITE-76 - CINE-76

	1999	2000	2001	2002	2003	2004	2005	2006	2007	2008
Total	.	.	.	.	77.580	.	.	63.209 [2]	.	.
X-0	.	.	.	.	2.700	.	.	4.279	.	.
1	.	.	.	.	15.611	.	.	13.832	.	.
2	.	.	.	.	35.862	.	.	25.755	.	.
3-7	.	.	.	.	23.407	.	.	18.808	.	.
?	.	.	.	.	.	.	.	0.435	.	.

Madagascar (B) [3]

Total unemployment - Chômage total - Desempleo total

Total - Total - Total — ISCED-76 - CITE-76 - CINE-76

	1999	2000	2001	2002	2003	2004	2005	2006	2007	2008
Total	.	.	.	.	383.0 [4]	.	274.3	.	.	.
X	.	.	.	.	124.1	.	63.1	.	.	.
0-1	.	.	.	.	163.5	.	120.3	.	.	.
2-3	.	.	.	.	72.2	.	65.3	.	.	.
5-7	.	.	.	.	23.2	.	25.6	.	.	.

Men - Hommes - Hombres — ISCED-76 - CITE-76 - CINE-76

	1999	2000	2001	2002	2003	2004	2005	2006	2007	2008
Total	.	.	.	.	149.8 [4]	.	100.4	.	.	.
X	.	.	.	.	39.8	.	17.3	.	.	.
0-1	.	.	.	.	68.4	.	43.1	.	.	.
2-3	.	.	.	.	29.9	.	25.9	.	.	.
5-7	.	.	.	.	11.7	.	14.1	.	.	.

Women - Femmes - Mujeres — ISCED-76 - CITE-76 - CINE-76

	1999	2000	2001	2002	2003	2004	2005	2006	2007	2008
Total	.	.	.	.	233.2 [4]	.	173.8	.	.	.
X	.	.	.	.	84.3	.	45.7	.	.	.
0-1	.	.	.	.	95.1	.	77.2	.	.	.
2-3	.	.	.	.	42.3	.	39.4	.	.	.
5-7	.	.	.	.	11.5	.	11.5	.	.	.

Maroc (BA) [5][6]

Total unemployment - Chômage total - Desempleo total

Total - Total - Total — ISCED-97 - CITE-97 - CINE-97

	1999	2000	2001	2002	2003	2004	2005	2006	2007	2008
Total	1 161.8	1 146.4	1 061.1	1 017.2	1 125.1	1 020.6	1 028.7	.	.	.
X	89.5	78.4	62.9	49.4	67.0	52.0	44.0	.	.	.
0	1.5	0.9	0.3	-	-	-	-	.	.	.
1	296.4	273.1	256.8	235.7	250.3	230.9	232.0	.	.	.
2	318.9	320.7	288.8	287.4	316.2	281.2	293.2	.	.	.
3-4	249.7	258.2	247.1	229.3	253.6	232.3	230.7	.	.	.
5-6	197.4	206.7	198.9	207.4	230.9	216.3	222.4	.	.	.
?	8.4	8.3	6.3	8.0	7.1	7.9	6.4	.	.	.

Men - Hommes - Hombres — ISCED-97 - CITE-97 - CINE-97

	1999	2000	2001	2002	2003	2004	2005	2006	2007	2008
Total	808.2	813.6	760.1	715.0	772.8	703.0	703.5	.	.	.
X	57.6	49.4	39.4	29.0	36.5	31.5	25.8	.	.	.
0	1.0	0.9	0.3	-	-	-	-	.	.	.
1	236.8	224.6	214.0	196.0	204.6	189.6	189.1	.	.	.
2	232.0	247.2	224.8	219.2	240.3	207.7	217.0	.	.	.
3-4	164.4	174.2	169.5	157.3	168.3	153.6	153.0	.	.	.
5-6	108.6	109.2	106.5	106.8	117.3	113.6	113.7	.	.	.
?	7.8	8.1	5.6	6.7	5.8	6.9	4.9	.	.	.

Explanatory notes: see p. 451.

[1] Persons aged 12 years and over. [2] Totals include persons still attending school. [3] Persons aged 6 years and over. [4] Totals include persons still attending school (incl. full-time tertiary students). [5] Persons aged 15 years and over. [6] Urban areas.

Notes explicatives: voir p. 454.

[1] Personnes âgées de 12 ans et plus. [2] Les totaux incluent les personnes encore en cours d'études. [3] Personnes âgées de 6 ans et plus. [4] Les totaux incluent les personnes encore en cours d'études (y compris les étudiants à plein temps de l'enseignement supérieur). [5] Personnes âgées de 15 ans et plus. [6] Régions urbaines.

Notas explicativas: véase p. 457.

[1] Personas de 12 años y más. [2] Los totales incluyen a las personas que siguen estudiando. [3] Personas de 6 años y más. [4] Los totales incluyen a las personas que siguen estudiando (incl. los estudiantes a tiempo completo de la enseñanza superior). [5] Personas de 15 años y más. [6] Areas urbanas.

UNEMPLOYMENT	CHÔMAGE	DESEMPLEO
By level of education	**Par niveau d'instruction**	**Por nivel de educación**

	Thousands							Milliers			Millares
	1999	2000	2001	2002	2003	2004	2005	2006	2007	2008

Maroc (BA) [1] [2] — Total unemployment - Chômage total - Desempleo total

Women - Femmes - Mujeres
ISCED-97 - CITE-97 - CINE-97

	1999	2000	2001	2002	2003	2004	2005	2006	2007	2008
Total	353.6	332.7	301.0	302.2	352.2	317.6	325.1			
X	31.9	29.0	23.5	20.3	30.4	20.5	18.1			
0	0.6	0.1	-	-	-	-	-			
1	59.6	48.5	42.8	39.7	45.8	42.3	42.9			
2	86.9	73.5	64.0	68.2	75.9	73.5	76.2			
3-4	85.3	84.0	77.6	72.0	85.3	78.6	77.7			
5-6	88.8	97.6	92.4	100.6	113.6	102.7	108.8			
?	0.5	0.1	0.7	1.3	1.2	1.0	1.5			

Mauritius (BA) [3] — Total unemployment - Chômage total - Desempleo total

Total - Total - Total
ISCED-97 - CITE-97 - CINE-97

	1999	2000	2001	2002	2003	2004	2005	2006	2007	2008
Total						45.1	52.1	50.1 |	46.8 [4]	40.4
X-0						0.7	0.6	0.4 |	0.7 [4]	0.7
1						14.2	18.7	17.8 |	14.4 [4]	12.3
2						5.4	6.6	3.1 |	6.0 [4]	5.9
3						22.5	23.4	26.7 |	22.7 [4]	19.4
5-6						2.3	2.8	2.1 |	3.0 [4]	2.1

Men - Hommes - Hombres
ISCED-97 - CITE-97 - CINE-97

	1999	2000	2001	2002	2003	2004	2005	2006	2007	2008
Total						20.3	20.3	19.5 |	18.6 [4]	14.6
X-0						0.2	0.1	0.1 |	0.2 [4]	0.2
1						7.0	7.3	8.0 |	6.5 [4]	4.9
2						3.0	2.7	1.2 |	2.7 [4]	2.8
3						9.1	9.0	9.4 |	7.7 [4]	5.7
5-6						1.0	1.2	0.8 |	1.5 [4]	1.0

Women - Femmes - Mujeres
ISCED-97 - CITE-97 - CINE-97

	1999	2000	2001	2002	2003	2004	2005	2006	2007	2008
Total						24.8	31.8	30.6 |	28.2 [4]	25.8
X-0						0.5	0.5	0.3 |	0.5 [4]	0.5
1						7.2	11.4	9.8 |	7.9 [4]	7.4
2						2.4	3.9	1.9 |	3.3 [4]	3.1
3						13.4	14.4	17.3 |	15.0 [4]	13.7
5-6						1.3	1.6	1.3 |	1.5 [4]	1.1

Mauritius (FB) [1] [5] — Registered unemployment - Chômage enregistré - Desempleo registrado

Total - Total - Total
ISCED-76 - CITE-76 - CINE-76 .... ISCED-97 - CITE-97 - CINE-97

	1999	2000	2001	2002	2003	2004	2005	2006	2007	2008	
Total	12.130	18.024 |	21.576	21.976	23.373	.	33.614	.	.	20.611	Total
X	0.082	0.110 |	0.117	.	0.061	.	.	.	.	.	X
1	4.033	6.390 |	.	.	.	.	10.344	.	.	4.976	X-0
2-3	8.015	11.524 |	8.096	.	.	.	.	.	.	2.586	0-1
		|	.	.	8.496	.	4.438	.	.	7.123	1
		|	.	.	8.224	.	10.864	.	.	4.457	2
		|	13.363	.	.	.	.	.	.	.	2-3
		|	.	.	6.592	.	5.912	.	.	1.142	3
		|	.	.	.	.	1.802	.	.	.	4
		|	.	.	.	.	0.3	.	.	0.3	5-6
		|	.	.	.	.	0.254	.	.	.	5

Men - Hommes - Hombres
ISCED-76 - CITE-76 - CINE-76 .... ISCED-97 - CITE-97 - CINE-97

	1999	2000	2001	2002	2003	2004	2005	2006	2007	2008	
Total	5.328	8.567 |	10.477	10.116	10.069	.	15.365	.	.	7.135	Total
X	0.046	0.063 |	0.078	.	0.030	.	.	.	.	.	X
1	2.160	3.696 |	.	.	.	.	6.294	.	.	2.354	X-0
2-3	3.122	4.808 |	4.898	.	.	.	.	.	.	0.913	0-1
		|	.	.	4.591	.	2.010	.	.	2.212	1
		|	.	.	3.432	.	4.649	.	.	1.205	2
		|	5.501	.	.	.	.	.	.	.	2-3
		|	.	.	2.016	.	1.753	.	.	0.318	3
		|	.	.	.	.	0.542	.	.	.	4
		|	.	.	.	.	0.1	.	.	0.1	5-6
		|	.	.	.	.	0.117	.	.	.	5

Women - Femmes - Mujeres
ISCED-76 - CITE-76 - CINE-76 .... ISCED-97 - CITE-97 - CINE-97

	1999	2000	2001	2002	2003	2004	2005	2006	2007	2008	
Total	6.802	9.457 |	11.099	11.860	13.304	.	18.249	.	.	13.476	Total
X	0.036	0.047 |	0.039	.	0.031	.	.	.	.	.	X
1	1.873	2.694 |	.	.	.	.	4.050	.	.	2.622	X-0
2-3	4.893	6.716 |	3.198	.	.	.	.	.	.	1.673	0-1
		|	.	.	3.905	.	2.427	.	.	4.911	1
		|	.	.	4.792	.	6.215	.	.	3.252	2
		|	7.862	.	.	.	.	.	.	.	2-3
		|	.	.	4.576	.	4.159	.	.	0.824	3
		|	.	.	.	.	1.261	.	.	.	4
		|	.	.	.	.	0.1	.	.	0.2	5-6
		|	.	.	.	.	0.137	.	.	.	5

Explanatory notes: see p. 451.

[1] Persons aged 15 years and over. [2] Urban areas. [3] Persons aged 16 years and over. [4] Prior to 2007: persons aged 15 years and over. [5] Excl. Rodrigues.

Notes explicatives: voir p. 454.

[1] Personnes âgées de 15 ans et plus. [2] Régions urbaines. [3] Personnes âgées de 16 ans et plus. [4] Avant 2006: personnes âgées de 15 ans et plus. [5] Non compris Rodriguez.

Notas explicativas: véase p. 457.

[1] Personas de 15 años y más. [2] Areas urbanas. [3] Personas de 16 años y más. [4] Antes de 2006: personas de 15 años y más. [5] Excl. Rodríguez.

By level of education   Par niveau d'instruction   Por nivel de educación

	Thousands / Milliers / Millares									
	1999	2000	2001	2002	2003	2004	2005	2006	2007	2008

South Africa (BA) [1][2] — Total unemployment - Chômage total - Desempleo total

Total - Total - Total
ISCED-97 - CITE-97 - CINE-97

	1999	2000	2001	2002	2003	2004	2005	2006	2007	2008
Total	3 158	4 162	4 655	4 936	4 434	4 135	4 487	4 391	3 945	4 075
X	151	199	206	188	142	121	152	154	106	98
0	-	6	10	4	3	4	5	4	-	
0-1										627
1	804	698	724	738	602	530	563	497	750	
2	914	1 541	1 701	1 825	1 627	1 560	1 607	1 617	678	
2-3										3 126
3	1 119	1 443	1 719	1 870	1 798	1 716	1 928	1 872	2 179	
4	-	25	25	34	29	31	31	37	44	161
5A-5B										28
5-6	125	233	246	249	215	154	183	198	178	
6										5
?	28	17	24	30	18	20	18	11	9	30

Men - Hommes - Hombres
ISCED-97 - CITE-97 - CINE-97

	1999	2000	2001	2002	2003	2004	2005	2006	2007	2008
Total	1 480	1 983	2 236	2 316	2 166	2 029	2 057	1 967	1 883	1 917
X	64	93	92	93	79	61	67	70	61	49
0	-	3	5	1	2	3	2	1	-	
0-1										357
1	413	383	398	409	336	296	295	263	419	
2	432	727	822	850	815	793	776	737	331	
2-3										1 418
3	486	653	797	832	820	775	814	791	967	
4		17	14	20	19	22	18	23	25	58
5A-5B										13
5-6	57	97	94	99	86	66	72	81	76	
6										4
?	19	10	14	12	10	14	13	2	5	18

Women - Femmes - Mujeres
ISCED-97 - CITE-97 - CINE-97

	1999	2000	2001	2002	2003	2004	2005	2006	2007	2008
Total	1 677	2 179	2 420	2 619	2 268	2 103	2 428	2 424	2 059	2 158
X	87	106	115	96	64	61	84	84	45	49
0	-	3	5	3	1	2	3	3	-	
0-1										270
1	391	315	326	328	266	234	267	234	331	
2	482	814	880	975	812	767	831	880	347	
2-3										1 709
3	633	790	922	1 037	978	937	1 112	1 081	1 211	
4		8	11	14	10	8	13	14	19	103
5A-5B										14
5-6	67	135	152	148	130	88	112	117	102	
6										1
?	9	7	9	18	8	6	5	9	4	11

Tunisie (BA) [3][4] — Total unemployment - Chômage total - Desempleo total

Total - Total - Total
ISCED-76 - CITE-76 - CINE-76

	1999	2000	2001	2002	2003	2004	2005	2006	2007	2008
Total	472.5	475.1	469.2	485.5	473.4	473.9	486.4	.	.	.
X	63.8	48.0	48.5	60.8	52.4	60.0	35.3			
0-1	236.0	216.6	220.3	216.1	209.0	200.3	201.5			
2-3	151.1	178.1	168.6	170.1	169.2	171.8	183.2			
5-7	21.2	31.4	31.5	38.6	42.8	40.8	66.2			
?	0.4	0.1	-	-	-	1.0	0.2			

Men - Hommes - Hombres
ISCED-76 - CITE-76 - CINE-76

	1999	2000	2001	2002	2003	2004	2005	2006	2007	2008
Total	345.1	347.4	341.4	351.6	334.7	322.7	328.8	.	.	.
X	43.3	34.3	31.7	39.9	30.5	38.2	25.4			
0-1	179.7	161.9	170.5	166.0	158.4	144.6	151.2			
2-3	110.0	133.6	121.5	123.6	122.0	119.8	122.6			
5-7	11.9	17.6	17.8	22.1	23.8	19.4	29.5			
?	0.2	-	-	-	-	0.7	0.1			

Women - Femmes - Mujeres
ISCED-76 - CITE-76 - CINE-76

	1999	2000	2001	2002	2003	2004	2005	2006	2007	2008
Total	127.5	127.7	127.8	133.9	138.6	151.2	157.6	.	.	.
X	20.6	13.7	16.8	20.9	21.9	21.8	9.8			
0-1	56.3	54.6	49.8	50.1	50.6	55.7	50.3			
2-3	41.1	45.5	47.1	46.4	47.2	52.0	60.7			
5-7	9.3	13.8	14.0	16.5	19.0	21.4	36.7			
?	0.2	-	-	-	-	0.3	0.1			

Explanatory notes: see p. 451.

[1] Persons aged 15 to 64 years. [2] Prior to 2008: persons aged 15 years and over; September of each year. [3] Persons aged 15 years and over. [4] 1999-2003: figures revised on the basis of the 2004 census results.

Notes explicatives: voir p. 454.

[1] Personnes âgées de 15 à 64 ans. [2] Avant 2008: personnes agées de 15 ans et plus; septembre de chaque année. [3] Personnes âgées de 15 ans et plus. [4] 1999-2003: données révisées sur la base des résultats du Recensement de 2004.

Notas explicativas: véase p. 457.

[1] Personas de 15 a 64 años. [2] Antes de 2008: personas de 15 años y más; Septiembre de cada año. [3] Personas de 15 años y más. [4] 1999-2003: datos revisados de acuerdo con los resultados del Censo de 2004.

3C

UNEMPLOYMENT	CHÔMAGE	DESEMPLEO
By level of education	**Par niveau d'instruction**	**Por nivel de educación**

	Thousands				Milliers				Millares	
	1999	2000	2001	2002	2003	2004	2005	2006	2007	2008

AMERICA-AMÉRIQUE-AMERICA

Argentina (BA) [1][2][3]   Total unemployment - Chômage total - Desempleo total

Total - Total - Total
ISCED-97 - CITE-97 - CINE-97

	1999	2000	2001	2002	2003	2004	2005	2006	2007	2008
Total	1 359.6	1 460.9	1 709.8	1 955.8	1 633.0 [4]	1 361.6	1 141.5	1 049.2 [5]		
X	9.7	9.1	10.0	14.7	10.9 [4]	5.1	6.4	5.3 [5]		
0	2.5	4.3	4.9	4.4	2.7 [4]	1.3	1.7	0.9 [5]		
1	132.9	133.7	154.1	156.7	142.9 [4]	100.0	70.1	68.9 [5]		
2	566.6	619.1	695.3	743.8	551.2 [4]	472.9	389.9	322.7 [5]		
3-4	436.9	472.8	570.8	668.3	592.6 [4]	513.3	454.8	438.5 [5]		
5	58.0	58.9	71.7	110.2	104.0 [4]	93.2	62.2	79.0 [5]		
6	147.7	157.5	196.9	249.7	213.3 [4]	158.8	147.6	127.3 [5]		
?	5.4	5.6	6.0	7.9	15.4 [4]	17.0	8.6	6.7 [5]		

Men - Hommes - Hombres
ISCED-97 - CITE-97 - CINE-97

	1999	2000	2001	2002	2003	2004	2005	2006	2007	2008
Total	764.9	809.9	1 021.3	1 175.2	824.8 [4]	687.6	561.7	488.9 [5]		
X	5.9	6.0	5.6	12.6	3.8 [4]	2.7	4.4	1.5 [5]		
0	2.2	3.4	4.1	3.9	0.5 [4]	0.5	0.6	0.4 [5]		
1	91.2	96.0	112.8	117.1	84.6 [4]	64.7	43.7	44.8 [5]		
2	354.8	369.9	465.8	505.5	315.7 [4]	257.5	213.9	178.0 [5]		
3-4	223.6	241.1	314.3	369.4	288.4 [4]	256.5	206.5	182.9 [5]		
5	15.2	15.7	22.3	29.2	29.8 [4]	23.3	19.7	23.2 [5]		
6	68.7	74.7	92.5	132.9	90.7 [4]	73.4	65.9	54.3 [5]		
?	3.4	3.1	3.8	4.6	9.6 [4]	9.1	6.9	3.9 [5]		

Women - Femmes - Mujeres
ISCED-97 - CITE-97 - CINE-97

	1999	2000	2001	2002	2003	2004	2005	2006	2007	2008
Total	594.7	651.0	688.4	780.6	808.2 [4]	673.9	579.8	560.3 [5]		
X	3.8	3.1	4.4	2.1	7.0 [4]	2.4	2.0	3.9 [5]		
0	0.3	0.8	0.8	0.6	0.5 [4]	0.8	1.1	0.4 [5]		
1	41.7	37.8	41.3	39.6	58.3 [4]	35.4	26.4	24.1 [5]		
2	211.7	249.1	229.5	238.4	235.5 [4]	215.3	176.0	144.7 [5]		
3-4	213.3	231.7	256.5	298.9	304.2 [4]	256.8	248.3	255.6 [5]		
5	42.8	43.2	49.5	81.0	74.2 [4]	69.9	42.5	55.9 [5]		
6	78.9	82.8	104.3	116.8	122.6 [4]	85.4	81.7	73.0 [5]		
?	2.0	2.5	2.2	3.3	5.8 [4]	7.9	1.7	2.8 [5]		

Bahamas (BA) [6][7]   Total unemployment - Chômage total - Desempleo total

Total - Total - Total
ISCED-97 - CITE-97 - CINE-97

	1999	2000	2001	2002	2003	2004	2005	2006	2007	2008
Total	12.28	.	11.37	15.28	18.83	17.99	18.18	13.83 [8]	14.61	.
X	0.42		0.17	0.36	0.56	1.37	1.04	0.84 [8]	0.20	
1	3.34		2.77	2.74	2.20	1.91	1.71	1.50 [8]	0.94	
2-3	7.44		7.59	10.06	14.52	13.60	14.42	10.17 [8]	12.11	
4	0.27		0.18	0.69	-	-	-	- [8]	-	
5A	0.51		0.41	0.74	0.94	0.59	0.67			
5-6								1.33 [8]	1.38	
5B	0.30		0.24	0.60	0.56	0.52	0.34			
?	-		-	0.09	0.05	-	-	- [8]	-	

Men - Hommes - Hombres
ISCED-97 - CITE-97 - CINE-97

	1999	2000	2001	2002	2003	2004	2005	2006	2007	2008
Total	4.96	.	5.73	7.56	8.78	8.50	8.38	6.38 [8]	6.44	.
X	0.19		0.14	0.28	0.29	0.62	0.70	0.46 [8]	-	
1	1.65		1.46	1.67	1.04	1.13	0.96	0.74 [8]	-	
2-3	2.68		3.71	4.66	6.76	6.40	6.37	4.69 [8]	5.43	
4	0.16		0.04	0.33	-	-	-	- [8]	-	
5A	0.12		0.17	0.27	0.48	0.12	0.25			
5-6								0.49 [8]	0.64	
5B	0.16		0.21	0.31	0.15	0.23	0.08			
?	-		-	-	0.05	-	-	- [8]	-	

Women - Femmes - Mujeres
ISCED-97 - CITE-97 - CINE-97

	1999	2000	2001	2002	2003	2004	2005	2006	2007	2008
Total	7.33	.	5.64	7.78	10.05	9.50	9.80	7.46 [8]	8.17	.
X	0.24		0.03	0.08	0.27	0.76	0.33	0.38 [8]	0.20	
1	1.69		1.31	1.06	1.16	0.78	0.75	0.76 [8]	0.57	
2-3	4.76		3.88	5.40	7.76	7.20	8.05	5.48 [8]	6.67	
4	0.11		0.15	0.35	-	-	-	- [8]	-	
5A	0.39		0.24	0.47	0.46	0.46	0.42			
5-6								0.85 [8]	0.74	
5B	0.15		0.03	0.29	0.40	0.29	0.25			
?	-		-	0.06	-	-	-	- [8]	-	

Explanatory notes: see p. 451.

[1] Persons aged 10 years and over. [2] 31 Urban agglomerations. [3] Second semester. [4] Methodology revised; data not strictly comparable; Prior to 2003: May and October. [5] Prior to 2006: 28 urban agglomerations. [6] Persons aged 15 years and over. [7] April of each year. [8] May.

Notes explicatives: voir p. 454.

[1] Personnes âgées de 10 ans et plus. [2] 31 agglomérations urbaines. [3] Second semestre. [4] Méthodologie révisée; les données ne sont pas strictement comparables; Avant 2003: mai et octobre. [5] Avant 2006: 28 agglomérations urbaines. [6] Personnes âgées de 15 ans et plus. [7] Avril de chaque année. [8] Mai.

Notas explicativas: véase p. 457.

[1] Personas de 10 años y más. [2] 31 aglomerados úrbanos. [3] Segundo semestre. [4] Metodología revisada; los datos no son estrictamente comparables; antes de 2003: mayo y octubre. [5] Antes de 2006: 28 aglomerados úrbanos [6] Personas de 15 años y más. [7] Abril de cada año. [8] Mayo.

By level of education · Par niveau d'instruction · Por nivel de educación

	Thousands			Milliers				Millares		
	1999	2000	2001	2002	2003	2004	2005	2006	2007	2008

Belize (BA) [1] [2] — Total unemployment - Chômage total - Desempleo total

Total - Total - Total
ISCED-76 - CITE-76 - CINE-76

	1999	2000	2001	2002	2003	2004	2005	2006	2007	2008
Total	11.455	.	.	.	.	.	12.197	.	.	.
X	2.475	.	.	.	.	.	0.549	.	.	.
0	-	.	.	.	.	.	2.382	.	.	.
1	6.675	.	.	.	.	.	5.150	.	.	.
2	-	.	.	.	.	.	1.282	.	.	.
3	1.755	.	.	.	.	.	2.125	.	.	.
5	0.410	.	.	.	.	.	0.504	.	.	.
6	-	.	.	.	.	.	0.101	.	.	.
7	-	.	.	.	.	.	0.047	.	.	.
9	-	.	.	.	.	.	0.057	.	.	.

Men - Hommes - Hombres
ISCED-76 - CITE-76 - CINE-76

	1999	2000	2001	2002	2003	2004	2005	2006	2007	2008
Total	5.310	.	.	.	.	.	5.217	.	.	.
X	1.120	.	.	.	.	.	0.222	.	.	.
0	-	.	.	.	.	.	1.011	.	.	.
1	3.425	.	.	.	.	.	2.437	.	.	.
2	-	.	.	.	.	.	0.491	.	.	.
3	0.550	.	.	.	.	.	0.786	.	.	.
5	0.120	.	.	.	.	.	0.157	.	.	.
6	-	.	.	.	.	.	0.045	.	.	.
7	-	.	.	.	.	.	0.030	.	.	.
9	-	.	.	.	.	.	0.039	.	.	.

Women - Femmes - Mujeres
ISCED-76 - CITE-76 - CINE-76

	1999	2000	2001	2002	2003	2004	2005	2006	2007	2008
Total	6.145	.	.	.	.	.	6.980	.	.	.
X	1.355	.	.	.	.	.	0.327	.	.	.
0	-	.	.	.	.	.	1.371	.	.	.
1	3.250	.	.	.	.	.	2.714	.	.	.
2	-	.	.	.	.	.	0.791	.	.	.
3	1.205	.	.	.	.	.	1.339	.	.	.
5	0.290	.	.	.	.	.	0.347	.	.	.
6	-	.	.	.	.	.	0.057	.	.	.
7	-	.	.	.	.	.	0.018	.	.	.
9	-	.	.	.	.	.	0.018	.	.	.

Brasil (BA) [3] [4] — Total unemployment - Chômage total - Desempleo total

Total - Total - Total
ISCED-97 - CITE-97 - CINE-97

	1999	2000	2001	2002	2003	2004	2005	2006	2007	2008
Total	.	.	7 853	7 958	8 640 [5]	8 264	8 953	8 210	8 060	.
X	.	.	488	402	453 [5]	409	376	331	309	.
0	.	.	799	756	738 [5]	643	621	560	533	.
1	.	.	2 509	2 380	2 380 [5]	2 195	2 358	2 018	1 799	.
2	.	.	1 959	2 014	2 321 [5]	2 215	2 439	2 219	2 175	.
3-4	.	.	1 828	2 140	2 438 [5]	2 509	2 823	2 757	2 880	.
5-6	.	.	205	214	262 [5]	247	289	298	330	.
?	.	.	66	52	48 [5]	46	47	27	34	.

Men - Hommes - Hombres
ISCED-97 - CITE-97 - CINE-97

	1999	2000	2001	2002	2003	2004	2005	2006	2007	2008
Total	.	.	3 675	3 685	3 973 [5]	3 591	3 859	3 510	3 391	.
X	.	.	274	220	249 [5]	221	189	181	157	.
0	.	.	415	394	396 [5]	306	313	286	280	.
1	.	.	1 305	1 209	1 222 [5]	1 049	1 130	974	880	.
2	.	.	896	922	1 051 [5]	959	1 070	952	925	.
3-4	.	.	688	822	940 [5]	944	1 031	1 016	1 016	.
5-6	.	.	68	90	94 [5]	92	108	91	119	.
?	.	.	29	27	20 [5]	21	18	9	14	.

Women - Femmes - Mujeres
ISCED-97 - CITE-97 - CINE-97

	1999	2000	2001	2002	2003	2004	2005	2006	2007	2008
Total	.	.	4 178	4 273	4 667 [5]	4 673	5 094	4 700	4 669	.
X	.	.	214	182	204 [5]	188	188	150	152	.
0	.	.	384	361	342 [5]	337	308	274	253	.
1	.	.	1 204	1 171	1 158 [5]	1 147	1 227	1 044	918	.
2	.	.	1 063	1 092	1 270 [5]	1 256	1 368	1 267	1 250	.
3-4	.	.	1 140	1 318	1 498 [5]	1 565	1 792	1 741	1 864	.
5-6	.	.	137	124	168 [5]	155	181	207	212	.
?	.	.	36	25	28 [5]	25	30	18	20	.

Explanatory notes: see p. 451.

[1] Persons aged 14 years and over. [2] April of each year. [3] Persons aged 10 years and over. [4] Sep. of each year. [5] Prior to 2003: Excl. rural population of Rondõnia, Acre, Amazonas, Roraima, Pará and Amapá.

Notes explicatives: voir p. 454.

[1] Personnes âgées de 14 ans et plus. [2] Avril de chaque année. [3] Personnes âgées de 10 ans et plus. [4] Sept. de chaque année. [5] Avant 2003: Non compris la population rurale de Rondõnia, Acre, Amazonas, Roraima, Pará et Amapá.

Notas explicativas: véase p. 457.

[1] Personas de 14 años y más. [2] Abril de cada año. [3] Personas de 10 años y más. [4] Sept. de cada año. [5] Antes de 2003: Excl. la población rural de Rondonia, Acre, Amazonas, Roraima, Pará y Amapá.

3C UNEMPLOYMENT — CHÔMAGE — DESEMPLEO

By level of education — Par niveau d'instruction — Por nivel de educación

Thousands — Milliers — Millares

	1999	2000	2001	2002	2003	2004	2005	2006	2007	2008
Canada (BA) [1][2]				Total unemployment - Chômage total - Desempleo total						
Total - Total - Total										
ISCED-97 - CITE-97 - CINE-97										
Total	1 181.6	1 082.8	1 163.6	1 268.9	1 286.2	1 235.3	1 172.8	1 108.4	1 079.4	1 119.3
X-1	85.8	79.5	77.3	78.1	81.4	70.8	68.9	65.3	61.4	57.7
2	308.5	278.0	282.2	306.3	291.3	278.4	248.6	249.0	238.0	237.1
3	366.3	343.6	352.1	392.7	397.3	389.3	366.4	330.9	327.2	343.6
4	134.1	114.7	127.6	128.9	128.5	128.0	119.8	118.1	116.5	114.9
5A.6	122.8	116.9	145.5	165.9	187.8	173.8	173.9	157.6	150.9	175.3
5B	164.1	150.0	178.9	196.9	199.9	195.0	195.2	187.5	185.4	190.7
Men - Hommes - Hombres										
ISCED-97 - CITE-97 - CINE-97										
Total	660.4	595.3	655.1	721.7	719.6	685.4	649.0	608.3	603.9	632.6
X-1	55.7	48.4	47.3	49.2	50.0	42.9	40.1	36.7	36.8	35.8
2	183.7	160.9	168.9	187.4	174.2	163.5	145.7	144.2	142.5	145.8
3	195.3	180.7	190.8	213.4	217.1	215.5	204.1	182.6	183.4	193.7
4	86.8	76.4	85.3	85.5	84.5	83.4	77.4	78.0	79.9	79.4
5A.6	65.2	61.4	76.7	89.5	101.0	89.0	90.7	77.3	75.3	86.7
5B	73.7	67.6	86.0	96.7	92.8	91.1	91.1	89.5	86.0	91.3
Women - Femmes - Mujeres										
ISCED-97 - CITE-97 - CINE-97										
Total	521.2	487.5	508.5	547.2	566.6	549.9	523.8	500.1	475.5	486.6
X-1	30.1	31.1	29.9	28.9	31.4	27.9	28.8	28.6	24.6	21.9
2	124.8	117.1	113.3	118.9	117.1	115.0	102.9	104.7	95.5	91.3
3	171.0	162.9	161.3	179.3	180.3	173.8	162.3	148.3	143.8	149.9
4	47.3	38.3	42.3	43.4	44.0	44.5	42.5	40.0	36.6	35.5
5A.6	57.6	55.5	68.8	76.5	86.8	84.9	83.3	80.3	75.6	88.7
5B	90.4	82.4	92.9	100.2	107.1	103.8	104.1	98.0	99.5	99.4
Cayman Islands (BA) [1][3]				Total unemployment - Chômage total - Desempleo total						
Total - Total - Total										
ISCED-97 - CITE-97 - CINE-97										
Total	.	.	.	.	.	.	.	.	.	1.549
X-1	.	.	.	.	.	.	.	.	.	0.087
2	.	.	.	.	.	.	.	.	.	0.372
3	.	.	.	.	.	.	.	.	.	0.732
4	.	.	.	.	.	.	.	.	.	0.016
5-6	.	.	.	.	.	.	.	.	.	0.321
?	.	.	.	.	.	.	.	.	.	0.020
Men - Hommes - Hombres										
ISCED-97 - CITE-97 - CINE-97										
Total	.	.	.	.	.	.	.	.	.	0.773
X-1	.	.	.	.	.	.	.	.	.	0.068
2	.	.	.	.	.	.	.	.	.	0.202
3	.	.	.	.	.	.	.	.	.	0.368
4	.	.	.	.	.	.	.	.	.	0.016
5-6	.	.	.	.	.	.	.	.	.	0.120
?	.	.	.	.	.	.	.	.	.	-
Women - Femmes - Mujeres										
ISCED-97 - CITE-97 - CINE-97										
Total	.	.	.	.	.	.	.	.	.	0.777
X-1	.	.	.	.	.	.	.	.	.	0.020
2	.	.	.	.	.	.	.	.	.	0.172
3	.	.	.	.	.	.	.	.	.	0.363
4	.	.	.	.	.	.	.	.	.	
5-6	.	.	.	.	.	.	.	.	.	0.201
?	.	.	.	.	.	.	.	.	.	0.020
Colombia (BA) [4][5][6]				Total unemployment - Chômage total - Desempleo total						
Total - Total - Total										
ISCED-76 - CITE-76 - CINE-76										
Total	.	.	2 708.8	2 848.6	2 797.3	2 462.0	2 260.6	2 428.0	2 089.2	2 245.7
X-0	.	.	62.2	103.3	85.6	59.3	43.1	64.9	51.4	52.2
1	.	.	649.0	730.4	665.8	558.8	479.1	551.3	454.7	470.6
2-3	.	.	630.3	649.6	581.2	517.6	1 301.3	1 346.6	1 176.3	1 205.3
5-7	.	.	413.0	418.3	475.3	442.5	433.6	423.5	406.1	517.6
?	.	.	954.4	947.0	989.4	883.8	3.4	41.6	0.8	-
Men - Hommes - Hombres										
ISCED-76 - CITE-76 - CINE-76										
Total	.	.	1 257.6	1 341.3	1 264.8	1 132.1	1 019.4	1 094.9	996.4	1 033.0
X-0	.	.	37.1	58.2	42.4	34.2	23.6	28.2	40.1	30.8
1	.	.	331.2	360.8	318.5	274.8	241.9	282.7	241.4	232.8
2-3	.	.	295.9	310.5	269.4	238.4	556.2	595.6	540.2	549.8
5-7	.	.	180.9	199.2	213.7	198.8	194.8	174.6	173.9	219.6
?	.	.	412.5	412.7	420.8	385.9	2.8	13.7	0.8	-

Explanatory notes: see p. 451. — Notes explicatives: voir p. 454. — Notas explicativas: véase p. 457.

[1] Persons aged 15 years and over. [2] Excl. residents of the Territories and indigenous persons living on reserves. [3] Oct. [4] From 2001, figures revised on the basis of the 2005 census results. [5] Persons aged 10 years and over. [6] Third quarter.

[1] Personnes âgées de 15 ans et plus. [2] Non compris les habitants des "Territoires" et les populations indigènes vivant dans les réserves. [3] Oct. [4] A partir de 2001, données révisées sur la base des résultats du recensement de 2005. [5] Personnes âgées de 10 ans et plus. [6] Troisième trimestre.

[1] Personas de 15 años y más. [2] Excl. a los habitantes de los "Territorios" y a las poblaciones indígenas que viven en reservas. [3] Oct. [4] A partir de 2001, datos revisados de acuerdocon los resultados del censo de 2005. [5] Personas de 10 años y más. [6] Tercer trimestre.

UNEMPLOYMENT — CHÔMAGE — DESEMPLEO 3C

By level of education — Par niveau d'instruction — Por nivel de educación

	Thousands — Milliers — Millares									
	1999	2000	2001	2002	2003	2004	2005	2006	2007	2008
Colombia (BA) [1][2][3]				Total unemployment - Chômage total - Desempleo total						
Women - Femmes - Mujeres										
ISCED-76 - CITE-76 - CINE-76										
Total	.	.	1 451.2	1 507.3	1 532.5	1 329.9	1 241.2	1 333.0	1 092.8	1 212.7
X-0	.	.	25.1	45.2	43.2	25.1	19.5	36.7	11.3	21.4
1	.	.	317.8	369.6	347.4	284.0	237.2	268.6	213.2	237.8
2-3	.	.	334.3	339.1	311.8	279.2	745.1	751.0	636.1	655.4
5-7	.	.	232.1	219.1	261.6	243.7	238.8	248.9	232.2	298.1
?	.	.	541.8	534.3	568.5	497.9	0.6	27.9	-	-
Costa Rica (BA) [4][5]				Total unemployment - Chômage total - Desempleo total						
Total - Total - Total										
ISCED-97 - CITE-97 - CINE-97										
Total	.	.	100.4	108.5	117.2	114.9	126.2	116.0	92.8	101.9
X	.	.	2.4	3.1	3.4	3.3	3.6	2.8	1.1	1.5
0	.	.	-	-	-	-	-	-	-	0.3
1	.	.	51.0	52.7	53.4	46.8	53.2	49.8	38.5	46.3
2	.	.	20.9	22.8	26.6	24.6	27.6	25.7	22.0	21.9
3	.	.	14.6	17.6	20.8	25.9	24.1	23.0	20.5	16.7
4	.	.	0.7	1.1	1.8	1.8	1.8	6.8	4.8	7.1
5A	.	.						5.0	3.4	6.1
5-6	.	.	10.0	10.2	10.7	11.3	15.1			
5B	.	.						2.0	2.5	1.8
6	.	.						0.5	-	0.2
?	.	.	0.8	0.7	0.6	0.4	0.6	0.4	-	0.1
Men - Hommes - Hombres										
ISCED-97 - CITE-97 - CINE-97										
Total	.	.	55.7	61.6	66.0	62.5	60.2	53.8	41.3	53.5
X	.	.	1.8	2.6	2.3	2.3	2.2	2.1	0.8	1.2
0	.	.	-	-	-	-	-	-	-	-
1	.	.	31.3	33.0	31.9	28.1	28.7	24.3	17.3	27.7
2	.	.	11.0	12.3	14.0	12.8	11.3	11.5	10.7	10.9
3	.	.	6.4	7.9	10.5	12.2	10.8	9.7	9.0	8.1
4	.	.	0.2	0.7	0.7	0.7	0.4	3.3	2.1	3.6
5A	.	.						1.4	0.7	1.1
5-6	.	.	4.4	4.2	6.1	5.6	6.3			
5B	.	.						0.8	0.7	0.8
6	.	.						0.5	-	-
?	.	.	0.6	0.6	0.4	0.4	0.5	0.1	-	0.1
Women - Femmes - Mujeres										
ISCED-97 - CITE-97 - CINE-97										
Total	.	.	44.6	46.9	51.2	52.4	66.0	62.3	51.5	48.4
X	.	.	0.6	0.5	1.1	1.0	1.4	0.7	0.3	0.3
0	.	.	-	-	-	-	-	-	-	0.3
1	.	.	19.7	19.7	21.4	18.7	24.5	25.5	21.2	18.6
2	.	.	9.9	10.5	12.6	11.9	16.4	14.1	11.3	11.0
3	.	.	8.1	9.7	10.2	13.8	13.4	13.3	11.5	8.6
4	.	.	0.6	0.4	1.1	1.2	1.4	3.5	2.7	3.5
5A	.	.						3.7	2.7	5.0
5-6	.	.	5.6	6.0	4.6	5.7	8.9			
5B	.	.						1.1	1.8	1.0
6	.	.						-	-	0.2
?	.	.	0.2	0.1	0.2	0.1	0.1	0.3	-	-
Cuba (BA) [6][7]				Total unemployment - Chômage total - Desempleo total						
Total - Total - Total										
ISCED-97 - CITE-97 - CINE-97										
Total	290.9	252.3	191.6	156.1	109.7	87.7	93.9	92.7	88.6	79.6 [8]
0								1.6	1.1	1.0 [8]
1	38.0	35.7	23.7	22.8	11.8	8.7	10.6	8.5	5.7	7.2 [8]
2								35.7	32.4	29.9 [8]
2-3	125.7	99.8	81.0	66.2	50.0	35.7	38.8			
3								27.1	29.8	25.7 [8]
4	118.2	110.0	81.6	63.0	43.5	39.2	40.2	16.8	16.6	12.9 [8]
5-6	9.1	6.6	5.3	4.0	4.3	4.1	4.3	4.6	4.1	2.9 [8]
Men - Hommes - Hombres										
ISCED-97 - CITE-97 - CINE-97										
Total	126.1	111.8	93.8	76.9	51.3	49.7	55.0	52.6	53.3	42.0 [8]
0								1.3	0.7	0.7 [8]
1	19.1	15.5	13.7	13.1	5.8	5.6	6.2	5.3	3.7	3.3 [8]
2								20.3	20.9	17.0 [8]
2-3	57.2	47.9	41.7	32.3	26.0	21.5	23.9			
3								14.9	16.9	12.9 [8]
4	45.4	44.8	35.5	29.2	17.3	20.0	22.0	9.4	9.2	6.8 [8]
5-6	4.5	3.5	2.9	2.4	2.2	2.5	2.9	2.7	2.3	1.3 [8]

Explanatory notes: see p. 451.

[1] From 2001, figures revised on the basis of the 2005 census results. [2] Persons aged 10 years and over. [3] Third quarter. [4] Persons aged 12 years and over. [5] July of each year. [6] Persons aged 15 years and over. [7] Dec. [8] February - April

Notes explicatives: voir p. 454.

[1] A partir de 2001, données révisées sur la base des résultats du recensement de 2005. [2] Personnes âgées de 10 ans et plus. [3] Troisième trimestre. [4] Personnes âgées de 12 ans et plus. [5] Juillet de chaque année. [6] Personnes âgées de 15 ans et plus. [7] Déc. [8] Février - Avril

Notas explicativas: véase p. 457.

[1] A partir de 2001, datos revisados de acuerdocon los resultados del censo de 2005. [2] Personas de 10 años y más. [3] Tercer trimestre. [4] Personas de 12 años y más. [5] Julio de cada año. [6] Personas de 15 años y más. [7] Dic. [8] Febrero - Abril

3C   UNEMPLOYMENT   CHÔMAGE   DESEMPLEO

By level of education   Par niveau d'instruction   Por nivel de educación

	Thousands / Milliers / Millares									
	1999	2000	2001	2002	2003	2004	2005	2006	2007	2008

Cuba (BA) [1][2]   Total unemployment - Chômage total - Desempleo total
Women - Femmes - Mujeres
ISCED-97 - CITE-97 - CINE-97

	1999	2000	2001	2002	2003	2004	2005	2006	2007	2008
Total	164.8	140.5	97.8	79.2	58.4	38.0	38.9	40.1	35.3	37.6 [3]
0	.	.	.	.	.	.	.	0.3	0.4	0.3 [3]
1	18.9	20.2	10.1	9.7	6.0	3.1	4.4	2.9	1.6	3.9 [3]
2	.	.	.	.	.	.	.	15.4	11.5	12.9 [3]
2-3	68.5	52.0	39.2	34.0	24.0	14.2	14.8	.	.	.
3	.	.	.	.	.	.	.	12.2	12.9	12.8 [3]
4	72.8	65.2	46.1	33.8	26.3	19.2	18.3	7.4	7.1	6.1 [3]
5-6	4.6	3.1	2.4	1.6	2.1	1.5	1.4	1.9	1.8	1.6 [3]

Chile (BA) [1][4]   Total unemployment - Chômage total - Desempleo total
Total - Total - Total
ISCED-76 - CITE-76 - CINE-76

	1999	2000	2001	2002	2003	2004	2005	2006	2007	2008
Total	529.1	489.4	469.4	468.7	453.1	494.7	440.4	409.9 [5]	510.8	.
X	4.0	2.9	3.2	2.2	2.9	3.2	1.8	2.7 [5]	0.9	.
0	-	-	-	-	0.2	-	-	- [5]	-	.
1-2	138.8	101.0	106.4	108.6	83.7	86.0	71.1	69.5 [5]	86.6	.
3	301.9	277.1	257.9	276.3	267.3	288.3	259.4	236.0 [5]	296.0	.
5	41.0	52.2	48.0	38.3	42.3	53.2	47.6	41.4 [5]	57.0	.
6-7	42.8	56.1	53.4	43.2	56.6	63.9	60.5	59.9 [5]	69.6	.
9	0.7	0.1	0.4	0.1	0.2	0.1	0.2	0.4 [5]	0.6	.

Men - Hommes - Hombres
ISCED-76 - CITE-76 - CINE-76

	1999	2000	2001	2002	2003	2004	2005	2006	2007	2008
Total	.	.	.	.	.	.	.	239.3	280.2	.
X	.	.	.	.	.	.	.	2.3	0.5	.
1-2	.	.	.	.	.	.	.	49.9	52.9	.
3	.	.	.	.	.	.	.	135.2	167.3	.
5	.	.	.	.	.	.	.	19.3	24.4	.
6-7	.	.	.	.	.	.	.	32.1	34.4	.
9	.	.	.	.	.	.	.	0.4	0.6	.

Women - Femmes - Mujeres
ISCED-76 - CITE-76 - CINE-76

	1999	2000	2001	2002	2003	2004	2005	2006	2007	2008
Total	.	.	.	.	.	.	.	170.6	230.6	.
X	.	.	.	.	.	.	.	0.4	0.4	.
1-2	.	.	.	.	.	.	.	19.6	33.6	.
3	.	.	.	.	.	.	.	100.8	128.8	.
5	.	.	.	.	.	.	.	22.1	32.6	.
6-7	.	.	.	.	.	.	.	27.8	35.2	.
9	.	.	.	.	.	.	.	-	-	.

República Dominicana (BA) [6]   Total unemployment - Chômage total - Desempleo total
Total - Total - Total
ISCED-76 - CITE-76 - CINE-76

	1999	2000	2001	2002	2003	2004	2005	2006	2007	2008
Total	.	.	.	.	.	723.7	715.8	661.4	654.0	.
X-0	.	.	.	.	.	36.3	32.0	23.0	26.8	.
1	.	.	.	.	.	315.5	301.3	247.8	229.0	.
2-5	.	.	.	.	.	262.5	264.4	279.8	291.2	.
6-9	.	.	.	.	.	109.4	118.2	110.8	107.1	.

Men - Hommes - Hombres
ISCED-76 - CITE-76 - CINE-76

	1999	2000	2001	2002	2003	2004	2005	2006	2007	2008
Total	.	.	.	.	.	252.5	269.6	233.5	240.7	.
X-0	.	.	.	.	.	10.9	12.4	5.2	11.0	.
1	.	.	.	.	.	109.7	117.7	90.4	88.3	.
2-5	.	.	.	.	.	97.0	97.3	105.1	109.6	.
6-9	.	.	.	.	.	35.0	42.1	32.7	31.8	.

Women - Femmes - Mujeres
ISCED-76 - CITE-76 - CINE-76

	1999	2000	2001	2002	2003	2004	2005	2006	2007	2008
Total	.	.	.	.	.	471.2	446.3	428.0	413.3	.
X-0	.	.	.	.	.	25.4	19.6	17.8	15.7	.
1	.	.	.	.	.	205.9	183.6	157.4	140.7	.
2-5	.	.	.	.	.	165.5	167.1	174.7	181.6	.
6-9	.	.	.	.	.	74.4	76.0	78.1	75.3	.

Ecuador (BA) [6][7][8]   Total unemployment - Chômage total - Desempleo total
Total - Total - Total
ISCED-97 - CITE-97 - CINE-97

	1999	2000	2001	2002	2003	2004	2005	2006	2007	2008
Total	543.5	333.1	450.9	352.9	461.1	362.1	333.6	341.8	.	.
X-0	8.6	7.4	9.9	6.9	6.4	6.0	5.3	8.1	.	.
1	155.1	83.7	120.7	108.8	147.6	104.2	95.9	104.5	.	.
2-4	285.4	172.3	229.3	164.9	207.3	172.7	157.5	148.5	.	.
5-6	94.5	69.8	91.1	71.6	99.8	79.2	74.9	80.6	.	.

Explanatory notes: see p. 451.
[1] Persons aged 15 years and over. [2] Dec. [3] February - April [4] Fourth quarter of each year. [5] Methodology revised; data not strictly comparable. [6] Persons aged 10 years and over. [7] Urban areas. [8] Nov. of each year.

Notes explicatives: voir p. 454.
[1] Personnes âgées de 15 ans et plus. [2] Déc. [3] Février - Avril [4] Quatrième trimestre de chaque année. [5] Méthodologie révisée; les données ne sont pas strictement comparables. [6] Personnes âgées de 10 ans et plus. [7] Régions urbaines. [8] Nov. de chaque année.

Notas explicativas: véase p. 457.
[1] Personas de 15 años y más. [2] Dic. [3] Febrero - Abril [4] Cuarto trimestre de cada año. [5] Metodología revisada; los datos no son estrictamente comparables. [6] Personas de 10 años y más. [7] Areas urbanas. [8] Nov. de cada año.

By level of education   Par niveau d'instruction   Por nivel de educación

	Thousands / Milliers / Millares									
	1999	2000	2001	2002	2003	2004	2005	2006	2007	2008
Ecuador (BA) [1] [2] [3]				Total unemployment - Chômage total - Desempleo total						
Men - Hommes - Hombres ISCED-97 - CITE-97 - CINE-97										
Total	239.5	138.3	169.0	136.2	.	160.7	143.3	143.4	.	.
X-0	5.8	4.0	2.9	3.9	.	3.8	2.5	3.6	.	.
1	78.5	35.3	48.6	45.7	.	53.4	43.3	50.6	.	.
2-4	120.8	73.6	84.5	58.6	.	71.8	65.3	58.9	.	.
5-6	34.3	25.4	33.0	27.4	.	31.7	32.2	30.4	.	.
Women - Femmes - Mujeres ISCED-97 - CITE-97 - CINE-97										
Total	304.0	194.8	282.0	216.7	.	201.4	190.3	198.4	.	.
X-0	2.7	3.4	6.9	2.9	.	2.2	2.8	4.5	.	.
1	76.6	48.4	72.1	63.1	.	50.8	52.6	53.9	.	.
2-4	164.5	98.7	144.8	106.2	.	100.9	92.2	89.7	.	.
5-6	60.2	44.4	58.1	44.2	.	47.5	42.7	50.3	.	.
Jamaica (BA) [4]				Total unemployment - Chômage total - Desempleo total						
Total - Total - Total ISCED-97 - CITE-97 - CINE-97										
Total	.	.	.	171.8	128.9	136.8	133.3	119.6	119.4	134.6
X	.	.	.	130.3	95.2	98.9	91.6	88.2	83.8	97.9
0	.	.	.	8.3	5.1	4.3	6.4	4.4	4.7	4.4
1	.	.	.	8.1	6.1	7.2	7.7	4.1	5.3	6.6
2	.	.	.	8.5	6.6	10.6	9.5	7.5	10.0	9.5
3	.	.	.	4.0	5.7	7.0	5.4	4.8	5.9	5.5
4	.	.	.	0.4	-	0.4	0.2	0.3	0.3	0.5
5	.	.	.	2.1	1.5	3.3	2.4	3.1	2.9	3.9
6	.	.	.	2.8	2.4	1.6	3.5	1.2	1.3	1.4
?	.	.	.	7.3	6.3	3.5	6.4	5.7	4.9	4.7
Men - Hommes - Hombres ISCED-97 - CITE-97 - CINE-97										
Total	.	.	.	65.7	47.6	54.0	50.0	48.0	37.8	52.8
X	.	.	.	51.3	36.4	41.3	37.9	38.6	27.6	41.0
0	.	.	.	2.6	1.2	0.9	0.5	0.6	0.8	1.0
1	.	.	.	1.5	2.1	3.3	2.6	1.1	2.3	2.2
2	.	.	.	2.8	1.6	3.2	2.9	2.3	2.4	2.7
3	.	.	.	1.5	2.0	2.5	1.9	1.6	1.2	1.8
4	.	.	.	0.2	-	0.1	0.2	0.3	0.2	0.3
5	.	.	.	0.7	1.0	1.2	0.7	0.9	0.9	1.8
6	.	.	.	0.9	0.7	0.6	0.9	0.2	0.1	0.2
?	.	.	.	4.2	2.6	0.9	2.4	2.1	2.2	1.7
Women - Femmes - Mujeres ISCED-97 - CITE-97 - CINE-97										
Total	.	.	.	106.1	81.3	82.8	83.3	71.6	81.6	81.8
X	.	.	.	79.0	58.8	57.5	53.7	49.6	56.2	56.9
0	.	.	.	5.7	3.9	3.4	5.9	3.8	3.9	3.4
1	.	.	.	6.6	4.0	4.0	5.1	3.0	3.0	4.4
2	.	.	.	5.7	5.0	7.4	6.6	5.2	7.6	6.8
3	.	.	.	2.5	3.7	4.5	3.5	3.2	4.7	3.7
4	.	.	.	0.2	-	0.2	0.0	0.0	0.1	0.2
5	.	.	.	1.4	0.5	2.2	1.7	2.2	2.0	2.1
6	.	.	.	1.9	1.7	1.0	2.6	1.0	1.2	1.2
?	.	.	.	3.1	3.7	2.6	4.0	3.6	2.7	3.0
México (BA) [4] [5]				Total unemployment - Chômage total - Desempleo total						
Total - Total - Total ISCED-97 - CITE-97 - CINE-97										
Total	954.2	998.9	996.1	1 145.6	1 195.6	1 539.8	1 482.5	1 377.7	1 505.2	1 593.3
X	27.6	39.5	28.9	31.9	31.1	36.7	34.5	40.1	27.1	36.5
1	250.6	249.2	259.5	287.2	267.6	345.9	331.1	304.3	305.7	341.0
2	273.9	302.4	279.7	337.8	373.0	449.4	435.1	406.8	457.8	479.6
3	109.3	147.9	158.6	160.8	185.3	238.1	262.1	260.1	280.6	336.7
4	76.2	77.3	66.8	77.6	70.7	100.1	98.2	81.5	88.9	65.1
5A	177.3	149.0	168.0	209.1	223.9	295.0	307.4	265.1	332.6	307.6
5B	30.9	28.5	29.3	32.6	38.1	66.0	9.0	10.3	6.1	12.5
6	8.4	5.1	4.8	8.6	6.2	8.7	4.6	8.6	6.2	14.1
?	0.0	0.0	0.4	0.0	0.0	0.0	0.5	1.0	0.2	0.1
Men - Hommes - Hombres ISCED-97 - CITE-97 - CINE-97										
Total	494.4	559.7	550.6	656.5	687.0	828.7	917.8	811.5	885.6	927.4
X	17.7	26.1	18.7	20.9	22.9	23.3	25.0	30.4	21.9	26.5
1	144.2	159.8	164.8	173.8	179.6	219.8	227.1	197.6	212.5	236.9
2	137.9	184.8	152.6	209.0	217.1	253.1	275.9	252.4	283.3	304.3
3	70.0	80.9	89.4	99.6	113.6	130.9	159.6	151.1	161.9	174.4
4	12.0	22.4	20.4	28.2	19.6	22.7	37.9	27.4	29.0	23.1
5A	95.4	69.8	89.2	106.4	111.8	148.1	184.9	142.7	170.6	152.3
5B	16.5	13.6	13.4	14.3	18.5	25.9	4.1	3.9	4.0	2.8
6	0.6	2.2	1.7	4.4	3.9	4.7	2.9	5.0	2.4	7.0
?	0.0	0.0	0.4	0.0	0.0	0.0	0.5	0.9	0.1	0.1

Explanatory notes: see p. 451.

[1] Persons aged 10 years and over. [2] Urban areas. [3] Nov. of each year. [4] Persons aged 14 years and over. [5] Second quarter of each year.

Notes explicatives: voir p. 454.

[1] Personnes âgées de 10 ans et plus. [2] Régions urbaines. [3] Nov. de chaque année. [4] Personnes âgées de 14 ans et plus. [5] Deuxième trimestre de chaque année.

Notas explicativas: véase p. 457.

[1] Personas de 10 años y más. [2] Areas urbanas. [3] Nov. de cada año. [4] Personas de 14 años y más. [5] Segundo trimestre de cada año.

3C

UNEMPLOYMENT	CHÔMAGE	DESEMPLEO
By level of education	Par niveau d'instruction	Por nivel de educación

	Thousands			Milliers				Millares		
	1999	2000	2001	2002	2003	2004	2005	2006	2007	2008

México (BA) [1][2]
Total unemployment - Chômage total - Desempleo total

Women - Femmes - Mujeres
ISCED-97 - CITE-97 - CINE-97

	1999	2000	2001	2002	2003	2004	2005	2006	2007	2008
Total	459.8	439.2	445.5	489.0	508.7	711.0	564.7	566.2	619.6	665.9
X	9.9	13.3	10.2	11.0	8.3	13.3	9.4	9.8	5.3	10.1
1	106.4	89.4	94.7	113.4	88.0	126.0	104.1	106.6	93.2	104.1
2	136.0	117.6	127.1	128.9	155.9	196.3	159.2	154.4	174.5	175.3
3	39.3	67.0	69.3	61.2	71.7	107.2	102.5	109.0	118.7	162.3
4	64.2	54.9	46.4	49.5	51.2	77.4	60.4	54.0	59.9	42.0
5A	81.9	79.2	78.8	102.7	111.8	146.8	122.6	122.4	162.0	155.3
5B	14.3	14.9	15.9	18.3	19.6	40.0	4.9	6.4	2.1	9.7
6	7.8	2.9	3.1	4.2	2.3	4.0	1.7	3.5	3.9	7.1
?	0.0	0.0	0.0	0.0	0.0	0.0	0.0	0.1	0.1	0.0

Netherlands Antilles (BA) [3][4][5]
Total unemployment - Chômage total - Desempleo total

Total - Total - Total
ISCED-97 - CITE-97 - CINE-97

	2007	2008
Total	7.659	6.486
X	0.383	0.459
0	0.044	0.020
1	0.923	0.871
2	4.028	3.140
3	1.939	1.575
4	0.342	0.367
?		0.054

Men - Hommes - Hombres
ISCED-97 - CITE-97 - CINE-97

	2007	2008
Total	3.044	2.482
X	0.080	0.209
0	0.025	0.020
1	0.296	0.398
2	1.816	1.158
3	0.677	0.516
4	0.150	0.152
?		0.029

Women - Femmes - Mujeres
ISCED-97 - CITE-97 - CINE-97

	2007	2008
Total	4.616	4.003
X	0.303	0.250
0	0.019	0.000
1	0.627	0.472
2	2.213	1.982
3	1.262	1.059
4	0.192	0.215
?		0.025

Nicaragua (BA)
Total unemployment - Chômage total - Desempleo total

Total - Total - Total
ISCED-76 - CITE-76 - CINE-76 [6][7] · · · ISCED-97 - CITE-97 - CINE-97 [8]

	1999	2000	2001	2002	2003	2004	2005	2006	2007	2008	
Total	46.9	84.3	101.9	135.3	160.5	138.0	122.5	114.5	.	.	Total
X	2.5	4.6	5.6	6.4	15.6	10.6	7.7	8.1			0
0	-	-	-	-	52.1	36.2	37.3	33.1			1
1	13.0	22.5	31.9	39.3	65.7	62.7	51.0	50.3			2-3
2	12.8	22.1	25.6	29.5		3.6	3.6	2.4			4
3	11.6	20.2	23.8	33.5	27.0 [9]	24.9	22.1	20.6			5
5	-	-	-				0.9				6
6	2.3	6.6	5.3	8.8							
7	4.7	8.3	9.7	17.8							
?	-	-	-	-							

Men - Hommes - Hombres
ISCED-76 - CITE-76 - CINE-76 [6][7] · · · ISCED-97 - CITE-97 - CINE-97 [8]

	1999	2000	2001	2002	2003	2004	2005	2006	2007	2008	
Total	27.6	49.5	64.2	84.0	97.1	74.2	73.4	74.1	.	.	Total
X	1.9	3.5	3.4	4.3	9.2	7.2	5.7	6.2			0
0	-	-	-	-	35.6	21.8	23.9	25.3			1
1	9.0	15.6	23.4	27.6	38.4	31.7	29.4	29.6			2-3
2	8.3	13.0	16.6	19.2		1.9	1.7	1.2			4
3	5.3	10.3	13.3	19.1	13.9 [9]	11.6	12.4	11.9			5
5	-	-	-				0.4				6
6	1.1	3.2	2.6	3.7							
7	2.1	4.0	5.0	10.0							
?	-	-	-	-							

Explanatory notes: see p. 451.

[1] Persons aged 14 years and over. [2] Second quarter of each year. [3] Persons aged 15 years and over. [4] Curaçao. [5] Oct. of each year. [6] 1993-1999: Oct.; 2000: Nov.; 2001: July. [7] 17 main cities of the country; 1993, 1994 and 1999: 8 main cities. [8] Persons aged 10 years and over. [9] Levels 4-5.

Notes explicatives: voir p. 454.

[1] Personnes âgées de 14 ans et plus. [2] Deuxième trimestre de chaque année. [3] Personnes âgées de 15 ans et plus. [4] Curaçao. [5] Oct. de chaque année. [6] 1993-1999: oct.; 2000: nov.; 2001: juillet. [7] 17 villes principales du pays; 1993, 1994 et 1999: 8 villes principales. [8] Personnes âgées de 10 ans et plus. [9] Niveaux 4-5.

Notas explicativas: véase p. 457.

[1] Personas de 14 años y más. [2] Segundo trimestre de cada año. [3] Personas de 15 años y más. [4] Curaçao. [5] Oct. de cada año. [6] 1993-1999: oct.; 2000: nov.; 2001: julio. [7] 17 ciudades principales del país; 1993, 1994 y 1999: 8 ciudades principales. [8] Personas de 10 años y más. [9] Niveles 4-5.

By level of education

Par niveau d'instruction

Por nivel de educación

	Thousands			Milliers				Millares		
	1999	2000	2001	2002	2003	2004	2005	2006	2007	2008

Nicaragua (BA)   Total unemployment - Chômage total - Desempleo total

Women - Femmes - Mujeres
ISCED-76 - CITE-76 - CINE-76 [1] [2]   ISCED-97 - CITE-97 - CINE-97 [3]

	1999	2000	2001	2002	2003	2004	2005	2006	2007	2008	
Total	19.2	34.7	37.7	51.3	63.4	63.8	49.1	40.3	.	.	Total
X	0.6	1.1	2.3	2.0	6.5	3.4	2.0	2.0	.	.	0
0	-	-	-	-	16.5	14.4	13.4	7.8	.	.	1
1	3.9	6.9	8.5	11.6	27.3	31.0	21.6	20.7	.	.	2-3
2	4.5	9.1	9.0	10.2	.	1.7	1.9	1.1	.	.	4
3	6.3	9.9	10.5	14.5	13.2 [4]	13.3	9.8	8.7	.	.	5
5	-	-	-	-	.	.	0.5	.	.	.	6
6	1.3	3.3	2.7	5.1							
7	2.6	4.4	4.7	7.8							
?	-	-	-	-							

Panamá (BA) [5] [6]   Total unemployment - Chômage total - Desempleo total

Total - Total - Total
ISCED-97 - CITE-97 - CINE-97

	1999	2000	2001	2002	2003	2004	2005	2006	2007	2008
Total	.	.	169.7	172.4	170.4	159.9	136.8	121.4	92.0	82.9
X			2.5	1.3	1.2	1.1	1.1	0.9	0.3	0.4
1			34.3	32.6	27.5	24.7	18.0	19.3	12.4	10.7
2			34.7	34.1	33.7	31.8	25.4	21.7	20.7	19.0
3			62.4	62.7	63.0	57.4	52.1	47.3	36.3	32.8
4			0.4	0.3	0.6	0.4	0.5	0.2	0.2	0.2
5-6			35.5	41.4	44.3	44.5	39.9	31.9	22.1	19.7

Men - Hommes - Hombres
ISCED-97 - CITE-97 - CINE-97

	1999	2000	2001	2002	2003	2004	2005	2006	2007	2008
Total	.	.	92.0	86.5	82.9	76.3	66.7	60.2	44.5	40.2
X			1.7	1.0	0.9	0.8	0.9	0.8	0.3	0.1
1			23.9	19.7	17.1	15.5	12.4	13.0	8.4	7.0
2			20.7	20.6	19.8	19.4	14.4	13.5	12.4	10.9
3			30.1	28.0	28.4	25.2	24.8	20.9	15.4	15.5
4			0.3	0.3	0.3	0.2	0.2	0.0	-	-
5-6			15.2	16.9	16.4	15.1	13.9	12.0	8.1	6.6

Women - Femmes - Mujeres
ISCED-97 - CITE-97 - CINE-97

	1999	2000	2001	2002	2003	2004	2005	2006	2007	2008
Total	.	.	77.8	85.9	87.4	83.6	70.2	61.1	47.5	42.7
X			0.8	0.4	0.3	0.3	0.2	0.1	0.1	0.3
1			10.4	12.9	10.4	9.2	5.6	6.3	4.0	3.8
2			14.0	13.4	13.9	12.4	11.0	8.3	8.4	8.0
3			32.3	34.7	34.6	32.1	27.2	26.4	20.9	17.3
4			0.1	-	0.3	0.2	0.3	0.2	0.2	0.2
5-6			20.2	24.4	27.9	29.4	26.0	19.9	14.0	13.1

Paraguay (BA) [7] [8]   Total unemployment - Chômage total - Desempleo total

Total - Total - Total
ISCED-97 - CITE-97 - CINE-97

	1999	2000	2001	2002	2003	2004	2005	2006	2007	2008
Total	.	.	.	.	.	.	.	.	161.2	170.6
X									3.6	2.9
1									52.1	53.2
2									28.3	38.0
3-4									61.2	53.6
5A									4.1	18.6
5B									11.8	4.3

Men - Hommes - Hombres
ISCED-97 - CITE-97 - CINE-97

	1999	2000	2001	2002	2003	2004	2005	2006	2007	2008
Total	.	.	.	.	.	.	.	.	74.6	83.9
X									1.2	1.0
1									25.3	28.0
2									15.7	24.3
3-4									24.4	22.7
5A									0.9	7.6
5B									7.0	0.5

Women - Femmes - Mujeres
ISCED-97 - CITE-97 - CINE-97

	1999	2000	2001	2002	2003	2004	2005	2006	2007	2008
Total	.	.	.	.	.	.	.	.	86.6	86.7
X									2.4	2.0
1									26.8	25.2
2									12.6	13.7
3-4									36.8	30.9
5A									3.2	11.0
5B									4.8	3.9

Explanatory notes: see p. 451.

[1] 1993-1999: Oct.; 2000: Nov.; 2001: July. [2] 17 main cities of the country; 1993, 1994 and 1999: 8 main cities. [3] Persons aged 10 years and over. [4] Levels 4-5. [5] Persons aged 15 years and over. [6] Aug. of each year. [7] Persons aged 10 years and over. [8] Fourth quarter.

Notes explicatives: voir p. 454.

[1] 1993-1999: oct.; 2000: nov.; 2001: juillet. [2] 17 villes principales du pays; 1993, 1994 et 1999: 8 villes principales. [3] Personnes âgées de 10 ans et plus. [4] Niveaux 4-5. [5] Personnes âgées de 15 ans et plus. [6] Août de chaque année. [7] Personnes âgées de 10 ans et plus. [8] Quatrième trimestre.

Notas explicativas: véase p. 457.

[1] 1993-1999: oct.; 2000: nov.; 2001: julio. [2] 17 ciudades principales del país; 1993, 1994 y 1999: 8 ciudades principales. [3] Personas de 10 años y más. [4] Niveles 4-5. [5] Personas de 15 años y más. [6] Agosto de cada año. [7] Personas de 10 años y más. [8] Cuarto trimestre.

UNEMPLOYMENT — CHÔMAGE — DESEMPLEO

By level of education — Par niveau d'instruction — Por nivel de educación

Thousands — Milliers — Millares

	1999	2000	2001	2002	2003	2004	2005	2006	2007	2008
Perú (BA) [1][2]				**Total unemployment - Chômage total - Desempleo total**						
Total - Total - Total										
ISCED-97 - CITE-97 - CINE-97										
Total				359.4 [3]	316.0 [4]	339.5	333.4	297.6	300.1	308.0
0				2.8 [3]	5.3 [4]	2.9	3.4	5.3	0.7	3.4
1				59.5 [3]	26.6 [4]	33.3	34.2	28.7	25.7	18.7
2				51.3 [3]	61.7 [4]	62.0	65.2	70.0	62.7	57.5
3-4				133.9 [3]	127.6 [4]	130.8	121.6	112.1	95.6	112.6
5A				53.3 [3]	37.6 [4]	60.9	51.1	38.5	59.4	69.0
5B				56.7 [3]	51.0 [4]	49.6	55.5	43.1	52.1	42.3
6				1.9 [3]	6.3 [4]	-	2.4	-	3.9	4.6
Men - Hommes - Hombres										
ISCED-97 - CITE-97 - CINE-97										
Total				194.0 [3]	182.5 [4]	159.4	155.4	136.3	139.1	131.3
0				1.4 [3]	3.8 [4]	-	-	0.7	-	0.7
1				28.5 [3]	10.0 [4]	15.8	19.9	15.0	7.5	3.0
2				30.1 [3]	39.1 [4]	33.3	27.2	42.4	39.2	22.7
3-4				72.6 [3]	84.3 [4]	60.9	59.3	47.2	42.4	49.1
5A				26.1 [3]	16.5 [4]	23.7	18.8	13.9	26.4	36.7
5B				33.3 [3]	23.7 [4]	25.8	27.8	17.1	20.8	15.8
6				1.9 [3]	5.0 [4]	-	2.4	-	2.8	3.3
Women - Femmes - Mujeres										
ISCED-97 - CITE-97 - CINE-97										
Total				165.4 [3]	133.6 [4]	180.1	178.0	161.3	161.0	176.6
0				1.4 [3]	1.5 [4]	2.9	3.4	4.6	0.7	2.7
1				31.0 [3]	16.5 [4]	17.5	14.3	13.8	18.1	15.7
2				21.2 [3]	22.6 [4]	28.7	37.9	27.7	23.5	34.8
3-4				61.3 [3]	43.3 [4]	69.9	62.3	64.8	53.3	63.5
5A				27.2 [3]	21.1 [4]	37.3	32.3	24.5	33.0	32.3
5B				23.4 [3]	27.3 [4]	23.8	27.7	26.0	31.3	26.5
6				- [3]	1.3 [4]	-	-	-	1.0	1.3
Trinidad and Tobago (BA) [5]				**Total unemployment - Chômage total - Desempleo total**						
Total - Total - Total										
ISCED-76 - CITE-76 - CINE-76										
Total	74.0	69.6	62.5	61.1				39.0	34.5	29.0
X	0.2	0.3	0.2	0.1						
X-0								0.1	-	0.2
0	1.5	1.9	1.2	1.2						
1	26.8	23.0	19.6	19.7				11.2	9.7	8.1
2	16.7	18.4	15.0	14.3						
2-3								26.4	23.4	19.1
3	28.2	25.2	25.6	24.8						
5	-	0.1	0.2	0.3						
5-7								1.2	1.4	1.5
6-7	0.6	0.7	0.6	0.8						
9	-	-	0.1	0.1				0.1	-	0.1
Men - Hommes - Hombres										
ISCED-76 - CITE-76 - CINE-76										
Total	37.9	36.2	30.7	27.9				16.4	14.4	12.9
X	0.1	0.2	0.1	0.1						
X-0								0.1	-	0.1
0	0.6	0.8	0.6	0.5						
1	15.3	13.4	10.8	10.4				4.5	3.9	3.6
2	8.0	9.8	6.8	5.8						
2-3								11.2	10.2	8.5
3	13.5	11.7	12.2	10.7						
5	-	-	-	0.1						
5-7								0.5	0.3	0.6
6-7	0.3	0.3	0.2	0.3						
9	-	-	-	-				-	-	0.1
Women - Femmes - Mujeres										
ISCED-76 - CITE-76 - CINE-76										
Total	36.1	33.4	31.8	33.3				22.6	20.1	16.1
X	0.1	0.1	0.1	-						
X-0										0.1
0	0.9	1.1	0.6	0.7						
1	11.5	9.6	8.8	9.5				6.7	5.8	4.5
2	8.7	8.6	8.2	8.5						
2-3								15.2	13.2	10.6
3	14.7	13.5	13.4	13.8						
5	-	0.1	0.2	0.2						
5-7								0.7	1.1	0.9
6-7	0.3	0.4	0.4	0.5						
9	-	-	0.1	0.1				0.1		

Explanatory notes: see p. 451.

[1] Persons aged 14 years and over. [2] Metropolitan Lima. [3] Fourth quarter. [4] May-Dec. [5] Persons aged 15 years and over.

Notes explicatives: voir p. 454.

[1] Personnes âgées de 14 ans et plus. [2] Lima métropolitaine. [3] Quatrième trimestre. [4] Mai-déc. [5] Personnes âgées de 15 ans et plus.

Notas explicativas: véase p. 457.

[1] Personas de 14 años y más. [2] Lima metropolitana. [3] Cuarto trimestre. [4] Mayo-dic. [5] Personas de 15 años y más.

	1999	2000	2001	2002	2003	2004	2005	2006	2007	2008
	Thousands			Milliers				Millares		

United States (BA) [1] [2]   Total unemployment - Chômage total - Desempleo total

Total - Total - Total
ISCED-76 - CITE-76 - CINE-76

	1999	2000	2001	2002	2003	2004	2005	2006	2007	2008
Total	3 676	3 537	4 351	5 695	6 028	5 511	5 070	4 648	4 735	6 094
X-2	817	771	883	1 064	1 109	1 062	967	866	886	1 092
3	1 310	1 285	1 537	1 985	2 069	1 890	1 798	1 652	1 682	2 166
5	906	879	1 098	1 522	1 629	1 462	1 349	1 267	1 275	1 678
6	458	430	601	796	869	775	687	628	633	806
7	185	172	233	327	351	323	268	235	258	352

Men - Hommes - Hombres
ISCED-76 - CITE-76 - CINE-76

	1999	2000	2001	2002	2003	2004	2005	2006	2007	2008
Total	1 870	1 800	2 323	3 105	3 368	2 980	2 617	2 426	2 538	3 377
X-2	426	398	476	613	648	602	514	498	523	682
3	661	675	846	1 087	1 161	1 049	973	914	951	1 270
5	434	422	552	771	863	732	636	575	610	839
6	244	212	323	450	491	422	364	315	323	404
7	106	93	125	184	205	175	130	124	132	181

Women - Femmes - Mujeres
ISCED-76 - CITE-76 - CINE-76

	1999	2000	2001	2002	2003	2004	2005	2006	2007	2008
Total	1 805	1 736	2 028	2 590	2 660	2 531	2 453	2 221	2 198	2 717
X-2	391	373	407	451	461	460	453	368	363	410
3	649	609	691	898	908	841	826	737	731	896
5	473	458	546	751	766	730	713	692	666	838
6	214	218	277	347	378	353	323	313	310	402
7	80	79	106	141	146	147	138	110	128	170

Uruguay (BA) [3]   Total unemployment - Chômage total - Desempleo total

Total - Total - Total
ISCED-76 - CITE-76 - CINE-76

	1999	2000	2001	2002	2003	2004	2005	2006	2007	2008
Total	.	.	193.2	211.3	.	.	154.9 ǀ	167.0 [4]	149.0	.
X	.	.	0.6	0.3	.	.	0.2 ǀ	0.7 [4]	0.4	.
1	.	.	51.9	56.6	.	.	36.8 ǀ	45.6 [4]	42.6	.
2	.	.	46.1	59.1	.	.	49.6 ǀ	49.4 [4]	45.5	.
3	.	.	41.0	66.1	.	.	45.5 ǀ	46.6 [4]	40.2	.
5	.	.	28.1	6.9	.	.	5.5 ǀ	6.8 [4]	4.0	.
6	.	.	2.9	.	.	.	17.1 ǀ	17.5 [4]	16.6	.
6-7	.	.	.	22.4	.	.	.	.	.	.
7	.	.	22.7	.	.	.	0.2 ǀ	0.3 [4]	-	.

Men - Hommes - Hombres
ISCED-76 - CITE-76 - CINE-76

	1999	2000	2001	2002	2003	2004	2005	2006	2007	2008
Total	.	.	80.4	93.3	.	.	65.4 ǀ	70.0 [4]	60.0	.
X	.	.	0.2	0.2	.	.	0.1 ǀ	0.3 [4]	0.2	.
1	.	.	22.6	27.1	.	.	16.6 ǀ	19.6 [4]	17.0	.
2	.	.	20.1	28.9	.	.	22.9 ǀ	23.1 [4]	20.1	.
3	.	.	14.4	27.0	.	.	17.8 ǀ	18.5 [4]	15.0	.
5	.	.	14.1	1.5	.	.	1.3 ǀ	1.6 [4]	1.0	.
6	.	.	0.7	.	.	.	6.5 ǀ	6.7 [4]	6.7	.
6-7	.	.	.	8.6	.	.	.	.	.	.
7	.	.	8.2	.	.	.	0.1 ǀ	0.2 [4]	-	.

Women - Femmes - Mujeres
ISCED-76 - CITE-76 - CINE-76

	1999	2000	2001	2002	2003	2004	2005	2006	2007	2008
Total	.	.	112.8	118.0	.	.	89.5 ǀ	96.9 [4]	89.3	.
X	.	.	0.4	0.1	.	.	0.1 ǀ	0.3 [4]	0.2	.
1	.	.	29.3	29.5	.	.	20.2 ǀ	26.0 [4]	25.6	.
2	.	.	26.0	30.2	.	.	26.7 ǀ	26.3 [4]	25.4	.
3	.	.	26.5	39.1	.	.	27.7 ǀ	28.1 [4]	25.2	.
5	.	.	14.0	5.4	.	.	4.2 ǀ	5.2 [4]	3.1	.
6	.	.	2.2	.	.	.	10.6 ǀ	10.8 [4]	9.9	.
6-7	.	.	.	13.9	.	.	.	.	.	.
7	.	.	14.4	.	.	.	0.1 ǀ	0.1 [4]	-	.

ASIA-ASIE-ASIA

Armenia (BA) [5]   Total unemployment - Chômage total - Desempleo total

Total - Total - Total
ISCED-97 - CITE-97 - CINE-97

	1999	2000	2001	2002	2003	2004	2005	2006	2007	2008
Total	.	.	.	.	.	.	.	.	470.9	.
X-0	.	.	.	.	.	.	.	.	0.5	.
1	.	.	.	.	.	.	.	.	3.7	.
2	.	.	.	.	.	.	.	.	38.9	.
3	.	.	.	.	.	.	.	.	210.5	.
4	.	.	.	.	.	.	.	.	118.2	.
5A	.	.	.	.	.	.	.	.	18.6	.
5B	.	.	.	.	.	.	.	.	79.5	.
6	.	.	.	.	.	.	.	.	1.0	.

Explanatory notes: see p. 451.   Notes explicatives: voir p. 454.   Notas explicativas: véase p. 457.

[1] Persons with diploma only. [2] Persons aged 25 years and over. [3] Persons aged 14 years and over. [4] Prior to 2006: urban areas. [5] Persons aged 16 years and over.

[1] Diplômés seulement. [2] Personnes âgées de 25 ans et plus. [3] Personnes âgées de 14 ans et plus. [4] Avant 2006: régions urbaines. [5] Personnes âgées de 16 ans et plus.

[1] Personas con diploma solamente. [2] Personas de 25 años y más. [3] Personas de 14 años y más. [4] Antes de 2006: areas urbanas. [5] Personas de 16 años y más.

3C

UNEMPLOYMENT	CHÔMAGE	DESEMPLEO
By level of education	Par niveau d'instruction	Por nivel de educación

	Thousands				Milliers				Millares	
	1999	2000	2001	2002	2003	2004	2005	2006	2007	2008

Armenia (BA) [1]

Total unemployment - Chômage total - Desempleo total

Men - Hommes - Hombres
ISCED-97 - CITE-97 - CINE-97

	1999	2000	2001	2002	2003	2004	2005	2006	2007	2008
Total									183.7	
X-0									0.2	
1									2.6	
2									21.8	
3									86.9	
4									33.9	
5A									7.3	
5B									30.5	
6									0.4	

Women - Femmes - Mujeres
ISCED-97 - CITE-97 - CINE-97

	1999	2000	2001	2002	2003	2004	2005	2006	2007	2008
Total									287.2	
X-0									0.4	
1									1.0	
2									17.0	
3									123.6	
4									84.3	
5A									11.3	
5B									48.9	
6									0.6	

Armenia (FB) [2][3]

Registered unemployment - Chômage enregistré - Desempleo registrado

Total - Total - Total
ISCED-97 - CITE-97 - CINE-97

	1999	2000	2001	2002	2003	2004	2005	2006	2007	2008
Total	174.9	153.9	138.4	127.3	118.6	108.6	89.0	84.6	75.1	74.7
1									0.6	0.7
1-2	12.4	10.5	8.6	7.1	6.4	5.7	5.5	4.9		
2									3.2	3.1
3									38.0	37.0
3-4	142.4	125.0	112.7	104.2	96.8	88.5	71.0	67.5		
4									23.4	22.6
5A									1.0	2.2
5-6	20.1	18.4	17.1	16.0	15.4	14.4	12.5	12.2		
5B									8.9	9.2
6									-	-

Men - Hommes - Hombres
ISCED-97 - CITE-97 - CINE-97

	1999	2000	2001	2002	2003	2004	2005	2006	2007	2008
Total									19.8	18.3
1									0.3	0.3
2									1.4	1.3
3									9.0	8.9
4									6.6	5.2
5A									0.3	0.3
5B									2.3	2.1
6									-	-

Women - Femmes - Mujeres
ISCED-97 - CITE-97 - CINE-97

	1999	2000	2001	2002	2003	2004	2005	2006	2007	2008
Total									55.2	56.4
1									0.3	0.3
2									1.9	1.8
3									28.9	28.0
4									16.8	17.3
5A									0.7	1.8
5B									6.6	7.1
6									-	-

Azerbaijan (BA) [4]

Total unemployment - Chômage total - Desempleo total

Total - Total - Total
ISCED-97 - CITE-97 - CINE-97

	1999	2000	2001	2002	2003	2004	2005	2006	2007	2008
Total					404.7			291.2	281.1	261.4
X-0					0.5			-	-	-
1					2.6			1.0	1.5	-
2					33.4			7.5	16.2	22.8
3					300.1			217.0	187.6	160.9
4					34.6			27.5	34.1	44.5
5-6					33.5			38.3	41.8	33.2

Men - Hommes - Hombres
ISCED-97 - CITE-97 - CINE-97

	1999	2000	2001	2002	2003	2004	2005	2006	2007	2008
Total					210.5			157.0	169.9	156.9
X-0					0.3			-	-	-
1					1.4			0.4	1.0	-
2					15.2			3.5	11.4	14.8
3					160.7			118.1	115.4	85.5
4					12.7			11.4	15.3	28.7
5-6					20.2			23.8	26.9	27.9

Explanatory notes: see p. 451.

[1] Persons aged 16 years and over. [2] Persons aged 16 to 63 years. [3] Dec. of each year. [4] Persons aged 15 years and over.

Notes explicatives: voir p. 454.

[1] Personnes âgées de 16 ans et plus. [2] Personnes âgées de 16 à 63 ans. [3] Déc. de chaque année. [4] Personnes âgées de 15 ans et plus.

Notas explicativas: véase p. 457.

[1] Personas de 16 años y más. [2] Personas de 16 a 63 años de edad. [3] Dic. de cada año. [4] Personas de 15 años y más.

By level of education   Par niveau d'instruction   Por nivel de educación

	Thousands			Milliers				Millares		
	1999	2000	2001	2002	2003	2004	2005	2006	2007	2008

Azerbaijan (BA) [1]   Total unemployment - Chômage total - Desempleo total

Women - Femmes - Mujeres
ISCED-97 - CITE-97 - CINE-97

	1999	2000	2001	2002	2003	2004	2005	2006	2007	2008
Total	.	.	.	.	194.2	.	.	134.2	111.2	104.5
X-0	.	.	.	.	0.2	.	.	-	-	-
1	.	.	.	.	1.2	.	.	0.6	0.5	-
2	.	.	.	.	18.2	.	.	4.0	4.8	8.0
3	.	.	.	.	139.4	.	.	98.9	72.2	75.4
4	.	.	.	.	21.9	.	.	16.1	18.8	15.8
5-6	.	.	.	.	13.3	.	.	14.5	14.9	5.3

Azerbaijan (FB) [1][2]   Registered unemployment - Chômage enregistré - Desempleo registrado

Total - Total - Total
ISCED-97 - CITE-97 - CINE-97

	1999	2000	2001	2002	2003	2004	2005	2006	2007	2008
Total	45.2	43.7	48.4	51.0	54.4	55.9	56.3	53.9	50.7	44.5
X-0,2	3.0	2.1	2.2	2.6	2.8	2.6	2.5	1.6	1.2	1.0
3	13.9	14.9	17.1	17.1	17.7	17.5	17.0	16.9	14.7	10.8
4	15.2	14.8	16.8	18.0	18.9	19.4	19.6	17.9	17.3	15.9
5-6	13.0	11.9	12.4	13.3	15.1	16.5	17.3	17.5	17.4	16.8

Men - Hommes - Hombres
ISCED-97 - CITE-97 - CINE-97

	1999	2000	2001	2002	2003	2004	2005	2006	2007	2008
Total	19.6	19.3	21.8	23.1	25.3	26.7	27.3	26.3	25.3	23.6
X-0,2	1.0	0.8	0.9	1.0	1.1	1.2	1.1	0.8	0.6	0.5
3	5.2	5.7	7.1	7.2	7.5	7.3	7.1	6.8	6.1	5.1
4	6.6	6.6	7.3	7.7	8.0	8.4	8.5	7.9	7.7	7.3
5-6	6.8	6.1	6.5	7.1	8.7	9.8	10.6	10.9	10.9	10.7

Women - Femmes - Mujeres
ISCED-97 - CITE-97 - CINE-97

	1999	2000	2001	2002	2003	2004	2005	2006	2007	2008
Total	25.6	24.5	26.6	27.9	29.1	29.3	29.1	27.5	25.3	20.9
X-0,2	2.0	1.2	1.3	1.5	1.6	1.4	1.3	0.8	0.6	0.5
3	8.8	9.2	10.0	9.9	10.2	10.2	9.9	10.1	8.5	5.7
4	8.6	8.2	9.5	10.3	10.9	11.0	11.1	10.0	9.6	8.6
5-6	6.2	5.8	5.9	6.1	6.3	6.7	6.7	6.6	6.5	6.0

Bahrain (FB) [1][3]   Work applicants - Demandeurs d'emploi - Solicitantes

Total - Total - Total
ISCED-76 - CITE-76 - CINE-76

	1999	2000	2001	2002	2003	2004	2005	2006	2007	2008
Total	3.754	6.160	.	8.735	11.778	6.293	6.441	6.805	9.536	.
X	0.060	0.102	.	0.431	0.943	0.312	0.199	0.047	0.128	.
0	-	-	.	-	-	-	-	0.102	0.441	.
1	0.567	0.812	.	1.264	1.515	0.738	0.693	0.203	0.366	.
2	0.953	1.606	.	1.998	2.649	1.308	1.199	0.927	1.801	.
3	1.419	2.432	.	3.442	4.615	2.587	2.548	3.005	3.703	.
5	0.399	0.636	.	0.659	1.081	0.678	0.810	0.962	1.000	.
6	0.356	0.553	.	0.746	0.731	0.569	0.879	1.411	2.009	.
7	-	0.012	.	0.022	0.021	0.006	0.015	0.035	0.011	.
9	-	-	.	0.173	0.223	0.095	0.098	0.092	0.077	.
?	-	0.007	.	-	-	-	-	0.021	-	.

Men - Hommes - Hombres
ISCED-76 - CITE-76 - CINE-76

	1999	2000	2001	2002	2003	2004	2005	2006	2007	2008
Total	2.639	4.183	.	4.377	6.034	3.077	2.898	1.525	1.240	.
X	0.052	0.083	.	0.246	0.331	0.129	0.129	0.016	0.024	.
0	-	-	.	-	-	-	-	0.052	0.091	.
1	0.514	0.744	.	0.964	1.196	0.577	0.565	0.113	0.111	.
2	0.826	1.368	.	1.178	1.644	0.808	0.713	0.345	0.239	.
3	0.909	1.488	.	1.412	2.124	1.171	1.084	0.612	0.461	.
5	0.175	0.249	.	0.226	0.378	0.230	0.212	0.170	0.130	.
6	0.163	0.239	.	0.188	0.151	0.069	0.099	0.143	0.135	.
7	-	0.009	.	0.019	0.019	0.004	0.006	0.017	0.006	.
9	-	-	.	0.144	0.191	0.089	0.090	0.052	0.043	.
?	-	0.003	.	-	-	-	-	0.005	-	.

Women - Femmes - Mujeres
ISCED-76 - CITE-76 - CINE-76

	1999	2000	2001	2002	2003	2004	2005	2006	2007	2008
Total	1.115	1.977	.	4.358	5.744	3.216	3.543	5.280	8.296	.
X	0.008	0.019	.	0.185	0.612	0.183	0.070	0.031	0.104	.
0	-	-	.	-	-	-	-	0.050	0.350	.
1	0.053	0.068	.	0.300	0.319	0.161	0.128	0.090	0.255	.
2	0.127	0.238	.	0.820	1.005	0.500	0.486	0.582	1.562	.
3	0.510	0.944	.	2.030	2.491	1.416	1.464	2.393	3.242	.
5	0.224	0.387	.	0.433	0.703	0.448	0.598	0.792	0.870	.
6	0.193	0.314	.	0.558	0.580	0.500	0.780	1.268	1.874	.
7	-	0.003	.	0.003	0.002	0.002	0.009	0.018	0.005	.
9	-	-	.	0.029	0.032	0.006	0.008	0.040	0.034	.
?	-	0.004	.	-	-	-	-	0.016	-	.

Explanatory notes: see p. 451.   Notes explicatives: voir p. 454.   Notas explicativas: véase p. 457.

[1] Persons aged 15 years and over. [2] Dec. of each year. [3] Jan.   [1] Personnes âgées de 15 ans et plus. [2] Déc. de chaque année. [3] Janv.   [1] Personas de 15 años y más. [2] Dic. de cada año. [3] Enero.

	Thousands			Milliers				Millares		
	1999	2000	2001	2002	2003	2004	2005	2006	2007	2008

Georgia (BA) [1] — Total unemployment - Chômage total - Desempleo total

Total - Total - Total
ISCED-97 - CITE-97 - CINE-97

	1999	2000	2001	2002	2003	2004	2005	2006	2007	2008
Total	277.5	212.2	235.6	265.0	235.9	257.6	279.3	274.5	261.0	315.8
X-1	3.6	1.9	2.4	0.5	0.9	0.4	0.9	1.3	0.4	0.5
2	10.8	11.7	7.3	12.0	9.1	14.6	12.4	12.8	12.9	14.0
3	89.7	69.9	83.3	100.7	83.4	89.6	88.8	86.8	83.0	112.0
4	69.7	53.0	61.0	54.2	50.0	58.7	67.6	64.0	54.1	65.2
5-6	98.5	70.2	81.2	96.1	91.2	93.9	108.5	109.6	110.5	123.8
?	4.6	5.6	0.4	1.5	1.3	0.6	1.0	-	-	0.3

Men - Hommes - Hombres
ISCED-97 - CITE-97 - CINE-97

	1999	2000	2001	2002	2003	2004	2005	2006	2007	2008
Total	160.0	116.7	126.9	155.5	124.2	143.2	159.2	165.4	143.7	172.4
X-1	1.8	0.8	1.2	0.2	0.8	0.4	0.7	0.9	0.1	0.4
2	6.4	6.5	5.9	7.2	5.1	10.3	9.8	8.5	8.2	10.1
3	60.3	41.9	50.2	68.0	48.5	53.5	58.3	61.6	53.6	74.8
4	33.7	24.7	28.6	25.7	23.5	27.3	29.1	29.8	23.3	26.3
5-6	55.2	40.2	40.8	53.4	45.4	51.7	61.0	64.5	58.4	60.7
?	2.6	2.6	0.1	1.0	0.9	0.1	0.3	-	-	0.2

Women - Femmes - Mujeres
ISCED-97 - CITE-97 - CINE-97

	1999	2000	2001	2002	2003	2004	2005	2006	2007	2008
Total	117.4	95.5	108.7	109.5	111.7	114.4	120.1	109.1	117.3	143.4
X-1	1.8	1.1	1.1	0.3	0.1	-	0.3	0.4	0.3	0.2
2	4.4	5.2	1.4	4.8	4.0	4.3	2.7	4.3	4.7	4.0
3	29.4	28.0	33.0	32.7	34.9	36.1	30.5	25.2	29.4	37.2
4	36.0	28.3	32.4	28.5	26.5	31.4	38.5	34.0	30.7	38.9
5-6	43.3	30.0	40.4	42.7	45.8	42.1	47.5	45.1	52.1	63.1
?	2.0	2.9	0.3	0.5	0.4	0.5	0.7	-	-	0.1

Hong Kong, China (BA) [1] [2] — Total unemployment - Chômage total - Desempleo total

Total - Total - Total
ISCED-97 - CITE-97 - CINE-97

	1999	2000	2001	2002	2003	2004	2005	2006	2007	2008
Total	207.5	166.9	174.3	254.2	275.2	239.2	197.6	171.1	145.7	130.1
X	4.4	2.9	2.5	3.8	4.7	4.1	2.9	2.4	1.7	1.4
0	-	-	-	-	-	-	-	-	-	-
1	43.4	34.8	34.5	51.5	57.1	51.6	40.3	31.1	24.8	20.4
2	56.1	45.2	46.9	67.0	75.7	63.9	50.3	43.1	34.8	29.1
3	78.3	64.5	66.0	95.5	98.1	86.0	71.3	64.7	54.5	51.3
4	5.6	5.4	5.4	8.3	9.9	8.9	7.4	6.5	6.0	5.7
5A	14.1	9.7	13.3	18.1	18.4	16.1	16.6	15.3	15.3	14.4
5B	4.3	3.2	3.9	7.4	7.3	5.3	5.7	5.5	5.9	5.4
6	1.3	1.2	1.9	2.6	4.1	3.3	3.3	2.5	2.8	2.5

Men - Hommes - Hombres
ISCED-97 - CITE-97 - CINE-97

	1999	2000	2001	2002	2003	2004	2005	2006	2007	2008
Total	140.6	109.6	117.8	164.0	180.0	151.8	127.5	110.2	89.2	79.4
X	2.9	2.1	1.7	2.3	2.9	2.2	1.7	1.6	1.0	1.0
0	-	-	-	-	-	-	-	-	-	-
1	33.3	26.2	26.7	36.2	40.7	34.4	28.2	21.5	16.3	13.6
2	43.4	33.1	35.3	47.4	55.0	44.2	35.8	30.6	23.2	19.7
3	45.8	37.1	39.4	55.4	57.2	50.3	42.7	39.0	31.8	29.3
4	3.5	3.1	3.4	4.9	5.8	5.7	4.3	3.9	3.5	3.3
5A	8.2	5.4	7.9	11.4	11.1	9.6	9.3	8.7	8.9	8.0
5B	2.8	2.0	2.4	4.8	4.6	3.4	3.6	3.3	3.1	3.0
6	0.7	0.6	1.0	1.6	2.6	2.2	2.0	1.6	1.5	1.6

Women - Femmes - Mujeres
ISCED-97 - CITE-97 - CINE-97

	1999	2000	2001	2002	2003	2004	2005	2006	2007	2008
Total	66.9	57.3	56.5	90.1	95.3	87.4	70.1	60.8	56.5	50.7
X	1.4	0.8	0.8	1.5	1.8	1.9	1.1	0.8	0.7	0.4
0	-	-	-	-	-	-	-	-	-	-
1	10.1	8.6	7.8	15.2	16.4	17.2	12.1	9.6	8.4	6.8
2	12.8	12.2	11.6	19.6	20.7	19.7	14.4	12.5	11.7	9.4
3	32.6	27.4	26.6	40.0	40.9	35.8	28.6	25.7	22.7	22.0
4	2.0	2.3	2.0	3.4	4.0	3.2	3.1	2.6	2.6	2.5
5A	5.9	4.3	5.3	6.7	7.3	6.5	7.3	6.5	6.4	6.3
5B	1.4	1.2	1.5	2.6	2.7	2.0	2.1	2.2	2.9	2.4
6	0.5	0.6	0.9	1.1	1.6	1.1	1.3	0.9	1.3	0.9

India (FB) [3] [4] — Work applicants - Demandeurs d'emploi - Solicitantes

Total - Total - Total
ISCED-76 - CITE-76 - CINE-76

	1999	2000	2001	2002	2003	2004	2005	2006	2007	2008
Total	40 371	41 344	41 996	41 171	41 389	40 458	39 348	.	.	
X-2	11 712	12 190	11 625	11 616	11 182	12 154	11 402	.	.	
3	16 275	16 694	17 370	16 826	17 020	15 501	14 833	.	.	
5	7 223	7 348	7 699	7 635	7 882	7 541	7 727	.	.	
6	4 510	4 356	4 518	4 291	4 515	4 435	4 422	.	.	
7	651	756	783	803	789	826	964	.	.	

Explanatory notes: see p. 451.
[1] Persons aged 15 years and over. [2] Excl. marine, military and institutional populations. [3] Persons aged 14 years and over. [4] Dec. of each year.

Notes explicatives: voir p. 454.
[1] Personnes âgées de 15 ans et plus. [2] Non compris le personnel militaire, de la marine et la population institutionnelle. [3] Personnes âgées de 14 ans et plus. [4] Déc. de chaque année.

Notas explicativas: véase p. 457.
[1] Personas de 15 años y más. [2] Excl. el personal militar y de la marina, y la población institucional. [3] Personas de 14 años y más. [4] Dic. de cada año.

	Thousands			Milliers				Millares		
	1999	2000	2001	2002	2003	2004	2005	2006	2007	2008

India (FB) [1] [2] — Work applicants - Demandeurs d'emploi - Solicitantes

Men - Hommes - Hombres
ISCED-76 - CITE-76 - CINE-76

	1999	2000	2001	2002	2003	2004	2005	2006	2007	2008
Total	30 438	30 887	31 111	30 521	30 636	29 746	28 742	.	.	.
X-2	9 503	9 645	9 265	8 888	8 462	8 772	8 337	.	.	.
3	12 099	12 346	12 864	12 645	12 722	11 608	10 970	.	.	.
5	5 368	5 455	5 646	5 619	5 915	5 730	5 752	.	.	.
6	3 092	2 985	3 074	2 874	3 081	3 125	3 095	.	.	.
7	376	456	261	495	455	511	588	.	.	.

Women - Femmes - Mujeres
ISCED-76 - CITE-76 - CINE-76

	1999	2000	2001	2002	2003	2004	2005	2006	2007	2008
Total	9 933	10 457	10 885	10 650	10 752	10 712	10 606	.	.	.
X-2	2 209	2 545	2 360	2 728	2 719	3 383	3 065	.	.	.
3	4 176	4 348	4 506	4 181	4 298	3 893	3 863	.	.	.
5	1 855	1 893	2 053	2 016	1 967	1 810	1 975	.	.	.
6	1 418	1 371	1 444	1 417	1 434	1 310	1 327	.	.	.
7	275	300	522	308	334	315	376	.	.	.

Indonesia (BA) [3] [4] — Total unemployment - Chômage total - Desempleo total

Total - Total - Total
ISCED-76 - CITE-76 - CINE-76

	1999	2000	2001	2002	2003	2004	2005	2006	2007	2008
Total	6 030.3	5 813.2	8 005.0	9 132.1	9 939.3	10 251.4	11 899.3 [5]	10 932.0	10 011.1	9 394.5
X	.	29.0	278.3	214.7	352.5	336.0	264.5 [5]	170.7	94.3	103.2
X-0	278.5	.	.	.	.	.	.	.	.	.
0	.	192.2	573.1	653.6	710.4	668.3	673.5 [5]	611.3	438.5	443.8
1	1 151.3	1 217.0	1 893.6	2 353.3	2 495.9	2 275.3	2 729.9 [5]	2 589.7	2 179.8	2 100.0
2	1 159.5	1 367.9	1 786.3	2 146.5	2 458.9	2 690.9	3 151.2 [5]	2 730.0	2 264.2	1 974.0
3	2 886.2	2 546.4	2 933.5	3 244.1	3 472.9	3 695.5	4 376.1 [5]	4 156.7	4 070.6	3 812.5
5	243.9	54.3	95.6	86.6	79.6	92.8	101.0 [5]	94.4	176.0	136.7
6	.	130.4	155.5	163.9	123.2	144.5	207.5 [5]	183.6	221.2	226.0
6-7	310.9	.	.	.	.	.	.	.	.	.
7	.	276.1	289.1	269.4	245.9	348.1	395.5 [5]	395.6	566.6	598.3

Men - Hommes - Hombres
ISCED-76 - CITE-76 - CINE-76

	1999	2000	2001	2002	2003	2004	2005	2006	2007	2008
Total	3 524.2	3 340.7	4 032.4	4 727.8	5 100.1	5 345.7	6 292.4 [5]	5 772.6	5 571.9	5 245.1
X	.	11.5	78.9	57.9	114.7	126.5	101.4 [5]	38.2	42.3	37.9
X-0	168.3	.	.	.	.	.	.	.	.	.
0	.	109.4	232.9	269.5	262.2	305.7	316.2 [5]	270.1	244.8	246.2
1	669.4	716.4	934.5	1 156.3	1 245.9	1 188.2	1 438.1 [5]	1 334.4	1 228.3	1 155.3
2	703.6	821.2	922.0	1 166.2	1 296.0	1 415.5	1 721.8 [5]	1 513.2	1 293.6	1 102.1
3	1 712.1	1 462.5	1 612.3	1 837.9	1 967.3	2 054.6	2 401.4 [5]	2 328.0	2 356.5	2 260.7
5	99.5	26.9	34.5	31.7	39.8	36.1	35.5 [5]	33.4	56.8	48.7
6	.	58.3	71.1	73.6	62.2	69.1	99.2 [5]	79.6	92.3	103.3
6-7	171.3	.	.	.	.	.	.	.	.	.
7	.	134.6	146.3	134.5	112.0	150.0	178.9 [5]	175.8	257.4	290.9

Women - Femmes - Mujeres
ISCED-76 - CITE-76 - CINE-76

	1999	2000	2001	2002	2003	2004	2005	2006	2007	2008
Total	2 506.1	2 472.6	3 972.6	4 404.3	4 839.2	4 905.7	5 606.8 [5]	5 159.4	4 439.2	4 149.5
X	.	17.6	199.4	156.8	237.9	209.5	163.1 [5]	132.5	52.0	65.3
X-0	110.2	100.4	539.7	.	.	.	.	.	.	.
0	.	82.9	340.2	384.1	448.2	362.5	357.3 [5]	341.2	193.7	197.6
1	481.9	500.6	959.0	1 197.0	1 250.0	1 087.1	1 291.8 [5]	1 255.3	951.5	944.7
2	455.9	546.7	864.3	980.3	1 163.0	1 275.5	1 429.5 [5]	1 216.9	970.6	871.9
3	1 174.1	1 083.9	1 321.2	1 406.2	1 505.6	1 640.9	1 974.7 [5]	1 828.7	1 714.0	1 551.8
5	144.4	27.4	61.2	54.8	39.8	56.7	65.5 [5]	61.0	119.2	88.0
6	.	72.1	84.4	90.2	61.0	75.3	108.3 [5]	104.1	128.9	122.7
6-7	139.7	.	.	.	.	.	.	.	.	.
7	.	141.5	142.8	134.9	133.9	198.1	216.7 [5]	219.7	309.2	307.4

Iran, Islamic Rep. of (BA) [6] — Total unemployment - Chômage total - Desempleo total

Total - Total - Total
ISCED-97 - CITE-97 - CINE-97

	1999	2000	2001	2002	2003	2004	2005	2006	2007	2008
Total	.	.	.	.	.	.	2 577	2 549	2 407	2 316
X	.	.	.	.	.	.	3	3	2	.
1	.	.	.	.	.	.	529	516	471	424
2	.	.	.	.	.	.	586	610	558	542
3	.	.	.	.	.	.	931	867	794	741
5A	.	.	.	.	.	.	.	.	.	410
5A,6	.	.	.	.	.	.	343	347	381	.
5B	.	.	.	.	.	.	185	205	201	199
6	.	.	.	.	.	.	.	.	.	1
?	.	.	.	.	.	.	98	94	79	76

Explanatory notes: see p. 451.

[1] Persons aged 14 years and over. [2] Dec. of each year. [3] Persons aged 15 years and over. [4] Aug. of each year. [5] Nov. [6] Persons aged 10 years and over.

Notes explicatives: voir p. 454.

[1] Personnes âgées de 14 ans et plus. [2] Déc. de chaque année. [3] Personnes âgées de 15 ans et plus. [4] Août de chaque année. [5] Nov. [6] Personnes âgées de 10 ans et plus.

Notas explicativas: véase p. 457.

[1] Personas de 14 años y más. [2] Dic. de cada año. [3] Personas de 15 años y más. [4] Agosto de cada año. [5] Nov. [6] Personas de 10 años y más.

3C

UNEMPLOYMENT	CHÔMAGE	DESEMPLEO
By level of education	**Par niveau d'instruction**	**Por nivel de educación**

	Thousands			Milliers					Millares	
	1999	2000	2001	2002	2003	2004	2005	2006	2007	2008

Iran, Islamic Rep. of (BA) [1] — Total unemployment - Chômage total - Desempleo total

Men - Hommes - Hombres
ISCED-97 - CITE-97 - CINE-97

	2005	2006	2007	2008
Total	1 768	1 791	1 694	1 646
X	2	2	1	
1	461	466	424	385
2	507	544	503	485
3	564	547	534	521
5A				152
5A,6	141	129	130	
5B	92	102	101	103
6				1
?	88	87	70	69

Women - Femmes - Mujeres
ISCED-97 - CITE-97 - CINE-97

	2005	2006	2007	2008
Total	810	758	714	670
X	1	1	1	
1	68	50	46	40
2	78	66	55	56
3	367	321	260	220
5A				258
5A,6	203	218	251	
5B	93	103	100	96
6				0
?	10	7	9	7

Israel (BA) [2] — Total unemployment - Chômage total - Desempleo total

Total - Total - Total
ISCED-76 - CITE-76 - CINE-76 ... ISCED-97 - CITE-97 - CINE-97

ISCED-76	1999	2000	2001	2002	2003	2004	2005	2006	2007	2008	ISCED-97
Total	208.5	213.8	234.0	262.4	279.8	277.7	246.4	236.1	211.8	180.4	Total
X	1.4	-	2.3	2.3	-	3.8	2.5	3.3	2.2		X
1	22.0										0
2	27.8	29.4	25.2	28.8	30.0	28.9	26.7	26.5	25.9	18.3	1
3	88.0	28.1	30.9	29.6	33.4	32.8	30.6	29.5	27.1	21.5	2
5	45.7	100.2	113.7	126.8	136.9	134.8	120.4	118.2	103.1	86.6	3
6	23.4	28.2	31.1	39.4	41.1	39.7	31.8	29.8	27.8	28.2	5A
9	0.2	23.7	28.5	32.5	34.1	33.6	31.4	25.6	22.7	22.5	5B
		-	-	-	-	-	-				6
						2.8					?

Men - Hommes - Hombres
ISCED-76 - CITE-76 - CINE-76 ... ISCED-97 - CITE-97 - CINE-97

ISCED-76	1999	2000	2001	2002	2003	2004	2005	2006	2007	2008	ISCED-97
Total	108.8	111.7	120.9	138.4	142.8	136.5	124.9	118.5	104.8	90.8	Total
X	1.0	-	-	-	-	1.6	-	2.0	-		X
1	17.6										0
2	18.8	22.3	18.0	21.3	21.5	20.0	19.4	18.6	18.2	13.2	1
3	40.3	17.3	19.1	19.6	20.7	18.4	19.5	17.9	16.1	14.3	2
5	19.4	46.9	53.7	60.4	65.4	62.7	57.2	53.5	47.8	38.3	3
6	11.5	12.8	14.1	18.2	18.1	17.6	12.5	14.3	11.9	13.1	5A
9	0.1	10.0	13.0	15.4	14.4	14.2	14.0	10.7	8.4	10.3	5B
			-								6
											?

Women - Femmes - Mujeres
ISCED-76 - CITE-76 - CINE-76 ... ISCED-97 - CITE-97 - CINE-97

ISCED-76	1999	2000	2001	2002	2003	2004	2005	2006	2007	2008	ISCED-97
Total	99.7	102.1	113.0	124.0	137.1	141.2	121.5	117.6	107.0	89.6	Total
X	0.4	-	-	-	-	2.2	-	1.3	-		X
1	4.4										0
2	9.0	7.0	7.3	7.5	8.4	8.8	7.4	7.9	7.7	5.1	1
3	47.7	10.8	11.8	10.0	12.7	14.4	11.1	11.6	11.0	7.1	2
5	26.3	53.3	59.9	66.4	71.4	72.1	63.2	64.7	55.3	48.3	3
6	11.9	15.5	16.9	21.2	23.0	22.0	19.2	15.6	15.9	15.1	5A
9	0.1	13.7	15.5	17.1	19.7	19.4	17.4	14.9	14.3	12.2	5B
			-								6
											?

Japan (BA) [2][3] — Total unemployment - Chômage total - Desempleo total

Total - Total - Total
ISCED-76 - CITE-76 - CINE-76

	1999	2000	2001	2002	2003	2004	2005	2006	2007	2008
Total	3 010	3 180	3 110	3 430 [4]	3 430	3 070	2 880	2 680	2 500	2 560
X										
1-2	700	720	670							
1-3				2 440 [4]	2 430	2 160	1 990	1 830	1 680	1 710
3	1 540	1 570	1 660	[4]						
5	440	420	380	500 [4]	500	430	430	400	390	420
6-7	330	310	390	500 [4]	500	470	450	450	430	430

Explanatory notes: see p. 451.

[1] Persons aged 10 years and over. [2] Persons aged 15 years and over. [3] Refer only to persons graduated from school. [4] Prior to 2002: Special Labour Force Survey, february of each year.

Notes explicatives: voir p. 454.

[1] Personnes âgées de 10 ans et plus. [2] Personnes âgées de 15 ans et plus. [3] Se rapportent seulement aux personnes diplômées de l'école. [4] Avant 2002: Enquête spécial sur la main-d'oeuvre, février de chaque année.

Notas explicativas: véase p. 457.

[1] Personas de 10 años y más. [2] Personas de 15 años y más. [3] Se refieren solamente de las personas con diploma. [4] Antes de 2002: encuesta especial sobre la fuerza de trabajo, febrero de cada año.

	Thousands			Milliers				Millares		
	1999	2000	2001	2002	2003	2004	2005	2006	2007	2008

Japan (BA) [1] [2] — Total unemployment - Chômage total - Desempleo total

Men - Hommes - Hombres
ISCED-76 - CITE-76 - CINE-76

	1999	2000	2001	2002	2003	2004	2005	2006	2007	2008
Total	1 820	1 990	1 880	2 090 [3]	2 110	1 880	1 740	1 640	1 490	1 530
X										
1-2	510	500	480	. [3]	.					
1-3				1 550	1 540	1 370	1 260	1 130	1 040	1 060
3	920	950	950	. [3]						
5	130	160	130	170 [3]	190	150	150	160	140	160
6-7	260	330	310	380 [3]	370	360	320	350	320	310

Women - Femmes - Mujeres
ISCED-76 - CITE-76 - CINE-76

	1999	2000	2001	2002	2003	2004	2005	2006	2007	2008
Total	1 190	1 230	1 230	1 340 [3]	1 320	1 190	1 140	1 040	1 000	1 030
X										
1-2	190	220	180	. [3]						
1-3				890	890	790	730	700	640	650
3	620	620	710	. [3]						
5	310	270	250	330 [3]	310	280	280	240	250	260
6-7	70	80	80	120 [3]	120	120	130	100	110	120

Kazakhstan (BA) [1] — Total unemployment - Chômage total - Desempleo total

Total - Total - Total
ISCED-97 - CITE-97 - CINE-97

	1999	2000	2001	2002	2003	2004	2005	2006	2007	2008
Total	.	.	780.3	690.8	672.1	658.8	640.7	625.4	597.2	557.8
1	.	.	83.4	54.2	53.4	48.4	42.3	44.5	37.3	36.4
2	.	.	338.4	289.1	273.4	262.4	255.2	234.4	228.1	215.4
3	.	.	258.0	263.0	247.2	251.4	233.3	230.2	219.2	182.2
4	.	.	24.7	16.9	22.8	27.3	35.7	35.2	30.7	39.0
5B	.	.	75.7	67.6	75.4	69.3	74.3	81.1	81.9	84.8

Men - Hommes - Hombres
ISCED-97 - CITE-97 - CINE-97

	1999	2000	2001	2002	2003	2004	2005	2006	2007	2008
Total	.	.	338.0	283.8	281.4	281.1	270.6	262.5	244.5	226.5
1	.	.	44.8	27.5	28.2	24.6	20.5	20.9	19.7	16.7
2	.	.	153.6	123.8	122.4	118.1	112.3	104.2	96.9	92.0
3	.	.	95.2	98.5	95.7	99.8	93.9	93.7	89.5	68.6
4	.	.	11.9	7.2	9.0	13.6	14.0	17.8	13.6	20.8
5B	.	.	32.4	26.9	26.1	24.9	29.9	25.9	24.9	28.4

Women - Femmes - Mujeres
ISCED-97 - CITE-97 - CINE-97

	1999	2000	2001	2002	2003	2004	2005	2006	2007	2008
Total	.	.	442.4	407.0	390.7	377.8	370.1	362.9	352.7	331.4
1	.	.	38.6	26.7	25.2	23.8	21.8	23.6	17.6	19.7
2	.	.	184.8	165.3	151.0	144.3	142.8	130.2	131.3	123.4
3	.	.	162.8	164.5	151.5	151.5	139.4	136.5	129.7	113.6
4	.	.	12.8	9.7	13.9	13.7	21.7	17.4	17.1	18.3
5B	.	.	43.3	40.7	49.3	44.4	44.4	55.3	57.0	56.4

Korea, Republic of (BA) [1] — Total unemployment - Chômage total - Desempleo total

Total - Total - Total
ISCED-97 - CITE-97 - CINE-97

	1999	2000	2001	2002	2003	2004	2005	2006	2007	2008
Total	1 374	979 [4]	899	752	818	860	887	827	783	769
0-1	141	98 [4]	80	55	50	59	64	54	47	49
2	219	146 [4]	123	93	82	90	90	82	72	69
3	734	505 [4]	462	380	432	460	472	420	389	384
5A,6	165	123 [4]	129	126	147	147	144	164	153	162
5B	116	107 [4]	104	98	106	105	117	108	123	106

Men - Hommes - Hombres
ISCED-97 - CITE-97 - CINE-97

	1999	2000	2001	2002	2003	2004	2005	2006	2007	2008
Total	926	647 [4]	591	491	508	534	553	533	517	505
0-1	86	56 [4]	49	32	29	35	38	34	30	31
2	149	100 [4]	84	62	51	57	62	56	47	49
3	495	334 [4]	299	249	273	294	295	281	263	261
5A,6	126	91 [4]	97	91	97	95	95	103	100	104
5B	70	66 [4]	61	57	58	53	63	59	76	60

Women - Femmes - Mujeres
ISCED-97 - CITE-97 - CINE-97

	1999	2000	2001	2002	2003	2004	2005	2006	2007	2008
Total	442	332 [4]	308	261	310	326	334	294	266	265
0-1	55	42 [4]	31	23	21	23	26	20	17	18
2	70	47 [4]	40	31	32	33	27	26	25	21
3	238	170 [4]	163	130	159	166	177	138	125	122
5A,6	39	32 [4]	32	36	50	52	50	61	52	58
5B	45	41 [4]	43	41	48	52	54	49	46	46

Explanatory notes: see p. 451.

[1] Persons aged 15 years and over. [2] Refer only to persons graduated from school. [3] Prior to 2002: Special Labour Force Survey, february of each year. [4] Estimates based on the 2000 Population Census results.

Notes explicatives: voir p. 454.

[1] Personnes âgées de 15 ans et plus. [2] Se rapportent seulement aux personnes diplômées de l'école. [3] Avant 2002: Enquête spécial sur la main-d'oeuvre, février de chaque année. [4] Estimations basées sur les résultats du Recensement de la population de 2000.

Notas explicativas: véase p. 457.

[1] Personas de 15 años y más. [2] Se refieren solamente de las personas con diploma. [3] Antes de 2002: encuesta especial sobre la fuerza de trabajo, febrero de cada año. [4] Estimaciones basadas en los resultados del Censo de población de 2000.

3C

UNEMPLOYMENT	CHÔMAGE	DESEMPLEO
By level of education	Par niveau d'instruction	Por nivel de educación

	Thousands				Milliers				Millares	
	1999	2000	2001	2002	2003	2004	2005	2006	2007	2008

Kuwait (FD) [1] — Registered unemployment - Chômage enregistré - Desempleo registrado

Total - Total - Total
ISCED-97 - CITE-97 - CINE-97

	1999	2000	2001	2002	2003	2004	2005	2006	2007	2008
Total	8.921	9.305	9.464	15.053	18.061	25.919	25.698	24.921	.	.
X	3.543	3.759	3.833	3.980	4.038	6.866	7.149	7.323		
1					1.533	1.808	1.710	1.699		
1-2	3.983	4.170	4.247	4.141						
2					2.399	2.977	3.058	3.146		
3					5.233	6.431	7.414	5.080		
3-4.5B	1.144	1.142	1.129	6.013						
4					2.189	4.311	2.967	5.230		
5A.6	0.247	0.231	0.251	0.919						
5					2.600	3.436	3.328	2.385		
6					0.012	0.012	0.011	0.013		
?	0.004	0.003	0.004	-	0.057	0.078	0.061	0.045		

Men - Hommes - Hombres
ISCED-97 - CITE-97 - CINE-97

	1999	2000	2001	2002	2003	2004	2005	2006	2007	2008
Total	7.264	7.467	7.584	9.443	10.129	12.722	12.836	11.874		
X	2.772	2.891	2.962	2.991	2.868	3.823	3.854	3.856		
1					1.277	1.403	1.316	1.280		
1-2	3.511	3.593	3.639	3.459						
2					1.970	2.445	2.499	2.473		
3					2.652	3.034	3.468	2.333		
3-4.5B	0.754	0.815	0.833	2.715						
4					0.650	1.049	0.840	1.279		
5A.6	0.157	0.152	0.148	0.278						
5					0.686	0.931	0.833	0.625		
6					0.011	0.011	0.009	0.010		
?	0.002	-	0.002	-	0.015	0.026	0.017	0.018		

Women - Femmes - Mujeres
ISCED-97 - CITE-97 - CINE-97

	1999	2000	2001	2002	2003	2004	2005	2006	2007	2008
Total	1.657	1.838	1.880	5.610	7.932	13.197	12.862	13.047		
X	0.771	0.868	0.871	0.989	1.170	3.043	3.295	3.467		
1					0.256	0.405	0.394	0.419		
1-2	0.472	0.577	0.608	0.682						
2					0.429	0.532	0.559	0.673		
3					2.581	3.397	3.946	2.747		
3-4.5B	0.329	0.311	0.296	3.298						
4					1.539	3.262	2.127	3.951		
5A.6	0.083	0.079	0.103	0.641						
5					1.914	2.505	2.495	1.760		
6					0.001	0.001	0.002	0.003		
?	0.002	0.003	0.002	-	0.042	0.052	0.044	0.027		

Kyrgyzstan (BA) [2][3] — Total unemployment - Chômage total - Desempleo total

Total - Total - Total
ISCED-97 - CITE-97 - CINE-97

	1999	2000	2001	2002	2003	2004	2005	2006	2007	2008
Total	.	.	.	.	265.5	212.3	185.7	183.5	188.9	.
1					3.0	3.7	4.7	3.4	5.5	
2					33.4	17.5	13.6	20.6	19.7	
3					136.4	132.3	118.5	106.2	117.3	
4					59.9	35.6	29.1	28.1	28.3	
5A					32.7	23.3	19.8	25.2	18.2	

Men - Hommes - Hombres
ISCED-97 - CITE-97 - CINE-97

	1999	2000	2001	2002	2003	2004	2005	2006	2007	2008
Total					132.6	113.1	98.8	95.7	101.4	
1					1.6	2.3	3.9	2.4	3.7	
2					16.4	10.6	8.4	12.7	11.5	
3					73.0	74.5	64.1	56.2	63.5	
4					26.3	13.7	11.9	12.3	13.6	
5A					15.3	12.0	10.3	12.2	9.2	

Women - Femmes - Mujeres
ISCED-97 - CITE-97 - CINE-97

	1999	2000	2001	2002	2003	2004	2005	2006	2007	2008
Total					132.9	99.2	86.9	87.8	87.5	
1					1.5	1.4	0.8	1.1	1.8	
2					17.0	6.9	5.2	7.9	8.2	
3					63.4	57.7	54.3	50.0	53.8	
4					33.6	21.9	17.2	15.8	14.6	
5A					17.4	11.3	9.4	13.1	8.9	

Kyrgyzstan (FB) [2] — Registered unemployment - Chômage enregistré - Desempleo registrado

Total - Total - Total
ISCED-76 - CITE-76 - CINE-76

	1999	2000	2001	2002	2003	2004	2005	2006	2007	2008
Total	54.7	58.3	60.5	60.2	57.4	58.2	68.0	73.4	71.3	.
1	5.6	5.9	5.7	5.8	6.3	5.1	7.7	7.5	7.9	
2	12.6	12.0	14.2	12.5	12.5	13.2	15.2	16.2	14.6	
3	30.5	34.7	34.5	36.5	33.6	34.1	37.5	42.6	42.6	
5	5.9	5.7	6.1	5.4	5.0	5.7	7.6	7.0	6.3	

Explanatory notes: see p. 451.

[1] June of each year. [2] Persons aged 15 years and over. [3] Nov. of each year.

Notes explicatives: voir p. 454.

[1] Juin de chaque année. [2] Personnes âgées de 15 ans et plus. [3] Nov. de chaque année.

Notas explicativas: véase p. 457.

[1] Junio de cada año. [2] Personas de 15 años y más. [3] Nov. de cada año.

	Thousands				Milliers				Millares	
	1999	2000	2001	2002	2003	2004	2005	2006	2007	2008

Kyrgyzstan (FB) [1] Registered unemployment - Chômage enregistré - Desempleo registrado

Men - Hommes - Hombres
ISCED-76 - CITE-76 - CINE-76

	1999	2000	2001	2002	2003	2004	2005	2006	2007	2008
Total	24.2	27.1	28.0	27.6	26.5	26.8	33.2	35.5	35.5	.
1	2.6	2.8	2.5	2.4	3.3	2.1	3.8	3.7	3.6	.
2	5.6	5.0	5.9	5.3	5.0	5.6	7.1	7.3	6.6	.
3	13.7	17.0	17.0	17.7	16.2	16.8	17.9	21.6	22.7	.
5	2.3	2.3	2.5	2.2	2.1	2.2	3.3	3.0	2.6	.

Women - Femmes - Mujeres
ISCED-76 - CITE-76 - CINE-76

	1999	2000	2001	2002	2003	2004	2005	2006	2007	2008
Total	30.6	31.2	32.5	32.6	30.9	31.4	34.9	37.9	35.8	.
1	3.1	3.1	3.1	3.4	3.0	3.0	3.9	3.9	4.3	.
2	7.0	7.0	8.2	7.2	7.5	7.6	8.1	9.0	8.0	.
3	16.8	17.7	17.5	18.8	17.4	17.4	19.6	21.0	19.9	.
5	3.7	3.5	3.6	3.2	3.0	3.5	4.2	4.1	3.7	.

Liban (B) [1] Total unemployment - Chômage total - Desempleo total

Total - Total - Total
ISCED-97 - CITE-97 - CINE-97

	1999	2000	2001	2002	2003	2004	2005	2006	2007	2008
Total	.	.	.	.	.	94.4	.	.	110.4	.
X	.	.	.	.	.	6.0	.	.	3.0	.
0	.	.	.	.	.	0.0	.	.	2.6	.
1	.	.	.	.	.	26.7	.	.	24.6	.
2	.	.	.	.	.	24.8	.	.	25.6	.
3	.	.	.	.	.	17.0	.	.	21.7	.
5-6	.	.	.	.	.	20.0	.	.	32.8	.

Men - Hommes - Hombres
ISCED-97 - CITE-97 - CINE-97

	1999	2000	2001	2002	2003	2004	2005	2006	2007	2008
Total	.	.	.	.	.	67.3	.	.	79.3	.
X	.	.	.	.	.	4.7	.	.	2.4	.
0	.	.	.	.	.	0.0	.	.	2.1	.
1	.	.	.	.	.	22.3	.	.	20.5	.
2	.	.	.	.	.	18.7	.	.	19.7	.
3	.	.	.	.	.	11.6	.	.	15.8	.
5-6	.	.	.	.	.	10.0	.	.	18.7	.

Women - Femmes - Mujeres
ISCED-97 - CITE-97 - CINE-97

	1999	2000	2001	2002	2003	2004	2005	2006	2007	2008
Total	.	.	.	.	.	27.1	.	.	31.1	.
X	.	.	.	.	.	1.3	.	.	0.6	.
0	.	.	.	.	.	0.0	.	.	0.5	.
1	.	.	.	.	.	4.4	.	.	4.1	.
2	.	.	.	.	.	6.1	.	.	5.9	.
3	.	.	.	.	.	5.4	.	.	5.8	.
5-6	.	.	.	.	.	10.0	.	.	14.2	.

Macau, China (BA) [2] Total unemployment - Chômage total - Desempleo total

Total - Total - Total
ISCED-76 - CITE-76 - CINE-76

	1999	2000	2001	2002	2003	2004	2005	2006	2007	ISCED-97 - CITE-97 - CINE-97
Total	13.2	14.2	14.0	13.7	13.1	11.2	10.3	10.4	9.5	10.1 Total
X-0	2.2	2.4	0.3	0.2	0.2	0.1	0.1	0.1	0.2	0.2 X
1	5.1	5.2	1.8	1.8	1.6	1.4	1.1	1.0	0.6	0.6 0
2	3.7	4.1	4.8	4.8	5.0	4.0	3.3	2.8	2.6	2.7 1
3	1.4	1.6	4.1	4.3	3.5	3.2	3.2	3.3	3.0	2.8 2
5	0.1	0.1	2.0	2.0	1.8	1.6	1.7	2.0	2.1	2.2 3
6-7	0.8	0.8	0.8	0.6	0.8	0.7	0.8	1.1	0.8	1.3 5A,6
9	-	-	0.1	0.1	0.2	0.1	0.1	0.2	0.1	0.3 5B
			-	0.0	0.0	0.0	0.0	0.0	0.0	0.0 ?

Men - Hommes - Hombres
ISCED-76 - CITE-76 - CINE-76

	1999	2000	2001	2002	2003	2004	2005	2006	2007	ISCED-97 - CITE-97 - CINE-97
Total	9.1	9.8	9.5	9.1	8.3	6.8	5.8	5.6	5.6	5.7 Total
X-0	1.5	1.5	0.2	0.1	0.1	0.1	0.1	0.1	0.1	0.1 X
1	3.6	3.9	1.2	1.3	1.2	1.0	0.5	0.5	0.3	0.4 0
2	2.6	2.8	3.4	3.1	3.3	2.7	2.0	1.7	1.8	1.8 1
3	0.9	1.1	2.9	2.8	2.2	1.8	1.7	1.8	1.8	1.5 2
5	0.1	0.1	1.2	1.3	1.0	0.9	0.9	0.8	1.1	1.2 3
6-7	0.4	0.3	0.6	0.4	0.5	0.3	0.5	0.6	0.4	0.6 5A,6
9	-	-	0.1	-	0.1	0.1	-	0.1	0.1	0.1 5B
			-	0.0	0.0	0.0	0.0	0.0	0.0	0.0 ?

Women - Femmes - Mujeres
ISCED-76 - CITE-76 - CINE-76

	1999	2000	2001	2002	2003	2004	2005	2006	2007	ISCED-97 - CITE-97 - CINE-97
Total	4.2	4.4	4.5	4.6	4.8	4.4	4.5	4.8	3.9	4.3 Total
X-0	0.7	0.9	0.1	0.1	0.1	0.1	0.1	-	0.1	0.1 X
1	1.5	1.3	0.5	0.5	0.4	0.4	0.5	0.4	0.3	0.2 0
2	1.1	1.3	1.4	1.7	1.6	1.3	1.3	1.1	0.8	0.9 1
3	0.6	0.5	1.3	1.4	1.4	1.4	1.4	1.5	1.2	1.3 2
5	-	-	0.8	0.7	0.9	0.7	0.8	1.2	0.9	1.0 3
6-7	0.4	0.4	0.3	0.2	0.4	0.4	0.3	0.5	0.4	0.7 5A,6
9	-	-	-	-	0.1	-	0.1	0.1	0.1	0.2 5B
			-	0.0	0.0	0.0	0.0	0.0	0.0	0.0 ?

Explanatory notes: see p. 451.   Notes explicatives: voir p. 454.   Notas explicativas: véase p. 457.

[1] Persons aged 15 years and over. [2] Persons aged 14 years and over.   [1] Personnes âgées de 15 ans et plus. [2] Personnes âgées de 14 ans et plus.   [1] Personas de 15 años y más. [2] Personas de 14 años y más.

UNEMPLOYMENT   CHÔMAGE   DESEMPLEO

By level of education   Par niveau d'instruction   Por nivel de educación

	1999	2000	2001	2002	2003	2004	2005	2006	2007	2008
	Thousands				Milliers				Millares	

Malaysia (BA) [1]
Total unemployment - Chômage total - Desempleo total

Total - Total - Total
ISCED-97 - CITE-97 - CINE-97

	1999	2000	2001	2002	2003	2004	2005	2006	2007	2008
Total	313.7	286.9	342.4	343.5	369.8	366.6	368.1	353.6	351.4	368.5
X	7.6	10.0	9.8	13.6	13.4	11.1	9.5	10.7	7.7	14.2
1	47.7	43.8	46.0	46.4	45.7	48.7	42.2	41.0	39.0	38.2
2-3	214.5	189.3	236.0	220.5	240.9	230.2	229.6	215.1	216.5	224.3
5-6	43.9	43.7	50.5	63.0	69.9	76.6	86.8	86.7	88.2	91.7

Men - Hommes - Hombres
ISCED-97 - CITE-97 - CINE-97

	1999	2000	2001	2002	2003	2004	2005	2006	2007	2008
Total	212.3	182.7	212.3	210.5	235.8	224.7	230.4	224.9	216.4	223.5
X	4.9	6.0	5.5	7.0	9.2	6.9	5.4	6.6	5.1	8.2
1	37.1	31.7	33.4	33.9	33.7	35.7	31.0	30.3	26.5	25.9
2-3	147.7	125.7	150.2	139.5	157.3	147.0	152.7	146.8	143.5	144.6
5-6	21.9	19.3	23.1	30.0	35.6	35.0	41.3	41.2	41.2	44.8

Women - Femmes - Mujeres
ISCED-97 - CITE-97 - CINE-97

	1999	2000	2001	2002	2003	2004	2005	2006	2007	2008
Total	101.4	104.2	130.1	133.1	134.0	142.0	137.7	128.7	135.0	145.0
X	2.7	4.0	4.3	6.6	4.2	4.2	4.1	4.1	2.6	6.0
1	9.9	12.1	12.5	12.5	12.0	13.0	11.2	10.7	12.5	12.4
2-3	66.7	63.6	85.9	81.0	83.5	83.2	76.9	68.3	72.9	79.7
5-6	22.0	24.5	27.5	32.9	34.3	41.6	45.5	45.5	47.0	46.9

Mongolia (E) [2][3]
Registered unemployment - Chômage enregistré - Desempleo registrado

Total - Total - Total
ISCED-97 - CITE-97 - CINE-97

	1999	2000	2001	2002	2003	2004	2005	2006	2007	2008
Total	39.8	38.6	40.3	30.9	33.3	35.6	32.9	32.9	29.9	29.8
X	1.1	1.1	0.8	0.2	0.3	0.3	0.2	0.2	0.2	0.2
1	3.0	2.4	2.6	1.5	1.8	1.8	1.6	1.5	1.1	1.0
2	10.1	9.4	9.2	9.7	10.2	10.7	9.6	9.4	8.1	7.4
3	9.6	9.3	8.7	9.6	11.0	12.6	11.9	12.4	12.3	12.6
4	9.4	9.4	11.3	3.8	3.6	3.7	3.3	2.8	2.2	2.0
5A	4.6	4.9	5.2	3.4	3.3	3.1	2.7	2.4	2.0	1.9
5B	1.9	2.1	2.4	2.7	3.1	3.5	3.6	4.2	4.0	4.7

Pakistan (BA) [4][5]
Total unemployment - Chômage total - Desempleo total

Total - Total - Total
ISCED-76 - CITE-76 - CINE-76

	1999	2000	2001	2002	2003	2004	2005	2006	2007	2008
Total	.	3 117	3 181	3 506	3 594	3 499	3 566	3 103	2 680	.
X	.	1 529	1 561	1 574	1 614	1 429	1 457	1 358	1 203	.
0	.	64	65	122	125	142	145	104	83	.
2	.	470	480	516	529	459	468	479	384	.
3	.	406	414	430	441	432	440	316	306	.
5	.	389	397	480	492	566	577	459	389	.
6	.	136	139	184	189	223	227	182	163	.
7	.	117	119	182	186	228	232	195	146	.
9	.	6	6	18	18	20	20	10	6	.

Men - Hommes - Hombres
ISCED-76 - CITE-76 - CINE-76

	1999	2000	2001	2002	2003	2004	2005	2006	2007	2008
Total	.	2 040	2 082	2 381	2 441	2 461	2 508	2 166	1 807	.
X	.	773	790	850	872	786	801	752	634	.
0	.	56	57	106	109	125	128	86	68	.
2	.	362	370	407	417	358	365	389	296	.
3	.	345	352	367	376	390	397	281	267	.
5	.	306	312	370	379	464	473	376	309	.
6	.	104	106	132	136	172	175	138	125	.
7	.	89	90	136	136	157	160	136	102	.
9	.	5	5	13	13	9	9	7	6	.

Women - Femmes - Mujeres
ISCED-76 - CITE-76 - CINE-76

	1999	2000	2001	2002	2003	2004	2005	2006	2007	2008
Total	.	1 077	1 099	1 125	1 153	1 038	1 058	937	873	.
X	.	756	771	724	742	643	656	606	569	.
0	.	8	8	16	16	17	17	18	15	.
2	.	108	110	109	112	101	103	90	88	.
3	.	61	62	63	65	42	43	35	39	.
5	.	83	85	110	113	102	104	82	80	.
6	.	32	33	52	53	51	52	45	38	.
7	.	28	29	46	47	71	72	58	44	.
9	.	1	1	5	5	11	11	3	-	.

Explanatory notes: see p. 451.

[1] Persons aged 15 to 64 years. [2] Persons aged 16 years and over. [3] Dec. of each year. [4] Persons aged 10 years and over. [5] Jan.

Notes explicatives: voir p. 454.

[1] Personnes âgées de 15 à 64 ans. [2] Personnes âgées de 16 ans et plus. [3] Déc. de chaque année. [4] Personnes âgées de 10 ans et plus. [5] Janv.

Notas explicativas: véase p. 457.

[1] Personas de 15 a 64 años. [2] Personas de 16 años y más. [3] Dic. de cada año. [4] Personas de 10 años y más. [5] Enero.

By level of education   Par niveau d'instruction   Por nivel de educación

	Thousands / Milliers / Millares									
	1999	2000	2001	2002	2003	2004	2005	2006	2007	2008

Philippines (BA) [1]   Total unemployment - Chômage total - Desempleo total

Total - Total - Total
ISCED-97 - CITE-97 - CINE-97

	1999	2000	2001	2002	2003	2004	2005	2006	2007	2008
Total	3 017	3 459	3 653	3 874	3 936	4 249	2 748 [2]	2 829	2 653	2 716
X	53	66	73	73	78	100	20 [2]	19	18	14
0-1	283	339	346	359	387	417	182 [2]	187	184	173
2	373	416	431	440	437	462	236 [2]	242	217	207
3	469	532	579	575	588	635	365 [2]	375	355	338
4	820	931	1 000	1 084	1 072	1 191	858 [2]	918	867	899
5A	562	631	642	695	709	739	550 [2]	571	534	574
5B,6	434	508	581	648	664	707	536 [2]	518	479	512
?	25	38	-	-	-	-	- [2]	-	-	-

Men - Hommes - Hombres
ISCED-97 - CITE-97 - CINE-97

	1999	2000	2001	2002	2003	2004	2005	2006	2007	2008
Total	1 852	2 113	2 174	2 295	2 343	2 558	1 685 [2]	1 798	1 675	1 714
X	27	33	35	35	41	52	10 [2]	11	12	11
0-1	188	221	221	232	252	279	130 [2]	143	139	132
2	239	273	266	274	271	295	162 [2]	174	155	152
3	308	352	391	392	387	410	252 [2]	266	253	245
4	508	573	609	653	644	712	518 [2]	569	531	557
5A	344	384	374	401	417	456	342 [2]	361	337	351
5B,6	221	252	279	311	333	354	271 [2]	274	249	268
?	17	26	-	-	-	-	- [2]	-	-	-

Women - Femmes - Mujeres
ISCED-97 - CITE-97 - CINE-97

	1999	2000	2001	2002	2003	2004	2005	2006	2007	2008
Total	1 165	1 346	1 478	1 579	1 592	1 692	1 062 [2]	1 031	978	1 002
X	26	33	38	39	37	48	10 [2]	7	7	4
0-1	94	118	126	128	135	138	52 [2]	44	45	41
2	133	144	165	166	166	166	74 [2]	68	62	55
3	161	180	189	183	201	224	113 [2]	109	102	94
4	313	357	391	432	428	479	340 [2]	349	335	342
5A	217	247	268	294	293	283	209 [2]	210	197	223
5B,6	213	256	302	337	332	353	265 [2]	243	230	244
?	8	12	-	-	-	-	- [2]	-	-	-

Saudi Arabia (BA) [1]   Total unemployment - Chômage total - Desempleo total

Total - Total - Total
ISCED-97 - CITE-97 - CINE-97

	1999	2000	2001	2002	2003	2004	2005	2006	2007	2008
Total	254.054	273.637	281.148	328.644	.	.	.	501.901 [3]	463.313	418.062
X-0	22.362	26.715	29.353	22.675	.	.	.	5.382 [3]	2.423	2.790
1	57.464	57.202	48.205	68.671	.	.	.	75.455 [3]	58.233	36.868
2	54.149	48.504	52.321	57.169	.	.	.	76.902 [3]	63.098	56.144
3	57.842	73.372	82.170	89.616	.	.	.	143.240 [3]	159.152	125.185
4	22.099	19.179	17.071	24.510	.	.	.	46.257 [3]	47.648	42.249
5A	40.138	48.320	51.909	65.355	.	.	.			
5	.	.	.		.	.	.	154.042 [3]	131.129	154.055
5B	-	-	-	0.848	.	.	.			
6	-	0.345	0.119	-	.	.	.	0.623 [3]	1.630	0.771

Men - Hommes - Hombres
ISCED-97 - CITE-97 - CINE-97

	1999	2000	2001	2002	2003	2004	2005	2006	2007	2008
Total	183.780	194.329	202.568	224.979	.	.	.	319.060 [3]	295.473	250.402
X-0	18.941	26.358	27.849	22.263	.	.	.	5.239 [3]	2.423	2.684
1	53.197	54.950	45.813	65.473	.	.	.	73.116 [3]	55.942	35.162
2	49.161	45.226	47.835	51.653	.	.	.	73.690 [3]	59.591	54.047
3	42.833	49.906	62.642	65.037	.	.	.	105.294 [3]	123.150	105.102
4	6.960	3.365	3.628	5.993	.	.	.	24.574 [3]	30.073	25.012
5A	12.688	14.524	14.801	14.258	.	.	.			
5	.	.	.		.	.	.	37.147 [3]	23.462	28.344
5B	-	-	-	0.302	.	.	.			
6	-	-	-	-	.	.	.	- [3]	0.832	0.051

Women - Femmes - Mujeres
ISCED-97 - CITE-97 - CINE-97

	1999	2000	2001	2002	2003	2004	2005	2006	2007	2008
Total	70.274	79.308	78.580	103.665	.	.	.	182.841 [3]	167.840	167.660
X-0	3.421	0.357	1.504	0.412	.	.	.	0.143 [3]	-	0.106
1	4.267	2.252	2.392	3.198	.	.	.	2.239 [3]	2.291	1.706
2	4.988	3.278	4.486	5.316	.	.	.	3.212 [3]	3.507	2.097
3	15.009	23.466	19.528	24.579	.	.	.	37.946 [3]	36.002	20.083
4	15.139	15.814	13.443	18.517	.	.	.	21.683 [3]	17.575	17.237
5A	27.450	33.796	37.108	51.097	.	.	.			
5	.	.	.		.	.	.	116.895 [3]	107.667	125.711
5B	-	-	-	0.346	.	.	.			
6	-	0.345	0.119	-	.	.	.	0.623 [3]	0.798	0.720

Explanatory notes: see p. 451.

[1] Persons aged 15 years and over. [2] Definitions revised; data not strictly comparable. [3] April.

Notes explicatives: voir p. 454.

[1] Personnes âgées de 15 ans et plus. [2] Définitions révisées; les données ne sont pas strictement comparables. [3] Avril.

Notas explicativas: véase p. 457.

[1] Personas de 15 años y más. [2] Definiciones revisadas; los datos no son estrictamente comparables. [3] Abril.

	Thousands			Milliers				Millares		
	1999	2000	2001	2002	2003	2004	2005	2006	2007	2008

Singapore (BA) [1] [2]   Total unemployment - Chômage total - Desempleo total

Total - Total - Total
ISCED-97 - CITE-97 - CINE-97

	1999	2000	2001	2002	2003	2004	2005	2006	2007	2008
Total	77.5	.	61.9	94.2	101.0	101.3	.	84.5	74.8	76.2
X-1	20.4	.	14.8	21.6	20.0	18.5	.	14.0	11.5	11.0
2	13.6	.	10.7	15.6	16.4	15.4	.	13.7	11.9	9.7
3	21.3	.	16.5	24.7	25.4	26.1	.	22.7	19.3	17.3
4 [3]	12.9	.	12.1	17.2	20.1	22.5	.	17.5	16.6	19.4
6	9.4	.	7.8	15.2	19.0	18.8	.	16.2	15.5	18.8

Men - Hommes - Hombres
ISCED-97 - CITE-97 - CINE-97

	1999	2000	2001	2002	2003	2004	2005	2006	2007	2008
Total	44.3	.	35.7	55.3	57.6	56.8	.	44.7	40.0	39.6
X-1	13.7	.	9.9	14.4	13.2	12.8	.	8.4	7.3	6.7
2	8.6	.	6.5	11.0	11.6	10.1	.	8.4	7.3	5.7
3	11.3	.	9.1	13.8	13.2	13.7	.	11.2	9.8	8.0
4 [3]	5.8	.	6.0	8.4	9.5	10.7	.	8.6	8.7	10.7
6	4.8	.	4.2	7.7	10.0	9.5	.	8.1	7.0	8.6

Women - Femmes - Mujeres
ISCED-97 - CITE-97 - CINE-97

	1999	2000	2001	2002	2003	2004	2005	2006	2007	2008
Total	33.3	.	26.2	39.0	43.4	44.5	.	39.5	34.8	36.6
X-1	6.7	.	4.8	7.2	6.8	5.8	.	5.6	4.2	4.3
2	5.0	.	4.3	4.6	4.8	5.3	.	5.3	4.6	4.0
3	10.0	.	7.5	10.9	12.2	12.3	.	11.5	9.5	9.3
4 [3]	7.1	.	6.0	8.8	10.6	11.8	.	9.0	7.9	8.7
6	4.6	.	3.6	7.5	9.0	9.3	.	8.1	8.5	10.3

Sri Lanka (BA) [4] [5]   Total unemployment - Chômage total - Desempleo total

Total - Total - Total
ISCED-97 - CITE-97 - CINE-97

	1999	2000	2001	2002	2003	2004	2005	2006	2007	2008
Total	.	.	.	.	.	.	.	493.4	447.0	394.0
X-1	.	.	.	.	.	.	.	22.5	19.7	16.5
2	.	.	.	.	.	.	.	206.7	183.3	162.2
3-4	.	.	.	.	.	.	.	131.3	98.5	90.0
5-6	.	.	.	.	.	.	.	132.9	145.6	125.4

Men - Hommes - Hombres
ISCED-97 - CITE-97 - CINE-97

	1999	2000	2001	2002	2003	2004	2005	2006	2007	2008
Total	.	.	.	.	.	.	.	226.7	209.7	175.3
X-1	.	.	.	.	.	.	.	14.2	12.1	9.2
2	.	.	.	.	.	.	.	110.9	103.7	91.5
3-4	.	.	.	.	.	.	.	60.2	51.4	38.0
5-6	.	.	.	.	.	.	.	41.4	42.5	36.4

Women - Femmes - Mujeres
ISCED-97 - CITE-97 - CINE-97

	1999	2000	2001	2002	2003	2004	2005	2006	2007	2008
Total	.	.	.	.	.	.	.	266.8	237.3	218.7
X-1	.	.	.	.	.	.	.	8.3	7.6	7.2
2	.	.	.	.	.	.	.	95.8	79.5	70.7
3-4	.	.	.	.	.	.	.	71.1	47.0	51.9
5-6	.	.	.	.	.	.	.	91.5	103.1	89.0

Syrian Arab Republic (BA) [6]   Total unemployment - Chômage total - Desempleo total

Total - Total - Total
ISCED-97 - CITE-97 - CINE-97

	1999	2000	2001	2002	2003	2004	2005	2006	2007	2008
Total	.	.	.	637.8	.	.	.	.	454.8	.
X	.	.	.	33.4	.	.	.	.	.	.
0	.	.	.	.	.	.	.	.	52.0	.
1	.	.	.	396.0	.	.	.	.	163.1	.
2	.	.	.	83.6	.	.	.	.	73.1	.
3	.	.	.	65.4	.	.	.	.	84.5	.
4	.	.	.	.	.	.	.	.	54.1	.
5-6	.	.	.	.	.	.	.	.	28.0	.
5A.6	.	.	.	20.0	.	.	.	.	.	.
5B	.	.	.	42.2	.	.	.	.	.	.
?	.	.	.	0.1	.	.	.	.	.	.

Men - Hommes - Hombres
ISCED-97 - CITE-97 - CINE-97

	1999	2000	2001	2002	2003	2004	2005	2006	2007	2008
Total	.	.	.	.	.	.	.	.	237.3	.
0	.	.	.	.	.	.	.	.	36.7	.
1	.	.	.	.	.	.	.	.	100.4	.
2	.	.	.	.	.	.	.	.	35.7	.
3	.	.	.	.	.	.	.	.	31.9	.
4	.	.	.	.	.	.	.	.	18.8	.
5-6	.	.	.	.	.	.	.	.	13.8	.

Explanatory notes: see p. 451.

[1] The data refer to the residents (Singapore citizens and permanent residents) aged 15 years and over. [2] June. [3] Levels 4-5. [4] Persons aged 10 years and over. [5] Excl. Northern and Eastern provinces. [6] Persons aged 15 years and over.

Notes explicatives: voir p. 454.

[1] Les données se réfèrent aux résidents (citoyens de Singapour et résidents permanents) âgés de 15 ans et plus. [2] Juin. [3] Niveaux 4-5. [4] Personnes âgées de 10 ans et plus. [5] Non compris les provinces du Nord et de l'Est. [6] Personnes âgées de 15 ans et plus.

Notas explicativas: véase p. 457.

[1] Los datos se refieren a los residentes (ciudadanos de Singapur y residentes permanentes) de 15 años y más. [2] Junio. [3] Niveles 4-5. [4] Personas de 10 años y más. [5] Excl. las provincias del Norte y del Este. [6] Personas de 15 años y más.

By level of education | Par niveau d'instruction | Por nivel de educación

	Thousands / Milliers / Millares									
	1999	2000	2001	2002	2003	2004	2005	2006	2007	2008

Syrian Arab Republic (BA) [1] — Total unemployment - Chômage total - Desempleo total

Women - Femmes - Mujeres
ISCED-97 - CITE-97 - CINE-97

	1999	2000	2001	2002	2003	2004	2005	2006	2007	2008
Total	.	.	.	.	.	.	.	.	217.5	.
0	.	.	.	.	.	.	.	.	15.2	.
1	.	.	.	.	.	.	.	.	62.7	.
2	.	.	.	.	.	.	.	.	37.5	.
3	.	.	.	.	.	.	.	.	52.6	.
4	.	.	.	.	.	.	.	.	35.4	.
5-6	.	.	.	.	.	.	.	.	14.1	.

Taiwan, China (BA) [1] — Total unemployment - Chômage total - Desempleo total

Total - Total - Total
ISCED-76 - CITE-76 - CINE-76

	1999	2000	2001	2002	2003	2004	2005	2006	2007	2008
Total	283	293	450	515	503	454	428	411	419	450
X	3	2	2	3	3	1	1	-	-	-
1	34	34	57	59	60	46	35	29	26	.
1-2	.	.	.	.	.	.	.	.	.	100
2	61	65	105	110	105	86	76	63	63	.
3	26	27	44	50	48	42	41	37	37	40
5	85	90	138	165	159	142	131	128	129	126
6	45	44	64	76	73	70	68	65	61	64
7	29	31	40	51	55	66	77	89	102	120

Tajikistan (FB) [1] — Registered unemployment - Chômage enregistré - Desempleo registrado

Total - Total - Total
ISCED-97 - CITE-97 - CINE-97

	1999	2000	2001	2002	2003	2004	2005	2006	2007	2008
Total	49.7	43.2	42.9	46.7	42.9	38.8	43.6	46.5	51.7	.
0-2	6.9	7.0	6.7	8.8	9.0	20.1	24.6	27.6	34.4	.
3	31.8	28.3	26.3	29.3	25.1	11.7	11.4	10.9	7.9	.
4	7.2	5.9	8.0	6.5	6.5	4.9	5.9	6.0	7.0	.
5-6	3.8	1.9	2.0	2.1	2.3	2.2	1.7	2.1	2.4	.

Men - Hommes - Hombres
ISCED-97 - CITE-97 - CINE-97

	1999	2000	2001	2002	2003	2004	2005	2006	2007	2008
Total	23.4	20.4	20.2	21.0	19.7	16.9	19.8	21.2	23.4	.
0-2	5.5	3.3	3.5	4.4	5.0	8.6	11.9	11.6	15.4	.
3	12.2	13.4	12.1	12.8	10.8	5.1	4.6	5.7	3.4	.
4	5.4	2.8	3.8	2.7	2.9	1.9	2.4	2.9	3.4	.
5-6	0.3	0.9	0.9	1.0	1.0	1.4	0.9	1.2	1.3	.

Women - Femmes - Mujeres
ISCED-97 - CITE-97 - CINE-97

	1999	2000	2001	2002	2003	2004	2005	2006	2007	2008
Total	26.3	22.8	22.7	25.7	23.2	21.9	23.8	25.3	28.3	.
0-2	1.4	3.7	3.2	4.4	4.0	11.5	12.7	16.0	19.0	.
3	19.6	14.9	14.2	16.5	14.3	6.6	6.8	5.2	4.5	.
4	1.8	3.1	4.2	3.8	3.6	3.0	3.5	3.1	3.6	.
5-6	3.5	1.0	1.1	1.3	0.8	0.8	0.8	0.9	1.1	.

Thailand (BA) [1][2] — Total unemployment - Chômage total - Desempleo total

Total - Total - Total
ISCED-97 - CITE-97 - CINE-97

	1999	2000	2001	2002	2003	2004	2005	2006	2007	2008
Total	.	.	.	.	543.7	548.9	495.8	449.9	442.3	450.9
X	.	.	.	.	70.5	68.8	68.2	56.3	61.5	40.1
1	.	.	.	.	109.7	121.9	87.5	90.0	76.2	87.6
2	.	.	.	.	107.0	97.8	109.5	113.5	103.1	99.7
3	.	.	.	.	87.1	124.5	84.1	84.2	76.8	93.1
4	.	.	.	.	168.4	134.8	145.6	104.1	124.3	129.3
5	.	.	.	.	0.8	0.7	0.2	0.1	-	-
6	.	.	.	.	0.5	0.6	0.7	1.6	0.4	1.1

Men - Hommes - Hombres
ISCED-97 - CITE-97 - CINE-97

	1999	2000	2001	2002	2003	2004	2005	2006	2007	2008
Total	.	.	.	.	314.7	324.2	289.9	259.7	258.1	268.1
X	.	.	.	.	34.7	30.3	38.6	33.5	29.0	21.4
1	.	.	.	.	81.3	91.3	61.8	55.8	53.1	60.0
2	.	.	.	.	66.1	58.3	70.1	72.9	63.0	65.4
3	.	.	.	.	50.9	84.5	52.0	48.4	48.0	52.4
4	.	.	.	.	80.6	58.8	67.2	47.7	64.6	68.0
5	.	.	.	.	0.5	0.6	-	0.1	-	-
6	.	.	.	.	0.5	0.6	-	1.4	0.4	1.1

Women - Femmes - Mujeres
ISCED-97 - CITE-97 - CINE-97

	1999	2000	2001	2002	2003	2004	2005	2006	2007	2008
Total	.	.	.	.	229.0	224.7	206.0	190.2	184.2	182.8
X	.	.	.	.	35.8	38.5	29.5	22.9	32.5	18.7
1	.	.	.	.	28.4	30.6	25.8	34.2	23.1	27.6
2	.	.	.	.	40.9	39.5	39.4	40.6	40.1	34.3
3	.	.	.	.	36.2	40.0	32.1	35.9	28.8	40.7
4	.	.	.	.	87.8	76.0	78.4	56.4	59.7	61.5
5	.	.	.	.	-	-	-	-	-	-
6	.	.	.	.	-	-	0.7	0.3	-	0.1

Explanatory notes: see p. 451.   Notes explicatives: voir p. 454.   Notas explicativas: véase p. 457.

[1] Persons aged 15 years and over. [2] Third quarter.   [1] Personnes âgées de 15 ans et plus. [2] Troisième trimestre.   [1] Personas de 15 años y más. [2] Tercer trimestre.

	Thousands / Milliers / Millares									
	1999	2000	2001	2002	2003	2004	2005	2006	2007	2008

United Arab Emirates (BA) [1] [2]   Total unemployment - Chômage total - Desempleo total

Total - Total - Total
ISCED-97 - CITE-97 - CINE-97

	1999	2000	2001	2002	2003	2004	2005	2006	2007	2008
Total	.	.	.	.	.	.	.	.	.	77.106
X	.	.	.	.	.	.	.	.	.	0.997
0	.	.	.	.	.	.	.	.	.	2.472
1	.	.	.	.	.	.	.	.	.	5.677
2	.	.	.	.	.	.	.	.	.	9.507
3	.	.	.	.	.	.	.	.	.	25.689
4	.	.	.	.	.	.	.	.	.	7.182
5A	.	.	.	.	.	.	.	.	.	22.693
5B	.	.	.	.	.	.	.	.	.	1.074
6	.	.	.	.	.	.	.	.	.	1.815

Men - Hommes - Hombres
ISCED-97 - CITE-97 - CINE-97

	1999	2000	2001	2002	2003	2004	2005	2006	2007	2008
Total	.	.	.	.	.	.	.	.	.	30.254
X	.	.	.	.	.	.	.	.	.	0.650
0	.	.	.	.	.	.	.	.	.	2.137
1	.	.	.	.	.	.	.	.	.	4.725
2	.	.	.	.	.	.	.	.	.	6.318
3	.	.	.	.	.	.	.	.	.	9.241
4	.	.	.	.	.	.	.	.	.	1.763
5A	.	.	.	.	.	.	.	.	.	5.061
5B	.	.	.	.	.	.	.	.	.	0.130
6	.	.	.	.	.	.	.	.	.	0.229

Women - Femmes - Mujeres
ISCED-97 - CITE-97 - CINE-97

	1999	2000	2001	2002	2003	2004	2005	2006	2007	2008
Total	.	.	.	.	.	.	.	.	.	46.852
X	.	.	.	.	.	.	.	.	.	0.347
0	.	.	.	.	.	.	.	.	.	0.335
1	.	.	.	.	.	.	.	.	.	0.952
2	.	.	.	.	.	.	.	.	.	3.189
3	.	.	.	.	.	.	.	.	.	16.448
4	.	.	.	.	.	.	.	.	.	5.419
5A	.	.	.	.	.	.	.	.	.	17.632
5B	.	.	.	.	.	.	.	.	.	0.944
6	.	.	.	.	.	.	.	.	.	1.586

West Bank and Gaza Strip (BA) [3]   Total unemployment - Chômage total - Desempleo total

Total - Total - Total
ISCED-97 - CITE-97 - CINE-97

	1999	2000	2001	2002	2003	2004	2005	2006	2007	2008
Total	79.000	98.836	170.544 [4]	217.532	194.321	212.157	194.658	206.150	183.689	227.993
X	9.108	11.995	19.173 [4]	22.937	20.050	20.031	17.822	19.236	14.808	17.005
1	18.627	24.711	46.989 [4]	58.238	48.562	52.596	45.128	46.868	39.151	46.341
2	22.377	30.063	55.973 [4]	74.559	63.298	71.483	62.297	68.310	60.604	76.368
3	11.059	12.597	24.711 [4]	33.238	28.127	27.869	25.944	27.773	26.038	32.517
5A	8.707	10.895	8.808 [4]	11.789	13.239	15.736	15.359	14.323	29.374	37.288
5B	8.801	8.228	14.607 [4]	16.543	20.302	23.861	27.607	28.769	13.113	17.574
6	0.321	0.346	0.281 [4]	0.228	0.654	0.580	0.500	0.871	0.601	0.901

Men - Hommes - Hombres
ISCED-97 - CITE-97 - CINE-97

	1999	2000	2001	2002	2003	2004	2005	2006	2007	2008
Total	66.101	85.399	158.016 [4]	201.518	172.224	185.786	164.569	175.153	153.676	190.126
X	8.801	11.667	18.712 [4]	22.128	19.365	19.412	16.976	17.996	14.763	16.153
1	18.069	23.904	46.342 [4]	57.270	47.210	50.937	43.727	45.179	38.199	45.425
2	20.893	28.890	55.014 [4]	72.138	61.320	69.098	58.977	65.525	57.876	73.628
3	9.756	11.428	24.060 [4]	31.663	25.920	26.347	24.125	25.781	24.740	30.350
5A	4.476	5.503	5.654 [4]	7.373	7.032	8.271	7.881	7.621	11.959	14.866
5B	3.836	3.802	7.980 [4]	10.749	10.806	11.220	12.469	12.387	6.139	9.114
6	0.271	0.204	0.252 [4]	0.196	0.571	0.502	0.414	0.664	0.001	0.591

Women - Femmes - Mujeres
ISCED-97 - CITE-97 - CINE-97

	1999	2000	2001	2002	2003	2004	2005	2006	2007	2008
Total	12.899	13.437	12.528 [4]	16.014	22.097	26.371	30.088	30.997	30.013	37.866
X	0.307	0.328	0.461 [4]	0.808	0.685	0.619	0.846	1.240	1.596	0.852
1	0.558	0.807	0.647 [4]	0.968	1.352	1.659	1.401	1.689	0.001	0.916
2	1.483	1.173	0.958 [4]	2.422	1.977	2.386	3.320	2.785	2.728	2.740
3	1.303	1.169	0.651 [4]	1.575	2.297	1.522	1.820	1.991	1.299	2.167
5A	4.231	5.393	3.154 [4]	4.415	6.207	7.465	7.478	6.701	17.415	22.422
5B	4.965	4.426	6.627 [4]	5.794	9.496	12.641	15.138	16.382	6.974	8.460
6	0.050	0.142	0.029 [4]	0.032	0.084	0.078	0.086	0.208	0.000	0.309

Explanatory notes: see p. 451.

[1] February. [2] Persons aged 15 years and over. [3] Persons aged 10 years and over. [4] Prior to 2001: persons aged 15 years and over.

Notes explicatives: voir p. 454.

[1] Février. [2] Personnes âgées de 15 ans et plus. [3] Personnes âgées de 10 ans et plus. [4] Avant 2001: personnes agées de 15 ans et plus.

Notas explicativas: véase p. 457.

[1] Febrero. [2] Personas de 15 años y más. [3] Personas de 10 años y más. [4] Antes de 2001: personas de 15 años y más.

UNEMPLOYMENT

CHÔMAGE

DESEMPLEO

3C

By level of education

Par niveau d'instruction

Por nivel de educación

	Thousands				Milliers				Millares	
	1999	2000	2001	2002	2003	2004	2005	2006	2007	2008

EUROPE-EUROPE-EUROPA

Albania (FB) [1] [2]   Registered unemployment - Chômage enregistré - Desempleo registrado

Total - Total - Total
ISCED-97 - CITE-97 - CINE-97

	1999	2000	2001	2002	2003	2004	2005	2006	2007	2008
Total	239.8	215.1	180.5	172.4	163.0	157.0	153.3	149.8	.	.
X-1	114.8	104.6	89.3	87.3	86.9	84.1	81.8	81.3	.	.
2-3	118.0	104.6	87.1	82.3	73.5	70.2	68.6	65.1	.	.
5-6	7.0	5.9	4.1	2.8	2.6	2.7	2.8	3.4	.	.

Austria (BA) [1]   Total unemployment - Chômage total - Desempleo total

Total - Total - Total
ISCED-97 - CITE-97 - CINE-97

	1999	2000	2001	2002	2003	2004	2005	2006	2007	2008
Total	.	.	142.5	161.0	168.8 [3]	194.6 [4]	207.7	195.6	185.6	162.3
0-2	.	.	55.3	62.4	69.2 [3]	78.2 [4]	86.7	84.0	70.5	60.9
3	.	.	75.7	85.3	84.9 [3]	94.2 [4]	100.2	93.3	84.6	76.0
4	.	.	6.4	8.8	9.1 [3]	13.0 [4]	14.1	12.6	12.1	12.4
5A	.	.	.	.	.	.	.	.	11.9	9.1
5A,6	.	.	5.1	4.0	5.6 [3]	9.2 [4]	6.7	5.7	.	.
5B	.	.	.	.	.	.	.	.	5.3	3.5
6	.	.	.	.	.	.	.	.	1.2	0.4

Men - Hommes - Hombres
ISCED-97 - CITE-97 - CINE-97

	1999	2000	2001	2002	2003	2004	2005	2006	2007	2008
Total	.	.	77.0	91.7	94.7 [3]	98.0 [4]	107.8	97.1	89.7	81.8
0-2	.	.	29.6	34.6	37.3 [3]	37.8 [4]	45.0	40.3	32.6	28.4
3	.	.	41.7	49.8	49.2 [3]	48.5 [4]	53.4	48.3	43.5	41.0
4	.	.	3.0	5.0	4.4 [3]	5.8 [4]	5.9	5.2	4.8	5.7
5A	.	.	.	.	.	.	.	.	5.7	4.9
5A,6	.	.	2.7	2.3	3.8 [3]	5.9 [4]	3.5	3.3	.	.
5B	.	.	.	.	.	.	.	.	2.7	1.7
6	.	.	.	.	.	.	.	.	0.4	0.2

Women - Femmes - Mujeres
ISCED-97 - CITE-97 - CINE-97

	1999	2000	2001	2002	2003	2004	2005	2006	2007	2008
Total	.	.	65.5	69.3	74.3 [3]	96.6 [4]	100.0	98.5	95.8	80.5
0-2	.	.	25.7	28.3	32.1 [3]	40.7 [4]	41.6	43.7	37.9	32.4
3	.	.	34.0	35.5	35.7 [3]	45.7 [4]	46.9	45.0	41.0	35.0
4	.	.	3.4	3.8	4.7 [3]	7.0 [4]	8.3	7.4	7.3	6.7
5A	.	.	.	.	.	.	.	.	6.2	4.2
5A,6	.	.	2.4	1.7	1.8 [3]	3.2 [4]	3.2	2.4	.	.
5B	.	.	.	.	.	.	.	.	2.6	1.8
6	.	.	.	.	.	.	.	.	0.8	0.3

Belarus (FB) [2] [5]   Registered unemployment - Chômage enregistré - Desempleo registrado

Total - Total - Total
ISCED-76 - CITE-76 - CINE-76

	1999	2000	2001	2002	2003	2004	2005	2006	2007	2008
Total	95.4	95.8	102.9	130.5	136.1	83.0	67.9	52.0	44.1	37.3
X-2	7.3	7.2	8.1	12.1	12.4	8.5	7.0	5.3	4.4	3.8
3	14.8	14.0	15.7	22.7	24.6	33.7	26.8	20.8	17.2	14.4
5	61.4	60.9	64.7	79.1	82.6	30.1	26.1	20.2	17.4	14.8
6-7	11.9	13.7	14.4	16.6	16.5	10.7	8.0	5.7	5.1	4.3

Men - Hommes - Hombres
ISCED-76 - CITE-76 - CINE-76

	1999	2000	2001	2002	2003	2004	2005	2006	2007	2008
Total	34.2	37.6	40.9	47.8	46.1	25.5	21.1	17.7	15.2	14.7
X-2	2.5	2.3	2.8	4.2	4.1	3.0	2.2	1.8	1.6	1.4
3	3.5	4.0	4.0	5.3	5.4	8.6	6.8	5.9	5.0	5.0
5	21.9	24.3	27.0	29.3	28.2	9.0	8.3	7.4	6.3	6.2
6-7	6.3	7.0	7.1	9.0	8.4	5.1	3.8	2.6	2.3	2.1

Women - Femmes - Mujeres
ISCED-76 - CITE-76 - CINE-76

	1999	2000	2001	2002	2003	2004	2005	2006	2007	2008
Total	61.2	58.2	62.0	82.7	90.0	57.5	46.8	34.3	28.9	22.6
X-2	4.8	4.9	5.3	7.9	8.3	5.7	4.8	3.5	2.8	2.4
3	11.3	10.0	11.7	17.4	19.2	25.1	20.0	14.9	12.2	9.4
5	39.5	36.6	37.7	49.8	54.4	21.1	17.8	12.8	11.1	8.6
6-7	5.6	6.7	7.3	7.6	8.1	5.6	4.2	3.1	2.8	2.2

Explanatory notes: see p. 451.

[1] Persons aged 15 years and over. [2] Dec. of each year. [3] Prior to 2003: May and November of each year. [4] Methodology revised; data not strictly comparable. [5] Men aged 16 to 59 years; women aged 16 to 54 years.

Notes explicatives: voir p. 454.

[1] Personnes âgées de 15 ans et plus. [2] Déc. de chaque année. [3] Avant 2003: mai et novembre de chaque année. [4] Méthodologie révisée; les données ne sont pas strictement comparables. [5] Hommes âgés de 16 à 59 ans; femmes âgées de 16 à 54 ans.

Notas explicativas: véase p. 457.

[1] Personas de 15 años y más. [2] Dic. de cada año. [3] Antes de 2003: mayo y noviembre de cada año. [4] Metodología revisada; los datos no son estrictamente comparables. [5] Hombres de 16 a 59 años; mujeres de 16 a 54 años.

UNEMPLOYMENT CHÔMAGE DESEMPLEO

By level of education Par niveau d'instruction Por nivel de educación

	Thousands			Milliers					Millares	
	1999	2000	2001	2002	2003	2004	2005	2006	2007	2008

Belgique (BA) [1] — Total unemployment - Chômage total - Desempleo total

Total - Total - Total
ISCED-97 - CITE-97 - CINE-97

	1999	2000	2001	2002	2003	2004	2005	2006	2007	2008
Total	.	.	286.4	332.1	364.3	380.3	391.0	383.2	353.0	333.7
X-0	.	.	.	.	.	.	.	.	27.2	22.2
0-1	.	.	56.1	65.7	66.2	65.4	70.8	69.6	.	.
1	.	.	.	.	.	.	.	.	30.9	32.5
2	.	.	75.0	85.8	92.8	94.6	94.4	91.9	88.7	80.5
3	.	.	102.6	115.6	133.8	141.2	145.5	140.7	134.7	127.9
4	.	.	3.1	5.0	5.0	4.8	8.0	5.5	6.6	7.3
5A	.	.	22.9	28.6	30.4	32.0	37.8	33.1	33.8	28.0
5B	.	.	26.2	31.0	35.3	41.6	33.7	41.5	30.6	34.5
6	.	.	0.4	0.4	0.8	0.8	0.8	0.9	0.5	0.8

Men - Hommes - Hombres
ISCED-97 - CITE-97 - CINE-97

	1999	2000	2001	2002	2003	2004	2005	2006	2007	2008
Total	.	.	147.9	168.1	193.0	191.4	196.4	191.0	174.4	170.4
X-0	.	.	.	.	.	.	.	.	15.0	13.5
0-1	.	.	34.1	37.3	40.9	38.5	40.6	38.2	.	.
1	.	.	.	.	.	.	.	.	18.1	19.8
2	.	.	40.8	46.2	53.1	49.6	48.0	50.7	45.6	43.3
3	.	.	49.0	54.7	64.6	66.4	70.2	66.3	62.7	60.5
4	.	.	1.3	2.4	2.4	1.2	3.0	2.1	2.0	2.9
5A	.	.	11.8	15.5	16.8	18.1	15.2	17.5	15.0	12.0
5B	.	.	10.5	12.1	14.8	17.2	18.7	15.6	15.7	18.2
6	.	.	0.4	0.1	0.6	0.4	0.6	0.5	0.3	0.3

Women - Femmes - Mujeres
ISCED-97 - CITE-97 - CINE-97

	1999	2000	2001	2002	2003	2004	2005	2006	2007	2008
Total	.	.	138.4	164.0	171.3	188.9	194.6	192.2	178.6	163.2
X-0	.	.	.	.	.	.	.	.	12.2	8.7
0-1	.	.	22.0	28.4	25.4	26.9	30.2	31.4	.	.
1	.	.	.	.	.	.	.	.	12.8	12.7
2	.	.	34.2	39.6	39.8	44.9	46.4	41.1	43.1	37.3
3	.	.	53.6	60.9	69.2	74.7	75.4	74.4	71.9	67.4
4	.	.	1.7	2.6	2.5	3.6	5.0	3.4	4.6	4.4
5A	.	.	11.1	13.1	13.6	13.9	22.6	15.6	18.8	16.0
5B	.	.	15.7	18.9	20.5	24.4	15.0	25.9	14.9	16.3
6	.	.	-	0.3	0.2	0.4	0.2	0.4	0.2	0.5

Bosnia and Herzegovina (BA) [1] — Total unemployment - Chômage total - Desempleo total

Total - Total - Total
ISCED-76 - CITE-76 - CINE-76

	1999	2000	2001	2002	2003	2004	2005	2006	2007	2008
Total								366	347	272
X-1								93	90	67
2								257	242	191
3-7								16	14	13 [2]

Men - Hommes - Hombres
ISCED-76 - CITE-76 - CINE-76

	1999	2000	2001	2002	2003	2004	2005	2006	2007	2008
Total								215	203	156
X-1								57	52	40
2								150	144	112
3-7								8	7	5 [2]

Women - Femmes - Mujeres
ISCED-76 - CITE-76 - CINE-76

	1999	2000	2001	2002	2003	2004	2005	2006	2007	2008
Total								151	144	116
X-1								36	39	27
2								107	98	80
3-7								8	7	9 [2]

Bulgaria (BA) [3] — Total unemployment - Chômage total - Desempleo total

Total - Total - Total
ISCED-97 - CITE-97 - CINE-97

	1999	2000	2001	2002	2003	2004	2005	2006	2007	2008
Total	486.7 [4]	559.0 [4]	661.1 [4]	599.2 [4]	449.1	399.8	334.2	305.7	240.2	199.7
X-1	35.5 [4]	42.3 [4]	44.8 [4]	40.5 [4]	33.9	35.3	34.6	26.9	24.3	21.8
2	165.4 [4]	171.1 [4]	197.7 [4]	174.6 [4]	133.5	115.7	94.4	95.5	76.0	63.1
3-4	249.0 [4]	298.4 [4]	350.7 [4]	322.1 [4]	228.3	203.4	170.6	150.5	119.3	94.7
5A	27.0 [4]	31.4 [4]	45.2 [4]	18.4 [4]	.	.	.	.	.	.
5A.6	.	.	.	.	41.0	35.8	28.5	27.0	17.0	16.2
5B	9.8 [4]	15.7 [4]	22.6 [4]	43.5 [4]	12.3	9.6	6.0	5.8	3.6	3.9

Men - Hommes - Hombres
ISCED-97 - CITE-97 - CINE-97

	1999	2000	2001	2002	2003	2004	2005	2006	2007	2008
Total	258.6 [4]	306.3 [4]	363.2 [4]	328.7 [4]	246.1	221.6	182.5	156.4	120.7	103.9
X-1	16.9 [4]	20.8 [4]	23.1 [4]	21.3 [4]	17.8	19.3	18.5	12.9	12.9	12.2
2	94.6 [4]	98.3 [4]	118.0 [4]	104.4 [4]	82.8	69.7	55.2	51.8	36.3	33.0
3-4	131.7 [4]	166.4 [4]	195.5 [4]	179.9 [4]	126.2	116.0	94.3	79.1	63.3	51.6
5A	12.3 [4]	15.9 [4]	19.4 [4]	5.1 [4]	.	.	.	.	.	.
5A.6	.	.	.	.	15.7	14.1	12.6	10.9	7.1	6.0
5B	3.1 [4]	4.8 [4]	7.3 [4]	18.0 [4]	3.5	2.3	1.9	1.7	1.1	1.2

Explanatory notes: see p. 451.

[1] Persons aged 15 years and over. [2] Estimate not sufficiently reliable. [3] Persons aged 15 to 74 years. [4] June.

Notes explicatives: voir p. 454.

[1] Personnes âgées de 15 ans et plus. [2] Estimation pas suffisamment fiable. [3] Personnes âgées de 15 à 74 ans. [4] Juin.

Notas explicativas: véase p. 457.

[1] Personas de 15 años y más. [2] Estimación no suficientemente fiable. [3] Personas de 15 a 74 años. [4] Junio.

UNEMPLOYMENT — CHÔMAGE — DESEMPLEO

By level of education — Par niveau d'instruction — Por nivel de educación

	Thousands — Milliers — Millares									
	1999	2000	2001	2002	2003	2004	2005	2006	2007	2008

Bulgaria (BA) [1] — Total unemployment - Chômage total - Desempleo total

Women - Femmes - Mujeres
ISCED-97 - CITE-97 - CINE-97

	1999	2000	2001	2002	2003	2004	2005	2006	2007	2008
Total	228.1 [2]	252.6 [2]	297.8 [2]	270.4 [2]	203.0	178.2	151.6	149.3	119.5	95.8
X-1	18.6 [2]	21.5 [2]	21.7 [2]	19.3 [2]	16.1	16.0	16.1	14.0	11.3	9.6
2	70.9 [2]	72.8 [2]	79.7 [2]	70.2 [2]	50.8	46.0	39.2	43.7	39.8	30.2
3-4	117.2 [2]	131.9 [2]	155.2 [2]	142.2 [2]	102.1	87.4	76.3	71.4	56.0	43.1
5A	14.7 [2]	15.5 [2]	25.9 [2]	13.2 [2]	.	.	.	.	.	.
5A,6	.	.	.	.	25.3	21.6	15.9	16.1	9.9	10.2
5B	6.7 [2]	10.8 [2]	15.3 [2]	25.5 [2]	8.8	7.2	4.1	4.1	2.6	2.8

Bulgaria (FB) [3] [4] — Registered unemployment - Chômage enregistré - Desempleo registrado

Total - Total - Total
ISCED-97 - CITE-97 - CINE-97

	1999	2000	2001	2002	2003	2004	2005	2006	2007	2008
Total	610.6	682.8	662.3	602.5	500.7	450.6	397.3	337.8	255.9	232.3
X-1	.	.	.	.	101.3	101.9	187.1	94.0	71.6	70.3
X-2	338.9	375.4	379.5	340.7	.	.	.	.	.	.
2	.	.	.	.	185.9	165.2	52.6	114.1	83.2	59.4
3-4	235.4	260.8	243.5	222.3	180.0	154.2	132.2	108.7	84.0	82.4
5-6	36.2	46.6	39.3	39.6	33.5	29.2	25.4	20.9	17.1	20.2

Men - Hommes - Hombres
ISCED-97 - CITE-97 - CINE-97

	1999	2000	2001	2002	2003	2004	2005	2006	2007	2008
Total	284.5	323.4	321.1	281.1	227.1	201.6	171.8	140.0	100.0	86.7
X-1	.	.	.	.	43.9	44.5	83.5	38.2	27.5	25.6
X-2	166.6	189.4	193.9	167.2	.	.	.	.	.	.
2	.	.	.	.	92.2	81.1	26.0	52.4	35.1	24.0
3-4	105.8	120.0	114.8	101.5	80.3	66.6	54.5	43.0	31.9	31.0
5-6	12.0	14.0	12.4	12.4	10.7	9.3	7.8	6.5	5.3	6.0

Women - Femmes - Mujeres
ISCED-97 - CITE-97 - CINE-97

	1999	2000	2001	2002	2003	2004	2005	2006	2007	2008
Total	326.0	359.4	341.2	321.5	273.6	249.0	225.5	197.8	156.0	145.6
X-1	.	.	.	.	57.5	57.4	103.6	55.8	44.1	44.7
X-2	172.3	186.0	185.6	173.5	.	.	.	.	.	.
2	.	.	.	.	93.7	84.1	26.5	61.7	48.1	35.3
3-4	129.6	140.8	128.7	120.8	99.7	87.6	77.7	65.8	52.1	51.4
5-6	24.2	32.6	26.9	27.1	22.8	19.9	17.6	14.5	11.7	14.2

Croatia (BA) [5] — Total unemployment - Chômage total - Desempleo total

Total - Total - Total
ISCED-97 - CITE-97 - CINE-97

	1999	2000	2001	2002	2003	2004	2005	2006	2007	2008
Total	.	.	.	.	255.7	249.7	229.1	198.7	171.0	149.2
X-1	.	.	.	.	8.7	5.8	4.5	4.8	4.1 [6]	- [7]
2	.	.	.	.	47.6	47.8	37.9	35.6	30.8 [6]	27.2 [6]
3-4	.	.	.	.	173.1	170.7	166.3	137.4	115.9	102.6
5A	.	.	.	.	15.5	15.2	12.4	10.9	11.0 [6]	8.6 [6]
5B	.	.	.	.	8.9	9.2	8.2	8.3	9.2 [6]	7.6 [6]
6	.	.	.	.	-	-	-	-	-	-
?	.	.	.	.	1.9	1.0	-	-	- [7]	- [7]

Men - Hommes - Hombres
ISCED-97 - CITE-97 - CINE-97

	1999	2000	2001	2002	2003	2004	2005	2006	2007	2008
Total	.	.	.	.	127.7	120.0	114.4	94.4	81.6	67.9
X-1	.	.	.	.	5.8	2.4	2.3	3.3	2.1 [6]	.
2	.	.	.	.	23.4	22.8	18.6	17.0	14.3 [6]	13.0 [6]
3-4	.	.	.	.	87.1	82.8	84.0	65.7	56.3	45.9
5A	.	.	.	.	5.8	7.0	5.5	4.2	4.3 [6]	3.9 [6]
5B	.	.	.	.	4.4	4.5	4.0	3.1	4.6 [6]	3.5 [6]
6	.	.	.	.	-	-	-	-	-	-
?	.	.	.	.	1.1	0.5	-	-	- [7]	- [7]

Women - Femmes - Mujeres
ISCED-97 - CITE-97 - CINE-97

	1999	2000	2001	2002	2003	2004	2005	2006	2007	2008
Total	.	.	.	.	128.1	129.7	114.7	104.2	89.4	81.3
X-1	.	.	.	.	2.9	3.4	2.1	1.5	2.0 [6]	.
2	.	.	.	.	24.2	25.0	19.2	18.6	16.5 [6]	14.1 [6]
3-4	.	.	.	.	86.0	87.9	82.3	71.7	59.5	56.7
5A	.	.	.	.	9.7	8.2	6.9	6.7	6.8 [6]	4.7 [6]
5B	.	.	.	.	4.5	4.7	4.2	5.3	4.6 [6]	4.1 [6]
6	.	.	.	.	-	-	-	-	-	-
?	.	.	.	.	0.8	0.5	-	-	- [7]	- [7]

Explanatory notes: see p. 451.

[1] Persons aged 15 to 74 years. [2] June. [3] Men aged 16 to 60 years; women aged 16 to 55 years. After 1999, age limits vary according to the year. [4] Dec. of each year. [5] Persons aged 15 years and over. [6] Estimate not sufficiently reliable. [7] Not indicated due to lack of statistical reliability.

Notes explicatives: voir p. 454.

[1] Personnes âgées de 15 à 74 ans. [2] Juin. [3] Hommes âgés de 16 à 60 ans; femmes âgées de 16 à 55 ans. Après 1999, les limites d'âge varient selon l'année. [4] Déc. de chaque année. [5] Personnes âgées de 15 ans et plus. [6] Estimation pas suffisamment fiable. [7] Non indiqué en raison du manque de fiabilité statistique.

Notas explicativas: véase p. 457.

[1] Personas de 15 a 74 años. [2] Junio. [3] Hombres de 16 a 60 años; mujeres de 16 a 55 años. Después de 1999, los límites de edad varían según el año. [4] Dic. de cada año. [5] Personas de 15 años y más. [6] Estimación no suficientemente fiable. [7] No se indica por la falta de confiabilidad estadística.

By level of education — **Par niveau d'instruction** — **Por nivel de educación**

	Thousands				Milliers				Millares	
	1999	2000	2001	2002	2003	2004	2005	2006	2007	2008

Croatia (FB) [1]   Registered unemployment - Chômage enregistré - Desempleo registrado

Total - Total - Total
ISCED-97 - CITE-97 - CINE-97

Total	.	.	.	.	318.7	317.6	307.9	293.2	254.5	240.5
X-0	.	.	.	.	5.3	4.8	4.3	4.1	3.8	3.7
1	.	.	.	.	16.9	15.5	15.2	15.3	14.0	13.2
2	.	.	.	.	74.2	70.9	71.9	70.3	64.1	60.4
3	.	.	.	.	200.8	205.3	195.0	182.1	154.8	145.7
5A	.	.	.	.	8.5	8.7	9.2	9.2	7.9	7.8
5B	.	.	.	.	10.1	10.1	11.0	11.3	9.6	9.3
6	.	.	.	.	2.8	2.3	1.2	0.8	0.4	0.3

Men - Hommes - Hombres
ISCED-97 - CITE-97 - CINE-97

Total	.	.	.	.	132.4	132.5	125.5	115.6	97.8	90.5
X-0	.	.	.	.	1.7	1.6	1.4	1.4	1.2	1.1
1	.	.	.	.	8.4	7.8	7.5	7.4	6.7	6.2
2	.	.	.	.	29.9	28.3	28.2	26.5	23.4	21.3
3	.	.	.	.	84.2	86.9	80.6	72.6	60.1	55.6
5A	.	.	.	.	3.1	3.2	3.2	3.1	2.8	2.7
5B	.	.	.	.	3.7	3.7	3.9	4.0	3.5	3.4
6	.	.	.	.	1.4	1.1	0.6	0.4	0.1	0.1

Women - Femmes - Mujeres
ISCED-97 - CITE-97 - CINE-97

Total	.	.	.	.	186.3	185.1	182.4	177.6	156.7	150.0
X-0	.	.	.	.	3.6	3.2	2.9	2.7	2.6	2.6
1	.	.	.	.	8.5	7.7	7.7	7.9	7.3	7.0
2	.	.	.	.	44.3	42.6	43.7	43.8	40.7	39.1
3	.	.	.	.	116.6	118.4	114.4	109.5	94.7	90.1
5A	.	.	.	.	5.4	5.5	6.0	6.1	5.1	5.1
5B	.	.	.	.	6.4	6.4	7.1	7.3	6.1	5.9
6	.	.	.	.	1.4	1.2	0.6	0.4	0.3	0.2

Cyprus (BA) [2][3]   Total unemployment - Chômage total - Desempleo total

Total - Total - Total
ISCED-97 - CITE-97 - CINE-97

Total	.	13.0	10.8	.	14.1	16.7	19.5	17.0	15.4	14.5
X-0	.	0.6	0.4	.	0.2	0.6	0.2	0.1	0.1	0.2
1	.	3.2	1.8	.	2.6	3.2	3.3	2.0	2.2	1.9
2	.	1.3	1.5	.	2.3	2.9	2.9	2.5	1.8	2.0
3	.	4.7	4.3	.	4.7	5.4	7.4	6.2	6.1	5.8
4	.	0.3	0.2	.	0.2	0.4	0.6	0.7	0.4	0.3
5A	.	1.1	1.4	.	2.4	2.7	3.6	3.3	3.3	2.9
5B	.	1.6	1.0	.	1.7	1.4	1.5	2.0	1.5	1.3
6	.	0.1	0.1	.	0.1	-	-	0.1	-	0.1

Men - Hommes - Hombres
ISCED-97 - CITE-97 - CINE-97

Total	.	4.9	4.7	.	7.1	7.0	9.0	8.0	7.3	7.0
X-0	.	0.4	0.1	.	0.1	0.5	0.1	0.0	0.0	0.1
1	.	1.2	0.8	.	1.4	1.4	1.7	0.9	1.2	1.1
2	.	0.5	0.8	.	1.1	1.4	1.7	1.4	0.9	0.9
3	.	1.8	2.0	.	2.7	2.4	3.7	3.6	3.6	3.1
4	.	0.1	-	.	0.1		0.1	0.1	0.0	0.0
5A	.	0.5	0.4	.	1.2	0.8	1.5	1.5	1.2	1.1
5B	.	0.4	0.4	.	0.4	0.5	0.4	0.5	0.4	0.6
6	.	0.1	0.1	.	0.1	-	-	-	-	0.1

Women - Femmes - Mujeres
ISCED-97 - CITE-97 - CINE-97

Total	.	8.1	6.0	.	7.0	9.7	10.4	9.0	8.1	7.6
X-0	.	0.2	0.3	.	0.1	0.1	0.1	0.1	0.1	0.1
1	.	2.1	1.0	.	1.2	1.8	1.7	1.1	1.0	0.9
2	.	0.8	0.7	.	1.1	1.6	1.2	1.1	0.9	1.1
3	.	2.9	2.3	.	2.0	3.0	3.7	2.7	2.5	2.6
4	.	0.3	0.2	.	0.1	0.4	0.6	0.6	0.4	0.2
5A	.	0.6	0.9	.	1.1	1.9	2.1	1.8	2.0	1.9
5B	.	1.2	0.6	.	1.3	0.9	1.1	1.5	1.1	0.7
6	.	-	-	.	-	-	-	0.1	-	-

Cyprus (FB) [2][3]   Registered unemployment - Chômage enregistré - Desempleo registrado

Total - Total - Total
ISCED-97 - CITE-97 - CINE-97

Total	11.375	10.934	9.546	10.561	11.961	12.650	13.153	12.824	12.017	11.541
X-0	0.075	0.066	0.036	0.036	0.040	0.044	0.032	0.021	0.022	0.021
1	3.360	3.077	2.293	2.308	2.608	2.822	2.948	2.695	2.538	2.583
2	1.249	1.258	0.975	1.077	1.257	1.346	1.528	1.395	1.199	1.152
3-4	4.582	4.721	4.343	4.915	5.534	5.727	5.763	5.842	5.390	4.942
5A								1.684	1.732	1.821	1.857
5A.6	1.050	0.872	0.960	1.167	1.331	1.457				
5B	1.059	0.939	0.940	1.059	1.192	1.254	1.184	1.118	1.027	0.970
6							0.015	0.020	0.020	0.017

Explanatory notes: see p. 451.

Notes explicatives: voir p. 454.

Notas explicativas: véase p. 457.

[1] 31st Dec. of each year. [2] Government-controlled area. [3] Persons aged 15 years and over.

[1] 31 déc. de chaque année. [2] Région sous contrôle gouvernemental. [3] Personnes âgées de 15 ans et plus.

[1] 31 dic. de cada año. [2] Area controlada por el gobierno. [3] Personas de 15 años y más.

By level of education — Par niveau d'instruction — Por nivel de educación

	Thousands			Milliers				Millares		
	1999	2000	2001	2002	2003	2004	2005	2006	2007	2008

Cyprus (FB) [1] [2]

Registered unemployment - Chômage enregistré - Desempleo registrado

Men - Hommes - Hombres
ISCED-97 - CITE-97 - CINE-97

	1999	2000	2001	2002	2003	2004	2005	2006	2007	2008
Total	5.580	5.266	4.535	4.692	5.113	5.415	5.819	5.737	5.210	4.929
X-0	0.039	0.033	0.014	0.017	0.016	0.016	0.013	0.012	0.013	0.011
1	1.628	1.415	0.994	0.917	0.972	1.083	1.320	1.271	1.145	1.174
2	0.705	0.666	0.506	0.531	0.584	0.621	0.792	0.689	0.574	0.540
3-4	2.232	2.307	2.159	2.263	2.484	2.597	2.568	2.705	2.425	2.168
5A	.	.	.	.	.	.	0.694	0.677	0.701	0.711
5A,6	0.523	0.431	0.471	0.566	0.589	0.624				
5B	0.453	0.412	0.391	0.399	0.463	0.475	0.425	0.368	0.339	0.314
6	.	.	.	.	.	.	0.009	0.015	0.013	0.011

Women - Femmes - Mujeres
ISCED-97 - CITE-97 - CINE-97

	1999	2000	2001	2002	2003	2004	2005	2006	2007	2008
Total	5.795	5.668	5.011	5.869	6.848	7.235	7.334	7.087	6.808	6.612
X-0	0.036	0.033	0.022	0.019	0.024	0.028	0.019	0.009	0.009	0.010
1	1.732	1.662	1.299	1.391	1.636	1.739	1.628	1.424	1.394	1.409
2	0.544	0.592	0.469	0.546	0.668	0.725	0.736	0.706	0.625	0.612
3-4	2.350	2.414	2.184	2.652	3.050	3.130	3.195	3.138	2.965	2.774
5A	.	.	.	.	.	.	0.990	1.055	1.120	1.146
5A,6	0.527	0.441	0.489	0.601	0.742	0.833				
5B	0.606	0.527	0.549	0.660	0.729	0.779	0.759	0.749	0.688	0.655
6	.	.	.	.	.	.	0.006	0.005	0.007	0.005

Czech Republic (BA) [2]

Total unemployment - Chômage total - Desempleo total

Total - Total - Total
ISCED-97 - CITE-97 - CINE-97

	1999	2000	2001	2002	2003	2004	2005	2006	2007	2008
Total	454	455	418	374	399	426	410	371	276	230
X-0	7	4	6	1	-	-	-	-	-	-
1	.	.	.	.	.	.	.	.	.	.
1-2	103	116	108	91	93	105	99			
2								91	73	68
3								258	188	147
3-4	328	318	290	269	291	306	295			
4								4	2	2
5A								16	11	12
5-6	17	16	15	14	14	15	17			
5B								2	1	1

Men - Hommes - Hombres
ISCED-97 - CITE-97 - CINE-97

	1999	2000	2001	2002	2003	2004	2005	2006	2007	2008
Total	211	212	193	169	175	201	187	169	124	103
X-0	3	2	3	-	-	-	-	-	-	-
1	.	.	.	.	.	.	.	.	.	.
1-2	47	55	50	42	41	47	46			
2								41	33	30
3								117	83	65
3-4	153	146	133	120	126	145	132			
4								2	-	1
5A								9	7	6
5-6	8	8	8	7	7	9	9			
5B								-	-	1

Women - Femmes - Mujeres
ISCED-97 - CITE-97 - CINE-97

	1999	2000	2001	2002	2003	2004	2005	2006	2007	2008
Total	243	243	225	205	224	225	223	202	153	127
X-0	3	1	3	1	-	-	-	-	-	-
1	.	.	.	.	.	.	.	.	.	.
1-2	56	61	59	48	52	58	53			
2								50	40	38
3								141	106	82
3-4	175	172	157	149	165	161	162			
4								2	1	1
5A								7	5	5
5-6	9	8	7	7	7	6	8			
5B								1	1	1

Czech Republic (FB) [2] [3]

Registered unemployment - Chômage enregistré - Desempleo registrado

Total - Total - Total
ISCED-76 - CITE-76 - CINE-76

	1999	2000	2001	2002	2003	2004	2005	2006	2007	2008
Total	488	457	462	514	542	542	510	449	355	352
X-2	146	145	148	162	170	166	156	141	112	106
3-5	326	299	300	336	355	358	337	292	229	230
6-9	16	13	14	16	17	18	17	16	14	16

Men - Hommes - Hombres
ISCED-76 - CITE-76 - CINE-76

	1999	2000	2001	2002	2003	2004	2005	2006	2007	2008
Total	240	228	230	257	270	266	244	210	164	168
X-2	69	70	71	79	82	79	72	65	49	48
3-5	163	150	151	169	178	177	163	136	107	112
6-9	8	8	8	9	10	10	9	9	8	8

Explanatory notes: see p. 451.

[1] Government-controlled area. [2] Persons aged 15 years and over. [3] Dec. of each year.

Notes explicatives: voir p. 454.

[1] Région sous contrôle gouvernemental. [2] Personnes âgées de 15 ans et plus. [3] Déc. de chaque année.

Notas explicativas: véase p. 457.

[1] Area controlada por el gobierno. [2] Personas de 15 años y más. [3] Dic. de cada año.

3C

UNEMPLOYMENT	CHÔMAGE	DESEMPLEO
By level of education	Par niveau d'instruction	Por nivel de educación

	Thousands				Milliers				Millares	
	1999	2000	2001	2002	2003	2004	2005	2006	2007	2008

Czech Republic (FB) [1] [2] — Registered unemployment - Chômage enregistré - Desempleo registrado

Women - Femmes - Mujeres
ISCED-76 - CITE-76 - CINE-76

	1999	2000	2001	2002	2003	2004	2005	2006	2007	2008
Total	248	229	232	257	272	276	266	239	191	184
X-2	77	75	77	83	88	87	84	76	63	58
3-5	163	149	149	167	177	181	174	156	122	118
6-9	8	5	6	7	7	8	8	7	6	8

Denmark (BA) [3] — Total unemployment - Chômage total - Desempleo total

Total - Total - Total
ISCED-97 - CITE-97 - CINE-97

	1999	2000	2001	2002	2003	2004	2005	2006	2007	2008
Total					157.559	162.552	143.296	117.896	114.539	98.380
X-0					2.709	2.825	-	-	-	-
1					0.695	1.107	-	-	-	-
2					43.155	41.046	39.681	35.996	41.065	34.917
3					68.383	75.586	64.203	45.102	40.218	36.637
4					0.142	0.090	-	-	-	-
5A					30.600	27.853	26.728	24.015	21.142	16.508
5B					11.442	13.389	8.111	7.741	5.203	3.971
6					0.277	0.212	4.573	-	-	-
?					0.157	0.440	-	5.042	6.911	5.643

Men - Hommes - Hombres
ISCED-97 - CITE-97 - CINE-97

	1999	2000	2001	2002	2003	2004	2005	2006	2007	2008
Total					75.735	79.867	69.433	53.421	55.079	47.077
X-0					1.558	2.140	-	-	-	-
1					0.366	0.292	-	-	-	-
2					21.514	21.681	21.506	17.103	21.186	17.962
3					32.967	35.677	29.480	20.455	17.949	16.445
4					-	0.050	-	-	-	-
5A					12.970	11.501	12.029	8.949	9.044	7.854
5B					6.063	7.967	3.795	3.676	2.003	2.631
6					0.140	0.158	2.623	-	-	-
?					0.157	0.404	-	3.238	4.897	2.185

Women - Femmes - Mujeres
ISCED-97 - CITE-97 - CINE-97

	1999	2000	2001	2002	2003	2004	2005	2006	2007	2008
Total					81.825	82.686	73.863	64.475	59.346	51.303
X-0					1.151	0.685	-	-	-	-
1					0.329	0.816	-	-	-	-
2					21.641	19.365	18.175	18.893	19.878	16.954
3					35.416	39.911	34.723	24.647	22.268	20.192
4					0.142	0.040	-	-	-	-
5A					17.630	16.353	14.699	15.066	12.098	8.654
5B					5.379	5.425	4.316	4.065	3.200	1.340
6					0.137	0.054	1.950	-	-	-
?					-	0.036	-	1.804	2.016	3.458

España (BA) [4] — Total unemployment - Chômage total - Desempleo total

Total - Total - Total
ISCED-97 - CITE-97 - CINE-97

	1999	2000	2001	2002	2003	2004	2005	2006	2007	2008
Total	2 722.2	2 496.4	1 904.4[5]	2 155.3	2 242.2	2 213.6	1 912.5[5]	1 837.1	1 833.9	2 590.6
X-0	186.5	27.7	21.1[5]	19.2	23.5	26.7	17.2[5]	16.0	21.1	32.5
1	578.5	668.0	463.7[5]	507.3	496.5	470.4	369.3[5]	341.5	362.9	583.0
2	845.8	772.8	619.1[5]	703.2	750.0	734.6	661.8[5]	649.1	642.4	929.9
3	520.6	480.4	378.8[5]	432.3	464.3	475.3	420.0[5]	418.9	431.1	583.7
4	-	1.4	2.5[5]	3.5	4.1	3.7	1.8[5]	1.3	2.3	2.0
5A	-	356.4	273.3[5]	322.8	333.8	332.9	292.5[5]	267.0	238.4	283.2
5	590.0									
5B		186.8	144.0[5]	163.6	167.1	167.5	147.8[5]	138.6	131.5	173.0
6	0.9	2.9	1.9[5]	3.6	2.9	2.7	2.2[5]	4.6	4.1	3.3

Men - Hommes - Hombres
ISCED-97 - CITE-97 - CINE-97

	1999	2000	2001	2002	2003	2004	2005	2006	2007	2008
Total	1 158.3	1 037.4	828.1[5]	929.3	976.4	970.8	862.9[5]	791.5	815.2	1 311.0
X-0	105.4	11.8	11.8[5]	9.5	11.9	12.9	7.6[5]	7.8	11.0	19.3
1	304.4	349.9	242.5[5]	263.5	253.3	241.2	198.4[5]	171.9	185.9	350.2
2	361.2	318.8	283.3[5]	316.9	338.1	343.1	305.0[5]	293.2	289.8	486.3
3	191.2	170.6	145.9[5]	162.1	185.1	186.2	170.4[5]	161.2	177.8	265.1
4	-	0.5	1.1[5]	1.6	1.3	0.9	1.2[5]	0.5	1.0	0.7
5A	-	118.6	91.5[5]	109.9	120.6	119.4	113.8[5]	93.9	90.2	111.2
5	195.7									
5B		66.0	51.0[5]	64.4	64.1	65.6	65.8[5]	60.7	57.4	77.3
6	0.3	1.4	1.0[5]	1.6	2.3	1.5	0.8[5]	2.3	2.1	0.9

Explanatory notes: see p. 451.

[1] Persons aged 15 years and over. [2] Dec. of each year. [3] Persons aged 15 to 66 years. [4] Persons aged 16 to 74 years. [5] Methodology revised; data not strictly comparable.

Notes explicatives: voir p. 454.

[1] Personnes âgées de 15 ans et plus. [2] Déc. de chaque année. [3] Personnes âgées de 15 à 66 ans. [4] Personnes âgées de 16 à 74 ans. [5] Méthodologie révisée; les données ne sont pas strictement comparables.

Notas explicativas: véase p. 457.

[1] Personas de 15 años y más. [2] Dic. de cada año. [3] Personas de 15 a 66 años. [4] Personas de 16 a 74 años. [5] Metodología revisada; los datos no son estrictamente comparables.

	Thousands — Milliers — Millares									
	1999	2000	2001	2002	2003	2004	2005	2006	2007	2008

España (BA) [1] — Total unemployment - Chômage total - Desempleo total

Women - Femmes - Mujeres
ISCED-97 - CITE-97 - CINE-97

	1999	2000	2001	2002	2003	2004	2005	2006	2007	2008
Total	1 563.9	1 458.9	1 076.3 [2]	1 226.0	1 265.8	1 242.9	1 049.7 [2]	1 045.6	1 018.7	1 279.6
X-0	81.1	16.0	9.3 [2]	9.7	11.7	13.8	9.6 [2]	8.2	10.1	13.2
1	274.1	318.2	221.2 [2]	243.8	243.3	229.2	170.9 [2]	169.7	177.0	232.8
2	484.5	454.1	335.9 [2]	386.3	412.0	391.5	356.7 [2]	355.9	352.5	443.6
3	329.3	309.9	232.9 [2]	270.2	279.2	289.1	249.6 [2]	257.8	253.3	318.6
4	.	0.9	1.4 [2]	1.8	2.9	2.8	0.7 [2]	0.8	1.3	1.3
5A	.	237.9	181.8 [2]	212.9	213.3	213.4	178.6 [2]	173.1	148.2	172.0
5	394.3	.	.	.	.	.	.	.	.	.
5B	.	120.8	93.1 [2]	99.2	103.1	102.0	82.0 [2]	77.8	74.2	95.7
6	0.6	1.5	0.9 [2]	2.0	0.6	1.2	1.5 [2]	2.4	2.0	2.5

España (FB) [1] — Registered unemployment - Chômage enregistré - Desempleo registrado

Total - Total - Total
ISCED-97 - CITE-97 - CINE-97

	1999	2000	2001	2002	2003	2004	2005	2006	2007	2008
Total	.	.	.	.	.	.	2 069.9	2 039.4	2 039.0	2 539.9
X-0	.	.	.	.	.	.	48.9	47.6	19.2	29.3
1	.	.	.	.	.	.	211.0	301.9	345.7	462.9
2	.	.	.	.	.	.	1 195.7	1 105.0	1 106.8	1 395.1
3	.	.	.	.	.	.	317.2	306.1	300.8	351.8
4	.	.	.	.	.	.	0.6	1.1	1.0	1.2
5A	.	.	.	.	.	.	192.4	176.7	167.2	184.1
5B	.	.	.	.	.	.	103.5	100.0	97.2	114.4
6	.	.	.	.	.	.	0.5	1.1	1.1	1.2

Men - Hommes - Hombres
ISCED-97 - CITE-97 - CINE-97

	1999	2000	2001	2002	2003	2004	2005	2006	2007	2008
Total	.	.	.	.	.	.	818.0	788.2	791.8	1 147.0
X-0	.	.	.	.	.	.	21.0	20.3	8.9	16.1
1	.	.	.	.	.	.	98.8	136.3	155.2	237.5
2	.	.	.	.	.	.	500.1	446.1	447.9	666.9
3	.	.	.	.	.	.	108.1	102.3	100.6	129.9
4	.	.	.	.	.	.	0.2	0.4	0.3	0.5
5A	.	.	.	.	.	.	56.8	51.3	48.7	57.0
5B	.	.	.	.	.	.	32.8	31.0	29.8	38.6
6	.	.	.	.	.	.	0.2	0.4	0.4	0.5

Women - Femmes - Mujeres
ISCED-97 - CITE-97 - CINE-97

	1999	2000	2001	2002	2003	2004	2005	2006	2007	2008
Total	.	.	.	.	.	.	1 251.8	1 251.2	1 247.2	1 393.0
X-0	.	.	.	.	.	.	27.9	27.3	10.3	13.2
1	.	.	.	.	.	.	112.3	165.6	190.6	225.3
2	.	.	.	.	.	.	695.7	658.8	658.8	728.2
3	.	.	.	.	.	.	209.1	203.8	200.2	221.8
4	.	.	.	.	.	.	0.4	0.8	0.7	0.8
5A	.	.	.	.	.	.	135.5	125.3	118.5	127.2
5B	.	.	.	.	.	.	70.6	69.0	67.4	75.8
6	.	.	.	.	.	.	0.3	0.6	0.6	0.7

Estonia (BA) [3] — Total unemployment - Chômage total - Desempleo total

Total - Total - Total
ISCED-97 - CITE-97 - CINE-97

	1999	2000	2001	2002	2003	2004	2005	2006	2007	2008
Total	80.5	89.9	83.1	67.2	66.2	63.6	52.2	40.5	32.0	38.4
X-1	1.7	1.2	2.0	1.4	0.9	1.4	-	-	-	.
2	16.0	18.1	14.0	12.7	11.0	11.9	8.2	8.9	7.4	8.5
3	46.0	50.6	46.1	36.5	34.9	34.2	29.5	21.6	17.4	19.9
4	4.8	5.5	6.0	4.8	5.9	5.3	4.1	1.7	1.1	2.4
5A	5.5	8.0	7.1	5.7	7.7	5.5	6.3	4.2	2.4	3.9
5B,6	6.4	6.4	7.9	6.0	5.6	5.2	4.1	3.4	2.9	3.0

Men - Hommes - Hombres
ISCED-97 - CITE-97 - CINE-97

	1999	2000	2001	2002	2003	2004	2005	2006	2007	2008
Total	45.7	49.5	43.7	36.1	34.2	34.7	28.9	21.3	18.9	20.2
X-1	-	-	-	-	-	1.0	-	-	-	.
2	10.2	11.8	8.1	8.2	6.9	8.0	5.5	5.7	5.1	5.1
3	27.7	29.4	26.1	19.4	19.3	18.7	16.4	11.0	10.4	10.9
4	2.6	2.5	1.6	2.1	2.3	2.6	2.2	1.1	0.6	0.9
5A	1.8	3.1	3.2	3.0	3.5	3.1	3.0	1.6	1.1	1.5
5B,6	2.1	1.5	3.0	2.2	1.7	1.2	1.8	1.4	1.1	1.3

Women - Femmes - Mujeres
ISCED-97 - CITE-97 - CINE-97

	1999	2000	2001	2002	2003	2004	2005	2006	2007	2008
Total	34.8	40.5	39.3	31.0	32.0	28.9	23.3	19.2	13.1	18.1
X-1	-	-	-	-	-	0.4	-	-	-	.
2	5.8	6.3	5.8	4.5	4.2	3.9	2.7	3.1	2.3	3.4
3	18.3	21.2	19.9	17.1	15.7	15.5	13.2	10.6	7.0	8.9
4	2.2	2.9	4.3	2.7	3.6	2.7	1.9	0.6	0.5	1.4
5A	3.7	4.8	3.9	2.7	4.2	2.4	3.3	2.6	1.3	2.4
5B,6	4.3	4.9	4.9	3.8	3.8	4.0	2.3	2.0	1.8	1.7

Explanatory notes: see p. 451.

[1] Persons aged 16 to 74 years. [2] Methodology revised; data not strictly comparable. [3] Persons aged 15 to 74 years.

Notes explicatives: voir p. 454.

[1] Personnes âgées de 16 à 74 ans. [2] Méthodologie révisée; les données ne sont pas strictement comparables. [3] Personnes âgées de 15 à 74 ans.

Notas explicativas: véase p. 457.

[1] Personas de 16 a 74 años. [2] Metodología revisada; los datos no son estrictamente comparables. [3] Personas de 15 a 74 años.

UNEMPLOYMENT   CHÔMAGE   DESEMPLEO

By level of education   Par niveau d'instruction   Por nivel de educación

Thousands — Milliers — Millares

	1999	2000	2001	2002	2003	2004	2005	2006	2007	2008
Finland (BA) [1]				Total unemployment - Chômage total - Desempleo total						
Total - Total - Total										
ISCED-97 - CITE-97 - CINE-97										
Total	261	254	238	237	235	229	220	204	183	172
0-2	102	95	91	93	93	82	78	74	65	63
3-4	117	118	109	111	108	106	103	97	84	78
5A	13	14	13	11	12	17	18	17	15	18
5B	28	26	25	21	21	22	20	16	18	12
6	-	-	-	-	1	1	1	-	1	-
Men - Hommes - Hombres										
ISCED-97 - CITE-97 - CINE-97										
Total	130	123	117	123	124	118	111	101	90	85
0-2	53	49	47	49	50	44	41	39	35	34
3-4	63	59	55	60	59	57	54	49	42	39
5A	6	6	5	5	6	7	8	7	5	7
5B	9	10	9	6	9	9	7	6	8	4
6	-	-	-	-	1	1	1	-	-	-
Women - Femmes - Mujeres										
ISCED-97 - CITE-97 - CINE-97										
Total	131	131	121	114	111	111	109	103	93	87
0-2	50	46	44	44	43	38	37	35	30	29
3-4	55	60	54	51	49	49	49	48	43	39
5A	7	8	7	6	6	10	10	10	10	11
5B	19	17	15	13	12	14	13	10	10	8
6	-	-	-	-	-	-	-	-	-	-
France (BA) [2]				Total unemployment - Chômage total - Desempleo total						
Total - Total - Total										
ISCED-97 - CITE-97 - CINE-97										
Total	.	.	.	.	2 295	2 408	2 429	2 435	2 222	2 070
X-0	.	.	.	.	28	38	29	20	15	12
1	.	.	.	.	274	262	266	276	254	211
2	.	.	.	.	647	682	696	698	633	606
3	.	.	.	.	918	967	963	973	877	860
4	.	.	.	.	2	3	4	6	2	3
5A	.	.	.	.	265	286	275	274	262	232
5B	.	.	.	.	148	163	189	181	170	140
6	.	.	.	.	12	8	8	7	9	6
Men - Hommes - Hombres										
ISCED-97 - CITE-97 - CINE-97										
Total	.	.	.	.	1 097	1 153	1 163	1 175	1 092	1 018
X-0	.	.	.	.	16	19	14	11	8	6
1	.	.	.	.	133	127	131	137	122	108
2	.	.	.	.	329	356	350	349	343	322
3	.	.	.	.	422	432	450	455	412	415
4	.	.	.	.	2	1	1	1	-	-
5A	.	.	.	.	133	138	130	130	121	109
5B	.	.	.	.	59	78	83	87	80	55
6	.	.	.	.	3	2	3	4	5	3
Women - Femmes - Mujeres										
ISCED-97 - CITE-97 - CINE-97										
Total	.	.	.	.	1 198	1 255	1 266	1 260	1 130	1 053
X-0	.	.	.	.	12	19	14	9	7	6
1	.	.	.	.	141	134	135	138	132	103
2	.	.	.	.	317	326	346	349	290	285
3	.	.	.	.	497	536	513	518	465	445
4	.	.	.	.	1	2	3	5	2	3
5A	.	.	.	.	132	148	145	144	141	123
5B	.	.	.	.	88	84	105	94	90	85
6	.	.	.	.	9	6	5	3	3	3
Germany (BA) [2]				Total unemployment - Chômage total - Desempleo total						
Total - Total - Total										
ISCED-97 - CITE-97 - CINE-97										
Total	3 503	3 127 [3]	3 150	3 486 [4]	4 023 [3]	4 388 [5][1]	4 583 [6]	4 263	3 608	3 141
X-1	163	147 [3]	116	165 [4]	211 [3]	207 [5][1]	304 [6]	308	279	252
2	848	746 [3]	728	777 [4]	890 [3]	983 [5][1]	1 086 [6]	1 077	916	763
3	1 906	1 746 [3]	1 813	1 997 [4]	2 257 [3]	2 476 [5][1]	2 445 [6]	2 218	1 874	1 644
4	108	85 [3]	91	118 [4]	151 [3]	179 [5][1]	193 [6]	182	157	130
5A	227	189 [3]	192	199 [4]	225 [3]	233 [5][1]	305 [6]	280	241	215
5B	240	205 [3]	198	221 [4]	255 [3]	290 [5][1]	234 [6]	186	131	120
6	11	9 [3]	13	11 [4]	25 [3]	19 [5][1]	15 [6]	11	10	10
?	-	-	-	-	-	-	-	-	-	7

Explanatory notes: see p. 451.

[1] Persons aged 15 to 74 years. [2] Persons aged 15 years and over. [3] May. [4] Prior to 2002: April of each year. [5] March. [6] Methodology revised; data not strictly comparable.

Notes explicatives: voir p. 454.

[1] Personnes âgées de 15 à 74 ans. [2] Personnes âgées de 15 ans et plus. [3] Mai. [4] Avant 2002: avril de chaque année. [5] Mars. [6] Méthodologie révisée; les données ne sont pas strictement comparables.

Notas explicativas: véase p. 457.

[1] Personas de 15 a 74 años. [2] Personas de 15 años y más. [3] Mayo. [4] Antes del 2002: abril de cada año. [5] Marzo. [6] Metodología revisada; los datos no son estrictamente comparables.

	Thousands			Milliers				Millares		
	1999	2000	2001	2002	2003	2004	2005	2006	2007	2008

Germany (BA) [1]

Total unemployment - Chômage total - Desempleo total

Men - Hommes - Hombres
ISCED-97 - CITE-97 - CINE-97

	1999	2000	2001	2002	2003	2004	2005	2006	2007	2008
Total	1 905	1 691 [2]	1 753	1 982 [3]	2 311 [2]	2 551 [4]	2 574 [5]	2 348	1 944	1 640
X-1	107	93 [2]	75	108 [3]	136 [2]	136 [4]	187 [5]	188	165	149
2	453	400 [2]	406	431 [3]	518 [2]	571 [4]	604 [5]	574	493	418
3	1 012	931 [2]	999	1 133 [3]	1 287 [2]	1 436 [4]	1 370 [5]	1 226	1 000	876
4	56	40 [2]	45	61 [3]	85 [2]	96 [4]	96 [5]	93	85	64
5A	127	103 [2]	109	114 [3]	123 [2]	135 [4]	173 [5]	158	129	110
5B	143	118 [2]	112	129 [3]	146 [2]	167	137 [5]	102	66	64
6	7	6 [2]	7	6 [3]	16 [2]	11 [4]	8 [5]	6	6	5
?	-	-	-	-	-	-	-	-	-	-

Women - Femmes - Mujeres
ISCED-97 - CITE-97 - CINE-97

	1999	2000	2001	2002	2003	2004	2005	2006	2007	2008
Total	1 599	1 435 [2]	1 397	1 504 [3]	1 703 [2]	1 836 [4]	2 009 [5]	1 915	1 664	1 451
X-1	55	54 [2]	41	56 [3]	75 [2]	71 [4]	117 [5]	119	113	103
2	396	346 [2]	322	346 [3]	373 [2]	412 [4]	483 [5]	503	422	345
3	894	815 [2]	814	864 [3]	970 [2]	1 040 [4]	1 076 [5]	992	875	768
4	52	44 [2]	46	57 [3]	66 [2]	83 [4]	97 [5]	89	72	65
5A	100	86 [2]	82	85 [3]	101 [2]	98 [4]	132 [5]	122	112	106
5B	98	87 [2]	86	92 [3]	109 [2]	124 [4]	97 [5]	84	65	57
6	-	- [2]	5	5 [3]	9 [2]	8 [4]	7 [5]	5	4	-
?	-	-	-	-	-	-	-	-	-	-

Greece (BA) [1][6]

Total unemployment - Chômage total - Desempleo total

Total - Total - Total
ISCED-97 - CITE-97 - CINE-97

	1999	2000	2001	2002	2003	2004	2005	2006	2007	2008
Total	543.3	519.3	478.4	462.1	441.8	492.7	466.7	427.4	398.0	357.1
X-0	5.3	3.2	2.6	1.3	0.4	3.2	1.9	1.2	1.8	3.7
1	120.3	111.5	96.7	88.5	86.6	92.9	82.6	71.6	68.1	55.3
2	68.8	63.5	68.3	65.4	54.4	59.9	61.2	52.8	48.6	43.5
3	210.5	210.7	188.2	181.4	175.0	182.1	171.5	160.5	145.0	125.0
4	59.4	56.2	52.3	54.3	55.8	61.8	60.3	55.4	47.8	49.5
5A	52.7	50.8	48.8	44.7	47.2	60.8	60.4	51.7	51.9	48.3
5B	26.1	23.1	20.5	26.1	22.2	31.2	28.6	33.2	33.9	31.0
6	0.3	0.3	0.9	0.3	0.3	0.7	0.3	1.1	1.0	0.7

Men - Hommes - Hombres
ISCED-97 - CITE-97 - CINE-97

	1999	2000	2001	2002	2003	2004	2005	2006	2007	2008
Total	212.8	207.2	191.4	180.5	170.8	181.7	166.8	160.9	144.0	136.6
X-0	1.7	1.1	1.1	0.6	0.2	1.2	0.5	0.7	0.7	1.7
1	50.0	49.4	40.8	38.9	35.7	39.3	32.6	31.2	29.7	23.0
2	33.0	31.1	32.9	30.5	22.1	26.1	29.8	25.5	18.7	17.7
3	80.6	82.5	76.5	72.2	68.1	66.2	59.6	56.4	51.3	51.4
4	18.0	16.6	14.6	13.9	19.9	18.1	15.0	17.0	14.0	14.0
5A	18.9	19.2	16.6	15.2	15.9	21.0	19.6	18.5	19.3	17.1
5B	10.5	7.1	8.3	9.2	8.7	9.3	9.6	11.0	10.1	11.4
6	-	0.1	0.6	0.1	0.1	0.6	-	0.7	0.2	0.3

Women - Femmes - Mujeres
ISCED-97 - CITE-97 - CINE-97

	1999	2000	2001	2002	2003	2004	2005	2006	2007	2008
Total	330.5	312.1	287.0	281.6	271.0	311.0	299.9	266.5	254.0	220.5
X-0	3.6	2.1	1.6	0.8	0.2	2.0	1.4	0.5	1.1	2.1
1	70.2	62.1	55.9	49.6	50.8	53.6	50.0	40.4	38.4	32.3
2	35.7	32.4	35.4	34.9	32.3	33.8	31.5	27.3	29.9	25.8
3	129.9	128.2	111.7	109.2	106.9	116.0	111.8	104.1	93.6	73.6
4	41.4	39.6	37.6	40.4	35.9	43.7	45.3	38.4	33.9	35.5
5A	33.8	31.5	32.2	29.5	31.3	39.8	40.7	33.3	32.6	31.2
5B	15.5	16.0	12.3	17.0	13.5	21.9	19.0	22.2	23.8	19.6
6	0.3	0.2	0.3	0.2	0.1	0.2	0.3	0.4	0.8	0.4

Hungary (BA) [7]

Total unemployment - Chômage total - Desempleo total

Total - Total - Total
ISCED-76 - CITE-76 - CINE-76   ISCED-97 - CITE-97 - CINE-97

	1999	2000	2001	2002	2003	2004	2005	2006	2007	2008	
Total	284.7	262.5	232.9	238.8 [8]	244.5	252.9	303.9	316.8	311.9	329.2	Total
1	9.7	6.7	6.5	7.2 [8]	7.6	6.0	7.2	9.5	9.3	8.6	1
2	90.5	78.5	76.0	76.9 [8]	74.2	72.7	84.7	93.3	94.0	102.6	2
3	175.4	166.6	129.7	131.4 [8]	145.8	150.6	183.9	185.2	175.8	186.0	3
5	6.5	7.3	11.1	10.2 [8]	3.8	4.6	5.0	4.9	7.4	6.3	4
6	2.6	3.4	9.3	12.9 [8]	12.6	18.5	22.4	22.3	23.2	2.0	5A
			0.3	0.1 [8]	0.4	0.3	0.6	1.5	2.2	23.3	5B
			-	0.1 [8]	0.1	0.2	0.1	0.1	0.0	0.3	6

Explanatory notes: see p. 451.

[1] Persons aged 15 years and over. [2] May. [3] Prior to 2002: April of each year. [4] March. [5] Methodology revised; data not strictly comparable. [6] Second quarter of each year. [7] Persons aged 15 to 74 years. [8] Estimates based on the 2001 Population Census results.

Notes explicatives: voir p. 454.

[1] Personnes âgées de 15 ans et plus. [2] Mai. [3] Avant 2002: avril de chaque année. [4] Mars. [5] Méthodologie révisée; les données ne sont pas strictement comparables. [6] Deuxième trimestre de chaque année. [7] Personnes âgées de 15 à 74 ans. [8] Estimations basées sur les résultats du Recensement de la population de 2001.

Notas explicativas: véase p. 457.

[1] Personas de 15 años y más. [2] Mayo. [3] Antes del 2002: abril de cada año. [4] Marzo. [5] Metodología revisada; los datos no son estrictamente comparables. [6] Segundo trimestre de cada año. [7] Personas de 15 a 74 años. [8] Estimaciones basadas en los resultados del Censo de población de 2001.

ILO YEARBOOK OF LABOUR STATISTICS 2009   *ANNUAIRE DES STATISTIQUES DU TRAVAIL DU BIT 2009*   *ANUARIO DE ESTADISTICAS DEL TRABAJO DEL OIT 2009*   **589**

	UNEMPLOYMENT	CHÔMAGE	DESEMPLEO
	By level of education	**Par niveau d'instruction**	**Por nivel de educación**

Hungary (BA) [1] — Total unemployment - Chômage total - Desempleo total

	1999	2000	2001	2002	2003	2004	2005	2006	2007	2008	

Men - Hommes - Hombres
ISCED-76 - CITE-76 - CINE-76 · ISCED-97 - CITE-97 - CINE-97

	1999	2000	2001	2002	2003	2004	2005	2006	2007	2008	
Total	170.7	159.5	142.7	138.0[2]	138.5	136.8	159.1	164.6	164.2	174.3	Total
1	6.3	4.6	4.1	4.8[2]	5.2	4.4	4.8	5.5	5.4	4.4	1
2	52.6	47.8	48.4	45.8[2]	41.9	42.0	46.3	49.4	51.9	56.9	2
3	107.0	101.6	79.8	78.2[2]	83.9	82.1	96.8	96.6	93.9	100.3	3
5	3.1	3.6	6.3	4.6[2]	1.8	1.6	2.0	2.2	3.1	2.9	4
6	1.7	1.9	4.0	4.6[2]	5.6	6.6	8.9	9.8	9.0	0.8	5A
			0.1	-[2]	0.1	0.1	0.3	1.0	0.9	8.7	5B
			-	-[2]	-	-	0.0	0.1	0.0	0.3	6

Women - Femmes - Mujeres
ISCED-76 - CITE-76 - CINE-76 · ISCED-97 - CITE-97 - CINE-97

	1999	2000	2001	2002	2003	2004	2005	2006	2007	2008	
Total	114.0	103.0	90.2	100.8[2]	106.0	116.1	144.8	152.2	147.7	154.9	Total
1	3.4	2.1	2.4	2.4[2]	2.4	1.6	2.4	4.0	3.9	4.2	1
2	37.9	30.7	27.6	31.1[2]	32.3	30.7	38.4	43.9	42.1	45.7	2
3	68.4	65.0	49.9	53.2[2]	61.9	68.5	87.1	88.6	81.9	85.7	3
5	3.4	3.7	4.8	5.6[2]	2.0	3.0	3.0	2.7	4.3	3.5	4
6	0.9	1.5	5.3	8.3[2]	7.0	11.9	13.5	12.5	14.2	1.2	5A
			0.2	0.1[2]	0.3	0.2	0.3	0.5	1.3	14.5	5B
			-	0.1[2]	0.1	0.2	0.1	0.0	0.0	0.0	6

Ireland (BA) [3] — Total unemployment - Chômage total - Desempleo total

Total - Total - Total
ISCED-76 - CITE-76 - CINE-76 [4] · ISCED-97 - CITE-97 - CINE-97 [5]

	1999	2000	2001	2002	2003	2004	2005	2006	2007	2008	
Total	96.9	.	.	77.1	82.6	84.6	86.5	92.8	100.3	115.4	Total
X	0.2	.	.	-	-	-	-	-	-	-	X
0	0.5	.	.	19.8	17.0	17.3	17.2	16.1	16.5	15.3	1
1	29.8	.	.	18.3	21.5	23.9	21.7	21.2	24.4	28.9	2
2	29.1	.	.	18.8	19.6	20.4	21.1	24.5	27.0	34.4	3
3	20.2	.	.	6.9	7.3	7.8	8.2	9.7	9.9	10.6	4
5	11.9	.	.	6.3	8.1	7.3	8.8	9.7	9.9	10.8	5A
6	2.4	.	.	4.7	6.5	5.6	6.0	7.2	8.7	9.2	5B
7	1.3	.	.	-	-	-	-	-	-	1.3	6
9	1.6	.	.	1.4	2.0	1.8	2.7	3.9	3.9	4.4	?

Men - Hommes - Hombres
ISCED-76 - CITE-76 - CINE-76 [4] · ISCED-97 - CITE-97 - CINE-97 [5]

	1999	2000	2001	2002	2003	2004	2005	2006	2007	2008	
Total	59.4	.	.	48.8	51.9	54.6	53.7	56.0	60.0	77.9	Total
X	0.1	.	.	-	-	-	-	-	0.0	-	X
0	0.4	.	.	15.4	13.5	13.5	13.3	12.3	12.1	12.8	1
1	22.3	.	.	12.1	14.8	16.6	14.7	13.7	16.0	22.9	2
2	17.8	.	.	13.3	14.8	16.6	14.7	13.7	16.0	22.4	3
3	10.5	.	.	3.2	3.7	4.3	4.5	4.4	4.5	6.3	4
5	5.3	.	.	3.9	4.7	3.9	4.6	5.8	6.1	5.6	5A
6	1.3	.	.	2.7	3.3	2.8	2.7	3.6	3.8	4.8	5B
7	0.7	.	.	-	0.0	-	-	-	-	-	6
9	0.9	.	.	-	1.1	1.2	1.4	2.8	2.5	2.3	?

Women - Femmes - Mujeres
ISCED-76 - CITE-76 - CINE-76 [4] · ISCED-97 - CITE-97 - CINE-97 [5]

	1999	2000	2001	2002	2003	2004	2005	2006	2007	2008	
Total	37.5	.	.	28.4	30.6	30.0	32.9	36.8	40.3	37.5	Total
X	0.1	.	.	-	-	-	0.0	-	-	-	X
0	-	.	.	4.4	3.5	3.7	4.0	3.8	4.4	2.5	1
1	7.4	.	.	6.2	6.6	7.3	7.0	7.5	8.4	6.1	2
2	11.3	.	.	8.5	9.3	8.4	9.1	10.9	12.0	12.0	3
3	9.7	.	.	3.8	3.6	3.5	3.7	5.3	5.0	4.3	4
5	6.6	.	.	2.4	3.4	3.4	4.2	4.5	3.8	5.2	5A
6	1.1	.	.	2.0	3.2	2.9	3.3	3.7	4.9	4.4	5B
7	0.6	.	.	0.0	-	-	-	-	-	-	6
9	0.7	.	.	-	-	-	1.3	1.1	1.4	2.1	?

Italy (BA) [3] — Total unemployment - Chômage total - Desempleo total

Total - Total - Total
ISCED-76 - CITE-76 - CINE-76 · ISCED-97 - CITE-97 - CINE-97

	1999	2000	2001	2002	2003	2004	2005	2006	2007	2008	
Total	2 669	2 495	2 267	2 163	.	1 960[6]	1 889	1 673	1 506	1 692	Total
X	50	47	41	35	.	33[6]	32	26	22	21	X
1	320	283	246	228	.	200[6]	164	139	112	129	1
2	1 075	1 006	868	841	.	783[6]	745	649	589	669	2
3	1 041	990	879	831	.	715[6]	697	636	578	656	3
5	24	22	71	65	.	45[6]	37	32	34	26	4
6	156	145	141	138	.	171[6]	200	183	161	182	5A
7	3	3	20	22	.	11[6]	12	7	8	6	5B
			2	3	.	1[6]	1		1	2	6

Explanatory notes: see p. 451.

[1] Persons aged 15 to 74 years. [2] Estimates based on the 2001 Population Census results. [3] Persons aged 15 years and over. [4] April of each year. [5] Second quarter of each year. [6] Methodology revised; data not strictly comparable.

Notes explicatives: voir p. 454.

[1] Personnes âgées de 15 à 74 ans. [2] Estimations basées sur les résultats du Recensement de la population de 2001. [3] Personnes âgées de 15 ans et plus. [4] Avril de chaque année. [5] Deuxième trimestre de chaque année. [6] Méthodologie révisée; les données ne sont pas strictement comparables.

Notas explicativas: véase p. 457.

[1] Personas de 15 a 74 años. [2] Estimaciones basadas en los resultados del Censo de población de 2001. [3] Personas de 15 años y más. [4] Abril de cada año. [5] Segundo trimestre de cada año. [6] Metodología revisada; los datos no son estrictamente comparables.

By level of education   Par niveau d'instruction   Por nivel de educación

	Thousands		Milliers				Millares				
	1999	2000	2001	2002	2003	2004	2005	2006	2007	2008	

Italy (BA) [1] — Total unemployment - Chômage total - Desempleo total

Men - Hommes - Hombres
ISCED-76 - CITE-76 - CINE-76 → ISCED-97 - CITE-97 - CINE-97

	1999	2000	2001	2002	2003	2004	2005	2006	2007	2008	
Total	1 266	1 179	1 066	1 016	.	925 [2]	902	801	722	820	Total
X	32	29	25	20	.	18 [2]	18	12	12	13	X
1	180	158	139	126	.	115 [2]	94	82	67	77	1
2	548	526	454	437	.	399 [2]	391	338	313	360	2
3	438	405	360	350	.	308 [2]	307	288	258	296	3
5	8	7	25	23	.	18 [2]	13	10	13	10	4
6	58	53	54	51	.	63 [2]	73	67	56	62	5A
7	1	2	8	9	.	4 [2]	6	2	4	3	5B
			1	1	.	0 [2]	1	1	0	0	6

Women - Femmes - Mujeres
ISCED-76 - CITE-76 - CINE-76 → ISCED-97 - CITE-97 - CINE-97

	1999	2000	2001	2002	2003	2004	2005	2006	2007	2008	
Total	1 404	1 316	1 201	1 147	.	1 036 [2]	986	873	784	872	Total
X	18	18	15	16	.	15 [2]	14	14	11	8	X
1	140	125	106	102	.	85 [2]	70	57	44	52	1
2	527	480	414	404	.	384 [2]	354	311	276	310	2
3	603	584	518	481	.	407 [2]	390	348	321	360	3
5	16	15	46	42	.	27 [2]	24	22	21	16	4
6	98	92	87	87	.	109 [2]	127	116	105	120	5A
7	2	1	13	13	.	7 [2]	7	5	5	3	5B
			1	1	.	1 [2]	0	0	1	2	6

Latvia (BA) [3] — Total unemployment - Chômage total - Desempleo total

Total - Total - Total
ISCED-97 - CITE-97 - CINE-97

	1999	2000	2001	2002	2003	2004	2005	2006	2007	2008	
Total	.	.	144.7	134.5	119.2	118.6	99.1	79.9	72.1	91.6	
X	.	.	-	-	-	-	-	-	-	-	
0	.	.	-	-	-	-	-	-	-	-	
1	.	.	3.5	2.8	1.9	1.7	1.8	2.2	1.7	-	
2	.	.	36.6	31.3	27.2	24.9	21.6	21.2	15.8	20.9	
3	.	.	70.0	59.4	62.9	67.7	54.8	41.0	39.3	53.0	
4	.	.	22.4	28.2	16.7	13.6	10.2	4.9	3.9	2.9	
5	.	.	11.6	12.4	10.4	10.4	10.6	10.6	10.5	13.0	
6	.	.	-	-	-	-	-	-	-	-	
?	.	.	-	-	-	-	-	-	-	-	

Men - Hommes - Hombres
ISCED-97 - CITE-97 - CINE-97

	1999	2000	2001	2002	2003	2004	2005	2006	2007	2008	
Total	.	.	81.9	74.9	61.7	61.7	52.8	43.7	39.4	50.3	
X	.	.	-	-	-	-	-	-	-	-	
0	.	.	-	-	-	-	-	-	-	-	
1	.	.	-	-	-	-	-	-	-	-	
2	.	.	25.2	23.2	18.4	14.5	13.4	14.2	10.6	14.5	
3	.	.	38.2	30.7	31.3	36.4	28.8	22.2	20.7	29.5	
4	.	.	11.5	13.1	6.2	4.7	4.6	2.0	2.1	-	
5	.	.	4.7	5.8	4.7	4.6	4.3	3.9	4.0	3.8	
6	.	.	-	-	-	-	-	-	-	-	
?	.	.	-	-	-	-	-	-	-	-	

Women - Femmes - Mujeres
ISCED-97 - CITE-97 - CINE-97

	1999	2000	2001	2002	2003	2004	2005	2006	2007	2008	
Total	.	.	62.7	59.6	57.5	56.9	46.2	36.2	32.7	41.4	
X	.	.	-	-	-	-	-	-	-	-	
0	.	.	-	-	-	-	-	-	-	-	
1	.	.	-	-	-	-	-	-	-	-	
2	.	.	11.4	8.1	8.8	10.4	8.2	7.0	5.2	6.4	
3	.	.	31.8	28.7	31.6	31.3	26.0	18.7	18.6	23.5	
4	.	.	10.9	15.1	10.6	8.9	5.6	2.9	1.8	-	
5	.	.	6.9	6.6	5.7	5.8	6.2	6.7	6.5	9.1	
6	.	.	-	-	-	-	-	-	-	-	
?	.	.	-	-	-	-	-	-	-	-	

Latvia (FB) [4] [5] — Registered unemployment - Chômage enregistré - Desempleo registrado

Total - Total - Total
ISCED-97 - CITE-97 - CINE-97

	1999	2000	2001	2002	2003	2004	2005	2006	2007	2008	
Total	.	.	.	.	90.6	90.8	78.5	68.9	52.3	.	
X-1	.	.	.	.	1.7	1.8	1.5	1.3	1.0	.	
2	.	.	.	.	19.5	20.0	16.8	14.2	10.4	.	
3	.	.	.	.	49.3	52.7	45.3	38.8	28.8	.	
4	.	.	.	.	7.7	6.9	5.6	4.4	4.2	.	
5	.	.	.	.	6.4	7.0	6.7	6.7	6.3	.	
6	.	.	.	.	0.0	0.0	0.0	0.0	0.0	.	
?	.	.	.	.	6.0	2.5	2.6	3.5	1.6	.	

Explanatory notes: see p. 451.
[1] Persons aged 15 years and over. [2] Methodology revised; data not strictly comparable. [3] Persons aged 15 to 74 years. [4] Age limits vary according to the year. [5] 31st Dec. of each year.

Notes explicatives: voir p. 454.
[1] Personnes âgées de 15 ans et plus. [2] Méthodologie révisée; les données ne sont pas strictement comparables. [3] Personnes âgées de 15 à 74 ans. [4] Les limites d'âge varient selon l'année. [5] 31 déc. de chaque année.

Notas explicativas: véase p. 457.
[1] Personas de 15 años y más. [2] Metodología revisada; los datos no son estrictamente comparables. [3] Personas de 15 a 74 años. [4] Los límites de edad varían según el año. [5] 31 dic. de cada año.

UNEMPLOYMENT	CHÔMAGE	DESEMPLEO
By level of education	**Par niveau d'instruction**	**Por nivel de educación**

	Thousands				Milliers				Millares	
	1999	2000	2001	2002	2003	2004	2005	2006	2007	2008

Latvia (FB) [1][2] — Registered unemployment - Chômage enregistré - Desempleo registrado

Men - Hommes - Hombres
ISCED-97 - CITE-97 - CINE-97

	1999	2000	2001	2002	2003	2004	2005	2006	2007	2008
Total	.	.	.	.	37.6	37.3	31.5	27.0	20.1	.
X-1					0.8	0.8	0.7	0.5	0.4	.
2					9.4	9.4	7.6	6.3	4.5	.
3					20.0	21.4	18.1	15.2	11.1	.
4					2.4	2.2	1.7	1.3	1.4	.
5					2.1	2.3	2.1	2.0	2.0	.
6					0.0	0.0	0.0	0.0	0.0	.
?					3.0	1.2	1.3	1.7	0.7	.

Women - Femmes - Mujeres
ISCED-97 - CITE-97 - CINE-97

	1999	2000	2001	2002	2003	2004	2005	2006	2007	2008
Total	.	.	.	.	53.0	53.5	47.0	42.0	32.2	.
X-1					0.9	1.0	0.9	0.7	0.6	.
2					10.1	10.6	9.2	7.9	5.9	.
3					29.3	31.4	27.1	23.7	17.6	.
4					5.3	4.7	3.9	3.1	2.8	.
5					4.3	4.7	4.6	4.7	4.3	.
6					0.0	0.0	0.0	0.0	0.0	.
?					3.1	1.2	1.4	1.9	0.9	.

Lithuania (BA) [3] — Total unemployment - Chômage total - Desempleo total

Total - Total - Total
ISCED-97 - CITE-97 - CINE-97

	1999	2000	2001	2002	2003	2004	2005	2006	2007	2008
Total	249.0	273.7	284.0	224.4	203.9	184.4	132.9	89.3	69.0	94.3
1	4.1	5.5	4.9	2.4	3.1	2.8	2.2	1.3	0.7	1.3
2	33.3	40.8	40.8	35.9	29.9	24.8	19.6	12.3	9.1	12.8
3	140.9	149.5	129.8	101.5	95.0	77.8	59.5	42.6	34.4	44.0
4	51.6	58.6	74.6	57.7	48.5	48.6	32.8	20.9	14.2	19.8
5A	19.2	19.3	19.0	16.6	18.5	18.5	11.0	8.3	5.9	9.9
5B	-	-	14.9	10.5	8.9	11.9	7.7	3.8	4.7	6.4

Men - Hommes - Hombres
ISCED-97 - CITE-97 - CINE-97

	1999	2000	2001	2002	2003	2004	2005	2006	2007	2008
Total	140.5	158.5	165.6	121.1	105.4	90.6	67.1	46.7	34.6	49.5
1	3.2	4.8	3.9	2.2	2.3	2.2	1.9	1.0	0.4	0.8
2	22.0	26.6	28.7	22.3	19.3	14.9	12.5	8.0	5.6	8.3
3	85.4	90.9	80.2	59.1	49.6	41.3	31.8	24.5	18.7	25.9
4	22.2	27.1	35.7	25.9	22.1	19.9	12.7	8.2	5.7	8.1
5A	7.6	9.2	10.0	7.4	7.7	6.6	5.2	3.6	2.5	4.2
5B	-	-	7.2	4.2	4.4	5.7	3.1	1.4	1.6	2.3

Women - Femmes - Mujeres
ISCED-97 - CITE-97 - CINE-97

	1999	2000	2001	2002	2003	2004	2005	2006	2007	2008
Total	108.5	115.2	118.4	103.3	98.4	93.8	65.8	42.6	34.3	44.8
1	0.9	0.7	1.1	0.1	0.7	0.6	0.4	0.3	0.3	0.5
2	11.3	14.2	12.1	13.6	10.7	9.9	7.2	4.3	3.4	4.6
3	55.3	58.6	49.7	42.3	45.3	36.5	27.6	18.1	15.7	18.1
4	29.4	31.5	38.9	31.7	26.4	28.7	20.1	12.7	8.4	11.8
5A	11.6	10.1	9.0	9.2	10.8	11.9	5.9	4.8	3.3	5.7
5B	-	-	7.7	6.3	4.5	6.2	4.7	2.4	3.2	4.1

Lithuania (FB) [2][4] — Registered unemployment - Chômage enregistré - Desempleo registrado

Total - Total - Total
ISCED-97 - CITE-97 - CINE-97

	1999	2000	2001	2002	2003	2004	2005	2006	2007	2008
Total	177.4	225.9	224.0	191.2	158.8	126.4	87.2	79.3	69.7	95.0
1	.	.	.	8.6	7.7	6.0	3.9	3.6	3.0	4.6
2	60.5	76.2	68.1	37.9	29.7	22.6	14.3	13.1	11.8	16.8
3	80.0	103.3	108.6	102.6	85.4	68.5	46.7	42.1	37.1	50.7
5A	8.1	10.2	10.3	9.3	8.6	7.2	6.3	6.6	6.4	9.7
5B	28.8	36.2	37.0	32.8	27.4	22.1	16.0	13.9	11.4	13.2

Men - Hommes - Hombres
ISCED-97 - CITE-97 - CINE-97

	1999	2000	2001	2002	2003	2004	2005	2006	2007	2008
Total	94.6	123.1	117.7	95.1	73.7	53.8	33.9	29.9	27.4	49.0
1	.	.	.	6.4	5.5	3.8	2.3	2.1	1.7	3.1
2	30.6	39.8	32.5	23.3	17.3	11.9	7.1	6.3	5.9	10.4
3	49.4	65.1	68.0	50.9	39.5	29.4	18.4	15.8	14.5	26.3
5A	3.3	4.1	3.8	3.4	2.9	2.3	1.9	2.1	2.1	4.0
5B	11.3	14.1	13.4	11.1	8.5	6.4	4.2	3.6	3.2	5.2

Women - Femmes - Mujeres
ISCED-97 - CITE-97 - CINE-97

	1999	2000	2001	2002	2003	2004	2005	2006	2007	2008
Total	82.8	102.8	106.3	96.1	85.1	72.6	53.3	49.4	42.3	46.0
1	.	.	.	2.2	2.2	2.2	1.6	1.5	1.3	1.5
2	29.9	36.4	35.6	14.6	12.4	10.7	7.2	6.8	5.9	6.4
3	30.6	38.2	40.7	51.7	45.9	39.1	28.3	26.3	22.6	24.4
5A	4.8	6.0	6.4	5.9	5.7	4.9	4.4	4.5	4.3	5.7
5B	17.5	22.1	23.4	21.7	18.9	15.7	11.8	10.3	8.2	8.0

Explanatory notes: see p. 451.

[1] Age limits vary according to the year. [2] 31st Dec. of each year. [3] Persons aged 15 years and over. [4] Persons aged 16 to 64 years.

Notes explicatives: voir p. 454.

[1] Les limites d'âge varient selon l'année. [2] 31 déc. de chaque année. [3] Personnes âgées de 15 ans et plus. [4] Personnes âgées de 16 à 64 ans.

Notas explicativas: véase p. 457.

[1] Los límites de edad varían según el año. [2] 31 dic. de cada año. [3] Personas de 15 años y más. [4] Personas de 16 a 64 años.

By level of education   Par niveau d'instruction   Por nivel de educación

Thousands — Milliers — Millares

Luxembourg (FB) [1]

Registered unemployment - Chômage enregistré - Desempleo registrado

Total - Total - Total
ISCED-76 - CITE-76 - CINE-76

	1999	2000	2001	2002	2003	2004	2005	2006	2007	2008
Total	5.351	4.964	4.927	5.823	7.587	8.716	9.845	9.487	9.623	9.916
0-2	3.006	2.726	2.536	2.715	3.535	4.172	4.935	4.807	4.989	5.151
3	1.807	1.720	1.747	2.151	2.734	3.193	3.557	3.394	3.371	3.404
5-7	0.524	0.503	0.629	0.938	1.295	1.301	1.275	1.171	1.110	1.167
?	0.014	0.014	0.015	0.019	0.023	0.050	0.078	0.115	0.153	0.194

Men - Hommes - Hombres
ISCED-76 - CITE-76 - CINE-76

	1999	2000	2001	2002	2003	2004	2005	2006	2007	2008
Total	.	2.630	2.616	3.162	4.128	4.743	5.438	4.950	4.932	5.202
0-2	.	1.429	1.347	1.453	1.939	2.313	2.796	2.593	2.651	2.821
3	.	0.912	0.916	1.167	1.447	1.707	1.929	1.722	1.686	1.730
5-7	.	0.282	0.345	0.535	0.728	0.706	0.692	0.606	0.559	0.591
?	.	0.007	0.008	0.007	0.013	0.017	0.021	0.029	0.036	0.059

Women - Femmes - Mujeres
ISCED-76 - CITE-76 - CINE-76

	1999	2000	2001	2002	2003	2004	2005	2006	2007	2008
Total	.	2.333	2.312	2.661	3.459	3.973	4.407	4.537	4.691	4.714
0-2	.	1.297	1.189	1.261	1.596	1.859	2.139	2.213	2.337	2.330
3	.	0.808	0.831	0.984	1.287	1.486	1.629	1.673	1.686	1.674
5-7	.	0.221	0.285	0.403	0.566	0.595	0.584	0.565	0.551	0.575
?	.	0.007	0.007	0.012	0.010	0.033	0.056	0.086	0.117	0.135

Malta (BA)

Total unemployment - Chômage total - Desempleo total

Total - Total - Total
ISCED-76 - CITE-76 - CINE-76 [2][3]   ISCED-97 - CITE-97 - CINE-97 [4]

ISCED-76	1999	2000	2001	2002	2003	2004	2005	2006	2007	2008	ISCED-97
Total	7.695	.	10.164	10.875	12.596	11.518	11.745	11.925	10.729	10.389	Total
1	4.249	.	2.193	2.485	1.724	1.590	1.608	1.708	1.800	1.667	1
2	2.117	.	6.672	6.930	9.737	7.719	8.072	7.991	6.825	7.206	2
3	0.980	.	-	-	-	.	0.678	0.974	0.947	0.615	3
5	0.294	.	-	-	-	1.662	.	.	.	.	3-6
6-7	0.055	.	.	.	.	.	0.619	0.519	.	0.546	4
?	-	.	.	.	.	.	.	.	.	0.355	5A
			.	.	.	.	0.502	-	-	.	5B

Men - Hommes - Hombres
ISCED-76 - CITE-76 - CINE-76 [2][3]   ISCED-97 - CITE-97 - CINE-97 [4]

ISCED-76	1999	2000	2001	2002	2003	2004	2005	2006	2007	2008	ISCED-97
Total	6.611	.	6.626	6.715	8.502	7.080	7.279	7.242	6.474	6.442	Total
1	3.807	.	2.006	1.909	-	1.188	1.252	1.339	1.306	1.214	1
2	1.924	.	3.918	4.066	6.217	4.748	5.007	4.706	4.063	4.380	2
3	0.687	.	-	.	.	.	-	0.401	0.463	0.296	3
5	0.161	.	-	-	.	1.131	.	.	.	.	3-6
6-7	0.032	.	.	.	.	.	0.574	0.468	-	0.363	4
?	-	.	.	.	.	.	.	.	.	0.189	5A
			.	.	.	.	.	.	-	.	5B

Women - Femmes - Mujeres
ISCED-76 - CITE-76 - CINE-76 [2][3]   ISCED-97 - CITE-97 - CINE-97 [4]

ISCED-76	1999	2000	2001	2002	2003	2004	2005	2006	2007	2008	ISCED-97
Total	1.084	.	3.538	4.160	4.094	4.438	4.466	4.683	4.255	3.947	Total
1	0.442	.	0.187	0.576	-	0.402	0.356	0.369	0.494	0.453	1
2	0.193	.	2.754	2.864	3.520	2.791	3.065	3.285	2.762	2.826	2
3	0.293	.	.	.	.	.	-	0.573	0.484	0.319	3
5	0.133	.	-	-	.	0.531	.	.	.	.	3-6
6-7	0.023	.	.	.	.	.	0.045	0.051	-	0.183	4
?	-	.	.	.	.	.	.	.	.	0.166	5A
			.	.	.	.	.	.	.	.	5B

Netherlands (BA) [5]

Total unemployment - Chômage total - Desempleo total

Total - Total - Total
ISCED-97 - CITE-97 - CINE-97

	1999	2000	2001	2002	2003	2004	2005	2006	2007	2008
Total	279	246	204	252	332	411	425	354	300	257
X	-	-	-	-	4	7	7	6	4	3
0	6	5	3	4	5	5	4	3	2	4
1	47	43	37	38	45	51	50	47	37	30
2	89	73	67	77	94	115	121	96	87	78
3	89	77	60	81	113	146	155	132	112	88
4	7	6	6	6	9	11	11	9	7	6
5A	30	32	24	38	53	68	73	57	48	43
5B	10	9	7	6	6	8	7	3	3	5
6	-	-	-	-			2	.	.	

Explanatory notes: see p. 451.

[1] Persons aged 16 to 64 years. [2] Persons aged 16 years and over. [3] Dec. of each year. [4] Persons aged 15 years and over. [5] Persons aged 15 to 64 years.

Notes explicatives: voir p. 454.

[1] Personnes âgées de 16 à 64 ans. [2] Personnes âgées de 16 ans et plus. [3] Déc. de chaque année. [4] Personnes âgées de 15 ans et plus. [5] Personnes âgées de 15 à 64 ans.

Notas explicativas: véase p. 457.

[1] Personas de 16 a 64 años. [2] Personas de 16 años y más. [3] Dic. de cada año. [4] Personas de 15 años y más. [5] Personas de 15 a 64 años.

UNEMPLOYMENT — CHÔMAGE — DESEMPLEO

By level of education — Par niveau d'instruction — Por nivel de educación

Thousands — Milliers — Millares

	1999	2000	2001	2002	2003	2004	2005	2006	2007	2008

Netherlands (BA) [1] — Total unemployment - Chômage total - Desempleo total

Men - Hommes - Hombres
ISCED-97 - CITE-97 - CINE-97

	1999	2000	2001	2002	2003	2004	2005	2006	2007	2008
Total	128	111	94	126	178	219	220	174	143	128
X	-	-	-	-	2	4	3	4	2	-
0	4	3	2	2	3	3	2	2	2	3
1	23	20	19	22	26	28	27	23	20	17
2	37	30	33	37	49	57	58	44	39	37
3	40	32	24	40	58	77	80	64	52	42
4	3	2	2	2	4	5	6	4	3	3
5A	14	18	10	20	32	41	40	31	24	23
5B	6	5	3	3	4	4	2	2	2	3
6										

Women - Femmes - Mujeres
ISCED-97 - CITE-97 - CINE-97

	1999	2000	2001	2002	2003	2004	2005	2006	2007	2008
Total	151	135	111	125	153	192	205	180	157	128
X	-	-	-	-	3	4	3	3	2	.
0	2	-	-	2	2	2	.	.	.	.
1	24	23	18	16	19	23	24	23	17	14
2	52	44	34	40	45	58	63	52	49	41
3	49	45	36	42	55	69	75	67	60	46
4	4	4	4	5	5	6	5	5	4	3
5A	16	15	14	18	21	27	32	26	24	21
5B	4	4	4	2	4	2	.	2	.	2
6										

Norway (BA) — Total unemployment - Chômage total - Desempleo total

Total - Total - Total
ISCED-76 - CITE-76 - CINE-76 [2]   ISCED-97 - CITE-97 - CINE-97 [3]

	1999	2000	2001	2002	2003	2004	2005	2006	2007	2008	
Total	75	81	84	92	107	106	111	84 [4]	63	67	Total
2	19	19	3	3	3	1	3	3 [4]	2	2	0
3	41	43	-	-	-	-	-	-	-	-	1
5	6	7	21	23	24	23	27	18 [4]	16	33	2
6	4	7	42	47	55	56	58	45 [4]	30	19	3
7	3	3	2	1	2	2	2	2 [4]	1	1	4
9	2	2	14	16	18	20	17	13 [4]	10	9	5
			3	2	4	3	4	3 [4]	3	3	6

Men - Hommes - Hombres
ISCED-76 - CITE-76 - CINE-76 [2]   ISCED-97 - CITE-97 - CINE-97 [3]

	1999	2000	2001	2002	2003	2004	2005	2006	2007	2008	
Total	42	46	46	52	62	62	61	45 [4]	34	38	Total
2	10	10	2	2	1	1	1	1 [4]	1	1	0
3	24	25	-	-	-	-	-	-	-	-	1
5	4	4	11	13	14	15	15	11 [4]	9	20	2
6	2	3	24	27	32	32	32	23 [4]	17	11	3
7	2	1	1	1	1	1	2	2 [4]	1	-	4
9	1	1	7	9	9	10	9	6 [4]	5	4	5
			1	3	2		2	2 [4]	2	1	6

Women - Femmes - Mujeres
ISCED-76 - CITE-76 - CINE-76 [2]   ISCED-97 - CITE-97 - CINE-97 [3]

	1999	2000	2001	2002	2003	2004	2005	2006	2007	2008	
Total	33	35	38	41	45	45	49	39 [4]	29	30	Total
2	9	9	1	1	1	1	1	2 [4]	1	1	0
3	17	18	-	-	-	-	-	-	-	-	1
5	2	2	9	10	9	9	12	7 [4]	7	13	2
6	2	4	18	20	23	24	25	22 [4]	13	8	3
7	1	1	1	1	1	1	1	1 [4]	-	-	4
9	1	1	7	7	9	10	9	6 [4]	5	5	5
			1	2	1		1	1 [4]	2	2	6

Poland (BA) [3] — Total unemployment - Chômage total - Desempleo total

Total - Total - Total
ISCED-97 - CITE-97 - CINE-97

	1999	2000	2001	2002	2003	2004	2005	2006	2007	2008
Total	.	.	3 170	3 431	3 329	3 230	3 045	2 344	1 619	1 211
1-2			605	642	590	580	538	400	266	193
3			2 338	2 513	2 431	2 331	2 183	1 663	1 131	819
4			95	101	104	104	94	77	54	51
5-6			132	174	203	215	231	205	168	147

Men - Hommes - Hombres
ISCED-97 - CITE-97 - CINE-97

	1999	2000	2001	2002	2003	2004	2005	2006	2007	2008
Total	.	.	1 583	1 779	1 741	1 681	1 553	1 202	831	599
1-2			328	362	333	328	309	234	158	115
3			1 184	1 331	1 293	1 239	1 135	865	598	415
4			23	23	28	27	23	22	15	15
5-6			47	63	86	87	86	81	60	55

Explanatory notes: see p. 451.
[1] Persons aged 15 to 64 years. [2] Persons aged 16 to 74 years. [3] Persons aged 15 to 74 years. [4] Prior to 2006: persons aged 16 to 74 years.

Notes explicatives: voir p. 454.
[1] Personnes âgées de 15 à 64 ans. [2] Personnes âgées de 16 à 74 ans. [3] Personnes âgées de 15 à 74 ans. [4] Avant 2006: personnes âgées de 16 à 74 ans.

Notas explicativas: véase p. 457.
[1] Personas de 15 a 64 años. [2] Personas de 16 a 74 años. [3] Personas de 15 a 74 años. [4] Antes de 2006: personas de 16 a 74 años.

	Thousands			Milliers				Millares		
	1999	2000	2001	2002	2003	2004	2005	2006	2007	2008
Poland (BA) [1]				*Total unemployment - Chômage total - Desempleo total*						
Women - Femmes - Mujeres										
ISCED-97 - CITE-97 - CINE-97										
Total	.	.	1 587	1 652	1 588	1 550	1 493	1 142	788	612
1-2	.	.	277	280	257	252	229	166	109	78
3	.	.	1 154	1 183	1 138	1 093	1 048	798	533	405
4	.	.	71	78	76	77	71	55	39	36
5-6	.	.	85	111	117	128	145	124	108	92
Poland (FB) [2] [3]				*Registered unemployment - Chômage enregistré - Desempleo registrado*						
Total - Total - Total										
ISCED-76 - CITE-76 - CINE-76										
Total	2 349.8	2 702.6	3 115.1	3 217.0	3 175.7	2 999.6	2 773.0	2 309.4	1 746.6	1 473.8
1	778.9	903.8	1 014.0	1 044.1	1 028.3	970.6	898.8	751.1	564.6	448.3
3-5	1 523.2	1 729.4	2 000.6	2 046.3	2 007.1	1 879.6	1 721.8	1 417.5	1 061.8	900.7
6-7	47.7	69.4	100.5	126.6	140.3	149.4	152.4	140.7	120.2	124.8
Men - Hommes - Hombres										
ISCED-76 - CITE-76 - CINE-76										
Total	1 042.5	1 211.0	1 473.0	1 571.2	1 541.0	1 431.1	1 286.6	1 003.7	729.3	640.4
1	385.7	448.4	524.7	558.5	550.5	519.2	471.8	375.1	272.5	225.2
3-5	639.8	738.3	910.8	965.0	939.0	859.5	763.3	582.7	417.8	373.5
6-7	17.0	24.3	37.5	47.7	51.5	52.4	51.5	45.9	38.9	41.7
Women - Femmes - Mujeres										
ISCED-76 - CITE-76 - CINE-76										
Total	1 307.3	1 491.6	1 642.1	1 645.8	1 634.7	1 568.5	1 486.4	1 305.7	1 017.3	833.4
1	393.2	455.4	489.3	485.6	477.8	451.4	427.0	376.1	292.1	223.1
3-5	883.4	991.1	1 089.8	1 081.3	1 068.1	1 020.1	958.6	834.8	643.9	527.2
6-7	30.7	45.1	63.0	78.9	88.8	97.0	100.8	94.8	81.3	83.1
Portugal (BA) [4]				*Total unemployment - Chômage total - Desempleo total*						
Total - Total - Total										
ISCED-97 - CITE-97 - CINE-97										
Total	225.8	205.5	213.5	270.5	342.3	365.0	422.3	427.8	448.6	427.1
X-0	12.2	8.2	10.4	11.1	13.4	12.2	14.5	16.5	14.6	14.4
1	118.6	112.4	110.5	137.3	172.1	182.7	206.6	206.1	207.5	180.2
2	43.4	40.4	44.9	58.8	70.0	80.1	90.0	84.9	98.2	107.2
3	33.8	29.2	30.0	37.2	49.9	50.6	61.0	68.0	64.5	63.4
4 [5]	-	-	-	-	-	1.5	3.8	4.0	4.5	4.3
5A	13.5	11.1	13.5	20.2	30.0	30.9	38.3	39.9	50.0	48.0
5B	-	-	-	4.6	6.3	5.9	7.3	6.9	7.6	5.0
6 [5]	-	-	-	-	-	1.0	0.6	1.5	1.7	4.5
Men - Hommes - Hombres										
ISCED-97 - CITE-97 - CINE-97										
Total	108.9	89.3	91.6	121.4	160.9	172.9	198.1	194.8	196.8	194.3
X-0	5.9	2.7	4.1	4.5	7.6	6.3	7.7	7.7	7.6	8.4
1	61.8	53.5	51.4	66.4	86.3	90.8	100.8	99.9	98.0	94.1
2	21.2	17.8	18.2	27.6	34.2	40.0	46.0	39.4	44.7	47.7
3	13.5	10.3	12.9	16.4	20.8	21.4	25.7	29.8	26.7	26.0
4 [5]	-	-	-	-	-	0.9	1.4	2.5	2.1	1.7
5A	5.0	4.0	3.8	4.5	9.2	10.6	13.4	12.1	13.1	13.2
5B [5]	-	-	-	-	-	2.4	3.2	3.1	3.6	1.9
6 [5]	-	-	-	-	-	0.4	0.1	0.3	0.9	1.5
Women - Femmes - Mujeres										
ISCED-97 - CITE-97 - CINE-97										
Total	116.8	116.2	121.9	149.1	181.4	192.2	224.1	233.1	251.8	232.7
X-0	6.3	5.5	6.3	6.6	5.8	5.9	6.8	8.8	7.0	6.0
1	56.8	58.9	59.0	71.0	85.8	91.9	106.0	106.2	109.3	86.1
2	22.2	22.6	26.6	31.3	35.8	40.1	44.1	45.5	53.5	59.5
3	20.3	18.9	17.1	20.8	29.1	29.3	35.3	38.2	37.8	37.4
4 [5]	-	-	-	-	-	0.6	2.4	1.5	2.4	2.5
5A	8.4	7.1	9.7	15.6	20.8	20.3	25.0	27.8	36.9	34.8
5B [5]	-	-	-	-	-	3.5	4.2	3.8	4.0	3.1
6 [5]	-	-	-	-	-	0.5	0.5	1.2	0.9	3.1
Roumanie (BA) [4]				*Total unemployment - Chômage total - Desempleo total*						
Total - Total - Total										
ISCED-97 - CITE-97 - CINE-97										
Total	789.9	821.2	749.9	845.2 [6]	691.7	799.5	704.4	728.4	641.0	575.5
X	10.3	9.6	8.5	8.6 [6]	4.6	12.9	9.3	10.7	12.2	13.7
1	29.9	27.4	22.9	34.5 [6]	24.6	40.8	31.3	35.8	33.7	34.5
2	141.4	136.8	131.6	170.8 [6]	139.7	167.2	131.0	143.1	131.4	128.0
3	557.3	582.6	521.6	560.7 [6]	459.7	513.8	462.4	467.7	408.3	348.5
4	21.3	28.1	23.9	23.8 [6]	25.8	21.1	24.0	21.7	16.4	12.3
5A	22.5	29.3	33.8	37.9 [6]	28.5	35.0	36.3	36.7	31.2	32.2
5B	6.9	7.0	7.3	8.6 [6]	8.6	8.3	9.9	12.7	7.8	6.3

Explanatory notes: see p. 451.   Notes explicatives: voir p. 454.   Notas explicativas: véase p. 457.

[1] Persons aged 15 to 74 years. [2] Men aged 18 to 64 years; women aged 18 to 59 years (with the exception of juvenile graduates). [3] 31st Dec. of each year. [4] Persons aged 15 years and over. [5] Data not reliable; coefficient of variation greater than 20%. [6] Estimates based on the 2002 Population Census results.

[1] Personnes âgées de 15 à 74 ans. [2] Hommes âgés de 18 à 64 ans; femmes âgées de 18 à 59 ans (à l'exception des jeunes diplômés). [3] 31 déc. de chaque année. [4] Personnes âgées de 15 ans et plus. [5] Données non fiables; coefficient de variation supérieur à 20%. [6] Estimations basées sur les résultats du Recensement de la population de 2002.

[1] Personas de 15 a 74 años. [2] Hombres de 18 a 64 años; mujeres de 18 a 59 años (salvo los jovenes diplomados universitarios). [3] 31 dic. de cada año. [4] Personas de 15 años y más. [5] Datos no fiables; coeficiente de variación superior a 20%. [6] Estimaciones basadas en los resultados del Censo de población de 2002.

	Thousands / Milliers / Millares									
	1999	2000	2001	2002	2003	2004	2005	2006	2007	2008
Roumanie (BA) [1]	Total unemployment - Chômage total - Desempleo total									
Men - Hommes - Hombres ISCED-97 - CITE-97 - CINE-97										
Total	462.5	481.6	436.0	494.0[2]	408.0	490.7	420.3	452.4	398.7	369.2
X	5.9	6.8	5.8	5.5[2]	2.9	9.6	7.2	7.6	9.3	11.9
1	21.7	19.7	15.9	23.7[2]	17.5	30.3	24.0	26.5	24.9	27.2
2	86.4	77.2	80.8	104.7[2]	85.2	106.6	77.0	94.9	84.4	89.0
3	323.9	342.9	301.2	326.0[2]	267.6	314.5	278.8	290.9	252.6	217.4
4	9.9	14.8	11.6	11.6[2]	13.5	10.8	11.7	11.0	8.7	8.3
5A	11.5	17.6	16.9	17.4[2]	16.2	14.8	16.8	16.1	15.2	15.4
5B	2.9	2.2	3.6	4.7[2]	4.7	3.9	4.6	6.2	3.6	-
Women - Femmes - Mujeres ISCED-97 - CITE-97 - CINE-97										
Total	327.3	339.5	313.9	351.1[2]	283.7	308.7	284.1	276.0	242.3	206.3
X	4.3	2.7	2.6	3.0[2]	-	3.3	2.1	3.1	2.9	1.8
1	8.1	7.7	7.0	10.7[2]	7.0	10.5	7.3	9.3	8.8	7.3
2	55.0	59.6	50.8	66.0[2]	54.5	60.6	54.0	48.3	47.0	39.0
3	233.4	239.6	220.3	234.6[2]	192.0	199.2	183.6	177.6	155.7	131.1
4	11.4	13.2	12.3	12.2[2]	12.2	10.3	12.3	10.7	7.7	4.0
5A	10.9	11.6	16.9	20.5[2]	12.2	20.1	19.5	20.6	16.0	16.8
5B	4.0	4.7	3.7	3.9[2]	3.8	4.4	5.3	6.5	4.2	6.3
Roumanie (FB) [1][3]	Registered unemployment - Chômage enregistré - Desempleo registrado									
Total - Total - Total ISCED-97 - CITE-97 - CINE-97										
Total	1 130.3	1 007.1	826.9	760.6	658.9	557.9	523.0	460.5	367.8	403.4
1-2	832.3	725.9	599.1	584.5	494.9	420.2	418.4	369.8	290.3	311.9
3-4	265.3	248.8	199.7	152.1	136.2	109.1	84.8	73.2	61.7	70.8
5-6	32.7	32.4	28.1	24.0	27.8	28.6	19.7	17.5	15.8	20.7
Men - Hommes - Hombres ISCED-97 - CITE-97 - CINE-97										
Total	600.2	535.5	445.8	421.1	372.6	323.3	303.7	269.0	201.2	216.2
1-2	474.1	417.1	351.6	343.3	296.2	261.2	257.2	228.5	169.4	180.2
3-4	110.3	103.3	81.2	67.3	64.0	49.9	38.2	33.2	25.5	28.5
5-6	15.7	15.0	13.0	10.5	12.4	12.3	8.4	7.4	6.3	7.5
Women - Femmes - Mujeres ISCED-97 - CITE-97 - CINE-97										
Total	530.1	471.6	381.1	339.5	286.3	234.6	219.2	191.4	166.6	187.2
1-2	358.2	308.7	247.6	241.2	198.7	159.0	161.2	141.3	120.9	131.8
3-4	155.0	145.5	118.5	84.9	72.2	59.2	46.7	40.0	36.2	42.3
5-6	17.0	17.4	15.1	13.5	15.4	16.4	11.3	10.1	9.5	13.2
Russian Federation (BA) [4]	Total unemployment - Chômage total - Desempleo total									
Total - Total - Total ISCED-97 - CITE-97 - CINE-97										
Total	9 436	7 700	6 424	5 698	5 959	5 675	5 263	5 312	4 588	4 791
1	295	198	91	67	75	72	66	72	64	73
2	1 285	1 084	901	777	818	787	747	758	565	557
3	2 890	2 425	2 149	1 921	1 939	1 896	1 755	1 783	1 646	1 595
4	1 044	940	811	763	1 055	1 021	976	975	839	935
5A	2 675	2 028	1 636	1 436	1 268	1 126	1 028	996	825	926
5B	274	268	185	167	155	179	146	142	133	158
6	972	757	650	567	649	595	545	585	517	548
Men - Hommes - Hombres ISCED-97 - CITE-97 - CINE-97										
Total	4 939	4 057	3 450	3 014	3 121	2 975	2 725	2 811	2 453	2 542
1	193	137	66	42	50	50	38	43	44	47
2	765	664	556	488	511	492	457	477	352	347
3	1 611	1 311	1 207	1 049	1 054	1 011	946	960	911	873
4	609	536	504	449	631	615	591	581	515	577
5A	1 171	923	740	641	498	443	393	405	342	388
5B	130	136	77	72	79	88	67	75	63	71
6	459	350	299	272	297	276	234	269	226	238
Women - Femmes - Mujeres ISCED-97 - CITE-97 - CINE-97										
Total	4 497	3 643	2 974	2 685	2 838	2 699	2 538	2 501	2 136	2 250
1	102	61	25	25	25	22	28	29	20	25
2	520	420	346	290	307	294	291	281	213	209
3	1 279	1 113	942	872	885	885	808	823	735	722
4	435	404	306	314	424	407	385	394	323	358
5A	1 503	1 105	896	795	770	683	636	592	483	538
5B	145	133	109	95	76	90	80	67	70	87
6	513	407	350	295	352	319	310	316	291	310

Explanatory notes: see p. 451. Notes explicatives: voir p. 454. Notas explicativas: véase p. 457.

[1] Persons aged 15 years and over. [2] Estimates based on the 2002 Population Census results. [3] Dec. of each year. [4] Persons aged 15 to 72 years.

[1] Personnes âgées de 15 ans et plus. [2] Estimations basées sur les résultats du Recensement de la population de 2002. [3] Déc. de chaque année. [4] Personnes âgées de 15 à 72 ans.

[1] Personas de 15 años y más. [2] Estimaciones basadas en los resultados del Censo de población de 2002. [3] Dic. de cada año. [4] Personas de 15 a 72 años.

By level of education   Par niveau d'instruction   Por nivel de educación

	Thousands / Milliers / Millares									
	1999	2000	2001	2002	2003	2004	2005	2006	2007	2008

Russian Federation (FB) [1]   Registered unemployment - Chômage enregistré - Desempleo registrado

Total - Total - Total
ISCED-97 - CITE-97 - CINE-97

	1999	2000	2001	2002	2003	2004	2005	2006	2007	2008
Total	.	1 037	1 123	1 500	1 639	1 920	1 830	1 742	1 553	1 522
1									94.0	88.0
1-2	.	139	154	212	257	334	317	314		
2									207.0	198.0
3	.	316	343	490	562	651	610	580	516	479
4	.	191	209	278	294	352	332	318	295	296
5A-5B	.	258	273	341	348	378	360	338	286	279
6	.	130	140	172	169	194	198	182	155	183

Men - Hommes - Hombres
ISCED-97 - CITE-97 - CINE-97

	1999	2000	2001	2002	2003	2004	2005	2006	2007	2008
Total	.	322	360	487	533	647	630	609	570	604
1									38.0	36.0
1-2	.	61	67	86	105	141	135	137		
2									92.0	92.0
3	.	105	118	174	198	234	223	216	203	204
4	.	66	73	96	98	121	116	113	110	127
5A-5B	.	51	56	75	77	87	87	82	76	83
6	.	39	44	55	52	61	64	57	51	61

Women - Femmes - Mujeres
ISCED-97 - CITE-97 - CINE-97

	1999	2000	2001	2002	2003	2004	2005	2006	2007	2008
Total	.	715	763	1 013	1 106	1 273	1 200	1 133	983	918
1									56.0	52.0
1-2	.	78	87	126	152	193	182	177		
2									115.0	106.0
3	.	211	225	316	364	417	387	364	313	275
4	.	125	136	182	196	231	216	205	185	169
5A-5B	.	207	217	266	271	291	273	256	210	195
6	.	91	96	117	117	133	134	125	104	121

San Marino (E) [2][3]   Registered unemployment - Chômage enregistré - Desempleo registrado

Total - Total - Total
ISCED-76 - CITE-76 - CINE-76   ISCED-97 - CITE-97 - CINE-97

	1999	2000	2001	2002	2003	2004	2005	2006	2007	2008	
Total	0.423	.	0.514	0.710	0.628	0.577	0.671	0.595	0.573	0.713	Total
1	0.012	.	0.018	0.034	0.025	0.021	0.020	0.015	0.010	0.016	1
2	0.087	.	0.103	0.215	0.270	0.231	0.203	0.172	0.154	0.229	2
3	0.045	.	0.271	0.301	0.190	0.167	0.257	0.219	0.233	0.293	3-4
5	0.184	.	0.087	0.030	0.120	0.126	0.152	0.141	0.133	0.120	5A,6
6	0.011	.	0.020	0.129	0.021	0.032	0.039	0.047	0.041	0.050	5B
7	0.084	.	0.015	0.001	0.002	-	-	0.001	0.002	0.005	?

Men - Hommes - Hombres
ISCED-76 - CITE-76 - CINE-76   ISCED-97 - CITE-97 - CINE-97

	1999	2000	2001	2002	2003	2004	2005	2006	2007	2008	
Total	0.121	.	0.164	0.184	0.174	0.133	0.180	0.144	0.153	0.197	Total
1	0.007	.	0.007	0.007	0.007	0.010	0.006	0.006	0.003	0.010	1
2	0.020	.	0.032	0.050	0.065	0.036	0.051	0.041	0.040	0.061	2
3	0.010	.	0.086	0.079	0.060	0.053	0.081	0.052	0.074	0.091	3-4
5	0.053	.	0.030	0.010	0.033	0.022	0.033	0.032	0.024	0.021	5A,6
6	0.003	.	0.006	0.038	0.007	0.012	0.009	0.013	0.012	0.012	5B
7	0.028	.	0.003	-	0.002	-	-	-	-	0.002	?

Women - Femmes - Mujeres
ISCED-76 - CITE-76 - CINE-76   ISCED-97 - CITE-97 - CINE-97

	1999	2000	2001	2002	2003	2004	2005	2006	2007	2008	
Total	0.302	.	0.350	0.526	0.454	0.444	0.491	0.451	0.420	0.516	Total
1	0.005	.	0.011	0.027	0.018	0.011	0.014	0.009	0.007	0.006	1
2	0.067	.	0.071	0.165	0.205	0.195	0.152	0.131	0.114	0.168	2
3	0.035	.	0.185	0.222	0.130	0.114	0.176	0.167	0.159	0.202	3-4
5	0.131	.	0.057	0.020	0.087	0.104	0.119	0.109	0.109	0.099	5A,6
6	0.008	.	0.014	0.091	0.014	0.020	0.030	0.034	0.029	0.038	5B
7	0.056	.	0.012	0.001	-	-	-	0.001	0.002	0.003	?

Slovakia (BA) [2][4]   Total unemployment - Chômage total - Desempleo total

Total - Total - Total
ISCED-76 - CITE-76 - CINE-76   ISCED-97 - CITE-97 - CINE-97

	1999	2000	2001	2002	2003	2004	2005	2006	2007	2008	
Total	416.8	485.2	508.0	486.9	459.2	481.0	427.5	353.4	291.9	257.5	Total
0-1	89.0	95.7	0.3	-	-		0.2	0.9	0.2	0.3	0
2-3	315.2	374.0	5.6	6.2	6.6	7.9	8.1	10.2	5.2	2.6	1
5-7	12.7	15.5	95.1	94.2	99.9	108.0	107.9	88.9	80.0	69.1	2
			391.9	372.5	336.4	345.0	292.1	240.7	190.5	170.4	3-4
			13.2	12.8	14.7	18.4	17.2	12.2	14.1	13.9	5A
			1.6	1.2	1.7	2.1	1.9	0.7	1.5	1.2	5B
			0.2	0.1	-	-	-	-	0.2	-	6

Explanatory notes: see p. 451.   Notes explicatives: voir p. 454.   Notas explicativas: véase p. 457.

[1] Dec. of each year. [2] Persons aged 15 years and over. [3] Dec. [4] Excl. persons on child-care leave.

[1] Déc. de chaque année. [2] Personnes âgées de 15 ans et plus. [3] Déc. [4] Non compris les personnes en congé parental.

[1] Dic. de cada año. [2] Personas de 15 años y más. [3] Dic. [4] Excl. las personas con licencia parental.

UNEMPLOYMENT	CHÔMAGE	DESEMPLEO
By level of education	Par niveau d'instruction	Por nivel de educación

	Thousands				Milliers				Millares	
	1999	2000	2001	2002	2003	2004	2005	2006	2007	2008

Slovakia (BA) [1][2] — Total unemployment - Chômage total - Desempleo total

Men - Hommes - Hombres
ISCED-76 - CITE-76 - CINE-76 … ISCED-97 - CITE-97 - CINE-97

	1999	2000	2001	2002	2003	2004	2005	2006	2007	2008	
Total	226.6	265.5	282.5	263.9	246.5	250.0	223.6	179.5	143.5	124.6	Total
0-1	45.7	50.2	0.2	-	-	-	0.1	0.4	-	0.2	0
2-3	174.4	205.8	3.3	4.0	3.8	4.5	4.3	5.8	3.0	1.6	1
5-7	6.7	9.5	50.5	48.7	50.8	53.6	56.6	45.4	40.6	35.1	2
			220.7	204.8	184.7	182.0	153.4	122.5	94.0	81.3	3-4
			7.4	5.8	6.6	9.9	8.9	5.2	5.3	6.0	5A
			0.6	0.6	0.6	0.3	0.4	0.1	0.4	0.3	5B
			-	-	-	-	-	-	0.2	-	6

Women - Femmes - Mujeres
ISCED-76 - CITE-76 - CINE-76 … ISCED-97 - CITE-97 - CINE-97

	1999	2000	2001	2002	2003	2004	2005	2006	2007	2008	
Total	190.3	219.7	225.4	223.0	212.7	231.0	203.8	173.9	148.3	132.8	Total
0-1	43.4	45.5	0.2	-	-	-	0.1	0.4	0.2	0.1	0
2-3	140.9	168.2	2.4	2.2	2.8	3.4	3.8	4.4	2.2	0.9	1
5-7	6.1	6.0	44.7	45.5	49.1	54.0	51.4	43.4	39.4	33.9	2
			171.2	167.8	151.6	163.0	138.7	118.2	96.5	89.1	3-4
			5.8	7.0	8.2	8.5	8.3	7.0	8.8	7.9	5A
			1.0	0.7	1.2	1.8	1.6	0.7	1.1	1.0	5B
			0.2	0.1	0.1	-	-	-	-	-	6

Slovakia (FB) [1][3] — Registered unemployment - Chômage enregistré - Desempleo registrado

Total - Total - Total
ISCED-97 - CITE-97 - CINE-97

	1999	2000	2001	2002	2003	2004	2005	2006	2007	2008
Total	535.2	506.5	533.7	504.1	452.2	383.2	333.8	273.4	239.9	248.5
0-1	13.1	12.9	16.4	17.7	16.7	14.7	14.9	16.7	16.0	15.7
2	152.0	136.9	152.9	148.6	131.3	113.0	104.1	91.1	80.4	76.4
3-4	354.6	341.0	348.6	321.7	288.8	242.5	203.3	155.1	132.8	143.8
5A	13.9	13.9	14.0	14.0	13.6	11.1	9.8	8.9	8.9	10.0
5B	1.5	1.7	1.7	2.0	1.7	1.8	1.6	1.5	1.7	2.4
6	0.1	0.1	0.1	0.1	0.1	0.1	0.1	0.1	0.1	0.2

Men - Hommes - Hombres
ISCED-97 - CITE-97 - CINE-97

	1999	2000	2001	2002	2003	2004	2005	2006	2007	2008
Total	299.1	275.0	295.0	277.3	247.8	193.1	164.1	130.7	112.8	119.8
0-1	7.3	7.0	9.3	10.2	9.6	8.0	8.0	8.9	8.3	8.3
2	80.8	69.7	80.1	78.4	68.9	54.6	49.8	42.4	36.7	35.1
3-4	202.4	189.9	197.2	180.4	161.3	124.1	100.7	74.6	63.1	70.8
5A	8.0	7.7	7.6	7.5	7.3	5.8	5.0	4.3	4.2	4.8
5B	0.6	0.7	0.7	0.7	0.6	0.6	0.5	0.5	0.5	0.7
6	-	-	0.1	0.1	0.1	-	0.1	-	-	0.1

Women - Femmes - Mujeres
ISCED-97 - CITE-97 - CINE-97

	1999	2000	2001	2002	2003	2004	2005	2006	2007	2008
Total	236.1	231.5	238.7	226.8	204.4	190.1	169.7	142.7	127.1	128.7
0-1	5.8	5.8	7.1	7.5	7.1	6.7	6.8	7.8	7.7	7.4
2	71.2	67.3	72.8	70.2	62.4	58.5	54.3	48.7	43.7	41.3
3-4	152.3	151.1	151.4	141.3	127.5	118.3	102.6	80.5	69.7	73.0
5A	5.9	6.3	6.4	6.5	6.3	5.3	4.8	4.6	4.7	5.2
5B	0.9	1.0	1.0	1.3	1.1	1.2	1.1	1.0	1.2	1.7
6						0.1	0.1	0.1	0.1	0.1

Slovenia (BA) [1][4] — Total unemployment - Chômage total - Desempleo total

Total - Total - Total
ISCED-76 - CITE-76 - CINE-76 [5] … ISCED-97 - CITE-97 - CINE-97

	1999	2000	2001	2002	2003	2004	2005	2006	2007	2008	
Total	71	69	57	58	63	61	58	61	48	43	Total
X	-	-	-	-	-	-	-	-	-	1	0
1	2	3	4	2	3	2	1	1	2	1	1
2	18	19	15	14	15	14	12	12	10	9	2
3	46	44	36	39	41	39	40	41	29	25	3-4
5	4	1	1	-	-	2	2	2	4	4	5A
6	1	2	2	2	2	3	3	5	2	3	5B
7	-	-	-	-	-	-	-				

Men - Hommes - Hombres
ISCED-76 - CITE-76 - CINE-76 [5] … ISCED-97 - CITE-97 - CINE-97

	1999	2000	2001	2002	2003	2004	2005	2006	2007	2008	
Total	37	36	29	30	32	31	30	28	20	20	Total
X	-	-	-	-	-	-	-	-	-	-	0
1	1	2	3	1	2	1	-	-	1	-	1
2	9	10	7	7	8	9	8	6	6	4	2
3	25	24	19	21	18	19	19	18	11	12	3-4
5	2	-	-	-	-	-	-	1	2	2	5A
6	-	-	1	-	1	1	1	2	1	1	5B
7	-	-	-	-	-	-	-				

Explanatory notes: see p. 451.

[1] Persons aged 15 years and over. [2] Excl. persons on child-care leave. [3] 31st Dec. of each year. [4] Second quarter of each year. [5] Figures under 6000 are rough estimates.

Notes explicatives: voir p. 454.

[1] Personnes âgées de 15 ans et plus. [2] Non compris les personnes en congé parental. [3] 31 déc. de chaque année. [4] Deuxième trimestre de chaque année. [5] Les chiffres en dessous de 6000 sont des estimations imprécises.

Notas explicativas: véase p. 457.

[1] Personas de 15 años y más. [2] Excl. las personas con licencia parental. [3] 31 dic. de cada año. [4] Segundo trimestre de cada año. [5] Las cifras de menos de 6000 son estimaciones aproximativas.

| By level of education | Par niveau d'instruction | Por nivel de educación |

	Thousands			Milliers				Millares		
	1999	2000	2001	2002	2003	2004	2005	2006	2007	2008

Slovenia (BA) [1] [2] Total unemployment - Chômage total - Desempleo total

Women - Femmes - Mujeres
ISCED-76 - CITE-76 - CINE-76 [3]   ISCED-97 - CITE-97 - CINE-97

	1999	2000	2001	2002	2003	2004	2005		2006	2007	2008	
Total	34	33	28	27	31	30	28	|	33	28	23	Total
X	-	-	-	-	-	-	-	|	-	-	-	0
1	1	2	1	-	1	1	-	|	1	1	-	1
2	9	9	8	8	7	6	5	|	5	4	5	2
3	21	20	17	18	19	20	20	|	23	18	14	3-4
5	2	1	1	-	-	-	-	|	1	3	2	5A
6	1	1	1	2	3	2	2	|	3	2	2	5B
7	-	-	-	-	-	-	-	|				

Slovenia (FB) [1] [4] Registered unemployment - Chômage enregistré - Desempleo registrado

Total - Total - Total
ISCED-76 - CITE-76 - CINE-76

	1999	2000	2001	2002	2003	2004	2005	2006	2007	2008
Total	.	106.601	101.857	102.634	97.674	93.420	.	.	.	.
1	.	50.353	47.923	48.237	43.162	38.060	.	.	.	.
2	.	29.033	27.278	27.015	24.960	22.890	.	.	.	.
3	.	22.423	21.947	22.426	23.627	24.600	.	.	.	.
5	.	2.592	2.238	2.118	2.086	2.133	.	.	.	.
6-7	.	2.200	2.471	2.858	3.839	4.582	.	.	.	.

Men - Hommes - Hombres
ISCED-76 - CITE-76 - CINE-76

	1999	2000	2001	2002	2003	2004	2005	2006	2007	2008
Total	.	52.507	50.164	50.106	46.075	43.561	.	.	.	.
1	.	24.950	24.219	24.542	21.646	19.482	.	.	.	.
2	.	15.630	14.443	14.074	12.424	11.338	.	.	.	.
3	.	9.508	9.280	9.295	9.604	10.108	.	.	.	.
5	.	1.368	1.147	1.049	1.007	0.994	.	.	.	.
6-7	.	1.051	1.075	1.146	1.395	1.639	.	.	.	.

Women - Femmes - Mujeres
ISCED-76 - CITE-76 - CINE-76

	1999	2000	2001	2002	2003	2004	2005	2006	2007	2008
Total	.	54.094	51.693	52.528	51.598	49.856	.	.	.	.
1	.	25.403	23.704	23.678	21.515	18.581	.	.	.	.
2	.	13.403	12.835	12.941	12.536	11.555	.	.	.	.
3	.	12.915	12.667	13.131	14.024	14.490	.	.	.	.
5	.	1.224	1.091	1.069	1.079	1.139	.	.	.	.
6-7	.	1.149	1.396	1.712	2.444	2.943	.	.	.	.

Suisse (BA) [1] [2] Total unemployment - Chômage total - Desempleo total

Total - Total - Total
ISCED-97 - CITE-97 - CINE-97

	1999	2000	2001	2002	2003	2004	2005	2006	2007	2008
Total	122	106	101	119	170	179	185	169	156	147
1-2	39	32	34	33	45	51	52	48	45	41
3-4	65	61	52	65	93	97	99	91	83	79
5-6	17	13	14	22	32	30	32	29	28	26

Men - Hommes - Hombres
ISCED-97 - CITE-97 - CINE-97

	1999	2000	2001	2002	2003	2004	2005	2006	2007	2008
Total	59	51	38	62	86	89	88	78	68	66
1-2	18	17	16	18	22	24	23	21	20	18
3-4	33	26	16	30	43	47	46	41	33	34
5-6	8	7	5	14	21	18	18	16	15	14

Women - Femmes - Mujeres
ISCED-97 - CITE-97 - CINE-97

	1999	2000	2001	2002	2003	2004	2005	2006	2007	2008
Total	62	55	63	57	84	89	97	91	88	80
1-2	21	15	17	15	23	27	29	28	25	22
3-4	33	35	37	35	50	50	53	50	50	45
5-6	8	5	9	8	11	12	15	13	13	12

Sweden (BA) Total unemployment - Chômage total - Desempleo total

Total - Total - Total
ISCED-76 - CITE-76 - CINE-76 [5]   ISCED-97 - CITE-97 - CINE-97 [6]

	1999	2000		2001	2002	2003	2004		2005	2006	2007	2008	
Total	241	203	|	175	176	217	246	|	270 [7]	246	298	305	Total
1	24	21	|	14	13	13	14	|	17 [7]	13	14	15	1
2	53	48	|	36	33	40	43	|	53 [7]	54	82	84	2
3	122	99	|	92	91	111	129	|	130 [7]	116	119	118	3
5	24	20	|	7	8	11	14	|	17 [7]	12	18	19	4
6-7	14	12	|	14	17	23	28	|	30 [7]	31	34	32	5A
9	4	4	|	8	9	14	14	|	15 [7]	14	16	17	5B
			|	1	1	2	2	|	3 [7]	2	1	1	6
			|	3	4	3	3	|	4 [7]	4	12	18	?

Explanatory notes: see p. 451.

[1] Persons aged 15 years and over. [2] Second quarter of each year. [3] Figures under 6000 are rough estimates. [4] 31st Dec. of each year. [5] Persons aged 16 to 64 years. [6] Persons aged 15 to 74 years; prior to 2007: 16 to 64 years. [7] Methodology revised; data not strictly comparable.

Notes explicatives: voir p. 454.

[1] Personnes âgées de 15 ans et plus. [2] Deuxième trimestre de chaque année. [3] Les chiffres en dessous de 6000 sont des estimations imprécises. [4] 31 déc. de chaque année. [5] Personnes âgées de 16 à 64 ans. [6] Personnes âgées de 15 à 74 ans; avant 2007: 16 à 64 ans. [7] Méthodologie révisée; les données ne sont pas strictement comparables.

Notas explicativas: véase p. 457.

[1] Personas de 15 años y más. [2] Segundo trimestre de cada año. [3] Las cifras de menos de 6000 son estimaciones aproximativas. [4] 31 dic. de cada año. [5] Personas de 16 a 64 años. [6] Personas de 15 a 74 años; antes de 2007: 16 a 64 años. [7] Metodología revisada; los datos no son estrictamente comparables.

UNEMPLOYMENT	CHÔMAGE	DESEMPLEO
By level of education	Par niveau d'instruction	Por nivel de educación

	Thousands			Milliers					Millares		
	1999	2000	2001	2002	2003	2004	2005	2006	2007	2008	

Sweden (BA)

Total unemployment - Chômage total - Desempleo total

Men - Hommes - Hombres
ISCED-76 - CITE-76 - CINE-76 [1]   ISCED-97 - CITE-97 - CINE-97 [2]

	1999	2000	2001	2002	2003	2004	2005	2006	2007	2008	
Total	133	114	99	101	123	137	148 [3]	131	149	152	Total
1	14	12	8	7	7	9	10 [3]	7	7	7	1
2	29	26	21	19	22	24	29 [3]	30	41	44	2
3	66	57	53	53	63	72	74 [3]	62	60	60	3
5	13	11	4	5	7	9	10 [3]	7	9	10	4
6-7	9	7	7	10	14	14	14 [3]	15	17	15	5A
9	2	2	4	5	7	7	7 [3]	6	7	8	5B
			-	1	1	1	2 [3]	1	1	1	6
			2	2	2	2	2 [3]	2	6	8	?

Women - Femmes - Mujeres
ISCED-76 - CITE-76 - CINE-76 [1]   ISCED-97 - CITE-97 - CINE-97 [2]

	1999	2000	2001	2002	2003	2004	2005	2006	2007	2008	
Total	107	89	76	76	94	109	123 [3]	114	148	152	Total
1	10	9	6	6	6	5	7 [3]	6	7	8	1
2	24	22	15	14	18	19	24 [3]	23	41	40	2
3	56	42	39	38	49	57	56 [3]	54	59	58	3
5	11	9	3	3	4	5	7 [3]	5	8	9	4
6-7	5	5	7	7	9	14	17 [3]	16	17	17	5A
9	2	2	4	4	7	7	8 [3]	8	9	9	5B
			-	-	1	1	1 [3]	1	-	-	6
			1	2	1	1	2 [3]	1	6	10	?

Sweden (FB) [1]

Registered unemployment - Chômage enregistré - Desempleo registrado

Total - Total - Total
ISCED-97 - CITE-97 - CINE-97

	1999	2000	2001	2002	2003	2004	2005	2006	2007	2008
Total		.	.	185.838	223.023	239.201	241.434	210.891	169.516	150.384
X				0.015	0.002	0.001	0.009	0.033	0.032	0.002
1				20.683	24.736	26.493	26.346	22.732	18.938	16.789
2				31.664	35.024	36.468	37.436	34.200	29.637	26.342
3				86.081	102.658	111.481	113.882	98.069	78.124	69.139
4				12.709	15.781	15.879	15.431	13.849	10.534	9.290
5				33.746	43.473	47.277	46.502	40.297	30.801	27.572
6				0.940	1.349	1.603	1.828	1.711	1.450	1.250

Men - Hommes - Hombres
ISCED-97 - CITE-97 - CINE-97

	1999	2000	2001	2002	2003	2004	2005	2006	2007	2008
Total		.	.	105.418	127.430	135.090	132.000	114.169	90.268	80.903
X				0.009	0.001		0.003	0.009	0.009	0.003
1				12.700	15.421	16.567	16.052	13.710	10.914	9.594
2				18.607	20.697	21.407	21.318	19.469	16.818	15.242
3				48.985	58.901	63.322	62.813	53.585	42.075	37.863
4				6.788	8.491	8.513	7.958	6.938	5.229	4.608
5				17.771	23.086	24.302	22.749	19.465	14.442	12.898
6				0.558	0.832	0.981	1.107	0.992	0.781	0.695

Women - Femmes - Mujeres
ISCED-97 - CITE-97 - CINE-97

	1999	2000	2001	2002	2003	2004	2005	2006	2007	2008
Total		.	.	80.420	95.593	104.111	109.435	96.722	79.248	69.481
X				0.006	0.001	0.001	0.007	0.024	0.023	0.001
1				7.983	9.314	9.926	10.294	9.022	8.024	7.193
2				13.057	14.327	15.061	16.119	14.731	12.819	11.100
3				37.096	43.757	48.159	51.068	44.484	36.050	31.276
4				5.921	7.290	7.367	7.473	6.911	5.305	4.682
5				15.975	20.387	22.975	23.753	20.832	16.357	14.674
6				0.382	0.517	0.622	0.722	0.719	0.670	0.555

Turkey (BA) [4]

Total unemployment - Chômage total - Desempleo total

Total - Total - Total
ISCED-97 - CITE-97 - CINE-97

	1999	2000	2001	2002	2003	2004	2005	2006	2007	2008
Total	1 830	1 495	1 967	2 464	2 493	2 498	2 519	2 446	2 377	2 611
X	45	68	60	79	113	57	60	55	55	64
1	791	627	891	1 091	1 113	972	955	899	803	871
2	241	191	254	329	332	364	412	416	424	501
3-4	566	424	551	653	582	730	708	688	675	679
5-6	155	143	164	266	290	317	287	293	311	362
?	34	42	46	44	64	59	97	95	109	134

Men - Hommes - Hombres
ISCED-97 - CITE-97 - CINE-97

	1999	2000	2001	2002	2003	2004	2005	2006	2007	2008
Total	1 312	1 111	1 485	1 826	1 830	1 878	1 867	1 776	1 716	1 877
X	33	40	45	48	58	44	42	43	43	47
1	633	527	736	917	916	827	796	735	672	716
2	175	157	199	264	272	300	342	333	340	403
3-4	358	275	371	416	384	483	452	431	415	423
5-6	86	80	93	145	153	172	152	156	153	179
?	27	32	39	36	48	52	83	78	93	109

Explanatory notes: see p. 451.

[1] Persons aged 16 to 64 years. [2] Persons aged 15 to 74 years; prior to 2007: 16 to 64 years. [3] Methodology revised; data not strictly comparable. [4] Persons aged 15 years and over.

Notes explicatives: voir p. 454.

[1] Personnes âgées de 16 à 64 ans. [2] Personnes âgées de 15 à 74 ans; avant 2007: 16 à 64 ans. [3] Méthodologie révisée; les données ne sont pas strictement comparables. [4] Personnes âgées de 15 ans et plus.

Notas explicativas: véase p. 457.

[1] Personas de 16 a 64 años. [2] Personas de 15 a 74 años; antes de 2007: 16 a 64 años. [3] Metodología revisada; los datos no son estrictamente comparables. [4] Personas de 15 años y más.

By level of education — Par niveau d'instruction — Por nivel de educación

	Thousands			Milliers			Millares			
	1999	2000	2001	2002	2003	2004	2005	2006	2007	2008

Turkey (BA) [1] — Total unemployment - Chômage total - Desempleo total

Women - Femmes - Mujeres
ISCED-97 - CITE-97 - CINE-97

	1999	2000	2001	2002	2003	2004	2005	2006	2007	2008
Total	518	387	482	638	663	620	652	670	661	734
X	12	28	15	31	55	13	18	12	12	17
1	158	100	155	174	197	145	159	164	131	155
2	66	34	55	65	60	64	70	83	84	98
3-4	208	149	180	237	198	246	256	257	260	256
5-6	69	63	71	121	137	144	135	137	158	183
?	7	10	7	8	16	7	15	17	16	25

Turkey (FB) [2] [3] — Registered unemployment - Chômage enregistré - Desempleo registrado

Total - Total - Total
ISCED-76 - CITE-76 - CINE-76

	1999	2000	2001	2002	2003	2004	2005	2006	2007	2008
Total	487.5	730.5	718.7	464.2	587.5	811.9	881.3	1 061.9	696.5	987.8
X	3.7	3.4	3.6	2.7	4.3	5.2	6.2	9.3	10.5	22.0
0	5.6	5.3	5.1	4.8	11.0	13.1	14.9	17.6	16.9	24.5
1	210.5	186.4	195.3	140.4	221.2	268.0	342.8	402.7	.	.
1-2	.	.	.	.	.	.	.	.	313.2	445.5
2	75.4	117.3	108.8	72.8	82.8	96.7	120.7	140.7	.	.
3	169.0	352.5	336.9	194.9	149.2	227.9	338.0	416.0	312.3	422.8
5-7	23.4	65.6	69.0	48.6	119.0	201.0	58.6	75.6	43.7	73.1

Men - Hommes - Hombres
ISCED-76 - CITE-76 - CINE-76

	1999	2000	2001	2002	2003	2004	2005	2006	2007	2008
Total	413.8	591.9	582.9	379.8	469.4	611.4	656.2	782.7	520.1	724.3
X	2.9	2.7	2.7	2.0	2.9	3.4	3.8	6.8	5.4	10.9
0	4.4	4.2	4.1	3.7	7.9	9.2	10.1	13.0	11.8	16.4
1	191.9	169.6	176.9	126.3	193.1	226.2	281.1	296.8	.	.
1-2	.	.	.	.	.	.	.	.	257.9	362.1
2	68.0	106.1	98.1	64.9	73.3	83.1	100.7	103.7	.	.
3	131.4	267.6	257.1	151.9	112.3	158.1	227.0	306.7	219.4	291.9
5-7	15.3	41.9	44.0	31.0	80.0	131.4	33.6	55.7	25.6	43.0

Women - Femmes - Mujeres
ISCED-76 - CITE-76 - CINE-76

	1999	2000	2001	2002	2003	2004	2005	2006	2007	2008
Total	73.7	138.6	135.8	84.5	118.0	200.6	225.0	279.2	176.4	263.5
X	0.9	0.8	0.9	0.7	1.4	1.8	2.4	2.4	5.0	11.1
0	1.2	1.1	1.0	1.1	3.2	3.9	4.8	4.6	5.1	8.1
1	18.6	16.8	18.4	14.1	28.1	41.8	61.8	105.9	.	.
1-2	.	.	.	.	.	.	.	.	55.3	83.4
2	7.4	11.3	10.7	7.9	9.4	13.6	20.1	37.0	.	.
3	37.6	84.9	79.8	43.1	36.9	69.8	111.0	109.4	92.9	130.9
5-7	8.1	23.7	25.0	17.6	39.0	69.6	25.0	19.9	18.1	30.0

Ukraine (BA) [4] — Total unemployment - Chômage total - Desempleo total

Total - Total - Total
ISCED-76 - CITE-76 - CINE-76

	1999	2000	2001	2002	2003	2004	2005	2006	2007	2008
Total	2 614.3	2 655.8	2 455.0	2 140.7	2 008.0	1 906.7	1 600.8	1 515.0	1 417.6	1 425.1
1	20.6	15.5	7.7	5.6	3.1	12.0	5.2	1.6	1.1	0.5
2	222.9	214.2	200.6	145.0	125.7	245.6	169.7	133.1	120.0	105.0
3	1 518.2	1 540.7	1 445.9	1 288.7	1 214.1	1 035.1	852.3	793.8	739.9	753.3
5	550.9	560.2	499.8	449.4	423.6	401.0	375.8	372.9	321.8	349.5
6-7	301.7	325.2	301.0	252.0	241.5	213.0	197.8	213.6	234.8	216.8

Men - Hommes - Hombres
ISCED-76 - CITE-76 - CINE-76

	1999	2000	2001	2002	2003	2004	2005	2006	2007	2008
Total	1 346.5	1 357.4	1 263.0	1 106.5	1 055.7	1 001.6	862.5	804.1	770.7	768.9
1	12.1	11.5	5.9	4.7	2.6	7.3	2.5	0.8	0.4	0.1
2	130.8	129.9	122.7	86.7	76.9	143.8	111.3	83.7	84.0	66.6
3	848.8	860.5	809.3	729.6	694.4	565.9	490.3	445.9	428.3	447.6
5	210.8	207.8	184.9	163.9	161.9	180.6	160.5	154.7	142.8	141.0
6-7	144.0	147.7	140.2	121.6	119.9	104.0	97.9	119.0	115.2	113.6

Women - Femmes - Mujeres
ISCED-76 - CITE-76 - CINE-76

	1999	2000	2001	2002	2003	2004	2005	2006	2007	2008
Total	1 267.8	1 298.4	1 192.0	1 034.2	952.3	905.1	738.3	710.9	646.9	656.2
1	8.5	4.0	1.8	0.9	0.5	4.7	2.7	0.8	0.7	0.4
2	92.1	84.3	77.9	58.3	48.8	101.8	58.4	49.4	36.0	38.4
3	669.4	680.2	636.6	559.1	519.7	469.2	362.0	347.9	311.6	305.7
5	340.1	352.4	314.9	285.5	261.7	220.4	215.3	218.2	179.0	208.5
6-7	157.7	177.5	160.8	130.4	121.6	109.0	99.9	94.6	119.6	103.2

Explanatory notes: see p. 451.

[1] Persons aged 15 years and over. [2] Persons aged 14 years and over. [3] Dec. of each year. [4] Persons aged 15-70 years.

Notes explicatives: voir p. 454.

[1] Personnes âgées de 15 ans et plus. [2] Personnes âgées de 14 ans et plus. [3] Déc. de chaque année. [4] Personnes âgées de 15 à 70 ans.

Notas explicativas: véase p. 457.

[1] Personas de 15 años y más. [2] Personas de 14 años y más. [3] Dic. de cada año. [4] Personas de 15 á 70 años.

UNEMPLOYMENT   CHÔMAGE   DESEMPLEO

By level of education   Par niveau d'instruction   Por nivel de educación

	Thousands / Milliers / Millares									
	1999	2000	2001	2002	2003	2004	2005	2006	2007	2008

Ukraine (FB) [1] [2]   Registered unemployment - Chômage enregistré - Desempleo registrado

Total - Total - Total
ISCED-76 - CITE-76 - CINE-76

	1999	2000	2001	2002	2003	2004	2005	2006	2007	2008
Total	1 174.5	1 155.2	1 008.1	1 034.2	988.9	981.8	881.5	759.5	642.3	844.9
1	3.6	3.3	2.8	3.1	3.1	2.5	2.0	1.4	1.0	1.3
2	56.9	58.3	53.7	62.2	64.1	61.6	53.1	39.7	31.8	40.1
3	339.1	333.3	301.7	319.7	311.0	324.1	295.4	237.7	195.2	241.2
5	378.5	368.9	321.4	330.8	314.9	312.0	279.2	249.9	213.5	289.9
6-7	396.4	391.4	328.5	318.4	295.8	281.6	251.8	230.8	200.8	272.4

United Kingdom (BA) [3] [4]   Total unemployment - Chômage total - Desempleo total

Total - Total - Total
ISCED-76 - CITE-76 - CINE-76

	1999	2000	2001	2002	2003	2004	2005	2006	2007	2008
Total	1 710	1 559	1 423	1 472	1 420	1 394	1 397	1 649	1 621	1 643
X-1	423	372	349	335	290	292	280	307	315	304
2	310	298	254	264	271	226	229	291	280	305
3	737	679	617	634	622	639	646	770	760	764
6-7	129	108	117	148	147	139	142	173	163	157
9	111	102	86	91	90	98	100	108	103	113

Men - Hommes - Hombres
ISCED-76 - CITE-76 - CINE-76

	1999	2000	2001	2002	2003	2004	2005	2006	2007	2008
Total	1 047	942	861	892	867	824	817	959	930	969
X-1	268	236	218	219	190	188	180	196	197	188
2	180	179	149	160	166	136	135	166	165	194
3	453	406	375	369	363	358	357	440	426	442
6-7	74	63	71	92	97	85	88	94	91	83
9	72	58	48	52	51	57	57	63	51	62

Women - Femmes - Mujeres
ISCED-76 - CITE-76 - CINE-76

	1999	2000	2001	2002	2003	2004	2005	2006	2007	2008
Total	663	617	562	580	553	570	580	690	691	674
X-1	155	136	131	116	101	104	101	111	118	116
2	130	119	105	104	106	90	94	124	115	111
3	284	273	241	265	258	281	288	330	334	322
6-7	55	45	46	55	50	54	54	79	73	73
9	39	44	39	40	38	41	43	46	51	52

OCEANIA-OCÉANIE-OCEANIA

Australia (BA) [5] [6]   Total unemployment - Chômage total - Desempleo total

Total - Total - Total
ISCED-76 - CITE-76 - CINE-76   ISCED-97 - CITE-97 - CINE-97

	1999	2000	2001	2002	2003	2004	2005	2006	2007	2008	
Total	685.5	641.6	666.2 [7]	622.4	615.0	557.5	538.6 |	516.5	459.1	472.6	Total
X-1	1.3	0.4	1.2 [7]	0.8	0.9	0.1	0.8 |	71.2	65.6	66.5	X-1
2	317.6	284.3	361.5 [7]	322.0	307.7	269.2	277.1 |	172.0	154.7	157.6	2
3	273.6	261.7	209.9 [7]	195.9	196.6	182.5	156.8 |	177.3	148.6	150.6	3
5	43.2	42.6	40.7 [7]	49.9	46.6	42.2	43.3 |	12.9	8.1	8.3	4B
6	37.3	38.8	39.3 [7]	41.8	44.5	44.2	44.4 |	57.5	52.3	54.3	5A.6
7	12.6	13.9	13.6 [7]	12.0	18.7	19.3	16.1 |	25.6	29.8	35.4	5B

Men - Hommes - Hombres
ISCED-76 - CITE-76 - CINE-76   ISCED-97 - CITE-97 - CINE-97

	1999	2000	2001	2002	2003	2004	2005	2006	2007	2008	
Total	395.8	356.6	372.5 [7]	361.2	336.4	305.8	288.3 |	280.1	233.2	245.4	Total
X-1	1.3	0.4	0.9 [7]	0.8	0.3	0.1	0.6 |	43.8	35.2	37.7	X-1
2	185.6	161.5	195.9 [7]	189.9	171.4	154.7	153.3 |	94.4	78.7	81.3	2
3	161.6	144.4	128.5 [7]	117.9	105.9	97.3	82.6 |	99.7	79.3	81.8	3
5	20.7	20.0	20.1 [7]	22.5	22.5	20.6	18.5 |	5.5	5.0	2.9	4B
6	20.9	22.6	21.7 [7]	21.8	25.5	22.8	23.5 |	25.8	23.1	26.4	5A.6
7	5.7	7.8	5.4 [7]	8.4	10.8	10.3	9.6 |	10.9	11.9	15.4	5B

Women - Femmes - Mujeres
ISCED-76 - CITE-76 - CINE-76   ISCED-97 - CITE-97 - CINE-97

	1999	2000	2001	2002	2003	2004	2005	2006	2007	2008	
Total	289.7	285.0	293.7 [7]	261.1	278.6	251.7	250.3 |	236.3	226.0	227.2	Total
X-1	-	-	0.4 [7]	-	0.7	0.2	0.2 |	27.4	30.4	28.8	X-1
2	131.9	122.9	165.6 [7]	132.0	136.3	114.6	123.8 |	77.6	76.0	76.4	2
3	112.0	117.2	81.3 [7]	78.0	90.6	85.1	74.2 |	77.6	69.3	68.8	3
5	22.5	22.7	20.6 [7]	27.5	24.1	21.6	24.8 |	7.4	3.1	5.4	4B
6	16.4	16.2	17.6 [7]	20.0	19.0	21.3	20.9 |	31.6	29.2	27.9	5A.6
7	6.9	6.1	8.2 [7]	3.7	7.8	9.0	6.5 |	14.7	17.9	20.0	5B

Explanatory notes: see p. 451.

[1] Men aged 16 to 59 years; women aged 16 to 54 years. [2] 31st Dec. of each year. [3] Persons aged 16 years and over. [4] Second quarter. [5] Persons aged 15 years and over. [6] May of each year. [7] Data coded under the new Australian Standard Classification of Education (ASCED).

Notes explicatives: voir p. 454.

[1] Hommes âgés de 16 à 59 ans; femmes âgées de 16 à 54 ans. [2] 31 déc. de chaque année. [3] Personnes âgées de 16 ans et plus. [4] Deuxième trimestre. [5] Personnes âgées de 15 ans et plus. [6] Mai de chaque année. [7] Les données sont codées selon la nouvelle Classification australienne type de l'éducation ("ASCED").

Notas explicativas: véase p. 457.

[1] Hombres de 16 a 59 años; mujeres de 16 a 54 años. [2] 31 dic. de cada año. [3] Personas de 16 años y más. [4] Segundo trimestre. [5] Personas de 15 años y más. [6] Mayo de cada año. [7] Los datos se codifican según la nueva Clasificación Australiana Normalizada de la Educación ("ASCED").

By level of education — **Par niveau d'instruction** — **Por nivel de educación**

	Thousands			Milliers			Millares			
	1999	2000	2001	2002	2003	2004	2005	2006	2007	2008
New Zealand (BA)[1]				Total unemployment - Chômage total - Desempleo total						
Total - Total - Total										
ISCED-97 - CITE-97 - CINE-97										
Total	127.8	113.4	102.3	102.5	93.9	84.9[2]	82.6	85.4	82.8	95.0
X	43.8	39.4	33.2	31.8	27.0	26.7[2]	26.5	26.2	26.1	29.1
X-0	43.8	39.4	33.2	31.8	27.0	.	.	.	.	.
X-0,2	.	.	.	.	.	25.0	24.6	24.6	24.4	.
1	0.7	0.7	0.5	0.6	0.8	-	-	.	.	.
2	0.2	0.3	0.4	0.4	0.6	.	.	.	.	.
3	27.3	24.5	23.1	22.1	20.0	28.5[2]	29.4	28.8	27.6	31.8
4	38.1	31.4	29.8	29.9	28.4	3.6[2]	2.6	4.6	4.3	5.4
5A	6.6	7.2	6.3	7.7	7.3	9.5[2]	8.1	9.2	8.9	9.5
5B	3.8	3.5	3.1	3.1	2.9	10.7[2]	10.9	10.6	9.9	11.8
6	2.1	2.8	2.3	2.2	3.3	2.1[2]	1.8	2.8	3.0	3.1
?[3]	5.2	3.6	3.7	4.5	3.5	3.0[2]	3.1	3.3	3.0	4.4
Men - Hommes - Hombres										
ISCED-97 - CITE-97 - CINE-97										
Total	72.4	63.4	56.2	54.6	48.0	40.7[2]	40.9	42.3	41.0	49.8
X	26.3	24.6	19.9	18.9	15.2	13.7[2]	14.1	14.0	14.3	17.0
X-0	26.3	24.6	19.9	18.9	15.2	.	.	.	.	.
X-0,2	.	.	.	.	.	12.8	12.9	13.0	13.4	.
1	0.4	0.3	0.3	0.4	0.5	-	-	.	.	.
2	0.2	0.1	0.2	0.2	0.2	.	.	.	.	.
3	13.5	.	11.9	11.0	10.1	13.3[2]	13.7	13.5	12.9	16.1
4	22.8	17.0	16.4	15.0	13.2	2.8[2]	2.3	3.6	3.0	4.2
5A	3.9	3.9	3.1	4.3	4.4	4.5[2]	4.1	4.4	4.5	4.3
5B	1.5	1.1	1.0	0.0	0.9	3.5[2]	4.4	4.0	3.4	4.8
6	1.3	1.7	1.5	1.3	1.8	1.2[2]	1.1	1.1	1.5	1.6
?[3]	2.5	2.1	2.1	2.5	1.8	1.2[2]	1.3	1.6	1.4	1.8
Women - Femmes - Mujeres										
ISCED-97 - CITE-97 - CINE-97										
Total	55.4	50.0	46.1	47.9	45.9	44.2[2]	41.6	43.1	41.7	45.2
X	17.5	14.8	13.3	12.9	11.8	13.1[2]	12.4	12.2	11.8	12.0
X-0	17.5	14.8	13.3	12.9	11.8	.	.	.	.	.
X-0,2	.	.	.	.	.	12.2	11.7	11.4	11.0	.
1	0.3	0.4	0.2	0.2	0.3	-	-	.	.	.
2	0.1	0.2	0.2	0.2	0.4	.	.	.	.	.
3	13.8	11.8	11.2	11.1	10.0	15.2[2]	15.7	15.3	14.6	15.8
4	15.3	14.4	13.5	15.0	15.3	-	-	-	1.3	1.2
5A	2.7	3.3	3.1	3.4	3.0	5.0[2]	4.1	4.8	4.4	5.2
5B	2.2	2.4	2.1	2.2	2.0	7.1[2]	6.5	6.5	6.5	7.0
6	0.8	1.2	0.8	0.9	1.5	-	-	1.6	1.6	1.5
?[3]	2.7	1.5	1.6	2.0	1.7	1.8[2]	1.8	1.7	1.5	2.6

Explanatory notes: see p. 451.

[1] Persons aged 15 years and over. [2] Methodology revised; data not strictly comparable. [3] Incl. overseas qualifications.

Notes explicatives: voir p. 454.

[1] Personnes âgées de 15 ans et plus. [2] Méthodologie révisée; les données ne sont pas strictement comparables. [3] Y compris les qualifications étrangères.

Notas explicativas: véase p. 457.

[1] Personas de 15 años y más. [2] Metodología revisada; los datos no son estrictamente comparables. [3] Incl. las calificaciones extranjeras.

By economic activity — **Par activité économique** — **Por actividad económica**

	Thousands			Milliers				Millares		
	1999	2000	2001	2002	2003	2004	2005	2006	2007	2008

AFRICA-AFRIQUE-AFRICA

Egypt (BA) [1][2]   Total unemployment - Chômage total - Desempleo total

Total - Total - Total
ISIC 3 - CITI 3 - CIIU 3

	1999	2000	2001	2002	2003	2004	2005	2006	2007	2008
Total	1 480.5	1 698.0	1 783.0	2 020.6	2 240.7	2 153.9	2 450.0	2 434.5	2 134.9	.
UB	1 374.3	1 578.8	1 634.4	1 865.5	2 134.1	2 043.6	2 257.4	2 201.2	1 966.1	.
A	4.6	4.8	8.7	7.8	5.2	4.0	13.9	18.9	6.9	.
B	0.4	-	0.3	-	0.2	-	2.5	-	0.9	.
C	0.6	0.6	0.5	2.7	1.8	1.0	3.2	0.2	0.2	.
D	16.5	24.2	20.6	17.0	19.7	15.9	23.2	31.0	23.4	.
E	0.4	0.3	1.6	0.5	0.1	0.2	-	0.5	0.3	.
F	23.5	19.7	24.8	14.1	17.6	12.0	34.8	34.9	22.5	.
G	23.4	27.8	36.3	42.4	32.0	41.0	53.9	50.5	34.8	.
H	2.0	4.2	4.6	1.7	7.2	3.1	7.4	12.3	7.1	.
I	5.1	1.6	6.0	3.7	3.5	5.8	10.5	14.7	6.5	.
J	0.5	-	0.6	-	0.4	0.2	-	0.5	0.2	.
K	4.1	4.4	7.3	6.1	5.5	6.1	8.7	10.7	7.7	.
L	2.5	1.4	1.8	1.5	0.6	0.8	1.4	3.4	1.6	.
M	5.5	5.2	5.9	3.9	6.9	7.4	10.1	13.6	10.9	.
N	0.8	0.6	1.2	0.5	1.1	3.7	1.6	3.7	1.3	.
O	0.3	2.6	0.9	3.0	0.9	4.6	3.6	3.2	2.7	.
P	-	0.7	0.3	-	0.4	0.3	0.4	0.2	0.5	.
Q	.	.	.	.	.	.	.	0.2	-	.
X	15.8	21.4	27.2	50.3	3.5	4.2	17.2	35.0	41.1	.

Men - Hommes - Hombres
ISIC 3 - CITI 3 - CIIU 3

	1999	2000	2001	2002	2003	2004	2005	2006	2007	2008
Total	726.2	743.5	851.8	983.2	1 186.7	942.6	1 194.5	1 207.6	1 077.4	.
UB	648.4	659.0	753.0	895.4	1 104.3	861.1	1 034.5	1 018.7	944.7	.
A	4.4	4.3	7.7	6.0	4.6	4.0	13.9	18.3	6.7	.
B	0.4	-	0.3	-	0.2	-	2.5	-	0.9	.
C	0.6	0.3	0.5	1.1	1.4	0.7	3.0	0.2	0.2	.
D	13.0	17.0	16.1	9.9	13.4	12.7	18.8	22.7	18.5	.
E	0.4	0.3	1.3	0.5	0.1	0.2	-	0.5	0.3	.
F	21.6	19.7	22.5	14.1	17.3	11.5	34.4	34.0	21.8	.
G	16.9	19.7	21.9	24.5	21.6	27.5	43.0	42.7	28.8	.
H	1.5	4.2	4.0	1.1	7.0	3.1	7.2	12.3	6.4	.
I	4.6	1.6	5.7	3.4	3.2	4.3	10.3	13.6	5.6	.
J	0.5	-	0.3	-	0.3	0.1	-	-	0.2	.
K	3.9	2.3	4.3	5.0	4.2	4.5	6.9	7.6	5.9	.
L	1.4	0.5	0.8	1.1	0.6	0.7	0.4	1.8	0.9	.
M	2.0	2.0	1.3	2.1	4.3	3.9	3.2	4.8	3.2	.
N	0.5	0.3	0.3	0.3	0.3	0.7	0.2	0.5	0.4	.
O	0.3	2.1	0.6	2.6	0.9	3.5	3.2	3.0	1.2	.
P	-	0.7	-	-	0.4	0.3	0.2	0.2	0.3	.
Q	.	.	.	.	.	.	.	0.2	-	.
X	5.7	9.6	11.2	16.1	2.6	3.8	12.6	26.7	31.4	.

Women - Femmes - Mujeres
ISIC 3 - CITI 3 - CIIU 3

	1999	2000	2001	2002	2003	2004	2005	2006	2007	2008
Total	754.3	954.5	931.2	1 037.4	1 054.0	1 211.3	1 255.5	1 226.9	1 057.5	.
UB	725.9	919.8	881.4	970.1	1 029.8	1 182.5	1 222.9	1 182.5	1 021.4	.
A	0.2	0.5	1.0	1.8	0.6	-	-	0.6	0.2	.
B									-	.
C	.	0.3	.	1.6	0.4	0.3	0.2	.	-	.
D	3.5	7.2	4.5	7.1	6.3	3.2	4.4	8.3	4.9	.
E	-	-	0.3	-	-	-	-	-	-	.
F	1.9	-	2.3	-	0.3	0.5	0.4	0.9	0.7	.
G	6.5	8.1	14.4	17.9	10.4	13.5	10.9	7.8	6.0	.
H	0.5	-	0.6	0.6	0.2	-	0.2	-	0.7	.
I	0.5	-	0.3	0.3	0.3	1.5	0.2	1.1	0.9	.
J	-	-	0.3	-	0.1	0.1	-	0.5	-	.
K	0.2	2.1	3.0	1.1	1.3	1.6	1.8	3.1	1.8	.
L	1.1	0.9	1.0	0.4	-	0.1	1.0	1.6	0.7	.
M	3.5	3.2	4.6	1.8	2.6	3.5	6.9	8.8	7.7	.
N	0.3	0.3	0.9	0.2	0.8	3.0	1.4	3.2	0.9	.
O	-	0.5	0.3	0.4	-	1.1	0.4	0.2	1.5	.
P	-	-	0.3	-	-	.	0.2	-	0.2	.
Q	.	.	.	.	.	.	.	.	-	.
X	10.1	11.8	16.0	34.2	0.9	0.4	4.6	8.3	9.9	.

Explanatory notes: see p. 451.
[1] Persons aged 15 to 64 years. [2] May and Nov.

Notes explicatives: voir p. 454.
[1] Personnes âgées de 15 à 64 ans. [2] Mai et nov.

Notas explicativas: véase p. 457.
[1] Personas de 15 a 64 años. [2] Mayo y nov.

3D

UNEMPLOYMENT	CHÔMAGE	DESEMPLEO
By economic activity	Par activité économique	Por actividad económica

	Thousands				Milliers				Millares	
	1999	2000	2001	2002	2003	2004	2005	2006	2007	2008

Maroc (BA) [1] — Total unemployment - Chômage total - Desempleo total

Total - Total - Total
ISIC 3 - CITI 3 - CIIU 3

	1999	2000	2001	2002	2003	2004	2005	2006	2007	2008
Total	.	.	.	1 202.7	1 299.0	1 192.5	1 226.4	.	.	.
UB	.	.	.	625.6	681.1	598.8	600.1	.	.	.
A-B	.	.	.	71.0	68.9	56.4	76.3	.	.	.
C	.	.	.	2.2	1.5	2.1	1.3	.	.	.
D	.	.	.	168.7	167.4	168.4	166.4	.	.	.
E	.	.	.	0.7	2.0	2.2	2.5	.	.	.
F	.	.	.	94.0	98.9	100.9	108.2	.	.	.
G	.	.	.	106.2	.	.	.	.	.	.
G-H	.	.	.	.	117.6	146.0	148.4	.	.	.
H	.	.	.	26.3	.	.	.	.	.	.
I	.	.	.	24.1	29.0	26.3	26.6	.	.	.
J-K	.	.	.	13.9	15.8	15.9	17.7	.	.	.
L	.	.	.	14.5	.	.	.	.	.	.
L-Q	.	.	.	.	115.9	74.3	77.8	.	.	.
M-Q	.	.	.	54.5	.	.	.	.	.	.
X	.	.	.	1.0	0.8	1.1	1.1	.	.	.

Men - Hommes - Hombres
ISIC 3 - CITI 3 - CIIU 3

	1999	2000	2001	2002	2003	2004	2005	2006	2007	2008
Total	.	.	.	878.4	922.4	851.2	877.6	.	.	.
UB	.	.	.	418.6	442.0	382.6	386.6	.	.	.
A-B	.	.	.	62.0	58.9	49.1	64.5	.	.	.
C	.	.	.	2.0	1.5	2.1	1.3	.	.	.
D	.	.	.	109.0	104.2	111.1	105.7	.	.	.
E	.	.	.	0.7	1.7	2.2	2.2	.	.	.
F	.	.	.	92.0	96.6	99.5	107.2	.	.	.
G	.	.	.	96.8	.	.	.	.	.	.
G-H	.	.	.	.	100.2	125.1	128.9	.	.	.
H	.	.	.	21.5	.	.	.	.	.	.
I	.	.	.	21.7	25.2	22.8	23.7	.	.	.
J-K	.	.	.	7.9	9.0	9.0	11.3	.	.	.
L	.	.	.	12.2	.	.	.	.	.	.
L-Q	.	.	.	.	82.5	46.7	45.4	.	.	.
M-Q	.	.	.	33.1	.	.	.	.	.	.
X	.	.	.	0.8	0.6	0.8	0.8	.	.	.

Women - Femmes - Mujeres
ISIC 3 - CITI 3 - CIIU 3

	1999	2000	2001	2002	2003	2004	2005	2006	2007	2008
Total	.	.	.	324.3	376.6	341.4	348.8	.	.	.
UB	.	.	.	207.0	239.1	216.2	213.5	.	.	.
A-B	.	.	.	9.0	10.0	7.3	11.8	.	.	.
C	.	.	.	0.2	-	0.0	0.0	.	.	.
D	.	.	.	59.7	63.2	57.3	60.7	.	.	.
E	.	.	.	-	0.3	0.0	0.3	.	.	.
F	.	.	.	2.0	2.2	1.5	1.0	.	.	.
G	.	.	.	9.4	.	.	.	.	.	.
G-H	.	.	.	.	17.5	20.9	19.5	.	.	.
H	.	.	.	4.7	.	.	.	.	.	.
I	.	.	.	2.4	3.8	3.5	2.9	.	.	.
J-K	.	.	.	6.0	6.8	6.9	6.4	.	.	.
L	.	.	.	2.3	.	.	.	.	.	.
L-Q	.	.	.	.	33.4	27.4	32.4	.	.	.
M-Q	.	.	.	21.4	.	.	.	.	.	.
X	.	.	.	0.2	0.2	0.3	0.3	.	.	.

Mauritius (BA) [2] — Total unemployment - Chômage total - Desempleo total

Total - Total - Total
ISIC 3 - CITI 3 - CIIU 3

	1999	2000	2001	2002	2003	2004	2005	2006	2007	2008
Total	.	.	.	.	.	45.1	52.1	50.1	46.8 [3]	40.4
UB	.	.	.	.	.	18.7	19.4	15.8	16.9 [3]	12.7
A	.	.	.	.	.	0.5	1.7	2.0	1.1 [3]	1.3
B	.	.	.	.	.	0.2	-	0.1	0.1 [3]	0.1
C	.	.	.	.	.	-	0.1	0.1	0.1 [3]	0.0
D	.	.	.	.	.	10.3	13.4	13.2	11.0 [3]	9.8
E	.	.	.	.	.	0.1	0.1	0.1	0.0 [3]	0.0
F	.	.	.	.	.	4.2	3.7	4.7	4.5 [3]	3.0
G	.	.	.	.	.	3.7	4.8	5.1	3.7 [3]	5.0
H	.	.	.	.	.	1.9	2.2	2.1	2.0 [3]	2.5
I	.	.	.	.	.	1.2	1.0	1.0	1.2 [3]	0.8
J	.	.	.	.	.	0.1	0.3	0.2	0.3 [3]	0.3
K	.	.	.	.	.	0.9	0.9	1.5	1.3 [3]	1.1
L	.	.	.	.	.	0.1	0.4	0.2	0.2 [3]	0.3
M	.	.	.	.	.	0.7	0.6	0.8	0.9 [3]	0.6
N	.	.	.	.	.	0.1	0.3	0.3	0.4 [3]	0.3
O	.	.	.	.	.	1.1	0.8	0.8	0.9 [3]	0.6
P	.	.	.	.	.	1.2	2.3	1.9	2.2 [3]	2.0
Q	.	.	.	.	.	0.1	0.1	0.2	0.0 [3]	0.0
X	.	.	.	.	.	0.1	0.1	0.2	0.0 [3]	

Explanatory notes: see p. 451.

[1] Persons aged 15 years and over. [2] Persons aged 16 years and over. [3] Prior to 2007: persons aged 15 years and over.

Notes explicatives: voir p. 454.

[1] Personnes âgées de 15 ans et plus. [2] Personnes âgées de 16 ans et plus. [3] Avant 2006: personnes âgées de 15 ans et plus.

Notas explicativas: véase p. 457.

[1] Personas de 15 años y más. [2] Personas de 16 años y más. [3] Antes de 2006: personas de 15 años y más.

By economic activity — **Par activité économique** — **Por actividad económica**

	Thousands — Milliers — Millares									
	1999	2000	2001	2002	2003	2004	2005	2006	2007	2008

Mauritius (BA) [1] — Total unemployment - Chômage total - Desempleo total

Men - Hommes - Hombres
ISIC 3 - CITI 3 - CIIU 3

	1999	2000	2001	2002	2003	2004	2005	2006	2007	2008
Total	.	.	.	.	.	20.3	20.3	19.5	18.6 [2]	14.6
UB	.	.	.	.	.	7.7	7.2	5.0	4.9 [2]	3.8
A	.	.	.	.	.	0.4	0.9	1.2	0.7 [2]	0.8
B	.	.	.	.	.	0.2	-	0.1	0.1 [2]	0.1
C	.	.	.	.	.	-	0.1	0.1	0.1 [2]	0.0
D	.	.	.	.	.	3.2	3.3	2.7	3.0 [2]	2.2
E	.	.	.	.	.	0.1	0.1	0.1	0.0 [2]	0.0
F	.	.	.	.	.	4.1	3.6	4.7	4.4 [2]	2.9
G	.	.	.	.	.	1.4	1.9	1.9	1.5 [2]	1.9
H	.	.	.	.	.	0.9	1.1	1.0	1.2 [2]	0.9
I	.	.	.	.	.	0.9	0.8	0.7	0.7 [2]	0.6
J	.	.	.	.	.	-	0.1	-	0.1 [2]	0.1
K	.	.	.	.	.	0.7	0.6	0.9	0.7 [2]	0.6
L	.	.	.	.	.	0.1	0.2	0.1	0.2 [2]	0.2
M	.	.	.	.	.	-	0.1	0.1	0.2 [2]	0.1
N	.	.	.	.	.	-	-	-	0.1 [2]	0.1
O	.	.	.	.	.	0.5	0.2	0.4	0.4 [2]	0.1
P	.	.	.	.	.	0.1	0.1	0.4	0.3 [2]	0.2
Q	.	.	.	.	.			0.1	0.0 [2]	0.0
X	.	.	.	.	.	-	-	-	0.0 [2]	.

Women - Femmes - Mujeres
ISIC 3 - CITI 3 - CIIU 3

	1999	2000	2001	2002	2003	2004	2005	2006	2007	2008
Total	.	.	.	.	.	24.8	31.8	30.6	28.2 [2]	25.8
UB	.	.	.	.	.	11.0	12.2	10.8	12.0 [2]	8.9
A	.	.	.	.	.	0.1	0.8	0.8	0.4 [2]	0.5
B	.	.	.	.	.	-	-	-	0.0 [2]	0.0
C	.	.	.	.	.	-	-	-	0.0 [2]	0.0
D	.	.	.	.	.	7.1	10.1	10.5	8.0 [2]	7.6
E	.	.	.	.	.	-	-	-	0.0 [2]	0.0
F	.	.	.	.	.	0.1	0.1	-	0.1 [2]	0.1
G	.	.	.	.	.	2.3	2.9	3.2	2.2 [2]	3.1
H	.	.	.	.	.	1.0	1.1	1.1	0.8 [2]	1.6
I	.	.	.	.	.	0.3	0.2	0.3	0.5 [2]	0.2
J	.	.	.	.	.	0.1	0.2	0.2	0.2 [2]	0.2
K	.	.	.	.	.	0.2	0.3	0.6	0.6 [2]	0.5
L	.	.	.	.	.	-	0.2	0.1	0.0 [2]	0.1
M	.	.	.	.	.	0.7	0.5	0.7	0.7 [2]	0.5
N	.	.	.	.	.	0.1	0.3	0.3	0.3 [2]	0.2
O	.	.	.	.	.	0.6	0.6	0.4	0.5 [2]	0.5
P	.	.	.	.	.	1.1	2.2	1.5	1.9 [2]	1.8
Q	.	.	.	.	.	0.1	0.1	0.1	0.0 [2]	0.0
X	.	.	.	.	.	0.1	0.1	0.1	0.0 [2]	.

South Africa (BA) [3][4] — Total unemployment - Chômage total - Desempleo total

Total - Total - Total
ISIC 3 - CITI 3 - CIIU 3

	1999	2000	2001	2002	2003	2004	2005	2006	2007	2008
Total	.	4 162	4 655	4 936	4 434	4 135	4 487	4 391	3 945	4 075
UB	.	2 278	2 555	2 967	2 671	2 461	2 945	2 603	2 170	1 726
A-B	.	122	139	114	129	130	126	180	136	111
C	.	80	89	73	65	57	50	45	38	29
D	.	346	457	411	325	337	295	304	285	247
E	.	17	21	14	10	10	12	13	12	11
F	.	170	208	188	182	178	147	167	216	285
G-H	.	412	461	431	398	377	366	431	419	459
I	.	82	100	93	80	81	59	57	71	85
J-K	.	123	149	149	140	133	122	157	141	185
L-O	.	173	162	179	169	123	143	153	162	173
P	.	278	303	301	260	239	215	272	287	237
Q	.	25	10	13	4	8	6	9	8	1
X	.	56	-	-	-	-	-	-	-	527

Men - Hommes - Hombres
ISIC 3 - CITI 3 - CIIU 3

	1999	2000	2001	2002	2003	2004	2005	2006	2007	2008
Total	.	1 983	2 236	2 316	2 166	2 029	2 057	1 967	1 883	1 917
UB	.	1 004	1 141	1 305	1 218	1 124	1 295	1 133	996	744
A-B	.	63	68	48	54	64	55	68	59	49
C	.	77	84	71	63	56	46	41	35	26
D	.	202	275	249	191	200	175	171	191	149
E	.	16	17	11	7	6	6	9	9	7
F	.	157	193	175	169	168	131	145	190	249
G-H	.	179	188	175	184	172	152	168	164	180
I	.	73	77	74	71	65	40	44	56	63
J-K	.	63	87	81	91	76	62	94	68	96
L-O	.	84	72	78	77	55	61	48	56	58
P	.	26	27	40	39	37	31	40	57	46
Q	.	14	4	6	2	5	3	6	3	-
X	.	24	-	-	-	-	-	-	-	249

Explanatory notes: see p. 451.

[1] Persons aged 16 years and over. [2] Prior to 2007: persons aged 15 years and over. [3] Persons aged 15 to 64 years. [4] Prior to 2008: persons aged 15 years and over; September of each year.

Notes explicatives: voir p. 454.

[1] Personnes âgées de 16 ans et plus. [2] Avant 2006: personnes âgées de 15 ans et plus. [3] Personnes âgées de 15 à 64 ans. [4] Avant 2008: personnes agées de 15 ans et plus; septembre de chaque année.

Notas explicativas: véase p. 457.

[1] Personas de 16 años y más. [2] Antes de 2006: personas de 15 años y más. [3] Personas de 15 a 64 años. [4] Antes de 2008: personas de 15 años y más; Septiembre de cada año.

3D UNEMPLOYMENT — CHÔMAGE — DESEMPLEO

By economic activity — Par activité économique — Por actividad económica

	Thousands / Milliers / Millares									
	1999	2000	2001	2002	2003	2004	2005	2006	2007	2008

South Africa (BA) [1] [2] — Total unemployment - Chômage total - Desempleo total
Women - Femmes - Mujeres
ISIC 3 - CITI 3 - CIIU 3

	1999	2000	2001	2002	2003	2004	2005	2006	2007	2008
Total	.	2 179	2 420	2 619	2 268	2 103	2 428	2 424	2 059	2 158
UB	.	1 274	1 414	1 661	1 454	1 333	1 648	1 470	1 173	982
A-B	.	59	71	66	75	66	71	112	76	62
C	.	3	5	3	2	1	4	4	4	2
D	.	145	182	162	134	137	120	133	93	98
E	.	2	4	3	3	3	6	4	4	3
F	.	13	15	12	14	11	17	22	26	36
G-H	.	233	272	256	215	205	214	263	255	279
I	.	8	23	19	9	16	18	13	16	22
J-K	.	60	62	68	48	57	59	63	73	89
L-O	.	89	90	101	91	68	82	105	106	115
P	.	252	276	261	220	202	184	232	230	191
Q	.	11	.6	7	2	3	3	3	4	1
X	.	34	-	-	-	-	-	-	-	278

AMERICA-AMÉRIQUE-AMERICA

Argentina (BA) [3] [4] [5] — Total unemployment - Chômage total - Desempleo total
Total - Total - Total
ISIC 3 - CITI 3 - CIIU 3

	1999	2000	2001	2002	2003	2004	2005	2006	2007	2008
Total	1 359.6	1 460.9	1 709.8	1 955.8	1 633.0 [6]	1 361.6	1 141.5	1 049.2 [7]	.	.
UB	166.3	173.2	189.5	239.9	228.1 [6]	196.7	137.6	134.0 [7]	.	.
A	9.0	8.8	13.0	18.0	15.1 [6]	14.3	12.1	6.8 [7]	.	.
B	0.5	0.4	1.2	2.4	0.4 [6]	0.8	1.3	0.8 [7]	.	.
C	2.1	1.5	2.9	2.8	2.2 [6]	1.2	0.5	1.6 [7]	.	.
D	183.8	192.7	246.2	233.9	163.3 [6]	144.6	121.2	112.8 [7]	.	.
E	4.2	6.2	5.5	5.5	1.9 [6]	1.5	0.3	1.2 [7]	.	.
F	234.3	247.7	304.2	358.8	233.1 [6]	199.3	164.7	141.5 [7]	.	.
G	220.9	233.5	274.5	319.8	206.2 [6]	185.9	157.7	148.1 [7]	.	.
H	49.9	68.1	78.5	84.9	57.5 [6]	53.7	43.4	46.2 [7]	.	.
I	83.3	87.8	104.6	121.1	80.7 [6]	70.7	57.7	51.8 [7]	.	.
J	21.7	19.6	16.9	27.2	17.4 [6]	10.9	11.2	13.6 [7]	.	.
K	83.7	82.9	115.9	116.8	97.5 [6]	68.2	66.5	76.3 [7]	.	.
L	25.5	39.2	35.1	37.2	16.0 [6]	13.9	12.6	6.5 [7]	.	.
M	25.7	27.6	38.6	38.0	34.5 [6]	24.0	21.8	15.1 [7]	.	.
N	37.8	39.4	48.6	51.0	27.2 [6]	26.3	24.1	17.6 [7]	.	.
O	56.7	70.4	75.9	96.6	65.6 [6]	42.0	42.3	45.7 [7]	.	.
P	151.4	158.7	153.7	193.6	179.9 [6]	157.6	146.5	121.8 [7]	.	.
Q	-	-	-	-	0.3 [6]	0.5	0.6	- [7]	.	.
X [8]	3.0	3.4	5.2	8.3	206.0 [6]	149.1	119.3	107.9 [7]	.	.

Men - Hommes - Hombres
ISIC 3 - CITI 3 - CIIU 3

	1999	2000	2001	2002	2003	2004	2005	2006	2007	2008
Total	764.9	809.9	1 021.3	1 175.2	824.8 [6]	687.6	561.7	488.9 [7]	.	.
UB	69.5	66.7	79.1	103.4	86.3 [6]	76.0	59.7	56.6 [7]	.	.
A	7.9	7.1	10.9	17.3	12.5 [6]	12.0	10.8	4.7 [7]	.	.
B	0.5	0.4	1.1	2.4	0.4 [6]	0.8	1.3	0.8 [7]	.	.
C	1.9	1.2	2.2	2.7	2.2 [6]	1.1	0.5	1.0 [7]	.	.
D	114.0	121.6	167.2	163.6	91.3 [6]	73.1	62.8	56.9 [7]	.	.
E	3.3	5.5	5.1	4.5	1.7 [6]	1.0	0.3	1.2 [7]	.	.
F [8]	230.8	241.8	298.8	354.0	230.3 [6]	197.4	161.5	134.8 [7]	.	.
G	119.6	125.6	156.9	183.9	112.7 [6]	98.0	78.9	72.5 [7]	.	.
H	20.2	33.9	42.4	34.9	26.8 [6]	24.9	19.9	20.4 [7]	.	.
I	70.9	70.4	86.4	95.1	62.7 [6]	53.3	45.3	33.3 [7]	.	.
J	12.0	8.2	7.2	13.0	10.9 [6]	4.7	2.5	4.9 [7]	.	.
K	38.3	42.6	59.6	71.6	52.1 [6]	42.2	36.9	46.3 [7]	.	.
L	12.8	19.3	19.1	22.2	8.4 [6]	5.4	5.2	2.3 [7]	.	.
M	4.8	3.0	9.5	7.3	7.4 [6]	5.3	3.8	2.9 [7]	.	.
N	7.2	7.1	7.1	9.6	2.4 [6]	3.3	2.3	4.3 [7]	.	.
O	29.5	32.3	42.6	50.2	28.9 [6]	19.5	17.2	16.9 [7]	.	.
P	18.8	20.5	23.2	34.6	24.6 [6]	25.6	20.4	3.6 [7]	.	.
Q	-	-	-	-	- [6]	0.3	0.6	- [7]	.	.
X	2.9	2.6	3.0	5.0	63.4 [6]	43.5	31.7	25.7 [7]	.	.

Explanatory notes: see p. 451.

[1] Persons aged 15 to 64 years. [2] Prior to 2008: persons aged 15 years and over; September of each year. [3] Persons aged 10 years and over. [4] 31 Urban agglomerations. [5] Second semester. [6] Methodology revised; data not strictly comparable; Prior to 2003: May and October. [7] Prior to 2006: 28 urban agglomerations. [8] Prior to 2003: May and october.

Notes explicatives: voir p. 454.

[1] Personnes âgées de 15 à 64 ans. [2] Avant 2008: personnes âgées de 15 ans et plus; septembre de chaque année. [3] Personnes âgées de 10 ans et plus. [4] 31 agglomérations urbaines. [5] Second semestre. [6] Méthodologie révisée; les données ne sont pas strictement comparables; Avant 2003: mai et octobre. [7] Avant 2006: 28 agglomérations urbaines. [8] Avant 2003: Mai et octobre.

Notas explicativas: véase p. 457.

[1] Personas de 15 a 64 años. [2] Antes de 2008: personas de 15 años y más; Septiembre de cada año. [3] Personas de 10 años y más. [4] 31 aglomerados úrbanos. [5] Segundo semestre. [6] Metodología revisada; los datos no son estrictamente comparables; antes de 2003: mayo y octubre. [7] Antes de 2006: 28 aglomerados úrbanos [8] Antes de 2003: Mayo y octubre.

Thousands — Milliers — Millares

Argentina (BA) [1] [2] [3]   Total unemployment - Chômage total - Desempleo total

Women - Femmes - Mujeres
ISIC 3 - CITI 3 - CIIU 3

	1999	2000	2001	2002	2003	2004	2005	2006	2007	2008
Total	594.7	651.0	688.4	780.6	808.2 [4]	673.9	579.8	560.3 [5]	.	.
UB	96.8	106.5	110.4	136.5	141.8 [4]	120.6	77.9	77.4 [5]	.	.
A	1.1	1.7	2.1	0.8	2.6 [4]	2.3	1.4	2.1 [5]	.	.
B	-	-	0.1	-	- [4]	-	-	- [5]	.	.
C	0.2	0.3	0.7	0.1	- [4]	0.1	-	0.6 [5]	.	.
D	69.8	71.0	78.9	70.3	72.0 [4]	71.4	58.4	55.9 [5]	.	.
E	0.9	0.7	0.4	0.9	0.1 [4]	0.4	-	- [5]	.	.
F	3.4	5.9	5.4	4.8	2.8 [4]	1.9	3.1	6.7 [5]	.	.
G	101.3	107.8	117.6	136.0	93.5 [4]	87.8	78.9	75.6 [5]	.	.
H	29.7	34.3	36.1	50.0	30.7 [4]	28.7	23.5	25.8 [5]	.	.
I	12.4	17.4	18.2	25.9	18.1 [4]	17.3	12.4	18.5 [5]	.	.
J	9.6	11.4	9.7	14.2	6.5 [4]	6.2	8.7	8.6 [5]	.	.
K	45.4	40.3	56.2	45.2	45.5 [4]	26.0	29.6	30.1 [5]	.	.
L	12.7	19.9	16.0	15.0	7.7 [4]	8.4	7.3	4.3 [5]	.	.
M	20.9	24.5	29.1	30.7	27.2 [4]	18.7	18.0	12.1 [5]	.	.
N	30.5	32.3	41.4	41.3	24.8 [4]	22.9	21.8	13.3 [5]	.	.
O	27.2	38.1	33.3	46.4	36.7 [4]	22.5	25.1	28.8 [5]	.	.
P	132.5	138.2	130.5	159.0	155.3 [4]	132.0	126.1	118.2 [5]	.	.
Q	-	-	-	-	0.3 [4]	0.3	-	- [5]	.	.
X	0.1	0.8	2.1	3.3	142.6 [4]	105.5	87.7	82.3 [5]	.	.

Bahamas (BA) [6] [7]   Total unemployment - Chômage total - Desempleo total

Total - Total - Total
ISIC 2 - CITI 2 - CIIU 2

	1999	2000	2001	2002	2003	2004	2005	2006	2007	2008
Total	.	.	11.33	15.28	18.83	.	.	.	14.61	.
UB	.	.	2.13	2.38	3.44	.	.	.	2.40	.
1	.	.	0.07	0.65	0.70	.	.	.	0.37	.
2	.	.	0.04	-	0.03	.	.	.	0.03	.
3	.	.	0.44	0.51	0.63	.	.	.	0.62	.
4	.	.	-	0.06	0.09	.	.	.	0.15	.
5	.	.	2.33	3.12	3.62	.	.	.	2.27	.
6	.	.	3.13	4.35	5.97	.	.	.	5.31	.
7	.	.	0.49	0.75	0.33	.	.	.	0.39	.
8	.	.	0.90	0.96	1.03	.	.	.	1.09	.
9	.	.	1.49	2.14	2.61	.	.	.	1.90	.
0	.	.	0.33	0.36	0.39	.	.	.	0.09	.

Men - Hommes - Hombres
ISIC 2 - CITI 2 - CIIU 2

	1999	2000	2001	2002	2003	2004	2005	2006	2007	2008
Total	.	.	5.72	7.56	8.78	.	.	.	6.44	.
UB	.	.	0.90	0.85	0.98	.	.	.	0.66	.
1	.	.	0.07	0.51	0.50	.	.	.	0.37	.
2	.	.	0.04	-	0.03	.	.	.	0.03	.
3	.	.	0.38	0.25	0.33	.	.	.	0.46	.
4	.	.	-	0.06	0.03	.	.	.	0.12	.
5	.	.	2.15	2.94	3.51	.	.	.	2.15	.
6	.	.	0.83	1.51	1.93	.	.	.	1.46	.
7	.	.	0.31	0.40	0.23	.	.	.	0.24	.
8	.	.	0.24	0.49	0.47	.	.	.	0.31	.
9	.	.	0.59	0.43	0.59	.	.	.	0.59	.
0	.	.	0.21	0.12	0.19	.	.	.	0.06	.

Women - Femmes - Mujeres
ISIC 2 - CITI 2 - CIIU 2

	1999	2000	2001	2002	2003	2004	2005	2006	2007	2008
Total	.	.	5.61	7.72	10.05	.	.	.	8.17	.
UB	.	.	1.22	1.53	2.46	.	.	.	1.74	.
1	.	.	-	0.14	0.20	.	.	.	-	.
2	.	.	-	-	-	.	.	.	-	.
3	.	.	0.06	0.26	0.31	.	.	.	0.17	.
4	.	.	-	-	0.06	.	.	.	0.03	.
5	.	.	0.18	0.18	0.09	.	.	.	0.12	.
6	.	.	2.30	2.84	4.04	.	.	.	3.85	.
7	.	.	0.18	0.35	0.09	.	.	.	0.14	.
8	.	.	0.66	0.47	0.56	.	.	.	0.78	.
9	.	.	0.90	1.71	2.02	.	.	.	1.31	.
0	.	.	0.12	0.23	0.20	.	.	.	0.03	.

Explanatory notes: see p. 451.

[1] Persons aged 10 years and over. [2] 31 Urban agglomerations. [3] Second semester. [4] Methodology revised; data not strictly comparable; Prior to 2003: May and October. [5] Prior to 2006: 28 urban agglomerations. [6] Persons aged 15 years and over. [7] April of each year.

Notes explicatives: voir p. 454.

[1] Personnes âgées de 10 ans et plus. [2] 31 agglomérations urbaines. [3] Second semestre. [4] Méthodologie révisée; les données ne sont pas strictement comparables; Avant 2003: mai et octobre. [5] Avant 2006: 28 agglomérations urbaines. [6] Personnes âgées de 15 ans et plus. [7] Avril de chaque année.

Notas explicativas: véase p. 457.

[1] Personas de 10 años y más. [2] 31 aglomerados úrbanos. [3] Segundo semestre. [4] Metodología revisada; los datos no son estrictamente comparables; antes de 2003: mayo y octubre. [5] Antes de 2006: 28 aglomerados úrbanos [6] Personas de 15 años y más. [7] Abril de cada año.

UNEMPLOYMENT CHÔMAGE DESEMPLEO

By economic activity Par activité économique Por actividad económica

	Thousands				Milliers				Millares	
	1999	2000	2001	2002	2003	2004	2005	2006	2007	2008

Canada (BA) [1][2] — Total unemployment - Chômage total - Desempleo total

Total - Total - Total
ISIC 3 - CITI 3 - CIIU 3

	1999	2000	2001	2002	2003	2004	2005	2006	2007	2008
Total	1 181.6	1 082.8	1 163.6	1 268.9	1 286.2	1 235.3	1 172.8	1 108.4	1 079.4	1 119.3
A	38.9	34.2	34.5	34.4	35.6	32.4	32.1	29.0	25.8	26.7
B	6.1	6.2	8.0	8.5	7.2	8.0	7.5	6.8	6.6	5.8
C	13.1	9.0	9.7	11.5	11.4	8.9	8.7	10.0	10.3	13.1
D	125.9	111.2	145.5	151.7	144.0	136.7	132.2	130.6	131.8	133.7
E	2.5	2.6	2.7	3.2	3.2	2.7	2.4	2.0	2.0	2.7
F	90.1	79.4	84.0	92.7	92.0	89.1	82.3	83.4	83.9	87.9
G	127.0	116.5	123.3	141.4	140.7	139.8	134.3	121.8	125.8	132.5
H	77.8	71.6	71.0	82.8	96.3	83.1	81.0	76.9	79.9	80.7
I	47.0	44.0	50.6	58.2	52.8	51.1	42.7	34.4	36.0	35.8
J	12.6	14.3	12.8	15.7	15.7	14.6	14.6	12.5	12.9	12.3
K	91.9	89.5	104.6	116.7	125.2	114.8	107.1	99.7	100.4	108.4
L	27.0	21.6	25.8	23.1	23.5	25.1	23.7	23.8	20.4	19.6
M	32.8	31.9	34.3	37.7	41.5	44.4	39.3	40.2	44.1	42.4
N	34.1	31.9	33.9	35.7	38.2	43.3	36.3	34.2	31.6	33.4
O	42.6	41.1	39.3	51.5	51.4	43.2	43.5	45.6	42.0	48.5
P	10.5	6.2	5.2	7.6	7.0	7.9	4.1	5.1	4.1	3.0
Q	-	-	-	-	-	-	-	-	-	-
X	401.0	371.1	378.2	396.7	400.4	390.4	380.6	352.1	321.5	332.6

Men - Hommes - Hombres
ISIC 3 - CITI 3 - CIIU 3

	1999	2000	2001	2002	2003	2004	2005	2006	2007	2008
Total	660.4	595.3	655.1	721.7	719.6	685.4	649.0	608.3	603.9	632.6
A	29.9	25.0	26.2	25.5	24.3	22.8	21.9	20.3	18.2	17.8
B	5.2	5.0	6.5	7.3	5.8	6.2	6.2	5.3	5.1	4.8
C	11.9	7.9	8.9	10.4	10.0	7.9	7.6	8.3	8.8	11.2
D	81.1	71.3	95.2	102.5	95.5	91.7	86.5	86.8	86.2	92.3
E	1.7	2.1	2.4	2.2	2.4	2.2	1.5	-	1.6	1.6
F	83.6	73.7	78.9	85.8	85.0	84.0	76.6	77.7	77.8	77.7
G	73.9	62.6	67.5	77.6	76.7	76.7	74.4	68.0	68.2	75.9
H	33.7	29.3	30.9	38.2	42.7	34.6	37.1	32.9	36.0	36.7
I	32.0	29.8	34.6	43.1	36.0	34.0	30.9	24.7	26.4	27.0
J	4.0	4.6	5.6	6.2	5.9	4.7	6.3	3.9	4.5	5.2
K	52.7	50.0	59.0	66.3	70.7	67.8	62.1	60.2	57.3	64.1
L	14.5	11.2	12.6	10.6	10.5	10.8	12.6	12.4	10.6	10.2
M	11.3	10.2	11.6	13.2	14.7	14.7	12.6	10.9	13.4	11.1
N	5.5	5.4	5.9	5.4	7.3	9.2	6.5	5.1	5.0	6.5
O	20.9	21.1	21.3	27.4	26.6	21.8	20.5	22.2	20.3	23.4
P	0.7	0.8	0.6	0.8	0.6	0.7	0.5	0.1	0.2	0.3
Q	-	-	-	-	-	-	-	-	-	-
X	197.5	185.1	187.3	199.0	204.7	195.6	185.2	168.1	164.3	166.7

Women - Femmes - Mujeres
ISIC 3 - CITI 3 - CIIU 3

	1999	2000	2001	2002	2003	2004	2005	2006	2007	2008
Total	521.2	487.5	508.5	547.2	566.6	549.9	523.8	500.1	475.5	486.6
A	9.1	9.2	8.4	8.9	11.3	9.5	10.1	8.7	7.6	8.9
B	0.9	1.2	1.5	1.2	1.4	1.7	1.3	1.5	1.5	1.0
C	1.2	1.1	0.8	1.1	1.4	1.0	1.1	1.8	1.5	2.0
D	44.9	40.0	50.3	49.2	48.5	45.0	45.7	43.8	45.6	41.4
E	0.8	0.5	0.3	1.0	0.8	0.5	0.9	-	0.4	1.1
F	6.5	5.6	5.2	6.8	6.9	5.1	5.7	5.7	6.2	10.2
G	53.1	53.9	55.8	63.7	64.1	63.0	60.0	53.8	57.7	56.6
H	44.1	42.3	40.1	44.5	53.5	48.5	43.8	44.0	43.9	44.1
I	15.1	14.2	16.0	15.1	16.9	17.1	11.8	9.7	9.6	8.8
J	8.7	9.7	7.2	9.5	9.8	10.0	8.3	8.6	8.5	7.1
K	39.3	39.6	45.6	50.3	54.5	46.9	45.1	39.5	43.1	44.3
L	12.5	10.4	13.1	12.5	12.9	14.3	11.1	11.5	9.9	9.4
M	21.5	21.7	22.7	24.4	26.9	29.7	26.7	29.3	30.7	31.4
N	28.6	26.5	28.0	30.3	30.9	34.0	29.9	29.0	26.6	26.9
O	21.6	20.1	18.0	24.0	24.9	21.4	23.0	23.4	21.7	25.1
P	9.8	5.4	4.6	6.8	6.4	7.2	3.6	5.0	3.9	2.7
Q	-	-	-	-	-	-	-	-	-	-
X	203.5	186.0	190.9	197.7	195.7	194.7	195.5	184.0	157.1	165.9

Colombia (BA) [3][4][5] — Total unemployment - Chômage total - Desempleo total

Total - Total - Total
ISIC 3 - CITI 3 - CIIU 3

	1999	2000	2001	2002	2003	2004	2005	2006	2007	2008
Total	·	·	2 224.4	2 320.4	2 255.5	1 952.8	1 831.8	1 902.3	1 677.6	1 786.0
UB			484.4	528.3	541.7	509.2	428.8	522.5	411.7	459.7
A			149.7	176.0	183.6	164.5	161.5	175.0	160.7	155.2
C			12.3	12.5	20.1	11.3	9.9	6.9	7.1	13.9
D			316.6	335.2	331.5	270.6	266.3	193.9	216.5	212.6
E			14.6	9.7	16.5	7.0	12.6	8.3	10.8	11.5
F			242.2	283.5	222.2	171.3	172.0	163.3	156.3	163.8
G			625.0	568.7	528.2	478.6	486.4	403.7	459.7	489.4
I			134.2	151.3	149.6	156.6	123.3	104.8	121.5	126.4
J			34.5	42.1	31.8	33.8	30.0	18.8	22.8	26.1
K			107.5	98.9	127.2	101.0	91.1	97.0	104.5	126.7
N			584.7	640.8	640.4	557.2	477.9	448.6	410.7	452.5
X			3.1	1.7	4.4	0.9	0.7	282.0	6.9	7.9

Explanatory notes: see p. 451.

[1] Persons aged 15 years and over. [2] Excl. residents of the Territories and indigenous persons living on reserves. [3] From 2001, figures revised on the basis of the 2005 census results. [4] Persons aged 10 years and over. [5] Third quarter.

Notes explicatives: voir p. 454.

[1] Personnes âgées de 15 ans et plus. [2] Non compris les habitants des "Territoires" et les populations indigènes vivant dans les réserves. [3] A partir de 2001, données révisées sur la base des résultats du recensement de 2005. [4] Personnes âgées de 10 ans et plus. [5] Troisième trimestre.

Notas explicativas: véase p. 457.

[1] Personas de 15 años y más. [2] Excl. a los habitantes de los "Territorios" y a las poblaciones indígenas que viven en reservas. [3] A partir de 2001, datos revisados de acuerdocon los resultados del censo de 2005. [4] Personas de 10 años y más. [5] Tercer trimestre.

By economic activity — Par activité économique — Por actividad económica

	Thousands			Milliers				Millares		
	1999	2000	2001	2002	2003	2004	2005	2006	2007	2008

Colombia (BA) [1][2][3] Total unemployment - Chômage total - Desempleo total

Men - Hommes - Hombres
ISIC 3 - CITI 3 - CIIU 3

	1999	2000	2001	2002	2003	2004	2005	2006	2007	2008
Total	.	.	1 068.2	1 122.3	1 042.2	931.5	843.7	885.6	824.9	846.2
UB	.	.	189.4	219.0	222.6	200.6	175.7	208.3	171.4	186.8
A	.	.	109.6	130.2	144.6	126.1	122.0	136.3	131.9	120.6
C	.	.	8.7	11.6	14.0	10.4	8.3	6.5	6.6	9.7
D	.	.	149.0	158.4	127.7	124.9	118.5	84.6	96.6	103.6
E	.	.	13.1	5.9	14.7	5.7	7.3	6.1	7.2	10.4
F	.	.	231.3	267.7	201.5	162.9	163.7	156.5	148.6	155.3
G	.	.	255.5	234.6	196.6	185.2	179.9	144.7	187.9	191.9
I	.	.	113.6	124.8	115.0	122.7	85.9	78.7	91.8	88.7
J	.	.	11.4	20.9	13.7	18.8	8.6	8.7	8.5	10.9
K	.	.	57.7	46.4	62.5	52.2	43.9	46.1	47.2	62.6
N	.	.	115.7	121.8	151.8	121.7	105.7	96.5	94.8	88.1
X	.	.	2.7	-	-	0.8	-	120.9	3.9	4.6

Women - Femmes - Mujeres
ISIC 3 - CITI 3 - CIIU 3

	1999	2000	2001	2002	2003	2004	2005	2006	2007	2008
Total	.	.	1 156.2	1 198.1	1 213.3	1 021.3	988.2	1 016.7	852.6	939.8
UB	.	.	295.0	309.2	319.2	308.5	253.1	314.2	240.2	272.9
A	.	.	40.1	45.7	39.1	38.4	39.5	38.6	28.8	34.6
C	.	.	3.6	0.8	6.1	0.9	1.6	0.5	0.6	4.2
D	.	.	167.6	176.8	203.7	145.7	147.8	109.3	119.9	109.0
E	.	.	1.5	3.8	1.8	1.3	5.3	2.2	3.6	1.1
F	.	.	10.9	15.9	20.6	8.4	8.4	6.8	7.7	8.5
G	.	.	369.5	334.1	331.6	293.4	306.5	259.0	271.8	297.5
I	.	.	20.6	26.5	34.6	33.9	37.4	26.2	29.7	37.7
J	.	.	23.1	21.2	18.1	15.0	21.4	10.2	14.3	15.1
K	.	.	49.8	52.5	64.8	48.8	47.2	50.8	57.3	64.2
N	.	.	469.0	519.0	488.5	435.5	372.3	352.2	315.9	364.4
X	.	.	0.5	1.7	4.4	0.1	0.7	161.0	2.9	3.3

Costa Rica (BA) [4][5] Total unemployment - Chômage total - Desempleo total

Total - Total - Total
ISIC 3 - CITI 3 - CIIU 3

	1999	2000	2001	2002	2003	2004	2005	2006	2007	2008
Total	.	71.9	100.4	.	117.2	114.9	126.2	116.0	92.8	101.9
UB	.	11.7	15.9	.	22.1	21.8	24.6	27.7	20.6	16.3
A	.	10.9	13.0	.	11.9	8.6	10.8	10.1	9.6	10.8
B	.	0.6	0.4	.	0.5	0.5	1.1	0.2	0.2	0.3
C	.	0.3	0.4	.	0.2	0.3	0.2	0.1	-	0.1
D	.	8.6	17.9	.	14.7	16.1	16.9	13.7	10.4	11.9
E	.	0.3	0.8	.	0.5	0.8	0.6	0.8	0.5	0.2
F	.	6.7	9.5	.	12.2	11.4	9.6	10.9	5.2	11.6
G	.	10.1	15.0	.	18.6	19.0	19.3	15.8	14.6	15.1
H	.	4.8	6.2	.	8.0	6.8	10.1	7.4	6.6	6.7
I	.	1.8	2.5	.	2.7	3.7	4.1	2.4	4.2	5.8
J	.	0.4	1.3	.	2.2	0.8	1.2	1.7	0.5	1.3
K	.	0.3	4.5	.	6.4	5.4	5.9	4.6	4.4	6.5
L	.	-	1.5	.	3.0	1.6	1.9	1.7	1.2	0.4
M	.	0.4	2.4	.	1.8	2.7	2.6	2.9	3.0	2.5
N	.	1.4	0.9	.	1.5	2.3	2.4	2.6	0.9	1.5
O	.	6.6	2.0	.	2.9	2.9	2.7	1.6	3.8	2.5
P	.	6.1	5.5	.	7.2	9.0	11.5	11.7	6.4	7.7
Q	.	-	0.1	.	0.2	-	-	-	0.2	.
X	.	1.0	0.4	.	0.6	1.1	0.7	0.2	0.4	0.7

Men - Hommes - Hombres
ISIC 3 - CITI 3 - CIIU 3

	1999	2000	2001	2002	2003	2004	2005	2006	2007	2008
Total	.	41.2	55.8	.	66.0	62.5	60.2	53.8	41.3	53.5
UB	.	5.9	7.5	.	10.3	10.9	8.5	10.8	9.1	7.7
A	.	9.0	10.4	.	9.1	6.6	8.1	6.9	6.2	8.3
B	.	0.6	0.3	.	0.5	0.4	1.0	0.2	0.2	0.3
C	.	0.3	0.4	.	0.2	0.3	0.2	0.1	-	0.1
D	.	4.5	9.4	.	8.6	10.0	8.9	6.9	4.4	5.4
E	.	0.3	0.5	.	0.4	0.6	0.6	0.4	0.2	0.2
F	.	6.7	9.1	.	12.1	11.0	9.6	10.8	5.2	11.4
G	.	4.6	7.3	.	9.8	9.5	9.1	7.2	6.1	8.0
H	.	1.6	1.9	.	2.6	2.3	2.1	1.7	1.4	2.3
I	.	1.4	2.4	.	2.6	2.7	2.8	1.5	3.1	4.5
J	.	-	0.8	.	0.7	0.3	0.1	1.1	0.2	0.6
K	.	0.2	3.2	.	3.4	2.9	3.4	1.8	2.7	2.5
L	.	.	0.8	.	1.4	1.5	0.9	1.2	0.8	0.1
M	.	0.4	0.4	.	0.7	0.9	1.1	0.5	0.5	0.3
N	.	0.9	0.1	.	0.5	0.4	1.2	0.9	-	0.4
O	.	3.9	0.9	.	1.4	0.9	1.2	1.1	1.0	0.7
P	.	0.1	0.2	.	0.3	0.5	0.7	0.6	0.2	0.3
Q	.	-	0.1	.	0.2	-	-	-	-	.
X	.	0.9	0.1	.	0.6	0.8	0.5	0.2	0.3	0.5

Explanatory notes: see p. 451.

[1] From 2001, figures revised on the basis of the 2005 census results. [2] Persons aged 10 years and over. [3] Third quarter. [4] Persons aged 12 years and over. [5] July of each year.

Notes explicatives: voir p. 454.

[1] A partir de 2001, données révisées sur la base des résultats du recensement de 2005. [2] Personnes âgées de 10 ans et plus. [3] Troisième trimestre. [4] Personnes âgées de 12 ans et plus. [5] Juillet de chaque année.

Notas explicativas: véase p. 457.

[1] A partir de 2001, datos revisados de acuerdo con los resultados del censo de 2005. [2] Personas de 10 años y más. [3] Tercer trimestre. [4] Personas de 12 años y más. [5] Julio de cada año.

	Thousands				Milliers				Millares	
	1999	2000	2001	2002	2003	2004	2005	2006	2007	2008

Costa Rica (BA) [1][2]   Total unemployment - Chômage total - Desempleo total

Women - Femmes - Mujeres
ISIC 3 - CITI 3 - CIIU 3

	1999	2000	2001	2002	2003	2004	2005	2006	2007	2008
Total	.	30.8	44.6	.	51.2	52.4	66.0	62.3	51.5	48.4
UB	.	5.9	8.4	.	11.8	10.9	16.1	16.9	11.5	8.7
A	.	1.9	2.6	.	2.7	2.1	2.6	3.2	3.4	2.5
B	.	-	0.1	.	-	0.1	0.1	-	-	-
C	.	-	-	.	-	-	-	-	-	-
D	.	4.1	8.4	.	6.0	6.1	8.0	6.8	6.1	6.6
E	.	-	0.3	.	0.1	0.2	-	0.4	0.3	-
F	.	-	0.3	.	0.2	0.4	0.0	0.1	-	0.2
G	.	5.5	7.8	.	8.8	9.5	10.1	8.6	8.5	7.1
H	.	3.2	4.3	.	5.4	4.5	8.0	5.7	5.1	4.4
I	.	0.3	0.1	.	0.1	1.0	1.2	0.9	1.1	1.4
J	.	0.4	0.5	.	1.5	0.5	1.1	0.6	0.4	0.7
K	.	0.1	1.4	.	3.0	2.4	2.5	2.8	1.7	4.0
L	.	-	0.8	.	1.2	0.1	1.0	0.5	0.5	0.3
M	.	-	2.0	.	1.1	1.9	1.5	2.4	2.5	2.2
N	.	0.5	0.9	.	1.0	1.9	1.3	1.8	0.9	1.1
O	.	2.7	1.1	.	1.5	1.9	1.5	0.6	2.9	1.8
P	.	6.1	5.3	.	6.9	8.6	10.8	11.0	6.2	7.4
Q	.	-	0.1	.	-	-	-	-	0.2	-
X	.	0.1	0.3	.	-	0.3	0.2	0.1	0.2	0.2

Chile (BA) [3][4]   Total unemployment - Chômage total - Desempleo total

Total - Total - Total
ISIC 2 - CITI 2 - CIIU 2

	1999	2000	2001	2002	2003	2004	2005	2006	2007	2008
Total	529.1	489.4	469.4	468.7	453.1	494.7	440.4 ǀ	409.9 s	510.7	544.7
UB	79.1	75.9	72.5	75.8	71.3	74.3	89.4 ǀ	67.6 s	91.5	72.3
1	28.4	29.2	28.1	31.3	24.2	26.6	23.0 ǀ	28.1 s	27.1	29.1
2	4.9	4.2	6.2	3.5	2.7	3.4	3.3 ǀ	3.2 s	5.9	7.3
3	77.5	71.8	59.3	62.2	61.3	66.8	50.6 ǀ	55.2 s	60.3	58.7
4	2.3	3.7	4.7	3.5	1.6	2.5	2.2 ǀ	1.4 s	3.6	3.9
5	75.2	75.7	72.3	68.9	65.7	59.3	53.3 ǀ	58.0 s	57.3	79.9
6	98.3	83.1	80.6	86.9	78.6	87.3	75.1 ǀ	69.4 s	92.0	108.4
7	32.8	28.5	28.8	30.0	35.5	36.7	34.4 ǀ	31.0 s	38.4	40.2
8	43.3	44.0	42.5	36.8	41.0	46.3	34.8 ǀ	36.7 s	52.7	55.2
9	87.4	73.3	74.5	69.8	71.2	91.5	74.3 ǀ	59.4 s	81.3	89.8

Men - Hommes - Hombres
ISIC 2 - CITI 2 - CIIU 2

	1999	2000	2001	2002	2003	2004	2005	2006	2007	2008
Total	322.9	312.5	302.6	298.5	279.2	280.8	248.2 ǀ	239.3 s	280.1	306.7
UB	40.4	37.2	38.8	41.1	35.7	39.4	44.9 ǀ	31.6 s	39.9	31.9
1	21.8	23.0	24.2	26.2	18.5	18.7	16.4 ǀ	21.5 s	18.4	21.8
2	4.7	3.8	5.3	3.1	2.2	3.2	3.1 ǀ	2.8 s	5.1	6.6
3	53.7	50.2	45.1	46.5	42.3	42.9	31.4 ǀ	37.2 s	38.2	34.9
4	2.2	3.7	3.9	2.6	1.0	2.0	1.7 ǀ	1.2 s	3.0	3.0
5	72.6	73.5	70.6	64.6	64.5	55.5	51.4 ǀ	54.4 s	54.5	76.2
6	48.1	42.1	38.6	40.5	38.3	39.0	32.0 ǀ	26.6 s	45.8	50.8
7	27.5	21.1	22.3	22.9	26.2	26.8	22.5 ǀ	23.7 s	27.2	27.1
8	22.5	25.7	23.4	20.6	22.6	23.0	17.4 ǀ	17.9 s	22.2	24.4
9	29.5	32.3	30.4	30.5	28.0	30.3	27.4 ǀ	22.4 s	25.8	30.0

Women - Femmes - Mujeres
ISIC 2 - CITI 2 - CIIU 2

	1999	2000	2001	2002	2003	2004	2005	2006	2007	2008
Total	206.2	176.9	166.9	170.2	173.9	213.9	192.2 ǀ	170.6 s	230.6	238.0
UB	38.6	38.8	33.6	34.7	35.6	34.9	44.5 ǀ	36.0 s	51.9	40.3
1	6.6	6.2	3.9	5.2	5.8	7.9	6.7 ǀ	6.7 s	8.6	7.2
2	0.2	0.5	1.0	0.4	0.5	0.2	0.2 ǀ	0.3 s	0.8	0.7
3	23.9	21.5	14.2	15.7	19.0	23.8	19.2 ǀ	18.0 s	22.1	23.8
4	0.1	-	0.8	0.9	0.7	0.5	0.5 ǀ	0.1 s	0.6	0.9
5	2.6	2.2	1.7	4.3	1.2	3.9	1.9 ǀ	3.6 s	2.8	3.7
6	50.2	41.0	41.9	46.4	40.3	48.2	43.1 ǀ	42.8 s	46.8	57.6
7	5.2	7.4	6.5	7.2	9.2	9.9	11.9 ǀ	7.3 s	11.2	13.1
8	20.8	18.3	19.1	16.2	18.4	23.3	17.4 ǀ	18.8 s	30.5	30.8
9	58.0	41.1	44.1	39.3	43.2	61.3	46.9 ǀ	37.0 s	55.4	59.8

Explanatory notes: see p. 451.

[1] Persons aged 12 years and over. [2] July of each year.
[3] Persons aged 15 years and over. [4] Fourth quarter of each year.
[5] Methodology revised; data not strictly comparable.

Notes explicatives: voir p. 454.

[1] Personnes âgées de 12 ans et plus. [2] Juillet de chaque année.
[3] Personnes âgées de 15 ans et plus. [4] Quatrième trimestre de chaque année. [5] Méthodologie révisée; les données ne sont pas strictement comparables.

Notas explicativas: véase p. 457.

[1] Personas de 12 años y más. [2] Julio de cada año. [3] Personas de 15 años y más. [4] Cuarto trimestre de cada año. [5] Metodología revisada; los datos no son estrictamente comparables.

By economic activity   Par activité économique   Por actividad económica

	Thousands			Milliers				Millares		
	1999	2000	2001	2002	2003	2004	2005	2006	2007	2008

República Dominicana (BA) [1]   Total unemployment - Chômage total - Desempleo total

Total - Total - Total
ISIC 3 - CITI 3 - CIIU 3

	1999	2000	2001	2002	2003	2004	2005	2006	2007	2008
Total	477.9	491.4	556.3	596.3	619.7	723.7	715.8	661.4	654.0	.
UB	253.2	175.8	199.9	233.5	244.0	-	-	300.3	317.1	.
A-B	10.2	16.3	17.9	17.1	13.8	.	.	.	.	.
A	.	.	.	.	.	11.0	11.2	10.7	10.5	.
B	.	.	.	.	.	-	0.4	0.3	0.3	.
C	1.1	1.3	1.7	0.9	0.8	1.8	1.1	0.5	0.0	.
D	60.5	80.6	84.8	84.0	93.1	83.7	91.8	91.3	70.5	.
E	1.6	3.9	4.7	4.4	2.3	3.4	4.6	4.3	4.2	.
F	19.7	21.2	21.7	23.9	23.2	22.5	26.0	22.2	16.3	.
G	41.2	54.4	68.2	64.1	69.1	67.4	68.2	68.1	60.4	.
H	14.8	23.1	25.4	30.5	32.6	36.2	38.3	36.2	34.0	.
I	8.2	11.4	16.3	13.9	13.9	16.8	12.8	14.9	13.1	.
J	2.8	5.0	5.9	9.1	8.2	9.3	10.2	7.4	6.8	.
K	.	.	.	.	.	11.8	12.8	8.1	9.8	.
K,M-N	10.2	14.2	16.4	15.5	13.4	.	.	.	.	.
L	54.3	84.4	93.3	99.3	105.3	19.6	20.5	10.4	14.0	.
M	.	.	.	.	.	16.8	16.4	8.8	9.4	.
N	.	.	.	.	.	14.8	11.7	8.1	11.3	.
O	.	.	.	.	.	29.5	32.2	26.0	28.5	.
P	.	.	.	.	.	46.5	56.8	43.2	47.7	.
Q	.	.	.	.	.	-	0.2	0.6	-	.
X	-	-	-	-	-	332.7	300.7	-	-	.

Men - Hommes - Hombres
ISIC 3 - CITI 3 - CIIU 3

	1999	2000	2001	2002	2003	2004	2005	2006	2007	2008
Total	175.8	174.7	208.0	215.5	243.0	252.5	269.6	233.5	240.7	.
UB	61.2	50.2	55.5	66.9	84.1	-	-	83.7	108.9	.
A-B	8.8	11.4	14.2	15.8	11.1	.	.	.	.	.
A	.	.	.	.	.	8.6	9.9	9.3	8.0	.
B	.	.	.	.	.	-	0.4	0.3	0.3	.
C	1.1	0.8	1.4	0.7	0.8	1.8	1.1	0.5	0.0	.
D	29.3	32.2	37.9	34.2	39.6	32.3	38.8	38.5	31.3	.
E	2.0	2.0	3.1	3.4	1.9	2.8	2.8	2.6	2.6	.
F	19.1	20.1	21.1	22.9	21.6	21.3	24.0	20.4	15.9	.
G	22.6	23.5	31.6	27.9	34.3	31.6	32.5	38.9	27.4	.
H	6.6	6.8	6.6	9.8	11.6	11.8	10.0	10.8	13.0	.
I	7.7	6.2	11.5	9.6	9.8	11.3	8.9	8.3	8.6	.
J	0.2	1.6	2.2	3.6	4.3	4.8	4.1	1.9	2.4	.
K	.	.	.	.	.	4.3	5.0	2.5	3.9	.
K,M-N	5.7	9.2	7.8	7.7	6.3	.	.	.	.	.
L	11.9	10.7	15.0	13.1	17.5	9.9	11.5	6.3	5.8	.
M	.	.	.	.	.	3.8	2.8	1.5	1.9	.
N	.	.	.	.	.	2.5	1.4	1.5	2.2	.
O	.	.	.	.	.	6.8	7.6	5.2	6.7	.
P	.	.	.	.	.	1.2	1.2	0.6	1.5	.
Q	.	.	.	.	.	-	0.2	0.6	-	.
X	-	-	-	-	-	97.8	107.4	-	-	.

Women - Femmes - Mujeres
ISIC 3 - CITI 3 - CIIU 3

	1999	2000	2001	2002	2003	2004	2005	2006	2007	2008
Total	302.1	316.8	348.2	380.8	376.8	471.2	446.3	428.0	413.3	.
UB	192.0	125.6	144.4	166.6	159.9	-	-	216.6	208.2	.
A-B	1.3	4.9	3.7	1.4	2.7	.	.	.	.	.
A	.	.	.	.	.	2.4	1.3	1.4	2.4	.
B	.	.	.	.	.	.	.	.	.	.
C	.	0.5	0.2	0.2	.	-	-	-	-	.
D	31.3	48.3	46.9	49.8	53.5	51.4	53.0	52.9	39.2	.
E	0.2	1.9	1.6	1.1	0.4	0.5	1.8	1.7	1.6	.
F	0.6	1.0	0.6	1.0	1.6	1.3	2.0	1.8	0.4	.
G	18.6	30.9	36.7	36.3	34.8	35.8	35.7	29.2	33.0	.
H	8.2	16.3	18.8	20.8	21.0	24.4	28.3	25.5	21.0	.
I	0.5	5.2	4.7	4.3	4.1	5.5	3.9	6.6	4.5	.
J	2.7	3.4	3.6	5.5	3.8	4.5	6.1	5.5	4.4	.
K	.	.	.	.	.	7.5	7.7	5.7	5.9	.
K,M-N	4.4	5.0	8.5	7.8	7.1	.	.	.	.	.
L	42.3	73.8	78.4	86.2	87.9	9.7	9.0	4.0	8.1	.
M	.	.	.	.	.	13.1	13.6	7.2	7.6	.
N	.	.	.	.	.	12.3	10.3	6.6	9.1	.
O	.	.	.	.	.	22.7	24.6	20.7	21.8	.
P	.	.	.	.	.	45.3	55.6	42.6	46.2	.
Q	.	.	.	.	.	.	.	.	.	.
X	-	-	-	-	-	234.9	193.4	-	-	.

Explanatory notes: see p. 451.   Notes explicatives: voir p. 454.   Notas explicativas: véase p. 457.

[1] Persons aged 10 years and over.   [1] Personnes âgées de 10 ans et plus.   [1] Personas de 10 años y más.

	Thousands					Milliers				Millares
	1999	2000	2001	2002	2003	2004	2005	2006	2007	2008

Ecuador (BA) [1][2][3]   Total unemployment - Chômage total - Desempleo total

Total - Total - Total
ISIC 3 - CITI 3 - CIIU 3

Total	543.5	333.1	450.9 [4]	352.9	461.1	362.1	333.6	341.8	.	.
UB	177.2	133.4	173.9 [4]	138.3	192.4	123.0	137.7	125.8	.	.
A	13.5	6.9	13.5 [4]	13.0	21.0	12.6	10.6	8.3	.	.
B	7.3	3.7	6.6 [4]	4.1	5.4	4.2	4.1	5.5	.	.
C	1.7	1.6	1.3 [4]	0.7	1.9	0.9	1.8	1.8	.	.
D	69.8	31.6	35.2 [4]	35.9	48.8	33.1	31.7	32.6	.	.
E	2.5	1.9	1.1 [4]	1.5	2.2	0.9	0.9	1.9	.	.
F	46.0	18.1	15.9 [4]	21.7	30.9	30.0	20.1	21.3	.	.
G	82.7	50.5	74.5 [4]	49.1	53.3	57.9	51.2	56.2	.	.
H	15.1	9.3	14.6 [4]	10.6	12.2	12.2	15.5	14.6	.	.
I	20.7	12.6	11.7 [4]	8.7	15.1	15.0	8.5	15.7	.	.
J	7.9	3.5	6.3 [4]	3.7	5.2	3.5	2.9	1.6	.	.
K	20.7	10.8	4.6 [4]	9.8	16.0	12.0	8.3	6.5	.	.
L	12.8	10.1	11.6 [4]	5.9	10.4	7.8	5.3	8.1	.	.
M	10.7	9.5	10.4 [4]	12.2	6.9	9.6	4.3	10.6	.	.
N	11.0	4.9	8.8 [4]	4.5	7.7	5.5	4.8	7.3	.	.
O	8.6	5.5	13.4 [4]	4.8	10.5	14.3	8.5	7.1	.	.
P	35.3	19.4	36.0 [4]	28.3	21.3	19.5	17.4	16.8	.	.
Q	-	-	0.3 [4]	-	-	0.1	0.1	-	.	.
X	-	-	11.5 [4]	-	-	-	-	-	.	.

Men - Hommes - Hombres
ISIC 3 - CITI 3 - CIIU 3

Total	239.5	138.3	169.0 [4]	136.2	.	160.7	143.3	143.4	.	.
UB	52.0	47.1	54.3 [4]	38.8	.	47.2	48.2	38.5	.	.
A	9.6	5.0	10.3 [4]	9.6	.	10.2	6.7	6.8	.	.
B	5.4	1.8	4.5 [4]	2.7	.	3.6	2.8	3.4	.	.
C	1.5	1.2	1.3 [4]	0.7	.	0.6	1.5	1.7	.	.
D	38.7	15.4	18.3 [4]	18.1	.	17.6	19.0	17.7	.	.
E	1.9	1.6	0.5 [4]	1.1	.	0.8	0.9	1.7	.	.
F	43.2	17.2	14.1 [4]	20.6	.	28.4	19.0	20.7	.	.
G	33.2	18.4	26.0 [4]	17.0	.	18.2	20.9	23.3	.	.
H	4.7	1.4	4.5 [4]	3.2	.	4.0	2.8	3.6	.	.
I	15.5	10.1	9.0 [4]	6.3	.	11.0	6.4	12.0	.	.
J	2.9	1.2	2.2 [4]	1.6	.	2.1	1.5	0.2	.	.
K	12.9	5.7	1.1 [4]	5.3	.	6.3	4.7	4.9	.	.
L	7.8	6.2	7.0 [4]	4.2	.	4.4	3.0	3.3	.	.
M	2.4	1.9	1.9 [4]	2.6	.	0.9	0.9	1.9	.	.
N	2.3	0.5	2.0 [4]	0.3	.	0.4	0.7	0.6	.	.
O	4.0	2.8	4.3 [4]	3.0	.	4.0	2.6	2.1	.	.
P	1.7	0.9	0.6 [4]	1.0	.	1.0	1.8	0.9	.	.
Q	-	-	0.1 [4]	-	.	-	0.1	-	.	.
X	-	-	7.0 [4]	-	.	-	-	-	.	.

Women - Femmes - Mujeres
ISIC 3 - CITI 3 - CIIU 3

Total	304.0	194.8	282.0 [4]	216.7	.	201.4	190.3	198.4	.	.
UB	125.4	86.3	119.6 [4]	99.5	.	75.8	89.5	87.3	.	.
A	4.0	1.8	3.1 [4]	3.4	.	2.4	4.0	1.5	.	.
B	1.9	1.9	2.1 [4]	1.4	.	0.6	1.3	2.0	.	.
C	0.2	0.4	0.0 [4]	-	.	0.3	0.3	0.1	.	.
D	31.0	16.2	16.9 [4]	17.8	.	15.5	12.7	14.9	.	.
E	0.5	0.3	0.6 [4]	0.4	.	0.0	0.0	0.2	.	.
F	2.8	0.9	1.8 [4]	1.1	.	1.6	1.1	0.6	.	.
G	49.5	32.0	48.5 [4]	32.1	.	39.7	30.3	33.0	.	.
H	10.5	7.9	10.1 [4]	7.3	.	8.2	12.7	10.9	.	.
I	5.1	2.5	2.7 [4]	2.5	.	4.0	2.2	3.7	.	.
J	5.1	2.3	4.1 [4]	2.2	.	1.4	1.3	1.5	.	.
K	7.7	5.1	3.5 [4]	4.5	.	5.8	3.5	1.6	.	.
L	5.0	3.8	4.5 [4]	1.7	.	3.4	2.3	4.8	.	.
M	8.3	7.7	8.4 [4]	9.6	.	8.7	3.4	8.7	.	.
N	8.8	4.4	6.8 [4]	4.2	.	5.0	4.0	6.7	.	.
O	4.6	2.7	9.0 [4]	1.8	.	10.3	5.9	5.0	.	.
P	33.6	18.5	35.4 [4]	27.3	.	18.6	15.6	15.9	.	.
Q	-	-	0.2 [4]	-	.	0.1	0.0	-	.	.
X	-	-	4.5 [4]	-	.	-	-	-	.	.

Explanatory notes: see p. 451.

[1] Persons aged 10 years and over. [2] Urban areas. [3] Nov. of each year. [4] July.

Notes explicatives: voir p. 454.

[1] Personnes âgées de 10 ans et plus. [2] Régions urbaines. [3] Nov. de chaque année. [4] Juillet.

Notas explicativas: véase p. 457.

[1] Personas de 10 años y más. [2] Areas urbanas. [3] Nov. de cada año. [4] Julio.

UNEMPLOYMENT — CHÔMAGE — DESEMPLEO — 3D

By economic activity — Par activité économique — Por actividad económica

	Thousands			Milliers			Millares			
	1999	2000	2001	2002	2003	2004	2005	2006	2007	2008

El Salvador (BA) [1] [2] — Total unemployment - Chômage total - Desempleo total

Total - Total - Total
ISIC 3 - CITI 3 - CIIU 3

	1999	2000	2001	2002	2003	2004	2005	2006	2007	2008
Total	163.3	164.4	170.3	147.4	169.4	164.0	177.6	164.2	166.6	.
UB	29.3	26.9	27.1	20.6	23.1	27.2	32.4	23.0	25.7	.
A	38.0	41.5	34.8	26.8	50.1	41.5	32.7	55.3	49.9	.
B	0.7	0.7	2.3	0.4	1.4	0.6	0.2	0.7	0.5	.
C	0.3	0.3	0.2	0.2	0.2	0.1	-	-	0.0	.
D	23.8	21.8	25.3	25.3	18.2	19.9	21.9	17.2	15.4	.
E	1.2	0.3	0.4	0.4	0.5	0.2	0.5	0.2	0.3	.
F	20.8	22.0	24.1	26.5	29.4	31.6	35.9	24.2	23.6	.
G-H	20.4	21.9	26.6	17.8	20.4	19.4	26.8	20.6	22.2	.
I	7.7	10.0	8.1	8.0	6.3	7.0	9.0	5.5	7.1	.
J-K	5.0	5.6	5.7	5.3	6.1	4.8	6.3	5.5	6.9	.
L	3.8	4.9	4.7	4.8	3.1	1.7	2.3	3.0	4.9	.
M	2.1	1.8	0.8	2.9	1.4	1.7	1.5	1.1	1.6	.
N-O	6.2	3.3	4.9	4.7	5.2	5.1	3.7	3.4	4.2	.
P	4.1	3.1	5.2	3.8	3.9	3.2	4.4	4.5	4.2	.
X	-	0.3	-	-	-	-	-	-	-	.

Men - Hommes - Hombres
ISIC 3 - CITI 3 - CIIU 3

	1999	2000	2001	2002	2003	2004	2005	2006	2007	2008
Total	120.2	129.5	119.6	113.7	134.5	127.3	129.6	123.9	126.6	.
UB	17.5	17.9	16.6	12.8	14.3	17.8	17.2	12.1	15.7	.
A	33.3	38.2	29.7	25.4	45.9	39.4	29.6	49.6	44.8	.
B	0.7	0.7	2.1	0.4	1.3	0.5	0.2	0.7	0.5	.
C	0.3	0.3	0.2	0.2	0.2	-	-	-	0.0	.
D	16.0	16.4	17.4	18.7	13.7	12.3	14.3	12.5	11.4	.
E	1.2	0.3	0.2	0.2	0.5	0.2	0.5	0.2	0.2	.
F	20.7	21.9	24.1	26.3	29.3	31.2	35.6	24.0	23.4	.
G-H	13.5	14.0	11.7	11.2	11.9	11.3	15.8	10.2	13.6	.
I	7.5	9.4	7.0	6.8	5.8	6.7	8.3	5.2	6.3	.
J-K	4.0	3.7	3.7	3.7	4.4	2.8	3.8	4.4	4.9	.
L	2.6	3.9	4.2	4.0	2.8	0.9	1.8	2.1	2.6	.
M	0.5	0.9	0.4	1.1	0.8	0.8	0.5	0.5	1.0	.
N-O	2.4	1.4	1.6	2.5	3.5	2.9	1.2	1.4	1.7	.
P	0.1	0.2	0.6	0.3	0.3	0.5	0.6	1.0	0.4	.
X	-	0.3	-	-	-	-	-	-	-	.

Women - Femmes - Mujeres
ISIC 3 - CITI 3 - CIIU 3

	1999	2000	2001	2002	2003	2004	2005	2006	2007	2008
Total	43.2	34.9	50.7	33.7	34.9	36.7	48.1	40.4	40.0	.
UB	11.8	9.0	10.5	7.8	8.8	9.4	15.1	10.9	10.0	.
A	4.7	3.3	5.1	1.3	4.2	2.1	3.2	5.7	5.0	.
B	-	-	0.2	-	0.1	0.0	-	-	-	.
C	-	-	-	-	-	0.1	-	-	-	.
D	7.8	5.4	7.9	6.6	4.6	7.6	7.5	4.7	4.0	.
E	-	-	0.2	0.1	-	-	-	0.0	0.1	.
F	0.1	0.1	0.1	0.2	0.1	0.4	0.3	0.1	0.2	.
G-H	6.9	7.9	14.9	6.6	8.5	8.1	11.0	10.4	8.3	.
I	0.3	0.6	1.1	1.1	0.5	0.3	0.6	0.3	1.1	.
J-K	1.0	2.0	2.0	1.7	1.7	1.9	2.5	1.1	2.0	.
L	1.1	1.0	0.4	0.8	0.4	0.9	0.5	0.9	2.3	.
M	1.6	0.9	0.4	1.7	0.6	0.9	1.0	0.6	0.6	.
N-O	3.8	1.9	3.3	2.2	1.7	2.3	2.5	2.0	2.5	.
P	4.0	2.9	4.6	3.5	3.6	2.6	3.8	3.6	3.9	.
X	-	-	-	-	-	-	-	-	-	.

Honduras (BA) [1] [3] — Total unemployment - Chômage total - Desempleo total

Total - Total - Total
ISIC 2 - CITI 2 - CIIU 2

	1999	2000	2001	2002	2003	2004	2005	2006	2007	2008
Total	89.3	.	103.4 [4]	.	.	153.2 [5]	107.8	.	.	.
UB	19.0	.	21.3 [4]	.	.	35.0 [5]	29.6	.	.	.
1	11.0	.	7.8 [4]	.	.	14.4 [5]	8.1	.	.	.
2	-	.	0.2 [4]	.	.	0.2 [5]	0.7	.	.	.
3	18.7	.	21.9 [4]	.	.	24.7 [5]	19.0	.	.	.
4	0.1	.	1.5 [4]	.	.	0.8 [5]	0.8	.	.	.
5	9.8	.	13.7 [4]	.	.	18.8 [5]	11.6	.	.	.
6	12.8	.	15.1 [4]	.	.	24.6 [5]	18.5	.	.	.
7	2.8	.	4.4 [4]	.	.	4.6 [5]	3.0	.	.	.
8	2.9	.	3.1 [4]	.	.	4.3 [5]	2.1	.	.	.
9	12.3	.	14.3 [4]	.	.	25.2 [5]	14.2	.	.	.
0	.	.	- [4]	.	.	0.4 [5]	-	.	.	.

Explanatory notes: see p. 451.

[1] Persons aged 10 years and over. [2] Dec. [3] March of each year. [4] Sep. [5] May.

Notes explicatives: voir p. 454.

[1] Personnes âgées de 10 ans et plus. [2] Déc. [3] Mars de chaque année. [4] Sept. [5] Mai.

Notas explicativas: véase p. 457.

[1] Personas de 10 años y más. [2] Dic. [3] Marzo de cada año. [4] Sept. [5] Mayo.

UNEMPLOYMENT — CHÔMAGE — DESEMPLEO

By economic activity — Par activité économique — Por actividad económica

Thousands — Milliers — Millares

Honduras (BA) [1][2] — Total unemployment - Chômage total - Desempleo total

Men - Hommes - Hombres
ISIC 2 - CITI 2 - CIIU 2

	1999	2000	2001	2002	2003	2004	2005	2006	2007	2008
Total	56.6	.	.	.	.	81.0 [3]	55.2	.	.	.
UB	10.4					13.6 [3]	13.0			
1	9.1					13.0 [3]	5.7			
2	-					0.2 [3]	0.7			
3	11.9					12.3 [3]	8.2			
4	-					0.8 [3]	0.8			
5	9.8					18.2 [3]	11.0			
6	6.8					10.4 [3]	8.2			
7	2.1					3.5 [3]	2.5			
8	1.3					2.4 [3]	1.2			
9	5.3					6.2 [3]	3.7			
0	-					0.4 [3]	-			

Women - Femmes - Mujeres
ISIC 2 - CITI 2 - CIIU 2

	1999	2000	2001	2002	2003	2004	2005	2006	2007	2008
Total	32.6	.	.	.	.	72.2 [3]	52.6	.	.	.
UB	8.6					48.6 [3]	16.6			
1	1.9					1.4 [3]	2.4			
2	-					- [3]	-			
3	6.9					12.4 [3]	10.8			
4	0.1					- [3]	-			
5	-					0.7 [3]	0.6			
6	6.0					14.2 [3]	10.3			
7	0.7					1.2 [3]	0.5			
8	1.6					1.9 [3]	0.9			
9	7.0					19.0 [3]	10.5			
0	-					- [3]	-			

Jamaica (BA) [4] — Total unemployment - Chômage total - Desempleo total

Total - Total - Total
ISIC 2 - CITI 2 - CIIU 2

	1999	2000	2001	2002	2003	2004	2005	2006	2007	2008
Total	175.2	171.8	165.4 [5]	171.8	128.9	136.8	133.3	119.6	119.4	134.6
UB	54.7	48.4	50.9 [5]	51.1	29.7	35.7	29.8	25.9	28.3	26.2
1	6.0	5.8	5.0 [5]	4.1	5.0	6.2	5.4	5.1	3.9	3.5
2	0.2	0.6	0.5 [5]	0.7	0.2	1.2	0.5	0.7	0.5	0.7
3	18.8	19.5	16.4 [5]	18.7	11.3	9.6	10.1	8.4	6.7	8.1
4	1.0	0.6	0.2 [5]	0.5	0.4	0.7	0.3	1.2	0.6	0.2
5	13.0	16.3	19.0 [5]	17.8	16.0	15.7	15.3	15.5	14.2	21.3
6	37.3	38.5	34.7 [5]	36.7	31.7	35.4	38.4	30.3	36.8	36.7
7	5.0	5.3	4.6 [5]	5.2	3.9	5.3	4.3	5.4	4.3	5.9
8	5.8	5.9	4.1 [5]	5.4	5.0	4.3	3.6	3.8	3.6	4.1
9	29.6	29.4	28.0 [5]	29.9	24.3	21.7	24.3	22.0	19.3	26.7
0	4.0	1.7	2.3 [5]	1.7	1.4	1.0	1.3	1.3	1.2	1.2

Men - Hommes - Hombres
ISIC 2 - CITI 2 - CIIU 2

	1999	2000	2001	2002	2003	2004	2005	2006	2007	2008
Total	61.4	62.5	63.4 [5]	65.7	47.6	54.0	50.0	48.0	37.8	52.8
UB	18.8	17.3	17.8 [5]	18.1	11.3	13.3	10.3	8.3	7.2	8.0
1	3.0	3.2	2.4 [5]	1.5	1.8	2.9	2.4	2.4	1.8	1.7
2	0.1	0.4	0.3 [5]	0.4	0.2	1.0	0.5	0.6	0.3	0.4
3	6.8	6.5	5.4 [5]	7.1	4.0	4.7	4.4	4.0	2.1	4.2
4	0.7	0.3	0.1 [5]	0.4	0.1	0.3	0.2	1.0	0.4	0.1
5	12.0	14.5	17.5 [5]	16.2	14.2	13.9	13.6	13.8	11.9	19.4
6	7.7	8.6	6.9 [5]	8.4	5.8	8.0	8.4	6.4	7.0	8.1
7	3.8	3.8	3.5 [5]	4.0	2.8	4.0	3.4	4.4	2.5	4.0
8	1.5	2.3	1.7 [5]	2.4	2.3	1.5	1.2	1.4	1.3	2.3
9	5.9	4.9	6.9 [5]	6.8	4.2	3.7	4.8	5.3	2.8	4.4
0	1.2	0.8	1.0 [5]	0.4	0.9	0.7	0.8	0.4	0.5	0.2

Women - Femmes - Mujeres
ISIC 2 - CITI 2 - CIIU 2

	1999	2000	2001	2002	2003	2004	2005	2006	2007	2008
Total	113.8	109.2	102.1 [5]	106.1	81.3	82.8	83.0	71.6	81.6	81.8
UB	35.9	31.1	33.1 [5]	33.0	18.4	22.4	19.5	17.6	21.1	18.2
1	3.0	2.6	2.6 [5]	2.6	3.2	3.3	3.0	2.7	2.1	1.8
2	0.1	0.2	0.2 [5]	0.3	-	0.2	0.0	0.1	0.2	0.3
3	12.0	13.1	11.0 [5]	11.6	7.3	4.9	5.7	4.4	4.6	3.9
4	0.3	0.2	0.1 [5]	0.1	0.3	0.4	0.1	0.2	0.2	0.1
5	1.0	1.8	1.5 [5]	1.6	1.8	1.8	1.7	1.7	2.3	1.9
6	29.6	30.0	27.8 [5]	28.3	25.9	27.4	30.0	23.9	29.8	28.6
7	1.2	1.5	1.1 [5]	1.2	1.1	1.2	0.9	1.0	1.8	1.9
8	4.3	3.5	2.5 [5]	3.0	2.7	2.8	2.4	2.4	2.3	1.8
9	23.7	24.4	21.1 [5]	23.1	20.1	18.1	19.5	16.7	16.5	22.3
0	2.8	0.9	1.3 [5]	1.3	0.5	0.3	0.5	0.9	0.7	1.0

Explanatory notes: see p. 451.
[1] Persons aged 10 years and over. [2] March of each year. [3] May.
[4] Persons aged 14 years and over. [5] First and second quarters.

Notes explicatives: voir p. 454.
[1] Personnes âgées de 10 ans et plus. [2] Mars de chaque année. [3] Mai. [4] Personnes âgées de 14 ans et plus. [5] Premier et deuxième trimestres.

Notas explicativas: véase p. 457.
[1] Personas de 10 años y más. [2] Marzo de cada año. [3] Mayo. [4] Personas de 14 años y más. [5] Primero y secondo trimestres.

	Thousands			Milliers				Millares		
	1999	2000	2001	2002	2003	2004	2005	2006	2007	2008

México (BA) [1] [2]

Total unemployment - Chômage total - Desempleo total

Total - Total - Total
ISIC 3 - CITI 3 - CIIU 3

	1999	2000	2001	2002	2003	2004	2005	2006	2007	2008
Total	954.2	998.9	996.1	1 145.6	1 195.6	1 539.8	1 482.5	1 377.7	.	.
UB	95.5	98.2	105.9	108.2	129.1	171.2	183.1	177.4	.	.
A	42.9	60.9	57.1	60.6	60.4	63.4	47.0	44.4	.	.
B	1.5	1.3	0.9	2.6	2.6	0.9	2.5	1.8	.	.
C	2.7	3.3	2.8	1.1	1.6	3.5	5.7	3.0	.	.
D	175.8	167.9	181.7	197.4	232.2	241.3	210.2	183.6	.	.
E	0.9	0.8	1.1	3.3	2.0	3.1	2.4	2.5	.	.
F	62.0	70.7	83.2	87.3	88.1	119.3	168.1	153.3	.	.
G	145.9	162.0	142.0	209.8	192.1	276.3	194.7	205.8	.	.
H	49.5	50.5	45.2	61.1	61.8	75.4	73.2	78.3	.	.
I	25.3	30.5	37.0	41.2	39.3	40.7	46.0	44.7	.	.
J	5.4	8.8	6.2	12.8	5.4	4.2	14.1	7.9	.	.
K	42.6	32.9	47.9	54.9	46.6	73.6	81.0	70.6	.	.
L	23.6	46.7	38.0	30.4	21.1	35.4	51.3	39.8	.	.
M	22.1	11.1	17.8	21.6	25.3	25.4	25.4	23.1	.	.
N	10.0	14.6	18.1	17.6	15.5	16.6	12.6	10.9	.	.
O	31.3	30.1	28.8	30.4	37.4	50.0	33.6	31.7	.	.
P	56.8	38.9	38.3	33.1	29.9	53.5	40.4	36.6	.	.
Q	0.0	0.0	0.0	0.0	0.0	0.0	0.0	5.7	.	.
X	160.7	169.8	144.4	172.3	205.2	285.9 ‖	291.1 [3]	256.6	.	.

Men - Hommes - Hombres
ISIC 3 - CITI 3 - CIIU 3

	1999	2000	2001	2002	2003	2004	2005	2006	2007	2008
Total	494.4	559.7	550.6	656.5	687.0	828.7	813.3	811.7	.	.
UB	33.9	38.9	33.6	39.3	48.7	72.8	84.9	79.0	.	.
A	32.1	48.6	43.9	49.7	49.3	52.3	42.5	39.8	.	.
B	1.5	1.3	0.8	1.9	2.6	0.7	2.5	1.4	.	.
C	2.7	3.3	2.7	1.1	1.5	3.3	4.9	2.9	.	.
D	97.5	97.4	103.0	118.3	134.9	127.3	143.8	111.9	.	.
E	0.9	0.5	0.7	2.7	1.7	2.2	1.2	1.4	.	.
F	59.1	68.6	80.1	83.2	85.3	113.4	162.9	147.3	.	.
G	79.2	101.5	82.0	138.4	113.3	167.8	128.2	122.5	.	.
H	13.7	27.8	25.0	26.2	29.3	37.1	37.6	38.1	.	.
I	18.6	24.0	33.2	34.3	35.7	32.8	42.4	39.2	.	.
J	4.1	4.3	4.1	8.6	3.8	1.1	8.2	3.7	.	.
K	28.7	16.7	27.0	27.1	21.6	43.0	62.5	41.2	.	.
L	16.3	28.5	20.5	18.2	15.0	21.0	36.3	22.7	.	.
M	7.0	1.7	5.4	8.5	8.5	12.0	10.4	8.5	.	.
N	0.3	2.7	2.4	2.9	3.3	2.7	2.5	1.4	.	.
O	23.6	19.1	18.7	21.6	23.4	30.7	20.1	18.3	.	.
P	11.1	6.1	3.9	2.6	3.5	5.3	4.4	3.6	.	.
Q	0.0	0.0	0.0	0.0	0.0	0.0	0.0	5.7	.	.
X	64.1	68.9	63.4	71.9	105.7	103.4 ‖	122.6 [3]	122.9	.	.

Women - Femmes - Mujeres
ISIC 3 - CITI 3 - CIIU 3

	1999	2000	2001	2002	2003	2004	2005	2006	2007	2008
Total	459.8	439.2	445.5	489.0	508.7	711.0	598.4	566.3	.	.
UB	61.6	59.3	72.2	68.9	80.4	98.4	98.3	98.5	.	.
A	10.8	12.3	13.1	10.9	11.1	11.2	4.6	4.5	.	.
B	0.0	0.0	0.1	0.7	0.0	0.2	0.0	0.5	.	.
C	0.0	0.0	0.1	0.0	0.1	0.2	0.9	0.1	.	.
D	78.3	70.5	78.8	79.1	97.3	114.0	66.5	71.7	.	.
E	0.0	0.4	0.4	0.6	0.3	0.9	1.2	1.0	.	.
F	2.9	2.1	3.1	4.1	2.8	5.8	5.2	6.0	.	.
G	66.7	60.5	60.0	71.4	78.8	108.5	66.5	83.4	.	.
H	35.8	22.7	20.1	34.9	32.5	38.3	35.6	40.2	.	.
I	6.7	6.5	3.8	6.9	3.6	7.9	3.5	5.5	.	.
J	1.3	4.5	2.0	4.1	1.7	3.2	5.9	4.2	.	.
K	13.9	16.2	20.9	27.7	25.1	30.7	18.5	29.4	.	.
L	7.3	18.2	17.5	12.3	6.1	14.4	15.0	17.1	.	.
M	15.0	9.4	12.5	13.1	16.7	13.4	15.0	14.6	.	.
N	9.7	11.9	15.6	14.7	12.2	13.9	10.2	9.5	.	.
O	7.6	11.0	10.1	8.7	14.0	19.3	13.5	13.5	.	.
P	45.8	32.8	34.3	30.5	26.5	48.2	36.0	33.0	.	.
Q	0.0	0.0	0.0	0.0	0.0	0.0	0.0	0.0	.	.
X	96.5	100.9	81.0	100.4	99.5	182.5 ‖	168.5 [3]	133.7	.	.

Explanatory notes: see p. 451.

[1] Persons aged 14 years and over. [2] Second quarter of each year. [3] Begenning 2005: excluded, persons in unemployment that finished its last work for more than one year.

Notes explicatives: voir p. 454.

[1] Personnes âgées de 14 ans et plus. [2] Deuxième trimestre de chaque année. [3] A partir de 2005: non compris les chômeurs n'ayant pas travaillé depuis plus de 1 an.

Notas explicativas: véase p. 457.

[1] Personas de 14 años y más. [2] Segundo trimestre de cada año. [3] A partir de 2005: excluye a los desempleados que terminaron su último trabajo hace más de un año.

	UNEMPLOYMENT	CHÔMAGE	DESEMPLEO
	By economic activity	Par activité économique	Por actividad económica

	Thousands			Milliers					Millares	
	1999	2000	2001	2002	2003	2004	2005	2006	2007	2008

Panamá (BA) [1] [2] — Total unemployment - Chômage total - Desempleo total

Total - Total - Total
ISIC 3 - CITI 3 - CIIU 3

	1999	2000	2001	2002	2003	2004	2005	2006	2007	2008
Total	128.0	147.0	169.7	172.4	170.4	159.9	136.8	121.4	92.0	82.9
UB	27.9	33.7	40.6	30.6	36.3	28.9	23.7	17.4	15.2	14.0
A	3.3	3.9	6.5	5.5	4.8	4.8	3.8	4.5	2.2	2.0
B	0.7	1.0	0.8	0.7	0.5	0.4	0.1	0.5	0.1	0.2
C	0.2	0.1	0.5	0.2	0.2	0.6	0.3	0.3	0.0	-
D	11.6	11.5	14.3	14.2	13.1	12.3	10.8	9.9	6.3	5.6
E	1.1	0.8	0.9	1.4	1.0	0.9	0.6	0.5	0.9	0.1
F	13.4	16.1	18.5	21.8	14.8	18.4	17.4	16.1	10.2	11.4
G	22.1	26.3	30.5	34.6	33.9	30.8	26.3	23.8	20.2	16.6
H	6.4	7.5	8.8	9.3	10.7	9.9	8.5	7.3	5.4	6.2
I	5.7	7.0	8.0	7.0	9.0	8.8	5.1	5.8	4.2	3.4
J	1.8	1.8	2.0	3.9	2.5	2.4	2.4	1.5	1.7	1.8
K	5.7	6.7	5.9	7.3	6.9	6.9	6.6	7.8	4.6	5.0
L	4.1	6.5	6.2	6.0	6.4	5.3	6.9	5.3	2.6	2.9
M	2.3	2.7	2.7	2.8	3.7	3.5	3.3	3.9	3.5	1.2
N	1.6	1.4	1.9	1.8	2.5	2.9	4.1	1.6	1.3	1.4
O	6.7	8.3	7.5	8.8	9.5	7.7	7.0	6.3	5.2	4.1
P	12.7	11.6	13.0	16.5	13.8	15.0	10.0	8.8	8.5	6.9
Q	0.5	0.2	0.8	0.3	0.6	0.3	0.1	0.2	-	-
X	-	0.1	1.0	-	-	-	-	-	-	-

Men - Hommes - Hombres
ISIC 3 - CITI 3 - CIIU 3

	1999	2000	2001	2002	2003	2004	2005	2006	2007	2008
Total	62.1	77.7	92.0	86.5	82.9	76.3	66.7	60.2	44.5	40.2
UB	10.7	15.9	19.6	13.4	16.8	11.9	9.0	5.6	5.9	4.8
A	3.0	3.7	6.1	4.7	4.6	4.0	3.0	4.2	2.1	1.6
B	0.5	0.8	0.7	0.6	0.4	0.4	0.1	0.5	0.1	0.2
C	0.1	-	0.5	0.1	0.2	0.6	0.3	0.3	-	-
D	6.7	7.7	9.8	8.5	8.3	6.7	6.8	5.9	4.3	4.2
E	0.8	0.6	0.5	1.0	0.7	0.4	0.5	0.3	0.7	0.1
F	13.1	15.6	17.8	20.6	14.0	17.6	17.0	15.1	9.8	11.2
G	10.4	12.7	15.2	15.8	15.2	13.1	11.8	9.3	8.9	7.8
H	2.0	1.8	2.5	1.4	2.9	2.3	2.0	1.9	1.6	1.5
I	4.3	5.2	6.3	5.4	6.3	6.7	4.1	5.2	2.9	2.4
J	0.6	0.7	0.8	2.1	1.4	0.9	1.0	0.7	1.0	0.6
K	3.3	4.2	3.5	4.2	2.7	3.6	3.4	3.9	2.0	2.3
L	1.8	3.5	3.0	2.9	2.6	1.5	2.8	2.4	1.0	1.0
M	0.4	0.5	0.5	0.6	0.7	0.6	0.7	0.9	1.1	0.2
N	0.5	0.2	0.4	0.2	0.9	0.6	0.9	0.3	0.2	0.4
O	3.4	4.1	4.0	4.6	4.4	4.3	3.0	3.4	2.9	1.7
P	0.3	0.3	0.1	0.3	0.5	0.9	0.4	0.4	0.2	0.3
Q	0.3	0.2	0.5	0.2	0.4	0.1	-	-	-	-
X	-	0.1	1.0	-	-	-	-	-	-	-

Women - Femmes - Mujeres
ISIC 3 - CITI 3 - CIIU 3

	1999	2000	2001	2002	2003	2004	2005	2006	2007	2008
Total	65.9	69.3	77.8	85.9	87.4	83.6	70.2	61.1	47.5	42.7
UB	17.2	17.8	21.1	17.2	19.5	16.9	14.7	11.8	9.2	9.2
A	0.4	0.2	0.3	0.4	0.3	0.8	0.7	0.3	0.2	0.5
B	0.2	0.2	0.2	0.1	0.1	-	-	-	-	-
C	0.1	0.1	-	0.1	-	0.1	-	-	-	-
D	4.9	3.8	4.5	5.7	4.8	5.5	4.0	4.0	2.0	1.5
E	0.3	0.2	0.4	0.4	0.3	0.5	0.1	0.2	0.2	-
F	0.3	0.5	0.7	1.2	0.8	0.9	0.5	1.0	0.4	0.2
G	11.8	13.6	15.3	18.8	18.7	17.6	14.5	14.5	11.3	8.9
H	4.4	5.7	6.3	8.0	7.8	7.5	6.5	5.4	3.8	4.7
I	1.4	1.8	1.7	1.5	2.7	2.1	1.0	0.6	1.3	1.0
J	1.2	1.1	1.2	1.9	1.1	1.5	1.4	0.8	0.7	1.1
K	2.4	2.5	2.4	3.1	4.2	3.3	3.2	3.9	2.6	2.7
L	2.3	3.0	3.2	3.2	3.8	3.8	4.2	3.0	1.6	1.9
M	1.9	2.2	2.2	2.2	3.0	3.0	2.6	3.0	2.4	1.0
N	1.1	1.2	1.5	1.6	1.7	2.3	3.2	1.4	1.2	1.0
O	3.3	4.2	3.5	4.3	5.1	3.4	3.9	2.9	2.4	2.4
P	12.4	11.3	12.9	16.2	13.3	14.1	9.6	8.4	8.3	6.6
Q	0.2	-	0.3	0.1	0.2	0.2	0.1	0.2	-	-
X	-	-	-	-	-	-	-	-	-	-

Paraguay (BA) [3] [4] — Total unemployment - Chômage total - Desempleo total

Total - Total - Total
ISIC 3 - CITI 3 - CIIU 3

	1999	2000	2001	2002	2003	2004	2005	2006	2007	2008
Total	.	.	.	.	.	.	.	.	161.2	170.6
UB	.	.	.	.	.	.	.	.	48.6	42.9
A-B	.	.	.	.	.	.	.	.	2.0	4.7
C	.	.	.	.	.	.	.	.	0.3	1.4
D	.	.	.	.	.	.	.	.	14.1	13.1
E	.	.	.	.	.	.	.	.	0.6	1.1
F	.	.	.	.	.	.	.	.	14.8	17.5
G-H	.	.	.	.	.	.	.	.	26.6	31.5
I	.	.	.	.	.	.	.	.	6.4	8.3
J-K	.	.	.	.	.	.	.	.	4.8	3.0
L-Q	.	.	.	.	.	.	.	.	43.0	47.1

Explanatory notes: see p. 451.

[1] Persons aged 15 years and over. [2] Aug. of each year. [3] Persons aged 10 years and over. [4] Fourth quarter.

Notes explicatives: voir p. 454.

[1] Personnes âgées de 15 ans et plus. [2] Août de chaque année. [3] Personnes âgées de 10 ans et plus. [4] Quatrième trimestre.

Notas explicativas: véase p. 457.

[1] Personas de 15 años y más. [2] Agosto de cada año. [3] Personas de 10 años y más. [4] Cuarto trimestre.

By economic activity — Par activité économique — Por actividad económica

Thousands — Milliers — Millares	1999	2000	2001	2002	2003	2004	2005	2006	2007	2008
Paraguay (BA) [1][2] — Total unemployment - Chômage total - Desempleo total										
Men - Hommes - Hombres ISIC 3 - CITI 3 - CIIU 3										
Total	.	.	.	.	.	.	.	.	74.6	83.9
UB	.	.	.	.	.	.	.	.	19.7	20.7
A-B	.	.	.	.	.	.	.	.	1.5	3.5
C	.	.	.	.	.	.	.	.	0.3	0.8
D	.	.	.	.	.	.	.	.	10.7	7.2
E	.	.	.	.	.	.	.	.	0.4	0.6
F	.	.	.	.	.	.	.	.	14.5	17.5
G-H	.	.	.	.	.	.	.	.	12.8	17.6
I	.	.	.	.	.	.	.	.	4.1	6.1
J-K	.	.	.	.	.	.	.	.	2.1	1.4
L-Q	.	.	.	.	.	.	.	.	8.5	8.6
Women - Femmes - Mujeres ISIC 3 - CITI 3 - CIIU 3										
Total	.	.	.	.	.	.	.	.	86.6	86.7
UB	.	.	.	.	.	.	.	.	28.9	22.2
A-B	.	.	.	.	.	.	.	.	0.5	1.2
C	.	.	.	.	.	.	.	.	-	0.6
D	.	.	.	.	.	.	.	.	3.4	5.9
E	.	.	.	.	.	.	.	.	0.2	0.5
F	.	.	.	.	.	.	.	.	0.4	-
G-H	.	.	.	.	.	.	.	.	13.8	13.9
I	.	.	.	.	.	.	.	.	2.3	2.2
J-K	.	.	.	.	.	.	.	.	2.7	1.6
L-Q	.	.	.	.	.	.	.	.	34.5	38.5
Perú (BA) [3][4] — Total unemployment - Chômage total - Desempleo total										
Total - Total - Total ISIC 3 - CITI 3 - CIIU 3										
Total	.	.	.	359.4 [2]	316.0 [5]	339.5	333.4	297.6	300.1	308.0
UB	.	.	.	57.6 [2]	52.9 [5]	36.7	62.9	57.7	61.3	48.4
A	.	.	.	3.0 [2]	3.2 [5]	0.8	1.1	1.7	1.1	3.1
B	.	.	.	2.0 [2]	4.6 [5]	0.6	-	2.6	0.3	-
C	.	.	.	5.2 [2]	3.7 [5]	-	1.2	-	2.6	2.4
D	.	.	.	68.3 [2]	40.9 [5]	55.9	55.6	37.1	35.8	55.9
E	.	.	.	4.4 [2]	- [5]	2.4	2.9	0.5	-	2.3
F	.	.	.	39.1 [2]	30.3 [5]	32.7	23.6	21.2	19.4	11.1
G	.	.	.	54.4 [2]	44.0 [5]	42.7	31.9	46.3	46.3	47.7
H	.	.	.	16.1 [2]	18.7 [5]	19.4	23.8	21.1	20.9	21.9
I	.	.	.	11.5 [2]	19.1 [5]	28.0	26.1	16.6	17.6	15.7
J	.	.	.	4.7 [2]	9.6 [5]	5.5	5.6	0.8	4.6	5.2
K	.	.	.	19.5 [2]	21.2 [5]	14.0	28.1	20.5	14.5	24.0
L	.	.	.	16.0 [2]	15.1 [5]	11.4	14.8	15.7	14.7	16.7
M	.	.	.	13.9 [2]	8.3 [5]	18.5	13.8	13.4	21.6	7.4
N	.	.	.	9.0 [2]	6.3 [5]	8.6	10.7	3.8	4.9	4.9
O	.	.	.	12.4 [2]	21.9 [5]	28.8	14.3	18.6	19.1	23.6
P	.	.	.	22.2 [2]	16.2 [5]	33.5	17.0	19.8	15.4	17.8
Men - Hommes - Hombres ISIC 3 - CITI 3 - CIIU 3										
Total	.	.	.	194.0 [2]	182.5 [5]	159.4	155.4	136.3	139.1	131.3
UB	.	.	.	34.8 [2]	31.7 [5]	18.3	22.8	30.0	31.8	24.9
A	.	.	.	0.6 [2]	1.6 [5]	0.8	1.1	0.7	1.1	0.9
B	.	.	.	2.0 [2]	0.6 [5]	0.6	-	2.6	0.3	-
C	.	.	.	5.2 [2]	1.1 [5]	-	1.2	-	1.8	2.4
D	.	.	.	35.3 [2]	27.7 [5]	29.1	35.8	16.3	15.0	27.3
E	.	.	.	4.4 [2]	- [5]		2.9	-	-	2.3
F	.	.	.	38.2 [2]	30.3 [5]	32.7	20.7	19.7	19.4	10.0
G	.	.	.	24.5 [2]	22.8 [5]	15.8	14.4	19.3	16.6	18.9
H	.	.	.	4.8 [2]	6.8 [5]	5.5	2.2	3.3	5.2	5.7
I	.	.	.	9.3 [2]	15.7 [5]	21.5	11.7	14.1	11.1	9.9
J	.	.	.	3.9 [2]	2.7 [5]	1.0	4.1	-	1.1	-
K	.	.	.	10.5 [2]	11.8 [5]	8.1	18.0	8.0	10.6	13.0
L	.	.	.	7.6 [2]	7.9 [5]	4.0	6.3	5.2	5.8	6.4
M	.	.	.	3.0 [2]	- [5]	5.0	1.4	3.2	10.4	1.0
N	.	.	.	3.0 [2]	3.5 [5]	1.4	3.1	1.2	0.4	-
O	.	.	.	6.9 [2]	15.0 [5]	15.2	9.5	10.1	8.4	8.7
P	.	.	.	- [2]	3.2 [5]	0.3	-	2.6	-	-

Explanatory notes: see p. 451.
[1] Persons aged 10 years and over. [2] Fourth quarter. [3] Persons aged 14 years and over. [4] Metropolitan Lima. [5] May-Dec.

Notes explicatives: voir p. 454.
[1] Personnes âgées de 10 ans et plus. [2] Quatrième trimestre. [3] Personnes âgées de 14 ans et plus. [4] Lima métropolitaine. [5] Mai-déc.

Notas explicativas: véase p. 457.
[1] Personas de 10 años y más. [2] Cuarto trimestre. [3] Personas de 14 años y más. [4] Lima metropolitana. [5] Mayo-dic.

	Thousands			Milliers					Millares	
	1999	2000	2001	2002	2003	2004	2005	2006	2007	2008

Perú (BA) [1][2] — Total unemployment - Chômage total - Desempleo total

Women - Femmes - Mujeres
ISIC 3 - CITI 3 - CIIU 3

Total	.	.	.	165.4 [3]	133.6 [4]	180.1	178.0	161.3	161.0	176.6
UB	.	.	.	22.8 [3]	21.2 [4]	18.4	40.1	27.7	29.5	23.5
A	.	.	.	2.4 [3]	1.6 [4]	-	-	1.0	-	2.2
B	.	.	.	- [3]	4.1 [4]	-	-	-	-	-
C	.	.	.	- [3]	2.6 [4]	-	-	-	0.7	-
D	.	.	.	33.0 [3]	13.1 [4]	26.8	19.7	20.8	20.9	28.6
E	.	.	.	- [3]	- [4]	2.4	-	0.5	-	-
F	.	.	.	0.9 [3]	- [4]	-	2.9	1.6	-	1.1
G	.	.	.	29.9 [3]	21.1 [4]	26.9	17.6	27.1	29.7	28.7
H	.	.	.	11.3 [3]	11.8 [4]	13.9	21.6	17.8	15.6	16.2
I	.	.	.	2.2 [3]	3.4 [4]	6.5	14.4	2.5	6.5	5.8
J	.	.	.	0.8 [3]	6.9 [4]	4.5	1.5	0.8	3.5	5.2
K	.	.	.	9.0 [3]	9.4 [4]	5.9	10.0	12.5	3.9	11.0
L	.	.	.	8.4 [3]	7.2 [4]	7.4	8.5	10.5	8.8	10.3
M	.	.	.	10.9 [3]	8.3 [4]	13.5	12.3	10.3	11.3	6.4
N	.	.	.	6.0 [3]	2.8 [4]	7.2	7.6	2.6	4.5	4.9
O	.	.	.	5.5 [3]	6.9 [4]	13.5	4.8	8.5	10.7	14.9
P	.	.	.	22.2 [3]	13.1 [4]	33.2	17.0	17.3	15.4	17.8

Puerto Rico (BA) [5][6] — Total unemployment - Chômage total - Desempleo total

Total - Total - Total
ISIC 2 - CITI 2 - CIIU 2

Total	152	131	145	163	164	145	160	156	152	158
UB	10	8	8	9	10	8	9	9	10	12
1	4	5	5	4	4	4	4	3	4	3
3	24	20	23	27	24	17	17	19	21	20
4	-	-	-	-	-	-	-	-	-	1
5	25	25	27	29	28	27	29	25	24	25
6 [7]	30	25	28	31	35	32	36	33	34	34
7	4	4	4	5	4	4	4	3	4	4
8	2	1	3	2	2	3	2	2	2	3
9 [8]	53	44	49	57	57	51	59	62	53	56

Men - Hommes - Hombres
ISIC 2 - CITI 2 - CIIU 2

Total	101	90	97	101	99	92	97	90	93	97
UB	4	3	4	4	4	4	4	4	5	6
1	4	4	5	4	3	4	4	3	3	3
3	14	13	14	14	13	9	9	10	13	13
4	-	-	-	-	-	-	-	-	-	-
5	24	24	26	28	27	25	28	24	23	24
6 [7]	17	15	15	16	17	16	18	15	18	17
7	4	3	3	4	3	3	3	2	2	3
8	1	1	1	1	1	1	1	1	1	1
9 [8]	34	27	30	32	30	29	31	31	28	31

Women - Femmes - Mujeres
ISIC 2 - CITI 2 - CIIU 2

Total	51	42	48	62	65	53	63	66	59	60
UB	6	5	4	5	6	4	5	5	5	6
1	1	1	-	-	-	-	-	-	-	-
3	10	7	10	13	12	8	8	9	8	7
4	-	-	-	-	-	-	-	-	-	-
5	1	1	1	2	1	1	1	1	1	1
6 [7]	12	11	13	15	19	16	18	17	17	17
7	1	1	1	1	1	1	1	1	1	1
8	1	-	1	1	1	1	1	1	1	2
9 [8]	19	16	19	25	25	22	29	31	25	25

Trinidad and Tobago (BA) [9] — Total unemployment - Chômage total - Desempleo total

Total - Total - Total
ISIC 2 - CITI 2 - CIIU 2

Total	74.0	69.6	62.4	61.1	62.4	51.1	49.7	39.1	34.5	29.0
1	2.6	3.5	1.8	1.5	2.7	3.0	1.7	1.0	1.1	0.9
2	2.6	1.9	1.9	2.5	1.6 [10]	1.3 [10]	1.8 [10]	1.1 [10]	1.3 [10]	0.9 [10]
3	7.1	6.4	6.3	5.7	5.8	4.4	3.4	3.1	1.8	2.0
4	0.5	0.2	0.2	0.3	0.2 [11]	0.6 [11]	0.2 [11]	0.3 [11]	0.1 [11]	0.2 [11]
5	22.7	23.1	19.1	20.8	20.2	15.5	17.4	14.0	13.0	10.7
6	14.9	13.8	13.6	12.4	12.0	8.9	9.4	7.0	6.4	5.7
7	2.3	2.6	2.3	1.9	2.2	1.8	1.7	1.3	1.1	0.7
8	3.4	2.8	2.8	3.0	3.0	2.6	2.1	1.5	1.5	1.7
9	17.3	15.0	13.9	12.1	14.1	12.4	11.5	9.7	7.9	6.2
0	0.3	0.3	0.5	1.0	0.6	0.5	0.5	0.4	0.4	0.1

Explanatory notes: see p. 451.

[1] Persons aged 14 years and over. [2] Metropolitan Lima. [3] Fourth quarter. [4] May-Dec. [5] Excl. persons temporarily laid off. [6] Persons aged 16 years and over. [7] Excl. hotels. [8] Incl. hotels. [9] Persons aged 15 years and over. [10] Incl. petroleum and gas extraction. [11] Excl. gas.

Notes explicatives: voir p. 454.

[1] Personnes âgées de 14 ans et plus. [2] Lima métropolitaine. [3] Quatrième trimestre. [4] Mai-déc. [5] Non compris les personnes temporairement mises à pied. [6] Personnes âgées de 16 ans et plus. [7] Non compris les hôtels. [8] Y compris les hôtels. [9] Personnes âgées de 15 ans et plus. [10] Y compris l'extraction du pétrole et du gaz. [11] Non compris le gaz.

Notas explicativas: véase p. 457.

[1] Personas de 14 años y más. [2] Lima metropolitana. [3] Cuarto trimestre. [4] Mayo-dic. [5] Excl. las personas temporalmente despedidas. [6] Personas de 16 años y más. [7] Excl. hoteles. [8] Incl. hoteles. [9] Personas de 15 años y más. [10] Incl. extracción de petróleo y gas. [11] Excl. gas.

By economic activity — **Par activité économique** — **Por actividad económica**

	Thousands			Milliers			Millares			
	1999	2000	2001	2002	2003	2004	2005	2006	2007	2008

Trinidad and Tobago (BA) [1]   Total unemployment - Chômage total - Desempleo total

Men - Hommes - Hombres
ISIC 2 - CITI 2 - CIIU 2

	1999	2000	2001	2002	2003	2004	2005	2006	2007	2008
Total	37.9	36.1	30.7	27.9	29.8	23.4	21.3	16.4	14.4	12.8
1	2.3	2.8	1.4	1.2	2.4	2.5	1.5	0.8	0.8	0.7
2	2.1	1.5	1.3	1.7	1.2 [2]	1.0 [2]	1.1 [2]	0.6 [2]	1.1 [2]	0.6 [2]
3	3.7	3.3	3.6	3.2	3.4	2.8	2.1	1.7	0.9	1.2
4	0.2	0.2	0.1	0.2	0.1 [3]	0.2 [3]	- [3]	0.2 [3]	- [3]	- [3]
5	16.9	16.6	13.7	12.9	13.1	9.1	9.4	7.4	6.8	5.9
6	3.9	3.6	3.7	2.8	2.8	1.8	2.0	1.6	1.5	1.4
7	1.7	1.5	1.5	1.1	1.3	1.1	1.0	0.9	0.7	0.4
8	1.4	1.0	1.1	1.2	1.0	0.9	0.7	0.6	0.6	0.8
9	5.5	5.4	4.0	3.3	4.1	3.7	3.3	2.5	1.8	1.9
0	0.1	0.2	0.3	0.4	0.2	0.3	0.2	0.2	0.2	-

Women - Femmes - Mujeres
ISIC 2 - CITI 2 - CIIU 2

	1999	2000	2001	2002	2003	2004	2005	2006	2007	2008
Total	36.1	33.5	31.7	33.2	32.6	27.7	28.4	22.7	20.1	16.1
1	0.3	0.7	0.4	0.3	0.3	0.5	0.2	0.2	0.3	0.2
2	0.5	0.4	0.6	0.8	0.4 [2]	0.3 [2]	0.7 [2]	0.5 [2]	0.2 [2]	0.3 [2]
3	3.4	3.1	2.7	2.5	2.4	1.6	1.3	1.4	0.9	0.8
4	0.3	-	0.1	0.1	0.1 [3]	0.4 [3]	0.2 [3]	0.1 [3]	0.1 [3]	0.2 [3]
5	5.8	6.5	5.4	7.9	7.1	6.4	8.0	6.6	6.2	4.8
6	11.0	10.2	9.9	9.6	9.2	7.1	7.4	5.4	4.9	4.3
7	0.6	1.1	0.8	0.8	0.9	0.7	0.7	0.4	0.4	0.3
8	2.0	1.8	1.7	1.8	2.0	1.7	1.4	0.9	0.9	0.9
9	11.8	9.6	9.9	8.8	10.0	8.7	8.2	7.2	6.1	4.3
0	0.2	0.1	0.2	0.6	0.4	0.2	0.3	0.2	0.2	-

United States (BA) [4]   Total unemployment - Chômage total - Desempleo total

Total - Total - Total
ISIC 2 - CITI 2 - CIIU 2

	1999	2000	2001	2002	2003	2004	2005	2006	2007	2008	ISIC 3 - CITI 3 - CIIU 3
Total	5 880	5 655	6 742	8 378 |	8 774	8 149	7 591	7 001	7 078	8 924	Total
UB	469	431	453	536 |	641	686	666	616	627	766	UB
1	215	193	232	247 |	153	143	119	109	91	138	A-B
2	34	21	27	33 |	37	22	20	22	26	26	C
3	750	741	1 034	1 278 |	1 174	976	823	707	715	965	D
4	26	24	27	36 |	35	22	18	19	17	29	E
5	564	545	649	846 |	899	876	810	760	858	1 165	F
6	1 457	1 413	1 583	1 980 |	1 271	1 228	1 168	1 062	1 016	1 244	G
7	249	255	334	454 |	864	839	786	728	758	927	H
8	685	680	865	1 063 |	291	255	248	245	252	330	I
9	1 411	1 337	1 521	1 884 |	226	233	189	187	198	273	J
0	19	14	16	22 |	1 230	1 045	970	923	924	1 155	K
				|	154	151	144	101	133	139	L
				|	357	326	335	312	329	376	M
				|	575	573	573	522	511	593	N
				|	839	744	722	688	623	791	O-X

Men - Hommes - Hombres
ISIC 2 - CITI 2 - CIIU 2

	1999	2000	2001	2002	2003	2004	2005	2006	2007	2008	ISIC 3 - CITI 3 - CIIU 3
Total	3 066	2 954	3 663	4 597 |	4 906	4 456	4 059	3 753	3 882	5 033	Total
UB	219	216	217	274 |	320	346	359	312	343	393	UB
1	157	139	173	185 |	106	108	85	78	64	104	A-B
2	30	20	24	29 |	30	19	19	19	21	24	C
3	437	428	632	787 |	751	616	518	440	444	625	D
4	20	20	16	24 |	24	15	14	12	11	19	E
5	518	502	602	783 |	836	805	744	698	784	1 090	F
6	659	651	769	954 |	655	609	572	522	500	607	G
7	169	166	230	287 |	394	375	334	322	336	412	H
8	330	319	427	525 |	229	193	178	176	184	249	I
9	511	484	558	729 |	92	86	64	75	75	105	J
0	16	11	14	19 |	672	580	511	500	512	662	K
				|	77	75	69	44	65	68	L
				|	118	105	102	100	110	119	M
				|	115	107	99	96	95	104	N
				|	465	389	391	359	338	450	O-X

Explanatory notes: see p. 451.

[1] Persons aged 15 years and over. [2] Incl. petroleum and gas extraction. [3] Excl. gas. [4] Persons aged 16 years and over.

Notes explicatives: voir p. 454.

[1] Personnes âgées de 15 ans et plus. [2] Y compris l'extraction du pétrole et du gaz. [3] Non compris le gaz. [4] Personnes âgées de 16 ans et plus.

Notas explicativas: véase p. 457.

[1] Personas de 15 años y más. [2] Incl. extracción de petróleo y gas. [3] Excl. gas. [4] Personas de 16 años y más.

3D — UNEMPLOYMENT — CHÔMAGE — DESEMPLEO

By economic activity — Par activité économique — Por actividad económica

Thousands — Milliers — Millares

United States (BA) [1]
Women - Femmes - Mujeres
ISIC 2 - CITI 2 - CIIU 2 (1999–2002) — ISIC 3 - CITI 3 - CIIU 3 (2003–2008)

Total unemployment - Chômage total - Desempleo total

ISIC 2	1999	2000	2001	2002	2003	2004	2005	2006	2007	2008	ISIC 3
Total	2 814	2 701	3 079	3 781	3 868	3 694	3 531	3 247	3 196	3 891	Total
UB	250	215	236	262	321	340	306	304	285	374	UB
1	58	55	59	62	47	36	34	30	27	33	A-B
2	4	1	3	4	7	2	1	4	4	2	C
3	313	314	402	491	423	360	305	267	271	340	D
4	6	4	11	12	11	8	4	7	5	10	E
5	46	43	47	63	63	71	66	62	74	76	F
6	797	762	814	1 026	616	619	595	540	516	637	G
7	81	88	104	167	470	463	453	405	422	515	H
8	355	364	438	538	62	62	70	69	68	81	I
9	900	852	963	1 155	134	147	125	112	122	168	J
0	3	3	2	3	558	465	459	422	410	493	K
					78	75	75	56	67	71	L
					239	221	233	212	219	257	M
					460	466	474	426	416	489	N
					373	355	331	331	290	345	O-X

Uruguay (BA) [2]

Total unemployment - Chômage total - Desempleo total

Total - Total - Total
ISIC 3 - CITI 3 - CIIU 3

	1999	2000	2001	2002	2003	2004	2005	2006	2007	2008
Total	.	167.7	193.2	211.3	208.5	.	154.9	167.0 [3]	149.3	.
UB	.	34.2	35.3	35.7	38.2	.	27.4	33.8 [3]	28.3	.
A-C	.	6.7	4.6	5.2	5.4	.	3.2	10.3 [3]	10.2	.
D-E	.	25.4	14.7	17.3	12.5	.	7.4	19.3 [3]	16.7	.
F	.	14.2	12.3	17.5	15.5	.	8.1	11.9 [3]	11.0	.
G-H	.	32.3	22.5	25.4	21.3	.	13.4	29.6 [3]	26.7	.
I	.	4.7	4.3	3.8	3.9	.	2.9	4.6 [3]	4.7	.
J-K	.	10.7	10.8	11.1	10.1	.	6.2	11.4 [3]	9.6	.
L	.	3.2	1.2	1.3	1.2	.	0.6	3.4 [3]	2.4	.
M	.	2.6	1.8	1.9	1.9	.	0.6	3.7 [3]	3.1	.
N	.	4.5	3.0	3.7	3.7	.	2.9	5.5 [3]	4.6	.
O,Q	.	5.2	4.6	4.0	3.5	.	3.1	6.4 [3]	6.3	.
P	.	23.7	16.4	18.2	17.6	.	12.8	26.7 [3]	25.8	.
X	.	.	61.7 [4]	66.3 [4]	73.7 [4]	.	66.2 [4]	0.3 [3]	-	.

Men - Hommes - Hombres
ISIC 3 - CITI 3 - CIIU 3

	1999	2000	2001	2002	2003	2004	2005	2006	2007	2008
Total	.	74.7	80.4	93.3	92.2	.	65.4	70.0 [3]	60.0	.
UB	.	14.9	14.9	14.3	17.3	.	11.2	13.9 [3]	11.9	.
A-C	.	4.9	3.9	4.4	4.3	.	2.9	7.6 [3]	7.1	.
D-E	.	12.2	7.8	10.1	6.9	.	4.2	8.9 [3]	7.3	.
F	.	13.8	12.1	17.2	15.2	.	7.7	11.5 [3]	10.2	.
G-H	.	15.1	11.9	13.9	12.1	.	7.2	12.1 [3]	10.4	.
I	.	3.2	3.2	2.9	3.4	.	2.5	3.4 [3]	3.1	.
J-K	.	4.2	5.5	6.1	5.7	.	3.0	5.7 [3]	4.9	.
L	.	2.2	0.6	1.0	0.6	.	0.4	2.0 [3]	1.1	.
M	.	0.5	0.4	0.2	0.3	.	0.1	0.5 [3]	0.5	.
N	.	0.4	0.3	0.4	0.6	.	0.4	0.6 [3]	0.4	.
O,Q	.	2.2	2.0	1.8	1.4	.	1.2	2.6 [3]	2.0	.
P	.	1.0	0.5	1.1	0.8	.	1.0	1.0 [3]	1.1	.
X	.	.	17.2 [4]	19.9 [4]	23.6 [4]	.	23.6 [4]	0.2 [3]	-	.

Women - Femmes - Mujeres
ISIC 3 - CITI 3 - CIIU 3

	1999	2000	2001	2002	2003	2004	2005	2006	2007	2008
Total	.	93.0	112.8	118.0	116.2	.	89.5	96.9 [3]	89.3	.
UB	.	19.2	20.4	21.4	20.9	.	16.1	19.9 [3]	16.3	.
A-C	.	1.8	0.7	0.8	1.2	.	0.4	2.7 [3]	3.1	.
D-E	.	13.2	7.0	7.2	5.6	.	3.2	10.4 [3]	9.5	.
F	.	0.5	0.2	0.3	0.3	.	0.4	0.3 [3]	0.8	.
G-H	.	17.2	10.6	11.5	9.2	.	6.2	17.5 [3]	16.2	.
I	.	1.4	1.0	0.9	0.4	.	0.4	1.2 [3]	1.6	.
J-K	.	6.5	5.3	5.0	4.4	.	3.3	5.7 [3]	4.7	.
L	.	1.0	0.5	0.3	0.5	.	0.1	1.4 [3]	1.3	.
M	.	2.2	1.4	1.7	1.6	.	0.4	3.2 [3]	2.5	.
N	.	4.1	2.8	3.3	3.1	.	2.6	4.9 [3]	4.3	.
O,Q	.	2.9	2.5	2.1	2.0	.	1.9	3.8 [3]	4.3	.
P	.	22.8	15.9	17.1	16.8	.	11.8	25.6 [3]	24.7	.
X	.	.	44.5 [4]	46.4 [4]	50.1 [4]	.	42.3 [4]	0.1 [3]	-	.

Explanatory notes: see p. 451. — Notes explicatives: voir p. 454. — Notas explicativas: véase p. 457.

[1] Persons aged 16 years and over. [2] Persons aged 14 years and over. [3] Prior to 2006: urban areas. [4] Incl. the unemployed whose last job was 1 year ago or over.

[1] Personnes âgées de 16 ans et plus. [2] Personnes âgées de 14 ans et plus. [3] Avant 2006: régions urbaines. [4] Y compris les chômeurs dont le dernier emploi date de 1 an ou plus.

[1] Personas de 16 años y más. [2] Personas de 14 años y más. [3] Antes de 2006: areas urbanas. [4] Incl. los desempleados cuyo último trabajo fue hace 1 año o más.

| By economic activity | Par activité économique | Por actividad económica |

Thousands		Milliers						Millares	
1999	2000	2001	2002	2003	2004	2005	2006	2007	2008

ASIA-ASIE-ASIA

Azerbaijan (BA) [1] Total unemployment - Chômage total - Desempleo total

Total - Total - Total
ISIC 3 - CITI 3 - CIIU 3

	1999	2000	2001	2002	2003	2004	2005	2006	2007	2008
Total	.	.	.	.	.	.	.	.	.	261.4
A	.	.	.	.	.	.	.	.	.	7.7
B	.	.	.	.	.	.	.	.	.	0.2
C	.	.	.	.	.	.	.	.	.	9.6
D	.	.	.	.	.	.	.	.	.	59.4
E	.	.	.	.	.	.	.	.	.	16.4
F	.	.	.	.	.	.	.	.	.	59.3
G	.	.	.	.	.	.	.	.	.	30.0
H	.	.	.	.	.	.	.	.	.	4.1
I	.	.	.	.	.	.	.	.	.	18.9
J	.	.	.	.	.	.	.	.	.	3.3
K	.	.	.	.	.	.	.	.	.	17.1
L	.	.	.	.	.	.	.	.	.	5.2
M	.	.	.	.	.	.	.	.	.	8.9
N	.	.	.	.	.	.	.	.	.	10.8
O	.	.	.	.	.	.	.	.	.	10.6

Men - Hommes - Hombres
ISIC 3 - CITI 3 - CIIU 3

	1999	2000	2001	2002	2003	2004	2005	2006	2007	2008
Total	.	.	.	.	.	.	.	.	.	156.9
A	.	.	.	.	.	.	.	.	.	4.6
B	.	.	.	.	.	.	.	.	.	0.1
C	.	.	.	.	.	.	.	.	.	5.8
D	.	.	.	.	.	.	.	.	.	35.7
E	.	.	.	.	.	.	.	.	.	9.9
F	.	.	.	.	.	.	.	.	.	35.6
G	.	.	.	.	.	.	.	.	.	18.0
H	.	.	.	.	.	.	.	.	.	2.4
I	.	.	.	.	.	.	.	.	.	11.3
J	.	.	.	.	.	.	.	.	.	2.0
K	.	.	.	.	.	.	.	.	.	10.2
L	.	.	.	.	.	.	.	.	.	3.1
M	.	.	.	.	.	.	.	.	.	5.3
N	.	.	.	.	.	.	.	.	.	6.5
O	.	.	.	.	.	.	.	.	.	6.4

Women - Femmes - Mujeres
ISIC 3 - CITI 3 - CIIU 3

	1999	2000	2001	2002	2003	2004	2005	2006	2007	2008
Total	.	.	.	.	.	.	.	.	.	104.5
A	.	.	.	.	.	.	.	.	.	3.1
B	.	.	.	.	.	.	.	.	.	0.1
C	.	.	.	.	.	.	.	.	.	3.8
D	.	.	.	.	.	.	.	.	.	23.7
E	.	.	.	.	.	.	.	.	.	6.6
F	.	.	.	.	.	.	.	.	.	23.7
G	.	.	.	.	.	.	.	.	.	12.0
H	.	.	.	.	.	.	.	.	.	1.6
I	.	.	.	.	.	.	.	.	.	7.5
J	.	.	.	.	.	.	.	.	.	1.3
K	.	.	.	.	.	.	.	.	.	6.8
L	.	.	.	.	.	.	.	.	.	2.1
M	.	.	.	.	.	.	.	.	.	3.6
N	.	.	.	.	.	.	.	.	.	4.3
O	.	.	.	.	.	.	.	.	.	4.2

Hong Kong, China (BA) [2] [3] Total unemployment - Chômage total - Desempleo total

Total - Total - Total
ISIC 2 - CITI 2 - CIIU 2

	1999	2000	2001	2002	2003	2004	2005	2006	2007	2008
Total	207.5	166.9	174.3	254.2	275.2	239.2	197.6	171.1	145.7	130.1
UB	23.9	17.6	16.1	24.7	23.2	23.4	20.1	18.7	17.0	15.7
1	-	-	-	0.5	-	-	-	-	-	-
2	-	-	-	-	-	-	-	-	-	-
3	27.1	19.0	18.1	22.7	22.4	17.7	15.0	11.6	9.6	8.6
4	-	-	-	-	-	-	-	-	-	-
5	41.1	34.3	35.0	53.4	61.3	50.1	39.2	33.8	25.0	19.4
6	64.3	54.5	57.0	83.1	88.0	75.3	63.4	55.7	49.1	45.5
7	19.0	14.8	15.9	19.8	24.0	19.7	17.9	15.1	12.9	12.6
8	15.0	12.1	15.1	23.1	25.5	22.7	18.3	16.7	13.9	13.1
9	16.3	14.0	16.8	26.9	30.2	29.6	23.2	19.0	17.7	14.8

Explanatory notes: see p. 451.

Notes explicatives: voir p. 454.

Notas explicativas: véase p. 457.

[1] Men aged 15 to 61 years; women aged 15 to 56 years. [2] Excl. marine, military and institutional populations. [3] Persons aged 15 years and over.

[1] Hommes âgés de 15 à 61 ans; femmes âgées de 15 à 56 ans. [2] Non compris le personnel militaire, de la marine et la population institutionnelle. [3] Personnes âgées de 15 ans et plus.

[1] Hombres de 15 a 61 años; mujeres de 15 a 56 años. [2] Excl. el personal militar y de la marina, y la población institucional. [3] Personas de 15 años y más.

UNEMPLOYMENT CHÔMAGE DESEMPLEO

By economic activity Par activité économique Por actividad económica

	Thousands					Milliers			Millares	
	1999	2000	2001	2002	2003	2004	2005	2006	2007	2008

Hong Kong, China (BA) [1] [2] — Total unemployment - Chômage total - Desempleo total

Men - Hommes - Hombres
ISIC 2 - CITI 2 - CIIU 2

Total	140.6	109.6	117.8	164.0	180.0	151.8	127.5	110.2	89.2	79.4
UB	11.7	8.2	8.3	10.4	9.9	9.5	9.1	8.9	7.7	7.4
1	-		-		-		-		-	-
2				.		.		.		
3	18.5	12.8	12.2	14.0	14.6	11.1	9.5	7.1	5.9	4.9
4	-		-		-		-		-	-
5	39.9	33.3	33.9	51.8	58.8	47.6	38.0	32.5	24.2	18.7
6	34.9	28.4	30.8	43.5	45.4	37.5	33.4	28.6	24.3	23.1
7	16.0	12.5	13.8	16.3	20.4	17.0	15.2	13.2	10.6	10.4
8	10.0	7.4	9.9	15.2	16.8	15.5	12.6	11.4	8.5	8.7
9	9.0	6.7	8.6	12.4	13.5	13.2	9.3	8.3	7.7	6.0

Women - Femmes - Mujeres
ISIC 2 - CITI 2 - CIIU 2

Total	66.9	57.3	56.5	90.1	95.3	87.4	70.1	60.8	56.5	50.7
UB	12.2	9.4	7.9	14.3	13.3	13.9	11.0	9.8	9.3	8.3
1	-		-		-		-		-	-
2				.		.		.		
3	8.6	6.3	5.9	8.7	7.8	6.6	5.5	4.5	3.7	3.7
4	-		-		-		-		-	-
5	1.2	1.0	1.1	1.5	2.5	2.5	1.3	1.2	0.9	0.7
6	29.4	26.2	26.2	39.6	42.6	37.8	29.9	27.2	24.8	22.4
7	3.0	2.3	2.2	3.5	3.6	2.8	2.7	2.0	2.2	2.2
8	5.0	4.7	5.1	7.8	8.7	7.2	5.7	5.4	5.3	4.4
9	7.3	7.3	8.1	14.5	16.7	16.4	13.9	10.7	10.0	8.9

Iran, Islamic Rep. of (BA) [3] — Total unemployment - Chômage total - Desempleo total

Total - Total - Total
ISIC 3 - CITI 3 - CIIU 3

							2005	2006	2007	2008
Total							1 519	1 589	1 487	1 301
UB							1 156	1 054	999	1 091
A							115	133	107	82
B							4	3	4	2
C							11	9	8	6
D							302	314	251	228
E							12	11	8	6
F							310	331	317	302
G							157	171	160	136
H							17	18	21	22
I							106	108	124	95
J							8	8	7	6
K							38	37	36	40
L							328	347	354	301
M							43	42	35	30
N							29	27	22	18
O							34	26	29	25
P							3	2	2	1
Q							0	0	0	0
X							0	1	1	1

Men - Hommes - Hombres
ISIC 3 - CITI 3 - CIIU 3

							2005	2006	2007	2008
Total							1 346	1 416	1 333	1 181
UB							509	462	431	535
A							108	125	98	77
B							4	3	4	2
C							11	9	8	6
D							245	261	209	198
E							11	10	7	5
F							306	328	314	299
G							142	155	144	126
H							16	17	20	20
I							103	103	118	90
J							7	5	5	4
K							26	25	24	29
L							319	336	341	290
M							17	14	13	11
N							9	8	9	7
O							20	15	19	16
P							1	1	0	0
Q							0	0	0	0
X							0	1	1	1

Explanatory notes: see p. 451.

[1] Excl. marine, military and institutional populations. [2] Persons aged 15 years and over. [3] Persons aged 10 years and over.

Notes explicatives: voir p. 454.

[1] Non compris le personnel militaire, de la marine et la population institutionnelle. [2] Personnes âgées de 15 ans et plus. [3] Personnes âgées de 10 ans et plus.

Notas explicativas: véase p. 457.

[1] Excl. el personal militar y de la marina, y la población institucional. [2] Personas de 15 años y más. [3] Personas de 10 años y más.

By economic activity   **Par activité économique**   **Por actividad económica**

	Thousands			Milliers			Millares			
	1999	2000	2001	2002	2003	2004	2005	2006	2007	2008

Iran, Islamic Rep. of (BA) [1]   Total unemployment - Chômage total - Desempleo total

Women - Femmes - Mujeres
ISIC 3 - CITI 3 - CIIU 3

	1999	2000	2001	2002	2003	2004	2005	2006	2007	2008
Total	.	.	.	.	.	.	172	173	154	120
UB	.	.	.	.	.	.	647	592	568	557
A	.	.	.	.	.	.	7	7	9	6
B	.	.	.	.	.	.	0	0	0	0
C	.	.	.	.	.	.	0	0	0	0
D	.	.	.	.	.	.	57	52	42	30
E	.	.	.	.	.	.	1	1	1	1
F	.	.	.	.	.	.	3	3	3	3
G	.	.	.	.	.	.	15	17	15	11
H	.	.	.	.	.	.	1	1	2	2
I	.	.	.	.	.	.	3	5	6	5
J	.	.	.	.	.	.	1	3	2	2
K	.	.	.	.	.	.	12	12	12	11
L	.	.	.	.	.	.	9	11	13	11
M	.	.	.	.	.	.	26	27	23	19
N	.	.	.	.	.	.	20	19	14	11
O	.	.	.	.	.	.	14	12	10	9
P	.	.	.	.	.	.	2	2	1	1
Q	.	.	.	.	.	.	0	0	0	0
X	.	.	.	.	.	.	0	0	0	0

Israel (BA) [2]   Total unemployment - Chômage total - Desempleo total

Total - Total - Total
ISIC 3 - CITI 3 - CIIU 3

	1999	2000	2001	2002	2003	2004	2005	2006	2007	2008
Total	208.5	213.8	234.0	262.4	279.8	277.7	246.4	236.1	211.8	180.4
UB	95.5	107.6	107.1	129.2	154.5	163.4	139.5	135.8	118.6	94.7
A	2.1	2.4	3.0	2.2	-	2.1	2.1	-	-	-
B	.	0.0	.	.	.	.	0.0	0.0	.	0.0
C	.	.	.	.	.	.	.	.	.	0.0
D	22.4	20.1	26.1	27.5	22.3	17.8	17.2	13.5	12.1	14.5
E	.	.	.	.	.	.	.	.	.	.
F	15.7	11.2	11.1	11.0	9.2	8.0	5.9	5.9	5.6	4.7
G	18.8	18.6	20.5	22.3	19.5	19.9	19.9	19.6	17.0	15.9
H	8.5	8.4	12.0	12.3	10.2	11.8	8.3	10.4	10.1	7.9
I	6.1	5.8	8.4	8.3	8.3	7.0	7.6	6.2	7.4	6.8
J	-	-	3.1	3.4	3.4	2.7	2.8	2.9	-	-
K	12.3	11.5	17.3	20.0	21.4	15.6	15.7	15.7	14.9	14.4
L	2.8	2.2	-	2.5	-	-	2.4	-	-	-
M	6.8	7.6	7.4	8.6	10.4	9.8	8.8	6.7	7.3	6.0
N	6.2	6.0	5.7	6.3	6.9	6.7	6.4	6.8	5.5	4.5
O	5.1	6.8	5.5	4.7	5.9	6.0	5.2	5.2	4.0	3.8
P	2.6	2.1	2.7	2.2	2.7	3.2	2.6	2.4	-	-
Q	0.0	.	.	0.0	0.0	0.0	0.0	0.0	.	0.0
X	-	-	-	-	-	-	-	-	2.2	-

Men - Hommes - Hombres
ISIC 3 - CITI 3 - CIIU 3

	1999	2000	2001	2002	2003	2004	2005	2006	2007	2008
Total	108.8	111.7	120.9	138.4	142.8	136.5	124.9	118.5	104.8	90.8
UB	45.9	53.0	52.3	66.3	76.8	77.2	68.5	68.7	58.5	44.8
A	-	-	-	-	-	-	-	-	-	.
B	.	.	.	.	.	.	.	.	.	0.0
C	.	.	.	.	.	.	.	.	.	0.0
D	14.2	13.5	16.5	17.7	15.1	12.7	11.3	9.1	8.1	10.0
E	.	.	.	.	.	.	.	.	.	.
F	14.5	10.7	10.3	10.0	8.3	7.5	5.7	5.4	5.2	4.3
G	9.9	8.6	10.0	10.5	10.1	8.6	9.7	8.9	8.5	7.8
H	4.3	4.6	6.9	6.3	4.6	6.3	4.9	5.3	5.2	4.6
I	4.1	3.5	5.3	5.8	5.0	4.3	5.6	3.7	4.0	4.4
J	.	.	1.0	1.1	1.1	.	0.8	0.9	.	.
K	5.7	5.8	9.1	10.5	12.1	8.5	8.1	8.5	7.0	7.2
L	-	-	-	-	-	-	-	-	-	-
M	1.5	1.8	1.6	2.0	2.2	2.1	2.1	1.1	0.9	1.6
N	1.1	1.4	1.0	1.4	1.6	1.2	1.3	1.5	1.1	1.0
O	2.6	3.7	2.6	2.5	2.5	3.4	3.2	2.4	2.5	2.0
P	0.1	0.1	0.2	0.1	0.3	0.2	0.3	0.1	0.0	0.0
Q	.	.	.	.	.	.	.	.	0.0	.
X	.	.	-	.	.	.	.	.	-	.

Explanatory notes: see p. 451.   Notes explicatives: voir p. 454.   Notas explicativas: véase p. 457.

[1] Persons aged 10 years and over. [2] Persons aged 15 years and over.   [1] Personnes âgées de 10 ans et plus. [2] Personnes âgées de 15 ans et plus.   [1] Personas de 10 años y más. [2] Personas de 15 años y más.

3D   UNEMPLOYMENT   CHÔMAGE   DESEMPLEO

By economic activity   Par activité économique   Por actividad económica

	Thousands				Milliers				Millares	
	1999	2000	2001	2002	2003	2004	2005	2006	2007	2008

Israel (BA) [1]   Total unemployment - Chômage total - Desempleo total

Women - Femmes - Mujeres
ISIC 3 - CITI 3 - CIIU 3

	1999	2000	2001	2002	2003	2004	2005	2006	2007	2008
Total	99.7	102.1	113.0	124.0	137.1	141.2	121.5	117.6	107.0	89.6
UB	49.6	54.6	54.8	62.9	77.7	86.2	71.0	67.1	60.1	49.9
A	.	.	.	.	-	-	-	.	.	.
B	0.0	.	0.0	.	0.0	0.0	.	.	0.0	0.0
C	.	0.0	0.0	0.0	0.0	.	0.0	0.0	0.0	0.0
D	8.1	6.6	9.6	9.9	7.3	5.1	5.9	4.5	4.0	4.5
E	.	.	.	0.0	.	.	.	.	0.0	.
F	1.2	0.4	0.8	0.9	0.9	0.5	0.2	0.5	0.4	0.4
G	8.8	10.1	10.5	11.9	9.4	11.3	10.3	10.7	8.5	8.1
H	4.1	3.7	5.0	6.0	5.6	5.5	3.4	5.1	4.9	3.3
I	2.0	2.3	3.2	2.5	3.3	2.7	2.0	2.5	3.5	2.3
J	-	-	2.2	2.3	2.4	-	2.0	2.0	-	-
K	6.5	5.7	8.1	9.5	9.3	7.1	7.6	7.2	7.9	7.2
L	-	-	-	-	-	-	-	-	-	-
M	5.3	5.8	5.8	6.6	8.2	7.6	6.8	5.7	6.4	4.4
N	5.1	4.6	4.7	4.9	5.2	5.5	5.1	5.3	4.4	3.5
O	2.5	3.0	2.8	2.2	3.4	2.5	2.0	2.8	1.5	1.9
P	2.5	2.1	2.5	2.2	2.3	3.0	2.3	2.3	-	-
Q	.	.	0.0	.	.	.	.	.	.	.
X	.	.	.	.	.	.	.	.	.	.

Japan (BA) [1]   Total unemployment - Chômage total - Desempleo total

Total - Total - Total
ISIC 2 - CITI 2 - CIIU 2   ISIC 3 - CITI 3 - CIIU 3 [2]

	1999	2000	2001	2002	2003	2004	2005	2006	2007	2008	
Total	3 170	3 200	3 400	3 590 [3]	2 640	2 310	2 140	1 990	1 870	1 910	Total
UB	970	1 100	1 340	830 [3]	270	270	240	220	200	190	UB
1	10	10	-	20 [3]	20	10	10	20	10	10	A
3	480	470	380	600 [3]	0	0	0	0	0	0	B
5	200	210	180	260 [3]	0	0	0	0	0	0	C
6 [4]	480	490	460	620 [3]	510	390	330	310	270	280	D [4]
7	170	130	110	200 [3]	10	20	10	0	0	10	E
8	90	80	60	290 [5]	270	240	190	170	150	150	F
9 [6]	430	420	370	390 [3]	440	370	360	350	320	330	G [6]
0	300	270	280	380 [3]	180	170	140	120	130	130	H
					630	560	570	540	540	570	I.K.O [7]
					60	60	50	40	40	40	J
					30	20	30	30	20	20	L
					50	40	40	30	40	30	M
					120	110	120	120	110	110	N
					50	50	40	40	30	40	X

Men - Hommes - Hombres
ISIC 2 - CITI 2 - CIIU 2   ISIC 3 - CITI 3 - CIIU 3 [2]

	1999	2000	2001	2002	2003	2004	2005	2006	2007	2008	
Total	1 940	1 960	2 090	2 190 [3]	1 590	1 400	1 240	1 150	1 070	1 100	Total
UB	570	610	800	440 [3]	170	170	150	140	130	130	UB
1	10	-	-	10 [3]	10	10	10	10	10	10	A
3	290	330	240	390 [3]	0	0	0	0	0	0	B
5	180	180	150	230 [3]	0	0	0	0	0	0	C
6 [4]	230	260	210	300 [3]	340	260	220	200	180	180	D [4]
7	140	110	80	160 [3]	10	10	0	0	0	0	E
8	40	30	30	150 [5]	240	210	170	150	130	140	F
9 [6]	220	220	180	170 [3]	220	200	180	170	150	150	G [6]
0	210	250	240	340 [3]	80	70	60	50	50	60	H
					410	350	370	330	340	350	I.K.O [7]
					30	20	20	20	20	20	J
					10	10	10	10	10	10	L
					20	20	10	10	10	10	M
					20	20	10	20	20	10	N
					40	30	30	20	20	30	X

Explanatory notes: see p. 451.

[1] Persons aged 15 years and over. [2] Refer only to unemployed who left the previous job in the past 3 years. [3] Prior to 2002: Special Labour Force Survey, february of each year. [4] Excl. publishing. [5] Incl. activities not adequately defined. [6] Excl. repair of motor vehicles, motor cycles and personal and household goods. [7] Incl. repair of motor vehicles, motor cycles and personal and household goods.

Notes explicatives: voir p. 454.

[1] Personnes âgées de 15 ans et plus. [2] Se rapportent seulement aux chômeurs dont le dernier travail date de moins de 3 ans. [3] Avant 2002: Enquête spécial sur la main-d'oeuvre, février de chaque année. [4] Non compris l'édition. [5] Y compris les activités mal désignées. [6] Non compris réparation de véhicules automobiles, de motocycles et de biens personnels etdomestiques. [7] Y compris réparation de véhicules automobiles, de motocycles et de biens personnels et domestiques.

Notas explicativas: véase p. 457.

[1] Personas de 15 años y más. [2] Se refieren solamente de las desempleados cuyo último trabajo fue hace menos de 3 años. [3] Antes de 2002: encuesta especial sobre la fuerza de trabajo, febrero de cada año. [4] Excl. las editoriales. [5] Incl. actividades no bien especificadas. [6] Excl. reparación de vehículos automotores, motocicletas, efectos personals y enseres domesticos. [7] Incl. reparación de vehículos automotores, motocicletas, efectos personals y enseres domesticos.

UNEMPLOYMENT — CHÔMAGE — DESEMPLEO 3D

By economic activity — Par activité économique — Por actividad económica

	Thousands — Milliers — Millares										
	1999	2000	2001	2002	2003	2004	2005	2006	2007	2008	

Japan (BA) [1]

Women - Femmes - Mujeres
ISIC 2 - CITI 2 - CIIU 2 (left labels) / ISIC 3 - CITI 3 - CIIU 3 [2] (right labels)

Total unemployment - Chômage total - Desempleo total

Left	1999	2000	2001	2002	2003	2004	2005	2006	2007	2008	Right
Total	1 230	1 230	1 310	1 400 [3]	1 050	910	900	830	800	820	Total
UB	400	480	540	450 [3]	100	100	90	70	70	60	UB
1	-	-	-	10 [3]	-	10	-	0	0	0	A
3	200	140	140	210 [3]	0	0	0	0	0	0	B
5	30	30	30	40 [3]	0	0	0	0	0	-	C
6 [4]	240	220	250	320 [3]	170	130	110	100	90	100	D [4]
7	20	20	20	40 [3]	-	10	10	0	0	0	E
8	60	50	30	140 [5]	30	20	20	20	20	20	F
9 [6]	210	200	190	210 [3]	220	170	190	180	170	190	G [6]
0	80	50	50	10 [3]	100	90	70	70	80	70	H
					230	210	230	220	200	220	I,K,O [7]
					30	40	30	20	30	20	J
					20	10	20	10	10	10	L
					20	20	20	20	30	20	M
					100	90	110	100	90	100	N
					10	10	10	10	10	10	X

Korea, Republic of (BA) [1]

Total - Total - Total
ISIC 3 - CITI 3 - CIIU 3

Total unemployment - Chômage total - Desempleo total

	1999	2000	2001	2002	2003	2004	2005	2006	2007	2008
Total	1 353	979 [8]	899	752	818	860	887	827	783	.
UB	92	66 [8]	58	46	72	53	42	44	41	.
A	18	12 [8]	11	7	5	5	6	4	4	.
B	3	2 [8]	2	1	1	1	2	1	1	.
C	1	- [8]	-	1	0	1	1	0	0	.
D	193	150 [8]	138	116	115	124	136	119	113	.
E	2	1 [8]	1	2	1	0	1	1	1	.
F	219	132 [8]	110	76	88	110	117	105	92	.
G	191	138 [8]	127	107	125	120	116	97	97	.
H	139	96 [8]	91	84	77	85	82	64	65	.
I	43	39 [8]	36	28	29	30	29	30	23	.
J	26	18 [8]	16	13	17	14	11	13	12	.
K	60	53 [8]	54	58	60	68	66	70	72	.
L	68	42 [8]	24	14	11	10	12	12	10	.
M	31	26 [8]	27	25	28	30	26	22	21	.
N	11	8 [8]	11	10	11	14	14	14	13	.
O	40	43 [8]	47	42	45	48	52	59	53	.
P	9	5 [8]	4	5	4	4	3	3	3	.
Q	-	- [8]	-	-	-	-	1	1	0	.
X	207	149 [8]	141	118	129	143	171	172	159	.

Men - Hommes - Hombres
ISIC 3 - CITI 3 - CIIU 3

	1999	2000	2001	2002	2003	2004	2005	2006	2007	2008
Total	911	647 [8]	591	491	508	534	553	533	517	.
UB	56	41 [8]	34	29	41	29	22	23	25	.
A	13	9 [8]	8	5	4	3	4	3	2	.
B	3	2 [8]	2	1	0	1	1	1	1	.
C	1	- [8]	-	1	0	1	1	0	0	.
D	135	102 [8]	93	82	77	79	91	82	81	.
E	-	1 [8]	1	1	0	0	1	0	1	.
F	204	124 [8]	105	70	83	103	110	98	85	.
G	126	84 [8]	74	67	68	68	64	61	62	.
H	65	46 [8]	47	41	36	33	37	27	31	.
I	38	34 [8]	32	23	23	27	24	25	20	.
J	14	11 [8]	8	6	9	6	5	7	6	.
K	43	35 [8]	37	39	40	46	43	45	48	.
L	45	23 [8]	11	7	6	5	5	6	5	.
M	10	10 [8]	12	9	8	10	10	7	8	.
N	5	2 [8]	3	3	2	3	3	2	2	.
O	23	29 [8]	32	28	32	31	31	40	35	.
P	-	- [8]	1	-	0	0	0	0	1	.
Q	-	0 [8]	-	0	0	0	1	1	0	.
X	127	94 [8]	91	79	79	89	100	107	104	.

Explanatory notes: see p. 451.

[1] Persons aged 15 years and over. [2] Refer only to unemployed who left the previous job in the past 3 years. [3] Prior to 2002: Special Labour Force Survey, february of each year. [4] Excl. publishing. [5] Incl. activities not adequately defined. [6] Excl. repair of motor vehicles, motor cycles and personal and household goods. [7] Incl. repair of motor vehicles, motor cycles and personal and household goods. [8] Estimates based on the 2000 Population Census results.

Notes explicatives: voir p. 454.

[1] Personnes âgées de 15 ans et plus. [2] Se rapportent seulement aux chômeurs dont le dernier travail date de moins de 3 ans. [3] Avant 2002: Enquête spécial sur la main-d'oeuvre, février de chaque année. [4] Non compris l'édition. [5] Y compris les activités mal désignées. [6] Non compris réparation de véhicules automobiles, de motocycles et de biens personnels etdomestiques. [7] Y compris réparation de véhicules automobiles, de motocycles et de biens personnels et domestiques. [8] Estimations basées sur les résultats du Recensement de la population de 2000.

Notas explicativas: véase p. 457.

[1] Personas de 15 años y más. [2] Se refieren solamente de las desempleados cuyo último trabajo fue hace menos de 3 años. [3] Antes de 2002: encuesta especial sobre la fuerza de trabajo, febrero de cada año. [4] Excl. las editoriales. [5] Incl. actividades no bien especificadas. [6] Excl. reparación de vehículos automotores, motocicletas, efectos personals y enseres domesticos. [7] Incl. reparación de vehículos automotores, motocicletas, efectos personals y enseres domesticos. [8] Estimaciones basadas en los resultados del Censo de población de 2000.

UNEMPLOYMENT — CHÔMAGE — DESEMPLEO

By economic activity — Par activité économique — Por actividad económica

	Thousands			Milliers					Millares	
	1999	2000	2001	2002	2003	2004	2005	2006	2007	2008

Korea, Republic of (BA) [1] — Total unemployment - Chômage total - Desempleo total

Women - Femmes - Mujeres
ISIC 3 - CITI 3 - CIIU 3

	1999	2000	2001	2002	2003	2004	2005	2006	2007	2008
Total	448	332 [2]	308	261	307	326	334	294	266	.
UB	37	25 [2]	24	17	31	23	20	21	16	.
A	5	3 [2]	3	1	2	2	2	2	2	.
B	-	- [2]	-	-	-	0	0	0	0	.
C	.	- [2]	-	-	-	-	0	0	0	.
D	58	48 [2]	46	34	38	45	45	37	33	.
E	-	- [2]	-	-	1	0	0	0	1	.
F	14	7 [2]	5	6	5	7	8	7	6	.
G	65	54 [2]	53	40	57	52	51	37	35	.
H	73	50 [2]	44	43	42	52	45	37	35	.
I	5	6 [2]	4	4	6	3	5	5	2	.
J	12	7 [2]	8	7	8	8	6	6	6	.
K	18	18 [2]	18	19	20	23	23	25	24	.
L	24	19 [2]	13	7	5	6	7	6	5	.
M	20	16 [2]	14	17	19	20	16	15	14	.
N	6	5 [2]	8	7	8	10	11	11	11	.
O	17	14 [2]	15	14	14	17	21	19	18	.
P	9	4 [2]	4	4	4	4	3	2	3	.
Q	-	- [2]	-	-	-	-	0	0	0	.
X	79	55 [2]	50	39	50	54	71	65	55	.

Kyrgyzstan (BA) [1] [3] — Total unemployment - Chômage total - Desempleo total

Total - Total - Total
ISIC 3 - CITI 3 - CIIU 3

	1999	2000	2001	2002	2003	2004	2005	2006	2007	2008
Total	.	.	.	265.5	212.3	185.7	183.5	188.9	.	.
UB	.	.	.	104.9	85.6	76.9	66.9	68.7	.	.
A	.	.	.	19.8	25.6	20.1	25.5	24.1	.	.
B	.	.	.	-	0.1	-	-	-	.	.
C	.	.	.	3.1	1.4	0.8	1.0	1.2	.	.
D	.	.	.	39.2	22.9	16.7	17.4	16.6	.	.
E	.	.	.	3.0	1.8	2.7	3.3	3.2	.	.
F	.	.	.	15.1	12.1	12.3	11.4	15.4	.	.
G	.	.	.	18.7	16.1	16.8	19.4	25.3	.	.
H	.	.	.	4.6	6.9	5.6	7.4	9.2	.	.
I	.	.	.	8.7	9.0	7.0	6.2	4.9	.	.
J	.	.	.	0.7	0.6	0.4	0.2	0.3	.	.
K	.	.	.	4.1	2.5	2.6	2.1	1.1	.	.
L	.	.	.	11.1	7.9	7.0	6.2	5.7	.	.
M	.	.	.	14.4	7.9	7.3	7.4	5.8	.	.
N	.	.	.	10.2	7.6	3.6	4.2	2.6	.	.
O	.	.	.	6.8	3.6	5.2	3.9	4.3	.	.
P	.	.	.	1.2	0.5	0.7	0.7	0.4	.	.
Q	.	.	.	-	0.2	0.0	0.2	0.0	.	.

Men - Hommes - Hombres
ISIC 3 - CITI 3 - CIIU 3

	1999	2000	2001	2002	2003	2004	2005	2006	2007	2008
Total	.	.	.	132.6	113.1	98.8	95.7	101.4	.	.
UB	.	.	.	54.0	42.6	36.1	32.2	33.2	.	.
A	.	.	.	14.0	17.0	13.1	13.9	14.1	.	.
B	.	.	.	-	-	-	-	-	.	.
C	.	.	.	1.5	1.1	0.8	0.9	1.2	.	.
D	.	.	.	19.0	10.4	7.0	8.2	8.6	.	.
E	.	.	.	2.7	1.6	2.6	3.1	3.1	.	.
F	.	.	.	12.3	10.7	11.6	10.9	15.1	.	.
G	.	.	.	7.6	7.3	8.4	8.2	10.0	.	.
H	.	.	.	-	1.7	0.9	1.9	2.6	.	.
I	.	.	.	6.1	8.0	5.8	5.2	4.7	.	.
J	.	.	.	-	0.1	0.1	0.1	0.1	.	.
K	.	.	.	1.1	1.5	1.3	1.1	0.5	.	.
L	.	.	.	6.0	5.8	5.3	5.1	3.8	.	.
M	.	.	.	1.9	1.4	1.6	1.7	1.5	.	.
N	.	.	.	3.3	1.7	0.8	0.9	0.8	.	.
O	.	.	.	2.4	1.8	3.3	1.6	2.1	.	.
P	.	.	.	0.8	0.2	0.2	0.3	0.2	.	.
Q	.	.	.	-	0.2	-	0.2	0.2	.	.

Explanatory notes: see p. 451.

[1] Persons aged 15 years and over. [2] Estimates based on the 2000 Population Census results. [3] Nov. of each year.

Notes explicatives: voir p. 454.

[1] Personnes âgées de 15 ans et plus. [2] Estimations basées sur les résultats du Recensement de la population de 2000. [3] Nov. de chaque année.

Notas explicativas: véase p. 457.

[1] Personas de 15 años y más. [2] Estimaciones basadas en los resultados del Censo de población de 2000. [3] Nov. de cada año.

By economic activity — **Par activité économique** — **Por actividad económica**

Thousands — Milliers — Millares

	1999	2000	2001	2002	2003	2004	2005	2006	2007	2008

Kyrgyzstan (BA) [1][2]
Women - Femmes - Mujeres
ISIC 3 - CITI 3 - CIIU 3
Total unemployment - Chômage total - Desempleo total

	1999	2000	2001	2002	2003	2004	2005	2006	2007	2008
Total	.	.	.	132.9	99.2	86.9	87.8	87.5	.	.
UB	.	.	.	50.9	43.0	40.8	34.6	35.6	.	.
A	.	.	.	5.8	8.6	7.0	11.6	10.0	.	.
B	.	.	.	-	0.1	-	-	-	.	.
C	.	.	.	1.6	0.4	-	0.1	0.0	.	.
D	.	.	.	20.2	12.6	9.7	9.2	8.1	.	.
E	.	.	.	0.3	0.3	0.1	0.2	0.1	.	.
F	.	.	.	2.8	1.4	0.7	0.5	0.3	.	.
G	.	.	.	11.1	8.8	8.4	11.2	15.3	.	.
H	.	.	.	4.6	5.2	4.7	5.5	6.7	.	.
I	.	.	.	2.7	1.0	1.2	1.0	0.2	.	.
J	.	.	.	0.7	0.5	0.3	0.1	0.2	.	.
K	.	.	.	3.0	1.0	1.3	1.0	0.6	.	.
L	.	.	.	5.1	2.0	1.7	1.0	1.9	.	.
M	.	.	.	12.5	6.5	5.7	5.7	4.2	.	.
N	.	.	.	6.9	5.9	2.8	3.3	1.9	.	.
O	.	.	.	4.4	1.7	1.9	2.4	2.2	.	.
P	.	.	.	0.4	0.3	0.5	0.4	0.2	.	.
Q	.	.	.	-	-	-	-	0.0	.	.

Macau, China (BA) [3]
Total - Total - Total
ISIC 3 - CITI 3 - CIIU 3
Total unemployment - Chômage total - Desempleo total

	1999	2000	2001	2002	2003	2004	2005	2006	2007	2008
Total	13.2	14.2	14.0	13.7	13.1	11.2	10.3	10.4	9.5	10.1
UB	1.3	1.0	1.0	1.1	1.1	1.2	1.3	1.1	1.3	1.4
A	-	-	-	-	-	-	0.1	-	0.1	.
B	0.0	0.0	0.0	-	-	-	0.0	0.0	-	.
A-C	.	.	.	.	.	.	.	.	.	-
C	0.0	-	0.0	0.0	0.0	0.0	0.0	-	0.0	.
D	2.2	1.9	2.5	2.6	2.4	2.0	1.9	1.6	1.1	0.8
E	0.0	0.0	-	0.0	0.0	0.0	-	-	0.0	0.0
F	3.6	4.3	3.4	2.7	2.2	1.3	1.2	1.4	1.7	2.0
G	1.6	1.8	2.0	2.1	2.0	1.9	1.5	1.5	1.5	1.3
H	1.9	2.0	2.1	2.4	2.4	2.1	1.4	1.7	1.4	1.5
I	0.7	0.6	0.7	0.7	0.6	0.5	0.5	0.5	0.3	0.3
J	0.3	0.3	0.1	0.2	0.1	0.1	-	0.1	0.1	0.1
K	0.5	0.6	0.6	0.5	0.7	0.4	0.5	0.6	0.5	0.7
L	0.1	0.1	0.1	-	0.2	-	0.1	-	-	0.1
M	0.2	0.2	0.2	0.1	0.2	0.2	0.2	0.2	0.1	0.1
N	0.1	0.1	0.1	-	0.1	0.1	0.2	0.1	0.1	-
O	0.7	1.0	1.1	1.0	1.0	1.1	1.2	1.4	1.1	1.7
P	0.1	0.3	0.1	0.2	0.2	0.1	0.2	0.1	0.1	0.2
Q	0.0	0.0	0.0	0.0	0.0	0.0	0.0	0.0	0.0	0.0
X	0.0	0.0	0.0	0.0	0.0	0.0	0.0	0.0	-	0.0

Men - Hommes - Hombres
ISIC 3 - CITI 3 - CIIU 3

	1999	2000	2001	2002	2003	2004	2005	2006	2007	2008
Total	9.1	9.8	9.5	9.1	8.3	6.8	5.8	5.6	5.6	5.7
UB	0.7	0.6	0.6	0.8	0.7	0.8	0.7	0.6	0.8	0.7
A	0.0	-	-	0.0	-	-	-	0.0	-	.
B	0.0	0.0	0.0	-	-	-	0.0	0.0	0.0	.
A-C	.	.	.	.	.	.	.	.	.	0.0
C	0.0	0.0	0.0	0.0	0.0	0.0	0.0	-	0.0	.
D	1.2	1.0	1.4	1.3	1.0	0.9	0.6	0.6	0.4	0.4
E	0.0	0.0	-	0.0	0.0	0.0	0.0	-	0.0	0.0
F	3.4	4.1	3.2	2.6	2.1	1.3	1.1	1.2	1.5	1.7
G	1.0	0.9	1.0	1.1	1.0	0.9	0.8	0.6	0.7	0.5
H	1.2	1.2	1.3	1.5	1.7	1.4	0.8	0.9	0.7	0.7
I	0.4	0.5	0.6	0.5	0.5	0.4	0.4	0.3	0.2	0.2
J	0.1	0.1	0.1	0.1	-	0.1	-	0.1	-	0.1
K	0.4	0.4	0.4	0.3	0.5	0.4	0.4	0.4	0.4	0.4
L	0.1	0.1	0.1	-	0.1	-	-	0.0	-	-
M	0.1	0.1	0.1	0.1	0.1	-	0.1	0.1	-	-
N	-	-	-	0.0	-	-	0.0	0.0	-	-
O	0.5	0.6	0.6	0.6	0.5	0.6	0.8	0.8	0.6	0.9
P	-	-	-	-	-	0.0	-	0.0	-	0.1
Q	0.0	0.0	0.0	0.0	0.0	0.0	0.0	0.0	0.0	0.0
X	0.0	0.0	0.0	0.0	0.0	0.0	0.0	0.0	-	0.0

Explanatory notes: see p. 451.

[1] Persons aged 15 years and over. [2] Nov. of each year. [3] Persons aged 14 years and over.

Notes explicatives: voir p. 454.

[1] Personnes âgées de 15 ans et plus. [2] Nov. de chaque année. [3] Personnes âgées de 14 ans et plus.

Notas explicativas: véase p. 457.

[1] Personas de 15 años y más. [2] Nov. de cada año. [3] Personas de 14 años y más.

3D UNEMPLOYMENT · CHÔMAGE · DESEMPLEO

By economic activity · Par activité économique · Por actividad económica

	Thousands · Milliers · Millares									
	1999	2000	2001	2002	2003	2004	2005	2006	2007	2008

Macau, China (BA) [1]

Total unemployment - Chômage total - Desempleo total
Women - Femmes - Mujeres
ISIC 3 - CITI 3 - CIIU 3

	1999	2000	2001	2002	2003	2004	2005	2006	2007	2008
Total	4.2	4.4	4.5	4.6	4.8	4.4	4.5	4.8	3.9	4.3
UB	0.6	0.4	0.3	0.4	0.4	0.5	0.6	0.5	0.5	0.7
A	-	-		-					-	
B	0.0	0.0	0.0	0.0	0.0	0.0	0.0	0.0	-	
A-C										-
C	0.0		0.0	0.0	0.0	0.0	0.0	0.0	0.0	
D	1.0	0.9	1.0	1.4	1.4	1.1	1.3	1.1	0.7	0.5
E	0.0	0.0	0.0	0.0	0.0	0.0	-	0.0	0.0	0.0
F	0.2	0.2	0.2	0.1	0.1	-	0.1	0.2	0.2	0.3
G	0.6	0.9	0.9	0.9	0.9	1.0	0.7	0.9	0.8	0.8
H	0.7	0.8	0.8	0.9	0.7	0.7	0.7	0.8	0.6	0.7
I	0.3	0.2	0.2	0.1	0.1	0.1	0.1	0.1	0.1	-
J	0.2	0.2	0.1	0.1	0.1	-	0.0	-	0.1	-
K	0.1	0.1	0.2	0.2	0.2	0.1	0.1	0.1	0.2	0.2
L	-	0.0	-	-	-	-	-	-	-	-
M	0.1	0.2	0.2	-	0.1	0.1	0.1	0.2	0.1	0.1
N	-	0.1	-	-	0.1	0.1	0.2	0.1	0.1	0.0
O	0.2	0.4	0.5	0.4	0.5	0.5	0.5	0.6	0.5	0.8
P	0.1	0.2	0.1	0.1	0.2	0.1	0.1	0.1	0.1	0.2
Q	0.0	0.0	0.0	0.0	0.0	0.0	0.0	0.0	0.0	0.0
X	0.0	0.0	0.0	0.0	0.0	0.0	0.0	0.0	-	0.0

Pakistan (BA) [2][3]

Total unemployment - Chômage total - Desempleo total
Total - Total - Total
ISIC 2 - CITI 2 - CIIU 2

	1999	2000	2001	2002	2003	2004	2005	2006	2007	2008
Total	2 334	3 127	3 181	3 506	3 594	3 499	3 566	3 103	2 680	.
UB	2 117	2 658	2 704	3 013	3 089	2 923	2 979	2 683	2 427	.
1	33	101	102	81	83	91	93	56	26	.
2	3	1	1	1	1	-	-	2	1	.
3	34	92	93	104	107	139	142	104	65	.
4	2	4	4	4	4	4	4	4	3	.
5	21	66	67	83	85	102	104	79	37	.
6	28	58	59	61	62	72	73	66	40	.
7	45	37	38	61	63	64	65	28	20	.
8	2	5	6	5	5	9	9	3	9	.
9	49	104	106	92	94	94	96	78	51	.
0	-	1	1	1	1	1	1	-	1	.

Men - Hommes - Hombres
ISIC 2 - CITI 2 - CIIU 2

	1999	2000	2001	2002	2003	2004	2005	2006	2007	2008
Total	1 419	2 046	2 082	2 381	2 441	2 461	2 508	2 166	1 807	.
UB	1 229	1 625	1 654	1 939	1 988	1 984	2 022	1 806	1 582	.
1	26	90	90	71	72	47	48	48	16	.
2	3	1	1	1	1	-	-	2	1	.
3	30	79	80	88	90	119	122	85	58	.
4	2	4	4	4	4	4	4	4	3	.
5	19	65	66	80	82	100	102	78	36	.
6	26	56	57	59	61	63	64	66	40	.
7	45	37	38	60	62	62	63	27	20	.
8	2	5	6	5	5	8	8	3	9	.
9	37	83	85	73	75	73	74	46	41	.
0	-	1	1	1	1	1	1	-	1	.

Women - Femmes - Mujeres
ISIC 2 - CITI 2 - CIIU 2

	1999	2000	2001	2002	2003	2004	2005	2006	2007	2008
Total	915	1 081	1 099	1 125	1 153	1 038	1 058	937	873	.
UB	888	1 033	1 050	1 074	1 101	939	957	878	845	.
1	7	11	12	10	11	44	45	8	10	.
2	-	-	-	-	-	-	-	-	-	.
3	4	13	13	16	17	20	20	19	7	.
4	-	-	-	-	-	-	-	-	-	.
5	2	1	1	3	3	2	2	-	1	.
6	2	2	2	2	1	9	9	-	-	.
7	-	-	-	1	1	2	2	-	-	.
8	-	-	-	-	-	1	1	-	-	.
9	12	21	21	19	19	21	22	32	10	.
0	-	-	-	-	-	-	-	-	-	.

Explanatory notes: see p. 451.

[1] Persons aged 14 years and over. [2] Persons aged 10 years and over. [3] Jan.

Notes explicatives: voir p. 454.

[1] Personnes âgées de 14 ans et plus. [2] Personnes âgées de 10 ans et plus. [3] Janv.

Notas explicativas: véase p. 457.

[1] Personas de 14 años y más. [2] Personas de 10 años y más. [3] Enero.

By economic activity   **Par activité économique**   **Por actividad económica**

	Thousands			Milliers				Millares		
	1999	2000	2001	2002	2003	2004	2005	2006	2007	2008

Pakistan (FB) [1]   **Work applicants - Demandeurs d'emploi - Solicitantes**

Total - Total - Total
ISIC 2 - CITI 2 - CIIU 2

	1999	2000	2001	2002	2003	2004	2005	2006	2007	2008
Total	217	469	477	493	505	576	587	420	.	.
1	33	101	102	81	83	91	93	56	.	.
2	3	1	1	1	1	-	-	2	.	.
3	34	92	93	104	107	139	142	104	.	.
4	2	4	4	4	4	4	4	4	.	.
5	21	66	67	83	85	102	104	79	.	.
6	28	58	59	61	63	72	73	66	.	.
7	45	37	38	61	62	64	65	28	.	.
8	2	5	6	5	5	9	9	3	.	.
9	49	104	106	92	94	94	96	78	.	.
0	-	-	1	1	1	1	1	-	.	.

Men - Hommes - Hombres
ISIC 2 - CITI 2 - CIIU 2

	1999	2000	2001	2002	2003	2004	2005	2006	2007	2008
Total	190	421	428	442	453	477	486	360	.	.
1	26	90	90	71	73	47	48	48	.	.
2	3	1	1	1	1	-	-	2	.	.
3	30	79	80	88	91	119	122	85	.	.
4	2	4	4	4	4	4	4	4	.	.
5	19	65	66	80	82	100	102	79	.	.
6	26	56	57	59	61	63	64	66	.	.
7	45	37	38	60	61	62	63	27	.	.
8	2	5	6	5	5	8	8	3	.	.
9	37	83	85	73	74	73	74	46	.	.
0	-	-	1	1	1	1	1	-	.	.

Women - Femmes - Mujeres
ISIC 2 - CITI 2 - CIIU 2

	1999	2000	2001	2002	2003	2004	2005	2006	2007	2008
Total	27	48	49	51	52	99	101	60	.	.
1	7	11	12	10	10	44	45	8	.	.
3	4	13	13	16	16	20	20	19	.	.
5	2	1	1	3	3	2	2	-	.	.
6	2	2	2	2	2	9	9	-	.	.
7	-	-	-	1	1	2	2	1	.	.
8	-	-	-	-	-	1	1	-	.	.
9	12	21	21	19	20	21	22	32	.	.

Singapore (BA) [2][3]   **Total unemployment - Chômage total - Desempleo total**

Total - Total - Total
ISIC 3 - CITI 3 - CIIU 3   ISIC 4 - CITI 4 - CIIU 4

	1999	2000	2001	2002	2003	2004	2005	2006	2007	2008	
Total	77.5	.	61.9 [4]	94.2	101.0	101.3	.	84.2	74.8	76.2	Total
UB	9.4	.	6.2 [4]	9.1	8.4	8.3	.	6.0	6.7	7.0	UB
A-C,E,X	1.0	.	0.3 [4]	0.9	0.6	0.5	.	0.7	0.8	0.9	B,D,E,X
D	17.1	.	12.4 [4]	18.1	17.5	16.9	.	12.2	12.2	12.2	C
F	6.5	.	5.5 [4]	8.0	7.9	7.5	.	5.0	3.8	3.0	F
G	12.7	.	9.9 [4]	14.8	16.5	16.4	.	15.2	10.5	11.4	G
H	6.4	.	5.9 [4]	8.0	9.7	10.6	.	6.3	6.2	5.8	H
I	6.8	.	5.5 [4]	9.0	11.2	10.1	.	8.7	8.3	8.0	I
J	2.6	.	2.1 [4]	4.4	5.0	4.0	.	4.5	3.4	4.0	J
K	7.1	.	8.2 [4]	12.4	13.9	13.9	.	3.6	2.7	4.0	K
L,M	2.7	.	2.0 [4]	3.3	4.2	6.1	.	1.2	1.2	1.2	L
N	1.5	.	1.0 [4]	1.7	1.9	2.0	.	2.7	3.5	3.9	M
O-Q	3.8	.	2.9 [4]	4.6	4.1	4.9	.	5.9	5.1	5.1	N
								5.7	5.4	4.1	O-P
								2.4	1.4	2.1	Q
								4.1	3.6	3.6	R-U

Men - Hommes - Hombres
ISIC 3 - CITI 3 - CIIU 3   ISIC 4 - CITI 4 - CIIU 4

	1999	2000	2001	2002	2003	2004	2005	2006	2007	2008	
Total	44.3	.	35.7 [4]	55.3	57.6	56.8	.	44.7	40.0	39.6	Total
UB	3.4	.	2.7 [4]	3.7	3.5	3.6	.	2.6	3.3	3.0	UB
A-C,E,X	0.7	.	0.2 [4]	0.8	0.3	0.3	.	0.5	0.5	0.7	B,D,E,X
D	10.0	.	6.6 [4]	10.3	10.5	9.7	.	6.5	6.2	7.4	C
F	5.7	.	4.9 [4]	7.1	6.8	6.5	.	4.0	3.2	2.5	F
G	7.1	.	4.9 [4]	8.1	9.2	8.8	.	7.5	5.4	5.7	G
H	3.5	.	3.4 [4]	5.1	5.3	5.9	.	4.7	4.9	3.9	H
I	4.9	.	4.2 [4]	6.8	7.7	6.9	.	4.9	4.1	4.1	I
J	1.2	.	1.0 [4]	2.0	2.4	1.6	.	2.4	1.8	1.9	J
K	3.7	.	4.6 [4]	6.9	7.6	7.9	.	1.5	1.3	1.6	K
L,M	1.3	.	0.9 [4]	1.2	1.6	2.5	.	0.8	0.6	0.8	L
N	0.4	.	0.4 [4]	0.4	0.4	0.3	.	1.3	1.6	1.7	M
O-Q	2.4	.	1.8 [4]	2.9	2.4	2.9	.	3.4	2.9	2.9	N
								2.4	2.3	1.8	O-P
								0.5	0.3	0.4	Q
								1.8	1.8	1.4	R-U

Explanatory notes: see p. 451.

[1] Persons aged 18 to 60 years. [2] The data refer to the residents (Singapore citizens and permanent residents) aged 15 years and over. [3] June. [4] Methodology revised; data not strictly comparable.

Notes explicatives: voir p. 454.

[1] Personnes âgées de 18 à 60 ans. [2] Les données se réfèrent aux résidents (citoyens de Singapour et résidents permanents) âgés de 15 ans et plus. [3] Juin. [4] Méthodologie révisée; les données ne sont pas strictement comparables.

Notas explicativas: véase p. 457.

[1] Personas de 18 a 60 años. [2] Los datos se refieren a los residentes (ciudadanos de Singapur y residentes permanentes) de 15 años y más. [3] Junio. [4] Metodología revisada; los datos no son estrictamente comparables.

	Thousands			Milliers					Millares		
	1999	2000	2001	2002	2003	2004	2005	2006	2007	2008	

Singapore (BA) [1][2] **Total unemployment - Chômage total - Desempleo total**

Women - Femmes - Mujeres
ISIC 3 - CITI 3 - CIIU 3 / ISIC 4 - CITI 4 - CIIU 4

ISIC 3	1999	2000	2001	2002	2003	2004	2005	2006	2007	2008	ISIC 4
Total	33.3	.	26.2 [3]	39.0	43.4	44.5	.	39.5	34.8	36.6	Total
UB	6.0	.	3.5 [3]	5.4	4.9	4.7	.	3.4	3.4	4.0	UB
A-C,E,X	0.3	.	0.1 [3]	0.1	0.3	0.2	.	0.2	0.3	0.2	B.D.E.X
D	7.0	.	5.7 [3]	7.8	7.0	7.2	.	5.7	6.0	4.8	C
F	0.9	.	0.6 [3]	0.9	1.1	0.9	.	1.1	0.6	0.5	F
G	5.6	.	5.0 [3]	6.7	7.4	7.7	.	7.7	5.1	5.8	G
H	2.9	.	2.5 [3]	2.9	4.4	4.8	.	1.7	1.3	1.9	H
I	1.9	.	1.2 [3]	2.3	3.4	3.2	.	3.8	4.2	3.9	I
J	1.4	.	1.1 [3]	2.4	2.6	2.4	.	2.1	1.7	2.1	J
K	3.3	.	3.6 [3]	5.5	6.3	6.0	.	2.1	1.5	2.3	K
L,M	1.3	.	1.2 [3]	2.0	2.6	3.7	.	0.4	0.6	0.5	L
N	1.1	.	0.6 [3]	1.3	1.6	1.7	.	1.4	1.9	2.2	M
O-Q	1.5	.	1.1 [3]	1.7	1.7	2.0	.	2.6	2.2	2.2	N
							.	3.2	3.1	2.3	O-P
							.	1.9	1.2	1.7	Q
							.	2.3	1.8	2.2	R-U

United Arab Emirates (BA) [4][5] **Total unemployment - Chômage total - Desempleo total**

Total - Total - Total
ISIC 3 - CITI 3 - CIIU 3

	1999	2000	2001	2002	2003	2004	2005	2006	2007	2008
Total	.	.	.	.	.	.	.	.	.	77.108
UB	.	.	.	.	.	.	.	.	.	63.307
A	.	.	.	.	.	.	.	.	.	0.193
C	.	.	.	.	.	.	.	.	.	0.276
D	.	.	.	.	.	.	.	.	.	0.833
E	.	.	.	.	.	.	.	.	.	0.088
F	.	.	.	.	.	.	.	.	.	0.911
G	.	.	.	.	.	.	.	.	.	0.853
H	.	.	.	.	.	.	.	.	.	0.199
I	.	.	.	.	.	.	.	.	.	0.589
J	.	.	.	.	.	.	.	.	.	0.520
K	.	.	.	.	.	.	.	.	.	1.081
L	.	.	.	.	.	.	.	.	.	5.383
M	.	.	.	.	.	.	.	.	.	1.812
N	.	.	.	.	.	.	.	.	.	0.619
O	.	.	.	.	.	.	.	.	.	0.257
P	.	.	.	.	.	.	.	.	.	0.057
Q	.	.	.	.	.	.	.	.	.	0.010
X	.	.	.	.	.	.	.	.	.	0.120

Men - Hommes - Hombres
ISIC 3 - CITI 3 - CIIU 3

	1999	2000	2001	2002	2003	2004	2005	2006	2007	2008
Total	.	.	.	.	.	.	.	.	.	30.254
UB	.	.	.	.	.	.	.	.	.	21.473
A	.	.	.	.	.	.	.	.	.	0.113
C	.	.	.	.	.	.	.	.	.	0.276
D	.	.	.	.	.	.	.	.	.	0.351
E	.	.	.	.	.	.	.	.	.	0.088
F	.	.	.	.	.	.	.	.	.	0.569
G	.	.	.	.	.	.	.	.	.	0.501
H	.	.	.	.	.	.	.	.	.	0.199
I	.	.	.	.	.	.	.	.	.	0.280
J	.	.	.	.	.	.	.	.	.	0.297
K	.	.	.	.	.	.	.	.	.	0.612
L	.	.	.	.	.	.	.	.	.	4.921
M	.	.	.	.	.	.	.	.	.	0.133
N	.	.	.	.	.	.	.	.	.	0.184
O	.	.	.	.	.	.	.	.	.	0.070
P	.	.	.	.	.	.	.	.	.	0.057
Q	.	.	.	.	.	.	.	.	.	0.010
X	.	.	.	.	.	.	.	.	.	0.120

Explanatory notes: see p. 451.

[1] The data refer to the residents (Singapore citizens and permanent residents) aged 15 years and over. [2] June. [3] Methodology revised; data not strictly comparable. [4] February. [5] Persons aged 15 years and over.

Notes explicatives: voir p. 454.

[1] Les données se réfèrent aux résidents (citoyens de Singapour et résidents permanents) âgés de 15 ans et plus. [2] Juin. [3] Méthodologie révisée; les données ne sont pas strictement comparables. [4] Février. [5] Personnes âgées de 15 ans et plus.

Notas explicativas: véase p. 457.

[1] Los datos se refieren a los residentes (ciudadanos de Singapur y residentes permanentes) de 15 años y más. [2] Junio. [3] Metodología revisada; los datos no son estrictamente comparables. [4] Febrero. [5] Personas de 15 años y más.

UNEMPLOYMENT	CHÔMAGE	DESEMPLEO	**3D**
By economic activity	Par activité économique	Por actividad económica	

	Thousands			Milliers				Millares		
	1999	2000	2001	2002	2003	2004	2005	2006	2007	2008

United Arab Emirates (BA) [1] [2]　　　　Total unemployment - Chômage total - Desempleo total

Women - Femmes - Mujeres
ISIC 3 - CITI 3 - CIIU 3

	1999	2000	2001	2002	2003	2004	2005	2006	2007	2008
Total	.	.	.	.	.	.	.	.	.	46.854
UB	.	.	.	.	.	.	.	.	.	41.834
A	.	.	.	.	.	.	.	.	.	0.080
C	.	.	.	.	.	.	.	.	.	-
D	.	.	.	.	.	.	.	.	.	0.482
E	.	.	.	.	.	.	.	.	.	-
F	.	.	.	.	.	.	.	.	.	0.342
G	.	.	.	.	.	.	.	.	.	0.352
H	.	.	.	.	.	.	.	.	.	-
I	.	.	.	.	.	.	.	.	.	0.309
J	.	.	.	.	.	.	.	.	.	0.223
K	.	.	.	.	.	.	.	.	.	0.469
L	.	.	.	.	.	.	.	.	.	0.462
M	.	.	.	.	.	.	.	.	.	1.679
N	.	.	.	.	.	.	.	.	.	0.435
O	.	.	.	.	.	.	.	.	.	0.187
P	.	.	.	.	.	.	.	.	.	-
Q	.	.	.	.	.	.	.	.	.	-
X	.	.	.	.	.	.	.	.	.	-

EUROPE-EUROPE-EUROPA

Austria (BA) [2]　　　　Total unemployment - Chômage total - Desempleo total

Total - Total - Total
ISIC 3 - CITI 3 - CIIU 3

	1999	2000	2001	2002	2003	2004	2005	2006	2007	2008
Total	146.7	138.8	142.5	161.0	168.8 [3]	194.6 [4]	207.7	195.6	185.6	162.3
UB	5.7	10.1	7.2	7.0	8.1 [3]	28.3 [4]	30.7	28.9	28.7	25.3
A	3.1	3.7	4.1	3.3	3.9 [3]	2.4 [4]	2.0	2.4	2.6	1.8
C	0.4	0.2	0.2	0.1	0.3 [3]	0.3 [4]	0.1	0.5	0.1	0.1
D	32.7	28.0	28.0	32.3	32.2 [3]	29.7 [4]	34.2	28.8	26.0	21.5
E	0.4	0.2	0.2	0.8	0.6 [3]	0.1 [4]	0.3	0.1	0.3	0.2
F	23.7	20.5	21.4	25.0	24.2 [3]	18.1 [4]	18.2	19.3	16.8	12.5
G	27.1	25.8	27.4	31.9	32.3 [3]	31.8 [4]	35.8	30.0	32.3	31.1
H	15.0	13.5	14.6	16.5	16.4 [3]	20.5 [4]	19.9	19.3	17.2	16.8
I	7.2	6.3	7.8	9.1	9.3 [3]	8.6 [4]	10.6	10.8	8.6	9.2
J	2.8	1.9	2.7	3.5	4.0 [3]	4.0 [4]	4.2	2.6	2.5	1.9
K	10.7	10.7	11.7	16.5	15.9 [3]	16.4 [4]	16.6	18.3	17.1	15.5
L	2.9	2.4	2.4	3.0	3.4 [3]	4.7 [4]	4.3	4.0	5.1	3.7
M	2.0	2.6	3.3	4.1	3.0 [3]	3.8 [4]	3.5	3.7	3.5	2.6
N	5.8	6.0	6.5	7.2	7.0 [3]	6.6 [4]	8.3	7.5	7.6	6.0
O	6.3	6.3	4.2	7.4	7.5 [3]	7.7 [4]	7.4	10.4	9.4	6.8
P	0.9	0.6	0.9	0.3	0.3 [3]	0.2 [4]	0.4	1.0	0.3	0.3
Q	-	-	0.1	-	0.1 [3]	0.1 [4]	-	0.3	-	0.0
X	-	-	-	-	- [3]	11.2 [4]	11.5	7.5	7.4	7.2

Men - Hommes - Hombres
ISIC 3 - CITI 3 - CIIU 3

	1999	2000	2001	2002	2003	2004	2005	2006	2007	2008
Total	81.7	73.8	77.0	91.7	94.7 [3]	98.0 [4]	107.8	97.1	89.7	81.8
UB	2.2	4.4	3.4	3.4	3.8 [3]	11.7 [4]	14.9	13.2	12.4	11.2
A	1.3	1.7	1.9	1.8	2.1 [3]	1.2 [4]	1.0	1.5	1.3	1.1
C	0.4	0.2	0.2	0.1	0.1 [3]	0.3 [4]	0.1	0.4	0.1	0.1
D	21.1	17.3	18.0	20.7	21.8 [3]	19.5 [4]	22.8	19.2	16.1	14.5
E	0.2	0.2	0.1	0.5	0.2 [3]	- [4]	0.2	0.1	0.3	0.2
F	21.5	19.1	19.6	23.3	22.1 [3]	16.8 [4]	16.7	16.6	15.0	11.6
G	11.3	10.3	11.9	15.1	15.5 [3]	14.3 [4]	15.9	12.9	13.8	13.3
H	5.5	4.2	5.3	6.2	6.2 [3]	5.5 [4]	6.1	5.7	6.6	6.5
I	4.7	4.7	5.4	6.7	7.0 [3]	6.6 [4]	8.0	7.8	5.9	6.4
J	1.2	0.6	0.8	1.2	1.8 [3]	1.8 [4]	2.4	1.0	0.7	0.9
K	5.9	5.7	5.0	7.3	6.1 [3]	8.5 [4]	8.2	8.5	6.8	6.2
L	1.2	1.4	1.4	1.4	1.5 [3]	3.0 [4]	2.8	1.8	2.6	2.5
M	0.6	0.8	0.8	1.3	0.8 [3]	1.1 [4]	0.5	0.6	0.7	0.9
N	1.1	0.8	1.7	2.7	1.7 [3]	1.2 [4]	1.5	1.4	1.6	1.8
O	3.4	2.6	1.3	3.4	3.7 [3]	2.7 [4]	3.1	4.7	3.7	2.3
P	-	-	0.1	0.1	0.2 [3]	- [4]	-	-	-	0.1
Q	-	-	-	-	- [3]	- [4]	-	0.3	-	0.0
X	-	-	-	-	- [3]	3.9 [4]	3.7	1.4	2.1	2.3

Explanatory notes: see p. 451.

[1] February. [2] Persons aged 15 years and over. [3] Prior to 2003: May and November of each year. [4] Methodology revised; data not strictly comparable.

Notes explicatives: voir p. 454.

[1] Février. [2] Personnes âgées de 15 ans et plus. [3] Avant 2003: mai et novembre de chaque année. [4] Méthodologie révisée; les données ne sont pas strictement comparables.

Notas explicativas: véase p. 457.

[1] Febrero. [2] Personas de 15 años y más. [3] Antes de 2003: mayo y noviembre de cada año. [4] Metodología revisada; los datos no son estrictamente comparables.

UNEMPLOYMENT	CHÔMAGE	DESEMPLEO
By economic activity	**Par activité économique**	**Por actividad económica**

	Thousands				Milliers				Millares	
	1999	2000	2001	2002	2003	2004	2005	2006	2007	2008

Austria (BA) [1]

Total unemployment - Chômage total - Desempleo total

Women - Femmes - Mujeres
ISIC 3 - CITI 3 - CIIU 3

	1999	2000	2001	2002	2003	2004	2005	2006	2007	2008
Total	65.0	65.0	65.5	69.3	74.3 [2]	96.6 [3]	100.0	98.5	95.8	80.5
UB	3.5	5.7	3.8	3.6	4.3 [2]	16.6 [3]	15.8	15.7	16.3	14.1
A	1.8	2.1	2.2	1.5	1.8 [2]	1.3 [3]	1.0	0.9	1.3	0.7
C	-	-	-	-	- [2]	- [3]	-	0.1	0.1	-
D	11.5	10.7	10.1	11.6	10.4 [2]	10.2 [3]	11.5	9.6	9.9	7.1
E	0.3	-	0.1	0.3	0.4 [2]	0.1 [3]	0.1	0.1	-	-
F	2.2	1.4	1.8	1.7	2.1 [2]	1.3 [3]	1.5	2.7	1.9	0.9
G	15.8	15.5	15.4	16.8	16.8 [2]	17.5 [3]	19.9	17.1	18.5	17.8
H	9.5	9.3	9.2	10.3	10.3 [2]	15.0 [3]	13.8	13.6	10.6	10.4
I	2.4	1.6	2.3	2.4	2.3 [2]	2.0 [3]	2.6	3.0	2.7	2.8
J	1.6	1.2	1.8	2.3	2.2 [2]	2.2 [3]	1.8	1.5	1.7	1.1
K	4.8	5.0	6.7	9.2	9.8 [2]	7.9 [3]	8.4	9.9	10.3	9.3
L	1.7	1.1	1.0	1.5	1.9 [2]	1.7 [3]	1.5	2.2	2.6	1.2
M	1.5	1.9	2.5	2.8	2.2 [2]	2.8 [3]	3.0	3.1	2.8	1.7
N	4.7	5.2	4.8	4.5	5.3 [2]	5.4 [3]	6.7	6.1	5.9	4.2
O	2.8	3.7	2.9	4.0	3.8 [2]	5.0 [3]	4.3	5.7	5.7	4.4
P	0.9	0.6	0.8	0.2	0.6 [2]	0.2 [3]	0.4	1.0	0.3	0.2
Q	-	-	0.1	-	0.1 [2]	0.1 [3]	-	-	-	-
X	-	-	-	-	- [2]	7.3 [3]	7.8	6.1	5.3	4.8

Austria (FB) [1]

Registered unemployment - Chômage enregistré - Desempleo registrado

Total - Total - Total
ISIC 3 - CITI 3 - CIIU 3 / ISIC 4 - CITI 4 - CIIU 4

ISIC 3	1999	2000	2001	2002	2003	2004	2005	2006	2007	2008	ISIC 4
Total	221.7	194.3	203.9	232.4	240.1	243.9	252.7	239.2	222.1	212.3	Total
A	3.9	3.5	3.6	3.9	3.8	3.9	4.1	4.0	3.6	1.5	A
B	0.1	0.1	0.1	0.1	0.1	0.1	-	-	-	0.8	B
C	0.7	0.6	0.7	0.8	0.8	0.9	1.0	1.0	0.9	22.2	C
D	41.8	35.0	35.4	41.9	42.5	41.8	42.5	38.5	34.5	0.2	D
E	0.4	0.4	0.5	0.5	0.5	0.5	0.5	0.5	0.5	0.7	E
F	39.1	36.1	39.8	43.0	42.6	42.1	42.7	39.9	35.3	24.3	F
G	41.6	34.9	35.5	40.3	40.9	41.6	42.4	39.9	37.4	33.0	G
H	32.4	29.3	29.7	31.9	32.8	34.5	36.0	34.9	33.5	11.1	H
I	8.9	7.7	8.3	9.4	9.9	10.3	10.8	10.4	9.4	28.8	I
J	2.8	2.4	2.3	2.7	2.9	2.8	2.9	2.7	2.6	3.4	J
K	15.1	13.3	14.3	17.0	18.4	19.2	20.5	20.2	19.4	2.4	K
L	8.5	7.2	6.7	7.3	7.4	7.2	7.1	6.6	6.2	2.5	L
M	2.3	2.0	2.0	2.2	2.3	2.5	2.7	2.6	2.6	6.6	M
N	6.4	5.7	5.5	6.2	6.6	7.0	7.4	7.5	7.5	33.3	N
O	9.4	8.7	9.0	10.9	12.5	13.4	14.2	13.3	13.2	7.2	O
P	0.6	0.5	0.5	0.5	0.5	0.5	0.6	0.6	0.5	3.0	P
Q	0.1	0.1	0.2	0.2	0.2	0.2	0.2	0.2	0.2	11.3	Q
X	7.5	6.9	9.8	13.6	15.3	15.4	17.3	16.3	14.9	3.1	R
										6.0	S
										0.3	T
										0.1	U
										10.6	X

Men - Hommes - Hombres
ISIC 3 - CITI 3 - CIIU 3 / ISIC 4 - CITI 4 - CIIU 4

ISIC 3	1999	2000	2001	2002	2003	2004	2005	2006	2007	2008	ISIC 4
Total	121.5	107.5	115.3	134.4	139.7	140.3	144.2	135.8	124.3	118.8	Total
A	2.3	2.1	2.2	2.4	2.4	2.4	2.5	2.5	2.2	0.9	A
B	-	-	-	-	-	-	-	-	-	0.7	B
C	0.6	0.5	0.6	0.7	0.7	0.8	0.8	0.9	0.8	14.3	C
D	25.8	21.7	22.4	27.3	28.1	27.2	27.7	25.0	22.3	0.2	D
E	0.3	0.3	0.3	0.4	0.4	0.4	0.4	0.4	0.4	0.5	E
F	34.7	32.3	36.0	38.9	38.7	38.2	38.8	36.3	31.9	22.3	F
G	18.7	15.7	16.4	19.4	20.0	20.0	20.2	18.9	17.4	14.7	G
H	11.1	10.1	10.5	11.9	12.7	13.3	13.8	13.4	12.8	8.5	H
I	6.6	5.8	6.2	7.1	7.4	7.7	8.1	7.8	7.0	10.9	I
J	1.6	1.3	1.2	1.5	1.6	1.5	1.5	1.4	1.4	2.0	J
K	6.8	5.9	6.4	8.1	9.0	9.5	10.1	10.0	9.8	1.2	K
L	4.4	3.7	3.5	3.9	3.9	3.8	3.7	3.4	3.2	1.1	L
M	0.6	0.5	0.5	0.6	0.7	0.7	0.8	0.8	0.8	3.0	M
N	1.4	1.2	1.2	1.4	1.6	1.7	1.7	1.8	1.8	21.2	N
O	3.7	3.5	3.7	4.6	5.4	5.8	6.1	5.7	5.6	3.3	O
P	0.0	0.0	0.0	0.0	0.0	0.1	0.1	0.1	0.1	1.3	P
Q	0.1	0.1	0.1	0.1	0.1	0.1	0.1	0.1	0.1	4.0	Q
X	2.7	2.7	3.9	6.0	7.0	7.0	7.9	7.3	6.7	1.7	R
										2.0	S
										0.1	T
										-	U
										5.1	X

Explanatory notes: see p. 451.

[1] Persons aged 15 years and over. [2] Prior to 2003: May and November of each year. [3] Methodology revised; data not strictly comparable.

Notes explicatives: voir p. 454.

[1] Personnes âgées de 15 ans et plus. [2] Avant 2003: mai et novembre de chaque année. [3] Méthodologie révisée; les données ne sont pas strictement comparables.

Notas explicativas: véase p. 457.

[1] Personas de 15 años y más. [2] Antes de 2003: mayo y noviembre de cada año. [3] Metodología revisada; los datos no son estrictamente comparables.

	Thousands				Milliers				Millares		
	1999	2000	2001	2002	2003	2004	2005	2006	2007	2008	

Austria (FB) [1]   Registered unemployment - Chômage enregistré - Desempleo registrado

Women - Femmes - Mujeres
ISIC 3 - CITI 3 - CIIU 3   ISIC 4 - CITI 4 - CIIU 4

	1999	2000	2001	2002	2003	2004	2005	2006	2007		2008	
Total	100.2	86.8	88.6	98.0	100.4	103.6	108.4	103.4	97.9	|	93.4	Total
A	1.5	1.4	1.4	1.5	1.5	1.5	1.6	1.5	1.4	|	0.6	A
B	-	-	-	-	-	-	-	-	-	|	0.1	B
C	0.1	0.1	0.1	0.1	0.1	0.1	0.1	0.1	0.1	|	7.9	C
D	16.1	13.3	13.0	14.6	14.5	14.5	14.8	13.5	12.3	|	0.1	D
E	0.1	0.1	0.1	0.1	0.1	0.1	0.1	0.1	0.1	|	0.2	E
F	4.4	3.8	3.9	4.1	3.9	3.9	3.9	3.6	3.4	|	2.0	F
G	22.9	19.1	19.1	20.9	20.9	21.6	22.2	21.0	20.0	|	18.3	G
H	21.3	19.2	19.2	20.0	20.1	21.2	22.1	21.5	20.7	|	2.6	H
I	2.3	2.0	2.1	2.3	2.5	2.2	2.7	2.6	2.3	|	17.9	I
J	1.2	1.1	1.1	1.2	1.3	1.3	1.4	1.3	1.2	|	1.4	J
K	8.4	7.3	7.8	8.9	9.4	9.8	10.4	10.2	9.6	|	1.2	K
L	4.0	3.4	3.2	3.4	3.5	3.4	3.4	3.2	3.0	|	1.4	L
M	1.7	1.5	1.5	1.6	1.6	1.8	1.9	1.8	1.8	|	3.6	M
N	5.0	4.4	4.3	4.8	5.0	5.4	5.7	5.7	5.7	|	12.1	N
O	5.7	5.2	5.4	6.3	7.0	7.6	8.1	7.6	7.5	|	3.9	O
P	0.6	0.5	0.4	0.5	0.5	0.5	0.5	0.5	0.4	|	1.8	P
Q	0.1	0.1	0.1	0.1	0.1	0.1	0.1	0.1	0.1	|	7.3	Q
X	4.8	4.3	5.9	7.5	8.3	8.4	9.4	8.9	8.2	|	1.4	R
										|	4.0	S
										|	0.2	T
										|	-	U
										|	5.6	X

Belgique (BA) [1]   Total unemployment - Chômage total - Desempleo total

Total - Total - Total
ISIC 3 - CITI 3 - CIIU 3

	1999	2000	2001	2002	2003	2004	2005	2006	2007	2008
Total	.	.	286.4	332.1	364.3	380.3	391.0	383.2	353.0	333.7
UB	.	.	105.0	118.7	123.4	125.5	84.2	80.9	79.0	74.0
A	.	.	1.6	2.4	2.9	4.3	3.3	2.8	3.8	4.3
B	.	.	-	0.1	0.2	-	0.1	0.1	.	.
C	.	.	1.0	0.5	1.1	0.6	0.7	0.7	0.1	0.1
D	.	.	37.0	47.4	52.8	52.0	50.9	49.6	38.9	39.1
E	.	.	0.9	1.0	0.9	2.3	1.7	1.2	1.1	1.4
F	.	.	13.8	15.9	18.7	18.9	19.1	18.4	18.8	17.2
G	.	.	37.9	37.9	43.9	47.1	48.2	45.3	42.7	39.6
H	.	.	12.4	16.7	17.7	19.1	20.2	21.1	20.1	18.0
I	.	.	12.7	14.0	15.6	16.9	18.3	18.6	15.0	13.5
J	.	.	4.2	4.4	4.0	5.6	5.2	4.9	4.5	4.6
K	.	.	15.8	21.6	28.2	21.7	25.8	26.0	26.2	24.7
L	.	.	9.6	10.5	12.2	14.4	14.6	16.6	13.8	12.7
M	.	.	7.6	8.1	10.2	14.4	13.3	14.2	12.5	12.7
N	.	.	14.1	18.9	18.2	22.6	21.8	19.5	21.8	19.0
O	.	.	10.6	12.2	12.0	12.6	17.4	15.0	15.6	11.9
P	.	.	1.8	1.0	2.0	1.3	1.6	1.5	2.3	2.3
Q	.	.	0.6	0.7	0.4	1.0	1.1	0.9	1.0	1.0
X	.	.	-	-	-	-	43.5	45.9	35.8	37.3

Men - Hommes - Hombres
ISIC 3 - CITI 3 - CIIU 3

	1999	2000	2001	2002	2003	2004	2005	2006	2007	2008
Total	.	.	147.9	168.1	193.0	191.4	196.4	191.0	174.4	170.4
UB	.	.	50.0	54.4	58.4	55.0	40.6	35.0	33.3	35.5
A	.	.	1.2	1.5	1.9	3.3	1.7	1.8	2.8	3.5
B	.	.	-	0.1	0.2	-	0.1	0.1	.	.
C	.	.	1.0	0.4	1.0	0.5	0.7	0.5	0.1	0.1
D	.	.	24.6	30.9	35.5	34.1	32.9	31.0	27.2	25.7
E	.	.	0.7	0.7	0.7	1.3	1.2	1.0	0.8	1.0
F	.	.	12.7	15.0	17.7	17.6	17.4	17.3	17.8	16.4
G	.	.	17.0	16.4	19.8	20.8	22.7	22.1	19.2	18.2
H	.	.	6.4	7.4	8.6	8.0	9.4	9.8	9.6	9.0
I	.	.	9.1	10.4	11.8	12.1	12.0	13.7	10.6	9.9
J	.	.	1.8	1.8	1.8	2.7	2.0	1.9	1.8	1.7
K	.	.	8.5	11.6	16.1	11.9	12.6	12.7	13.2	11.9
L	.	.	4.9	5.5	5.7	7.3	7.2	8.8	5.9	7.5
M	.	.	2.5	1.4	3.1	5.0	3.2	3.7	3.2	3.5
N	.	.	2.3	4.0	3.7	5.1	5.9	4.8	5.4	4.2
O	.	.	4.7	6.2	6.1	6.2	7.8	6.4	6.8	6.0
P	.	.	0.2	-	0.6	0.3	0.2	0.3	0.4	0.2
Q	.	.	0.3	0.2	0.2	0.3	0.5	0.2	0.4	0.4
X	.	.	-	-	-	-	18.2	20.0	15.9	15.7

Explanatory notes: see p. 451.   Notes explicatives: voir p. 454.   Notas explicativas: véase p. 457.

[1] Persons aged 15 years and over.   [1] Personnes âgées de 15 ans et plus.   [1] Personas de 15 años y más.

UNEMPLOYMENT   CHÔMAGE   DESEMPLEO

By economic activity   Par activité économique   Por actividad económica

	Thousands — Milliers — Millares									
	1999	2000	2001	2002	2003	2004	2005	2006	2007	2008

Belgique (BA) [1]

Total unemployment - Chômage total - Desempleo total

Women - Femmes - Mujeres
ISIC 3 - CITI 3 - CIIU 3

	1999	2000	2001	2002	2003	2004	2005	2006	2007	2008
Total			138.4	164.0	171.3	188.9	194.6	192.2	178.6	163.2
UB			55.1	64.3	64.9	70.5	43.6	45.9	45.6	38.5
A			0.3	0.8	1.0	1.0	1.5	1.0	1.0	0.9
B			..	-	-	-	-	-	-	-
C			-	0.1	0.1	0.1	0.1	0.1	0.0	0.0
D			12.4	16.4	17.3	18.0	18.0	18.6	11.8	13.4
E			0.2	0.4	0.3	1.0	0.5	0.2	0.3	0.5
F			1.1	0.9	1.0	1.2	1.7	1.2	1.0	0.8
G			20.9	21.5	24.1	26.3	25.5	23.2	23.5	21.4
H			6.0	9.4	9.1	11.2	10.8	11.3	10.5	9.0
I			3.6	3.5	3.7	4.8	6.3	4.9	4.4	3.6
J			2.4	2.6	2.2	2.9	3.1	3.0	2.7	2.9
K			7.3	10.0	12.1	9.8	13.2	13.3	13.0	12.8
L			4.7	5.0	6.4	7.1	7.4	7.8	7.9	5.2
M			5.1	6.8	7.1	9.5	10.1	10.5	9.3	9.2
N			11.8	14.9	14.5	17.5	16.0	14.7	16.4	14.7
O			5.9	6.0	6.0	6.4	9.6	8.6	8.8	5.9
P			1.6	1.0	1.3	1.0	1.4	1.2	1.9	2.2
Q			0.2	0.5	0.2	0.7	0.6	0.7	0.6	0.6
X			-	-	-	-	25.3	25.9	19.9	21.6

Bulgaria (BA) [2]

Total unemployment - Chômage total - Desempleo total

Total - Total - Total
ISIC 3 - CITI 3 - CIIU 3 .... ISIC 4 - CITI 4 - CIIU 4

ISIC 3	1999	2000	2001	2002	2003	2004	2005	2006	2007	2008	ISIC 4
Total	559.0[3]		661.1[3]	599.2[3]	449.1	399.8	334.2	305.7	240.2|	199.7	Total
UB	103.2[3]		153.9[3]	139.1[3]	99.6	87.7	74.2	65.9	53.2|	41.7	UB
A-B				34.4[3]	25.5	23.4	24.7	24.2	19.4|	17.4	A
A	53.0[3]		40.1[3]							1.1	B
B	0.3[3]		0.7[3]							29.1	C
C	7.9[3]		5.5[3]	8.0[3]	4.9	4.1	3.9	3.1	1.3|	0.9	D
D	159.6[3]		143.2[3]	117.6[3]	83.9	71.1	59.8	50.8	33.2|	7.0	E
E	2.6[3]		3.1[3]	3.7[3]	2.8	2.1	2.2	2.5	1.7|	15.5	F
F	33.3[3]		37.3[3]	38.2[3]	25.8	25.2	20.3	17.9	14.6|	16.7	G
G	55.0[3]		52.7[3]	50.5[3]	40.6	36.8	28.2	25.9	18.5|	4.3	H
H	26.1[3]		24.3[3]	22.1[3]	20.6	19.1	17.2	15.2	11.1|	9.3	I
I	24.6[3]		25.8[3]	17.5[3]	16.5	15.3	12.6	12.7	8.7|	2.3	J
J	4.8[3]		3.7[3]	3.7[3]	2.0	2.0	1.4	0.6	0.3|	1.0	K
K	7.3[3]		10.1[3]	11.4[3]	10.3	10.4	6.6	6.1	4.1|	0.1	L
L	29.5[3]		31.6[3]	29.2[3]	20.6	16.9	11.5	9.8	9.0|	1.1	M
M	18.2[3]		20.7[3]	20.4[3]	14.0	11.6	8.9	9.6	7.6|	7.1	N
N	14.3[3]		17.0[3]	15.5[3]	10.3	8.1	7.2	5.2	5.2|	7.6	O
O	17.8[3]		17.5[3]	16.1[3]						5.5	P
O-Q					14.3	17.2	17.5	19.1	17.5|	3.7	Q
P	0.1[3]		0.1[3]	-[3]						1.2	R
Q	0.1[3]		-[3]							1.8	S-U
X	1.4[3]		73.9[3]	71.8[3]	57.7	48.9	38.0	37.4	34.9|	25.2	X

Men - Hommes - Hombres
ISIC 3 - CITI 3 - CIIU 3 .... ISIC 4 - CITI 4 - CIIU 4

ISIC 3	1999	2000	2001	2002	2003	2004	2005	2006	2007	2008	ISIC 4
Total	306.3[3]		363.2[3]	328.7[3]	246.1	221.6	182.5	156.4	120.7|	103.9	Total
UB	63.4[3]		86.7[3]	81.8[3]	59.7	48.7	41.2	34.1	29.3|	24.9	UB
A-B				20.7[3]	15.9	15.5	15.3	14.8	10.4|	10.3	A
A	31.0[3]		25.2[3]							0.8	B
B	0.1[3]		0.7[3]							12.5	C
C	6.4[3]		4.5[3]	6.7[3]	3.8	3.3	3.1	2.5	1.0|	0.6	D
D	78.8[3]		78.2[3]	62.1[3]	42.3	36.6	29.8	21.9	13.9|	3.0	E
E	1.9[3]		2.4[3]	3.3[3]	2.0	1.5	1.6	1.8	1.2|	14.7	F
F	29.1[3]		32.7[3]	34.1[3]	22.1	23.2	18.5	16.3	13.5|	6.1	G
G	26.8[3]		25.6[3]	22.8[3]	18.2	18.4	13.3	11.0	7.5|	3.4	H
H	10.9[3]		10.0[3]	8.3[3]	7.0	6.4	6.9	5.5	4.0|	2.7	I
I	16.6[3]		19.5[3]	12.3[3]	11.6	11.8	9.2	8.1	6.0|	1.3	J
J	1.8[3]		0.2[3]	1.2[3]	0.5	0.7	0.6	0.1	0.1|	0.3	K
K	3.4[3]		5.0[3]	6.6[3]	5.9	6.0	4.0	3.8	2.6|	0.5	L
L	16.7[3]		17.7[3]	17.4[3]	11.6	10.1	6.0	5.4	4.7|	3.6	M
M	5.9[3]		5.9[3]	3.7[3]	3.2	2.7	2.1	2.2	1.3|	4.4	N
N	3.5[3]		3.2[3]	3.6[3]	2.6	1.6	1.9	1.0	0.8|	0.8	O
O	9.3[3]		9.2[3]	8.8[3]						1.0	Q
O-Q					7.8	9.2	8.9	8.4	7.6|	0.4	R
P	-[3]		-[3]	-[3]						0.4	S-U
Q	-[3]		-[3]	-[3]						12.1	X
X	1.0[3]		36.6[3]	35.2[3]	31.9	25.8	20.1	19.5	17.1|		X

Explanatory notes: see p. 451.   Notes explicatives: voir p. 454.   Notas explicativas: véase p. 457.

[1] Persons aged 15 years and over. [2] Persons aged 15 to 74 years. [3] June. — [1] Personnes âgées de 15 ans et plus. [2] Personnes âgées de 15 à 74 ans. [3] Juin. — [1] Personas de 15 años y más. [2] Personas de 15 a 74 años. [3] Junio.

| By economic activity | Par activité économique | Por actividad económica |

Thousands			Milliers			Millares			
1999	2000	2001	2002	2003	2004	2005	2006	2007	2008

Bulgaria (BA) [1] — Total unemployment - Chômage total - Desempleo total

Women - Femmes - Mujeres
ISIC 3 - CITI 3 - CIIU 3 / ISIC 4 - CITI 4 - CIIU 4

	1999	2000	2001	2002	2003	2004	2005	2006	2007	2008	
Total	.	252.6 [2]	297.8 [2]	270.4 [2]	203.0	178.2	151.6	149.3	119.5 [1]	95.8	Total
UB	.	39.8 [2]	67.2 [2]	57.3 [2]	40.0	39.1	33.0	31.8	24.0 [1]	16.8	UB
A-B	.	.	.	13.7 [2]	9.6	8.0	9.4	9.4	9.0 [1]	7.1	A
A	.	22.0 [2]	14.9 [2]	.	.	.	.	.	. [1]	0.2	B
B	.	0.1 [2]	- [2]	.	.	.	.	.	. [1]	16.5	C
C	.	1.5 [2]	1.0 [2]	1.2 [2]	1.2	0.7	0.8	0.6	0.3 [1]	0.3	D
D	.	80.8 [2]	65.1 [2]	55.5 [2]	41.6	34.4	29.9	28.9	19.3 [1]	4.0	E
E	.	0.7 [2]	0.7 [2]	0.5 [2]	0.9	0.6	0.6	0.8	0.4 [1]	0.8	F
F	.	4.2 [2]	4.6 [2]	4.0 [2]	3.6	2.1	1.8	1.6	1.2 [1]	10.6	G
G	.	28.2 [2]	27.1 [2]	27.7 [2]	22.4	18.4	14.8	14.9	11.0 [1]	0.9	H
H	.	15.1 [2]	14.3 [2]	13.8 [2]	13.6	12.7	10.3	9.7	7.1 [1]	6.7	I
I	.	8.0 [2]	6.3 [2]	5.2 [2]	4.9	3.5	3.4	4.7	2.7 [1]	1.0	J
J	.	3.0 [2]	3.4 [2]	2.6 [2]	1.5	1.4	0.8	0.5	0.3 [1]	0.7	K
K	.	3.9 [2]	5.0 [2]	4.8 [2]	4.2	4.2	2.6	2.2	1.5 [1]	0.1	L
L	.	12.7 [2]	13.9 [2]	11.8 [2]	8.9	6.9	5.5	4.4	4.4 [1]	0.6	M
M	.	12.4 [2]	14.8 [2]	16.7 [2]	10.8	8.9	6.8	7.4	6.3 [1]	3.5	N
N	.	10.7 [2]	13.8 [2]	11.8 [2]	7.7	6.4	5.3	4.2	4.4 [1]	3.3	O
O	.	8.6 [2]	8.3 [2]	7.2 [2]	.	.	.	.	. [1]	4.6	P
O-Q	.	.	.	.	6.5	8.0	8.6	10.7	9.8 [1]	2.7	Q
P	.	0.1 [2]	0.1 [2]	.	.	.	.	.	. [1]	0.8	R
Q	.	0.1 [2]	- [2]	- [2]	.	.	.	.	. [1]	1.4	S-U
X	.	0.7 [2]	37.3 [2]	36.6 [2]	25.8	23.1	17.9	17.8	17.7 [1]	13.1	X

Croatia (BA) [3] — Total unemployment - Chômage total - Desempleo total

Total - Total - Total
ISIC 3 - CITI 3 - CIIU 3

	1999	2000	2001	2002	2003	2004	2005	2006	2007	2008
Total	.	.	.	.	255.7	249.7	229.1	198.7	171.0	149.2
UB	.	.	.	.	85.0	79.3	67.1	59.5	49.3 [4]	45.9
A	.	.	.	.	7.4	8.2	7.6	6.1	6.9 [4]	5.8 [4]
D	.	.	.	.	47.7	48.0	47.7	37.7	35.4 [4]	29.5 [4]
F	.	.	.	.	19.4	16.2	14.2	16.2	13.5 [4]	8.7 [4]
G	.	.	.	.	34.5	34.3	35.2	28.4	22.3 [4]	21.3 [4]
H	.	.	.	.	25.0	25.2	18.2	19.2	16.7 [4]	14.5 [4]
I	.	.	.	.	8.9	8.2	9.2	5.8	7.6 [4]	7.5 [4]
J	.	.	.	.	2.2	2.2	2.3	4.1	3.0 [4]	.
K	.	.	.	.	4.3	6.0	5.9	6.1	4.0 [4]	.
L	.	.	.	.	5.2	6.4	5.6	3.5	3.0 [4]	.
M	.	.	.	.	3.9	3.7	3.8	2.7	2.0 [4]	.
N	.	.	.	.	3.5	3.2	3.2	2.8	1.0 [4]	.
O	.	.	.	.	4.7	5.1	5.5	4.6	5.0 [4]	.
P	.	.	.	.	2.1	1.9	1.4	2.0	1.3 [4]	.

Men - Hommes - Hombres
ISIC 3 - CITI 3 - CIIU 3

	1999	2000	2001	2002	2003	2004	2005	2006	2007	2008
Total	.	.	.	.	127.7	120.0	114.4	94.4	81.6	67.9
UB	.	.	.	.	40.4	37.1	31.6	26.3	21.4 [4]	20.0 [4]
A	.	.	.	.	4.7	5.2	4.5	3.3	4.4 [4]	.
D	.	.	.	.	23.4	21.9	25.5	18.3	14.8 [4]	13.0 [4]
F	.	.	.	.	18.0	14.9	13.1	14.8	12.8 [4]	8.1 [4]
G	.	.	.	.	13.7	12.4	13.8	10.1	7.3 [4]	7.2 [4]
H	.	.	.	.	10.1	9.2	7.5	7.5	7.0 [4]	4.4 [4]
I	.	.	.	.	6.4	6.2	7.2	4.5	5.9 [4]	5.8 [4]
J	.	.	.	.	-	0.6	0.8	1.5	1.5 [4]	.
K	.	.	.	.	2.2	3.0	2.7	3.0	2.0 [4]	.
L	.	.	.	.	3.2	4.2	3.6	0.9	1.0 [4]	.
M	.	.	.	.	0.4	0.9	0.8	0.9	1.0 [4]	.
N	.	.	.	.	0.5	0.5	0.9	0.5	1.0 [4]	.
O	.	.	.	.	2.5	2.1	1.9	2.3	1.0 [4]	.
P	.	.	.	.	-	0.5	0.9	0.5	0.5 [4]	.

Women - Femmes - Mujeres
ISIC 3 - CITI 3 - CIIU 3

	1999	2000	2001	2002	2003	2004	2005	2006	2007	2008
Total	.	.	.	.	128.1	129.7	114.7	104.2	89.4	81.3
UB	.	.	.	.	44.6	42.1	35.4	33.2	27.9 [4]	25.9 [4]
A	.	.	.	.	2.7	3.0	3.1	2.8	2.5 [4]	.
D	.	.	.	.	24.3	26.1	22.1	19.4	20.6 [4]	16.5 [4]
F	.	.	.	.	1.4	1.3	1.1	1.4	0.7 [4]	0.6 [4]
G	.	.	.	.	20.8	21.9	21.5	18.4	15.0 [4]	14.1 [4]
H	.	.	.	.	14.8	16.0	10.7	12.3	9.7 [4]	10.1 [4]
I	.	.	.	.	2.5	1.9	2.0	1.3	1.7 [4]	1.7 [4]
J	.	.	.	.	-	1.6	1.7	2.6	1.5 [4]	.
K	.	.	.	.	2.1	2.9	3.3	3.1	2.0 [4]	.
L	.	.	.	.	2.0	2.2	2.0	2.6	2.0 [4]	.
M	.	.	.	.	3.6	2.8	2.9	1.8	1.0 [4]	.
N	.	.	.	.	3.0	2.7	2.3	2.3	- [5]	.
O	.	.	.	.	2.2	3.0	3.6	2.3	4.0 [4]	.
P	.	.	.	.	-	1.4	0.5	1.5	0.8 [4]	.

Explanatory notes: see p. 451.

[1] Persons aged 15 to 74 years. [2] June. [3] Persons aged 15 years and over. [4] Estimate not sufficiently reliable. [5] Not indicated due to lack of statistical reliability.

Notes explicatives: voir p. 454.

[1] Personnes âgées de 15 à 74 ans. [2] Juin. [3] Personnes âgées de 15 ans et plus. [4] Estimation pas suffisamment fiable. [5] Non indiqué en raison du manque de fiabilité statistique.

Notas explicativas: véase p. 457.

[1] Personas de 15 a 74 años. [2] Junio. [3] Personas de 15 años y más. [4] Estimación no suficientemente fiable. [5] No se indica por la falta de confiabilidad estadística.

By economic activity   **Par activité économique**   **Por actividad económica**

	Thousands				Milliers				Millares		
	1999	2000	2001	2002	2003	2004	2005	2006	2007	2008	

Croatia (FB) ¹   Registered unemployment - Chômage enregistré - Desempleo registrado

Total - Total - Total
ISIC 3 - CITI 3 - CIIU 3   ISIC 4 - CITI 4 - CIIU 4

	1999	2000	2001	2002	2003	2004	2005	2006	2007	2008	
Total	342.0	378.0	395.0	366.0	318.0	318.0	308.0	293.2	254.5	240.5	Total
UB	99.3	105.1	106.8	92.0	76.8	74.5	69.6	65.6	51.7	44.9	UB
A	11.3	12.2	12.1	12.2	11.7	12.2	12.0	10.5	9.3	8.8	A
B	0.5	0.5	0.5	0.6	0.5	0.5	0.5	0.5	0.5	0.5	B
C	1.1	1.1	1.0	0.8	0.6	0.7	0.7	0.6	0.5	48.1	C
D	64.2	72.6	75.5	74.2	66.0	64.1	61.2	56.2	50.1	0.3	D
E	1.1	1.3	1.3	1.2	1.0	1.0	0.9	0.9	0.8	1.6	E
F	24.8	28.3	28.5	24.6	20.2	21.4	20.5	18.7	16.3	15.6	F
G	44.7	52.3	55.1	53.6	48.2	49.7	49.0	46.6	41.3	38.7	G
H	35.2	38.7	41.9	35.5	30.5	30.5	30.5	31.2	27.5	5.4	H
I	11.4	11.6	11.5	10.3	8.9	9.0	9.5	9.0	8.1	26.2	I
J	2.7	3.1	3.0	2.6	2.5	2.4	2.2	2.1	2.0	2.3	J
K	12.0	12.6	12.7	12.0	10.5	11.1	11.6	12.9	12.1	2.0	K
L	5.9	6.4	7.7	7.7	6.0	5.0	4.8	4.5	4.2	0.7	L
M	5.2	5.7	6.0	5.7	4.8	4.6	4.7	4.5	4.0	5.6	M
N	6.6	6.9	6.8	6.0	4.8	4.7	4.6	4.4	3.8	7.1	N
O	10.6	12.3	13.2	14.2	13.7	13.8	13.2	12.5	10.9	4.4	O
P	4.7	7.4	10.9	12.7	11.7	12.2	12.1	12.2	11.3	4.0	P
Q	0.4	0.5	0.5	0.4	0.3	0.2	0.2	0.2	0.2	3.4	Q
R										1.5	R
S										14.7	S
T										4.7	T
U										0.1	U

Men - Hommes - Hombres
ISIC 3 - CITI 3 - CIIU 3

	1999	2000	2001	2002	2003	2004	2005	2006	2007	2008
Total	162.0	177.0	180.0	160.0	132.0	133.0	126.0	115.6	97.8	90.5
UB	46.8	49.3	50.1	40.7	32.2	30.6	27.7	25.4	19.4	16.3
A	7.0	7.5	7.3	7.3	6.8	6.9	6.7	5.6	4.7	4.4
B	0.4	0.4	0.4	0.4	0.3	0.3	0.3	0.3	0.3	0.2
C	0.9	0.9	0.8	0.6	0.5	1.6	0.6	0.4	0.4	0.3
D	31.1	35.9	36.3	34.2	28.7	28.1	26.3	23.3	20.3	19.4
E	0.9	1.0	1.0	1.0	0.8	0.8	0.7	0.7	0.6	0.6
F	21.9	24.8	24.5	20.6	16.5	17.8	16.6	14.8	12.6	11.8
G	15.8	18.3	18.7	18.4	16.3	17.4	16.8	15.6	13.5	12.6
H	10.6	11.5	12.4	9.6	7.9	8.1	7.9	8.3	7.1	6.8
I	8.5	8.6	8.2	7.0	5.6	5.6	5.9	5.3	4.7	4.2
J	0.8	0.8	0.7	0.7	0.6	0.6	0.5	0.5	0.5	0.5
K	5.5	5.8	5.5	4.9	4.3	4.7	4.7	5.2	4.8	4.9
L	3.2	3.5	4.5	4.7	3.6	2.8	2.5	2.4	2.2	2.2
M	1.0	1.0	0.9	0.9	0.8	0.7	0.8	0.7	0.7	0.7
N	1.2	1.3	1.3	1.1	0.9	0.9	0.9	0.8	0.7	0.7
O	5.1	5.8	6.1	6.0	5.0	5.2	4.9	4.6	4.0	3.6
P	0.7	1.2	1.5	1.8	1.5	1.5	1.4	1.4	1.2	1.2
Q	0.2	0.3	0.3	0.2	0.2	0.1	0.1	0.1	0.1	0.1

Women - Femmes - Mujeres
ISIC 3 - CITI 3 - CIIU 3

	1999	2000	2001	2002	2003	2004	2005	2006	2007	2008
Total	180.0	201.0	215.0	206.0	186.0	185.0	182.0	177.6	156.7	150.0
UB	52.5	55.8	56.7	51.3	44.6	43.9	41.9	40.2	32.3	28.6
A	4.3	4.6	4.8	4.9	4.9	5.3	5.3	4.9	4.6	4.5
B	0.1	0.1	0.1	0.2	0.2	0.2	0.2	0.2	0.2	0.2
C	0.2	0.2	0.2	0.2	0.1	0.1	0.1	0.2	0.1	0.1
D	33.1	36.7	39.4	40.0	37.3	36.0	34.9	32.9	29.8	29.8
E	0.2	0.3	0.3	0.2	0.2	0.2	0.2	0.2	0.2	0.2
F	2.9	3.5	4.0	4.0	3.7	3.6	3.9	3.9	3.7	3.7
G	28.9	34.0	36.4	35.2	31.9	32.3	32.2	31.0	27.8	26.7
H	24.6	27.2	29.5	25.9	22.6	22.4	22.6	22.9	20.4	19.5
I	2.9	3.0	3.3	3.3	3.3	3.4	3.6	3.7	3.4	3.4
J	1.9	2.3	2.3	1.9	1.9	1.8	1.7	1.6	1.5	1.4
K	6.5	6.8	7.2	7.1	6.2	6.4	6.9	7.7	7.3	7.8
L	2.7	2.9	3.2	3.0	2.4	2.2	2.3	2.1	2.0	2.1
M	4.2	4.7	5.1	4.8	4.0	3.9	3.9	3.8	3.3	3.3
N	5.4	5.6	5.5	4.9	3.9	3.8	3.7	3.6	3.1	2.9
O	5.5	6.5	7.1	8.2	8.7	8.6	8.3	7.9	6.9	6.5
P	4.0	6.3	9.4	10.9	10.2	10.7	10.7	10.8	10.1	9.2
Q	0.2	0.2	0.2	0.2	0.1	0.1	0.1	0.1	0.1	0.1

Explanatory notes: see p. 451.   Notes explicatives: voir p. 454.   Notas explicativas: véase p. 457.

¹ 31st Dec. of each year.   ¹ 31 déc. de chaque année.   ¹ 31 dic. de cada año.

UNEMPLOYMENT

By economic activity

CHÔMAGE

Par activité économique

DESEMPLEO

Por actividad económica

3D

	Thousands			Milliers			Millares			
	1999	2000	2001	2002	2003	2004	2005	2006	2007	2008

Cyprus (BA) [1] [2] — Total unemployment - Chômage total - Desempleo total

Total - Total - Total
ISIC 3 - CITI 3 - CIIU 3

	1999	2000	2001	2002	2003	2004	2005	2006	2007	2008
Total	16.9	14.5	12.8	10.8	14.1	16.7	19.5	17.0	15.4	14.5
UB	3.5	3.7	3.2	1.6	2.9	3.1	4.1	3.4	3.3	2.4
A	0.1	-	0.1	0.2	0.3	0.2	0.2	0.3	0.5	0.3
B	-	-	0.1	-	0.1	-	-	-	-	-
C	-	-	0.1	-	-	0.1	0.1	0.1	0.1	0.0
D	3.1	3.2	1.7	1.8	1.6	2.2	2.2	1.5	1.4	1.1
E	-	-	-	-	-	-	0.0	-	-	-
F	2.7	2.1	1.4	0.7	1.2	1.5	2.1	1.7	1.2	1.3
G	2.6	2.4	2.7	2.3	2.3	2.8	3.0	2.8	2.5	2.6
H	1.7	1.1	1.6	1.3	2.6	2.4	2.7	2.7	2.6	2.7
I	0.5	0.3	0.3	0.7	0.8	0.9	0.8	1.1	1.0	0.5
J	0.2	0.1	0.2	0.2	0.2	0.1	0.1	0.2	0.0	0.2
K	1.0	0.5	0.7	0.4	0.7	0.8	1.0	0.7	0.7	1.1
L	0.4	0.1	0.3	0.3	0.3	0.5	0.4	0.3	0.3	0.3
M	0.3	0.3	0.2	0.6	0.2	0.7	1.0	0.6	0.4	0.7
N	0.5	0.3	0.3	0.2	0.2	0.4	0.4	0.5	0.3	0.4
O	0.3	0.3	0.1	0.6	0.6	0.9	1.1	0.9	0.8	0.9
P	0.1	0.1	0.1	-	-	0.2	0.2	0.1	0.0	0.0
Q	0.1	0.2	0.1	-	-	-	0.0	0.1	0.3	0.1

Men - Hommes - Hombres
ISIC 3 - CITI 3 - CIIU 3

	1999	2000	2001	2002	2003	2004	2005	2006	2007	2008
Total	7.7	5.5	4.8	4.7	7.1	7.0	9.0	8.0	7.3	7.0
UB	1.2	0.8	0.7	0.7	1.4	0.9	1.6	1.5	1.5	1.0
A	0.1	-	0.1	0.2	0.2	0.2	0.2	0.2	0.3	0.3
B	-	-	0.1	-	0.1	-	-	-	-	-
C	-	-	0.1	-	-	0.1	0.1	0.1	0.1	0.0
D	1.0	1.3	0.4	0.7	0.7	1.2	1.1	0.8	0.9	0.6
E	-	-	-	-	-	-	0.0	-	-	-
F	2.4	1.9	1.2	0.7	1.0	1.4	2.0	1.6	1.1	1.2
G	1.0	0.5	1.0	1.0	1.0	0.9	1.2	1.3	1.0	1.2
H	1.2	0.3	0.7	0.3	1.2	0.8	1.3	1.1	0.8	1.2
I	0.3	0.2	0.2	0.4	0.6	0.6	0.3	0.6	0.5	0.3
J	-	0.1	-	0.2	0.1	0.1	0.1	0.2	0.0	0.1
K	0.2	0.2	0.1	0.1	0.2	0.2	0.4	0.2	0.3	0.2
L	0.1	-	0.1	0.1	0.2	0.1	0.1	0.1	0.0	0.2
M	-	-	0.1	0.1	-	0.1	0.0	0.0	0.1	0.2
N	0.1	0.1	-	0.1	0.1	0.1	0.1	0.0	0.1	0.0
O	0.1	0.1	0.1	0.3	0.2	0.4	0.6	0.4	0.3	0.4
P	-	0.0	-	-	-	-	-	-	-	0.0
Q	0.1	0.1	0.1	-	-	-	-	0.0	0.2	0.0

Women - Femmes - Mujeres
ISIC 3 - CITI 3 - CIIU 3

	1999	2000	2001	2002	2003	2004	2005	2006	2007	2008
Total	9.1	8.9	8.1	6.0	7.0	9.7	10.4	9.0	8.1	7.6
UB	2.4	2.9	2.5	0.9	1.5	2.2	2.5	1.9	1.8	1.4
A	-	-	-	-	0.1	-	0.1	0.2	0.1	-
B	.	.	.	.	.	.	.	.	.	.
C	-	-	0.1	-	-	0.1	.	-	-	-
D	2.0	1.8	1.2	1.1	1.0	1.0	1.1	0.7	0.5	0.5
E	.	.	.	.	.	.	.	.	.	.
F	0.2	0.2	0.2	-	0.1	0.1	0.1	0.1	0.0	0.1
G	1.6	1.9	1.6	1.3	1.3	1.9	1.8	1.5	1.5	1.4
H	0.5	0.8	0.9	1.0	1.4	1.6	1.4	1.6	1.7	1.5
I	0.2	0.1	0.1	0.3	0.2	0.3	0.4	0.5	0.5	0.3
J	0.2	-	0.2	-	0.1	-	-	0.0	-	0.1
K	0.8	0.2	0.6	0.3	0.5	0.5	0.6	0.4	0.4	0.8
L	0.2	0.1	0.1	0.2	0.1	0.3	0.3	0.2	0.3	0.1
M	0.3	0.3	0.1	0.4	0.2	0.5	1.0	0.6	0.4	0.5
N	0.4	0.2	0.3	0.1	0.2	0.3	0.4	0.5	0.2	0.3
O	0.2	0.2	0.1	0.3	0.4	0.5	0.5	0.6	0.5	0.5
P	0.1	0.1	0.1	-	-	0.2	0.2	0.1	0.0	0.0
Q	-	0.1	-	-	-	-	0.0	0.0	0.1	0.0

Explanatory notes: see p. 451.

Notes explicatives: voir p. 454.

Notas explicativas: véase p. 457.

[1] Government-controlled area. [2] Persons aged 15 years and over.

[1] Région sous contrôle gouvernemental. [2] Personnes âgées de 15 ans et plus.

[1] Area controlada por el gobierno. [2] Personas de 15 años y más.

3D UNEMPLOYMENT   CHÔMAGE   DESEMPLEO

By economic activity   Par activité économique   Por actividad económica

	Thousands					Milliers				Millares	
	1999	2000	2001	2002	2003	2004	2005	2006	2007	2008	

Cyprus (FB) [1][2]   Registered unemployment - Chômage enregistré - Desempleo registrado

Total - Total - Total
ISIC 2 - CITI 2 - CIIU 2 .... ISIC 3 - CITI 3 - CIIU 3

	1999	2000	2001	2002	2003	2004	2005	2006	2007	2008	
Total	11.375	10.934	9.546	10.561	11.961	12.650	13.153	12.824	12.017	11.541	Total
UB	0.579	0.712	0.805	0.768	0.912	0.922	0.060	0.077	0.079	0.074	A
1	0.156	0.154	0.081	0.075	0.083	0.075	0.020	0.010	0.009	0.005	B
2	0.013	0.016	0.027	0.032	0.029	0.037	0.048	0.028	0.014	0.014	C
3	2.661	2.246	1.540	1.657	1.684	1.586	1.602	1.685	1.280	1.150	D
4	0.048	0.037	0.006	0.007	0.010	0.012	0.059	0.067	0.063	0.032	E
5	1.709	1.326	0.758	0.657	0.685	0.780	1.070	1.114	0.963	0.902	F
6	3.080	3.171	3.018	3.653	4.568	4.894	2.290	2.274	2.099	2.029	G
7	0.480	0.531	0.551	0.569	0.590	0.642	2.429	1.946	1.958	1.845	H
8	0.540	0.444	0.491	0.690	0.734	0.700	0.663	0.715	0.559	0.474	I
9	2.109	2.298	2.269	2.455	2.667	3.004	0.221	0.281	0.190	0.184	J
							0.543	0.596	0.591	0.655	K
							1.838	1.671	1.937	1.843	L
							0.629	0.660	0.598	0.601	M
							0.151	0.156	0.185	0.191	N
							0.533	0.512	0.490	0.482	O
							0.039	0.032	0.040	0.037	P
							0.015	0.016	0.013	0.011	Q
							0.945	0.982	0.978	1.013	X

Men - Hommes - Hombres
ISIC 2 - CITI 2 - CIIU 2 .... ISIC 3 - CITI 3 - CIIU 3

	1999	2000	2001	2002	2003	2004	2005	2006	2007	2008	
Total	5.580	5.266	4.535	4.692	5.113	5.415	5.819	5.737	5.210	4.929	Total
UB	0.223	0.280	0.352	0.327	0.386	0.401	0.025	0.034	0.036	0.032	A
1	0.112	0.100	0.039	0.036	0.035	0.032	0.017	0.008	0.006	0.004	B
2	0.012	0.015	0.025	0.026	0.023	0.033	0.043	0.024	0.013	0.010	C
3	0.911	0.812	0.627	0.624	0.613	0.618	0.625	0.696	0.511	0.469	D
4	0.043	0.035	0.004	0.005	0.007	0.010	0.051	0.060	0.055	0.029	E
5	1.610	1.247	0.694	0.586	0.602	0.691	0.978	1.013	0.806	0.789	F
6	1.166	1.165	1.117	1.351	1.656	1.747	0.847	0.812	0.737	0.673	G
7	0.292	0.340	0.353	0.317	0.325	0.329	0.854	0.658	0.641	0.592	H
8	0.199	0.157	0.188	0.259	0.263	0.254	0.353	0.366	0.292	0.259	I
9	1.012	1.117	1.136	1.164	1.203	1.302	0.098	0.135	0.094	0.085	J
							0.186	0.220	0.225	0.271	K
							1.054	1.013	1.131	1.043	L
							0.070	0.078	0.072	0.064	M
							0.009	0.006	0.012	0.015	N
							0.197	0.197	0.192	0.175	O
							0.002	0.001	-	-	P
							0.006	0.006	0.004	0.002	Q
							0.405	0.410	0.383	0.419	X

Women - Femmes - Mujeres
ISIC 2 - CITI 2 - CIIU 2 .... ISIC 3 - CITI 3 - CIIU 3

	1999	2000	2001	2002	2003	2004	2005	2006	2007	2008	
Total	5.795	5.668	5.011	5.869	6.848	7.235	7.334	7.087	6.808	6.612	Total
UB	0.356	0.432	0.453	0.441	0.526	0.521	0.035	0.044	0.043	0.043	A
1	0.044	0.054	0.042	0.039	0.048	0.043	0.003	0.002	0.003	0.001	B
2	0.001	0.001	0.002	0.006	0.006	0.004	0.005	0.004	0.001	0.004	C
3	1.750	1.434	0.913	1.033	1.071	0.968	0.977	0.989	0.769	0.682	D
4	0.005	0.002	0.002	0.002	0.003	0.002	0.008	0.007	0.008	0.002	E
5	0.100	0.079	0.064	0.071	0.083	0.089	0.092	0.101	0.130	0.113	F
6	1.913	2.006	1.902	2.302	2.912	3.147	1.443	1.462	1.362	1.356	G
7	0.188	0.191	0.198	0.252	0.265	0.313	1.575	1.288	1.317	1.253	H
8	0.341	0.287	0.303	0.431	0.471	0.446	0.310	0.349	0.267	0.215	I
9	1.097	1.181	1.133	1.291	1.464	1.702	0.123	0.146	0.096	0.099	J
							0.357	0.376	0.366	0.384	K
							0.784	0.658	0.806	0.800	L
							0.559	0.582	0.526	0.537	M
							0.142	0.151	0.172	0.177	N
							0.336	0.316	0.297	0.307	O
							0.037	0.031	0.040	0.037	P
							0.009	0.010	0.009	0.009	Q
							0.540	0.572	0.595	0.594	X

Explanatory notes: see p. 451.

[1] Government-controlled area. [2] Persons aged 15 years and over.

Notes explicatives: voir p. 454.

[1] Région sous contrôle gouvernemental. [2] Personnes âgées de 15 ans et plus.

Notas explicativas: véase p. 457.

[1] Area controlada por el gobierno. [2] Personas de 15 años y más.

By economic activity   Par activité économique   Por actividad económica

	1999	2000	2001	2002	2003	2004	2005	2006	2007	2008
Thousands				Milliers				Millares		

Czech Republic (BA) [1] — Total unemployment - Chômage total - Desempleo total

Total - Total - Total
ISIC 3 - CITI 3 - CIIU 3

	1999	2000	2001	2002	2003	2004	2005	2006	2007	2008
Total	454	455	418	374	399	426	410	371	276	230
UB	70	70	65	63	63	68	69	61	40	36
A-B	21	19	17	15	14	17	16	12	9	.
A	.	.	.	.	.	.	.	.	.	6
B	.	.	.	.	.	.	.	.	.	0
C	12	11	9	8	7	7	7	6	5	3
D	127	120	108	95	107	110	97	94	69	58
E	4	4	3	3	3	3	3	2	1	1
F	39	39	32	28	28	30	25	25	16	17
G	56	58	52	45	49	52	49	46	33	23
H	23	23	22	16	21	22	24	18	15	11
I	20	20	16	14	17	19	18	16	11	9
J	4	6	6	4	4	4	5	4	3	3
K	1	15	11	10	10	11	12	10	10	9
L	12	12	10	11	12	15	16	13	11	7
M	9	9	9	9	8	8	10	8	7	6
N	13	12	11	12	14	14	11	13	10	8
O	13	13	14	12	14	17	17	9	8	8
P	1	-	-	-	-	-	1	-	-	.
X	20	25	32	29	29	29	31	33	29	23

Men - Hommes - Hombres
ISIC 3 - CITI 3 - CIIU 3

	1999	2000	2001	2002	2003	2004	2005	2006	2007	2008
Total	211	212	193	169	175	201	187	169	124	103
UB	32	35	33	29	30	38	36	29	19	16
A-B	10	9	9	8	8	9	9	6	4	.
A	.	.	.	.	.	.	.	.	.	3
B	.	.	.	.	.	.	.	.	.	0
C	9	8	7	7	6	6	6	6	4	2
D	56	55	51	42	45	47	42	44	31	24
E	3	2	2	2	1	2	2	2	1	1
F	35	34	28	25	26	28	24	23	15	16
G	17	16	15	12	12	16	13	12	9	6
H	8	7	8	6	6	6	8	7	5	3
I	12	12	9	8	10	12	11	9	7	5
J	1	1	1	1	1	1	1	1	1	1
K	6	6	5	4	5	5	5	5	4	4
L	7	7	6	7	7	10	9	7	6	5
M	1	1	2	2	1	2	1	1	2	1
N	2	1	1	1	2	3	2	2	2	1
O	6	6	6	7	6	7	8	5	4	4
P	-	-	-	-	-	-	-	-	-	.
X	6	9	11	11	9	9	8	11	10	9

Women - Femmes - Mujeres
ISIC 3 - CITI 3 - CIIU 3

	1999	2000	2001	2002	2003	2004	2005	2006	2007	2008
Total	243	243	225	205	224	225	223	202	153	127
UB	38	34	32	34	33	30	32	32	21	20
A-B	12	10	8	7	7	9	6	6	5	.
A	.	.	.	.	.	.	.	.	.	3
B	.	.	.	.	.	.	.	.	.	0
C	3	2	2	2	1	1	1	1	-	0
D	71	65	57	53	62	63	55	50	38	33
E	1	1	1	1	2	1	1	-	-	0
F	3	4	5	3	2	2	1	2	1	1
G	40	42	37	33	38	36	36	34	24	17
H	15	15	15	11	14	15	16	11	10	8
I	7	8	7	6	6	8	7	7	4	4
J	3	5	5	3	3	3	4	4	2	2
K	6	9	6	5	5	6	7	5	5	5
L	5	5	4	4	5	5	6	6	5	2
M	8	8	7	8	7	6	8	7	6	5
N	11	11	10	10	12	11	9	10	8	7
O	6	7	9	6	7	9	9	5	3	4
P	1	-	-	-	1	-	1	-	-	.
X	13	16	20	19	19	20	23	21	20	14

Explanatory notes: see p. 451.   Notes explicatives: voir p. 454.   Notas explicativas: véase p. 457.

[1] Persons aged 15 years and over.   [1] Personnes âgées de 15 ans et plus.   [1] Personas de 15 años y más.

3D

UNEMPLOYMENT	CHÔMAGE	DESEMPLEO
By economic activity	Par activité économique	Por actividad económica

	Thousands			Milliers					Millares	
	1999	2000	2001	2002	2003	2004	2005	2006	2007	2008

Denmark (BA) [1] — Total unemployment - Chômage total - Desempleo total

Total - Total - Total
ISIC 3 - CITI 3 - CIIU 3

	1999	2000	2001	2002	2003	2004	2005	2006	2007	2008
Total		131.074		134.026	157.559	162.552	143.296	117.896	114.539	98.380
UB		17.403		20.972	28.820	26.928	26.686	23.579	24.096	15.485
A		3.525		2.938	3.419	4.159	-	-	-	-
B		0.113		0.252	0.133	0.264	-	-	-	-
C		0.230		-	0.130	0.105	-	-	-	-
D		26.510		22.201	30.196	29.522	24.735	14.985	13.707	15.201
E		0.209		0.340	0.130	0.320	-	-	-	-
F		6.683		8.396	7.753	9.077	7.615	4.433	4.534	5.061
G		15.001		18.427	17.846	18.907	16.248	13.212	15.425	16.622
H		5.620		5.546	7.020	6.860	6.422	5.820	6.720	6.835
I		8.102		7.975	7.958	8.364	7.377	6.655	6.133	5.082
J		1.772		2.088	1.611	1.815	-	-	-	-
K		9.699		12.607	12.568	11.638	10.024	9.634	11.736	8.245
L		4.090		3.905	3.890	5.023	3.824	-	-	-
M		6.464		6.996	8.546	8.556	7.589	5.787	5.993	4.650
N		15.539		13.578	18.393	21.903	17.872	17.640	14.241	9.157
O		6.915		5.278	7.555	7.680	7.925	6.352	5.106	4.940
P		0.506		0.375	0.092	0.351	-	-	-	-
Q		0.252		0.036	0.015	0.056	-	-	-	-
X		2.442		1.815	1.488	1.024	6.979	10.000	6.848	-

Men - Hommes - Hombres
ISIC 3 - CITI 3 - CIIU 3

	1999	2000	2001	2002	2003	2004	2005	2006	2007	2008
Total		61.246		66.021	75.734	79.867	69.433	53.421	55.079	47.077
UB		8.349		10.678	14.148	15.457	12.564	11.312	11.731	7.031
A		2.025		1.238	2.232	2.763	-	-	-	-
B		0.113		0.252	0.116	0.231	-	-	-	-
C		0.205		-	0.130	0.105	-	-	-	-
D		13.730		12.947	18.338	17.731	15.490	9.313	7.453	8.743
E		0.177		0.041	0.041	0.116	-	-	-	-
F		5.199		7.342	6.856	8.396	6.667	3.539	4.060	4.177
G		7.906		7.979	7.415	7.132	7.298	6.049	7.739	7.412
H		2.034		2.409	2.703	2.756	2.714	1.806	-	2.576
I		5.674		5.508	4.419	5.660	4.865	3.886	4.216	-
J		0.672		0.549	0.631	0.380	-	-	-	-
K		4.574		7.237	6.560	6.019	4.958	4.863	5.781	3.998
L		1.694		1.322	1.256	1.874	-	-	-	-
M		2.301		2.748	2.984	2.954	3.427	3.000	3.000	-
N		2.892		2.079	3.419	4.442	3.514	3.040	2.783	1.754
O		2.354		2.678	3.406	3.268	3.027	2.133	2.000	-
P				-	-	0.022	-	-	-	-
Q		0.038		0.019		0.056	-	-	-	-
X		1.308		0.994	1.080	0.505	4.909	4.480	6.315	-

Women - Femmes - Mujeres
ISIC 3 - CITI 3 - CIIU 3

	1999	2000	2001	2002	2003	2004	2005	2006	2007	2008
Total		69.828		68.005	81.825	82.686	73.863	64.475	59.460	51.303
UB		9.054		10.294	14.672	11.471	14.123	12.267	12.365	8.454
A		1.500		1.700	1.187	1.396	-	-	-	-
B		-		-	0.017	0.033	-	-	-	-
C		0.025		-	-		-	-	-	-
D		12.780		9.254	11.858	11.792	9.245	5.672	6.255	6.459
E		0.032		0.298	0.088	0.203	-	-	-	-
F		1.484		1.054	0.897	0.681	0.948	0.894	0.474	0.884
G		7.095		10.448	10.431	11.775	8.950	7.163	7.686	9.210
H		3.586		3.136	4.317	4.104	3.708	4.014	6.719	4.259
I		2.428		2.466	3.538	2.703	2.512	2.769	1.917	-
J		1.099		1.538	0.980	1.436	-	-	-	-
K		5.125		5.371	6.007	5.619	5.067	4.771	5.955	4.247
L		2.396		2.583	2.634	3.148	3.822	-	-	-
M		4.163		4.248	5.561	5.602	4.162	2.787	2.993	-
N		12.648		11.799	14.974	17.461	14.358	14.600	11.458	7.403
O		4.561		2.600	4.149	4.412	4.898	4.219	3.106	-
P		0.506		0.375	0.092	0.329	-	-	-	-
Q		0.213		0.018	0.015	-	-	-	-	-
X		1.133		0.822	0.407	0.520	2.070	5.520	0.533	-

Explanatory notes: see p. 451.	Notes explicatives: voir p. 454.	Notas explicativas: véase p. 457.
[1] Persons aged 15 to 66 years.	[1] Personnes âgées de 15 à 66 ans.	[1] Personas de 15 a 66 años.

By economic activity   Par activité économique   Por actividad económica

	Thousands			Milliers			Millares			
	1999	2000	2001	2002	2003	2004	2005	2006	2007	2008

España (BA) [1]   Total unemployment - Chômage total - Desempleo total

Total - Total - Total
ISIC 3 - CITI 3 - CIIU 3

	1999	2000	2001 [2]	2002	2003	2004	2005 [2]	2006	2007	2008
Total	2 722.2	2 496.4	1 904.4	2 155.3	2 242.2	2 213.7	1 912.4	1 837.1	1 833.9	2 590.6
UB	626.2	519.3	333.3	358.7	374.2	336.2	246.5	206.7	198.1	231.7
A	210.3	211.9	159.1	176.3	177.6	174.6	105.7	87.1	93.6	134.8
B	5.4	4.4	3.0	2.9	3.9	4.1	1.8	3.6	3.3	2.7
C	3.8	3.7	1.6	2.6	3.7	3.2	1.5	1.2	1.0	3.1
D	231.8	214.5	200.6	232.8	246.0	239.2	156.4	141.0	131.9	206.7
E	3.2	5.2	3.9	4.2	4.9	5.0	3.4	4.0	2.7	4.0
F	201.8	197.7	179.1	209.2	210.7	209.2	151.9	161.7	183.4	418.5
G	250.1	235.5	198.2	237.1	248.5	247.0	176.1	166.3	177.9	237.7
H	150.9	150.5	127.0	143.6	165.6	169.3	117.6	134.3	141.9	188.8
I	47.3	53.3	50.2	63.8	60.9	64.3	46.3	52.3	51.2	68.2
J	22.4	20.3	15.8	16.9	18.2	15.6	12.4	10.2	7.9	18.4
K	107.9	95.7	88.6	106.9	123.0	134.9	90.2	91.6	96.9	135.1
L	88.9	88.9	55.2	83.6	79.8	81.3	52.9	60.2	50.1	71.0
M	48.2	50.7	47.5	53.9	54.8	46.9	31.4	26.7	29.8	39.7
N	78.6	79.4	61.4	65.8	73.4	72.8	49.6	51.4	49.1	59.3
O	67.6	69.7	59.5	67.0	67.0	79.3	55.5	56.4	53.7	70.3
P	59.7	60.8	50.3	55.4	60.2	61.3	41.3	57.3	55.1	65.0
Q	0.1	0.4	0.5	0.1	0.7	-	0.6	0.3	0.1	-
X [3]	518.0	434.7	269.9	274.9	269.3	269.4	571.5	525.0	506.2	635.6

Men - Hommes - Hombres
ISIC 3 - CITI 3 - CIIU 3

	1999	2000	2001 [2]	2002	2003	2004	2005 [2]	2006	2007	2008
Total	1 158.3	1 037.4	828.1	929.4	976.4	970.8	862.9	791.5	815.2	1 311.0
UB	207.9	173.0	110.4	128.7	140.5	128.4	90.0	75.5	76.7	92.4
A	117.7	111.3	82.5	89.5	87.4	84.1	53.5	43.3	50.6	72.8
B	5.1	4.1	2.8	2.5	3.4	3.6	1.5	3.1	2.5	2.7
C	3.0	3.2	1.4	2.4	3.5	2.6	1.4	1.1	0.8	2.9
D	131.4	117.1	111.2	124.8	138.3	134.2	97.2	85.6	77.7	134.1
E	2.4	3.0	2.3	3.5	3.9	3.3	2.4	3.1	1.8	3.2
F	182.4	178.4	168.2	193.9	195.3	195.8	145.6	156.1	175.7	406.0
G	97.7	87.3	77.0	85.3	88.1	91.8	68.5	60.6	66.4	99.4
H	64.0	60.2	52.4	52.7	56.0	60.2	41.1	50.0	52.1	68.9
I	30.9	32.0	33.0	41.9	41.7	42.3	31.5	33.3	33.5	48.6
J	8.4	9.3	5.3	7.1	10.1	6.0	5.8	4.1	2.8	7.5
K	32.9	31.6	32.3	39.3	46.3	48.7	37.7	34.6	35.0	54.1
L	39.4	37.3	23.0	32.3	30.5	33.5	23.0	22.6	19.2	29.4
M	12.1	13.9	12.8	12.2	16.5	14.7	10.1	5.2	7.9	11.6
N	10.2	10.7	7.8	7.9	12.9	8.7	8.5	7.2	8.2	10.7
O	32.1	26.7	22.9	25.7	25.4	32.7	26.0	21.7	23.5	31.9
P	4.7	4.6	3.2	4.0	3.2	5.3	5.2	5.7	6.0	6.2
Q	0.1	-	0.2	0.1	0.2	-	0.3	0.2	-	-
X [3]	176.3	134.0	79.5	75.7	73.7	75.2	213.8	178.5	174.8	228.6

Women - Femmes - Mujeres
ISIC 3 - CITI 3 - CIIU 3

	1999	2000	2001 [2]	2002	2003	2004	2005 [2]	2006	2007	2008
Total	1 564.0	1 459.0	1 076.4	1 226.0	1 265.8	1 242.9	1 049.7	1 045.6	1 018.7	1 279.6
UB	418.3	346.3	223.0	230.0	233.7	207.9	156.5	131.2	121.4	139.3
A	92.7	100.6	76.6	86.8	90.2	90.6	52.2	43.8	43.0	62.0
B	0.3	0.3	0.2	0.4	0.6	0.5	0.4	0.5	0.7	0.1
C	0.8	0.5	0.2	0.2	0.3	0.6	0.1	0.1	0.2	0.3
D	100.5	97.4	89.4	108.0	107.7	105.0	59.2	55.4	54.3	72.5
E	0.9	2.3	1.6	0.7	1.0	1.7	1.0	1.0	0.9	0.8
F	19.4	19.3	10.9	15.3	15.5	13.4	6.3	5.6	7.7	12.5
G	152.3	148.2	121.3	151.8	160.4	155.3	107.7	105.6	111.5	138.2
H	87.0	90.3	74.6	90.9	109.6	109.2	76.6	84.3	89.8	119.9
I	16.5	21.2	17.2	21.9	19.2	22.0	14.9	18.9	17.7	19.6
J	14.1	11.0	10.4	9.8	8.2	9.7	6.7	6.1	5.1	10.9
K	75.0	64.2	56.3	67.6	76.7	86.2	52.6	56.9	62.0	81.0
L	49.5	51.6	32.2	51.3	49.3	47.8	29.9	37.6	30.9	41.6
M	36.2	36.8	34.7	41.6	38.3	32.2	21.3	21.5	21.9	28.0
N	68.4	68.7	53.6	57.9	60.5	64.1	41.1	44.2	40.9	48.6
O	35.4	43.0	36.6	41.3	41.7	46.6	29.5	34.6	30.2	38.4
P	55.0	56.2	47.1	51.3	57.1	56.0	36.1	51.6	49.2	58.8
Q	-	0.4	0.3	-	0.5	-	0.3	0.1	-	-
X [3]	341.7	300.7	190.4	199.3	195.6	194.2	357.7	346.5	331.4	407.0

Explanatory notes: see p. 451.

[1] Persons aged 16 to 74 years. [2] Methodology revised; data not strictly comparable. [3] Unemployed whose last job was 3 years ago and over.

Notes explicatives: voir p. 454.

[1] Personnes âgées de 16 à 74 ans. [2] Méthodologie révisée; les données ne sont pas strictement comparables. [3] Chômeurs dont le dernier travail date de 3 ans ou plus.

Notas explicativas: véase p. 457.

[1] Personas de 16 a 74 años. [2] Metodología revisada; los datos no son estrictamente comparables. [3] Desempleados cuyo último trabajo fue hace 3 años o más.

UNEMPLOYMENT — CHÔMAGE — DESEMPLEO

By economic activity — Par activité économique — Por actividad económica

	Thousands / Milliers / Millares									
	1999	2000	2001	2002	2003	2004	2005	2006	2007	2008

España (FB) [1] — Registered unemployment - Chômage enregistré - Desempleo registrado

Total - Total - Total
ISIC 3 - CITI 3 - CIIU 3

	1999	2000	2001	2002	2003	2004	2005	2006	2007	2008
Total							2 069.9	2 039.4	2 039.0	2 539.9
UB							225.6	224.4	222.8	240.3
A							54.2	58.8	60.5	79.9
B							5.2	4.9	4.4	4.9
C							5.3	6.9	7.2	7.5
D							289.2	275.6	263.1	308.7
E							4.1	4.2	4.1	4.7
F							231.4	222.2	234.8	401.8
G							287.5	275.0	269.5	324.2
H							180.4	177.7	178.8	214.8
I							59.7	52.7	50.7	66.3
J							11.6	11.0	10.8	12.9
K							363.4	387.3	407.5	512.8
L							135.8	129.3	121.9	134.0
M							47.1	43.4	40.7	44.3
N							62.9	60.3	58.1	63.3
O							96.9	94.9	94.0	108.6
P							9.4	10.6	9.8	10.8
Q							0.2	0.2	0.2	0.2

Men - Hommes - Hombres
ISIC 3 - CITI 3 - CIIU 3

	1999	2000	2001	2002	2003	2004	2005	2006	2007	2008
Total							818.0	788.2	791.8	1 146.9
UB							57.4	55.4	53.0	64.4
A							24.2	26.3	26.9	41.3
B							4.4	4.1	3.6	4.0
C							3.9	4.9	5.1	5.5
D							123.2	114.3	108.2	142.8
E							2.8	2.8	2.7	3.2
F							195.1	186.6	200.4	362.2
G							86.7	79.7	76.8	104.5
H							53.3	51.9	51.4	67.2
I							35.9	31.2	30.1	43.2
J							4.4	4.1	3.9	4.8
K							130.6	137.3	145.0	202.1
L							43.6	40.7	38.2	45.1
M							11.0	10.1	9.3	11.0
N							8.1	7.6	7.1	8.1
O							31.5	29.5	28.6	35.4
P							1.7	1.7	1.4	1.8
Q							0.1	0.1	0.1	0.1

Women - Femmes - Mujeres
ISIC 3 - CITI 3 - CIIU 3

	1999	2000	2001	2002	2003	2004	2005	2006	2007	2008
Total							1 251.8	1 251.2	1 247.2	1 393.0
UB							168.2	169.0	169.8	175.9
A							30.0	32.5	33.7	38.7
B							0.8	0.8	0.8	0.9
C							1.4	2.0	2.1	1.9
D							166.0	161.4	154.9	165.9
E							1.3	1.4	1.4	1.5
F							36.3	35.6	34.4	39.5
G							200.8	195.3	192.7	219.7
H							127.0	125.8	127.4	147.6
I							23.8	21.5	20.6	23.1
J							7.2	7.0	6.9	8.1
K							232.9	249.9	262.6	310.6
L							92.1	88.7	83.7	88.8
M							36.1	33.3	31.4	33.3
N							54.8	52.7	51.0	55.2
O							65.4	65.5	65.4	73.1
P							7.7	8.9	8.3	9.0
Q							0.2	0.2	0.1	0.1

Estonia (BA) [2] — Total unemployment - Chômage total - Desempleo total

Total - Total - Total
ISIC 3 - CITI 3 - CIIU 3

	1999	2000	2001	2002	2003	2004	2005	2006	2007	2008
Total	80.5	89.9 [3]	83.1	67.2	66.2	63.6	52.2	40.5	32.0	38.4
UB	8.8	12.4 [3]	12.4	10.9	12.5	14.0	12.1	10.2	8.3	7.3
A-B	8.2	9.6 [3]	7.3	4.7	5.3	4.9	2.9	2.1	2.3	2.2
C-F	31.3	30.4 [3]	29.9	24.8	21.5	19.4	16.9	16.7	12.7	13.6
G-Q	27.6	37.5 [3]	33.4	26.8	27.0	25.4	20.3	11.6	8.7	15.1

Men - Hommes - Hombres
ISIC 3 - CITI 3 - CIIU 3

	1999	2000	2001	2002	2003	2004	2005	2006	2007	2008
Total	45.7	49.5 [3]	43.7	36.1	34.2	34.7	28.9	21.3	18.9	20.2
UB	3.7	5.4 [3]	5.1	5.3	6.2	8.0	7.3	4.7	5.2	4.0
A-B	6.2	6.5 [3]	5.2	3.3	3.6	4.0	2.4	1.4	1.3	1.5
C-F	20.4	21.0 [3]	19.3	16.8	14.4	11.9	10.0	10.9	8.8	9.8
G-Q	13.3	16.6 [3]	14.1	10.7	10.0	10.8	9.1	4.3	3.7	4.8

Explanatory notes: see p. 451.   Notes explicatives: voir p. 454.   Notas explicativas: véase p. 457.

[1] Persons aged 16 to 74 years. [2] Persons aged 15 to 74 years. [3] Prior to 2000: second quarter of each year.

[1] Personnes âgées de 16 à 74 ans. [2] Personnes âgées de 15 à 74 ans. [3] Avant 2000: deuxième trimestre de chaque année.

[1] Personas de 16 a 74 años. [2] Personas de 15 a 74 años. [3] Antes de 2000: segundo trimestre de cada año.

By economic activity — Par activité économique — Por actividad económica

	Thousands / Milliers / Millares									
	1999	2000	2001	2002	2003	2004	2005	2006	2007	2008

Estonia (BA) [1] — Total unemployment - Chômage total - Desempleo total

Women - Femmes - Mujeres
ISIC 3 - CITI 3 - CIIU 3

	1999	2000	2001	2002	2003	2004	2005	2006	2007	2008
Total	34.8	40.5 [2]	39.3	31.0	32.0	28.9	23.3	19.2	13.1	18.1
UB	5.1	7.1 [2]	7.3	5.6	6.3	6.0	4.8	5.5	3.1	3.3
A-B	2.0	3.1 [2]	2.1	1.4	1.7	0.9	0.5	0.7	1.0	0.7
C-F	11.0	9.4 [2]	10.6	7.9	7.0	7.4	6.8	5.8	3.9	3.7
G-Q	14.3	20.9 [2]	19.3	16.1	16.9	14.6	11.2	7.3	5.0	10.3

Finland (BA) [1] — Total unemployment - Chômage total - Desempleo total

Total - Total - Total
ISIC 3 - CITI 3 - CIIU 3

	1999	2000	2001	2002	2003	2004	2005	2006	2007	2008
Total	261	253	238	237	235	229	220	204	183	172 [3]
UB	86	79	78	79	84	80	80	80	68	23 [3]
A	9	8	6	5	4	4	4	4	3	4 [3]
C	1	1	1	1	.	.	.	.	.	.
D	27	23	25	27	28	23	23	20	16	20 [3]
E	1	-	1	-	1	1	1	-	1	- [3]
F	21	20	19	20	17	16	14	12	10	11 [3]
G	16	16	17	18	16	16	16	13	13	19 [3]
H	8	9	7	7	6	6	6	5	5	7 [3]
I	8	7	6	8	8	8	7	7	5	6 [3]
J	2	1	1	1	1	1	1	1	1	1 [3]
K	17	16	17	18	17	19	16	15	14	16 [3]
L	7	7	5	5	6	5	4	3	3	3 [3]
M	11	11	9	7	7	9	9	8	7	8 [3]
N	29	30	29	25	23	22	22	20	18	18 [3]
O	15	16	15	15	14	14	15	13	12	14 [3]
P	1	1	1	1	1	1	2	2	2	3 [3]
X	2	8	1	2	2	2	1	1	5	19 [3]

Men - Hommes - Hombres
ISIC 3 - CITI 3 - CIIU 3

	1999	2000	2001	2002	2003	2004	2005	2006	2007	2008
Total	130	122	117	123	124	118	111	101	90	85 [3]
UB	37	34	34	37	40	38	36	37	30	11 [3]
A	6	5	4	4	3	2	3	3	2	2 [3]
C	1	1	1	-	.	.	.	.	.	.
D	19	15	15	19	19	15	15	13	11	13 [3]
E	1	-	-	-	1	1	-	-	-	- [3]
F	20	19	18	19	17	15	13	11	9	11 [3]
G	8	7	9	9	8	9	9	7	7	8 [3]
H	2	3	3	2	2	2	2	1	2	2 [3]
I	6	5	4	5	5	6	5	5	4	4 [3]
J	1	-	-	-	-	-	-	1	-	- [3]
K	9	9	10	11	10	11	9	8	7	9 [3]
L	3	3	3	2	3	2	2	2	1	1 [3]
M	4	4	3	2	2	2	3	2	2	2 [3]
N	5	5	6	5	5	4	4	4	4	3 [3]
O	7	7	6	7	8	6	8	6	6	5 [3]
P	-	-	-	-	-	1	1	1	1	2 [3]
X	1	5	1	1	1	1	1	-	3	10 [3]

Women - Femmes - Mujeres
ISIC 3 - CITI 3 - CIIU 3

	1999	2000	2001	2002	2003	2004	2005	2006	2007	2008
Total	131	131	121	114	111	111	109	103	93	87 [3]
UB	49	45	44	42	44	42	44	43	38	12 [3]
A	3	3	2	1	1	2	1	1	1	2 [3]
C	-	-	-	-	.	.	.	.	.	.
D	8	8	10	8	9	8	8	7	5	7 [3]
E	-	-	-	-	.	.	.	.	.	- [3]
F	1	1	1	1	1	1	1	1	1	- [3]
G	8	9	8	9	8	8	7	6	6	10 [3]
H	6	6	5	5	4	4	4	4	3	5 [3]
I	2	3	2	3	2	2	2	2	1	2 [3]
J	1	1	1	-	1	1	1	-	-	1 [3]
K	8	7	7	6	7	7	7	7	7	7 [3]
L	4	4	3	3	4	4	2	1	2	2 [3]
M	7	8	6	5	5	6	6	6	5	6 [3]
N	24	25	23	20	18	18	18	16	14	15 [3]
O	8	9	9	8	6	7	7	7	7	9 [3]
P	1	1	1	1	1	-	1	1	1	1 [3]
X	1	3	1	1	1	1	-	1	2	9 [3]

Explanatory notes: see p. 451.

[1] Persons aged 15 to 74 years. [2] Prior to 2000: second quarter of each year. [3] Methodology revised; data not strictly comparable.

Notes explicatives: voir p. 454.

[1] Personnes âgées de 15 à 74 ans. [2] Avant 2000: deuxième trimestre de chaque année. [3] Méthodologie révisée; les données ne sont pas strictement comparables.

Notas explicativas: véase p. 457.

[1] Personas de 15 a 74 años. [2] Antes de 2000: segundo trimestre de cada año. [3] Metodología revisada; los datos no son estrictamente comparables.

By economic activity **Par activité économique** **Por actividad económica**

	Thousands							Milliers		Millares
	1999	2000	2001	2002	2003	2004	2005	2006	2007	2008

Germany (BA) [1] — Total unemployment - Chômage total - Desempleo total

Total - Total - Total
ISIC 3 - CITI 3 - CIIU 3

	1999	2000	2001	2002	2003	2004	2005	2006	2007	2008
Total	3 503	3 127 [2]	3 150	3 486 [3]	4 023 [2]	4 388 [4]	4 583 [5]	4 279	3 608	3 141
UB	240	214 [2]	197	228 [3]	258 [2]	310 [4]	459 [5]	455	386	336
A-B	159	142 [2]	147	151 [3]	169 [2]	187 [4]	168 [5]	149	129	110
C								18	15	10
C-D	944	759 [2]	739	818 [3]	956 [2]	1 018 [4]	927 [5]	840	669	
D								822	654	552
E	21	18 [2]	27	21 [3]	17 [2]	27 [4]	25 [5]	21	14	15
F	500	460 [2]	527	529 [3]	623 [2]	676 [4]	597 [5]	505	401	329
G								600	502	445
G-H	631	566 [2]	549	625 [3]	733 [2]	808 [4]	892 [5]	850	726	
H								250	224	206
I	160	142 [2]	148	180 [3]	191 [2]	214 [4]	223 [5]	209	172	155
J	46	38 [2]	39	47 [3]	57 [2]	55 [4]	62 [5]	56	44	37
K	181	185 [2]	187	246 [3]	328 [2]	346 [4]	386 [5]	372	340	318
L								149	129	112
L-N	157	162 [2]	139	429 [3]	483 [2]	525 [4]	586 [5]	565	501	
M								124	111	103
N								292	261	211
O								237	203	185
O-Q	464	441 [2]	451	212 [3]	207 [2]	219 [4]	259 [5]	257	224	
P								18	18	15

Men - Hommes - Hombres
ISIC 3 - CITI 3 - CIIU 3

	1999	2000	2001	2002	2003	2004	2005	2006	2007	2008
Total	1 905	1 691 [2]	1 754	1 982 [3]	2 316 [2]	2 551 [4]	2 574 [5]	2 358	1 944	1 690
UB	122	105 [2]	97	113 [3]	142 [2]	164 [4]	227 [5]	228	194	157
A-B	86	80 [2]	84	75 [3]	98 [2]	112 [4]	109 [5]	95	77	70
C								14	11	7
C-D	554	469 [2]	446	509 [3]	605 [2]	643 [4]	588 [5]	513	403	
D								499	392	329
E	14	13 [2]	20	15 [3]	10 [2]	19 [4]	17 [5]	15	10	9
F	443	405 [2]	476	478 [3]	562 [2]	618 [4]	542 [5]	461	364	304
G								263	217	197
G-H	253	218 [2]	215	268 [3]	313 [2]	339 [4]	392 [5]	372	310	
H								109	93	85
I	108	93 [2]	99	131 [3]	137 [2]	154 [4]	160 [5]	153	123	111
J	20	15 [2]	13	15 [3]	22 [2]	24 [4]	24 [5]	21	19	15
K	86	88 [2]	92	129 [3]	174 [2]	178 [4]	193 [5]	191	170	165
L								86	76	65
L-N	76	74 [2]	68	150 [3]	163 [2]	192 [4]	205 [5]	200	179	
M								42	37	33
N								72	66	58
O								106	91	80
O-Q	143	131 [2]	144	99 [3]	90 [2]	102 [4]	117 [5]	108	95	
P								2	1	2

Women - Femmes - Mujeres
ISIC 3 - CITI 3 - CIIU 3

	1999	2000	2001	2002	2003	2004	2005	2006	2007	2008
Total	1 598	1 436 [2]	1 396	1 504 [3]	1 707 [2]	1 836 [4]	2 009 [5]	1 921	1 664	1 451
UB	118	109 [2]	100	115 [3]	116 [2]	146 [4]	231 [5]	226	192	179
A-B	73	62 [2]	63	76 [3]	71 [2]	75 [4]	59 [5]	54	52	40
C								4	4	3
C-D	390	290 [2]	293	309 [3]	351 [2]	375 [4]	339 [5]	327	266	
D								323	262	223
E	7	5 [2]	7	6 [3]	8 [2]	8 [4]	8 [5]	6	5	6
F	57	55 [2]	51	51 [3]	61 [2]	58 [4]	55 [5]	44	37	25
G								338	285	248
G-H	378	348 [2]	334	357 [3]	420 [2]	469 [4]	500 [5]	479	416	
H								141	131	121
I	52	49 [2]	49	49 [3]	54 [2]	60 [4]	63 [5]	56	49	44
J	26	23 [2]	26	32 [3]	36 [2]	31 [4]	38 [5]	35	25	22
K	95	97 [2]	95	117 [3]	154 [2]	168 [4]	193 [5]	181	170	153
L								63	53	47
L-N	81	88 [2]	71	279 [3]	320 [2]	333 [4]	381 [5]	365	322	
M								82	74	70
N								220	195	153
O								130	112	105
O-Q	321	310 [2]	307	113 [3]	117 [2]	117 [4]	142 [5]	147	130	
P								16	17	13

Explanatory notes: see p. 451.

[1] Persons aged 15 years and over. [2] May. [3] Prior to 2002: April of each year. [4] March. [5] Methodology revised; data not strictly comparable.

Notes explicatives: voir p. 454.

[1] Personnes âgées de 15 ans et plus. [2] Mai. [3] Avant 2002: avril de chaque année. [4] Mars. [5] Méthodologie révisée; les données ne sont pas strictement comparables.

Notas explicativas: véase p. 457.

[1] Personas de 15 años y más. [2] Mayo. [3] Antes del 2002: abril de cada año. [4] Marzo. [5] Metodología revisada; los datos no son estrictamente comparables.

By economic activity — Par activité économique — Por actividad económica

Thousands — Milliers — Millares

Greece (BA) [1][2] Total unemployment - Chômage total - Desempleo total

Total - Total - Total
ISIC 3 - CITI 3 - CIIU 3 ... ISIC 4 - CITI 4 - CIIU 4

	1999	2000	2001	2002	2003	2004	2005	2006	2007	2008	
Total	543.3	519.3	478.4	462.1	441.8	492.7	466.7	427.4	398.0	357.1	Total
UB	257.6	240.4	229.7	190.7	184.0	212.6	178.6	156.8	139.9	130.3	UB
A	11.5	8.3	7.2	3.9	5.9	7.6	4.6	3.4	5.7	5.7	A
B	0.1	0.4	0.3	1.2	0.2	0.9	1.3	0.6	0.4	1.0	B
C	1.4	2.0	1.3	1.4	0.6	0.8	1.6	0.7	1.3	34.2	C
D	70.2	63.8	53.0	53.9	51.8	49.7	52.4	48.3	40.4	1.2	D
E	1.1	1.3	0.7	1.3	1.5	1.1	1.6	1.7	1.9	3.0	E
F	15.4	15.4	14.2	13.5	14.0	15.2	15.0	13.0	14.9	14.2	F
G	50.3	48.3	46.5	46.9	41.4	51.8	53.9	52.0	44.2	36.5	G
H	31.0	37.2	32.8	40.7	36.7	33.0	37.1	37.9	37.1	6.7	H
I	13.8	15.5	12.7	18.0	15.8	15.6	14.6	15.2	14.0	37.3	I
J	3.2	3.0	3.8	3.6	4.6	5.0	7.4	6.0	3.6	4.6	J
K	12.5	10.3	12.0	14.4	13.5	16.9	16.7	18.1	20.2	3.8	K
L	9.2	10.5	10.6	9.6	13.4	12.1	17.3	15.4	13.1	0.2	L
M	11.0	8.3	8.4	7.6	7.2	10.7	11.6	8.9	9.9	8.6	M
N	8.1	7.1	5.9	9.5	9.3	7.8	8.6	9.1	9.3	5.2	N
O	11.5	10.6	9.4	12.1	11.6	14.4	15.5	15.9	14.0	11.9	O
P	4.2	3.4	4.0	4.9	4.1	5.2	3.9	2.9	4.7	6.4	P
Q	0.3	0.3	0.3	-	-	-	-	0.1	-	9.8	Q
X	30.9	33.3	25.9	28.7	26.2	32.3	25.1	21.3	23.3	5.2	R
										3.7	S
										4.3	T
										-	U
										23.3	X

Men - Hommes - Hombres
ISIC 3 - CITI 3 - CIIU 3 ... ISIC 4 - CITI 4 - CIIU 4

	1999	2000	2001	2002	2003	2004	2005	2006	2007	2008	
Total	212.8	207.2	191.4	180.5	170.8	181.7	166.8	160.9	144.0	136.6	Total
UB	87.4	82.2	78.2	69.2	65.1	67.3	47.4	51.3	43.0	44.4	UB
A	6.5	4.8	3.9	2.0	3.7	4.4	3.1	1.7	3.7	3.2	A
B	0.1	0.4	0.3	0.8	0.2	0.5	0.8	0.4	0.2	0.8	B
C	1.1	1.6	1.1	0.9	0.6	0.5	1.5	0.6	0.8	15.9	C
D	33.5	29.2	25.5	23.7	21.1	21.4	24.1	22.7	17.5	0.7	D
E	0.8	1.0	0.6	0.9	1.3	1.1	1.3	1.6	1.5	2.2	E
F	14.9	15.0	13.6	13.1	12.7	14.9	14.3	12.2	14.1	13.9	F
G	18.5	19.6	21.5	16.1	16.0	20.3	20.2	19.6	17.2	13.9	G
H	12.8	16.9	15.9	17.3	15.6	14.3	14.0	14.1	14.1	5.1	H
I	11.1	11.4	7.9	10.8	9.2	11.1	10.0	8.3	7.6	15.7	I
J	0.8	0.4	1.3	1.6	1.4	1.7	1.9	2.6	1.2	2.1	J
K	4.0	2.9	3.8	4.8	4.1	5.2	6.9	6.0	6.1	0.8	K
L	5.0	5.7	4.9	5.1	6.8	4.8	7.1	6.2	5.4	0.2	L
M	2.8	1.7	1.3	1.6	1.3	1.8	2.6	1.3	2.1	2.0	M
N	0.7	1.1	1.2	0.9	0.9	1.2	1.5	1.0	0.4	1.9	N
O	5.3	4.5	4.4	5.6	5.8	5.0	5.5	7.1	5.7	3.9	O
P	0.3	0.2	0.3	0.2	0.1	-	-	0.4	0.1	1.7	P
Q	0.3	0.2	0.3	-	-	-	-	0.1	-	1.3	Q
X	7.1	8.4	5.6	5.9	5.2	6.1	4.6	3.6	3.4	2.5	R
										0.4	S
										-	T
										-	U
										4.0	X

Women - Femmes - Mujeres
ISIC 3 - CITI 3 - CIIU 3 ... ISIC 4 - CITI 4 - CIIU 4

	1999	2000	2001	2002	2003	2004	2005	2006	2007	2008	
Total	330.5	312.1	287.0	281.6	271.0	311.0	299.9	266.5	254.0	220.5	Total
UB	170.2	158.2	151.5	121.5	118.9	145.3	131.2	105.5	96.9	85.9	UB
A	5.0	3.5	3.2	1.9	2.2	3.2	1.5	1.7	2.0	2.4	A
B	-	-	-	0.4	-	0.4	0.6	0.2	0.2	0.3	B
C	0.3	0.4	0.2	0.5	-	0.3	0.1	0.1	0.5	18.2	C
D	36.7	34.6	27.4	30.2	30.7	28.3	28.3	25.6	23.0	0.5	D
E	0.3	0.3	0.1	0.5	0.2	-	0.3	0.1	0.4	0.7	E
F	0.5	0.4	0.5	0.5	1.3	0.3	0.6	0.9	0.7	0.3	F
G	31.8	28.7	25.0	30.8	25.5	31.5	33.7	32.5	27.1	22.6	G
H	18.2	20.3	16.9	23.3	21.2	18.7	23.1	23.8	23.0	1.7	H
I	2.7	4.1	4.8	7.1	6.6	4.5	4.6	6.9	6.3	21.5	I
J	2.4	2.6	2.6	2.0	3.2	3.4	5.5	3.3	2.4	2.5	J
K	8.6	7.4	8.2	9.6	9.4	11.7	9.9	12.1	14.1	3.0	K
L	4.3	4.8	5.7	4.5	6.7	7.3	10.1	9.2	7.7	-	L
M	8.2	6.6	7.1	6.0	5.9	8.8	8.9	7.6	7.7	6.6	M
N	7.4	5.9	4.6	8.6	8.4	6.5	7.1	8.2	8.9	3.3	N
O	6.2	6.1	5.0	6.5	5.8	9.5	10.0	8.8	8.4	8.0	O
P	4.0	3.2	3.7	4.8	4.0	5.2	3.9	2.5	4.6	4.7	P
Q	-	0.1	-	-	-	-	-	-	-	8.6	Q
X	23.8	24.8	20.3	22.9	21.0	26.2	20.5	17.8	19.9	2.7	R
										3.3	S
										4.3	T
										-	U
										19.3	X

Explanatory notes: see p. 451.
[1] Persons aged 15 years and over. [2] Second quarter of each year.

Notes explicatives: voir p. 454.
[1] Personnes âgées de 15 ans et plus. [2] Deuxième trimestre de chaque année.

Notas explicativas: véase p. 457.
[1] Personas de 15 años y más. [2] Segundo trimestre de cada año.

By economic activity Par activité économique Por actividad económica

	Thousands			Milliers					Millares	
	1999	2000	2001	2002	2003	2004	2005	2006	2007	2008

Hungary (BA) [1] Total unemployment - Chômage total - Desempleo total

Total - Total - Total
ISIC 3 - CITI 3 - CIIU 3

	1999	2000	2001	2002	2003	2004	2005	2006	2007	2008
Total	284.7	262.5	232.9	238.8 [2]	244.5	252.9	303.9	316.8	311.9	329.2
UB	41.2	38.1	31.1	33.5 [2]	35.7	38.5	46.7	47.9	46.9	50.6
A-B	18.2	13.3	13.8	12.2 [2]	10.7	9.6	11.0	9.8	10.3	12.6
C	2.6	2.7	1.7	1.2 [2]	0.8	0.6	0.6	0.5	0.5	0.4
D	69.1	62.6	55.1	56.9 [2]	59.3	57.3	72.9	73.4	63.2	69.9
E	4.4	3.4	2.6	2.3 [2]	2.1	1.7	2.5	1.5	3.0	1.9
F	23.6	22.1	20.2	20.3 [2]	19.1	18.4	21.5	23.9	25.2	30.2
G	30.5	28.8	25.4	27.1 [2]	27.1	31.8	37.5	36.8	34.7	32.3
H	10.8	11.2	10.8	10.9 [2]	9.5	11.7	14.1	15.0	14.0	12.4
I	13.7	10.6	9.7	7.9 [2]	8.2	8.1	11.2	11.9	9.7	14.8
J	3.3	3.7	3.0	2.1 [2]	1.7	1.9	2.2	2.5	2.6	2.5
K	9.1	7.8	7.5	9.0 [2]	9.5	10.6	14.6	13.9	12.3	11.3
L	19.2	17.8	17.1	17.9 [2]	18.2	19.4	22.7	28.9	33.1	35.4
M	9.2	5.0	3.9	6.9 [2]	6.8	6.2	6.0	7.8	8.9	7.8
N	6.9	6.8	5.8	5.1 [2]	5.8	6.5	8.0	8.2	9.5	8.4
O	8.0	8.9	9.3	9.4 [2]	6.8	6.5	6.5	9.0	11.8	10.1
P	0.2	0.2	0.1	0.1 [2]	-	-	-	0.1	0.1	0.1
Q	0.2	0.4	-	- [2]	-	-	0.1	0.2	0.0	0.0
X	15.5	19.1	15.8	16.0 [2]	23.2	24.1	25.8	25.5	26.1	28.4

Men - Hommes - Hombres
ISIC 3 - CITI 3 - CIIU 3

	1999	2000	2001	2002	2003	2004	2005	2006	2007	2008
Total	170.7	159.5	142.7	138.0 [2]	138.5	136.8	159.1	164.6	164.2	174.3
UB	25.5	23.1	17.7	18.4 [2]	19.9	22.4	26.3	25.9	23.3	25.6
A-B	13.2	10.6	11.0	9.1 [2]	8.1	6.8	8.1	6.7	7.5	8.9
C	2.3	2.4	1.5	1.1 [2]	0.7	0.6	0.6	0.4	0.4	0.4
D	40.2	36.9	34.0	32.5 [2]	32.1	28.9	36.7	35.8	31.0	36.5
E	3.3	2.8	2.2	2.0 [2]	1.6	1.5	1.8	1.1	2.1	1.2
F	22.4	21.2	19.1	18.5 [2]	18.3	17.5	20.3	22.3	23.8	27.9
G	13.1	13.0	11.6	13.0 [2]	11.8	13.1	15.2	15.0	14.7	12.0
H	4.5	5.8	4.7	4.6 [2]	3.6	4.3	4.2	3.7	4.1	3.5
I	9.4	7.3	7.2	6.4 [2]	5.6	4.9	6.8	7.5	7.0	10.8
J	0.8	0.5	0.6	0.4 [2]	0.5	0.5	0.7	0.8	1.1	0.3
K	4.9	4.7	4.8	4.6 [2]	5.6	5.5	6.6	7.6	6.1	6.1
L	13.8	13.2	13.2	12.6 [2]	12.8	13.4	14.4	18.2	22.0	22.1
M	1.9	1.1	0.7	1.7 [2]	1.3	1.3	1.4	2.0	2.4	2.1
N	2.5	2.2	1.5	1.3 [2]	1.9	2.0	2.4	2.2	2.1	1.1
O	5.4	5.2	5.9	5.3 [2]	4.1	4.0	3.1	4.4	5.6	3.6
P	-	0.1	0.1	0.1 [2]	-	-	-	-	0.0	0.0
Q	-	0.1	-	- [2]	-	-	-	0.1	-	-
X	7.5	9.4	6.9	6.4 [2]	10.6	10.1	10.5	10.9	11.0	12.2

Women - Femmes - Mujeres
ISIC 3 - CITI 3 - CIIU 3

	1999	2000	2001	2002	2003	2004	2005	2006	2007	2008
Total	114.0	103.0	90.2	100.3 [2]	106.0	116.1	144.8	152.2	147.7	154.9
UB	15.7	15.0	13.4	15.1 [2]	15.8	16.1	20.4	22.0	23.6	25.0
A-B	5.0	2.7	2.8	3.1 [2]	2.6	2.8	2.9	3.1	2.8	3.7
C	0.3	0.3	0.2	0.1 [2]	0.1	-	0.0	0.1	0.1	0.0
D	28.9	25.7	21.1	24.4 [2]	27.2	28.4	36.2	37.6	32.2	33.4
E	1.1	0.6	0.4	0.3 [2]	0.5	0.2	0.7	0.4	0.9	0.7
F	1.2	0.9	1.1	1.8 [2]	0.8	0.9	1.2	1.6	1.4	2.3
G	17.4	15.8	13.8	14.1 [2]	15.3	18.7	22.3	21.8	20.0	20.3
H	6.3	5.4	6.1	6.3 [2]	5.9	7.4	9.9	11.3	9.9	8.9
I	4.3	3.3	2.5	1.5 [2]	2.6	3.2	4.4	4.4	2.7	4.0
J	2.5	3.2	2.4	1.7 [2]	1.2	1.4	1.5	1.7	1.5	2.2
K	4.2	3.1	2.7	4.4 [2]	3.9	5.1	8.0	6.3	6.2	5.2
L	5.4	4.6	3.9	5.3 [2]	5.4	6.0	8.3	10.7	11.1	13.3
M	6.3	3.9	3.2	5.2 [2]	5.5	4.9	4.6	5.8	6.5	5.7
N	4.4	4.6	4.3	3.8 [2]	3.9	4.5	5.6	6.0	7.4	7.3
O	2.6	3.8	3.4	4.1 [2]	2.7	2.5	3.4	4.6	6.2	6.6
P	0.2	0.1	-	- [2]	-	-	-	0.1	0.1	0.1
Q	0.2	0.3	-	- [2]	-	-	0.1	0.1	0.0	0.0
X	8.0	9.7	8.9	9.6 [2]	12.6	14.0	15.3	14.6	15.1	16.2

Explanatory notes: see p. 451.

[1] Persons aged 15 to 74 years. [2] Estimates based on the 2001 Population Census results.

Notes explicatives: voir p. 454.

[1] Personnes âgées de 15 à 74 ans. [2] Estimations basées sur les résultats du Recensement de la population de 2001.

Notas explicativas: véase p. 457.

[1] Personas de 15 a 74 años. [2] Estimaciones basadas en los resultados del Censo de población de 2001.

	Thousands			Milliers				Millares		
	1999	2000	2001	2002	2003	2004	2005	2006	2007	2008

Italy (BA) [1] — Total unemployment - Chômage total - Desempleo total

Total - Total - Total
ISIC 3 - CITI 3 - CIIU 3

	1999	2000	2001	2002	2003	2004	2005	2006	2007	2008
Total	2 669	2 495	2 267	2 163	2 096	1 960 [2]	1 889	1 673	1 506	1 692
UB	1 411	1 326	1 183	1 101	1 064	635 [2]	634	567	471	505
A	127	108	100	97	101	66 [2]	58	53	52	62
B	2	2	3	2	2	2 [2]	2	2	1	1
C	3	2	3	3	2	1 [2]	2	2	1	1
D	206	181	152	160	154	219 [2]	229	190	164	191
E	4	3	2	2	4	3 [2]	2	1	2	3
F	139	129	115	108	95	135 [2]	134	116	116	135
G	165	140	130	125	117	183 [2]	171	150	150	166
H	82	83	79	82	82	137 [2]	134	108	102	119
I	43	46	42	34	37	48 [2]	51	42	40	47
J	11	10	10	10	8	14 [2]	13	9	9	9
K	54	51	50	49	48	106 [2]	96	97	87	96
L	59	55	47	43	39	28 [2]	24	22	22	23
M	39	33	33	33	34	47 [2]	43	35	34	38
N	33	28	24	24	25	38 [2]	38	34	29	34
O	65	58	52	54	50	71 [2]	74	71	72	75
P	21	17	16	14	13	31 [2]	32	25	27	30
Q	1	1	1	-	-	1 [2]	1	1	1	2
X	206	223	224	222	222	195 [2]	153	150	126	156

Men - Hommes - Hombres
ISIC 3 - CITI 3 - CIIU 3

	1999	2000	2001	2002	2003	2004	2005	2006	2007	2008
Total	1 266	1 179	1 066	1 016	996	925 [2]	902	801	722	820
UB	627	589	512	475	480	263 [2]	266	250	204	215
A	60	54	49	48	48	38 [2]	31	28	29	36
B	2	2	2	2	1	2 [2]	2	2	1	1
C	2	2	3	1	1	1 [2]	2	2	1	1
D	105	96	80	91	86	127 [2]	135	111	95	115
E	2	2	2	1	3	2 [2]	1	1	1	2
F	132	121	108	103	91	130 [2]	130	111	111	128
G	82	67	65	57	52	89 [2]	81	75	71	80
H	38	39	37	36	37	61 [2]	59	45	46	53
I	30	31	28	22	22	32 [2]	35	29	29	36
J	5	5	4	5	3	5 [2]	6	4	2	4
K	20	18	20	19	18	48 [2]	41	41	34	37
L	26	25	23	22	19	15 [2]	11	9	12	13
M	6	5	5	6	7	9 [2]	10	7	8	8
N	7	7	6	5	6	7 [2]	6	5	6	6
O	28	23	23	25	22	29 [2]	29	28	27	26
P	2	2	3	2	1	2 [2]	2	2	2	2
Q	-	1	-	-	-	0 [2]	1	0	1	1
X	89	91	97	97	98	65 [2]	54	53	44	57

Women - Femmes - Mujeres
ISIC 3 - CITI 3 - CIIU 3

	1999	2000	2001	2002	2003	2004	2005	2006	2007	2008
Total	1 404	1 316	1 201	1 147	1 100	1 036 [2]	986	873	784	872
UB	784	737	671	626	584	371 [2]	368	317	267	290
A	67	54	50	49	53	28 [2]	27	25	24	26
B	-	-	-	-	-	0 [2]	0	0	0	.
C	-	-	1	1	1	0 [2]	0	0	1	.
D	100	85	72	69	69	93 [2]	94	78	69	76
E	1	1	1	1	1	1 [2]	0	0	1	1
F	7	8	6	5	3	5 [2]	4	5	5	6
G	83	73	65	68	65	94 [2]	89	76	79	86
H	44	44	42	46	45	76 [2]	75	63	56	66
I	13	15	14	12	15	16 [2]	16	13	11	12
J	6	5	7	5	5	9 [2]	7	5	7	5
K	34	33	30	30	30	58 [2]	55	56	53	59
L	33	30	24	22	19	14 [2]	12	13	10	10
M	33	28	28	27	28	39 [2]	33	28	26	31
N	25	21	18	19	19	31 [2]	33	29	23	28
O	36	35	28	28	28	43 [2]	45	44	45	49
P	18	15	14	12	12	29 [2]	30	23	25	28
Q	1	-	1	-	-	0 [2]	0	0	0	0
X	118	132	127	126	124	130 [2]	99	97	82	99

Latvia (BA) [3] — Total unemployment - Chômage total - Desempleo total

Total - Total - Total
ISIC 3 - CITI 3 - CIIU 3

	1999	2000	2001	2002	2003	2004	2005	2006	2007	2008
Total	161.4	158.7	144.7	134.5 [4]	119.2	118.6	99.1	79.9	72.1	91.6
UB	19.9	17.5	16.8	20.4 [4]	13.8	14.1	13.1	15.3	11.9	11.3
A-B	6.1	7.6	6.0	9.3 [4]	6.3	5.4	5.0	3.1	4.3	-
C-F	36.7	36.6	35.3	38.3 [4]	35.1	33.4	23.1	18.8	20.7	23.8
G-Q	42.9	46.3	39.2	44.6 [4]	47.5	45.4	39.4	30.5	26.3	23.7
X	55.8	50.8	47.4	21.9 [4]	16.5	20.4	18.4	12.2	8.8	31.3

Explanatory notes: see p. 451.   Notes explicatives: voir p. 454.   Notas explicativas: véase p. 457.

[1] Persons aged 15 years and over. [2] Methodology revised; data not strictly comparable. [3] Persons aged 15 to 74 years. [4] Prior to 2002: persons aged 15 years and over.

[1] Personnes âgées de 15 ans et plus. [2] Méthodologie révisée; les données ne sont pas strictement comparables. [3] Personnes âgées de 15 à 74 ans. [4] Avant 2002: personnes agées de 15 ans et plus.

[1] Personas de 15 años y más. [2] Metodología revisada; los datos no son estrictamente comparables. [3] Personas de 15 a 74 años. [4] Antes de 2002: personas de 15 años y más.

UNEMPLOYMENT — CHÔMAGE — DESEMPLEO

By economic activity — Par activité économique — Por actividad económica

Thousands — Milliers — Millares

Latvia (BA) [1] — Total unemployment - Chômage total - Desempleo total

Men - Hommes - Hombres
ISIC 3 - CITI 3 - CIIU 3

	1999	2000	2001	2002	2003	2004	2005	2006	2007	2008
Total	88.7	87.0	81.9	74.9 [2]	61.7	61.7	52.8	43.7	39.4	50.3
UB	12.4	9.8	9.1	10.3 [2]	7.1	7.4	7.3	7.5	6.0	5.6
A-B	-	5.7	-	7.5 [2]	4.3	-	3.2	-	-	-
C-F	23.0	25.6	24.6	24.4 [2]	22.4	22.0	15.5	12.9	14.4	17.9
G-Q	21.6	21.0	17.7	18.8 [2]	19.3	17.6	15.3	14.0	9.7	10.1
X	26.8	24.9	25.4	13.9 [2]	8.5	10.3	11.6	7.1	6.2	15.7

Women - Femmes - Mujeres
ISIC 3 - CITI 3 - CIIU 3

	1999	2000	2001	2002	2003	2004	2005	2006	2007	2008
Total	72.7	71.7	62.7	59.6 [2]	57.5	56.9	46.2	36.2	32.7	41.4
UB	7.5	7.7	7.7	10.1 [2]	6.7	6.7	5.8	7.8	5.9	5.7
A-B	-	1.9	-	1.8 [2]	1.9	-	1.8	-	-	-
C-F	13.6	11.0	10.6	13.9 [2]	12.7	11.3	7.6	6.0	6.3	5.9
G-Q	21.3	25.3	21.5	25.8 [2]	28.2	27.8	24.1	16.5	16.6	13.6
X	29.0	25.9	22.0	8.0 [2]	8.0	10.0	6.9	5.1	2.6	15.7

Lithuania (BA) [3] — Total unemployment - Chômage total - Desempleo total

Total - Total - Total
ISIC 3 - CITI 3 - CIIU 3

	1999	2000	2001	2002	2003	2004	2005	2006	2007	2008
Total	249.0	273.7	284.0	224.4	203.9	184.4	132.9	89.3	69.0	94.3
UB [4]	63.4	57.2	66.9	51.5	56.7	49.9	37.2	26.1	14.5	21.4
A	22.6	17.2	23.5	16.0	15.2	12.0	8.3	6.1	3.6	4.7
B	0.2	1.2	0.3	0.4	0.6	0.2	0.0	0.1	0.1	0.2
C	0.8	1.5	1.7	0.8	0.8	0.5	0.2	0.5	0.6	0.1
D	51.8	58.2	57.6	45.2	36.4	35.1	22.9	14.2	13.9	17.2
E	2.2	3.7	2.5	2.5	1.3	1.4	0.6	0.7	0.6	0.3
F	27.1	35.3	31.0	23.0	19.9	16.8	13.1	9.4	7.9	15.4
G	35.4	44.3	42.3	36.7	30.5	27.9	20.6	11.5	10.6	11.8
H	8.7	7.0	4.0	5.2	5.8	5.2	3.3	3.4	2.9	2.8
I	15.4	14.0	14.9	14.8	9.2	7.1	6.4	3.2	3.3	4.8
J	0.6	2.5	1.4	1.6	1.7	1.0	1.4	0.3	0.2	0.3
K	2.4	4.0	3.9	3.3	3.1	2.4	2.4	2.0	3.1	4.6
L	4.1	5.8	10.8	6.6	5.2	6.5	3.9	2.0	1.7	3.1
M	6.6	7.2	9.4	5.6	5.3	5.8	3.8	3.2	2.1	3.3
N	2.9	7.4	5.5	3.4	4.2	6.3	2.4	2.2	1.4	2.0
O	4.8	6.4	7.7	7.1	7.4	5.7	5.9	4.2	2.1	2.0
P	-	0.6	0.5	0.5	0.7	0.5	0.4	0.2	0.2	0.2

Men - Hommes - Hombres
ISIC 3 - CITI 3 - CIIU 3

	1999	2000	2001	2002	2003	2004	2005	2006	2007	2008
Total	140.5	158.5	165.6	121.1	105.4	90.6	67.1	46.7	34.6	49.5
UB [4]	29.6	34.8	37.0	26.1	27.0	22.9	16.0	12.2	6.7	10.2
A	17.7	12.4	17.1	9.6	9.2	8.1	5.4	3.4	2.3	3.7
B	-	1.1	0.2	0.3	0.5	0.2	-	0.1	0.1	0.2
C	-	1.3	1.0	0.6	0.8	0.4	0.1	0.1	0.2	0.1
D	28.7	29.4	31.2	24.2	16.5	17.8	11.7	7.1	7.5	9.0
E	2.1	2.3	1.7	1.8	1.0	0.6	0.4	0.7	0.5	0.2
F	25.2	32.8	28.0	20.7	18.3	15.8	12.3	9.2	7.6	13.3
G	17.3	21.2	18.4	14.2	11.7	10.8	7.4	4.0	3.6	4.1
H	1.1	1.4	1.0	1.0	1.0	0.9	0.6	1.6	0.6	0.4
I	9.9	8.6	10.4	9.7	6.4	4.8	4.7	2.1	1.8	3.2
J	-	0.6	0.3	0.4	0.5	0.1	0.3	0.1	-	0.2
K	2.0	2.4	2.6	1.7	1.4	1.1	1.2	0.5	1.4	2.0
L	2.2	2.4	6.9	3.7	2.8	3.1	2.8	1.5	0.6	0.9
M	1.9	2.9	4.5	2.4	2.6	1.0	1.6	1.6	0.8	0.6
N	0.7	2.0	1.1	1.0	0.8	0.6	0.5	0.6	0.1	0.2
O	2.1	2.9	3.5	3.3	4.3	2.4	2.0	1.9	0.6	1.1
P	-	0.5		0.2	0.6		0.1	-	-	-

Women - Femmes - Mujeres
ISIC 3 - CITI 3 - CIIU 3

	1999	2000	2001	2002	2003	2004	2005	2006	2007	2008
Total	108.5	115.2	118.4	103.3	98.4	93.8	65.8	42.6	34.3	44.8
UB [4]	33.8	22.4	30.0	25.4	29.6	27.0	21.3	13.9	7.9	11.2
A	5.0	4.8	6.5	6.3	5.9	4.0	2.9	2.7	1.3	1.0
B	0.2	0.1	0.1	0.1	0.1	-	-	-	-	0.0
C	0.8	0.2	0.6	0.1	-	-	0.1	0.4	0.4	0.0
D	23.0	28.8	26.4	21.0	19.9	17.4	11.2	7.2	6.4	8.1
E	0.1	1.4	0.8	0.7	0.2	0.8	0.2	-	0.1	0.1
F	1.9	2.5	3.0	2.4	1.6	1.0	0.9	0.2	0.4	2.2
G	18.1	23.1	23.9	22.5	18.8	17.1	13.1	7.5	6.8	7.7
H	7.7	5.7	2.9	4.1	4.8	4.2	2.7	1.8	2.3	2.3
I	5.6	5.4	4.5	5.1	2.8	2.3	1.7	1.1	1.5	1.6
J	0.6	1.9	1.2	1.2	1.1	0.9	1.2	0.2	0.1	0.1
K	0.3	1.6	1.3	1.6	1.7	1.3	1.2	1.5	1.7	2.6
L	1.9	3.4	3.9	2.9	2.4	3.4	1.1	0.5	1.1	2.2
M	4.6	4.4	4.9	3.2	2.7	4.9	2.1	1.6	1.3	2.7
N	2.3	5.4	4.4	2.4	3.4	5.6	1.9	1.6	1.3	1.8
O	2.6	3.6	4.2	3.9	3.1	3.3	3.9	2.3	1.5	0.9
P	-	0.6	-	0.3	0.1	0.5	0.3	0.2	0.2	0.2

Explanatory notes: see p. 451.

[1] Persons aged 15 to 74 years. [2] Prior to 2002: persons aged 15 years and over. [3] Persons aged 15 years and over. [4] Incl. the unemployed whose last job was 8 years ago or over.

Notes explicatives: voir p. 454.

[1] Personnes âgées de 15 à 74 ans. [2] Avant 2002: personnes âgées de 15 ans et plus. [3] Personnes âgées de 15 ans et plus. [4] Y compris les chômeurs dont le dernier emploi date de 8 ans ou plus.

Notas explicativas: véase p. 457.

[1] Personas de 15 a 74 años. [2] Antes de 2002: personas de 15 años y más. [3] Personas de 15 años y más. [4] Incl. los desempleados cuyo último trabajo fue hace 8 años o más.

By economic activity   Par activité économique   Por actividad económica

	Thousands			Milliers				Millares		
	1999	2000	2001	2002	2003	2004	2005	2006	2007	2008
Lithuania (FB) [1][2]			Registered unemployment - Chômage enregistré - Desempleo registrado							
Total - Total - Total										
ISIC 3 - CITI 3 - CIIU 3										
Total	177.4	225.9	224.0	191.2	158.8	126.4	87.2	79.3	69.7	95.0
UB	16.7	18.9	16.9	18.0	13.1	9.3	6.2	6.0	5.9	7.0
A	27.1	30.8	29.3	25.6	19.9	16.8	10.5	8.2	5.4	6.2
C-E	39.4	53.6	54.6	46.9	39.7	30.4	21.4	20.1	17.8	25.3
F	18.0	16.0	17.9	13.0	10.4	8.2	5.3	4.7	4.7	12.0
G-H	30.3	36.8	39.8	30.0	22.0	17.1	13.5	12.8	12.0	18.2
I	10.9	10.0	12.2	8.2	6.9	5.1	3.4	3.0	2.8	4.4
K	2.5	5.6	4.5	5.8	5.5	4.5	3.4	3.5	3.6	5.7
L	4.0	5.7	5.8	5.7	6.0	6.2	5.2	5.0	4.1	4.0
M	5.8	6.4	7.0	4.6	5.0	4.5	3.4	3.0	2.6	2.7
N	3.7	4.5	5.5	3.8	3.7	3.1	2.5	2.1	1.6	1.6
O	19.0	37.6	30.5	29.6	26.6	21.2	12.4	10.9	9.2	7.9
Men - Hommes - Hombres										
ISIC 3 - CITI 3 - CIIU 3										
Total	94.6	123.1	117.7	95.1	73.7	53.8	33.9	29.9	27.4	49.0
UB	7.8	9.1	8.1	9.0	6.4	4.0	2.5	2.4	2.5	3.5
A	16.4	19.5	18.7	14.9	10.6	8.1	4.7	3.5	2.4	3.1
C-E	21.2	29.5	29.0	22.0	17.4	12.4	7.8	7.2	6.5	12.4
F	13.4	12.0	13.7	11.0	8.8	6.8	4.3	3.9	4.0	10.8
G-H	11.1	15.8	14.1	11.1	8.4	5.9	3.8	3.5	3.4	7.0
I	7.6	6.7	8.9	4.5	3.6	2.4	1.5	1.3	1.3	2.8
K	1.4	2.8	2.2	2.7	2.3	1.7	1.2	1.2	1.4	2.7
L	2.4	3.9	3.8	3.1	3.1	2.9	2.2	2.0	1.6	1.6
M	2.1	2.4	2.1	1.8	1.7	1.4	1.0	0.8	0.6	0.9
N	1.3	1.4	1.4	1.0	0.8	0.5	0.4	0.3	0.2	0.3
O	9.7	20.0	15.7	14.0	10.6	7.7	4.5	3.8	3.5	3.9
Women - Femmes - Mujeres										
ISIC 3 - CITI 3 - CIIU 3										
Total	82.8	102.8	106.3	96.1	85.1	72.6	53.3	49.4	42.3	46.0
UB	8.9	9.8	8.8	9.0	6.7	5.3	3.7	3.6	3.4	3.5
A	10.7	11.3	10.6	10.7	9.3	8.7	5.8	4.7	3.0	3.1
C-E	18.2	24.1	25.6	24.9	22.3	18.0	13.6	12.9	11.3	12.9
F	4.5	4.0	4.2	2.0	1.6	1.4	1.0	0.8	0.7	1.2
G-H	19.3	21.0	25.7	18.9	13.6	11.2	9.7	9.3	8.6	11.2
I	3.3	3.3	3.3	3.7	3.3	2.7	1.9	1.7	1.5	1.6
K	1.1	2.8	2.3	3.1	3.2	2.8	2.2	2.3	2.2	3.0
L	1.6	1.8	2.1	2.6	2.9	3.3	3.0	3.0	2.5	2.4
M	3.7	4.0	4.9	2.8	3.3	3.1	2.4	2.2	2.0	1.8
N	2.4	3.1	4.1	2.8	2.9	2.6	2.1	1.8	1.4	1.3
O	9.2	17.6	14.8	15.6	16.0	13.5	7.9	7.1	5.7	4.0
Malta (BA) [3]			Total unemployment - Chômage total - Desempleo total							
Total - Total - Total										
ISIC 3 - CITI 3 - CIIU 3										
Total	.	10.151	10.164	.	.	11.518	11.750	11.925	10.729	10.389
UB	.	3.091	4.344	.	.	5.059	5.104	3.515	2.857	2.592
A	.	-	0.041	.	.	-	-	-	-	0.027
B	.	-	0.059	.	.	-	-	-	-	-
C	.	0.298	0.207	.	.	-	-	-	-	0.092
D	.	2.045	2.784	.	.	2.457	2.754	2.637	2.533	2.228
E	.	0.136	-	.	.	-	-	-	-	-
F	.	1.172	0.924	.	.	0.912	0.851	0.848	0.795	0.932
G	.	0.758	1.264	.	.	0.877	1.115	1.212	1.273	1.226
H	.	0.750	0.822	.	.	1.534	0.915	1.113	1.438	1.123
I	.	0.749	0.338	.	.	-	-	-	0.427	0.336
J	.	0.221	-	.	.	-	-	-	-	0.090
K	.	0.069	0.211	.	.	-	0.535	-	-	0.512
L	.	0.118	0.062	.	.	-	-	-	-	0.198
M	.	0.061	0.073	.	.	-	-	-	-	0.202
N	.	0.108	0.073	.	.	-	-	-	-	0.174
O	.	0.336	0.162	.	.	-	-	0.597	-	0.280
P	.	.	.	.	.	.	.	.	.	.
Q	.	0.054	-	.	.	-	-	-	-	-
X	.	.	.	.	.	.	.	.	.	0.212

Explanatory notes: see p. 451.

[1] Persons aged 16 to 64 years. [2] 31st Dec. of each year. [3] Persons aged 15 years and over.

Notes explicatives: voir p. 454.

[1] Personnes âgées de 16 à 64 ans. [2] 31 déc. de chaque année. [3] Personnes âgées de 15 ans et plus.

Notas explicativas: véase p. 457.

[1] Personas de 16 a 64 años. [2] 31 dic. de cada año. [3] Personas de 15 años y más.

	Thousands					Milliers				Millares
	1999	2000	2001	2002	2003	2004	2005	2006	2007	2008

Malta (BA) [1]   Total unemployment - Chômage total - Desempleo total

Men - Hommes - Hombres
ISIC 3 - CITI 3 - CIIU 3

	1999	2000	2001	2002	2003	2004	2005	2006	2007	2008
Total	.	7.628	6.626	.	.	7.080	7.279	7.242	6.474	6.442
UB	.	2.159	2.308	.	.	2.289	2.358	2.031	1.747	1.485
A	.	-	0.041	.	.	-	-	-	-	0.012
B	.	-	0.059	.	.	-	-	-	-	-
C	.	0.298	0.207	.	.	-	-	-	-	0.077
D	.	1.244	1.630	.	.	1.502	1.702	1.385	1.295	1.284
E	.	0.076	-	.	.	-	-	-	-	-
F	.	1.172	0.924	.	.	0.882	0.836	0.811	0.795	0.896
G	.	0.633	0.556	.	.	0.703	0.723	0.680	0.559	0.682
H	.	0.509	0.628	.	.	0.696	0.576	0.635	0.948	0.650
I	.	0.684	0.274	.	.	-	-	-	-	0.198
J	.	0.115	-	.	.	-	-	-	-	0.015
K	.	-	0.072	.	.	-	-	-	-	0.383
L	.	0.118	-	.	.	-	-	-	-	0.176
M	.	0.061	-	.	.	-	-	-	-	0.104
N	.	0.050	-	.	.	-	-	-	-	0.025
O	.	0.268	0.108	.	.	-	-	-	-	0.207
P	.	.	.	.	.	.	.	.	.	.
Q	.	0.054	-	.	.	.	.	.	.	.
X	.	.	.	.	.	.	.	.	.	0.126

Women - Femmes - Mujeres
ISIC 3 - CITI 3 - CIIU 3

	1999	2000	2001	2002	2003	2004	2005	2006	2007	2008
Total	.	2.523	3.538	.	.	4.438	4.466	4.683	4.255	3.947
UB	.	0.932	2.036	.	.	2.770	2.746	1.484	1.110	2.797
A	.	-	0.000	.	.	-	-	-	-	0.015
B	.	-	0.000	.	.	-	-	-	-	-
C	.	.	.	.	.	.	.	.	.	0.015
D	.	0.801	1.154	.	.	0.855	1.052	1.252	1.238	0.944
E	.	0.060	-	.	.	-	-	-	-	-
F	.	-	-	.	.	0.030	0.015	0.037	0.000	0.036
G	.	0.124	0.708	.	.	0.174	0.392	0.532	0.714	0.544
H	.	0.241	0.194	.	.	0.838	0.339	0.478	0.490	0.473
I	.	0.065	0.064	.	.	-	-	-	-	0.138
J	.	0.105	-	.	.	-	-	-	-	0.075
K	.	0.069	0.139	.	.	-	-	-	-	0.129
L	.	-	0.062	.	.	-	-	-	-	0.022
M	.	-	0.062	.	.	-	-	-	-	0.098
N	.	0.057	0.073	.	.	-	-	-	-	0.149
O	.	0.068	0.054	.	.	-	-	-	-	0.073
P	.	.	.	.	.	.	.	.	.	.
Q	.	.	.	.	.	.	.	.	.	.
X	.	.	.	.	.	.	.	.	.	0.086

Moldova, Republic of (BA) [1]   Total unemployment - Chômage total - Desempleo total

Total - Total - Total
ISIC 3 - CITI 3 - CIIU 3

	1999	2000	2001	2002	2003	2004	2005	2006	2007	2008
Total	187.2	140.1	117.7	110.0	117.1	116.5	103.7	99.9	66.7	51.7
UB	43.2	30.5	27.6	27.3	25.8	28.4	27.3	29.3	20.2	14.9
A	25.3	15.8	12.9	13.7	19.0	17.9	13.8	12.0	4.5	3.4
B	0.2	0.1	0.2	0.1	-	0.2	0.1	0.1	0.0	-
C	0.5	0.3	0.3	-	0.1	0.1	0.1	0.1	0.2	0.2
D	30.7	22.4	19.4	16.1	14.4	12.4	10.9	10.8	8.0	6.0
E	3.4	2.1	2.0	1.4	1.6	1.6	1.0	1.3	0.7	0.5
F	16.7	11.5	9.2	8.6	7.9	7.4	6.8	8.3	5.5	4.7
G	16.6	14.5	9.7	9.3	9.5	9.9	8.8	8.6	6.3	4.0
H	4.0	3.4	2.8	1.7	1.9	1.9	1.7	1.1	0.8	1.6
I	10.9	8.2	6.2	4.6	5.2	4.5	3.8	2.9	2.4	2.4
J	1.1	1.0	0.6	0.5	0.4	0.5	0.7	0.1	0.3	0.3
K	2.2	2.4	2.2	1.5	1.9	1.4	1.1	1.5	0.8	0.9
L	5.2	4.6	3.7	3.2	3.8	3.2	2.8	1.8	2.2	2.3
M	7.8	7.3	5.5	5.6	4.2	3.9	2.4	2.9	1.3	1.4
N	5.2	4.4	2.7	3.3	2.6	2.4	1.4	1.4	0.5	0.9
O	5.2	4.2	2.7	1.9	1.6	2.1	2.0	1.3	1.1	0.9
P	0.3	0.3	0.2	0.1	0.3	0.1	0.3	0.4	0.3	0.3
Q	.	.	.	.	.	.	.	.	.	.
X	8.7	7.0	9.9	11.0	16.8	18.4	18.7	16.2	11.6	7.2

Explanatory notes: see p. 451.
[1] Persons aged 15 years and over.

Notes explicatives: voir p. 454.
[1] Personnes âgées de 15 ans et plus.

Notas explicativas: véase p. 457.
[1] Personas de 15 años y más.

By economic activity   Par activité économique   Por actividad económica

	Thousands			Milliers				Millares		
	1999	2000	2001	2002	2003	2004	2005	2006	2007	2008

Moldova, Republic of (BA) [1]   Total unemployment - Chômage total - Desempleo total

Men - Hommes - Hombres
ISIC 3 - CITI 3 - CIIU 3

	1999	2000	2001	2002	2003	2004	2005	2006	2007	2008
Total	113.6	80.6	70.1	64.4	69.9	70.1	59.8	61.7	41.5	30.0
UB	27.3	17.6	16.1	16.2	14.6	16.5	14.3	17.3	12.4	7.0
A	17.4	11.1	9.6	8.5	13.1	10.4	8.6	7.7	3.3	2.5
B	0.2	0.1	0.2	0.1	-	0.2	0.1	0.1	0.0	-
C	0.5	0.3	0.3	-	0.1	0.1	0.1	0.1	0.1	0.1
D	15.3	11.7	10.5	8.7	7.9	7.8	6.9	7.2	4.3	3.7
E	2.9	1.8	1.6	1.0	1.3	1.2	0.8	1.1	0.6	0.5
F	13.8	9.3	7.0	7.7	6.8	6.5	6.2	7.5	4.9	4.3
G	8.3	6.7	4.8	4.6	4.2	4.7	3.1	4.2	3.3	2.2
H	1.1	1.0	0.6	0.5	0.6	0.5	0.4	0.5	0.3	0.3
I	9.8	6.9	5.4	4.0	4.5	4.1	3.6	2.5	2.0	2.0
J	0.5	0.3	0.2	0.1	-	0.5	0.6	0.0	0.3	0.2
K	1.3	1.4	1.3	1.0	1.2	0.9	0.7	0.9	0.8	0.9
L	3.7	2.9	2.3	2.3	2.7	2.0	1.5	1.2	1.4	1.3
M	2.0	2.2	1.6	1.6	1.2	1.6	0.9	1.1	0.4	0.5
N	1.8	1.0	0.9	1.1	0.7	0.7	0.4	0.6	0.2	0.2
O	2.8	2.3	1.6	0.8	1.2	1.1	1.1	0.7	0.8	0.5
P	0.1	0.0	0.0	-	-	-	0.1	0.1	0.1	0.1
Q	.	.	.	.	.	.	.	.	.	.
X	4.8	4.1	6.3	6.3	9.9	11.5	10.4	8.9	6.1	3.9

Women - Femmes - Mujeres
ISIC 3 - CITI 3 - CIIU 3

	1999	2000	2001	2002	2003	2004	2005	2006	2007	2008
Total	73.6	59.5	47.6	45.4	47.2	46.4	43.9	38.2	25.2	21.8
UB	15.9	12.8	11.5	11.1	11.3	11.8	13.0	12.1	7.8	7.9
A	7.9	4.7	3.4	5.2	5.9	7.5	5.2	4.3	1.2	0.9
B	-	-	-	-	-	-	-	0.0	0.0	-
C	-	-	-	-	-	-	-	0.0	0.0	0.1
D	15.4	10.7	8.9	7.4	6.5	4.7	4.0	3.6	3.8	2.3
E	0.5	0.3	0.4	0.4	0.3	0.4	0.1	0.2	0.1	0.1
F	3.0	2.3	2.3	0.9	1.1	1.0	0.6	0.8	0.6	0.4
G	8.4	7.8	4.9	4.7	5.3	5.2	5.7	4.4	3.0	1.8
H	2.9	2.4	2.2	1.3	1.4	1.4	1.2	0.6	0.4	1.3
I	1.1	1.4	0.9	0.6	0.7	0.3	0.2	0.3	0.3	0.4
J	0.6	0.7	0.4	0.5	0.4	-	0.1	0.1	0.0	0.0
K	0.9	1.0	0.9	0.5	0.7	0.5	0.4	0.5	0.0	-
L	1.4	1.7	1.3	0.9	1.1	1.2	1.3	0.6	0.8	1.0
M	5.8	5.0	4.0	4.0	3.0	2.4	1.6	1.9	0.9	1.0
N	3.3	3.4	1.9	2.2	2.0	1.7	1.0	0.8	0.3	0.7
O	2.4	2.0	1.1	1.1	0.5	1.0	0.8	0.6	0.2	0.4
P	0.2	0.3	0.1	0.1	0.3	0.1	0.2	0.2	0.2	0.2
Q	.	.	.	.	.	.	.	.	.	.
X	3.9	2.9	3.6	4.7	6.7	6.9	8.4	7.3	5.5	3.4

Poland (BA) [2]   Total unemployment - Chômage total - Desempleo total

Total - Total - Total
ISIC 3 - CITI 3 - CIIU 3   ISIC 4 - CITI 4 - CIIU 4

	1999	2000	2001	2002	2003	2004	2005	2006	2007	2008	
Total	2 391 [3]	2 785	3 170 [4]	3 431	3 329	3 230	3 045	2 344	1 619	1 211	Total
UB	498 [3]	597	703 [4]	773	769	727	709	541	361	250	UB
A	94 [3]	96	106 [4]	88	76	92	89	65	37	30	A
B	- [3]	-	- [4]	-	-	-	-	-	-	5	B
C	25 [3]	26	25 [4]	23	18	15	11	10	6	198	C
D	499 [3]	559	595 [4]	642	612	582	512	398	265	-	D
E	14 [3]	20	19 [4]	17	15	17	15	11	8	8	E
F	243 [3]	254	322 [4]	361	337	316	279	178	114	90	F
G	319 [3]	371	438 [4]	465	440	415	383	296	205	159	G
H	61 [3]	66	83 [4]	89	82	76	66	58	43	33	H
I	63 [3]	79	99 [4]	117	98	87	76	62	50	36	I
J	19 [3]	28	32 [4]	31	28	29	29	24	15	12	J
K	38 [3]	52	81 [4]	98	93	100	95	76	58	13	K
L	69 [3]	70	72 [4]	94	93	89	80	71	53	5	L
M	37 [3]	44	43 [4]	46	55	50	51	45	34	16	M
N	63 [3]	84	84 [4]	82	67	59	58	45	33	36	N
O	55 [3]	72	68 [4]	77	78	71	63	54	40	45	O
P	6 [3]	4	8 [4]	8	5	7	6	7	4	30	P
Q	- [3]	-	- [4]	-	-	-	-	-	-	26	Q
X	285 [3]	360	390 [4]	419	459	497	520	402	288	9	R
										12	S
										-	T
										191	X

---

[1] Persons aged 15 years and over. [2] Persons aged 15 to 74 years. [3] First and fourth quarters. [4] Prior to 2001: persons aged 15 years and over.

[1] Personnes âgées de 15 ans et plus. [2] Personnes âgées de 15 à 74 ans. [3] Premier et quatrième trimestres. [4] Avant 2001: personnes agées de 15 ans et plus.

[1] Personas de 15 años y más. [2] Personas de 15 a 74 años. [3] Primero y cuarto trimestres. [4] Antes de 2001: personas de 15 años y más.

3D UNEMPLOYMENT — CHÔMAGE — DESEMPLEO

By economic activity — Par activité économique — Por actividad económica

Thousands — Milliers — Millares

Poland (BA) [1]

Total unemployment - Chômage total - Desempleo total

Men - Hommes - Hombres — ISIC 3 - CITI 3 - CIIU 3

	1999[2]	2000	2001[3]	2002	2003	2004	2005	2006	2007
Total	1 147	1 344	1 583	1 779	1 741	1 681	1 553	1 202	831
UB	215	265	327	381	387	351	336	276	182
A	56	57	65	59	52	62	57	41	21
B	-	-	-	-	-	-	-	-	-
C	22	23	22	19	16	12	10	9	5
D	248	288	317	361	345	333	290	226	167
E	10	15	16	15	13	14	14	9	6
F	227	239	306	344	318	295	263	170	111
G	102	128	169	180	168	167	151	111	80
H	16	11	21	21	19	17	20	19	14
I	47	59	77	90	72	67	57	47	35
J	5	8	8	8	6	6	6	6	-
K	21	31	40	52	55	55	54	39	28
L	39	35	36	47	48	47	40	33	25
M	9	14	10	9	12	14	13	11	9
N	7	15	11	12	14	15	13	10	5
O	27	37	30	41	46	37	34	29	21
P	-	-	-	-	-	-	-	-	-
Q	-	-	-	-	-	-	-	-	-
X	93	118	124	137	167	186	193	165	117

ISIC 4 - CITI 4 - CIIU 4 (2008):

	2008
Total	599
UB	121
A	18
B	-
C	113
D	-
E	6
F	87
G	58
H	24
I	9
J	7
K	-
L	-
M	8
N	18
O	20
P	9
Q	5
R	-
S	-
T	-
X	74

Women - Femmes - Mujeres — ISIC 3 - CITI 3 - CIIU 3

	1999[2]	2000	2001[3]	2002	2003	2004	2005	2006	2007
Total	1 244	1 440	1 587	1 652	1 588	1 550	1 493	1 142	788
UB	283	332	376	392	382	376	373	265	180
A	38	39	41	29	25	31	32	24	16
B	-	-	-	-	-	-	-	-	-
C	2	2	4	4	2	3	-	-	-
D	251	272	278	282	267	248	222	172	99
E	3	5	2	2	2	-	-	-	-
F	16	16	16	17	19	20	16	7	-
G	218	243	269	284	272	248	232	184	125
H	45	55	62	68	64	59	46	40	29
I	16	20	22	26	26	21	19	15	15
J	14	21	24	22	21	24	23	19	13
K	17	21	41	45	38	45	41	37	30
L	30	35	36	47	45	42	41	38	29
M	28	30	32	37	43	36	38	34	26
N	56	68	73	71	53	44	45	36	28
O	28	35	38	36	32	34	29	25	19
P	5	4	7	7	-	7	6	6	-
Q	-	-	-	-	-	-	-	-	-
X	191	242	266	282	292	311	326	237	172

ISIC 4 - CITI 4 - CIIU 4 (2008):

	2008
Total	612
UB	129
A	12
B	-
C	85
D	-
E	-
F	-
G	101
H	9
I	27
J	5
K	9
L	-
M	8
N	17
O	25
P	21
Q	21
R	5
S	9
T	-
X	117

Poland (FB) [4]

Registered unemployment - Chômage enregistré - Desempleo registrado

Total - Total - Total — ISIC 3 - CITI 3 - CIIU 3

	1999	2000	2001	2002	2003	2004	2005	2006	2007	2008
Total	2 349.8	2 702.6	3 115.1	3 217.0	3 175.7	2 999.6	2 773.0	2 309.4	1 746.6	1 473.8
UB	556.9	643.3	739.4	767.3	764.2	708.2	656.6	545.3	404.8	328.9
A	103.0	100.7	105.0	103.5	99.9	94.3	87.1	72.3	53.7	41.2
B	1.3	1.4	1.8	1.8	1.8	1.5	1.7	1.3	1.0	0.7
C	19.1	16.9	16.6	15.8	14.3	12.2	10.7	8.3	5.9	4.2
D	505.3	554.6	625.3	622.9	592.6	542.4	497.6	408.0	303.9	267.7
E	12.6	11.5	13.2	13.5	13.4	12.8	11.4	9.2	7.0	5.5
F	188.9	204.2	252.1	265.8	251.6	223.1	194.0	143.4	104.9	88.0
G	341.0	369.6	419.3	429.6	429.4	412.4	379.2	320.4	237.7	191.7
H	47.5	52.0	60.8	61.8	61.0	58.4	54.0	46.1	34.9	28.5
I	52.4	55.2	67.9	70.4	67.8	63.7	57.8	46.8	34.7	28.9
J	13.3	14.0	16.8	18.1	19.0	19.0	17.1	15.2	11.3	9.7
K	50.5	59.4	74.1	84.0	86.7	83.8	81.7	70.2	55.9	50.3
L	130.8	134.6	142.1	159.8	162.0	158.3	143.6	122.2	98.1	82.7
M	36.2	39.6	41.2	40.3	40.5	40.2	38.3	34.6	27.6	22.8
N	63.9	74.1	78.7	74.4	74.1	70.0	65.5	56.5	43.5	33.3
O	137.4	149.8	189.8	207.8	220.4	210.9	189.4	161.4	121.5	102.8
P	21.3	15.6	14.9	13.1	12.1	11.5	10.5	8.8	7.4	5.4
Q	0.3	0.2	0.3	0.3	0.2	0.2	0.1	0.1	0.1	0.1
X	68.1	205.9	255.8	266.8	264.7	276.7	276.7	239.1	192.7	181.5

Explanatory notes: see p. 451.

[1] Persons aged 15 to 74 years. [2] First and fourth quarters. [3] Prior to 2001: persons aged 15 years and over. [4] 31st Dec. of each year.

Notes explicatives: voir p. 454.

[1] Personnes âgées de 15 à 74 ans. [2] Premier et quatrième trimestres. [3] Avant 2001: personnes agées de 15 ans et plus. [4] 31 déc. de chaque année.

Notas explicativas: véase p. 457.

[1] Personas de 15 a 74 años. [2] Primero y cuarto trimestres. [3] Antes de 2001: personas de 15 años y más. [4] 31 dic. de cada año.

By economic activity — **Par activité économique** — **Por actividad económica**

	Thousands			Milliers				Millares		
	1999	2000	2001	2002	2003	2004	2005	2006	2007	2008

Poland (FB) [1] — Registered unemployment - Chômage enregistré - Desempleo registrado

Men - Hommes - Hombres
ISIC 3 - CITI 3 - CIIU 3

	1999	2000	2001	2002	2003	2004	2005	2006	2007	2008
Total	1 042.5	1 211.0	1 473.0	1 571.2	1 541.0	1 431.1	1 286.6	1 003.7	729.3	640.4
UB	212.8	256.2	308.1	337.2	334.5	300.0	267.8	204.8	142.2	117.8
A	49.8	48.7	52.2	54.2	52.4	49.4	45.1	35.9	25.8	20.6
B	0.7	0.9	1.3	1.3	1.3	1.1	1.2	1.0	0.7	0.5
C	14.4	12.2	12.0	11.6	10.4	8.7	7.6	5.8	4.0	3.1
D	210.6	237.2	286.0	294.8	276.4	251.8	226.0	175.0	125.2	118.4
E	9.5	8.8	10.1	10.3	10.2	9.6	8.5	6.8	5.1	4.1
F	168.2	180.9	226.4	239.5	225.6	199.1	172.1	124.5	90.5	77.2
G	101.4	116.6	142.1	151.8	149.1	140.5	124.9	98.2	68.6	59.4
H	8.2	9.1	12.0	13.6	13.4	13.1	11.5	9.1	6.5	5.5
I	32.7	34.4	44.2	45.4	42.9	39.3	35.3	27.2	19.4	17.2
J	3.5	3.2	4.0	4.8	4.7	4.9	4.0	3.3	2.3	2.1
K	24.4	29.0	37.4	43.0	44.2	41.9	40.2	32.2	24.5	22.0
L	80.1	80.1	86.9	93.4	99.9	98.0	88.3	72.4	56.4	47.0
M	9.1	10.2	11.2	11.5	11.6	11.6	10.6	9.0	6.9	5.8
N	11.4	12.1	12.9	13.3	13.9	13.5	13.0	10.5	7.8	6.1
O	67.9	71.6	95.3	107.1	113.0	106.5	92.2	75.0	54.2	46.7
P	2.7	2.0	2.1	2.0	1.8	1.9	1.6	1.2	1.1	1.0
Q	0.1	0.1	0.2	0.2	0.1	0.3	-	-	-	-
X	35.0	97.7	128.6	136.2	135.6	139.9	136.7	111.9	88.0	85.6

Women - Femmes - Mujeres
ISIC 3 - CITI 3 - CIIU 3

	1999	2000	2001	2002	2003	2004	2005	2006	2007	2008
Total	1 307.3	1 491.6	1 642.1	1 645.8	1 634.7	1 568.5	1 486.4	1 305.7	1 017.3	833.4
UB	344.1	387.1	431.3	430.1	429.7	408.2	388.9	340.5	262.6	211.1
A	53.2	52.0	52.8	49.3	47.5	44.9	42.0	36.4	28.0	20.5
B	0.6	0.5	0.5	0.5	0.5	0.4	0.4	0.4	0.3	0.2
C	4.7	4.7	4.6	4.2	3.9	3.4	3.1	2.6	1.9	1.1
D	294.7	317.4	339.3	328.0	316.2	290.6	271.6	233.1	178.8	149.3
E	3.1	2.7	3.1	3.2	3.2	3.2	2.9	2.5	1.8	1.4
F	20.7	23.3	25.7	26.2	26.0	24.0	22.0	18.9	14.4	10.8
G	239.6	253.0	277.2	277.8	280.3	271.9	254.2	222.2	169.0	132.3
H	32.3	42.9	48.8	48.2	47.6	45.3	42.5	37.0	28.4	23.0
I	19.7	20.8	23.7	25.0	24.9	24.4	22.5	19.6	15.3	11.6
J	9.8	10.8	12.8	13.3	14.3	14.1	13.1	11.9	9.0	7.5
K	26.1	30.4	36.7	41.0	42.5	41.8	41.5	38.0	31.4	28.2
L	50.7	54.5	55.2	66.4	62.1	60.3	55.3	49.8	41.7	35.7
M	27.1	29.4	30.0	28.8	28.9	28.6	27.7	25.6	20.7	17.0
N	52.5	62.0	65.8	61.1	60.2	56.5	52.5	46.0	35.7	27.1
O	69.5	78.2	94.5	100.7	100.4	104.3	97.2	86.4	67.3	56.1
P	18.6	13.6	12.8	11.1	10.3	9.6	9.0	7.6	6.3	4.4
Q	0.2	0.1	0.1	0.1	0.1	0.2	0.1	0.1	0.1	-
X	33.1	108.2	127.2	130.8	129.1	136.8	140.0	127.1	104.7	95.9

Portugal (BA) [2] — Total unemployment - Chômage total - Desempleo total

Total - Total - Total
ISIC 3 - CITI 3 - CIIU 3 / ISIC 4 - CITI 4 - CIIU 4

	1999	2000	2001	2002	2003	2004	2005	2006	2007	2008	
Total	225.8	205.5	213.5	270.5	342.3	365.0	422.3	427.8	448.6 |	427.1	Total
UB	33.6	27.3	34.6	41.1	46.3	49.2	58.7	58.8	61.5 |	58.4	UB
A	7.7	5.6	8.5	8.9	11.0	8.9	9.6	10.0	11.1 |	9.4	A
B	-	-	-	-	-	-	1.0	0.7	1.1 |	0.9 [3]	B
C	-	-	-	-	-	-	1.1	1.4	0.6 |	88.2	C
D	55.2	48.9	51.4	67.5	82.0	91.4	117.5	118.4	112.2 |	0.8 [3]	D
E	-	-	-	-	-	1.3	0.8	0.7	0.8 |	3.8 [3]	E
F	23.4	17.4	18.8	26.1	41.5	42.5	43.0	43.5	49.9 |	57.9	F
G	30.7	32.8	31.8	36.1	46.4	51.9	59.0	59.6	64.7 |	57.0	G
H	18.4	19.1	17.6	20.5	28.5	27.3	30.2	32.9	32.8 |	11.2	H
I	6.5	7.4	5.3	12.6	13.5	13.3	13.7	16.2	15.5 |	36.3	I
J	-	-	-	-	-	2.5	3.2	1.7	3.0 |	7.8	J
K	12.5	12.7	12.4	14.4	21.7	21.5	26.6	26.0	24.0 |	2.6 [3]	K
L	5.8	5.5	6.1	6.2	8.0	8.5	8.2	10.8	11.5 |	1.6 [3]	L
M	7.9	7.3	9.5	11.9	12.6	11.2	14.3	14.9	18.6 |	8.8	M
N	7.3	6.6	5.7	7.4	9.4	13.0	15.0	15.0	17.3 |	15.7	N
O	9.4	7.5	5.2	7.0	10.6	12.7	12.6	10.7	14.3 |	9.3	O
P	-	-	-	5.8	6.2	8.5	7.8	6.2	9.1 |	17.2	P
Q	-	-	-	-	-	-	-	0.3	0.3 |	17.5	Q
X	-	-	-	-	-	-	-	-	- |	4.1 [3]	R
									|	10.4	S
									|	8.2	T

Explanatory notes: see p. 451.

Notes explicatives: voir p. 454.

Notas explicativas: véase p. 457.

[1] 31st Dec. of each year. [2] Persons aged 15 years and over. [3] Data not reliable; coefficient of variation greater than 20%.

[1] 31 déc. de chaque année. [2] Personnes âgées de 15 ans et plus. [3] Données non fiables; coefficient de variation supérieur à 20%.

[1] 31 dic. de cada año. [2] Personas de 15 años y más. [3] Datos no fiables; coeficiente de variación superior a 20%.

Thousands · Milliers · Millares	1999	2000	2001	2002	2003	2004	2005	2006	2007	2008	

Portugal (BA) [1] — Total unemployment - Chômage total - Desempleo total

Men - Hommes - Hombres
ISIC 3 - CITI 3 - CIIU 3 ... ISIC 4 - CITI 4 - CIIU 4

ISIC 3	1999	2000	2001	2002	2003	2004	2005	2006	2007	2008	ISIC 4
Total	108.9	89.3	91.6	121.4	160.9	172.9	198.1	194.8	196.8	194.3	Total
UB	13.6	11.0	13.6	19.1	21.3	22.0	22.9	25.6	23.2	23.8	UB
A	1.8	-	2.7	4.7	4.1	3.4	3.8	4.0	4.0	3.4[2]	A
B	-	-	-	-	-	-	0.9	0.7	0.9	0.8[2]	B
C	-	-	-	-	-	-	0.9	1.0	0.5	39.3	C
D	30.0	22.4	22.8	26.9	35.4	41.7	53.6	48.2	43.5	0.8[2]	D
E	-	-	-	-	-	-	0.7	0.6	0.6	2.9[2]	E
F	22.3	15.6	17.1	24.5	38.8	40.2	41.5	40.4	45.2	54.5	F
G	14.9	15.8	11.7	13.9	19.0	23.3	26.6	26.1	29.5	22.8	G
H	4.6	4.0[2]	6.2	7.2	9.8	8.2	8.6	8.4	9.6	9.0	H
I	-	4.7	-	9.0	9.2	8.8	9.3	12.1	12.1	11.6	I
J	-	-	-	-	-	1.1	1.5	1.0	1.5	3.7[2]	J
K	5.3	4.5	5.4	6.3	11.3	9.8	11.6	11.3	9.8	1.0[2]	K
L	-	-	-	-	3.1[2]	3.9[2]	4.6	6.3	4.8	0.5[2]	L
M	2.5	1.9	1.4	1.3	1.9	2.1	3.1	2.6	3.8	3.1[2]	M
N	0.6	0.6	0.8	0.3	0.7	1.8	2.4	1.5	2.4	5.5	N
O	4.7	2.8[2]	-	2.1[2]	3.4[2]	4.0[2]	5.7	4.7	5.2	3.4[2]	O
P	-	-	-	0.1	0.3	0.2	0.3	0.1	-	2.6[2]	P
Q	-	-	-	-	-	-	-	0.2	0.1	1.4[2]	Q
X	-	-	-	-	-	-	-	-	-	1.0[2]	R
										3.4[2]	S
										0.1[2]	T

Women - Femmes - Mujeres
ISIC 3 - CITI 3 - CIIU 3 ... ISIC 4 - CITI 4 - CIIU 4

ISIC 3	1999	2000	2001	2002	2003	2004	2005	2006	2007	2008	ISIC 4
Total	116.9	116.2	122.0	149.1	181.4	192.2	224.1	233.1	251.8	232.7	Total
UB	20.0	16.3	21.0	22.0	25.0	27.2	35.8	33.2	38.2	34.6	UB
A	5.9	-	5.8	5.1	6.9	5.5	5.8	6.1	7.2	5.9	A
B	-	-	-	-	-	-	0.1	-	0.3	0.1[2]	B
C	-	-	-	-	-	-	0.2	0.4	0.1	48.9	C
D	25.1	26.5	28.7	40.6	46.6	49.7	63.9	70.2	68.7	0.9[2]	E
E	-	-	-	-	-	-	0.1	-	0.2	3.5[2]	F
F	-	-	-	-	-	2.3[2]	1.5[2]	3.1[2]	4.7	34.2	G
G	15.8	17.1	20.1	22.1	27.4	28.6	32.5	33.5	35.3	2.2[2]	H
H	13.8	15.1	11.4	13.2	18.7	19.0	21.5	24.4	23.2	24.7	I
I	-	-	-	-	-	4.5	4.4[2]	4.1[2]	3.4[2][1]	4.1[2]	J
J	-	-	-	-	-	1.3	1.7	0.7	1.5	1.7[2]	K
K	7.1	8.2	7.1	8.1	10.4	11.7	14.9	14.8	14.3	1.1[2]	L
L	-	-	-	-	4.9	4.6	3.5[2]	4.6	6.7	5.7	M
M	5.4	5.4	8.1	10.6	10.7	9.0	11.2	12.3	14.8	10.2	N
N	6.7	6.0	4.9	7.1	8.7	11.2	12.6	13.4	15.0	5.9	O
O	4.7	4.7	-	4.9	7.2	8.7	6.9	6.1	9.1	14.6	P
P	-	-	-	5.7	5.9	8.3	7.5	6.1	9.1	16.1	Q
Q	-	-	-	-	-	-	-	0.2	0.2	3.1[2]	R
X	-	-	-	-	-	-	-	-	-	7.0	S
										8.1	T

Roumanie (BA) [1] — Total unemployment - Chômage total - Desempleo total

Total - Total - Total
ISIC 3 - CITI 3 - CIIU 3

ISIC 3	1999	2000	2001	2002	2003	2004	2005	2006	2007	2008
Total	789.9	821.2	749.9	845.2[3]	691.7	799.5	704.5	728.4	641.0	575.5
UB	272.6	280.2	250.8	287.7[3]	232.5	306.5	238.9	273.4	268.9	246.7
A	69.4	61.2	65.4	92.2[3]	48.1	36.9	50.4	45.8	34.5	34.4
B	-	-	-	-[3]	-	-	-	-	-	-
C	22.9	14.0	10.9	12.5[3]	7.0	11.2	8.3	9.1	7.8	-
D	202.7	200.8	174.9	170.8[3]	150.9	158.1	153.4	149.7	120.5	94.1
E	6.8	12.4	7.7	6.3[3]	5.2	7.0	-	-	-	-
F	44.7	43.0	38.6	50.6[3]	42.6	41.8	35.0	41.0	30.7	31.9
G	58.4	73.6	59.5	63.0[3]	52.0	55.2	52.4	47.4	37.1	34.2
H	14.9	14.7	15.7	13.0[3]	11.7	15.1	15.1	10.9	11.3	11.8
I	23.4	25.7	25.6	20.2[3]	20.4	19.2	18.9	19.7	16.9	11.7
J	2.4	2.8	3.5	-[3]	-	-	-	-	-	-
K	5.2	4.6	6.8	6.6[3]	8.2	10.1	9.2	11.4	8.1	6.8
L	18.9	20.9	18.6	23.8[3]	20.8	13.4	15.0	15.0	9.3	7.4
M	5.6	7.7	7.2	5.3[3]	4.4	-	-	-	-	-
N	3.2	6.8	5.8	6.2[3]	5.4	-	-	-	-	-
O-Q	10.3	10.8	10.3	11.3[3]	8.8	10.0	12.1	12.8	11.4	12.1
X [4]	27.5	40.4	47.5	73.2[3]	71.5	102.3	76.7	74.8	71.3	71.6

Explanatory notes: see p. 451.

[1] Persons aged 15 years and over. [2] Data not reliable; coefficient of variation greater than 20%. [3] Estimates based on the 2002 Population Census results. [4] Incl. the unemployed whose last job was 8 years ago or over, except for 1994-1996.

Notes explicatives: voir p. 454.

[1] Personnes âgées de 15 ans et plus. [2] Données non fiables; coefficient de variation supérieur à 20%. [3] Estimations basées sur les résultats du Recensement de la population de 2002. [4] Y compris les chômeurs dont le dernier emploi date de 8 ans ou plus, sauf pour 1994-1996.

Notas explicativas: véase p. 457.

[1] Personas de 15 años y más. [2] Datos no fiables; coeficiente de variación superior a 20%. [3] Estimaciones basadas en los resultados del Censo de población de 2002. [4] Incl. los desempleados cuyo último trabajo fue hace 8 años o más, excepto por 1994-1996.

By economic activity — Par activité économique — Por actividad económica

	Thousands			Milliers				Millares		
	1999	2000	2001	2002	2003	2004	2005	2006	2007	2008

Roumanie (BA) [1]   Total unemployment - Chômage total - Desempleo total

Men - Hommes - Hombres
ISIC 3 - CITI 3 - CIIU 3

	1999	2000	2001	2002	2003	2004	2005	2006	2007	2008
Total	462.5	481.6	436.0	494.0 [2]	408.0	490.7	420.3	452.4	398.7	369.2
UB	149.3	156.9	136.5	151.6 [2]	124.8	178.2	139.5	158.6	161.9	154.4
A	46.9	45.0	45.2	67.8 [2]	37.4	28.9	30.7	35.2	24.6	27.2
B	-	-	-	- [2]	-	-	-	-	-	-
C	19.0	11.5	9.3	10.4 [2]	6.2	10.1	7.3	7.8	-	-
D	109.9	106.8	98.6	96.1 [2]	83.5	94.9	85.3	87.2	70.5	51.0
E	6.0	9.8	5.8	4.9 [2]	4.2	-	-	-	-	-
F	40.0	37.1	34.1	44.8 [2]	38.2	37.7	31.5	39.0	28.9	30.3
G	22.4	32.9	22.7	24.8 [2]	22.8	24.9	24.1	21.6	17.7	16.8
H	5.4	5.1	4.9	4.0 [2]	3.2	6.6	5.7	2.8	4.2	3.8
I	19.5	22.9	22.6	15.4 [2]	14.3	13.5	13.9	13.7	12.4	8.9
J	-	-	-	- [2]	-	-	-	-	-	-
K	3.8	2.5	3.9	3.7 [2]	4.5	7.1	6.7	8.8	-	-
L	16.4	18.0	14.8	19.0 [2]	17.6	10.0	10.8	11.1	6.9	-
M	1.1	1.7	2.8	- [2]	-	-	-	-	-	-
N	-	3.0	-	- [2]	-	-	-	-	-	-
O-Q	5.8	6.4	6.1	5.7 [2]	4.6	-	-	8.2	-	-
X [3]	13.7	19.6	25.4	41.4 [2]	42.8	64.5	49.9	49.6	48.6	53.1

Women - Femmes - Mujeres
ISIC 3 - CITI 3 - CIIU 3

	1999	2000	2001	2002	2003	2004	2005	2006	2007	2008
Total	327.3	339.5	313.9	351.1 [2]	283.7	308.7	284.1	276.0	242.3	206.3
UB	123.3	123.3	114.3	136.1 [2]	107.7	128.2	99.4	114.8	107.0	92.3
A	22.5	16.1	20.2	24.4 [2]	10.7	8.0	19.7	10.5	9.9	7.2
B	-	-	-	- [2]	-	-	-	-	-	-
C	3.8	2.5	-	2.1 [2]	-	-	0.1	1.3	-	-
D	92.7	94.0	76.2	74.7 [2]	67.5	63.1	68.1	62.5	50.0	43.1
E	-	2.5	-	- [2]	-	-	-	-	-	-
F	4.6	5.9	4.5	5.8 [2]	4.4	-	3.5	2.0	1.8	1.6
G	35.9	40.7	36.7	38.1 [2]	29.1	30.3	28.3	25.7	19.4	17.4
H	9.5	9.6	10.7	8.9 [2]	8.5	8.5	9.4	8.1	7.1	8.0
I	3.9	2.7	3.0	4.8 [2]	6.0	-	5.0	6.0	4.5	2.8
J	-	-	2.8	- [2]	-	-	-	-	-	-
K	-	2.1	2.8	2.8 [2]	3.7	-	2.5	2.6	-	-
L	2.4	2.8	3.8	4.7 [2]	3.1	-	4.2	3.9	2.4	-
M	4.4	6.0	4.3	3.4 [2]	2.8	-	-	-	-	-
N	-	3.7	4.2	4.4 [2]	4.4	-	-	-	-	-
O-Q	4.5	4.4	4.2	5.6 [2]	4.2	10.0	-	4.6	-	-
X [3]	13.8	20.7	22.1	31.7 [2]	28.6	37.8	26.8	25.2	22.7	18.5

Russian Federation (BA) [4]   Total unemployment - Chômage total - Desempleo total

Total - Total - Total
ISIC 3 - CITI 3 - CIIU 3

	1999	2000	2001	2002	2003	2004	2005	2006	2007	2008
Total	.	7 700	.	5 698	5 959	5 675	5 263	5 312	4 588	4 791
UB	.	1 577	.	1 249	1 383	1 396	1 371	1 602	1 468	1 366
A	.	686	.	623	675	622	575	648	543	554
B	.	31	.	15	24	27	22	22	22	15
C	.	116	.	95	90	86	94	71	54	69
D	.	1 472	.	1 004	994	904	793	709	579	606
E	.	109	.	74	91	91	83	92	68	88
F	.	505	.	345	401	401	377	335	292	329
G	.	905	.	745	757	722	686	627	497	588
H	.	173	.	122	145	116	111	98	91	102
I	.	498	.	361	356	345	294	276	246	272
J	.	80	.	36	33	23	19	20	23	31
K	.	163	.	134	209	204	183	177	146	167
L	.	327	.	203	217	192	164	172	149	152
M	.	419	.	273	277	273	230	203	192	195
N	.	238	.	181	182	160	145	136	108	138
O	.	396	.	237	125	111	112	120	111	116
P	.	5	.	1	-	-	3	2	1	1
Q	.	1	.	-	-	-	-	-	-	1

Explanatory notes: see p. 451.

[1] Persons aged 15 years and over. [2] Estimates based on the 2002 Population Census results. [3] Incl. the unemployed whose last job was 8 years ago or over, except for 1994-1996. [4] Persons aged 15 to 72 years.

Notes explicatives: voir p. 454.

[1] Personnes âgées de 15 ans et plus. [2] Estimations basées sur les résultats du Recensement de la population de 2002. [3] Y compris les chômeurs dont le dernier emploi date de 8 ans ou plus, sauf pour 1994-1996. [4] Personnes âgées de 15 à 72 ans.

Notas explicativas: véase p. 457.

[1] Personas de 15 años y más. [2] Estimaciones basadas en los resultados del Censo de población de 2002. [3] Incl. los desempleados cuyo último trabajo fue hace 8 años o más, excepto por 1994-1996. [4] Personas de 15 a 72 años.

UNEMPLOYMENT — CHÔMAGE — DESEMPLEO

By economic activity — Par activité économique — Por actividad económica

	Thousands / Milliers / Millares									
	1999	2000	2001	2002	2003	2004	2005	2006	2007	2008
Russian Federation (BA) [1]				Total unemployment - Chômage total - Desempleo total						
Men - Hommes - Hombres										
ISIC 3 - CITI 3 - CIIU 3										
Total	.	4 057	.	3 014	3 121	2 975	2 725	2 811	2 453	2 542
UB	.	810	.	606	687	685	648	818	752	686
A	.	449	.	413	433	408	375	432	360	384
B	.	27	.	10	21	21	16	16	18	12
C	.	81	.	74	71	65	73	51	39	51
D	.	806	.	541	534	484	420	387	309	344
E	.	79	.	54	73	64	60	64	51	66
F	.	398	.	276	321	322	318	276	246	272
G	.	345	.	289	268	259	245	230	194	204
H	.	37	.	25	39	20	19	14	13	15
I	.	349	.	271	250	252	217	195	184	183
J	.	14	.	7	9	7	4	6	5	10
K	.	81	.	77	131	121	121	103	80	95
L	.	222	.	135	142	130	94	103	95	96
M	.	89	.	59	65	56	56	43	40	43
N	.	46	.	37	31	37	24	27	23	30
O	.	220	.	139	46	44	36	46	44	49
P	.	4	.	1	-	-	-	-	-	-
Q	.	1	.	-	-	-	-	1	-	1
Women - Femmes - Mujeres										
ISIC 3 - CITI 3 - CIIU 3										
Total	.	3 643	.	2 685	2 838	2 699	2 538	2 501	2 136	2 250
UB	.	767	.	642	695	711	723	784	716	681
A	.	237	.	210	242	214	201	216	183	170
B	.	3	.	5	3	7	7	7	3	2
C	.	34	.	21	19	21	21	19	15	18
D	.	666	.	463	459	421	373	322	270	262
E	.	30	.	20	19	27	23	29	16	23
F	.	107	.	70	80	79	59	60	45	57
G	.	560	.	456	489	463	441	397	303	383
H	.	137	.	97	106	96	92	84	78	87
I	.	149	.	90	105	93	78	81	62	89
J	.	66	.	29	24	16	15	14	19	22
K	.	81	.	57	79	83	61	74	66	72
L	.	105	.	68	75	62	70	70	54	55
M	.	330	.	214	212	217	174	160	151	152
N	.	192	.	144	151	123	121	109	85	108
O	.	176	.	98	79	67	76	74	67	69
P	.	1	.	-	-	-	3	2	-	1
Q	.	-	.	-	-	-	-	-	-	-
Serbia (BA) [2][3]				Total unemployment - Chômage total - Desempleo total						
Total - Total - Total										
ISIC 3 - CITI 3 - CIIU 3										
Total	.	.	.	.	.	665.4	719.9	693.0	585.5	445.4
UB	.	.	.	.	.	238.2	282.3	299.7	233.1	187.9
A	.	.	.	.	.	19.2	21.9	14.1	19.8	11.0
B	.	.	.	.	.	-	-	0.9	1.2	1.4
C	.	.	.	.	.	1.2	3.6	2.9	1.9	1.9
D	.	.	.	.	.	151.7	161.1	162.4	139.2	96.3
E	.	.	.	.	.	4.1	4.8	1.8	2.5	1.1
F	.	.	.	.	.	28.8	26.8	27.7	21.7	15.8
G	.	.	.	.	.	103.7	101.0	93.2	77.5	60.8
H	.	.	.	.	.	33.0	27.9	17.4	19.6	14.4
I	.	.	.	.	.	15.3	21.0	12.3	13.2	14.1
J	.	.	.	.	.	9.9	8.8	6.6	5.8	4.7
K	.	.	.	.	.	12.9	9.4	6.4	10.9	6.2
L	.	.	.	.	.	12.4	16.4	13.1	12.8	8.0
M	.	.	.	.	.	7.6	10.2	9.5	4.9	3.9
N	.	.	.	.	.	8.9	7.1	10.9	11.0	6.3
O	.	.	.	.	.	17.7	15.6	13.2	9.1	11.4
P	.	.	.	.	.	1.0	1.5	0.8	1.2	0.2
Q	.	.	.	.	.	-	0.4	-	-	0.2

Explanatory notes: see p. 451.
[1] Persons aged 15 to 72 years. [2] Persons aged 15 years and over. [3] Oct.

Notes explicatives: voir p. 454.
[1] Personnes âgées de 15 à 72 ans. [2] Personnes âgées de 15 ans et plus. [3] Oct.

Notas explicativas: véase p. 457.
[1] Personas de 15 a 72 años. [2] Personas de 15 años y más. [3] Oct.

Thousands			Milliers				Millares		
1999	2000	2001	2002	2003	2004	2005	2006	2007	2008

Serbia (BA) [1][2]   **Total unemployment - Chômage total - Desempleo total**

Men - Hommes - Hombres
ISIC 3 - CITI 3 - CIIU 3

	1999	2000	2001	2002	2003	2004	2005	2006	2007	2008
Total	.	.	.	.	.	303.2	329.8	339.8	289.8	217.5
UB	.	.	.	.	.	103.4	123.9	136.4	112.7	87.0
A	.	.	.	.	.	11.9	13.1	9.8	13.7	6.4
B	.	.	.	.	.	-	-	0.9	0.8	1.4
C	.	.	.	.	.	1.2	3.3	2.6	1.9	1.8
D	.	.	.	.	.	77.1	77.2	88.3	71.9	49.0
E	.	.	.	.	.	2.4	4.0	1.8	2.0	0.8
F	.	.	.	.	.	23.4	21.5	23.4	18.2	14.9
G	.	.	.	.	.	34.4	31.4	33.0	25.0	24.5
H	.	.	.	.	.	11.0	9.7	6.2	9.6	4.2
I	.	.	.	.	.	10.7	16.5	11.2	10.7	10.6
J	.	.	.	.	.	2.0	4.2	1.5	1.6	2.3
K	.	.	.	.	.	6.1	3.7	2.7	4.0	2.8
L	.	.	.	.	.	7.4	10.7	11.7	9.3	3.8
M	.	.	.	.	.	2.0	2.3	0.7	2.2	1.1
N	.	.	.	.	.	1.3	1.2	2.3	2.3	0.6
O	.	.	.	.	.	8.7	6.3	7.4	4.0	6.2
P	.	.	.	.	.	0.3	0.8	-	-	-
Q	.	.	.	.	.	-	-	-	-	0.2

Women - Femmes - Mujeres
ISIC 3 - CITI 3 - CIIU 3

	1999	2000	2001	2002	2003	2004	2005	2006	2007	2008
Total	.	.	.	.	.	362.2	390.1	353.2	295.7	227.9
UB	.	.	.	.	.	134.8	158.4	163.3	120.4	100.9
A	.	.	.	.	.	7.3	8.7	4.4	6.1	4.6
B	.	.	.	.	.	-	-	-	0.4	-
C	.	.	.	.	.	-	0.3	0.3	-	0.1
D	.	.	.	.	.	74.6	83.9	74.0	67.3	47.2
E	.	.	.	.	.	1.7	0.8	-	0.5	0.3
F	.	.	.	.	.	5.3	5.3	4.3	3.6	0.9
G	.	.	.	.	.	69.3	69.6	60.2	52.5	36.3
H	.	.	.	.	.	22.0	18.2	11.3	10.1	10.2
I	.	.	.	.	.	4.7	4.5	1.1	2.6	3.6
J	.	.	.	.	.	7.9	4.6	5.1	4.2	2.5
K	.	.	.	.	.	6.8	5.7	3.6	6.9	3.4
L	.	.	.	.	.	5.0	5.7	1.4	3.6	4.2
M	.	.	.	.	.	5.6	7.9	8.9	2.7	2.7
N	.	.	.	.	.	7.6	5.9	8.6	8.7	5.7
O	.	.	.	.	.	8.9	9.3	5.8	5.1	5.1
P	.	.	.	.	.	0.7	0.8	0.8	1.2	0.2
Q	.	.	.	.	.	-	0.4	-	-	-

Slovakia (BA) [1][3]   **Total unemployment - Chômage total - Desempleo total**

Total - Total - Total
ISIC 3 - CITI 3 - CIIU 3

	1999	2000	2001	2002	2003	2004	2005	2006	2007	2008
Total	416.8	485.2	508.0	486.9	459.2	481.0	427.5	353.4	291.9	257.5
UB	94.0	104.2	109.4	107.9	95.8	100.0	101.3	89.0	70.1	64.5
A-B	30.3	31.3	30.8	29.8	32.7	33.2	28.6	21.3	13.7	11.4
C	2.5	3.6	3.9	1.9	3.1	4.4	2.0	1.7	1.8	0.7
D	84.3	106.5	102.2	94.6	91.2	90.6	77.7	63.3	52.9	48.8
E	2.7	4.0	4.2	2.8	2.4	3.0	2.9	1.2	0.5	0.9
F	43.8	49.4	49.5	41.8	37.6	33.8	27.2	20.1	15.0	12.5
G	33.3	43.3	48.3	42.7	35.6	38.3	30.5	25.4	22.6	21.5
H	12.1	15.0	18.0	16.0	14.3	15.8	12.8	10.1	8.7	7.0
I	9.1	12.3	14.7	11.4	10.6	12.4	11.0	7.8	6.6	6.1
J	1.6	2.2	2.3	1.9	2.5	2.9	3.3	2.0	1.0	1.7
K	7.5	8.7	11.7	9.4	8.1	8.9	7.5	5.9	3.4	3.1
L	18.2	14.6	10.4	11.0	11.6	13.0	10.7	8.6	8.5	6.5
M	4.5	6.7	8.1	6.8	5.7	8.3	8.3	6.1	6.9	5.8
N	7.8	10.2	10.5	9.8	10.2	14.7	11.3	10.0	7.2	6.4
O	8.7	10.1	42.6	51.5	46.5	35.4	25.4	13.2	9.4	7.9
P	0.4	0.7	1.5	0.5	1.1	1.2	1.2	0.2	1.1	0.7
Q	-	-	-	-	0.1	0.1	-	-	-	-
X	56.2	62.8	40.0	47.2	50.2	64.5	65.6	67.8	62.8	52.1

Explanatory notes: see p. 451.   Notes explicatives: voir p. 454.   Notas explicativas: véase p. 457.

[1] Persons aged 15 years and over. [2] Oct. [3] Excl. persons on child-care leave.   [1] Personnes âgées de 15 ans et plus. [2] Oct. [3] Non compris les personnes en congé parental.   [1] Personas de 15 años y más. [2] Oct. [3] Excl. las personas con licencia parental.

3D

UNEMPLOYMENT	CHÔMAGE	DESEMPLEO
By economic activity	Par activité économique	Por actividad económica

	Thousands								Milliers	Millares
	1999	2000	2001	2002	2003	2004	2005	2006	2007	2008

Slovakia (BA) [1] [2] Total unemployment - Chômage total - Desempleo total

Men - Hommes - Hombres
ISIC 3 - CITI 3 - CIIU 3

Total	226.6	265.5	282.5	263.9	246.5	250.0	223.6	179.5	143.5	124.6
UB	49.5	56.7	59.7	56.8	49.6	54.0	52.2	45.9	36.5	32.4
A-B	20.1	20.5	20.3	20.5	21.4	21.7	19.3	14.5	9.0	7.3
C	2.4	3.3	3.5	1.3	2.8	3.9	1.1	1.2	1.5	0.7
D	42.9	54.5	56.5	52.4	48.7	46.3	37.1	31.0	22.9	24.0
E	2.4	3.7	3.8	2.3	1.9	2.2	2.1	0.5	0.2	0.7
F	41.6	47.0	46.6	39.0	35.1	31.3	26.0	18.9	14.9	12.4
G	11.2	14.5	16.1	13.4	11.9	11.0	10.4	6.4	6.8	7.3
H	5.1	4.8	6.8	5.9	4.8	4.6	3.7	3.1	2.6	1.8
I	6.1	8.5	9.2	7.0	7.0	7.0	7.3	5.5	4.4	3.7
J	0.4	0.4	0.9	0.5	0.4	0.6	1.0	0.6	0.1	0.3
K	3.5	5.0	7.1	6.2	5.1	4.9	4.4	4.3	2.4	1.7
L	11.5	10.1	5.4	4.3	4.9	7.8	5.7	3.7	4.0	2.7
M	0.9	1.7	2.3	2.4	1.9	2.5	2.4	1.2	1.2	1.2
N	1.9	1.2	1.1	1.5	2.6	2.7	2.4	1.0	1.1	1.7
O	3.8	5.9	27.9	31.3	28.5	22.1	16.8	8.2	5.1	3.7
P	-	0.1	0.3	0.1	0.3	0.3	-	-	0.2	-
Q	-	-	-	-	0.1	0.1	-	-	-	-
X	23.3	27.9	15.1	19.1	19.7	27.4	31.7	33.6	30.7	23.1

Women - Femmes - Mujeres
ISIC 3 - CITI 3 - CIIU 3

Total	190.2	219.7	225.5	223.0	212.7	231.0	203.8	173.9	148.4	132.8
UB	44.5	47.6	49.7	51.1	46.2	46.3	49.1	43.0	33.6	32.0
A-B	10.2	10.8	10.5	9.3	11.3	11.6	9.2	6.7	4.7	4.2
C	0.1	0.2	0.5	0.7	0.4	0.5	0.9	0.5	0.1	-
D	41.4	52.1	45.7	42.2	42.5	44.4	40.6	32.3	30.0	24.8
E	0.3	0.3	0.4	0.5	0.5	0.8	0.8	0.7	0.3	0.2
F	2.2	2.4	2.9	2.8	2.5	2.6	1.2	1.2	0.1	0.2
G	22.1	28.8	32.1	29.3	23.6	27.3	20.1	19.0	15.8	14.2
H	7.1	10.2	11.2	10.0	9.5	11.2	9.2	7.0	6.2	5.2
I	3.0	3.8	5.4	4.4	3.6	5.5	3.7	2.3	2.1	2.4
J	1.3	1.9	1.4	1.4	2.1	2.3	2.3	1.5	0.7	1.4
K	4.1	3.7	4.6	3.3	3.0	4.0	3.1	1.6	1.0	1.4
L	6.7	4.5	5.1	6.7	6.7	5.3	4.9	4.9	4.6	3.8
M	3.6	5.0	5.8	4.5	3.9	5.8	5.9	5.0	5.7	4.6
N	5.9	8.9	9.3	8.4	7.7	12.0	8.9	8.9	6.1	4.6
O	4.8	4.3	14.8	20.2	18.0	13.4	8.7	5.1	4.3	4.2
P	0.4	0.6	1.2	0.4	0.8	1.0	1.2	0.2	0.9	0.7
Q	-	-	-	-	-	-	-	-	-	-
X	33.0	34.9	25.0	28.1	30.5	37.1	33.9	34.3	32.2	29.0

Slovakia (FB) [1] [3] Registered unemployment - Chômage enregistré - Desempleo registrado

Total - Total - Total
ISIC 3 - CITI 3 - CIIU 3

Total	535.2	506.5	533.7	504.1	452.2	383.2	333.8	273.4	239.9	248.5
UB	173.3	170.3	163.8	153.5	127.9	125.6	126.9	114.4	105.0	121.5
A	48.9	44.2	41.1	38.5	39.5	28.1	21.5	16.1	12.7	10.1
B	0.1	-	-	-	-	-	-	-	-	-
C	3.7	2.6	2.5	2.2	2.4	1.8	1.4	1.0	0.9	1.1
D	88.9	77.1	74.1	65.7	64.5	53.0	42.9	31.1	27.4	30.5
E	1.1	0.9	0.8	0.9	1.1	1.1	0.9	0.7	0.8	0.7
F	62.9	53.5	47.7	41.8	38.5	26.3	20.5	14.8	11.8	11.3
G	32.2	33.6	32.1	29.1	25.1	21.1	17.1	13.4	11.3	10.5
H	10.8	11.1	11.5	11.2	9.9	7.8	6.5	5.5	4.8	4.2
I	9.7	10.1	10.9	10.9	10.7	8.0	5.9	4.3	3.4	3.5
J	2.1	2.1	2.2	2.8	2.2	1.7	1.4	1.1	0.9	0.9
K	8.4	8.1	8.3	7.3	6.1	5.1	4.4	3.3	3.2	3.5
L	36.1	40.1	80.0	82.5	70.0	55.0	43.8	34.2	29.2	24.3
M	6.8	7.0	5.9	5.6	5.0	6.2	5.0	3.8	3.3	2.8
N	9.3	8.3	9.2	8.8	8.8	8.2	6.4	5.0	4.2	3.5
O	40.0	37.1	43.2	43.0	40.1	33.9	29.0	24.6	20.9	20.0
P	0.4	0.3	0.2	0.2	0.2	0.2	0.1	0.1	0.1	0.1
Q	0.5	0.1	0.2	0.1	0.2	0.1	0.1	-	-	-

Explanatory notes: see p. 451.

[1] Persons aged 15 years and over. [2] Excl. persons on child-care leave. [3] 31st Dec. of each year.

Notes explicatives: voir p. 454.

[1] Personnes âgées de 15 ans et plus. [2] Non compris les personnes en congé parental. [3] 31 déc. de chaque année.

Notas explicativas: véase p. 457.

[1] Personas de 15 años y más. [2] Excl. las personas con licencia parental. [3] 31 dic. de cada año.

By economic activity · Par activité économique · Por actividad económica

Thousands · Milliers · Millares

Slovenia (BA) [1] [2] — Total unemployment - Chômage total - Desempleo total

Total - Total - Total

ISIC 3 - CITI 3 - CIIU 3	1999	2000	2001	2002	2003	2004	2005	2006	2007	2008	ISIC 4 - CITI 4 - CIIU 4
Total	71	69	57	58	63	61	58	61	48	43	Total
UB	19	22	16	16	17	16	14	18	13	11	UB
A	1	1	1	-	-	-	1	-	1	1	A
C	-	-	-	-	-	-	-	-	-	-	B
D	26	22	17	21	21	18	17	17	12	11	C
E	-	-	1	-	-	-	-	-	-	-	D
F	4	5	4	3	5	5	5	4	3	-	E
G	8	6	5	6	7	7	7	6	5	5	F
H	3	3	4	3	4	2	3	4	3	5	G
I	2	2	1	2	2	2	1	1	-	-	H
J	-	1	-	-	-	-	-	1	-	3	I
K	2	2	1	3	3	2	3	3	3	-	J
L	-	1	1	-	-	1	-	2	1	-	K
M	1	1	-	-	1	2	2	1	3	-	L
N	1	1	2	2	1	1	2	2	1	1	M
O	2	1	1	-	1	2	1	1	2	1	N
X	1	-	2	-	-	-	-	-	1	1	O
										1	P
										1	Q
										-	R
										-	S
										-	T
										-	U
										1	X

Men - Hommes - Hombres

ISIC 3 - CITI 3 - CIIU 3	1999	2000	2001	2002	2003	2004	2005	2006	2007	2008	ISIC 4 - CITI 4 - CIIU 4
Total	37	36	29	30	32	31	30	28	20	20	Total
UB	9	10	8	7	8	5	7	8	5	4	UB
A	-	1	1	-	-	-	-	-	1	-	A
C	-	-	-	-	-	-	-	-	-	-	B
D	15	12	9	11	9	10	9	9	6	6	C
E	-	-	-	-	-	-	-	-	-	-	D
F	3	5	4	3	4	5	5	4	3	-	E
G	3	3	2	3	4	3	3	2	1	4	F
H	1	1	1	1	2	-	-	1	1	1	G
I	2	1	1	1	1	2	-	1	-	-	H
J	-	-	-	-	-	-	-	-	-	1	I
K	1	-	1	1	1	1	1	1	-	-	J
L	-	1	1	-	-	1	-	-	-	-	K
M	-	-	-	-	-	-	-	-	1	-	L
N	-	-	-	-	-	-	-	-	-	1	M
O	1	1	-	-	-	-	-	-	1	-	N
X	1	-	1	-	-	-	-	-	-	-	O
										-	P
										-	Q
										-	R
										-	S
										-	T
										-	U
										-	X

Women - Femmes - Mujeres

ISIC 3 - CITI 3 - CIIU 3	1999	2000	2001	2002	2003	2004	2005	2006	2007	2008	ISIC 4 - CITI 4 - CIIU 4
Total	34	33	28	28	31	30	28	33	28	23	Total
UB	10	12	8	8	9	11	7	10	8	7	UB
A	-	-	-	-	-	-	-	-	-	1	A
C	-	-	-	-	-	-	-	-	-	-	B
D	12	10	8	9	12	9	8	8	6	5	C
E	-	-	-	-	-	-	-	-	-	-	D
F	-	1	-	-	-	-	-	1	-	-	E
G	5	3	3	3	3	4	4	4	4	3	F
H	2	2	3	2	2	1	2	3	2	3	G
I	1	-	-	-	-	-	-	-	-	-	H
J	-	-	-	-	-	-	-	-	-	2	I
K	1	2	1	2	2	1	2	2	2	-	J
L	-	1	1	-	-	-	-	1	1	-	K
M	1	-	-	-	-	1	2	1	1	-	L
N	1	1	2	1	-	-	1	2	1	-	M
O	1	-	-	-	-	1	7	1	1	-	N
X	-	-	1	-	-	-	-	-	1	-	O
										1	P
										1	Q
										-	R
										-	S
										-	T
										-	U
										-	X

Explanatory notes: see p. 451.

[1] Persons aged 15 years and over. [2] Second quarter of each year.

Notes explicatives: voir p. 454.

[1] Personnes âgées de 15 ans et plus. [2] Deuxième trimestre de chaque année.

Notas explicativas: véase p. 457.

[1] Personas de 15 años y más. [2] Segundo trimestre de cada año.

3D UNEMPLOYMENT · CHÔMAGE · DESEMPLEO

By economic activity · Par activité économique · Por actividad económica

Thousands · Milliers · Millares

Suisse (BA) [1][2]

Total unemployment - Chômage total - Desempleo total
Total - Total - Total
ISIC 3 - CITI 3 - CIIU 3

	1999	2000	2001	2002	2003	2004	2005	2006	2007	2008
Total	.	.	.	.	170	179	185	169	156	147
A-B	.	.	.	.	3[3]	3[3]	2[3]	.[4]	.[4]	3[3]
C-E	.	.	.	.	32	31	28	28	22	18
F	.	.	.	.	9	11	8	7	7	6
G	.	.	.	.	23	25	28	24	23	18
H	.	.	.	.	15	17	15	19	14	15
I	.	.	.	.	9	7	11	8	7[3]	7[3]
J	.	.	.	.	7	9	9	4[3]	3[3]	4[3]
K	.	.	.	.	18	19	17	17	18	14
L,Q	.	.	.	.	4[3]	6[3]	5[3]	5[3]	4[3]	3[3]
M	.	.	.	.	6	4[3]	6	5	4[3]	9
N	.	.	.	.	13	13	12	13	12	12
O-P	.	.	.	.	6	9	11	10	12	11
X	.	.	.	.	26	24	32	26	28	24

Sweden (BA) [5]

Total unemployment - Chômage total - Desempleo total
Total - Total - Total
ISIC 3 - CITI 3 - CIIU 3 / ISIC 4 - CITI 4 - CIIU 4

ISIC 3	1999	2000	2001	2002	2003	2004	2005	2006	2007	2008	ISIC 4
Total	241	203	175	176	217	246	270[6]	246	298	305	Total
UB	29	23	17	16	17	20	42[6]	40	75	83	UB
A-B	7	6	4	4	4	4	5[6]	4	3	3	A
C	1	1	-	-	-	-	-[6]	-	-	1	B
D	41	33	30	29	35	39	38[6]	29	29	26	C
E	1	1	-	-	-	1	-[6]	1	1	1	D
F	17	14	10	11	14	16	14[6]	12	11	1	E
G	30	25	20	22	26	30	30[6]	30	30	11	F
H	12	10	10	12	14	17	17[6]	16	19	30	G
I	12	10	9	9	12	15	14[6]	12	13	11	H
J	1	1	1	1	2	2	2[6]	2	2	19	I
K	20	18	20	25	35	38	33[6]	30	36	5	J
L,Q	8	8	8	7	6	7	7[6]	6	9	2	K
M	14	13	11	11	18	19	21[6]	19	20	3	L
N	30	22	19	19	18	22	25[6]	23	25	11	M
O-P	16	15	12	10	12	13	14[6]	14	15	23	N
X	3	3	2	2	2	3	8[6]	8	9	9	O
										20	P
										26	Q
										6	R
										7	S
										10	X

Men - Hommes - Hombres
ISIC 3 - CITI 3 - CIIU 3 / ISIC 4 - CITI 4 - CIIU 4

ISIC 3	1999	2000	2001	2002	2003	2004	2005	2006	2007	2008	ISIC 4
Total	133	114	99	101	123	137	148[6]	131	149	152	Total
UB	16	13	9	8	9	10	24[6]	22	36	39	UB
A-B	5	4	3	3	3	3	3[6]	3	1	1	A
C	1	1	-	-	-	-	-[6]	-	-	-	B
D	28	23	21	20	25	28	25[6]	20	20	17	C
E	1	-	-	-	-	-	-[6]	-	-	-	D
F	16	13	9	10	13	15	13[6]	11	10	1	E
G	16	13	11	12	15	16	15[6]	16	14	10	F
H	6	5	5	6	7	8	10[6]	8	9	15	G
I	8	7	6	6	8	10	10[6]	8	10	8	H
J	-	-	-	-	1	1	1[6]	1	1	8	I
K	13	11	12	15	22	23	19[6]	17	21	3	J
L,Q	4	3	4	3	3	2	3[6]	3	4	1	K
M	6	6	5	5	7	7	7[6]	6	5	2	L
N	5	4	4	5	4	5	6[6]	5	5	5	M
O-P	9	8	6	6	6	6	7[6]	7	7	13	N
X	2	2	1	1	1	2	4[6]	5	5	5	O
										6	P
										6	Q
										3	R
										3	S
										6	X

Explanatory notes: see p. 451.

[1] Persons aged 15 years and over. [2] Second quarter of each year. [3] Relative statistical reliability. [4] Not indicated due to lack of statistical reliability. [5] Persons aged 15 to 74 years; prior to 2007: 16 to 64 years. [6] Methodology revised; data not strictly comparable.

Notes explicatives: voir p. 454.

[1] Personnes âgées de 15 ans et plus. [2] Deuxième trimestre de chaque année. [3] Fiabilité statistique relative. [4] Non indiqué en raison du manque de fiabilité statistique. [5] Personnes âgées de 15 à 74 ans; avant 2007: 16 à 64 ans. [6] Méthodologie révisée; les données ne sont pas strictement comparables.

Notas explicativas: véase p. 457.

[1] Personas de 15 años y más. [2] Segundo trimestre de cada año. [3] Confiabilidad estadística relativa. [4] No se indica por la falta de confiabilidad estadística. [5] Personas de 15 a 74 años; antes de 2007: 16 a 64 años. [6] Metodología revisada; los datos no son estrictamente comparables.

UNEMPLOYMENT — CHÔMAGE — DESEMPLEO 3D

By economic activity — Par activité économique — Por actividad económica

	Thousands — Milliers — Millares									
	1999	2000	2001	2002	2003	2004	2005	2006	2007	2008

Sweden (BA) [1]
Total unemployment - Chômage total - Desempleo total

Women - Femmes - Mujeres — ISIC 3 - CITI 3 - CIIU 3 (1999–2007)

	1999	2000	2001	2002	2003	2004	2005	2006	2007
Total	107	89	76	76	94	109	123 [2]	114	148
UB	13	10	8	8	8	10	18 [2]	19	39
A-B	2	2	1	1	1	1	2 [2]	1	1
C	-	-	-	-	-	-	- [2]	-	-
D	13	10	9	9	10	11	13 [2]	9	9
E	-	-	-	-	-	1	- [2]	-	-
F	1	1	1	1	1	1	1 [2]	1	1
G	14	12	9	10	11	14	15 [2]	14	16
H	6	5	5	6	7	9	7 [2]	8	10
I	4	3	3	3	4	5	3 [2]	4	4
J	1	1	-	-	1	1	1 [2]	1	1
K	7	7	8	10	13	15	14 [2]	13	15
L,Q	4	5	4	4	3	5	4 [2]	4	5
M	8	7	6	6	11	12	14 [2]	12	15
N	25	18	15	14	14	17	18 [2]	17	20
O-P	7	7	6	4	6	7	7 [2]	7	8
X	1	1	1	1	1	1	5 [2]	4	4

ISIC 4 - CITI 4 - CIIU 4 (2008)

	2008
Total	152
UB	44
A	1
B	-
C	9
D	-
E	-
F	1
G	15
H	3
I	11
J	2
K	1
L	1
M	6
N	10
O	4
P	13
Q	19
R	3
S	4
X	4

Turkey (BA) [3]
Total unemployment - Chômage total - Desempleo total

Total - Total - Total — ISIC 3 - CITI 3 - CIIU 3

	1999	2000	2001	2002	2003	2004	2005	2006	2007	2008
Total	.	1 497	1 967	2 464	2 493	2 498	2 519	2 446	2 377	2 611
UB	.	467	477	513	480	612	553	490	430	394
A-B	.	.	.	.	.	.	167	182	167	181
A	.	124	132	168	221	179	.	.	.	.
B	.	1	1	1	-	3	.	.	.	.
C	.	4	5	9	96	10	11	10	10	13
D	.	258	417	513	463	468	494	480	463	525
E	.	2	2	5	3	5	6	6	2	5
F	.	199	311	383	398	359	360	332	352	412
G	.	152	244	307	301	301	325	332	336	384
H	.	102	120	163	164	163	179	182	165	196
I	.	57	68	126	112	118	111	115	116	119
J	.	12	19	26	22	18	22	18	19	20
K	.	30	50	76	62	71	71	81	94	105
L	.	21	27	31	30	43	48	39	38	38
M	.	13	20	30	23	35	41	48	47	58
N	.	13	16	26	21	29	34	33	35	40
O	.	32	49	69	76	63	.	.	.	.
O-Q							97	99	102	121
P	.	8	9	19	19	21	.	.	.	.

Men - Hommes - Hombres — ISIC 3 - CITI 3 - CIIU 3

	1999	2000	2001	2002	2003	2004	2005	2006	2007	2008
Total	.	1 111	1 485	1 826	1 830	1 878	1 867	1 777	1 716	1 878
UB	.	282	273	279	262	361	306	261	222	195
A-B	.	.	.	.	.	.	138	147	133	141
A	.	89	107	121	156	143	.	.	.	.
B	.	1	1	1	-	3	.	.	.	.
C	.	4	5	9	60	10	11	9	9	12
D	.	199	320	380	334	358	366	351	342	378
E	.	1	2	4	5	5	5	5	2	4
F	.	194	304	375	389	352	352	325	343	402
G	.	118	189	238	227	228	243	236	235	270
H	.	90	107	147	141	144	160	159	140	163
I	.	51	61	113	100	106	104	102	102	104
J	.	6	11	14	11	9	11	10	10	9
K	.	20	30	44	41	47	48	50	61	66
L	.	18	23	24	24	35	39	32	29	30
M	.	4	8	10	8	13	15	19	12	19
N	.	5	5	9	6	8	9	11	12	11
O	.	26	37	56	65	51	.	.	.	.
O-Q							61	60	64	74
P	.	2	2	2	3	5	.	.	.	.

Explanatory notes: see p. 451.

[1] Persons aged 15 to 74 years; prior to 2007: 16 to 64 years. [2] Methodology revised; data not strictly comparable. [3] Persons aged 15 years and over.

Notes explicatives: voir p. 454.

[1] Personnes âgées de 15 à 74 ans; avant 2007: 16 à 64 ans. [2] Méthodologie révisée; les données ne sont pas strictement comparables. [3] Personnes âgées de 15 ans et plus.

Notas explicativas: véase p. 457.

[1] Personas de 15 a 74 años; antes de 2007: 16 a 64 años. [2] Metodología revisada; los datos no son estrictamente comparables. [3] Personas de 15 años y más.

3D UNEMPLOYMENT CHÔMAGE DESEMPLEO

By economic activity — Par activité économique — Por actividad económica

	Thousands — Milliers — Millares									
	1999	2000	2001	2002	2003	2004	2005	2006	2007	2008

Turkey (BA) [1] — Total unemployment - Chômage total - Desempleo total

Women - Femmes - Mujeres
ISIC 3 - CITI 3 - CIIU 3

	1999	2000	2001	2002	2003	2004	2005	2006	2007	2008
Total	.	387	482	638	663	620	652	671	660	733
UB	.	186	204	234	218	251	248	230	208	199
A-B	.						29	35	34	40
A	.	35	25	47	65	35	.			
C	.	-	-	-	36	-	.	1	1	1
D	.	59	97	133	129	110	129	129	121	147
E	.	1	-	1	1	-	-	1	-	1
F	.	5	7	8	9	6	8	7	9	10
G	.	34	55	69	74	73	82	96	101	114
H	.	12	13	16	23	19	18	24	25	33
I	.	6	7	13	12	12	7	13	14	15
J	.	6	8	12	11	8	11	8	9	11
K	.	10	20	32	21	23	24	31	33	39
L	.	3	4	7	6	8	9	7	9	8
M	.	9	12	20	15	23	26	29	35	39
N	.	8	11	17	15	21	25	22	23	29
O	.	6	12	13	11	12				
O-Q	.						36	38	38	47
P	.	6	7	17	16	16				

Ukraine (BA) [2] — Total unemployment - Chômage total - Desempleo total

Total - Total - Total
ISIC 3 - CITI 3 - CIIU 3

	1999	2000	2001	2002	2003	2004	2005	2006	2007	2008
Total	2 614.3	2 655.8	2 455.0	2 140.7	2 008.0	1 906.7	1 600.8	1 515.0	1 417.6	1 425.1
UB	604.1	540.1	481.0	397.1	341.0	467.0	366.2	332.9	327.8	312.6
A	156.6	191.6	214.4	175.9	260.0	304.9	221.6	218.6	194.7	176.4
B	4.8	3.2	1.3	2.2	2.9	3.1	3.5	1.3	3.1	1.4
C	82.6	56.8	63.3	47.2	53.7	28.7	20.1	20.5	29.8	28.9
D	633.8	665.4	616.1	562.1	464.8	353.1	298.9	263.4	234.1	231.8
E	21.1	40.6	46.8	38.1	37.1	35.7	31.5	36.9	26.7	33.6
F	217.6	189.2	176.3	148.2	143.8	114.4	122.2	102.6	107.9	146.9
G	277.4	297.4	272.1	252.9	242.4	204.7	199.4	211.2	178.9	197.2
H	20.4	59.9	69.9	61.5	48.6	51.2	32.5	35.4	45.1	36.8
I	166.0	160.1	124.6	110.1	98.0	79.4	75.9	59.3	50.2	57.5
J	23.4	20.6	21.2	16.5	16.7	12.0	9.5	6.9	13.8	13.9
K	42.0	58.9	46.6	40.8	45.6	41.5	35.7	30.2	19.2	26.3
L	95.1	100.3	82.5	78.3	74.7	52.7	54.1	68.4	61.1	31.4
M	125.6	120.8	103.5	99.4	86.8	76.4	56.7	57.1	57.2	51.6
N	67.5	87.2	72.9	65.1	48.3	49.8	35.1	37.3	37.6	45.8
O	75.3	63.2	62.0	43.8	42.5	28.8	36.4	32.8	28.1	30.6
P	1.0	0.5	0.5	1.5	1.1	3.3	1.5	0.2	2.3	2.4

Men - Hommes - Hombres
ISIC 3 - CITI 3 - CIIU 3

	1999	2000	2001	2002	2003	2004	2005	2006	2007	2008
Total	1 346.5	1 357.4	1 263.0	1 106.5	1 055.7	1 001.6	862.5	804.1	770.7	768.9
UB	315.8	264.7	250.8	204.8	167.2	268.3	202.4	168.0	175.8	172.3
A	107.1	125.0	143.2	112.8	159.0	170.5	136.1	142.3	122.5	106.4
B	3.2	3.2	1.3	2.1	2.8	1.9	3.5	0.8	2.9	1.4
C	57.2	41.2	45.9	35.2	40.0	17.2	10.8	12.7	22.8	24.9
D	293.6	331.1	292.7	285.2	246.9	180.4	160.9	136.5	115.1	115.2
E	13.5	29.8	33.3	25.2	24.3	21.3	20.6	23.2	20.6	17.6
F	162.5	147.6	135.1	119.0	115.7	81.1	104.7	91.6	99.3	129.5
G	116.9	112.5	101.5	95.4	94.8	89.6	79.7	81.5	76.6	79.0
H	6.4	11.0	18.1	11.3	11.5	15.6	8.3	5.0	9.2	10.3
I	116.4	116.8	92.5	77.5	69.3	45.5	49.7	38.0	35.3	34.9
J	3.5	3.6	7.7	5.1	6.7	2.6	2.3	4.6	6.0	4.7
K	18.0	28.4	22.1	23.0	26.2	23.1	17.6	16.5	9.0	10.5
L	56.9	60.9	48.7	43.8	37.5	26.8	24.7	41.5	36.1	11.4
M	27.0	23.5	25.6	27.3	24.7	26.8	15.8	19.1	16.4	18.0
N	14.5	25.5	18.3	19.6	11.1	18.4	10.0	9.9	11.3	17.8
O	33.9	32.4	25.8	19.2	17.7	11.6	15.4	12.9	10.8	15.0
P	0.1	0.2	0.4	-	0.3	0.9	-	-	1.0	-

Women - Femmes - Mujeres
ISIC 3 - CITI 3 - CIIU 3

	1999	2000	2001	2002	2003	2004	2005	2006	2007	2008
Total	1 267.8	1 298.4	1 192.0	1 034.2	952.3	905.1	738.3	710.9	646.9	656.2
UB	288.3	275.4	230.2	192.3	173.8	198.7	163.8	164.9	152.0	140.3
A	49.5	66.6	71.2	63.1	101.0	134.4	85.5	76.3	72.2	70.0
B	1.6	-	-	0.1	0.1	1.2		0.5	0.2	-
C	25.4	15.6	17.4	12.0	13.7	11.5	9.3	7.8	7.0	4.0
D	340.2	334.3	323.4	276.9	217.9	172.7	138.0	126.9	119.0	116.6
E	7.6	10.8	13.5	12.9	12.8	14.4	10.9	13.7	6.1	16.0
F	55.1	41.6	41.2	29.2	28.1	33.3	17.5	11.0	8.6	17.4
G	160.5	184.9	170.6	157.5	147.6	115.1	119.7	129.7	102.3	118.2
H	14.0	48.9	51.8	50.2	37.1	35.6	24.2	30.4	35.9	26.5
I	49.6	43.3	32.1	32.6	28.7	33.9	26.2	21.3	14.9	22.6
J	19.9	17.0	13.5	11.4	10.0	9.4	7.2	2.3	7.8	9.2
K	24.0	30.5	24.5	17.8	19.4	18.4	18.1	13.7	10.2	15.8
L	38.2	39.4	33.8	34.5	37.2	25.9	29.4	26.9	25.0	20.0
M	98.6	97.3	77.9	72.1	62.1	49.6	40.9	38.0	40.8	33.6
N	53.0	61.7	54.6	45.5	37.2	31.4	25.1	27.4	26.3	28.0
O	41.4	30.8	36.2	24.6	24.8	17.2	21.0	19.9	17.3	15.6
P	0.9	0.3	0.1	1.5	0.8	2.4	1.5	0.2	1.3	2.4

Explanatory notes: see p. 451.   Notes explicatives: voir p. 454.   Notas explicativas: véase p. 457.

[1] Persons aged 15 years and over. [2] Persons aged 15-70 years.   [1] Personnes âgées de 15 ans et plus. [2] Personnes âgées de 15 à 70 ans.   [1] Personas de 15 años y más. [2] Personas de 15 á 70 años.

By economic activity — Par activité économique — Por actividad económica

	Thousands			Milliers				Millares		
	1999	2000	2001	2002	2003	2004	2005	2006	2007	2008

United Kingdom (BA) [1] [2] — Total unemployment - Chômage total - Desempleo total

Total - Total - Total
ISIC 3 - CITI 3 - CIIU 3

	1999	2000	2001	2002	2003	2004	2005	2006	2007	2008
Total	1 710	1 559	1 423	1 472	1 420	1 394	1 397	1 649	1 621	1 643
UB	289	275	265	251	266	291	304	360	385	397
A	13	18	17	10	12	12	15	11	8	10
B	2	2	1	2	2	2	1	-	-	-
C	8	4	5	5	2	5	2	2	3	4
D	301	254	229	232	217	183	173	188	173	183
E	11	7	5	7	5	5	7	5	7	6
F	133	129	88	100	88	96	85	107	97	107
G	204	203	175	196	191	175	192	238	249	243
H	100	88	93	88	96	99	90	116	123	96
I	84	65	79	80	78	79	82	74	73	97
J	33	28	20	36	38	34	39	34	27	31
K	129	114	101	133	121	98	106	144	121	105
L	32	28	29	28	28	28	36	38	37	44
M	54	43	36	36	37	40	40	49	47	51
N	70	67	54	69	67	74	73	90	94	97
O	69	55	56	64	62	58	50	65	65	72
P	3	7	7	5	4	7	4	3	4	4
Q	4	3	2	-	-	-	-	-	-	-
X	172	167	161	131	106	110	97	122	108	97

Men - Hommes - Hombres
ISIC 3 - CITI 3 - CIIU 3

	1999	2000	2001	2002	2003	2004	2005	2006	2007	2008
Total	1 047	942	861	892	867	824	817	959	930	969
UB	165	155	152	150	141	164	180	218	208	239
A	11	16	14	8	11	9	13	9	6	7
B	1	2	1	2	2	2	1	-	-	-
C	7	2	4	5	1	5	2	2	3	3
D	225	189	170	175	166	137	127	149	133	138
E	8	6	2	7	4	4	5	3	3	2
F	125	123	83	95	81	88	79	100	93	102
G	112	112	102	99	114	97	97	118	135	132
H	50	45	47	43	51	45	48	52	58	46
I	67	50	60	58	60	63	61	57	54	73
J	14	12	10	19	21	18	25	22	14	16
K	79	70	58	82	81	60	60	89	75	63
L	17	14	16	16	14	15	18	17	23	26
M	23	14	12	15	11	12	13	15	17	14
N	14	11	13	16	18	18	16	17	20	23
O	37	33	29	35	34	35	25	31	36	39
P	-	3	3	2	-	2	2	2	2	-
Q	1	3	-	-	-	-	-	-	-	-
X	89	82	81	69	58	52	44	57	50	46

Women - Femmes - Mujeres
ISIC 3 - CITI 3 - CIIU 3

	1999	2000	2001	2002	2003	2004	2005	2006	2007	2008
Total	663	617	562	580	553	570	580	690	691	674
UB	125	120	113	101	125	127	124	142	177	158
A	2	2	3	2	1	3	2	2	2	2
B	-	-	-	-	-	-	-	-	-	-
C	-	1	-	-	-	-	-	-	-	-
D	76	66	59	58	51	46	46	39	40	45
E	3	1	3	-	-	-	2	2	3	4
F	8	6	5	5	7	7	6	7	4	5
G	91	91	73	97	78	78	95	120	114	112
H	50	43	46	45	45	54	42	65	65	50
I	18	15	19	22	18	16	21	17	19	23
J	18	16	10	17	17	16	14	12	12	15
K	50	45	42	52	40	38	46	55	46	43
L	15	14	13	12	14	13	18	21	14	18
M	31	29	24	21	26	28	27	34	30	37
N	56	57	41	53	49	56	57	73	74	74
O	32	23	27	29	28	24	25	34	29	33
P	2	4	4	3	3	5	2	-	3	3
Q	2	-	2	-	-	-	-	-	-	-
X	84	85	80	63	49	57	53	66	57	52

Explanatory notes: see p. 451.
[1] Persons aged 16 years and over. [2] Second quarter.

Notes explicatives: voir p. 454.
[1] Personnes âgées de 16 ans et plus. [2] Deuxième trimestre.

Notas explicativas: véase p. 457.
[1] Personas de 16 años y más. [2] Segundo trimestre.

	Thousands				Milliers				Millares	
	1999	2000	2001	2002	2003	2004	2005	2006	2007	2008

OCEANIA-OCÉANIE-OCEANIA

Australia (BA) [1,2]   Total unemployment - Chômage total - Desempleo total

Total - Total - Total
ISIC 3 - CITI 3 - CIIU 3

	1999	2000	2001	2002	2003	2004	2005	2006	2007	2008
Total	654.9	607.5	648.0	631.2	596.0	554.7	529.0	517.7	487.5	470.9
UB	144.4	129.9	97.9	104.2	102.9	102.6	102.0	105.4	108.5	100.1
A	18.5	16.2	21.9	20.6	20.7	16.0	15.8	14.6	12.4	10.3
B	1.8	1.5	1.5	0.8	1.2	1.2	0.6	0.5	0.8	0.6
C	3.2	2.2	3.5	3.1	1.9	1.2	2.6	2.0	2.0	2.1
D	52.0	49.8	58.2	52.2	46.0	42.5	43.8	38.0	38.7	32.3
E	1.6	1.9	2.7	2.0	1.1	1.2	1.4	1.2	1.4	1.1
F	32.9	32.1	40.8	31.5	29.9	29.5	30.4	27.7	27.4	27.8
G	58.7	52.8	74.7	69.7	65.7	61.4	61.1	65.5	54.8	53.6
H	20.6	22.8	47.5	45.8	42.5	46.7	37.1	38.3	38.0	37.0
I	14.5	17.5	26.5	23.2	21.2	18.0	14.8	15.4	17.0	16.5
J	6.5	5.9	9.0	9.3	8.7	8.8	7.8	6.4	7.7	9.0
K	28.3	30.2	47.4	45.2	40.6	36.7	35.3	31.9	32.7	35.6
L	11.6	8.8	15.4	16.2	15.6	12.5	11.8	11.8	9.3	10.6
M	8.3	8.0	12.0	14.2	14.5	13.9	14.9	13.2	11.7	11.1
N	13.9	11.6	17.7	18.5	19.3	18.6	19.0	19.8	19.6	18.7
O	13.0	12.2	20.4	16.5	16.3	15.8	15.4	14.1	13.9	13.0
P	0.8	0.3	0.7	0.5	0.4	0.2	0.1	0.3	0.2	-
Q	-	0.3								
X	221.6	203.5	248.0	261.7	250.5	230.5	217.0	216.9	199.9	191.6

Men - Hommes - Hombres
ISIC 3 - CITI 3 - CIIU 3

	1999	2000	2001	2002	2003	2004	2005	2006	2007	2008
Total	379.5	347.7	373.7	360.9	324.9	299.4	283.1	277.5	245.7	236.9
UB	71.7	63.8	49.0	53.5	52.2	49.4	51.3	54.1	50.7	49.9
A	13.2	11.0	15.6	15.0	14.0	12.2	11.4	10.2	8.3	6.6
B	1.5	1.4	1.4	0.8	1.0	1.2	0.5	0.5	0.8	0.6
C	2.8	2.1	2.8	2.7	1.6	1.2	2.3	1.8	2.0	1.5
D	40.9	38.6	42.7	39.6	33.7	31.1	30.3	28.0	28.3	23.8
E	1.5	1.7	2.1	1.6	0.8	1.0	0.7	0.7	0.9	0.6
F	31.1	30.4	38.9	29.7	27.8	27.5	28.7	26.0	24.7	26.1
G	34.1	32.3	42.2	38.1	35.3	32.4	32.1	34.9	28.6	25.0
H	11.0	11.9	22.1	20.9	18.1	19.7	17.1	16.5	14.6	14.2
I	11.6	14.1	20.1	17.3	15.0	13.8	10.2	11.6	11.9	11.7
J	3.0	2.9	4.1	4.3	4.0	4.2	3.6	2.6	3.4	4.0
K	17.9	17.4	27.5	27.6	23.1	20.3	19.1	17.7	15.5	19.7
L	7.6	5.2	9.4	9.8	8.8	7.4	6.8	6.6	4.9	6.1
M	3.6	3.2	4.4	5.1	4.6	4.3	4.6	5.1	4.6	3.7
N	3.5	2.7	4.1	3.9	4.2	3.9	4.8	4.7	4.3	3.5
O	7.5	6.9	10.3	9.4	8.8	9.3	8.0	5.5	5.6	6.4
P	0.2	0.1	0.2	0.3	-	0.0	-	-	0.0	-
Q	-	-								
X	115.1	101.7	125.9	134.9	124.1	109.7	103.1	105.2	87.7	83.4

Women - Femmes - Mujeres
ISIC 3 - CITI 3 - CIIU 3

	1999	2000	2001	2002	2003	2004	2005	2006	2007	2008
Total	275.4	259.8	274.3	270.3	271.1	255.4	245.9	240.1	241.7	234.0
UB	72.7	66.1	48.9	50.7	50.7	53.1	50.8	51.3	57.8	50.2
A	5.4	5.2	6.3	5.6	6.7	3.8	4.4	4.3	4.2	3.7
B	0.2	0.1	0.1	-	0.1	-	0.1	0.0	0.1	-
C	0.4	0.1	0.6	0.4	0.3	0.0	0.3	0.2	0.0	0.7
D	11.1	11.2	15.5	12.6	12.3	11.4	13.5	10.0	10.4	8.6
E	0.1	0.2	0.5	0.4	0.3	0.2	0.7	0.4	0.5	0.4
F	1.7	1.7	2.0	1.8	2.1	2.0	1.7	1.7	2.7	1.7
G	24.6	20.5	32.5	31.7	30.4	29.0	29.0	30.6	26.3	28.6
H	9.6	10.8	25.4	24.9	24.4	27.0	20.0	21.8	23.4	22.8
I	2.9	3.4	6.4	5.9	6.2	4.2	4.7	3.9	5.1	4.8
J	3.5	3.0	4.9	5.0	4.8	4.6	4.2	3.8	4.3	5.0
K	10.4	12.8	19.9	17.6	17.5	16.4	16.2	14.2	17.2	15.8
L	4.0	3.6	6.0	6.4	6.8	5.1	5.1	5.3	4.4	4.5
M	4.7	4.7	7.6	9.1	9.8	9.6	10.3	8.1	7.1	7.4
N	10.3	8.9	13.7	14.5	15.1	14.7	14.2	15.1	15.4	15.2
O	5.4	5.3	10.1	7.1	7.5	6.6	7.4	8.6	8.3	6.6
P	0.6	0.2	0.6	0.2	0.4	0.1	0.1	0.3	0.1	-
Q	-	-								
X	106.7	101.9	122.1	126.8	126.4	120.8	114.0	111.7	112.2	108.2

Explanatory notes: see p. 451.   Notes explicatives: voir p. 454.   Notas explicativas: véase p. 457.

[1] Excl. armed forces. [2] Persons aged 15 years and over.   [1] Non compris les forces armées. [2] Personnes âgées de 15 ans et plus.   [1] Excl. las fuerzas armadas. [2] Personas de 15 años y más.

By economic activity · **Par activité économique** · **Por actividad económica**

	Thousands				Milliers			Millares		
	1999	2000	2001	2002	2003	2004	2005	2006	2007	2008

New Zealand (BA) [1] — Total unemployment - Chômage total - Desempleo total

Total - Total - Total
ISIC 3 - CITI 3 - CIIU 3

	1999	2000	2001	2002	2003	2004	2005	2006	2007	2008
Total	127.8	113.4	102.3	102.5	97.8 [2]	84.9	82.5	85.4	82.8	95.0
UB	15.5	12.4	12.5	12.1	12.3 [2]	12.3	11.6	12.5	14.3	15.7
A	12.9	11.0	10.5	11.4	9.0 [2]	6.9	7.6	6.4	6.3	6.1
B	-	-	-	-	- [2]	-	-	-	-	-
C	-	-	-	-	- [2]	-	-	-	-	-
D	16.7	14.8	11.9	11.4	10.3 [2]	9.8	8.3	8.3	8.1	8.1
E	-	-	-	-	- [2]	-	-	-	-	-
F	8.3	7.1	5.6	5.8	5.0 [2]	4.0	4.9	4.0	4.2	6.5
G	15.4	14.5	13.0	13.2	12.7 [2]	11.3	12.5	13.4	13.0	15.2
H	10.3	8.9	7.8	8.8	8.0 [2]	6.4	7.1	6.8	6.8	7.0
I	4.7	4.3	4.9	4.0	4.2 [2]	3.1	3.6	3.9	2.5	3.8
J	1.7	1.4	1.1	1.1	1.4 [2]	-	1.0	-	-	1.1
K	8.0	7.5	6.9	8.0	7.3 [2]	7.4	5.8	7.3	6.8	7.1
L	3.8	3.7	3.1	2.8	3.7 [2]	2.9	2.7	2.4	2.5	2.7
M	4.2	4.6	4.6	4.2	4.2 [2]	4.4	4.1	3.2	3.2	3.9
N	4.9	3.8	4.8	4.6	4.6 [2]	3.6	3.2	4.9	3.6	3.5
O	5.1	4.7	3.7	4.1	4.3 [2]	3.8	3.5	3.5	3.3	4.9
P	1.0	1.1	1.0	-	- [2]	-	-	-	-	-
Q	.	.	.	.	.	.	.	.	.	.
X	14.1	12.5	10.0	9.2	9.3 [2]	7.2	5.9	7.7	7.1	8.7

Men - Hommes - Hombres
ISIC 3 - CITI 3 - CIIU 3

	1999	2000	2001	2002	2003	2004	2005	2006	2007	2008
Total	72.4	63.4	56.2	54.6	49.3 [2]	40.7	40.9	42.3	41.0	49.8
UB	7.7	6.4	6.6	6.3	6.4 [2]	5.5	5.7	6.0	7.2	8.4
A	8.9	7.1	6.4	7.1	5.1 [2]	4.1	4.7	3.7	3.6	3.7
B	-	-	-	-	- [2]	-	-	-	-	-
C	-	-	-	-	- [2]	-	-	-	-	-
D	12.5	10.2	9.1	7.7	6.8 [2]	5.9	5.0	5.8	5.3	5.7
E	-	-	-	-	- [2]	-	-	-	-	-
F	7.7	6.5	5.1	5.3	4.7 [2]	3.6	4.3	3.8	3.7	5.9
G	7.8	8.7	7.3	6.4	6.5 [2]	5.1	6.0	6.3	5.7	7.6
H	4.2	3.4	2.6	3.3	2.5 [2]	2.0	1.4	2.5	2.4	2.6
I	3.5	2.9	3.5	2.8	2.6 [2]	1.9	2.6	2.5	1.6	2.4
J	-	-	-	-	- [2]	-	-	-	-	-
K	4.8	3.6	3.6	4.6	4.0 [2]	3.7	3.3	3.6	3.9	3.4
L	2.2	2.3	1.6	1.6	1.6 [2]	1.5	1.4	1.3	1.1	1.2
M	1.6	1.6	1.8	1.5	1.4 [2]	1.4	-	-	1.0	1.3
N	-	-	1.1	-	- [2]	-	-	-	-	-
O	2.7	2.5	2.1	2.2	1.8 [2]	1.5	1.6	1.6	1.8	2.8
P	-	-	-	-	- [2]	-	-	-	-	.
Q	.	.	.	.	.	.	.	.	.	.
X	6.3	5.8	4.4	3.8	3.9 [2]	2.8	2.8	3.3	3.1	3.6

Women - Femmes - Mujeres
ISIC 3 - CITI 3 - CIIU 3

	1999	2000	2001	2002	2003	2004	2005	2006	2007	2008
Total	55.4	50.0	46.1	47.9	48.5 [2]	44.2	41.6	43.1	41.7	45.2
UB	7.8	6.0	5.9	5.8	5.9 [2]	6.7	6.0	6.5	7.0	7.3
A	4.0	3.9	4.1	4.3	3.9 [2]	2.8	3.0	2.7	2.7	2.4
B	-	-	-	-	- [2]	.	.	-	.	-
C	-	-	-	-	- [2]	.	.	.	.	.
D	4.1	4.5	2.9	3.6	3.5 [2]	3.9	3.3	2.5	2.9	2.4
E	-	-	-	-	- [2]	-	-	-	-	-
F	-	-	-	-	- [2]	-	-	-	-	-
G	7.6	5.8	5.7	6.8	6.2 [2]	6.2	6.5	7.1	7.2	7.7
H	6.1	5.5	5.2	5.5	5.6 [2]	4.5	5.7	4.3	4.4	4.4
I	1.3	1.5	1.5	1.2	1.6 [2]	1.2	1.0	1.4	-	1.5
J	1.1	-	-	-	- [2]	-	-	-	-	-
K	3.2	3.9	3.3	3.4	3.4 [2]	3.7	2.5	3.7	2.9	3.7
L	1.6	1.4	1.5	1.2	3.0 [2]	1.4	1.3	1.1	1.3	1.5
M	2.6	3.0	2.8	2.8	2.8 [2]	3.0	3.2	2.3	2.2	2.6
N	4.2	3.1	3.7	3.7	3.7 [2]	2.8	2.9	4.2	3.3	2.8
O	2.4	2.1	1.7	1.9	2.5 [2]	2.3	1.9	1.9	1.5	2.2
P	-	1.0	-	-	-	-	-	-	-	-
Q	.	.	.	.	.	.	.	.	.	.
X	7.8	6.7	5.6	5.4	5.4 [2]	4.4	3.2	4.4	4.0	5.1

Explanatory notes: see p. 451.

[1] Persons aged 15 years and over. [2] Methodology revised; data not strictly comparable.

Notes explicatives: voir p. 454.

[1] Personnes âgées de 15 ans et plus. [2] Méthodologie révisée; les données ne sont pas strictement comparables.

Notas explicativas: véase p. 457.

[1] Personas de 15 años y más. [2] Metodología revisada; los datos no son estrictamente comparables.

	Thousands			Milliers				Millares		
	1999	2000	2001	2002	2003	2004	2005	2006	2007	2008

AFRICA-AFRIQUE-AFRICA

Egypt (BA) [1] [2]   Total unemployment - Chômage total - Desempleo total

Total - Total - Total
ISCO-88 - CITP-88 - CIUO-88

	1999	2000	2001	2002	2003	2004	2005	2006	2007	2008
Total	1 480.5	1 698.0	1 783.0	2 020.6	2 240.7	2 153.9	2 450.0	2 435.0	2 134.9	.
UB	1 374.3	1 578.8	1 634.4	1 865.5	2 134.1	2 043.6	2 257.4	2 201.0	1 966.1	.
1	2.7	1.8	4.3	4.8	1.0	2.2	1.8	3.5	1.8	.
2	10.6	10.7	15.5	14.1	17.0	14.8	17.5	23.4	20.4	.
3	8.4	7.5	9.3	11.9	8.3	8.4	8.8	13.2	8.7	.
4	4.5	4.5	5.8	7.7	4.2	8.5	6.3	8.2	6.6	.
5	20.2	27.8	34.3	37.1	36.0	38.4	49.2	56.9	32.5	.
6	5.7	5.5	10.2	8.7	6.0	4.3	19.5	18.8	7.8	.
7	34.0	36.1	36.6	22.8	25.9	21.8	54.6	51.8	35.2	.
8	5.3	6.8	9.3	5.4	6.4	8.4	13.7	20.3	13.5	.
9	4.0	2.0	2.9	2.4	1.8	3.5	7.2	8.9	6.4	.
X	10.8	16.5	20.5	40.5	-	-	13.8	28.3	35.5	.

Men - Hommes - Hombres
ISCO-88 - CITP-88 - CIUO-88

	1999	2000	2001	2002	2003	2004	2005	2006	2007	2008
Total	726.2	743.5	851.8	983.2	1 186.7	942.6	1 194.5	1 208.0	1 077.4	.
UB	648.4	659.0	753.0	895.4	1 104.3	861.1	1 034.5	1 019.0	944.7	.
1	2.2	0.6	2.8	2.6	0.8	1.9	1.6	3.3	1.8	.
2	6.6	6.9	7.2	9.4	13.2	10.7	10.7	13.1	11.7	.
3	5.6	4.7	4.6	8.1	6.1	4.2	5.2	6.5	4.3	.
4	2.2	3.0	3.6	4.8	2.9	5.0	4.6	5.4	3.2	.
5	13.2	19.3	21.5	21.1	24.2	25.1	37.9	48.4	26.6	.
6	5.5	5.0	9.1	5.8	5.5	4.2	19.1	18.2	7.6	.
7	31.3	32.0	33.3	19.9	24.0	20.2	52.4	47.3	33.9	.
8	5.1	5.7	7.1	3.9	3.9	6.8	11.9	17.7	9.8	.
9	4.0	2.0	2.9	2.4	1.8	3.4	7.2	8.7	6.2	.
X	2.1	5.3	6.6	10.0	-	-	9.3	20.4	27.4	.

Women - Femmes - Mujeres
ISCO-88 - CITP-88 - CIUO-88

	1999	2000	2001	2002	2003	2004	2005	2006	2007	2008
Total	754.3	954.5	931.2	1 037.4	1 054.0	1 211.3	1 255.5	1 227.0	1 057.5	.
UB	725.9	919.8	881.4	970.1	1 029.8	1 182.5	1 222.9	1 183.0	1 021.4	.
1	0.5	1.2	1.4	2.2	0.2	0.3	0.2	0.2	-	.
2	4.0	3.8	8.3	4.7	3.8	4.1	6.8	10.3	8.7	.
3	2.8	2.8	4.7	3.8	2.2	4.2	3.6	6.7	4.4	.
4	2.3	1.5	2.2	2.9	1.3	3.5	1.7	2.8	3.4	.
5	7.0	8.5	12.8	16.0	11.8	13.3	11.3	8.5	5.9	.
6	0.2	0.5	1.1	2.9	0.5	0.1	0.4	0.6	0.2	.
7	2.7	4.1	3.3	2.9	1.9	1.6	2.2	4.5	1.3	.
8	0.2	1.1	2.2	1.5	2.5	1.6	1.8	2.6	3.7	.
9	-	-	-	-	-	0.1	-	0.2	0.2	.
X	8.7	11.2	13.9	30.5	-	-	4.5	7.9	8.1	.

Maroc (BA) [3]   Total unemployment - Chômage total - Desempleo total

Total - Total - Total
ISCO-88 - CITP-88 - CIUO-88

	1999	2000	2001	2002	2003	2004	2005	2006	2007	2008
Total	.	.	.	.	.	1 192.5	1 226.4	.	.	.
UB	.	.	.	.	.	598.8	600.1	.	.	.
1	.	.	.	.	.	2.6	1.8	.	.	.
2	.	.	.	.	.	7.1	7.4	.	.	.
3	.	.	.	.	.	83.1	80.3	.	.	.
4	.	.	.	.	.	111.8	110.7	.	.	.
5	.	.	.	.	.	27.6	24.8	.	.	.
6	.	.	.	.	.	52.8	69.4	.	.	.
7	.	.	.	.	.	221.5	245.5	.	.	.
8	.	.	.	.	.	27.7	28.0	.	.	.
9	.	.	.	.	.	196.7	200.7	.	.	.
X	.	.	.	.	.	461.6	457.8	.	.	.

Men - Hommes - Hombres
ISCO-88 - CITP-88 - CIUO-88

	1999	2000	2001	2002	2003	2004	2005	2006	2007	2008
Total	.	.	.	.	.	851.2	877.6	.	.	.
UB	.	.	.	.	.	382.6	386.6	.	.	.
1	.	.	.	.	.	2.2	1.7	.	.	.
2	.	.	.	.	.	4.8	4.6	.	.	.
3	.	.	.	.	.	43.2	41.2	.	.	.
4	.	.	.	.	.	66.0	67.3	.	.	.
5	.	.	.	.	.	26.3	23.9	.	.	.
6	.	.	.	.	.	47.0	60.3	.	.	.
7	.	.	.	.	.	163.5	182.9	.	.	.
8	.	.	.	.	.	26.9	25.5	.	.	.
9	.	.	.	.	.	161.3	160.8	.	.	.
X	.	.	.	.	.	310.0	309.3	.	.	.

Explanatory notes: see p. 451.   Notes explicatives: voir p. 454.   Notas explicativas: véase p. 457.

[1] Persons aged 15 to 64 years. [2] May and Nov. [3] Persons aged 15 years and over.   [1] Personnes âgées de 15 à 64 ans. [2] Mai et nov. [3] Personnes âgées de 15 ans et plus.   [1] Personas de 15 a 64 años. [2] Mayo y nov. [3] Personas de 15 años y más.

	Thousands					Milliers				Millares
	1999	2000	2001	2002	2003	2004	2005	2006	2007	2008

Maroc (BA) [1]   Total unemployment - Chômage total - Desempleo total

Women - Femmes - Mujeres
ISCO-88 - CITP-88 - CIUO-88

	1999	2000	2001	2002	2003	2004	2005	2006	2007	2008
Total	.	.	.	.	.	341.4	348.8	.	.	.
UB	.	.	.	.	.	216.2	213.5	.	.	.
1	.	.	.	.	.	0.4	0.1	.	.	.
2	.	.	.	.	.	2.3	2.8	.	.	.
3	.	.	.	.	.	40.0	39.1	.	.	.
4	.	.	.	.	.	45.7	43.5	.	.	.
5	.	.	.	.	.	1.3	0.9	.	.	.
6	.	.	.	.	.	5.8	9.1	.	.	.
7	.	.	.	.	.	58.1	62.5	.	.	.
8	.	.	.	.	.	0.8	2.4	.	.	.
9	.	.	.	.	.	35.5	39.9	.	.	.
X	.	.	.	.	.	151.6	148.6	.	.	.

Mauritius (FB) [1][2]   Registered unemployment - Chômage enregistré - Desempleo registrado

Total - Total - Total
ISCO-88 - CITP-88 - CIUO-88

	1999	2000	2001	2002	2003	2004	2005	2006	2007	2008
Total	12.1	18.0	21.6	.	23.4	.	33.6	.	.	20.6
UB	3.0	4.4	5.0	.	5.4	.	6.4	.	.	4.4
1	0.0	0.0	0.0	.	.	.	0.1	.	.	0.1
1-3	.	.	.	.	0.8	.	.	.	.	.
2	0.1	0.0	0.0	.	.	.	0.3	.	.	0.2
3	0.4	0.6	0.7	.	.	.	1.0	.	.	1.1
4	2.0	2.9	3.4	.	4.0	.	5.3	.	.	3.7
5	0.7	1.0	1.3	.	1.7	.	2.9	.	.	2.2
6	0.1	0.1	0.2	.	0.2	.	0.3	.	.	0.2
7	2.9	4.2	4.9	.	.	.	7.3	.	.	3.3
7-8	.	.	.	.	7.9	.	.	.	.	.
8	1.3	2.0	2.7	.	.	.	4.1	.	.	2.1
9	1.7	2.7	3.3	.	3.3	.	6.0	.	.	3.3

Men - Hommes - Hombres
ISCO-88 - CITP-88 - CIUO-88

	1999	2000	2001	2002	2003	2004	2005	2006	2007	2008
Total	5.3	8.6	10.5	.	10.1	.	15.4	.	.	7.1
UB	1.0	1.5	1.6	.	1.5	.	1.8	.	.	1.1
1	0.0	0.0	0.0	.	.	.	0.0	.	.	0.0
1-3	.	.	.	.	0.3	.	.	.	.	.
2	0.0	0.0	0.0	.	.	.	0.1	.	.	0.1
3	0.1	0.2	0.3	.	.	.	0.3	.	.	0.3
4	0.4	0.6	0.7	.	0.7	.	1.0	.	.	0.7
5	0.3	0.5	0.7	.	0.7	.	1.2	.	.	0.7
6	0.1	0.1	0.2	.	0.2	.	0.3	.	.	0.2
7	1.4	2.3	2.9	.	.	.	4.2	.	.	1.5
7-8	.	.	.	.	4.4	.	.	.	.	.
8	0.8	1.3	1.7	.	.	.	2.4	.	.	1.0
9	1.2	2.0	2.5	.	2.3	.	4.0	.	.	1.7

Women - Femmes - Mujeres
ISCO-88 - CITP-88 - CIUO-88

	1999	2000	2001	2002	2003	2004	2005	2006	2007	2008
Total	6.8	9.5	11.1	.	13.3	.	18.2	.	.	13.5
UB	2.0	2.9	3.4	.	3.9	.	4.6	.	.	3.3
1	0.0	-	-	.	.	.	0.0	.	.	0.0
1-3	.	.	.	.	0.6	.	.	.	.	.
2	0.0	0.0	0.0	.	.	.	0.2	.	.	0.1
3	0.3	0.4	0.5	.	.	.	0.7	.	.	0.8
4	1.7	2.3	2.7	.	3.3	.	4.3	.	.	3.1
5	0.4	0.5	0.7	.	1.0	.	1.7	.	.	1.5
6	0.0	0.0	0.0	.	0.0	.	0.0	.	.	0.0
7	1.5	1.9	2.1	.	.	.	3.1	.	.	1.8
7-8	.	.	.	.	3.6	.	.	.	.	.
8	0.5	0.7	1.0	.	.	.	1.8	.	.	1.1
9	0.5	0.7	0.8	.	1.0	.	1.9	.	.	1.7

South Africa (BA) [3][4]   Total unemployment - Chômage total - Desempleo total

Total - Total - Total
ISCO-88 - CITP-88 - CIUO-88

	1999	2000	2001	2002	2003	2004	2005	2006	2007	2008
Total	.	4 162	4 655	4 936	4 434	4 135	4 487	4 391	3 945	4 075
UB	.	2 278	2 555	2 967	2 671	2 461	2 945	2 603	2 170	1 726
1	.	26	25	29	24	20	21	19	23	32
2	.	16	14	11	15	10	11	18	20	30
3	.	76	87	96	63	60	69	92	69	82
4	.	155	211	203	175	166	147	160	155	184
5	.	265	311	258	249	215	220	250	254	265
6	.	37	43	57	21	17	32	75	50	7
7	.	315	345	313	270	259	237	258	307	320
8	.	202	278	244	196	207	166	141	153	132
9	.	717	779	748	747	718	637	766	736	770
X	.	75	5	8	3	4	2	8	6	527

Explanatory notes: see p. 451.

[1] Persons aged 15 years and over. [2] Excl. Rodrigues. [3] Persons aged 15 to 64 years. [4] Prior to 2008: persons aged 15 years and over; September of each year.

Notes explicatives: voir p. 454.

[1] Personnes âgées de 15 ans et plus. [2] Non compris Rodriguez. [3] Personnes âgées de 15 à 64 ans. [4] Avant 2008: personnes âgées de 15 ans et plus; septembre de chaque année.

Notas explicativas: véase p. 457.

[1] Personas de 15 años y más. [2] Excl. Rodríguez. [3] Personas de 15 a 64 años. [4] Antes de 2008: personas de 15 años y más; Septiembre de cada año.

By occupation   **Par profession**   **Por ocupación**

Thousands — Milliers — Millares

South Africa (BA) [1] [2]

Total unemployment - Chômage total - Desempleo total

Men - Hommes - Hombres
ISCO-88 - CITP-88 - CIUO-88

	1999	2000	2001	2002	2003	2004	2005	2006	2007	2008
Total	.	1 983	2 236	2 316	2 166	2 029	2 057	1 967	1 883	1 917
UB	.	1 004	1 141	1 305	1 218	1 124	1 295	1 133	996	744
1	.	17	17	19	14	13	10	13	15	18
2	.	9	5	4	9	5	8	12	7	16
3	.	33	41	54	30	31	35	44	29	40
4	.	44	67	62	60	45	43	30	29	48
5	.	120	154	106	130	116	106	115	129	110
6	.	30	35	49	10	9	16	25	19	4
7	.	268	292	261	236	217	182	189	249	267
8	.	162	206	180	146	157	130	108	116	107
9	.	260	272	270	311	308	231	289	291	315
X	.	36	3	5	2	3	1	7	3	248

Women - Femmes - Mujeres
ISCO-88 - CITP-88 - CIUO-88

	1999	2000	2001	2002	2003	2004	2005	2006	2007	2008
Total	.	2 179	2 420	2 619	2 268	2 103	2 428	2 424	2 059	2 158
UB	.	1 274	1 414	1 661	1 454	1 333	1 648	1 470	1 173	982
1	.	10	8	10	10	7	11	5	8	15
2	.	7	9	7	6	4	4	7	13	15
3	.	43	47	42	33	29	34	49	41	42
4	.	111	144	140	115	121	104	130	126	136
5	.	145	157	152	119	99	114	135	125	155
6	.	8	7	7	11	7	16	50	31	2
7	.	47	53	53	34	41	54	69	59	53
8	.	40	72	63	50	49	36	33	36	26
9	.	457	507	478	432	410	406	477	444	454
X	.	37	2	4	1	1	1	-	3	278

AMERICA-AMÉRIQUE-AMERICA

Argentina (BA) [3] [4] [5]

Total unemployment - Chômage total - Desempleo total

Total - Total - Total
ISCO-88 - CITP-88 - CIUO-88

	1999	2000	2001	2002	2003	2004	2005	2006	2007	2008
Total	1 359.6	1 460.9	1 709.8	1 955.8	1 633.0 [6]	1 361.6	1 141.5	1 037.9 [7]	.	.
UB	166.3	173.2	189.5	239.9	228.1 [6]	196.7	137.6	134.0 [7]	.	.
1	13.8	19.0	24.1	27.7	1.3 [6]	0.6	-	- [7]	.	.
2	20.4	26.4	25.3	29.4	29.8 [6]	13.4	16.2	12.9 [7]	.	.
3	101.4	103.1	129.5	158.0	106.7 [6]	72.6	54.5	52.7 [7]	.	.
4	76.5	85.0	115.1	122.0	72.1 [6]	73.1	61.7	79.8 [7]	.	.
5	195.6	196.4	244.1	268.7	285.9 [6]	231.5	189.7	193.7 [7]	.	.
6	19.0	25.5	27.9	43.8	8.8 [6]	6.6	3.2	1.9 [7]	.	.
7	290.2	305.7	386.7	427.7	261.3 [6]	218.5	173.0	156.5 [7]	.	.
8	80.0	77.1	99.1	108.2	67.5 [6]	72.2	64.8	49.4 [7]	.	.
9	387.2	438.9	456.2	515.1	349.3 [6]	311.3	305.6	250.6 [7]	.	.
0	0.9	1.6	0.9	0.2	0.1 [6]	0.4	0.8	0.5 [7]	.	.
X	8.3	9.1	11.3	15.2	222.2 [6]	164.7	134.4	105.9 [7]	.	.

Men - Hommes - Hombres
ISCO-88 - CITP-88 - CIUO-88

	1999	2000	2001	2002	2003	2004	2005	2006	2007	2008
Total	764.9	809.9	1 021.3	1 175.2	824.8 [6]	687.6	561.7	483.4 [7]	.	.
UB	69.5	66.7	79.1	103.4	86.3 [6]	76.0	59.7	56.6 [7]	.	.
1	9.2	15.0	20.2	21.9	0.6 [6]	0.3	-	- [7]	.	.
2	11.9	14.5	11.7	14.1	13.8 [6]	6.0	8.4	7.2 [7]	.	.
3	44.7	45.7	65.9	80.2	51.1 [6]	35.9	26.0	21.8 [7]	.	.
4	30.6	31.5	43.6	44.2	25.2 [6]	30.9	23.7	27.5 [7]	.	.
5	75.8	71.7	102.9	122.5	130.2 [6]	102.3	71.0	75.8 [7]	.	.
6	17.9	22.6	25.3	42.7	8.4 [6]	4.9	3.1	1.8 [7]	.	.
7	250.3	260.9	344.5	386.9	227.9 [6]	180.5	139.5	126.7 [7]	.	.
8	67.2	67.6	88.5	96.3	51.6 [6]	50.0	42.5	34.5 [7]	.	.
9	182.7	208.1	232.8	253.3	156.5 [6]	148.0	144.3	105.4 [7]	.	.
0	0.9	1.5	0.8	0.2	0.1 [6]	0.4	0.3	0.5 [7]	.	.
X	4.4	4.0	6.1	9.6	73.1 [6]	52.3	43.1	25.5 [7]	.	.

Women - Femmes - Mujeres
ISCO-88 - CITP-88 - CIUO-88

	1999	2000	2001	2002	2003	2004	2005	2006	2007	2008
Total	594.7	651.0	688.4	780.6	808.2 [6]	673.9	579.8	554.5 [7]	.	.
UB	96.8	106.5	110.4	136.5	141.8 [6]	120.6	77.9	77.4 [7]	.	.
1	4.6	4.0	3.9	5.8	0.7 [6]	0.2	-	- [7]	.	.
2	8.6	11.9	13.6	15.3	15.9 [6]	7.4	7.8	5.6 [7]	.	.
3	56.7	57.4	63.6	77.8	55.7 [6]	36.7	28.6	30.9 [7]	.	.
4	45.9	53.5	71.5	77.7	46.9 [6]	42.3	38.1	52.3 [7]	.	.
5	119.8	124.8	141.2	146.3	155.6 [6]	129.3	118.7	117.9 [7]	.	.
6	1.2	2.9	2.7	1.1	0.4 [6]	1.6	0.1	0.2 [7]	.	.
7	40.0	44.8	42.3	40.7	33.3 [6]	38.0	33.4	29.7 [7]	.	.
8	12.8	9.4	10.6	11.8	15.9 [6]	22.3	22.3	14.9 [7]	.	.
9	204.5	230.7	223.4	261.8	192.8 [6]	163.3	161.2	145.2 [7]	.	.
0	-	0.0	0.1	0.0	- [6]	-	0.5	- [7]	.	.
X	3.9	5.0	5.2	5.6	149.1 [6]	112.3	91.3	80.5 [7]	.	.

Explanatory notes: see p. 451.   Notes explicatives: voir p. 454.   Notas explicativas: véase p. 457.

[1] Persons aged 15 to 64 years. [2] Prior to 2008: persons aged 15 years and over; September of each year. [3] Persons aged 10 years and over. [4] 31 Urban agglomerations. [5] Second semester. [6] Methodology revised; data not strictly comparable; Prior to 2003: May and October. [7] Prior to 2006: 28 urban agglomerations.

[1] Personnes âgées de 15 à 64 ans. [2] Avant 2008: personnes âgées de 15 ans et plus; septembre de chaque année. [3] Personnes âgées de 10 ans et plus. [4] 31 agglomérations urbaines. [5] Second semestre. [6] Méthodologie révisée; les données ne sont pas strictement comparables; Avant 2003: mai et octobre. [7] Avant 2006: 28 agglomérations urbaines.

[1] Personas de 15 a 64 años. [2] Antes de 2008: personas de 15 años y más; Septiembre de cada año. [3] Personas de 10 años y más. [4] 31 aglomerados úrbanos. [5] Segundo semestre. [6] Metodología revisada; los datos no son estrictamente comparables; antes de 2003: mayo y octubre. [7] Antes de 2006: 28 aglomerados úrbanos

	Thousands				Milliers				Millares	
	1999	2000	2001	2002	2003	2004	2005	2006	2007	2008

Bahamas (BA) [1] [2]

Total unemployment - Chômage total - Desempleo total

Total - Total - Total
ISCO-88 - CITP-88 - CIUO-88

	1999	2000	2001	2002	2003	2004	2005	2006	2007	2008
Total	12.29	.	11.33	15.28	18.83	17.99	18.17	13.83 [3]	14.62	.
UB	2.58	.	2.13	2.38	3.44	4.33	3.21	1.94 [3]	2.40	.
1	0.17	.	0.39	0.39	0.79	0.26	0.57	0.53 [3]	0.41	.
2	0.04	.	0.10	0.21	0.09	0.18	0.23	0.05 [3]	0.24	.
3	0.30	.	0.50	0.77	0.44	0.63	0.57	0.40 [3]	0.71	.
4	1.01	.	1.21	1.87	2.14	1.53	1.87	1.48 [3]	1.59	.
5	2.10	.	1.81	2.30	3.57	3.19	3.83	3.11 [3]	2.99	.
6	0.56	.	-	0.56	0.21	0.18	0.13	0.18 [3]	0.19	.
7	1.56	.	1.55	2.60	2.49	1.96	2.32	1.73 [3]	1.95	.
8	-	.	0.41	0.58	0.48	0.42	0.27	0.54 [3]	0.43	.
9	3.56	.	2.81	3.23	4.82	5.13	4.89	3.74 [3]	3.63	.
X	0.40	.	0.43	0.39	0.38	0.18	0.30	0.14 [3]	0.09	.

Men - Hommes - Hombres
ISCO-88 - CITP-88 - CIUO-88

	1999	2000	2001	2002	2003	2004	2005	2006	2007	2008
Total	4.96	.	5.72	7.56	8.78	8.49	8.37	6.37 [3]	6.45	.
UB	0.62	.	0.90	0.85	0.98	1.25	1.02	0.44 [3]	0.66	.
1	0.07	.	0.24	0.19	0.47	0.17	0.21	0.27 [3]	0.19	.
2	0.04	.	0.06	0.12	0.06	0.03	0.06	0.02 [3]	0.06	.
3	0.15	.	0.14	0.33	0.14	0.21	0.14	0.21 [3]	0.34	.
4	0.04	.	0.14	0.37	0.15	0.08	0.19	0.22 [3]	0.06	.
5	0.39	.	0.38	0.58	1.05	0.72	0.99	0.71 [3]	0.72	.
6	0.56	.	-	0.53	0.21	0.18	0.13	0.12 [3]	0.19	.
7	1.29	.	1.49	2.40	2.36	1.96	2.23	1.59 [3]	1.89	.
8	-	.	0.35	0.35	0.37	0.29	0.24	0.42 [3]	0.40	.
9	1.58	.	1.74	1.70	2.82	3.48	2.99	2.26 [3]	1.89	.
X	0.22	.	0.28	0.15	0.18	0.11	0.19	0.12 [3]	0.06	.

Women - Femmes - Mujeres
ISCO-88 - CITP-88 - CIUO-88

	1999	2000	2001	2002	2003	2004	2005	2006	2007	2008
Total	7.33	.	5.61	7.72	10.05	9.50	9.80	7.46 [3]	8.17	.
UB	1.96	.	1.22	1.53	2.46	3.07	2.19	1.50 [3]	1.74	.
1	0.10	.	0.15	0.21	0.32	0.09	0.36	0.26 [3]	0.22	.
2	-	.	0.15	0.09	0.03	0.15	0.17	0.03 [3]	0.17	.
3	0.14	.	0.24	0.44	0.30	0.42	0.44	0.19 [3]	0.37	.
4	0.97	.	1.07	1.50	1.99	1.45	1.68	1.25 [3]	1.52	.
5	1.71	.	1.43	1.72	2.52	2.47	2.84	2.40 [3]	2.28	.
6	-	.	-	0.03	-	-	-	0.06 [3]	-	.
7	0.27	.	0.06	0.21	0.13	-	0.09	0.14 [3]	0.06	.
8	-	.	0.06	0.23	0.11	0.13	0.03	0.11 [3]	0.03	.
9	1.98	.	1.07	1.53	1.99	1.65	1.90	1.48 [3]	1.75	.
X	0.18	.	0.15	0.23	0.20	0.06	0.10	0.02 [3]	0.03	.

Canada (BA) [1] [4]

Total unemployment - Chômage total - Desempleo total

Total - Total - Total
ISCO-88 - CITP-88 - CIUO-88

	1999	2000	2001	2002	2003	2004	2005	2006	2007	2008
Total	1 181.6	1 082.8	1 163.6	1 268.9	1 286.2	1 235.3	1 172.8	1 108.4	1 079.4	1 119.3
1	32.7	30.7	30.3	34.7	34.0	32.7	36.1	30.4	25.9	30.8
2	59.3	58.6	69.4	75.0	82.5	71.8	67.0	61.6	63.6	69.1
3	65.9	60.7	75.7	82.0	79.8	74.5	75.5	70.8	77.2	73.3
4	101.4	87.9	101.3	116.4	116.7	114.6	105.3	102.6	101.9	104.5
5	133.4	122.5	122.1	144.1	160.4	151.2	132.5	126.7	129.6	134.2
6	34.1	30.2	30.4	31.3	30.8	30.1	29.6	25.0	23.8	23.0
7	105.6	91.6	102.8	117.8	111.8	108.2	97.8	96.7	95.6	99.2
8	104.5	93.8	116.1	118.2	109.4	104.0	99.8	99.1	102.2	102.1
9	142.6	134.8	136.0	150.8	159.6	156.2	146.7	141.4	136.4	148.6
X	401.0	371.1	378.2	396.7	400.4	390.4	380.6	352.1	321.5	332.6

Men - Hommes - Hombres
ISCO-88 - CITP-88 - CIUO-88

	1999	2000	2001	2002	2003	2004	2005	2006	2007	2008
Total	660.4	595.3	655.1	721.7	719.6	685.4	649.0	608.3	603.9	632.6
1	20.6	19.1	18.1	22.0	20.7	20.8	22.1	17.4	14.1	19.9
2	28.5	27.4	36.0	37.7	44.2	35.4	33.9	29.7	32.0	32.1
3	30.8	26.2	34.2	39.9	37.6	31.0	33.1	29.6	32.5	34.4
4	25.0	20.9	27.5	32.6	30.5	31.6	33.3	29.6	28.9	31.6
5	50.7	44.8	49.9	60.0	61.4	56.9	52.4	49.7	52.0	55.1
6	28.2	23.5	23.7	25.1	23.1	23.7	22.5	18.4	17.3	17.1
7	98.1	85.1	94.3	106.4	102.7	98.6	89.4	88.1	87.3	89.3
8	77.9	69.6	84.5	89.7	79.8	78.2	72.0	74.2	78.3	79.0
9	102.1	93.1	98.6	107.9	114.4	112.3	104.0	101.9	95.7	106.1
X	197.5	185.1	187.3	199.0	204.7	195.6	185.2	168.1	164.3	166.7

Explanatory notes: see p. 451.

[1] Persons aged 15 years and over. [2] April of each year. [3] May. [4] Excl. residents of the Territories and indigenous persons living on reserves.

Notes explicatives: voir p. 454.

[1] Personnes âgées de 15 ans et plus. [2] Avril de chaque année. [3] Mai. [4] Non compris les habitants des "Territoires" et les populations indigènes vivant dans les réserves.

Notas explicativas: véase p. 457.

[1] Personas de 15 años y más. [2] Abril de cada año. [3] Mayo. [4] Excl. a los habitantes de los "Territorios" y a las poblaciones indígenas que viven en reservas.

By occupation   Par profession   Por ocupación

	Thousands			Milliers				Millares		
	1999	2000	2001	2002	2003	2004	2005	2006	2007	2008

Canada (BA) [1] [2]   Total unemployment - Chômage total - Desempleo total

Women - Femmes - Mujeres
ISCO-88 - CITP-88 - CIUO-88

	1999	2000	2001	2002	2003	2004	2005	2006	2007	2008
Total	521.2	487.5	508.5	547.2	566.6	549.9	523.8	500.1	475.5	486.6
1	12.0	11.6	12.2	12.7	13.3	12.0	14.0	13.0	11.7	10.9
2	30.8	31.1	33.3	37.3	38.4	36.4	33.1	31.9	31.6	37.0
3	35.1	34.5	41.5	42.1	42.3	43.5	42.4	41.2	44.7	38.8
4	76.4	67.1	73.7	83.7	86.2	83.0	72.0	73.0	73.1	72.9
5	82.7	77.6	72.2	84.2	99.0	94.3	80.2	76.9	77.7	79.2
6	5.9	6.7	6.6	6.2	7.7	6.3	7.1	6.6	6.5	6.0
7	7.5	6.5	8.5	11.3	9.0	9.5	8.4	8.6	8.3	9.8
8	26.6	24.2	31.7	28.5	29.6	25.8	27.8	25.0	23.8	23.1
9	40.5	41.8	37.4	42.9	45.2	43.9	42.7	39.5	40.7	42.5
X	203.5	186.0	190.9	197.7	195.7	194.7	195.5	184.0	157.1	165.9

Colombia (BA) [3] [4] [5]   Total unemployment - Chômage total - Desempleo total

Total - Total - Total
ISCO-68 - CITP-68 - CIUO-68

	1999	2000	2001	2002	2003	2004	2005	2006	2007	2008
Total	.	.	2 708.8	2 848.6	2 797.3	2 462.0	2 260.6	2 428.0	2 089.2	2 245.7
UB	.	.	484.4	528.3	541.7	509.2	428.8	525.6	411.7	459.7
0/1	.	.	223.4	247.1	266.1	227.4	216.2	119.7	121.8	128.5
2	.	.	23.5	33.1	45.0	41.0	37.1	26.5	25.3	37.6
3	.	.	485.6	457.4	449.3	381.9	378.1	193.7	221.2	251.2
4	.	.	536.3	516.6	531.4	503.3	496.5	239.3	297.8	296.5
5	.	.	653.9	717.8	682.3	610.9	538.1	447.1	408.4	466.4
6	.	.	109.2	153.7	169.5	122.0	117.0	151.9	145.3	137.5
7/8/9	.	.	654.0	698.1	605.9	536.6	446.7	422.7	440.3	448.5
X	.	.	23.0	24.8	47.8	39.0	30.9	827.2	429.1	479.7

Men - Hommes - Hombres
ISCO-68 - CITP-68 - CIUO-68

	1999	2000	2001	2002	2003	2004	2005	2006	2007	2008
Total	.	.	1 257.6	1 341.3	1 264.8	1 132.1	1 019.4	1 094.9	996.4	1 033.0
UB	.	.	189.4	219.0	222.6	200.6	175.7	209.3	171.4	186.8
0/1	.	.	100.0	120.9	118.6	96.3	100.9	50.2	60.0	63.6
2	.	.	9.6	18.2	24.5	21.1	17.0	9.3	14.5	15.9
3	.	.	207.8	210.3	182.4	165.3	155.8	76.7	86.0	86.8
4	.	.	152.0	156.2	159.7	136.9	140.5	72.2	92.2	92.9
5	.	.	146.4	151.7	139.2	135.7	128.9	84.4	84.7	92.0
6	.	.	90.3	113.5	142.4	99.1	99.9	120.8	121.7	111.5
7/8/9	.	.	530.7	556.1	460.8	440.8	347.2	334.6	352.3	368.7
X	.	.	20.8	14.4	37.1	36.9	29.2	346.8	185.0	201.6

Women - Femmes - Mujeres
ISCO-68 - CITP-68 - CIUO-68

	1999	2000	2001	2002	2003	2004	2005	2006	2007	2008
Total	.	.	1 451.2	1 507.3	1 532.5	1 329.9	1 241.2	1 333.0	1 092.8	1 212.7
UB	.	.	295.0	309.2	319.2	308.5	253.1	316.3	240.2	272.9
0/1	.	.	123.4	126.2	147.5	131.1	115.3	69.6	61.9	64.9
2	.	.	13.9	14.9	20.5	19.9	20.1	17.2	10.9	21.7
3	.	.	277.7	247.1	266.8	216.6	222.3	117.1	135.2	164.4
4	.	.	384.3	360.4	371.7	366.3	356.0	167.1	205.6	203.5
5	.	.	507.5	566.1	543.1	475.3	409.2	362.6	323.7	374.4
6	.	.	18.9	40.1	27.1	22.8	17.1	31.1	23.5	26.0
7/8/9	.	.	123.4	142.0	145.1	95.8	99.5	88.0	88.0	79.7
X	.	.	2.2	10.4	10.6	2.1	1.7	480.4	244.1	278.1

Costa Rica (BA) [6] [7]   Total unemployment - Chômage total - Desempleo total

Total - Total - Total
ISCO-88 - CITP-88 - CIUO-88

	1999	2000	2001	2002	2003	2004	2005	2006	2007	2008
Total	.	71.9	100.4	.	117.2	114.9	126.2	116.0	92.8	101.9
UB	.	11.7	15.9	.	22.1	21.8	24.6	27.7	20.6	16.3
1	.	1.4	2.4	.	3.2	2.4	3.3	0.2	0.1	0.6
2	.	0.8	0.2	.	0.6	0.5	1.1	3.3	2.9	4.3
3	.	1.6	6.9	.	8.0	9.8	6.8	8.3	4.3	6.6
4	.	3.8	9.0	.	7.8	9.5	9.0	6.8	12.4	9.5
5	.	23.1	14.8	.	21.6	18.0	25.8	21.0	17.6	16.6
6	.	0.5	1.4	.	1.2	1.5	1.7	0.7	0.6	0.7
7	.	13.1	8.0	.	8.9	8.5	10.8	8.3	4.6	8.1
8	.	12.9	9.0	.	7.4	7.7	8.6	6.4	5.8	8.0
9	.	2.6	32.6	.	35.6	34.5	33.9	33.3	23.7	30.9
X	.	0.3	0.2	.	0.7	0.6	0.4	0.0	0.4	0.3

Explanatory notes: see p. 451.

[1] Persons aged 15 years and over. [2] Excl. residents of the Territories and indigenous persons living on reserves. [3] From 2001, figures revised on the basis of the 2005 census results. [4] Persons aged 10 years and over. [5] Third quarter. [6] Persons aged 12 years and over. [7] July of each year.

Notes explicatives: voir p. 454.

[1] Personnes âgées de 15 ans et plus. [2] Non compris les habitants des "Territoires" et les populations indigènes vivant dans les réserves. [3] A partir de 2001, données révisées sur la base des résultats du recensement de 2005. [4] Personnes âgées de 10 ans et plus. [5] Troisième trimestre. [6] Personnes âgées de 12 ans et plus. [7] Juillet de chaque année.

Notas explicativas: véase p. 457.

[1] Personas de 15 años y más. [2] Excl. a los habitantes de los "Territorios" y a las poblaciones indígenas que viven en reservas. [3] A partir de 2001, datos revisados de acuerdocon los resultados del censo de 2005. [4] Personas de 10 años y más. [5] Tercer trimestre. [6] Personas de 12 años y más. [7] Julio de cada año.

	Thousands						Milliers			Millares	
	1999	2000	2001	2002	2003	2004	2005	2006	2007	2008

Costa Rica (BA) [1] [2] — Total unemployment - Chômage total - Desempleo total

Men - Hommes - Hombres
ISCO-88 - CITP-88 - CIUO-88

Total	.	41.2	55.8	.	66.0	62.5	60.2	53.8	41.3	53.5
UB	.	5.9	7.5	.	10.3	10.9	8.5	10.8	9.1	7.7
1	.	0.8	0.9	.	2.4	1.3	2.1	0.2	-	0.1
2	.	0.6	0.1	.	0.4	0.1	0.5	1.2	0.6	0.8
3	.	1.2	3.1	.	4.0	5.7	3.7	3.8	2.1	3.7
4	.	1.0	3.2	.	3.7	4.0	2.5	2.6	3.7	4.7
5	.	8.0	6.5	.	8.9	6.8	7.2	6.5	4.0	5.2
6	.	0.5	1.4	.	1.1	1.3	1.7	0.5	0.6	0.7
7	.	10.9	7.5	.	7.9	7.6	10.6	7.5	3.8	7.4
8	.	10.8	4.7	.	4.7	5.0	4.2	3.8	3.3	3.3
9	.	1.1	20.7	.	21.9	19.3	19.1	16.8	13.7	19.5
X	.	0.3	0.2	.	0.7	0.6	0.3	0.0	0.4	0.3

Women - Femmes - Mujeres
ISCO-88 - CITP-88 - CIUO-88

Total	.	30.8	44.6	.	51.2	52.4	66.0	62.3	51.5	48.4
UB	.	5.9	8.4	.	11.8	10.9	16.1	16.9	11.5	8.7
1	.	0.6	1.6	.	0.9	1.2	1.2	-	0.1	0.5
2	.	0.2	0.2	.	0.2	0.4	0.5	2.1	2.2	3.6
3	.	0.4	3.9	.	3.9	4.1	3.1	4.6	2.2	2.8
4	.	2.8	5.7	.	4.2	5.5	6.5	4.2	8.7	4.8
5	.	15.1	8.2	.	12.8	11.2	18.7	14.5	13.5	11.3
6	.	-	-	.	0.1	0.2	0.0	0.1	-	-
7	.	2.2	0.5	.	1.0	1.0	0.3	0.8	0.8	0.7
8	.	2.1	4.3	.	2.7	2.7	4.5	2.6	2.4	4.6
9	.	1.5	11.9	.	13.7	15.2	14.8	16.4	10.0	11.3
X	.	-	-	.	-	-	0.2	-	-	-

Chile (BA) [3] [4] — Total unemployment - Chômage total - Desempleo total

Total - Total - Total
ISCO-68 - CITP-68 - CIUO-68

Total	529.1	489.4	469.4	468.7	453.1	494.7	440.4 [‖]	409.9 [5]	510.8	544.7
UB	79.1	75.9	72.5	75.8	71.3	74.3	89.4 [‖]	67.6 [5]	91.5	72.3
0/1	20.2	25.7	27.4	20.5	26.4	26.1	20.8 [‖]	21.2 [5]	29.0	35.4
2	3.1	3.2	5.0	5.7	4.9	6.7	7.3 [‖]	5.5 [5]	4.0	5.5
3	87.6	79.1	76.6	80.7	76.7	90.3	75.2 [‖]	70.6 [5]	84.1	94.9
4	52.8	49.6	42.9	44.5	39.0	49.4	38.7 [‖]	41.3 [5]	49.6	52.1
5	72.5	58.9	58.3	55.0	56.8	72.7	53.6 [‖]	50.1 [5]	78.7	82.9
6	28.5	29.2	27.0	30.9	24.3	26.0	23.0 [‖]	27.1 [5]	26.6	26.8
7/8/9	184.2	167.4	159.5	154.8	153.6	149.0	131.7 [‖]	126.6 [5]	146.3	174.0
X	1.1	0.4	0.3	0.9	0.1	0.3	0.8 [‖]	- [5]	1.0	0.9

Men - Hommes - Hombres
ISCO-68 - CITP-68 - CIUO-68

Total	322.9	312.5	302.6	298.5	279.2	280.8	248.2 [‖]	239.3 [5]	280.2	306.7
UB	40.4	37.2	38.8	41.1	35.7	39.4	44.9 [‖]	31.6 [5]	39.6	31.9
0/1	11.1	15.6	12.8	11.4	15.0	10.2	11.9 [‖]	10.0 [5]	13.5	15.6
2	2.5	2.4	4.4	4.8	4.0	5.5	4.2 [‖]	3.9 [5]	2.6	3.4
3	39.6	39.3	33.2	37.3	31.8	39.0	29.8 [‖]	32.5 [5]	33.9	36.9
4	21.5	21.9	18.0	17.5	16.9	18.2	12.5 [‖]	14.5 [5]	21.9	19.8
5	20.5	23.5	24.8	21.5	22.5	24.7	17.5 [‖]	16.9 [5]	29.5	30.7
6	22.0	23.3	23.9	25.8	19.3	18.3	15.9 [‖]	20.5 [5]	18.8	20.0
7/8/9	164.2	149.0	146.4	138.2	134.1	125.3	110.6 [‖]	109.4 [5]	119.4	147.4
X	1.1	0.4	0.3	0.9	0.1	0.3	0.8 [‖]	- [5]	0.9	0.9

Women - Femmes - Mujeres
ISCO-68 - CITP-68 - CIUO-68

Total	206.2	176.9	166.9	170.2	173.9	213.9	192.2 [‖]	170.6 [5]	230.6	238.0
UB	38.6	38.8	33.6	34.7	35.6	34.9	44.5 [‖]	36.0 [5]	51.9	40.3
0/1	9.1	10.2	14.6	9.2	11.4	15.9	9.0 [‖]	11.2 [5]	15.6	19.8
2	0.7	0.7	0.6	0.9	0.9	1.2	3.0 [‖]	1.6 [5]	1.4	2.1
3	48.0	39.9	43.4	43.4	44.9	51.3	45.4 [‖]	38.1 [5]	50.2	58.0
4	31.3	27.7	24.8	26.9	22.2	31.2	26.2 [‖]	26.7 [5]	27.6	32.3
5	52.0	35.4	33.5	33.5	34.3	48.0	36.0 [‖]	33.1 [5]	49.2	52.2
6	6.5	5.8	3.1	5.1	5.0	7.8	7.0 [‖]	6.6 [5]	7.8	6.8
7/8/9	20.0	18.4	13.1	16.5	19.5	23.7	21.1 [‖]	17.2 [5]	26.9	26.6
X	-	-	-	-	-	-	- [‖]	- [5]	0.1	-

UNEMPLOYMENT — CHÔMAGE — DESEMPLEO — 3E

By occupation — Par profession — Por ocupación

	Thousands			Milliers				Millares		
	1999	2000	2001	2002	2003	2004	2005	2006	2007	2008

República Dominicana (BA) [1]   Total unemployment - Chômage total - Desempleo total

Total - Total - Total
ISCO-88 - CITP-88 - CIUO-88

	1999	2000	2001	2002	2003	2004	2005	2006	2007	2008
Total	477.9	491.4	556.3	596.3	619.7	723.7	715.8	661.4	654.0	.
UB	253.2	175.8	199.9	233.5	244.0	332.7	300.7	300.3	317.1	.
1	2.4	4.1	5.3	6.2	5.1	6.3	5.8	4.5	4.6	.
2	11.6	12.5	10.4	10.0	11.3	13.5	12.5	9.8	8.8	.
3	9.9	20.9	25.4	24.7	28.7	33.2	32.2	27.0	23.0	.
4	25.6	42.3	46.0	52.8	51.5	54.3	60.9	48.4	49.4	.
5	39.8	56.1	63.8	67.1	74.4	79.3	76.7	71.2	66.7	.
6	2.6	6.3	9.1	9.1	8.1	5.8	6.0	4.6	3.7	.
7	30.0	39.0	48.7	47.0	47.2	43.5	47.6	47.8	35.1	.
8	37.8	48.7	49.6	49.6	57.7	53.5	60.5	63.5	51.4	.
9	65.0	85.9	98.3	96.4	91.8	100.4	111.7	83.0	93.7	.
0	.	.	.	.	.	1.2	1.5	1.3	0.6	.

Men - Hommes - Hombres
ISCO-88 - CITP-88 - CIUO-88

	1999	2000	2001	2002	2003	2004	2005	2006	2007	2008
Total	175.8	174.7	208.0	215.5	243.0	252.5	269.6	233.5	240.7	.
UB	61.2	50.2	55.5	67.0	84.1	97.8	107.4	83.7	108.9	.
1	0.8	1.9	2.8	3.1	3.3	4.1	2.4	1.1	2.5	.
2	5.1	5.3	4.6	4.3	4.8	4.9	5.9	2.8	2.8	.
3	5.4	6.1	9.6	7.3	10.2	12.9	13.6	12.0	7.6	.
4	6.7	8.3	11.6	8.4	9.7	11.0	12.1	9.4	7.4	.
5	19.4	17.1	18.1	22.9	26.0	26.8	22.6	26.7	23.4	.
6	2.3	4.9	8.3	8.6	7.6	4.7	5.3	4.3	3.5	.
7	24.6	32.2	41.7	39.1	41.6	38.1	42.5	39.9	30.8	.
8	20.0	19.3	23.9	20.2	24.5	22.4	24.7	29.3	25.1	.
9	30.2	29.3	32.0	34.5	31.2	28.9	31.5	22.9	28.1	.
0	.	.	.	.	.	1.0	1.4	1.3	0.6	.

Women - Femmes - Mujeres
ISCO-88 - CITP-88 - CIUO-88

	1999	2000	2001	2002	2003	2004	2005	2006	2007	2008
Total	302.1	316.8	348.2	380.8	376.8	471.2	446.3	428.0	413.3	.
UB	192.0	125.6	144.4	166.6	159.9	234.9	193.4	216.6	208.2	.
1	1.6	2.2	2.5	3.0	1.9	2.2	3.4	3.4	2.1	.
2	6.4	7.1	5.8	5.6	6.4	8.7	6.6	7.0	6.0	.
3	4.4	14.8	15.8	17.4	18.4	20.3	18.6	15.0	15.4	.
4	18.9	34.0	34.0	44.4	41.7	43.3	48.8	39.0	42.0	.
5	20.4	39.0	45.7	44.2	48.4	52.5	54.1	44.4	43.2	.
6	0.3	1.4	0.8	0.5	0.5	1.1	0.6	0.3	0.2	.
7	5.3	6.7	7.0	8.0	5.6	5.4	5.0	7.9	4.3	.
8	17.9	29.4	25.4	29.3	33.2	31.1	35.7	34.2	26.3	.
9	34.8	56.0	66.4	61.8	60.6	71.5	80.1	60.2	65.6	.
0	.	.	.	.	.	0.2	0.1	-	-	.

Ecuador (BA) [1] [2] [3]   Total unemployment - Chômage total - Desempleo total

Total - Total - Total
ISCO-88 - CITP-88 - CIUO-88

	1999	2000	2001	2002	2003	2004	2005	2006	2007	2008
Total	543.5	333.1	450.9 [4]	352.9	461.1	362.1	333.6	341.8	.	.
UB	177.2	133.4	173.9 [4]	138.3	192.4	123.0	137.7	125.8	.	.
1	3.8	6.0	3.7 [4]	1.9	2.8	3.2	3.6	3.9	.	.
2	17.3	11.7	12.9 [4]	11.8	11.6	12.3	6.7	9.9	.	.
3	19.0	13.7	13.0 [4]	10.2	16.9	15.9	13.9	17.4	.	.
4	55.7	30.8	32.5 [4]	26.4	28.0	28.0	16.9	20.6	.	.
5	69.0	39.7	54.6 [4]	48.8	61.8	54.2	51.5	53.5	.	.
6	9.8	1.9	8.2 [4]	5.2	3.4	5.8	3.1	3.5	.	.
7	73.3	30.2	33.0 [4]	42.4	57.4	47.4	32.2	32.4	.	.
8	28.0	15.7	14.0 [4]	9.6	18.5	13.1	9.0	10.3	.	.
9	88.6	50.0	104.5 [4]	57.5	67.8	57.7	58.7	64.4	.	.
0	1.6	0.0	0.8 [4]	0.9	0.5	1.7	0.2	0.1	.	.

Men - Hommes - Hombres
ISCO-88 - CITP-88 - CIUO-88

	1999	2000	2001	2002	2003	2004	2005	2006	2007	2008
Total	239.5	138.3	169.0 [4]	136.2	215.0	160.7	143.3	143.4	.	.
UB	52.0	47.1	54.3 [4]	38.8	74.7	47.2	48.2	38.5	.	.
1	2.2	3.6	3.2 [4]	1.4	.	1.4	2.0	3.0	.	.
2	7.8	4.9	5.1 [4]	4.1	.	4.9	3.9	2.8	.	.
3	8.8	4.5	3.6 [4]	2.8	.	4.8	6.4	8.0	.	.
4	13.0	5.6	4.4 [4]	7.6	.	9.2	5.4	5.8	.	.
5	22.8	14.4	16.6 [4]	16.5	.	13.7	15.7	17.2	.	.
6	7.7	1.1	7.0 [4]	3.7	.	5.5	2.3	3.2	.	.
7	60.3	23.1	25.5 [4]	32.0	.	36.6	25.5	25.0	.	.
8	21.6	10.7	11.0 [4]	7.9	.	11.1	7.9	8.5	.	.
9	41.6	23.4	38.0 [4]	20.8	.	24.5	25.9	31.3	.	.
0	1.6	0.0	0.3 [4]	0.6	.	1.7	0.0	0.1	.	.

Explanatory notes: see p. 451.
[1] Persons aged 10 years and over. [2] Urban areas. [3] Nov. of each year. [4] July.

Notes explicatives: voir p. 454.
[1] Personnes âgées de 10 ans et plus. [2] Régions urbaines. [3] Nov. de chaque année. [4] Juillet.

Notas explicativas: véase p. 457.
[1] Personas de 10 años y más. [2] Areas urbanas. [3] Nov. de cada año. [4] Julio.

	Thousands					Milliers			Millares	
	1999	2000	2001	2002	2003	2004	2005	2006	2007	2008

Ecuador (BA) [1][2][3]   Total unemployment - Chômage total - Desempleo total

Women - Femmes - Mujeres
ISCO-88 - CITP-88 - CIUO-88

	1999	2000	2001	2002	2003	2004	2005	2006	2007	2008
Total	304.0	194.8	282.0 [4]	216.7	246.1	201.4	190.3	198.4	.	.
UB	125.4	86.3	119.6 [4]	99.5	117.8	75.8	89.5	87.3	.	.
1	1.6	2.3	0.5 [4]	0.5	.	1.7	1.6	0.9	.	.
2	9.4	6.8	7.8 [4]	7.7	.	7.4	2.8	7.1	.	.
3	10.2	9.2	9.4 [4]	7.4	.	11.1	7.5	9.3	.	.
4	42.7	25.2	28.1 [4]	18.7	.	18.7	11.5	14.8	.	.
5	46.2	25.3	38.1 [4]	32.3	.	40.5	35.9	36.3	.	.
6	2.1	0.8	1.1 [4]	1.5	.	0.3	0.8	0.3	.	.
7	13.0	7.2	7.4 [4]	10.3	.	10.7	6.6	7.4	.	.
8	6.5	5.0	3.0 [4]	1.8	.	2.0	1.0	1.9	.	.
9	46.8	26.6	66.4 [4]	36.6	.	33.2	32.9	33.1	.	.
0	-	0.0	0.5 [4]	0.4	.	-	0.2	-	.	.

El Salvador (BA) [1][5]   Total unemployment - Chômage total - Desempleo total

Total - Total - Total
ISCO-88 - CITP-88 - CIUO-88

	1999	2000	2001	2002	2003	2004	2005	2006	2007	2008
Total	163.3	164.4	170.3	147.4	169.4	164.0	177.6	164.2	166.6	.
UB	29.3	26.9	27.1	20.6	23.1	27.2	32.4	23.0	25.7	.
1	1.1	0.4	0.1	0.2	0.3	0.4	0.3	1.0	1.0	.
2	3.4	1.7	1.5	2.0	1.7	2.1	2.9	1.3	3.7	.
3	8.8	7.7	6.4	8.5	8.0	8.9	6.8	7.4	6.1	.
4	8.2	9.8	7.4	11.3	6.8	4.6	9.4	6.2	10.8	.
5	12.5	12.0	15.4	10.1	12.4	11.8	15.2	12.3	12.7	.
6	1.3	8.9	11.0	1.3	22.8	18.9	4.6	23.0	22.1	.
7	19.6	22.9	31.1	22.6	24.4	23.1	29.4	20.6	19.8	.
8	11.4	13.0	11.2	12.1	9.7	13.9	13.9	9.9	6.4	.
9	67.5	60.7	58.8	58.7	60.2	52.8	62.5	59.6	57.6	.
X	0.3	0.3	0.3	-	0.0	0.3	0.2	-	0.6	.

Men - Hommes - Hombres
ISCO-88 - CITP-88 - CIUO-88

	1999	2000	2001	2002	2003	2004	2005	2006	2007	2008
Total	120.2	129.5	119.6	113.7	134.5	127.3	129.6	123.9	126.6	.
UB	17.5	17.9	16.6	12.8	14.3	17.8	17.2	12.1	15.7	.
1	0.7	0.2	0.1	0.1	0.3	0.4	0.3	0.3	0.3	.
2	2.1	1.6	1.1	1.3	1.4	1.3	1.6	0.5	2.0	.
3	5.2	5.0	3.6	5.5	5.4	4.2	3.5	5.9	3.8	.
4	4.5	4.5	3.2	5.9	3.8	1.8	2.5	3.1	6.6	.
5	5.5	5.9	6.9	5.2	5.5	5.8	8.7	4.2	6.4	.
6	1.2	8.6	10.2	1.3	21.5	18.5	4.4	22.2	20.8	.
7	18.1	21.8	26.2	21.8	23.7	22.1	28.1	19.7	18.1	.
8	8.4	10.3	8.3	9.6	7.1	9.7	10.0	8.0	5.3	.
9	56.4	53.3	43.0	50.2	51.6	45.4	52.9	47.9	47.1	.
X	0.3	0.3	0.3	-	0.0	0.3	0.2	-	0.6	.

Women - Femmes - Mujeres
ISCO-88 - CITP-88 - CIUO-88

	1999	2000	2001	2002	2003	2004	2005	2006	2007	2008
Total	43.2	34.9	50.7	33.7	34.9	36.7	48.1	40.4	40.0	.
UB	11.8	9.0	10.5	7.8	8.8	9.4	15.1	10.9	10.0	.
1	0.4	0.2	-	0.0	0.1	0.1	-	0.7	0.8	.
2	1.3	0.2	0.4	0.7	0.3	0.8	1.3	0.7	1.7	.
3	3.5	2.7	2.8	3.0	2.6	4.7	3.2	1.5	2.3	.
4	3.6	5.3	4.2	5.4	3.0	2.7	6.9	3.1	4.2	.
5	6.9	6.1	8.5	5.0	6.8	5.9	6.5	8.1	6.4	.
6	0.1	0.3	0.8	-	1.4	0.4	0.2	0.8	1.3	.
7	1.5	1.1	4.9	0.8	0.7	1.0	1.3	0.9	1.8	.
8	3.0	2.7	2.9	2.4	2.6	4.2	3.9	1.9	1.0	.
9	11.1	7.4	15.8	8.6	8.6	7.4	9.7	11.7	10.6	.
X	-	-	-	-	-	-	-	-	-	.

Honduras (BA) [1][6]   Total unemployment - Chômage total - Desempleo total

Total - Total - Total
ISCO-68 - CITP-68 - CIUO-68

	1999	2000	2001	2002	2003	2004	2005	2006	2007	2008
Total	89.3	.	103.4 [7]	.	.	153.2 [8]	107.8	.	.	.
UB	19.0	.	21.3 [7]	.	.	35.0 [8]	29.6	.	.	.
0/1	3.8	.	6.2 [7]	.	.	8.1 [8]	.	.	.	.
2	1.2	.	2.7 [7]	.	.	2.6 [8]	2.7	.	.	.
3	7.2	.	6.1 [7]	.	.	8.6 [8]	6.6	.	.	.
4	7.6	.	7.4 [7]	.	.	11.7 [8]	11.0	.	.	.
5	8.7	.	8.5 [7]	.	.	22.7 [8]	12.6	.	.	.
6	9.7	.	6.8 [7]	.	.	13.8 [8]	6.1	.	.	.
7/8/9	32.2	.	44.3 [7]	.	.	50.2 [8]	35.0	.	.	.
X	-	.	- [7]	.	.	0.4 [8]	3.9	.	.	.

Explanatory notes: see p. 451.   Notes explicatives: voir p. 454.   Notas explicativas: véase p. 457.

[1] Persons aged 10 years and over. [2] Urban areas. [3] Nov. of each year. [4] July. [5] Dec. [6] March of each year. [7] Sep. [8] May.

[1] Personnes âgées de 10 ans et. plus. [2] Régions urbaines. [3] Nov. de chaque année. [4] Juillet. [5] Déc. [6] Mars de chaque année. [7] Sept. [8] Mai.

[1] Personas de 10 años y más. [2] Areas urbanas. [3] Nov. de cada año. [4] Julio. [5] Dic. [6] Marzo de cada año. [7] Sept. [8] Mayo.

UNEMPLOYMENT — CHÔMAGE — DESEMPLEO

By occupation — Par profession — Por ocupación

	1999	2000	2001	2002	2003	2004	2005	2006	2007	2008
	Thousands			Milliers				Millares		

Honduras (BA) [1] [2] — Total unemployment - Chômage total - Desempleo total

Men - Hommes - Hombres
ISCO-68 - CITP-68 - CIUO-68

	1999	2000	2001	2002	2003	2004	2005	2006	2007	2008
Total	56.7	.	.	.	.	81.0 [3]	55.2	.	.	.
UB	10.4	.	.	.	.	13.6 [3]	13.0	.	.	.
0/1	1.2	.	.	.	.	2.6 [3]		.	.	.
2	0.4	.	.	.	.	0.8 [3]	1.5	.	.	.
3	2.2	.	.	.	.	3.1 [3]	3.2	.	.	.
4	3.4	.	.	.	.	4.0 [3]	4.1	.	.	.
5	4.3	.	.	.	.	5.3 [3]	2.6	.	.	.
6	8.1	.	.	.	.	12.9 [3]	5.0	.	.	.
7/8/9	26.8	.	.	.	.	38.3 [3]	23.4	.	.	.
X	-	.	.	.	.	0.4 [3]	2.3	.	.	.

Women - Femmes - Mujeres
ISCO-68 - CITP-68 - CIUO-68

	1999	2000	2001	2002	2003	2004	2005	2006	2007	2008
Total	32.6	.	.	.	.	72.2 [3]	52.6	.	.	.
UB	8.6	.	.	.	.	21.4 [3]	16.6	.	.	.
0/1	2.6	.	.	.	.	5.5 [3]	.	.	.	.
2	0.8	.	.	.	.	1.8 [3]	1.2	.	.	.
3	5.0	.	.	.	.	5.5 [3]	3.4	.	.	.
4	4.2	.	.	.	.	7.8 [3]	7.0	.	.	.
5	4.5	.	.	.	.	17.4 [3]	10.0	.	.	.
6	1.7	.	.	.	.	0.9 [3]	1.1	.	.	.
7/8/9	5.4	.	.	.	.	11.9 [3]	11.7	.	.	.
X	-	.	.	.	.	- [3]	1.7	.	.	.

Jamaica (BA) [4] — Total unemployment - Chômage total - Desempleo total

Total - Total - Total
ISCO-88 - CITP-88 - CIUO-88

	1999	2000	2001	2002	2003	2004	2005	2006	2007	2008
Total	175.2	171.8	165.4 [5]	171.8	128.9	136.8	133.3	119.6	119.4	134.6
UB	54.7	48.4	50.9 [5]	51.1	29.7	35.7	29.8	25.9	28.3	26.2
1-3	11.5	14.0	9.2 [5]	11.1	8.1	8.3	10.4	7.0	7.6	8.7
4	17.2	16.8	14.0 [5]	13.9	13.4	14.3	13.7	13.3	14.9	12.6
5	29.3	29.9	27.2 [5]	32.3	26.6	26.1	29.9	24.9	29.7	32.2
6	2.8	2.2	2.2 [5]	1.9	1.7	2.5	2.9	3.0	2.7	2.9
7	15.8	19.6	21.7 [5]	22.6	16.1	15.9	15.8	15.7	10.1	16.0
8	10.1	10.3	7.7 [5]	10.2	6.7	5.3	5.3	6.7	5.8	6.1
9	30.5	29.5	30.4 [5]	27.5	25.7	27.7	24.5	22.3	19.6	28.9
X	3.6	1.0	2.3 [5]	1.2	0.9	1.0	1.0	0.8	0.7	1.0

Men - Hommes - Hombres
ISCO-88 - CITP-88 - CIUO-88

	1999	2000	2001	2002	2003	2004	2005	2006	2007	2008
Total	61.4	62.5	63.4 [5]	65.7	47.6	54.0	50.0	48.0	37.8	52.8
UB	18.8	17.3	17.8 [5]	18.1	11.3	13.3	10.3	8.3	7.2	8.0
1-3	3.5	3.6	2.2 [5]	3.6	2.5	3.4	3.7	2.2	2.2	2.9
4	1.8	2.2	2.0 [5]	2.8	2.0	2.5	1.8	2.2	2.6	2.3
5	6.0	6.2	5.5 [5]	6.9	4.4	4.4	4.9	4.5	5.2	5.2
6	1.6	1.3	1.2 [5]	0.7	0.5	1.1	1.9	1.5	1.2	2.1
7	12.8	16.5	18.5 [5]	18.7	14.2	13.5	13.6	14.3	9.0	14.6
8	4.3	3.7	2.3 [5]	4.6	2.7	3.2	3.1	4.1	2.9	4.3
9	11.6	11.2	12.9 [5]	9.9	9.6	11.9	10.1	10.6	7.3	13.2
X	1.1	0.6	1.2 [5]	0.4	0.4	0.7	0.6	0.3	0.2	0.2

Women - Femmes - Mujeres
ISCO-88 - CITP-88 - CIUO-88

	1999	2000	2001	2002	2003	2004	2005	2006	2007	2008
Total	113.8	109.2	102.1 [5]	106.1	81.3	82.8	83.3	71.6	81.6	81.8
UB	35.9	31.1	33.1 [5]	33.0	18.4	22.4	19.5	17.6	21.1	18.2
1-3	7.9	10.5	7.0 [5]	7.5	5.6	4.9	6.7	4.8	5.4	5.8
4	15.4	14.6	12.1 [5]	11.1	11.4	11.8	11.9	11.1	12.3	10.3
5	23.3	23.7	21.7 [5]	25.4	22.2	21.7	25.0	20.4	24.5	27.0
6	1.2	0.8	1.1 [5]	1.2	1.2	1.4	1.0	1.5	1.5	0.8
7	3.0	3.2	3.2 [5]	3.9	1.9	2.4	2.2	1.4	1.1	1.4
8	5.8	6.6	5.5 [5]	5.6	4.0	2.1	2.2	2.6	2.9	1.8
9	18.9	18.3	17.5 [5]	17.6	16.1	15.8	14.4	11.7	12.3	15.7
X	2.5	0.5	1.2 [5]	0.8	0.5	0.3	0.4	0.5	0.5	0.8

Explanatory notes: see p. 451.

[1] Persons aged 10 years and over. [2] March of each year. [3] May. [4] Persons aged 14 years and over. [5] First and second quarters.

Notes explicatives: voir p. 454.

[1] Personnes âgées de 10 ans et plus. [2] Mars de chaque année. [3] Mai. [4] Personnes âgées de 14 ans et plus. [5] Premier et deuxième trimestres.

Notas explicativas: véase p. 457.

[1] Personas de 10 años y más. [2] Marzo de cada año. [3] Mayo. [4] Personas de 14 años y más. [5] Primero y secondo trimestres.

	UNEMPLOYMENT		CHÔMAGE			DESEMPLEO		

By occupation — Par profession — Por ocupación

	Thousands				Milliers				Millares	
	1999	2000	2001	2002	2003	2004	2005	2006	2007	2008

México (BA) [1] [2] — Total unemployment - Chômage total - Desempleo total

Total - Total - Total
ISCO-88 - CITP-88 - CIUO-88

	1999	2000	2001	2002	2003	2004	2005	2006	2007	2008
Total	954.2	998.9	996.1	1 145.6	1 195.6	1 539.8	1.211.7	1 377.7	.	.
UB	95.5	98.2	105.9	108.2	129.1	171.2	183.1	177.4	.	.
1	4.7	10.7	12.2	15.9	9.5	13.6	15.3	10.2	.	.
2	33.5	18.5	31.6	34.7	33.6	49.6	41.1	34.2	.	.
3	83.5	82.4	81.0	98.9	97.9	106.3	123.8	99.4	.	.
4	69.1	76.6	75.0	84.0	86.8	112.7	109.4	111.2	.	.
5	103.3	116.6	105.8	128.0	135.0	198.2	160.4	178.1	.	.
6	40.3	59.0	56.2	58.5	57.2	60.4	47.8	44.6	.	.
7	102.1	109.2	119.1	129.8	140.3	162.7	180.5	154.2	.	.
8	74.7	70.5	94.4	106.5	99.2	95.0	108.6	108.2	.	.
9	197.8	191.8	178.7	219.4	219.8	292.3	239.4	228.7	.	.
0	2.2	1.9	1.2	0.9	0.8	0.9	1.5	1.0	.	.
X	147.4	163.5	135.0	160.8	186.3	276.8	271.5	230.4	.	.

Men - Hommes - Hombres
ISCO-88 - CITP-88 - CIUO-88

	1999	2000	2001	2002	2003	2004	2005	2006	2007	2008
Total	494.4	559.7	550.6	656.5	687.0	828.7	813.3	811.7	.	.
UB	33.9	38.9	33.6	39.3	48.7	72.8	84.9	79.0	.	.
1	4.4	8.6	10.6	12.5	7.7	9.5	11.8	6.1	.	.
2	25.1	8.7	18.3	17.3	15.5	24.7	28.4	18.9	.	.
3	42.2	45.9	47.8	64.1	48.3	67.0	80.9	63.0	.	.
4	15.6	29.3	28.2	30.6	32.4	50.1	55.5	43.1	.	.
5	41.5	53.6	48.5	59.2	66.8	83.3	88.5	94.9	.	.
6	31.1	47.0	40.6	48.4	48.5	51.2	43.9	41.3	.	.
7	76.8	88.0	87.1	97.9	109.3	129.5	152.6	125.8	.	.
8	48.8	49.5	71.6	74.1	66.6	58.3	90.7	82.9	.	.
9	119.2	125.1	108.6	149.9	153.3	186.3	174.0	155.9	.	.
0	2.2	1.9	1.2	0.9	0.8	0.9	1.5	1.0	.	.
X	53.6	63.2	54.7	62.3	89.0	95.1	105.2	99.8	.	.

Women - Femmes - Mujeres
ISCO-88 - CITP-88 - CIUO-88

	1999	2000	2001	2002	2003	2004	2005	2006	2007	2008
Total	459.8	439.2	445.5	489.0	508.7	711.0	398.4	566.3	.	.
UB	61.6	59.3	72.2	68.9	80.4	98.4	98.3	98.5	.	.
1	0.3	2.2	1.5	3.4	1.8	4.0	3.5	4.1	.	.
2	8.4	9.8	13.4	17.4	18.1	24.9	12.7	15.3	.	.
3	41.3	36.6	33.2	34.7	49.6	39.3	43.0	36.4	.	.
4	53.5	47.3	46.9	53.4	54.3	62.6	53.9	68.2	.	.
5	61.8	63.0	57.3	68.8	68.2	114.9	72.0	83.2	.	.
6	9.2	12.0	15.7	10.1	8.7	9.2	4.0	3.4	.	.
7	25.4	21.2	32.0	31.9	31.1	33.2	27.9	28.5	.	.
8	25.9	21.1	22.8	32.4	32.7	36.7	17.9	25.3	.	.
9	78.6	66.7	70.1	69.5	66.4	105.9	65.4	72.8	.	.
0	0.0	0.0	0.0	0.0	0.0	0.0	0.0	0.0	.	.
X	93.8	100.2	80.3	98.5	97.3	181.8	166.3	130.6	.	.

Panamá (BA) [4] [5] — Total unemployment - Chômage total - Desempleo total

Total - Total - Total
ISCO-88 - CITP-88 - CIUO-88

	1999	2000	2001	2002	2003	2004	2005	2006	2007	2008
Total	.	147.0	169.7	172.4	170.4	159.9	136.8	121.4	92.0	82.9
UB	.	33.7	40.6	30.6	36.3	28.9	23.7	17.4	15.2	14.0
1	.	7.4	1.4	2.3	1.4	1.3	1.6	1.7	0.6	1.1
2	.	3.6	3.7	5.3	5.9	5.6	5.7	5.0	3.9	3.1
3	.	18.9	5.0	4.4	4.8	4.8	4.5	3.9	3.1	2.5
4	.	14.8	20.5	23.7	26.7	25.4	22.4	18.6	12.3	11.7
5	.	5.0	27.3	30.6	31.2	28.5	24.5	19.6	16.3	16.6
6	.	4.7	6.7	5.2	4.9	4.6	3.4	4.6	2.6	2.0
7	.	26.6	20.5	22.4	18.1	16.3	15.5	14.3	8.7	10.6
8	.	5.6	8.0	6.5	6.4	6.8	5.7	5.0	3.3	2.7
9	.	26.5	35.9	41.3	34.6	37.5	29.9	31.2	26.0	18.6
X	.	0.2	0.1	-	-	-	-	-	-	-

Men - Hommes - Hombres
ISCO-88 - CITP-88 - CIUO-88

	1999	2000	2001	2002	2003	2004	2005	2006	2007	2008
Total	.	77.7	92.0	86.5	82.9	76.3	66.7	60.2	44.5	40.2
UB	.	15.9	19.6	13.4	16.8	11.9	9.0	5.6	5.9	4.8
1	.	3.4	0.6	0.6	0.6	0.8	0.8	1.0	0.4	0.4
2	.	2.4	1.0	1.8	2.1	1.9	2.2	1.9	1.5	1.3
3	.	3.7	3.2	2.5	2.7	2.4	2.5	1.9	1.7	1.1
4	.	5.1	5.4	5.2	6.0	5.4	4.6	4.5	2.6	2.2
5	.	4.8	10.0	10.1	10.5	9.2	7.6	5.8	4.9	4.6
6	.	4.7	6.4	4.7	4.6	4.3	2.8	4.3	2.5	1.7
7	.	24.0	18.7	20.9	16.8	14.8	14.4	12.5	7.6	9.8
8	.	4.4	6.9	5.7	5.1	5.8	4.6	4.2	2.9	2.6
9	.	9.2	20.2	21.5	17.7	19.9	18.0	18.5	14.4	11.7
X	.	0.2	0.1	-	-	-	-	-	-	-

Explanatory notes: see p. 451.

Notes explicatives: voir p. 454.

Notas explicativas: véase p. 457.

[1] Persons aged 14 years and over. [2] Second quarter of each year. [3] Begenning 2005: excluded, persons in unemployment that finished its last work for more than one year. [4] Persons aged 15 years and over. [5] Aug. of each year.

[1] Personnes âgées de 14 ans et plus. [2] Deuxième trimestre de chaque année. [3] A partir de 2005: non compris les chômeurs n'ayant pas travaillé depuis plus de 1 an. [4] Personnes âgées de 15 ans et plus. [5] Août de chaque année.

[1] Personas de 14 años y más. [2] Segundo trimestre de cada año. [3] A partir de 2005: excluye a los desempleados que terminaron su último trabajo hace más de un año. [4] Personas de 15 años y más. [5] Agosto de cada año.

By occupation — Par profession — Por ocupación

Thousands			Milliers				Millares		
1999	2000	2001	2002	2003	2004	2005	2006	2007	2008

Panamá (BA) [1] [2] — Total unemployment - Chômage total - Desempleo total

Women - Femmes - Mujeres
ISCO-88 - CITP-88 - CIUO-88

	1999	2000	2001	2002	2003	2004	2005	2006	2007	2008
Total	.	69.3	77.8	85.9	87.3	83.6	70.2	61.1	47.5	42.7
UB	.	17.8	21.1	17.2	19.5	17.0	14.7	11.8	9.2	9.2
1	.	4.1	0.8	1.8	0.8	0.5	0.8	0.7	0.3	0.8
2	.	1.2	2.8	3.4	3.8	3.8	3.5	3.1	2.3	1.8
3	.	15.2	1.8	1.9	2.1	2.4	1.9	2.0	1.3	1.4
4	.	9.7	15.1	18.6	20.7	20.0	17.8	14.1	9.7	9.5
5	.	0.2	17.3	20.6	20.7	19.3	16.9	13.8	11.4	12.0
6	.	-	0.4	0.5	0.3	0.4	0.5	0.3	0.2	0.3
7	.	2.5	1.8	1.5	1.3	1.5	1.1	1.8	1.1	0.8
8	.	1.2	1.1	0.7	1.3	1.1	1.1	0.8	0.4	0.1
9	.	17.4	15.7	19.7	16.9	17.6	11.9	12.8	11.6	6.8
X	.	-	0.1	-	-	-	-	-	-	-

Paraguay (BA) [3] [4] — Total unemployment - Chômage total - Desempleo total

Total - Total - Total
ISCO-88 - CITP-88 - CIUO-88

	1999	2000	2001	2002	2003	2004	2005	2006	2007	2008
Total	.	.	.	.	.	.	.	.	161.2	170.6
UB									48.6	42.9
1									4.0	1.3
2									2.0	2.0
3									4.9	4.7
4									9.2	9.9
5									20.9	22.5
6									3.1	2.5
7									17.7	23.7
8									7.1	7.0
9									43.8	54.2

Men - Hommes - Hombres
ISCO-88 - CITP-88 - CIUO-88

	1999	2000	2001	2002	2003	2004	2005	2006	2007	2008
Total	.	.	.	.	.	.	.	.	74.6	83.9
UB									19.7	20.7
1									2.0	1.0
2									1.1	0.8
3									2.9	1.8
4									3.0	4.9
5									5.3	7.9
6									2.7	2.0
7									15.4	18.8
8									7.1	6.3
9									15.4	19.6

Women - Femmes - Mujeres
ISCO-88 - CITP-88 - CIUO-88

	1999	2000	2001	2002	2003	2004	2005	2006	2007	2008
Total	.	.	.	.	.	.	.	.	86.6	86.7
UB									28.9	22.2
1									2.0	0.3
2									0.8	1.2
3									2.0	2.9
4									6.1	4.9
5									15.6	14.6
6									0.5	0.4
7									2.3	4.8
8										0.7
9									28.4	34.6

Perú (BA) [5] [6] [7] — Total unemployment - Chômage total - Desempleo total

Total - Total - Total
ISCO-88 - CITP-88 - CIUO-88

	1999	2000	2001	2002	2003	2004	2005	2006	2007	2008
Total	.	.	.	359.0 [8]	386.0 [9]	394.4 [10]	437.1 [11]	350.9 [8]	291.6 [11]	277.4 [12]
UB	.	.	.	34.5 [8]	58.2 [9]	72.2 [10]	54.2 [11]	45.7 [8]	32.6 [11]	22.6 [12]
1	.	.	.	6.1 [8]	1.6 [9]	2.0 [10]	2.0 [11]	1.8 [8]	0.3 [11]	1.2 [12]
2	.	.	.	26.7 [8]	21.6 [9]	20.7 [10]	17.2 [11]	19.1 [8]	19.3 [11]	18.0 [12]
3	.	.	.	20.4 [8]	20.7 [9]	33.3 [10]	34.0 [11]	33.8 [8]	16.9 [11]	26.0 [12]
4	.	.	.	30.5 [8]	37.5 [9]	40.7 [10]	55.3 [11]	40.8 [8]	38.9 [11]	37.2 [12]
5	.	.	.	54.6 [8]	54.7 [9]	65.0 [10]	86.6 [11]	70.1 [8]	56.6 [11]	69.3 [12]
6	.	.	.	2.8 [8]	2.3 [9]	1.1 [10]	2.6 [11]	1.3 [8]	0.6 [11]	0.5 [12]
7	.	.	.	48.5 [8]	27.9 [9]	41.0 [10]	51.4 [11]	44.8 [8]	33.8 [11]	30.2 [12]
8	.	.	.	40.7 [8]	40.6 [9]	31.6 [10]	44.2 [11]	27.4 [8]	27.6 [11]	18.4 [12]
9	.	.	.	93.5 [8]	116.8 [9]	86.0 [10]	88.9 [11]	64.8 [8]	64.7 [11]	54.1 [12]
0	.	.	.	0.9 [8]	4.2 [9]	0.8 [10]	0.7 [11]	1.3 [8]	0.4 [11]	- [12]

Explanatory notes: see p. 451.

[1] Persons aged 15 years and over. [2] Aug. of each year. [3] Persons aged 10 years and over. [4] Fourth quarter. [5] Persons aged 14 years and over. [6] Metropolitan Lima. [7] Excl. conscripts. [8] October. [9] July. [10] Aug. [11] September. [12] Aug.-Oct.

Notes explicatives: voir p. 454.

[1] Personnes âgées de 15 ans et plus. [2] Août de chaque année. [3] Personnes âgées de 10 ans et plus. [4] Quatrième trimestre. [5] Personnes âgées de 14 ans et plus. [6] Lima métropolitaine. [7] Non compris les conscrits. [8] Octobre. [9] Juillet. [10] Août. [11] Septembre. [12] Août-oct.

Notas explicativas: véase p. 457.

[1] Personas de 15 años y más. [2] Agosto de cada año. [3] Personas de 10 años y más. [4] Cuarto trimestre. [5] Personas de 14 años y más. [6] Lima metropolitana. [7] Excl. los conscriptos. [8] Octubre. [9] Julio. [10] Agosto. [11] Septiembre. [12] Agosto-oct.

3E — UNEMPLOYMENT / CHÔMAGE / DESEMPLEO

By occupation / Par profession / Por ocupación

Thousands / Milliers / Millares

	1999	2000	2001	2002	2003	2004	2005	2006	2007	2008
Perú (BA) [1][2][3]				**Total unemployment - Chômage total - Desempleo total**						
Men - Hommes - Hombres ISCO-88 - CITP-88 - CIUO-88										
Total	.	.	.	173.4 [4]	187.9 [5]	207.0 [6]	209.9 [7]	155.7 [4]	143.8 [7]	118.8 [8]
UB	.	.	.	12.4 [4]	30.3 [5]	39.2 [6]	22.1 [7]	16.0 [4]	15.7 [7]	8.5 [8]
1	.	.	.	5.2 [4]	1.6 [5]	1.2 [6]	2.0 [7]	0.8 [4]	0.3 [7]	0.9 [8]
2	.	.	.	16.0 [4]	8.1 [5]	8.9 [6]	3.2 [7]	9.2 [4]	8.3 [7]	6.1 [8]
3	.	.	.	6.9 [4]	8.7 [5]	16.6 [6]	16.1 [7]	18.2 [4]	12.0 [7]	13.1 [8]
4	.	.	.	11.8 [4]	10.7 [5]	18.2 [6]	20.5 [7]	16.6 [4]	14.4 [7]	9.8 [8]
5	.	.	.	17.9 [4]	19.2 [5]	22.3 [6]	29.6 [7]	17.2 [4]	20.1 [7]	18.1 [8]
6	.	.	.	2.8 [4]	2.3 [5]	1.1 [6]	1.6 [7]	1.3 [4]	0.6 [7]	0.5 [8]
7	.	.	.	29.8 [4]	16.0 [5]	26.6 [6]	34.0 [7]	28.0 [4]	23.2 [7]	16.9 [8]
8	.	.	.	36.1 [4]	40.6 [5]	28.7 [6]	40.0 [7]	25.7 [4]	24.7 [7]	17.3 [8]
9	.	.	.	33.5 [4]	46.2 [5]	43.3 [6]	40.2 [7]	21.6 [4]	24.1 [7]	27.6 [8]
0	.	.	.	0.9 [4]	4.2 [5]	0.8 [6]	0.7 [7]	1.3 [4]	0.4 [7]	- [8]
Women - Femmes - Mujeres ISCO-88 - CITP-88 - CIUO-88										
Total	.	.	.	185.7 [4]	198.1 [5]	187.4 [6]	227.2 [7]	195.2 [4]	147.9 [7]	158.7 [8]
UB	.	.	.	22.1 [4]	27.9 [5]	33.0 [6]	32.1 [7]	29.7 [4]	16.9 [7]	14.0 [8]
1	.	.	.	0.9 [4]	- [5]	0.8 [6]	- [7]	1.0 [4]	- [7]	0.3 [8]
2	.	.	.	10.7 [4]	13.5 [5]	11.8 [6]	14.0 [7]	9.8 [4]	11.0 [7]	11.9 [8]
3	.	.	.	13.5 [4]	12.0 [5]	16.7 [6]	18.0 [7]	15.6 [4]	4.8 [7]	12.9 [8]
4	.	.	.	18.7 [4]	26.8 [5]	22.5 [6]	34.7 [7]	24.2 [4]	24.5 [7]	27.4 [8]
5	.	.	.	36.7 [4]	35.5 [5]	42.7 [6]	57.1 [7]	52.9 [4]	36.5 [7]	51.2 [8]
6	.	.	.	- [4]	- [5]	- [6]	1.0 [7]	- [4]	- [7]	- [8]
7	.	.	.	18.6 [4]	11.9 [5]	14.4 [6]	17.3 [7]	16.8 [4]	10.6 [7]	13.3 [8]
8	.	.	.	4.6 [4]	- [5]	2.9 [6]	4.2 [7]	1.7 [4]	2.9 [7]	1.1 [8]
9	.	.	.	59.9 [4]	70.6 [5]	42.7 [6]	48.7 [7]	43.3 [4]	40.6 [7]	26.6 [8]
0	.	.	.	- [4]	- [5]	- [6]	- [7]	- [4]	- [7]	- [8]
Puerto Rico (BA) [9][10]				**Total unemployment - Chômage total - Desempleo total**						
Total - Total - Total ISCO-88 - CITP-88 - CIUO-88										
Total	152	131	145	163	164	145	160	156	152	158
UB	10	8	8	9	10	8	9	9	10	12
1	6	5	6	5	5	5	6	8	9	7
2	5	4	6	6	6	5	6	12	9	8
3	4	3	4	4	3	3	3	3	3	2
4	18	17	18	23	23	20	24	22	19	22
5 [11]	33	28	33	38	41	37	39	38	38	38
6	8	8	8	8	8	7	8	7	8	7
7	27	23	26	28	27	25	26	25	22	22
8	25	21	24	28	25	20	20	20	19	20
9 [12]	16	14	14	15	16	15	17	12	15	18
Men - Hommes - Hombres ISCO-88 - CITP-88 - CIUO-88										
Total	101	90	97	101	99	92	97	90	93	97
UB	4	3	4	4	4	4	4	4	5	6
1	4	3	4	3	3	3	3	4	4	3
2	3	2	3	3	2	2	4	4	4	3
3	2	1	2	2	2	2	2	1	1	1
4	5	4	4	5	4	5	4	4	5	5
5 [11]	20	18	20	20	20	20	20	19	19	20
6	7	7	7	8	7	6	8	7	7	7
7	26	23	26	28	27	24	25	25	21	22
8	16	15	16	17	16	13	12	12	13	14
9 [12]	15	13	13	13	14	13	15	11	13	16
Women - Femmes - Mujeres ISCO-88 - CITP-88 - CIUO-88										
Total	51	42	48	62	65	53	63	66	59	60
UB	6	5	4	5	6	4	5	5	5	6
1	2	2	2	2	2	2	3	4	4	4
2	3	3	4	4	4	3	3	8	5	5
3	2	2	2	2	2	1	2	2	2	1
4	14	13	13	18	18	15	19	18	14	16
5 [11]	12	10	14	18	20	17	20	19	20	19
6	1	1	-	-	-	1	1	-	-	-
7	-	-	-	-	-	-	-	-	-	-
8	8	6	8	11	10	7	8	8	6	6
9 [12]	1	1	2	2	2	2	2	1	1	2

Explanatory notes: see p. 451.

[1] Persons aged 14 years and over. [2] Metropolitan Lima. [3] Excl. conscripts. [4] October. [5] July. [6] Aug. [7] September. [8] Aug.-Oct. [9] Excl. persons temporarily laid off. [10] Persons aged 16 years and over. [11] Incl. sales and services elementary occupations. [12] Excl. sales and services elementary occupations.

Notes explicatives: voir p. 454.

[1] Personnes âgées de 14 ans et plus. [2] Lima métropolitaine. [3] Non compris les conscrits. [4] Octobre. [5] Juillet. [6] Août. [7] Septembre. [8] Août-oct. [9] Non compris les personnes temporairement mises à pied. [10] Personnes âgées de 16 ans et plus. [11] Y compris les employés non qualifiés des services et de la vente. [12] Non compris les employés non qualifiés des services et de la vente.

Notas explicativas: véase p. 457.

[1] Personas de 14 años y más. [2] Lima metropolitana. [3] Excl. los conscriptos. [4] Octubre. [5] Julio. [6] Agosto. [7] Septiembre. [8] Agosto-oct. [9] Excl. las personas temporalmente despedidas. [10] Personas de 16 años y más. [11] Incl. los trabajadores no calificados de ventas y servicios. [12] Excl. los trabajadores no calificados de ventas y servicios.

By occupation   Par profession   Por ocupación

	Thousands			Milliers				Millares		
	1999	2000	2001	2002	2003	2004	2005	2006	2007	2008

Saint Lucia (BA) [1]   Total unemployment - Chômage total - Desempleo total

Total - Total - Total
ISCO-88 - CITP-88 - CIUO-88

	1999	2000	2001	2002	2003	2004	2005	2006	2007	2008
Total	13.220	12.535	.	14.990	18.205	16.527	.	.	.	.
1	0.185	0.175	.	0.175	0.297	0.167	.	.	.	.
2	0.185	0.080	.	0.270	0.217	0.212	.	.	.	.
3	0.260	0.380	.	0.175	0.310	0.225	.	.	.	.
4	0.855	0.900	.	0.640	0.760	0.670	.	.	.	.
5	2.275	1.765	.	1.185	1.845	1.792	.	.	.	.
6	0.230	0.235	.	0.115	0.215	0.225	.	.	.	.
7	1.630	1.270	.	1.565	2.197	1.625	.	.	.	.
8	0.620	0.565	.	0.795	0.460	0.470	.	.	.	.
9	1.915	2.290	.	2.490	2.567	2.442	.	.	.	.
X	5.065	4.875	.	7.580	9.335	8.697	.	.	.	.

Men - Hommes - Hombres
ISCO-88 - CITP-88 - CIUO-88

	1999	2000	2001	2002	2003	2004	2005	2006	2007	2008
Total	6.065	5.070	.	6.710	7.557	7.382	.	.	.	.
1	0.075	0.045	.	0.095	0.132	0.070	.	.	.	.
2	0.020	0.020	.	0.125	0.055	0.017	.	.	.	.
3	0.145	0.105	.	0.120	0.097	0.142	.	.	.	.
4	0.165	0.115	.	0.060	0.050	0.127	.	.	.	.
5	0.635	0.355	.	0.170	0.432	0.640	.	.	.	.
6	0.190	0.115	.	0.055	0.152	0.177	.	.	.	.
7	1.420	0.965	.	1.425	1.722	1.230	.	.	.	.
8	0.280	0.285	.	0.335	0.292	0.100	.	.	.	.
9	1.000	0.960	.	1.175	1.117	1.192	.	.	.	.
X	2.135	2.105	.	3.150	3.505	3.685	.	.	.	.

Women - Femmes - Mujeres
ISCO-88 - CITP-88 - CIUO-88

	1999	2000	2001	2002	2003	2004	2005	2006	2007	2008
Total	7.155	7.465	.	8.280	10.647	9.563	.	.	.	.
1	0.110	0.130	.	0.080	0.165	0.097	.	.	.	.
2	0.165	0.060	.	0.145	0.162	0.195	.	.	.	.
3	0.115	0.275	.	0.055	0.212	0.082	.	.	.	.
4	0.690	0.785	.	0.580	0.710	0.542	.	.	.	.
5	1.640	1.410	.	1.015	1.412	1.152	.	.	.	.
6	0.040	0.120	.	0.060	0.062	0.047	.	.	.	.
7	0.210	0.305	.	0.140	0.475	0.395	.	.	.	.
8	0.340	0.280	.	0.460	0.352	0.370	.	.	.	.
9	0.915	1.330	.	1.315	1.515	1.250	.	.	.	.
X	2.930	2.770	.	4.430	5.580	5.445	.	.	.	.

Trinidad and Tobago (BA) [1]   Total unemployment - Chômage total - Desempleo total

Total - Total - Total
ISCO-88 - CITP-88 - CIUO-88

	1999	2000	2001	2002	2003	2004	2005	2006	2007	2008
Total	74.0	69.6	62.4	61.1	62.4	51.1	49.7	.	.	.
1	0.7	0.5	0.7	0.6	0.5	0.6	0.7	.	.	.
2	0.1	0.4	0.4	0.3	0.4	0.4	0.6	.	.	.
3	2.3	2.6	2.6	2.9	2.7	2.5	2.0	.	.	.
4	9.8	9.2	7.8	9.3	8.1	7.6	7.9	.	.	.
5,0	12.0	12.7	12.0	11.3	11.3	9.2	8.3	.	.	.
6	0.4	0.3	0.4	0.1	0.1	0.2	0.2	.	.	.
7	12.3	12.9	10.6	9.4	8.3	7.4	5.8	.	.	.
8	3.4	2.5	3.3	2.4	2.7	1.8	2.0	.	.	.
9	32.6	28.2	24.3	24.0	27.5	21.1	22.0	.	.	.
X	0.1	0.3	0.3	0.9	0.7	0.4	0.3	.	.	.

Men - Hommes - Hombres
ISCO-88 - CITP-88 - CIUO-88

	1999	2000	2001	2002	2003	2004	2005	2006	2007	2008
Total	37.9	36.1	30.7	27.9	29.8	23.4	21.3	.	.	.
1	0.4	0.2	0.4	0.2	0.4	0.3	0.4	.	.	.
2	0.1	0.1	0.2	0.1	0.2	0.2	0.3	.	.	.
3	0.7	0.9	0.7	0.9	1.1	1.2	0.9	.	.	.
4	1.4	1.4	1.2	1.5	1.1	1.0	1.3	.	.	.
5,0	2.3	2.4	2.1	1.9	1.7	1.3	1.3	.	.	.
6	0.4	0.3	0.3	0.1	0.1	0.2	0.2	.	.	.
7	10.9	11.5	9.7	8.6	7.7	6.8	5.2	.	.	.
8	2.2	1.9	2.3	1.8	2.1	1.5	1.7	.	.	.
9	19.3	17.3	13.6	12.4	14.9	10.8	9.9	.	.	.
X	-	0.1	0.2	0.4	0.3	0.2	0.1	.	.	.

Women - Femmes - Mujeres
ISCO-88 - CITP-88 - CIUO-88

	1999	2000	2001	2002	2003	2004	2005	2006	2007	2008
Total	36.1	33.5	31.7	33.2	32.6	27.7	28.4	.	.	.
1	0.3	0.3	0.3	0.4	0.1	0.3	0.3	.	.	.
2	-	0.3	0.2	0.2	0.2	0.2	0.3	.	.	.
3	1.6	1.7	1.9	2.0	1.6	1.3	1.1	.	.	.
4	8.4	7.8	6.6	7.8	7.0	6.6	6.6	.	.	.
5,0	9.7	10.3	9.9	9.4	9.6	7.9	7.0	.	.	.
6	-	-	0.1	-	-	-	-	.	.	.
7	1.4	1.4	0.9	0.8	0.6	0.6	0.6	.	.	.
8	1.2	0.6	1.0	0.6	0.6	0.3	0.3	.	.	.
9	13.3	10.9	10.7	11.6	12.6	10.3	12.1	.	.	.
X	0.1	0.2	0.1	0.5	0.4	0.2	0.2	.	.	.

Explanatory notes: see p. 451.   Notes explicatives: voir p. 454.   Notas explicativas: véase p. 457.

[1] Persons aged 15 years and over.   [1] Personnes âgées de 15 ans et plus.   [1] Personas de 15 años y más.

	Thousands								Milliers / Millares	
	1999	2000	2001	2002	2003	2004	2005	2006	2007	2008

United States (BA) [1]   Total unemployment - Chômage total - Desempleo total

Total - Total - Total
ISCO-68 - CITP-68 - CIUO-68 · · · · · · · ISCO-88 - CITP-88 - CIUO-88

	1999	2000	2001	2002	2003	2004	2005	2006	2007	2008	
Total	5 880	5 655	6 742	8 378	8 774	8 149	7 591	7 001	7 078	8 924	Total
UB	469	431	453	536	641	686	666	616	627	766	UB
0/1	495	466	615	815	627	544	464	427	429	619	1
2	376	356	491	717	929	801	708	638	662	844	2-3
3	662	684	772	968	1 076	1 025	946	856	804	1 026	4
4	714	684	794	1 001	2 676	2 529	2 461	2 297	2 356	2 749	5
5	1 081	1 023	1 150	1 369	136	132	103	101	89	112	6
6	249	215	259	275	2 664	2 401	2 210	2 033	2 091	2 783	7-8
7/8/9	1 814	1 782	2 192	2 675	.	.	33	33	20	25	X
X [2]	19	14	16	22							

Men - Hommes - Hombres
ISCO-68 - CITP-68 - CIUO-68 · · · · · · · ISCO-88 - CITP-88 - CIUO-88

	1999	2000	2001	2002	2003	2004	2005	2006	2007	2008	
Total	3 066	2 954	3 663	4 597	4 906	4 456	4 059	3 753	3 882	5 033	Total
UB	219	216	217	274	320	346	359	312	343	393	UB
0/1	237	204	313	423	339	301	250	227	220	335	1
2	191	185	255	363	463	380	308	268	289	359	2-3
3	152	166	197	235	323	319	277	245	248	307	4
4	253	244	307	412	1 177	1 063	1 004	949	994	1 210	5
5	416	403	470	558	82	89	69	69	57	79	6
6	182	157	191	215	2 180	1 930	1 764	1 654	1 715	2 331	7-8
7/8/9	1 400	1 367	1 701	2 098	.	.	28	29	16	19	X
X [2]	16	11	14	19							

Women - Femmes - Mujeres
ISCO-68 - CITP-68 - CIUO-68 · · · · · · · ISCO-88 - CITP-88 - CIUO-88

	1999	2000	2001	2002	2003	2004	2005	2006	2007	2008	
Total	2 814	2 701	3 079	3 781	3 868	3 694	3 531	3 247	3 196	3 891	Total
UB	250	215	236	262	321	340	306	304	285	374	UB
0/1	257	262	302	392	288	243	214	200	209	284	1
2	184	171	237	354	466	421	400	370	373	486	2-3
3	510	518	575	733	753	705	669	610	556	719	4
4	462	440	487	589	1 499	1 467	1 457	1 348	1 361	1 539	5
5	665	620	680	811	53	44	35	32	32	33	6
6	67	59	68	60	483	472	445	380	377	453	7-8
7/8/9	414	415	491	577	.	.	5	3	3	3	X
X [2]	3	3	2	3							

Uruguay (BA) [3]   Total unemployment - Chômage total - Desempleo total

Total - Total - Total
ISCO-88 - CITP-88 - CIUO-88

	1999	2000	2001	2002	2003	2004	2005	2006	2007	2008
Total	.	167.7	193.2	211.3	208.5	.	154.9	167.0 [4]	149.0	.
UB	.	34.2	35.3	35.7	38.2	.	27.4	33.8 [4]	28.3	.
1	.	2.2	1.0	1.5	1.2	.	1.2	2.2 [4]	2.6	.
2	.	2.6	2.0	2.5	2.8	.	1.9	4.5 [4]	3.2	.
3	.	4.9	3.3	3.3	3.1	.	4.8	5.1 [4]	4.3	.
4	.	14.8	9.4	8.5	7.2	.	14.5	13.1 [4]	10.9	.
5	.	29.9	21.9	24.7	22.8	.	2.5	31.0 [4]	28.6	.
6	.	2.7	2.2	3.9	3.9	.	9.0	4.1 [4]	2.1	.
7	.	24.2	16.2	23.8	20.3	.	2.7	18.6 [4]	13.7	.
8	.	9.2	5.7	5.6	4.3	.	24.1	6.7 [4]	5.8	.
9	.	41.7	34.1	35.2	30.8	.	21.1	47.2 [4]	49.4	.
0	.	1.2	0.4	0.3	0.1	.	0.6	0.6 [4]	0.4	.
X	.	.	61.7 [5]	66.3	73.7	.	45.1	0.1 [4]	-	.

Men - Hommes - Hombres
ISCO-88 - CITP-88 - CIUO-88

	1999	2000	2001	2002	2003	2004	2005	2006	2007	2008
Total	.	74.7	80.4	93.3	92.2	.	65.4	70.0 [4]	60.0	.
UB	.	14.9	14.9	14.3	17.3	.	11.2	13.9 [4]	11.9	.
1	.	1.1	0.6	0.9	0.6	.	0.4	1.1 [4]	1.4	.
2	.	0.8	0.8	0.8	0.9	.	1.1	1.4 [4]	1.0	.
3	.	2.2	1.8	1.9	1.6	.	2.1	2.8 [4]	2.1	.
4	.	3.4	2.6	2.6	2.2	.	2.9	3.8 [4]	2.7	.
5	.	7.3	5.4	5.8	6.7	.	2.2	5.0 [4]	4.1	.
6	.	2.5	2.0	3.6	3.6	.	7.9	3.6 [4]	1.8	.
7	.	18.3	13.6	21.0	17.7	.	2.0	14.8 [4]	10.4	.
8	.	5.6	4.1	4.4	3.5	.	11.5	4.3 [4]	3.7	.
9	.	17.5	16.9	17.8	14.4	.	10.7	18.6 [4]	20.5	.
0	.	1.2	0.4	0.3	0.1	.	0.3	0.6 [4]	0.4	.
X	.	.	17.2 [5]	19.9	23.6	.	12.9	- [4]	-	.

Explanatory notes: see p. 451.

[1] Persons aged 16 years and over. [2] Unemployed whose last job was in the armed forces. [3] Persons aged 14 years and over. [4] Prior to 2006: urban areas. [5] Incl. the unemployed whose last job was 1 year ago or over.

Notes explicatives: voir p. 454.

[1] Personnes âgées de 16 ans et plus. [2] Chômeurs dont le dernier emploi était dans les forces armées. [3] Personnes âgées de 14 ans et plus. [4] Avant 2006: régions urbaines. [5] Y compris les chômeurs dont le dernier emploi date de 1 an ou plus.

Notas explicativas: véase p. 457.

[1] Personas de 16 años y más. [2] Desempleados que estaban empleados anteriormente en las fuerzas armadas. [3] Personas de 14 años y más. [4] Antes de 2006: areas urbanas. [5] Incl. los desempleados cuyo último trabajo fue hace 1 año o más.

By occupation   Par profession   Por ocupación

	Thousands			Milliers				Millares		
	1999	2000	2001	2002	2003	2004	2005	2006	2007	2008

Uruguay (BA) [1]   Total unemployment - Chômage total - Desempleo total

Women - Femmes - Mujeres
ISCO-88 - CITP-88 - CIUO-88

	1999	2000	2001	2002	2003	2004	2005	2006	2007	2008
Total	.	93.0	112.8	118.0	116.2	.	89.5	96.9 [2]	89.3	.
UB	.	19.2	20.4	21.4	20.9	.	16.1	19.9 [2]	16.3	.
1	.	1.2	0.4	0.5	0.5	.	0.8	1.1 [2]	1.2	.
2	.	1.9	1.3	1.7	1.9	.	0.8	3.2 [2]	2.2	.
3	.	2.7	1.5	1.4	1.5	.	2.7	2.3 [2]	2.1	.
4	.	11.4	6.8	5.9	5.1	.	11.6	9.2 [2]	8.2	.
5	.	22.6	16.5	18.9	16.1	.	0.2	26.0 [2]	24.5	.
6	.	0.2	0.2	0.3	0.3	.	1.1	0.5 [2]	0.3	.
7	.	5.9	2.6	2.8	2.6	.	0.6	3.8 [2]	3.2	.
8	.	3.6	1.6	1.2	0.7	.	12.5	2.3 [2]	2.1	.
9	.	24.2	17.2	17.4	16.4	.	10.4	28.6 [2]	29.0	.
0	.	-	-	-	-	.	0.3	- [2]	0.1	.
X	.	.	44.5 [3]	46.4	50.1	.	32.3	0.1 [2]	-	.

Venezuela, Rep. Bolivariana de (BA) [4] [5]   Total unemployment - Chômage total - Desempleo total

Total - Total - Total
ISCO-68 - CITP-68 - CIUO-68

	1999	2000	2001	2002	2003	2004	2005	2006	2007	2008
Total	1 483.4	1 365.8	1 419.2	1 887.7	2 014.9	1 687.7	1 374.3	1 143.7	928.2	872.9
UB	143.2	135.1	139.8	157.9	165.1	143.2	122.7	99.5	86.7	75.4
0/1	86.5	100.7	89.3	119.2	137.4	109.4	93.9	87.5	72.9	71.4
2	26.2	27.1	27.4	29.2	36.7	43.7	57.1	25.8	18.4	20.4
3	137.6	121.5	133.6	158.2	163.2	124.3	105.3	90.8	74.6	67.2
4	192.5	156.2	205.9	315.1	354.3	271.4	208.6	183.8	130.6	123.4
5	249.6	222.5	274.0	369.2	413.5	354.7	261.8	233.7	171.6	152.0
6	78.7	81.3	72.6	108.1	100.6	89.8	75.9	55.7	45.2	38.4
7/8/9	511.0	465.1	433.3	570.3	571.4	479.1	408.6	328.1	303.6	295.6
X	58.1	56.2	43.2	60.5	72.7	72.1	40.3	38.9	24.6	29.1

Men - Hommes - Hombres
ISCO-68 - CITP-68 - CIUO-68

	1999	2000	2001	2002	2003	2004	2005	2006	2007	2008
Total	882.3	821.2	788.1	1 017.1	1 034.2	900.9	762.4	618.9	536.7	506.3
UB	48.1	54.9	55.3	57.5	57.2	53.2	47.4	34.8	35.8	28.4
0/1	28.7	30.4	29.0	43.0	49.4	40.2	30.9	28.6	23.8	20.3
2	19.7	17.9	17.1	20.3	22.1	26.5	32.2	15.4	10.9	13.5
3	34.2	34.5	38.1	41.4	42.3	33.5	29.3	23.1	21.7	21.8
4	73.8	64.4	74.7	111.2	118.7	89.8	70.7	64.9	48.2	40.0
5	116.0	100.1	104.2	116.9	119.9	114.4	100.9	87.6	64.6	57.3
6	75.3	75.6	66.0	102.6	94.5	84.4	69.2	50.8	41.1	36.0
7/8/9	463.8	415.3	385.4	503.4	502.1	427.5	362.5	296.4	280.6	276.2
X	22.7	28.2	18.4	21.0	28.1	31.4	19.3	17.4	10.0	12.8

Women - Femmes - Mujeres
ISCO-68 - CITP-68 - CIUO-68

	1999	2000	2001	2002	2003	2004	2005	2006	2007	2008
Total	601.1	544.6	631.1	870.6	980.7	786.8	611.9	524.8	391.5	366.6
UB	95.1	80.2	84.5	100.4	107.9	90.0	75.3	64.7	50.9	47.0
0/1	57.9	70.3	60.4	76.2	88.0	69.2	63.0	58.9	49.1	51.1
2	6.5	9.3	10.4	8.9	14.5	17.3	24.9	10.4	7.5	7.0
3	103.3	87.0	95.5	116.8	120.9	90.8	76.0	67.7	52.9	45.4
4	118.8	91.8	131.2	203.9	235.6	181.5	137.9	118.9	82.5	83.3
5	133.5	122.3	169.7	252.3	293.7	240.3	160.9	146.1	106.9	94.7
6	3.4	5.7	6.7	5.5	6.2	5.4	6.8	4.9	4.0	2.4
7/8/9	47.2	49.8	47.9	67.0	69.4	51.5	46.1	31.7	23.0	19.4
X	35.4	28.1	24.8	39.5	44.6	40.7	21.0	21.5	14.6	16.3

ASIA-ASIE-ASIA

Azerbaijan (FB) [6] [7]   Registered unemployment - Chômage enregistré - Desempleo registrado

Total - Total - Total
ISCO-88 - CITP-88 - CIUO-88

	1999	2000	2001	2002	2003	2004	2005	2006	2007	2008
Total	.	.	.	.	.	.	56.3	53.9	50.7	44.5
1	.	.	.	.	.	.	1.4	1.3	1.3	1.0
2	.	.	.	.	.	.	7.5	7.2	7.1	6.5
3	.	.	.	.	.	.	9.6	9.2	9.1	8.5
4	.	.	.	.	.	.	7.1	6.4	6.0	5.8
5	.	.	.	.	.	.	5.7	5.7	6.3	5.9
6	.	.	.	.	.	.	4.9	5.0	4.6	4.1
7	.	.	.	.	.	.	7.6	6.8	5.1	4.1
8	.	.	.	.	.	.	3.3	3.4	3.4	2.8
9	.	.	.	.	.	.	7.1	6.2	4.9	2.7
0	.	.	.	.	.	.	2.2	2.6	2.9	3.1

Explanatory notes: see p. 451.   Notes explicatives: voir p. 454.   Notas explicativas: véase p. 457.

[1] Persons aged 14 years and over. [2] Prior to 2006: urban areas. [3] Incl. the unemployed whose last job was 1 year ago or over. [4] Persons aged 15 years and over. [5] Second semester. [6] Men aged 15 to 61 years; women aged 15 to 56 years. [7] Dec. of each year.

[1] Personnes âgées de 14 ans et plus. [2] Avant 2006: régions urbaines. [3] Y compris les chômeurs dont le dernier emploi date de 1 an ou plus. [4] Personnes âgées de 15 ans et plus. [5] Second semestre. [6] Hommes âgés de 15 à 61 ans; femmes âgées de 15 à 56 ans. [7] Déc. de chaque année.

[1] Personas de 14 años y más. [2] Antes de 2006: areas urbanas. [3] Incl. los desempleados cuyo último trabajo fue hace 1 año o más. [4] Personas de 15 años y más. [5] Segundo semestre. [6] Hombres de 15 a 61 años; mujeres de 15 a 56 años. [7] Dic. de cada año.

	Thousands					Milliers				Millares
	1999	2000	2001	2002	2003	2004	2005	2006	2007	2008

Azerbaijan (FB) [1][2]   Registered unemployment - Chômage enregistré - Desempleo registrado

Men - Hommes - Hombres
ISCO-88 - CITP-88 - CIUO-88

	1999	2000	2001	2002	2003	2004	2005	2006	2007	2008
Total	.	.	.	.	.	.	27.3	26.3	25.3	23.6
1	.	.	.	.	.	.	0.9	0.8	0.8	0.7
2	.	.	.	.	.	.	3.8	3.4	3.4	3.2
3	.	.	.	.	.	.	4.4	4.1	4.0	3.8
4	.	.	.	.	.	.	3.4	3.2	3.0	2.8
5	.	.	.	.	.	.	2.3	2.1	2.5	2.4
6	.	.	.	.	.	.	2.8	2.7	2.4	2.3
7	.	.	.	.	.	.	3.5	3.1	2.3	2.1
8	.	.	.	.	.	.	1.8	2.0	2.0	1.8
9	.	.	.	.	.	.	2.2	2.3	2.0	1.5
0	.	.	.	.	.	.	2.2	2.5	2.9	3.1

Women - Femmes - Mujeres
ISCO-88 - CITP-88 - CIUO-88

	1999	2000	2001	2002	2003	2004	2005	2006	2007	2008
Total	.	.	.	.	.	.	29.1	27.5	25.3	20.9
1	.	.	.	.	.	.	0.5	0.5	0.4	0.3
2	.	.	.	.	.	.	3.7	3.8	3.7	3.4
3	.	.	.	.	.	.	5.2	5.2	5.1	4.7
4	.	.	.	.	.	.	3.6	3.2	3.1	3.0
5	.	.	.	.	.	.	3.4	3.6	3.7	3.5
6	.	.	.	.	.	.	2.1	2.3	2.1	1.8
7	.	.	.	.	.	.	4.1	3.6	2.8	2.1
8	.	.	.	.	.	.	1.6	1.4	1.4	1.0
9	.	.	.	.	.	.	4.9	4.0	2.9	1.2
0	.	.	.	.	.	.	0.0	0.0	0.0	0.0

Bahrain (FB) [3][4]   Work applicants - Demandeurs d'emploi - Solicitantes

Total - Total - Total
ISCO-68 - CITP-68 - CIUO-68

	1999	2000	2001	2002	2003	2004	2005	2006	2007	2008
Total	.	6.160	.	8.735	11.778	6.293	6.441	.	.	.
0/1	.	0.758	.	1.207	1.383	0.919	1.258	.	.	.
2	.	0.007	.	0.027	0.029	0.013	0.012	.	.	.
3	.	1.585	.	3.217	4.104	2.365	2.527	.	.	.
4	.	0.475	.	0.575	0.990	0.593	0.480	.	.	.
5	.	0.654	.	0.954	1.791	0.681	0.613	.	.	.
6	.	0.012	.	0.022	0.016	0.008	0.010	.	.	.
7/8/9	.	2.668	.	2.733	3.465	1.694	1.525	.	.	.
X	.	0.001	.	-	-	0.020	0.016	.	.	.

Men - Hommes - Hombres
ISCO-68 - CITP-68 - CIUO-68

	1999	2000	2001	2002	2003	2004	2005	2006	2007	2008
Total	.	4.183	.	.	.	3.077	2.898	.	.	.
0/1	.	0.352	.	.	.	0.268	0.278	.	.	.
2	.	0.006	.	.	.	0.010	0.009	.	.	.
3	.	0.650	.	.	.	0.714	0.679	.	.	.
4	.	0.227	.	.	.	0.207	0.159	.	.	.
5	.	0.589	.	.	.	0.541	0.499	.	.	.
6	.	0.011	.	.	.	0.007	0.010	.	.	.
7/8/9	.	2.347	.	.	.	1.322	1.258	.	.	.
X	.	0.001	.	.	.	0.008	0.006	.	.	.

Women - Femmes - Mujeres
ISCO-68 - CITP-68 - CIUO-68

	1999	2000	2001	2002	2003	2004	2005	2006	2007	2008
Total	.	1.977	.	.	.	3.216	3.543	.	.	.
0/1	.	0.406	.	.	.	0.651	0.980	.	.	.
2	.	0.001	.	.	.	0.003	0.003	.	.	.
3	.	0.935	.	.	.	1.651	1.848	.	.	.
4	.	0.248	.	.	.	0.386	0.321	.	.	.
5	.	0.065	.	.	.	0.140	0.114	.	.	.
6	.	0.001	.	.	.	0.001	0.000	.	.	.
7/8/9	.	0.321	.	.	.	0.372	0.267	.	.	.
X	.	-	.	.	.	0.012	0.010	.	.	.

Hong Kong, China (BA) [3][5]   Total unemployment - Chômage total - Desempleo total

Total - Total - Total
ISCO-88 - CITP-88 - CIUO-88

	1999	2000	2001	2002	2003	2004	2005	2006	2007	2008
Total	207.5	166.9	174.3	254.2	275.2	239.2	197.6	171.1	145.7	130.1
UB	23.9	17.6	16.1	24.7	23.2	23.4	20.1	18.7	17.0	15.7
1	5.7	3.9	5.2	8.4	6.7	5.3	6.1	4.6	4.3	3.4
2	2.6	2.1	3.7	4.8	5.0	4.5	4.1	3.2	3.5	3.3
3	18.7	13.4	17.1	25.8	26.5	22.3	18.0	17.1	15.9	14.3
4	25.7	21.3	21.4	30.0	30.1	25.5	22.5	19.5	17.8	17.9
5	36.6	34.1	33.3	47.3	55.3	46.8	39.0	33.3	28.2	26.7
6	-	-	-	-	-	-	-	-	-	-
7	40.2	32.5	31.6	46.9	51.7	41.2	31.9	27.3	19.4	15.5
8	16.5	11.5	12.1	15.0	17.7	15.3	11.7	9.9	7.2	6.6
9	37.2	30.3	33.6	51.0	58.7	54.6	43.8	37.3	32.3	26.7

Explanatory notes: see p. 451.

[1] Men aged 15 to 61 years; women aged 15 to 56 years. [2] Dec. of each year. [3] Persons aged 15 years and over. [4] Jan. [5] Excl. marine, military and institutional populations.

Notes explicatives: voir p. 454.

[1] Hommes âgés de 15 à 61 ans; femmes âgées de 15 à 56 ans. [2] Déc. de chaque année. [3] Personnes âgées de 15 ans et plus. [4] Janv. [5] Non compris le personnel militaire, de la marine et la population institutionnelle.

Notas explicativas: véase p. 457.

[1] Hombres de 15 a 61 años; mujeres de 15 a 56 años. [2] Dic. de cada año. [3] Personas de 15 años y más. [4] Enero. [5] Excl. el personal militar y de la marina, y la población institucional.

UNEMPLOYMENT — CHÔMAGE — DESEMPLEO — 3E

By occupation — Par profession — Por ocupación

	Thousands			Milliers				Millares		
	1999	2000	2001	2002	2003	2004	2005	2006	2007	2008

Hong Kong, China (BA) [1] [2] — Total unemployment - Chômage total - Desempleo total

Men - Hommes - Hombres
ISCO-88 - CITP-88 - CIUO-88

	1999	2000	2001	2002	2003	2004	2005	2006	2007	2008
Total	140.6	109.6	117.8	164.0	180.0	151.8	127.5	110.2	89.2	79.4
UB	11.7	8.2	8.3	10.4	9.9	9.5	9.1	8.9	7.7	7.4
1	4.9	3.1	4.2	6.8	4.9	4.2	4.8	3.3	2.9	2.5
2	1.8	1.5	2.7	3.5	3.5	3.1	3.0	2.4	2.6	2.4
3	13.1	9.0	11.3	18.1	18.4	15.3	12.0	11.1	10.2	9.2
4	8.5	6.6	7.1	9.0	8.6	8.5	7.2	6.4	6.4	5.5
5	19.7	17.2	16.9	22.8	28.1	22.3	20.1	17.1	12.8	13.5
6	-	-	-	-	-	-	-	-	-	-
7	38.8	31.5	31.0	45.9	50.9	40.1	31.3	26.8	18.9	14.8
8	13.2	9.2	9.6	11.4	14.2	12.3	9.3	7.9	5.8	5.3
9	28.6	23.1	26.5	36.0	41.0	36.5	30.5	26.0	21.9	18.8

Women - Femmes - Mujeres
ISCO-88 - CITP-88 - CIUO-88

	1999	2000	2001	2002	2003	2004	2005	2006	2007	2008
Total	66.9	57.3	56.5	90.1	95.3	87.4	70.1	60.8	56.5	50.7
UB	12.2	9.4	7.9	14.3	13.3	13.9	11.0	9.8	9.3	8.3
1	0.9	0.8	0.9	1.6	1.7	1.1	1.3	1.3	1.4	0.9
2	0.8	0.6	1.0	1.3	1.4	1.4	1.2	0.8	0.9	0.9
3	5.5	4.4	5.7	7.8	8.1	7.0	6.0	6.0	5.7	5.2
4	17.2	14.7	14.3	21.1	21.4	17.1	15.3	13.0	11.4	12.4
5	16.9	16.9	16.4	24.5	27.2	24.6	18.9	16.2	15.3	13.2
6	-	-	.	-	-	-	-	-	-	-
7	1.3	1.0	0.6	0.9	0.9	1.1	0.6	-	-	0.7
8	3.4	2.3	2.5	3.6	3.5	3.0	2.4	2.0	1.5	1.3
9	8.6	7.2	7.1	15.1	17.7	18.1	13.4	11.3	10.4	7.9

India (FB) [3] [4] — Work applicants - Demandeurs d'emploi - Solicitantes

Total - Total - Total
ISCO-68 - CITP-68 - CIUO-68

	1999	2000	2001	2002	2003	2004	2005	2006	2007	2008
Total	40 371	41 344	41 996	41 171	41 389	40 458	39 348	41 466	39 116	.
0/1	2 678	3 637	3 640	3 569	3 588	3 507	3 411	3 594	3 391	.
2	18	34	33	32	33	32	31	33	31	.
3	2 516	2 627	2 719	2 666	2 680	2 620	2 548	2 685	2 533	.
4	7	10	98	96	96	94	91	96	91	.
5	383	688	478	468	421	460	474	472	445	.
6	125	97	104	102	103	100	98	103	97	.
7/8/9	8 974	2 900	4 500	4 412	4 435	4 335	4 216	4 443	4 191	.
X [5]	25 672	31 351	30 424	29 827	29 984	29 310	28 506	30 040	28 337	.

Men - Hommes - Hombres
ISCO-68 - CITP-68 - CIUO-68

	1999	2000	2001	2002	2003	2004	2005	2006	2007	2008
Total	30 438	30 887	31 111	30 521	30 636	29 746	28 742	29 685	26 788	.
0/1	1 749	2 560	2 321	2 277	2 284	2 208	2 125	2 166	1 896	.
2	9	17	18	17	18	17	16	16	14	.
3	1 976	1 751	1 968	1 931	1 937	1 880	1 815	1 871	1 681	.
4	6	8	88	86	87	84	81	86	80	.
5	277	370	344	337	339	329	344	327	294	.
6	99	76	77	75	75	73	71	73	66	.
7/8/9	7 032	2 743	3 864	3 790	3 807	3 709	3 596	3 755	3 471	.
X [5]	19 292	23 361	22 433	22 008	22 090	21 446	20 720	21 391	19 286	.

Women - Femmes - Mujeres
ISCO-68 - CITP-68 - CIUO-68

	1999	2000	2001	2002	2003	2004	2005	2006	2007	2008
Total	9 933	10 457	10 885	10 650	10 752	10 712	10 606	11 781	12 328	.
0/1	929	1 078	1 320	1 291	1 304	1 299	1 286	1 428	1 495	.
2	9	17	15	15	15	15	15	16	17	.
3	540	876	752	736	743	740	733	814	852	.
4	1	2	10	10	10	10	10	11	11	.
5	105	318	134	131	132	132	130	145	151	.
6	26	21	28	27	27	27	27	30	31	.
7/8/9	1 942	156	636	622	628	626	620	688	720	.
X [5]	6 380	7 990	7 991	7 819	7 894	7 864	7 786	8 649	9 051	.

Explanatory notes: see p. 451.

[1] Excl. marine, military and institutional populations. [2] Persons aged 15 years and over. [3] Persons aged 14 years and over. [4] Dec. of each year. [5] Incl. persons seeking their first job.

Notes explicatives: voir p. 454.

[1] Non compris le personnel militaire, de la marine et la population institutionnelle. [2] Personnes âgées de 15 ans et plus. [3] Personnes âgées de 14 ans et plus. [4] Déc. de chaque année. [5] Y compris les personnes en quête de leur premier emploi.

Notas explicativas: véase p. 457.

[1] Excl. el personal militar y de la marina, y la población institucional. [2] Personas de 15 años y más. [3] Personas de 14 años y más. [4] Dic. de cada año. [5] Incl. las personas en busca de su primer empleo.

UNEMPLOYMENT — CHÔMAGE — DESEMPLEO

By occupation — Par profession — Por ocupación

	Thousands — Milliers — Millares									
	1999	2000	2001	2002	2003	2004	2005	2006	2007	2008
Iran, Islamic Rep. of (BA) [1]										
Total - Total - Total										
ISCO-88 - CITP-88 - CIUO-88										
Total	.	.	.	.	.	.	1 519	1 589	1 487	1 301
UB	.	.	.	.	.	.	1 156	1 054	999	1 091
1	.	.	.	.	.	.	24	22	19	15
2	.	.	.	.	.	.	60	69	63	45
3	.	.	.	.	.	.	68	68	66	49
4	.	.	.	.	.	.	72	79	70	61
5	.	.	.	.	.	.	145	149	141	126
6	.	.	.	.	.	.	62	68	57	40
7	.	.	.	.	.	.	349	346	292	264
8	.	.	.	.	.	.	154	150	157	131
9	.	.	.	.	.	.	300	329	315	294
X	.	.	.	.	.	.	285	308	307	276
Men - Hommes - Hombres										
ISCO-88 - CITP-88 - CIUO-88										
Total	.	.	.	.	.	.	1 346	1 416	1 333	1 181
UB	.	.	.	.	.	.	509	462	431	535
1	.	.	.	.	.	.	20	18	16	13
2	.	.	.	.	.	.	29	30	28	22
3	.	.	.	.	.	.	51	49	50	39
4	.	.	.	.	.	.	37	39	37	30
5	.	.	.	.	.	.	121	127	120	110
6	.	.	.	.	.	.	60	65	52	37
7	.	.	.	.	.	.	314	319	265	244
8	.	.	.	.	.	.	147	146	154	129
9	.	.	.	.	.	.	285	316	305	285
X	.	.	.	.	.	.	284	307	306	273
Women - Femmes - Mujeres										
ISCO-88 - CITP-88 - CIUO-88										
Total	.	.	.	.	.	.	172	173	154	120
UB	.	.	.	.	.	.	647	592	568	557
1	.	.	.	.	.	.	4	4	3	2
2	.	.	.	.	.	.	32	39	34	22
3	.	.	.	.	.	.	17	20	17	11
4	.	.	.	.	.	.	35	40	32	31
5	.	.	.	.	.	.	24	22	21	16
6	.	.	.	.	.	.	2	3	4	2
7	.	.	.	.	.	.	35	27	27	20
8	.	.	.	.	.	.	7	4	3	3
9	.	.	.	.	.	.	15	13	10	9
X	.	.	.	.	.	.	1	1	1	3
Israel (BA) [2]										
Total - Total - Total										
ISCO-88 - CITP-88 - CIUO-88										
Total	208.5	213.8	233.9	262.4	279.9	277.7	246.4	236.1	211.8	180.4
UB	95.5	107.6	107.1	129.2	154.5	163.4	139.5	135.8	118.6	94.7
1	3.2	4.2	6.9	6.8	8.5	5.2	4.5	4.5	5.3	5.9
2	5.3	5.1	6.1	7.8	8.9	7.4	6.5	5.7	5.9	4.7
3	11.0	12.2	16.6	18.1	17.9	14.6	13.8	13.8	13.0	13.7
4	20.1	18.8	20.7	22.1	20.1	19.6	18.0	18.9	17.7	13.9
5	20.8	19.2	24.0	25.9	26.6	25.7	24.9	23.6	21.8	17.6
6	-	2.3	2.3	-	-	-	-	-	-	-
7	19.6	16.2	16.6	17.2	12.7	11.9	10.1	8.7	8.5	9.0
8	13.3	10.5	14.0	14.7	11.5	10.4	12.2	7.3	7.9	9.8
9	16.8	16.8	18.7	18.1	17.3	17.6	15.1	16.0	10.7	9.8
Men - Hommes - Hombres										
ISCO-88 - CITP-88 - CIUO-88										
Total	108.8	111.7	120.9	138.4	142.8	136.5	124.9	118.5	104.8	90.8
UB	45.9	53.0	52.3	66.3	76.8	77.2	68.5	68.7	58.5	44.8
1	2.2	2.7	4.2	5.0	6.2	2.9	2.7	2.6	2.9	3.9
2	2.8	2.6	3.2	4.2	5.1	3.5	2.9	2.3	2.6	2.5
3	5.2	5.2	8.5	9.1	7.9	7.9	6.9	6.8	6.1	6.3
4	4.9	4.8	4.7	5.2	4.8	4.1	4.9	5.3	4.4	3.5
5	7.0	6.4	8.4	8.9	10.3	8.9	8.7	7.7	7.8	6.4
6	-	-	-	-	-	-	-	-	-	
7	18.5	15.1	15.8	16.1	12.0	11.3	9.6	7.9	8.2	8.3
8	10.1	7.8	9.6	10.6	8.3	8.6	9.6	6.1	6.3	7.8
9	9.9	11.7	12.1	10.9	9.9	10.6	9.8	9.7	6.5	6.5

Total unemployment - Chômage total - Desempleo total

Explanatory notes: see p. 451. Notes explicatives: voir p. 454. Notas explicativas: véase p. 457.

[1] Persons aged 10 years and over. [2] Persons aged 15 years and over. [1] Personnes âgées de 10 ans et plus. [2] Personnes âgées de 15 ans et plus. [1] Personas de 10 años y más. [2] Personas de 15 años y más.

UNEMPLOYMENT CHÔMAGE DESEMPLEO

By occupation Par profession Por ocupación

	Thousands			Milliers				Millares		
	1999	2000	2001	2002	2003	2004	2005	2006	2007	2008

Israel (BA) [1] — Total unemployment - Chômage total - Desempleo total

Women - Femmes - Mujeres
ISCO-88 - CITP-88 - CIUO-88

	1999	2000	2001	2002	2003	2004	2005	2006	2007	2008
Total	99.7	102.1	113.0	124.0	137.1	141.2	121.5	117.6	107.0	89.6
UB	49.6	54.6	54.8	62.9	77.7	86.2	71.0	67.1	60.1	49.9
1	-	-	2.7	-	2.4	2.3	-	-	2.4	2.0
2	2.5	2.5	2.9	3.6	3.8	3.9	3.6	3.4	3.4	2.2
3	5.8	7.0	8.2	8.9	10.0	6.7	6.9	7.0	6.9	7.5
4	15.2	14.0	16.0	16.9	15.3	15.5	13.1	13.7	13.3	10.4
5	13.8	12.8	15.6	17.0	16.3	16.7	16.2	15.9	14.0	11.2
6	-	-	-	-	0.0	-	-	-	-	.
7	-	-	-	-	-	-	-	-	-	-
8	3.2	2.7	4.4	4.1	3.1	-	2.6	-	-	2.1
9	6.9	5.1	6.6	7.2	7.3	7.1	5.3	6.2	4.2	3.3

Japan (BA) [1][2] — Total unemployment - Chômage total - Desempleo total

Total - Total - Total
ISCO-68 - CITP-68 - CIUO-68

	1999	2000	2001	2002	2003	2004	2005	2006	2007	2008
Total	2 640	2 640	2 570	2 730 [3]	2 640	2 310	2 140	1 990	1 870	1 910
UB	170	180	230	290 [3]	270	270	240	220	200	190
0/1	150	190	160	180 [3]	190	180	160	150	130	130
2	40	40	40	30 [3]	30	20	20	10	10	10
3	530	520	450	460 [3]	470	400	380	370	350	350
4	400	400	410	440 [3]	380	320	320	310	280	290
5 [4]	300	240	330	280 [3]	310	280	270	240	240	230
6	20	30	20	20 [3]	20	20	20	20	20	20
7/8/9 [5]	1 030	1 040	930	980 [3]	940	780	700	630	590	650
X	.		.		.		.		.	

Men - Hommes - Hombres
ISCO-68 - CITP-68 - CIUO-68

	1999	2000	2001	2002	2003	2004	2005	2006	2007	2008
Total	1 540	1 600	1 510	1 620 [3]	1 590	1 400	1 240	1 150	1 070	1 100
UB	90	110	150	170 [3]	170	170	150	140	130	130
0/1	60	90	70	80 [3]	100	100	70	70	60	60
2	40	40	40	30 [3]	20	20	20	10	10	10
3	150	160	150	140 [3]	150	120	110	130	110	110
4	220	230	220	270 [3]	220	190	180	180	160	160
5 [4]	160	120	160	140 [3]	140	130	140	110	100	110
6	10	10	10	20 [3]	20	10	10	20	10	10
7/8/9 [5]	810	840	710	750 [3]	730	620	550	460	450	490
X	.		.		.		.		.	

Women - Femmes - Mujeres
ISCO-68 - CITP-68 - CIUO-68

	1999	2000	2001	2002	2003	2004	2005	2006	2007	2008
Total	1 070	1 010	1 060	1 110 [3]	1 050	910	900	830	800	820
UB	70	70	80	120 [3]	100	100	90	70	70	60
0/1	90	90	90	90 [3]	90	80	100	80	70	60
2	-	0	0	0 [3]	0	0	0	0	0	-
3	370	350	300	320 [3]	310	280	270	250	250	250
4	180	170	190	180 [3]	160	120	140	120	120	130
5 [4]	140	130	170	140 [3]	160	150	130	130	140	130
6	0	0	0	0 [3]	0	0	0	0	0	0
7/8/9 [5]	220	200	230	240 [3]	200	170	150	160	130	170
X	.		.		.		.		.	

Korea, Republic of (BA) [1] — Total unemployment - Chômage total - Desempleo total

Total - Total - Total
ISCO-88 - CITP-88 - CIUO-88

	1999	2000	2001	2002	2003	2004	2005	2006	2007	2008
Total	1 353	979 [6]	899	752	818	860	887	827	783	.
UB	92	66 [6]	58	46	72	53	42	44	41	.
1	17	9 [6]	9	7	9	6	7	6	6	.
2	16	20 [6]	23	29	28	33	28	27	24	.
3	92	63 [6]	58	52	56	56	56	55	59	.
4	109	97 [6]	90	89	108	102	99	91	87	.
5	257	203 [6]	196	178	172	183	176	151	142	.
6	12	8 [6]	8	6	4	3	5	3	3	.
7	213	130 [6]	105	75	78	96	103	89	82	.
8	96	80 [6]	77	56	58	65	72	73	69	.
9	242	153 [6]	133	97	104	121	127	118	111	.
X	207	149 [6]	141	118	130	143	172	172	159	.

Explanatory notes: see p. 451.

[1] Persons aged 15 years and over. [2] Refer only to unemployed who left the previous job in the past 3 years. [3] Prior to 2002: Special Labour Force Survey, february of each year. [4] Excl. cleaners. [5] Incl. cleaners. [6] Estimates based on the 2000 Population Census results.

Notes explicatives: voir p. 454.

[1] Personnes âgées de 15 ans et plus. [2] Se rapportent seulement aux chômeurs dont le dernier travail date de moins de 3 ans. [3] Avant 2002: Enquête spécial sur la main-d'oeuvre, février de chaque année. [4] Non compris les nettoyeurs. [5] Y compris les nettoyeurs. [6] Estimations basées sur les résultats du Recensement de la population de 2000.

Notas explicativas: véase p. 457.

[1] Personas de 15 años y más. [2] Se refieren solamente de las desempleados cuyo último trabajo fue hace menos de 3 años. [3] Antes de 2002: encuesta especial sobre la fuerza de trabajo, febrero de cada año. [4] Excl. los limpiadores. [5] Incl. los limpiadores. [6] Estimaciones basadas en los resultados del Censo de población de 2000.

UNEMPLOYMENT   CHÔMAGE   DESEMPLEO

By occupation   Par profession   Por ocupación

Thousands   Milliers   Millares

Korea, Republic of (BA) [1]

Total unemployment - Chômage total - Desempleo total

Men - Hommes - Hombres
ISCO-88 - CITP-88 - CIUO-88

	1999	2000	2001	2002	2003	2004	2005	2006	2007	2008
Total	911	647 [2]	591	491	508	534	553	533	517	.
UB	56	41 [2]	34	29	41	29	22	23	25	.
1	16	9 [2]	8	7	8	6	7	6	5	.
2	12	11 [2]	12	15	12	17	14	12	12	.
3	65	44 [2]	40	35	38	37	36	36	40	.
4	52	45 [2]	38	43	48	43	37	40	38	.
5	124	100 [2]	98	91	83	82	84	74	72	.
6	10	7 [2]	7	5	3	3	4	2	2	.
7	192	114 [2]	93	65	68	84	93	82	76	.
8	87	72 [2]	69	50	52	57	60	62	61	.
9	172	111 [2]	99	71	76	88	95	90	81	.
X	127	94 [2]	91	79	79	89	100	107	104	.

Women - Femmes - Mujeres
ISCO-88 - CITP-88 - CIUO-88

	1999	2000	2001	2002	2003	2004	2005	2006	2007	2008
Total	442	332 [2]	308	261	310	326	334	294	266	.
UB	37	25 [2]	24	17	31	23	20	21	16	.
1	-	- [2]	1	-	1	0	0	0	1	.
2	4	9 [2]	11	14	15	16	14	15	12	.
3	28	19 [2]	18	17	18	18	20	19	19	.
4	57	52 [2]	52	45	60	59	62	51	49	.
5	134	103 [2]	98	87	89	101	93	77	70	.
6	2	1 [2]	1	-	1	0	1	1	1	.
7	21	16 [2]	12	9	10	12	10	7	6	.
8	10	9 [2]	8	6	6	8	12	10	8	.
9	70	43 [2]	34	26	28	33	32	28	30	.
X	78	55 [2]	50	39	50	54	71	65	55	.

Kyrgyzstan (BA) [1] [3]

Total unemployment - Chômage total - Desempleo total

Total - Total - Total
ISCO-88 - CITP-88 - CIUO-88

	1999	2000	2001	2002	2003	2004	2005	2006	2007	2008
Total	.	.	.	265.5	212.3	185.7	183.5	188.9	.	.
UB	.	.	.	76.3	85.6	76.9	66.9	68.7	.	.
1	.	.	.	8.5	2.3	0.2	0.5	1.3	.	.
2	.	.	.	26.4	7.6	7.9	8.8	6.5	.	.
3	.	.	.	26.8	12.4	10.6	7.6	7.0	.	.
4	.	.	.	7.2	4.5	4.3	2.8	1.5	.	.
5	.	.	.	26.1	23.0	22.9	28.1	30.6	.	.
6	.	.	.	10.3	20.2	16.6	24.4	22.7	.	.
7	.	.	.	37.7	27.1	23.6	25.1	29.7	.	.
8	.	.	.	26.3	17.4	11.3	8.1	10.3	.	.
9	.	.	.	20.0	12.2	11.4	11.1	10.6	.	.

Men - Hommes - Hombres
ISCO-88 - CITP-88 - CIUO-88

	1999	2000	2001	2002	2003	2004	2005	2006	2007	2008
Total	.	.	.	132.6	113.1	98.8	95.7	101.4	.	.
UB	.	.	.	39.1	42.6	36.1	32.2	33.2	.	.
1	.	.	.	5.0	1.6	0.2	0.4	1.0	.	.
2	.	.	.	11.2	2.8	3.8	4.0	3.3	.	.
3	.	.	.	7.3	4.6	4.8	2.5	2.5	.	.
4	.	.	.	0.7	1.9	1.1	0.4	0.3	.	.
5	.	.	.	5.3	6.4	7.7	10.3	8.8	.	.
6	.	.	.	6.8	12.1	9.8	13.3	12.6	.	.
7	.	.	.	23.0	17.6	17.5	17.4	23.2	.	.
8	.	.	.	22.2	15.4	11.1	7.4	9.5	.	.
9	.	.	.	11.9	8.1	6.7	7.8	6.9	.	.

Women - Femmes - Mujeres
ISCO-88 - CITP-88 - CIUO-88

	1999	2000	2001	2002	2003	2004	2005	2006	2007	2008
Total	.	.	.	132.9	99.2	86.9	87.8	87.5	.	.
UB	.	.	.	37.2	43.0	40.8	34.6	35.6	.	.
1	.	.	.	3.5	0.7	-	0.2	0.3	.	.
2	.	.	.	15.2	4.8	4.2	4.8	3.2	.	.
3	.	.	.	19.5	7.9	5.8	5.1	4.5	.	.
4	.	.	.	6.5	2.6	3.1	2.4	1.2	.	.
5	.	.	.	20.8	16.6	15.1	17.8	21.7	.	.
6	.	.	.	3.4	8.1	6.9	11.1	10.0	.	.
7	.	.	.	14.7	9.4	6.1	7.6	6.5	.	.
8	.	.	.	4.1	2.0	0.2	0.8	0.8	.	.
9	.	.	.	8.1	4.1	4.7	3.3	3.7	.	.

Explanatory notes: see p. 451.

[1] Persons aged 15 years and over. [2] Estimates based on the 2000 Population Census results. [3] Nov. of each year.

Notes explicatives: voir p. 454.

[1] Personnes âgées de 15 ans et plus. [2] Estimations basées sur les résultats du Recensement de la population de 2000. [3] Nov. de chaque année.

Notas explicativas: véase p. 457.

[1] Personas de 15 años y más. [2] Estimaciones basadas en los resultados del Censo de población de 2000. [3] Nov. de cada año.

	Thousands			Milliers				Millares		
	1999	2000	2001	2002	2003	2004	2005	2006	2007	2008

Liban (B) [1]   Total unemployment - Chômage total - Desempleo total

Total - Total - Total
ISCO-88 - CITP-88 - CIUO-88

	1999	2000	2001	2002	2003	2004	2005	2006	2007	2008
Total	.	.	.	.	.	94.4	.	.	110.4	.
UB	.	.	.	.	.	50.0	.	.	52.4	.
1	.	.	.	.	.	3.6	.	.	4.8	.
2	.	.	.	.	.	2.3	.	.	2.7	.
3	.	.	.	.	.	3.4	.	.	3.8	.
4	.	.	.	.	.	3.8	.	.	3.6	.
5	.	.	.	.	.	8.1	.	.	14.6	.
6	.	.	.	.	.	0.3	.	.	0.8	.
7	.	.	.	.	.	10.8	.	.	15.0	.
8	.	.	.	.	.	3.8	.	.	3.7	.
9	.	.	.	.	.	6.7	.	.	7.0	.
0	.	.	.	.	.	1.2	.	.	1.9	.
X	.	.	.	.	.	0.4	.	.	0.0	.

Men - Hommes - Hombres
ISCO-88 - CITP-88 - CIUO-88

	1999	2000	2001	2002	2003	2004	2005	2006	2007	2008
Total	.	.	.	.	.	67.3	.	.	79.3	.
UB	.	.	.	.	.	30.9	.	.	33.4	.
1	.	.	.	.	.	3.4	.	.	4.8	.
2	.	.	.	.	.	1.6	.	.	1.9	.
3	.	.	.	.	.	2.1	.	.	1.4	.
4	.	.	.	.	.	2.5	.	.	2.2	.
5	.	.	.	.	.	5.5	.	.	10.0	.
6	.	.	.	.	.	0.2	.	.	0.8	.
7	.	.	.	.	.	10.3	.	.	13.1	.
8	.	.	.	.	.	3.6	.	.	3.7	.
9	.	.	.	.	.	5.8	.	.	6.1	.
0	.	.	.	.	.	1.1	.	.	1.9	.
X	.	.	.	.	.	0.4	.	.	0.0	.

Women - Femmes - Mujeres
ISCO-88 - CITP-88 - CIUO-88

	1999	2000	2001	2002	2003	2004	2005	2006	2007	2008
Total	.	.	.	.	.	27.1	.	.	31.1	.
UB	.	.	.	.	.	19.1	.	.	18.9	.
1	.	.	.	.	.	0.3	.	.	0.0	.
2	.	.	.	.	.	0.7	.	.	0.8	.
3	.	.	.	.	.	1.3	.	.	2.4	.
4	.	.	.	.	.	1.3	.	.	1.4	.
5	.	.	.	.	.	2.7	.	.	4.6	.
6	.	.	.	.	.	0.1	.	.	0.0	.
7	.	.	.	.	.	0.5	.	.	1.9	.
8	.	.	.	.	.	0.2	.	.	0.1	.
9	.	.	.	.	.	1.0	.	.	1.0	.
0	.	.	.	.	.	0.1	.	.	0.0	.
X	.	.	.	.	.	0.0	.	.	0.0	.

Macau, China (BA) [2]   Total unemployment - Chômage total - Desempleo total

Total - Total - Total
ISCO-88 - CITP-88 - CIUO-88

	1999	2000	2001	2002	2003	2004	2005	2006	2007	2008
Total	13.2	14.2	14.0	13.7	13.1	11.2	10.3	10.4	9.5	10.1
UB	1.3	1.0	1.0	1.1	1.1	1.2	1.3	1.1	1.3	1.4
1	0.4	0.3	0.3	0.4	0.4	0.3	0.4	0.2	0.1	0.2
2	0.1	0.1	0.1	-	-	0.1	0.1	0.2	0.1	0.1
3	0.5	0.5	0.4	0.5	0.3	0.5	0.2	0.4	0.3	0.2
4	1.6	1.5	1.8	1.5	1.7	1.4	1.3	1.5	1.3	1.8
5	2.3	2.7	3.0	3.0	3.0	3.2	2.4	2.9	2.4	2.1
6	0.1	-	-	-	0.1	-	0.1	0.1	0.1	0.1
7	3.4	4.1	3.3	3.0	2.2	1.3	1.2	1.3	1.3	1.4
8	1.2	1.1	1.4	1.6	1.2	1.1	1.2	0.9	0.8	0.5
9	2.6	2.8	2.8	2.5	3.0	2.1	2.1	1.8	1.6	2.2
X	0.0	0.0	0.0	0.0	0.0	0.0	0.0	0.0	0.0	0.0

Men - Hommes - Hombres
ISCO-88 - CITP-88 - CIUO-88

	1999	2000	2001	2002	2003	2004	2005	2006	2007	2008
Total	9.1	9.8	9.5	9.1	8.3	6.8	5.8	5.6	5.6	5.7
UB	0.7	0.6	0.6	0.8	0.7	0.8	0.7	0.6	0.8	0.7
1	0.3	0.2	0.2	0.4	0.3	0.2	0.3	0.1	0.1	0.2
2	-	0.1	0.1	-	-	-	-	0.1	-	-
3	0.4	0.3	0.3	0.3	0.2	0.3	0.2	0.2	0.2	0.2
4	0.5	0.5	0.7	0.6	0.7	0.5	0.5	0.6	0.5	0.7
5	1.4	1.6	1.7	1.5	1.7	1.9	1.3	1.5	1.1	1.1
6	-	-	-	-	-	-	0.1	0.0	0.1	-
7	3.2	3.9	3.1	2.8	2.0	1.0	0.9	1.0	1.3	1.4
8	0.8	0.7	0.8	0.9	0.5	0.6	0.5	0.4	0.4	0.3
9	1.7	1.8	1.9	1.7	2.1	1.5	1.2	0.9	1.0	1.1
X	0.0	0.0	0.0	0.0	0.0	0.0	0.0	0.0	0.0	0.0

Explanatory notes: see p. 451.   Notes explicatives: voir p. 454.   Notas explicativas: véase p. 457.

[1] Persons aged 15 years and over. [2] Persons aged 14 years and over.   [1] Personnes âgées de 15 ans et plus. [2] Personnes âgées de 14 ans et plus.   [1] Personas de 15 años y más. [2] Personas de 14 años y más.

	UNEMPLOYMENT	CHÔMAGE	DESEMPLEO
	By occupation	Par profession	Por ocupación

	Thousands				Milliers				Millares	
	1999	2000	2001	2002	2003	2004	2005	2006	2007	2008

Macau, China (BA) [1] — Total unemployment - Chômage total - Desempleo total
Women - Femmes - Mujeres
ISCO-88 - CITP-88 - CIUO-88

	1999	2000	2001	2002	2003	2004	2005	2006	2007	2008
Total	4.2	4.4	4.5	4.6	4.8	4.4	4.5	4.8	3.9	4.3
UB	0.6	0.4	0.3	0.4	0.4	0.5	0.6	0.5	0.5	0.7
1	-	-	-	-	0.1	-	0.1	0.1	-	0.1
2	-	-	-	-	0.0	0.1	-	0.1	0.1	0.1
3	0.1	0.2	0.1	0.1	0.1	0.2	0.1	0.1	0.1	0.1
4	1.0	1.0	1.1	0.9	1.0	0.8	0.8	0.9	0.8	1.1
5	0.9	1.2	1.3	1.4	1.3	1.3	1.1	1.4	1.3	1.1
6	-	-	-	-	-	-	-	0.1	-	-
7	0.2	0.2	0.2	0.2	0.2	0.3	0.2	0.2	0.1	0.1
8	0.4	0.4	0.6	0.7	0.7	0.6	0.7	0.5	0.4	0.2
9	0.8	1.0	0.8	0.8	0.9	0.6	0.9	0.9	0.6	1.0
X	0.0	0.0	0.0	0.0	0.0	0.0	0.0	0.0	0.0	0.0

Pakistan (BA) [2][3] — Total unemployment - Chômage total - Desempleo total
Total - Total - Total
ISCO-88 - CITP-88 - CIUO-88

	1999	2000	2001	2002	2003	2004	2005	2006	2007	2008
Total	2 334	3 127	3 181	3 506	3 594	3 499	3 566	3 103	2 680	.
UB	2 117	2 658	2 704	3 013	3 089	2 923	2 979	2 683	2 427	.
1	15	36	37	26	27	51	52	45	22	.
2	10	12	13	15	15	7	7	5	6	.
3	5	39	40	24	25	45	46	41	21	.
4	8	13	13	18	18	19	19	17	7	.
5	35	67	68	62	64	77	79	41	44	.
6	19	61	62	57	58	35	36	20	10	.
7	32	127	129	125	128	121	123	93	51	.
8	13	29	29	38	39	48	49	23	19	.
9	80	85	86	128	131	173	176	132	73	.
0	-	-	-	-	-	-	-	1	-	.

Men - Hommes - Hombres
ISCO-88 - CITP-88 - CIUO-88

	1999	2000	2001	2002	2003	2004	2005	2006	2007	2008
Total	1 419	2 046	2 082	2 381	2 441	2 461	2 508	2 166	1 807	.
UB	1 229	1 625	1 654	1 939	1 988	1 984	2 022	1 806	1 582	.
1	12	36	37	26	27	47	48	45	22	.
2	3	4	5	10	11	6	6	5	5	.
3	4	32	33	13	15	29	30	15	14	.
4	8	13	13	18	18	19	19	16	7	.
5	33	65	66	58	59	73	75	38	44	.
6	18	54	55	57	57	30	31	19	9	.
7	29	112	113	109	111	99	100	75	40	.
8	13	29	29	38	38	46	47	23	19	.
9	70	76	77	113	117	128	130	123	65	.
0	-	-	-	-	-	-	-	1	-	.

Women - Femmes - Mujeres
ISCO-88 - CITP-88 - CIUO-88

	1999	2000	2001	2002	2003	2004	2005	2006	2007	2008
Total	915	1 081	1 099	1 125	1 153	1 038	1 058	937	873	.
UB	888	1 033	1 050	1 074	1 101	939	957	878	845	.
1	3	-	-	-	-	4	4	1	-	.
2	7	8	8	4	4	1	1	-	1	.
3	1	7	7	10	10	16	16	26	7	.
4	-	-	-	-	-	-	-	1	-	.
5	2	2	2	5	5	4	4	3	-	.
6	1	7	7	1	1	5	5	1	1	.
7	3	15	16	16	17	22	23	18	11	.
8	-	-	-	1	1	2	2	-	-	.
9	10	9	9	14	14	45	46	8	8	.
0	-	-	-	-	-	-	-	-	-	.

Philippines (BA) [4] — Total unemployment - Chômage total - Desempleo total
Total - Total - Total
ISCO-88 - CITP-88 - CIUO-88

	1999	2000	2001	2002	2003	2004	2005	2006	2007	2008
Total	.	.	3 653	3 874	3 936	4 249	2 748 [5]	2 829	2 653	2 716
UB			1 449	1 286	1 359	1 453	756 [5]	725	729	674
1			68	89	91	106	62 [5]	61	52	58
2			72	81	80	89	48 [5]	53	48	55
3			71	85	93	97	81 [5]	86	73	79
4			149	180	175	187	168 [5]	170	146	173
5			311	401	403	444	383 [5]	405	373	440
6			171	172	179	191	67 [5]	82	80	67
7			380	408	376	373	263 [5]	278	256	246
8			199	235	242	274	198 [5]	207	186	195
9			760	920	921	1 010	713 [5]	751	697	719
X			24	17	17	25	9 [5]	13	13	11

Explanatory notes: see p. 451.

[1] Persons aged 14 years and over. [2] Persons aged 10 years and over. [3] Jan. [4] Persons aged 15 years and over. [5] Definitions revised; data not strictly comparable.

Notes explicatives: voir p. 454.

[1] Personnes âgées de 14 ans et plus. [2] Personnes âgées de 10 ans et plus. [3] Janv. [4] Personnes âgées de 15 ans et plus. [5] Définitions révisées; les données ne sont pas strictement comparables.

Notas explicativas: véase p. 457.

[1] Personas de 14 años y más. [2] Personas de 10 años y más. [3] Enero. [4] Personas de 15 años y más. [5] Definiciones revisadas; los datos no son estrictamente comparables.

	Thousands			Milliers				Millares		
	1999	2000	2001	2002	2003	2004	2005	2006	2007	2008

Philippines (BA) [1]   Total unemployment - Chômage total - Desempleo total

Men - Hommes - Hombres — ISCO-88 - CITP-88 - CIUO-88

	1999	2000	2001	2002	2003	2004	2005	2006	2007	2008
Total	.	.	2 174	2 295	2 343	2 558	1 685 [2]	1 798	1 675	1 714
UB	.	.	790	695	744	792	420 [2]	405	405	373
1	.	.	39	48	53	60	36 [2]	38	32	39
2	.	.	31	32	32	35	17 [2]	24	21	24
3	.	.	40	46	50	56	46 [2]	47	39	45
4	.	.	55	62	64	73	69 [2]	70	60	71
5	.	.	143	185	186	208	192 [2]	211	185	229
6	.	.	138	141	147	165	57 [2]	72	69	59
7	.	.	288	312	292	289	212 [2]	230	210	205
8	.	.	173	197	204	230	162 [2]	163	150	151
9	.	.	458	565	558	630	467 [2]	529	494	509
X	.	.	19	12	14	21	8 [2]	10	11	8

Women - Femmes - Mujeres — ISCO-88 - CITP-88 - CIUO-88

	1999	2000	2001	2002	2003	2004	2005	2006	2007	2008
Total	.	.	1 478	1 579	1 592	1 692	1 062 [2]	1 031	978	1 002
UB	.	.	658	591	615	662	335 [2]	320	325	301
1	.	.	28	41	38	46	25 [2]	23	20	19
2	.	.	41	49	48	54	31 [2]	28	27	31
3	.	.	31	39	44	41	36 [2]	38	34	34
4	.	.	94	118	111	114	99 [2]	100	86	101
5	.	.	167	216	218	236	191 [2]	194	188	211
6	.	.	33	31	32	26	10 [2]	10	12	8
7	.	.	92	96	84	84	51 [2]	48	46	41
8	.	.	26	38	38	44	36 [2]	44	36	44
9	.	.	302	355	363	380	246 [2]	222	203	209
X	.	.	4	5	3	5	1 [2]	4	2	2

Singapore (BA) [3][4]   Total unemployment - Chômage total - Desempleo total

Total - Total - Total — ISCO-88 - CITP-88 - CIUO-88

	1999	2000	2001	2002	2003	2004	2005	2006	2007	2008
Total	77.5	.	61.9	94.2	101.0	101.3	.	84.2	74.8	76.2
UB	9.4	.	6.2	9.1	8.4	8.3	.	6.0	6.7	7.0
1	4.4	.	4.2	7.0	8.6	7.5	.	6.9	6.1	6.7
2	3.3	.	3.8	6.3	9.0	8.9	.	6.0	6.2	6.4
3	9.1	.	7.6	12.8	13.7	13.0	.	12.1	10.7	10.7
4	13.3	.	9.9	14.4	16.9	17.5	.	15.2	13.0	13.3
5	13.2	.	10.0	14.1	15.4	16.0	.	14.7	12.1	14.7
6	0.4	.	-	0.1	.	.	.	0.1	-	-
7	6.9	.	5.7	7.9	6.2	7.5	.	4.5	4.0	3.2
8	11.2	.	8.1	13.2	11.7	10.6	.	8.8	7.2	6.3
9	5.9	.	6.0	9.1	11.1	11.6	.	9.6	8.2	7.8
0-X	0.5	.	0.3	0.3	0.1	0.3	.	0.2	0.6	0.2

Men - Hommes - Hombres — ISCO-88 - CITP-88 - CIUO-88

	1999	2000	2001	2002	2003	2004	2005	2006	2007	2008
Total	44.3	.	35.7	55.3	57.6	56.8	.	44.7	40.0	39.6
UB	3.4	.	2.7	3.7	3.5	3.6	.	2.6	3.3	3.0
1	3.8	.	3.4	5.3	6.6	5.4	.	4.8	4.6	4.1
2	2.0	.	2.4	3.7	5.8	5.2	.	3.5	2.9	3.3
3	5.7	.	4.2	7.3	7.3	6.5	.	6.3	5.6	5.7
4	3.9	.	2.9	4.2	4.5	4.8	.	4.4	3.3	3.4
5	7.4	.	5.1	8.2	8.3	8.4	.	7.3	6.5	7.9
6	0.3	.	-	0.1	.	.	.	0.1	-	-
7	6.5	.	5.1	7.3	5.7	6.9	.	4.0	3.6	3.0
8	7.0	.	4.9	8.4	8.2	7.4	.	5.2	4.7	4.3
9	4.1	.	4.6	6.7	7.6	8.2	.	6.2	5.1	4.8
0-X	0.4	.	0.3	0.3	0.1	0.2	.	0.2	0.5	0.2

Women - Femmes - Mujeres — ISCO-88 - CITP-88 - CIUO-88

	1999	2000	2001	2002	2003	2004	2005	2006	2007	2008
Total	33.3	.	26.2	39.0	43.4	44.5	.	39.5	34.8	36.6
UB	6.0	.	3.5	5.4	4.9	4.7	.	3.4	3.4	4.0
1	0.6	.	0.7	1.7	2.0	2.1	.	2.1	1.6	2.7
2	1.3	.	1.4	2.6	3.2	3.7	.	2.5	3.3	3.0
3	3.5	.	3.4	5.5	6.5	6.5	.	5.8	5.1	5.0
4	9.4	.	7.0	10.1	12.4	12.7	.	10.8	9.7	9.9
5	5.8	.	4.8	5.9	7.1	7.6	.	7.4	5.6	6.8
6	0.1	.	-	.	.	.	.	-	-	-
7	0.4	.	0.6	0.5	0.5	0.6	.	0.5	0.5	0.2
8	4.2	.	3.3	4.8	3.4	3.2	.	3.6	2.5	2.0
9	1.9	.	1.4	2.4	3.5	3.4	.	3.4	3.1	3.0
0-X	0.1	.	-	.	.	.	.	-	-	-

Explanatory notes: see p. 451.

[1] Persons aged 15 years and over. [2] Definitions revised; data not strictly comparable. [3] The data refer to the residents (Singapore citizens and permanent residents) aged 15 years and over. [4] June.

Notes explicatives: voir p. 454.

[1] Personnes âgées de 15 ans et plus. [2] Définitions révisées; les données ne sont pas strictement comparables. [3] Les données se réfèrent aux résidents (citoyens de Singapour et résidents permanents) âgés de 15 ans et plus. [4] Juin.

Notas explicativas: véase p. 457.

[1] Personas de 15 años y más. [2] Definiciones revisadas; los datos no son estrictamente comparables. [3] Los datos se refieren a los residentes (ciudadanos de Singapur y residentes permanentes) de 15 años y más. [4] Junio.

3E

UNEMPLOYMENT	CHÔMAGE	DESEMPLEO
By occupation	Par profession	Por ocupación

	Thousands			Milliers					Millares		
	1999	2000	2001	2002	2003	2004	2005	2006	2007	2008	

Thailand (BA) — Total unemployment - Chômage total - Desempleo total

Total - Total - Total
ISCO-68 - CITP-68 - CIUO-68 [1] [2]   ISCO-88 - CITP-88 - CIUO-88 [2] [3]

	1999	2000	2001	2002	2003	2004	2005	2006	2007	2008	
Total	985.7	812.6	.	616.3	543.7	548.9	495.8	449.9	442.3	450.9	Total
UB	211.7	245.1	.	236.0	217.3	232.9	180.6	189.0	165.9	180.8	UB
0/1	26.2	35.8	.	5.9	7.7	9.1	4.8	6.8	6.4	3.2	1
2	10.7	12.0	.	9.2	5.0	7.9	9.9	4.0	3.1	7.2	2
3	36.1	27.5	.	15.4	20.4	18.3	17.4	9.2	8.9	11.9	3
4	54.8	38.2	.	23.5	27.6	21.6	26.3	17.8	23.5	24.5	4
5	39.6	31.1	.	59.3	41.8	41.0	47.3	36.2	47.5	41.7	5
6	322.6	178.4	.	88.6	56.1	59.3	26.1	32.7	28.4	25.8	6
7/8/9	282.4	243.1	.	54.5	56.4	37.9	63.4	57.8	56.3	46.0	7
X	0.2	-	.	39.8	46.9	49.3	46.6	36.2	42.5	44.8	8
				84.0	63.7	70.0	73.3	56.1	59.1	64.5	9
				-	0.7	1.6	-	4.0	0.7	0.5	X

Men - Hommes - Hombres
ISCO-68 - CITP-68 - CIUO-68 [1] [2]   ISCO-88 - CITP-88 - CIUO-88 [2] [3]

	1999	2000	2001	2002	2003	2004	2005	2006	2007	2008	
Total	546.4	454.5	.	372.1	314.7	324.2	289.9	259.7	258.1	268.1	Total
UB	118.6	137.0	.	132.2	109.7	131.2	96.6	100.6	101.3	97.2	UB
0/1	15.1	17.7	.	4.4	3.7	8.8	2.5	2.0	3.6	2.0	1
2	10.2	8.8	.	3.4	3.4	5.3	6.0	3.0	1.5	3.3	2
3	9.8	11.3	.	8.7	8.5	6.6	7.7	6.3	3.9	4.8	3
4	27.6	21.4	.	8.5	9.4	9.0	8.2	6.2	9.6	6.7	4
5	16.2	12.9	.	34.6	23.7	13.8	23.0	17.1	20.6	20.8	5
6	142.2	69.2	.	45.2	33.7	31.7	15.1	19.3	11.4	9.6	6
7/8/9	205.9	175.4	.	45.7	45.2	33.0	48.7	47.6	42.9	42.2	7
X	0.3	-	.	32.4	36.1	39.4	36.1	18.8	26.2	35.7	8
				57.0	40.5	43.8	45.9	36.9	37.1	45.3	9
				-	0.7	1.6	-	1.9	-	0.5	X

Women - Femmes - Mujeres
ISCO-68 - CITP-68 - CIUO-68 [1] [2]   ISCO-88 - CITP-88 - CIUO-88 [2] [3]

	1999	2000	2001	2002	2003	2004	2005	2006	2007	2008	
Total	439.3	358.0	.	244.2	229.0	224.7	206.0	190.2	184.2	182.8	Total
UB	91.3	108.0	.	103.8	107.6	101.7	84.0	88.4	64.6	83.6	UB
0/1	11.1	18.1	.	1.5	4.0	0.3	2.3	4.8	2.8	1.2	1
2	0.5	3.2	.	5.8	1.7	2.6	3.9	1.0	1.6	3.9	2
3	26.3	16.2	.	6.6	11.9	11.7	9.7	2.9	5.0	7.1	3
4	27.2	16.8	.	15.1	18.1	12.6	18.1	11.7	13.9	17.8	4
5	23.4	18.2	.	24.7	18.1	27.2	24.3	19.1	26.9	20.9	5
6	180.4	109.2	.	43.4	22.3	27.6	11.0	13.4	17.0	16.2	6
7/8/9	76.5	67.7	.	8.8	11.3	4.9	14.7	10.2	13.4	3.8	7
X	0.2	-	.	7.4	10.8	9.9	10.6	17.4	16.3	9.1	8
				26.9	23.2	26.2	27.4	19.2	22.0	19.2	9
				-	-	-	-	2.1	0.7	-	X

United Arab Emirates (BA) [3] [4] — Total unemployment - Chômage total - Desempleo total

Total - Total - Total
ISCO-88 - CITP-88 - CIUO-88

	1999	2000	2001	2002	2003	2004	2005	2006	2007	2008
Total	.	.	.	.	.	.	.	.	.	77.109
UB	.	.	.	.	.	.	.	.	.	63.307
1										0.353
2										1.704
3										3.593
4										2.466
5										1.592
6										0.062
7										1.136
8										0.379
9										2.429
X										0.088

Men - Hommes - Hombres
ISCO-88 - CITP-88 - CIUO-88

	1999	2000	2001	2002	2003	2004	2005	2006	2007	2008
Total	.	.	.	.	.	.	.	.	.	30.254
UB	.	.	.	.	.	.	.	.	.	21.473
1										0.332
2										0.613
3										1.375
4										1.067
5										1.329
6										0.062
7										1.136
8										0.379
9										2.400
X										0.088

Explanatory notes: see p. 451.

[1] Persons aged 13 years and over. [2] Third quarter. [3] Persons aged 15 years and over. [4] February.

Notes explicatives: voir p. 454.

[1] Personnes âgées de 13 ans et plus. [2] Troisième trimestre. [3] Personnes âgées de 15 ans et plus. [4] Février.

Notas explicativas: véase p. 457.

[1] Personas de 13 años y más. [2] Tercer trimestre. [3] Personas de 15 años y más. [4] Febrero.

692   ILO YEARBOOK OF LABOUR STATISTICS 2009   ANNUAIRE DES STATISTIQUES DU TRAVAIL DU BIT 2009   ANUARIO DE ESTADISTICAS DEL TRABAJO DEL OIT 2009

By occupation — **Par profession** — **Por ocupación**

Thousands				Milliers				Millares		
	1999	2000	2001	2002	2003	2004	2005	2006	2007	2008

United Arab Emirates (BA) [1][2]   Total unemployment - Chômage total - Desempleo total

Women - Femmes - Mujeres
ISCO-88 - CITP-88 - CIUO-88

	1999	2000	2001	2002	2003	2004	2005	2006	2007	2008
Total	.	.	.	.	.	.	.	.	.	46.855
UB	.	.	.	.	.	.	.	.	.	41.834
1	.	.	.	.	.	.	.	.	.	0.021
2	.	.	.	.	.	.	.	.	.	1.091
3	.	.	.	.	.	.	.	.	.	2.218
4	.	.	.	.	.	.	.	.	.	1.399
5	.	.	.	.	.	.	.	.	.	0.263
6	.	.	.	.	.	.	.	.	.	-
7	.	.	.	.	.	.	.	.	.	-
8	.	.	.	.	.	.	.	.	.	-
9	.	.	.	.	.	.	.	.	.	0.029
X	.	.	.	.	.	.	.	.	.	-

EUROPE-EUROPE-EUROPA

Austria (BA) [2]   Total unemployment - Chômage total - Desempleo total

Total - Total - Total
ISCO-88 - CITP-88 - CIUO-88

	1999	2000	2001	2002	2003	2004	2005	2006	2007	2008
Total	146.7	138.8	142.5	161.0	168.8 [3]	194.6 [4]	207.7	195.6	185.6	162.3
UB	5.7	10.1	7.2	7.0	8.1 [3]	28.3 [4]	30.7	28.9	28.7	25.3
1	4.2	3.3	3.0	3.8	5.7 [3]	5.2 [4]	5.8	6.2	5.0	4.8
2	5.7	4.8	4.0	7.0	5.4 [3]	7.2 [4]	7.9	7.5	7.4	4.9
3	11.4	10.0	9.8	13.1	15.0 [3]	21.3 [4]	23.3	22.4	19.8	17.0
4	17.9	14.9	14.7	18.4	19.7 [3]	19.2 [4]	18.6	19.6	20.9	14.7
5	27.6	26.6	31.9	33.5	34.6 [3]	30.0 [4]	32.7	29.8	27.9	29.6
6	1.9	2.6	2.9	2.1	2.8 [3]	1.8 [4]	2.0	2.2	2.1	1.4
7	32.5	29.5	29.0	35.8	33.2 [3]	25.9 [4]	27.3	23.7	21.0	17.4
8	15.1	15.2	14.5	13.9	16.3 [3]	12.0 [4]	11.3	12.7	8.9	9.4
9	24.6	21.8	25.5	33.0	27.7 [3]	26.9 [4]	35.0	34.9	36.1	30.6
0	0.1	-	0.1	0.3	0.2 [3]	0.2 [4]	0.3	0.0	0.4	0.1
X	-	-	-	-	- [3]	16.5 [4]	12.8	7.5	7.4	7.2

Men - Hommes - Hombres
ISCO-88 - CITP-88 - CIUO-88

	1999	2000	2001	2002	2003	2004	2005	2006	2007	2008
Total	81.7	73.8	77.0	91.7	94.7 [3]	98.0 [4]	107.8	97.1	89.7	81.8
UB	2.2	4.4	3.4	3.4	3.8 [3]	11.7 [4]	14.9	13.2	12.4	11.2
1	3.1	2.0	1.9	2.9	4.0 [3]	3.2 [4]	3.7	4.4	3.5	3.0
2	2.5	2.4	1.9	3.3	2.5 [3]	3.9 [4]	4.7	3.2	3.4	2.4
3	6.6	4.9	4.9	7.7	8.8 [3]	11.6 [4]	11.7	11.1	10.0	10.2
4	5.7	4.2	3.8	5.5	5.9 [3]	5.0 [4]	5.8	6.2	5.8	3.8
5	9.9	8.7	11.6	13.4	13.9 [3]	9.3 [4]	10.0	7.6	8.4	8.7
6	0.9	1.5	1.4	1.2	0.9 [3]	1.0 [4]	1.0	1.2	0.9	0.7
7	27.5	25.6	25.4	31.5	29.5 [3]	24.0 [4]	23.9	20.8	18.8	16.1
8	11.8	10.9	10.8	10.0	12.0 [3]	10.0 [4]	9.2	10.2	7.5	7.6
9	11.5	9.2	11.9	15.9	12.5 [3]	10.9 [4]	18.2	17.8	16.6	15.8
0	0.1	-	-	0.3	0.2 [3]	0.2 [4]	0.3	0.0	0.4	0.1
X	-	-	-	-	- [3]	7.1 [4]	4.3	1.4	2.1	2.3

Women - Femmes - Mujeres
ISCO-88 - CITP-88 - CIUO-88

	1999	2000	2001	2002	2003	2004	2005	2006	2007	2008
Total	65.0	65.0	65.5	69.3	74.3 [3]	96.6 [4]	100.0	98.5	95.8	80.5
UB	3.5	5.7	3.8	3.6	4.3 [3]	16.6 [4]	15.8	15.7	16.3	14.1
1	1.1	1.3	1.0	1.0	1.7 [3]	2.0 [4]	2.1	1.7	1.5	1.8
2	3.2	2.4	2.2	3.8	2.9 [3]	3.3 [4]	3.2	4.3	4.0	2.5
3	4.8	5.1	4.8	5.4	6.3 [3]	9.7 [4]	11.6	11.3	9.8	6.8
4	12.2	10.7	10.9	12.9	13.8 [3]	14.2 [4]	12.8	13.4	15.1	10.9
5	17.7	17.9	20.4	20.1	20.7 [3]	20.7 [4]	22.7	22.2	19.5	20.9
6	1.0	1.1	1.4	0.9	1.3 [3]	0.8 [4]	1.0	1.0	1.2	0.8
7	5.0	3.9	3.5	4.3	3.7 [3]	1.9 [4]	3.4	2.9	2.2	1.4
8	3.3	4.3	3.8	3.9	4.3 [3]	2.0 [4]	2.2	2.6	1.4	1.8
9	13.1	12.6	13.7	17.1	15.2 [3]	16.0 [4]	16.9	17.1	19.5	14.8
0	.	.	.	.	. [3]	. [4]	.	.	.	0.0
X	-	-	-	-	- [3]	9.4 [4]	8.3	6.1	5.3	4.8

Austria (FB) [2]   Registered unemployment - Chômage enregistré - Desempleo registrado

Total - Total - Total
ISCO-68 - CITP-68 - CIUO-68

	1999	2000	2001	2002	2003	2004	2005	2006	2007	2008
Total	221.7	194.3	203.9	232.4	240.1	243.9	252.7	.	.	.
0/1	19.2	17.0	17.8	21.7	23.4	24.3	24.6	.	.	.
2	0.9	0.9	0.8	1.2	1.4	1.6	1.6	.	.	.
3	32.5	27.2	28.0	32.7	33.7	33.5	33.6	.	.	.
4	22.9	19.3	19.8	22.9	24.1	24.7	25.8	.	.	.
5	43.6	37.7	40.0	43.5	45.7	48.6	51.4	.	.	.
6	4.2	3.9	4.0	4.2	4.3	4.4	4.6	.	.	.
7/8/9	98.0	86.8	93.4	106.0	107.3	106.6	110.7	.	.	.
X	0.1	0.1	0.1	0.2	0.3	0.3	0.3	.	.	.

Explanatory notes: see p. 451.

Notes explicatives: voir p. 454.

Notas explicativas: véase p. 457.

[1] February. [2] Persons aged 15 years and over. [3] Prior to 2003: May and November of each year. [4] Methodology revised; data not strictly comparable.

[1] Février. [2] Personnes âgées de 15 ans et plus. [3] Avant 2003: mai et novembre de chaque année. [4] Méthodologie révisée; les données ne sont pas strictement comparables.

[1] Febrero. [2] Personas de 15 años y más. [3] Antes de 2003: mayo y noviembre de cada año. [4] Metodología revisada; los datos no son estrictamente comparables.

	Thousands — Milliers — Millares									
	1999	2000	2001	2002	2003	2004	2005	2006	2007	2008

Austria (FB) [1] — Registered unemployment - Chômage enregistré - Desempleo registrado

Men - Hommes - Hombres
ISCO-68 - CITP-68 - CIUO-68

	1999	2000	2001	2002	2003	2004	2005	2006	2007	2008
Total	121.5	107.5	115.3	134.4	139.7	140.3	144.2	.	.	.
0/1	9.3	8.1	8.6	11.4	12.5	12.6	12.4	.	.	.
2	0.6	0.5	0.5	0.7	0.9	0.9	1.0	.	.	.
3	9.9	8.2	8.4	10.1	10.7	10.5	10.2	.	.	.
4	7.6	6.4	6.6	8.1	8.6	8.8	8.9	.	.	.
5	13.0	11.6	12.2	14.0	15.1	16.1	17.0	.	.	.
6	2.6	2.4	2.5	2.6	2.7	2.8	2.9	.	.	.
7/8/9	78.2	69.9	76.4	87.5	89.2	88.5	91.7	.	.	.
X	0.1	0.1	0.1	0.1	0.1	0.1	0.1	.	.	.

Women - Femmes - Mujeres
ISCO-68 - CITP-68 - CIUO-68

	1999	2000	2001	2002	2003	2004	2005	2006	2007	2008
Total	100.2	86.8	88.6	98.0	100.4	103.6	108.4	.	.	.
0/1	9.9	8.9	9.2	10.4	10.9	11.7	12.2	.	.	.
2	0.3	0.3	0.3	0.5	0.6	0.6	0.7	.	.	.
3	22.9	18.8	19.4	22.6	23.0	23.1	23.4	.	.	.
4	15.3	12.9	13.9	14.9	15.4	15.9	16.9	.	.	.
5	30.7	27.5	27.8	29.5	30.6	32.4	34.4	.	.	.
6	1.6	1.5	1.5	1.5	1.6	1.6	1.7	.	.	.
7/8/9	19.7	16.9	17.1	18.6	18.1	18.1	19.0	.	.	.
X	0.1	0.1	0.1	0.1	0.2	0.2	0.2	.	.	.

Belgique (BA) [1] — Total unemployment - Chômage total - Desempleo total

Total - Total - Total
ISCO-88 - CITP-88 - CIUO-88

	1999	2000	2001	2002	2003	2004	2005	2006	2007	2008
Total	.	.	286.4	332.1	364.0	380.3	390.3	383.2	353.0	333.7
UB	.	.	105.0	118.7	123.4	125.5	130.3	80.9	79.0	74.0
1	.	.	11.4	12.3	13.7	14.3	14.8	12.7	12.0	11.8
2	.	.	13.9	16.3	20.0	22.2	21.3	23.9	22.8	21.2
3	.	.	12.1	16.9	17.8	22.3	23.0	22.9	19.0	14.8
4	.	.	24.9	32.9	33.7	33.5	37.3	35.6	33.9	31.1
5	.	.	36.0	38.1	43.3	47.9	47.5	48.7	48.3	44.1
6	.	.	1.5	3.0	3.2	4.9	5.3	4.4	4.7	4.4
7	.	.	25.0	30.5	31.8	35.2	33.0	33.2	28.2	27.0
8	.	.	16.7	22.9	29.0	24.7	27.5	28.1	20.6	23.3
9	.	.	39.4	39.8	48.0	49.1	51.3	45.6	48.7	44.2
0	.	.	0.4	0.3	0.5	0.3	-	0.5	0.3	0.5
X	.	.	0.1	0.4	-	-	-	46.6	35.6	37.3

Men - Hommes - Hombres
ISCO-88 - CITP-88 - CIUO-88

	1999	2000	2001	2002	2003	2004	2005	2006	2007	2008
Total	.	.	147.9	168.1	193.0	191.4	196.0	191.0	174.4	170.4
UB	.	.	50.0	54.4	58.4	55.0	60.3	35.0	33.3	35.5
1	.	.	6.5	7.4	8.8	9.1	9.0	7.8	7.1	6.8
2	.	.	6.3	6.1	10.0	10.6	7.5	9.6	8.5	10.1
3	.	.	6.9	9.9	10.4	12.5	12.3	12.2	11.1	9.2
4	.	.	9.1	9.5	11.6	9.4	11.5	12.3	12.6	10.5
5	.	.	11.5	11.7	12.5	13.4	16.0	16.6	15.7	14.1
6	.	.	1.1	2.3	2.6	3.9	3.7	3.1	3.7	3.6
7	.	.	22.4	26.6	29.2	31.4	29.8	29.7	25.6	24.4
8	.	.	13.0	17.9	20.2	17.5	19.5	19.0	15.8	16.8
9	.	.	21.1	21.9	28.7	27.9	27.5	24.7	24.8	23.1
0	.	.	0.2	0.2	0.4	0.3	-	0.4	0.3	0.5
X	.	.	-	0.3	-	-	-	20.5	15.9	15.7

Women - Femmes - Mujeres
ISCO-88 - CITP-88 - CIUO-88

	1999	2000	2001	2002	2003	2004	2005	2006	2007	2008
Total	.	.	138.4	164.0	171.3	188.9	194.3	192.2	178.6	163.2
UB	.	.	55.1	64.3	64.9	70.5	70.0	45.9	45.6	38.5
1	.	.	4.9	4.9	4.9	5.1	5.5	4.9	4.8	4.9
2	.	.	7.6	10.2	10.0	11.6	13.8	14.3	14.3	11.1
3	.	.	5.2	7.0	7.3	9.8	10.5	10.7	7.9	5.6
4	.	.	15.8	23.4	22.0	24.0	26.0	23.3	21.3	20.7
5	.	.	24.5	26.4	30.8	34.5	31.8	32.1	32.5	29.9
6	.	.	0.4	0.7	0.6	1.0	1.6	1.3	1.0	0.8
7	.	.	2.6	3.9	2.6	3.8	4.0	3.5	2.5	2.6
8	.	.	3.7	5.0	8.7	7.1	8.0	9.2	4.8	6.5
9	.	.	18.3	17.9	19.3	21.1	24.0	20.9	24.0	21.0
0	.	.	0.1	0.1	0.1	-	-	0.1	-	-
X	.	.	0.1	0.0	-	-	-	26.1	19.7	21.6

Explanatory notes: see p. 451.
[1] Persons aged 15 years and over.

Notes explicatives: voir p. 454.
[1] Personnes âgées de 15 ans et plus.

Notas explicativas: véase p. 457.
[1] Personas de 15 años y más.

By occupation — Par profession — Por ocupación

	Thousands / Milliers / Millares									
	1999	2000	2001	2002	2003	2004	2005	2006	2007	2008

Bulgaria (BA) [1] — Total unemployment - Chômage total - Desempleo total

Total - Total - Total
ISCO-88 - CITP-88 - CIUO-88

	1999	2000	2001	2002	2003	2004	2005	2006	2007	2008
Total	.	559.0 [2]	661.1 [2]	599.2 [2]	449.1	399.8	334.2	305.7	240.2	199.7
UB	.	103.2 [2]	153.9 [2]	139.1 [2]	99.6	87.8	74.2	65.9	53.2	41.7
1	.	11.4 [2]	13.1 [2]	10.2 [2]	8.9	7.9	5.2	4.2	2.2	2.9
2	.	18.9 [2]	24.7 [2]	21.2 [2]	14.6	12.4	9.5	9.0	6.1	5.6
3	.	38.0 [2]	38.8 [2]	35.4 [2]	25.7	19.7	13.6	13.1	9.7	9.3
4	.	27.0 [2]	30.9 [2]	22.9 [2]	22.0	16.5	14.2	11.8	9.2	6.1
5	.	57.9 [2]	58.2 [2]	59.4 [2]	47.7	44.1	34.2	32.2	25.7	22.8
6	.	22.9 [2]	14.3 [2]	13.7 [2]	9.8	7.2	8.1	8.1	5.1	5.5
7	.	91.1 [2]	79.9 [2]	75.9 [2]	48.6	42.8	36.8	31.7	22.0	20.5
8	.	76.8 [2]	73.0 [2]	61.3 [2]	43.5	41.3	33.5	27.0	19.8	14.8
9	.	107.8 [2]	97.0 [2]	88.2 [2]	70.4	69.0	65.7	65.2	51.7	44.3
X [3]	.	3.7 [2]	77.4 [2]	71.9 [2]	57.7	51.1	39.2	37.5	35.5	26.2

Men - Hommes - Hombres
ISCO-88 - CITP-88 - CIUO-88

	1999	2000	2001	2002	2003	2004	2005	2006	2007	2008
Total	.	306.3 [2]	363.2 [2]	328.7 [2]	246.1	221.6	182.5	156.4	120.7	103.9
UB	.	63.4 [2]	86.7 [2]	81.8 [2]	59.7	48.7	41.2	34.1	29.3	24.9
1	.	8.5 [2]	9.7 [2]	6.3 [2]	5.6	5.4	3.6	2.7	1.4	1.9
2	.	7.6 [2]	8.2 [2]	7.9 [2]	5.2	4.3	3.8	2.4	1.8	1.1
3	.	15.3 [2]	13.5 [2]	14.2 [2]	10.9	7.7	5.9	6.3	4.7	4.8
4	.	6.9 [2]	8.1 [2]	5.8 [2]	4.7	4.8	4.0	2.9	2.0	1.6
5	.	17.6 [2]	21.1 [2]	18.5 [2]	15.6	15.1	10.9	10.7	8.0	6.3
6	.	9.1 [2]	6.5 [2]	5.4 [2]	3.7	3.6	4.0	4.3	2.2	2.8
7	.	65.0 [2]	61.1 [2]	57.0 [2]	36.8	33.4	28.6	21.5	15.1	14.4
8	.	53.1 [2]	55.9 [2]	46.5 [2]	30.6	29.6	23.2	17.1	12.9	9.3
9	.	56.8 [2]	52.5 [2]	49.7 [2]	41.0	41.4	36.1	34.2	25.5	23.9
X [3]	.	3.0 [2]	39.9 [2]	35.5 [2]	31.8	27.7	21.2	20.0	17.8	12.9

Women - Femmes - Mujeres
ISCO-88 - CITP-88 - CIUO-88

	1999	2000	2001	2002	2003	2004	2005	2006	2007	2008
Total	.	252.6 [2]	297.8 [2]	270.4 [2]	203.0	178.2	151.6	149.3	119.5	95.8
UB	.	39.8 [2]	67.2 [2]	57.3 [2]	40.0	39.1	33.0	31.8	24.0	16.8
1	.	2.8 [2]	3.4 [2]	3.8 [2]	3.3	2.5	1.6	1.5	0.8	1.0
2	.	11.3 [2]	16.5 [2]	13.3 [2]	9.4	8.1	5.7	6.6	4.2	4.5
3	.	22.7 [2]	25.4 [2]	21.2 [2]	14.8	12.1	7.7	6.7	5.0	4.5
4	.	20.1 [2]	22.8 [2]	17.2 [2]	17.3	11.7	10.2	8.9	7.3	4.5
5	.	40.4 [2]	37.1 [2]	40.8 [2]	32.1	29.0	23.3	21.5	17.6	16.5
6	.	13.9 [2]	7.7 [2]	8.2 [2]	6.1	3.7	4.1	3.8	2.9	2.7
7	.	26.1 [2]	18.8 [2]	18.9 [2]	11.8	9.4	8.2	10.3	6.9	6.1
8	.	23.7 [2]	17.1 [2]	14.8 [2]	12.9	11.7	10.3	9.8	6.9	5.5
9	.	51.0 [2]	44.5 [2]	38.4 [2]	29.3	27.6	29.6	31.0	26.2	20.4
X [3]	.	0.8 [2]	37.5 [2]	36.4 [2]	25.8	23.4	17.8	17.5	17.7	13.3

Croatia (BA) [4] — Total unemployment - Chômage total - Desempleo total

Total - Total - Total
ISCO-88 - CITP-88 - CIUO-88

	1999	2000	2001	2002	2003	2004	2005	2006	2007	2008
Total	.	.	.	.	255.7	249.7	229.1	198.7	171.0	149.2
UB					85.0	79.3	67.1	59.5	49.3 [5]	45.9
1					4.6	3.4	3.9	3.7	3.0 [5]	.
2					3.6	5.1	5.4	4.4	3.5 [5]	.
3					13.7	11.8	16.0	10.8	11.2 [5]	8.5 [5]
4					19.1	18.3	19.1	12.8	11.2 [5]	11.6 [5]
5					45.9	46.8	41.0	37.2	31.0 [5]	28.6 [5]
6					2.3	2.5	2.0	0.5	1.0 [5]	.
7					27.2	22.3	23.0	19.7	17.1 [5]	14.4 [5]
8					23.0	22.9	22.6	21.2	18.5 [5]	15.0 [5]
9					28.6	34.8	26.4	26.4	23.7 [5]	18.3 [5]
0					2.4	2.2	1.7	2.5	1.5 [5]	.

Men - Hommes - Hombres
ISCO-88 - CITP-88 - CIUO-88

	1999	2000	2001	2002	2003	2004	2005	2006	2007	2008
Total	.	.	.	.	127.7	120.0	114.4	94.4	81.6	67.9
UB					40.4	37.1	31.6	26.3	21.4 [5]	20.0 [5]
1					3.9	2.9	2.8	2.0	2.0 [5]	.
2					0.9	2.6	2.8	2.5	3.0 [5]	.
3					7.9	5.8	9.9	5.1	5.5 [5]	4.6 [5]
4					4.2	4.5	5.4	3.1	3.0 [5]	3.8 [5]
5					16.4	14.5	13.6	11.7	9.8 [5]	7.7 [5]
6					1.6	1.8	1.1	0.6	1.0 [5]	.
7					22.7	19.0	20.2	16.8	14.5 [5]	11.9 [5]
8					12.2	11.8	11.8	12.1	9.0 [5]	7.0 [5]
9					15.1	17.4	13.5	13.7	11.4 [5]	8.4 [5]
0					2.4	2.2	1.4	1.0	1.0 [5]	.

Explanatory notes: see p. 451.

[1] Persons aged 15 to 74 years. [2] June. [3] Incl. the armed forces. [4] Persons aged 15 years and over. [5] Estimate not sufficiently reliable.

Notes explicatives: voir p. 454.

[1] Personnes âgées de 15 à 74 ans. [2] Juin. [3] Y compris les forces armées. [4] Personnes âgées de 15 ans et plus. [5] Estimation pas suffisamment fiable.

Notas explicativas: véase p. 457.

[1] Personas de 15 a 74 años. [2] Junio. [3] Incl. las fuerzas armadas. [4] Personas de 15 años y más. [5] Estimación no suficientemente fiable.

UNEMPLOYMENT CHÔMAGE DESEMPLEO

By occupation Par profession Por ocupación

	Thousands				Milliers				Millares	
	1999	2000	2001	2002	2003	2004	2005	2006	2007	2008

Croatia (BA) [1] Total unemployment - Chômage total - Desempleo total

Women - Femmes - Mujeres
ISCO-88 - CITP-88 - CIUO-88

Total	.	.	.	.	128.1	129.7	114.7	104.2	89.4 [2]	81.3
UB	.	.	.	.	44.6	42.1	35.4	33.2	27.9 [2]	25.9 [2]
1	.	.	.	.	0.7	0.5	1.1	1.7	1.0 [2]	.
2	.	.	.	.	2.7	2.5	2.6	2.9	0.5 [2]	.
3	.	.	.	.	5.8	5.9	6.1	5.7	5.7 [2]	3.8 [2]
4	.	.	.	.	14.9	13.9	13.7	9.7	8.2 [2]	7.8 [2]
5	.	.	.	.	29.5	32.3	27.4	25.5	21.2 [2]	20.9 [2]
6	.	.	.	.	1.1	0.7	0.9	0.8	- [3]	.
7	.	.	.	.	4.5	3.4	2.7	2.8	2.6 [2]	2.5 [2]
8	.	.	.	.	10.8	11.0	10.7	9.2	9.1 [2]	8.1 [2]
9	.	.	.	.	13.5	17.4	12.9	12.7	12.3 [2]	9.9 [2]
0	.	.	.	.	0.1	-	0.3	1.5	0.5 [2]	.

Croatia (FB) [4] Registered unemployment - Chômage enregistré - Desempleo registrado

Total - Total - Total
ISCO-88 - CITP-88 - CIUO-88

Total	.	.	.	.	318.0	318.0	307.8	293.2	254.5	240.5
UB	.	.	.	.	76.8	74.5	69.6	65.6	51.7	44.9
1	.	.	.	.	0.2	0.4	0.3	0.3	0.2	0.2
2	.	.	.	.	6.5	6.8	6.4	6.3	5.5	5.4
3	.	.	.	.	25.8	25.5	21.7	21.0	18.2	17.5
4	.	.	.	.	30.8	30.4	29.7	29.1	26.4	25.6
5	.	.	.	.	49.8	53.3	53.6	51.1	44.6	42.0
6	.	.	.	.	2.0	2.1	2.0	1.8	1.7	1.6
7	.	.	.	.	41.1	40.7	36.1	32.2	28.0	26.5
8	.	.	.	.	24.1	22.4	19.3	17.1	14.8	14.1
9	.	.	.	.	61.5	61.5	69.3	68.9	63.4	62.5
0	.	.	.	.	0.1	0.1	-	-	-	-

Men - Hommes - Hombres
ISCO-88 - CITP-88 - CIUO-88

Total	.	.	.	.	132.0	133.0	124.4	115.5	97.8	90.5
UB	.	.	.	.	32.4	30.6	27.7	25.4	19.4	16.3
1	.	.	.	.	0.2	0.2	0.2	0.2	0.1	0.2
2	.	.	.	.	2.5	2.6	2.3	2.3	2.0	2.1
3	.	.	.	.	11.0	11.4	10.0	9.6	8.3	8.1
4	.	.	.	.	5.8	6.1	6.1	6.0	5.5	5.4
5	.	.	.	.	12.6	14.2	13.8	12.9	11.0	10.0
6	.	.	.	.	0.8	0.9	0.9	0.8	0.8	0.7
7	.	.	.	.	28.1	28.7	26.1	23.1	19.7	18.2
8	.	.	.	.	13.6	14.3	13.6	11.9	9.9	9.4
9	.	.	.	.	25.6	23.5	24.5	23.4	21.1	20.1
0	.	.	.	.	0.1	0.1	-	-	-	-

Women - Femmes - Mujeres
ISCO-88 - CITP-88 - CIUO-88

Total	.	.	.	.	186.0	185.0	183.5	177.6	156.7	150.0
UB	.	.	.	.	44.6	43.9	41.9	40.2	32.3	28.6
1	.	.	.	.	0.1	0.1	0.1	0.1	0.1	0.1
2	.	.	.	.	4.1	4.3	4.1	4.0	3.5	3.3
3	.	.	.	.	14.7	14.1	11.7	11.4	9.9	9.5
4	.	.	.	.	25.1	24.3	23.6	23.0	20.9	20.2
5	.	.	.	.	37.4	39.1	39.8	38.2	33.6	32.0
6	.	.	.	.	1.2	1.1	1.1	1.0	0.9	0.9
7	.	.	.	.	12.8	12.0	10.0	9.1	8.3	8.3
8	.	.	.	.	10.4	8.2	5.7	5.2	4.9	4.7
9	.	.	.	.	35.9	38.0	44.8	45.5	42.3	42.4
0	.	.	.	.	-	-	-	-	-	-

Cyprus (BA) [1] [5] Total unemployment - Chômage total - Desempleo total

Total - Total - Total
ISCO-88 - CITP-88 - CIUO-88

Total	.	14.5	12.8	10.8	14.1	16.7	19.5	17.0	15.4	14.5
UB	.	3.7	3.2	1.6	2.9	3.1	4.1	3.4	3.3	2.4
1	.	0.1	0.2	0.2	0.3	0.2	0.2	0.2	0.2	0.1
2	.	0.3	0.3	0.7	0.6	0.7	1.1	0.8	0.8	1.0
3	.	0.9	1.0	0.7	1.4	1.4	1.4	1.6	0.9	1.0
4	.	1.0	1.3	2.2	1.7	2.2	2.4	2.0	1.6	1.6
5	.	2.3	2.3	1.5	2.9	3.5	3.4	3.4	3.4	3.6
6	.	-	-	0.1	0.1	0.1	0.1	0.1	0.1	0.0
7	.	2.3	1.4	0.8	1.0	1.6	1.9	1.6	1.3	1.2
8	.	1.3	0.9	0.7	0.6	1.1	1.1	0.6	0.8	0.6
9	.	2.6	2.3	2.2	2.6	2.9	3.8	3.3	2.9	2.9
0	.	-	-	0.0	-	-	-	-	0.0	0.0

Explanatory notes: see p. 451.

[1] Persons aged 15 years and over. [2] Estimate not sufficiently reliable. [3] Not indicated due to lack of statistical reliability. [4] 31st Dec. of each year. [5] Government-controlled area.

Notes explicatives: voir p. 454.

[1] Personnes âgées de 15 ans et plus. [2] Estimation pas suffisamment fiable. [3] Non indiqué en raison du manque de fiabilité statistique. [4] 31 déc. de chaque année. [5] Région sous contrôle gouvernemental.

Notas explicativas: véase p. 457.

[1] Personas de 15 años y más. [2] Estimación no suficientemente fiable. [3] No se indica por la falta de confiabilidad estadística. [4] 31 dic. de cada año. [5] Area controlada por el gobierno.

UNEMPLOYMENT — CHÔMAGE — DESEMPLEO

By occupation — Par profession — Por ocupación

Thousands / Milliers / Millares	1999	2000	2001	2002	2003	2004	2005	2006	2007	2008

Cyprus (BA) [1][2] Total unemployment - Chômage total - Desempleo total

Men - Hommes - Hombres
ISCO-88 - CITP-88 - CIUO-88

	1999	2000	2001	2002	2003	2004	2005	2006	2007	2008
Total	.	5.5	4.8	4.7	7.1	7.0	9.0	8.0	7.3	7.0
UB	.	0.8	0.7	0.7	1.4	0.9	1.6	1.5	1.5	1.0
1	.	0.1	0.1	0.1	0.2	0.1	0.2	0.2	0.2	0.1
2	.	0.1	0.1	0.3	0.4	0.3	0.3	0.3	0.3	0.2
3	.	0.4	0.5	0.6	0.8	0.7	0.9	0.9	0.5	0.7
4	.	0.2	0.2	0.5	0.6	0.5	0.4	0.4	0.3	0.4
5	.	0.3	0.7	0.5	1.2	0.9	1.1	1.2	1.1	1.4
6	.	-	-	0.1	0.1	0.1	0.1	0.1	0.0	0.0
7	.	2.2	1.2	0.8	1.0	1.5	1.8	1.6	1.3	1.1
8	.	0.5	0.3	0.3	0.4	0.7	0.8	0.5	0.7	0.6
9	.	0.9	0.9	0.9	1.0	1.3	2.0	1.5	1.4	1.5
0	.	-	-	-	-	-	-	-	0.0	-

Women - Femmes - Mujeres
ISCO-88 - CITP-88 - CIUO-88

	1999	2000	2001	2002	2003	2004	2005	2006	2007	2008
Total	.	8.9	8.1	6.0	7.0	9.7	10.4	9.0	8.1	7.6
UB	.	2.9	2.5	0.9	1.5	2.2	2.5	1.9	1.8	1.4
1	.	-	0.1	0.1	0.1	0.1	0.0	0.1	-	-
2	.	0.2	0.2	0.4	0.2	0.4	0.8	0.5	0.4	0.7
3	.	0.5	0.5	0.1	0.6	0.6	0.5	0.8	0.4	0.3
4	.	0.9	1.2	1.7	1.1	1.7	1.9	1.6	1.3	1.2
5	.	1.9	1.6	1.0	1.7	2.6	2.3	2.1	2.3	2.3
6	.	-	-	-	-	-	0.0	0.1	0.0	-
7	.	0.1	0.1	-	-	0.1	0.1	0.1	0.1	0.1
8	.	0.8	0.6	0.4	0.2	0.4	0.4	0.0	0.1	0.0
9	.	1.6	1.4	1.3	1.6	1.6	1.8	1.8	1.5	1.4
0	.	-	-	0.0	-	-	-	-	-	0.0

Cyprus (FB) [1][2] Registered unemployment - Chômage enregistré - Desempleo registrado

Total - Total - Total
ISCO-88 - CITP-88 - CIUO-88

	1999	2000	2001	2002	2003	2004	2005	2006	2007	2008
Total	11.375	10.934	9.546	10.561	11.961	12.650	13.153	12.824	12.017	11.541
UB	0.579	0.712	0.805	0.768	0.912	0.922	0.878	0.983	0.978	1.013
1	0.250	0.261	0.266	0.290	0.352	0.400	0.424	0.353	0.313	0.291
2	0.761	0.705	0.680	0.752	0.805	0.848	0.922	0.951	1.107	1.202
3	1.137	1.041	1.050	1.218	1.308	1.412	1.458	1.438	1.295	1.048
4	1.418	1.325	1.232	1.567	1.725	1.862	1.879	1.774	1.632	1.545
5	1.475	1.559	1.511	1.849	2.255	2.489	2.384	2.235	2.227	2.251
6	0.052	0.054	0.034	0.033	0.034	0.042	0.042	0.034	0.038	0.034
7	2.100	1.778	1.125	1.008	1.046	1.085	1.376	1.414	1.066	0.989
8	1.209	1.001	0.555	0.592	0.610	0.560	0.577	0.547	0.440	0.405
9	2.385	2.490	2.276	2.473	2.882	2.993	3.130	3.040	2.867	2.718
0	0.009	0.009	0.013	0.013	0.032	0.037	0.084	0.058	0.056	0.046

Men - Hommes - Hombres
ISCO-88 - CITP-88 - CIUO-88

	1999	2000	2001	2002	2003	2004	2005	2006	2007	2008
Total	5.580	5.266	4.535	4.692	5.113	5.415	5.819	5.737	5.210	4.929
UB	0.223	0.280	0.352	0.327	0.386	0.401	0.338	0.411	0.383	0.419
1	0.201	0.202	0.207	0.227	0.276	0.300	0.329	0.269	0.233	0.215
2	0.322	0.298	0.294	0.342	0.334	0.320	0.340	0.332	0.400	0.412
3	0.634	0.579	0.564	0.626	0.632	0.698	0.710	0.674	0.626	0.520
4	0.364	0.321	0.303	0.312	0.326	0.368	0.342	0.332	0.304	0.278
5	0.657	0.710	0.675	0.829	0.943	0.999	0.893	0.809	0.804	0.799
6	0.049	0.050	0.032	0.032	0.032	0.041	0.041	0.034	0.036	0.031
7	1.797	1.523	0.937	0.830	0.870	0.928	1.210	1.241	0.948	0.882
8	0.466	0.471	0.332	0.326	0.341	0.329	0.364	0.387	0.334	0.295
9	0.859	0.826	0.829	0.831	0.942	0.994	1.167	1.193	1.092	1.053
0	0.008	0.007	0.011	0.011	0.031	0.036	0.084	0.057	0.051	0.027

Women - Femmes - Mujeres
ISCO-88 - CITP-88 - CIUO-88

	1999	2000	2001	2002	2003	2004	2005	2006	2007	2008
Total	5.795	5.668	5.011	5.869	6.848	7.235	7.334	7.087	6.808	6.612
UB	0.356	0.432	0.453	0.441	0.526	0.521	0.540	0.572	0.595	0.594
1	0.049	0.059	0.059	0.063	0.076	0.100	0.095	0.084	0.080	0.077
2	0.439	0.407	0.386	0.410	0.471	0.528	0.582	0.619	0.707	0.790
3	0.503	0.462	0.486	0.592	0.676	0.714	0.748	0.764	0.669	0.528
4	1.053	1.004	0.929	1.255	1.399	1.494	1.537	1.442	1.328	1.267
5	0.817	0.849	0.836	1.020	1.312	1.490	1.191	1.426	1.423	1.452
6	0.003	0.004	0.002	0.001	0.002	0.001	0.001	-	0.002	0.004
7	0.304	0.255	0.188	0.178	0.176	0.157	0.166	0.173	0.118	0.107
8	0.743	0.530	0.223	0.266	0.269	0.231	0.213	0.160	0.106	0.110
9	1.527	1.664	1.447	1.642	1.940	1.999	1.963	1.847	1.775	1.665
0	0.001	0.002	0.002	0.002	0.001	0.001	-	0.001	0.005	0.019

Explanatory notes: see p. 451. Notes explicatives: voir p. 454. Notas explicativas: véase p. 457.

[1] Government-controlled area. [2] Persons aged 15 years and over. [1] Région sous contrôle gouvernemental. [2] Personnes âgées de 15 ans et plus. [1] Area controlada por el gobierno. [2] Personas de 15 años y más.

UNEMPLOYMENT   CHÔMAGE   DESEMPLEO

By occupation   Par profession   Por ocupación

	Thousands					Milliers				Millares
	1999	2000	2001	2002	2003	2004	2005	2006	2007	2008

Czech Republic (BA) [1] — Total unemployment - Chômage total - Desempleo total

Total - Total - Total
ISCO-88 - CITP-88 - CIUO-88

	1999	2000	2001	2002	2003	2004	2005	2006	2007	2008
Total	454	455	418	374	399	426	410	371	276	230
UB	70	70	65	63	63	68	69	61	40	37
1	9	6	6	4	3	6	6	6	4	3
2	11	13	11	9	10	9	9	9	6	8
3	37	38	31	28	29	34	33	30	21	17
4	28	29	25	20	25	22	20	18	15	11
5	65	65	64	54	61	59	61	54	41	31
6	11	9	8	7	7	9	8	5	5	3
7	78	79	67	59	62	68	56	55	42	32
8	52	45	43	39	46	47	45	42	27	24
9	73	76	66	60	64	75	72	57	46	40
0	1	1	1	-	-	1	1	-	-	-
X	19	25	32	29	29	29	31	33	29	23

Men - Hommes - Hombres
ISCO-88 - CITP-88 - CIUO-88

	1999	2000	2001	2002	2003	2004	2005	2006	2007	2008
Total	211	212	193	169	175	201	187	169	124	103
UB	32	35	33	29	30	38	36	29	19	16
1	5	3	3	2	2	3	3	3	3	1
2	5	4	4	3	4	5	4	4	3	5
3	14	14	10	11	11	15	11	10	8	7
4	5	4	5	3	4	3	4	3	3	2
5	18	15	16	14	12	12	14	14	9	.8
6	4	4	3	3	3	4	4	2	1	2
7	59	58	51	45	45	49	40	43	30	22
8	31	27	25	21	25	27	25	24	16	13
9	33	37	31	27	29	36	36	26	21	17
0	1	1	1	-	-	1	1	-	-	-
X	6	9	11	11	9	9	8	11	10	9

Women - Femmes - Mujeres
ISCO-88 - CITP-88 - CIUO-88

	1999	2000	2001	2002	2003	2004	2005	2006	2007	2008
Total	243	243	225	205	224	225	223	202	153	127
UB	38	34	32	34	33	30	32	32	21	20
1	4	3	3	2	1	3	3	2	1	2
2	7	9	7	6	6	4	5	5	3	4
3	23	24	21	17	18	19	22	21	12	10
4	24	24	20	17	21	19	15	15	12	9
5	46	49	49	40	49	47	47	41	32	23
6	7	5	5	5	4	5	4	3	3	1
7	20	21	16	14	17	19	16	13	11	10
8	21	18	17	18	21	20	20	18	11	11
9	40	39	35	33	35	39	37	31	25	23
0	-	-	-	-	-	-	-	-	-	-
X	13	16	20	19	19	19	23	21	20	14

Denmark (BA) [2] — Total unemployment - Chômage total - Desempleo total

Total - Total - Total
ISCO-88 - CITP-88 - CIUO-88

	1999	2000	2001	2002	2003	2004	2005	2006	2007	2008
Total	.	131.074	.	134.026	157.559	162.552	143.296	117.896	114.539	98.380
UB	.	17.403	.	20.972	28.820	26.928	26.686	23.579	24.096	15.485
1	.	5.488	.	4.451	5.790	4.263	4.263	4.819	3.633	3.693
2	.	8.118	.	10.720	12.815	11.810	10.664	8.935	7.333	7.636
3	.	15.110	.	17.443	19.028	21.564	17.233	15.435	11.643	11.587
4	.	15.307	.	13.362	14.591	16.409	13.643	11.288	6.750	8.290
5	.	21.391	.	21.045	22.208	27.444	23.690	21.778	17.028	17.796
6	.	1.619	.	1.482	1.534	3.085	-	-	-	-
7	.	10.222	.	11.744	14.567	14.472	10.267	6.727	4.262	6.449
8	.	9.274	.	8.312	12.736	12.186	11.244	6.454	5.682	6.655
9	.	24.849	.	23.238	24.135	23.960	22.468	16.450	15.919	19.044
0	.	0.509	.	0.472	0.396	0.040	-	-	-	-
X	.	1.784	.	0.786	0.938	0.390	2.764	2.431	18.193	-

Men - Hommes - Hombres
ISCO-88 - CITP-88 - CIUO-88

	1999	2000	2001	2002	2003	2004	2005	2006	2007	2008
Total	.	61.246	.	66.021	75.734	79.867	69.433	53.421	55.079	47.077
UB	.	8.349	.	10.678	14.148	15.457	12.564	11.312	11.731	7.031
1	.	3.859	.	3.450	4.360	2.486	4.263	2.530	1.155	2.405
2	.	4.095	.	6.185	7.016	6.146	6.121	3.828	3.753	4.053
3	.	6.272	.	8.337	7.933	10.199	7.308	7.126	4.624	4.556
4	.	3.147	.	3.017	2.762	3.888	3.628	2.666	1.899	2.971
5	.	4.621	.	4.108	4.465	6.259	5.846	4.611	5.007	4.077
6	.	1.132	.	1.040	1.237	2.298	-	-	-	-
7	.	8.913	.	10.327	12.926	13.080	8.859	5.732	4.262	5.761
8	.	5.808	.	5.057	8.086	7.092	7.290	4.401	4.537	4.407
9	.	13.374	.	12.795	11.766	12.765	13.090	8.783	9.263	10.071
0	.	0.509	.	0.432	0.396	0.020	-	-	-	-
X	.	1.167	.	0.596	0.639	0.179	0.093	2.431	8.848	-

Explanatory notes: see p. 451.   Notes explicatives: voir p. 454.   Notas explicativas: véase p. 457.

[1] Persons aged 15 years and over. [2] Persons aged 15 to 66 years.   [1] Personnes âgées de 15 ans et plus. [2] Personnes âgées de 15 à 66 ans.   [1] Personas de 15 años y más. [2] Personas de 15 a 66 años.

	Thousands			Milliers				Millares		
	1999	2000	2001	2002	2003	2004	2005	2006	2007	2008
Denmark (BA) [1]			Total unemployment - Chômage total - Desempleo total							
Women - Femmes - Mujeres										
ISCO-88 - CITP-88 - CIUO-88										
Total	.	69.828	.	68.005	81.825	82.686	73.863	64.475	59.460	51.303
UB	.	9.054	.	10.294	14.672	11.471	14.123	12.267	12.365	8.454
1	.	1.630	.	1.002	1.430	1.777	-	2.289	2.478	1.288
2	.	4.023	.	4.535	5.799	5.664	4.543	5.107	3.580	3.583
3	.	8.837	.	9.106	11.095	11.365	9.925	8.308	7.019	7.031
4	.	12.160	.	10.345	11.829	12.521	10.015	8.622	4.851	5.319
5	.	16.771	.	16.937	17.743	21.186	17.845	17.167	12.021	13.719
6	.	0.487	.	0.442	0.298	0.788	-	-	-	-
7	.	1.308	.	1.417	1.641	1.392	1.408	0.995	-	0.688
8	.	3.466	.	3.256	4.650	5.094	3.954	2.053	1.145	2.248
9	.	11.474	.	10.443	12.369	11.196	9.379	7.667	6.656	8.973
0	.	-	.	0.040	-	0.020	-	-	-	-
X	.	0.617	.	0.189	0.299	0.212	2.671	-	9.345	-
España (BA) [2]			Total unemployment - Chômage total - Desempleo total							
Total - Total - Total										
ISCO-88 - CITP-88 - CIUO-88										
Total	2 722.2	2 496.4	1 904.4 [3]	2 155.3	2 242.2	2 213.6	1 912.4 [3]	1 837.1	1 833.9	2 590.6
UB	626.2	519.3	333.3 [3]	358.7	374.2	336.2	246.5 [3]	206.7	198.1	231.7
1	30.1	29.0	18.3 [3]	29.2	24.5	28.2	14.2 [3]	17.7	16.8	23.3
2	77.2	82.5	69.9 [3]	76.8	90.1	87.1	56.5 [3]	57.1	49.7	63.7
3	87.8	96.1	89.0 [3]	108.4	110.8	122.9	81.7 [3]	83.5	75.3	119.4
4	150.4	132.6	107.6 [3]	136.4	145.9	136.4	93.6 [3]	97.6	94.1	123.0
5	316.4	306.2	249.7 [3]	296.2	316.9	315.0	238.4 [3]	241.7	262.4	328.9
6	35.9	32.4	24.2 [3]	24.7	27.3	29.5	19.0 [3]	13.4	14.9	19.7
7	221.3	213.7	190.4 [3]	227.2	229.0	225.3	169.8 [3]	166.5	183.2	386.1
8	105.4	98.8	101.9 [3]	113.8	113.1	113.7	79.8 [3]	80.9	82.9	142.0
9	552.4	549.0	448.8 [3]	506.6	538.7	547.5	340.3 [3]	344.9	349.3	515.3
0	1.0	2.1	1.5 [3]	2.7	2.6	2.7	1.3 [3]	2.0	1.0	1.9
X [4]	518.0	434.7	269.9 [3]	274.9	269.3	269.4	571.5 [3]	525.0	506.2	635.6
Men - Hommes - Hombres										
ISCO-88 - CITP-88 - CIUO-88										
Total	1 158.3	1 037.4	828.0 [3]	929.4	976.4	970.8	862.9 [3]	791.5	815.2	1 311.0
UB	207.9	173.0	110.3 [3]	128.7	140.5	128.3	90.0 [3]	75.5	76.7	92.4
1	16.7	17.3	9.3 [3]	15.2	14.4	17.3	7.7 [3]	10.0	9.3	14.4
2	25.2	28.9	23.3 [3]	25.2	38.6	36.3	23.9 [3]	19.3	18.8	26.1
3	44.6	44.0	44.9 [3]	50.0	51.4	59.4	40.8 [3]	37.8	38.4	57.5
4	36.6	32.4	27.7 [3]	34.3	36.0	31.5	27.5 [3]	22.1	25.7	30.4
5	95.9	81.4	68.2 [3]	76.3	80.6	80.5	69.2 [3]	66.3	73.2	97.7
6	27.0	23.0	16.7 [3]	17.9	18.6	18.3	13.2 [3]	9.8	11.5	15.9
7	185.2	176.6	160.5 [3]	193.0	195.9	191.8	148.4 [3]	146.5	162.7	360.6
8	72.0	64.5	67.4 [3]	76.3	77.3	75.6	56.5 [3]	60.0	57.5	108.2
9	270.0	260.4	219.0 [3]	234.7	247.6	254.8	170.9 [3]	164.0	165.8	277.6
0	0.9	2.0	1.3 [3]	2.2	1.9	1.8	1.1 [3]	1.6	0.8	1.8
X [4]	176.3	134.0	79.5 [3]	75.7	73.7	75.2	213.8 [3]	178.5	174.8	228.6
Women - Femmes - Mujeres										
ISCO-88 - CITP-88 - CIUO-88										
Total	1 564.0	1 459.0	1 076.3 [3]	1 225.9	1 265.8	1 242.9	1 049.6 [3]	1 045.6	1 018.7	1 279.6
UB	418.3	346.3	223.0 [3]	230.0	233.7	207.9	156.5 [3]	131.2	121.4	139.3
1	13.4	11.7	9.0 [3]	14.0	10.0	10.9	6.4 [3]	7.7	7.4	8.9
2	52.0	53.6	46.6 [3]	51.6	51.4	50.8	32.6 [3]	37.8	31.0	37.6
3	43.2	52.2	44.1 [3]	58.4	59.4	63.5	40.9 [3]	45.7	36.8	61.9
4	113.7	100.2	80.0 [3]	102.1	110.0	104.9	66.1 [3]	75.5	68.4	92.6
5	220.5	224.8	181.5 [3]	219.9	236.3	234.5	169.2 [3]	175.4	189.2	231.2
6	8.9	9.4	7.5 [3]	6.8	8.7	11.3	5.9 [3]	3.7	3.4	3.8
7	36.0	37.1	29.8 [3]	34.2	33.1	33.5	21.4 [3]	20.0	20.4	25.6
8	33.7	34.2	34.5 [3]	37.4	35.8	38.1	23.3 [3]	20.9	25.4	33.8
9	282.4	288.7	229.9 [3]	271.9	291.2	292.6	169.4 [3]	180.9	183.5	237.7
0	0.1	0.1	0.2 [3]	0.5	0.7	0.9	0.3 [3]	0.4	0.2	0.1
X [4]	341.7	300.7	190.4 [3]	199.3	195.6	194.2	357.7 [3]	346.5	331.4	407.0
España (FB) [2]			Registered unemployment - Chômage enregistré - Desempleo registrado							
Total - Total - Total										
ISCO-88 - CITP-88 - CIUO-88										
Total	.	.	.	.	.	.	2 069.9	2 039.4	2 039.0	2 539.9
1	.	.	.	.	.	.	20.7	20.6	20.8	24.1
2	.	.	.	.	.	.	158.7	140.1	127.6	137.6
3	.	.	.	.	.	.	153.5	151.5	150.0	179.4
4	.	.	.	.	.	.	270.5	263.1	257.9	295.9
5	.	.	.	.	.	.	427.0	430.4	431.8	497.0
6	.	.	.	.	.	.	50.9	48.4	47.4	58.5
7	.	.	.	.	.	.	251.8	245.8	255.5	402.4
8	.	.	.	.	.	.	138.1	138.1	138.6	182.8
9	.	.	.	.	.	.	597.7	600.0	608.0	760.6
0	.	.	.	.	.	.	1.0	1.5	1.4	1.6

Explanatory notes: see p. 451.   Notes explicatives: voir p. 454.   Notas explicativas: véase p. 457.

[1] Persons aged 15 to 66 years. [2] Persons aged 16 to 74 years. [3] Methodology revised; data not strictly comparable. [4] Unemployed whose last job was 3 years ago and over.

[1] Personnes âgées de 15 à 66 ans. [2] Personnes âgées de 16 à 74 ans. [3] Méthodologie révisée; les données ne sont pas strictement comparables. [4] Chômeurs dont le dernier travail date de 3 ans ou plus.

[1] Personas de 15 a 66 años. [2] Personas de 16 a 74 años. [3] Metodología revisada; los datos no son estrictamente comparables. [4] Desempleados cuyo último trabajo fue hace 3 años o más.

3E   UNEMPLOYMENT   CHÔMAGE   DESEMPLEO

By occupation   Par profession   Por ocupación

	Thousands					Milliers				Millares
	1999	2000	2001	2002	2003	2004	2005	2006	2007	2008

España (FB) [1]   Registered unemployment - Chômage enregistré - Desempleo registrado

Men - Hommes - Hombres
ISCO-88 - CITP-88 - CIUO-88

	1999	2000	2001	2002	2003	2004	2005	2006	2007	2008
Total	.	.	.	.	.	.	818.0	788.2	791.8	1 146.9
1	.	.	.	.	.	.	16.1	15.5	15.4	17.7
2	.	.	.	.	.	.	49.9	43.3	39.9	46.1
3	.	.	.	.	.	.	74.3	72.9	72.1	90.2
4	.	.	.	.	.	.	55.5	51.2	49.0	58.1
5	.	.	.	.	.	.	79.2	77.3	76.1	96.7
6	.	.	.	.	.	.	29.6	28.2	27.6	36.9
7	.	.	.	.	.	.	202.0	197.4	208.2	352.3
8	.	.	.	.	.	.	77.1	77.9	79.9	120.1
9	.	.	.	.	.	.	233.5	223.6	222.6	327.7
0	.	.	.	.	.	.	0.8	1.1	1.0	1.2

Women - Femmes - Mujeres
ISCO-88 - CITP-88 - CIUO-88

	1999	2000	2001	2002	2003	2004	2005	2006	2007	2008
Total	.	.	.	.	.	.	1 251.8	1 251.2	1 247.2	1 393.0
1	.	.	.	.	.	.	4.7	5.0	5.4	6.3
2	.	.	.	.	.	.	108.7	96.8	87.8	91.6
3	.	.	.	.	.	.	79.1	78.6	77.8	89.3
4	.	.	.	.	.	.	215.0	211.9	208.9	237.8
5	.	.	.	.	.	.	347.8	353.2	355.7	400.2
6	.	.	.	.	.	.	21.3	20.1	19.8	21.6
7	.	.	.	.	.	.	49.8	48.5	47.2	50.1
8	.	.	.	.	.	.	60.9	60.2	58.7	62.8
9	.	.	.	.	.	.	364.2	376.5	385.4	432.9
0	.	.	.	.	.	.	0.3	0.4	0.4	0.4

Estonia (BA) [2]   Total unemployment - Chômage total - Desempleo total

Total - Total - Total
ISCO-88 - CITP-88 - CIUO-88

	1999	2000	2001	2002	2003	2004	2005	2006	2007	2008
Total	89.9 [3]	83.1	67.2	66.2	63.6	52.2	40.5	32.0	38.4	
UB	12.4 [3]	12.4	10.9	12.5	14.0	12.1	10.2	8.3	7.3	
1	4.5 [3]	2.9	2.1	3.2	1.8	2.0	-	-	1.4	
2	2.9 [3]	2.7	1.5	2.2	2.0	2.4	-	-	1.7	
3	6.6 [3]	7.5	4.2	5.9	4.9	1.8	1.6	1.4	2.6	
4	3.0 [3]	4.9	3.8	1.8	2.0	1.8	-	-	2.2	
5	12.0 [3]	10.3	10.2	9.0	9.9	6.8	4.6	4.1	4.8	
6	3.3 [3]	2.0	1.6	1.5	1.2	0.9	-	-	-	
7	17.8 [3]	16.2	13.4	11.6	10.6	10.1	8.2	6.5	7.0	
8	14.4 [3]	13.5	8.6	7.5	8.3	8.2	7.3	4.9	4.6	
9	13.0 [3]	10.5	10.9	11.0	9.0	6.1	4.9	4.2	5.8	
0	-	-	-	-	-	-	-	-	-	

Men - Hommes - Hombres
ISCO-88 - CITP-88 - CIUO-88

	1999	2000	2001	2002	2003	2004	2005	2006	2007	2008
Total	49.5 [3]	43.7	36.1	34.2	34.7	28.9	21.3	18.9	20.2	
UB	5.4 [3]	5.1	5.3	6.2	8.0	7.3	4.7	5.2	4.0	
1	- [3]	-	-	-	0.3	1.0	-	-	-	
2	- [3]	-	1.1	2.0	1.7	1.7	-	-	-	
3	1.2 [3]	2.8	1.1	2.0	1.7	0.8	-	-	0.8	
4	- [3]	-	1.1	0.4	0.9	1.0	-	-	0.5	
5	3.0 [3]	1.9	1.7	1.7	2.9	1.0	-	-	0.9	
6	1.8 [3]	1.1	-	-	0.2	0.3	-	-	-	
7	14.7 [3]	13.2	11.4	9.5	7.7	7.6	6.8	5.7	6.4	
8	11.6 [3]	9.5	6.6	5.9	6.5	5.0	4.2	3.0	2.8	
9	7.6 [3]	6.1	6.2	5.3	4.8	3.2	2.7	2.5	2.7	
0	-	-	-	-	-	-	-	-	-	

Women - Femmes - Mujeres
ISCO-88 - CITP-88 - CIUO-88

	1999	2000	2001	2002	2003	2004	2005	2006	2007	2008
Total	40.5 [3]	39.3	31.0	32.0	28.9	23.3	19.2	18.9	18.1	
UB	7.1 [3]	7.3	5.6	6.3	6.0	4.8	5.5	5.2	3.3	
1	- [3]	-	-	-	1.5	1.0	-	-	-	
2	- [3]	-	0.4	0.2	0.3	0.7	-	-	-	
3	5.4 [3]	4.7	3.1	3.9	3.2	1.0	-	-	1.8	
4	- [3]	-	2.7	1.4	1.1	0.8	-	-	1.7	
5	9.0 [3]	8.3	8.6	7.3	7.0	5.8	-	-	3.9	
6	1.5 [3]	0.9	-	-	1.0	0.6	-	-	-	
7	3.1 [3]	3.0	1.9	2.1	2.8	2.5	1.4	5.7	0.6	
8	2.9 [3]	4.0	2.0	1.6	1.8	3.2	3.0	3.0	1.8	
9	5.4 [3]	4.5	4.7	5.7	4.2	2.9	2.1	2.5	3.1	
0	-	-	-	-	-	-	-	-	-	

Explanatory notes: see p. 451.

[1] Persons aged 16 to 74 years. [2] Persons aged 15 to 74 years.
[3] Prior to 2000: second quarter of each year.

Notes explicatives: voir p. 454.

[1] Personnes âgées de 16 à 74 ans. [2] Personnes âgées de 15 à 74 ans. [3] Avant 2000: deuxième trimestre de chaque année.

Notas explicativas: véase p. 457.

[1] Personas de 16 a 74 años. [2] Personas de 15 a 74 años. [3] Antes de 2000: segundo trimestre de cada año.

UNEMPLOYMENT — CHÔMAGE — DESEMPLEO

By occupation — Par profession — Por ocupación

Thousands — Milliers — Millares	1999	2000	2001	2002	2003	2004	2005	2006	2007	2008

Finland (BA) [1]

Total unemployment - Chômage total - Desempleo total

Total - Total - Total
ISCO-88 - CITP-88 - CIUO-88

	1999	2000	2001	2002	2003	2004	2005	2006	2007	2008
Total	.	253	238	237	235	228	220	204	183	172 [2]
UB	.	79	78	79	84	80	80	80	68	23 [2]
1	.	4	4	5	6	5	6	4	4	4 [2]
2	.	10	9	10	11	11	14	10	10	13 [2]
3	.	17	19	17	14	17	15	14	12	15 [2]
4	.	16	14	13	14	13	11	10	9	10 [2]
5	.	33	29	27	27	25	23	24	20	24 [2]
6	.	11	9	8	9	6	6	6	6	6 [2]
7	.	30	30	32	31	29	27	21	18	20 [2]
8	.	16	15	16	16	14	13	12	10	12 [2]
9	.	33	31	29	26	27	26	23	21	28 [2]
X	.	3	-	-	-	-	-	-	4	17 [2]

Men - Hommes - Hombres
ISCO-88 - CITP-88 - CIUO-88

	1999	2000	2001	2002	2003	2004	2005	2006	2007	2008
Total	.	122	117	123	124	118	111	101	90	85 [2]
UB	.	34	34	37	40	38	36	37	30	11 [2]
1	.	3	3	3	4	4	4	3	3	2 [2]
2	.	4	4	5	5	5	7	5	5	6 [2]
3	.	8	8	8	7	9	7	6	5	6 [2]
4	.	4	3	3	3	3	3	3	2	3 [2]
5	.	6	5	5	5	4	4	5	4	4 [2]
6	.	7	7	6	6	4	3	3	3	3 [2]
7	.	26	27	29	29	27	24	18	16	18 [2]
8	.	12	11	12	11	10	10	10	8	9 [2]
9	.	15	15	15	13	13	13	11	10	14 [2]
X	.	2	-	-	-	-	-	-	3	9 [2]

Women - Femmes - Mujeres
ISCO-88 - CITP-88 - CIUO-88

	1999	2000	2001	2002	2003	2004	2005	2006	2007	2008
Total	.	131	121	114	111	111	109	103	93	87 [2]
UB	.	45	44	42	44	42	44	43	38	12 [2]
1	.	1	1	1	2	1	2	1	1	1 [2]
2	.	6	5	5	5	6	7	5	5	7 [2]
3	.	9	10	9	7	8	8	8	6	9 [2]
4	.	12	11	10	10	10	8	7	7	7 [2]
5	.	27	24	23	21	21	19	19	16	20 [2]
6	.	4	3	2	2	2	3	3	3	3 [2]
7	.	4	3	2	2	2	3	3	2	2 [2]
8	.	4	4	4	5	4	3	2	2	3 [2]
9	.	18	16	15	13	14	13	12	11	14 [2]
X	.	1	-	-	-	-	-	-	2	8 [2]

Germany (BA) [3]

Total unemployment - Chômage total - Desempleo total

Total - Total - Total
ISCO-88 - CITP-88 - CIUO-88

	1999	2000	2001	2002	2003	2004	2005	2006	2007	2008
Total	3 503	3 127 [4]	3 150	3 486 [5]	4 023 [4]	4 385 [6]	.	4 279 [2]	3 608	3 141
UB	240	214 [4]	197	228 [5]	258 [4]	310 [6]	.	455 [2]	386	336
1	107	86 [4]	81	135 [5]	171 [4]	183 [6]	.	173 [2]	143	125
2	179	153 [4]	150	162 [5]	197 [4]	216 [6]	.	185 [2]	154	126
3	410	379 [4]	360	373 [5]	440 [4]	452 [6]	.	444 [2]	377	305
4	352	318 [4]	319	336 [5]	401 [4]	430 [6]	.	408 [2]	341	296
5	404	368 [4]	371	408 [5]	457 [4]	517 [6]	.	595 [2]	545	488
6	104	87 [4]	86	93 [5]	106 [4]	108 [6]	.	103 [2]	86	75
7	761	674 [4]	712	778 [5]	918 [4]	1 025 [6]	.	812 [2]	631	526
8	335	276 [4]	293	322 [5]	382 [4]	388 [6]	.	390 [2]	302	265
9	481	452 [4]	463	501 [5]	544 [4]	618 [6]	.	633 [2]	571	530
0	12	14 [4]	13	20 [5]	18 [4]	22 [6]	.	19 [2]	15	14
X	118	106 [4]	105	130 [5]	130 [4]	116 [6]	.	62 [2]	57	56

Men - Hommes - Hombres
ISCO-88 - CITP-88 - CIUO-88

	1999	2000	2001	2002	2003	2004	2005	2006	2007	2008
Total	1 905	1 691 [4]	1 754	1 982 [5]	2 316 [4]	2 543 [6]	.	2 358 [2]	1 944	1 690
UB	122	105 [4]	97	113 [5]	142 [4]	164 [6]	.	228 [2]	194	157
1	75	58 [4]	57	74 [5]	94 [4]	107 [6]	.	91 [2]	80	66
2	107	84 [4]	88	91 [5]	116 [4]	128 [6]	.	106 [2]	89	69
3	143	130 [4]	138	149 [5]	179 [4]	180 [6]	.	183 [2]	155	130
4	96	81 [4]	85	101 [5]	115 [4]	134 [6]	.	124 [2]	101	93
5	86	85 [4]	79	103 [5]	117 [4]	125 [6]	.	159 [2]	145	131
6	56	45 [4]	46	47 [5]	57 [4]	66 [6]	.	60 [2]	48	46
7	633	572 [4]	604	676 [5]	795 [4]	897 [6]	.	702 [2]	543	452
8	246	206 [4]	223	250 [5]	297 [4]	304 [6]	.	302 [2]	228	207
9	265	254 [4]	267	286 [5]	307 [4]	352 [6]	.	346 [2]	312	294
0	12	14 [4]	12	20 [5]	18 [4]	21 [6]	.	19 [2]	15	13
X	64	57 [4]	58	72 [5]	79 [4]	65 [6]	.	38 [2]	34	32

Explanatory notes: see p. 451.
[1] Persons aged 15 to 74 years. [2] Methodology revised; data not strictly comparable. [3] Persons aged 15 years and over. [4] May. [5] Prior to 2002: April of each year. [6] March.

Notes explicatives: voir p. 454.
[1] Personnes âgées de 15 à 74 ans. [2] Méthodologie révisée; les données ne sont pas strictement comparables. [3] Personnes âgées de 15 ans et plus. [4] Mai. [5] Avant 2002: avril de chaque année. [6] Mars.

Notas explicativas: véase p. 457.
[1] Personas de 15 a 74 años. [2] Metodología revisada; los datos no son estrictamente comparables. [3] Personas de 15 años y más. [4] Mayo. [5] Antes del 2002: abril de cada año. [6] Marzo.

3E

UNEMPLOYMENT	CHÔMAGE	DESEMPLEO
By occupation	Par profession	Por ocupación

	Thousands					Milliers				Millares
	1999	2000	2001	2002	2003	2004	2005	2006	2007	2008

Germany (BA) [1]

Total unemployment - Chômage total - Desempleo total

Women - Femmes - Mujeres
ISCO-88 - CITP-88 - CIUO-88

	1999	2000	2001	2002	2003	2004	2005	2006	2007	2008
Total	1 598	1 436 [2]	1 396	1 504 [3]	1 707 [2]	1 841 [4]	.	1 921 [5]	1 664	1 451
UB	118	109 [2]	100	115 [3]	116 [2]	146 [4]	.	226 [5]	192	179
1	32	28 [2]	24	61 [3]	77 [2]	76 [4]	.	83 [5]	62	60
2	72	69 [2]	62	71 [3]	82 [2]	87 [4]	.	78 [5]	65	57
3	267	249 [2]	222	224 [3]	261 [2]	272 [4]	.	260 [5]	222	175
4	256	237 [2]	234	235 [3]	286 [2]	296 [4]	.	284 [5]	239	204
5	318	283 [2]	292	305 [3]	340 [2]	392 [4]	.	436 [5]	399	357
6	48	42 [2]	40	46 [3]	49 [2]	42 [4]	.	43 [5]	39	28
7	128	102 [2]	108	102 [3]	123 [2]	128 [4]	.	110 [5]	89	74
8	89	70 [2]	70	72 [3]	85 [2]	84 [4]	.	88 [5]	73	58
9	216	198 [2]	196	215 [3]	238 [2]	267 [4]	.	287 [5]	259	236
0	-	- [2]	-	1 [3]	- [2]	1 [4]	.	- [5]	1	1
X	54	49 [2]	47	58 [3]	51 [2]	51 [4]	.	25 [5]	24	24

Germany (FB) [6]

Registered unemployment - Chômage enregistré - Desempleo registrado

Total - Total - Total
ISCO-88 - CITP-88 - CIUO-88

	1999	2000	2001	2002	2003	2004	2005	2006	2007	2008
Total	4 101	3 890	3 853	4 061	4 377	4 381	4 493	4 107	3 440	2 973
1	126	120	125	139	150	144	137	114	94	82
2	192	177	174	190	214	211	196	161	119	100
3	444	410	398	423	474	483	477	404	307	261
4	556	528	518	541	585	572	543	495	398	329
5	513	497	499	521	571	590	639	627	565	497
6	52	51	52	54	58	58	54	45	40	35
7	539	519	541	607	667	664	640	477	334	294
8	446	408	397	418	444	440	516	476	455	394
9	1 228	1 174	1 146	1 165	1 213	1 218	1 202	1 136	980	852
X	6	5	3	2	1	1	89	172	148	129

Men - Hommes - Hombres
ISCO-88 - CITP-88 - CIUO-88

	1999	2000	2001	2002	2003	2004	2005	2006	2007	2008
Total	2 161	2 053	2 064	2 240	2 446	2 449	2 411	2 142	1 734	1 523
1	92	87	91	100	108	102	96	79	60	55
2	116	105	102	114	130	128	117	96	70	59
3	178	162	157	175	201	202	192	167	128	110
4	116	111	110	121	133	133	125	113	91	79
5	100	96	102	115	133	140	152	151	133	122
6	21	21	21	23	25	26	25	22	20	18
7	473	458	481	544	601	601	579	427	294	261
8	300	275	272	295	321	323	344	336	317	278
9	761	735	725	751	793	795	744	665	552	481
X	4	3	2	1	1	1	37	86	69	59

Women - Femmes - Mujeres
ISCO-88 - CITP-88 - CIUO-88

	1999	2000	2001	2002	2003	2004	2005	2006	2007	2008
Total	1 940	1 836	1 789	1 821	1 931	1 933	2 082	1 964	1 706	1 450
1	34	33	34	39	43	42	41	35	33	27
2	76	72	72	76	84	84	79	64	49	41
3	266	248	241	248	273	281	285	238	179	151
4	440	417	408	420	452	439	418	382	307	250
5	413	400	398	406	438	450	487	475	432	375
6	31	31	30	31	32	32	29	23	20	17
7	66	61	60	63	66	63	61	50	41	33
8	145	133	124	123	123	118	171	140	138	115
9	467	439	421	414	420	423	458	471	428	371
X	2	2	1	1	0	0	53	86	79	70

Greece (BA) [1] [7]

Total unemployment - Chômage total - Desempleo total

Total - Total - Total
ISCO-88 - CITP-88 - CIUO-88

	1999	2000	2001	2002	2003	2004	2005	2006	2007	2008
Total	543.3	519.3	478.4	462.1	441.8	492.7	466.7	427.4	398.0	357.1
UB	257.6	240.4	229.7	190.7	184.0	212.6	178.6	156.8	139.9	130.3
1	10.9	11.7	10.6	8.9	8.2	13.1	11.9	10.1	8.2	7.4
2	16.4	13.3	12.5	12.6	12.6	17.6	19.8	14.3	17.4	12.6
3	16.8	14.7	13.6	20.2	16.5	20.7	21.7	18.8	16.7	14.9
4	29.2	33.7	32.1	39.9	35.1	36.2	45.1	44.2	39.4	30.9
5	56.2	56.6	52.2	62.1	58.6	61.0	59.5	66.5	60.4	53.6
6	8.3	4.9	3.9	3.1	4.7	3.5	3.6	2.2	3.0	3.7
7	59.6	52.2	44.4	38.9	38.6	39.3	44.5	38.1	33.3	26.6
8	22.1	26.0	20.5	22.2	19.6	22.2	22.2	18.9	20.0	19.6
9	34.6	32.2	32.8	34.6	37.1	33.5	34.7	35.8	35.6	33.8
X	31.6	33.5	26.1	28.7	26.9	33.0	25.2	21.7	24.1	23.8

Explanatory notes: see p. 451.

[1] Persons aged 15 years and over. [2] May. [3] Prior to 2002: April of each year. [4] March. [5] Methodology revised; data not strictly comparable. [6] Persons aged 15 to 64 years. [7] Second quarter of each year.

Notes explicatives: voir p. 454.

[1] Personnes âgées de 15 ans et plus. [2] Mai. [3] Avant 2002: avril de chaque année. [4] Mars. [5] Méthodologie révisée; les données ne sont pas strictement comparables. [6] Personnes âgées de 15 à 64 ans. [7] Deuxième trimestre de chaque année.

Notas explicativas: véase p. 457.

[1] Personas de 15 años y más. [2] Mayo. [3] Antes del 2002: abril de cada año. [4] Marzo. [5] Metodología revisada; los datos no son estrictamente comparables. [6] Personas de 15 a 64 años. [7] Segundo trimestre de cada año.

By occupation — Par profession — Por ocupación

	Thousands			Milliers				Millares		
	1999	2000	2001	2002	2003	2004	2005	2006	2007	2008

Greece (BA) [1] [2] — Total unemployment - Chômage total - Desempleo total

Men - Hommes - Hombres
ISCO-88 - CITP-88 - CIUO-88

	1999	2000	2001	2002	2003	2004	2005	2006	2007	2008
Total	212.8	207.2	191.4	180.5	170.8	181.7	166.8	160.9	144.0	136.6
UB	87.4	82.2	78.2	69.2	65.1	67.3	47.4	51.3	43.0	44.4
1	6.8	7.8	6.9	5.4	4.7	7.8	7.6	6.6	5.3	4.3
2	5.3	4.0	4.4	2.8	3.9	5.9	7.1	5.0	6.1	3.7
3	8.5	7.1	6.9	9.3	6.0	8.1	8.4	7.1	5.3	5.2
4	7.7	8.2	8.6	9.7	9.4	7.0	9.8	10.0	7.9	7.0
5	16.7	21.4	20.0	20.4	21.6	22.9	20.6	22.9	21.1	18.4
6	4.8	3.2	2.2	2.0	3.6	2.4	3.3	1.4	2.0	2.3
7	38.0	34.4	29.0	25.4	22.9	26.2	29.5	24.9	23.3	18.3
8	16.4	17.5	14.8	15.4	12.0	15.4	15.0	13.0	13.7	14.3
9	13.5	12.7	14.5	15.0	15.7	11.9	13.4	14.7	12.1	14.3
X	7.8	8.7	5.7	5.9	5.8	6.8	4.7	3.9	4.2	4.5

Women - Femmes - Mujeres
ISCO-88 - CITP-88 - CIUO-88

	1999	2000	2001	2002	2003	2004	2005	2006	2007	2008
Total	330.5	312.1	287.0	281.6	271.0	311.0	299.9	266.5	254.0	220.5
UB	170.2	158.2	151.5	121.5	118.9	145.3	131.2	105.5	96.9	85.9
1	4.1	3.9	3.6	3.5	3.5	5.3	4.3	3.4	2.9	3.1
2	11.0	9.3	8.1	9.9	8.7	11.7	12.6	9.4	11.3	8.9
3	8.2	7.7	6.6	10.9	10.5	12.6	13.3	11.7	11.4	9.8
4	21.5	25.6	23.4	30.2	25.6	29.1	35.3	34.2	31.5	23.9
5	39.6	35.2	32.2	41.7	36.9	38.0	38.9	43.6	39.4	35.1
6	3.5	1.7	1.7	1.1	1.0	1.1	0.3	0.7	1.0	1.5
7	21.6	17.8	15.4	13.5	15.8	13.2	15.0	13.2	9.9	8.3
8	5.8	8.5	5.7	6.7	7.6	6.7	7.2	5.9	6.3	5.3
9	21.0	19.6	18.3	19.6	21.4	21.6	21.3	21.2	23.5	19.5
X	23.8	24.8	20.4	22.9	21.0	26.2	20.5	17.8	19.9	19.3

Hungary (BA) [3] — Total unemployment - Chômage total - Desempleo total

Total - Total - Total
ISCO-88 - CITP-88 - CIUO-88

	1999	2000	2001	2002	2003	2004	2005	2006	2007	2008
Total	284.7	262.5	232.9	238.8 [4]	244.5	252.9	303.9	316.8	311.9	329.2
UB	41.2	38.1	31.1	33.5 [4]	35.7	38.5	46.7	47.9	46.9	50.6
1	4.0	4.1	4.8	4.7 [4]	3.9	4.6	5.5	5.7	5.5	4.8
2	6.4	3.6	4.0	5.1 [4]	4.0	6.5	6.6	7.6	9.0	7.9
3	16.5	16.3	11.5	13.6 [4]	12.6	15.9	19.7	21.5	20.0	19.8
4	15.4	10.4	12.8	8.7 [4]	10.0	9.7	12.7	14.9	12.7	12.7
5	34.7	35.5	28.8	31.8 [4]	32.7	36.3	43.9	40.4	42.4	41.2
6	9.7	6.9	8.1	7.3 [4]	5.9	5.7	6.4	7.0	8.6	9.8
7	65.6	59.9	48.4	47.8 [4]	47.6	44.9	53.7	55.7	49.1	53.0
8	30.2	26.7	27.3	29.1 [4]	29.4	27.6	36.3	35.9	34.8	39.3
9	45.0	41.4	40.1	41.0 [4]	39.1	38.4	45.4	53.9	55.9	61.0
0	0.5	0.5	0.2	0.2 [4]	0.4	0.7	1.2	0.8	0.9	0.7
X	15.5	19.1	15.8	16.0 [4]	23.2	24.1	25.8	25.5	26.1	28.4

Men - Hommes - Hombres
ISCO-88 - CITP-88 - CIUO-88

	1999	2000	2001	2002	2003	2004	2005	2006	2007	2008
Total	170.7	159.5	142.7	138.0 [4]	138.5	136.8	159.1	164.6	164.2	174.3
UB	25.5	23.1	17.7	18.4 [4]	19.9	22.4	26.3	25.9	23.3	25.6
1	2.5	2.2	2.9	2.6 [4]	2.8	2.7	2.9	2.6	3.1	2.2
2	2.7	1.9	1.9	1.6 [4]	1.6	1.6	2.7	3.0	3.5	3.2
3	5.8	6.2	5.1	4.6 [4]	4.0	5.0	7.2	7.6	6.6	5.9
4	0.6	0.8	3.8	0.9 [4]	0.9	0.9	0.7	1.7	1.6	0.8
5	16.1	17.4	12.4	14.1 [4]	13.6	14.8	16.2	13.7	15.5	14.3
6	7.1	5.4	6.1	5.5 [4]	4.4	4.2	4.3	4.3	6.4	6.6
7	52.2	47.4	40.2	38.9 [4]	37.9	33.7	40.7	40.9	37.8	41.7
8	21.9	19.2	18.6	18.3 [4]	18.4	16.9	19.2	19.9	21.0	24.9
9	28.3	26.0	26.9	26.6 [4]	24.0	23.9	27.3	33.3	33.6	36.2
0	0.5	0.5	0.2	0.1 [4]	0.4	0.6	1.1	0.8	0.8	0.7
X	7.5	9.4	6.9	6.4 [4]	10.6	10.1	10.5	10.9	11.0	12.2

Women - Femmes - Mujeres
ISCO-88 - CITP-88 - CIUO-88

	1999	2000	2001	2002	2003	2004	2005	2006	2007	2008
Total	114.0	103.0	90.2	100.8 [4]	106.0	116.1	144.8	152.2	147.7	154.9
UB	15.7	15.0	13.4	15.1 [4]	15.8	16.1	20.4	22.0	23.6	25.0
1	1.5	1.9	1.9	2.1 [4]	1.1	1.9	2.6	3.1	2.4	2.6
2	3.7	1.7	2.1	3.5 [4]	2.4	4.9	3.9	4.6	5.5	4.7
3	10.7	10.1	6.4	9.0 [4]	8.6	10.9	12.5	13.9	13.4	13.9
4	14.8	9.6	9.0	7.8 [4]	9.1	8.8	12.0	13.2	11.1	11.9
5	18.6	18.1	16.4	17.7 [4]	19.1	21.5	27.7	26.7	26.9	26.9
6	2.6	1.5	2.0	1.8 [4]	1.5	1.5	2.1	2.7	2.2	3.2
7	13.4	12.5	8.2	8.9 [4]	9.7	11.2	13.0	14.8	11.3	11.3
8	8.3	7.5	8.7	10.8 [4]	11.0	10.7	17.1	16.0	13.8	14.4
9	16.7	15.4	13.2	14.4 [4]	15.1	14.5	18.1	20.6	22.3	24.8
0	-	-	-	0.1 [4]	-	0.1	0.1	0.0	0.1	0.0
X	8.0	9.7	8.9	9.6 [4]	12.6	14.0	15.3	14.6	15.1	16.2

Explanatory notes: see p. 451.

[1] Persons aged 15 years and over. [2] Second quarter of each year. [3] Persons aged 15 to 74 years. [4] Estimates based on the 2001 Population Census results.

Notes explicatives: voir p. 454.

[1] Personnes âgées de 15 ans et plus. [2] Deuxième trimestre de chaque année. [3] Personnes âgées de 15 à 74 ans. [4] Estimations basées sur les résultats du Recensement de la population de 2001.

Notas explicativas: véase p. 457.

[1] Personas de 15 años y más. [2] Segundo trimestre de cada año. [3] Personas de 15 a 74 años. [4] Estimaciones basadas en los resultados del Censo de población de 2001.

	Thousands / Milliers / Millares									
	1999	2000	2001	2002	2003	2004	2005	2006	2007	2008

Italy (BA) [1] — Total unemployment - Chômage total - Desempleo total

Total - Total - Total
ISCO-88 - CITP-88 - CIUO-88

	1999	2000	2001	2002	2003	2004	2005	2006	2007	2008
Total	2 669	2 495	2 267	2 163	2 096	1 960 [2]	1 889	1 673	1 506	1 692
UB	1 411	1 326	1 183	1 101	1 064	635 [2]	634	567	471	505
1	7	7	6	6	6	36 [2]	39	30	29	31
2	41	40	40	39	38	34 [2]	36	32	30	34
3	88	77	70	73	75	119 [2]	118	114	106	115
4	92	84	77	73	65	124 [2]	121	104	100	116
5	214	202	182	184	181	246 [2]	234	209	200	217
6	23	18	25	25	14	17 [2]	16	12	13	14
7	216	188	166	158	144	218 [2]	217	195	178	205
8	93	83	73	70	73	93 [2]	103	79	75	86
9	270	240	213	205	208	239 [2]	215	178	173	209
0	3	2	2	3	2	3 [2]	3	3	4	4
X	212	229	229	227	227	195 [2]	153	150	126	156

Men - Hommes - Hombres
ISCO-88 - CITP-88 - CIUO-88

	1999	2000	2001	2002	2003	2004	2005	2006	2007	2008
Total	1 266	1 179	1 066	1 016	996	925 [2]	902	801	722	820
UB	627	589	512	475	480	263 [2]	266	250	204	215
1	5	5	5	5	4	21 [2]	21	21	18	17
2	12	11	14	12	10	14 [2]	17	16	12	13
3	43	35	33	36	32	55 [2]	56	46	44	52
4	26	23	24	26	23	38 [2]	38	36	33	41
5	79	78	69	68	66	86 [2]	77	66	71	73
6	14	13	15	14	10	12 [2]	12	8	8	12
7	169	149	132	126	114	176 [2]	179	154	139	165
8	61	54	49	51	50	62 [2]	70	54	53	60
9	135	126	112	103	105	129 [2]	111	93	93	112
0	3	2	2	2	2	3 [2]	3	3	3	3
X	92	94	99	99	100	65 [2]	54	53	44	57

Women - Femmes - Mujeres
ISCO-88 - CITP-88 - CIUO-88

	1999	2000	2001	2002	2003	2004	2005	2006	2007	2008
Total	1 404	1 316	1 201	1 147	1 100	1 036 [2]	986	873	784	872
UB	784	737	671	626	584	371 [2]	368	317	267	290
1	3	2	2	2	2	15 [2]	18	10	11	13
2	29	29	27	27	27	20 [2]	20	16	18	21
3	45	42	37	37	43	64 [2]	62	67	62	63
4	65	61	53	47	42	86 [2]	82	68	67	75
5	135	124	113	116	115	160 [2]	157	143	129	144
6	9	5	10	10	5	5 [2]	4	4	4	3
7	47	39	33	32	30	42 [2]	38	41	39	40
8	32	29	24	19	22	31 [2]	33	25	22	26
9	135	114	101	102	102	111 [2]	104	85	80	97
0	-	-	-	-	-	0 [2]	0	0	0	1
X	120	135	130	128	127	130 [2]	99	97	82	99

Latvia (BA) [3] — Total unemployment - Chômage total - Desempleo total

Total - Total - Total
ISCO-88 - CITP-88 - CIUO-88

	1999	2000	2001	2002	2003	2004	2005	2006	2007	2008
Total	161.4	158.7	144.7	134.5 [4]	119.2	118.6	99.1	79.9	72.1	91.6
UB	19.9	17.5	16.8	20.4 [4]	13.8	14.1	13.1	15.3	11.9	11.3
1	5.2	3.1	3.4	4.5 [4]	4.4	4.1	5.0	-	-	-
2	4.8	3.5	4.7	3.7 [4]	3.2	3.4	2.3	3.1	2.6	3.3
3	7.7	7.2	4.9	7.5 [4]	7.5	5.5	4.5	6.8	7.2	6.2
4	4.0	5.0	3.1	5.8 [4]	4.9	6.0	4.4	-	2.6	2.2
5	11.6	15.5	14.9	13.5 [4]	16.3	15.2	13.3	10.0	7.4	6.5
6	-	-	-	2.8 [4]	2.1	2.6	1.8	2.0	-	-
7	20.8	22.2	18.9	20.4 [4]	17.3	18.7	14.4	10.9	10.7	11.0
8	11.7	12.8	11.0	12.5 [4]	12.3	11.8	8.3	6.0	5.3	6.6
9	17.8	18.9	17.8	21.2 [4]	20.8	16.6	13.3	10.1	11.9	11.8
X	55.8	50.9	47.4	21.9 [4]	16.5	20.4	18.4	12.2	8.8	31.1

Men - Hommes - Hombres
ISCO-88 - CITP-88 - CIUO-88

	1999	2000	2001	2002	2003	2004	2005	2006	2007	2008
Total	88.7	87.0	81.9	74.9 [4]	61.7	61.7	52.8	43.7	39.4	50.3
UB	12.4	9.8	9.1	10.3 [4]	7.1	7.4	7.3	7.5	6.0	5.6

Women - Femmes - Mujeres
ISCO-88 - CITP-88 - CIUO-88

	1999	2000	2001	2002	2003	2004	2005	2006	2007	2008
Total	72.7	71.7	62.7	59.6 [4]	57.5	56.9	46.2	36.2	32.7	41.4
UB	7.5	7.7	7.7	10.1 [4]	6.7	6.7	5.8	7.8	5.9	5.7

Explanatory notes: see p. 451.

[1] Persons aged 15 years and over. [2] Methodology revised; data not strictly comparable. [3] Persons aged 15 to 74 years. [4] Prior to 2002: persons aged 15 years and over.

Notes explicatives: voir p. 454.

[1] Personnes âgées de 15 ans et plus. [2] Méthodologie révisée; les données ne sont pas strictement comparables. [3] Personnes âgées de 15 à 74 ans. [4] Avant 2002: personnes agées de 15 ans et plus.

Notas explicativas: véase p. 457.

[1] Personas de 15 años y más. [2] Metodología revisada; los datos no son estrictamente comparables. [3] Personas de 15 a 74 años. [4] Antes de 2002: personas de 15 años y más.

By occupation — Par profession — Por ocupación

	Thousands			Milliers				Millares		
	1999	2000	2001	2002	2003	2004	2005	2006	2007	2008

Latvia (FB) [1] [2]   Registered unemployment - Chômage enregistré - Desempleo registrado

Total - Total - Total
ISCO-88 - CITP-88 - CIUO-88

Total	109.5	93.3	91.6	89.7	90.6	90.8	78.5	68.9	52.3	.
UB	5.2	5.1	5.2	5.1	6.9	7.6	8.4	7.2	3.6	.
1	3.0	2.5	2.6	2.5	2.5	2.4	2.3	2.2	2.2	.
2	5.1	3.6	3.6	3.4	3.4	3.3	3.1	3.0	3.0	.
3	7.8	6.7	5.9	5.7	5.2	5.4	5.1	5.1	4.8	.
4	6.6	5.6	5.3	5.2	5.1	5.2	4.7	4.5	3.2	.
5	15.0	13.8	14.4	14.7	14.4	14.2	12.5	11.3	8.7	.
6	4.5	3.3	3.2	3.3	3.1	3.4	2.1	1.9	1.5	.
7	19.0	15.2	14.8	14.0	13.7	13.4	10.8	9.7	7.3	.
8	14.5	12.4	12.1	11.1	10.9	10.9	8.6	7.4	5.5	.
9	28.6	24.9	24.5	24.6	25.4	25.0	20.8	16.7	12.5	.
0	0.1	0.1	0.1	0.1	0.0	0.0	0.0	0.0	0.0	.

Men - Hommes - Hombres
ISCO-88 - CITP-88 - CIUO-88

Total	46.7	39.5	39.1	37.0	37.6	37.3	31.5	27.0	20.1	.
UB	1.8	1.6	1.6	1.5	2.1	2.1	2.4	2.0	0.9	.
1	1.3	1.1	1.1	1.0	1.1	1.1	1.0	1.0	1.0	.
2	0.9	0.7	0.7	0.7	0.8	0.9	0.8	0.8	0.8	.
3	1.8	1.6	1.5	1.5	1.5	1.6	1.5	1.5	1.5	.
4	0.7	0.7	0.6	0.6	0.6	0.7	0.6	0.6	0.4	.
5	2.5	2.3	2.3	2.2	2.2	2.1	2.0	1.7	1.2	.
6	1.5	1.2	1.2	1.1	1.0	1.1	0.7	0.5	0.4	.
7	12.4	10.0	9.8	9.1	8.8	8.6	6.9	6.1	4.7	.
8	11.2	9.5	9.4	8.6	8.3	8.1	6.6	5.7	4.1	.
9	12.4	10.8	10.8	10.6	11.1	11.0	8.9	6.9	5.0	.
0	0.1	0.1	0.1	0.1	0.0	0.0	0.0	0.0	0.0	.

Women - Femmes - Mujeres
ISCO-88 - CITP-88 - CIUO-88

Total	62.8	53.8	52.6	52.7	53.0	53.5	47.0	42.0	32.2	.
UB	3.5	3.5	3.6	3.6	4.9	5.5	6.0	5.2	2.7	.
1	1.7	1.5	1.5	1.5	1.4	1.4	1.3	1.2	1.1	.
2	4.2	2.9	2.8	2.6	2.6	2.5	2.3	2.2	2.1	.
3	6.0	5.0	4.4	4.1	3.7	3.8	3.6	3.6	3.4	.
4	5.9	5.0	4.7	4.6	4.4	4.4	4.0	3.8	2.8	.
5	12.5	11.5	12.1	12.6	12.1	12.1	10.5	9.6	7.5	.
6	3.0	2.2	2.0	2.1	2.0	2.3	1.4	1.3	1.1	.
7	6.6	5.2	5.0	5.0	5.0	4.8	3.9	3.6	2.6	.
8	3.3	3.0	2.7	2.6	2.6	2.7	2.0	1.7	1.4	.
9	16.2	14.1	13.7	14.0	14.2	14.0	11.9	9.8	7.5	.
0	0.0	0.0	0.0	0.0	0.0	0.0	0.0	0.0	0.0	.

Lithuania (BA) [3]   Total unemployment - Chômage total - Desempleo total

Total - Total - Total
ISCO-88 - CITP-88 - CIUO-88

Total	249.0	273.7	284.0	224.4	203.9	184.4	132.9	89.3	69.0	94.3
UB [4]	63.4	57.2	66.9	51.5	56.7	49.9	37.2	26.1	14.5	21.4
1	7.4	11.3	6.4	4.3	3.5	2.5	3.0	2.0	2.6	2.9
2	11.2	8.0	9.8	7.7	8.4	12.0	6.4	2.9	4.5	5.5
3	7.0	10.9	11.9	10.5	9.1	9.3	4.1	3.1	3.2	5.2
4	9.7	13.1	9.4	9.0	5.5	4.1	3.7	2.5	2.1	4.2
5	25.9	33.3	32.2	27.9	24.6	22.2	14.9	9.5	7.9	8.8
6	10.2	4.3	8.7	6.2	5.0	3.4	2.3	2.5	0.8	1.2
7	53.2	56.1	59.4	48.5	39.7	33.8	20.8	15.5	13.6	20.0
8	28.6	35.3	33.4	21.6	16.1	13.6	11.6	8.3	4.5	5.5
9	32.2	44.1	45.0	36.7	35.3	33.6	28.9	16.8	15.3	19.4
0	0.1	0.1	0.9	0.6	-	-	-	0.2	-	-

Men - Hommes - Hombres
ISCO-88 - CITP-88 - CIUO-88

Total	140.5	158.5	165.6	121.1	105.4	90.6	67.1	46.7	34.6	49.5
UB [4]	29.6	34.8	37.0	26.1	27.0	22.9	16.0	12.2	6.7	10.2
1	4.9	7.1	4.2	2.1	1.7	0.9	1.6	1.0	1.8	1.5
2	3.6	2.6	3.6	2.8	2.9	3.5	2.9	0.7	1.8	1.1
3	2.7	4.1	5.3	4.3	3.8	4.5	1.3	1.1	0.4	1.6
4	1.4	1.6	1.7	1.5	0.9	0.4	0.5	0.5	0.2	1.5
5	5.0	7.3	6.3	6.4	4.2	5.0	3.2	1.2	1.0	1.7
6	8.0	2.4	6.0	3.3	2.7	2.5	1.6	1.0	0.3	0.9
7	40.5	41.2	45.2	33.6	27.3	23.9	13.5	11.3	10.4	15.1
8	25.0	28.8	28.6	17.7	13.1	10.0	10.0	7.1	3.7	4.5
9	19.7	28.5	26.8	22.6	21.9	17.0	16.6	10.4	8.3	11.5
0	0.1	0.1	0.9	0.6	-	-	-	0.2	-	-

Explanatory notes: see p. 451.

[1] Age limits vary according to the year. [2] 31st Dec. of each year. [3] Persons aged 15 years and over. [4] Incl. the unemployed whose last job was 8 years ago or over.

Notes explicatives: voir p. 454.

[1] Les limites d'âge varient selon l'année. [2] 31 déc. de chaque année. [3] Personnes âgées de 15 ans et plus. [4] Y compris les chômeurs dont le dernier emploi date de 8 ans ou plus.

Notas explicativas: véase p. 457.

[1] Los límites de edad varían según el año. [2] 31 dic. de cada año. [3] Personas de 15 años y más. [4] Incl. los desempleados cuyo último trabajo fue hace 8 años o más.

	Thousands				Milliers				Millares	
	1999	2000	2001	2002	2003	2004	2005	2006	2007	2008

Lithuania (BA) [1] — Total unemployment - Chômage total - Desempleo total

Women - Femmes - Mujeres
ISCO-88 - CITP-88 - CIUO-88

	1999	2000	2001	2002	2003	2004	2005	2006	2007	2008
Total	108.5	115.2	118.4	103.3	98.4	93.8	65.8	42.6	34.3	44.8
UB [2]	33.8	22.4	30.0	25.4	29.6	27.0	21.3	13.9	7.9	11.2
1	2.5	4.2	2.2	2.2	1.8	1.7	1.4	1.0	0.8	1.4
2	7.6	5.5	6.2	4.9	5.6	8.5	3.5	2.2	2.7	4.4
3	4.3	6.7	6.5	6.2	5.3	4.9	2.8	1.9	2.8	3.6
4	8.3	11.5	7.7	7.5	4.6	3.7	3.2	2.0	1.9	2.8
5	20.9	25.9	25.8	21.5	20.4	17.2	11.7	8.3	6.9	7.1
6	2.2	1.9	2.7	2.9	2.3	0.9	0.8	1.5	0.5	0.3
7	12.7	14.9	14.2	14.9	12.5	9.9	7.3	4.2	3.1	5.0
8	3.7	6.5	4.9	3.9	3.0	3.6	1.6	1.2	0.8	1.0
9	12.5	15.6	18.2	14.0	13.3	16.5	12.3	6.3	7.0	7.9
0	.	.	.	.	.	.	.	.	.	.

Lithuania (FB) [3] [4] — Registered unemployment - Chômage enregistré - Desempleo registrado

Total - Total - Total
ISCO-88 - CITP-88 - CIUO-88

	1999	2000	2001	2002	2003	2004	2005	2006	2007	2008
Total	.	.	.	191.2	158.8	126.4	87.2	79.3	69.7	95.0
UB	.	.	.	18.0	13.1	9.3	6.2	6.0	5.9	7.0
1	.	.	.	7.1	6.3	3.5	2.6	2.6	2.5	3.6
2	.	.	.	6.5	5.7	5.3	4.5	3.9	3.7	4.8
3	.	.	.	8.5	7.0	5.7	4.1	3.8	3.7	4.9
4	.	.	.	6.6	6.1	5.2	3.5	3.3	2.8	3.2
5	.	.	.	21.0	19.3	15.3	10.7	10.1	8.8	10.2
6	.	.	.	4.5	4.2	2.2	1.6	1.4	1.1	1.2
7	.	.	.	37.6	31.1	20.5	13.7	13.0	12.3	21.1
8	.	.	.	21.3	16.6	11.7	7.2	6.2	4.9	8.6
9	.	.	.	58.8	48.4	47.7	32.9	28.9	24.0	30.4
0	.	.	.	1.3	1.0	0.0	0.2	0.1	0.0	.

Men - Hommes - Hombres
ISCO-88 - CITP-88 - CIUO-88

	1999	2000	2001	2002	2003	2004	2005	2006	2007	2008
Total	.	.	.	95.1	73.7	53.8	33.9	29.9	27.4	49.0
UB	.	.	.	9.0	6.4	4.0	2.5	2.4	2.5	3.5
1	.	.	.	3.4	2.7	1.3	1.0	1.0	1.1	1.9
2	.	.	.	1.5	1.1	0.8	0.8	0.7	0.7	1.4
3	.	.	.	3.2	2.4	1.9	1.2	1.1	1.0	1.7
4	.	.	.	1.1	0.8	0.6	0.4	0.4	0.4	0.6
5	.	.	.	3.4	3.1	2.1	1.2	1.1	1.2	2.0
6	.	.	.	1.2	1.1	0.9	0.6	0.5	0.4	0.5
7	.	.	.	20.3	15.5	11.9	7.3	6.6	6.8	15.1
8	.	.	.	17.1	12.9	8.8	5.2	4.3	3.6	7.1
9	.	.	.	33.6	26.7	21.5	13.5	11.7	9.7	15.2
0	.	.	.	1.3	1.0	0.0	0.2	0.1	0.0	.

Women - Femmes - Mujeres
ISCO-88 - CITP-88 - CIUO-88

	1999	2000	2001	2002	2003	2004	2005	2006	2007	2008
Total	.	.	.	96.1	85.1	72.6	53.3	49.4	42.3	46.0
UB	.	.	.	9.0	6.7	5.3	3.7	3.6	3.4	3.5
1	.	.	.	3.7	3.6	2.2	1.6	1.6	1.4	1.7
2	.	.	.	5.0	4.6	4.5	3.7	3.2	3.0	3.4
3	.	.	.	5.3	4.6	3.8	2.9	2.7	2.7	3.2
4	.	.	.	5.5	5.3	4.6	3.1	2.9	2.4	2.6
5	.	.	.	17.6	16.2	13.2	9.5	9.0	7.6	8.2
6	.	.	.	3.3	3.1	1.3	1.0	0.9	0.7	0.7
7	.	.	.	17.3	15.6	8.6	6.4	6.4	5.5	6.0
8	.	.	.	4.2	3.7	2.9	2.0	1.9	1.3	1.5
9	.	.	.	25.2	21.7	26.2	19.4	17.2	14.3	15.2
0	.	.	.	0.0	0.0	0.0	0.0	0.0	0.0	.

Malta (BA) [1] — Total unemployment - Chômage total - Desempleo total

Total - Total - Total
ISCO-88 - CITP-88 - CIUO-88

	1999	2000	2001	2002	2003	2004	2005	2006	2007	2008
Total	.	10.151	10.164	.	.	11.518	11.750	11.925	10.729	10.389
UB	.	3.091	4.344	.	.	5.059	5.104	3.515	2.857	2.592
1	.	0.054	0.130	.	.	-	-	-	-	0.167
2	.	0.172	-	.	.	-	-	-	-	0.100
3	.	0.189	0.202	.	.	-	0.706	0.593	-	0.449
4	.	0.524	0.431	.	.	-	0.698	0.976	0.685	0.497
5	.	0.942	1.029	.	.	1.411	1.310	1.690	2.055	1.750
6	.	-	0.161	.	.	-	-	-	-	0.086
7	.	1.543	1.371	.	.	1.493	1.123	1.106	0.965	0.988
8	.	1.974	1.961	.	.	1.568	1.920	1.952	1.653	1.491
9	.	1.662	1.662	.	.	1.889	1.824	1.618	1.649	1.901
0	.	.	.	.	.	-	-	-	-	.
X	.	.	.	.	.	.	.	.	.	0.2

Explanatory notes: see p. 451. Notes explicatives: voir p. 454. Notas explicativas: véase p. 457.

[1] Persons aged 15 years and over. [2] Incl. the unemployed whose last job was 8 years ago or over. [3] Persons aged 16 to 64 years. [4] 31st Dec. of each year.

[1] Personnes âgées de 15 ans et plus. [2] Y compris les chômeurs dont le dernier emploi date de 8 ans ou plus. [3] Personnes âgées de 16 à 64 ans. [4] 31 déc. de chaque année.

[1] Personas de 15 años y más. [2] Incl. los desempleados cuyo último trabajo fue hace 8 años o más. [3] Personas de 16 a 64 años. [4] 31 dic. de cada año.

UNEMPLOYMENT — CHÔMAGE — DESEMPLEO

By occupation — Par profession — Por ocupación

Thousands — Milliers — Millares

	1999	2000	2001	2002	2003	2004	2005	2006	2007	2008
Malta (BA) [1]					Total unemployment - Chômage total - Desempleo total					
Men - Hommes - Hombres ISCO-88 - CITP-88 - CIUO-88										
Total	.	7.628	6.626	.	.	7.080	7.279	7.242	6.474	6.442
UB	.	2.159	2.308	.	.	2.289	2.358	2.031	1.747	1.485
1	.	0.054	.	.	.	-	-	-	-	0.087
2	.	0.172	-	.	.	-	-	-	-	0.029
3	.	-	0.072	.	.	-	-	-	-	0.240
4	.	0.176	0.074	.	.	-	-	-	-	0.142
5	.	0.757	0.635	.	.	0.897	0.773	0.906	1.050	0.907
6	.	-	0.161	.	.	-	-	-	-	0.056
7	.	1.543	1.298	.	.	1.464	1.123	1.028	0.886	0.917
8	.	1.370	0.880	.	.	0.766	0.979	0.942	0.799	0.768
9	.	1.397	1.379	.	.	-	1.470	1.234	1.156	1.534
0	.	.	.	.	.	-	-	-	.	.
X	.	.	.	.	.	.	.	.	.	0.2
Women - Femmes - Mujeres ISCO-88 - CITP-88 - CIUO-88										
Total	.	2.523	3.538	.	.	4.438	4.466	4.683	4.255	3.947
UB	.	0.932	2.036	.	.	2.770	2.746	1.484	1.110	1.107
1	.	-	0.130	.	.	-	-	-	-	0.080
2	.	.	.	.	.	.	.	.	.	0.071
3	.	0.189	0.130	.	.	-	-	-	-	0.209
4	.	0.348	0.357	.	.	-	-	0.666	-	0.355
5	.	0.185	0.394	.	.	0.514	0.537	0.784	1.005	0.843
6	.	.	.	.	.	.	.	.	.	0.030
7	.	-	0.073	.	.	0.029	0.000	0.078	0.079	0.071
8	.	0.604	1.081	.	.	0.802	0.941	1.010	0.854	0.723
9	.	0.265	0.283	.	.	-	0.354	0.384	0.493	0.367
0	.	-	-	.	.	-	-	-	-	.
X	.	.	.	.	.	.	.	.	.	0.0
Moldova, Republic of (BA) [1]					Total unemployment - Chômage total - Desempleo total					
Total - Total - Total ISCO-88 - CITP-88 - CIUO-88										
Total	187.2	140.1	117.7	110.0	117.1	116.5	103.7	99.9	66.7	51.7
UB	43.2	30.5	27.6	27.3	25.8	28.4	27.3	29.3	20.2	14.9
1	5.0	3.8	2.8	2.7	2.9	1.8	1.4	1.7	1.6	1.2
2	9.9	8.9	7.6	7.5	6.6	6.5	3.5	4.2	2.5	3.1
3	12.4	9.8	7.4	7.0	5.4	4.5	4.1	3.5	2.3	2.3
4	4.0	3.1	2.4	2.1	1.5	1.1	0.8	0.9	0.6	0.8
5	16.7	15.8	10.2	9.1	10.2	9.9	9.4	7.8	5.5	5.6
6	14.0	8.8	6.9	7.1	10.1	11.2	9.7	4.8	1.7	1.1
7	30.5	20.6	17.6	14.4	13.1	12.4	11.0	11.1	8.4	7.0
8	21.0	13.6	11.8	8.0	9.4	7.1	5.6	7.6	3.6	3.0
9	21.6	17.9	13.3	13.4	14.9	14.8	12.0	12.9	8.1	5.2
0	0.3	0.2	-	0.1	0.4	0.5	0.2	0.0	0.6	0.4
X	8.7	7.0	10.1	11.0	16.8	18.4	18.7	16.2	11.6	7.2
Men - Hommes - Hombres ISCO-88 - CITP-88 - CIUO-88										
Total	113.6	80.6	70.1	64.4	69.9	70.1	59.8	61.7	41.5	30.0
UB	27.3	17.6	16.1	16.2	14.6	16.5	14.3	17.3	12.4	7.0
1	3.7	2.7	1.9	1.6	2.0	1.3	1.0	1.1	1.3	1.0
2	4.3	4.3	3.5	3.9	2.8	2.5	1.3	2.0	1.4	0.9
3	5.1	4.0	2.4	2.4	2.2	1.8	2.1	1.7	1.3	1.0
4	0.9	0.3	0.1	0.2	0.1	0.4	0.3	0.1	0.1	0.4
5	5.5	4.2	2.9	3.4	3.5	3.1	2.5	3.0	2.3	2.3
6	8.1	5.7	4.7	3.9	6.3	5.8	5.6	3.1	1.0	0.6
7	20.9	13.3	11.7	9.9	9.1	9.5	8.4	8.7	5.9	5.6
8	19.2	12.8	11.4	7.7	8.6	6.8	5.2	7.3	3.3	2.9
9	13.4	11.5	8.9	8.7	10.4	10.4	8.5	8.4	6.0	4.2
0	0.3	0.1	-	0.1	0.4	0.5	0.1	0.0	0.4	0.2
X	4.8	4.1	6.5	6.3	9.9	11.5	10.4	8.9	6.1	3.9
Women - Femmes - Mujeres ISCO-88 - CITP-88 - CIUO-88										
Total	73.6	59.5	47.6	45.4	47.2	46.4	43.9	38.2	25.2	21.8
UB	15.9	12.8	11.5	11.1	11.3	11.8	13.0	12.1	7.8	7.9
1	1.3	1.1	0.8	1.1	1.0	0.5	0.3	0.5	0.3	0.3
2	5.6	4.6	4.1	3.6	3.7	4.0	2.2	2.2	1.1	2.1
3	7.3	5.8	5.0	4.6	3.2	2.7	2.0	1.8	1.0	1.3
4	3.1	2.8	2.3	1.9	1.4	0.7	0.5	0.8	0.5	0.4
5	11.2	11.6	7.3	5.6	6.7	6.8	6.9	4.7	3.2	3.3
6	5.8	3.2	2.2	3.2	3.9	5.4	4.1	1.8	0.7	0.5
7	9.6	7.4	5.9	4.6	4.0	2.9	2.7	2.3	2.5	1.4
8	1.7	0.8	0.5	0.4	0.8	0.3	0.3	0.3	0.3	0.1
9	8.1	6.5	4.4	4.8	4.4	4.5	3.5	4.4	2.2	1.0
0	-	0.1	-	-	-	-	0.1	0.0	0.3	0.1
X	3.9	2.9	3.6	4.7	6.7	6.9	8.4	7.3	5.5	3.4

Explanatory notes: see p. 451.
[1] Persons aged 15 years and over.

Notes explicatives: voir p. 454.
[1] Personnes âgées de 15 ans et plus.

Notas explicativas: véase p. 457.
[1] Personas de 15 años y más.

	UNEMPLOYMENT	CHÔMAGE	DESEMPLEO
	By occupation	Par profession	Por ocupación

	Thousands				Milliers				Millares	
	1999	2000	2001	2002	2003	2004	2005	2006	2007	2008

Norway (FB) [1] Registered unemployment - Chômage enregistré - Desempleo registrado

Total - Total - Total
ISCO-88 - CITP-88 - CIUO-88

	1999	2000	2001	2002	2003	2004	2005	2006	2007	2008
Total	60	63	63	75	93	92	83	63 [2]	46	43
1	1	2	2	4	5	6	5	4 [2]	3	2
2	2	2	2	4	5	5	5	4 [2]	3	2
3	5	6	6	8	10	10	9	7 [2]	5	4
4	7	7	7	8	10	10	9	7 [2]	5	4
5	13	13	15	16	20	21	21	17 [2]	13	11
6	1	1	2	1	2	2	2	1 [2]	1	1
7	7	8	7	8	12	11	9	6 [2]	4	5
8	7	8	7	8	10	9	8	6 [2]	4	4
9	8	8	9	12	13	11	10	8 [2]	6	5
0	0	0	1	2	3	3	3	2 [2]	1	1
X	8	7	4	4	4	3	4	3 [2]	3	3

Men - Hommes - Hombres
ISCO-88 - CITP-88 - CIUO-88

	1999	2000	2001	2002	2003	2004	2005	2006	2007	2008
Total	34	36	36	43	54	52	46	33 [2]	24	24
1	1	1	2	3	4	4	3	2 [2]	2	1
2	1	1	1	2	3	3	3	2 [2]	1	1
3	3	3	3	4	5	5	4	3 [2]	2	2
4	2	2	3	3	4	4	3	3 [2]	2	2
5	4	4	5	6	7	8	7	6 [2]	4	4
6	1	1	1	1	1	1	1	1 [2]	1	1
7	6	7	7	8	11	10	8	5 [2]	4	4
8	5	6	6	6	7	7	6	4 [2]	3	3
9	4	4	5	7	7	6	5	4 [2]	3	3
0	0	0	1	2	2	3	2	1 [2]	1	1
X	5	5	3	2	2	2	2	2 [2]	1	2

Women - Femmes - Mujeres
ISCO-88 - CITP-88 - CIUO-88

	1999	2000	2001	2002	2003	2004	2005	2006	2007	2008
Total	26	26	27	33	39	39	38	30 [2]	22	19
1	0	0	1	1	2	2	2	1 [2]	1	1
2	1	1	1	1	2	2	2	2 [2]	1	1
3	2	2	3	3	4	5	4	3 [2]	3	2
4	4	4	4	5	6	6	6	4 [2]	3	2
5	9	9	10	11	13	14	14	11 [2]	9	7
6	0	0	0	0	0	0	0	0 [2]	-	-
7	1	1	1	1	1	1	1	1 [2]	-	-
8	2	2	2	2	2	2	2	1 [2]	1	1
9	4	4	4	5	6	5	5	4 [2]	3	2
0	0	0	0	0	1	1	1	0 [2]	-	-
X	2	2	1	2	2	1	2	2 [2]	1	2

Poland (BA) [1] Total unemployment - Chômage total - Desempleo total

Total - Total - Total
ISCO-88 - CITP-88 - CIUO-88

	1999	2000	2001	2002	2003	2004	2005	2006	2007	2008
Total	2 391 [3]	2 785	3 170 [4]	3 431	3 329	3 230	3 045	2 344	1 619	1 211
UB	498 [3]	597	703 [4]	773	769	727	709	541	361	250
1	38 [3]	41	49 [4]	51	48	53	45	42	27	16
2	28 [3]	40	40 [4]	53	59	52	63	55	43	38
3	97 [3]	138	147 [4]	164	160	145	118	98	80	71
4	132 [3]	150	168 [4]	185	168	159	149	118	80	71
5	296 [3]	342	398 [4]	421	410	387	348	284	182	153
6	50 [3]	49	48 [4]	41	36	39	35	30	14	10
7	503 [3]	546	611 [4]	683	620	582	502	357	249	183
8	154 [3]	179	207 [4]	239	230	222	199	147	89	73
9	307 [3]	339	405 [4]	397	362	363	354	267	201	155
0	3 [3]	4	4 [4]	5	6	-	5	-	-	-
X [5]	285 [3]	360	390 [4]	419	459	497	520	402	288	191

Men - Hommes - Hombres
ISCO-88 - CITP-88 - CIUO-88

	1999	2000	2001	2002	2003	2004	2005	2006	2007	2008
Total	1 147 [3]	1 344	1 583 [4]	1 779	1 741	1 681	1 553	1 202	831	599
UB	215 [3]	265	327 [4]	381	387	351	336	276	182	121
1	22 [3]	24	31 [4]	33	29	34	25	23	16	10
2	10 [3]	11	11 [4]	18	22	18	22	21	14	16
3	31 [3]	46	57 [4]	68	65	55	48	37	30	24
4	28 [3]	41	42 [4]	50	48	49	40	31	24	23
5	60 [3]	70	92 [4]	102	110	112	103	78	53	38
6	27 [3]	27	29 [4]	25	25	27	23	19	8	6
7	367 [3]	406	472 [4]	543	491	462	401	283	202	147
8	129 [3]	151	175 [4]	197	189	177	158	118	76	61
9	161 [3]	182	219 [4]	220	202	205	200	149	105	78
0	3 [3]	4	4 [4]	5	6	-	5	-	-	-
X [5]	93 [3]	118	124 [4]	137	167	186	194	165	117	74

Explanatory notes: see p. 451.

[1] Persons aged 15 to 74 years. [2] Prior to 2006: persons aged 16 to 74 years. [3] First and fourth quarters. [4] Prior to 2001: persons aged 15 years and over. [5] Incl. the unemployed whose last job was 8 years ago or over.

Notes explicatives: voir p. 454.

[1] Personnes âgées de 15 à 74 ans. [2] Avant 2006: personnes âgées de 16 à 74 ans. [3] Premier et quatrième trimestres. [4] Avant 2001: personnes âgées de 15 ans et plus. [5] Y compris les chômeurs dont le dernier emploi date de 8 ans ou plus.

Notas explicativas: véase p. 457.

[1] Personas de 15 a 74 años. [2] Antes de 2006: personas de 16 a 74 años. [3] Primero y cuarto trimestres. [4] Antes de 2001: personas de 15 años y más. [5] Incl. los desempleados cuyo último trabajo fue hace 8 años o más.

By occupation   Par profession   Por ocupación

	Thousands			Milliers				Millares		
	1999	2000	2001	2002	2003	2004	2005	2006	2007	2008

Poland (BA) [1]   Total unemployment - Chômage total - Desempleo total
Women - Femmes - Mujeres
ISCO-88 - CITP-88 - CIUO-88

	1999	2000	2001	2002	2003	2004	2005	2006	2007	2008
Total	1 244 [2]	1 440	1 587 [3]	1 652	1 588	1 550	1 493	1 142	788	612
UB	283 [2]	332	376 [3]	392	382	376	373	265	180	129
1	16 [2]	17	19 [3]	19	19	19	20	19	11	6
2	18 [2]	29	28 [3]	36	36	34	41	34	29	22
3	67 [2]	92	90 [3]	96	96	90	70	61	50	47
4	103 [2]	109	126 [3]	134	120	110	109	86	56	48
5	237 [2]	271	306 [3]	319	300	275	245	207	128	115
6	23 [2]	22	19 [3]	16	11	12	12	11	6	4
7	135 [2]	140	138 [3]	140	129	121	101	73	47	36
8	25 [2]	29	32 [3]	42	42	45	41	30	14	11
9	146 [2]	157	186 [3]	178	160	158	154	119	96	77
0	-	-	-	-	-	-	-	-	-	-
X [4]	191 [2]	242	266 [3]	282	292	311	326	237	172	117

Portugal (BA) [5]   Total unemployment - Chômage total - Desempleo total
Total - Total - Total
ISCO-88 - CITP-88 - CIUO-88

	1999	2000	2001	2002	2003	2004	2005	2006	2007	2008
Total	225.8	205.5	213.5	270.5	342.3	365.0	422.3	427.8	448.6	427.1
UB	33.6	27.6	34.6	41.1	46.3	49.2	58.7	58.8	61.5	58.4
1	5.2	4.8	4.9	6.0	8.1	11.1	12.4	9.7	11.8	9.7
2	8.1	7.2	7.8	13.2	14.5	14.3	14.6	18.2	21.2	20.0
3	12.0	14.2	13.9	13.7	17.9	21.5	22.8	28.7	28.1	26.9
4	25.1	25.0	22.9	30.3	41.4	42.3	45.9	41.6	43.0	42.8
5	39.1	37.9	34.1	37.4	50.7	53.6	61.1	63.2	77.7	74.0
6	-	-	-	4.6	5.0	3.4 [6]	5.9	7.5	6.8	5.8
7	42.2	34.4	36.8	50.1	68.2	77.1	86.2	88.1	86.5	83.8
8	18.7	18.6	19.7	27.5	33.5	33.0	43.5	45.0	41.7	36.4
9	39.1	33.9	34.4	45.7	55.8	57.6	70.2	65.8	69.2	67.7
0 [6]	-	-	-	-	-	2.0	0.9	1.2	1.2	1.5

Men - Hommes - Hombres
ISCO-88 - CITP-88 - CIUO-88

	1999	2000	2001	2002	2003	2004	2005	2006	2007	2008
Total	108.9	89.3	91.6	121.4	160.9	172.9	198.1	194.8	196.8	194.3
UB	13.6	11.0	13.6	19.1	21.3	22.0	22.9	25.6	23.3	23.8
1	-	-	-	-	5.2	6.0	6.1	5.5	6.0	6.3
2	-	-	1.5 [6]	3.2 [6]	5.1	5.3	5.7	5.8	8.4	6.0
3	6.6	6.3	6.0	7.2	11.4	14.3	14.7	17.4	14.6	13.7
4	10.0	8.1	9.0	10.0	11.4	13.1	16.8	14.4	17.2	14.7
5	10.7	8.9	7.3	9.7	12.2	12.3	14.1	13.8	20.9	15.2
6 [6]	-	-	-	-	-	2.0	2.9	3.8	2.4	3.1
7	29.9	24.1	25.8	32.6	47.6	51.8	56.1	53.4	52.9	63.1
8	12.2	13.1	11.0	15.7	19.2	20.8	28.7	27.5	23.4	23.1
9	16.6	10.2	10.9	16.2	23.8	23.6	29.4	26.5	26.4	24.0
0 [6]	-	-	-	-	-	1.8	0.7	1.1	1.2	1.4

Women - Femmes - Mujeres
ISCO-88 - CITP-88 - CIUO-88

	1999	2000	2001	2002	2003	2004	2005	2006	2007	2008
Total	116.9	116.2	122.0	149.1	181.4	192.2	224.1	233.1	251.8	232.7
UB	20.0	16.3	21.0	22.0	25.0	27.2	35.8	33.2	38.2	34.6
1	-	-	-	-	2.9 [6]	5.1	6.3	4.2 [6]	5.8	3.5 [6]
2	-	-	6.3	10.0	9.4	9.0	9.0	12.4	12.8	14.0
3	5.4	7.9	7.9	6.5	6.5	7.2	8.1	11.3	13.4	13.2
4	15.1	16.8	14.0	20.3	30.0	29.2	29.1	27.2	25.8	28.1
5	28.4	28.9	26.8	27.6	38.5	41.3	47.0	49.4	56.7	58.8
6 [6]	-	-	-	-	-	1.4	3.0	3.6	4.4	2.7
7	12.3	10.3	11.0	17.5	20.6	25.4	30.1	34.8	33.6	20.7
8	6.5	5.5	8.7	11.8	14.3	12.2	14.8	17.5	18.3	13.3
9	22.5	23.7	23.4	29.6	32.0	34.0	40.7	39.4	42.8	43.7
0 [6]	-	-	-	-	-	-	0.2	0.1	-	0.1

Roumanie (BA) [5]   Total unemployment - Chômage total - Desempleo total
Total - Total - Total
ISCO-88 - CITP-88 - CIUO-88

	1999	2000	2001	2002	2003	2004	2005	2006	2007	2008
Total	789.9	821.2	749.9	845.2 [7]	691.7	799.5	704.5	728.4	641.0	575.5
UB	272.6	280.2	250.8	287.7 [7]	232.5	306.5	238.9	273.4	268.9	246.7
1	4.6	6.0	4.4	5.0 [7]	2.1	-	-	-	-	-
2	9.3	11.1	15.4	13.4 [7]	9.1	10.8	12.1	9.4	8.3	7.3
3	31.0	37.4	31.9	28.3 [7]	26.5	24.8	28.4	24.2	17.5	12.4
4	25.8	25.6	20.7	22.9 [7]	18.7	18.9	19.6	15.2	11.9	14.1
5	52.1	57.0	57.2	57.9 [7]	47.7	53.6	52.8	49.4	36.7	35.9
6	42.5	35.5	30.5	58.3 [7]	22.3	16.0	28.1	20.2	11.3	11.4
7	169.5	169.9	143.6	149.6 [7]	130.7	134.8	126.1	118.7	92.5	74.6
8,0,X [8]	101.4	131.7	123.6	149.6 [7]	133.5	165.9	134.9	137.7	121.9	110.4
9	80.7	66.4	71.3	72.1 [7]	68.1	64.8	60.7	77.4	69.3	59.6

Explanatory notes: see p. 451.

[1] Persons aged 15 to 74 years. [2] First and fourth quarters. [3] Prior to 2001: persons aged 15 years and over. [4] Incl. the unemployed whose last job was 8 years ago or over. [5] Persons aged 15 years and over. [6] Data not reliable; coefficient of variation greater than 20%. [7] Estimates based on the 2002 Population Census results. [8] Incl. the unemployed whose last job was 8 years ago or over, except for 1994-1996.

Notes explicatives: voir p. 454.

[1] Personnes âgées de 15 à 74 ans. [2] Premier et quatrième trimestres. [3] Avant 2001: personnes âgées de 15 ans et plus. [4] Y compris les chômeurs dont le dernier emploi date de 8 ans ou plus. [5] Personnes âgées de 15 ans et plus. [6] Données non fiables; coefficient de variation supérieur à 20%. [7] Estimations basées sur les résultats du Recensement de la population de 2002. [8] Y compris les chômeurs dont le dernier emploi date de 8 ans ou plus, sauf pour 1994-1996.

Notas explicativas: véase p. 457.

[1] Personas de 15 a 74 años. [2] Primero y cuarto trimestres. [3] Antes de 2001: personas de 15 años y más. [4] Incl. los desempleados cuyo último trabajo fue hace 8 años o más. [5] Personas de 15 años y más. [6] Datos no fiables; coeficiente de variación superior a 20%. [7] Estimaciones basadas en los resultados del Censo de población de 2002. [8] Incl. los desempleados cuyo último trabajo fue hace 8 años o más, excepto por 1994-1996.

UNEMPLOYMENT CHÔMAGE DESEMPLEO

By occupation Par profession Por ocupación

	Thousands				Milliers				Millares	
	1999	2000	2001	2002	2003	2004	2005	2006	2007	2008
Roumanie (BA) [1]				Total unemployment - Chômage total - Desempleo total						
Men - Hommes - Hombres										
ISCO-88 - CITP-88 - CIUO-88										
Total	462.5	481.6	436.0	494.0 [2]	408.0	490.7	420.3	452.4	398.7	369.2
UB	149.3	156.9	136.5	151.6 [2]	124.8	178.2	139.5	158.6	161.9	154.4
1	3.9	5.2	3.2	3.3 [2]	1.4	-	-	-	-	-
2	4.5	6.8	9.2	7.6 [2]	6.5	-	5.4	-	-	-
3	12.6	16.5	13.2	12.5 [2]	11.0	10.5	12.1	11.3	7.5	5.4
4	9.3	6.8	5.7	7.5 [2]	3.9	4.2	3.8	3.4	3.9	3.1
5	12.6	15.8	16.0	15.7 [2]	14.9	19.6	19.2	17.3	12.0	12.6
6	28.2	24.1	20.6	40.6 [2]	14.9	11.5	14.5	15.1	7.9	9.0
7	119.8	119.3	105.8	109.1 [2]	93.6	103.5	93.2	88.1	69.1	54.7
8,0,X [3]	62.8	86.1	78.6	0.0 [2]	88.5	111.6	92.1	96.6	85.6	79.8
9	59.1	43.7	46.7	48.4 [2]	48.1	43.9	38.4	55.6	44.3	42.4
Women - Femmes - Mujeres										
ISCO-88 - CITP-88 - CIUO-88										
Total	327.3	339.5	313.9	351.1 [2]	283.7	308.7	284.1	276.0	242.3	206.3
UB	123.3	123.3	114.3	136.1 [2]	107.7	128.2	99.4	114.8	107.0	92.3
1	-	-	-	1.7 [2]	-	-	-	-	-	-
2	4.8	4.2	6.1	5.8 [2]	2.5	-	6.7	-	-	-
3	18.4	20.9	18.6	15.7 [2]	15.5	14.2	16.2	12.9	9.9	7.0
4	16.5	18.7	14.9	15.3 [2]	14.7	14.7	15.8	11.8	8.0	11.0
5	39.4	41.1	41.1	42.2 [2]	32.8	33.9	33.6	32.1	24.7	23.3
6	14.2	11.3	9.8	17.6 [2]	7.3	-	13.6	5.1	3.4	2.4
7	49.7	50.6	37.8	40.5 [2]	37.1	31.3	32.9	30.6	23.4	19.9
8,0,X [3]	34.9	45.5	45.1	0.0 [2]	45.1	54.3	42.7	40.5	36.3	30.6
9	21.5	22.7	24.5	23.7 [2]	19.9	20.9	22.3	21.8	24.9	17.2
Russian Federation (BA) [4]				Total unemployment - Chômage total - Desempleo total						
Total - Total - Total										
ISCO-88 - CITP-88 - CIUO-88										
Total	9 436	7 700	6 424	5 698	5 959	5 675	5 263	5 312	4 588	4 791
1	178	162	102	78	133	150	148	115	80	92
2	803	611	523	450	341	303	250	237	219	247
3	1 229	927	729	669	490	465	384	356	314	349
4	303	292	200	165	159	130	119	109	93	85
5	1 168	948	817	756	716	695	631	623	509	602
6	178	164	144	160	161	176	154	186	154	146
7	1 886	1 507	1 241	1 020	941	876	785	732	603	634
8	1 276	1 056	849	806	705	645	579	519	422	485
9	1 336	1 124	976	817	931	839	842	834	726	785
X	1 078	909	842	776	1 383	1 396	1 371	1 602	1 468	1 366
Men - Hommes - Hombres										
ISCO-88 - CITP-88 - CIUO-88										
Total	4 939	4 057	3 450	3 014	3 121	2 975	2 725	2 811	2 453	2 542
1	99	96	59	47	84	92	77	67	42	53
2	320	239	201	189	128	118	87	83	88	95
3	370	281	230	197	160	162	132	111	115	124
4	27	22	25	20	16	17	10	11	7	9
5	293	243	205	183	159	143	125	145	126	140
6	84	79	74	74	78	92	76	99	80	88
7	1 344	1 065	899	736	681	628	580	527	437	463
8	1 122	930	768	722	618	562	509	461	378	444
9	723	608	551	456	509	476	481	488	429	441
X	558	495	437	390	687	685	648	818	752	686
Women - Femmes - Mujeres										
ISCO-88 - CITP-88 - CIUO-88										
Total	4 497	3 643	2 974	2 685	2 838	2 699	2 538	2 501	2 136	2 250
1	79	66	43	31	49	58	71	49	38	39
2	483	371	322	262	213	184	163	153	131	152
3	859	647	499	472	331	303	252	245	200	224
4	277	271	175	146	143	112	109	98	86	76
5	874	705	612	573	557	551	506	478	384	463
6	94	85	71	85	83	85	78	87	74	58
7	542	442	342	284	260	248	205	204	166	172
8	154	126	81	85	87	84	70	58	44	42
9	613	516	424	361	421	363	361	345	297	344
X	520	414	405	386	695	711	723	784	716	681

Explanatory notes: see p. 451.

[1] Persons aged 15 years and over. [2] Estimates based on the 2002 Population Census results. [3] Incl. the unemployed whose last job was 8 years ago or over, except for 1994-1996. [4] Persons aged 15 to 72 years.

Notes explicatives: voir p. 454.

[1] Personnes âgées de 15 ans et plus. [2] Estimations basées sur les résultats du Recensement de la population de 2002. [3] Y compris les chômeurs dont le dernier emploi date de 8 ans ou plus, sauf pour 1994-1996. [4] Personnes âgées de 15 à 72 ans.

Notas explicativas: véase p. 457.

[1] Personas de 15 años y más. [2] Estimaciones basadas en los resultados del Censo de población de 2002. [3] Incl. los desempleados cuyo último trabajo fue hace 8 años o más, excepto por 1994-1996. [4] Personas de 15 a 72 años.

By occupation — Par profession — Por ocupación

	Thousands			Milliers				Millares		
	1999	2000	2001	2002	2003	2004	2005	2006	2007	2008

Serbia (BA) [1] [2]   Total unemployment - Chômage total - Desempleo total

Total - Total - Total
ISCO-88 - CITP-88 - CIUO-88

	1999	2000	2001	2002	2003	2004	2005	2006	2007	2008
Total	.	.	.	.	.	.	.	.	585.5	445.4
UB	.	.	.	.	.	.	.	.	233.1	187.9
1	.	.	.	.	.	.	.	.	4.8	8.4
2	.	.	.	.	.	.	.	.	12.4	10.5
3	.	.	.	.	.	.	.	.	57.3	34.6
4	.	.	.	.	.	.	.	.	27.3	19.9
5	.	.	.	.	.	.	.	.	81.6	58.8
6	.	.	.	.	.	.	.	.	5.2	2.5
7	.	.	.	.	.	.	.	.	74.5	60.5
8	.	.	.	.	.	.	.	.	36.8	24.4
9	.	.	.	.	.	.	.	.	48.1	36.2
0	.	.	.	.	.	.	.	.	4.3	1.8

Men - Hommes - Hombres
ISCO-88 - CITP-88 - CIUO-88

	1999	2000	2001	2002	2003	2004	2005	2006	2007	2008
Total	.	.	.	.	.	.	.	.	289.8	217.5
UB	.	.	.	.	.	.	.	.	112.7	87.0
1	.	.	.	.	.	.	.	.	3.4	4.9
2	.	.	.	.	.	.	.	.	2.8	3.6
3	.	.	.	.	.	.	.	.	22.6	14.3
4	.	.	.	.	.	.	.	.	11.8	8.2
5	.	.	.	.	.	.	.	.	24.8	18.8
6	.	.	.	.	.	.	.	.	4.0	1.4
7	.	.	.	.	.	.	.	.	47.1	41.0
8	.	.	.	.	.	.	.	.	26.8	19.3
9	.	.	.	.	.	.	.	.	29.9	17.4
0	.	.	.	.	.	.	.	.	3.9	1.8

Women - Femmes - Mujeres
ISCO-88 - CITP-88 - CIUO-88

	1999	2000	2001	2002	2003	2004	2005	2006	2007	2008
Total	.	.	.	.	.	.	.	.	295.7	227.9
UB	.	.	.	.	.	.	.	.	120.4	100.9
1	.	.	.	.	.	.	.	.	1.5	3.5
2	.	.	.	.	.	.	.	.	9.5	7.0
3	.	.	.	.	.	.	.	.	34.7	20.3
4	.	.	.	.	.	.	.	.	15.5	11.7
5	.	.	.	.	.	.	.	.	56.8	40.1
6	.	.	.	.	.	.	.	.	1.2	1.1
7	.	.	.	.	.	.	.	.	27.4	19.4
8	.	.	.	.	.	.	.	.	10.0	5.0
9	.	.	.	.	.	.	.	.	18.2	18.9
0	.	.	.	.	.	.	.	.	0.5	-

Slovakia (BA) [1] [3]   Total unemployment - Chômage total - Desempleo total

Total - Total - Total
ISCO-88 - CITP-88 - CIUO-88

	1999	2000	2001	2002	2003	2004	2005	2006	2007	2008
Total	416.8	485.2	508.0	486.9	459.2	481.0	427.5	353.4	291.9	257.5
UB	94.0	104.2	109.4	107.9	95.8	100.0	101.3	89.0	70.1	64.5
1	5.8	6.8	6.4	4.7	4.5	4.7	5.2	2.4	2.6	1.6
2	7.2	6.2	6.1	6.7	5.2	8.1	6.8	5.1	4.7	5.1
3	22.8	29.0	31.1	30.0	27.6	32.0	26.4	16.4	13.3	13.8
4	13.3	15.7	19.6	15.8	16.5	16.2	13.2	11.1	8.4	7.6
5	38.6	51.3	57.8	52.4	46.1	53.0	38.0	34.1	30.0	25.5
6	7.3	6.9	6.4	5.5	6.1	6.2	5.2	4.8	3.5	3.4
7	67.9	85.1	83.3	66.4	65.1	63.7	50.9	36.6	32.3	26.8
8	40.7	52.0	49.8	49.5	43.5	46.4	40.6	32.3	26.5	23.9
9	63.1	65.3	98.4	100.9	98.8	85.2	72.9	53.8	37.0	33.4
0	.	.	.	0.5	0.7	2.0	1.4	1.3	1.0	0.1
X	56.2	62.8	39.9	46.8	49.5	63.2	65.6	66.7	62.4	52.1

Men - Hommes - Hombres
ISCO-88 - CITP-88 - CIUO-88

	1999	2000	2001	2002	2003	2004	2005	2006	2007	2008
Total	226.6	265.5	282.5	263.9	246.5	250.0	223.6	179.5	143.5	124.6
UB	49.5	56.7	59.7	56.8	49.6	54.0	52.2	45.9	36.5	32.4
1	3.6	4.5	4.0	2.9	3.0	3.0	3.1	1.6	1.8	1.0
2	3.1	2.8	2.1	2.5	2.6	3.3	2.2	1.6	1.7	1.6
3	6.7	10.4	10.8	10.6	9.5	10.0	9.0	5.0	4.1	5.0
4	3.5	4.2	5.6	3.4	3.1	2.9	3.5	3.3	2.5	2.0
5	11.4	13.4	15.4	13.5	13.0	12.2	9.6	6.5	5.8	6.2
6	3.8	3.8	3.2	3.2	3.1	2.8	2.1	2.4	1.7	1.5
7	54.0	66.6	69.2	55.5	51.1	50.2	38.8	26.4	22.5	18.5
8	28.7	36.6	34.8	33.3	30.5	30.6	24.6	21.6	16.5	15.3
9	39.0	38.9	62.8	63.0	61.2	52.8	46.0	31.8	19.5	18.1
0	.	.	.	0.5	0.6	1.5	1.0	0.8	0.7	-
X	23.3	27.9	15.0	18.9	19.2	26.6	31.7	32.9	30.5	23.1

Explanatory notes: see p. 451.

[1] Persons aged 15 years and over. [2] Oct. [3] Excl. persons on child-care leave.

Notes explicatives: voir p. 454.

[1] Personnes âgées de 15 ans et plus. [2] Oct. [3] Non compris les personnes en congé parental.

Notas explicativas: véase p. 457.

[1] Personas de 15 años y más. [2] Oct. [3] Excl. las personas con licencia parental.

UNEMPLOYMENT · CHÔMAGE · DESEMPLEO

By occupation · Par profession · Por ocupación

Thousands · Milliers · Millares

	1999	2000	2001	2002	2003	2004	2005	2006	2007	2008
Slovakia (BA) [1][2]				**Total unemployment - Chômage total - Desempleo total**						
Women - Femmes - Mujeres										
ISCO-88 - CITP-88 - CIUO-88										
Total	190.2	219.7	225.5	223.0	212.7	231.0	203.8	173.9	148.4	132.8
UB	44.5	47.6	49.7	51.1	46.2	46.3	49.1	43.0	33.6	32.0
1	2.3	2.4	2.4	1.8	1.5	1.8	2.1	0.9	0.9	0.6
2	4.1	3.3	3.9	4.2	2.6	4.7	4.6	3.5	3.0	3.5
3	16.1	18.6	20.2	19.4	18.1	22.0	17.4	11.4	9.2	8.8
4	9.8	11.5	14.0	12.4	13.4	13.2	9.8	7.9	6.0	5.6
5	27.2	38.0	42.4	38.9	33.1	40.7	28.4	27.7	24.3	19.3
6	3.5	3.2	3.3	2.2	3.0	3.4	3.1	2.4	1.8	1.9
7	13.9	18.5	14.1	10.9	14.1	13.5	12.2	10.2	9.8	8.3
8	12.0	15.5	15.0	16.3	12.9	15.8	16.1	10.7	10.1	8.6
9	24.1	26.4	35.6	38.0	37.6	32.4	26.9	22.0	17.6	15.3
0	.	.	.	.	0.1	0.5	0.3	0.6	0.4	0.1
X	33.0	34.9	24.9	27.8	30.3	36.6	33.9	33.8	32.0	29.0
Slovakia (FB) [1][3]				**Registered unemployment - Chômage enregistré - Desempleo registrado**						
Total - Total - Total										
ISCO-88 - CITP-88 - CIUO-88										
Total	535.2	506.5	533.7	504.1	452.2	383.2	333.8	273.4	239.9	248.5
UB	173.3	170.3	163.8	153.5	127.9	125.6	126.9	114.4	105.0	121.5
1	3.9	3.2	2.9	2.7	2.6	2.0	1.8	1.8	1.8	1.8
2	9.8	9.8	8.6	7.2	6.5	5.8	4.7	3.8	3.8	3.4
3	31.1	28.4	27.8	25.5	24.6	20.8	15.9	12.3	11.3	11.1
4	19.2	18.3	17.8	17.1	16.0	13.8	10.8	8.3	7.6	7.9
5	41.0	42.3	42.6	41.4	38.1	32.6	27.6	22.3	18.9	16.9
6	11.0	9.6	9.4	8.6	9.0	6.9	5.5	4.3	3.6	3.1
7	79.3	66.7	61.7	56.7	54.2	41.8	32.7	23.3	19.7	19.4
8	30.4	26.7	25.5	23.9	25.9	19.7	15.6	10.9	9.7	11.9
9	136.2	131.2	173.6	167.4	147.2	114.0	92.2	71.9	58.4	51.5
0	-	-	-	0.1	0.2	0.2	0.1	0.1	0.1	
Slovenia (BA) [1][4]				**Total unemployment - Chômage total - Desempleo total**						
Total - Total - Total										
ISCO-88 - CITP-88 - CIUO-88										
Total	71	69	57	58	63	62	58	61	48	43
UB	19	22	16	16	17	16	14	18	13	11
1	2	1	1	1	2	1	2	1	1	1
2	1	1	1	2	2	2	2	3	3	2
3	7	5	4	5	4	5	5	5	5	2
4	6	5	5	4	4	3	4	4	2	4
5	9	7	6	6	7	6	7	7	6	5
6	1	1	-	-	-	-	-	-	-	-
7	7	9	6	9	8	7	7	7	4	5
8	16	14	10	11	12	11	10	9	6	5
9	4	5	6	4	6	7	6	6	6	5
0	-	-	-	-	-	-	-	-	-	1
X	-	1	2	-	-	-	-	1	1	-
Men - Hommes - Hombres										
ISCO-88 - CITP-88 - CIUO-88										
Total	37	36	29	30	32	31	30	28	20	20
UB	9	10	8	7	8	6	7	8	5	4
1	1	-	1	1	1	-	2	1	1	1
2	-	-	-	-	1	-	1	2	1	1
3	4	2	2	2	2	3	2	2	2	1
4	2	2	2	2	2	1	2	1	1	1
5	3	2	2	1	3	2	2	1	1	1
6	1	-	-	-	-	-	-	-	-	-
7	7	9	6	8	7	6	6	6	4	4
8	9	8	5	5	5	6	5	4	3	3
9	2	2	3	2	2	4	3	2	2	3
0	-	-	-	-	-	-	-	-	-	-
X	-	-	1	-	-	-	-	1	-	.
Women - Femmes - Mujeres										
ISCO-88 - CITP-88 - CIUO-88										
Total	34	33	28	28	31	30	28	33	28	23
UB	10	12	8	8	9	11	7	10	8	7
1	1	-	-	-	-	-	-	-	-	-
2	-	-	-	1	-	1	1	1	2	1
3	3	2	2	3	2	2	3	3	3	1
4	4	4	4	3	2	2	3	2	2	3
5	6	4	5	4	5	4	5	6	5	4
6	-	-	-	-	-	-	-	-	-	-
7	-	-	1	1	-	1	1	1	1	1
8	7	6	5	6	7	5	5	5	3	2
9	2	3	3	3	3	3	3	4	4	3
0	-	-	-	-	-	-	-	-	-	-
X	-	-	1	-	-	-	-	-	-	-

Explanatory notes: see p. 451.

[1] Persons aged 15 years and over. [2] Excl. persons on child-care leave. [3] 31st Dec. of each year. [4] Second quarter of each year.

Notes explicatives: voir p. 454.

[1] Personnes âgées de 15 ans et plus. [2] Non compris les personnes en congé parental. [3] 31 déc. de chaque année. [4] Deuxième trimestre de chaque année.

Notas explicativas: véase p. 457.

[1] Personas de 15 años y más. [2] Excl. las personas con licencia parental. [3] 31 dic. de cada año. [4] Segundo trimestre de cada año.

	Thousands			Milliers				Millares		
	1999	2000	2001	2002	2003	2004	2005	2006	2007	2008

Suisse (BA) [1] [2]

Total unemployment - Chômage total - Desempleo total

Total - Total - Total
ISCO-88 - CITP-88 - CIUO-88

	1999	2000	2001	2002	2003	2004	2005	2006	2007	2008
Total	.	.	.	119	170	179	185	169	156	147
1	.	.	.	8	9	10	10	7	6	8
2	.	.	.	14	19	17	17	14	14	16
3	.	.	.	12	21	21	24	21	19	19
4	.	.	.	15	21	32	29	25	20	18
5	.	.	.	19	27	28	29	33	28	24
6	.	.	.	. [3]	3 [4]	4 [4]	2 [4]	3 [4]	2 [4]	3 [4]
7	.	.	.	17	27	25	22	19	19	17
8	.	.	.	8	9	10	11	10	8	6
9	.	.	.	6	9	8	9	10	11	12
X	.	.	.	19	26	24	31	27	28	24

Men - Hommes - Hombres
ISCO-88 - CITP-88 - CIUO-88

	1999	2000	2001	2002	2003	2004	2005	2006	2007	2008
Total	.	.	.	.	86	89	88	78	68	66
1	.	.	.	.	6	7	7	3 [4]	3 [4]	5 [4]
2	.	.	.	.	12	10	10	8	8	10
3	.	.	.	.	9	9	9	8	6 [4]	7 [4]
4	.	.	.	.	8	12	11	8	6 [4]	5 [4]
5	.	.	.	.	7	8	9	11	8	7
6	.	.	.	.	. [3]	2 [4]	. [3]	. [3]	. [3]	. [3]
7	.	.	.	.	21	20	17	16	14	13
8	.	.	.	.	6	6	9	8	5 [4]	4 [4]
9	.	.	.	.	3 [4]	3 [4]	4 [4]	4 [4]	5 [4]	5 [4]
X	.	.	.	.	12	12	11	10	11	9

Women - Femmes - Mujeres
ISCO-88 - CITP-88 - CIUO-88

	1999	2000	2001	2002	2003	2004	2005	2006	2007	2008
Total	.	.	.	.	84	89	97	91	88	80
1	.	.	.	.	3 [4]	3 [4]	3 [4]	3 [4]	3 [4]	2 [4]
2	.	.	.	.	6	7	7	6	6	6
3	.	.	.	.	13	12	15	13	13	12
4	.	.	.	.	13	20	18	17	14	13
5	.	.	.	.	19	21	20	21	20	17
7	.	.	.	.	6	5	5	4 [4]	5	4 [4]
8	.	.	.	.	3 [4]	4 [4]	2 [4]	2 [4]	3 [4]	2 [4]
9	.	.	.	.	5	5	5	7	7	7
X	.	.	.	.	14	11	20	17	17	16

Sweden (BA) [5]

Total unemployment - Chômage total - Desempleo total

Total - Total - Total
ISCO-88 - CITP-88 - CIUO-88

	1999	2000	2001	2002	2003	2004	2005	2006	2007	2008
Total	241	203	175	176	217	246	270 [6]	246	298	305
UB	29	23	17	16	17	20	42 [6]	40	75	83
1	5	3	2	4	4	5	5 [6]	4	4	4
2	17	14	15	17	24	24	24 [6]	23	22	18
3	23	20	17	19	25	28	29 [6]	24	24	24
4	24	21	19	20	27	29	25 [6]	21	26	26
5	45	36	33	33	39	48	53 [6]	49	58	57
6	7	7	6	4	5	7	7 [6]	6	5	5
7	32	28	24	23	29	30	26 [6]	25	24	22
8	32	26	21	22	26	29	29 [6]	22	23	24
9	28	24	18	16	19	23	23 [6]	23	28	32
X	-	-	2	2	2	2	7 [6]	7	8	9

Men - Hommes - Hombres
ISCO-88 - CITP-88 - CIUO-88

	1999	2000	2001	2002	2003	2004	2005	2006	2007	2008
Total	133	114	99	101	123	137	148 [6]	131	149	152
UB	16	13	9	8	9	10	24 [6]	22	36	39
1	4	3	2	3	3	4	4 [6]	3	3	3
2	10	9	9	9	14	13	12 [6]	11	11	10
3	14	12	11	12	16	15	17 [6]	13	13	13
4	7	6	6	7	8	11	8 [6]	7	10	10
5	12	10	10	11	12	16	18 [6]	17	17	16
6	5	5	4	3	3	4	5 [6]	4	4	3
7	30	26	22	21	26	28	24 [6]	23	23	21
8	25	20	16	18	21	23	21 [6]	17	18	18
9	12	11	8	7	10	10	11 [6]	11	12	15
X	-	-	1	2	1	2	2 [6]	4	4	5

(A vertical break line separates 2004 and 2005 columns for Sweden, indicating revised methodology.)

Explanatory notes: see p. 451.

[1] Persons aged 15 years and over. [2] Second quarter of each year. [3] Not indicated due to lack of statistical reliability. [4] Relative statistical reliability. [5] Persons aged 15 to 74 years; prior to 2007: 16 to 64 years. [6] Methodology revised; data not strictly comparable.

Notes explicatives: voir p. 454.

[1] Personnes âgées de 15 ans et plus. [2] Deuxième trimestre de chaque année. [3] Non indiqué en raison du manque de fiabilité statistique. [4] Fiabilité statistique relative. [5] Personnes âgées de 15 à 74 ans; avant 2007: 16 à 64 ans. [6] Méthodologie révisée; les données ne sont pas strictement comparables.

Notas explicativas: véase p. 457.

[1] Personas de 15 años y más. [2] Segundo trimestre de cada año. [3] No se indica por la falta de confiabilidad estadística. [4] Confiabilidad estadística relativa. [5] Personas de 15 a 74 años; antes de 2007: 16 a 64 años. [6] Metodología revisada; los datos no son estrictamente comparables.

	Thousands					Milliers			Millares	
	1999	2000	2001	2002	2003	2004	2005	2006	2007	2008

Sweden (BA) [1]

Total unemployment - Chômage total - Desempleo total

Women - Femmes - Mujeres
ISCO-88 - CITP-88 - CIUO-88

	1999	2000	2001	2002	2003	2004	2005	2006	2007	2008
Total	107	89	76	76	94	109	123 [2]	114	148	152
UB	14	10	8	7	8	9	18 [2]	19	39	44
1	1	-	-	1	1	1	1 [2]	2	2	1
2	8	6	6	7	9	11	11 [2]	12	11	9
3	9	8	6	7	9	13	12 [2]	11	11	12
4	16	14	13	13	18	18	17 [2]	15	16	16
5	33	26	23	22	27	32	35 [2]	33	41	40
6	2	2	2	2	2	2	1 [2]	2	1	2
7	2	2	2	2	2	2	2 [2]	2	2	1
8	7	7	5	4	5	6	8 [2]	5	5	6
9	16	13	10	9	10	12	12 [2]	12	17	17
X	-	-	1	1	1	1	4 [2]	3	4	4

Turkey (BA) [3]

Total unemployment - Chômage total - Desempleo total

Total - Total - Total
ISCO-88 - CITP-88 - CIUO-88

	1999	2000	2001	2002	2003	2004	2005	2006	2007	2008
Total	.	.	1 967	2 464	2 493	2 498	2 519	2 446	2 377	2 611
UB	.	.	477	513	480	612	553	490	430	394
1	.	.	79	90	77	83	89	79	78	91
2	.	.	42	61	61	62	71	77	85	95
3	.	.	95	117	104	116	121	116	120	133
4	.	.	71	155	133	140	151	154	175	197
5	.	.	215	299	295	292	303	334	314	358
6	.	.	64	51	87	62	58	49	50	51
7	.	.	467	541	503	457	474	430	427	496
8	.	.	152	227	218	244	254	261	227	254
9	.	.	305	407	532	430	445	456	471	542

Men - Hommes - Hombres
ISCO-88 - CITP-88 - CIUO-88

	1999	2000	2001	2002	2003	2004	2005	2006	2007	2008
Total	.	.	1 485	1 826	1 830	1 878	1 867	1 777	1 716	1 877
UB	.	.	273	279	262	361	306	261	222	195
1	.	.	62	76	67	75	83	68	69	75
2	.	.	25	32	37	35	37	38	36	47
3	.	.	61	71	60	71	70	70	73	78
4	.	.	28	66	54	58	63	68	70	76
5	.	.	170	238	228	224	228	240	221	255
6	.	.	55	38	57	51	49	38	39	42
7	.	.	411	485	453	422	429	392	393	455
8	.	.	143	206	189	218	224	226	197	218
9	.	.	259	334	421	364	379	376	396	436

Women - Femmes - Mujeres
ISCO-88 - CITP-88 - CIUO-88

	1999	2000	2001	2002	2003	2004	2005	2006	2007	2008
Total	.	.	482	638	663	620	652	669	660	734
UB	.	.	204	234	218	251	248	230	208	199
1	.	.	17	14	10	8	7	11	9	16
2	.	.	17	29	24	27	34	40	49	48
3	.	.	34	46	44	45	51	46	47	55
4	.	.	43	89	79	82	88	86	104	121
5	.	.	45	61	67	68	75	93	93	103
6	.	.	9	13	30	12	9	11	11	9
7	.	.	56	56	50	36	45	38	34	41
8	.	.	9	21	29	26	30	35	30	36
9	.	.	46	73	111	66	66	79	75	106

Turkey (FB) [4][5]

Registered unemployment - Chômage enregistré - Desempleo registrado

Total - Total - Total
ISCO-68 - CITP-68 - CIUO-68

	1999	2000	2001	2002	2003	2004	2005	2006	2007	2008
Total	487.5	730.5	718.7	464.2	587.5	811.9	881.3	1 061.9	696.5	987.8
0/1	24.8	80.4	80.8	43.1	49.2	82.9	70.0	87.6	12.0	75.5
2	4.2	10.8	12.2	11.7	21.0	40.5	42.6	49.4	48.5	57.8
3	100.6	178.7	174.3	109.1	128.1	207.6	190.3	206.1	126.3	161.1
4	0.5	0.7	0.8	2.3	6.9	10.2	14.3	21.0	70.6	83.0
5	13.2	15.9	15.3	15.9	25.7	31.6	41.7	54.7	27.8	41.4
6	0.6	0.8	0.8	0.8	1.5	1.8	2.2	2.8	1.7	2.9
7/8/9	143.7	265.9	259.0	159.5	156.1	198.2	219.4	283.4	98.0	157.2
X	200.0	177.3	175.4	122.0	198.8	239.1	300.9	356.9	311.7	409.0

Explanatory notes: see p. 451.

[1] Persons aged 15 to 74 years; prior to 2007: 16 to 64 years. [2] Methodology revised; data not strictly comparable. [3] Persons aged 15 years and over. [4] Persons aged 14 years and over. [5] Dec. of each year.

Notes explicatives: voir p. 454.

[1] Personnes âgées de 15 à 74 ans; avant 2007: 16 à 64 ans. [2] Méthodologie révisée; les données ne sont pas strictement comparables. [3] Personnes âgées de 15 ans et plus. [4] Personnes âgées de 14 ans et plus. [5] Déc. de chaque année.

Notas explicativas: véase p. 457.

[1] Personas de 15 a 74 años; antes de 2007: 16 a 64 años. [2] Metodología revisada; los datos no son estrictamente comparables. [3] Personas de 15 años y más. [4] Personas de 14 años y más. [5] Dic. de cada año.

UNEMPLOYMENT — CHÔMAGE — DESEMPLEO

By occupation — Par profession — Por ocupación

	Thousands — Milliers — Millares									
	1999	2000	2001	2002	2003	2004	2005	2006	2007	2008
Turkey (FB) [1][2]	*Registered unemployment - Chômage enregistré - Desempleo registrado*									
Men - Hommes - Hombres										
ISCO-68 - CITP-68 - CIUO-68										
Total	413.8	591.9	582.9	379.8	469.4	611.4	656.2	782.7	520.1	724.3
0/1	17.0	50.6	50.5	28.0	33.1	54.4	44.3	46.6	8.3	53.2
2	2.9	6.6	7.4	7.2	13.9	26.5	28.1	32.5	26.6	32.1
3	65.5	111.0	110.3	71.3	82.3	122.7	109.8	119.7	88.9	108.8
4	0.4	0.5	0.5	1.6	4.6	6.6	9.2	13.6	38.2	42.2
5	12.5	14.5	13.9	14.4	22.6	26.3	33.7	44.2	20.3	28.3
6	0.6	0.7	0.7	0.7	1.3	1.6	2.0	2.6	1.6	2.7
7/8/9	138.9	253.1	246.8	152.2	143.3	175.8	186.7	236.0	85.2	136.8
X	176.0	155.0	152.7	104.4	168.3	197.5	242.4	287.5	250.9	320.3
Women - Femmes - Mujeres										
ISCO-68 - CITP-68 - CIUO-68										
Total	73.7	138.6	135.8	84.9	118.0	200.6	225.0	279.2	176.4	263.5
0/1	7.8	29.9	30.3	15.1	16.0	28.6	25.7	41.0	3.6	22.3
2	1.3	4.2	4.8	4.4	7.2	14.1	14.5	16.8	21.8	25.7
3	35.1	67.7	64.0	37.9	45.8	84.8	80.4	86.4	37.3	52.3
4	0.1	0.2	0.2	0.7	2.3	3.5	5.1	7.5	32.3	40.8
5	0.6	1.4	1.5	1.4	3.2	5.3	8.0	10.5	7.5	13.1
6	0.0	0.1	0.1	0.6	1.9	0.2	0.2	0.2	0.1	0.2
7/8/9	4.8	12.8	12.2	7.3	12.8	22.5	32.7	47.5	12.8	20.5
X	24.0	22.3	22.8	17.6	30.5	41.6	58.5	69.4	60.8	88.7
Ukraine (BA) [3]	*Total unemployment - Chômage total - Desempleo total*									
Total - Total - Total										
ISCO-88 - CITP-88 - CIUO-88										
Total	2 614.3	2 655.8	2 455.0	2 140.7	2 008.0	1 906.7	1 600.8	1 515.0	1 417.6	1 425.1
UB	604.1	540.1	481.0	397.1	341.0	467.0	366.2	332.9	327.8	312.6
1	82.8	93.4	98.6	83.5	70.5	50.3	56.2	45.9	38.7	40.7
2	179.8	181.6	157.7	131.4	117.0	94.2	73.1	101.0	75.8	71.3
3	335.1	316.8	264.9	206.3	185.0	172.2	133.8	130.8	114.3	99.5
4	97.8	104.4	103.0	89.4	85.6	61.5	51.4	45.3	51.4	53.0
5	278.4	293.6	277.6	265.0	247.8	229.6	204.4	206.0	204.0	205.3
6	27.5	42.7	48.0	39.0	55.9	65.4	42.8	25.0	26.5	32.9
7	399.6	421.9	372.9	348.1	323.1	240.6	217.9	170.7	165.7	210.3
8	365.9	400.1	365.8	322.9	304.8	266.6	199.5	199.7	169.5	175.4
9	243.3	261.2	285.5	258.0	277.3	259.3	255.5	257.7	243.9	224.1
Men - Hommes - Hombres										
ISCO-88 - CITP-88 - CIUO-88										
Total	1 346.5	1 357.4	1 263.0	1 106.5	1 055.7	1 001.6	862.5	804.1	770.7	768.9
UB	315.8	264.7	250.8	204.8	167.2	268.3	202.4	168.0	175.8	172.3
1	53.0	55.6	55.8	46.2	42.3	28.3	30.4	29.5	21.7	23.0
2	61.9	55.4	55.2	50.6	44.8	41.4	24.0	48.3	37.5	35.2
3	137.3	132.9	106.6	82.4	79.1	73.6	54.4	57.3	50.7	41.6
4	11.2	15.4	13.0	8.6	12.4	17.5	5.1	6.6	9.4	5.9
5	67.7	68.5	69.6	66.2	64.3	74.0	59.3	56.3	67.7	59.0
6	13.1	18.2	21.5	15.5	20.7	30.4	18.2	11.9	9.3	11.6
7	294.4	313.0	280.2	266.0	252.9	165.5	177.3	143.3	142.0	172.7
8	258.0	287.6	253.4	227.6	221.4	169.1	143.6	133.0	120.0	118.9
9	134.1	146.1	156.9	138.6	150.6	133.5	147.8	149.9	136.6	128.7
Women - Femmes - Mujeres										
ISCO-88 - CITP-88 - CIUO-88										
Total	1 267.8	1 298.4	1 192.0	1 034.2	952.3	905.1	738.3	710.9	646.9	656.2
UB	288.3	275.4	230.2	192.3	173.8	198.7	163.8	164.9	152.0	140.3
1	29.8	37.8	42.8	37.3	28.2	22.0	25.8	16.4	17.0	17.7
2	117.9	126.2	102.5	80.8	72.2	52.8	49.1	52.7	38.3	36.1
3	197.8	183.9	158.3	123.9	105.9	98.6	79.4	73.5	63.6	57.9
4	86.6	89.0	90.0	80.8	73.2	44.0	46.3	38.7	42.0	47.1
5	210.7	225.1	208.0	198.8	183.5	155.6	145.1	149.7	136.3	146.3
6	14.4	24.5	26.5	23.5	35.2	35.0	24.6	13.1	17.2	21.3
7	105.2	108.9	92.7	82.1	70.2	75.1	40.6	27.4	23.7	37.6
8	107.9	112.5	112.4	95.3	83.4	97.5	55.9	66.7	49.5	56.5
9	109.2	115.1	128.6	119.4	126.7	125.8	107.7	107.8	107.3	95.4
United Kingdom (BA) [4][5]	*Total unemployment - Chômage total - Desempleo total*									
Total - Total - Total										
ISCO-88 - CITP-88 - CIUO-88										
Total	.	.	1 423	1 472	1 420	1 394	1 397	1 649	1 621	1 643
UB	.	.	265	251	266	291	304	360	385	397
1	.	.	80	99	108	81	78	99	90	93
2	.	.	45	56	60	55	49	57	54	49
3	.	.	62	93	97	76	74	82	83	99
4	.	.	92	118	113	96	115	123	105	97
5	.	.	159	185	173	189	193	237	236	245
6,9	.	.	288	287	254	258	265	317	326	323
7	.	.	132	127	121	127	105	121	126	121
8	.	.	148	132	130	119	118	133	114	123
X	.	.	153	123	99	102	95	118	103	96

Explanatory notes: see p. 451.

[1] Persons aged 14 years and over. [2] Dec. of each year. [3] Persons aged 15-70 years. [4] Persons aged 16 years and over. [5] Second quarter.

Notes explicatives: voir p. 454.

[1] Personnes âgées de 14 ans et plus. [2] Déc. de chaque année. [3] Personnes âgées de 15 à 70 ans. [4] Personnes âgées de 16 ans et plus. [5] Deuxième trimestre.

Notas explicativas: véase p. 457.

[1] Personas de 14 años y más. [2] Dic. de cada año. [3] Personas de 15 á 70 años. [4] Personas de 16 años y más. [5] Segundo trimestre.

	Thousands				Milliers				Millares	
	1999	2000	2001	2002	2003	2004	2005	2006	2007	2008

United Kingdom (BA) [1] [2]   Total unemployment - Chômage total - Desempleo total

Men - Hommes - Hombres
ISCO-88 - CITP-88 - CIUO-88

Total	.	.	861	892	867	824	817	959	930	969
UB	.	.	152	150	141	164	180	218	208	239
1	.	.	56	69	78	53	51	70	55	62
2	.	.	30	41	45	38	30	35	31	33
3	.	.	41	63	63	49	40	48	48	54
4	.	.	25	37	37	25	40	38	34	31
5	.	.	48	60	63	58	56	74	74	75
6.9	.	.	198	192	169	174	184	193	217	212
7	.	.	121	120	112	119	97	115	117	111
8	.	.	114	100	105	96	95	112	96	106
X	.	.	76	61	53	47	42	54	49	46

Women - Femmes - Mujeres
ISCO-88 - CITP-88 - CIUO-88

Total	.	.	562	580	553	570	580	690	691	674
UB	.	.	113	101	125	127	124	142	177	158
1	.	.	24	30	29	28	27	29	35	31
2	.	.	15	15	15	17	19	22	23	16
3	.	.	21	30	34	27	33	34	34	45
4	.	.	67	81	75	71	76	86	71	66
5	.	.	111	126	109	130	137	162	162	170
6.9	.	.	89	96	85	84	80	123	109	111
7	.	.	12	7	9	8	8	7	8	10
8	.	.	33	32	25	23	23	21	18	17
X	.	.	77	62	46	54	53	63	54	50

OCEANIA-OCÉANIE-OCEANIA

Australia (BA) [3] [4]   Total unemployment - Chômage total - Desempleo total

Total - Total - Total
ISCO-88 - CITP-88 - CIUO-88

Total	654.9	607.5	648.0	631.2	596.0	554.7	529.0	517.7	487.5	470.9
UB	144.4	129.9	97.9	104.2	102.9	102.6	102.0	105.4	108.5	100.1
1	17.1	19.7	15.3	18.1	18.3	17.0	14.9	18.1	18.0	18.0
2	21.6	20.8	30.3	31.6	31.8	29.2	26.4	25.7	23.6	26.2
3	23.4	22.7	30.8	28.5	26.1	22.9	25.1	22.7	23.1	21.9
4	36.2	32.7	54.2	50.4	49.7	43.0	40.8	40.9	42.7	38.6
5	42.7	38.7	82.4	77.4	74.1	70.2	65.4	66.2	62.0	61.2
6	7.4	6.9	7.5	6.3	5.7	5.5	6.2	5.7	6.0	5.3
7	52.7	51.7	53.9	45.1	34.9	36.1	35.4	32.0	32.2	31.8
8	42.0	38.9	38.9	33.1	28.4	25.6	28.4	23.8	22.8	20.4
9	42.7	41.3	86.7	79.1	76.5	74.7	69.4	65.6	57.1	55.9
X	224.7	204.2	248.0	261.7	250.5	230.5	217.0	216.9	199.9	191.6

Men - Hommes - Hombres
ISCO-88 - CITP-88 - CIUO-88

Total	379.5	347.7	373.7	360.9	324.9	299.4	283.1	277.5	245.7	236.9
UB	71.7	63.8	49.0	53.5	52.2	49.4	51.3	54.1	50.7	49.9
1	11.2	11.5	9.7	12.6	12.1	11.3	9.2	11.2	11.3	10.1
2	12.4	13.2	17.6	17.5	17.9	15.7	13.1	12.1	10.1	13.4
3	12.6	10.5	18.8	15.7	13.8	12.5	11.8	10.3	9.5	9.8
4	14.7	14.5	18.5	17.6	15.3	13.3	11.6	13.7	13.8	12.0
5	16.7	16.6	32.7	29.8	27.6	26.0	24.7	23.4	20.6	20.0
6	6.9	5.8	6.7	5.6	4.7	5.0	5.2	4.9	4.7	3.9
7	48.7	48.1	50.9	42.4	32.7	34.4	33.1	29.5	30.5	30.1
8	37.9	34.7	33.1	28.9	24.1	21.4	24.4	19.9	18.9	16.1
9	29.9	27.2	59.9	56.0	52.7	50.0	46.9	47.3	38.6	38.1
X	116.8	102.0	125.9	134.9	124.1	109.7	103.1	105.2	87.7	83.4

Women - Femmes - Mujeres
ISCO-88 - CITP-88 - CIUO-88

Total	275.4	259.8	274.3	270.3	271.1	255.4	245.9	240.1	241.7	234.0
UB	72.7	66.1	48.9	50.7	50.7	53.1	50.8	51.3	57.8	50.2
1	5.9	8.2	5.6	5.5	6.2	5.7	5.8	6.8	6.7	7.9
2	9.2	7.7	12.7	14.1	14.0	13.5	13.3	13.6	13.4	12.8
3	10.8	12.2	12.0	12.8	12.3	10.4	13.3	12.5	13.7	12.1
4	21.5	18.2	35.7	32.8	34.4	29.8	29.1	27.2	28.9	26.6
5	26.1	22.1	49.7	47.6	46.5	44.2	40.7	42.8	41.4	41.2
6	0.4	1.2	0.8	0.7	1.0	0.5	1.0	0.8	1.3	1.4
7	4.1	3.6	3.0	2.7	2.2	1.7	2.3	2.5	1.7	1.7
8	4.1	4.2	5.9	4.1	4.2	4.2	4.0	3.9	3.9	4.3
9	12.7	14.1	26.8	23.1	23.7	24.7	22.5	18.3	18.5	17.8
X	107.9	102.2	122.1	126.8	126.4	120.8	114.0	111.7	112.2	108.2

Explanatory notes: see p. 451.

[1] Persons aged 16 years and over. [2] Second quarter. [3] Excl. armed forces. [4] Persons aged 15 years and over.

Notes explicatives: voir p. 454.

[1] Personnes âgées de 16 ans et plus. [2] Deuxième trimestre. [3] Non compris les forces armées. [4] Personnes âgées de 15 ans et plus.

Notas explicativas: véase p. 457.

[1] Personas de 16 años y más. [2] Segundo trimestre. [3] Excl. las fuerzas armadas. [4] Personas de 15 años y más.

By occupation **Par profession** **Por ocupación**

	Thousands			Milliers				Millares		
	1999	2000	2001	2002	2003	2004	2005	2006	2007	2008

New Zealand (BA) [1]   Total unemployment - Chômage total - Desempleo total

Total - Total - Total
ISCO-88 - CITP-88 - CIUO-88

	1999	2000	2001	2002	2003	2004	2005	2006	2007	2008
Total	127.8	113.4	102.3	102.5	97.8 [2]	84.9	82.5	85.4	82.8	95.0
UB	15.9	12.8	12.7	12.4	12.3 [2]	12.3	11.6	12.5	14.3	15.7
1	4.5	3.8	4.4	4.3	3.1 [2]	3.1	3.2	3.9	4.0	3.9
2	5.3	5.5	4.5	5.8	5.5 [2]	4.6	3.8	4.5	4.6	6.2
3	7.3	8.4	6.9	6.6	5.5 [2]	4.6	5.2	5.1	4.3	5.9
4	9.5	9.4	8.0	8.4	9.9 [2]	8.1	8.4	8.3	7.8	7.8
5	21.0	18.5	17.7	19.5	18.0 [2]	16.3	16.4	16.1	15.0	17.3
6	13.3	11.3	10.4	10.9	9.4 [2]	7.2	7.5	6.4	6.3	6.0
7	8.5	6.3	6.6	5.3	4.3 [2]	3.1	3.0	4.7	4.8	5.5
8	12.1	10.8	8.9	8.5	7.9 [2]	7.1	7.7	6.2	5.2	6.6
9	17.2	15.2	12.9	12.5	12.8 [2]	11.6	10.4	10.5	9.7	11.6
X	13.7	11.9	9.6	8.5	9.0 [2]	7.0	5.6	7.5	6.7	8.4

Men - Hommes - Hombres
ISCO-88 - CITP-88 - CIUO-88

	1999	2000	2001	2002	2003	2004	2005	2006	2007	2008
Total	72.4	63.4	56.2	54.6	49.3 [2]	40.7	40.9	42.3	41.0	49.8
UB	7.9	6.6	6.5	6.4	6.4 [2]	5.5	5.7	6.0	7.2	8.4
1	2.9	2.1	2.7	2.8	1.7 [2]	1.6	2.1	2.3	2.2	2.4
2	2.6	2.7	2.1	3.1	3.0 [2]	2.3	1.8	1.6	2.0	2.8
3	3.6	5.0	3.3	3.4	2.8 [2]	2.2	2.4	2.3	1.6	2.3
4	2.2	2.7	2.3	2.3	2.7 [2]	2.2	2.6	2.2	2.7	1.8
5	7.7	6.9	6.0	6.5	5.6 [2]	4.7	4.2	5.0	4.5	6.3
6	9.4	7.5	6.9	6.9	5.7 [2]	4.4	4.5	4.1	4.0	4.1
7	8.0	6.0	6.0	4.9	3.9 [2]	2.8	2.8	4.4	4.6	5.0
8	9.9	8.4	7.4	6.6	5.4 [2]	4.8	5.6	5.4	3.7	5.7
9	12.3	10.4	8.8	8.6	8.5 [2]	7.6	6.9	5.9	5.5	7.5
X	6.1	5.4	4.1	3.3	3.7 [2]	2.5	2.5	3.3	2.9	3.4

Women - Femmes - Mujeres
ISCO-88 - CITP-88 - CIUO-88

	1999	2000	2001	2002	2003	2004	2005	2006	2007	2008
Total	55.4	50.0	46.1	47.9	48.5 [2]	44.2	41.6	43.1	41.7	45.2
UB	8.0	6.2	6.1	6.0	5.9 [2]	6.7	6.0	6.5	7.0	7.3
1	1.6	1.6	1.8	1.5	1.4 [2]	1.4	1.1	1.6	1.8	1.4
2	2.7	2.8	2.4	2.7	2.4 [2]	2.3	3.0	3.0	2.6	3.4
3	3.7	3.4	3.6	3.2	2.8 [2]	2.4	2.8	2.8	2.7	3.6
4	7.2	6.7	5.7	6.2	7.3 [2]	5.9	5.8	6.1	5.1	6.0
5	13.2	11.5	11.7	13.0	12.5 [2]	11.6	12.2	11.1	10.5	11.0
6	3.9	3.8	3.4	4.0	3.7 [2]	2.8	3.0	2.3	2.2	1.9
7	-	-	-	-	-	-	-	-	-	-
8	2.3	2.4	1.5	1.9	2.5 [2]	2.2	2.1	-	1.4	1.0
9	4.9	4.8	4.1	4.0	4.4 [2]	4.0	3.4	4.6	4.2	4.1
X	7.6	6.5	5.4	5.2	5.3 [2]	4.5	3.1	4.2	3.8	5.0

Explanatory notes: see p. 451.

[1] Persons aged 15 years and over. [2] Methodology revised; data not strictly comparable.

Notes explicatives: voir p. 454.

[1] Personnes âgées de 15 ans et plus. [2] Méthodologie révisée; les données ne sont pas strictement comparables.

Notas explicativas: véase p. 457.

[1] Personas de 15 años y más. [2] Metodología revisada; los datos no son estrictamente comparables.

Hours of work

Durée du travail

Horas de trabajo

Hours of work

The hours of work relate to any period of time spent by persons in the performance of activities which contribute to the production of goods and services within the general production boundary as defined by the United Nations System of National Accounts.

The various types of statistics on hours of work presented in Chapter 4 are indicated in the tables by the following codes[1]:

(a) Hours actually worked
(b) Hours paid for
(c) Hours usually worked
(d) Normal hours of work

The series generally relate to employees of both sexes, irrespective of age. Data by sex are presented in around half of the series.

Definitions

Since 1962, there are international statistical standards only for the *hours actually* worked and the *normal hours of work* concepts, adopted by the Tenth International Conference of Labour Statisticians[2]. These are confined to persons in paid employment and describe work situations that are more typical for production workers in manufacturing establishments. While they have served as a guide to countries when producing national estimates, many national definitions have now become more comprehensive. These international standards are currently being revised to improve the coverage of persons and work activities, and to better reflect diverse working time arrangements. New international standards are expected to be adopted by the forthcoming 18th International Conference of Labour Statisticians in 2008, that will include other concepts such as *hours usually worked* and *hours paid for*. The following paragraphs provide definitional elements for these concepts as they are being measured by many countries.

The concept of *hours actually worked* relates to the time that persons in employment spend on work activities during a specified reference period, comprising:
(a) time spent directly on production (producing goods and services, including paid and unpaid overtime);
(b) time spent to facilitate production, necessary to work activities or to enhance the performance of persons (design, prepare, maintain the workplace, procedures, tools, including receipts, time sheets, reports), changing time (donning necessary work clothing), transporting activities (door to door, bringing agricultural produce to market) and work-related training;
(c) time spent in-between main activities (awaiting customers, stand-by for reasons such as lack of supply of work or power, machinery breakdown, accident), travel time to meetings or work assignments, active on-call duty (as for health and technical service professional);
(d) resting time (short rest or refreshment breaks including tea, coffee or prayer breaks).

Hours actually worked excludes time not worked, whether paid or unpaid, such as:

(a) annual leave, public holidays, sick leave, parental leave, etc.;
(b) meal breaks;
(c) time spent on travel from home to work and vice versa, also known as commuter travel, that is not actually time spent working.

Hours actually worked covers all types of workers, whether in self-employment jobs or in paid employment jobs; it may be paid or unpaid and carried out in any location, including the street, field, home, etc.

The *hours paid for* concept covers workers in paid employment and comprises all hours, whether worked or not, that have been paid by the employer. When compared to the *hours actually worked* of employees, it covers all paid hours, even those not worked, such as paid annual vacation, public holidays, paid sick leave, other paid leave, and excludes all unpaid time worked (for example, unpaid overtime).

The concept of *normal hours of work* covers a subset of persons in paid employment (e.g. those covered by labour laws and regulations) and relates to the hours in a day, week or year that they are expected to be at the disposal of their employer according to legislation, collective agreements or arbitral awards. When compared to the *hours actually worked* of employees, *normal hours of work* excludes all overtime (paid and unpaid) but includes all time which is paid at normal rates even if not worked.

The *hours usually worked* relates to the hours actually most commonly worked per week by persons in paid and self-employment during a long reference period such as a month, season, or other long period, i.e., the typical value of the weekly hours worked. As compared to the *normal hours of work*, all usual overtime is included in *hours usually worked*. All time worked not on a usual basis is therefore excluded.

Sources

In general, hours of work data are obtained from two main sources, namely establishment surveys or censuses and household sample surveys. Two other sources are official national estimates or administrative records of social insurance schemes. These sources are identified in the tables as a code in parentheses to the right of the country name. The source codes are explained in page XVI.

The first source relates to payroll data derived from establishment sample surveys or censuses, that often furnish at the same time statistics on wages and on employment. These statistics often relate to *hours paid for* and, to a lesser extent, to *hours actually worked*. Statistics derived from establishment-based surveys tend to have limited worker coverage, as they cover employees or a subset of them (e.g., wage earners or salaried employees) or who work in establishments above a certain size or in certain industries only. The coverage of the statistics may therefore be importantly limited in countries where most workers are engaged, for example, in small sized establishments or in self-employment jobs. These types of limitations are indicated in footnotes.

The second main source relates to labour force sample surveys or other household based surveys. Statistics derived from this source often relate to *hours actually worked*, and sometimes to the *hours usually worked*. In theory they cover the employed population as a whole, including the self-employed. Some statistics from labour force surveys relate to the hours of work in the main job only. This and other types of limitation are indicated in footnotes.

Worker coverage

The statistics presented in Tables 4A and 4B relate to *employees*, as defined by the International Standard Classification of Status in Employment, ICSE-93. When statistics are derived from labour force surveys, they can refer to *total employment*. When they are derived from establishment surveys, they can refer to a subgroup of employees, namely to *wage earners* or to *salaried employees*. Some countries further limit worker coverage to "adults", "skilled" or "unskilled" employees, in which case it is specified as a footnote. There are no international definitions for *wage earners* or for *salaried employees*. The former are generally equated with "manual", "production" or "blue collar" workers, and the latter with "white collar workers".

Worker coverage is indicated at the centre of the page for each series.

Time units

The series are presented on the basis of the average number of hours of work per week; in a few cases hours per day or per month are shown. These exceptions are indicated in footnotes.

Averaging methods

For statistics derived from establishment surveys, average hours actually worked or average hours paid for per week or per month are normally compiled by dividing the total number of hours actually worked or paid for during a week or a month by the average number of workers on the payrolls during the same period. Average hours actually worked or paid for per day are generally compiled by dividing the total number of hours actually worked or paid for during a week, fortnight or month by the total number of days actually worked or paid for during the same period.

In labour force surveys, average hours actually worked are normally derived by dividing the hours actually worked by all persons in employment (or all employees) by the number of persons in employment (or employees). In these calculations, persons absent from work during the whole survey reference week should be included in the calculation. In some series, however, they are excluded to better reflect a "typical" work week, in which case this is indicated in a footnote. In deriving averages, statistics may be based on one single point in time (i.e., when the survey is carried out once in the year), on a set of points in time (i.e., monthly or quarterly surveys) or on continuous observations (i.e., surveys that cover all weeks in a year). The more points in time are involved in the calculation, the less the estimate will be affected by seasonal fluctuations, annual and sick leave actually taken during the year as well as by variations in strike activity.

Comparability issues

In making comparisons of statistics on hours of work, it should be borne in mind that the data are influenced by the averaging method used, the number of data points used, and practices regarding the number of days normally worked per week, regulations and customs regarding weekend and overtime work, the extent of absence from work, etc.. They will also be affected by industrial and job coverage. Statistics that exclude workers in agriculture, where hours worked follow different patterns than in other industries, will not be comparable with those that include them. Similarly, statistics that relate to the main job only will be lower than statistics that cover multiple jobs[3].

4A Hours of work, by economic activity

The data shown in this table refer to, in principle, the average hours of work according to the broadest economic activity distinctions of all major divisions or categories of the International Standard Industrial Classification of all economic activities, ISIC. Three versions of ISIC are used to present statistics, ISIC rev.2, ISIC rev.3 and ISIC rev.4[4]. Major Divisions (for ISIC rev. 2) or Tabulation Categories (for ISIC rev. 3 and ISIC rev.4) are shown as codes with an indication of the classification which is used, and the name corresponding to each code is given in the Appendix. Where the national divisions or categories differ from the international groups, this is indicated in footnotes.

4B Hours of work in manufacturing

This table shows average hours of work in manufacturing by major group (in ISIC rev. 2) or division (in ISIC rev.3 and ISIC rev.4) in the manufacturing industry. Where the national major groups or divisions differ from the international groups, this is indicated in footnotes.

Notes

[1]. For the full set of statistical time series on hours of work held in the ILO data base, see the ILO Department of Statistics statistical dissemination website: (http://laborsta.ilo.org).

[2]. For the full text of the resolution, see ILO: *Current international recommendations on labour statistics* (Geneva, 2000) or the ILO Department of Statistics' website (www.ilo.org/public/english/bureau/stat).

[3]. For information on the differences in scope, definitions and methods of calculation, etc., used for the various national series, see ILO: *Sources and Methods: Labour Statistics* (formerly *Statistical Sources and Methods*), Vol. 2 : ~ Employment, wages, hours of work and labour cost (establishment surveys)~ , second edition (Geneva, 1995); Vol. 3 : ~ Economically active population, employment, unemployment and hours of work (household surveys)~ , second edition (Geneva, 1990); Vol. 4 : ~ Employment, unemployment, wages and hours of work (administrative records and related sources)~ (Geneva, 1989). All these volumes can be consulted online at our statistical website http://laborsta.ilo.org.

[4]. The detailed classifications can be consulted on the UN Statistical Division website at: http://unstats.un.org/unsd/class/default.htm.

Durée du travail

La durée du travail couvre toutes les périodes que les personnes dédient à des activités qui contribuent à la production des biens et services se trouvant dans la frontière générale de production définie par le Système de Comptes Nationaux des Nations Unies. Les divers types de statistiques sur la durée du travail présentées dans le Chapitre 4 sont indiqués dans les tableaux avec les codes suivants[1] :

(a) Heures réellement effectuées
(b) Heures rémunérées
(c) Heures habituellement travaillées
(d) Durée normale du travail

Les séries se réfèrent généralement aux salariés des deux sexes, sans considération d'âge. Des données par sexe sont présentées dans à peu prés la moitié des séries.

Définitions

Depuis 1962, des normes statistiques internationales existent uniquement pour les concepts des *heures réellement effectuées* et pour la *durée normale de travail*, adoptées par la dixième Conférence internationale des statisticiens du travail[2]. Elles sont confinées aux salariés et décrivent les situations de travail typiques des travailleurs de la production dans des établissements industriels. Bien qu'elles aient servi de guide pour les pays voulant produire des estimations nationales, beaucoup de définitions nationales sont maintenant devenues plus complètes. Ces normes internationales sont en train d'être révisées pour améliorer leur couverture des travailleurs et des activités de travail, ainsi que pour mieux refléter les divers arrangements du travail. De nouvelles normes internationales pourront être adoptées par la 18ème Conférence internationale des statisticiens du travail en 2008, qui inclura aussi des concepts sur les *heures habituelles du travail* et les *heures rémunérées*. Les paragraphes suivants montrent des définitions pour chacun des concepts tels qu'ils sont mesurés par les pays.

Le concept des heures de *travail réellement effectuées* se réfère au temps que les personnes employées dédient à des activités du travail pendant une période de référence spécifiée, et incluent:
(a) le temps dédié directement à la production (consacré à produire des biens et des services, incluant le temps supplémentaire payé et non payé);
(b) le temps dédié à faciliter la production, nécessaire aux activités de travail ou à améliorer la productivité des travailleurs (consacré à la conception, préparation, entretien du lieu de travail, procédures, outils, incluant les reçus, fiches de durée d'opérations et rapports), activités de transport (pour le travail à domicile, transport des produits sur le marché) et formation liée au travail;
(c) le temps entre les activités principales (temps morts, en raison, par exemple, du manque occasionnel de travail ou d'électricité, d'arrêts de machines, d'accidents), temps de voyage pour des réunions ou assignations de travail, temps de garde (pour le personnel de santé et les services techniques professionnels) ;
(d) le temps de repos (courtes périodes de repos ou rafraîchissement, y compris les arrêts du travail pour collation ou prière).

Les *heures de travail réellement effectuées* excluent le temps non travaillé, payé ou non payé, tel que:
(a) les congés annuels payés, congés parentaux, jours fériés payés, congés de maladie;
(b) les pauses pour les repas;
(c) le temps consacré aux trajets entre le domicile et le lieu de travail et vice versa, qui ne peut pas être considéré comme temps de travail.

Le concept des *heures de travail réellement effectuées* couvre tous les types de travailleurs indépendants et salariés ; elles peuvent être payés ou non et peuvent être faites dans n'importe quel endroit, y compris la rue, les champs, la maison, etc.

Le concept des *heures rémunérées* couvre les salariés et se réfère aux heures qui sont payées par l'employeur, effectuées ou non. Quand on les compare avec les *heures réellement effectuées* des salariés, elles incluent toutes les heures payées même si elles n'ont pas été effectuées, telles que les congés annuels, les jours fériés payés, les congés de maladie payés et autres congés payés, en excluant toutes les heures effectuées non payées (par exemple les heures supplémentaires non payées).

Le concept de la durée normale du travail couvre un sous groupe de salariés (ceux qui sont couverts par la législation et la réglementation du travail), se référent aux heures par jour, semaine ou année pendant lesquelles les travailleurs sont à la disposition de leur employeur selon ladite législation. Quand on les compare aux *heures réellement effectuées*, la *durée normale de travail* exclue les heures supplémentaires (payées ou non) mais inclue le temps non effectué qui est payé à des taux normaux de rémunération.

Le concept des heures habituellement travaillées est lié avec les heures réellement effectuées hebdomadairement par les indépendants et les salariés qui sont les plus communes pendant une période longue de référence tel que le mois, la saison ou autre longue période. Elles sont donc la valeur type des heures de travail hebdomadaires. Quand on le compare à la durée normale du travail, les heures habituellement travaillées incluent les heures supplémentaires habituelles et excluent les heures non travaillés habituellement.

Sources

En général, les statistiques de la durée du travail sont principalement tirées de deux types de sources: les enquêtes par sondage auprès des établissements et les enquêtes auprès des ménages. Deux autres sources sont les estimations officielles et les registres administratifs d'assurances sociales. Ces sources sont indiquées sous forme de code entre parenthèse à côté du nom du pays. Les codes des sources sont expliqués en page XVI.

La première source provient des bordereaux de salaire utilisés dans les enquêtes ou les recensements auprès des établissements qui fournissent fréquemment des données sur les salaires et sur l'emploi. Ces statistiques se réfèrent souvent aux *heures rémunérées* et dans une moindre mesure aux *heures réellement effectuées*. Les statistiques dérivées des enquêtes auprès des établissements ont souvent une couverture des travailleurs limitée, couvrant les salariés ou un sous groupe de salariés, par exemple, les ouvriers ou employés qui travaillent dans des établissements d'une certaine taille ou dans certaines industries. La couverture des statistiques peut être de ce fait considérablement limitée dans les pays où la plupart des travailleurs sont dans de petits établissements ou sont des indépendants. Ce type de limitation est indiqué dans les notes. Le second type de source est les enquêtes par sondage auprès des ménages. Les statistiques tirées de ce type de source se réfèrent habituellement aux *heures réellement effectuées* et parfois aux *heures habituellement travaillées*. Ces enquêtes sont capables en théorie de couvrir toute la population occupée, incluant les travailleurs indépendants. Certaines séries se réfèrent seulement aux heures de travail dans l'emploi principal. Ceci est indiqué dans les notes de bas de page.

Couverture des travailleurs

Les statistiques dans les tableaux 4A et 4B se réfèrent aux salariés, tels qu'ils sont définis par la Classification Internationale de la Situation dans l'Emploi (CISE-93). Dans quelques cas, quand les statistiques sont tirées des enquêtes des forces du travail, elles peuvent se référer à l'emploi total, et quand elles sont tirées des enquêtes auprès des établissements, elles peuvent couvrir un sous groupe de salariés, tel que les ouvriers ou les employés. Des pays limitent la couverture des travailleur encore plus, en ne couvrant que les « adultes », les travailleurs « qualifiés » ou « non qualifiés ». Ces spécifications sont présentées dans des notes de bas de page. Il n'y a pas de définition internationale pour les ouvriers ni pour les employés. Le premier groupe est généralement identifié aux travailleurs manuels ou de la production, tandis que le second et identifié aux travailleurs de bureau.

L'information sur la couverture des travailleurs se présente au centre de la première ligne de chaque tableau.

Unités de temps

Les tableaux montrent généralement la moyenne du nombre d'heures de travail par semaine, mais dans quelques cas les heures par jour ou par mois sont présentées. Ces exceptions sont indiquées dans les notes de bas de page.

Méthodes de calcul de la moyenne

Pour les statistiques tirées des enquêtes auprès des établissements, le nombre moyen d'heures de travail (réellement effectuées ou rémunérées) par semaine ou par mois est généralement obtenu en divisant le nombre total d'heures (réellement effectuées ou rémunérées) pendant une semaine ou un mois par le nombre moyen de travailleurs figurant sur les bordereaux de salaires pendant la même période. La durée moyenne de la journée de travail effectuée ou rémunérée est généralement obtenue en divisant le nombre total d'heures (réellement effectuées ou rémunérées) pendant une semaine, une quinzaine ou un mois par le nombre total de journées réellement effectuées ou rémunérées pendant la même période.

Pour les statistiques tirées des enquêtes auprès des ménages, le nombre moyen d'heures de travail réellement effectuées est généralement obtenu en divisant les heures de travail de toutes les personnes actives occupées (ou de tous les salariés) durant la période de référence par le nombre des personnes actives occupées (ou des salariés) dans la même période Dans ces calculs, les personnes absentes du travail pendant toute la semaine de référence doivent être inclus dans le calcul. Dans quelques séries elles sont exclues, néanmoins, pour mieux refléter la semaine « typique ». Dans ce cas, ceci est indiqué dans les notes de bas de page.

Dans le calcul des moyennes, les statistiques peuvent être basées sur une seule observation (quand l'enquête se déroule une fois par année), sur un ensemble d'observations (quand l'enquête est mensuelle ou trimestrielle) ou par des observations continuelles (quand l'enquête couvre toutes les semaines de l'année). Plus il y a de points dans le calcul, moins grande sera l'influence des variations saisonnières et dans l'activité syndicale, ainsi que dans les congés annuels et de maladie effectivement pris pendant l'année.

Questions de comparabilité

En comparant les statistiques relatives à la durée du travail, il ne faut pas perdre de vue que ces données sont influencées par la méthode utilisé pour calculer la moyenne, par le nombre d'observations utilisées, et par les différentes

pratiques, en ce qui concerne le nombre de journées normalement effectuées par semaine, les règlements et les usages concernant le travail du week-end et les heures supplémentaires, les absence du travail, etc. Elles seront aussi affectées par la couverture industrielle et des emplois. Les statistiques qui excluent les travailleurs dans l'agriculture, où les heures de travail suivent des comportements différents des autres industries, ne seront pas comparables avec les statistiques qui les incluent. De façon similaire, les statistiques qui couvrent seulement l'emploi principal seront plus basses que les statistiques qui couvrent tous les emplois[3].

4A Durée du travail, par activité économique

Les données présentées dans ce tableau se réfèrent à la durée moyenne des heures du travail selon les groupes industriels les plus amples de la Classification internationale type par industrie de toutes les branches d'activité économique, CITI. On utilise trois versions de la CITI pour présenter les statistiques, la CITI Rév.2, la CITI Rév.3 et la CITI Rév.4[4]. Les branches principales (pour la CITI Rév.2) et les catégories de tabulation (pour la CITI Rév.3 et la CITI Rév.4) apparaissent sous forme de codes avec une indication de la version utilisée, le texte correspondant à chaque code est donné en annexe. Quand les branches ou catégories nationales ne correspondent pas aux groupes internationaux, ceci est signalé dans les notes de bas de page.

4B Durée du travail dans les industries manufacturières

Ce tableau présente la durée du travail moyenne par travailleur pour l'ensemble des industries manufacturières et par grand groupe (CITI rev. 2) ou branche (CITI rev. 3) d'industrie. Quand les branches ou catégories nationales ne correspondent pas aux groupes internationaux, ceci est signalé dans les notes de bas de page.

Notes

[1] L'ensemble des séries statistiques sur la durée du travail disponibles au BIT peut être visualisé sur LABORSTA, le site de diffusion statistique du Département de statistique : http://laborsta.ilo.org

[2] Pour le texte intégral de la résolution, voir BIT: *Recommandations internationales en vigueur sur les statistiques du travail* (Genève, 2000) ou le site Web du Département de statistique du BIT (www.ilo.org/public/french/bureau/stat)

[3] Pour des renseignements sur les différences de portée, définitions et méthodes de calcul, etc., utilisées pour les diverses séries nationales, voir BIT: *Sources et méthodes: statistiques du travail* (précédemment *Sources et méthodes statistiques*), vol. 2 «Emploi, salaires, durée du travail et coût de la main-d'oeuvre (enquêtes auprès des établissements)», deuxième édition (Genève, 1995); vol. 3 «Population active, emploi, chômage et durée du travail (enquête auprès des ménages)», deuxième édition (Genève, 1991), publié sous forme de Document de travail; vol. 4 «Emploi, chômage, salaires et durée du travail (documents administratifs et sources assimilées)» (Genève, 1989), publié sous forme de Document de travail. Tous ces volumes peuvent être consultées sur LABORSTA.

[4] Ces classifications peuvent être consultées sur le site web de la Division Statistique des Nations Unis à : http://unstats.un.org/unsd/class/default.htm

Horas de trabajo

Las horas de trabajo se refieren a todo período de tiempo dedicado por las personas a actividades que contribuyen a la producción de bienes y servicios dentro de los límites de producción definidos por el Sistema de Cuentas Nacionales de las Naciones Unidas.

Los diversos tipos de estadísticas sobre las horas de trabajo presentados en el Capítulo 4 se indican en los cuadros con los siguientes códigos[1]:

(a) Horas efectivamente trabajadas
(b) Horas pagadas
(c) Horas habitualmente trabajadas
(d) Horas normales de trabajo

Las series cubren generalmente a los asalariados de ambos sexos, independientemente de su edad. Alrededor de la mitad de las series presentan datos separadamente para hombres y mujeres.

Definiciones

Desde 1962 existen normas estadísticas internacionales únicamente para las horas efectivamente trabajadas y las horas normales de trabajo, adoptadas por la décima Conferencia Internacional de Estadísticos del Trabajo[2]. Están confinadas a los trabajadores asalariados y describen situaciones de trabajo que son típicas de los trabajadores de producción en establecimientos manufactureros. Estas normas sirven de guía para los países cuando producen sus estimaciones nacionales, pero ahora las definiciones nacionales son mucho más completas. Es por esta razón que se están revisando estas normas internacionales para mejorar la cobertura de trabajadores y de situaciones de trabajo, así como para reflejar mejor los diversos arreglos de trabajo. Se espera que la 18ª Conferencia Internacional de Estadísticas del Trabajo adopte nuevas normas internacionales que incluirán también conceptos tales como las horas habitualmente trabajadas y las horas pagadas. Los siguientes párrafos proveen definiciones para cada uno de estos conceptos tal como se miden comúnmente en los países.

El concepto de las horas efectivamente trabajadas se refiere al tiempo que las personas ocupadas dedican a actividades laborales durante un período de referencia especificado, incluyendo:
(a) tiempo dedicado directamente a la producción (produciendo bienes y servicios, incluyendo las horas extraordinarias pagadas y no pagadas);
(b) tiempo dedicado a facilitar la producción, necesario para las actividades laborales o para mejorar la eficiencia de las personas (diseñando, preparando y manteniendo el lugar de trabajo, procedimientos, herramientas, incluyendo recibos, fichas de tiempos e informes), tiempo para cambiar de ropa, actividades de transporte (de puerta en puerta, trayendo productos agrícolas al mercado) y formación relacionada con el trabajo;
(c) tiempo entre actividades principales (esperando clientes, tiempo muerto por razones tales como la falta ocasional de trabajo o electricidad, paro de máquinas, o accidentes), tiempo de viaje para atender reuniones o asignaciones de trabajo, tiempo de guardia (como para los trabajadores de la salud o de servicios técnicos);
(d) tiempo de reposo (breves períodos de descanso o refrescamiento incluidas las interrupciones para tomar té, café o rezar.

Las horas efectivamente trabajadas excluyen el tiempo no trabajado, que sean pagado o no, tales como:
(a) las vacaciones pagadas, días feriados pagados, ausencias por enfermedad o maternidad;
(b) las interrupciones para las comidas;
(c) el tiempo dedicado a ir desde el domicilio del trabajador al lugar de trabajo y viceversa, que no es tiempo dedicado a trabajar.

Las horas efectivamente trabajadas cubren a todos los tipos de trabajadores, que sean independientes o asalariados; pueden ser pagadas o no y llevarse a cabo en cualquier lugar, incluyendo la calle, el campo, el domicilio del trabajador, etc.

El concepto de las horas pagadas abarca a los trabajadores con un empleo asalariado y cubren todas las horas, trabajadas o no, que han sido pagadas por el empleador. Cuando se comparan con las horas efectivamente trabajadas por los asalariados, incluye todas las horas pagadas, aun las que no se trabajan, tales como las vacaciones anuales, los días feriados, ausencias por motivo de enfermedad y otros permisos pagados, y excluye todas las horas trabajadas pero no pagadas (por ejemplo, las horas extraordinarias no pagadas).

El concepto de horas normales de trabajo abarca a un subconjunto de los asalariados, esto es, los que están cubiertos por la legislación o reglamentos laborales, y se relaciona con las horas diarias, semanales o anuales que se espera que estos asalariados estén a la disposición de su empleador, de acuerdo con dicha legislación, acuerdo colectivo o laudos arbitrales. Cuando se compara con las horas efectivamente trabajadas de los asalariados, las horas normales excluyen todo el tiempo extraordinario (pagado y no pagado) pero incluyen todo el tiempo pagado con tasas normales aun cuando no se trabaja.

Las horas habitualmente trabajadas se relacionan con las horas semanales más comúnmente trabajadas por personas con empleo asalariado o independiente durante un período de referencia largo, tal como un mes, una estación o cualquier otro período largo, esto es, es el valor típico de las horas de trabajo semanales. Cuando se comparan con las horas normales de trabajo, las horas habitualmente trabajadas incluyen todas las horas extraordinarias habituales. Todo el tiempo no trabajado de manera habitual queda por ende excluido.

Fuentes

En general, las estadísticas de horas de trabajo se obtienen principalmente de dos fuentes, las encuestas de establecimientos y las encuestas de hogares. Otras fuentes son las estimaciones oficiales o registros administrativos de la seguridad social. La información sobre la fuente se presenta en forma de código en paréntesis a la par del nombre del país. Los códigos de las distintas fuentes se explican en la página XVI.

La primera fuente proviene de nóminas de salarios obtenidas por censos o encuestas por muestra a los establecimientos que, generalmente, también reúnen estadísticas de salarios y empleo. Estas estadísticas se refieren usualmente a las horas pagadas y en menor medida a las horas efectivamente trabajadas. Las estadísticas derivadas de estas encuestas o censos suelen tener una cobertura de trabajadores limitada a ciertos grupos de asalariados (por ejemplo, obreros y empleados) o que trabajan en establecimientos de cierto tamaño o solo en ciertas industrias. La falta de cobertura de trabajadores puede ser un problema importante en los países en donde la mayoría de los trabajadores trabajan en establecimientos pequeños o son independientes. Las cuestiones de cobertura se indican en notas al pié de página.

El segundo tipo de fuente se refiere a las encuestas de hogares. Las estadísticas derivadas de esta fuente se relacionan comúnmente a las horas efectivamente trabajadas y a veces a las horas habitualmente trabajadas. Pueden cubrir a toda la población ocupada, incluyendo a los trabajadores independientes. Algunas estadísticas de encuestas de la fuerza de trabajo se relacionan con las horas trabajadas en el empleo principal solamente. Este tipo de información se indica en notas al pie de página.

Cobertura de trabajadores

Las estadísticas de los Cuadros 4A y 4B se refieren a los asalariados en su conjunto, tal como se definen en la Clasificación Internacional de la Situación en el Empleo, CISE-93. Algunas series que se derivan de encuestas de hogares, se refieren a todos los ocupados y cuando se derivan de encuestas de establecimientos, a solo un subconjunto de asalariados, por ejemplo a los obreros o a los empleados. Algunos países limitan la cobertura de trabajadores aún más, incluyendo solo a los "adultos", a los trabajadores "calificados" o a los "no calificados", en cuyo caso se especifica en una nota al pie de página. No existe una definición internacional de obrero ni de empleado. El primer grupo generalmente se refiere a los asalariados manuales o de la producción y el segundo a los trabajadores de oficina.

Unidades de tiempo

Las series generalmente muestran el número promedio de horas de trabajo por semana, pero en algunos casos se muestran las horas por día o por mes. Esto se indica en notas al pie de página.

Cálculo de promedios

Para las estadísticas derivadas de encuestas de establecimientos, las horas promedio efectivamente trabajadas o pagadas por semana o por mes se calculan generalmente dividiendo el total de las horas (pagadas o trabajadas) por el promedio de trabajadores en la nómina de salarios durante el mismo período. Las horas (pagadas o trabajadas) promedio por día se calculan generalmente dividiendo el total de las horas durante el mes o quincena por el total de días efectivamente trabajados o pagados durante el mismo período.

En las encuestas de hogares el promedio de las horas efectivamente trabajadas se derivan generalmente dividiendo las horas efectivamente trabajadas por el número total de personas ocupadas (o asalariadas) durante el mismo período, usualmente una semana de referencia. En estos cálculos, las personas ausentes del trabajo durante toda la semana de referencia deberían incluirse. Algunas series las excluyen para reflejar mejor una semana "típica" de trabajo, en cuyo caso se indica en una nota.

Estos cálculos pueden basarse en una sola observación en el año (cuando la encuesta se efectúa una vez por año), en un conjunto de observaciones (en encuestas mensuales o trimestrales) o en observaciones continuas (esto es, en encuestas que cubren todas las semanas del año). Mientras más puntos en el tiempo incluya el cálculo del promedio, menor será el efecto de las fluctuaciones estacionales y las variaciones en la actividad sindical así como de las ausencias debidas a las vacaciones o la enfermedad.

Cuestiones de comparabilidad

Al comparar las estadísticas sobre horas de trabajo cabe tener presente que varían en función del método utilizado para calcular el promedio, el número de observaciones utilizadas para su cálculo, y las prácticas laborales relativas al número normal de días de trabajo por semana, de disposiciones reglamentarias y costumbres relativas al trabajo durante el fin de semana y de las horas extraordinarias, la amplitud de las ausencias del trabajo, etc. También estarán afectadas por la cobertura de industrias y empleos. Las estadísticas que excluyen trabajadores en la agricultura, donde las horas de trabajo varían según las estaciones, no serán comparables con las estadísticas que los incluyen. De igual manera, las estadísticas que se refieren al empleo principal solamente serán inferiores a las que cubren todos los empleos[3].

4A Horas de trabajo, por actividad económica

Las series de este cuadro se refieren al promedio de las horas de trabajo según los grupos más generales de la actividad económica de la Clasificación Industrial Internacional Uniforme de todas las actividades económicas, CIIU. Se utilizan tres versiones de la CIIU, la CIIU Rev.2, la CIIU Rev.3 y la CIIU Rev.4[4]. Las grandes divisiones (para la CIIU rev. 2) y las categorías de tabulación (para la CIIU rev.3 y para la CIIU Rev.4) se indican mediante códigos con mención de la versión utilizada; el título correspondiente a cada código figura en anexo. Las notas de pie de página indican las diferencias entre las divisiones o categorías nacionales y los grupos internacionales.

4B Horas de trabajo en las industrias manufactureras

Las series que se presentan en este cuadro muestran el promedio de las horas de trabajo en las industrias manufactureras según grandes grupos (cuando se utiliza la CIIU rev. 2) o agrupaciones (CIIU rev. 3). Las notas de pie de página indican las diferencias entre las divisiones o categorías nacionales y los grupos internacionales.

Notas
[1]. El conjunto completo de series de horas de trabajo se encuentra en el sitio estadístico LABORSTA en http://laborsta.ilo.org.
[2]. Para el texto completo de la Resolución, véase OIT: Recomendaciones internacionales de actualidad en estadísticas del trabajo (Ginebra, 2000) o el sitio Web del Departamento de Estadística de la OIT www.ilo.org/public/french/bureau/stat).
[3]. Para más amplia información sobre las diferencias de alcance, definiciones y métodos de cálculo, etc., que utilizan las diversas series nacionales, véase OIT: Fuentes y Métodos: Estadísticas del Trabajo (anteriormente Fuentes y Métodos Estadísticos), vol.2: «Empleo, salarios, horas de trabajo y costo de la mano de obra (encuestas de establecimientos)», segunda edición (Ginebra, 1995); vol.3: «Población económicamente activa, empleo, desempleo y horas de trabajo (encuestas de hogares)», segunda edición (Ginebra, 1992), publicado como Documento de trabajo; vol.4: «Empleo, desempleo, salarios y horas de trabajo (registros administrativos y fuentes conexas)» (Ginebra, 1989). Todas estas publicaciones se pueden consultar en nuestra base de datos en línea en http://laborsta.ilo.org.
[4]. Estas clasificaciones se encuentran en el sitio web de la División Estadística de las Naciones Unidas en http://unstats.un.org/unsd/class/default.htm.

By economic activity   **Par activité économique**   **Por actividad económica**

	Per week			Par semaine				Por semana		
	1999	2000	2001	2002	2003	2004	2005	2006	2007	2008

AFRICA-AFRIQUE-AFRICA

Egypt (CA) (b) [1][2]   **Wage earners - Ouvriers - Obreros**

Total men and women - Total hommes et femmes - Total hombres y mujeres
ISIC 3 - CITI 3 - CIIU 3

	1999	2000	2001	2002	2003	2004	2005	2006	2007	2008
Total	56	54	54	53	56	55	56	55	55	.
A-B	53	54	.	55	54	54	56	57	57	.
C-Q	56	54	53	55	56	55	56	55	55	.
A	53	54	53	55	54	54	57	58	57	.
B	56	56	59	53	54	52	52	50	49	.
C	52	49	52	53	52	50	52	50	52	.
D	57	55	54	55	57	56	57	56	56	.
E	52	53	53	51	53	53	52	52	52	.
F	51	52	50	51	51	50	51	51	51	.
G	54	52	53	53	55	54	55	55	55	.
H	59	57	56	58	57	58	58	57	58	.
I	60	55	55	55	57	56	56	56	57	.
J	50	50	47	51	50	50	50	51	51	.
K	55	53	51	53	55	59	54	55	55	.
L	.	.	.	.	.	.	.	.	.	.
M	52	50	49	52	51	52	52	.	51	.
N	53	53	52	54	53	53	54	54	55	.
O	55	51	51	.	53	52	53	54	54	.
P	.	.	.	.	.	.	.	.	.	.

Men - Hommes - Hombres
ISIC 3 - CITI 3 - CIIU 3

	1999	2000	2001	2002	2003	2004	2005	2006	2007	2008
Total	56	54	53	53	55	54	56	55	55	.
A-B	53	54	55	55	54	54	56	57	57	.
C-Q	56	54	53	54	55	54	56	55	55	.
A	53	54	53	54	54	54	57	58	57	.
B	56	56	59	53	53	52	52	50	49	.
C	52	49	52	53	52	50	52	50	52	.
D	57	55	54	55	56	55	57	56	56	.
E	52	53	53	51	53	53	53	52	52	.
F	51	52	50	51	51	50	51	51	51	.
G	54	52	53	53	55	54	55	54	55	.
H	59	57	56	58	57	58	58	57	58	.
I	60	55	55	55	57	56	56	55	57	.
J	50	50	47	51	50	50	50	51	51	.
K	54	52	51	53	55	58	54	55	55	.
L	.	.	.	.	.	.	.	.	.	.
M	52	50	49	51	50	51	53	53	51	.
N	53	55	53	55	53	54	54	54	55	.
O	55	52	50	53	51	52	54	54	54	.
P	.	.	.	.	.	.	.	.	.	.

Women - Femmes - Mujeres
ISIC 3 - CITI 3 - CIIU 3

	1999	2000	2001	2002	2003	2004	2005	2006	2007	2008
Total	56	56	55	53	57	56	57	57	57	.
A-B	56	55	61	61	56	49	58	59	59	.
C-Q	56	56	55	56	57	56	58	57	56	.
A	56	55	61	61	56	49	58	59	59	.
B	58	.	58	58	57	57	.	.	.	.
C	58	61	50	.	.	.	.	.	62	.
D	56	56	56	57	58	57	57	58	57	.
E	52	57	53	51	53	52	52	55	51	.
F	56	51	53	53	53	52	50	57	54	.
G	55	55	55	54	54	54	55	55	55	.
H	56	57	55	57	57	56	57	57	59	.
I	62	53	56	56	57	59	58	59	59	.
J	50	52	47	54	46	47	48	47	52	.
K	64	56	51	45	53	63	55	54	54	.
L	.	.	.	.	.	.	.	.	.	.
M	53	51	50	52	53	52	52	52	51	.
N	53	52	50	53	52	53	54	54	55	.
O	54	49	53	53	63	52	52	53	53	.

Explanatory notes: see p. 721.   Notes explicatives: voir p. 723.   Notas explicativas: véase p. 725.

[1] Establishments with 10 or more persons employed. [2] Oct. of each year.   [1] Etablissements occupant 10 personnes et plus. [2] Oct. de chaque année.   [1] Establecimientos con 10 y más trabajadores. [2] Oct. de cada año.

	Per week				Par semaine			Por semana		
	1999	2000	2001	2002	2003	2004	2005	2006	2007	2008

Ethiopia (BA) (a) [1]   **Total employment - Emploi total - Empleo total**

Total men and women - Total hommes et femmes - Total hombres y mujeres
ISIC 3 - CITI 3 - CIIU 3

	1999	2000	2001	2002	2003	2004	2005	2006	2007	2008
Total	.	.	.	.	.	43	28	.	.	.
A-B	.	.	.	.	.	35	27	.	.	.
C-Q	.	.	.	.	.	44	.	.	.	.
A	.	.	.	.	.	35	.	.	.	.
B	.	.	.	.	.	40	.	.	.	.
C	.	.	.	.	.	39	34	.	.	.
D	.	.	.	.	.	39	28	.	.	.
E	.	.	.	.	.	45	45	.	.	.
F	.	.	.	.	.	41	38	.	.	.
G	.	.	.	.	.	43	33	.	.	.
H	.	.	.	.	.	46	34	.	.	.
I	.	.	.	.	.	51	51	.	.	.
J	.	.	.	.	.	43	45	.	.	.
K	.	.	.	.	.	42	45	.	.	.
L	.	.	.	.	.	44	43	.	.	.
M-N	.	.	.	.	.	.	39	.	.	.
N	.	.	.	.	.	40	.	.	.	.
O	.	.	.	.	.	41	45	.	.	.
P	.	.	.	.	.	56	38	.	.	.
Q	.	.	.	.	.	53	55	.	.	.
X	.	.	.	.	.	47	36	.	.	.

Men - Hommes - Hombres
ISIC 3 - CITI 3 - CIIU 3

	1999	2000	2001	2002	2003	2004	2005	2006	2007	2008
Total	.	.	.	.	.	44	34	.	.	.
A-B	.	.	.	.	.	37	32	.	.	.
C-Q	.	.	.	.	.	45	.	.	.	.
A	.	.	.	.	.	37	.	.	.	.
B	.	.	.	.	.	41	.	.	.	.
C	.	.	.	.	.	39	38	.	.	.
D	.	.	.	.	.	45	41	.	.	.
E	.	.	.	.	.	46	47	.	.	.
F	.	.	.	.	.	40	39	.	.	.
G	.	.	.	.	.	46	40	.	.	.
H	.	.	.	.	.	56	52	.	.	.
I	.	.	.	.	.	52	52	.	.	.
J	.	.	.	.	.	45	47	.	.	.
K	.	.	.	.	.	42	45	.	.	.
L	.	.	.	.	.	46	47	.	.	.
M-N	.	.	.	.	.	.	40	.	.	.
N	.	.	.	.	.	41	.	.	.	.
O	.	.	.	.	.	41	47	.	.	.
P	.	.	.	.	.	62	41	.	.	.
Q	.	.	.	.	.	55	62	.	.	.
X	.	.	.	.	.	50	39	.	.	.

Women - Femmes - Mujeres
ISIC 3 - CITI 3 - CIIU 3

	1999	2000	2001	2002	2003	2004	2005	2006	2007	2008
Total	.	.	.	.	.	41	22	.	.	.
A-B	.	.	.	.	.	30	20	.	.	.
C-Q	.	.	.	.	.	42	.	.	.	.
A	.	.	.	.	.	29	.	.	.	.
B	.	.	.	.	.	39	.	.	.	.
C	.	.	.	.	.	42	26	.	.	.
D	.	.	.	.	.	32	23	.	.	.
E	.	.	.	.	.	39	39	.	.	.
F	.	.	.	.	.	43	34	.	.	.
G	.	.	.	.	.	40	29	.	.	.
H	.	.	.	.	.	43	32	.	.	.
I	.	.	.	.	.	40	39	.	.	.
J	.	.	.	.	.	36	42	.	.	.
K	.	.	.	.	.	41	45	.	.	.
L	.	.	.	.	.	39	35	.	.	.
M-N	.	.	.	.	.	.	36	.	.	.
N	.	.	.	.	.	38	.	.	.	.
O	.	.	.	.	.	42	41	.	.	.
P	.	.	.	.	.	56	32	.	.	.
Q	.	.	.	.	.	44	54	.	.	.
X	.	.	.	.	.	45	30	.	.	.

Explanatory notes: see p. 721.   Notes explicatives: voir p. 723.   Notas explicativas: véase p. 725.

[1] Urban areas.   [1] Régions urbaines.   [1] Areas urbanas.

HOURS OF WORK — DURÉE DU TRAVAIL — HORAS DE TRABAJO

4A

By economic activity — Par activité économique — Por actividad económica

	Per week / Par semaine / Por semana									
	1999	2000	2001	2002	2003	2004	2005	2006	2007	2008

Mauritius (BA) (a) — Total employment - Emploi total - Empleo total

Total men and women - Total hommes et femmes - Total hombres y mujeres
ISIC 3 - CITI 3 - CIIU 3

	1999	2000	2001	2002	2003	2004	2005	2006	2007	2008
Total	.	.	.	.	.	.	39	39	.	.
A-B	.	.	.	.	.	.	.	.	45	.
A	.	.	.	.	.	.	.	.	45	.
B	.	.	.	.	.	.	.	.	45	.
C	.	.	.	.	.	.	42	42	.	.
D	.	.	.	.	.	.	43	43	45	.
E	.	.	.	.	.	.	42	41	45	.
F	.	.	.	.	.	.	38	38	45	.
G	.	.	.	.	.	.	42	42	45	.
H	.	.	.	.	.	.	45	44	48	.
I	.	.	.	.	.	.	42	43	45	.
J	.	.	.	.	.	.	37	38	45	.
K	.	.	.	.	.	.	47	46	45	.
L	.	.	.	.	.	.	40	39	.	.
M	.	.	.	.	.	.	26	28	.	.
N	.	.	.	.	.	.	39	41	.	.
O	.	.	.	.	.	.	39	38	.	.
P	.	.	.	.	.	.	27	27	48	.
Q	.	.	.	.	.	.	40	40	.	.
X	.	.	.	.	.	.	.	.	.	.

Men - Hommes - Hombres
ISIC 3 - CITI 3 - CIIU 3

	1999	2000	2001	2002	2003	2004	2005	2006	2007	2008
Total	.	.	.	.	.	.	41	41	.	.
A-B	.	.	.	.	.	.	.	.	45	.
A	.	.	.	.	.	.	.	.	45	.
B	.	.	.	.	.	.	.	.	45	.
C	.	.	.	.	.	.	42	44	.	.
D	.	.	.	.	.	.	43	44	.	.
E	.	.	.	.	.	.	43	41	.	.
F	.	.	.	.	.	.	38	38	.	.
G	.	.	.	.	.	.	42	42	.	.
H	.	.	.	.	.	.	48	46	.	.
I	.	.	.	.	.	.	43	43	.	.
J	.	.	.	.	.	.	38	39	.	.
K	.	.	.	.	.	.	50	49	.	.
L	.	.	.	.	.	.	42	41	.	.
M	.	.	.	.	.	.	28	30	.	.
N	.	.	.	.	.	.	39	43	.	.
O	.	.	.	.	.	.	40	39	.	.
P	.	.	.	.	.	.	36	39	.	.
Q	.	.	.	.	.	.	37	41	.	.
X	.	.	.	.	.	.	.	.	.	.

Women - Femmes - Mujeres
ISIC 3 - CITI 3 - CIIU 3

	1999	2000	2001	2002	2003	2004	2005	2006	2007	2008
Total	.	.	.	.	.	.	35	35	.	.
A-B	.	.	.	.	.	.	.	.	45	.
A	.	.	.	.	.	.	.	.	45	.
B	.	.	.	.	.	.	.	.	45	.
C	.	.	.	.	.	.	.	.	.	.
D	.	.	.	.	.	.	42	42	.	.
E	.	.	.	.	.	.	30	35	.	.
F	.	.	.	.	.	.	36	37	.	.
G	.	.	.	.	.	.	40	41	.	.
H	.	.	.	.	.	.	40	39	.	.
I	.	.	.	.	.	.	38	39	.	.
J	.	.	.	.	.	.	35	36	.	.
K	.	.	.	.	.	.	37	38	.	.
L	.	.	.	.	.	.	34	33	.	.
M	.	.	.	.	.	.	24	25	.	.
N	.	.	.	.	.	.	39	38	.	.
O	.	.	.	.	.	.	38	35	.	.
P	.	.	.	.	.	.	25	25	.	.
Q	.	.	.	.	.	.	45	38	.	.

Explanatory notes: see p. 721.   Notes explicatives: voir p. 723.   Notas explicativas: véase p. 725.

4A

HOURS OF WORK	DURÉE DU TRAVAIL	HORAS DE TRABAJO
By economic activity	Par activité économique	Por actividad económica

	Per week				Par semaine			Por semana		
	1999	2000	2001	2002	2003	2004	2005	2006	2007	2008

AMERICA-AMÉRIQUE-AMERICA

Argentina (BA) (a) [1] [2] [3]
Total employment - Emploi total - Empleo total

Total men and women - Total hommes et femmes - Total hombres y mujeres
ISIC 3 - CITI 3 - CIIU 3

	1999	2000	2001	2002	2003[4]	2004[4]	2005	2006	2007	2008
Total	42.8	42.2	41.4	39.2	40.0	40.7	41.5			
C-Q	42.6	42.0	41.2	38.9	40.0	40.8	41.5			
C	55.3	59.1	60.8	56.7	53.2	53.3	54.4			
D	45.8	45.4	44.6	42.6	42.8	42.8	44.3			
E	43.3	44.6	42.3	42.3	44.1	43.6	44.1			
F	44.2	42.3	41.4	38.0	38.5	39.9	41.1			
G	50.3	49.4	48.8	47.1	46.6	47.2	46.9			
H	48.6	48.1	46.1	44.7	44.3	44.4	45.2			
I	55.4	53.3	53.2	51.4	51.5	51.3	52.3			
J	45.0	44.8	43.9	44.2	43.3	43.6	42.8			
K	44.0	44.0	43.4	41.1	42.5	41.3	42.4			
L	39.4	39.1	38.7	36.7	37.7	39.9	41.8			
M	26.4	26.0	26.0	25.5	27.7	28.8	29.1			
N	39.2	39.2	38.6	35.9	33.7	36.1	37.4			
O	38.6	39.5	37.5	33.5	35.2	36.7	37.5			
P	29.5	28.8	28.2	27.4	28.3	26.2	26.9			
Q	43.6	40.8	37.6	35.6	41.9		55.8			

Men - Hommes - Hombres
ISIC 3 - CITI 3 - CIIU 3

	1999	2000	2001	2002	2003[4]	2004[4]	2005	2006	2007	2008
Total	47.1	46.5	45.8	43.7	44.8	45.6	46.3			
C-Q	46.9	46.3	45.6	43.4	44.8	45.6	46.3			
C	56.1	59.8	62.0	57.7	54.5	54.2	57.3			
D	47.9	47.6	47.0	45.4	46.2	46.8	47.8			
E	43.9	45.5	43.4	42.9	44.6	44.2	44.7			
F	44.3	42.4	41.5	38.0	38.6	40.0	41.2			
G	51.3	50.5	50.0	48.5	48.6	49.3	49.0			
H	52.7	52.6	50.2	49.0	45.4	48.6	48.9			
I	57.0	54.6	54.7	52.5	53.3	52.9	54.1			
J	46.8	46.2	45.3	45.5	44.1	44.4	44.3			
K	47.5	47.1	46.8	44.4	45.2	44.0	45.7			
L	41.8	41.8	41.5	39.6	41.4	44.2	45.2			
M	30.9	30.5	30.1	28.9	31.1	32.5	34.2			
N	41.7	42.6	42.4	40.1	40.1	43.1	46.2			
O	40.4	41.5	39.5	36.5	40.8	40.9	42.2			
P	28.0	26.1	26.0	22.0	27.9	23.8	24.8			
Q	43.3	42.8	44.0	40.0	53.5		71.0			

Women - Femmes - Mujeres
ISIC 3 - CITI 3 - CIIU 3

	1999	2000	2001	2002	2003[4]	2004[4]	2005	2006	2007	2008
Total	36.1	35.6	34.9	32.9	33.4	34.0	34.7			
C-Q	36.0	35.6	34.9	32.9	33.5	34.1	34.8			
C	45.3	42.1	42.1	42.9	41.7	41.7	46.3			
D	39.0	38.8	37.8	34.5	35.9	34.3	36.3			
E	39.2	38.3	37.6	39.6	42.8	41.5	39.2			
F	40.0	37.8	37.5	34.4	34.2	33.7	37.2			
G	48.3	47.2	46.5	44.5	42.9	43.7	43.2			
H	43.8	42.8	41.6	39.4	42.6	40.0	40.8			
I	42.6	44.1	42.1	42.7	40.0	41.2	42.4			
J	42.2	42.4	41.7	42.2	42.1	42.2	40.8			
K	37.5	38.2	37.6	35.2	36.5	36.4	36.9			
L	34.9	34.3	34.0	32.1	31.8	33.2	36.9			
M	25.1	24.7	24.8	24.5	26.8	27.8	27.5			
N	37.9	37.6	36.9	34.1	31.0	33.0	34.0			
O	35.5	36.2	33.9	29.4	28.7	31.7	32.1			
P	29.5	28.9	28.4	27.7	28.4	26.4	27.0			
Q	43.8	39.2	33.3	35.0	31.6		31.7			

Explanatory notes: see p. 721.

[1] 28 urban agglomerations. [2] Persons aged 10 years and over. [3] Second semester of each year. [4] Prior to 2003: May and October.

Notes explicatives: voir p. 723.

[1] 28 agglomérations urbaines. [2] Personnes âgées de 10 ans et plus. [3] Second semestre de chaque année. [4] Avant 2003: mai et octobre.

Notas explicativas: véase p. 725.

[1] 28 aglomerados úrbanos. [2] Personas de 10 años y más. [3] Segundo semestre de cada año. [4] Antes de 2003: mayo y octubre.

By economic activity	Par activité économique	Por actividad económica

	Per week			Par semaine				Por semana		
	1999	2000	2001	2002	2003	2004	2005	2006	2007	2008

Argentina (BA) (a) [1][2][3]   Employees - Salariés - Asalariados

Total men and women - Total hommes et femmes - Total hombres y mujeres
ISIC 3 - CITI 3 - CIIU 3

Total	41.6	41.1	40.5	38.3	39.5 [4]	40.1	40.8	.	.	.
C-Q	41.5	40.8	40.3	38.0	39.5 [4]	40.1	40.9	.	.	.
C	56.3	59.9	60.8	57.0	53.1 [4]	53.2	55.1	.	.	.
D	46.4	46.1	45.4	44.1	44.8 [4]	44.4	45.3	.	.	.
E	43.1	44.4	42.2	42.3	42.8 [4]	42.2	44.1	.	.	.
F	46.6	45.2	45.1	42.6	40.7 [4]	42.1	44.2	.	.	.
G	47.2	46.5	46.4	45.2	45.5 [4]	45.1	45.3	.	.	.
H	47.8	46.7	45.1	44.1	42.8 [4]	43.1	43.7	.	.	.
I	55.8	53.7	54.1	52.5	52.0 [4]	51.4	52.3	.	.	.
J	44.9	44.7	44.1	44.0	43.3 [4]	43.0	42.5	.	.	.
K	43.1	43.9	43.3	41.0	43.6 [4]	41.8	42.3	.	.	.
L	39.4	39.1	38.7	36.7	37.7 [4]	39.9	41.8	.	.	.
M	26.7	26.2	26.3	25.7	28.3 [4]	29.8	30.1	.	.	.
N	39.6	39.8	39.1	36.0	33.9 [4]	35.9	37.5	.	.	.
O	39.8	40.3	39.3	34.0	37.1 [4]	38.5	38.5	.	.	.
P	30.6	29.9	29.4	28.7	28.6 [4]	26.6	27.2	.	.	.
Q	43.6	40.8	37.6	35.6	41.9 [4]	.	55.8	.	.	.

Men - Hommes - Hombres
ISIC 3 - CITI 3 - CIIU 3

Total	46.7	46.3	45.9	43.9	45.2 [4]	45.8	46.6	.	.	.
C-Q	46.6	46.1	45.7	43.6	45.3 [4]	45.8	46.7	.	.	.
C	57.1	60.7	61.9	58.0	54.5 [4]	54.1	57.2	.	.	.
D	47.6	47.6	47.1	45.9	47.0 [4]	47.1	47.7	.	.	.
E	43.7	45.3	43.3	42.9	45.4 [4]	44.4	44.6	.	.	.
F	46.9	45.6	45.3	42.9	40.8 [4]	42.3	44.3	.	.	.
G	49.7	49.1	48.8	47.9	48.1 [4]	47.4	48.4	.	.	.
H	49.8	49.6	46.7	46.8	43.8 [4]	46.3	46.8	.	.	.
I	57.6	55.2	55.9	53.9	54.0 [4]	53.2	54.4	.	.	.
J	46.8	46.2	45.4	45.3	44.2 [4]	43.5	43.8	.	.	.
K	47.3	47.6	47.9	45.7	47.7 [4]	45.0	46.6	.	.	.
L	41.9	41.9	41.5	39.7	41.4 [4]	44.2	45.2	.	.	.
M	31.3	30.6	30.4	29.2	31.2 [4]	33.9	35.1	.	.	.
N	41.7	43.1	42.9	39.6	40.1 [4]	42.7	46.6	.	.	.
O	41.7	42.5	41.8	37.8	42.0 [4]	42.8	42.2	.	.	.
P	34.8	31.0	34.4	31.4	38.1 [4]	32.6	27.9	.	.	.
Q	43.3	42.8	44.0	40.0	53.5 [4]	.	71.0	.	.	.

Women - Femmes - Mujeres
ISIC 3 - CITI 3 - CIIU 3

Total	34.5	34.0	33.5	31.7	32.5 [4]	32.9	33.6	.	.	.
C-Q	34.5	34.0	33.4	31.6	32.5 [4]	33.0	33.7	.	.	.
C	45.5	42.1	42.0	42.9	41.7 [4]	41.7	48.8	.	.	.
D	41.8	40.7	39.7	37.5	38.6 [4]	37.1	38.8	.	.	.
E	39.2	38.3	37.6	39.6	42.8 [4]	41.5	39.2	.	.	.
F	38.7	36.0	39.1	34.3	37.8 [4]	35.0	39.4	.	.	.
G	42.2	41.3	41.4	39.8	40.2 [4]	40.4	38.9	.	.	.
H	45.0	43.1	42.8	40.5	41.1 [4]	39.3	40.0	.	.	.
I	42.5	44.0	42.1	42.1	39.7 [4]	40.6	41.8	.	.	.
J	42.2	42.4	42.0	42.2	41.8 [4]	42.2	40.8	.	.	.
K	36.9	37.9	36.9	34.3	36.2 [4]	36.9	35.9	.	.	.
L	34.9	34.3	34.0	32.1	31.9 [4]	33.2	36.9	.	.	.
M	25.5	24.9	25.0	24.7	27.5 [4]	28.6	28.4	.	.	.
N	38.7	38.5	37.6	34.6	31.4 [4]	33.1	34.3	.	.	.
O	36.3	36.6	34.8	29.2	30.9 [4]	33.0	33.6	.	.	.
P	30.5	29.9	29.2	28.7	28.4 [4]	26.5	27.2	.	.	.
Q	43.8	39.2	33.3	35.0	31.6 [4]	.	31.7	.	.	.

Bermuda (CA) (a) [5]   Employees - Salariés - Asalariados

Total men and women - Total hommes et femmes - Total hombres y mujeres
ISIC 3 - CITI 3 - CIIU 3

Total	.	.	.	.	29.0	33.0	33.0	34.1	33.0	.
A-B	.	.	.	33.0	33.0	35.0	34.0	36.6	35.0	.
A	.	.	.	37.0	37.0	39.0	38.0	39.4	38.0	.
B	.	.	.	18.0	18.0	19.0	20.0	22.8	22.0	.
C	.	.	.	40.0	40.0	31.0	30.0	28.8	36.0	.
D	.	.	.	34.0	29.0	33.0	35.0	35.6	35.0	.
E	.	.	.	41.0	33.0	31.0	31.0	31.8	40.0	.
F	.	.	.	38.0	32.0	38.0	39.0	39.4	38.0	.
G	.	.	.	.	30.0	33.0	34.0	33.9	34.0	.
H	.	.	.	36.0	30.0	35.0	35.0	37.6	36.0	.
I	.	.	.	35.0	33.0	35.0	35.0	36.0	35.0	.
J	.	.	.	33.0	24.0	33.0	33.0	42.3	33.0	.
K	.	.	.	31.0	28.0	31.0	32.0	33.1	33.0	.
L	.	.	.	27.0	27.0	29.0	30.0	25.7	26.0	.
M	.	.	.	17.0	16.0	18.0	21.0	20.7	22.0	.
N	.	.	.	31.0	29.0	29.0	33.0	32.8	29.0	.
O	.	.	.	30.0	26.0	28.0	29.0	28.9	29.0	.
P	.	.	.	28.0	27.0	29.0	30.0	29.5	30.0	.
Q	.	.	.	34.0	27.0	33.0	34.0	33.9	34.0	.

Explanatory notes: see p. 721.

Notes explicatives: voir p. 723.

Notas explicativas: véase p. 725.

[1] 28 urban agglomerations. [2] Persons aged 10 years and over. [3] Second semester of each year. [4] Prior to 2003: May and October. [5] Aug. of each year.

[1] 28 agglomérations urbaines. [2] Personnes âgées de 10 ans et plus. [3] Second semestre de chaque année. [4] Avant 2003: mai et octobre. [5] Août de chaque année.

[1] 28 aglomerados úrbanos. [2] Personas de 10 años y más. [3] Segundo semestre de cada año. [4] Antes de 2003: mayo y octubre. [5] Agosto de cada año.

HOURS OF WORK — DURÉE DU TRAVAIL — HORAS DE TRABAJO

By economic activity — Par activité économique — Por actividad económica

	Per week			Par semaine				Por semana		
	1999	2000	2001	2002	2003	2004	2005	2006	2007	2008

Bermuda (CA) (a) [1] — Employees - Salariés - Asalariados

Men - Hommes - Hombres
ISIC 3 - CITI 3 - CIIU 3

	1999	2000	2001	2002	2003	2004	2005	2006	2007	2008
Total	.	.	.	36.0	32.0	35.0	36.0	36.9	36.0	
A-B	.	.	.	33.0	33.0	39.0	38.0	37.1	36.0	
A	.	.	.	38.0	38.0	39.0	38.0	40.0	38.0	.
B	.	.	.	18.0	18.0	19.0	20.0	23.1	23.0	
F	.	.	.	38.0	33.0	39.0	39.0	39.9	39.0	
G	.	.	.	36.0	32.0	36.0	37.0	36.5	37.0	
H	.	.	.	39.0	36.0	38.0	38.0	41.2	40.0	
I	.	.	.	37.0	35.0	37.0	37.0	37.6	37.0	
J	.	.	.	33.0	25.0	34.0	33.0	42.0	34.0	
K	.	.	.	34.0	31.0	34.0	35.0	35.6	35.0	
L	.	.	.	33.0	33.0	34.0	34.0	31.8	32.0	
M	.	.	.	15.0	13.0	16.0	19.0	20.0	22.0	
N	.	.	.	33.0	30.0	30.0	36.0	34.7	31.0	
O	.	.	.	32.0	28.0	30.0	30.0	29.9	30.0	
P	.	.	.	31.0	31.0	33.0	32.0	33.1	34.0	
Q	.	.	.	35.0	29.0	34.0	35.0	35.0	35.0	

Women - Femmes - Mujeres
ISIC 3 - CITI 3 - CIIU 3

	1999	2000	2001	2002	2003	2004	2005	2006	2007	2008
Total	.	.	.	30.0	25.0	29.0	30.0	31.1	30.0	
A-B	.	.	.	27.0	27.0	29.0	20.0	31.2	29.0	
A	.	.	.	27.0	27.0	32.0	34.0	33.1	31.0	
B	.	.	.	21.0	21.0	16.0	19.0	18.1	14.0	
D	.	.	.	31.0	26.0	29.0	32.0	32.4	32.0	
E	.	.	.	37.0	17.0	19.0	17.0	18.4	33.0	
F	.	.	.	32.0	27.0	31.0	32.0	31.8	31.0	
G	.	.	.	32.0	27.0	31.0	31.0	31.2	31.0	
H	.	.	.	32.0	30.0	31.0	30.0	32.8	31.0	
I	.	.	.	31.0	28.0	32.0	32.0	32.7	32.0	
J	.	.	.	32.0	23.0	32.0	32.0	42.4	32.0	
K	.	.	.	29.0	25.0	29.0	29.0	30.8	31.0	
L	.	.	.	23.0	21.0	25.0	25.0	20.0	20.0	
M	.	.	.	17.0	17.0	19.0	21.0	20.9	22.0	
N	.	.	.	30.0	28.0	29.0	33.0	32.2	29.0	
O	.	.	.	29.0	25.0	27.0	28.0	28.2	29.0	
P	.	.	.	27.0	26.0	28.0	29.0	28.9	29.0	
Q	.	.	.	32.0	25.0	32.0	32.0	33.1	33.0	

Bolivia (BA) (b) — Total employment - Emploi total - Empleo total

Total men and women - Total hommes et femmes - Total hombres y mujeres
ISIC 3 - CITI 3 - CIIU 3

	1999	2000	2001	2002	2003	2004	2005	2006	2007	2008
Total	42.8	46.7	39.6	42.9	.	42.5 [2]	44.2	43.3	44.4	
A [3]	38.4	43.4	35.8	37.6	.	38.4 [2]	38.4	38.6	38.9	
B [4]	43.9	41.8	15.6	23.1	.	43.7 [2]	45.1	42.7	53.8	
C	47.7	49.7	49.7	49.3	.	48.4 [2]	48.2	50.6	49.5	
D	43.9	47.0	39.8	45.4	.	43.2 [2]	46.4	45.2	46.7	
E	45.9	55.6	45.4	49.3	.	51.1 [2]	48.6	52.7	43.7	
F	48.4	50.8	46.9	49.6	.	47.9 [2]	49.5	50.7	49.8	
G	48.2	52.1	41.8	49.5	.	46.6 [2]	51.4	50.2	51.7	
H	46.2	50.2	43.6	43.9	.	40.5 [2]	46.0	41.5	42.6	
I	57.6	58.5	54.5	58.9	.	57.7 [2]	59.3	56.3	56.7	
J	47.9	50.9	48.1	46.6	.	46.5 [2]	47.8	43.0	45.0	
K	41.7	46.5	42.1	49.8	.	44.6 [2]	46.2	46.0	48.9	
L	47.1	54.2	48.9	50.2	.	51.3 [2]	46.3	48.4	49.2	
M	28.8	31.7	27.7	28.6	.	26.4 [2]	30.8	29.7	30.7	
N	45.2	46.5	42.1	41.0	.	41.7 [2]	46.3	41.2	44.6	
O	33.9	33.6	32.2	35.2	.	31.0 [2]	37.7	37.1	37.7	
P	50.6	52.6	49.3	53.1	.	50.8 [2]	52.6	50.5	47.2	
Q	40.0	68.3	40.0	44.2	.	42.4 [2]	42.1	40.0	54.2	

Men - Hommes - Hombres
ISIC 3 - CITI 3 - CIIU 3

	1999	2000	2001	2002	2003	2004	2005	2006	2007	2008
Total	44.5	48.6	42.2	45.2	.	45.0 [2]	46.7	45.4	46.8	.
A [3]	39.4	45.1	38.3	39.8	.	39.8 [2]	40.1	39.4	40.6	.
B [4]	45.7	44.0	17.8	25.6	.	44.3 [2]	43.8	55.2	54.0	
C	47.8	50.3	49.9	51.5	.	49.3 [2]	49.0	51.1	49.7	
D	48.8	49.6	44.9	49.5	.	48.4 [2]	49.4	49.9	50.4	
E	46.5	57.1	46.0	50.7	.	51.7 [2]	50.3	52.9	44.7	
F	48.4	50.9	47.2	50.0	.	48.2 [2]	50.2	50.7	49.9	
G	48.5	53.8	42.3	49.1	.	47.4 [2]	54.3	50.2	51.4	
H	49.3	54.2	42.0	47.7	.	43.1 [2]	55.1	41.8	46.6	
I	58.5	59.6	55.8	60.1	.	58.7 [2]	60.2	58.1	57.7	
J	48.9	53.1	49.5	47.9	.	49.2 [2]	48.6	46.1	46.4	
K	42.4	48.1	45.5	50.8	.	48.7 [2]	49.3	46.5	50.9	
L	49.0	58.7	50.7	51.6	.	53.6 [2]	48.1	51.3	49.8	
M	30.1	32.8	29.0	32.1	.	27.1 [2]	32.8	31.6	34.0	
N	44.7	51.8	41.7	44.0	.	39.9 [2]	49.4	46.0	46.1	
O	35.3	39.9	37.8	42.6	.	35.3 [2]	43.8	42.4	40.4	
P	44.2	44.6	49.1	49.9	.	47.6 [2]	66.0	40.8	49.3	
Q	40.0	84.0	40.0	38.0	.	45.0 [2]	42.0	40.0	70.0	.

Explanatory notes: see p. 721.   Notes explicatives: voir p. 723.   Notas explicativas: véase p. 725.

[1] Aug. of each year. [2] Continued Household survey, 2003-2004. [3] Excl. forestry. [4] Incl. forestry.

[1] Août de chaque année. [2] Enquête continue des Ménages, 2003-2004. [3] Non compris la sylviculture. [4] Y compris la sylviculture.

[1] Agosto de cada año. [2] Encuesta continua de hogares, 2003-2004. [3] Excl. la silvicultura. [4] Incl. silvicultura.

By economic activity — **Par activité économique** — **Por actividad económica**

	Per week			Par semaine				Por semana		
	1999	2000	2001	2002	2003	2004	2005	2006	2007	2008

Bolivia (BA) (b) — Total employment - Emploi total - Empleo total

Women - Femmes - Mujeres
ISIC 3 - CITI 3 - CIIU 3

	1999	2000	2001	2002	2003	2004	2005	2006	2007	2008
Total	40.8	44.1	36.4	39.9	.	39.4 [1]	41.1	40.8	41.4	.
A [2]	37.2	41.0	32.6	34.3	.	36.9 [1]	36.4	37.7	37.0	.
B [3]	31.7	30.1	10.7	18.9	.	36.8 [1]	52.4	12.0	42.0	.
C	46.7	45.0	47.5	29.8	.	33.2 [1]	44.1	44.7	43.7	.
D	37.1	42.9	32.4	38.8	.	35.9 [1]	41.3	38.5	39.8	.
E	40.0	43.8	43.4	41.8	.	44.8 [1]	42.3	48.0	37.6	.
F	47.0	47.1	36.0	41.4	.	39.5 [1]	41.7	52.0	44.4	.
G	48.1	51.2	41.4	49.7	.	46.0 [1]	49.7	50.3	51.8	.
H	45.1	49.1	44.2	42.8	.	39.9 [1]	43.4	41.5	41.5	.
I	40.9	47.2	44.9	43.7	.	45.8 [1]	51.0	45.2	48.7	.
J	46.9	46.3	43.4	44.8	.	42.7 [1]	47.4	38.6	42.7	.
K	40.5	41.6	35.0	48.1	.	36.5 [1]	41.0	44.9	44.4	.
L	41.3	39.8	42.0	45.7	.	44.7 [1]	42.5	41.4	47.5	.
M	27.3	30.8	26.7	25.5	.	25.8 [1]	29.1	28.3	28.4	.
N	45.4	42.5	42.6	39.3	.	42.9 [1]	44.8	38.6	43.7	.
O	32.3	27.8	27.5	28.8	.	27.4 [1]	32.5	31.9	35.5	.
P	50.9	53.1	49.4	53.5	.	50.9 [1]	52.2	51.2	47.1	.
Q	0.0	60.1	0.0	50.8	.	40.5 [1]	44.0	0.0	51.2	.

Brasil (BA) (c) [4][5] — Employees - Salariés - Asalariados

Total men and women - Total hommes et femmes - Total hombres y mujeres
ISIC 3 - CITI 3 - CIIU 3

	1999	2000	2001	2002	2003	2004	2005	2006	2007	2008
Total	.	.	.	42.2 [6]	42.0 [6]	41.9	41.7	41.4	41.3	.
A-B	.	.	.	46.1 [6]	45.9 [6]	45.3	44.5	44.1	43.8	.
C-Q	.	.	.	41.8 [6]	41.6 [6]	41.5	41.4	41.2	41.1	.
A	.	.	.	46.0 [6]	45.8 [6]	45.2	44.4	44.0	43.8	.
B	.	.	.	53.0 [6]	52.9 [6]	51.4	49.1	48.2	47.5	.
C	.	.	.	44.7 [6]	44.8 [6]	46.2	45.0	45.2	44.9	.
D	.	.	.	44.2 [6]	44.2 [6]	44.1	43.9	43.9	43.6	.
E	.	.	.	42.0 [6]	42.1 [6]	42.0	41.7	41.4	41.4	.
F	.	.	.	44.8 [6]	44.6 [6]	44.6	44.1	43.9	43.7	.
G	.	.	.	45.5 [6]	45.4 [6]	45.1	44.9	45.0	44.6	.
H	.	.	.	45.4 [6]	45.2 [6]	45.1	44.9	44.7	44.1	.
I	.	.	.	47.2 [6]	47.1 [6]	46.6	46.5	46.4	45.9	.
J	.	.	.	39.3 [6]	39.6 [6]	39.2	39.2	39.0	39.3	.
K	.	.	.	42.4 [6]	42.0 [6]	42.3	42.2	41.6	41.6	.
L	.	.	.	39.6 [6]	39.3 [6]	39.1	39.1	38.8	38.9	.
M	.	.	.	32.5 [6]	33.0 [6]	32.8	32.5	32.6	33.0	.
N	.	.	.	39.1 [6]	39.0 [6]	39.1	39.0	39.0	38.8	.
O	.	.	.	40.3 [6]	40.5 [6]	40.4	40.1	39.8	39.3	.
P	.	.	.	39.0 [6]	38.0 [6]	37.8	37.6	36.9	36.8	.
Q	.	.	.	42.9 [6]	35.2 [6]	39.4	36.8	35.5	43.3	.
X	.	.	.	39.5 [6]	40.7 [6]	39.9	43.2	42.2	41.0	.

Men - Hommes - Hombres
ISIC 3 - CITI 3 - CIIU 3

	1999	2000	2001	2002	2003	2004	2005	2006	2007	2008
Total	.	.	.	44.8 [6]	44.6 [6]	44.4	44.1	43.8	43.6	.
A-B	.	.	.	46.7 [6]	46.5 [6]	45.9	45.0	44.6	44.2	.
C-Q	.	.	.	44.4 [6]	44.3 [6]	44.1	44.6	43.7	43.6	.
A	.	.	.	46.6 [6]	46.3 [6]	45.8	44.9	44.5	44.2	.
B	.	.	.	53.1 [6]	53.0 [6]	51.5	50.3	48.4	47.4	.
C	.	.	.	44.8 [6]	45.2 [6]	46.6	45.2	45.5	45.3	.
D	.	.	.	44.9 [6]	44.8 [6]	44.6	44.6	44.4	44.1	.
E	.	.	.	42.6 [6]	42.5 [6]	42.8	42.5	42.0	42.1	.
F	.	.	.	45.0 [6]	44.8 [6]	44.7	44.3	44.0	43.9	.
G	.	.	.	46.6 [6]	46.2 [6]	45.9	45.7	45.7	45.4	.
H	.	.	.	45.7 [6]	45.7 [6]	45.8	45.5	45.5	44.7	.
I	.	.	.	48.2 [6]	48.0 [6]	47.7	47.7	47.5	47.0	.
J	.	.	.	40.6 [6]	40.5 [6]	40.0	40.2	39.8	40.4	.
K	.	.	.	44.1 [6]	43.6 [6]	43.8	43.8	43.0	43.3	.
L	.	.	.	41.4 [6]	41.2 [6]	40.9	40.9	40.5	40.5	.
M	.	.	.	35.5 [6]	35.9 [6]	35.7	34.7	35.0	35.4	.
N	.	.	.	40.3 [6]	39.8 [6]	40.3	40.5	39.5	39.7	.
O	.	.	.	41.3 [6]	41.5 [6]	41.3	40.7	40.8	39.8	.
P	.	.	.	45.0 [6]	45.2 [6]	45.0	44.2	42.7	43.5	.
Q	.	.	.	42.9 [6]	37.1 [6]	41.8	38.5	41.3	46.0	.
X	.	.	.	40.9 [6]	42.3 [6]	40.6	44.3	43.9	40.8	.

Explanatory notes: see p. 721.

[1] Continued Household survey, 2003-2004. [2] Excl. forestry. [3] Incl. forestry. [4] Persons aged 10 years and over. [5] Sep. of each year. [6] Excl. rural population of Rondônia, Acre, Amazonas, Roraima, Pará and Amapá.

Notes explicatives: voir p. 723.

[1] Enquête continue des Ménages, 2003-2004. [2] Non compris la sylviculture. [3] Y compris la sylviculture. [4] Personnes âgées de 10 ans et plus. [5] Sept. de chaque année. [6] Non compris la population rurale de Rondônia, Acre, Amazonas, Roraima, Pará et Amapá.

Notas explicativas: véase p. 725.

[1] Encuesta continua de hogares, 2003-2004. [2] Excl. la silvicultura. [3] Incl. silvicultura. [4] Personas de 10 años y más. [5] Sept. de cada año. [6] Excl. la población rural de Rondonia, Acre, Amazonas, Roraima, Pará y Amapá.

HOURS OF WORK   DURÉE DU TRAVAIL   HORAS DE TRABAJO

By economic activity   Par activité économique   Por actividad económica

	Per week				Par semaine				Por semana	
	1999	2000	2001	2002	2003	2004	2005	2006	2007	2008

Brasil (BA) (c) [1] [2]   **Employees - Salariés - Asalariados**

Women - Femmes - Mujeres
ISIC 3 - CITI 3 - CIIU 3

	1999	2000	2001	2002	2003	2004	2005	2006	2007	2008
Total	.	.	.	38.8 [3]	38.7 [3]	38.6	38.5	38.4	38.3	.
A-B	.	.	.	41.7 [3]	40.9 [3]	40.5	39.8	39.9	40.5	.
C-Q	.	.	.	38.8 [3]	38.6 [3]	38.6	38.5	38.4	38.3	.
A	.	.	.	41.6 [3]	40.9 [3]	40.5	39.4	39.9	40.5	.
B	.	.	.	45.3 [3]	45.9 [3]	49.6	25.4	35.5	50.0	.
C	.	.	.	43.3 [3]	40.7 [3]	42.0	43.2	41.4	41.5	.
D	.	.	.	42.5 [3]	42.7 [3]	42.7	42.4	42.7	42.3	.
E	.	.	.	39.1 [3]	40.4 [3]	37.3	37.7	38.8	38.2	.
F	.	.	.	39.4 [3]	40.0 [3]	41.3	40.5	40.4	39.0	.
G	.	.	.	43.7 [3]	43.9 [3]	43.8	43.5	43.8	43.2	.
H	.	.	.	45.1 [3]	44.7 [3]	44.4	44.3	44.0	43.7	.
I	.	.	.	41.3 [3]	41.6 [3]	40.1	41.0	41.0	40.7	.
J	.	.	.	37.9 [3]	38.7 [3]	38.3	38.4	38.3	38.1	.
K	.	.	.	39.4 [3]	39.3 [3]	39.7	39.3	39.2	38.9	.
L	.	.	.	36.2 [3]	36.1 [3]	36.2	36.2	35.9	36.3	.
M	.	.	.	31.8 [3]	32.2 [3]	32.0	31.8	31.9	32.3	.
N	.	.	.	38.8 [3]	38.8 [3]	38.8	38.6	38.9	38.6	.
O	.	.	.	39.1 [3]	39.5 [3]	39.4	39.4	38.9	38.8	.
P	.	.	.	38.5 [3]	37.5 [3]	37.3	37.2	36.5	36.4	.
Q	.	.	.	43.0 [3]	33.7 [3]	37.1	35.4	32.5	36.8	.
X	.	.	.	35.4 [3]	38.3 [3]	38.4	40.8	38.0	41.3	.

Canada (DA) (b) [4] [5]   **Wage earners - Ouvriers - Obreros**

Total men and women - Total hommes et femmes - Total hombres y mujeres
ISIC 3 - CITI 3 - CIIU 3

	1999	2000	2001	2002	2003	2004	2005	2006	2007	2008
Total	31.6	31.6	31.1	30.8	31.0	30.9	30.9	30.9	30.5	30.4
C-Q	31.5	31.5	31.0	30.8	31.0	30.9	30.8	30.8	30.4	30.4
A [6]	39.6	38.8	38.3	37.6	37.8	37.4	38.9	39.3	39.4	39.7
C	40.9	42.1	40.4	40.0	41.6	39.9	41.1	39.6	40.2	38.5
D	38.8	38.8	38.2	38.3	38.1	37.9	37.9	37.9	38.0	37.2
E	38.6	38.4	39.7	40.3	39.2	38.5	38.4	39.1	38.8	38.8
F	37.6	37.3	37.6	36.6	37.2	37.2	36.7	36.5	37.2	37.1
G	29.4	28.6	29.1	28.7	28.9	28.9	28.7	28.6	28.2	28.3
H	24.3	25.4	23.5	23.2	23.4	23.5	23.0	23.8	23.3	23.3
I	35.1	35.7	35.0	34.5	34.1	34.1	35.1	35.2	34.0	34.3
J	29.0	29.4	29.0	28.1	29.4	29.1	28.8	29.7	29.0	29.7
K	31.1	30.2	30.0	29.3	29.6	30.1	30.2	30.6	30.3	30.0
L	30.6	35.0	30.3	31.5	31.9	30.8	31.6	30.8	30.9	30.8
M	24.3	25.7	22.8	25.0	26.6	26.2	25.9	24.4	24.1	25.8
N	28.1	28.6	27.9	27.7	28.3	28.6	28.7	28.6	28.1	28.6
O	24.8	24.9	25.5	25.1	26.2	25.6	25.2	23.3	24.1	25.2

Cayman Islands (BA) (a)   **Total employment - Emploi total - Empleo total**

Total men and women - Total hommes et femmes - Total hombres y mujeres
ISIC 3 - CITI 3 - CIIU 3

	1999	2000	2001	2002	2003	2004	2005	2006	2007	2008
Total	.	.	.	.	.	.	.	.	.	41.8
A-B	.	.	.	.	.	.	.	.	.	41.6
C-D	.	.	.	.	.	.	.	.	.	41.8
E	.	.	.	.	.	.	.	.	.	43.2
F	.	.	.	.	.	.	.	.	.	43.8
G	.	.	.	.	.	.	.	.	.	41.7
H	.	.	.	.	.	.	.	.	.	40.3
I	.	.	.	.	.	.	.	.	.	38.1
J	.	.	.	.	.	.	.	.	.	40.6
K	.	.	.	.	.	.	.	.	.	43.4
L	.	.	.	.	.	.	.	.	.	41.3
M-N	.	.	.	.	.	.	.	.	.	40.6
N	.	.	.	.	.	.	.	.	.	.
O	.	.	.	.	.	.	.	.	.	41.0
P	.	.	.	.	.	.	.	.	.	43.0
Q	.	.	.	.	.	.	.	.	.	.
X	.	.	.	.	.	.	.	.	.	43.2

Explanatory notes: see p. 721.

[1] Persons aged 10 years and over. [2] Sep. of each year. [3] Excl. rural population of Rondônia, Acre, Amazonas, Roraima, Pará and Amapá. [4] Employees paid by the hour. [5] Incl. overtime. [6] Excl. agriculture and hunting.

Notes explicatives: voir p. 723.

[1] Personnes âgées de 10 ans et plus. [2] Sept. de chaque année. [3] Non compris la population rurale de Rondônia, Acre, Amazonas, Roraima, Pará et Amapá. [4] Salariés rémunérés à l'heure. [5] Y compris les heures supplémentaires. [6] Non compris l'agriculture et la chasse.

Notas explicativas: véase p. 725.

[1] Personas de 10 años y más. [2] Sept. de cada año. [3] Excl. la población rural de Rondonia, Acre, Amazonas, Roraima, Pará y Amapá. [4] Asalariados remunerados por hora. [5] Incl. las horas extraordinarias. [6] Excl. agricultura y caza.

	Per week / Par semaine / Por semana									
	1999	2000	2001	2002	2003	2004	2005	2006	2007	2008

Cayman Islands (BA) (a) — Total employment - Emploi total - Empleo total

Men - Hommes - Hombres
ISIC 3 - CITI 3 - CIIU 3

	1999	2000	2001	2002	2003	2004	2005	2006	2007	2008
Total	.	.	.	.	.	.	.	.	.	42.9
A-B	.	.	.	.	.	.	.	.	.	41.6
C-D	.	.	.	.	.	.	.	.	.	42.5
E	.	.	.	.	.	.	.	.	.	44.9
F	.	.	.	.	.	.	.	.	.	44.1
G	.	.	.	.	.	.	.	.	.	43.4
H	.	.	.	.	.	.	.	.	.	41.7
I	.	.	.	.	.	.	.	.	.	38.1
J	.	.	.	.	.	.	.	.	.	40.7
K	.	.	.	.	.	.	.	.	.	45.6
L	.	.	.	.	.	.	.	.	.	41.2
M-N	.	.	.	.	.	.	.	.	.	39.8
O	.	.	.	.	.	.	.	.	.	41.9
P	.	.	.	.	.	.	.	.	.	43.4
X	.	.	.	.	.	.	.	.	.	44.9

Women - Femmes - Mujeres
ISIC 3 - CITI 3 - CIIU 3

	1999	2000	2001	2002	2003	2004	2005	2006	2007	2008
Total	.	.	.	.	.	.	.	.	.	40.7
A-B	.	.	.	.	.	.	.	.	.	41.8
C-D	.	.	.	.	.	.	.	.	.	38.6
E	.	.	.	.	.	.	.	.	.	39.9
F	.	.	.	.	.	.	.	.	.	40.7
G	.	.	.	.	.	.	.	.	.	40.2
H	.	.	.	.	.	.	.	.	.	38.9
I	.	.	.	.	.	.	.	.	.	37.9
J	.	.	.	.	.	.	.	.	.	40.6
K	.	.	.	.	.	.	.	.	.	41.3
L	.	.	.	.	.	.	.	.	.	41.4
M-N	.	.	.	.	.	.	.	.	.	40.8
N	.	.	.	.	.	.	.	.	.	.
O	.	.	.	.	.	.	.	.	.	40.1
P	.	.	.	.	.	.	.	.	.	43.0
X	.	.	.	.	.	.	.	.	.	41.1

Colombia (BA) (a) [1][2][3] — Employees - Salariés - Asalariados

Total men and women - Total hommes et femmes - Total hombres y mujeres
ISIC 3 - CITI 3 - CIIU 3

	1999	2000	2001	2002	2003	2004	2005	2006	2007	2008
Total	.	.	.	42.4	42.3	43.6	44.2	46.8	46.0 [3]	.
C-Q	.	.	.	44.2	43.8	43.8	44.5	47.1	47.0 [3]	.
A	.	.	.	41.0	40.6	42.0	41.2	43.9	42.5 [3]	.
C	.	.	.	46.7	45.9	43.9	42.4	46.7	49.9 [3]	.
D	.	.	.	41.6	41.6	42.7	43.6	46.6	45.1 [3]	.
E	.	.	.	46.6	45.5	47.0	47.0	47.6	49.1 [3]	.
F	.	.	.	44.8	43.3	43.6	45.1	47.8	46.7 [3]	.
G	.	.	.	44.9	44.4	45.5	46.0	49.1	48.1 [3]	.
I	.	.	.	50.6	50.2	49.8	51.7	55.1	54.0 [3]	.
J	.	.	.	42.3	42.4	40.2	43.3	43.8	44.6 [3]	.
K	.	.	.	42.2	41.4	42.4	42.6	45.7	43.9 [3]	.
O	.	.	.	38.2	39.3	38.9	39.0	41.9	42.0 [3]	.
X	.	.	.	52.0	59.9	32.7	45.4	45.4	41.7 [3]	.

Men - Hommes - Hombres
ISIC 3 - CITI 3 - CIIU 3

	1999	2000	2001	2002	2003	2004	2005	2006	2007	2008
Total	.	.	.	45.9	46.0	45.8	46.3	48.6	48.5 [3]	.
C-Q	.	.	.	46.6	46.6	46.0	46.6	49.0	49.2 [3]	.
A	.	.	.	43.2	44.1	44.2	43.3	45.6	44.1 [3]	.
C	.	.	.	47.6	48.4	45.4	43.5	47.2	50.1 [3]	.
D	.	.	.	46.5	46.4	46.3	47.1	49.5	49.2 [3]	.
E	.	.	.	47.5	47.3	47.9	47.5	49.1	49.6 [3]	.
F	.	.	.	44.9	43.3	43.7	45.2	47.9	46.8 [3]	.
G	.	.	.	48.2	48.0	48.2	48.9	52.5	51.8 [3]	.
I	.	.	.	52.3	52.1	51.4	53.2	56.5	55.9 [3]	.
J	.	.	.	43.7	45.8	41.6	45.1	43.1	45.4 [3]	.
K	.	.	.	46.8	45.5	46.1	46.1	48.5	48.2 [3]	.
O	.	.	.	42.0	42.9	43.2	42.6	46.5	45.7 [3]	.
X	.	.	.	52.2	60.9	42.4	44.4	49.5	39.2 [3]	.

Explanatory notes: see p. 721.

[1] Excl. armed forces. [2] Persons aged 10 years and over. [3] Third quarter.

Notes explicatives: voir p. 723.

[1] Non compris les forces armées. [2] Personnes âgées de 10 ans et plus. [3] Troisième trimestre.

Notas explicativas: véase p. 725.

[1] Excl. las fuerzas armadas. [2] Personas de 10 años y más. [3] Tercer trimestre.

	Per week / Par semaine / Por semana									
	1999	2000	2001	2002	2003	2004	2005	2006	2007	2008

Colombia (BA) (a) [1][2][3] — Employees - Salariés - Asalariados
Women - Femmes - Mujeres
ISIC 3 - CITI 3 - CIIU 3

	1999	2000	2001	2002	2003	2004	2005	2006	2007	2008
Total	.	.	.	37.3	37.1	38.9	39.4	42.3	45.7 [3]	.
C-Q	.	.	.	39.5	39.1	39.9	40.5	43.5	43.5 [3]	.
A	.	.	.	28.6	24.5	29.3	29.6	30.9	33.2 [3]	.
C	.	.	.	42.5	39.3	40.7	35.7	43.0	48.1 [3]	.
D	.	.	.	36.8	36.2	38.2	39.6	42.8	40.0 [3]	.
E	.	.	.	41.7	40.0	43.6	45.0	41.8	46.4 [3]	.
F	.	.	.	42.0	43.9	42.0	41.5	44.9	43.2 [3]	.
G	.	.	.	40.9	40.4	42.6	42.8	45.3	44.1 [3]	.
I	.	.	.	37.9	39.2	40.7	43.8	48.8	46.9 [3]	.
J	.	.	.	40.9	39.1	39.1	41.7	44.4	43.9 [3]	.
K	.	.	.	35.9	35.5	35.6	37.2	41.0	38.8 [3]	.
O	.	.	.	36.5	37.9	36.9	37.5	39.9	40.4 [3]	.
X	.	.	.	51.7	54.0	18.5	48.0	37.2	51.7 [3]	.

Costa Rica (BA) (a) [4] — Total employment - Emploi total - Empleo total
Total men and women - Total hommes et femmes - Total hombres y mujeres
ISIC 3 - CITI 3 - CIIU 3

	1999	2000	2001	2002	2003	2004	2005	2006	2007	2008
Total	46.8	46.6	47.0	47.0	47.0	45.6	45.1	45.1	46.5	46.9
A-B	45.5	45.1	46.0	.	47.0	43.5	42.9	43.4	45.3	46.3
C-Q	47.1	46.9	47.0	47.0	47.0	46.0	45.5	45.4	46.6	46.3
A	45.2	44.6	45.0	.	46.0	43.1	42.6	43.0	44.9	45.9
B	58.8	64.6	62.0	.	65.0	55.1	52.9	54.6	57.2	59.8
C	48.5	59.5	47.0	54.0	51.0	49.9	49.9	57.7	58.6	52.1
D	49.1	48.9	49.0	50.0	49.0	47.4	46.7	46.1	47.6	47.4
E	48.5	49.3	49.0	48.0	49.0	47.5	48.5	49.6	51.0	49.2
F	51.8	52.1	52.0	52.0	53.0	51.3	51.5	50.8	52.2	52.7
G	49.8	48.8	49.0	49.0	49.0	46.4	45.9	46.2	47.4	48.3
H	49.5	48.9	48.0	49.0	48.0	47.8	46.8	48.4	49.0	49.7
I	52.5	51.0	53.0	53.0	52.0	52.7	52.2	51.5	53.2	53.0
J	46.8	46.2	48.0	48.0	.	46.7	46.6	46.9	47.3	47.9
K	44.5	49.9	48.0	50.0	49.0	46.2	46.6	46.4	46.9	46.3
L	.	.	48.0	47.0	47.0	47.3	48.8	47.0	47.8	48.0
M	40.7	40.6	40.0	39.0	39.0	38.9	39.6	39.4	40.9	40.6
N	45.4	45.3	48.0	47.0	46.0	46.0	46.5	45.3	47.7	47.4
O	47.6	47.8	43.0	43.0	43.0	39.2	36.8	37.6	38.2	39.5
P	35.6	35.6	38.0	38.0	36.0	35.0	34.0	34.3	34.6	34.9
Q	48.3	50.4	49.0	47.0	48.0	45.1	44.7	50.1	53.2	49.1
X	46.8	43.5	48.0	49.0	49.0	45.4	43.5	42.5	46.2	47.9

Men - Hommes - Hombres
ISIC 3 - CITI 3 - CIIU 3

	1999	2000	2001	2002	2003	2004	2005	2006	2007	2008
Total	49.0	48.8	50.0	50.0	49.0	48.7	48.3	48.2	49.9	50.4
A-B	45.5	45.6	46.0	47.0	.	44.1	43.8	44.0	46.2	46.7
C-Q	50.1	49.9	50.0	50.0	50.0	49.8	49.6	49.2	50.7	46.7
A	45.3	45.1	46.0	46.0	.	43.7	43.4	43.5	45.6	46.3
B	58.7	65.9	63.0	56.0	.	56.1	53.9	55.4	59.1	60.8
C	49.2	61.7	52.0	57.0	57.0	49.9	51.1	59.1	57.8	54.7
D	50.5	49.6	51.0	51.0	50.0	50.6	50.3	49.4	51.0	51.3
E	48.9	50.1	50.0	49.0	50.0	48.0	48.7	50.7	52.7	50.7
F	51.8	52.4	52.0	53.0	53.0	51.5	51.6	51.0	52.7	52.9
G	50.6	50.7	50.0	51.0	51.0	49.6	49.3	49.5	51.0	51.7
H	51.1	52.0	51.0	51.0	50.0	53.3	52.1	52.9	52.4	54.2
I	54.2	52.4	55.0	54.0	54.0	53.6	53.3	52.7	54.3	54.5
J	48.1	47.4	49.0	50.0	47.0	47.1	47.7	47.6	47.8	50.1
K	48.2	54.9	51.0	53.0	54.0	50.1	48.9	49.2	50.2	50.1
L	.	.	50.0	49.0	49.0	49.2	50.4	48.4	50.1	49.7
M	41.0	42.1	43.0	42.0	41.0	40.5	41.6	41.2	41.9	42.9
N	49.1	47.5	50.0	48.0	47.0	47.3	47.9	46.7	50.1	48.9
O	49.3	49.2	46.0	44.0	45.0	43.7	40.1	41.1	43.1	43.8
P	37.1	33.1	46.0	45.0	50.0	38.9	40.6	35.1	37.0	42.8
Q	49.8	51.8	50.0	48.0	50.0	45.9	47.4	56.8	54.4	54.9
X	46.7	43.7	48.0	52.0	49.0	46.4	41.5	45.5	48.4	49.7

Explanatory notes: see p. 721.

[1] Excl. armed forces. [2] Persons aged 10 years and over. [3] Third quarter. [4] Main occupation; July of each year.

Notes explicatives: voir p. 723.

[1] Non compris les forces armées. [2] Personnes âgées de 10 ans et plus. [3] Troisième trimestre. [4] Occupation principale; juillet de chaque année.

Notas explicativas: véase p. 725.

[1] Excl. las fuerzas armadas. [2] Personas de 10 años y más. [3] Tercer trimestre. [4] Ocupación principal; julio de cada año.

	Per week			Par semaine				Por semana		
	1999	2000	2001	2002	2003	2004	2005	2006	2007	2008

Costa Rica (BA) (a) [1]   Total employment - Emploi total - Empleo total

Women - Femmes - Mujeres
ISIC 3 - CITI 3 - CIIU 3

Total	42.7	42.3	43.0	43.0	42.0	39.6	39.1	39.6	40.5	40.9
A-B	45.2	40.2	41.0	44.0	.	37.9	36.3	39.0	40.3	43.0
C-Q	42.5	42.4	43.0	43.0	42.0	39.7	39.2	39.6	40.5	43.0
A	45.1	40.3	41.0	44.0	.	37.5	36.3	38.9	40.3	43.0
B	60.0	26.3	24.0	48.0	.	47.0	37.5	41.7	39.6	42.2
C	43.0	42.0	24.0	22.0	13.0	49.8	45.1	48.0	64.3	40.0
D	45.8	47.2	47.0	47.0	47.0	39.4	38.2	38.8	40.4	40.2
E	44.8	44.4	45.0	45.0	48.0	45.0	47.1	45.3	44.4	43.9
F	46.3	44.4	41.0	43.0	50.0	45.2	44.2	42.7	38.7	47.1
G	48.2	45.5	46.0	45.0	45.0	40.1	39.5	40.3	40.8	42.2
H	48.0	45.8	46.0	47.0	46.0	43.3	42.8	45.1	46.6	46.5
I	42.7	43.1	43.0	47.0	45.0	45.5	44.8	42.8	46.0	45.0
J	44.5	44.3	46.0	46.0	44.0	46.0	44.9	45.8	46.7	45.9
K	35.6	44.2	42.0	42.0	39.0	37.6	41.1	40.6	39.4	39.3
L	.	.	45.0	44.0	45.0	44.4	45.7	44.3	44.2	45.1
M	40.6	39.9	39.0	38.0	38.0	38.3	38.8	38.8	40.4	39.7
N	42.4	43.7	47.0	46.0	45.0	45.1	45.6	44.4	46.3	46.5
O	43.0	43.4	38.0	41.0	40.0	35.2	33.2	33.9	33.4	34.6
P	35.5	35.7	38.0	37.0	36.0	34.6	33.4	34.2	34.2	34.4
Q	45.7	39.7	45.0	42.0	45.0	44.1	43.7	46.2	48.0	44.2
X	47.0	43.0	47.0	44.0	50.0	40.3	50.8	39.5	41.0	44.9

Cuba (F) (a)   Employees - Salariés - Asalariados

Total men and women - Total hommes et femmes - Total hombres y mujeres
ISIC 2 - CITI 2 - CIIU 2

2-9	41	41	41	41	41	41	41	42	41	39
1	43	43	42	43	42	43	42	42	41	.
2	42	42	41	45	43	42	44	43	47	40
3	41	41	41	40	40	41	41	42	41	41
4	46	39	35	40	38	42	42	41	41	40
5	48	46	35	45	45	45	46	45	43	43
6	40	41	41	40	42	41	41	45	41	40
7	39	41	41	41	40	41	43	41	52	43
8	41	40	39	40	40	40	42	44	45	39
9	40	40	40	41	40	40	40	41	41	36

Chile (BA) (a) [2][3]   Total employment - Emploi total - Empleo total

Total men and women - Total hommes et femmes - Total hombres y mujeres
ISIC 2 - CITI 2 - CIIU 2

Total	43.5 [4]	44.1 [4]	43.7	43.8	43.5 [4]	42.9	42.1	42.1	41.7	40.6
2-9	43.3 [4]	43.9 [4]	43.6	43.7	43.2 [4]	42.8	42.0	42.2	41.6	40.5
1	44.7 [4]	45.3 [4]	44.8	44.8	45.1 [4]	44.0	42.8	41.5	42.2	41.2
2	47.2 [4]	47.4 [4]	47.6	48.1	47.8 [4]	47.0	45.8	46.4	45.3	45.5
3	43.2 [4]	43.6 [4]	43.6	44.1	43.3 [4]	43.0	42.0	42.0	41.7	40.3
4	45.2 [4]	44.2 [4]	45.2	46.0	46.4 [4]	46.8	44.1	43.2	43.2	42.2
5	43.4 [4]	42.9 [4]	42.6	43.3	43.1 [4]	43.2	42.9	42.7	43.1	41.5
6	45.5 [4]	46.7 [4]	46.7	46.1	45.9 [4]	44.6	43.6	43.9	42.9	42.1
7	46.8 [4]	47.2 [4]	46.9	46.7	46.1 [4]	46.4	45.9	46.2	45.2	44.3
8	43.7 [4]	44.4 [4]	44.0	44.4	43.7 [4]	43.8	42.8	42.4	42.1	41.2
9	40.7 [4]	41.4 [4]	40.6	40.9	40.4 [4]	39.9	39.4	39.4	38.8	37.4

Men - Hommes - Hombres
ISIC 2 - CITI 2 - CIIU 2

Total	44.5 [4]	45.1 [4]	44.7	44.9	44.5 [4]	44.0	43.2	43.3	43.3	42.1
2-9	44.4 [4]	45.0 [4]	44.7	44.9	44.3 [4]	44.0	43.2	43.6	43.2	42.2
1	44.9 [4]	45.6 [4]	45.1	45.0	45.3 [4]	44.1	43.3	41.9	42.7	41.7
2	47.3 [4]	47.5 [4]	47.7	48.2	48.0 [4]	46.9	46.0	46.6	45.3	45.5
3	44.7 [4]	45.1 [4]	45.3	45.7	45.1 [4]	44.8	43.6	43.9	43.4	42.1
4	45.3 [4]	45.1 [4]	46.1	46.5	47.4 [4]	47.4	44.4	44.1	43.8	42.8
5	43.4 [4]	42.9 [4]	42.6	43.2	43.1 [4]	43.1	42.9	42.6	43.1	41.6
6	46.7 [4]	48.1 [4]	48.0	47.7	47.1 [4]	46.5	45.3	45.9	45.1	44.4
7	47.3 [4]	47.8 [4]	47.3	47.1	46.5 [4]	47.0	46.4	47.2	46.1	45.0
8	44.9 [4]	45.3 [4]	45.3	46.0	44.8 [4]	44.8	43.9	43.4	43.0	42.6
9	41.0 [4]	42.0 [4]	41.1	41.3	41.1 [4]	40.2	39.7	39.9	39.8	38.7

Explanatory notes: see p. 721.

[1] Main occupation; July of each year. [2] Excl. armed forces. [3] Persons aged 15 years and over. [4] Oct.-Dec.

Notes explicatives: voir p. 723.

[1] Occupation principale; juillet de chaque année. [2] Non compris les forces armées. [3] Personnes âgées de 15 ans et plus. [4] Oct.-déc.

Notas explicativas: véase p. 725.

[1] Ocupación principal; julio de cada año. [2] Excl. las fuerzas armadas. [3] Personas de 15 años y más. [4] Oct.-dic.

	Per week				Par semaine				Por semana	
	1999	2000	2001	2002	2003	2004	2005	2006	2007	2008

Chile (BA) (a) [1][2]   **Total employment - Emploi total - Empleo total**

Women - Femmes - Mujeres
ISIC 2 - CITI 2 - CIIU 2

	1999	2000	2001	2002	2003	2004	2005	2006	2007	2008
Total	41.5[3]	42.1[3]	41.7	41.8	41.5[3]	40.8	40.1	40.0	39.1	38.0
2-9	41.4[3]	42.0[3]	41.6	41.7	41.3[3]	40.6	40.1	40.0	39.1	37.9
1	43.2[3]	43.1[3]	43.3	43.4	44.1[3]	43.9	40.4	39.6	39.8	39.1
2	44.1[3]	41.9[3]	45.7	46.7	45.3[3]	48.7	41.4	44.6	44.7	46.2
3	39.0[3]	39.4[3]	38.8	39.4	38.1[3]	38.1	37.7	36.9	36.8	35.8
4	44.8[3]	40.0[3]	40.2	42.2	39.7[3]	44.1	43.1	37.8	39.4	39.8
5	43.8[3]	43.7[3]	44.4	46.3	43.6[3]	44.7	42.8	44.4	42.3	39.4
6	44.0[3]	45.0[3]	45.1	44.1	44.6[3]	42.5	41.7	41.8	40.6	39.9
7	42.9[3]	43.2[3]	44.3	43.8	44.0[3]	42.7	43.0	40.8	40.4	40.9
8	41.7[3]	42.8[3]	41.9	42.0	41.9[3]	42.1	41.1	40.8	40.7	39.1
9	40.4[3]	40.9[3]	40.1	40.5	39.8[3]	39.6	39.1	39.1	38.1	36.5

República Dominicana (BA) (c)   **Total employment - Emploi total - Empleo total**

Total men and women - Total hommes et femmes - Total hombres y mujeres
ISIC 3 - CITI 3 - CIIU 3

	1999	2000	2001	2002	2003	2004	2005	2006	2007	2008
Total						40.1	40.2	42.2	39.6	
A-B						38.5	38.2	21.1	38.4	
C-Q						40.4	40.5	40.8	40.6	
A						37.1	37.1	21.1	35.0	
B						38.9	39.7	20.0	38.3	
C						41.1	46.8	46.0	44.7	
D						42.0	43.0		42.7	
E						41.6	41.0		40.7	
F						41.7	40.7		42.3	
G						42.5	41.9	43.5	41.5	
H						41.4	40.9	41.0	40.7	
I						43.0	41.9		43.3	
J						41.1	41.6	41.0	43.4	
K						40.6	39.4	37.5	40.0	
L						39.8	40.2	41.4	39.6	
M						33.7	34.2	37.5	34.3	
N						39.5	39.1	37.5	38.4	
O						36.6	36.2	37.5	35.2	
P						42.1	43.4	37.5	41.3	
Q						40.1	37.2	37.5	40.9	
X										

Men - Hommes - Hombres
ISIC 3 - CITI 3 - CIIU 3

	1999	2000	2001	2002	2003	2004	2005	2006	2007	2008
A-B						38.5	38.2	21.1	38.4	
C-Q						42.2	41.6	41.9	42.1	
A						38.1	36.8	22.1	38.5	
B						38.9	39.7	20.0	38.3	
C		47.1	45.9	44.8	48.5	44.1	45.6	47.7	46.4	
D		46.7	46.4	45.1	45.9	43.4	45.3	42.8	44.0	
E		46.7	46.4	45.1	45.9	42.9	42.8	39.7	43.0	
F		47.4	46.2	45.4	45.7	42.8	42.4	42.9	42.0	
G		44.8	43.6	43.1	41.5	44.2	43.6	43.9	43.0	
H		48.7	47.3	46.7	45.0	44.1	43.9	43.9	44.1	
I		45.8	45.6	45.9	45.5	44.3	43.8	41.5	43.0	
J		50.0	49.7	48.1	47.2	42.5	42.4	43.1	44.6	
K		43.9	46.0	44.2	43.6	42.5	41.0	39.7	41.5	
L		39.7	40.7	40.4	40.1	43.6	42.7	42.1	42.2	
M		47.5	46.4	43.8	44.2	35.6	35.3	36.6	35.7	
N						40.7	41.0	41.2	39.3	
O						37.6	37.5	38.3	36.3	
P						45.0	47.2	43.2	43.9	
Q						39.5	30.0		43.0	
X										

Explanatory notes: see p. 721.   Notes explicatives: voir p. 723.   Notas explicativas: véase p. 725.

[1] Excl. armed forces. [2] Persons aged 15 years and over. [3] Oct.-Dec.   [1] Non compris les forces armées. [2] Personnes âgées de 15 ans et plus. [3] Oct.-déc.   [1] Excl. las fuerzas armadas. [2] Personas de 15 años y más. [3] Oct.-dic.

By economic activity — Par activité économique — Por actividad económica

	Per week			Par semaine				Por semana		
	1999	2000	2001	2002	2003	2004	2005	2006	2007	2008

República Dominicana (BA) (c) — Total employment - Emploi total - Empleo total

Women - Femmes - Mujeres
ISIC 3 - CITI 3 - CIIU 3

	1999	2000	2001	2002	2003	2004	2005	2006	2007	2008
Total	.	39.1	38.4	38.1	38.1	38.5	39.2	37.5	37.5	.
A-B	.	.	.	.	.	.	.	.	.	.
C-Q	.	.	.	.	.	38.7	39.3	37.8	39.1	.
A	.	.	.	.	.	36.2	37.5	20.0	31.5	.
B	.	.	.	.	.	.	.	.	.	.
C	.	.	.	40.0	.	38.0	48.0	35.9	43.0	.
D	.	43.2	42.4	41.9	42.4	40.5	40.6	41.0	41.4	.
E	.	41.9	43.5	38.0	40.7	40.2	39.2	39.6	38.4	.
F	.	46.5	42.2	45.9	38.3	40.6	39.0	40.9	42.6	.
G	.	41.0	39.5	39.6	37.9	40.8	40.3	40.0	40.1	.
H	.	38.4	38.4	38.3	39.2	38.6	37.8	36.1	37.3	.
I	.	41.7	42.4	42.5	41.2	41.6	40.0	42.6	43.7	.
J	.	38.3	36.1	36.6	40.4	39.8	40.8	40.5	42.2	.
K	.	36.4	36.7	36.6	36.7	38.7	37.7	36.2	38.5	.
L	.	38.6	37.3	36.0	35.6	35.9	37.7	36.2	36.9	.
N	.	.	.	.	.	38.3	37.1	37.5	37.5	.
O	.	.	.	.	.	35.6	34.8	35.0	34.1	.
P	.	.	.	.	.	39.2	39.5	38.7	38.6	.
Q	.	.	.	.	.	40.7	44.4	34.1	38.8	.
X	.	.	.	.	.	.	.	.	.	.

República Dominicana (BA) (c) — Employees - Salariés - Asalariados

Total men and women - Total hommes et femmes - Total hombres y mujeres
ISIC 3 - CITI 3 - CIIU 3

	1999	2000	2001	2002	2003	2004	2005	2006	2007	2008
Total	44.9	43.1	42.7	41.7	.	42.0	43.1	42.0	43.0	.
C	41.5	47.1	45.9	44.5	48.5	45.1	.	.	.	.
D	46.2	45.4	45.1	44.0	44.8	44.4	.	.	.	.
E	47.0	46.2	45.6	44.1	44.7	44.0	.	.	.	.
F	45.7	.	43.6	.	41.4	43.9	.	.	.	.
G	46.6	.	.	.	.	43.3	.	.	.	.
H	47.3	41.7	41.7	41.4	42.4	42.6	.	.	.	.
I	52.5	.	.	.	.	47.0	.	.	.	.
J	42.2	41.0	40.8	40.4	42.0	41.9	.	.	.	.
K	41.2	37.6	38.2	37.9	37.9	38.1	.	.	.	.
L	42.9	.	.	.	.	.	.	.	.	.

Men - Hommes - Hombres
ISIC 3 - CITI 3 - CIIU 3

	1999	2000	2001	2002	2003	2004	2005	2006	2007	2008
Total	.	45.1	44.7	43.5	43.5	43.8	.	.	.	.

Ecuador (BA) (a) — Total employment - Emploi total - Empleo total

Total men and women - Total hommes et femmes - Total hombres y mujeres
ISIC 3 - CITI 3 - CIIU 3

	1999	2000	2001	2002	2003	2004	2005	2006	2007	2008
Total	.	.	.	.	.	38	44	43	.	.
A-B	.	.	.	.	.	.	41	.	.	.
C-Q	.	.	.	.	.	44	44	.	.	.
A	.	.	.	.	.	55	39	39	.	.
B	.	.	.	.	.	54	53	47	.	.
C	.	.	.	.	.	45	53	54	.	.
D	.	.	.	.	.	45	45	46	.	.
E	.	.	.	.	.	43	48	44	.	.
F	.	.	.	.	.	45	42	42	.	.
G	.	.	.	.	.	44	44	43	.	.
H	.	.	.	.	.	50	46	44	.	.
I	.	.	.	.	.	47	50	50	.	.
J	.	.	.	.	.	46	45	44	.	.
K	.	.	.	.	.	47	48	47	.	.
L	.	.	.	.	.	38	47	46	.	.
M	.	.	.	.	.	44	38	38	.	.
N	.	.	.	.	.	33	43	43	.	.
O	.	.	.	.	.	44	34	33	.	.
P	.	.	.	.	.	44	41	43	.	.
Q	.	.	.	.	.	44	48	44	.	.

Explanatory notes: see p. 721. Notes explicatives: voir p. 723. Notas explicativas: véase p. 725.

HOURS OF WORK DURÉE DU TRAVAIL HORAS DE TRABAJO

By economic activity Par activité économique Por actividad económica

	Per week					Par semaine			Por semana	
	1999	2000	2001	2002	2003	2004	2005	2006	2007	2008

Ecuador (BA) (a) — Total employment - Emploi total - Empleo total

Men - Hommes - Hombres
ISIC 3 - CITI 3 - CIIU 3

	1999	2000	2001	2002	2003	2004	2005	2006	2007	2008
Total	.	.	.	.	.	39	46	46	.	.
A-B	.	.	.	.	.	.	43	.	.	.
C-Q	.	.	.	.	.	47	47	.	.	.
A	.	.	.	.	.	56	41	41	.	.
B	.	.	.	.	.	55	54	51	.	.
C	.	.	.	.	.	49	53	55	.	.
D	.	.	.	.	.	45	48	48	.	.
E	.	.	.	.	.	43	49	44	.	.
F	.	.	.	.	.	48	43	42	.	.
G	.	.	.	.	.	47	47	45	.	.
H	.	.	.	.	.	51	50	48	.	.
I	.	.	.	.	.	49	51	51	.	.
J	.	.	.	.	.	49	45	45	.	.
K	.	.	.	.	.	49	50	51	.	.
L	.	.	.	.	.	41	48	48	.	.
M	.	.	.	.	.	47	40	40	.	.
N	.	.	.	.	.	44	46	46	.	.
O	.	.	.	.	.	50	40	41	.	.
P	.	.	.	.	.	44	56	45	.	.
Q	.	.	.	.	.	47	49	.	.	.

Women - Femmes - Mujeres
ISIC 3 - CITI 3 - CIIU 3

	1999	2000	2001	2002	2003	2004	2005	2006	2007	2008
Total	.	.	.	.	.	31	40	40	.	.
A-B	.	.	.	.	.	.	36	.	.	.
C-Q	.	.	.	.	.	40	40	.	.	.
A	.	.	.	.	.	50	32	32	.	.
B	.	.	.	.	.	39	49	44	.	.
C	.	.	.	.	.	38	50	53	.	.
D	.	.	.	.	.	44	40	41	.	.
E	.	.	.	.	.	43	40	43	.	.
F	.	.	.	.	.	42	39	36	.	.
G	.	.	.	.	.	43	42	41	.	.
H	.	.	.	.	.	41	44	42	.	.
I	.	.	.	.	.	45	43	44	.	.
J	.	.	.	.	.	40	44	43	.	.
K	.	.	.	.	.	42	41	38	.	.
L	.	.	.	.	.	36	43	43	.	.
M	.	.	.	.	.	42	37	36	.	.
N	.	.	.	.	.	25	41	41	.	.
O	.	.	.	.	.	44	29	28	.	.
P	.	.	.	.	.	40	40	43	.	.
Q	.	.	.	.	.	39	48	44	.	.

El Salvador (DA) (a) [1] — Wage earners - Ouvriers - Obreros

Total men and women - Total hommes et femmes - Total hombres y mujeres
ISIC 2 - CITI 2 - CIIU 2

	1999	2000	2001	2002	2003	2004	2005	2006	2007	2008	ISIC 3 - CITI 3 - CIIU 3
3	48.2	.	44.0	44.0	44.0	44.0	44.0	44.0	44.0	44.0	A-B
6	46.0	.	45.0	52.0	48.0	47.0	48.0	50.0	48.0	53.0	D
		.	45.0	46.0	46.0	48.0	50.0	45.0	46.0	45.0	G-H

Men - Hommes - Hombres
ISIC 2 - CITI 2 - CIIU 2

	1999	2000	2001	2002	2003	2004	2005	2006	2007	2008	ISIC 3 - CITI 3 - CIIU 3
3	48.6	48.0	44.0	44.0	44.0	44.0	44.0	44.0	44.0	44.0	A-B
6	45.5	47.0	46.0	51.0	49.0	48.0	49.0	50.0	50.0	51.0	D
			45.0	47.0	46.0	48.0	54.0	45.0	46.0	45.0	G-H

Women - Femmes - Mujeres
ISIC 2 - CITI 2 - CIIU 2

	1999	2000	2001	2002	2003	2004	2005	2006	2007	2008	ISIC 3 - CITI 3 - CIIU 3
3	47.7	49.0	44.0	44.0	44.0	44.0	44.0	44.0	44.0	44.0	A-B
6	46.6	46.0	45.0	54.0	47.0	46.0	47.0	49.0	47.0	55.0	D
			45.0	45.0	45.0	48.0	45.0	44.0	46.0	45.0	G-H

Explanatory notes: see p. 721. Notes explicatives: voir p. 723. Notas explicativas: véase p. 725.

[1] Urban areas. [1] Régions urbaines. [1] Areas urbanas.

By economic activity   **Par activité économique**   **Por actividad económica**

	Per week			Par semaine			Por semana		
	1999	2000	2001	2002	2003	2004	2005	2006	2007	2008

Guyana (DA) (b)   **Salaried employees - Employés - Empleados**

Total men and women - Total hommes et femmes - Total hombres y mujeres
ISIC 3 - CITI 3 - CIIU 3

	1999	2000	2001	2002	2003	2004	2005	2006	2007	2008
C-Q	.	.	.	.	38	.	.	45	48 [1]	.
C	.	.	.	.	48	.	.	42	48 [1]	.
D	.	.	.	.	45	.	.	45	55 [1]	.
E	.	.	.	.	44	.	.	42	42 [1]	.
F	.	.	.	.	.	.	.	60	62 [1]	.
G	.	.	.	.	41	.	.	42	38 [1]	.
H	.	.	.	.	51	.	.	46	54 [1]	.
I	.	.	.	.	45	.	.	50	44 [1]	.
J	.	.	.	.	46	.	.	46	40 [1]	.
K	.	.	.	.	44	.	.	40	. [1]	.
L	.	.	.	.	40	.	.	41	43 [1]	.
M	.	.	.	.	40	.	.	35	42 [1]	.
N	.	.	.	.	41	.	.	46	44 [1]	.

México (BA) (d) [2] [3]   **Employees - Salariés - Asalariados**

Total men and women - Total hommes et femmes - Total hombres y mujeres
ISIC 3 - CITI 3 - CIIU 3

	1999	2000	2001	2002	2003	2004	2005	2006	2007	2008
Total	44.9	43.9	43.5	44.2	43.3	43.6 |	45.2 [4]	44.1	43.9	44.5
A-B	45.4	44.1	43.2	43.3	41.3	40.6 |	40.4 [4]	39.6	38.9	42.0
C-Q	44.8	43.9	43.5	44.3	43.5	43.8 |	45.4 [4]	44.4	44.1	44.7
A	45.2	43.9	43.0	43.1	41.1	40.5 |	40.4 [4]	39.6	39.0	41.9
B	55.8	50.0	50.2	50.8	47.7	48.0 |	40.9 [4]	38.3	37.5	46.6
C	48.4	50.2	48.3	47.0	48.0	47.4 |	50.9 [4]	51.0	50.9	52.9
D	45.5	44.4	44.0	45.2	44.4	44.8 |	46.5 [4]	45.4	45.5	46.4
E	43.5	40.6	41.2	42.7	41.7	42.2 |	43.5 [4]	43.0	42.3	43.3
F	47.7	46.0	45.3	46.3	45.1	45.1 |	47.1 [4]	46.2	46.3	46.9
G	46.8	45.7	45.5	46.5	45.7	45.6 |	48.5 [4]	47.7	47.2	48.0
H	47.9	47.0	47.2	46.9	46.1	46.3 |	46.5 [4]	46.3	46.2	46.1
I	52.6	51.7	51.1	52.3	51.8	53.0 |	59.1 [4]	54.8	54.4	55.1
J	42.8	42.3	42.4	42.8	41.9	42.8 |	44.8 [4]	43.8	43.2	44.5
K	48.6	44.9	45.8	46.6	46.1	46.5 |	47.7 [4]	46.2	45.7	46.1
L	46.8	45.4	45.3	46.2	45.2	46.8 |	46.6 [4]	45.5	45.1	46.1
M	31.4	31.4	31.2	31.7	31.1	32.1 |	32.3 [4]	31.2	31.3	31.1
N	39.5	39.7	39.5	39.6	39.5	39.8 |	39.9 [4]	39.2	39.0	39.9
O	42.0	43.4	41.8	42.7	42.5	42.4 |	44.2 [4]	42.7	41.9	42.1
P	39.8	39.2	37.7	38.0	36.3	35.0 |	35.6 [4]	35.2	34.1	34.6
Q	.	56.5	45.6	.	.	36.1 |	45.7 [4]	37.8	44.6	64.3
X	.	.	.	.	.	|	.	.	.	.

Men - Hommes - Hombres
ISIC 3 - CITI 3 - CIIU 3

	1999	2000	2001	2002	2003	2004	2005	2006	2007	2008
Total	47.2	46.2	45.7	46.5	45.6	46.0 |	47.6 [4]	46.9	46.6	47.2
A-B	45.8	44.5	43.7	43.6	41.7	41.2 |	41.8 [4]	40.8	40.3	42.2
C-Q	47.4	46.5	46.0	46.9	46.1	46.7 |	48.3 [4]	47.6	47.2	47.8
A	45.6	44.4	43.5	43.5	41.6	41.0 |	41.8 [4]	40.9	40.3	42.2
B	56.0	50.0	50.6	51.2	49.8	48.7 |	42.2 [4]	38.7	38.5	47.0
C	49.1	51.1	49.1	47.7	48.9	48.0 |	52.2 [4]	51.9	51.8	54.2
D	46.5	45.6	45.2	46.2	45.3	45.9 |	47.8 [4]	46.3	46.6	47.4
E	44.3	40.9	41.9	43.1	42.2	43.0 |	43.5 [4]	43.9	43.2	44.0
F	47.8	46.1	45.3	46.4	45.1	45.2 |	47.1 [4]	46.4	46.3	47.0
G	48.9	47.9	47.6	48.5	47.5	47.9 |	48.5 [4]	49.5	48.6	49.5
H	49.8	48.2	48.3	48.3	47.6	47.3 |	46.5 [4]	48.5	47.7	47.7
I	53.8	52.9	52.3	53.6	52.9	54.1 |	59.1 [4]	56.3	56.0	56.6
J	43.6	44.1	43.5	43.7	43.2	43.5 |	44.8 [4]	44.7	45.1	45.4
K	52.0	48.3	49.3	50.1	49.3	49.4 |	47.7 [4]	50.0	48.6	49.4
L	50.1	49.1	48.6	49.5	48.3	50.6 |	46.6 [4]	49.0	48.5	49.6
M	33.7	33.3	33.5	34.1	32.9	33.9 |	32.3 [4]	33.2	33.4	32.7
N	40.3	40.6	40.6	41.1	41.6	41.9 |	39.9 [4]	40.3	40.2	40.8
O	43.0	44.9	42.1	43.5	43.6	43.4 |	44.2 [4]	43.5	42.8	42.7
P	46.8	45.7	44.5	45.4	44.9	46.3 |	35.6 [4]	45.5	46.2	45.1
Q	.	54.3	44.8	.	.	27.0 |	45.7 [4]	33.4	48.6	65.0
X	.	.	.	.	.	|	.	.	.	.

Explanatory notes: see p. 721.

Notes explicatives: voir p. 723.

Notas explicativas: véase p. 725.

[1] July. [2] Persons aged 14 years and over. [3] Second quarter of each year. [4] Revised averages based on 2005 Population and Housing Census results; data not comparable.

[1] Juillet. [2] Personnes âgées de 14 ans et plus. [3] Deuxième trimestre de chaque année. [4] Moyennes révisées sur la base des résultats du recensement de population et de l'habitat de 2005;les données ne sont pas comparables

[1] Julio. [2] Personas de 14 años y más. [3] Segundo trimestre de cada año. [4] Promedios revisados de acuerdo con los resultados del censo de población y Vivienda de 2005; datos no comparables.

4A HOURS OF WORK — DURÉE DU TRAVAIL — HORAS DE TRABAJO

By economic activity — Par activité économique — Por actividad económica

	Per week				Par semaine				Por semana	
	1999	2000	2001	2002	2003	2004	2005	2006	2007	2008

México (BA) (d) [1][2] — Employees - Salariés - Asalariados

Women - Femmes - Mujeres
ISIC 3 - CITI 3 - CIIU 3

	1999	2000	2001	2002	2003	2004	2005[3]	2006	2007	2008
Total	40.2	39.5	39.1	39.8	38.9	39.0	39.8	39.3	39.3	40.0
A-B	41.6	39.9	37.9	39.3	35.0	35.1	30.2	30.4	29.0	39.0
C-Q	40.2	39.5	39.2	39.8	39.0	39.1	39.8	39.3	39.4	40.0
A	41.5	39.9	37.9	39.2	35.2	35.2	35.2	30.4	29.1	38.9
B	50.7	50.8	44.8	47.5	27.9	31.0	30.6	31.3	22.8	42.4
C	41.7	42.2	41.9	42.6	40.6	42.4	42.4	42.8	39.4	43.6
D	43.4	42.1	41.7	43.2	42.6	42.4	44.1	43.6	43.4	44.5
E	38.2	38.7	37.4	40.4	39.0	38.1	40.4	38.9	38.0	39.3
F	43.4	43.3	43.0	43.9	42.5	42.2	45.2	42.6	45.5	43.7
G	42.1	41.1	41.2	42.3	41.8	40.9	43.2	44.2	44.5	45.1
H	45.7	45.7	45.9	45.5	44.5	45.3	44.9	44.2	44.7	44.6
I	43.9	41.7	42.9	42.6	41.4	43.5	43.1	43.7	43.1	44.1
J	41.5	40.5	40.7	41.6	40.3	41.8	43.2	42.7	41.0	43.7
K	43.4	39.5	40.1	41.3	40.8	41.6	42.4	40.7	41.4	41.6
L	39.5	37.6	38.3	39.3	38.7	39.2	39.9	38.6	38.8	39.7
M	29.7	30.0	29.6	30.0	29.8	30.8	31.0	29.9	30.0	30.0
N	39.2	39.2	39.0	39.0	38.5	39.0	39.3	38.7	38.5	39.5
O	40.5	40.6	41.3	41.3	40.8	40.7	41.4	39.5	40.6	41.1
P	39.0	38.3	36.9	37.1	35.0	33.7	34.3	33.3	33.0	33.7
Q	.	57.2	50.0	.	.	40.0	42.3	40.0	40.8	54.8
X										

Panamá (BA) (a) [4][5] — Total employment - Emploi total - Empleo total

Total men and women - Total hommes et femmes - Total hombres y mujeres
ISIC 3 - CITI 3 - CIIU 3

	1999	2000	2001	2002	2003	2004	2005	2006	2007	2008
Total	.	.	43.5	43.4	43.5	43.1	43.4	43.3	43.1	40.8
A-B	.	.	41.5	42.1	40.9	39.9	39.7	39.8	39.3	38.8
C-Q	.	.	43.7	43.5	43.7	43.3	43.7	43.6	43.5	40.9
A	.	.	41.0	41.1	39.9	39.3	39.2	39.2	38.6	38.2
B	.	.	49.1	59.8	57.6	51.8	52.7	52.0	51.8	54.7
C	.	.	45.8	42.2	45.2	54.5	49.0	49.4	47.7	47.2
D	.	.	45.1	45.4	46.2	45.9	45.9	45.6	45.6	43.0
E	.	.	41.7	43.5	42.9	44.1	45.5	43.7	44.0	43.2
F	.	.	44.7	42.4	43.5	44.8	45.2	45.0	45.3	41.5
G	.	.	46.1	46.7	46.5	46.0	46.7	46.0	45.8	41.8
H	.	.	45.0	46.0	46.4	44.1	44.6	45.1	44.7	41.6
I	.	.	44.6	44.8	44.0	44.1	44.4	45.4	44.1	44.1
J	.	.	43.0	43.5	42.7	42.5	43.5	43.7	43.8	41.3
K	.	.	44.7	44.8	45.7	44.9	46.1	45.4	46.1	42.0
L	.	.	42.6	42.6	43.1	41.8	41.9	42.5	42.3	40.9
M	.	.	39.1	38.2	38.1	38.0	38.1	38.6	38.5	38.0
N	.	.	41.1	41.5	41.3	41.1	41.2	41.5	41.9	41.4
O	.	.	41.6	42.3	43.4	43.1	43.0	42.8	42.4	37.7
P	.	.	43.8	41.4	42.0	41.8	40.2	38.7	38.4	36.0
Q	.	.	46.1	41.0	45.7	44.2	43.0	43.4	41.6	39.3
X	.	.	.	40.0	.	.	.	.	.	.

Men - Hommes - Hombres
ISIC 3 - CITI 3 - CIIU 3

	1999	2000	2001	2002	2003	2004	2005	2006	2007	2008
Total	.	.	44.4	44.4	44.5	44.3	44.6	44.5	44.3	42.3
A-B	.	.	41.5	42.2	40.8	39.8	40.0	39.8	39.2	39.0
C-Q	.	.	44.9	44.8	45.1	45.0	45.3	45.2	45.1	42.8
A	.	.	40.9	41.1	39.8	39.2	39.6	39.1	38.5	38.3
B	.	.	50.4	63.1	58.0	53.4	52.9	52.8	51.8	54.8
C	.	.	45.8	42.1	45.2	54.5	49.0	49.6	47.8	47.8
D	.	.	45.6	45.8	46.5	47.1	46.6	46.1	46.3	43.5
E	.	.	42.5	44.0	42.8	44.5	46.0	44.3	44.0	44.1
F	.	.	44.7	42.5	43.6	44.8	45.3	45.1	45.5	41.4
G	.	.	46.4	47.1	46.9	46.4	46.9	46.3	46.3	43.1
H	.	.	47.0	47.4	47.7	47.1	45.4	47.2	46.8	45.3
I	.	.	45.4	45.4	44.7	45.0	45.3	46.3	44.7	45.0
J	.	.	44.3	44.1	43.4	43.7	44.3	44.3	43.8	42.0
K	.	.	45.8	47.3	49.3	48.4	49.9	48.2	48.1	44.7
L	.	.	44.1	43.9	44.6	42.9	43.3	43.6	43.6	42.8
M	.	.	40.3	38.9	38.8	38.3	38.6	38.9	39.2	38.4
N	.	.	41.2	41.2	42.4	41.5	41.9	42.0	42.6	42.9
O	.	.	43.2	43.0	43.0	45.6	43.9	43.6	41.8	40.3
P	.	.	46.2	42.8	42.9	42.8	40.0	38.9	41.7	38.7
Q	.	.	45.6	41.0	50.0	42.6	40.0	44.7	41.2	40.0
X	.	.	.	40.0	.	.	.	.	.	.

Explanatory notes: see p. 721.

[1] Persons aged 14 years and over. [2] Second quarter of each year. [3] Revised averages based on 2005 Population and Housing Census results; data not comparable. [4] Persons aged 15 years and over. [5] Aug. of each year.

Notes explicatives: voir p. 723.

[1] Personnes âgées de 14 ans et plus. [2] Deuxième trimestre de chaque année. [3] Moyennes révisées sur la base des résultats du recensement de population et de l'habitat de 2005; les données ne sont pas comparables [4] Personnes âgées de 15 ans et plus. [5] Août de chaque année.

Notas explicativas: véase p. 725.

[1] Personas de 14 años y más. [2] Segundo trimestre de cada año. [3] Promedios revisados de acuerdo con los resultados del censo de población y Vivienda de 2005; datos no comparables. [4] Personas de 15 años y más. [5] Agosto de cada año.

By economic activity   **Par activité économique**   **Por actividad económica**

	Per week				Par semaine				Por semana	
	1999	2000	2001	2002	2003	2004	2005	2006	2007	2008

Panamá (BA) (a) [1] [2]   Total employment - Emploi total - Empleo total

Women - Femmes - Mujeres
ISIC 3 - CITI 3 - CIIU 3

	1999	2000	2001	2002	2003	2004	2005	2006	2007	2008
Total	.	.	42.1	41.9	42.0	41.3	41.5	41.3	41.4	38.4
A-B	.	.	42.4	38.0	43.6	42.7	32.5	41.6	41.6	35.0
C-Q	.	.	42.1	41.9	42.0	41.3	41.6	41.3	41.4	38.5
A	.	.	43.1	41.2	43.3	43.2	32.2	41.9	40.7	34.8
B	.	.	39.2	14.2	48.0	40.5	45.4	37.8	51.9	48.5
C	.	.	44.9	56.0	45.0	.	48.0	47.0	46.1	43.2
D	.	.	43.3	44.0	45.0	42.0	43.3	43.8	43.4	41.4
E	.	.	38.9	41.1	43.4	40.9	43.0	41.4	44.2	40.9
F	.	.	43.2	39.9	41.9	43.7	43.5	43.0	40.8	42.6
G	.	.	45.5	45.9	45.7	45.5	46.3	45.3	45.0	40.0
H	.	.	42.9	44.6	45.0	40.7	43.9	43.4	42.7	38.7
I	.	.	41.9	43.0	41.6	41.6	41.1	42.4	41.8	39.6
J	.	.	42.2	43.1	42.3	41.8	43.0	43.2	43.9	40.9
K	.	.	42.3	40.0	40.0	40.4	39.4	40.0	43.2	38.4
L	.	.	40.4	40.8	40.9	40.3	39.9	40.9	40.4	38.3
M	.	.	38.6	37.9	37.7	37.9	37.8	38.5	38.2	37.8
N	.	.	41.0	41.6	40.5	40.9	40.9	41.3	41.5	40.6
O	.	.	39.4	41.2	43.8	39.9	41.9	41.8	43.0	34.6
P	.	.	43.6	41.2	41.9	41.6	40.2	38.7	38.0	35.7
Q	.	.	46.7	.	41.5	60.0	43.9	40.0	42.3	39.0

Paraguay (BA) (c) [3]   Employees - Salariés - Asalariados

Total men and women - Total hommes et femmes - Total hombres y mujeres
ISIC 3 - CITI 3 - CIIU 3

	1999	2000	2001	2002	2003	2004	2005	2006	2007	2008
Total	.	.	.	.	.	.	.	.	48.8	48.0
A-B	.	.	.	.	.	.	.	.	52.0	49.3
C-Q	.	.	.	.	.	.	.	.	48.6	47.9
C	.	.	.	.	.	.	.	.	50.7	56.0
D	.	.	.	.	.	.	.	.	52.3	53.1
E	.	.	.	.	.	.	.	.	46.8	44.6
F	.	.	.	.	.	.	.	.	54.1	51.2
G-H	.	.	.	.	.	.	.	.	53.2	54.0
I	.	.	.	.	.	.	.	.	53.8	53.7
J-K	.	.	.	.	.	.	.	.	48.5	46.8
L-Q	.	.	.	.	.	.	.	.	42.8	40.9

Men - Hommes - Hombres
ISIC 3 - CITI 3 - CIIU 3

	1999	2000	2001	2002	2003	2004	2005	2006	2007	2008
Total	.	.	.	.	.	.	.	.	52.0	51.6
A-B	.	.	.	.	.	.	.	.	53.0	50.9
C-Q	.	.	.	.	.	.	.	.	51.9	51.6
C	.	.	.	.	.	.	.	.	50.7	56.9
D	.	.	.	.	.	.	.	.	53.0	54.5
E	.	.	.	.	.	.	.	.	48.2	45.9
F	.	.	.	.	.	.	.	.	54.2	51.2
G-H	.	.	.	.	.	.	.	.	54.0	55.2
I	.	.	.	.	.	.	.	.	55.0	55.2
J-K	.	.	.	.	.	.	.	.	54.3	50.2
L-Q	.	.	.	.	.	.	.	.	45.2	43.8

Women - Femmes - Mujeres
ISIC 3 - CITI 3 - CIIU 3

	1999	2000	2001	2002	2003	2004	2005	2006	2007	2008
Total	.	.	.	.	.	.	.	.	43.6	42.0
A-B	.	.	.	.	.	.	.	.	37.4	37.3
C-Q	.	.	.	.	.	.	.	.	43.6	51.6
C	.	.	.	.	.	.	.	.	.	30.0
D	.	.	.	.	.	.	.	.	49.3	46.7
E	.	.	.	.	.	.	.	.	31.2	38.7
F	.	.	.	.	.	.	.	.	41.2	33.6
G-H	.	.	.	.	.	.	.	.	51.1	51.2
I	.	.	.	.	.	.	.	.	46.8	43.0
J-K	.	.	.	.	.	.	.	.	39.2	39.5
L-Q	.	.	.	.	.	.	.	.	41.7	39.6

Explanatory notes: see p. 721.

[1] Persons aged 15 years and over. [2] Aug. of each year. [3] Fourth quarter of each year.

Notes explicatives: voir p. 723.

[1] Personnes âgées de 15 ans et plus. [2] Août de chaque année. [3] Quatrième trimestre de chaque année.

Notas explicativas: véase p. 725.

[1] Personas de 15 años y más. [2] Agosto de cada año. [3] Cuarto trimestre de cada año.

By economic activity · Par activité économique · Por actividad económica

	Per week / Par semaine / Por semana									
	1999	2000	2001	2002	2003	2004	2005	2006	2007	2008

Perú (B) (b) [1] [2] [3] — Wage earners - Ouvriers - Obreros
Total men and women - Total hommes et femmes - Total hombres y mujeres
ISIC 3 - CITI 3 - CIIU 3

	1999	2000	2001	2002	2003	2004	2005	2006	2007	2008
Total	.	.	53.0 [4]	54.1	55.7 [4]	54.5	54.9	54.5	52.9	53.1
A-B	.	.	40.6 [4]	47.3	62.2 [4]	63.0	54.4	50.4	45.9	55.5
C-Q	.	.	53.3 [4]	54.3	55.4 [4]	54.3	54.9	54.6	53.1	53.0
A	.	.	40.0 [4]	45.7	61.4 [4]	62.6	52.3	50.0	44.7	52.2
B	.	.	50.4 [4]	56.0	65.1 [4]	66.6	62.0	53.0	55.3	74.6
C	.	.	70.0 [4]	62.7	. [4]	54.5	49.5	57.5	59.2	67.4
D	.	.	54.6 [4]	53.6	55.9 [4]	53.7	54.8	54.1	54.5	53.4
E	.	.	65.7 [4]	63.8	54.3 [4]	44.3	57.9	52.3	58.4	50.0
F	.	.	47.8 [4]	51.2	50.0 [4]	50.7	48.6	52.0	49.6	50.9
G	.	.	51.6 [4]	54.5	56.4 [4]	52.2	57.3	57.5	49.7	51.0
H	.	.	54.2 [4]	56.9	57.6 [4]	58.1	54.3	54.2	48.6	50.7
I	.	.	60.5 [4]	63.6	62.5 [4]	68.4	67.9	63.2	62.4	62.9
J	.	.	.	54.0	.	.	.	42.2		
K	.	.	49.0 [4]	51.7	56.3 [4]	54.0	55.9	57.3	51.9	49.6
L	.	.	49.7 [4]	44.9	50.7 [4]	48.8	51.7	46.7	45.7	45.3
M	.	.	61.9 [4]	40.9	55.5 [4]	40.2	48.1	57.5	41.8	45.9
N	.	.	31.0 [4]	33.2	40.6 [4]	34.5	36.1	30.7	26.4	
O	.	.	48.8 [4]	53.7	54.6 [4]	54.5	55.4	51.6	47.8	48.7
P	.	.			40.0 [4]					
Q	.	.	50.0 [4]		35.0 [4]	69.0	.	.	.	.

Perú (D) (b) [1] [5] — Wage earners - Ouvriers - Obreros
Total men and women - Total hommes et femmes - Total hombres y mujeres
ISIC 3 - CITI 3 - CIIU 3

	1999	2000	2001	2002	2003	2004	2005	2006	2007	2008
Total	50.2	49.9	50.1 [6]	44.7 [2]	49.4	45.0	48.0	49.3	47.8	49.7
C-Q	50.3	49.8	50.2 [6]	44.6 [2]	49.3	45.0	48.2	49.6	48.0	49.6
C	45.7	47.8	48.7 [6]	46.2 [2]	52.7	43.7	48.3	46.1	47.3	56.4
D	49.6	49.1	49.3 [6]	43.2 [2]	49.0	46.3	48.9	49.9	48.2	50.0
E	48.6	48.7	48.4 [6]	43.0 [2]	47.1	41.1	45.2	46.5	44.7	43.1
F	51.7	48.6	52.0 [6]	48.2 [2]	51.8	48.9	52.2	51.8	47.5	50.9
G	49.7	49.0	48.9 [6]	43.2 [2]	49.8	44.3	46.8	47.5	48.0	48.8
H	47.3	47.1	47.8 [6]	42.2 [2]	41.6	39.5	45.6	46.8	48.1	47.1
I	51.1	49.6	48.3 [6]	45.4 [2]	47.4	40.4	43.1	44.9	47.3	45.1
J	51.3	42.4	47.3 [6]	40.5 [2]	44.7	37.4	48.0	39.3	42.9	48.0
K	52.8	52.9	53.6 [6]	48.2 [2]	53.7	45.3	49.6	53.6	50.0	51.3
M	49.4	48.5	47.5 [6]	40.2 [2]	48.3	41.8	44.4	46.7	45.2	48.3
N	48.2	48.0	46.0 [6]	40.9 [2]	47.5	39.7	45.3	48.0	47.8	48.7
O	47.8	48.4	47.4 [6]	43.2 [2]	47.0	43.1	43.5	44.3	43.8	46.4

Puerto Rico (DA) (b) [7] — Wage earners - Ouvriers - Obreros
Total men and women - Total hommes et femmes - Total hombres y mujeres
ISIC 2 - CITI 2 - CIIU 2

	1999	2000	2001	2002	2003	2004	2005	2006	2007	2008
3	41.0	40.6	39.9	40.6	40.9	41.0	40.8	40.5	40.9	40.6

United States (BA) (a) — Employees - Salariés - Asalariados
Total men and women - Total hommes et femmes - Total hombres y mujeres
ISIC 3 - CITI 3 - CIIU 3

	1999	2000	2001	2002	2003	2004	2005	2006	2007	2008
A [8]	41.1	41.0	40.6	40.5	42.6	43.4	43.6	42.8	42.1	42.3

Men - Hommes - Hombres
ISIC 3 - CITI 3 - CIIU 3

	1999	2000	2001	2002	2003	2004	2005	2006	2007	2008
A [8]	43.2	43.1	42.9	42.4	44.8	46.3	45.9	45.1	43.9	44.1

Women - Femmes - Mujeres
ISIC 3 - CITI 3 - CIIU 3

	1999	2000	2001	2002	2003	2004	2005	2006	2007	2008
A [8]	34.8	34.7	34.5	35.0	35.3	33.9	35.1	34.9	34.6	35.9

Explanatory notes: see p. 721.

[1] Figures at the desaggregated level are not representative because of the small sample size. [2] Metropolitan Lima. [3] Fourth quarter. [4] May-Dec. [5] Second quarter. [6] Average of the first three quarters. [7] Persons aged 15 years and over; prior to 1998: 14 years and over. [8] Excl. hunting and forestry.

Notes explicatives: voir p. 723.

[1] Chiffres non représentatifs au niveau desagrégé en raison de la faible taille de l'échantillonage. [2] Lima métropolitaine. [3] Quatrième trimestre. [4] Mai-déc. [5] Deuxième trimestre. [6] Moyenne des trois premiers trimestres. [7] Personnes âgées de 15 ans et plus; avant 1998: 14 ans et plus. [8] Non compris la chasse et la sylviculture.

Notas explicativas: véase p. 725.

[1] Cifras no reprentativas al nivel de desagregación debidas al pequeño tamaño muestral. [2] Lima metropolitana. [3] Cuarto trimestre. [4] Mayo-dic. [5] Segundo trimestre. [6] Promedio de los tres primeros trimestres. [7] Personas de 15 años y más; antes de 1998: 14 años y más. [8] Excl. caza y silvicultura.

By economic activity   Par activité économique   Por actividad económica

	Per week			Par semaine				Por semana		
	1999	2000	2001	2002	2003	2004	2005	2006	2007	2008

United States (DA) (a) [1][2]   **Employees - Salariés - Asalariados**

Total men and women - Total hommes et femmes - Total hombres y mujeres
ISIC 3 - CITI 3 - CIIU 3

	1999	2000	2001	2002	2003	2004	2005	2006	2007	2008
Total	34.3	34.3	34.0	33.9	33.7	33.7	33.8	33.9	33.9	33.6
C	45.4	45.5	45.5	43.9	44.4	45.4	46.4	46.3	46.2	45.3
D	41.4	41.3	40.3	40.5	40.4	40.8	40.7	41.1	41.2	40.8
E	42.0	42.0	41.4	40.9	41.1	40.9	41.1	41.4	42.4	42.7
F	39.0	39.2	38.7	38.4	38.4	38.3	38.6	39.0	39.0	38.5
H	26.2	26.2	25.8	25.8	25.6	25.6	25.7	25.8	25.6	25.4
N	32.0	32.1	32.3	32.3	32.5	32.7	32.9	32.8	32.8	32.8

Uruguay (BA) (a)   **Employees - Salariés - Asalariados**

Total men and women - Total hommes et femmes - Total hombres y mujeres
ISIC 3 - CITI 3 - CIIU 3

	1999	2000	2001	2002	2003	2004	2005	2006	2007	2008
Total	.	39.2	41.2	40.5	40.2	40.6	40.3	40.2	39.3	.
A-B	.	47.0	49.9	.	.	.	.	48.6	47.2	.
C-Q	.	38.9	40.8	40.2	39.9	40.2	39.9	39.3	39.9	.
C	.	47.2	47.3	48.1	47.2	48.2	.	.	.	.
D-E	.	42.4	45.0	43.9	43.8	45.1	44.7	45.3	45.0	.
F	.	42.0	45.3	44.4	44.0	44.3	44.3	45.3	44.9	.
G-H	.	43.1	44.8	44.8	44.3	44.2	43.9	44.2	43.6	.
I	.	45.9	47.7	47.3	46.9	47.3	47.5	47.5	47.6	.
J-K	.	39.1	40.4	40.2	40.2	39.8	40.7	38.8	38.7	.
L	.	42.2	44.7	43.5	43.0	43.4	43.3	43.6	43.7	.
M	.	26.6	29.7	29.5	30.0	29.6	29.5	29.8	29.2	.
N	.	34.4	37.2	36.9	37.4	37.3	36.9	36.7	36.4	.
O,Q	.	36.5	36.2	38.2	35.1	35.8	35.8	35.8	35.6	.
P	.	31.5	31.4	31.3	31.7	31.6	39.6	30.5	29.5	.
X	.	.	.	.	.	.	.	.	.	.

Men - Hommes - Hombres
ISIC 3 - CITI 3 - CIIU 3

	1999	2000	2001	2002	2003	2004	2005	2006	2007	2008
Total	.	43.8	45.7	45.0	44.3	44.8	44.9	44.0	45.1	.
A-B	.	48.4	52.0	.	.	.	.	49.9	48.5	.
C-Q	.	43.5	45.3	44.6	44.0	44.5	44.5	44.9	44.6	.
C	.	47.7	48.8	50.1	47.2	47.2	.	.	.	.
D-E	.	43.7	45.9	44.9	44.6	46.2	46.0	46.5	46.2	.
F	.	42.3	45.5	44.7	44.2	44.6	44.6	45.5	45.2	.
G-H	.	45.2	46.2	46.2	45.9	45.2	45.2	45.7	45.0	.
I	.	47.5	49.3	48.6	48.2	40.3	49.3	49.5	49.6	.
J-K	.	42.8	42.7	43.5	42.4	42.6	43.7	40.7	40.7	.
L	.	45.6	48.2	46.1	45.5	46.3	46.2	46.8	47.5	.
M	.	31.7	33.9	32.3	32.7	33.0	32.4	33.6	32.5	.
N	.	36.3	38.8	37.7	37.3	38.2	37.9	39.1	37.8	.
O,Q	.	38.1	38.4	40.5	36.8	37.4	37.6	37.6	37.5	.
P	.	45.3	45.5	44.7	42.2	44.1	41.0	44.7	44.6	.
X	.	.	.	.	.	.	.	.	.	.

Women - Femmes - Mujeres
ISIC 3 - CITI 3 - CIIU 3

	1999	2000	2001	2002	2003	2004	2005	2006	2007	2008
Total	.	33.7	35.9	35.5	35.7	35.6	35.2	35.0	35.0	.
A-B	.	33.4	37.5	.	.	.	.	41.3	39.8	.
C-Q	.	33.6	35.8	35.4	35.6	35.5	35.2	35.2	34.9	.
C	.	35.0	36.5	20.0	.	.	.	.	.	.
D-E	.	39.4	42.8	41.6	42.0	42.4	41.9	42.6	42.4	.
F	.	34.6	38.0	39.1	39.2	38.3	33.1	38.2	35.1	.
G-H	.	39.8	42.6	42.8	41.9	42.5	41.9	42.1	41.9	.
I	.	37.7	40.1	40.8	40.8	47.3	41.3	40.4	40.5	.
J-K	.	35.2	37.5	36.6	37.8	36.4	36.9	36.7	36.8	.
L	.	34.8	37.4	37.7	37.9	37.2	37.7	37.0	36.7	.
M	.	25.2	28.5	28.8	29.3	28.6	28.7	28.6	28.2	.
N	.	33.7	36.7	36.6	37.4	37.0	36.6	36.0	36.0	.
O,Q	.	33.9	33.3	34.7	32.7	33.5	33.7	33.5	33.3	.
P	.	30.5	30.6	30.3	30.7	30.7	28.7	29.2	28.1	.
X	.	.	.	.	.	.	.	.	.	.

Explanatory notes: see p. 721.

[1] National classification not strictly compatible with ISIC. [2] Not all employees covered; only production and non-supervisory workers; private sector.

Notes explicatives: voir p. 723.

[1] Classification nationale non strictement compatible avec la CITI. [2] Non couverts tous les salariés: seulement travailleurs à la production et ceux sans activité de surveillance; secteur privé.

Notas explicativas: véase p. 725.

[1] Clasificación nacional no estrictamente compatible con la CIIU. [2] Todos asalariados no cubiertos; sólo trabajaodores de la producción y los sin funciones de supervisión; sector privado.

4A — HOURS OF WORK / DURÉE DU TRAVAIL / HORAS DE TRABAJO

By economic activity — Par activité économique — Por actividad económica

	Per week — Par semaine — Por semana									
	1999	2000	2001	2002	2003	2004	2005	2006	2007	2008

Venezuela, Rep. Bolivariana de (BA) (a) Total employment - Emploi total - Empleo total

Total men and women - Total hommes et femmes - Total hombres y mujeres
ISIC 2 - CITI 2 - CIIU 2

	1999	2000	2001	2002	2003	2004	2005	2006	2007	2008
Total	.	.	.	.	.	.	.	.	41	41 [1]
1	.	.	.	.	.	.	.	.	41	41 [1]
2	.	.	.	.	.	.	.	.	43	43 [1]
3	.	.	.	.	.	.	.	.	40	41 [1]
4	.	.	.	.	.	.	.	.	42	42 [1]
5	.	.	.	.	.	.	.	.	41	41 [1]
6	.	.	.	.	.	.	.	.	40	39 [1]
7	.	.	.	.	.	.	.	.	45	45 [1]
8	.	.	.	.	.	.	.	.	43	43 [1]
9	.	.	.	.	.	.	.	.	39	39 [1]
0	.	.	.	.	.	.	.	.	41	40 [1]

Men - Hommes - Hombres
ISIC 2 - CITI 2 - CIIU 2

	1999	2000	2001	2002	2003	2004	2005	2006	2007	2008
Total	.	.	.	.	.	.	.	.	43	43 [1]
1	.	.	.	.	.	.	.	.	42	42 [1]
2	.	.	.	.	.	.	.	.	44	43 [1]
3	.	.	.	.	.	.	.	.	42	43 [1]
4	.	.	.	.	.	.	.	.	42	42 [1]
5	.	.	.	.	.	.	.	.	41	41 [1]
6	.	.	.	.	.	.	.	.	44	43 [1]
7	.	.	.	.	.	.	.	.	46	46 [1]
8	.	.	.	.	.	.	.	.	45	45 [1]
9	.	.	.	.	.	.	.	.	41	41 [1]
0	.	.	.	.	.	.	.	.	42	41 [1]

Women - Femmes - Mujeres
ISIC 2 - CITI 2 - CIIU 2

	1999	2000	2001	2002	2003	2004	2005	2006	2007	2008
Total	.	.	.	.	.	.	.	.	37	37 [1]
1	.	.	.	.	.	.	.	.	35	35 [1]
2	.	.	.	.	.	.	.	.	40	42 [1]
3	.	.	.	.	.	.	.	.	36	36 [1]
4	.	.	.	.	.	.	.	.	41	41 [1]
5	.	.	.	.	.	.	.	.	41	40 [1]
6	.	.	.	.	.	.	.	.	37	36 [1]
7	.	.	.	.	.	.	.	.	41	41 [1]
8	.	.	.	.	.	.	.	.	39	39 [1]
9	.	.	.	.	.	.	.	.	37	36 [1]
0	.	.	.	.	.	.	.	.	40	38 [1]

Virgin Islands (US) (DA) (b) Wage earners - Ouvriers - Obreros

Total men and women - Total hommes et femmes - Total hombres y mujeres
ISIC 3 - CITI 3 - CIIU 3

	1999	2000	2001	2002	2003	2004	2005	2006	2007	2008
D	.	.	43.9	43.7	42.8	46.4	43.7	43.8	42.2	43.3

ASIA-ASIE-ASIA

Armenia (BA) (a) [2] Total employment - Emploi total - Empleo total

Total men and women - Total hommes et femmes - Total hombres y mujeres
ISIC 3 - CITI 3 - CIIU 3

	1999	2000	2001	2002	2003	2004	2005	2006	2007	2008
Total	.	.	43.0	43.0	44.0	44.6	48.7	45.4	38.0	.
A-B	.	.	47.8	37.0	36.9	39.0	41.0	34.6	24.5	.
C-Q	.	.	41.9	44.7	46.4	47.2	51.2	49.1	45.2	.
A	.	.	47.9	37.0	37.4	39.1	40.9	34.3	24.8	.
B	.	.	15.5	35.5	24.5	.	45.5	40.9	34.5	.
C	.	.	48.0	47.7	39.9	37.3	54.1	49.9	44.2	.
D	.	.	41.0	44.7	45.4	50.8	52.8	47.3	46.0	.
E	.	.	45.7	42.7	45.3	44.8	52.2	49.4	45.6	.
F	.	.	50.2	53.8	59.9	50.8	62.0	56.4	47.3	.
G	.	.	56.1	58.2	57.7	54.8	71.1	59.1	50.8	.
H	.	.	54.9	70.8	53.3	60.9	62.3	50.4	54.5	.
I	.	.	46.4	49.0	50.3	51.5	41.7	39.6	49.9	.
J	.	.	47.2	46.3	48.8	42.7	43.8	52.9	45.8	.
K	.	.	39.6	49.5	40.8	41.5	50.7	44.0	44.6	.
L	.	.	44.1	46.1	45.3	45.1	36.4	41.6	48.3	.
M	.	.	28.1	30.2	30.0	32.0	47.8	48.2	34.7	.
N	.	.	38.3	38.6	37.4	42.9	39.9	50.1	42.4	.
O	.	.	33.7	39.1	42.3	38.6	30.5	40.6	42.1	.
P	.	.	35.5	33.5	.	11.8	30.5	48.7	30.6	.
Q	.	.	.	45.5	45.5	.	.	39.1	42.2	.

Explanatory notes: see p. 721. Notes explicatives: voir p. 723. Notas explicativas: véase p. 725.

[1] First semester. [2] Employed persons and at work. [1] Premier semestre. [2] Personnes pourvues d'un emploi et au travail [1] Primer semestre. [2] Personas con empleo y trabajando.

By economic activity   Par activité économique   Por actividad económica

	Per week			Par semaine				Por semana		
	1999	2000	2001	2002	2003	2004	2005	2006	2007	2008

Armenia (BA) (a) [1]   Total employment - Emploi total - Empleo total

Men - Hommes - Hombres
ISIC 3 - CITI 3 - CIIU 3

Total	.	.	46.7	47.3	48.1	49.3	52.8	47.1	41.8	.
A-B	.	.	47.4	38.4	37.9	44.3	43.9	35.4	27.3	.
C-Q	.	.	46.6	50.2	51.7	51.4	55.3	50.8	47.9	.
A	.	.	47.6	38.4	38.9	44.4	43.8	34.9	27.2	.
B	.	.	15.5	35.5	24.5	.	45.5	42.6	41.8	.
C	.	.	50.7	48.8	41.5	37.0	55.9	49.9	44.1	.
D	.	.	41.4	44.5	46.2	55.0	55.2	47.6	47.8	.
E	.	.	47.1	44.1	46.3	45.8	52.3	49.4	45.7	.
F	.	.	50.9	54.0	60.4	51.3	63.5	57.5	47.3	.
G	.	.	56.6	59.4	57.7	56.7	.	62.9	51.3	.
H	.	.	53.3	.	63.4	58.9	65.4	48.9	55.9	.
I	.	.	46.4	50.4	53.5	54.7	41.1	40.6	51.0	.
J	.	.	50.8	55.8	53.2	40.5	48.0	55.8	48.0	.
K	.	.	41.9	50.6	48.5	44.1	53.5	45.2	44.8	.
L	.	.	47.7	49.7	48.2	47.8	39.2	43.3	49.8	.
M	.	.	33.4	38.9	35.7	36.6	49.5	44.1	36.7	.
N	.	.	44.2	44.2	40.2	54.4	40.1	55.1	48.4	.
O	.	.	34.7	41.8	46.2	42.1	45.5	25.3	43.2	.
P	.	.	.	38.8	45.5	.	45.5	35.5	32.8	.
Q	.	.	.	.	.	.	.	42.0	46.4	.
X	.	.	.	.	.	.	.	.	.	.

Women - Femmes - Mujeres
ISIC 3 - CITI 3 - CIIU 3

Total	.	.	38.5	37.5	38.5	37.7	42.6	43.0	33.3	.
A-B	.	.	48.3	34.8	35.2	32.9	38.0	33.6	22.8	.
C-Q	.	.	36.6	38.2	39.5	40.5	44.5	46.6	41.1	.
A	.	.	48.3	34.8	35.2	32.9	38.0	33.7	22.8	.
B	.	.	.	.	.	.	.	30.5	14.0	.
C	.	.	38.8	35.5	37.2	38.0	51.0	49.8	44.7	.
D	.	.	40.2	45.1	44.3	41.1	40.5	45.2	42.8	.
E	.	.	34.5	34.7	40.1	39.0	45.5	46.4	45.0	.
F	.	.	25.5	40.5	41.9	35.5	59.3	54.2	43.6	.
G	.	.	55.1	56.1	57.8	51.6	35.5	53.2	50.0	.
H	.	.	56.3	67.7	45.1	.	48.1	59.1	53.0	.
I	.	.	46.4	41.3	40.3	41.0	43.0	38.8	44.2	.
J	.	.	41.5	36.8	43.5	43.8	35.5	50.4	43.2	.
K	.	.	34.3	45.5	31.0	37.7	44.5	42.1	44.3	.
L	.	.	38.9	39.5	39.5	38.7	35.6	41.3	44.0	.
M	.	.	26.8	28.3	28.7	30.6	47.1	48.8	34.3	.
N	.	.	36.9	37.3	36.9	39.4	39.6	43.5	41.0	.
O	.	.	32.4	35.7	38.7	35.8	15.5	50.8	40.4	.
P	.	.	35.5	29.4	.	11.8	15.5	57.5	30.2	.
Q	.	.	.	45.5	.	.	.	37.2	34.3	.
X	.	.	.	.	.	.	.	.	.	.

Azerbaijan (DA) (a) [2]   Employees - Salariés - Asalariados

Total men and women - Total hommes et femmes - Total hombres y mujeres
ISIC 3 - CITI 3 - CIIU 3

Total	.	.	.	.	.	.	.	.	152.9	151.5
A-B	.	.	.	.	.	.	.	.	148.7	149.6
C-Q	.	.	.	.	.	.	.	.	148.9	151.6
A	.	.	.	.	.	.	.	.	153.6	149.4
B	.	.	.	.	.	.	.	.	125.0	163.8
C	.	.	.	.	.	.	.	.	149.2	154.7
D	.	.	.	.	.	.	.	.	142.3	135.8
E	.	.	.	.	.	.	.	.	160.3	154.4
F	.	.	.	.	.	.	.	.	138.5	169.6
G	.	.	.	.	.	.	.	.	160.2	155.3
H	.	.	.	.	.	.	.	.	170.2	147.2
I	.	.	.	.	.	.	.	.	157.3	156.6
J	.	.	.	.	.	.	.	.	158.7	154.4
K	.	.	.	.	.	.	.	.	153.1	157.0
L	.	.	.	.	.	.	.	.	162.5	160.3
M	.	.	.	.	.	.	.	.	145.6	145.8
N	.	.	.	.	.	.	.	.	147.1	145.8
O	.	.	.	.	.	.	.	.	154.9	157.9

Explanatory notes: see p. 721.   Notes explicatives: voir p. 723.   Notas explicativas: véase p. 725.

[1] Employed persons and at work. [2] Per month.   [1] Personnes pourvues d'un emploi et au travail [2] Par mois.   [1] Personas con empleo y trabajando. [2] Por mes.

	HOURS OF WORK	DURÉE DU TRAVAIL	HORAS DE TRABAJO
	By economic activity	Par activité économique	Por actividad económica

	Per week				Par semaine				Por semana	
	1999	2000	2001	2002	2003	2004	2005	2006	2007	2008

Azerbaijan (DA) (a) [1] — Employees - Salariés - Asalariados

Men - Hommes - Hombres
ISIC 3 - CITI 3 - CIIU 3

	1999	2000	2001	2002	2003	2004	2005	2006	2007	2008
Total	.	.	.	.	.	.	.	.	165.8	152.5
A-B									157.0	148.7
C-Q									232.1	152.7
A									156.8	148.5
B									130.0	158.5
C									153.9	155.5
D									158.7	135.0
E									168.6	155.4
F									145.9	170.1
G									164.7	153.7
H									172.8	142.3
I									172.4	156.4
J									175.9	157.6
K									184.6	155.2
L									171.8	160.5
M									158.0	145.8
N									160.0	145.8
O									168.0	157.0

Women - Femmes - Mujeres
ISIC 3 - CITI 3 - CIIU 3

	1999	2000	2001	2002	2003	2004	2005	2006	2007	2008
Total	.	.	.	.	.	.	.	.	97.5	150.2
A-B									118.9	152.9
C-Q									78.1	150.1
A									119.7	152.4
B									92.4	179.2
C									121.6	149.2
D									96.1	138.5
E									124.8	149.4
F									71.9	163.4
G									151.8	159.0
H									169.0	157.7
I									114.0	157.0
J									107.2	148.4
K									62.3	160.1
L									138.8	159.8
M									129.8	145.8
N									125.6	145.8
O									118.3	158.7

China (DA) (a) [2][3] — Employees - Salariés - Asalariados

Total men and women - Total hommes et femmes - Total hombres y mujeres
ISIC 3 - CITI 3 - CIIU 3

	1999	2000	2001	2002	2003	2004	2005	2006	2007	2008
Total	.	.	.	.	45.4	45.5	47.8	47.3	45.5	.
A-B					44.1	42.9	42.9	41.9	38.2	.
C					44.1	45.4	47.5	47.8	46.1	.
D					46.4	46.9	51.1	50.4	49.4	.
E					42.2	42.4	43.4	43.5	43.2	.
F					48.4	48.0	51.6	51.3	49.7	.
G					49.2	50.1	52.5	50.9		.
H					50.1	49.1	53.9	54.4	52.1	.
I					46.1	46.5	49.9	50.0	41.0	.
64					43.1	43.6	45.6	46.3	45.1	.
J					41.1	41.7	42.4	42.6	42.4	.
K					46.3	45.2	45.8	46.4	45.0	.
73					42.2	42.2	42.7	42.5	42.2	.
70					42.2	42.4	45.8	45.8	45.7	.
L					40.9	41.1	42.2	42.0	41.8	.
M					41.0	41.1	42.3	42.4	41.7	.
N										.
O										.
93					47.5	47.0	52.3	52.1	50.2	.
P										.
Q					34.6	43.0	43.4	47.8	40.0	.

Explanatory notes: see p. 721. Notes explicatives: voir p. 723. Notas explicativas: véase p. 725.

[1] Per month. [2] Urban areas. [3] Nov. of each year. [1] Par mois. [2] Régions urbaines. [3] Nov. de chaque année. [1] Por mes. [2] Areas urbanas. [3] Nov. de cada año.

	Per week / Par semaine / Por semana									
	1999	2000	2001	2002	2003	2004	2005	2006	2007	2008

China (DA) (a) [1][2] — Employees - Salariés - Asalariados

Men - Hommes - Hombres — ISIC 3 - CITI 3 - CIIU 3

	1999	2000	2001	2002	2003	2004	2005	2006	2007	2008
Total	.	.	.	.	45.8	46.0	48.7	48.3	46.8	.
A-B	.	.	.	.	45.4	44.4	45.0	44.4	40.9	.
C	.	.	.	.	44.5	45.9	48.2	48.8	46.9	.
D	.	.	.	.	46.2	46.5	51.0	50.3	49.6	.
E	.	.	.	.	42.5	42.6	43.9	43.9	43.8	.
F	.	.	.	.	49.1	48.6	52.2	51.9	50.3	.
G	.	.	.	.	49.6	50.6	52.9	53.0	51.4	.
H	.	.	.	.	50.7	49.8	54.5	54.9	52.6	.
I	.	.	.	.	46.8	47.3	50.8	51.0	49.9	.
J	.	.	.	.	41.2	41.8	42.7	42.8	42.6	.
74	.	.	.	.	46.4	45.5	46.7	47.5	45.9	.
73	.	.	.	.	42.5	42.4	43.1	43.0	42.6	.
70	.	.	.	.	42.4	42.8	46.6	46.6	46.1	.
L	.	.	.	.	40.9	41.1	42.2	42.0	41.8	.
M	.	.	.	.	41.0	41.1	42.3	42.4	41.7	.
O	.	.	.	.	42.0	43.0	44.6	45.3	44.2	.
92	.	.	.	.	43.2	44.1	46.4	47.3	45.7	.
93	.	.	.	.	47.9	47.7	52.7	52.7	51.0	.
Q	.	.	.	.	34.5	44.6	44.7	53.8	.	.

Women - Femmes - Mujeres — ISIC 3 - CITI 3 - CIIU 3

	1999	2000	2001	2002	2003	2004	2005	2006	2007	2008
Total	.	.	.	.	44.9	44.0	46.7	45.9	44.0	.
A-B	.	.	.	.	42.8	41.2	40.8	39.4	35.6	.
C	.	.	.	.	42.9	43.6	44.8	44.1	43.2	.
D	.	.	.	.	46.6	47.5	51.3	50.5	49.2	.
E	.	.	.	.	41.6	41.9	42.2	42.4	41.9	.
F	.	.	.	.	45.2	44.3	47.7	47.9	46.0	.
G	.	.	.	.	48.9	49.7	52.2	52.0	50.4	.
H	.	.	.	.	49.6	48.6	53.4	53.9	51.6	.
I	.	.	.	.	43.5	43.3	45.6	45.4	45.0	.
64	.	.	.	.	42.8	42.9	45.3	46.0	44.5	.
J	.	.	.	.	40.9	41.6	42.2	42.3	42.2	.
K	.	.	.	.	.	.	.	.	.	.
74	.	.	.	.	46.3	44.9	44.4	44.5	43.8	.
73	.	.	.	.	41.7	42.0	41.8	41.6	41.6	.
70	.	.	.	.	41.8	41.9	44.5	44.4	44.8	.
L	.	.	.	.	40.5	40.7	41.3	41.3	41.2	.
M	.	.	.	.	40.8	41.0	42.0	42.1	41.6	.
O	.	.	.	.	41.7	42.7	43.9	44.5	43.7	.
92	.	.	.	.	43.1	44.1	46.1	46.0	44.6	.
93	.	.	.	.	47.1	46.3	51.9	51.4	49.2	.
Q	.	.	.	.	34.6	39.7	41.7	40.0	40.0	.

Hong Kong, China (BA) (a) [3][4] — Total employment - Emploi total - Empleo total

Total men and women - Total hommes et femmes - Total hombres y mujeres — ISIC 2 - CITI 2 - CIIU 2

	1999	2000	2001	2002	2003	2004	2005	2006	2007	2008
Total	46.0	46.6	46.5	46.9	46.6	47.1	46.9	46.3	46.6	45.6
2-9	46.0	46.6	46.5	46.9	46.6	47.1	46.9	46.3	46.6	45.5
1	52.8	51.6	48.9	53.4	53.3	51.5	48.4	46.6	47.2	48.8
2	-	-	-	-	-	-	-	-	-	-
3	45.0	45.3	45.4	45.6	45.4	46.5	46.4	45.5	45.8	44.6
4	41.7	43.3	42.5	42.5	42.3	42.7	42.5	42.4	42.5	41.6
5	41.9	41.9	41.9	41.5	41.3	42.6	42.6	42.1	43.1	41.8
6	47.8	48.2	48.0	48.5	48.4	48.7	48.3	47.3	47.7	46.7
7	46.4	47.1	46.8	47.4	47.0	48.0	47.6	47.2	47.4	46.2
8	45.2	46.4	45.9	46.8	46.7	47.0	47.1	46.3	46.2	45.1
9	46.2	47.0	47.1	47.1	46.4	46.3	46.4	46.1	46.4	45.4

Men - Hommes - Hombres — ISIC 2 - CITI 2 - CIIU 2

	1999	2000	2001	2002	2003	2004	2005	2006	2007	2008
Total	46.8	47.3	47.1	47.5	47.3	48.0	47.8	47.1	47.4	46.3
2-9	46.7	47.2	47.1	47.4	47.3	47.9	47.8	47.1	47.4	46.3
1	53.5	53.0	50.3	53.7	51.9	53.2	48.9	47.0	47.6	50.3
2	-	-	-	-	-	-	-	-	-	-
3	46.7	46.8	47.0	47.3	47.0	48.1	48.1	47.2	47.7	46.0
4	42.2	43.7	42.7	42.7	42.8	43.0	42.8	42.6	43.0	42.3
5	41.9	41.9	41.8	41.4	41.3	42.7	42.6	42.1	43.2	42.0
6	49.8	50.2	50.0	50.8	50.7	50.9	50.5	49.3	49.8	48.8
7	47.6	48.3	48.2	48.8	48.4	49.4	49.1	48.8	49.1	48.0
8	47.3	48.4	48.1	49.1	48.9	49.1	49.1	48.3	48.2	47.1
9	44.8	45.6	45.0	44.6	44.3	44.5	44.3	44.3	44.2	43.2

Explanatory notes: see p. 721. — Notes explicatives: voir p. 723. — Notas explicativas: véase p. 725.

[1] Urban areas. [2] Nov. of each year. [3] Excl. marine, military and institutional populations. [4] Persons aged 15 years and over.

[1] Régions urbaines. [2] Nov. de chaque année. [3] Non compris le personnel militaire, de la marine et la population institutionnelle. [4] Personnes âgées de 15 ans et plus.

[1] Areas urbanas. [2] Nov. de cada año. [3] Excl. el personal militar y de la marina, y la población institucional. [4] Personas de 15 años y más.

HOURS OF WORK
DURÉE DU TRAVAIL
HORAS DE TRABAJO

By economic activity
Par activité économique
Por actividad económica

	Per week				Par semaine				Por semana	
	1999	2000	2001	2002	2003	2004	2005	2006	2007	2008

Hong Kong, China (BA) (a) [1] [2]   Total employment - Emploi total - Empleo total

Women - Femmes - Mujeres
ISIC 2 - CITI 2 - CIIU 2

Total	45.0	45.7	45.8	46.1	45.8	46.0	45.9	45.4	45.6	44.7
2-9	44.9	45.7	45.8	46.1	45.8	46.0	45.9	45.4	45.6	44.7
1	51.3	48.6	45.4	52.6	56.1	47.7	47.4	45.9	46.6	45.5
2										
3	42.0	42.4	42.3	42.6	42.3	43.5	43.2	42.4	42.4	41.7
4	37.3	40.0	41.1	41.6	39.6	40.9	41.3	41.4	40.4	38.1
5	41.4	41.8	42.3	42.2	41.7	42.1	42.4	42.1	42.6	40.3
6	45.5	46.0	45.8	46.3	46.1	46.4	46.1	45.4	45.6	44.8
7	41.4	42.4	41.8	42.2	41.9	42.6	42.1	41.6	41.6	40.4
8	42.0	43.5	42.8	43.4	43.5	43.9	44.2	43.6	43.6	42.4
9	47.1	47.7	48.3	48.3	47.5	47.3	47.4	47.1	47.4	46.5

Hong Kong, China (BA) (a) [1] [2] [3]   Employees - Salariés - Asalariados

Total men and women - Total hommes et femmes - Total hombres y mujeres
ISIC 2 - CITI 2 - CIIU 2

Total	45.6	46.2	46.1	46.6	46.4	47.0	46.9	46.3	46.6	45.6
2-9	45.6	46.2	46.1	46.6	46.4	47.0	46.9	46.3	46.6	45.6
1	48.4	47.4	47.5	47.9	50.7	49.0	48.3	44.7	43.5	47.1
2	-	-	-	-	-	-	-	-	-	-
3	44.6	44.9	44.9	45.2	45.0	46.3	46.3	45.3	45.7	44.4
4	41.7	43.3	42.5	42.5	42.3	42.7	42.5	42.4	42.5	41.6
5	41.4	41.4	41.4	41.4	41.5	42.6	42.5	42.2	43.1	41.7
6	47.0	47.5	47.3	47.8	47.5	48.0	47.8	46.8	47.1	46.3
7	45.1	46.0	45.6	46.2	45.8	47.0	46.7	46.3	46.6	45.4
8	45.1	46.4	45.9	46.9	46.9	47.2	47.3	46.5	46.5	45.4
9	46.6	47.2	47.4	47.5	47.0	47.2	47.2	46.9	47.2	46.2

Men - Hommes - Hombres
ISIC 2 - CITI 2 - CIIU 2

Total	46.1	46.7	46.5	47.0	46.9	47.6	47.5	46.9	47.2	46.2
2-9	46.1	46.7	46.5	47.0	46.9	47.6	47.5	46.9	47.2	46.2
1	50.8	48.6	49.6	49.1	51.5	54.7	49.2	44.1	44.2	48.9
2	-	-	-	-	-	-	-	-	-	-
3	46.3	46.6	46.7	47.0	46.7	48.3	48.1	47.3	47.8	46.0
4	42.2	43.7	42.7	42.7	42.8	43.0	42.8	42.6	43.0	42.3
5	41.5	41.4	41.4	41.3	41.5	42.6	42.5	42.2	43.1	41.9
6	49.1	49.6	49.3	50.0	49.8	50.3	49.9	48.8	49.3	48.5
7	46.3	47.1	46.9	47.6	47.2	48.4	48.2	48.0	48.5	47.3
8	47.4	48.5	48.2	49.2	49.3	49.5	49.4	48.6	48.5	47.4
9	44.7	45.4	44.7	44.6	44.4	44.8	44.7	44.6	44.6	43.6

Women - Femmes - Mujeres
ISIC 2 - CITI 2 - CIIU 2

Total	44.9	45.7	45.7	46.2	45.9	46.3	46.2	45.7	45.9	45.0
2-9	44.9	45.7	45.7	46.2	45.9	46.3	46.2	45.7	45.9	45.0
1	42.7	45.4	42.7	45.1	49.1	32.3	47.0	45.7	42.7	43.5
2	-	-	-	-	-	-	-	-	-	-
3	41.9	42.3	42.2	42.6	42.2	43.4	43.1	42.2	42.3	41.6
4	37.3	40.0	41.1	41.6	39.6	40.9	41.3	41.4	40.4	38.1
5	41.2	41.6	42.0	42.2	41.9	42.3	42.4	42.3	42.8	40.3
6	44.9	45.6	45.4	45.8	45.6	46.0	45.9	45.1	45.3	44.5
7	41.2	42.4	41.6	42.1	41.9	42.8	42.2	41.6	41.7	40.5
8	41.9	43.4	42.7	43.5	43.5	44.0	44.3	43.7	43.7	42.6
9	47.6	48.2	48.7	49.0	48.3	48.4	48.3	47.9	48.4	47.4

India (DA) (a) [4]   Employees - Salariés - Asalariados

Total men and women - Total hommes et femmes - Total hombres y mujeres
ISIC 2 - CITI 2 - CIIU 2

3	46.6	47.2	46.7	46.9	47.1	47.0	47.2	46.9		

Men - Hommes - Hombres
ISIC 2 - CITI 2 - CIIU 2

3	46.7	46.5	46.7	46.9	47.0	47.0	47.2	46.9		

Women - Femmes - Mujeres
ISIC 2 - CITI 2 - CIIU 2

3	46.1	47.8	46.6	46.9	47.2	47.1	47.2	46.7		

Explanatory notes: see p. 721.

[1] Excl. marine, military and institutional populations. [2] Persons aged 15 years and over. [3] incl. outworkers. [4] Dec. of each year.

Notes explicatives: voir p. 723.

[1] Non compris le personnel militaire, de la marine et la population institutionnelle. [2] Personnes âgées de 15 ans et plus. [3] Y compris les travailleurs externes. [4] Déc. de chaque année.

Notas explicativas: véase p. 725.

[1] Excl. el personal militar y de la marina, y la población institucional. [2] Personas de 15 años y más. [3] Incl. los trabajadores fuera del establecimiento. [4] Dic. de cada año.

By economic activity   **Par activité économique**   **Por actividad económica**

	Per week — Par semaine — Por semana									
	1999	2000	2001	2002	2003	2004	2005	2006	2007	2008

India (FD) (a) [1] — Employees - Salariés - Asalariados

Total men and women - Total hommes et femmes - Total hombres y mujeres
ISIC 2 - CITI 2 - CIIU 2

	1999	2000	2001	2002	2003	2004	2005	2006	2007	2008
2 [2]	46.2	47.5	46.5	45.8	46.3	47.3	45.9	45.4	.	.
4	47.0	47.5	47.0	47.1	47.3	47.3	47.3	46.4	.	.
5	.	47.0	47.2	46.5	47.0	46.9	47.8	49.0	.	.
6	46.6	46.7	46.6	46.7	46.9	46.8	47.7	46.7	.	.
7	45.5	46.3	45.8	45.7	45.9	46.2	46.6	45.0	.	.
8	43.8	45.7	47.1	46.3	49.2	47.9	46.9	49.0	.	.
9	45.9	46.6	46.7	46.0	46.2	46.0	46.6	46.9	.	.

Men - Hommes - Hombres
ISIC 2 - CITI 2 - CIIU 2

	1999	2000	2001	2002	2003	2004	2005	2006	2007	2008
2 [2]	.	46.7	46.5	46.3	46.9	47.6	46.2	46.1	.	.
4	47.0	47.0	47.0	47.1	47.3	47.3	47.3	46.4	.	.
5	45.7	46.6	47.2	46.5	46.9	46.9	47.8	49.0	.	.
6	46.6	46.0	46.6	46.7	46.9	46.8	47.7	46.7	.	.
7	45.5	45.2	45.8	45.7	46.0	46.3	46.6	44.9	.	.
8	43.5	43.5	47.1	46.2	49.3	48.4	47.0	49.0	.	.
9	45.9	45.3	46.7	46.1	46.2	46.0	46.3	46.8	.	.

Women - Femmes - Mujeres
ISIC 2 - CITI 2 - CIIU 2

	1999	2000	2001	2002	2003	2004	2005	2006	2007	2008
2	.	47.6	46.5	42.5	44.4	46.6	43.6	41.6	.	.
4	46.3	48.0	46.6	46.7	47.2	47.2	47.3	46.5	.	.
5	46.5	47.4	45.2	44.5	49.5	46.5	48.0	.	.	.
6	46.4	47.4	46.5	46.6	46.5	46.2	45.9	46.7	.	.
7	45.4	47.4	45.7	45.7	45.7	45.9	46.1	46.5	.	.
8	46.2	48.0	46.7	46.8	48.7	46.7	46.5	.	.	.
9	45.9	48.9	46.6	45.8	45.7	46.0	47.6	47.6	.	.

Indonesia (BA) (a) [3] [4] — Total employment - Emploi total - Empleo total

Total men and women - Total hommes et femmes - Total hombres y mujeres
ISIC 3 - CITI 3 - CIIU 3

	1999	2000	2001	2002	2003	2004	2005	2006	2007	2008
Total	.	38.4	38.9	38.5	38.5	39.5	39.2 [5]	39.5	41.0	41.0
A-B	.	30.6	31.1	30.8	30.9	31.2	31.4 [5]	30.9	.	.
A	.	30.0	30.7	30.3	30.4	30.6	31.0 [5]	30.4	32.8	32.9
B	.	43.9	41.9	42.8	45.1	46.7	42.1 [5]	43.8	44.4	44.0
C	.	43.8	42.0	41.9	42.9	44.0	44.0 [5]	43.6	45.2	44.4
D	.	43.1	43.4	42.8	43.3	44.0	43.6 [5]	43.3	44.1	43.8
E	.	43.1	43.9	41.9	40.2	42.5	41.7 [5]	41.5	43.5	44.0
F	.	46.5	46.5	46.4	46.8	47.0	46.4 [5]	46.5	46.9	47.0
G	.	46.4	46.9	46.5	46.9	47.9	47.8 [5]	48.4	49.4	49.4
H	.	46.3	49.1	49.6	50.1	51.4	50.1 [5]	49.8	50.3	49.9
I	.	50.9	49.9	50.1	50.8	51.7	50.8 [5]	50.3	49.8	49.1
J	.	42.5	42.5	42.9	43.4	43.0	43.0 [5]	42.9	44.0	43.7
K	.	42.0	44.3	44.2	45.4	46.4	42.1 [5]	44.1	44.4	42.3
L	.	41.1	40.4	40.2	40.7	40.6	40.5 [5]	40.8	42.3	41.7
M	.	34.3	33.7	34.3	33.9	34.0	34.3 [5]	33.8	35.0	34.5
N	.	41.4	38.3	40.7	39.5	39.8	40.2 [5]	40.6	41.1	40.8
O	.	41.0	41.6	42.7	41.7	41.7	43.3 [5]	43.5	44.1	43.1
P	.	49.0	45.5	44.5	45.4	45.8	44.0 [5]	48.5	50.9	51.6
Q	.	.	35.1	30.0	46.0	36.7	53.3 [5]	42.8	39.8	42.4
X	.	.	51.1	47.0	39.5	46.3	35.0 [5]	43.7	42.9	42.8

Men - Hommes - Hombres
ISIC 3 - CITI 3 - CIIU 3

	1999	2000	2001	2002	2003	2004	2005	2006	2007	2008
Total	.	41.1	41.2	40.7	40.8	41.7	41.3 [5]	41.3	43.0	42.8
A-B	.	34.2	34.5	33.9	34.0	34.3	34.1 [5]	33.7	.	.
A	.	33.4	34.0	33.3	33.3	33.4	33.6 [5]	33.1	35.7	35.6
B	.	45.4	42.5	43.9	46.2	47.5	43.3 [5]	45.3	45.6	45.4
C	.	45.7	44.0	43.7	43.8	45.4	45.6 [5]	44.6	46.5	45.6
D	.	45.9	46.1	45.3	45.5	46.3	45.9 [5]	45.9	46.7	46.5
E	.	43.3	43.9	41.8	40.1	42.7	41.7 [5]	41.9	44.3	44.2
F	.	46.7	46.6	46.3	46.8	47.0	46.4 [5]	46.5	46.9	47.0
G	.	48.4	48.5	48.0	48.9	49.4	49.5 [5]	49.8	50.0	49.6
H	.	49.7	50.2	49.2	50.3	51.6	52.5 [5]	50.9	52.4	52.6
I	.	51.0	50.0	50.3	50.8	51.8	50.9 [5]	50.5	50.3	49.9
J	.	42.9	42.7	43.5	44.2	43.5	43.6 [5]	43.7	45.3	45.0
K	.	43.0	44.9	45.3	45.7	47.1	42.0 [5]	44.9	45.5	43.9
L	.	41.6	40.9	40.7	41.2	41.2	41.0 [5]	41.4	43.0	42.5
M	.	36.1	35.3	35.8	35.2	35.1	36.1 [5]	35.2	37.6	37.1
N	.	40.9	39.3	42.4	41.4	41.1	41.0 [5]	40.8	42.6	42.0
O	.	44.7	42.0	43.7	42.1	43.2	44.3 [5]	44.8	46.5	45.4
P	.	45.3	45.2	44.2	44.8	45.3	43.0 [5]	46.4	48.6	47.0
Q	.	.	40.0	.	51.5	35.0	58.9 [5]	42.1	39.8	42.6
X	.	.	64.4	43.4	39.6	54.3	38.5 [5]	45.8	46.3	45.7

Explanatory notes: see p. 721.

[1] Dec. of each year. [2] Excl. coal mining and petroleum production. [3] Persons aged 15 years and over. [4] Aug. of each year. [5] Nov.

Notes explicatives: voir p. 723.

[1] Déc. de chaque année. [2] Non compris l'extraction du charbon et la production de pétrole. [3] Personnes âgées de 15 ans et plus. [4] Août de chaque année. [5] Nov.

Notas explicativas: véase p. 725.

[1] Dic. de cada año. [2] Excl. la explotación de minas de carbón y la producción de petróleo. [3] Personas de 15 años y más. [4] Agosto de cada año. [5] Nov.

HOURS OF WORK — DURÉE DU TRAVAIL — HORAS DE TRABAJO

By economic activity — Par activité économique — Por actividad económica

	Per week / Par semaine / Por semana									
	1999	2000	2001	2002	2003	2004	2005	2006	2007	2008

Indonesia (BA) (a) [1] [2]   Total employment - Emploi total - Empleo total

Women - Femmes - Mujeres
ISIC 3 - CITI 3 - CIIU 3

	1999	2000	2001	2002	2003	2004	2005	2006	2007	2008
Total	.	34.0	34.9	34.5	34.5	35.6	35.3 [3]	36.1	37.6	38.2
A-B	.	25.1	25.5	25.5	25.6	25.9	26.3 [3]	25.6	.	.
A	.	25.0	25.5	25.5	25.6	25.9	26.2 [3]	25.6	28.1	28.7
B	.	30.2	33.9	26.3	28.1	31.5	27.0 [3]	28.9	29.6	29.2
C	.	35.0	32.6	29.8	37.3	36.2	35.1 [3]	35.7	35.9	35.2
D	.	39.2	39.7	39.3	40.4	40.4	40.3 [3]	39.6	40.5	40.3
E	.	41.0	43.4	42.0	40.6	40.4	40.7 [3]	38.2	37.5	42.0
F	.	40.9	44.6	47.1	46.8	44.9	46.3 [3]	44.5	43.8	44.6
G	.	44.0	45.2	44.7	44.7	46.2	45.7 [3]	46.8	48.8	49.2
H	.	44.0	47.7	50.3	49.8	51.2	47.7 [3]	48.8	48.4	47.9
I	.	48.3	47.4	46.1	49.1	48.4	46.9 [3]	46.8	43.7	42.6
J	.	41.5	42.0	41.4	41.8	41.7	41.6 [3]	41.3	41.6	41.0
K	.	39.1	42.5	39.9	44.7	44.1	42.7 [3]	41.6	40.3	37.7
L	.	39.3	38.6	38.7	38.6	38.6	38.4 [3]	38.7	39.2	38.5
M	.	32.2	32.1	32.7	32.6	32.8	32.6 [3]	32.5	32.8	32.5
N	.	41.8	37.5	39.4	38.2	38.9	39.6 [3]	40.4	40.1	40.1
O	.	35.1	40.6	39.3	40.4	35.9	39.1 [3]	40.4	37.3	37.3
P	.	51.4	46.0	44.9	46.1	46.3	44.7 [3]	49.4	51.7	53.0
Q	.	.	34.2	30.0	43.6	39.0	48.4 [3]	45.0	39.8	41.1
X	.	.	34.9	54.0	36.4	37.9	28.9 [3]	38.0	34.8	35.6

Israel (BA) (a) [1] [4]   Total employment - Emploi total - Empleo total

Total men and women - Total hommes et femmes - Total hombres y mujeres
ISIC 3 - CITI 3 - CIIU 3

	1999	2000	2001	2002	2003	2004	2005	2006	2007	2008
Total	40.0	40.5	39.8	40.0	39.6	39.2	39.1	39.1	39.3	39.1
A-B	44.3	44.9	45.7	44.1	45.0	44.5	44.4	43.7	44.1	.
C-Q	39.9	40.4	39.7	39.9	39.5	39.1	39.0	39.0	39.2	39.0
A	44.5	44.9	45.7	44.2	45.0	44.5	44.3	43.6	44.3	44.7
C	48.6	46.9	45.0	43.5	47.9	49.6	44.3	46.6	46.5	45.1
D	43.9	44.7	43.9	44.4	43.9	44.0	44.0	43.9	43.9	43.6
E	45.7	44.7	43.7	44.0	44.4	44.1	43.3	42.9	43.2	43.5
F	44.7	45.3	44.5	45.4	44.3	43.6	43.5	43.8	43.9	43.9
G	42.9	42.7	42.2	42.3	41.9	41.5	41.1	41.3	41.6	41.0
H	40.2	40.8	40.2	39.2	39.5	38.1	37.9	37.2	38.2	37.1
I	43.9	44.8	44.1	43.5	42.8	42.4	42.5	43.7	43.3	42.6
J	40.3	40.2	39.9	40.8	40.6	39.7	40.3	39.7	39.8	40.0
K	41.0	41.8	41.0	41.1	40.9	40.3	40.0	40.0	40.3	40.1
L	42.0	42.4	42.3	42.5	42.6	42.7	42.8	41.8	42.0	41.6
M	31.2	30.7	30.3	30.9	30.3	30.6	30.5	30.3	30.5	30.3
N	34.6	34.9	33.9	33.8	33.4	32.6	32.6	33.1	33.6	33.3
O	35.0	34.4	35.3	35.5	35.0	35.2	35.5	34.8	35.3	35.7
P	27.7	30.4	28.8	31.6	33.3	31.5	31.8	31.2	30.8	33.2
Q	.	.	.	35.2	.	.	.	.	.	.
X	42.2	42.9	41.4	41.8	41.7	41.5	41.8	41.7	42.3	42.3

Men - Hommes - Hombres
ISIC 3 - CITI 3 - CIIU 3

	1999	2000	2001	2002	2003	2004	2005	2006	2007	2008
Total	44.7	45.2	44.6	44.6	44.1	43.7	43.8	43.7	44.0	43.5
A-B	46.1	46.5	47.5	45.8	47.1	46.1	45.5	45.3	45.7	.
C-Q	44.7	45.2	44.5	44.6	44.1	43.6	43.8	43.7	43.9	43.4
A	46.4	46.6	47.5	45.8	47.1	46.1	45.4	45.2	45.9	46.7
B	-	-	.	-	.	.	.	.	.	-
C	50.1	48.2	44.8	44.1	47.1	49.6	44.5	46.9	48.1	45.7
D	45.8	46.6	45.6	46.1	45.5	45.5	45.8	45.4	45.8	45.1
E	46.7	46.3	45.1	45.2	45.6	45.4	44.8	44.1	43.9	45.0
F	45.2	45.9	45.2	46.0	44.9	44.1	43.9	44.3	44.4	44.6
G	47.2	47.0	46.6	46.5	46.2	45.5	45.7	45.6	45.9	45.0
H	44.0	44.3	43.6	42.7	43.3	42.1	41.1	40.6	41.3	41.5
I	46.1	47.3	46.5	45.9	44.8	44.8	44.8	46.1	45.3	44.9
J	43.5	43.9	44.0	44.4	44.9	42.9	42.8	42.8	43.4	42.9
K	44.3	45.2	44.5	44.4	44.5	43.1	43.3	43.4	43.7	43.1
L	45.2	45.3	45.4	46.1	45.5	46.2	45.7	45.6	45.3	44.9
M	35.7	35.1	34.6	35.4	33.8	34.3	34.6	34.6	34.6	33.8
N	43.5	44.4	42.1	41.6	40.4	39.6	41.0	41.0	41.5	41.1
O	39.4	38.9	40.2	39.8	38.8	39.1	40.5	39.7	40.9	39.9
P	33.6	36.4	36.1	40.5	42.2	38.8	44.4	40.1	39.7	48.4
Q	-	.	37.2	.	.	.	.	.	.	.
X	44.9	45.6	.	44.5	43.5	43.8	44.4	43.9	44.7	45.0

Explanatory notes: see p. 721.   Notes explicatives: voir p. 723.   Notas explicativas: véase p. 725.

[1] Persons aged 15 years and over. [2] Aug. of each year. [3] Nov. [4] Excl. armed forces.

[1] Personnes âgées de 15 ans et plus. [2] Août de chaque année. [3] Nov. [4] Non compris les forces armées.

[1] Personas de 15 años y más. [2] Agosto de cada año. [3] Nov. [4] Excl. las fuerzas armadas.

Per week — Par semaine — Por semana

Israel (BA) (a) [1] [2] — Total employment - Emploi total - Empleo total

Women - Femmes - Mujeres
ISIC 3 - CITI 3 - CIIU 3

	1999	2000	2001	2002	2003	2004	2005	2006	2007	2008
Total	34.1	34.5	33.9	34.2	34.0	33.7	33.3	33.4	33.6	33.7
A-B	37.9	37.3	34.8	35.6	36.6	36.9	39.4	35.7	34.9	.
C-Q	34.0	34.5	33.9	34.2	34.0	33.7	33.3	33.4	33.6	33.7
A	38.1	37.1	34.9	36.1	36.6	36.9	39.4	35.7	35.0	35.7
C	.	.	.	.	.	-	.	.	.	.
D	39.0	39.8	39.4	39.9	39.4	39.9	39.2	39.6	39.1	39.8
E	40.8	37.2	38.0	38.7	38.5	39.2	37.6	36.6	40.5	38.1
F	37.5	36.5	36.2	38.1	36.6	37.9	37.4	37.2	37.4	35.5
G	36.1	36.4	35.8	36.3	35.7	35.2	34.3	35.4	35.3	35.3
H	35.2	36.2	35.3	34.4	34.2	32.5	32.8	32.0	33.6	30.9
I	37.7	38.7	37.6	37.1	37.2	36.5	36.9	37.7	38.3	37.1
J	37.8	37.4	37.0	38.1	37.5	37.7	38.4	37.6	37.5	38.0
K	36.6	37.3	36.4	36.5	35.9	36.0	35.0	35.2	35.5	35.8
L	37.8	38.7	38.0	37.9	38.8	38.1	39.0	36.8	37.8	37.7
M	29.6	29.3	28.8	29.4	29.2	29.4	29.3	28.9	29.2	29.2
N	31.7	31.8	31.2	31.4	31.1	30.4	30.2	30.8	31.2	30.9
O	30.5	29.8	30.1	31.3	31.4	31.0	29.9	29.9	29.4	30.7
P	26.8	29.6	28.2	30.7	32.2	31.0	31.0	30.2	30.0	31.7
Q	.	.	.	.	.	.	.	.	.	.
X	35.7	37.2	35.7	35.5	37.1	35.9	36.1	38.3	37.8	37.7

Japan (BA) (a) — All persons engaged - Effectif occupé - Efectivo ocupado

Total men and women - Total hommes et femmes - Total hombres y mujeres
ISIC 2 - CITI 2 - CIIU 2   ISIC 3 - CITI 3 - CIIU 3

ISIC 2	1999	2000	2001	2002	2003	2004	2005	2006	2007	2008	ISIC 3
Total	42.3	42.7	42.2	42.2	42.0	42.0	41.8	41.7	41.1	40.7	Total
2-9 [3]	42.5	43.0	42.4	42.3	42.1	42.2	41.9	41.8	41.2	40.9	C-Q [3]
1 [4]	37.6	37.1	37.7	40.6	37.9	37.9	38.2	37.9	37.7	37.8	A
13 [5]	43.2	45.8	44.7	43.8	43.4	41.5	42.2	43.0	44.4	42.0	B
2	44.5	44.2	44.9	44.5	44.9	45.8	44.8	43.0	44.3	43.7	C
3	42.7	43.7	42.8	43.1	43.1	43.5	43.5	43.5	42.9	42.4	D [6]
4	41.0	41.8	40.8	41.0	40.5	41.0	41.4	42.3	41.2	41.0	E
5	45.0	45.8	45.3	45.5	45.4	45.7	45.5	45.2	44.7	44.5	F
6 [7]	42.7	42.7	42.3	42.0	42.1	41.9	41.3	40.9	40.4	40.1	G [8]
7	46.6	47.0	46.6	46.6	40.6	40.2	39.6	39.4	38.5	38.1	H
8 [9]	.	42.8	41.9	42.0	47.9	48.0	48.0	47.4	46.9	46.7	I [10]
9 [11]	.	40.7	40.1	40.1	42.8	42.5	42.1	42.5	41.6	41.4	J
					43.0	43.3	43.0	43.3	43.0	42.6	L
					37.2	37.8	37.9	38.2	37.9	38.0	M
					38.1	38.4	38.0	38.1	37.5	37.3	N
					39.0	39.6	39.9	39.1	38.7	38.5	X [12]

Men - Hommes - Hombres
ISIC 2 - CITI 2 - CIIU 2   ISIC 3 - CITI 3 - CIIU 3

ISIC 2	1999	2000	2001	2002	2003	2004	2005	2006	2007	2008	ISIC 3
Total	46.6	47.3	46.7	46.8	46.6	46.7	46.5	46.3	45.6	45.3	Total
2-9 [3]	46.9	47.6	47.0	47.0	46.8	46.9	46.7	46.5	45.8	45.5	C-Q [3]
1 [4]	40.7	40.1	40.9	44.9	40.8	40.8	41.0	40.7	40.6	40.8	A
13 [5]	45.8	48.1	47.3	46.6	46.0	44.4	45.0	46.5	47.6	44.3	B
2	45.5	45.2	45.6	45.3	46.0	47.2	46.2	44.4	44.5	44.6	C
3	46.0	47.1	46.2	46.4	46.4	46.7	46.6	46.7	45.8	45.2	D [6]
4	41.7	42.6	41.5	41.6	41.3	41.5	41.8	42.9	41.6	41.5	E
5	46.8	47.7	47.2	47.5	47.4	47.8	47.5	47.2	46.7	46.5	F
6 [7]	49.8	50.2	49.8	49.5	49.1	49.0	48.5	47.9	47.3	47.0	G [8]
7	49.1	49.6	49.3	49.3	49.6	49.4	48.3	48.4	47.6	46.9	H
8 [9]	.	47.8	46.8	47.2	50.3	50.4	50.6	50.0	49.5	49.4	I [10]
9 [11]	.	45.6	45.0	45.0	48.0	47.7	47.2	47.4	46.2	46.2	J
					44.5	44.7	44.6	44.7	44.4	44.1	L
					41.7	42.1	42.4	42.8	42.5	42.5	M
					44.1	44.5	44.3	44.3	43.8	43.8	N
					44.0	44.3	44.1	42.8	42.9	43.2	X [12]

Explanatory notes: see p. 721.

[1] Excl. armed forces. [2] Persons aged 15 years and over. [3] Incl. fishing. [4] Excl. fishing. [5] Fishing. [6] Excl. publishing. [7] Excl. hotels. [8] Excl. repair of motor vehicles, motor cycles and personal and household goods. [9] Excl. business services. [10] Excl. communications. [11] Incl. business services and hotels. [12] Incl. repair of motor vehicles, motor cycles and personal and household goods, divisions 71, 73 and 74.

Notes explicatives: voir p. 723.

[1] Non compris les forces armées. [2] Personnes âgées de 15 ans et plus. [3] Y compris la pêche. [4] Non compris la pêche. [5] Pêche. [6] Non compris l'édition. [7] Non compris les hôtels. [8] Non compris réparation de véhicules automobiles, de motocycles et de biens personnels etdomestiques. [9] Non compris les services aux entreprises. [10] Non compris les communications. [11] Y compris les services aux entreprises et les hôtels. [12] Non compris la réparation de véhicules automobiles, de motocycles et de biens personnels et domestiques, divisions 71, 73 et 74.

Notas explicativas: véase p. 725.

[1] Excl. las fuerzas armadas. [2] Personas de 15 años y más. [3] Incl. la pesca. [4] Excl. la pesca. [5] Pesca. [6] Excl. las editoriales. [7] Excl. hoteles. [8] Excl. reparación de vehículos automotores, motocicletas, efectos personals y enseres domesticos. [9] Excl. servicios para las empresas. [10] Excl. las comunicaciones. [11] Incl. servicios para empresas y hoteles. [12] Excl. la reparación de vehículos automotores, motocicletas, efectos personales y enseresdomesticos, divisiones 71, 73 y 74.

4A

| HOURS OF WORK | DURÉE DU TRAVAIL | HORAS DE TRABAJO |
| By economic activity | Par activité économique | Por actividad económica |

	Per week								Por semana		
					Par semaine						
	1999	2000	2001	2002	2003	2004	2005	2006	2007	2008	

Japan (BA) (a) — All persons engaged - Effectif occupé - Efectivo ocupado

Women - Femmes - Mujeres
ISIC 2 - CITI 2 - CIIU 2 / ISIC 3 - CITI 3 - CIIU 3

	1999	2000	2001	2002	2003	2004	2005	2006	2007	2008	
Total	36.0	36.1	35.7	35.5	35.3	35.4	35.1	35.1	34.6	34.4	Total
2-9 [1]	36.1	36.3	35.7	35.5	35.4	35.4	35.1	35.2	34.7	34.4	C-Q [1]
1 [2]	34.2	33.7	34.2	34.7	34.4	34.3	34.7	34.2	34.0	34.0	A
13 [3]	36.6	40.1	38.1	36.6	36.6	33.4	35.1	34.0	36.1	36.3	B
2	38.4	37.7	39.1	38.5	39.3	39.1	38.6	35.8	36.9	39.1	C
3	36.6	37.3	36.4	36.6	36.6	36.9	36.7	36.9	36.4	36.1	D [4]
4	36.4	36.7	36.5	36.6	35.7	37.4	37.7	37.4	37.0	35.7	E
5	35.0	35.7	34.7	34.6	34.0	34.1	33.7	33.4	33.3	32.8	F
6 [5]	35.9	35.7	35.3	34.9	35.1	34.8	34.3	34.1	33.7	33.4	G [6]
7	35.7	35.8	35.5	35.3	34.4	33.9	33.5	33.2	32.4	31.9	H
8 [7]		37.2	36.5	36.2	35.2	35.1	35.4	34.9	34.5	34.0	I [8]
9 [9]		36.2	35.8	35.6	37.5	37.6	37.1	37.7	37.0	36.8	J
					37.3	34.6	37.0	37.9	38.0	37.1	L
					33.2	33.8	34.1	34.4	34.0	34.2	M
					36.3	36.5	36.1	36.2	35.4	35.3	N
					32.9	33.5	34.7	34.4	33.2	32.2	X [10]

Japan (BA) (a) — Employees - Salariés - Asalariados

Total men and women - Total hommes et femmes - Total hombres y mujeres
ISIC 3 - CITI 3 - CIIU 3

	2003	2004	2005	2006	2007	2008
Total	42.2	42.2	42.0	41.9	41.3	40.9
C-Q	42.2	42.3	42.0	41.9	41.3	40.9
A	40.0	39.2	39.7	40.7	40.4	40.4
B	45.5	45.9	45.8	46.6	47.7	43.3
C	45.0	46.0	44.9	43.0	44.3	43.7
D [4]	43.6	44.0	44.0	44.1	43.3	42.8
E	40.5	41.0	41.4	42.3	41.2	41.0
F	46.1	46.5	46.2	45.9	45.3	45.2
G [6]	41.4	41.1	40.7	40.3	39.8	39.6
H	37.2	36.9	36.3	36.4	35.8	35.1
I [8]	48.1	48.0	48.1	47.5	47.0	46.7
J	43.0	42.8	42.4	42.7	41.8	41.6
K						
L	43.0	43.3	43.0	43.3	43.0	42.6
M	39.1	39.7	39.5	39.9	39.5	39.4
N	38.2	38.4	38.1	38.1	37.4	37.3
O						
X	39.6	40.1	40.2	39.3	39.5	39.2

Men - Hommes - Hombres
ISIC 3 - CITI 3 - CIIU 3

	2003	2004	2005	2006	2007	2008
Total	46.8	46.9	46.7	46.6	45.9	45.5
C-Q	46.8	47.0	46.7	46.6	45.9	45.5
A	44.5	43.3	44.0	44.9	44.6	44.6
B	48.9	48.2	48.0	50.3	52.8	46.4
C	46.1	47.4	46.3	44.4	45.5	44.5
D [4]	46.5	46.8	46.8	46.9	46.0	45.3
E	41.3	41.5	41.8	42.9	41.6	41.5
F	47.9	48.4	48.0	47.8	47.2	47.2
G [6]	48.6	48.5	48.1	47.6	46.9	46.6
H	46.8	46.7	45.3	45.5	44.9	44.1
I [8]	50.5	50.5	50.7	50.2	49.6	49.5
J	48.4	48.1	47.7	47.7	46.5	46.5
K						
L	44.5	44.7	44.6	44.7	44.4	44.1
M	42.3	42.9	43.1	43.4	42.9	42.9
N	44.2	44.4	44.3	44.3	43.8	43.6
O						
X	44.3	44.5	44.4	42.8	43.5	43.8

Explanatory notes: see p. 721.

[1] Incl. fishing. [2] Excl. fishing. [3] Fishing. [4] Excl. publishing. [5] Excl. hotels. [6] Excl. repair of motor vehicles, motor cycles and personal and household goods. [7] Excl. business services. [8] Excl. communications. [9] Incl. business services and hotels. [10] Incl. repair of motor vehicles, motor cycles and personal and household goods, divisions 71, 73 and 74.

Notes explicatives: voir p. 723.

[1] Y compris la pêche. [2] Non compris la pêche. [3] Pêche. [4] Non compris l'édition. [5] Non compris les hôtels. [6] Non compris réparation de véhicules automobiles, de motocycles et de biens personnels etdomestiques. [7] Non compris les services aux entreprises. [8] Non compris les communications. [9] Y compris les services aux entreprises et les hôtels. [10] Non compris la réparation de véhicules automobiles, de motocycles et de biens personnels et domestiques, divisions 71, 73 et 74.

Notas explicativas: véase p. 725.

[1] Incl. la pesca. [2] Excl. la pesca. [3] Pesca. [4] Excl. las editoriales. [5] Excl. hoteles. [6] Excl. reparación de vehículos automotores, motocicletas, efectos personals y enseres domesticos. [7] Excl. servicios para las empresas. [8] Excl. las comunicaciones. [9] Incl. servicios para empresas y hoteles. [10] Excl. la reparación de vehículos automotores, motocicletas, efectos personales y enseresdomesticos, divisiones 71, 73 y 74.

By economic activity   Par activité économique   Por actividad económica

	Per week / Par semaine / Por semana									
	1999	2000	2001	2002	2003	2004	2005	2006	2007	2008

Japan (BA) (a) — Employees - Salariés - Asalariados

Women - Femmes - Mujeres
ISIC 3 - CITI 3 - CIIU 3

	1999	2000	2001	2002	2003	2004	2005	2006	2007	2008
Total	.	.	.	.	35.4	35.5	35.2	35.4	34.8	34.5
C-Q	.	.	.	.	35.4	35.5	35.2	35.4	34.8	34.5
A	.	.	.	.	34.4	34.1	34.0	35.7	35.4	35.2
B	.	.	.	.	33.0	35.3	37.0	32.5	30.0	33.9
C	.	.	.	.	39.3	39.1	38.6	35.8	36.9	39.1
D [1]	.	.	.	.	37.5	37.8	37.6	37.7	37.1	36.8
E	.	.	.	.	35.7	37.4	37.7	37.4	37.0	35.7
F	.	.	.	.	35.9	35.7	35.9	35.4	35.0	34.5
G [2]	.	.	.	.	34.1	33.8	33.4	33.4	33.0	32.8
H	.	.	.	.	30.7	30.3	30.1	30.5	29.8	29.2
I [3]	.	.	.	.	35.5	35.4	35.5	35.1	34.6	34.1
J	.	.	.	.	37.8	37.9	37.3	37.9	37.2	37.0
K	.	.	.	.						
L	.	.	.	.	37.3	37.6	37.0	37.9	38.0	37.1
M	.	.	.	.	35.9	36.5	36.3	36.7	36.2	36.3
N	.	.	.	.	36.6	36.8	36.4	36.5	35.7	35.5
O	.	.	.	.						
X	.	.	.	.	33.9	34.5	35.0	35.0	34.0	33.1

Japan (DA) (a) — Employees - Salariés - Asalariados

Total men and women - Total hommes et femmes - Total hombres y mujeres
ISIC 3 - CITI 3 - CIIU 3

	1999	2000	2001	2002	2003	2004	2005	2006	2007	2008
C-Q	.	.	.	.	.	.	35.2	35.4	35.6	35.3
C	.	.	.	.	.	.	38.2	38.0	38.2	37.9
D	.	.	.	.	.	.	38.5	38.7	38.7	38.2
E	.	.	.	.	.	.	35.9	36.5	36.7	36.4
F	.	.	.	.	.	.	39.4	40.2	40.2	40.3
G	.	.	.	.	.	.	31.7	32.2	32.7	32.6
H	.	.	.	.	.	.	28.6	28.1	28.3	28.2
I	.	.	.	.	.	.				
J	.	.	.	.	.	.	34.8	35.4	35.2	35.0
K	.	.	.	.	.	.				
L	.	.	.	.	.	.				
M	.	.	.	.	.	.	30.0	30.3	31.8	31.4
N	.	.	.	.	.	.	34.2	34.3	33.7	33.6

Men - Hommes - Hombres
ISIC 3 - CITI 3 - CIIU 3

	1999	2000	2001	2002	2003	2004	2005	2006	2007	2008
C-Q	.	.	.	.	.	.	38.0	38.3	38.5	38.1
C	.	.	.	.	.	.	38.5	38.3	38.6	38.4
D	.	.	.	.	.	.	39.8	40.1	40.2	39.6
E	.	.	.	.	.	.	36.3	36.9	37.2	36.9
F	.	.	.	.	.	.	39.9	40.7	40.8	41.0
G	.	.	.	.	.	.	36.0	36.6	37.2	36.9
H	.	.	.	.	.	.	33.4	33.2	32.9	32.4
I	.	.	.	.	.	.				
J	.	.	.	.	.	.	36.4	37.0	36.8	36.6
K	.	.	.	.	.	.				
L	.	.	.	.	.	.				
M	.	.	.	.	.	.	31.2	31.7	33.3	32.9
N	.	.	.	.	.	.	35.2	35.3	34.7	34.6

Women - Femmes - Mujeres
ISIC 3 - CITI 3 - CIIU 3

	1999	2000	2001	2002	2003	2004	2005	2006	2007	2008
C-Q	.	.	.	.	.	.	30.9	31.1	31.2	31.1
C	.	.	.	.	.	.	35.1	34.9	35.6	34.7
D	.	.	.	.	.	.	34.8	35.1	34.6	34.3
E	.	.	.	.	.	.	32.7	33.3	33.5	33.1
F	.	.	.	.	.	.	35.4	36.0	36.0	35.7
G	.	.	.	.	.	.	28.2	28.5	28.8	28.8
H	.	.	.	.	.	.	24.7	24.2	24.6	24.4
I	.	.	.	.	.	.				
J	.	.	.	.	.	.	32.7	33.3	33.3	33.0
K	.	.	.	.	.	.				
L	.	.	.	.	.	.				
M	.	.	.	.	.	.	28.4	28.7	29.6	29.2
N	.	.	.	.	.	.	33.9	33.9	33.4	33.3
O	.	.	.	.	.	.				
P	.	.	.	.	.	.				

Explanatory notes: see p. 721.

[1] Excl. publishing. [2] Excl. repair of motor vehicles, motor cycles and personal and household goods. [3] Excl. communications.

Notes explicatives: voir p. 723.

[1] Non compris l'édition. [2] Non compris réparation de véhicules automobiles, de motocycles et de biens personnels etdomestiques. [3] Non compris les communications.

Notas explicativas: véase p. 725.

[1] Excl. las editoriales. [2] Excl. reparación de vehículos automotores, motocicletas, efectos personals y enseres domesticos. [3] Excl. las comunicaciones.

4A

HOURS OF WORK

By economic activity

DURÉE DU TRAVAIL

Par activité économique

HORAS DE TRABAJO

Por actividad económica

	Per week				Par semaine				Por semana	
	1999	2000	2001	2002	2003	2004	2005	2006	2007	2008

Jordan (DA) (b) [1] [2] Employees - Salariés - Asalariados

Total men and women - Total hommes et femmes - Total hombres y mujeres
ISIC 3 - CITI 3 - CIIU 3

C	247	248	249	248	251	251	249	256	241	.
D	234	258	256	258	256	256	259	253	256	
E	227	257	229	251	245	226	224	230	231	
F	251	250	248	252	247	249	250	247	249	
G	271	272	273	250	275	260	284	260	257	
H	272	278	284	266	271	271	268	271	256	
I	243	255	244	250	252	251	253	250	252	
J	236	239	243	240	246	239	245	246	239	
K	253	257	253	247	253	257	251	247	248	
L	216	223	219	220	222	215	214	206	214	
M	217	217	219	216	216	217	205	217	223	
N	243	247	224	238	245	228	227	231	228	
O	253	254	268	246	256	251	.	256	251	.

Men - Hommes - Hombres
ISIC 3 - CITI 3 - CIIU 3

C	247	248	249	248	251	251	249	256	241	.
D	236	260	257	260	257	257	261	255	255	
E	228	258	229	251	245	226	224	230	231	
F	252	251	248	252	247	249	250	247	249	
G	272	274	275	274	275	260	286	262	258	
H	273	278	285	274	271	272	269	271	256	
I	244	256	243	251	252	251	254	250	252	
J	237	240	245	241	246	240	245	247	239	
K	258	260	252	252	253	258	252	247	249	
L	217	223	219	220	222	215	213	206	213	
M	222	221	221	226	219	223	212	220	229	
N	244	247	225	245	245	226	226	234	228	
O	255	254	271	264	258	256	255	263	253	.

Women - Femmes - Mujeres
ISIC 3 - CITI 3 - CIIU 3

C	245	245	247	248	248	246	246	249	.	.
D	222	251	250	250	248	256	254	248	.	
E	207	255	235	251	245	222	225	230	.	
F	248	249	244	248	242	248	249	247	.	
G	258	253	252	250	252	261	261	245	.	
H	250	257	258	266	270	268	252	251	.	
I	235	250	247	250	249	250	248	248	.	
J	235	237	239	240	246	239	246	246	.	
K	236	247	254	247	253	254	247	248	.	
L	212	221	220	220	224	220	219	207	.	
M	212	214	216	216	214	212	199	215	.	
N	242	246	224	238	244	230	228	228	.	
O	244	255	259	246	250	240	257	237	.	.

Korea, Republic of (DA) (a) [3] Employees - Salariés - Asalariados

Total men and women - Total hommes et femmes - Total hombres y mujeres
ISIC 3 - CITI 3 - CIIU 3

C	44.4	44.6	43.8	44.9	45.0	43.2	43.7	43.4	43.4	41.1 [4]
C-X	47.9	47.5	47.0	46.2	45.9	45.7	45.1	44.2	43.5	40.9 [4]
D	50.1	49.3	48.3	47.7	47.6	47.4	46.9	46.0	45.5	43.7 [4]
E	48.7	48.3	49.1	47.7	47.9	45.7	42.4	42.0	41.6	40.3 [4]
F	45.1	44.4	44.4	43.9	43.3	43.4	42.7	41.6	41.2	38.8 [4]
G	45.8	44.7	44.6	44.2	43.6	43.2	42.9	42.1	41.3	38.9 [4]
H	45.7	46.5	47.1	46.0	45.5	45.9	47.5	46.7	46.3	40.7 [4]
I	50.0	49.5	49.1	47.9	47.4	47.3	45.8	45.1	44.0	40.3 [4]
J	43.3	42.9	42.7	41.8	40.2	40.0	39.2	38.7	38.5	37.2 [4]
K	47.7	47.4	47.3	47.2	47.0	46.0	46.0	44.2	43.2	40.7 [4]
L	.	.	.	.	.	.	.	.	.	.
M	45.1	45.9	44.6	41.9	41.5	41.4	40.8	40.0	39.2	36.8 [4]
N	45.0	45.0	45.1	44.2	43.7	43.3	42.9	42.0	41.7	38.8 [4]
O	45.7	44.8	45.4	44.8	44.5	44.4	44.1	43.7	43.0	41.2 [4]
P	.	.	.	.	.	.	.	.	.	.
Q	.	.	.	.	.	.	.	.	.	.
X	.	.	.	.	.	.	.	.	.	.

Explanatory notes: see p. 721.

[1] Per month. [2] Oct. of each year. [3] Establishments with 10 or more permanent employees. [4] Methodology revised; data not strictly comparable.

Notes explicatives: voir p. 723.

[1] Par mois. [2] Oct. de chaque année. [3] Etablissements occupant 10 salariés permanents ou plus. [4] Méthodologie révisée; les données ne sont pas strictement comparables.

Notas explicativas: véase p. 725.

[1] Por mes. [2] Oct. de cada año. [3] Establecimientos con 10 y más asalariados permanentes. [4] Metodología revisada; los datos no son estrictamente comparables.

	Per week / Par semaine / Por semana									
	1999	2000	2001	2002	2003	2004	2005	2006	2007	2008

Korea, Republic of (DA) (a) [1]   Employees - Salariés - Asalariados

Men - Hommes - Hombres
ISIC 3 - CITI 3 - CIIU 3

	1999	2000	2001	2002	2003	2004	2005	2006	2007	2008
C	44.1	44.4	43.5	44.7	45.0	43.0	43.8	43.4	43.5	.
C-X	48.2	47.8	47.4	46.6	46.3	46.0	45.6	44.6	43.9	.
D	49.8	49.2	48.3	47.6	47.6	47.3	47.0	46.0	45.5	.
E	49.0	48.6	49.4	47.9	48.2	45.9	42.6	42.1	41.8	.
F	45.2	44.4	44.4	44.0	43.4	43.5	42.7	41.6	41.3	.
G	45.7	44.9	44.6	44.0	43.4	43.0	43.0	42.4	41.7	.
H	45.4	46.0	46.4	46.0	45.5	45.7	47.0	46.1	45.4	.
I	50.6	50.2	49.8	49.2	48.9	48.8	46.2	45.6	44.6	.
J	43.4	42.7	42.8	43.7	43.0	41.4	39.3	38.8	38.6	.
K	48.7	48.5	48.6	48.4	48.3	47.7	47.7	45.7	44.4	.
L	.	.	.	.	.	.	.	.	.	.
M	45.5	47.1	46.0	42.9	42.5	42.3	41.2	40.3	39.5	.
N	44.5	44.6	44.4	44.2	43.5	43.1	42.6	41.6	41.4	.
O	45.9	44.9	45.5	44.9	44.6	44.5	44.3	43.9	43.3	.
P	.	.	.	.	.	.	.	.	.	.
Q	.	.	.	.	.	.	.	.	.	.
X	.	.	.	.	.	.	.	.	.	.

Women - Femmes - Mujeres
ISIC 3 - CITI 3 - CIIU 3

	1999	2000	2001	2002	2003	2004	2005	2006	2007	2008
C	47.1	46.5	46.9	47.2	46.0	45.3	43.3	43.6	42.7	.
C-X	47.3	46.7	46.0	45.3	44.9	44.7	44.1	43.1	42.5	.
D	50.7	49.8	48.4	47.9	47.7	47.6	46.9	46.1	45.4	.
E	45.6	45.2	46.4	45.5	45.6	43.8	41.1	40.6	40.5	.
F	44.4	44.2	44.2	43.4	42.6	42.9	42.6	41.4	41.1	.
G	46.0	44.5	44.7	44.5	43.9	43.7	42.6	41.5	40.6	.
H	46.0	47.0	47.9	46.0	45.5	46.1	48.1	47.3	47.1	.
I	45.0	43.9	44.0	44.2	43.7	43.6	42.6	41.5	40.8	.
J	43.2	43.2	42.5	41.0	39.9	39.7	39.1	38.7	38.5	.
K	44.1	43.7	43.6	43.5	43.3	43.4	41.5	40.6	40.2	.
L	.	.	.	.	.	.	.	.	.	.
M	44.3	43.5	42.5	41.0	41.0	41.0	40.5	39.7	38.9	.
N	45.4	45.3	45.4	44.3	43.8	43.4	43.1	42.2	41.9	.
O	45.2	44.6	45.2	44.3	44.3	44.1	43.7	43.1	42.3	.
P	.	.	.	.	.	.	.	.	.	.
Q	.	.	.	.	.	.	.	.	.	.
X	.	.	.	.	.	.	.	.	.	.

Korea, Republic of (DA) (a) [1] [2]   Employees - Salariés - Asalariados

Total men and women - Total hommes et femmes - Total hombres y mujeres
ISIC 3 - CITI 3 - CIIU 3

	1999	2000	2001	2002	2003	2004	2005	2006	2007	2008
C	.	.	.	.	.	.	.	.	37.3	39.8
C-X	.	.	.	.	.	.	.	.	40.1	39.4
D	.	.	.	.	.	.	.	.	42.5	43.1
E	.	.	.	.	.	.	.	.	40.7	40.1
F	.	.	.	.	.	.	.	.	37.0	36.0
G	.	.	.	.	.	.	.	.	38.8	38.2
H	.	.	.	.	.	.	.	.	40.8	39.7
I	.	.	.	.	.	.	.	.	42.3	39.3
J	.	.	.	.	.	.	.	.	36.9	36.7
K	.	.	.	.	.	.	.	.	39.4	39.8
M	.	.	.	.	.	.	.	.	31.6	32.1
N	.	.	.	.	.	.	.	.	39.4	38.3
O	.	.	.	.	.	.	.	.	38.7	38.4

Kyrgyzstan (CA) (a)   Employees - Salariés - Asalariados

Total men and women - Total hommes et femmes - Total hombres y mujeres
ISIC 3 - CITI 3 - CIIU 3

	1999	2000	2001	2002	2003	2004	2005	2006	2007	2008
Total	35.9	34.8	35.7	35.3	35.2	36.3	35.7	.	.	.
A-B	.	35.6	38.4	37.4	37.4	37.8	37.4	.	.	.
C-Q	35.8	34.8	35.5	35.2	35.0	36.3	35.7	.	.	.
A	36.9	35.6	38.4	37.3	37.4	37.8	37.4	.	.	.
B	.	32.3	31.7	39.2	37.0	39.8	36.1	.	.	.
C	30.7	32.1	34.1	35.6	33.8	35.9	34.5	.	.	.
D	32.2	32.3	33.2	33.2	34.1	34.4	34.5	.	.	.
E	34.7	34.5	35.5	35.1	36.0	35.1	35.3	.	.	.
F	35.3	35.7	36.0	35.1	35.3	36.7	35.2	.	.	.
G	37.9	35.1	35.3	38.7	35.7	34.7	36.3	.	.	.
H	37.6	35.6	37.3	37.8	33.5	36.6	39.1	.	.	.
I	33.5	32.6	33.9	34.4	32.5	33.9	33.7	.	.	.
J	36.0	35.9	36.7	36.3	35.3	36.0	35.5	.	.	.
K	36.9	35.6	36.2	37.3	36.3	37.0	35.5	.	.	.
L	37.3	36.3	36.9	36.0	34.6	37.5	36.5	.	.	.
M	36.4	34.4	35.8	34.3	34.7	36.4	35.6	.	.	.
N	38.1	37.0	36.6	36.8	37.1	37.5	37.2	.	.	.
O	36.2	35.4	34.0	36.0	35.7	36.6	35.6	.	.	.

Explanatory notes: see p. 721.   Notes explicatives: voir p. 723.   Notas explicativas: véase p. 725.

[1] Establishments with 10 or more permanent employees. [2] Incl. daily and temporary employees.   [1] Etablissements occupant 10 salariés permanents ou plus. [2] Y compris les salaries journaliers et temporaires.   [1] Establecimientos con 10 y más asalariados permanentes. [2] Incl. los asalariados diarios y temporales.

By economic activity   Par activité économique   Por actividad económica

	Per week						Par semaine		Por semana	
	1999	2000	2001	2002	2003	2004	2005	2006	2007	2008

Macau, China (BA) (a) [1]   Total employment - Emploi total - Empleo total

Total men and women - Total hommes et femmes - Total hombres y mujeres
ISIC 3 - CITI 3 - CIIU 3

	1999	2000	2001	2002	2003	2004	2005	2006	2007	2008
Total	48.3	48.1	48.1	47.8	47.3	48.0	47.5	47.1	46.9	46.9
C-Q	48.3	48.1	48.1	47.9	47.3	48.0	47.5	47.1	46.9	46.9
C	43.2	47.0	47.0	44.5	47.0	57.0	52.0	54.4	52.8	
D	48.8	48.2	48.0	47.8	47.2	47.4	47.5	47.2	47.3	47.7
E	42.4	43.0	42.9	43.3	41.7	41.9	42.4	42.7	41.8	41.8
F	44.7	45.1	45.9	44.6	45.2	46.2	46.6	47.1	47.1	46.4
G	52.1	52.5	53.4	52.9	52.0	54.1	49.3	48.9	48.8	48.6
H	55.5	56.3	57.9	55.5	53.0	54.0	51.4	49.8	48.7	48.1
I	47.1	47.1	47.4	47.0	47.0	47.6	47.2	47.0	47.1	46.7
J	43.8	43.7	43.8	43.9	43.0	44.2	43.3	43.2	43.2	43.0
K	49.9	53.1	53.6	54.2	51.6	52.4	48.8	48.4	48.0	48.3
L	38.5	38.8	38.9	39.1	39.0	39.6	39.2	39.1	38.9	38.6
M	41.6	40.8	41.5	41.3	40.6	41.2	42.2	41.7	41.9	42.6
N	44.6	42.1	43.6	43.3	43.4	44.5	43.3	44.3	43.3	43.7
O	55.1	54.9	55.0	53.9	52.2	53.3	49.1	47.4	47.0	46.9
P	60.6	56.2	55.7	55.2	55.9	58.5	48.9	51.5	48.7	50.0

Men - Hommes - Hombres
ISIC 3 - CITI 3 - CIIU 3

	1999	2000	2001	2002	2003	2004	2005	2006	2007	2008
Total	48.1	48.0	48.2	47.9	47.5	48.3	47.7	47.3	47.1	47.0
C-Q	48.1	48.0	48.2	47.9	47.5	48.3	47.7	47.3	47.1	47.0
C	43.2		47.0	44.5	47.0	57.0	52.0	54.4	52.8	
D	48.2	48.2	48.0	48.1	47.4	47.7	48.0	47.7	47.5	48.2
E	43.0	43.1	43.4	43.6	42.2	42.1	42.5	42.8	42.1	42.3
F	44.6	45.1	45.9	44.8	45.2	46.3	46.6	47.2	47.4	46.5
G	52.5	53.2	54.2	53.5	53.4	55.0	50.0	49.2	49.3	48.8
H	58.4	58.2	57.4	57.2	53.0	54.4	51.7	49.6	48.9	48.2
I	47.9	47.9	47.9	47.5	47.7	48.3	48.0	47.8	48.5	47.3
J	44.4	44.8	44.4	43.9	43.0	44.2	43.6	43.2	43.6	43.4
K	59.3	59.9	59.6	61.1	60.0	60.3	53.6	52.8	50.6	49.9
L	39.2	39.6	39.3	40.0	39.8	40.5	40.3	40.0	39.4	39.1
M	41.8	40.1	41.0	40.9	40.6	41.0	41.8	41.6	41.2	41.8
N	43.0	42.8	43.3	42.8	44.6	45.3	42.9	42.8	42.7	44.7
O	54.9	54.9	55.3	53.3	52.8	54.5	49.2	47.5	47.0	46.9
P	58.6	58.4	53.5	56.8	56.5	64.9	56.2	55.1	48.4	54.8

Women - Femmes - Mujeres
ISIC 3 - CITI 3 - CIIU 3

	1999	2000	2001	2002	2003	2004	2005	2006	2007	2008
Total	48.6	48.2	48.0	47.8	47.1	47.7	47.3	46.9	46.6	46.8
C-Q	48.6	48.2	48.0	47.8	47.1	47.7	47.3	46.9	46.6	46.8
C		47.0								
D	49.1	48.3	48.0	47.8	47.1	47.3	47.3	46.9	47.2	47.2
E	38.8	40.7	41.2	39.7	40.3	40.8	42.2	35.5	40.6	40.1
F	45.8	45.2	45.3	42.6	45.2	45.3	46.4	46.3	45.4	44.9
G	51.7	51.8	52.7	52.1	50.7	52.8	48.9	48.7	48.2	48.4
H	54.0	54.5	58.4	54.1	53.0	53.6	51.2	50.0	48.6	48.0
I	45.4	45.4	46.5	46.0	45.5	45.9	45.6	45.1	44.3	45.1
J	43.3	43.0	43.4	43.8	43.0	44.3	43.1	43.2	42.9	42.8
K	46.4	47.0	47.0	47.2	46.8	47.0	46.9	46.8	46.1	46.5
L	37.4	37.5	38.0	37.8	37.8	38.2	36.4	38.0	38.2	37.9
M	41.5	41.1	41.7	41.5	40.6	41.4	42.3	41.7	42.2	43.0
N	45.0	41.9	43.8	43.6	43.0	44.1	43.4	44.8	43.6	43.4
O	55.4	54.9	54.6	54.5	51.7	52.0	49.0	47.3	46.9	46.9
P	60.7	55.8	56.1	54.9	55.9	56.9	48.8	51.3	48.7	49.8

Malaysia (BA) (a)   Total employment - Emploi total - Empleo total

Total men and women - Total hommes et femmes - Total hombres y mujeres
ISIC 3 - CITI 3 - CIIU 3

	1999	2000	2001	2002	2003	2004	2005	2006	2007	2008
Total	.	.	47.7	48.3	48.1	47.4	48.2	48.0	47.3	46.9
A	.	.	40.3	41.0	40.5	40.0	41.3	40.4	39.1	40.0
B	.	.	50.5	48.4	48.1	47.6	50.4	48.4	47.0	44.5
C	.	.	50.2	53.2	50.8	51.6	51.9	52.3	51.0	51.0
D	.	.	48.8	49.3	49.1	48.8	49.6	49.6	49.1	48.8
E	.	.	46.7	46.7	46.9	45.7	46.9	45.4	46.2	45.1
F	.	.	48.9	49.4	49.3	48.4	48.9	48.7	48.5	47.6
G	.	.	51.3	51.7	51.5	50.7	51.3	51.3	50.5	50.6
H	.	.	51.5	51.6	51.3	51.5	51.1	51.6	51.0	49.2
I	.	.	51.4	52.0	51.7	51.2	51.6	51.9	50.9	50.7
J	.	.	46.3	46.3	46.2	44.7	46.0	45.6	45.8	44.9
K	.	.	48.3	48.2	48.7	47.9	49.3	49.4	49.0	48.9
L	.	.	45.5	46.2	45.9	44.5	45.6	44.3	44.8	44.3
M	.	.	35.3	36.0	36.3	34.9	37.1	36.5	36.6	34.8
N	.	.	46.8	46.5	46.7	46.4	46.6	46.3	45.7	44.7
O	.	.	48.1	48.0	47.9	46.8	47.7	47.8	47.5	47.5
P	.	.	66.0	67.9	68.7	67.8	68.8	68.2	67.2	65.9

Explanatory notes: see p. 721.   Notes explicatives: voir p. 723.   Notas explicativas: véase p. 725.

[1] Median.   [1] Médiane.   [1] Mediana.

By economic activity   **Par activité économique**   **Por actividad económica**

	Per week			Par semaine				Por semana		
	1999	2000	2001	2002	2003	2004	2005	2006	2007	2008

Malaysia (BA) (a)   Total employment - Emploi total - Empleo total

Men - Hommes - Hombres
ISIC 3 - CITI 3 - CIIU 3

	1999	2000	2001	2002	2003	2004	2005	2006	2007	2008
Total	.	.	48.4	48.9	48.6	47.9	48.7	48.4	47.8	47.5
A	.	.	41.6	42.4	41.9	41.2	42.6	41.3	42.0	41.2
B	.	.	50.9	48.9	48.2	47.7	50.7	48.5	47.3	44.7
C	.	.	50.8	53.9	51.2	51.6	52.9	52.9	51.7	52.0
D	.	.	50.1	50.7	50.2	49.9	50.6	50.6	50.2	50.1
E	.	.	46.9	47.0	47.1	46.0	47.0	45.7	46.5	45.1
F	.	.	49.1	49.6	49.5	48.5	49.1	48.9	48.6	47.7
G	.	.	51.5	51.9	51.8	50.9	51.4	51.4	50.6	50.6
H	.	.	52.9	53.1	52.7	53.6	52.6	53.4	52.5	50.7
I	.	.	52.3	52.8	52.6	52.2	52.5	52.8	51.8	51.6
J	.	.	47.0	46.8	46.7	45.0	46.5	45.9	46.3	45.3
K	.	.	49.8	49.7	50.3	49.6	51.0	51.2	50.9	50.8
L	.	.	46.5	47.4	47.0	45.4	46.4	45.2	45.7	45.2
M	.	.	37.4	38.6	38.6	37.7	39.4	38.9	38.3	36.8
N	.	.	46.5	47.0	46.6	46.6	46.8	46.4	46.7	44.3
O	.	.	48.4	48.9	48.3	47.2	47.9	48.3	47.1	47.6
P	.	.	48.8	49.4	49.2	50.4	52.7	47.3	49.6	45.0

Women - Femmes - Mujeres
ISIC 3 - CITI 3 - CIIU 3

	1999	2000	2001	2002	2003	2004	2005	2006	2007	2008
Total	.	.	46.4	47.1	47.1	46.3	47.4	47.1	46.5	45.8
A	.	.	37.4	37.6	37.3	36.7	37.7	37.6	35.7	36.3
B	.	.	39.4	33.8	44.8	42.9	43.0	43.7	40.1	38.7
C	.	.	46.8	46.0	46.9	51.4	45.4	48.6	47.4	46.9
D	.	.	46.8	47.4	47.6	47.1	48.1	48.0	47.3	46.8
E	.	.	45.6	43.9	45.9	44.0	46.2	43.8	44.7	45.0
F	.	.	46.6	47.0	46.9	47.3	47.3	46.4	46.4	45.7
G	.	.	50.7	51.3	50.8	50.2	51.1	51.1	50.1	50.6
H	.	.	49.9	50.1	49.9	49.3	49.5	49.5	49.3	47.6
I	.	.	45.9	46.9	46.7	45.6	46.9	47.5	46.5	45.9
J	.	.	45.5	45.9	45.7	44.5	45.5	45.3	45.2	44.6
K	.	.	45.9	45.9	46.0	45.2	46.5	46.5	46.0	46.0
L	.	.	42.1	42.9	42.8	42.1	43.4	41.9	42.4	42.0
M	.	.	33.8	34.3	34.8	33.3	35.7	35.2	35.6	33.7
N	.	.	46.9	46.2	46.7	46.3	46.5	46.2	45.2	44.8
O	.	.	47.6	46.8	47.4	46.2	47.4	47.2	47.9	47.5
P	.	.	67.2	69.1	70.1	68.8	69.9	70.0	68.6	68.6

Myanmar (DA) (a) [1] [2]   Employees - Salariés - Asalariados

Total men and women - Total hommes et femmes - Total hombres y mujeres
ISIC 2 - CITI 2 - CIIU 2

	1999	2000	2001	2002	2003	2004	2005	2006	2007	2008
2-9	.	7.9	8.0	8.0	8.0	8.0	8.0	8.0	8.0	8.0
2 [3]	7.9	7.9	8.0	8.0	8.0	8.0	8.0	8.0	8.0	8.0
3	7.9	8.0	8.0	8.0	8.0	8.0	8.0	8.0	8.0	8.0
5	7.9	7.8	8.0	8.0	8.0	8.0	8.0	8.0	8.0	8.0
7 [4]	7.9	8.0	8.0	8.0	8.0	8.0	8.0	8.0	8.0	8.0

Philippines (BA) (a) [5]   Total employment - Emploi total - Empleo total

Total men and women - Total hommes et femmes - Total hombres y mujeres
ISIC 3 - CITI 3 - CIIU 3

	1999	2000	2001	2002	2003	2004	2005	2006	2007	2008
Total	.	.	40.5	40.8	41.6	41.6	41.6	41.2 [6]	41.7	.
A-B	34.4	33.8	34.2	31.1	32.6	32.1	32.5	31.5 [6]	32.2	.
C-Q	.	.	44.3	44.3	44.5	45.1	44.8	44.7 [6]	.	.
A	33.7	32.9	29.1	29.1	31.9	31.2	31.9	30.8 [6]	31.5	.
B	41.7	41.0	34.1	33.8	38.0	38.9	37.7	37.1 [6]	37.7	.
C	.	.	41.2	43.0	43.0	45.0	41.7	44.0 [6]	44.9	.
D	.	.	43.2	43.6	44.1	44.4	44.8	44.4 [6]	44.9	.
E	.	.	44.8	43.4	44.2	45.6	44.5	45.0 [6]	45.4	.
F	.	.	42.8	43.1	43.6	43.5	43.3	43.0 [6]	43.9	.
G	.	.	48.9	49.7	50.3	50.7	50.0	49.8 [6]	50.2	.
H	.	.	48.7	49.7	50.3	50.6	50.3	49.7 [6]	49.3	.
I	.	.	48.5	48.4	49.3	49.9	49.4	49.2 [6]	50.0	.
J	.	.	42.5	41.7	42.4	43.1	42.1	42.6 [6]	43.1	.
K	.	.	45.9	46.8	48.6	48.0	47.4	48.4 [6]	48.4	.
L	.	.	40.1	40.1	41.3	41.0	40.6	39.7 [6]	39.9	.
M	.	.	39.9	40.2	39.8	40.4	40.2	39.9 [6]	40.2	.
N	.	.	40.9	42.0	41.1	41.6	40.7	41.6 [6]	42.8	.
O	.	.	37.0	36.4	36.4	38.1	35.8	36.8 [6]	36.5	.
P	.	.	54.8	54.8	54.9	54.5	55.6	54.6 [6]	54.1	.
Q	.	.	45.3	41.2	38.3	40.0	45.7	42.1 [6]	44.5	.

Explanatory notes: see p. 721.

[1] Regular employees. [2] Per day. [3] Metal mining. [4] Excl. storage and communication; incl. sea transport. [5] Oct. of each year. [6] Methodology revised; data not strictly comparable.

Notes explicatives: voir p. 723.

[1] Salariés stables. [2] Par jour. [3] Extraction de minerais métalliques. [4] Non compris les entrepôts et communications; y compris les transports maritimes. [5] Oct. de chaque année. [6] Méthodologie révisée; les données ne sont pas strictement comparables.

Notas explicativas: véase p. 725.

[1] Asalariados estables. [2] Por día. [3] Extracción de minerales metálicos. [4] Excl. almacenaje y comunicaciones; incl. los transportes marítimos. [5] Oct. de cada año. [6] Metodología revisada; los datos no son estrictamente comparables.

			Per week			Par semaine				Por semana	
	1999	2000	2001	2002	2003	2004	2005	2006	2007	2008

Philippines (BA) (a) [1] Total employment - Emploi total - Empleo total

Men - Hommes - Hombres
ISIC 3 - CITI 3 - CIIU 3

	1999	2000	2001	2002	2003	2004	2005	2006	2007	2008
Total	.	.	40.2	40.4	41.5	41.4	41.4	40.9 [2]	41.4	.
A-B	37.0	36.2	36.1	33.4	35.0	34.4	34.9	33.9 [2]	34.5	.
C-Q	.	.	44.9	44.8	45.7	45.7	45.7	45.4 [2]	.	.
A	36.2	35.3	33.4	33.2	34.4	33.6	34.2	33.2 [2]	33.8	.
B	42.4	41.6	38.4	39.7	38.8	39.7	38.7	38.1 [2]	38.7	.
C	.	.	41.8	43.6	43.4	46.2	43.1	45.1 [2]	45.4	.
D	.	.	45.0	45.4	45.8	46.2	46.4	45.9 [2]	46.2	.
E	.	.	45.3	43.6	44.4	46.4	44.8	45.7 [2]	45.5	.
F	.	.	42.8	43.1	43.6	43.5	43.3	43.0 [2]	43.9	.
G	.	.	46.3	47.0	48.3	48.1	48.1	47.5 [2]	48.0	.
H	.	.	47.4	48.8	49.5	49.0	49.0	49.0 [2]	47.6	.
I	.	.	48.8	48.6	49.6	50.2	49.6	49.5 [2]	50.3	.
J	.	.	43.2	42.2	43.0	43.7	42.8	43.3 [2]	44.0	.
K	.	.	47.8	48.8	50.5	49.8	50.2	50.7 [2]	51.0	.
L	.	.	42.4	42.6	43.8	43.6	43.0	42.3 [2]	42.2	.
M	.	.	40.9	41.3	41.2	41.9	41.7	41.1 [2]	41.2	.
N	.	.	44.1	45.5	45.7	44.1	43.8	43.5 [2]	45.1	.
O	.	.	40.6	39.0	40.3	41.8	40.0	39.8 [2]	39.4	.
P	.	.	50.9	52.8	52.4	51.7	52.7	52.1 [2]	51.2	.
Q	.	.	46.8	40.0	43.4	40.0	46.6	42.8 [2]	43.0	.

Women - Femmes - Mujeres
ISIC 3 - CITI 3 - CIIU 3

	1999	2000	2001	2002	2003	2004	2005	2006	2007	2008
Total	.	.	41.0	41.3	41.8	42.1	42.0	41.7 [2]	42.1	.
A-B	27.3	26.5	28.3	24.4	25.6	24.9	25.8	24.5 [2]	25.4	.
C-Q	.	.	42.4	42.8	42.7	43.1	43.0	42.3 [2]	.	.
A	27.2	26.3	24.7	24.9	25.5	24.8	25.9	24.6 [2]	25.3	.
B	30.2	32.4	29.8	28.0	27.8	27.5	25.4	22.5 [2]	25.9	.
C	.	.	33.5	35.5	37.9	34.5	33.5	31.4 [2]	39.2	.
D	.	.	41.2	41.5	41.9	42.1	42.9	42.5 [2]	42.8	.
E	.	.	42.7	42.3	43.3	42.7	43.5	41.9 [2]	45.1	.
F	.	.	43.5	44.8	45.1	45.0	44.8	42.5 [2]	44.2	.
G	.	.	50.5	51.4	51.7	52.5	51.3	51.3 [2]	51.7	.
H	.	.	49.6	50.5	50.8	52.0	51.3	50.3 [2]	50.7	.
I	.	.	42.3	44.3	43.7	44.4	46.5	45.0 [2]	45.9	.
J	.	.	42.0	41.3	41.8	42.7	41.6	42.1 [2]	42.5	.
K	.	.	42.5	43.0	44.3	44.1	41.7	43.9 [2]	43.9	.
L	.	.	36.3	36.3	37.0	36.5	36.6	35.3 [2]	36.3	.
M	.	.	39.6	39.8	39.4	39.9	39.7	39.5 [2]	39.8	.
N	.	.	39.7	40.7	39.6	40.7	39.4	40.8 [2]	41.9	.
O	.	.	34.0	34.0	32.8	34.0	31.6	33.7 [2]	33.7	.
P	.	.	55.5	55.1	55.2	55.0	56.1	55.1 [2]	54.6	.
Q	.	.	43.8	42.0	35.4	40.0	43.9	40.0 [2]	48.0	.

Philippines (BA) (a) Employees - Salariés - Asalariados

Total men and women - Total hommes et femmes - Total hombres y mujeres
ISIC 3 - CITI 3 - CIIU 3

	1999	2000	2001	2002	2003	2004	2005	2006	2007	2008
Total	44.9	45.4	44.0	44.1	44.3	44.3	45.0	44.3	44.4	44.8
A-B	37.8	38.4	36.5	35.9	36.8	36.5	36.9	35.9	36.9	36.6
C-Q	46.5	46.9	45.7	45.8	45.9	45.9	46.6	46.1	46.0	46.5
A	37.8	38.4	35.4	34.8	35.5	35.3	35.5	34.8	35.8	35.4
B	45.0	47.2	45.2	44.9	47.0	45.8	47.6	44.3	45.5	45.6
C	46.7	47.3	44.1	43.4	43.2	45.0	43.8	42.3	42.4	43.8
D	44.4	44.9	46.0	46.3	46.5	46.5	47.5	46.9	46.6	47.4
E	44.3	44.7	43.8	43.7	43.9	44.4	45.2	44.2	44.0	44.7
F	48.3	49.0	43.0	43.0	43.0	43.1	43.7	43.0	43.5	44.4
G	49.8	50.4	47.7	48.3	48.2	48.0	48.6	48.2	47.7	48.6
H	46.3	46.4	47.9	48.7	48.8	48.0	49.3	49.0	47.7	49.2
I	45.9	46.0	49.0	48.9	48.8	49.4	49.5	48.9	49.5	50.4
J	37.2	42.7	42.6	42.2	42.5	42.4	42.9	42.8	42.8	43.7
K	.	.	48.3	49.0	49.8	49.6	50.5	49.9	49.8	49.8
L	.	.	39.8	40.2	40.6	40.0	40.5	39.9	39.3	39.0
M	.	.	39.5	39.5	39.6	39.2	40.0	39.2	39.2	39.6
N	.	.	41.8	42.6	41.4	41.5	42.9	42.6	42.9	43.6
O	.	.	39.9	39.9	38.9	38.9	38.5	38.5	39.4	40.8
P	.	.	56.3	55.2	54.5	54.4	54.9	54.1	53.3	53.8
Q	.	.	45.0	41.3	41.1	43.1	44.6	47.3	42.8	42.7

Explanatory notes: see p. 721.   Notes explicatives: voir p. 723.   Notas explicativas: véase p. 725.

[1] Oct. of each year. [2] Methodology revised; data not strictly comparable.

[1] Oct. de chaque année. [2] Méthodologie révisée; les données ne sont pas strictement comparables.

[1] Oct. de cada año. [2] Metodología revisada; los datos no son estrictamente comparables.

By economic activity   Par activité économique   Por actividad económica

	Per week			Par semaine				Por semana		
	1999	2000	2001	2002	2003	2004	2005	2006	2007	2008

Philippines (BA) (a)   Employees - Salariés - Asalariados

Men - Hommes - Hombres
ISIC 3 - CITI 3 - CIIU 3

	1999	2000	2001	2002	2003	2004	2005	2006	2007	2008
Total	44.8	45.2	43.8	43.9	44.2	44.2	44.8	44.1	44.2	44.6
A-B	39.2	39.7	37.8	37.2	38.0	37.7	38.2	37.1	37.9	37.7
C-Q	46.4	46.8	45.5	45.7	46.0	46.0	46.5	46.0	46.0	46.7
A	39.2	39.7	36.5	36.0	36.5	36.3	36.5	35.8	36.6	36.3
B	45.1	47.2	45.2	44.9	47.4	46.3	48.1	44.9	45.8	46.1
C	47.0	47.6	44.3	43.8	43.9	45.2	44.1	42.8	42.7	43.9
D	44.7	45.1	46.2	46.4	46.8	46.8	47.5	46.9	46.7	47.6
E	44.2	44.7	44.0	43.8	44.1	45.0	45.5	44.6	44.2	45.0
F	47.7	48.2	43.0	43.0	43.0	43.1	43.7	43.0	43.5	44.4
G	50.1	50.7	46.9	47.5	47.7	47.5	48.1	47.6	47.2	48.1
H	48.3	48.5	47.5	47.4	47.7	46.6	48.0	48.0	46.5	48.1
I	44.9	45.1	49.2	49.2	49.1	49.7	49.8	49.2	49.8	50.9
J	36.3	42.2	43.5	43.2	43.5	43.1	43.7	43.4	43.3	44.5
K	.	.	50.1	51.2	51.6	51.9	52.9	52.6	52.3	51.8
L	.	.	42.1	42.7	43.0	42.4	42.9	42.7	41.9	41.6
M	.	.	40.7	40.5	41.2	40.4	41.3	40.3	40.5	40.7
N	.	.	45.5	46.8	45.2	46.0	45.9	45.0	45.2	45.8
O	.	.	41.1	41.8	41.1	41.1	40.6	40.5	40.6	41.3
P	.	.	53.6	52.7	52.9	52.0	52.1	52.2	51.0	52.0
Q	.	.	40.5	41.7	41.0	45.5	45.7	47.8	41.9	42.7

Women - Femmes - Mujeres
ISIC 3 - CITI 3 - CIIU 3

	1999	2000	2001	2002	2003	2004	2005	2006	2007	2008
Total	45.1	45.7	44.5	44.5	44.6	44.5	45.3	44.8	44.7	45.1
A-B	33.1	33.7	32.1	31.3	32.3	31.7	31.9	31.3	32.9	32.1
C-Q	46.6	47.0	45.9	46.0	45.9	45.8	46.7	46.1	45.9	46.4
A	33.1	33.7	31.9	31.1	32.2	31.7	31.9	31.4	32.8	32.1
B	42.5	47.3	45.5	45.3	36.5	32.2	33.7	26.5	38.0	32.3
C	46.2	47.0	41.4	38.7	33.7	41.3	36.5	33.9	38.3	42.1
D	42.3	43.7	45.9	46.2	46.1	46.0	47.5	46.9	46.4	47.0
E	45.5	46.3	42.9	43.0	43.2	41.6	43.5	42.0	43.5	42.6
F	49.1	49.9	43.6	46.1	43.8	44.2	45.8	43.8	43.6	45.3
G	45.7	46.0	48.8	49.3	49.0	48.6	49.4	49.0	48.3	49.2
H	43.6	43.8	48.3	49.9	49.9	49.4	50.7	49.9	48.8	50.2
I	46.6	46.8	45.8	45.1	45.4	45.4	46.3	46.3	46.2	46.6
J	55.3	44.4	42.0	41.6	41.8	41.9	42.2	42.3	42.4	43.2
K	.	.	45.1	45.1	45.6	44.4	45.0	44.7	45.0	45.9
L	.	.	36.0	36.2	36.5	35.9	36.3	35.4	35.3	34.9
M	.	.	39.0	39.2	39.1	38.8	39.5	38.8	38.8	39.2
N	.	.	40.4	40.9	40.3	40.0	41.9	41.8	42.1	42.7
O	.	.	38.8	38.0	36.5	36.1	35.9	35.8	37.6	40.0
P	.	.	56.8	55.6	54.8	54.8	55.5	54.5	53.7	54.2
Q	.	.	49.8	40.9	41.2	41.4	43.3	45.7	45.7	42.6

Philippines (DB) (a) [1]   Employees - Salariés - Asalariados

Total men and women - Total hommes et femmes - Total hombres y mujeres
ISIC 3 - CITI 3 - CIIU 3

	1999	2000	2001	2002	2003	2004	2005	2006	2007	2008
C	46.3	.	53.9	.	44.3	.	51.1	.	.	.
C-F	50.0	.	49.4	.	49.4	.	48.6	.	.	.
D	49.3	.	49.2	.	49.4	.	48.6	.	.	.
E	47.6	.	46.8	.	46.4	.	46.0	.	.	.
F	55.9	.	51.2	.	51.9	.	50.1	.	.	.

Men - Hommes - Hombres
ISIC 3 - CITI 3 - CIIU 3

	1999	2000	2001	2002	2003	2004	2005	2006	2007	2008
C	46.5	.	54.0	.	44.3	.	51.1	.	.	.
C-F	50.6	.	49.2	.	49.2	.	48.9	.	.	.
D	49.4	.	48.7	.	49.0	.	48.8	.	.	.
E	47.6	.	46.8	.	46.4	.	46.0	.	.	.
F	56.0	.	51.3	.	51.9	.	50.1	.	.	.

Women - Femmes - Mujeres
ISIC 3 - CITI 3 - CIIU 3

	1999	2000	2001	2002	2003	2004	2005	2006	2007	2008
C	40.3	.	49.7	.	43.2	.	52.8	.	.	.
C-F	49.2	.	49.6	.	49.8	.	48.3	.	.	.
D	49.2	.	49.6	.	49.8	.	48.3	.	.	.
E	47.4	.	47.3	.	45.6	.	45.4	.	.	.
F	46.8	.	44.6	.	51.8	.	47.1	.	.	.

Explanatory notes: see p. 721.   Notes explicatives: voir p. 723.   Notas explicativas: véase p. 725.

[1] Establishments with 20 or more persons employed.   [1] Etablissements occupant 20 personnes et plus.   [1] Establecimientos con 20 y más trabajadores.

4A

HOURS OF WORK	DURÉE DU TRAVAIL	HORAS DE TRABAJO
By economic activity	Par activité économique	Por actividad económica

	Per week				Par semaine				Por semana	
	1999	2000	2001	2002	2003	2004	2005	2006	2007	2008

Qatar (BA) (a) [1] — Employees - Salariés - Asalariados

Total men and women - Total hommes et femmes - Total hombres y mujeres
ISIC 3 - CITI 3 - CIIU 3

	1999	2000	2001	2002	2003	2004	2005	2006	2007	2008
Total								50	50	
C								45	44	
D								54	53	
E								42	42	
F								53	54	
G								54	53	
H								56	59	
I								47	47	
J								42	41	
K								52	51	
L								39	38	
M								37	37	
N								42	40	
O								46	44	
P								62	62	
Q								43	42	

Men - Hommes - Hombres
ISIC 3 - CITI 3 - CIIU 3

	1999	2000	2001	2002	2003	2004	2005	2006	2007	2008
Total								50	50	
A									55	
B									51	
C								46	44	
D								55	53	
E								42	42	
F								53	54	
G								54	54	
H								56	59	
I								48	48	
J								42	41	
K								52	52	
L								40	38	
M								39	38	
N								43	41	
O								48	44	
P								60	61	
Q								44	42	

Women - Femmes - Mujeres
ISIC 3 - CITI 3 - CIIU 3

	1999	2000	2001	2002	2003	2004	2005	2006	2007	2008
Total								52	52	
C								43	40	
D								46	44	
E								39	39	
F								47	47	
G								50	49	
H								53	50	
I								42	44	
J								40	40	
K								47	45	
L								37	36	
M								36	36	
N								41	39	
O								41	43	
P								64	63	
Q								39	41	

Singapore (CA) (b) — Employees - Salariés - Asalariados

Total men and women - Total hommes et femmes - Total hombres y mujeres
ISIC 3 - CITI 3 - CIIU 3

	1999	2000	2001	2002	2003	2004	2005	2006	2007	2008
Total	46.8	47.0	46.2	46.0	46.0	46.3	46.5	46.2 [2]	46.3	
A-B,D-E,X		46.5	47.4	46.2	45.8	46.5	46.7	45.3 [2]	45.2	
C	57.3	52.1	. [3]		55.7			. [2]		
D		50.0	48.7	49.0	49.2	49.8	50.2	50.5 [2]	50.6	
E	44.7	46.0	. [3]	45.0	44.3	.	44.3	. [2]		
F		51.5	50.9	50.6	51.1	51.7	51.9	51.9 [2]	52.2	
G		43.7	43.3	43.1	43.1	43.4	43.5	43.2 [2]	43.5	
H		40.9	40.3	38.9	38.4	38.4	38.6	38.9 [2]	39.8	
I [4]		46.7	46.2	45.8	45.7	45.7	45.9	45.9 [2]	45.6	
64		42.7	42.4	42.3	42.1	42.0	42.0	41.9 [2]	41.9	
J		43.2	43.0	42.6	42.6	42.9	42.8	42.3 [2]	42.0	
K		45.0	44.5	44.3	44.8	44.7	45.2	44.2 [2]	44.4	
74		51.5	51.2	50.4	50.1	50.3	50.9	50.8 [2]	49.5	
73		43.9	43.4	43.1	43.2	43.5	43.5	44.0 [2]	44.0	
L,M		38.1	37.9	37.6	38.1	37.9	39.0	41.4 [2]	41.5	
N		41.9	41.8	41.9	41.8	41.9	42.3	42.1 [2]	42.1	
O		43.5	43.7	43.2	43.0	43.2	43.3	43.0 [2]	42.7	
Q	42.8	42.8						. [2]		

Explanatory notes: see p. 721.   Notes explicatives: voir p. 723.   Notas explicativas: véase p. 725.

[1] October. [2] Prior to 2006: establishments with 25 or more persons in the private sector only. [3] Confidential. [4] Excl. communications.

[1] Octobre. [2] Avant 2006: établissements occupant 25 personnes et plus dans le secteur privé seulement. [3] Confidentiel. [4] Non compris les communications.

[1] Octubre. [2] Antes de 2006: establecimientos con 25 o más personas del sector privado solo. [3] Confidencial. [4] Excl. las comunicaciones.

By economic activity — Par activité économique — Por actividad económica

	Per week				Par semaine			Por semana		
	1999	2000	2001	2002	2003	2004	2005	2006	2007	2008

Singapore (DA) (b) [1]
Employees - Salariés - Asalariados

Total men and women - Total hommes et femmes - Total hombres y mujeres
ISIC 4 - CITI 4 - CIIU 4

Total	.	47.0	46.2	46.0	46.0	46.3	46.5	46.2 [2]	46.3	46.3
A,B,D,E	.	46.5	47.4	46.2	45.8	46.5	46.7	45.3 [2]	45.2	45.3
C	.	50.0	48.7	49.0	49.2	49.8	50.2	50.5 [2]	50.6	50.2
F	.	51.5	50.9	50.6	51.1	51.7	51.9	51.9 [2]	52.2	52.4
G	.	43.7	43.3	43.1	43.1	43.4	43.5	43.2 [2]	43.5	43.8
H	.	46.7	46.2	45.8	45.7	45.7	45.9	45.9 [2]	45.6	46.0
I	.	40.9	40.3	38.9	38.4	38.4	38.6	38.9 [2]	39.8	41.2
J	.	42.7	42.4	42.3	42.1	42.0	42.0	41.9 [2]	41.9	41.8
K	.	43.2	43.0	42.6	42.6	42.9	42.8	42.3 [2]	42.0	41.7
L	.	45.0	44.5	44.3	44.8	44.7	45.2	44.2 [2]	44.4	44.3
M	.	43.9	43.4	43.1	43.2	43.5	43.5	44.0 [2]	44.0	44.1
N	.	51.5	51.2	50.4	50.1	50.3	50.9	50.8 [2]	49.5	48.8
O-P	.	38.2	37.9	37.6	38.1	37.9	39.0	41.4 [2]	41.5	41.4
Q	.	41.9	41.8	41.9	41.8	41.9	42.3	42.1 [2]	42.1	41.9
R-U	.	43.5	43.7	43.2	43.0	43.2	43.3	43.0 [2]	42.7	43.0

Sri Lanka (DA) (b) [3]
Wage earners - Ouvriers - Obreros

Total men and women - Total hommes et femmes - Total hombres y mujeres
ISIC 2 - CITI 2 - CIIU 2

Total [4]	49.1	50.3	50.3	46.5	47.8	47.0	46.9	47.1	49.9	47.7
2-9 [4]	53.1	52.9	54.2	50.8	51.8	51.5	51.7	51.0	54.2	50.2
1	40.3	44.9	43.0	39.9	40.4	38.6	39.5	41.3	42.5	44.0
3	53.8	53.0	53.7	49.0	51.1	50.7	49.6	49.2	53.0	48.9
5	42.2	46.0	51.6	48.1	42.4	42.5	42.6	52.8	63.3	53.6
6	48.6	50.8	48.9	52.6	54.6	63.7	60.6	55.5	55.8	56.1
7 [5]	49.0	57.7	51.3	46.1	45.8	46.3	49.8	47.2	48.4	49.9

Men - Hommes - Hombres
ISIC 2 - CITI 2 - CIIU 2

Total [4]	49.5	51.7	50.5	46.8	48.3	47.1	46.3	49.1	49.3	49.7
2-9	53.2	53.9	54.4	50.9	52.0	51.6	51.8	51.4	54.1	52.9
1	41.1	47.6	43.1	40.2	41.4	38.8	37.3	46.0	40.7	44.6
3	54.2	53.5	54.1	49.2	51.4	50.8	49.9	49.9	53.1	51.6
5	42.2	46.0	51.6	48.1	42.4	42.5	42.6	52.8	63.3	56.0
6	48.6	50.8	48.9	52.6	54.6	63.7	60.6	55.5	55.8	57.8
7	49.0	57.7	51.3	46.1	45.9	46.3	49.8	47.2	48.4	47.1

Women - Femmes - Mujeres
ISIC 2 - CITI 2 - CIIU 2

Total [4]	47.4	48.1	48.5	43.6	45.7	45.5	46.9	44.9	50.5	45.8
2-9 [4]	51.4	51.9	52.2	47.9	49.7	49.7	51.7	49.2	54.3	47.8
1	39.6	42.1	42.8	38.7	39.5	38.4	41.7	37.2	44.2	43.5
3	51.3	50.3	50.5	44.3	48.0	48.4	48.8	48.4	52.9	46.2
5	42.2	49.0	51.6	48.1	42.4	42.5	42.6	.	.	51.2
6	48.6	49.1	48.9	52.5	54.6	63.7	60.6	55.5	55.8	54.4

Taiwan, China (DA) (a) [6]
Employees - Salariés - Asalariados

Total men and women - Total hommes et femmes - Total hombres y mujeres
ISIC 2 - CITI 2 - CIIU 2 / ISIC 3 - CITI 3 - CIIU 3

Total	190.2	190.1	180.3	181.4	181.2	183.5	181.9	180.9	180.5	179.7	C-Q
2	189.6	189.2	186.9	188.6	186.2	184.3	181.0	182.7	184.0	184.2	C
3	199.1	198.7	184.4	187.6	188.3	190.6	188.8	187.3	187.3	184.7	D
4	181.7	181.2	171.6	171.3	170.3	172.2	171.1	171.6	171.3	172.7	E [7]
5	185.5	187.8	181.7	176.5	175.6	177.3	177.7	178.1	176.9	176.4	F
6	183.4	183.2	177.8	177.1	176.0	180.1	177.6	175.3	174.8	175.9	G
7	188.5	187.7	178.4	178.7	177.1	169.2	174.0	173.6	172.5	172.3	H
8 [8]	175.7	174.2	167.0	169.2	168.7	182.5	180.8	179.9	179.4	179.1	I [9]
9	191.5	190.4	184.3	184.5	.	169.1	168.0	168.6	167.1	167.5	J
						185.4	186.1	182.6	177.9	180.3	K [8]
						176.3	176.0	175.3	175.1	174.4	N
						185.2	184.5	186.3	184.7	181.4	92
						199.9	199.5	201.2	201.5	200.0	93

Explanatory notes: see p. 721.
[1] From 2006: all establishments in the public sector and those with 25 or more persons employed in the private sector. [2] Before 2006: excl. public sector. [3] March and Sep. of each year. [4] Excl. major divisions 4, 8 and 9. [5] Excl. storage and communication. [6] Per month. [7] Excl. water supply. [8] Excl. business services. [9] Excl. communications.

Notes explicatives: voir p. 723.
[1] A partir de 2006: établissements du secteur public et ceux occupant 25 personnes ou plus dans le secteur privé. [2] Avant 2006: non compris le secteur public. [3] Mars et sept. de chaque année. [4] Non compris les branches 4, 8 et 9. [5] Non compris les entrepôts et communications. [6] Par mois. [7] Non compris l'approvisionnement de l'eau. [8] Non compris les services aux entreprises. [9] Non compris les communications.

Notas explicativas: véase p. 725.
[1] Desde 2006: establecimientos del sector público y los que emplean 25 o más trabajadores en el sector privado. [2] Antes de 2006: excl. el sector público. [3] Marzo y sept. de cada año. [4] Excl. las grandes divisiones 4, 8 y 9. [5] Excl. almacenaje y comunicaciones. [6] Por mes. [7] Excl. el suministro del agua. [8] Excl. servicios para las empresas. [9] Excl. las comunicaciones.

4A | HOURS OF WORK | DURÉE DU TRAVAIL | HORAS DE TRABAJO

By economic activity — Par activité économique — Por actividad económica

	Per week — Par semaine — Por semana									
	1999	2000	2001	2002	2003	2004	2005	2006	2007	2008

Taiwan, China (DA) (a) [1] — Employees - Salariés - Asalariados

Men - Hommes - Hombres
ISIC 3 - CITI 3 - CIIU 3

	1999	2000	2001	2002	2003	2004	2005	2006	2007	2008
C-Q	.	.	.	.	.	185.7	183.8	183.0	182.4	181.9
C	.	.	.	.	.	184.9	181.7	183.1	184.5	185.4
D	.	.	.	.	.	192.9	190.6	189.4	189.4	186.8
E [2]	.	.	.	.	.	172.5	171.4	171.9	171.7	173.2
F	.	.	.	.	.	178.0	178.2	178.9	177.9	177.8
G	.	.	.	.	.	180.4	177.4	174.9	174.4	176.6
H	.	.	.	.	.	168.9	172.7	173.6	172.9	172.4
I [3]	.	.	.	.	.	186.1	184.4	183.6	182.7	182.3
J	.	.	.	.	.	171.4	169.8	169.7	167.9	168.0
K [4]	.	.	.	.	.	188.4	191.2	187.7	181.6	185.3
N	.	.	.	.	.	176.0	176.6	175.7	174.5	173.5
92	.	.	.	.	.	186.3	183.9	186.0	184.3	180.9
93	.	.	.	.	.	195.2	195.6	196.2	195.5	193.7

Women - Femmes - Mujeres
ISIC 3 - CITI 3 - CIIU 3

	1999	2000	2001	2002	2003	2004	2005	2006	2007	2008
C-Q	.	.	.	.	.	180.9	179.6	178.5	178.0	177.1
C	.	.	.	.	.	181.8	178.2	181.0	182.3	180.0
D	.	.	.	.	.	187.5	186.2	184.7	184.5	181.9
E [2]	.	.	.	.	.	169.7	168.6	169.3	169.0	169.2
F	.	.	.	.	.	173.3	174.7	173.6	171.7	169.9
G	.	.	.	.	.	179.8	177.8	175.8	175.2	175.3
H	.	.	.	.	.	169.4	174.9	173.7	172.2	172.3
I [3]	.	.	.	.	.	173.3	172.2	171.5	171.3	171.5
J	.	.	.	.	.	167.7	166.8	167.8	166.7	167.1
K [4]	.	.	.	.	.	181.7	179.9	176.8	173.8	175.0
N	.	.	.	.	.	176.3	175.9	175.1	175.2	174.7
92	.	.	.	.	.	184.1	185.0	186.6	185.2	182.0
93	.	.	.	.	.	203.4	202.3	204.6	205.6	204.2

West Bank and Gaza Strip (BA) (a) [5] — Employees - Salariés - Asalariados

Total men and women - Total hommes et femmes - Total hombres y mujeres
ISIC 3 - CITI 3 - CIIU 3

	1999	2000	2001	2002	2003	2004	2005	2006	2007	2008
Total	44.2	43.1	42.2	41.1	42.0	42.9	42.3	41.6	41.3	42.2
A-B	44.5	42.6	38.9	38.9	40.6	41.7	41.4	39.1	34.9	37.1
C-Q	44.1	43.1	42.2	41.2	42.1	43.0	42.4	41.7	41.6	42.4
C	51.1	45.9	44.8	42.0	49.1	48.2	45.5	44.6	47.6	38.4
D	46.2	45.7	43.6	42.4	44.2	45.3	45.1	44.7	43.8	44.1
E	46.1	43.7	44.3	42.5	42.2	45.5	43.3	43.3	45.8	44.8
F	43.6	42.2	40.5	39.7	41.5	42.0	40.9	39.0	38.7	39.0
G	48.4	47.7	46.2	44.1	47.9	50.3	50.1	49.6	48.7	47.7
H	48.4	47.4	46.9	46.4	47.6	49.0	48.9	47.0	46.0	48.0
I	49.8	50.8	49.8	44.8	47.6	48.4	47.4	46.0	46.1	47.0
J	46.5	43.5	42.5	40.4	42.3	42.5	41.6	42.8	41.6	40.2
K	45.7	44.8	43.3	43.8	42.7	46.0	44.3	43.1	44.4	45.2
L	44.2	43.1	42.9	42.4	42.7	42.8	42.0	41.8	43.2	44.2
M	36.4	35.5	36.0	36.0	34.9	35.3	34.9	34.0	33.4	36.0
N	43.4	42.8	43.3	42.2	42.4	42.2	41.6	41.4	41.0	43.2
O	43.8	43.4	43.1	41.4	42.0	44.5	42.7	40.8	41.1	43.0
P	38.2	42.4	51.7	48.5	59.4	43.7	40.0	.	32.7	.
Q	40.9	43.1	42.3	41.0	41.3	41.7	40.1	40.1	40.1	41.5

Men - Hommes - Hombres
ISIC 3 - CITI 3 - CIIU 3

	1999	2000	2001	2002	2003	2004	2005	2006	2007	2008
Total	44.8	43.7	42.7	41.7	42.8	43.8	37.4	42.4	42.4	43.1
A-B	44.7	42.8	38.5	38.6	40.6	41.7	41.4	38.8	34.8	37.0
C-Q	44.8	43.7	42.9	41.8	42.9	43.9	43.3	42.5	42.7	43.4
C	51.5	45.9	44.8	42.0	49.1	48.2	45.5	44.6	47.6	38.7
D	46.5	45.9	43.8	42.5	44.2	45.4	45.2	44.9	44.3	44.2
E	46.1	43.7	44.8	42.5	42.7	45.5	43.5	43.6	45.8	44.9
F	43.6	42.2	40.4	39.7	41.5	42.0	40.9	39.0	38.7	39.0
G	48.5	47.9	46.6	44.3	48.2	50.9	50.6	49.9	49.0	47.9
H	48.7	47.5	47.1	46.4	47.7	49.1	49.1	47.2	46.5	48.2
I	50.0	51.0	50.0	44.9	47.9	48.9	47.7	46.3	46.4	47.3
J	47.0	44.0	43.2	41.6	43.7	42.8	42.1	43.2	42.2	40.8
K	47.3	46.3	43.6	44.3	43.3	46.4	45.0	44.6	46.1	46.8
L	44.5	43.4	43.2	42.6	43.0	43.1	42.2	42.1	43.8	44.8
M	37.8	36.5	37.0	37.2	36.0	36.5	36.1	34.9	34.5	36.9
N	43.9	43.7	44.3	43.4	43.7	43.2	43.1	43.4	43.1	44.7
O	44.4	44.2	43.7	41.9	42.4	45.5	44.1	41.7	42.2	44.2
P	28.7	42.7	42.3	44.0	41.5	55.5	.	.	38.4	.
Q	41.6	44.4	42.3	41.3	40.8	41.9	41.1	40.8	40.6	42.0

Explanatory notes: see p. 721.

[1] Per month. [2] Excl. water supply. [3] Excl. communications. [4] Excl. business services. [5] Persons aged 15 years and over.

Notes explicatives: voir p. 723.

[1] Par mois. [2] Non compris l'approvisionnement de l'eau. [3] Non compris les communications. [4] Non compris les services aux entreprises. [5] Personnes âgées de 15 ans et plus.

Notas explicativas: véase p. 725.

[1] Por mes. [2] Excl. el suministro del agua. [3] Excl. las comunicaciones. [4] Excl. servicios para las empresas. [5] Personas de 15 años y más.

	Per week			Par semaine			Por semana			
	1999	2000	2001	2002	2003	2004	2005	2006	2007	2008

West Bank and Gaza Strip (BA) (a) [1]   Employees - Salariés - Asalariados

Women - Femmes - Mujeres
ISIC 3 - CITI 3 - CIIU 3

	1999	2000	2001	2002	2003	2004	2005	2006	2007	2008
Total	39.2	38.9	38.8	37.8	37.8	38.3	43.2	37.1	35.7	38.2
A-B	40.5	37.8	42.7	42.6	41.2	41.7	42.3	44.1	37.6	40.1
C-Q	39.2	38.8	38.7	37.7	37.7	38.3	37.4	36.9	35.7	38.1
C	24.0		.							
D	43.8	44.2	42.8	42.0	44.3	44.1	43.8	43.8	41.3	43.3
E	.		39.8	42.1	38.4	.	39.2	37.6	.	.
F	41.6	41.4	46.8	47.1	43.1	45.4	41.3	36.1	38.1	.
G	46.0	43.3	41.2	40.4	43.0	43.5	44.2	45.9	44.7	44.9
H	40.3	44.9	39.9	48.0	39.7	45.7	37.7	36.7	31.2	.
I	45.8	47.1	43.4	40.8	39.9	40.8	41.3	42.0	37.4	.
J	45.1	42.2	41.5	37.5	37.4	41.6	40.0	41.6	39.5	38.6
K	40.9	41.3	42.7	41.4	41.3	45.3	42.1	39.4	38.9	40.0
L	40.4	39.9	40.3	40.2	39.4	39.5	38.5	38.4	36.0	38.0
M	34.6	34.2	34.9	34.6	33.7	33.9	33.7	33.0	32.2	35.1
N	42.7	41.4	41.5	40.1	40.2	40.5	39.4	38.4	37.1	41.0
O	39.1	39.9	40.9	38.2	40.8	41.2	37.4	36.6	36.7	38.9
P	48.0	42.2	52.8	51.1	65.6	39.1	40.0	.	31.1	.
Q	38.3	39.9	42.3	39.8	43.1	40.9	37.6	37.9	39.0	40.3

EUROPE-EUROPE-EUROPA

Albania (DB) (a) [2]   Wage earners - Ouvriers - Obreros

Total men and women - Total hommes et femmes - Total hombres y mujeres
ISIC 3 - CITI 3 - CIIU 3

	1999	2000	2001	2002	2003	2004	2005	2006	2007	2008
C-D	139.2	139.2	138.5	138.1	138.5	139.8	.	.	.	.

Austria (BA) (a)   Employees - Salariés - Asalariados

Total men and women - Total hommes et femmes - Total hombres y mujeres
ISIC 3 - CITI 3 - CIIU 3

	1999	2000	2001	2002	2003	2004	2005	2006	2007	2008
Total	35.6	35.5	35.3	35.3	36.5	35.8	34.9	34.8	34.6	34.3
A-B	38.2	38.1	38.7	37.7	37.9	50.0	47.1	47.4	44.7	42.9
C-Q	.	.	.	35.4	35.8	34.9	34.1	34.1	34.0	33.8
A	.	.	.	.	.	50.1	47.1	47.4	44.7	42.9
B	.	.	.	.	.	.	.	.	.	.
C	35.6	36.6	37.0	37.6	37.5	37.3	36.0	39.1	37.1	37.5
D	36.7	36.6	36.5	36.8	36.9	36.0	35.2	35.6	35.6	35.5
E	36.6	36.8	37.4	37.3	35.7	35.7	34.1	33.9	34.3	35.0
F	36.9	37.1	36.8	37.2	37.6	36.1	35.7	36.1	36.1	35.9
G	34.1	33.9	33.8	33.8	34.7	34.4	33.0	33.2	33.2	33.1
H	36.5	36.2	35.4	35.7	38.2	37.9	37.4	37.7	37.4	36.8
I	38.0	38.0	38.0	37.5	38.1	38.4	37.8	37.2	37.6	36.8
J	35.8	35.7	35.2	.	35.4	34.8	34.2	34.4	33.6	34.5
K	34.5	34.2	34.0	34.0	36.0	34.4	33.5	33.6	33.1	33.3
L	36.9	36.5	36.5	36.7	36.1	35.8	34.7	34.7	34.6	34.5
M	32.0	32.5	32.9	33.1	33.2	30.3	29.2	28.2	27.9	29.0
N	34.0	33.8	33.6	33.3	33.1	32.5	31.9	30.8	30.5	30.5
O	35.0	34.5	34.4	34.4	34.6	34.2	32.6	31.9	32.0	31.4
P	24.6	24.0	.	21.6	20.3	19.4	19.6	17.4	20.1	15.1
Q	39.3	36.9	39.3	37.8	36.1	37.5	37.9	37.6	37.0	36.9

Men - Hommes - Hombres
ISIC 3 - CITI 3 - CIIU 3

	1999	2000	2001	2002	2003	2004	2005	2006	2007	2008
Total	38.4	38.3	38.3	38.4	39.6	39.6	38.8	38.9	38.6	38.3
A-B	39.8	39.9	40.9	40.1	39.3	53.3	50.7	50.8	48.1	46.3
C-Q	.	.	.	38.4	39.0	38.8	38.1	38.2	38.1	37.9
A	.	.	.	.	39.3	53.4	50.7	50.8	48.1	46.2
B	.	.	.	.	33.2	.	.	.	.	.
C	36.4	38.7	38.3	38.5	38.9	38.4	36.8	39.6	37.9	39.6
D	37.8	37.7	37.6	38.0	38.1	37.7	36.9	37.4	37.4	37.2
E	37.4	37.6	38.1	37.6	36.2	36.5	35.4	35.2	35.3	35.9
F	37.4	37.6	37.6	37.8	38.2	37.0	36.8	37.2	37.2	37.3
G	38.8	38.3	38.5	38.7	39.7	39.7	38.9	39.0	38.4	38.4
H	40.5	40.0	40.2	40.0	42.9	44.5	43.6	43.3	43.6	42.3
I	39.4	39.7	39.4	38.9	39.9	40.5	39.9	39.0	40.0	38.8
J	39.9	39.5	39.0	39.4	39.2	38.6	38.8	38.9	38.2	38.8
K	39.4	39.3	39.1	39.0	41.0	40.7	39.6	39.8	38.7	38.1
L	39.4	38.9	39.2	39.1	39.0	39.2	38.2	38.7	38.7	38.4
M	35.4	36.5	35.9	36.5	36.5	34.2	33.1	32.6	32.7	33.0
N	39.4	39.3	38.9	39.2	40.0	40.4	39.4	38.6	37.6	38.0
O	39.0	38.8	38.9	39.4	38.3	38.9	37.9	36.8	37.1	36.8
P	32.8	29.7	27.5	27.1	27.8	43.8	39.1	24.7	26.0	15.1
Q	40.3	38.8	40.6	39.4	37.6	40.2	40.2	38.5	41.2	40.9

Explanatory notes: see p. 721.

[1] Persons aged 15 years and over. [2] Per month.

Notes explicatives: voir p. 723.

[1] Personnes âgées de 15 ans et plus. [2] Par mois.

Notas explicativas: véase p. 725.

[1] Personas de 15 años y más. [2] Por mes.

HOURS OF WORK — DURÉE DU TRAVAIL — HORAS DE TRABAJO

By economic activity — Par activité économique — Por actividad económica

	Per week				Par semaine				Por semana		
	1999	2000	2001	2002	2003	2004	2005	2006	2007	2008	

Austria (BA) (a) — Employees - Salariés - Asalariados

Women - Femmes - Mujeres
ISIC 3 - CITI 3 - CIIU 3

	1999	2000	2001	2002	2003	2004	2005	2006	2007	2008
Total	31.7	31.6	31.5	31.5	32.5	30.9	29.9	29.8	29.5	29.4
A-B	35.0	34.0	34.7	33.7	35.3	46.2	43.2	43.4	40.7	38.8
C-Q				31.4	31.6	29.9	29.1	28.9	28.8	28.9
A					35.3	46.2	42.9	43.4	40.7	38.9
B										
C	28.6	28.0	27.8	28.3	28.4	27.9	31.6	35.9	32.2	30.2
D	33.3	33.2	33.5	33.1	33.1	31.0	30.1	30.3	30.1	30.2
E	30.8	32.5	33.1	35.1	32.0	31.2	27.8	27.9	30.4	31.1
F	30.0	29.9	28.6	29.3	29.2	28.4	27.2	27.1	27.7	26.6
G	30.2	30.3	30.1	30.0	30.5	29.4	28.0	28.3	28.4	28.4
H	34.3	34.2	32.9	33.5	35.5	33.9	33.5	34.6	33.9	33.6
I	32.8	32.3	33.1	32.9	32.5	31.6	31.4	31.4	31.0	30.3
J	31.2	31.5	31.2	31.8	31.6	30.8	29.3	29.5	28.6	30.1
K	30.7	30.0	29.9	30.1	30.4	27.9	27.3	27.0	27.0	27.8
L	33.0	32.9	32.4	33.1	32.1	30.8	29.8	29.3	29.1	29.4
M	30.4	30.6	31.4	31.6	31.8	28.4	27.4	26.3	26.0	27.2
N	32.5	32.0	32.0	31.6	30.9	29.9	29.2	28.4	28.3	28.2
O	31.8	31.3	30.9	30.6	31.7	30.1	28.2	28.1	27.9	27.1
P	24.3	23.9	22.6	21.5	20.1	18.4	18.8	17.2	19.7	15.1
Q	38.0	35.3	38.5	36.3	34.9	34.2	35.4	36.5	31.9	34.7

Austria (DB) (a) [1] — Employees - Salariés - Asalariados

Total men and women - Total hommes et femmes - Total hombres y mujeres
ISIC 3 - CITI 3 - CIIU 3 — ISIC 4 - CITI 4 - CIIU 4

	1999	2000	2001	2002	2003	2004	2005	2006	2007	2008	
C-D	140.4	140.2	139.6	138.9	139.4	140.5	139.7	140.0 |	.	138.9	B-C
C-F	139.9	139.8	139.2	138.8	139.5	140.6	139.9	140.1 |	.	139.6	B-F
E	140.3	140.6	141.4	140.5	138.7	138.9	138.4	138.9 |	.	137.2	D
F	138.4	138.4	137.5	137.9	139.9	140.9	140.6	140.5 |	.	141.3	E
								|	.	141.9	F

Austria (DB) (b) [1] — Employees - Salariés - Asalariados

Total men and women - Total hommes et femmes - Total hombres y mujeres
ISIC 3 - CITI 3 - CIIU 3 — ISIC 4 - CITI 4 - CIIU 4

	1999	2000	2001	2002	2003	2004	2005	2006	2007	2008	
C-D	167.7	167.4	167.2	166.2	165.7	166.3	165.7	165.4 |	.	165.8	B-C
C-F	167.6	167.5	167.4	166.7	166.1	166.7	166.0	165.6 |	.	166.0	B-F
E	170.4	171.5	171.9	171.8	170.0	170.7	169.4	170.0 |	.	169.1	D
F	167.1	167.2	167.3	167.3	166.5	167.4	166.4	165.4 |	.	167.8	E
								|	.	166.2	F

Belarus (D) (a) [1] — Employees - Salariés - Asalariados

Total men and women - Total hommes et femmes - Total hombres y mujeres
ISIC 3 - CITI 3 - CIIU 3

	1999	2000	2001	2002	2003	2004	2005	2006	2007	2008
Total	159	157	156	155	156	160	159	159	158	158
A-B	176	175	175	175	176	179	178	178	176	177
C-Q	155	153	153	152	153	156	155	155	155	155

Belgique (DA) (b) [2] — Employees - Salariés - Asalariados

Total men and women - Total hommes et femmes - Total hombres y mujeres
ISIC 3 - CITI 3 - CIIU 3

	1999	2000	2001	2002	2003	2004	2005	2006	2007	2008
C	35.2	35.6	37.4	37.6	36.7	33.6	32.8	36.1	35.6	.
D	34.4	35.7	36.6	37.1	36.2	34.0	33.2	35.3	35.0	.
E	35.5	37.2	38.4	38.8	38.4	35.8	35.1	36.9	32.8	.
F	35.1	34.5	37.2	36.6	36.6	34.7	33.1	35.5	34.8	.
G	32.8	33.3	34.0	34.3	34.0	32.3	31.5	32.8	32.2	.
H	24.1	24.5	26.0	26.6	24.6	24.2	24.0	26.2	25.0	.
I	36.0	35.7	37.9	38.6	37.5	35.5	34.0	35.5	34.9	.
J	33.4	34.9	36.1	35.8	35.5	32.6	32.5	33.6	33.6	.
K	32.0	33.8	34.5	35.4	34.8	32.4	31.7	32.8	31.5	.
M								20.9		.
N								29.7		.
O								32.4		.

Explanatory notes: see p. 721.
[1] Per month. [2] Oct. of each year.

Notes explicatives: voir p. 723.
[1] Par mois. [2] Oct. de chaque année.

Notas explicativas: véase p. 725.
[1] Por mes. [2] Oct. de cada año.

HOURS OF WORK

By economic activity

DURÉE DU TRAVAIL

Par activité économique

HORAS DE TRABAJO

Por actividad económica

4A

	Per week / Par semaine / Por semana									
	1999	2000	2001	2002	2003	2004	2005	2006	2007	2008

Belgique (DA) (b) [1] Employees - Salariés - Asalariados

Men - Hommes - Hombres
ISIC 3 - CITI 3 - CIIU 3

	1999	2000	2001	2002	2003	2004	2005	2006	2007	2008
C	35.5	35.7	37.8	37.7	36.6	33.9	32.9	36.2	35.5	.
D	35.1	36.4	37.3	37.8	36.9	34.8	33.8	36.1	35.8	.
E	36.0	37.7	39.1	39.2	38.9	36.1	35.6	37.3	32.9	.
F	35.2	34.6	37.3	36.7	36.8	34.9	33.2	35.6	35.0	.
G	35.1	35.7	37.1	37.1	36.5	34.3	33.9	35.2	34.7	.
H	25.3	25.8	27.3	28.1	25.5	25.7	25.1	28.0	27.1	.
I	36.8	36.3	38.7	39.3	38.3	36.5	34.7	36.1	35.6	.
J	34.9	36.2	37.7	37.7	37.2	34.1	33.9	35.2	35.3	.
K	34.3	36.2	37.0	36.8	36.4	34.3	33.5	34.9	34.2	.
M	.	.	.	.	.	.	.	22.0	.	.
N	.	.	.	.	.	.	.	33.8	.	.
O	.	.	.	.	.	.	.	34.4	.	.

Women - Femmes - Mujeres
ISIC 3 - CITI 3 - CIIU 3

	1999	2000	2001	2002	2003	2004	2005	2006	2007	2008
C	31.4	33.4	33.2	36.6	37.3	30.8	30.6	35.6	36.3	.
D	31.8	33.1	34.0	34.7	33.7	31.0	31.0	32.6	32.4	.
E	32.9	35.0	35.3	37.0	36.8	34.8	33.6	35.5	32.4	.
F	32.6	32.9	34.3	34.8	34.6	31.5	32.2	33.9	32.6	.
G	29.8	30.4	30.5	31.2	31.1	29.8	28.8	29.8	29.1	.
H	23.0	23.4	24.8	25.2	23.8	22.9	23.0	24.3	23.1	.
I	33.3	33.9	35.4	36.2	35.0	32.2	32.1	33.6	32.9	.
J	31.6	33.5	34.4	33.9	33.6	30.9	30.8	31.8	32.0	.
K	29.2	31.0	32.3	33.5	33.4	29.8	29.6	29.9	28.4	.
M	.	.	.	.	.	.	.	20.3	.	.
N	.	.	.	.	.	.	.	28.7	.	.
O	.	.	.	.	.	.	.	30.3	.	.

Belgique (DA) (b) [1][2] Employees - Salariés - Asalariados

Total men and women - Total hommes et femmes - Total hombres y mujeres
ISIC 3 - CITI 3 - CIIU 3

	1999	2000	2001	2002	2003	2004	2005	2006	2007	2008
C-Q	.	.	.	.	.	.	.	.	.	.
C	37.0	35.8	36.7	36.6	35.8	35.5	35.8	36.6	36.3	.
D	36.6	36.5	35.9	36.5	35.8	36.7	36.5	36.4	36.5	.
E	37.7	37.8	37.5	37.6	37.2	38.1	38.2	37.4	33.2	.
F	36.8	34.8	36.2	35.6	35.6	36.8	35.8	35.9	35.6	.
G	37.6	36.2	36.3	36.7	34.9	37.3	37.5	36.3	36.2	.
H	32.7	34.4	34.9	35.6	33.5	35.1	34.8	33.0	34.2	.
I	39.1	37.2	37.6	38.4	37.6	39.3	38.5	37.3	37.4	.
J	36.5	36.4	36.1	36.2	36.0	36.1	37.1	36.0	36.0	.
K	37.1	37.1	37.2	36.9	36.3	37.2	37.3	36.1	35.2	.
M	.	.	.	.	.	.	.	27.6	.	.
N	.	.	.	.	.	.	.	36.2	.	.
O	.	.	.	.	.	.	.	36.2	.	.

Men - Hommes - Hombres
ISIC 3 - CITI 3 - CIIU 3

	1999	2000	2001	2002	2003	2004	2005	2006	2007	2008
C-Q	.	.	.	.	.	.	.	.	.	.
C	36.9	35.8	36.6	36.6	35.6	35.3	35.8	36.4	36.2	.
D	36.9	36.7	36.1	36.6	35.9	36.9	36.7	36.6	36.7	.
E	37.8	37.9	37.6	37.7	37.4	38.1	38.4	37.6	33.1	.
F	36.8	34.7	36.1	35.5	35.6	36.7	35.6	35.8	35.5	.
G	37.8	36.7	36.6	36.7	35.9	37.3	37.7	36.6	36.5	.
H	33.9	34.9	35.1	36.0	33.3	35.6	35.2	34.1	34.5	.
I	39.4	37.3	37.9	38.7	37.8	39.7	38.7	37.4	37.6	.
J	36.8	36.5	36.3	36.4	36.2	36.3	37.3	36.3	36.2	.
K	37.3	37.3	37.3	36.9	36.2	37.2	37.6	36.4	35.6	.
M	.	.	.	.	.	.	.	36.6	.	.
N	.	.	.	.	.	.	.	36.9	.	.
O	.	.	.	.	.	.	.	36.4	.	.

Women - Femmes - Mujeres
ISIC 3 - CITI 3 - CIIU 3

	1999	2000	2001	2002	2003	2004	2005	2006	2007	2008
C-Q	.	.	.	.	.	.	.	.	.	.
C	37.7	36.6	37.4	36.6	38.6	37.8	36.6	37.8	37.9	.
D	35.1	35.5	34.9	35.9	35.4	35.4	35.8	35.4	35.4	.
E	37.1	37.3	37.1	37.2	36.7	37.9	37.7	36.8	33.5	.
F	37.2	38.1	37.8	37.5	37.6	37.9	38.9	37.5	37.8	.
G	37.1	35.2	35.5	36.9	33.2	37.3	37.0	35.6	35.5	.
H	31.4	33.9	34.7	35.1	33.8	34.5	34.2	31.5	33.8	.
I	37.7	36.7	36.6	37.3	36.8	37.4	37.7	37.0	36.6	.
J	36.0	36.2	35.8	36.0	35.7	35.9	36.7	35.6	35.8	.
K	36.8	36.6	37.1	36.9	36.4	37.1	36.9	35.5	34.5	.
M	.	.	.	.	.	.	.	26.5	.	.
N	.	.	.	.	.	.	.	36.0	.	.
O	.	.	.	.	.	.	.	35.3	.	.

Explanatory notes: see p. 721. Notes explicatives: voir p. 723. Notas explicativas: véase p. 725.

[1] Oct. of each year. [2] Full-time employees only. [1] Oct. de chaque année. [2] Salariés à plein temps seulement. [1] Oct. de cada año. [2] Asalariados a tiempo completo solamente.

4A HOURS OF WORK — DURÉE DU TRAVAIL — HORAS DE TRABAJO

By economic activity — Par activité économique — Por actividad económica

	Per week — Par semaine — Por semana										
	1999	2000	2001	2002	2003	2004	2005	2006	2007	2008	

Bulgaria (CA) (a) — Employees - Salariés - Asalariados

Total men and women - Total hommes et femmes - Total hombres y mujeres
ISIC 3 - CITI 3 - CIIU 3 [1]

ISIC 3	1999	2000	2001	2002	2003	2004	2005	2006	2007	2008	ISIC 4
Total	.	33	34	34	33	34	34	34	34	.	Total
A-B	.	35	35	35	35	35	35	35	35	.	A
C-Q	.	33	34	33	33	34	32	31	32	.	B
A	.	35	35	35	35	35	34	34	34	.	B-U
B	.	34	34	34	34	35	34	34	34	.	C
C	.	32	32	32	32	32	33	34	34	.	D
D	.	33	33	33	33	34	33	33	33	.	E
E	.	32	33	33	33	33	34	35	35	.	F
F	.	34	34	34	34	34	35	35	35	.	G
G	.	36	36	35	34	34	34	34	34	.	H
H	.	34	35	34	33	34	34	35	35	.	I
I	.	34	34	34	34	34	34	35	34	.	J
J	.	34	35	35	34	34	35	34	33	.	K
K	.	34	34	34	34	34	34	33	34	.	L
L	.	35	34	34	34	34	34	33	34	.	M
M	.	32	31	31	31	31	33	34	34	.	N
N	.	33	33	33	33	33	34	34	34	.	O
O	.	34	34	34	34	34	31	31	30	.	P
							33	32	32	.	Q
							34	33	34	.	R
							34	33	34	.	S

(ISIC 4 - CITI 4 - CIIU 4)

Croatia (BA) (a) [2][3] — Employees - Salariés - Asalariados

Total men and women - Total hommes et femmes - Total hombres y mujeres
ISIC 3 - CITI 3 - CIIU 3

ISIC 3	1999	2000	2001	2002	2003	2004	2005	2006	2007	2008
Total	41.9↓	41.9↓	41.5↓	41.5↓	41.5↓	41.5	41.3↓	41.2	41.2	40.9
A-B	42.8↓	43.4↓	41.6↓	42.1↓	42.1↓	41.8	42.0↓	42.2	41.1	41.6
C-Q	41.9↓	41.8↓	41.5↓	41.5↓	41.5↓	41.5	41.3↓	41.2	41.1	40.8
A	41.8↓	42.0↓	41.7↓	42.4↓	41.5↓	41.2	41.8↓	42.2	.	41.2
B							42.9↓	41.5	.	
C										42.2
D	41.6↓	41.5↓	41.3↓	41.3↓	41.3↓	41.4	41.0↓	41.2	41.0	40.6
E	41.3↓	40.5↓	40.2↓	40.4↓	40.3↓	40.3	40.4↓	40.2	.	40.2
F	44.6↓	44.4↓	43.2↓	43.1↓	43.8↓	43.3	43.3↓	43.1	43.1	42.4
G	42.2↓	42.0↓	42.4↓	41.8↓	41.9↓	41.9	41.5↓	41.2	40.8	41.0
H	43.7↓	44.3↓	44.7↓	44.7↓	44.0↓	43.5	43.4↓	43.3	42.4	42.8
I	43.2↓	44.3↓	41.9↓	43.1↓	42.4↓	42.7	42.8↓	42.1	42.2	42.0
J	41.3↓	40.9↓	40.1↓	40.5↓	40.7↓	40.3	40.4↓	40.4	.	39.7
K	41.5↓	40.5↓	41.4↓	41.0↓	40.7↓	40.5	40.6↓	40.8	40.3	39.9
L	41.7↓	40.9↓	40.8↓	40.6↓	40.1↓	40.7	40.4↓	40.3	40.3	40.1
M	39.0↓	39.9↓	39.0↓	39.0↓	39.2↓	39.0	39.2↓	39.3	38.8	38.9
N	41.5↓	41.0↓	39.9↓	40.8↓	40.5↓	40.5	40.8↓	40.5	40.6	40.5
O	40.1↓	40.8↓	40.0↓	40.1↓	41.4↓	41.0	39.9↓	39.9	40.8	40.4

Men - Hommes - Hombres
ISIC 3 - CITI 3 - CIIU 3

ISIC 3	1999	2000	2001	2002	2003	2004	2005	2006	2007	2008
Total	42.8↓	42.5↓	42.3↓	42.2↓	42.2↓	42.1	41.9↓	41.8	41.7	41.4
A-B	43.6↓	43.5↓	42.2↓	42.3↓	42.6↓	42.1	42.0↓	42.4	.	41.8
C-Q	42.7↓	42.5↓	42.3↓	42.2↓	42.2↓	42.0	41.9↓	41.7	41.7	41.4
A	42.3↓	42.2↓	42.3↓	42.4↓	41.8↓	41.4	41.9↓	42.3	.	41.2
B							42.9↓	43.5	.	
C										42.4
D	42.0↓	41.7↓	41.7↓	41.5↓	41.4↓	41.6	41.3↓	41.4	41.2	40.8
E	41.5↓	40.5↓	40.1↓	40.5↓	40.3↓	40.5	40.4↓	40.4	.	40.3
F	45.2↓	45.0↓	43.5↓	43.7↓	44.2↓	43.5	43.8↓	43.4	43.4	42.6
G	42.7↓	42.1↓	43.2↓	42.4↓	42.4↓	42.0	41.8↓	41.6	41.5	41.3
H	44.9↓	43.8↓	48.0↓	45.6↓	44.9↓	44.2	42.9↓	44.0	.	43.5
I	44.0↓	45.7↓	42.7↓	43.9↓	43.2↓	43.5	43.2↓	42.7	42.9	42.5
J	.	42.1↓	39.6↓	40.9↓	40.5↓	40.9	40.6↓	40.9	.	39.3
K	42.2↓	41.0↓	42.4↓	42.3↓	41.4↓	40.9	41.5↓	41.5	.	41.0
L	42.6↓	41.6↓	41.4↓	41.1↓	40.6↓	40.9	40.8↓	40.5	40.8	40.3
M	40.0↓	40.5↓	38.7↓	40.0↓	39.1↓	39.3	39.0↓	39.6	.	39.3
N	42.1↓	42.9↓	42.0↓	42.0↓	40.6↓	41.4	41.2↓	40.7	.	41.5
O	40.3↓	40.3↓	40.6↓	40.5↓	42.8↓	41.2	40.0↓	39.5	.	40.2

Explanatory notes: see p. 721.

[1] Official estimates. [2] Persons aged 15 years and over. [3] Excl. conscripts. [4] Second semester.

Notes explicatives: voir p. 723.

[1] Estimations officielles. [2] Personnes âgées de 15 ans et plus. [3] Non compris les conscrits. [4] Second semestre.

Notas explicativas: véase p. 725.

[1] Estimaciones oficiales. [2] Personas de 15 años y más. [3] Excl. los conscriptos. [4] Segundo semestre.

By economic activity — Par activité économique — Por actividad económica

	Per week — Par semaine — Por semana									
	1999	2000	2001	2002	2003	2004	2005	2006	2007	2008

Croatia (BA) (a) [1][2] — Employees - Salariés - Asalariados
Women - Femmes - Mujeres
ISIC 3 - CITI 3 - CIIU 3

	1999	2000	2001	2002	2003	2004	2005	2006	2007	2008
Total	40.9[3]	41.0[3]	40.4[3]	40.6[3]	40.7[3]	40.7	40.6[3]	40.5	40.3	40.2
A-B	40.4[3]	43.2[3]	40.4[3]	41.7[3]	40.7[3]	40.7	41.7[3]	41.4	.	40.9
C-Q	40.9[3]	41.0[3]	40.4[3]	40.6[3]	40.7[3]	40.5	40.6[3]	40.5	40.2	40.2
A	40.1[3]	41.5[3]	40.4[3]	42.4[3]	40.6[3]	40.6	41.5[3]	42.0	.	41.0
B	.	.	.	.	.	.	43.1[3]	.	.	.
D	40.9[3]	41.1[3]	40.7[3]	41.1[3]	41.1[3]	41.0	40.6[3]	40.9	40.8	40.2
E	.[3]	40.4[3]	40.4[3]	40.1[3]	40.3[3]	39.7	40.5[3]	39.7	.	39.6
F	.[3]	41.3[3]	40.2[3]	38.4[3]	39.5[3]	41.5	39.1[3]	39.8	.	40.0
G	41.8[3]	42.0[3]	41.7[3]	41.3[3]	41.5[3]	41.8	41.3[3]	40.9	40.4	40.7
H	42.8[3]	44.8[3]	42.6[3]	43.9[3]	43.3[3]	42.9	43.7[3]	42.8	.	42.2
I	40.4[3]	40.6[3]	39.0[3]	40.8[3]	40.1[3]	39.7	41.3[3]	39.9	.	39.9
J	41.0[3]	40.3[3]	40.3[3]	40.4[3]	40.7[3]	40.0	40.3[3]	40.1	.	39.9
K	40.9[3]	40.1[3]	40.4[3]	39.6[3]	40.1[3]	39.8	39.4[3]	39.9	.	38.9
L	40.1[3]	39.7[3]	39.8[3]	39.9[3]	39.3[3]	40.4	39.9[3]	40.1	39.6	39.8
M	38.7[3]	39.7[3]	39.0[3]	38.7[3]	39.3[3]	38.9	39.2[3]	39.2	38.7	38.7
N	41.3[3]	40.4[3]	39.5[3]	40.5[3]	40.4[3]	40.3	40.7[3]	40.5	40.4	40.3
O	39.7[3]	41.1[3]	39.4[3]	39.5[3]	40.2[3]	40.8	39.8[3]	40.3	.	40.6

Croatia (CA) (a) — Employees - Salariés - Asalariados
Total men and women - Total hommes et femmes - Total hombres y mujeres
ISIC 3 - CITI 3 - CIIU 3

	1999	2000	2001	2002	2003	2004	2005	2006	2007	2008
Total	143	143	143	142	143[4]	144	143	142	141	.
A-B	143	143	142	141	142[4]	143	141	140	138	.
C-Q	146	143	144	143	143[4]	144	143	142	141	.
A	143	143	142	141	143[4]	142	140	140	138	.
B	151	152	154	144	143[4]	149	148	145	146	.
C	139	142	145	145	146[4]	142	142	141	141	.
D	139	139	140	139	141[4]	143	142	140	139	.
E	149	137	141	140	140[4]	142	140	139	139	.
F	149	148	147	145	145[4]	146	147	146	145	.
G	152	152	150	148	148[4]	148	147	146	144	.
H	146	149	149	146	150[4]	149	148	146	145	.
I	143	142	141	140	142[4]	143	143	142	141	.
J	140	139	142	141	141[4]	143	143	140	138	.
K	151	151	148	147	148[4]	148	147	147	147	.
L	144	142	142	142	139[4]	142	138	137	136	.
M	142	141	141	141	140[4]	141	139	137	136	.
N	138	139	141	140	142[4]	141	139	137	137	.
O	146	145	144	143	143[4]	144	143	142	142	.
Q	.	.	.	.	.[4]	.	.	.	.	.

Cyprus (DA) (b) [5][6] — Employees - Salariés - Asalariados
Total men and women - Total hommes et femmes - Total hombres y mujeres
ISIC 3 - CITI 3 - CIIU 3

	1999	2000	2001	2002	2003	2004	2005	2006	2007	2008
Total	40.1	40.0	40.0	39.9	39.7	39.8	39.9	39.9	.	.
A-B	40.6	39.7	41.3	41.2	43.3	40.3	40.6	40.7	.	.
C-Q	40.1	40.0	40.0	39.8	39.7	39.8	39.9	39.9	.	.
A	40.2	39.8	41.3	41.2	43.4	40.4	40.6	40.6	.	.
B	42.5	38.5	38.6	38.3	38.3	38.5	39.8	45.8	.	.
C	43.9	42.6	42.8	43.6	43.8	46.3	44.1	43.4	.	.
D	40.5	40.2	40.5	40.0	40.1	40.0	39.9	40.4	.	.
E	38.6	39.2	39.3	38.7	38.5	38.8	39.3	39.3	.	.
F	40.3	40.4	40.3	40.6	39.8	40.3	40.1	39.2	.	.
G	40.1	40.1	40.0	40.3	40.2	40.4	40.2	40.0	.	.
H	38.6	38.9	38.9	38.8	38.8	39.3	40.8	40.8	.	.
I	42.0	42.0	41.9	41.1	40.5	40.3	39.9	40.3	.	.
J	39.0	38.7	38.4	38.3	38.3	38.2	38.2	38.3	.	.
K	40.6	40.4	40.6	39.7	39.9	40.0	40.1	40.0	.	.
L	39.4	39.4	39.3	39.3	39.8	39.9	39.9	39.9	.	.
M	38.1	38.2	38.1	38.2	38.1	37.9	38.4	38.3	.	.
N	42.9	42.7	42.5	42.6	40.8	40.6	40.7	40.9	.	.
O	39.7	39.4	40.1	39.5	39.5	39.5	39.6	39.7	.	.

Explanatory notes: see p. 721.

[1] Persons aged 15 years and over. [2] Excl. conscripts. [3] Second semester. [4] Prior to 2003: excl. employees of the Ministries of International Affairs and Defence. [5] Adults. [6] Oct. of each year.

Notes explicatives: voir p. 723.

[1] Personnes âgées de 15 ans et plus. [2] Non compris les conscrits. [3] Second semestre. [4] Avant 2003: non compris les salariés des ministères de l'Intérieur et de la Défense. [5] Adultes. [6] Oct. de chaque année.

Notas explicativas: véase p. 725.

[1] Personas de 15 años y más. [2] Excl. los conscriptos. [3] Segundo semestre. [4] Antes de 2003: excl. los asalariados de los ministerios del Interior y de la Defensa. [5] Adultos. [6] Oct. de cada año.

HOURS OF WORK · DURÉE DU TRAVAIL · HORAS DE TRABAJO

By economic activity · Par activité économique · Por actividad económica

	Per week				Par semaine				Por semana	
	1999	2000	2001	2002	2003	2004	2005	2006	2007	2008

Cyprus (DA) (b) [1][2] — Employees - Salariés - Asalariados

Men - Hommes - Hombres
ISIC 3 - CITI 3 - CIIU 3

	1999	2000	2001	2002	2003	2004	2005	2006	2007	2008
Total	40.5	40.3	40.3	40.2	40.1	40.2	40.1	40.2	.	.
A-B	41.0	40.0	41.8	41.8	45.3	40.9	41.1	41.8	.	.
C-Q	40.5	40.3	40.3	40.2	40.0	40.2	40.1	40.2	.	.
A	40.5	40.4	41.8	41.9	45.5	41.0	41.2	41.6	.	.
B	42.7	38.5	38.6	38.4	38.4	38.6	40.0	47.0	.	.
C	44.3	42.9	43.1	43.9	44.1	46.7	44.5	43.9	.	.
D	41.1	40.5	40.9	40.3	40.3	40.8	40.2	41.0	.	.
E	38.7	39.3	39.5	38.8	38.6	38.9	39.4	39.6	.	.
F	40.5	40.6	40.5	40.8	40.0	40.4	40.3	39.2	.	.
G	40.0	40.0	39.9	40.5	40.6	40.8	40.2	40.4	.	.
H	38.5	38.6	38.5	38.6	38.7	39.3	40.4	40.8	.	.
I	43.1	43.3	42.7	41.9	41.2	41.0	40.5	41.0	.	.
J	39.0	38.8	38.6	38.4	38.4	38.4	38.4	38.5	.	.
K	41.7	41.2	41.8	40.1	40.5	40.7	40.7	40.2	.	.
L	39.7	39.8	39.6	39.8	39.8	39.9	40.0	40.0	.	.
M	38.6	38.8	38.5	38.5	38.4	38.2	38.9	38.7	.	.
N	42.4	42.8	42.1	42.5	41.4	40.7	41.0	41.9	.	.
O	39.7	39.4	40.5	39.9	40.0	39.9	39.8	40.0	.	.

Women - Femmes - Mujeres
ISIC 3 - CITI 3 - CIIU 3

	1999	2000	2001	2002	2003	2004	2005	2006	2007	2008
Total	39.6	39.6	39.6	39.4	39.3	39.2	39.7	39.5	.	.
A-B	39.9	39.2	40.7	40.3	40.8	39.6	39.9	39.3	.	.
C-Q	39.6	39.6	39.6	39.4	39.3	39.2	39.7	39.5	.	.
A	39.9	39.2	40.7	40.3	40.8	39.6	39.9	39.3	.	.
B	39.8	38.6	38.7	38.0	38.0	38.0	38.1	38.0	.	.
C	38.3	38.6	37.9	38.9	38.9	39.5	38.8	38.7	.	.
D	39.6	39.9	39.8	39.5	39.7	38.8	39.5	39.4	.	.
E	38.1	38.1	38.2	38.1	38.1	38.1	38.6	38.3	.	.
F	38.6	38.6	38.4	38.4	38.4	38.3	38.4	38.4	.	.
G	40.3	40.3	40.0	40.0	39.7	40.1	40.2	39.6	.	.
H	38.7	39.2	39.2	39.0	38.9	39.3	41.1	40.8	.	.
I	39.7	39.3	40.4	39.6	39.3	39.1	38.8	39.1	.	.
J	39.0	38.5	38.3	38.2	38.2	38.1	38.1	38.2	.	.
K	39.6	39.6	39.8	39.4	39.6	39.5	39.7	39.9	.	.
L	38.6	38.6	38.8	38.6	39.8	39.9	39.9	39.8	.	.
M	37.8	37.8	37.9	38.1	38.0	37.8	38.1	38.1	.	.
N	43.1	42.7	42.6	42.6	40.6	40.5	40.6	40.5	.	.
O	39.8	39.3	39.5	39.1	38.8	38.9	39.3	39.3	.	.

Czech Republic (DA) (a) [3] — Wage earners - Ouvriers - Obreros

Total men and women - Total hommes et femmes - Total hombres y mujeres
ISIC 3 - CITI 3 - CIIU 3

	1999	2000	2001	2002	2003	2004	2005	2006	2007	2008
C	39.0	39.3	39.4	39.5	39.6	39.7	39.1	39.5	39.5	.
D	41.0	40.7	40.7	40.7	40.7	40.6	40.5	40.5	40.4	.
E	39.9	38.9	39.0	39.4	39.7	39.1	39.6	39.7	39.6	.

España (BA) (a) [4][5] — Total employment - Emploi total - Empleo total

Total men and women - Total hommes et femmes - Total hombres y mujeres
ISIC 3 - CITI 3 - CIIU 3

	1999	2000	2001	2002	2003	2004	2005	2006	2007	2008
Total	36.2	35.9	35.9	35.7	35.4	35.2	34.8	35.0	34.7	34.7
A-B	42.6	42.1	41.6	41.6	40.6	40.7	39.3	39.8	39.6	39.5
C-Q	35.7	35.4	35.5	35.3	35.1	34.9	34.6	34.8	34.5	34.5
A	42.6	42.1	41.4	41.6	40.7	40.8	39.8	40.2	40.1	40.0
B	41.8	41.6	44.5	41.7	39.2	39.6	29.5	32.1	30.8	28.4
C	35.4	34.8	35.4	36.7	36.3	35.7	38.5	37.3	37.7	38.2
D	36.3	36.1	36.3	36.0	36.0	35.8	36.2	36.5	36.1	36.0
E	35.2	35.0	35.2	35.2	35.3	35.4	35.7	35.5	35.1	34.6
F	37.5	37.2	37.2	37.4	37.1	37.2	38.0	38.3	37.9	37.8
G	37.9	37.6	37.8	37.4	36.9	36.8	36.2	36.4	36.1	36.3
H	41.4	41.3	41.2	40.3	40.2	39.6	38.6	39.1	38.2	38.5
I	38.6	37.8	38.3	37.7	37.8	37.5	37.2	37.2	37.7	36.6
J	35.9	35.5	35.8	35.4	35.4	35.1	35.2	35.3	33.7	35.2
K	34.7	34.3	34.4	34.3	34.4	34.0	34.0	33.8	33.7	33.5
L	33.5	32.8	33.1	32.9	32.9	32.3	31.4	31.6	31.3	31.2
M	25.6	25.9	25.3	25.7	25.4	25.2	25.4	25.7	25.4	25.9
N	33.8	33.4	33.0	33.0	32.9	32.7	31.3	31.8	31.6	31.7
O	34.5	34.4	34.7	34.6	33.6	33.4	32.6	33.2	32.5	32.6
P	26.2	25.8	26.5	27.3	27.0	27.3	26.1	25.8	25.9	26.2
Q	43.5	42.0	38.6	38.8	35.9	21.8	23.1	29.1	30.2	35.2

Explanatory notes: see p. 721.

Notes explicatives: voir p. 723.

Notas explicativas: véase p. 725.

[1] Adults. [2] Oct. of each year. [3] Enterprises with 20 or more employees. [4] Excl. compulsory military service. [5] Persons aged 16 years and over.

[1] Adultes. [2] Oct. de chaque année. [3] Entreprises occupant 20 salariés et plus. [4] Non compris les militaires du contingent. [5] Personnes âgées de 16 ans et plus.

[1] Adultos. [2] Oct. de cada año. [3] Empresas con 20 y más asalariados. [4] Excl. a los militares en servicio obligatorio. [5] Personas de 16 años y más.

	Per week / Par semaine / Por semana									
	1999	2000	2001	2002	2003	2004	2005	2006	2007	2008

España (BA) (a) [1][2]   Total employment - Emploi total - Empleo total

Men - Hommes - Hombres
ISIC 3 - CITI 3 - CIIU 3

	1999	2000	2001	2002	2003	2004	2005	2006	2007	2008
Total	38.2	37.8	38.0	37.7	37.5	37.4	37.7	37.9	37.5	37.5
A-B	43.8	43.4	43.1	42.7	42.0	42.3	41.4	41.7	41.6	41.2
C-Q	37.7	37.4	37.6	37.3	37.2	37.0	37.4	37.7	37.3	37.3
A	43.7	43.3	42.7	42.5	41.9	42.3	41.8	42.1	42.0	41.7
B	45.4	44.5	47.5	44.7	42.2	42.7	34.5	34.3	33.7	31.3
C	35.3	34.8	35.7	37.0	36.7	35.8	39.3	37.7	38.4	38.4
D	36.9	36.8	37.0	36.7	36.8	36.6	37.3	37.5	37.2	37.0
E	35.4	35.3	35.6	35.2	35.8	35.9	36.8	35.7	35.9	35.7
F	37.6	37.4	37.4	37.6	37.3	37.4	38.4	38.7	38.3	38.2
G	39.9	39.5	39.8	39.3	39.2	39.0	39.3	39.3	39.2	39.6
H	44.7	44.8	44.9	43.6	43.7	42.8	42.1	43.2	42.2	42.4
I	39.8	39.0	39.5	38.9	38.9	38.7	39.1	38.9	38.8	38.2
J	37.1	36.6	37.4	36.7	36.5	36.4	37.1	37.4	36.5	37.2
K	37.7	37.5	37.7	37.5	37.6	37.4	38.5	38.2	37.9	37.6
L	34.5	33.7	33.9	33.7	33.8	33.1	32.5	32.8	32.3	32.7
M	27.1	27.3	26.8	26.9	26.9	26.9	27.2	27.3	27.2	27.9
N	35.4	35.4	35.3	35.3	35.4	35.2	34.6	35.1	34.4	34.7
O	36.6	36.1	36.3	36.0	35.3	35.2	34.6	35.3	33.9	34.3
P	37.9	36.7	37.4	36.5	34.7	34.4	36.4	34.0	33.8	35.1
Q	47.0	43.3	40.9	36.5	40.5	16.8	32.1	35.1	38.3	45.8

Women - Femmes - Mujeres
ISIC 3 - CITI 3 - CIIU 3

	1999	2000	2001	2002	2003	2004	2005	2006	2007	2008
Total	32.7	32.5	32.5	32.4	32.1	31.9	30.6	31.0	30.8	30.9
A-B	39.0	38.3	37.2	38.5	37.0	36.3	33.4	35.2	34.5	34.8
C-Q	32.7	32.2	32.2	32.2	31.9	31.9	30.5	30.9	30.7	30.8
A	39.6	38.7	37.6	38.9	37.4	36.7	34.4	35.6	35.0	35.4
B	14.2	24.0	25.0	25.1	22.6	22.4	17.5	25.0	21.4	16.7
C	36.3	34.8	30.6	32.5	31.3	35.1	32.1	32.6	32.1	35.9
D	34.5	34.0	34.1	33.9	33.5	33.7	33.0	33.4	32.9	33.0
E	33.5	32.8	32.8	35.2	32.8	33.1	31.6	34.5	32.1	30.9
F	33.8	33.3	32.8	33.3	34.1	33.1	30.4	31.1	31.2	31.5
G	35.4	35.1	35.4	35.0	34.3	34.3	32.9	33.3	32.8	32.9
H	37.4	37.2	37.2	37.0	36.7	36.4	35.5	35.7	35.1	35.4
I	33.3	32.9	33.6	33.2	33.3	33.2	31.1	32.0	32.0	31.7
J	33.6	33.6	33.5	33.6	33.5	33.2	33.0	32.9	32.6	32.9
K	31.1	30.9	30.9	30.9	31.1	30.7	29.6	29.5	29.6	29.6
L	31.7	31.4	31.7	31.4	31.5	30.9	29.8	30.0	29.8	29.2
M	24.8	25.0	24.3	24.9	24.6	24.4	24.4	24.8	24.4	24.8
N	33.1	32.5	32.2	32.1	32.1	31.9	30.1	30.6	30.7	30.8
O	32.4	32.7	33.1	33.1	32.0	31.7	30.7	31.2	31.2	31.2
P	24.6	24.4	25.2	26.3	26.2	26.6	25.0	25.1	25.2	25.4
Q	38.9	35.8	30.7	39.7	32.9	24.9	14.5	23.1	22.5	18.6

Estonia (DA) (a)   Employees - Salariés - Asalariados

Total men and women - Total hommes et femmes - Total hombres y mujeres
ISIC 3 - CITI 3 - CIIU 3

	1999	2000	2001	2002	2003	2004	2005	2006	2007	2008
Total	34.7	34.8	35.2	34.9	34.5	34.8	34.8	34.7	34.7	34.3
A-B	35.8	36.0	37.1	37.0	36.1	36.4	36.3	35.8	36.3	35.5
C-Q	34.6	34.7	35.1	34.8	34.4	34.7	34.8	34.7	34.7	34.2
A	35.7	36.0	37.1	37.1	36.2	36.4	36.4	35.8	36.3	35.5
B	36.6	36.5	36.5	35.0	35.2	36.5	35.5	34.7	35.7	34.6
C	27.8	30.2	33.3	33.3	32.9	33.0	30.9	30.6	32.3	32.5
D	33.8	34.2	34.2	34.5	34.1	34.3	34.2	34.2	34.0	33.6
E	34.7	34.8	35.1	35.0	34.5	34.6	34.8	34.4	34.2	34.3
F	34.6	34.5	35.0	34.6	34.5	34.9	35.4	35.3	35.1	34.1
G	35.8	35.9	36.4	36.0	35.8	36.1	36.0	35.8	35.7	35.2
H	36.3	36.3	36.2	36.3	33.6	35.2	35.3	35.3	35.2	34.0
I	35.4	35.4	36.0	36.0	35.7	35.9	35.8	35.8	36.0	35.5
J	35.8	35.2	35.7	34.7	34.7	34.6	35.3	34.9	34.5	33.8
K	36.4	36.8	37.2	36.5	36.0	36.5	36.3	36.3	36.6	36.2
L	35.0	34.3	34.4	34.4	34.0	34.2	34.0	33.9	34.1	33.6
M	32.0	32.0	32.5	31.9	31.6	31.8	31.6	31.6	31.2	31.3
N	36.1	36.4	35.9	34.4	34.3	34.9	35.6	34.9	34.8	34.2
O	35.3	35.2	35.8	35.3	34.9	35.2	35.4	35.2	35.2	35.1

Explanatory notes: see p. 721.   Notes explicatives: voir p. 723.   Notas explicativas: véase p. 725.

[1] Excl. compulsory military service. [2] Persons aged 16 years and over.

[1] Non compris les militaires du contingent. [2] Personnes âgées de 16 ans et plus.

[1] Excl. a los militares en servicio obligatorio. [2] Personas de 16 años y más.

HOURS OF WORK

By economic activity

DURÉE DU TRAVAIL

Par activité économique

HORAS DE TRABAJO

Por actividad económica

	Per week				Par semaine				Por semana	
	1999	2000	2001	2002	2003	2004	2005	2006	2007	2008

Finland (BA) (a)   **Employees - Salariés - Asalariados**

Total men and women - Total hommes et femmes - Total hombres y mujeres
ISIC 3 - CITI 3 - CIIU 3

	1999	2000	2001	2002	2003	2004	2005	2006	2007	2008
Total	36.5	36.3	36.3	36.0	35.9	36.0	36.1	35.9	35.9	36.3
A-B	37.7	37.3	37.9	37.6	37.2	37.3	38.2	37.5	36.4	37.7
C-Q	.	.	.	.	.	.	.	.	.	36.2
A	37.6	37.2	38.0	37.6	37.2	37.3	38.2	37.5	36.5	37.9
B	44.0	40.4	35.2	36.2	35.5	41.9	39.5	35.6	32.7	26.4
C	39.3	39.9	38.6	39.2	39.7	40.6	40.7	42.4	41.0	45.1
D	38.1	38.0	37.8	37.6	37.5	37.5	37.8	37.8	37.7	38.2
E	37.9	37.8	37.6	36.8	37.2	37.2	37.3	38.1	36.8	37.5
F	38.9	39.0	38.9	38.6	39.0	38.8	38.6	38.7	38.5	38.9
G	35.9	35.4	34.9	34.9	35.0	34.7	34.8	34.4	34.8	35.0
H	32.9	32.4	32.9	32.6	32.5	32.5	32.2	32.8	32.2	32.6
I	38.4	38.0	38.6	38.1	37.9	38.4	38.0	37.7	37.7	38.0
J	37.5	37.2	36.7	36.4	35.9	36.3	36.4	36.2	36.2	36.7
K	35.6	35.2	35.7	35.3	35.4	35.3	35.3	35.2	35.4	36.3
L	37.1	36.6	37.0	36.5	36.7	36.9	36.8	36.5	36.7	37.2
M	33.8	33.6	33.4	33.4	32.9	33.1	33.5	33.1	33.1	33.8
N	35.8	36.1	35.9	35.9	35.5	35.8	36.2	35.8	35.9	35.4
O	33.7	33.4	33.5	33.0	33.5	33.5	33.5	33.1	32.1	33.5
P	25.4	30.4	24.5	26.0	27.6	29.6	29.2	27.6	27.5	28.3
Q	36.2	36.3	38.7	38.5	40.3	38.0	37.0	36.4	39.5	37.4
X							35.1	32.6	33.9	33.7

Men - Hommes - Hombres
ISIC 3 - CITI 3 - CIIU 3

	1999	2000	2001	2002	2003	2004	2005	2006	2007	2008
Total	38.3	38.2	38.1	37.9	37.9	37.9	37.9	37.9	37.8	38.2
A-B	39.3	38.4	39.2	39.3	39.1	38.4	39.4	39.1	37.7	38.8
C-Q	.	.	.	.	.	.	.	.	.	38.2
A	39.2	38.3	39.3	39.3	39.1	38.3	39.3	39.2	37.8	38.9
B	44.3	40.9	37.1	40.9	36.6	43.1	41.1	35.6	34.0	31.4
C	39.7	40.9	38.7	39.2	40.0	41.1	42.1	43.2	41.1	45.9
D	38.6	38.7	38.5	38.2	38.1	38.1	38.4	38.4	38.3	38.8
E	38.4	38.3	38.2	37.1	37.5	37.6	37.9	38.6	37.5	38.2
F	39.3	39.4	39.3	39.0	39.4	39.2	38.9	39.0	38.8	39.2
G	39.0	38.4	37.8	38.0	37.7	37.6	37.7	37.4	37.7	37.7
H	33.6	33.7	34.4	35.2	34.5	32.8	33.7	34.9	34.3	33.7
I	40.0	39.5	40.2	39.2	39.6	40.1	39.3	39.3	39.1	39.6
J	41.0	40.0	39.9	39.8	38.9	38.9	38.5	39.2	38.9	38.8
K	37.3	37.0	37.2	36.9	37.2	37.0	37.1	37.0	37.1	37.7
L	39.0	38.7	39.3	38.4	38.5	39.1	38.8	38.6	39.1	39.3
M	35.3	35.1	34.5	34.6	34.1	34.5	34.4	34.5	34.0	35.6
N	36.9	36.9	36.3	37.6	37.7	36.6	36.9	36.9	37.5	35.7
O	34.9	36.3	35.6	35.0	35.7	36.0	35.2	35.9	34.9	36.0
P	18.2	25.2	17.0	19.2	30.7	33.4	34.1	35.1	34.2	33.8
Q	37.9	34.3	42.2	41.0	40.2	37.2	38.9	41.3	41.7	41.9
X							39.3	33.1	35.3	35.1

Women - Femmes - Mujeres
ISIC 3 - CITI 3 - CIIU 3

	1999	2000	2001	2002	2003	2004	2005	2006	2007	2008
Total	34.5	34.3	34.3	34.1	33.9	34.1	34.3	33.9	33.9	34.3
A-B	34.4	34.7	35.1	34.1	33.2	34.9	35.5	33.4	33.2	35.1
C-Q	.	.	.	.	.	.	.	.	.	34.3
A	34.3	34.6	35.2	34.1	33.1	34.9	35.5	33.4	33.3	35.6
B	36.0	39.2	30.9	33.1	34.8	35.0	37.1	35.6	30.1	19.5
C	37.8	36.3	38.1	38.6	36.5	34.8	28.7	35.4	39.6	39.2
D	36.7	36.2	36.3	36.4	36.0	36.0	36.3	36.4	36.1	36.5
E	35.7	36.1	36.0	35.7	36.4	35.6	35.2	36.6	34.9	35.3
F	33.4	34.1	34.0	33.2	34.4	33.6	34.4	34.4	34.0	35.6
G	32.8	32.5	31.9	32.0	32.4	31.9	31.9	31.6	32.1	32.2
H	32.7	31.9	32.3	31.6	31.9	32.4	31.7	32.1	31.5	32.3
I	34.9	34.2	34.6	34.7	33.8	34.0	34.8	33.6	34.4	34.2
J	36.0	36.1	35.2	35.1	34.7	35.1	35.4	34.9	35.0	35.8
K	33.5	32.9	33.7	33.1	33.0	33.2	33.2	33.2	33.4	34.6
L	35.2	34.6	34.8	34.7	35.0	34.9	34.9	34.7	34.6	35.5
M	33.0	32.9	32.8	32.9	32.2	32.3	32.9	32.3	32.6	32.8
N	35.6	36.0	35.9	35.6	35.2	35.7	36.1	35.7	35.6	35.4
O	32.9	31.4	31.7	31.4	31.7	31.6	32.2	31.1	30.2	31.7
P	25.7	30.6	25.1	26.9	27.2	25.9	25.0	22.9	21.9	22.6
Q	34.4	37.3	37.3	36.6	40.5	39.1	34.8	31.5	37.2	33.4
X							31.8	32.2	32.1	32.0

Explanatory notes: see p. 721.   Notes explicatives: voir p. 723.   Notas explicativas: véase p. 725.

	Per week				Par semaine				Por semana	
	1999	2000	2001	2002	2003	2004	2005	2006	2007	2008	

France (BA) (c) [1]   Employees - Salariés - Asalariados

Total men and women - Total hommes et femmes - Total hombres y mujeres
ISIC 3 - CITI 3 - CIIU 3 [2]   ISIC 4 - CITI 4 - CIIU 4

ISIC 3	1999	2000	2001	2002	2003	2004	2005	2006	2007	2008	ISIC 4
Total	39.66	38.95	38.36	38.28	36.63 [3]	37.06	37.30	37.24	37.49	37.5	Total
A-B	40.64	40.40	40.18	38.88	38.09 [3]	37.85	37.87	37.87	38.17	38.9	A
C-Q	39.64	.	38.33	37.68	36.61 [3]	37.05	37.29	37.23	37.48	37.3	B
A	.	.	.	.	37.31	37.29	37.43	37.45	37.65	37.5	B-U
B	.	.	.	.	57.52	55.86	51.13	52.71	50.89	37.3	C
C	40.73	39.98	39.28	38.24	35.99 [3]	36.56	38.05	40.15	41.70	36.8	D
D	39.65	38.63	37.93	37.40	36.19 [3]	36.78	37.05	37.05	37.20	36.0	E
E	39.23	36.64	36.65	36.28	34.35 [3]	35.78	35.78	35.68	36.05	37.5	F
F	40.14	39.58	38.96	38.11	36.98 [3]	37.24	37.50	37.28	37.33	38.0	G
G	40.83	39.59	39.01	38.05	37.45 [3]	37.77	37.76	37.84	37.91	38.6	H
H	43.30	42.52	41.61	41.04	40.79 [3]	40.46	41.74	40.57	41.14	40.2	I
I	40.29	39.43	38.11	37.92	36.95 [3]	37.29	37.63	38.03	38.16	38.3	J
J	40.27	39.58	38.55	38.26	36.50 [3]	37.37	37.33	37.59	37.69	38.0	K
K	41.00	40.08	39.60	38.85	37.25 [3]	38.13	38.47	38.29	38.24	38.7	L
L	39.76	39.60	39.40	37.83	36.84 [3]	37.05	37.35	36.99	37.60	38.9	M
M	.	.	.	.	32.79	33.39	33.76	33.35	34.20	37.0	N
M-Q	37.49	37.31	36.81	36.50	35.48 [3]	35.83	36.00	35.91	36.31	37.6	O
N	.	.	.	.	36.55	36.86	36.79	36.76	37.10	34.3	P
O	.	.	.	.	36.48	36.62	37.00	37.47	37.38	37.1	Q
P	.	.	.	.	37.50	36.93	37.90	37.89	36.84	36.9	R
Q	.	.	.	.	38.79	37.44	40.38	38.61	38.43	37.3	S
X	.	.	.	.	37.08	35.78	38.89	40.18	35.69	37.5	T
										40.3	U
										32.3	X

Men - Hommes - Hombres
ISIC 3 - CITI 3 - CIIU 3 [2]   ISIC 4 - CITI 4 - CIIU 4

ISIC 3	1999	2000	2001	2002	2003	2004	2005	2006	2007	2008	ISIC 4
Total	40.31	39.56	38.95	38.83	37.43 [3]	37.86	38.13	38.05	38.34	38.3	Total
A-B	40.94	41.01	40.81	39.35	38.74 [3]	38.57	38.28	38.27	38.88	40.1	A
C-Q	40.30	39.54	38.91	38.20	37.40 [3]	37.85	38.12	38.04	38.32	37.5	B
A	.	.	.	.	37.73	37.84	37.69	37.76	38.26	38.3	B-U
B	.	.	.	.	59.17	56.70	52.74	56.17	52.41	37.6	C
C	40.83	40.18	39.62	38.22	36.82 [3]	36.88	38.47	40.28	40.14	36.9	D
D	39.84	38.82	38.16	37.60	36.56 [3]	37.22	37.44	37.42	37.59	36.1	E
E	39.39	36.79	36.88	36.38	34.64 [3]	36.03	35.99	35.83	36.17	37.6	F
F	40.12	39.60	38.98	38.17	37.15 [3]	37.32	37.57	37.39	37.40	39.2	G
G	41.61	40.39	39.85	38.79	38.55 [3]	38.91	38.85	38.99	39.00	39.5	H
H	44.34	43.55	43.10	42.05	41.76 [3]	41.78	43.19	41.80	42.62	41.5	I
I	40.87	39.97	38.58	38.42	37.78 [3]	37.98	38.42	38.76	39.08	38.8	J
J	41.62	41.04	39.81	39.60	38.25 [3]	39.35	39.35	39.37	39.80	40.1	K
K	41.74	40.89	40.30	39.46	38.00 [3]	39.07	39.41	39.23	39.19	39.6	L
L	40.39	40.20	40.05	38.51	37.85 [3]	37.94	38.02	37.78	38.59	40.3	M
M	.	.	.	.	33.70	34.38	34.73	33.58	34.81	37.6	N
M-Q	37.68	37.57	37.00	36.65	36.19 [3]	36.29	36.82	36.54	37.19	38.4	O
N	.	.	.	.	37.25	37.01	37.50	37.91	38.14	35.0	P
O	.	.	.	.	37.42	37.46	38.44	38.27	38.60	37.2	Q
P	.	.	.	.	38.35	37.58	37.68	37.48	38.33	37.3	R
Q	.	.	.	.	38.78	39.27	41.98	39.80	38.27	39.3	S
X	.	.	.	.	37.29	37.15	38.50	41.49	37.56	37.3	T
										41.6	U
										32.8	X

Women - Femmes - Mujeres
ISIC 3 - CITI 3 - CIIU 3 [2]   ISIC 4 - CITI 4 - CIIU 4

ISIC 3	1999	2000	2001	2002	2003	2004	2005	2006	2007	2008	ISIC 4
Total	38.66	38.03	37.46	37.44	35.42 [3]	35.82	36.06	36.02	36.24	36.4	Total
A-B	39.54	38.46	38.11	37.36	35.86 [3]	35.77	36.52	36.19	35.67	35.4	A
C-Q	38.65	38.02	37.46	36.92	35.41 [3]	35.82	36.04	36.02	36.25	36.4	B
A	.	.	.	.	35.94	35.79	36.60	36.19	35.61	36.4	B-U
B	.	.	.	.	26.95	32.00	26.78	36.53	39.35	36.4	C
C	40.07	38.44	36.96	38.37	33.48	34.08	35.47	39.16	44.56	36.5	D
D	39.15	38.11	37.34	36.89	35.15 [3]	35.59	35.97	35.98	36.08	35.9	E
E	38.63	35.94	35.65	35.79	32.95	34.24	34.66	34.85	35.32	36.0	F
F	40.43	39.23	38.58	37.43	34.58 [3]	36.05	36.57	35.74	36.36	36.3	G
G	39.56	38.35	37.71	36.91	35.72 [3]	35.97	36.14	36.01	36.16	35.7	H
H	41.62	40.75	39.52	39.47	39.39 [3]	38.34	39.46	38.81	38.92	38.5	I
I	38.67	37.83	36.77	36.54	34.58 [3]	35.26	35.48	35.89	35.63	37.0	J
J	39.08	38.28	37.42	37.07	34.75 [3]	35.35	35.44	36.12	35.99	36.4	K
K	40.02	39.03	38.61	38.03	36.13 [3]	36.71	37.00	36.86	36.82	37.9	L
L	38.92	38.81	38.54	37.02	35.52 [3]	35.74	36.37	35.94	36.78	37.2	M
M	.	.	.	.	32.22 [3]	32.76	33.18	33.22	33.83	36.0	N
M-Q	37.39	37.19	36.72	36.43	35.10 [3]	35.59	35.59	35.62	35.89	36.6	O
N	.	.	.	.	36.33 [3]	36.82	36.57	36.43	36.78	33.9	P
O	.	.	.	.	35.47	35.82	35.60	36.62	36.22	37.1	Q
P	.	.	.	.	36.88	36.45	38.02	38.10	35.99	36.1	R
Q	.	.	.	.	38.79	35.49	39.18	37.69	38.65	35.9	S
X	.	.	.	.	36.74	33.86	39.68	37.84	35.05	37.6	T
										39.0	U
										31.2	X

Explanatory notes: see p. 721.
[1] Full-time employees. [2] Fourth quarter of each year. [3] Prior to 2003: March of each year.

Notes explicatives: voir p. 723.
[1] Salariés à plein temps. [2] Quatrième trimestre de chaque année. [3] Avant 2003: mars de chaque année.

Notas explicativas: véase p. 725.
[1] Asalariados a tiempo completo. [2] Cuarto trimestre de cada año. [3] Antes de 2003: marzo de cada año.

	HOURS OF WORK	DURÉE DU TRAVAIL	HORAS DE TRABAJO
	By economic activity	Par activité économique	Por actividad económica

	Per week				Par semaine				Por semana	
	1999	2000	2001	2002	2003	2004	2005	2006	2007	2008

France (BA) (c) [1] — **Employees - Salariés - Asalariados**

Total men and women - Total hommes et femmes - Total hombres y mujeres
ISIC 3 - CITI 3 - CIIU 3

	1999	2000	2001	2002	2003	2004	2005	2006	2007	2008
Total	37.27	35.61	35.77	35.24	34.21 [2]	34.52	34.72	34.65	34.90	35.00
A-B					36.05	35.68	35.83	35.33	35.32	36.03
C-Q	37.30	35.58	35.75	35.22	34.19 [2]	34.52	34.71	34.64	34.90	34.97
A					35.37	35.19	35.40	35.03	34.82	35.56
B					54.65	53.55	50.52	45.10	49.76	50.17
C	36.57	36.87	36.14	35.20	35.99 [2]	36.38	37.97	40.06	41.35	37.58
D	37.60	36.32	35.65	35.31	35.56 [2]	36.00	36.30	36.37	36.53	36.65
E	36.63	33.85	34.13	33.43	33.51 [2]	35.27	35.22	34.89	35.42	35.35
F	37.21	37.09	36.64	36.03	36.33 [2]	36.56	36.68	36.52	36.59	36.82
G	38.73	37.03	36.58	35.82	35.05 [2]	35.24	35.23	35.28	35.44	35.51
H	39.04	38.36	37.81	38.22	36.03 [2]	35.68	36.27	35.45	35.84	35.03
I	38.00	36.06	35.03	34.98	35.85 [2]	36.09	36.44	36.82	37.03	37.29
J	38.39	36.63	35.71	34.84	35.19 [2]	35.79	35.72	36.04	36.22	36.76
K	39.36	37.93	37.75	36.70	34.79 [2]	35.57	35.86	35.63	35.37	35.74
L	37.23	35.68	37.39	35.34	34.67 [2]	34.94	34.89	34.58	35.40	35.31
M	32.35	27.06	31.09	32.03	30.00 [2]	30.43	30.94	30.51	31.40	31.10
N	36.11	34.56	34.67	34.40	32.67 [2]	33.30	33.14	32.99	33.40	33.53
O	36.58	35.22	34.79	34.65	32.45 [2]	32.26	32.95	33.46	33.16	32.94
P	38.01	37.81	38.79	37.75	25.44 [2]	23.97	24.23	24.01	23.40	23.01
Q	38.48	35.66	38.69	40.60	34.41 [2]	35.70	38.75	37.58	37.00	40.88
X	33.24	29.42	30.77	41.52	32.98	31.73	34.93	35.74	31.23	35.41

Men - Hommes - Hombres
ISIC 3 - CITI 3 - CIIU 3

	1999	2000	2001	2002	2003	2004	2005	2006	2007	2008
Total	38.48	37.00	36.97	36.46	36.68 [2]	37.04	37.27	37.16	37.47	37.47
A-B					37.58	37.23	37.19	36.75	37.46	38.08
C-Q	38.54	36.96	36.95	36.45	36.67 [2]	37.04	37.27	37.17	37.47	37.44
A					36.68	36.57	36.61	36.29	36.83	37.52
B					56.06	54.28	52.05	50.79	51.59	50.17
C	36.11	36.79	36.42	34.90	36.82 [2]	36.77	38.47	40.28	40.94	38.05
D	38.12	36.90	36.27	35.81	36.36 [2]	36.93	37.18	37.21	37.44	37.42
E	37.12	34.25	34.49	33.76	34.38 [2]	35.79	35.65	35.62	36.13	35.89
F	37.20	37.19	36.70	36.12	37.01 [2]	37.13	37.30	37.12	37.11	37.27
G	40.28	38.79	38.21	37.64	37.88 [2]	38.06	37.94	38.04	38.14	38.30
H	40.66	39.63	39.49	39.46	38.93 [2]	38.99	39.65	38.57	39.38	37.62
I	38.95	37.07	35.76	35.74	37.31 [2]	37.49	37.94	38.22	38.46	38.74
J	41.13	38.95	37.60	37.39	37.78 [2]	39.04	38.92	38.92	39.36	39.74
K	41.06	39.29	39.21	38.14	37.08 [2]	38.15	38.29	38.10	38.08	38.27
L	38.14	36.59	38.63	36.70	37.18 [2]	37.27	37.24	36.91	37.80	37.67
M	33.79	28.30	32.69	34.06	31.83 [2]	32.45	32.69	31.52	32.86	32.38
N	37.86	36.63	36.47	36.38	35.54 [2]	35.42	35.84	36.21	36.45	35.94
O	38.54	36.54	36.28	36.60	35.11 [2]	34.58	36.19	35.69	35.67	35.43
P	38.10	36.95	36.78	32.86	35.21 [2]	34.22	33.70	33.22	32.81	30.94
Q	42.09	31.48	41.25	43.63	37.41 [2]	38.63	41.71	39.08	36.37	41.59
X	40.85	29.55	30.22	43.14	35.28 [2]	35.80	36.67	39.63	34.22	38.02

Women - Femmes - Mujeres
ISIC 3 - CITI 3 - CIIU 3

	1999	2000	2001	2002	2003	2004	2005	2006	2007	2008
Total	35.33	33.38	33.82	33.30	31.41 [2]	31.69	31.91	31.90	32.15	32.32
A-B					31.99 [2]	32.13	32.39	31.14	30.17	30.72
C-Q	35.35	33.38	33.81	33.28	31.41 [2]	31.70	31.91	31.91	32.17	32.34
A					32.02	32.13	32.43	31.33	30.14	30.72
B					26.95	32.00	26.78	23.86	33.35	
C	39.92	37.47	34.10	37.10	33.48 [2]	33.43	35.10	38.43	42.75	35.42
D	36.20	34.67	33.89	33.88	33.58 [2]	33.83	34.18	34.26	34.42	34.81
E	34.59	31.92	32.44	31.68	30.45 [2]	32.72	33.47	31.99	32.81	33.50
F	37.40	35.78	35.67	34.70	29.96 [2]	31.13	31.23	30.84	31.28	32.67
G	36.00	33.99	33.74	32.69	31.93 [2]	32.10	32.32	32.13	32.37	32.55
H	36.25	36.00	35.15	36.14	33.03 [2]	31.98	32.49	32.26	32.57	32.32
I	34.95	32.75	32.58	32.57	32.55 [2]	32.84	33.15	33.48	33.65	33.91
J	35.63	34.29	33.79	32.27	33.00 [2]	33.21	33.27	34.07	34.11	34.78
K	36.98	35.97	35.55	34.61	32.16 [2]	32.62	33.00	32.77	32.36	32.82
L	35.84	34.30	35.52	33.38	32.15 [2]	32.40	32.38	32.26	33.16	33.07
M	31.43	26.28	30.10	30.79	29.06 [2]	29.36	30.05	30.04	30.70	30.53
N	35.48	33.81	33.99	33.67	31.96 [2]	32.76	32.50	32.31	32.72	32.98
O	34.45	33.88	33.06	32.56	30.27 [2]	30.56	30.56	31.64	31.29	30.92
P	38.00	37.86	38.93	38.04	22.78 [2]	21.49	22.32	22.38	21.56	21.30
Q	34.57	38.81	36.23	38.36	30.96 [2]	33.01	36.72	36.50	37.53	40.33
X	12.97	29.22	39.00	39.29	30.25 [2]	27.99	32.44	31.48	27.33	32.30

Explanatory notes: see p. 721.   Notes explicatives: voir p. 723.   Notas explicativas: véase p. 725.

[1] All employees. [2] Prior to 2003: March of each year.   [1] Ensemble des salariés. [2] Avant 2003: mars de chaque année.   [1] Todos los asalariados. [2] Antes de 2003: marzo de cada año.

By economic activity

Par activité économique

Por actividad económica

	Per week / Par semaine / Por semana									
	1999	2000	2001	2002	2003	2004	2005	2006	2007	2008

Germany (DA) (b) — **Employees - Salariés - Asalariados**

Total men and women - Total hommes et femmes - Total hombres y mujeres
ISIC 3 - CITI 3 - CIIU 3

	1999	2000	2001	2002	2003	2004	2005	2006	2007	2008
C	.	.	.	.	.	.	.	.	40.4	40.3
D	.	.	.	.	.	.	.	.	38.4	38.4
E	.	.	.	.	.	.	.	.	38.1	38.2
F	.	.	.	.	.	.	.	.	39.1	39.0
G	.	.	.	.	.	.	.	.	39.1	39.2
H	.	.	.	.	.	.	.	.	39.3	39.3
I	.	.	.	.	.	.	.	.	40.1	40.3
J	.	.	.	.	.	.	.	.	38.5	38.6
K	.	.	.	.	.	.	.	.	38.8	38.9
L	.	.	.	.	.	.	.	.		
M	.	.	.	.	.	.	.	.	38.6	38.5
N	.	.	.	.	.	.	.	.	38.9	39.0
O	.	.	.	.	.	.	.	.	39.2	39.2

Men - Hommes - Hombres
ISIC 3 - CITI 3 - CIIU 3

	1999	2000	2001	2002	2003	2004	2005	2006	2007	2008
C	.	.	.	.	.	.	.	.	40.6	40.5
D	.	.	.	.	.	.	.	.	38.5	38.5
E	.	.	.	.	.	.	.	.	38.2	38.3
F	.	.	.	.	.	.	.	.	39.1	39.0
G	.	.	.	.	.	.	.	.	39.3	39.5
H	.	.	.	.	.	.	.	.	39.5	39.5
I	.	.	.	.	.	.	.	.	40.5	40.7
J	.	.	.	.	.	.	.	.	38.6	38.7
K	.	.	.	.	.	.	.	.	39.1	39.1
L	.	.	.	.	.	.	.	.		
M	.	.	.	.	.	.	.	.	38.9	38.8
N	.	.	.	.	.	.	.	.	39.2	39.4
O	.	.	.	.	.	.	.	.	39.5	39.6

Women - Femmes - Mujeres
ISIC 3 - CITI 3 - CIIU 3

	1999	2000	2001	2002	2003	2004	2005	2006	2007	2008
C	.	.	.	.	.	.	.	.	38.5	38.4
D	.	.	.	.	.	.	.	.	37.9	37.9
E	.	.	.	.	.	.	.	.	37.7	37.8
F	.	.	.	.	.	.	.	.	38.8	38.8
G	.	.	.	.	.	.	.	.	38.5	38.6
H	.	.	.	.	.	.	.	.	39.1	39.1
I	.	.	.	.	.	.	.	.	38.6	38.6
J	.	.	.	.	.	.	.	.	38.5	38.6
K	.	.	.	.	.	.	.	.	38.4	38.5
L	.	.	.	.	.	.	.	.		
M	.	.	.	.	.	.	.	.	38.3	38.2
N	.	.	.	.	.	.	.	.	38.8	38.9
O	.	.	.	.	.	.	.	.	38.6	38.6

Germany (DA) (b) — **Wage earners - Ouvriers - Obreros**

Total men and women - Total hommes et femmes - Total hombres y mujeres
ISIC 3 - CITI 3 - CIIU 3

	1999	2000	2001	2002	2003	2004	2005	2006	2007	2008
A [1]	203.7	194.2	192.0	195.4	197.3	198.8	196.0	191.9 [2]	.	.
C	40.6	41.0	40.8	41.5	40.8	41.1	40.8	41.6 [2]	.	.
D	37.5	37.9	37.8	37.6	37.7	37.6	37.6	37.9 [2]	.	.
E	38.7	38.7	38.7	38.7	38.7	38.5	38.5	38.4 [2]	.	.
F	39.7	39.2	39.2	38.8	38.9	38.9	39.0	39.9 [2]	.	.

Men - Hommes - Hombres
ISIC 3 - CITI 3 - CIIU 3

	1999	2000	2001	2002	2003	2004	2005	2006	2007	2008
A [1]	208.2	197.0	194.7	199.4	201.4	203.1	200.0	195.6 [2]	.	.
C	40.6	41.0	40.8	41.5	40.8	41.1	40.8	41.6 [2]	.	.
D	37.6	38.0	37.9	37.7	37.7	37.7	37.7	37.9 [2]	.	.
E	38.7	38.7	38.7	38.7	38.7	38.5	38.5	38.4 [2]	.	.
F	39.7	39.2	39.2	38.8	38.9	38.9	39.0	39.9 [2]	.	.

Women - Femmes - Mujeres
ISIC 3 - CITI 3 - CIIU 3

	1999	2000	2001	2002	2003	2004	2005	2006	2007	2008
A [1]	192.3	186.4	185.3	183.1	184.7	184.6	183.5	180.4 [2]	.	.
C	39.5	39.7	39.6	39.9	39.6	39.7	38.6	39.7 [2]	.	.
D	37.0	37.4	37.3	37.2	37.2	37.2	37.3	37.6 [2]	.	.
E	38.2	38.3	38.3	38.3	38.4	38.4	38.3	38.3 [2]	.	.
F	39.9	37.0	39.1	38.2	37.9	37.4	38.2	39.7 [2]	.	.

Explanatory notes: see p. 721.   Notes explicatives: voir p. 723.   Notas explicativas: véase p. 725.

[1] Permanent workers; per month. [2] Series discontinued.   [1] Travailleurs permanents; par mois. [2] Série arrêtée.   [1] Trabajadores permanentes; por mes. [2] Serie interrumpida.

	Per week				Par semaine				Por semana	
	1999	2000	2001	2002	2003	2004	2005	2006	2007	2008

Gibraltar (CA) (b) [1][2] Employees - Salariés - Asalariados

Total men and women - Total hommes et femmes - Total hombres y mujeres
ISIC 3 - CITI 3 - CIIU 3

	1999	2000	2001	2002	2003	2004	2005	2006	2007	2008
Total	43.1	43.0	43.7	43.2	42.0	41.7	41.6	41.9	41.7	.
C-Q	43.1	43.0	43.7	43.2	42.0	41.7	41.6	41.9	41.7	.
D	46.4	45.1	45.5	46.9	44.8	50.0	49.1	47.7	47.2	.
E	70.4	62.1	56.0	59.4	63.5	50.9	51.1	52.3	52.5	
F	42.5	43.4	43.5	42.9	43.5	41.0	41.8	42.3	41.9	
G	38.9	38.7	39.1	39.1	39.2	38.5	38.5	38.8	38.4	
H	40.6	39.4	40.4	39.9	39.1	38.9	38.5	39.3	37.8	
I	45.6	45.3	49.3	46.2	48.8	46.8	46.7	47.5	46.0	
J	36.9	33.9	38.5	37.0	39.4	39.1	34.7	37.4	36.9	
K	44.2	44.5	44.7	44.5	40.0	40.3	39.6	40.0	41.6	
L	48.2	46.2	48.8	63.8	51.7	47.5	49.2	50.9	48.6	
M	42.7	42.5	44.1	45.1	47.6	45.7	44.3	47.0	49.2	
N	48.9	52.0	.	52.1	49.5	50.7	47.0	47.4	47.1	
O	41.2	40.9	41.3	41.4	45.8	46.0	44.5	43.7	45.0	

Men - Hommes - Hombres
ISIC 3 - CITI 3 - CIIU 3

	1999	2000	2001	2002	2003	2004	2005	2006	2007	2008
Total	44.3	44.2	45.0	44.5	43.7	42.8	42.8	43.2	43.1	
C-Q	44.3	44.2	45.0	44.5	43.7	42.8	42.8	43.2	43.1	
D	47.1	45.6	46.0	47.5	45.4	50.7	50.1	48.9	48.3	
E	70.4	62.1	56.0	59.4	63.5	50.9	51.1	52.3	52.5	
F	42.7	43.6	43.6	43.1	43.6	41.1	41.9	42.4	42.1	
G	39.3	39.8	40.1	40.0	39.7	39.3	39.3	39.8	39.3	
H	41.7	41.5	41.2	40.9	39.7	39.6	39.3	40.0	39.2	
I	46.4	46.7	50.6	47.3	49.8	48.1	47.8	48.2	46.8	
J	36.4	36.2	39.7	38.4	44.5	40.0	.	37.9	39.1	
K	48.1	48.8	49.1	48.4	41.9	42.0	41.0	41.9	43.5	
L	49.8	47.5	50.6	67.3	54.3	49.5	49.8	53.0	49.3	
M	48.5	45.3	53.7	47.8	50.0	52.0	48.2	50.7	56.2	
N	55.8	56.5	56.9	61.7	60.0	59.6	53.6	53.3	55.3	
O	43.0	42.1	42.8	42.5	48.4	48.8	47.1	45.4	48.5	

Women - Femmes - Mujeres
ISIC 3 - CITI 3 - CIIU 3

	1999	2000	2001	2002	2003	2004	2005	2006	2007	2008
Total	39.9	39.2	39.6	39.2	39.2	38.5	38.1	38.4	37.2	
C-Q	39.9	39.2	39.6	39.2	39.2	38.5	38.1	38.4	37.2	
D	40.1	40.5	40.7	41.2	39.6	41.5	37.9	36.7	37.1	
F	38.4	37.1	39.0	37.7	39.5	38.0	37.6	37.1	34.8	
G	38.2	37.1	37.6	38.0	38.5	37.4	37.5	37.6	37.2	
H	38.6	38.0	39.2	38.5	38.1	38.0	37.4	38.4	36.0	
I	38.5	37.2	38.8	39.4	38.4	37.4	37.7	37.6	35.1	
J	37.1	32.3	37.3	37.0	37.7	37.7	34.7	36.6	35.4	
K	36.5	36.6	36.8	36.9	37.1	37.4	37.3	36.9	36.9	
L	41.9	41.2	42.5	44.5	42.6	39.6	45.6	42.0	44.5	
M	40.0	41.4	40.6	44.1	46.6	43.9	43.1	46.0	46.8	
N	47.9	50.7	49.8	48.3	46.0	46.5	43.7	43.5	40.4	
O	37.4	37.4	37.4	38.0	37.7	37.7	37.2	38.4	35.3	

Greece (BA) (a) Total employment - Emploi total - Empleo total

Total men and women - Total hommes et femmes - Total hombres y mujeres
ISIC 3 - CITI 3 - CIIU 3 [3][4][5]

	1999	2000	2001	2002	2003	2004	2005	2006	2007
Total	41.0	41.0	41.0	41.0	41.0	41.2	41.1	40.3	39.9
A-B	42.0	40.0	41.0	41.0	41.0	42.2	42.0	38.7	38.2
C-Q	41.0	41.0	41.0	41.0	41.0	41.0	41.1	40.5	40.1
A	42.0	40.0	41.0	41.0	41.0	42.0	41.1	38.6	38.0
B	47.0	43.0	45.0	47.0	47.0	45.2	51.3	43.4	45.8
C	42.0	39.0	41.0	40.0	41.0	42.5	41.0	42.0	41.8
D	42.0	43.0	42.0	42.0	42.0	42.3	42.3	42.1	42.0
E	39.0	39.0	39.0	39.0	39.0	40.5	38.7	38.9	38.9
F	41.0	41.0	41.0	41.0	42.0	42.1	42.0	41.0	41.5
G	45.0	45.0	44.0	45.0	45.0	44.7	44.6	43.6	43.4
H	50.0	48.0	48.0	49.0	49.0	47.7	47.8	47.6	47.0
I	46.0	46.0	46.0	45.0	45.0	45.3	45.7	45.5	44.6
J	39.0	39.0	39.0	39.0	39.0	38.9	39.1	38.5	38.5
K	42.0	42.0	41.0	42.0	41.0	41.8	41.4	41.3	40.2
L	39.0	39.0	38.0	38.0	38.0	38.7	38.4	37.8	37.2
M	23.0	26.0	24.0	26.0	25.0	25.3	24.7	24.6	23.6
N	39.0	38.0	38.0	38.0	38.0	38.6	38.5	38.4	37.6
O	40.0	40.0	41.0	41.0	41.0	40.0	40.4	39.3	39.1
P	36.0	37.0	37.0	38.0	38.0	38.8	39.2	39.0	38.7
Q	34.0	53.0	.	36.0	39.0	38.1	39.8	30.2	32.4

ISIC 4 - CITI 4 - CIIU 4 [4] (2008)

2008	
40.1	Total
38.6	A
42.2	B
40.3	B-U
41.8	C
38.5	D
38.2	E
41.0	F
43.7	G
46.1	H
47.2	I
39.0	J
38.5	K
46.2	L
40.7	M
39.2	N
37.6	O
23.8	P
38.0	Q
39.0	R
40.8	S
38.4	T
40.5	U
	X

Explanatory notes: see p. 721.

[1] Excl. part-time workers and juveniles. [2] Oct. of each year. [3] Persons aged 15 years and over. [4] Second quarter of each year. [5] Excl. conscripts.

Notes explicatives: voir p. 723.

[1] Non compris les travailleurs à temps partiel et les jeunes. [2] Oct. de chaque année. [3] Personnes âgées de 15 ans et plus. [4] Deuxième trimestre de chaque année. [5] Non compris les conscrits.

Notas explicativas: véase p. 725.

[1] Excl. los trabajadores a tempo parcial y los jóvenes. [2] Oct. de cada año. [3] Personas de 15 años y más. [4] Segundo trimestre de cada año. [5] Excl. los conscriptos.

By economic activity   **Par activité économique**   **Por actividad económica**

	Per week			Par semaine			Por semana			
	1999	2000	2001	2002	2003	2004	2005	2006	2007	2008	

Greece (BA) (a) — Total employment - Emploi total - Empleo total

Men - Hommes - Hombres
ISIC 3 - CITI 3 - CIIU 3 [1][2][3]   ISIC 4 - CITI 4 - CIIU 4 [2]

	1999	2000	2001	2002	2003	2004	2005	2006	2007	2008	
Total	43.0	43.0	43.0	43.0	43.0	43.3	43.3	42.5	42.3	42.3	Total
A-B	45.0	43.0	44.0	44.0	45.0	46.4	42.5	43.1	43.2	43.1	A
C-Q	43.0	43.0	43.0	43.0	43.0	38.0	42.9	42.5	42.1	42.7	B
A	45.0	43.0	44.0	44.0	45.0	46.4	46.0	43.0	43.0	42.2	B-U
B	47.0	45.0	45.0	48.0	48.0	45.8	51.7	44.5	47.1	42.7	C
C	42.0	39.0	41.0	40.0	41.0	42.6	41.1	42.3	41.8	39.0	D
D	43.0	43.0	43.0	43.0	43.0	43.3	43.2	42.9	43.0	38.5	E
E	39.0	39.0	39.0	39.0	39.0	41.3	39.2	38.9	39.1	41.1	F
F	41.0	41.0	42.0	41.0	42.0	42.1	42.0	41.1	41.5	45.7	G
G	46.0	46.0	46.0	47.0	47.0	46.1	46.2	45.4	45.4	47.4	H
H	52.0	51.0	50.0	51.0	51.0	50.7	50.9	50.4	49.3	49.8	I
I	47.0	47.0	47.0	46.0	46.0	46.8	47.1	47.2	46.4	39.5	J
J	40.0	40.0	40.0	40.0	40.0	40.1	40.1	40.1	39.4	39.3	K
K	44.0	44.0	43.0	44.0	43.0	44.0	43.6	43.8	42.3	44.4	L
L	40.0	39.0	39.0	40.0	39.0	39.5	39.1	38.9	38.5	42.7	M
M	25.0	28.0	25.0	27.0	27.0	26.7	25.5	25.9	24.5	41.9	N
N	40.0	40.0	40.0	40.0	40.0	40.1	39.8	39.8	39.7	38.3	O
O	40.0	41.0	41.0	41.0	41.0	40.6	41.4	40.2	39.8	24.9	P
P	41.0	45.0	43.0	37.0	42.0	43.9	47.6	43.9	40.9	39.7	Q
Q	36.0	53.0	.	38.0	40.0	39.8	39.8	40.0	31.8	40.3	R
										41.2	S
										37.8	T
										42.7	U
										.	X

Women - Femmes - Mujeres
ISIC 3 - CITI 3 - CIIU 3 [1][2][3]   ISIC 4 - CITI 4 - CIIU 4 [2]

	1999	2000	2001	2002	2003	2004	2005	2006	2007	2008	
Total	38.0	38.0	38.0	38.0	38.0	37.7	37.6	36.7	36.2	36.7	Total
A-B	37.0	36.0	37.0	36.0	37.0	36.3	39.9	32.8	31.4	32.3	A
C-Q	38.0	39.0	38.0	39.0	38.0	41.1	38.0	37.3	36.9	38.0	B
A	37.0	36.0	37.0	36.0	37.0	36.2	34.7	32.8	31.4	37.3	B-U
B	42.0	34.0	39.0	37.0	39.0	41.2	48.1	35.1	38.0	39.4	C
C	41.0	41.0	39.0	40.0	40.0	40.0	39.6	39.1	41.6	36.9	D
D	40.0	41.0	40.0	40.0	40.0	39.7	40.1	39.8	39.3	36.6	E
E	38.0	38.0	38.0	37.0	38.0	37.7	36.3	39.1	38.1	36.8	F
F	38.0	37.0	38.0	41.0	38.0	41.3	39.8	37.2	40.3	41.0	G
G	43.0	43.0	42.0	43.0	43.0	42.6	42.1	41.1	40.6	39.1	H
H	47.0	45.0	45.0	46.0	46.0	44.3	43.9	44.1	44.3	44.1	I
I	40.0	40.0	40.0	39.0	39.0	38.8	39.3	38.4	37.4	38.2	J
J	38.0	39.0	38.0	38.0	38.0	37.6	38.1	36.8	37.6	37.8	K
K	39.0	40.0	39.0	40.0	39.0	39.1	38.9	38.6	37.7	48.9	L
L	37.0	38.0	36.0	36.0	37.0	37.0	36.9	35.8	35.0	38.4	M
M	22.0	25.0	24.0	25.0	25.0	24.4	24.2	23.7	23.0	36.4	N
N	38.0	38.0	38.0	38.0	37.0	37.6	37.6	37.7	36.4	36.4	O
O	39.0	39.0	41.0	41.0	41.0	39.4	39.5	38.3	38.4	23.1	P
P	36.0	36.0	37.0	38.0	38.0	38.4	38.9	38.7	38.5	37.2	Q
Q	31.0	.	.	35.0	38.0	37.4	.	28.3	38.0	36.8	R
										40.5	S
										38.4	T
										32.3	U
										.	X

Hungary (DA) (a) [4][5][6] — Wage earners - Ouvriers - Obreros

Total men and women - Total hommes et femmes - Total hombres y mujeres
ISIC 3 - CITI 3 - CIIU 3

	1999	2000	2001	2002	2003	2004	2005	2006	2007	2008
C	146.5	148.5	148.2	148.4	150.1	151.9	152.9	152.5	147.7	152.6
D	149.6	149.6	147.2	147.3	148.1	150.5	150.2	149.9	148.2	148.8
E	144.7	145.2	144.5	144.5	145.7	148.2	147.4	146.4	145.8	147.8

Explanatory notes: see p. 721.

[1] Persons aged 15 years and over. [2] Second quarter of each year. [3] Excl. conscripts. [4] Full-time workers. [5] Enterprises with 5 or more employees. [6] Per month.

Notes explicatives: voir p. 723.

[1] Personnes âgées de 15 ans et plus. [2] Deuxième trimestre de chaque année. [3] Non compris les conscrits. [4] Travailleurs à plein temps. [5] Entreprises occupant 5 salariés et plus. [6] Par mois.

Notas explicativas: véase p. 725.

[1] Personas de 15 años y más. [2] Segundo trimestre de cada año. [3] Excl. los conscriptos. [4] Trabajadores a tiempo completo. [5] Empresas con 5 y más asalariados. [6] Por mes.

	HOURS OF WORK	DURÉE DU TRAVAIL	HORAS DE TRABAJO
	By economic activity	Par activité économique	Por actividad económica

	Per week				Par semaine				Por semana	
	1999	2000	2001	2002	2003	2004	2005	2006	2007	2008

Iceland (BA) (a)   Employees - Salariés - Asalariados

Total men and women - Total hommes et femmes - Total hombres y mujeres
ISIC 3 - CITI 3 - CIIU 3

	1999	2000	2001	2002	2003	2004	2005	2006	2007	2008
Total	40.6	40.9	40.3	40.0	39.2 ı	39.6	39.7	39.7	39.6	39.6
A-B	58.3	60.3	57.8	50.6	. ı	.	.	.	.	.
A	44.0	38.8	41.7	44.7	45.3	43.3	43.0	47.6	44.3	46.3
B	60.4	67.1	62.7	53.4	55.1	55.9	57.3	64.6	60.9	62.0
C	47.6	40.5	42.3	53.6	36.6 ı	42.7	63.6	59.8	61.3	53.5
D	42.7	43.5	43.5	42.3	41.1 ı	41.1	42.2	42.7	42.2	43.0
E	47.1	47.8	47.7	46.4	44.0 ı	46.6	44.9	43.9	42.1	43.8
F	47.4	50.1	48.4	48.0	46.8 ı	48.0	46.7	46.7	47.1	46.4
G	38.0	38.5	37.0	38.0	38.4 ı	38.8	39.3	38.9	38.9	38.2
H	33.6	32.6	32.7	34.1	36.8 ı	37.4	36.8	36.9	36.6	35.1
I	43.0	42.3	43.2	43.8	42.8 ı	42.1	43.1	42.6	41.6	41.6
J	40.4	41.7	40.9	40.0	39.8 ı	40.1	38.8	38.8	40.1	40.5
K	42.1	40.9	40.6	39.6	39.2 ı	39.7	38.6	39.6	40.3	40.0
L	43.5	43.9	43.2	43.8	41.4 ı	40.9	41.1	40.8	42.4	41.4
M	39.8	39.2	39.7	39.7	36.2 ı	35.9	36.8	35.9	34.7	35.8
N	33.3	33.4	33.2	33.9	33.3 ı	33.9	33.5	33.1	33.8	33.6
O	36.2	36.4	37.0	35.7	35.8 ı	36.8	37.5	36.0	35.7	36.6
P	.	.	55.0	.	. ı	.	.	.	.	.
Q	41.3	41.9	40.9	37.6	37.5 ı	37.0	37.4	40.5	34.2	24.0
X	.	.	.	.	43.5 ı	41.7	41.4	.	42.1	49.5

Men - Hommes - Hombres
ISIC 3 - CITI 3 - CIIU 3

	1999	2000	2001	2002	2003	2004	2005	2006	2007	2008
Total	47.9	48.1	46.8	45.9	44.2 ı	45.0	45.4	45.1	44.7	44.3
A-B	62.7	67.2	61.6	55.4	. ı	.	.	.	.	.
A	46.9	44.6	46.1	50.7	46.3	45.5	45.4	50.9	49.4	49.6
B	64.3	71.9	64.3	56.8	58.0	58.6	58.7	66.4	62.2	65.9
C	47.6	40.5	42.1	59.2	36.6 ı	43.0	63.6	59.8	61.3	53.5
D	47.2	47.5	47.2	45.4	43.8 ı	44.5	45.5	46.5	45.1	45.8
E	48.2	49.3	48.9	48.8	45.4 ı	47.8	46.4	45.6	44.2	45.0
F	48.2	50.8	48.8	49.3	47.2 ı	48.7	47.9	47.7	47.8	47.3
G	44.6	44.8	43.1	44.5	43.0 ı	43.9	45.0	43.1	43.8	42.5
H	42.5	37.6	38.1	38.6	40.1 ı	45.2	42.3	40.0	39.6	38.7
I	48.3	49.2	50.3	49.2	46.8 ı	45.9	46.7	46.2	45.8	44.3
J	48.3	46.1	47.1	44.9	42.8 ı	45.3	44.8	43.2	44.0	43.4
K	47.6	47.9	45.7	44.8	42.6 ı	44.2	42.4	43.3	43.5	42.5
L	48.3	49.8	49.3	47.6	45.9 ı	45.3	46.7	45.1	46.9	45.2
M	46.6	47.5	42.7	44.8	39.9 ı	40.5	39.7	38.3	36.1	37.1
N	41.8	39.5	36.6	41.5	37.9 ı	38.9	40.2	40.4	38.8	37.7
O	43.8	42.6	45.0	41.7	40.8 ı	41.2	43.0	40.0	41.5	41.6
P	.	.	55.0	.	. ı	.	.	.	.	.
Q	43.9	43.7	40.8	38.3	39.3 ı	37.6	37.9	39.4	39.6	40.0
X	.	.	.	.	. ı	47.6	40.2	.	44.0	58.7

Women - Femmes - Mujeres
ISIC 3 - CITI 3 - CIIU 3

	1999	2000	2001	2002	2003	2004	2005	2006	2007	2008
Total	33.2	33.6	33.8	34.3	34.1 ı	34.0	33.8	33.9	33.9	34.4
A-B	34.0	34.7	35.2	34.0	. ı	.	.	.	.	.
A	38.8	31.2	36.5	37.8	44.0	40.1	38.9	39.6	34.2	41.5
B	32.0	38.0	31.7	26.7	28.0	28.9	31.9	39.3	28.6	25.3
C	.	.	45.0	45.3	.	.	.	.	.	.
D	33.4	34.1	35.1	35.9	35.3 ı	34.2	35.1	33.9	35.3	36.0
E	40.0	42.1	43.3	40.2	36.9 ı	38.4	39.5	37.9	35.9	39.7
F	34.4	33.0	38.6	29.4	37.0 ı	37.6	34.2	34.7	26.2	35.9
G	31.0	32.1	30.3	31.1	33.0 ı	32.3	32.0	33.7	32.6	32.6
H	28.7	28.3	28.3	29.9	34.8 ı	32.0	32.3	33.7	34.6	32.1
I	35.9	34.2	34.9	36.5	36.2 ı	35.1	36.5	36.8	34.4	36.3
J	34.8	38.8	38.1	37.6	38.4 ı	38.0	36.4	36.4	37.6	38.5
K	35.5	32.8	33.7	34.0	34.3 ı	34.3	33.5	33.7	34.2	35.2
L	37.2	36.7	36.8	39.4	37.0 ı	37.3	35.5	36.6	37.8	37.7
M	36.6	36.1	38.4	37.7	34.2 ı	33.3	35.5	34.8	34.0	35.2
N	32.1	32.5	32.7	32.5	32.6 ı	33.0	32.4	32.0	33.0	32.9
O	31.0	31.5	28.7	31.1	30.4 ı	32.4	32.3	32.2	30.7	31.8
P	.	.	55.0	.	. ı	.	.	.	.	.
Q	31.8	37.7	41.2	36.1	33.6 ı	34.5	36.7	44.7	28.5	19.5
X	.	.	.	.	. ı	.	45.0	.	37.8	34.0

Explanatory notes: see p. 721.	Notes explicatives: voir p. 723.	Notas explicativas: véase p. 725.
[1] Prior to 2003: April and Nov. of each year.	[1] Avant 2003: avril et nov. de chaque année.	[1] Antes de 2003: abril y nov. de cada año.

By economic activity   **Par activité économique**   **Por actividad económica**

	Per week — Par semaine — Por semana									
	1999	2000	2001	2002	2003	2004	2005	2006	2007	2008

Ireland (BA) (c) [1]   **Total employment - Emploi total - Empleo total**

Total men and women - Total hommes et femmes - Total hombres y mujeres
ISIC 3 - CITI 3 - CIIU 3

	1999	2000	2001	2002	2003	2004	2005	2006	2007	2008
Total	38.1	38.0	37.9	37.8	37.2	37.0	36.9	36.6	36.4	36.1
A-B	53.9	53.4	53.8	54.2	52.5	52.8	53.1	51.9	51.6	49.2
C-Q	37.1	37.1	37.1	36.9	36.5	36.3	36.2	36.0	35.9	35.6
A	54.0	53.6	54.0	54.4	52.7	53.0	53.3	52.1	51.7	49.2
B	44.9	41.0	40.5	45.9	45.6	44.1	46.4	43.8	49.3	49.9
C	42.8	42.2	42.0	41.8	41.0	41.6	40.6	42.1	40.8	42.0
D	39.9	39.5	39.6	39.4	39.2	39.1	39.0	38.8	39.1	38.9
E	38.4	38.5	39.1	39.1	38.9	38.8	38.6	38.6	38.5	40.2
F	41.9	42.4	42.1	41.9	41.4	41.3	41.1	40.9	40.9	40.7
G	36.3	36.0	35.5	35.6	34.7	34.7	34.4	34.3	34.1	34.1
H	34.1	34.1	34.5	35.1	33.2	33.3	33.4	33.5	33.4	32.8
I	40.4	40.4	40.4	40.4	40.6	40.2	39.7	39.3	38.9	38.7
J	38.0	38.0	37.8	37.9	37.7	37.6	37.4	37.3	37.4	37.0
K	38.1	38.0	38.1	37.6	37.9	37.8	37.4	37.1	37.0	37.3
L	37.8	37.8	37.5	37.0	36.9	36.8	36.5	35.9	35.6	35.9
M	28.7	28.8	29.3	29.0	29.0	29.2	28.7	28.3	28.0	28.2
N	34.1	33.9	33.1	33.7	33.2	32.5	32.6	32.6	32.6	32.1
O	34.4	34.3	34.1	34.0	34.0	33.9	34.0	34.0	34.0	33.0
P	26.3	29.9	31.9	24.8	31.5	28.3	28.5	29.8	30.9	27.7
Q	40.5	42.2	36.1	41.0	39.5	39.2	35.7	38.7	34.4	38.3
X	33.5	34.6	33.8	35.2	32.8	35.7	35.0	34.6	31.1	33.4

Men - Hommes - Hombres
ISIC 3 - CITI 3 - CIIU 3

	1999	2000	2001	2002	2003	2004	2005	2006	2007	2008
Total	42.3	42.0	42.1	42.0	41.3	41.3	41.1	40.5	40.6	40.3
A-B	56.7	55.7	55.9	56.1	54.5	54.7	55.0	53.4	53.5	51.8
C-Q	40.8	40.7	40.9	40.8	40.3	40.3	40.2	39.7	39.9	39.6
A	56.8	55.9	56.2	56.3	54.6	55.0	55.2	53.6	53.5	51.8
B	47.1	41.8	40.2	46.5	47.4	44.1	46.5	44.6	51.6	51.6
C	43.1	42.6	42.7	42.3	41.6	42.5	41.3	42.8	41.5	42.8
D	41.3	40.9	41.0	40.9	40.7	40.7	40.4	40.2	40.5	40.2
E	40.3	40.0	40.1	40.2	39.7	40.5	40.2	39.8	39.6	41.3
F	42.3	42.7	42.5	42.3	41.9	41.8	41.6	41.3	41.4	41.2
G	41.0	40.5	40.4	40.6	39.7	39.9	39.4	39.2	38.7	38.5
H	40.3	39.8	40.5	40.7	38.3	37.9	37.5	37.4	37.4	36.9
I	42.0	42.0	42.0	42.5	42.0	41.9	41.5	41.1	40.4	40.4
J	40.7	40.8	40.9	40.9	40.7	41.0	41.1	40.5	41.2	40.7
K	41.6	41.4	42.1	41.3	41.5	40.9	41.1	40.5	40.8	40.7
L	40.2	40.1	40.0	39.5	39.3	39.4	39.7	38.6	38.7	39.0
M	31.4	31.9	32.6	32.2	32.6	32.9	32.1	31.8	32.0	32.2
N	42.0	41.2	41.1	41.5	40.3	40.0	40.3	38.8	39.4	38.7
O	38.6	37.4	37.4	37.9	38.0	38.4	38.4	36.5	38.5	36.8
P	40.5	44.6	47.7	45.3	41.7	37.7	39.6	41.3	42.0	40.5
Q	47.6	46.3	38.5	46.8	40.2	41.3	40.6	38.0	34.7	43.2
X	37.1	36.6	36.8	37.3	34.9	37.5	38.0	35.2	32.2	33.9

Women - Femmes - Mujeres
ISIC 3 - CITI 3 - CIIU 3

	1999	2000	2001	2002	2003	2004	2005	2006	2007	2008
Total	32.7	32.8	32.5	32.4	32.1	31.7	31.7	31.7	31.4	31.3
A-B	35.8	36.8	38.5	39.1	39.3	38.6	39.4	39.3	37.3	33.8
C-Q	32.6	32.7	32.4	32.4	32.0	31.7	31.6	31.6	31.4	31.2
A	35.7	36.9	38.4	39.1	39.4	38.5	39.4	39.4	37.3	33.7
B	38.9	34.5	41.8	40.3	34.8	43.8	39.0	37.6	38.1	39.7
C	38.3	35.7	35.0	34.5	30.3	34.7	35.4	35.4	34.7	33.7
D	37.1	36.7	36.4	36.2	36.0	35.9	36.1	35.8	35.9	35.8
E	34.3	32.7	34.8	33.9	34.1	32.9	33.3	34.0	34.7	35.0
F	33.8	35.7	35.1	34.8	34.0	32.6	32.5	32.7	33.0	32.5
G	31.4	31.2	30.6	30.9	30.2	29.7	29.9	29.7	29.5	29.8
H	30.3	30.5	30.7	31.0	29.6	29.5	30.6	30.6	30.5	30.0
I	36.4	36.1	36.5	35.4	36.6	35.1	34.3	34.1	34.0	33.5
J	36.0	36.1	35.7	35.9	35.6	35.2	34.7	35.2	35.0	34.5
K	34.2	34.4	33.9	33.7	33.9	34.2	33.5	33.2	33.1	33.6
L	34.4	34.8	34.5	34.2	34.2	33.8	33.8	33.3	32.9	33.2
M	27.4	27.4	27.8	27.7	27.5	27.7	27.4	26.9	26.6	26.8
N	32.2	32.2	31.4	31.9	31.6	30.9	31.0	31.5	31.1	30.9
O	31.0	31.7	31.3	31.1	31.0	30.2	30.6	31.8	30.4	29.8
P	24.7	28.6	30.2	23.3	28.9	27.1	26.6	29.0	30.1	27.1
Q	34.2	38.5	34.7	35.0	38.4	37.8	33.9	39.0	34.2	30.1
X	30.0	32.7	31.6	33.0	30.3	32.9	29.0	33.2	28.4	32.8

Ireland (DA) (b) [1][2][3]   **Wage earners - Ouvriers - Obreros**

Total men and women - Total hommes et femmes - Total hombres y mujeres
ISIC 3 - CITI 3 - CIIU 3

	1999	2000	2001	2002	2003	2004	2005	2006	2007	2008
A-B [4]	.	.	40.9	54.2	52.5	52.8	53.1	51.9	51.6	49.2
A [4]	.	.	.	54.5	52.7	53.0	53.3	52.1	51.7	49.2
B [4]	.	.	.	45.9	45.6	44.1	46.3	43.8	49.3	49.9
D [5]	40.5	40.7	39.9	36.9	36.5	36.3	36.2	36.0	35.9	35.6

Explanatory notes: see p. 721.   Notes explicatives: voir p. 723.   Notas explicativas: véase p. 725.

[1] Second quarter of each year. [2] Establishments with 10 or more persons employed. [3] Incl. juveniles. [4] Permanent workers. [5] Industrial workers.

[1] Deuxième trimestre de chaque année. [2] Etablissements occupant 10 personnes et plus. [3] Y compris les jeunes gens. [4] Travailleurs permanents. [5] Travailleurs de l'industrie.

[1] Segundo trimestre de cada año. [2] Establecimientos con 10 y más trabajadores. [3] Incl. los jóvenes. [4] Trabajadores permanentes. [5] Trabajadores industriales.

	Per week				Par semaine			Por semana		
	1999	2000	2001	2002	2003	2004	2005	2006	2007	2008
Ireland (DA) (b) [1][2][3]					Wage earners - Ouvriers - Obreros					
Men - Hommes - Hombres										
ISIC 3 - CITI 3 - CIIU 3										
A-B [4]				56.1	54.5	54.7	55.0	53.4	53.5	51.8
A [4]				56.3	54.6	55.0	55.2	53.6	53.5	51.8
B [4]				46.5	47.4	44.1	46.5	44.6	51.6	51.6
D [5]	42.2	42.1	41.3	40.8	40.3	40.3	40.2	39.7	39.9	39.6
Women - Femmes - Mujeres										
ISIC 3 - CITI 3 - CIIU 3										
A-B [4]				39.1	39.3	38.6	39.4	39.3	37.3	33.8
A [4]				39.1	39.4	38.5	39.4	39.4	37.3	33.7
B [4]				40.3	34.8	43.8	46.5	37.6	38.1	39.7
D [5]	37.3	38.0	36.8	32.3	32.0	31.7	31.7	31.6	31.4	31.2
Isle of Man (DA) (b) [6]					Employees - Salariés - Asalariados					
Total men and women - Total hommes et femmes - Total hombres y mujeres										
ISIC 3 - CITI 3 - CIIU 3										
Total	35.8	35.1	35.5	34.4	34.9	34.5	34.6	33.9	34.3	34.1
C-Q	35.8	35.1	35.5	34.5	34.9	34.4	34.7	33.9	34.4	34.1
A	42.4	40.7	39.6							
C	43.3									
D	40.7	39.2	37.9	39.8	38.6	39.6	39.7	39.0	38.6	38.3
E	40.1	36.0	37.0	37.7	39.9	40.1	38.6	38.4	39.0	34.1
F	47.0	43.5	41.9	43.2	44.1	40.3	39.7	41.6	44.0	41.8
G	35.2	33.9	34.3	30.9	31.6	33.4	34.1	33.6	31.6	32.9
H	35.5	37.2	31.1	33.2	30.9	32.1	36.6	29.4	30.4	30.9
I	41.7	41.3	39.1	40.1	38.6	41.3	40.2	40.5	41.3	38.6
J	34.6	34.7	35.2	34.7	35.2	33.7	34.6	34.5	34.1	34.7
K	36.6	34.9	33.6	37.1	35.0	34.4	35.4	33.9	35.0	34.6
L	38.4	37.3	34.7	36.2	37.7	35.0	35.2	36.0	37.7	36.0
M	25.5	23.2	26.3	25.0	26.7	25.9	20.8	23.0	27.2	22.4
N	34.1	33.5	35.5	32.9	32.8	34.6	34.3	33.0	34.4	35.4
O	30.7	31.7	33.8		29.7	27.3	32.9	31.9	27.4	30.9
P	29.3							37.5		
Men - Hommes - Hombres										
ISIC 3 - CITI 3 - CIIU 3										
Total	40.1	39.4	39.4	38.1	38.5	38.8	38.7	37.6	34.3	38.1
C-Q	40.0	39.4	39.4	38.1	38.5	38.8	38.7	37.5	34.4	38.1
C										
D	42.9	41.5	39.8	40.3	41.9	42.9	40.9	40.4	39.4	39.0
E	41.4	39.3	37.0	41.6	39.9	40.1	38.8	39.1	39.1	37.5
F	47.0	43.9	43.5	43.8	45.1	41.7	40.7	43.4	44.0	44.2
G	39.4	39.3	39.2	38.0	36.3	38.3	39.0	39.3	38.0	37.5
H	42.3	41.5	30.8	38.9	33.4	38.4	40.0	30.9	33.0	33.5
I	44.9	43.8	42.7	42.8	39.8	43.6	41.9	42.2	43.1	42.0
J	36.6	36.0	36.1	36.0	36.1	34.9	36.4	35.5	35.7	36.1
K	38.0	37.4	37.2	39.3	37.2	37.3	38.8	36.7	36.8	36.5
L	41.5	38.5	37.5	36.6	39.8	39.6	37.8	38.4	39.4	38.0
M	30.8	31.5	40.0	29.8	34.4	33.9	27.2	27.6	31.0	30.2
N	36.8	36.7	40.7	36.0	36.5	37.9	41.8	37.6	38.2	38.1
O	37.1	38.7	43.5	31.3	33.2	32.8	35.8	35.0	34.5	37.6
Women - Femmes - Mujeres										
ISIC 3 - CITI 3 - CIIU 3										
Total	31.5	31.1	31.5	30.8	31.2	30.2	30.4	30.4	30.8	30.4
C-Q	31.5	31.1	31.5	30.8	31.2	30.2	30.5	30.5	30.9	30.4
D	31.5	33.9	29.9	37.9	33.2	28.6	34.7	35.2	34.8	
E	33.0			31.0				33.5		
F			30.6					20.8		
G	30.9	29.4	29.9	24.7	27.4	28.6	29.8	28.7	25.8	37.7
H	30.3	33.8	31.2	24.5	28.4	24.2	32.4	28.1	28.2	27.7
I	36.1	36.0	33.9	33.2	36.0	36.1	34.5	37.1	38.3	33.4
J	33.2	33.8	34.6	33.7	34.5	33.0	33.4	33.7	32.7	33.6
K	35.3	33.6	30.7	35.1	33.4	31.2	31.9	30.8	33.4	33.1
L	34.2	35.4	27.1	35.5	33.7	29.3	31.7	32.6	35.0	33.3
M	23.0	20.0	19.9	22.9	24.0	23.9	19.1	21.3	25.0	20.4
N	33.1	32.6	34.5	32.1	31.4	33.7	32.1	31.6	33.4	34.7
O	24.1	26.8	25.9	25.3	27.0	22.3	29.2	27.8	20.3	29.0
P	29.3							37.5		

Explanatory notes: see p. 721.

Notes explicatives: voir p. 723.

Notas explicativas: véase p. 725.

[1] Establishments with 10 or more persons employed. [2] Incl. juveniles. [3] Second quarter of each year. [4] Permanent workers. [5] Industrial workers. [6] June of each year.

[1] Etablissements occupant 10 personnes et plus. [2] Y compris les jeunes gens. [3] Deuxième trimestre de chaque année. [4] Travailleurs permanents. [5] Travailleurs de l'industrie. [6] Juin de chaque année.

[1] Establecimientos con 10 y más trabajadores. [2] Incl. los jóvenes. [3] Segundo trimestre de cada año. [4] Trabajadores permanentes. [5] Trabajadores industriales. [6] Junio de cada año.

HOURS OF WORK

By economic activity

DURÉE DU TRAVAIL

Par activité économique

HORAS DE TRABAJO

Por actividad económica

4A

	Per week			Par semaine				Por semana		
	1999	2000	2001	2002	2003	2004	2005	2006	2007	2008

Italy (BA) (a) [1] **Total employment - Emploi total - Empleo total**

Total men and women - Total hommes et femmes - Total hombres y mujeres
ISIC 3 - CITI 3 - CIIU 3

Total	39.4	39.3	39.3	38.2	38.3	34.7 [2]	34.9	34.8	34.8	34.6
A-B	42.6	42.4	42.5	41.6	41.9	40.4 [2]	40.4	40.1	40.2	41.0
C-Q	39.2	39.1	39.1	38.2	38.1	34.4 [2]	34.6	34.5	34.5	34.3
A	42.6	42.4	42.4	41.5	41.8	40.6 [2]	40.5	40.1	40.2	41.0
B	43.3	43.8	44.5	43.4	45.5	35.1 [2]	37.4	40.2	40.3	40.0
C	40.3	40.5	40.2	39.5	39.7	36.2 [2]	37.7	37.6	37.1	36.8
D	40.6	40.5	40.5	39.4	39.2	35.8 [2]	36.1	36.1	36.3	35.9
E	39.0	39.0	39.1	38.1	38.1	35.8 [2]	36.3	36.3	36.4	36.1
F	41.5	41.5	41.6	40.6	40.5	36.6 [2]	37.0	37.4	37.2	36.6
G	42.8	42.6	42.5	41.4	41.3	38.4 [2]	38.9	38.4	38.2	37.9
H	43.4	42.9	42.9	42.4	42.3	39.7 [2]	39.3	39.2	38.8	38.4
I	40.3	40.2	40.4	39.6	39.5	37.2 [2]	37.2	37.1	37.5	36.9
J	38.7	38.7	38.7	37.6	37.5	35.2 [2]	35.0	34.9	35.1	35.5
K	39.6	39.3	39.4	38.3	38.0	33.8 [2]	34.1	34.2	34.4	34.0
L	35.9	35.8	35.9	35.1	35.1	32.7 [2]	32.9	32.7	32.7	33.0
M	27.8	27.9	27.9	27.1	27.2	22.5 [2]	22.7	22.6	22.4	22.3
N	36.4	36.4	36.4	35.5	35.5	31.5 [2]	31.6	31.3	31.2	31.1
O	38.2	38.2	38.5	37.7	37.4	32.7 [2]	32.9	32.6	32.4	32.4
P	30.1	31.6	31.3	31.2	30.9	22.8 [2]	23.9	25.0	25.5	26.4
Q	38.0	38.5	38.1	38.1	38.3	34.8 [2]	35.8	33.5	31.7	31.9

Men - Hommes - Hombres
ISIC 3 - CITI 3 - CIIU 3

Total	41.4	41.4	41.5	40.3	40.5	38.0 [2]	38.2	38.1	38.2	37.9
A-B	44.7	44.5	44.5	43.6	44.1	43.8 [2]	43.4	42.8	43.1	43.6
C-Q	41.2	41.2	41.3	40.3	40.3	37.7 [2]	37.9	37.8	37.9	37.5
A	44.7	44.5	44.4	43.6	44.0	44.0 [2]	43.6	42.8	43.1	43.7
B	43.6	44.3	44.8	44.0	46.1	36.7 [2]	38.2	41.3	42.1	41.1
C	40.8	41.0	40.8	40.2	40.4	36.8 [2]	38.4	37.9	37.8	37.4
D	41.6	41.6	41.7	40.5	40.4	37.5 [2]	37.9	37.9	38.1	37.6
E	39.4	39.5	39.6	38.5	38.5	36.4 [2]	37.0	36.9	36.9	36.5
F	41.9	41.8	42.0	41.0	40.9	37.2 [2]	37.4	37.8	37.6	37.1
G	44.7	44.6	44.5	43.4	43.4	41.6 [2]	42.0	41.3	41.4	41.0
H	46.1	46.0	46.4	45.8	45.9	45.3 [2]	45.1	44.5	44.1	43.8
I	41.2	41.2	41.3	40.6	40.6	38.6 [2]	38.7	38.7	39.1	38.4
J	40.2	40.2	40.2	39.1	38.8	37.8 [2]	37.4	37.2	37.6	38.0
K	42.6	42.5	42.6	41.4	41.1	38.0 [2]	38.3	38.3	38.6	38.0
L	36.8	36.7	36.8	36.1	36.2	34.1 [2]	34.2	34.1	34.0	34.2
M	29.6	29.9	30.0	29.3	29.4	25.2 [2]	25.0	25.3	25.5	25.2
N	38.2	38.3	38.5	37.5	37.4	35.4 [2]	35.1	35.0	34.6	34.8
O	40.2	40.1	40.4	39.5	39.4	35.7 [2]	36.1	36.0	35.7	35.7
P	43.2	44.4	43.2	42.1	41.3	35.8 [2]	34.0	33.9	31.3	33.3
Q	39.6	41.1	41.1	39.9	39.1	36.6 [2]	37.7	36.7	34.1	34.5

Women - Femmes - Mujeres
ISIC 3 - CITI 3 - CIIU 3

Total	35.6	35.4	35.4	34.5	34.5	29.8 [2]	30.1	29.9	29.8	29.8
A-B	37.7	37.7	38.0	36.7	36.6	33.8 [2]	34.2	34.3	34.0	35.1
C-Q	35.5	35.4	35.3	34.5	34.4	29.6 [2]	29.9	29.7	29.7	29.6
A	37.7	37.7	38.0	36.8	36.6	33.9 [2]	34.2	34.3	34.0	35.2
B	37.7	37.8	40.7	34.7	37.7	24.2 [2]	29.8	29.2	22.5	26.0
C	37.4	37.6	37.5	36.2	35.0	30.7 [2]	31.4	34.8	31.1	31.2
D	38.1	37.9	37.8	36.7	36.4	31.8 [2]	32.0	31.8	32.1	31.8
E	35.4	35.6	36.1	35.4	35.5	32.0 [2]	32.0	32.2	33.5	34.2
F	35.5	36.2	35.4	34.6	34.5	28.1 [2]	29.3	30.1	29.2	28.7
G	39.6	39.1	39.1	38.2	37.9	33.9 [2]	34.4	34.0	33.6	33.4
H	40.1	39.3	39.0	38.5	38.2	34.5 [2]	33.9	34.3	33.9	33.6
I	36.2	36.1	36.6	35.6	35.3	31.9 [2]	32.1	31.8	32.0	31.8
J	35.8	36.1	36.3	35.3	35.3	31.4 [2]	31.6	31.5	31.6	32.0
K	35.3	34.9	35.1	34.2	33.9	28.8 [2]	29.2	29.2	29.4	29.2
L	34.0	33.9	34.1	33.1	33.1	30.0 [2]	30.4	29.9	30.2	30.9
M	27.0	27.1	27.0	26.2	26.4	21.6 [2]	21.9	21.6	21.3	21.4
N	35.1	35.1	35.0	34.3	34.2	29.5 [2]	29.8	29.5	29.6	29.6
O	35.9	36.2	36.4	35.7	35.3	30.0 [2]	30.1	29.5	29.5	29.5
P	26.5	27.7	28.0	28.6	28.3	21.3 [2]	22.8	24.0	24.9	25.7
Q	35.3	34.9	35.2	35.9	37.1	32.1 [2]	32.5	29.5	29.3	28.2

Explanatory notes: see p. 721. Notes explicatives: voir p. 723. Notas explicativas: véase p. 725.

[1] Persons aged 15 years and over. [2] Revised methodology; data not strictly comparable. [1] Personnes âgées de 15 ans et plus. [2] Méthodologie révisée; les données ne sont pas strictement comparables. [1] Personas de 15 años y más. [2] Metodología revisada; datos no estrictamente comparables.

HOURS OF WORK	DURÉE DU TRAVAIL	HORAS DE TRABAJO
By economic activity	Par activité économique	Por actividad económica

	Per week				Par semaine			Por semana		
	1999	2000	2001	2002	2003	2004	2005	2006	2007	2008

Latvia (BA) (a) [1]   Total employment - Emploi total - Empleo total

Total men and women - Total hommes et femmes - Total hombres y mujeres
ISIC 3 - CITI 3 - CIIU 3

	1999	2000	2001	2002	2003	2004	2005	2006	2007	2008
Total	41.2	41.4	41.3	40.1	40.0	39.4	42.1	39.7	39.2	37.4
A-B	41.3	41.2	42.0	39.3	40.4	39.2	41.0	40.8	41.0	39.1
C-Q	41.2	41.4	41.2	40.2	39.9	39.5	42.0	39.6	39.0	37.2
A	41.2	41.1	42.0	39.5	40.4	39.2	40.9	40.9	40.9	39.0
B	46.6	45.5	44.2	35.4	42.1	38.5	44.1	37.4	45.0	39.0
C	-	-	-	43.9	37.9	35.9	34.9	49.1	40.9	41.0
D	40.4	41.0	41.2	40.4	40.4	40.6	40.9	40.4	38.7	37.1
E	40.3	39.7	40.0	40.6	39.3	39.3	39.2	39.7	38.4	38.7
F	43.1	42.4	44.4	42.9	43.9	42.6	42.7	42.6	41.4	40.2
G	44.8	44.7	43.3	43.0	42.3	41.8	41.3	40.3	39.3	38.0
H	42.9	46.0	45.4	42.3	46.0	43.6	40.4	39.5	40.4	37.2
I	41.9	43.2	42.5	43.0	41.5	40.5	42.1	40.6	40.8	38.6
J	38.1	39.8	40.1	38.5	38.2	38.1	37.3	39.1	36.6	37.4
K	40.9	41.7	40.1	39.6	38.8	37.9	39.6	40.2	39.4	36.8
L	41.3	41.0	41.6	39.8	39.8	38.9	40.2	38.7	38.8	36.6
M	35.5	36.1	35.8	32.7	31.3	32.8	32.6	33.3	35.0	32.5
N	41.2	39.7	40.4	39.9	38.0	38.5	40.0	39.7	38.5	37.1
O	41.0	39.9	38.4	37.5	37.4	35.4	38.2	38.3	36.9	35.2
P	28.6	26.9	-	30.3	32.2	30.5	30.7	31.8	33.0	34.3
Q	.	.	.	.	.	.	.	.	.	.
X	.	.	.	.	.	.	.	.	.	-

Men - Hommes - Hombres
ISIC 3 - CITI 3 - CIIU 3

	1999	2000	2001	2002	2003	2004	2005	2006	2007	2008
Total	42.7	42.7	43.1	42.0	41.9	41.4	42.1	41.6	40.9	39.1
A-B	41.6	41.3	43.1	40.6	41.7	41.1	42.2	41.4	42.3	40.0
C-Q	43.0	43.0	43.1	42.4	41.9	41.4	42.0	41.6	40.7	38.9
A	41.4	41.1	43.0	40.7	41.7	41.0	42.1	41.6	42.1	39.9
B	.	.	.	.	.	.	.	.	.	-
C	.	.	.	.	.	.	.	.	.	.
D	41.3	41.8	42.6	42.0	41.5	41.5	42.0	41.5	39.6	37.9
E	41.4	40.2	40.8	42.1	39.8	39.4	39.7	40.5	38.9	39.0
F	44.0	42.8	44.9	43.5	44.5	43.4	43.2	42.7	41.8	40.6
G	45.7	45.8	44.2	44.4	43.8	43.4	43.1	42.4	40.7	39.4
H	47.6	45.5	42.6	41.0	48.7	46.8	42.8	46.3	41.6	38.6
I	43.9	44.9	43.9	44.6	42.6	42.2	43.5	41.6	42.3	39.3
J	40.3	40.7	40.3	41.7	40.6	41.4	39.0	40.9	39.4	39.4
K	43.7	44.6	42.4	41.6	40.5	40.6	42.0	42.9	41.3	38.4
L	43.4	42.8	43.8	42.3	42.1	40.0	42.4	41.1	40.9	39.3
M	36.1	36.5	38.0	34.1	34.1	34.2	35.0	34.3	35.8	34.3
N	44.6	42.1	42.6	42.0	40.3	40.7	41.1	40.8	41.7	39.5
O	43.0	43.4	39.7	39.2	37.8	36.3	39.9	40.1	37.8	36.2
P	.	.	.	.	.	.	.	.	.	.
Q	.	.	.	.	.	.	.	.	.	.
X	.	.	.	.	.	.	.	.	.	-

Women - Femmes - Mujeres
ISIC 3 - CITI 3 - CIIU 3

	1999	2000	2001	2002	2003	2004	2005	2006	2007	2008
Total	39.6	40.0	39.6	38.0	37.9	37.4	37.9	37.7	37.4	35.7
A-B	41.0	41.0	40.3	37.1	38.0	35.9	38.6	39.7	38.9	37.3
C-Q	39.3	39.8	39.5	38.1	37.9	37.5	37.8	37.6	37.3	35.6
A	41.0	41.0	40.4	37.4	38.0	36.0	38.5	39.7	38.9	37.3
B	.	.	.	.	.	.	.	.	.	-
C	.	.	.	.	.	.	.	.	.	.
D	39.3	40.0	39.5	38.2	39.0	39.4	39.4	39.2	37.5	36.1
E	37.5	38.3	36.3	25.0	37.6	39.0	38.0	37.3	36.5	37.5
F	36.1	38.4	39.5	37.7	38.8	35.8	37.7	39.8	36.6	36.5
G	44.0	43.9	42.6	42.1	41.4	40.9	40.3	39.1	38.4	37.2
H	41.4	46.1	46.3	42.6	45.3	42.3	39.6	38.1	40.2	36.8
I	37.7	39.3	39.4	39.4	38.9	36.4	38.8	38.3	37.6	37.2
J	37.0	39.2	39.9	36.5	36.8	35.3	36.3	38.4	35.6	36.7
K	37.9	38.6	37.4	37.1	36.2	34.8	37.1	37.3	37.5	35.1
L	38.7	38.8	38.8	37.0	37.3	37.6	37.6	36.1	36.9	34.1
M	35.3	36.0	35.3	32.3	30.6	32.5	32.1	33.1	34.9	32.1
N	40.4	39.3	40.0	39.5	37.7	38.2	39.8	39.6	38.0	36.6
O	39.3	36.9	37.6	36.3	37.1	34.7	36.8	37.1	36.4	34.8
P	.	.	.	.	.	.	.	.	.	.
Q	.	.	.	.	.	.	.	.	.	.
X	.	.	.	.	.	.	.	.	.	-

Explanatory notes: see p. 721.	Notes explicatives: voir p. 723.	Notas explicativas: véase p. 725.
[1] On the main job.	[1] Emploi principal.	[1] Empleo principal.

	Per week			Par semaine			Por semana			
	1999	2000	2001	2002	2003	2004	2005	2006	2007	2008

Latvia (BA) (a) [1]   **Employees - Salariés - Asalariados**

Total men and women - Total hommes et femmes - Total hombres y mujeres
ISIC 3 - CITI 3 - CIIU 3

	1999	2000	2001	2002	2003	2004	2005	2006	2007	2008
Total	40.9	41.3	41.1	40.3	40.0	39.6	40.0	39.5	39.1	37.2
A-B	40.4	40.5	42.9	41.5	42.5	41.7	42.1	40.4	40.8	38.1
C-Q	40.9	41.3	41.0	40.2	39.8	39.4	39.8	39.5	39.0	37.2
A	39.5	40.3	42.7	42.0	42.4	41.7	40.9	40.5	40.6	37.7
B	51.8	-	-	36.1	41.5	39.8	44.1	39.0	45.2	39.6
C	-	-	-	45.1	37.8	35.8	34.9	49.1	41.2	41.0
D	40.3	40.8	40.9	40.5	40.3	40.4	40.8	40.4	38.8	37.1
E	40.4	39.7	39.7	40.5	39.1	39.3	39.2	39.8	38.3	38.7
F	42.4	42.4	43.8	42.6	43.8	42.3	42.4	42.7	41.4	40.1
G	44.4	44.8	42.9	43.0	42.3	41.9	41.2	40.3	39.2	37.9
H	43.1	45.8	45.3	42.6	45.4	42.6	40.4	39.2	40.2	36.9
I	41.8	43.2	42.4	42.7	41.4	40.5	42.1	40.2	40.7	38.5
J	39.0	39.7	39.9	38.1	38.2	37.6	36.8	39.0	36.7	37.3
K	40.5	41.7	39.7	40.1	39.5	37.5	39.6	39.6	39.3	36.7
L	41.3	40.9	41.6	39.9	39.8	38.9	40.3	38.8	38.8	36.6
M	35.5	36.1	35.8	32.7	31.4	32.7	32.7	33.2	34.9	32.6
N	41.0	39.9	40.3	40.0	37.9	38.3	39.8	39.6	38.7	37.3
O	40.3	39.7	39.2	37.7	37.9	36.6	38.3	37.9	37.4	35.5
P	-	-	-	32.1	36.2	26.8	31.5	34.7	35.4	37.8
Q	.	.	.	.	.	.	.	.	.	.
X	.	.	.	.	.	.	.	.	.	-

Men - Hommes - Hombres
ISIC 3 - CITI 3 - CIIU 3

	1999	2000	2001	2002	2003	2004	2005	2006	2007	2008
Total	42.4	42.6	42.8	42.3	41.9	41.4	42.1	41.5	40.8	38.9
A-B	40.9	40.9	43.9	42.1	42.9	42.6	43.4	41.6	41.8	39.4
C-Q	42.6	42.8	42.7	42.4	41.8	41.3	41.9	41.5	40.8	38.9
A	39.9	40.5	43.6	42.2	42.8	42.6	42.1	41.7	41.6	39.1
B	.	.	.	.	.	.	.	.	.	-
C	.	.	.	.	.	.	.	.	.	.
D	41.0	41.5	42.1	42.1	41.3	41.1	41.7	41.4	39.6	37.9
E	41.6	40.2	40.5	41.9	39.5	39.4	39.7	40.5	38.9	39.0
F	43.3	42.8	44.3	43.2	44.4	43.2	42.9	42.9	41.9	40.6
G	45.0	45.5	43.5	44.5	43.7	43.6	42.9	42.2	40.7	39.3
H	47.3	44.6	42.5	42.7	46.7	44.2	42.7	46.1	41.7	37.6
I	43.8	45.1	43.8	44.3	42.5	42.2	43.6	41.3	42.2	39.1
J	39.5	40.6	39.9	40.8	40.5	40.4	37.7	40.6	39.4	39.4
K	43.2	43.9	41.7	41.7	41.3	40.1	42.2	42.4	41.4	38.4
L	43.4	42.8	43.8	42.3	42.1	40.0	42.5	41.2	40.9	39.3
M	36.2	36.4	38.0	34.3	34.1	34.2	35.0	34.1	35.3	34.4
N	43.7	41.9	42.3	42.7	39.9	40.7	41.3	40.3	41.9	39.0
O	42.1	42.8	40.4	39.9	38.7	37.8	39.6	39.7	39.0	36.9
P	.	.	.	.	.	.	.	.	.	.
Q	.	.	.	.	.	.	.	.	.	-
X	.	.	.	.	.	.	.	.	.	-

Women - Femmes - Mujeres
ISIC 3 - CITI 3 - CIIU 3

	1999	2000	2001	2002	2003	2004	2005	2006	2007	2008
Total	39.3	39.9	39.5	38.2	38.1	37.6	37.8	37.5	37.4	35.6
A-B	38.8	39.7	40.0	39.7	41.5	38.6	37.9	36.7	38.2	34.9
C-Q	39.3	39.9	39.4	38.2	38.0	37.6	37.8	37.5	37.4	35.6
A	38.5	39.7	40.2	41.3	41.3	39.0	38.5	36.7	38.2	34.7
B	.	.	.	.	.	.	.	.	.	.
C	.	.	.	.	.	.	.	.	.	.
D	39.3	40.0	39.6	38.2	39.1	39.6	39.6	39.2	37.9	36.1
E	37.5	38.3	36.3	35.0	37.6	39.0	38.0	37.5	36.5	37.8
F	35.6	38.1	38.9	37.7	39.5	35.6	37.6	39.7	36.6	36.2
G	43.9	44.2	42.5	42.2	41.5	41.0	40.3	39.2	38.4	37.2
H	41.8	46.1	46.1	42.5	45.1	42.0	39.6	37.8	39.9	36.7
I	37.7	39.1	39.4	39.4	38.8	36.3	38.8	37.9	37.5	37.1
J	38.8	39.2	39.9	36.5	36.7	35.2	36.2	38.4	35.8	36.6
K	37.9	39.2	37.2	38.0	36.8	34.6	37.0	36.9	37.5	34.8
L	38.8	38.6	38.7	37.1	37.3	37.7	37.8	36.3	36.9	34.1
M	35.3	36.1	35.3	32.3	30.7	32.4	32.1	33.0	34.8	32.1
N	40.4	39.6	39.9	39.5	37.6	37.9	39.6	39.5	38.2	37.0
O	39.0	36.9	38.4	36.2	37.3	35.9	37.4	36.8	36.4	34.9
P	.	.	.	.	.	.	.	.	.	.
Q	.	.	.	.	.	.	.	.	.	-
X	.	.	.	.	.	.	.	.	.	-

Explanatory notes: see p. 721.   Notes explicatives: voir p. 723.   Notas explicativas: véase p. 725.

[1] On the main job.   [1] Emploi principal.   [1] Empleo principal.

HOURS OF WORK DURÉE DU TRAVAIL HORAS DE TRABAJO

By economic activity Par activité économique Por actividad económica

	Per week				Par semaine			Por semana		
	1999	2000	2001	2002	2003	2004	2005	2006	2007	2008

Lithuania (BA) (b) [1] [2] [3] **Employees - Salariés - Asalariados**

Total men and women - Total hommes et femmes - Total hombres y mujeres
ISIC 3 - CITI 3 - CIIU 3

	1999	2000	2001	2002	2003	2004	2005	2006	2007	2008
Total	39.3	39.0	38.7	38.5	38.2	38.5	38.6	38.5	38.8	39.1
A-B	38.5	38.3	38.9	36.9	37.8	37.7	38.6	38.0	37.9	39.1
C-Q	39.4	39.1	38.7	38.5	38.2	38.5	38.6	38.5	38.9	39.1
A	38.3	37.8	38.3	36.7	37.5	37.4	38.3	37.7	37.6	38.8
B	43.8	50.3	52.1	53.4	49.3	48.7	44.4	46.8	.	42.5
C	41.9	41.7	38.8	37.6	40.1	39.7	41.4	40.1	40.4	40.5
D	39.8	39.8	39.7	39.2	39.0	39.2	39.5	39.3	39.4	39.8
E	40.0	40.1	40.0	40.0	39.6	39.6	39.8	39.3	38.9	39.6
F	41.9	40.6	41.7	40.3	40.3	39.9	40.4	39.7	39.8	40.2
G	41.8	41.6	40.8	39.7	39.1	39.6	39.5	39.6	39.7	39.5
H	42.3	40.8	39.5	41.0	40.8	40.9	39.7	39.2	39.6	39.1
I	42.7	41.9	40.6	41.3	40.8	41.4	41.1	40.2	40.3	40.5
J	38.8	39.9	40.3	39.6	38.7	38.3	37.9	37.5	39.6	38.2
K	39.5	38.6	39.2	38.1	37.7	38.6	38.5	38.4	38.8	39.3
L	41.4	40.3	40.2	40.2	39.3	39.5	39.4	39.7	39.6	40.0
M	33.1	33.3	32.8	32.2	32.0	32.5	32.7	33.1	34.8	35.6
N	38.1	37.9	37.5	37.8	37.7	37.7	38.0	37.4	37.9	39.2
O	37.4	38.1	37.1	37.3	36.1	36.3	37.1	37.7	38.0	37.2
P	33.6	32.9	31.4	29.9	31.1	34.8	38.8	.	39.4	39.6
Q										

Men - Hommes - Hombres
ISIC 3 - CITI 3 - CIIU 3

	1999	2000	2001	2002	2003	2004	2005	2006	2007	2008
Total	40.6	40.2	40.4	39.7	39.5	39.7	39.9	39.4	39.7	39.9
A-B	39.7	38.5	39.7	36.8	37.8	38.2	38.7	38.3	38.0	39.6
C-Q	40.7	40.3	40.4	39.9	39.6	39.8	40.0	39.5	39.8	39.9
A	39.4	37.7	38.9	36.5	37.3	37.7	38.2	37.8	37.7	39.4
B	43.8	55.5	52.1	53.4	52.9	50.4	45.5	47.8	44.0	42.8
C	43.8	44.1	38.5	38.5	40.4	39.5	42.3	40.1	40.0	40.7
D	40.1	40.2	40.1	39.3	39.6	39.6	39.8	39.4	39.7	40.1
E	40.2	39.9	40.0	40.0	39.7	39.7	40.2	39.4	39.2	39.5
F	42.1	40.7	42.1	40.6	40.6	40.2	40.6	39.7	39.9	40.4
G	40.6	40.3	41.5	39.9	39.8	39.9	40.1	39.5	39.9	39.6
H	44.9	42.2	41.8	44.0	40.5	40.3	38.6	38.7	38.6	37.6
I	44.4	43.1	41.9	43.0	42.0	42.8	42.7	41.6	41.6	41.4
J	41.4	41.4	40.9	40.9	42.3	39.6	38.4	39.6	40.3	38.6
K	40.0	40.7	41.4	40.0	39.4	40.4	40.2	39.1	39.9	40.1
L	42.3	41.1	41.2	41.4	40.1	40.5	40.3	40.5	40.5	40.7
M	33.8	34.5	34.7	33.7	32.1	33.9	34.2	34.6	35.7	36.2
N	39.5	38.2	38.4	39.1	38.7	38.3	38.6	37.7	38.1	39.3
O	37.8	39.8	37.9	38.9	37.5	36.5	38.5	38.1	39.1	37.8
P	.	.	.	.	.	32.8	39.3	38.8	37.7	36.3
Q										

Women - Femmes - Mujeres
ISIC 3 - CITI 3 - CIIU 3

	1999	2000	2001	2002	2003	2004	2005	2006	2007	2008
Total	38.1	38.0	37.2	37.2	36.9	37.2	37.3	37.6	37.9	38.3
A-B	35.7	37.7	37.1	37.1	37.9	36.7	38.5	37.4	37.4	37.6
C-Q	38.2	38.0	37.2	37.2	36.8	37.3	37.3	37.6	37.9	38.4
A	35.7	37.9	37.1	37.1	38.0	36.6	38.4	37.4	37.4	37.6
B						20.0	41.0	20.0	30.0	29.2
C	40.0	39.3	40.0	36.2	39.2	40.5	28.5	40.0	42.9	40.0
D	39.5	39.4	39.4	39.1	38.4	38.9	39.2	39.1	39.0	39.4
E	39.4	40.4	40.1	40.3	39.4	39.0	38.5	39.0	38.1	39.7
F	39.5	39.7	37.1	38.0	38.0	37.7	38.9	38.9	37.9	38.5
G	42.9	42.7	40.2	39.5	38.5	39.4	39.0	39.7	39.5	39.4
H	41.6	40.2	39.0	40.5	40.8	41.0	40.0	39.3	39.8	39.3
I	39.0	39.1	37.6	36.9	37.4	37.2	37.0	36.8	36.9	38.1
J	37.6	38.7	39.8	38.5	36.8	37.7	37.6	36.4	39.4	38.0
K	38.9	36.0	36.9	36.2	36.1	36.5	36.3	37.5	37.8	38.3
L	40.2	39.2	39.0	38.9	38.0	38.2	38.5	38.8	38.6	39.2
M	32.9	33.0	32.3	31.8	31.9	32.1	32.1	32.7	34.6	35.4
N	37.9	37.9	37.3	37.6	37.6	37.6	37.8	37.3	37.8	39.2
O	37.2	36.3	36.7	35.8	35.1	36.2	36.3	37.3	37.4	36.9
P	42.2	32.9	40.0	35.4	37.7	38.9	38.7	38.3	41.0	40.6

Explanatory notes: see p. 721.   Notes explicatives: voir p. 723.   Notas explicativas: véase p. 725.

[1] On the main job. [2] Persons aged 15 years and over. [3] Excl. conscripts.   [1] Emploi principal. [2] Personnes âgées de 15 ans et plus. [3] Non compris les conscrits.   [1] Empleo principal. [2] Personas de 15 años y más. [3] Excl. los conscriptos.

Per week — Par semaine — Por semana

	1999	2000	2001	2002	2003	2004	2005	2006	2007	2008
Lithuania (DA) (b)				Employees - Salariés - Asalariados						
Total men and women - Total hommes et femmes - Total hombres y mujeres										
ISIC 3 - CITI 3 - CIIU 3										
Total	38.1	37.9	37.8	37.7	38.1	38.2	37.8	37.2	37.5	.
A-B	36.0	37.2	37.7	38.0	38.7	38.9	38.3	38.1	37.8	.
C-Q	38.2	38.0	37.8	37.7	38.1	38.2	37.8	37.2	37.5	.
A	36.0	37.1	37.7	38.0	38.7	38.9	38.3	38.1	37.8	.
B	38.7	38.4	38.2	38.6	39.5	39.0	38.8	37.8	37.9	.
C	39.1	38.7	38.7	38.9	39.0	39.1	38.6	37.9	38.0	.
D	38.8	38.6	38.6	38.6	38.8	39.0	38.5	37.8	37.9	.
E	38.7	38.5	38.3	38.4	38.9	38.6	38.4	37.5	37.7	.
F	38.8	38.6	38.6	38.7	38.9	39.1	38.5	37.8	37.9	.
G	38.8	38.5	38.5	38.5	38.8	39.1	38.4	37.7	37.9	.
H	38.7	38.5	38.5	38.6	38.8	39.0	38.5	37.8	37.9	.
I	39.1	39.1	39.0	38.8	39.0	39.1	38.7	38.0	38.2	.
J	38.7	38.5	38.4	38.6	38.9	39.0	38.7	37.6	37.9	.
K	38.7	38.5	38.5	38.4	38.6	39.1	38.6	37.8	38.0	.
L	39.0	38.6	38.6	38.6	38.8	39.0	38.5	37.8	38.0	.
M	35.8	35.5	34.7	33.9	34.6	34.4	34.1	34.1	34.8	.
N	37.9	37.8	37.7	37.6	38.1	38.3	37.8	37.4	37.5	.
O	38.1	37.9	37.8	38.0	38.4	38.8	38.6	37.6	37.7	.
Malta (BA) (a) [1] [2]				Total employment - Emploi total - Empleo total						
Total men and women - Total hommes et femmes - Total hombres y mujeres										
ISIC 3 - CITI 3 - CIIU 3										
Total	.	39.0	38.0	38.5	38.4	38.5	38.4	38.2	38.9	38.1
A-B	.	36.0	31.0	48.1	49.8	45.4	41.2	42.4	47.7	46.5
C-Q	.	38.0	37.0	38.3	38.2	38.4	38.3	38.1	38.7	37.9
A	.	37.0	45.0	49.7	51.6	47.7	41.7	44.1	48.1	47.6
B	.	14.0	17.0	.	.	34.0	38.5	.	.	38.3
C	.	38.0	32.0	.	.	.	.	.	.	48.9
D	.	41.0	40.0	40.0	38.7	39.4	40.2	39.2	40.3	39.4
E	.	40.0	36.0	38.1	38.5	40.3	39.8	38.9	39.5	39.6
F	.	39.0	39.0	38.3	38.8	39.2	39.2	39.8	40.1	40.1
G	.	41.0	39.0	42.2	39.6	39.4	39.2	39.4	39.0	39.2
H	.	38.0	37.0	35.5	36.6	36.6	34.9	36.3	37.9	36.9
I	.	40.0	40.0	40.2	39.7	39.3	38.0	39.3	40.5	37.8
J	.	38.0	39.0	36.2	39.1	39.0	39.2	38.8	37.6	38.8
K	.	41.0	41.0	38.4	37.5	38.7	39.3	38.3	39.1	37.8
L	.	39.0	39.0	39.6	40.3	40.5	40.6	39.6	40.0	39.4
M	.	35.0	30.0	29.5	31.6	31.9	32.2	31.4	31.2	31.7
N	.	39.0	37.0	37.0	36.6	38.0	38.1	37.5	38.1	37.3
O	.	37.0	35.0	38.1	38.6	37.2	35.4	36.7	37.0	35.5
P	.	23.0	40.0	.	.	.	.	.	.	19.9
Q	.	38.0	38.0	.	.	.	.	.	.	39.9
Men - Hommes - Hombres										
ISIC 3 - CITI 3 - CIIU 3										
Total	.	41.0	40.0	40.5	40.1	40.2	40.2	39.8	41.1	40.1
A-B	.	36.0	29.0	48.4	50.3	45.0	42.8	42.8	48.8	47.4
C-Q	.	41.0	39.0	40.3	39.8	40.0	40.0	39.7	40.9	39.9
A	.	44.0	43.0	.	52.4	47.5	43.5	44.5	49.4	48.7
B	.	27.0	14.0	.	.	34.2	39.1	.	.	38.3
C	.	38.0	32.0	.	.	.	.	.	.	49.1
D	.	42.0	41.0	40.9	39.6	40.2	41.2	39.9	41.1	39.9
E	.	40.0	36.0	39.2	38.8	40.5	40.0	38.9	39.8	39.7
F	.	39.0	39.0	38.5	38.8	39.3	39.2	39.8	40.1	40.2
G	.	43.0	42.0	44.6	42.0	40.9	41.7	41.0	41.1	41.6
H	.	40.0	40.0	37.5	38.9	38.7	37.3	38.1	40.6	39.0
I	.	41.0	41.0	41.2	40.6	40.2	38.4	40.3	41.9	38.9
J	.	40.0	40.0	37.9	40.5	39.6	40.2	40.6	40.4	40.9
K	.	44.0	43.0	39.6	40.1	40.4	41.1	39.6	42.5	40.2
L	.	41.0	39.0	40.5	41.3	41.3	41.4	40.3	41.7	40.4
M	.	38.0	32.0	33.5	33.8	34.9	34.8	34.1	34.0	33.7
N	.	43.0	39.0	41.1	35.9	40.8	41.0	40.4	42.5	41.1
O	.	39.0	38.0	39.7	40.0	39.9	37.5	37.8	39.9	37.3
P	.	40.0	40.0	.	.	.	.	.	.	.
Q	.	41.0	39.0	.	.	.	.	.	.	40.2

Explanatory notes: see p. 721.   Notes explicatives: voir p. 723.   Notas explicativas: véase p. 725.

[1] Persons aged 15 years and over. [2] Dec. of each year.   [1] Personnes âgées de 15 ans et plus. [2] Déc. de chaque année.   [1] Personas de 15 años y más. [2] Dic. de cada año.

4A

HOURS OF WORK	DURÉE DU TRAVAIL	HORAS DE TRABAJO
By economic activity	Par activité économique	Por actividad económica

	Per week			Par semaine				Por semana	
	1999	2000	2001	2002	2003	2004	2005	2006	2007	2008

Malta (BA) (a) [1] [2] — Total employment - Emploi total - Empleo total

Women - Femmes - Mujeres
ISIC 3 - CITI 3 - CIIU 3

	1999	2000	2001	2002	2003	2004	2005	2006	2007	2008
Total	.	35.0	34.0	34.2	34.8	34.8	34.4	34.8	34.2	34.2
A-B	.	15.0	33.0	.	.	.	.	.	.	34.1
C-Q	.	31.0	36.0	34.2	34.8	34.7	34.3	34.8	34.2	34.2
A	.	30.0	46.0	.	.	.	.	.	.	33.8
B	.	.	20.0	.	.	.	.	.	.	40.0
C	.	.	.	.	.	.	.	.	.	40.0
D	.	39.0	38.0	38.4	36.2	37.1	37.2	37.1	37.9	37.2
E	.	41.0	38.0	.	.	38.7	36.9	.	35.0	37.5
F	.	34.0	38.0	.	.	36.9	37.2	.	38.3	37.9
G	.	36.0	33.0	36.4	35.3	35.1	33.6	35.9	34.4	34.1
H	.	34.0	31.0	31.4	32.7	32.9	30.4	32.2	32.9	33.8
I	.	31.0	35.0	36.7	36.5	36.0	36.6	35.6	35.6	34.3
J	.	35.0	38.0	34.4	37.7	38.2	38.3	36.8	35.2	37.0
K	.	33.0	37.0	35.1	31.1	35.0	34.8	35.6	33.7	33.1
L	.	36.0	39.0	37.0	37.4	38.0	37.9	38.0	35.7	37.4
M	.	31.0	29.0	26.9	30.3	30.2	30.7	29.8	29.4	30.6
N	.	36.0	35.0	33.3	37.2	35.3	35.8	35.0	34.2	34.2
O	.	33.0	30.0	35.7	34.7	32.7	32.9	35.1	32.9	32.9
P	.	20.0	40.0	.	.	.	.	.	.	19.9
Q	.	32.0	38.0	.	.	.	.	.	.	39.3

Moldova, Republic of (CA) (a) [3] — Employees - Salariés - Asalariados

Total men and women - Total hommes et femmes - Total hombres y mujeres
ISIC 3 - CITI 3 - CIIU 3

	1999	2000	2001	2002	2003	2004	2005	2006	2007	2008
Total	26.6	28.1	28.9	29.9	30.3	30.9	30.7	30.1	31.0	31.4
A-B	21.4	23.8	23.4	24.1	23.6	24.5	23.8	22.6	23.5	25.3
C-Q	29.0	29.7	30.7	31.7	32.2	32.4	32.2	31.5	32.2	32.2
A	21.4	23.7	23.4	24.1	23.5	24.4	23.8	22.5	23.4	25.2
B	30.0	30.4	29.6	32.4	32.4	32.6	33.4	34.2	35.2	35.6
C	26.8	24.3	24.9	28.4	30.9	31.2	32.1	32.3	32.4	31.6
D	22.7	24.4	26.6	27.7	29.7	30.3	30.4	29.5	31.3	31.4
E	32.2	32.8	33.5	33.8	34.0	34.5	34.1	34.3	34.3	34.3
F	19.5	20.5	22.5	24.6	27.4	29.9	31.6	31.0	32.2	31.8
G	29.9	30.9	32.9	34.2	34.6	34.9	34.8	33.6	34.3	34.3
H	30.2	32.0	32.7	33.1	33.2	34.0	33.0	31.8	32.6	32.8
I	27.0	28.8	29.3	30.6	31.3	31.4	31.6	31.4	32.1	32.1
J	35.1	35.3	36.6	36.1	36.1	35.9	33.4	34.0	34.8	34.3
K	33.3	33.3	33.6	34.8	34.5	34.1	34.1	33.8	34.2	34.1
L	36.5	36.8	36.8	36.9	36.0	36.6	33.0	33.7	32.6	32.5
M	29.2	28.4	28.9	30.2	29.8	29.7	30.1	28.0	28.5	28.3
N	33.5	33.9	34.2	34.7	35.4	35.1	35.0	35.6	36.4	36.9
O	33.5	33.6	34.4	34.6	34.6	34.5	34.2	34.4	34.7	34.5

Netherlands (DA) (c) [2] [4] [5] — Employees - Salariés - Asalariados

Total men and women - Total hommes et femmes - Total hombres y mujeres
ISIC 3 - CITI 3 - CIIU 3

	1999	2000	2001	2002	2003	2004	2005	2006	2007	2008
Total	30.9	30.8	30.6	30.2	30.0	29.6	29.7	.	.	.
A-B	30.9	29.9	30.2	29.9	30.0	29.0	29.4	.	.	.
C-Q	30.9	30.8	30.6	30.3	30.0	29.6	29.7	.	.	.
C	38.7	38.7	38.6	38.6	38.4	38.2	38.0	.	.	.
D	36.1	36.0	35.8	35.6	35.5	35.0	35.2	.	.	.
E	36.5	36.4	36.6	36.4	36.4	36.3	36.3	.	.	.
F	37.9	37.7	37.7	37.7	37.5	36.5	37.3	.	.	.
G	29.3	29.0	28.9	28.4	28.2	27.7	27.7	.	.	.
H	22.9	22.9	22.7	21.5	22.2	19.7	21.0	.	.	.
I	33.6	33.8	33.4	33.4	32.7	32.3	32.6	.	.	.
J	34.2	34.1	33.4	33.4	33.3	32.9	33.0	.	.	.
K	29.9	30.1	30.1	29.9	29.7	29.9	29.7	.	.	.
L	33.8	33.7	33.5	33.4	33.2	33.2	33.1	.	.	.
M	29.3	28.9	29.2	29.2	29.1	28.9	29.0	.	.	.
N	25.1	25.0	24.8	24.5	24.4	24.4	24.2	.	.	.
O	28.0	27.9	28.2	28.1	27.9	27.0	27.2	.	.	.

Explanatory notes: see p. 721.

[1] Persons aged 15 years and over. [2] Dec. of each year. [3] Enterprises with 20 or more employees. [4] Full and part-time employees. [5] Excl. overtime.

Notes explicatives: voir p. 723.

[1] Personnes âgées de 15 ans et plus. [2] Déc. de chaque année. [3] Entreprises occupant 20 salariés et plus. [4] Salariés à temps complet et à temps partiel. [5] Non compris les heures supplémentaires.

Notas explicativas: véase p. 725.

[1] Personas de 15 años y más. [2] Dic. de cada año. [3] Empresas con 20 y más asalariados. [4] Asalariados a tiempo completo y a tiempo parcial. [5] Excl. las horas extraordinarias.

HOURS OF WORK

DURÉE DU TRAVAIL

HORAS DE TRABAJO

4A

By economic activity

Par activité économique

Por actividad económica

	Per week			Par semaine				Por semana		
	1999	2000	2001	2002	2003	2004	2005	2006	2007	2008

Netherlands (DA) (c) [1] [2] [3] — Employees - Salariés - Asalariados

Men - Hommes - Hombres
ISIC 3 - CITI 3 - CIIU 3

Total	35.0	34.9	34.8	34.6	34.3	33.8	34.1	.	.	.
A-B	33.4	32.6	33.0	32.9	33.2	31.9	32.3	.	.	.
C-Q	35.1	34.9	34.8	34.6	34.4	33.9	34.1	.	.	.
C	39.4	39.4	39.4	39.4	39.0		38.7	.	.	.
D	37.7	37.6	37.5	37.3	37.1	36.7	37.0	.	.	.
E	37.6	37.5	37.7	37.6	37.6	37.6	37.7	.	.	.
F	38.7	38.6	38.6	38.5	38.4	37.5	38.4	.	.	.
G	33.4	33.2	33.4	32.8	32.6	31.9	32.1	.	.	.
H	26.0	26.0	25.3	24.3	25.3	22.0	23.6	.	.	.
I	35.3	35.5	35.2	35.3	34.6	34.2	34.7	.	.	.
J	37.0	37.0	36.3	36.5	36.4	36.0	36.0	.	.	.
K	34.1	33.7	33.8	33.5	33.2	33.4	33.2	.	.	.
L	36.0	35.9	35.7	35.6	35.6	35.5	35.5	.	.	.
M	32.8	32.7	33.2	33.1	33.1	33.0	33.2	.	.	.
N	31.8	31.7	31.4	31.4	31.2	31.0	30.9	.	.	.
O	31.3	31.6	32.0	32.0	31.5	30.6	30.7	.	.	.

Women - Femmes - Mujeres
ISIC 3 - CITI 3 - CIIU 3

Total	25.2	25.3	25.1	24.8	24.6	24.4	24.3	.	.	.
A-B	24.3	23.3	22.3	22.2	21.6	21.1	21.8	.	.	.
C-Q	25.2	25.3	25.1	24.8	24.7	24.5	24.4	.	.	.
C	33.1	33.3	33.1	33.3	34.2	33.3	33.5	.	.	.
D	30.2	30.1	30.0	29.4	29.5	28.7	28.5	.	.	.
E	29.9	30.0	30.4	30.4	30.6	30.7	31.4	.	.	.
F	27.5	27.3	27.9	28.1	26.8	26.3	25.9	.	.	.
G	24.1	23.9	23.7	23.2	23.0	22.7	22.4	.	.	.
H	20.2	20.1	20.5	18.9	19.5	17.8	18.8	.	.	.
I	28.3	28.8	28.4	27.8	27.1	26.9	26.8	.	.	.
J	30.8	30.7	29.8	29.6	29.4	29.1	29.3	.	.	.
K	24.7	25.2	25.0	24.9	24.8	25.1	24.8	.	.	.
L	29.2	29.3	29.4	29.3	29.2	29.1	29.1	.	.	.
M	25.8	25.9	26.1	26.2	26.2	26.0	26.1	.	.	.
N	23.5	23.5	23.3	23.0	23.0	23.0	22.8	.	.	.
O	24.7	24.4	24.5	24.4	24.4	23.6	23.9	.	.	.

Netherlands (DA) (c) [2] [3] [4] — Employees - Salariés - Asalariados

Total men and women - Total hommes et femmes - Total hombres y mujeres
ISIC 3 - CITI 3 - CIIU 3

Total	38.4	38.4	38.4	38.4	38.4	38.4	38.4	.	.	.
A-B	38.6	38.6	38.8	38.5	38.8	38.7	.	.	.	.
C-Q	38.4	38.4	38.4	38.4	38.3	38.4	38.4	.	.	.
C	39.6	39.7	39.7	39.7	39.7	39.7	39.8	.	.	.
D	38.6	38.6	38.6	38.5	38.5	38.5	38.5	.	.	.
E	38.3	38.2	38.2	38.0	38.1	38.3	38.2	.	.	.
F	39.5	39.5	39.5	39.5	39.5	39.5	39.5	.	.	.
G	38.9	38.9	38.9	38.9	38.8	38.9	38.9	.	.	.
H	38.3	38.3	38.3	38.3	38.3	38.4	38.3	.	.	.
I	38.7	38.8	38.8	38.8	38.9	38.9	39.0	.	.	.
J	37.7	37.8	37.6	37.6	37.7	37.7	37.8	.	.	.
K	39.1	39.1	39.2	39.1	39.1	39.1	39.1	.	.	.
L	37.0	36.9	36.7	36.7	36.7	36.6	36.6	.	.	.
M	37.9	37.9	37.9	37.9	37.9	37.9	37.9	.	.	.
N	36.5	36.5	36.5	36.5	36.5	36.6	36.5	.	.	.
O	38.1	38.1	38.3	38.1	38.1	38.1	38.2	.	.	.

Men - Hommes - Hombres
ISIC 3 - CITI 3 - CIIU 3

Total	38.6	38.6	38.6	38.5	38.5	38.5	38.6	.	.	.
A-B	38.6	38.6	38.8	38.5	38.8	38.7	.	.	.	.
C-Q	38.6	38.6	38.6	38.5	38.5	38.5	38.5	.	.	.
C	39.6	39.7	39.7	39.7	39.7	39.8	39.8	.	.	.
D	38.6	38.6	38.6	38.5	38.5	38.5	38.6	.	.	.
E	38.3	38.2	38.2	38.0	38.1	38.3	38.2	.	.	.
F	39.5	39.5	39.5	39.5	39.5	39.5	39.5	.	.	.
G	39.1	39.0	39.0	39.0	38.9	39.1	39.0	.	.	.
H	38.3	38.3	38.3	38.3	38.4	38.4	38.3	.	.	.
I	38.7	38.8	38.8	38.8	38.9	38.9	39.0	.	.	.
J	37.8	37.9	37.8	37.8	37.8	37.9	37.9	.	.	.
K	39.1	39.1	39.2	39.2	39.2	39.2	39.2	.	.	.
L	37.1	37.0	36.8	36.7	36.7	36.7	36.7	.	.	.
M	38.0	38.1	38.1	38.1	38.1	38.0	38.1	.	.	.
N	36.5	36.5	36.5	36.5	36.5	36.6	36.6	.	.	.
O	38.1	38.2	38.4	38.3	38.2	38.3	38.3	.	.	.

Explanatory notes: see p. 721.

[1] Full and part-time employees. [2] Excl. overtime. [3] Dec. of each year. [4] Full-time employees only.

Notes explicatives: voir p. 723.

[1] Salariés à temps complet et à temps partiel. [2] Non compris les heures supplémentaires. [3] Déc. de chaque année. [4] Salariés à plein temps seulement.

Notas explicativas: véase p. 725.

[1] Asalariados a tiempo completo y a tiempo parcial. [2] Excl. las horas extraordinarias. [3] Dic. de cada año. [4] Asalariados a tiempo completo solamente.

	Per week / Par semaine / Por semana									
	1999	2000	2001	2002	2003	2004	2005	2006	2007	2008

Netherlands (DA) (c) [1][2][3]   **Employees - Salariés - Asalariados**

Women - Femmes - Mujeres
ISIC 3 - CITI 3 - CIIU 3

	1999	2000	2001	2002	2003	2004	2005	2006	2007	2008
Total	37.9	38.0	37.9	37.8	37.8	37.9	37.8			
A-B	38.3	38.5	38.7	38.4	38.7	38.3	.			
C-Q	37.9	37.9	37.9	37.8	37.8	37.9	37.8			
C	.	.	39.7	39.7	39.8	39.7	.			
D	38.5	38.3	38.4	38.3	38.3	38.3	38.3			
E	38.3	38.2	38.2	38.1	38.2	38.3	38.2			
F	39.4	39.4	39.5	39.5	39.5	39.4	39.5			
G	38.5	38.5	38.4	38.4	38.3	38.5	38.4			
H	38.3	38.4	38.4	38.3	38.3	38.3	38.2			
I	38.8	38.9	38.9	38.9	38.9	39.0	39.1			
J	37.5	37.5	37.3	37.2	37.2	37.3	37.4			
K	38.9	38.9	39.0	38.9	38.9	38.9	38.9			
L	36.5	36.5	36.5	36.4	36.4	36.3	36.3			
M	37.6	37.6	37.6	37.6	37.6	37.5	37.6			
N	36.5	36.5	36.5	36.4	36.4	36.6	36.5			
O	37.9	37.9	38.0	37.9	37.8	37.9	38.0			

Norway (BA) (a) [4]   **Employees - Salariés - Asalariados**

Total men and women - Total hommes et femmes - Total hombres y mujeres
ISIC 3 - CITI 3 - CIIU 3

	1999	2000	2001	2002	2003	2004	2005	2006	2007	2008
Total	35.4	35.1	34.9	34.8	34.6	34.6	34.9	34.5	34.4	34.4
A-B	42.8	43.1	43.4	42.8	42.3	42.4	41.9	42.3	41.8	41.9
C-Q	35.0	34.7	34.6	34.5	34.3	34.3	34.6	34.3	34.1	34.2
A	42.2	42.0	43.0	42.0	41.7	41.0	41.0	41.1	40.4	40.7
B	47.3	49.4	48.3	48.4	45.7	49.2	47.1	48.6	49.3	47.7
C	44.6	45.4	44.5	45.1	45.8	44.1	46.0	45.9	45.0	42.9
D	36.6	36.5	36.5	36.7	36.3	36.3	36.9	36.8	36.7	36.6
E	37.2	36.5	36.5	37.0	37.5	36.5	37.0	36.8	35.6	36.3
F	38.3	37.9	38.1	37.9	37.5	37.6	38.1	38.2	38.1	38.2
G	34.3	33.6	32.9	32.5	32.7	32.7	32.9	32.2	31.8	31.5
H	32.2	32.6	31.9	31.5	30.4	31.6	31.4	31.4	29.4	31.4
I	39.6	38.8	38.0	38.4	38.3	38.2	38.7	39.0	38.5	38.4
J	36.3	36.2	36.6	36.7	35.9	35.7	36.6	36.2	35.8	36.3
K	36.7	36.2	36.6	35.8	35.8	36.2	36.4	36.1	35.8	36.3
L	36.4	36.0	36.0	36.2	36.3	36.0	36.3	34.0	33.1	33.2
M	33.1	33.0	33.1	33.3	33.5	33.2	33.4	33.2	33.7	34.0
N	30.8	30.8	30.6	30.9	30.6	30.7	31.1	30.7	30.9	30.9
O	32.4	32.3	32.5	32.0	31.7	31.7	32.0	31.8	32.7	32.9
P	24.7	24.7	23.7	24.3	22.3	20.1	19.2	15.2	14.0	15.6
Q	22.5	22.0	.	47.4	37.9	47.0	34.9	.	30.0	38.5

Men - Hommes - Hombres
ISIC 3 - CITI 3 - CIIU 3

	1999	2000	2001	2002	2003	2004	2005	2006	2007	2008
Total	39.3	38.4	38.5	38.4	38.0	38.1	38.3	38.0	37.7	37.5
A-B	46.4	46.7	46.5	45.7	45.4	45.9	44.9	45.2	45.0	45.9
C-Q	38.9	38.3	38.5	38.0	37.6	37.7	38.0	37.6	37.4	37.2
A	45.8	45.7	45.6	44.4	44.9	44.4	43.8	44.0	43.7	45.1
B	48.9	51.2	50.8	50.8	47.3	52.0	49.7	51.3	50.8	48.9
C	46.8	47.0	46.0	46.6	47.8	45.9	47.2	47.5	46.9	44.6
D	38.3	38.0	38.0	38.1	37.8	38.0	38.5	38.3	38.1	38.1
E	38.3	37.4	37.8	37.5	37.4	37.4	37.0	37.5	35.9	36.9
F	39.4	38.8	38.8	38.6	38.0	38.3	38.7	39.0	38.7	38.6
G	38.3	37.4	36.7	36.6	36.4	36.5	36.6	36.0	35.6	35.0
H	37.2	36.8	35.5	36.2	34.1	35.2	34.6	35.3	31.7	34.5
I	42.2	41.5	40.5	40.9	40.3	39.9	40.5	41.1	40.6	40.4
J	38.3	38.1	38.7	38.9	38.5	37.7	38.7	38.1	37.1	37.8
K	39.7	39.0	38.8	38.0	38.2	38.3	38.6	38.3	38.2	38.1
L	38.2	37.9	38.2	38.4	38.3	38.1	38.3	34.7	33.9	33.5
M	36.1	35.6	35.5	36.3	35.9	36.0	35.9	35.8	36.5	35.9
N	36.5	36.4	36.1	35.5	35.1	35.9	35.5	34.7	35.1	35.1
O	37.5	35.9	36.4	35.7	35.3	35.4	34.7	34.4	36.3	34.9
P	.	15.7	23.7	.	.	27.9	23.9	23.2	21.4	19.4
Q	.	.	.	47.4	37.9	54.0	39.3	.	30.0	41.0

Explanatory notes: see p. 721.

[1] Full-time employees only. [2] Excl. overtime. [3] Dec. of each year.
[4] Persons aged 15 to 74 years; prior to 2006: 16 to 74 years.

Notes explicatives: voir p. 723.

[1] Salariés à plein temps seulement. [2] Non compris les heures supplémentaires. [3] Déc. de chaque année. [4] Personnes âgées de 15 à 74 ans: avant 2006: 16 à 74 ans.

Notas explicativas: véase p. 725.

[1] Asalariados a tiempo completo solamente. [2] Excl. las horas extraordinarias. [3] Dic. de cada año. [4] Personas de 15 a 74 años; antes de 2006: 16 a 74 años.

HOURS OF WORK

By economic activity

DURÉE DU TRAVAIL

Par activité économique

HORAS DE TRABAJO

Por actividad económica

4A

	Per week			Par semaine				Por semana		
	1999	2000	2001	2002	2003	2004	2005	2006	2007	2008

Norway (BA) (a) [1] — Employees - Salariés - Asalariados

Women - Femmes - Mujeres
ISIC 3 - CITI 3 - CIIU 3

	1999	2000	2001	2002	2003	2004	2005	2006	2007	2008
Total	30.6	30.6	30.5	30.4	30.4	30.3	30.8	30.4	30.4	30.8
A-B	32.3	32.5	33.6	33.1	32.8	31.1	31.7	31.3	30.5	30.0
C-Q	30.5	30.5	30.5	30.4	30.4	30.3	30.8	30.4	30.4	30.8
A	32.1	32.4	33.8	33.4	33.2	31.6	32.2	31.6	30.5	28.0
B	34.6	34.7	31.4	29.6	26.1	24.0	26.1	28.0	30.2	26.8
C	34.7	37.7	38.6	38.2	37.7	37.0	40.5	38.2	36.7	36.6
D	31.6	32.2	31.9	32.2	31.8	31.2	31.7	32.0	32.1	32.2
E	32.7	32.7	31.2	34.8	38.0	33.5	37.1	34.3	34.7	34.7
F	26.6	27.9	29.0	29.7	31.1	28.0	28.7	27.3	30.3	31.4
G	29.1	28.7	28.4	27.8	28.3	28.1	28.5	27.9	27.5	27.4
H	29.7	30.1	29.7	29.0	28.3	28.9	29.4	29.0	28.2	29.6
I	33.3	32.4	32.2	31.3	32.7	33.3	33.1	32.8	32.2	32.8
J	34.3	34.2	34.1	34.1	33.1	33.4	34.3	34.1	34.3	34.6
K	31.8	31.8	32.6	32.0	31.8	32.4	32.4	32.4	31.7	32.7
L	33.7	33.3	33.0	33.5	33.7	33.3	33.7	33.1	32.2	32.8
M	31.5	31.3	31.5	31.5	32.0	31.6	32.0	31.7	32.1	32.9
N	29.6	29.6	29.4	29.8	29.6	29.6	30.1	29.7	29.9	30.0
O	28.0	29.1	29.1	28.4	28.3	28.5	29.8	29.6	29.7	31.0
P	24.7	25.2	23.7	26.0	24.4	19.5	18.3	13.8	13.3	14.5
Q	22.5	22.0	.	.	.	.	41.5	30.4	.	.	37.8

Poland (BA) (a) — Employees - Salariés - Asalariados

Total men and women - Total hommes et femmes - Total hombres y mujeres
ISIC 3 - CITI 3 - CIIU 3 / ISIC 4 - CITI 4 - CIIU 4

ISIC 3	1999	2000	2001	2002	2003	2004	2005	2006	2007	2008	ISIC 4
Total	39.9 [2]	40.1	40.0	39.8	39.8	39.8	39.7	40.0	39.9	39.8	Total
A-B	. [2]	41.7	41.7	41.8	41.3	41.9	41.5	38.1	37.5	38.0	A
C-Q	. [2]	40.0	39.9	39.7	39.8	39.8	39.6	41.0	40.5	40.4	B
A	41.9 [2]	41.6	41.6	41.6	41.0	41.6	41.2	38.1	37.5	40.9	C
B	. [2]	44.3	46.3	47.4	48.9	48.7	48.4	44.1	47.2	39.6	D
C	40.2 [2]	40.4	40.4	40.6	40.8	40.7	41.0	41.0	40.9	40.2	E
D	41.2 [2]	41.3	41.2	41.0	41.1	41.2	41.2	42.0	41.4	44.2	F
E	40.6 [2]	40.8	40.2	40.2	40.2	40.1	40.0	40.0	40.0	41.7	G
F	43.1 [2]	43.1	43.3	43.2	43.4	43.8	43.8	45.0	44.7	43.5	H
G	41.3 [2]	41.2	41.2	40.9	41.1	40.9	40.6	43.0	42.3	41.1	I
H	40.6 [2]	40.3	40.7	40.2	40.6	40.8	40.5	42.0	42.0	40.8	J
I	42.4 [2]	42.4	42.3	42.1	42.8	43.0	42.9	44.0	43.9	39.5	K
J	40.2 [2]	39.8	39.6	39.7	39.7	39.4	39.5	40.0	39.4	38.2	L
K	39.0 [2]	39.5	39.9	39.7	39.5	39.6	39.2	40.0	40.0	40.2	M
L	40.4 [2]	40.8	40.3	40.1	40.2	40.4	40.0	40.0	39.4	39.0	N
M	30.0 [2]	30.4	30.0	30.0	30.3	29.9	29.8	30.0	30.6	39.3	O
N	39.2 [2]	39.2	38.9	38.9	39.4	38.9	39.0	39.0	38.8	31.4	P
O	37.7 [2]	38.6	38.4	38.1	37.9	37.5	37.6	38.0	38.1	38.6	Q
P	. [2]	36.0	26.1	26.6	30.0	.	32.0	30.0	29.7	36.1	R
Q	. [2]	.	.	.	.	.	.	40.0	40.0	39.0	S
X	.	.	.	.	.	.	44.3	41.0	39.4	33.2	T
											U
										41.3	X

Men - Hommes - Hombres
ISIC 3 - CITI 3 - CIIU 3 / ISIC 4 - CITI 4 - CIIU 4

ISIC 3	1999	2000	2001	2002	2003	2004	2005	2006	2007	2008	ISIC 4
Total	41.5 [2]	41.7	41.6	41.4	41.6	41.7	41.6	42.0	42.1	42.0	Total
A-B	. [2]	42.4	41.9	42.5	42.0	42.7	42.1	41.1	40.5	41.2	A
C-Q	. [2]	41.7	41.6	41.4	41.6	41.7	41.6	43.0	42.5	40.6	B
A	42.2 [2]	42.2	41.7	42.3	41.7	42.3	41.8	41.1	40.5	41.5	C
B	. [2]	45.4	47.6	48.5	49.8	49.4	49.1	45.7	48.3	39.7	D
C	40.1 [2]	40.4	40.4	40.7	41.0	40.9	41.2	41.0	41.0	40.7	E
D	41.7 [2]	41.8	41.6	41.4	41.6	41.7	41.8	42.0	42.1	44.6	F
E	41.0 [2]	41.1	40.3	40.5	40.5	40.4	40.3	40.0	40.1	43.4	G
F	43.7 [2]	43.5	43.7	43.6	43.9	44.2	44.2	45.0	45.1	44.8	H
G	43.1 [2]	42.5	42.6	42.3	42.6	42.7	42.3	44.0	44.2	43.5	I
H	42.1 [2]	40.5	41.6	41.3	40.8	40.4	40.8	44.0	44.8	41.7	J
I	43.3 [2]	43.4	43.5	43.1	43.8	44.2	44.1	45.0	45.1	41.8	K
J	42.2 [2]	41.3	40.6	40.9	41.3	39.9	40.5	41.0	41.2	39.1	L
K	40.3 [2]	41.0	41.6	41.2	40.9	41.1	40.7	42.0	42.1	42.0	M
L	41.8 [2]	42.2	41.5	41.2	41.7	41.8	41.2	41.0	40.4	41.5	N
M	31.9 [2]	32.7	31.7	32.0	32.1	31.5	31.6	32.0	31.8	40.3	O
N	40.3 [2]	41.4	40.6	40.8	41.1	40.1	40.8	41.0	40.5	33.3	P
O	39.1 [2]	40.0	40.2	39.4	39.4	38.6	39.1	39.0	39.3	40.4	Q
P	.	.	.	.	.	.	.	17.0	15.3	38.0	R
Q	.	.	.	.	.	.	.	40.0	40.0	41.3	S
X	.	.	.	.	.	.	.	45.0	43.1	21.0	T
											U
										42.3	X

Explanatory notes: see p. 721.

[1] Persons aged 15 to 74 years; prior to 2006: 16 to 74 years. [2] 4th quarter; holidays included.

Notes explicatives: voir p. 723.

[1] Personnes âgées de 15 à 74 ans: avant 2006: 16 à 74 ans. [2] 4e trimestre; y compris les heures de travail normales des salariés en vacance.

Notas explicativas: véase p. 725.

[1] Personas de 15 a 74 años; antes de 2006: 16 a 74 años. [2] 4o trimestre: incl. horas de las personas que están de vacaciones.

By economic activity   **Par activité économique**   **Por actividad económica**

	Per week				Par semaine				Por semana		
	1999	2000	2001	2002	2003	2004	2005	2006	2007	2008	

Poland (BA) (a)   **Employees - Salariés - Asalariados**

Women - Femmes - Mujeres
ISIC 3 - CITI 3 - CIIU 3   ISIC 4 - CITI 4 - CIIU 4

	1999	2000	2001	2002	2003	2004	2005	2006	2007	2008	
Total	37.9 ı	38.1	38.0	37.9	37.7	37.6	37.4	37.0	37.2 ı	37.2	Total
A-B	. ı	39.9	41.1	39.9	39.3	39.6	39.6	34.2	33.7 ı	34.0	A
C-Q	. ı	38.1	38.0	37.8	37.7	37.6	37.4	38.0	38.0 ı	39.3	B
A	41.0 ı	40.0	41.2	39.6	39.1	39.5	39.5	34.2	33.7 ı	39.8	C
B								32.9	42.3 ı	39.4	D
C	40.7 ı	40.3	40.2	39.9	39.3	39.4	39.4	40.0	39.8 ı	38.6	E
D	40.4 ı	40.5	40.5	40.2	40.1	40.1	40.1	40.0	40.0 ı	37.3	F
E	39.0 ı	39.8	39.7	39.2	38.8	38.9	38.5	39.0	39.4 ı	40.4	G
F	37.4 ı	38.6	38.8	39.3	39.2	38.6	38.0	39.0	38.2 ı	39.0	H
G	40.1 ı	40.3	40.2	39.9	39.9	39.5	39.4	41.0	40.7 ı	40.0	I
H	40.1 ı	40.2	40.3	39.8	40.5	40.9	40.3	41.0	40.9 ı	39.0	J
I	40.1 ı	40.0	39.5	39.8	40.1	39.9	39.6	39.0	39.3 ı	38.5	K
J	39.3 ı	39.2	39.2	39.2	39.2	39.2	39.1	39.0	38.7 ı	37.5	L
K	37.3 ı	37.5	37.5	37.5	37.4	37.4	37.1	38.0	37.3 ı	38.6	M
L	38.7 ı	39.1	38.8	38.8	38.7	39.0	38.8	38.0	38.3 ı	35.9	N
M	29.3 ı	29.6	29.5	29.4	29.7	29.4	29.3	30.0	30.2 ı	38.4	O
N	38.9 ı	38.7	38.6	38.5	39.0	38.7	38.6	38.0	38.4 ı	30.9	P
O	36.3 ı	37.3	36.6	36.6	36.5	36.4	36.1	37.0	37.2 ı	38.2	Q
P	. ı	35.6	26.5	27.8	30.8	30.9	31.9	33.0	30.2 ı	34.8	R
Q								40.0	. ı	37.5	S
X								33.0	19.0 ı	33.5	T
									ı		U
									ı	40.3	X

Portugal (BA) (a) [2] [3]   **Employees - Salariés - Asalariados**

Total men and women - Total hommes et femmes - Total hombres y mujeres
ISIC 3 - CITI 3 - CIIU 3

	1999	2000	2001	2002	2003	2004	2005	2006	2007	2008
Total	37.3	36.8	36.4	36.4	36.0	35.4	35.7	35.7	35.2	35.1
A-B	35.6	33.6	32.0	32.1	32.5	37.2	36.8	36.8	35.4	36.1
C-Q	37.6	37.3	37.1	37.0	36.5	35.4	35.7	35.7	35.2	35.1
A	35.3	33.3	31.7	31.9	32.1	36.3	35.8	36.1	35.3	35.7
B	45.2	43.4	41.3	37.9	44.4	44.2	44.4	41.8	36.6	40.4
C	42.2	39.7	39.0	38.4	37.9	37.3	38.0	39.1	36.9	39.3
D	37.1	37.0	36.9	36.8	36.4	36.1	36.6	36.8	35.9	36.1
E	36.5	36.8	35.9	35.9	35.1	35.1	34.1	35.1	36.4	36.0
F	39.3	39.0	38.9	38.2	37.9	37.6	38.2	37.9	37.7	37.4
G	41.1	40.4	39.9	39.8	39.0	37.7	37.8	37.5	37.2	36.7
H	46.8	46.1	45.4	46.2	45.3	39.8	39.2	39.3	39.0	39.1
I	39.4	39.1	39.3	39.5	38.6	37.0	37.0	37.5	37.7	36.6
J	35.8	34.6	34.5	35.5	35.4	36.1	35.0	34.9	35.2	34.9
K	36.6	36.8	36.7	36.6	36.9	35.4	35.2	36.4	34.8	35.4
L	35.6	34.7	34.1	33.9	33.9	33.7	34.2	34.0	33.5	33.1
M	28.9	28.7	29.2	29.2	28.9	28.7	29.3	29.2	29.3	29.1
N	35.5	35.5	35.2	35.2	33.8	34.0	34.3	34.1	33.8	34.5
O	36.4	36.8	35.9	36.3	35.3	35.1	35.3	35.3	35.1	34.1
P	28.3	26.5	27.5	27.3	26.9	27.6	28.2	28.0	27.5	26.6
Q	37.2	37.3	38.0	36.4	36.7	37.3	37.8	31.2	32.2	34.8

Men - Hommes - Hombres
ISIC 3 - CITI 3 - CIIU 3

	1999	2000	2001	2002	2003	2004	2005	2006	2007	2008
Total	39.5	38.9	38.5	38.4	38.0	37.3	37.6	37.4	37.0	36.8
A-B	38.3	36.1	34.7	34.8	35.5	39.0	38.6	38.1	37.2	38.1
C-Q	39.7	39.3	39.0	38.9	38.3	37.2	37.6	37.4	37.0	36.8
A	37.8	35.6	34.2	34.5	35.0	37.9	37.0	37.4	37.2	37.7
B	45.3	44.1	41.9	38.7	45.1	45.1	46.5	41.9	37.0	41.0
C	42.5	39.9	39.5	38.5	37.7	37.2	37.9	39.1	36.8	39.3
D	38.8	38.5	38.4	38.4	37.7	37.3	37.5	37.6	36.9	36.9
E	36.9	36.8	36.3	36.1	35.4	35.2	34.8	35.5	36.8	36.6
F	39.5	39.2	39.0	38.3	38.0	37.8	38.3	38.0	37.8	37.5
G	42.3	41.6	41.0	41.0	40.2	39.0	39.2	38.4	38.2	38.0
H	50.2	49.5	48.7	49.2	48.5	42.6	41.7	40.9	41.2	41.7
I	40.9	40.4	40.6	40.6	39.5	38.0	39.0	38.6	38.5	37.6
J	37.3	35.4	35.7	36.2	36.8	37.3	36.7	36.4	36.9	36.5
K	40.0	39.5	39.0	38.8	39.1	37.5	37.5	38.8	37.3	37.6
L	37.1	35.7	35.4	35.1	35.2	34.9	35.6	35.3	34.6	34.0
M	30.3	30.8	29.7	29.7	30.2	30.3	30.7	30.2	30.0	30.0
N	36.3	37.6	37.2	37.8	35.0	35.1	35.3	35.3	35.5	34.6
O	37.5	38.0	36.4	37.7	35.9	34.6	36.1	35.4	34.7	33.7
P	36.4	26.6	30.8	29.1	33.6	28.1	34.7	.	38.4	37.5
Q	38.7	37.8	40.0	36.2	36.6	38.6	37.6		36.4	34.9

Explanatory notes: see p. 721.

[1] 4th quarter; holidays included. [2] Persons aged 15 years and over. [3] Estimates based on the 2001 Population Census results.

Notes explicatives: voir p. 723.

[1] 4e trimestre; y compris les heures de travail normales des salariés en vacance. [2] Personnes âgées de 15 ans et plus. [3] Estimations basées sur les résultats du Recensement de la population de 2001.

Notas explicativas: véase p. 725.

[1] 4o trimestre: incl. horas de las personas que están de vacaciones. [2] Personas de 15 años y más. [3] Estimaciones basadas en los resultados del Censo de población de 2001.

HOURS OF WORK

By economic activity

DURÉE DU TRAVAIL

Par activité économique

HORAS DE TRABAJO

Por actividad económica

4A

	Per week / Par semaine / Por semana									
	1999	2000	2001	2002	2003	2004	2005	2006	2007	2008

Portugal (BA) (a) [1] [2]   Employees - Salariés - Asalariados

Women - Femmes - Mujeres
ISIC 3 - CITI 3 - CIIU 3

Total	34.6	34.2	33.9	33.9	33.6	33.4	33.5	33.8	33.3	33.2
A-B	32.9	31.1	29.4	29.4	29.3	33.0	33.6	33.7	31.1	31.7
C-Q	34.9	34.8	34.6	34.6	34.2	33.4	33.5	33.8	33.3	33.2
A	32.9	31.1	29.4	29.4	29.3	33.0	34.0	33.5	31.2	31.8
B	41.2	31.8	32.2	22.8	34.0	33.0	19.3	40.9	22.1	18.1
C	38.0	34.8	30.6	37.9	39.1	38.0	38.8	38.9	38.6	39.0
D	34.9	35.0	35.0	34.7	34.7	34.6	35.3	35.7	34.7	35.0
E	33.2	36.8	33.4	34.5	33.7	34.3	31.0	33.0	34.9	33.6
F	32.5	35.8	35.3	34.5	35.4	34.8	35.1	34.8	34.8	33.6
G	39.4	38.8	38.3	38.2	37.4	36.2	36.1	36.5	36.1	35.2
H	44.4	43.9	43.2	44.2	43.2	38.3	38.0	38.5	37.9	37.7
I	34.0	33.9	34.7	35.0	35.4	33.8	32.1	34.4	34.9	33.8
J	33.1	33.3	32.5	34.7	33.1	34.2	32.9	32.8	33.4	33.1
K	33.2	33.9	34.1	34.2	35.0	33.6	33.2	33.8	32.8	33.6
L	32.9	33.0	31.7	31.7	31.7	31.7	31.8	31.8	31.6	31.6
M	28.4	28.1	29.0	29.1	28.5	28.3	28.9	28.9	29.0	28.8
N	35.3	34.9	34.7	34.6	33.5	33.7	34.1	33.9	33.4	34.4
O	35.5	35.7	35.4	35.3	34.8	35.5	34.7	35.3	35.5	34.4
P	28.2	26.5	27.4	27.2	26.8	27.6	28.1	27.9	27.4	26.5
Q	33.6	36.9	34.6	37.4	37.1	35.8	38.0	27.4	26.2	34.6

Portugal (DA) (b)   Employees - Salariés - Asalariados

Total men and women - Total hommes et femmes - Total hombres y mujeres
ISIC 3 - CITI 3 - CIIU 3

C	39.6	39.4	39.5	38.4	37.8	39.6	40.1	40.4	40.7	40.5
D	39.3	39.5	39.4	38.5	37.9	39.5	39.9	40.1	40.1	40.2
E	38.1	34.6	36.0	36.6	36.0	37.6	37.3	37.7	38.4	38.5
F	39.3	39.5	39.4	38.6	38.2	39.6	40.1	40.2	40.3	.
G	39.5	39.6	39.6	38.5	38.0	39.5	39.8	39.8	39.9	40.0
H	39.5	39.8	39.7	38.6	38.1	39.6	40.0	40.0	40.1	40.0
I	39.8	37.9	38.6	38.8	38.3	39.7	39.6	39.7	40.5	40.7
J	34.5	35.4	35.0	34.3	33.9	34.8	35.0	35.5	35.8	36.1
K	38.9	39.0	39.0	38.3	37.8	39.1	39.4	39.4	39.7	40.1
M	35.6	35.7	35.7	34.2	33.9	34.6	34.2	34.5	34.6	35.4
N	38.1	38.2	38.2	36.7	36.1	37.5	37.9	38.2	38.2	38.7
O	38.1	37.9	38.0	37.3	36.9	37.7	37.6	38.1	37.8	38.4

Men - Hommes - Hombres
ISIC 3 - CITI 3 - CIIU 3

C	39.6	39.4	39.5	38.6	38.0	39.7	40.2	40.5	40.8	40.6
D	39.4	39.4	39.4	38.5	38.0	39.6	40.0	40.2	40.2	40.2
E	38.3	34.6	36.1	36.8	36.2	37.8	37.6	37.9	38.6	38.7
F	39.4	39.5	39.5	38.7	38.2	39.7	40.2	40.3	40.4	40.2
G	39.5	39.6	39.6	38.5	38.0	39.5	39.8	39.8	39.9	39.9
H	39.5	39.8	39.7	38.7	38.1	39.7	40.0	40.0	40.2	40.0
I	40.3	38.3	39.1	39.6	39.0	40.6	40.3	40.6	41.2	41.3
J	34.5	35.3	35.0	34.3	33.9	34.8	35.0	35.5	35.7	36.0
K	39.1	39.1	39.1	38.6	38.1	39.5	39.8	39.7	40.2	40.5
M	36.5	36.4	36.4	34.7	34.3	34.9	34.3	34.6	34.8	35.6
N	38.2	38.1	38.1	36.6	35.9	37.6	38.0	38.8	38.4	38.8
O	38.0	37.5	37.7	37.5	37.1	37.9	37.8	37.9	37.8	38.5

Women - Femmes - Mujeres
ISIC 3 - CITI 3 - CIIU 3

C	38.9	39.2	39.1	37.6	36.8	38.9	39.5	39.5	39.8	39.8
D	39.2	39.5	39.4	38.3	37.8	39.3	39.7	40.0	40.0	40.0
E	37.0	34.6	35.5	35.6	34.9	36.3	36.1	36.9	37.4	37.5
F	38.4	38.6	38.5	37.8	37.4	38.9	39.5	39.4	39.6	39.6
G	39.4	39.6	39.5	38.5	38.0	39.5	39.7	39.7	39.9	40.0
H	39.5	39.8	39.7	38.6	38.1	39.6	40.0	40.0	40.0	40.0
I	37.9	36.4	37.0	36.8	36.4	37.4	37.4	37.3	38.6	39.0
J	34.6	35.4	35.1	34.3	33.9	34.8	35.0	35.5	35.9	36.1
K	38.8	38.9	38.9	37.8	37.4	38.6	38.9	39.0	39.0	39.4
M	35.2	35.5	35.4	34.1	33.7	34.5	34.2	34.5	34.6	35.3
N	38.1	38.2	38.2	36.7	36.1	37.5	37.9	38.1	38.2	38.7
O	38.2	38.1	38.2	37.0	36.6	37.5	37.5	38.2	38.2	38.3

Explanatory notes: see p. 721.

[1] Persons aged 15 years and over. [2] Estimates based on the 2001 Population Census results.

Notes explicatives: voir p. 723.

[1] Personnes âgées de 15 ans et plus. [2] Estimations basées sur les résultats du Recensement de la population de 2001.

Notas explicativas: véase p. 725.

[1] Personas de 15 años y más. [2] Estimaciones basadas en los resultados del Censo de población de 2001.

HOURS OF WORK — DURÉE DU TRAVAIL — HORAS DE TRABAJO

By economic activity — Par activité économique — Por actividad económica

	Per week — Par semaine — Por semana									
	1999	2000	2001	2002	2003	2004	2005	2006	2007	2008

Roumanie (BA) (a) [1] — Total employment - Emploi total - Empleo total

Total men and women - Total hommes et femmes - Total hombres y mujeres
ISIC 3 - CITI 3 - CIIU 3

	1999	2000	2001	2002	2003	2004	2005	2006	2007	2008
Total	38.0	37.9	38.3	39.6[2]	39.4	39.4	39.4	39.1	39.7	39.6
A-B	34.8	34.4	34.3	35.9[2]	35.6	35.3	36.1	35.7	35.2	34.8
A					35.5	35.2	36.1	35.7	35.2	34.8
B	40.1	40.2	43.0	42.0[2]	42.7	46.0	42.2	39.3	42.2	39.7
C	39.0	39.1	39.8	39.9[2]	39.6	39.7	39.6	39.6	40.1	40.0
D	38.8	39.5	40.3	40.9[2]	40.9	40.8	40.6	40.3	41.6	41.4
E	40.1	40.2	40.5	41.1[2]	41.0	40.7	40.6	40.3	40.8	40.6
F	42.0	42.6	43.5	44.4[2]	43.7	43.0	42.7	42.4	43.2	42.9
G	43.8	43.7	43.0	44.5[2]	43.9	43.4	42.9	42.0	42.3	42.2
H	44.2	43.4	44.3	44.7[2]	43.9	43.8	43.5	42.8	43.5	43.0
I					43.1	42.8	42.7	42.2	42.8	42.8
J	40.2	40.3	40.3	40.1[2]	40.8	41.0	40.7	40.2	41.1	40.8
K	40.9	41.3	41.3	41.7[2]	42.4	41.5	40.6	40.4	41.2	40.9
L	40.4	40.9	41.0	41.3[2]	41.1	40.9	40.7	40.6	41.1	40.8
M	35.9	35.4	35.8	36.5[2]	36.3	36.2	35.5	35.8	38.7	38.4
N	40.1	40.1	40.3	40.7[2]	40.9	40.8	40.7	40.3	41.2	41.4
O-Q	39.0	39.2	39.5	40.2[2]	39.9	40.2	39.5	39.1	39.8	39.9

Men - Hommes - Hombres
ISIC 3 - CITI 3 - CIIU 3

	1999	2000	2001	2002	2003	2004	2005	2006	2007	2008
Total	39.6	39.6	39.8	41.0[2]	40.7	40.7	40.7	40.3	40.7	40.5
A-B	37.5	36.9	36.8	38.3[2]	37.7	37.4	37.8	37.3	37.0	36.9
A					37.6	37.4	37.8	37.3	37.0	36.9
B	40.1	40.3	43.0	42.1[2]	43.0	47.1	42.0	38.5	42.6	39.7
C	39.0	39.0	39.8	39.9[2]	39.5	39.7	39.5	39.6	40.1	40.0
D	39.5	40.0	40.5	41.2[2]	41.4	41.5	41.5	41.1	41.7	41.5
E	40.5	40.5	40.8	41.4[2]	41.2	41.0	40.9	40.6	40.9	40.6
F	42.3	43.0	43.8	44.8[2]	44.0	43.2	43.0	42.7	43.4	43.0
G	45.0	45.2	45.0	45.9[2]	45.0	44.6	44.3	43.2	42.7	42.5
H	45.4	45.4	46.5	45.6[2]	44.8	45.3	45.4	44.5	44.6	43.6
I					43.9	43.6	43.5	43.0	43.3	43.3
J	41.0	41.3	41.3	41.1[2]	41.9	42.9	42.2	41.4	41.5	41.0
K	41.7	42.4	42.3	43.2[2]	43.6	42.4	42.2	41.5	41.7	41.2
L	40.8	41.3	41.5	41.8[2]	41.5	41.2	41.2	40.9	41.2	41.0
M	36.1	36.1	36.8	37.8[2]	37.9	37.5	37.4	37.3	39.1	38.9
N	40.6	41.0	42.0	41.7[2]	41.1	41.9	41.0	40.9	41.3	41.6
O-Q	39.3	40.2	40.5	40.6[2]	40.2	40.8	40.0	39.5	39.6	39.5

Women - Femmes - Mujeres
ISIC 3 - CITI 3 - CIIU 3

	1999	2000	2001	2002	2003	2004	2005	2006	2007	2008
Total	36.0	36.0	36.3	37.8[2]	37.8	37.8	37.9	39.7	38.6	38.4
A-B	32.1	31.8	31.8	33.4[2]	33.2	32.9	34.3	33.9	33.3	32.6
A					33.2	32.9	34.3	33.9	33.3	32.6
B	40.0	40.0	40.0	20.0[2]	20.0	42.8	-	42.1	40.0	30.0
C	38.6	39.5	39.8	39.9[2]	40.4	39.8	40.2	39.7	40.1	40.0
D	38.0	38.8	39.8	40.5[2]	40.4	40.0	39.7	39.4	41.5	41.3
E	38.9	39.4	39.5	40.2[2]	40.4	39.7	39.5	39.2	40.5	40.5
F	39.7	40.0	40.5	41.0[2]	41.0	40.7	39.7	40.2	41.4	41.3
G	42.8	42.5	42.3	43.3[2]	42.9	42.5	41.7	40.9	42.0	41.9
H	43.6	42.2	43.5	44.3[2]	43.3	43.1	42.6	41.9	42.9	42.7
I					40.4	40.3	40.2	39.3	40.7	40.7
J	39.9	39.8	40.0	39.6[2]	40.1	40.0	39.9	39.7	40.9	40.8
K	39.9	39.8	39.3	39.6[2]	40.5	40.1	38.2	38.7	40.5	40.4
L	39.1	39.6	39.5	39.9[2]	40.0	40.0	40.0	40.0	40.8	40.4
M	35.8	35.1	35.5	35.9[2]	35.6	35.8	34.8	35.3	38.5	38.2
N	40.0	39.9	40.0	40.4[2]	40.8	40.6	40.5	40.1	41.2	41.4
O-Q	38.6	38.1	38.0	39.7[2]	39.5	39.6	39.1	38.6	40.0	40.3

Russian Federation (DA) (a) [3] — Employees - Salariés - Asalariados

Total men and women - Total hommes et femmes - Total hombres y mujeres
ISIC 3 - CITI 3 - CIIU 3

	2005	2006	2007	2008
Total	7.1[4]	7.1	7.1	7.0
A-B	7.5[4]	7.5	7.5	7.5
C-Q	7.0[4]	7.1	7.1	6.9
A	7.5[4]	7.5	7.5	7.5
B	7.2[4]	7.2	7.4	7.3
C	6.8[4]	6.8	6.9	6.9
D	6.9[4]	6.9	7.0	6.8
E	7.1[4]	7.1	7.1	7.1
F	7.1[4]	7.1	7.2	7.1
G	7.4[4]	7.4	7.4	7.2
H	7.3[4]	7.2	7.2	7.1
I	7.0[4]	7.0	7.0	7.0
J	7.3[4]	7.2	7.3	7.2
K	7.2[4]	7.2	7.2	7.1
L	7.2[4]	7.3	7.3	7.3
M	6.7[4]	6.7	6.7	6.7
N	7.3[4]	7.2	7.2	7.2
O	7.2[4]	7.2	7.1	7.1
Q	7.0[4]	7.3	7.2	7.4

Explanatory notes: see p. 721.

[1] Persons aged 15 years and over. [2] Methodology revised; data not strictly comparable. [3] Per day. [4] New series: data not comparable.

Notes explicatives: voir p. 723.

[1] Personnes âgées de 15 ans et plus. [2] Méthodologie révisée; les données ne sont pas strictement comparables. [3] Par jour. [4] Nouvelle série: données non comparables. .

Notas explicativas: véase p. 725.

[1] Personas de 15 años y más. [2] Metodología revisada; los datos no son estrictamente comparables. [3] Por día. [4] Nueva serie : datos no comparables.

By economic activity   **Par activité économique**   **Por actividad económica**

	Per week — Par semaine — Por semana										
	1999	2000	2001	2002	2003	2004	2005	2006	2007	2008	

San Marino (E) (a)   Employees - Salariés - Asalariados

Total men and women - Total hommes et femmes - Total hombres y mujeres
ISIC 2 - CITI 2 - CIIU 2   ISIC 3 - CITI 3 - CIIU 3

ISIC 2	1999	2000	2001	2002	2003	2004	2005	2006	2007	2008	ISIC 3
2-9[1]	42.1	.	.	.	39.1	39.1	.	.	.	.	Total
3	38.8	.	.	.	41.4	39.1	.	.	.	.	A-B
5	42.9	.	.	.	38.4	36.9	.	.	.	.	D
6	60.4	.	.	.	39.3	38.8	.	.	.	.	F
7	39.5	.	.	.	44.9	44.5	.	.	.	.	G
8	38.4	.	.	.	38.1	37.5	.	.	.	.	I
9	49.3	.	.	.	29.9	29.1	.	.	.	.	J
		.	.	.	37.3	36.6	.	.	.	.	M-O

Slovakia (CA) (a) [2] [3]   Employees - Salariés - Asalariados

Total men and women - Total hommes et femmes - Total hombres y mujeres
ISIC 3 - CITI 3 - CIIU 3

	1999	2000	2001	2002	2003	2004	2005	2006	2007	2008
Total	146	146	146	141	136	140	139	140	140	139
A	159	161	159	150	147	153	153	152	152	151
B	.	.	.	.	.	.	.	.	.	.
C	137	138	141	135	136	141	141	140	139	138
D	141	142	143	138	137	142	142	142	142	140
E	146	143	143	139	137	138	138	138	138	138
F	145	148	151	144	144	149	148	147	147	147
G	151	152	153	147	145	147	146	146	146	147
H	154	155	155	151	148	148	148	147	147	146
I	146	146	145	140	137	140	139	139	141	142
J	153	150	150	145	143	145	144	141	142	142
K	153	153	154	151	145	146	145	146	145	146
L	146	144	145	144	135	137	136	143	141	140
M	143	141	140	137	123	126	125	125	125	124
N	149	147	146	139	128	130	131	130	131	133
O	151	147	149	145	142	142	140	140	140	140

Slovenia (BA) (a) [4] [5]   Employees - Salariés - Asalariados

Total men and women - Total hommes et femmes - Total hombres y mujeres
ISIC 3 - CITI 3 - CIIU 3

	1999	2000	2001	2002	2003	2004	2005	2006	2007	2008
Total	40.4	40.5	35.2	37.2	37.4	36.5	36.2	39.9	34.9	.
A-B	49.1	48.7	37.0	45.6	44.8	41.4	42.4	40.4	38.2	.
C-Q	40.4	40.5	35.1	36.3	36.7	36.0	36.3	39.8	34.9	.
C	40.0	40.1	30.5	37.3	31.2	35.0	35.4	39.8	36.4	.
D	40.5	40.3	34.9	36.0	36.7	36.1	37.1	39.9	35.1	.
E	40.5	40.0	36.6	34.0	36.7	35.3	40.4	40.7	37.5	.
F	42.8	42.8	37.7	39.1	40.9	40.3	40.9	42.7	38.3	.
G	40.9	40.6	35.2	37.0	37.6	36.2	35.2	40.0	34.4	.
H	41.7	41.7	37.2	37.8	38.1	35.7	33.8	36.9	33.8	.
I	41.9	42.2	36.4	38.1	39.5	38.4	38.5	41.7	37.1	.
J	38.6	39.7	35.3	35.3	34.5	35.0	37.2	39.6	36.2	.
K	40.6	40.7	34.9	36.4	36.3	36.8	35.0	39.5	33.6	.
L	40.2	40.1	34.7	34.7	35.1	35.2	35.7	40.2	34.8	.
M	38.3	38.8	33.6	33.8	34.1	33.5	34.5	39.1	33.8	.
N	40.8	40.3	35.7	36.2	35.4	34.5	36.2	40.3	33.3	.
O	37.4	38.3	33.6	34.4	34.3	33.9	14.4	36.6	32.5	.
P	.	.	.	.	.	.	.	19.8	34.3	.
X	.	.	.	.	.	.	.	31.9	28.6	.

Men - Hommes - Hombres
ISIC 3 - CITI 3 - CIIU 3

	1999	2000	2001	2002	2003	2004	2005	2006	2007	2008
Total	41.1	41.0	36.2	38.9	39.3	38.5	38.1	40.6	36.7	.
A-B	50.5	50.2	39.1	46.6	46.4	43.0	43.7	40.0	37.7	.
C-Q	41.1	41.1	36.2	38.1	38.6	38.1	38.1	40.7	36.6	.
C	40.0	40.1	30.9	36.1	31.7	34.8	37.1	39.8	38.2	.
D	40.7	40.5	35.8	37.5	38.0	37.4	38.3	40.2	35.9	.
E	40.3	39.8	36.3	34.3	36.7	35.3	40.7	40.8	37.2	.
F	43.2	43.3	37.7	39.6	41.5	40.9	41.3	43.0	39.2	.
G	41.4	41.0	35.8	38.7	40.3	39.0	36.2	40.8	37.1	.
H	43.4	43.9	38.3	40.6	40.8	39.9	37.1	38.9	35.5	.
I	42.3	42.9	36.9	39.1	40.7	39.8	40.4	42.7	38.3	.
J	37.9	40.6	36.1	37.4	35.8	36.9	39.1	40.9	36.7	.
K	42.5	42.1	38.2	38.8	38.4	39.6	37.4	40.5	35.3	.
L	41.3	41.1	34.4	36.1	36.1	36.0	36.0	40.1	36.8	.
M	37.5	38.3	35.1	35.0	36.8	35.1	36.0	39.9	35.7	.
N	41.8	39.7	36.7	40.0	36.9	35.8	37.2	40.7	38.6	.
O	36.9	38.3	35.5	37.8	35.1	35.7	.	38.0	34.9	.
P	.	.	.	.	.	.	.	15.0	.	.
X	.	.	.	.	.	.	.	33.9	32.8	.

Explanatory notes: see p. 721.

[1] Excl. mining and quarrying. [2] Excl. enterprises with less than 20 employees. [3] Per month. [4] Persons aged 15 years and over. [5] Second quarter of each year.

Notes explicatives: voir p. 723.

[1] Non compris les industries extractives. [2] Non compris les entreprises occupant moins de 20 salariés. [3] Par mois. [4] Personnes âgées de 15 ans et plus. [5] Deuxième trimestre de chaque année.

Notas explicativas: véase p. 725.

[1] Excl. las minas y canteras. [2] Excl. las empresas con menos de 20 asalariados. [3] Por mes. [4] Personas de 15 años y más. [5] Segundo trimestre de cada año.

4A HOURS OF WORK — DURÉE DU TRAVAIL — HORAS DE TRABAJO

By economic activity — Par activité économique — Por actividad económica

	Per week				Par semaine			Por semana		
	1999	2000	2001	2002	2003	2004	2005	2006	2007	2008

Slovenia (BA) (a) [1][2] — Employees - Salariés - Asalariados

Women - Femmes - Mujeres
ISIC 3 - CITI 3 - CIIU 3

	1999	2000	2001	2002	2003	2004	2005	2006	2007	2008
Total	39.7	39.8	34.1	35.1	35.2	34.1	34.2	39.0	32.9	.
A-B	47.6	47.1	30.3	44.3	42.8	39.4	41.0	41.1	39.4	.
C-Q	39.7	39.8	34.1	34.1	34.5	33.7	34.2	39.0	32.8	.
C	.	40.0	27.0	.	23.8	36.3	25.6	39.5	27.3	.
D	40.1	40.2	33.7	33.7	34.7	34.0	35.1	39.5	33.9	.
E	41.3	40.7	39.0	32.2	36.8	34.9	39.1	40.7	38.9	.
F	38.9	39.1	37.4	33.9	35.1	33.3	35.5	39.8	29.4	.
G	40.4	40.3	34.6	35.5	35.3	33.8	34.4	39.3	32.2	.
H	40.6	40.1	36.6	36.1	36.1	32.9	31.8	36.0	33.0	.
I	40.7	40.4	35.1	34.9	34.9	33.3	33.2	39.1	33.5	.
J	38.9	39.3	34.8	34.0	34.0	34.1	35.0	38.8	35.9	.
K	38.8	39.2	31.2	33.3	33.8	33.5	32.4	38.2	31.6	.
L	39.0	39.2	34.9	33.3	34.3	34.4	35.4	40.3	32.4	.
M	38.5	39.0	33.1	33.4	33.2	33.0	34.0	38.9	33.3	.
N	40.5	40.5	35.4	35.0	35.1	34.3	36.0	40.2	32.0	.
O	37.9	38.4	31.6	31.2	33.5	31.8	14.4	35.0	29.5	.
P	.	.	.	.	.	.	.	20.1	34.3	.
X	.	.	.	.	.	.	.	30.4	24.4	.

Slovenia (BA) (c) [2] — Total employment - Emploi total - Empleo total

Total men and women - Total hommes et femmes - Total hombres y mujeres
ISIC 4 - CITI 4 - CIIU 4

	1999	2000	2001	2002	2003	2004	2005	2006	2007	2008
Total	.	.	.	.	.	.	.	.	.	40.4
A	.	.	.	.	.	.	.	.	.	40.6
B	.	.	.	.	.	.	.	.	.	40.0
B-U	.	.	.	.	.	.	.	.	.	40.7
C	.	.	.	.	.	.	.	.	.	40.7
D	.	.	.	.	.	.	.	.	.	39.7
E	.	.	.	.	.	.	.	.	.	39.4
F	.	.	.	.	.	.	.	.	.	43.4
G	.	.	.	.	.	.	.	.	.	40.3
H	.	.	.	.	.	.	.	.	.	43.1
I	.	.	.	.	.	.	.	.	.	38.8
J	.	.	.	.	.	.	.	.	.	40.0
K	.	.	.	.	.	.	.	.	.	41.1
L	.	.	.	.	.	.	.	.	.	43.5
M	.	.	.	.	.	.	.	.	.	39.8
N	.	.	.	.	.	.	.	.	.	39.6
O	.	.	.	.	.	.	.	.	.	40.4
P	.	.	.	.	.	.	.	.	.	38.4
Q	.	.	.	.	.	.	.	.	.	40.3
R	.	.	.	.	.	.	.	.	.	34.2
S	.	.	.	.	.	.	.	.	.	39.5
T	.	.	.	.	.	.	.	.	.	41.4
U	.	.	.	.	.	.	.	.	.	40.0
X	.	.	.	.	.	.	.	.	.	33.9

Men - Hommes - Hombres
ISIC 4 - CITI 4 - CIIU 4

	1999	2000	2001	2002	2003	2004	2005	2006	2007	2008
Total	.	.	.	.	.	.	.	.	.	41.5
A	.	.	.	.	.	.	.	.	.	41.4
B	.	.	.	.	.	.	.	.	.	40.0
B-U	.	.	.	.	.	.	.	.	.	41.5
C	.	.	.	.	.	.	.	.	.	41.0
D	.	.	.	.	.	.	.	.	.	39.7
E	.	.	.	.	.	.	.	.	.	39.2
F	.	.	.	.	.	.	.	.	.	43.8
G	.	.	.	.	.	.	.	.	.	41.5
H	.	.	.	.	.	.	.	.	.	43.8
I	.	.	.	.	.	.	.	.	.	40.4
J	.	.	.	.	.	.	.	.	.	41.3
K	.	.	.	.	.	.	.	.	.	42.8
L	.	.	.	.	.	.	.	.	.	50.3
M	.	.	.	.	.	.	.	.	.	41.8
N	.	.	.	.	.	.	.	.	.	40.9
O	.	.	.	.	.	.	.	.	.	40.9
P	.	.	.	.	.	.	.	.	.	38.9
Q	.	.	.	.	.	.	.	.	.	40.1
R	.	.	.	.	.	.	.	.	.	33.3
S	.	.	.	.	.	.	.	.	.	41.3
T	.	.	.	.	.	.	.	.	.	54.7
U	.	.	.	.	.	.	.	.	.	.
X	.	.	.	.	.	.	.	.	.	36.1

Explanatory notes: see p. 721.

[1] Persons aged 15 years and over. [2] Second quarter of each year.

Notes explicatives: voir p. 723.

[1] Personnes âgées de 15 ans et plus. [2] Deuxième trimestre de chaque année.

Notas explicativas: véase p. 725.

[1] Personas de 15 años y más. [2] Segundo trimestre de cada año.

	Per week / Par semaine / Por semana									
	1999	2000	2001	2002	2003	2004	2005	2006	2007	2008

Slovenia (BA) (c) [1] — Total employment - Emploi total - Empleo total
Women - Femmes - Mujeres
ISIC 4 - CITI 4 - CIIU 4

	1999	2000	2001	2002	2003	2004	2005	2006	2007	2008
Total	.	.	.	.	.	.	.	.	.	39.2
A	.	.	.	.	.	.	.	.	.	39.6
B	.	.	.	.	.	.	.	.	.	40.0
B-U	.	.	.	.	.	.	.	.	.	39.2
C	.	.	.	.	.	.	.	.	.	40.0
D	.	.	.	.	.	.	.	.	.	39.8
E	.	.	.	.	.	.	.	.	.	40.0
F	.	.	.	.	.	.	.	.	.	40.3
G	.	.	.	.	.	.	.	.	.	39.2
H	.	.	.	.	.	.	.	.	.	39.4
I	.	.	.	.	.	.	.	.	.	37.9
J	.	.	.	.	.	.	.	.	.	36.8
K	.	.	.	.	.	.	.	.	.	40.3
L	.	.	.	.	.	.	.	.	.	40.0
M	.	.	.	.	.	.	.	.	.	38.0
N	.	.	.	.	.	.	.	.	.	38.6
O	.	.	.	.	.	.	.	.	.	40.0
P	.	.	.	.	.	.	.	.	.	38.3
Q	.	.	.	.	.	.	.	.	.	40.4
R	.	.	.	.	.	.	.	.	.	35.4
S	.	.	.	.	.	.	.	.	.	38.7
T	.	.	.	.	.	.	.	.	.	31.0
U	.	.	.	.	.	.	.	.	.	40.0
X	.	.	.	.	.	.	.	.	.	32.2

Suisse (BA) (a) — Employees - Salariés - Asalariados
Total men and women - Total hommes et femmes - Total hombres y mujeres
ISIC 3 - CITI 3 - CIIU 3

	1999	2000	2001	2002	2003	2004	2005	2006	2007	2008
Total	36.4	36.4	36.2	35.6	35.6	36.1	36.0	36.0	36.1	35.9
A-B	40.3	41.9	42.2	38.8	37.2	40.4	38.1	40.1	39.7	38.0
C-Q	36.3	36.4	36.2	35.6	35.6	36.1	36.0	35.9	36.0	35.9
C	35.2	46.5	44.9	45.4	42.1	44.3	42.9	41.3	42.9	42.4
D	40.1	41.1	40.9	39.4	39.6	39.9	40.3	40.6	40.5	40.4
E	40.5	37.3	41.3	39.9	39.9	39.6	40.7	42.1	41.0	39.5
F	39.3	40.6	39.0	39.7	40.1	41.1	41.0	40.4	40.8	41.1
G	36.6	.	35.5	35.5	35.4	36.0	35.4	35.3	35.3	34.7
H	34.2	32.9	33.7	32.8	32.5	34.4	33.6	34.7	33.4	33.3
I	38.4	38.3	38.9	37.9	38.2	38.0	37.8	37.9	38.3	39.0
J	41.4	41.4	39.4	39.7	40.0	40.9	41.0	40.8	41.1	41.0
K	36.6	35.4	36.7	35.7	35.8	36.2	37.1	36.0	36.3	36.2
L	37.2	37.4	38.9	37.3	38.1	38.2	37.9	37.9	37.1	36.9
M	31.8	32.6	32.7	31.9	31.1	32.1	31.8	31.8	31.4	31.3
N	32.7	32.2	31.7	31.4	31.6	31.6	31.5	31.8	32.1	32.2
O	31.9	30.3	30.9	31.2	31.1	31.8	31.0	29.9	30.8	31.1
P	13.7	17.9	13.8	17.2	15.1	16.3	16.1	15.6	17.6	18.3
Q	42.9	49.5	37.3	41.1	36.7	40.0	39.1	39.7	40.5	40.6

Men - Hommes - Hombres
ISIC 3 - CITI 3 - CIIU 3

	1999	2000	2001	2002	2003	2004	2005	2006	2007	2008
Total	42.1	42.2	42.1	41.5	41.6	42.1	42.1	41.8	41.9	42.0
A-B	42.8	44.9	44.1	41.3	42.6	43.7	41.4	42.5	43.7	42.0
C-Q	42.1	42.2	42.1	41.5	41.6	42.1	42.1	41.8	41.8	42.0
C	35.2	46.5	44.9	47.5	45.0	45.8	45.1	44.3	43.1	45.7
D	42.5	43.3	43.2	41.9	41.9	42.5	42.8	43.1	42.9	43.1
E	41.6	38.5	43.2	42.4	41.5	42.3	43.0	43.7	43.9	41.7
F	41.3	42.2	41.3	41.1	41.8	42.7	42.5	41.8	42.4	42.6
G	42.9	42.9	42.2	42.1	42.6	42.7	42.5	42.1	41.7	41.4
H	44.6	41.3	40.2	41.5	39.5	42.0	40.7	42.0	40.4	39.8
I	42.2	42.0	42.5	41.6	42.1	41.6	41.7	42.0	42.2	42.6
J	45.5	45.9	43.2	44.1	44.8	44.7	44.7	44.1	45.2	45.6
K	42.8	41.3	42.0	41.8	41.2	41.8	42.8	41.5	41.8	42.1
L	42.5	42.3	43.6	42.1	42.6	43.0	43.1	43.4	42.2	42.5
M	38.5	39.2	39.6	38.8	38.7	40.2	39.9	38.8	37.8	38.9
N	42.3	42.7	41.1	41.1	40.8	40.9	40.4	39.8	39.3	40.5
O	38.7	38.0	38.9	39.1	39.5	39.1	38.1	36.4	38.3	37.8
P	18.1	23.2	17.7	22.3	17.5	23.1	26.9	23.7	31.6	34.9
Q	43.2	43.3	40.3	42.7	38.4	42.0	44.5	42.9	43.7	44.9

Explanatory notes: see p. 721.   Notes explicatives: voir p. 723.   Notas explicativas: véase p. 725.
[1] Second quarter of each year.   [1] Deuxième trimestre de chaque année.   [1] Segundo trimestre de cada año.

4A   HOURS OF WORK · DURÉE DU TRAVAIL · HORAS DE TRABAJO

By economic activity · Par activité économique · Por actividad económica

	Per week · Par semaine · Por semana									
	1999	2000	2001	2002	2003	2004	2005	2006	2007	2008

Suisse (BA) (a) — Employees · Salariés · Asalariados
Women · Femmes · Mujeres — ISIC 3 · CITI 3 · CIIU 3

	1999	2000	2001	2002	2003	2004	2005	2006	2007	2008
Total	29.5	29.5	29.4	29.0	28.8	29.3	29.1	29.3	29.4	29.1
A-B	29.9	30.9	33.7	32.6	25.1	32.9	29.9	34.9	30.3	27.7
C-Q	29.5	29.5	29.4	29.0	28.8	29.3	29.1	29.3	29.4	29.2
C				25.4	14.8	25.5	28.2	.	25.0	28.8
D	33.5	35.2	34.6	33.0	33.6	33.6	33.9	34.0	34.0	33.8
E	33.0	30.7	31.7	30.2	33.3	28.1	31.0	32.0	28.6	27.9
F	25.5	26.9	22.0	26.9	25.2	27.2	26.9	28.4	25.9	26.8
G	30.6	29.7	29.2	29.6	28.8	30.1	29.7	29.4	29.7	29.0
H	29.2	28.6	30.4	27.6	28.0	29.3	28.8	29.7	28.5	28.9
I	31.1	30.8	32.0	30.0	29.3	29.4	28.9	28.9	28.7	29.7
J	35.8	35.3	34.0	34.0	33.7	35.3	35.7	36.1	35.5	35.0
K	28.4	27.7	29.5	28.2	28.8	28.5	28.9	28.1	28.7	28.4
L	30.0	30.6	31.4	30.5	31.4	31.1	30.4	29.7	30.3	29.5
M	27.4	28.3	28.2	27.8	26.5	27.4	27.1	27.8	27.8	26.8
N	29.5	28.9	28.9	28.8	29.1	29.0	29.0	29.6	30.0	29.9
O	27.2	25.0	25.4	25.3	25.0	25.9	25.6	24.8	24.9	25.7
P	12.9	16.5	13.3	16.1	14.7	15.4	13.7	14.3	15.3	15.1
Q	42.7	54.0	31.0	37.8	34.6	38.0	34.1	36.6	37.5	37.0

Sweden (BA) (a) [1] — Total employment · Emploi total · Empleo total
Total men and women · Total hommes et femmes · Total hombres y mujeres — ISIC 3 · CITI 3 · CIIU 3

(Column 2008 and final label column correspond to ISIC 4 · CITI 4 · CIIU 4)

ISIC 3	1999	2000	2001	2002	2003	2004	2005	2006	2007	2008	ISIC 4
Total	.	.	37.0	36.6	36.2	36.1	36.6 [2]	36.4	37.0	36.1	Total
A-B	.	.	44.9	45.0	44.6	45.0	44.4 [2]	44.9	43.3	43.3	A
C-Q	36.7	36.9	36.8	36.4	36.0	35.9	36.4 [2]	36.3	35.9	41.5	B
A	.	.	44.6	44.9	44.5	44.9	44.4 [2]	44.8	43.2	35.9	B-U
B	.	.	55.0	49.0	49.4	54.2	44.1 [2]	50.2	49.3	37.6	C
C	.	.	42.1	42.3	40.8	40.7	42.9 [2]	42.1	44.4	38.6	D
C-E	37.8	37.8	38.2	38.0	37.5	37.5	37.9 [2]	37.7	37.7	38.0	E
D	.	.	38.2	37.9	37.5	37.5	37.9 [2]	37.7	37.6	38.8	F
E	.	.	38.6	38.4	37.5	37.4	38.8 [2]	38.0	37.4	35.6	G
F	39.3	39.1	39.3	39.0	38.6	38.8	39.3 [2]	39.3	39.0	37.8	H
G	.	.	37.1	36.7	36.2	36.2	36.7 [2]	36.5	35.9	34.5	I
H	.	.	36.6	36.4	35.7	35.3	34.8 [2]	35.2	34.6	37.7	J
I	38.8	38.6	38.4	38.1	38.0	37.7	38.6 [2]	38.2	37.9	36.3	K
J	.	.	36.8	36.3	35.3	35.4	36.1 [2]	35.7	35.5	35.5	L
J-K	.	.	.	.	36.3	36.3	37.1 [2]	36.8	36.3	37.2	M
K	.	.	37.6	37.0	36.4	36.5	37.2 [2]	37.0	36.4	34.7	N
L	.	.	37.3	37.0	36.8	36.4	36.8 [2]	36.6	36.5	36.1	O
L.Q	.	.	.	.	36.8	36.4	36.8 [2]	36.6	36.5	35.1	P
M	.	.	36.7	36.6	35.1 [3]	34.9	35.7 [2]	35.2	34.9	33.0	Q
N	.	.	33.4	33.2	33.5 [3]	33.0	33.0 [2]	33.2	32.9	32.8	R
O	.	.	34.9	34.9	34.1	33.9	34.6 [2]	34.5	34.0	34.9	S
P	.	.	28.4	22.7	23.1	14.3	29.8 [2]	36.0	31.2	31.7	T
Q	.	.	36.7	36.0	43.1	43.7	35.3 [2]	37.7	30.5	29.8	U
X	.	.	36.7	39.3	35.3	38.7	39.7 [2]	35.4	37.3	35.8	X

Men · Hommes · Hombres — ISIC 3 · CITI 3 · CIIU 3

ISIC 3	1999	2000	2001	2002	2003	2004	2005	2006	2007	2008	ISIC 4
Total	.	.	39.9	39.4	38.9	38.8	39.4 [2]	39.1	38.7	38.6	Total
A-B	.	.	47.8	47.4	46.6	47.1	46.5 [2]	46.6	45.3	45.0	A
C-Q	39.8	39.6	39.6	39.1	38.6	38.6	39.1 [2]	38.9	38.5	41.1	B
A	.	.	47.6	47.3	46.5	46.9	46.5 [2]	46.4	45.2	38.4	B-U
B	.	.	55.0	49.2	51.3	54.3	44.9 [2]	51.9	50.1	38.4	C
C	.	.	42.7	42.4	41.3	40.8	44.4 [2]	43.8	44.8	39.4	D
C-E	38.8	38.9	39.4	39.0	38.5	38.6	39.0 [2]	38.8	38.5	39.2	E
D	.	.	39.3	39.0	38.5	38.5	38.9 [2]	38.7	38.5	39.4	F
E	.	.	39.9	39.2	38.2	38.4	39.8 [2]	38.6	38.1	38.6	G
F	39.9	39.6	39.8	39.6	39.1	39.2	39.8 [2]	39.8	39.5	39.1	H
G	.	.	40.6	40.1	39.4	39.4	39.9 [2]	39.7	39.0	39.9	I
H	.	.	41.7	41.5	40.8	39.9	39.3 [2]	39.6	39.5	38.8	J
I	40.5	40.2	40.1	39.7	39.7	39.2	40.2 [2]	39.6	39.3	38.6	K
J	.	.	39.2	38.3	37.7	38.1	39.0 [2]	37.9	37.4	36.8	L
J-K	.	.	.	.	38.1	38.3	39.1 [2]	38.9	38.1	38.8	M
K	.	.	39.5	38.7	38.2	38.3	39.1 [2]	39.0	38.2	36.5	N
L	.	.	39.3	39.1	38.7	38.1	38.9 [2]	38.5	38.3	37.6	O
L.Q	.	.	.	.	38.7	38.2	38.9 [2]	38.4	38.2	37.8	P
M	.	.	38.8	38.6	37.7 [3]	37.4	38.4 [2]	38.1	37.4	36.2	Q
N	.	.	37.5	37.0	36.5 [3]	36.7	36.6 [2]	36.6	36.2	36.1	R
O	.	.	37.9	37.8	37.5	36.9	37.6 [2]	37.4	37.7	40.2	S
P	.	.	39.9	.	.	8.0	.	.	.	.	T
Q	.	.	41.5	37.7	42.0	45.1	26.4 [2]	36.0	31.2	28.2	U
X	.	.	39.0	40.2	38.1	39.0	41.6 [2]	38.4	38.9	36.8	X

Explanatory notes: see p. 721.

[1] Persons in main job and at work. [2] Methodology revised; data not strictly comparable. [3] 2003: revised industrial classification; data for tabulation categories M and N not comparable with averages of previous years.

Notes explicatives: voir p. 723.

[1] Personnes dans l'emploi principal et au travail. [2] Méthodologie révisée; les données ne sont pas strictement comparables. [3] 2003: classification industrielle révisée; données pour M et N non comparables à celles des années précédentes.

Notas explicativas: véase p. 725.

[1] Personas en el empleo principal y trabajando. [2] Metodología revisada; los datos no son estrictamente comparables. [3] 2003: clasificación industrial revisada; datos para M y N no comparables a los promedios de los años precedentes.

HOURS OF WORK — DURÉE DU TRAVAIL — HORAS DE TRABAJO

By economic activity — Par activité économique — Por actividad económica

	Per week / Par semaine / Por semana										
	1999	2000	2001	2002	2003	2004	2005	2006	2007	2008	

Sweden (BA) (a) [1] — Total employment - Emploi total - Empleo total

Women - Femmes - Mujeres
ISIC 3 - CITI 3 - CIIU 3 ... ISIC 4 - CITI 4 - CIIU 4

	1999	2000	2001	2002	2003	2004	2005	2006	2007	2008	
Total	.	.	33.6	33.4	33.0	32.9	33.3 [2]	33.3	33.0	33.0	Total
A-B	.	.	35.0	36.3	37.0	37.4	36.7 [2]	38.5	35.2	35.8	A
C-Q	33.6	33.7	33.6	33.4	33.0	32.9	33.3 [2]	33.2	32.9	44.1	B
A	.	.	35.0	36.3	37.1	37.3	36.7 [2]	38.6	35.2	33.0	B-U
B	.	.	.	37.3	20.6	50.3	39.7 [2]	.	.	34.8	C
C	.	.	38.6	41.2	37.5	39.0	29.8 [2]	27.9	41.3	35.7	D
C-E	34.5	34.5	34.7	34.6	34.3	34.2	34.7 [2]	34.5	36.4	31.5	E
D	.	.	34.7	34.6	34.3	34.2	34.6 [2]	34.5	35.0	32.6	F
E	.	.	35.3	36.0	35.3	34.7	36.5 [2]	36.3	35.3	31.6	G
F	33.3	33.3	32.2	32.7	32.2	32.7	31.9 [2]	32.4	32.3	33.8	H
G	.	.	32.4	32.0	31.6	31.4	32.2 [2]	32.1	31.7	30.0	I
H	.	.	32.3	31.7	31.3	31.3	30.8 [2]	31.3	30.1	35.1	J
I	34.1	34.2	34.1	33.7	33.5	33.6	33.6 [2]	34.1	33.7	34.0	K
J	.	.	34.7	34.6	33.3	33.1	33.7 [2]	33.9	33.4	33.0	L
J-K	.	.	.	.	33.5	33.3	34.0 [2]	33.6	33.5	34.6	M
K	.	.	34.1	33.9	33.5	33.4	34.1 [2]	33.5	33.5	32.5	N
L	.	.	35.3	35.2	34.9	34.8	34.9 [2]	35.1	34.9	34.9	O
L,Q	.	.	.	.	34.9	34.8	34.9 [2]	35.1	34.9	34.2	P
M	.	.	35.5	35.5		34.1 [3]	34.0	34.8 [2]	34.2	33.9	32.4	Q
N	.	.	32.7	32.5		32.4 [3]	32.2	32.2 [2]	32.5	32.3	29.3	R
O	.	.	32.3	32.1	31.1	31.2	31.9 [2]	32.0	30.9	31.4	S
P	.	.	25.8	24.0	23.1	15.1	32.7 [2]	34.6	30.6	30.9	T
Q	.	.	31.8	31.5	50.3	37.2	37.8 [2]	40.0	29.2	.	U
X	.	.	30.6	37.4	26.2	37.8	37.4 [2]	31.6	34.2	34.5	X

Sweden (BA) (a) [1] — Employees - Salariés - Asalariados

Total men and women - Total hommes et femmes - Total hombres y mujeres
ISIC 3 - CITI 3 - CIIU 3

	1999	2000	2001	2002	2003	2004	2005	2006	2007	2008
Total	.	.	36.1	35.8	35.4	35.3	35.6 [2]	35.5	35.2	35.3
A-B	37.5	38.7	38.5	38.9	38.6	38.2	37.9 [2]	38.2	37.9	37.3
C-Q	36.2	36.2	36.1	35.8	35.4	35.3	35.6 [2]	35.5	35.2	35.3
A	.	.	.	38.9	38.7	38.1	37.7 [2]	38.0	37.7	37.3
B	.	.	.	39.3	27.5	49.2	53.2 [2]	47.0	46.6	37.6
C	.	.	42.1	42.1	40.6	40.4	42.6 [2]	42.2	44.3	41.1
C-E	37.8	37.9	37.8	37.6	37.1	37.1	37.5 [2]	37.3	37.2	37.2
D	.	.	37.8	37.5	37.1	37.1	37.4 [2]	37.2	37.2	37.1
E	.	.	38.6	38.4	37.4	37.4	38.8 [2]	38.0	37.3	38.5
F	38.5	38.2	38.4	38.2	37.6	37.9	38.1 [2]	38.1	38.0	37.9
G	36.1	35.6	35.3	34.9	34.6	34.5	34.8 [2]	34.7	34.3	34.1
H	.	.	31.8	31.4	31.4	31.6	30.4 [2]	31.1	30.7	30.7
H,O-P	33.3	33.3	33.5	.	.	.	32.6 [2]	32.6	32.2	32.5
I	37.9	37.6	37.5	37.2	37.1	37.0	37.5 [2]	37.2	37.0	37.1
J	.	.	36.6	36.2	35.3	35.4	36.0 [2]	35.5	35.3	36.1
J-K	37.1	37.3	37.1	36.6	36.0	35.9	36.3 [2]	36.2	35.8	36.1
K	.	.	37.2	36.7	36.2	36.0	36.3 [2]	36.3	35.8	36.1
L	.	.	37.2	37.0	36.8	36.4	36.8 [2]	36.6	36.5	36.2
L,Q	37.5	37.2	37.2	37.0	36.8	36.4	36.8 [2]	36.6	36.5	36.1
M [4]	36.8	37.1	36.6	36.6	35.0 [3]	34.9	35.7 [2]	35.1	34.8	35.1
N	33.3	33.5	33.3	33.1	33.0 [3]	32.9	32.9 [2]	33.1	32.9	32.9
O	.	.	34.5	34.4	33.4	33.4	33.8 [2]	33.5	33.2	33.7
P	.	.	30.0	29.6	23.1	14.3	29.8 [2]	36.0	31.5	33.8
Q	.	.	36.7	36.0	43.1	43.7	35.3 [2]	37.7	30.5	29.8
X	.	.	36.5	38.9	33.0	38.6	39.3 [2]	34.3	35.8	37.8

Explanatory notes: see p. 721.

[1] Persons in main job and at work. [2] Methodology revised; data not strictly comparable. [3] 2003: revised industrial classification; data for tabulation categories M and N not comparable with averages of previous years. [4] Incl. research and development.

Notes explicatives: voir p. 723.

[1] Personnes dans l'emploi principal et au travail. [2] Méthodologie révisée; les données ne sont pas strictement comparables. [3] 2003: classification industrielle révisée; données pour M et N non comparables à celles des années précédentes. [4] Y compris recherche-développement.

Notas explicativas: véase p. 725.

[1] Personas en el empleo principal y trabajando. [2] Metodología revisada; los datos no son estrictamente comparables. [3] 2003: clasificación industrial revisada; datos para M y N no comparables a los promedios de los años precedentes. [4] Incl. investigación y desarrollo.

By economic activity   **Par activité économique**   **Por actividad económica**

	Per week / Par semaine / Por semana									
	1999	2000	2001	2002	2003	2004	2005	2006	2007	2008

Sweden (BA) (a) [1] — Employees - Salariés - Asalariados

Men - Hommes - Hombres
ISIC 3 - CITI 3 - CIIU 3

	1999	2000	2001	2002	2003	2004	2005	2006	2007	2008
Total			38.7	38.3	37.9	37.8	38.1 [2]	37.9	37.6	37.6
A-B	39.5	40.4	40.6	40.4	39.9	39.7	39.9 [2]	39.4	39.4	38.5
C-Q	39.0	38.8	38.7	38.3	37.8	37.8	38.0 [2]	37.8	37.6	37.6
A			40.5	40.4	39.9	39.6	39.7 [2]	39.1	39.2	38.5
B			50.9	39.7	36.6	49.0	66.4 [2]	51.4	48.5	37.6
C			42.7	42.2	41.1	40.5	44.1 [2]	43.9	44.7	40.6
C-E	38.9	39.0	38.9	38.5	38.1	38.1	38.5 [2]	38.2	38.0	37.9
D			38.9	38.5	38.0	38.1	38.4 [2]	38.1	37.9	37.8
E			39.8	39.2	38.1	38.4	39.8 [2]	38.7	38.0	39.3
F	39.1	38.8	38.9	38.7	38.1	38.4	38.7 [2]	38.6	38.6	38.4
G	39.7	39.0	38.6	38.2	37.7	37.6	37.7 [2]	37.7	37.3	37.1
H			34.9	34.2	34.4	34.6	32.3 [2]	33.5	33.7	33.6
H,O-P	36.5	36.6	36.5				34.9 [2]	35.2	35.7	36.4
I	39.5	39.2	38.9	38.7	38.6	38.3	39.0 [2]	38.4	38.2	38.2
J			38.9	38.2	37.6	38.1	38.9 [2]	37.7	37.2	38.2
J-K [3]	39.7	39.1	39.1	38.4	38.0	38.0	38.1 [2]	38.1	37.5	37.8
K [3]			39.1	38.4	38.1	38.0	38.0 [2]	38.2	37.5	37.8
L			39.2	39.1	38.7	38.1	38.9 [2]	38.5	38.3	37.6
L,Q	39.7	39.3	39.2	39.1	38.7	38.2	38.9 [2]	38.4	38.2	37.6
M [4]	38.9	38.9	38.9	38.6	37.6 [5]	37.3	38.4 [2]	37.9	37.3	37.7
N	37.8	37.9	37.4	36.9	36.4 [5]	36.5	36.4 [2]	36.2	35.8	35.9
O			37.2	37.2	36.5	36.4	36.2 [2]	36.0	36.8	37.8
P			39.9			8.0	[2]			
Q			41.5	37.7	42.0	45.1	26.4 [2]	36.0	31.2	28.2
X			38.4	39.3	35.4	39.0	41.5 [2]	37.0	36.7	38.1

Women - Femmes - Mujeres
ISIC 3 - CITI 3 - CIIU 3

	1999	2000	2001	2002	2003	2004	2005	2006	2007	2008
Total			33.3	33.2	32.8	32.7	33.0 [2]	32.9	32.7	35.3
A-B	32.2	33.7	31.9	33.4	33.9	32.4	32.1 [2]	34.4	32.3	33.3
C-Q	33.3	33.5	33.3	33.2	32.8	32.7	33.0 [2]	32.9	32.7	33.4
A			31.9	33.4	34.1	32.2	32.2 [2]	34.6	32.3	33.3
B				37.3	20.6	50.3	28.3 [2]			
C			38.6	41.2	37.5	39.0	29.8 [2]	27.9	41.3	44.2
C-E	34.5	34.5	34.7	34.6	34.2	34.0	34.5 [2]	34.4	34.9	34.7
D			34.6	34.5	34.1	34.0	34.4 [2]	34.3	34.9	34.7
E			35.3	36.0	35.3	34.7	36.5 [2]	36.3	35.3	35.7
F	32.6	32.5	32.6	32.7	32.3	32.8	30.8 [2]	32.4	32.7	33.0
G	31.7	31.7	31.3	30.9	30.7	30.6	31.1 [2]	30.9	30.7	30.3
H			29.7	29.4	29.4	29.5	29.1 [2]	29.3	28.5	28.7
H,O-P	30.8	30.6	31.1				30.7 [2]	30.5	29.4	29.2
I	34.2	34.1	34.1	33.7	33.4	33.6	33.4 [2]	34.0	33.7	34.2
J			34.8	34.6	33.3	33.1	33.7 [2]	33.9	33.4	34.0
J-K [3]	34.4	34.7	34.3	34.1	33.4	33.1	33.7 [2]	33.4	33.3	33.6
K [3]			34.2	34.0	33.4	33.1	33.7 [2]	33.3	33.3	33.5
L			35.3	35.2	34.9	34.8	34.9 [2]	35.1	34.9	34.9
L,Q	34.9	35.1	35.3	35.2	34.9	34.8	34.9 [2]	35.1	34.9	34.9
M [4]	35.6	36.0	35.5	35.6	34.1 [5]	34.1	34.8 [2]	34.1	33.9	34.2
N	32.6	32.8	32.6	32.5	32.4 [5]	32.2	32.2 [2]	32.4	32.3	32.3
O			31.9	31.8	30.4	30.5	31.6 [2]	31.2	30.0	29.6
P			27.6	29.6	23.1	15.1	32.7 [2]	34.6	30.9	33.1
Q			31.8	31.5	50.3	37.2	37.8 [2]	40.0	29.2	33.4
X			31.4	38.1	25.9	37.8	37.0 [2]	31.3	34.4	37.5

Turkey (BA) (a) — Total employment - Emploi total - Empleo total

Total men and women - Total hommes et femmes - Total hombres y mujeres
ISIC 2 - CITI 2 - CIIU 2 [6][7]   ISIC 3 - CITI 3 - CIIU 3

	1999	2000	2001	2002	2003	2004	2005	2006	2007	2008	
Total	45.2	46.5	48.6	48.7	48.7	49.3	51.4	51.3	49.3	49.7	Total
1	.	37.4	43.4	42.8	42.2	42.9	44.9	43.3	40.7	40.5	A-B
2	44.9	51.6	51.7	51.8	51.9	52.5	54.0	54.1	51.8	52.4	C-Q
3	48.1	40.4	45.9	45.6	45.1	46.0	48.2	47.4			A
4	39.4		40.7	40.1			41.3	39.0			B
5	49.6	47.4	48.3	48.1	48.3	51.5	51.9	51.5	50.7	52.3	C
6	58.1	51.3	51.4	51.9	52.2	52.1	53.7	54.0	51.8	52.8	D
7	51.6	43.7	43.1	43.5	43.1	42.1	45.0	46.0	43.5	45.3	E
8	40.8	51.3	51.1	49.8	50.7	52.2	53.4	54.3	51.9	52.2	F
9	40.8	56.6	57.0	57.9	57.5	58.0	59.8	59.8	57.0	57.8	G
		63.1	63.1	63.5	62.4	63.6	65.1	65.0	62.2	62.2	H
		53.5	54.0	52.8	53.4	55.1	56.2	56.0	53.8	53.4	I
		43.5	44.3	45.0	44.8	43.3	45.9	45.5	43.3	45.1	J
		50.2	50.6	50.6	50.2	50.2	51.4	51.3	48.9	49.9	K
		44.8	44.3	44.7	44.8	44.9	46.6	45.7	43.7	44.8	L
		37.5	37.4	36.8	37.3	37.3	38.4	38.9	37.0	38.7	M
		44.3	45.0	44.3	44.6	45.0	46.1	46.1	44.8	46.0	N
		52.2	52.6	51.7	51.9	54.2	52.4	53.2	51.1	51.2	O-Q
		46.9	46.1	43.2	43.9	44.5					P

Explanatory notes: see p. 721.

[1] Persons in main job and at work. [2] Methodology revised; data not strictly comparable. [3] Excl. research and development. [4] Incl. research and development. [5] 2003: revised industrial classification; data for tabulation categories M and N not comparable with averages of previous years. [6] Averages of Apr. and Oct. based on 2000 Population Census results. [7] Persons aged 15 years and over.

Notes explicatives: voir p. 723.

[1] Personnes dans l'emploi principal et au travail. [2] Méthodologie révisée; les données ne sont pas strictement comparables. [3] Non compris recherche-développement. [4] Y compris recherche-développement. [5] 2003: classification industrielle révisée; données pour M et N non comparables à celles des années précédentes. [6] Moyennes d'avr. et d'octobre révisées sur la base des résultats du recensement de population de 2000. [7] Personnes âgées de 15 ans et plus.

Notas explicativas: véase p. 725.

[1] Personas en el empleo principal y trabajando. [2] Metodología revisada; los datos no son estrictamente comparables. [3] Excl. investigación y desarrollo. [4] Incl. investigación y desarrollo. [5] 2003: clasificación industrial revisada; datos para M y N no comparables a los promedios de los años precedentes. [6] Promedios de abr. y oct. revisados de acuerdo con los resultados del censo de población de 2000. [7] Personas de 15 años y más.

By economic activity Par activité économique Por actividad económica

	Per week / Par semaine / Por semana										
	1999	2000	2001	2002	2003	2004	2005	2006	2007	2008	

Turkey (BA) (a) Total employment - Emploi total - Empleo total

Men - Hommes - Hombres
ISIC 2 - CITI 2 - CIIU 2 [1]   ISIC 3 - CITI 3 - CIIU 3

	1999	2000	2001	2002	2003	2004	2005	2006	2007	2008	
Total	49.2 [2]	49.6	51.1	51.3	51.3	52.0	54.1	54.2	52.0	52.5	Total
1	45.1 [2]	.	.	.	.	.	48.2	47.4	44.8	44.6	A-B
2	47.4 [2]	52.8	52.9	53.0	53.1	53.8	55.6	55.7	53.3	54.0	C-Q
3	50.5 [2]	40.4	45.9	45.6	45.1	46.0	48.2	47.4	.	.	A
4	42.6 [2]	47.9	43.0	45.3	54.1	55.6	.	.			B
5	50.5 [2]	47.5	48.5	48.8	48.4	51.5	52.0	51.7	50.9	52.5	C
6	60.0 [2]	52.6	52.6	53.1	53.3	53.3	55.1	55.3	53.1	54.0	D
7	53.4 [2]	43.9	43.3	43.7	43.2	42.4	45.4	46.4	43.8	45.6	E
8	43.5 [2]	51.4	51.2	49.8	50.7	52.3	53.5	54.4	52.0	52.3	F
9	44.0 [2]	57.3	57.7	58.6	58.2	58.9	60.9	61.0	58.1	59.1	G
		64.0	64.0	64.6	63.3	64.7	66.3	66.2	63.7	63.7	H
		54.1	54.5	53.1	53.8	55.6	56.7	56.5	54.4	54.0	I
		43.8	44.7	45.6	45.0	43.9	46.4	45.9	44.0	45.9	J
		51.1	51.6	51.6	50.9	51.3	52.9	52.5	50.1	51.2	K
		45.4	44.8	45.2	45.3	45.5	47.2	46.4	44.4	45.5	L
		38.5	38.2	37.7	38.5	38.2	39.3	40.0	38.2	39.7	M
		44.1	44.8	43.9	44.8	45.1	46.2	46.5	45.2	46.4	N
		52.5	52.6	51.9	51.9	54.7	56.8	56.9	55.3	55.4	O-Q
		60.0	59.6	57.8	59.0	59.5	.	.	.	.	P

Women - Femmes - Mujeres
ISIC 2 - CITI 2 - CIIU 2 [1]   ISIC 3 - CITI 3 - CIIU 3

	1999	2000	2001	2002	2003	2004	2005	2006	2007	2008	
Total	38.7 [2]	38.2	42.4	42.3	42.0	42.1	43.8	43.2	41.4	41.9	Total
1	37.9 [2]	33.9	40.7	40.1	39.4	39.4	41.3	39.0	36.5	36.2	A-B
2	32.0 [2]	45.0	45.3	45.0	45.8	45.8	46.5	47.2	45.1	46.1	C-Q
3	42.2 [2]	33.9	40.7	40.1	39.4	39.4	41.3	39.0	.	.	A
4	33.8 [2]	52.5	39.5	.	39.2	50.2	.	.			B
5	43.6 [2]	45.5	44.1	33.3	45.8	46.1	47.0	41.4	39.6	43.0	C
6	50.4 [2]	46.0	46.5	47.4	47.8	47.4	47.9	48.7	46.9	47.8	D
7	47.2 [2]	41.5	40.9	40.4	41.2	38.8	40.2	39.8	37.7	41.5	E
8	39.9 [2]	47.8	46.8	48.8	48.7	47.6	48.8	51.0	46.4	49.2	F
9	35.1 [2]	51.2	51.4	52.9	52.0	51.7	52.8	53.3	51.1	51.7	G
		53.1	53.7	53.0	53.4	53.5	55.5	56.1	52.7	53.0	H
		45.3	46.1	47.7	46.8	46.9	48.7	47.9	45.3	46.7	I
		43.1	43.4	43.8	44.4	42.3	45.0	44.6	42.2	43.9	J
		47.4	47.5	47.5	47.8	46.7	46.5	47.5	45.4	45.8	K
		41.0	40.8	40.8	41.1	39.9	41.5	40.9	39.4	40.8	L
		36.0	35.9	35.2	35.3	35.7	36.9	37.3	35.5	37.4	M
		44.6	45.2	44.7	44.3	44.9	46.0	45.7	44.4	45.8	N
		50.8	52.5	50.7	51.8	51.1	41.7	44.2	41.1	41.5	O-Q
		37.0	37.1	34.9	34.9	36.7	.	.	.	.	P

Ukraine (CA) (a) [3] Employees - Salariés - Asalariados

Total men and women - Total hommes et femmes - Total hombres y mujeres
ISIC 2 - CITI 2 - CIIU 2   ISIC 3 - CITI 3 - CIIU 3

	1999	2000	2001	2002	2003	2004	2005	2006	2007	2008	
Total	129	130	135	135	137	139	139	139	141	141	Total
2-9	125	139	140	137	134	140	140	140	143	146	A-B
1	147	128	134	135	137	139	139	139	141	140	C-Q
2	120	139	140	137	.	140	140	141	143	146	A
3	110	141	141	140	.	135	137	136	140	141	B
5	114	123	126	125	125	127	126	126	126	126	C
7	129	143	128	132	136	142	142	142	143	141	D
		143	146	147	147	148	147	146	147	147	E
		117	131	.	139	145	143	144	147	142	F
		139	143	144	144	148	149	150	151	150	G
		134	135	137	137	140	141	142	144	144	H
		133	137	139	140	142	142	142	143	142	I
		146	148	149	149	151	151	151	151	151	J
		137	143	144	145	147	146	146	148	148	K
		145	146	146	145	144	142	142	142	143	L
		120	122	121	122	122	122	122	122	124	M
		137	140	140	142	143	143	143	145	146	N
		128	131	133	134	136	136	137	138	140	O

Explanatory notes: see p. 721.   Notes explicatives: voir p. 723.   Notas explicativas: véase p. 725.

[1] Oct. of each year. [2] April. [3] Per month.   [1] Oct. de chaque année. [2] Avril. [3] Par mois.   [1] Oct. de cada año. [2] Abril. [3] Por mes.

HOURS OF WORK DURÉE DU TRAVAIL HORAS DE TRABAJO

By economic activity Par activité économique Por actividad económica

	Per week			Par semaine				Por semana			
	1999	2000	2001	2002	2003	2004	2005	2006	2007	2008	

Ukraine (CA) (a) [1] **Employees - Salariés - Asalariados**

Men - Hommes - Hombres
ISIC 2 - CITI 2 - CIIU 2 ..... ISIC 3 - CITI 3 - CIIU 3

	1999	2000	2001	2002	2003	2004	2005	2006	2007	2008	
Total	132	132	137	136	137	140	140	140	142	141	Total
2-9	126	129	136	137	133	139	138	139	142	145	A-B
1	149	140	141	136	137	140	140	140	142	141	C-Q
5	114	117	131	137	.	139	138	140	142	146	A
7	128	133	137	139	.	134	137	135	139	140	B
				120	120	122	121	121	122	121	C
				133	137	143	142	143	144	141	D
				148	147	148	147	147	147	148	E
				133	140	145	143	144	147	142	F
				145	145	149	150	150	152	150	G
				139	138	140	142	141	144	143	H
				138	141	143	143	143	145	144	I
				149	147	150	149	149	150	150	J
				145	145	147	147	147	149	148	K
				147	146	142	141	141	142	142	L
				122	122	123	123	123	124	125	M
				136	137	137	139	140	142	143	N
				134	135	137	138	138	140	142	O

Women - Femmes - Mujeres
ISIC 2 - CITI 2 - CIIU 2 ..... ISIC 3 - CITI 3 - CIIU 3

	1999	2000	2001	2002	2003	2004	2005	2006	2007	2008	
Total	127	128	132	135	136	139	139	138	140	140	Total
2-9	124	127	131	138	137	142	142	143	145	148	A-B
1	143	138	137	135	136	139	138	138	139	140	C-Q
5	116	120	130	138	137	142	143	143	145	148	A
7	131	135	136	142	136	137	138	139	143	144	B
				139	139	142	139	139	140	140	C
				130	135	141	141	140	142	140	D
				146	147	148	146	145	146	147	E
				136	138	141	142	143	145	143	F
				142	143	147	148	149	150	150	G
				136	137	140	141	142	144	145	H
				139	138	140	140	140	140	140	I
				149	150	152	151	152	152	151	J
				144	145	147	146	146	147	147	K
				144	144	145	143	143	143	143	L
				121	122	122	122	121	122	123	M
				141	143	144	143	144	145	146	N
				131	133	135	136	136	137	138	O

United Kingdom (DA) (b) [2][3] **Employees - Salariés - Asalariados**

Total men and women - Total hommes et femmes - Total hombres y mujeres
ISIC 3 - CITI 3 - CIIU 3

	1999	2000	2001	2002	2003	2004	2005	2006	2007	2008
Total	39.8	39.7	39.7	39.6	39.5	39.5	39.4	39.4	39.4	.
A-B	45.0	43.9	43.8	44.7	44.8	44.5	43.7	44.0	43.9	.
C-Q	39.7	39.7	39.7	39.5	39.5	39.5	39.4	39.4	39.4	.
A	45.0	43.9	43.7	44.7	44.9	44.5	43.7	44.1	43.9	.
B	43.4	44.4	45.4	43.4	42.9	43.5	43.1	42.2	43.6	.
C	44.9	44.1	44.0	43.2	45.3	43.4	43.5	42.6	44.1	.
D	41.2	41.3	41.3	41.0	40.9	41.0	40.6	40.7	40.9	.
E	39.9	39.4	39.9	39.9	39.6	40.0	39.3	40.3	39.7	.
F	44.0	44.2	44.1	43.4	43.4	43.1	43.0	43.1	43.0	.
G	40.6	40.4	40.5	40.5	40.4	40.4	40.3	40.4	40.3	.
H	40.6	40.4	40.6	40.7	40.7	41.1	40.9	41.0	41.0	.
I	43.7	43.5	43.0	42.7	43.0	42.6	42.9	42.3	42.2	.
J	36.4	36.3	36.4	36.3	36.1	36.3	36.0	36.1	36.2	.
K	39.5	39.4	39.4	39.3	39.3	39.3	39.1	39.3	39.2	.
L	38.1	38.0	38.3	38.5	39.1	39.2	39.2	39.2	39.0	.
M	34.9	35.0	35.3	35.5	35.6	35.6	35.5	35.6	35.7	.
N	38.5	38.4	38.6	38.5	38.5	38.6	38.7	38.6	38.4	.
O	40.2	39.7	40.0	39.6	39.4	39.8	40.0	39.9	39.6	.
P	.	41.9	41.4	44.2	42.8	42.0	43.4	43.6	40.8	.
Q	.	37.1	38.0	38.4	40.9	38.8	38.0	38.7	38.4	.

Explanatory notes: see p. 721.

[1] Per month. [2] April; full-time employees on adult rates. [3] Incl. overtime.

Notes explicatives: voir p. 723.

[1] Par mois. [2] Avril; salariés à plein temps rémunérés sur la base de taux de salaires pour adultes. [3] Y compris les heures supplémentaires.

Notas explicativas: véase p. 725.

[1] Por mes. [2] Abril; asalariados a tiempo completo pagados sobre la base de tasas de salarios para adultos. [3] Incl. las horas extraordinarias.

	Per week			Par semaine				Por semana		
	1999	2000	2001	2002	2003	2004	2005	2006	2007	2008

United Kingdom (DA) (b) [1][2]   **Employees - Salariés - Asalariados**

Men - Hommes - Hombres
ISIC 3 - CITI 3 - CIIU 3

Total	41.1	41.0	41.0	40.8	40.8	40.8	40.6	40.7	40.7	.
A-B	45.9	44.7	44.6	45.8	46.0	45.6	44.7	44.9	44.6	.
C-Q	41.1	41.0	41.0	40.8	40.8	40.8	40.6	40.6	40.6	.
A	45.9	44.7	44.6	45.8	46.1	45.6	44.7	45.0	44.6	.
B	43.5	44.6	.	44.1	43.4	45.4	43.4	43.1	44.2	.
C	45.8	44.8	44.8	44.1	46.5	44.4	44.4	43.6	45.0	.
D	41.9	42.0	41.9	41.6	41.5	41.6	41.2	41.3	41.5	.
E	40.5	39.9	40.4	40.6	40.1	40.5	39.9	41.1	40.3	.
F	44.6	44.8	44.7	44.0	44.0	43.7	43.5	43.6	43.6	.
G	41.6	41.4	41.5	41.5	41.5	41.4	41.2	41.3	41.2	.
H	41.5	41.3	41.6	41.7	41.8	42.1	41.8	41.8	42.0	.
I	44.8	44.6	44.1	43.7	44.0	43.5	43.8	43.3	43.2	.
J	36.5	36.3	36.5	36.4	36.3	36.4	36.2	36.3	36.3	.
K	40.5	40.3	40.3	40.2	40.1	40.2	39.9	40.2	40.1	.
L	38.9	38.7	38.9	39.1	40.0	40.1	40.1	40.0	39.8	.
M	36.1	36.1	36.4	36.6	36.7	36.6	36.5	36.6	36.7	.
N	39.7	39.6	39.9	39.8	39.4	39.5	39.7	39.5	39.4	.
O	41.6	41.0	41.1	40.7	40.4	40.9	41.1	40.8	40.5	.
P	.	40.9	43.2	42.7	41.6	43.3	47.9	47.4	43.8	.
Q	.	38.2	38.8	39.7	45.7	39.2	37.6	39.0	39.0	.

Women - Femmes - Mujeres
ISIC 3 - CITI 3 - CIIU 3

Total	37.5	37.4	37.5	37.5	37.4	37.5	37.4	37.6	37.4	.
A-B	40.6	40.2	39.5	39.8	39.6	39.1	39.1	40.4	40.8	.
C-Q	37.5	37.4	37.5	37.5	37.4	37.5	37.4	37.5	37.4	.
A	40.6	40.1	39.5	39.8	39.6	39.2	39.0	40.5	40.8	.
B	42.9	43.2	.	40.0	39.8	36.5	42.2	.	.	.
C	38.8	38.3	38.6	37.8	37.6	37.2	38.1	37.7	38.0	.
D	39.0	38.9	39.0	38.8	38.7	38.7	38.4	38.6	38.6	.
E	37.8	37.4	38.1	37.7	37.9	38.1	37.3	37.8	37.9	.
F	38.0	37.7	38.4	38.2	38.3	38.2	38.0	38.6	38.2	.
G	38.7	38.5	38.6	38.7	38.3	38.5	38.5	38.7	38.4	.
H	39.5	39.4	39.4	39.5	39.4	39.9	39.7	40.0	39.8	.
I	39.8	39.7	39.2	39.2	39.1	39.3	39.3	38.7	38.6	.
J	36.4	36.2	36.3	36.2	35.9	36.2	35.7	35.9	36.0	.
K	37.8	37.8	37.8	37.8	37.7	37.7	37.6	37.7	37.6	.
L	37.0	37.0	37.4	37.6	37.8	37.9	37.9	38.1	37.8	.
M	34.0	34.2	34.4	34.7	34.8	34.9	34.8	35.0	35.0	.
N	38.0	37.9	38.1	38.1	38.1	38.2	38.4	38.2	38.0	.
O	38.2	38.0	38.3	38.2	38.0	38.2	38.4	38.7	38.2	.
P	.	42.2	40.9	44.4	43.0	41.8	42.6	42.9	40.2	.
Q	.	36.7	37.5	37.8	38.0	38.5	38.3	38.4	38.0	.

OCEANIA-OCÉANIE-OCEANIA

Australia (BA) (a)   **Total employment - Emploi total - Empleo total**

Total men and women - Total hommes et femmes - Total hombres y mujeres
ISIC 3 - CITI 3 - CIIU 3

Total	.	.	34.9 [3]	34.9	34.7	34.7	34.7	34.6	34.6	34.5
A-B	.	.	42.5 [3]	41.9	41.4	41.0	40.5	41.0	41.5	42.0
C-Q	.	.	34.5 [3]	34.5	34.4	34.5	34.4	34.3	34.3	34.2
A	.	.	42.5 [3]	42.1	41.5	41.1	40.6	41.2	41.7	42.2
B	.	.	42.7 [3]	37.5	40.8	36.9	37.6	36.1	36.5	34.9
C	.	.	44.1 [3]	45.3	45.3	44.4	45.6	43.8	43.8	44.4
D	.	.	38.0 [3]	38.2	38.2	38.1	38.1	37.9	37.6	37.7
E	.	.	38.6 [3]	38.1	37.2	38.2	38.0	38.1	38.6	36.8
F	.	.	37.8 [3]	38.4	38.2	38.4	38.1	38.4	38.7	38.3
G	.	.	32.9 [3]	32.8	32.6	32.9	32.7	32.9	32.9	32.5
H	.	.	30.1 [3]	30.5	29.9	29.8	29.7	28.9	29.0	28.6
I	.	.	38.5 [3]	39.1	38.5	38.8	38.4	37.9	38.2	38.1
J	.	.	35.7 [3]	36.2	35.9	36.4	36.2	36.2	36.2	36.2
K	.	.	36.0 [3]	36.0	35.4	35.8	35.7	35.5	35.3	35.4
L	.	.	34.0 [3]	34.3	33.8	34.0	34.2	34.4	34.4	34.1
M	.	.	33.3 [3]	32.5	33.4	33.1	33.1	32.4	32.9	32.4
N	.	.	30.2 [3]	30.2	29.8	30.0	30.0	30.2	30.0	30.4
O	.	.	32.4 [3]	31.5	32.2	31.4	31.8	31.6	31.4	31.6
P	.	.	19.2 [3]	18.1	12.2	16.0	17.9	14.1	24.0	19.7
Q	.	.	.	.	.	.	.	.	.	.
X	.	.	.	.	.	.	.	.	.	.

Explanatory notes: see p. 721.   Notes explicatives: voir p. 723.   Notas explicativas: véase p. 725.

[1] April; full-time employees on adult rates. [2] Incl. overtime. [3] May, Aug. and Nov.

[1] Avril; salariés à plein temps rémunérés sur la base de taux de salaires pour adultes. [2] Y compris les heures supplémentaires. [3] Mai, août et nov.

[1] Abril; asalariados a tiempo completo pagados sobre la base de tasas de salarios para adultos. [2] Incl. las horas extraordinarias. [3] Mayo, agosto y nov.

HOURS OF WORK — DURÉE DU TRAVAIL — HORAS DE TRABAJO

By economic activity — Par activité économique — Por actividad económica

	Per week / Par semaine / Por semana									
	1999	2000	2001	2002	2003	2004	2005	2006	2007	2008

Australia (BA) (a) — Total employment - Emploi total - Empleo total

Men - Hommes - Hombres
ISIC 3 - CITI 3 - CIIU 3

	1999	2000	2001	2002	2003	2004	2005	2006	2007	2008
Total	.	.	39.7 [1]	39.6	39.4	39.3	39.2	39.1	39.0	38.9
A-B	.	.	48.6 [1]	47.4	46.7	46.4	45.7	46.2	47.0	47.1
C-Q	.	.	39.1 [1]	39.2	39.0	39.0	38.9	38.8	38.7	38.5
A	.	.	48.7 [1]	47.8	46.9	46.6	45.9	46.4	47.3	47.6
B	.	.	46.1 [1]	40.6	44.0	41.7	41.9	40.9	38.6	36.6
C	.	.	44.9 [1]	46.2	45.6	45.2	46.2	44.7	44.6	45.3
D	.	.	40.4 [1]	40.4	40.4	40.4	40.3	40.2	39.9	40.1
E	.	.	39.7 [1]	39.6	38.0	39.2	39.0	39.4	39.6	38.0
F	.	.	40.2 [1]	40.7	40.6	40.3	40.2	40.4	40.4	40.1
G	.	.	38.1 [1]	38.2	38.0	37.9	37.7	38.1	37.9	37.3
H	.	.	35.1 [1]	36.0	35.6	34.5	34.7	33.2	33.0	32.1
I	.	.	41.0 [1]	41.5	41.0	41.5	40.7	40.5	40.8	40.5
J	.	.	40.7 [1]	41.1	40.9	40.5	41.2	40.3	40.4	39.6
K	.	.	40.9 [1]	40.4	39.7	40.2	40.2	39.5	39.4	39.5
L	.	.	36.7 [1]	36.6	36.4	36.6	36.8	36.9	36.9	36.6
M	.	.	37.9 [1]	36.6	37.6	37.3	37.1	36.5	36.5	36.6
N	.	.	37.4 [1]	36.2	37.0	36.4	36.6	36.1	35.6	36.6
O	.	.	35.9 [1]	35.7	36.0	35.8	36.0	35.7	35.7	36.3
P	.	.	17.2 [1]	17.9	14.1	11.2	28.1	31.8	28.5	10.8
Q	.	.								
X	.	.								

Women - Femmes - Mujeres
ISIC 3 - CITI 3 - CIIU 3

	1999	2000	2001	2002	2003	2004	2005	2006	2007	2008
Total	.	.	29.0 [1]	29.0	28.8	29.0	29.1	29.1	29.2	29.2
A-B	.	.	29.6 [1]	29.5	29.2	29.4	28.7	29.6	29.3	30.3
C-Q	.	.	28.9 [1]	28.9	28.8	29.0	29.1	29.1	29.2	29.2
A	.	.	29.7 [1]	29.7	29.3	29.7	28.9	29.8	29.4	30.4
B	.	.	25.6 [1]	21.6	22.6	17.5	20.5	20.3	26.2	25.3
C	.	.	38.0 [1]	38.0	43.1	38.2	41.5	38.3	38.9	39.1
D	.	.	31.6 [1]	32.5	32.5	32.1	32.1	31.6	31.6	31.4
E	.	.	34.4 [1]	33.1	34.4	33.7	33.9	33.4	34.9	32.6
F	.	.	21.9 [1]	23.2	22.4	24.0	24.7	24.0	25.6	25.1
G	.	.	26.5 [1]	26.2	26.2	26.8	26.8	26.9	27.0	27.0
H	.	.	26.3 [1]	26.1	25.5	25.8	25.8	25.7	25.8	25.9
I	.	.	31.4 [1]	31.7	31.7	31.5	31.9	30.9	31.3	31.5
J	.	.	31.8 [1]	32.1	31.9	32.9	32.1	32.5	32.2	33.2
K	.	.	30.3 [1]	30.7	30.2	30.4	30.5	30.8	30.5	30.6
L	.	.	30.4 [1]	31.1	30.5	30.9	31.0	31.4	31.5	31.3
M	.	.	31.1 [1]	30.5	31.3	31.0	31.1	30.5	31.1	30.6
N	.	.	28.2 [1]	28.4	27.8	28.2	28.2	28.5	28.5	28.7
O	.	.	28.9 [1]	27.5	28.7	27.3	28.1	28.2	28.2	27.9
P	.	.	19.9 [1]	18.1	12.0	16.8	11.7	11.7	22.6	21.3
Q	.	.								
X	.	.								

New Zealand (BA) (a) [2] [3] — Total employment - Emploi total - Empleo total

Total men and women - Total hommes et femmes - Total hombres y mujeres
ISIC 3 - CITI 3 - CIIU 3

	1999	2000	2001	2002	2003	2004	2005	2006	2007	2008
Total	34.8	34.4	34.4	34.4	34.4 [4]	35.1 [5]	34.8	34.4	34.0	33.9
A-B	40.4	40.0	39.9	39.6	40.3 [4]	40.5 [5]	40.2	39.9	39.6	39.4
C-Q	34.2	33.9	33.9	33.9	33.9 [4]	34.6 [5]	34.4	34.0	33.6	33.5
A	40.4	39.9	39.8	39.7	40.3 [4]	40.6 [5]	40.2	39.9	39.6	39.4
B	41.3	43.4	42.4	37.2	37.2 [4]	37.5 [5]	38.8	40.4	35.0	44.6
C	42.3	41.4	41.0	43.7	45.1 [4]	45.7 [5]	43.2	45.2	44.5	46.0
D	38.1	37.0	37.4	37.9	38.0 [4]	38.4 [5]	38.0	37.8	37.5	37.3
E	41.4	38.0	37.0	37.8	37.4 [4]	38.8 [5]	38.6	37.9	37.9	39.2
F	39.3	38.4	38.8	38.7	38.8 [4]	39.6 [5]	39.2	37.9	38.1	37.8
G	33.8	33.7	33.7	33.2	33.4 [4]	34.5 [5]	34.3	33.7	33.3	32.8
H	30.3	29.9	30.3	30.1	30.8 [4]	29.5 [5]	29.9	29.9	29.2	30.2
I	38.7	38.6	37.8	37.7	37.9 [4]	39.4 [5]	39.4	38.2	37.9	37.3
J	34.5	34.5	34.4	35.1	34.9 [4]	34.5 [5]	34.5	35.0	35.3	35.6
K	34.1	34.3	34.6	34.5	34.6 [4]	35.4 [5]	34.7	34.2	33.5	33.6
L	35.2	34.8	34.8	35.6	34.9 [4]	35.5 [5]	35.5	34.7	34.7	34.2
M	28.8	28.6	29.3	28.6	28.6 [4]	29.5 [5]	29.7	29.3	28.6	28.6
N	28.7	28.3	28.6	29.0	28.6 [4]	29.6 [5]	29.2	29.6	29.4	29.7
O	31.0	31.8	30.5	32.3	28.8 [4]	29.7 [5]	29.4	29.0	28.7	29.7
P	18.0	19.0	16.1	16.5	16.1 [4]	18.9 [5]	17.7	16.1	21.8	24.5
Q	34.1	35.6	33.2	39.7						
X	28.7	29.5	29.4	27.7	27.6 [4]	32.3 [5]	31.2	31.4	32.1	32.7

Explanatory notes: see p. 721.

[1] May, Aug. and Nov. [2] Excl. armed forces. [3] Persons aged 15 years and over. [4] Change of industrial classification: estimates not strictly comparable. [5] Estimates based on the 2006 Population Census results thus not comparable with those for previous years.

Notes explicatives: voir p. 723.

[1] Mai, août et nov. [2] Non compris les forces armées. [3] Personnes âgées de 15 ans et plus. [4] Changement de classification industrielle: les estimations ne sont pas strictement comparables. [5] Estimations basées sur les résultats du Recensement de la population de 2006 donc non comparables à celles des années antérieures.

Notas explicativas: véase p. 725.

[1] Mayo, agosto y nov. [2] Excl. las fuerzas armadas. [3] Personas de 15 años y más. [4] Cambio de clasificación industrial: las estimaciones non son estrictamente comparables. [5] Estimaciones basadas en los resultados del Censo de población de 2006 y por eso no comparables a las de los anos anteriores.

By economic activity Par activité économique Por actividad económica

	Per week — Par semaine — Por semana									
	1999	2000	2001	2002	2003 [3]	2004 [4]	2005	2006	2007	2008

New Zealand (BA) (a) [1][2] Total employment - Emploi total - Empleo total

Men - Hommes - Hombres
ISIC 3 - CITI 3 - CIIU 3

	1999	2000	2001	2002	2003	2004	2005	2006	2007	2008
Total	39.8	39.2	39.3	39.2	39.1	39.8	39.5	38.9	38.6	38.3
A-B	46.3	45.9	45.3	44.5	45.4	45.9	45.9	45.4	44.6	45.1
C-Q	38.9	38.3	38.5	38.5	38.4	39.1	38.9	38.3	38.0	37.7
A	46.4	45.8	45.2	44.5	45.6	46.0	46.0	45.5	44.8	45.0
B	43.4	47.2	47.4	41.4	39.6	40.4	43.4	44.2	36.1	47.6
C	43.7	43.7	44.2	46.3	48.6	47.5	44.9	46.7	46.6	47.9
D	40.4	39.1	39.7	40.0	39.8	40.4	39.8	39.6	39.4	39.3
E	42.7	40.3	40.3	39.6	39.2	39.8	39.9	39.8	39.5	40.6
F	40.6	39.8	40.5	40.8	40.5	41.1	40.8	39.6	39.7	39.3
G	38.3	37.9	38.0	37.5	37.7	38.8	38.8	38.1	38.0	36.9
H	35.6	35.2	35.0	34.5	36.7	34.1	35.2	36.1	34.7	33.5
I	41.4	41.3	40.5	40.7	40.5	42.5	41.6	40.4	40.5	39.7
J	38.2	38.5	39.8	39.7	38.8	37.8	38.9	39.3	39.3	39.7
K	38.5	38.5	38.6	38.7	38.7	39.3	38.5	38.0	36.8	37.6
L	38.1	37.5	37.5	38.0	37.9	38.6	38.8	38.2	37.4	37.4
M	33.9	33.7	34.0	32.1	32.4	33.0	34.8	33.8	33.8	33.3
N	35.8	35.3	35.3	36.7	36.6	35.7	35.4	35.9	35.3	35.8
O	35.8	36.1	34.8	37.1	32.4	34.4	33.6	32.1	32.5	32.7
P	17.6	16.0	23.8	27.0	17.1	10.1	22.2	18.1	9.7	37.8
Q	37.1	33.9	40.4	42.1	. [3]	.	.	.	.	.
X	30.8	32.5	31.1	31.3	28.7	37.1	35.3	35.0	34.0	35.1

Women - Femmes - Mujeres
ISIC 3 - CITI 3 - CIIU 3

	1999	2000	2001	2002	2003	2004	2005	2006	2007	2008
Total	28.8	28.6	28.6	28.7	28.7	29.5	29.3	29.1	28.8	28.9
A-B	27.9	26.8	27.3	28.0	28.4	29.0	28.2	28.8	28.9	27.9
C-Q	28.9	28.7	28.7	28.7	28.8	29.6	29.3	29.1	28.7	28.9
A	28.0	26.9	27.4	28.1	28.5	29.1	28.2	28.7	28.9	27.8
B	26.5	16.5	22.8	18.5	24.2	20.6	23.0	31.6	30.7	30.3
C	30.2	26.6	24.5	31.6	28.3	23.7	31.3	37.3	33.4	32.2
D	32.7	32.0	31.7	32.4	33.2	33.6	33.2	33.0	32.7	32.7
E	36.4	31.7	29.3	32.3	31.4	35.3	35.4	33.1	31.5	33.1
F	27.9	24.7	23.5	23.6	25.1	27.0	25.8	25.4	25.8	25.6
G	28.1	28.6	28.6	28.0	28.5	29.3	29.3	28.8	28.1	28.2
H	27.0	26.6	27.4	27.1	27.3	27.1	26.9	26.8	26.0	27.9
I	32.9	32.1	31.5	31.2	31.9	32.3	34.2	33.5	31.4	31.4
J	31.7	31.6	31.1	31.7	32.0	32.2	31.2	31.3	31.9	32.5
K	28.9	29.4	29.7	29.2	29.5	30.6	30.0	29.7	29.8	29.3
L	32.5	32.0	32.4	33.3	32.0	32.5	32.2	31.6	32.0	31.3
M	26.8	26.8	27.4	27.1	27.0	28.1	27.7	27.4	26.4	26.8
N	27.1	26.9	27.1	27.4	27.0	28.2	28.0	28.3	28.3	28.4
O	27.2	28.4	26.9	28.3	25.9	26.2	26.4	26.6	25.7	26.9
P	18.0	19.3	15.1	15.7	15.5	19.6	17.3	15.8	22.8	23.7
Q	30.3	38.0	30.1	39.2	. [3]	.	.	.	.	.
X	25.9	27.0	27.2	24.0	27.2	27.4	26.3	27.5	29.3	28.4

Polynésie française (FD) (b) [5] Employees - Salariés - Asalariados

Men - Hommes - Hombres
ISIC 3 - CITI 3 - CIIU 3

	1999	2000	2001	2002	2003	2004	2005	2006	2007	2008
Total	153	153	155	156	153	.	.	.	.	.
A	138	139	138	136	137	.	.	.	.	.
B	150	151	151	146	147	.	.	.	.	.
C	156	155	152	155	153	.	.	.	.	.
D	156	157	160	161	158	.	.	.	.	.
E	172	172	172	171	170	.	.	.	.	.
F	146	144	146	147	146	.	.	.	.	.
G	159	158	158	158	159	.	.	.	.	.
H	145	144	145	144	144	.	.	.	.	.
I	154	156	155	157	152	.	.	.	.	.
J	166	166	166	166	166	.	.	.	.	.
K	142	141	142	141	139	.	.	.	.	.
L	159	160	168	172	161	.	.	.	.	.
M	158	159	146	149	149	.	.	.	.	.
N	159	157	155	156	156	.	.	.	.	.
O	139	133	135	137	138	.	.	.	.	.
P	94	91	85	85	117	.	.	.	.	.

Explanatory notes: see p. 721.

[1] Excl. armed forces. [2] Persons aged 15 years and over. [3] Change of industrial classification: estimates not strictly comparable. [4] Estimates based on the 2006 Population Census results thus not comparable with those for previous years. [5] Per month.

Notes explicatives: voir p. 723.

[1] Non compris les forces armées. [2] Personnes âgées de 15 ans et plus. [3] Changement de classification industrielle: les estimations ne sont pas strictement comparables. [4] Estimations basées sur les résultats du Recensement de la population de 2006 donc non comparables à celles des années antérieures. [5] Par mois.

Notas explicativas: véase p. 725.

[1] Excl. las fuerzas armadas. [2] Personas de 15 años y más. [3] Cambio de clasificación industrial: las estimaciones non son estrictamente comparables. [4] Estimaciones basadas en los resultados del Censo de población de 2006 y por eso no comparables a las de los anos anteriores. [5] Por mes.

4A

HOURS OF WORK

DURÉE DU TRAVAIL

HORAS DE TRABAJO

By economic activity

Par activité économique

Por actividad económica

	Per week				Par semaine				Por semana	
	1999	2000	2001	2002	2003	2004	2005	2006	2007	2008

Polynésie française (FD) (b) [1]   **Employees - Salariés - Asalariados**

Women - Femmes - Mujeres

ISIC 3 - CITI 3 - CIIU 3

	1999	2000	2001	2002	2003	2004	2005	2006	2007	2008
Total	140	139	141	141	139	.	.	.	.	.
A	123	125	123	124	127	.	.	.	.	.
B	148	147	143	142	146	.	.	.	.	.
C	138	137	141	138	135	.	.	.	.	.
D	145	144	145	145	146	.	.	.	.	.
E	168	168	163	164	163	.	.	.	.	.
F	128	122	124	131	128	.	.	.	.	.
G	150	148	147	147	148	.	.	.	.	.
H	136	136	134	135	135	.	.	.	.	.
I	145	147	147	147	145	.	.	.	.	.
J	158	158	159	158	160	.	.	.	.	.
K	125	123	123	123	121	.	.	.	.	.
L	151	151	160	160	151	.	.	.	.	.
M	150	149	134	133	139	.	.	.	.	.
N	148	147	148	148	148	.	.	.	.	.
O	127	127	127	128	130	.	.	.	.	.
P	60	59	58	59	58	.	.	.	.	.
Q	48	45	48	48	49	.	.	.	.	.

Explanatory notes: see p. 721.

[1] Per month.

Notes explicatives: voir p. 723.

[1] Par mois.

Notas explicativas: véase p. 725.

[1] Por mes.

In manufacturing   **Dans les industries manufacturières**   **En las industrias manufactureras**

Per week — Par semaine — Por semana

AFRICA-AFRIQUE-AFRICA

Egypt (CA) (b) [1][2]   **Wage earners - Ouvriers - Obreros**

Total men and women - Total hommes et femmes - Total hombres y mujeres
ISIC 3 - CITI 3 - CIIU 3

	1999	2000	2001	2002	2003	2004	2005	2006	2007	2008
Total	57	55	54	55	57	56	57	56	56	.
15	58	55	53	55	57	56	56	56	57	.
16	57	54	52	55	54	54	53	53	53	.
17	57	56	55	57	57	56	57	57	56	.
18	57	58	58	58	59	59	59	59	59	.
19	57	55	55	56	54	56	57	58	57	.
20	57	59	55	54	56	57	59	58	58	.
21	57	57	53	55	58	56	58	58	58	.
22	51	51	51	51	56	52	55	56	54	.
23	52	50	50	51	52	53	51	51	50	.
24	51	51	51	52	55	53	54	54	55	.
25	56	57	56	56	56	57	59	57	59	.
26	59	56	55	55	58	56	57	56	53	.
27	54	52	51	52	52	51	55	56	56	.
28	56	54	53	53	59	54	56	55	57	.
29	52	53	52	53	53	54	57	56	57	.
30	61	52	53	62	50	60	60	62	56	.
31	54	54	53	54	53	54	56	56	56	.
32	47	46	49	49	46	52	51	52	52	.
33	57	54	56	54	53	58	56	58	58	.
34	75	59	59	59	60	63	61	57	55	.
35	70	56	57	56	53	57	62	60	58	.
36	58	55	55	57	56	58	59	57	57	.
37	58	62	50	59	57	.	68	62	.	.

Men - Hommes - Hombres
ISIC 3 - CITI 3 - CIIU 3

	1999	2000	2001	2002	2003	2004	2005	2006	2007	2008
Total	57	55	54	55	56	55	57	56	56	.
15	58	55	53	55	57	55	56	56	56	.
16	55	54	53	54	54	54	53	53	53	.
17	57	56	55	57	57	56	57	57	56	.
18	57	58	59	58	59	58	59	59	59	.
19	57	55	55	56	55	55	57	58	57	.
20	57	59	55	54	56	57	59	58	58	.
21	57	57	53	55	58	55	58	58	58	.
22	51	51	51	51	56	52	55	56	54	.
23	51	50	50	51	52	53	51	51	50	.
24	52	51	52	52	56	53	54	54	55	.
25	56	57	55	56	55	57	59	57	59	.
26	59	56	55	55	58	56	57	56	53	.
27	54	52	51	52	52	51	55	56	56	.
28	56	54	53	53	59	54	56	55	57	.
29	52	53	52	53	53	54	57	56	57	.
30	61	52	53	62	50	60	60	62	58	.
31	54	54	53	54	53	54	56	56	56	.
32	47	47	49	50	45	52	51	52	53	.
33	56	53	56	53	51	57	56	58	58	.
34	75	59	59	59	60	63	61	57	55	.
35	70	56	57	56	53	57	62	60	58	.
36	58	55	55	57	56	58	59	57	57	.
37	58	62	58	59	54	.	68	62	.	.

Women - Femmes - Mujeres
ISIC 3 - CITI 3 - CIIU 3

	1999	2000	2001	2002	2003	2004	2005	2006	2007	2008
Total	56	56	56	57	58	57	57	58	57	.
15	60	56	55	55	62	57	58	58	57	.
16	64	58	51	58	55	56	53	53	51	.
17	56	56	55	57	55	56	56	57	56	.
18	57	58	58	59	59	59	59	59	59	.
19	59	54	56	55	51	58	56	58	59	.
20	54	62	51	54	58	58	62	61	57	.
21	57	58	54	58	57	58	58	59	62	.
22	56	52	56	56	56	57	58	59	59	.
23	55	47	54	54	54	53	49	53	53	.
24	49	50	50	51	52	53	55	54	54	.
25	58	57	57	56	60	58	58	56	57	.
26	59	56	55	57	61	60	60	61	53	.
27	51	49	52	51	50	57	58	.	37	.
28	56	55	57	52	57	56	58	57	59	.
29	52	58	58	53	55	53	56	54	56	.
30	.	52	53	63	50	60	61	.	44	.
31	53	58	50	57	51	55	47	55	57	.
32	44	44	45	48	51	51	43	51	44	.
33	60	57	56	56	58	62	58	57	57	.
34	72	55	59	62	59	61	57	54	60	.
35	71	50	55	50	57	59	58	59	62	.
36	56	57	55	56	52	58	56	61	58	.
37	56	62	42	54	59	.	68	.	.	.

Explanatory notes: see p. 721.   Notes explicatives: voir p. 723.   Notas explicativas: véase p. 725.

[1] Establishments with 10 or more persons employed. [2] Oct. of each year.   [1] Etablissements occupant 10 personnes et plus. [2] Oct. de chaque année.   [1] Establecimientos con 10 y más trabajadores. [2] Oct. de cada año.

In manufacturing Dans les industries manufacturières En las industrias manufactureras

	Per week								Por semana	
	1999	2000	2001	2002	2003	2004	2005	2006	2007	2008

Ethiopia (BA) (a) [1] Total employment - Emploi total - Empleo total

Total men and women - Total hommes et femmes - Total hombres y mujeres
ISIC 3 - CITI 3 - CIIU 3

	1999	2000	2001	2002	2003	2004	2005	2006	2007	2008
Total	.	.	.	.	.	39	28	.	.	.
15	.	.	.	.	.	42	25	.	.	.
16	.	.	.	.	.	41	26	.	.	.
17	.	.	.	.	.	35	30	.	.	.
18	.	.	.	.	.	41	34	.	.	.
19	.	.	.	.	.	46	38	.	.	.
20	.	.	.	.	.	40	30	.	.	.
21	.	.	.	.	.	39	48	.	.	.
22	.	.	.	.	.	48	48	.	.	.
23	.	.	.	.	.	42	51	.	.	.
24	.	.	.	.	.	49	44	.	.	.
25	.	.	.	.	.	46	51	.	.	.
26	.	.	.	.	.	46	36	.	.	.
27	.	.	.	.	.	43	38	.	.	.
28	.	.	.	.	.	44	39	.	.	.
29	.	.	.	.	.	41	41	.	.	.
30	.	.	.	.	.	41	32	.	.	.
31	.	.	.	.	.	29	46	.	.	.
32	.	.	.	.	.	44	38	.	.	.
33	.	.	.	.	.	29		.	.	.
34	.	.	.	.	.	51	50	.	.	.
35	.	.	.	.	.	45	49	.	.	.
36	.	.	.	.	.	41	26	.	.	.

Men - Hommes - Hombres
ISIC 3 - CITI 3 - CIIU 3

	1999	2000	2001	2002	2003	2004	2005	2006	2007	2008
Total	.	.	.	.	.	45	41	.	.	.
15	.	.	.	.	.	51	45	.	.	.
16	.	.	.	.	.	47	44	.	.	.
17	.	.	.	.	.	42	40	.	.	.
18	.	.	.	.	.	43	35	.	.	.
19	.	.	.	.	.	46	38	.	.	.
20	.	.	.	.	.		34	.	.	.
21	.	.	.	.	.	38	49	.	.	.
22	.	.	.	.	.	53	51	.	.	.
23	.	.	.	.	.	42	51	.	.	.
24	.	.	.	.	.	52	46	.	.	.
25	.	.	.	.	.	47	50	.	.	.
26	.	.	.	.	.	51	48	.	.	.
27	.	.	.	.	.	44	38	.	.	.
28	.	.	.	.	.	46	41	.	.	.
29	.	.	.	.	.	41	50	.	.	.
30	.	.	.	.	.	.	32	.	.	.
31	.	.	.	.	.	42	49	.	.	.
32	.	.	.	.	.	44	38	.	.	.
33	.	.	.	.	.	20	.	.	.	.
34	.	.	.	.	.	52	51	.	.	.
35	.	.	.	.	.	45	49	.	.	.
36	.	.	.	.	.	44	40	.	.	.

Women - Femmes - Mujeres
ISIC 3 - CITI 3 - CIIU 3

	1999	2000	2001	2002	2003	2004	2005	2006	2007	2008
Total	.	.	.	.	.	32	23	.	.	.
15	.	.	.	.	.	37	20	.	.	.
16	.	.	.	.	.	32	25	.	.	.
17	.	.	.	.	.	28	25	.	.	.
18	.	.	.	.	.	35	29	.	.	.
19	.	.	.	.	.	43	37	.	.	.
20	.	.	.	.	.	31	23	.	.	.
21	.	.	.	.	.	39	47	.	.	.
22	.	.	.	.	.	45	45	.	.	.
23	.	.	.	.	.	.	.	.	.	.
24	.	.	.	.	.	45	42	.	.	.
25	.	.	.	.	.	45	53	.	.	.
26	.	.	.	.	.	35	30	.	.	.
27	.	.	.	.	.	39	35	.	.	.
28	.	.	.	.	.	33	17	.	.	.
29	.	.	.	.	.	42	29	.	.	.
30	.	.	.	.	.	41	.	.	.	.
31	.	.	.	.	.	.	34	.	.	.
32	.	.	.	.	.	.	.	.	.	.
33	.	.	.	.	.	40	.	.	.	.
34	.	.	.	.	.	44	31	.	.	.
35	.	.	.	.	.	.	28	.	.	.
36	.	.	.	.	.	29	23	.	.	.

Mauritius (BA) (a) Total employment - Emploi total - Empleo total

Total men and women - Total hommes et femmes - Total hombres y mujeres
ISIC 3 - CITI 3 - CIIU 3

	1999	2000	2001	2002	2003	2004	2005	2006	2007	2008
Total	.	.	.	.	.	.	43	43	45	.

Explanatory notes: see p. 721. Notes explicatives: voir p. 723. Notas explicativas: véase p. 725.

[1] Urban areas. [1] Régions urbaines. [1] Areas urbanas.

In manufacturing   **Dans les industries manufacturières**   **En las industrias manufactureras**

Per week - Par semaine - Por semana

	1999	2000	2001	2002	2003	2004	2005	2006	2007	2008
Mauritius (BA) (a)				Total employment - Emploi total - Empleo total						
Men - Hommes - Hombres										
ISIC 3 - CITI 3 - CIIU 3										
Total	.	.	.	.	.	.	43	44	.	.
Women - Femmes - Mujeres										
ISIC 3 - CITI 3 - CIIU 3										
Total	.	.	.	.	.	.	42	42	.	.

AMERICA-AMÉRIQUE-AMERICA

Argentina (BA) (a) [1][2][3]   Total employment - Emploi total - Empleo total

Total men and women - Total hommes et femmes - Total hombres y mujeres
ISIC 3 - CITI 3 - CIIU 3

	1999	2000	2001	2002	2003	2004	2005	2006	2007	2008
Total	45.8	45.4	44.6	42.6	42.8 [4]	42.8	44.3	.	.	.
15	47.7	48.5	46.4	44.3	43.0 [4]	43.9	46.6	.	.	.
16	46.5	52.1	49.5	50.2	37.6 [4]	36.2	40.3	.	.	.
17	46.2	44.7	45.2	42.0	45.4 [4]	41.8	45.5	.	.	.
18	40.4	41.1	39.8	36.0	37.8 [4]	35.3	39.5	.	.	.
19	45.8	44.7	45.3	40.9	46.7 [4]	47.0	43.6	.	.	.
20	47.0	46.5	44.6	39.7	41.1 [4]	36.9	46.1	.	.	.
21	48.2	47.9	47.3	46.9	50.0 [4]	44.6	43.6	.	.	.
22	43.8	43.0	42.4	42.2	41.9 [4]	44.7	46.4	.	.	.
23	50.0	47.7	48.9	45.5	46.9 [4]	46.6	46.4	.	.	.
24	42.8	39.2	41.1	40.6	41.5 [4]	39.9	42.8	.	.	.
25	48.1	47.2	46.8	47.5	43.3 [4]	44.1	46.7	.	.	.
26	46.1	45.3	46.4	44.8	38.9 [4]	44.7	46.2	.	.	.
27	45.6	46.3	45.2	47.2	43.4 [4]	48.7	46.6	.	.	.
28	46.3	45.4	45.1	41.8	41.1 [4]	42.9	45.1	.	.	.
29	46.3	46.5	47.4	45.2	45.6 [4]	45.9	47.2	.	.	.
30	49.1	48.9	41.3	35.2	23.7 [4]	52.5	48.7	.	.	.
31	48.0	51.2	44.3	43.9	44.3 [4]	46.4	46.4	.	.	.
32	45.6	44.9	43.8	41.3	40.6 [4]	38.5	38.5	.	.	.
33	43.7	41.8	41.9	41.3	42.9 [4]	36.1	41.7	.	.	.
34	44.2	44.6	44.2	44.7	43.0 [4]	43.3	44.8	.	.	.
35	46.1	49.2	46.8	45.9	45.7 [4]	44.6	44.5	.	.	.
36	44.6	43.6	42.4	39.2	37.9 [4]	36.2	40.2	.	.	.
37	48.5	39.8	36.7	36.1	46.1 [4]	37.2	43.9	.	.	.

Men - Hommes - Hombres
ISIC 3 - CITI 3 - CIIU 3

	1999	2000	2001	2002	2003	2004	2005	2006	2007	2008
Total	47.9	47.6	47.0	45.4	46.2 [4]	46.8	47.8	.	.	.
15	50.7	51.1	49.5	48.7	47.4 [4]	47.8	50.8	.	.	.
16	47.8	52.5	49.9	48.9	37.6 [4]	36.2	43.8	.	.	.
17	48.5	47.6	47.4	46.6	52.0 [4]	48.5	52.1	.	.	.
18	49.4	48.9	48.5	42.0	50.9 [4]	47.4	46.0	.	.	.
19	46.1	45.7	46.3	41.4	49.1 [4]	49.3	46.7	.	.	.
20	47.3	47.0	45.0	40.0	41.4 [4]	37.1	47.0	.	.	.
21	49.4	49.3	48.5	47.3	51.9 [4]	55.4	44.2	.	.	.
22	46.3	44.5	45.2	43.8	45.3 [4]	46.2	49.6	.	.	.
23	49.3	48.5	49.2	45.4	46.9 [4]	47.0	46.0	.	.	.
24	47.2	47.9	48.3	46.7	45.1 [4]	47.5	47.0	.	.	.
25	49.6	48.2	48.3	49.4	44.4 [4]	45.1	47.9	.	.	.
26	46.7	46.3	46.7	44.3	39.3 [4]	45.4	48.6	.	.	.
27	45.7	46.3	45.5	47.1	43.0 [4]	48.9	46.4	.	.	.
28	46.6	45.6	45.6	41.9	41.7 [4]	43.4	45.6	.	.	.
29	47.1	47.3	47.9	45.4	45.8 [4]	46.5	48.8	.	.	.
30	52.8	50.3	41.1	33.2	23.7 [4]	52.5	48.4	.	.	.
31	48.2	50.6	44.2	44.0	45.1 [4]	47.4	46.9	.	.	.
32	45.4	44.9	44.8	41.1	40.8 [4]	36.1	40.7	.	.	.
33	42.9	43.3	44.2	46.7	45.1 [4]	37.0	45.0	.	.	.
34	44.5	44.7	45.1	45.0	43.4 [4]	43.5	45.4	.	.	.
35	46.9	50.0	48.4	48.1	48.9 [4]	48.1	47.1	.	.	.
36	45.8	45.3	43.7	42.1	41.8 [4]	42.4	47.0	.	.	.
37	49.1	41.5	37.8	37.6	46.0 [4]	35.5	41.4	.	.	.

Explanatory notes: see p. 721.

[1] 28 urban agglomerations. [2] Persons aged 10 years and over. [3] Second semester of each year. [4] Prior to 2003: May and October.

Notes explicatives: voir p. 723.

[1] 28 agglomérations urbaines. [2] Personnes âgées de 10 ans et plus. [3] Second semestre de chaque année. [4] Avant 2003: mai et octobre.

Notas explicativas: véase p. 725.

[1] 28 aglomerados úrbanos. [2] Personas de 10 años y más. [3] Segundo semestre de cada año. [4] Antes de 2003: mayo y octubre.

HOURS OF WORK — DURÉE DU TRAVAIL — HORAS DE TRABAJO

In manufacturing — Dans les industries manufacturières — En las industrias manufactureras

	Per week — Par semaine — Por semana									
	1999	2000	2001	2002	2003	2004	2005	2006	2007	2008

Argentina (BA) (a) [1] [2] [3] — Total employment - Emploi total - Empleo total

Women - Femmes - Mujeres
ISIC 3 - CITI 3 - CIIU 3

	1999	2000	2001	2002	2003	2004	2005	2006	2007	2008
Total	39.0	38.8	37.8	34.5	35.9 [4]	34.3	36.3	.	.	.
15	40.2	41.9	39.5	34.6	35.1 [4]	36.3	36.5	.	.	.
16	43.8	50.0	45.0	58.0	. [4]	47.9	34.5	.	.	.
17	40.5	38.2	40.5	33.1	37.9 [4]	32.3	36.6	.	.	.
18	37.4	38.9	36.7	33.9	34.2 [4]	34.9	37.0	.	.	.
19	44.9	42.2	42.7	39.6	43.5 [4]	45.3	35.8	.	.	.
20	33.7	30.5	39.3	35.7	37.9 [4]	32.1	33.3	.	.	.
21	40.7	43.4	43.9	44.6	33.1 [4]	26.1	41.9	.	.	.
22	36.4	38.5	36.1	38.0	35.0 [4]	36.9	38.2	.	.	.
23	61.7	41.7	46.7	46.7	. [4]	44.2	50.0	.	.	.
24	33.8	25.6	29.4	29.0	30.2 [4]	33.2	36.1	.	.	.
25	38.8	41.0	39.8	37.0	39.2 [4]	42.7	40.0	.	.	.
26	39.4	37.8	42.5	50.7	37.8 [4]	28.4	27.9	.	.	.
27	45.0	45.0	41.7	47.5	47.3 [4]	51.1	55.1	.	.	.
28	38.8	42.7	37.7	41.0	33.6 [4]	34.2	38.8	.	.	.
29	41.4	38.0	43.6	42.8	45.0 [4]	34.1	36.8	.	.	.
30	44.4	42.5	42.5	45.0	. [4]	70.0	50.0	.	.	.
31	46.7	56.0	45.0	43.8	40.3 [4]	44.3	44.0	.	.	.
32	46.1	44.7	42.2	42.1	40.3 [4]	50.1	35.5	.	.	.
33	48.4	38.4	34.1	27.0	37.5 [4]	42.5	34.8	.	.	.
34	39.4	42.1	33.9	38.3	37.7 [4]	36.6	35.8	.	.	.
35	33.5	38.0	36.2	31.0	29.0 [4]	37.1	34.8	.	.	.
36	34.6	34.5	35.3	26.7	30.4 [4]	24.7	32.2	.	.	.
37	30.0	35.1	33.7	28.3	48.0 [4]	32.7	56.0	.	.	.

Argentina (BA) (a) [1] [2] [3] — Employees - Salariés - Asalariados

Total men and women - Total hommes et femmes - Total hombres y mujeres
ISIC 3 - CITI 3 - CIIU 3

	1999	2000	2001	2002	2003	2004	2005	2006	2007	2008
Total	46.4	46.1	45.4	44.1	44.8 [4]	44.4	45.3	.	.	.
15	48.4	48.6	47.8	47.0	43.0 [4]	43.9	48.3	.	.	.
16	46.5	47.5	49.5	50.2	37.6 [4]	36.2	40.3	.	.	.
17	47.6	46.8	46.6	44.6	45.4 [4]	41.8	47.1	.	.	.
18	45.3	45.5	43.6	37.9	37.8 [4]	35.3	41.4	.	.	.
19	45.5	46.1	45.4	40.4	46.7 [4]	47.0	43.3	.	.	.
20	45.5	46.8	45.0	41.9	41.1 [4]	36.9	46.5	.	.	.
21	49.8	48.8	46.7	47.0	50.0 [4]	44.6	44.6	.	.	.
22	43.2	43.0	42.4	42.1	41.9 [4]	44.7	45.3	.	.	.
23	50.0	47.8	49.2	45.8	46.9 [4]	46.6	46.4	.	.	.
24	42.9	39.6	41.0	40.1	41.5 [4]	39.9	42.9	.	.	.
25	48.4	47.3	47.1	45.8	43.3 [4]	44.1	46.7	.	.	.
26	45.6	45.0	45.9	44.2	38.9 [4]	44.7	45.4	.	.	.
27	46.4	46.6	45.4	47.1	43.4 [4]	48.7	47.5	.	.	.
28	46.2	47.2	45.6	42.1	41.1 [4]	42.9	45.9	.	.	.
29	46.0	46.2	46.6	47.0	45.6 [4]	45.9	47.5	.	.	.
30	44.4	46.3	41.8	37.2	23.7 [4]	52.5	43.6	.	.	.
31	48.0	46.2	43.0	46.4	44.3 [4]	46.4	46.6	.	.	.
32	45.3	45.2	42.8	41.8	40.6 [4]	38.5	33.3	.	.	.
33	42.2	41.7	41.7	43.4	42.9 [4]	36.1	40.3	.	.	.
34	44.0	44.9	44.0	43.2	43.0 [4]	43.3	44.7	.	.	.
35	47.2	49.5	47.0	47.0	45.7 [4]	44.6	43.8	.	.	.
36	45.1	44.6	42.8	41.6	37.9 [4]	36.2	43.2	.	.	.
37	42.8	39.4	43.9	31.6	46.1 [4]	37.6	37.7	.	.	.

Men - Hommes - Hombres
ISIC 3 - CITI 3 - CIIU 3

	1999	2000	2001	2002	2003	2004	2005	2006	2007	2008
Total	47.6	47.6	47.1	45.9	47.0 [4]	47.1	47.7	.	.	.
15	49.5	49.9	49.1	48.4	48.1 [4]	46.7	50.4	.	.	.
16	47.8	47.0	49.9	48.9	37.6 [4]	36.2	43.8	.	.	.
17	48.6	48.2	47.5	47.0	51.8 [4]	48.3	51.8	.	.	.
18	50.2	49.1	46.9	41.7	49.8 [4]	48.8	45.5	.	.	.
19	45.4	47.2	45.4	41.3	48.8 [4]	46.5	45.2	.	.	.
20	45.9	47.0	45.0	42.2	43.0 [4]	39.4	46.9	.	.	.
21	50.3	49.5	48.3	47.2	51.5 [4]	53.4	46.2	.	.	.
22	45.9	44.6	46.0	44.8	45.5 [4]	46.7	47.7	.	.	.
23	49.3	48.7	49.5	45.8	46.9 [4]	46.6	46.0	.	.	.
24	47.3	47.8	48.2	46.2	44.5 [4]	47.1	46.9	.	.	.
25	49.9	48.1	48.0	47.3	42.5 [4]	45.5	48.0	.	.	.
26	45.9	45.2	45.9	43.8	37.5 [4]	45.5	46.4	.	.	.
27	46.2	46.7	45.5	47.1	42.8 [4]	48.7	47.2	.	.	.
28	46.7	47.5	46.4	42.8	44.0 [4]	44.9	46.4	.	.	.
29	46.9	47.1	46.9	47.4	44.6 [4]	47.0	49.5	.	.	.
30	44.5	47.4	41.7	35.3	40.0 [4]	45.4	43.6	.	.	.
31	48.0	46.9	43.0	47.3	45.4 [4]	44.1	46.9	.	.	.
32	45.9	45.2	43.5	41.6	42.5 [4]	54.7	30.2	.	.	.
33	41.8	43.1	46.2	45.4	45.1 [4]	40.0	41.8	.	.	.
34	44.2	44.9	44.8	43.4	43.3 [4]	42.5	45.4	.	.	.
35	47.5	50.4	48.5	48.4	48.7 [4]	46.5	46.4	.	.	.
36	45.3	45.2	43.9	43.3	45.1 [4]	42.1	48.6	.	.	.
37	42.8	39.6	43.5	34.7	. [4]	44.0	37.7	.	.	.

Explanatory notes: see p. 721.

Notes explicatives: voir p. 723.

Notas explicativas: véase p. 725.

[1] 28 urban agglomerations. [2] Persons aged 10 years and over. [3] Second semester of each year. [4] Prior to 2003: May and October.

[1] 28 agglomérations urbaines. [2] Personnes âgées de 10 ans et plus. [3] Second semestre de chaque année. [4] Avant 2003: mai et octobre.

[1] 28 aglomerados úrbanos. [2] Personas de 10 años y más. [3] Segundo semestre de cada año. [4] Antes de 2003: mayo y octubre.

In manufacturing — Dans les industries manufacturières — En las industrias manufactureras

Per week — Par semaine — Por semana

Argentina (BA) (a) [1][2][3] — Employees - Salariés - Asalariados

Women - Femmes - Mujeres
ISIC 3 - CITI 3 - CIIU 3

	1999	2000	2001	2002	2003	2004	2005	2006	2007	2008
Total	41.8	40.7	39.7	37.5	38.6[4]	37.1	38.8	.	.	.
15	44.3	43.8	43.5	42.2	39.3[4]	40.4	40.7	.	.	.
16	43.8	50.0	45.0	58.0	.[4]	36.0	34.5	.	.	.
17	43.5	41.4	42.9	36.3	42.4[4]	35.7	39.5	.	.	.
18	43.3	44.2	41.7	36.1	37.3[4]	34.1	39.5	.	.	.
19	45.8	42.9	45.5	38.1	45.8[4]	42.5	37.4	.	.	.
20	36.7	21.8	43.9	38.3	40.4[4]	42.6	37.2	.	.	.
21	45.2	45.9	41.1	45.0	34.0[4]	34.6	40.6	.	.	.
22	35.9	38.5	35.5	35.6	35.4[4]	39.7	39.1	.	.	.
23	61.7	41.7	46.7	46.7	.[4]	45.2	50.0	.	.	.
24	34.0	26.4	28.6	28.7	30.8[4]	30.1	36.5	.	.	.
25	39.2	41.7	43.0	37.6	34.1[4]	34.7	39.6	.	.	.
26	40.5	41.7	46.5	51.6	38.7[4]	39.3	29.7	.	.	.
27	60.0	42.5	42.5	47.5	47.3[4]	47.1	55.1	.	.	.
28	39.0	43.0	37.1	35.4	33.8[4]	38.1	41.7	.	.	.
29	40.8	36.6	44.2	42.5	46.6[4]	41.3	37.0	.	.	.
30	44.4	42.5	42.5	45.0	.[4]	52.0	.	.	.	.
31	48.4	39.0	43.3	43.8	40.2[4]	39.5	45.2	.	.	.
32	44.5	45.2	41.7	42.5	43.7[4]	48.3	35.5	.	.	.
33	46.3	39.2	26.8	35.8	38.9[4]	36.3	38.7	.	.	.
34	39.4	45.1	33.9	38.3	39.5[4]	41.0	35.8	.	.	.
35	40.0	38.0	37.4	27.5	29.0[4]	30.7	34.8	.	.	.
36	43.1	38.5	33.5	30.1	31.4[4]	28.6	35.6	.	.	.
37	.	39.0	48.0	24.8	48.0[4]	48.0	.	.	.	.

Bermuda (CA) (a) [5] — Employees - Salariés - Asalariados

Total men and women - Total hommes et femmes - Total hombres y mujeres
ISIC 3 - CITI 3 - CIIU 3

	1999	2000	2001	2002	2003	2004	2005	2006	2007	2008
Total	.	.	.	34.0	29.0	33.0	35.0	35.6	35.0	.
15	.	.	.	37.0	28.0	37.0	37.0	38.8	38.0	.
17	.	.	.	27.0	21.0	26.0	26.0	29.4	25.0	.
18	.	.	.	29.0	22.0	26.0	26.0	30.3	29.0	.
20	.	.	.	33.0	29.0	33.0	35.0	32.5	35.0	.
22	.	.	.	.	28.0	30.0	35.0	35.0	34.0	.
23	.	.	.	.	.	.	.	.	.	.
24	.	.	.	38.0	33.0	34.0	37.0	38.5	39.0	.
25	.	.	.	.	39.0	34.0	34.0	35.0	36.0	.
26	.	.	.	36.0	31.0	38.0	37.0	38.3	39.0	.
28	.	.	.	34.0	31.0	33.0	33.0	35.1	35.0	.
29	.	.	.	30.0	25.0	21.0	21.0	60.0	.	.
31	.	.	.	30.0	22.0	22.0	.	40.0	42.0	.
35	.	.	.	35.0	31.0	34.0	36.0	36.8	34.0	.
36	.	.	.	31.0	27.0	30.0	29.0	29.1	29.0	.
37	.	.	.	.	.	.	.	.	32.0	.

Men - Hommes - Hombres
ISIC 3 - CITI 3 - CIIU 3

	1999	2000	2001	2002	2003	2004	2005	2006	2007	2008
Total	.	.	.	36.0	30.0	35.0	36.0	36.9	37.0	.
15	.	.	.	38.0	29.0	39.0	39.0	40.0	40.0	.
17	.	.	.	32.0	19.0	31.0	29.0	33.7	34.0	.
18	.	.	.	26.0	21.0	29.0	31.0	31.3	36.0	.
20	.	.	.	34.0	29.0	33.0	36.0	34.0	36.0	.
22	.	.	.	34.0	29.0	31.0	35.0	35.8	36.0	.
24	.	.	.	38.0	36.0	35.0	36.0	38.1	38.0	.
25	.	.	.	38.0	39.0	34.0	33.0	34.2	35.0	.
26	.	.	.	37.0	32.0	39.0	38.0	40.4	39.0	.
28	.	.	.	35.0	32.0	33.0	33.0	36.0	35.0	.
29	.	.	.	43.0	45.0	29.0	29.0	60.0	.	.
31	.	.	.	37.0	26.0	26.0	.	40.0	43.0	.
35	.	.	.	35.0	31.0	34.0	36.0	37.0	34.0	.
36	.	.	.	34.0	27.0	32.0	31.0	29.6	31.0	.
37	.	.	.	.	.	.	.	.	31.0	.

Women - Femmes - Mujeres
ISIC 3 - CITI 3 - CIIU 3

	1999	2000	2001	2002	2003	2004	2005	2006	2007	2008
Total	.	.	.	31.0	26.0	29.0	32.0	32.4	32.0	.
15	.	.	.	32.0	25.0	31.0	30.0	33.6	33.0	.
17	.	.	.	23.0	22.0	21.0	23.0	22.1	18.0	.
18	.	.	.	30.0	24.0	22.0	21.0	29.0	21.0	.
20	.	.	.	25.0	25.0	27.0	27.0	21.0	27.0	.
22	.	.	.	32.0	27.0	29.0	34.0	34.2	32.0	.
24	.	.	.	37.0	26.0	30.0	38.0	40.0	40.0	.
25	.	.	.	40.0	40.0	.	40.0	40.0	40.0	.
26	.	.	.	32.0	30.0	32.0	31.0	30.5	39.0	.
28	.	.	.	32.0	22.0	30.0	34.0	28.7	38.0	.
29	.	.	.	.	5.0	5.0	5.0	.	.	.
31	.	.	.	.	10.0	10.0	.	40.0	40.0	.
35	.	.	.	34.0	34.0	34.0	36.0	35.5	34.0	.
36	.	.	.	27.0	26.0	28.0	27.0	27.9	26.0	.
37	.	.	.	.	.	.	.	.	35.0	.

Explanatory notes: see p. 721.

[1] 28 urban agglomerations. [2] Persons aged 10 years and over. [3] Second semester of each year. [4] Prior to 2003: May and October. [5] Last week of Aug. of each year.

Notes explicatives: voir p. 723.

[1] 28 agglomérations urbaines. [2] Personnes âgées de 10 ans et plus. [3] Second semestre de chaque année. [4] Avant 2003: mai et octobre. [5] Dernière semaine d'août de chaque année.

Notas explicativas: véase p. 725.

[1] 28 aglomerados úrbanos. [2] Personas de 10 años y más. [3] Segundo semestre de cada año. [4] Antes de 2003: mayo y octubre. [5] Ultima semana de agosto de cada año.

HOURS OF WORK   DURÉE DU TRAVAIL   HORAS DE TRABAJO

In manufacturing

Dans les industries manufacturières

En las industrias manufactureras

	Per week				Par semaine				Por semana	
	1999	2000	2001	2002	2003	2004	2005	2006	2007	2008
Bolivia (BA) (b)				**Total employment - Emploi total - Empleo total**						
Total men and women - Total hommes et femmes - Total hombres y mujeres										
ISIC 3 - CITI 3 - CIIU 3										
Total	43.9	47.0	39.8	45.4	.	43.2 ¹	46.4	45.2	46.7	.
Men - Hommes - Hombres										
ISIC 3 - CITI 3 - CIIU 3										
Total	48.8	49.6	44.9	49.5	.	48.4 ¹	49.4	49.9	50.4	.
Women - Femmes - Mujeres										
ISIC 3 - CITI 3 - CIIU 3										
Total	37.1	42.9	32.4	38.8	.	35.9 ¹	41.3	38.5	39.8	.
Brasil (BA) (c) ² ³				**Employees - Salariés - Asalariados**						
Total men and women - Total hommes et femmes - Total hombres y mujeres										
ISIC 3 - CITI 3 - CIIU 3										
Total	.	.	.	44.2 ⁴	44.2 ⁴	44.1	43.9	43.9	43.6	.
15	.	.	.	46.6 ⁴	46.1 ⁴	45.8	45.2	45.7	45.8	.
16	.	.	.	43.8 ⁴	44.1 ⁴	43.0	45.3	42.3	45.3	.
17	.	.	.	42.3 ⁴	42.8 ⁴	42.9	43.0	42.9	41.7	.
18	.	.	.	43.0 ⁴	43.3 ⁴	43.0	42.7	42.9	42.5	.
19	.	.	.	43.7 ⁴	43.3 ⁴	43.7	43.7	43.5	43.5	.
20	.	.	.	46.1 ⁴	46.3 ⁴	44.8	46.1	45.0	44.5	.
21	.	.	.	43.9 ⁴	43.9 ⁴	43.3	44.4	43.6	43.7	.
22	.	.	.	42.6 ⁴	41.8 ⁴	42.2	42.0	42.2	41.5	.
23	.	.	.	47.2 ⁴	48.2 ⁴	46.6	45.9	47.0	45.8	.
24	.	.	.	43.7 ⁴	44.1 ⁴	44.1	43.8	43.7	43.3	.
25	.	.	.	44.3 ⁴	43.6 ⁴	43.9	43.9	43.3	43.2	.
26	.	.	.	44.6 ⁴	44.9 ⁴	44.9	44.5	44.1	44.1	.
27	.	.	.	43.8 ⁴	44.0 ⁴	43.6	43.9	43.3	43.8	.
28	.	.	.	43.6 ⁴	43.8 ⁴	43.7	43.9	44.1	43.2	.
29	.	.	.	44.2 ⁴	44.2 ⁴	44.1	43.9	43.6	43.7	.
30	.	.	.	41.7 ⁴	41.8 ⁴	42.9	44.1	42.3	42.7	.
31	.	.	.	43.3 ⁴	43.6 ⁴	42.8	44.0	44.0	44.7	.
32	.	.	.	42.9 ⁴	43.1 ⁴	43.9	43.9	43.4	42.4	.
33	.	.	.	42.4 ⁴	41.9 ⁴	42.2	41.4	42.7	41.6	.
34	.	.	.	43.2 ⁴	43.5 ⁴	43.9	43.4	43.3	43.0	.
35	.	.	.	43.0 ⁴	44.8 ⁴	45.0	45.2	44.3	43.5	.
36	.	.	.	43.7 ⁴	43.0 ⁴	43.3	43.0	43.3	42.6	.
37	.	.	.	45.1 ⁴	42.7 ⁴	42.4	42.5	44.0	41.3	.
Men - Hommes - Hombres										
ISIC 3 - CITI 3 - CIIU 3										
Total	.	.	.	44.9 ⁴	44.8 ⁴	44.6	44.6	44.4	44.1	.
15	.	.	.	47.7 ⁴	46.9 ⁴	46.5	46.3	46.5	46.4	.
16	.	.	.	44.2 ⁴	45.0 ⁴	44.9	47.0	44.2	48.8	.
17	.	.	.	44.3 ⁴	44.4 ⁴	44.1	45.1	43.8	42.6	.
18	.	.	.	44.2 ⁴	43.6 ⁴	44.4	43.6	43.6	43.3	.
19	.	.	.	44.1 ⁴	43.9 ⁴	44.0	43.7	43.8	43.7	.
20	.	.	.	46.5 ⁴	46.7 ⁴	45.0	46.5	45.2	44.8	.
21	.	.	.	44.2 ⁴	44.6 ⁴	43.5	44.6	43.6	44.0	.
22	.	.	.	42.8 ⁴	42.3 ⁴	42.7	42.5	42.7	42.2	.
23	.	.	.	48.0 ⁴	48.5 ⁴	47.2	46.5	47.3	46.0	.
24	.	.	.	44.6 ⁴	44.8 ⁴	45.0	44.5	44.4	44.1	.
25	.	.	.	44.6 ⁴	44.2 ⁴	44.5	44.3	43.6	43.4	.
26	.	.	.	45.2 ⁴	45.1 ⁴	45.1	44.6	44.3	44.7	.
27	.	.	.	43.9 ⁴	44.4 ⁴	43.8	44.2	43.5	44.0	.
28	.	.	.	43.7 ⁴	43.8 ⁴	43.9	44.2	44.3	43.4	.
29	.	.	.	44.5 ⁴	44.5 ⁴	44.4	44.3	43.8	44.0	.
30	.	.	.	42.4 ⁴	41.7 ⁴	43.4	45.2	41.9	43.1	.
31	.	.	.	43.4 ⁴	43.9 ⁴	42.8	44.3	44.1	45.2	.
32	.	.	.	42.9 ⁴	43.2 ⁴	43.6	43.9	43.4	42.3	.
33	.	.	.	41.9 ⁴	41.6 ⁴	42.4	41.4	42.6	42.8	.
34	.	.	.	43.4 ⁴	43.7 ⁴	44.1	43.3	43.4	43.1	.
35	.	.	.	43.5 ⁴	45.1 ⁴	45.0	45.4	44.6	43.7	.
36	.	.	.	44.0 ⁴	43.8 ⁴	43.9	43.3	43.6	43.0	.
37	.	.	.	44.6 ⁴	42.1 ⁴	42.6	43.5	45.1	42.1	.

Explanatory notes: see p. 721.

¹ Continued Household survey, 2003-2004. ² Persons aged 10 years and over. ³ Sep. of each year. ⁴ Excl. rural population of Rondônia, Acre, Amazonas, Roraima, Pará and Amapá.

Notes explicatives: voir p. 723.

¹ Enquête continue des Ménages, 2003-2004. ² Personnes âgées de 10 ans et plus. ³ Sept. de chaque année. ⁴ Non compris la population rurale de Rondônia, Acre, Amazonas, Roraima, Pará et Amapá.

Notas explicativas: véase p. 725.

¹ Encuesta continua de hogares, 2003-2004. ² Personas de 10 años y más. ³ Sept. de cada año. ⁴ Excl. la población rural de Rondonia, Acre, Amazonas, Roraima, Pará y Amapá.

In manufacturing — Dans les industries manufacturières — En las industrias manufactureras

	Per week — Par semaine — Por semana									
	1999	2000	2001	2002	2003	2004	2005	2006	2007	2008

Brasil (BA) (c) [1][2]   Employees - Salariés - Asalariados

Women - Femmes - Mujeres
ISIC 3 - CITI 3 - CIIU 3

	1999	2000	2001	2002	2003	2004	2005	2006	2007	2008
Total	.	.	.	42.5 [3]	42.7 [3]	42.7	42.4	42.7	42.3	.
15	.	.	.	43.8 [3]	44.2 [3]	44.1	42.6	43.7	44.3	.
16	.	.	.	42.9 [3]	42.2 [3]	39.2	42.1	40.6	40.0	.
17	.	.	.	40.1 [3]	40.9 [3]	41.2	40.6	41.7	40.6	.
18	.	.	.	42.7 [3]	43.2 [3]	42.6	42.4	42.7	42.3	.
19	.	.	.	43.1 [3]	42.7 [3]	43.3	43.6	43.1	43.3	.
20	.	.	.	43.0 [3]	43.2 [3]	43.3	43.4	43.6	42.9	.
21	.	.	.	43.1 [3]	41.2 [3]	42.9	43.8	43.4	43.1	.
22	.	.	.	42.1 [3]	40.8 [3]	41.1	41.0	41.4	40.1	.
23	.	.	.	42.1 [3]	44.7 [3]	42.4	41.4	44.1	44.2	.
24	.	.	.	41.2 [3]	42.4 [3]	42.1	42.1	41.7	41.3	.
25	.	.	.	43.2 [3]	41.7 [3]	41.9	42.6	42.4	42.1	.
26	.	.	.	40.7 [3]	43.6 [3]	42.9	43.2	42.1	40.4	.
27	.	.	.	42.8 [3]	41.1 [3]	41.5	40.8	41.4	41.7	.
28	.	.	.	42.6 [3]	43.2 [3]	42.2	41.5	42.5	41.8	.
29	.	.	.	42.4 [3]	41.9 [3]	42.1	41.2	42.7	41.8	.
30	.	.	.	40.7 [3]	42.1 [3]	41.3	42.8	43.0	42.0	.
31	.	.	.	43.0 [3]	42.3 [3]	42.6	42.9	43.7	43.0	.
32	.	.	.	42.8 [3]	42.9 [3]	44.3	43.9	43.2	42.6	.
33	.	.	.	43.3 [3]	42.7 [3]	41.6	41.4	42.9	39.2	.
34	.	.	.	42.3 [3]	42.5 [3]	42.8	43.7	42.7	42.4	.
35	.	.	.	37.8 [3]	42.0 [3]	45.1	44.0	41.1	41.9	.
36	.	.	.	42.3 [3]	40.9 [3]	41.2	41.8	42.1	41.1	.
37	.	.	.	45.9 [3]	43.9 [3]	41.4	39.9	41.3	39.3	.

Canada (DA) (b) [4][5]   Wage earners - Ouvriers - Obreros

Total men and women - Total hommes et femmes - Total hombres y mujeres
ISIC 3 - CITI 3 - CIIU 3

	1999	2000	2001	2002	2003	2004	2005	2006	2007	2008
Total	38.8	38.8	38.2	38.3	38.1	37.9	37.9	37.9	38.0	37.2
15	36.4	35.3	36.5	37.2	37.6	36.1	35.9	36.5	36.4	35.3
16	43.3	40.4	38.1	34.8	37.5	38.7	42.3	44.5	41.3	.
17	36.9	37.8	40.4	39.0	39.3	36.9	37.2	36.1	37.8	34.2
18	36.7	37.4	38.3	36.6	37.2	34.9	36.8	37.1	38.6	34.8
19	37.2	37.3	37.5	36.7	36.3	33.6	35.0	35.3	37.3	33.3
20	39.3	40.1	38.3	38.3	37.4	37.7	38.1	36.8	38.0	37.0
21	39.9	39.7	39.4	39.6	38.8	39.0	38.4	38.8	38.3	37.3
22	34.6	34.3	32.5	34.0	33.6	32.9	33.1	32.4	32.8	34.0
23	39.8	43.1	40.7	39.7	40.8	40.4	39.0	38.2	39.3	39.9
24	39.2	41.6	38.4	38.4	38.9	38.8	38.0	37.9	38.8	39.4
25	38.9	38.8	39.3	40.0	39.3	40.7	40.8	39.7	38.7	38.5
26	40.0	39.8	36.7	38.1	40.0	38.4	38.6	37.8	37.7	37.5
27	40.5	40.3	40.7	39.8	39.3	39.6	39.8	39.2	40.6	40.5
28	39.7	39.6	39.6	38.8	38.2	38.4	38.2	38.5	39.0	37.0
29	40.3	40.5	40.0	40.5	39.9	40.0	40.0	39.6	37.7	37.5
30	37.7	38.3	37.9	38.8	37.1	37.4	38.3	38.9	39.6	38.9
31	38.4	38.8	37.0	38.3	38.5	38.4	38.0	37.6	37.8	38.3
32	38.9	40.0	35.5	35.9	35.8	35.0	36.2	37.5	38.1	37.5
33	38.2	38.0	36.3	37.7	38.2	36.7	36.9	37.9	37.7	37.0
34	41.3	41.0	39.8	40.2	39.6	39.9	39.3	39.4	39.8	37.1
34-35	41.4	41.0	39.9	39.9	39.4	39.8	39.5	39.6	39.9	38.4
35	41.7	40.8	40.1	39.0	38.8	39.6	40.0	40.4	40.1	39.4
36	37.9	38.3	37.7	36.3	36.3	36.7	36.4	37.8	39.0	38.7
37	37.0	36.2	34.4	35.3	35.6	34.6	35.5	37.2	36.3	36.3

Colombia (BA) (a) [1][6][7]   Employees - Salariés - Asalariados

Total men and women - Total hommes et femmes - Total hombres y mujeres
ISIC 3 - CITI 3 - CIIU 3

	1999	2000	2001	2002	2003	2004	2005	2006	2007	2008
Total	.	.	.	41.6	41.6	42.7	43.6	46.6	45.1 [7]	.

Men - Hommes - Hombres
ISIC 3 - CITI 3 - CIIU 3

	1999	2000	2001	2002	2003	2004	2005	2006	2007	2008
Total	.	.	.	46.5	46.4	46.3	47.1	49.5	49.2 [7]	.

Women - Femmes - Mujeres
ISIC 3 - CITI 3 - CIIU 3

	1999	2000	2001	2002	2003	2004	2005	2006	2007	2008
Total	.	.	.	36.8	36.2	38.2	39.6	42.8	40.0 [7]	.

Explanatory notes: see p. 721.

[1] Persons aged 10 years and over. [2] Sep. of each year. [3] Excl. rural population of Rondônia, Acre, Amazonas, Roraima, Pará and Amapá. [4] Employees paid by the hour. [5] Incl. overtime. [6] Excl. armed forces. [7] Third quarter.

Notes explicatives: voir p. 723.

[1] Personnes âgées de 10 ans et plus. [2] Sept. de chaque année. [3] Non compris la population rurale de Rondônia, Acre, Amazonas, Roraima, Pará et Amapá. [4] Salariés rémunérés à l'heure. [5] Y compris les heures supplémentaires. [6] Non compris les forces armées. [7] Troisième trimestre.

Notas explicativas: véase p. 725.

[1] Personas de 10 años y más. [2] Sept. de cada año. [3] Excl. la población rural de Rondonia, Acre, Amazonas, Roraima, Pará y Amapá. [4] Asalariados remunerados por hora. [5] Incl. las horas extraordinarias. [6] Excl. las fuerzas armadas. [7] Tercer trimestre.

Per week — Par semaine — Por semana

Costa Rica (BA) (a) [1] — Total employment - Emploi total - Empleo total

Total men and women - Total hommes et femmes - Total hombres y mujeres
ISIC 3 - CITI 3 - CIIU 3

	1999	2000	2001	2002	2003	2004	2005	2006	2007	2008
Total	49.1	48.9	49.0	50.0	49.0	47.4	46.7	46.1	47.6	47.4
15	49.8	49.9	51.0	52.0	50.0	51.0	50.5	49.3	50.2	49.7
16	50.5	.	.	57.0	47.0	56.0	60.0	.	49.1	48.0
17	45.3	48.8	48.0	49.0	48.0	46.0	34.7	37.6	37.1	37.4
18	48.9	47.7	48.0	48.0	48.0	47.0	35.5	36.0	37.4	37.7
19	46.7	51.2	49.0	48.0	40.0	45.0	45.5	45.8	51.2	44.9
20	49.7	47.7	52.0	50.0	49.0	50.0	47.9	50.1	48.1	49.4
21	55.7	50.9	52.0	51.0	53.0	55.0	52.9	52.1	53.5	53.5
22	44.2	48.9	51.0	47.0	48.0	49.0	47.2	46.5	51.5	46.8
23	45.8	45.6	.	40.0	.	.	40.0	.	51.3	48.0
24	50.0	46.7	46.0	47.0	49.0	50.0	47.7	48.9	49.8	48.3
25	50.6	50.2	50.0	49.0	51.0	53.0	50.3	48.9	51.3	53.7
26	49.5	49.6	49.0	49.0	50.0	50.0	42.8	50.3	51.4	50.2
27	48.9	60.0	53.0	54.0	47.0	48.0	50.0	46.9	54.8	54.1
28	50.9	48.9	49.0	51.0	49.0	50.0	50.2	46.4	49.7	48.0
29	56.2	44.8	47.0	50.0	50.0	51.0	46.7	47.4	46.7	45.1
30	47.0	50.0	49.0	52.0	48.0	52.0	55.4	.	45.1	48.0
31	46.9	44.4	47.0	49.0	48.0	47.0	49.2	46.0	45.9	48.3
32	48.2	47.7	48.0	49.0	47.0	46.0	49.6	46.2	48.2	47.1
33	48.0	47.7	48.0	48.0	48.0	48.0	49.7	49.4	46.3	48.1
34	54.4	52.8	49.0	49.0	45.0	50.0	54.2	54.8	53.4	49.1
35	46.1	50.9	48.0	48.0	53.0	47.0	51.2	51.9	48.8	48.4
36	47.9	48.8	48.0	49.0	49.0	48.0	46.4	44.5	49.1	50.5
37	37.9	54.4	50.0	50.0	49.0	66.0	60.1	35.3	40.8	43.1

Men - Hommes - Hombres
ISIC 3 - CITI 3 - CIIU 3

	1999	2000	2001	2002	2003	2004	2005	2006	2007	2008
Total	50.5	49.6	51.0	51.0	50.0	51.0	50.3	49.4	51.0	51.3
15	52.2	51.3	53.0	53.0	52.0	53.0	55.1	52.5	52.6	52.9
16	50.5	.	.	61.0	42.0	56.0	60.0	.	50.1	48.0
17	46.0	49.9	48.0	49.0	48.0	48.0	39.3	45.9	46.6	50.1
18	49.2	47.6	49.0	49.0	48.0	49.0	45.0	45.2	48.4	50.2
19	49.1	52.9	50.0	47.0	41.0	44.0	46.5	45.6	54.8	46.2
20	49.7	47.8	52.0	51.0	49.0	50.0	48.9	51.1	48.9	51.6
21	56.8	51.0	52.0	51.0	56.0	57.0	58.1	54.4	56.6	54.5
22	48.3	49.6	51.0	49.0	52.0	50.0	49.0	47.3	52.9	50.2
23	47.7	46.0	.	.	.	.	.	.	53.0	48.0
24	51.0	47.9	48.0	48.0	49.0	50.0	47.4	50.5	50.7	49.4
25	50.9	50.7	51.0	50.0	51.0	55.0	50.7	50.6	51.3	54.1
26	51.9	50.5	50.0	50.0	51.0	52.0	44.8	51.5	53.2	51.6
27	48.9	60.0	53.0	54.0	47.0	50.0	50.0	46.9	54.8	53.0
28	51.6	48.8	49.0	51.0	49.0	50.0	50.4	46.9	49.9	49.6
29	56.2	44.8	48.0	49.0	51.0	51.0	48.4	47.6	49.0	49.2
30	47.1	49.2	49.0	52.0	48.0	54.0	53.9	.	46.5	48.0
31	46.9	44.6	46.0	49.0	49.0	67.0	50.5	47.2	46.7	48.4
32	48.1	47.5	45.0	48.0	47.0	46.0	49.0	46.3	48.3	46.9
33	48.2	47.5	52.0	47.0	47.0	48.0	50.2	49.0	50.6	49.7
34	54.4	52.8	51.0	53.0	43.0	51.0	54.3	54.8	53.8	52.1
35	48.8	50.9	50.0	48.0	53.0	47.0	51.2	52.2	48.8	48.4
36	48.9	48.9	49.0	50.0	50.0	49.0	47.1	46.0	49.9	51.9
37	37.9	54.4	50.0	50.0	49.0	66.0	74.9	49.1	44.5	38.5

Women - Femmes - Mujeres
ISIC 3 - CITI 3 - CIIU 3

	1999	2000	2001	2002	2003	2004	2005	2006	2007	2008
Total	45.8	47.2	47.0	47.0	47.0	39.4	38.2	38.8	40.4	51.3
15	44.1	45.6	47.0	47.0	47.0	45.0	39.3	42.0	45.4	44.1
16	.	.	.	44.0	.	.	.	.	48.0	.
17	44.8	47.7	48.0	49.0	47.0	42.0	31.5	32.0	30.4	32.3
18	48.6	47.8	47.0	47.0	47.0	46.0	31.2	32.8	35.2	35.2
19	42.4	46.6	48.0	50.0	33.0	47.0	32.9	48.0	45.4	41.0
20	50.3	46.4	49.0	37.0	48.0	50.0	29.3	45.7	38.6	37.5
21	50.8	50.7	47.0	50.0	47.0	48.0	34.8	42.2	46.1	51.0
22	34.4	47.1	46.0	37.0	42.0	47.0	42.5	43.7	47.9	39.1
23	40.0	43.1	.	40.0	.	.	40.0	.	48.0	.
24	47.9	45.2	43.0	46.0	47.0	49.0	48.8	44.4	45.3	45.9
25	49.4	49.0	49.0	47.0	51.0	46.0	47.4	42.3	51.0	49.9
26	36.1	44.9	46.0	43.0	44.0	33.0	35.2	41.7	41.1	41.9
27	.	.	48.0	.	45.0	38.0	.	.	.	58.0
28	34.1	50.0	48.0	48.0	50.0	44.0	48.1	37.2	44.8	26.3
29	.	.	46.0	52.0	50.0	50.0	42.1	47.1	33.4	29.9
30	46.7	51.3	48.0	.	.	48.0	56.0	.	42.7	48.0
31	.	44.0	48.0	48.0	47.0	44.0	46.1	43.0	43.9	48.0
32	48.7	48.1	50.0	51.0	48.0	48.0	50.3	45.8	47.8	48.0
33	47.5	48.0	46.0	48.0	49.0	48.0	49.2	49.7	41.1	46.0
34	.	.	43.0	42.0	48.0	49.0	54.0	.	48.0	45.0
35	.	.	40.0	.	.	.	.	48.0	.	48.0
36	39.3	47.9	45.0	45.0	44.0	47.0	38.9	33.8	42.0	35.7
37	.	.	.	.	.	.	38.5	10.1	20.0	46.1

Explanatory notes: see p. 721.   Notes explicatives: voir p. 723.   Notas explicativas: véase p. 725.

[1] Main occupation; July of each year.   [1] Occupation principale; juillet de chaque année.   [1] Ocupación principal; julio de cada año.

In manufacturing — Dans les industries manufacturières — En las industrias manufactureras

Per week — Par semaine — Por semana

	1999	2000	2001	2002	2003	2004	2005	2006	2007	2008
Cuba (F) (a)					Employees - Salariés - Asalariados					
Total men and women - Total hommes et femmes - Total hombres y mujeres										
ISIC 2 - CITI 2 - CIIU 2										
Total	41	41	41	40	40	41	41	42	41	41
31	42	43	43	42	42	42	.	.	.	.
32	33	33	33	32	33	34	.	.	.	.
33	36	35	38	35	38	38	.	.	.	.
34	37	38	38	44	41	39	.	.	.	.
35	40	40	40	40	39	40	.	.	.	.
351	41	40	41	40	41	41	.	.	.	.
352	41	42	44	43	45	42	.	.	.	.
353	39	39	40	39	39	39	.	.	.	.
Chile (BA) (a) [1] [2]					Total employment - Emploi total - Empleo total					
Total men and women - Total hommes et femmes - Total hombres y mujeres										
ISIC 2 - CITI 2 - CIIU 2										
Total	43.2 [3]	43.6 [3]	43.6	44.1	43.3 [3]	43.0	42.0	42.0	41.7	40.3
Men - Hommes - Hombres										
ISIC 2 - CITI 2 - CIIU 2										
Total	44.7 [3]	45.1 [3]	45.3	45.7	45.1 [3]	44.8	43.6	43.9	43.4	42.1
Women - Femmes - Mujeres										
ISIC 2 - CITI 2 - CIIU 2										
Total	39.0 [3]	39.4 [3]	38.8	39.4	38.1 [3]	38.1	37.7	36.9	36.8	35.8
República Dominicana (BA) (c)					Total employment - Emploi total - Empleo total					
Total men and women - Total hommes et femmes - Total hombres y mujeres										
ISIC 3 - CITI 3 - CIIU 3										
Total	.	.	.	.	.	42.0	43.1	42.0	43.0	.
15	.	.	.	.	.	42.4	42.4	43.1	42.7	.
16	.	.	.	.	.	42.9	44.7	43.7	44.9	.
17	.	.	.	.	.	39.3	38.7	41.4	39.6	.
18	.	.	.	.	.	43.4	43.5	43.2	43.1	.
19	.	.	.	.	.	44.0	46.4	46.4	42.3	.
20	.	.	.	.	.	35.4	36.6	40.0	42.7	.
21	.	.	.	.	.	46.5	45.3	42.6	42.2	.
22	.	.	.	.	.	41.6	41.3	40.7	42.0	.
23	.	.	.	.	.	38.0	39.3	36.1	40.7	.
24	.	.	.	.	.	42.8	42.7	43.6	44.0	.
25	.	.	.	.	.	44.9	46.0	43.2	45.4	.
26	.	.	.	.	.	42.0	42.7	38.6	43.4	.
27	.	.	.	.	.	47.6	47.9	46.7	47.1	.
28	.	.	.	.	.	38.9	40.5	43.0	38.6	.
29	.	.	.	.	.	36.8	43.0	36.3	46.2	.
30	.	.	.	.	.	42.7	.	.	43.0	.
31	.	.	.	.	.	43.5	46.1	43.7	44.4	.
32	.	.	.	.	.	41.1	44.1	43.5	44.4	.
33	.	.	.	.	.	42.4	43.9	41.9	43.6	.
34	.	.	.	.	.	43.9	49.3	38.2	44.7	.
35	.	.	.	.	.	44.5	47.2	43.0	41.8	.
36	.	.	.	.	.	38.1	36.7	39.9	37.6	.
37	.	.	.	.	.	48.8	36.1	36.5	.	.
Men - Hommes - Hombres										
ISIC 3 - CITI 3 - CIIU 3										
Total	.	.	.	.	.	43.3	45.2	42.8	44.1	.
15	.	.	.	.	.	46.1	46.4	46.5	45.3	.
16	.	.	.	.	.	42.6	45.5	42.4	44.6	.
17	.	.	.	.	.	43.2	44.3	45.0	43.7	.
18	.	.	.	.	.	45.0	45.0	45.2	44.5	.
19	.	.	.	.	.	44.9	46.3	45.3	42.4	.
20	.	.	.	.	.	36.8	45.1	42.1	40.5	.
21	.	.	.	.	.	46.1	45.9	47.9	45.5	.
22	.	.	.	.	.	41.8	42.2	42.3	43.8	.
23	.	.	.	.	.	38.0	38.0	36.1	40.7	.
24	.	.	.	.	.	43.8	45.1	45.0	45.0	.
25	.	.	.	.	.	47.8	48.6	45.9	47.7	.
26	.	.	.	.	.	45.8	47.0	43.6	46.1	.
27	.	.	.	.	.	47.6	47.9	46.7	47.1	.
28	.	.	.	.	.	41.4	41.7	43.4	40.8	.
29	.	.	.	.	.	41.3	44.4	36.3	47.9	.
30	.	.	.	.	.	42.5	.	.	43.1	.
31	.	.	.	.	.	42.8	46.4	41.9	44.6	.
32	.	.	.	.	.	39.6	46.3	44.0	44.6	.
33	.	.	.	.	.	41.5	43.2	40.1	43.3	.
34	.	.	.	.	.	45.9	52.1	34.5	47.0	.
35	.	.	.	.	.	46.0	47.2	43.0	40.6	.
36	.	.	.	.	.	41.6	40.6	41.9	41.4	.
37	.	.	.	.	.	.	.	.	.	.

Explanatory notes: see p. 721.   Notes explicatives: voir p. 723.   Notas explicativas: véase p. 725.

[1] Excl. armed forces. [2] Persons aged 15 years and over. [3] Oct.-Dec.   [1] Non compris les forces armées. [2] Personnes âgées de 15 ans et plus. [3] Oct.-déc.   [1] Excl. las fuerzas armadas. [2] Personas de 15 años y más. [3] Oct.-dic.

HOURS OF WORK   DURÉE DU TRAVAIL   HORAS DE TRABAJO

In manufacturing   Dans les industries manufacturières   En las industrias manufactureras

	Per week					Par semaine			Por semana	
	1999	2000	2001	2002	2003	2004	2005	2006	2007	2008

República Dominicana (BA) (c)   Total employment - Emploi total - Empleo total

Women - Femmes - Mujeres
ISIC 3 - CITI 3 - CIIU 3

	1999	2000	2001	2002	2003	2004	2005	2006	2007	2008
Total	.	.	.	.	.	40.7	41.1	41.2	41.9	.
15	.	.	.	.	.	38.6	38.4	39.8	40.0	.
16	.	.	.	.	.	43.2	44.0	44.9	45.3	.
17	.	.	.	.	.	35.4	33.2	37.9	35.4	.
18	.	.	.	.	.	41.9	42.0	41.2	41.7	.
19	.	.	.	.	.	43.1	46.6	47.6	42.1	.
20	.	.	.	.	.	34.0	28.1	38.0	44.8	.
21	.	.	.	.	.	46.9	44.6	37.2	38.9	.
22	.	.	.	.	.	41.5	40.4	39.1	40.1	.
23	.	.	.	.	.	.	40.5			.
24	.	.	.	.	.	41.9	40.3	42.2	42.9	.
25	.	.	.	.	.	41.9	43.4	40.5	43.2	.
26	.	.	.	.	.	.				.
27	.	.	.	.	.	.				.
28	.	.	.	.	.	36.4	39.3	42.6	36.4	.
29	.	.	.	.	.	32.4	41.6	.	44.6	.
30	.	.	.	.	.	43.0	.	.	43.0	.
31	.	.	.	.	.	44.2	45.8	45.4	44.2	.
32	.	.	.	.	.	42.6	42.0	43.0	44.1	.
33	.	.	.	.	.	43.3	44.6	43.7	43.8	.
34	.	.	.	.	.	42.0	46.4	41.9	42.4	.
35	.	.	.	.	.	43.0	.	.	43.0	.
36	.	.	.	.	.	34.5	32.7	37.8	33.9	.
37	.	.	.	.	.	.				.

República Dominicana (BA) (c)   Employees - Salariés - Asalariados

Total men and women - Total hommes et femmes - Total hombres y mujeres
ISIC 3 - CITI 3 - CIIU 3

	1999	2000	2001	2002	2003	2004	2005	2006	2007	2008
Total	46.2	45.4	45.1	44.0	44.8	44.4				

Ecuador (BA) (a)   Total employment - Emploi total - Empleo total

Total men and women - Total hommes et femmes - Total hombres y mujeres
ISIC 3 - CITI 3 - CIIU 3

	1999	2000	2001	2002	2003	2004	2005	2006	2007	2008
Total	.	.	.	.	.	45	45	46	.	.
15	.	.	.	.	.	44	45	46	.	.
16	.	.	.	.	.	47	51	50	.	.
17	.	.	.	.	.	44	44	45	.	.
18	.	.	.	.	.	41	41	42	.	.
19	.	.	.	.	.	42	48	44	.	.
20	.	.	.	.	.	40	42	47	.	.
21	.	.	.	.	.	50	49	52	.	.
22	.	.	.	.	.	48	44	47	.	.
23	.	.	.	.	.	49	50	53	.	.
24	.	.	.	.	.	45	46	42	.	.
25	.	.	.	.	.	57	49	56	.	.
26	.	.	.	.	.	46	44	40	.	.
27	.	.	.	.	.	50	45	49	.	.
28	.	.	.	.	.	44	44	45	.	.
29	.	.	.	.	.	47	46	49	.	.
30	.	.	.	.	.	.			.	.
31	.	.	.	.	.	51	37	48	.	.
32	.	.	.	.	.	51	40	26	.	.
33	.	.	.	.	.	43	37	38	.	.
34	.	.	.	.	.	46	46	53	.	.
35	.	.	.	.	.	37	36	38	.	.
36	.	.	.	.	.	41	46	44	.	.
37	.	.	.	.	.	49	36	36	.	.

Explanatory notes: see p. 721.   Notes explicatives: voir p. 723.   Notas explicativas: véase p. 725.

HOURS OF WORK — DURÉE DU TRAVAIL — HORAS DE TRABAJO 4B

In manufacturing — Dans les industries manufacturières — En las industrias manufactureras

Per week — Par semaine — Por semana

	1999	2000	2001	2002	2003	2004	2005	2006	2007	2008
Ecuador (BA) (a)					Total employment - Emploi total - Empleo total					
Men - Hommes - Hombres										
ISIC 3 - CITI 3 - CIIU 3										
Total	.	.	.	.	.	45	48	48	.	.
15	.	.	.	.	.	53	53	54	.	.
16	.	.	.	.	.	57	47	55	.	.
17	.	.	.	.	.	49	47	48	.	.
18	.	.	.	.	.	50	46	48	.	.
19	.	.	.	.	.	44	51	44	.	.
20	.	.	.	.	.	41	42	48	.	.
21	.	.	.	.	.	59	48	52	.	.
22	.	.	.	.	.	51	47	48	.	.
23	.	.	.	.	.	49	51	56	.	.
24	.	.	.	.	.	49	49	44	.	.
25	.	.	.	.	.	58	50	58	.	.
26	.	.	.	.	.	48	47	42	.	.
27	.	.	.	.	.	49	45	50	.	.
28	.	.	.	.	.	44	45	45	.	.
29	.	.	.	.	.	47	45	51	.	.
30	.	.	.	.	.	.	.	.	.	.
31	.	.	.	.	.	49	39	48	.	.
32	.	.	.	.	.	51	29	26	.	.
33	.	.	.	.	.	65	37	38	.	.
34	.	.	.	.	.	46	47	53	.	.
35	.	.	.	.	.	41	36	38	.	.
36	.	.	.	.	.	44	48	46	.	.
37	.	.	.	.	.	51	40	39	.	.
Women - Femmes - Mujeres										
ISIC 3 - CITI 3 - CIIU 3										
Total	.	.	.	.	.	44	40	41	.	.
15	.	.	.	.	.	38	46	43	.	.
16	.	.	.	.	.	42	41	.	.	.
17	.	.	.	.	.	39	38	43	.	.
18	.	.	.	.	.	38	38	39	.	.
19	.	.	.	.	.	39	44	44	.	.
20	.	.	.	.	.	35	41	42	.	.
21	.	.	.	.	.	40	51	50	.	.
22	.	.	.	.	.	42	39	44	.	.
23	.	.	.	.	.	.	44	30	.	.
24	.	.	.	.	.	39	37	38	.	.
25	.	.	.	.	.	52	48	46	.	.
26	.	.	.	.	.	40	36	37	.	.
27	.	.	.	.	.	84	45	46	.	.
28	.	.	.	.	.	34	33	44	.	.
29	.	.	.	.	.	44	48	41	.	.
30	.	.	.	.	.	.	.	.	.	.
31	.	.	.	.	.	58	8	.	.	.
32	.	.	.	.	.	.	84	.	.	.
33	.	.	.	.	.	36	37	.	.	.
34	.	.	.	.	.	.	41	40	.	.
35	.	.	.	.	.	15	.	.	.	.
36	.	.	.	.	.	32	38	35	.	.
37	.	.	.	.	.	42	31	28	.	.
El Salvador (DA) (a) [1]					Wage earners - Ouvriers - Obreros					
Men - Hommes - Hombres										
ISIC 2 - CITI 2 - CIIU 2										
31	47.3	50.0	.	.	.	.	.	.	.	.
32	48.7	49.0	.	.	.	.	.	.	.	.
33	44.4	44.0	.	.	.	.	.	.	.	.
34	49.4	48.0	.	.	.	.	.	.	.	.
35	51.2	52.0	.	.	.	.	.	.	.	.
36	50.8	48.0	.	.	.	.	.	.	.	.
37	47.9	49.0	.	.	.	.	.	.	.	.
38	45.5	45.0	.	.	.	.	.	.	.	.
39	44.6	45.0	.	.	.	.	.	.	.	.
Women - Femmes - Mujeres										
ISIC 2 - CITI 2 - CIIU 2										
Total	.	.	.	.	.	.	.	.	.	.
31	45.0	48.0	.	.	.	.	.	.	.	.
32	47.7	48.0	.	.	.	.	.	.	.	.
33	39.5	44.0	.	.	.	.	.	.	.	.
34	53.9	48.0	.	.	.	.	.	.	.	.
35	46.2	48.0	.	.	.	.	.	.	.	.
36	53.4	44.0	.	.	.	.	.	.	.	.
37	41.3	44.0	.	.	.	.	.	.	.	.
38	45.7	44.0	.	.	.	.	.	.	.	.
39	44.3	45.0	.	.	.	.	.	.	.	.

Explanatory notes: see p. 721.   Notes explicatives: voir p. 723.   Notas explicativas: véase p. 725.

[1] Urban areas.   [1] Régions urbaines.   [1] Areas urbanas.

HOURS OF WORK   DURÉE DU TRAVAIL   HORAS DE TRABAJO

In manufacturing   Dans les industries manufacturières   En las industrias manufactureras

Per week — Par semaine — Por semana

	1999	2000	2001	2002	2003	2004	2005	2006	2007	2008
El Salvador (DA) (a) [1]					**Wage earners - Ouvriers - Obreros**					
Total men and women - Total hommes et femmes - Total hombres y mujeres										
ISIC 3 - CITI 3 - CIIU 3										
Total	.	.	45.0	52.0	46.0	47.0	48.0	50.0	48.0	53.0
15-16	.	.	.	58.0	49.0	49.0	48.0	56.0	51.0	49.0
17-19	.	.	45.0	52.0	46.0	46.0	47.0	48.0	46.0	64.0
20	.	.	.	46.0	43.0	47.0	44.0	47.0	44.0	44.0
21-22	.	.	46.0	52.0	50.0	50.0	39.0	58.0	51.0	48.0
23-25	.	.	50.0	51.0	50.0	49.0	42.0	46.0	52.0	53.0
26	.	.	42.0	53.0	47.0	48.0	44.0	45.0	47.0	45.0
27	.	.	47.0	50.0	47.0	45.0	51.0	44.0	68.0	49.0
28-34	.	.	45.0	43.0	43.0	48.0	45.0	47.0	46.0	47.0
36	.	.	.	.	.	.	.	.	.	48.0
Men - Hommes - Hombres										
ISIC 3 - CITI 3 - CIIU 3										
Total	.	.	46.0	51.0	47.0	48.0	49.0	50.0	50.0	51.0
15-16	.	.	46.0	.	48.0	51.0	50.0	56.0	52.0	49.0
17-19	.	.	45.0	48.0	47.0	47.0	47.0	48.0	48.0	59.0
21-22	.	.	47.0	52.0	46.0	52.0	37.0	60.0	50.0	48.0
23-25	.	.	50.0	52.0	51.0	50.0	40.0	46.0	53.0	55.0
26	.	.	42.0	53.0	47.0	47.0	44.0	45.0	48.0	45.0
27	.	.	47.0	50.0	47.0	45.0	51.0	44.0	68.0	50.0
28-34	.	.	45.0	42.0	43.0	48.0	44.0	46.0	46.0	47.0
36	.	.	44.0	46.0	45.0	48.0	44.0	48.0	46.0	49.0
Women - Femmes - Mujeres										
ISIC 3 - CITI 3 - CIIU 3										
Total	.	.	45.0	54.0	46.0	46.0	47.0	49.0	47.0	55.0
15-16	.	.	46.0	63.0	49.0	46.0	46.0	55.0	49.0	48.0
17-19	.	.	45.0	53.0	46.0	45.0	47.0	49.0	45.0	67.0
20	.	.	44.0	46.0	39.0	45.0	44.0	44.0	40.0	44.0
21-22	.	.	45.0	52.0	56.0	47.0	42.0	45.0	54.0	46.0
23-25	.	.	47.0	48.0	47.0	48.0	44.0	48.0	51.0	51.0
26	.	.	.	44.0	44.0	48.0	44.0	44.0	44.0	44.0
27	.	.	46.0	51.0	44.0	44.0	48.0	.	44.0	44.0
28-34	.	.	44.0	44.0	44.0	48.0	46.0	48.0	44.0	47.0
36	.	.	.	.	.	.	.	.	.	46.0
Guyana (DA) (b)					**Salaried employees - Employés - Empleados**					
Total men and women - Total hommes et femmes - Total hombres y mujeres										
ISIC 3 - CITI 3 - CIIU 3										
Total	.	.	.	.	45	.	.	45	55 [2]	.
México (BA) (d) [3][4]					**Employees - Salariés - Asalariados**					
Total men and women - Total hommes et femmes - Total hombres y mujeres										
ISIC 3 - CITI 3 - CIIU 3										
Total	45.5	44.4	44.0	45.2	44.5	44.8	46.5 [5]	45.4	45.5	46.4
15	48.8	47.5	46.9	47.6	47.8	47.3	49.5 [5]	48.1	47.8	48.5
16	44.2	44.2	44.5	47.4	46.2	45.0	.	.	.	.
17	42.6	41.8	41.4	42.2	40.2	41.7	46.3 [5]	44.5	44.3	45.3
18	44.4	43.3	42.9	44.3	44.3	44.0	. [5]	40.2	43.9	42.9
19	44.4	42.8	43.0	44.0	42.9	42.8	45.9 [5]	44.8	44.2	46.0
20	45.7	43.9	44.3	44.6	43.7	44.5	45.5 [5]	43.4	45.6	46.5
21	44.6	44.1	44.7	45.2	45.4	45.3	47.2 [5]	45.0	45.8	47.4
22	43.7	44.5	42.8	44.7	43.5	43.4	46.4 [5]	44.5	44.9	46.7
23	44.6	43.8	43.9	45.2	45.2	44.4	47.3 [5]	45.5	44.4	43.8
24	43.3	41.0	41.5	42.4	40.8	41.1	42.0 [5]	43.7	44.3	45.4
25	44.8	44.2	43.8	46.0	44.9	45.8	47.1 [5]	45.5	45.1	46.9
26	46.5	45.1	44.5	45.4	44.3	44.6	46.7 [5]	45.5	45.4	45.3
27	46.4	45.0	46.1	46.1	.	47.4	47.4 [5]	46.5	46.8	47.8
28	46.2	44.7	44.8	45.8	44.2	44.8	46.9 [5]	45.4	45.6	46.4
29	44.1	44.7	43.5	45.4	42.8	44.6	46.7 [5]	45.5	46.2	47.1
30	46.0	43.3	43.0	46.2	44.0	45.2	44.9 [5]	44.2	44.9	45.0
31	45.0	43.5	42.3	44.8	44.0	44.9	46.0 [5]	44.9	44.5	45.7
32	44.9	44.2	44.3	44.6	44.5	44.1	.	.	.	.
33	44.1	44.4	44.7	43.9	42.6	43.7	43.3 [5]	44.2	43.3	43.5
34	45.1	44.8	43.2	45.1	43.9	44.3	46.3 [5]	45.0	45.1	45.8
35	50.5	44.3	42.6	45.8	45.6	45.3	.	.	.	.
36	45.2	43.4	43.9	44.5	42.9	44.6	45.8 [5]	44.0	45.1	46.0
37	.	.	.	.	.	.	. [5]	.	.	.

Explanatory notes: see p. 721.

[1] Urban areas. [2] July. [3] Persons aged 14 years and over. [4] Second quarter of each year. [5] Revised averages based on 2005 Population and Housing Census results; data not comparable.

Notes explicatives: voir p. 723.

[1] Régions urbaines. [2] Juillet. [3] Personnes âgées de 14 ans et plus. [4] Deuxième trimestre de chaque année. [5] Moyennes révisées sur la base des résultats du recensement de population et de l'habitat de 2005;les données ne sont pas comparables

Notas explicativas: véase p. 725.

[1] Areas urbanas. [2] Julio. [3] Personas de 14 años y más. [4] Segundo trimestre de cada año. [5] Promedios revisados de acuerdo con los resultados del censo de población y Vivienda de 2005; datos no comparables.

In manufacturing   Dans les industries manufacturières   En las industrias manufactureras

	Per week / Par semaine / Por semana									
	1999	2000	2001	2002	2003	2004	2005	2006	2007	2008

México (BA) (d) [1] [2]   Employees - Salariés - Asalariados

Men - Hommes - Hombres
ISIC 3 - CITI 3 - CIIU 3

	1999	2000	2001	2002	2003	2004	2005	2006	2007	2008
Total	46.5	45.6	45.2	46.2	45.4	45.9	47.8 [3]	46.3	46.6	47.4
15	50.4	48.8	48.2	48.7	48.6	48.5	51.0 [3]	52.5	49.5	50.1
16	44.6	45.8	45.6	47.4	46.3	44.1	. [3]	.	.	.
17	44.1	43.9	44.4	45.5	43.8	45.0	46.9 [3]	43.8	45.1	45.9
18	46.1	45.4	44.8	45.9	46.0	45.8	47.5 [3]	46.6	46.3	48.1
19	45.5	44.2	44.3	44.8	44.2	44.1	47.4 [3]	46.2	45.7	47.0
20	46.1	44.3	45.1	45.2	43.7	45.1	46.2 [3]	44.0	46.4	47.1
21	45.2	45.0	45.0	46.0	45.8	47.1	48.5 [3]	46.4	46.8	48.0
22	44.6	45.4	43.5	45.7	44.5	44.4	46.5 [3]	45.1	45.5	48.1
23	45.6	45.3	45.6	45.6	45.8	45.3	48.1 [3]	52.9	44.7	44.6
24	45.7	44.9	44.0	44.8	44.4	45.2	45.7 [3]	44.5	45.3	46.5
25	44.4	45.4	44.2	46.4	45.4	47.0	48.8 [3]	46.0	45.8	48.1
26	46.8	45.6	45.3	45.7	44.8	44.7	47.3 [3]	49.7	45.8	45.8
27	46.7	46.7	45.3	46.2	46.0	48.0	47.4 [3]	47.5	47.7	48.3
28	46.4	45.0	45.0	46.1	44.4	45.0	47.3 [3]	45.8	46.0	46.5
29	44.7	45.1	43.9	45.7	43.3	45.1	47.6 [3]	46.1	46.6	47.9
30	46.9	42.2	42.1	47.5	43.5	45.0	45.8 [3]	44.5	45.5	45.5
31	45.7	44.0	42.7	45.0	44.6	45.0	46.6 [3]	44.8	45.8	46.7
32	44.9	44.6	44.7	44.9	45.2	44.9	. [3]	.	.	.
33	43.6	44.4	45.1	43.9	42.2	44.4	44.9 [3]	45.5	44.8	45.7
34	45.4	45.2	43.4	45.5	44.1	44.6	46.8 [3]	45.7	45.7	46.3
35	47.6	42.6	41.5	46.1	48.1	47.1	. [3]	.	.	.
36	46.0	44.3	44.8	45.1	43.2	45.0	.	44.2	45.8	46.3
37	.	.	.	.	.	.	.	.	.	.

Women - Femmes - Mujeres
ISIC 3 - CITI 3 - CIIU 3

	1999	2000	2001	2002	2003	2004	2005	2006	2007	2008
Total	43.4	42.1	41.7	43.2	42.6	42.5	44.1 [3]	43.6	43.4	44.5
15	44.7	44.5	43.7	45.2	45.8	44.5	46.1 [3]	44.7	44.4	45.2
16	42.5	41.0	40.0	47.4	45.3	47.0	. [3]	.	.	.
17	39.5	37.7	35.8	36.7	34.7	37.3	38.8 [3]	45.4	42.5	43.3
18	43.5	42.2	42.0	43.4	43.3	42.9	44.7 [3]	38.6	41.4	38.5
19	42.1	40.5	40.5	42.4	39.9	40.2	44.0 [3]	43.8	43.0	45.1
20	43.6	41.3	37.0	41.4	43.2	39.9	38.4 [3]	39.5	39.5	42.4
21	43.2	41.8	44.0	43.1	44.3	39.6	42.5 [3]	40.6	43.5	46.2
22	40.4	42.2	41.2	42.2	41.1	41.5	46.0 [3]	42.9	43.8	43.3
23	38.6	38.4	35.1	43.0	42.1	41.4	42.9 [3]	39.9	42.9	39.5
24	39.6	35.0	37.3	38.7	35.2	34.0	36.8 [3]	42.3	42.3	43.2
25	45.7	42.1	42.8	45.5	44.1	43.8	44.4 [3]	44.7	44.0	45.0
26	44.5	42.3	40.0	43.9	41.0	43.3	43.5 [3]	42.6	42.8	43.2
27	44.5	42.7	42.2	44.0	46.9	45.7	47.0 [3]	41.7	43.3	44.6
28	43.1	42.7	42.3	43.3	42.8	43.4	44.7 [3]	42.0	42.9	46.3
29	41.7	42.7	42.1	44.1	40.9	42.7	44.5 [3]	43.6	44.8	44.6
30	44.5	45.3	44.4	44.7	44.7	45.4	44.1 [3]	44.0	44.2	44.4
31	43.9	42.8	41.6	44.6	43.1	44.7	45.0 [3]	45.1	42.9	44.6
32	44.9	43.8	43.9	44.2	43.7	43.3	.	.	.	.
33	45.1	44.5	44.3	43.9	43.0	43.3	41.9 [3]	42.9	41.9	40.9
34	44.5	43.9	42.8	44.2	43.5	43.7	45.4 [3]	43.7	44.2	44.8
35	53.6	48.1	48.2	44.8	32.1	41.9	.	.	.	.
36	40.6	39.9	41.3	42.2	41.5	42.7	42.2 [3]	43.0	41.3	44.5
37	.	.	.	.	.	.	.	.	.	.

Panamá (BA) (a) [4] [5]   Total employment - Emploi total - Empleo total

Total men and women - Total hommes et femmes - Total hombres y mujeres
ISIC 3 - CITI 3 - CIIU 3

	1999	2000	2001	2002	2003	2004	2005	2006	2007	2008
Total	.	.	45.1	45.4	46.2	45.9	45.9	45.6	45.6	43.0

Men - Hommes - Hombres
ISIC 3 - CITI 3 - CIIU 3

	1999	2000	2001	2002	2003	2004	2005	2006	2007	2008
Total	.	.	45.6	45.8	46.5	47.1	46.6	46.1	46.3	43.5

Women - Femmes - Mujeres
ISIC 3 - CITI 3 - CIIU 3

	1999	2000	2001	2002	2003	2004	2005	2006	2007	2008
Total	.	.	43.3	44.0	45.0	42.0	43.3	43.8	43.4	41.4

Paraguay (BA) (c) [6]   Employees - Salariés - Asalariados

Total men and women - Total hommes et femmes - Total hombres y mujeres
ISIC 3 - CITI 3 - CIIU 3

	1999	2000	2001	2002	2003	2004	2005	2006	2007	2008
Total	.	.	.	.	.	.	.	.	52.3	53.1

Explanatory notes: see p. 721.

[1] Persons aged 14 years and over. [2] Second quarter of each year. [3] Revised averages based on 2005 Population and Housing Census results; data not comparable. [4] Persons aged 15 years and over. [5] Aug. of each year. [6] Fourth quarter of each year.

Notes explicatives: voir p. 723.

[1] Personnes âgées de 14 ans et plus. [2] Deuxième trimestre de chaque année. [3] Moyennes révisées sur la base des résultats du recensement de population et de l'habitat de 2005; les données ne sont pas comparables [4] Personnes âgées de 15 ans et plus. [5] Août de chaque année. [6] Quatrième trimestre de chaque année.

Notas explicativas: véase p. 725.

[1] Personas de 14 años y más. [2] Segundo trimestre de cada año. [3] Promedios revisados de acuerdo con los resultados del censo de población y Vivienda de 2005; datos no comparables. [4] Personas de 15 años y más. [5] Agosto de cada año. [6] Cuarto trimestre de cada año.

In manufacturing — **Dans les industries manufacturières** — **En las industrias manufactureras**

Per week — Par semaine — Por semana

	1999	2000	2001	2002	2003	2004	2005	2006	2007	2008

Paraguay (BA) (c) [1] — Employees - Salariés - Asalariados

Men - Hommes - Hombres
ISIC 3 - CITI 3 - CIIU 3

	1999	2000	2001	2002	2003	2004	2005	2006	2007	2008
Total									53.0	54.5

Women - Femmes - Mujeres
ISIC 3 - CITI 3 - CIIU 3

	1999	2000	2001	2002	2003	2004	2005	2006	2007	2008
Total									49.3	46.7

Perú (B) (b) [2][3][4] — Wage earners - Ouvriers - Obreros

Total men and women - Total hommes et femmes - Total hombres y mujeres
ISIC 3 - CITI 3 - CIIU 3

	1999	2000	2001	2002	2003	2004	2005	2006	2007	2008
Total			54.6 [5]	53.6	55.9 [5]	53.7	54.8	54.1	54.5	53.4
15			49.5 [5]	55.3	54.3 [5]	51.3	60.1	50.8	52.8	55.4
17			55.6 [5]	58.0	52.6 [5]	54.1	50.9	50.9	49.2	50.6
18			55.5 [5]	55.9	57.9 [5]	57.2	55.7	55.8	58.2	54.8
19			61.7 [5]	53.2	58.5 [5]	57.2	62.4	67.9	60.2	57.3
20				40.8	63.3 [5]	54.5	73.6	54.4	54.0	51.9
21			51.1 [5]	64.1	55.1 [5]	53.1	52.8	59.4	56.6	55.4
22			59.0 [5]	49.4	46.1 [5]	55.2	52.1	57.7	58.1	56.0
23			68.6 [5]		94.7 [5]					
24			50.4 [5]	49.5	50.2 [5]	48.1	49.9	48.3	59.7	58.1
25			62.5 [5]	59.8	52.6 [5]	56.8	63.0	55.0	53.5	55.3
26			60.1 [5]	55.9	62.1 [5]	49.1	44.5	55.4	57.3	53.0
27			41.0 [5]	54.9	72.0 [5]	53.5	49.4	41.0	59.0	43.5
28			49.8 [5]	48.2	55.0 [5]	54.4	57.5	56.3	52.4	52.9
29			61.6 [5]	51.2	60.0 [5]	51.3	53.1	52.3	51.0	47.1
30			48.0 [5]	50.0			45.8			44.5
31			13.9 [5]	55.0	53.1 [5]	48.0	44.0	59.8	60.8	59.2
33			72.0 [5]	55.0	48.0 [5]		44.5	58.0	41.2	54.0
34			59.5 [5]	54.1	. [5]	60.0	53.2	51.2	45.8	57.5
35			48.1 [5]	76.0	44.8 [5]	51.1	59.3	53.4	41.2	43.4
36			55.5 [5]	50.5	55.8 [5]	46.7	52.6	52.7	50.6	51.7

Perú (D) (b) [2][6] — Wage earners - Ouvriers - Obreros

Total men and women - Total hommes et femmes - Total hombres y mujeres
ISIC 3 - CITI 3 - CIIU 3

	1999	2000	2001	2002	2003	2004	2005	2006	2007	2008
Total	49.61	49.05	49.28 [7]	43.24 [3]	48.99	46.31	48.94	49.93	48.22	49.96
15	50.30	50.67	49.66 [7]	42.86 [3]	49.19	43.23	49.95	47.65	47.94	50.29
16	48.19	47.30	48.56 [7]	. [3]		40.00	41.58		47.36	.
17	47.58	46.75	47.92 [7]	43.53 [3]	48.99	48.90	50.49	51.45	49.88	49.96
18	52.52	50.48	51.45 [7]	45.09 [3]	53.24	52.65	48.70	51.79	48.63	49.02
19	48.12	43.92	45.78 [7]	40.48 [3]	46.31	37.66	41.91	44.51	41.49	48.35
20	55.20	52.87	49.72 [7]	.	50.34	46.98	48.06	44.70	44.49	48.38
21	62.08	57.95	61.69 [7]	60.64 [3]	51.05	47.46	63.08	61.17	49.67	49.00
22	50.28	49.26	46.54 [7]	41.46 [3]	50.62	53.29	54.70	53.53	41.00	52.79
23			. [7]			60.40				53.40
24	48.21	48.06	48.01 [7]	41.40 [3]	48.04	44.75	45.70	56.33	46.72	47.97
25	50.55	49.63	49.81 [7]	44.15 [3]	47.88	43.87	45.73	48.40	47.02	49.35
26	46.22	48.45	48.09 [7]	41.16 [3]	41.93	40.50	45.93	45.17	45.56	48.67
27	47.01	46.29	44.73 [7]	37.65	.	47.35	48.01	48.19	49.10	55.57
28	50.57	50.33	49.92 [7]	42.87 [3]	49.21	43.98	47.61	53.91	53.89	52.34
29	47.91	42.50	47.19 [7]	39.50 [3]	53.90	43.46	44.96	49.43	47.14	49.11
31	47.75	46.23	47.39 [7]	41.41 [3]	49.99	42.01	43.43	45.34	50.44	50.09
34	49.10	46.40	50.19 [7]	42.43 [3]	42.39	41.24	39.34	46.01	49.23	45.96
35	46.73	48.82	49.27 [7]	48.50 [3]	46.33	51.03	48.15	50.58	52.98	62.58
36	53.09	48.06	48.29 [7]	38.63 [3]	48.79	44.27	47.15	51.12	46.65	49.65

Explanatory notes: see p. 721.

[1] Fourth quarter of each year. [2] Figures at the desaggregated level are not representative because of the small sample size. [3] Metropolitan Lima. [4] Fourth quarter. [5] May-Dec. [6] Second quarter. [7] Average of the first three quarters.

Notes explicatives: voir p. 723.

[1] Quatrième trimestre de chaque année. [2] Chiffres non représentatifs au niveau desagrégé en raison de la faible taille de l'échantillonage. [3] Lima métropolitaine. [4] Quatrième trimestre. [5] Mai-déc. [6] Deuxième trimestre. [7] Moyenne des trois premiers trimestres.

Notas explicativas: véase p. 725.

[1] Cuarto trimestre de cada año. [2] Cifras no reprentativas al nivel de desagregación debidas al pequeño tamaño muestral. [3] Lima metropolitana. [4] Cuarto trimestre. [5] Mayo-dic. [6] Segundo trimestre. [7] Promedio de los tres primeros trimestres.

818

ILO YEARBOOK OF LABOUR STATISTICS 2009   *ANNUAIRE DES STATISTIQUES DU TRAVAIL DU BIT 2009*   *ANUARIO DE ESTADISTICAS DEL TRABAJO DEL OIT 2009*

In manufacturing   Dans les industries manufacturières   En las industrias manufactureras

Per week — Par semaine — Por semana

	1999	2000	2001	2002	2003	2004	2005	2006	2007	2008
Puerto Rico (DA) (b) [1]				**Wage earners - Ouvriers - Obreros**						
Total men and women - Total hommes et femmes - Total hombres y mujeres										
ISIC 2 - CITI 2 - CIIU 2										
Total	.	.	.	40.6	40.9	41.0	40.8	40.5	40.9	40.6
311-312	40.3	39.2	40.1	40.5	41.3	40.1	40.8	40.6	40.6	41.4
311-313	.	.	.	.	.	.	.	.	.	.
314 [2]	38.9	43.1	.	.	.	.	.	.	.	.
321 [2]	34.7	32.2	.	.	.	.	.	.	.	.
322	36.9	35.7	34.5	36.2	36.5	35.4	35.4	34.8	37.0	37.2
323 [2]	40.4	39.0	.	.	.	.	.	.	.	.
324 [2]	38.6	41.4	.	.	.	.	.	.	.	.
33 [2]	38.4	37.7	.	.	.	.	.	.	.	.
341 [2]	41.0	40.3	.	.	.	.	.	.	.	.
342 [2]	41.8	42.6	.	.	.	.	.	.	.	.
351-352	43.1	42.4	42.2	42.5	42.0	42.7	42.5	42.3	41.6	41.1
353-354 [2]	43.1	43.6	.	.	.	.	.	.	.	.
355-356	41.1	40.4	39.6	39.7	38.7	38.8	39.0	39.3	37.5	35.4
361 [3]	46.5	45.9	42.2	40.6	42.0	44.7	43.5	42.0	42.9	43.6
362	.	.	.	.	.	.	.	.	.	.
369	.	.	.	.	.	.	.	.	.	.
381	41.2	40.2	39.0	39.3	39.5	39.5	39.5	37.2	37.8	37.2
382 [2]	44.0	43.0	.	.	.	.	.	.	.	.
383	41.5	42.4	40.3	41.6	41.6	42.2	43.3	42.4	42.8	42.2
384 [2]	43.2	39.3	.	.	.	.	.	.	.	.
385	41.4	40.8	.	.	.	43.8	41.7	39.9	41.4	42.4
390 [2]	40.2	41.5	41.0	.	.	.	.	.	.	.
United States (DA) (a) [4][5]				**Employees - Salariés - Asalariados**						
Total men and women - Total hommes et femmes - Total hombres y mujeres										
ISIC 3 - CITI 3 - CIIU 3										
Total	41.4	41.3	40.3	40.5	40.4	40.8	40.7	41.1	41.2	40.8
16	38.2	40.3	39.2	39.8	38.4	38.8	41.2	41.3	39.6	41.6
18	35.4	35.7	36.0	36.7	35.6	36.1	35.8	36.5	37.2	36.4
19	37.2	37.5	36.4	37.5	39.3	38.4	38.4	38.9	38.2	37.5
20	41.3	41.0	40.2	39.9	40.4	40.7	40.0	39.8	39.4	38.6
21	43.6	42.8	42.1	41.9	41.5	42.1	42.5	42.9	43.1	42.9
23	42.6	42.7	43.8	43.0	44.5	44.9	45.5	45.0	44.1	44.6
24	42.7	42.2	41.9	42.3	42.4	42.8	42.3	42.5	41.9	41.5
25	41.3	40.8	40.0	40.6	40.4	40.4	40.0	40.6	41.3	41.0
26	42.1	41.6	41.6	42.0	42.2	42.4	42.2	43.0	42.3	42.1
27	43.8	44.2	42.4	42.4	42.3	43.1	43.1	43.6	42.9	42.2
28	41.7	41.9	40.6	40.6	40.7	41.1	41.0	41.4	41.6	41.3
37	38.2	38.0	38.2	38.3	38.8	39.3	39.7	41.2	43.0	42.4
Venezuela, Rep. Bolivariana de (BA) (a)				**Total employment - Emploi total - Empleo total**						
Total men and women - Total hommes et femmes - Total hombres y mujeres										
ISIC 2 - CITI 2 - CIIU 2										
Total	.	.	.	.	.	.	.	.	40	41 [6]
311-312	.	.	.	.	.	.	.	.	41	42 [6]
313	.	.	.	.	.	.	.	.	43	43 [6]
314	.	.	.	.	.	.	.	.	41	42 [6]
321	.	.	.	.	.	.	.	.	36	33 [6]
322	.	.	.	.	.	.	.	.	35	36 [6]
323	.	.	.	.	.	.	.	.	43	41 [6]
324	.	.	.	.	.	.	.	.	42	42 [6]
331	.	.	.	.	.	.	.	.	42	42 [6]
332	.	.	.	.	.	.	.	.	42	43 [6]
341	.	.	.	.	.	.	.	.	41	44 [6]
342	.	.	.	.	.	.	.	.	42	43 [6]
351	.	.	.	.	.	.	.	.	40	42 [6]
352	.	.	.	.	.	.	.	.	41	41 [6]
353	.	.	.	.	.	.	.	.	38	37 [6]
354	.	.	.	.	.	.	.	.	.	40 [6]
355	.	.	.	.	.	.	.	.	42	44 [6]
356	.	.	.	.	.	.	.	.	42	43 [6]
361	.	.	.	.	.	.	.	.	40	31 [6]
362	.	.	.	.	.	.	.	.	41	43 [6]
369	.	.	.	.	.	.	.	.	42	43 [6]
371	.	.	.	.	.	.	.	.	42	42 [6]
372	.	.	.	.	.	.	.	.	43	43 [6]
381	.	.	.	.	.	.	.	.	42	43 [6]
382	.	.	.	.	.	.	.	.	41	43 [6]
383	.	.	.	.	.	.	.	.	41	44 [6]
384	.	.	.	.	.	.	.	.	42	44 [6]
385	.	.	.	.	.	.	.	.	39	40 [6]
390	.	.	.	.	.	.	.	.	37	34 [6]

Explanatory notes: see p. 721.

[1] Persons aged 15 years and over; prior to 1998: 14 years and over. [2] March of each year. [3] Incl. major groups 362, 369. [4] National classification not strictly compatible with ISIC. [5] Not all employees covered; only production and non-supervisory workers; private sector. [6] First semester.

Notes explicatives: voir p. 723.

[1] Personnes âgées de 15 ans et plus; avant 1998: 14 ans et plus. [2] Mars de chaque année. [3] Y compris les classes 362, 369. [4] Classification nationale non strictement compatible avec la CITI. [5] Non couverts tous les salariés: seulement travailleurs à la production et ceux sans activité de surveillance; secteur privé. [6] Premier semestre.

Notas explicativas: véase p. 725.

[1] Personas de 15 años y más; antes de 1998: 14 años y más. [2] Marzo de cada año. [3] Incl. las agrupaciones 362, 369. [4] Clasificación nacional no estrictamente compatible con la CIIU. [5] Todos asalariados no cubiertos; sólo trabajaodores de la producción y los sin funciones de supervisión; sector privado. [6] Primer semestre.

4B

HOURS OF WORK
DURÉE DU TRAVAIL
HORAS DE TRABAJO

In manufacturing
Dans les industries manufacturières
En las industrias manufactureras

				Per week - Par semaine - Por semana						
	1999	2000	2001	2002	2003	2004	2005	2006	2007	2008

Venezuela, Rep. Bolivariana de (BA) (a) — Total employment - Emploi total - Empleo total

Men - Hommes - Hombres
ISIC 2 - CITI 2 - CIIU 2

	1999	2000	2001	2002	2003	2004	2005	2006	2007	2008
Total	.	.	.	.	.	.	.	.	42	43 [1]
311-312	.	.	.	.	.	.	.	.	44	44 [1]
313	.	.	.	.	.	.	.	.	43	44 [1]
314	.	.	.	.	.	.	.	.	42	44 [1]
321	.	.	.	.	.	.	.	.	40	
322	.	.	.	.	.	.	.	.	42	43 [1]
323	.	.	.	.	.	.	.	.	44	42 [1]
324	.	.	.	.	.	.	.	.	42	44 [1]
331	.	.	.	.	.	.	.	.	42	42 [1]
332	.	.	.	.	.	.	.	.	43	43 [1]
341	.	.	.	.	.	.	.	.	42	44 [1]
342	.	.	.	.	.	.	.	.	43	44 [1]
351	.	.	.	.	.	.	.	.	41	43 [1]
352	.	.	.	.	.	.	.	.	41	42 [1]
353	.	.	.	.	.	.	.	.	37	41 [1]
354	.	.	.	.	.	.	.	.		40 [1]
355	.	.	.	.	.	.	.	.	43	44 [1]
356	.	.	.	.	.	.	.	.	42	44 [1]
361	.	.	.	.	.	.	.	.		21 [1]
362	.	.	.	.	.	.	.	.	41	44 [1]
369	.	.	.	.	.	.	.	.	42	43 [1]
371	.	.	.	.	.	.	.	.	42	42 [1]
372	.	.	.	.	.	.	.	.	43	43 [1]
381	.	.	.	.	.	.	.	.	42	43 [1]
382	.	.	.	.	.	.	.	.	41	43 [1]
383	.	.	.	.	.	.	.	.	42	44 [1]
384	.	.	.	.	.	.	.	.	42	45 [1]
385	.	.	.	.	.	.	.	.	38	42 [1]
390	.	.	.	.	.	.	.	.	41	40 [1]

Women - Femmes - Mujeres
ISIC 2 - CITI 2 - CIIU 2

	1999	2000	2001	2002	2003	2004	2005	2006	2007	2008
Total	.	.	.	.	.	.	.	.	36	36 [1]
311-312	.	.	.	.	.	.	.	.	36	37 [1]
313	.	.	.	.	.	.	.	.	37	41 [1]
314	.	.	.	.	.	.	.	.	39	39 [1]
321	.	.	.	.	.	.	.	.	32	29 [1]
322	.	.	.	.	.	.	.	.	34	35 [1]
323	.	.	.	.	.	.	.	.	42	41 [1]
324	.	.	.	.	.	.	.	.	41	40 [1]
331	.	.	.	.	.	.	.	.	37	38 [1]
332	.	.	.	.	.	.	.	.	39	45 [1]
341	.	.	.	.	.	.	.	.	36	42 [1]
342	.	.	.	.	.	.	.	.	40	41 [1]
351	.	.	.	.	.	.	.	.	37	40 [1]
352	.	.	.	.	.	.	.	.	40	41 [1]
353	.	.	.	.	.	.	.	.	40	15 [1]
354	.	.	.	.	.	.	.	.		
355	.	.	.	.	.	.	.	.	38	40 [1]
356	.	.	.	.	.	.	.	.	42	41 [1]
361	.	.	.	.	.	.	.	.	40	39 [1]
362	.	.	.	.	.	.	.	.	40	40 [1]
369	.	.	.	.	.	.	.	.	40	41 [1]
371	.	.	.	.	.	.	.	.	41	42 [1]
372	.	.	.	.	.	.	.	.	41	40 [1]
381	.	.	.	.	.	.	.	.	41	39 [1]
382	.	.	.	.	.	.	.	.	41	41 [1]
383	.	.	.	.	.	.	.	.	40	42 [1]
384	.	.	.	.	.	.	.	.	41	40 [1]
385	.	.	.	.	.	.	.	.	41	33 [1]
390	.	.	.	.	.	.	.	.	34	31 [1]

Virgin Islands (US) (DA) (b) — Wage earners - Ouvriers - Obreros

Total men and women - Total hommes et femmes - Total hombres y mujeres
ISIC 3 - CITI 3 - CIIU 3

	1999	2000	2001	2002	2003	2004	2005	2006	2007	2008
Total	.	.	43.9	43.7	42.8	46.4	43.7	43.8	42.2	43.3

ASIA-ASIE-ASIA

Armenia (BA) (a) [2] — Total employment - Emploi total - Empleo total

Total men and women - Total hommes et femmes - Total hombres y mujeres
ISIC 3 - CITI 3 - CIIU 3

	1999	2000	2001	2002	2003	2004	2005	2006	2007	2008
Total	.	.	41.0	44.7	45.4	50.8	52.8 [3][1]	47.3 [4]	46.0	.

Men - Hommes - Hombres
ISIC 3 - CITI 3 - CIIU 3

	1999	2000	2001	2002	2003	2004	2005	2006	2007	2008
Total	.	.	41.4	44.5	46.2	55.0	55.2 [1]	47.6 [4]	47.8	.

Explanatory notes: see p. 721.

[1] First semester. [2] Employed persons and at work. [3] October-December. [4] Methodology revised; data not strictly comparable.

Notes explicatives: voir p. 723.

[1] Premier semestre. [2] Personnes pourvues d'un emploi et au travail [3] Octobre-Décembre. [4] Méthodologie révisée; les données ne sont pas strictement comparables.

Notas explicativas: véase p. 725.

[1] Primer semestre. [2] Personas con empleo y trabajando. [3] Octubre-diciembre. [4] Metodología revisada; los datos no son estrictamente comparables.

In manufacturing · Dans les industries manufacturières · En las industrias manufactureras

Per week · Par semaine · Por semana

	1999	2000	2001	2002	2003	2004	2005	2006	2007	2008
Armenia (BA) (a) [1]										

Total employment - Emploi total - Empleo total

Women - Femmes - Mujeres
ISIC 3 - CITI 3 - CIIU 3

	1999	2000	2001	2002	2003	2004	2005	2006	2007	2008
Total	.	.	40.2	45.1	44.3	41.1	40.5 ǀ	45.2 [2]	42.8	.

Azerbaijan (DA) (a)

Employees - Salariés - Asalariados

Total men and women - Total hommes et femmes - Total hombres y mujeres
ISIC 3 - CITI 3 - CIIU 3

	1999	2000	2001	2002	2003	2004	2005	2006	2007	2008
Total	.	.	.	.	.	.	.	.	.	32.6
15	.	.	.	.	.	.	.	.	.	34.1
16	.	.	.	.	.	.	.	.	.	36.0
17	.	.	.	.	.	.	.	.	.	29.5
18	.	.	.	.	.	.	.	.	.	34.3
19	.	.	.	.	.	.	.	.	.	31.2
20	.	.	.	.	.	.	.	.	.	34.9
21	.	.	.	.	.	.	.	.	.	35.9
22	.	.	.	.	.	.	.	.	.	33.0
23	.	.	.	.	.	.	.	.	.	34.9
24	.	.	.	.	.	.	.	.	.	32.4
25	.	.	.	.	.	.	.	.	.	34.7
26	.	.	.	.	.	.	.	.	.	34.2
27	.	.	.	.	.	.	.	.	.	26.1
28	.	.	.	.	.	.	.	.	.	34.6
29	.	.	.	.	.	.	.	.	.	32.4
30	.	.	.	.	.	.	.	.	.	29.4
31	.	.	.	.	.	.	.	.	.	29.9
32	.	.	.	.	.	.	.	.	.	33.5
33	.	.	.	.	.	.	.	.	.	32.3
34	.	.	.	.	.	.	.	.	.	33.0
35	.	.	.	.	.	.	.	.	.	33.7
36	.	.	.	.	.	.	.	.	.	32.4
37	.	.	.	.	.	.	.	.	.	34.5

Men - Hommes - Hombres
ISIC 3 - CITI 3 - CIIU 3

	1999	2000	2001	2002	2003	2004	2005	2006	2007	2008
Total	.	.	.	.	.	.	.	.	.	32.8
15	.	.	.	.	.	.	.	.	.	34.2
16	.	.	.	.	.	.	.	.	.	36.2
17	.	.	.	.	.	.	.	.	.	29.9
18	.	.	.	.	.	.	.	.	.	36.3
19	.	.	.	.	.	.	.	.	.	35.1
20	.	.	.	.	.	.	.	.	.	37.1
21	.	.	.	.	.	.	.	.	.	35.7
22	.	.	.	.	.	.	.	.	.	35.0
23	.	.	.	.	.	.	.	.	.	34.7
24	.	.	.	.	.	.	.	.	.	31.4
25	.	.	.	.	.	.	.	.	.	34.8
26	.	.	.	.	.	.	.	.	.	34.4
27	.	.	.	.	.	.	.	.	.	27.0
28	.	.	.	.	.	.	.	.	.	34.4
29	.	.	.	.	.	.	.	.	.	32.7
30	.	.	.	.	.	.	.	.	.	44.9
31	.	.	.	.	.	.	.	.	.	30.0
32	.	.	.	.	.	.	.	.	.	33.2
33	.	.	.	.	.	.	.	.	.	31.3
34	.	.	.	.	.	.	.	.	.	33.1
35	.	.	.	.	.	.	.	.	.	33.6
36	.	.	.	.	.	.	.	.	.	33.0
37	.	.	.	.	.	.	.	.	.	34.2

Explanatory notes: see p. 721.

[1] Employed persons and at work. [2] Methodology revised; data not strictly comparable.

Notes explicatives: voir p. 723.

[1] Personnes pourvues d'un emploi et au travail [2] Méthodologie révisée; les données ne sont pas strictement comparables.

Notas explicativas: véase p. 725.

[1] Personas con empleo y trabajando. [2] Metodología revisada; los datos no son estrictamente comparables.

HOURS OF WORK · DURÉE DU TRAVAIL · HORAS DE TRABAJO

In manufacturing · Dans les industries manufacturières · En las industrias manufactureras

Per week · Par semaine · Por semana

	1999	2000	2001	2002	2003	2004	2005	2006	2007	2008

Azerbaijan (DA) (a) — Employees - Salariés - Asalariados

Women - Femmes - Mujeres
ISIC 3 - CITI 3 - CIIU 3

	1999	2000	2001	2002	2003	2004	2005	2006	2007	2008
Total	.	.	.	.	.	.	.	.	.	32.0
15	.	.	.	.	.	.	.	.	.	33.9
16	.	.	.	.	.	.	.	.	.	35.2
17	.	.	.	.	.	.	.	.	.	29.0
18	.	.	.	.	.	.	.	.	.	33.4
19	.	.	.	.	.	.	.	.	.	25.6
20	.	.	.	.	.	.	.	.	.	27.4
21	.	.	.	.	.	.	.	.	.	36.1
22	.	.	.	.	.	.	.	.	.	30.1
23	.	.	.	.	.	.	.	.	.	35.2
24	.	.	.	.	.	.	.	.	.	34.0
25	.	.	.	.	.	.	.	.	.	34.4
26	.	.	.	.	.	.	.	.	.	32.6
27	.	.	.	.	.	.	.	.	.	21.6
28	.	.	.	.	.	.	.	.	.	35.3
29	.	.	.	.	.	.	.	.	.	31.3
30	.	.	.	.	.	.	.	.	.	10.0
31	.	.	.	.	.	.	.	.	.	29.6
32	.	.	.	.	.	.	.	.	.	34.5
33	.	.	.	.	.	.	.	.	.	35.6
34	.	.	.	.	.	.	.	.	.	32.8
35	.	.	.	.	.	.	.	.	.	34.5
36	.	.	.	.	.	.	.	.	.	29.7
37	.	.	.	.	.	.	.	.	.	35.1

China (DA) (a) [1] [2] — Employees - Salariés - Asalariados

Total men and women - Total hommes et femmes - Total hombres y mujeres
ISIC 3 - CITI 3 - CIIU 3

	1999	2000	2001	2002	2003	2004	2005	2006	2007	2008
Total	.	.	.	.	46.4	46.9	51.1	50.4	49.4	.

Men - Hommes - Hombres
ISIC 3 - CITI 3 - CIIU 3

	1999	2000	2001	2002	2003	2004	2005	2006	2007	2008
Total	.	.	.	.	46.2	46.5	51.0	50.3	49.6	.

Women - Femmes - Mujeres
ISIC 3 - CITI 3 - CIIU 3

	1999	2000	2001	2002	2003	2004	2005	2006	2007	2008
Total	.	.	.	.	46.6	47.5	51.3	50.5	49.2	.

Hong Kong, China (BA) (a) [3] [4] — Total employment - Emploi total - Empleo total

Total men and women - Total hommes et femmes - Total hombres y mujeres
ISIC 2 - CITI 2 - CIIU 2

	1999	2000	2001	2002	2003	2004	2005	2006	2007	2008
Total	45.0	45.3	45.4	45.6	45.4	46.5	46.4	45.5	45.8	44.6

Men - Hommes - Hombres
ISIC 2 - CITI 2 - CIIU 2

	1999	2000	2001	2002	2003	2004	2005	2006	2007	2008
Total	46.7	46.8	47.0	47.3	47.0	48.1	48.1	47.2	47.7	46.0
31	48.4	48.4	49.8	47.8	49.0	50.7	51.0	49.8	50.9	50.0
32	47.3	46.7	47.4	48.8	47.7	48.6	48.6	47.5	49.3	47.5
321	.	.	.	.	.	.	.	.	.	.
322	.	.	.	.	.	.	.	.	.	.
323-324										
33	46.2	44.9	47.0	43.0	43.8	47.2	50.0	45.7	46.5	42.9
34	47.6	47.9	47.8	47.3	47.1	49.0	48.3	47.7	48.2	46.4
35	47.1	46.4	46.9	46.9	47.2	48.3	47.4	46.5	47.4	44.6
351-354,36,390										
355	.	.	.	.	.	.	.	.	.	.
356	.	.	.	.	.	.	.	.	.	.
36	49.1	48.1	49.4	50.2	46.4	48.2	48.7	40.6	47.4	47.6
37	45.0	44.4	45.5	46.2	50.2	43.0	44.7	49.2	46.1	45.2
371-372,381,385										
38	45.7	46.5	46.2	46.9	46.4	47.1	47.6	46.8	46.3	44.7
382,384	.	.	.	.	.	.	.	.	.	.
383	.	.	.	.	.	.	.	.	.	.
39	44.5	45.1	45.2	45.5	46.7	45.5	44.8	44.8	45.7	44.1

Explanatory notes: see p. 721.

[1] Urban areas. [2] Nov. of each year. [3] Excl. marine, military and institutional populations. [4] Persons aged 15 years and over.

Notes explicatives: voir p. 723.

[1] Régions urbaines. [2] Nov. de chaque année. [3] Non compris le personnel militaire, de la marine et la population institutionnelle. [4] Personnes âgées de 15 ans et plus.

Notas explicativas: véase p. 725.

[1] Areas urbanas. [2] Nov. de cada año. [3] Excl. el personal militar y de la marina, y la población institucional. [4] Personas de 15 años y más.

822

ILO YEARBOOK OF LABOUR STATISTICS 2009 · *ANNUAIRE DES STATISTIQUES DU TRAVAIL DU BIT 2009* · *ANUARIO DE ESTADISTICAS DEL TRABAJO DEL OIT 2009*

In manufacturing / Dans les industries manufacturières / En las industrias manufactureras

Per week - Par semaine - Por semana

Hong Kong, China (BA) (a) [1][2] — Total employment - Emploi total - Empleo total
Women - Femmes - Mujeres
ISIC 2 - CITI 2 - CIIU 2

	1999	2000	2001	2002	2003	2004	2005	2006	2007	2008
Total	42.0	42.4	42.3	42.6	42.3	43.5	43.2	42.4	42.4	41.7
31	43.2	42.0	43.4	42.8	43.3	45.0	42.3	40.1	40.2	40.1
32	41.5	41.4	42.2	43.0	41.9	42.8	43.1	41.5	43.3	42.6
321	.	.	.	.	.	.	.	.	.	.
322	.	.	.	.	.	.	.	.	.	.
323-324	.	.	.	.	.	.	.	.	.	.
33	38.7	-	-	.	.	-	-	-	-	-
34	43.1	44.2	43.1	43.3	42.9	44.7	44.0	43.8	43.0	41.6
35	42.1	42.9	42.6	41.5	43.3	43.1	42.3	43.3	42.7	43.0
351-354,36,390	.	.	.	.	.	.	.	.	.	.
355	.	.	.	.	.	.	.	.	.	.
356	.	.	.	.	.	.	.	.	.	.
36	43.6	-	43.0	47.3	-	31.5	-	-	-	-
37	-	-	-	-	-	-	-	-	-	-
371-372,381,385	.	.	.	.	.	.	.	.	.	.
38	41.9	43.0	41.5	41.8	41.8	44.2	43.5	43.5	41.9	41.1
382,384	.	.	.	.	.	.	.	.	.	.
383	.	.	.	.	.	.	.	.	.	.
39	42.2	41.7	42.3	42.4	41.0	40.1	41.4	42.5	39.7	41.1

Hong Kong, China (BA) (a) [1][2][3] — Employees - Salariés - Asalariados
Total men and women - Total hommes et femmes - Total hombres y mujeres
ISIC 2 - CITI 2 - CIIU 2

	1999	2000	2001	2002	2003	2004	2005	2006	2007	2008
Total	44.6	44.9	44.9	45.2	45.0	46.3	46.3	45.3	45.7	44.4
31	46.6	46.3	47.2	45.6	46.4	48.2	47.7	45.6	46.1	45.4
32	43.8	43.4	44.2	45.1	44.2	45.1	45.5	44.4	45.7	44.7
33	44.7	44.1	45.2	43.0	43.4	50.6	50.1	45.9	45.9	41.6
34	45.8	46.5	46.1	45.8	45.8	47.5	46.9	46.0	46.1	44.5
35	44.8	44.9	45.0	44.7	45.4	45.8	45.3	45.4	45.0	42.9
36	47.7	47.7	48.1	49.4	45.4	44.7	47.9	40.9	46.5	47.0
37	44.2	44.3	45.5	46.7	48.2	43.3	42.4	48.9	44.9	45.9
38	44.2	45.2	44.4	45.0	44.8	46.5	46.7	46.0	45.6	44.3
39	43.5	43.8	43.7	44.1	44.3	44.4	43.3	43.1	43.3	43.2

Men - Hommes - Hombres
ISIC 2 - CITI 2 - CIIU 2

	1999	2000	2001	2002	2003	2004	2005	2006	2007	2008
Total	46.3	46.6	46.7	47.0	46.7	48.3	48.1	47.3	47.8	46.0
31	48.2	48.5	49.5	48.0	48.7	50.5	51.1	49.5	50.7	50.4
32	46.9	46.1	47.0	48.4	47.2	48.6	48.6	47.8	49.2	47.1
33	45.7	43.8	45.1	42.8	43.2	48.7	48.8	46.6	46.0	41.7
34	47.2	47.6	47.6	47.2	47.1	49.0	48.2	47.6	48.0	46.2
35	46.4	46.1	46.2	46.3	46.5	47.6	47.0	46.4	46.9	43.2
36	48.7	48.4	49.2	49.9	46.3	48.2	48.1	41.4	46.9	47.7
37	-	44.7	45.4	46.6	50.0	43.7	44.7	49.2	46.7	46.4
38	45.3	46.3	45.7	46.4	46.0	47.4	47.7	46.9	46.7	45.0
39	43.9	44.9	44.4	45.0	45.8	46.7	44.9	43.9	45.4	44.4

Women - Femmes - Mujeres
ISIC 2 - CITI 2 - CIIU 2

	1999	2000	2001	2002	2003	2004	2005	2006	2007	2008
Total	41.9	42.3	42.2	42.6	42.2	43.4	43.1	42.2	42.3	41.6
31	43.4	41.8	43.5	42.5	42.8	44.8	42.5	40.0	40.1	40.1
32	41.3	41.2	41.9	42.8	41.8	42.7	42.8	41.7	43.3	42.5
33	-	-	-	-	-	-	-	-	-	-
34	43.0	44.1	43.2	43.4	43.0	44.6	44.3	43.5	42.9	41.5
35	41.8	42.6	42.7	41.1	43.2	41.9	42.1	42.7	41.6	42.5
36	43.4	-	43.0	47.3	-	31.5	-	-	-	-
37	-	-	-	-	-	-	-	-	-	-
38	41.9	43.0	41.2	41.9	41.7	44.3	43.8	43.2	41.9	41.5
39	42.5	41.6	42.2	42.7	41.8	40.7	40.7	41.8	39.7	41.2

India (DA) (a) [4] — Employees - Salariés - Asalariados
Total men and women - Total hommes et femmes - Total hombres y mujeres
ISIC 2 - CITI 2 - CIIU 2

	1999	2000	2001	2002	2003	2004	2005	2006	2007	2008
Total	46.6	47.2	46.7	46.9	47.1	47.0	47.2	46.9	.	.
31	46.7	46.5	46.8	47.1	46.9	46.7	47.0	46.7	.	.
32	46.6	46.1	46.7	46.9	47.2	47.0	47.4	47.0	.	.
33	46.4	46.4	46.5	46.5	46.8	46.4	46.7	46.6	.	.
34	46.8	47.0	47.0	46.9	47.5	47.0	47.3	46.8	.	.
35	46.8	46.4	46.7	46.8	46.9	46.0	47.4	47.0	.	.
36	46.7	46.3	46.7	46.7	46.7	46.8	47.2	46.3	.	.
37	46.6	46.5	46.6	46.9	47.0	46.9	46.9	46.7	.	.
38	46.6	.	46.7	46.9	47.3	47.1	47.3	47.2	.	.
39	46.7	.	46.8	46.9	47.0	47.1	47.2	47.2	.	.

Explanatory notes: see p. 721.   Notes explicatives: voir p. 723.   Notas explicativas: véase p. 725.

[1] Excl. marine, military and institutional populations. [2] Persons aged 15 years and over. [3] incl. outworkers. [4] Dec. of each year.

[1] Non compris le personnel militaire, de la marine et la population institutionnelle. [2] Personnes âgées de 15 ans et plus. [3] Y compris les travailleurs externes. [4] Déc. de chaque année.

[1] Excl. el personal militar y de la marina, y la población institucional. [2] Personas de 15 años y más. [3] Incl. los trabajadores fuera del establecimiento. [4] Dic. de cada año.

	Per week / Par semaine / Por semana									
	1999	2000	2001	2002	2003	2004	2005	2006	2007	2008
India (DA) (a) [1]					*Employees - Salariés - Asalariados*					
Men - Hommes - Hombres										
ISIC 2 - CITI 2 - CIIU 2										
Total	46.7	46.5	46.7	46.9	47.0	47.0	47.2	46.9	.	.
31	46.7	46.5	46.8	47.1	46.9	46.7	47.0	46.7	.	.
32	46.6	46.1	46.7	46.9	47.2	47.0	47.4	47.0		
33	46.4	46.4	46.5	46.5	46.8	46.4	46.7	46.6		
34	46.8	47.0	47.0	46.9	47.5	47.0	47.3	46.8		
35	46.8	46.4	46.7	46.8	46.9	46.9	47.4	47.0		
36	46.7	46.3	46.7	46.7	46.7	46.8	47.2	46.3		
37	46.6	46.5	46.6	46.9	47.0	46.9	46.9	46.7		
38	46.6	.	46.7	46.9	47.3	47.1	47.3	47.2		
39	46.7	.	46.8	46.9	47.0	47.1	47.2	47.2		
Women - Femmes - Mujeres										
ISIC 2 - CITI 2 - CIIU 2										
Total	46.1	47.8	46.6	46.9	47.2	47.1	47.2	46.7		
31	46.2	46.4	46.5	46.5	46.6	46.3	46.8	46.5		
32	46.2	46.4	46.6	47.2	47.9	47.6	47.6	47.6		
33	40.5	46.4	46.8	46.5	47.8	46.5	46.3	46.4		
34	44.8	45.6	46.6	47.0	47.5	46.8	47.2	46.5		
35	46.3	46.1	46.6	46.7	47.2	47.1	47.4	46.4		
36	46.4	46.7	46.5	46.0	46.1	45.7	46.4	45.2		
37	45.3	46.5	46.3	46.6	46.9	46.9	47.0	46.7		
38	43.6	.	46.4	46.6	46.9	47.0	47.6	47.4		
39	45.9	.	46.6	46.9	47.0	47.6	47.3	47.2		
Indonesia (BA) (a) [2][3]					*Total employment - Emploi total - Empleo total*					
Total men and women - Total hommes et femmes - Total hombres y mujeres										
ISIC 3 - CITI 3 - CIIU 3										
Total	.	43.1	43.4	42.8	43.3	44.0	43.6 [4]	43.3	44.1	43.8
Men - Hommes - Hombres										
ISIC 3 - CITI 3 - CIIU 3										
Total	.	45.9	46.1	45.3	45.5	46.3	45.9 [4]	45.9	46.7	46.5
Women - Femmes - Mujeres										
ISIC 3 - CITI 3 - CIIU 3										
Total	.	39.2	39.7	39.3	40.4	40.4	40.3 [4]	39.6	40.5	40.3
Israel (BA) (a) [2][5]					*Total employment - Emploi total - Empleo total*					
Total men and women - Total hommes et femmes - Total hombres y mujeres										
ISIC 3 - CITI 3 - CIIU 3										
Total	43.9	44.7	43.9	44.4	43.9	44.0	44.0	43.9	43.9	43.6
15	44.8	45.5	45.0	45.0	44.2	44.8	44.0	44.4	44.0	43.1
16	.	.	.	.	.	.	.	.	.	.
17	43.8	43.0	43.5	42.6	43.8	42.9	44.4	44.8	43.1	42.8
18	40.0	42.8	39.8	40.7	41.5	41.6	39.2	39.2	39.2	36.5
19	39.5	41.5	.	.	.	.	.	.	.	.
20	44.0	46.5	44.7	43.5	41.7	46.5	41.3	44.8	43.5	43.3
21	43.0	45.0	42.3	46.0	42.4	42.1	44.8	42.0	43.1	42.3
22	40.1	39.6	40.9	39.9	38.3	39.9	39.7	39.9	39.8	40.7
23	.	45.5	44.6	44.7	.	48.4	43.8	.	.	44.1
24	43.3	44.6	42.0	43.0	44.1	43.2	44.9	43.4	43.0	43.1
25	44.7	45.3	45.1	45.1	43.6	44.7	45.5	44.6	45.6	46.2
26	46.6	47.0	45.7	47.1	47.6	44.9	45.5	43.9	45.4	45.7
27	47.4	47.2	44.5	47.9	45.0	47.1	44.2	48.8	41.5	43.6
28	45.2	45.1	44.9	45.7	44.8	44.2	45.3	45.8	45.6	45.5
29	44.7	46.4	45.7	46.7	45.1	44.3	44.3	44.4	45.7	44.4
30	43.2	46.3	43.5	45.0	46.1	43.6	44.4	44.7	43.1	45.7
31	44.7	45.0	44.6	44.7	43.4	42.1	44.1	42.1	42.1	41.6
32	44.4	46.3	44.6	45.3	45.7	46.0	45.1	44.9	45.9	45.1
32-33	44.4	46.3	44.6	45.3	45.7	46.0	45.1	44.9	45.9	
33	44.1	43.9	44.2	45.1	46.6	44.5	45.0	44.4	44.3	44.2
34	46.5	45.6	43.5	45.0	43.8	45.6	47.5	47.8	45.8	42.3
35	43.0	43.7	43.4	43.3	42.6	44.2	44.6	44.0	43.4	44.6
36	43.6	44.6	43.2	43.4	41.8	42.3	41.9	41.5	42.0	40.6
37	.	42.1	35.4	.	.	.	.	41.1	44.1	.

Explanatory notes: see p. 721.

[1] Dec. of each year. [2] Persons aged 15 years and over. [3] Aug. of each year. [4] Nov. [5] Excl. armed forces.

Notes explicatives: voir p. 723.

[1] Déc. de chaque année. [2] Personnes âgées de 15 ans et plus. [3] Août de chaque année. [4] Nov. [5] Non compris les forces armées.

Notas explicativas: véase p. 725.

[1] Dic. de cada año. [2] Personas de 15 años y más. [3] Agosto de cada año. [4] Nov. [5] Excl. las fuerzas armadas.

HOURS OF WORK   DURÉE DU TRAVAIL   HORAS DE TRABAJO   4B

In manufacturing   Dans les industries manufacturières   En las industrias manufactureras

Per week - Par semaine - Por semana

Israel (BA) (a) [1][2] — Total employment - Emploi total - Empleo total

Men - Hommes - Hombres
ISIC 3 - CITI 3 - CIIU 3

	1999	2000	2001	2002	2003	2004	2005	2006	2007	2008
Total	45.8	46.6	45.6	46.1	45.5	45.5	45.8	45.4	45.8	45.1
15	46.9	47.5	47.1	46.8	46.1	46.0	46.0	45.7	46.2	44.4
16	.	.	.	.	.	.	.	.	.	.
17	48.0	46.2	45.6	46.4	47.6	46.0	47.8	47.5	45.4	45.8
18	46.7	49.8	45.5	46.1	47.3	47.7	45.6	46.1	47.1	40.7
19	.	.	.	.	.	.	.	.	.	.
20	45.2	47.7	44.9	44.7	42.4	46.7	43.9	46.8	44.6	45.2
21	45.1	47.6	43.9	47.6	44.0	43.5	47.5	44.2	45.5	42.6
22	43.3	43.6	43.8	43.0	40.7	43.6	42.9	43.4	42.8	43.0
23		45.8	45.6	46.1		49.6				
24	45.1	46.5	43.5	45.5	46.4	45.0	46.2	45.2	45.3	45.6
25	47.0	46.4	46.2	46.1	44.6	46.2	46.8	45.7	47.2	47.7
26	48.2	48.9	47.0	47.9	48.6	46.2	46.6	44.9	46.7	46.9
27	48.4	49.6	46.2	49.2	46.2	47.7	44.6	50.6	43.3	44.1
28	46.2	46.4	46.1	46.8	45.7	45.3	46.7	47.1	47.0	46.4
29	45.4	47.4	46.7	47.7	46.4	45.1	45.2	45.2	46.8	45.6
30	44.1	47.8	43.9	46.6		44.7	44.8	46.4	44.2	45.6
31	45.8	46.6	46.1	45.1	45.0	43.8	45.3	43.6	43.2	41.1
32	45.6	48.3	46.4	46.8	47.5	47.3	46.6	45.6	47.4	46.4
32-33	45.6	48.3	46.4	46.8	47.5	47.3	46.6	45.6	47.4	
33	45.3	45.0	45.6	46.6	47.8	45.4	46.4	45.9	46.3	45.7
34	47.3	46.3	44.5	47.1	45.2	45.6	47.6	48.1	47.6	43.5
35	43.4	44.7	44.8	43.6	43.4	44.7	45.1	44.7	44.0	45.1
36	45.2	45.7	44.2	45.0	43.3	44.4	43.9	42.8	43.4	42.3
37	.	.	.	.	.	.	.	42.9	.	.

Women - Femmes - Mujeres
ISIC 3 - CITI 3 - CIIU 3

	1999	2000	2001	2002	2003	2004	2005	2006	2007	2008
Total	39.0	39.8	39.4	39.9	39.4	39.9	39.2	39.6	39.1	39.8
15	39.8	40.0	40.3	41.2	40.2	42.0	39.6	41.3	38.8	39.7
16	.	.	.	.	.	.	.	.	.	.
17	39.9	39.3	40.7	39.0	40.4	40.2	40.8	42.0	40.2	39.7
18	37.8	39.8	37.5	37.7	-	38.3	36.3	35.5	34.6	35.0
19						36.8				
20	.	.	.	.	.	.	.	.	.	.
21								36.8	38.8	41.7
22	35.4	34.7	36.3	33.7	34.3	34.5	34.7	34.8	35.5	37.3
23	.	.	.	.	.	.	.	.	.	.
24	39.7	40.8	39.3	38.9	40.6	40.1	42.6	40.4	39.5	39.2
25	39.1	41.5	41.6	41.8	40.4	40.6	40.7	41.3	40.5	41.8
26								37.9	.	39.2
27								41.2		
28	36.6	38.3	37.7	38.5	37.7	37.8	36.3	37.1	38.3	40.5
29	41.9	41.8	39.6	40.8	40.1	41.1	40.2	39.0	39.8	39.7
30			42.7							
31	40.3	40.6	39.1	42.9	38.3	37.8	40.7	38.0	39.5	42.8
32	42.2	43.0	41.5	42.5	42.2	43.7	42.2	43.7	43.1	43.0
32-33	42.2	43.0	41.5	42.5	42.2	43.7	42.2	43.7	43.1	
33	41.0	41.1	40.6	42.0	43.3	42.3	41.6	40.8	39.9	41.1
34	.	.	.	.	.	.	.	.	.	.
35	41.0	.	37.9	41.7	38.8	41.6	41.2	40.2	39.7	41.1
36	36.3	40.2	39.1	38.1	36.2	35.7	35.7	36.4	37.1	35.4

Japan (BA) (a) — All persons engaged - Effectif occupé - Efectivo ocupado

Total men and women - Total hommes et femmes - Total hombres y mujeres
ISIC 2 - CITI 2 - CIIU 2   ISIC 3 - CITI 3 - CIIU 3

	1999	2000	2001	2002	2003	2004	2005	2006	2007	2008	ISIC 3
Total	42.7	43.7	42.8	43.1	43.1	43.5	43.5	43.5	42.9	42.4	Total [3]
					41.2	41.3	41.2	41.2	40.8	40.7	15 [4]
					.	.	.	.	.	.	16
					43.0	43.2	42.7	42.1	41.3	42.0	17
					40.1	40.1	39.8	40.0	39.3	39.4	18 [5]
					40.9	39.2	40.0	41.2	43.9	40.8	19 [6]
					43.6	43.3	43.1	43.6	42.6	42.2	20 [7]
					42.3	42.1	42.1	42.1	41.9	41.5	21
					45.4	45.4	45.0	45.2	44.6	44.1	22 [3]
					42.8	45.4	44.0	44.0	44.9	43.3	23 [8]
					42.7	42.6	42.8	43.5	42.7	42.3	24
					42.8	42.7	43.2	42.8	41.9	41.7	25 [9]
					43.6	43.9	44.5	43.8	43.1	43.4	26
					44.4	44.9	45.0	44.9	43.9	43.9	27 [10]
					43.7	44.1	43.9	44.0	43.1	42.6	28
					45.3	45.8	45.4	45.6	44.5	44.1	29
					43.3	44.0	44.4	44.1	42.9	42.2	31
					.	.	.	.	.	.	32
					43.5	44.4	43.6	43.4	43.2	42.6	33
					44.1	44.7	45.3	45.6	44.8	43.5	34-35
					39.8	40.5	39.1	39.2	39.7	39.5	36 [11]

Explanatory notes: see p. 721.

[1] Excl. armed forces. [2] Persons aged 15 years and over. [3] Excl. publishing. [4] Excl. beverages. [5] Excl. dressing and dyeing of fur. [6] Incl. dressing and dying of fur. [7] Excl. articles of straw. [8] Excl. nuclear fuel. [9] Excl. rubber. [10] Excl. basic precious and non-ferrous metals. [11] Excl. furniture and articles of straw.

Notes explicatives: voir p. 723.

[1] Non compris les forces armées. [2] Personnes âgées de 15 ans et plus. [3] Non compris l'édition. [4] Non compris les boissons. [5] Non compris la préparation et teinture des fourrures. [6] Y compris la préparation et teinture des fourrures. [7] Non compris les articles de vannerie. [8] Non compris les combustibles nucléaires. [9] Non compris le caoutchouc. [10] Non compris les métaux de base et non ferreux. [11] Non compris les meubles et les articles de vannerie.

Notas explicativas: véase p. 725.

[1] Excl. las fuerzas armadas. [2] Personas de 15 años y más. [3] Excl. las editoriales. [4] Excl. las bebidas. [5] Excl. el adobo y teñida de pieles. [6] Incl. el adobo y teñida de pieles. [7] Excl. los artículos de paja. [8] Excl. el combustible nuclear. [9] Excl. el caucho. [10] Excl. los metales básicos y no ferrosos. [11] Excl. los muebles y los artículos de paja.

4B

HOURS OF WORK	DURÉE DU TRAVAIL	HORAS DE TRABAJO
In manufacturing	**Dans les industries manufacturières**	**En las industrias manufactureras**

	Per week			Par semaine				Por semana		
	1999	2000	2001	2002	2003	2004	2005	2006	2007	2008

Japan (BA) (a) — All persons engaged - Effectif occupé - Efectivo ocupado

Men - Hommes - Hombres
ISIC 2 - CITI 2 - CIIU 2   ISIC 3 - CITI 3 - CIIU 3

	1999	2000	2001	2002	2003	2004	2005	2006	2007	2008	
Total	46.0	47.1	46.2	46.4	46.4	46.7	46.6	46.7	45.8	45.2	Total [1]
					47.7	47.8	47.4	47.2	46.7	46.6	15 [2]
					46.9	47.2	46.9	45.6	44.5	44.7	17
					47.4	47.3	46.9	47.1	45.4	46.1	18 [3]
					46.5	45.0	46.4	46.2	48.6	46.9	19 [4]
					45.7	45.1	45.4	46.0	44.9	44.1	20 [5]
					45.2	45.1	45.4	45.2	44.7	44.2	21
					49.1	48.4	48.3	48.5	47.8	46.9	22 [1]
					43.2	45.8	44.7	45.1	45.7	43.9	23 [6]
					44.2	44.0	44.0	45.1	44.2	43.7	24
					47.0	46.4	47.2	47.1	45.9	45.5	25 [7]
					45.1	45.6	46.4	45.5	44.7	44.8	26
					45.0	45.4	45.8	45.6	44.4	44.5	27 [8]
					46.3	46.8	46.7	46.8	45.6	44.9	28
					47.4	47.8	47.3	47.6	46.5	46.0	29
					46.6	47.1	47.4	47.0	45.9	45.2	31
											32
					46.4	47.2	46.6	46.4	46.5	45.4	33
					45.4	46.2	46.5	46.8	45.8	44.3	34-35
					45.2	46.1	44.3	44.7	44.6	44.6	36 [9]

Women - Femmes - Mujeres
ISIC 2 - CITI 2 - CIIU 2   ISIC 3 - CITI 3 - CIIU 3

	1999	2000	2001	2002	2003	2004	2005	2006	2007	2008	
Total	36.6	37.3	36.4	36.6	36.6	36.9	36.7	36.9	36.4	36.1	Total [1]
					36.0	35.9	36.1	36.2	35.8	35.4	15 [2]
					38.2	38.1	37.4	37.3	36.6	37.6	17
					37.4	37.4	37.1	37.4	36.8	36.6	18 [3]
					34.6	33.5	33.2	35.3	38.4	33.9	19 [4]
					37.7	37.5	36.2	36.0	35.9	36.1	20 [5]
					36.0	35.4	34.7	35.3	35.5	35.0	21
					37.4	38.7	38.0	37.8	37.0	37.7	22 [1]
					38.5	40.4	40.0	38.8	39.7	36.9	23 [6]
					37.9	38.6	39.1	38.5	38.0	37.8	24
					35.6	36.5	36.0	35.6	35.4	35.1	25 [7]
					38.0	38.0	37.7	38.2	37.4	38.6	26
					38.7	38.9	39.1	39.8	38.8	37.8	27 [8]
					35.6	35.6	35.4	35.4	35.4	35.1	28
					36.1	36.9	36.6	37.0	36.0	35.7	29
					37.0	37.3	37.2	37.9	36.4	35.6	31
											32
					38.5	39.3	37.4	37.8	37.4	37.3	33
					38.1	37.9	38.5	39.0	38.7	38.3	34-35
					32.2	32.9	32.4	31.6	32.7	32.4	36 [9]

Japan (BA) (a) — Employees - Salariés - Asalariados

Total men and women - Total hommes et femmes - Total hombres y mujeres
ISIC 3 - CITI 3 - CIIU 3

	1999	2000	2001	2002	2003	2004	2005	2006	2007	2008
Total [1]	.	.	.	.	43.6	44.0	44.0	44.1	43.3	42.8
15 [2]	.	.	.	.	41.0	41.3	41.2	41.2	40.8	40.6
17	.	.	.	.	43.2	43.9	43.0	42.2	41.8	42.5
18 [3]	.	.	.	.	41.9	42.4	41.9	41.8	40.8	41.0
19 [4]	.	.	.	.	42.4	42.3	42.0	42.2	42.8	41.1
20 [5]	.	.	.	.	44.2	44.1	43.8	44.5	43.2	43.0
21	.	.	.	.	43.2	43.0	43.0	43.2	42.9	42.3
22 [1]	.	.	.	.	46.0	46.0	45.6	45.6	44.9	44.5
23 [6]	.	.	.	.	42.8	45.5	44.0	44.1	44.9	43.3
24	.	.	.	.	42.7	42.6	42.8	43.5	42.7	42.3
25 [7]	.	.	.	.	43.2	43.1	43.6	43.2	42.4	42.2
26	.	.	.	.	43.9	44.4	45.0	44.1	43.5	43.6
27 [8]	.	.	.	.	44.4	44.9	45.1	45.1	44.0	43.9
28	.	.	.	.	44.3	44.6	44.3	44.7	43.5	42.9
29	.	.	.	.	45.5	46.0	45.5	45.7	43.5	44.3
31	.	.	.	.	43.8	44.6	44.9	44.7	44.7	42.7
32										
33	.	.	.	.	43.6	44.6	43.6	43.5	43.4	42.8
34										
34-35	.	.	.	.	44.2	44.8	45.4	45.7	44.8	43.5
36 [9]	.	.	.	.	41.5	42.5	41.8	41.9	41.9	41.9

Explanatory notes: see p. 721.

[1] Excl. publishing. [2] Excl. beverages. [3] Excl. dressing and dyeing of fur. [4] Incl. dressing and dying of fur. [5] Excl. articles of straw. [6] Excl. nuclear fuel. [7] Excl. rubber. [8] Excl. basic precious and non-ferrous metals. [9] Excl. furniture and articles of straw.

Notes explicatives: voir p. 723.

[1] Non compris l'édition. [2] Non compris les boissons. [3] Non compris la préparation et teinture des fourrures. [4] Y compris la préparation et teinture des fourrures. [5] Non compris les articles de vannerie. [6] Non compris les combustibles nucléaires. [7] Non compris le caoutchouc. [8] Non compris les métaux de base et non ferreux. [9] Non compris les meubles et les articles de vannerie.

Notas explicativas: véase p. 725.

[1] Excl. las editoriales. [2] Excl. las bebidas. [3] Excl. el adobo y teñida de pieles. [4] Incl. el adobo y teñida de pieles. [5] Excl. los artículos de paja. [6] Excl. el combustible nuclear. [7] Excl. el caucho. [8] Excl. los metales básicos y no ferrosos. [9] Excl. los muebles y lós artículos de paja.

In manufacturing   Dans les industries manufacturières   En las industrias manufactureras

		Per week			Par semaine			Por semana	
1999	2000	2001	2002	2003	2004	2005	2006	2007	2008

Japan (BA) (a)   Employees - Salariés - Asalariados

Men - Hommes - Hombres
ISIC 3 - CITI 3 - CIIU 3

	1999	2000	2001	2002	2003	2004	2005	2006	2007	2008
Total [1]	.	.	.	.	46.5	46.8	46.8	46.9	46.0	45.3
15 [2]	.	.	.	.	47.6	47.9	47.5	47.3	46.8	46.7
17	.	.	.	.	46.4	47.2	46.5	44.9	44.4	44.6
18 [3]	.	.	.	.	47.7	48.6	47.8	48.0	46.2	46.6
19 [4]	.	.	.	.	46.3	47.5	46.9	45.8	46.5	46.5
20 [5]	.	.	.	.	46.1	45.8	45.8	46.4	45.2	44.7
21	.	.	.	.	45.9	45.6	45.6	45.8	45.2	44.8
22 [1]	.	.	.	.	49.4	48.8	48.8	48.8	48.1	47.3
23 [6]	.	.	.	.	43.2	45.8	44.7	44.9	45.7	43.9
24	.	.	.	.	44.2	44.0	44.0	45.1	44.2	43.7
25 [7]	.	.	.	.	47.0	46.5	47.2	47.1	46.1	45.7
26	.	.	.	.	45.4	45.9	46.5	45.5	44.9	44.9
27 [8]	.	.	.	.	44.9	45.4	45.8	45.7	44.5	44.5
28	.	.	.	.	46.6	47.0	46.8	47.1	45.7	45.0
29	.	.	.	.	47.5	47.8	47.3	47.2	46.5	46.0
31	.	.	.	.	46.7	47.3	47.5	.	46.1	45.4
32	.	.	.	.	47.2	.	.	.	.	.
33	.	.	.	.	46.4	47.1	46.4	46.5	46.4	45.6
34	.	.	.	.	.	.	.	.	.	.
34-35	.	.	.	.	45.4	46.2	46.6	46.8	45.8	44.3
36 [9]	.	.	.	.	45.5	47.0	46.3	46.4	45.6	45.6

Women - Femmes - Mujeres
ISIC 3 - CITI 3 - CIIU 3

	1999	2000	2001	2002	2003	2004	2005	2006	2007	2008
Total [1]	.	.	.	.	37.5	37.8	37.6	37.7	37.1	36.8
15 [2]	.	.	.	.	35.8	35.9	36.1	36.2	35.7	35.3
17	.	.	.	.	38.8	39.3	38.1	38.2	37.9	38.9
18 [3]	.	.	.	.	39.8	40.2	39.7	39.6	38.8	38.6
19 [4]	.	.	.	.	37.6	37.6	35.7	37.6	38.6	34.9
20 [5]	.	.	.	.	38.8	38.6	37.6	37.9	36.8	37.2
21	.	.	.	.	36.9	36.7	36.5	37.0	36.9	36.0
22 [1]	.	.	.	.	38.2	39.5	38.6	38.2	37.4	38.1
23 [6]	.	.	.	.	38.5	40.9	40.0	39.8	39.7	36.9
24	.	.	.	.	37.9	38.6	39.1	38.5	38.0	37.8
25 [7]	.	.	.	.	36.5	37.2	36.8	36.3	36.1	35.8
26	.	.	.	.	38.4	38.9	39.1	39.1	38.2	39.2
27 [8]	.	.	.	.	38.8	39.3	39.7	40.4	39.1	38.0
28	.	.	.	.	36.9	36.7	36.7	36.9	36.4	35.9
29	.	.	.	.	36.8	37.7	37.0	37.5	36.6	36.4
31	.	.	.	.	37.9	38.4	38.4	39.0	37.4	36.5
32	.	.	.	.	.	.	.	.	.	.
33	.	.	.	.	38.9	39.9	37.7	38.1	37.8	37.6
34	.	.	.	.	.	.	.	.	.	.
34-35	.	.	.	.	38.5	38.2	38.7	39.3	39.1	38.5
36 [9]	.	.	.	.	35.0	35.8	35.7	34.9	36.0	36.0

Japan (DA) (a) [10]   Employees - Salariés - Asalariados

Total men and women - Total hommes et femmes - Total hombres y mujeres
ISIC 3 - CITI 3 - CIIU 3

	1999	2000	2001	2002	2003	2004	2005	2006	2007	2008
Total	.	.	.	.	.	.	38.5	38.7	38.7	38.2
15	.	.	.	.	.	.	.	.	.	.
16	.	.	.	.	.	.	.	.	.	.
17	.	.	.	.	.	.	38.3	38.4	38.3	38.1
18	.	.	.	.	.	.	37.3	37.4	36.6	36.4
19	.	.	.	.	.	.	38.2	38.8	37.9	37.1
20	.	.	.	.	.	.	40.2	40.8	41.7	41.2
21	.	.	.	.	.	.	38.1	38.2	39.0	38.8
22	.	.	.	.	.	.	40.4	40.4	41.0	40.7
23	.	.	.	.	.	.	37.1	37.9	38.0	37.5
24	.	.	.	.	.	.	36.2	36.7	36.5	36.3
25	.	.	.	.	.	.	39.0	39.1	39.0	38.6
26	.	.	.	.	.	.	38.2	38.8	39.8	39.0
27	.	.	.	.	.	.	39.6	40.0	40.6	39.9
28	.	.	.	.	.	.	39.7	39.8	39.6	39.3
29	.	.	.	.	.	.	39.8	40.1	40.1	39.7
30	.	.	.	.	.	.	.	.	.	.
31	.	.	.	.	.	.	37.7	38.1	37.6	37.1
32	.	.	.	.	.	.	37.6	38.0	37.9	37.3
33	.	.	.	.	.	.	37.7	38.2	38.6	38.2
34	.	.	.	.	.	.	.	.	.	.
35	.	.	.	.	.	.	.	.	.	.
36	.	.	.	.	.	.	36.6	37.1	37.0	36.7
37	.	.	.	.	.	.	.	.	.	.

Explanatory notes: see p. 721.   Notes explicatives: voir p. 723.   Notas explicativas: véase p. 725.

[1] Excl. publishing. [2] Excl. beverages. [3] Excl. dressing and dyeing of fur. [4] Incl. dressing and dying of fur. [5] Excl. articles of straw. [6] Excl. nuclear fuel. [7] Excl. rubber. [8] Excl. basic precious and non-ferrous metals. [9] Excl. furniture and articles of straw. [10] Some divisions do not fully correspond to the classification.

[1] Non compris l'édition. [2] Non compris les boissons. [3] Non compris la préparation et teinture des fourrures. [4] Y compris la préparation et teinture des fourrures. [5] Non compris les articles de vannerie. [6] Non compris les combustibles nucléaires. [7] Non compris le caoutchouc. [8] Non compris les métaux de base et non ferreux. [9] Non compris les meubles et les articles de vannerie. [10] Certaines divisions ne correspondent pas strictement à la classification.

[1] Excl. las editoriales. [2] Excl. las bebidas. [3] Excl. el adobo y teñida de pieles. [4] Incl. el adobo y teñida de pieles. [5] Excl. los artículos de paja. [6] Excl. el combustible nuclear. [7] Excl. el caucho. [8] Excl. los metales básicos y no ferrosos. [9] Excl. los muebles y los artículos de paja. [10] Algunas divisiones no corresponden estrictamente a la clasificacion.

In manufacturing   **Dans les industries manufacturières**   **En las industrias manufactureras**

	Per week				Par semaine				Por semana	
	1999	2000	2001	2002	2003	2004	2005	2006	2007	2008

Japan (DA) (a) [1]   Employees - Salariés - Asalariados

Men - Hommes - Hombres
ISIC 3 - CITI 3 - CIIU 3

	1999	2000	2001	2002	2003	2004	2005	2006	2007	2008
Total							39.8	40.1	40.2	39.6
15										
16										
17							39.3	39.3	39.6	39.4
18							39.1	39.5	39.5	39.3
19							40.3	40.5	39.3	38.5
20							41.1	41.6	42.8	42.2
21							39.0	39.1	39.9	39.7
22							41.5	41.5	42.0	41.7
23							37.4	38.1	38.3	37.8
24							36.9	37.3	37.5	37.3
25							40.4	40.3	40.8	40.4
26							39.1	39.6	40.7	39.9
27							40.0	40.3	40.9	40.2
28							41.0	40.9	41.0	40.5
29							40.6	40.9	41.0	40.5
30										
31							38.9	39.3	38.8	38.2
32							38.6	39.0	39.0	38.4
33							39.1	39.5	40.0	39.4
34										
35										
36							38.4	39.2	38.8	38.5
37										

Women - Femmes - Mujeres
ISIC 3 - CITI 3 - CIIU 3

	1999	2000	2001	2002	2003	2004	2005	2006	2007	2008
Total							34.8	35.1	34.6	34.3
15										
16										
17							36.4	36.7	36.2	36.0
18							36.7	36.6	35.7	35.6
19							36.0	36.9	36.4	35.6
20							36.6	37.3	37.2	37.0
21							34.9	35.1	35.7	35.4
22							36.8	37.1	38.4	38.1
23							34.4	35.1	35.0	34.6
24							34.2	34.6	33.6	33.3
25							35.6	36.3	34.7	34.5
26							35.4	35.8	36.2	35.2
27							35.9	36.3	36.5	35.7
28							35.3	35.8	35.3	35.4
29							35.3	35.7	35.1	35.0
30										
31							34.3	34.8	34.1	33.7
32							34.6	34.7	34.3	33.7
33							34.5	35.3	35.3	35.1
34										
35										
36							33.2	33.3	33.6	33.1
37										

Jordan (DA) (b) [2] [3]   Employees - Salariés - Asalariados

Total men and women - Total hommes et femmes - Total hombres y mujeres
ISIC 3 - CITI 3 - CIIU 3

	1999	2000	2001	2002	2003	2004	2005	2006	2007	2008
Total	234	258	256	258	256	256	259	253	256	
15		273	265	269						
16		271	248	254						
17		246	254	256						
18		249	250	249						
19		261	252	243						
20		266	261	272						
21		256	250	249						
22		249	250	249						
23		248	247	248						
24		248	249	251						
25		261	249	255						
26		257	263							
27		256	248	247						
28		260	256	259						
29		251		249						
30		252	247							
31		253								
32		253								
33		271	249	250						
34		261	268	248						
36		261	256	271						

Explanatory notes: see p. 721.   Notes explicatives: voir p. 723.   Notas explicativas: véase p. 725.

[1] Some divisions do not fully correspond to the classification. [2] Per month. [3] Oct. of each year.   [1] Certaines divisions ne correspondent pas strictement à la classification. [2] Par mois. [3] Oct. de chaque année.   [1] Algunas divisiones no corresponden estrictamente a la clasificacion. [2] Por mes. [3] Oct. de cada año.

In manufacturing   Dans les industries manufacturières   En las industrias manufactureras

Per week — Par semaine — Por semana

Jordan (DA) (b) [1][2] — Employees - Salariés - Asalariados

Men - Hommes - Hombres
ISIC 3 - CITI 3 - CIIU 3

	1999	2000	2001	2002	2003	2004	2005	2006	2007	2008
Total	236	260	257	260	257	257	261	255	255	.
15	.	274	265	271	.	.	.	.	.	.
16	.	272	248	254	.	.	.	.	.	.
17	.	246	254	258	.	.	.	.	.	.
18	.	248	252	249	.	.	.	.	.	.
19	.	263	251	242	.	.	.	.	.	.
20	.	267	261	272	.	.	.	.	.	.
21	.	257	249	249	.	.	.	.	.	.
22	.	250	250	250	.	.	.	.	.	.
23	.	248	247	248	.	.	.	.	.	.
24	.	248	249	251	.	.	.	.	.	.
25	.	261	249	256	.	.	.	.	.	.
26	.	257	264	266	.	.	.	.	.	.
27	.	257	248	247	.	.	.	.	.	.
28	.	260	256	259	.	.	.	.	.	.
29	.	251	246	249	.	.	.	.	.	.
30	.	252	247	248	.	.	.	.	.	.
31	.	254	248	264	.	.	.	.	.	.
32	.	249	250	251	.	.	.	.	.	.
33	.	271	250	250	.	.	.	.	.	.
34	.	271	269	248	.	.	.	.	.	.
36	.	262	257	272	.	.	.	.	.	.

Women - Femmes - Mujeres
ISIC 3 - CITI 3 - CIIU 3

	1999	2000	2001	2002	2003	2004	2005	2006	2007	2008
Total	222	251	250	250	248	256	254	248	.	.
15	.	259	251	251	.	.	.	.	.	.
16	.	248	248	244	.	.	.	.	.	.
17	.	246	254	252	.	.	.	.	.	.
18	.	249	249	249	.	.	.	.	.	.
19	.	246	260	248	.	.	.	.	.	.
20	.	248	248	248	.	.	.	.	.	.
21	.	249	256	250	.	.	.	.	.	.
22	.	248	245	247	.	.	.	.	.	.
23	.	248	248	248	.	.	.	.	.	.
24	.	248	248	250	.	.	.	.	.	.
25	.	248	248	248	.	.	.	.	.	.
26	.	243	247	249	.	.	.	.	.	.
27	.	246	248	248	.	.	.	.	.	.
28	.	262	247	248	.	.	.	.	.	.
29	.	253	244	248	.	.	.	.	.	.
30	.	252	248	248	.	.	.	.	.	.
31	.	248	248	276	.	.	.	.	.	.
32	.	263	254	257	.	.	.	.	.	.
33	.	270	248	248	.	.	.	.	.	.
34	.	0	0	0	.	.	.	.	.	.
36	.	258	252	248	.	.	.	.	.	.

Korea, Republic of (DA) (a) [3] — Employees - Salariés - Asalariados

Total men and women - Total hommes et femmes - Total hombres y mujeres
ISIC 3 - CITI 3 - CIIU 3

	1999	2000	2001	2002	2003	2004	2005	2006	2007	2008
Total	50.1	49.3	48.3	47.7	47.6	47.4	46.9	46.0	45.4	43.7 [4]
15	51.7	52.1	52.1	49.5	48.8	48.4	47.8	47.1	46.3	46.4 [4]
16	44.9	47.6	49.5	45.0	43.4	40.4	42.1	41.8	42.0	41.1 [4]
17	54.8	54.0	53.3	51.0	50.3	49.7	49.3	48.8	48.7	46.2 [4]
18	47.5	47.4	47.0	46.5	45.3	45.3	45.1	43.8	43.2	40.5 [4]
19	51.7	50.8	50.3	48.1	45.9	45.2	44.0	43.3	42.7	42.6 [4]
20	51.2	48.5	49.0	48.7	49.2	48.4	49.6	49.3	48.2	52.5 [4]
21	51.6	50.4	50.0	49.7	49.3	49.4	49.5	48.4	47.5	45.1 [4]
22	47.5	47.9	46.9	45.8	45.3	45.8	45.5	44.9	44.1	41.0 [4]
23	42.9	43.7	44.2	43.3	43.9	43.6	42.1	41.1	40.8	39.8 [4]
24	47.3	46.4	45.8	44.2	44.6	44.6	44.2	42.8	42.7	40.1 [4]
25	51.1	51.0	49.6	51.0	51.6	51.4	50.4	48.8	47.9	45.8 [4]
26	51.1	50.4	50.9	49.9	49.0	48.6	48.6	47.8	46.6	41.4 [4]
27	53.1	50.4	50.7	51.7	52.2	51.8	48.3	48.5	47.2	43.7 [4]
28	51.5	50.3	49.1	48.4	47.9	47.8	47.9	47.6	47.1	47.3 [4]
29	49.6	49.2	47.9	47.1	46.8	47.1	47.5	46.6	45.2	43.7 [4]
30	46.7	45.8	45.4	45.4	45.6	43.4	44.2	42.9	44.2	42.6 [4]
31	49.7	49.1	49.0	47.7	47.1	47.0	46.6	45.5	44.8	44.2 [4]
32	52.0	49.0	46.5	46.9	47.0	46.6	44.9	44.0	44.1	44.1 [4]
33	46.2	46.3	45.7	45.8	44.9	45.3	44.4	44.6	42.9	43.0 [4]
34	46.4	46.5	44.2	45.2	46.7	47.0	48.6	46.7	46.6	43.6 [4]
35	46.7	49.0	47.1	46.2	46.1	45.9	45.2	45.4	45.3	43.8 [4]
36	48.7	47.8	47.3	46.7	46.5	46.4	46.1	44.7	44.3	42.2 [4]
37	51.9	49.5	50.7	49.0	49.5	49.0	46.0	46.0	45.6	49.6 [4]

Explanatory notes: see p. 721.

[1] Per month. [2] Oct. of each year. [3] Establishments with 10 or more permanent employees. [4] Methodology revised; data not strictly comparable.

Notes explicatives: voir p. 723.

[1] Par mois. [2] Oct. de chaque année. [3] Etablissements occupant 10 salariés permanents ou plus. [4] Méthodologie révisée; les données ne sont pas strictement comparables.

Notas explicativas: véase p. 725.

[1] Por mes. [2] Oct. de cada año. [3] Establecimientos con 10 y más asalariados permanentes. [4] Metodología revisada; los datos no son estrictamente comparables.

Korea, Republic of (DA) (a) [1] Employees - Salariés - Asalariados

Men - Hommes - Hombres
ISIC 3 - CITI 3 - CIIU 3

	1999	2000	2001	2002	2003	2004	2005	2006	2007	2008
Total	49.8	49.2	48.3	47.6	47.6	47.3	47.0	46.0	45.5	.
15	52.3	52.1	52.5	49.3	48.6	48.0	48.1	47.4	46.6	.
16	45.5	47.9	50.0	45.9	43.5	40.5	42.2	42.0	42.3	.
17	54.5	53.8	53.0	51.5	50.8	50.1	49.1	48.6	49.0	.
18	46.4	46.1	45.5	45.4	44.7	44.7	44.9	43.4	43.0	.
19	50.6	49.5	48.6	47.7	45.5	44.9	44.0	43.2	43.1	.
20	50.7	48.6	49.5	48.4	49.1	48.5	50.3	49.8	48.6	.
21	52.1	50.5	50.2	50.2	50.2	50.1	50.1	49.0	48.0	.
22	48.1	48.5	47.8	46.2	45.7	46.1	46.0	45.6	44.8	.
23	43.0	43.9	44.3	43.4	44.0	43.8	42.3	41.3	41.0	.
24	47.2	46.3	45.9	44.6	45.0	45.0	44.8	43.3	43.2	.
25	51.4	51.0	49.6	50.7	50.6	50.8	50.6	48.9	48.2	.
26	51.8	51.0	51.7	50.5	49.7	49.1	48.9	48.1	46.8	.
27	53.6	50.8	51.1	52.1	52.7	52.3	48.4	48.7	47.4	.
28	52.0	50.9	49.6	48.8	48.5	48.3	47.7	47.6	47.2	.
29	49.9	49.7	48.4	47.2	46.7	47.1	47.7	46.8	45.5	.
30	45.8	44.0	43.6	45.2	44.8	42.8	43.4	41.9	43.1	.
31	49.1	48.8	48.4	47.7	47.1	46.9	46.7	45.5	45.0	.
32	50.8	48.9	46.8	45.7	45.6	45.4	43.3	42.6	42.7	.
33	45.7	45.6	44.8	45.0	44.3	44.6	43.9	44.3	42.6	.
34	46.0	46.1	43.7	45.1	46.6	46.6	48.4	46.4	46.3	.
35	46.7	49.0	47.1	46.2	46.2	45.9	45.2	45.5	45.4	.
36	48.1	47.2	46.8	46.6	46.4	46.4	46.3	44.9	44.6	.
37	52.9	50.6	51.8	50.5	50.7	50.3	46.3	46.1	45.9	.

Women - Femmes - Mujeres
ISIC 3 - CITI 3 - CIIU 3

	1999	2000	2001	2002	2003	2004	2005	2006	2007	2008
Total	50.7	49.8	48.4	47.9	47.7	47.6	46.9	46.1	45.4	.
15	50.9	52.2	51.5	49.7	49.1	49.0	47.4	46.7	46.0	.
16	44.5	46.2	47.3	41.3	42.9	40.0	41.7	40.4	40.1	.
17	55.1	54.5	53.6	50.2	49.6	49.2	49.4	49.3	48.2	.
18	48.0	48.0	47.7	47.0	45.6	45.5	45.1	44.0	43.2	.
19	53.3	52.3	52.3	48.7	46.5	45.6	44.0	43.5	42.3	.
20	52.6	48.3	47.3	50.3	49.6	48.0	47.1	47.2	47.0	.
21	50.2	49.7	48.8	47.5	45.7	46.9	47.0	46.2	45.3	.
22	45.8	46.6	44.7	44.8	44.5	45.2	44.5	43.2	42.6	.
23	40.9	41.6	42.4	41.9	42.3	41.4	39.7	38.8	39.0	.
24	47.6	46.9	45.5	42.9	43.3	43.3	42.0	41.1	40.8	.
25	50.2	51.0	49.5	52.0	54.9	53.4	50.1	48.7	47.0	.
26	47.8	47.2	46.7	47.4	45.9	46.2	47.0	46.8	45.4	.
27	47.4	46.5	47.5	48.1	46.7	46.3	46.6	46.4	45.4	.
28	49.3	48.1	46.9	46.8	45.6	45.9	48.5	47.5	46.7	.
29	47.5	46.8	45.5	46.8	47.1	47.1	46.2	45.7	43.4	.
30	47.8	49.5	47.5	45.8	47.3	45.0	45.8	45.5	46.4	.
31	50.9	49.8	50.3	47.8	47.2	47.3	46.1	45.4	44.4	.
32	53.8	49.1	46.0	48.8	49.0	48.5	47.3	46.1	46.3	.
33	47.4	47.5	47.4	47.4	46.4	46.7	45.3	45.1	43.6	.
34	49.7	48.4	46.8	45.8	47.3	49.2	49.9	48.4	48.7	.
35	46.7	48.8	46.5	47.0	44.8	45.7	44.8	44.6	44.7	.
36	49.8	48.8	48.2	46.9	46.7	46.6	45.7	44.3	43.5	.
37	46.4	44.3	46.8	45.0	44.2	44.3	44.8	45.5	44.4	.

Korea, Republic of (DA) (a) [1] [2] Employees - Salariés - Asalariados

Total men and women - Total hommes et femmes - Total hombres y mujeres
ISIC 3 - CITI 3 - CIIU 3

	1999	2000	2001	2002	2003	2004	2005	2006	2007	2008
Total	.	.	.	.	.	.	.	.	42.5	43.1
15	.	.	.	.	.	.	.	.	45.2	45.1
16	.	.	.	.	.	.	.	.	41.6	40.6
17	.	.	.	.	.	.	.	.	43.9	45.8
18	.	.	.	.	.	.	.	.	39.5	39.8
19	.	.	.	.	.	.	.	.	39.6	42.1
20	.	.	.	.	.	.	.	.	49.8	52.1
21	.	.	.	.	.	.	.	.	45.2	44.8
22	.	.	.	.	.	.	.	.	39.8	39.7
23	.	.	.	.	.	.	.	.	40.3	39.7
24	.	.	.	.	.	.	.	.	41.6	39.6
25	.	.	.	.	.	.	.	.	46.7	45.5
26	.	.	.	.	.	.	.	.	44.1	40.9
27	.	.	.	.	.	.	.	.	42.7	43.4
28	.	.	.	.	.	.	.	.	46.2	47.2
29	.	.	.	.	.	.	.	.	43.0	42.5
30	.	.	.	.	.	.	.	.	42.6	42.2
31	.	.	.	.	.	.	.	.	43.5	43.3
32	.	.	.	.	.	.	.	.	41.2	43.7
33	.	.	.	.	.	.	.	.	42.0	41.8
34	.	.	.	.	.	.	.	.	44.4	43.4
35	.	.	.	.	.	.	.	.	41.3	43.2
36	.	.	.	.	.	.	.	.	42.1	40.4
37	.	.	.	.	.	.	.	.	42.9	49.3

Explanatory notes: see p. 721. Notes explicatives: voir p. 723. Notas explicativas: véase p. 725.

[1] Establishments with 10 or more permanent employees. [2] Incl. daily and temporary employees.

[1] Etablissements occupant 10 salariés permanents ou plus. [2] Y compris les salaries journaliers et temporaires.

[1] Establecimientos con 10 y más asalariados permanentes. [2] Incl. los asalariados diarios y temporales.

In manufacturing   Dans les industries manufacturières   En las industrias manufactureras

	Per week — Par semaine — Por semana									
	1999	2000	2001	2002	2003	2004	2005	2006	2007	2008

Kyrgyzstan (CA) (a)   Employees - Salariés - Asalariados

Total men and women - Total hommes et femmes - Total hombres y mujeres
ISIC 3 - CITI 3 - CIIU 3

	1999	2000	2001	2002	2003	2004	2005	2006	2007	2008
Total	32.2	32.3	33.2	33.2	34.1	34.4	34.5	.	.	.

Macau, China (BA) (a) [1]   Total employment - Emploi total - Empleo total

Total men and women - Total hommes et femmes - Total hombres y mujeres
ISIC 3 - CITI 3 - CIIU 3

	1999	2000	2001	2002	2003	2004	2005	2006	2007	2008
Total	48.8	48.2	48.0	47.8	47.2	47.4	47.5	47.2	47.3	47.7

Men - Hommes - Hombres
ISIC 3 - CITI 3 - CIIU 3

	1999	2000	2001	2002	2003	2004	2005	2006	2007	2008
Total	48.2	48.2	48.0	48.1	47.4	47.7	48.0	47.7	47.5	48.2

Women - Femmes - Mujeres
ISIC 3 - CITI 3 - CIIU 3

	1999	2000	2001	2002	2003	2004	2005	2006	2007	2008
Total	49.1	48.3	48.0	47.8	47.1	47.3	47.3	46.9	47.2	47.2

Malaysia (BA) (a)   Total employment - Emploi total - Empleo total

Total men and women - Total hommes et femmes - Total hombres y mujeres
ISIC 3 - CITI 3 - CIIU 3

	1999	2000	2001	2002	2003	2004	2005	2006	2007	2008
Total	.	.	48.8	49.3	49.1	48.8	49.6	49.6	49.1	48.8

Men - Hommes - Hombres
ISIC 3 - CITI 3 - CIIU 3

	1999	2000	2001	2002	2003	2004	2005	2006	2007	2008
Total	.	.	50.1	50.7	50.2	49.9	50.6	50.6	50.2	50.1

Women - Femmes - Mujeres
ISIC 3 - CITI 3 - CIIU 3

	1999	2000	2001	2002	2003	2004	2005	2006	2007	2008
Total	.	.	46.8	47.4	47.6	47.1	48.1	48.0	47.3	46.8

Myanmar (DA) (a) [2][3]   Employees - Salariés - Asalariados

Total men and women - Total hommes et femmes - Total hombres y mujeres
ISIC 2 - CITI 2 - CIIU 2

	1999	2000	2001	2002	2003	2004	2005	2006	2007	2008
Total	7.9	8.0	8.0	8.0	8.0	8.0	8.0	8.0	8.0	8.0

Philippines (BA) (a) [4]   Total employment - Emploi total - Empleo total

Total men and women - Total hommes et femmes - Total hombres y mujeres
ISIC 3 - CITI 3 - CIIU 3

	1999	2000	2001	2002	2003	2004	2005	2006	2007	2008
Total	.	.	43.2	43.6	44.1	44.4	44.8	44.4 [5]	44.7	.
15	.	.	44.3	44.8	44.8	45.5	46.5	44.9 [5]	45.5	.
16	.	.	46.9	49.9	47.1	50.8	49.7	48.0 [5]	47.4	.
17	.	.	38.5	39.9	38.9	37.8	38.9	38.7 [5]	37.3	.
18	.	.	40.6	41.7	43.0	43.1	43.9	44.2 [5]	43.6	.
19	.	.	47.4	45.7	46.1	47.6	47.3	46.7 [5]	47.2	.
20	.	.	39.2	39.1	38.9	38.3	39.0	38.6 [5]	40.3	.
21	.	.	47.3	48.6	47.2	47.0	50.8	44.7 [5]	48.2	.
22	.	.	44.0	45.6	47.2	47.6	47.9	45.2 [5]	46.4	.
23	.	.	45.7	51.3	47.6	45.8	45.9	46.7 [5]	51.7	.
24	.	.	46.3	45.3	46.0	47.8	47.8	46.8 [5]	48.8	.
25	.	.	46.5	49.8	48.6	50.5	48.9	52.4 [5]	48.9	.
26	.	.	43.6	41.0	41.8	44.3	43.7	42.9 [5]	42.3	.
27	.	.	45.7	45.7	47.7	48.7	46.5	47.9 [5]	47.5	.
28	.	.	44.0	43.9	45.1	43.4	44.1	44.5 [5]	44.7	.
29	.	.	46.0	46.5	46.4	46.8	47.4	46.2 [5]	46.1	.
30	.	.	45.5	47.6	50.3	47.9	50.5	46.7 [5]	48.0	.
31	.	.	48.1	47.7	48.2	48.7	49.2	49.0 [5]	46.4	.
32	.	.	48.2	48.1	48.3	49.0	49.2	49.6 [5]	49.4	.
33	.	.	47.6	44.2	48.0	48.3	47.7	47.2 [5]	45.8	.
34	.	.	47.0	47.1	47.6	47.0	46.8	45.2 [5]	46.3	.
35	.	.	47.8	48.7	45.1	46.7	44.4	46.2 [5]	46.0	.
36	.	.	40.3	42.1	43.3	44.0	41.7	42.8 [5]	43.8	.
37	.	.	40.7	46.5	41.3	39.2	43.2	44.6 [5]	54.7	.

Explanatory notes: see p. 721.   Notes explicatives: voir p. 723.   Notas explicativas: véase p. 725.

[1] Median. [2] Regular employees. [3] Per day. [4] Oct. of each year. [5] Methodology revised; data not strictly comparable.

[1] Médiane. [2] Salariés stables. [3] Par jour. [4] Oct. de chaque année. [5] Méthodologie révisée; les données ne sont pas strictement comparables.

[1] Mediana. [2] Asalariados estables. [3] Por día. [4] Oct. de cada año. [5] Metodología revisada; los datos no son estrictamente comparables.

4B HOURS OF WORK — DURÉE DU TRAVAIL — HORAS DE TRABAJO

In manufacturing — Dans les industries manufacturières — En las industrias manufactureras

Per week — Par semaine — Por semana

Philippines (BA) (a) [1] — Total employment - Emploi total - Empleo total

Men - Hommes - Hombres
ISIC 3 - CITI 3 - CIIU 3

	1999	2000	2001	2002	2003	2004	2005	2006	2007	2008
Total	.	.	45.0	45.4	45.8	46.2	46.4	45.9 [2]	46.2	.
15	.	.	45.0	46.1	46.1	46.6	47.2	46.1 [2]	46.0	.
16	.	.	47.3	50.6	46.6	52.0	51.3	48.0 [2]	49.2	.
17	.	.	42.8	43.6	44.0	47.5	46.0	47.0 [2]	42.1	.
18	.	.	44.5	44.8	46.7	46.1	48.0	47.2 [2]	46.9	.
19	.	.	49.6	48.0	46.8	47.2	48.2	46.6 [2]	49.0	.
20	.	.	42.7	43.7	43.5	43.0	44.0	43.1 [2]	45.2	.
21	.	.	47.6	49.5	49.2	48.2	51.6	45.3 [2]	50.3	.
22	.	.	45.4	45.7	47.1	47.8	47.7	46.5 [2]	47.2	.
23	.	.	45.8	51.5	48.3	46.3	49.2	48.2 [2]	55.4	.
24	.	.	47.5	45.9	46.2	48.6	48.5	47.7 [2]	48.8	.
25	.	.	46.5	49.3	49.1	51.3	48.6	52.7 [2]	48.4	.
26	.	.	44.2	42.2	42.7	44.7	44.0	43.3 [2]	42.9	.
27	.	.	45.6	45.4	48.9	48.8	47.2	47.9 [2]	47.6	.
28	.	.	43.9	43.6	45.3	43.4	44.4	44.6 [2]	44.7	.
29	.	.	45.5	46.6	46.3	46.6	47.4	45.9 [2]	46.2	.
30	.	.	40.5	46.6	50.6	49.6	47.0	47.8 [2]	48.9	.
31	.	.	48.4	45.5	47.6	48.5	46.9	48.9 [2]	46.6	.
32	.	.	47.9	48.1	48.2	49.1	48.3	47.9 [2]	48.3	.
33	.	.	46.7	41.2	45.6	45.7	46.4	43.8 [2]	42.6	.
34	.	.	46.3	47.0	47.2	46.1	46.8	44.9 [2]	46.3	.
35	.	.	48.5	48.3	44.1	46.6	44.9	46.6 [2]	45.7	.
36	.	.	43.3	44.0	44.2	45.4	43.4	44.8 [2]	45.6	.
37	.	.	41.2	46.5	37.0	41.0	42.9	41.7 [2]	58.8	.

Women - Femmes - Mujeres
ISIC 3 - CITI 3 - CIIU 3

	1999	2000	2001	2002	2003	2004	2005	2006	2007	2008
Total	.	.	41.2	41.5	41.9	42.1	42.9	42.5 [2]	42.8	.
15	.	.	43.0	41.9	42.1	43.4	45.0	42.7 [2]	44.2	.
16	.	.	46.6	48.0	48.1	46.5	45.2	48.0 [2]	38.0	.
17	.	.	36.7	38.3	36.8	34.5	36.8	35.1 [2]	35.6	.
18	.	.	39.7	40.8	41.9	42.1	42.7	43.2 [2]	42.5	.
19	.	.	45.2	43.4	45.3	47.9	46.3	47.0 [2]	45.2	.
20	.	.	35.7	34.0	32.6	32.4	33.6	33.7 [2]	34.1	.
21	.	.	46.6	46.4	43.8	45.1	49.5	43.8 [2]	44.2	.
22	.	.	41.0	45.0	47.4	47.2	48.3	42.0 [2]	44.2	.
23	.	.	44.5	48.0	46.3	44.3	40.9	43.8 [2]	45.1	.
24	.	.	43.7	43.8	45.7	46.2	46.1	45.2 [2]	48.8	.
25	.	.	46.6	50.7	46.7	47.6	50.0	51.7 [2]	49.8	.
26	.	.	41.0	37.0	39.0	41.6	41.9	40.7 [2]	38.8	.
27	.	.	48.0	48.0	37.0	48.2	42.9	48.0 [2]	46.6	.
28	.	.	44.8	46.3	41.0	43.9	39.7	42.3 [2]	45.0	.
29	.	.	47.9	46.0	46.9	47.9	47.1	49.5 [2]	45.8	.
30	.	.	48.4	48.1	50.1	46.8	53.5	45.6 [2]	47.2	.
31	.	.	47.7	49.8	48.9	48.8	50.8	49.2 [2]	46.2	.
32	.	.	48.3	48.1	48.3	48.9	49.6	50.3 [2]	49.9	.
33	.	.	48.4	46.4	49.4	49.9	48.4	49.8 [2]	47.0	.
34	.	.	49.5	48.0	49.7	50.2	48.2	46.3 [2]	46.3	.
35	.	.	43.5	51.5	52.9	48.0	41.0	43.4 [2]	48.0	.
36	.	.	35.9	38.7	41.2	40.9	38.4	39.5 [2]	39.5	.
37	.	.	36.4	46.4	42.8	36.5	43.5	46.8 [2]	52.4	.

Philippines (BA) (a) — Employees - Salariés - Asalariados

Total men and women - Total hommes et femmes - Total hombres y mujeres
ISIC 3 - CITI 3 - CIIU 3

	1999	2000	2001	2002	2003	2004	2005	2006	2007	2008
Total	44.4	44.9	46.0	46.3	46.5	46.5	47.5	46.9	46.6	47.4
15	47.4	48.0	46.9	47.2	47.2	47.1	47.3	47.0	47.0	47.7
16	45.9	46.6	46.8	49.7	47.6	47.9	48.2	46.0	46.5	47.3
17	44.8	45.8	44.2	43.6	44.6	43.9	44.9	42.5	42.8	44.9
18	47.0	47.5	45.9	46.7	47.1	46.6	48.2	47.7	46.9	47.8
19	47.2	47.3	46.3	46.2	45.2	46.3	48.7	47.5	48.0	47.5
20	46.3	46.4	43.3	43.6	44.0	45.1	45.9	45.0	45.3	45.4
21	46.9	47.4	46.2	47.7	46.0	45.6	48.4	46.9	47.9	48.2
22	47.8	48.5	45.1	45.8	46.6	46.7	47.6	45.0	45.3	47.1
23	44.4	45.7	43.7	47.7	47.3	46.0	47.2	46.0	47.0	47.8
24	.	.	46.1	45.8	46.2	46.1	47.3	46.6	46.9	46.5
25	.	.	47.9	48.9	47.8	49.2	50.4	51.3	50.0	49.7
26	.	.	43.8	44.4	44.8	45.2	44.4	46.1	44.5	45.7
27	.	.	46.7	46.6	46.7	47.0	48.0	46.5	46.7	47.6
28	.	.	45.0	44.5	45.8	45.8	46.2	44.7	45.2	46.2
29	.	.	46.5	46.7	46.8	45.6	47.9	47.3	46.5	47.3
30	.	.	46.8	47.9	48.0	47.9	49.9	48.1	46.0	47.7
31	.	.	46.7	47.7	47.6	46.8	48.6	47.8	46.1	46.8
32	.	.	47.7	48.3	48.7	47.9	49.5	49.4	48.3	48.7
33	.	.	47.6	47.9	47.6	48.2	49.4	47.9	47.6	48.6
34	.	.	45.5	47.4	46.6	46.4	46.5	45.8	46.6	48.7
35	.	.	46.1	45.2	45.5	46.2	47.3	44.5	45.5	48.2
36	.	.	45.3	44.3	44.3	45.1	46.2	45.5	22.0	45.9
37	.	.	43.0	47.4	44.9	40.8	44.4	42.2	42.7	48.0

Explanatory notes: see p. 721.

[1] Oct. of each year. [2] Methodology revised; data not strictly comparable.

Notes explicatives: voir p. 723.

[1] Oct. de chaque année. [2] Méthodologie révisée; les données ne sont pas strictement comparables.

Notas explicativas: véase p. 725.

[1] Oct. de cada año. [2] Metodología revisada; los datos no son estrictamente comparables.

	In manufacturing			Dans les industries manufacturières				En las industrias manufactureras		
	Per week			Par semaine				Por semana		
	1999	2000	2001	2002	2003	2004	2005	2006	2007	2008

Philippines (BA) (a)   Employees - Salariés - Asalariados

Men - Hommes - Hombres
ISIC 3 - CITI 3 - CIIU 3

	1999	2000	2001	2002	2003	2004	2005	2006	2007	2008
Total	44.7	45.1	46.2	46.4	46.8	46.8	47.5	46.9	46.7	47.6
15	47.9	48.2	46.8	47.1	47.5	47.1	47.0	46.9	47.0	48.0
16	47.0	47.3	46.7	50.1	47.9	49.1	48.4	45.8	46.5	49.0
17	44.9	46.1	46.0	44.8	46.4	47.1	48.5	46.9	44.6	47.5
18	47.3	47.7	46.4	47.8	48.5	47.4	49.0	48.4	47.7	49.1
19	48.2	47.6	47.5	47.5	45.8	46.9	50.3	48.6	49.9	47.5
20	46.5	46.3	44.1	44.6	45.3	46.3	47.2	46.6	46.1	46.9
21	46.8	47.4	46.6	49.1	47.6	47.6	50.5	48.2	50.4	49.7
22	46.7	47.9	45.3	46.1	46.9	46.6	47.4	44.8	46.0	47.0
23	46.2	47.1	43.9	47.9	48.2	47.2	47.2	46.7	49.1	46.7
24	.	.	46.7	46.4	46.8	46.3	47.8	46.5	47.5	46.9
25	.	.	48.1	49.0	48.5	49.6	50.5	51.2	50.3	50.1
26	.	.	44.2	44.0	44.7	45.4	44.2	45.6	44.2	45.6
27	.	.	46.9	46.4	46.5	47.0	48.1	46.6	46.6	47.6
28	.	.	45.1	44.3	45.7	45.6	46.2	44.5	45.3	46.2
29	.	.	46.2	46.5	46.8	45.5	48.1	47.8	46.7	47.3
30	.	.	44.5	46.8	46.9	48.1	47.9	49.0	46.0	48.3
31	.	.	47.5	46.4	47.3	46.5	47.4	47.7	45.5	46.5
32	.	.	46.9	48.7	48.4	47.9	48.7	48.6	47.6	48.3
33	.	.	47.6	47.1	46.0	45.9	48.5	47.3	47.8	50.2
34	.	.	45.0	47.5	46.4	46.2	46.3	45.3	46.0	48.8
35	.	.	45.8	45.0	44.8	46.3	47.4	44.5	45.0	48.4
36	.	.	45.6	45.3	44.9	45.7	46.9	46.1	21.7	46.3
37	.	.	42.5	47.2	45.9	42.2	46.9	46.0	44.4	48.0

Women - Femmes - Mujeres
ISIC 3 - CITI 3 - CIIU 3

	1999	2000	2001	2002	2003	2004	2005	2006	2007	2008
Total	42.3	43.7	45.9	46.2	46.1	46.0	47.5	46.9	46.4	47.0
15	46.2	47.3	47.2	47.3	46.3	47.1	48.0	47.3	47.1	46.9
16	45.5	46.3	46.9	49.0	47.0	45.9	48.0	46.3	46.6	44.3
17	44.5	44.8	43.2	42.7	43.3	41.9	42.6	39.6	41.7	43.4
18	46.3	47.1	45.7	46.3	46.7	46.3	47.9	47.5	46.6	47.3
19	45.5	46.9	45.1	45.1	44.5	45.7	46.7	46.1	45.7	47.5
20	44.9	46.7	41.0	40.5	40.0	41.8	43.0	42.0	43.6	41.8
21	47.7	47.7	45.5	45.0	43.0	42.7	44.5	44.7	43.7	45.9
22	49.0	49.1	44.8	44.9	45.9	46.9	47.9	45.5	43.9	47.2
23	42.5	44.1	41.1	46.2	43.6	41.7	47.2	44.2	40.5	50.2
24	.	.	44.9	44.8	45.4	45.6	46.4	46.9	45.8	45.8
25	.	.	47.4	48.7	46.2	48.2	50.2	51.5	49.6	48.8
26	.	.	42.1	46.9	45.0	44.2	45.2	48.8	46.7	46.2
27	.	.	45.0	47.9	48.4	47.1	47.0	45.8	48.6	47.7
28	.	.	44.1	46.8	47.1	48.4	46.5	48.1	45.2	47.3
29	.	.	47.5	47.1	46.5	45.9	47.3	45.0	45.4	47.3
30	.	.	48.4	48.4	48.6	47.7	51.1	47.1	46.1	47.1
31	.	.	46.0	48.6	47.8	47.1	49.5	48.0	46.8	47.1
32	.	.	48.1	48.2	48.9	47.9	49.9	49.7	48.7	49.0
33	.	.	47.6	48.3	48.5	49.4	49.8	48.1	47.5	47.5
34	.	.	47.6	47.2	47.5	47.5	47.4	47.2	48.8	48.1
35	.	.	48.4	46.8	50.1	44.8	46.7	44.5	48.2	47.0
36	.	.	44.5	42.3	42.7	43.7	44.9	44.2	22.8	44.7
37	.	.	44.3	48.0	43.2	38.7	38.3	38.1	40.6	48.1

Philippines (DB) (a) [1]   Employees - Salariés - Asalariados

Total men and women - Total hommes et femmes - Total hombres y mujeres
ISIC 3 - CITI 3 - CIIU 3

	1999	2000	2001	2002	2003	2004	2005	2006	2007	2008
Total	49.3	.	49.2	.	49.4	.	48.6	.	.	.
15	49.2	.	48.4	.	48.7	.	47.6	.	.	.
16	50.7	.	49.9	.	51.8	.	50.0	.	.	.
17	49.6	.	49.2	.	49.2	.	49.0	.	.	.
18	50.1	.	50.1	.	49.0	.	49.5	.	.	.
19	47.4	.	48.6	.	47.8	.	43.8	.	.	.
20	49.5	.	47.9	.	48.0	.	47.6	.	.	.
21	52.5	.	49.1	.	50.8	.	50.5	.	.	.
22	47.1	.	46.8	.	49.2	.	48.9	.	.	.
23	50.5	.	48.0	.	48.5	.	46.2	.	.	.
24	49.5	.	49.6	.	48.8	.	50.0	.	.	.
25	50.2	.	49.6	.	49.3	.	49.5	.	.	.
26	49.2	.	48.1	.	47.0	.	48.7	.	.	.
27	49.6	.	48.4	.	49.4	.	51.2	.	.	.
28	48.5	.	47.4	.	50.1	.	47.8	.	.	.
29	48.5	.	47.3	.	47.4	.	46.2	.	.	.
30	48.7	.	52.6	.	52.8	.	48.2	.	.	.
31	51.5	.	49.2	.	45.9	.	45.9	.	.	.
32	49.8	.	50.2	.	51.8	.	49.6	.	.	.
33	45.7	.	47.9	.	51.2	.	53.8	.	.	.
34	47.4	.	46.3	.	50.1	.	48.2	.	.	.
35	47.9	.	49.7	.	47.9	.	46.7	.	.	.
36	48.9	.	48.5	.	48.6	.	47.3	.	.	.
37	43.5	.	49.9	.	46.8	.	45.6	.	.	.

Explanatory notes: see p. 721.   Notes explicatives: voir p. 723.   Notas explicativas: véase p. 725.

[1] Establishments with 20 or more persons employed.   [1] Etablissements occupant 20 personnes et plus.   [1] Establecimientos con 20 y más trabajadores.

HOURS OF WORK — DURÉE DU TRAVAIL — HORAS DE TRABAJO

In manufacturing — Dans les industries manufacturières — En las industrias manufactureras

Per week — Par semaine — Por semana

	1999	2000	2001	2002	2003	2004	2005	2006	2007	2008
Philippines (DB) (a) [1]					Employees - Salariés - Asalariados					
Men - Hommes - Hombres										
ISIC 3 - CITI 3 - CIIU 3										
Total	49.4	.	48.7	.	49.0	.	48.8	.	.	.
15	50.1	.	48.6	.	49.0	.	48.9	.	.	.
16	54.3	.	52.9	.	54.5	.	53.5	.	.	.
17	49.6	.	49.6	.	48.8	.	49.0	.	.	.
18	50.0	.	49.9	.	49.4	.	49.1	.	.	.
19	46.0	.	48.4	.	45.9	.	44.0	.	.	.
20	49.9	.	47.5	.	48.2	.	47.5	.	.	.
21	54.5	.	49.1	.	50.8	.	50.7	.	.	.
22	47.0	.	47.3	.	49.0	.	49.0	.	.	.
23	50.9	.	48.0	.	48.6	.	47.0	.	.	.
24	49.2	.	49.6	.	48.9	.	50.3	.	.	.
25	50.7	.	49.1	.	49.6	.	49.8	.	.	.
26	49.1	.	47.8	.	46.8	.	48.8	.	.	.
27	49.1	.	48.5	.	49.5	.	51.6	.	.	.
28	47.1	.	47.6	.	50.0	.	48.4	.	.	.
29	47.9	.	47.2	.	48.7	.	47.8	.	.	.
30	51.4	.	52.0	.	48.5	.	49.1	.	.	.
31	51.1	.	49.0	.	46.6	.	46.3	.	.	.
32	50.2	.	49.8	.	50.3	.	50.0	.	.	.
33	44.0	.	48.9	.	49.4	.	55.7	.	.	.
34	47.1	.	45.5	.	48.9	.	48.0	.	.	.
35	47.8	.	49.7	.	47.9	.	46.7	.	.	.
36	49.2	.	48.2	.	48.8	.	46.9	.	.	.
37	41.9	.	49.0	.	44.4	.	47.1	.	.	.
Women - Femmes - Mujeres										
ISIC 3 - CITI 3 - CIIU 3										
Total	49.2	.	49.6	.	49.8	.	48.3	.	.	.
15	47.3	.	47.9	.	48.1	.	45.0	.	.	.
16	46.6	.	46.7	.	48.4	.	44.2	.	.	.
17	49.6	.	49.0	.	49.6	.	48.9	.	.	.
18	50.2	.	50.1	.	48.8	.	49.6	.	.	.
19	48.2	.	48.7	.	49.4	.	43.5	.	.	.
20	47.9	.	50.1	.	47.2	.	47.8	.	.	.
21	49.6	.	49.0	.	50.9	.	50.1	.	.	.
22	47.4	.	45.7	.	49.4	.	48.7	.	.	.
23	45.4	.	48.0	.	48.0	.	40.5	.	.	.
24	50.3	.	49.6	.	48.8	.	49.4	.	.	.
25	48.7	.	50.7	.	48.8	.	48.9	.	.	.
26	49.5	.	49.9	.	47.9	.	48.4	.	.	.
27	54.9	.	47.8	.	48.9	.	47.9	.	.	.
28	53.4	.	46.7	.	50.3	.	46.1	.	.	.
29	49.4	.	47.5	.	45.6	.	43.6	.	.	.
30	48.0	.	52.7	.	54.3	.	47.9	.	.	.
31	51.7	.	49.4	.	45.6	.	45.7	.	.	.
32	49.7	.	50.3	.	52.2	.	49.5	.	.	.
33	46.1	.	47.6	.	51.8	.	53.0	.	.	.
34	49.3	.	49.6	.	52.6	.	48.6	.	.	.
35	48.6	.	47.6	.	47.3	.	46.9	.	.	.
36	48.3	.	49.1	.	48.4	.	48.1	.	.	.
37	46.6	.	51.5	.	52.0	.	43.0	.	.	.
Qatar (BA) (a) [2]					Employees - Salariés - Asalariados					
Total men and women - Total hommes et femmes - Total hombres y mujeres										
ISIC 3 - CITI 3 - CIIU 3										
Total	.	.	.	.	.	.	.	54	53	.
Men - Hommes - Hombres										
ISIC 3 - CITI 3 - CIIU 3										
Total	.	.	.	.	.	.	.	55	53	.
Women - Femmes - Mujeres										
ISIC 3 - CITI 3 - CIIU 3										
Total	.	.	.	.	.	.	.	46	44	.

Explanatory notes: see p. 721.   Notes explicatives: voir p. 723.   Notas explicativas: véase p. 725.

[1] Establishments with 20 or more persons employed. [2] October.   [1] Etablissements occupant 20 personnes et plus. [2] Octobre.   [1] Establecimientos con 20 y más trabajadores. [2] Octubre.

HOURS OF WORK   DURÉE DU TRAVAIL   HORAS DE TRABAJO

In manufacturing   Dans les industries manufacturières   En las industrias manufactureras

	Per week - Par semaine - Por semana									
	1999	2000	2001	2002	2003	2004	2005	2006	2007	2008

Singapore (CA) (b) — Employees - Salariés - Asalariados

Total men and women - Total hommes et femmes - Total hombres y mujeres
ISIC 3 - CITI 3 - CIIU 3

	1999	2000	2001	2002	2003	2004	2005	2006	2007	2008
Total	.	50.0	48.7	49.0	49.2	49.8	50.2	50.5 ₁	50.6	.
15	.	46.9	47.4	47.6	47.6	47.2	47.4	47.5 ₁	47.5	.
16	.	45.9	45.4	46.6	46.5	46.3	46.7	46.6 ₁	46.3	.
17	.	47.3	47.2	46.1	46.7	47.0	47.1	46.4 ₁	47.2	.
18	.	45.8	46.6	48.0	48.7	49.6	50.7	50.6 ₁	50.8	.
19	.	50.2	49.3	50.5	49.4	49.7	49.3	50.0 ₁	50.3	.
20	.	46.7	48.6	48.9	46.6	46.3	47.7	50.6 ₁	49.7	.
21	.	46.9	46.2	45.5	46.8	50.3	48.1	49.2 ₁	51.0	.
22	.	52.7	50.1	49.8	51.0	50.9	51.4	51.6 ₁	51.3	.
23	.	51.3	48.9	49.8	51.0	50.9	51.4	51.4 ₁	51.0	.
24	.	43.9	44.0	43.9	43.3	44.6	44.7	44.6 ₁	44.2	.
25	.	46.1	45.3	45.0	45.2	45.8	45.6	45.9 ₁	46.1	.
26	.	45.8	46.0	45.7	46.0	44.8	44.3	44.5 ₁	44.7	.
27	.	50.7	48.7	49.1	49.9	50.7	50.6	50.5 ₁	50.2	.
28	.	54.2	51.4	51.0	51.1	52.0	51.5	51.0 ₁	51.8	.
29	.	51.2	50.8	50.7	50.4	51.3	52.0	56.0 ₁	50.4	.
29-30	.	51.0	49.8	50.1	50.4	51.5	51.9	. ₁	.	.
30	.	51.9	50.2	51.0	51.6	51.9	52.6	52.3 ₁	52.1	.
31	.	50.9	49.8	50.1	50.5	51.5	51.9	52.7 ₁	52.9	.
32	.	49.8	47.5	48.1	48.0	47.4	48.9	49.8 ₁	49.8	.
33	.	48.4	45.9	46.7	46.9	47.7	48.1	48.0 ₁	48.0	.
34	.	48.6	47.3	47.7	48.6	49.1	48.8	48.1 ₁	47.6	.
35	.	53.3	54.3	52.8	52.3	52.9	53.5	53.4 ₁	53.4	.
36	.	50.1	48.7	47.2	48.7	49.0	50.7	50.6 ₁	50.4	.
37	.	53.1	. ²	. ²			52.3	. ₁	.	.

Singapore (DA) (b) ³ — Employees - Salariés - Asalariados

Total men and women - Total hommes et femmes - Total hombres y mujeres
ISIC 4 - CITI 4 - CIIU 4

	1999	2000	2001	2002	2003	2004	2005	2006	2007	2008
Total	.	50.0	48.7	49.0	49.2	49.8	50.2 ⱡ	50.5 ⁴	50.6	50.2
10-12	.	46.8	47.3	47.4	47.4	47.1	47.4 ⱡ	47.4 ⁴	47.4	47.1
13-16,23-24,31-32	.	50.9	49.5	49.4	49.4	50.2	50.4 ⱡ	50.9 ⁴	50.8	50.8
17-18	.	51.6	49.2	49.8	50.7	51.0	51.3 ⱡ	51.5 ⁴	51.1	50.9
19-21	.	45.7	45.1	44.9	44.9	45.4	45.2 ⱡ	45.4 ⁴	45.5	45.4
22	.	50.7	48.7	49.1	49.9	50.7	50.6 ⱡ	50.5 ⁴	50.2	50.0
25	.	51.9	50.2	51.0	51.6	51.9	52.6 ⱡ	52.3 ⁴	52.1	51.6
26	.	48.6	47.3	47.7	48.6	49.1	48.8 ⱡ	48.1 ⁴	47.6	47.5
27	.	49.8	47.5	48.1	48.0	48.9	48.9 ⱡ	49.8 ⁴	49.8	48.7
28	.	50.9	49.8	50.1	50.5	51.5	51.9 ⱡ	52.7 ⁴	52.9	52.2
29-30	.	53.3	54.3	52.8	52.3	52.9	53.5 ⱡ	53.4 ⁴	53.4	53.1

Sri Lanka (DA) (b) ⁵ — Wage earners - Ouvriers - Obreros

Total men and women - Total hommes et femmes - Total hombres y mujeres
ISIC 2 - CITI 2 - CIIU 2

	1999	2000	2001	2002	2003	2004	2005	2006	2007	2008
Total	53.8	53.0	53.7	49.0	51.1	50.7	49.6	49.2	53.0	48.9

Men - Hommes - Hombres
ISIC 2 - CITI 2 - CIIU 2

	1999	2000	2001	2002	2003	2004	2005	2006	2007	2008
Total	54.2	53.5	54.1	49.2	51.4	50.8	49.9	49.9	53.1	51.6

Women - Femmes - Mujeres
ISIC 2 - CITI 2 - CIIU 2

	1999	2000	2001	2002	2003	2004	2005	2006	2007	2008
Total	51.3	50.3	50.5	44.3	48.0	48.4	48.8	48.4	52.9	46.2

Taiwan, China (DA) (a) ⁶ — Employees - Salariés - Asalariados

Total men and women - Total hommes et femmes - Total hombres y mujeres
ISIC 2 - CITI 2 - CIIU 2   ISIC 3 - CITI 3 - CIIU 3

	1999	2000	2001	2002	2003	2004	2005	2006	2007	2008	
Total	199.1	198.7	184.4	187.6	188.3 ⱡ	190.6	188.8	187.3	187.3	184.7	Total

Men - Hommes - Hombres
ISIC 3 - CITI 3 - CIIU 3

	1999	2000	2001	2002	2003	2004	2005	2006	2007	2008
Total	.	.	.	.	.	192.9	190.6	189.4	189.4	186.8

Women - Femmes - Mujeres
ISIC 3 - CITI 3 - CIIU 3

	1999	2000	2001	2002	2003	2004	2005	2006	2007	2008
Total	.	.	.	.	.	187.5	186.2	184.7	184.5	181.9

Explanatory notes: see p. 721.

¹ Prior to 2006: establishments with 25 or more persons in the private sector only. ² Confidential. ³ From 2006: all establishments in the public sector and those with 25 or more persons employed in the private sector. ⁴ Before 2006: excl. public sector. ⁵ March and Sep. of each year. ⁶ Per month.

Notes explicatives: voir p. 723.

¹ Avant 2006: établissements occupant 25 personnes et plus dans le secteur privé seulement. ² Confidentiel. ³ A partir de 2006: établissements du secteur public et ceux occupant 25 personnes ou plus dans le secteur privé. ⁴ Avant 2006: non compris le secteur public. ⁵ Mars et sept. de chaque année. ⁶ Par mois.

Notas explicativas: véase p. 725.

¹ Antes de 2006: establecimientos con 25 o más personas del sector privado solo. ² Confidencial. ³ Desde 2006: establecimientos del sector público y los que emplean 25 o más trabajadores en el sector privado. ⁴ Antes de 2006: excl. el sector público. ⁵ Marzo y sept. de cada año. ⁶ Por mes.

In manufacturing   **Dans les industries manufacturières**   **En las industrias manufactureras**

	Per week / Par semaine / Por semana									
	1999	2000	2001	2002	2003	2004	2005	2006	2007	2008

West Bank and Gaza Strip (BA) (a) [1]   **Employees - Salariés - Asalariados**

Total men and women - Total hommes et femmes - Total hombres y mujeres
ISIC 3 - CITI 3 - CIIU 3

	1999	2000	2001	2002	2003	2004	2005	2006	2007	2008
Total	46.2	45.7	43.6	42.4	44.2	45.3	45.1	44.7	43.8	44.1
15	48.9	48.1	46.4	45.7	47.1	46.3	49.1	49.3	50.3	46.9
16	50.6	45.0	45.7	47.2	44.3	50.1	48.7	44.7	48.6	.
17	47.9	45.7	40.6	40.5	47.0	47.8	41.9	42.2	39.1	44.3
18	44.6	43.0	41.0	39.2	39.7	42.5	42.7	42.3	40.6	43.3
19	47.2	44.4	45.2	42.6	46.2	43.6	41.4	40.5	41.4	44.6
20	47.0	48.1	41.6	40.1	41.6	46.1	47.4	46.6	37.9	40.8
21	47.4	46.8	41.7	49.2	45.9	47.1	46.4	47.6	51.8	.
22	46.4	45.9	46.1	45.1	47.1	45.7	46.3	46.8	43.7	46.3
23			45.0	48.0	59.3	39.0	35.5			
24	45.8	49.6	43.6	45.2	45.1	45.7	46.3	47.2	46.6	45.8
25	44.8	45.4	42.6	44.0	45.0	48.1	42.9	45.6	49.8	47.3
26	46.9	50.4	43.7	40.5	44.1	43.2	41.4	40.0	38.5	40.7
27	44.1	47.6	47.2	47.9	44.8	52.0	47.4	42.7	52.0	.
28	46.3	46.0	45.0	44.0	44.4	47.1	46.1	45.6	43.9	43.2
29	45.2	46.3	47.5	36.0	45.1	47.6	46.6	47.6	50.9	.
30		45.0	39.0	.	.		41.3		72.0	.
31	47.8	46.8	43.6	45.4	46.9	40.9	49.1	50.0	37.7	.
32	50.6	72.0	34.2		48.0	46.9				
33	48.1	49.4	45.9		48.0	48.0	50.4	51.7	43.5	
34	46.3	53.0	44.3	42.0	45.6	37.0	47.2	48.0	40.0	.
35										
36	45.7	45.6	43.5	42.3	45.0	48.8	47.6	46.5	45.8	43.4
37			.	.	.		43.6	40.6	35.8	.

Men - Hommes - Hombres
ISIC 3 - CITI 3 - CIIU 3

	1999	2000	2001	2002	2003	2004	2005	2006	2007	2008
Total	46.5	45.9	43.8	42.5	44.2	45.4	45.2	44.9	44.3	44.2
15	49.0	48.2	46.4	46.0	47.1	46.4	49.3	49.5	50.4	47.1
16	50.6	45.4	47.5	47.2	44.3	50.1	48.7	44.7	48.7	.
17	49.4	45.9	40.2	40.2	46.0	49.8	42.8	41.9	39.2	46.2
18	45.2	42.4	39.5	38.0	37.9	41.2	41.3	40.3	40.6	43.6
19	47.3	44.3	45.3	41.8	46.1	43.4	41.6	40.3	41.3	44.6
20	47.0	48.1	41.4	40.1	41.6	46.1	47.4	46.6	38.1	40.5
21	47.3	46.6	42.0	49.2	48.7	47.2	46.4	47.6	52.2	.
22	46.4	46.1	46.2	45.1	47.4	45.6	46.6	47.0	43.7	46.6
23		82.5	45.0	48.0	59.3	39.0				
24	45.5	50.9	43.5	44.4	44.1	45.3	46.2	49.0	48.9	45.9
25	44.8	45.4	42.5	43.6	45.0	48.2	42.9	45.6	49.8	47.3
26	46.9	50.4	43.7	40.4	44.2	43.2	41.3	40.0	38.5	40.7
27	44.1	47.6	47.5	47.9	44.8	52.0	47.4	42.7	52.0	.
28	46.3	46.0	45.4	44.0	44.4	47.1	46.1	45.6	43.9	43.1
29	45.2	46.3	47.5	36.9	45.1	47.6	50.3	47.9	50.9	.
30		45.0	.	.	.		41.3		72.0	.
31	47.8	46.8	43.6	45.4	46.9	43.0	49.1	51.7	37.7	.
32	50.6	72.0	34.2		48.0	46.9				
33	48.2	49.4	45.6		48.0	48.0	50.4	41.7	43.5	
34	46.3	53.0	44.3	42.0	45.6	37.0	47.2	48.0	40.0	.
35									45.7	.
36	45.6	45.6	43.5	42.3	44.9	48.9	47.9	46.7	35.8	43.5
37			.	.	.		43.6	40.6		

Women - Femmes - Mujeres
ISIC 3 - CITI 3 - CIIU 3

	1999	2000	2001	2002	2003	2004	2005	2006	2007	2008
Total	43.8	44.2	42.8	42.0	44.3	44.1	43.8	43.8	41.3	43.3
15	46.3	45.9	46.5	38.9	47.2	42.8	44.9	40.4	46.5	.
16		44.0	39.0	.	.				48.0	.
17	42.3	44.9	45.0	48.0	50.8	36.8	31.2	45.8	39.0	.
18	43.4	44.0	42.5	41.4	43.3	44.3	44.7	44.0	40.7	43.1
19	45.2	48.0	40.0	48.0	48.0	44.9	37.8	48.0	42.2	.
20		48.0	.	.	.				30.0	.
21	48.4	48.0	.	.	30.7	46.4			48.0	.
22	48.0	41.4	42.0		40.0	48.0	41.5	44.7	44.1	.
23			.	.	.		35.5			
24	48.0	42.7	44.2	46.8	48.0	46.8	46.3	44.8	42.5	.
25	48.0		48.0	46.7	.	42.0				
26		.	45.2	44.3	38.8		52.4	45.0	40.0	.
27			40.0	.	.					
28	48.0	37.5	.	.	45.9		53.9	42.0	42.0	.
29			.	24.0	.		19.5	42.0	.	.
30			39.0	.	.					
31			.	.	.		35.0		40.0	.
33	48.0		48.0	.	.					
36	51.0		44.8	42.2	56.1	45.1	35.6		51.5	.

Explanatory notes: see p. 721.   Notes explicatives: voir p. 723.   Notas explicativas: véase p. 725.

[1] Persons aged 15 years and over.   [1] Personnes âgées de 15 ans et plus.   [1] Personas de 15 años y más.

In manufacturing — Dans les industries manufacturières — En las industrias manufactureras

Per week — Par semaine — Por semana

	1999	2000	2001	2002	2003	2004	2005	2006	2007	2008

EUROPE-EUROPE-EUROPA

Austria (BA) (a) — Employees - Salariés - Asalariados

Total men and women - Total hommes et femmes - Total hombres y mujeres
ISIC 3 - CITI 3 - CIIU 3

	1999	2000	2001	2002	2003	2004	2005	2006	2007	2008
Total	36.7	36.6	36.5	36.8	36.9	35.9	35.2	35.6	35.6	35.5
15	37.8	37.1	37.1	37.8	37.7	36.5	35.5	36.0	35.0	35.5
16	32.7	33.2	32.8	34.7	37.0	37.3	34.3	39.1	38.4	37.6
17	35.1	35.6	36.1	35.2	36.6	34.3	33.7	32.2	34.3	34.9
18	34.6	33.7	35.8	36.9	37.0	28.8	31.7	33.2	33.2	30.3
19	35.1	34.8	36.4	37.5	36.5	34.9	34.5	38.5	35.0	34.4
20	36.9	36.9	37.8	38.4	37.7	37.3	35.1	36.0	37.5	35.9
21	36.8	36.6	37.6	36.7	36.0	36.2	35.0	36.3	35.0	34.5
22	37.1	35.3	36.0	35.8	36.0	35.5	33.8	33.5	34.2	33.4
23	36.5	38.3	39.4	37.0	40.2	37.0	38.5	35.9	34.3	36.3
24	37.1	37.1	36.2	37.1	37.3	35.7	34.7	34.8	34.8	34.7
25	37.2	35.7	36.7	36.2	35.2	36.8	35.2	36.0	35.1	35.9
26	36.3	36.2	36.4	37.3	35.7	36.5	35.4	35.6	35.6	35.4
27	36.8	36.7	36.8	36.5	36.5	34.7	34.2	36.2	35.7	35.4
28	36.6	36.7	37.2	37.4	36.6	35.4	35.1	35.2	35.8	36.1
29	36.9	36.7	37.1	37.3	37.3	36.7	36.2	36.3	36.1	35.9
30	37.0	36.7	38.0	39.1	35.6	37.4	36.9	36.8	35.3	33.6
31	35.2	35.4	35.5	36.5	35.9	35.9	32.8	35.6	35.7	34.0
32	38.0	36.9	37.4	37.3	37.1	36.8	37.0	37.5	35.6	37.9
33	36.3	36.3	37.6	36.7	36.3	35.3	34.4	34.4	34.8	34.6
34	36.7	37.7	37.3	37.3	37.4	35.7	35.3	35.8	36.2	36.0
35	36.9	36.9	38.2	37.1	35.8	37.6	36.6	35.2	36.4	36.0
36	36.2	36.9	37.5	38.2	38.1	36.1	36.1	35.9	35.5	35.3
37	31.9	40.4	36.9	40.4	26.8	29.2	35.9	40.8	36.2	36.8

Men - Hommes - Hombres
ISIC 3 - CITI 3 - CIIU 3

	1999	2000	2001	2002	2003	2004	2005	2006	2007	2008
Total	37.8	37.7	37.6	38.0	38.1	37.7	36.9	37.4	37.4	37.2
15	39.4	38.6	39.1	40.3	40.0	39.8	39.0	39.7	37.8	38.3
16	33.8	33.6	32.0	33.7	38.2	39.0	37.0	42.5	38.6	39.2
17	37.1	37.2	37.9	38.2	38.4	36.9	35.4	33.8	37.3	39.1
18	39.1	37.9	40.4	39.6	39.8	39.5	39.5	36.1	36.8	35.9
19	35.5	37.0	38.6	39.1	38.6	37.4	35.3	42.8	37.6	35.3
20	38.1	38.0	38.6	40.1	39.5	38.8	37.1	37.7	39.1	37.1
21	37.4	37.7	38.4	37.3	37.2	38.7	36.6	36.7	35.6	34.9
22	39.1	37.0	37.9	38.4	37.8	37.6	37.3	38.0	37.7	37.4
23	37.7	39.4	39.3	36.1	40.7	36.8	37.9	35.7	36.5	36.6
24	38.0	38.4	37.4	38.7	39.2	37.4	36.2	36.7	37.3	36.2
25	38.5	37.4	38.0	38.2	36.2	38.2	36.6	37.8	37.1	37.0
26	37.3	36.9	37.4	38.4	36.9	38.0	37.3	37.3	37.3	37.7
27	37.5	37.0	37.2	36.7	36.8	35.4	35.0	37.1	36.2	36.2
28	37.6	37.6	37.9	38.2	37.4	36.4	36.3	36.6	37.1	37.1
29	37.4	37.3	37.7	38.1	38.0	37.7	37.2	37.3	37.4	37.3
30	38.9	40.2	38.4	39.2	35.9	38.6	39.6	38.0	37.8	36.5
31	36.3	36.3	36.0	37.3	38.0	38.2	33.6	37.7	37.7	36.3
32	39.1	37.9	37.9	38.5	37.7	38.5	38.8	38.4	37.2	39.4
33	37.9	37.4	39.1	38.5	39.2	38.9	36.9	37.2	38.0	37.9
34	37.2	38.3	37.4	38.3	37.8	36.0	36.5	36.5	37.0	36.8
35	36.9	37.4	37.9	36.9	35.9	37.9	36.5	36.1	36.6	36.5
36	37.4	37.8	39.2	39.4	39.2	38.2	37.8	38.6	37.5	37.2
37	38.4	40.1	37.4	41.1	20.5	23.8	39.6	47.1	38.5	36.2

Women - Femmes - Mujeres
ISIC 3 - CITI 3 - CIIU 3

	1999	2000	2001	2002	2003	2004	2005	2006	2007	2008
Total	33.3	33.2	33.5	33.1	33.1	30.9	30.1	30.3	30.1	30.2
15	34.0	33.2	32.8	32.5	32.3	31.2	29.8	30.8	31.0	31.2
16	28.2	32.8	34.2	38.4	34.3	33.3	26.8	35.4	38.2	34.2
17	32.8	33.9	34.3	32.3	34.9	32.0	31.3	30.3	30.8	30.0
18	33.7	32.8	33.9	35.7	36.0	25.7	29.4	32.5	32.3	29.0
19	34.7	33.3	34.1	35.7	34.8	32.5	33.3	34.4	33.0	33.6
20	31.2	31.9	34.4	31.4	29.4	30.3	27.2	29.3	30.3	29.8
21	33.9	32.2	34.4	34.4	31.1	24.2	30.7	34.7	32.8	33.2
22	33.5	32.2	32.6	32.1	32.9	32.3	29.7	28.2	29.2	28.4
23	32.4	34.4	40.0	43.4	37.8	39.3	39.9	36.5	11.3	34.6
24	35.4	34.2	34.1	34.2	34.0	32.8	31.7	31.2	29.6	31.8
25	32.8	31.5	33.1	30.9	32.2	32.1	31.6	31.6	30.3	32.5
26	31.8	33.0	32.7	33.5	32.2	30.7	29.4	29.1	29.4	27.9
27	33.8	35.5	34.1	34.7	32.9	29.4	27.1	30.3	32.0	31.1
28	33.2	32.8	34.4	33.6	33.2	30.8	29.7	28.9	28.5	30.1
29	33.4	33.7	33.0	31.3	32.4	30.4	29.3	30.6	29.6	29.1
30	31.1	28.2	36.2	38.4	32.0	34.4	29.7	33.0	27.9	28.2
31	32.6	33.0	34.4	34.7	31.5	30.2	30.4	28.6	27.8	26.3
32	34.7	34.4	35.9	32.8	34.4	33.0	31.9	34.6	31.2	33.4
33	33.2	34.3	34.3	33.6	32.3	29.9	28.0	30.1	29.0	29.8
34	33.4	34.2	36.2	32.3	35.4	34.1	31.3	32.5	32.0	32.2
35	34.5	29.4	42.6	39.6	34.2	33.0	37.2	26.9	35.2	34.6
36	31.0	32.8	29.9	32.4	32.6	28.6	29.2	27.8	27.0	27.8
37	.	42.5	35.0	24.8	37.1	32.1	24.3	23.0	29.5	38.2

Explanatory notes: see p. 721.   Notes explicatives: voir p. 723.   Notas explicativas: véase p. 725.

HOURS OF WORK — DURÉE DU TRAVAIL — HORAS DE TRABAJO

In manufacturing — Dans les industries manufacturières — En las industrias manufactureras

Per week — Par semaine — Por semana

Austria (DB) (a) [1] — Employees - Salariés - Asalariados

Total men and women - Total hommes et femmes - Total hombres y mujeres

ISIC 3 - CITI 3 - CIIU 3 ⟶ ISIC 4 - CITI 4 - CIIU 4

	1999	2000	2001	2002	2003	2004	2005	2006	2007	2008	ISIC 4
Total[2]	140.4	140.2	139.6	138.9	139.4	140.5	139.7	140.0	.	138.9	Total[2]
15	142.3	140.9	140.2	139.5	137.7	137.1	136.7	136.0		137.0	10
16	137.2	131.9	134.3	138.7	133.7	134.3	130.0	130.3		141.9	11
17	137.1	135.7	136.6	135.6	136.3	138.0	135.8	134.9		133.1	12
18	134.0	134.6	133.8	131.9	136.8	138.4	134.3	133.7		134.2	13
19	137.6	136.4	136.8	133.6	136.3	139.4	141.3	136.4		133.5	14
20	143.1	142.5	142.3	143.0	141.8	142.3	142.1	140.6		136.0	15
21	140.3	139.9	138.6	137.4	136.5	138.3	138.1	138.9		139.9	16
22	136.6	136.4	137.0	137.5	138.1	137.8	138.6	139.1		136.9	17
23	134.6	131.8	132.6	127.8	128.6	133.4	129.5	128.0		145.4	18
24	137.1	137.3	137.4	138.2	140.2	139.0	137.4	137.3		129.4	19
25	140.9	140.1	140.1	139.7	140.0	139.3	138.0	139.3		135.1	20
26	140.4	139.6	138.9	138.9	139.1	140.9	140.6	140.5		135.5	21
27	137.9	139.3	136.9	135.8	136.8	139.0	136.7	137.3		138.9	22
28	141.0	140.6	140.1	140.2	140.6	142.2	141.3	142.4		139.6	23
29	141.8	143.0	141.8	141.0	141.9	143.2	142.5	142.3		135.9	24
30	135.2	140.1	137.6	138.1	141.1	138.0	138.4	134.6		139.6	25
31	142.6	143.7	141.5	140.7	140.2	143.9	142.0	143.4		138.3	26
32	142.1	141.8	140.2	132.8	138.6	145.3	144.5	144.1		140.5	27
33	139.2	141.7	140.4	139.7	138.6	139.9	136.9	137.2		141.4	28
34	136.9	136.4	138.9	138.9	138.4	138.4	139.5	142.6		137.3	29
35	147.0	146.2	144.5	145.7	146.1	148.1	141.5	143.0		146.2	30
36	140.8	140.0	139.3	139.1	139.1	139.1	138.9	139.0		140.1	31
37	145.3	149.8	150.9	146.7	147.9	149.8	149.2	146.7		137.1	32
										139.2	33

Austria (DB) (b) [1] — Employees - Salariés - Asalariados

Total men and women - Total hommes et femmes - Total hombres y mujeres

ISIC 3 - CITI 3 - CIIU 3 ⟶ ISIC 4 - CITI 4 - CIIU 4

	1999	2000	2001	2002	2003	2004	2005	2006	2007	2008	ISIC 4
Total[2]	167.7	167.4	167.2	166.2	165.7	166.3	165.7	165.4	.	165.8	Total[2]
15	165.0	164.3	163.1	162.5	160.3	161.1	160.8	159.8		160.6	10
16	170.8	171.6	169.8	171.5	168.0	167.9	164.6	166.5		168.2	11
17	164.8	163.1	164.7	163.2	162.7	163.2	160.9	160.0		165.6	12
18	160.7	161.4	161.4	159.1	162.0	161.0	157.8	157.0		160.6	13
19	166.0	164.7	165.8	165.0	166.5	167.2	167.9	165.6		157.8	14
20	169.3	169.0	168.6	168.8	167.5	167.4	167.5	165.5		166.4	15
21	167.7	167.4	166.8	165.9	164.6	165.4	165.3	165.6		166.1	16
22	159.9	159.2	160.3	160.1	160.6	160.3	160.7	160.6		165.2	17
23	166.8	164.7	164.3	158.6	160.2	161.5	160.7	159.0		169.0	18
24	164.2	164.3	163.8	163.4	163.7	162.9	161.8	161.7		158.9	19
25	168.2	167.2	168.1	168.3	166.9	166.4	165.6	166.7		162.3	20
26	169.1	168.9	168.6	168.1	167.2	168.8	168.3	168.4		161.2	21
27	170.3	170.7	169.3	168.4	168.5	169.3	167.9	167.7		167.3	22
28	169.1	168.6	168.3	168.0	167.6	168.6	167.9	167.6		167.8	23
29	170.1	170.5	170.5	168.9	169.1	170.2	169.1	168.7		168.5	24
30	153.9	160.3	158.5	157.9	160.8	159.1	161.8	160.0		166.6	25
31	170.0	171.0	169.1	168.2	166.6	168.1	167.1	167.5		162.6	26
32	167.8	167.4	167.0	158.6	162.3	164.6	166.1	164.8		165.0	27
33	163.2	164.9	164.0	163.2	162.1	162.5	160.1	159.7		168.8	28
34	167.6	166.1	168.9	169.5	168.2	167.4	167.5	168.2		167.5	29
35	176.2	175.3	173.5	174.1	172.6	170.0	167.5	167.7		168.3	30
36	168.2	167.4	167.3	166.4	165.5	165.3	164.7	164.4		165.5	31
37	168.6	173.7	176.8	175.8	176.9	173.8	172.3	172.3		164.0	32
										164.7	33

Belgique (DA) (b) [3] — Employees - Salariés - Asalariados

Total men and women - Total hommes et femmes - Total hombres y mujeres

ISIC 3 - CITI 3 - CIIU 3

	1999	2000	2001	2002	2003	2004	2005	2006	2007
Total	34.4	35.7	36.6	37.1	36.2	34.0	33.2	35.3	35.0
15	32.5	34.4	35.3	35.7	34.4	32.0	32.1	33.6	33.2
16	32.7	34.3	35.8	35.5	34.3	31.5	29.8	30.9	31.8
17	32.7	34.7	34.8	35.3	34.0	31.0	30.6	32.3	32.9
18	27.2	27.5	31.6	32.6	29.3	26.4	28.1	31.7	29.7
19	32.1	34.7	32.0	35.4	31.6	29.7	30.0	32.8	32.3
20	34.9	35.9	36.3	37.7	37.2	33.6	34.3	35.3	34.4
21	33.8	34.8	35.1	35.8	34.4	32.5	32.4	34.1	34.0
22	34.6	35.1	36.2	35.7	35.5	33.0	32.8	34.7	34.6
23	37.1	37.6	39.4	39.3	39.0	36.1	37.1	37.5	36.9
24	36.1	36.5	38.1	38.5	38.0	35.5	35.0	36.8	36.0
25	35.1	36.1	37.1	38.2	37.3	34.4	33.8	35.8	35.5
26	34.7	35.7	36.2	37.0	35.8	34.4	33.3	35.6	36.0
27	35.1	37.8	39.2	39.5	38.6	36.4	34.7	36.3	36.2
28	34.8	35.9	37.0	37.5	36.4	34.4	33.3	36.6	36.0
29	34.6	36.0	36.9	37.5	36.4	33.5	33.0	35.7	35.5
30	33.9	35.5	39.1	38.4	38.1	34.6	34.9	35.5	33.9
31	34.5	35.5	36.5	37.7	36.6	34.3	33.1	35.3	35.1
32	35.9	36.6	36.7	37.3	37.7	34.6	33.7	36.9	36.6
33	34.2	36.1	36.8	37.1	36.6	34.1	32.5	36.4	35.9
34	35.5	36.7	36.9	37.0	36.5	36.2	33.7	35.7	35.9
35	35.1	35.7	36.0	36.8	36.2	33.2	32.3	35.8	36.0
36	33.8	35.2	35.6	37.0	34.6	32.4	31.8	33.9	32.8
37	32.9	35.2	35.5	36.6	34.1	33.8	33.4	35.4	36.3

Explanatory notes: see p. 721. — Notes explicatives: voir p. 723. — Notas explicativas: véase p. 725.

[1] Per month. [2] Incl. mining and quarrying. [3] Oct. of each year. — [1] Par mois. [2] Y compris les industries extractives. [3] Oct. de chaque année. — [1] Por mes. [2] Incl. las minas y canteras. [3] Oct. de cada año.

In manufacturing — Dans les industries manufacturières — En las industrias manufactureras

Per week — Par semaine — Por semana

	1999	2000	2001	2002	2003	2004	2005	2006	2007	2008
Belgique (DA) (b) [1]					Employees - Salariés - Asalariados					
Men - Hommes - Hombres										
ISIC 3 - CITI 3 - CIIU 3										
Total	35.1	36.4	37.3	37.8	36.9	34.8	33.8	36.1	35.8	.
15	33.5	35.7	36.4	36.9	35.7	33.3	33.0	34.8	34.2	.
16	35.3	36.5	37.9	37.7	37.2	34.4	32.9	34.6	35.7	.
17	33.5	35.7	35.9	36.2	34.9	33.1	31.5	34.1	34.2	.
18	33.7	32.9	36.4	36.7	30.0	34.3	32.5	33.7	27.2	.
19	33.3	36.4	34.8	37.2	34.4	31.9	33.0	34.7	35.2	.
20	35.5	36.4	36.9	38.1	37.6	34.1	34.6	35.6	35.1	.
21	33.8	34.9	35.2	35.9	34.7	32.9	32.7	34.3	34.4	.
22	35.4	35.5	36.4	36.3	35.9	33.7	33.5	35.6	35.3	.
23	37.4	37.7	39.5	39.4	39.1	36.4	37.6	37.6	37.1	.
24	36.8	37.0	38.5	39.1	38.7	36.1	35.6	37.5	36.9	.
25	35.5	36.4	37.6	38.7	37.6	34.9	34.3	36.5	36.0	.
26	34.8	35.8	36.6	37.1	35.9	34.8	33.4	35.9	36.2	.
27	35.1	37.9	39.3	39.7	38.8	36.6	34.7	36.3	36.3	.
28	35.1	36.3	37.4	37.8	36.9	34.7	33.6	36.9	36.5	.
29	34.8	36.3	37.3	37.8	36.6	33.6	33.2	35.9	35.8	.
30	35.4	36.9	40.2	39.5	39.1	36.3	36.1	37.9	36.9	.
31	35.1	35.9	37.2	38.1	37.1	35.1	33.8	36.1	36.1	.
32	36.6	37.6	38.5	38.8	39.3	35.7	35.1	38.0	37.6	.
33	35.1	37.5	38.5	39.0	38.2	35.8	34.1	37.7	37.5	.
34	35.8	37.1	37.3	37.3	36.8	36.5	33.9	35.9	36.1	.
35	35.2	35.8	36.1	37.0	36.4	33.5	32.4	35.9	36.1	.
36	34.5	36.0	36.7	37.8	35.7	33.7	33.0	34.7	33.6	.
37	33.5	36.5	35.8	37.4	37.2	34.3	34.3	36.2	37.1	.
Women - Femmes - Mujeres										
ISIC 3 - CITI 3 - CIIU 3										
Total	31.8	33.1	34.0	34.7	33.7	31.0	31.0	32.6	32.4	.
15	30.1	31.5	32.8	33.0	31.7	29.2	30.0	31.0	31.0	.
16	30.6	32.4	33.8	34.1	31.9	29.8	28.1	28.9	29.3	.
17	31.5	32.9	33.0	34.0	32.8	27.8	29.2	29.5	30.9	.
18	25.8	26.6	30.7	31.8	29.2	24.8	27.0	31.2	30.3	.
19	30.6	32.8	28.6	33.8	29.5	27.8	27.0	30.6	29.2	.
20	30.7	33.5	32.8	34.9	34.5	30.3	32.2	32.7	30.9	.
21	33.5	34.3	34.8	35.4	33.0	31.0	31.4	33.1	32.4	.
22	33.1	34.4	35.8	34.5	34.8	31.9	31.7	33.2	33.3	.
23	35.0	37.0	38.5	38.4	38.3	34.8	35.5	37.1	35.7	.
24	33.7	34.8	36.8	36.9	36.1	33.9	33.2	34.7	33.7	.
25	33.8	34.6	35.4	36.3	36.3	32.8	31.7	33.3	33.4	.
26	33.2	34.8	33.1	36.0	34.5	30.9	32.2	33.7	34.4	.
27	35.8	36.6	37.5	37.7	36.0	34.8	33.8	34.9	34.5	.
28	32.4	32.4	33.6	35.4	33.1	31.8	31.2	33.2	32.1	.
29	32.6	34.4	33.8	35.4	34.9	32.5	31.9	34.2	33.2	.
30	29.3	31.3	37.3	36.4	35.2	32.3	32.4	32.4	29.8	.
31	32.0	34.2	33.8	36.0	34.7	31.6	30.7	32.9	32.2	.
32	34.4	34.6	32.8	34.3	34.6	32.0	30.8	34.2	34.0	.
33	32.1	32.8	33.6	33.8	33.4	31.2	29.5	33.3	32.6	.
34	33.2	33.9	33.9	35.0	34.8	33.5	31.9	34.0	34.4	.
35	32.3	33.7	35.4	33.2	33.4	29.9	31.4	33.8	34.4	.
36	31.3	32.6	32.6	34.7	31.4	28.7	28.9	30.9	31.0	.
37	31.2	32.4	34.8	33.4	27.1	32.3	30.1	32.9	31.6	.
Belgique (DA) (b) [1][2]					Employees - Salariés - Asalariados					
Total men and women - Total hommes et femmes - Total hombres y mujeres										
ISIC 3 - CITI 3 - CIIU 3										
Total	36.6	36.5	35.9	36.5	35.8	36.7	36.5	36.4	36.5	.
15	35.5	36.0	35.5	35.9	35.1	35.6	36.3	35.5	35.3	.
16	35.8	36.1	35.7	36.3	35.0	35.3	35.1	35.3	35.6	.
17	34.8	35.4	33.9	35.0	33.5	33.6	33.6	33.8	34.9	.
18	29.0	28.6	30.9	33.1	29.7	28.4	31.2	34.6	32.7	.
19	34.9	35.6	31.5	35.9	33.8	33.5	34.3	33.7	34.1	.
20	37.0	36.5	35.3	36.9	36.2	36.1	37.4	36.2	35.7	.
21	35.6	35.1	34.0	34.8	33.5	34.7	35.3	34.6	35.0	.
22	36.9	36.0	35.5	35.4	35.4	36.1	36.4	36.0	36.1	.
23	38.9	37.9	38.0	37.9	37.7	38.8	39.6	37.7	37.6	.
24	38.6	37.4	37.3	37.9	37.5	38.4	38.6	38.0	37.7	.
25	37.2	36.6	36.3	37.2	36.6	37.0	37.4	37.0	36.9	.
26	36.6	36.1	35.2	35.9	35.0	36.7	36.2	36.4	37.1	.
27	36.9	38.0	37.8	38.1	37.4	38.7	37.5	36.6	37.0	.
28	36.7	36.5	36.1	36.5	35.8	36.7	36.1	37.1	37.1	.
29	36.6	36.4	35.9	36.4	35.6	36.0	36.1	36.3	36.3	.
30	35.8	35.8	38.0	37.5	38.1	37.4	38.6	37.0	36.4	.
31	36.3	36.0	36.1	37.1	35.9	36.8	36.2	36.7	36.6	.
32	38.0	37.3	36.2	37.2	37.5	37.4	37.1	37.8	38.1	.
33	36.4	37.2	36.5	37.2	37.0	37.7	36.9	37.6	37.8	.
34	37.2	37.4	36.5	36.4	36.2	38.2	36.6	36.4		.
35	37.1	35.9	34.7	35.9	35.4	35.7	35.4	37.0	37.0	.
36	36.0	35.8	35.0	36.4	34.1	35.3	35.0	35.1	34.3	.
37	35.1	36.3	35.0	35.8	34.5	36.9	37.0	36.0	38.2	.

Explanatory notes: see p. 721.
[1] Oct. of each year. [2] Full-time employees only.

Notes explicatives: voir p. 723.
[1] Oct. de chaque année. [2] Salariés à plein temps seulement.

Notas explicativas: véase p. 725.
[1] Oct. de cada año. [2] Asalariados a tiempo completo solamente.

HOURS OF WORK DURÉE DU TRAVAIL HORAS DE TRABAJO

In manufacturing / Dans les industries manufacturières / En las industrias manufactureras

Per week — Par semaine — Por semana

Belgique (DA) (b) [1][2] Employees - Salariés - Asalariados

Men - Hommes - Hombres
ISIC 3 - CITI 3 - CIIU 3

	1999	2000	2001	2002	2003	2004	2005	2006	2007	2008
Total	36.9	36.7	36.1	36.6	35.9	36.9	36.7	36.6	36.7	.
15	35.7	36.2	35.5	36.1	35.0	35.8	36.4	35.7	35.4	.
16	36.9	36.6	36.7	37.0	35.9	36.7	36.6	36.4	36.6	.
17	35.4	35.9	34.7	35.5	33.8	35.0	34.2	35.0	35.8	.
18	36.0	36.1	35.5	36.5	34.7	36.5	36.3	35.1	33.3	.
19	35.3	36.5	33.3	36.0	33.9	33.9	36.0	35.0	35.9	.
20	37.2	36.5	35.5	36.9	36.2	36.1	37.4	36.2	36.0	.
21	35.5	35.0	33.9	34.6	33.5	34.7	35.3	34.6	35.1	.
22	37.1	35.9	35.1	35.4	35.0	36.0	36.3	36.1	36.0	.
23	39.0	37.8	38.0	37.8	37.7	38.9	39.7	37.8	37.7	.
24	38.8	37.3	37.2	37.9	37.4	38.4	38.7	38.1	38.0	.
25	37.3	36.6	36.4	37.2	36.5	37.1	37.4	37.2	37.1	.
26	36.5	36.0	35.3	35.8	34.9	36.8	36.1	36.5	37.1	.
27	36.8	38.0	37.7	38.1	37.4	38.6	37.5	36.6	37.0	.
28	36.8	36.6	36.2	36.5	35.8	36.7	36.1	37.2	37.1	.
29	36.7	36.4	36.1	36.4	35.4	35.8	36.1	36.3	36.4	.
30	37.4	36.9	38.6	38.2	38.3	38.1	39.3	38.7	37.2	.
31	36.5	36.0	36.4	37.2	36.0	37.0	36.4	36.9	37.1	.
32	38.3	37.7	37.2	37.6	37.9	37.7	37.8	38.6	38.5	.
33	36.9	37.7	37.3	37.7	37.1	38.1	37.3	38.1	38.3	.
34	37.3	37.5	36.6	36.4	36.1	38.4	36.5	36.4	36.7	.
35	37.3	35.9	34.7	35.9	35.5	35.8	35.4	37.1	37.1	.
36	36.3	36.1	35.5	36.6	34.6	35.7	35.4	35.3	34.3	.
37	35.3	36.9	34.9	36.0	36.1	37.1	37.3	36.5	38.7	.

Women - Femmes - Mujeres
ISIC 3 - CITI 3 - CIIU 3

	1999	2000	2001	2002	2003	2004	2005	2006	2007	2008
Total	35.1	35.5	34.9	35.9	35.4	35.4	35.8	35.4	35.4	.
15	34.7	35.3	35.3	35.3	35.3	35.2	36.0	35.0	34.9	.
16	34.6	35.5	34.5	35.8	34.1	34.0	33.3	34.5	34.6	.
17	33.7	34.3	32.6	34.3	33.0	30.9	32.8	31.7	33.2	.
18	27.4	27.3	30.1	32.4	29.0	26.4	29.6	34.4	32.6	.
19	34.4	34.5	28.7	35.8	33.7	32.9	32.0	31.9	31.5	.
20	35.7	36.9	33.8	37.3	37.2	36.4	36.8	36.5	34.0	.
21	36.0	35.5	34.8	35.6	33.6	35.1	35.3	34.7	34.5	.
22	36.3	36.2	36.1	35.3	36.6	36.4	36.8	35.8	36.4	.
23	38.5	38.7	38.4	38.3	38.1	38.4	39.4	37.4	37.4	.
24	37.9	37.7	37.9	37.7	37.6	38.3	38.0	37.4	36.7	.
25	36.5	36.5	35.9	37.1	37.2	37.0	37.3	36.5	36.0	.
26	37.0	36.8	34.4	37.3	36.0	35.2	37.3	35.9	37.2	.
27	39.7	39.0	39.6	38.6	38.6	40.2	37.3	36.3	37.0	.
28	35.9	35.9	35.0	36.7	35.6	36.8	36.2	35.8	36.2	.
29	35.9	36.2	34.8	36.0	37.0	37.2	36.1	36.2	35.1	.
30	30.8	32.1	36.9	36.0	37.2	36.0	36.7	33.9	33.9	.
31	35.2	36.1	34.9	37.0	35.5	35.9	35.3	36.2	34.9	.
32	37.3	36.5	33.5	36.2	36.4	36.3	35.2	35.6	37.0	.
33	34.9	35.7	34.8	36.0	36.5	36.6	35.8	36.0	36.4	.
34	36.4	36.7	36.3	36.0	36.7	36.3	37.1	36.5	36.2	.
35	34.9	35.6	35.0	35.6	33.5	33.9	35.6	36.3	36.1	.
36	34.8	34.7	33.5	35.6	32.4	33.3	33.7	34.1	34.4	.
37	34.4	34.9	35.1	34.6	28.8	36.1	35.8	34.1	35.2	.

Bulgaria (CA) (a) Employees - Salariés - Asalariados

Total men and women - Total hommes et femmes - Total hombres y mujeres
ISIC 3 - CITI 3 - CIIU 3 [3]   ISIC 4 - CITI 4 - CIIU 4

	1999	2000	2001	2002	2003	2004	2005	2006	2007	2008	
Total	.	33	33	33	33	34 |	34	34	34	.	Total
15	.	35	34	35	34	34 |	35	34	35	.	11
16	.	32	33	34	34	33 |	35	35	35	.	12
17	.	33	33	33	33	33 |	34	33	34	.	13
18	.	34	34	33	34	33 |	33	33	34	.	14
19	.	33	33	34	34	33 |	33	33	34	.	15
20	.	34	35	34	34	34 |	33	33	33	.	16
21	.	33	33	33	33	34 |	34	34	34	.	17
22	.	35	35	35	35	35 |	34	34	35	.	18
23	.	29	30	29	.	. |	35	33	34	.	19
24	.	32	33	33	33	33 |	34	34	34	.	20
25	.	33	33	33	34	34 |	33	34	34	.	21
26	.	34	34	34	34	34 |	34	34	34	.	22
27	.	31	31	31	32	33 |	34	34	35	.	23
28	.	33	34	34	33	34 |	33	33	33	.	24
29	.	31	32	32	32	33 |	33	33	34	.	25
30	.	34	33	35	34	36 |	34	34	34	.	26
31	.	32	33	32	33	33 |	33	34	33	.	27
32	.	32	33	33	33	33 |	34	34	34	.	28
33	.	32	33	33	33	34 |	34	34	35	.	29
34	.	33	34	34	33	34 |	35	34	33	.	30
35	.	33	33	33	33	34 |	34	34	35	.	31
36	.	34	34	34	34	34 |	34	34	34	.	32
37	.	38	38	36	36	36 |	33	33	34	.	33

Explanatory notes: see p. 721.
[1] Full-time employees only. [2] Oct. of each year. [3] Official estimates.

Notes explicatives: voir p. 723.
[1] Salariés à plein temps seulement. [2] Oct. de chaque année. [3] Estimations officielles.

Notas explicativas: véase p. 725.
[1] Asalariados a tiempo completo solamente. [2] Oct. de cada año. [3] Estimaciones oficiales.

In manufacturing

Dans les industries manufacturières

En las industrias manufactureras

	Per week			Par semaine				Por semana			
	1999	2000	2001	2002	2003	2004	2005	2006	2007	2008	

Croatia (BA) (a) [1][2]   **Employees - Salariés - Asalariados**

Total men and women - Total hommes et femmes - Total hombres y mujeres
ISIC 3 - CITI 3 - CIIU 3

Total	41.6 [3]	41.5 [3]	41.3 [3]	41.3 [3]	41.3 [3]	41.4	41.0 [3]	41.2	41.0	40.6	

Men - Hommes - Hombres
ISIC 3 - CITI 3 - CIIU 3

Total	42.0 [3]	41.7 [3]	41.7 [3]	41.5 [3]	41.4 [3]	41.6	41.3 [3]	41.4	41.2	40.8	

Women - Femmes - Mujeres
ISIC 3 - CITI 3 - CIIU 3

Total	40.9 [3]	41.1 [3]	40.7 [3]	41.1 [3]	41.1 [3]	41.0	40.6 [3]	40.9	40.8	40.2	

Croatia (CA) (a)   **Employees - Salariés - Asalariados**

Total men and women - Total hommes et femmes - Total hombres y mujeres
ISIC 3 - CITI 3 - CIIU 3

	1999	2000	2001	2002	2003	2004	2005	2006	2007	2008
Total	139	139	140	139	141	142	142	140	139	.
15	140	139	139	142	141	142	142	140	138	.
16	136	133	145	140	141	156	150	149	142	.
17	133	135	139	139	141	141	141	140	137	.
18	129	133	134	133	135	138	135	132	133	.
19	138	137	138	135	141	141	143	139	139	.
20	143	140	144	140	143	144	146	144	144	.
21	139	142	139	143	141	138	141	143	139	.
22	148	146	144	146	145	146	145	144	143	.
23	138	140	140	141	141	142	140	140	136	.
24	140	138	140	139	140	143	142	142	139	.
25	146	144	146	145	145	145	146	145	144	.
26	144	144	145	143	147	146	146	142	142	.
27	133	134	136	132	135	142	134	136	132	.
28	145	144	142	144	143	146	146	145	142	.
29	141	140	145	142	145	144	145	144	143	.
30	156	155	155	151	150	153	153	146	154	.
31	136	138	140	137	143	142	141	140	138	.
32	138	160	151	147	150	149	146	144	147	.
33	153	154	149	150	148	150	146	146	146	.
34	137	134	138	138	139	141	140	136	135	.
35	133	134	132	130	129	134	133	135	134	.
36	141	140	138	138	141	145	142	140	141	.
37	151	150	144	146	146	148	147	147	151	.

Cyprus (DA) (b) [4][5]   **Employees - Salariés - Asalariados**

Total men and women - Total hommes et femmes - Total hombres y mujeres
ISIC 3 - CITI 3 - CIIU 3

	1999	2000	2001	2002	2003	2004	2005	2006	2007	2008
Total	40.5	40.2	40.5	40.0	40.1	40.0	39.9	40.4	.	.
15	41.1	40.9	41.3	41.2	40.8	39.9	39.7	40.2	.	.
16	39.2	41.6	37.7	37.2	37.9	38.8	38.0	39.4	.	.
17	38.6	38.4	39.7	39.1	39.0	39.2	38.9	40.1	.	.
18	39.4	39.9	38.2	39.1	39.1	38.0	38.8	38.3	.	.
19	38.3	38.2	38.5	38.1	38.4	39.2	39.5	37.7	.	.
20	39.2	38.4	40.1	38.2	38.0	38.1	38.2	40.9	.	.
21	38.6	38.7	39.6	38.9	38.5	38.3	38.6	38.2	.	.
22	42.5	44.5	42.7	39.4	40.1	40.6	40.4	42.3	.	.
23	41.2	42.8	43.4	43.1	48.4	49.8	41.7	.	.	.
24	43.0	40.5	40.0	39.6	39.9	39.6	44.0	41.0	.	.
25	39.9	39.0	39.3	39.7	39.7	39.3	39.5	39.2	.	.
26	46.4	41.4	42.3	42.3	41.9	42.9	42.0	43.5	.	.
27	38.6	38.7	38.5	42.2	39.3	39.8	38.0	40.2	.	.
28	38.9	39.0	40.9	40.1	42.0	43.1	40.3	40.3	.	.
29	38.6	39.2	38.3	39.1	38.5	39.0	39.7	38.8	.	.
31	39.0	39.4	38.2	38.7	38.9	40.5	39.5	39.9	.	.
32	.	.	.	.	.	.	.	38.0	.	.
33	39.0	39.2	38.9	39.1	41.3	40.9	40.4	39.2	.	.
34	38.9	39.0	40.1	38.7	38.9	39.1	39.0	39.5	.	.
35	38.6	38.7	39.8	39.5	40.9	40.0	38.2	37.3	.	.
36	39.3	40.5	40.1	39.1	39.0	39.2	39.4	38.9	.	.
37	43.4	40.8	39.4	39.4	39.4	39.5	40.0	40.1	.	.

Explanatory notes: see p. 721.   Notes explicatives: voir p. 723.   Notas explicativas: véase p. 725.

[1] Persons aged 15 years and over. [2] Excl. conscripts. [3] Second semester. [4] Adults. [5] Oct. of each year.

[1] Personnes âgées de 15 ans et plus. [2] Non compris les conscrits. [3] Second semestre. [4] Adultes. [5] Oct. de chaque année.

[1] Personas de 15 años y más. [2] Excl. los conscriptos. [3] Segundo semestre. [4] Adultos. [5] Oct. de cada año.

In manufacturing — Dans les industries manufacturières — En las industrias manufactureras

	1999	2000	2001	2002	2003	2004	2005	2006	2007	2008

Per week — Par semaine — Por semana

Cyprus (DA) (b) [1] [2] — Employees - Salariés - Asalariados

Men - Hommes - Hombres
ISIC 3 - CITI 3 - CIIU 3

	1999	2000	2001	2002	2003	2004	2005	2006	2007	2008
Total	41.1	40.5	40.9	40.3	40.3	40.8	40.2	41.0	.	.
15	41.5	41.3	41.2	41.3	40.5	40.5	39.9	40.5	.	.
16	40.5	42.4	38.4	38.0	38.2	39.3	38.0	39.0	.	.
17	38.8	38.3	38.1	39.6	40.2	40.4	39.3	43.2	.	.
18	38.5	38.6	38.5	39.2	38.7	38.1	38.4	38.1	.	.
19	38.9	38.1	38.5	38.1	38.2	40.4	40.1	38.3	.	.
20	39.3	38.3	40.1	38.2	37.9	38.1	38.2	40.9	.	.
21	38.9	39.0	39.6	39.2	38.7	38.4	38.8	38.2	.	.
22	43.8	46.7	44.7	39.9	40.8	41.8	40.9	44.6	.	.
23	41.4	43.1	43.8	43.4	49.1	50.9	41.9	.	.	.
24	42.6	39.9	40.0	39.9	40.6	39.9	42.4	40.6	.	.
25	40.2	38.9	39.5	39.7	40.1	39.4	40.0	39.4	.	.
26	47.7	41.9	42.8	42.9	42.4	43.6	42.5	44.3	.	.
27	38.6	38.8	38.6	42.8	39.5	40.0	38.0	40.5	.	.
28	39.0	39.2	41.2	40.3	42.2	43.7	40.5	40.5	.	.
29	38.4	39.3	38.3	39.1	38.3	39.0	39.9	38.8	.	.
31	39.2	39.9	38.7	39.0	39.1	41.4	39.9	40.4	.	.
32	.	.	.	.	.	.	.	38.0	.	.
33	39.3	39.3	38.7	39.6	42.4	41.6	41.2	39.8	.	.
34	39.0	39.2	40.5	38.7	39.0	39.0	39.3	39.2	.	.
35	38.5	38.7	39.8	39.5	40.9	40.0	38.2	37.2	.	.
36	39.6	40.6	40.6	39.3	39.2	39.4	39.8	39.2	.	.
37	43.5	40.8	39.5	39.4	39.4	39.5	40.0	40.2	.	.

Women - Femmes - Mujeres
ISIC 3 - CITI 3 - CIIU 3

	1999	2000	2001	2002	2003	2004	2005	2006	2007	2008
Total	39.6	39.9	39.8	39.5	39.7	38.8	39.5	39.4	.	.
15	40.4	40.4	41.4	41.0	41.3	39.2	39.5	39.8	.	.
16	38.0	40.9	37.1	36.6	37.7	38.4	38.0	39.8	.	.
17	38.6	38.4	40.2	39.0	38.6	38.9	38.8	38.3	.	.
18	39.6	40.1	38.2	39.1	39.2	38.0	38.8	38.3	.	.
19	38.0	38.2	38.5	38.1	38.6	38.2	39.0	37.2	.	.
20	39.1	38.7	40.5	38.1	39.0	38.4	38.2	40.5	.	.
21	38.1	38.3	39.7	38.5	38.3	38.3	38.3	38.2	.	.
22	40.8	41.7	40.5	38.9	39.3	39.3	39.9	39.8	.	.
23	37.7	39.0	39.7	39.7	40.8	37.9	39.7	.	.	.
24	43.4	41.1	40.0	39.3	39.4	39.3	45.7	41.4	.	.
25	39.2	39.4	38.8	39.6	38.7	39.0	38.3	38.8	.	.
26	38.6	38.5	39.1	38.4	38.3	38.5	38.6	38.0	.	.
27	38.0	38.0	38.0	38.0	38.1	38.0	38.0	38.2	.	.
28	38.6	37.9	39.2	39.2	40.6	39.3	39.0	38.5	.	.
29	39.2	38.8	38.3	39.0	39.2	38.8	39.1	39.0	.	.
31	38.6	38.0	37.0	38.1	38.3	38.4	38.4	38.1	.	.
32	.	.	.	.	.	.	.	38.0	.	.
33	38.7	39.0	39.0	38.7	40.5	40.4	39.7	38.5	.	.
34	38.5	38.4	39.1	38.7	38.7	39.2	38.0	40.2	.	.
35	39.2	39.2	39.5	.	.	.	.	37.4	.	.
36	38.5	40.2	39.0	38.5	38.6	38.7	38.4	37.9	.	.
37	40.0	39.8	38.0	39.8	39.8	40.0	40.0	40.0	.	.

Czech Republic (DA) (a) [3] — Wage earners - Ouvriers - Obreros

Total men and women - Total hommes et femmes - Total hombres y mujeres
ISIC 3 - CITI 3 - CIIU 3

	1999	2000	2001	2002	2003	2004	2005	2006	2007	2008
Total	41.0	40.7	40.7	40.7	40.7	40.6	40.5	40.5	40.4	.
15	42.5	42.0	42.4	42.1	42.0	41.9	41.5	41.7	41.4	.
17	38.0	38.1	38.3	37.7	38.3	38.1	38.6	39.5	39.5	.
18	40.5	39.8	39.7	39.7	38.2	39.3	38.5	39.4	38.1	.
19	39.8	39.8	38.0	40.0	40.3	40.2	38.5	39.1	39.4	.
20	41.8	41.0	40.1	40.3	41.1	40.5	39.6	40.2	40.1	.
21	41.3	40.2	41.6	42.0	41.8	41.9	41.8	41.9	41.8	.
22	42.3	42.4	42.7	40.9	40.1	40.1	39.8	40.0	40.6	.
23	.	.	.	.	.	.	.	.	.	.
24	40.0	39.2	39.2	41.0	39.4	39.4	39.1	39.0	38.9	.
25	41.2	41.4	41.3	40.0	40.1	40.0	39.8	40.6	40.7	.
26	41.8	42.3	41.3	42.8	41.7	41.5	40.6	40.5	40.3	.
27	39.8	39.4	40.4	38.6	40.4	39.9	40.2	40.7	39.9	.
28	41.5	40.5	40.4	40.2	39.9	40.2	40.0	40.1	40.2	.
29	41.8	41.7	41.8	42.3	42.1	41.9	41.4	41.1	41.0	.
30	.	.	.	.	.	.	.	.	.	.
31	40.9	40.9	40.7	40.4	40.0	40.0	41.0	40.3	40.5	.
32	39.4	39.9	41.3	41.3	41.4	41.4	40.0	39.9	40.4	.
33	40.2	39.2	40.4	38.4	39.7	39.5	40.8	40.8	40.2	.
34	41.8	41.8	40.9	41.7	40.5	41.4	41.2	41.3	41.1	.
35	42.2	41.4	41.2	42.8	40.3	40.3	41.3	41.2	41.0	.
36	40.4	39.3	39.8	40.3	39.8	40.1	40.3	40.0	39.8	.
37	.	40.7	40.5	41.0	38.9	40.9	.	.	40.2	.

Explanatory notes: see p. 721.

Notes explicatives: voir p. 723.

Notas explicativas: véase p. 725.

[1] Adults. [2] Oct. of each year. [3] Enterprises with 20 or more employees.

[1] Adultes. [2] Oct. de chaque année. [3] Entreprises occupant 20 salariés et plus.

[1] Adultos. [2] Oct. de cada año. [3] Empresas con 20 y más asalariados.

In manufacturing **Dans les industries manufacturières** **En las industrias manufactureras**

	Per week / Par semaine / Por semana									
	1999	2000	2001	2002	2003	2004	2005	2006	2007	2008

España (BA) (a) [1] [2] Total employment - Emploi total - Empleo total

Total men and women - Total hommes et femmes - Total hombres y mujeres
ISIC 3 - CITI 3 - CIIU 3

	1999	2000	2001	2002	2003	2004	2005	2006	2007	2008
Total	36.3	36.1	36.3	36.0	36.0	35.8	36.2	36.5	36.1	36.0
15	38.3	37.6	38.1	37.5	37.6	37.2	36.9	37.3	37.3	36.9
16	34.8	35.1	36.1	35.3	35.4	34.3	32.0	37.0	34.9	32.1
17	35.3	35.5	34.6	34.8	35.8	34.7	36.0	35.3	35.0	34.5
18	35.9	34.6	34.3	34.0	34.5	34.6	34.3	34.1	34.1	34.0
19	36.0	36.6	37.2	37.1	35.1	35.5	35.5	37.8	36.6	35.4
20	36.2	36.8	37.0	36.6	36.6	36.8	36.7	38.1	36.8	36.5
21	36.1	35.9	37.1	37.1	36.5	36.6	35.4	36.0	37.4	35.7
22	35.7	35.8	36.4	35.0	35.4	35.3	35.2	35.8	35.0	35.3
23	37.3	35.4	36.0	35.1	36.8	36.2	38.1	37.1	35.9	37.0
24	36.3	35.7	35.6	35.7	36.0	35.9	35.8	36.1	35.2	35.1
25	35.6	35.4	36.2	36.0	36.0	35.3	36.3	35.4	35.3	35.3
26	37.1	36.6	37.1	37.1	36.8	36.9	37.4	37.6	37.1	36.7
27	35.6	35.6	35.5	35.3	35.0	34.6	35.7	36.1	36.2	36.5
28	36.4	36.7	36.4	36.1	36.4	36.5	37.2	36.9	36.5	36.6
29	36.1	35.4	35.6	35.8	36.0	35.6	36.5	36.7	36.0	36.0
30	36.3	35.1	36.2	35.6	35.4	33.6	38.2	37.1	36.6	43.5
31	35.9	35.6	35.5	35.5	35.8	35.7	35.7	35.6	34.9	36.1
32	35.3	36.5	37.1	35.1	35.2	36.9	33.7	34.2	35.3	35.6
33	36.5	37.7	36.1	35.3	35.5	35.3	36.4	36.9	35.0	36.4
34	34.5	34.8	34.4	34.6	34.1	34.2	34.1	35.4	34.7	33.8
35	36.1	36.2	36.4	35.1	35.2	34.1	37.2	37.5	36.4	36.7
36	36.9	36.1	37.0	36.3	36.2	36.3	36.2	36.7	36.5	36.1
37	37.8	37.7	36.1	36.3	35.6	35.4	37.1	37.3	34.1	35.8

Men - Hommes - Hombres
ISIC 3 - CITI 3 - CIIU 3

	1999	2000	2001	2002	2003	2004	2005	2006	2007	2008
Total	36.9	36.8	37.0	36.7	36.8	36.6	37.3	37.5	37.2	37.0
15	39.7	39.1	39.5	38.9	39.2	38.4	39.0	39.4	39.2	38.6
16	36.0	35.1	36.7	35.6	36.2	33.7	33.3	40.4	37.3	38.5
17	36.0	36.8	35.5	36.5	38.6	35.7	38.0	37.3	36.8	36.1
18	39.5	37.2	37.6	37.4	37.6	37.5	38.7	36.7	38.3	37.4
19	38.3	37.9	39.3	39.1	38.0	37.8	37.2	39.4	37.8	37.5
20	36.7	37.2	37.5	36.9	36.9	37.3	37.5	38.7	37.7	37.0
21	35.9	35.8	37.8	37.7	36.7	36.7	36.1	37.0	37.0	36.2
22	36.1	37.1	37.5	35.9	37.0	36.0	36.8	36.7	36.1	36.8
23	37.1	35.0	36.1	35.6	36.6	35.9	38.8	38.0	37.0	37.0
24	36.7	36.7	36.4	36.3	36.6	36.9	37.1	37.1	36.2	36.4
25	36.2	35.5	36.5	36.1	36.2	35.7	36.9	35.9	36.5	36.4
26	37.5	36.9	37.3	37.4	37.1	37.4	38.2	38.3	38.0	37.4
27	35.5	35.6	35.5	35.4	35.1	35.0	35.8	36.1	36.3	36.6
28	36.7	37.1	36.7	36.5	37.2	37.0	38.1	37.7	37.2	37.4
29	36.3	35.9	36.0	36.2	36.7	36.1	37.1	37.5	36.6	36.5
30	36.6	35.0	36.6	36.9	36.5	34.3	38.5	37.9	36.9	45.6
31	36.1	36.1	36.1	36.2	36.3	36.4	36.2	36.4	36.1	36.5
32	36.9	37.1	37.7	35.4	35.5	37.6	34.0	34.4	36.6	36.5
33	37.4	38.8	37.0	36.2	36.0	35.7	38.0	38.8	36.9	37.3
34	34.5	34.8	34.7	34.8	34.3	34.7	34.6	35.6	35.4	34.4
35	36.2	36.3	36.6	35.2	35.2	34.2	37.1	37.8	36.5	37.0
36	37.2	37.0	37.7	36.6	36.8	37.0	37.2	37.7	38.0	37.4
37	38.1	38.7	36.5	36.9	35.9	35.5	36.6	37.7	36.5	35.6

Women - Femmes - Mujeres
ISIC 3 - CITI 3 - CIIU 3

	1999	2000	2001	2002	2003	2004	2005	2006	2007	2008
Total	34.5	34.0	34.1	33.9	33.5	33.7	33.0	33.5	32.8	33.0
15	35.0	34.3	35.1	34.5	34.3	34.7	33.2	33.7	34.1	34.2
16	33.4	35.1	35.3	34.9	34.5	35.2	29.7	29.6	32.6	28.0
17	34.2	33.8	33.5	32.8	32.5	33.0	32.9	32.8	32.8	32.5
18	34.8	33.8	33.3	33.1	33.3	33.7	33.0	33.1	32.7	32.9
19	33.1	34.9	34.4	34.9	32.0	32.8	32.9	35.3	35.0	32.4
20	32.5	33.4	33.8	34.2	33.9	33.3	31.2	34.2	30.4	32.2
21	37.2	36.4	33.6	34.3	35.7	36.0	33.1	33.4	38.8	32.8
22	34.4	33.0	34.2	33.1	31.8	33.9	32.3	34.0	32.7	32.6
23	39.4	38.4	35.5	32.9	38.1	38.7	35.4	31.2	31.0	37.5
24	35.3	33.7	34.1	34.5	34.7	34.2	33.2	34.0	33.4	32.8
25	33.5	35.0	35.1	35.7	35.5	34.1	34.2	33.1	31.4	32.0
26	34.5	34.7	35.7	35.1	34.9	34.2	33.1	33.6	32.2	33.1
27	35.7	36.1	35.8	33.6	34.5	28.8	34.7	36.1	34.6	35.8
28	32.6	33.9	33.5	32.5	31.0	32.8	30.9	31.2	31.6	31.5
29	34.3	32.1	33.4	33.3	31.6	32.3	33.4	32.4	32.7	33.1
30	35.1	35.5	35.4	33.2	33.6	32.7	37.4	34.4	36.1	35.4
31	35.2	34.2	34.4	33.7	33.8	33.5	33.7	33.1	31.6	34.8
32	30.1	35.3	35.8	34.3	34.4	35.1	33.1	33.7	32.3	33.5
33	33.4	34.5	34.2	31.8	34.2	34.6	33.4	33.5	31.8	34.9
34	34.3	34.9	32.6	33.5	33.1	31.9	32.1	34.1	31.8	31.3
35	34.4	34.6	35.1	34.2	35.5	33.1	38.0	34.8	35.9	35.1
36	35.3	32.0	33.7	35.1	33.6	33.2	31.8	32.6	30.0	30.2
37	33.4	32.7	34.3	34.0	34.7	34.9	38.4	35.9	25.0	36.8

Explanatory notes: see p. 721. Notes explicatives: voir p. 723. Notas explicativas: véase p. 725.

[1] Excl. compulsory military service. [2] Persons aged 16 years and over. [1] Non compris les militaires du contingent. [2] Personnes âgées de 16 ans et plus. [1] Excl. a los militares en servicio obligatorio. [2] Personas de 16 años y más.

HOURS OF WORK   DURÉE DU TRAVAIL   HORAS DE TRABAJO

In manufacturing   Dans les industries manufacturières   En las industrias manufactureras

	Per week / Par semaine / Por semana									
	1999	2000	2001	2002	2003	2004	2005	2006	2007	2008

Estonia (DA) (a) [1]   Employees - Salariés - Asalariados

Total men and women - Total hommes et femmes - Total hombres y mujeres
ISIC 3 - CITI 3 - CIIU 3

	1999	2000	2001	2002	2003	2004	2005	2006	2007	2008
Total	33.8	33.9	33.8	34.0	33.7	34.0	33.7	33.8	33.4	33.2
15	34.3	34.8	34.9	34.5	34.1	34.5	34.6	34.6	34.1	34.0
15-16	34.3	34.8	34.9	34.5	34.1	34.5	34.6	34.6	34.1	34.0
17	31.5	33.0	33.2	32.9	32.6	33.0	32.3	32.5	30.9	31.7
18	32.2	32.7	33.0	32.9	32.8	33.1	32.9	32.5	32.3	32.0
19	32.3	32.1	33.0	33.5	33.5	32.5	32.8	32.7	33.0	31.9
20	35.5	34.6	34.6	35.5	34.5	34.2	34.1	33.8	33.3	32.5
21	38.4	40.5	40.6	39.1	37.3	38.0	37.5	36.6	36.0	36.2
22	35.3	35.4	35.0	35.3	35.1	34.6	34.8	34.9	34.9	34.3
23-24	33.2	33.2	34.1	33.1	34.6	34.7	35.8	37.0	36.7	36.0
25	34.9	36.0	35.5	36.1	34.8	34.7	34.0	33.3	33.2	32.5
26	33.7	34.4	34.3	34.4	33.9	34.9	34.7	34.4	33.9	32.9
27-28	33.5	34.0	34.4	34.1	33.7	33.4	33.9	33.9	33.5	33.3
29	32.5	34.1	34.2	34.6	33.7	34.7	34.3	34.7	34.7	34.0
30	.	.	.	.	.	.	.	.	.	.
31	32.7	33.8	32.9	34.4	33.9	34.9	33.7	34.2	33.6	33.6
32	29.6	30.6	.	31.4	32.6	33.0	31.7	32.1	30.9	33.3
33	33.9	34.7	34.4	35.2	34.9	34.5	34.3	34.1	33.5	33.1
34-35	33.9	33.5	33.7	33.7	32.9	33.9	33.4	33.5	33.3	32.9
36	33.1	33.7	34.0	33.9	33.6	34.1	33.4	33.0	32.7	32.3
37	.	.	.	.	.	.	.	.	.	.

Finland (BA) (a)   Employees - Salariés - Asalariados

Total men and women - Total hommes et femmes - Total hombres y mujeres
ISIC 3 - CITI 3 - CIIU 3

	1999	2000	2001	2002	2003	2004	2005	2006	2007	2008
Total	38.1	38.0	37.8	37.6	37.5	37.5	37.8	37.8	37.7	38.2
15	37.6	36.7	37.0	36.8	36.7	36.9	37.4	37.1	36.0	37.3
16	39.7	37.0	37.8	32.3	20.0	.	.	.	.	.
17	36.4	35.5	36.9	37.7	37.7	37.1	38.0	36.8	37.1	39.4
18	36.7	37.7	37.3	36.9	38.4	36.3	36.0	36.4	35.8	38.6
19	36.0	38.7	36.9	38.3	36.1	38.5	38.1	37.0	34.8	39.5
20	38.7	38.7	38.4	37.6	37.8	37.7	37.8	38.1	37.7	39.1
21	37.0	36.4	36.6	37.2	36.5	36.0	37.0	36.9	37.3	39.0
22	35.6	35.6	35.2	35.2	35.2	35.5	36.4	35.2	35.3	37.1
23	37.7	39.7	38.5	37.5	37.3	37.9	38.8	37.7	40.3	40.6
24	38.5	37.6	38.3	.	37.3	38.4	38.5	37.2	37.2	39.0
25	37.8	38.2	37.1	37.2	36.7	38.4	37.6	38.3	37.1	38.9
26	38.1	38.9	38.4	37.9	38.5	38.2	37.4	38.6	38.1	39.2
27	37.6	37.2	37.4	36.6	37.6	37.5	37.9	38.3	36.6	38.4
28	38.8	38.2	38.4	39.0	38.1	37.5	38.4	38.8	38.5	39.5
29	39.6	39.4	39.6	38.7	39.1	38.4	38.5	38.7	39.4	39.6
30	38.8	37.4	37.5	37.4	38.3	34.8	33.8	43.2	37.1	38.7
31	38.0	38.3	38.0	38.0	37.9	38.8	38.4	38.2	37.2	38.9
32	38.3	38.1	37.7	38.1	37.7	38.4	38.3	38.2	38.4	39.5
33	38.1	38.4	39.4	38.1	36.4	37.7	37.9	37.6	37.2	39.1
34	39.2	40.3	38.5	39.3	37.6	37.7	37.6	38.6	39.4	39.8
35	39.2	39.9	38.8	37.7	39.4	37.1	.	.	38.2	39.1
36	38.5	38.9	37.9	38.2	37.8	37.4	37.6	38.7	38.2	39.0
37	32.7	32.6	37.5	34.9	37.2	42.0	38.7	37.7	36.5	39.0

Men - Hommes - Hombres
ISIC 3 - CITI 3 - CIIU 3

	1999	2000	2001	2002	2003	2004	2005	2006	2007	2008
Total	38.6	38.7	38.5	38.2	38.1	38.1	38.4	38.4	38.3	38.5
15	39.5	38.1	38.0	37.6	37.5	37.9	38.2	38.2	37.3	38.2
16	39.8	32.4	40.0	24.0	20.0	.	.	.	.	.
17	37.4	35.7	37.5	38.0	38.6	38.3	40.6	37.9	37.7	39.5
18	41.4	41.6	39.8	36.2	42.5	32.8	34.8	37.0	33.5	-
19	36.9	38.9	38.0	39.5	36.9	40.3	38.5	39.4	34.0	38.0
20	39.0	39.2	38.9	38.2	38.4	38.1	38.0	38.6	38.2	39.5
21	36.9	36.3	36.6	36.8	36.6	35.9	36.9	36.7	37.4	39.0
22	35.8	37.1	35.9	36.7	35.6	36.8	37.2	35.7	36.0	37.2
23	37.8	40.1	37.3	37.9	37.4	38.4	39.1	36.4	40.3	39.9
24	39.1	38.1	39.3	37.8	37.4	40.0	39.3	37.6	37.7	40.0
25	38.6	39.2	37.6	37.5	37.4	38.7	38.0	39.1	37.2	39.4
26	38.6	39.5	38.5	38.1	39.1	38.4	37.9	38.9	38.6	39.7
27	37.5	37.3	37.4	36.9	38.1	37.8	38.0	38.2	36.4	38.4
28	39.2	39.3	38.9	39.2	38.4	37.8	38.8	39.0	38.9	39.8
29	40.0	39.9	39.9	39.0	39.7	38.9	39.0	39.0	39.8	39.9
30	38.5	37.2	38.5	37.2	38.0	35.1	37.8	46.1	37.3	37.3
31	38.6	38.4	38.6	38.6	38.9	39.1	39.5	39.0	37.6	38.9
32	38.2	38.5	37.9	38.2	38.0	38.8	38.9	38.6	38.7	39.6
33	38.2	38.4	40.4	38.8	36.5	39.0	38.5	38.0	37.7	39.3
34	39.4	41.0	39.0	39.9	37.7	38.2	38.5	39.0	39.7	39.9
35	39.5	40.1	39.6	37.9	39.4	37.4	.	.	38.4	39.4
36	38.7	39.8	38.8	38.7	38.1	38.5	38.7	39.4	39.3	39.2
37	38.3	35.1	37.5	34.9	37.2	42.0	38.7	38.3	36.5	38.9

Explanatory notes: see p. 721.   Notes explicatives: voir p. 723.   Notas explicativas: véase p. 725.

[1] Enterprises with 50 or more employees, state-owned and municipal enterprises, institutions and organisations.   [1] Entreprises occupant 50 salariés et plus, entreprises d'Etat et municipales, institutions et organisations.   [1] Empresas con 50 y más asalariados, empresas estatales y municipales, instituciones y organisaciones.

In manufacturing

Dans les industries manufacturières

En las industrias manufactureras

	Per week			Par semaine				Por semana			
	1999	2000	2001	2002	2003	2004	2005	2006	2007	2008	

Finland (BA) (a) — Employees - Salariés - Asalariados

Women - Femmes - Mujeres
ISIC 3 - CITI 3 - CIIU 3

	1999	2000	2001	2002	2003	2004	2005	2006	2007	2008
Total	36.7	36.2	36.3	36.4	36.0	36.0	36.3	36.4	36.1	36.5
15	36.0	35.4	35.9	35.8	35.7	35.7	36.6	35.9	34.5	36.4
16	39.3	40.0	37.2	35.5	.	.	.	.	.	.
17	35.8	35.4	36.5	37.6	36.9	36.1	36.5	35.9	36.7	39.3
18	35.9	37.2	37.1	37.0	37.2	36.6	36.3	36.3	36.2	38.7
19	35.0	38.6	36.2	37.7	35.2	36.7	37.8	36.3	34.9	-
20	37.1	36.8	36.3	35.1	35.3	36.3	37.1	35.9	35.1	36.8
21	37.3	36.7	36.7	38.4	36.2	36.5	37.4	37.5	37.1	39.0
22	35.3	33.8	34.4	33.9	34.7	34.0	35.5	34.7	34.5	36.9
23	37.6	38.4	44.2	35.7	36.3	36.8	38.2	42.1	40.5	41.7
24	37.7	36.8	37.0	37.0	37.2	35.8	36.7	36.4	36.5	36.6
25	36.1	36.3	36.1	36.6	35.0	37.6	36.7	36.5	36.7	37.7
26	35.9	36.5	37.6	36.9	36.0	37.5	35.3	37.6	36.2	36.7
27	38.0	36.5	37.3	35.1	33.9	35.6	37.3	39.0	37.8	38.4
28	35.9	36.0	35.6	37.5	36.1	36.0	36.8	37.6	36.3	37.4
29	36.8	35.8	37.1	36.8	35.6	35.9	35.7	36.7	37.1	37.9
30	39.2	38.1	35.1	38.0	39.5	34.2	27.2	37.3	36.6	42.9
31	36.8	38.1	36.6	36.9	35.7	37.9	35.4	35.6	36.0	38.9
32	38.5	37.5	37.3	37.8	37.2	37.4	36.7	37.4	37.8	39.2
33	37.7	38.5	37.4	36.3	36.1	35.4	36.7	36.6	36.3	38.7
34	37.8	36.4	36.2	35.1	36.1	30.2	31.1	35.8	37.7	39.3
35	36.2	37.9	31.4	36.1	38.7	35.2	.	.	35.9	36.1
36	38.0	36.6	35.5	37.2	37.2	35.1	35.1	37.0	36.1	38.6
37	25.8	28.6	.	.	.	.	38.0	30.5	38.0	.

France (BA) (c) [1] — Employees - Salariés - Asalariados

Total men and women - Total hommes et femmes - Total hombres y mujeres
ISIC 3 - CITI 3 - CIIU 3 [2] .... ISIC 4 - CITI 4 - CIIU 4

	1999	2000	2001	2002	2003	2004	2005	2006	2007	2008	
Total	.	.	.	.	36.19	36.78	37.05	37.05	37.20 |	37.6	Total
15	.	.	.	.	37.53	37.03	37.14	37.44	37.61 |	38.4	10
16	.	.	.	.	33.82	34.56	34.60	33.51	35.70 |	36.3	11
17	.	.	.	.	35.24	36.06	37.04	35.80	36.80 |	35.8	12
18	.	.	.	.	36.46	35.89	35.34	37.56	37.20 |	37.7	13
19	.	.	.	.	35.05	35.48	36.12	35.76	37.19 |	39.6	14
20	.	.	.	.	36.96	36.76	36.36	36.76	36.53 |	37.4	15
21	.	.	.	.	35.47	36.80	36.45	35.93	35.26 |	37.3	16
22	.	.	.	.	36.38	36.86	37.48	37.86	36.13 |	37.7	17
23	.	.	.	.	35.87	37.18	36.10	38.73	37.43 |	38.4	18
24	.	.	.	.	36.04	37.81	38.19	36.99	37.26 |	37.0	19
25	.	.	.	.	35.81	36.56	37.11	36.05	37.10 |	37.2	20
26	.	.	.	.	35.79	36.64	36.30	36.53	37.00 |	38.1	21
27	.	.	.	.	35.88	36.23	36.28	37.20	37.29 |	37.1	22
28	.	.	.	.	36.40	36.30	36.33	36.78	36.93 |	36.8	23
29	.	.	.	.	36.06	36.56	37.13	36.94	37.55 |	36.3	24
30	.	.	.	.	37.13	38.90	41.19	39.76	39.77 |	37.3	25
31	.	.	.	.	35.36	36.18	36.85	37.73	36.86 |	38.9	26
32	.	.	.	.	35.68	37.14	37.90	37.51	37.93 |	37.9	27
33	.	.	.	.	37.27	37.73	38.02	38.53	38.23 |	38.2	28
34	.	.	.	.	35.41	36.47	36.94	36.44	37.26 |	37.2	29
35	.	.	.	.	36.34	37.55	37.33	37.40	37.31 |	37.7	30
36	.	.	.	.	34.68	36.14	37.07	36.23	36.61 |	37.0	31
37	.	.	.	.	36.46	36.83	36.15	37.76	36.96 |	36.8	32
									|	37.7	33

Men - Hommes - Hombres
ISIC 3 - CITI 3 - CIIU 3 [2] .... ISIC 4 - CITI 4 - CIIU 4

	1999	2000	2001	2002	2003	2004	2005	2006	2007	2008	
Total	.	.	.	.	36.56	37.22	37.44	37.42	37.61 |	37.6	Total
15	.	.	.	.	38.39	37.52	37.72	37.84	38.35 |	38.4	10
16	.	.	.	.	33.15	34.78	40.00	32.71	35.00 |	36.3	11
17	.	.	.	.	35.95	36.87	37.52	36.59	38.29 |	35.8	12
18	.	.	.	.	40.61	39.90	40.18	41.09	39.12 |	37.7	13
19	.	.	.	.	35.03	35.24	36.21	36.60	40.74 |	39.6	14
20	.	.	.	.	37.10	36.76	36.34	36.94	36.49 |	37.4	15
21	.	.	.	.	35.63	37.09	36.26	36.13	34.64 |	37.3	16
22	.	.	.	.	36.53	37.60	37.99	38.36	37.08 |	37.7	17
23	.	.	.	.	35.94	37.43	35.62	39.06	37.32 |	38.4	18
24	.	.	.	.	36.14	38.51	39.19	37.42	37.44 |	37.0	19
25	.	.	.	.	36.18	36.97	37.40	36.42	37.66 |	37.2	20
26	.	.	.	.	35.98	36.66	36.69	36.83	37.39 |	38.1	21
27	.	.	.	.	35.92	36.43	36.39	37.29	37.43 |	37.1	22
28	.	.	.	.	36.60	36.76	36.57	37.01	37.21 |	36.8	23
29	.	.	.	.	36.40	36.93	37.35	37.20	37.88 |	36.3	24
30	.	.	.	.	37.78	42.09	43.62	41.36	40.77 |	37.3	25
31	.	.	.	.	36.23	36.99	37.46	38.23	37.62 |	38.9	26
32	.	.	.	.	36.20	38.24	38.60	38.45	39.39 |	37.9	27
33	.	.	.	.	37.93	38.38	38.91	39.32	38.75 |	38.2	28
34	.	.	.	.	35.68	36.55	37.25	36.74	37.35 |	37.2	29
35	.	.	.	.	36.54	37.85	37.56	37.66	37.34 |	37.7	30
36	.	.	.	.	35.32	36.71	37.35	36.67	36.56 |	37.0	31
37	.	.	.	.	36.04	37.28	36.25	38.43	37.47 |	36.8	32
									|	37.7	33

Explanatory notes: see p. 721.

Notes explicatives: voir p. 723.

Notas explicativas: véase p. 725.

[1] Full-time employees. [2] Fourth quarter of each year.

[1] Salariés à plein temps. [2] Quatrième trimestre de chaque année.

[1] Asalariados a tiempo completo. [2] Cuarto trimestre de cada año.

HOURS OF WORK   DURÉE DU TRAVAIL   HORAS DE TRABAJO

In manufacturing   Dans les industries manufacturières   En las industrias manufactureras

	Per week			Par semaine				Por semana		
	1999	2000	2001	2002	2003	2004	2005	2006	2007	2008

France (BA) (c) [1]   Employees - Salariés - Asalariados

Women - Femmes - Mujeres
ISIC 3 - CITI 3 - CIIU 3 [2]   ISIC 4 - CITI 4 - CIIU 4

	1999	2000	2001	2002	2003	2004	2005	2006	2007	2008	
Total	.	.	.	.	35.15	35.59	35.97	35.98	36.08 |	36.4	Total
15	.	.	.	.	35.88	36.06	36.06	36.61	36.41 |	36.0	10
16	.	.	.	.	35.59	34.09	34.04	34.03	36.43 |	34.2	11
17	.	.	.	.	34.42	34.90	36.43	34.53	35.07 |	38.8	12
18	.	.	.	.	34.84	34.30	33.59	36.55	36.63 |	36.5	13
19	.	.	.	.	35.06	35.58	36.06	34.94	34.11 |	35.1	14
20	.	.	.	.	36.00	36.74	36.56	35.88	36.67 |	36.5	15
21	.	.	.	.	35.01	35.96	37.04	35.44	36.63 |	36.5	16
22	.	.	.	.	36.10	35.91	36.67	37.02	34.87 |	37.9	17
23	.	.	.	.	35.39	35.33	41.03	35.90	40.03 |	36.1	18
24	.	.	.	.	35.86	36.76	36.53	36.28	37.03 |	36.6	19
25	.	.	.	.	34.91	35.50	36.37	35.04	35.49 |	36.3	20
26	.	.	.	.	34.54	36.55	34.78	35.12	35.12 |	40.7	21
27	.	.	.	.	35.47	32.97	35.21	36.53	36.27 |	35.1	22
28	.	.	.	.	35.45	34.13	34.91	35.38	35.21 |	36.8	23
29	.	.	.	.	34.45	34.61	35.74	35.48	35.55 |	36.9	24
30	.	.	.	.	36.03	33.12	35.42	35.23	34.49 |	36.3	25
31	.	.	.	.	33.07	34.82	35.68	36.45	35.05 |	35.6	26
32	.	.	.	.	34.46	35.07	36.58	35.78	35.41 |	35.9	27
33	.	.	.	.	35.58	36.01	35.84	36.78	36.97 |	34.3	28
34	.	.	.	.	34.04	36.00	35.17	34.95	36.78 |	38.0	29
35	.	.	.	.	35.34	36.11	36.12	36.30	37.12 |	37.1	30
36	.	.	.	.	33.43	34.96	36.57	35.40	36.70 |	35.6	31
37	.	.	.	.	38.53	34.70	35.43	34.14	35.73 |	35.8	32
									|	37.8	33

France (BA) (c) [3]   Employees - Salariés - Asalariados

Total men and women - Total hommes et femmes - Total hombres y mujeres
ISIC 3 - CITI 3 - CIIU 3

	1999	2000	2001	2002	2003	2004	2005	2006	2007	2008
Total	37.60	36.32	35.65	35.31 |	35.56 [4]	36.00	36.30	36.37	36.53	36.65
15	37.71	35.38	35.15	34.67 |	36.48 [4]	35.55	35.76	36.07	36.23	36.07
16	36.11	33.72	30.87	30.69 |	33.82 [4]	34.56	34.60	33.51	35.70	36.50
17	36.00	34.84	35.28	35.02 |	34.59 [4]	35.15	35.27	34.95	36.00	36.77
18	36.58	35.60	34.56	34.99 |	34.78 [4]	34.43	33.80	36.48	36.26	35.50
19	38.17	35.24	34.70	35.67 |	34.88 [4]	33.42	34.83	34.39	36.19	36.77
20	36.08	35.85	36.03	34.08 |	36.34 [4]	36.01	35.69	36.06	36.40	36.60
21	36.99	36.55	34.58	34.32 |	34.99 [4]	36.21	35.50	35.86	35.20	38.15
22	38.90	36.66	36.29	35.76 |	35.18 [4]	35.22	36.08	36.52	35.26	35.66
23	39.18	36.72	33.75	33.94 |	35.31 [4]	36.32	36.10	38.47	36.11	36.02
24	38.00	36.53	35.31	35.59 |	35.21 [4]	37.20	37.53	36.33	36.57	37.28
25	37.09	36.17	35.01	35.21 |	35.25 [4]	36.23	36.82	35.52	36.58	36.17
26	37.24	35.40	35.42	34.90 |	35.20 [4]	36.10	36.10	36.02	36.34	36.70
27	35.92	35.56	34.50	34.66 |	35.37 [4]	35.57	36.09	37.07	37.14	36.35
28	38.08	37.37	36.08	35.42 |	35.92 [4]	35.68	35.84	36.19	36.35	36.76
29	37.17	36.82	36.67	36.12 |	35.70 [4]	36.03	36.46	36.58	37.14	37.20
30	41.32	37.95	38.09	36.89 |	36.30 [4]	38.49	41.02	39.61	39.50	40.90
31	37.58	36.70	35.69	35.19 |	35.20 [4]	35.78	36.59	37.20	36.39	36.67
32	37.31	36.94	35.38	35.45 |	35.15 [4]	36.64	37.36	36.83	37.22	35.78
33	39.06	37.58	38.10	37.54 |	36.78 [4]	37.19	37.24	38.00	37.67	37.29
34	37.07	36.40	35.24	35.00 |	35.27 [4]	36.22	36.59	36.16	36.95	37.07
35	38.30	36.13	36.21	35.98 |	35.61 [4]	36.78	36.62	36.92	36.90	37.01
36	38.78	35.42	35.87	34.79 |	33.76 [4]	35.44	36.29	35.87	36.11	35.99
37	38.16	39.17	34.25	36.46 |	36.18 [4]	35.12	34.49	35.40	34.82	37.43

Men - Hommes - Hombres
ISIC 3 - CITI 3 - CIIU 3

	1999	2000	2001	2002	2003	2004	2005	2006	2007	2008
Total	38.12	36.90	36.27	35.81 |	36.36 [4]	36.93	37.18	37.21	37.44	37.42
15	38.72	35.99	36.04	35.03 |	38.09 [4]	36.94	37.13	37.43	37.88	37.83
16	35.32	32.05	35.60	41.64 |	33.15 [4]	34.78	40.00	32.71	35.00	35.80
17	35.61	35.58	35.50	36.20 |	35.92 [4]	36.84	37.09	36.59	38.29	37.73
18	39.07	39.17	39.27	41.12 |	40.10 [4]	39.29	38.43	40.57	39.12	37.76
19	38.83	37.17	35.92	35.86 |	35.03 [4]	30.27	35.50	36.60	40.56	37.47
20	36.66	36.07	36.08	34.08 |	36.99 [4]	36.55	36.09	36.53	36.43	36.82
21	37.06	36.44	34.89	34.52 |	35.22 [4]	36.98	36.20	36.40	34.67	38.26
22	39.79	37.54	36.56	36.63 |	35.93 [4]	36.60	37.56	37.47	36.55	36.61
23	38.67	36.30	33.75	34.38 |	35.81 [4]	37.04	35.62	39.06	36.73	36.25
24	38.66	37.17	36.25	36.01 |	35.82 [4]	38.36	39.16	37.42	37.44	37.19
25	37.07	36.75	35.42	36.04 |	35.85 [4]	36.82	37.22	36.24	37.56	37.09
26	37.49	35.67	35.78	34.82 |	35.98 [4]	36.62	36.69	36.82	37.35	37.20
27	36.17	36.04	34.70	34.68 |	35.48 [4]	36.01	36.22	37.19	37.37	36.36
28	38.10	37.62	36.37	35.74 |	36.49 [4]	36.52	36.27	36.75	37.07	37.28
29	37.64	37.48	37.37	36.66 |	36.21 [4]	36.73	37.15	37.08	37.72	37.99
30	43.67	37.12	40.54	39.50 |	37.76 [4]	41.74	43.62	41.36	40.77	41.26
31	38.85	37.24	36.65	36.23 |	36.20 [4]	36.87	37.44	38.08	37.48	38.04
32	38.44	39.04	37.47	36.92 |	36.13 [4]	38.06	38.49	38.33	39.12	36.91
33	39.98	38.67	38.94	38.28 |	37.93 [4]	38.33	38.66	39.30	38.71	38.17
34	37.49	36.70	35.61	35.34 |	35.56 [4]	36.38	37.16	36.61	37.29	37.21
35	38.34	36.46	36.51	36.23 |	36.49 [4]	37.73	37.46	37.52	37.03	37.46
36	39.41	35.53	35.88	34.64 |	35.08 [4]	36.55	36.67	36.56	36.48	36.94
37	38.12	39.78	34.33	37.91 |	35.88 [4]	37.06	35.74	37.78	37.17	38.13

Explanatory notes: see p. 721.   Notes explicatives: voir p. 723.   Notas explicativas: véase p. 725.

[1] Full-time employees. [2] Fourth quarter of each year. [3] All employees. [4] Prior to 2003: March of each year.   [1] Salariés à plein temps. [2] Quatrième trimestre de chaque année. [3] Ensemble des salariés. [4] Avant 2003: mars de chaque année.   [1] Asalariados a tiempo completo. [2] Cuarto trimestre de cada año. [3] Todos los asalariados. [4] Antes de 2003: marzo de cada año.

| In manufacturing | Dans les industries manufacturières | En las industrias manufactureras |

	Per week			Par semaine			Por semana		
	1999	2000	2001	2002	2003	2004	2005	2006	2007	2008

France (BA) (c) [1] — Employees - Salariés - Asalariados

Women - Femmes - Mujeres
ISIC 3 - CITI 3 - CIIU 3

	1999	2000	2001	2002	2003	2004	2005	2006	2007	2008
Total	36.20	34.67	33.89	33.88	33.58 [2]	33.83	34.18	34.26	34.42	34.81
15	35.69	34.11	33.30	33.84	33.84 [2]	33.34	33.62	33.82	33.99	33.58
16	37.23	37.05	27.45	19.28	35.59 [2]	34.09	34.04	34.03	36.43	38.84
17	36.47	33.92	34.98	33.74	33.19 [2]	33.07	33.44	32.81	33.65	35.57
18	35.84	34.59	33.51	33.47	32.95 [2]	32.71	32.31	35.36	35.48	34.69
19	37.64	33.67	33.90	35.54	34.82 [2]	34.99	34.40	32.67	32.74	36.25
20	33.59	34.78	35.66	34.07	32.79 [2]	32.65	33.33	33.97	36.31	35.23
21	36.83	36.91	33.66	33.73	34.34 [2]	34.41	33.79	34.65	36.31	37.88
22	37.14	34.95	35.73	34.25	33.99 [2]	33.67	34.18	35.11	33.71	34.44
23	41.93	38.66	33.84	30.34	32.64 [2]	32.63	41.03	34.78	30.77	34.84
24	36.84	35.40	33.71	34.90	34.29 [2]	35.64	35.19	34.77	35.59	37.39
25	37.13	34.46	33.90	32.95	33.83 [2]	34.79	35.83	33.79	34.16	34.02
26	36.29	34.29	33.97	35.31	31.25 [2]	34.15	34.01	32.91	32.73	34.50
27	33.99	31.50	32.88	34.53	34.50 [2]	30.20	34.85	36.15	35.59	36.31
28	37.94	35.65	34.51	33.52	33.67 [2]	32.33	33.61	33.29	32.80	34.10
29	34.83	33.67	32.58	33.40	33.47 [2]	32.94	32.98	34.21	34.09	33.39
30	33.88	40.22	32.19	32.09	34.20 [2]	32.93	34.96	34.74	33.42	39.19
31	34.48	35.32	33.50	32.78	32.72 [2]	34.15	35.10	35.23	34.09	33.80
32	35.72	33.55	31.46	32.88	33.12 [2]	34.18	35.39	34.35	34.27	33.49
33	36.79	34.98	36.14	35.43	34.16 [2]	34.53	34.10	35.40	35.47	35.73
34	34.69	34.64	33.24	33.29	33.86 [2]	35.44	33.79	34.10	36.37	36.33
35	38.07	34.15	34.47	34.64	32.22 [2]	33.08	33.08	34.75	36.12	35.04
36	37.35	35.15	35.83	35.25	31.48 [2]	33.33	35.63	34.69	35.44	34.00
37	38.52	36.63	33.81	30.08	37.39 [2]	29.20	28.58	28.09	31.03	34.69

Germany (DA) (b) — Employees - Salariés - Asalariados

Total men and women - Total hommes et femmes - Total hombres y mujeres
ISIC 3 - CITI 3 - CIIU 3

	1999	2000	2001	2002	2003	2004	2005	2006	2007	2008
Total	.	.	.	.	.	.	.	.	38.4	38.4
15	.	.	.	.	.	.	.	.	39.5	39.6
16	.	.	.	.	.	.	.	.	37.9	38.0
17	.	.	.	.	.	.	.	.	38.7	38.5
18	.	.	.	.	.	.	.	.	37.6	38.0
19	.	.	.	.	.	.	.	.	39.4	39.2
20	.	.	.	.	.	.	.	.	39.7	39.8
21	.	.	.	.	.	.	.	.	38.8	38.6
22	.	.	.	.	.	.	.	.	37.7	37.7
23	.	.	.	.	.	.	.	.	38.6	38.6
24	.	.	.	.	.	.	.	.	38.6	38.6
25	.	.	.	.	.	.	.	.	39.1	39.3
26	.	.	.	.	.	.	.	.	39.7	39.6
27	.	.	.	.	.	.	.	.	37.5	37.2
28	.	.	.	.	.	.	.	.	39.0	38.9
29	.	.	.	.	.	.	.	.	38.4	38.3
30	.	.	.	.	.	.	.	.	39.0	39.1
31	.	.	.	.	.	.	.	.	38.1	38.0
32	.	.	.	.	.	.	.	.	38.2	38.3
33	.	.	.	.	.	.	.	.	38.4	38.4
34	.	.	.	.	.	.	.	.	36.9	36.9
35	.	.	.	.	.	.	.	.	37.9	38.1
36	.	.	.	.	.	.	.	.	38.6	38.6
37	.	.	.	.	.	.	.	.	41.0	41.1

Men - Hommes - Hombres
ISIC 3 - CITI 3 - CIIU 3

	1999	2000	2001	2002	2003	2004	2005	2006	2007	2008
Total	.	.	.	.	.	.	.	.	38.5	38.5
15	.	.	.	.	.	.	.	.	39.9	40.1
16	.	.	.	.	.	.	.	.	38.1	38.1
17	.	.	.	.	.	.	.	.	39.0	38.8
18	.	.	.	.	.	.	.	.	38.0	38.3
19	.	.	.	.	.	.	.	.	39.5	39.3
20	.	.	.	.	.	.	.	.	39.8	39.9
21	.	.	.	.	.	.	.	.	38.9	38.7
22	.	.	.	.	.	.	.	.	37.8	37.8
23	.	.	.	.	.	.	.	.	38.7	38.6
24	.	.	.	.	.	.	.	.	38.6	38.6
25	.	.	.	.	.	.	.	.	39.2	39.5
26	.	.	.	.	.	.	.	.	39.9	39.7
27	.	.	.	.	.	.	.	.	37.6	37.2
28	.	.	.	.	.	.	.	.	39.2	39.1
29	.	.	.	.	.	.	.	.	38.5	38.5
30	.	.	.	.	.	.	.	.	39.2	39.2
31	.	.	.	.	.	.	.	.	38.3	38.3
32	.	.	.	.	.	.	.	.	38.3	38.5
33	.	.	.	.	.	.	.	.	38.6	38.7
34	.	.	.	.	.	.	.	.	36.9	37.0
35	.	.	.	.	.	.	.	.	38.0	38.1
36	.	.	.	.	.	.	.	.	38.6	38.7
37	.	.	.	.	.	.	.	.	41.2	41.4

Explanatory notes: see p. 721.
[1] All employees. [2] Prior to 2003: March of each year.

Notes explicatives: voir p. 723.
[1] Ensemble des salariés. [2] Avant 2003: mars de chaque année.

Notas explicativas: véase p. 725.
[1] Todos los asalariados. [2] Antes de 2003: marzo de cada año.

HOURS OF WORK   DURÉE DU TRAVAIL   HORAS DE TRABAJO

In manufacturing   Dans les industries manufacturières   En las industrias manufactureras

	Per week				Par semaine				Por semana	
	1999	2000	2001	2002	2003	2004	2005	2006	2007	2008

Germany (DA) (b)   Employees - Salariés - Asalariados

Women - Femmes - Mujeres
ISIC 3 - CITI 3 - CIIU 3

	1999	2000	2001	2002	2003	2004	2005	2006	2007	2008
Total	.	.	.	.	.	.	.	.	37.9	37.9
15	.	.	.	.	.	.	.	.	38.7	38.8
16	.	.	.	.	.	.	.	.	37.6	37.8
17	.	.	.	.	.	.	.	.	38.3	37.9
18	.	.	.	.	.	.	.	.	37.4	37.9
19	.	.	.	.	.	.	.	.	39.2	39.0
20	.	.	.	.	.	.	.	.	38.7	38.7
21	.	.	.	.	.	.	.	.	38.2	38.1
22	.	.	.	.	.	.	.	.	37.5	37.6
23	.	.	.	.	.	.	.	.	38.4	38.4
24	.	.	.	.	.	.	.	.	38.4	38.5
25	.	.	.	.	.	.	.	.	38.8	38.8
26	.	.	.	.	.	.	.	.	38.6	38.5
27	.	.	.	.	.	.	.	.	36.8	36.7
28	.	.	.	.	.	.	.	.	37.9	37.8
29	.	.	.	.	.	.	.	.	37.1	37.1
30	.	.	.	.	.	.	.	.	38.4	38.6
31	.	.	.	.	.	.	.	.	37.3	37.2
32	.	.	.	.	.	.	.	.	37.8	37.8
33	.	.	.	.	.	.	.	.	37.8	37.9
34	.	.	.	.	.	.	.	.	36.6	36.6
35	.	.	.	.	.	.	.	.	37.4	37.5
36	.	.	.	.	.	.	.	.	38.3	38.2
37	.	.	.	.	.	.	.	.	40.0	39.7

Germany (DA) (b)   Wage earners - Ouvriers - Obreros

Total men and women - Total hommes et femmes - Total hombres y mujeres
ISIC 3 - CITI 3 - CIIU 3

	1999	2000	2001	2002	2003	2004	2005	2006	2007	2008
Total	37.5	37.9	37.8	37.6	37.7	37.6	37.6	37.9 [1]	.	.
15	40.3	40.3	40.1	40.0	40.1	39.9	39.9	39.9 [1]	.	.
16	38.2	38.2	38.1	38.1	37.9	37.9	37.7	38.1 [1]	.	.
17	38.3	38.8	38.6	38.4	38.6	38.4	38.5	38.8 [1]	.	.
18	37.0	37.5	37.3	37.4	37.5	37.4	37.7	37.9 [1]	.	.
19	39.1	39.4	39.3	38.9	39.0	38.8	38.8	39.4 [1]	.	.
20	39.1	39.6	39.2	39.3	39.3	39.7	39.9	40.2 [1]	.	.
21	38.6	38.9	38.4	38.2	38.2	38.2	38.3	38.5 [1]	.	.
22	37.6	37.9	37.6	37.4	37.2	37.5	37.8	37.8 [1]	.	.
23	39.1	39.0	39.0	39.0	38.9	38.9	39.1	39.1 [1]	.	.
24	38.2	38.3	38.2	38.2	38.2	38.2	38.3	38.5 [1]	.	.
25	38.9	39.0	38.8	38.7	38.7	38.7	38.8	39.1 [1]	.	.
26	40.0	40.1	39.7	39.3	39.4	39.6	39.7	40.0 [1]	.	.
27	37.1	37.7	37.5	37.2	37.4	37.5	37.4	37.6 [1]	.	.
28	38.2	38.7	38.6	38.2	38.4	38.4	38.3	38.8 [1]	.	.
29	37.3	37.5	37.6	37.1	37.1	37.2	37.4	37.7 [1]	.	.
30	36.5	37.3	37.1	36.8	37.0	37.3	37.6	38.1 [1]	.	.
31	36.6	37.0	36.9	36.6	36.7	36.9	37.1	37.3 [1]	.	.
32	36.6	36.6	36.0	36.0	36.5	36.7	36.9	37.2 [1]	.	.
33	36.7	37.2	37.3	37.1	37.0	37.0	37.2	37.4 [1]	.	.
34	34.9	35.3	35.6	36.1	36.1	35.5	35.2	35.4 [1]	.	.
35	37.5	37.6	37.8	37.3	37.2	37.2	37.2	37.4 [1]	.	.
36	37.6	37.8	37.7	37.2	37.2	37.2	37.4	37.9 [1]	.	.
37	42.1	42.0	41.9	41.7	42.0	42.0	42.0	42.1 [1]	.	.

Men - Hommes - Hombres
ISIC 3 - CITI 3 - CIIU 3

	1999	2000	2001	2002	2003	2004	2005	2006	2007	2008
Total	37.6	38.0	37.9	37.7	37.7	37.7	37.7	37.9 [1]	.	.
15	40.8	40.8	40.5	40.3	40.4	40.3	40.2	40.2 [1]	.	.
16	38.2	38.1	38.1	38.0	37.8	37.9	37.8	38.3 [1]	.	.
17	38.7	39.1	38.8	38.6	38.8	38.6	38.6	38.8 [1]	.	.
18	38.3	38.8	38.3	38.1	38.5	38.4	38.7	38.9 [1]	.	.
19	39.6	39.7	39.6	39.3	39.4	38.8	39.0	39.8 [1]	.	.
20	39.3	39.7	39.3	39.4	39.4	39.9	40.0	40.4 [1]	.	.
21	38.8	39.2	38.6	38.4	38.4	38.4	38.4	38.6 [1]	.	.
22	37.7	38.0	37.6	37.5	37.2	37.5	37.9	37.8 [1]	.	.
23	39.1	38.9	39.0	39.0	38.9	38.9	39.1	39.1 [1]	.	.
24	38.2	38.3	38.2	38.2	38.2	38.2	38.3	38.5 [1]	.	.
25	39.0	39.2	38.9	38.8	38.9	38.8	38.9	39.2 [1]	.	.
26	40.3	40.3	39.9	39.6	39.4	39.8	39.9	40.2 [1]	.	.
27	37.1	37.7	37.5	37.3	37.4	37.5	37.4	37.7 [1]	.	.
28	38.4	38.9	38.8	38.4	38.5	38.5	38.5	38.9 [1]	.	.
29	37.4	37.6	37.8	37.2	37.2	37.3	37.5	37.8 [1]	.	.
30	36.6	37.3	37.2	36.8	37.0	37.4	37.7	38.2 [1]	.	.
31	36.7	37.2	37.1	36.8	36.9	37.1	37.3	37.5 [1]	.	.
32	37.1	36.8	36.1	36.2	36.6	36.8	37.0	37.2 [1]	.	.
33	36.9	37.4	37.5	37.2	37.0	37.0	37.2	37.4 [1]	.	.
34	35.0	35.3	35.6	36.2	36.1	35.5	35.2	35.4 [1]	.	.
35	37.5	37.6	37.8	37.3	37.2	37.2	37.2	37.4 [1]	.	.
36	37.6	37.9	37.7	37.2	37.2	37.2	37.3	37.9 [1]	.	.
37	42.3	42.2	42.0	41.8	42.1	42.1	42.0	42.2 [1]	.	.

Explanatory notes: see p. 721.   Notes explicatives: voir p. 723.   Notas explicativas: véase p. 725.
[1] Series discontinued.   [1] Série arrêtée.   [1] Serie interrumpida.

In manufacturing
Dans les industries manufacturières
En las industrias manufactureras

	Per week / Par semaine / Por semana									
	1999	2000	2001	2002	2003	2004	2005	2006	2007	2008

Germany (DA) (b) Wage earners - Ouvriers - Obreros

Women - Femmes - Mujeres
ISIC 3 - CITI 3 - CIIU 3

	1999	2000	2001	2002	2003	2004	2005	2006	2007	2008
Total	37.0	37.4	37.3	37.2	37.2	37.2	37.3	37.6 [1]	.	.
15	38.9	39.0	39.0	38.9	39.0	38.9	39.0	39.0 [1]	.	.
16	38.3	38.2	38.1	38.2	38.0	37.9	37.5	37.5 [1]	.	.
17	37.6	38.4	38.3	38.0	38.1	38.1	38.5	38.7 [1]	.	.
18	36.7	37.3	37.0	37.2	37.2	37.2	37.4	37.5 [1]	.	.
19	38.7	39.2	39.0	38.6	38.6	38.8	38.6	39.0 [1]	.	.
20	37.4	38.1	37.6	37.7	37.6	37.7	37.9	38.3 [1]	.	.
21	37.4	37.3	37.1	37.0	37.1	37.0	37.3	37.6 [1]	.	.
22	37.0	37.4	37.3	37.2	37.1	37.3	37.6	37.7 [1]	.	.
23	39.6	39.1	39.0	39.0	38.9	38.9	39.3	39.1 [1]	.	.
24	38.0	38.3	38.3	38.2	38.2	38.2	38.3	38.4 [1]	.	.
25	38.4	38.4	38.3	38.1	38.1	38.0	38.4	38.6 [1]	.	.
26	38.1	38.2	37.9	37.4	37.3	38.0	37.9	38.2 [1]	.	.
27	36.8	37.4	37.2	37.1	37.2	37.3	37.0	37.2 [1]	.	.
28	36.8	37.5	37.3	37.2	37.2	37.2	37.2	37.8 [1]	.	.
29	36.0	36.2	36.2	36.0	36.0	36.1	36.1	36.5 [1]	.	.
30	36.3	37.2	37.1	36.9	37.1	37.2	37.4	37.9 [1]	.	.
31	36.3	36.6	36.4	36.2	36.4	36.5	36.7	36.9 [1]	.	.
32	36.1	36.4	35.9	35.8	36.3	36.6	36.8	37.1 [1]	.	.
33	36.3	36.9	37.1	36.9	36.8	36.9	37.1	37.4 [1]	.	.
34	34.4	35.2	35.3	35.8	35.7	35.1	34.9	35.2 [1]	.	.
35	36.9	37.2	37.0	36.7	36.8	36.7	36.7	37.2 [1]	.	.
36	37.5	37.6	37.7	37.2	37.3	37.2	37.6	38.0 [1]	.	.
37	39.7	40.0	40.0	39.9	40.0	40.1	40.5	40.4 [1]	.	.

Gibraltar (CA) (b) [2] [3] Employees - Salariés - Asalariados

Total men and women - Total hommes et femmes - Total hombres y mujeres
ISIC 3 - CITI 3 - CIIU 3

	1999	2000	2001	2002	2003	2004	2005	2006	2007	2008
Total	46.4	45.1	45.5	46.9	44.8	50.0	49.1	47.7	47.1	.

Men - Hommes - Hombres
ISIC 3 - CITI 3 - CIIU 3

	1999	2000	2001	2002	2003	2004	2005	2006	2007	2008
Total	47.1	45.6	46.0	47.5	45.4	50.7	50.1	48.9	48.3	.

Women - Femmes - Mujeres
ISIC 3 - CITI 3 - CIIU 3

	1999	2000	2001	2002	2003	2004	2005	2006	2007	2008
Total	40.1	40.5	40.7	41.2	39.6	41.5	37.9	36.7	37.1	.

Greece (BA) (a) Total employment - Emploi total - Empleo total

Total men and women - Total hommes et femmes - Total hombres y mujeres
ISIC 3 - CITI 3 - CIIU 3 [4] [5] [6] | ISIC 4 - CITI 4 - CIIU 4 [5]

	1999	2000	2001	2002	2003	2004	2005	2006	2007	2008	
Total	42.0	43.0	42.0	42.0	42.0	42.3	42.3	42.1	42.0 [1]	41.8	Total
15	45.0	44.0	43.0	44.0	44.0	43.9	43.8	43.8	44.7 [1]	43.7	10
16	41.0	39.0	40.0	36.0	39.0	37.8	39.7	38.8	35.7 [1]	40.8	11
17	41.0	41.0	41.0	40.0	41.0	40.8	40.7	42.0	39.5 [1]	37.1	12
18	40.0	41.0	41.0	41.0	41.0	40.6	41.2	40.6	40.2 [1]	40.1	13
19	41.0	43.0	41.0	43.0	39.0	42.5	40.9	38.7	40.1 [1]	40.6	14
20	45.0	44.0	45.0	44.0	44.0	44.5	45.1	44.5	44.5 [1]	40.8	15
21	40.0	40.0	43.0	42.0	39.0	40.8	40.6	41.3	37.1 [1]	42.8	16
22	42.0	43.0	42.0	40.0	41.0	41.7	41.6	40.9	40.3 [1]	38.9	17
23	40.0	40.0	41.0	39.0	39.0	40.8	40.5	39.3	40.0 [1]	41.9	18
24	40.0	40.0	40.0	41.0	40.0	40.5	39.7	39.4	39.7 [1]	41.0	19
25	41.0	41.0	41.0	42.0	41.0	39.5	40.9	40.0	39.3 [1]	39.9	20
26	43.0	42.0	42.0	43.0	42.0	42.5	42.1	42.0	42.6 [1]	40.3	21
27	43.0	41.0	41.0	39.0	41.0	41.3	40.4	39.4	39.4 [1]	39.5	22
28	43.0	43.0	42.0	43.0	43.0	43.5	42.2	42.5	43.1 [1]	41.7	23
29	42.0	42.0	40.0	42.0	42.0	41.9	42.3	40.7	40.6 [1]	42.7	24
30	40.0	38.0	42.0	43.0	39.0	39.0	40.0	40.0	25.0 [1]	42.7	25
31	40.0	41.0	39.0	41.0	41.0	42.3	40.1	40.1	41.0 [1]	37.5	26
32	39.0	41.0	41.0	36.0	39.0	41.2	39.2	39.0	38.6 [1]	39.4	27
33	40.0	44.0	42.0	39.0	42.0	43.2	41.9	40.6	41.2 [1]	41.7	28
34	39.0	40.0	43.0	37.0	40.0	39.3	42.9	45.5	41.8 [1]	42.5	29
35	39.0	42.0	40.0	41.0	40.0	39.1	42.8	40.9	40.2 [1]	38.5	30
36	43.0	43.0	44.0	44.0	44.0	43.6	43.8	44.8	43.8 [1]	43.4	31
37	40.0	40.0	40.0	38.0	40.0	40.0	40.0	41.8	39.9 [1]	40.3	32
									[1]	43.6	33

Explanatory notes: see p. 721. Notes explicatives: voir p. 723. Notas explicativas: véase p. 725.

[1] Series discontinued. [2] Excl. part-time workers and juveniles. [3] Oct. of each year. [4] Persons aged 15 years and over. [5] Second quarter of each year. [6] Excl. conscripts.

[1] Série arrêtée. [2] Non compris les travailleurs à temps partiel et les jeunes. [3] Oct. de chaque année. [4] Personnes âgées de 15 ans et plus. [5] Deuxième trimestre de chaque année. [6] Non compris les conscrits.

[1] Serie interrumpida. [2] Excl. los trabajadores a tiempo parcial y los jóvenes. [3] Oct. de cada año. [4] Personas de 15 años y más. [5] Segundo trimestre de cada año. [6] Excl. los conscriptos.

HOURS OF WORK — DURÉE DU TRAVAIL — HORAS DE TRABAJO

In manufacturing — Dans les industries manufacturières — En las industrias manufactureras

Per week — Par semaine — Por semana

Greece (BA) (a) — Total employment - Emploi total - Empleo total

Men - Hommes - Hombres
ISIC 3 - CITI 3 - CIIU 3 [1] [2] [3]   ISIC 4 - CITI 4 - CIIU 4 [2]

	1999	2000	2001	2002	2003	2004	2005	2006	2007	2008	
Total	43.0	43.0	43.0	43.0	43.0	43.3	43.2	42.9	43.0 |	42.7	Total
15	46.0	45.0	44.0	45.0	45.0	45.2	45.2	44.7	45.9 |	45.1	10
16	41.0	40.0	40.0	36.0	43.0	36.9	40.2	38.2	38.4 |	40.7	11
17	43.0	42.0	42.0	40.0	42.0	41.8	41.6	43.0	40.7 |	36.0	12
18	42.0	44.0	42.0	44.0	43.0	43.5	43.5	43.1	43.8 |	41.5	13
19	42.0	44.0	43.0	45.0	41.0	44.6	42.3	39.6	40.4 |	43.9	14
20	45.0	44.0	45.0	44.0	44.0	44.8	45.6	44.8	44.9 |	42.2	15
21	40.0	41.0	43.0	42.0	40.0	41.0	40.7	42.2	38.8 |	43.4	16
22	43.0	44.0	44.0	42.0	42.0	43.4	43.0	41.4	41.5 |	40.1	17
23	41.0	41.0	41.0	41.0	39.0	40.9	40.4	39.2	40.5 |	42.8	18
24	41.0	41.0	40.0	42.0	41.0	41.9	39.4	39.7	40.9 |	41.3	19
25	42.0	42.0	41.0	42.0	42.0	40.9	41.0	40.3	40.1 |	40.5	20
26	43.0	43.0	43.0	43.0	42.0	43.2	42.7	41.9	42.9 |	41.2	21
27	43.0	41.0	40.0	39.0	42.0	41.7	40.4	39.6	39.7 |	40.4	22
28	44.0	44.0	43.0	44.0	43.0	43.7	42.5	43.2	43.9 |	42.2	23
29	42.0	42.0	41.0	42.0	43.0	42.2	42.5	41.6	41.3 |	42.9	24
30	40.0	39.0	42.0	43.0	38.0	39.0	40.0	40.0	25.0 |	43.2	25
31	40.0	42.0	39.0	42.0	42.0	42.9	40.7	40.6	41.6 |	36.9	26
32	38.0	41.0	41.0	35.0	41.0	40.7	39.4	39.2	38.1 |	40.0	27
33	41.0	44.0	41.0	39.0	42.0	43.8	43.1	42.7	41.5 |	41.5	28
34	41.0	42.0	43.0	36.0	39.0	39.3	43.0	46.7	42.4 |	42.7	29
35	39.0	42.0	40.0	41.0	40.0	39.1	43.2	41.3	40.1 |	38.8	30
36	44.0	44.0	44.0	44.0	45.0	44.6	44.9	45.9	44.4 |	43.8	31
37	40.0	40.0	40.0	38.0	.	40.0	40.0	41.8	42.3 |	43.0	32
									|	43.8	33

Women - Femmes - Mujeres
ISIC 3 - CITI 3 - CIIU 3 [1] [2] [3]   ISIC 4 - CITI 4 - CIIU 4 [2]

	1999	2000	2001	2002	2003	2004	2005	2006	2007	2008	
Total	40.0	41.0	40.0	40.0	40.0	39.7	40.1	39.8	39.3 |	39.4	Total
15	42.0	43.0	42.0	42.0	42.0	41.6	41.6	42.1	42.8 |	41.6	10
16	41.0	38.0	40.0	36.0	34.0	39.3	38.7	39.4	33.3 |	41.3	11
17	39.0	39.0	38.0	41.0	40.0	39.2	39.5	40.1	36.8 |	39.2	12
18	40.0	40.0	40.0	40.0	40.0	39.0	39.8	39.0	38.2 |	38.2	13
19	40.0	41.0	39.0	40.0	36.0	38.6	38.8	37.3	39.7 |	37.6	14
20	42.0	43.0	43.0	43.0	38.0	37.4	37.5	38.1	36.0 |	38.4	15
21	38.0	40.0	44.0	39.0	37.0	40.3	39.7	39.4	33.6 |	34.4	16
22	41.0	41.0	40.0	37.0	41.0	39.3	38.6	39.9	38.0 |	35.6	17
23	40.0	38.0	39.0	31.0	40.0	40.1	41.4	40.0	38.2 |	40.2	18
24	39.0	38.0	38.0	40.0	39.0	38.3	40.3	39.0	37.7 |	39.1	19
25	38.0	40.0	42.0	41.0	39.0	37.2	40.6	39.2	35.3 |	38.3	20
26	38.0	38.0	39.0	40.0	38.0	38.5	37.6	43.4	39.1 |	39.1	21
27	41.0	40.0	44.0	41.0	32.0	37.7	39.2	36.6	37.2 |	37.2	22
28	37.0	38.0	38.0	38.0	41.0	41.5	40.0	37.7	37.0 |	37.2	23
29	39.0	41.0	38.0	39.0	38.0	39.6	40.6	36.4	35.7 |	41.3	24
30	40.0	32.0	40.0		40.0		40.0		|	38.7	25
31	40.0	41.0	40.0	39.0	36.0	39.7	38.0	38.6	39.1 |	39.2	26
32	40.0	41.0	39.0	40.0	35.0	45.4	37.8	37.9	40.6 |	36.2	27
33	37.0	43.0	44.0	40.0	42.0	41.6	40.0	35.6	40.2 |	43.3	28
34	35.0	35.0	40.0	38.0	42.0		40.0	32.0	35.6 |	40.0	29
35	37.0	41.0	39.0	40.0	40.0	39.1	39.9	36.5	40.8 |	36.3	30
36	38.0	40.0	41.0	42.0	40.0	38.3	38.6	38.6	39.5 |	41.2	31
37	40.0	40.0	40.0	40.0	40.0	.	.	.	28.7 |	35.3	32
									|	43.0	33

Hungary (DA) (a) [4] [5] [6] — Wage earners - Ouvriers - Obreros

Total men and women - Total hommes et femmes - Total hombres y mujeres
ISIC 3 - CITI 3 - CIIU 3

	1999	2000	2001	2002	2003	2004	2005	2006	2007	2008
Total	149.6	149.6	147.2	147.3	148.1	150.5	150.2	149.9	148.2	148.8
15	154.0	154.3	152.0	150.4	151.2	152.7	152.9	152.4	150.9	152.3
16	143.4	141.0	144.2	144.0	149.1	145.6	156.8	153.3	149.3	144.7
17	147.3	146.4	146.4	146.8	148.2	152.5	150.5	148.4	144.1	145.8
18	143.1	143.9	141.1	139.7	140.9	145.1	144.5	145.8	143.6	144.4
19	147.1	145.8	144.3	143.5	142.4	144.9	149.6	147.4	147.5	147.7
20	151.8	150.4	149.0	146.3	147.8	150.3	148.7	148.9	149.9	150.3
21	150.9	150.3	150.0	150.3	148.1	151.0	149.4	149.3	145.7	148.5
22	161.7	159.2	156.3	152.1	152.2	156.3	154.4	154.0	151.3	152.5
23	144.7	149.4	147.5	144.3	140.2	141.4	140.1	138.6	137.3	139.8
24	143.1	144.5	142.7	142.1	143.0	146.3	144.8	143.4	142.9	145.1
25	150.8	150.9	146.5	147.2	150.1	151.5	149.0	149.5	147.1	148.2
26	147.6	147.8	147.1	146.2	147.0	149.4	149.3	149.0	146.8	147.1
27	147.8	146.9	146.5	147.2	144.3	145.4	146.8	146.8	147.1	149.3
28	151.5	150.7	149.2	148.1	149.0	151.3	150.6	150.3	148.5	151.0
29	149.4	147.9	146.3	148.8	148.6	151.1	150.9	150.7	148.9	149.6
30	151.0	150.7	146.4	152.7	150.6	156.2	150.4	144.6	149.1	147.5
31	151.2	151.3	146.2	148.0	150.2	152.0	150.3	147.8	147.8	146.6
32	149.4	149.8	145.0	147.3	149.7	150.9	152.3	154.0	148.8	148.7
33	148.5	149.9	147.4	149.9	151.1	152.0	149.9	149.5	149.4	149.7
34	149.7	150.8	147.0	147.3	147.1	150.1	150.8	151.3	149.5	148.1
35	146.2	146.0	142.8	143.9	142.5	145.3	144.3	147.0	143.8	143.2
36	150.8	149.8	149.0	148.5	147.9	151.0	152.0	152.1	149.0	148.4
37	149.1	150.7	152.8	147.3	152.9	155.2	152.1	153.6	152.6	156.8

Explanatory notes: see p. 721.

[1] Persons aged 15 years and over. [2] Second quarter of each year. [3] Excl. conscripts. [4] Full-time workers. [5] Enterprises with 5 or more employees. [6] Per month.

Notes explicatives: voir p. 723.

[1] Personnes âgées de 15 ans et plus. [2] Deuxième trimestre de chaque année. [3] Non compris les conscrits. [4] Travailleurs à plein temps. [5] Entreprises occupant 5 salariés et plus. [6] Par mois.

Notas explicativas: véase p. 725.

[1] Personas de 15 años y más. [2] Segundo trimestre de cada año. [3] Excl. los conscriptos. [4] Trabajadores a tiempo completo. [5] Empresas con 5 y más asalariados. [6] Por mes.

In manufacturing   Dans les industries manufacturières   En las industrias manufactureras

Per week — Par semaine — Por semana

Iceland (BA) (a) — Employees - Salariés - Asalariados

Total men and women - Total hommes et femmes - Total hombres y mujeres
ISIC 3 - CITI 3 - CIIU 3

	1999	2000	2001	2002	2003	2004	2005	2006	2007	2008
Total	42.7	43.5	43.5	42.3	41.1 [1]	41.1	42.2	42.7	42.2	43.0
15	42.2	42.2	42.2	41.4	40.9 [1]	40.7	41.9	42.0	41.0	42.2
17	46.1	47.7	43.3	46.1	40.0 [1]	47.0	43.6	37.1	46.7	47.7
18	36.2	41.5	36.8	37.0	35.6 [1]	37.1	33.0	29.6	39.5	.
19	.	.	.	40.0	45.4 [1]	.	.	.	20.0	.
20	50.5	44.3	45.1	31.9	46.7 [1]	42.0	45.3	48.5	44.7	44.0
21	45.9	41.9	45.0	42.8	43.0 [1]	41.0	43.7	27.8	50.4	59.8
22	38.8	44.1	42.2	38.1	33.8 [1]	35.5	38.6	37.7	40.2	38.1
24	41.8	43.4	43.4	43.7	44.3 [1]	39.9	39.7	40.9	34.8	41.4
25	36.7	42.1	40.5	37.9	39.8 [1]	34.5	42.2	44.2	43.3	42.9
26	52.3	49.0	51.2	49.3	45.5 [1]	51.0	50.0	53.8	45.1	47.5
27	41.3	41.6	42.6	43.4	43.1 [1]	39.1	41.9	40.3	43.6	45.6
28	44.6	45.6	46.3	47.8	45.6 [1]	43.6	46.6	47.1	45.1	45.6
29	47.2	49.2	56.1	46.5	44.1 [1]	48.6	40.9	44.4	45.7	44.9
31	.	60.0	54.2	51.3	46.6 [1]	27.8	44.9	46.1	44.2	42.2
32	.	.	.	.	.	.	.	.	.	46.5
33	* 46.6	45.3	42.5	46.5	37.4 [1]	38.8	38.6	34.9	43.6	40.3
34	.	.	34.0	48.0	36.1 [1]	50.6	39.5	.	47.6	.
35	54.4	43.5	49.5	47.7	43.1 [1]	42.6	42.6	48.5	52.4	39.9
36	41.8	44.1	43.6	37.7	43.3 [1]	42.1	38.5	41.4	39.0	45.5
37	44.4	47.6	48.0	45.3	. [1]	.	49.1	50.0	.	.

Men - Hommes - Hombres
ISIC 3 - CITI 3 - CIIU 3

	1999	2000	2001	2002	2003	2004	2005	2006	2007	2008
Total	47.2	47.5	47.2	45.4	43.8 [1]	44.5	45.5	46.5	45.1	45.8
15	47.9	47.9	47.3	45.0	45.3 [1]	46.0	47.4	47.5	44.8	46.1
17	49.2	52.0	44.3	48.3	44.7 [1]	51.0	46.5	43.1	46.5	50.2
18	48.3	52.0	44.9	52.0	38.7 [1]	45.0	46.6	40.0	42.4	.
20	53.5	44.8	45.3	31.9	46.6 [1]	45.4	47.7	52.7	48.5	45.5
21	45.9	41.9	45.9	43.4	45.0 [1]	40.2	43.7	.	50.4	59.8
22	42.2	48.4	47.1	42.9	34.7 [1]	39.1	39.6	40.2	44.0	40.6
24	45.7	46.9	47.1	48.3	46.3 [1]	43.2	39.3	44.4	31.5	44.5
25	44.5	43.6	40.5	38.4	39.6 [1]	35.4	44.3	45.4	43.9	43.8
26	52.5	51.9	51.2	50.6	48.4 [1]	52.0	50.9	55.0	48.7	48.9
27	43.1	42.2	42.6	42.2	43.7 [1]	39.1	42.1	41.1	44.1	46.7
28	46.1	48.8	47.1	47.8	46.0 [1]	45.0	47.8	47.1	46.9	47.7
29	48.5	49.2	56.1	50.3	44.5 [1]	49.6	43.8	46.2	46.5	45.3
31	.	60.0	59.1	54.0	47.5 [1]	27.8	38.6	.	.	42.2
32	.	.	.	.	.	.	.	.	.	46.5
33	49.7	47.0	43.5	47.5	39.4 [1]	42.5	40.2	37.9	47.1	42.0
34	.	.	34.0	48.0	36.1 [1]	50.6	47.1	.	47.6	.
35	54.4	45.2	52.2	49.8	43.1 [1]	42.6	42.6	50.2	53.6	44.2
36	43.7	44.9	43.8	38.9	43.3 [1]	42.1	38.4	44.2	40.2	46.1
37	44.4	47.6	48.0	45.3	. [1]	.	49.1	50.0	.	.

Women - Femmes - Mujeres
ISIC 3 - CITI 3 - CIIU 3

	1999	2000	2001	2002	2003	2004	2005	2006	2007	2008
Total	33.4	34.1	35.1	35.9	35.3 [1]	34.2	35.1	33.9	35.3	36.0
15	33.9	34.1	35.6	36.6	35.4 [1]	34.7	34.2	32.7	35.1	35.3
17	40.8	39.9	41.8	42.2	29.8 [1]	29.5	.	28.7	48.0	42.7
18	32.4	33.0	30.9	34.9	33.9 [1]	31.8	29.3	24.7	38.3	.
19	.	.	.	40.0	. [1]	.	.	.	.	.
20	25.8	40.0	42.5	.	. [1]	22.8	31.7	34.1	28.9	25.0
21	.	.	40.0	40.0	. [1]	.	.	.	.	.
22	32.6	35.6	29.6	27.3	32.6 [1]	29.9	36.8	34.5	34.0	34.1
24	37.0	33.1	38.4	38.3	41.7 [1]	37.4	39.9	38.7	37.0	38.4
25	18.4	22.0	.	36.1	47.0 [1]	30.9	25.6	36.4	40.8	38.0
26	49.9	26.7	.	25.0	35.3 [1]	42.1	39.1	38.4	30.7	36.7
27	34.5	39.1	42.8	47.8	39.4 [1]	.	40.5	36.7	41.4	41.8
28	26.0	14.8	38.2	.	37.2 [1]	30.8	27.6	46.7	27.0	18.6
29	20.0	.	.	46.0	40.8 [1]	41.3	27.6	34.8	35.6	41.5
31	.	.	40.0	40.0	. [1]	.	.	.	.	.
32	.	.	.	.	.	.	.	.	.	.
33	33.0	36.0	37.0	40.0	34.2 [1]	34.5	37.5	29.7	38.7	20.0
35	.	20.0	15.0	14.0	. [1]	.	42.5	39.8	42.1	29.4
36	22.8	25.0	40.0	30.6	. [1]	.	.	33.1	34.9	41.7

Explanatory notes: see p. 721.   Notes explicatives: voir p. 723.   Notas explicativas: véase p. 725.

[1] Prior to 2003: April and Nov. of each year.   [1] Avant 2003: avril et nov. de chaque année.   [1] Antes de 2003: abril y nov. de cada año.

4B HOURS OF WORK — DURÉE DU TRAVAIL — HORAS DE TRABAJO

In manufacturing — Dans les industries manufacturières — En las industrias manufactureras

Per week — Par semaine — Por semana

	1999	2000	2001	2002	2003	2004	2005	2006	2007	2008

Ireland (BA) (c) [1] — Total employment - Emploi total - Empleo total

Total men and women - Total hommes et femmes - Total hombres y mujeres
ISIC 3 - CITI 3 - CIIU 3

	1999	2000	2001	2002	2003	2004	2005	2006	2007	2008
Total	39.9	39.5	39.6	39.4	39.2	39.2	39.0	38.8	39.1	38.9
15	40.1	39.5	39.6	39.5	39.1	39.4	38.8	38.4	38.7	38.6
16	38.2	39.4	38.0	38.5	35.4	37.4	38.8	38.7	34.0	35.5
17	38.0	38.6	37.7	37.2	37.2	36.8	36.2	36.3	35.7	38.5
18	37.9	35.8	33.8	35.3	34.5	35.3	35.0	35.6	35.1	35.3
19	38.3	37.2	40.8	38.3	.	.	37.8	37.6	33.3	.
20	41.3	39.1	40.6	40.4	41.3	40.9	41.3	41.4	40.9	40.1
21	39.4	40.3	40.3	38.5	38.6	38.1	38.0	37.5	39.1	37.9
22	38.7	38.6	38.9	38.4	37.7	37.8	37.9	37.3	38.7	37.3
23	39.6	42.2	39.4	41.7	41.1	38.4	40.6	38.8	39.3	40.5
24	40.0	39.7	39.9	39.5	39.5	39.2	39.0	38.6	39.0	39.1
25	40.1	40.1	40.4	39.9	39.0	38.5	39.0	39.3	38.7	39.9
26	40.7	40.7	39.8	39.7	40.0	39.5	39.8	40.3	40.8	39.8
27	40.2	40.7	40.3	40.8	40.3	39.0	39.2	40.2	40.1	40.7
28	40.8	40.3	40.3	40.2	40.4	40.6	40.4	39.8	39.9	39.9
29	41.0	40.8	40.9	41.5	40.3	40.0	39.9	39.0	39.0	40.0
30	39.5	39.8	39.8	39.6	39.4	39.9	39.5	39.5	39.7	39.6
31	39.9	39.1	39.1	38.6	39.1	39.5	38.5	40.8	40.7	39.5
32	39.3	39.0	39.5	39.0	39.2	39.5	39.8	39.1	39.3	38.8
33	38.8	38.6	38.5	38.4	37.8	37.9	38.2	37.9	37.8	37.4
34	39.8	39.4	38.4	39.3	39.3	40.0	40.0	38.1	38.4	38.6
35	42.7	40.6	41.0	40.0	40.4	39.9	41.0	40.2	41.3	38.8
36	40.4	39.4	39.6	39.6	39.4	39.3	38.7	39.2	39.9	38.8
37	37.4	38.6	39.5	38.7	41.9	34.9	40.6	37.3	40.8	40.9

Men - Hommes - Hombres
ISIC 3 - CITI 3 - CIIU 3

	1999	2000	2001	2002	2003	2004	2005	2006	2007	2008
Total	41.3	40.9	41.0	40.9	40.7	40.7	40.4	40.2	40.5	40.2
15	41.5	41.5	41.3	41.0	40.0	41.0	40.2	39.6	40.2	39.6
16	39.8	40.8	38.9	40.8	39.6	38.6	38.5	38.6	36.2	39.0
17	40.3	41.1	39.7	39.7	40.3	40.7	40.4	39.4	39.4	41.2
18	41.2	38.6	40.9	40.0	38.2	40.5	39.3	40.4	40.6	40.9
19	40.7	39.6	43.5	39.6	39.3	40.8	40.6	47.0	40.0	.
20	41.8	40.0	41.4	41.4	42.4	41.8	41.8	41.6	41.7	40.8
21	40.2	41.4	41.5	40.1	40.0	39.6	39.6	39.0	40.9	39.3
22	40.1	40.7	40.6	40.6	39.6	39.8	39.9	39.9	40.4	38.9
23	40.3	42.2	39.4	41.9	42.5	42.7	41.3	41.3	39.3	40.6
24	41.4	40.7	41.3	41.0	40.8	40.5	40.5	40.6	40.2	40.9
25	41.3	41.1	41.3	41.1	40.0	40.2	39.9	40.0	40.1	40.8
26	41.9	41.7	40.6	40.7	41.1	41.0	40.4	40.9	41.4	40.6
27	40.7	40.8	40.5	41.0	40.5	40.4	39.8	40.7	40.8	41.1
28	41.1	41.1	41.2	40.8	41.4	41.3	41.3	40.3	40.8	41.0
29	42.0	41.5	41.8	42.9	41.3	41.2	40.8	39.6	40.0	40.7
30	40.3	40.6	40.7	40.5	40.5	41.0	39.8	40.6	40.4	39.7
31	41.0	40.3	40.5	39.2	40.6	41.0	39.9	41.9	42.6	40.1
32	40.7	40.3	40.9	40.4	40.7	40.8	40.3	40.2	40.4	40.4
33	40.7	40.1	40.4	40.1	40.3	39.9	40.2	39.6	39.5	39.5
34	40.9	40.3	39.3	40.5	40.0	41.1	41.2	38.6	39.5	39.3
35	42.9	40.6	41.6	41.2	41.4	40.5	41.5	40.3	41.5	39.5
36	41.8	40.7	41.2	41.6	41.3	40.7	40.9	40.8	41.0	40.0
37	41.3	40.8	40.6	41.3	44.2	34.7	41.5	38.4	42.6	42.0

Women - Femmes - Mujeres
ISIC 3 - CITI 3 - CIIU 3

	1999	2000	2001	2002	2003	2004	2005	2006	2007	2008
Total	37.1	36.7	36.4	36.2	36.0	35.9	36.1	35.8	35.9	35.8
15	36.4	35.6	35.4	35.7	36.7	36.1	36.0	35.8	35.9	36.4
16	34.9	37.7	36.4	33.8	30.2	32.6	39.5	39.0	28.2	28.0
17	35.0	36.2	35.5	33.5	32.5	33.2	31.8	31.5	32.1	35.0
18	36.7	34.8	31.6	32.6	33.0	32.2	33.4	33.2	31.9	32.7
19	33.7	33.6	36.9	36.9	36.2	41.0	30.9	33.0	29.4	.
20	37.9	33.9	35.8	33.3	34.4	34.5	37.6	38.7	31.4	36.5
21	37.4	38.1	37.1	34.5	35.7	32.8	35.4	34.3	33.5	32.0
22	36.3	34.6	35.7	34.0	34.6	34.3	34.3	32.5	35.7	34.7
23	35.0	.	.	40.0	22.0	32.7	37.2	33.4	.	40.0
24	38.2	38.2	37.6	37.4	37.1	37.3	37.1	35.9	37.3	36.2
25	37.0	37.5	37.2	36.9	35.7	34.8	35.2	37.2	32.2	35.3
26	35.7	36.1	35.8	35.0	36.0	35.3	36.6	37.7	37.1	34.2
27	35.8	39.4	38.4	39.1	39.2	33.3	34.8	35.0	29.1	36.1
28	37.6	35.6	34.3	34.6	34.7	35.5	34.3	36.4	34.1	33.9
29	36.1	37.9	37.2	37.4	36.4	34.4	35.3	36.2	33.9	34.5
30	38.5	38.7	38.2	38.0	37.8	37.7	38.9	37.6	38.0	39.5
31	38.4	37.5	37.4	37.6	36.9	36.6	35.6	38.1	36.4	38.2
32	37.5	37.0	37.4	36.9	37.1	36.7	38.6	36.6	37.2	36.3
33	37.5	37.6	37.0	36.9	35.7	36.2	36.5	36.4	36.1	35.1
34	37.7	38.0	36.5	37.1	37.9	36.9	38.0	37.2	37.0	37.1
35	40.5	41.1	39.4	36.7	35.1	37.3	37.6	38.8	39.8	34.4
36	35.9	36.4	35.8	33.9	34.5	35.0	33.1	33.4	35.1	33.6
37	32.2	32.8	35.4	24.2	35.6	35.2	35.7	34.7	35.7	37.3

Explanatory notes: see p. 721.

Notes explicatives: voir p. 723.

Notas explicativas: véase p. 725.

[1] Second quarter of each year.

[1] Deuxième trimestre de chaque année.

[1] Segundo trimestre de cada año.

In manufacturing   Dans les industries manufacturières   En las industrias manufactureras

	Per week / Par semaine / Por semana									
	1999	2000	2001	2002	2003	2004	2005	2006	2007	2008

Ireland (DA) (b)   **Wage earners - Ouvriers - Obreros**

Total men and women - Total hommes et femmes - Total hombres y mujeres
ISIC 3 - CITI 3 - CIIU 3

	1999	2000	2001	2002	2003	2004	2005	2006	2007	2008
Total	.	.	.	39.0	39.0	39.0	39.0	39.0	39.1	38.9
15	.	.	.	40.0	39.0	39.0	39.0	38.0	38.7	38.6
16	.	.	.	39.0	35.0	37.0	39.0	39.0	34.0	35.5
17	.	.	.	37.0	35.0	37.0	36.0	36.0	35.7	38.5
18	.	.	.	35.0	35.0	35.0	35.0	36.0	35.1	35.3
19	.	.	.	38.0	40.0	36.0	38.0	38.0	33.3	.
20	.	.	.	40.0	41.0	41.0	41.0	41.0	40.9	40.1
21	.	.	.	39.0	39.0	38.0	38.0	38.0	39.1	37.9
22	.	.	.	38.0	38.0	38.0	38.0	37.0	38.7	37.3
23	.	.	.	42.0	41.0	38.0	41.0	39.0	39.3	40.5
24	.	.	.	40.0	40.0	39.0	39.0	39.0	39.0	39.1
25	.	.	.	40.0	39.0	39.0	39.0	39.0	38.7	39.9
26	.	.	.	40.0	40.0	40.0	40.0	40.0	40.8	39.8
27	.	.	.	41.0	40.0	39.0	39.0	40.0	40.1	40.7
28	.	.	.	40.0	40.0	41.0	40.0	40.0	39.9	39.9
29	.	.	.	42.0	40.0	40.0	40.0	39.0	39.0	40.0
30	.	.	.	40.0	39.0	40.0	40.0	40.0	39.7	39.6
31	.	.	.	39.0	39.0	40.0	39.0	41.0	40.7	39.5
32	.	.	.	39.0	39.0	40.0	40.0	39.0	39.3	38.8
33	.	.	.	38.0	38.0	38.0	38.0	38.0	37.8	37.4
34	.	.	.	39.0	39.0	40.0	40.0	38.0	38.4	38.6
35	.	.	.	40.0	40.0	40.0	41.0	40.0	41.3	38.8
36	.	.	.	40.0	39.0	39.0	39.0	39.0	39.9	38.8
37	.	.	.	39.0	42.0	35.0	41.0	37.0	40.8	40.9

Men - Hommes - Hombres
ISIC 3 - CITI 3 - CIIU 3

	1999	2000	2001	2002	2003	2004	2005	2006	2007	2008
Total	.	.	.	.	.	.	.	.	40.5	40.2
15	.	.	.	.	.	.	.	.	40.2	39.6
16	.	.	.	.	.	.	.	.	36.2	39.0
17	.	.	.	.	.	.	.	.	39.4	41.2
18	.	.	.	.	.	.	.	.	40.6	40.9
19	.	.	.	.	.	.	.	.	40.0	.
20	.	.	.	.	.	.	.	.	41.7	40.8
21	.	.	.	.	.	.	.	.	40.9	39.3
22	.	.	.	.	.	.	.	.	40.4	38.9
23	.	.	.	.	.	.	.	.	39.3	40.6
24	.	.	.	.	.	.	.	.	40.2	40.9
25	.	.	.	.	.	.	.	.	40.1	40.8
26	.	.	.	.	.	.	.	.	41.4	40.6
27	.	.	.	.	.	.	.	.	40.8	41.1
28	.	.	.	.	.	.	.	.	40.8	41.0
29	.	.	.	.	.	.	.	.	40.0	40.7
30	.	.	.	.	.	.	.	.	40.4	39.7
31	.	.	.	.	.	.	.	.	42.6	40.1
32	.	.	.	.	.	.	.	.	40.4	40.4
33	.	.	.	.	.	.	.	.	39.5	39.5
34	.	.	.	.	.	.	.	.	39.5	39.3
35	.	.	.	.	.	.	.	.	41.5	39.5
36	.	.	.	.	.	.	.	.	41.0	40.0
37	.	.	.	.	.	.	.	.	42.6	42.0

Women - Femmes - Mujeres
ISIC 3 - CITI 3 - CIIU 3

	1999	2000	2001	2002	2003	2004	2005	2006	2007	2008
Total	.	.	.	.	.	.	.	.	35.9	35.8
15	.	.	.	.	.	.	.	.	35.9	36.4
16	.	.	.	.	.	.	.	.	28.2	28.0
17	.	.	.	.	.	.	.	.	32.1	35.0
18	.	.	.	.	.	.	.	.	31.9	32.7
19	.	.	.	.	.	.	.	.	29.4	.
20	.	.	.	.	.	.	.	.	31.4	36.5
21	.	.	.	.	.	.	.	.	33.5	32.0
22	.	.	.	.	.	.	.	.	35.7	34.7
23	.	.	.	.	.	.	.	.	.	40.0
24	.	.	.	.	.	.	.	.	37.3	36.2
25	.	.	.	.	.	.	.	.	32.2	35.3
26	.	.	.	.	.	.	.	.	37.1	34.2
27	.	.	.	.	.	.	.	.	29.1	36.1
28	.	.	.	.	.	.	.	.	34.1	33.9
29	.	.	.	.	.	.	.	.	33.9	34.5
30	.	.	.	.	.	.	.	.	38.0	39.5
31	.	.	.	.	.	.	.	.	36.4	38.2
32	.	.	.	.	.	.	.	.	37.2	36.3
33	.	.	.	.	.	.	.	.	36.1	35.1
34	.	.	.	.	.	.	.	.	37.0	37.1
35	.	.	.	.	.	.	.	.	39.8	34.4
36	.	.	.	.	.	.	.	.	35.1	33.6
37	.	.	.	.	.	.	.	.	35.7	37.3

Isle of Man (DA) (b) [1]   **Employees - Salariés - Asalariados**

Total men and women - Total hommes et femmes - Total hombres y mujeres
ISIC 3 - CITI 3 - CIIU 3

	1999	2000	2001	2002	2003	2004	2005	2006	2007	2008
Total	40.7	39.2	37.9	39.8	38.6	39.6	39.7	39.0	38.6	38.3

Explanatory notes: see p. 721.   Notes explicatives: voir p. 723.   Notas explicativas: véase p. 725.

[1] June of each year.   [1] Juin de chaque année.   [1] Junio de cada año.

4B

HOURS OF WORK	DURÉE DU TRAVAIL	HORAS DE TRABAJO
In manufacturing	Dans les industries manufacturières	En las industrias manufactureras

	Per week				Par semaine			Por semana	
1999	2000	2001	2002	2003	2004	2005	2006	2007	2008

Isle of Man (DA) (b) [1]   Employees - Salariés - Asalariados

Men - Hommes - Hombres
ISIC 3 - CITI 3 - CIIU 3

	1999	2000	2001	2002	2003	2004	2005	2006	2007	2008
Total	42.9	41.5	39.8	40.3	41.9	42.9	40.9	40.4	39.4	39.0

Women - Femmes - Mujeres
ISIC 3 - CITI 3 - CIIU 3

	1999	2000	2001	2002	2003	2004	2005	2006	2007	2008
Total	31.5	33.9	29.9	37.9	33.2	28.6	34.7	35.2	34.8	.

Italy (BA) (a) [2]   Total employment - Emploi total - Empleo total

Total men and women - Total hommes et femmes - Total hombres y mujeres
ISIC 3 - CITI 3 - CIIU 3

	1999	2000	2001	2002	2003	2004	2005	2006	2007	2008
Total	40.6	40.5	40.5	39.4	39.2	35.8 [3]	36.1	36.1	36.3	35.9
15	42.2	42.2	41.8	41.0	40.8	38.3 [3]	38.2	37.8	38.2	38.0
16	38.5	39.1	37.6	39.2	37.6	34.9 [3]	34.6	32.1	32.9	37.2
17	39.5	39.2	39.2	38.0	37.8	33.7 [3]	34.1	34.3	33.9	32.5
18	39.9	39.5	39.5	38.2	37.9	32.8 [3]	33.2	33.1	34.1	34.1
19	39.8	39.8	40.2	38.8	38.8	33.4 [3]	35.3	34.5	35.1	34.3
20	42.1	41.8	41.7	40.9	40.7	37.0 [3]	38.3	37.5	37.8	37.6
21	39.9	39.7	40.0	38.9	39.3	36.0 [3]	36.2	35.4	36.9	35.6
22	40.4	40.6	40.2	39.2	39.0	35.1 [3]	36.1	35.4	35.1	35.6
23	41.0	39.9	40.4	39.5	39.4	38.4 [3]	37.2	38.7	35.6	37.8
24	40.0	40.0	40.1	39.2	38.8	35.9 [3]	36.4	35.7	34.7	36.2
25	40.0	40.0	39.9	38.9	38.7	34.8 [3]	35.2	35.8	36.3	35.3
26	40.4	40.4	40.6	39.4	39.3	36.6 [3]	37.0	36.8	36.8	36.4
27	40.5	40.5	40.7	39.4	39.4	35.9 [3]	36.5	36.2	36.7	36.5
28	40.8	40.6	40.6	39.8	39.6	36.2 [3]	36.8	37.3	37.1	36.9
29	40.6	40.7	40.8	39.4	39.2	36.4 [3]	36.3	36.2	36.8	36.0
30	39.9	39.6	40.3	39.2	38.8	35.9 [3]	35.2	33.9	33.4	34.9
31	40.6	40.4	40.6	39.2	39.1	36.2 [3]	36.2	35.7	35.9	35.9
32	39.8	40.1	40.4	38.4	38.8	33.4 [3]	33.5	34.3	34.5	34.1
33	40.4	40.2	39.9	38.9	38.8	34.7 [3]	35.3	35.5	35.6	36.1
34	40.6	40.4	40.5	39.7	39.3	34.7 [3]	34.9	35.4	36.3	34.9
35	40.3	40.7	40.6	38.9	39.0	36.6 [3]	36.7	37.1	37.1	36.8
36	41.3	41.3	41.1	39.7	39.5	35.4 [3]	35.9	36.5	36.5	35.2
37	41.4	41.3	42.3	39.4	38.3	37.6 [3]	34.8	35.1	35.1	33.9

Men - Hommes - Hombres
ISIC 3 - CITI 3 - CIIU 3

	1999	2000	2001	2002	2003	2004	2005	2006	2007	2008
Total	41.6	41.6	41.7	40.5	40.4	37.5 [3]	37.9	37.9	38.1	37.6
15	43.4	43.6	43.3	42.4	42.1	40.4 [3]	40.6	40.1	40.4	40.3
16	38.8	41.0	39.6	40.6	38.8	36.0 [3]	34.8	32.6	32.8	35.6
17	41.5	41.2	41.4	40.0	40.2	36.1 [3]	36.9	37.1	36.4	35.4
18	43.3	42.6	43.0	41.2	40.9	37.4 [3]	36.8	38.8	39.2	37.8
19	41.5	41.5	41.8	39.8	39.9	36.1 [3]	38.1	37.6	37.3	36.4
20	42.9	42.7	42.5	41.6	41.5	38.0 [3]	39.2	38.8	39.2	38.9
21	40.4	40.4	40.9	39.8	40.1	37.1 [3]	37.7	36.8	38.2	36.9
22	41.6	41.8	41.5	40.3	40.5	37.4 [3]	38.5	37.9	37.5	37.8
23	41.3	40.1	40.7	39.6	39.9	38.9 [3]	37.7	39.1	35.6	38.1
24	40.6	40.6	40.8	39.9	39.6	37.1 [3]	37.6	36.9	36.2	37.1
25	40.9	40.9	40.9	39.8	39.8	36.3 [3]	36.7	37.5	37.8	36.6
26	41.4	41.4	41.6	40.7	40.5	38.0 [3]	38.5	37.8	38.1	37.8
27	40.8	40.9	41.2	39.8	39.8	36.7 [3]	37.0	36.8	37.3	36.9
28	41.7	41.5	41.5	40.8	40.5	37.8 [3]	38.4	38.5	38.3	38.0
29	41.3	41.5	41.6	40.1	40.0	37.6 [3]	37.5	37.7	37.9	37.1
30	40.8	40.2	41.4	40.3	39.5	38.5 [3]	37.2	35.9	36.6	37.6
31	41.6	41.4	41.7	40.4	40.4	37.8 [3]	37.9	37.3	38.1	37.9
32	40.9	41.0	41.6	39.3	39.5	35.9 [3]	35.6	36.7	36.7	35.4
33	41.9	42.0	41.9	40.5	40.5	37.0 [3]	37.3	37.3	37.7	38.7
34	40.9	40.8	40.8	39.9	39.7	35.4 [3]	35.9	36.3	37.1	36.1
35	40.6	41.1	41.0	39.5	39.5	36.8 [3]	37.3	37.7	37.8	37.3
36	42.5	42.4	42.4	41.1	40.9	37.2 [3]	37.7	38.3	38.7	37.2
37	42.4	43.2	43.4	39.9	39.3	41.1 [3]	35.2	35.8	36.7	35.8

Explanatory notes: see p. 721.

[1] June of each year. [2] Persons aged 15 years and over. [3] Revised methodology; data not strictly comparable.

Notes explicatives: voir p. 723.

[1] Juin de chaque année. [2] Personnes âgées de 15 ans et plus. [3] Méthodologie révisée; les données ne sont pas strictement comparables.

Notas explicativas: véase p. 725.

[1] Junio de cada año. [2] Personas de 15 años y más. [3] Metodología revisada; datos no estrictamente comparables.

In manufacturing   Dans les industries manufacturières   En las industrias manufactureras

	Per week — Par semaine — Por semana									
	1999	2000	2001	2002	2003	2004	2005	2006	2007	2008

Italy (BA) (a) [1] — Total employment - Emploi total - Empleo total

Women - Femmes - Mujeres
ISIC 3 - CITI 3 - CIIU 3

	1999	2000	2001	2002	2003	2004	2005	2006	2007	2008
Total	38.1	37.9	37.8	36.7	36.4	31.8 [2]	32.0	31.8	32.1	31.8
15	39.5	39.3	38.7	38.1	38.3	34.5 [2]	34.0	33.9	34.4	34.0
16	37.8	34.6	34.4	36.5	35.4	33.4 [2]	34.2	30.6	33.3	39.0
17	38.0	37.7	37.5	36.4	36.1	31.7 [2]	31.7	31.8	31.8	30.4
18	38.7	38.5	38.3	37.2	36.8	31.6 [2]	32.2	31.6	32.6	33.0
19	37.8	37.8	38.3	37.7	37.6	30.6 [2]	32.6	31.7	32.8	32.0
20	37.2	37.5	37.6	36.2	35.1	30.9 [2]	32.4	30.2	30.4	30.4
21	38.2	37.3	37.0	36.5	36.9	32.4 [2]	31.7	31.4	32.8	32.3
22	37.6	37.7	37.3	36.9	36.0	30.7 [2]	31.0	30.9	31.0	31.7
23	38.1	38.0	38.5	39.0	36.7	33.0 [2]	32.5	35.3	34.7	34.4
24	38.4	38.2	38.4	37.2	36.5	33.1 [2]	33.6	33.1	31.5	34.2
25	37.9	37.9	37.5	36.9	36.5	31.4 [2]	31.5	31.3	32.4	31.8
26	37.6	37.3	37.6	35.6	35.9	31.1 [2]	31.3	32.4	31.3	30.7
27	38.1	37.7	37.5	36.5	36.7	30.0 [2]	33.2	31.8	32.8	32.5
28	37.0	36.7	36.7	35.5	35.6	30.9 [2]	29.7	31.4	30.7	30.8
29	37.9	37.4	37.6	36.4	36.0	31.2 [2]	31.6	30.7	32.0	31.3
30	37.2	37.8	37.9	36.2	37.1	31.1 [2]	30.8	28.9	27.1	29.2
31	38.1	37.9	37.8	35.8	35.7	32.6 [2]	32.0	31.6	31.1	30.8
32	37.6	38.3	37.4	36.2	36.9	29.3 [2]	29.7	28.8	29.7	30.7
33	37.4	36.5	36.4	35.5	35.1	31.0 [2]	31.8	32.3	31.9	31.4
34	39.1	39.0	39.5	38.6	37.1	32.0 [2]	31.2	31.4	33.2	30.4
35	37.9	38.3	37.3	35.2	36.4	35.1 [2]	32.5	32.2	32.5	33.6
36	37.7	38.0	37.6	36.1	35.9	31.5 [2]	31.9	32.1	31.6	30.4
37	34.5	32.4	34.7	37.2	33.8	25.6 [2]	32.9	33.0	29.0	27.7

Latvia (BA) (a) [3] — Total employment - Emploi total - Empleo total

Total men and women - Total hommes et femmes - Total hombres y mujeres
ISIC 3 - CITI 3 - CIIU 3

	1999	2000	2001	2002	2003	2004	2005	2006	2007	2008
Total	40.4	41.0	41.2	40.4	40.4	40.6	40.9	40.4	38.7	37.1

Men - Hommes - Hombres
ISIC 3 - CITI 3 - CIIU 3

| Total | 41.3 | 41.8 | 42.6 | 42.0 | 41.5 | 41.5 | 42.0 | 41.5 | 39.6 | 37.9 |

Women - Femmes - Mujeres
ISIC 3 - CITI 3 - CIIU 3

| Total | 39.3 | 40.0 | 39.5 | 38.2 | 39.0 | 39.4 | 39.4 | 39.2 | 37.5 | 36.1 |

Latvia (BA) (a) [3] — Employees - Salariés - Asalariados

Total men and women - Total hommes et femmes - Total hombres y mujeres
ISIC 3 - CITI 3 - CIIU 3

| Total | 40.3 | 40.8 | 40.9 | 40.5 | 40.3 | 40.4 | 40.8 | 40.4 | 38.8 | 37.1 |

Men - Hommes - Hombres
ISIC 3 - CITI 3 - CIIU 3

| Total | 41.0 | 41.5 | 42.1 | 42.1 | 41.3 | 41.1 | 41.7 | 41.4 | 39.6 | 37.9 |

Women - Femmes - Mujeres
ISIC 3 - CITI 3 - CIIU 3

| Total | 39.3 | 40.0 | 39.6 | 38.2 | 39.1 | 39.6 | 39.6 | 39.2 | 37.9 | 36.1 |

Lithuania (BA) (b) [1][3][4] — Employees - Salariés - Asalariados

Total men and women - Total hommes et femmes - Total hombres y mujeres
ISIC 3 - CITI 3 - CIIU 3

| Total | 39.8 | 39.8 | 39.7 | 39.2 | 39.0 | 39.2 | 39.5 | 39.3 | 39.4 | 39.8 |

Men - Hommes - Hombres
ISIC 3 - CITI 3 - CIIU 3

| Total | 40.1 | 40.2 | 40.1 | 39.3 | 39.6 | 39.6 | 39.8 | 39.4 | 39.7 | 40.1 |

Women - Femmes - Mujeres
ISIC 3 - CITI 3 - CIIU 3

| Total | 39.5 | 39.4 | 39.4 | 39.1 | 38.4 | 38.9 | 39.2 | 39.1 | 39.0 | 39.4 |

Explanatory notes: see p. 721.

[1] Persons aged 15 years and over. [2] Revised methodology; data not strictly comparable. [3] On the main job. [4] Excl. conscripts.

Notes explicatives: voir p. 723.

[1] Personnes âgées de 15 ans et plus. [2] Méthodologie révisée; les données ne sont pas strictement comparables. [3] Emploi principal. [4] Non compris les conscrits.

Notas explicativas: véase p. 725.

[1] Personas de 15 años y más. [2] Metodología revisada; datos no estrictamente comparables. [3] Empleo principal. [4] Excl. los conscriptos.

HOURS OF WORK	DURÉE DU TRAVAIL	HORAS DE TRABAJO
In manufacturing	**Dans les industries manufacturières**	**En las industrias manufactureras**
Per week	Par semaine	Por semana

	1999	2000	2001	2002	2003	2004	2005	2006	2007	2008
Lithuania (DA) (b)					**Employees - Salariés - Asalariados**					
Total men and women - Total hommes et femmes - Total hombres y mujeres										
ISIC 3 - CITI 3 - CIIU 3										
Total	38.8	38.6	38.6	38.6	38.8	39.0	38.5	37.8	37.9	.
15	39.0	38.9	38.8	38.7	39.0	39.1	38.5	37.8	37.9	.
16	.	.	.	.	.	.	.	.	.	.
17	37.6	37.9	38.2	38.2	38.4	38.6	38.5	37.7	37.8	.
18	38.9	38.9	38.6	38.7	38.9	39.0	38.4	37.8	37.9	.
19	39.0	38.7	38.7	38.7	38.9	39.0	38.7	37.8	37.8	.
20	38.9	38.7	38.6	38.6	38.9	39.0	38.5	37.9	38.0	.
21	39.0	38.8	38.7	38.6	38.8	39.0	38.5	37.2	37.4	.
22	38.8	38.4	38.5	38.6	38.8	39.1	38.4	38.0	38.1	.
23	.	.	.	.	.	.	.	.	.	.
24	38.8	38.7	38.4	38.9	39.2	39.1	38.6	38.1	38.0	.
25	38.8	38.6	38.7	38.6	38.8	39.1	38.5	37.9	37.9	.
26	38.9	38.8	38.6	38.7	38.9	39.1	38.6	37.9	38.0	.
27	38.8	38.7	38.6	38.6	38.9	38.9	38.4	37.7		.
28	38.9	38.5	38.5	38.6	38.8	39.1	38.4	37.7	37.9	.
29	38.7	38.1	38.1	38.6	38.8	38.9	38.4	37.7	37.8	.
30	38.9	39.0	38.9	38.1	38.4	39.0	38.7	38.1	38.0	.
31	38.8	38.8	38.7	38.8	38.9	39.0	38.9	38.2	37.9	.
32	39.0	38.2	38.4	38.3	38.8	38.8	38.4	37.8	37.9	.
33	38.6	38.6	38.7	38.6	38.8	38.9	38.5	37.7	37.9	.
34	39.0	38.8	39.2	38.9	38.7	38.9	38.4	37.6	38.3	.
35	39.1	38.7	39.4	38.6	38.8	39.0	38.5	37.9	38.0	.
36	38.8	38.5	38.6	38.7	38.8	39.0	38.5	37.8	37.9	.
37	38.9	36.1	37.6	37.7	37.8	38.4	38.4	37.7	37.9	.
Malta (BA) (a) [1] [2]					**Total employment - Emploi total - Empleo total**					
Total men and women - Total hommes et femmes - Total hombres y mujeres										
ISIC 3 - CITI 3 - CIIU 3										
Total	.	41.0	40.0	40.0	38.7	39.4	40.2	39.2	40.3	39.4
15	.	40.0	41.0	40.0	40.6	40.2	42.1	39.3	40.9	40.2
16	.	49.0	38.0	.	.	.	.	.	.	34.9
17	.	41.0	40.0	.	.	.	.	.	.	35.1
18	.	42.0	38.0	39.3	39.1	40.0	39.5	38.8	37.4	39.2
19	.	38.0	38.0	.	.	.	.	.	.	40.0
20	.	44.0	.	.	.	.	.	.	.	43.2
21	.	43.0	40.0	.	.	.	.	.	.	38.8
22	.	38.0	40.0	.	40.4	40.2	38.3	38.0	40.2	39.4
23	.	60.0	41.0	.	.	.	.	.	.	30.0
24	.	42.0	39.0	.	.	37.2	38.7	39.3	39.4	38.2
25	.	41.0	41.0	40.4	.	37.1	37.0	40.6	39.6	38.9
26	.	42.0	42.0	.	.	39.6	41.6	41.6	38.9	39.1
27	.	44.0	39.0	.	.	38.4	40.3	.	.	40.6
28	.	41.0	45.0	.	.	40.5	42.8	38.8	39.2	36.1
29	.	.	42.0	.	.	.	.	40.7	40.3	40.0
30	.	34.0	.	.	.	.	.	.	.	39.0
31	.	.	41.0	.	.	38.5	40.1	39.8	40.0	40.0
32	.	42.0	.	40.5	35.7	38.3	40.4	38.3	41.8	39.6
33	.	42.0	36.0	.	.	40.1	38.9	.	40.2	39.6
34	.	44.0	40.0	.	.	.	.	40.0	.	36.2
35	.	40.0	41.0	40.3	40.2	39.9	40.6	38.8	41.6	39.4
36	.	.	41.0	36.7	37.0	39.1	39.9	39.6	40.3	39.4
37	.	41.0	.	.	.	.	.	.	.	.
Men - Hommes - Hombres										
ISIC 3 - CITI 3 - CIIU 3										
Total	.	42.0	41.0	40.9	39.6	40.2	41.2	39.9	41.1	39.9
15	.	41.0	43.0	40.3	43.2	41.6	43.7	40.3	42.0	40.8
16	.	53.0	37.0	.	.	.	.	.	.	34.9
17	.	42.0	42.0	.	.	.	.	.	.	34.2
18	.	49.0	37.0	.	.	41.3	40.1	.	41.4	40.5
19	.	37.0	.	.	.	.	.	.	.	40.0
20	.	44.0	.	.	.	.	.	.	.	44.0
21	.	42.0	40.0	.	.	.	.	.	.	35.1
22	.	41.0	40.0	.	.	40.8	40.3	39.1	41.5	39.9
23	.	60.0	41.0	.	.	.	.	.	.	.
24	.	44.0	42.0	.	.	37.6	40.5	40.0	40.4	38.2
25	.	41.0	40.0	.	.	39.7	39.1	41.0	40.6	40.3
26	.	43.0	43.0	.	.	39.6	41.6	42.7	40.3	39.8
27	.	44.0	39.0	.	.	.	.	.	.	40.7
28	.	40.0	45.0	.	.	41.7	44.4	39.3	39.1	37.4
29	.	40.0	43.0	.	.	.	.	40.8	40.5	40.0
30	.	32.0	.	.	.	.	.	.	.	39.0
31	.	41.0	41.0	.	.	.	.	40.3	40.4	40.2
32	.	42.0	39.0	.	36.8	38.3	40.4	39.6	43.2	39.8
33	.	47.0	42.0	.	.	41.8	38.5	38.0	40.2	40.6
34	.	47.0	40.0	.	.	.	.	.	.	40.0
35	.	40.0	41.0	40.3	40.2	39.9	40.6	38.7	41.7	39.4
36	.	42.0	41.0	36.2	37.8	39.4	40.2	39.7	40.1	40.6
37	.	41.0	.	.	.	.	.	.	.	.

Explanatory notes: see p. 721.   Notes explicatives: voir p. 723.   Notas explicativas: véase p. 725.

[1] Persons aged 15 years and over. [2] Dec. of each year.   [1] Personnes âgées de 15 ans et plus. [2] Déc. de chaque année.   [1] Personas de 15 años y más. [2] Dic. de cada año.

HOURS OF WORK — DURÉE DU TRAVAIL — HORAS DE TRABAJO

In manufacturing — Dans les industries manufacturières — En las industrias manufactureras

Per week — Par semaine — Por semana

	1999	2000	2001	2002	2003	2004	2005	2006	2007	2008
Malta (BA) (a) [1][2]				Total employment - Emploi total - Empleo total						
Women - Femmes - Mujeres										
ISIC 3 - CITI 3 - CIIU 3										
Total	.	39.0	38.0	38.4	36.2	37.1	37.2	37.1	37.9	37.2
15	.	33.0	31.0	.	.	34.0	33.2	34.4	35.8	35.5
16	.	40.0	40.0	.	.	.	.	.	.	.
17	.	40.0	35.0	.	.	.	.	.	.	40.0
18	.	41.0	39.0	39.1	.	39.0	38.6	38.2	35.7	37.8
19	.	40.0	38.0	.	.	.	.	.	.	.
20	.	45.0	.	.	.	.	.	.	.	40.0
21	.	44.0	40.0	.	.	.	.	.	.	70.0
22	.	31.0	40.0	.	.	38.3	35.5	35.3	35.5	37.5
23	.	.	.	.	.	.	.	.	.	30.0
24	.	37.0	32.0	.	.	.	.	.	.	38.3
25	.	41.0	42.0	.	.	.	.	.	.	36.1
26	.	24.0	40.0	.	.	.	.	.	.	19.3
27	.	.	.	.	.	.	.	.	.	40.0
28	.	47.0	40.0	.	.	.	.	.	.	21.7
29	.	40.0	40.0	.	.	.	.	.	.	40.0
30	.	36.0	.	.	.	.	.	.	.	.
31	.	43.0	40.0	.	.	.	.	38.4	38.9	39.6
32	.	37.0	41.0	.	34.5	38.4	40.6	36.4	40.4	39.1
33	.	40.0	27.0	.	.	38.9	39.0	37.4	40.2	38.9
34	.	40.0	.	.	.	.	.	.	.	20.0
35	.	.	42.0	.	.	.	.	.	.	40.0
36	.	40.0	40.0	.	.	.	.	.	.	33.8
37	.	.	.	.	.	.	.	.	.	.
Moldova, Republic of (CA) (a) [3]				Employees - Salariés - Asalariados						
Total men and women - Total hommes et femmes - Total hombres y mujeres										
ISIC 3 - CITI 3 - CIIU 3										
Total	22.7	24.4	26.6	27.7	29.7	30.3	30.4	29.5	31.3	31.4
15	24.8	24.9	26.8	28.4	30.5	30.6	31.2	28.9	30.3	31.2
16	29.0	29.9	30.0	24.3	23.6	24.3	24.2	23.0	26.0	26.2
17	20.9	23.3	29.8	28.1	29.3	30.9	28.7	28.9	31.2	31.7
18	21.7	25.5	26.8	27.8	29.6	30.3	30.4	30.6	32.6	32.3
19	20.3	25.4	25.2	27.7	28.7	29.3	25.6	29.5	32.3	30.9
20	28.6	30.5	30.1	31.3	32.7	33.4	32.0	24.8	27.5	30.9
21	24.1	27.0	23.7	32.2	32.8	32.9	31.8	29.9	33.3	27.6
22	29.0	30.7	33.1	34.0	34.9	35.7	35.1	33.5	35.0	34.9
23	.	.	.	.	.	.	.	24.0	.	39.0
24	26.3	29.8	27.1	28.9	31.4	32.8	31.7	32.0	32.5	33.3
25	19.3	21.0	29.3	28.5	29.4	33.1	34.1	34.0	34.9	34.3
26	21.7	25.4	27.4	29.5	31.9	32.8	33.3	32.3	33.6	33.4
27	21.9	16.0	20.8	25.6	28.9	23.8	25.7	27.8	26.9	27.6
28	21.1	23.6	26.3	27.3	28.6	30.2	29.9	30.5	33.2	32.2
29	18.9	21.4	23.7	25.5	28.1	28.8	28.4	28.7	30.0	28.5
30	20.1	30.2	34.8	33.6	32.3	30.6	28.6	32.9	34.0	34.5
31	19.1	19.0	16.9	16.7	20.6	22.7	26.4	24.5	30.5	32.0
32	12.8	13.0	13.2	11.8	14.2	17.6	26.9	32.7	31.5	33.3
33	18.4	20.5	21.3	22.7	24.4	24.0	22.4	25.2	25.6	23.9
34	.	.	38.8	38.8	38.9	35.4	23.4	32.7	22.9	20.0
35	23.9	24.7	25.3	24.3	27.7	30.4	33.4	32.8	34.6	33.0
36	24.3	27.9	30.0	31.3	33.8	31.5	31.7	31.7	31.9	32.3
37	37.2	37.4	30.9	30.8	36.0	31.7	32.1	32.1	34.0	30.2
Netherlands (DA) (c) [2][4][5]				Employees - Salariés - Asalariados						
Total men and women - Total hommes et femmes - Total hombres y mujeres										
ISIC 3 - CITI 3 - CIIU 3										
Total	36.1	36.0	35.8	35.6	35.5	35.0	35.2	.	.	.
15-16	33.7	33.9	33.7	33.5	33.8	32.7	33.1	.	.	.
17	34.3	35.3	35.4	34.6	33.9	33.4	33.5	.	.	.
18	31.9	32.7	29.8	28.5	30.8	29.3	29.6	.	.	.
19	35.5	34.7	34.3	35.2	35.7	33.6	33.9	.	.	.
20	36.1	35.9	35.9	35.8	35.8	35.7	36.1	.	.	.
21	35.7	35.5	35.6	35.5	35.5	35.3	35.4	.	.	.
22	33.5	33.3	33.6	33.3	33.2	32.6	32.7	.	.	.
23	38.5	38.2	38.1	38.1	38.0	38.1	38.1	.	.	.
24	37.8	37.6	37.5	37.3	37.2	36.9	37.1	.	.	.
25	37.1	37.2	37.0	37.0	36.6	36.5	36.8	.	.	.
26	37.4	37.2	37.1	36.6	36.3	36.3	36.1	.	.	.
27	37.7	37.2	37.3	37.1	37.0	36.9	37.0	.	.	.
28	37.6	37.6	37.6	36.9	36.7	36.2		.	.	.
29	38.0	37.8	37.6	37.5	37.3	37.1	36.5	.	.	.
30-31	37.8	37.9	37.2	36.8	36.9	37.1		.	.	.
32-33	37.6	37.6	37.7	37.4	37.2	36.5	36.9	.	.	.
34	37.8	37.6	37.4	37.5	37.1	37.2	37.2	.	.	.
35	37.6	37.4	37.6	37.3	37.4	37.2	37.1	.	.	.
36-37	35.2	34.6	34.0	33.9	33.4	32.8	33.0	.	.	.

Explanatory notes: see p. 721.

[1] Persons aged 15 years and over. [2] Dec. of each year. [3] Enterprises with 20 or more employees. [4] Full and part-time employees. [5] Excl. overtime.

Notes explicatives: voir p. 723.

[1] Personnes âgées de 15 ans et plus. [2] Déc. de chaque année. [3] Entreprises occupant 20 salariés et plus. [4] Salariés à temps complet et à temps partiel. [5] Non compris les heures supplémentaires.

Notas explicativas: véase p. 725.

[1] Personas de 15 años y más. [2] Dic. de cada año. [3] Empresas con 20 y más asalariados. [4] Asalariados a tiempo completo y a tiempo parcial. [5] Excl. las horas extraordinarias.

In manufacturing — Dans les industries manufacturières — En las industrias manufactureras

	Per week				Par semaine			Por semana		
	1999	2000	2001	2002	2003	2004	2005	2006	2007	2008

Netherlands (DA) (c) [1][2][3]   Employees - Salariés - Asalariados

Men - Hommes - Hombres
ISIC 3 - CITI 3 - CIIU 3

	1999	2000	2001	2002	2003	2004	2005	2006	2007	2008
Total	37.7	37.6	37.5	37.3	37.1	36.7	37.0	.	.	.
15-16	37.0	37.0	36.6	36.7	36.4	35.7	36.3	.	.	.
17	37.1	37.6	37.8	37.7	37.1	37.1	37.7	.	.	.
18	.	.	33.2	34.6	35.9	34.0	32.8	.	.	.
19	37.9	38.1	38.6	38.7	38.6	37.5	38.0	.	.	.
20	37.1	36.9	37.0	36.7	37.0	37.1	37.4	.	.	.
21	36.5	36.5	36.6	36.6	36.6	36.2	36.6	.	.	.
22	35.8	35.5	35.8	35.7	35.5	35.0	35.3	.	.	.
23	38.7	38.9	38.7	38.7	38.6	38.9	38.8	.	.	.
24	38.8	38.7	38.7	38.5	38.5	38.4	38.6	.	.	.
25	38.4	38.6	38.5	38.6	38.3	37.9	38.2	.	.	.
26	38.2	38.0	38.0	37.6	37.5	37.3	37.5	.	.	.
27	38.0	37.6	37.7	37.5	37.4	37.4	37.5	.	.	.
28	38.4	38.5	38.6	38.2	37.8	37.3	37.9	.	.	.
29	38.8	38.7	38.6	38.5	38.4	38.2	38.1	.	.	.
30-31	38.9	38.9	38.4	38.2	38.6	38.5	37.9	.	.	.
32-33	39.1	39.1	39.1	38.9	38.8	38.2	38.7	.	.	.
34	38.2	38.4	38.2	38.2	37.9	38.0	38.1	.	.	.
35	38.3	38.1	38.1	38.0	38.1	37.8	38.1	.	.	.
36-37	36.1	35.7	35.2	35.0	34.6	33.9	34.4	.	.	.

Women - Femmes - Mujeres
ISIC 3 - CITI 3 - CIIU 3

	1999	2000	2001	2002	2003	2004	2005	2006	2007	2008
Total	30.2	30.1	30.0	29.4	29.5	28.7	28.5	.	.	.
15-16	26.5	27.2	27.7	27.1	28.1	26.1	26.2	.	.	.
17	29.9	30.4	30.8	28.3	27.6	26.8	25.9	.	.	.
18	31.0	30.1	27.6	25.6	28.4	27.1	27.8	.	.	.
19	.	.	28.0	28.8	29.9	26.7	26.5	.	.	.
20	.	.	26.8	27.3	27.1	24.3	26.1	.	.	.
21	31.6	30.8	29.9	29.5	29.3	30.3	28.6	.	.	.
22	29.2	29.2	29.3	28.9	28.9	28.4	28.1	.	.	.
23	.	.	33.0	33.9	33.5	33.3	33.3	.	.	.
24	33.7	33.3	33.3	33.0	32.8	32.1	32.3	.	.	.
25	31.9	31.4	30.5	30.5	29.6	31.0	30.7	.	.	.
26	31.4	30.6	29.7	28.5	27.1	28.4	27.2	.	.	.
27	33.1	32.6	32.7	31.8	32.3	31.6	31.5	.	.	.
28	29.8	29.8	29.9	26.8	28.2	27.6	26.7	.	.	.
29	31.8	31.4	29.7	29.6	29.4	29.1	28.6	.	.	.
30-31	33.1	33.1	32.1	31.0	28.9	30.5	29.9	.	.	.
32-33	33.1	33.0	33.2	32.4	31.9	30.5	31.2	.	.	.
34	33.8	30.6	30.9	32.1	29.7	29.3	28.9	.	.	.
35	29.6	29.8	32.9	31.3	30.5	31.3	28.1	.	.	.
36-37	31.5	30.7	30.2	30.6	30.0	29.4	19.0	.	.	.

Netherlands (DA) (c) [2][3][4]   Employees - Salariés - Asalariados

Total men and women - Total hommes et femmes - Total hombres y mujeres
ISIC 3 - CITI 3 - CIIU 3

	1999	2000	2001	2002	2003	2004	2005	2006	2007	2008
Total	38.6	38.6	38.6	38.5	38.5	38.5	38.5	.	.	.
15-16	38.4	38.3	38.3	38.4	38.4	38.4	38.5	.	.	.
17	38.3	38.4	38.4	38.5	38.6	38.6	38.7	.	.	.
18	38.2	38.1	38.2	38.0	38.0	38.6	38.5	.	.	.
19	39.5	39.6	39.7	39.6	39.5	39.5	39.5	.	.	.
20	38.5	38.2	38.4	38.4	38.6	38.5	38.4	.	.	.
21	37.0	37.0	37.1	37.0	37.0	37.3	37.2	.	.	.
22	36.9	37.0	37.1	37.0	37.0	37.1	37.2	.	.	.
23	38.7	39.0	39.0	39.0	38.9	39.2	39.1	.	.	.
24	39.2	39.2	39.2	39.2	39.2	39.2	39.2	.	.	.
25	39.1	39.1	39.3	39.2	39.2	39.2	39.1	.	.	.
26	38.7	38.7	38.8	38.6	38.8	38.8	38.8	.	.	.
27	38.4	38.0	38.1	38.0	37.8	37.8	37.8	.	.	.
28	39.3	39.4	39.3	39.3	39.3	39.2	39.3	.	.	.
29	39.4	39.4	39.4	39.5	39.5	39.5	39.4	.	.	.
30-31	39.3	39.3	39.3	39.3	39.3	39.3	39.3	.	.	.
32-33	39.6	39.6	39.6	39.5	39.7	39.6	39.6	.	.	.
34	39.0	38.9	38.9	38.8	38.8	39.0	38.9	.	.	.
35	39.1	39.0	39.1	39.1	39.0	39.0	39.0	.	.	.
36-37	37.8	37.4	37.2	37.1	37.0	36.8	37.0	.	.	.

Explanatory notes: see p. 721.

[1] Full and part-time employees. [2] Excl. overtime. [3] Dec. of each year. [4] Full-time employees only.

Notes explicatives: voir p. 723.

[1] Salariés à temps complet et à temps partiel. [2] Non compris les heures supplémentaires. [3] Déc. de chaque année. [4] Salariés à plein temps seulement.

Notas explicativas: véase p. 725.

[1] Asalariados a tiempo completo y a tiempo parcial. [2] Excl. las horas extraordinarias. [3] Dic. de cada año. [4] Asalariados a tiempo completo solamente.

In manufacturing   Dans les industries manufacturières   En las industrias manufactureras

	Per week			Par semaine				Por semana		
	1999	2000	2001	2002	2003	2004	2005	2006	2007	2008

Netherlands (DA) (c) [1][2][3]   Employees - Salariés - Asalariados

Men - Hommes - Hombres
ISIC 3 - CITI 3 - CIIU 3

	1999	2000	2001	2002	2003	2004	2005	2006	2007	2008
Total	38.6	38.6	38.6	38.5	38.5	38.5	38.6	.	.	.
15-16	38.4	38.3	38.3	38.4	38.4	38.4	38.5	.	.	.
17	38.4	38.5	38.5	38.5	38.7	38.7	38.8	.	.	.
18	.	.	38.5	38.0	38.2	38.7	38.7	.	.	.
19	39.5	39.7	39.7	39.6	39.6	39.5	39.5	.	.	.
20	38.5	38.2	38.4	38.4	38.5	38.5	38.4	.	.	.
21	36.9	37.0	37.1	37.0	37.0	37.2	37.1	.	.	.
22	36.9	37.0	37.0	37.0	36.9	37.0	37.1	.	.	.
23	38.7	39.0	39.0	39.0	38.9	39.1	39.1	.	.	.
24	39.1	39.1	39.1	39.2	39.1	39.2	39.2	.	.	.
25	39.1	39.1	39.3	39.2	39.2	39.2	39.1	.	.	.
26	38.7	38.6	38.8	38.6	38.7	38.8	38.8	.	.	.
27	38.3	38.0	38.0	38.0	37.8	37.8	37.7	.	.	.
28	39.3	39.4	39.3	39.3	39.3	39.2	39.3	.	.	.
29	39.4	39.4	39.4	39.5	39.5	39.5	39.4	.	.	.
30-31	39.3	39.3	39.3	39.3	39.3	39.3	39.3	.	.	.
32-33	39.6	39.6	39.7	39.5	39.7	39.6	39.6	.	.	.
34	38.9	38.9	38.9	38.8	38.8	39.0	38.9	.	.	.
35	39.1	39.0	39.1	39.1	39.0	39.0	39.0	.	.	.
36-37	37.8	38.5	37.3	37.1	37.0	36.9	37.1	.	.	.

Women - Femmes - Mujeres
ISIC 3 - CITI 3 - CIIU 3

	1999	2000	2001	2002	2003	2004	2005	2006	2007	2008
Total	38.5	38.3	38.4	38.3	38.3	38.3	38.3	.	.	.
15-16	38.4	38.2	38.3	38.5	38.5	38.5	38.5	.	.	.
17	38.0	38.0	37.9	38.1	38.1	38.2	38.2	.	.	.
18	.	.	37.8	37.9	37.8	38.5	38.3	.	.	.
19	.	.	39.6	39.4	39.2	39.5	39.5	.	.	.
20	.	.	38.6	38.3	39.7	39.4	39.6	.	.	.
21	37.4	37.3	37.2	37.2	37.3	38.5	37.6	.	.	.
22	37.1	37.1	37.3	37.1	37.1	37.2	37.4	.	.	.
23	.	.	39.0	39.2	39.2	39.5	39.5	.	.	.
24	39.6	39.5	39.4	39.5	39.5	39.5	39.5	.	.	.
25	39.3	39.2	39.5	39.2	39.5	39.1	39.2	.	.	.
26	.	38.9	39.2	38.9	38.8	38.6	39.0	.	.	.
27	.	39.1	39.2	39.2	39.1	38.9	38.9	.	.	.
28	39.3	39.0	39.4	39.3	39.3	39.2	39.6	.	.	.
29	39.5	39.5	39.5	39.4	39.4	39.4	39.3	.	.	.
30-31	39.1	39.3	39.4	39.2	39.2	39.2	39.4	.	.	.
32-33	39.5	39.5	39.5	39.6	39.6	39.5	39.6	.	.	.
34	39.3	39.1	39.1	39.0	39.0	39.1	39.0	.	.	.
35	39.2	39.2	39.2	39.2	38.9	39.2	39.2	.	.	.
36-37	37.6	37.2	36.9	36.9	36.8	36.6	36.6	.	.	.

Norway (BA) (a) [4]   Employees - Salariés - Asalariados

Total men and women - Total hommes et femmes - Total hombres y mujeres
ISIC 3 - CITI 3 - CIIU 3

	1999	2000	2001	2002	2003	2004	2005	2006	2007	2008
Total	36.6	36.5	36.5	36.7	36.3	36.3	36.9	36.8	36.7	36.6
15	35.9	35.1	34.9	35.4	35.9	34.8	35.2	36.2	34.9	34.9
16	35.4	30.3	30.8	30.0	32.2	28.2	35.6	33.6	29.8	38.7
17	37.1	35.7	32.2	34.4	31.9	27.3	28.7	33.9	35.8	35.3
18	33.5	33.7	33.9	33.6	35.5	32.2	32.0	29.5	33.6	31.8
19	35.2	33.9	36.4	49.3	31.4	30.8	32.8	37.7	26.2	20.8
20	36.1	37.3	37.8	36.3	35.0	35.9	36.9	36.9	36.7	37.5
21	36.5	37.5	38.2	37.4	37.0	36.0	37.0	35.9	34.8	34.0
22	32.8	32.3	33.4	32.6	32.4	33.4	34.5	34.3	35.0	34.0
23	37.0	36.1	36.0	39.7	51.2	43.2	35.7	39.7	41.0	36.1
24	37.7	38.0	36.4	37.4	37.1	37.4	37.5	36.0	35.8	36.4
25	38.2	38.2	36.9	37.5	37.6	36.6	38.2	36.5	34.6	35.9
26	37.6	37.3	39.0	38.5	36.1	36.3	36.3	35.0	36.8	35.0
27	36.4	37.3	36.0	36.6	36.4	35.4	36.7	37.0	36.7	37.5
28	37.3	38.1	37.1	37.4	35.9	37.3	38.2	37.4	36.2	37.7
29	38.2	38.2	37.6	38.6	37.4	38.5	38.4	38.4	38.2	37.6
30	39.3	39.4	38.8	36.6	25.0	38.0	38.0	34.8	33.9	37.5
31	37.6	36.6	36.7	35.7	37.5	37.3	38.2	38.0	37.6	38.7
32	37.0	37.4	37.2	37.9	40.4	38.2	37.5	34.7	38.5	35.4
33	37.0	37.0	38.9	39.2	39.0	38.4	39.0	38.4	37.2	37.0
34	36.9	37.6	37.7	36.1	36.5	38.3	38.9	36.1	34.5	37.3
35	40.0	39.7	40.0	40.4	39.3	40.5	40.4	40.4	40.9	40.6
36	34.4	34.3	34.6	35.8	34.1	34.0	34.8	34.5	35.8	35.3
37	37.3	39.2	35.6	37.0	43.0	37.2	39.0	38.5	39.8	41.2

Explanatory notes: see p. 721.   Notes explicatives: voir p. 723.   Notas explicativas: véase p. 725.

[1] Full-time employees only. [2] Excl. overtime. [3] Dec. of each year. [4] Persons aged 15 to 74 years; prior to 2006: 16 to 74 years.

[1] Salariés à plein temps seulement. [2] Non compris les heures supplémentaires. [3] Déc. de chaque année. [4] Personnes âgées de 15 à 74 ans: avant 2006: 16 à 74 ans.

[1] Asalariados a tiempo completo solamente. [2] Excl. las horas extraordinarias. [3] Dic. de cada año. [4] Personas de 15 a 74 años; antes de 2006: 16 a 74 años.

HOURS OF WORK DURÉE DU TRAVAIL HORAS DE TRABAJO

In manufacturing Dans les industries manufacturières En las industrias manufactureras

	Per week				Par semaine				Por semana	
	1999	2000	2001	2002	2003	2004	2005	2006	2007	2008

Norway (BA) (a) [1] Employees - Salariés - Asalariados

Men - Hommes - Hombres
ISIC 3 - CITI 3 - CIIU 3

	1999	2000	2001	2002	2003	2004	2005	2006	2007	2008
Total	38.3	38.0	38.0	38.1	37.8	38.0	38.5	38.3	38.1	38.1
15	38.6	37.8	37.5	37.7	38.2	37.2	38.0	38.2	37.1	37.2
16	38.0	27.7	36.8	34.3	36.5	32.6	36.0	33.6	26.5	38.7
17	39.8	37.3	37.4	37.8	32.7	30.8	31.8	38.1	37.4	36.3
18	51.2	37.7	35.9	39.7	39.2	32.3	36.6	30.0	38.7	40.1
19	40.8	36.2	39.7	54.9	35.0	33.6	33.8	37.7	41.8	
20	37.8	38.9	39.2	37.7	36.5	37.7	38.5	38.1	38.4	38.4
21	36.9	38.3	38.7	37.9	37.7	36.9	38.1	37.0	36.4	37.2
22	35.0	33.3	34.6	33.2	33.2	34.1	35.7	35.3	35.7	35.4
23	37.8	36.6	36.0	40.3	51.2	43.2	35.4	39.9	42.4	36.8
24	39.1	39.3	37.3	38.0	37.7	38.3	38.5	36.5	37.0	37.6
25	39.1	39.1	37.2	37.9	38.1	37.4	38.6	37.7	35.7	37.4
26	38.7	38.5	39.9	39.2	37.5	38.3	38.4	37.7	38.1	35.6
27	36.4	37.5	36.4	37.2	37.0	36.2	37.4	37.5	37.1	37.9
28	38.7	39.3	37.9	38.2	37.4	38.9	39.4	38.9	37.1	38.2
29	39.1	39.2	38.5	39.3	38.0	39.3	38.9	39.0	38.9	38.4
30	35.6	44.5	41.1	36.6	25.0	38.0	38.0	34.8	33.9	37.5
31	38.6	37.0	37.4	36.1	39.0	38.3	38.4	38.6	38.4	40.1
32	39.5	38.2	38.5	39.0	41.6	39.7	39.3	36.7	38.7	36.2
33	37.7	38.4	40.5	39.8	40.5	39.8	40.8	39.9	39.7	38.7
34	36.9	37.7	37.8	36.8	37.1	39.9	39.4	37.4	35.7	37.4
35	40.6	39.9	40.6	41.7	40.3	41.1	41.1	41.0	41.9	41.6
36	37.3	35.8	37.3	39.6	37.6	36.5	38.0	37.4	36.4	35.2
37	38.9	39.2	35.6	36.4	43.0	37.3	39.9	40.9	42.0	43.2

Women - Femmes - Mujeres
ISIC 3 - CITI 3 - CIIU 3

	1999	2000	2001	2002	2003	2004	2005	2006	2007	2008
Total	31.6	32.2	31.9	32.2	31.8	31.2	31.7	32.0	32.1	32.2
15	31.4	30.8	30.6	31.1	32.6	31.2	.	31.2	30.5	31.2
16	34.3	32.3	19.3	10.0	15.0	21.8	29.9	.	37.5	.
17	34.3	34.2	28.0	31.9	31.1	24.2	27.2	30.2	34.5	34.3
18	30.5	33.2	33.7	32.3	34.2	32.2	30.1	29.2	32.5	30.5
19	28.4	18.5	35.3	30.0	18.7	18.2	18.8	.	20.6	20.8
20	25.0	29.2	31.4	28.4	28.2	27.3	28.6	30.7	29.3	32.8
21	34.8	34.5	36.8	35.8	34.8	32.9	34.0	32.0	29.5	25.3
22	29.3	30.6	31.0	31.3	30.8	32.2	32.8	32.9	33.5	31.9
23	30.9	28.2	35.8	30.2	.	.	39.3	38.9	32.0	33.8
24	33.1	34.6	34.0	35.9	35.3	34.3	34.4	34.4	32.3	33.6
25	34.1	33.8	34.0	34.5	33.1	32.7	36.6	29.1	30.0	30.6
26	32.5	30.4	35.6	36.5	31.2	29.6	31.4	28.6	31.3	31.5
27	36.3	36.0	33.2	31.2	31.7	31.9	33.9	34.3	33.7	33.9
28	29.7	29.0	29.7	32.4	28.2	27.8	30.0	28.5	27.8	32.5
29	32.5	30.5	29.5	33.0	33.3	30.9	31.0	33.2	32.2	31.2
30	46.1	34.4	32.5	.						
31	31.9	34.4	35.0	34.8	29.3	31.4	36.6	35.0	34.5	33.9
32	33.8	35.5	33.7	33.8	33.6	29.8	32.8	32.0	38.1	34.0
33	35.2	33.9	33.9	36.8	35.1	35.2	35.0	36.0	33.0	33.5
34	36.9	35.9	35.4	31.4	32.7	26.7	35.6	29.0	28.0	37.2
35	34.9	38.2	34.7	31.6	32.2	33.6	34.7	35.1	33.4	33.0
36	29.1	32.2	31.7	30.8	28.5	30.3	30.3	29.7	34.8	35.5
37				42.4	.	36.0	35.2	32.6	33.7	36.6

Poland (BA) (a) Employees - Salariés - Asalariados

Total men and women - Total hommes et femmes - Total hombres y mujeres
ISIC 3 - CITI 3 - CIIU 3 ISIC 4 - CITI 4 - CIIU 4

	1999	2000	2001	2002	2003	2004	2005	2006	2007	2008	
Total	41.2 [2]	41.3	41.2	41.0	41.1	41.2	41.2	42.0	41.4 |	40.9	Total

Men - Hommes - Hombres
ISIC 3 - CITI 3 - CIIU 3 ISIC 4 - CITI 4 - CIIU 4

	1999	2000	2001	2002	2003	2004	2005	2006	2007	2008	
Total	41.7 [2]	41.8	41.6	41.4	41.6	41.7	41.8	42.0	42.1 |	41.5	Total

Women - Femmes - Mujeres
ISIC 3 - CITI 3 - CIIU 3 ISIC 4 - CITI 4 - CIIU 4

	1999	2000	2001	2002	2003	2004	2005	2006	2007	2008	
Total	40.4 [2]	40.5	40.5	40.2	40.1	40.1	40.1	40.0	40.0 |	39.8	Total

Explanatory notes: see p. 721.

[1] Persons aged 15 to 74 years; prior to 2006: 16 to 74 years. [2] 4th quarter; holidays included.

Notes explicatives: voir p. 723.

[1] Personnes âgées de 15 à 74 ans: avant 2006: 16 à 74 ans. [2] 4e trimestre; y compris les heures de travail normales des salariés en vacance.

Notas explicativas: véase p. 725.

[1] Personas de 15 a 74 años; antes de 2006: 16 a 74 años. [2] 4o trimestre: incl. horas de las personas que están de vacaciones.

In manufacturing   **Dans les industries manufacturières**   **En las industrias manufactureras**

Per week   Par semaine   Por semana

Portugal (BA) (a) [1] [2]   **Employees - Salariés - Asalariados**

Total men and women - Total hommes et femmes - Total hombres y mujeres
ISIC 3 - CITI 3 - CIIU 3

	1999	2000	2001	2002	2003	2004	2005	2006	2007	2008
Total	37.1	37.0	36.9	36.8	36.4	36.1	36.6	36.8	35.9	36.1
15	39.8	39.0	39.0	39.3	39.3	37.2	38.1	37.8	37.2	36.8
16	39.6	37.7	36.7	28.5	37.7	34.6	34.4	38.0	31.1	31.2
17	34.7	34.0	34.8	35.2	34.9	35.2	35.9	36.1	35.2	35.1
18	35.4	35.2	35.6	35.5	35.5	35.2	36.2	36.4	35.4	35.1
19	36.7	36.7	36.2	34.9	34.2	35.6	36.0	35.9	35.0	35.2
20	37.8	37.2	36.9	37.3	36.9	36.1	35.3	36.3	36.0	36.6
21	36.2	36.2	36.8	36.3	35.0	37.2	37.7	36.7	36.8	37.7
22	37.4	38.1	36.9	37.1	37.6	35.3	36.7	37.7	37.0	36.3
23	35.0	38.1	39.7	38.4	32.5	36.9	37.8	37.4	37.1	37.0
24	37.1	36.8	35.2	36.0	35.0	36.8	37.0	36.8	36.7	36.3
25	37.3	35.6	37.7	38.4	37.0	37.0	37.4	37.4	35.0	36.3
26	37.7	37.5	37.0	35.9	36.5	36.4	37.1	37.4	35.3	35.7
27	39.0	38.9	37.0	37.1	35.0	37.4	36.9	37.2	36.9	37.0
28	37.9	38.1	38.3	38.1	37.0	37.0	36.8	36.5	36.0	36.1
29	37.8	37.5	38.1	37.4	36.3	36.7	38.1	37.0	35.4	36.5
30	40.9	42.4	40.8	32.6	33.3	34.0	35.7	37.4	41.9	36.7
31	36.3	36.2	35.5	37.0	35.1	35.2	35.8	35.6	35.7	35.4
32	36.6	39.2	37.3	34.6	37.4	35.1	34.5	37.3	36.2	35.9
33	37.6	33.5	36.7	39.2	34.9	35.5	34.9	35.1	37.6	36.8
34	36.7	37.0	36.0	36.7	36.3	36.1	35.9	36.8	35.6	35.7
35	35.0	38.1	38.3	36.8	35.7	36.3	34.5	36.2	37.6	38.8
36	38.4	39.5	38.5	37.7	37.7	36.2	36.7	37.1	35.3	37.4
37	40.4	38.9	41.3	38.4	35.5	37.7	36.1	34.8	37.6	38.1

Men - Hommes - Hombres
ISIC 3 - CITI 3 - CIIU 3

	1999	2000	2001	2002	2003	2004	2005	2006	2007	2008
Total	38.8	38.5	38.4	38.4	37.7	37.3	37.5	37.6	36.9	36.9
15	42.0	40.8	40.9	41.5	41.4	38.9	39.8	39.0	38.6	37.7
16	39.8	39.2	38.7	28.0	37.7	34.5	33.8	38.7	34.4	30.1
17	38.0	35.3	36.1	37.3	36.7	36.6	37.5	37.3	37.0	36.5
18	37.5	39.0	39.2	37.8	37.6	37.3	36.3	37.9	37.9	36.8
19	38.8	38.4	38.6	38.1	35.9	36.9	37.0	36.7	35.5	35.0
20	38.8	38.2	37.6	38.1	37.7	36.7	35.8	36.6	36.6	37.5
21	37.1	37.5	37.8	37.2	35.7	36.6	38.6	37.5	37.4	38.1
22	38.2	38.7	37.9	37.5	37.5	37.2	37.7	38.8	37.5	37.0
23	34.9	41.1	40.6	39.6	33.2	38.1	38.3	36.5	38.4	39.0
24	37.7	37.4	37.1	36.8	36.3	38.4	38.0	37.9	37.0	36.9
25	38.3	36.6	38.0	38.7	38.7	38.2	38.0	38.7	35.5	37.0
26	38.7	37.4	38.4	37.3	37.3	37.3	37.9	37.9	36.0	36.3
27	39.5	39.0	37.7	37.3	33.7	37.3	37.3	37.6	37.3	37.2
28	38.6	38.9	38.6	38.6	37.3	37.6	37.1	36.8	36.3	36.6
29	38.5	38.0	39.2	38.6	37.2	37.2	38.1	36.9	36.5	36.6
30	41.4	40.0	40.0	40.0	40.0	37.2	35.4	37.0	42.2	35.5
31	38.1	37.1	36.8	38.2	36.5	37.0	36.8	37.7	35.8	35.9
32	39.1	40.6	38.9	35.7	39.0	36.5	37.5	39.9	36.2	37.1
33	37.2	36.9	37.2	39.0	37.1	37.5	35.5	37.4	40.0	36.8
34	37.9	38.3	36.9	37.6	36.5	37.1	36.8	37.1	37.0	36.6
35	35.1	38.2	38.6	36.9	35.6	37.0	35.0	37.2	38.1	38.9
36	39.2	40.5	39.3	38.9	38.8	36.4	37.7	38.3	36.8	38.1
37	41.1	43.4	43.8	36.4	37.6	38.1	38.2	32.9	37.4	37.7

Women - Femmes - Mujeres
ISIC 3 - CITI 3 - CIIU 3

	1999	2000	2001	2002	2003	2004	2005	2006	2007	2008
Total	34.9	35.0	35.0	34.7	34.7	34.6	35.3	35.7	34.7	35.0
15	37.3	37.1	36.8	36.2	36.3	35.4	36.1	36.7	36.0	36.1
16	38.4	33.3	35.8	28.6	.	34.9	35.3	32.0	19.6	38.0
17	32.4	33.0	33.8	33.9	33.7	34.1	34.8	35.1	34.0	34.3
18	35.1	34.6	34.9	35.2	35.3	34.9	36.1	36.2	35.2	34.9
19	35.1	35.6	34.8	33.2	33.2	34.7	35.3	35.4	34.7	35.3
20	33.8	33.8	34.1	34.0	33.0	34.4	33.5	35.1	34.4	34.6
21	34.2	33.0	33.5	33.3	33.1	38.6	35.5	34.7	35.9	36.1
22	35.8	36.9	34.8	36.1	38.0	32.1	35.0	36.1	36.2	34.9
23	35.7	27.4	37.5	37.2	30.8	33.0	35.6	40.2	32.9	31.9
24	36.0	36.0	32.9	35.1	33.0	34.7	35.6	35.1	36.3	35.6
25	35.1	33.9	37.1	37.7	33.6	34.4	36.1	34.8	34.0	34.9
26	35.6	38.0	33.1	32.8	35.0	34.6	35.3	36.5	33.7	34.1
27	36.3	38.2	33.3	36.1	38.5	38.4	35.0	34.6	33.0	35.9
28	33.8	33.3	35.9	34.3	35.5	34.1	35.3	35.2	34.6	32.8
29	35.3	35.6	34.9	32.7	33.3	34.9	38.1	37.0	31.0	35.5
30	35.0	45.1	41.1	30.9	26.0	26.5	36.8	37.8	40.2	43.5
31	34.6	35.3	35.3	35.9	33.1	33.8	35.1	33.5	35.4	34.4
32	34.1	37.7	36.5	34.0	35.6	33.9	31.5	34.9	36.2	34.7
33	37.9	30.3	35.9	39.6	31.6	33.7	34.1	30.3	32.8	36.8
34	34.6	34.1	34.3	35.2	35.9	33.4	33.6	36.1	32.4	33.9
35	31.6	36.1	36.9	36.2	37.0	32.0	31.7	29.9	35.3	38.2
36	35.1	35.9	36.3	34.1	34.7	35.8	33.9	34.5	31.7	36.0
37	35.0	34.7	38.6	44.0	33.5	37.1	32.9	40.0	38.3	39.6

Explanatory notes: see p. 721.

[1] Persons aged 15 years and over. [2] Estimates based on the 2001 Population Census results.

Notes explicatives: voir p. 723.

[1] Personnes âgées de 15 ans et plus. [2] Estimations basées sur les résultats du Recensement de la population de 2001.

Notas explicativas: véase p. 725.

[1] Personas de 15 años y más. [2] Estimaciones basadas en los resultados del Censo de población de 2001.

HOURS OF WORK DURÉE DU TRAVAIL HORAS DE TRABAJO

In manufacturing	Dans les industries manufacturières	En las industrias manufactureras
Per week	Par semaine	Por semana

	1999	2000	2001	2002	2003	2004	2005	2006	2007	2008

Portugal (DA) (b) — Employees - Salariés - Asalariados

Total men and women - Total hommes et femmes - Total hombres y mujeres
ISIC 3 - CITI 3 - CIIU 3

	1999	2000	2001	2002	2003	2004	2005	2006	2007	2008
Total	39.3	39.5	39.4	38.5	37.9	39.5	39.9	40.1	40.1	40.2
15	39.6									
15-16		39.5	38.3	38.5	38.0	39.5	40.1	40.2	40.2	
16	38.9									
17	39.1									
17-18		39.6	38.1	38.3	37.8	39.3	39.8	40.0	40.1	40.1
18	39.3									
19	39.4	39.7	38.0	38.2	37.8	39.2	39.7	40.0	40.0	40.0
20	39.2	39.6	38.3	38.5	38.0	39.6	39.8	40.1	40.1	
21	39.3									
21-22		38.9	38.0	38.2	37.7	39.0	39.4	39.5	39.7	39.7
22	38.9									
23	39.8	39.9	36.6	36.8	36.3	37.5	37.4	37.2	36.8	37.8
24	39.3	38.9	38.4	38.6	38.1	39.5	39.4	40.1	40.0	40.3
25	39.5	39.5	38.8	39.0	38.6	39.7	40.0	40.1	40.3	40.3
26	39.4	39.4	38.2	38.5	37.8	39.9	40.1	40.2	40.1	40.1
27										
27-28		39.5	38.3	38.5	38.1	39.4	40.0	40.0	40.0	40.3
28	39.5									
29	39.5	39.5	38.5	38.7	38.1	39.8	40.3	40.2	40.1	40.4
30	38.0									
30-33		39.5	38.7	38.9	38.4	40.0	40.3	41.0	40.7	40.8
31	40.6									
32	36.1									
33	39.2									
34	39.3									
34-35		38.9	38.2	38.3	37.9	39.6	40.1	40.6	40.7	40.5
35	39.6									
36	39.5									
36-37		39.6	38.1	38.3	37.8	39.3	39.6	39.9	40.1	40.0
37	40.4									

Men - Hommes - Hombres
ISIC 3 - CITI 3 - CIIU 3

	1999	2000	2001	2002	2003	2004	2005	2006	2007	2008
Total	39.4	39.4	39.4	38.5	38.0	39.6	40.0	40.2	40.2	40.2
15	39.6									
15-16			38.4	38.6	38.1	39.7	40.2	40.3	40.3	40.2
16	38.8									
17	39.2									
17-18		39.4	38.1	38.4	37.8	39.5	39.9	40.1	40.2	40.2
18	39.5									
19	39.4	39.7	38.1	38.2	37.9	39.2	39.8	39.9	39.9	39.9
20	39.3	39.6	38.4	38.6	38.1	39.7	39.9	40.1	40.2	40.0
21	39.4									
21-22		38.9	38.1	38.4	37.8	39.2	39.6	39.6	39.9	39.8
22	38.9									
23	40.0	39.9	37.2	37.4	36.9	38.1	37.9	37.7	37.4	38.7
24	39.6	39.0	38.6	38.9	38.3	39.7	39.6	40.3	40.3	40.5
25	39.6	39.5	39.0	39.2	38.8	39.9	40.0	40.2	40.5	40.4
26	39.5	39.4	38.4	38.6	37.9	40.0	40.1	40.2	40.1	40.1
27	39.5									
27-28		39.5	38.3	38.5	38.0	39.4	40.0	40.1	40.0	40.3
28	39.5									
29	39.6	39.5	38.6	38.9	38.2	39.9	40.4	40.3	40.2	40.4
30	37.8									
30-33		39.6	38.8	39.0	38.5	40.1	40.8	41.2	40.9	40.8
31	39.9									
32	38.1									
33	39.1									
34	39.3									
34-35		38.9	38.2	38.3	37.9	39.6	40.2	40.8	40.8	40.6
35	39.7									
36	39.6									
36-37		39.7	38.0	38.2	37.7	39.4	39.6	39.9	40.1	40.0
37	40.7									

Explanatory notes: see p. 721. Notes explicatives: voir p. 723. Notas explicativas: véase p. 725.

In manufacturing / Dans les industries manufacturières / En las industrias manufactureras

Per week / Par semaine / Por semana									
1999	2000	2001	2002	2003	2004	2005	2006	2007	2008

Portugal (DA) (b) — Employees - Salariés - Asalariados

Women - Femmes - Mujeres
ISIC 3 - CITI 3 - CIIU 3

	1999	2000	2001	2002	2003	2004	2005	2006	2007	2008
Total	39.2	39.5	39.4	38.3	37.8	39.3	39.7	40.0	40.0	40.0
15	39.6	.	.	.	.	.	.	.	.	.
15-16	.	.	38.2	38.4	38.0	39.4	39.9	40.1	40.2	40.2
16	39.2	.	.	.	.	.	.	.	.	.
17	39.1	.	.	.	.	.	.	.	.	.
17-18	.	39.6	38.1	38.3	37.8	39.3	39.7	40.0	40.0	40.0
18	39.3	.	.	.	.	.	.	.	.	.
19	39.4	39.7	38.0	38.2	37.8	39.1	39.7	40.0	40.0	40.0
20	38.9	39.5	37.9	38.2	37.5	39.5	39.5	39.9	39.8	40.0
21	39.2	.	.	.	.	.	.	.	.	.
21-22	.	38.9	37.7	37.9	37.4	38.7	39.0	38.2	39.3	39.3
22	38.7	.	.	.	.	.	.	.	.	.
23	36.9	40.0	34.4	34.6	34.1	35.4	35.5	35.5	35.4	35.6
24	38.7	38.7	38.0	38.3	37.7	39.0	39.1	39.9	39.7	39.9
25	39.3	39.5	38.4	38.5	38.1	39.5	39.9	39.9	40.0	40.1
26	39.2	39.4	38.0	38.2	37.6	39.6	39.9	40.0	39.9	39.9
27	39.6	.	.	.	.	.	.	.	.	.
27-28	.	39.3	38.4	38.6	38.1	39.3	39.8	39.8	40.0	40.0
28	39.1	.	.	.	.	.	.	.	.	.
29	39.3	39.4	38.0	38.2	37.7	39.4	39.6	39.7	39.7	40.0
30	38.6	.	.	.	.	.	.	.	.	.
30-33	.	39.3	38.6	38.8	38.2	39.9	39.9	40.9	40.5	40.7
31	40.6	.	.	.	.	.	.	.	.	.
32	34.6	.	.	.	.	.	.	.	.	.
33	39.4	.	.	.	.	.	.	.	.	.
34	39.1	.	.	.	.	.	.	.	.	.
34-35	.	39.0	38.3	38.4	38.1	39.6	39.7	40.2	40.4	40.3
35	38.4	.	.	.	.	.	.	.	.	.
36	39.3	.	.	.	.	.	.	.	.	.
36-37	.	39.4	38.2	38.4	37.9	39.2	39.7	39.9	40.0	39.9
37	39.6	.	.	.	.	.	.	.	.	.

Roumanie (BA) (a) [1] — Total employment - Emploi total - Empleo total

Total men and women - Total hommes et femmes - Total hombres y mujeres
ISIC 3 - CITI 3 - CIIU 3

	1999	2000	2001	2002	2003	2004	2005	2006	2007	2008
Total	38.8	39.5	40.3 |	40.9 [2]	40.9	40.8	40.6	40.3	41.6	41.4

Men - Hommes - Hombres
ISIC 3 - CITI 3 - CIIU 3

	1999	2000	2001	2002	2003	2004	2005	2006	2007	2008
Total	39.5	40.0	40.5 |	41.2 [2]	41.4	41.5	41.5	41.1	41.7	41.5

Women - Femmes - Mujeres
ISIC 3 - CITI 3 - CIIU 3

	1999	2000	2001	2002	2003	2004	2005	2006	2007	2008
Total	38.0	38.8	39.8 |	40.5 [2]	40.4	40.0	39.7	39.4	41.5	41.3

Russian Federation (DA) (a) [3] — Employees - Salariés - Asalariados

Total men and women - Total hommes et femmes - Total hombres y mujeres
ISIC 3 - CITI 3 - CIIU 3

	1999	2000	2001	2002	2003	2004	2005	2006	2007	2008
Total	.	.	.	.	.	.	| 6.9 [4]	6.9	7.0	6.8
15	.	.	.	.	.	.	| 7.2 [4]	7.2	7.2	7.1
16	.	.	.	.	.	.	| 7.0 [4]	6.8	7.0	7.0
17	.	.	.	.	.	.	| 6.6 [4]	6.6	6.6	6.6
18	.	.	.	.	.	.	| 7.0 [4]	7.0	7.2	7.0
19	.	.	.	.	.	.	| 6.8 [4]	7.0	6.9	6.8
20	.	.	.	.	.	.	| 7.1 [4]	7.1	7.2	7.0
21	.	.	.	.	.	.	| 7.0 [4]	7.0	7.1	7.0
22	.	.	.	.	.	.	| 7.1 [4]	7.0	7.2	7.1
23	.	.	.	.	.	.	| 6.9 [4]	6.9	6.9	6.8
24	.	.	.	.	.	.	| 7.0 [4]	6.9	6.8	6.8
25	.	.	.	.	.	.	| 7.0 [4]	7.0	7.0	6.7
26	.	.	.	.	.	.	| 7.1 [4]	7.1	7.1	6.9
27	.	.	.	.	.	.	| 6.9 [4]	6.9	6.9	6.7
28	.	.	.	.	.	.	| 7.0 [4]	7.0	7.0	6.7
29	.	.	.	.	.	.	| 6.9 [4]	6.9	6.9	6.7
30	.	.	.	.	.	.	| 6.7 [4]	6.6	7.0	6.9
31	.	.	.	.	.	.	| 6.8 [4]	6.8	6.9	6.7
32	.	.	.	.	.	.	| 6.7 [4]	6.8	7.0	6.8
33	.	.	.	.	.	.	| 6.9 [4]	7.0	7.0	6.9
34	.	.	.	.	.	.	| 6.7 [4]	6.9	6.9	6.5
35	.	.	.	.	.	.	| 6.8 [4]	6.8	6.9	6.8
36	.	.	.	.	.	.	| 7.1 [4]	7.0	7.1	7.0
37	.	.	.	.	.	.	| 7.2 [4]	7.1	7.1	6.9

Explanatory notes: see p. 721.

[1] Persons aged 15 years and over. [2] Methodology revised; data not strictly comparable. [3] Per day. [4] New series: data not comparable.

Notes explicatives: voir p. 723.

[1] Personnes âgées de 15 ans et plus. [2] Méthodologie révisée; les données ne sont pas strictement comparables. [3] Par jour. [4] Nouvelle série: données non comparables. .

Notas explicativas: véase p. 725.

[1] Personas de 15 años y más. [2] Metodología revisada; los datos no son estrictamente comparables. [3] Por día. [4] Nueva serie : datos no comparables.

	Per week — Par semaine — Por semana									
	1999	2000	2001	2002	2003	2004	2005	2006	2007	2008

San Marino (E) (a) — Employees - Salariés - Asalariados

Total men and women - Total hommes et femmes - Total hombres y mujeres
ISIC 2 - CITI 2 - CIIU 2

	1999	2000	2001	2002	2003	2004	2005	2006	2007	2008
Total	38.8			40.3	38.4	36.9				
311-313	44.5			42.8	42.1	35.6				
321	37.9			38.6	36.5	37.4				
322	36.1			38.9	36.3	35.6				
323	38.4			39.0	41.5	34.2				
324	36.0			38.4	25.0	36.6				
331	43.3			42.0	39.2	37.7				
332	39.1			38.6	37.0	37.6				
341	41.9			39.3	38.0	34.2				
342	39.8			40.8	39.6	32.9				
352	40.5			41.5	38.9	38.0				
355	39.1			38.6	38.5	42.1				
356	38.3			40.8	38.3	37.9				
36	41.0			41.3	39.5	38.8				
372					32.0	44.1				
381-383	37.8			39.3	37.9	36.7				
384	32.7			41.7	45.8	35.0				
385	40.1			42.4	34.3	34.7				
390	43.5			57.9	39.1	38.2				

Slovakia (CA) (a) [1] [2] — Employees - Salariés - Asalariados

Total men and women - Total hommes et femmes - Total hombres y mujeres
ISIC 3 - CITI 3 - CIIU 3

	1999	2000	2001	2002	2003	2004	2005	2006	2007	2008
Total	141	142	143	138	137	142	142	142	142	140
15	147	146	148	143	141	146	146	145	145	144
16					138					
17	133	135	136	132	129	138	138	138	137	137
18	134	136	137	131	129	137	135	136	135	132
19	135	136	138	136	133	135	137	138	134	132
20	139	144	141	138	136	144	144	143	142	138
21	149	147	147	140	137	143	141	142	142	142
22	151	148	152	147	144	148	148	147	147	148
23	144	144	144	138	134	136	134	136	137	137
24	141	142	142	134	136	140	139	139	139	136
25	143	145	147	140	141	144	145	144	144	140
26	144	144	145	139	138	143	143	142	142	142
27	138	140	138	132	130	135	134	134	133	132
28	143	145	145	141	141	145	145	145	144	142
29	140	143	143	139	139	145	145	145	144	141
30	147	147	153	147	152	164	182	143	145	143
31	140	144	146	140	138	143	143	142	145	141
32	136	143	142	139	135	141	141	149	145	141
33	140	145	148	142	136	145	144	144	141	140
34	145	150	149	145	143	143	143	144	146	142
35	129	127	140	132	135	141	136	138	145	148
36	137	142	144	140	139	143	144	144	144	139
37	146	146	158	149	152	156	146	144	140	135

Slovenia (BA) (a) [3] [4] — Employees - Salariés - Asalariados

Total men and women - Total hommes et femmes - Total hombres y mujeres
ISIC 3 - CITI 3 - CIIU 3

	1999	2000	2001	2002	2003	2004	2005	2006	2007	2008
Total	40.5	40.3	34.9	36.0	36.7	36.1	37.1	39.9	35.1	
15	40.4	40.7	35.4	37.2	37.7	37.4	38.7	39.3	34.5	
16	38.8	38.4	40.0	41.2	36.4	21.7		40.0	40.0	
17	40.3	40.3	34.1	33.9	36.9	32.0	35.9	40.6	34.4	
18	40.5	40.4	32.0	31.9	34.0	35.0	34.6	39.0	34.2	
19	40.4	39.8	36.2	36.9	35.5	35.9	39.4	40.2	34.2	
20	40.8	40.3	35.3	38.0	37.2	36.8	38.2	40.1	38.0	
21	40.8	40.0	37.7	36.1	37.6	31.5	36.4	39.5	39.4	
22	40.7	39.6	34.7	36.0	34.5	35.9	34.5	36.2	34.7	
23		40.0	40.0	36.1				40.0	40.0	
24	41.1	40.7	35.8	35.6	37.6	35.8	35.7	40.9	35.4	
25	40.6	40.5	37.7	36.5	37.4	34.3	36.1	39.6	33.7	
26	40.7	41.0	36.9	35.6	36.2	37.5	39.7	40.6	35.8	
27	40.1	40.4	35.5	36.9	37.3	38.4	37.1	39.7	33.9	
28	40.5	40.7	35.2	36.4	37.4	37.4	39.3	40.1	34.5	
29	40.5	41.3	35.2	38.0	36.8	37.3	38.0	40.3	36.6	
30		41.9	42.1	41.4	42.2	31.1		48.4	0.0	
31	39.6	39.9	32.5	34.9	36.0	34.9	37.7	40.4	32.9	
32	40.8	40.1	36.2	31.4	36.1	38.1	35.8	39.8	34.1	
33	40.9	38.6	33.0	37.3	36.8	37.6	38.6	39.5	36.1	
34	40.4	39.4	35.0	38.9	37.4	36.2	36.4	40.4	37.0	
35	40.8	40.5	29.8	32.4	34.1		38.6	40.6	36.3	
36	40.6	40.1	35.3	36.0	36.8	36.2	38.0	39.8	34.8	
37	40.1	40.0	38.7	40.6	37.9	41.0	42.8	43.2	38.5	

Explanatory notes: see p. 721.

[1] Excl. enterprises with less than 20 employees. [2] Per month. [3] Persons aged 15 years and over. [4] Second quarter of each year.

Notes explicatives: voir p. 723.

[1] Non compris les entreprises occupant moins de 20 salariés. [2] Par mois. [3] Personnes âgées de 15 ans et plus. [4] Deuxième trimestre de chaque année.

Notas explicativas: véase p. 725.

[1] Excl. las empresas con menos de 20 asalariados. [2] Por mes. [3] Personas de 15 años y más. [4] Segundo trimestre de cada año.

In manufacturing Dans les industries manufacturières En las industrias manufactureras

	Per week			Par semaine				Por semana		
	1999	2000	2001	2002	2003	2004	2005	2006	2007	2008

Slovenia (BA) (a) [1][2] — Employees - Salariés - Asalariados

Men - Hommes - Hombres
ISIC 3 - CITI 3 - CIIU 3

	1999	2000	2001	2002	2003	2004	2005	2006	2007	2008
Total	40.7	40.5	35.8	37.5	38.0	37.4	38.3	40.2	35.9	.
15	40.8	41.1	36.8	38.4	39.4	39.1	37.5	40.6	35.3	.
16	.	40.0	40.0	40.0	.	31.8	.	.	40.0	.
17	40.4	40.3	34.8	35.4	38.5	32.5	37.6	40.8	37.7	.
18	40.6	38.9	29.0	35.3	33.7	38.8	38.0	40.7	32.1	.
19	40.4	39.4	38.6	39.5	36.6	35.5	41.4	40.5	37.8	.
20	41.0	40.6	36.1	39.4	38.4	37.8	38.6	39.9	37.5	.
21	41.3	40.3	37.9	38.1	39.4	32.0	39.2	39.1	39.4	.
22	40.6	39.7	35.0	36.7	37.0	36.6	37.8	34.1	33.8	.
23	.	40.0	40.0	36.1	.	.	.	40.0	40.0	.
24	41.7	41.0	36.9	36.9	36.4	34.4	39.9	40.7	35.6	.
25	40.8	40.2	38.7	36.7	37.7	34.3	36.8	39.9	33.8	.
26	41.5	40.6	37.9	36.3	36.9	38.3	40.5	40.5	38.9	.
27	40.5	40.6	36.5	36.8	37.1	39.4	38.3	39.5	33.7	.
28	40.5	40.7	35.8	37.2	37.5	38.8	40.3	40.3	35.5	.
29	40.8	41.3	33.9	38.5	37.3	39.1	39.2	40.7	36.8	.
30	.	42.7	42.5	41.0	40.0	31.1	.	48.4	.	.
31	39.7	40.0	35.0	36.3	38.4	35.9	37.5	40.8	32.8	.
32	40.4	40.6	40.2	38.1	37.4	39.2	36.7	40.5	35.3	.
33	41.7	38.8	31.2	38.4	41.7	36.8	41.3	41.1	38.9	.
34	40.5	39.4	34.0	38.7	39.8	37.2	36.4	40.4	37.8	.
35	41.0	40.7	32.6	34.1	33.5	38.0	40.3	40.7	38.5	.
36	40.7	40.4	35.8	37.9	40.4	36.7	38.8	40.4	35.0	.
37	40.1	40.0	38.4	40.6	37.9	41.7	42.6	43.2	37.8	.

Women - Femmes - Mujeres
ISIC 3 - CITI 3 - CIIU 3

	1999	2000	2001	2002	2003	2004	2005	2006	2007	2008
Total	40.1	40.2	33.7	33.7	34.7	34.0	35.1	39.5	33.9	.
15	39.6	40.2	33.0	35.5	35.5	35.3	40.3	37.9	33.4	.
16	.	37.5	40.0	44.0	36.4	18.4	.	40.0	40.0	.
17	39.0	40.3	33.8	33.3	36.2	31.8	35.3	40.5	32.4	.
18	40.5	40.7	32.5	31.2	34.1	34.3	33.6	38.8	34.5	.
19	40.4	40.1	35.1	35.5	34.9	36.3	37.2	40.1	30.7	.
20	40.3	39.6	33.1	33.8	32.0	31.2	36.8	40.7	39.2	.
21	40.1	39.6	37.4	32.1	35.0	30.8	30.7	40.3	39.2	.
22	40.9	39.3	34.3	35.1	30.2	35.2	32.1	38.9	35.9	.
23	.	40.0	.	.	.	.	.	.	.	.
24	40.2	40.2	34.4	33.9	38.9	37.7	30.2	41.1	35.2	.
25	40.2	40.8	36.2	36.0	36.6	34.5	34.8	39.0	33.4	.
26	39.7	41.7	34.3	33.8	34.5	36.0	38.4	40.6	30.1	.
27	36.5	39.2	29.2	37.1	38.2	31.0	32.7	40.2	36.3	.
28	40.3	40.6	33.0	32.8	37.3	31.7	34.4	39.4	30.6	.
29	39.8	41.2	37.9	36.8	35.4	32.0	33.7	39.0	35.8	.
30	.	40.0	40.0	45.0	45.0	.	.	40.0	.	.
31	39.5	39.8	30.2	33.7	33.1	33.9	38.0	40.0	33.1	.
32	41.6	39.2	32.8	20.7	34.1	36.7	34.0	38.6	32.2	.
33	40.0	38.4	35.2	36.6	33.0	38.7	36.6	38.6	34.3	.
34	40.2	39.5	39.0	39.7	32.9	34.2	36.3	40.3	34.9	.
35	.	40.0	19.5	26.7	37.6	40.0	35.8	40.0	0.0	.
36	40.5	39.5	34.6	32.9	29.1	34.8	36.2	38.6	34.3	.
37	.	.	40.0	.	.	37.4	44.3	.	40.0	.

Slovenia (BA) (c) [2] — Total employment - Emploi total - Empleo total

Total men and women - Total hommes et femmes - Total hombres y mujeres
ISIC 4 - CITI 4 - CIIU 4

	1999	2000	2001	2002	2003	2004	2005	2006	2007	2008
Total	.	.	.	.	.	.	.	.	.	40.7
10	.	.	.	.	.	.	.	.	.	40.5
11	.	.	.	.	.	.	.	.	.	40.9
12	.	.	.	.	.	.	.	.	.	
13	.	.	.	.	.	.	.	.	.	40.7
14	.	.	.	.	.	.	.	.	.	39.9
15	.	.	.	.	.	.	.	.	.	41.0
16	.	.	.	.	.	.	.	.	.	41.9
17	.	.	.	.	.	.	.	.	.	39.7
18	.	.	.	.	.	.	.	.	.	40.3
19	.	.	.	.	.	.	.	.	.	40.0
20	.	.	.	.	.	.	.	.	.	41.6
21	.	.	.	.	.	.	.	.	.	41.3
22	.	.	.	.	.	.	.	.	.	40.9
23	.	.	.	.	.	.	.	.	.	40.7
24	.	.	.	.	.	.	.	.	.	41.6
25	.	.	.	.	.	.	.	.	.	40.2
26	.	.	.	.	.	.	.	.	.	40.8
27	.	.	.	.	.	.	.	.	.	40.4
28	.	.	.	.	.	.	.	.	.	42.1
29	.	.	.	.	.	.	.	.	.	40.4
30	.	.	.	.	.	.	.	.	.	41.6
31	.	.	.	.	.	.	.	.	.	40.0
32	.	.	.	.	.	.	.	.	.	38.0
33	.	.	.	.	.	.	.	.	.	40.8

Explanatory notes: see p. 721.

[1] Persons aged 15 years and over. [2] Second quarter of each year.

Notes explicatives: voir p. 723.

[1] Personnes âgées de 15 ans et plus. [2] Deuxième trimestre de chaque année.

Notas explicativas: véase p. 725.

[1] Personas de 15 años y más. [2] Segundo trimestre de cada año.

HOURS OF WORK — DURÉE DU TRAVAIL — HORAS DE TRABAJO

In manufacturing — **Dans les industries manufacturières** — **En las industrias manufactureras**

	Per week — Par semaine — Por semana									
	1999	2000	2001	2002	2003	2004	2005	2006	2007	2008

Slovenia (BA) (c) [1] — Total employment - Emploi total - Empleo total

Men - Hommes - Hombres
ISIC 4 - CITI 4 - CIIU 4

	1999	2000	2001	2002	2003	2004	2005	2006	2007	2008
Total	.	.	.	.	.	.	.	.	.	41.1
10	.	.	.	.	.	.	.	.	.	41.0
11	.	.	.	.	.	.	.	.	.	40.6
12	.	.	.	.	.	.	.	.	.	.
13	.	.	.	.	.	.	.	.	.	41.6
14	.	.	.	.	.	.	.	.	.	40.7
15	.	.	.	.	.	.	.	.	.	41.6
16	.	.	.	.	.	.	.	.	.	43.1
17	.	.	.	.	.	.	.	.	.	39.6
18	.	.	.	.	.	.	.	.	.	40.2
19	.	.	.	.	.	.	.	.	.	40.0
20	.	.	.	.	.	.	.	.	.	41.6
21	.	.	.	.	.	.	.	.	.	41.5
22	.	.	.	.	.	.	.	.	.	40.8
23	.	.	.	.	.	.	.	.	.	40.8
24	.	.	.	.	.	.	.	.	.	41.4
25	.	.	.	.	.	.	.	.	.	40.5
26	.	.	.	.	.	.	.	.	.	41.3
27	.	.	.	.	.	.	.	.	.	40.6
28	.	.	.	.	.	.	.	.	.	42.6
29	.	.	.	.	.	.	.	.	.	40.8
30	.	.	.	.	.	.	.	.	.	41.8
31	.	.	.	.	.	.	.	.	.	40.3
32	.	.	.	.	.	.	.	.	.	39.2
33	.	.	.	.	.	.	.	.	.	41.5

Women - Femmes - Mujeres
ISIC 4 - CITI 4 - CIIU 4

	1999	2000	2001	2002	2003	2004	2005	2006	2007	2008
Total	.	.	.	.	.	.	.	.	.	40.0
10	.	.	.	.	.	.	.	.	.	40.0
11	.	.	.	.	.	.	.	.	.	41.5
12	.	.	.	.	.	.	.	.	.	.
13	.	.	.	.	.	.	.	.	.	40.3
14	.	.	.	.	.	.	.	.	.	39.7
15	.	.	.	.	.	.	.	.	.	40.6
16	.	.	.	.	.	.	.	.	.	38.5
17	.	.	.	.	.	.	.	.	.	40.0
18	.	.	.	.	.	.	.	.	.	40.5
19	.	.	.	.	.	.	.	.	.	.
20	.	.	.	.	.	.	.	.	.	41.7
21	.	.	.	.	.	.	.	.	.	41.2
22	.	.	.	.	.	.	.	.	.	41.0
23	.	.	.	.	.	.	.	.	.	40.5
24	.	.	.	.	.	.	.	.	.	42.7
25	.	.	.	.	.	.	.	.	.	38.9
26	.	.	.	.	.	.	.	.	.	39.9
27	.	.	.	.	.	.	.	.	.	40.1
28	.	.	.	.	.	.	.	.	.	40.0
29	.	.	.	.	.	.	.	.	.	40.2
30	.	.	.	.	.	.	.	.	.	40.0
31	.	.	.	.	.	.	.	.	.	39.1
32	.	.	.	.	.	.	.	.	.	37.1
33	.	.	.	.	.	.	.	.	.	37.3

Suisse (BA) (a) — Employees - Salariés - Asalariados

Total men and women - Total hommes et femmes - Total hombres y mujeres
ISIC 3 - CITI 3 - CIIU 3

	1999	2000	2001	2002	2003	2004	2005	2006	2007	2008
Total	40.1	41.1	40.9	39.4	39.6	39.9	40.3	40.6	40.5	40.4

Men - Hommes - Hombres
ISIC 3 - CITI 3 - CIIU 3

	1999	2000	2001	2002	2003	2004	2005	2006	2007	2008
Total	42.5	43.3	43.2	41.9	41.9	42.5	42.8	43.1	42.9	43.1

Women - Femmes - Mujeres
ISIC 3 - CITI 3 - CIIU 3

	1999	2000	2001	2002	2003	2004	2005	2006	2007	2008
Total	33.5	35.2	34.6	33.0	33.6	33.6	33.9	34.0	34.0	33.8

Explanatory notes: see p. 721. Notes explicatives: voir p. 723. Notas explicativas: véase p. 725.

[1] Second quarter of each year. [1] Deuxième trimestre de chaque année. [1] Segundo trimestre de cada año.

In manufacturing

Dans les industries manufacturières

En las industrias manufactureras

	Per week / Par semaine / Por semana									
	1999	2000	2001	2002	2003	2004	2005	2006	2007	2008

Suisse (FA) (d) [1][2] — Employees - Salariés - Asalariados

Total men and women - Total hommes et femmes - Total hombres y mujeres
ISIC 3 - CITI 3 - CIIU 3

	1999	2000	2001	2002	2003	2004	2005	2006	2007	2008
Total	41.3	41.3	41.2	41.2	41.2	41.2	41.2	41.2	41.2	41.2
15	42.2	42.1	42.1	42.1	42.1	42.1	42.2	42.2	42.2	42.2
16	40.2	40.2	40.3	40.2	40.2	40.1	40.1	40.1	40.2	40.1
17	42.1	42.0	42.0	42.0	41.9	41.9	41.9	42.0	42.1	42.0
18	41.8	41.7	41.5	41.5	41.2	41.3	41.1	40.8	40.9	40.9
19	42.0	42.0	42.0	40.6	42.0	42.0	41.9	41.7	41.5	41.7
20	42.4	42.4	42.3	42.2	42.0	42.0	42.0	42.2	42.2	42.2
21	41.6	41.6	41.5	41.5	41.4	41.4	41.5	41.3	41.3	41.3
22	40.6	40.6	40.5	40.5	40.5	40.5	40.5	40.4	40.5	40.5
23	40.7	40.7	40.7	40.8	40.9	40.8	40.8	40.8	40.6	41.3
24	40.8	40.8	40.8	40.9	41.0	40.9	40.9	40.8	40.8	40.8
25	41.9	41.9	41.8	41.8	41.8	41.7	41.8	41.7	41.7	41.7
26	42.1	42.1	42.0	42.2	42.1	42.1	42.1	41.7	41.8	41.9
27	41.7	41.7	41.6	41.6	41.5	41.4	41.4	40.8	41.0	41.0
28	41.6	41.6	41.5	41.5	41.4	41.3	41.3	41.5	41.5	41.5
29	40.9	40.8	40.8	40.8	40.8	40.8	40.9	41.0	41.0	41.0
30	40.9	40.8	40.8	40.8	40.8	40.8	40.9	41.2	41.3	41.6
31	40.9	40.9	40.8	40.8	40.7	40.7	40.8	41.1	41.1	40.9
32	40.9	40.9	40.8	40.8	40.7	40.7	40.8	41.0	40.9	40.9
33	40.7	40.7	40.7	40.7	40.6	40.6	40.6	40.5	40.5	40.4
34	40.9	40.8	40.8	40.8	40.8	40.8	40.9	41.2	41.2	41.1
35	40.9	40.8	40.8	40.8	40.8	40.8	40.9	41.0	41.0	41.1
36-37	42.0	42.0	41.9	41.9	41.7	41.7	41.6	42.0	41.9	41.9

Sweden (BA) (a) [3] — Total employment - Emploi total - Empleo total

Total men and women - Total hommes et femmes - Total hombres y mujeres
ISIC 3 - CITI 3 - CIIU 3 · ISIC 4 - CITI 4 - CIIU 4

	1999	2000	2001	2002	2003	2004	2005	2006	2007	2008	ISIC 4
Total	.	.	38.2	37.9	37.5	37.5 |	37.9 [4]	37.7	37.6 |	37.6	Total
15	.	.	37.6	37.6	36.5	37.3 |	37.7 [4]	36.7	36.7 |	36.4	10
16	.	.	31.3	34.0	32.3	36.6 |	38.1 [4]	38.4	36.6 |	37.6	11
17	.	.	37.4	37.7	37.4	35.7 |	35.5 [4]	35.9	37.6 |	33.7	12
18-19	.	.	38.0	37.2	38.8	35.2 |	37.2 [4]	34.4	. |	35.2	13
20	.	.	38.3	38.6	38.4	38.4 |	38.4 [4]	38.8	38.3 |	36.2	14
21	.	.	37.9	37.7	37.5	36.4 |	38.5 [4]	37.9	37.1 |	38.5	15
22	.	.	36.5	35.4	35.1	35.8 |	36.4 [4]	35.0	36.1 |	37.9	16
23	.	.	38.5	37.8	38.6	39.4 |	37.2 [4]	38.0	35.8 |	37.4	17
24	.	.	38.3	37.9	37.4	37.7 |	37.1 [4]	37.3	37.1 |	37.7	18
25	.	.	37.7	38.0	37.6	36.3 |	38.4 [4]	37.8	37.6 |	41.3	19
26	.	.	38.1	38.0	38.5	39.0 |	36.5 [4]	37.9	38.5 |	37.8	20
27	.	.	37.0	36.6	36.9	37.1 |	37.1 [4]	37.5	37.0 |	38.4	21
28	.	.	38.8	38.6	37.9	38.0 |	38.2 [4]	38.2	38.5 |	37.1	22
29	.	.	39.1	39.0	38.6	38.3 |	39.0 [4]	38.7	38.1 |	37.8	23
30	.	.	38.7	37.8	37.7	38.5 |	40.0 [4]	37.5	36.6 |	37.2	24
31	.	.	37.2	37.5	37.5	37.4 |	38.4 [4]	38.5	39.1 |	38.2	25
32	.	.	38.3	38.1	37.4	37.9 |	38.2 [4]	37.7	38.3 |	37.4	26
33	.	.	39.2	38.2	37.6	36.6 |	37.4 [4]	38.1	36.7 |	36.9	27
34	.	.	38.5	37.8	37.1	37.8 |	38.4 [4]	38.1	37.7 |	38.0	28
35	.	.	39.2	39.0	37.9	37.6 |	37.8 [4]	37.7	37.9 |	37.6	29
36	.	.	37.4	37.5	37.4	37.1 |	36.0 [4]	37.2	37.7 |	38.5	30
37	.	.	39.4	40.0	37.9	37.2 |	34.9 [4]	40.0	37.4 |	37.4	31
									|	36.2	32
									|	39.2	33

Men - Hommes - Hombres
ISIC 3 - CITI 3 - CIIU 3 · ISIC 4 - CITI 4 - CIIU 4

	1999	2000	2001	2002	2003	2004	2005	2006	2007	2008	ISIC 4
Total	.	.	39.3	39.0	38.5	38.5 |	38.9 [4]	38.7	38.5 |	38.4	Total
15	.	.	39.5	38.9	38.1	39.2 |	39.7 [4]	38.5	37.6 |	37.7	10
16	.	.	36.8	31.0	36.2	44.3 |	37.7 [4]	37.6	38.7 |	38.7	11
17	.	.	37.5	38.5	39.8	38.5 |	36.0 [4]	38.5	39.4 |	.	12
18-19	.	.	39.9	39.4	40.1	37.0 |	43.4 [4]	39.2	39.3 |	38.3	13
20	.	.	39.1	39.8	39.3	39.3 |	39.1 [4]	39.4	39.0 |	42.3	14
21	.	.	38.7	38.4	38.4	37.5 |	39.1 [4]	38.5	37.7 |	40.2	15
22	.	.	38.6	37.7	36.4	36.9 |	37.8 [4]	36.0	37.2 |	38.5	16
23	.	.	39.9	38.0	40.1	40.1 |	41.4 [4]	41.8	36.0 |	37.6	17
24	.	.	39.4	39.0	38.3	39.2 |	38.3 [4]	38.7	38.1 |	39.0	18
25	.	.	39.0	39.3	38.8	37.5 |	39.3 [4]	39.5	38.7 |	43.0	19
26	.	.	38.8	38.7	39.4	39.6 |	37.7 [4]	39.3	39.5 |	37.6	20
27	.	.	37.6	36.9	37.3	37.2 |	36.9 [4]	37.8	37.5 |	40.0	21
28	.	.	40.1	39.6	38.8	39.1 |	39.2 [4]	39.0	39.4 |	37.8	22
29	.	.	39.9	39.7	39.2	38.9 |	39.9 [4]	39.4	38.7 |	39.0	23
30	.	.	40.6	39.3	39.5	38.7 |	42.0 [4]	39.9	37.7 |	37.6	24
31	.	.	38.9	39.0	38.8	39.0 |	39.3 [4]	39.4	39.9 |	39.1	25
32	.	.	39.4	39.8	38.1	38.3 |	38.7 [4]	37.7	38.2 |	38.1	26
33	.	.	40.6	39.1	38.5	37.6 |	38.3 [4]	39.4	37.6 |	37.9	27
34	.	.	39.1	38.3	37.5	38.5 |	38.7 [4]	38.4	38.3 |	38.6	28
35	.	.	39.9	39.3	38.6	37.9 |	38.7 [4]	38.4	38.2 |	38.1	29
36	.	.	39.4	39.2	39.5	39.1 |	37.6 [4]	38.5	38.5 |	38.8	30
37	.	.	39.4	40.0	39.0	39.3 |	36.5 [4]	39.7	39.9 |	38.6	31
									|	37.9	32
									|	40.1	33

Explanatory notes: see p. 721.

[1] Full-time employees only. [2] Accident insurance records. [3] Persons in main job and at work. [4] Methodology revised; data not strictly comparable.

Notes explicatives: voir p. 723.

[1] Salariés à plein temps seulement. [2] Fichiers d'assurances accidents. [3] Personnes dans l'emploi principal et au travail. [4] Méthodologie révisée; les données ne sont pas strictement comparables.

Notas explicativas: véase p. 725.

[1] Asalariados a tiempo completo solamente. [2] Registros del seguro de accidentes. [3] Personas en el empleo principal y trabajando. [4] Metodología revisada; los datos no son estrictamente comparables.

HOURS OF WORK — DURÉE DU TRAVAIL — HORAS DE TRABAJO

In manufacturing — Dans les industries manufacturières — En las industrias manufactureras

	Per week				Par semaine				Por semana	
	1999	2000	2001	2002	2003	2004	2005	2006	2007	2008

Sweden (BA) (a) [1] — Total employment - Emploi total - Empleo total

Women - Femmes - Mujeres
ISIC 3 - CITI 3 - CIIU 3   ISIC 4 - CITI 4 - CIIU 4

	1999	2000	2001	2002	2003	2004	2005	2006	2007	2008	
Total	.	.	34.7	34.6	34.3	34.2	34.6 [2]	34.5	35.0	34.8	Total
15			34.2	35.0	33.2	33.8	33.5 [2]	33.1	35.2	34.2	10
16			28.3	38.9	22.3	25.1	38.5 [2]	.	.	33.8	11
17			37.3	36.4	32.8	32.0	34.8 [2]	32.5	35.2		12
18-19			36.9	35.6	38.0	34.4	32.2 [2]	31.7	35.5	32.3	13
20			33.8	32.1	33.5	32.4	33.4 [2]	35.1	34.7	34.2	14
21			35.6	35.1	34.2	32.3	36.1 [2]	35.3	35.0	33.5	15
22			33.0	31.9	32.8	33.9	34.5 [2]	33.4	34.6	34.2	16
23			35.1	37.2	34.0	38.3	33.5 [2]	30.2	34.4	36.7	17
24			36.2	36.2	36.2	35.6	35.3 [2]	35.0	35.5	34.4	18
25			34.9	34.8	34.3	32.9	36.1 [2]	33.7	34.7	.	19
26			35.4	35.2	34.9	37.1	31.9 [2]	32.9	33.6	38.3	20
27			34.2	35.2	34.6	36.4	38.2 [2]	36.1	34.5	36.3	21
28			32.3	33.1	33.0	31.9	32.9 [2]	33.7	33.5	34.7	22
29			35.1	35.1	35.1	35.0	33.7 [2]	35.1	35.0	30.8	23
30			34.6	34.3	32.9	38.1	34.6 [2]	32.8	35.1	35.1	24
31			33.7	34.2	33.6	33.4	35.5 [2]	35.5	36.5	33.9	25
32			36.6	35.4	36.0	37.1	36.8 [2]	37.5	38.7	35.6	26
33			36.1	35.9	34.9	33.6	35.5 [2]	37.5	34.8	34.0	27
34			36.2	35.8	35.7	35.3	37.0 [2]	37.0	35.2	35.1	28
35			35.6	36.9	34.2	35.9	33.4 [2]	34.3	36.3	36.0	29
36			31.7	31.8	32.8	33.1	32.2 [2]	34.1	35.3	37.1	30
37			40.7	.	28.6	27.3	19.6 [2]	.	31.6	34.2	31
										33.2	32
										33.0	33

Sweden (BA) (a) [1] — Employees - Salariés - Asalariados

Total men and women - Total hommes et femmes - Total hombres y mujeres
ISIC 3 - CITI 3 - CIIU 3

	1999	2000	2001	2002	2003	2004	2005	2006	2007	2008
Total	.	.	37.8	37.5	37.1	37.1	37.4 [2]	37.2	37.2	37.1
15	30.9	30.5	37.1	37.1	35.9	36.7	36.6 [2]	35.9	35.8	35.5
16	39.6	26.1	31.4	34.0	32.3	36.6	37.5 [2]	37.2	36.6	33.7
17	29.2	29.4	36.9	37.3	37.2	35.2	35.6 [2]	34.1	35.8	34.8
18-19	31.2	30.5	36.2	35.1	37.9	33.0	37.9 [2]	34.3	35.0	35.7
20	31.8	.	37.7	37.6	37.6	37.3	37.6 [2]	37.8	37.3	37.3
21	30.9	30.2	37.9	37.7	37.6	36.3	38.5 [2]	37.8	37.1	37.4
22	29.3	29.2	35.8	34.7	34.5	34.9	35.5 [2]	33.9	35.4	34.9
23	30.0	29.2	38.5	37.8	38.6	39.4	37.6 [2]	38.1	35.8	39.4
24	32.0	32.1	38.1	37.9	37.4	37.7	37.4 [2]	37.2	37.3	37.8
25	30.6	30.9	37.1	37.4	37.3	35.9	37.8 [2]	37.0	37.1	36.5
26	32.3	31.5	37.8	37.5	37.4	38.5	35.9 [2]	37.4	37.9	37.2
27	31.4	31.6	36.9	36.4	36.8	37.1	36.9 [2]	37.4	36.9	37.1
28	31.7	31.1	38.1	38.1	37.2	37.1	37.5 [2]	37.2	37.6	37.4
29	33.1	32.9	38.8	38.6	38.4	37.9	38.7 [2]	38.4	37.9	37.9
30	30.4	30.3	38.6	37.4	36.9	38.3	37.0 [2]	36.5	35.5	35.2
31	33.0	32.5	37.4	37.2	37.3	37.3	38.0 [2]	38.1	38.7	37.5
32	30.7	31.6	38.2	38.1	37.4	37.9	38.0 [2]	37.6	38.2	37.4
33	32.9	32.1	38.6	38.1	37.4	36.5	37.4 [2]	37.9	37.0	37.6
34	32.0	31.4	38.5	37.8	37.1	37.8	38.0 [2]	37.9	37.5	37.3
35	32.7	32.9	39.0	38.4	37.7	37.6	37.4 [2]	37.6	37.7	37.6
36	31.1	31.5	36.1	36.3	35.8	35.8	35.5 [2]	36.7	36.7	36.6
37	35.9	32.0	37.3	38.1	36.3	37.2	34.9 [2]	39.3	36.7	38.1

Men - Hommes - Hombres
ISIC 3 - CITI 3 - CIIU 3

	1999	2000	2001	2002	2003	2004	2005	2006	2007	2008
Total	.	.	38.9	38.5	38.0	38.1	38.4 [2]	38.1	37.9	37.8
15	33.3	33.4	38.8	38.2	37.3	38.5	38.4 [2]	37.4	36.5	36.9
16	38.2	30.3	37.0	31.0	36.2	44.3	37.7 [2]	37.6	38.7	34.9
17	30.6	31.1	37.2	38.6	39.9	37.5	36.1 [2]	36.7	37.6	38.3
18-19	35.7	34.9	37.8	36.7	40.8	36.2	42.4 [2]	38.4	36.0	37.6
20	33.0	31.8	38.3	38.6	38.5	38.3	38.3 [2]	38.4	37.8	37.8
21	32.0	30.9	38.8	38.4	38.6	37.4	39.0 [2]	38.4	37.7	37.6
22	31.2	31.6	37.7	36.6	35.6	35.8	36.4 [2]	34.3	35.8	35.5
23	33.3	30.5	39.9	38.0	40.1	40.1	42.6 [2]	42.1	36.0	40.5
24	34.2	34.2	39.1	39.0	38.2	39.2	38.6 [2]	38.7	38.1	37.9
25	32.7	32.6	38.4	38.6	38.4	37.0	38.5 [2]	38.4	38.0	37.2
26	33.9	31.8	38.4	38.0	38.4	39.5	36.8 [2]	38.7	38.8	38.2
27	32.2	31.8	37.5	36.7	37.2	37.2	36.7 [2]	37.6	37.4	37.5
28	33.0	32.5	39.3	39.0	38.0	38.1	38.5 [2]	37.9	38.3	38.2
29	34.0	34.1	39.5	39.3	38.9	38.5	39.6 [2]	39.1	38.6	38.6
30	32.9	33.4	40.5	38.9	38.6	38.4	38.0 [2]	38.8	35.8	35.8
31	34.7	34.2	39.0	38.5	38.7	39.0	38.9 [2]	39.0	39.5	38.4
32	33.2	33.2	39.2	39.7	38.0	38.2	38.8 [2]	39.1	38.2	37.9
33	35.7	35.2	39.7	39.0	38.3	37.6	38.4 [2]	38.1	38.1	38.7
34	33.1	32.5	39.0	38.3	37.4	38.5	38.3 [2]	38.1	38.1	37.7
35	33.0	33.2	39.7	38.6	38.3	37.9	38.2 [2]	38.2	38.0	38.1
36	34.1	33.6	37.9	38.0	38.0	37.7	37.7 [2]	38.1	37.5	37.8
37	34.6	31.7	37.3	38.1	37.3	38.5	36.5 [2]	38.8	39.4	38.4

Explanatory notes: see p. 721.

[1] Persons in main job and at work. [2] Methodology revised; data not strictly comparable.

Notes explicatives: voir p. 723.

[1] Personnes dans l'emploi principal et au travail. [2] Méthodologie révisée; les données ne sont pas strictement comparables.

Notas explicativas: véase p. 725.

[1] Personas en el empleo principal y trabajando. [2] Metodología revisada; los datos no son estrictamente comparables.

HOURS OF WORK — DURÉE DU TRAVAIL — HORAS DE TRABAJO — 4B

In manufacturing — Dans les industries manufacturières — En las industrias manufactureras

Per week — Par semaine — Por semana

Sweden (BA) (a) [1] — Employees - Salariés - Asalariados

Women - Femmes - Mujeres
ISIC 3 - CITI 3 - CIIU 3

	1999	2000	2001	2002	2003	2004	2005	2006	2007	2008
Total	.	.	34.6	34.5	34.1	34.0	34.3 [2]	34.3	34.9	34.7
15	26.3	25.6	33.9	34.8	32.9	33.7	33.1 [2]	33.0	34.6	32.9
16	44.1	22.8	28.3	38.9	22.3	25.1	36.2 [2]	.	.	32.4
17	27.1	26.6	36.5	35.1	32.5	32.0	35.0 [2]	30.0	32.9	30.7
18-19	29.6	28.4	35.1	33.9	36.4	31.6	32.1 [2]	31.5	34.4	33.1
20	25.6	27.5	34.5	32.7	32.9	31.2	33.4 [2]	35.0	34.8	34.3
21	27.0	27.7	35.6	35.1	34.2	32.3	36.0 [2]	35.2	35.0	36.6
22	26.5	25.5	33.0	32.0	32.8	33.4	34.3 [2]	33.2	34.9	34.1
23	18.1	23.7	35.1	37.2	34.0	38.3	33.5 [2]	30.2	34.4	31.5
24	28.5	28.8	36.3	36.3	36.2	35.6	35.4 [2]	35.0	35.8	37.5
25	26.1	27.5	34.4	34.8	34.3	32.8	36.1 [2]	33.7	34.7	34.6
26	27.9	30.6	35.1	35.1	33.0	34.3	32.2 [2]	32.5	33.7	31.2
27	26.8	20.8	34.2	35.2	34.6	36.4	38.2 [2]	36.1	34.5	35.1
28	27.0	25.5	32.5	33.5	33.1	31.8	32.7 [2]	33.5	33.3	33.8
29	28.9	27.8	35.1	35.1	35.2	34.9	33.7 [2]	35.0	35.0	34.9
30	25.7	25.0	34.2	33.8	32.9	38.1	34.6 [2]	32.8	35.1	33.6
31	27.5	27.8	34.0	34.2	33.4	33.3	35.1 [2]	35.1	36.2	34.7
32	27.0	28.9	36.6	35.4	36.0	37.1	35.7 [2]	37.4	38.3	36.4
33	27.5	27.6	36.1	35.9	34.9	33.6	35.1 [2]	35.2	34.6	35.7
34	27.5	26.7	36.0	35.8	35.7	35.3	37.0 [2]	37.0	35.2	35.8
35	30.9	31.2	35.6	36.9	34.1	35.7	33.4 [2]	34.4	36.2	34.5
36	24.8	25.5	31.0	30.5	31.1	32.1	30.3 [2]	33.0	34.4	33.8
37	40.0	40.0	40.7	.	28.6	30.6	19.6 [2]	.	31.6	.

Turkey (BA) (a) — Total employment - Emploi total - Empleo total

Total men and women - Total hommes et femmes - Total hombres y mujeres
ISIC 2 - CITI 2 - CIIU 2 [3] [4]   ISIC 3 - CITI 3 - CIIU 3

	1999	2000	2001	2002	2003	2004	2005	2006	2007	2008	
Total	48.1	51.3	51.4	51.9	52.2	52.1	53.7	54.0	51.8	52.8	Total
		54.2	54.2	56.5	57.1	57.5	58.7	59.3	56.9	57.5	15
		43.9	44.5	43.5	43.4	45.1	46.5	47.1	45.6	46.1	16
		47.8	47.3	48.3	49.1	47.9	48.6	49.3	47.4	48.7	17
		52.5	53.4	53.5	53.5	52.9	54.5	55.1	52.9	54.5	18
		54.1	54.0	55.5	55.9	54.0	56.1	55.6	53.5	55.7	19
		51.2	52.1	54.0	54.3	51.4	54.7	55.3	52.0	51.9	20
		49.8	49.6	49.7	50.4	51.8	53.2	52.1	50.2	51.3	21
		52.5	53.0	54.4	53.1	54.4	55.0	54.2	51.0	53.1	22
		45.4	46.5	44.3	45.3	44.0	44.8	46.0	45.6	49.5	23
		48.8	49.9	49.8	49.4	50.4	51.1	50.8	49.1	49.6	24
		51.6	53.5	52.6	53.0	53.0	55.1	55.0	52.9	54.8	25
		50.9	51.2	51.4	51.7	52.5	54.2	55.0	52.4	52.8	26
		49.5	50.4	50.3	49.3	50.3	52.4	52.6	50.6	51.4	27
		52.9	53.6	52.8	53.3	52.9	55.0	55.5	52.4	53.1	28
		50.8	49.6	49.9	50.3	51.0	52.9	52.9	50.2	51.4	29
										50.8	47.7	30
		50.4	.	50.7	50.2	49.5	52.7	53.3	51.7	51.0	31
		49.1	49.3	51.1	50.7	50.3	53.1	51.0	47.3	50.1	32
		51.9	50.8	51.7	50.8	50.1	52.1	53.5	49.2	50.9	33
		49.0	49.3	48.4	48.7	49.3	51.2	51.5	49.2	50.0	34
		46.3	45.5	47.3	47.2	49.9	49.4	49.7	48.9	50.4	35
		53.4	54.0	54.7	55.1	53.6	55.3	55.8	53.7	53.9	36
										50.1	52.4	37

Men - Hommes - Hombres
ISIC 2 - CITI 2 - CIIU 2 [5]   ISIC 3 - CITI 3 - CIIU 3

	1999	2000	2001	2002	2003	2004	2005	2006	2007	2008	
Total	50.5 [6]	52.6	52.6	53.1	53.3	53.3	55.1	55.3	53.1	54.0	Total
		55.5	55.4	57.9	57.9	58.6	60.4	60.7	58.3	59.1	15
		44.1	44.1	44.6	43.5	44.6	46.1	46.8	46.2	46.5	16
		51.7	51.2	52.3	53.3	52.3	54.3	54.6	53.1	54.7	17
		54.3	54.8	54.9	55.1	54.3	56.2	56.3	54.0	55.7	18
		54.6	54.5	56.3	56.6	54.7	56.4	55.9	54.2	56.2	19
		51.9	52.4	54.0	54.6	52.5	54.9	55.5	52.1	52.4	20
		50.4	49.9	49.3	50.5	52.0	53.4	52.6	51.0	51.6	21
		53.4	53.7	55.2	53.7	55.2	55.8	55.2	52.2	54.2	22
		45.6	46.2	44.4	45.3	44.4	45.1	46.8	45.7	50.2	23
		49.1	50.5	50.3	49.7	51.0	51.7	51.3	49.9	50.4	24
		52.1	53.8	52.7	53.1	53.3	55.4	55.6	53.2	55.1	25
		51.4	51.4	51.6	52.0	52.8	54.5	55.4	52.8	53.2	26
		49.5	50.6	50.4	49.3	50.4	52.4	52.9	50.9	51.5	27
		53.0	53.8	52.9	53.4	53.0	55.3	55.7	52.7	53.6	28
		51.1	50.0	50.1	50.6	51.2	53.2	53.2	50.5	51.8	29
										49.8	47.6	30
		51.1	49.8	50.9	50.5	50.0	53.3	54.3	52.5	51.7	31
		49.8	49.6	52.9	51.4	51.1	54.6	51.4	48.2	50.9	32
		52.5	51.0	52.2	51.3	50.6	52.5	54.8	50.2	52.0	33
		49.2	49.3	48.4	48.9	49.3	51.5	51.7	49.5	50.1	34
		46.3	45.5	47.4	47.4	50.0	49.5	49.3	49.1	50.5	35
		53.8	54.3	55.0	55.4	54.0	55.8	56.4	54.2	54.5	36
										51.2	52.2	37

Explanatory notes: see p. 721.

[1] Persons in main job and at work. [2] Methodology revised; data not strictly comparable. [3] Averages of Apr. and Oct. based on 2000 Population Census results. [4] Persons aged 15 years and over. [5] Oct. of each year. [6] April.

Notes explicatives: voir p. 723.

[1] Personnes dans l'emploi principal et au travail. [2] Méthodologie révisée; les données ne sont pas strictement comparables. [3] Moyennes d'avr. et d'octobre révisées sur la base des résultats du recensement de population de 2000. [4] Personnes âgées de 15 ans et plus. [5] Oct. de chaque année. [6] Avril.

Notas explicativas: véase p. 725.

[1] Personas en el empleo principal y trabajando. [2] Metodología revisada; los datos no son estrictamente comparables. [3] Promedios de abr. y oct. revisados de acuerdo con los resultados del censo de población de 2000. [4] Personas de 15 años y más. [5] Oct. de cada año. [6] Abril.

In manufacturing — Dans les industries manufacturières — En las industrias manufactureras

Per week — Par semaine — Por semana

Turkey (BA) (a) — Total employment - Emploi total - Empleo total

Women - Femmes - Mujeres
ISIC 2 - CITI 2 - CIIU 2 [1]

ISIC 3 - CITI 3 - CIIU 3

	1999	2000	2001	2002	2003	2004	2005	2006	2007	2008	
Total	42.2 [2]	46.0	46.5	47.4	47.8	47.4	47.9	48.7	46.9	47.8	Total
		45.9	45.8	48.1	51.5	51.3	50.0	51.2	50.2	50.2	15
		43.1	45.9	41.0	43.0	46.9	48.2	49.5	42.7	44.7	16
		41.3	41.2	42.6	43.1	42.6	41.6	42.0	39.1	40.2	17
		49.8	51.3	51.8	51.4	50.8	52.0	53.4	51.2	52.7	18
		48.5	45.4	48.4	47.8	48.3	53.0	51.8	46.7	51.8	19
		43.1	45.3	52.6	44.6	36.7	50.1	50.8	50.1	42.5	20
		44.9	46.3	51.9	49.6	51.0	51.4	47.5	44.2	49.5	21
		48.1	49.7	50.0	49.3	48.7	47.8	48.4	43.6	48.2	22
		43.2	52.2	41.7	45.1	42.4	41.5	40.9	44.5	42.6	23
		48.0	47.4	48.3	48.0	48.1	48.7	48.8	46.2	46.8	24
		46.8	50.7	51.5	51.7	50.0	51.8	49.7	50.0	50.7	25
		45.9	49.5	48.7	47.2	48.6	49.8	49.6	47.0	48.8	26
		48.2	46.4	45.1	47.5	47.8	50.7	46.4	46.7	49.2	27
		49.7	49.5	48.7	50.6	49.9	47.1	52.0	47.8	46.6	28
		46.5	45.2	48.2	46.8	49.2	48.9	48.8	46.2	47.2	29
									57.3	48.3	30
		47.6	48.4	49.6	47.6	45.2	49.2	48.3	47.0	46.4	31
		47.1	46.9	46.0	47.3	46.8	45.4	49.0	44.0	46.6	32
		49.3	49.0	49.3	49.3	48.5	50.7	46.9	46.0	48.4	33
		46.8	49.5	48.0	46.0	48.7	47.4	49.7	46.4	48.1	34
		46.8	43.5	45.3	44.0	46.6	47.4	53.9	39.3	50.0	35
		42.9	48.8	49.5	51.0	48.4	47.6	49.0	48.4	47.4	36
									31.1	56.0	37

Ukraine (CA) (a) [3] — Employees - Salariés - Asalariados

Total men and women - Total hommes et femmes - Total hombres y mujeres
ISIC 2 - CITI 2 - CIIU 2

ISIC 3 - CITI 3 - CIIU 3

	1999	2000	2001	2002	2003	2004	2005	2006	2007	2008	
Total	110	143	128	132	136	142	142	142	143	141	Total
311-312	119	123	133	137	140	144	145	145	146	145	15
313	122	137	135	137	142	149	155	152	148	145	16
314	138	79	93	100	104	124	123	126	131	131	17
321	60	114	129	129	131	138	136	138	139	139	18
322	98	86	101	112	126	131	134	135	138	137	19
323	92	107	123	135	140	145	145	146	146	144	20
324	66	128	135	138	139	146	145	147	149	146	21
331	111	139	144	146	145	146	147	147	147	146	22
332	90	141	145	143	143	144	143	144	143	143	23
341	116	128	134	134	137	142	143	142	143	142	24
342	130	113	128	128	133	142	143	143	144	139	25
351	123	120	128	134	139	144	144	143	146	142	26
352	113	140	142	142	144	146	145	144	145	140	27
353	138	106	120	128	135	140	141	140	143	139	28
354	139	114	127	129	134	140	139	138	141	138	29
355	109	76	106	115	120	129	132	136	142	141	30
356	104	101	117	121	128	137	138	138	140	136	31
361	126	76	93	103	112	125	124	126	133	131	32
362	120	100	117	122	125	132	134	134	135	135	33
369	114	103	111	119	136	146	141	146	149	139	34
371	134	117	128	133	137	141	139	139	141	139	35
372	126	100	110	125	132	140	143	145	146	143	36
381	118	142	143	142	144	149	147	149	150	143	37
382	106										
383	96										
384	98										
385	79										
390	122										

Men - Hommes - Hombres
ISIC 3 - CITI 3 - CIIU 3

	1999	2000	2001	2002	2003	2004	2005	2006	2007	2008
Total				133	137	143	142	143	144	141
15				137	140	144	145	147	146	146
16				142	145	154	159	154	147	146
17				104	106	126	126	127	132	131
18				127	129	130	135	134	132	133
19				121	131	132	131	132	138	138
20				136	140	145	146	146	146	143
21				142	143	147	147	149	152	146
22				147	145	146	148	148	147	146
23				141	142	144	144	144	143	143
24				137	139	143	139	144	146	144
25				130	136	143	145	145	146	141
26				136	141	146	146	145	148	143
27				140	141	144	144	144	145	138
28				130	137	142	142	141	144	140
29				129	134	141	139	139	141	138
30				120	125	134	135	138	145	143
31				125	131	140	139	140	141	136
32				108	115	127	127	127	134	135
33				122	125	131	136	136	137	137
34				122	138	145	141	148	150	140
35				134	138	143	140	140	143	141
36				127	135	143	144	146	146	143
37				143	146	150	148	148	150	142

Explanatory notes: see p. 721.   Notes explicatives: voir p. 723.   Notas explicativas: véase p. 725.

[1] Oct. of each year. [2] April. [3] Per month.   [1] Oct. de chaque année. [2] Avril. [3] Par mois.   [1] Oct. de cada año. [2] Abril. [3] Por mes.

In manufacturing   Dans les industries manufacturières   En las industrias manufactureras

	Per week / Par semaine / Por semana									
	1999	2000	2001	2002	2003	2004	2005	2006	2007	2008

Ukraine (CA) (a) [1]   Employees - Salariés - Asalariados

Women - Femmes - Mujeres
ISIC 3 - CITI 3 - CIIU 3

	1999	2000	2001	2002	2003	2004	2005	2006	2007	2008
Total	.	.	.	130	135	141	141	140	142	140
15	.	.	.	137	141	144	144	144	145	144
16	.	.	.	131	138	142	148	148	148	145
17	.	.	.	98	104	123	122	125	131	132
18	.	.	.	129	131	139	136	138	139	140
19	.	.	.	107	124	131	135	137	138	137
20	.	.	.	132	140	145	144	145	146	144
21	.	.	.	132	133	143	141	144	144	145
22	.	.	.	145	145	147	146	147	147	146
23	.	.	.	145	143	144	142	143	143	142
24	.	.	.	130	134	141	147	141	141	139
25	.	.	.	124	129	139	140	141	141	137
26	.	.	.	130	136	142	142	140	143	140
27	.	.	.	145	150	148	147	145	145	143
28	.	.	.	124	130	136	139	139	141	137
29	.	.	.	128	133	140	138	136	139	137
30	.	.	.	109	114	123	128	133	138	139
31	.	.	.	116	124	134	137	135	138	135
32	.	.	.	99	110	123	121	126	131	126
33	.	.	.	120	124	132	132	133	133	133
34	.	.	.	113	132	146	141	143	147	137
35	.	.	.	132	136	137	139	138	139	136
36	.	.	.	122	128	137	141	142	144	142
37	.	.	.	139	139	147	146	150	150	144

United Kingdom (DA) (b) [2][3]   Employees - Salariés - Asalariados

Total men and women - Total hommes et femmes - Total hombres y mujeres
ISIC 3 - CITI 3 - CIIU 3

	1999	2000	2001	2002	2003	2004	2005	2006	2007	2008
Total	41.2	41.3	41.3	41.0	40.9	41.0	40.6	40.7	40.9	.
15	42.4	42.3	42.2	42.0	42.1	41.8	41.9	41.6	41.6	.
16	37.5	36.7	38.1	38.6	38.6	37.4	36.2	37.4	36.3	.
17	40.9	41.2	41.0	41.2	40.8	41.1	41.2	41.0	40.8	.
18	39.0	39.2	38.9	39.0	39.1	39.1	39.2	38.8	40.4	.
19	40.7	40.7	39.7	39.9	39.8	39.6	39.8	39.8	39.8	.
20	43.5	43.3	43.5	43.2	43.5	43.1	42.2	42.6	42.9	.
21	41.9	41.9	41.6	41.4	41.1	41.6	40.5	40.6	40.5	.
22	39.4	39.1	39.2	39.0	39.0	39.0	38.6	38.5	38.5	.
23	40.2	41.0	40.6	39.8	39.2	39.7	38.9	39.3	39.1	.
24	39.3	39.1	39.3	39.3	38.9	38.8	38.7	38.9	39.1	.
25	42.1	41.9	42.0	42.0	41.9	41.6	40.9	41.5	41.3	.
26	42.4	42.4	42.2	41.8	42.7	42.5	42.3	42.6	42.5	.
27	41.3	41.9	41.7	41.4	41.5	41.1	41.3	41.4	42.2	.
28	43.0	43.3	43.2	42.7	42.6	42.9	42.5	42.4	42.6	.
29	41.4	41.6	41.7	41.2	41.4	41.5	41.2	41.5	41.6	.
30	39.7	39.9	39.7	39.4	39.8	40.0	39.3	39.3	39.8	.
31	40.7	40.9	40.9	40.2	40.3	41.1	40.2	40.5	40.6	.
32	40.0	40.2	39.7	39.2	39.5	39.4	39.5	39.5	39.9	.
33	39.6	39.4	40.0	39.7	39.7	40.2	39.2	39.1	39.2	.
34	41.7	42.2	41.9	41.7	40.8	41.4	40.1	40.6	41.0	.
35	41.7	41.1	41.3	40.1	39.8	39.9	39.9	40.0	40.6	.
36	41.8	42.0	42.1	41.9	41.2	41.5	41.2	41.0	41.2	.
37	44.8	47.6	46.4	46.1	46.0	44.6	45.9	46.2	44.3	.

Men - Hommes - Hombres
ISIC 3 - CITI 3 - CIIU 3

	1999	2000	2001	2002	2003	2004	2005	2006	2007	2008
Total	41.9	42.0	41.9	41.6	41.5	41.6	41.2	41.3	41.5	.
15	43.4	43.2	43.0	42.8	43.0	42.6	42.6	42.3	42.2	.
16	37.8	36.9	38.4	39.3	40.0	38.2	36.4	38.1	36.6	.
17	41.8	42.4	42.1	42.0	41.6	42.3	42.3	41.8	42.2	.
18	39.4	40.0	40.6	40.7	41.0	40.0	39.5	40.0	43.4	.
19	41.6	41.6	40.3	40.1	41.3	40.6	40.4	40.5	41.1	.
20	44.0	43.8	44.1	43.7	44.1	43.5	42.7	43.0	43.3	.
21	42.7	42.9	42.4	42.2	41.8	42.2	41.2	41.1	41.1	.
22	40.3	40.0	39.8	39.8	39.8	39.7	39.3	39.2	39.2	.
23	40.6	41.3	40.9	40.0	39.3	39.9	39.2	39.4	39.4	.
24	39.6	39.5	39.6	39.8	39.4	39.2	39.1	39.5	39.8	.
25	42.7	42.4	42.5	42.5	42.4	42.1	41.4	42.1	41.8	.
26	43.1	43.0	42.9	42.4	43.5	43.2	42.9	43.1	43.0	.
27	41.6	42.3	42.1	41.7	41.8	41.4	41.6	41.8	42.4	.
28	43.6	43.9	43.8	43.1	43.1	43.4	43.0	42.7	43.2	.
29	41.8	42.0	42.1	41.6	41.8	42.0	41.5	41.9	42.0	.
30	39.9	40.0	39.9	39.4	39.8	40.0	39.4	39.4	38.9	.
31	41.1	41.4	41.3	40.5	40.7	41.5	40.8	40.9	40.9	.
32	40.1	40.3	39.8	39.4	39.7	39.6	39.6	39.7	39.9	.
33	39.9	39.7	40.3	40.1	39.9	40.6	39.5	39.4	39.6	.
34	42.0	42.6	42.2	41.9	41.0	41.6	40.2	40.7	41.3	.
35	42.0	41.3	41.6	40.3	40.0	40.2	40.0	40.2	40.8	.
36	42.7	42.8	42.9	42.6	41.8	42.3	42.0	41.6	41.8	.
37	45.1	.	.	46.5	.	44.9	46.5	46.8	44.9	.

Explanatory notes: see p. 721.

[1] Per month. [2] April; full-time employees on adult rates. [3] Incl. overtime.

Notes explicatives: voir p. 723.

[1] Par mois. [2] Avril; salariés à plein temps rémunérés sur la base de taux de salaires pour adultes. [3] Y compris les heures supplémentaires.

Notas explicativas: véase p. 725.

[1] Por mes. [2] Abril; asalariados a tiempo completo pagados sobre la base de tasas de salarios para adultos. [3] Incl. las horas extraordinarias.

HOURS OF WORK	DURÉE DU TRAVAIL	HORAS DE TRABAJO
In manufacturing	Dans les industries manufacturières	En las industrias manufactureras

	Per week				Par semaine				Por semana	
	1999	2000	2001	2002	2003	2004	2005	2006	2007	2008

United Kingdom (DA) (b) [1] [2] Employees - Salariés - Asalariados

Women - Femmes - Mujeres
ISIC 3 - CITI 3 - CIIU 3

Total	39.0	38.9	39.0	38.8	38.7	38.7	38.4	38.6	38.6	.
15	40.1	39.9	40.0	40.0	40.0	39.9	39.9	40.0	40.2	.
16	36.6	35.9	37.1	36.2	35.3	35.9	35.7	35.5	35.6	.
17	39.2	39.1	39.0	39.2	39.1	38.3	38.4	39.1	37.9	.
18	38.8	38.8	38.0	38.2	37.9	38.4	39.1	38.1	39.0	.
19	38.7	39.2	38.8	39.5	36.9	37.8	38.4	38.4	37.6	.
20	38.9	38.9	38.7	39.3	38.8	39.4	37.8	38.5	39.2	.
21	39.1	38.7	38.7	38.6	38.5	39.5	38.3	38.3	38.2	.
22	37.5	37.5	37.8	37.3	37.4	37.5	37.2	37.0	37.3	.
23	38.6	39.4	38.7	38.6	38.9	38.4	38.0	39.0	37.9	.
24	38.5	38.1	38.4	38.1	37.9	37.9	37.7	37.6	37.6	.
25	39.9	40.0	40.0	39.9	39.4	39.2	38.5	39.0	38.8	.
26	39.2	39.7	39.2	38.9	38.5	38.8	38.5	38.9	38.8	.
27	37.7	38.0	37.9	38.1	37.7	38.0	37.6	37.2	38.7	.
28	38.8	39.4	39.4	39.5	39.0	39.2	38.5	39.4	38.3	.
29	38.7	38.8	38.8	38.5	38.3	38.6	38.9	39.0	38.5	.
30	39.0	39.5	39.1	39.2	39.8	39.9	39.1	39.0	39.1	.
31	39.4	39.2	39.6	39.1	39.2	39.5	38.3	39.0	39.6	.
32	39.8	39.8	39.3	38.8	39.1	39.0	39.3	39.2	39.7	.
33	38.9	38.6	39.0	38.6	38.8	38.9	37.9	38.1	38.0	.
34	39.0	39.1	39.5	39.4	39.2	39.4	38.5	39.4	38.0	.
35	38.9	38.6	39.0	37.9	37.7	37.6	38.1	38.1	38.8	.
36	39.1	39.4	39.3	39.5	39.0	38.8	38.5	38.8	38.7	.
37	39.3	.	.	37.7	.	39.3	38.8	40.5	39.5	.

OCEANIA-OCÉANIE-OCEANIA

Australia (BA) (a) Total employment - Emploi total - Empleo total

Total men and women - Total hommes et femmes - Total hombres y mujeres
ISIC 3 - CITI 3 - CIIU 3

Total	.	.	38.0 [3]	38.2	38.2	38.1	38.1	37.9	37.6	37.7
15	.	.	36.8 [3]	36.7	36.2	37.4	37.4	36.3	36.2	36.3
16	.	.	40.2 [3]	41.1	38.9	32.8	35.9	44.7	39.3	42.2
17	.	.	37.0 [3]	36.0	36.1	36.8	35.8	34.9	35.1	34.8
18	.	.	35.4 [3]	36.8	35.8	35.8	37.4	34.9	35.5	33.8
19	.	.	41.8 [3]	40.1	35.9	38.9	41.3	34.8	37.2	32.6
20	.	.	39.5 [3]	38.9	39.5	39.3	39.6	39.4	38.2	38.6
21	.	.	37.9 [3]	37.6	38.6	39.1	37.6	39.7	36.1	38.2
22	.	.	35.1 [3]	36.5	35.4	35.7	35.8	35.2	35.5	35.3
23	.	.	40.2 [3]	38.3	38.2	37.0	41.7	39.9	36.1	37.5
24	.	.	38.5	40.1	39.3	38.9	36.2	38.8	37.1	37.5
25	.	.	39.2 [3]	39.6	39.0	37.8	37.3	38.3	38.7	38.7
26	.	.	39.3 [3]	39.6	39.9	39.4	40.4	39.0	39.6	41.5
27	.	.	39.9 [3]	39.5	39.3	38.4	39.6	40.2	40.2	40.2
28	.	.	39.6 [3]	39.5	40.2	40.0	39.2	38.8	39.0	39.4
29	.	.	40.8 [3]	39.8	40.2	41.4	39.9	40.1	39.8	39.9
30	.	.	38.2 [3]	39.2	39.1	37.2	38.3	39.8	38.7	38.9
31	.	.	38.5 [3]	38.5	39.0	40.1	38.1	39.6	38.1	37.9
32	.	.	.	.	.	.	.	.	.	.
33	.	.	38.1 [3]	36.8	38.8	36.6	35.7	37.1	37.0	38.9
34	.	.	38.3 [3]	38.4	39.3	38.7	38.8	38.6	38.8	37.2
35	.	.	39.3 [3]	39.8	39.8	39.7	40.6	40.0	39.1	40.9
36	.	.	37.6 [3]	38.6	39.0	37.8	38.3	38.0	38.8	38.2
37	.	.	.	.	.	.	.	.	.	.

Men - Hommes - Hombres
ISIC 3 - CITI 3 - CIIU 3

Total	.	.	40.4 [3]	40.4	40.4	40.4	40.3	40.2	39.9	.
15	.	.	39.5 [3]	39.6	38.8	40.3	40.3	39.8	39.7	.
16	.	.	43.2 [3]	42.5	37.1	37.0	36.6	49.0	41.1	.
17	.	.	39.3 [3]	38.8	40.1	41.1	38.7	40.8	37.4	.
18	.	.	39.9 [3]	41.7	39.4	39.3	41.9	38.0	38.2	.
19	.	.	45.5 [3]	40.3	37.7	44.6	47.2	38.4	40.5	.
20	.	.	40.9 [3]	40.6	40.6	40.6	41.0	41.2	39.9	.
21	.	.	40.1 [3]	38.1	40.8	40.7	40.0	40.7	37.9	.
22	.	.	39.2 [3]	39.3	38.7	38.6	38.4	38.0	38.0	.
23	.	.	40.9 [3]	39.0	40.8	37.5	43.1	41.0	37.9	.
24	.	.	40.6 [3]	41.4	41.7	41.4	38.8	40.7	39.0	.
25	.	.	40.9 [3]	40.7	41.4	39.7	38.9	40.0	40.2	.
26	.	.	41.2 [3]	41.8	41.0	41.7	41.7	40.1	40.9	.
27	.	.	40.9 [3]	40.6	40.3	39.3	40.8	41.1	41.2	.
28	.	.	41.0 [3]	41.4	41.8	41.5	40.7	40.6	40.3	.
29	.	.	42.3 [3]	41.4	41.7	43.5	41.5	41.4	41.3	.
30	.	.	40.1 [3]	40.8	40.6	38.4	41.0	41.6	39.5	.
31	.	.	39.8 [3]	40.1	39.9	42.3	39.1	40.1	40.1	.
32	.	.	.	.	.	.	.	.	.	.
33	.	.	41.1 [3]	38.6	40.3	39.7	39.0	41.2	38.6	.
34	.	.	39.5 [3]	39.5	40.8	39.5	39.6	39.3	39.8	.
35	.	.	40.6 [3]	40.6	40.7	40.1	41.2	41.1	40.3	.
36	.	.	40.8 [3]	40.9	40.8	40.0	40.4	40.4	40.4	.
37	.	.	.	.	.	.	.	.	.	.

Explanatory notes: see p. 721.

[1] April; full-time employees on adult rates. [2] Incl. overtime. [3] May, Aug. and Nov.

Notes explicatives: voir p. 723.

[1] Avril; salariés à plein temps rémunérés sur la base de taux de salaires pour adultes. [2] Y compris les heures supplémentaires. [3] Mai, août et nov.

Notas explicativas: véase p. 725.

[1] Abril; asalariados a tiempo completo pagados sobre la base de tasas de salarios para adultos. [2] Incl. las horas extraordinarias. [3] Mayo, agosto y nov.

	In manufacturing			Dans les industries manufacturières				En las industrias manufactureras		

	Per week			Par semaine				Por semana		
	1999	2000	2001	2002	2003	2004	2005	2006	2007	2008

Australia (BA) (a) — Total employment - Emploi total - Empleo total

Women - Femmes - Mujeres
ISIC 3 - CITI 3 - CIIU 3

	1999	2000	2001	2002	2003	2004	2005	2006	2007	2008
Total	.	.	31.6 [1]	32.5	32.5	32.1	32.1	31.6	31.6	31.4
15	.	.	31.4 [1]	31.2	31.5	31.4	31.5	30.0	29.9	29.9
16	.	.	36.6 [1]	37.6	42.2	19.1	34.4	34.6	37.0	0.0
17	.	.	34.0 [1]	33.0	32.4	33.6	33.0	29.6	32.3	34.0
18	.	.	33.2 [1]	34.4	34.2	34.2	35.2	33.6	33.9	31.0
19	.	.	21.9 [1]	39.2	31.6	30.2	30.3	32.6	30.3	29.8
20	.	.	30.0 [1]	28.9	32.2	29.0	31.0	29.1	27.3	32.0
21	.	.	31.4 [1]	36.3	33.0	34.5	30.8	36.5	31.0	32.6
22	.	.	30.5 [1]	32.3	31.0	31.7	32.4	31.7	32.0	32.1
23	.	.	35.9 [1]	33.8	31.6	34.4	35.9	35.3	23.8	35.4
24	.	.	34.7 [1]	37.8	35.2	34.2	32.1	35.7	34.5	35.3
25	.	.	34.7 [1]	36.5	32.6	33.3	33.1	33.8	34.3	36.6
26	.	.	29.7 [1]	29.7	35.0	29.1	32.8	34.1	33.2	30.3
27	.	.	29.3 [1]	28.9	29.4	31.3	30.0	31.5	32.0	31.0
28	.	.	31.2 [1]	29.1	32.2	30.7	30.9	29.4	31.0	28.8
29	.	.	32.8 [1]	32.2	33.4	30.6	31.1	32.4	31.0	33.2
30	.	.	34.1 [1]	35.2	35.7	35.0	32.6	33.9	35.6	34.7
31	.	.	33.8 [1]	33.7	36.3	33.1	34.5	38.2	31.0	33.3
32	.	.	.	.	.	.	.	.	.	.
33	.	.	31.8 [1]	33.2	35.1	30.3	30.7	31.5	34.3	33.7
34	.	.	31.1 [1]	32.5	33.0	35.0	34.6	34.2	33.7	31.3
35	.	.	26.2 [1]	29.7	32.0	35.9	34.3	30.0	28.2	27.4
36	.	.	27.6 [1]	29.4	32.7	30.4	29.9	29.3	32.0	29.0
37	.	.	.	.	.	.	.	.	.	.

New Zealand (BA) (a) [2] [3] — Total employment - Emploi total - Empleo total

Total men and women - Total hommes et femmes - Total hombres y mujeres
ISIC 3 - CITI 3 - CIIU 3

	1999	2000	2001	2002	2003	2004	2005	2006	2007	2008
Total	38.1	37.0	37.4	37.9 |	38.0 [4]|	38.4 [5]	38.0	37.8	37.5	37.3
15-16	37.4	37.2	37.3	37.3 |	38.3 [4]|	37.7 [5]	37.7	37.6	37.0	37.6
17	38.4	35.9	33.8	36.6	.	.	.	.	.	.
17-19	.	.	.	.	35.6	36.2	35.6	35.7	34.3	34.5
18	34.8	33.3	33.4	33.9	.	.	.	.	.	.
19	40.0	37.6	38.5	39.3	.	.	.	.	.	.
20	39.5	38.3	40.5	39.0	.	.	.	.	.	.
20-21	.	.	.	.	39.7 |	41.3 [5]	39.7	40.2	40.2	38.7
21	38.5	39.8	39.5	38.3	.	.	.	.	.	.
22	34.3	33.0	31.8	34.7 |	34.9 [4]|	34.8 [5]	35.7	34.6	34.4	33.7
23	38.2	35.6	40.9	42.5	.	.	.	.	.	.
23-25	.	.	.	.	37.4 |	39.2 [5]	39.0	39.1	38.9	37.8
24	39.9	36.3	36.3	37.5	. |	.	.	.	.	.
25	39.6	37.2	36.7	38.1	.	.	.	.	.	.
26	40.4	37.3	38.6	39.6 |	38.6 [4]|	40.5 [5]	38.3	39.3	40.9	40.0
27	39.6	40.7	41.2	41.2	.	.	.	.	.	.
27-28	.	.	.	.	38.4 |	39.6 [5]	38.9	38.8	38.4	38.7
28	39.6	38.4	39.3	39.2	.	.	.	.	.	.
29	39.5	36.5	38.9	41.0	.	.	.	.	.	.
29-35	.	.	.	.	38.9 |	39.3 [5]	39.3	38.1	38.1	37.9
31	38.7	37.9	36.9	37.5	.	.	.	.	.	.
33	33.8	.	34.2	.	.	.	.	.	.	.
34-35	40.6	37.8	39.6	39.0	.	.	.	.	.	.
36	36.2	36.9	37.3	37.8 |	38.6 [4]|	38.8 [5]	36.2	36.5	36.5	35.6

Men - Hommes - Hombres
ISIC 3 - CITI 3 - CIIU 3

	1999	2000	2001	2002	2003	2004	2005	2006	2007	2008
Total	40.4	39.1	39.7	40.0 |	39.8 [4]|	40.4 [5]	39.8	39.6	39.4	39.3
15-16	39.8	39.2	39.1	39.3 |	39.7 [4]|	39.3 [5]	39.2	38.7	38.5	39.4
17	40.9	38.8	38.5	40.7	.	.	.	.	.	.
17-19	.	.	.	.	39.5 |	40.7 [5]	39.2	40.1	38.2	37.9
18	43.2	41.1	41.6	38.6	.	.	.	.	.	.
19	41.6	40.2	41.6	39.8	.	.	.	.	.	.
20	41.1	39.5	41.4	40.3	.	.	.	.	.	.
20-21	.	.	.	.	41.0 |	42.9	41.3	41.4	41.0	39.5
21	40.1	41.5	41.8	40.0	.	.	.	.	.	.
22	36.5	35.1	34.2	37.8 |	38.5 [4]|	36.6 [5]	37.9	38.5	35.9	36.5
23	38.3	36.7	42.4	44.0	.	.	.	.	.	.
23-25	.	.	.	.	38.8 |	40.8 [5]	39.9	39.9	40.5	39.9
24	42.0	39.4	40.2	40.9	.	.	.	.	.	.
25	40.9	39.0	38.0	38.9	.	.	.	.	.	.
26	41.6	39.1	40.5	42.2 |	39.7 [4]|	42.1 [5]	40.7	42.3	43.2	40.5
27	40.6	41.1	41.5	42.2	.	.	.	.	.	.
27-28	.	.	.	.	39.7 |	41.3 [5]	39.9	40.3	39.7	40.6
28	41.6	40.0	41.0	40.4	.	.	.	.	.	.
29	41.8	38.2	41.2	42.3	.	.	.	.	.	.
29-35	.	.	.	.	40.2 |	40.8 [5]	41.0	39.5	39.6	39.4
31	40.2	39.5	38.0	38.3	.	.	.	.	.	.
33	34.6	26.4	30.9	35.0	.	.	.	.	.	.
34-35	41.8	38.7	40.1	40.0	.	.	.	.	.	.
36	38.6	39.1	39.8	39.5 |	40.4 [4]|	40.3 [5]	37.5	38.4	38.8	37.9

Explanatory notes: see p. 721.

[1] May, Aug. and Nov. [2] Excl. armed forces. [3] Persons aged 15 years and over. [4] Change of industrial classification: estimates not strictly comparable. [5] Estimates based on the 2006 Population Census results thus not comparable with those for previous years.

Notes explicatives: voir p. 723.

[1] Mai, août et nov. [2] Non compris les forces armées. [3] Personnes âgées de 15 ans et plus. [4] Changement de classification industrielle: les estimations ne sont pas strictement comparables. [5] Estimations basées sur les résultats du Recensement de la population de 2006 donc non comparables à celles des années antérieures.

Notas explicativas: véase p. 725.

[1] Mayo, agosto y nov. [2] Excl. las fuerzas armadas. [3] Personas de 15 años y más. [4] Cambio de clasificación industrial: las estimaciones non son estrictamente comparables. [5] Estimaciones basadas en los resultados del Censo de población de 2006 y por eso no comparables a las de los anos anteriores.

4B

HOURS OF WORK	DURÉE DU TRAVAIL	HORAS DE TRABAJO
In manufacturing	Dans les industries manufacturières	En las industrias manufactureras

	Per week			Par semaine				Por semana		
	1999	2000	2001	2002	2003	2004	2005	2006	2007	2008

New Zealand (BA) (a) [1] [2] — Total employment - Emploi total - Empleo total

Women - Femmes - Mujeres
ISIC 3 - CITI 3 - CIIU 3

	1999	2000	2001	2002	2003	2004	2005	2006	2007	2008
Total	32.7	32.0	31.7	32.4 |	33.2 [3]|	33.6 [4]	33.2	33.0	32.7	32.7
15-16	32.9	33.2	33.5	33.2 |	34.9 [3]|	34.8 [4]	34.7	35.4	34.2	34.6
17	35.0	32.4	29.5	31.2						
17-19					32.8 |	33.2	33.1	32.3	30.8	31.9
18	32.5	31.6	31.6	32.5						
19	35.5	33.1	31.2	37.2						
20	32.2	31.2	35.2	31.0						
20-21					33.7 |	33.8	31.0	34.2	34.8	34.5
21	34.2	35.3	34.3	32.5						
22	31.3	30.5	28.7	30.5 |	30.6 [3]|	32.5 [4]	33.3	30.4	32.5	30.4
23	34.8		29.5	26.1						
23-25					33.7 |	34.7 [4]	36.3	36.8	35.4	33.7
24	35.1	30.1	30.2	32.6						
25	34.6	31.7	32.6	35.5						
26	34.9	30.1	31.4	28.3 |	34.2 [3]|	33.1 [4]	23.8	23.6	32.0	38.7
27	35.0	37.8	34.9	32.7						
27-28					32.4 |	31.2	29.6	29.1	29.8	29.5
28	30.8	30.8	29.6	32.6						
29	28.1	26.3	27.1	32.3						
29-35					33.6 |	33.2	31.5	32.1	31.1	31.7
31	35.0	34.6	34.6	34.8						
33	29.8	24.3	38.5	36.0						
34-35	31.8	31.7	36.4	31.2						
36	30.4	29.4	30.2	32.5 |	33.4 [3]|	33.4 [4]	31.6	31.0	31.0	30.3

Polynésie française (FD) (b) [5] — Employees - Salariés - Asalariados

Men - Hommes - Hombres
ISIC 3 - CITI 3 - CIIU 3

	1999	2000	2001	2002	2003	2004	2005	2006	2007	2008
Total	156	157	160	161	158					
15	154	153	154	158	155					
17	166	167	166	164	165					
18	138	101	152	138	152					
19	152	157	158	156	160					
20	157	157	159	158	154					
21	153	162	165	168	163					
22	158	164	165	165	165					
23										
24	167	161	165	165	163					
25	167	165	166	163	163					
26	171	173	170	174	166					
27	166	160	162	163	162					
28	150	156	163	164	159					
29	158	162	167	172	168					
31	161	159	158	164	162					
32										
33	147	148	146	154	157					
34	167	167	165	164	163					
35	159	160	159	161	159					
36	146	152	154	151	152					
37	159	154	156	141	136					

Women - Femmes - Mujeres
ISIC 3 - CITI 3 - CIIU 3

	1999	2000	2001	2002	2003	2004	2005	2006	2007	2008
Total	145	144	145	145	146					
15	145	144	143	144	144					
17	152	155	152	147	151					
18	130	105	119	137	134					
19	131	122	140	140	140					
20	144	137	139	140	141					
21	132	124	138	129	132					
22	145	149	154	153	154					
24	155	151	155	154	155					
25	165	158	155	148	155					
26	144	153	143	137	118					
27	159	157	164	169	163					
28	145	142	149	148	149					
29	145	142	137	153	159					
31	101	106	114	116	132					
32										
33	132	132	136	136	131					
34	126	128	128	128	105					
35	150	153	159	156	154					
36	144	142	141	138	139					

Explanatory notes: see p. 721.

[1] Excl. armed forces. [2] Persons aged 15 years and over. [3] Change of industrial classification: estimates not strictly comparable. [4] Estimates based on the 2006 Population Census results thus not comparable with those for previous years. [5] Per month.

Notes explicatives: voir p. 723.

[1] Non compris les forces armées. [2] Personnes âgées de 15 ans et plus. [3] Changement de classification industrielle: les estimations ne sont pas strictement comparables. [4] Estimations basées sur les résultats du Recensement de la population de 2006 donc non comparables à celles des années antérieures. [5] Par mois.

Notas explicativas: véase p. 725.

[1] Excl. las fuerzas armadas. [2] Personas de 15 años y más. [3] Cambio de clasificación industrial: las estimaciones non son estrictamente comparables. [4] Estimaciones basadas en los resultados del Censo de población de 2006 y por eso no comparables a las de los anos anteriores. [5] Por mes.

Wages

Salaires

Salarios

Wages

The Resolution concerning an integrated system of wages statistics adopted by the Twelfth International Conference of Labour Statisticians (Geneva, 1973) [1] defines earnings and wage rates as follows:

8. The concept of earnings, as applied in wages statistics, relates to remuneration in cash and in kind paid to employees, as a rule at regular intervals, for time worked or work done together with remuneration for time not worked, such as for annual vacation, other paid leave or holidays. Earnings exclude employers' contributions in respect of their employees paid to social security and pension schemes and also the benefits received by employees under these schemes. Earnings also exclude severance and termination pay.

9. Statistics of earnings should relate to employees' gross remuneration, i.e. the total before any deductions are made by the employer in respect of taxes, contributions of employees to social security and pension schemes, life insurance premiums, union dues and other obligations of employees.

10. (i) Earnings should include: direct wages and salaries, remuneration for time not worked (excluding severance and termination pay), bonuses and gratuities and housing and family allowances paid by the employer directly to this employee.
(a) Direct wages and salaries for time worked, or work done, cover: (i) straight time pay of time-rated workers; (ii) incentive pay of time-rated workers; (iii) earnings of piece workers (excluding overtime premiums); (iv) premium pay for overtime, shift, night and holiday work; (v) commissions paid to sales and other personnel. Included are: premiums for seniority and special skills, geographical zone differentials, responsibility premiums, dirt, danger and discomfort allowances, payments under guaranteed wage systems, cost-of-living allowances and other regular allowances.
(b) Remuneration for time not worked comprises direct payments to employees in respect of public holidays, annual vacations and other time off with pay granted by the employer.
(c) Bonuses and gratuities cover seasonal and end-of-year bonuses, additional payments in respect of vacation period (supplementary to normal pay) and profit-sharing bonuses.
(ii) Statistics of earnings should distinguish cash earnings from payments in kind.
...

12. Wage rates should include basic wages, cost-of-living allowances and other guaranteed and regularly paid allowances, but exclude overtime payments, bonuses and gratuities, family allowances and other social security payments made by employers. *Ex gratia* payments in kind, supplementary to normal wage rates, are also excluded.

13. Statistics of wage rates fixed by or in pursuance of laws or regulations, collective agreements or arbitral awards (which are generally minimum or standard rates) should be clearly distinguished from statistics referring to wage rates actually paid to individual workers. Each of these types of wage rates is useful for particular purposes.

14. Time rates of wages for normal periods of work should be distinguished from special and other rates such as piece rates, overtime rates, premium rates for work on holidays and shift rates.

The statistics of wages presented in tables 5A and 5B are, in general, *average earnings* per worker or, in some cases, *average wage rates*. Occasionally wage indices are given in the absence of absolute wage data. Some of the series cover wage earners (i.e. manual or production workers) only, while others refer to salaried employees (i.e. non-manual workers), or all employees (i.e. wage earners and salaried employees). Where they refer to specific groups of workers (e.g. adults, skilled or unskilled workers), this is indicated in footnotes. Unless otherwise stated, the series cover workers of both sexes, irrespective of age. Data by sex are presented whenever possible.

The data on *average earnings* are mostly obtained from payroll data and derived from establishment sample surveys or censuses often furnishing at the same time data on hours of work and on employment. In a few cases, *average earnings* are compiled on the basis of social insurance statistics, collective agreements or other sources. The types of sources used are listed on page XVI.

Earnings data from payrolls of establishments usually refer to cash payments received from employers (before deduction of taxes and social security contributions payable by workers) and include remuneration for normal working hours; overtime pay; remuneration for time not worked (public holidays, annual vacation, sick leave and other paid leave); bonuses and gratuities; cost-of-living allowances and special premiums (such as end-of-year bonuses). When earnings include the value of payments in kind and family allowances, this is indicated in a footnote. Statistics of earnings derived from social insurance records usually yield lower averages than payroll data because overtime pay, incentive pay and the like
may be excluded as well as wages exceeding a certain upper limit.

Statistics of wage rates are in most cases based on collective agreements, arbitral awards or other wage-fixing decisions, which generally specify minimum rates for particular occupations or groups of workers. In some countries rates actually paid correspond closely to these minima. In countries where the fixing of wage rates is widespread, series of average wage rates in particular industries or groups of industries are calculated, using as weights the numerical importance in a given year of the different occupations for which rates are available in the industries covered. Data on wage rates usually refer only to rates for adults working normal hours, and therefore payments for overtime and other supplementary wage elements are not taken into account; cost-of-living allowances, however, are often included, and other allowances fixed in the wage-setting process, such as housing allowances, are sometimes included. Some countries obtain average *rates actually paid* (straight-time earnings) from establishment payrolls in the same way as average earnings are obtained. Rates actually paid usually cover the remuneration on the basis of normal time worked, both for normal and overtime hours, but exclude incentive pay and other bonuses as well as the premium part of overtime pay. Rates actually paid are sometimes also gathered by labour inspectors.

The different types of wages statistics are indicated in the tables by the following codes:

(E.G.) *Earnings*
(R.T.) *Wage rates*
(h.) *per hour*
(d.j.) *per day*
(w.s.) *per week*
(m.) *per month*

Earnings data show fluctuations which reflect the influence both of changes in wage rates and supplementary wage payments. Weekly, daily and monthly earnings are in addition much dependent on variations in hours of work. Statistics of wage rates do not reflect the influence of changes in wage supplements nor the influence of variations in hours of work. The fluctuations of average earnings obtained from global payrolls are also influenced by changes in the employment structure, i.e. the relative importance of males, females, unskilled and skilled labour, full-time and part-time workers etc., while average wage rates are normally compiled using the employment structure of a given year as weights. Average hourly earnings are generally higher than hourly rates because the former include overtime payments, premiums, bonuses and allowances which do not enter into statistics of wage rates. Average weekly or monthly earnings should also be higher than the corresponding rates, but may sometimes fall short of wage rates because of loss of working time through sickness, other absences or part-time work. In making comparisons between wage series, account must be taken of differences in concepts, scope, methods of compilation and of presentation of the data.

It should be borne in mind that figures of wages do not reflect workers' disposable or net earnings, since they generally represent the gross wages, before deductions such as those for taxes or social security contributions.

International comparisons should take into account differences between countries in the prices of consumer goods and services, as well as the need for a common currency and appropriate exchange rates, while analyses of wage changes over time should take into account changes in the relevant consumer prices during that time.

For further information, see ILO: *An integrated system of wages statistics: A manual on methods* (Geneva, 1979). For information on the differences in scope, definitions and methods of calculation, etc., used for the various national series, see ILO: *Sources and Methods: Labour Statistics* (formerly *Statistical Sources and Methods*), Vol. 2: "Employment, wages, hours of work and labour cost (establishment surveys)", second edition (Geneva, 1995) and Vol. 4: "Employment, unemployment, wages and hours of work (administrative records and related sources)" (Geneva, 1989).

Table 5A

Wages, by economic activity

The data shown in this table cover, in principle, all major divisions or categories of economic activity. Divisions or categories are shown as codes with an indication of the classification which is used, and the name corresponding to each code is given in the Appendix.

Where certain divisions or categories are only represented by certain of the groups composing them, this is indicated in footnotes.

In most cases, for a given country, the statistics of wages for different activities are drawn from the same source and cover the same categories of workers. The type of source of the series is shown as a code in parentheses following the name of the country, and the coverage in terms of categories of workers is shown on the first line of the table. Where the statistics are derived from different sources or where two or more series with different coverage are supplied, the series are shown separately.

In making comparisons of data on wages in agriculture and in other activities, it should be borne in mind that the methods of payment and the types of labour contracts and arrangements in agriculture are often quite different from those in other activities. Wherever possible, a distinction is made between permanent workers, seasonal workers and regular or casual day workers. In most cases, the statistics refer to total wages which are paid entirely in cash or to the money part of the wages only, although the workers receive payments in kind in addition. In a few cases, the value of meals and/or lodging furnished is included. Whenever possible, if earnings include the value of payments in kind, this is indicated in a footnote.

International comparisons of wages are subject to greater reservations with respect to agriculture than for other activities. The nature of the work carried out by the different categories of agricultural workers and the length of the working day and week also show considerable variation from one country to another. Seasonal fluctuations in agricultural wages are more important in some countries than in others. The methods followed in the different countries for estimating the money value of the payments in kind is not uniform.

Table 5B

Wages in manufacturing

This table shows *average wages* per worker in manufacturing as a whole and by major industry group or division. As far as possible, the different industries have been arranged according to the *International Standard Industrial Classification of all economic activities (ISIC) Revision 2, 3 or 4* (see Appendix) with the corresponding codes. Any differences are indicated in footnotes.

Note

1 For the full text of the resolution, see ILO: *Current international recommendations on labour statistics* (Geneva, 2000) or the ILO Department of Statistics' web site (www.ilo.org/public/english/bureau/stat).

Salaires

La résolution concernant un système intégré de statistiques des salaires, adoptée par la douzième Conférence internationale des statisticiens du travail (Genève, 1973)[1], définit les gains et les taux de salaire de la manière suivante:

8. Aux fins des statistiques des salaires, le concept de gains s'entend de la rémunération en espèces et en nature versée aux salariés, en règle générale à intervalles réguliers, au titre des heures de travail effectuées ou du travail accompli, ainsi que de la rémunération afférente aux heures non effectuées, par exemple pour le congé annuel, d'autres congés payés ou les jours fériés. Les gains ne comprennent pas les contributions que les employeurs versent pour leurs salariés aux régimes de sécurité sociale et de pensions, non plus que les prestations reçues par les salariés dans le cadre de ces régimes. Sont également exclues les indemnités de licenciement et de cessation de service.

9. Les statistiques des gains devraient être établies sur la base de la rémunération brute des salariés, c'est-à-dire le montant total avant toute déduction effectuée par l'employeur au titre des impôts, des cotisations des salariés aux régimes de sécurité sociale et de pensions, des primes d'assurance vie, des cotisations syndicales et d'autres obligations des salariés.

10. (1) Les gains devraient comprendre: les salaires et traitements directs, la rémunération des heures non effectuées (à l'exclusion des indemnités de licenciement et de cessation de service), les primes et gratifications, les allocations de logement et les allocations familiales payées directement par l'employeur à son salarié:

a) les salaires et traitements directs pour les heures de travail effectuées ou pour le travail accompli couvrent: i) les paiements aux taux normaux des travailleurs rémunérés au temps; ii) les primes de stimulation pour les travailleurs rémunérés au temps; iii) les gains des travailleurs aux pièces (à l'exclusion des majorations pour heures supplémentaires); iv) les majorations pour heures supplémentaires, travail par équipes et de nuit et heures effectuées les jours fériés; v) les commissions payées au personnel de vente et à d'autres membres du personnel. Sont également compris: les primes pour ancienneté et qualifications spéciales, les primes compensatoires pour tenir compte de la zone géographique, les primes de responsabilité, les allocations pour un travail salissant, dangereux ou pénible, les versements effectués dans le cadre de systèmes de salaire garanti, les allocations de vie chère et d'autres allocations régulières;

b) la rémunération des heures non effectuées comprend les paiements faits directement aux travailleurs au titre des jours fériés officiels, des congés annuels et d'autres congés payés accordés par l'employeur;

c) les primes et gratifications couvrent les primes saisonnières et les primes de fin d'année, les primes de vacances (s'ajoutant à la rémunération normale) et les primes de participation aux bénéfices.

(2) Les statistiques des gains devraient établir une distinction entre les gains en espèces et les paiements en nature.

...

12. Les taux de salaire devraient comprendre les salaires de base, les allocations de vie chère et les autres allocations garanties et versées régulièrement, mais exclure la rémunération des heures supplémentaires, les primes et gratifications, les allocations familiales et les autres versements de sécurité sociale effectués par les employeurs. Les avantages en nature accordés par l'employeur à titre gracieux et qui s'ajoutent aux taux normaux de salaire sont également exclus.

13. Les statistiques des taux de salaire fixés par les lois ou règlements, les conventions collectives ou les sentences arbitrales (qui sont en général des taux minima ou uniformes) devraient être nettement différenciées des statistiques des taux de salaire effectivement versés aux travailleurs pris individuellement. Chacun de ces types de taux de salaire est utile à certaines fins.

14. Il convient de distinguer les taux de salaire au temps correspondant aux périodes normales de travail des taux spéciaux et autres comme les taux aux pièces, les taux des heures supplémentaires, les taux majorés pour le travail effectué les jours fériés et les taux pour le travail posté.

Les statistiques des salaires présentées dans les tableaux 5A et 5B sont en général celles des gains moyens par travailleur ou, dans quelques cas, celles des *taux de salaire moyens*. Exceptionnellement, ce sont les indices des salaires qui sont reproduits, à défaut de données absolues sur les salaires. Certaines séries couvrent uniquement les ouvriers (travailleurs manuels ou travailleurs à la production) tandis que d'autres se rapportent aux employés (travailleurs non manuels) ou à l'ensemble des salariés (ouvriers et employés). Quand elles se réfèrent à des groupes spécifiques de travailleurs (adultes, travailleurs spécialisés ou travailleurs non spécialisés), ce fait est indiqué en notes de bas de page. Les séries couvrent, sauf indication contraire, les ouvriers (hommes et femmes), sans distinction d'âge. Dans la mesure du possible, les données sont publiées par sexe.

Les données sur les *gains moyens* sont généralement tirées des bordereaux de salaires et proviennent d'enquêtes par sondage auprès des établissements ou de recensements qui, fréquemment, fournissent à la fois des données sur la durée du travail et sur l'emploi. Dans quelques cas, les *gains moyens* sont calculés à partir des statistiques d'assurances sociales, des conventions collectives et d'autres sources. Les types de sources utilisées sont détaillés page XVI.

Les données sur les *gains*, tirées des bordereaux de salaires des établissements, correspondent en général aux paiements en espèces de l'employeur (avant déduction des impôts et des cotisations de sécurité sociale à la charge des travailleurs) et comprennent la rémunération pour les heures normales de travail; le paiement des heures supplémentaires; la rémunération pour les heures de travail payées, mais non effectuées (jours fériés, congés annuels, congés de maladie et autres congés payés); les primes et gratifications, les allocations de cherté de vie et les versements spéciaux (par exemple les gratifications de fin d'année). Lorsque les gains comprennent également la valeur des paiements en nature et les allocations familiales, ce fait est indiqué en note de bas de page. Les statistiques des gains calculées à partir des registres d'assurances sociales fournissent généralement des moyennes inférieures à celles qui sont obtenues à partir des bordereaux de salaires, les heures supplémentaires, les primes de stimulation, etc., pouvant être exclues, de même que les salaires qui dépassent un certain niveau.

Les *statistiques des taux de salaire* se fondent le plus souvent sur les conventions collectives, les décisions d'arbitrage ou les décisions d'autorités réglementant les salaires, qui spécifient généralement des taux minima pour des professions particulières ou des catégories de travailleurs déterminées. Dans quelques pays, les taux effectivement payés sont très proches de ces minima. Dans d'autres, où il est d'usage de fixer des taux de salaire, on calcule les séries des taux de salaire moyens dans des branches d'activité économique particulières ou dans des groupes de branches d'activité, en pondérant ces taux suivant l'importance numérique que revêtent, au cours d'une année donnée, les différentes professions pour lesquelles on connaît les taux appliqués dans les branches d'activité couvertes par ces statistiques. Les données relatives aux taux de salaire ne concernent généralement que les taux de rémunération des adultes travaillant pendant l'horaire normal. Par conséquent, il n'est pas tenu compte de la rémunération des heures supplémentaires et des autres éléments qui s'ajoutent au salaire; cependant, les allocations de cherté de vie sont souvent comprises dans les calculs, de même que d'autres allocations déterminées par la procédure de fixation des salaires, par exemple l'indemnité de logement. Dans quelques pays, on obtient les *taux* moyens *effectivement payés* (rémunération au temps exclusivement) en utilisant les bordereaux de salaires des établissements, de la même façon que pour les gains moyens. En général, les taux effectivement payés comprennent la rémunération calculée sur la base de la durée normale du travail, aussi bien pour les heures supplémentaires que pour la durée normale du travail, mais ils ne tiennent pas compte des primes de stimulation et d'autres versements spéciaux, pas plus que de la part de la rémunération des heures supplémentaires correspondant aux primes. Parfois, ce sont les inspecteurs du travail qui prennent note des taux effectivement payés.

Les différents types de statistiques des salaires sont indiqués dans les tableaux par les codes suivants:

(E.G.) *Gains*
(R.T.) *Taux de salaire*
(h.) *par heure*
(d.j.) *par jour*
(w.s.) *par semaine*
(m.) *par mois*

Les données concernant les gains sont sujettes à des fluctuations qui traduisent des changements survenus aussi bien dans les taux de salaire que dans les paiements supplémentaires. En outre, les gains journaliers, hebdomadaires et mensuels dépendent très fortement des variations de la durée du travail. Par contre, les statistiques des taux de salaire ne subissent pas l'influence des changements affectant les suppléments de salaire, ni celle des variations de la durée du travail. Les fluctuations des gains moyens obtenus à partir de l'ensemble des bordereaux de salaires sont également influencées par les changements survenus dans la structure de l'emploi, c'est-à-dire par l'importance relative des travailleurs, des travailleuses, de la main-d'œuvre non qualifiée et de la main-d'œuvre qualifiée, des travailleurs à plein temps et à temps partiel, etc., tandis que les taux de salaire moyens sont calculés le plus souvent en prenant la structure de l'emploi d'une année donnée comme coefficient de pondération. Les gains horaires moyens sont généralement plus élevés que les taux de salaire horaires, les premiers comprenant la rémunération des heures supplémentaires, les gratifications, les primes et les allocations, qui n'entrent pas dans les statistiques des taux de salaire. Les gains hebdomadaires ou mensuels moyens devraient aussi être plus élevés que les taux de salaire correspondants, mais il arrive qu'ils leur soient inférieurs en raison des heures de travail perdues du fait de la maladie, des autres absences ou du travail à temps partiel. Lorsqu'on fait une comparaison entre des séries concernant les salaires, il y a lieu de tenir compte des différences que peuvent présenter les notions, la portée

économique, les méthodes d'établissement des séries et la présentation des données.

Toutefois, il convient de garder présent à l'esprit que les données de salaires ne reflètent pas les gains nets ou disponibles des travailleurs et qu'elles se réfèrent généralement aux gains bruts, avant toute déduction telle qu'impôts ou cotisations de sécurité sociale.

Lors de comparaisons internationales, il convient de tenir compte des différences, entre les pays, des prix à la consommation des biens et services et de la nécessité d'avoir une monnaie de référence et des taux de change appropriés; par contre, les analyses de l'évolution dans le temps des salaires devraient tenir compte des évolutions des prix à la consommation, pour les mêmes catégories de travailleurs, au cours de la même période.

Pour de plus amples informations, voir BIT: *Un système intégré de statistiques de salaires: manuel de méthodologie* (Genève, 1980). Pour des renseignements sur les différences de portée, définitions et méthodes de calcul, etc., utilisées pour les diverses séries nationales, voir BIT: *Sources et méthodes: statistiques du travail* (précédemment *Sources et méthodes statistiques*), vol. 2 «Emploi, salaires, durée du travail et coût de la main-d'œuvre (enquêtes auprès des établissements)» deuxième édition (Genève, 1995); vol. 4 «Emploi, chômage, salaires et durée du travail (documents administratifs et sources assimilées)» (Genève, 1989). Le volume 4 est disponible sous forme brochée uniquement en anglais, mais une édition française non brochée peut être obtenue sur demande auprès du Département de statistique.

Tableau 5A

Salaires, par activité économique

Les données publiées dans ce tableau couvrent en principe toutes les branches ou catégories d'activité économique. Les branches ou les catégories apparaissent sous forme de codes avec indication de la classification utilisée et le nom correspondant à chaque code est donné en annexe. Lorsque certaines branches ou catégories ne sont représentées que par une partie seulement des classes qui les composent, ce fait est précisé en notes de bas de page.

Dans la plupart des cas, pour un pays donné, les statistiques des salaires de diverses branches d'activité économique sont extraites de la même source et couvrent les mêmes catégories de travailleurs. Le type de source des séries apparaît sous forme de codes entre parenthèses placés après le nom du pays et la portée en termes de catégories de travailleurs couverts est précisée sur la première ligne du tableau. Si les statistiques sont tirées de sources différentes ou lorsque deux ou plusieurs séries de portée différente sont fournies, les séries sont présentées séparément.

Lorsque l'on fait une comparaison des données sur les salaires dans l'agriculture et dans d'autres secteurs d'activité, il convient de garder présent à l'esprit que les modes de rémunération, les types de contrat et les dispositions prises dans l'agriculture sont souvent très différents de ceux qui prévalent dans les autres branches d'activité économique. Lorsque c'est possible, on établit une distinction entre les travailleurs permanents, les travailleurs saisonniers et les travailleurs journaliers réguliers ou occasionnels. Dans la plupart des cas, les statistiques se réfèrent aux salaires totaux payés entièrement en espèces ou seulement à la partie du salaire payée en espèces bien que les travailleurs reçoivent en outre des prestations en nature. Parfois, la valeur des repas et du logement fournis par l'employeur est incluse. Si les gains incluent les paiements en nature, ce fait sera mentionné, lorsque c'est possible, en notes de bas de page.

Les comparaisons internationales des salaires sont sujettes à de plus grandes réserves pour l'agriculture que pour les autres branches d'activité. La nature du travail effectué par les différentes catégories de travailleurs agricoles et la durée de la journée de travail ou de la semaine de travail présentent également des différences considérables d'un pays à l'autre. Les fluctuations saisonnières des salaires agricoles sont plus accusées dans certains pays que dans d'autres. Les méthodes suivies dans les différents pays pour estimer la valeur nominale des paiements en nature accusent un manque d'uniformité.

Tableau 5B

Salaires dans les industries manufacturières

Ce tableau présente les *salaires moyens* par travailleur pour l'ensemble des industries manufacturières et par grand groupe ou branche d'industrie. Dans la mesure du possible, les différentes industries manufacturières ont été ordonnées conformément à la *Classification internationale type, par industrie, de toutes les branches d'activité économique (CITI) Révisions 2, 3* ou 4 (voir annexe) avec indication du numéro de code correspondant. Les divergences sont précisées en notes de bas de page.

Note

1 Pour le texte intégral de la résolution, voir BIT: *Recommandations internationales en vigueur sur les statistiques du travail* (Genève, 2000) ou le site Web du Département de statistique du BIT (www.ilo.org/public/french/bureau/stat).

Salarios

La Resolución sobre un sistema integrado de estadísticas de salarios adoptada por la duodécima Conferencia Internacional de Estadísticos del Trabajo (Ginebra, 1973)[1] da las definiciones siguientes:

8. El concepto de ganancias, aplicado a las estadísticas de salarios, se refiere a la remuneración en efectivo y en especie pagada a los trabajadores, en general a intervalos regulares, por el tiempo trabajado o el trabajo realizado, junto con la remuneración por períodos de tiempo no trabajados, tales como vacaciones anuales y otros permisos o días feriados. Las ganancias excluyen las contribuciones que el empleador paga respecto de sus trabajadores a los regímenes de seguridad social y de pensiones, así como las prestaciones recibidas de esos regímenes por los trabajadores. También excluyen las indemnizaciones por despido y por terminación del contrato de trabajo.

9. Las estadísticas de ganancias deberían referirse a la remuneración bruta, o sea al total pagado antes de todo descuento realizado por el empleador por concepto de impuestos, cotizaciones de los trabajadores a los regímenes de seguridad social y pensiones, primas del seguro de vida, cotizaciones sindicales y otras obligaciones del trabajador.

10. (1) Las ganancias incluirán: salarios y sueldos directos, remuneración por períodos de tiempo no trabajados (con exclusión de la indemnización por despido y terminación del contrato de trabajo), primas y gratificaciones, subsidios de vivienda y asignaciones familiares pagadas por el empleador directamente al trabajador.

a) Los salarios y sueldos directos por el tiempo trabajado o el trabajo realizado incluyen: i) salario básico por tiempo normal trabajado; ii) incentivos pagados a los trabajadores remunerados por tiempo; iii) ganancias de los trabajadores a destajo (excluidos los suplementos por horas extraordinarias); iv) suplemento por cumplimiento de horas extraordinarias, trabajo por turnos, trabajo nocturno y en días feriados; v) comisiones pagadas al personal de ventas y otros empleados. Se incluyen: primas por antigüedad, por calificaciones especiales y por diferencias debidas a las zonas geográficas, primas de responsabilidad y por trabajos sucios, peligrosos y penosos; pagos efectuados de acuerdo con los sistemas de salario garantizado; asignaciones de costo de vida y otras asignaciones regulares.

b) La remuneración por períodos de tiempo no trabajados comprenden los pagos directos a los trabajadores por días feriados públicos, vacaciones anuales y otros períodos no trabajados remunerados por el empleador.

c) Las primas y gratificaciones abarcan las primas estacionales y de fin de año (aguinaldos), pagos adicionales por vacaciones como complemento de la paga normal de las mismas y primas de participación en los beneficios.
(2) Las estadísticas de ganancias deberían distinguir entre los pagos en efectivo y los pagos en especie.
...

12. Las tasas de salarios deberían incluir los salarios básicos, el valor de las asignaciones por costo de vida y otros subsidios garantizados y pagados regularmente, pero deberían excluir los pagos por horas extraordinarias, primas y gratificaciones, asignaciones familiares y otros pagos de seguridad social a cargo de los empleadores. Las asignaciones concedidas graciosamente en especie, como complemento de las tasas normales de salarios, deben ser también excluidas.

13. Asimismo, deberían distinguirse claramente las estadísticas de tasas de salarios (generalmente tasas mínimas o corrientes) fijadas por la ley o los reglamentos, los contratos colectivos o laudos arbitrales, o en aplicación de los mismos, de las estadísticas que se refieren a las tasas de salarios efectivamente pagadas a los trabajadores en forma individual. Cada uno de estos tipos de tasas de salarios es útil y responde a propósitos particulares.

14. Las tasas de salario por tiempo durante los períodos normales de trabajo deberían distinguirse de las tasas especiales y de otro tipo, tales como las pagadas por trabajo a destajo, por horas extraordinarias y como suplemento por trabajo nocturno y en días feriados, y por trabajo por turnos.

Las estadísticas de los cuadros 5A y 5B son, generalmente, de ganancias medias por trabajador y, en algunos casos, de *tasas medias de salarios*. Ocasionalmente, si faltan cifras absolutas, se reproducen índices de salarios. Algunas series sólo comprenden obreros (es decir, trabajadores manuales o de la producción), mientras que otras se refieren a los empleados (es decir, trabajadores no manuales) o a todos los asalariados (es decir, obreros y empleados). En notas de pie de página se señala si se refieren a grupos específicos de trabajadores (como adultos, trabajadores calificados o no calificados). Salvo indicación expresa en contrario, las series se refieren tanto a trabajadores como a trabajadoras, con independencia de su edad. Siempre que es posible, los datos se presentan desglosados por sexo.

Las estadísticas sobre *ganancias medias* se obtienen principalmente de los datos sobre nóminas reunidos por censos o encuestas por muestra a los establecimientos que, generalmente, también informan sobre horas de trabajo y empleo. En unos pocos casos las *ganancias medias* se fundan en estadísticas de la seguridad social, convenios colectivos u otras fuentes. Las distintas fuentes se indican en la página XVI.

Los datos sobre dichas *ganancias*, obtenidos de las nóminas de salarios, se refieren en general a los pagos en efectivo del empleador (antes de deducir los impuestos y las cotizaciones de la seguridad social a cargo de los trabajadores) y comprenden la remuneración de las horas normales de trabajo; el pago de las horas extraordinarias; la remuneración de las horas de trabajo pagadas pero no efectuadas (días feriados, vacaciones anuales, ausencias por motivo de enfermedad y otros permisos pagados); las primas y gratificaciones, las asignaciones por carestía de vida y pagos especiales (por ejemplo, las gratificaciones de fin de año). Cuando las ganancias comprenden también el valor de los pagos en especie y las asignaciones familiares, se indica el hecho en una nota a pie de página. Las estadísticas de las ganancias calculadas sobre la base de los registros del seguro social suelen arrojar promedios más bajos que los obtenidos basándose en las nóminas de salarios, ya que aquéllos pueden excluir los pagos por horas extraordinarias, primas de estímulo, etc., así como también los salarios que sobrepasan de determinado límite.

Las *estadísticas de tasas de salarios* se basan de ordinario en los contratos colectivos, en las decisiones arbitrales o en otros procedimientos de fijación de salarios, donde generalmente se especifican las tasas mínimas en determinadas ocupaciones o para grupos particulares de trabajadores. En algunos países las tasas realmente pagadas se aproximan mucho a esos mínimos. En países donde está muy generalizada la práctica de fijar las tasas de salarios, se calculan las series de las tasas medias de salarios en determinadas industrias o grupos de industrias utilizando como ponderaciones las cifras correspondientes a la importancia numérica en un año dado de las diferentes ocupaciones sobre las cuales se dispone de tasas en las industrias comprendidas en las estadísticas. Las estadísticas de tasas de salarios se refieren generalmente sólo a las tasas para los adultos que trabajan las horas normales, y por lo mismo no se incluyen los pagos por horas extraordinarias y por suplementos de salarios. En cambio, con frecuencia se incluyen en las estadísticas tanto las asignaciones por carestía de vida como otras asignaciones determinadas por el sistema de fijación de salarios (por ejemplo, los subsidios de vivienda). Algunos países establecen promedios de *tasas efectivamente pagadas* (ganancias de tiempo seguido) sirviéndose de las nóminas de pagos de establecimientos y utilizando el mismo método que para las ganancias medias. Las tasas efectivamente pagadas comprenden en general la remuneración del tiempo normalmente trabajado, es decir, las horas ordinarias y las extraordinarias, pero excluyen las primas de estímulo y otras gratificaciones, como también la porción correspondiente a las primas en la remuneración por horas extraordinarias. Las tasas efectivamente pagadas son compiladas a veces por los inspectores del trabajo.

Los diferentes tipos de estadísticas de salarios se distinguen en los cuadros por medio de las claves siguientes:

(E.G.) *Ganancias*
(R.T.) *Tasas de salarios*
(h.) *por hora*
(d.j.) *por día*
(w.s.) *por semana*
(m.) *por mes*

Los datos sobre las ganancias presentan fluctuaciones que reflejan la influencia tanto de los cambios en las tasas de salarios como en los demás suplementos de los salarios. Además, las ganancias diarias, semanales o mensuales dependen en gran parte de las variaciones en el promedio de horas de trabajo. Las estadísticas de las tasas de salarios no revelan la influencia de las modificaciones de los suplementos de los salarios ni la influencia de las variaciones de las horas de trabajo. Las fluctuaciones de las ganancias medias que se obtienen de las nóminas de salarios globales dependen también de los cambios en la estructura del empleo, es decir, la mayor o menor importancia relativa que tengan los hombres y las mujeres, los trabajadores no calificados y los trabajadores calificados, los trabajadores a tiempo completo y a tiempo parcial, etc.; las tasas medias de salarios se calculan ordinariamente utilizando como ponderación la estructura del empleo en un año determinado. Las ganancias medias por hora son ordinariamente mayores que las tasas por hora, ya que las primeras incluyen el pago de las horas extraordinarias, las primas, las bonificaciones y otras gratificaciones que no se incluyen en las estadísticas de tasas de salarios. Las ganancias medias por semana o por mes deberían ser más elevadas que sus correspondientes tasas, pero a veces pueden no superar dichas tasas de salarios por razón de la pérdida de tiempo laborable a causa de enfermedad, absentismo o trabajo a tiempo parcial. Al hacer comparaciones entre las series de salarios se deben tener presentes las diferencias de conceptos, alcance, métodos de compilación y de presentación de las estadísticas.

Sin embargo, se debería tener presente que los datos sobre salarios no reflejan las ganancias netas o disponibles de los trabajadores y que se refieren más bien a las ganancias brutas, antes de cualquier deducción de los impuestos o de las cotizaciones de la seguridad social.

En las comparaciones internacionales, se deberían tener en cuenta las diferencias existentes entre los países, los precios del consumo de los bienes y servicios y la necesidad de disponer de una moneda de referencia y de tasas de cambio adecuadas; en cambio, en los análisis sobre la evolución a través del tiempo de los salarios se debería tener en cuenta la evolución de los precios del consumo, para las mismas categorías de trabajadores, durante el mismo período.

Para más amplias informaciones, véase OIT: *Un sistema integrado de estadísticas de salarios: Manual metodológico* (Ginebra, 1992). (La edición española puede solicitarse al Departamento de Estadística de la OIT.) Para información sobre las diferencias de alcance, definiciones y métodos de cálculo, etc., utilizados para las diversas series nacionales, véase OIT: *Fuentes y Métodos: Estadísticas del trabajo* (anteriormente Fuentes y Métodos Estadísticos), vol. 2: «Empleo, salarios, horas de trabajo y costo de la mano de obra (encuestas de establecimientos)», segunda edición (Ginebra, 1995), y vol. 4: «Empleo, desempleo, salarios y horas de trabajo (registros administrativos y fuentes conexas)» (Ginebra, 1989). El volumen 4 sólo se publicó en rústica en inglés. Sin embargo, una edición española puede solicitarse al Departamento de Estadística.

Cuadro 5A

Salarios, por actividad económica

Los datos de este cuadro abarcan, en principio, todas las grandes divisiones y categorías de tabulación de la actividad económica. Estas categorías o divisiones se indican mediante códigos con mención de la clasificación utilizada; la designación correspondiente a cada código figura en anexo. En notas de pie de página se señala si las divisiones o categorías sólo comprenden algunos de los grupos que las componen.

Generalmente, para un país dado, la mayoría de las estadísticas sobre los salarios de las diversas actividades tienen la misma fuente y abarcan los mismos grupos de trabajadores. La clase de fuente de las series se indica mediante un código entre paréntesis, a continuación del nombre del país, mientras que los grupos de trabajadores abarcados se señalan en la primera línea del cuadro. Cuando las estadísticas provienen de fuentes diferentes, o cuando el alcance de dos o más series es distinto, se las presenta por separado.

Al comparar datos sobre los salarios de la agricultura con los de otras actividades, se debiera tener presente que los sistemas de pago, las clases de contratos y los acuerdos de trabajo del sector agrícola difieren con frecuencia de los que predominan en los demás. Siempre que es posible, se distingue entre trabajadores permanentes y estacionales y entre jornaleros de plantilla y ocasionales. La mayoría de las estadísticas se refieren al salario total pagado íntegramente en metálico o a la parte del mismo pagada en efectivo, aun cuando los trabajadores reciban complementos en especie. En unos pocos casos se incluye el valor de los alimentos y/o del alojamiento que proporciona el empleador. Siempre que es posible se indica en notas de pie de página si las ganancias incluyen el valor de los pagos en especie.

Las comparaciones internacionales de salarios en la agricultura están sujetas a mayores reservas que en las demás actividades económicas. La naturaleza del trabajo realizado por las distintas clases de trabajadores agrícolas, así como el número de horas de trabajo por día y por semana, también presentan grandes variaciones según los países. Las fluctuaciones estacionales de los salarios agrícolas son más importantes en algunos países que en otros. Los métodos seguidos por los distintos países para estimar el valor monetario de las remuneraciones en especie no son uniformes.

Cuadro 5B

Salarios en las industrias manufactureras

Este cuadro muestra *promedios de los salarios* por trabajador de las industrias manufactureras, en su conjunto y por grandes grupos o agrupaciones. En la medida de lo posible, las distintas industrias se han dispuesto según la *Clasificación Internacional Industrial Uniforme de Todas las Actividades Económicas (CIIU), Revisiones 2, 3 o 4* (véase Apéndice), con sus códigos correspondientes. Toda diferencia al respecto se señala en notas de pie de página.

Nota

1 Para el texto completo de la Resolución, véase OIT: *Recomendaciones internacionales de actualidad en estadísticas del trabajo* (Ginebra, 2000) o el sitio Web del Departamento de Estadística de la OIT (www.ilo.org/public/spanish/bureau/stat).

	1999	2000	2001	2002	2003	2004	2005	2006	2007	2008

AFRICA-AFRIQUE-AFRICA

Botswana (DA) [1]   Employees - Salariés - Asalariados   E.G./m. - Pula

Total men and women - Total hommes et femmes - Total hombres y mujeres
ISIC 3 - CITI 3 - CIIU 3

	1999	2000	2001	2002	2003	2004	2005	2006	2007	2008
A [2]	.	.	.	.	.	.	.	1 010	.	.
C	.	.	.	.	.	.	.	6 936	.	.
D	.	.	.	.	.	.	.	1 590	.	.
E [3]	.	.	.	.	.	.	.	7 777	.	.
F	.	.	.	.	.	.	.	2 698	.	.
G	.	.	.	.	.	.	.	2 065	.	.
H	.	.	.	.	.	.	.	1 208	.	.
I	.	.	.	.	.	.	.	3 842	.	.
J	.	.	.	.	.	.	.	9 191	.	.
70	.	.	.	.	.	.	.	4 179	.	.
M	.	.	.	.	.	.	.	4 179	.	.
N	.	.	.	.	.	.	.	4 154	.	.
O	.	.	.	.	.	.	.	1 966	.	.

Men - Hommes - Hombres
ISIC 3 - CITI 3 - CIIU 3

	1999	2000	2001	2002	2003	2004	2005	2006	2007	2008
A	.	.	.	.	.	.	.	1 081	.	.
C	.	.	.	.	.	.	.	6 435	.	.
D	.	.	.	.	.	.	.	2 053	.	.
E	.	.	.	.	.	.	.	7 881	.	.
F	.	.	.	.	.	.	.	2 818	.	.
G	.	.	.	.	.	.	.	2 452	.	.
H	.	.	.	.	.	.	.	1 711	.	.
I	.	.	.	.	.	.	.	3 717	.	.
J	.	.	.	.	.	.	.	11 799	.	.
70	.	.	.	.	.	.	.	4 349	.	.
M	.	.	.	.	.	.	.	6 652	.	.
N	.	.	.	.	.	.	.	5 079	.	.
O	.	.	.	.	.	.	.	2 282	.	.

Women - Femmes - Mujeres
ISIC 3 - CITI 3 - CIIU 3

	1999	2000	2001	2002	2003	2004	2005	2006	2007	2008
A	.	.	.	.	.	.	.	912	.	.
C	.	.	.	.	.	.	.	6 930	.	.
D	.	.	.	.	.	.	.	1 134	.	.
E	.	.	.	.	.	.	.	7 358	.	.
F	.	.	.	.	.	.	.	2 037	.	.
G	.	.	.	.	.	.	.	1 625	.	.
H	.	.	.	.	.	.	.	988	.	.
I	.	.	.	.	.	.	.	4 142	.	.
J	.	.	.	.	.	.	.	7 448	.	.
70	.	.	.	.	.	.	.	3 728	.	.
M	.	.	.	.	.	.	.	4 560	.	.
N	.	.	.	.	.	.	.	3 793	.	.
O	.	.	.	.	.	.	.	1 735	.	.

Egypt (CA) [4][5]   Wage earners - Ouvriers - Obreros   E.G./w.s. - Pound

Total men and women - Total hommes et femmes - Total hombres y mujeres
ISIC 3 - CITI 3 - CIIU 3

	1999	2000	2001	2002	2003	2004	2005	2006	2007	2008
Total	143	162	154	163	174	190	207	229	252	.
A-B	89	89	73	106	93	281	138	142	146	.
C-Q	129	163	154	164	175	188	207	229	.	.
A	89	89	73	108	92	290	144	143	143	.
B	89	88	71	89	105	111	114	131	173	.
C	262	421	353	276	357	530	472	535	593	.
D	121	125	136	147	150	162	179	203	220	.
E	104	494	165	174	219	203	275	339	339	.
F	114	192	157	165	182	212	236	244	285	.
G	135	156	161	171	179	194	210	241	243	.
H	96	104	111	118	121	128	156	149	178	.
I	132	138	190	197	211	215	247	286	301	.
J	201	215	237	253	285	320	367	359	480	.
K	302	261	288	277	278	225	386	227	246	.
L	.	.	.	.	.	.	.	.	.	.
M	101	111	91	98	86	124	93	98	111	.
N	71	77	85	79	115	87	86	130	132	.
O	87	105	97	104	132	138	154	133	137	.
P	.	.	.	.	.	.	.	.	.	.

Explanatory notes: see p. 877.   Notes explicatives: voir p. 879.   Notas explicativas: véase p. 882.

[1] Sep. of each year. [2] Excl. hunting and forestry. [3] Excl. gas. [4] Establishments with 10 or more persons employed. [5] Oct. of each year.

[1] Sept. de chaque année. [2] Non compris la chasse et la sylviculture. [3] Non compris le gaz. [4] Etablissements occupant 10 personnes et plus. [5] Oct. de chaque année.

[1] Sept. de cada año. [2] Excl. caza y silvicultura. [3] Excl. gas. [4] Establecimientos con 10 y más trabajadores. [5] Oct. de cada año.

	1999	2000	2001	2002	2003	2004	2005	2006	2007	2008

Egypt (CA) [1][2] Wage earners - Ouvriers - Obreros E.G./w.s. - Pound

Men - Hommes - Hombres
ISIC 3 - CITI 3 - CIIU 3

	1999	2000	2001	2002	2003	2004	2005	2006	2007	2008
Total	148	169	157	167	179	193	215	236	261	.
A-B	88	92	74	108	96	287	135	141	145	.
C-Q	131	169	158	253	179	191	215	236	.	.
A	88	92	74	111	95	295	141	142	145	.
B	89	88	70	88	106	110	113	236	143	.
C	261	420	355	271	354	536	472	534	593	.
D	125	131	142	154	157	168	187	210	231	.
E	103	515	164	173	217	199	273	334	339	.
F	114	192	155	163	181	210	235	242	281	.
G	137	159	163	175	181	197	214	248	247	.
H	96	104	111	117	120	128	156	148	176	.
I	127	130	184	187	205	209	240	279	295	.
J	199	213	234	251	280	314	360	356	469	.
K	313	277	296	284	291	229	395	225	246	.
L										
M	116	139	106	118	93	144	100	104	115	.
N	87	93	101	93	185	106	102	170	157	.
O	89	103	96	107	128	141	156	136	138	.
P										

Women - Femmes - Mujeres
ISIC 3 - CITI 3 - CIIU 3

	1999	2000	2001	2002	2003	2004	2005	2006	2007	2008
Total	116	125	133	139	149	169	167	188	203	.
A-B	90	70	64	81	67	133	163	160	151	.
C-Q	115	125	133	140	149	169	167	188	203	.
A	90	70	62	79	62	136	169	167	142	.
B	92	88	95	103	101	112	130	128	186	.
C	293	443	325	502	401	460	321	592	197	.
D	94	87	97	104	104	126	134	159	153	.
E	109	279	171	179	236	232	292	387	347	.
F	118	204	187	197	199	234	266	274	339	.
G	123	138	154	150	167	184	187	204	220	.
H	99	102	111	125	135	132	148	168	205	.
I	177	221	247	281	270	264	304	367	365	.
J	206	224	248	258	302	341	390	368	520	.
K	232	196	227	223	216	203	322	242	245	.
L										
M	91	93	82	86	82	112	89	94	109	.
N	62	66	73	68	68	74	75	96	113	.
O	76	119	101	92	151	127	144	118	129	.
P										

Mauritius (CA) [1][3] Employees - Salariés - Asalariados E.G./m. - Rupee

Total men and women - Total hommes et femmes - Total hombres y mujeres
ISIC 3 - CITI 3 - CIIU 3

	1999	2000	2001	2002	2003	2004	2005	2006	2007	2008
Total	7 494	8 178	8 701	9 159	9 826	11 103	12 067	12 632	13 397	14 438
A-B	5 916	6 602	7 581	7 959	8 734	9 334	9 824	10 019	10 409	10 958
C-Q	7 714	8 390	8 854	9 279	9 938	11 263	12 255	12 632	13 646	14 684
A	5 825	6 477	7 488	7 840	8 589	9 095	9 671	9 874	10 290	10 829
B	9 978	11 600	11 563	11 916	13 276	14 685	13 232	13 233	13 839	13 997
C	3 627	3 889	4 655	5 155	5 441	5 496	5 588	5 895	6 340	6 735
D	5 142	5 544	5 856	6 155	6 668	7 299	7 798	8 214	8 622	8 979
E	12 152	13 515	15 663	17 518	17 347	18 456	19 457	22 016	24 125	24 449
F	7 832	8 746	8 972	9 280	10 147	11 465	12 042	13 047	14 143	15 457
G	8 940	9 584	10 573	10 762	11 236	12 032	12 772	13 547	14 387	15 786
H	7 074	7 401	7 799	8 034	8 402	8 947	9 881	10 561	11 325	11 550
I	10 019	11 502	12 000	12 788	13 830	15 189	15 982	16 664	17 472	19 824
J	13 488	14 814	16 538	17 179	17 734	20 225	21 478	22 692	24 504	27 413
K	8 850	9 958	10 800	11 241	11 690	12 003	12 822	13 447	13 880	15 231
L	9 577	10 146	10 674	11 020	11 232	13 960	15 066	14 535	15 497	16 880
M	10 609	11 280	11 299	11 728	12 524	13 993	15 008	16 216	16 682	17 287
N	10 061	11 256	12 360	12 082	12 812	15 134	16 628	17 306	18 866	19 571
O	7 847	8 271	8 488	8 751	9 839	10 846	11 427	12 298	12 513	13 173

Explanatory notes: see p. 877. Notes explicatives: voir p. 879. Notas explicativas: véase p. 882.

[1] Establishments with 10 or more persons employed. [2] Oct. of each year. [3] March of each year.

[1] Etablissements occupant 10 personnes et plus. [2] Oct. de chaque année. [3] Mars de chaque année.

[1] Establecimientos con 10 y más trabajadores. [2] Oct. de cada año. [3] Marzo de cada año.

By economic activity — Par activité économique — Por actividad económica

	1999	2000	2001	2002	2003	2004	2005	2006	2007	2008

Seychelles (FA) Employees - Salariés - Asalariados E.G./m. - Rupee

Total men and women - Total hommes et femmes - Total hombres y mujeres
ISIC 3 - CITI 3 - CIIU 3

	1999	2000	2001	2002	2003	2004	2005	2006	2007	2008
Total	3 274	3 343	3 417	3 465 I	3 603 [1]	3 708	3 750	3 938	4 015	4 645
A-B [2]	3 025	3 046	3 097	3 259	2 910	3 040	3 001	3 276	3 417	3 498
B	.	.	.	.	2 826	3 148	2 979	3 104	3 739	4 612
C	2 746	2 814	2 882	2 875 I	4 625 [3]	5 114	5 331	5 475	5 469	7 086
D	2 962	3 067	3 235	3 300	2 986	3 042	3 314	3 350	3 306	4 100
E	3 678	3 539	3 607	3 803	3 780	3 747	3 809	4 582	4 316	4 747
F	.	.	.	.	2 668	3 035	2 964	2 949	2 953	3 554
G	2 544	2 689	2 584	2 617	2 757	2 857	2 856	2 963	3 073	3 527
H	2 389	2 517	2 770	2 779 I	3 308 [4]	3 413	3 346	3 672	3 972	4 838
I	4 396	4 547	4 611	4 958 I	4 723 [5]	5 158	5 132	5 370	5 688	6 510
J	.	.	.	.	4 991	5 052	5 293	5 713	5 768	6 513
J-K	3 824	3 796	3 934	3 994	.	.	.	.	.	.
K	.	.	.	.	4 190	3 659	3 554	3 613	3 907	4 874
L	3 807	3 886	3 949	4 032	4 116	4 065	4 166	4 434	4 228	4 696
M	.	.	.	.	3 391	3 640	3 767	4 315	4 390	4 771
N	.	.	.	.	4 126	4 253	4 346	4 740	4 749	5 132
O	3 321	3 420	3 423	3 395	3 805	3 815	3 906	3 828	3 855	4 517
X	2 597	2 865	2 907	2 838	.	.	.	.	.	.

AMERICA-AMÉRIQUE-AMERICA

Argentina (DB) [6][7] Wage earners - Ouvriers - Obreros E.G./h. - Peso

Total men and women - Total hommes et femmes - Total hombres y mujeres
ISIC 3 - CITI 3 - CIIU 3

	1999	2000	2001	2002	2003	2004	2005	2006	2007	2008
D	4.20	4.27	4.33	4.46	5.06	6.30	7.63	9.72	.	

Bermuda (CA) [8] Employees - Salariés - Asalariados E.G./m. - Dollar

Total men and women - Total hommes et femmes - Total hombres y mujeres
ISIC 3 - CITI 3 - CIIU 3

	1999	2000	2001	2002	2003	2004	2005	2006	2007	2008
Total	.	.	.	.	.	3 838	3 912	4 222	4 442	.
C-Q	.	.	.	.	.	3 853	3 921	4 235	4 455	.
A	.	.	.	.	.	3 500	3 023	3 181	3 288	.
B	.	.	.	.	.	.	.	4 500	.	.
C	.	.	.	.	.	.	.	.	.	.
D	.	.	.	.	.	4 167	3 561	3 692	3 950	.
E	.	.	.	.	.	4 000	4 804	4 793	4 907	.
F	.	.	.	.	.	4 306	4 405	4 392	.	.
G	.	.	.	.	.	3 294	3 051	3 166	3 356	.
H	.	.	.	.	.	2 477	2 623	2 787	2 746	.
I	.	.	.	.	.	3 455	3 914	3 990	4 113	.
J	.	.	.	.	.	3 833	4 357	4 625	4 945	.
K	.	.	.	.	.	3 929	3 898	4 553	4 978	.
L	.	.	.	.	.	4 650	4 502	4 640	4 709	.
M	.	.	.	.	.	5 333	5 784	6 132	6 332	.
N	.	.	.	.	.	4 071	3 935	4 144	4 383	.
O	.	.	.	.	.	3 250	3 313	3 281	3 407	.
P	.	.	.	.	.	.	.	2 500	2 679	.
Q	.	.	.	.	.	5 650	5 567	6 862	7 361	.

Men - Hommes - Hombres
ISIC 3 - CITI 3 - CIIU 3

	1999	2000	2001	2002	2003	2004	2005	2006	2007	2008
Total	.	.	.	.	.	4 028	4 016	4 365	4 533	.
C-Q	.	.	.	.	.	4 077	4 037	4 390	4 557	.
A	.	.	.	.	.	3 500	2 993	3 154	3 247	.
B	.	.	.	.	.	.	.	4 500	.	.
C	.	.	.	.	.	.	.	.	.	.
D	.	.	.	.	.	4 333	3 691	3 792	4 101	.
E	.	.	.	.	.	4 500	4 811	4 813	5 468	.
F	.	.	.	.	.	4 417	4 428	4 409	4 558	.
G	.	.	.	.	.	4 000	3 636	3 696	3 850	.
H	.	.	.	.	.	2 575	2 744	2 942	2 862	.
I	.	.	.	.	.	3 833	4 197	4 279	4 385	.
J	.	.	.	.	.	4 250	5 876	6 555	7 068	.
K	.	.	.	.	.	3 500	3 970	5 093	5 396	.
L	.	.	.	.	.	4 900	4 404	4 545	4 649	.
M	.	.	.	.	.	5 750	5 919	6 322	6 440	.
N	.	.	.	.	.	7 500	3 889	4 269	4 432	.
O	.	.	.	.	.	3 875	3 581	3 577	3 724	.
P	.	.	.	.	.	.	.	2 625	.	.
Q	.	.	.	.	.	7 125	6 278	10 645	11 562	.

Explanatory notes: see p. 877.

[1] Prior to 2003: Incl. hotels and non tourism-related transport, storage and communication. [2] Excl. hunting. [3] Prior to 2003: incl. construction. [4] Prior to 2003: excl. hotels. [5] Prior to 2003: tourism-related [6] Local units with 10 or more workers. [7] Production and related workers. [8] Last week of Aug. of each year.

Notes explicatives: voir p. 879.

[1] Avant 2003: y compris les hotels et les transports, entrepôts et communications non liés au tourisme. [2] Non compris la chasse. [3] Avant 2003: y compris la construction. [4] Avant 2003: non compris les hôtels. [5] Avant 2003: liés au tourisme. [6] Unités locales occupant 10 ouvriers et plus. [7] Ouvriers à la production et assimilés. [8] Dernière semaine d'août de chaque année.

Notas explicativas: véase p. 882.

[1] Antes de 2003: incl. hoteles y transporte, almacenamiento y comunicaciones no relacionados con el turismo. [2] Excl. la caza. [3] Antes de 2003: incl. construcción. [4] Antes de 2003: excl. hoteles. [5] Antes de 2003: relacionados con el turismo. [6] Unidades locales con 10 y más obreros. [7] Obreros manufactureros y trabajadores asimilados. [8] Ultima semana de agosto de cada año.

5A

WAGES	SALAIRES	SALARIOS
By economic activity	Par activité économique	Por actividad económica

	1999	2000	2001	2002	2003	2004	2005	2006	2007	2008

Bermuda (CA) [1] Employees - Salariés - Asalariados E.G./m. - Dollar

Women - Femmes - Mujeres
ISIC 3 - CITI 3 - CIIU 3

	1999	2000	2001	2002	2003	2004	2005	2006	2007	2008
Total						3 655	3 819	4 062	4 333	
C-Q						3 655	3 819	4 063	4 335	
A							3 357	3 600	3 666	
C										
D						2 375	3 347	3 490	3 740	
E						3 500	4 750	4 647	4 907	
F						3 500	4 015	4 016	4 427	
G						2 889		2 719	2 829	
H						2 167	2 450	2 573	2 607	
I						3 000	3 633	3 668	3 745	
J						3 750	4 070	4 257	4 565	
K						4 071	3 854	4 340	4 739	
L						4 400	4 565	4 794	4 824	
M						4 500	5 700	6 056	6 289	
N						3 875	3 951	4 116	4 370	
O						2 917	3 048	2 989	3 139	
P								2 464	2 678	
Q						5 111	5 294	5 812	6 158	

Bolivia (F) Employees - Salariés - Asalariados R.T./m. - Boliviano

Total men and women - Total hommes et femmes - Total hombres y mujeres
ISIC 3 - CITI 3 - CIIU 3

	1999	2000	2001	2002	2003	2004	2005	2006	2007	2008
C-Q						2 270	2 333	2 358	2 410	2 520 [2]
C						1 306	1 777	1 986	1 957	2 030 [2]
11						6 265	4 109	4 158	4 267	4 359 [2]
14						1 306	1 777	1 986	1 957	2 030 [2]
E						4 502	4 687	4 956	5 066	5 415 [2]
F						1 802	1 721	1 806	1 787	1 901 [2]
G						1 993	1 955	1 943	2 000	2 175 [2]
H [3]						1 564	1 625	1 622	1 654	1 774 [2]
I [4]						2 660	2 703	2 686	2 869	3 049 [2]
64						5 937	6 123	5 959	5 660	5 702 [2]
J						4 419	4 316	4 293	4 202	4 236 [2]
K						2 383	2 665	2 695	2 812	2 966 [2]
N						1 411	1 506	1 604	1 633	1 742 [2]
O						1 633	1 486	1 743	1 824	2 036 [2]

Men - Hommes - Hombres
ISIC 3 - CITI 3 - CIIU 3

	1999	2000	2001	2002	2003	2004	2005	2006	2007	2008
C-Q						2 297	2 351	2 367	2 417	2 523 [2]
C						1 272	1 727	1 927	1 899	1 991 [2]
11						5 881	3 765	3 837	3 993	4 039 [2]
14						1 272	1 727	1 927	1 899	1 991 [2]
E						4 495	4 661	4 929	5 054	5 410 [2]
F						1 785	1 686	1 773	1 765	1 882 [2]
G						2 016	2 009	1 989	2 077	2 239 [2]
H [3]						1 556	1 584	1 561	1 626	1 787 [2]
I [4]						2 807	2 844	2 804	3 048	3 225 [2]
64						6 376	6 602	6 386	6 026	6 089 [2]
J						5 133	5 083	5 039	4 849	4 838 [2]
K						2 572	2 884	2 799	2 932	3 052 [2]
N						1 683	1 877	2 069	2 144	2 201 [2]
O						1 847	1 749	1 972	2 050	2 268 [2]

Women - Femmes - Mujeres
ISIC 3 - CITI 3 - CIIU 3

	1999	2000	2001	2002	2003	2004	2005	2006	2007	2008
C-Q						2 185	2 277	2 332	2 387	2 509 [2]
11						9 593	9 377	9 410	8 565	9 554 [2]
14						1 824	2 505	2 846	3 059	2 987 [2]
E						4 557	4 885	5 161	5 156	5 449 [2]
F						2 042	2 354	2 434	2 227	2 354 [2]
G						1 934	1 821	1 831	1 829	2 023 [2]
H [3]						1 579	1 709	1 736	1 706	1 749 [2]
I [4]						2 198	2 260	2 315	2 385	2 539 [2]
64						4 820	5 070	5 064	4 882	4 879 [2]
J						3 405	3 281	3 317	3 377	3 466 [2]
K						1 973	2 265	2 470	2 531	2 754 [2]
N						1 231	1 298	1 372	1 395	1 523 [2]
O						1 321	1 151	1 409	1 436	1 616 [2]

Explanatory notes: see p. 877.

[1] Last week of Aug. of each year. [2] First semester. [3] Excl. restaurants. [4] Excl. communications.

Notes explicatives: voir p. 879.

[1] Dernière semaine d'août de chaque année. [2] Premier semestre. [3] Excl. restaurants. [4] Non compris les communications.

Notas explicativas: véase p. 882.

[1] Ultima semana de agosto de cada año. [2] Primer semestre. [3] Excl. restaurantes. [4] Excl. las comunicaciones.

	1999	2000	2001	2002	2003	2004	2005	2006	2007	2008

Canada (DA) [1] [2]   **Wage earners - Ouvriers - Obreros**   E.G./h. - Dollar

Total men and women - Total hommes et femmes - Total hombres y mujeres
ISIC 3 - CITI 3 - CIIU 3

	1999	2000	2001	2002	2003	2004	2005	2006	2007	2008
Total	16.04	16.48	16.34	16.65	17.17	17.69	18.30	18.76	19.48	20.16
C-Q	16.01	16.45	16.28	16.61	17.14	17.65	18.27	18.74	19.47	20.15
A [3]	19.93	20.61	25.36	22.30	22.71	23.11	22.37	22.34	21.37	21.87
C	25.51	24.90	24.65	24.58	25.91	25.95	28.02	29.23	31.63	31.52
D	17.79	18.26	18.36	18.59	19.36	19.99	20.53	20.50	21.58	21.95
E	24.88	25.76	29.14	30.82	32.80	32.58	33.00	33.61	34.77	34.51
F	20.51	21.31	20.76	22.02	22.26	22.31	23.11	23.75	24.63	26.49
G	13.08	13.92	12.71	12.85	13.49	13.78	14.25	14.94	15.07	15.51
H	8.78	9.22	9.29	9.65	9.83	10.16	10.48	10.64	11.24	11.89
I	18.49	18.50	18.45	18.88	20.23	20.36	21.62	21.70	23.34	22.46
I3 0B	19.93	20.61	21.02	21.70	22.19	23.21	22.86	23.00	22.20	
J	15.66	16.82	16.83	15.89	17.42	17.11	18.16	20.17	20.95	22.48
K	14.62	15.26	14.49	14.56	14.62	15.29	16.11	16.42	16.91	18.48
L	16.24	15.73	17.63	19.07	19.23	19.47	19.09	20.78	22.89	23.12
M	11.82	12.32	15.82	15.81	15.39	15.54	14.87	16.52	18.90	18.03
N	18.46	18.84	19.24	19.75	20.02	21.40	22.13	22.70	23.41	24.03
O	12.57	13.20	12.97	12.77	13.24	13.08	14.29	14.48	15.52	16.86

Canada (DA) [2]   **Employees - Salariés - Asalariados**   E.G./w.s. - Dollar

Total men and women - Total hommes et femmes - Total hombres y mujeres
ISIC 3 - CITI 3 - CIIU 3

	1999	2000	2001	2002	2003	2004	2005	2006	2007	2008
Total	640.47	655.55	656.74	672.68	690.79	709.41	737.29	755.50	788.17	810.45
C-Q	639.59	654.57	655.80	671.89	690.01	708.53	736.63	754.89	787.71	810.04
A [3]	773.42	810.15	815.52	809.81	847.06	894.01	883.89	902.28	907.41	935.84
C	1 101.04	1 137.37	1 152.59	1 138.06	1 219.00	1 278.11	1 296.35	1 325.73	1 437.44	1 527.98
D	780.44	794.81	796.69	818.64	837.36	860.63	895.40	904.66	939.63	947.38
E	1 018.23	1 029.28	1 159.26	1 236.15	1 275.34	1 261.08	1 298.32	1 350.66	1 421.49	1 424.73
F	782.63	808.06	790.11	819.64	847.87	846.38	877.34	900.32	961.16	1 014.51
G	532.34	538.48	526.35	526.32	540.97	551.86	573.31	591.18	607.11	621.49
H	259.54	273.30	265.85	279.33	277.00	287.18	288.45	299.73	318.40	331.11
I	739.47	747.57	756.51	779.75	805.92	843.60	859.48	858.33	896.61	909.57
J	830.21	844.28	833.71	866.92	885.43	905.63	933.86	966.38	1 010.76	1 014.68
K	664.53	697.55	710.06	725.50	727.25	732.99	777.23	798.78	847.53	878.31
L	761.05	781.15	782.01	844.53	867.71	894.04	925.45	951.03	1 007.53	1 040.51
M	664.74	673.88	685.38	700.62	727.02	750.52	779.60	808.15	834.62	862.64
N	544.79	562.39	568.41	577.69	609.87	635.03	667.40	687.72	705.55	743.94
O	448.10	459.28	478.33	487.44	505.03	527.13	551.07	557.80	582.79	605.69

Colombia (BA) [4] [5] [6]   **Employees - Salariés - Asalariados**   E.G./m. - Peso

Total men and women - Total hommes et femmes - Total hombres y mujeres
ISIC 3 - CITI 3 - CIIU 3

	1999	2000	2001	2002	2003	2004	2005	2006	2007	2008
Total	.	.	.	352 448	410 396	624 656	677 332	681 543	657 756	.
C-Q	.	.	.	558 119	558 523	645 673	723 314	721 353	885 833	.
A	.	.	.	154 854	228 835	435 499	263 495	323 247	323 267	.
C	.	.	.	843 623	393 245	554 518	804 373	602 954	1 060 428	.
D	.	.	.	353 590	442 510	468 406	506 020	608 137	694 244	.
E	.	.	.	680 694	752 123	807 008	1 022 357	766 487	1 264 793	.
F	.	.	.	325 269	369 112	453 493	439 672	510 135	545 936	.
G	.	.	.	294 082	367 401	424 241	444 668	491 831	539 798	.
I	.	.	.	423 901	490 871	518 390	510 846	570 420	653 935	.
J	.	.	.	866 114	1 030 009	1 225 920	1 307 901	1 195 873	1 264 278	.
K	.	.	.	753 892	678 335	762 579	823 728	965 133	1 049 838	.
O	.	.	.	481 910	503 101	596 502	650 261	781 209	899 250	.
X	.	.	.	545 841	254 530	.	339 204	477 038	629 403	.

Men - Hommes - Hombres
ISIC 3 - CITI 3 - CIIU 3

	1999	2000	2001	2002	2003	2004	2005	2006	2007	2008
Total	.	.	.	377 576	439 929	705 816	767 999	777 056	899 250	.
C-Q	.	.	.	619 704	639 067	733 908	822 922	826 674	992 440	.
A	.	.	.	166 964	242 236	452 986	273 686	330 493	321 007	.
C	.	.	.	911 873	474 735	692 837	806 749	630 027	993 928	.
D	.	.	.	457 189	531 791	557 571	605 537	707 408	847 898	.
E	.	.	.	660 417	723 920	875 223	1 025 210	756 146	1 362 844	.
F	.	.	.	315 758	360 653	445 988	432 051	496 899	526 053	.
G	.	.	.	356 051	441 443	496 942	535 929	570 411	647 511	.
I	.	.	.	426 502	472 528	508 742	516 362	591 230	672 639	.
J	.	.	.	866 536	1 239 040	1 350 620	1 640 523	1 498 191	1 389 348	.
K	.	.	.	908 312	779 307	828 090	885 783	1 033 280	1 338 518	.
O	.	.	.	674 704	728 188	849 159	958 155	1 156 478	1 153 220	.
X	.	.	.	366 407	328 064	.	197 872	452 948	690 402	.

Explanatory notes: see p. 877.   Notes explicatives: voir p. 879.   Notas explicativas: véase p. 882.

[1] Employees paid by the hour. [2] Incl. overtime. [3] Excl. agriculture and hunting. [4] Excl. armed forces. [5] Persons aged 10 years and over. [6] Fourth quarter.

[1] Salariés rémunérés à l'heure. [2] Y compris les heures supplémentaires. [3] Non compris l'agriculture et la chasse. [4] Non compris les forces armées. [5] Personnes âgées de 10 ans et plus. [6] Quatrième trimestre.

[1] Asalariados remunerados por hora. [2] Incl. las horas extraordinarias. [3] Excl. agricultura y caza. [4] Excl. las fuerzas armadas. [5] Personas de 10 años y más. [6] Cuarto trimestre.

	1999	2000	2001	2002	2003	2004	2005	2006	2007	2008

Colombia (BA) [1] [2] [3]

Employees - Salariés - Asalariados E.G./m. - Peso

Women - Femmes - Mujeres
ISIC 3 - CITI 3 - CIIU 3

	1999	2000	2001	2002	2003	2004	2005	2006	2007	2008
Total	.	.	.	317 784	369 430	531 403	622 050	610 361	608 984	
C-Q				513 265	510 373	556 632	669 534	649 612	842 561	
A				91 094	134 663	304 338	194 692	257 096	338 950	
C				533 799	172 383	275 935	787 282	411 329	1 493 385	
D				258 415	347 588	365 782	394 964	473 334	505 713	
E				801 363	859 504	532 297	1 010 184	805 431	894 490	
F				564 485	521 570	625 386	681 662	878 966	1 038 930	
G				226 606	283 870	341 957	345 484	402 215	419 708	
I				406 104	598 474	574 609	480 981	479 447	583 934	
J				865 749	845 712	1 140 961	1 060 548	919 739	1 164 655	
K				558 628	544 099	655 979	734 662	851 768	702 165	
O				404 242	420 160	496 782	530 037	624 282	780 068	
X				792 373			723 000	514 152	419 787	

Costa Rica (BA) [4]

Employees - Salariés - Asalariados E.G./h. - Colón

Total men and women - Total hommes et femmes - Total hombres y mujeres
ISIC 3 - CITI 3 - CIIU 3

	1999	2000	2001	2002	2003	2004	2005	2006	2007	2008
Total	.	.	667.2	730.3	793.0	862.0	943.9	1 017.3	1 221.6	1 336.3
A-B			354.3	410.2	430.0	513.3	540.3	604.6	686.5	778.3
C-Q			719.5	781.8	851.1	914.9	1 007.4	1 074.5	1 294.6	1 413.6
A			353.0	402.6	429.0	514.3	537.5	607.7	683.8	784.7
B			410.0	647.3	460.7	481.8	634.4	532.3	753.0	596.5
C			454.8	652.7	598.8	716.9	804.9	816.7	869.7	1 042.2
D			617.2	700.8	758.8	768.5	953.0	993.3	1 210.2	1 272.1
E			929.0	1 084.6	1 151.2	1 203.8	1 428.1	1 302.3	1 894.9	2 063.2
F			537.0	511.5	593.2	598.5	668.7	698.3	870.0	964.7
G			576.6	658.0	690.8	739.0	778.5	878.4	1 037.7	1 145.6
H			517.3	490.1	569.9	607.8	700.9	728.3	920.6	940.9
I			717.2	740.4	792.6	898.0	946.6	1 092.2	1 327.6	1 449.4
J			1 165.6	1 360.3	1 374.1	1 574.4	1 886.2	2 123.7	2 346.1	2 380.1
K			794.6	813.3	757.2	925.2	1 024.2	949.1	1 462.4	1 370.4
L			1 032.4	1 069.4	1 185.8	1 276.1	1 509.6	1 813.9	1 959.8	2 179.5
M			1 103.4	1 218.9	1 320.2	1 446.7	1 512.9	1 524.6	1 912.3	2 118.3
N			987.2	1 121.4	1 408.8	1 406.3	1 330.2	1 633.4	1 742.1	2 114.3
O			824.5	830.9	1 048.2	1 003.0	1 178.2	1 077.3	1 230.3	1 444.3
P			366.5	373.3	395.6	410.6	475.3	429.7	606.0	557.5
Q			1 421.3	1 323.5	1 337.9	1 793.9	2 799.6	2 829.9	3 276.3	3 859.3
X								1 241.5	1 214.9	919.2

Men - Hommes - Hombres
ISIC 3 - CITI 3 - CIIU 3

	1999	2000	2001	2002	2003	2004	2005	2006	2007	2008
Total	.	.	646.6	724.9	771.1	851.6	952.2	1 009.8	1 236.5	1 336.9
A-B			350.6	413.0	430.5	514.4	544.2	602.0	690.1	790.8
C-Q			722.5	800.7	852.6	927.3	1 047.4	1 088.3	1 344.3	1 440.6
A			349.1	404.6	429.4	515.3	541.6	605.8	687.6	798.8
B			414.0	657.8	461.4	484.6	628.8	525.9	746.3	595.0
C			462.9	671.2	583.6	735.9	823.6	830.3	898.4	1 075.3
D			626.8	742.3	780.2	795.8	1 006.1	1 028.5	1 325.5	1 345.6
E			935.7	1 053.6	1 183.0	1 138.8	1 477.8	1 133.3	1 658.9	1 943.8
F			509.9	505.9	592.4	597.0	664.9	691.7	857.5	959.3
G			595.9	709.0	715.8	790.0	809.0	907.2	1 092.8	1 215.9
H			551.2	591.6	638.1	630.7	803.7	813.8	1 059.8	1 006.1
I			702.3	728.6	761.1	861.9	900.1	1 040.1	1 303.9	1 438.9
J			1 281.2	1 410.9	1 509.7	1 742.5	2 178.7	2 339.3	2 500.6	2 686.7
K			715.7	785.2	703.1	899.0	1 005.1	889.6	1 460.7	1 390.3
L			999.4	1 034.3	1 134.5	1 262.1	1 454.3	1 803.4	1 940.5	2 081.8
M			1 114.7	1 332.6	1 365.3	1 585.3	1 580.3	1 529.1	2 215.9	2 340.8
N			1 212.6	1 272.4	1 541.2	1 817.5	1 563.6	1 898.3	1 889.4	2 371.5
O			887.0	886.9	1 094.1	963.2	1 308.8	1 077.6	1 309.6	1 621.8
P			344.8	413.9	500.9	470.5	563.6	679.9	718.9	726.4
Q			1 438.2	1 437.9	1 057.9	1 822.9	5 847.4	3 733.5	3 850.4	3 400.6
X								1 312.8	1 384.0	842.2

Explanatory notes: see p. 877.

[1] Excl. armed forces. [2] Persons aged 10 years and over. [3] Fourth quarter. [4] Main occupation; July of each year.

Notes explicatives: voir p. 879.

[1] Non compris les forces armées. [2] Personnes âgées de 10 ans et plus. [3] Quatrième trimestre. [4] Occupation principale; juillet de chaque année.

Notas explicativas: véase p. 882.

[1] Excl. las fuerzas armadas. [2] Personas de 10 años y más. [3] Cuarto trimestre. [4] Ocupación principal; julio de cada año.

	1999	2000	2001	2002	2003	2004	2005	2006	2007	2008

Costa Rica (BA) [1] — Employees - Salariés - Asalariados — E.G./h. - Colón

Women - Femmes - Mujeres
ISIC 3 - CITI 3 - CIIU 3

	1999	2000	2001	2002	2003	2004	2005	2006	2007	2008
Total	.	.	703.4	739.9	832.5	881.4	929.4	1 031.7	1 197.4	1 335.3
A-B	.	.	390.6	385.4	426.0	502.8	510.1	622.3	666.9	703.0
C-Q	.	.	715.1	753.9	848.7	895.1	948.0	1 051.0	1 124.1	1 368.9
A	.	.	391.3	385.5	425.9	504.5	506.1	620.5	663.5	703.0
B	.	.	328.7	377.7	430.1	461.5	696.1	1 268.9	833.3	686.8
C	.	.	418.6	466.5	683.0	666.1	750.7	712.5	700.9	853.3
D	.	.	597.3	594.4	703.6	688.6	793.6	890.3	923.4	1 091.4
E	.	.	901.1	1 177.1	989.3	1 568.9	1 135.3	2 008.0	2 721.6	2 602.5
F	.	.	1 024.0	742.4	656.9	661.2	811.3	1 041.0	1 208.7	1 153.6
G	.	.	533.9	548.8	635.1	634.7	718.0	814.7	930.8	995.8
H	.	.	428.7	408.1	511.5	586.9	616.1	649.6	821.6	888.5
I	.	.	790.2	814.3	925.0	1 078.5	1 174.0	1 415.2	1 428.4	1 498.1
J	.	.	980.3	1 277.8	1 160.9	1 236.6	1 389.3	1 764.8	2 183.1	2 071.9
K	.	.	950.6	870.2	884.1	988.2	1 066.3	1 087.4	1 465.7	1 329.5
L	.	.	1 089.6	1 120.8	1 269.9	1 296.9	1 613.3	1 835.2	1 990.8	2 353.5
M	.	.	1 098.9	1 176.6	1 302.4	1 392.6	1 485.6	1 522.6	1 777.3	2 030.9
N	.	.	856.0	1 030.4	1 330.3	1 162.0	1 187.4	1 472.0	1 662.5	1 974.5
O	.	.	728.1	727.2	965.0	1 060.5	969.0	1 076.8	1 129.3	1 088.6
P	.	.	368.0	370.4	386.9	404.6	469.0	404.0	594.4	543.5
Q	.	.	1 389.8	1 074.7	1 949.6	1 686.4	1 636.8	2 198.4	.	.
X	.	.	.	.	.	.	.	1 133.7	960.7	1 046.2

Costa Rica (BA) [1] — Total employment - Emploi total - Empleo total — E.G./m. - Colón

Total men and women - Total hommes et femmes - Total hombres y mujeres
ISIC 3 - CITI 3 - CIIU 3

	1999	2000	2001	2002	2003	2004	2005	2006	2007	2008
Total	95 235	106 272	132 037	.	.	166 804	385 737	.	.	576 699
A-B	63 670	67 356	69 044	.	.	104 127	104 837	.	.	104 060
C-Q	102 437	114 871	142 611	.	.	176 143	410 211	.	.	610 069
A	63 612	66 649	67 875	.	.	103 729	103 933	.	.	103 660
B	66 574	98 345	115 054	.	.	116 991	133 939	.	.	116 991
C	95 007	79 978	94 719	.	.	.	340 120	.	.	451 267
D	97 775	108 777	128 207	.	.	.	393 518	.	.	549 285
E	140 227	144 971	205 401	.	.	.	600 681	.	.	893 365
F	86 358	98 250	118 724	.	.	.	280 787	.	.	415 040
G	94 139	105 136	119 521	.	.	.	323 876	.	.	494 827
H	79 413	87 728	101 638	.	.	.	282 022	.	.	405 696
I	112 454	130 199	157 507	.	.	.	374 279	.	.	626 393
J	200 421	196 919	241 912	.	.	.	818 375	.	.	1 028 839
K	116 691	170 473	148 988	.	.	.	393 553	.	.	591 402
L	.	.	210 018	.	.	.	622 638	.	.	939 842
M	144 789	154 408	187 571	.	.	.	616 694	.	.	917 237
N	135 259	149 809	227 552	.	.	.	558 009	.	.	915 482
O	117 193	130 204	133 364	.	.	.	451 285	.	.	619 193
P	31 446	37 645	44 240	.	.	.	157 868	.	.	239 346
Q	182 982	192 153	299 037	.	.	.	.	.	.	1 671 059
X	81 340	119 689	105 131	.	.	.	355 693	.	.	382 168

Men - Hommes - Hombres
ISIC 3 - CITI 3 - CIIU 3

	1999	2000	2001	2002	2003	2004	2005	2006	2007	2008
Total	100 530	111 081	137 032	.	.	172 119	385 754	.	.	577 400
A-B	63 854	68 432	69 724	.	.	105 238	106 681	.	.	105 163
C-Q	113 135	125 265	154 364	.	.	186 878	419 519	.	.	622 140
A	63 803	67 638	68 412	.	.	104 788	105 715	.	.	104 711
B	66 229	101 110	118 662	.	.	120 273	136 593	.	.	120 273
C	100 847	82 244	106 251	.	.	164 302	344 799	.	.	465 626
D	106 594	115 642	135 707	.	.	173 054	410 986	.	.	580 373
E	141 648	148 973	203 659	.	.	234 278	617 856	.	.	841 684
F	85 639	98 214	115 983	.	.	130 974	279 822	.	.	412 639
G	100 093	115 576	126 884	.	.	161 398	335 112	.	.	526 493
H	95 139	97 171	119 882	.	.	136 263	318 109	.	.	434 659
I	114 293	129 302	158 394	.	.	186 259	350 981	.	.	621 599
J	223 838	211 326	270 957	.	.	358 908	938 950	.	.	1 159 447
K	109 624	177 521	146 064	.	.	175 174	387 799	.	.	600 013
L	.	.	210 432	.	.	254 822	589 412	.	.	898 186
M	168 028	176 698	215 497	.	.	253 857	609 858	.	.	1 013 565
N	166 286	164 063	294 026	.	.	275 589	642 194	.	.	1 026 863
O	112 217	130 486	153 954	.	.	177 752	484 091	.	.	702 237
P	43 834	57 863	67 294	.	.	78 834	194 591	.	.	314 546
Q	194 382	196 602	311 338	.	.	354 902	.	.	.	1 472 439
X	82 034	131 541	120 741	.	.	240 882	384 205	.	.	374 601

Explanatory notes: see p. 877.   Notes explicatives: voir p. 879.   Notas explicativas: véase p. 882.

[1] Main occupation; July of each year.   [1] Occupation principale; juillet de chaque année.   [1] Ocupación principal; julio de cada año.

	1999	2000	2001	2002	2003	2004	2005	2006	2007	2008

Costa Rica (BA) [1]   Total employment - Emploi total - Empleo total   E.G./m. - Colón

Women - Femmes - Mujeres
ISIC 3 - CITI 3 - CIIU 3

	1999	2000	2001	2002	2003	2004	2005	2006	2007	2008
Total	84 934	97 042	123 233	.	.	156 834	385 702	.	.	575 389
A-B	61 813	56 958	62 267			93 200	90 431			93 200
C-Q	86 141	99 176	125 521			159 145	393 797			590 068
A	61 721	57 241	62 597			93 197	90 149			93 197
B	85 648	24 148	34 163			93 274	103 400			93 274
C	53 474	66 147	43 506			144 255	323 528			369 467
D	77 969	93 773	112 596			135 471	335 824			472 590
E	129 795	119 321	212 707			312 666	496 741			1 126 865
F	134 520	99 349	168 510			137 614	326 812			499 516
G	82 878	86 650	103 243			121 288	299 569			427 891
H	65 482	79 034	82 932			105 324	249 233			382 506
I	100 705	135 087	153 194			205 362	508 604			648 687
J	160 484	173 176	195 350			242 101	599 907			897 139
K	136 835	162 593	154 814			170 992	432 268			573 711
L			209 296			246 605	691 281			1 013 865
M	134 420	144 462	176 319			226 963	619 572			879 380
N	109 685	138 349	189 361			234 723	501 509			854 969
O	130 704	129 381	101 635			157 730	395 241			457 582
P	30 674	36 558	42 522			54 511	154 265			233 167
Q	159 782	170 924	276 099			322 433	.			1 891 770
X	79 097	91 461	81 379			130 000	223 109			393 407

Cuba (FD) [2]   Employees - Salariés - Asalariados   E.G./m. - Peso

Total men and women - Total hommes et femmes - Total hombres y mujeres
ISIC 2 - CITI 2 - CIIU 2

	1999	2000	2001	2002	2003	2004	2005	2006	2007	2008
1	212	224 [3]	240	254	276	297	332	387	420	444
2	254	265 [3]	272	308	315	353	407	540	544	562
3	225	242 [3]	255	263	275	290	338	404	433	430
4	230	244 [3]	269	319	314	339	398	496	508	517
5	262	286 [3]	304	322	339	349	400	478	497	522
6	180	189 [3]	204	213	225	230	280	334	353	365
7	212	232 [3]	264	259	280	295	331	406	418	427
8	234	260 [3]	277	296	317	332	402	477	493	445
9	233	249 [3]	259	267	276	285	331	378	398	385

Chile (DA) [4]   Employees - Salariés - Asalariados   E.G./m. - Peso

Total men and women - Total hommes et femmes - Total hombres y mujeres
ISIC 2 - CITI 2 - CIIU 2 [5]   ISIC 3 - CITI 3 - CIIU 3 [5]

ISIC2	1999	2000	2001	2002	2003	2004	2005	2006	2007	2008	ISIC3
2-9	226 049	237 283	246 980	256 258	264 508	273 715	276 882	295 257	314 221	347 263	C-Q
2	428 748	450 706	473 035	478 088	509 695	569 769	542 954		870 512	965 547	C
3	203 540	208 257	213 394	218 740	221 860	229 575	242 160	300 948	315 408	351 684	D
4	466 682	470 875	489 617	516 025	542 745	598 926	558 639	626 603	646 444	714 028	E
5	148 640	161 155	166 612	168 130	161 580	161 662	156 569	269 536	284 906	324 152	F
6	178 439	182 398	189 516	193 531	198 078	196 217	198 618	258 354	284 467	316 799	G
7	214 181	238 671	245 192	249 767	263 142	270 437	270 735	187 058	188 469	202 916	H
8	419 402	440 821	464 145	491 970	507 580	510 268	521 617	296 486	318 341	350 221	I
9	245 640	257 644	272 889	293 652	305 296	318 267	325 303	592 288	591 879	634 728	J
								240 041	258 813	275 122	K
								452 831	501 860	557 568	L
								383 675	390 481	434 096	M
								308 164	337 848	366 819	N
								294 318	323 550	359 010	O

República Dominicana (BA)   Employees - Salariés - Asalariados   E.G./h. - Peso

Total men and women - Total hommes et femmes - Total hombres y mujeres
ISIC 3 - CITI 3 - CIIU 3

	1999	2000	2001	2002	2003	2004	2005	2006	2007	2008
Total	27.5	29.6	31.3	31.3	37.7	41.7				
A [6]	20.8	.	.	.	.	.				
C	73.3	39.1	44.4	48.0	41.5	26.1				
D	27.1	24.1	28.2	29.4	32.7	50.8				
E	30.6	33.3	34.7	34.9	51.4	39.4				
F	27.1	36.0	38.6	38.6	46.2	73.4				
G	27.6	29.8	31.8	34.0	36.7	51.6				
H	31.4	32.1	30.5	29.9	34.5	41.5				
I [7]	26.4	33.1	34.7	32.6	37.0	35.0				
J	46.9	53.4	53.4	48.3	69.0	48.2				
K	35.6	36.0	34.9	35.8	44.4	69.1				
L	29.1	28.6	37.2	36.8	44.6	45.5				

Explanatory notes: see p. 877.   Notes explicatives: voir p. 879.   Notas explicativas: véase p. 882.

[1] Main occupation; July of each year. [2] State sector (civilian). [3] Incl. employment-related allowances received from the State. [4] Incl. family allowances and the value of payments in kind. [5] April of each year. [6] Excl. hunting and forestry. [7] Excl. storage.

[1] Occupation principale; juillet de chaque année. [2] Secteur d'Etat (civils). [3] Y compris les allocations en espèces liées à l'emploi et reçues de l'Etat. [4] Y compris les allocations familiales et la valeur des paiements en nature. [5] Avril de chaque année. [6] Non compris la chasse et la sylviculture. [7] Non compris les entrepôts.

[1] Ocupación principal; julio de cada año. [2] Sector de Estado (civil). [3] Incl. las prestaciones monetarias relacionadas con el empleo y pagadas por el Estado. [4] Incl. las asignaciones familiares y el valor de los pagos en especie. [5] Abril de cada año. [6] Excl. caza y silvicultura. [7] Excl. almacenaje.

WAGES — SALAIRES — SALARIOS

By economic activity — Par activité économique — Por actividad económica

	1999	2000	2001	2002	2003	2004	2005	2006	2007	2008

El Salvador (BA) — Employees - Salariés - Asalariados — E.G./m. - US dollar

Total men and women - Total hommes et femmes - Total hombres y mujeres
ISIC 3 - CITI 3 - CIIU 3

	1999	2000	2001	2002	2003	2004	2005	2006	2007	2008
Total	1 969.35	2 073.25	2 108.02	243.71	232.00	234.01	246.70	247.40	.	.
A	801.45	822.44	770.78	93.46	92.78	102.00	.	.	.	.
B	1 490.44	1 604.48	2 050.70	188.87	166.04	188.00	.	.	.	.
C	1 311.85	2 736.29	1 498.37	160.69	366.09	216.90	225.00	122.30	.	.
D	1 746.61	1 789.97	1 750.43	208.70	209.56	211.34	229.00	235.10	.	.
E	3 412.92	3 736.09	4 004.74	394.59	366.36	430.16	392.00	534.50	.	.
F	1 911.51	2 042.43	2 125.04	235.24	230.19	221.09	227.50	227.30	.	.
H	2 032.24	2 145.45	2 139.20	247.33	232.24	239.71	241.70	251.70	.	.
I	2 710.71	3 054.53	3 123.76	313.96	349.34	351.89	336.80	322.30	.	.
J	3 266.81	3 081.67	3 779.60	365.40	334.67	301.45	359.30	382.10	.	.
L	3 373.63	3 601.05	3 564.59	399.85	403.18	433.05	429.90	439.20	.	.
M	3 121.90	3 147.99	3 304.95	484.58	377.97	376.05	394.70	442.90	.	.
O	2 267.36	2 126.11	2 269.46	241.32	244.76	250.78	260.90	312.10	.	.
P	653.67	732.38	716.75	82.69	89.22	95.18	109.00	126.20	.	.
Q	3 718.18	6 218.33	3 649.07	484.65	1 335.69	322.46			.	.

Men - Hommes - Hombres
ISIC 3 - CITI 3 - CIIU 3

	1999	2000	2001	2002	2003	2004	2005	2006	2007	2008
Total	2 178.30	2 287.29	2 349.74	277.58	258.31	255.12	270.60	260.20	.	.
A	806.27	828.93	773.14	92.96	93.49	101.80	.	.	.	.
B	1 532.64	1 617.61	2 189.33	196.93	172.10	194.10	.	.	.	.
C	1 311.85	2 736.29	1 498.37	157.52	381.45	216.89	225.90	222.00	.	.
D	2 157.83	2 241.07	2 117.37	253.79	249.58	261.75	280.60	284.80	.	.
E	3 446.02	3 698.95	4 091.57	416.52	355.93	431.08	381.00	546.90	.	.
F	1 857.69	2 026.03	2 044.31	227.97	226.59	218.57	227.60	223.10	.	.
H	2 560.21	2 586.76	2 795.22	329.32	295.42	286.34	296.90	288.40	.	.
I	2 693.18	3 034.73	3 039.67	305.00	342.35	348.98	332.90	315.20	.	.
J	3 098.04	2 988.88	3 836.92	368.64	332.30	283.78	357.70	377.40	.	.
L	3 164.72	3 364.50	3 354.99	386.53	394.21	407.40	417.00	401.80	.	.
M	3 272.38	3 150.81	3 494.30	644.22	382.74	413.77	400.40	465.10	.	.
O	2 988.75	2 644.54	2 587.32	299.63	288.70	301.92	325.10	452.60	.	.
P	995.74	1 217.84	1 022.52	118.96	121.26	138.95	160.20	218.20	.	.
Q	3 012.12	6 764.27	2 302.81	576.39	1 285.86	342.91			.	.

Women - Femmes - Mujeres
ISIC 3 - CITI 3 - CIIU 3

	1999	2000	2001	2002	2003	2004	2005	2006	2007	2008
Total	1 706.12	1 809.79	1 803.58	204.59	199.90	206.75	217.30	230.30	.	.
A	765.41	756.39	739.05	101.15	86.30	104.60	.	.	.	.
B	921.69	1 349.82	667.27	69.47	91.09	139.10	.	.	.	.
C				297.00	149.00	217.00	173.00	.	.	.
D	1 337.08	1 370.44	1 370.53	167.69	171.23	162.54	178.10	181.30	.	.
E	2 804.34	4 657.12	1 603.94	244.68	427.94	419.26	456.70	436.30	.	.
F	3 349.62	3 276.87	5 390.33	498.60	432.43	328.12	222.20	368.20	.	.
H	1 670.09	1 837.80	1 699.52	194.69	191.13	207.52	202.50	227.80	.	.
I	2 924.63	3 305.30	3 925.19	405.43	420.90	377.05	369.40	409.20	.	.
J	3 545.16	3 284.11	3 679.64	359.36	339.86	350.74	362.50	390.90	.	.
L	3 929.34	4 142.72	4 132.31	431.69	428.04	512.43	460.80	537.50	.	.
M	3 040.14	3 146.35	3 191.91	387.09	375.12	355.99	392.20	431.00	.	.
N					.				.	.
O	1 845.65	1 891.19	2 048.26	208.13	215.92	221.22	224.00	244.10	.	.
P	618.61	697.89	689.94	78.99	85.13	90.92	103.50	110.60	.	.
Q	4 247.49	3 927.40	9 724.22	352.59	1 387.60	275.00			.	.

El Salvador (DA) [2] — Wage earners - Ouvriers - Obreros — E.G./h. - US dollar

Total men and women - Total hommes et femmes - Total hombres y mujeres
ISIC 2 - CITI 2 - CIIU 2

	1999	2000	2001	2002	2003	2004	2005	2006	2007	2008	ISIC 3 - CITI 3 - CIIU 3
3	10.68	10.09	.	1.21	1.25	1.43	1.45	1.23	1.28	1.58	D
6	10.43	10.62	9.22	1.59	1.35	1.39	1.34	1.27	1.29	1.69	G-H

Men - Hommes - Hombres
ISIC 2 - CITI 2 - CIIU 2

	1999	2000	2001	2002	2003	2004	2005	2006	2007	2008	ISIC 3 - CITI 3 - CIIU 3
1	2.70	2.70	2.70	0.31	0.31	0.31	0.31	0.34	0.38	0.41	A
3	12.05	11.37	10.34	1.33	1.47	1.70	1.52	1.36	1.30	1.67	D
6	11.37	11.36	10.16	1.89	1.43	1.55	1.44	1.38	1.36	1.78	G-H

Women - Femmes - Mujeres
ISIC 2 - CITI 2 - CIIU 2

	1999	2000	2001	2002	2003	2004	2005	2006	2007	2008	ISIC 3 - CITI 3 - CIIU 3
1	2.70	2.70	2.70	0.31	0.31	0.31	0.31	0.34	0.38	0.41	A
3	9.20	9.00	9.53	.	1.23	1.20	1.23	1.13	1.11	1.40	D
6	9.31	9.56	9.18	1.07	1.27	1.11	1.20	1.14	1.18	1.58	G-H

Explanatory notes: see p. 877.
[1] Prior to 2002: colones; 8.75 colones=1 US dollar. [2] Urban areas.

Notes explicatives: voir p. 879.
[1] Avant 2002: colones; 8.75 colones=1 dollar EU. [2] Régions urbaines.

Notas explicativas: véase p. 882.
[1] Antes de 2002: colones; 8.75 colones=1 dólar EU. [2] Areas urbanas.

5A WAGES — SALAIRES — SALARIOS

By economic activity — Par activité économique — Por actividad económica

	1999	2000	2001	2002	2003	2004	2005	2006	2007	2008
Guatemala (FA)					Employees - Salariés - Asalariados					E.G./m. - Quetzal

Total men and women - Total hommes et femmes - Total hombres y mujeres
ISIC 2 - CITI 2 - CIIU 2

	1999	2000	2001	2002	2003	2004	2005	2006	2007	2008
Total	1 567.78	1 724.80	1 859.80	1 992.78	2 113.91	2 223.23	2 329.16	2 454.24	2 564.12	2 677.93
2-9	1 775.00	1 925.88						3 036.30		
1	770.72	845.53	968.45	1 074.88	1 149.71	1 175.86	1 309.28	1 406.12	1 469.79	1 551.99
2	2 670.03	3 044.07	2 978.73	3 552.63	3 589.85	3 689.53	3 997.56	4 556.15	4 601.60	4 843.00
3	1 602.25	1 655.25	1 732.27	1 837.32	1 911.44	2 100.06	2 199.65	2 482.09	2 579.44	2 737.21
4	2 394.08	2 789.15	3 157.75	3 371.77	3 907.92	4 281.02	4 361.30	4 659.28	5 024.78	5 327.62
5	1 357.90	1 346.64	1 436.87	1 390.43	1 533.48	1 556.69	1 698.35	1 864.55	1 942.63	2 053.94
6	1 948.20	2 063.84	2 161.67	2 258.46	2 407.47	2 505.09	2 632.97	2 747.64	2 871.48	2 991.87
7	2 106.13	2 382.91	2 430.78	2 536.61	2 725.39	2 765.46	2 985.59	3 188.19	3 309.26	3 465.59
8 [1]										
9 [2]	1 763.27	1 976.13	2 105.56	2 255.62	2 386.57	2 471.51	2 537.02	2 574.87	2 681.80	2 760.70

Guyana (DA) [3]					Employees - Salariés - Asalariados					E.G./m. - Dollar

Total men and women - Total hommes et femmes - Total hombres y mujeres
ISIC 3 - CITI 3 - CIIU 3

	1999	2000	2001	2002	2003	2004	2005	2006	2007	2008
Total					53 910	73 922		62 624	77 750	
C						128 708		81 805	116 951	
D					29 678	47 800		55 615	47 150	
E								66 545	147 740	
F					70 600			67 686	60 345	
G									36 729	
H					22 131	46 788		30 000	36 817	
I								62 153	69 567	
J					71 040	106 489		72 210	103 327	
L					76 105	39 828		72 596	87 129	
M								46 007	71 743	

México (BA) [4][5]					Employees - Salariés - Asalariados					E.G./m. - Nuevo peso

Total men and women - Total hommes et femmes - Total hombres y mujeres
ISIC 3 - CITI 3 - CIIU 3

	1999	2000	2001	2002	2003	2004	2005	2006	2007	2008
Total	2 384.9	2 938.5	3 320.1	3 553.5	3 796.7	3 969.7	4 173.8	4 425.9	4 716.3	4 800.9
A-B	1 249.0	1 449.3	1 720.4	1 798.1	1 990.0	2 086.4	2 271.0	2 379.9	2 522.9	2 690.9
C-Q	2 520.4	3 101.3	3 488.2	3 736.3	3 972.0	4 147.7	4 346.2	4 617.6	4 898.3	4 979.5
A	1 218.9	1 411.4	1 686.2	1 778.2	1 953.5	2 066.8	2 229.9	2 342.8	2 494.1	2 661.0
B	2 487.7	2 912.6	3 114.5	2 956.8	3 575.5	2 959.4	3 899.7	4 013.5	4 157.0	4 379.1
C	6 195.2	6 254.7	7 317.2	7 249.6	8 453.3	6 919.4	8 287.8	9 509.1	10 010.3	10 580.4
D	2 388.0	2 930.5	3 393.7	3 551.5	3 752.6	3 887.4	4 140.3	4 422.6	4 689.2	4 679.3
E	3 166.1	4 224.5	4 591.6	5 375.9	5 498.5	6 235.4	5 951.4	6 689.0	7 391.0	7 151.7
F	1 942.8	2 494.7	3 057.7	3 388.3	3 499.0	3 754.2	3 972.2	4 278.1	4 476.8	4 750.5
G	2 023.8	2 538.4	2 912.3	3 134.9	3 363.9	3 427.8	3 726.7	3 971.1	4 154.0	4 236.4
H	2 086.2	2 166.9	2 470.3	2 830.4	2 905.8	3 071.2	3 330.9	3 519.4	3 760.6	3 893.2
I	3 076.0	3 694.6	4 027.2	4 146.8	4 484.8	4 678.5	4 795.9	5 151.9	5 647.3	5 854.9
J	5 201.9	6 597.4	7 570.9	7 087.1	7 099.4	7 689.7	7 773.7	8 087.7	8 876.9	8 976.4
K	2 662.6	3 874.9	4 175.4	4 526.8	4 721.3	5 011.0	4 658.1	5 039.7	5 155.0	5 181.2
L	3 319.5	4 236.7	4 497.1	4 887.2	5 246.7	5 611.3	5 812.4	6 130.9	6 498.4	6 565.3
M	3 535.9	4 418.7	4 686.2	5 016.3	5 451.0	5 620.5	5 938.1	6 267.7	6 549.6	6 640.9
N	3 818.8	4 086.1	4 518.5	4 961.9	5 539.4	5 578.7	5 929.8	6 315.7	6 620.5	6 741.2
O	2 163.9	2 883.7	3 150.6	3 313.9	3 658.8	3 899.1	4 031.9	4 150.6	4 622.8	4 556.4
P	965.8	1 225.8	1 429.3	1 649.7	1 796.0	1 847.8	1 980.9	2 167.7	2 340.7	2 401.1
Q										
X										

Men - Hommes - Hombres
ISIC 3 - CITI 3 - CIIU 3

	1999	2000	2001	2002	2003	2004	2005	2006	2007	2008
Total	2 533.2	3 134.9	3 543.8	3 785.7	4 025.3	4 210.2	4 441.0	4 696.8	5 043.6	5 131.7
A-B	1 248.6	1 465.9	1 725.7	1 807.4	2 011.4	2 115.1	2 268.5	2 399.9	2 551.8	2 706.3
C-Q	2 752.1	3 396.9	3 822.0	4 088.4	4 310.4	4 496.2	4 735.2	5 014.9	5 350.5	5 441.4
A	1 216.2	1 425.1	1 690.2	1 788.2	1 973.2	2 094.1	2 227.2	2 361.0	2 522.3	2 675.4
B	2 496.1	2 951.1	3 153.2	2 953.4	3 714.1	2 996.3	3 986.6	4 016.0	4 187.5	4 444.2
C	6 369.8	6 163.5	7 397.0	7 275.5	8 585.8	6 544.1	8 272.9	9 528.5	9 799.7	10 586.1
D	2 644.2	3 279.9	3 774.6	3 978.6	4 157.2	4 260.1	4 625.6	4 839.5	5 242.5	5 172.2
E	3 107.5	4 165.4	4 695.3	5 506.9	5 490.2	6 317.9	5 852.6	6 750.0	7 651.4	7 233.0
F	1 935.7	2 467.5	3 017.9	3 354.7	3 439.5	3 685.1	3 811.9	4 235.9	4 431.4	4 670.0
G	2 154.5	2 770.3	3 168.4	3 414.7	3 635.6	3 784.8	4 073.9	4 304.8	4 514.5	4 529.7
H	2 502.3	2 399.0	2 830.7	3 270.0	3 275.0	3 465.8	3 716.9	4 042.2	4 170.0	4 528.9
I	3 066.2	3 699.1	3 984.5	4 099.0	4 416.2	4 658.8	4 821.6	5 115.5	5 694.0	5 844.1
J	6 410.9	8 013.1	8 832.3	8 143.8	8 685.6	8 709.5	9 298.9	8 884.9	10 239.8	9 781.8
K	2 689.9	4 200.7	4 481.9	4 871.4	5 016.5	5 501.9	5 085.5	5 383.9	5 410.4	5 662.2
L	3 425.0	4 350.6	4 514.9	5 018.7	5 330.3	5 719.9	5 858.8	6 224.9	6 551.1	6 887.1
M	3 801.7	5 132.7	5 221.1	5 697.0	6 065.9	6 117.4	6 649.4	6 995.8	7 315.3	7 391.6
N	5 378.3	5 413.2	5 917.0	6 451.3	7 277.3	6 745.6	7 554.3	8 207.4	8 391.3	8 541.6
O	2 516.5	3 063.3	3 603.3	3 522.7	4 092.2	4 517.4	4 349.9	4 533.1	5 031.3	5 026.9
P	1 460.4	1 755.0	2 138.4	2 520.2	2 801.0	2 675.3	2 879.1	3 349.5	3 555.5	3 578.1
Q										
X										

Explanatory notes: see p. 877. — Notes explicatives: voir p. 879. — Notas explicativas: véase p. 882.

[1] Private sector. [2] Public sector. [3] July. [4] Persons aged 14 years and over. [5] Second quarter of each year. — [1] Secteur privé. [2] Secteur public. [3] Juillet. [4] Personnes âgées de 14 ans et plus. [5] Deuxième trimestre de chaque année. — [1] Sector privado. [2] Sector público. [3] Julio. [4] Personas de 14 años y más. [5] Segundo trimestre de cada año.

| **By economic activity** | **Par activité économique** | **Por actividad económica** | |

	1999	2000	2001	2002	2003	2004	2005	2006	2007	2008

México (BA) [1] [2]   Employees - Salariés - Asalariados   E.G./m. - Nuevo peso

Women - Femmes - Mujeres
ISIC 3 - CITI 3 - CIIU 3

	1999	2000	2001	2002	2003	2004	2005	2006	2007	2008
Total	2 091.7	2 563.7	2 894.6	3 118.3	3 354.1	3 522.8	3 713.6	3 956.8	4 157.1	4 239.0
A-B	1 253.0	1 293.3	1 663.0	1 695.1	1 727.8	1 815.8	2 295.9	2 199.7	2 252.8	2 529.4
C-Q	2 117.3	2 599.8	2 924.4	3 150.8	3 386.7	3 564.3	3 743.7	3 998.8	4 196.0	4 270.9
A	1 245.0	1 285.5	1 643.7	1 666.8	1 710.8	1 813.5	2 257.2	2 179.6	2 232.1	2 510.5
B	2 232.7	2 010.5	2 611.7	2 985.3	2 295.1	2 066.9	3 336.4	3 966.0	3 778.6	3 655.7
C	4 533.8	7 105.9	6 642.9	7 098.5	7 278.0	10 234.5	8 387.0	9 338.8	11 684.4	10 534.0
D	1 842.4	2 247.5	2 646.8	2 723.9	2 918.9	3 133.6	3 217.5	3 628.3	3 651.1	3 715.3
E	3 567.2	4 529.4	4 001.5	4 608.3	5 543.4	5 832.2	6 540.1	6 406.7	6 141.9	6 741.2
F	2 204.8	3 231.1	4 147.9	4 289.3	5 901.2	5 401.2	7 548.5	5 372.3	5 657.0	6 574.1
G	1 734.5	2 042.4	2 368.7	2 536.6	2 774.9	2 715.4	3 049.5	3 307.6	3 491.1	3 685.9
H	1 579.1	1 904.8	2 077.5	2 366.6	2 525.6	2 667.7	2 943.8	3 035.6	3 346.2	3 313.1
I	3 144.3	3 658.2	4 311.7	4 522.0	5 115.5	4 850.1	4 583.3	5 432.5	5 292.5	5 933.7
J	3 497.4	5 140.6	5 701.2	5 663.3	5 255.7	6 404.2	6 171.1	7 202.7	7 293.1	8 204.5
K	2 620.4	3 378.7	3 673.9	4 002.1	4 234.2	4 132.9	4 024.6	4 536.9	4 763.9	4 534.5
L	3 084.0	3 997.6	4 458.7	4 613.1	5 063.1	5 392.8	5 724.7	5 947.8	6 399.6	5 989.5
M	3 339.5	3 909.1	4 304.8	4 557.4	5 023.6	5 264.2	5 485.1	5 818.0	6 045.4	6 142.0
N	3 062.4	3 487.9	3 855.3	4 277.2	4 727.3	5 105.0	5 226.4	5 600.6	5 941.4	5 999.5
O	1 680.8	2 573.9	2 466.9	2 974.2	3 036.6	2 930.4	3 556.9	3 650.9	3 991.6	3 855.4
P	911.3	1 163.1	1 342.7	1 543.5	1 649.8	1 756.2	1 896.5	2 066.2	2 247.2	2 296.7
Q	.	.	.	.	.	.	.	.	.	.
X	.	.	.	.	.	.	.	.	.	.

Nicaragua (DA)   Employees - Salariés - Asalariados   E.G./h. - Córdoba

Total men and women - Total hommes et femmes - Total hombres y mujeres
ISIC 2 - CITI 2 - CIIU 2

	1999	2000	2001	2002	2003	2004	2005	2006	2007	2008
Total	.	10.62	11.90	12.88	13.98	15.14	17.50	.	.	.
2-9	12.00	13.80	14.60	15.25	15.70	16.30	18.40	19.90	.	.
2	11.00	14.98	17.48	19.11	19.11	19.11	21.30	23.80	.	.
3	12.00	13.24	13.45	13.46	13.48	13.49	13.70	13.90	.	.
4	11.00	11.34	12.60	16.06	18.81	19.21	22.40	24.60	.	.
5	11.00	12.18	12.43	14.64	14.40	15.54	15.70	16.00	.	.
6	13.00	15.28	17.89	19.03	19.37	19.43	21.40	22.90	.	.
7	13.00	15.61	16.61	17.63	16.66	16.71	18.20	19.60	.	.
8	25.00	28.53	33.07	34.58	39.54	41.55	44.40	44.90	.	.
9	11.00	12.95	13.99	14.26	14.48	16.15	19.30	22.30	.	.

Nicaragua (DA)   Employees - Salariés - Asalariados   E.G./m. - Córdoba

Total men and women - Total hommes et femmes - Total hombres y mujeres
ISIC 2 - CITI 2 - CIIU 2

	1999	2000	2001	2002	2003	2004	2005	2006	2007	2008
Total	2 282.3	2 585.0	2 896.9	3 135.0	3 388.0	3 686.0	4 266.0	4 926.0	.	.
2-9	3 038.0	3 357.0	3 559.0	3 712.0	3 812.0	3 971.0	4 476.0	4 853.0	.	.
1 [3]	632.9	749.5	703.9	748.0	779.0	813.0	.	.	.	.
2	3 092.2	3 644.1	4 254.3	4 649.0	4 649.0	4 651.0	5 192.0	5 800.0	.	.
3	3 097.7	3 221.9	3 272.9	3 276.0	3 279.0	3 283.0	3 331.0	3 393.0	.	.
4 [4]	2 617.7	2 759.8	3 064.5	3 894.0	4 579.0	4 675.0	5 453.0	5 994.0	.	.
5	2 620.0	2 962.8	3 025.0	3 075.0	3 505.0	3 782.0	3 811.0	3 901.0	.	.
6	3 173.1	3 717.6	4 353.8	4 630.0	4 715.0	4 730.0	5 218.0	5 580.0	.	.
7	3 201.0	3 798.3	4 042.0	4 046.0	4 056.0	4 065.0	4 422.0	4 758.0	.	.
8	6 116.7	6 943.1	8 048.1	8 415.0	9 623.0	10 110.0	10 793.0	10 925.0	.	.
9	2 585.8	3 151.3	3 404.5	3 471.0	3 524.0	3 930.0	4 700.0	5 438.0	.	.

Panamá (BA) [5] [6] [7]   Total employment - Emploi total - Empleo total   E.G./h. - Balboa

Total men and women - Total hommes et femmes - Total hombres y mujeres
ISIC 3 - CITI 3 - CIIU 3

	1999	2000	2001	2002	2003	2004	2005	2006	2007	2008
Total	.	.	.	2.2	2.2	2.2	2.6	2.6	2.3	2.4
A-B	.	.	1.4	1.0	1.0	0.9	1.0	1.0	1.0	1.1
C-Q	.	.	.	.	.	.	2.8	2.7	2.4	2.5
A	.	.	1.3	0.9	1.0	0.9	1.0	1.0	1.0	1.1
B	.	.	1.6	1.4	1.7	1.6	1.5	1.5	1.3	1.5
C	.	.	.	1.8	2.1	1.3	1.5	1.5	1.6	1.9
D	.	.	.	1.8	1.7	1.9	2.2	2.2	2.2	2.0
E	.	.	.	3.3	3.5	3.7	4.9	4.9	3.3	3.0
F	.	.	.	1.7	1.9	1.8	1.9	1.9	2.0	2.2
G	.	.	.	1.9	1.9	1.9	2.1	2.1	1.9	2.1
H	.	.	.	1.3	1.3	1.3	1.4	1.4	1.4	1.6
I	.	.	.	4.0	4.4	4.1	5.5	5.5	3.7	3.9
J	.	.	.	3.6	3.6	3.6	4.4	4.4	4.2	4.2
K	.	.	.	2.4	2.3	2.2	2.6	2.6	2.5	2.6
L	.	.	.	2.9	3.0	3.0	3.3	3.3	3.0	3.2
M	.	.	.	3.2	3.2	3.3	3.8	3.8	3.3	3.6
N	.	.	.	3.2	3.5	3.9	4.4	4.4	4.0	4.1
O	.	.	.	1.9	1.7	1.9	2.0	2.0	1.9	2.1
P	.	.	.	0.6	0.7	0.7	0.9	0.9	0.8	0.9
Q	.	.	.	2.8	7.0	3.1	4.9	4.9	9.6	3.0
X	.	.	.	1.4	.	.	.	.	.	.

Explanatory notes: see p. 877.

[1] Persons aged 14 years and over. [2] Second quarter of each year. [3] Agricultural and livestock production, agricultural services. [4] Excl. gas. [5] Persons aged 15 years and over. [6] Median. [7] Aug. of each year.

Notes explicatives: voir p. 879.

[1] Personnes âgées de 14 ans et plus. [2] Deuxième trimestre de chaque année. [3] Production agricole, élevage et activités annexes de l'agriculture. [4] Non compris le gaz. [5] Personnes âgées de 15 ans et plus. [6] Médiane. [7] Août de chaque année.

Notas explicativas: véase p. 882.

[1] Personas de 14 años y más. [2] Segundo trimestre de cada año. [3] Producción agropecuaria y servicios agrícolas. [4] Excl. gas. [5] Personas de 15 años y más. [6] Mediana. [7] Agosto de cada año.

5A

WAGES	SALAIRES	SALARIOS
By economic activity	Par activité économique	Por actividad económica

	1999	2000	2001	2002	2003	2004	2005	2006	2007	2008

Panamá (BA) [1][2][3] Total employment - Emploi total - Empleo total E.G./h. - Balboa

Men - Hommes - Hombres
ISIC 3 - CITI 3 - CIIU 3

	1999	2000	2001	2002	2003	2004	2005	2006	2007	2008
Total	.	.	.	2.2	2.3	2.2	2.6	2.6	2.3	2.4
A-B	.	.	1.4	0.9	1.0	0.9	1.0	1.0	1.0	1.1
C-Q	.	.	.	.	.	.	2.8	2.8	2.4	2.6
A	.	.	1.3	0.9	1.0	0.9	1.0	1.0	1.0	1.1
B	.	.	1.6	1.4	1.7	1.7	1.5	1.5	1.3	1.5
C	.	.	.	1.8	2.1	1.3	1.6	1.6	1.6	1.9
D	.	.	.	1.8	1.7	1.9	2.1	2.1	2.2	2.1
E	.	.	.	3.2	3.6	3.7	5.2	5.2	2.6	2.6
F	.	.	.	1.7	1.8	1.8	1.9	1.9	2.0	2.2
G	.	.	.	1.9	1.9	1.9	2.3	2.3	1.8	2.1
H	.	.	.	1.3	1.5	1.4	1.6	1.6	1.5	1.6
I	.	.	.	4.2	4.4	4.4	5.4	5.4	3.8	4.0
J	.	.	.	3.9	3.3	3.6	3.7	3.7	4.4	4.4
K	.	.	.	2.3	2.2	1.9	2.3	2.3	2.4	2.4
L	.	.	.	2.9	3.0	3.0	3.4	3.4	3.1	3.2
M	.	.	.	3.3	3.4	3.7	3.9	3.9	3.4	3.8
N	.	.	.	3.9	4.3	5.2	5.7	5.7	4.6	4.5
O	.	.	.	2.0	1.8	1.9	2.2	2.2	2.0	2.1
P	.	.	.	0.8	0.8	0.9	0.9	0.9	0.9	1.2
Q	.	.	.	2.8	10.5	3.0	2.0	2.0	11.7	3.3
X	.	.	.	1.4	.	3.0	.	.	.	.

Women - Femmes - Mujeres
ISIC 3 - CITI 3 - CIIU 3

	1999	2000	2001	2002	2003	2004	2005	2006	2007	2008
Total	.	.	.	2.1	2.1	2.1	2.5	2.5	2.3	2.5
A-B	.	.	1.3	1.7	1.4	1.1	1.0	1.0	1.5	1.6
C-Q	.	.	.	.	.	.	2.6	2.6	2.3	2.5
A	.	.	1.2	1.6	1.3	1.2	1.0	1.0	1.5	1.6
B	.	.	1.6	1.3	1.7	0.9	0.8	0.8	1.2	2.0
C	.	.	.	1.2	1.0	.	1.0	1.0	2.0	2.7
D	.	.	.	1.9	1.8	2.1	2.7	2.7	2.1	2.0
E	.	.	.	3.4	3.1	3.2	3.1	3.1	4.9	4.1
F	.	.	.	2.1	2.6	2.1	2.4	2.4	2.9	2.9
G	.	.	.	1.8	1.9	2.0	1.9	1.9	2.0	2.1
H	.	.	.	1.3	1.2	1.2	1.3	1.3	1.3	1.5
I	.	.	.	3.6	4.0	3.3	5.8	5.8	3.2	3.4
J	.	.	.	3.3	3.7	3.5	4.8	4.8	4.0	4.0
K	.	.	.	2.8	2.5	2.7	3.3	3.3	2.8	3.0
L	.	.	.	3.0	3.0	3.1	3.1	3.1	2.9	3.2
M	.	.	.	3.1	3.2	3.1	3.8	3.8	3.2	3.5
N	.	.	.	2.7	3.0	3.1	3.6	3.6	3.6	3.8
O	.	.	.	1.7	1.6	1.9	1.8	1.8	1.8	2.1
P	.	.	.	0.6	0.6	0.6	0.9	0.9	0.8	0.8
Q	.	.	.	.	3.0	3.9	5.7	5.7	6.6	2.8

Paraguay (BA) Employees - Salariés - Asalariados E.G./m. - Guarani

Total men and women - Total hommes et femmes - Total hombres y mujeres
ISIC 2 - CITI 2 - CIIU 2 | ISIC 3 - CITI 3 - CIIU 3 [4][5]

	1999	2000	2001	2002	2003				2007	2008	
Total	.	787 514	736 269	801 083	869 822		.	.	6 415.5	6 871.7	Total
1	.	417 673	368 186	771 037	638 090		.	.	3 782.8	4 038.3	A-B
2	.	864 958	522 286	431 291	728 903		.	.	6 601.2	7 115.8	C-Q
3	.	813 765	639 988	739 738	816 428		.	.	4 121.1	6 488.9	C
4	.	4 074 972	3 927 595	2 351 453	2 278 239		.	.	5 399.1	5 907.1	D
5	.	738 188	614 883	705 600	794 481		.	.	13 112.8	23 814.5	E
6	.	851 370	984 318	724 802	944 575		.	.	4 565.5	4 395.7	F
7	.	1 806 235	1 211 482	1 073 978	1 293 563		.	.	6 374.2	5 901.9	G-H
8	.	1 482 153	1 393 135	1 470 650	1 734 162		.	.			I
9	.	773 946	732 030	768 144	844 737		.	.	8 303.8	10 209.2	J-K
							.	.	7 095.5	7 795.7	L-Q

Men - Hommes - Hombres
ISIC 2 - CITI 2 - CIIU 2 | ISIC 3 - CITI 3 - CIIU 3 [4][5]

	1999	2000	2001	2002	2003				2007	2008	
Total	.	899 758	855 861	953 288	989 453		.	.	6 392.9	7 011.2	Total
1	.	480 995	426 571	930 422	699 513		.	.	3 838.7	4 086.2	A-B
2	.	874 958	522 286	446 200	728 903		.	.	6 675.3	7 385.6	C-Q
3	.	995 539	746 213	880 891	966 821		.	.	4 121.1	3 976.9	C
4	.	4 176 014	3 996 227	2 463 508	2 431 563		.	.	5 550.4	5 827.6	D
5	.	739 274	587 590	701 304	781 439		.	.	13 653.5	24 945.8	E
6	.	921 347	1 277 733	852 686	1 150 072		.	.	4 526.5	4 370.2	F
7	.	1 897 426	1 226 136	1 098 041	1 308 524		.	.	5 922.1	6 029.9	G-H
8	.	1 726 343	1 474 254	1 761 082	1 790 333		.	.	7 230.5	8 118.5	I
9	.	1 031 829	926 805	995 568	1 081 704		.	.	8 004.6	10 183.5	J-K
							.	.	9 109.7	10 439.7	L-Q

Explanatory notes: see p. 877.

[1] Persons aged 15 years and over. [2] Median. [3] Aug. of each year. [4] Fourth quarter of each year. [5] Figures in thousands.

Notes explicatives: voir p. 879.

[1] Personnes âgées de 15 ans et plus. [2] Médiane. [3] Août de chaque année. [4] Quatrième trimestre de chaque année. [5] Données en milliers.

Notas explicativas: véase p. 882.

[1] Personas de 15 años y más. [2] Mediana. [3] Agosto de cada año. [4] Cuarto trimestre de cada año. [5] Cifras en millares.

	1999	2000	2001	2002	2003	2004	2005	2006	2007	2008	

Paraguay (BA) — Employees - Salariés - Asalariados — E.G./m. - Guarani

Women - Femmes - Mujeres
ISIC 2 - CITI 2 - CIIU 2   ISIC 3 - CITI 3 - CIIU 3 [1][2]

	1999	2000	2001	2002	2003	2004	2005	2006	2007	2008	
Total	.	606 598	557 454	552 478	681 531		.	.	.	6 452.3	6 641.1	Total
1	.	221 125	220 271	219 549	448 589		.	.	.	2 970.0	3 647.3	A-B
2	.	.	.	253 743	.		.	.	.	6 491.5	6 711.4	C-Q
3	.	402 798	408 608	453 064	514 766		.	.	.	.	.	C
4	.	3 578 950	3 287 027	.	1 670 943		.	.	.	4 745.9	6 303.2	D
5	.	374 454	2 170 582	883 867	1 586 582		.	.	.	7 360.5	17 592.2	E
6	.	771 212	636 986	572 404	668 328		.	.	.	8 337.0	7 385.2	F
7	.	1 143 255	1 078 510	946 289	1 194 304		.	.	.	7 465.2	5 614.8	G-H
8	.	1 020 905	1 189 597	960 467	1 619 267		.	.	.	9 819.2	8 788.7	I
9	.	642 134	646 345	635 910	721 483		.	.	.	8 778.0	10 269.4	J-K
							.	.	.	6 139.7	6 625.2	L-Q

Perú (B) [3] — Wage earners - Ouvriers - Obreros — R.T./h. - Nuevo sol

Total men and women - Total hommes et femmes - Total hombres y mujeres
ISIC 3 - CITI 3 - CIIU 3

	1999	2000	2001	2002	2003	2004	2005	2006	2007	2008
Total	.	.	.	2.6	2.7	2.7	2.8	3.0	3.3	3.7
A-B	.	.	.	1.9	1.9	2.1	2.1	2.2	2.5	2.9
C-Q	.	.	.	2.7	2.9	2.8	2.9	3.1	3.4	3.7
A	.	.	.	1.9	1.8	1.9	1.9	2.0	2.1	2.5
B	.	.	.	2.2	2.8	3.3	3.5	4.3	4.5	5.0
C	.	.	.	8.3	9.4	9.1	12.3	11.0	9.0	10.0
D	.	.	.	2.5	2.7	2.7	2.6	2.9	3.4	3.6
E	.	.	.	4.9	4.6	5.2	4.1	5.6	5.1	5.5
F	.	.	.	2.9	3.0	2.6	2.8	3.0	3.5	3.9
G	.	.	.	2.2	2.1	2.1	2.3	2.4	2.6	2.8
H	.	.	.	2.5	2.1	2.0	2.2	2.3	2.3	2.5
I	.	.	.	2.3	2.4	2.4	2.2	2.5	2.7	3.0
K	.	.	.	3.2	2.9	2.9	3.4	3.3	3.8	4.4
L	.	.	.	3.0	3.3	2.9	3.0	3.1	3.3	4.1
M	.	.	.	2.7	3.2	3.5	3.0	3.7	3.3	3.8
N	.	.	.	1.4	2.4	1.6	3.1	2.1	3.7	4.2
O	.	.	.	2.4	2.6	2.2	2.1	2.5	2.6	3.2

Perú (B) [3] — Salaried employees - Employés - Empleados — R.T./h. - Nuevo sol

Total men and women - Total hommes et femmes - Total hombres y mujeres
ISIC 3 - CITI 3 - CIIU 3

	1999	2000	2001	2002	2003	2004	2005	2006	2007	2008
Total	.	.	.	6.5	6.9	6.0	6.1	6.4	6.6	7.2
A-B	.	.	.	7.1	5.2	5.8	4.2	5.3	5.8	6.0
C-Q	.	.	.	6.5	7.0	6.0	6.1	6.4	6.6	7.2
A	.	.	.	4.2	5.3	4.6	4.2	4.1	4.9	6.0
B	.	.	.	12.1	.	.	.	.	.	.
C	.	.	.	17.4	17.4	18.4	26.9	17.3	16.6	20.7
D	.	.	.	11.4	10.6	9.8	6.4	8.0	7.9	9.1
E	.	.	.	10.5	14.3	9.5	12.1	9.1	13.0	12.7
F	.	.	.	18.8	22.7	13.3	7.0	20.0	8.7	12.8
G	.	.	.	4.5	4.3	3.2	3.9	3.4	4.4	4.0
H	.	.	.	3.3	3.1	3.3	3.1	2.9	3.0	3.6
I	.	.	.	8.2	7.0	5.1	5.4	6.1	5.6	5.9
J	.	.	.	15.7	15.8	8.0	9.8	12.8	10.6	11.7
K	.	.	.	6.2	6.5	5.2	8.5	5.5	6.4	6.5
L	.	.	.	5.8	6.6	6.8	6.4	7.0	7.0	8.2
M	.	.	.	5.9	6.9	6.6	6.0	7.5	7.6	7.9
N	.	.	.	5.4	6.3	6.8	7.4	7.0	8.8	8.4
O	.	.	.	6.4	5.3	3.5	5.1	5.0	4.9	5.8

Puerto Rico (DA) — Wage earners - Ouvriers - Obreros — E.G./h. - US dollar

Total men and women - Total hommes et femmes - Total hombres y mujeres
ISIC 2 - CITI 2 - CIIU 2

	1999	2000	2001	2002	2003	2004	2005	2006	2007	2008
3	8.93	9.39	9.84	10.30	10.46	10.84	11.10	11.48	11.94	12.09

United States (BA) [4] — Employees - Salariés - Asalariados — E.G./w.s. - Dollar

Total men and women - Total hommes et femmes - Total hombres y mujeres
ISIC 3 - CITI 3 - CIIU 3

	1999	2000	2001	2002	2003	2004	2005	2006	2007	2008
A [5]	340	347	371	374	397	.	402	422	412	444

Men - Hommes - Hombres
ISIC 3 - CITI 3 - CIIU 3

	1999	2000	2001	2002	2003	2004	2005	2006	2007	2008
A [5]	342	351	375	381	408	.	420	436	418	454

Women - Femmes - Mujeres
ISIC 3 - CITI 3 - CIIU 3

	1999	2000	2001	2002	2003	2004	2005	2006	2007	2008
A [5]	332	332	360	345	354	.	323	.	383	416

Explanatory notes: see p. 877.   Notes explicatives: voir p. 879.   Notas explicativas: véase p. 882.

[1] Fourth quarter of each year. [2] Figures in thousands. [3] Urban areas. [4] Median. [5] Excl. hunting and forestry.

[1] Quatrième trimestre de chaque année. [2] Données en milliers. [3] Régions urbaines. [4] Médiane. [5] Non compris la chasse et la sylviculture.

[1] Cuarto trimestre de cada año. [2] Cifras en millares. [3] Areas urbanas. [4] Mediana. [5] Excl. caza y silvicultura.

WAGES SALAIRES SALARIOS

By economic activity Par activité économique Por actividad económica

	1999	2000	2001	2002	2003	2004	2005	2006	2007	2008

United States (DA) [1] [2] Employees - Salariés - Asalariados E.G./h. - Dollar

Total men and women - Total hommes et femmes - Total hombres y mujeres
ISIC 3 - CITI 3 - CIIU 3

	1999	2000	2001	2002	2003	2004	2005	2006	2007	2008
Total	13.49	14.02	14.54	14.97	15.37	15.69	16.13	16.76	17.43	18.08
C	16.76	16.94	17.33	17.53	17.90	18.44	19.04	20.28	21.43	23.01
E	22.03	22.75	23.58	23.96	24.77	25.61	26.68	27.40	27.88	28.84
F	16.80	17.48	18.00	18.52	18.95	19.23	19.46	20.02	20.95	21.87
G										
H	7.56	7.92	8.13	8.31	8.50	8.65	8.80	9.19	9.82	10.23
I										
64										
N	13.48	13.98	14.67	15.32	15.88	16.45	17.05	17.75	18.48	19.25
O										

Uruguay (D) [3] Employees - Salariés - Asalariados E.G./h. - Peso

Indices, total - Indices, total - Índices, total
ISIC 3 - CITI 3 - CIIU 3

	1999	2000	2001	2002	2003	2004	2005	2006	2007	2008
Total									90.61	101.17
C-Q									90.61	101.17
D									90.45	100.48
F									92.55	104.53
G									89.56	99.88
H									91.02	100.95
I									91.69	101.30
J									91.95	100.83
K									89.70	101.56
M									91.27	101.07
N									90.17	102.36

Virgin Islands (US) (DA) Wage earners - Ouvriers - Obreros E.G./h. - US dollar

Total men and women - Total hommes et femmes - Total hombres y mujeres
ISIC 3 - CITI 3 - CIIU 3

	1999	2000	2001	2002	2003	2004	2005	2006	2007	2008
D			22.57	22.98	23.37	23.35	23.49	26.53	26.35	28.05

ASIA-ASIE-ASIA

Armenia (DA) Employees - Salariés - Asalariados E.G./m. - Dram

Total men and women - Total hommes et femmes - Total hombres y mujeres
ISIC 3 - CITI 3 - CIIU 3

	1999	2000	2001	2002	2003	2004	2005	2006	2007	2008
Total	20 157	22 706	24 483	27 324	34 783	43 445	52 060	62 293	74 227	92 759
A-B		14 830	16 875	18 536	25 155	30 473	34 914	46 146	58 697	68 178
C-Q	20 290	22 906	24 637	27 472	34 903	43 613	52 271	62 436	74 385	93 039
A		14 827		18 544	25 153	30 442	34 971	46 393	59 147	68 451
B		15 614	17 819	15 622	27 687	32 671	31 437	39 835	42 994	39 069
C				58 545	88 305	96 325	106 725	128 279	160 499	201 496
D	24 515	29 307	35 848	30 061	41 881	48 191	54 536	61 490	71 834	92 559
E				58 937	68 796	82 882	95 392	98 417		117 834
F	35 261	41 445	41 484	44 789	50 991	59 121	68 780	84 951	97 569	123 947
G	20 490	20 254	20 315	24 203	33 335	35 962	42 248	42 771	51 944	64 759
H				36 380	49 895	48 475	41 992		54 611	72 970
I	35 306	38 821	43 466	50 234	52 966	57 504	64 329		87 447	114 426
J	70 766	90 686	98 732	109 664	133 483	152 991	174 918	205 454	227 970	281 808
K	17 422	16 373	18 729	27 526	31 909	38 331	48 581	66 320	100 155	122 955
L	29 168	32 548	36 034	38 612	53 465	67 243	75 250	76 328	88 093	109 936
M	10 116	12 604	12 659	15 016	19 293	29 164	38 636	45 986	54 334	64 116
N	11 575	13 029	13 045	13 070	15 002	19 770	27 848	38 757	44 394	56 160
O	13 955	17 457	17 946	24 370	28 578	31 695	34 444	41 201	49 011	60 991

Men - Hommes - Hombres
ISIC 3 - CITI 3 - CIIU 3

	1999	2000	2001	2002	2003	2004	2005	2006	2007	2008
Total		29 208	33 921	41 452	49 831	57 043	66 301	81 581	96 802	
A-B		15 235	16 814	19 547	25 480	31 598	36 885	49 756	64 006	
C-Q		29 720	34 481	42 092	50 358	57 558	66 883	81 977	97 318	
A								49 827	64 232	
B								46 062	45 139	
C								146 842	181 298	
D								78 214	88 692	
E								103 947	113 992	
F								90 484	104 392	
G								53 215	64 000	
H								82 309	77 967	
I								77 228	94 471	
J								282 173	304 290	
K								76 832	122 753	
L								89 605	103 995	
M								54 174	62 293	
N								51 872	56 568	
O								50 970	59 628	

Explanatory notes: see p. 877.

[1] National classification not strictly compatible with ISIC. [2] Not all employees covered; only production and non-supervisory workers; private sector. [3] Index base: July 2008 = 100.

Notes explicatives: voir p. 879.

[1] Classification nationale non strictement compatible avec la CITI. [2] Non couverts tous les salariés: seulement travailleurs à la production et ceux sans activité de surveillance; secteur privé. [3] Indices base: juillet 2008 = 100.

Notas explicativas: véase p. 882.

[1] Clasificación nacional no estrictamente compatible con la CIIU. [2] Todos asalariados no cubiertos; sólo trabajaodores de la producción y los sin funciones de supervisión; sector privado. [3] Indices base: julio 2008 = 100.

	1999	2000	2001	2002	2003	2004	2005	2006	2007	2008

Armenia (DA) Employees - Salariés - Asalariados E.G./m. - Dram

Women - Femmes - Mujeres
ISIC 3 - CITI 3 - CIIU 3

	1999	2000	2001	2002	2003	2004	2005	2006	2007	2008
Total	.	15 160	15 528	16 865	20 990	30 485	38 131	48 319	58 101	.
A-B	.	9 839	14 029	15 507	18 573	26 659	31 319	39 153	49 995	.
C-Q	.	15 205	15 542	16 902	21 006	30 511	38 177	48 355	58 141	.
A	.	.	.	.	.	.	.	39 237	50 089	.
B	.	.	.	.	.	.	.	35 000	40 000	.
C	.	.	.	.	.	.	.	79 474	96 119	.
D	.	.	.	.	.	.	.	46 410	54 844	.
E	.	.	.	.	.	.	.	77 484	112 777	.
F	.	.	.	.	.	.	.	63 859	79 658	.
G	.	.	.	.	.	.	.	39 243	47 056	.
H	.	.	.	.	.	.	.	65 969	61 148	.
I	.	.	.	.	.	.	.	83 184	80 254	.
J	.	.	.	.	.	.	.	144 673	172 311	.
K	.	.	.	.	.	.	.	50 146	76 552	.
L	.	.	.	.	.	.	.	59 886	68 973	.
M	.	.	.	.	.	.	.	43 502	51 951	.
N	.	.	.	.	.	.	.	34 817	40 681	.
O	.	.	.	.	.	.	.	33 241	41 789	.

Azerbaijan (DA) Employees - Salariés - Asalariados E.G./m. - Manat

Total men and women - Total hommes et femmes - Total hombres y mujeres
ISIC 3 - CITI 3 - CIIU 3

	1999	2000	2001	2002	2003	2004	2005[1]	2006	2007	2008
Total	184 367.5	221 606.0	259 990.7	315 406.7	386 974.2	497 081.2	123.6	149.0	215.8	274.4
A-B	64 960.4	68 743.3	78 414.9	89 430.0	115 016.9	149 619.1	41.6	52.5	86.7	114.5
C-Q	197 780.9	222 654.7	266 867.1	322 215.2	395 379.8	507 577.2	126.0	155.4	219.6	279.2
A	65 122.1	69 080.6	78 936.0	89 929.7	115 691.5	149 246.3	41.5	52.5	86.8	114.7
B	53 280.1	52 102.7	53 666.9	60 498.9	71 502.6	170 192.7	46.2	52.7	82.8	104.6
C	630 124.2	814 539.6	1 090 745.1	1 290 457.7	1 444 922.7	2 256 347.3	505.2	633.7	845.5	1 011.4
D	244 087.1	284 272.3	303 163.6	348 815.6	445 436.5	491 330.2	115.3	140.5	190.5	251.6
E	222 512.3	267 931.8	323 365.0	324 612.3	365 989.9	438 625.7	121.7	146.7	210.0	287.4
F	428 473.2	416 662.9	436 923.8	545 130.8	771 948.4	1 090 795.8	237.6	298.7	381.4	406.1
G	117 943.1	119 283.6	149 648.1	460 195.3	484 681.4	588 810.8	119.5	128.7	173.7	211.3
H	343 351.1	314 857.7	419 446.6	483 945.5	508 524.6	563 061.6	157.9	164.6	212.3	265.4
I	249 870.1	292 421.0	330 280.7	368 286.4	439 961.2	565 867.1	137.7	175.4	250.4	329.4
J	590 960.9	632 625.7	723 605.5	1 020 095.7	979 800.6	1 086 523.5	314.1	545.8	709.1	812.6
K	274 926.2	334 051.4	540 074.1	661 511.7	857 532.7	1 015 480.4	299.2	383.0	504.7	527.9
L	181 745.7	194 527.5	223 421.1	260 728.8	314 920.7	434 061.0	134.5	158.6	210.6	288.0
M	141 532.0	156 065.4	165 224.6	169 057.6	211 396.1	256 400.9	66.0	87.0	145.4	214.4
N	71 098.1	73 395.0	80 629.5	90 009.8	109 515.6	148 195.0	45.3	69.4	94.7	130.9
O	98 737.3	113 968.1	137 059.6	150 125.7	178 967.6	216 404.5	77.2	78.8	140.0	182.7

Men - Hommes - Hombres
ISIC 3 - CITI 3 - CIIU 3

	1999	2000	2001	2002	2003	2004	2005	2006	2007	2008
Total	.	.	.	.	.	.	.	.	277.1	324.6
A-B	.	.	.	.	.	.	.	.	82.3	114.8
C-Q	.	.	.	.	.	.	.	.	284.8	333.2
A	.	.	.	.	.	.	.	.	82.2	114.9
B	.	.	.	.	.	.	.	.	66.8	104.9
C	.	.	.	.	.	.	.	.	872.6	1 029.0
D	.	.	.	.	.	.	.	.	212.7	253.9
E	.	.	.	.	.	.	.	.	220.8	293.3
F	.	.	.	.	.	.	.	.	401.2	371.9
G	.	.	.	.	.	.	.	.	177.9	214.3
H	.	.	.	.	.	.	.	.	216.0	257.8
I	.	.	.	.	.	.	.	.	274.1	355.8
J	.	.	.	.	.	.	.	.	831.0	877.5
K	.	.	.	.	.	.	.	.	675.3	643.8
L	.	.	.	.	.	.	.	.	223.4	296.4
M	.	.	.	.	.	.	.	.	185.7	257.0
N	.	.	.	.	.	.	.	.	146.0	167.8
O	.	.	.	.	.	.	.	.	189.4	238.6

Women - Femmes - Mujeres
ISIC 3 - CITI 3 - CIIU 3

	1999	2000	2001	2002	2003	2004	2005	2006	2007	2008
Total	.	.	.	.	.	.	.	.	140.0	184.5
A-B	.	.	.	.	.	.	.	.	116.1	92.9
C-Q	.	.	.	.	.	.	.	.	140.5	185.8
A	.	.	.	.	.	.	.	.	117.8	93.0
B	.	.	.	.	.	.	.	.	62.1	87.4
C	.	.	.	.	.	.	.	.	689.4	826.0
D	.	.	.	.	.	.	.	.	128.1	151.4
E	.	.	.	.	.	.	.	.	163.5	232.6
F	.	.	.	.	.	.	.	.	197.8	220.7
G	.	.	.	.	.	.	.	.	164.0	199.1
H	.	.	.	.	.	.	.	.	211.2	241.9
I	.	.	.	.	.	.	.	.	181.3	210.1
J	.	.	.	.	.	.	.	.	479.3	573.8
K	.	.	.	.	.	.	.	.	205.7	269.2
L	.	.	.	.	.	.	.	.	180.4	231.1
M	.	.	.	.	.	.	.	.	129.8	186.0
N	.	.	.	.	.	.	.	.	80.4	112.6
O	.	.	.	.	.	.	.	.	106.5	126.4

Explanatory notes: see p. 877. Notes explicatives: voir p. 879. Notas explicativas: véase p. 882.

[1] New denomination of AZM; 1 AZN=5000 AZM. [1] Nouvelle dénomination de l'AZM; 1 AZN = 5000 AZM. [1] Nueva denominación del AZM; 1 AZN = 5000 AZM.

	1999	2000	2001	2002	2003	2004	2005	2006	2007	2008	

Bahrain (FA) [1] All persons engaged - Effectif occupé - Efectivo ocupado E.G./m. - Dinar

Total men and women - Total hommes et femmes - Total hombres y mujeres
ISIC 3 - CITI 3 - CIIU 3

Total	.	.	.	.	.	.	.	.	.	247	
A-B	.	.	.	.	.	.	.	.	.	76	
C-Q	.	.	.	.	.	.	.	.	.	249	
A	.	.	.	.	.	.	.	.	.	121	
B	.	.	.	.	.	.	.	.	.	54	
C	.	.	.	.	.	.	.	.	.	218	
D	.	.	.	.	.	.	.	.	.	253	
E	.	.	.	.	.	.	.	.	.	933	
F	.	.	.	.	.	.	.	.	.	105	
G	.	.	.	.	.	.	.	.	.	182	
H	.	.	.	.	.	.	.	.	.	126	
I	.	.	.	.	.	.	.	.	.	553	
J	.	.	.	.	.	.	.	.	.	1 484	
K	.	.	.	.	.	.	.	.	.	390	
L	.	.	.	.	.	.	.	.	.	1 320	
M	.	.	.	.	.	.	.	.	.	437	
N	.	.	.	.	.	.	.	.	.	364	
O	.	.	.	.	.	.	.	.	.	111	
P	.	.	.	.	.	.	.	.	.	151	
Q	.	.	.	.	.	.	.	.	.	573	
X	.	.	.	.	.	.	.	.	.	272	

Men - Hommes - Hombres
ISIC 3 - CITI 3 - CIIU 3

Total	.	.	.	.	.	.	.	.	.	237	
A-B	.	.	.	.	.	.	.	.	.	73	
C-Q	.	.	.	.	.	.	.	.	.	239	
A	.	.	.	.	.	.	.	.	.	116	
B	.	.	.	.	.	.	.	.	.	53	
C	.	.	.	.	.	.	.	.	.	215	
D	.	.	.	.	.	.	.	.	.	254	
E	.	.	.	.	.	.	.	.	.	939	
F	.	.	.	.	.	.	.	.	.	102	
G	.	.	.	.	.	.	.	.	.	176	
H	.	.	.	.	.	.	.	.	.	122	
I	.	.	.	.	.	.	.	.	.	567	
J	.	.	.	.	.	.	.	.	.	1 692	
K	.	.	.	.	.	.	.	.	.	385	
L	.	.	.	.	.	.	.	.	.	1 470	
M	.	.	.	.	.	.	.	.	.	548	
N	.	.	.	.	.	.	.	.	.	103	
O	.	.	.	.	.	.	.	.	.	434	
P	.	.	.	.	.	.	.	.	.	147	
Q	.	.	.	.	.	.	.	.	.	559	
X	.	.	.	.	.	.	.	.	.	265	

Women - Femmes - Mujeres
ISIC 3 - CITI 3 - CIIU 3

Total	.	.	.	.	.	.	.	.	.	344	
A-B	.	.	.	.	.	.	.	.	.	207	
C-Q	.	.	.	.	.	.	.	.	.	345	
A	.	.	.	.	.	.	.	.	.	218	
B	.	.	.	.	.	.	.	.	.	89	
C	.	.	.	.	.	.	.	.	.	307	
D	.	.	.	.	.	.	.	.	.	252	
E	.	.	.	.	.	.	.	.	.	826	
F	.	.	.	.	.	.	.	.	.	202	
G	.	.	.	.	.	.	.	.	.	240	
H	.	.	.	.	.	.	.	.	.	148	
I	.	.	.	.	.	.	.	.	.	492	
J	.	.	.	.	.	.	.	.	.	935	
K	.	.	.	.	.	.	.	.	.	418	
L	.	.	.	.	.	.	.	.	.	315	
M	.	.	.	.	.	.	.	.	.	357	
N	.	.	.	.	.	.	.	.	.	292	
O	.	.	.	.	.	.	.	.	.	135	
P	.	.	.	.	.	.	.	.	.	211	
Q	.	.	.	.	.	.	.	.	.	641	
X	.	.	.	.	.	.	.	.	.	298	

Explanatory notes: see p. 877. Notes explicatives: voir p. 879. Notas explicativas: véase p. 882.

[1] Private sector. [1] Secteur privé. [1] Sector privado.

	1999	2000	2001	2002	2003	2004	2005	2006	2007	2008

Bahrain (FA) [1]   Employees - Salariés - Asalariados   E.G./m. - Dinar

Total men and women - Total hommes et femmes - Total hombres y mujeres
ISIC 2 - CITI 2 - CIIU 2

	1999	2000	2001	2002	2003	2004	2005	2006	2007	2008
Total	239	242	234	236	228	223	213	206	213	.
2-9	240	243	235	238	229	224	214	207	215	.
1	.	.	.	.	115	111	.	76	72	.
2	157	147	129	130	.	.	60	52	117	.
3	227	231	215	228	230	234	228	219	225	.
4	193	195	198	207	321	335	335	367	403	.
5	117	117	117	119	112	109	105	107	108	.
6	170	169	169	169	167	164	155	142	151	.
7	454	464	465	484	492	521	496	511	520	.
8	823	835	839	861	879	860	859	857	915	.
9	263	267	246	223	207	203	197	189	196	.
0		228	262	275	577	572	549	491	540	.

Men - Hommes - Hombres
ISIC 2 - CITI 2 - CIIU 2

	1999	2000	2001	2002	2003	2004	2005	2006	2007	2008
Total	240	243	237	238	228	221	209	200	205	.
2-9	242	245	238	239	229	222	210	202	207	.
1	.	.	.	.	112	107	.	74	70	.
2	149	140	122	122	.	.	60	52	95	.
3	250	255	241	252	250	249	239	226	230	.
4	193	195	198	207	322	336	337	368	404	.
5	116	116	116	118	110	107	103	105	105	.
6	171	170	170	170	167	163	153	139	144	.
7	491	502	501	517	514	545	527	536	549	.
8	896	907	910	930	948	920	922	922	979	.
9	260	264	242	215	196	191	185	176	183	.
0	260	231	262	273	593	651	607	592	653	.

Women - Femmes - Mujeres
ISIC 2 - CITI 2 - CIIU 2

	1999	2000	2001	2002	2003	2004	2005	2006	2007	2008
Total	231	237	218	224	227	242	243	253	287	.
2-9	232	233	218	224	227	242	243	253	287	.
1	.	.	.	.	225	247	.	223	232	.
2	302	216	155	162	.	.	.	.	225	.
3	109	107	100	111	125	138	145	155	177	.
4	186	191	196	199	293	322	299	343	392	.
5	137	139	140	146	154	161	166	172	188	.
6	162	163	161	163	164	169	167	167	213	.
7	321	330	332	354	389	411	373	402	402	.
8	584	597	604	621	641	646	631	627	681	.
9	278	282	264	262	251	254	250	249	262	.
0	278	203	258	297	520	371	420	313	343	.

China (DA) [2]   Employees - Salariés - Asalariados   E.G./m. - Yuan

Total men and women - Total hommes et femmes - Total hombres y mujeres
ISIC 3 - CITI 3 - CIIU 3

	1999	2000	2001	2002	2003	2004	2005	2006	2007	2008
Total	695.50	780.92	905.83	1 035.17	1 170.00	1 335.00	1 530.33	1 750.08	2 077.67	2 435.75
A-B	402.67	432.00	478.42	533.17	580.80	634.30	692.40	785.80	923.80	1 079.83
C [3]	626.75	695.00	798.83	918.08	1 140.17	1 406.17	1 718.83	2 027.92	2 364.75	2 867.08
D	649.50	729.17	814.50	916.75	1 041.33	1 169.42	1 313.08	1 497.17	1 740.33	2 016.00
E	959.42	1 069.17	1 215.83	1 370.00	1 562.67	1 817.08	2 089.42	2 397.08	2 817.42	3 267.00
F	665.17	727.92	790.33	856.58	956.50	1 064.17	1 194.83	1 367.17	1 565.42	1 793.92
G-H [4]	534.75	599.17	682.67	783.17	.	.	1 270.08	1 478.00	1 740.67	2 128.17
I	915.92	1 026.58	1 180.58	1 337.00	1 331.08 [5]	1 531.75	1 779.33	2 051.92	2 369.50	2 733.00
J	1 003.83	1 123.17	1 356.42	1 594.58	1 871.42	2 248.50	2 685.67	3 273.33	4 119.58	5 153.42
K	958.75	1 051.33	1 174.67	1 291.75	1 431.83	1 559.33	1 715.08	1 881.50	2 202.08	2 527.25
L [6]	748.17	836.92	1 011.83	1 164.58	1 294.42	1 467.42	1 708.75	1 906.92	2 347.58	2 746.25
M [7]	709.17	790.17	954.33	1 107.50	1 199.92	1 356.42	1 539.17	1 761.17	2 180.17	2 515.42
N [8]	805.33	910.83	1 077.75	1 232.92	.	.	.	.	.	.

[1] Private sector. [2] State-owned units, urban collective-owned units and other ownership units. [3] Mining only. [4] Incl. catering. [5] Excl. communications. [6] State organs, social organizations. [7] Incl. cultural, art, radio and television activities. [8] Incl. sporting activities and activities of membership organizations n.e.c.

[1] Secteur privé. [2] Unités d'Etat, unités collectives urbaines et autres. [3] Mines seulement. [4] Y compris la restauration. [5] Non compris les communications. [6] Organes d'Etat, organisations sociales. [7] Y compris les activités culturelles, artistiques, radiophoniques et télévisuelles. [8] Y compris activités sportives et activités associatives diverses.

[1] Sector privado. [2] Unidades estatales, unidades colectivas y otras. [3] Minas solamente. [4] Incl. la restauración. [5] Excl. las comunicaciones. [6] Organos estatales, organizaciones sociales. [7] Incl. actividades culturales, artísticas, radiofónicas y televisuales. [8] Incl. actividades deportivas y actividades de asociaciones n.c.p.

WAGES — **SALAIRES** — **SALARIOS**

By economic activity — Par activité économique — Por actividad económica

	1999	2000	2001	2002	2003	2004	2005	2006	2007	2008
Georgia (CA)					Employees - Salariés - Asalariados					E.G./m. - Lari
Total men and women - Total hommes et femmes - Total hombres y mujeres										
ISIC 3 - CITI 3 - CIIU 3										
Total	67.5	72.3	94.6	113.5	125.9	156.6	204.2	277.9	368.1	
A-B	27.7	27.9	29.3	42.2	47.6	67.8	127.6	146.1	184.4	
C-Q	80.1	79.0	95.6	114.7	127.0	157.8	205.1	279.1	369.6	
A	27.8	27.8	29.3	40.8	47.6	68.0	128.9	148.1		
B		18.1		29.1	46.2	60.7	93.0	94.4	168.8	
C	52.8	.	.	192.2	218.7	179.5	210.8	352.3	657.7	
D	87.4	99.3	120.8	143.4	152.5	183.8	212.1	260.5	357.7	
E	145.1	.	212.1	214.3	250.2	259.2	341.5	398.2	533.8	
F	141.1	.	145.9	176.1	206.2	264.5	296.4	391.0	494.5	
G	35.6	47.0	57.4	72.8	85.5	107.9	173.6	246.4	355.5	
H	30.2	40.4	50.1	51.5	56.6	70.3	108.2	196.5	238.4	
I	.	138.5	141.1	171.7	191.1	229.1	265.7	391.3	492.3	
J	304.5	313.4	428.7	429.6	530.5	739.3	1 049.2	779.0	1 014.5	
K	72.6	76.5	88.2	92.0	110.3	125.5	210.8	284.2	405.8	
L	84.9	88.5	105.9	141.2	132.0	192.4	342.4	448.0	585.4	
M	44.0	.	.	56.5	68.5	88.7	92.5	122.1	153.0	
N	32.9	32.1	45.6	55.6	76.8	80.3	99.5	143.3	206.4	
O	54.4	66.9	75.3	82.1	72.3	123.2	113.4	175.6	260.6	
Q	465.9	320.5				340.4				
Men - Hommes - Hombres										
ISIC 3 - CITI 3 - CIIU 3										
Total	90.9	95.9	125.2	150.1	163.0	200.7	267.9	362.0	475.6	
A-B	33.6	31.0	35.3	44.4	48.4	66.7	134.4	152.8	191.3	
C-Q	94.5	87.9	127.3	152.7	165.2	203.3	270.1	364.5	478.8	
A	33.8	31.0	35.3	41.1	48.3	66.8	136.0	155.8	166.9	
B	8.8	18.1	23.7	27.9	54.3	61.7	96.9	95.5	177.1	
C	54.0	119.3	156.6	199.5	226.2	189.6	224.5	367.7	645.0	
D	101.1	111.2	141.5	165.1	174.9	210.2	243.5	293.7	411.0	
E	152.8	173.3	213.9	219.7	257.0	267.4	354.2	422.6	559.0	
F	149.3	139.0	149.2	181.9	215.4	266.4	303.3	399.2	503.2	
G	41.8	53.8	63.7	84.4	97.5	116.6	205.5	303.1	445.5	
H	34.7	49.1	54.8	57.6	63.0	79.5	130.5	266.7	329.5	
I	97.4	136.2	151.9	185.3	208.3	252.2	288.9	421.2	519.5	
J	397.2	472.4	488.9	492.3	607.6	833.1	1 077.2	1 356.4	1 190.4	
K	83.1	84.2	107.0	113.7	135.2	155.2	257.6	327.4	447.8	
L	95.7	94.5	125.0	163.0	151.4	214.6	374.9	482.8	622.2	
M	54.9	57.1	58.5	71.1	86.7	112.8	109.5	141.8	191.4	
N	50.3	55.4	58.1	72.0	105.9	102.9	130.0	219.1	298.0	
O	72.2	90.1	104.9	114.3	99.1	163.9	140.3	201.4	324.5	
Q	428.0	310.4	316.1			295.5				
Women - Femmes - Mujeres										
ISIC 3 - CITI 3 - CIIU 3										
Total	47.4	58.8	63.5	75.7	85.7	108.0	131.1	177.6	240.2	
A-B	18.2	21.2	27.0	36.7	44.6	71.9	104.7	130.4	166.1	
C-Q	48.2	60.0	64.0	76.1	86.0	108.2	131.3	177.6	240.6	
A	18.2	21.2	25.3	39.7	45.1	72.2	105.5	130.9	166.9	
B	14.2	18.1	27.0	35.8	25.2	54.6	67.4	83.3	102.8	
C	43.4	87.3	153.0	167.1	192.4	133.8	148.7	287.6	727.6	
D	63.3	69.3	82.7	101.6	108.4	132.2	147.7	191.8	246.4	
E	116.2	137.0	205.9	198.0	226.2	231.4	299.4	320.1	470.5	
F	72.9	81.8	112.8	120.5	124.3	245.0	204.1	250.4	341.0	
G	29.2	47.0	52.6	60.1	72.6	97.1	134.2	181.8	254.2	
H	26.2	40.4	45.0	46.1	51.1	63.1	91.3	150.6	181.4	
I	91.0	138.5	113.7	137.2	145.6	169.3	197.9	301.2	407.5	
J	246.9	313.4	382.6	381.6	473.3	660.3	1 025.0	449.1	878.1	
K	57.0	57.8	65.4	70.0	83.3	94.6	148.1	203.3	316.4	
L	69.0	88.5	73.2	99.1	93.9	147.8	259.6	354.3	467.0	
M	40.0	45.5	49.5	52.0	62.7	81.4	87.3	116.5	142.1	
N	28.5	32.1	42.5	51.7	69.1	74.4	91.7	125.3	181.6	
O	47.1	49.9	53.0	59.7	53.6	90.2	94.3	154.6	207.3	
Q	516.5	324.8	344.1			412.4				
Hong Kong, China (DA)					Wage earners - Ouvriers - Obreros					R.T./d.j. - Dollar
Total men and women - Total hommes et femmes - Total hombres y mujeres										
ISIC 2 - CITI 2 - CIIU 2										
2-9 [1]	403.3	397.5	412.5	401.3	408.5	398.6	370.0	419.6	440.8	453.3
3	334.7	335.4	342.6	326.1	322.2	324.3	279.0	321.7	342.8	341.2
7 [2]	526.0	504.9	507.7	508.6	496.5	491.3	503.7	507.0	511.2	522.4
8	418.5	437.3	455.1	432.8	426.0	417.6	417.1	432.0	447.4	462.2
9 [3]	532.7	531.4	549.9	524.6	518.4	525.8	500.4	518.9	548.0	533.2
Men - Hommes - Hombres										
ISIC 2 - CITI 2 - CIIU 2										
2-9 [1]	480.2	475.5	480.8	476.0	469.2	451.4	397.3	482.4	491.7	502.1
3	422.6	428.8	428.5	419.2	406.1	380.4	282.4	420.8	436.4	430.3
7 [2]	529.1	507.5	511.1	510.5	497.4	491.9	504.4	507.6	510.9	523.5
8	418.5	437.1	462.7	432.8	426.1	417.7	417.1	432.0	447.4	462.2
9 [3]	532.7	531.4	549.9	524.6	518.4	525.8	500.4	518.9	548.0	533.2

Explanatory notes: see p. 877.

[1] Excl. major divisions 2, 5 and 6. [2] Excl. storage and communication. [3] Excl. community and social services.

Notes explicatives: voir p. 879.

[1] Non compris les branches 2, 5 et 6. [2] Non compris les entrepôts et communications. [3] Non compris les services fournis à la collectivité et services sociaux.

Notas explicativas: véase p. 882.

[1] Excl. las grandes divisiones 2, 5 y 6. [2] Excl. almacenaje y comunicaciones. [3] Excl. los servicios comunales y sociales.

WAGES

SALAIRES

SALARIOS

5A

By economic activity

Par activité économique

Por actividad económica

	1999	2000	2001	2002	2003	2004	2005	2006	2007	2008	
Hong Kong, China (DA)					Wage earners - Ouvriers - Obreros						R.T./d.j. - Dollar
Women - Femmes - Mujeres											
ISIC 2 - CITI 2 - CIIU 2											
2-9 [1]	275.0	283.2	291.0	277.8	274.4	289.8	287.0	269.9	283.0	274.2	
3	268.9	278.1	280.6	268.2	262.7	280.0	273.8	256.9	259.6	259.9	
Hong Kong, China (DA)					Salaried employees - Employés - Empleados						R.T./m. - Dollar
Total men and women - Total hommes et femmes - Total hombres y mujeres											
ISIC 2 - CITI 2 - CIIU 2											
2-9 [2]	11 560.9	11 573.7	11 449.0	11 069.8	10 854.3	10 534.6	10 671.1	10 985.1	11 378.5	11 358.9	
3	11 853.0	11 869.7	12 133.1	11 950.7	11 508.8	11 498.1	11 622.0	11 972.4	11 878.0	11 881.3	
6	11 802.2	11 959.3	12 046.4	11 745.0	11 580.8	11 385.1	11 704.9	11 912.6	11 916.3	12 032.5	
7 [3]	13 322.0	12 799.8	13 191.6	13 381.7	13 037.2	12 711.3	13 303.6	12 772.8	13 061.1	14 101.2	
8	11 697.4	11 429.4	11 311.8	10 571.8	10 645.4	9 830.9	9 815.3	10 239.3	11 195.0	10 799.4	
9	6 659.0	6 749.6	6 405.7	6 179.2	5 972.9	6 053.4	5 934.3	6 000.3	6 570.1	6 600.0	
Men - Hommes - Hombres											
ISIC 2 - CITI 2 - CIIU 2											
2-9 [2]	12 141.0	12 105.3	11 905.0	11 619.0	11 269.8	11 025.0	11 016.0	11 391.9	11 759.3	11 792.0	
3	12 893.2	12 697.1	12 929.7	12 810.2	12 082.7	11 880.7	12 248.6	12 483.3	12 596.7	12 470.3	
6	12 784.6	12 938.5	13 076.3	12 867.8	12 526.3	12 299.3	12 599.4	12 856.4	12 797.2	12 803.0	
7 [3]	14 340.9	13 509.9	13 768.4	14 296.0	14 056.1	13 586.5	14 032.0	13 524.7	13 962.0	15 094.3	
8	10 702.4	10 547.5	10 438.2	9 606.4	9 703.1	9 110.3	8 988.4	9 422.4	10 094.0	10 011.9	
9	7 773.2	7 649.5	7 162.9	6 993.0	6 479.7	6 536.4	6 444.1	6 493.3	6 820.6	6 710.4	
Women - Femmes - Mujeres											
ISIC 2 - CITI 2 - CIIU 2											
2-9 [2]	10 952.1	11 011.9	10 969.3	10 518.2	10 445.8	10 052.4	10 319.5	10 596.5	11 015.2	10 943.0	
3	10 846.7	11 101.4	11 395.0	11 123.2	11 021.1	11 139.3	11 015.0	11 552.3	11 282.4	11 335.9	
6	10 941.7	11 115.0	11 204.5	10 852.0	10 836.7	10 640.6	10 998.1	11 192.9	11 217.6	11 404.3	
7 [3]	11 707.5	11 634.8	12 274.2	12 059.8	11 657.0	11 538.6	12 212.3	11 721.8	11 800.8	12 719.0	
8	13 390.2	13 107.7	13 054.8	12 554.1	12 319.7	11 320.0	11 579.2	11 803.6	13 113.1	12 257.9	
9	5 843.5	6 061.8	5 886.2	5 688.7	5 617.7	5 791.8	5 576.3	5 686.5	6 429.5	6 536.9	
Hong Kong, China (FD) [4]					Wage earners - Ouvriers - Obreros						R.T./d.j. - Dollar
Total men and women - Total hommes et femmes - Total hombres y mujeres											
ISIC 2 - CITI 2 - CIIU 2											
5	810.1	814.3	806.3	794.7	797.6	745.1	705.3	687.7	666.7	649.0	
India (DA) [5]					Wage earners - Ouvriers - Obreros						E.G./m. - Rupee
Total men and women - Total hommes et femmes - Total hombres y mujeres											
ISIC 2 - CITI 2 - CIIU 2											
3	1 548.5	1 280.8	1 893.2	1 158.6	1 078.9	1 731.8	1 234.4	3 525.9	.	.	
India (FD) [6] [7]					Wage earners - Ouvriers - Obreros						E.G./d.j. - Rupee
Total men and women - Total hommes et femmes - Total hombres y mujeres											
ISIC 2 - CITI 2 - CIIU 2											
29	1 004.00	1 084.00	1 047.00	1 073.00	1 064.00	1 097.00	1 075.00	1 122.00	.	.	
India (FD) [7] [8]					Employees - Salariés - Asalariados						E.G./w.s. - Rupee
Total men and women - Total hommes et femmes - Total hombres y mujeres											
ISIC 2 - CITI 2 - CIIU 2											
21	1 758.00	1 842.00	2 279.00	2 393.00	2 512.00	2 686.00	2 976.00	3 235.00	.	.	

Explanatory notes: see p. 877.

[1] Excl. major divisions 2, 5 and 6. [2] Excl. major divisions 2 and 5. [3] Excl. storage and communication. [4] Government project workers. [5] Fluctuations due to various changes in workers' coverage. [6] Excl. coal mining and petroleum production. [7] Dec. of each year. [8] Coal mining.

Notes explicatives: voir p. 879.

[1] Non compris les branches 2, 5 et 6. [2] Non compris les branches 2 et 5. [3] Non compris les entrepôts et communications. [4] Travailleurs de projets de l'Etat. [5] Fluctuations dues aux divers changements de couverture des travailleurs. [6] Non compris l'extraction du charbon et la production de pétrole. [7] Déc. de chaque année. [8] Mines de charbon.

Notas explicativas: véase p. 882.

[1] Excl. las grandes divisiones 2, 5 y 6. [2] Excl. las grandes divisiones 2 y 5. [3] Excl. almacenaje y comunicaciones. [4] Trabajadores de proyectos del Estado. [5] Fluctuaciones debidas a varios cambios de lacobertura de los trabajadores. [6] Excl. la explotación de minas de carbón y la producción de petróleo. [7] Dic. de cada año. [8] Minas de carbón.

WAGES   SALAIRES   SALARIOS

By economic activity   **Par activité économique**   **Por actividad económica**

Indonesia (BA) [1] [2]   **Salaried employees - Employés - Empleados**   R.T./m. - Rupiah

Total men and women - Total hommes et femmes - Total hombres y mujeres

ISIC 2 - CITI 2 - CIIU 2   ISIC 3 - CITI 3 - CIIU 3

	1999	2000	2001	2002	2003	2004	2005	2006	2007	2008	
Total	346 950	473 078	276 080	313 848	335 581	380 754	394 996 [3]	473 078	908 834	976 923	Total
1	190 513	156 190	86 285	96 321	97 160	115 464	124 493 [4]	156 190	423 754	532 187	A
2	575 930	960 989	464 988	607 095	665 859	711 766	784 107 [4]	960 989	697 472	751 678	B
3	303 251	578 669	370 078	426 769	482 658	522 445	562 456 [4]	578 669	1 477 670	1 751 750	C
4	572 662	1 162 922	736 496	895 556	1 001 218	1 044 142	1 111 644 [4]	1 162 922	836 337	868 886	D
5	339 148	743 929	426 622	507 945	572 203	617 751	656 536 [4]	743 929	1 423 137	1 829 703	E
6	332 217	518 297	280 147	335 703	357 606	397 461	412 629 [4]	518 297	838 031	899 440	F
7	422 168	781 174	525 332	569 787	600 914	666 130	660 226 [4]	781 174	858 918	963 734	G
8	559 196	1 478 933	907 575	1 026 783	1 036 905	1 254 947	1 197 123 [4]	1 478 933	859 749	903 701	H
9	436 796	969 637	611 963	705 871	809 686	834 244 [5]	858 474	969 637	1 135 124	1 231 933	I
0	.	377 430	215 012	550 950	400 239	487 239	366 765 [4]	377 430	1 739 052	1 847 103	J
									1 465 469	1 554 825	K
									1 702 926	1 835 326	L
									1 357 794	1 435 115	M
									1 500 878	1 577 417	N
									798 522	833 436	O
									463 824	548 863	P
									2 552 906	2 590 854	Q
									663 274	858 913	X

Men - Hommes - Hombres

ISIC 2 - CITI 2 - CIIU 2   ISIC 3 - CITI 3 - CIIU 3

	1999	2000	2001	2002	2003	2004	2005	2006	2007	2008	
Total	384 005	547 253	333 677	375 954	400 982	455 607	464 095 [4]	547 253	982 450	1 055 123	Total
1	230 553	201 689	118 173	128 559	128 908	154 740	160 722 [4]	201 689	488 642	611 822	A
2	584 970	1 017 849	535 540	665 083	725 223	805 855	893 990 [4]	1 017 849	710 443	762 594	B
3	346 783	703 109	455 108	519 691	589 464	634 963	688 765 [4]	703 109	1 530 024	1 817 840	C
4	571 030	1 199 281	708 596	909 214	997 603	1 057 583	1 134 464 [4]	1 199 281	947 627	993 430	D
5	336 339	739 647	428 389	508 461	572 194	618 668	654 405 [4]	739 647	1 450 034	1 871 136	E
6	366 142	634 308	361 131	435 094	463 477	508 319	514 798 [4]	634 308	833 233	894 826	F
7	423 417	772 290	524 961	566 111	597 684	667 487	661 052 [4]	772 290	937 509	1 002 157	G
8	581 880	1 487 351	922 629	1 086 843	1 075 030	1 311 227	1 218 775 [4]	1 487 351	980 039	1 018 697	H
9	486 855	1 120 608	688 290	786 101	902 401	943 329	973 876 [4]	1 120 608	1 118 949	1 232 618	I
0	.	360 728	281 364	730 203	393 774	746 766	443 097 [4]	360 728	1 857 294	1 886 640	J
									1 519 629	1 549 224	K
									1 754 422	1 874 465	L
									1 484 330	1 551 906	M
									1 698 049	1 776 309	N
									831 748	854 122	O
									691 281	750 963	P
									2 594 959	2 299 935	Q
									697 486	874 116	X

Women - Femmes - Mujeres

ISIC 2 - CITI 2 - CIIU 2   ISIC 3 - CITI 3 - CIIU 3

	1999	2000	2001	2002	2003	2004	2005	2006	2007	2008	
Total	269 550	335 766	178 365	203 808	218 762	243 921	264 446 [4]	335 766	747 277	814 142	Total
1	124 964	69 040	33 650	41 298	42 620	46 893	56 922	69 040	301 205	380 427	A
2	448 534	521 832	131 340	228 062	260 547	218 293	178 522 [4]	521 832	479 034	589 435	B
3	226 675	400 200	254 880	294 309	334 071	352 530	381 853	400 200	849 474	976 403	C
4	598 546	871 555	969 634	773 539	1 044 238	906 743	847 304 [4]	871 555	655 915	678 723	D
5	409 288	903 269	368 065	490 174	572 476	581 332	752 099 [4]	903 269	1 242 621	1 380 203	E
6	276 068	383 407	194 266	223 503	238 224	269 856	291 583 [4]	383 407	1 020 843	1 097 027	F
7	404 130	945 797	534 723	670 739	689 765	629 350	633 963	945 797	721 606	896 673	G
8	506 167	1 458 517	861 181	859 009	937 470	1 086 438	1 138 102 [4]	1 458 517	678 668	750 754	H
9	356 935	778 593	494 415	581 009	661 287	675 251	693 756	778 593	1 301 344	1 225 032	I
0	.	420 736	134 244	200 000	544 017	210 822	232 507 [4]	420 736	1 530 195	1 769 778	J
									1 248 535	1 574 480	K
									1 501 175	1 685 042	L
									1 247 962	1 339 050	M
									1 382 652	1 449 927	N
									661 299	752 203	O
									393 346	499 490	P
									2 483 410	3 935 062	Q
									527 393	801 003	X

Explanatory notes: see p. 877.

[1] Persons aged 15 years and over. [2] Aug. of each year. [3] Nov. [4] November. [5] August.

Notes explicatives: voir p. 879.

[1] Personnes âgées de 15 ans et plus. [2] Août de chaque année. [3] Nov. [4] Novembre. [5] Août.

Notas explicativas: véase p. 882.

[1] Personas de 15 años y más. [2] Agosto de cada año. [3] Nov. [4] Noviembre. [5] Agosto.

	1999	2000	2001	2002	2003	2004	2005	2006	2007	2008

Israel (FA) [1] [2]   Employees - Salariés - Asalariados   E.G./m. - New shekel

Total men and women - Total hommes et femmes - Total hombres y mujeres
ISIC 3 - CITI 3 - CIIU 3

	1999	2000	2001	2002	2003	2004	2005	2006	2007	2008
Total	6 323	6 791	7 082	7 023	6 859	7 050 [3]	7 219	7 466	.	.
A-B	3 603	3 838	4 166	4 200	4 192	4 333 [3]	4 421	4 585	.	.
C-Q	6 413	6 882	7 167	7 109	6 942	7 127 [3]	7 303	7 551	.	.
C-D	8 286	8 738	9 138	9 226	9 288	9 529 [3]	9 911	10 370	.	.
E	13 753	14 962	15 342	15 716	15 428	15 545 [3]	16 775	18 305	.	.
F	5 274	5 667	5 946	5 991	5 818	5 978 [3]	5 996	6 163	.	.
G	5 873	6 297	6 537	6 429	6 296	6 318 [3]	6 468	6 613	.	.
H	3 316	3 485	3 517	3 452	3 478	3 477 [3]	3 522	3 621	.	.
I	8 327	8 544	8 704	8 733	8 579	8 534 [3]	8 663	8 883	.	.
J	11 167	12 651	13 214	12 552	12 247	13 024 [3]	13 609	14 989	.	.
K	5 861	6 764	7 061	6 801	6 588	6 868 [3]	7 282	7 639	.	.
L	8 776	9 183	11 062	11 362	10 935	11 645 [3]	11 362	11 835	.	.
M	5 211	5 478	5 724	5 806	5 546	5 738 [3]	5 745	5 867	.	.
N	5 428	5 669	5 827	5 787	5 684	5 913 [3]	5 988	6 042	.	.
O	4 585	4 868	4 961	4 943	4 712	5 019 [3]	5 123	5 146	.	.

Israel (FA) [4]   Wage earners - Ouvriers - Obreros   E.G./m. - New shekel

Total men and women - Total hommes et femmes - Total hombres y mujeres
ISIC 3 - CITI 3 - CIIU 3

	1999	2000	2001	2002	2003	2004	2005	2006	2007	2008
Total	.	.	.	.	.	.	7 324	7 576	7 749	8 075
A	.	.	.	.	.	.	4 801	4 927	4 992	5 269
C	.	.	.	.	.	.	15 614	17 498	19 303	20 590
D	.	.	.	.	.	.	9 848	10 297	10 602	10 886
E	.	.	.	.	.	.	16 816	18 346	18 281	19 693
F	.	.	.	.	.	.	6 287	6 473	6 659	7 137
G	.	.	.	.	.	.	6 470	6 617	6 794	7 023
H	.	.	.	.	.	.	3 488	3 575	3 658	3 765
I	.	.	.	.	.	.	8 676	8 891	8 931	9 116
J	.	.	.	.	.	.	13 597	14 966	14 906	15 732
K	.	.	.	.	.	.	7 344	7 696	8 015	8 513
L	.	.	.	.	.	.	11 364	11 845	12 082	12 381
M	.	.	.	.	.	.	5 746	5 868	6 004	6 375
N	.	.	.	.	.	.	6 231	6 329	6 492	6 705
O	.	.	.	.	.	.	5 072	5 076	5 230	5 343

Japan (DA)   Employees - Salariés - Asalariados   E.G./m. - Yen

Total men and women - Total hommes et femmes - Total hombres y mujeres
ISIC 4 - CITI 4 - CIIU 4

	1999	2000	2001	2002	2003	2004	2005	2006	2007	2008
B	300 400	299 100	295 100	293 700	285 200	292 400	302 900	306 900	301 900	298 800
C	291 100	293 100	297 500	296 400	296 500	293 100	292 100	299 600	296 800	293 400
F	320 800	320 800	325 900	313 800	316 900	319 400	321 400	323 400	321 100	316 700
G	.	.	.	.	.	308 400 [5]	306 100	295 700	295 500	305 300
I	.	.	.	.	.	245 600	239 400	240 500	239 500	244 600
J	.	.	.	.	.	353 400	358 100	367 900	372 400	355 000
K	352 900	355 000	364 200	355 600	360 300	366 300	373 300	373 100	377 300	368 600
L	337 100	335 600	333 600	345 400	348 600	350 800	334 000	335 800	339 300	327 000
P	.	.	.	.	.	378 500	393 100	381 800	382 900	376 800
Q	.	.	.	.	.	272 400	276 500	272 400	269 800	273 900

Men - Hommes - Hombres
ISIC 4 - CITI 4 - CIIU 4

	1999	2000	2001	2002	2003	2004	2005	2006	2007	2008
B	314 100	313 400	307 800	305 800	297 900	305 800	316 300	319 300	314 300	313 000
C	327 700	328 100	331 400	328 300	327 800	323 100	323 800	332 300	328 500	322 600
F	337 700	337 600	342 400	328 200	331 500	333 500	336 200	338 500	336 100	330 300
G	.	.	.	.	.	341 200 [5]	348 300	336 800	336 300	345 700
I	.	.	.	.	.	275 600	276 600	278 200	274 300	277 600
J	.	.	.	.	.	375 500	386 800	392 600	400 000	378 600
K	458 500	460 500	465 500	458 700	459 800	462 900	472 600	477 300	477 400	463 500
L	380 600	376 200	377 800	382 600	387 000	384 800	373 300	373 100	379 900	362 100
P	.	.	.	.	.	440 500	449 800	440 400	441 900	434 100
Q	.	.	.	.	.	371 400	371 700	365 700	355 000	361 000

Women - Femmes - Mujeres
ISIC 4 - CITI 4 - CIIU 4

	1999	2000	2001	2002	2003	2004	2005	2006	2007	2008
B	204 700	205 900	203 200	205 100	199 200	205 500	208 000	212 500	206 000	196 300
C	189 000	190 700	195 000	195 600	195 800	194 100	190 900	194 600	197 700	198 000
F	207 800	208 000	211 200	212 500	212 200	212 900	212 300	216 900	211 800	216 300
G	.	.	.	.	.	222 400 [5]	212 200	209 200	215 600	214 800
I	.	.	.	.	.	192 400	181 400	183 100	184 500	188 400
J	.	.	.	.	.	269 300	267 800	279 900	282 000	272 300
K	238 500	236 900	241 300	239 300	243 400	246 700	249 900	251 800	257 900	259 300
L	228 200	230 500	222 100	237 900	244 700	247 800	236 200	238 800	239 900	239 400
P	.	.	.	.	.	296 600	304 600	296 000	299 800	294 500
Q	.	.	.	.	.	241 600	243 300	242 700	242 100	243 900

Explanatory notes: see p. 877.   Notes explicatives: voir p. 879.   Notas explicativas: véase p. 882.

[1] Incl. workers from the Judea, Samaria and Gaza areas. [2] Incl. payments subject to income tax. [3] From 2004: new sample; data not strictly comparable. [4] Israeli workers only. [5] Wholesale and retail trade.

[1] Y compris les travailleurs des régions de Judée, Samarie et Gaza. [2] Y compris les versements soumis à l'impôt sur le revenu. [3] A partir de 2004: nouvel échantillon; données non strictement comparables. [4] Travailleurs israéliens seulement. [5] Commerce de gros et de détail.

[1] Incl. los trabajadores de las regiones de Judea, Samaria y Gaza. [2] Incl. los pagos sometidos al impuesto sobre la renta. [3] A partir de 1983: nueva muestra; datos no estrictamente comparables. [4] Trabajadores israelíes solamente. [5] Comercio al por mayor y por menor.

	1999	2000	2001	2002	2003	2004	2005	2006	2007	2008
Japan (DA) [1] [2]					Employees - Salariés - Asalariados					E.G./m. - Yen

Total men and women - Total hommes et femmes - Total hombres y mujeres
ISIC 3 - CITI 3 - CIIU 3

	1999	2000	2001	2002	2003	2004	2005	2006	2007	2008
C	300 400	299 100	295 100	293 700	285 200	292 400	302 900	306 900	301 900	298 800
D	291 100	293 100	297 500	296 400	296 500	293 100	292 100	299 600	296 800	293 400
E	392 500	397 400	400 600	399 200	399 500	399 600	406 900	403 600	405 700	398 700
F	320 800	320 800	325 900	313 800	316 900	319 400	321 400	323 400	321 100	316 700
G [3]						308 400	306 100	295 700	295 500	305 300
H						245 600	239 400	240 500	239 500	244 600
J	352 900	355 000	364 200	355 600	360 300	366 300	373 300	373 100	377 300	368 600
M						378 500	393 100	381 800	382 900	376 800
N						272 400	276 500	272 400	269 800	273 900

Men - Hommes - Hombres
ISIC 3 - CITI 3 - CIIU 3

	1999	2000	2001	2002	2003	2004	2005	2006	2007	2008
C	314 100	313 400	307 800	305 800	297 900	305 800	316 300	319 300	314 300	313 000
D	327 700	328 100	331 400	328 300	327 800	323 100	323 800	332 300	328 500	322 600
E	408 300	412 900	416 400	415 100	414 100	411 900	420 300	416 300	418 000	411 000
F	337 700	337 600	342 400	328 200	331 500	333 500	336 200	338 500	336 100	330 300
G [3]						341 200	348 300	336 800	336 300	345 700
H						275 600	276 600	278 200	274 300	277 600
J	458 500	460 500	465 500	458 700	459 800	462 900	472 600	477 300	477 400	463 500
M						440 500	449 800	440 400	441 900	434 100
N						371 400	371 700	365 700	355 000	361 000

Women - Femmes - Mujeres
ISIC 3 - CITI 3 - CIIU 3

	1999	2000	2001	2002	2003	2004	2005	2006	2007	2008
C	204 700	205 900	203 200	205 100	199 200	205 500	208 000	212 500	206 000	196 300
D	189 000	190 700	195 000	195 600	195 800	194 100	190 900	194 600	197 700	198 000
E	274 100	276 900	286 600	281 300	284 600	289 300	297 300	291 500	296 000	292 200
F	207 800	208 000	211 200	212 500	212 200	212 900	212 300	216 900	211 800	216 300
G [3]						222 400	212 200	209 200	215 600	214 800
H						192 400	181 400	183 100	184 500	188 400
J	238 500	236 900	241 300	239 300	243 400	246 700	249 900	251 800	257 900	259 300
M						296 600	304 600	296 000	299 800	294 500
N						241 600	243 300	242 700	242 100	243 900

	1999	2000	2001	2002	2003	2004	2005	2006	2007	2008
Japan (F) [4] [5]					Wage earners - Ouvriers - Obreros					E.G./d.j. - Yen

Men - Hommes - Hombres
ISIC 2 - CITI 2 - CIIU 2

	1999	2000	2001	2002	2003	2004	2005	2006	2007	2008
I [6]	8 729	8 652	8 659	8 663	8 671	8 649	8 653	8 653		

Women - Femmes - Mujeres
ISIC 2 - CITI 2 - CIIU 2

	1999	2000	2001	2002	2003	2004	2005	2006	2007	2008
I [6]	6 505	6 495	6 506	6 517	6 522	6 520	6 527	6 538		

	1999	2000	2001	2002	2003	2004	2005	2006	2007	2008
Jordan (DA) [7]					Employees - Salariés - Asalariados					E.G./m. - Dinar

Total men and women - Total hommes et femmes - Total hombres y mujeres
ISIC 3 - CITI 3 - CIIU 3

	1999	2000	2001	2002	2003	2004	2005	2006	2007	2008
C	370.0	328.0	378.0	423.1	421.0	428.0	440.0	479.0	519.0	
D	172.0	189.0	185.0	186.7	198.0	186.0	203.0	211.0	237.0	
E	263.0	265.0	275.0	277.4	276.0	313.0	337.0	391.0	404.0	
F	202.0	223.0		239.6	260.0	250.0	284.0	296.0	344.0	
G	155.0	172.0	169.0	165.6	173.0	169.0	202.0	209.0	226.0	
H	146.0	157.0	154.0	157.8	168.0	177.0	201.0	255.0	236.0	
I	253.0	298.0	319.0	373.7	349.0	336.0	419.0	415.0	444.0	
J	450.0	460.0	471.0	480.9	477.0	537.0	594.0	609.0	628.0	
K	225.0	231.0	244.0	289.6	264.0	271.0	274.0	253.0	329.0	
L	206.0	206.0	212.0	218.0	220.0	236.0	247.0	255.0	268.0	
M	245.0	255.0	259.0	265.1	280.0	306.0	308.0	329.0	359.0	
N	245.0	248.0	257.0	252.1	267.0	273.0	276.0	290.0	315.0	
O	179.0	173.0	187.0	172.1	178.0	193.0	190.0	260.0	263.0	

Explanatory notes: see p. 877.

[1] Regular scheduled cash earnings. [2] Private sector; establishments with 10 or more regular employees; June of each year. [3] Excl. repair of motor vehicles, motor cycles and personal and household goods. [4] Casual day workers. [5] Year ending in March of the year indicated. [6] Excl. fishing. [7] Oct. of each year.

Notes explicatives: voir p. 879.

[1] Gains en espèce tarifés réguliers. [2] Secteur privé; établissements occupant 10 salariés stables ou plus; juin de chaque années. [3] Non compris réparation de véhicules automobiles, de motocycles et de biens personnels etdomestiques. [4] Journaliers occasionnels. [5] Année se terminant en mars de l'année indiquée. [6] Non compris la pêche. [7] Oct. de chaque année.

Notas explicativas: véase p. 882.

[1] Ganancias en especie tarifadas regulares. [2] Sector privado; establecimientos con 10 y mas asalariados estables; junio de cada año. [3] Excl. reparación de vehículos automotores, motocicletas, efectos personals y enseres domesticos. [4] Jornaleros ocasionales. [5] Año que termina en marzo del año indicado. [6] Excl. la pesca. [7] Oct. de cada año.

	1999	2000	2001	2002	2003	2004	2005	2006	2007	2008

Jordan (DA) [1]　　　　　　　Employees - Salariés - Asalariados　　　　　　　E.G./m. - Dinar

Men - Hommes - Hombres
ISIC 3 - CITI 3 - CIIU 3

	1999	2000	2001	2002	2003	2004	2005	2006	2007	2008
C	371.0	328.0	378.0	424.3	421.0	429.0	439.0	476.0	518.0	.
C-O	227.0	234.0	238.0	246.0	250.0	250.0	273.0	291.0	315.0	.
D	180.0	198.0	195.0	196.0	208.0	201.0	222.0	234.0	254.0	.
E	265.0	267.0	276.0	278.5	278.0	315.0	339.0	393.0	409.0	.
F	203.0	225.0	236.0	240.4	261.0	251.0	283.0	297.0	344.0	.
G	155.0	174.0	169.0	163.4	179.0	168.0	187.0	210.0	229.0	.
H	144.0	155.0	152.0	155.8	168.0	174.0	199.0	251.0	235.0	.
I	256.0	299.0	313.0	370.6	347.0	334.0	418.0	408.0	430.0	.
J	487.0	494.0	506.0	518.4	512.0	582.0	644.0	651.0	676.0	.
K	246.0	249.0	257.0	293.9	295.0	285.0	277.0	241.0	358.0	.
L	205.0	206.0	213.0	219.1	221.0	235.0	246.0	254.0	266.0	.
M	283.0	304.0	301.0	317.3	330.0	383.0	371.0	397.0	425.0	.
N	295.0	304.0	316.0	305.9	326.0	319.0	328.0	338.0	374.0	.
O	184.0	194.0	195.0	180.7	187.0	215.0	208.0	282.0	275.0	.

Women - Femmes - Mujeres
ISIC 3 - CITI 3 - CIIU 3

	1999	2000	2001	2002	2003	2004	2005	2006	2007	2008
C	335.0	337.0	372.0	390.6	403.0	399.0	471.0	554.0	533.0	.
C-O	201.0	201.0	211.0	219.0	226.0	218.0	231.0	249.0	277.0	.
D	123.0	131.0	126.0	129.3	136.0	130.0	136.0	142.0	174.0	.
E	222.0	229.0	256.0	254.9	253.0	283.0	301.0	352.0	339.0	.
F	168.0	191.0	231.0	213.6	241.0	216.0	341.0	281.0	321.0	.
G	151.0	152.0	171.0	190.8	166.0	178.0	204.0	200.0	206.0	.
H	181.0	219.0	202.0	205.5	186.0	229.0	427.0	369.0	262.0	.
I	233.0	288.0	366.0	396.7	365.0	352.0	473.0	462.0	528.0	.
J	349.0	370.0	379.0	385.2	393.0	425.0	258.0	512.0	517.0	.
K	154.0	168.0	197.0	280.9	188.0	232.0	256.0	320.0	242.0	.
L	210.0	206.0	207.0	211.1	216.0	242.0	256.0	258.0	277.0	.
M	209.0	213.0	221.0	221.9	248.0	237.0	255.0	269.0	306.0	.
N	193.0	194.0	197.0	195.3	212.0	215.0	225.0	236.0	255.0	.
O	154.0	122.0	149.0	136.5	151.0	151.0	160.0	204.0	225.0	.

Kazakhstan (DA)　　　　　　　Employees - Salariés - Asalariados　　　　　　　E.G./m. - Tenge

Total men and women - Total hommes et femmes - Total hombres y mujeres
ISIC 3 - CITI 3 - CIIU 3

	1999	2000	2001	2002	2003	2004	2005	2006	2007	2008
Total	11 864	14 374	17 303	20 323	23 128	28 329	33 807	40 800	52 500	60 805
C-Q	.	.	.	.	.	.	.	.	.	.
A	3 896	5 657	6 851	8 163	9 567	11 978	15 000	18 800	24 700	31 407
B	4 798	6 812	7 562	8 685	10 481	10 999	14 600	18 300	25 300	28 894
C	24 659	32 059	36 625	40 045	45 594	54 305	65 800	75 900	89 800	109 933
D	13 821	17 717	19 982	22 130	24 823	30 234	35 400	43 600	54 400	65 874
E	15 651	17 290	20 026	21 594	23 339	26 899	30 800	37 000	46 000	55 995
F	15 905	21 017	26 805	32 453	34 473	38 622	47 900	55 700	70 800	81 573
G	10 766	12 961	15 366	18 931	22 797	27 595	33 500	40 200	49 300	59 330
H	13 736	15 979	21 511	32 743	40 012	44 925	47 400	48 700	56 800	64 382
I	14 696	18 788	24 412	28 969	34 140	41 637	49 000	58 900	70 400	83 012
J	33 392	36 140	41 686	50 460	55 207	64 532	79 500	97 500	121 600	138 544
K	12 338	16 672	22 132	29 329	36 624	40 628	50 700	60 500	78 200	93 557
L	11 308	11 758	14 970	16 930	18 045	26 031	31 200	35 600	45 600	47 276
M	8 149	8 512	9 937	12 863	14 406	17 964	20 300	24 000	31 900	34 454
N	6 821	7 267	8 288	10 863	12 112	15 195	18 000	21 300	33 100	35 775
O	10 097	12 857	16 873	21 078	24 175	29 510	39 100	43 100	52 300	61 369
Q	.	.	77 537	136 093	146 435	139 888	137 500	167 200	177 200	173 860

Men - Hommes - Hombres
ISIC 3 - CITI 3 - CIIU 3

	1999	2000	2001	2002	2003	2004	2005	2006	2007	2008
Total	14 034	17 603	21 511	24 847	28 476	34 648	41 840	49 737	62 629	73 508
C-Q	.	.	.	.	.	.	.	.	.	.
A	3 636	5 942	7 300	8 708	10 217	12 978	15 950	20 116	26 704	34 084
B	3 224	7 567	8 272	9 137	11 160	11 528	15 476	19 471	26 646	30 714
C	26 343	34 146	39 839	43 189	49 157	58 548	70 936	81 643	96 249	117 867
D	14 991	19 510	22 184	24 479	27 515	33 542	39 411	48 460	60 529	73 457
E	16 548	18 363	21 500	23 174	25 111	28 977	33 070	39 888	49 599	60 346
F	16 795	22 070	28 054	34 035	35 776	39 569	48 943	56 351	72 146	83 407
G	12 012	14 713	16 677	20 905	25 335	31 131	36 991	44 917	54 533	66 094
H	17 583	22 561	26 952	49 531	62 680	65 740	69 113	68 946	79 982	90 832
I	15 476	20 137	26 637	31 669	37 304	45 409	53 041	62 879	74 522	87 342
J	45 625	48 646	56 048	68 329	73 446	87 571	105 845	126 706	157 070	178 649
K	14 042	19 308	25 073	33 717	42 607	45 349	55 702	65 513	82 560	97 807
L	12 296	12 794	16 831	18 505	19 801	28 390	34 125	38 795	49 634	51 670
M	8 990	9 280	11 322	14 383	16 280	21 000	22 943	26 507	34 605	37 255
N	7 269	8 345	9 617	12 833	14 157	17 427	20 937	24 705	37 521	39 834
O	12 781	15 619	20 573	25 429	29 752	37 054	52 247	55 287	65 435	75 816
Q	79 656	50 292	91 754	149 397	157 626	153 226	155 361	206 493	209 397	188 825

Explanatory notes: see p. 877.　　　Notes explicatives: voir p. 879.　　　Notas explicativas: véase p. 882.

[1] Oct. of each year.　　　[1] Oct. de chaque année.　　　[1] Oct. de cada año.

WAGES   SALAIRES   SALARIOS

By economic activity   Par activité économique   Por actividad económica

	1999	2000	2001	2002	2003	2004	2005	2006	2007	2008

Kazakhstan (DA) — Employees - Salariés - Asalariados — E.G./m. - Tenge

Women - Femmes - Mujeres
ISIC 3 - CITI 3 - CIIU 3

	1999	2000	2001	2002	2003	2004	2005	2006	2007	2008
Total	9 485	10 819	12 635	15 340	17 304	21 445	25 564	30 984	41 202	46 922
A	3 989	4 725	5 444	6 518	7 734	9 869	12 248	15 387	19 495	24 698
B	5 400	4 282	5 353	7 069	8 297	9 504	12 241	15 369	21 064	22 428
C	19 420	25 229	26 911	30 279	34 376	40 459	48 626	56 617	68 427	82 517
D	11 433	13 981	15 597	17 433	19 382	23 433	27 190	33 432	41 452	49 764
E	13 366	14 539	16 428	17 755	19 176	22 052	25 541	30 588	38 149	46 423
F	12 176	15 982	19 923	23 238	26 841	33 133	41 793	51 578	61 985	70 437
G	9 542	11 081	13 540	16 262	19 397	22 749	28 776	34 273	42 667	51 208
H	12 404	13 973	18 749	24 247	27 831	33 800	36 773	38 825	46 177	52 137
I	13 074	16 012	20 083	23 725	28 065	34 431	41 258	50 804	61 784	73 749
J	27 010	29 395	33 698	40 324	45 121	52 541	65 304	82 095	102 255	116 749
K	10 203	13 275	17 817	22 879	26 909	32 372	40 761	50 381	68 942	84 616
L	9 752	10 032	11 777	14 183	15 067	22 227	26 479	30 596	39 306	40 540
M	7 888	8 274	9 494	12 355	13 772	16 916	19 427	23 075	31 008	33 506
N	6 725	7 042	8 015	10 472	11 696	14 739	17 456	20 631	32 148	34 952
O	7 587	10 156	13 299	16 936	18 927	22 371	27 211	32 362	40 246	47 914
Q	54 727	45 356	65 174	116 968	133 845	122 739	111 285	106 783	138 243	157 899

Korea, Republic of (DA) [1][2] — Employees - Salariés - Asalariados — E.G./m. - Won

Total men and women - Total hommes et femmes - Total hombres y mujeres
ISIC 3 - CITI 3 - CIIU 3

	1999	2000	2001	2002	2003	2004	2005	2006	2007	2008
C	1 563.0	1 679.0	1 745.0	1 938.0	2 229.0	2 398.0	2 474.7	2 544.9	2 767.7	2 640.0
C-X	1 544.0	1 668.0	1 752.0	1 948.0	2 127.4	2 254.9	2 404.4	2 541.9	2 683.2	2 809.9
D	1 443.0	1 568.0	1 659.0	1 857.0	2 018.0	2 209.3	2 387.6	2 522.5	2 688.4	2 758.7
E	2 304.0	2 458.0	2 835.0	3 206.0	3 648.7	3 838.2	4 101.3	4 307.4	4 648.8	4 017.1
F	1 576.0	1 701.0	1 687.0	1 859.0	2 072.4	2 129.9	2 123.1	2 319.2	2 436.7	2 875.4
G	1 426.0	1 548.0	1 725.0	1 888.0	2 089.0	2 175.0	2 408.4	2 542.6	2 693.3	2 889.4
H	1 052.0	1 106.0	1 174.0	1 364.0	1 438.6	1 512.7	1 600.0	1 615.1	1 622.3	1 929.1
I	1 555.0	1 744.0	.	1 652.3	1 835.5	1 926.4	2 111.0	2 381.9	2 520.2	2 659.6
J	2 185.0	2 396.0	2 592.0	2 940.0	3 310.0	3 539.0	3 748.1	4 077.0	4 403.4	3 906.7
K	1 404.0	1 495.0	1 550.0	1 753.0	1 854.0	1 985.0	2 114.0	2 290.2	2 424.1	2 556.8
L										
M	1 831.0	1 932.4	1 947.8	2 392.7	2 559.8	2 696.4	2 724.3	2 874.8	2 893.0	3 182.7
N	1 530.8	.	1 707.6	1 824.4	1 953.1	2 059.2	2 259.0	2 460.9	2 544.2	2 597.0
O	1 575.0	1 756.0	1 772.0	1 868.9	2 059.3	2 143.5	2 224.3	2 262.7	2 362.1	2 475.6
P										
Q										

Men - Hommes - Hombres
ISIC 3 - CITI 3 - CIIU 3

	1999	2000	2001	2002	2003	2004	2005	2006	2007	2008
C	1 635.0	1 742.0	1 815.0	2 029.0	2 322.8	2 498.6	2 556.4	2 644.0	2 865.7	
C-X	1 735.0	1 885.0	1 976.0	2 193.0	2 406.4	2 557.5	2 719.3	2 870.9	3 039.2	
D	1 650.0	1 790.0	1 889.0	2 118.0	2 304.6	2 521.4	2 715.7	2 847.4	3 025.6	
E	2 401.0	2 575.0	2 977.0	3 368.0	3 817.0	4 067.8	4 350.3	4 571.9	4 895.5	
F	1 678.0	1 815.0	1 792.0	1 979.0	2 199.8	2 261.6	2 245.6	2 463.9	2 587.0	
G	1 609.0	1 766.0	1 972.0	2 162.0	2 398.7	2 498.0	2 737.4	2 899.5	3 088.9	
H	1 258.0	1 322.0	1 420.0	1 670.0	1 756.5	1 850.4	1 932.2	1 972.5	1 992.5	
I	1 594.0	1 800.0	1 825.0	1 971.2	2 178.5	2 228.1	2 392.6	2 425.2	2 567.7	
J	2 717.7	3 016.6	3 235.8	3 627.0	4 007.6	4 259.6	4 489.5	4 893.1	5 251.4	
K	1 540.0	1 660.0	1 728.0	3 627.3	4 007.6	4 259.6	2 364.0	2 583.5	2 760.9	
L										
M	2 158.6	2 249.6	2 361.8	2 856.4	3 113.7	3 336.5	3 367.6	3 545.2	3 659.2	
N	2 001.0	2 084.0	2 298.4	2 468.8	2 705.7	2 853.0	3 300.6	3 576.0	3 731.0	
O	1 841.0	2 093.0	2 033.0	2 078.9	2 296.0	2 396.1	2 484.8	2 543.8	2 643.4	
P										
Q										

Women - Femmes - Mujeres
ISIC 3 - CITI 3 - CIIU 3

	1999	2000	2001	2002	2003	2004	2005	2006	2007	2008
C	881.6	946.8	1 019.3	1 103.4	1 208.7	1 275.1	1 414.6	1 399.0	1 596.3	
C-X	1 090.0	1 178.0	1 257.0	1 393.0	1 500.9	1 579.4	1 696.9	1 811.5	1 908.3	
D	918.0	1 036.0	1 096.0	1 187.0	1 291.2	1 382.8	1 525.4	1 643.2	1 742.1	
E	1 295.0	1 336.0	1 595.0	1 798.0	2 048.3	2 115.3	2 280.0	2 379.6	2 723.2	
F	909.0	980.0	1 045.0	1 116.0	1 313.7	1 304.7	1 379.7	1 422.3	1 535.9	
G	1 026.0	1 112.0	1 214.0	1 330.0	1 490.3	1 540.6	1 701.1	1 798.4	1 893.9	
H	854.0	915.0	966.0	1 115.0	1 189.1	1 253.4	1 325.5	1 349.6	1 350.8	
I	1 256.5	1 329.0	1 431.9	1 611.1	1 775.1	1 778.9	1 974.7	2 123.6	2 248.3	
J	1 554.0	1 704.0	1 886.0	2 076.0	2 777.2	2 425.6	2 630.6	2 852.2	3 103.1	
K	938.0	994.0	1 072.0	1 268.5	1 323.1	1 400.8	1 479.7	1 572.0	1 633.6	
L										
M	1 375.0	1 409.0	1 459.0	1 840.6	1 902.5	1 969.7	1 990.0	2 124.5	2 126.1	
N	1 274.0	1 330.0	1 428.2	1 535.8	1 635.1	1 749.0	1 852.1	2 025.3	2 113.9	
O	1 016.0	1 115.0	1 120.1	1 308.0	1 413.8	1 475.4	1 557.3	1 591.2	1 690.1	
P										
Q										

Explanatory notes: see p. 877.

[1] Figures in thousands. [2] Establishments with 5 or more regular employees.

Notes explicatives: voir p. 879.

[1] Données en milliers. [2] Establissements occupant 5 salariés stables et plus.

Notas explicativas: véase p. 882.

[1] Cifras en millares. [2] Establecimientos con 5 y más asalariados estables.

WAGES

SALAIRES

SALARIOS

5A

By economic activity

Par activité économique

Por actividad económica

	1999	2000	2001	2002	2003	2004	2005	2006	2007	2008

Korea, Republic of (DA) [1][2]   Employees - Salariés - Asalariados   E.G./m. - Won

Total men and women - Total hommes et femmes - Total hombres y mujeres
ISIC 3 - CITI 3 - CIIU 3

	1999	2000	2001	2002	2003	2004	2005	2006	2007	2008
C	1 581.1	1 702.3	1 779.6	1 994.0	2 304.0	2 457.0	2 536.9	2 615.6	2 834.7	2 724.0
C-X	1 599.2	1 727.3	1 824.8	2 036.0	2 228.0	2 373.0	2 524.9	2 666.6	2 823.2	2 891.4
D	1 475.5	1 601.5	1 702.4	1 907.0	2 074.0	2 280.0	2 458.0	2 594.8	2 772.4	2 757.8
E	2 327.6	2 489.8	2 875.4	3 243.0	3 661.0	3 860.0	4 138.0	4 353.6	4 703.1	4 006.6
F	1 690.9	1 839.8	1 834.7	2 063.0	2 287.0	2 352.0	2 373.8	2 576.5	2 730.6	3 140.5
G	1 471.2	1 597.6	1 826.7	1 979.0	2 215.0	2 301.0	2 573.5	2 717.9	2 883.0	3 018.4
H	1 191.8	1 251.2	1 335.8	1 527.0	1 615.0	1 686.0	1 781.1	1 830.0	1 851.2	1 948.0
I	1 575.7	1 771.5	1 802.7	1 954.0	2 156.0	2 203.0	2 361.0	2 405.9	2 545.9	2 638.6
J	2 215.9	2 448.1	2 646.1	3 027.1	3 395.2	3 646.2	3 854.3	4 198.2	4 531.7	3 959.0
K	1 445.0	1 532.8	1 596.7	1 827.4	1 924.5	2 066.2	2 197.7	2 387.0	2 539.0	2 593.6
M	2 018.7	2 095.8	2 137.7	2 596.9	2 849.9	3 053.1	3 051.6	3 192.1	3 231.8	3 367.5
N	1 604.3	1 671.2	1 804.0	1 944.6	2 078.1	2 191.7	2 403.1	2 592.7	2 675.9	2 693.7
O	1 686.2	1 889.1	1 893.9	2 039.8	2 256.1	2 345.4	2 422.5	2 456.1	2 549.7	2 577.8
P	.	.	.	1 944.6	2 078.1	2 191.7	2 403.1	.	.	.
Q	.	.	.	2 413.7	2 755.8	2 874.5	2 840.6	.	.	.

Men - Hommes - Hombres
ISIC 3 - CITI 3 - CIIU 3

	1999	2000	2001	2002	2003	2004	2005	2006	2007	2008
C	1 650.3	1 763.8	1 849.6	2 084.0	2 391.6	2 549.9	2 618.1	2 713.1	2 929.5	.
C-X	1 786.1	1 938.0	2 044.3	2 280.7	2 503.5	2 668.4	2 837.5	2 992.0	3 176.3	.
D	1 686.3	1 826.4	1 936.4	2 177.0	2 369.7	2 599.8	2 798.6	2 931.9	3 123.6	.
E	2 420.9	2 604.3	3 018.6	3 404.0	3 830.2	4 082.8	4 384.5	4 615.7	4 952.8	.
F	1 785.3	1 941.2	1 938.5	2 180.0	2 412.1	2 480.8	2 505.4	2 718.2	2 883.5	.
G	1 671.0	1 839.8	2 117.9	2 302.0	2 581.5	2 676.4	2 966.8	3 137.8	3 335.0	.
H	1 351.9	1 427.8	1 543.1	1 797.0	1 896.7	1 989.1	2 101.8	2 189.9	2 253.1	.
I	1 609.5	1 818.6	1 840.9	1 988.5	2 196.6	2 247.2	2 404.3	2 434.5	2 578.4	.
J	2 763.2	3 087.0	3 312.5	3 748.0	4 104.0	4 375.0	4 612.5	5 027.3	5 413.4	.
K	1 575.0	1 692.9	1 777.3	1 994.8	2 129.0	2 304.9	2 448.1	2 689.7	2 892.5	.
L										
M	2 263.4	2 333.5	2 465.8	2 973.9	3 270.8	3 509.7	3 555.7	3 731.7	3 855.5	.
N	2 052.9	2 130.7	2 356.6	2 566.0	2 814.4	2 995.5	3 402.4	3 640.6	3 762.6	.
O	1 942.8	2 217.2	2 147.7	2 237.8	2 484.2	2 584.5	2 661.4	2 726.6	2 830.4	.
P	.	.	.	.	.	.	.	.	.	.
Q	.	.	.	.	.	.	.	.	.	.

Women - Femmes - Mujeres
ISIC 3 - CITI 3 - CIIU 3

	1999	2000	2001	2002	2003	2004	2005	2006	2007	2008
C	881.6	946.8	1 019.3	1 103.0	1 208.7	1 324.9	1 421.3	1 397.7	1 612.2	.
C-X	1 130.9	1 224.8	1 315.0	1 458.0	1 573.6	1 662.7	1 777.6	1 898.4	2 005.0	.
D	933.1	1 055.8	1 121.3	1 211.0	1 320.0	1 419.7	1 556.1	1 675.6	1 785.3	.
E	1 325.5	1 372.8	1 623.9	1 837.0	2 062.0	2 150.4	2 323.4	2 431.4	2 765.5	.
F	960.5	1 064.8	1 125.0	1 243.0	1 438.7	1 422.7	1 525.7	1 580.8	1 692.2	.
G	1 048.1	1 134.7	1 255.0	1 366.0	1 544.4	1 595.8	1 750.1	1 869.3	1 991.2	.
H	986.2	1 051.8	1 113.1	1 258.0	1 341.8	1 382.6	1 442.1	1 491.9	1 510.7	.
I	1 290.7	1 386.6	1 496.8	1 686.0	1 859.0	1 876.0	2 055.1	2 216.9	2 341.3	.
J	1 574.2	1 737.8	1 929.9	2 129.6	2 323.7	2 490.3	2 688.4	2 879.3	3 142.3	.
K	949.3	1 002.5	1 087.1	1 310.0	1 351.0	1 432.0	1 534.1	1 620.0	1 682.2	.
L										
M	1 584.2	1 594.7	1 651.3	2 069.7	2 225.3	2 364.2	2 300.9	2 433.2	2 436.2	.
N	1 341.7	1 418.7	1 519.5	1 633.0	1 736.7	1 845.5	1 977.0	2 143.5	2 239.4	.
O	1 079.7	1 189.3	1 178.0	1 448.4	1 551.6	1 616.4	1 719.6	1 729.5	1 829.8	.
P	.	.	.	.	.	.	.	.	.	.
Q	.	.	.	.	.	.	.	.	.	.

Korea, Republic of (DA) [1][3]   Employees - Salariés - Asalariados   E.G./m. - Won

Total men and women - Total hommes et femmes - Total hombres y mujeres
ISIC 3 - CITI 3 - CIIU 3

	1999	2000	2001	2002	2003	2004	2005	2006	2007	2008
C	.	.	.	.	.	.	.	.	2 632.0	2 593.1
C-X	.	.	.	.	.	.	.	.	2 566.0	2 639.7
D	.	.	.	.	.	.	.	.	2 662.5	2 679.1
E	.	.	.	.	.	.	.	.	3 872.3	3 953.1
F	.	.	.	.	.	.	.	.	2 319.9	2 476.7
G	.	.	.	.	.	.	.	.	2 604.5	2 779.0
H	.	.	.	.	.	.	.	.	1 727.0	1 824.6
I	.	.	.	.	.	.	.	.	2 442.6	2 588.5
J	.	.	.	.	.	.	.	.	3 646.1	3 722.0
K	.	.	.	.	.	.	.	.	2 191.2	2 382.1
M	.	.	.	.	.	.	.	.	2 715.5	2 732.7
N	.	.	.	.	.	.	.	.	2 491.5	2 550.1
O	.	.	.	.	.	.	.	.	2 200.3	2 283.6

Explanatory notes: see p. 877.

[1] Figures in thousands. [2] Establishments with 10 or more regular employees. [3] Incl. temporary and daily employees of the establishments with 5 or more permanent employees.

Notes explicatives: voir p. 879.

[1] Données en milliers. [2] Etablissements occupant 10 salariés stables ou plus. [3] Y compris salariés temporaires et journaliers des etablissements occupant 5 salariés ou plus.

Notas explicativas: véase p. 882.

[1] Cifras en millares. [2] Establecimientos con 10 y más asalariados estables. [3] Incl. asalariados diarios y temporales de los establecimientos con 5 y más asalariados.

5A — WAGES / SALAIRES / SALARIOS

By economic activity / Par activité économique / Por actividad económica

Korea, Republic of (DA) [1][2]

Employees - Salariés - Asalariados

Total men and women - Total hommes et femmes - Total hombres y mujeres
ISIC 3 - CITI 3 - CIIU 3

E.G./m. - Won

	1999	2000	2001	2002	2003	2004	2005	2006	2007	2008
C										
C-X									2 673.7	2 631.1
D									2 627.0	2 711.6
E									2 696.5	2 675.9
F									3 904.8	3 948.7
G									2 431.6	2 645.0
H									2 658.3	2 869.1
I									1 788.6	1 842.5
J									2 451.0	2 564.3
K									3 683.6	3 717.4
L									2 310.4	2 452.3
M									0.0	
N									2 834.6	2 791.6
O									2 580.6	2 626.7
									2 274.7	2 312.1

Kyrgyzstan (CA)

Employees - Salariés - Asalariados

Total men and women - Total hommes et femmes - Total hombres y mujeres
ISIC 3 - CITI 3 - CIIU 3

E.G./m. - Som

	1999	2000	2001	2002	2003	2004	2005	2006	2007	2008
Total	1 049.90	1 227.00	1 455.10	1 684.40	1 916.00	2 240.00	2 612.00	3 270.00	3 970.00	
A-B [3]				776.20	878.00	903.80	1 041.20	1 259.10	1 788.20	
C-Q	1 108.70	1 279.60	1 598.20	1 738.60	1 978.60	2 311.00	2 682.00	3 473.00	4 039.00	
A [3]	450.20	591.10	703.90	775.90	878.00	903.50	1 040.90	1 203.40	1 733.20	
B [3]					833.50	870.50	1 084.80	1 172.10	1 852.00	1 471.30
C	1 699.00	2 240.40	1 893.20	2 050.70	2 163.90	2 415.00	2 927.00	3 964.00	4 609.00	
D	1 962.30	2 020.10	2 390.60	2 833.50	3 182.60	3 759.00	4 230.00	6 211.00	6 254.00	
E	1 868.40	2 097.10	2 644.80	3 391.90	3 752.40	4 116.00	4 410.00	5 340.00	6 315.00	
F	1 537.50	1 816.40	1 818.70	1 984.20	2 111.10	2 213.00	2 388.00	2 886.00	3 613.00	
G	830.90	1 089.40	1 199.60	1 399.00	1 615.70	1 901.00	2 081.00	2 288.00	3 142.00	
H	1 277.60	1 712.40	1 719.30	2 580.60	2 781.20	2 915.00	3 415.00	3 243.00	4 191.00	
I	1 301.10	1 722.70	2 054.60	2 417.30	2 833.50	2 480.00	4 108.00	5 141.00	6 497.00	
J	3 056.00	4 240.10	4 717.20	5 146.30	5 489.10	7 507.00	9 555.00	10 948.00	10 791.00	
K	1 152.70	1 429.10	1 715.80	1 879.90	2 199.90	2 521.00	2 981.00	3 492.00	4 576.00	
L	1 262.40	1 653.40	2 273.10	2 403.50	2 792.30	3 132.00	3 525.00	3 753.00	4 469.00	
M	607.50	715.10	866.10	976.40	1 128.20	1 346.00	1 622.00	1 955.00	2 676.00	
N	516.20	579.00	692.50	799.50	943.30	1 126.00	1 386.00	1 750.00	2 541.00	
O	765.40	994.80	1 081.20	1 238.60	1 392.80	1 684.00	1 933.00	2 243.00	2 536.00	

Macau, China (BA) [4]

Total employment - Emploi total - Empleo total

Total men and women - Total hommes et femmes - Total hombres y mujeres
ISIC 3 - CITI 3 - CIIU 3

E.G./m. - Pataca

	1999	2000	2001	2002	2003	2004	2005	2006	2007	2008
Total	4 920	4 822	4 658	4 672	4 801	5 167	5 773	6 701	7 800	8 000
C-Q	4 917	4 816	4 663	4 676	4 805	5 173	5 775	6 706	7 800	8 000
C	10 751	4 251	5 251	4 501	13 591	11 751	6 251	7 642	7 500	
D	2 921	2 960	2 758	2 758	2 834	2 983	3 101	3 140	4 000	4 000
E	11 726	11 631	9 955	12 648	11 010	11 546	12 969	13 417	14 100	15 000
F	4 660	4 351	4 300	4 145	4 593	4 967	5 922	7 521	8 500	10 000
G	4 711	4 533	4 445	4 430	4 355	4 550	4 888	5 576	6 000	7 000
H	4 443	4 099	4 005	4 054	4 074	4 272	4 468	4 885	5 500	6 100
I	5 675	5 649	5 630	5 851	5 802	5 958	6 455	6 924	7 800	8 500
J	7 549	7 726	7 696	7 923	8 588	8 159	8 691	8 825	9 800	11 000
K	4 385	3 957	3 823	3 731	3 700	3 712	4 198	4 675	5 500	5 600
L	13 767	13 742	13 805	13 745	14 019	13 895	14 521	14 793	14 900	18 000
M	9 526	9 095	8 672	8 690	9 084	8 975	9 503	9 636	9 900	12 000
N	7 914	9 137	9 831	7 756	7 904	9 669	9 705	8 029	9 900	10 000
O	6 494	6 156	6 187	5 965	6 466	7 080	7 837	9 537	11 600	12 000
P	2 940	2 816	2 846	2 813	2 752	2 674	2 609	2 543	2 500	2 700

Men - Hommes - Hombres
ISIC 3 - CITI 3 - CIIU 3

	1999	2000	2001	2002	2003	2004	2005	2006	2007	2008
Total	5 877	5 791	5 572	5 670	5 736	5 979	6 820	7 713	8 700	9 500
C-Q	5 873	5 784	5 575	5 276	5 743	5 981	6 823	7 716	8 800	9 500
C	10 751		5 251	4 501	13 591	11 751	6 251	7 642	7 500	
D	4 738	4 690	4 527	4 469	4 363	4 829	4 765	5 462	6 500	5 300
E	11 613	12 021	10 532	12 890	10 563	11 492	14 278	14 116	14 200	15 000
F	4 687	4 335	4 290	4 110	4 569	4 970	5 994	7 646	8 800	10 000
G	5 480	4 947	4 758	4 824	4 809	4 904	5 724	5 964	7 100	7 500
H	5 551	5 480	4 873	5 027	4 879	5 079	5 630	6 311	6 800	8 000
I	5 689	5 661	5 650	5 793	5 847	5 903	6 559	7 097	7 800	8 500
J	8 762	8 597	8 554	9 572	9 726	8 800	9 670	9 548	10 100	14 500
K	4 246	3 954	3 797	3 753	3 776	3 736	4 285	4 610	5 400	6 000
L	13 481	13 613	13 440	13 498	13 709	13 666	13 921	14 599	14 800	18 000
M	10 116	9 794	9 704	9 477	9 673	9 758	9 956	9 977	12 900	15 000
N	9 451	9 948	11 603	8 881	8 972	11 836	11 295	9 329	13 000	12 000
O	6 551	6 607	6 474	6 660	6 668	7 241	7 924	9 654	11 600	12 000
P	5 551	5 803	4 778	4 282	3 501	3 615	4 801	5 568	6 700	6 000

Explanatory notes: see p. 877.

[1] Incl. temporary and daily employees of the establishments with 10 or more permanent employees. [2] Figures in thousands. [3] Incl. the value of housing. [4] Median.

Notes explicatives: voir p. 879.

[1] Y compris salariés temporaires et journaliers des établissements occupant 10 salariés ou plus. [2] Données en milliers. [3] Y compris la valeur du logement. [4] Médiane.

Notas explicativas: véase p. 882.

[1] Incl. asalariados diarios y temporales de los establecimientos con 10 y más asalariados. [2] Cifras en millares. [3] Incl. el valor de vivienda. [4] Mediana.

	1999	2000	2001	2002	2003	2004	2005	2006	2007	2008

Macau, China (BA) [1] — Total employment - Emploi total - Empleo total — E.G./m. - Pataca

Women - Femmes - Mujeres
ISIC 3 - CITI 3 - CIIU 3

	1999	2000	2001	2002	2003	2004	2005	2006	2007	2008
Total	3 835	3 867	3 692	3 766	3 887	4 210	4 559	5 194	6 100	7 000
C-Q	3 834	3 865	3 693	3 767	3 890	4 216	4 572	5 205	6 300	7 000
C	.	4 251	.	.	.	.	.	.	.	.
D	2 510	2 613	2 429	2 430	2 542	2 652	2 795	2 698	3 100	3 500
E	12 938	11 620	9 298	9 021	11 501	11 848	8 267	12 167	14 000	13 000
F	4 436	4 509	4 471	4 418	4 904	4 945	5 414	5 750	6 600	7 500
G	4 044	3 876	3 886	3 858	3 808	3 926	4 324	4 821	5 200	6 000
H	3 745	3 606	3 524	3 570	3 573	3 732	3 915	4 313	4 900	6 000
I	5 616	5 602	5 567	6 168	5 687	6 391	5 905	6 578	7 700	8 500
J	7 062	7 322	7 274	7 570	7 633	7 768	8 006	8 624	9 700	10 000
K	4 672	3 965	3 878	3 675	3 513	3 656	4 024	4 743	5 700	5 500
L	14 730	14 352	15 541	15 385	15 280	14 791	15 898	15 902	16 100	18 200
M	9 170	8 755	8 287	8 591	8 875	8 597	8 771	8 995	9 700	11 000
N	6 886	8 117	9 403	6 652	7 064	8 485	8 910	7 853	8 700	9 000
O	6 368	5 708	5 851	5 553	5 944	6 880	7 739	8 708	11 500	12 000
P	2 904	2 756	2 792	2 773	2 735	2 646	2 582	2 500	2 500	2 700

Macau, China (DA) — Employees - Salariés - Asalariados — E.G./m. - Pataca

Total men and women - Total hommes et femmes - Total hombres y mujeres
ISIC 3 - CITI 3 - CIIU 3

	1999	2000	2001	2002	2003	2004	2005	2006	2007	2008
D [2]	.	4 044	4 102	3 970	4 010	4 178	4 390	4 652	4 990	5 447
E [2]	.	17 831	17 891	18 247	18 520	17 913	18 660	19 483	20 790	22 129
G [3]	.	5 422	5 391	5 427	6 748	7 180	7 593	8 595	9 294	10 310
H [2]	.	5 064	5 092	5 231	5 147	5 528	5 597	8 678	9 127	10 114
I [4]	.	9 289	9 496	10 025	11 868	12 710	16 830	17 098	18 575	20 111
J [2]	.	11 936	12 159	12 503	12 656	12 887	13 378	14 709	15 539	17 687
K [3]	.	.	.	.	.	.	.	6 418	7 244	8 498
O [3]	.	.	.	.	.	11 321	11 881	14 132	15 060	15 968

Men - Hommes - Hombres
ISIC 3 - CITI 3 - CIIU 3

	1999	2000	2001	2002	2003	2004	2005	2006	2007	2008
D [2]	.	5 411	5 382	5 250	5 335	5 750	5 961	6 193	6 716	7 072
E [2]	.	18 319	18 212	18 651	19 123	18 864	19 550	20 333	21 483	22 927
G [3]	.	5 918	5 754	5 991	7 421	7 913	8 455	9 533	10 019	11 138
H [2]	.	5 922	6 037	6 223	6 091	6 547	6 777	7 899	11 116	12 037
I [4]	.	10 362	10 543	11 162	13 175	13 939	18 395	18 354	20 269	21 505
J [2]	.	14 580	14 887	15 496	15 734	16 235	17 121	18 669	19 756	22 158
K [3]	.	.	.	.	.	.	.	6 182	7 030	8 281
O [3]	.	.	.	.	.	12 040	12 835	15 220	15 814	16 759

Women - Femmes - Mujeres
ISIC 3 - CITI 3 - CIIU 3

	1999	2000	2001	2002	2003	2004	2005	2006	2007	2008
D [2]	.	3 606	3 683	3 575	3 584	3 689	3 860	4 074	4 272	4 689
E [2]	.	15 513	16 369	16 380	15 936	14 255	15 378	16 256	18 097	19 044
G [3]	.	4 951	5 043	4 883	6 065	6 516	6 874	7 711	8 610	9 614
H [2]	.	4 263	4 243	4 336	4 312	4 598	4 947	.	7 269	8 234
I [4]	.	7 721	7 948	8 275	9 887	10 752	13 769	14 597	15 428	17 368
J [2]	.	9 930	10 110	10 229	10 340	10 462	10 705	11 899	12 684	14 767
K [3]	.	.	.	.	.	.	.	7 432	8 313	9 561
O [3]	.	.	.	.	.	10 510	10 844	13 062	14 349	15 251

Mongolia (DA) [5] — Employees - Salariés - Asalariados — E.G./m. - Tughriks

Total men and women - Total hommes et femmes - Total hombres y mujeres
ISIC 3 - CITI 3 - CIIU 3

	1999	2000	2001	2002	2003	2004	2005	2006	2007	2008
Total	.	62.3 [6]	65.2	71.3	81.5	93.1	101.2	127.7	173.0	274.2
A-B	.	48.4 [6]	50.3	45.7	37.3	.	.	.	.	.
C-Q	.	58.2 [6]	63.0	70.6	80.9	91.8	103.3	.	.	.
A	.	48.4 [6]	56.3	46.2	48.0	52.6	52.8	.	90.5	158.1
B	.	.	.	45.1	26.6	.	.	.	.	.
C	.	59.3 [6]	57.3	77.4	88.7	89.7	122.8	146.1	219.7	328.6
D	.	66.0 [6]	.	68.7	82.7	92.8	100.5	124.1	160.2	268.0
E	.	72.8 [6]	77.5	81.0	97.1	111.8	119.6	139.5	165.7	240.9
F	.	70.2 [6]	73.7	90.6	85.9	99.6	110.9	.	167.7	223.2
G	.	51.1 [6]	54.9	57.6	64.6	73.8	73.0	85.7	123.1	193.8
H	.	62.9 [6]	70.8	80.4	88.0	100.4	116.1	.	153.2	.
I	.	78.4 [6]	84.1	90.9	106.1	109.0	112.4	129.7	174.1	255.6
J	.	47.3 [6]	59.2	83.2	103.8	125.4	163.9	255.5	361.9	471.4
K	.	50.5 [6]	58.7	55.3	65.3	66.0	68.3	.	132.4	.
L	.	56.7 [6]	59.3	66.5	78.2	94.4	106.2	.	194.0	327.3
M	.	59.2 [6]	60.8	64.5	77.5	88.2	92.8	.	174.3	289.2
N	.	43.7 [6]	48.4	51.5	60.8	79.9	84.6	116.5	166.0	295.8
O	.	38.7 [6]	47.9	50.7	53.7	62.4	68.4	91.3	147.1	213.9

Explanatory notes: see p. 877.

[1] Median. [2] Third quarter of each year. [3] Fourth quarter of each year. [4] Fourth quarter of each year; excl. 63 since 2005. [5] Figures in thousands. [6] Fourth quarter.

Notes explicatives: voir p. 879.

[1] Médiane. [2] Troisième trimestre de chaque année. [3] Quatrième trimestre de chaque année. [4] Quatrième trimestre de chaque année; non compris 63 depuis 2005. [5] Données en milliers. [6] Quatrième trimestre.

Notas explicativas: véase p. 882.

[1] Mediana. [2] Tercer trimestre de cada año. [3] Cuarto trimestre de cada año. [4] Cuarto trimestre de cada año; excl. 63 desde 2005. [5] Cifras en millares. [6] Cuarto trimestre.

5A

WAGES	SALAIRES	SALARIOS
By economic activity	Par activité économique	Por actividad económica

	1999	2000	2001	2002	2003	2004	2005	2006	2007	2008

Mongolia (DA) [1]   Employees - Salariés - Asalariados   E.G./m. - Tughriks

Men - Hommes - Hombres
ISIC 3 - CITI 3 - CIIU 3

	1999	2000	2001	2002	2003	2004	2005	2006	2007	2008
Total	.	64.7 [2]	69.2	75.6	86.9	98.3	110.0	131.8	186.7	291.3
A-B	.	52.9 [2]	60.6	44.8	39.7			.	.	.
C-Q	.	60.0 [2]	65.1	72.8	84.4	93.7	108.7	.	.	.
A	.	52.9 [2]	60.6	45.2	49.4	52.9	57.7	64.0	96.0	163.4
B	.	. [2]	.	44.5	29.9	.	.	.	.	.
C	.	60.0 [2]	60.3	79.4	91.0	94.4	127.3	154.4	230.1	343.7
D	.	60.0 [2]	65.9	69.3	86.9	98.1	114.9	142.7	189.4	315.9
E	.	74.5 [2]	80.1	83.2	99.8	114.1	121.4	139.9	168.6	259.4
F	.	71.7 [2]	75.6	92.8	87.6	103.2	113.2	125.0	170.8	219.7
G	.	52.5 [2]	56.2	63.0	70.4	75.8	81.7	94.1	125.3	194.8
H	.	65.4 [2]	75.5	88.2	96.9	97.4	122.1	111.3	158.2	206.9
I	.	80.9 [2]	88.6	94.8	108.7	108.6	113.5	133.8	187.4	284.7
J	.	48.0 [2]	55.4	81.0	103.6	122.0	176.5	273.8	398.5	549.8
K	.	53.4 [2]	58.3	55.4	67.1	62.7	67.3	87.5	136.4	255.8
L	.	59.9 [2]	62.8	68.1	80.7	97.8	108.7	136.4	200.6	334.2
M	.	62.0 [2]	59.7	61.7	79.8	92.5	100.6	86.2	179.7	302.1
N	.	51.5 [2]	57.3	54.6	66.3	87.5	97.7	133.6	217.0	348.8
O	.	40.3 [2]	50.3	54.6	57.9	64.6	68.1	86.1	146.5	218.7

Women - Femmes - Mujeres
ISIC 3 - CITI 3 - CIIU 3

	1999	2000	2001	2002	2003	2004	2005	2006	2007	2008
Total	.	59.8 [2]	61.0	71.3	76.0	88.0	92.3	117.3	159.3	258.1
A-B	.	41.0 [2]	34.1	47.6	33.5	.	.	.	.	.
C-Q	.	55.9 [2]	60.5	67.5	77.0	88.4	97.8	.	.	.
A	.	41.0 [2]	34.1	49.0	44.7	51.6	46.1	61.6	83.9	145.4
B	.	. [2]	.	46.1	22.3	.	.	.	.	.
C	.	56.6 [2]	49.4	69.3	79.8	71.3	105.7	111.1	178.0	271.2
D	.	70.0 [2]	64.8	68.2	75.6	89.1	88.9	105.2	135.6	225.2
E	.	67.2 [2]	70.6	75.2	90.0	105.4	116.8	138.1	159.6	214.3
F	.	65.4 [2]	67.0	82.9	80.2	87.5	102.5	127.9	156.6	230.7
G	.	49.8 [2]	53.4	52.1	58.6	72.2	67.0	81.4	121.6	190.7
H	.	61.6 [2]	67.7	76.7	83.9	101.9	113.7	125.3	151.1	197.5
I	.	75.3 [2]	78.8	86.7	103.3	109.4	111.2	121.4	157.9	228.6
J	.	46.9 [2]	63.7	85.0	103.9	128.4	155.5	247.2	334.2	442.7
K	.	45.7 [2]	61.7	55.3	63.4	69.5	68.9	89.4	129.7	254.1
L	.	50.7 [2]	57.0	63.8	73.6	88.4	100.4	134.9	180.7	322.2
M	.	58.2 [2]	61.1	65.5	76.7	86.9	90.5	120.9	172.6	280.6
N	.	42.5 [2]	46.8	51.0	59.7	78.5	82.0	110.8	155.4	284.3
O	.	37.0 [2]	45.0	45.6	48.7	60.0	68.7	92.1	147.6	210.2

Myanmar (DA) [3] [4]   Employees - Salariés - Asalariados   R.T./h. - Kyat

Men - Hommes - Hombres
ISIC 2 - CITI 2 - CIIU 2

	1999	2000	2001	2002	2003	2004	2005	2006	2007	2008
2 [5]	.	13.14	24.92	28.04	31.88	34.98	36.89	117.28	155.63	172.16
3	.	13.51	18.98	20.82	22.84	29.89	31.89	94.00	132.74	180.55
5	.	10.94	33.42	34.29	34.70	39.56	41.08	134.33	183.50	186.43
7 [6]	.	13.02	20.66	23.69	24.37	30.37	32.40	107.80	146.74	178.82

Women - Femmes - Mujeres
ISIC 2 - CITI 2 - CIIU 2

	1999	2000	2001	2002	2003	2004	2005	2006	2007	2008
2 [5]	.	15.45	24.13	28.94	32.88	34.38	36.09	112.63	165.43	185.63
3	.	20.79	17.45	19.56	20.31	27.18	28.36	90.61	116.31	158.60
5	.	12.37	39.58	40.88	41.40	42.58	42.66	128.31	169.35	176.62
7 [6]	.	17.77	18.50	20.92	24.18	31.76	32.26	106.74	139.37	158.23

Philippines (BA) [7]   Wage earners - Ouvriers - Obreros   R.T./d.j. - Peso

Total men and women - Total hommes et femmes - Total hombres y mujeres
ISIC 2 - CITI 2 - CIIU 2

	1999	2000	2001	2002	2003	2004	2005	2006	2007	2008
I	131.25	132.50	132.55	138.72	143.73	149.88	158.60	.	.	.

Men - Hommes - Hombres
ISIC 2 - CITI 2 - CIIU 2

	1999	2000	2001	2002	2003	2004	2005	2006	2007	2008
I	137.47	138.92	139.52	143.67	147.93	152.95	161.88	.	.	.

Women - Femmes - Mujeres
ISIC 2 - CITI 2 - CIIU 2

	1999	2000	2001	2002	2003	2004	2005	2006	2007	2008
I	114.19	117.40	117.61	118.71	127.09	134.10	142.21	.	.	.

Explanatory notes: see p. 877.   Notes explicatives: voir p. 879.   Notas explicativas: véase p. 882.

[1] Figures in thousands. [2] Fourth quarter. [3] Regular employees. [4] March and Sep. of each year. [5] Metal mining. [6] Excl. storage and communication; incl. sea transport. [7] Rice, corn, coconut and sugar cane.

[1] Données en milliers. [2] Quatrième trimestre. [3] Salariés stables. [4] Mars et sept. de chaque année. [5] Extraction de minerais métalliques. [6] Non compris les entrepôts et communications; y compris les transports maritimes. [7] Riz, maïs, noix de coco et canne à sucre.

[1] Cifras en millares. [2] Cuarto trimestre. [3] Asalariados estables. [4] Marzo y sept. de cada año. [5] Extracción de minerales metálicos. [6] Excl. almacenaje y comunicaciones; incl. los transportes marítimos. [7] Arroz, maíz, coco y caña de azúcar.

	1999	2000	2001	2002	2003	2004	2005	2006	2007	2008
Philippines (BA)					Employees - Salariés - Asalariados					R.T./d.j. - Peso

Total men and women - Total hommes et femmes - Total hombres y mujeres
ISIC 3 - CITI 3 - CIIU 3

	1999	2000	2001	2002	2003	2004	2005	2006	2007	2008
Total	.	.	222.3	226.4	230.1	234.1	245.4	261.9	266.6	278.9
A-B	.	.	110.4	110.6	112.5	117.8	122.2	132.3	132.7	138.9
C-Q	.	.	245.0	249.5	253.7	258.1	267.9	286.2	292.4	305.7
A	.	.	108.8	109.1	110.9	116.3	120.5	130.2	130.6	136.7
B	.	.	125.6	125.1	129.1	133.5	143.1	157.2	159.4	166.2
C	.	.	225.3	228.9	212.4	185.6	207.9	200.5	205.1	242.3
D	.	.	226.2	229.0	237.4	239.4	246.6	265.0	277.2	289.6
E	.	.	334.3	350.3	348.2	367.9	421.6	440.1	460.7	457.4
F	.	.	209.8	213.7	219.4	225.8	235.9	264.2	256.1	267.8
G	.	.	199.1	199.4	210.8	213.5	217.5	227.3	242.5	249.9
H	.	.	202.8	201.4	210.4	221.2	221.8	237.0	242.6	251.3
I	.	.	230.1	228.2	237.3	246.3	284.4	326.4	344.2	357.1
J	.	.	389.4	402.5	409.0	426.0	446.1	491.7	473.4	495.8
K	.	.	307.6	296.1	306.0	318.4	320.2	361.5	378.0	412.3
L	.	.	334.9	358.6	369.5	366.7	396.2	414.9	411.6	415.5
M	.	.	423.2	440.1	437.2	445.8	441.0	459.0	460.8	487.5
N	.	.	349.7	364.3	338.5	366.8	373.2	392.3	400.2	417.3
O	.	.	202.9	211.4	225.2	239.6	252.0	268.2	272.6	287.9
P	.	.	107.9	108.7	110.3	111.6	108.4	113.5	121.1	122.6
Q	.	.	536.9	590.8	593.0	510.9	536.9	440.1	1 089.3	726.1

Men - Hommes - Hombres
ISIC 3 - CITI 3 - CIIU 3

	1999	2000	2001	2002	2003	2004	2005	2006	2007	2008
Total	.	.	219.0	223.4	228.6	232.0	245.8	264.8	268.8	279.2
A-B	.	.	114.7	114.2	116.0	121.7	126.4	138.3	137.6	143.3
C-Q	.	.	247.1	252.6	258.8	262.6	275.8	297.8	303.7	315.3
A	.	.	113.1	112.8	115.2	120.5	124.8	136.3	135.4	141.0
B	.	.	125.8	124.8	123.0	132.4	142.4	158.2	160.0	166.8
C	.	.	221.9	210.7	210.1	186.5	207.3	200.6	204.3	238.8
D	.	.	237.2	238.9	246.3	247.7	254.0	270.5	290.9	299.1
E	.	.	327.3	344.3	343.9	357.2	418.7	434.8	456.0	453.5
F	.	.	208.1	212.5	217.8	224.3	234.3	263.0	253.9	265.6
G	.	.	207.9	212.2	220.8	221.9	227.5	236.5	254.0	258.8
H	.	.	218.6	223.3	232.3	241.6	241.3	259.1	269.9	278.9
I	.	.	222.6	220.6	228.3	234.7	263.4	294.8	314.7	328.6
J	.	.	370.8	395.9	425.1	429.2	447.5	525.8	463.4	487.7
K	.	.	293.9	286.0	297.2	304.3	305.5	337.6	348.5	381.5
L	.	.	336.2	357.4	372.9	369.6	400.2	426.7	421.7	416.9
M	.	.	385.7	408.3	418.0	415.4	419.1	423.5	450.2	476.4
N	.	.	379.5	380.4	348.3	376.6	385.8	405.3	417.3	436.1
O	.	.	242.4	249.7	253.6	264.4	277.7	292.4	285.7	299.9
P	.	.	154.9	158.4	160.2	167.7	170.2	183.5	173.8	188.0
Q	.	.	405.2	547.9	436.9	546.7	592.5	430.6	1 143.4	813.9

Women - Femmes - Mujeres
ISIC 3 - CITI 3 - CIIU 3

	1999	2000	2001	2002	2003	2004	2005	2006	2007	2008
Total	.	.	227.5	231.1	232.5	237.5	244.7	257.6	263.4	278.6
A-B	.	.	96.0	98.3	100.2	103.2	106.8	109.7	114.6	122.4
C-Q	.	.	242.1	245.4	246.6	251.7	257.4	271.1	277.5	293.1
A	.	.	95.6	97.9	97.3	102.3	106.0	109.4	114.2	122.0
B	.	.	121.0	137.5	276.7	160.5	159.4	131.1	145.4	151.9
C	.	.	269.3	425.3	245.0	172.0	223.9	200.3	214.2	301.8
D	.	.	210.6	215.3	225.0	227.4	236.5	257.4	257.9	275.8
E	.	.	368.8	383.3	369.9	419.5	436.9	468.2	484.8	480.1
F	.	.	287.0	286.2	302.4	315.8	317.8	337.7	375.5	387.4
G	.	.	187.9	183.1	197.6	202.6	204.3	215.4	227.3	238.4
H	.	.	186.6	179.4	188.4	200.3	201.0	213.5	214.6	222.4
I	.	.	329.3	321.5	342.1	380.8	430.7	505.4	507.3	502.1
J	.	.	402.8	407.5	395.8	423.3	445.1	465.3	481.4	501.8
K	.	.	333.5	316.2	327.3	353.8	355.0	410.5	439.5	474.3
L	.	.	332.9	360.6	363.4	361.1	388.5	392.4	393.6	413.0
M	.	.	437.2	450.5	443.4	455.7	448.0	471.0	464.4	491.2
N	.	.	338.8	357.6	335.3	363.1	368.5	387.0	393.5	409.3
O	.	.	168.5	178.2	197.0	211.8	224.3	239.9	256.0	272.9
P	.	.	99.7	100.6	102.2	102.6	97.8	101.5	111.8	111.1
Q	.	.	684.5	624.0	676.4	491.3	467.6	477.8	942.2	535.1

Explanatory notes: see p. 877.   Notes explicatives: voir p. 879.   Notas explicativas: véase p. 882.

Philippines (DB) [1] [2] — Employees - Salariés - Asalariados

E.G./m. - Peso

Total men and women - Total hommes et femmes - Total hombres y mujeres
ISIC 3 - CITI 3 - CIIU 3

	1999	2000	2001	2002	2003	2004	2005	2006	2007	2008
Total	9 086		10 719		12 422		13 919			
A-B	4 472		5 490		6 270		7 460			
C-Q	9 313		10 690		12 730		13 105			
A	4 359		5 452		6 271		7 312			
B	5 068		5 695		6 265		8 227			
C	9 083		13 298		15 125		16 105			
D	8 347 [3]		9 936		11 166		12 973			
E	17 003		21 163		21 965		25 602			
F	6 884		7 438		8 065		10 060			
G	8 338		8 891		9 029		9 240			
H	6 162		6 685		7 444		8 021			
I	13 473		15 097		19 632		22 237			
J	20 958		29 075		33 350		37 413			
K	8 396		9 881		10 672		12 434			
M	8 582		9 641		12 353		13 769			
N	6 863		8 861		10 368		10 922			
O	9 847		12 101		14 327		15 989			

Qatar (BA) [4] — Employees - Salariés - Asalariados

R.T./m. - Riyal

Total men and women - Total hommes et femmes - Total hombres y mujeres
ISIC 3 - CITI 3 - CIIU 3

	1999	2000	2001	2002	2003	2004	2005	2006	2007	2008
Total								5 206	6 318	
B									2 357	
C								11 685	15 788	
D								3 677	5 060	
E								8 249	11 175	
F								3 477	3 985	
G								3 135	3 740	
H								2 823	3 833	
I								6 920	7 583	
J								8 787	11 630	
K								4 983	6 362	
L								8 731	11 772	
M								7 949	9 830	
N								7 675	9 494	
O								6 525	8 760	
P								1 649	1 792	
Q								14 775	18 080	

Men - Hommes - Hombres
ISIC 3 - CITI 3 - CIIU 3

	1999	2000	2001	2002	2003	2004	2005	2006	2007	2008
Total								5 611	6 884	
A									2 048	
C								11 987	16 404	
D								3 668	5 027	
E								8 438	11 526	
F								3 418	3 940	
G								3 109	3 607	
H								2 682	3 766	
I								7 158	7 721	
J								9 994	13 211	
K								4 934	6 288	
L								9 085	12 258	
M									11 065	
N								8 872	11 224	
O									9 252	
P								1 701	1 771	
Q								16 281	19 397	

Women - Femmes - Mujeres
ISIC 3 - CITI 3 - CIIU 3

	1999	2000	2001	2002	2003	2004	2005	2006	2007	2008
Total								4 131	4 939	
C								7 637	11 364	
D								4 092	7 118	
E								6 264	8 194	
F								7 365	7 242	
G								3 659	5 702	
H								3 820	5 425	
I								5 638	6 644	
J								6 106	8 929	
K									7 246	
L								6 741	9 485	
M								7 448	9 300	
N								6 684	8 379	
O								4 893	7 128	
P								1 610	1 804	
Q								8 750	11 828	

Explanatory notes: see p. 877.

[1] Computed on the basis of annual wages. [2] Establishments with 20 or more persons employed. [3] Before 1999: establishments with 10 or more persons employed. [4] October.

Notes explicatives: voir p. 879.

[1] Calculés sur la base de salaires annuels. [2] Etablissements occupant 20 personnes et plus. [3] Avant 1999: établissements occupant 10 personnes et plus. [4] Octobre.

Notas explicativas: véase p. 882.

[1] Calculados en base a los salarios anuales. [2] Establecimientos con 20 y más trabajadores. [3] Antes de 1999: establecimientos con 10 y más trabajadores. [4] Octubre.

By economic activity   Par activité économique   Por actividad económica

	1999	2000	2001	2002	2003	2004	2005	2006	2007	2008
Singapore (F)					Employees - Salariés - Asalariados					E.G./m. - Dollar
Total men and women - Total hommes et femmes - Total hombres y mujeres										
ISIC 3 - CITI 3 - CIIU 3										
Total	2 813	3 063	3 134	3 158	3 213	3 329	3 444 [1]	3 554	3 773	3 977
D	2 803	3 036	3 117	3 154	3 265	3 350	3 495 [1]	3 618	3 764	3 955
F	2 226	2 333	2 330	2 384	2 411	2 453	2 513 [1]	2 517	2 646	2 861
G	2 561	2 721	2 752	2 780	2 831	2 890	3 017 [1]	3 101	3 262	3 441
H	1 291	1 332	1 339	1 312	1 283	1 298	1 333 [1]	1 381	1 442	1 504
I	2 836	3 105	3 283	3 166	3 297	3 439	3 610 [1]	3 938	4 222	.
J	4 528	4 931	5 131	5 307	5 393	5 639	5 949 [1]	6 291	6 768	7 153
K	3 056	3 281	3 332	3 357	3 352	3 389	3 477 [1]	3 314	3 518	.
L-Q	2 955	3 336	3 340	3 384	3 409	3 668	3 686 [1]	3 831	4 074	4 168
Men - Hommes - Hombres										
ISIC 3 - CITI 3 - CIIU 3										
Total	3 222	3 518	3 606	3 632	3 698	3 825	3 962 [1]	4 081	4 335	4 560
D	3 384	3 653	3 752	3 762	3 881	3 969	4 111 [1]	4 218	4 359	4 559
F	2 414	2 550	2 563	2 624	2 656	2 687	2 759 [1]	2 774	2 929	3 174
G	2 942	3 145	3 193	3 247	3 323	3 396	3 558 [1]	3 677	3 885	4 110
H	1 479	1 519	1 527	1 497	1 461	1 458	1 498 [1]	1 551	1 618	1 697
I	3 037	3 339	3 522	3 389	3 532	3 684	3 904 [1]	4 245	4 566	.
J	6 121	6 557	6 731	6 988	7 077	7 387	7 776 [1]	8 231	8 637	8 906
K	3 445	3 723	3 782	3 805	3 792	3 834	3 914 [1]	3 704	3 928	.
L-Q	3 450	3 956	3 966	4 015	4 035	4 347	4 395 [1]	4 622	5 000	5 048
Women - Femmes - Mujeres										
ISIC 3 - CITI 3 - CIIU 3										
Total	2 327	2 530	2 588	2 617	2 662	2 773	2 865 [1]	2 966	3 148	3 332
D	2 007	2 181	2 226	2 283	2 374	2 442	2 563 [1]	2 682	2 815	2 974
F	1 749	1 800	1 780	1 823	1 852	1 915	1 950 [1]	1 931	2 010	2 157
G	2 101	2 224	2 245	2 256	2 292	2 343	2 439 [1]	2 497	2 616	2 753
H	1 121	1 163	1 169	1 149	1 131	1 160	1 190 [1]	1 232	1 288	.
I	2 443	2 663	2 840	2 753	2 867	3 004	3 102 [1]	3 427	3 649	.
J	3 579	3 925	4 116	4 239	4 316	4 511	4 769 [1]	5 039	5 468	5 886
K	2 628	2 807	2 854	2 872	2 874	2 907	2 998 [1]	2 905	3 089	.
L-Q	2 532	2 816	2 813	2 863	2 897	3 123	3 131 [1]	3 236	3 391	3 531
Sri Lanka (DA) [2]					Wage earners - Ouvriers - Obreros					E.G./h. - Rupee
Total men and women - Total hommes et femmes - Total hombres y mujeres										
ISIC 2 - CITI 2 - CIIU 2										
Total [3]	18.83	20.41	22.34	25.93	27.22	29.56	31.57	35.12	38.75	45.33
2-9 [3]	21.86	24.27	26.25	29.80	30.99	34.59	36.13	39.29	45.70	50.02
3	22.03	24.86	27.10	31.93	33.21	35.47	36.87	39.85	45.36	49.88
5	29.81	32.43	29.95	29.48	37.08	46.77	51.23	44.50	40.71	38.09
6	20.97	24.37	24.68	30.58	25.87	26.41	36.62	36.94	42.47	51.51
7	20.99	20.67	22.58	24.30	23.63	33.58	27.76	37.50	44.19	54.21
Men - Hommes - Hombres										
ISIC 2 - CITI 2 - CIIU 2										
Total [3]	19.11	21.01	22.60	26.26	27.60	30.23	32.09	35.71	39.28	47.79
2-9 [3]	22.09	24.41	26.50	29.92	31.27	34.80	36.28	39.47	46.26	54.26
3	22.29	25.28	27.48	32.09	33.61	35.79	37.08	39.95	46.09	55.15
5	29.81	32.43	29.95	29.48	37.08	46.77	51.23	44.50	40.70	38.16
6	20.97	24.37	24.68	30.58	25.87	26.41	36.62	36.94	42.47	51.66
7	20.99	20.67	22.58	24.30	23.63	33.58	27.76	37.50	44.19	60.22
Women - Femmes - Mujeres										
ISIC 2 - CITI 2 - CIIU 2										
Total [3]	16.36	18.45	19.94	23.67	24.66	26.87	29.76	33.52	37.51	42.68
2-9 [3]	18.74	21.71	23.75	27.63	28.08	32.29	34.25	36.82	44.70	45.23
3	18.10	20.36	22.59	28.03	28.90	31.17	35.09	39.08	42.95	44.61
5	.	32.43	29.95	29.48	37.08	46.77	51.23	.	.	38.03
6	.	22.63	24.68	30.58	25.87	26.41	32.62	36.94	42.47	51.36
7	.	.	.	.	.	.	.	.	.	48.21
Sri Lanka (DA) [2]					Wage earners - Ouvriers - Obreros					E.G./d.j. - Rupee
Total men and women - Total hommes et femmes - Total hombres y mujeres										
ISIC 2 - CITI 2 - CIIU 2										
Total [3]	163.33	182.04	192.21	221.06	242.81	253.50	277.98	305.29	342.81	392.60
2-9 [3]	193.91	220.09	233.86	261.38	283.71	298.57	318.99	354.93	414.49	438.15
1 [4]	96.89	104.12	112.11	128.72	138.43	152.94	178.47	206.33	201.75	307.11
3	199.20	222.48	230.66	273.10	306.28	308.98	336.49	356.11	412.19	432.55
5	241.11	285.99	263.12	259.63	269.64	335.70	416.75	424.55	408.37	336.71
6	174.97	197.20	207.75	254.45	230.59	248.37	287.98	324.34	368.97	487.45
7	188.14	161.49	218.32	211.78	208.86	286.39	266.41	341.29	368.45	415.37

Explanatory notes: see p. 877.

[1] Methodology revised; data not strictly comparable. [2] March and Sep. of each year. [3] Excl. major divisions 4, 8 and 9. [4] Tea plantations.

Notes explicatives: voir p. 879.

[1] Méthodologie révisée; les données ne sont pas strictement comparables. [2] Mars et sept. de chaque année. [3] Non compris les branches 4, 8 et 9. [4] Plantations de thé.

Notas explicativas: véase p. 882.

[1] Metodología revisada; los datos no son estrictamente comparables. [2] Marzo y sept. de cada año. [3] Excl. las grandes divisiones 4, 8 y 9. [4] Plantaciones de té.

5A WAGES — SALAIRES — SALARIOS

By economic activity — Par activité économique — Por actividad económica

	1999	2000	2001	2002	2003	2004	2005	2006	2007	2008

Sri Lanka (DA) [1]   Wage earners - Ouvriers - Obreros   E.G./d.j. - Rupee

Men - Hommes - Hombres
ISIC 2 - CITI 2 - CIIU 2

	1999	2000	2001	2002	2003	2004	2005	2006	2007	2008
Total [2]	166.79	183.03	194.68	227.71	246.60	258.22	281.89	311.41	348.99	433.65
2-9 [2]	196.98	220.17	235.49	264.67	287.15	300.68	324.30	356.13	419.70	489.11
1 [3]	99.48	107.46	115.44	140.35	141.43	161.93	183.30	220.63	208.32	322.70
3	203.91	222.61	233.12	278.13	311.22	312.06	338.06	357.47	418.96	489.15
5	241.11	285.99	263.12	259.63	269.64	335.70	416.75	424.55	408.37	371.08
6	174.97	202.72	207.75	254.45	230.59	248.37	287.98	324.34	368.97	504.18
7	188.14	161.49	218.32	211.78	208.86	286.39	266.41	341.29	368.45	437.49

Women - Femmes - Mujeres
ISIC 2 - CITI 2 - CIIU 2

	1999	2000	2001	2002	2003	2004	2005	2006	2007	2008
Total								287.87	331.16	349.43
2-9 [2]	173.37	196.54	209.49	244.36	247.67	275.51	292.88	325.43	403.93	380.80
1 [3]	94.30	100.79	108.79	117.09	135.41	143.96	173.91	192.03	195.20	291.53
3	165.75	185.58	201.31	235.07	252.98	270.00	327.87	346.17	394.36	375.95
5	241.11	285.99	263.12	259.63	269.64	335.70	416.75			
6	174.97	192.68	207.75	254.45	230.59	248.37	287.98	324.34	368.97	470.72

Taiwan, China (DA)   Employees - Salariés - Asalariados   E.G./m. - New dollar

Total men and women - Total hommes et femmes - Total hombres y mujeres
ISIC 3 - CITI 3 - CIIU 3

	1999	2000	2001	2002	2003	2004	2005	2006	2007	2008
C-Q	40 842	41 861	41 960	41 530	42 065	42 685	43 163	43 493	44 414	44 424
C						46 307	47 671	53 344	51 057	51 499
D						40 657	41 858	42 393	43 169	43 105
E [4]						94 525	91 184	97 230	98 448	89 296
F						37 916	38 450	39 168	40 327	40 792
G						39 819	39 545	39 380	39 475	39 980
H						24 813	25 121	24 960	25 500	26 747
I [5]						46 986	48 618	48 460	49 234	49 800
J						66 671	65 113	69 054	75 732	71 319
K [6]						39 781	38 819	38 313	37 877	40 343
N						55 341	55 603	55 429	56 603	58 122
92						29 662	29 898	31 303	31 499	32 053

Men - Hommes - Hombres
ISIC 2 - CITI 2 - CIIU 2   (ISIC 3 - CITI 3 - CIIU 3)

	1999	2000	2001	2002	2003	2004	2005	2006	2007	2008	
2	45 507	46 944	47 768	47 802		47 472	47 836	48 021	48 903	49 065	C-Q
3	44 092	45 211	44 616	44 122		49 899	51 865	58 391	56 162	57 092	C
4	92 822	92 547	97 617	93 828		46 866	48 024	48 521	49 400	49 219	D
5	39 742	40 559	39 322	38 503		97 103	93 678	99 852	101 160	91 811	E [4]
6	42 594	43 083	42 151	40 825		39 763	40 266	40 928	42 106	42 505	F
7	53 286	54 628	56 510	54 196		43 867	42 899	42 660	42 709	43 268	G
8 [6]	63 970	65 322	65 318	67 425		27 348	27 855	27 380	28 140	29 230	H
9	47 029	50 041	50 850	48 715		49 366	51 492	51 602	51 888	52 908	I [5]
						73 657	72 142	75 231	82 536	80 222	J
						43 836	41 932	40 806	39 993	43 309	K [6]
						94 122	92 454	92 550	94 213	97 384	N
						36 048	35 866	37 722	37 814	38 805	92
						33 904	34 933	34 968	34 290	33 264	93

Women - Femmes - Mujeres
ISIC 2 - CITI 2 - CIIU 2   (ISIC 3 - CITI 3 - CIIU 3)

	1999	2000	2001	2002	2003	2004	2005	2006	2007	2008	
2	26 402	27 756	29 073	29 581		36 845	37 480	38 035	39 032	38 870	C-Q
3	28 586	29 751	29 319	29 795		30 291	30 708	34 436	33 143	32 093	C
4	73 429	72 048	76 816	75 194		31 931	33 110	33 749	34 401	34 389	D
5	29 244	29 788	28 893	27 560		75 931	73 387	78 573	79 724	72 461	E [4]
6	31 690	32 756	33 865	33 877		29 128	30 004	30 803	31 568	31 895	F
7	44 286	45 450	47 810	42 920		35 955	36 672	36 180	36 306	36 754	G
8 [6]	51 355	52 015	55 455	57 326		23 046	23 249	23 295	23 688	25 064	H
9	35 799	36 752	36 849	36 958		41 214	41 907	41 184	42 905	42 412	I [5]
						62 205	60 730	65 262	71 566	65 907	J
						34 811	35 022	35 359	35 529	37 170	K [6]
						44 591	45 590	45 607	46 706	47 929	N
						23 479	24 120	25 073	25 193	25 255	92
						26 032	27 141	29 919	26 988	26 714	93

Explanatory notes: see p. 877.

[1] March and Sep. of each year. [2] Excl. major divisions 4, 8 and 9. [3] Tea plantations. [4] Excl. water supply. [5] Excl. communications. [6] Excl. business services.

Notes explicatives: voir p. 879.

[1] Mars et sept. de chaque année. [2] Non compris les branches 4, 8 et 9. [3] Plantations de thé. [4] Non compris l'approvisionnement de l'eau. [5] Non compris les communications. [6] Non compris les services aux entreprises.

Notas explicativas: véase p. 882.

[1] Marzo y sept. de cada año. [2] Excl. las grandes divisiones 4, 8 y 9. [3] Plantaciones de té. [4] Excl. el suministro del agua. [5] Excl. las comunicaciones. [6] Excl. servicios para las empresas.

	1999	2000	2001	2002	2003	2004	2005	2006	2007	2008

Tajikistan (CA)   Employees - Salariés - Asalariados   E.G./m. - Somoni

Total men and women - Total hommes et femmes - Total hombres y mujeres
ISIC 3 - CITI 3 - CIIU 3

	1999	2000	2001	2002	2003	2004	2005	2006	2007	2008
Total	.	15.6	23.5	32.6	44.6	61.8	83.6	116.3	163.3	.
A [1]	.	7.8	13.7	18.9	26.9	35.6	38.4	43.0	52.5	.
F	.	38.9	55.4	74.8	100.0	154.9	198.8	319.0	467.8	.
G	.	16.9	23.1	32.7	46.1	59.6	78.9	106.9	144.5	.
I [2]	.	31.0	48.9	69.6	101.0	144.2	181.0	232.3	394.0	.
64	.	38.4	59.6	95.2	149.0	222.7	288.0	555.9	482.6	.
70	.	25.4	34.5	47.3	48.0	79.7	115.0	194.1	197.1	.
N	.	6.7	8.8	13.0	17.1	23.8	40.9	56.0	77.1	.
92	.	11.5	18.3	24.2	33.8	41.8	59.0	84.3	105.8	.
93	.	16.4	23.4	34.8	44.8	67.9	105.7	132.2	166.5	.

Thailand (BA)   Employees - Salariés - Asalariados   R.T./m. - Baht

Total men and women - Total hommes et femmes - Total hombres y mujeres
ISIC 3 - CITI 3 - CIIU 3

	1999	2000	2001	2002	2003	2004	2005	2006	2007	2008
Total	.	.	5 562.9	6 445.7	5 839.6	.	.	7 978.5	7 357.4	.
A	.	.	2 091.7	5 629.7	2 345.5	.	.	3 079.3	3 284.3	.
B	.	.	4 154.0	3 444.0	4 492.4	.	.	5 006.4	5 258.0	.
C	.	.	10 829.7	5 223.3	5 329.8	7 745.6	7 935.7	8 265.8	9 325.0	.
D	.	.	6 064.6	6 795.3	6 432.2	6 129.0	6 407.4	6 941.6	6 999.2	.
E	.	.	12 135.1	5 512.0	10 473.5	11 819.0	12 366.2	18 230.0	14 613.9	.
F	.	.	4 622.1	6 898.8	4 728.7	4 773.9	4 863.3	5 649.2	5 477.8	.
G	.	.	6 555.7	6 300.8	6 662.2	6 546.5	6 726.7	7 399.2	7 455.6	.
H	.	.	5 100.6	6 873.3	5 174.2	5 335.9	5 489.5	6 055.6	6 011.1	.
I	.	.	8 308.3	6 325.3	9 448.8	9 740.5	9 843.5	13 088.0	11 745.9	.
J	.	.	16 929.7	6 651.2	16 641.8	16 897.9	18 780.3	18 479.9	18 364.0	.
K	.	.	8 919.3	5 969.3	8 736.1	9 561.6	10 010.3	11 058.1	10 792.6	.
L	.	.	.	.	.	20 894.2	28 944.5	12 236.0	11 924.5	.
M	.	.	8 798.8	5 074.9	9 345.3	8 509.3	9 840.1	16 413.5	13 531.8	.
N	.	.	9 573.5	7 750.4	8 936.9	11 284.3	11 070.7	11 043.8	10 177.9	.
O	.	.	6 776.5	6 241.7	6 172.1	5 667.3	6 510.3	6 937.5	6 825.6	.
P	.	.	3 747.5	5 398.9	4 009.3	4 186.8	4 206.3	4 792.7	4 903.1	.
Q	.	.	.	.	.	20 287.1	19 039.3	12 275.0	33 664.2	.
X	.	.	.	.	.	11 163.7	12 986.5	11 522.0	11 087.3	.

West Bank and Gaza Strip (BA) [3] [4]   Employees - Salariés - Asalariados   E.G./d.j. - New shekel

Total men and women - Total hommes et femmes - Total hombres y mujeres
ISIC 3 - CITI 3 - CIIU 3

	1999	2000	2001	2002	2003	2004	2005	2006	2007	2008
Total	75.4	77.1	73.1	75.3	74.2	75.0	79.3	84.4	83.9	91.4
C	84.5	96.7	84.2	87.5	104.6	96.9	86.7	84.9	94.9	91.2
D	65.4	68.8	68.0	70.1	68.5	66.8	74.0	77.7	71.1	81.4
E	93.1	93.7	95.2	109.4	107.1	108.3	101.8	110.3	105.4	113.6
F	97.4	101.6	97.3	100.4	94.8	88.1	90.5	97.9	102.1	119.7
G	69.8	73.1	74.3	75.8	71.0	71.9	75.3	73.8	72.3	72.5
H	89.8	96.2	87.8	89.9	103.3	94.8	96.9	106.8	100.7	129.8
I	69.9	76.6	68.4	72.2	71.1	77.6	81.3	75.9	73.6	100.0
J	88.6	88.1	98.8	107.6	123.8	113.3	99.8	89.7	111.1	85.6
K	86.9	91.3	77.1	92.8	76.2	79.7	93.0	94.3	87.8	101.4
L	58.1	57.4	58.4	61.9	61.2	66.3	70.1	79.2	78.7	82.5
M	68.8	69.6	69.3	72.6	74.0	78.0	81.0	86.7	87.0	87.7
N	66.0	71.5	78.1	79.8	80.0	78.7	83.6	92.4	89.7	98.7
O	73.5	74.1	62.1	85.1	62.4	69.1	72.6	69.0	80.3	102.5
P	85.2	61.4	34.4	54.1	46.0	44.5	36.4	93.5	82.9	.
Q	101.2	91.4	92.4	81.4	100.5	105.4	104.9	109.2	102.1	101.7
X	.	.	.	.	.	.	.	87.9	.	.

Men - Hommes - Hombres
ISIC 3 - CITI 3 - CIIU 3

	1999	2000	2001	2002	2003	2004	2005	2006	2007	2008
Total	78.0	80.1	75.5	78.0	76.4	77.4	81.4	86.6	86.2	94.2
C	85.4	96.6	84.0	85.4	104.6	96.9	86.7	84.9	94.9	91.5
D	69.3	73.2	73.5	74.7	71.7	70.9	77.8	81.8	76.4	86.6
E	93.2	93.8	95.8	120.9	110.5	110.0	102.7	112.8	105.4	116.1
F	97.6	101.6	97.5	100.5	94.8	88.1	90.6	98.0	102.2	119.6
G	70.4	74.8	75.1	76.8	72.3	74.7	77.6	76.2	73.7	74.3
H	90.4	97.2	88.2	90.3	104.3	95.7	97.2	107.5	100.9	130.5
I	70.2	76.3	68.5	72.3	71.0	78.1	82.0	76.9	73.4	99.4
J	96.1	95.5	117.2	119.5	133.7	125.5	101.6	89.1	101.2	92.0
K	87.6	106.5	86.1	99.6	83.6	90.0	96.2	104.2	90.5	112.4
L	58.2	57.6	58.5	62.1	61.3	66.3	69.8	79.0	78.7	82.5
M	76.4	78.3	78.1	79.5	80.8	86.3	90.1	95.8	96.7	94.4
N	71.1	77.0	85.7	85.8	89.6	87.2	91.7	104.4	99.8	107.0
O	77.0	78.3	63.5	86.8	65.6	72.8	77.8	73.0	84.8	109.0
P	69.2	93.7	82.0	30.0	48.3	54.8				.
Q	106.2	91.7	93.9	79.6	95.6	107.9	109.1	103.0	100.6	104.8
X	.	.	.	.	.	.	.	89.7	.	23.1

Explanatory notes: see p. 877.   Notes explicatives: voir p. 879.   Notas explicativas: véase p. 882.

[1] Excl. hunting, forestry and fishing. [2] Transport only. [3] Persons aged 15 years and over. [4] Net earnings.   [1] Non compris la chasse, la sylviculture et la pêche. [2] Transports seulement. [3] Personnes âgées de 15 ans et plus. [4] Gains nets.   [1] Excl. caza, silvicultura y pesca. [2] Transportes sólo. [3] Personas de 15 años y más. [4] Ganancias netas.

	1999	2000	2001	2002	2003	2004	2005	2006	2007	2008

West Bank and Gaza Strip (BA) [1] [2] — Employees - Salariés - Asalariados — E.G./d.j. - New shekel

Women - Femmes - Mujeres
ISIC 3 - CITI 3 - CIIU 3

	1999	2000	2001	2002	2003	2004	2005	2006	2007	2008
Total	55.4	55.5	57.1	63.0	63.3	64.5	68.6	73.3	72.6	78.2
C	26.9	100.0								
D	32.4	36.0	35.2	36.8	41.6	30.8	40.8	44.5	40.4	43.4
E			89.8	69.3	79.1	30.8	78.8	65.8		
F	73.3	79.6	76.2	73.9	90.6	101.8	63.2	72.5	85.0	
G	58.8	44.9	61.5	55.8	52.1	42.0	46.3	46.2	51.3	44.7
H	70.0	80.5	76.6	54.6	51.5	35.3	75.0	53.5	89.9	
I	65.2	82.0	64.0	70.9	72.8	71.2	66.6	63.8	79.4	
J	67.4	69.5	69.8	77.7	85.9	80.1	94.1	91.4	144.6	65.5
K	85.0	56.8	57.6	64.5	55.6	61.3	83.4	67.6	78.4	63.5
L	57.5	55.1	56.8	59.7	59.3	67.2	74.8	82.4	78.1	81.4
M	59.2	57.7	58.7	64.6	66.2	69.0	71.6	77.3	77.2	81.8
N	57.9	62.8	64.4	70.3	63.3	64.4	72.2	73.8	71.7	86.3
O	48.1	53.4	54.8	73.1	52.4	57.9	53.4	51.5	61.4	79.4
P	101.8	38.0	28.2	56.6	45.4	36.5	36.4		55.9	
Q	81.7	90.4	84.2	87.9	121.5	97.5	93.5	125.9	106.1	93.4
X										

EUROPE-EUROPE-EUROPA

Albania (CA) — Employees - Salariés - Asalariados — E.G./m. - Lek

Total men and women - Total hommes et femmes - Total hombres y mujeres
ISIC 3 - CITI 3 - CIIU 3

	1999	2000	2001	2002	2003	2004	2005	2006	2007	2008
C	13 750	14 999	17 003	19 250	23 459					
C-I	12 118	13 355	14 820							
D	10 734	11 708	14 056	14 334	16 572	17 559	18 333	19 750		
E	14 162	15 439	15 444	18 084	20 858	21 636	22 417	24 167		
F	10 936	12 489	13 416	15 014	15 017	16 055	17 333	19 167		
G	10 901	10 889	12 856	13 924	14 118	15 711	17 583	20 667		
H [3]	10 718	13 012	13 140	14 453	18 159	14 391	15 833	17 250		
I	14 503	16 225	18 124	23 434	27 030	27 439	28 167	31 333		
K							23 333	24 417		
O-P							17 333	18 250		

Andorre (F) — Employees - Salariés - Asalariados — E.G./m. - Euro

Total men and women - Total hommes et femmes - Total hombres y mujeres
ISIC 3 - CITI 3 - CIIU 3

	1999	2000	2001	2002	2003	2004	2005	2006	2007	2008
Total	1 185.4	1 249.0	1 321.8	1 391.5	1 458.5	1 542.9	1 624.0	1 726.5	1 810.7	
A-B	827.7	842.7	912.7	966.4	964.2	1 045.1	1 137.8	1 253.9	1 299.9	
C-Q	1 187.3	1 251.0	1 323.4	1 393.0	1 460.2	1 544.6	1 625.6	1 728.1	1 812.4	
A					964.2	1 045.1	1 137.8	1 253.9	1 299.6	
C										
D	1 189.3	1 260.5	1 334.2	1 424.3	1 508.9	1 585.9	1 680.3	1 801.6	1 902.5	
E	2 064.2	2 186.0	2 315.0	2 361.3	2 588.4	2 695.9	2 798.0	2 919.1	3 054.2	
F	1 255.3	1 328.1	1 400.8	1 461.2	1 536.5	1 610.4	1 705.3	1 835.5	1 904.8	
G	1 075.1	1 123.0	1 180.0	1 247.5	1 312.1	1 399.1	1 461.8	1 518.3	1 596.1	
H	907.3	957.1	1 025.3	1 118.6	1 147.6	1 227.7	1 288.5	1 350.8	1 410.2	
I	1 202.9	1 268.6	1 349.9	1 409.8	1 481.7	1 591.3	1 739.9	1 820.1	1 940.5	
J	2 325.3	2 512.4	2 635.0	2 726.6	2 963.5	3 151.4	3 267.6	3 719.1	4 057.2	
K	1 126.9	1 193.5	1 273.8	1 349.0	1 397.3	1 514.6	1 570.2	1 653.3	1 734.0	
L	1 599.5	1 645.2	1 734.3	1 774.3	1 838.7	1 909.0	1 997.7	2 097.2	2 208.9	
M	1 293.2	1 476.6	1 538.7	1 559.3	1 674.6	1 706.4	1 737.8	1 846.0	1 904.8	
N	1 307.5	1 333.1	1 382.5	1 464.4	1 557.4	1 653.6	1 741.5	1 906.1	1 964.0	
O	1 021.7	1 078.0	1 136.9	1 243.4	1 300.2	1 377.9	1 457.5	1 530.7	1 557.8	
P	649.1	698.7	741.1	791.6	830.4	907.4	986.8	1 023.7	1 087.8	
Q	831.9	1 013.7	1 227.2	1 193.9	1 290.8	1 283.5	1 425.7	1 560.4	1 616.5	
X	814.9	895.5	995.9	1 085.0	1 060.7	1 131.3	1 224.6	1 056.2	1 075.3	

Men - Hommes - Hombres
ISIC 3 - CITI 3 - CIIU 3

	1999	2000	2001	2002	2003	2004	2005	2006	2007	2008
Total					1 678.9	1 775.9	1 871.7	1 996.4	2 098.4	
A-B					1 083.5	1 160.1	1 249.0	1 366.4	1 388.6	
C-Q					1 681.2	1 778.3	1 874.1	1 998.8	2 101.3	
A					1 083.5	1 160.1	1 249.0	1 366.4	1 388.6	
C										
D					1 680.0	1 778.2	1 894.8	2 024.5	2 108.9	
E					2 859.8	2 972.7	3 087.6	3 202.3	3 324.1	
F					1 578.0	1 654.3	1 752.3	1 885.6	1 952.4	
G					1 534.9	1 635.7	1 713.2	1 772.9	1 864.8	
H					1 289.8	1 382.4	1 447.1	1 505.4	1 579.7	
I					1 617.2	1 740.8	1 905.4	2 002.8	2 129.0	
J					3 578.2	3 873.6	4 041.8	4 688.6	5 288.7	
K					1 660.4	1 830.5	1 882.0	2 008.7	2 106.9	
L					2 067.7	2 145.1	2 267.5	2 354.4	2 483.1	
M					1 882.7	1 942.2	2 037.6	2 141.8	2 241.7	
N					2 265.6	2 422.1	2 557.3	2 743.9	2 774.2	
O					1 558.5	1 633.8	1 733.1	1 828.8	1 865.4	
P					1 222.8	1 248.1	1 389.2	1 462.6	1 473.9	
Q					1 582.8	1 445.4	1 508.6	1 458.9	1 529.3	
X					1 520.9	1 836.9	2 045.5	1 393.3	1 461.5	

Explanatory notes: see p. 877. — Notes explicatives: voir p. 879. — Notas explicativas: véase p. 882.

[1] Persons aged 15 years and over. [2] Net earnings. [3] Incl. division 74 of tabulation category K and divisions 90, 93 of tabulation category O.

[1] Personnes âgées de 15 ans et plus. [2] Gains nets. [3] Y compris la division 74 de la catégorie de classement K et les divisions 90, 93 de la catégorie de classement O.

[1] Personas de 15 años y más. [2] Ganancias netas. [3] Incl. la división 74 de la categoría de tabulación K y las divisiones 90, 93 de la categoría de tabulación O.

Andorre (F)

Employees - Salariés - Asalariados   E.G./m. - Euro

Women - Femmes - Mujeres
ISIC 3 - CITI 3 - CIIU 3

	1999	2000	2001	2002	2003	2004	2005	2006	2007	2008
Total	.	.	.	.	1 191.5	1 261.5	1 325.7	1 408.0	1 480.9	.
A-B	.	.	.	.	781.6	847.0	954.1	1 083.1	1 149.0	.
C-Q	.	.	.	.	1 192.7	1 262.7	1 326.7	1 409.0	1 481.8	.
A	.	.	.	.	781.6	847.0	954.1	1 083.1	1 149.0	.
C	.	.	.	.	.	.	.	.	.	.
D	.	.	.	.	1 165.3	1 215.5	1 263.0	1 367.4	1 503.1	.
E	.	.	.	.	1 651.6	1 739.9	1 799.6	1 951.0	2 166.8	.
F	.	.	.	.	1 059.9	1 123.6	1 202.0	1 305.0	1 407.2	.
G	.	.	.	.	1 099.6	1 172.1	1 224.5	1 281.2	1 345.0	.
H	.	.	.	.	1 020.2	1 093.4	1 154.4	1 219.8	1 269.2	.
I	.	.	.	.	1 192.7	1 295.2	1 413.5	1 471.2	1 581.8	.
J	.	.	.	.	2 058.7	2 157.9	2 250.9	2 472.6	2 621.3	.
K	.	.	.	.	1 133.1	1 200.7	1 253.9	1 304.1	1 369.3	.
L	.	.	.	.	1 636.4	1 701.6	1 765.0	1 867.9	1 975.5	.
M	.	.	.	.	1 599.1	1 625.8	1 638.6	1 751.2	1 798.6	.
N	.	.	.	.	1 376.3	1 454.3	1 528.4	1 691.0	1 748.8	.
O	.	.	.	.	1 065.5	1 118.9	1 192.2	1 265.1	1 290.3	.
P	.	.	.	.	795.5	863.4	929.9	987.8	1 050.9	.
Q	.	.	.	.	1 029.4	1 113.7	1 343.3	1 649.5	1 738.6	.
X	.	.	.	.	927.7	948.7	1 015.0	1 000.7	1 018.2	.

Austria (DB) [1]

Employees - Salariés - Asalariados   E.G./h. - Euro

Total men and women - Total hommes et femmes - Total hombres y mujeres
ISIC 3 - CITI 3 - CIIU 3   ISIC 4 - CITI 4 - CIIU 4

	1999	2000	2001	2002	2003	2004	2005	2006	2007	2008	
C-D	12.38	12.68	13.03	13.44	13.75	14.00	14.40	14.85	15.25 |	15.80	B-C
C-F	12.28	12.57	12.91	13.31	13.64	13.89	14.30	14.65	15.05 |	15.64	B-F
E	16.87	17.08	17.39	17.68	18.30	18.65	19.25	19.81	20.40 |	21.89	D
F	11.19	11.48	11.78	12.15	12.54	12.78	13.18	13.30	13.69 |	13.56	E
									|	14.47	F

Austria (FE)

Wage earners - Ouvriers - Obreros   R.T./m. - Euro

Men - Hommes - Hombres
ISIC 3 - CITI 3 - CIIU 3

	1999	2000	2001	2002	2003	2004	2005	2006	2007	2008
A-B [2]	14 819	15 079	15 451 |	1 164 [3]	.	1 214	.	.	.	.

Women - Femmes - Mujeres
ISIC 3 - CITI 3 - CIIU 3

	1999	2000	2001	2002	2003	2004	2005	2006	2007	2008
A-B [2]	14 624	14 880	15 247 |	1 149 [3]	.	1 198	.	.	.	.

Belarus (D) [4]

Employees - Salariés - Asalariados   E.G./m. - B. roubles

Total men and women - Total hommes et femmes - Total hombres y mujeres [5]
ISIC 3 - CITI 3 - CIIU 3

	1999	2000	2001	2002	2003	2004	2005	2006	2007	2008
Total	34 588	87 [6]	165	220	297	430	556	659	785	987
A-B	19 494	53 [6]	97	120	158	255	329	400	485	667
C-Q	37 682	94 [6]	178	238	320	458	592	701	831	1 035

Men - Hommes - Hombres [5]
ISIC 3 - CITI 3 - CIIU 3

	1999	2000	2001	2002	2003	2004	2005	2006	2007	2008
Total	38 541	97 [6]	182	246	334	478	626	738	887	1 148
A-B	19 885	54 [6]	101	124	163	264	336	406	500	694
C-Q	44 015	109 [6]	204	277	375	528	690	813	969	1 240

Women - Femmes - Mujeres [5]
ISIC 3 - CITI 3 - CIIU 3

	1999	2000	2001	2002	2003	2004	2005	2006	2007	2008
Total	31 051	79 [6]	150	199	266	388	495	589	695	848
A-B	18 295	50 [6]	91	114	149	239	318	391	462	624
C-Q	32 709	83 [6]	158	209	279	405	514	611	720	871

Explanatory notes: see p. 877.

[1] Per hour paid. [2] Incl. the value of payments in kind; permanent workers. [3] Prior to 2002: ATS; 1 Euro=13.7603 ATS. [4] Dec. of each year. [5] Figures in thousands. [6] New denomination of the rouble: 1 new rouble = 1000 old roubles.

Notes explicatives: voir p. 879.

[1] Par heure rémunérée. [2] Y compris la valeur des paiements en nature; travailleurs permanents. [3] Avant 2002: ATS; 1 Euro=13,7603 ATS. [4] Déc. de chaque année. [5] Données en milliers. [6] Nouvelle dénomination du rouble: 1 nouveau rouble = 1000 anciens roubles.

Notas explicativas: véase p. 882.

[1] Por hora pagada. [2] Incl. el valor de los pagos en especie; trabajadores permanentes. [3] Antes de 2002: ATS; 1 Euro=13,7603 ATS. [4] Dic. de cada año. [5] Cifras en millares. [6] Nueva denominación del rublo: 1 nuevo rublo = 1000 antiguos rublos.

	1999	2000	2001	2002	2003	2004	2005	2006	2007	2008

Belgique (DA) [1] — **Employees - Salariés - Asalariados** — E.G./h. - Euro

Total men and women - Total hommes et femmes - Total hombres y mujeres
ISIC 3 - CITI 3 - CIIU 3

	1999	2000	2001	2002	2003	2004	2005	2006	2007	2008
C	13	13	13	14	15	15	16	16	16	.
D	13	13	14	14	15	16	16	16	17	.
E	19	19	19	19	20	20	20	20	21	.
F	11	12	12	13	13	13	14	14	14	.
G	12	12	13	13	13	14	14	15	15	.
H	8	9	9	10	10	10	11	11	12	.
I	12	12	13	13	14	14	15	16	16	.
J	17	18	18	19	19	21	21	22	22	.
K	14	14	14	15	15	16	16	17	17	.
M	.	.	.	.	.	.	.	21	.	.
N	.	.	.	.	.	.	.	15	.	.
O	.	.	.	.	.	.	.	15	.	.
P	.	.	.	.	.	.	.	.	.	.

Men - Hommes - Hombres
ISIC 3 - CITI 3 - CIIU 3

	1999	2000	2001	2002	2003	2004	2005	2006	2007	2008
C	12.9	12.9	13.5	13.9	14.6	15.2	15.9	15.7	16.1	.
D	13.6	14.0	14.5	14.9	15.5	16.1	16.6	16.9	17.2	.
E	19.7	19.8	20.0	20.2	20.4	20.7	21.0	21.3	21.9	.
F	11.5	11.7	12.4	12.8	13.1	13.5	14.0	14.1	14.4	.
G	13.0	13.5	14.1	14.1	14.8	15.3	15.6	16.0	16.4	.
H	8.9	9.1	9.6	10.0	10.5	11.0	11.4	12.1	12.2	.
I	12.3	12.8	13.3	13.9	14.2	14.8	15.1	15.7	15.8	.
J	19.4	19.7	20.9	21.2	21.7	23.2	23.9	24.2	24.7	.
K	15.5	15.6	16.0	16.6	16.9	17.6	18.0	18.6	18.8	.
M	.	.	.	.	.	.	.	23.4	.	.
N	.	.	.	.	.	.	.	15.6	.	.
O	.	.	.	.	.	.	.	16.4	.	.

Women - Femmes - Mujeres
ISIC 3 - CITI 3 - CIIU 3

	1999	2000	2001	2002	2003	2004	2005	2006	2007	2008
C	13.2	13.3	13.5	13.9	14.6	15.1	15.4	15.8	16.1	.
D	10.9	11.4	12.0	12.3	12.7	13.6	14.0	14.5	14.7	.
E	15.0	15.4	15.5	15.8	15.9	15.9	16.2	16.8	16.8	.
F	10.4	10.5	11.4	11.7	12.3	12.9	13.2	13.9	14.0	.
G	10.0	10.3	10.7	11.0	11.4	11.7	12.2	13.2	13.5	.
H	8.0	8.3	8.7	9.2	9.7	9.8	9.9	10.6	10.9	.
I	10.9	11.4	12.1	12.6	12.8	13.3	13.8	14.9	15.2	.
J	14.4	15.0	15.6	15.9	16.5	18.0	18.4	18.9	19.3	.
K	11.6	11.9	12.2	13.1	13.6	14.0	14.2	14.3	14.6	.
M	.	.	.	.	.	.	.	20.3	.	.
N	.	.	.	.	.	.	.	14.7	.	.
O	.	.	.	.	.	.	.	13.8	.	.

Belgique (DA) [1] — **Employees - Salariés - Asalariados** — E.G./m. - Euro

Total men and women - Total hommes et femmes - Total hombres y mujeres
ISIC 3 - CITI 3 - CIIU 3
Total

	1999	2000	2001	2002	2003	2004	2005	2006	2007	2008
C	2 137	2 166	2 253	2 342	2 399	2 481	2 583	2 605	2 622	.
D	2 189	2 261	2 350	2 391	2 520	2 609	2 660	2 695	2 740	.
E	3 111	3 153	3 345	3 384	3 170	3 214	3 282	3 319	3 365	.
F	1 981	2 007	2 127	2 169	2 268	2 305	2 349	2 388	2 436	.
G	1 829	1 893	1 992	1 962	2 089	2 140	2 162	2 260	2 308	.
H	1 114	1 068	1 174	1 166	1 208	1 232	1 294	1 528	1 528	.
I	2 019	2 066	2 163	2 198	2 315	2 342	2 397	2 496	2 508	.
J	2 684	2 755	2 872	3 047	3 003	3 221	3 253	3 295	3 301	.
K	2 146	2 234	2 214	2 409	2 363	2 448	2 555	2 617	2 631	.
L	.	.	.	.	.	.	.	.	.	.
M	.	.	.	.	.	.	.	2 312	.	.
N	.	.	.	.	.	.	.	2 040	.	.
O	.	.	.	.	.	.	.	2 295	.	.

Men - Hommes - Hombres
ISIC 3 - CITI 3 - CIIU 3
Total

	1999	2000	2001	2002	2003	2004	2005	2006	2007	2008
C	2 158	2 174	2 264	2 347	2 397	2 483	2 599	2 609	2 626	.
D	2 312	2 378	2 464	2 513	2 653	2 737	2 784	2 815	2 869	.
E	3 280	3 363	3 574	3 588	3 508	3 776	3 713	3 530	3 592	.
F	2 001	2 032	2 149	2 197	2 291	2 328	2 372	2 405	2 455	.
G	2 144	2 240	2 373	2 304	2 429	2 540	2 563	2 588	2 641	.
H	1 227	1 178	1 294	1 287	1 318	1 380	1 396	1 712	1 718	.
I	2 108	2 153	2 247	2 262	2 412	2 366	2 492	2 571	2 575	.
J	3 120	3 191	3 363	3 327	3 497	3 735	3 743	3 793	3 859	.
K	2 533	2 596	2 644	2 725	2 793	2 958	2 963	3 001	3 065	.
L	.	.	.	.	.	.	.	.	.	.
M	.	.	.	.	.	.	.	2 553	.	.
N	.	.	.	.	.	.	.	2 407	.	.
O	.	.	.	.	.	.	.	2 593	.	.

Explanatory notes: see p. 877.	Notes explicatives: voir p. 879.	Notas explicativas: véase p. 882.
[1] Oct. of each year.	[1] Oct. de chaque année.	[1] Oct. de cada año.

920

ILO YEARBOOK OF LABOUR STATISTICS 2009   *ANNUAIRE DES STATISTIQUES DU TRAVAIL DU BIT 2009*   *ANUARIO DE ESTADISTICAS DEL TRABAJO DEL OIT 2009*

	1999	2000	2001	2002	2003	2004	2005	2006	2007	2008

Belgique (DA) [1]   Employees - Salariés - Asalariados   E.G./m. - Euro

Women - Femmes - Mujeres
ISIC 3 - CITI 3 - CIIU 3
Total

	1999	2000	2001	2002	2003	2004	2005	2006	2007	2008
C	1 886	2 064	2 135	2 285	2 411	2 471	2 542	2 577	2 578	
D	1 739	1 830	1 945	1 944	2 051	2 160	2 218	2 251	2 279	
E	2 281	2 241	2 376	2 512	2 116	2 378	2 637	2 662	2 654	
F	1 635	1 617	1 748	1 791	1 918	1 979	2 041	2 156	2 185	
G	1 427	1 480	1 556	1 583	1 682	1 716	1 733	1 840	1 872	
H	1 007	967	1 059	1 058	1 084	1 107	1 200	1 342	1 347	
I	1 721	1 789	1 901	1 981	1 999	2 043	2 144	2 263	2 281	
J	2 127	2 255	2 315	2 337	2 447	2 648	2 685	2 719	2 754	
K	1 659	1 788	1 830	1 970	1 988	2 081	2 118	2 130	2 146	
L	.	.	.	.	.	.	.			
M	.	.	.	.	.	.	.	2 183	.	
N	.	.	.	.	.	.	.	1 945	.	
O	.	.	.	.	.	.	.	1 970	.	.

Belgique (DA) [1][2]   Employees - Salariés - Asalariados   E.G./h. - Euro

Total men and women - Total hommes et femmes - Total hombres y mujeres
ISIC 3 - CITI 3 - CIIU 3

	1999	2000	2001	2002	2003	2004	2005	2006	2007	2008
C-Q	.	14	14	14	15	16	16	.	.	.
C	13	13	13	14	15	15	16	16	.	.
D	13	13	14	14	15	16	16	16	.	.
E	19	19	20	20	19	21	22	21	.	.
F	11	12	12	13	13	13	14	14	.	.
G	12	13	14	14	14	15	15	16	.	.
H	9	10	10	10	11	11	11	12	.	.
I	12	13	13	13	14	14	15	16	.	.
J	18	18	19	19	20	22	22	22	.	.
K	15	15	15	16	15	17	17	18	.	.
M	.	.	.	.	.	.	.	15	.	.
N	.	.	.	.	.	.	.	15	.	.
O	.	.	.	.	.	.	.	16	.	.

Men - Hommes - Hombres
ISIC 3 - CITI 3 - CIIU 3

	1999	2000	2001	2002	2003	2004	2005	2006	2007	2008
C-Q	14	14	15	15	16	16	17	.	.	.
C	13	13	13	14	15	15	16	16	.	.
D	14	14	14	15	16	16	17	17	.	.
E	20	20	21	21	21	23	24	22	.	.
F	11	12	12	13	13	13	14	14	.	.
G	13	14	15	14	15	16	16	16	.	.
H	10	10	11	11	12	11	11	13	.	.
I	12	13	13	13	14	14	15	16	.	.
J	19	20	21	21	22	24	24	24	.	.
K	16	16	16	17	17	18	19	19	.	.
M	.	.	.	.	.	.	.	16	.	.
N	.	.	.	.	.	.	.	16	.	.
O	.	.	.	.	.	.	.	17	.	.

Women - Femmes - Mujeres
ISIC 3 - CITI 3 - CIIU 3

	1999	2000	2001	2002	2003	2004	2005	2006	2007	2008
C-Q	11	12	13	13	13	14	14	.	.	.
C	13	13	14	14	15	17	15	17	.	.
D	11	11	12	12	13	14	14	15	.	.
E	15	14	15	15	12	14	16	16	.	.
F	11	11	12	12	13	13	13	14	.	.
G	11	11	12	12	12	13	13	14	.	.
H	8	9	10	10	10	10	10	11	.	.
I	11	12	12	13	13	14	14	15	.	.
J	14	15	15	16	16	18	18	19	.	.
K	13	13	13	14	13	15	15	16	.	.
M	.	.	.	.	.	.	.	15	.	.
N	.	.	.	.	.	.	.	15	.	.
O	.	.	.	.	.	.	.	14	.	.

Explanatory notes: see p. 877.   Notes explicatives: voir p. 879.   Notas explicativas: véase p. 882.

[1] Oct. of each year. [2] Full-time employees only.   [1] Oct. de chaque année. [2] Salariés à plein temps seulement.   [1] Oct. de cada año. [2] Asalariados a tiempo completo solamente.

5A WAGES · SALAIRES · SALARIOS

By economic activity · Par activité économique · Por actividad económica

	1999	2000	2001	2002	2003	2004	2005	2006	2007	2008

Bosnia and Herzegovina (DA) [1] — Employees - Salariés - Asalariados — E.G./m. - Marka

Total men and women - Total hommes et femmes - Total hombres y mujeres
ISIC 3 - CİTI 3 - CIIU 3

	1999	2000	2001	2002	2003	2004	2005	2006	2007	2008
Total	550.80	606.94	651.85	709.86	770.85	784.58	819.93	887.07		
A								820.17		
B								589.38		
C								771.23		
D								672.78		
E								1 521.90		
F								642.15		
G								747.69		
H								639.08		
I								1 128.25		
J								1 696.40		
K								896.57		
L								1 169.47		
M								901.82		
N								1 009.06		
O								916.90		

Bulgaria (CA) — Employees - Salariés - Asalariados — E.G./m. - Leva

Total men and women - Total hommes et femmes - Total hombres y mujeres
ISIC 3 - CİTI 3 - CIIU 3 [2] | ISIC 4 - CITI 4 - CIIU 4

ISIC 3	1999	2000	2001	2002	2003	2004	2005	2006	2007	2008	ISIC 4
Total	201	225	240	258	273	292	324	360	431	524	Total
A-B	165	181	185	192	200	216	523	590	711	877	B
C-Q	203	227	242	260	276	295	327	363	434	527	B-U
A	165	181	186	192	203	216	288	319	381	471	C
B	103	105	108	112	125	148	657	751	871	1 075	D
C	304	368	389	417	431	486	318	363	435	549	E
D	203	219	227	236	246	262	267	298	354	446	F
E	406	412	444	464	511	541	251	288	349	388	G
F	203	204	213	215	232	245	359	391	474	594	H
G	151	158	167	180	201	217	202	222	267	325	I
H	147	140	150	155	162	172	557	698	875	914	J
I	249	271	294	310	342	355	755	824	964	1 237	K
J	361	442	510	553	626	680	299	352	438	519	L
K	180	213	228	240	249	271	370	415	551	647	M
L	243	305	336	395	432	470	183	215	263	386	N
M	171	213	232	269	297	321	478	531	637	764	O
N	156	190	218	255	297	330	339	378	433	580	P
O	146	186	209	227	194	206	377	388	461	571	Q
							297	318	386	475	R
							267	278	319	374	S

Men - Hommes - Hombres
ISIC 3 - CITI 3 - CIIU 3 [2] | ISIC 4 - CITI 4 - CIIU 4

ISIC 3	1999	2000	2001	2002	2003	2004	2005	2006	2007	2008	ISIC 4
Total	227	256	273	290	303	321	356	393	469		Total
A-B	174		198	204	213	229	551	610	740		B
C-Q	232	261	277	295	307	326	361	398	474		B-U
A	174	193	198	204	214	229	343	377	451		C
B	100	101	110	114	126	150	723	790	906		D
C	318	384	406	435	450	515	343	385	465		E
D	232	257	271	284	293	311	267	297	352		F
E	426	439	467	488	535	564	284	325	394		G
F	208	210	218	218	234	245	372	404	490		H
G	165	182	192	209	228	247	222	244	295		I
H	151	152	169	173	180	191	619	785	965		J
I	255	281	302	318	352	364	878	975	1 184		K
J	394	481	570	613	725	810	319	386	485		L
K	175	216	234	244	251	271	401	448	609		M
L	271	346	373	445	472	504	187	216	260		N
M	193	262	272	320	344	375	519	570	694		O
N	190	244	277	332	388	424	400	442	504		P
O	158	208	232	248	204	217	506	496	588		Q
							317	340	435		R
							295	311	358		S

Explanatory notes: see p. 877.

[1] Data refer to the Federation of Bosnia and Herzegovina. [2] Employees under labour contract.

Notes explicatives: voir p. 879.

[1] Les données se réfèrent à la Fédération de Bosnie-Herzégovine. [2] Salariés sous contrat de travail.

Notas explicativas: véase p. 882.

[1] Los datos se refieren a la Federación de Bosnia y Herzegovina. [2] Asalariados bajo contrato de trabajo.

By economic activity — Par activité économique — Por actividad económica

Bulgaria (CA)

Employees - Salariés - Asalariados E.G./m. - Leva

Women - Femmes - Mujeres
ISIC 3 - CITI 3 - CIIU 3 [1] | ISIC 4 - CITI 4 - CIIU 4

	1999	2000	2001	2002	2003	2004	2005	2006	2007	2008	
Total	175	194	209	227	246	265	293	327	391	.	Total
A-B	142	151	157	165	177	188	397	500	587	.	B
C-Q	176	195	210	229	247	266	294	329	393	.	B-U
A	142	151	157	166	177	188	235	262	312	.	C
B	111	124	100	106	121	141	497	646	764	.	D
C	252	303	317	338	347	364	269	316	375	.	E
D	172	181	185	192	203	216	266	303	369	.	F
E	349	339	380	397	446	475	223	255	309	.	G
F	179	177	186	198	224	243	328	359	433	.	H
G	138	137	146	156	178	192	192	212	253	.	I
H	144	132	140	145	153	162	482	592	761	.	J
I	236	251	277	293	324	335	693	753	865	.	K
J	343	420	478	521	574	615	279	320	394	.	L
K	188	208	220	235	245	272	340	385	502	.	M
L	223	276	310	360	404	447	175	214	269	.	N
M	165	199	221	255	284	307	451	504	599	.	O
N	147	175	203	236	274	305	322	361	414	.	P
O	137	168	190	208	184	196	344	360	428	.	Q
							280	298	343	.	R
							250	260	298	.	S

Croatia (DA) [2]

Employees - Salariés - Asalariados E.G./m. - Kuna

Total men and women - Total hommes et femmes - Total hombres y mujeres
ISIC 3 - CITI 3 - CIIU 3

	1999	2000	2001	2002	2003	2004	2005	2006	2007	2008
Total	4 551	4 869	5 061	5 366	5 599	5 916	6 192	6 575	6 995	.
A-B	3 806	4 237	4 083	4 383	4 521	4 807	5 039	5 525	5 986	.
C-Q	4 578	4 891	5 096	5 402	5 628	5 944	6 220	6 600	7 019	.
A	3 821	4 272	4 108	4 421	4 550	4 854	5 083	5 571	6 032	.
B	3 005	2 909	3 302	3 578	3 953	3 848	4 220	4 620	5 156	.
C	4 615	5 089	5 696	5 942	6 192	6 478	6 923	7 405	7 989	.
D	3 869	4 100	4 465	4 794	4 952	5 189	5 452	5 833	6 161	.
E	5 113	5 382	5 480	5 700	6 041	6 510	6 715	7 150	7 647	.
F	3 630	3 663	3 975	4 549	4 644	4 859	5 107	5 412	5 754	.
G	3 580	3 875	4 151	4 616	4 766	5 043	5 292	5 686	6 073	.
H	3 610	3 859	4 126	4 406	4 753	5 032	5 303	5 583	5 958	.
I	4 908	5 461	5 799	6 300	6 378	6 748	7 035	7 475	7 875	.
J	6 998	7 634	8 106	8 853	8 944	9 292	9 994	10 359	10 924	.
K	5 093	5 290	5 380	5 634	5 925	6 346	6 776	7 335	7 878	.
L	6 185	6 409	5 995	6 073	6 435	6 802	7 040	7 437	8 071	.
M	4 624	5 093	5 245	5 381	5 862	6 302	6 409	6 681	7 166	.
N	5 789	6 368	6 346	6 407	6 589	6 899	7 327	7 680	8 212	.
O	4 994	5 153	5 308	5 583	5 751	6 193	6 451	6 577	7 080	.

Men - Hommes - Hombres
ISIC 3 - CITI 3 - CIIU 3

	1999	2000	2001	2002	2003	2004	2005	2006	2007	2008
Total	.	.	.	.	5 868	6 206	6 492	6 909	7 344	.
A-B	.	.	.	.	4 633	4 921	5 131	5 711	6 192	.
C-Q	.	.	.	.	5 913	6 250	6 537	6 948	7 381	.
A	.	.	.	.	4 665	4 975	5 178	5 764	6 247	.
B	.	.	.	.	4 050	3 931	4 330	4 765	5 296	.
C	.	.	.	.	6 198	6 511	6 918	7 372	7 958	.
D	.	.	.	.	5 412	5 680	5 969	6 377	6 734	.
E	.	.	.	.	6 122	6 583	6 780	7 216	7 708	.
F	.	.	.	.	4 648	4 837	5 072	5 346	5 679	.
G	.	.	.	.	5 226	5 530	5 825	6 290	6 723	.
H	.	.	.	.	5 229	5 541	5 787	6 108	6 501	.
I	.	.	.	.	6 374	6 831	7 100	7 580	7 993	.
J	.	.	.	.	10 776	11 187	12 115	12 788	13 497	.
K	.	.	.	.	6 274	6 689	7 143	7 662	8 199	.
L	.	.	.	.	6 824	7 218	7 512	7 925	8 593	.
M	.	.	.	.	6 670	7 369	7 460	7 730	8 297	.
N	.	.	.	.	8 031	8 270	8 970	9 614	10 290	.
O	.	.	.	.	6 045	6 531	6 740	7 130	7 486	.

Explanatory notes: see p. 877.
[1] Employees under labour contract. [2] Excl. employees in craft and trade.

Notes explicatives: voir p. 879.
[1] Salariés sous contrat de travail. [2] Non compris les salariés dans l'artisanat et dans le commerce.

Notas explicativas: véase p. 882.
[1] Asalariados bajo contrato de trabajo. [2] Excl. los asalariados en el artesanado y el comercio.

5A

WAGES	SALAIRES	SALARIOS
By economic activity	Par activité économique	Por actividad económica

	1999	2000	2001	2002	2003	2004	2005	2006	2007	2008

Croatia (DA) [1] Employees - Salariés - Asalariados E.G./m. - Kuna

Women - Femmes - Mujeres
ISIC 3 - CITI 3 - CIIU 3

	1999	2000	2001	2002	2003	2004	2005	2006	2007	2008
Total	.	.	.	.	5 251	5 540	5 806	6 149	6 549	.
A-B	.	.	.	.	4 162	4 443	4 752	4 957	5 365	.
C-Q	.	.	.	.	5 267	5 555	5 820	6 165	6 564	.
A	.	.	.	.	4 187	4 477	4 792	4 994	5 398	.
B	.	.	.	.	3 493	3 429	3 687	3 982	4 419	.
C	.	.	.	.	6 162	6 319	6 952	7 572	8 146	.
D	.	.	.	.	4 196	4 359	4 560	4 874	5 148	.
E	.	.	.	.	5 700	6 212	6 446	6 883	7 398	.
F	.	.	.	.	4 621	5 016	5 371	5 923	6 366	.
G	.	.	.	.	4 280	4 528	4 733	5 057	5 396	.
H	.	.	.	.	4 364	4 603	4 895	5 135	5 495	.
I	.	.	.	.	6 388	6 535	6 866	7 206	7 573	.
J	.	.	.	.	8 188	8 497	9 088	9 327	9 809	.
K	.	.	.	.	5 417	5 829	6 230	6 842	7 376	.
L	.	.	.	.	5 759	6 134	6 356	6 759	7 368	.
M	.	.	.	.	5 577	5 931	6 052	6 326	6 785	.
N	.	.	.	.	6 146	6 460	6 804	7 102	7 582	.
O	.	.	.	.	5 377	5 765	6 084	6 340	6 586	.

Cyprus (DA) [2] [3] [4] Employees - Salariés - Asalariados E.G./h. - Pound

Total men and women - Total hommes et femmes - Total hombres y mujeres
ISIC 3 - CITI 3 - CIIU 3

	1999	2000	2001	2002	2003	2004	2005	2006	2007	2008
Total	4.85	5.16	5.48	5.70	6.13	6.25	6.50	6.83	.	.
A-B	3.05	3.37	3.42	3.45	3.70	3.73	3.83	4.14	.	.
C-Q	4.90	5.18	5.51	5.73	6.16	6.28	6.54	6.86	.	.
A	2.99	3.28	3.40	3.45	3.70	3.72	3.82	4.13	.	.
B	3.36	3.92	4.62	3.77	3.91	4.26	4.60	4.87	.	.
C	5.16	6.10	6.34	5.86	6.35	5.29	6.90	7.24	.	.
D	3.86	4.02	4.25	4.45	4.64	4.83	4.93	5.01	.	.
E	6.16	6.72	6.80	6.63	7.35	7.50	7.79	8.60	.	.
F	5.04	5.27	5.67	6.13	6.49	6.59	7.15	7.19	.	.
G	3.78	4.02	4.17	4.07	4.30	4.38	4.48	4.94	.	.
H	4.33	4.56	4.74	4.49	4.64	4.62	4.52	4.68	.	.
I	5.54	5.97	6.13	6.40	7.45	7.72	8.17	8.20	.	.
J	6.65	7.06	7.56	7.89	8.68	9.26	9.88	10.73	.	.
K	4.42	4.74	4.84	5.89	6.13	6.26	6.69	8.08	.	.
L	6.00	6.31	6.44	6.90	7.26	7.26	7.53	7.86	.	.
M	7.83	8.35	8.48	9.02	9.84	9.81	10.14	10.81	.	.
N	5.98	6.49	6.41	6.66	7.54	7.59	7.91	8.39	.	.
O	4.94	5.20	5.31	5.57	5.96	6.09	6.52	6.86	.	.

Men - Hommes - Hombres
ISIC 3 - CITI 3 - CIIU 3

	1999	2000	2001	2002	2003	2004	2005	2006	2007	2008
Total	5.41	5.72	6.08	6.35	6.84	6.97	7.24	7.53	.	.
A-B	3.54	3.97	4.18	4.08	4.31	4.36	4.42	4.89	.	.
C-Q	5.47	5.76	6.11	6.38	6.88	7.01	7.28	7.55	.	.
A	3.59	3.97	4.16	4.09	4.32	4.36	4.41	4.89	.	.
B	3.35	3.95	4.78	3.79	3.94	4.36	4.73	4.99	.	.
C	5.25	6.15	6.34	5.91	6.44	5.42	6.98	7.24	.	.
D	4.66	4.83	4.94	5.24	5.43	5.68	5.77	5.68	.	.
E	6.31	6.87	7.07	6.85	7.58	7.72	8.01	9.87	.	.
F	5.08	5.31	5.72	6.15	6.52	6.63	7.19	7.17	.	.
G	4.50	4.78	5.12	5.00	5.27	5.35	5.45	6.00	.	.
H	4.94	5.18	5.52	5.34	5.68	5.67	5.34	5.55	.	.
I	6.03	6.44	6.82	7.05	8.35	8.67	9.16	9.26	.	.
J	7.63	8.19	8.85	9.26	10.20	10.81	11.56	12.33	.	.
K	5.30	5.55	5.67	7.20	7.26	7.37	7.95	10.19	.	.
L	6.31	6.63	6.89	7.31	7.66	7.60	7.91	8.25	.	.
M	8.87	9.37	9.61	10.17	10.94	10.87	11.14	11.91	.	.
N	6.59	7.13	7.08	7.54	9.72	9.79	10.13	10.98	.	.
O	5.61	5.94	5.90	6.28	6.65	6.65	7.02	7.55	.	.

Women - Femmes - Mujeres
ISIC 3 - CITI 3 - CIIU 3

	1999	2000	2001	2002	2003	2004	2005	2006	2007	2008
Total	4.09	4.37	4.74	4.90	5.25	5.36	5.60	5.91	.	.
A-B	2.33	2.50	2.44	2.62	2.89	2.90	3.07	3.16	.	.
C-Q	4.13	4.35	4.77	4.93	5.28	5.40	5.64	5.94	.	.
A	2.30	2.47	2.43	2.62	2.89	2.90	3.07	3.16	.	.
B	3.44	3.51	3.52	3.60	3.68	3.58	3.74	4.08	.	.
C	3.84	5.29	6.34	4.98	4.95	3.06	5.45	7.20	.	.
D	2.79	2.94	3.16	3.19	3.39	3.50	3.60	3.70	.	.
E	4.56	5.10	5.33	5.38	6.03	6.27	6.55	7.12	.	.
F	4.77	4.77	5.12	5.88	6.23	6.20	6.63	7.46	.	.
G	2.81	3.00	3.15	3.09	3.25	3.35	3.45	3.62	.	.
H	3.75	3.98	4.12	3.82	3.82	3.79	3.87	4.00	.	.
I	4.56	5.05	4.88	5.24	5.83	6.01	6.37	6.19	.	.
J	5.59	5.82	6.42	6.69	7.34	7.90	8.40	9.43	.	.
K	3.63	4.01	4.26	4.98	5.34	5.48	5.81	6.13	.	.
L	5.24	5.55	5.59	6.12	6.51	6.61	6.82	7.27	.	.
M	7.17	7.71	7.90	8.43	9.27	9.26	9.62	10.34	.	.
N	5.76	6.25	6.20	6.39	6.87	6.91	7.23	7.52	.	.
O	4.18	4.37	4.55	4.67	5.08	5.37	5.88	5.90	.	.

Explanatory notes: see p. 877.

Notes explicatives: voir p. 879.

Notas explicativas: véase p. 882.

[1] Excl. employees in craft and trade. [2] Adults. [3] Incl. family allowances and the value of payments in kind. [4] Oct. of each year.

[1] Non compris les salariés dans l'artisanat et dans le commerce. [2] Adultes. [3] Y compris les allocations familiales et la valeur des paiements en nature. [4] Oct. de chaque année.

[1] Excl. los asalariados en el artesanado y el comercio. [2] Adultos. [3] Incl. las asignaciones familiares y el valor de los pagos en especie. [4] Oct. de cada año.

| By economic activity | Par activité économique | Por actividad económica |

	1999	2000	2001	2002	2003	2004	2005	2006	2007	2008
Cyprus (DA) [1][2][3]					Wage earners - Ouvriers - Obreros					E.G./h. - Pound

Total men and women - Total hommes et femmes - Total hombres y mujeres
ISIC 3 - CITI 3 - CIIU 3

	1999	2000	2001	2002	2003	2004	2005	2006	2007	2008
Total	3.74	3.87	4.11	4.37	4.63	4.63	4.87	5.29	.	.
C-Q	3.77	3.90	4.15	4.42	4.67	4.68	4.92	5.34	.	.
A	.	.	3.30	3.48	3.75	3.49	3.75	4.10	.	.
C	4.85	5.06	5.45	4.96	5.54	5.95	6.38	6.55	.	.
D	3.39	3.50	3.72	3.94	4.13	4.22	4.32	4.85	.	.
E	2.62	2.84	2.89	2.94	3.38	3.51	3.65	3.96	.	.
F	4.31	4.54	4.62	5.03	5.23	5.32	5.70	5.67	.	.
G	3.83	3.77	4.01	4.23	4.59	4.08	4.53	5.14	.	.
H	2.48	2.61	2.71	2.86	3.20	3.30	2.41	3.51	.	.
I	3.94	3.50	4.28	4.92	5.42	5.36	5.77	6.30	.	.
J	3.08	3.10	.	.	.	.	.	.	.	.
K	3.47	4.09	4.63	2.91	2.95	2.96	3.62	3.30	.	.
L	4.17	4.42	4.62	4.82	5.06	5.12	5.55	5.83	.	.
M	3.39	3.60	3.79	3.80	4.31	4.09	4.31	4.52	.	.
N	3.80	4.08	4.23	4.48	4.79	4.71	5.14	5.53	.	.
O	3.69	3.99	4.51	4.69	5.00	4.72	5.05	4.95	.	.

Men - Hommes - Hombres
ISIC 3 - CITI 3 - CIIU 3

	1999	2000	2001	2002	2003	2004	2005	2006	2007	2008
Total	4.20	4.34	4.50	4.85	5.13	5.14	5.40	5.64	.	.
C-Q	4.21	4.35	4.50	4.85	5.13	5.16	5.41	5.64	.	.
A	.	.	4.66	4.74	4.95	4.38	4.81	5.49	.	.
C	4.90	5.11	5.45	4.96	5.54	5.95	6.38	6.55	.	.
D	4.13	4.22	4.25	4.62	4.84	4.99	5.06	5.34	.	.
E	2.62	2.85	2.90	2.94	3.38	3.52	3.66	3.96	.	.
F	4.34	4.57	4.64	5.05	5.25	5.34	5.72	5.68	.	.
G	4.18	4.21	4.38	4.68	5.12	4.52	4.99	5.59	.	.
H	2.61	3.08	3.33	4.95	6.03	6.32	2.86	5.26	.	.
I	3.90	3.55	4.28	4.92	5.42	5.35	5.78	6.34	.	.
J	3.25	3.30	.	.	.	.	.	.	.	.
K	3.65	4.28	4.96	2.99	2.81	2.89	3.64	6.32	.	.
L	4.39	4.65	4.89	5.10	5.34	5.43	5.88	6.07	.	.
M	4.06	4.39	4.67	4.30	5.31	5.02	4.91	6.18	.	.
N	4.23	4.54	4.75	4.96	5.32	5.22	5.71	6.07	.	.
O	4.11	4.53	4.76	4.93	5.27	5.01	5.39	5.51	.	.

Women - Femmes - Mujeres
ISIC 3 - CITI 3 - CIIU 3

	1999	2000	2001	2002	2003	2004	2005	2006	2007	2008
Total	2.73	2.81	2.99	2.99	3.18	3.13	3.34	3.76	.	.
C-Q	2.76	2.84	3.06	3.04	3.21	3.16	3.38	3.85	.	.
A	.	.	2.35	2.59	2.90	2.87	3.00	3.12	.	.
C	2.38	2.67	.	.	.	.	.	.	.	.
D	2.55	2.68	2.78	2.72	2.86	2.86	2.99	3.22	.	.
E	2.60	2.67	2.78	2.88	3.35	3.37	3.45	.	.	.
F	3.37	3.57	3.89	4.16	4.50	4.39	4.70	5.08	.	.
G	3.12	2.87	3.01	3.02	3.17	2.90	3.28	3.70	.	.
H	2.42	2.38	2.44	1.96	1.99	1.99	2.21	2.62	.	.
I	4.64	2.73	4.23	4.97	5.32	5.66	5.54	5.96	.	.
J	3.00	3.00	.	.	.	.	.	.	.	.
K	2.84	3.42	3.82	2.73	3.29	3.14	3.58	2.32	.	.
L	3.04	3.20	3.34	3.49	3.73	3.64	3.98	4.89	.	.
M	2.93	3.07	3.26	3.50	3.70	3.53	3.94	4.04	.	.
N	3.55	3.82	3.98	4.25	4.53	4.46	4.86	5.17	.	.
O	3.15	3.30	3.44	3.67	3.88	3.47	3.63	4.07	.	.

	1999	2000	2001	2002	2003	2004	2005	2006	2007	2008
Cyprus (DA) [1][2][3]					Wage earners - Ouvriers - Obreros					E.G./w.s. - Pound

Total men and women - Total hommes et femmes - Total hombres y mujeres
ISIC 3 - CITI 3 - CIIU 3

	1999	2000	2001	2002	2003	2004	2005	2006	2007	2008
Total	.	.	167.62	178.36	187.92	188.42	196.58	211.61	.	.
C-Q	.	.	169.37	180.27	188.99	190.65	198.70	213.78	.	.
A	108.91	.	130.24	137.50	165.00	140.54	151.16	160.43	.	.
C	.	.	239.40	225.45	257.01	297.83	299.05	287.75	.	.
D	.	.	152.42	157.34	165.74	169.41	171.75	200.62	.	.
E	.	.	116.12	113.80	130.00	139.32	147.09	166.13	.	.
F	.	.	189.43	209.16	210.95	217.00	231.34	221.72	.	.
G	.	.	153.59	171.87	194.26	178.50	175.17	201.20	.	.
H	.	.	121.52	136.14	119.82	119.42	116.80	135.05	.	.
I	.	.	187.41	211.93	239.77	233.94	247.59	274.18	.	.
K	.	.	202.43	118.14	138.90	143.82	170.83	163.99	.	.
L	.	.	180.45	187.04	194.67	198.82	215.43	232.31	.	.
M	.	.	139.31	128.81	170.06	156.98	167.05	171.70	.	.
N	.	.	162.57	171.69	183.43	180.24	196.49	214.77	.	.
O	.	.	184.38	188.22	210.15	196.87	199.78	192.46	.	.

Explanatory notes: see p. 877.

[1] Adults. [2] Incl. family allowances and the value of payments in kind. [3] Oct. of each year.

Notes explicatives: voir p. 879.

[1] Adultes. [2] Y compris les allocations familiales et la valeur des paiements en nature. [3] Oct. de chaque année.

Notas explicativas: véase p. 882.

[1] Adultos. [2] Incl. las asignaciones familiares y el valor de los pagos en especie. [3] Oct. de cada año.

By economic activity — **Par activité économique** — **Por actividad económica**

	1999	2000	2001	2002	2003	2004	2005	2006	2007	2008

Cyprus (DA) [1][2][3] — **Wage earners - Ouvriers - Obreros** — E.G./w.s. - Pound

Men - Hommes - Hombres
ISIC 3 - CITI 3 - CIIU 3

	1999	2000	2001	2002	2003	2004	2005	2006	2007	2008
Total	.	.	185.24	198.78	210.01	212.26	218.85	227.33	.	.
C-Q	.	.	185.38	199.11	209.46	213.09	219.44	227.60	.	.
A	146.88	.	179.86	185.88	231.69	179.36	195.59	214.62	.	.
C	213.18	.	239.40	225.45	257.01	297.83	299.05	287.75	.	.
D	185.85	.	176.64	186.29	194.91	203.27	202.86	223.09	.	.
E	103.13	.	117.44	114.09	130.13	140.19	148.19	166.13	.	.
F	176.97	.	190.39	210.28	211.77	218.16	232.51	222.33	.	.
G	167.75	.	175.11	193.13	221.79	202.85	192.88	228.29	.	.
H	102.70	.	146.00	199.92	241.33	240.00	142.62	200.00	.	.
I	183.69	.	188.19	212.63	241.17	234.63	248.91	279.94	.	.
K	146.33	.	222.37	124.96	139.47	148.78	177.56	173.50	.	.
L	170.74	.	191.66	198.37	205.52	211.44	228.63	243.79	.	.
M	152.68	.	175.48	134.90	218.71	194.26	195.40	234.84	.	.
N	164.89	.	183.98	191.03	205.51	201.52	219.81	238.60	.	.
O	162.70	.	196.10	198.73	223.12	212.09	214.16	215.75	.	.

Women - Femmes - Mujeres
ISIC 3 - CITI 3 - CIIU 3

	1999	2000	2001	2002	2003	2004	2005	2006	2007	2008
Total	.	.	116.43	118.91	123.55	118.95	131.43	142.83	.	.
C-Q	.	.	118.84	120.67	124.18	119.61	132.76	145.86	.	.
A	88.87	.	95.29	103.42	118.03	113.20	119.86	122.26	.	.
D	100.16	.	109.04	105.51	113.49	108.77	115.55	125.08	.	.
E	94.64	.	105.37	109.34	127.96	126.05	130.24	.	.	.
F	128.69	.	146.76	159.10	174.42	165.38	179.30	195.62	.	.
G	116.70	.	95.50	114.51	119.97	112.78	127.37	113.65	.	.
H	98.57	.	110.90	108.47	67.10	67.10	105.60	102.00	.	.
I	195.48	.	171.27	197.49	210.88	219.63	220.41	227.04	.	.
K	111.85	.	153.47	101.39	137.50	131.64	154.31	135.02	.	.
L	114.47	.	127.39	133.45	143.32	139.12	152.99	187.15	.	.
M	106.49	.	117.27	125.10	140.42	134.26	149.78	153.66	.	.
N	135.61	.	152.30	162.41	172.84	170.03	185.30	198.99	.	.
O	119.17	.	134.61	143.63	155.11	132.24	138.76	155.67	.	.

Cyprus (DA) [1][2][3] — **Salaried employees - Employés - Empleados** — E.G./m. - Pound

Total men and women - Total hommes et femmes - Total hombres y mujeres
ISIC 3 - CITI 3 - CIIU 3

	1999	2000	2001	2002	2003	2004	2005	2006	2007	2008
Total	916.42	973.97	998.64	1 032.54	1 108.29	1 134.69	1 183.44	1 227.06	.	.
A-B	.	.	681.70	644.71	682.28	720.75	706.26	788.80	.	.
C-Q	919.56	976.85	1 000.72	1 035.06	1 111.05	1 137.37	1 186.56	1 229.25	.	.
A	.	.	677.67	645.62	683.78	721.19	702.41	780.66	.	.
B	.	.	772.17	624.20	648.49	710.96	792.72	971.51	.	.
C	1 083.92	1 344.76	1 396.05	1 300.53	1 322.87	733.01	1 331.39	1 456.52	.	.
D	776.00	806.00	814.54	842.02	876.56	928.36	936.84	887.24	.	.
E	1 075.87	1 189.40	1 195.21	1 190.62	1 312.47	1 343.89	1 410.22	1 498.53	.	.
F	1 204.65	1 259.75	1 248.45	1 330.30	1 435.73	1 471.31	1 612.62	1 592.54	.	.
G	661.10	707.92	726.26	708.91	741.75	768.52	783.35	855.54	.	.
H	732.69	774.53	810.34	769.28	796.26	803.02	810.64	838.23	.	.
I	1 053.51	1 159.01	1 151.99	1 170.95	1 342.62	1 389.20	1 454.23	1 459.51	.	.
J	1 128.84	1 186.88	1 258.62	1 309.50	1 440.81	1 534.65	1 637.25	1 780.80	.	.
K	781.90	842.04	852.71	1 031.11	1 072.27	1 094.24	1 173.41	1 415.03	.	.
L	1 108.30	1 167.18	1 151.50	1 241.06	1 324.70	1 320.91	1 367.16	1 426.55	.	.
M	1 297.59	1 389.34	1 405.79	1 500.11	1 631.81	1 618.88	1 694.42	1 794.78	.	.
N	1 258.08	1 359.05	1 318.17	1 370.68	1 489.27	1 492.28	1 552.59	1 580.76	.	.
O	878.94	914.57	946.82	983.83	1 040.00	1 076.09	1 169.28	1 202.85	.	.

Men - Hommes - Hombres
ISIC 3 - CITI 3 - CIIU 3

	1999	2000	2001	2002	2003	2004	2005	2006	2007	2008
Total	1 027.98	1 090.86	1 147.22	1 186.28	1 279.10	1 308.24	1 359.42	1 403.74	.	.
A-B	.	.	725.70	683.03	725.60	767.00	738.06	839.90	.	.
C-Q	1 033.03	1 095.78	1 151.59	1 191.43	1 284.76	1 313.79	1 365.85	1 408.05	.	.
A	.	.	722.14	685.66	729.05	768.86	734.15	831.36	.	.
B	.	.	798.87	628.92	654.68	728.87	818.45	1 015.39	.	.
C	1 109.76	1 368.88	1 459.32	1 383.00	1 410.01	768.86	1 405.57	1 511.07	.	.
D	919.00	954.00	967.18	1 005.67	1 038.88	1 108.16	1 104.98	1 035.12	.	.
E	1 104.80	1 220.09	1 251.88	1 245.00	1 368.99	1 398.62	1 465.68	1 581.69	.	.
F	1 231.52	1 292.61	1 331.41	1 400.74	1 517.24	1 560.89	1 717.68	1 649.07	.	.
G	788.58	841.92	900.35	882.90	923.87	951.83	964.09	1 056.33	.	.
H	832.58	870.96	930.59	892.95	947.71	959.30	942.80	983.00	.	.
I	1 190.05	1 306.65	1 348.73	1 351.50	1 572.95	1 633.22	1 706.17	1 700.52	.	.
J	1 293.89	1 379.87	1 477.61	1 538.65	1 697.47	1 796.68	1 922.93	2 054.12	.	.
K	957.14	1 012.24	1 028.99	1 290.74	1 301.71	1 323.91	1 429.08	1 816.04	.	.
L	1 186.86	1 247.22	1 260.73	1 350.82	1 421.89	1 401.64	1 454.43	1 530.66	.	.
M	1 486.71	1 581.38	1 609.35	1 704.51	1 827.69	1 804.76	1 886.35	2 001.31	.	.
N	1 425.18	1 559.80	1 514.28	1 644.83	2 130.13	2 101.21	2 179.72	2 270.77	.	.
O	999.09	1 045.95	1 091.41	1 154.78	1 205.58	1 214.86	1 299.98	1 332.06	.	.

Explanatory notes: see p. 877.

Notes explicatives: voir p. 879.

Notas explicativas: véase p. 882.

[1] Adults. [2] Incl. family allowances and the value of payments in kind. [3] Oct. of each year.

[1] Adultes. [2] Y compris les allocations familiales et la valeur des paiements en nature. [3] Oct. de chaque année.

[1] Adultos. [2] Incl. las asignaciones familiares y el valor de los pagos en especie. [3] Oct. de cada año.

926

ILO YEARBOOK OF LABOUR STATISTICS 2009   ANNUAIRE DES STATISTIQUES DU TRAVAIL DU BIT 2009   ANUARIO DE ESTADISTICAS DEL TRABAJO DEL OIT 2009

	1999	2000	2001	2002	2003	2004	2005	2006	2007	2008

Cyprus (DA) [1] [2] [3]   Salaried employees - Employés - Empleados   E.G./m. - Pound

Women - Femmes - Mujeres
ISIC 3 - CITI 3 - CIIU 3

	1999	2000	2001	2002	2003	2004	2005	2006	2007	2008
Total	757.58	807.55	846.41	875.02	933.30	956.87	1 003.15	1 034.73	.	.
A-B			503.30	489.30	506.60	533.19	577.30	581.60		
C-Q	758.48	808.56	847.32	876.04	934.43	957.99	1 004.27	1 035.66		
A			500.85	486.39	503.78	531.62	576.18	579.05		
B			589.71	591.98	606.19	588.60	616.91	671.68		
C	686.21	973.55	1 040.59	837.21	833.38	531.62	914.64	1 207.29		
D	545.00	556.00	593.22	604.33	641.07	667.51	692.89	654.75		
E	767.69	862.43	899.60	906.94	1 017.69	1 058.42	1 120.93	1 182.29		
F	893.63	879.45	892.81	1 028.32	1 086.32	1 087.30	1 162.22	1 316.22		
G	489.64	527.69	552.65	535.39	560.13	585.70	603.09	626.31		
H	638.15	683.27	712.38	668.54	672.88	675.71	702.98	722.20		
I	784.09	867.69	854.20	897.65	993.97	1 019.84	1 072.87	1 049.38		
J	948.72	976.27	1 065.36	1 107.28	1 214.31	1 303.42	1 385.15	1 559.88		
K	624.97	689.62	735.53	858.53	919.76	941.58	1 003.47	1 060.06		
L	919.04	974.35	968.75	1 057.43	1 162.10	1 185.85	1 221.16	1 293.54		
M	1 177.95	1 267.85	1 301.03	1 394.93	1 531.01	1 523.22	1 595.65	1 706.99		
N	1 196.53	1 285.10	1 266.01	1 297.77	1 318.83	1 330.32	1 385.79	1 375.49		
O	743.65	766.61	794.72	804.01	865.83	930.11	1 031.79	1 023.07		

Czech Republic (DA)   Employees - Salariés - Asalariados   E.G./m. - Koruna

Total men and women - Total hommes et femmes - Total hombres y mujeres
ISIC 3 - CITI 3 - CIIU 3

	1999	2000	2001	2002	2003	2004	2005	2006	2007	2008
Total	12 165	12 918	13 996	14 999	15 936	17 006	17 827	18 976	20 333 [4]	.
A-B	9 659	10 323	11 206	11 512	11 908	12 865	13 591	14 395	15 786 [4]	
C-Q	12 294	13 040	14 120	15 153	16 106	17 168	17 985	19 139	20 483 [4]	
A	9 641	10 307	11 189	11 493	11 888	12 841	13 571	14 374	15 773 [4]	
B	11 568	11 877	12 835	13 397	13 670	14 891	15 465	16 295	17 044 [4]	
C	15 639	16 601	17 751	18 846	19 640	21 203	22 156	24 003	25 759 [4]	
D	11 897	12 780	13 699	14 589	15 329	16 560	17 337	18 482	19 761 [4]	
E	16 001	17 049	18 369	19 714	21 226	22 463	24 035	26 027	27 887 [4]	
F	12 041	12 509	13 566	14 188	15 216	16 040	16 547	17 637	18 781 [4]	
G	11 411	12 471	13 246	13 991	14 718	15 927	16 711	17 856	19 365 [4]	
H	6 684	7 048	7 887	8 610	9 314	9 855	10 067	10 845	11 476 [4]	
I	13 125	14 143	15 340	16 413	17 268	18 482	19 362	20 444	21 560 [4]	
J	22 868	25 383	28 531	30 862	32 643	34 857	36 824	39 198	41 030 [4]	
K	13 651	14 057	15 292	16 338	17 355	18 379	19 352	20 328	22 049 [4]	
L	14 806	15 059	16 445	18 077	19 483	20 527	21 882	22 965	24 636 [4]	
M	10 966	11 220	12 395	13 577	15 251	15 969	17 081	18 116	19 374 [4]	
N	10 844	11 422	12 857	14 419	15 520	16 163	16 670	17 984	19 107 [4]	
O	10 593	10 926	11 770	12 581	13 510	14 232	14 986	16 076	16 972 [4]	

Denmark (CA) [5] [6]   Employees - Salariés - Asalariados   E.G./h. - Krone

Total men and women - Total hommes et femmes - Total hombres y mujeres
ISIC 3 - CITI 3 - CIIU 3

	1999	2000	2001	2002	2003	2004	2005	2006	2007	2008
C-Q	191.53	197.84	211.13	215.57	223.74	224.38	234.11	242.70	255.70	.
C	242.41	239.63	240.02	269.01	274.12	284.54	293.18	328.34	322.45	
D	182.34	188.59	199.10	207.02	215.34	217.15	226.63	235.63	248.81	
E	222.69	229.57	239.28	253.20	265.38	265.47	291.88	304.41	310.70	
F	180.86	188.56	200.60	206.14	211.49	215.25	223.07	233.80	244.87	
G	181.79	188.16	199.99	205.04	212.04	209.88	220.22	224.65	238.27	
H	154.50	153.13	162.55	165.67	171.13	176.23	177.51	178.49	191.93	
I	197.17	206.03	218.12	208.75	219.98	216.04	228.41	231.84	243.89	
J	227.94	238.14	262.81	273.81	282.85	289.80	302.79	314.83	332.04	
K	208.31	219.11	230.53	238.85	247.05	248.40	260.04	269.04	281.68	
M	178.00	181.22	196.13	198.24	203.33	204.99	211.41	218.75	231.87	
N	176.35	177.70	194.51	194.82	208.86	205.05	210.38	214.34	228.51	
O	206.83	207.91	224.38	225.96	233.15	231.36	240.19	251.53	272.61	

Men - Hommes - Hombres
ISIC 3 - CITI 3 - CIIU 3

	1999	2000	2001	2002	2003	2004	2005	2006	2007	2008
C-Q	204.90	210.71	223.63	227.26	235.16	236.51	247.04	256.14	268.29	.
C	246.36	242.07	243.25	271.58	277.88	289.16	297.01	329.78	327.56	
D	192.24	197.59	207.70	215.25	223.82	226.08	235.50	244.60	258.48	
E	233.96	243.07	251.85	264.85	279.93	278.40	303.57	318.92	324.38	
F	182.92	190.54	202.64	208.17	213.26	217.09	224.78	235.86	246.84	
G	200.63	205.42	217.94	222.58	227.93	227.59	238.85	243.87	257.21	
H	167.74	165.15	175.02	175.65	180.53	186.54	188.02	188.12	193.65	
I	205.70	215.09	228.10	216.21	227.40	223.23	236.91	239.59	251.29	
J	261.65	271.89	301.13	306.79	316.08	325.38	344.30	356.81	377.65	
K	234.40	245.65	257.61	265.41	273.04	273.64	288.74	297.79	306.45	
M	190.55	191.85	208.32	207.16	211.82	214.06	220.10	226.99	239.60	
N	193.34	194.11	211.88	210.34	225.85	220.49	225.83	226.92	242.69	
O	222.52	223.15	239.83	241.82	249.23	245.34	255.61	266.87	288.16	

Explanatory notes: see p. 877.   Notes explicatives: voir p. 879.   Notas explicativas: véase p. 882.

[1] Adults. [2] Incl. family allowances and the value of payments in kind. [3] Oct. of each year. [4] Estimates. [5] Excl. young people aged less than 18 years and trainees. [6] Private sector.

[1] Adultes. [2] Y compris les allocations familiales et la valeur des paiements en nature. [3] Oct. de chaque année. [4] Estimations. [5] Non compris les jeunes gens âgés de moins de 18 ans et les apprentis. [6] Secteur privé.

[1] Adultos. [2] Incl. las asignaciones familiares y el valor de los pagos en especie. [3] Oct. de cada año. [4] Estimaciones. [5] Excl. los jovenenes de menos de 18 años y los aprendices. [6] Sector privado.

5A

WAGES	SALAIRES	SALARIOS
By economic activity	Par activité économique	Por actividad económica

	1999	2000	2001	2002	2003	2004	2005	2006	2007	2008

Denmark (CA) [1] [2]   Employees - Salariés - Asalariados   E.G./h. - Krone

Women - Femmes - Mujeres
ISIC 3 - CITI 3 - CIIU 3

	1999	2000	2001	2002	2003	2004	2005	2006	2007	2008
C-Q	168.45	174.17	187.67	192.89	201.52	201.62	208.92	217.13	230.08	.
C	210.47	217.25	213.18	244.15	244.77	251.53	261.65	318.45	288.48	.
D	160.30	166.74	178.77	186.83	194.52	196.80	204.72	213.44	223.72	.
E	183.09	189.74	197.32	216.74	228.95	227.14	252.03	262.39	272.28	.
F	159.15	165.68	177.95	184.39	192.23	194.28	203.47	211.17	222.70	.
G	151.99	158.37	168.68	175.35	182.95	179.81	188.52	192.59	205.36	.
H	141.95	143.75	152.81	158.25	163.58	167.07	168.72	170.52	189.70	.
I	176.50	185.53	196.10	191.24	203.35	200.48	207.79	212.87	224.87	.
J	197.97	205.79	227.20	241.85	250.42	255.37	262.52	274.18	288.18	.
K	171.41	179.62	190.86	199.21	207.98	209.76	217.30	226.56	240.31	.
M	169.78	173.58	187.85	192.06	197.41	198.68	205.36	213.10	226.17	.
N	170.51	172.22	188.10	189.00	202.01	198.88	204.20	209.50	223.02	.
O	189.84	190.95	206.98	209.26	216.45	216.59	223.50	234.26	255.14	.

España (DA) [3]   Employees - Salariés - Asalariados   E.G./h. - Euro

Total men and women - Total hommes et femmes - Total hombres y mujeres
ISIC 3 - CITI 3 - CIIU 3

	1999	2000	2001	2002	2003	2004	2005	2006	2007	2008
C-Q [1]	9.25	9.47	9.83	10.24	10.70	11.10	11.40	11.89	12.41	13.02
C	11.95	11.97	12.28	12.98	13.50	13.70	14.10	14.63	14.85	15.76
D	9.75	10.04	10.46	10.97	11.50	12.00	12.40	12.90	13.35	14.05
E	15.47	15.98	16.46	17.54	18.60	19.40	20.30	21.26	21.62	22.13
F	7.56	7.90	8.23	8.61	9.05	9.47	9.69	10.14	10.67	11.27
G	7.51	7.95	8.30	8.68	8.91	9.31	9.64	10.01	10.28	10.65
H	6.20	6.43	6.83	7.08	7.21	7.43	7.63	7.98	8.25	8.57
I	10.74	10.87	11.28	11.37	12.00	12.20	12.70	13.01	13.35	14.17
J	17.56	18.53	19.53	19.98	20.80	21.80	22.80	23.50	24.57	25.40
K	8.07	8.48	9.09	9.72	10.20	10.50	10.80	11.44	12.00	12.45
M	.	12.43	12.20	13.11	13.60	14.50	15.40	15.93	16.46	16.88
N	.	11.78	12.16	12.40	13.30	13.90	14.40	15.26	16.50	17.17
O	.	8.78	8.94	9.44	9.91	9.90	10.20	10.57	11.08	11.59

España (DA) [5]   Employees - Salariés - Asalariados   E.G./h. - Euro

Total men and women - Total hommes et femmes - Total hombres y mujeres
ISIC 3 - CITI 3 - CIIU 3

	1999	2000	2001	2002	2003	2004	2005	2006	2007	2008
C-Q [1]	8.10	8.29	8.60	8.96	9.26	9.53	9.85	10.30	10.78	11.33
C	10.74	10.73	11.01	11.63	12.20	12.30	12.40	12.76	12.97	14.00
D	8.45	8.67	9.02	9.47	9.78	10.10	10.50	10.96	11.39	12.01
E	13.38	13.79	14.41	15.12	15.60	16.00	16.80	17.38	17.62	18.29
F	6.82	7.09	7.43	7.80	8.12	8.46	8.68	9.11	9.56	10.04
G	6.67	6.96	7.23	7.53	7.73	7.96	8.22	8.58	8.86	9.22
H	5.60	5.85	6.20	6.51	6.54	6.71	6.93	7.31	7.53	7.79
I	9.24	9.28	9.56	9.71	10.10	10.40	11.00	11.35	11.68	12.27
J	14.18	14.93	15.47	15.73	16.20	16.80	17.40	18.12	18.68	19.54
K	7.17	7.62	8.13	8.68	9.08	9.18	9.48	10.01	10.58	11.06
M	.	11.13	11.02	11.77	12.20	12.90	13.80	14.20	14.88	15.20
N	.	10.56	11.03	11.18	11.90	12.40	12.80	13.59	14.53	15.16
O	.	7.81	7.97	8.39	8.73	8.77	8.93	9.29	9.81	10.31

Estonia (DA)   Employees - Salariés - Asalariados   E.G./m. - Kroon

Total men and women - Total hommes et femmes - Total hombres y mujeres
ISIC 3 - CITI 3 - CIIU 3

	1999	2000	2001	2002	2003	2004	2005	2006	2007	2008
Total	4 440	4 907	5 510	6 144	6 723	7 287	8 073	9 407	11 336	12 912
A-B	2 888	3 301	3 868	4 382	4 631	5 293	6 133	.	.	.
C-Q	4 518	4 973	5 574	6 226	6 802	7 365	.	.	.	.
A	2 823	3 283	3 863	4 361	4 639	5 340	6 214	.	.	.
01	.	.	.	3 896	4 242	4 799	5 626	6 808	8 609	9 938
02	.	.	.	5 219	5 912	7 267	8 365	9 105	11 014	13 678
B	3 496	3 552	3 936	4 701	4 493	4 430	4 575	7 107	9 212	10 419
C	5 152	5 869	6 843	7 458	8 149	8 687	8 734	10 070	12 920	14 988
D	4 117	4 772	5 149	5 665	6 177	6 696	7 526	8 844	10 651	11 935
E	5 705	5 916	6 727	7 321	8 000	8 482	9 630	10 385	12 560	15 044
F	3 877	4 379	5 232	5 891	6 684	7 468	8 480	10 075	13 020	14 029
G	4 302	4 706	5 359	5 885	6 737	6 915	7 401	9 111	10 961	12 314
H	2 336	3 054	3 771	3 551	4 180	4 535	5 421	6 148	7 146	8 226
I	5 534	6 027	6 468	7 074	7 362	8 048	8 859	10 126	12 545	13 696
J	9 786	10 889	12 249	13 258	14 556	14 998	16 384	16 915	21 205	23 899
K	5 014	4 980	6 299	8 122	8 090	9 332	9 724	11 433	12 248	13 965
L	5 715	6 287	6 958	7 844	8 524	9 224	10 101	11 482	14 301	16 600
M	3 964	4 187	4 770	5 366	5 873	6 475	7 219	7 949	9 393	11 319
N	4 154	4 387	4 768	4 983	5 729	6 524	7 900	9 026	11 051	13 258
O	3 840	4 189	4 696	5 044	5 463	6 244	6 970	7 862	9 556	11 035

Explanatory notes: see p. 877.   Notes explicatives: voir p. 879.   Notas explicativas: véase p. 882.

[1] Excl. young people aged less than 18 years and trainees. [2] Private sector. [3] Incl. overtime payments and irregular gratuities. [4] Excl. categories L, P and Q; before 2000, excl. categories L-Q. [5] Excl. irregular gratuities.

[1] Non compris les jeunes gens âgés de moins de 18 ans et les apprentis. [2] Secteur privé. [3] Y compris la rémunération des heures supplémentaires et les gratifications versées irrégulièrement. [4] Non compris les catégories L, P et Q; avant 2000: non compris les catégories L-Q. [5] Non compris les gratifications versées irrégulièrement.

[1] Excl. los jovenenes de menos de 18 años y los aprendices. [2] Sector privado. [3] Incl. los pagos por horas extraordinarias y las gratificaciones pagadas irregularmente. [4] Excl. las categorías L, P y Q; antes de 2000: excl. las categorías L-Q. [5] Excl. las gratificaciones pagadas irregularmente.

WAGES   SALAIRES   SALARIOS   5A

By economic activity   Par activité économique   Por actividad económica

	1999	2000	2001	2002	2003	2004	2005	2006	2007	2008

Finland (CA)   Wage earners - Ouvriers - Obreros   E.G./h. - Euro

Total men and women - Total hommes et femmes - Total hombres y mujeres
ISIC 3 - CITI 3 - CIIU 3

	1999	2000	2001	2002	2003	2004	2005	2006	2007	2008
A[1]	44.22	44.30		8.03[2]	8.27	8.64	9.10	9.78	9.92	10.20	10.49

Men - Hommes - Hombres
ISIC 3 - CITI 3 - CIIU 3

	1999	2000	2001	2002	2003	2004	2005	2006	2007	2008
A[1]	45.53	45.31		8.24[2]	8.30	8.69	9.26	10.03	10.21	10.47	10.80

Women - Femmes - Mujeres
ISIC 3 - CITI 3 - CIIU 3

	1999	2000	2001	2002	2003	2004	2005	2006	2007	2008
A[1]	40.59	41.86		7.55[2]	8.23	8.57	8.78	9.29	9.48	9.82	10.17

Finland (DA) [3][4]   Wage earners - Ouvriers - Obreros   E.G./h. - Euro

Total men and women - Total hommes et femmes - Total hombres y mujeres
ISIC 3 - CITI 3 - CIIU 3

	1999	2000	2001	2002	2003	2004	2005	2006	2007	2008
C-Q	.	.	.	.	.	.	13.36	13.78	14.12	.
C	14.48	15.34	15.25	15.42	16.85[5]	17.52		14.64[6]	14.65	15.46	
D	.	.	.	.	.	.	13.85	14.53	15.14	.
E	.	.	.	.	.	.	14.93	15.37	15.82	.
F	11.22	11.88	12.29	12.64	13.00[5]	13.34		14.05[6]	14.39	14.85	
G	.	.	.	.	.	.	12.56	12.82	13.42	.
H	.	.	.	.	.	.	11.76	11.28	10.95	.
I	.	.	.	.	.	.	12.18	12.41	12.89	.
J	.	.	.	.	.	.	12.75	11.57	11.65	.
K	.	.	.	.	.	.	11.09	11.66	10.66	.
L	.	.	.	.	.	.	11.22	11.63	11.68	.
M	.	.	.	.	.	.	18.70	20.63	24.05	.
N	.	.	.	.	.	.	15.37	9.29	8.39	.
O	.	.	.	.	.	.	11.63	11.76	12.38	.

Men - Hommes - Hombres
ISIC 3 - CITI 3 - CIIU 3

	1999	2000	2001	2002	2003	2004	2005	2006	2007	2008
C-Q	.	.	.	.	.	.	13.95	14.41	14.79	.
C	.	.	.	.	.	.	14.76	14.77	15.51	.
D	.	.	.	.	.	.	14.40	15.10	15.69	.
E	.	.	.	.	.	.	15.08	15.52	15.99	.
F	11.28	11.95	12.36	12.71	13.07[5]	13.42		14.17[6]	14.55	14.98	
G	.	.	.	.	.	.	13.02	13.35	13.95	.
H	.	.	.	.	.	.	12.10	13.94	11.39	.
I	.	.	.	.	.	.	12.51	12.70	13.14	.
J	.	.	.	.	.	.	12.13	10.75	11.68	.
K	.	.	.	.	.	.	12.70	13.32	11.97	.
L	.	.	.	.	.	.	11.09	11.52	12.02	.
M	.	.	.	.	.	.	16.89	17.28	22.81	.
N	.	.	.	.	.	.	11.83	8.90	8.31	.
O	.	.	.	.	.	.	12.15	12.25	12.97	.

Women - Femmes - Mujeres
ISIC 3 - CITI 3 - CIIU 3

	1999	2000	2001	2002	2003	2004	2005	2006	2007	2008
C-Q	.	.	.	.	.	.	11.53	11.71	11.86	.
C	.	.	.	.	.	.	11.43	11.54	13.19	.
D	.	.	.	.	.	.	12.17	12.59	13.13	.
E	.	.	.	.	.	.	11.91	12.31	11.99	.
F	8.56	8.96	9.35	9.68	9.86[5]	10.23		10.99[6]	10.88	11.87	
G	.	.	.	.	.	.	10.47	10.58	11.00	.
H	.	.	.	.	.	.	11.37	10.02	10.74	.
I	.	.	.	.	.	.	10.90	11.20	11.86	.
J	.	.	.	.	.	.	13.03	12.27	11.63	.
K	.	.	.	.	.	.	9.90	10.30	9.68	.
L	.	.	.	.	.	.	11.64	12.07	11.00	.
M	.	.	.	.	.	.	20.95	23.43	24.83	.
N	.	.	.	.	.	.	19.02	9.86	8.49	.
O	.	.	.	.	.	.	11.09	11.22	11.67	.

Explanatory notes: see p. 877.

[1] Agriculture and hunting not fully covered. [2] Prior to 2001: FIM; 1 Euro = 5.94573 FIM. [3] Private sector. [4] Fourth quarter of each year. [5] From 2003: excl. seasonal and end-of-year bonuses. [6] Prior to 2005: data collected from organised employers only; data are not comparable.

Notes explicatives: voir p. 879.

[1] L'agriculture et la chasse ne sont pas complètement couvertes. [2] Avant 2001: FIM; 1 Euro = 5,94573 FIM. [3] Secteur privé. [4] Quatrième trimestre de chaque année. [5] A partir de 2003: non compris les primes saisonnières et de fin d'année. [6] Avant 2005: données collectées auprès des employeurs organisés seulement; les données ne sont pas comparables.

Notas explicativas: véase p. 882.

[1] Agricultura y casa no están completamente cubiertas. [2] Antes de 2001: FIM; 1 Euro = 5,94573 FIM. [3] Sector privado. [4] Cuarto trimestre de cada año. [5] A partir de 2003: excl. las primas temporales y de fin de año. [6] Antes de 2005: datos recopilados de empleadores organizados sólo. datos no son comparables.

WAGES — SALAIRES — SALARIOS

By economic activity — Par activité économique — Por actividad económica

	1999	2000	2001	2002	2003	2004	2005	2006	2007	2008

Finland (DA) [1][2] — Employees - Salariés - Asalariados — E.G./m. - Euro

Total men and women - Total hommes et femmes - Total hombres y mujeres
ISIC 3 - CITI 3 - CIIU 3

	1999	2000	2001[3]	2002	2003	2004[4]	2005	2006	2007	2008
C-Q	12 044	12 658	2 209	2 290	2 372	2 459	2 555	2 636	2 735	.
C	11 615	12 875	2 312	2 318	2 459	2 504	2 736	2 707	2 897	.
D	12 510	13 124	2 275	2 357	2 463	2 564	2 641	2 788	2 915	.
E	13 071	13 655	2 414	2 539	2 638	2 716	2 892	2 953	3 137	.
F	11 670	12 305	2 140	2 196	2 299	2 368	2 492	2 578	2 663	.
G	11 649	12 088	2 196	2 223	2 357	2 435	2 543	2 582	2 639	.
H	9 344	9 627	1 721	1 806	1 865	1 914	1 963	1 992	2 060	.
I	12 141	12 454	2 151	2 275	2 385	2 429	2 510	2 553	2 697	.
J	14 016	16 210	2 740	2 871	2 799	2 930	3 062	3 176	3 301	.
K	13 000	13 773	2 395	2 466	2 536	2 624	2 718	2 826	2 959	.
L	11 961	12 436	2 222	2 310	2 392	2 508	2 589	2 707	2 814	.
M	12 779	13 355	2 366	2 452	2 530	2 621	2 746	2 783	2 934	.
N	10 640	11 137	1 924	2 032	2 078	2 157	2 254	2 321	2 387	.
O	11 008	11 607	2 040	2 137	2 176	2 262	2 314	2 364	2 372	.

Men - Hommes - Hombres
ISIC 3 - CITI 3 - CIIU 3

	1999	2000	2001[3]	2002	2003	2004[4]	2005	2006	2007	2008
C-Q	13 363	14 110	2 441	2 519	2 621	2 708	2 813	2 924	3 037	.
C	11 709	13 268	2 379	2 372	2 523	2 556	2 805	2 744	2 960	.
D	13 305	13 939	2 402	2 475	2 581	2 685	2 772	2 921	3 048	.
E	13 698	14 283	2 550	2 676	2 782	2 865	3 030	3 098	3 297	.
F	11 790	12 457	2 165	2 225	2 327	2 393	2 522	2 605	2 686	.
G	13 320	13 969	2 474	2 467	2 634	2 710	2 844	2 886	2 945	.
H	10 250	10 418	1 893	2 014	2 084	2 133	2 167	2 191	2 280	.
I	12 688	13 047	2 243	2 346	2 497	2 541	2 628	2 661	2 808	.
J	19 921	23 292	3 815	4 008	3 865	4 035	4 244	4 368	4 505	.
K	14 698	15 636	2 703	2 784	2 817	2 908	3 009	3 132	3 287	.
L	13 565	14 127	2 503	2 617	2 713	2 830	2 914	3 074	3 185	.
M	14 238	14 500	2 627	2 711	2 797	2 877	3 002	3 066	3 206	.
N	14 406	14 377	2 636	2 859	2 867	2 929	3 056	3 251	3 299	.
O	12 540	13 260	2 297	2 382	2 447	2 527	2 609	2 657	2 657	.

Women - Femmes - Mujeres
ISIC 3 - CITI 3 - CIIU 3

	1999	2000	2001[3]	2002	2003	2004[4]	2005	2006	2007	2008
C-Q	10 612	11 116	1 957	2 041	2 107	2 190	2 275	2 344	2 434	.
C	10 270	10 313	1 933	2 029	2 112	2 182	2 225	2 461	2 537	.
D	10 683	11 239	1 969	2 063	2 160	2 252	2 315	2 447	2 568	.
E	10 521	11 062	1 931	2 065	2 157	2 213	2 436	2 497	2 667	.
F	9 969	10 357	1 803	1 826	1 940	2 036	2 141	2 273	2 403	.
G	9 783	10 114	1 879	1 939	2 007	2 091	2 171	2 225	2 284	.
H	9 044	9 361	1 661	1 738	1 779	1 836	1 892	1 930	1 988	.
I	10 917	11 198	1 950	2 106	2 141	2 201	2 275	2 319	2 449	.
J	12 256	13 291	2 338	2 408	2 423	2 524	2 623	2 711	2 835	.
K	10 922	11 530	2 023	2 096	2 182	2 241	2 333	2 422	2 526	.
L	10 544	11 003	1 974	2 052	2 126	2 231	2 312	2 408	2 522	.
M	11 978	12 508	2 221	2 306	2 381	2 476	2 603	2 635	2 788	.
N	10 211	10 691	1 845	1 937	1 988	2 067	2 162	2 216	2 286	.
O	9 880	10 527	1 856	1 953	1 981	2 066	2 110	2 160	2 175	.

France (F) [5] — Employees - Salariés - Asalariados — E.G./h. - Euro

Total men and women - Total hommes et femmes - Total hombres y mujeres
ISIC 3 - CITI 3 - CIIU 3

	1999	2000	2001	2002	2003	2004	2005	2006	2007	2008
C	15.70	16.60	16.40	17.00	18.20	16.30	16.74	17.40	17.70	.
C-K	13.00	13.60	14.30	14.90	15.30	15.80	16.15	16.70	17.20	.
D	13.40	14.10	14.70	15.30	15.90	16.40	16.77	17.30	17.90	.
E	16.20	16.80	18.70	19.00	19.30	19.90	21.19	22.70	23.70	.
F	11.60	12.00	12.70	13.50	13.90	14.30	14.62	15.10	15.50	.
G	11.70	12.30	12.70	13.20	13.70	14.00	14.39	14.70	15.20	.
H	9.00	9.40	9.70	10.20	10.60	10.90	11.32	11.70	12.10	.
I	12.40	12.80	13.40	13.80	14.30	14.60	14.95	15.60	16.10	.
J	19.10	20.10	21.70	21.90	22.20	23.10	23.55	24.40	26.00	.
K	14.00	14.70	15.50	16.40	16.80	17.10	17.54	18.00	18.50	.

Men - Hommes - Hombres
ISIC 3 - CITI 3 - CIIU 3

	1999	2000	2001	2002	2003	2004	2005	2006	2007	2008
C	15.90	16.80	16.50	17.00	18.20	16.40	16.83	17.40	17.70	.
C-K	13.90	14.60	15.30	16.00	16.40	16.90	17.23	17.80	18.30	.
D	14.30	15.00	15.60	16.20	16.80	17.30	17.65	18.20	18.80	.
E	16.90	17.50	19.30	19.60	19.90	20.60	21.78	23.30	24.40	.
F	11.60	12.00	12.70	13.60	13.90	14.30	14.61	15.10	15.50	.
G	13.10	13.80	14.30	14.90	15.40	15.70	16.09	16.40	16.90	.
H	9.70	10.00	10.40	11.00	11.30	11.60	12.03	12.40	12.80	.
I	12.60	13.20	13.70	14.10	14.60	14.90	15.20	15.90	16.30	.
J	23.60	24.80	27.20	27.50	27.90	29.20	29.67	31.00	33.60	.
K	15.60	16.40	17.30	18.30	18.60	19.00	19.38	19.80	20.40	.

Explanatory notes: see p. 877.

[1] Full-time employees. [2] Fourth quarter of each year. [3] Prior to 2001: FIM; 1 Euro = 5.94573 FIM. [4] From 2003: excl. seasonal and end-of-year bonuses. [5] Incl. managerial staff and intermediary occupations.

Notes explicatives: voir p. 879.

[1] Salariés à plein temps. [2] Quatrième trimestre de chaque année. [3] Avant 2001: FIM; 1 Euro = 5,94573 FIM. [4] A partir de 2003: non compris les primes saisonnières et de fin d'année. [5] Y compris les cadres et les professions intermédiaires.

Notas explicativas: véase p. 882.

[1] Asalariados a tiempo completo. [2] Cuarto trimestre de cada año. [3] Antes de 2001: FIM; 1 Euro = 5,94573 FIM. [4] A partir de 2003: excl. las primas temporales y de fin de año. [5] Incl. el personal directivo y las ocupaciones intermediarias.

	1999	2000	2001	2002	2003	2004	2005	2006	2007	2008

France (F) [1]　　　　　Employees - Salariés - Asalariados　　　　　E.G./h. - Euro

Women - Femmes - Mujeres
ISIC 3 - CITI 3 - CIIU 3

	1999	2000	2001	2002	2003	2004	2005	2006	2007	2008
C	14.50	15.00	15.90	17.10	18.30	15.80	16.00	16.90	17.50	.
C-K	11.20	11.70	12.30	12.90	13.30	13.70	14.12	14.60	15.10	.
D	11.20	11.80	12.40	13.00	13.50	14.00	14.48	15.00	15.60	.
E	13.70	14.30	16.50	17.00	17.20	17.60	19.14	20.60	21.40	.
F	11.50	11.80	12.30	13.30	13.70	14.20	14.65	15.10	15.60	.
G	9.90	10.30	10.70	11.20	11.60	11.90	12.27	12.60	13.10	.
H	8.30	8.60	8.90	9.40	9.70	10.00	10.50	10.90	11.20	.
I	11.60	12.00	12.70	13.00	13.60	13.90	14.32	14.90	15.50	.
J	15.20	16.00	17.10	17.40	17.70	18.20	18.72	19.20	20.20	.
K	11.80	12.40	13.00	13.70	14.10	14.50	14.99	15.50	15.90	.

France (F)　　　　　Wage earners - Ouvriers - Obreros　　　　　E.G./h. - Euro

Total men and women - Total hommes et femmes - Total hombres y mujeres
ISIC 3 - CITI 3 - CIIU 3

	1999	2000	2001	2002	2003	2004	2005	2006	2007	2008
C	10.20	10.50	10.20	12.30	12.90	12.40	12.58	13.60	13.40	.
C-K	9.30	9.70	10.10	11.00	11.40	11.70	11.96	12.30	12.60	.
D	9.70	10.20	10.60	11.50	12.00	12.30	12.56	12.90	13.30	.
E	11.70	12.40	13.30	14.00	13.90	16.90	17.70	15.90	16.80	.
F	9.20	9.50	10.00	11.30	11.60	12.00	12.30	12.70	13.00	.
G	8.60	9.00	9.40	10.20	10.60	10.80	11.10	11.40	11.80	.
H	8.20	8.50	8.80	9.30	9.60	10.10	10.48	10.90	11.10	.
I	9.40	9.90	10.30	10.90	11.40	11.50	11.75	12.40	12.60	.
J	10.00	9.90	11.00	12.10	12.70	13.00	13.44	14.20	14.30	.
K	8.50	9.00	9.50	10.10	10.30	10.60	10.91	11.20	11.50	.

Men - Hommes - Hombres
ISIC 3 - CITI 3 - CIIU 3

	1999	2000	2001	2002	2003	2004	2005	2006	2007	2008
C	10.20	10.50	10.20	12.40	12.90	12.40	12.60	13.60	13.40	.
C-K	9.50	9.90	10.40	11.30	11.60	11.90	12.23	12.60	12.90	.
D	10.10	10.60	11.10	12.00	12.40	12.80	13.01	13.40	13.80	.
E	11.80	12.50	13.40	14.20	14.10	17.10	17.88	16.00	17.10	.
F	9.20	9.50	10.00	11.30	11.60	12.00	12.31	12.70	13.00	.
G	8.70	9.10	9.50	10.30	10.70	10.90	11.21	11.50	11.90	.
H	8.40	8.60	8.90	9.40	9.80	10.20	10.62	11.00	11.30	.
I	9.50	9.90	10.30	11.00	11.40	11.50	11.81	12.40	12.70	.
J	11.20	10.90	12.40	13.30	14.00	14.40	14.85	15.80	16.00	.
K	8.90	9.40	9.90	10.50	10.80	11.00	11.38	11.70	12.00	.

Women - Femmes - Mujeres
ISIC 3 - CITI 3 - CIIU 3

	1999	2000	2001	2002	2003	2004	2005	2006	2007	2008
C	8.70	9.00	8.70	10.30	11.10	11.80	11.94	12.40	12.80	.
C-K	8.10	8.50	8.90	9.70	9.90	10.30	10.59	10.80	11.20	.
D	8.30	8.70	9.10	10.00	10.30	10.70	10.99	11.30	11.70	.
E	8.40	9.40	9.40	10.70	10.70	15.40	16.63	13.20	14.10	.
F	7.80	8.20	8.40	9.10	9.60	10.10	11.08	10.80	11.10	.
G	7.80	8.10	8.50	9.20	9.60	9.80	10.22	10.50	10.80	.
H	7.50	7.80	8.00	8.50	8.90	9.30	9.80	10.20	10.40	.
I	8.40	8.80	9.60	10.20	10.50	10.50	10.98	11.60	12.00	.
J	8.40	8.50	8.90	10.60	10.90	11.10	11.51	12.00	12.10	.
K	7.70	8.10	8.50	9.30	9.30	9.50	9.80	10.10	10.40	.

Germany (DA)　　　　　Employees - Salariés - Asalariados　　　　　E.G./h. - Euro

Total men and women - Total hommes et femmes - Total hombres y mujeres
ISIC 3 - CITI 3 - CIIU 3

	1999	2000	2001	2002	2003	2004	2005	2006	2007	2008
C	.	.	.	.	.	.	.	.	18.00	18.72
D	.	.	.	.	.	.	.	.	19.09	19.51
E	.	.	.	.	.	.	.	.	22.99	23.74
F	.	.	.	.	.	.	.	.	15.03	15.49
G	.	.	.	.	.	.	.	.	16.60	16.96
H	.	.	.	.	.	.	.	.	10.95	11.10
I	.	.	.	.	.	.	.	.	15.39	15.73
J	.	.	.	.	.	.	.	.	22.95	23.75
K	.	.	.	.	.	.	.	.	17.80	18.42
L	.	.	.	.	.	.	.	.	.	
M	.	.	.	.	.	.	.	.	18.03	18.57
N	.	.	.	.	.	.	.	.	17.41	17.75
O	.	.	.	.	.	.	.	.	17.13	17.65

Explanatory notes: see p. 877.　　　Notes explicatives: voir p. 879.　　　Notas explicativas: véase p. 882.

[1] Incl. managerial staff and intermediary occupations.　　[1] Y compris les cadres et les professions intermédiaires.　　[1] Incl. el personal directivo y las ocupaciones intermediarias.

5A

WAGES	SALAIRES	SALARIOS
By economic activity	Par activité économique	Por actividad económica

	1999	2000	2001	2002	2003	2004	2005	2006	2007	2008

Germany (DA) — Employees - Salariés - Asalariados — E.G./h. - Euro

Men - Hommes - Hombres
ISIC 3 - CITI 3 - CIIU 3

	1999	2000	2001	2002	2003	2004	2005	2006	2007	2008
C									18.10	18.82
D									20.01	20.46
E									23.72	24.49
F									15.11	15.58
G									17.82	18.17
H									11.98	12.12
I									15.48	15.81
J									25.95	26.86
K									19.08	19.72
L										
M									19.03	19.59
N									21.21	21.60
O									18.90	19.58

Women - Femmes - Mujeres
ISIC 3 - CITI 3 - CIIU 3

	1999	2000	2001	2002	2003	2004	2005	2006	2007	2008
C									16.66	17.42
D									15.27	15.61
E									19.49	20.19
F									13.87	14.26
G									14.01	14.35
H									9.91	10.08
I									15.00	15.36
J									19.00	19.66
K									15.01	15.54
L										
M									17.28	17.82
N									15.41	15.72
O									14.38	14.68

Germany (DA) — Wage earners - Ouvriers - Obreros — E.G./h. - Euro

Total men and women - Total hommes et femmes - Total hombres y mujeres
ISIC 3 - CITI 3 - CIIU 3

	1999	2000	2001	2002	2003	2004	2005	2006	2007	2008
A[1]	14.47	14.63	7.76 [2]	7.68	7.60	7.80	7.83	7.94 [3]		
C	26.04	26.31	13.66 [2]	13.96	14.29	14.60	14.76	14.81 [3]		
D	27.53	27.78	14.42 [2]	14.72	15.09	15.40	15.60	15.74 [3]		
E	30.71	30.83	16.13 [2]	16.50	17.07	17.61	18.16	18.55 [3]		
F	25.22	25.02	13.06 [2]	13.39	13.71	13.87	13.90	13.79 [3]		

Men - Hommes - Hombres
ISIC 3 - CITI 3 - CIIU 3

	1999	2000	2001	2002	2003	2004	2005	2006	2007	2008
A[1]	14.87	14.93	8.00 [2]	7.82	7.71	7.92	7.99	8.10 [3]		
C	26.08	26.35	13.68 [2]	13.99	14.31	14.61	14.78	14.82 [3]		
D	28.79	29.10	15.09 [2]	15.37	15.74	16.04	16.24	16.37 [3]		
E	30.90	31.04	16.22 [2]	16.59	17.17	17.71	18.26	18.65 [3]		
F	25.23	25.03	13.07 [2]	13.40	13.72	13.87	13.90	13.79 [3]		

Women - Femmes - Mujeres
ISIC 3 - CITI 3 - CIIU 3

	1999	2000	2001	2002	2003	2004	2005	2006	2007	2008
A[1]	13.36	13.77	7.11 [2]	7.20	7.21	7.34	7.31	7.42 [3]		
C	22.66	21.81	11.16 [2]	11.36	11.88	12.60	13.26	13.23 [3]		
D	21.44	21.39	11.10 [2]	11.37	11.64	11.89	12.02	12.10 [3]		
E	24.39	24.21	12.69 [2]	13.13	13.57	13.93	14.05	14.34 [3]		
F	19.44	20.39	10.20 [2]	10.74	11.70	11.59	11.85	11.53 [3]		

Germany (FA) — Wage earners - Ouvriers - Obreros — R.T./h. - Euro

Total men and women - Total hommes et femmes - Total hombres y mujeres
ISIC 3 - CITI 3 - CIIU 3

	1999	2000	2001	2002	2003	2004	2005	2006	2007	2008
A									9.13	

Gibraltar (CA) [4][5] — Wage earners - Ouvriers - Obreros — E.G./w.s. - Pound

Total men and women - Total hommes et femmes - Total hombres y mujeres
ISIC 2 - CITI 2 - CIIU 2

	1999	2000	2001	2002	2003	2004	2005	2006	2007	2008
2-9 [6]	246.49	243.91	264.12	263.12	275.80	271.73	290.60			
3	320.01	291.57	299.49	311.25	323.75	400.58	419.09			
4	460.74	419.84	398.20	453.62	609.05	598.23	667.44			
5	266.45	263.75	316.59	308.71	341.39	301.26	335.97			
6	197.90	202.52	201.23	205.07	208.34	211.28	220.95			
7	241.67	251.40	281.87	273.29	302.98	303.75	305.71			
8	235.53		232.14	225.00	213.95	263.33	268.96			
9	262.52	255.93	278.52	265.02	305.56	280.14	253.86			

Explanatory notes: see p. 877.

[1] Permanent workers. [2] Prior to 2001: DEM; 1 Euro = 1.95583 DEM. [3] Series discontinued. [4] Excl. part-time workers and juveniles. [5] Oct. of each year. [6] Excl. mining and quarrying.

Notes explicatives: voir p. 879.

[1] Travailleurs permanents. [2] Avant 2001: DEM; 1 Euro = 1,95583 DEM. [3] Série arrêtée. [4] Non compris les travailleurs à temps partiel et les jeunes. [5] Oct. de chaque année. [6] Non compris les industries extractives.

Notas explicativas: véase p. 882.

[1] Trabajadores permanentes. [2] Antes de: DEM; 1 Euro = 1,95583 DEM. [3] Serie interrumpida. [4] Excl. los trabajadores a tempo parcial y los jóvenes. [5] Oct. de cada año. [6] Excl. las minas y canteras.

Gibraltar (CA) [1][2] — Wage earners - Ouvriers - Obreros — E.G./w.s. - Pound

Men - Hommes - Hombres

ISIC 2 - CITI 2 - CIIU 2   ISIC 3 - CITI 3 - CIIU 3

	1999	2000	2001	2002	2003	2004	2005	2006	2007	2008	
2-9[3]	262.75	258.39	284.98	285.22	300.44	292.56	316.44	347.28	341.47	.	Total
3	332.55	299.82	306.40	339.48	333.23	414.25	433.32	347.28	341.47	.	C-Q
4	460.74	419.84	398.20	453.62	609.05	598.23	667.44	447.42	437.20	.	D
5	268.68	265.46	318.02	310.99	343.64	301.93	337.51	636.04	650.80	.	E
6	207.06	213.35	213.65	221.31	225.33	226.68	238.95	343.52	353.80	.	F
7	247.26	260.70	290.98	280.27	312.32	313.57	341.99	258.91	264.80	.	G
8	270.10	257.31	264.80	225.98	231.06	276.12	279.84	226.00	228.00	.	H
9	284.44	273.90	301.92	293.21	334.74	305.98	329.28	341.45	359.90	.	I
								1 366.10	853.40	.	J
								286.33	352.10	.	K
								447.02	457.30	.	L
								384.33	459.00	.	M
								417.96	461.70	.	N
								554.67	371.80	.	O

Women - Femmes - Mujeres

ISIC 2 - CITI 2 - CIIU 2   ISIC 3 - CITI 3 - CIIU 3

	1999	2000	2001	2002	2003	2004	2005	2006	2007	2008	
2-9[3]	198.40	200.45	199.37	196.95	203.80	210.50	216.39	234.16	230.00	.	Total
3	210.39	213.83	233.90	237.05	235.47	249.73	259.98	234.16	230.00	.	C-Q
5	207.18	208.41	256.04	229.77	254.18	279.19	287.33	253.71	267.90	.	D
6	182.54	186.68	184.12	183.38	184.60	190.62	196.98	.	.	.	E
7	192.48	197.78	210.88	228.03	203.17	232.95	231.11	316.47	280.50	.	F
8	179.04	251.69	174.51	223.75	188.12	238.31	249.74	211.12	222.20	.	G
9	223.71	216.16	230.08	215.66	265.43	239.64	244.22	191.09	184.90	.	H
								219.63	212.40	.	I
								347.80	307.70	.	J
								208.01	212.40	.	K
								307.85	354.30	.	L
								344.32	368.40	.	M
								306.57	318.90	.	N
								341.90	242.40	.	O

Gibraltar (CA) [1][2] — Wage earners - Ouvriers - Obreros — E.G./h. - Pound

Total men and women - Total hommes et femmes - Total hombres y mujeres

ISIC 3 - CITI 3 - CIIU 3

	1999	2000	2001	2002	2003	2004	2005	2006	2007	2008
C-Q[3]	5.69	5.66	6.02	6.06	6.45	6.49	6.49	7.52	7.51	.
D	6.83	6.44	6.56	7.02	7.21	7.96	8.42	8.85	8.76	.
E	6.54	6.76	7.11	7.64	9.59	11.75	13.06	12.16	12.39	.
F	6.26	6.07	7.28	7.18	7.85	7.35	8.04	8.11	8.40	.
G	5.22	5.50	5.37	5.47	5.56	5.76	6.00	6.10	6.42	.
H	4.50	4.48	4.49	4.62	4.74	4.83	5.16	5.35	5.51	.
I	5.30	5.54	5.71	5.91	6.19	6.48	7.04	7.00	7.57	.
J	6.25	10.48	6.05	5.66	5.99	8.61	7.08	26.27	13.95	.
K	5.27	5.32	5.14	5.22	5.31	5.40	5.92	6.39	7.43	.
L	5.81	5.89	6.06	5.80	6.91	7.73	8.01	8.22	9.07	.
M	5.19	5.42	5.89	5.53	7.11	7.25	7.59	7.51	7.95	.
N	5.09	4.74	5.12	5.30	6.28	6.90	7.44	7.36	8.10	.
O	5.61	5.28	5.43	5.64	6.07	6.48	6.81	11.42	7.46	.

Men - Hommes - Hombres

ISIC 3 - CITI 3 - CIIU 3

	1999	2000	2001	2002	2003	2004	2005	2006	2007	2008
C-Q[3]	5.93	5.85	6.33	6.41	6.88	6.84	7.39	8.04	7.92	.
D	7.01	6.56	6.65	7.15	7.22	8.14	8.56	9.05	8.92	.
E	6.54	6.76	7.11	7.64	9.59	11.75	13.06	12.16	12.40	.
F	6.29	6.09	7.29	7.22	7.88	7.35	8.06	8.10	8.40	.
G	5.38	5.54	5.56	5.79	5.98	6.06	6.45	6.51	6.74	.
H	4.69	4.82	4.65	4.87	4.99	5.07	5.37	5.65	5.82	.
I	5.32	5.58	5.75	5.93	6.27	6.52	7.15	7.08	7.69	.
J	5.97	5.17	6.78	5.08	5.20	10.48	.	36.04	21.83	.
K	5.67	5.35	5.39	5.36	5.51	5.59	6.35	6.85	8.09	.
L	5.98	6.06	6.25	5.90	7.14	7.92	8.14	8.43	9.28	.
M	5.29	6.30	5.78	5.40	6.68	7.21	7.55	7.58	8.17	.
N	5.11	5.25	5.69	5.63	6.75	7.22	8.12	7.84	8.35	.
O	5.70	5.35	5.56	5.73	6.30	6.82	7.24	12.22	7.66	.

Women - Femmes - Mujeres

ISIC 3 - CITI 3 - CIIU 3

	1999	2000	2001	2002	2003	2004	2005	2006	2007	2008
C-Q[3]	4.97	5.11	5.03	5.02	5.20	5.47	5.68	6.10	6.18	.
D	5.25	5.26	5.73	5.74	5.92	5.99	6.86	6.91	7.22	.
F	5.39	5.46	6.57	6.09	6.43	7.35	7.64	8.53	8.06	.
G	4.96	5.44	5.10	5.05	4.98	5.34	5.43	5.61	5.97	.
H	4.15	4.02	4.26	4.29	4.38	4.56	4.85	4.98	5.14	.
I	5.00	5.32	5.44	5.79	5.29	6.23	6.13	5.84	6.05	.
J	6.35	14.30	5.31	5.97	6.25	5.50	7.08	9.50	8.69	.
K	4.45	5.28	4.70	4.94	4.98	5.07	5.24	5.64	5.76	.
L	5.15	5.25	5.43	5.24	6.09	7.00	7.11	7.33	7.96	.
M	5.15	5.06	5.92	5.57	7.28	7.26	7.60	7.49	7.87	.
N	5.09	4.59	4.94	5.17	6.11	6.75	7.10	7.05	7.89	.
O	5.43	5.06	5.10	5.38	5.36	5.48	5.58	8.90	6.87	.

Explanatory notes: see p. 877.   Notes explicatives: voir p. 879.   Notas explicativas: véase p. 882.

[1] Excl. part-time workers and juveniles. [2] Oct. of each year. [3] Excl. mining and quarrying.   [1] Non compris les travailleurs à temps partiel et les jeunes. [2] Oct. de chaque année. [3] Non compris les industries extractives.   [1] Excl. los trabajadores a tempo parcial y los jóvenes. [2] Oct. de cada año. [3] Excl. las minas y canteras.

	1999	2000	2001	2002	2003	2004	2005	2006	2007	2008

Greece (DA)   Employees - Salariés - Asalariados   E.G./m. - Euro

Total men and women - Total hommes et femmes - Total hombres y mujeres
ISIC 3 - CITI 3 - CIIU 3

	1999	2000	2001	2002	2003	2004	2005	2006	2007	2008
C-Q								1 930		
C								1 606		
D								1 801		
E								3 346		
F								1 465		
G								1 490		
H								2 271		
I								2 321		
J								2 524		
K								1 685		
M								2 082		
N								2 007		
O								1 953		

Hungary (DA) [1] [2]   Employees - Salariés - Asalariados   E.G./m. - Forint

Total men and women - Total hommes et femmes - Total hombres y mujeres
ISIC 3 - CITI 3 - CIIU 3

	1999	2000	2001	2002	2003	2004	2005	2006	2007	2008
Total	76 973	87 566	103 280	122 266	138 003	145 187	159 461	168 002	180 568	198 942
A-B	52 664	59 538	72 128	83 649	89 215	96 905	102 392	110 117	121 527	133 628
C-Q	78 367	89 014	104 727	123 939	139 969	147 010	161 560	169 947	182 474	201 056
A	52 696	59 587	72 234	83 754	89 339	97 008	102 457	110 288	121 700	133 948
B	49 764	55 229	63 269	74 745	78 998	88 628	96 715	97 245	108 445	111 460
C	96 372	114 479	127 641	135 808	149 869	159 715	174 625	191 954	200 547	229 675
D	76 099	88 551	101 700	114 297	124 770	136 992	147 234	156 813	171 564	184 185
E	104 164	119 557	136 325	156 028	173 209	192 754	208 922	227 132	245 284	265 713
F	57 762	65 164	77 303	87 633	94 674	99 970	108 143	114 734	127 202	145 474
G	68 299	76 122	89 958	103 094	116 239	122 459	132 091	140 311	153 863	171 692
H	49 856	54 807	67 952	79 750	87 962	90 081	96 862	96 027	107 818	122 322
I	88 294	98 806	114 539	129 735	142 700	157 648	171 602	180 651	192 717	207 990
J	167 311	190 346	216 859	241 431	276 283	325 464	347 692	408 706	412 281	433 259
K	85 068	98 737	117 790	133 697	145 315	155 325	162 408	164 025	175 350	216 484
L	92 149	103 460	130 747	168 260	184 799	181 250	207 824	225 053	252 862	267 323
M	72 710	81 485	97 428	128 934	162 349	158 330	181 695	190 845	192 289	203 485
N	58 874	68 065	78 762	103 249	130 304	129 417	144 234	151 870	158 932	169 856
O	70 211	79 860	92 471	111 432	128 851	137 261	149 532	157 620	173 119	187 372

Men - Hommes - Hombres
ISIC 3 - CITI 3 - CIIU 3

	1999	2000	2001	2002	2003	2004	2005	2006	2007	2008
Total	84 649	96 563	113 311	131 413	146 496	155 183	168 327	176 359	191 767	.
A-B	54 703	61 878	75 092	86 171	91 838	99 928	105 176	112 841	124 812	.
C-Q	87 200	99 230	115 925	134 255	149 733	158 239	171 719	179 427	194 896	.
A	54 764	61 950	75 244	86 301	92 026	100 086	105 283	113 050	125 052	.
B	49 764	56 147	63 648	75 907	77 996	88 444	96 644	98 256	108 277	.
C	98 638	117 556	131 514	136 961	153 690	163 072	180 063	194 867	203 912	.
D	86 866	100 351	115 830	127 916	140 244	153 396	164 230	175 199	191 595	.
E	110 074	125 952	143 449	163 369	181 730	200 788	217 315	237 123	255 573	.
F	57 055	64 694	76 272	85 530	93 042	98 000	105 980	110 720	125 253	.
G	74 601	84 370	98 281	112 090	127 473	136 103	146 203	151 576	170 011	.
H	58 143	63 674	76 625	86 729	95 052	97 057	102 208	95 969	115 513	.
I	88 418	99 401	114 889	129 398	141 665	156 250	170 569	179 375	193 016	.
J	249 185	280 017	332 222	364 091	428 362	489 181	508 188	603 052	579 790	.
K	89 465	106 044	123 924	139 860	155 096	168 084	172 241	172 911	187 356	.
L	101 487	114 500	142 739	186 255	206 487	198 665	225 426	247 262	270 365	.
M	90 122	101 605	121 677	154 542	194 099	187 086	212 602	222 187	227 003	.
N	70 374	80 053	92 902	120 000	150 159	148 350	163 945	173 298	183 600	.
O	74 296	85 420	97 227	114 806	131 567	141 050	153 395	163 587	180 413	.

Women - Femmes - Mujeres
ISIC 3 - CITI 3 - CIIU 3

	1999	2000	2001	2002	2003	2004	2005	2006	2007	2008
Total	68 431	77 761	92 217	111 725	128 488	133 846	149 208	157 923	167 293	.
A-B	46 127	52 214	62 923	75 435	80 787	87 012	93 041	100 750	110 257	.
C-Q	69 056	78 412	92 898	112 499	129 437	134 713	150 211	158 862	168 186	.
A	46 100	52 223	62 936	75 489	80 757	87 012	93 010	100 833	110 265	.
B	49 764	51 079	61 209	69 076	84 851	89 631	97 111	91 989	109 361	.
C	80 122	94 792	103 885	127 755	124 225	136 021	145 206	174 804	178 667	.
D	61 898	72 962	82 761	94 882	102 585	112 946	121 082	128 302	139 856	.
E	86 744	100 543	114 812	133 833	147 614	169 116	183 831	197 423	212 361	.
F	63 333	68 739	85 663	106 875	108 109	116 601	126 974	157 231	142 959	.
G	62 127	68 293	81 448	93 144	104 172	107 775	116 372	127 040	136 030	.
H	45 334	49 897	62 845	75 391	83 595	85 653	93 202	96 075	102 536	.
I	88 003	97 457	113 733	130 530	145 301	161 171	174 264	184 082	191 924	.
J	137 119	156 052	173 436	195 889	218 893	259 221	281 277	326 840	342 784	.
K	78 864	89 625	109 708	125 141	132 414	137 351	148 268	150 607	158 409	.
L	82 146	92 201	118 702	147 468	163 414	164 102	190 699	203 839	235 241	.
M	67 664	75 598	90 500	121 293	153 365	150 025	172 386	181 555	181 912	.
N	55 474	64 569	74 636	98 427	124 598	124 020	138 665	145 650	151 620	.
O	65 333	73 245	86 671	107 386	125 506	132 612	144 727	150 182	163 800	.

Explanatory notes: see p. 877.   Notes explicatives: voir p. 879.   Notas explicativas: véase p. 882.

[1] Full-time employees. [2] Enterprises with 5 or more employees.   [1] Salariés à plein temps. [2] Entreprises occupant 5 salariés et plus.   [1] Asalariados a tiempo completo. [2] Empresas con 5 y más asalariados.

	1999	2000	2001	2002	2003	2004	2005	2006	2007	2008

Iceland (DA) [1]   Employees - Salariés - Asalariados   E.G./h. - Krona

Total men and women - Total hommes et femmes - Total hombres y mujeres
ISIC 3 - CITI 3 - CIIU 3

C-Q [2]	1 056	1 184	1 289	1 392	1 468	1 549	1 796	1 989	2 261	2 334
D	986	1 083	1 219	1 336	1 404	1 494	1 622	1 762	1 946	2 033
F	1 590	1 996	1 819	1 894	1 834	1 779	1 928	2 055	2 214	2 333
G	1 009	1 154	1 256	1 310	1 395	1 472	1 670	1 755	1 899	1 910
I	1 092	1 209	1 356	1 447	1 554	1 711	1 797	1 937	2 129	2 276
J	.	.	.	.	.	.	2 698	3 145	3 857	3 743

Men - Hommes - Hombres
ISIC 3 - CITI 3 - CIIU 3

C-Q [2]	1 231	1 389	1 495	1 593	1 656	1 737	2 021	2 225	2 531	2 568
D	1 132	1 242	1 383	1 496	1 568	1 670	1 812	1 961	2 131	2 216
F	1 629	2 048	1 859	1 920	1 840	1 776	1 929	2 057	2 218	2 335
G	1 172	1 343	1 456	1 505	1 589	1 675	1 906	1 975	2 120	2 104
I	1 347	1 509	1 722	1 791	1 897	2 104	2 103	2 250	2 480	2 637
J	.	.	.	.	.	.	4 665	5 170	6 594	5 957

Women - Femmes - Mujeres
ISIC 3 - CITI 3 - CIIU 3

C-Q [2]	818	901	997	1 083	1 150	1 231	1 448	1 614	1 816	1 938
D	760	833	941	1 074	1 122	1 200	1 312	1 425	1 597	1 675
F	-	-	-	-	-	-	-	-	-	-
G	826	920	1 011	1 065	1 137	1 210	1 323	1 428	1 542	1 646
I	888	967	1 048	1 121	1 202	1 302	1 470	1 588	1 751	1 864
J	.	.	.	.	.	.	1 880	2 150	2 410	2 557

Iceland (DA) [3]   Employees - Salariés - Asalariados   E.G./m. - Krona

Total men and women - Total hommes et femmes - Total hombres y mujeres
ISIC 3 - CITI 3 - CIIU 3

C-Q [2]	211 000	231 000	253 800	267 000	286 000	306 000	356 000	396 000	447 000	463 000
D	210 000	228 000	253 000	269 000	283 000	304 000	331 000	361 000	390 000	407 000
F	247 000	283 000	302 000	315 000	335 000	354 000	393 000	430 000	457 000	492 000
G	198 000	221 000	239 000	249 000	267 000	283 000	325 000	346 000	377 000	379 000
I	221 000	239 000	262 000	274 000	295 000	321 000	343 000	367 000	402 000	429 000
J	.	.	.	.	.	.	492 000	568 000	704 000	672 000

Men - Hommes - Hombres
ISIC 3 - CITI 3 - CIIU 3

C-Q [2]	239 000	260 000	284 000	296 000	314 000	337 000	396 000	440 000	496 000	509 000
D	238 000	256 000	282 000	297 000	312 000	335 000	365 000	398 000	426 000	443 000
F	248 000	285 000	305 000	318 000	336 000	355 000	396 000	433 000	461 000	495 000
G	225 000	247 000	264 000	273 000	291 000	311 000	356 000	380 000	411 000	412 000
I	267 000	291 000	320 000	329 000	352 000	386 000	399 000	421 000	465 000	489 000
J	.	.	.	.	.	.	812 000	893 000	1 145 000	1 023 000

Women - Femmes - Mujeres
ISIC 3 - CITI 3 - CIIU 3

C-Q [2]	153 000	168 000	187 000	200 000	214 000	231 000	275 000	305 000	343 000	366 000
D	145 000	160 000	180 000	200 000	212 000	231 000	254 000	272 000	303 000	318 000
F	-	-	-	-	-	-	-	-	-	-
G	148 000	167 000	188 000	196 000	210 000	222 000	249 000	263 000	285 000	305 000
I	168 000	180 000	193 000	202 000	216 000	232 000	262 000	282 000	305 000	324 000
J	.	.	.	.	.	.	339 000	384 000	435 000	455 000

Ireland (DA) [4][5]   Wage earners - Ouvriers - Obreros   E.G./h. - Euro

Total men and women - Total hommes et femmes - Total hombres y mujeres
ISIC 3 - CITI 3 - CIIU 3

C	11.36	12.05	14.97	15.60	17.11	17.04	16.43	15.91	.	.
D	9.80	10.50	11.61	12.50	12.85	13.56	13.95	14.45	.	.
E	13.48	14.46	17.69	19.52	21.35	22.98	23.47	26.03	.	.

Ireland (DA) [6][7]   Employees - Salariés - Asalariados   E.G./w.s. - Euro

Total men and women - Total hommes et femmes - Total hombres y mujeres
ISIC 3 - CITI 3 - CIIU 3

C	555.39	584.19	653.43	705.88	743.17	789.34	780.71	781.53	.	.
D	462.26	498.19	543.91	569.77	603.54	632.82	659.38	678.26	.	.
E	665.23	726.08	796.88	905.03	982.91	1 048.82	1 084.50	1 179.31	.	.

Explanatory notes: see p. 877.

[1] Adults. [2] Manufacturing, construction, trade and transport. [3] Full-time adult employees. [4] Incl. juveniles. [5] Sep. of each year. [6] Adult and non-adult rates of pay. [7] Establishments with 10 or more persons employed.

Notes explicatives: voir p. 879.

[1] Adultes. [2] Industries manufacturières, construction, commerce et transport. [3] Salariés adultes à plein temps. [4] Y compris les jeunes gens. [5] Sept. de chaque année. [6] Salariés rémunérés sur la base de taux de salaires pour adultes et non-adultes. [7] Etablissements occupant 10 personnes et plus.

Notas explicativas: véase p. 882.

[1] Adultos. [2] Industrías manufactureras, construcción, comercio y transporte. [3] Asalariados adultos a tiempo completo. [4] Incl. los jóvenes. [5] Sept. de cada año. [6] Asalariados pagados sobre la base de tasas de salarios para adultos y no adultos. [7] Establecimientos con 10 y más trabajadores.

WAGES	SALAIRES	SALARIOS
By economic activity	Par activité économique	Por actividad económica

	1999	2000	2001	2002	2003	2004	2005	2006	2007	2008

Ireland (DA) [1]   Wage earners - Ouvriers - Obreros   E.G./h. - Euro

Total men and women - Total hommes et femmes - Total hombres y mujeres
ISIC 3 - CITI 3 - CIIU 3

	1999	2000	2001	2002	2003	2004	2005	2006	2007	2008
C	11.68	12.11	14.08	15.44	16.51	17.33	16.42			
C-E	10.05	10.66	11.76	12.69	13.37	14.02	14.43			
D	9.79	10.40	11.47	12.29	12.87	13.45	13.94			
E	14.10	15.11	16.88	19.68	20.94	22.91	23.40			

Men - Hommes - Hombres
ISIC 3 - CITI 3 - CIIU 3

C	11.83	12.29	14.29	15.76	16.72	17.48	16.55	16.38		
D	10.74	11.35	12.41	13.26	13.76	14.36	14.81	15.26		
E	14.45	15.53	17.48	20.32	21.51	23.58	24.41	27.17		

Women - Femmes - Mujeres
ISIC 3 - CITI 3 - CIIU 3

C	6.97	7.73	10.29	8.80	10.08	11.42	11.92	11.81		
D	8.00	8.55	9.43	10.06	10.74	11.13	11.63	12.28		
E	9.26	11.04	11.13	12.43	13.18	15.91	17.71	21.74		

Ireland (DA) [1] [2]   Wage earners - Ouvriers - Obreros   E.G./w.s. - Euro

Total men and women - Total hommes et femmes - Total hombres y mujeres
ISIC 3 - CITI 3 - CIIU 3

	1999	2000	2001	2002	2003	2004	2005	2006	2007	2008
C	524.20	549.32	631.67	700.40	715.68	746.60	741.78	730.49		
C-E	409.28	436.20	470.96	501.51	535.74	560.77	580.88	601.21		
D	396.55	423.24	456.97	483.02	511.78	534.24	557.57	575.21		
E	616.61	650.24	716.61	838.45	924.47	1 007.52	1 005.58	1 134.88		

Men - Hommes - Hombres
ISIC 3 - CITI 3 - CIIU 3

C	533.68	561.61	645.93	721.15	727.57	755.26	750.26	744.70		
C-E	467.29	492.48	529.03	561.06	593.81	620.48	637.59			
D	452.97	477.73	512.38	538.38	564.90	588.91	609.91	624.45		
E	637.60	673.95	749.94	874.49	959.62	1 049.02	1 057.60	1 182.02		

Women - Femmes - Mujeres
ISIC 3 - CITI 3 - CIIU 3

C	267.91	289.31	399.45	314.38	365.24	405.30	452.61	421.99		
C-E	298.17	324.86	347.39	365.24	393.87	407.16	430.75			
D	298.17	324.72	347.32	365.19	393.78	406.83	430.23	451.13		
E	309.80	375.07	351.58	390.11	428.04	503.76	610.18	722.42		

Isle of Man (DA) [3]   Employees - Salariés - Asalariados   E.G./h. - Pound

Total men and women - Total hommes et femmes - Total hombres y mujeres
ISIC 3 - CITI 3 - CIIU 3

	1999	2000	2001	2002	2003	2004	2005	2006	2007	2008
Total	9.76	9.51	9.97	10.80	11.25	11.84		13.20	13.50	14.07
C-Q	9.78	9.53	10.02	10.83	11.24	11.86	11.72	13.20	13.70	14.09
A	7.33	6.88	7.10	7.58						
C	6.64									
D	9.08	8.53	9.02	10.26	9.65	10.35	10.56	11.00	12.00	12.88
E	10.58	9.08	10.73	18.25	11.33	10.13	12.67	14.80	17.10	19.03
F	7.30	7.61	9.12	9.57	10.31	10.33	11.39	11.80	10.00	10.89
G	6.90	6.27	6.47	7.20	6.96	8.59	8.09	8.80	8.60	9.73
H	5.93	5.96	5.05	6.57	6.31	6.59	7.40	10.50	8.50	8.11
I	8.93	9.72	8.45	10.03	11.47	10.43	11.46	12.50	12.40	14.09
J	11.53	12.52	12.77	13.05	14.01	14.78	13.73	14.80	17.40	16.69
K	10.02	9.86	10.65	10.86	13.20	12.83	12.43	15.70	14.00	16.42
L	10.07	10.29	11.29	11.55	12.26	13.83	13.29	15.30	15.70	15.67
M	15.90	11.15	9.69	13.45	14.36	13.60	13.59	15.40	17.40	15.88
N	8.82	8.94	10.64	10.43	10.79	11.47	11.49	14.40	12.90	14.15
O	6.19	6.48	7.81	7.17	8.02	8.06	9.16	10.00	8.60	8.54
P	4.14							11.00		

Explanatory notes: see p. 877.	Notes explicatives: voir p. 879.	Notas explicativas: véase p. 882.
[1] Establishments with 10 or more persons employed. [2] Wage-earners on adult rates of pay. [3] June of each year.	[1] Etablissements occupant 10 personnes et plus. [2] Ouvriers rémunérés sur la base de taux de salaire pour adultes. [3] Juin de chaque année.	[1] Establecimientos con 10 y más trabajadores. [2] Obreros remunerados sobre la base de tasas de salarios para adultos. [3] Junio de cada año.

	1999	2000	2001	2002	2003	2004	2005	2006	2007	2008

Isle of Man (DA) [1] — Employees - Salariés - Asalariados — E.G./h. - Pound

Men - Hommes - Hombres
ISIC 3 - CITI 3 - CIIU 3

	1999	2000	2001	2002	2003	2004	2005	2006	2007	2008
Total	10.78	10.60	11.09	11.78	12.21	12.79	12.74	14.80	14.30	14.91
C-Q	10.84	10.64	11.19	11.82	12.22	12.85	12.77	14.90	14.50	14.95
A	.									
C	6.89									
D	9.45	9.19	9.15	10.91	10.95	10.25	10.87	11.10	12.70	12.58
E	10.86	8.71	10.73	14.17	11.33	10.15	13.14	13.90	17.30	17.34
F	7.30	7.65	9.40	9.61	10.31	10.49	11.55	12.00	10.20	10.79
G	7.99	7.34	7.31	7.56	6.96	9.04	8.77	10.20	9.10	10.05
H	6.71	6.88	5.27	6.59	6.31	6.48	7.59	14.50	9.30	7.01
I	9.94	10.84	8.89	10.50	11.47	10.73	11.58	13.70	12.80	15.46
J	14.41	15.81	16.43	15.42	14.01	18.61	16.35	18.00	18.60	20.36
K	11.65	11.50	12.63	12.75	13.20	14.19	14.76	18.70	15.70	15.00
L	11.13	10.74	12.47	12.96	12.26	15.17	14.72	16.20	17.60	15.56
M	19.77	14.83	9.87	16.00	14.36	18.31	21.25	19.40	20.00	20.70
N	8.94	10.35	14.05	12.45	10.79	12.34	12.55	18.00	14.50	18.74
O	7.03	6.14	8.40	8.44	8.02	9.32	8.68	10.20	9.10	7.51

Women - Femmes - Mujeres
ISIC 3 - CITI 3 - CIIU 3

	1999	2000	2001	2002	2003	2004	2005	2006	2007	2008
Total	8.69	8.47	8.80	9.81	10.24	10.92	10.63	11.70	12.80	13.31
C-Q	8.69	8.47	8.83	9.83	10.24	10.92	10.65	11.70	12.90	13.32
A	.									
D	7.52	6.76	8.51	7.72	7.52	10.67	9.22	10.70	9.00	14.20
E	9.11							20.80		
F			7.06	8.58	6.37	9.13		9.00		
G	5.78	5.38	5.71	6.89	6.14	8.15	7.50	7.70	8.10	9.37
H	5.33	5.23	4.97	6.53	5.97	6.73	7.16	7.10	7.80	9.49
I	7.10	7.42	7.81	8.85	9.89	9.76	11.08	10.30	11.80	11.97
J	9.45	10.31	10.29	11.19	12.91	12.21	11.92	12.70	16.50	13.82
K	8.61	9.02	9.10	9.18	9.17	11.38	10.10	12.40	12.50	17.53
L	8.63	9.59	8.10	9.14	9.88	12.18	11.33	13.90	12.70	15.84
M	14.10	9.71	9.61	12.36	15.06	12.38	11.60	13.90	16.00	14.62
N	8.77	8.55	9.81	9.89	10.22	11.20	11.17	13.30	12.50	12.84
O	5.33	6.71	7.33	5.91	7.84	6.93	9.75	9.70	8.00	8.83
P	4.14							11.00		

Isle of Man (DA) [1] — Employees - Salariés - Asalariados — E.G./w.s. - Pound

Total men and women - Total hommes et femmes - Total hombres y mujeres
ISIC 3 - CITI 3 - CIIU 3

	1999	2000	2001	2002	2003	2004	2005	2006	2007	2008
Total	344.59	349.57	368.72	382.53	415.44	420.76	429.00	464.50	480.40	497.55
C-Q	344.94	349.98	369.88	383.61	415.30	421.44	431.00	465.00	488.30	498.37
A	307.08	279.99	304.47							
C	291.37									
D	377.05	366.94	361.40	392.03	409.56	412.44	441.00	445.80	482.40	539.99
E	414.81	320.60	432.01	685.94	475.81	484.20	500.00	594.50	677.30	626.60
F	348.75	346.40	376.62	420.73	478.27	440.91	454.00	487.00	452.00	470.65
G	254.17	224.53	241.34	224.61	238.35	271.49	304.00	320.70	281.60	322.29
H	216.59	217.12	165.43	229.18	209.06	213.47	276.00	242.00	242.00	223.68
I	365.70	424.43	343.14	425.68	451.24	458.50	492.00	527.40	525.20	556.84
J	404.06	453.71	463.75	465.59	508.22	519.00	516.00	528.70	611.60	591.74
K	364.78	357.41	375.59	417.29	498.81	.	457.00	570.10	508.00	592.91
L	395.48	392.58	417.29	431.36	493.38	504.42	489.00	578.00	638.70	583.31
M	351.74	272.66	238.52	343.86	385.96	363.20	305.00	388.90	475.90	385.96
N	293.52	331.71	400.85	369.75	387.65	431.68	420.00	522.20	482.30	566.44
O	206.45	212.53	280.43	214.84	253.04	248.89	324.00	321.80	259.00	270.65
P	117.94							405.50		

Men - Hommes - Hombres
ISIC 3 - CITI 3 - CIIU 3

	1999	2000	2001	2002	2003	2004	2005	2006	2007	2008
Total	413.10	423.70	445.83	452.06	494.96	503.48	511.00	555.20	550.50	585.28
C-Q	415.08	425.02	448.88	453.44	495.37	505.77	513.00	555.80	561.40	586.74
A	307.08									
C	.									
D	408.91	407.28	381.54	417.32	504.51	455.38	468.00	463.20	518.20	545.39
E	437.14	345.67	432.01	587.83	475.81	484.20	522.00	582.80	684.80	658.49
F	348.75	350.95	397.61	428.10	495.31	464.11	466.00	513.20	461.90	497.57
G	317.85	295.44	299.73	304.21	307.22	338.67	384.00	409.20	367.40	385.98
H	278.64	263.50	158.57	265.48	241.55	253.55	307.00	312.40	265.50	234.16
I	426.02	493.91	396.13	471.98	520.72	503.26	525.00	598.30	570.40	650.58
J	526.82	597.76	612.58	562.85	566.62	668.11	640.00	646.00	700.60	749.61
K	435.35	437.63	475.74	527.78	748.97	428.98	582.00	725.90	603.50	635.41
L	463.76	419.00	485.80	485.48	567.53	504.42	563.00	652.90	722.00	611.38
M	397.76	420.10	393.66	445.71	400.11	363.20	558.00	547.30	601.50	630.12
N	336.08	407.74	619.35	482.03	494.17	431.68	551.00	705.10	590.30	767.88
O	273.89	247.46	365.98	280.92	294.84	248.89	333.00	356.80	333.60	304.57

Explanatory notes: see p. 877. Notes explicatives: voir p. 879. Notas explicativas: véase p. 882.

[1] June of each year. [1] Juin de chaque année. [1] Junio de cada año.

5A

	WAGES	SALAIRES	SALARIOS
	By economic activity	Par activité économique	Por actividad económica

	1999	2000	2001	2002	2003	2004	2005	2006	2007	2008

Isle of Man (DA) [1] — Employees - Salariés - Asalariados — E.G./w.s. - Pound

Women - Femmes - Mujeres
ISIC 3 - CITI 3 - CIIU 3

	1999	2000	2001	2002	2003	2004	2005	2006	2007	2008
Total	272.96	278.66	288.92	312.18	332.29	340.34	344.00	380.10	408.10	418.32
C-Q	272.96	278.73	289.83	313.45	332.29	340.34	346.00	381.00	413.70	418.95
A										
D	241.11	258.21	278.31	292.82	253.85	265.24	325.00	401.10	323.00	
E	295.74							670.80		
F			223.75	262.30				191.80		
G	188.89	165.63	188.93	154.18	177.75	205.68	234.00	245.10	203.80	250.31
H	169.32	180.68	167.84	174.72	176.57	163.38	237.00	179.80	223.20	210.43
I	256.54	282.32	267.67	309.94	307.31	358.20	383.00	385.80	448.40	411.55
J	315.23	357.26	362.84	389.66	464.15	419.21	431.00	452.20	537.30	468.44
K	303.61	315.91	297.69	318.43	318.69	361.45	333.00	397.80	423.50	559.98
L	301.83	351.75	231.90	339.36	352.26	372.24	386.00	470.90	509.00	543.04
M	330.33	215.32	166.12	300.22	381.15	304.45	240.00	328.80	407.50	322.41
N	278.86	310.17	350.63	339.99	349.85	402.86	381.00	466.00	454.60	508.88
O	135.96	188.23	211.99			219.60	167.54	312.00	275.90	184.30	260.96
P	117.94							405.50		

Italy (FE) — Wage earners - Ouvriers - Obreros — R.T./h. - Euro

Indices, total - Indices, total - Índices, total
ISIC 3 - CITI 3 - CIIU 3

	1999	2000	2001	2002	2003	2004	2005	2006	2007	2008
Total	110.5	112.4	89.1 [2]	91.1	93.4	96.0	99.2	102.0	104.6	108.0
C-Q	110.9	113.2	89.0 [2]	91.1	93.3	96.0	99.1	102.0	104.6	108.1
A	106.8	106.8	89.9 [2]	91.0	94.4	95.1	100.0	101.5	105.1	105.9
C	112.1	113.1	90.2 [2]	92.2	94.0	96.6	99.5	101.9	105.8	108.6
D	110.9	113.1	89.2 [2]	91.7	94.0	96.7	99.4	102.7	105.6	109.1
E	108.4	108.5	92.4 [2]	94.2	95.9	97.7	99.6	100.7	105.0	108.4
F	111.1	114.2	86.3 [2]	88.4	90.7	94.7	99.3	102.2	106.6	110.8
G	114.3	116.6	87.8 [2]	90.7	92.7	94.3	99.2	100.7	102.9	104.9
H	110.3	112.1	90.8 [2]	91.5	93.1	97.0	99.3	100.5	101.6	107.5
I	107.7	108.1	90.5 [2]	91.1	93.3	95.3	97.8	101.5	103.9	107.6
K	108.4	110.0	87.0 [2]	88.4	91.6	95.4	99.0	101.2	103.3	105.5
M			88.6 [2]	90.6	92.9	96.5	98.6	100.2	101.4	108.7
N			89.8 [2]	92.4	93.6	94.2	99.0	100.0	106.0	106.0

Italy (FE) — Salaried employees - Employés - Empleados — R.T./h. - Euro

Indices, total - Indices, total - Índices, total
ISIC 3 - CITI 3 - CIIU 3

	1999	2000	2001	2002	2003	2004	2005	2006	2007	2008
Total	111.9	114.1	90.2 [2]	91.9	93.8	96.5	99.5	102.6	104.5	108.3
C-Q	111.7	113.8	90.3 [2]	92.0	93.8	96.5	99.5	102.5	104.5	108.3
C	114.5	116.1	92.1 [2]	93.7	95.2	97.6	99.3	101.7	105.7	109.3
D	112.1	114.4	89.0 [2]	91.5	93.9	96.9	99.5	103.0	106.0	109.8
E	109.2	109.3	91.0 [2]	93.2	95.1	97.3	99.7	100.8	105.6	109.2
F	109.2	111.7	88.9 [2]	91.2	93.6	96.0	99.5	102.4	105.8	109.0
G	115.1	117.5	87.1 [2]	90.2	92.3	94.0	99.1	100.8	103.1	105.3
H	111.7	113.5	90.9 [2]	91.6	93.2	97.1	99.3	100.5	101.6	107.6
I	108.9	109.2	90.1 [2]	90.8	92.5	96.6	98.9	102.0	104.5	107.9
J	109.2	110.9	89.3 [2]	91.1	93.4	94.9	97.9	100.1	100.6	106.0
K	114.6	117.0	87.3 [2]	88.7	91.5	95.1	98.9	101.3	103.5	105.9
L			91.0 [2]	92.1	93.4	96.0	100.0	102.7	104.9	108.9
M	110.7	113.7	93.4 [2]	93.5	96.1	99.5	99.9	105.1	105.3	110.4
N	114.0	118.5	91.2 [2]	94.2	94.5	97.6	99.7	102.3	105.2	108.4

Jersey (DA) [1] [3] [4] — Employees - Salariés - Asalariados — E.G./w.s. - Pound

Total men and women - Total hommes et femmes - Total hombres y mujeres
ISIC 3 - CITI 3 - CIIU 3

	1999	2000	2001	2002	2003	2004	2005	2006	2007	2008
Total	390	410	440	460	480	490	520	540	580	
A [5]	300	320	340	330	320	330		340	340	
D	400	420	450	460	480	500	530	530	550	
E	450	470	490	520	540	570	610	630	650	
F	410	420	450	470	480	500	520	520	550	
G	290	310	320	340	350	360	380	390	410	
H	230	240	260	270	280	290	300	300	320	
I	460	480	520	540	570	600	610	660	690	
J	500	540	580	630	660	680	710	740	770	
74	280	300	320	340	360	370	390	480	520	
L	530	570	600	620	640	650	700	720	760	

Explanatory notes: see p. 877.

[1] June of each year. [2] Index of hourly wage rates (Dec.2005=100). [3] Approximate levels since survey aims at measuring changes; excl. bonuses. [4] Full-time equivalent employees. [5] Excl. hunting and forestry.

Notes explicatives: voir p. 879.

[1] Juin de chaque année. [2] Indice des taux de salaire horaire (déc.2005=100). [3] Niveaux approximatifs étant donné que l'enquête vise à mesurer l'évolution; non compris les primes. [4] Salariés en équivalents à plein temps. [5] Non compris la chasse et la sylviculture.

Notas explicativas: véase p. 882.

[1] Junio de cada año. [2] Indice de las tasas de salario por hora (dic.2005=100). [3] Niveles aproximativos ya que la encuesta tiene por objectivo medir cambios; excl. las primas. [4] Asalariados en equivalentes a tiempo completo. [5] Excl. caza y silvicultura.

| | | | |

By economic activity | **Par activité économique** | **Por actividad económica**

	1999	2000	2001	2002	2003	2004	2005	2006	2007	2008	
Latvia (DA) [1]					Employees - Salariés - Asalariados						E.G./m. - Lat

Total men and women - Total hommes et femmes - Total hombres y mujeres
ISIC 3 - CITI 3 - CIIU 3

	1999	2000	2001	2002	2003	2004	2005	2006	2007	2008
Total	132.61	141.75	149.14	161.24	177.21	194.89	225.64	269.02	353.83	453.23
A-B	91.40	104.67	109.03	124.27	141.65	166.77	192.06	228.58	311.77	385.63
C-Q	134.31	142.75	149.86	162.24	178.14	195.58	226.44	269.99	354.75	454.67
A	90.88	105.89	109.83	126.65	144.31	170.82	195.57	231.53	315.03	390.27
B	99.75	85.30	99.72	94.00	105.42	124.53	146.97	195.46	267.62	325.66
C	134.08	137.25	141.53	172.71	193.90	218.05	233.63	283.32	392.17	488.95
D	128.97	135.13	140.34	145.51	159.26	176.36	200.26	239.62	315.03	394.04
E	186.56	203.82	209.76	232.55	257.08	269.53	313.52	370.99	538.71	620.79
F	122.46	124.18	125.67	127.09	142.68	160.04	181.43	239.80	323.32	414.19
G	99.83	106.59	112.06	120.57	135.96	159.06	182.26	221.41	296.65	380.81
H	80.31	84.01	94.28	99.76	107.83	125.22	137.66	168.76	223.55	283.81
I	182.13	190.59	198.54	202.39	224.12	227.21	265.64	307.03	371.59	490.09
J	310.71	357.92	396.69	450.18	460.69	462.43	588.00	701.56	860.95	1 094.27
K	152.08	161.75	174.95	190.01	195.46	214.83	239.05	290.22	377.72	485.44
L	167.50	181.55	188.79	207.45	223.75	257.49	308.15	355.85	490.45	622.17
M	111.57	121.40	137.99	157.87	179.26	192.64	226.05	254.73	327.14	432.00
N	113.01	118.64	121.43	135.42	157.67	183.64	207.79	267.38	365.60	459.89
O	119.74	123.46	128.48	139.72	151.76	160.70	189.59	227.73	318.98	401.13

Men - Hommes - Hombres
ISIC 3 - CITI 3 - CIIU 3

	1999	2000	2001	2002	2003	2004	2005	2006	2007	2008
Total	148.10	160.45	166.41	178.70	194.46	211.71	249.13	295.96	385.41	491.83
A-B	95.34	111.11	116.46	130.57	149.51	172.25	199.13	238.57	326.97	403.47
C-Q	151.18	162.54	171.32	180.51	196.11	213.06	250.79	297.89	387.15	494.42
A	94.87	113.46	115.96	134.61	153.92	178.34	204.25	242.04	332.78	410.89
B	101.20	85.25	101.66	94.19	105.48	123.80	147.96	206.87	262.58	326.72
C	134.97	143.12	145.92	182.59	201.35	226.75	242.72	299.62	415.08	515.49
D	137.48	146.00	150.86	157.28	172.78	192.14	217.93	263.07	350.27	430.19
E	194.65	212.50	219.61	243.89	269.32	282.54	348.22	389.76	566.68	653.41
F	125.56	126.93	127.92	128.63	143.49	159.49	183.07	242.17	326.93	424.44
G	116.89	128.65	133.71	142.83	160.85	188.36	214.92	268.76	350.52	444.97
H	97.03	105.99	118.60	118.49	127.88	148.99	173.20	209.67	262.33	339.78
I	194.07	204.11	209.01	214.70	239.36	235.26	282.44	318.66	384.89	509.34
J	427.64	491.44	538.84	637.06	645.22	642.59	870.97	985.25	1 240.98	1 580.47
K	164.89	180.90	192.97	211.77	212.64	232.07	269.49	317.15	408.18	515.53
L	165.10	181.75	188.45	206.68	220.34	261.77	318.99	357.20	488.87	622.80
M	118.29	133.26	151.34	168.31	189.04	198.68	242.38	275.39	351.39	501.80
N	127.12	133.67	140.32	155.98	182.95	200.69	231.35	300.78	418.83	527.96
O	141.19	144.94	154.70	164.12	175.64	184.55	225.96	277.89	379.24	461.79

Women - Femmes - Mujeres
ISIC 3 - CITI 3 - CIIU 3

	1999	2000	2001	2002	2003	2004	2005	2006	2007	2008
Total	118.48	126.16	133.39	145.59	161.69	179.20	204.06	243.80	323.48	417.30
A-B	83.50	94.46	100.85	112.23	126.59	155.78	178.25	208.33	282.40	351.08
C-Q	119.39	126.53	134.88	146.18	162.30	179.57	204.44	244.34	324.08	418.23
A	83.25	94.42	99.55	112.68	127.20	156.89	179.60	211.29	282.19	352.36
B	91.93	85.63	83.57	93.77	104.16	128.67	142.54	148.94	285.77	321.10
C	129.80	112.59	123.16	132.18	159.59	181.28	195.27	215.27	295.88	381.38
D	118.52	122.92	127.13	131.05	141.96	155.85	177.27	208.95	269.73	346.68
E	164.44	180.17	183.41	201.81	224.69	236.46	223.50	322.79	468.15	539.77
F	107.10	111.39	114.89	119.32	138.26	163.07	172.33	226.07	301.48	358.15
G	88.08	92.97	95.52	104.39	118.42	136.33	156.90	186.66	254.60	332.65
H	74.25	78.07	84.05	92.96	99.80	115.53	125.06	154.33	207.34	264.01
I	161.98	169.85	180.43	181.95	198.47	213.35	235.80	282.76	345.74	453.25
J	240.52	280.94	313.95	343.69	362.21	369.24	443.28	555.19	680.47	870.47
K	137.08	145.24	154.13	165.20	176.27	194.75	206.38	259.78	342.47	451.22
L	170.46	181.30	189.18	208.31	227.51	252.77	296.85	354.52	491.91	621.58
M	109.79	118.55	134.75	155.28	176.85	191.09	221.99	249.62	321.13	415.12
N	110.06	115.56	117.49	131.20	152.61	179.83	202.76	260.07	354.58	446.11
O	102.59	107.21	109.41	122.31	134.91	143.98	164.73	194.92	277.89	360.22

Liechtenstein (F) [2]					Employees - Salariés - Asalariados						E.G./m. - Swiss franc

Total men and women - Total hommes et femmes - Total hombres y mujeres
ISIC 3 - CITI 3 - CIIU 3

	1999	2000	2001	2002	2003	2004	2005	2006	2007	2008
Total	.	.	.	.	.	.	5 819	.	.	.
A-B	.	.	.	.	.	.	4 353	.	.	.
E	.	.	.	.	.	.	6 257	.	.	.
F	.	.	.	.	.	.	5 265	.	.	.
G	.	.	.	.	.	.	4 983	.	.	.
H	.	.	.	.	.	.	3 676	.	.	.
I	.	.	.	.	.	.	5 417	.	.	.
J	.	.	.	.	.	.	7 732	.	.	.
K	.	.	.	.	.	.	5 467	.	.	.
L,Q	.	.	.	.	.	.	7 026	.	.	.
M	.	.	.	.	.	.	8 656	.	.	.
N	.	.	.	.	.	.	5 356	.	.	.
O	.	.	.	.	.	.	5 404	.	.	.
P	.	.	.	.	.	.	4 093	.	.	.

Explanatory notes: see p. 877. | Notes explicatives: voir p. 879. | Notas explicativas: véase p. 882.

[1] First quarter of each year. [2] Median. | [1] Premier trimestre de chaque année. [2] Médiane. | [1] Primer trimestre de cada año. [2] Mediana.

	WAGES	SALAIRES	SALARIOS
	By economic activity	Par activité économique	Por actividad económica

	1999	2000	2001	2002	2003	2004	2005	2006	2007	2008

Liechtenstein (F) [1] Employees - Salariés - Asalariados E.G./m. - Swiss franc

Men - Hommes - Hombres
ISIC 3 - CITI 3 - CIIU 3

	1999	2000	2001	2002	2003	2004	2005	2006	2007	2008
Total							6 381			
A-B							4 536			
E							6 558			
F							5 295			
G							5 505			
H							4 280			
I							5 416			
J							9 917			
K							6 166			
L,Q							8 030			
M							9 777			
N							7 131			
O							6 700			
P										

Women - Femmes - Mujeres
ISIC 3 - CITI 3 - CIIU 3

	1999	2000	2001	2002	2003	2004	2005	2006	2007	2008
Total							5 092			
A-B										
E										
F							4 688			
G							4 478			
H							3 497			
I							5 417			
J							6 201			
K							4 670			
M							7 461			
N							5 151			
O							4 615			
P							4 000			

Lithuania (DA) [2][3] Employees - Salariés - Asalariados E.G./h. - Litas

Total men and women - Total hommes et femmes - Total hombres y mujeres
ISIC 3 - CITI 3 - CIIU 3

	1999	2000	2001	2002	2003	2004	2005	2006	2007	2008
Total	6.49 [4]	6.41	6.47	6.80	7.08	7.45	8.29	9.77	11.60	13.76
A-B	5.94 [4]	4.34	4.52	4.83	5.14	5.62	6.24	7.32	9.18	11.03
C-Q	6.50 [4]	6.49	6.54	6.87	7.14	7.51	8.35	9.84	11.67	13.83
A	6.07 [4]	4.36	4.54	4.87	5.17	5.58	6.21	7.27	9.14	10.99
B	3.59 [4]	3.53	3.45	3.50	4.49	6.18	6.80	8.14	10.00	11.78
C	6.72 [4]	7.51	8.66	8.77	9.37	9.55	10.25	12.00	14.46	17.36
D	6.16 [4]	6.21	6.33	6.48	6.60	6.87	7.61	8.94	11.01	12.82
E	8.30 [4]	8.34	8.64	9.00	9.34	10.01	11.26	12.66	14.41	16.66
F	5.84 [4]	5.76	5.82	6.24	6.23	7.47	7.96	10.59	13.38	14.77
G	5.39 [4]	5.61	5.94	6.46	6.50	6.64	7.56	9.12	11.05	12.72
H	4.58 [4]	4.32	4.37	4.16	4.41	4.58	5.15	5.55	6.81	8.25
I	6.94 [4]	6.80	7.32	7.29	7.86	7.72	8.55	9.57	11.43	13.71
J	12.85 [4]	12.22	13.32	14.76	15.50	15.32	16.88	19.18	22.25	25.01
K	7.30 [4]	8.15	6.34	7.16	7.61	8.11	9.21	10.39	12.07	15.18
L	9.11 [4]	9.11	8.92	9.83	10.58	11.33	12.10	14.08	15.11	18.50
M	6.47 [4]	6.28	6.28	6.41	6.59	7.21	8.08	8.92	10.24	12.61
N	5.24 [4]	5.13	5.21	5.40	5.49	5.94	7.20	9.38	11.05	13.34
O	5.76 [4]	5.21	5.60	5.98	6.01	6.34	6.89	8.15	9.44	11.33

Men - Hommes - Hombres
ISIC 3 - CITI 3 - CIIU 3

	1999	2000	2001	2002	2003	2004	2005	2006	2007	2008
Total	7.10 [4]	7.01	7.06	7.43	7.74	8.10	8.97	10.63	12.85	15.17
A-B	5.96 [4]	4.48	4.67	4.95	5.35	5.83	6.55	7.70	9.70	11.72
C-Q	6.50 [4]	7.15	7.19	7.56	7.84	8.20	9.07	10.74	12.96	15.28
A	6.10 [4]	4.50	4.70	4.99	5.39	5.79	6.52	7.65	9.66	11.69
B	3.64 [4]	3.56	3.51	3.55	4.59	6.25	6.91	8.23	10.33	12.11
C	6.92 [4]	7.69	8.82	8.84	9.45	9.58	10.32	12.19	14.77	17.73
D	6.90 [4]	6.92	7.11	7.24	7.48	7.74	8.58	10.16	12.70	14.88
E	8.71 [4]	8.74	9.00	9.38	9.67	10.33	11.67	13.13	14.99	17.36
F	5.91 [4]	5.84	5.89	6.29	6.24	7.50	7.98	10.73	13.65	14.93
G	5.93 [4]	6.10	6.65	7.09	7.26	7.33	8.45	10.15	12.70	14.50
H	5.50 [4]	4.78	4.71	4.52	5.07	4.85	5.92	6.44	7.75	9.56
I	7.21 [4]	7.09	7.73	7.51	7.94	7.83	8.70	9.70	11.57	13.89
J	16.24 [4]	15.61	17.42	19.71	21.30	21.36	24.18	27.36	32.15	36.32
K	7.96 [4]	9.43	6.73	7.71	8.23	8.87	9.95	10.91	12.47	16.60
L	9.44 [4]	9.51	9.36	10.49	10.85	11.68	12.39	14.42	15.50	19.16
M	6.44 [4]	6.01	6.14	6.20	6.64	7.00	7.89	8.95	10.17	12.71
N	5.89 [4]	5.76	5.96	6.32	6.46	7.01	8.50	11.40	13.66	16.53
O	6.21 [4]	5.63	6.04	6.61	6.63	7.00	7.52	8.77	10.75	12.79

Explanatory notes: see p. 877.

[1] Median. [2] Excl. individual unincorporated enterprises. [3] All employees converted into full-time units. [4] April.

Notes explicatives: voir p. 879.

[1] Médiane. [2] Non compris les entreprises individuelles non constituées en société. [3] Ensemble des salariés convertis en unités à plein temps. [4] Avril.

Notas explicativas: véase p. 882.

[1] Mediana. [2] Excl. las empresas individuales no constituidas en sociedad. [3] Todos los asalariados convertidos en unidades a tiempo completo. [4] Abril.

	1999	2000	2001	2002	2003	2004	2005	2006	2007	2008

Lithuania (DA) [1][2] — Employees - Salariés - Asalariados — E.G./h. - Litas

Women - Femmes - Mujeres
ISIC 3 - CITI 3 - CIIU 3

	1999	2000	2001	2002	2003	2004	2005	2006	2007	2008
Total	5.93 [3]	5.88	5.92	6.23	6.45	6.81	7.62	8.91	10.37	12.41
A-B	5.84 [3]	4.02	4.18	4.58	4.73	5.19	5.67	6.63	8.24	9.79
C-Q	5.93 [3]	5.92	5.96	6.27	6.48	6.84	7.66	8.95	10.41	12.45
A	5.98 [3]	4.03	4.19	4.61	4.75	5.18	5.66	6.61	8.24	9.79
B	3.37 [3]	3.44	3.17	3.28	3.99	5.71	6.19	7.60	8.37	10.10
C	5.96 [3]	6.78	7.96	8.44	8.98	9.44	9.90	11.03	12.90	15.43
D	5.35 [3]	5.47	5.51	5.67	5.79	5.92	6.50	7.52	9.01	10.41
E	7.01 [3]	7.13	7.51	7.82	8.28	9.00	10.00	11.28	12.76	14.67
F	5.36 [3]	5.29	5.38	5.92	6.15	7.17	7.78	9.50	11.34	13.56
G	4.89 [3]	5.22	5.28	5.85	5.68	5.88	6.68	8.09	9.50	11.18
H	4.22 [3]	4.13	4.23	4.01	4.18	4.46	4.87	5.27	6.56	7.87
I	6.34 [3]	6.22	6.54	6.84	7.67	7.46	8.22	9.27	11.12	13.30
J	10.77 [3]	10.26	11.01	12.13	12.65	12.55	13.78	15.92	18.44	20.79
K	6.64 [3]	6.79	5.90	6.61	6.99	7.28	8.44	9.87	11.64	13.63
L	8.64 [3]	8.56	8.39	9.11	10.23	10.92	11.75	13.69	14.68	17.81
M	6.48 [3]	6.37	6.32	6.47	6.57	7.28	8.15	8.91	10.26	12.59
N	5.12 [3]	5.01	5.06	5.21	5.29	5.73	6.94	8.99	10.57	12.72
O	5.36 [3]	4.82	5.15	5.35	5.42	5.75	6.32	7.60	8.37	10.15

Lithuania (DA) [2] — Employees - Salariés - Asalariados — E.G./m. - Litas

Total men and women - Total hommes et femmes - Total hombres y mujeres
ISIC 3 - CITI 3 - CIIU 3

	1999	2000	2001	2002	2003	2004	2005	2006	2007	2008
Total	987	971	982	1 014	1 073	1 149	1 276	1 496	1 802	2 174
A-B	648	691	713	761	802	894	977	1 145	1 419	1 739
C-Q	987	971	982	1 014	1 073	1 157	1 285	1 506	1 813	2 185
A	649	694	716	764	806	887	973	1 139	1 411	1 734
B	584	573	582	689	702	990	1 046	1 256	1 550	1 835
C	1 191	1 296	1 435	1 499	1 568	1 618	1 732	1 989	2 380	2 869
D	963	955	963	982	1 016	1 085	1 184	1 387	1 727	2 035
E	1 377	1 377	1 438	1 486	1 585	1 691	1 862	2 067	2 355	2 732
F	1 031	943	918	933	1 003	1 075	1 289	1 665	2 146	2 408
G	781	763	764	792	882	1 006	1 111	1 332	1 646	1 960
H	584	531	526	541	581	656	732	828	1 034	1 256
I	1 107	1 080	1 080	1 116	1 179	1 250	1 318	1 466	1 754	2 141
J	1 980	2 072	2 222	2 442	2 503	2 560	2 765	3 122	3 638	4 136
K	1 122	1 123	1 136	1 157	1 213	1 257	1 450	1 643	1 914	2 440
L	1 563	1 463	1 513	1 628	1 750	1 867	2 024	2 313	2 491	3 065
M	943	927	929	948	990	1 017	1 145	1 296	1 536	1 943
N	834	824	844	861	891	967	1 155	1 471	1 759	2 148
O	871	844	864	890	925	1 042	1 113	1 277	1 501	1 826

Luxembourg (CA) [4] — Wage earners - Ouvriers - Obreros — E.G./h. - Euro

Total men and women - Total hommes et femmes - Total hombres y mujeres
ISIC 3 - CITI 3 - CIIU 3

	1999	2000	2001	2002	2003	2004	2005	2006	2007	2008
C	12.42	12.54	12.96	13.49	13.74	14.20	14.73	14.77	14.90	15.63
D	12.22	12.54	12.62	13.10	13.49	14.18	14.68	14.67	14.82	15.08
E	16.41	16.96	17.20	18.06	19.21	19.42	20.07	19.98	20.21	20.81
F	10.73	11.18	11.53	11.93	12.31	12.70	13.11	13.14	13.48	13.85
G	9.62	9.99	10.26	10.66	10.99	11.52	11.91	11.89	12.21	12.53
H	8.28	8.68	9.02	9.26	9.75	10.30	10.91	10.93	11.27	11.51
I	.	.	.	.	.	.	.	.	.	14.2
J	11.30	11.18	11.68	11.43	12.58	13.10	12.25	13.63	15.88	14.81
K	.	.	.	.	.	.	.	.	.	12.0
M	.	.	.	.	.	.	.	.	.	13.9
N	.	.	.	.	.	.	.	.	.	13.5
O	.	.	.	.	.	.	.	.	.	13.1

Men - Hommes - Hombres
ISIC 3 - CITI 3 - CIIU 3

	1999	2000	2001	2002	2003	2004	2005	2006	2007	2008
C	12.44	12.57	12.99	13.51	13.76	14.22	14.75	14.79	14.94	15.63
D	12.74	13.06	13.11	13.61	14.02	14.71	15.19	15.18	15.31	15.57
E	16.61	17.06	17.33	18.16	19.39	19.80	20.38	20.29	20.48	21.06
F	10.76	11.20	11.55	11.95	12.33	12.72	13.13	13.16	13.51	13.87
G	10.31	10.66	10.93	11.40	11.73	12.28	12.62	12.56	12.89	13.21
H	8.92	9.35	9.74	9.99	10.49	11.19	11.92	11.97	12.33	12.61
I	.	.	.	.	.	.	.	.	.	14.2
J	11.73	11.80	12.69	11.94	13.88	14.92	12.63	14.16	16.21	15.30
K	.	.	.	.	.	.	.	.	.	12.9
M	.	.	.	.	.	.	.	.	.	17.7
N	.	.	.	.	.	.	.	.	.	12.6
O	.	.	.	.	.	.	.	.	.	15.2

Explanatory notes: see p. 877.

[1] Excl. individual unincorporated enterprises. [2] All employees converted into full-time units. [3] April. [4] Oct. of each year.

Notes explicatives: voir p. 879.

[1] Non compris les entreprises individuelles non constituées en société. [2] Ensemble des salariés convertis en unités à plein temps. [3] Avril. [4] Oct. de chaque année.

Notas explicativas: véase p. 882.

[1] Excl. las empresas individuales no constituidas en sociedad. [2] Todos los asalariados convertidos en unidades a tiempo completo. [3] Abril. [4] Oct. de cada año.

Luxembourg (CA) [1] — Wage earners - Ouvriers - Obreros — E.G./h. - Euro

Women - Femmes - Mujeres
ISIC 3 - CITI 3 - CIIU 3

	1999	2000	2001	2002	2003	2004	2005	2006	2007	2008
C										
D	8.70	9.35	9.47	9.80	10.22	10.58	11.07	10.96	11.12	11.35
E	11.43	12.39	12.64	13.06	13.39	13.36	13.90	14.34	15.04	15.51
F	8.68	9.49	9.84	9.71	10.20	10.58	10.91	10.93	11.23	11.67
G	8.01	8.43	8.73	8.90	9.32	9.80	10.23	10.22	10.48	10.76
H	7.56	7.96	8.30	8.46	8.94	9.34	9.85	9.84	10.17	10.41
I										14.6
J	9.92	8.85	9.74	10.18	10.71	10.96	11.51	12.87	13.90	13.56
K										10.3
M										12.2
N										13.9
O										11.8

Luxembourg (CA) [1] — Salaried employees - Employés - Empleados — E.G./m. - Euro

Total men and women - Total hommes et femmes - Total hombres y mujeres
ISIC 3 - CITI 3 - CIIU 3

	1999	2000	2001	2002	2003	2004	2005	2006	2007	2008
C	3 171	3 131	3 152	3 309	3 655	3 702	3 852	3 934	4 276	4 261
D	3 680	3 727	3 816	3 941	4 090	4 189	4 334	4 374	4 506	4 650
E	4 337	4 349	4 460	4 566	4 512	4 754	4 930	4 902	5 101	5 332
F	2 915	3 012	3 103	3 171	3 543	3 396	3 523	3 580	3 646	3 761
G	2 393	2 512	2 587	2 631	2 724	2 791	2 895	2 918	3 012	3 092
H	2 311	2 408	2 477	2 496	2 574	2 782	2 795	2 869	2 952	3 033
I										4 282
J	3 689	3 820	4 041	4 211	4 391	4 569	4 760	4 799	4 965	5 196
K										4 044
M										4 755
N										4 141
O										4 047

Men - Hommes - Hombres
ISIC 3 - CITI 3 - CIIU 3

	1999	2000	2001	2002	2003	2004	2005	2006	2007	2008
C										
D	3 944	3 995	4 104	4 251	4 412	4 510	4 663	4 710	4 876	5 007
E	4 460	4 432	4 573	4 672	4 587	4 858	5 031	5 053	5 278	5 508
F	3 208	3 291	3 405	3 544	3 961	3 709	3 852	3 944	4 007	4 131
G	2 924	3 074	3 178	3 259	3 376	3 452	3 561	3 599	3 696	3 802
H	2 600	2 716	2 775	2 934	3 035	3 163	3 170	3 208	3 304	3 435
I										4 656
J	4 167	4 331	4 593	4 758	4 956	5 206	5 421	5 474	5 666	5 948
K										4 443
M										5 145
N										5 160
O										4 539

Women - Femmes - Mujeres
ISIC 3 - CITI 3 - CIIU 3

	1999	2000	2001	2002	2003	2004	2005	2006	2007	2008
C										
D	2 535	2 621	2 710	2 782	2 911	3 030	3 185	3 229	3 280	3 489
E	3 552	3 603	3 563	3 707	3 835	4 051	4 247	3 989	4 093	4 310
F	2 130	2 248	2 306	2 306	2 399	2 501	2 592	2 617	2 704	2 800
G	1 804	1 887	1 971	1 965	2 024	2 084	2 180	2 205	2 297	2 361
H	1 978	2 040	2 130	2 020	2 092	2 315	2 346	2 459	2 532	2 569
I										3 204
J	3 001	3 101	3 261	3 397	3 523	3 653	3 802	3 835	3 970	4 129
K										3 306
M										4 410
N										3 722
O										3 409

Macedonia, The Former Yugoslav Rep. of (DA) [2] — Employees - Salariés - Asalariados — E.G./m. - Denar

Total men and women - Total hommes et femmes - Total hombres y mujeres
ISIC 3 - CITI 3 - CIIU 3

	1999	2000	2001	2002	2003	2004	2005	2006	2007	2008
Total			10 552	11 279	11 824	12 293	12 597	13 517	14 584	16 096
A			9 400	9 432	9 993	9 692	10 042	10 401	10 740	11 929
B			8 215	7 956	7 231	10 259	12 772	12 905	10 565	9 466
C			11 096	12 840	13 238	13 826	14 718	16 004	16 327	17 842
D			9 577	9 944	10 028	10 486	10 298	10 624	11 653	12 613
E			14 215	14 580	15 041	15 410	16 072	19 368	19 626	20 741
F			8 056	8 318	8 760	9 353	9 782	9 912	10 564	11 867
G			10 583	10 758	11 842	12 279	12 920	13 329	13 951	14 788
H			8 792	8 832	9 321	10 420	10 844	11 209	11 639	12 830
I			13 055	14 305	14 683	15 116	15 995	16 904	17 779	19 568
J			21 051	22 281	23 515	25 209	26 095	26 575	28 419	30 651
K			13 239	13 723	14 205	13 436	13 524	13 700	14 906	16 086
L			10 481	11 606	12 911	13 636	15 392	16 028	17 160	19 385
M			9 632	10 844	11 544	11 606	11 677	12 437	13 957	15 381
N			10 115	11 024	11 865	12 042	12 141	12 517	13 320	15 185
O			11 038	11 743	12 025	12 204	12 323	12 662	13 553	14 392

Explanatory notes: see p. 877. Notes explicatives: voir p. 879. Notas explicativas: véase p. 882.

[1] Oct. of each year. [2] Net earnings. [1] Oct. de chaque année. [2] Gains nets. [1] Oct. de cada año. [2] Ganancias netas.

Malta (BA)   Total employment - Emploi total - Empleo total   E.G./h. - Lira

Total men and women - Total hommes et femmes - Total hombres y mujeres
ISIC 3 - CITI 3 - CIIU 3

	1999	2000	2001	2002	2003	2004	2005	2006	2007	2008
Total	.	2.2	2.4	2.4	2.5	2.6	2.6	2.7	2.8	6.9 [1]
A-B	.	1.6	.	.	.	2.0	2.3	2.4	2.5	5.4 [1]
C-Q	.	2.2	2.4	2.4	2.5	2.6	2.6	2.7	.	7.0 [1]
A	.	1.6	.	.	.	2.1	2.3	2.4	2.5	5.9 [1]
B	.	1.6	.	.	.	2.1	2.3	2.4	.	6.8 [1]
C	.	1.4	.	.	.	.	.	2.0	.	5.6 [1]
D	.	2.1	2.2	2.3	2.3	2.3	2.4	2.6	2.6	6.4 [1]
E	.	2.3	2.4	2.5	2.6	2.5	2.7	2.8	2.9	6.9 [1]
F	.	2.0	2.1	2.1	2.1	2.2	2.3	2.3	2.4	5.8 [1]
G	.	2.0	2.2	2.1	2.2	2.2	2.2	2.3	2.5	6.1 [1]
H	.	2.0	2.1	2.1	2.3	2.4	2.3	2.3	2.4	6.1 [1]
I	.	2.7	2.7	2.8	2.8	2.8	2.9	3.0	3.1	7.5 [1]
J	.	2.8	2.8	3.0	3.3	3.4	3.5	3.6	3.7	8.6 [1]
K	.	2.5	2.9	2.2	2.6	2.7	2.8	2.9	3.1	7.5 [1]
L	.	2.1	2.4	2.6	2.6	2.6	2.6	2.8	2.7	6.9 [1]
M	.	2.6	3.0	3.4	3.2	3.5	3.5	3.7	3.6	9.3 [1]
N	.	2.2	2.3	2.5	2.6	2.5	2.5	2.8	2.7	6.9 [1]
O	.	2.2	2.2	2.1	2.4	2.3	2.5	2.5	2.7	6.8 [1]
P	.	1.6	.	2.2	.	.	.	.	.	4.3 [1]
Q	.	2.0	.	.	.	.	.	.	.	9.7 [1]

Men - Hommes - Hombres
ISIC 3 - CITI 3 - CIIU 3

	1999	2000	2001	2002	2003	2004	2005	2006	2007	2008
Total	.	2.3	2.4	2.5	2.5	2.6	2.6	2.7	2.9	7.0 [1]
A-B	.	1.6	.	.	.	2.1	2.3	2.4	2.4	5.3 [1]
C-Q	.	2.2	2.4	2.5	2.5	2.6	2.6	2.7	2.9	7.0 [1]
A	.	1.6	.	.	.	2.1	2.3	2.4	2.4	5.8 [1]
B	.	1.6	.	.	.	.	.	.	.	7.0 [1]
C	.	1.5	.	.	.	.	.	.	.	5.5 [1]
D	.	2.2	2.3	2.4	2.4	2.4	2.5	2.6	2.7	6.6 [1]
E	.	2.3	2.4	2.6	2.6	2.5	2.7	2.8	2.9	6.9 [1]
F	.	2.0	2.1	2.1	2.1	2.2	2.3	2.3	2.4	5.8 [1]
G	.	2.2	2.3	2.2	2.2	2.2	2.3	2.4	2.6	6.2 [1]
H	.	2.1	2.2	2.1	2.4	2.5	2.4	2.3	2.5	6.2 [1]
I	.	2.7	2.8	2.9	2.9	2.9	2.9	3.0	3.2	7.6 [1]
J	.	3.2	2.9	3.2	3.6	3.7	3.8	3.9	4.4	10.0 [1]
K	.	2.6	2.9	2.3	2.7	2.7	2.9	2.9	3.1	8.0 [1]
L	.	2.1	2.5	2.6	2.7	2.6	2.6	2.8	2.7	6.8 [1]
M	.	2.7	2.9	3.5	3.4	3.7	3.5	3.7	3.8	10.0 [1]
N	.	2.2	2.4	2.6	2.7	2.6	2.6	2.9	2.9	7.2 [1]
O	.	2.1	2.4	2.1	2.5	2.3	2.7	2.6	3.0	7.0 [1]
P	.	1.6	.	.	.	.	.	.	.	
Q	.	2.0	.	.	.	.	.	.	.	8.7 [1]

Women - Femmes - Mujeres
ISIC 3 - CITI 3 - CIIU 3

	1999	2000	2001	2002	2003	2004	2005	2006	2007	2008
Total	.	2.0	2.3	2.4	2.5	2.6	2.6	2.7	2.7	6.9 [1]
A-B	.	2.4	.	.	.	.	.	.	.	6.3 [1]
C-Q	.	1.9	2.3	2.4	2.5	2.6	2.6	2.7	2.7	6.9 [1]
A	.	2.4	.	.	.	.	.	.	.	6.7 [1]
B	.	.	.	.	.	.	.	.	.	5.1 [1]
C	.	.	.	.	.	.	.	.	.	5.6 [1]
D	.	1.8	1.9	2.1	2.2	2.2	2.2	2.3	2.3	5.8 [1]
E	.	2.1	2.3	.	.	.	2.7	2.9	.	6.1 [1]
F	.	2.2	1.8	.	.	.	2.4	2.3	2.3	6.0 [1]
G	.	1.6	2.0	1.9	2.1	2.1	2.2	2.1	2.2	5.9 [1]
H	.	2.0	1.8	2.0	2.2	2.3	2.2	2.3	2.3	5.9 [1]
I	.	2.1	2.1	2.4	2.5	2.5	2.6	2.9	2.7	7.1 [1]
J	.	2.3	2.7	2.8	3.0	3.0	3.2	3.3	3.2	7.4 [1]
K	.	1.7	3.0	2.0	.	2.6	2.5	2.8	3.1	6.8 [1]
L	.	2.1	2.1	2.4	2.4	2.5	2.6	2.7	2.8	7.0 [1]
M	.	2.6	3.1	3.3	3.0	3.3	3.5	3.7	3.6	8.8 [1]
N	.	2.2	2.1	2.4	2.5	2.4	2.5	2.7	2.6	6.6 [1]
O	.	2.2	1.8	2.1	.	2.5	2.3	2.5	2.3	6.5 [1]
P	.	1.5	.	2.2	.	.	.	.	.	4.3 [1]
Q	.	.	.	.	.	.	.	.	.	11.8 [1]

Explanatory notes: see p. 877.
[1] Euros; 1 Euro=0.429300 MTL.

Notes explicatives: voir p. 879.
[1] Euros; 1 Euro=0.429300 MTL.

Notas explicativas: véase p. 882.
[1] Euros; 1 Euro=0.429300MTL.

By economic activity — Par activité économique — Por actividad económica

Moldova, Republic of (CA) [1]

Employees - Salariés - Asalariados — E.G./m. - Leu

Total men and women - Total hommes et femmes - Total hombres y mujeres
ISIC 3 - CITI 3 - CIIU 3

	1999	2000	2001	2002	2003	2004	2005	2006	2007	2008
Total	304.6	407.9	543.7	691.5	890.8	1 103.1	1 318.7	1 697.1	2 065.0	2 529.7
A-B	173.2	252.1	315.4	394.1	499.0	643.6	745.6	916.2	1 099.7	1 483.5
C-Q	355.3	456.6	605.8	766.6	975.9	1 191.4	1 416.3	1 803.0	2 175.6	2 638.0
A	172.8	251.7	315.1	393.8	498.6	642.6	744.0	914.5	1 098.6	1 484.4
B	285.7	338.5	387.9	455.1	585.7	860.2	1 043.1	1 191.0	1 281.0	1 367.7
C	464.3	577.5	767.2	1 008.0	1 190.0	1 598.9	2 037.3	2 623.8	3 098.3	3 739.7
D	492.6	677.7	813.1	971.8	1 216.1	1 417.8	1 651.6	1 914.5	2 314.1	2 762.8
E	621.8	720.0	889.0	1 134.9	1 534.7	1 946.6	2 323.6	2 872.3	3 595.8	4 316.4
F	426.2	539.8	682.8	838.1	1 194.0	1 639.1	1 972.8	2 429.1	2 967.6	3 468.9
G	319.0	394.6	531.1	641.7	794.9	1 051.0	1 228.1	1 555.2	2 088.7	2 530.7
H	277.3	375.8	484.7	571.3	827.4	975.0	1 150.5	1 384.6	1 759.5	2 111.9
I	455.3	635.0	860.8	1 054.5	1 453.5	1 786.3	2 142.9	2 549.1	3 039.5	3 533.1
J	1 672.5	2 523.1	2 278.4	2 564.4	2 926.4	3 254.8	3 450.6	3 863.3	4 648.3	5 446.3
K	436.1	554.0	728.1	889.6	1 133.4	1 382.0	1 671.4	2 051.7	2 583.6	3 215.6
L	438.8	517.7	742.3	989.1	1 049.9	1 204.6	1 363.6	2 164.3	2 389.0	2 802.4
M	193.0	247.7	336.9	463.3	610.2	710.7	881.8	1 209.3	1 351.2	1 670.5
N	186.7	230.1	314.6	439.1	578.8	844.7	1 016.7	1 333.5	1 703.2	2 265.5
O	235.4	295.8	390.9	505.3	671.4	801.9	1 010.9	1 302.2	1 600.3	2 013.9

Montenegro (DA)

Employees - Salariés - Asalariados — E.G./m. - New Dinar

Total men and women - Total hommes et femmes - Total hombres y mujeres
ISIC 3 - CITI 3 - CIIU 3

	1999	2000	2001	2002	2003	2004	2005	2006	2007	2008
Total										
A									497	609
B									446	584
C									196	197
D									725	833
E									530	615
F									701	783
G									430	519
H									301	345
I									388	445
J									659	757
K									1 156	1 268
L									438	531
M									506	669
N									433	570
O									427	576
P									431	532
Q										

Netherlands (DA) [2][3]

Employees - Salariés - Asalariados — E.G./h. - Euro

Total men and women - Total hommes et femmes - Total hombres y mujeres
ISIC 3 - CITI 3 - CIIU 3

	1999	2000	2001	2002	2003	2004	2005
Total	33.16	34.52	16.60 [4]	17.25	17.80	18.18	18.44
A-B	26.72	27.61	13.34 [4]	13.58	14.27	15.03	14.55
C-Q	33.26	34.63	16.65 [4]	17.30	17.85	18.22	18.49
C	49.12	52.39	25.01 [4]	26.72	27.45	27.71	29.41
D	33.32	34.42	16.52 [4]	17.14	17.78	18.24	18.50
E	44.03	45.98	22.52 [4]	22.81	23.73	23.98	24.20
F	33.15	34.11	16.59 [4]	17.12	17.64	18.31	18.42
G	28.58	29.48	14.08 [4]	14.56	15.08	15.32	15.72
H	23.28	23.82	11.51 [4]	11.78	11.91	11.96	12.56
I	32.41	33.03	15.89 [4]	16.18	16.70	17.20	17.17
J	39.58	42.42	20.71 [4]	21.97	22.58	23.16	23.86
K	32.67	35.22	16.94 [4]	17.57	18.30	18.59	18.51
L	39.45	41.00	19.56 [4]	20.21	20.75	21.09	21.59
M	40.36	41.53	19.96 [4]	20.60	21.01	21.13	21.45
N	32.81	34.22	16.51 [4]	17.37	17.67	17.93	18.39
O	31.98	33.05	15.67 [4]	16.37	17.07	17.45	17.91

Men - Hommes - Hombres
ISIC 3 - CITI 3 - CIIU 3

	1999	2000	2001	2002	2003	2004	2005
Total	35.97	37.41	17.88 [4]	18.53	19.15	19.59	19.80
A-B	27.73	28.89	13.80 [4]	18.61	14.78	15.62	15.25
C-Q	36.12	37.56	17.96 [4]	18.61	19.22	19.66	19.88
C	50.54	53.89	25.72 [4]	27.49	28.16	28.55	30.37
D	34.69	35.83	17.20 [4]	17.81	18.45	18.87	19.13
E	45.02	47.00	23.01 [4]	23.40	24.35	24.67	25.17
F	33.45	34.41	16.67 [4]	17.25	17.81	18.47	18.57
G	32.21	33.35	15.72 [4]	16.25	16.78	17.16	17.46
H	25.13	25.48	12.37 [4]	12.57	12.60	12.68	13.42
I	33.62	34.37	16.50 [4]	16.71	17.24	17.79	17.73
J	46.33	49.40	23.91 [4]	25.20	25.72	26.44	27.22
K	36.69	39.22	18.58 [4]	19.24	20.05	20.26	20.13
L	41.37	42.96	20.53 [4]	21.17	21.71	22.04	22.49
M	44.06	45.82	21.96 [4]	22.69	23.10	23.20	23.58
N	41.25	43.55	20.99 [4]	21.95	22.58	23.14	23.63
O	35.24	36.56	17.13 [4]	18.12	18.71	18.98	19.80

Explanatory notes: see p. 877.

[1] Enterprises with 20 or more employees. [2] Excl. overtime payments. [3] Dec. of each year. [4] Prior to 2001: NLG; 1 Euro = 2.20371 NLG.

Notes explicatives: voir p. 879.

[1] Entreprises occupant 20 salariés et plus. [2] Non compris la rémunération des heures supplémentaires. [3] Déc. de chaque année. [4] Avant 2001: NLG; 1 Euro = 2,20371 NLG.

Notas explicativas: véase p. 882.

[1] Empresas con 20 y más asalariados. [2] Excl. los pagos por horas extraordinarias. [3] Dic. de cada año. [4] Antes de 2001: NLG; 1 Euro = 2,20371 NLG.

By economic activity   **Par activité économique**   **Por actividad económica**

	1999	2000	2001	2002	2003	2004	2005	2006	2007	2008

Netherlands (DA) [1] [2]   Employees - Salariés - Asalariados   E.G./h. - Euro

Women - Femmes - Mujeres
ISIC 3 - CITI 3 - CIIU 3

	1999	2000	2001	2002	2003	2004	2005	2006	2007	2008
Total	27.86	29.30	14.30 [3]	15.00	15.49	15.81	16.17	.	.	.
A-B	22.96	23.31	11.44 [3]	11.88	12.27	12.61	11.94	.	.	.
C-Q	27.91	29.36	14.33 [3]	15.03	15.51	15.83	16.21	.	.	.
C	36.54	39.23	18.85 [3]	20.57	22.07	21.26	22.24	.	.	.
D	26.90	27.96	13.53 [3]	14.14	14.73	15.36	15.61	.	.	.
E	36.74	38.64	19.11 [3]	19.05	20.09	20.03	20.12	.	.	.
F	27.41	29.20	15.30 [3]	15.18	14.97	15.96	15.97	.	.	.
G	22.31	23.18	11.34 [3]	11.75	12.26	12.25	12.76	.	.	.
H	21.19	21.94	10.60 [3]	10.85	11.15	11.19	11.60	.	.	.
I	27.89	28.25	13.70 [3]	14.21	14.74	15.02	15.14	.	.	.
J	29.88	32.40	16.05 [3]	17.08	17.78	18.14	18.81	.	.	.
K	25.73	28.18	13.91 [3]	14.52	15.03	15.48	15.49	.	.	.
L	34.67	36.20	17.34 [3]	18.08	18.68	19.09	19.73	.	.	.
M	35.67	37.15	18.00 [3]	18.64	19.08	19.28	19.62	.	.	.
N	30.01	31.40	15.18 [3]	16.03	16.25	16.45	16.93	.	.	.
O	27.84	28.90	13.88 [3]	14.24	15.08	15.59	15.71	.	.	.

Netherlands (DA) [1] [2] [4]   Employees - Salariés - Asalariados   E.G./m. - Euro

Total men and women - Total hommes et femmes - Total hombres y mujeres
ISIC 3 - CITI 3 - CIIU 3

	1999	2000	2001	2002	2003	2004	2005	2006	2007	2008
Total	5 028	5 220	2 517 [3]	2 623	2 712	2 792	2 836	.	.	.
A-B	.	.	2 041 [3]	2 040	2 150	2 264	2 197	.	.	.
C-Q	5 044	5 236	2 524 [3]	2 632	2 721	2 800	2 846	.	.	.
C	7 230	7 680	3 697 [3]	3 957	4 052	4 241	4 413	.	.	.
D	4 797	4 958	2 392 [3]	2 487	2 572	2 637	2 689	.	.	.
E	6 171	6 427	3 162 [3]	3 244	3 411	3 459	3 530	.	.	.
F	4 658	4 802	2 348 [3]	2 440	2 501	2 598	2 627	.	.	.
G	4 549	4 684	2 230 [3]	2 336	2 419	2 487	2 523	.	.	.
H	3 816	3 792	1 815 [3]	1 856	1 927	1 962	2 018	.	.	.
I	4 824	4 937	2 370 [3]	2 418	2 498	2 582	2 575	.	.	.
J	5 817	6 257	3 059 [3]	3 266	3 370	3 495	3 613	.	.	.
K	5 623	5 905	2 811 [3]	2 926	3 031	3 142	3 164	.	.	.
L	5 573	5 776	2 782 [3]	2 877	2 953	2 994	3 058	.	.	.
M	5 853	6 029	2 978 [3]	3 076	3 166	3 182	3 221	.	.	.
N	5 060	5 285	2 556 [3]	2 688	2 794	2 884	2 972	.	.	.
O	4 847	5 018	2 378 [3]	2 537	2 641	2 654	2 773	.	.	.

Men - Hommes - Hombres
ISIC 3 - CITI 3 - CIIU 3

	1999	2000	2001	2002	2003	2004	2005	2006	2007	2008
Total	5 276	5 481	2 634 [3]	2 737	2 926	2 904	2 944	.	.	.
A-B	.	.	2 069 [3]	2 082	2 188	2 306	2 248	.	.	.
C-Q	5 296	5 502	2 644 [3]	2 749	2 837	2 914	2 956	.	.	.
C	7 387	7 834	3 772 [3]	4 034	4 130	4 336	4 508	.	.	.
D	4 932	5 099	2 458 [3]	2 549	2 634	2 692	2 740	.	.	.
E	6 247	6 504	3 200 [3]	3 287	3 458	3 514	3 620	.	.	.
F	4 684	4 827	2 353 [3]	2 448	2 515	2 610	2 637	.	.	.
G	4 886	5 058	2 389 [3]	2 490	2 568	2 642	2 676	.	.	.
H	4 019	4 004	1 946 [3]	1 978	1 989	2 060	2 118	.	.	.
I	4 962	5 089	2 437 [3]	2 476	2 555	2 643	2 630	.	.	.
J	6 603	7 064	3 417 [3]	3 609	3 701	3 828	3 955	.	.	.
K	6 046	6 339	2 992 [3]	3 114	3 231	3 325	3 352	.	.	.
L	5 776	5 983	2 884 [3]	2 978	3 050	3 087	3 145	.	.	.
M	6 233	6 490	3 199 [3]	3 303	3 400	3 410	3 444	.	.	.
N	5 998	6 330	3 046 [3]	3 189	3 298	3 389	3 471	.	.	.
O	5 135	5 306	2 500 [3]	2 681	2 777	2 760	2 913	.	.	.

Women - Femmes - Mujeres
ISIC 3 - CITI 3 - CIIU 3

	1999	2000	2001	2002	2003	2004	2005	2006	2007	2008
Total	4 102	4 287	2 094 [3]	2 201	2 290	2 373	2 429	.	.	.
A-B	.	.	1 781 [3]	1 675	1 769	1 833	1 726	.	.	.
C-Q	4 109	4 293	2 096 [3]	2 205	2 293	2 376	2 434	.	.	.
C	.	.	2 834 [3]	3 065	3 278	3 254	.	.	.	.
D	3 870	4 001	1 944 [3]	2 039	2 123	2 221	2 282	.	.	.
E	5 175	5 451	2 691 [3]	2 749	2 901	2 865	2 862	.	.	.
F	3 859	4 112	2 219 [3]	2 215	2 110	2 245	2 322	.	.	.
G	3 504	3 590	1 738 [3]	1 832	1 914	1 955	1 994	.	.	.
H	3 377	3 374	1 589 [3]	1 617	1 792	1 762	1 799	.	.	.
I	4 040	4 131	2 007 [3]	2 082	2 149	2 207	2 237	.	.	.
J	4 222	4 577	2 262 [3]	2 432	2 535	2 631	2 737	.	.	.
K	4 314	4 612	2 232 [3]	2 315	2 375	2 529	2 536	.	.	.
L	4 744	4 942	2 392 [3]	2 502	2 589	2 649	2 738	.	.	.
M	4 964	5 154	2 554 [3]	2 655	2 737	2 769	2 824	.	.	.
N	4 202	4 396	2 138 [3]	2 250	2 342	2 420	2 519	.	.	.
O	4 182	4 386	2 093 [3]	2 178	2 306	2 391	2 440	.	.	.

Explanatory notes: see p. 877.

[1] Excl. overtime payments. [2] Dec. of each year. [3] Prior to 2001: NLG; 1 Euro = 2.20371 NLG. [4] Full-time employees only.

Notes explicatives: voir p. 879.

[1] Non compris la rémunération des heures supplémentaires. [2] Déc. de chaque année. [3] Avant 2001: NLG; 1 Euro = 2,20371 NLG. [4] Salariés à plein temps seulement.

Notas explicativas: véase p. 882.

[1] Excl. los pagos por horas extraordinarias. [2] Dic. de cada año. [3] Antes de 2001: NLG; 1 Euro = 2,20371 NLG. [4] Asalariados a tiempo completo solamente.

WAGES	SALAIRES	SALARIOS
By economic activity	Par activité économique	Por actividad económica

Norway (DA) [1,2] — Employees - Salariés - Asalariados — E.G./m. - Krone

Total men and women - Total hommes et femmes - Total hombres y mujeres
ISIC 3 - CITI 3 - CIIU 3

	1999	2000	2001	2002	2003	2004	2005	2006	2007	2008
C-Q	23 176	24 404	25 364	27 586	28 120	29 120	30 127	31 559	33 394	35 401
B				24 572	25 283	26 129	27 334	29 585	31 439	33 643
C	33 483	35 376	38 248	40 429	41 424	42 929	43 908	46 882	50 076	52 137
D	22 441	23 388	24 426	25 991	26 944	27 920	28 908	30 162	31 983	33 977
E	22 595	23 714	25 103	27 969	29 863	31 812	33 079	34 492	38 222	41 079
F	22 211	23 182	24 252	25 702	26 100	27 017	28 056	29 211	30 957	32 783
G	22 595	23 922	25 091	26 376	27 254	28 088	29 318	30 792	32 351	33 528
H			19 802	20 872	21 734	22 403	23 008	23 750	24 811	25 932
I	23 377	24 498	25 655	26 871	27 594	28 398	29 563	31 201	32 844	35 113
J	27 227	28 687	31 459	33 285	34 262	35 673	38 656	41 448	44 013	48 774
K	27 613	29 027	30 412	32 013	33 207	33 748	34 593	35 844	37 718	39 462
L	21 932	23 313	24 310	26 124	27 006	28 099	28 849	30 206	31 764	33 981
M [3]	23 266	24 063	25 445	26 894	27 847	28 999	30 075	30 851	32 297	34 395
N	19 945	20 784	21 740	22 874	24 111	24 732	25 644	26 606	28 148	29 622
O	23 938	25 211	26 264	28 102	28 905	29 964	31 014	32 393	34 254	35 997

Men - Hommes - Hombres
ISIC 3 - CITI 3 - CIIU 3

	1999	2000	2001	2002	2003	2004	2005	2006	2007	2008
C-Q	24 393	25 678	26 937	28 741	29 512	30 524	31 567	33 059	35 035	37 051
B				25 158	25 578	26 370	27 538	29 825	31 700	34 010
C	34 696	36 612	39 588	41 297	42 208	43 980	44 916	47 816	50 920	53 171
D	23 039	23 964	25 006	26 623	27 625	28 588	29 513	30 767	32 710	34 638
E	22 908	24 021	25 450	28 341	30 377	32 398	33 524	35 189	38 890	41 895
F	22 307	23 248	24 314	25 782	26 147	27 049	28 081	29 220	30 986	32 786
G	23 926	25 347	26 464	27 652	28 542	29 363	30 683	32 234	34 097	35 148
H	17 837	18 503	21 072	22 155	23 189	23 712	24 493	25 179	26 344	27 352
I	24 310	25 381	26 536	27 670	28 402	29 175	30 300	31 957	33 695	35 974
J	30 756	32 489	35 920	37 902	39 070	40 631	44 303	48 136	51 456	57 817
K	30 016	31 587	33 034	34 583	35 698	36 045	36 962	38 232	40 333	42 031
L	23 271	24 906	25 972	27 807	28 844	29 970	30 788	32 236	33 820	36 211
M [3]	24 979	25 751	27 384	28 640	29 459	30 782	31 910	32 673	33 820	36 880
N	21 991	23 148	23 774	25 425	26 899	27 920	28 924	30 149	34 599	33 372
O	25 425	26 937	27 820	29 799	30 556	31 699	32 630	34 181	36 465	38 085

Women - Femmes - Mujeres
ISIC 3 - CITI 3 - CIIU 3

	1999	2000	2001	2002	2003	2004	2005	2006	2007	2008
C-Q	20 788	21 951	23 134	24 508	25 429	26 445	27 397	28 691	30 306	32 282
B				21 709	23 508	24 296	25 853	27 925	29 655	31 622
C	27 883	29 387	32 190	35 777	37 498	38 260	39 380	42 589	46 303	47 663
D	20 017	21 091	22 051	23 483	24 260	25 290	26 432	27 649	29 124	31 301
E	20 709	21 589	22 768	26 952	26 952	28 829	30 663	31 794	35 461	37 917
F	20 564	21 911	23 032	24 177	25 175	26 359	27 556	29 050	30 419	32 724
G	19 607	20 659	21 905	23 116	24 105	24 983	25 842	27 204	28 319	29 868
H	16 659	17 291	18 711	19 832	20 459	21 326	21 816	22 581	23 525	24 742
I	20 905	22 031	22 977	24 380	25 015	25 958	27 268	28 685	30 136	32 149
J	23 131	24 403	26 271	27 809	28 463	29 782	31 855	33 435	35 291	38 295
K	23 060	24 202	25 608	26 998	28 067	28 702	29 581	30 877	32 628	34 364
L	20 673	21 934	22 911	24 717	25 523	26 633	27 379	28 712	30 282	32 423
M [3]	21 278	22 110	23 108	24 761	25 890	27 066	28 137	28 768	30 178	32 057
N	19 028	19 686	20 777	21 679	22 931	23 450	24 362	25 273	26 672	28 207
O	21 968	22 930	24 232	25 756	26 622	27 638	28 885	30 085	31 505	33 413

Poland (DA) [4] — Employees - Salariés - Asalariados — E.G./m. - Zloty

Total men and women - Total hommes et femmes - Total hombres y mujeres
ISIC 3 - CITI 3 - CIIU 3

	1999	2000	2001	2002	2003	2004	2005	2006	2007	2008
Total	1 697.10	1 893.70	2 045.10	2 097.83	2 185.02	2 273.44	2 360.62	2 475.88	2 672.58	2 943.88
A-B	1 542.19	1 688.95	1 863.67	1 936.00	1 969.12	2 112.58				
C-Q	1 699.50	1 896.80	2 047.90	2 099.91	2 187.61	2 275.27	2 362.30	2 477.20	2 682.12	2 939.77
A	1 553.98	1 711.82	1 861.35	1 958.87	1 983.38	2 133.76	2 345.01	2 377.31	2 593.94	2 880.76
B	1 350.55	1 355.23	1 428.16	1 452.46	1 650.13	1 612.17	1 773.07	1 796.87	1 921.30	2 034.71
C	2 944.23	3 210.05	3 509.34	3 693.14	3 767.69	4 062.42	4 347.13	4 570.24	4 882.55	5 409.98
D	1 598.89	1 756.43	1 866.51	1 911.52	1 980.73	2 053.65	2 123.63	2 245.95	2 450.66	2 679.87
E	2 304.81	2 562.91	2 792.18	2 909.40	2 999.87	3 145.20	3 284.83	3 451.37	3 737.19	4 126.87
F	1 558.25	1 705.82	1 745.39	1 760.48	1 810.14	1 844.57	1 906.52	2 041.17	2 252.10	2 501.14
G	1 472.99	1 589.92	1 722.71	1 726.66	1 831.34	1 874.68	1 921.89	2 014.17	2 193.53	2 400.58
H	1 208.79	1 301.49	1 354.89	1 370.84	1 457.12	1 473.04	1 512.58	1 559.26	1 660.94	1 816.81
I	1 886.35	2 144.35	2 348.28	2 458.58	2 481.31	2 539.88	2 591.93	2 650.03	2 803.28	3 104.21
J	2 689.68	3 257.70	3 644.16	3 818.14	3 916.37	4 096.58	4 244.57	4 474.46	4 882.36	5 117.19
K	1 890.22	2 133.36	2 322.52	2 230.53	2 279.12	2 363.87	2 483.81	2 612.61	2 834.24	3 103.30
L	2 180.08	2 432.44	2 639.36	2 717.51	2 788.12	2 926.05	3 060.70	3 214.66	3 368.99	3 794.04
M	1 530.26	1 835.03	1 982.37	2 072.85	2 195.17	2 348.96	2 471.02	2 573.12	2 711.88	2 965.39
N	1 341.05	1 479.88	1 641.82	1 717.22	1 804.31	1 866.15	1 954.12	2 101.82	2 463.50	2 868.25
O	1 700.84	1 891.52	1 901.07	1 891.73	2 165.41	2 218.59	2 294.91	2 385.28	2 506.74	2 749.52

Explanatory notes: see p. 877.

[1] Only remuneration in cash; excl. overtime payments. [2] Full-time employees. [3] Private education. [4] Incl. the value of payments in kind.

Notes explicatives: voir p. 879.

[1] Seulement rémunération en espèces; non compris les paiements pour heures supplémentaires. [2] Salariés à plein temps. [3] Enseignement privé. [4] Y compris la valeur des paiements en nature.

Notas explicativas: véase p. 882.

[1] Sólo remuneración en efectivo; excl. los pagos por horas extraordinarias. [2] Asalariados a tiempo completo. [3] Enseñanza privada. [4] Incl. el valor de los pagos en especie.

	1999	2000	2001	2002	2003	2004	2005	2006	2007	2008

Portugal (DA) — Employees - Salariés - Asalariados — E.G./m. - Euro

Total men and women - Total hommes et femmes - Total hombres y mujeres
ISIC 3 - CITI 3 - CIIU 3

C-Q										
C	152 498	157 211	159 514	862 [1]	890	914	921	913	975	1 020
D	122 327	126 923	133 939	705 [1]	775	806	837	868	893	932
E	236 604	246 604	263 145	1 387 [1]	1 283	1 334	1 410	1 496	1 603	1 690
F	119 270	129 923	141 675	743 [1]	733	763	798	836	879	914
G	136 156	138 666	146 040	762 [1]	821	854	902	938	949	982
H	93 858	97 768	103 089	530 [1]	592	612	636	651	666	689
I	206 416	224 071	239 605	1 244 [1]	1 354	1 388	1 446	1 489	1 539	1 628
J	302 402	316 583	336 185	1 688 [1]	1 821	1 888	1 938	2 025	2 088	2 171
K	173 365	174 469	177 540	949 [1]	1 094	1 154	1 210	1 262	1 305	1 331
L										
M	145 694	160 455	143 215	979 [1]	1 038	1 062	1 066	1 098	1 157	1 189
N	116 647	121 310	148 636	660 [1]	728	741	778	824	866	898
O	172 651	170 443	152 779	908 [1]	1 065	1 117	1 137	1 183	1 233	1 270

Men - Hommes - Hombres
ISIC 3 - CITI 3 - CIIU 3

C-Q										
C	152 327	157 041	159 717	865 [1]	895	913	919	909	975	1 019
D	146 138	151 422	159 822	840 [1]	905	934	968	1 003	1 026	1 065
E	238 278	249 517	265 971	1 401 [1]	1 287	1 333	1 411	1 512	1 616	1 706
F	118 839	129 106	140 736	738 [1]	730	755	792	832	874	902
G	151 164	152 204	161 777	841 [1]	918	949	1 005	1 038	1 051	1 078
H	105 457	110 698	116 718	604 [1]	693	724	741	779	795	821
I	205 415	222 723	238 853	1 246 [1]	1 360	1 397	1 463	1 507	1 554	1 645
J	329 202	348 821	371 711	1 868 [1]	2 017	2 113	2 170	2 265	2 342	2 437
K	206 696	204 440	198 102	1 048 [1]	1 297	1 323	1 379	1 433	1 503	1 521
L										
M	179 920	191 654	156 956	1 103 [1]	1 219	1 277	1 288	1 317	1 382	1 400
N	164 540	162 520	186 942	934 [1]	1 125	1 020	1 093	1 163	1 243	1 269
O	223 635	226 362	201 400	1 212 [1]	1 366	1 450	1 487	1 535	1 608	1 663

Women - Femmes - Mujeres
ISIC 3 - CITI 3 - CIIU 3

C-Q										
C	154 289	158 764	157 735	843 [1]	849	940	946	951	973	1 022
D	94 057	98 574	103 835	547 [1]	596	622	648	672	696	729
E	227 752	232 111	248 899	1 316 [1]	1 264	1 340	1 403	1 417	1 542	1 608
F	124 563	139 627	152 841	803 [1]	.	836	843	869	928	980
G	111 551	116 758	121 954	640 [1]	688	726	762	791	810	849
H	85 316	87 719	92 382	472 [1]	520	527	550	562	583	607
I	210 560	229 206	242 312	1 235 [1]	1 335	1 361	1 399	1 439	1 494	1 575
J	254 218	263 369	282 878	1 442 [1]	1 517	1 554	1 599	1 675	1 792	1 871
K	138 762	143 893	151 831	829 [1]	884	943	991	1 044	1 047	1 072
L										
M	134 186	149 143	135 863	934 [1]	966	987	990	1 025	1 077	1 114
N	110 705	115 430	141 004	628 [1]	673	698	732	769	804	841
O	130 568	127 564	128 191	680 [1]	800	845	888	931	952	963

Portugal (DA) — Wage earners - Ouvriers - Obreros — E.G./h. - Euro

Total men and women - Total hommes et femmes - Total hombres y mujeres
ISIC 3 - CITI 3 - CIIU 3

C	.	808.00	846.00	450.00	4.43 [2]	4.67	4.66	4.52	4.84	5.07
D	.	620.00	673.00	375.00	3.67 [2]	3.83	3.88	3.98	4.08	4.25
E	.	1 382.00	1 345.00	644.00	6.38 [2]	6.63	6.83	7.42	7.70	8.16
F	.	624.00	666.00	363.00	3.61 [2]	3.66	3.72	3.94	4.10	4.29
G	.	649.00	706.00	395.00	3.91 [2]	4.02	4.09	4.15	4.31	4.38
H	.	555.00	613.00	349.00	3.53 [2]	3.50	3.74	3.78	3.99	4.04
I	.	1 100.00	1 125.00	580.00	5.74 [2]	5.82	5.82	5.74	6.19	6.20
J	.	1 519.00	1 640.00	909.00	9.17 [2]	9.15	10.11	10.19	10.69	11.49
K	.	639.00	736.00	440.00	4.22 [2]	4.47	4.53	4.57	4.34	4.66
M	.	576.00	653.00	383.00	3.78 [2]	3.90	4.00	4.23	4.22	4.69
N	.	549.00	601.00	338.00	3.41 [2]	3.39	3.58	3.59	3.71	3.84
O	.	838.00	861.00	446.00	4.42 [2]	4.64	5.04	5.15	4.46	5.07

Men - Hommes - Hombres
ISIC 3 - CITI 3 - CIIU 3

C	.	816.00	854.00	454.00	4.46 [2]	4.71	4.68	4.55	4.87	5.11
D	.	731.00	784.00	430.00	4.22 [2]	4.39	4.46	4.58	4.65	4.82
E	.	1 389.00	1 351.00	645.00	6.39 [2]	6.64	7.10	7.44	7.71	8.17
F	.	625.00	666.00	363.00	3.61 [2]	3.66	3.71	3.94	4.11	4.29
G	.	684.00	747.00	420.00	4.15 [2]	4.25	4.30	4.35	4.52	4.56
H	.	608.00	697.00	414.00	4.21 [2]	4.12	4.19	4.39	4.61	4.79
I	.	1 105.00	1 130.00	583.00	5.77 [2]	5.84	5.84	5.74	6.21	6.22
J	.	1 694.00	1 795.00	971.00	9.91 [2]	9.76	11.05	11.00	11.38	12.20
K	.	694.00	789.00	464.00	4.54 [2]	4.65	4.74	4.92	4.74	4.94
M	.	643.00	765.00	473.00	4.60 [2]	5.05	5.02	4.73	5.08	4.94
N	.	649.00	697.00	384.00	4.03 [2]	3.75	3.96	4.02	4.19	4.37
O	.	1 074.00	1 032.00	484.00	4.90 [2]	5.21	5.79	5.96	5.11	5.58

Explanatory notes: see p. 877.   Notes explicatives: voir p. 879.   Notas explicativas: véase p. 882.

[1] Prior to 2002: PTE; 1 Euro= 200.482 PTE. [2] Prior to 2003: PTE; 1 Euro= 200.482 PTE.   [1] Avant 2002: PTE; 1 Euro= 200.482 PTE. [2] Avant 2003: PTE; 1 Euro= 200.482 PTE.   [1] Antes de 2002: PTE; 1 Euro= 200.482 PTE. [2] Antes de 2003: PTE; 1 Euro= 200.482 PTE.

5A

WAGES	SALAIRES	SALARIOS
By economic activity	Par activité économique	Por actividad económica

	1999	2000	2001	2002	2003	2004	2005	2006	2007	2008

Portugal (DA) — Wage earners - Ouvriers - Obreros — E.G./h. - Euro

Women - Femmes - Mujeres
ISIC 3 - CITI 3 - CIIU 3

	1999	2000	2001	2002	2003	2004	2005	2006	2007	2008
C	.	650.00	637.00	308.00	3.20	3.43	3.78	3.41	3.97	3.97
D	.	500.00	536.00	294.00	2.89	3.00	3.02	3.09	3.19	3.33
E	.	925.00	1 003.00	558.00	5.60	5.52	5.61	6.21	7.11	7.20
F	.	543.00	614.00	358.00	3.09	3.72	3.14	3.11	3.22	3.52
G	.	522.00	558.00	305.00	2.96	3.14	3.25	3.23	3.23	3.37
H	.	512.00	551.00	303.00	3.03	3.09	3.34	3.23	3.54	3.50
I	.	913.00	960.00	513.00	4.98	5.41	5.53	5.54	5.78	5.74
J	.	1 135.00	1 240.00	696.00	7.10	6.77	7.25	8.00	8.41	9.24
K	.	537.00	612.00	360.00	3.23	3.73	3.67	3.23	3.10	3.49
M	.	549.00	614.00	354.00	3.46	3.68	3.78	4.10	4.06	4.64
N	.	535.00	583.00	325.00	3.24	3.30	3.50	3.49	3.52	3.69
O	.	580.00	645.00	370.00	3.57	3.39	3.49	3.49	3.27	3.62

Roumanie (DA) — Employees - Salariés - Asalariados — E.G./m. - Leu

Total men and women - Total hommes et femmes - Total hombres y mujeres
ISIC 3 - CITI 3 - CIIU 3

	1999	2000	2001	2002	2003	2004	2005	2006	2007	2008
Total	1 921 754	2 840 449	4 220 357	5 320 559	6 637 868	8 183 317	968 [2]	1 146	1 396	.
A-B	1 495 929	2 068 006	3 035 646	3 829 075	4 902 186	6 283 470	670 [2]	802	983	
C-Q	1 944 731	2 875 155	4 271 421	5 375 086	6 698 273	8 247 396	978 [2]	1 156	1 407	
A	1 500 933	2 073 607	3 038 632	3 840 409	4 919 793	6 306 044	673 [2]	805	987	
B	1 165 022	1 668 773	2 792 973	3 099 076	3 905 880	4 913 670	509 [2]	647	771	
C	3 107 090	4 929 204	7 551 094	9 549 382	11 569 478	13 635 993	1 659 [2]	2 024	2 469	
D	1 712 748	2 535 223	3 734 701	4 632 583	5 804 147	7 196 971	829 [2]	950	1 146	
E	3 242 415	4 680 032	7 079 013	8 502 781	10 548 925	12 475 737	1 537 [2]	1 801	2 141	
F	1 734 648	2 383 968	3 550 631	4 443 484	5 659 688	7 006 512	814 [2]	936	1 180	
G	1 312 790	1 980 792	3 069 603	3 774 878	4 948 992	5 924 848	748 [2]	862	1 104	
H	1 118 890	1 764 833	2 871 275	3 349 208	4 275 387	5 375 749	583 [2]	693	861	
I	2 598 086	3 899 789	5 956 865	7 763 485	9 491 978	11 215 201	1 243 [2]	1 420	1 680	
J	5 872 067	8 211 322	11 949 723	15 926 966	19 937 440	25 097 516	2 789 [2]	3 078	3 575	
K	1 934 730	2 976 181	4 288 709	5 494 962	6 544 102	8 138 102	940 [2]	1 102	1 486	
L	2 708 414	4 174 866	5 911 602	7 300 538	9 902 913	12 039 545	1 538 [2]	2 112	2 681	
M	1 740 196	2 705 154	3 966 768	5 309 849	6 566 394	8 940 044	1 110 [2]	1 443	1 601	
N	1 850 581	2 287 269	3 592 630	4 378 503	5 550 256	6 955 768	869 [2]	1 085	1 265	
O	1 672 886	2 542 210	3 599 274	4 830 549	5 880 895	7 333 822	863 [2]	985	1 177	
Q										

Men - Hommes - Hombres
ISIC 3 - CITI 3 - CIIU 3

	1999	2000	2001	2002	2003	2004	2005	2006	2007	2008
Total	.	.	.	.	7 273 615	8 859 646	1 037 [2]	1 222	1 468	.
A-B					4 979 275	6 288 298	680 [2]	807	986	
C-Q					7 388 966	8 978 382	1 054 [2]	1 240	1 487	
A					5 002 132	6 319 364	684 [2]	811	981	
B					3 836 550	4 761 001	500 [2]	635	753	
C					11 810 981	13 888 744	1 679 [2]	2 045	2 491	
D					6 662 800	8 167 249	945 [2]	1 087	1 302	
E					10 976 047	12 896 439	1 573 [2]	1 832	2 157	
F					5 625 554	6 956 726	809 [2]	931	1 166	
G					5 711 254	6 872 959	860 [2]	1 002	1 230	
H					4 847 639	6 242 370	650 [2]	767	943	
I					9 428 550	11 176 732	1 255 [2]	1 464	1 689	
J					23 651 321	28 116 855	3 140 [2]	3 581	4 003	
K					6 387 003	7 766 185	911 [2]	1 060	1 433	
L					10 392 064	12 238 094	1 566 [2]	2 125	2 538	
M					7 288 344	10 229 068	1 222 [2]	1 616	1 840	
N					6 420 125	8 021 523	980 [2]	1 264	1 509	
O					6 220 280	7 818 984	912 [2]	1 043	1 282	
Q										

Women - Femmes - Mujeres
ISIC 3 - CITI 3 - CIIU 3

	1999	2000	2001	2002	2003	2004	2005	2006	2007	2008
Total	.	.	.	.	5 906 760	7 433 008	891 [2]	1 062	1 312	.
A-B					4 656 252	6 271 564	642 [2]	787	972	
C-Q					5 928 721	7 456 541	895 [2]	1 066	1 317	
A					4 659 607	6 273 628	643 [2]	788	973	
B					4 330 895	5 980 293	568 [2]	705	879	
C					10 126 216	12 155 410	1 549 [2]	1 904	2 340	
D					4 915 058	6 203 325	710 [2]	807	976	
E					9 323 768	11 276 133	1 432 [2]	1 711	2 093	
F					5 891 209	7 356 692	843 [2]	966	1 280	
G					4 258 129	5 132 423	646 [2]	737	979	
H					3 952 634	4 923 557	548 [2]	649	811	
I					9 653 448	11 311 996	1 213 [2]	1 312	1 659	
J					18 022 768	23 661 166	2 628 [2]	2 846	3 380	
K					6 849 930	8 856 435	992 [2]	1 177	1 580	
L					9 558 296	11 899 804	1 518 [2]	2 103	2 795	
M					6 246 092	8 357 928	1 058 [2]	1 363	1 493	
N					5 282 947	6 671 798	839 [2]	1 036	1 198	
O					5 492 964	6 786 894	806 [2]	920	1 057	
Q										

Explanatory notes: see p. 877.
[1] Prior to 2003: PTE; 1 Euro= 200.482 PTE. [2] New denomination: 1 leu = 10 000 old lei.

Notes explicatives: voir p. 879.
[1] Avant 2003: PTE; 1 Euro= 200,482 PTE. [2] Nouvelle dénomination: 1 leu = 10 000 anciens lei.

Notas explicativas: véase p. 882.
[1] Antes de 2003: PTE; 1 Euro= 200,482 PTE. [2] Nueva denominación: 1 leu = 10 000 antiguos lei.

	1999	2000	2001	2002	2003	2004	2005	2006	2007	2008

Russian Federation (DA) — Employees - Salariés - Asalariados — E.G./m. - Rouble

Total men and women - Total hommes et femmes - Total hombres y mujeres
ISIC 3 - CITI 3 - CIIU 3

	1999	2000	2001	2002	2003	2004	2005	2006	2007	2008
Total	.	.	.	.	.	.	8 555	10 634	13 593	17 290
A-B	.	.	.	.	.	.	3 839	4 820	6 441	8 056
C-Q	.	.	.	.	.	.	8 907	11 010	13 997	33 204
A	.	.	.	.	.	.	3 646	4 569	6 144	8 475
B	.	.	.	.	.	.	10 234	12 311	14 797	19 499
C	.	.	.	.	.	.	19 727	23 145	28 108	33 206
D	.	.	.	.	.	.	8 421	10 199	12 879	16 050
E	.	.	.	.	.	.	10 637	12 828	15 587	19 057
F	.	.	.	.	.	.	9 043	10 869	14 333	18 574
G	.	.	.	.	.	.	6 552	8 235	11 476	14 927
H	.	.	.	.	.	.	6 033	7 522	9 339	11 536
I	.	.	.	.	.	.	11 351	13 390	16 452	20 761
J	.	.	.	.	.	.	22 728	27 886	34 880	41 872
K	.	.	.	.	.	.	10 237	12 763	16 642	21 275
L	.	.	.	.	.	.	10 999	13 477	16 896	21 344
M	.	.	.	.	.	.	5 430	6 983	8 778	11 317
N	.	.	.	.	.	.	5 906	8 060	10 037	13 049
O	.	.	.	.	.	.	6 291	7 996	10 392	13 539
Q	.	.	.	.	.	.	18 922	26 990	30 339	36 083

San Marino (E) — Employees - Salariés - Asalariados — E.G./m. - Euro

Total men and women - Total hommes et femmes - Total hombres y mujeres
ISIC 3 - CITI 3 - CIIU 3

	1999	2000	2001	2002	2003	2004	2005	2006	2007	2008
Total	.	.	3 287 274	1 832 [1]	1 971	1 967	2 035	2 071	.	.
C-Q	.	.	3 288 024	1 832 [1]	1 971	1 968	2 037	2 073	.	.
A	.	.	2 896 760	1 570 [1]	1 471	1 620	1 173	1 325	.	.
D	.	.	3 289 004	1 868 [1]	1 922	1 900	1 934	2 021	.	.
F	.	.	3 407 188	1 840 [1]	1 854	1 868	1 871	1 951	.	.
G	.	.	3 076 946	990 [1]	1 692	1 676	1 765	1 753	.	.
H	.	.	2 616 557	1 335 [1]	1 562	1 867	1 555	1 398	.	.
I	.	.	3 372 942	1 791 [1]	1 785	1 838	1 876	1 911	.	.
J	.	.	5 330 090	3 161 [1]	3 184	3 358	3 386	3 471	.	.
K	.	.					1 716	1 757	.	.
L	.	.		2 251 [1]	2 234	2 219	2 392	2 511	.	.
M	.	.		2 057 [1]	1 976	2 009	1 982	2 037	.	.
N	.	.		2 429 [1]	2 484	2 533	2 511	2 615	.	.
O	.	.	912 666	1 633 [1]	1 548	1 526	1 681	1 701	.	.

Serbia (DA) [2] — Employees - Salariés - Asalariados — E.G./m. - New Dinar

Total men and women - Total hommes et femmes - Total hombres y mujeres
ISIC 3 - CITI 3 - CIIU 3

	1999	2000	2001	2002	2003	2004	2005	2006	2007	2008
Total	.	.	.	.	16 612	20 555	25 514	31 745	38 744	45 674
A	.	.	.	.	13 129	15 569	20 301	25 951	29 680	37 204
B	.	.	.	.	15 378	17 840	24 085	23 724	21 699	29 113
C	.	.	.	.	22 091	26 352	30 745	38 992	48 978	55 835
D	.	.	.	.	12 996	16 065	20 366	25 830	30 620	36 540
E	.	.	.	.	23 778	29 426	35 590	42 488	53 128	57 886
F	.	.	.	.	15 175	18 443	22 389	28 219	34 944	42 271
G	.	.	.	.	13 704	17 444	22 621	28 926	34 685	42 367
H	.	.	.	.	11 689	14 037	17 665	21 516	25 844	30 234
I	.	.	.	.	20 113	24 561	29 737	36 029	41 568	48 758
J	.	.	.	.	34 601	43 870	56 348	70 864	82 041	91 023
K	.	.	.	.	20 251	24 730	32 076	37 039	47 154	52 116
L	.	.	.	.	22 742	27 207	33 210	40 542	47 728	54 273
M	.	.	.	.	1 823	21 688	27 265	33 166	40 286	48 299
N	.	.	.	.	18 817	23 064	26 792	32 790	42 900	48 864
O	.	.	.	.	19 707	24 191	28 846	33 866	38 641	44 281

Slovakia (CA) [3] — Employees - Salariés - Asalariados — E.G./m. - Koruna

Total men and women - Total hommes et femmes - Total hombres y mujeres
ISIC 3 - CITI 3 - CIIU 3

	1999	2000	2001	2002	2003	2004	2005	2006	2007	2008
Total	10 728	11 430	12 365	13 511	14 365	15 825	17 274	18 761	20 146	21 782
A-B	8 380	9 020	9 750	10 413	10 942	12 211	13 163	14 294	15 766	17 169
A			.	10 410	10 940	12 210	13 162	14 292	15 763	17 167
C	11 988	13 361	14 470	15 595	16 251	17 700	18 923	20 081	22 219	25 066
D	10 758	11 722	12 908	13 837	14 873	16 378	17 604	18 817	20 024	21 449
E	14 349	15 967	17 984	19 516	21 061	23 911	26 009	27 727	29 769	31 834
F	9 899	10 541	11 047	11 547	12 001	13 083	13 867	14 558	15 561	16 753
G	11 530	12 660	13 394	14 117	14 641	16 182	17 525	18 822	20 035	21 998
H	8 804	9 491	10 096	10 982	11 808	12 342	13 280	14 170	15 045	15 481
I	11 563	12 455	13 626	14 553	15 300	16 900	18 340	19 532	21 270	22 419
J	19 955	22 150	24 409	27 094	29 088	33 064	34 950	38 305	40 871	42 342
K	13 108	14 095	15 547	17 102	17 940	19 698	21 550	23 770	25 129	27 441
L	13 052	13 780	14 662	16 509	17 508	19 240	21 049	23 953	25 637	27 887
M	8 400	8 990	9 450	10 934	11 984	12 895	14 224	15 439	16 632	18 043
N	9 100	9 318	10 380	12 020	12 430	12 865	13 946	15 130	17 540	19 627
O	9 423	8 283	8 879	10 220	11 120	12 310	13 344	14 171	15 442	16 909

Explanatory notes: see p. 877. — Notes explicatives: voir p. 879. — Notas explicativas: véase p. 882.

[1] Prior to 2002: ITL; 1 Euro=1936.27 ITL. [2] Excl. Kosovo and Metohia. [3] Excl. enterprises with less than 20 employees.

[1] Avant 2002: ITL; 1 Euro=1936,27 ITL. [2] N.c. Kosovo et Metohia. [3] Non compris les entreprises occupant moins de 20 salariés.

[1] Antes de 2002: ITL; 1 Euro=1936,27 ITL. [2] Excl. Kosovo y Metohia. [3] Excl. las empresas con menos de 20 asalariados.

	WAGES	SALAIRES	SALARIOS
	By economic activity	**Par activité économique**	**Por actividad económica**

	1999	2000	2001	2002	2003	2004	2005	2006	2007	2008

Slovenia (D) — Employees - Salariés - Asalariados — E.G./m. - Euro

Total men and women - Total hommes et femmes - Total hombres y mujeres
ISIC 3 - CITI 3 - CIIU 3

	1999	2000	2001	2002	2003	2004	2005	2006	2007	2008
Total	173 245	191 669	214 561	235 436	253 200	267 571	277 279 [1]	290 635 [1]	1 285 [2]	1 391
A-B	161 212	171 550	185 269	196 453	207 343	217 351	224 099 [1]	236 665 [1]	1 069 [2]	1 161
C-Q	173 405	191 919	214 896	235 869	253 687	268 067	277 793 [1]	291 111 [1]	1 287 [2]	1 393
A	161 367	171 669	185 550	196 299	207 565	217 554	224 225 [1]	236 681 [1]	1 069 [2]	1 163
B	154 290	166 131	172 752	183 110	197 567	207 828	218 670 [1]	236 027 [1]	1 063 [2]	1 103
C	193 169	218 705	248 031	274 202	298 122	326 739	344 670 [1]	360 110 [1]	1 608 [2]	1 826
D	144 110	161 296	178 596	196 220	211 060	226 029	238 985 [1]	252 162 [1]	1 124 [2]	1 208
E	200 429	219 212	250 000	276 788	299 812	324 344	353 836 [1]	373 473 [1]	1 657 [2]	1 805
F	147 510	159 541	173 179	188 882	204 316	218 781	224 794 [1]	238 698 [1]	1 061 [2]	1 141
G	162 907	173 119	189 609	207 040	222 101	237 002	244 880 [1]	258 521 [1]	1 161 [2]	1 251
H	139 145	150 527	165 159	178 073	189 230	200 054	202 895 [1]	211 873 [1]	937 [2]	1 018
I	186 849	208 417	232 483	251 515	272 238	290 603	299 377 [1]	310 080 [1]	1 368 [2]	1 475
J	255 147	279 107	313 370	339 900	370 832	392 954	413 896 [1]	443 595 [1]	1 986 [2]	2 101
K	186 301	207 803	233 439	253 928	273 716	288 965	292 763 [1]	304 295 [1]	1 361 [2]	1 483
L	223 914	244 662	278 826	299 889	321 502	322 912	333 302 [1]	343 572 [1]	1 507 [2]	1 691
M	192 089	220 572	255 222	288 029	309 968	326 002	340 967 [1]	357 301 [1]	1 550 [2]	1 659
N	203 098	224 575	253 131	295 319	308 013	312 423	316 827 [1]	325 245 [1]	1 400 [2]	1 571
O	228 012	245 579	273 443	293 759	307 184	325 541	325 159 [1]	332 137 [1]	1 440 [2]	1 532

Suisse (DA) [3] — Employees - Salariés - Asalariados — E.G./m. - Franc

Total men and women - Total hommes et femmes - Total hombres y mujeres
ISIC 3 - CITI 3 - CIIU 3

	2000	2002	2004	2006
C-Q	5 937	6 184	6 385	6 617
A	4 904	4 494	4 300	4 254
C	5 601	5 933	6 120	6 128
D	5 862	6 155	6 349	6 527
E	7 332	7 485	7 577	7 935
F	5 382	5 665	5 767	5 869
G	5 468	5 517	5 700	5 861
H	3 859	3 968	4 139	4 192
I	5 929	5 989	6 299	6 439
J	8 239	8 816	9 161	10 253
K	7 508	7 525	7 669	7 914
L	7 778	7 757	8 044	8 286
M	7 172	7 286	7 511	7 525
N	5 418	5 765	5 940	6 112
O	5 454	5 716	6 301	6 337

Men - Hommes - Hombres
ISIC 3 - CITI 3 - CIIU 3

	2000	2002	2004	2006
C-Q	6 487	6 773	6 975	7 234
A	5 148	4 629	4 441	4 402
C	5 634	5 992	6 155	6 134
D	6 296	6 552	6 726	6 915
E	7 556	7 703	7 781	8 155
F	5 408	5 697	5 798	5 905
G	6 285	6 364	6 546	6 703
H	4 151	4 249	4 394	4 454
I	6 207	6 232	6 539	6 688
J	9 671	10 235	10 740	12 017
K	8 332	8 461	8 528	8 827
L	8 124	8 013	8 263	8 502
M	7 936	8 002	8 245	8 252
N	6 341	6 687	6 986	7 210
O	6 288	6 632	7 254	7 288

Women - Femmes - Mujeres
ISIC 3 - CITI 3 - CIIU 3

	2000	2002	2004	2006
C-Q	4 844	5 116	5 314	5 517
A	4 095	3 989	3 749	3 674
C	5 246	5 297	5 703	6 061
D	4 550	4 926	5 162	5 353
E	5 729	5 956	6 096	6 437
F	4 983	5 183	5 310	5 354
G	4 370	4 506	4 687	4 863
H	3 560	3 714	3 899	3 951
I	5 132	5 305	5 592	5 698
J	6 166	6 695	6 788	7 483
K	5 829	5 857	6 041	6 242
L	6 599	6 899	7 294	7 580
M	6 275	6 504	6 710	6 765
N	5 110	5 461	5 602	5 755
O	4 577	4 891	5 315	5 397

Explanatory notes: see p. 877.

[1] Beginning 2005, methodology revised: excl. family allowances and the value of payments in kind. [2] Prior to 2007: SIT; 1 Euro = 239.64 SIT. [3] Standardised monthly earnings (40 hours x 4,3 weeks).

Notes explicatives: voir p. 879.

[1] A partir de 2005, méthodologie révisée: non compris les allocations familiales et la valeur des paiments en nature. [2] Avant 2007: SIT; 1 Euro = 239,64 SIT. [3] Gains mensuels standardisés (40 heures x 4,3semaines).

Notas explicativas: véase p. 882.

[1] A partir de 2005: metodología revisada: excl. las asignaciones familiares y el valor de los pagos en especie. [2] Antes de 2007: SIT; 1 Euro = 239,64 SIT. [3] Ganancias medias estandardizadas (40 horas x 4,3 semanas).

By economic activity **Par activité économique** **Por actividad económica**

	1999	2000	2001	2002	2003	2004	2005	2006	2007	2008	

Sweden (DA) [1][2]   Wage earners - Ouvriers - Obreros   E.G./h. - Krona

Total men and women - Total hommes et femmes - Total hombres y mujeres
ISIC 3 - CITI 3 - CIIU 3 [3]   ISIC 4 - CITI 4 - CIIU 4

ISIC3	1999	2000	2001	2002	2003	2004	2005	2006	2007	2008	ISIC4
Total	102.81	106.80	110.90	114.00	118.10	121.80	124.70	128.50	133.80	138.90	Total
A-B	93.47	96.00	100.10	103.50	106.70	111.20	113.30	116.40	123.60	124.90	A
C	123.68	128.60	132.70	138.10	139.80	147.00	151.10	161.60	169.10	173.30	B
D	106.85	111.30	114.90	118.20	122.00	126.10	129.90	133.80	139.50	145.20	C
E	111.66	117.30	124.60	125.10	132.50	134.00	140.80	146.80	154.20	154.00	D
F	112.96	118.00	123.50	128.00	131.30	135.30	137.40	141.30	147.30	143.80	D-E
G	96.34	99.30	104.20	107.50	112.30	116.50	118.90	122.80	129.50	153.00	F
H	85.73	88.70	91.70	95.30	99.20	102.60	104.00	108.50	112.50	132.90	G
I	101.01	106.50	110.30	113.30	118.10	121.80	122.30	128.70	131.90	139.50	H
K	94.36	98.40	104.90	106.00	109.90	112.30	116.50	118.90	121.70	116.80	I
M	95.98	96.70	101.60	103.40	100.90	104.80	108.50	112.00	116.50	144.80	J
N	100.31	101.60	108.10	110.10	113.30	115.90	116.50	119.70	123.10	133.40	L
O	96.00	98.50	100.40	104.20	108.80	.	113.20	116.70	121.30	141.60	M
										126.90	M-N
										124.70	N
										119.00	P
										131.70	Q
										121.00	R
										123.00	R-U
										124.30	S-U

Men - Hommes - Hombres
ISIC 3 - CITI 3 - CIIU 3 [3]   ISIC 4 - CITI 4 - CIIU 4

ISIC3	1999	2000	2001	2002	2003	2004	2005	2006	2007	2008	ISIC4
Total	105.65	110.20	114.20	117.50	121.60	125.50	128.40	132.20	137.40	143.10	Total
A-B	94.82	97.40	101.70	105.30	108.60	112.90	115.00	118.10	126.10	127.30	A
C	124.61	129.60	133.90	139.00	140.90	147.70	151.70	162.10	169.50	173.80	B
D	108.69	113.30	116.90	120.20	124.10	128.40	132.20	136.10	142.10	147.70	C
E	112.41	119.30	128.10	125.60	133.40	134.60	141.10	147.10	154.90	154.20	D
F	113.97	118.30	123.90	128.30	131.60	135.70	137.80	141.60	147.80	144.00	D-E
G	98.45	102.20	106.90	109.80	115.50	119.20	121.60	125.30	131.30	153.70	F
H	87.33	91.50	94.40	98.40	101.70	104.50	106.70	112.10	114.70	135.50	G
I	101.56	107.10	110.80	113.80	118.60	122.50	124.90	129.10	132.60	140.00	H
K	97.97	102.70	108.30	110.20	114.80	118.50	121.00	124.00	124.80	119.50	I
M	99.77	101.90	105.50	105.60	105.60	111.00	112.00	116.00	119.60	146.60	J
N	103.97	104.90	105.50	109.40	114.70	114.40	117.90	120.30	124.10	135.70	L
O	99.53	100.70	102.70	106.70	111.80	115.40	114.70	119.30	123.60	146.10	M
										131.50	M-N
										129.20	N
										125.00	P
										132.60	Q
										121.90	R
										123.50	R-U
										125.00	S-U

Women - Femmes - Mujeres
ISIC 3 - CITI 3 - CIIU 3 [3]   ISIC 4 - CITI 4 - CIIU 4

ISIC3	1999	2000	2001	2002	2003	2004	2005	2006	2007	2008	ISIC4
Total	93.98	96.80	100.90	103.70	107.30	110.80	113.50	117.30	123.00	127.40	Total
A-B	85.07	88.50	91.70	94.20	97.00	102.90	105.00	107.90	113.40	115.80	A
C	94.66	108.60	113.20	121.80	122.10	135.20	140.70	156.10	164.80	168.20	B
D	99.56	103.40	106.60	109.40	112.90	116.80	119.90	124.10	128.60	134.40	C
E	94.05	101.80	108.50	114.40	122.90	122.00	133.50	.	135.20	148.30	D
F	88.87	96.50	100.80	104.40	113.40	111.60	111.40	119.50	125.10	136.90	D-E
G	93.37	95.50	100.70	104.30	108.00	112.60	115.10	119.60	127.10	120.70	F
H	84.54	86.90	90.10	93.40	97.60	101.30	102.30	105.70	110.80	129.90	G
I	95.50	100.60	105.30	108.50	112.20	114.60	118.80	124.00	125.50	134.50	H
K	86.69	90.90	96.70	97.60	100.40	99.60	105.90	107.70	114.20	115.00	I
M	93.69	94.00	99.50	101.90	98.50	102.10	107.10	110.20	115.10	140.20	J
N	98.74	100.50	108.90	110.30	112.80	116.40	116.00	119.50	122.80	122.80	L
O	91.46	95.10	97.00	100.40	104.70	108.30	110.50	112.60	118.10	132.90	M
										118.90	M-N
										116.90	N
										116.80	P
										131.40	Q
										119.50	R
										122.30	R-U
										123.70	S-U

Explanatory notes: see p. 877.

[1] Private sector; Sep. of each year. [2] Excl. holidays, sick-leave and overtime payments. [3] Adults; prior to 1998: 2nd quarter of each year; 1998-2000: Sept-Oct. of each year.

Notes explicatives: voir p. 879.

[1] Secteur privé; sept. de chaque année. [2] Non compris les versements pour les vacances, congés maladie ainsi que la rémunération des heures supplémentaires. [3] Adultes; avant 1998: 2ème trimestre de chaque année; 1998-2000: sept.-oct. de chaque année.

Notas explicativas: véase p. 882.

[1] Sector privado; sept. de cada ano. [2] Excl. los pagos por vacancias, licencias de enfermedad, y pagos por horas extraordinarias. [3] Adultos; antes de 1998: segundo trimestre de cada año; 1998-2000:sept-oct. de cada año.

5A

WAGES	SALAIRES	SALARIOS
By economic activity	Par activité économique	Por actividad económica

	1999	2000	2001	2002	2003	2004	2005	2006	2007	2008
Turkey (DA)				**Employees - Salariés - Asalariados**						**E.G./m. - Lira**

Total men and women - Total hommes et femmes - Total hombres y mujeres
ISIC 3 - CITI 3 - CIIU 3

	1999	2000	2001	2002	2003	2004	2005	2006	2007	2008
C-Q	.	.	.	600 643	821 291	964 949	996 967	.	.	.
C	.	.	.	1 343 969	1 494 573	1 614 847	1 662 493	.	.	.
D	.	.	.	680 172	865 658	1 023 118	1 108 419	.	.	.
E	.	.	.	1 459 114	1 928 223	2 112 793	2 379 679	.	.	.
F	.	.	.	425 638	568 255	668 341	667 752	.	.	.
G	.	.	.	388 987	599 801	760 292	773 843	.	.	.
H	.	.	.	355 531	495 226	643 201	684 936	.	.	.
I	.	.	.	1 011 419	1 337 931	1 443 124	1 389 117	.	.	.
K	.	.	.	314 885	714 332	863 616	943 030	.	.	.
M	.	.	.	353 087	904 740	1 032 848	1 151 154	.	.	.
N	.	.	.	364 352	662 554	887 933	1 037 164	.	.	.
O	.	.	.	233 020	585 766	815 241	848 716	.	.	.

Ukraine (CA)				**Employees - Salariés - Asalariados**						**E.G./m. - Hryvnia**

Total men and women - Total hommes et femmes - Total hombres y mujeres
ISIC 3 - CITI 3 - CIIU 3

	1999	2000	2001	2002	2003	2004	2005	2006	2007	2008
Total	177.5	230.1	311.1	376.4	462.3	589.6	806.2	1 041.5	1 351.1	1 806.3
A-B	101.9	114.3	155.1	183.7	220.2	311.9	437.7	580.9	769.9	1 098.9
C-Q	195.7	257.1	343.6	411.9	499.4	625.5	847.7	1 086.1	1 400.0	1 859.3
A	101.8	113.9	154.5	182.9	219.2	311.0	436.8	580.5	770.6	1 101.4
B	110.0	146.5	203.6	241.6	290.6	374.7	499.0	606.7	721.3	913.1
C	302.0	393.4	516.7	609.9	701.3	910.0	1 245.8	1 535.9	1 970.5	2 681.2
D	191.3	270.7	368.3	441.3	552.9	700.6	905.1	1 137.3	1 456.4	1 849.0
E	293.0	370.7	475.8	562.1	651.3	766.9	969.0	1 228.1	1 576.8	2 110.6
F	206.7	260.2	362.4	427.5	546.3	708.7	894.0	1 139.5	1 486.0	1 832.4
G	174.9	225.5	283.6	330.4	393.7	508.7	713.2	898.2	1 144.5	1 513.6
H	141.2	178.2	234.8	286.1	339.6	429.4	566.5	735.1	943.9	1 221.4
I	240.7	335.3	459.9	572.5	685.0	843.1	1 057.5	1 328.2	1 669.7	2 207.0
J	410.1	559.6	833.2	976.1	1 051.2	1 258.0	1 553.3	2 049.6	2 770.1	3 747.0
K	205.4	277.7	372.6	473.1	526.8	666.8	900.0	1 193.3	1 594.8	2 085.4
L	224.6	335.3	396.1	495.0	576.9	691.0	1 086.7	1 578.4	1 851.9	2 581.2
M	141.2	156.5	224.1	267.4	340.5	429.5	640.6	806.3	1 059.6	1 447.8
N	129.5	138.2	182.7	223.5	279.0	351.2	517.1	657.9	870.5	1 177.4
O	143.4	162.1	210.6	246.5	298.7	399.6	619.6	828.1	1 090.3	1 511.3

Men - Hommes - Hombres
ISIC 2 - CITI 2 - CIIU 2   ISIC 3 - CITI 3 - CIIU 3

	1999	2000	2001	2002	2003	2004	2005	2006	2007	2008	
Total	205.7	269.2	367.5	447.1	552.0	707.0	952.7	1 216.3	1 578.1	2 080.4	Total
2-9	240.0	317.4	427.8	189.9	227.9	327.3	457.5	604.5	801.6	1 144.9	A-B
1	104.4	117.8	145.8	513.7	622.7	778.2	1 034.1	1 303.7	1 672.9	2 183.0	C-Q
5	216.0	281.1	394.9	188.9	226.6	326.2	456.5	604.4	803.0	1 149.0	A
7	263.0	368.5	515.9	245.4	296.1	381.6	511.2	610.1	720.0	904.5	B
				707.7	815.3	1 054.7	1 437.4	1 757.5	2 252.6	3 067.4	C
				509.0	640.8	809.0	1 042.3	1 302.1	1 667.0	2 103.2	D
				614.9	709.1	836.3	1 058.5	1 349.5	1 724.3	2 311.3	E
				450.1	576.8	751.9	935.8	1 184.1	1 535.2	1 883.1	F
				374.9	441.9	585.3	815.2	1 017.9	1 284.2	1 678.8	G
				367.8	430.2	540.3	697.2	873.9	1 116.0	1 377.7	H
				636.8	771.3	947.0	1 185.1	1 488.8	1 886.7	2 473.6	I
				1 437.3	1 517.5	1 667.3	2 029.6	2 644.6	3 635.7	4 762.9	J
				488.9	579.1	723.4	974.2	1 274.2	1 673.5	2 164.8	K
				557.1	643.1	792.5	1 292.4	1 811.6	2 130.0	2 898.3	L
				313.8	408.1	494.1	746.1	920.2	1 206.9	1 630.4	M
				252.2	319.6	396.0	585.7	730.5	991.6	1 306.9	N
				290.6	350.6	489.8	784.6	1 030.2	1 347.0	1 829.1	O

Women - Femmes - Mujeres
ISIC 2 - CITI 2 - CIIU 2   ISIC 3 - CITI 3 - CIIU 3

	1999	2000	2001	2002	2003	2004	2005	2006	2007	2008	
Total	148.9	190.9	256.2	309.8	378.8	484.7	675.4	885.1	1 150.3	1 564.7	Total
2-9	158.6	204.0	271.4	172.6	206.1	283.2	399.6	534.7	707.8	1 007.7	A-B
1	94.3	107.6	159.7	326.4	396.1	501.1	694.8	906.3	1 173.2	1 590.4	C-Q
5	179.0	228.3	319.6	172.2	205.6	282.7	399.2	534.2	707.7	1 008.1	A
7	207.8	287.2	381.7	226.2	270.0	344.3	445.7	591.4	726.5	951.1	B
				353.4	403.0	528.0	729.1	933.7	1 914.0	1 574.9	C
				358.9	443.5	562.9	727.0	920.0	1 175.3	1 503.5	D
				473.2	552.7	649.6	819.4	1 027.5	1 334.5	1 784.8	E
				355.7	443.6	561.7	740.4	966.3	1 289.3	1 623.9	F
				296.3	353.6	441.3	617.1	780.7	1 005.6	1 349.2	G
				260.5	309.5	390.8	519.6	683.1	874.6	1 158.4	H
				481.3	563.3	697.5	878.3	1 100.9	1 361.8	1 822.5	I
				767.0	837.2	1 069.1	1 332.5	1 783.5	2 386.1	3 279.2	J
				386.3	474.7	611.7	826.5	1 110.3	1 512.6	2 001.4	K
				439.8	517.4	643.0	987.5	1 462.7	1 714.2	2 424.2	L
				252.2	318.5	408.7	608.3	771.0	1 014.6	1 392.4	M
				217.1	270.2	341.6	502.6	642.3	845.1	1 149.7	N
				220.0	268.1	345.9	519.9	704.3	930.9	1 311.1	O

Explanatory notes: see p. 877.   Notes explicatives: voir p. 879.   Notas explicativas: véase p. 882.

By economic activity   Par activité économique   Por actividad económica

	1999	2000	2001	2002	2003	2004	2005	2006	2007	2008

United Kingdom (BA) [1]   Employees - Salariés - Asalariados   E.G./h. - Pound

Total men and women - Total hommes et femmes - Total hombres y mujeres
ISIC 3 - CITI 3 - CIIU 3

	1999	2000	2001	2002	2003	2004	2005	2006	2007	2008
Total	8.19	8.64	9.09	9.46	9.74	10.27	10.60	10.96	11.41	11.77
A-B	5.33	5.74	6.54	6.24	6.89	6.70	7.29	7.80	8.93	8.18
C,E	9.92	10.94	11.75	11.52	12.60	12.02	13.46	14.04	14.07	14.80
D	8.34	8.90	9.31	9.91	10.27	10.49	11.16	11.37	11.74	12.32
F	8.16	8.62	9.10	9.43	10.07	10.52	10.61	11.53	11.49	12.08
G-H	5.80	6.04	6.43	6.88	6.73	7.29	7.40	7.41	7.81	7.95
I	8.09	8.60	9.04	9.22	9.35	10.15	10.42	10.99	11.48	11.60
J-K	10.77	11.39	11.99	12.28	13.00	13.60	13.72	14.18	14.87	15.41
L-N	8.79	9.15	9.52	9.76	10.15	10.81	11.27	11.55	11.99	12.29
O-Q	6.61	6.93	7.03	8.02	8.18	8.43	8.57	9.23	9.62	10.07

Men - Hommes - Hombres
ISIC 3 - CITI 3 - CIIU 3

	1999	2000	2001	2002	2003	2004	2005	2006	2007	2008
Total	9.30	9.78	10.26	10.64	10.88	11.53	11.80	12.15	12.61	13.03
A-B	5.50	6.09	6.58	6.60	6.88	6.93	7.48	8.08	8.85	8.31
C,E	10.56	11.93	12.73	11.77	12.87	12.96	13.82	14.99	14.63	15.69
D	8.97	9.55	9.90	10.44	10.83	10.95	11.57	11.80	12.33	12.89
F	8.20	8.71	9.20	9.57	10.16	10.90	10.88	11.85	11.49	12.16
G-H	6.74	7.19	7.55	8.06	7.69	8.30	8.47	8.35	8.73	8.93
I	8.49	8.97	9.38	9.49	9.70	10.62	10.76	11.33	11.70	11.99
J-K	12.74	13.33	14.11	14.45	15.09	16.35	16.09	16.14	17.05	17.47
L-N	10.87	11.12	11.57	11.86	12.05	13.01	13.39	14.04	14.40	14.74
O-Q	8.00	7.77	7.84	8.72	9.22	9.58	9.40	9.99	10.91	11.30

Women - Femmes - Mujeres
ISIC 3 - CITI 3 - CIIU 3

	1999	2000	2001	2002	2003	2004	2005	2006	2007	2008
Total	7.01	7.41	7.85	8.22	8.53	8.94	9.34	9.71	10.15	10.45
A-B	4.92	4.94	6.45	5.55	6.93	5.96	6.92	7.26	9.10	7.89
C,E	8.04	7.86	8.45	10.67	11.30	9.58	12.21	11.63	12.75	12.49
D	6.59	7.09	7.62	8.36	8.62	9.17	9.96	10.05	10.05	10.73
F	7.85	8.10	8.31	8.53	9.58	8.32	8.96	9.58	11.48	11.38
G-H	5.05	5.18	5.55	5.89	5.92	6.37	6.47	6.58	6.95	7.03
I	7.09	7.47	8.09	8.50	8.40	8.78	9.53	9.93	10.80	10.58
J-K	8.66	9.28	9.66	9.86	10.61	10.61	10.98	11.96	12.46	13.09
L-N	7.86	8.29	8.67	8.90	9.33	9.87	10.33	10.52	10.95	11.23
O-Q	5.60	6.22	6.44	7.45	7.35	7.32	7.85	8.44	8.41	8.82

United Kingdom (BA) [1]   Employees - Salariés - Asalariados   E.G./w.s. - Pound

Total men and women - Total hommes et femmes - Total hombres y mujeres
ISIC 3 - CITI 3 - CIIU 3

	1999	2000	2001	2002	2003	2004	2005	2006	2007	2008
Total	368	386	404	419	432	451	464	476	497	514
A-B	245	267	294	297	319	298	332	359	396	367
C,E	442	473	502	501	545	548	582	563	583	639
D	355	377	395	414	431	437	467	477	491	513
F	363	375	396	415	424	459	454	494	492	515
G-H	292	306	315	343	332	359	360	354	371	381
I	366	390	402	408	411	444	460	479	492	499
J-K	464	487	510	517	555	571	573	583	622	647
L-N	376	386	402	414	429	452	468	479	500	513
O-Q	306	327	315	366	389	378	381	412	440	446

Men - Hommes - Hombres
ISIC 3 - CITI 3 - CIIU 3

	1999	2000	2001	2002	2003	2004	2005	2006	2007	2008
Total	408	427	444	460	474	496	506	516	540	561
A-B	258	285	304	308	330	311	350	374	389	381
C,E	475	521	538	525	572	592	605	607	625	682
D	382	405	421	438	456	462	486	495	517	521
F	368	381	404	423	436	472	465	507	498	521
G-H	329	352	358	387	371	397	397	392	404	421
I	384	407	417	421	428	459	478	489	501	525
J-K	542	561	587	594	635	669	655	650	709	725
L-N	448	455	473	490	498	527	548	563	588	608
O-Q	353	347	351	382	429	418	411	437	484	486

Women - Femmes - Mujeres
ISIC 3 - CITI 3 - CIIU 3

	1999	2000	2001	2002	2003	2004	2005	2006	2007	2008
Total	300	316	333	350	362	376	393	410	427	439
A-B	190	195	251	261	239	220	277	313	422	328
C,E	318	296	353	412	378	400	475	429	480	499
D	264	283	301	326	340	348	393	406	401	425
F	303	317	319	337	315	335	361	379	442	422
G-H	235	237	249	274	274	296	298	289	311	313
I	303	320	338	358	348	375	397	437	458	414
J-K	351	375	393	401	431	424	443	477	492	531
L-N	324	337	354	363	381	401	414	428	443	453
O-Q	246	293	270	344	340	317	336	370	367	381

Explanatory notes: see p. 877.   Notes explicatives: voir p. 879.   Notas explicativas: véase p. 882.

[1] Full-time employees.   [1] Salariés à plein temps.   [1] Asalariados a tiempo completo.

WAGES

SALAIRES

SALARIOS

By economic activity

Par activité économique

Por actividad económica

	1999	2000	2001	2002	2003	2004	2005	2006	2007	2008
United Kingdom (DA) [1][2][3]					**Employees - Salariés - Asalariados**					**E.G./h. - Pound**

Total men and women - Total hommes et femmes - Total hombres y mujeres
ISIC 3 - CITI 3 - CIIU 3

	1999	2000	2001	2002	2003	2004	2005	2006	2007	2008
Total	10.26	10.71	11.33	11.94	12.32	12.80	13.11	13.56	13.96	.
A-B	6.47	6.64	6.97	7.54	7.63	8.03	8.40	8.66	9.01	.
C-Q	10.29	10.75	11.36	11.97	12.35	12.63	13.15	13.59	13.99	.
A	6.42	6.59	6.92	7.52	7.59	8.14	8.35	8.61	9.04	.
B	8.38	8.42	8.76	8.08	9.15	9.63	10.22	10.55	8.25	.
C	11.24	12.21	13.21	13.68	14.51	14.60	15.14	17.60	17.20	.
D	9.76	10.10	10.66	11.12	11.65	12.03	12.51	12.87	13.20	.
E	12.54	13.23	13.33	13.61	14.17	14.78	15.57	15.50	15.90	.
F	9.01	9.52	10.10	10.75	11.28	11.82	12.21	12.84	13.20	.
G	8.79	9.10	9.55	9.95	10.27	10.74	10.56	11.04	11.40	.
H	6.48	6.76	6.97	7.27	7.64	7.87	7.91	8.37	8.51	.
I	9.53	9.87	10.30	10.83	11.07	11.84	11.85	12.38	13.00	.
J	15.33	16.19	17.27	18.49	18.29	19.18	19.50	19.91	20.90	.
K	11.79	12.43	13.53	14.36	14.47	15.02	15.09	15.59	16.10	.
L	10.69	11.01	11.42	11.87	12.01	12.67	13.39	13.68	14.10	.
M	11.68	12.00	12.43	12.94	13.52	13.86	14.60	14.95	15.30	.
N	9.38	9.93	10.56	11.10	11.60	12.30	12.99	13.37	13.80	.
O	9.66	10.26	10.61	11.82	12.34	12.96	12.60	13.13	13.00	.
P	.	6.96	6.98	6.84	7.31	7.21	8.26	9.09	9.06	.
Q	.	11.24	11.33	14.79	13.56	14.21	.	14.63	17.30	.

Men - Hommes - Hombres
ISIC 3 - CITI 3 - CIIU 3

	1999	2000	2001	2002	2003	2004	2005	2006	2007	2008
Total	11.03	11.50	12.16	12.83	13.21	13.67	13.98	14.54	14.90	.
A-B	6.60	6.75	7.05	7.66	7.77	8.10	8.58	8.82	9.12	.
C-Q	11.08	11.55	12.21	12.88	13.26	13.49	14.04	14.59	14.95	.
A	6.55	6.70	7.01	7.65	7.73	8.24	8.54	8.79	9.18	.
B	8.41	8.42	.	8.02	9.02	9.54	10.28	9.92	7.10	.
C	11.43	12.48	13.43	13.81	14.43	14.72	15.23	17.97	17.17	.
D	10.31	10.62	11.21	11.62	12.13	12.50	12.97	13.36	13.71	.
E	13.25	13.87	14.06	14.42	14.87	15.45	16.22	16.23	16.86	.
F	9.08	9.59	10.21	10.88	11.44	11.95	12.35	13.06	13.38	.
G	9.69	9.98	10.41	10.92	11.19	11.68	11.40	11.90	12.24	.
H	7.10	7.44	7.71	7.98	8.41	8.37	8.54	9.12	9.09	.
I	9.74	10.11	10.51	10.98	11.20	12.01	12.04	12.52	13.11	.
J	19.56	20.51	21.78	23.53	22.95	23.86	24.11	24.35	25.56	.
K	12.91	13.64	14.91	15.81	15.86	16.25	16.42	16.96	17.53	.
L	11.64	11.98	12.55	12.96	13.06	13.68	14.56	14.74	15.30	.
M	12.45	12.76	13.19	13.79	14.40	14.73	15.56	16.10	16.47	.
N	11.88	12.51	13.34	13.82	14.73	15.55	16.87	17.56	17.75	.
O	10.37	11.32	11.73	13.17	13.90	14.51	13.72	14.29	14.09	.
P	.	10.76	.	.	9.26	.	.	11.42	11.70	12.20	.
Q	.	.	.	14.68	.	.	.	16.67	19.69	.

Women - Femmes - Mujeres
ISIC 3 - CITI 3 - CIIU 3

	1999	2000	2001	2002	2003	2004	2005	2006	2007	2008
Total	8.84	9.22	9.79	10.32	10.71	11.26	11.64	11.99	12.38	.
A-B	5.78	6.08	6.51	6.89	6.91	7.50	7.45	7.91	8.45	.
C-Q	8.85	9.24	9.80	10.33	10.72	11.12	11.65	12.00	12.39	.
A	5.72	6.03	6.42	6.84	6.83	7.59	7.37	7.80	8.26	.
B	.	.	.	.	.	.	.	.	.	.
C	9.73	9.82	11.35	12.67	15.08	13.73	14.52	15.40	17.42	.
D	7.68	8.02	8.52	9.04	9.64	10.02	10.52	10.78	10.99	.
E	9.89	10.57	10.78	10.75	11.23	11.88	13.14	12.88	12.53	.
F	8.18	8.61	8.95	9.34	9.69	10.56	10.82	10.78	11.47	.
G	7.00	7.28	7.71	8.02	8.39	8.82	8.90	9.36	9.77	.
H	5.72	5.89	6.05	6.32	6.65	7.20	7.11	7.40	7.77	.
I	8.70	8.96	9.51	10.27	10.49	11.16	11.01	11.83	12.34	.
J	10.75	11.23	12.12	12.81	12.90	13.62	14.01	14.47	15.30	.
K	9.67	10.10	10.96	11.55	11.82	12.57	12.58	12.99	13.36	.
L	9.13	9.43	9.55	10.05	10.35	11.06	11.61	12.08	12.42	.
M	11.08	11.40	11.83	12.27	12.81	13.19	13.90	14.15	14.46	.
N	8.41	8.90	9.44	9.99	10.33	10.94	11.47	11.74	12.18	.
O	8.57	8.65	8.95	9.84	9.97	10.62	10.88	11.34	11.13	.
P	.	6.19	6.35	6.61	6.96	6.47	7.63	8.58	8.47	.
Q	.	11.29	.	14.85	13.95	12.26	11.00	12.73	15.51	.

Explanatory notes: see p. 877.

Notes explicatives: voir p. 879.

Notas explicativas: véase p. 882.

[1] April; full-time employees on adult rates. [2] Results with imputation and weighting. [3] Incl. overtime payments.

[1] Avril; salariés à plein temps rémunérés sur la base de taux de salaires pour adultes. [2] Résultats après imputation et pondération. [3] Y compris la rémunération des heures supplémentaires.

[1] Abril; asalariados a tiempo completo pagados sobre la base de tasas de salarios para adultos. [2] Resultados después imputación y ponderación. [3] Incl. los pagos por horas extraordinarias.

	1999	2000	2001	2002	2003	2004	2005	2006	2007	2008
United Kingdom (DA) [1][2][3]					Employees - Salariés - Asalariados					E.G./w.s. - Pound

Total men and women - Total hommes et femmes - Total hombres y mujeres
ISIC 3 - CITI 3 - CIIU 3

	1999	2000	2001	2002	2003	2004	2005	2006	2007	2008
Total	407.90	452.20	449.80	472.20	487.60	506.10	517.00	534.90	549.80	.
A-B	.	.	.	.	.	.	366.70	381.30	396.00	.
A	288.80	289.20	.	336.10	340.50	362.50	364.70	379.70	397.00	.
B	364.10	374.20	397.70	350.70	392.70	419.00	440.60	445.10	359.40	.
C	504.00	538.20	581.10	591.70	657.00	633.50	657.90	749.90	757.60	.
D	402.70	417.20	439.90	455.60	476.50	493.10	508.00	524.20	539.30	.
E	500.00	520.80	532.10	543.00	561.50	591.90	612.20	624.80	630.80	.
F	396.70	420.80	445.60	466.40	498.80	509.40	524.60	553.00	567.90	.
G	356.80	368.10	386.80	403.60	414.60	433.30	425.20	445.60	459.50	.
H	262.90	273.20	.	295.90	311.30	323.80	323.50	343.30	349.20	.
I	416.00	429.80	443.00	462.30	476.30	504.30	508.00	523.40	546.50	.
J	558.40	587.50	628.80	671.00	660.60	696.30	701.30	719.70	757.00	.
K	465.80	489.60	533.10	564.40	568.50	590.60	589.30	612.80	632.00	.
L	407.60	419.00	437.90	456.70	469.90	496.60	525.00	536.60	549.70	.
M	407.60	419.70	.	459.60	481.60	493.60	518.60	532.20	544.80	.
N	361.30	381.00	407.70	427.70	446.80	474.90	503.20	515.90	528.00	.
O	388.00	407.50	424.00	468.40	486.80	515.40	503.80	524.10	512.50	.
P	.	292.00	288.80	302.00	312.50	303.10	358.40	396.30	369.10	.
Q	.	417.20	431.00	568.10	554.50	550.60	.	566.00	664.50	.

Men - Hommes - Hombres
ISIC 3 - CITI 3 - CIIU 3

	1999	2000	2001	2002	2003	2004	2005	2006	2007	2008
Total	.	471.80	470.10	523.40	539.30	557.40	568.10	589.80	606.10	.
A-B	.	.	.	.	.	.	383.60	396.10	406.30	.
A	300.90	299.70	297.30	350.50	356.20	375.40	381.90	395.20	409.20	.
B	366.00	357.70	.	353.40	391.40	433.20	445.70	428.20	313.90	.
C	523.60	559.10	600.50	608.80	671.20	653.70	675.40	783.40	773.00	.
D	431.70	445.60	464.90	482.90	503.02	519.40	533.80	551.40	568.70	.
E	536.10	552.80	565.20	584.70	595.70	626.10	647.30	666.50	678.40	.
F	404.80	429.80	451.90	478.50	503.08	521.50	537.60	569.80	582.60	.
G	402.90	413.50	391.50	453.70	464.40	483.20	469.50	491.10	504.80	.
H	294.90	307.50	233.70	332.90	351.90	352.50	357.20	381.40	382.00	.
I	436.20	451.00	455.50	480.40	493.50	522.00	527.70	541.80	565.70	.
J	713.20	745.50	781.70	855.90	832.10	869.20	872.40	884.90	928.40	.
K	523.00	549.40	557.70	635.30	636.70	652.50	654.90	681.60	702.80	.
L	452.30	436.70	471.20	506.00	522.50	547.90	583.60	589.40	609.80	.
M	449.20	460.40	434.10	504.30	528.80	539.30	568.40	589.20	603.70	.
N	471.90	495.60	479.90	549.90	581.10	614.80	669.50	693.00	699.30	.
O	431.30	463.90	427.00	536.30	562.20	593.10	563.60	582.50	570.10	.
P	.	440.00	.	.	.	.	.	.	.	.
Q	.	.	.	582.00	594.70	721.80	.	650.80	768.00	.

Women - Femmes - Mujeres
ISIC 3 - CITI 3 - CIIU 3

	1999	2000	2001	2002	2003	2004	2005	2006	2007	2008
Total	331.20	344.90	367.10	386.80	400.70	422.10	435.70	450.00	463.10	.
A-B	.	.	.	.	.	.	291.60	320.00	344.40	.
A	231.90	242.00	253.50	272.30	270.80	297.50	287.60	316.10	337.10	.
B	.	.	258.40	.	.	.	.	.	.	.
C	378.10	376.40	437.60	478.60	566.50	511.00	552.50	580.30	661.50	.
D	299.30	312.10	332.20	350.80	372.80	388.10	404.30	415.90	423.80	.
E	373.60	395.40	410.90	405.10	426.00	453.00	490.20	486.50	474.70	.
F	311.00	324.50	343.90	356.90	370.80	403.80	411.50	415.70	438.00	.
G	270.60	280.20	297.20	310.10	321.60	339.30	343.20	361.80	375.50	.
H	225.70	231.70	238.50	249.80	262.20	287.20	282.40	295.90	309.40	.
I	346.30	355.30	372.90	402.90	410.00	439.00	432.80	458.10	476.50	.
J	391.00	406.60	440.50	463.70	463.70	492.50	500.00	519.60	550.30	.
K	365.30	381.60	414.60	436.30	446.40	474.50	472.80	490.20	502.50	.
L	333.70	349.00	357.70	377.60	390.90	418.90	440.20	460.00	469.30	.
M	377.10	389.60	407.10	425.70	445.90	460.20	484.00	494.80	506.50	.
N	320.00	337.20	359.90	380.10	394.00	417.90	440.30	448.90	463.10	.
O	327.70	328.40	343.10	375.70	379.10	405.70	417.90	438.30	424.90	.
P	.	261.10	259.80	293.60	299.10	270.40	325.40	368.30	341.10	.
Q	.	414.60	.	561.70	530.60	472.60	420.80	488.80	.	.

Explanatory notes: see p. 877.

[1] April; full-time employees on adult rates. [2] Results with imputation and weighting. [3] Incl. overtime payments.

Notes explicatives: voir p. 879.

[1] Avril; salariés à plein temps rémunérés sur la base de taux de salaires pour adultes. [2] Résultats après imputation et pondération. [3] Y compris la rémunération des heures supplémentaires.

Notas explicativas: véase p. 882.

[1] Abril; asalariados a tiempo completo pagados sobre la base de tasas de salarios para adultos. [2] Resultados después imputación y ponderación. [3] Incl. los pagos por horas extraordinarias.

WAGES · SALAIRES · SALARIOS

By economic activity · Par activité économique · Por actividad económica

	1999	2000	2001	2002	2003	2004	2005	2006	2007	2008

OCEANIA-OCÉANIE-OCEANIA

Australia (DA) [1][2]   Employees - Salariés - Asalariados   E.G./h. - Dollar

Total men and women - Total hommes et femmes - Total hombres y mujeres
ISIC 3 - CITI 3 - CIIU 3

	1999	2000	2001	2002	2003	2004	2005	2006	2007	2008
C-Q	.	19.86	.	21.40	.	22.48	.	25.65	.	.
C	.	25.56	.	28.19	.	32.08	.	34.98	.	.
D	.	18.16	.	20.45	.	22.77	.	25.36	.	.
E	.	22.17	.	26.10	.	28.22	.	31.57	.	.
F	.	18.19	.	21.76	.	23.11	.	24.33	.	.
G	.	16.47	.	17.68	.	19.11	.	22.55	.	.
H	.	14.67	.	15.92	.	17.28	.	19.22	.	.
I	.	20.43	.	22.04	.	22.86	.	26.80	.	.
J	.	21.05	.	24.63	.	27.81	.	29.48	.	.
K	.	19.55	.	21.05	.	22.75	.	26.77	.	.
L	.	22.69	.	24.17	.	26.05	.	29.51	.	.
M	.	21.73	.	24.14	.	25.15	.	29.30	.	.
N	.	19.53	.	18.49	.	20.50	.	24.42	.	.
O	.	17.96	.	19.76	.	21.21	.	24.68	.	.

Men - Hommes - Hombres
ISIC 3 - CITI 3 - CIIU 3

	1999	2000	2001	2002	2003	2004	2005	2006	2007	2008
C-Q	.	21.07	.	22.30	.	22.86	.	27.10	.	.
C	.	27.05	.	29.18	.	32.58	.	35.84	.	.
D	.	19.13	.	20.82	.	23.40	.	26.11	.	.
E	.	23.50	.	26.70	.	29.41	.	33.17	.	.
F	.	19.58	.	22.01	.	23.47	.	24.89	.	.
G	.	17.01	.	18.36	.	20.20	.	22.84	.	.
H	.	14.76	.	16.16	.	17.63	.	19.16	.	.
I	.	22.19	.	22.51	.	24.29	.	28.53	.	.
J	.	22.99	.	26.85	.	30.43	.	34.52	.	.
K	.	21.85	.	22.59	.	24.67	.	29.42	.	.
L	.	23.51	.	25.51	.	26.98	.	31.04	.	.
M	.	22.74	.	26.52	.	27.03	.	31.03	.	.
N	.	21.27	.	19.42	.	25.08	.	29.44	.	.
O	.	18.29	.	20.50	.	21.73	.	25.80	.	.

Women - Femmes - Mujeres
ISIC 3 - CITI 3 - CIIU 3

	1999	2000	2001	2002	2003	2004	2005	2006	2007	2008
C-Q	.	18.48	.	20.00	.	19.76	.	23.29	.	.
C	.	23.31	.	25.63	.	27.49	.	27.09	.	.
D	.	16.80	.	18.45	.	19.94	.	23.45	.	.
E	.	20.83	.	24.10	.	24.76	.	26.93	.	.
F	.	15.83	.	19.23	.	18.98	.	20.88	.	.
G	.	15.83	.	17.25	.	18.23	.	20.56	.	.
H	.	14.58	.	15.64	.	16.93	.	19.16	.	.
I	.	18.43	.	19.16	.	21.53	.	23.23	.	.
J	.	19.10	.	20.80	.	22.36	.	25.11	.	.
K	.	17.17	.	20.02	.	20.90	.	24.17	.	.
L	.	21.86	.	21.90	.	24.32	.	27.84	.	.
M	.	20.84	.	23.19	.	24.56	.	28.23	.	.
N	.	18.10	.	17.81	.	19.45	.	23.25	.	.
O	.	17.62	.	19.23	.	21.31	.	23.29	.	.

New Zealand (DA) [3][4][5]   Employees - Salariés - Asalariados   E.G./h. - Dollar

Total men and women - Total hommes et femmes - Total hombres y mujeres
ISIC 3 - CITI 3 - CIIU 3

	1999	2000	2001	2002	2003	2004	2005	2006	2007	2008
C	22.24	20.81	21.74	24.43	26.25	26.74	27.01	29.19	29.78	30.67
C-O [6]	17.27	17.60	18.15	18.81	19.25	20.17	20.55	21.65	22.66	23.69
D	16.51	16.97	17.50	18.10	18.50	19.29	19.58	20.51	21.45	22.40
E	21.01	23.96	24.65	26.83	27.74	28.43	29.61	32.13	32.81	34.78
F	15.31	15.91	16.66	16.68	17.20	18.03	18.38	19.12	20.79	21.87
G	14.73	15.20	15.41	16.02	16.18	16.88	17.05	17.90	18.73	19.51
H	12.00	11.62	12.13	12.36	12.55	13.09	13.35	13.46	14.21	14.99
I	17.55	17.73	18.17	18.90	18.55	19.63	20.08	21.68	21.82	23.19
J	22.79	23.40	24.68	25.31	26.66	28.10	28.78	29.27	31.07	30.99
K	19.98	19.98	20.72	21.62	22.30	23.02	23.26	25.01	25.93	26.55
L	21.00	21.20	22.37	23.00	23.67	25.12	25.96	26.79	27.98	30.10
M	19.79	20.55	21.08	23.08	23.91	24.48	26.14	28.90	29.28	30.31
N	17.87	18.08	18.35	18.98	19.51	20.52	21.16	22.60	23.79	25.25
O	17.46	17.42	18.05	18.16	19.26	19.69	20.25	20.10	21.28	22.73

Explanatory notes: see p. 877.

[1] Full-time adult non-managerial employees. [2] May of each year. [3] Full-time equivalent employees. [4] Establishments with the equivalent of more than 0.5 full-time paid employees. [5] Feb. of each year. [6] Tabulations categories L and M not fully covered.

Notes explicatives: voir p. 879.

[1] Salariés adultes à plein temps, non compris les cadres dirigeants. [2] Mai de chaque année. [3] Salariés en équivalents à plein temps. [4] Etablissements occupant plus de l'équivalent de 0.5 salarié à plein temps. [5] Fév. de chaque année. [6] Catégories de classement L et M pas complètement couvertes.

Notas explicativas: véase p. 882.

[1] Asalariados adultos a tiempo completo, excl. el personal directivo. [2] Mayo de cada año. [3] Asalariados en equivalentes a tiempo completo. [4] Establecimientos con más del equivalente de 0.5 asalariado a tiempo completo. [5] Febr. de cada año. [6] Categorías de tabulación L y M no están completamente cubiertas.

WAGES			**SALAIRES**			**SALARIOS**				**5A**

By economic activity   Par activité économique   Por actividad económica

	1999	2000	2001	2002	2003	2004	2005	2006	2007	2008
New Zealand (DA) [1] [2] [3]				Employees - Salariés - Asalariados						E.G./h. - Dollar

Men - Hommes - Hombres
ISIC 3 - CITI 3 - CIIU 3

	1999	2000	2001	2002	2003	2004	2005	2006	2007	2008
C	22.49	21.12	22.05	24.95	26.76	27.23	27.43	29.66	30.12	31.02
C-O [4]	18.59	18.90	19.56	20.24	20.69	21.54	21.89	23.01	24.11	25.09
D	17.41	17.87	18.40	19.06	19.54	20.24	20.54	21.52	22.54	23.54
E	21.65	25.00	26.64	28.91	30.02	30.61	32.27	34.77	35.64	37.75
F	15.39	16.04	16.87	16.82	17.34	18.16	18.54	19.23	20.93	21.96
G	16.31	16.63	16.93	17.76	17.68	18.41	18.68	19.59	20.36	21.38
H	12.89	12.37	13.03	13.47	13.52	14.17	14.56	14.35	15.10	15.74
I	18.07	18.18	18.56	19.42	19.28	20.29	20.86	22.57	22.90	24.46
J	29.64	29.78	32.54	33.13	34.61	36.56	37.29	37.26	39.66	39.05
K	23.12	22.64	23.47	24.55	25.18	26.43	26.17	28.42	29.30	29.61
L	23.83	23.25	24.88	25.44	26.08	27.47	28.51	29.28	30.66	32.75
M	21.60	22.94	23.67	25.15	26.20	26.54	27.83	29.66	30.77	32.23
N	24.63	25.47	25.08	26.86	27.54	28.86	29.34	31.95	32.88	34.39
O	20.08	20.15	20.42	20.07	22.17	21.67	22.82	22.37	23.72	24.84

Women - Femmes - Mujeres
ISIC 3 - CITI 3 - CIIU 3

	1999	2000	2001	2002	2003	2004	2005	2006	2007	2008
C	19.57	17.64	18.73	20.21	22.05	22.97	23.75	24.47	26.42	27.26
C-O [4]	15.58	15.94	16.40	17.05	17.51	18.50	18.88	19.97	20.86	21.92
D	13.89	14.44	14.93	15.30	15.51	16.55	16.84	17.62	18.47	19.16
E	18.85	20.82	19.37	21.09	21.83	22.65	23.01	25.56	25.92	27.59
F	14.34	14.09	14.72	15.19	15.90	16.73	16.62	17.90	19.15	20.93
G	12.59	13.22	13.36	13.68	14.20	14.80	14.89	15.63	16.40	16.89
H	11.36	11.10	11.75	11.56	11.91	12.32	12.49	12.84	13.63	14.43
I	16.38	16.67	17.21	17.64	16.89	18.06	18.27	19.74	19.33	20.42
J	18.29	19.46	19.63	20.40	21.51	22.44	22.99	23.67	25.18	25.74
K	16.95	17.37	17.97	18.71	19.40	19.85	20.35	21.54	22.53	23.47
L	18.51	18.79	19.61	20.49	21.19	22.64	23.37	24.30	25.29	27.40
M	18.86	19.23	19.72	21.99	22.76	23.46	25.26	28.48	28.48	29.32
N	16.36	16.57	16.89	17.36	17.89	18.79	19.42	20.70	21.87	23.29
O	14.76	14.92	15.85	16.21	16.23	17.77	17.91	18.23	19.16	20.86

Explanatory notes: see p. 877.

[1] Full-time equivalent employees. [2] Establishments with the equivalent of more than 0.5 full-time paid employees. [3] Feb. of each year. [4] Tabulations categories L and M not fully covered.

Notes explicatives: voir p. 879.

[1] Salariés en équivalents à plein temps. [2] Etablissements occupant plus de l'équivalent de 0.5 salarié à plein temps. [3] Fév. de chaque année. [4] Catégories de classement L et M pas complètement couvertes.

Notas explicativas: véase p. 882.

[1] Asalariados en equivalentes a tiempo completo. [2] Establecimientos con más del equivalente de 0.5 asalariado a tiempo completo. [3] Febr. de cada año. [4] Categorías de tabulación L y M no están completamente cubiertas.

WAGES — SALAIRES — SALARIOS

In manufacturing — Dans les industries manufacturières — En las industrias manufactureras

	1999	2000	2001	2002	2003	2004	2005	2006	2007	2008

AFRICA-AFRIQUE-AFRICA

Botswana (DA) [1]   Employees - Salariés - Asalariados   E.G./m. - Pula

Total men and women - Total hommes et femmes - Total hombres y mujeres
ISIC 3 - CITI 3 - CIIU 3

	1999	2000	2001	2002	2003	2004	2005	2006	2007	2008
Total	.	.	.	.	.	.	.	1 590	.	.

Men - Hommes - Hombres
ISIC 3 - CITI 3 - CIIU 3

Total	.	.	.	.	.	.	.	2 053	.	.

Women - Femmes - Mujeres
ISIC 3 - CITI 3 - CIIU 3

Total	.	.	.	.	.	.	.	1 134	.	.

Botswana (DA) [1]   Employees - Salariés - Asalariados   E.G./m. - Pula

Total men and women - Total hommes et femmes - Total hombres y mujeres
ISIC 3 - CITI 3 - CIIU 3

	1999	2000	2001	2002	2003	2004	2005	2006	2007	2008
15	1 186	1 296	1 268	1 373	1 481	1 592	1 586	1 846	2 058	.
17	559	618	578	590	574	713	599	662	849	.
18	421	420	452	510	481	736	623	750	689	.
19	448	490	579	581	589	627	616	880	637	.
20	616	677	868	842	811	859	879	888	921	.
21	522	730	665	665	665	897	811	937	1 101	.
22	885	798	1 962	755	1 682	2 278	3 174	1 630	1 887	.
24	1 304	1 139	1 123	1 356	1 597	2 175	2 311	2 206	2 378	.
25	897	1 084	978	1 223	1 276	1 153	1 747	1 813	1 841	.
26	663	1 044	764	1 077	1 253	949	1 950	1 236	1 385	.
27	464	578	632	610	610	750	750	750	760	.
28	632	652	848	898	850	1 512	905	1 658	1 274	.
29	832	1 171	1 113	1 670	1 523	1 224	1 233	1 392	1 424	.
30	.	.	.	.	.	.	.	1 628	1 909	.
31	.	681	605	1 186	1 715	775	775	.	.	.
32	.	434	.	455	710	3 506	5 237	2 725	2 725	.
33	765	486	922	669	877	904	904	1 287	1 281	.
34	2 949	1 091	1 170	2 432	1 626	1 133	1 335	2 109	2 012	.
35	.	622	1 149	.	.	.	.	705	.	.
36	470	585	967	898	1 020	952	939	711	1 003	.
37	.	.	.	420	.	.	2 299	.	.	.

Men - Hommes - Hombres
ISIC 3 - CITI 3 - CIIU 3

	1999	2000	2001	2002	2003	2004	2005	2006	2007	2008
15	1 233	1 477	1 498	1 577	1 624	1 747	1 733	1 701	2 372	.
17	772	815	764	773	776	961	833	851	1 060	.
18	475	497	499	554	532	766	617	1 551	868	.
19	494	492	703	668	732	718	670	2 069	835	.
20	552	664	861	804	807	888	893	877	905	.
21	523	790	676	676	676	977	881	1 057	1 022	.
22	881	851	1 748	990	2 450	2 306	2 735	2 171	3 082	.
24	1 571	1 283	1 129	1 400	1 687	2 262	2 453	2 330	2 520	.
25	1 117	1 384	1 164	1 577	1 545	1 515	1 971	2 780	2 790	.
26	793	1 153	764	1 288	1 377	1 015	2 547	1 367	1 518	.
27	457	575	639	616	616	786	786	788	792	.
28	652	648	962	1 015	969	1 725	995	1 638	1 334	.
29	923	1 171	1 035	1 960	1 701	1 409	1 449	1 494	1 536	.
30	.	.	.	.	.	.	.	1 950	3 748	.
31	.	1 027	750	1 499	2 015	775	775	.	.	.
32	.	522	.	421	898	5 400	6 892	2 927	2 927	.
33	1 363	533	1 046	622	750	1 100	1 100	1 607	1 508	.
34	3 116	1 023	1 246	2 628	1 585	1 144	1 271	2 002	1 964	.
35	.	739	1 141	.	.	.	.	705	.	.
36	544	846	1 452	1 448	1 301	1 171	1 144	1 160	1 336	.
37	.	.	.	472	.	.	2 299	.	.	.

Explanatory notes: see p. 877.	Notes explicatives: voir p. 879.	Notas explicativas: véase p. 882.
[1] Sep. of each year.	[1] Sept. de chaque année.	[1] Sept. de cada año.

5B

WAGES	SALAIRES	SALARIOS
In manufacturing	Dans les industries manufacturières	En las industrias manufactureras

	1999	2000	2001	2002	2003	2004	2005	2006	2007	2008

Botswana (DA) [1]   Employees - Salariés - Asalariados   E.G./m. - Pula

Women - Femmes - Mujeres
ISIC 3 - CITI 3 - CIIU 3

	1999	2000	2001	2002	2003	2004	2005	2006	2007	2008
15	1 083	913	885	1 003	1 161	1 287	1 285	2 108	1 509	.
17	464	496	484	495	484	576	409	530	664	.
18	414	420	446	500	475	732	432	677	674	.
19	414	489	566	564	569	616	474	614	608	.
20	1 022	733	895	974	823	744	815	910	972	.
21	522	676	657	657	657	839	765	867	1 145	.
22	888	753	2 076	642	1 132	2 253	3 890	1 318	1 232	.
24	1 015	887	1 100	1 266	1 388	1 932	1 943	1 962	2 162	.
25	507	681	690	748	909	745	1 309	880	917	.
26	497	800	763	756	943	816	815	954	1 045	.
27	555	608	574	551	551	500	500	550	500	.
28	515	684	603	659	615	706	693	1 759	1 104	.
29	626	.	1 418	1 260	1 311	881	882	1 108	1 208	.
30	.	.	.	.	.	.	.	1 370	1 092	.
31	.	574	556	1 052	1 365					
32	.	328	.	506	617	1 613	1 100	500	500	.
33	729	450	813	707	973	864	864	886	940	.
34	2 007	1 501	619	1 481	1 947	888	2 049	2 596	3 186	.
35	.	535	1 188							
36	389	490	725	755	925	803	565	603	829	.
37	.	.	.	280	.	.	2 299	.	.	.

Egypt (CA) [2][3]   Wage earners - Ouvriers - Obreros   E.G./w.s. - Pound

Total men and women - Total hommes et femmes - Total hombres y mujeres
ISIC 3 - CITI 3 - CIIU 3

	1999	2000	2001	2002	2003	2004	2005	2006	2007	2008
Total	121	125	136	147	150	162	179	203	220	.
15	95	95	111	113	108	116	134	154	173	.
16	119	134	135	136	133	178	200	233	218	.
17	95	91	104	116	123	129	135	152	166	.
18	69	60	70	71	71	80	94	96	110	.
19	66	79	74	77	75	80	91	98	105	.
20	78	72	96	101	113	90	123	138	151	.
21	99	110	123	125	132	142	170	167	194	.
22	170	178	257	201	189	223	205	204	259	.
23	259	346	381	345	392	369	459	543	480	.
24	152	171	174	193	198	255	285	345	282	.
25	82	81	84	81	89	94	109	128	186	.
26	152	153	142	169	156	196	197	176	207	.
27	182	208	214	237	293	311	385	386	470	.
28	137	112	133	150	155	161	211	210	228	.
29	127	132	142	152	165	151	152	195	222	.
30	554	76	106	252	108	61	147	124	183	.
31	140	141	120	158	211	233	230	195	237	.
32	158	150	196	182	149	319	169	397	397	.
33	100	237	97	175	136	145	140	164	198	.
34	157	149	149	180	199	216	214	220	243	.
35	138	134	158	169	193	185	211	416	474	.
36	79	92	93	102	100	89	109	109	138	.
37	52	56	46	116	46	.	58	66	.	.

Men - Hommes - Hombres
ISIC 3 - CITI 3 - CIIU 3

	1999	2000	2001	2002	2003	2004	2005	2006	2007	2008
Total	125	131	142	154	157	168	187	210	231	.
15	99	98	114	117	110	119	138	159	176	.
16	127	140	144	144	144	195	219	247	235	.
17	96	95	108	121	127	135	141	157	173	.
18	80	72	77	85	81	87	101	111	124	.
19	70	82	80	80	83	87	99	102	106	.
20	76	74	97	100	113	91	123	138	152	.
21	101	113	127	129	138	146	173	165	197	.
22	168	177	258	197	186	218	202	205	253	.
23	261	349	385	349	398	375	468	557	491	.
24	152	173	177	198	201	244	281	323	291	.
25	84	84	85	82	91	98	113	132	193	.
26	153	153	143	172	158	198	201	183	210	.
27	182	208	214	237	294	313	385	387	472	.
28	142	112	133	151	160	163	213	212	229	.
29	127	132	144	157	165	159	154	202	219	.
30	564	79	95	238	108	66	145	124	176	.
31	141	142	122	159	212	234	229	196	242	.
32	156	149	197	184	156	332	168	412	411	.
33	105	243	101	188	151	149	141	163	201	.
34	157	149	149	180	196	215	213	220	243	.
35	138	135	159	169	195	185	213	416	475	.
36	79	92	94	103	100	89	109	108	138	.
37	50	57	52	116	60	.	72	66	.	.

Explanatory notes: see p. 877.

[1] Sep. of each year. [2] Establishments with 10 or more persons employed. [3] Oct. of each year.

Notes explicatives: voir p. 879.

[1] Sept. de chaque année. [2] Etablissements occupant 10 personnes et plus. [3] Oct. de chaque année.

Notas explicativas: véase p. 882.

[1] Sept. de cada año. [2] Establecimientos con 10 y más trabajadores. [3] Oct. de cada año.

	1999	2000	2001	2002	2003	2004	2005	2006	2007	2008

Egypt (CA) [1] [2]   **Wage earners - Ouvriers - Obreros**   E.G./w.s. - Pound

Women - Femmes - Mujeres
ISIC 3 - CITI 3 - CIIU 3

	1999	2000	2001	2002	2003	2004	2005	2006	2007	2008
Total	94	87	97	104	104	126	134	159	153	.
15	72	73	89	86	89	95	109	117	140	.
16	76	92	87	93	77	95	113	144	135	.
17	90	71	81	91	98	96	105	121	132	.
18	63	53	65	61	65	75	89	86	99	.
19	49	58	48	58	43	55	56	76	98	.
20	105	53	78	113	102	74	122	139	125	.
21	76	71	76	75	78	86	117	191	156	.
22	204	189	237	235	226	271	233	186	313	.
23	238	298	322	284	315	288	365	384	372	.
24	152	158	158	189	183	317	307	468	238	.
25	60	61	70	64	66	60	67	75	91	.
26	137	145	113	114	138	165	143	121	170	.
27	171	194	204	213	235	253	364	293	336	.
28	71	114	122	135	81	119	152	171	200	.
29	129	116	120	87	147	87	107	103	278	.
30	366	61	167	291	112	56	160	119	236	.
31	130	124	102	140	199	226	247	181	179	.
32	165	154	192	172	122	209	174	325	314	.
33	74	208	71	116	84	111	136	166	174	.
34	185	145	156	185	284	271	261	226	247	.
35	121	117	132	197	151	172	170	400	445	.
36	81	77	74	92	93	96	112	143	153	.
37	62	30	39	145	36	.	40	.	.	.

Mauritius (CA) [1] [3]   **Employees - Salariés - Asalariados**   E.G./m. - Rupee

Total men and women - Total hommes et femmes - Total hombres y mujeres
ISIC 3 - CITI 3 - CIIU 3

	1999	2000	2001	2002	2003	2004	2005	2006	2007	2008
Total	5 142	5 544	5 856	6 155	6 668	7 299	7 798	8 214	8 622	8 979
15-16	7 166	7 756	8 088	8 398	9 265	9 627	10 059	10 225	10 574	10 690
17	6 010	6 159	6 844	7 414	6 809	7 201	7 902	7 924	8 649	9 538
18	4 272	4 529	4 761	4 960	5 441	5 955	6 311	6 639	6 996	7 227
19	4 671	5 145	5 820	5 931	7 036	7 270	7 180	7 158	7 481	8 191
20	5 714	6 243	6 101	5 851	6 759	7 880	7 932	8 232	8 501	8 748
21	5 005	5 203	5 811	5 975	6 687	6 978	6 845	7 156	8 019	8 889
22	8 608	9 058	9 588	10 179	10 649	12 079	12 121	12 877	13 437	13 997
23-24	7 426	7 860	8 356	8 660	9 739	11 038	11 563	11 810	12 805	13 021
25	5 507	6 119	6 232	6 687	7 459	7 641	8 125	8 904	9 165	9 308
26	7 484	8 559	9 662	8 919	10 086	11 212	11 530	12 284	13 043	13 647
27	6 707	7 502	7 959	9 611	10 605	11 672	9 999	10 439	11 085	12 169
28	7 381	7 292	8 207	8 072	9 158	9 156	9 312	10 124	10 105	10 796
29-30	9 130	11 766	14 554	12 426	13 390	14 185	14 703	14 430	15 052	16 024
31	7 654	8 843	9 076	8 702	8 838	9 457	10 373	11 123	11 031	11 632
32	7 128	6 920	6 712	6 388	7 001	7 379	7 316	8 445	9 110	10 171
33	5 406	5 692	6 201	6 671	6 964	7 413	8 024	8 357	8 377	8 812
34-35	6 235	6 993	8 505	8 567	8 780	9 076	8 436	10 718	10 922	11 020
36-37	4 837	5 536	6 028	6 078	6 222	6 567	7 313	7 561	7 725	8 013

Seychelles (FA)   **Employees - Salariés - Asalariados**   E.G./m. - Rupee

Total men and women - Total hommes et femmes - Total hombres y mujeres
ISIC 3 - CITI 3 - CIIU 3

	1999	2000	2001	2002	2003	2004	2005	2006	2007	2008
Total	2 962	3 067	3 235	3 300	2 986	3 042	3 314	3 350	3 306	4 100

Explanatory notes: see p. 877.   Notes explicatives: voir p. 879.   Notas explicativas: véase p. 882.

[1] Establishments with 10 or more persons employed. [2] Oct. of each year. [3] March of each year.   [1] Etablissements occupant 10 personnes et plus. [2] Oct. de chaque année. [3] Mars de chaque année.   [1] Establecimientos con 10 y más trabajadores. [2] Oct. de cada año. [3] Marzo de cada año.

WAGES

SALAIRES

SALARIOS

In manufacturing

Dans les industries manufacturières

En las industrias manufactureras

	1999	2000	2001	2002	2003	2004	2005	2006	2007	2008

AMERICA-AMÉRIQUE-AMERICA

Argentina (DB) [1][2] — Wage earners - Ouvriers - Obreros — E.G./h. - Peso

Total men and women - Total hommes et femmes - Total hombres y mujeres
ISIC 3 - CITI 3 - CIIU 3

	1999	2000	2001	2002	2003	2004	2005	2006	2007	2008
Total	4.20	4.27	4.33	4.46	5.06	6.30	7.63	9.72	.	
15	3.61	3.62	3.64	3.79	4.36	5.60	6.85	8.64	.	
16	6.49	6.12	5.89	5.44	6.57	7.31	7.65	9.74	.	
17	3.13	3.16	3.10	3.11	3.56	4.72	5.67	7.13	.	
18	2.37	2.35	2.31	2.56	2.97	4.14	4.84	5.82	.	
19	3.17	3.12	3.10	3.13	3.62	4.96	6.15	7.59	.	
20	2.65	2.68	2.76	2.81	3.31	4.47	5.49	7.02	.	
21	4.47	4.59	4.66	4.88	5.52	6.58	7.81	9.78	.	
22	6.34	6.61	6.82	6.74	7.37	8.71	10.13	12.40	.	
23	10.60	11.30	11.60	11.87	14.10	15.91	18.15	22.15	.	
24	5.50	5.54	5.97	5.81	6.63	7.88	9.19	11.90	.	
25	4.32	4.23	4.19	4.31	4.93	6.52	8.08	10.20	.	
26	4.48	4.50	4.60	4.74	5.35	6.41	7.84	9.96	.	
27	5.59	5.82	5.97	6.12	7.07	8.79	10.32	13.74	.	
28	3.77	3.98	4.19	4.15	4.77	6.03	7.27	9.58	.	
29	4.46	4.49	4.66	4.85	5.34	6.41	7.65	10.09	.	
30	4.85	5.11	5.41	5.83	6.91	8.36	9.08	10.48	.	
31	4.36	4.33	4.47	4.61	5.10	6.52	8.13	10.59	.	
32	7.43	8.01	7.71	7.16	7.66	9.23	10.77	13.86	.	
33	3.98	4.15	4.14	4.04	4.27	5.46	6.41	8.12	.	
34	5.75	6.04	6.37	6.69	7.33	8.30	10.83	13.78	.	
35	4.67	4.75	4.83	4.89	5.77	7.21	8.51	11.11	.	
36	3.14	3.17	3.14	3.17	3.54	4.61	5.61	7.25	.	

Bermuda (CA) [3] — Employees - Salariés - Asalariados — E.G./m. - Dollar

Total men and women - Total hommes et femmes - Total hombres y mujeres
ISIC 3 - CITI 3 - CIIU 3

	1999	2000	2001	2002	2003	2004	2005	2006	2007	2008
Total	.	.	.	.	.	4 167	3 561	3 692	3 950	.

Men - Hommes - Hombres
ISIC 3 - CITI 3 - CIIU 3

	1999	2000	2001	2002	2003	2004	2005	2006	2007	2008
Total	.	.	.	.	.	4 333	3 691	3 792	4 101	.

Women - Femmes - Mujeres
ISIC 3 - CITI 3 - CIIU 3

	1999	2000	2001	2002	2003	2004	2005	2006	2007	2008
Total	.	.	.	.	.	2 375	3 347	3 490	3 740	.

Canada (DA) [4][5] — Wage earners - Ouvriers - Obreros — E.G./h. - Dollar

Total men and women - Total hommes et femmes - Total hombres y mujeres
ISIC 3 - CITI 3 - CIIU 3

	1999	2000	2001	2002	2003	2004	2005	2006	2007	2008
Total	17.79	18.26	18.36	18.59	19.36	19.99	20.53	20.50	21.58	21.95
15	15.20	15.60	15.72	15.44	16.21	16.67	17.90	16.77	18.44	17.44
16	24.92	24.46	25.16	26.32	27.26	24.48	23.00	23.23	22.11	
17	12.54	13.35	12.25	13.69	13.28	13.87	14.17	14.77	14.98	16.39
18	10.98	11.50	10.56	12.29	12.16	12.55	12.27	12.77	12.76	13.56
19	11.26	11.71	11.07	12.79	12.63	12.96	12.31	12.57	12.50	13.72
20	17.69	18.09	16.43	18.33	18.84	18.64	20.10	19.92	20.71	20.41
21	22.45	23.04	22.32	22.97	24.00	23.80	25.77	23.81	25.12	25.78
22	15.79	16.44	17.06	17.09	17.24	18.18	18.31	19.04	20.62	20.22
23	21.54	19.56	21.03	21.65	22.72	21.78	23.96	24.77	24.74	24.91
24	18.71	18.48	19.46	20.06	22.00	20.88	22.56	23.35	23.29	22.85
25	16.16	16.96	16.93	16.42	16.57	17.20	16.91	16.58	17.83	18.53
26	17.57	17.65	19.57	18.96	20.21	20.42	20.91	21.19	23.84	23.02
27	22.58	22.59	23.59	24.29	24.75	26.14	26.21	26.57	28.45	27.65
28	17.89	18.06	18.06	17.81	18.82	20.39	20.19	20.20	21.13	22.89
29	18.93	19.97	21.05	20.00	20.71	21.39	21.79	22.34	23.08	24.69
30	16.51	16.43	16.88	18.38	18.97	19.34	19.38	20.22	19.88	20.70
31	16.11	17.27	17.56	17.22	17.45	17.86	19.14	20.65	20.89	18.79
32	17.36	18.23	18.91	18.02	18.32	19.15	19.46	20.14	20.06	21.63
33	16.70	17.36	17.50	16.56	17.61	17.92	18.70	19.32	19.57	20.98
34	22.98	23.12	24.35	25.04	25.98	26.69	26.59	26.86	27.93	24.50
34-35	22.42	22.58	23.60	24.33	25.32	26.00	25.78	26.11	27.23	27.18
35	20.89	21.06	21.49	22.11	23.10	23.73	23.22	23.86	25.12	25.48
36	14.31	15.12	15.11	14.62	16.02	15.83	16.17	16.17	16.38	17.47
37	12.72	13.10	13.28	14.64	16.27	16.01	16.36	16.02	16.28	18.31

Explanatory notes: see p. 877.

Notes explicatives: voir p. 879.

Notas explicativas: véase p. 882.

[1] Local units with 10 or more workers. [2] Production and related workers. [3] Last week of Aug. of each year. [4] Employees paid by the hour. [5] Incl. overtime.

[1] Unités locales occupant 10 ouvriers et plus. [2] Ouvriers à la production et assimilés. [3] Dernière semaine d'août de chaque année. [4] Salariés rémunérés à l'heure. [5] Y compris les heures supplémentaires.

[1] Unidades locales con 10 y más obreros. [2] Obreros manufactureros y trabajadores asimilados. [3] Ultima semana de agosto de cada año. [4] Asalariados remunerados por hora. [5] Incl. las horas extraordinarias.

	1999	2000	2001	2002	2003	2004	2005	2006	2007	2008

Canada (DA) [1]   Employees - Salariés - Asalariados   E.G./w.s. - Dollar

Total men and women - Total hommes et femmes - Total hombres y mujeres
ISIC 3 - CITI 3 - CIIU 3

	1999	2000	2001	2002	2003	2004	2005	2006	2007	2008
Total	780.44	794.81	796.69	818.64	837.36	860.63	895.40	904.66	939.63	947.38
15	643.52	663.31	661.04	658.58	690.78	702.39	760.49	772.68	806.89	776.07
16	1 169.22	1 128.41	1 095.52	1 094.88	1 157.43	1 166.36	1 275.60	1 306.20	1 222.68	.
17	559.23	587.65	570.73	609.87	603.36	616.21	633.91	645.55	704.16	663.46
18	483.71	497.43	478.33	520.90	523.83	534.38	545.08	566.67	604.36	569.02
19	485.08	505.76	481.07	534.49	532.09	527.74	521.53	534.31	574.66	538.85
20	742.64	760.71	706.51	756.17	759.94	773.44	845.26	805.44	831.89	842.83
21	951.57	948.80	969.42	1 019.07	1 007.93	1 019.53	1 087.60	1 054.34	1 077.94	1 073.99
22	708.22	730.20	714.98	759.00	755.57	778.12	811.22	855.73	874.60	888.99
23	1 066.30	1 075.73	1 118.01	1 108.59	1 126.30	1 114.98	1 176.89	1 232.63	1 218.97	1 277.22
24	925.81	944.07	956.48	989.42	1 025.84	1 012.70	1 058.31	1 122.22	1 108.17	1 113.85
25	714.27	717.39	741.90	773.16	767.24	806.35	836.40	799.71	829.56	825.33
26	751.64	763.65	773.28	793.89	844.81	834.16	888.43	905.16	961.87	1 008.48
27	979.83	980.49	998.24	1 026.45	1 038.58	1 090.66	1 116.13	1 106.74	1 207.30	1 180.95
28	767.44	774.18	774.39	766.90	785.32	830.66	829.60	839.22	903.29	960.13
29	862.36	895.30	916.89	920.17	906.67	933.46	958.47	1 003.49	987.60	1 038.02
30	852.02	861.19	922.02	1 019.65	1 069.57	1 112.96	1 116.15	1 112.13	1 159.62	1 120.81
31	833.99	836.74	840.50	854.41	921.32	915.50	978.16	1 004.93	1 054.98	1 070.60
32	947.15	934.26	994.76	1 029.28	1 038.66	1 063.76	1 097.18	1 099.10	1 148.18	1 146.66
33	813.21	841.70	864.72	852.97	867.68	882.68	907.59	910.05	967.74	996.62
34	998.67	1 006.45	1 006.78	1 053.97	1 072.10	1 112.82	1 120.59	1 103.40	1 156.63	1 121.28
34-35	980.86	988.66	985.77	1 023.81	1 055.35	1 092.53	1 101.23	1 095.06	1 142.66	1 114.48
35	936.91	946.31	936.01	949.36	1 012.61	1 040.00	1 052.05	1 074.58	1 108.83	1 008.02
36	594.96	632.22	635.19	615.82	682.13	727.96	716.98	730.00	747.47	763.42
37	576.14	601.00	603.63	686.59	704.42	710.03	713.42	722.23	740.20	816.32

Colombia (BA) [2][3][4]   Employees - Salariés - Asalariados   E.G./m. - Peso

Total men and women - Total hommes et femmes - Total hombres y mujeres
ISIC 3 - CITI 3 - CIIU 3

	1999	2000	2001	2002	2003	2004	2005	2006	2007	2008
Total	.	.	.	353 590	442 510	468 406	506 020	608 137	694 244	.

Men - Hommes - Hombres
ISIC 3 - CITI 3 - CIIU 3

Total	.	.	.	457 189	531 791	557 571	605 537	707 408	847 898	.

Women - Femmes - Mujeres
ISIC 3 - CITI 3 - CIIU 3

Total	.	.	.	258 415	347 588	365 782	394 964	473 333	505 713	.

Costa Rica (BA) [5]   Employees - Salariés - Asalariados   E.G./h. - Colón

Total men and women - Total hommes et femmes - Total hombres y mujeres
ISIC 3 - CITI 3 - CIIU 3

	1999	2000	2001	2002	2003	2004	2005	2006	2007	2008
Total	.	.	.	.	.	.	953.0	993.3	1 210.2	1 195.1
15	.	.	.	.	.	.	931.6	974.3	1 361.0	1 350.1
16	.	.	.	.	.	.	.	.	.	1 611.3
17	.	.	.	.	.	.	811.2	699.6	1 557.9	1 443.4
18	.	.	.	.	.	.	712.2	699.0	762.8	1 928.6
19	.	.	.	.	.	.	1 133.0	693.0	715.6	1 257.6
20	.	.	.	.	.	.	785.0	723.7	692.8	1 399.4
21	.	.	.	.	.	.	900.3	940.5	1 241.7	1 621.1
22	.	.	.	.	.	.	1 000.4	1 090.0	1 308.2	969.4
23	.	.	.	.	.	.	1 516.4	.	2 007.6	1 146.7
24	.	.	.	.	.	.	1 561.9	1 741.6	1 628.6	1 957.1
25	.	.	.	.	.	.	949.1	1 148.6	1 294.8	1 283.1
26	.	.	.	.	.	.	852.3	977.4	1 220.4	1 876.4
27	.	.	.	.	.	.	1 548.8	887.2	841.9	1 348.2
28	.	.	.	.	.	.	757.3	717.4	947.0	1 007.8
29	.	.	.	.	.	.	927.4	981.7	1 214.1	977.6
30	.	.	.	.	.	.	735.6	.	1 460.2	799.2
31	.	.	.	.	.	.	1 019.2	1 244.7	987.4	933.9
32	.	.	.	.	.	.	1 000.0	1 459.8	1 550.6	2 152.0
33	.	.	.	.	.	.	1 158.6	1 013.2	1 197.9	1 535.4
34	.	.	.	.	.	.	737.8	677.7	754.4	964.7
35	.	.	.	.	.	.	1 272.1	1 194.8	2 319.6	1 069.3
36	.	.	.	.	.	.	649.1	657.3	743.1	1 582.3
37	.	.	.	.	.	.	571.0	438.3	511.9	997.8

Explanatory notes: see p. 877.   Notes explicatives: voir p. 879.   Notas explicativas: véase p. 882.

[1] Incl. overtime. [2] Excl. armed forces. [3] Persons aged 10 years and over. [4] Fourth quarter. [5] Main occupation; July of each year.

[1] Y compris les heures supplémentaires. [2] Non compris les forces armées. [3] Personnes âgées de 10 ans et plus. [4] Quatrième trimestre. [5] Occupation principale; juillet de chaque année.

[1] Incl. las horas extraordinarias. [2] Excl. las fuerzas armadas. [3] Personas de 10 años y más. [4] Cuarto trimestre. [5] Ocupación principal; julio de cada año.

WAGES SALAIRES SALARIOS

In manufacturing Dans les industries manufacturières En las industrias manufactureras

	1999	2000	2001	2002	2003	2004	2005	2006	2007	2008

Costa Rica (BA) [1] — Employees - Salariés - Asalariados — E.G./h. - Colón

Men - Hommes - Hombres
ISIC 3 - CITI 3 - CIIU 3

	1999	2000	2001	2002	2003	2004	2005	2006	2007	2008
Total							1 006.1	1 028.5	1 325.5	1 209.1
15							991.8	1 026.3	1 599.3	1 446.7
16										1 494.6
17							910.4	753.5	1 993.9	1 443.4
18							828.4	722.5	815.0	1 946.6
19							1 168.0	717.1	688.3	1 263.7
20							787.4	723.1	697.7	1 377.2
21							905.4	984.9	1 354.8	1 945.1
22							1 044.9	1 071.3	1 254.6	957.0
23									2 191.8	1 184.6
24							1 527.2	1 869.5	1 634.0	3 031.2
25							994.6	1 217.8	1 340.2	1 418.8
26							862.3	858.2	1 267.9	1 993.2
27							1 548.8	887.2	841.9	1 700.9
28							749.1	668.0	933.1	1 038.1
29							957.3	811.1	1 237.0	977.6
30							1 393.3		1 125.7	795.6
31							988.0	1 382.7	1 156.3	641.5
32							1 281.4	1 552.6	1 595.9	2 008.8
33							1 506.5	1 188.9	1 440.0	1 506.1
34							1 008.1	677.7	756.9	959.3
35							1 272.1	1 194.8	2 319.6	1 064.4
36							673.5	640.7	724.1	1 632.4
37							571.0	454.3	511.9	1 080.5

Women - Femmes - Mujeres
ISIC 3 - CITI 3 - CIIU 3

	1999	2000	2001	2002	2003	2004	2005	2006	2007	2008
Total							793.6	890.3	923.4	1 144.0
15							748.2	811.3	849.0	1 110.8
16									847.1	1 863.4
17							634.9	611.7	839.1	
18							600.3	684.3	743.3	1 888.8
19							359.6	412.1	730.3	1 184.3
20							553.7	732.5	623.0	1 616.9
21							863.8	571.5	984.7	738.3
22							876.4	1 148.3	1 404.0	1 135.8
23							1 516.4		1 639.0	791.6
24							1 663.8	1 335.3	1 603.2	1 354.2
25							688.7	822.6	889.8	857.6
26							793.7		914.5	1 542.0
27										889.2
28							861.8	1 349.6	1 113.7	923.8
29							855.6	1 173.9	990.1	
30							584.0		2 353.9	856.6
31							1 083.7	982.6	645.2	1 325.8
32							707.5		1 471.7	2 865.5
33							710.4	873.8	822.9	1 616.7
34							222.2		721.7	1 153.6
35										1 145.4
36							457.8	829.0	912.5	1 430.5
37										890.1

Costa Rica (BA) [1] — Total employment - Emploi total - Empleo total — E.G./m. - Colón

Total men and women - Total hommes et femmes - Total hombres y mujeres
ISIC 3 - CITI 3 - CIIU 3

	1999	2000	2001	2002	2003	2004	2005	2006	2007	2008
Total	97 774	108 777	128 207				393 518			549 285
15	98 273	116 660	134 820				382 671			574 222
16	168 045									
17	98 241	108 552	106 003				359 594			420 171
18	81 532	92 380	94 142				279 151			373 456
19	113 317	95 027	108 732				456 092			469 011
20	75 897	97 895	93 423				276 621			336 051
21	120 092	116 895	154 361				388 564			584 596
22	107 554	106 892	197 004				415 239			697 701
23	236 175	217 718					656 593			625 000
24	132 570	104 803	128 769				639 018			835 102
25	103 108	124 728	158 310				398 858			544 560
26	106 852	118 129	203 724				346 977			588 790
27	57 109	101 099	175 080				639 339			701 917
28	116 530	91 319	108 158				320 611			419 745
29	136 315	105 752	147 470				394 813			496 530
30	120 394	152 890	108 011				311 597			847 411
31	54 777	100 651	150 099				443 135			555 568
32	114 676	107 911	160 658				420 688			812 500
33	110 027	101 147	108 535				509 730			583 759
34	80 088	233 524	120 084				318 944			436 369
35	107 917	126 482	211 367				538 856			423 284
36	69 345	84 951	104 859				256 464			339 968
37	78 711	108 861	78 978				213 875			404 393

Explanatory notes: see p. 877.   Notes explicatives: voir p. 879.   Notas explicativas: véase p. 882.

[1] Main occupation; July of each year.   [1] Occupation principale; juillet de chaque année.   [1] Ocupación principal; julio de cada año.

WAGES

In manufacturing

SALAIRES

Dans les industries manufacturières

SALARIOS

En las industrias manufactureras

5B

	1999	2000	2001	2002	2003	2004	2005	2006	2007	2008

Costa Rica (BA) [1] — Total employment - Emploi total - Empleo total — E.G./m. - Colón

Men - Hommes - Hombres
ISIC 3 - CITI 3 - CIIU 3

	1999	2000	2001	2002	2003	2004	2005	2006	2007	2008
Total	106 594	115 642	135 707	.	.	.	410 986	.	.	580 373
15	110 821	120 750	141 964	.	.	.	401 753	.	.	633 021
16	168 045	.	21 650							
17	132 549	104 884	108 132	.	.	.	405 031	.	.	503 625
18	96 167	106 726	100 377	.	.	.	298 818	.	.	414 567
19	135 571	101 623	117 037	.	.	.	471 465	.	.	523 183
20	76 463	100 017	94 200	.	.	.	277 041	.	.	337 984
21	119 756	121 120	166 399	.	.	.	390 371	.	.	626 403
22	105 672	109 248	201 044	.	.	.	443 646	.	.	647 167
23	198 706	202 121	.	.	.	.	.	.	.	625 000
24	145 008	121 571	121 979	.	.	.	631 303	.	.	842 861
25	107 324	131 325	154 019	.	.	.	415 399	.	.	547 203
26	106 569	121 345	193 994	.	.	.	341 785	.	.	577 788
27	57 109	101 099	172 816	.	.	.	639 339	.	.	842 225
28	119 606	89 344	104 803	.	.	.	316 409	.	.	414 372
29	136 315	105 752	162 600	.	.	.	401 276	.	.	512 941
30	125 826	193 980	119 193	.	.	.	600 392	.	.	1 312 521
31	54 777	113 022	157 286	.	.	.	413 239	.	.	614 320
32	131 747	120 911	204 803	.	.	.	535 183	.	.	863 038
33	125 949	125 996	116 723	.	.	.	665 146	.	.	736 510
34	80 088	233 524	131 034	.	.	.	435 009	.	.	449 477
35	116 101	126 482	209 517	.	.	.	538 856	.	.	423 284
36	70 809	84 671	105 153	.	.	.	262 701	.	.	338 074
37	78 711	108 861	78 978	.	.	.	213 875	.	.	277 778

Women - Femmes - Mujeres
ISIC 3 - CITI 3 - CIIU 3

	1999	2000	2001	2002	2003	2004	2005	2006	2007	2008
Total	77 969	93 773	112 596	.	.	.	335 824	.	.	472 590
15	70 257	104 315	116 857	.	.	.	312 474	.	.	453 279
16	.	.	.	.	.	.	.	.	.	.
17	74 593	112 271	104 297	.	.	.	271 658	.	.	373 885
18	71 620	83 453	90 010	.	.	.	260 048	.	.	353 681
19	76 811	74 462	73 514	.	.	.	155 724	.	.	320 161
20	64 513	64 861	77 457	.	.	.	239 760	.	.	180 417
21	121 361	96 563	77 692	.	.	.	372 938	.	.	480 955
22	112 006	101 566	177 755	.	.	.	330 399	.	.	806 843
23	350 000	339 780	.	.	.	.	656 593	.	.	-
24	110 903	84 635	139 426	.	.	.	661 238	.	.	817 866
25	86 826	108 281	172 957	.	.	.	297 276	.	.	512 816
26	108 585	94 279	258 516	.	.	.	378 939	.	.	700 128
27	.	.	190 110	.	.	.	.	.	.	319 680
28	52 144	113 351	180 375	.	.	.	373 145	.	.	491 795
29	.	.	94 330	.	.	.	377 550	.	.	342 772
30	109 812	98 195	85 648	.	.	.	252 885	.	.	586 367
31	.	67 011	119 075	.	.	.	511 582	.	.	371 320
32	63 978	77 689	140 417	.	.	.	303 726	.	.	667 691
33	81 172	67 891	103 566	.	.	.	299 913	.	.	385 035
34	.	.	67 320	.	.	.	96 222	.	.	400 000
35	.	.	220 000	.	.	.	.	.	.	-
36	57 092	87 879	103 320	.	.	.	198 870	.	.	370 891
37	.	.	.	.	.	.	.	.	.	574 074

Cuba (FD) [2] — Employees - Salariés - Asalariados — E.G./m. - Peso

Total men and women - Total hommes et femmes - Total hombres y mujeres
ISIC 2 - CITI 2 - CIIU 2

	1999	2000	2001	2002	2003	2004	2005	2006	2007	2008
Total	225	242 [3]	255	263	275	290	338	404	433	430
31	228	247 [3]	259	268	278	292	343	404	426	444
32	168	163 [3]	177	176	184	193	237	286	323	314
33	185	186 [3]	218	244	258	274	322	410	426	448
34	199	208 [3]	228	252	296	306	304	399	413	434
35	239	265 [3]	269	288	296	302	349	435	482	498
36	215	232 [3]	246	286	274	283	316	436	477	482
37	333	346 [3]	360	340	314	384	394	543	567	556
38	347	263 [3]	277	280	310	327	377	446	471	471

Explanatory notes: see p. 877.

[1] Main occupation; July of each year. [2] State sector (civilian).
[3] Incl. employment-related allowances received from the State.

Notes explicatives: voir p. 879.

[1] Occupation principale; juillet de chaque année. [2] Secteur d'Etat (civils). [3] Y compris les allocations en espèces liées à l'emploi et reçues de l'Etat.

Notas explicativas: véase p. 882.

[1] Ocupación principal; julio de cada año. [2] Sector de Estado (civil). [3] Incl. las prestaciones monetarias relacionadas con el empleo y pagadas por el Estado.

5B

WAGES	SALAIRES	SALARIOS
In manufacturing	Dans les industries manufacturières	En las industrias manufactureras

	1999	2000	2001	2002	2003	2004	2005	2006	2007	2008

Chile (DA) [1] — Employees - Salariés - Asalariados — E.G./m. - Peso

Total men and women - Total hommes et femmes - Total hombres y mujeres
ISIC 2 - CITI 2 - CIIU 2 [2] / ISIC 3 - CITI 3 - CIIU 3 [2]

	1999	2000	2001	2002	2003	2004	2005	2006	2007	2008	
Total	203 540	208 257	213 394	218 740	221 860	229 575	242 160	300 948	315 408	351 684	Total
31	189 213	197 152	204 992	209 371	215 294	217 682	235 174				
32	143 160	136 719	135 880	137 726	136 138	138 516	134 754				
33	169 797	173 721	171 786	168 968	178 042	184 283	187 632				
34	364 712	370 351	387 942	406 246	409 630	436 671	414 753				
35	296 662	308 516	313 805	318 805	312 819	338 562	345 558				
36	249 775	254 626	261 989	270 705	270 479	281 712	305 962				
37	212 198	218 738	225 564	241 022	250 687	259 226	292 590				
38	172 927	184 990	178 695	179 460	175 054	153 706	152 909				

República Dominicana (BA) — Employees - Salariés - Asalariados — E.G./h. - Peso

Total men and women - Total hommes et femmes - Total hombres y mujeres
ISIC 3 - CITI 3 - CIIU 3

	1999	2000	2001	2002	2003	2004
Total	27.1	24.1	28.2	29.4	32.7	50.8

El Salvador (BA) — Employees - Salariés - Asalariados — E.G./m. - US dollar

Total men and women - Total hommes et femmes - Total hombres y mujeres
ISIC 3 - CITI 3 - CIIU 3

	1999	2000	2001	2002	2003	2004	2005	2006
Total	1 746.61	1 789.97	1 750.43	208.70 [3]	209.56	211.34	229.00	235.10

Men - Hommes - Hombres
ISIC 3 - CITI 3 - CIIU 3

	1999	2000	2001	2002	2003	2004	2005	2006
Total	2 157.83	2 241.07	2 117.37	253.79 [3]	249.58	261.75	280.60	284.80

Women - Femmes - Mujeres
ISIC 3 - CITI 3 - CIIU 3

	1999	2000	2001	2002	2003	2004	2005	2006
Total	1 337.08	1 370.44	1 370.53	167.69 [3]	171.23	162.54	178.10	181.30

El Salvador (DA) [4] — Wage earners - Ouvriers - Obreros — E.G./h. - US dollar

Total men and women - Total hommes et femmes - Total hombres y mujeres
ISIC 2 - CITI 2 - CIIU 2 / ISIC 3 - CITI 3 - CIIU 3

	1999	2000	2001	2002	2003	2004	2005	2006	2007	2008	
Total	10.68	10.09		1.21 [3]	1.25	1.43	1.45	1.23	1.28	1.58	Total

Men - Hommes - Hombres
ISIC 2 - CITI 2 - CIIU 2 / ISIC 3 - CITI 3 - CIIU 3

	1999	2000	2001	2002	2003	2004	2005	2006	2007	2008	
Total	12.05	11.37	10.34	1.33 [3]	1.47	1.70	1.52	1.36	1.30	1.67	Total

Women - Femmes - Mujeres
ISIC 2 - CITI 2 - CIIU 2 / ISIC 3 - CITI 3 - CIIU 3

	1999	2000	2001	2002	2003	2004	2005	2006	2007	2008	
Total	9.20	9.00	9.53	[3]	1.23	1.20	1.23	1.13	1.11	1.40	Total

El Salvador (DA) [4] — Wage earners - Ouvriers - Obreros — E.G./h. - US dollar

Men - Hommes - Hombres
ISIC 2 - CITI 2 - CIIU 2

	1999	2000	2001	2002	2003	2004	2005	2006	2007	2008
31	11.83	12.88	9.87	1.39 [3]	1.78	1.89	1.77	2.00	1.00	1.51
32	9.64	9.47	8.38	1.19 [3]	1.33	1.30	1.23	1.00	1.00	1.10
33	8.46	9.48	15.50	1.39 [3]	1.00	0.89	1.68	1.00	1.00	1.34
34	14.26	16.44	10.68	1.75 [3]	1.92	2.70	1.57	2.00	2.00	2.81
35	13.07	12.00	11.40	1.23 [3]	1.38	1.55	1.55	1.00	1.00	1.85
36	15.01	10.25	10.69	1.15 [3]	1.49	1.85	1.55	1.00	1.00	1.62
37	12.77	13.18	11.98	1.38 [3]	1.00	1.25	1.07	1.00	1.00	1.44
38	11.20	9.79	10.15	1.57 [3]	1.43	3.14	1.39	1.00	2.00	1.45
39	12.80	11.52	10.76	1.40 [3]	1.27	1.50	1.43	1.00	2.00	1.65

Explanatory notes: see p. 877.

[1] Incl. family allowances and the value of payments in kind. [2] April of each year. [3] Prior to 2002: colones; 8.75 colones=1 US dollar. [4] Urban areas.

Notes explicatives: voir p. 879.

[1] Y compris les allocations familiales et la valeur des paiements en nature. [2] Avril de chaque année. [3] Avant 2002: colones; 8.75 colones=1 dollar EU. [4] Régions urbaines.

Notas explicativas: véase p. 882.

[1] Incl. las asignaciones familiares y el valor de los pagos en especie. [2] Abril de cada año. [3] Antes de 2002: colones; 8.75 colones=1 dólar EU. [4] Areas urbanas.

	1999	2000	2001	2002	2003	2004	2005	2006	2007	2008

El Salvador (DA) [1] — Wage earners - Ouvriers - Obreros — E.G./h. - US dollar

Women - Femmes - Mujeres
ISIC 2 - CITI 2 - CIIU 2

	1999	2000	2001	2002	2003	2004	2005	2006	2007	2008
31	10.19	10.11	10.43	0.90 [2]	1.04	1.18	1.39	1.00	1.00	1.17
32	8.67	8.81	7.60	0.98 [2]	1.27	1.20	1.39	1.00	1.00	1.02
33	8.11	10.18	10.61	2.00 [2]	1.00	0.95	1.66	1.00	1.00	1.32
34	11.14	10.00	10.49	1.21 [2]	1.10	1.16	1.11	2.00	1.00	3.74
35	11.19	10.18	10.32	1.13 [2]	1.20	1.23	1.41	1.00	2.00	2.29
36	14.74	10.01	.	1.39 [2]	1.11	1.27	1.05	2.00	.	3.55
37	16.75	38.18	11.78	1.53 [2]	0.93	0.84	0.86	1.00	1.00	2.77
38	9.63	10.90	10.20	0.82 [2]	1.09	1.20	1.07	1.00	1.00	1.00
39	10.80	7.25	11.73	0.98 [2]	1.04	1.30	1.07	1.00	1.00	1.20

Guatemala (FA) — Employees - Salariés - Asalariados — E.G./m. - Quetzal

Total men and women - Total hommes et femmes - Total hombres y mujeres
ISIC 2 - CITI 2 - CIIU 2

	1999	2000	2001	2002	2003	2004	2005	2006	2007	2008
Total	1 602.25	1 655.25	1 732.27	1 837.32	1 911.44	2 100.06	2 199.65	2 482.09	2 579.44	2 737.21

Guyana (DA) [3] — Employees - Salariés - Asalariados — E.G./m. - Dollar

Total men and women - Total hommes et femmes - Total hombres y mujeres
ISIC 3 - CITI 3 - CIIU 3

	1999	2000	2001	2002	2003	2004	2005	2006	2007	2008
Total	.	.	.	.	29 678	47 800	.	55 615	47 150	.

México (BA) [4] [5] — Employees - Salariés - Asalariados — E.G./m. - Nuevo peso

Total men and women - Total hommes et femmes - Total hombres y mujeres
ISIC 3 - CITI 3 - CIIU 3

	1999	2000	2001	2002	2003	2004	2005	2006	2007	2008
Total	2 403.3	2 944.1	3 399.8	3 554.8	3 757.3	3 887.9	4 140.3	4 422.6	4 689.2	4 679.3
15	2 118.4	2 761.3	3 036.3	3 245.4	3 547.6	3 554.0	4 061.8	3 944.2	4 264.0	4 092.0
16	2 426.7	4 646.8	3 499.1	3 824.0	6 153.6	3 053.9	.	.	.	.
17	2 116.1	2 512.7	2 600.1	2 942.4	3 465.2	3 211.2	3 856.7	3 775.7	4 123.6	4 211.4
18	1 690.3	2 092.4	2 288.3	2 427.2	2 621.6	2 743.7	2 635.9	3 136.5	3 129.1	3 819.1
19	1 868.7	2 319.4	2 562.5	2 977.6	3 600.6	3 238.8	3 071.8	3 313.1	3 560.3	3 659.3
20	1 801.6	2 484.2	2 729.1	2 927.0	3 257.7	3 246.2	3 693.1	3 339.1	3 890.2	3 997.8
21	3 359.1	3 446.0	3 566.9	3 927.9	3 639.4	4 285.8	4 584.1	4 903.3	5 187.7	5 092.7
22	2 212.1	2 920.5	4 329.1	3 989.2	4 039.5	4 335.6	5 167.7	4 627.8	5 554.5	5 145.2
23	4 905.1	5 872.9	6 793.4	8 335.5	8 880.0	8 052.6	9 758.9	11 479.6	9 635.5	11 392.0
24	4 125.2	3 955.4	4 823.4	4 700.2	5 646.6	4 854.7	5 362.4	6 530.4	7 164.1	7 068.0
25	2 326.5	3 143.4	4 108.3	3 660.3	3 714.8	4 021.7	4 003.4	4 755.3	4 802.1	4 707.1
26	2 390.2	2 588.5	2 833.2	3 593.4	3 501.9	3 766.4	3 980.1	4 378.2	5 158.4	4 516.4
27	3 446.8	4 296.4	5 311.5	5 430.8	5 374.5	5 373.8	5 132.6	6 379.9	5 901.4	6 193.2
28	2 087.2	2 712.2	3 091.9	3 325.1	3 535.8	3 917.7	4 248.2	4 413.9	4 357.4	4 674.8
29	3 511.3	3 919.6	4 671.9	4 379.8	4 409.4	5 338.4	5 543.2	6 470.1	5 389.9	5 926.8
30	2 683.6	3 730.2	4 758.7	4 713.6	7 304.9	3 547.3	5 109.1	5 216.8	5 629.1	5 450.5
31	2 799.1	3 643.3	4 297.8	4 064.2	4 263.6	4 203.3	4 564.7	5 225.1	5 666.6	5 315.7
32	2 933.7	3 702.6	4 118.3	4 354.0	4 357.7	4 567.5	.	.	.	.
33	2 933.8	3 656.8	4 188.4	4 138.3	4 618.8	4 519.8	2 918.9	3 521.4	3 890.3	3 760.2
34	2 916.8	3 522.3	4 009.6	4 193.2	4 322.0	4 836.2	4 555.0	4 821.0	5 138.6	5 359.1
35	2 498.7	2 097.7	2 789.6	2 645.2	2 996.8	3 624.8	.	.	.	.
36	1 929.4	2 528.1	2 777.3	2 972.2	3 024.0	3 598.7	3 713.7	3 732.9	3 880.1	4 111.3
37	.	.	.	.	.	.	.	.	.	.

Men - Hommes - Hombres
ISIC 3 - CITI 3 - CIIU 3

	1999	2000	2001	2002	2003	2004	2005	2006	2007	2008
Total	2 681.5	3 297.6	3 789.6	3 988.9	4 176.6	4 273.8	4 625.6	4 839.5	5 242.5	5 172.2
15	2 389.1	3 063.9	3 376.2	3 668.9	3 973.4	3 893.4	4 540.7	4 244.5	4 841.2	4 575.6
16	2 101.8	5 615.0	3 561.7	3 932.5	6 378.8	2 231.4	.	.	.	.
17	2 430.3	2 944.7	3 061.3	3 446.3	4 106.1	3 902.6	3 969.6	4 023.6	4 394.7	4 551.1
18	2 005.4	2 668.0	2 710.4	3 074.8	3 030.7	3 115.1	3 521.6	4 135.8	3 677.4	4 572.9
19	2 074.7	2 624.2	2 976.1	3 287.7	3 881.3	3 655.9	3 605.7	3 763.7	4 419.6	4 375.4
20	1 872.4	2 574.0	2 826.2	2 975.0	3 276.1	3 392.6	3 800.2	3 379.6	4 012.9	4 182.4
21	4 124.3	3 832.0	3 879.4	4 205.5	3 929.0	4 668.1	4 989.3	5 375.5	5 558.8	5 746.7
22	2 321.3	2 998.0	4 550.3	4 374.0	4 092.4	4 337.3	5 321.4	4 546.9	5 919.0	5 220.9
23	4 875.9	6 365.3	7 030.0	8 442.6	9 137.2	8 336.8	9 758.1	11 588.5	9 825.6	11 811.7
24	5 212.1	4 564.6	5 032.5	5 297.5	6 777.2	5 657.3	6 200.1	6 997.8	7 907.7	7 760.2
25	2 598.7	3 455.0	4 452.8	4 139.6	4 329.4	4 419.5	4 608.2	5 259.8	5 435.3	4 883.0
26	2 412.9	2 670.8	2 960.4	3 722.8	3 564.0	3 709.7	4 055.5	4 464.7	5 275.5	4 611.4
27	3 458.2	4 252.8	5 285.1	5 447.6	5 497.1	5 571.7	5 247.3	6 574.5	6 341.8	6 454.7
28	2 090.7	2 744.3	3 103.4	3 362.4	3 571.8	4 003.9	4 339.8	4 402.6	4 459.5	4 692.6
29	3 729.2	4 142.5	4 848.6	4 591.6	4 656.8	5 608.7	5 709.2	6 863.0	5 737.4	6 066.3
30	3 029.5	4 476.4	5 065.4	5 405.3	8 958.6	2 943.6	6 239.3	6 145.5	6 955.1	6 599.7
31	3 037.1	4 206.0	4 904.4	4 749.8	4 868.6	4 824.3	5 510.9	6 224.7	7 039.1	6 427.1
32	3 642.4	4 718.7	5 196.2	5 165.5	5 231.8	5 232.7	.	.	.	.
33	3 041.4	3 999.5	5 238.2	4 471.2	5 429.9	5 255.4	3 489.2	4 127.5	4 461.0	4 227.8
34	3 246.1	3 980.5	4 548.9	4 586.3	4 820.4	5 377.4	5 129.1	5 337.0	5 647.9	6 015.9
35	3 234.3	1 876.5	2 791.8	2 685.9	2 943.0	3 473.2	.	.	.	.
36	1 970.0	2 559.5	2 869.1	3 105.1	3 103.0	3 618.7	3 703.0	3 751.6	3 923.5	4 128.3
37	.	.	.	.	.	.	.	.	.	.

Explanatory notes: see p. 877.

[1] Urban areas. [2] Prior to 2002: colones; 8.75 colones=1 US dollar. [3] July. [4] Persons aged 14 years and over. [5] Second quarter of each year.

Notes explicatives: voir p. 879.

[1] Régions urbaines. [2] Avant 2002: colones; 8.75 colones=1 dollar EU. [3] Juillet. [4] Personnes âgées de 14 ans et plus. [5] Deuxième trimestre de chaque année.

Notas explicativas: véase p. 882.

[1] Areas urbanas. [2] Antes de 2002: colones; 8.75 colones=1 dólar EU. [3] Julio. [4] Personas de 14 años y más. [5] Segundo trimestre de cada año.

	WAGES			SALAIRES				SALARIOS		
	In manufacturing			**Dans les industries manufacturières**				**En las industrias manufactureras**		

	1999	2000	2001	2002	2003	2004	2005	2006	2007	2008
México (BA) [1] [2]					**Employees - Salariés - Asalariados**					**E.G./m. - Nuevo peso**
Women - Femmes - Mujeres										
ISIC 3 - CITI 3 - CIIU 3										
Total	1 829.6	2 259.4	2 646.1	2 714.7	2 911.7	3 114.6	3 217.5	3 628.3	3 651.1	3 715.3
15	1 485.6	2 045.8	2 231.3	2 298.6	2 562.6	2 787.3	3 017.4	3 302.0	3 107.9	3 102.4
16	3 817.4	2 298.7	3 270.1	2 899.3	4 052.8	4 968.4				
17	1 466.1	1 673.8	1 759.3	2 118.8	2 494.2	2 231.6	3 523.8	3 193.4	3 461.8	3 186.9
18	1 528.6	1 781.8	2 089.2	2 128.8	2 383.5	2 515.9	1 923.8	2 508.7	2 561.3	3 199.9
19	1 450.1	1 794.7	1 861.5	2 314.5	2 964.1	2 396.1	2 628.5	2 944.2	2 866.5	3 032.6
20	1 318.0	1 915.9	1 843.1	2 655.1	2 988.6	1 999.2	2 628.4	3 069.0	2 995.5	2 561.4
21	1 517.0	2 343.0	2 869.5	3 298.7	2 905.7	3 105.5	3 049.4	3 516.0	4 376.2	3 794.5
22	1 854.3	2 745.8	3 843.1	3 137.2	3 894.9	4 331.9	4 735.7	4 817.1	4 815.8	4 969.0
23	5 089.4	4 129.8	5 558.7	7 711.2	7 530.0	6 992.9	9 764.2	10 454.7	8 508.6	8 479.4
24	2 596.0	3 036.5	4 455.0	3 782.1	3 985.9	3 606.5	4 249.1	5 681.6	5 710.2	5 725.6
25	1 729.7	2 617.3	3 365.2	2 888.9	2 758.6	3 351.2	3 135.3	3 932.6	3 919.2	4 432.0
26	2 238.8	2 187.5	2 159.6	2 811.3	3 087.0	4 266.6	3 497.1	3 832.1	4 331.9	4 081.6
27	3 364.3	4 853.6	5 506.2	5 163.7	4 473.1	3 867.7	4 291.5	5 421.3	4 218.8	4 713.6
28	2 045.7	2 464.6	2 988.5	3 059.2	3 277.6	3 212.0	3 787.6	4 512.9	3 586.5	4 541.6
29	2 650.9	2 940.2	3 856.9	3 543.1	3 571.3	4 432.1	5 152.5	5 242.9	4 373.1	5 488.6
30	2 192.4	2 492.7	4 295.6	4 075.4	5 485.1	4 121.3	4 122.6	4 334.3	4 332.1	4 050.0
31	2 280.4	2 854.2	3 250.4	3 006.3	3 195.4	3 032.9	3 241.7	3 755.5	3 946.5	4 111.8
32	2 347.7	2 779.5	3 147.1	3 361.4	3 414.4	3 906.4				
33	2 716.9	3 157.7	3 054.6	3 760.3	3 874.9	4 047.7	2 401.5	2 923.9	3 337.6	3 241.7
34	2 186.9	2 513.8	2 920.2	3 381.1	3 279.4	3 768.6	3 432.1	3 941.3	4 310.6	4 104.5
35	1 693.0	2 641.4	2 777.1	2 479.4	3 447.3	3 917.9				
36	1 714.1	2 407.9	2 501.7	2 484.5	2 666.7	3 492.6	3 807.2	3 633.0	3 627.6	3 999.1
37										
Nicaragua (DA)					**Employees - Salariés - Asalariados**					**E.G./h. - Córdoba**
Total men and women - Total hommes et femmes - Total hombres y mujeres										
ISIC 2 - CITI 2 - CIIU 2										
Total					13.5	13.5	13.7	13.9		
31					13.1	13.1	13.1	14.4		
32					8.2	8.6	8.9	9.3		
33					15.1	15.1	15.1	15.1		
34					23.6	23.6	24.5	24.5		
35					14.7	15.2	15.7	16.2		
36					19.2	19.2	19.4	19.4		
38					12.2	13.2	14.2	10.8		
39					5.1	6.4	8.0	8.6		
Nicaragua (DA)					**Employees - Salariés - Asalariados**					**E.G./m. - Córdoba**
Total men and women - Total hommes et femmes - Total hombres y mujeres										
ISIC 2 - CITI 2 - CIIU 2										
Total					3 279	3 283	3 331	3 393		
31	3 051	3 181	3 184	3 184	3 184	3 184	3 184	3 502		
32	1 683	1 751	1 840	1 950	2 006	2 081	2 160	2 259		
33	3 076	3 458	3 581	3 668	3 668	3 668	3 668	3 668		
34	4 567	5 629	5 734	5 734	5 734	5 734	5 956	5 961		
35	2 961	3 318	3 553	3 570	3 570	3 686	3 817	3 936		
36	4 475	4 570	4 619	4 668	4 668	4 668	4 720	4 730		
37		2 892	2 955	2 955						
38	2 641				2 957	3 222	3 456	2 629		
39					1 230	1 554	1 938	2 088		
Panamá (BA) [3] [4] [5]					**Total employment - Emploi total - Empleo total**					**E.G./h. - Balboa**
Total men and women - Total hommes et femmes - Total hombres y mujeres										
ISIC 3 - CITI 3 - CIIU 3										
Total				1.8	1.7	1.9	2.2	2.2	2.2	2.0
Men - Hommes - Hombres										
ISIC 3 - CITI 3 - CIIU 3										
Total				1.8	1.7	1.9	2.1	2.1	2.2	2.1
Women - Femmes - Mujeres										
ISIC 3 - CITI 3 - CIIU 3										
Total				1.9	1.8	2.1	2.7	2.7	2.1	2.0
Paraguay (BA)					**Employees - Salariés - Asalariados**					**E.G./m. - Guarani**
Total men and women - Total hommes et femmes - Total hombres y mujeres										
ISIC 2 - CITI 2 - CIIU 2									ISIC 3 - CITI 3 - CIIU 3 [6] [7]	
Total		813 765	639 988	739 738	816 428				5 399.1	5 907.1
										Total

Explanatory notes: see p. 877.

[1] Persons aged 14 years and over. [2] Second quarter of each year. [3] Persons aged 15 years and over. [4] Median. [5] Aug. of each year. [6] Fourth quarter of each year. [7] Figures in thousands.

Notes explicatives: voir p. 879.

[1] Personnes âgées de 14 ans et plus. [2] Deuxième trimestre de chaque année. [3] Personnes âgées de 15 ans et plus. [4] Médiane. [5] Août de chaque année. [6] Quatrième trimestre de chaque année. [7] Données en milliers.

Notas explicativas: véase p. 882.

[1] Personas de 14 años y más. [2] Segundo trimestre de cada año. [3] Personas de 15 años y más. [4] Mediana. [5] Agosto de cada año. [6] Cuarto trimestre de cada año. [7] Cifras en millares.

	1999	2000	2001	2002	2003	2004	2005	2006	2007	2008	

Paraguay (BA) — Employees - Salariés - Asalariados — E.G./m. - Guarani

Men - Hommes - Hombres
ISIC 2 - CITI 2 - CIIU 2 / ISIC 3 - CITI 3 - CIIU 3 [1] [2]

	1999	2000	2001	2002	2003	2004	2005	2006	2007	2008	
Total	.	995 539	746 213	880 891	966 821 I	.	.	.	5 550.4	5 827.6	Total

Women - Femmes - Mujeres
ISIC 2 - CITI 2 - CIIU 2 / ISIC 3 - CITI 3 - CIIU 3 [1] [2]

	1999	2000	2001	2002	2003	2004	2005	2006	2007	2008	
Total	.	402 798	408 608	453 064	514 766 I	.	.	.	4 745.9	6 303.2	Total

Perú (B) [3] — Wage earners - Ouvriers - Obreros — R.T./h. - Nuevo sol

Total men and women - Total hommes et femmes - Total hombres y mujeres
ISIC 3 - CITI 3 - CIIU 3

	1999	2000	2001	2002	2003	2004	2005	2006	2007	2008
Total	.	.	.	2.5	2.7	2.7	2.6	2.9	3.4	3.6

Perú (B) [3] — Salaried employees - Employés - Empleados — R.T./h. - Nuevo sol

Total men and women - Total hommes et femmes - Total hombres y mujeres
ISIC 3 - CITI 3 - CIIU 3

	1999	2000	2001	2002	2003	2004	2005	2006	2007	2008
Total	.	.	.	11.4	10.6	9.8	6.4	8.0	7.9	9.1

Puerto Rico (DA) — Wage earners - Ouvriers - Obreros — E.G./h. - US dollar

Total men and women - Total hommes et femmes - Total hombres y mujeres
ISIC 2 - CITI 2 - CIIU 2

	1999	2000	2001	2002	2003	2004	2005	2006	2007	2008
Total	.	.	9.8	10.3	10.5	10.8	11.1	11.5	11.9	12.1
311-312	8.0	8.3	8.1	8.6	9.1	9.3	9.8	9.9	9.9	10.0
311-313 [4]	.	.	.	.	.	.	.	.	.	.
314 [4]	9.36	10.21	.	.	.	.	.	.	.	.
321 [4]	6.73	6.80	.	.	.	.	.	.	.	.
322 [4]	5.95	5.99	6.46	6.53	6.45	6.43	6.44	6.60	6.66	7.46
323 [4]	5.96	5.82	.	.	.	.	.	.	.	.
324 [4]	6.22	6.16	.	.	.	.	.	.	.	.
33 [4]	6.07	6.56	.	.	.	.	.	.	.	.
341 [4]	8.48	8.64	.	.	.	.	.	.	.	.
342 [4]	9.40	9.26	.	.	.	.	.	.	.	.
351-352 [4]	12.95	13.49	14.22	14.40	14.65	15.24	15.90	16.44	17.19	17.54
353-354 [4]	14.05	14.59	.	.	.	.	.	.	.	.
355-356 [4]	8.25	8.63	8.57	8.85	8.66	8.84	9.20	9.19	9.49	10.00
361 [4]	9.65	9.99	10.80	10.87	10.45	10.13	10.79	10.67	11.43	11.97
362	.	.	.	.	.	.	.	.	.	.
369	.	.	.	.	.	.	.	.	.	.
381 [4]	7.43	7.78	7.72	8.08	8.49	9.06	9.07	9.36	8.93	9.49
382 [4]	7.83	8.21	.	.	.	.	.	.	.	.
383 [4]	8.65	9.34	8.13	8.35	8.54	9.08	9.58	9.96	10.28	10.73
384 [4]	7.13	7.23	.	.	.	.	.	.	.	.
385 [4]	8.73	9.10	9.23	9.58	10.08	10.14	10.15	10.12	10.43	10.73
390 [4]	7.56	7.49	.	.	.	.	.	.	.	.

United States (DA) [5] [6] — Employees - Salariés - Asalariados — E.G./h. - Dollar

Total men and women - Total hommes et femmes - Total hombres y mujeres
ISIC 3 - CITI 3 - CIIU 3

	1999	2000	2001	2002	2003	2004	2005	2006	2007	2008
Total	13.85	14.32	14.76	15.29	15.74	16.14	16.56	16.81	17.26	17.74
16	17.49	18.24	18.50	18.95	20.36	21.15	21.33	23.05	25.86	26.21
18	8.35	8.61	8.83	9.11	9.58	9.77	10.26	10.65	11.05	11.40
19	9.93	10.35	10.69	11.00	11.66	11.63	11.50	11.44	12.04	12.96
20	11.18	11.63	11.99	12.33	12.71	13.03	13.16	13.39	13.68	14.20
21	15.58	15.91	16.38	16.85	17.33	17.91	17.99	18.01	18.44	18.88
23	22.22	22.80	22.90	23.04	23.63	24.39	24.47	24.11	25.21	27.46
24	16.40	17.09	17.57	17.97	18.50	19.17	19.67	19.60	19.55	19.49
25	12.25	12.70	13.21	13.55	14.18	14.59	14.80	14.97	15.39	15.85
26	13.97	14.53	14.86	15.40	15.76	16.25	16.61	16.59	16.93	16.90
27	16.00	16.64	17.06	17.68	18.13	18.57	18.94	19.36	19.66	20.18
28	13.34	13.77	14.19	14.68	15.01	15.31	15.80	16.17	16.53	16.99
31	.	.	.	.	.	.	.	.	.	.
37	11.09	11.63	12.43	12.71	12.56	13.21	13.56	14.31	14.51	13.89

Explanatory notes: see p. 877.

[1] Fourth quarter of each year. [2] Figures in thousands. [3] Urban areas. [4] March of each year. [5] National classification not strictly compatible with ISIC. [6] Not all employees covered; only production and non-supervisory workers; private sector.

Notes explicatives: voir p. 879.

[1] Quatrième trimestre de chaque année. [2] Données en milliers. [3] Régions urbaines. [4] Mars de chaque année. [5] Classification nationale non strictement compatible avec la CITI. [6] Non couverts tous les salariés: seulement travailleurs à la production et ceux sans activité de surveillance; secteur privé.

Notas explicativas: véase p. 882.

[1] Cuarto trimestre de cada año. [2] Cifras en millares. [3] Areas urbanas. [4] Marzo de cada año. [5] Clasificación nacional no estrictamente compatible con la CIIU. [6] Todos asalariados no cubiertos; sólo trabajaodores de la producción y los sin funciones de supervisión; sector privado.

5B

WAGES

In manufacturing

SALAIRES

Dans les industries manufacturières

SALARIOS

En las industrias manufactureras

	1999	2000	2001	2002	2003	2004	2005	2006	2007	2008	
Uruguay (D) [1]					Employees - Salariés - Asalariados						E.G./h.
Indices, total - Indices, total - Índices, total											
ISIC 3 - CITI 3 - CIIU 3											
Total									90.45	100.48	
15									90.88	101.04	
17									92.45	101.03	
18									89.01	98.65	
19									89.71	101.65	
20										102.61	
21									90.47	100.45	
22									90.04	100.06	
24									88.77	98.27	
25									88.49	100.85	
26									90.88	101.09	
28									92.14	101.92	
34									90.86	101.36	
36										103.45	
Virgin Islands (US) (DA)					Wage earners - Ouvriers - Obreros						E.G./h. - US dollar
Total men and women - Total hommes et femmes - Total hombres y mujeres											
ISIC 3 - CITI 3 - CIIU 3											
Total			22.57	22.98	23.37	23.35	23.49	26.53	26.35	28.05	

ASIA-ASIE-ASIA

	1999	2000	2001	2002	2003	2004	2005	2006	2007	2008	
Armenia (DA)					Employees - Salariés - Asalariados						E.G./m. - Dram
Total men and women - Total hommes et femmes - Total hombres y mujeres											
ISIC 3 - CITI 3 - CIIU 3											
Total	24 515	29 307	35 848	30 061	41 881	48 191	54 536	61 490	71 834	92 559	
15								59 221	67 933		
16								100 926	101 988		
17								40 665	41 742		
18								33 542	41 834		
19								34 074	49 538		
20								56 417	39 263		
21								47 302	51 584		
22								61 294	57 937		
23								30 933			
24								60 006	75 410		
25								40 633	49 166		
26								66 753	82 953		
27								102 699	117 674		
28								52 917	58 590		
29								52 585	56 880		
30								43 330			
31								56 617	64 494		
32								36 757	45 764		
33								67 115	76 414		
34								29 683			
35											
36								64 983	62 460		
37								19 519			
Men - Hommes - Hombres											
ISIC 3 - CITI 3 - CIIU 3											
Total								78 214	88 692		
Women - Femmes - Mujeres											
ISIC 3 - CITI 3 - CIIU 3											
Total								46 410	54 844		

Explanatory notes: see p. 877.
[1] Index base: July 2008 = 100.

Notes explicatives: voir p. 879.
[1] Indices base: juillet 2008 = 100.

Notas explicativas: véase p. 882.
[1] Indices base: julio 2008 = 100.

WAGES

In manufacturing

SALAIRES

Dans les industries manufacturières

SALARIOS

En las industrias manufactureras

5B

	1999	2000	2001	2002	2003	2004	2005	2006	2007	2008

Azerbaijan (DA)   Employees - Salariés - Asalariados   E.G./m. - Manat

Total men and women - Total hommes et femmes - Total hombres y mujeres
ISIC 3 - CITI 3 - CIIU 3

	1999	2000	2001	2002	2003	2004	2005	2006	2007	2008
Total	244 087	284 272	303 164	348 816	445 437	491 330	115 [1]	141	192	252
15	138 586	146 622	174 615	177 373	208 970	251 087	64 [1]	80	124	154
16	121 468	355 781	507 951	623 647	701 416	730 758	166 [1]	170	244	268
17	165 236	166 058	137 592	152 862	197 655	221 487	64 [1]	73	96	155
18	82 662	100 892	137 360	108 302	132 824	106 893	36 [1]	40	105	143
19	117 884	80 638	219 184	180 493	181 442	203 386	54 [1]	61	126	166
20	69 371	61 015	76 690	99 694	98 616	122 115	52 [1]	79	129	165
21	70 163	51 581	73 599	97 027	149 794	203 975	49 [1]	87	126	142
22	174 764	200 148	197 453	203 239	209 223	267 038	69 [1]	79	109	132
23	431 267	478 303	460 916	475 219	515 458	631 898	160 [1]	235	341	482
24	217 240	271 129	295 068	343 053	401 676	500 519	118 [1]	155	180	215
25	121 891	236 768	169 206	143 474	148 357	265 858	60 [1]	79	127	183
26	208 702	474 974	382 547	444 571	572 860	602 505	122 [1]	139	226	276
27	127 752	219 472	551 935	521 866	702 085	803 437	190 [1]	228	258	322
28	345 519	315 716	323 010	409 139	1 173 789	947 294	171 [1]	209	288	386
29	241 819	304 530	333 379	310 119	343 732	396 911	98 [1]	121	178	228
30	100 198	141 060	160 791	135 337	146 501	212 823	79 [1]	85	195	225
31	232 960	289 577	347 798	217 398	192 698	269 832	84 [1]	94	136	180
32	150 444	161 805	184 286	228 197	267 725	309 451	61 [1]	71	137	174
33	158 508	230 382	250 844	268 156	248 884	305 987	73 [1]	107	163	208
34	72 957	98 729	117 005	128 213	168 016	379 784	66 [1]	115	140	182
35	349 747	556 840	563 069	774 789	810 246	807 501	212 [1]	248	288	429
36	85 422	93 166	109 656	119 260	159 878	179 416	58 [1]	58	91	128
37	117 137	147 418	478 966	471 306	496 652	456 871	62 [1]	127	235	214

Men - Hommes - Hombres
ISIC 3 - CITI 3 - CIIU 3

	1999	2000	2001	2002	2003	2004	2005	2006	2007	2008
Total	.	.	.	.	.	.	.	.	.	283.2
15	.	.	.	.	.	.	.	.	.	177.7
16	.	.	.	.	.	.	.	.	.	244.0
17	.	.	.	.	.	.	.	.	.	172.5
18	.	.	.	.	.	.	.	.	.	314.3
19	.	.	.	.	.	.	.	.	.	180.8
20	.	.	.	.	.	.	.	.	.	202.1
21	.	.	.	.	.	.	.	.	.	140.0
22	.	.	.	.	.	.	.	.	.	139.5
23	.	.	.	.	.	.	.	.	.	570.1
24	.	.	.	.	.	.	.	.	.	267.6
25	.	.	.	.	.	.	.	.	.	190.9
26	.	.	.	.	.	.	.	.	.	292.6
27	.	.	.	.	.	.	.	.	.	334.5
28	.	.	.	.	.	.	.	.	.	409.8
29	.	.	.	.	.	.	.	.	.	235.5
30	.	.	.	.	.	.	.	.	.	330.7
31	.	.	.	.	.	.	.	.	.	189.1
32	.	.	.	.	.	.	.	.	.	169.3
33	.	.	.	.	.	.	.	.	.	218.2
34	.	.	.	.	.	.	.	.	.	171.4
35	.	.	.	.	.	.	.	.	.	453.5
36	.	.	.	.	.	.	.	.	.	131.6
37	.	.	.	.	.	.	.	.	.	211.4

Women - Femmes - Mujeres
ISIC 3 - CITI 3 - CIIU 3

	1999	2000	2001	2002	2003	2004	2005	2006	2007	2008
Total	.	.	.	.	.	.	.	.	.	159.0
15	.	.	.	.	.	.	.	.	.	95.5
16	.	.	.	.	.	.	.	.	.	176.0
17	.	.	.	.	.	.	.	.	.	123.5
18	.	.	.	.	.	.	.	.	.	70.6
19	.	.	.	.	.	.	.	.	.	144.9
20	.	.	.	.	.	.	.	.	.	43.7
21	.	.	.	.	.	.	.	.	.	144.5
22	.	.	.	.	.	.	.	.	.	121.8
23	.	.	.	.	.	.	.	.	.	325.7
24	.	.	.	.	.	.	.	.	.	129.8
25	.	.	.	.	.	.	.	.	.	146.7
26	.	.	.	.	.	.	.	.	.	167.9
27	.	.	.	.	.	.	.	.	.	258.1
28	.	.	.	.	.	.	.	.	.	257.5
29	.	.	.	.	.	.	.	.	.	195.0
30	.	.	.	.	.	.	.	.	.	97.6
31	.	.	.	.	.	.	.	.	.	148.3
32	.	.	.	.	.	.	.	.	.	190.3
33	.	.	.	.	.	.	.	.	.	168.3
34	.	.	.	.	.	.	.	.	.	334.9
35	.	.	.	.	.	.	.	.	.	250.9
36	.	.	.	.	.	.	.	.	.	106.3
37	.	.	.	.	.	.	.	.	.	222.3

Explanatory notes: see p. 877.   Notes explicatives: voir p. 879.   Notas explicativas: véase p. 882.

[1] New denomination of AZM; 1 AZN=5000 AZM.   [1] Nouvelle dénomination de l'AZM; 1 AZN = 5000 AZM.   [1] Nueva denominación del AZM; 1 AZN = 5000 AZM.

	1999	2000	2001	2002	2003	2004	2005	2006	2007	2008
Bahrain (FA) [1]				All persons engaged - Effectif occupé - Efectivo ocupado						E.G./m. - Dinar
Total men and women - Total hommes et femmes - Total hombres y mujeres										
ISIC 3 - CITI 3 - CIIU 3										
Total										253
Men - Hommes - Hombres										
ISIC 3 - CITI 3 - CIIU 3										
Total										254
Women - Femmes - Mujeres										
ISIC 3 - CITI 3 - CIIU 3										
Total										252
Bahrain (FA) [1]				Employees - Salariés - Asalariados						E.G./m. - Dinar
Total men and women - Total hommes et femmes - Total hombres y mujeres										
ISIC 2 - CITI 2 - CIIU 2										
Total	227	231	215	228	230	234	228	219	225	
Men - Hommes - Hombres										
ISIC 2 - CITI 2 - CIIU 2										
Total	250	255	241	252	250	249	239	226	230	
Women - Femmes - Mujeres										
ISIC 2 - CITI 2 - CIIU 2										
Total	109	107	100	111	125	138	145	155	177	
China (DA) [2]				Employees - Salariés - Asalariados						E.G./m. - Yuan
Total men and women - Total hommes et femmes - Total hombres y mujeres										
ISIC 3 - CITI 3 - CIIU 3										
Total	649.50	729.17	814.50	916.75	1 041.33	1 169.42	1 313.08	1 497.17	1 740.33	2 016.00
Georgia (CA)				Employees - Salariés - Asalariados						E.G./m. - Lari
Total men and women - Total hommes et femmes - Total hombres y mujeres										
ISIC 3 - CITI 3 - CIIU 3										
Total	87.4	99.3	120.8	143.4	152.5	183.9	212.1	260.5	368.1	
15	70.9	81.7	96.9	121.6	139.8	170.8	192.5	234.3	299.1	
16	66.2	61.4	354.3	387.7	359.0	745.9	667.2	641.4	908.9	
17	57.4	64.6	130.3	115.2	70.5	93.9	110.0	220.6	265.6	
18	44.2	66.7	69.4	99.1	92.7	120.0	114.6	179.0	209.9	
19	45.1	65.3	53.8	60.0	52.9	60.0	90.9	88.8	227.9	
20	42.8	50.0	44.1	68.1	71.3	68.8	92.9	99.8	174.4	
21	80.1	88.3	94.9	98.8	51.5	108.5	112.3	190.3	222.9	
22	59.6	66.2	75.2	88.6	84.9	85.6	130.1	190.9	278.4	
23	324.8	334.1	337.7	136.1	83.4	158.4	208.4	413.0		
24	101.5	140.7	154.5	186.7	212.7	221.4	257.3	352.1	475.3	
25	97.5	121.1	110.8	130.4	83.0	170.5	192.7	373.5	439.2	
26	108.0	123.5	139.5	181.6	171.0	198.9	242.6	245.2	416.5	
27	75.8	119.8	115.7	143.6	165.1	210.5	258.8	333.4	379.1	
28	85.5	88.4	97.1	129.9	128.0	159.2	225.3	209.1	387.5	
29	94.6	98.1	80.5	78.4	79.4	100.1	245.1	527.2	657.6	
30	28.1	54.7	69.2	88.5	186.2	110.8				
31	96.4	93.6	118.4	85.4	100.4	121.8	142.0		351.1	
32	50.2	50.1	64.7	49.2	53.2	28.6	135.2	636.9	629.6	
33	20.4	42.3	66.3	59.0	70.9	72.7	156.5	137.2	216.1	
34	101.5	106.9	107.6	95.1	118.4	82.4	102.4	180.6	150.3	
35	139.2	139.8	180.3	218.9	218.0	249.9	291.2	347.8	447.4	
36	74.7	63.0	73.9	74.4	100.8	95.3	121.1	185.6	297.5	
37	62.8	57.2	84.6	93.2	77.6	163.2	223.9	106.7	94.5	

Explanatory notes: see p. 877.

[1] Private sector. [2] State-owned units, urban collective-owned units and other ownership units.

Notes explicatives: voir p. 879.

[1] Secteur privé. [2] Unités d'Etat, unités collectives urbaines et autres.

Notas explicativas: véase p. 882.

[1] Sector privado. [2] Unidades estatales, unidades colectivas y otras.

972

ILO YEARBOOK OF LABOUR STATISTICS 2009 · *ANNUAIRE DES STATISTIQUES DU TRAVAIL DU BIT 2009* · *ANUARIO DE ESTADISTICAS DEL TRABAJO DEL OIT 2009*

WAGES   SALAIRES   SALARIOS   5B

In manufacturing   Dans les industries manufacturières   En las industrias manufactureras

	1999	2000	2001	2002	2003	2004	2005	2006	2007	2008
Georgia (CA)					Employees - Salariés - Asalariados					E.G./m. - Lari
Men - Hommes - Hombres										
ISIC 3 - CITI 3 - CIIU 3										
Total	101.1	111.2	141.5	165.1	174.9	210.2	243.5	293.7	475.6	.
15	82.1	93.2	135.9	144.2	167.5	196.0	225.1	269.6	357.9	.
16	66.4	63.5	296.2	402.9	380.9	770.0	800.5	612.1	1 046.6	.
17	64.7	86.1	122.7	158.4	82.5	104.3	113.7	278.6	401.6	.
18	46.2	67.7	63.3	69.8	78.7	74.2	118.4	182.9	273.2	.
19	44.3	63.7	52.0	60.6	56.6	56.0	102.0	86.9	207.5	.
20	46.3	37.1	44.2	70.1	73.7	71.5	96.7	99.5	175.1	.
21	86.5	92.6	129.0	107.0	54.8	.	119.6	213.0	248.7	.
22	69.1	75.2	99.6	103.1	91.3	118.7	151.9	215.3	336.2	.
23	403.6	334.7	340.6	134.6	77.6	152.3	217.0	591.3	95.5	.
24	116.5	167.6	214.7	217.0	236.0	271.3	318.6	425.0	532.8	.
25	115.4	130.9	142.9	142.9	86.4	185.2	227.6	425.7	521.9	.
26	119.0	131.8	189.1	194.6	183.0	210.5	253.5	261.1	418.6	.
27	79.8	156.7	153.7	162.1	189.4	227.6	277.6	345.5	413.5	.
28	96.0	93.7	119.7	141.6	131.0	178.9	239.8	219.0	407.7	.
29	107.5	128.6	130.7	84.0	85.7	108.5	276.8	589.4	724.2	.
30	33.5	62.1	93.9	104.6	238.5	125.2	.	.	.	.
31	126.0	129.0	130.2	91.3	110.8	132.2	172.2	428.7	406.9	.
32	56.5	59.2	61.6	52.4	55.8	27.7	152.2	162.9	655.5	.
33	20.5	43.8	77.2	65.2	80.1	91.9	206.4	164.6	292.9	.
34	109.6	107.1	109.5	102.3	121.3	78.8	101.4	189.2	156.5	.
35	156.6	161.3	211.8	239.9	236.6	266.6	315.2	380.6	486.8	.
36	74.1	70.9	77.1	80.8	117.1	106.2	123.9	193.0	303.8	.
37	64.3	60.9	87.1	94.8	78.1	169.1	229.7	114.0	100.3	.
Women - Femmes - Mujeres										
ISIC 3 - CITI 3 - CIIU 3										
Total	63.3	69.3	82.7	101.6	108.4	132.2	147.7	.	240.2	.
15	54.9	64.0	86.1	87.1	94.4	131.1	141.4	.	209.1	.
16	66.0	59.5	383.1	350.8	309.6	683.7	302.7	.	505.0	.
17	49.0	56.7	138.7	86.4	44.7	80.9	105.2	.	108.0	.
18	43.4	66.3	71.2	103.9	95.0	124.5	113.6	.	201.9	.
19	46.5	67.9	58.2	54.6	44.3	70.6	68.8	.	249.4	.
20	20.3	54.0	42.2	48.8	49.2	44.5	65.7	.	168.8	.
21	66.4	60.0	62.3	79.5	40.1	86.9	85.0	.	168.2	.
22	52.8	52.2	70.7	77.5	80.4	67.1	112.1	.	230.4	.
23	200.6	205.5	215.2	141.9	99.2	180.7	174.2	.	306.8	.
24	81.4	106.0	113.5	146.3	181.4	151.5	172.2	.	404.3	.
25	63.0	67.9	66.9	89.5	74.6	116.9	111.0	.	182.9	.
26	70.6	96.1	108.5	116.5	118.2	140.6	186.6	.	404.8	.
27	61.0	62.4	65.3	89.2	93.9	146.9	177.8	.	215.8	.
28	43.7	46.0	72.4	77.9	115.1	47.3	123.2	.	245.2	.
29	53.6	68.1	60.9	61.9	59.5	67.0	126.5	.	251.5	.
30	15.1	31.0	35.0	47.5	58.9	56.6	.	.	.	.
31	31.1	53.0	85.7	70.1	79.0	100.2	98.9	.	198.3	.
32	34.7	38.3	74.1	42.9	48.5	32.6	77.9	.	465.3	.
33	20.3	24.3	40.9	54.2	61.5	49.4	71.2	.	124.0	.
34	67.7	68.8	95.0	68.3	101.5	111.7	110.3	.	128.9	.
35	100.2	106.7	88.6	147.9	140.9	189.4	219.0	.	309.9	.
36	76.0	50.0	58.4	59.3	65.9	70.5	114.0	.	279.2	.
37	45.6	48.2	65.4	81.8	71.7	78.7	141.4	.	72.5	.
Hong Kong, China (DA)					Wage earners - Ouvriers - Obreros					R.T./d.j. - Dollar
Total men and women - Total hommes et femmes - Total hombres y mujeres										
ISIC 2 - CITI 2 - CIIU 2										
Total	334.7	335.4	342.6	326.1	322.2	324.3	279.0	321.7	342.8	341.2
311-312	.	.	.	.	.	.	.	.	.	.
321	308.6	314.0	334.4	311.0	303.9	313.7	311.1	301.8	298.7	351.4
322	254.9	263.8	261.5	254.2	250.6	269.3	266.9	249.2	227.1	199.5
324	.	.	.	.	.	.	.	.	.	.
332	.	.	.	.	.	.	.	.	.	.
341	487.0	467.1	403.5	389.3	.	.	392.6	392.6	352.8	410.9
342	447.8	456.0	460.0	444.3	415.0	379.9	396.5	425.9	424.8	414.9
356	307.1	337.9	311.0	295.9	298.1	.	.	.	306.6	306.0
381	417.3	394.5	361.8	357.1	.	.	285.3	314.5	368.0	405.9
383	316.4	319.8	327.4	327.5	302.1	320.5	.	.	303.1	304.6
384	.	.	.	.	.	.	.	.	.	.
385	327.2	306.2	329.6	323.4	.	.	.	.	317.7	351.4
390	473.2	475.1	467.5	442.8	466.6	434.1	486.6	529.5	532.0	519.5

Explanatory notes: see p. 877.   Notes explicatives: voir p. 879.   Notas explicativas: véase p. 882.

	WAGES			SALAIRES			SALARIOS		
	In manufacturing			Dans les industries manufacturières			En las industrias manufactureras		

	1999	2000	2001	2002	2003	2004	2005	2006	2007	2008
Hong Kong, China (DA)					Wage earners - Ouvriers - Obreros					R.T./d.j. - Dollar
Men - Hommes - Hombres										
ISIC 2 - CITI 2 - CIIU 2										
Total	422.6	428.8	428.5	419.2	406.1	380.4	282.4	420.8	436.4	430.3
311-312										
321	345.0	361.7	375.7	367.9	344.4	356.0	365.5	376.2	383.0	388.3
322	348.9	369.6	369.4	390.1	439.8			249.4		371.5
324										
332										
341	490.4	478.4	415.1	396.3			412.2	415.2	417.0	435.4
342	465.9	472.6	475.7	459.2	442.6	397.2	403.5	439.0	456.9	439.8
356	376.5	404.9	385.8	370.4					369.5	373.0
381	438.6	406.7	403.1	386.8			369.5	370.2	379.5	436.9
383	422.9	419.9	389.9	396.2	368.4	349.2			372.4	365.9
384										
385		374.7	375.9	379.9		384.3			380.6	411.5
390	489.1	493.5	488.7	455.5	483.2	449.7	505.3	552.1	541.9	526.6
Women - Femmes - Mujeres										
ISIC 2 - CITI 2 - CIIU 2										
Total	268.9	278.1	280.6	268.2	262.7	280.0	273.8	256.9	259.6	259.9
311-312										
321	272.0	277.0	296.9	281.8	275.4			270.6	262.8	330.6
322	241.8	251.2	249.7	240.4	234.9	254.7	258.6	240.9	220.0	195.8
324										
332										
341										257.8
342	357.8	359.6	376.0	366.0	319.7	303.9	342.1	342.9	311.2	319.3
356	236.1	236.4	242.7	224.8			231.8	208.4	206.2	226.1
381									276.3	288.4
383	285.6	297.1	302.1	295.6	277.9	304.3			275.2	260.2
384										
385	307.1	281.0	314.7	294.7		298.4			288.9	298.3
390	355.6	395.3	370.1	384.8	396.6	367.1	393.2	387.0	432.2	466.2
Hong Kong, China (DA)					Salaried employees - Employés - Empleados					R.T./m. - Dollar
Total men and women - Total hommes et femmes - Total hombres y mujeres										
ISIC 2 - CITI 2 - CIIU 2										
Total	11 853.0	11 869.7	12 133.1	11 950.7	11 508.8	11 498.1	11 622.0	11 972.4	11 878.0	11 881.3
Men - Hommes - Hombres										
ISIC 2 - CITI 2 - CIIU 2										
Total	12 893.2	12 697.1	12 929.7	12 810.2	12 082.7	11 880.7	12 248.6	12 483.3	12 596.7	12 470.3
Women - Femmes - Mujeres										
ISIC 2 - CITI 2 - CIIU 2										
Total	10 846.7	11 101.4	11 395.0	11 123.2	11 021.1	11 139.3	11 015.0	11 552.3	11 282.4	11 335.9
India (DA) [1]					Wage earners - Ouvriers - Obreros					E.G./m. - Rupee
Total men and women - Total hommes et femmes - Total hombres y mujeres										
ISIC 2 - CITI 2 - CIIU 2										
Total	1 548.5	1 280.8	1 893.2	1 158.6	1 078.9	1 731.8	1 234.4	3 525.9		
31						2 733.5	1 042.8	3 525.9		
321	1 708.5	1 447.6	1 447.6	1 136.6	1 388.5	1 413.4	1 432.5	4 345.2		
322,324	1 279.3	1 118.8	1 266.8	891.8	1 342.3	1 182.9	2 033.9			
323	1 663.3	1 734.9	1 595.3		859.2	620.7	660.2	573.1		
331	2 101.5	1 316.7	1 183.9	814.5	1 198.1	1 192.9	1 272.9	3 343.6		
332	1 247.2			1 286.0	1 182.7	1 372.9	1 352.3	4 716.8		
341	1 341.2	1 398.5	1 274.8	1 330.7	776.2	1 103.3	1 148.5	4 758.6		
342	955.3			1 328.1	1 225.6	1 429.0	1 380.2	6 676.9		
351-352	1 548.1	1 187.2	695.4	1 166.1	1 065.8	1 249.5		4 874.6		
354	1 854.7	1 719.8	1 641.7	712.9	1 049.6	1 506.8	1 377.2	5 671.2		
355	1 679.5	1 353.6	1 292.5	1 077.9	2 580.1	1 462.6	1 518.2	6 361.1		
36	1 568.0	925.8	1 264.3	1 198.7	901.7	1 305.0	1 288.9	2 678.5		
37	1 652.5	1 649.0	1 666.6	1 227.0	1 156.8	1 564.5	1 540.4	2 693.1		
381	1 535.4	1 546.2	1 666.1	1 029.7	1 194.6	1 460.1	1 473.2	5 675.0		
382										
382-383	1 606.7	1 260.1	1 805.7	1 715.8	1 354.0	1 468.3	1 466.2	3 272.3		
383										
384	1 759.3	1 325.2	1 502.5	1 846.9	1 399.5	1 532.4	1 545.1	5 322.6		
390	1 515.9	1 326.6		1 130.1	1 945.7	2 078.7	1 350.5	4 357.2		

Explanatory notes: see p. 877.　　　　Notes explicatives: voir p. 879.　　　　Notas explicativas: véase p. 882.

[1] Fluctuations due to various changes in workers' coverage.　　[1] Fluctuations dues aux divers changements de couverture des travailleurs.　　[1] Fluctuaciones debidas a varios cambios de lacobertura de los trabajadores.

WAGES — SALAIRES — SALARIOS

In manufacturing — Dans les industries manufacturières — En las industrias manufactureras

Indonesia (BA) [1][2] Salaried employees - Employés - Empleados R.T./m. - Rupiah

Total men and women - Total hommes et femmes - Total hombres y mujeres

ISIC 2 - CITI 2 - CIIU 2 / ISIC 3 - CITI 3 - CIIU 3

ISIC 2	1999	2000	2001	2002	2003	2004	2005	2006	2007	2008	ISIC 3
Total	.	.	498 956	556 553	685 878	749 404	748 160	801 965	836 337	868 886	Total
311-312	.	.	603 569	863 363	803 869	897 934	954 772 [3]	876 629	758 443	775 891	15
313	.	.	851 865	905 993	729 522	912 731	890 417	1 043 189	519 494	582 818	16
314	.	.	587 080	1 042 375	1 006 980	993 854	1 292 817 [3]	837 000	692 881	728 062	17
321	.	.	792 431	744 610	910 668	1 033 169	1 205 591	1 185 493	717 320	737 690	18
322	.	.	439 553	1 128 232	1 186 238	1 235 337	171 250 [3]	1 662 717	792 284	760 541	19
323	.	.	680 041	818 185	1 049 297	1 058 502	1 080 373 [3]	1 198 665	750 540	750 936	20
331	.	.	990 201	1 163 042	1 250 000	1 714 156	576 756 [3]	1 015 452	1 056 512	1 142 057	21
332	.	.	1 284 356	456 014	899 227	559 656	859 905 [3]	1 017 258	1 137 438	1 120 594	22
341	.	.	822 900	1 058 372	1 139 133	1 309 639	1 531 368 [3]	2 335 581	4 480 298	3 728 349	23
342	.	.	952 174	751 865	1 054 493	1 577 278	1 188 937 [3]	1 793 570	1 341 333	1 436 521	24
351	.	.	918 579	738 421	736 921	945 712	1 144 456 [3]	1 316 159	984 889	976 403	25
352	.	.	419 843	1 495 614	.	1 683 663	1 400 872 [3]	4 236 478	682 468	659 366	26
353	.	.	818 477	1 362 727	800 000	0	2 412 779 [3]	3 285 852	1 480 009	1 750 530	27
361	.	.	334 411	410 182	447 572	472 384	511 073 [3]	581 248	938 089	1 002 246	28
369	.	.	556 324	569 661	745 375	1 147 516	305 425 [3]	490 504	1 113 008	1 385 896	29
371	.	.	51 908	1 315 514	742 092	434 054	422 860 [3]	580 858	3 163 233	1 676 587	30
372	.	.	52 205	182 688	762 500	1 021 149	2 007 673 [3]	378 632	1 289 110	1 144 180	31
									1 453 107	1 541 547	32
									1 284 383	1 135 207	33
									1 556 140	1 716 995	34
									1 433 946	1 602 276	35
									705 331	704 098	36
									609 828	824 091	37

Men - Hommes - Hombres

ISIC 2 - CITI 2 - CIIU 2 / ISIC 3 - CITI 3 - CIIU 3

ISIC 2	1999	2000	2001	2002	2003	2004	2005	2006	2007	2008	ISIC 3
Total	.	.	509 893	581 120	678 484	778 471	790 055 [3]	852 057	947 627	993 430	Total
311-312	.	.	624 257	903 561	803 986	838 920	954 772 [3]	865 429	899 345	903 602	15
313	.	.	915 035	1 008 038	797 416	956 523	1 060 638 [3]	1 104 382	774 884	808 834	16
314	.	.	587 080	774 426	961 739	946 359	1 510 637 [3]	837 000	837 713	890 037	17
321	.	.	729 500	776 476	951 713	1 091 824	1 326 660 [3]	1 394 411	812 174	824 098	18
322	.	.	717 617	1 020 948	1 067 949	1 703 660	400 000 [3]	1 899 955	787 427	786 272	19
323	.	.	654 860	913 387	1 142 444	1 102 171	1 248 654 [3]	1 247 120	806 054	796 921	20
331	.	.	887 542	1 163 042	.	1 714 156	772 881 [3]	1 082 292	1 181 135	1 290 465	21
332	.	.	1 814 815	578 593	915 453	533 098	800 000 [3]	1 136 938	1 131 400	1 098 986	22
341	.	.	810 230	1 034 520	1 133 167	1 314 457	1 588 829 [3]	2 379 296	4 727 344	3 798 668	23
342	.	.	975 259	724 565	1 062 923	1 810 817	1 289 378 [3]	1 822 072	1 483 970	1 612 657	24
351	.	.	921 289	738 421	730 110	945 712	1 149 320 [3]	1 298 855	1 089 496	1 056 908	25
352	.	.	419 843	1 904 799	.	1 683 663	1 400 872 [3]	4 236 478	736 908	726 968	26
353	.	.	818 477	1 362 727	800 000	.	2 062 272 [3]	3 285 852	1 460 848	1 770 129	27
361	.	.	348 129	431 817	477 415	497 426	521 570 [3]	611 427	945 493	1 043 306	28
369	.	.	691 399	649 324	810 341	1 337 793	477 899 [3]	558 214	1 156 584	1 475 802	29
371	.	.	.	1 000 000	742 092	573 275	583 681 [3]	580 858		1 956 504	30
372	.	.	.	224 255	750 000	1 021 149	3 872 520 [3]	347 493	1 423 664	1 256 758	31
									1 327 450	1 867 594	32
									1 131 627	1 121 321	33
									1 528 086	1 720 551	34
									1 445 062	1 612 165	35
									760 941	771 336	36
									776 832	977 576	37

Women - Femmes - Mujeres

ISIC 2 - CITI 2 - CIIU 2 / ISIC 3 - CITI 3 - CIIU 3

ISIC 2	1999	2000	2001	2002	2003	2004	2005	2006	2007	2008	ISIC 3
Total	.	.	468 571	458 828	703 693	625 725	635 486 [3]	654 719	655 915	678 723	Total
311-312	.	.	555 144	692 619	803 270	3 653 465	[3]	916 066	531 659	576 994	15
313	.	.	689 168	670 883	579 236	803 923	740 191 [3]	931 488	437 119	509 417	16
314	.	.	.	1 585 332	1 160 000	1 500 000	773 023 [3]	.	548 352	591 999	17
321	.	.	887 629	691 070	827 404	919 806	1 052 995 [3]	942 869	662 141	692 097	18
322	.	.	116 054	1 500 000	1 746 729	818 413	1 195 076 [3]		797 899	728 716	19
323	.	.	720 880	667 234	990 274	952 014	930 188 [3]	1 082 721	566 115	577 926	20
331	.	.	1 153 852	.	1 250 000	.	400 000 [3]	796 921	800 401	792 117	21
332	.	.	300 000	357 853	859 950	615 625	868 500 [3]	926 805	1 156 518	1 182 405	22
341	.	.	918 295	1 362 355	1 225 099	1 270 303	939 907 [3]	2 011 136	2 441 556	2 804 723	23
342	.	.	500 000	1 630 000	894 378	554 832	681 065 [3]	1 637 626	1 044 941	1 087 013	24
351	.	.	850 000	.	949 239	.	1 031 848 [3]	1 714 500	783 687	806 385	25
352	.	.	.	475 000	.	.	[3]	.	475 454	429 288	26
353	.	.	.	.	.	.	3 800 000 [3]	.	1 748 839	1 527 210	27
361	.	.	265 675	279 782	316 492	319 987	427 814 [3]	426 819	885 220	760 219	28
369	.	.	369 965	402 192	604 819	549 064	170 897 [3]	415 522	943 887	1 134 341	29
371	.	.	51 908	1 500 000	.	230 868	270 000 [3]	.	1 412 720	1 511 904	30
372	.	.	108 965	54 729	775 000	.	303 445 [3]	600 000	1 060 370	928 065	31
									1 544 285	1 358 347	32
									1 450 544	1 161 977	33
									1 867 957	1 688 801	34
									1 321 663	1 486 651	35
									534 617	515 621	36
									370 273	387 963	37

Explanatory notes: see p. 877. Notes explicatives: voir p. 879. Notas explicativas: véase p. 882.

[1] Persons aged 15 years and over. [2] Aug. of each year. [3] November. — [1] Personnes âgées de 15 ans et plus. [2] Août de chaque année. [3] Novembre. — [1] Personas de 15 años y más. [2] Agosto de cada año. [3] Noviembre.

5B

WAGES	SALAIRES	SALARIOS
In manufacturing	Dans les industries manufacturières	En las industrias manufactureras

	1999	2000	2001	2002	2003	2004	2005	2006	2007	2008

Israel (FA) [1] — Wage earners - Ouvriers - Obreros — E.G./m. - New shekel

Total men and women - Total hommes et femmes - Total hombres y mujeres
ISIC 3 - CITI 3 - CIIU 3

	2005	2006	2007	2008
Total	9 915	10 377	10 694	10 982
15	6 838	7 094	7 241	7 543
17	7 025	7 486	7 929	8 174
18	4 886	4 918	4 895	4 994
19	5 564	5 846	5 842	6 110
20	6 798	6 942	7 268	7 306
21	7 643	7 968	8 245	8 517
22	7 466	7 586	7 819	8 011
23	19 967	21 190	26 517	23 545
24	12 180	12 679	13 226	14 048
25	7 738	8 134	8 381	8 537
26	8 610	8 897	9 282	9 848
27	9 006	9 180	9 336	9 608
28	7 908	8 602	8 497	8 743
29	10 626	11 145	11 606	12 314
31	9 002	9 008	9 162	9 626
32	14 309	14 970	15 759	15 482
33	17 369	17 884	18 117	18 265
34	13 729	13 931	13 953	13 817
36	6 520	6 719	7 035	7 290

Japan (DA) — Employees - Salariés - Asalariados — E.G./m. - Yen

Total men and women - Total hommes et femmes - Total hombres y mujeres
ISIC 4 - CITI 4 - CIIU 4

	1999	2000	2001	2002	2003	2004	2005	2006	2007	2008
Total	291 100	293 100	297 500	296 400	296 500	293 100	292 100	299 600	296 800	293 400

Men - Hommes - Hombres
ISIC 4 - CITI 4 - CIIU 4

	1999	2000	2001	2002	2003	2004	2005	2006	2007	2008
Total	327 700	328 100	331 400	328 300	327 800	323 100	323 800	332 300	328 500	322 600

Women - Femmes - Mujeres
ISIC 4 - CITI 4 - CIIU 4

	1999	2000	2001	2002	2003	2004	2005	2006	2007	2008
Total	189 000	190 700	195 000	195 600	195 800	194 100	190 900	194 600	197 700	198 000

Japan (DA) [2][3] — Employees - Salariés - Asalariados — E.G./m. - Yen

Total men and women - Total hommes et femmes - Total hombres y mujeres
ISIC 3 - CITI 3 - CIIU 3

	1999	2000	2001	2002	2003	2004	2005	2006	2007	2008
Total	291 100	293 100	297 500	296 400	296 500	293 100	292 100	299 600	296 800	293 400

Men - Hommes - Hombres
ISIC 3 - CITI 3 - CIIU 3

	1999	2000	2001	2002	2003	2004	2005	2006	2007	2008
Total	327 700	328 100	331 400	328 300	327 800	323 100	323 800	332 300	328 500	322 600

Women - Femmes - Mujeres
ISIC 3 - CITI 3 - CIIU 3

	1999	2000	2001	2002	2003	2004	2005	2006	2007	2008
Total	189 000	190 700	195 000	195 600	195 800	194 100	190 900	194 600	197 700	198 000

Explanatory notes: see p. 877.

[1] Israeli workers only. [2] Regular scheduled cash earnings. [3] Private sector; establishments with 10 or more regular employees; June of each year.

Notes explicatives: voir p. 879.

[1] Travailleurs israéliens seulement. [2] Gains en espèce tarifés réguliers. [3] Secteur privé; établissements occupant 10 salariés stables ou plus; juin de chaque années.

Notas explicativas: véase p. 882.

[1] Trabajadores israelíes solamente. [2] Ganancias en especie tarifadas regulares. [3] Sector privado; establecimientos con 10 y mas asalariados estables; junio de cada año.

In manufacturing	Dans les industries manufacturières	En las industrias manufactureras

	1999	2000	2001	2002	2003	2004	2005	2006	2007	2008

Jordan (DA) [1] — Employees - Salariés - Asalariados — E.G./m. - Dinar

Total men and women - Total hommes et femmes - Total hombres y mujeres
ISIC 3 - CITI 3 - CIIU 3

	1999	2000	2001	2002	2003	2004	2005	2006	2007	2008
Total	172.0	189.0	185.0	186.7	198.0	186.0	203.0	211.0	237.0	.
15	133.6	160.7	163.2	166.4	173.0	182.0	193.0	.	.	.
16	138.1	216.4	228.1	272.5	273.0	295.0	319.0	.	.	.
17	146.4	167.9	166.4	158.0	175.0	190.0	196.0	.	.	.
18	110.9	118.4	116.4	116.6	121.0	128.0	126.0	.	.	.
19	93.9	132.3	148.6	151.2	148.0	161.0	154.0	.	.	.
20	114.8	87.9	104.4	130.1	171.0	144.0	161.0	.	.	.
21	263.0	186.1	212.2	187.5	213.0	216.0	268.0	.	.	.
22	206.9	238.8	233.7	243.2	243.0	235.0	297.0	.	.	.
23	368.4	385.6	395.6	398.1	448.0	333.0	400.0	.	.	.
24	229.7	216.6	249.2	249.3	278.0	293.0	322.0	.	.	.
25	160.8	161.1	162.0	181.2	195.0	184.0	213.0	.	.	.
26	203.7	218.7	187.3	183.8	212.0	178.0	223.0	.	.	.
27	200.1	214.1	235.3	226.7	243.0	245.0	262.0	.	.	.
28	145.8	138.8	184.4	155.5	160.0	160.0	179.0	.	.	.
29	131.0	199.6	195.4	201.8	218.0	218.0	231.0	.	.	.
30	.	.	.	.	.	487.0	340.0	.	.	.
31	198.9	214.8	203.8	224.9	224.0	231.0	244.0	.	.	.
32	182.4	165.9	136.9	198.0	267.0	136.0	212.0	.	.	.
33	166.0	164.4	.	215.4	218.0	245.0	231.0	.	.	.
34	79.0	213.7	223.2	197.2	196.0	220.0	224.0	.	.	.
35	265.5	322.0	354.1	356.1	354.0	212.0	402.0	.	.	.
36	128.7	148.4	160.4	159.7	159.0	176.0	227.0	.	.	.
37	.	77.5	.	.	.	125.0	205.0	.	.	.

Men - Hommes - Hombres
ISIC 3 - CITI 3 - CIIU 3

	1999	2000	2001	2002	2003	2004	2005	2006	2007	2008
Total	180.0	198.0	195.0	196.0	208.0	201.0	222.0	234.0	254.0	.
15	136.5	165.6	164.4	168.9	176.0	186.0	197.0	.	.	.
16	132.9	217.3	231.4	271.5	274.0	294.0	315.0	.	.	.
17	166.2	179.2	183.1	178.0	204.0	202.0	212.0	.	.	.
18	150.0	145.2	140.2	147.9	141.0	151.0	150.0	.	.	.
19	92.6	135.6	159.0	155.0	154.0	162.0	159.0	.	.	.
20	114.8	87.7	104.5	130.0	173.0	144.0	159.0	.	.	.
21	212.0	192.6	222.6	193.7	220.0	221.0	271.0	.	.	.
22	206.8	245.0	238.0	243.5	250.0	239.0	293.0	.	.	.
23	368.3	386.3	396.1	397.7	447.0	333.0	401.0	.	.	.
24	253.2	282.9	257.5	264.3	324.0	309.0	350.0	.	.	.
25	163.7	162.5	162.6	182.1	200.0	188.0	218.0	.	.	.
26	203.1	217.0	187.6	182.9	206.0	178.0	222.0	.	.	.
27	197.7	213.6	235.8	226.7	244.0	245.0	262.0	.	.	.
28	146.1	139.0	184.8	155.5	161.0	165.0	179.0	.	.	.
29	127.3	198.3	195.3	201.8	217.0	215.0	231.0	.	.	.
30	.	.	.	.	.	522.0	335.0	.	.	.
31	202.5	220.0	227.4	224.9	223.0	232.0	247.0	.	.	.
32	186.5	168.1	138.4	198.0	269.0	130.0	214.0	.	.	.
33	175.6	176.1	175.6	215.4	230.0	263.0	252.0	.	.	.
34	75.9	216.8	222.1	197.2	195.0	217.0	224.0	.	.	.
35	265.5	322.0	354.1	356.1	354.0	212.0	409.0	.	.	.
36	130.9	151.3	162.0	159.7	161.0	176.0	226.0	.	.	.
37	.	77.5	.	.	.	125.0	205.0	.	.	.

Women - Femmes - Mujeres
ISIC 3 - CITI 3 - CIIU 3

	1999	2000	2001	2002	2003	2004	2005	2006	2007	2008
Total	123.0	131.0	126.0	129.3	136.0	130.0	136.0	142.0	174.0	.
15	102.4	115.9	140.8	137.9	135.0	139.0	142.0	.	.	.
16	245.3	199.1	116.6	301.2	260.0	320.0	417.0	.	.	.
17	88.3	126.8	113.9	107.6	112.0	140.0	131.0	.	.	.
18	83.9	101.0	101.0	97.1	102.0	114.0	109.0	.	.	.
19	106.2	79.9	94.8	113.8	93.0	140.0	123.0	.	.	.
20	135.0	104.4	100.0	140.0	140.0	210.0	331.0	.	.	.
21	.	134.9	132.8	134.3	147.0	158.0	245.0	.	.	.
22	208.6	191.6	193.7	239.1	201.0	194.0	320.0	.	.	.
23	369.6	341.5	365.6	427.1	448.0	326.0	335.0	.	.	.
24	139.4	185.9	206.9	189.6	184.0	225.0	224.0	.	.	.
25	113.0	132.0	153.8	116.5	126.0	140.0	153.0	.	.	.
26	249.1	290.4	179.1	236.1	361.0	209.0	282.0	.	.	.
27	295.0	233.3	213.0	226.0	194.0	232.0	269.0	.	.	.
28	130.2	126.2	148.5	151.1	137.0	113.0	188.0	.	.	.
29	196.0	221.7	197.9	194.4	259.0	281.0	229.0	.	.	.
30	.	147.9	102.9	.	.	280.0	390.0	.	.	.
31	136.4	129.4	125.6	205.6	263.0	183.0	178.0	.	.	.
32	134.6	135.5	123.8	159.3	249.0	160.0	197.0	.	.	.
33	120.4	162.2	260.8	229.6	177.0	159.0	184.0	.	.	.
34	164.0	.	.	236.1	212.0	278.0	225.0	.	.	.
35	.	.	.	.	.	.	234.0	.	.	.
36	101.7	113.3	131.1	132.4	141.0	172.0	234.0	.	.	.
37	.	.	.	.	.	.	178.0	.	.	.

Explanatory notes: see p. 877. | Notes explicatives: voir p. 879. | Notas explicativas: véase p. 882.

[1] Oct. of each year. | [1] Oct. de chaque année. | [1] Oct. de cada año.

WAGES	SALAIRES	SALARIOS
In manufacturing	Dans les industries manufacturières	En las industrias manufactureras

	1999	2000	2001	2002	2003	2004	2005	2006	2007	2008

Kazakhstan (DA)   Employees - Salariés - Asalariados   E.G./m. - Tenge

Total men and women - Total hommes et femmes - Total hombres y mujeres
ISIC 3 - CITI 3 - CIIU 3

Total	1999	2000	2001	2002	2003	2004	2005	2006	2007	2008
15	10 469	11 545	12 847	14 909	17 320	21 698	.	.	.	.
16	72 215	.	96 823	102 387	103 145	103 995	.	.	.	.
17	7 431	8 446	.	10 963	11 779	14 057	.	.	.	.
18	4 441	6 296	6 537	7 830	10 259	12 311	.	.	.	.
19	6 076	.	9 615	.	12 546	15 533	.	.	.	.
20	6 367	7 735	8 215	.	14 272	15 952	.	.	.	.
21	11 600	14 399	28 789	23 940	29 932	36 305	.	.	.	.
22	14 007	16 837	20 989	26 022	31 339	34 352	.	.	.	.
23	30 600	41 813	49 683	50 939	58 099	56 705	.	.	.	.
24	11 833	12 122	14 705	17 683	22 675	24 196	.	.	.	.
25	9 822	12 772	13 692	15 986	15 700	23 022	.	.	.	.
26	9 386	12 817	16 522	19 621	22 835	27 455	.	.	.	.
27	17 848	23 439	24 925	27 688	30 304	35 824	.	.	.	.
28	8 494	10 778	13 800	20 824	29 181	23 933	.	.	.	.
29	8 004	10 806	13 848	16 566	22 279	26 938	.	.	.	.
30	3 936	4 281	5 811	7 211	26 532	31 890	.	.	.	.
31	10 065	12 439	16 693	18 497	23 841	26 923	.	.	.	.
32	14 491	.	27 801	36 759	56 957	52 445	.	.	.	.
33	10 207	15 803	17 063	20 025	20 386	20 573	.	.	.	.
34	7 735	.	11 625	14 958	20 409	22 670	.	.	.	.
35	12 199	14 555	17 515	19 484	23 162	31 398	.	.	.	.
36	9 270	16 346	19 587	9 331	12 976	16 919	.	.	.	.
37	17 704	20 181	.	19 657	23 209	32 426	.	.	.	.

Men - Hommes - Hombres
ISIC 3 - CITI 3 - CIIU 3

Total	1999	2000	2001	2002	2003	2004	2005	2006	2007	2008
15	.	12 358	14 336	16 207	19 549	24 306	.	.	.	.
16	.	89 795	94 669	89 872	102 721	105 115	.	.	.	.
17	.	8 861	9 321	11 967	13 231	14 753	.	.	.	.
18	.	5 260	.	7 583	11 796	14 559	.	.	.	.
19	.	6 556	8 875	11 167	11 435	16 564	.	.	.	.
20	.	7 603	8 202	10 579	15 000	15 949	.	.	.	.
21	.	15 438	33 541	25 089	32 378	41 281	.	.	.	.
22	.	20 556	27 220	31 321	38 009	39 260	.	.	.	.
23	.	45 933	52 824	53 736	60 225	60 012	.	.	.	.
24	.	13 333	16 624	19 059	24 530	26 078	.	.	.	.
25	.	13 856	15 183	17 543	17 536	26 387	.	.	.	.
26	.	13 878	17 886	20 900	24 398	29 071	.	.	.	.
27	.	25 681	27 411	29 951	33 161	39 828	.	.	.	.
28	.	11 084	14 722	20 463	31 725	24 604	.	.	.	.
29	.	11 115	14 750	17 493	24 302	29 423	.	.	.	.
30	.	3 833	5 676	3 833	37 483	33 312	.	.	.	.
31	.	13 455	19 399	20 423	26 423	28 933	.	.	.	.
32	.	25 850	33 067	43 188	65 547	60 178	.	.	.	.
33	.	17 433	19 443	23 766	24 172	22 793	.	.	.	.
34	.	10 563	12 420	17 500	22 202	23 454	.	.	.	.
35	.	15 490	18 715	20 385	24 696	33 372	.	.	.	.
36	.	14 044	17 141	8 086	12 339	16 288	.	.	.	.
37	.	19 754	20 377	19 429	24 009	33 503	.	.	.	.

Women - Femmes - Mujeres
ISIC 3 - CITI 3 - CIIU 3

Total	1999	2000	2001	2002	2003	2004	2005	2006	2007	2008
15	.	10 572	11 713	13 337	15 828	18 525	.	.	.	.
16	.	91 333	101 172	124 556	104 017	101 841	.	.	.	.
17	.	7 842	8 214	9 669	9 755	12 781	.	.	.	.
18	.	6 742	7 400	7 991	9 875	11 751	.	.	.	.
19	.	7 254	10 082	11 041	13 613	14 535	.	.	.	.
20	.	8 271	8 886	10 784	11 962	15 963	.	.	.	.
21	.	12 799	19 950	20 315	21 611	27 294	.	.	.	.
22	.	14 428	17 548	22 323	26 241	30 832	.	.	.	.
23	.	32 162	42 185	43 324	52 013	49 359	.	.	.	.
24	.	9 788	12 184	15 028	19 210	20 749	.	.	.	.
25	.	9 358	10 249	12 030	12 113	16 361	.	.	.	.
26	.	10 050	13 625	16 028	18 434	22 648	.	.	.	.
27	.	17 681	18 849	21 966	23 123	26 098	.	.	.	.
28	.	9 713	11 543	21 514	22 628	21 597	.	.	.	.
29	.	9 777	11 551	13 439	16 855	20 346	.	.	.	.
30	.	5 451	8 102	11 467	15 580	28 276	.	.	.	.
31	.	9 791	11 339	12 976	17 297	20 789	.	.	.	.
32	.	24 904	19 955	28 662	44 978	40 274	.	.	.	.
33	.	12 373	12 974	13 838	15 040	17 331	.	.	.	.
34	.	11 246	10 256	11 359	16 543	20 633	.	.	.	.
35	.	11 490	14 062	16 292	18 325	25 022	.	.	.	.
36	.	22 040	25 505	12 703	14 621	18 516	.	.	.	.
37	.	21 643	23 471	21 337	20 252	29 119	.	.	.	.

Explanatory notes: see p. 877.   Notes explicatives: voir p. 879.   Notas explicativas: véase p. 882.

In manufacturing

Dans les industries manufacturières

En las industrias manufactureras

	1999	2000	2001	2002	2003	2004	2005	2006	2007	2008

Korea, Republic of (DA) [1] [2] — Employees - Salariés - Asalariados — E.G./m. - Won

Total men and women - Total hommes et femmes - Total hombres y mujeres
ISIC 3 - CITI 3 - CIIU 3

	1999	2000	2001	2002	2003	2004	2005	2006	2007	2008
Total	1 443.0	1 568.0	1 659.0	1 857.0	2 018.0	2 209.0	2 387.6	2 522.5	2 688.0	2 758.7
15	1 354.0	1 545.0	1 690.0	1 796.0	1 912.0	2 002.0	2 067.0	2 179.4	2 288.0	2 362.2
16	2 553.0	3 481.0	3 525.0	3 322.0	3 768.0	3 868.0	3 763.1	4 561.7	4 991.0	4 543.7
17	1 114.0	1 199.0	1 312.0	1 449.0	1 532.0	1 548.0	1 779.2	1 816.8	1 844.0	1 988.0
18	958.0	1 042.0	1 120.0	1 247.0	1 364.0	1 436.0	1 738.5	1 920.5	2 014.0	2 116.5
19	1 100.0	1 164.0	1 269.0	1 382.0	1 506.0	1 630.0	1 819.5	1 926.0	2 054.0	2 220.2
20	1 182.0	1 294.0	1 380.0	1 558.0	1 703.0	1 770.0	1 905.0	1 958.8	2 106.0	2 160.4
21	1 509.0	1 624.0	1 714.0	1 914.0	2 069.0	2 118.0	2 292.2	2 387.6	2 431.0	2 762.1
22	1 589.0	1 779.0	1 952.0	1 930.0	2 074.0	2 096.0	2 184.9	2 229.4	2 241.0	2 531.2
23	2 513.0	2 598.0	2 825.0	3 212.0	3 626.0	4 732.0	5 430.9	5 523.5	5 512.0	4 538.7
24	1 891.0	2 083.0	2 240.0	2 400.0	2 732.0	3 003.0	2 979.5	3 114.9	3 273.0	2 989.9
25	1 335.0	1 464.0	1 554.0	1 703.0	1 826.0	1 926.0	2 056.7	2 198.7	2 338.0	2 656.5
26	1 496.0	1 588.0	1 875.0	1 857.0	2 067.0	2 206.0	2 302.3	2 398.1	2 497.0	2 614.4
27	1 667.0	1 741.0	1 743.0	2 023.0	2 185.0	2 485.0	2 819.0	2 945.4	3 131.0	2 958.5
28	1 301.0	1 479.0	1 553.0	1 642.0	1 743.0	1 788.0	1 870.0	2 030.0	2 146.0	2 632.7
29	1 449.0	1 608.0	1 737.0	1 757.0	1 932.0	2 114.0	2 329.6	2 554.5	2 734.0	2 846.6
30	1 334.0	1 781.0	1 742.0	1 805.0	1 962.0	2 157.0	2 267.0	2 853.3	2 700.0	2 510.0
31	1 214.0	1 312.0	1 301.0	1 690.0	1 866.0	2 018.0	2 043.3	2 137.7	2 282.0	2 327.6
32	1 485.0	1 561.0	1 667.0	1 999.0	2 145.0	2 484.0	2 630.1	2 702.8	2 933.0	2 987.7
33	1 511.0	1 639.0	1 748.0	1 592.0	1 752.0	1 875.0	2 069.6	2 115.7	2 351.0	2 554.9
34	1 724.0	1 802.0	1 803.0	2 226.0	2 450.0	2 739.0	2 949.8	3 032.3	3 251.0	3 557.1
35	1 934.0	2 066.0	1 895.0	2 684.0	2 678.0	2 967.0	3 436.2	3 533.3	3 918.0	3 529.8
36	1 136.0	1 233.0	1 324.0	1 445.0	1 557.0	1 646.0	1 925.6	2 066.4	2 278.0	2 292.0
37	1 352.0	1 489.0	1 659.0	1 475.0	1 564.0	1 626.0	1 750.8	1 783.3	1 997.0	2 066.3

Men - Hommes - Hombres
ISIC 3 - CITI 3 - CIIU 3

	1999	2000	2001	2002	2003	2004	2005	2006	2007	2008
Total	1 650.0	1 790.0	1 889.0	2 118.0	2 304.6	2 521.4	2 715.7	2 847.4	3 025.6	.
15	1 685.0	1 937.0	2 146.0	2 214.0	2 357.9	2 505.6	2 612.9	2 717.5	2 819.1	.
16	2 595.0	3 649.0	3 778.0	3 593.0	3 858.3	3 983.3	3 875.1	4 663.6	5 045.3	.
17	1 315.0	1 418.0	1 543.0	1 729.0	1 847.7	1 841.8	2 144.0	2 147.6	2 150.7	.
18	1 405.0	1 541.0	1 637.0	1 759.0	1 933.8	2 044.5	2 428.8	2 718.4	2 846.7	.
19	1 305.0	1 405.0	1 559.0	1 652.0	1 818.8	1 959.1	2 226.1	2 291.4	2 466.8	.
20	1 266.0	1 393.0	1 490.0	1 653.0	1 823.5	1 898.7	2 043.0	2 095.6	2 231.7	.
21	1 650.0	1 796.0	1 878.0	2 074.0	2 257.9	2 302.0	2 512.1	2 606.5	2 661.9	.
22	1 792.0	2 012.0	2 214.0	2 150.0	2 335.0	2 350.5	2 466.3	2 465.7	2 480.3	.
23	2 571.0	2 668.0	2 895.0	3 338.0	3 739.1	4 934.9	5 650.8	5 767.0	5 797.2	.
24	2 098.0	2 304.0	2 473.0	2 689.0	3 061.7	3 341.2	3 282.7	3 404.2	3 574.8	.
25	1 493.0	1 637.0	1 771.0	1 883.0	2 017.1	2 141.6	2 289.2	2 457.5	2 602.0	.
26	1 644.0	1 734.0	2 029.0	2 014.0	2 239.8	2 376.9	2 474.0	2 572.1	2 681.9	.
27	1 723.0	1 806.0	1 818.0	2 100.0	2 275.9	2 585.6	2 942.5	3 067.5	3 267.7	.
28	1 399.0	1 610.0	1 675.0	1 788.0	1 916.0	1 948.2	2 009.7	2 178.5	2 316.3	.
29	1 540.0	1 714.0	1 859.0	1 899.0	2 083.7	2 270.7	2 510.7	2 750.0	2 961.0	.
30	1 628.0	2 093.0	2 060.0	2 087.0	2 260.0	2 426.4	2 638.0	3 244.1	3 107.6	.
31	1 393.0	1 473.0	1 460.0	2 003.0	2 193.6	2 344.3	2 342.7	2 424.5	2 606.4	.
32	1 760.0	1 789.0	1 946.0	2 375.0	2 580.2	3 016.1	3 155.7	3 223.4	3 465.2	.
33	1 761.0	1 932.0	1 995.0	1 852.0	2 042.4	2 174.0	2 366.3	2 429.1	2 709.4	.
34	1 816.0	1 913.0	1 925.0	2 382.0	2 645.8	2 943.2	3 171.9	3 252.1	3 475.3	.
35	1 975.0	2 105.0	1 931.0	2 747.0	2 753.7	3 036.1	3 539.3	3 638.9	4 046.9	.
36	1 261.0	1 395.0	1 489.0	1 607.0	1 743.3	1 847.4	2 129.4	2 258.9	2 476.2	.
37	1 440.0	1 590.0	1 791.0	1 636.0	1 677.3	1 761.1	1 873.7	1 915.2	2 141.8	.

Women - Femmes - Mujeres
ISIC 3 - CITI 3 - CIIU 3

	1999	2000	2001	2002	2003	2004	2005	2006	2007	2008
Total	918.0	1 036.0	1 096.0	1 187.0	1 291.2	1 382.8	1 525.4	1 643.2	1 742.1	.
15	877.0	1 017.0	1 083.0	1 164.0	1 243.7	1 324.4	1 363.1	1 465.1	1 551.1	.
16	2 303.0	2 549.0	2 333.0	2 174.0	3 308.7	3 252.2	3 157.9	3 752.5	4 577.5	.
17	879.0	953.0	1 024.0	1 053.0	1 103.2	1 143.8	1 248.6	1 305.2	1 351.4	.
18	755.0	842.0	899.0	1 000.0	1 089.1	1 164.7	1 419.4	1 522.5	1 584.4	.
19	790.0	848.0	923.0	1 014.0	1 094.4	1 171.7	1 304.8	1 407.3	1 475.8	.
20	929.0	973.0	978.0	1 150.0	1 272.3	1 229.2	1 385.4	1 452.9	1 610.6	.
21	841.0	1 022.0	1 036.0	1 240.0	1 342.1	1 401.0	1 372.4	1 465.9	1 494.0	.
22	1 076.0	1 224.0	1 361.0	1 443.0	1 556.5	1 624.2	1 643.9	1 723.5	1 736.4	.
23	1 393.0	1 629.0	1 631.0	1 782.0	1 887.4	2 900.8	2 909.4	2 845.1	3 011.8	.
24	1 137.0	1 207.0	1 340.0	1 453.0	1 609.8	1 762.0	1 937.6	2 121.2	2 159.8	.
25	818.0	919.0	971.0	1 157.0	1 251.7	1 303.4	1 378.1	1 479.8	1 572.8	.
26	840.0	929.0	1 072.0	1 168.0	1 291.6	1 388.0	1 447.2	1 513.3	1 600.2	.
27	961.0	1 035.0	1 087.0	1 182.0	1 264.0	1 384.1	1 567.0	1 649.2	1 785.1	.
28	857.0	967.0	1 035.0	1 046.0	1 087.6	1 145.8	1 323.3	1 431.1	1 516.6	.
29	950.0	1 065.0	1 132.0	1 160.0	1 230.2	1 352.4	1 381.5	1 569.0	1 633.2	.
30	926.0	1 170.0	1 344.0	1 231.0	1 330.4	1 437.0	1 611.3	1 781.8	1 907.0	.
31	835.0	947.0	948.0	1 049.0	1 190.6	1 275.3	1 339.9	1 434.7	1 562.5	.
32	1 053.0	1 224.0	1 237.0	1 401.0	1 525.0	1 644.9	1 822.7	1 946.0	2 091.5	.
33	991.0	1 096.0	1 226.0	1 079.0	1 164.6	1 254.4	1 431.0	1 463.7	1 605.9	.
34	1 085.0	1 176.0	1 115.0	1 237.0	1 323.0	1 452.1	1 626.5	1 683.5	1 812.9	.
35	1 264.0	1 550.0	1 319.0	1 681.0	1 795.1	1 943.2	1 990.7	2 007.8	2 264.1	.
36	883.0	948.0	967.0	1 084.0	1 143.5	1 131.2	1 447.5	1 568.9	1 659.4	.
37	849.0	1 012.0	1 146.0	1 051.0	1 068.4	1 125.1	1 265.0	1 295.0	1 439.9	.

Explanatory notes: see p. 877.

[1] Figures in thousands. [2] Establishments with 5 or more regular employees.

Notes explicatives: voir p. 879.

[1] Données en milliers. [2] Establissements occupant 5 salariés stables et plus.

Notas explicativas: véase p. 882.

[1] Cifras en millares. [2] Establecimientos con 5 y más asalariados estables.

5B

WAGES	SALAIRES	SALARIOS
In manufacturing	Dans les industries manufacturières	En las industrias manufactureras

	1999	2000	2001	2002	2003	2004	2005	2006	2007	2008

Korea, Republic of (DA) [1][2] — Employees - Salariés - Asalariados — E.G./m. - Won

Total men and women - Total hommes et femmes - Total hombres y mujeres
ISIC 3 - CITI 3 - CIIU 3

	1999	2000	2001	2002	2003	2004	2005	2006	2007	2008
Total	1 475.5	1 601.5	1 702.4	1 907.0	2 074.0	2 279.7	2 458.0	2 594.8	2 772.0	2 757.8
15	1 391.1	1 596.0	1 758.0	1 851.0	1 959.3	2 066.7	2 119.0	2 229.1	2 354.0	2 371.8
16	2 552.8	3 481.5	3 525.0	3 322.0	3 767.8	3 867.8	3 763.1	4 560.6	4 996.0	4 518.9
17	1 110.6	1 200.6	1 316.3	1 453.0	1 542.2	1 551.5	1 791.1	1 850.1	1 877.0	1 976.0
18	962.5	1 038.6	1 126.6	1 258.0	1 378.8	1 439.5	1 697.0	1 882.9	2 052.0	2 158.5
19	1 081.0	1 147.5	1 272.7	1 403.0	1 545.6	1 677.1	1 852.1	1 954.6	2 083.0	2 266.7
20	1 238.5	1 348.5	1 502.1	1 649.0	1 811.3	1 884.6	2 004.3	2 063.4	2 213.0	2 220.6
21	1 562.6	1 675.3	1 773.9	1 994.0	2 146.4	2 198.1	2 435.3	2 550.7	2 573.0	2 867.4
22	1 669.0	1 875.0	2 076.0	2 028.0	2 172.3	2 178.8	2 286.4	2 328.2	2 372.0	2 574.0
23	2 520.2	2 608.5	2 848.5	3 244.0	3 676.4	4 785.6	5 523.6	5 605.4	5 601.0	4 578.0
24	1 923.7	2 116.0	2 277.6	2 438.0	2 798.4	3 079.9	3 041.4	3 173.9	3 342.0	3 035.2
25	1 367.3	1 491.1	1 598.9	1 754.0	1 882.3	1 993.4	2 109.0	2 256.2	2 395.0	2 671.8
26	1 532.0	1 630.1	1 944.2	1 892.0	2 120.4	2 268.0	2 380.4	2 473.4	2 567.0	2 653.5
27	1 685.5	1 754.3	1 753.9	2 042.0	2 213.2	2 535.9	2 869.9	2 995.1	3 178.0	2 930.4
28	1 330.3	1 507.1	1 598.9	1 700.0	1 809.0	1 858.2	1 885.3	2 080.1	2 211.0	2 665.5
29	1 481.1	1 645.3	1 791.3	1 808.0	1 986.3	2 177.5	2 394.9	2 620.0	2 835.0	2 882.0
30	1 346.0	1 789.4	1 727.3	1 814.0	1 976.9	2 173.9	2 284.0	2 888.8	2 731.0	2 510.9
31	1 232.8	1 343.4	1 330.0	1 730.0	1 900.1	2 059.7	2 094.2	2 187.3	2 327.0	2 352.2
32	1 500.0	1 573.3	1 681.0	2 018.0	2 167.6	2 508.0	2 645.4	2 714.3	2 948.0	2 995.7
33	1 538.9	1 682.5	1 824.8	1 618.0	1 793.8	1 933.3	2 121.8	2 156.3	2 391.0	2 572.9
34	1 742.6	1 824.1	1 827.2	2 251.0	2 479.9	2 771.8	2 990.2	3 070.3	3 303.0	3 615.8
35	1 943.3	2 079.6	1 905.4	2 719.0	2 703.3	2 995.0	3 463.1	3 559.5	3 952.0	3 534.2
36	1 159.6	1 272.9	1 378.3	1 463.0	1 586.5	1 674.7	2 075.2	2 184.7	2 400.0	2 398.1
37	1 404.4	1 539.3	1 676.4	1 481.0	1 606.5	1 658.5	1 698.7	1 730.7	1 892.0	2 003.1

Men - Hommes - Hombres
ISIC 3 - CITI 3 - CIIU 3

	1999	2000	2001	2002	2003	2004	2005	2006	2007	2008
Total	1 686.3	1 826.0	1 936.0	2 177.0	2 369.7	2 599.8	2 798.6	2 931.9	3 123.6	.
15	1 729.0	1 998.5	2 227.7	2 284.8	2 419.6	2 598.4	2 685.8	2 786.2	2 913.1	.
16	2 594.8	3 648.6	3 777.9	3 593.3	3 858.4	3 983.2	3 875.1	4 662.8	5 048.4	.
17	1 307.0	1 412.8	1 541.3	1 739.0	1 858.7	1 837.6	2 158.6	2 191.0	2 193.4	.
18	1 449.8	1 585.6	1 712.1	1 825.0	1 974.7	2 071.0	2 437.1	2 746.7	2 937.2	.
19	1 291.4	1 391.2	1 563.7	1 686.0	1 866.5	2 017.5	2 279.3	2 353.4	2 524.5	.
20	1 337.2	1 463.8	1 615.5	1 742.0	1 949.4	2 029.0	2 141.6	2 205.5	2 357.2	.
21	1 701.1	1 847.4	1 940.9	2 157.0	2 342.8	2 389.3	2 654.4	2 777.9	2 827.5	.
22	1 871.6	2 121.7	2 359.7	2 261.0	2 453.6	2 434.3	2 563.9	2 571.2	2 618.2	.
23	2 577.8	2 678.0	2 913.7	3 369.0	3 782.7	4 986.1	5 731.6	5 843.8	5 883.0	.
24	2 131.4	2 337.8	2 521.1	2 731.0	3 128.6	3 421.2	3 351.2	3 472.1	3 647.2	.
25	1 528.8	1 667.0	1 823.7	1 948.0	2 083.6	2 217.4	2 364.6	2 530.1	2 663.5	.
26	1 682.5	1 777.8	2 100.4	2 051.0	2 300.9	2 446.9	2 558.2	2 652.1	2 751.6	.
27	1 746.6	1 817.0	1 829.1	2 116.0	2 299.1	2 628.8	2 992.5	3 115.9	3 313.4	.
28	1 430.9	1 641.1	1 723.8	1 854.0	1 990.5	2 022.7	2 022.3	2 230.1	2 392.6	.
29	1 570.2	1 748.1	1 914.4	1 958.0	2 145.6	2 336.6	2 576.4	2 816.8	3 079.2	.
30	1 636.4	2 100.6	2 047.9	2 103.0	2 277.5	2 442.4	2 659.7	3 284.4	3 156.3	.
31	1 411.8	1 499.5	1 470.6	2 039.0	2 228.6	2 385.7	2 398.4	2 477.6	2 652.0	.
32	1 780.1	1 800.9	1 960.8	2 396.0	2 611.7	3 052.0	3 186.2	3 244.6	3 491.5	.
33	1 797.2	1 990.9	2 108.3	1 903.0	2 089.0	2 252.3	2 447.5	2 498.3	2 783.7	.
34	1 832.1	1 932.1	1 948.4	2 406.0	2 673.2	2 972.9	3 208.0	3 282.7	3 518.4	.
35	1 982.2	2 110.8	1 937.9	2 779.0	2 776.6	3 060.0	3 561.6	3 662.4	4 079.0	.
36	1 299.0	1 443.8	1 571.0	1 628.0	1 775.0	1 869.0	2 303.7	2 387.9	2 601.7	.
37	1 478.5	1 637.3	1 802.4	1 680.0	1 738.5	1 813.0	1 836.7	1 876.9	2 049.2	.

Women - Femmes - Mujeres
ISIC 3 - CITI 3 - CIIU 3

	1999	2000	2001	2002	2003	2004	2005	2006	2007	2008
Total	933.1	1 055.8	1 121.3	1 211.0	1 320.0	1 419.7	1 556.1	1 675.6	1 785.3	.
15	894.7	1 045.8	1 124.3	1 193.0	1 266.9	1 354.9	1 389.1	1 493.8	1 586.1	.
16	2 303.4	2 549.5	2 332.7	2 174.0	3 308.0	3 252.2	3 157.9	3 744.7	4 595.0	.
17	879.7	959.7	1 032.4	1 053.0	1 107.7	1 146.1	1 242.2	1 313.5	1 361.9	.
18	746.5	828.6	888.2	1 006.0	1 096.8	1 165.4	1 360.9	1 441.9	1 604.7	.
19	783.5	840.6	826.9	1 031.0	1 133.2	1 215.4	1 318.9	1 416.5	1 486.0	.
20	973.0	1 010.1	1 062.8	1 241.0	1 354.3	1 294.7	1 448.6	1 488.2	1 671.3	.
21	860.4	1 043.2	1 051.4	1 282.0	1 369.6	1 413.2	1 459.2	1 554.8	1 547.3	.
22	1 131.5	1 279.2	1 427.4	1 498.0	1 604.2	1 682.7	1 732.1	1 798.0	1 831.1	.
23	1 400.3	1 640.5	1 667.3	1 809.0	1 947.6	2 949.2	3 031.7	2 917.1	3 080.7	.
24	1 154.7	1 220.7	1 353.6	1 468.0	1 644.0	1 806.3	1 974.4	2 155.8	2 206.9	.
25	835.5	935.7	996.8	1 180.0	1 279.5	1 341.0	1 393.6	1 518.7	1 622.8	.
26	854.8	944.3	1 106.6	1 185.0	1 304.4	1 402.8	1 501.2	1 567.0	1 658.9	.
27	970.9	1 044.6	1 092.2	1 192.0	1 279.4	1 425.4	1 573.4	1 637.4	1 785.6	.
28	873.8	985.3	1 060.1	1 069.0	1 124.6	1 196.4	1 353.3	1 481.8	1 563.7	.
29	980.7	1 105.5	1 178.2	1 195.0	1 264.1	1 401.6	1 423.4	1 587.1	1 657.4	.
30	943.0	1 181.7	1 351.7	1 238.0	1 343.7	1 454.0	1 626.0	1 798.5	1 923.4	.
31	850.6	979.0	996.0	1 080.0	1 222.5	1 317.2	1 376.6	1 476.8	1 611.6	.
32	1 063.1	1 236.3	1 250.7	1 416.0	1 542.2	1 660.3	1 830.3	1 953.5	2 097.8	.
33	1 006.6	1 117.6	1 265.7	1 099.0	1 196.3	1 294.5	1 464.8	1 498.1	1 631.0	.
34	1 102.1	1 195.6	1 130.9	1 252.0	1 341.0	1 476.9	1 659.2	1 723.2	1 864.4	.
35	1 286.8	1 625.1	1 354.7	1 733.0	1 834.5	1 995.0	2 032.3	2 038.0	2 293.8	.
36	899.2	970.7	985.4	1 119.0	1 193.1	1 195.6	1 548.8	1 657.7	1 735.8	.
37	899.5	1 071.2	1 213.1	954.0	1 039.6	1 113.4	1 108.8	1 154.2	1 296.3	.

Explanatory notes: see p. 877.

[1] Figures in thousands. [2] Establishments with 10 or more regular employees.

Notes explicatives: voir p. 879.

[1] Données en milliers. [2] Etablissements occupant 10 salariés stables ou plus.

Notas explicativas: véase p. 882.

[1] Cifras en millares. [2] Establecimientos con 10 y más asalariados estables.

980

ILO YEARBOOK OF LABOUR STATISTICS 2009   *ANNUAIRE DES STATISTIQUES DU TRAVAIL DU BIT 2009*   *ANUARIO DE ESTADISTICAS DEL TRABAJO DEL OIT 2009*

In manufacturing / Dans les industries manufacturières / En las industrias manufactureras

	1999	2000	2001	2002	2003	2004	2005	2006	2007	2008

Korea, Republic of (DA) [1][2] Employees - Salariés - Asalariados E.G./m. - Won

Total men and women - Total hommes et femmes - Total hombres y mujeres
ISIC 3 - CITI 3 - CIIU 3

	1999	2000	2001	2002	2003	2004	2005	2006	2007	2008
Total	.	.	.	.	.	.	.	.	2 662.5	2 679.1
15	.	.	.	.	.	.	.	.	2 153.2	2 213.9
16	.	.	.	.	.	.	.	.	4 257.6	4 469.4
17	.	.	.	.	.	.	.	.	1 829.6	1 950.9
18	.	.	.	.	.	.	.	.	1 930.1	2 033.9
19	.	.	.	.	.	.	.	.	2 018.3	2 184.1
20	.	.	.	.	.	.	.	.	2 128.2	2 133.8
21	.	.	.	.	.	.	.	.	2 445.1	2 059.1
22	.	.	.	.	.	.	.	.	2 345.1	2 441.1
23	.	.	.	.	.	.	.	.	4 728.1	4 520.5
24	.	.	.	.	.	.	.	.	2 954.3	2 933.4
25	.	.	.	.	.	.	.	.	2 425.9	2 628.3
26	.	.	.	.	.	.	.	.	2 379.6	2 569.5
27	.	.	.	.	.	.	.	.	3 093.5	2 925.0
28	.	.	.	.	.	.	.	.	2 292.4	2 623.5
29	.	.	.	.	.	.	.	.	2 783.0	2 761.0
30	.	.	.	.	.	.	.	.	2 760.8	2 472.7
31	.	.	.	.	.	.	.	.	2 354.1	2 216.9
32	.	.	.	.	.	.	.	.	2 533.4	2 925.2
33	.	.	.	.	.	.	.	.	2 343.5	2 447.2
34	.	.	.	.	.	.	.	.	3 082.5	3 510.3
35	.	.	.	.	.	.	.	.	3 688.7	3 400.7
36	.	.	.	.	.	.	.	.	2 179.6	2 167.0
37	.	.	.	.	.	.	.	.	1 794.4	2 050.1

Korea, Republic of (DA) [2][3] Employees - Salariés - Asalariados E.G./m. - Won

Total men and women - Total hommes et femmes - Total hombres y mujeres
ISIC 3 - CITI 3 - CIIU 3

	1999	2000	2001	2002	2003	2004	2005	2006	2007	2008
Total	.	.	.	.	.	.	.	.	2 696.5	2 675.9
15	.	.	.	.	.	.	.	.	2 168.6	2 211.2
16	.	.	.	.	.	.	.	.	4 261.4	4 445.1
17	.	.	.	.	.	.	.	.	1 823.7	1 936.1
18	.	.	.	.	.	.	.	.	1 978.1	2 092.5
19	.	.	.	.	.	.	.	.	2 049.7	2 224.8
20	.	.	.	.	.	.	.	.	2 162.3	2 186.8
21	.	.	.	.	.	.	.	.	2 724.6	2 832.8
22	.	.	.	.	.	.	.	.	2 396.8	2 457.6
23	.	.	.	.	.	.	.	.	4 767.8	4 565.8
24	.	.	.	.	.	.	.	.	2 974.1	2 974.4
25	.	.	.	.	.	.	.	.	2 442.8	2 636.3
26	.	.	.	.	.	.	.	.	2 404.5	2 604.5
27	.	.	.	.	.	.	.	.	3 109.3	2 895.2
28	.	.	.	.	.	.	.	.	2 307.2	2 651.5
29	.	.	.	.	.	.	.	.	2 801.5	2 786.5
30	.	.	.	.	.	.	.	.	2 757.7	2 470.8
31	.	.	.	.	.	.	.	.	2 379.2	2 221.8
32	.	.	.	.	.	.	.	.	2 537.2	2 931.2
33	.	.	.	.	.	.	.	.	2 360.0	2 446.6
34	.	.	.	.	.	.	.	.	3 105.5	3 566.0
35	.	.	.	.	.	.	.	.	3 693.1	3 407.3
36	.	.	.	.	.	.	.	.	2 217.8	2 225.7
37	.	.	.	.	.	.	.	.	1 721.3	1 991.5

Explanatory notes: see p. 877.

[1] Incl. temporary and daily employees of the establishments with 5 or more permanent employees. [2] Figures in thousands. [3] Incl. temporary and daily employees of the establishments with 10 or more permanent employees.

Notes explicatives: voir p. 879.

[1] Y compris salariés temporaires et journaliers des etablissements occupant 5 salariés ou plus. [2] Données en milliers. [3] Y compris salaritemporaires et journalier s des établissements occupant 10 salariés ou plus.

Notas explicativas: véase p. 882.

[1] Incl. asalariados diarios y temporales de los establecimientos con 5 y más asalariados. [2] Cifras en millares. [3] Incl. asalariados diarios y temporales de los establecimientos con 10 y más asalariados.

WAGES   SALAIRES   SALARIOS

In manufacturing   Dans les industries manufacturières   En las industrias manufactureras

	1999	2000	2001	2002	2003	2004	2005	2006	2007	2008

Kyrgyzstan (CA)   Employees - Salariés - Asalariados   E.G./m. - Som

Total men and women - Total hommes et femmes - Total hombres y mujeres
ISIC 3 - CITI 3 - CIIU 3

	1999	2000	2001	2002	2003	2004	2005	2006	2007	2008
Total	1 962.30	2 020.10	2 390.60	2 834.00	3 182.60	3 758.60	4 229.60	6 211.00	6 254.00	.
15	1 489.56	1 601.90	1 752.20	2 045.00	2 244.40	2 642.60	2 910.90	3 222.00	3 835.00	.
16	2 175.76	2 681.10	3 307.10	4 327.00	5 846.10	7 151.20	10 004.50	11 125.00	13 165.00	.
17	888.20	1 162.80	1 296.20	1 338.00	1 510.40	1 607.30	2 075.10	2 279.00	2 477.00	.
18	653.11	690.30	695.40	745.70	916.00	871.20	825.10	1 093.00	1 455.00	.
19	1 081.13	1 394.40	1 406.30	1 304.00	1 587.10	1 826.90	1 900.30	2 069.00	1 869.00	.
20	454.54	521.20	617.40	736.70	928.40	1 164.80	1 802.40	1 909.00	2 651.00	.
21	1 196.46	1 069.00	1 375.10	1 700.00	3 800.40	3 240.60	2 836.80	3 156.00	4 268.00	.
22	1 667.54	2 166.70	2 469.80	2 455.00	2 673.80	2 848.50	3 064.60	3 289.00	3 799.00	.
23	3 523.39	4 014.40	4 085.30	3 901.00	4 036.20	6 080.90	10 714.90	12 329.00	13 033.00	.
24	1 527.08	1 398.90	1 529.30	2 111.00	1 986.50	2 271.00	2 885.80	3 541.00	3 966.00	.
25	819.76	1 372.10	1 363.40	1 451.00	1 955.10	1 827.50	1 636.80	2 617.00	2 902.00	.
26	1 274.15	1 419.90	2 180.50	2 484.00	3 023.60	3 801.10	4 493.80	5 179.00	5 913.00	.
27	1 595.73	5 048.10	7 955.20	14 054.00	14 261.00	16 794.50	17 442.00	31 043.00	26 549.00	.
28	997.30	1 057.60	1 397.40	1 626.00	1 794.20	2 191.90	2 416.10	2 753.00	3 010.00	.
29	935.60	1 314.70	1 548.60	1 625.00	1 883.80	2 962.60	3 772.30	4 477.00	5 763.00	.
30	826.93	1 069.30	873.10	1 003.00	1 660.60	1 776.00	1 541.10	1 457.00	1 616.00	.
31	1 362.71	1 678.10	1 987.50	2 363.00	2 998.70	3 251.00	3 205.40	3 580.00	4 949.00	.
32	884.12	1 058.30	1 435.10	1 669.00	1 902.30	2 531.60	3 167.70	4 574.00	5 447.00	.
33	1 983.19	1 798.10	2 298.50	2 908.00	3 753.50	2 417.70	3 212.80	4 613.00	4 959.00	.
34	1 690.15	1 728.00	2 741.50	2 826.00	2 493.30	3 180.90	3 799.80	2 884.00	4 973.00	.
35	802.27	3 494.40	3 537.80	3 739.00	5 013.30	2 705.30	1 576.00	3 029.00	3 534.00	.
36	807.52	929.20	1 006.60	1 232.00	1 386.80	1 274.60	1 344.40	1 517.00	1 808.00	.
37	1 019.19	1 170.60	1 175.40	1 083.00	888.10	789.00	1 781.30	1 714.00	1 235.00	.

Macau, China (BA) [1]   Total employment - Emploi total - Empleo total   E.G./m. - Pataca

Total men and women - Total hommes et femmes - Total hombres y mujeres
ISIC 3 - CITI 3 - CIIU 3

	1999	2000	2001	2002	2003	2004	2005	2006	2007	2008
Total	2 921	2 960	2 758	2 758	2 834	2 983	3 101	3 140	4 000	4 000

Men - Hommes - Hombres
ISIC 3 - CITI 3 - CIIU 3

	1999	2000	2001	2002	2003	2004	2005	2006	2007	2008
Total	4 738	4 690	4 527	4 469	4 363	4 829	4 765	5 462	6 500	5 300

Women - Femmes - Mujeres
ISIC 3 - CITI 3 - CIIU 3

	1999	2000	2001	2002	2003	2004	2005	2006	2007	2008
Total	2 510	2 613	2 429	2 430	2 542	2 652	2 795	2 698	3 100	3 500

Macau, China (DA)   Employees - Salariés - Asalariados   E.G./m. - Pataca

Total men and women - Total hommes et femmes - Total hombres y mujeres
ISIC 3 - CITI 3 - CIIU 3

	1999	2000	2001	2002	2003	2004	2005	2006	2007	2008
Total [2]	.	4 044	4 102	3 970	4 010	4 178	4 390	4 652	4 990	5 447
17	.	4 249	4 443	4 356	4 232	4 319	4 486	4 963	5 655	5 472
18	.	3 754	3 784	3 707	.	3 830	3 974	4 110	4 197	4 764
36	.	5 031	5 111	.	.	.	.	.	.	.

Men - Hommes - Hombres
ISIC 3 - CITI 3 - CIIU 3

	1999	2000	2001	2002	2003	2004	2005	2006	2007	2008
Total [2]	.	5 411	5 382	5 250	5 335	5 750	5 961	6 193	6 716	7 072
17	.	5 149	5 220	5 527	5 349	5 714	5 647	6 243	6 984	6 960
18	.	4 975	4 906	4 883	.	5 112	5 224	5 127	4 197	6 042
36	.	6 148	6 133	5 670	.	.	.	.	.	.

Women - Femmes - Mujeres
ISIC 3 - CITI 3 - CIIU 3

	1999	2000	2001	2002	2003	2004	2005	2006	2007	2008
Total [2]	.	3 606	3 683	3 575	3 584	3 689	3 860	4 074	4 272	4 689
17	.	3 916	4 161	3 984	3 828	3 844	4 066	4 443	5 035	4 792
18	.	3 502	3 543	3 462	.	3 569	3 726	3 877	3 947	4 415
36	.	3 889	3 998	3 796	.	.	.	.	.	.

Mongolia (DA) [3]   Employees - Salariés - Asalariados   E.G./m. - Tughriks

Total men and women - Total hommes et femmes - Total hombres y mujeres
ISIC 3 - CITI 3 - CIIU 3

	1999	2000	2001	2002	2003	2004	2005	2006	2007	2008
Total	.	66.0 [4]	.	68.7	82.7	92.8	100.5	124.1	160.2	268.0

Men - Hommes - Hombres
ISIC 3 - CITI 3 - CIIU 3

	1999	2000	2001	2002	2003	2004	2005	2006	2007	2008
Total	.	60.0 [4]	65.9	69.3	86.9	98.1	114.9	142.7	189.4	315.9

Explanatory notes: see p. 877.   Notes explicatives: voir p. 879.   Notas explicativas: véase p. 882.

[1] Median. [2] Third quarter of each year. [3] Figures in thousands. [4] Fourth quarter.   [1] Médiane. [2] Troisième trimestre de chaque année. [3] Données en milliers. [4] Quatrième trimestre.   [1] Mediana. [2] Tercer trimestre de cada año. [3] Cifras en millares. [4] Cuarto trimestre.

In manufacturing   Dans les industries manufacturières   En las industrias manufactureras

	1999	2000	2001	2002	2003	2004	2005	2006	2007	2008

Mongolia (DA) [1]   Employees - Salariés - Asalariados   E.G./m. - Tughriks

Women - Femmes - Mujeres
ISIC 3 - CITI 3 - CIIU 3

	1999	2000	2001	2002	2003	2004	2005	2006	2007	2008
Total	.	70.0 [2]	64.8	68.2	75.6	89.1	88.9	105.2	135.6	225.2

Myanmar (DA) [3]   Employees - Salariés - Asalariados   R.T./h. - Kyat

Total men and women - Total hommes et femmes - Total hombres y mujeres [4]
ISIC 2 - CITI 2 - CIIU 2

	1999	2000	2001	2002	2003	2004	2005	2006	2007	2008
311-312	4.83	4.80	8.35	11.86	13.96	18.66	20.68	44.04	133.91	141.17
313	6.39	6.63	10.60	9.33	12.16	12.17	12.20	61.38	157.77	164.49
314	5.13	5.13	10.15	9.53	9.07	12.78	13.07	57.02	148.42	179.38
321	4.48	4.99	6.27	6.28	10.17	11.12	12.92	47.44	147.30	149.48
322-324	5.39	10.87	10.87	11.67	11.92	12.07	13.30	68.78	113.72	162.61
323	4.57	4.69	4.93	4.96	7.53	10.74	11.87	56.27	163.93	170.84
324	4.65	10.87	10.87	11.67	11.92	12.07	12.30	68.78	113.72	162.61
331	4.72	8.01	10.13	10.32	11.19	15.36	16.00	51.62	147.75	175.82
341	4.68	11.07	11.07	11.91	13.83	14.37	15.27	64.04	155.02	160.19
342	3.52	17.28	26.41	26.80	28.33	39.70	40.54	80.43	137.23	167.73
351	4.40	4.75	6.77	6.99	7.16	10.61	11.06	71.31	122.81	176.94
352	4.87	7.50	5.89	5.89	7.33	10.36	11.27	47.96	111.96	126.01
353	4.05	25.01	26.29	26.28	26.27	25.04	26.57	41.48	125.81	145.69
354	5.14	7.36	12.12	12.98	14.01	15.38	16.89	76.91	159.97	165.32
355	4.51	4.78	4.78	4.99	6.58	10.45	10.60	43.48	116.68	129.73
356	4.56	4.47	7.45	7.45	8.14	15.90	17.27	68.11	145.48	164.87
361	3.84	3.89	3.84	5.99	8.60	12.49	14.42	44.81	157.08	161.85
362	3.68	7.39	14.66	14.65	16.83	16.83	16.90	49.10	156.78	158.88
369	3.72	11.07	11.07	12.39	13.10	13.35	14.67	56.48	156.32	160.11
371	4.15	4.36	6.62	6.83	9.54	16.21	18.73	61.78	111.48	139.58
372	4.56	4.55	6.03	9.26	11.30	11.85	12.46	55.43	136.24	140.96
381	4.34	4.99	7.57	9.98	11.93	14.82	16.97	67.54	125.19	130.98
384	3.89	10.49	17.09	17.20	20.63	22.04	24.76	43.68	177.60	178.67

Men - Hommes - Hombres [5]
ISIC 2 - CITI 2 - CIIU 2

	1999	2000	2001	2002	2003	2004	2005	2006	2007	2008
Total	.	13.51	18.98	20.82	22.84	29.89	31.89	94.00	132.74	180.55

Women - Femmes - Mujeres [5]
ISIC 2 - CITI 2 - CIIU 2

	1999	2000	2001	2002	2003	2004	2005	2006	2007	2008
Total	.	20.79	17.45	19.56	20.31	27.18	28.36	90.61	116.31	158.60

Philippines (BA)   Employees - Salariés - Asalariados   R.T./d.j. - Peso

Total men and women - Total hommes et femmes - Total hombres y mujeres
ISIC 3 - CITI 3 - CIIU 3

	1999	2000	2001	2002	2003	2004	2005	2006	2007	2008
Total	.	.	226.2	229.0	237.4	239.4	246.6	265.0	277.2	289.6
15	.	.	203.8	214.0	209.1	212.3	223.2	231.1	238.0	248.3
16	.	.	278.5	310.0	305.9	292.9	341.7	362.1	379.0	439.8
17	.	.	202.1	191.4	213.8	208.6	213.6	202.9	216.4	217.3
18	.	.	190.9	197.8	209.4	213.3	221.3	228.2	237.6	248.8
19	.	.	190.4	188.1	215.4	209.6	212.4	219.2	240.6	253.2
20	.	.	172.2	171.9	186.2	178.2	172.0	179.3	189.7	194.7
21	.	.	220.3	238.5	232.0	208.3	237.4	259.7	257.7	262.1
22	.	.	284.4	272.9	304.6	294.3	305.1	335.4	338.8	380.7
23	.	.	328.0	344.3	345.1	441.5	515.4	617.3	557.2	441.9
24	.	.	366.0	350.6	376.6	385.2	363.1	446.5	420.9	480.7
25	.	.	274.2	270.7	274.5	264.1	275.9	296.3	317.5	332.2
26	.	.	227.5	232.6	230.9	233.7	231.9	321.2	269.3	289.5
27	.	.	254.4	275.2	255.8	282.0	289.5	328.3	340.2	332.9
28	.	.	215.4	216.8	230.1	232.3	251.1	262.9	328.9	286.1
29	.	.	257.7	280.3	272.4	261.7	283.4	305.5	304.1	337.3
30	.	.	321.1	288.0	317.9	299.3	339.3	387.7	353.4	368.8
31	.	.	278.7	270.3	289.7	330.3	323.6	341.3	349.8	379.9
32	.	.	274.0	275.5	295.2	299.3	299.9	317.3	354.1	355.2
33	.	.	266.0	277.3	309.7	291.1	262.1	294.2	355.7	392.2
34	.	.	268.8	300.8	304.5	331.0	323.9	346.5	373.4	384.1
35	.	.	226.6	234.1	258.5	252.2	279.0	305.7	303.7	342.7
36	.	.	191.3	188.4	203.5	212.2	221.3	233.6	224.3	248.1
37	.	.	180.0	172.8	136.6	185.6	284.0	200.4	202.0	215.8

Explanatory notes: see p. 877.   Notes explicatives: voir p. 879.   Notas explicativas: véase p. 882.

[1] Figures in thousands. [2] Fourth quarter. [3] March and Sep. of each year. [4] Temporary workers. [5] Regular employees.

[1] Données en milliers. [2] Quatrième trimestre. [3] Mars et sept. de chaque année. [4] Travailleurs temporaires. [5] Salariés stables.

[1] Cifras en millares. [2] Cuarto trimestre. [3] Marzo y sept. de cada año. [4] Trabajadores temporales. [5] Asalariados estables.

	WAGES		SALAIRES			SALARIOS			
	In manufacturing		Dans les industries manufacturières			En las industrias manufactureras			

	1999	2000	2001	2002	2003	2004	2005	2006	2007	2008
Philippines (BA)				Employees - Salariés - Asalariados						R.T./d.j. - Peso
Men - Hommes - Hombres										
ISIC 3 - CITI 3 - CIIU 3										
Total	.	.	237.2	238.9	246.3	247.7	254.0	270.5	290.9	299.1
15	.	.	206.7	220.4	211.4	219.2	226.3	234.3	240.9	252.9
16	.	.	308.9	358.0	335.8	306.4	358.9	377.1	395.6	483.6
17	.	.	236.8	207.7	240.6	252.2	250.9	250.1	263.5	263.0
18	.	.	220.3	239.0	251.9	242.5	248.4	254.9	272.5	280.5
19	.	.	202.0	204.4	217.4	224.9	213.1	228.3	252.4	272.3
20	.	.	185.2	180.6	196.3	193.2	183.2	199.6	208.9	218.6
21	.	.	220.0	251.0	257.0	233.6	250.8	277.1	272.9	306.0
22	.	.	281.1	276.3	292.5	283.6	299.5	332.6	335.9	368.9
23	.	.	310.6	332.7	340.4	437.4	470.9	622.7	509.9	400.9
24	.	.	371.8	348.2	377.8	364.2	348.2	386.5	433.4	469.7
25	.	.	276.8	276.1	276.7	263.9	281.7	300.0	328.0	342.0
26	.	.	232.4	226.7	225.8	234.0	228.7	249.7	264.8	279.2
27	.	.	249.9	265.2	259.5	280.8	287.7	328.8	341.5	331.1
28	.	.	214.9	222.2	230.5	231.2	247.7	258.8	326.8	281.8
29	.	.	262.8	269.7	277.4	263.7	282.6	302.9	303.5	326.6
30	.	.	406.3	381.4	356.0	305.6	364.4	427.7	359.0	384.1
31	.	.	316.1	302.0	325.3	373.7	356.8	364.1	369.3	376.2
32	.	.	331.5	307.4	336.2	337.6	338.8	363.9	426.5	400.6
33	.	.	308.9	328.6	365.4	321.9	300.2	330.6	496.5	485.1
34	.	.	266.3	290.7	302.3	311.2	323.5	351.6	388.3	382.0
35	.	.	221.0	229.6	246.0	247.3	272.2	306.3	296.2	344.5
36	.	.	196.8	193.6	212.9	218.2	231.7	239.1	236.7	258.7
37	.	.	208.0	163.4	147.1	220.2	267.2	228.0	222.2	262.2
Women - Femmes - Mujeres										
ISIC 3 - CITI 3 - CIIU 3										
Total	.	.	210.6	215.3	225.0	227.4	236.5	257.4	257.9	275.8
15	.	.	196.7	197.5	203.3	194.7	215.6	223.6	231.4	237.9
16	.	.	240.5	249.3	258.3	269.8	314.0	332.8	325.1	355.3
17	.	.	182.4	179.7	194.7	182.1	190.6	172.4	187.9	188.3
18	.	.	183.5	186.0	196.6	203.2	212.4	219.8	225.5	237.9
19	.	.	179.6	172.8	213.6	193.6	211.6	207.9	227.0	235.9
20	.	.	135.3	144.6	155.6	141.5	148.7	140.5	146.0	140.4
21	.	.	220.9	214.9	186.6	169.9	213.5	230.4	232.0	196.3
22	.	.	292.1	262.5	331.8	318.2	316.8	340.9	345.0	401.8
23	.	.	545.9	454.5	364.5	456.3	673.8	602.7	704.8	536.9
24	.	.	351.9	355.1	374.7	425.5	391.3	555.4	396.6	504.8
25	.	.	269.1	260.7	269.5	264.5	262.1	287.8	296.0	307.2
26	.	.	202.5	267.1	253.9	232.1	248.9	693.5	295.5	349.7
27	.	.	297.5	345.1	227.7	291.4	303.3	323.7	323.0	344.9
28	.	.	221.6	168.1	224.8	245.3	307.1	330.9	361.9	351.6
29	.	.	242.7	306.5	252.0	253.1	287.3	318.2	307.3	384.7
30	.	.	267.4	254.2	296.5	295.8	323.2	340.4	345.9	355.4
31	.	.	249.6	247.7	261.9	290.3	297.4	317.5	328.2	384.1
32	.	.	248.9	262.6	275.5	281.2	282.1	297.9	318.9	333.0
33	.	.	238.3	250.2	277.9	274.3	241.9	276.6	294.1	334.2
34	.	.	280.3	339.0	316.4	397.4	325.2	332.0	314.9	391.3
35	.	.	274.4	269.2	346.9	318.5	322.9	302.2	348.0	327.3
36	.	.	179.0	178.1	181.0	198.5	198.5	221.2	197.9	219.8
37	.	.	113.1	204.6	120.1	135.9	379.9	171.0	182.7	136.3
Philippines (DB) [1] [2]				Employees - Salariés - Asalariados						E.G./m. - Peso
Total men and women - Total hommes et femmes - Total hombres y mujeres										
ISIC 3 - CITI 3 - CIIU 3										
Total	8 347 [3]	.	9 936	.	11 166	.	12 973	.	.	.
Qatar (BA) [4]				Employees - Salariés - Asalariados						R.T./m. - Riyal
Total men and women - Total hommes et femmes - Total hombres y mujeres										
ISIC 3 - CITI 3 - CIIU 3										
Total	.	.	.	.	.	.	.	3 677	5 060	.
Men - Hommes - Hombres										
ISIC 3 - CITI 3 - CIIU 3										
Total	.	.	.	.	.	.	.	3 668	5 027	.
Women - Femmes - Mujeres										
ISIC 3 - CITI 3 - CIIU 3										
Total	.	.	.	.	.	.	.	4 092	7 118	.

Explanatory notes: see p. 877.

[1] Computed on the basis of annual wages. [2] Establishments with 20 or more persons employed. [3] Before 1999: establishments with 10 or more persons employed. [4] October.

Notes explicatives: voir p. 879.

[1] Calculés sur la base de salaires annuels. [2] Etablissements occupant 20 personnes et plus. [3] Avant 1999: établissements occupant 10 personnes et plus. [4] Octobre.

Notas explicativas: véase p. 882.

[1] Calculados en base a los salarios anuales. [2] Establecimientos con 20 y más trabajadores. [3] Antes de 1999: establecimientos con 10 y más trabajadores. [4] Octubre.

	1999	2000	2001	2002	2003	2004	2005	2006	2007	2008	
Singapore (F)					Employees - Salariés - Asalariados						E.G./m. - Dollar
Total men and women - Total hommes et femmes - Total hombres y mujeres											
ISIC 3 - CITI 3 - CIIU 3											
Total	2 803	3 036	3 117	3 154	3 265	3 350 ⎮	3 495 ⏐	3 618	3 764	3 955	
Men - Hommes - Hombres											
ISIC 3 - CITI 3 - CIIU 3											
Total	3 384	3 653	3 752	3 762	3 881	3 969 ⎮	4 111 ⏐	4 218	4 359	4 559	
Women - Femmes - Mujeres											
ISIC 3 - CITI 3 - CIIU 3											
Total	2 007	2 181	2 226	2 283	2 374	2 442 ⎮	2 563 ⏐	2 682	2 815	2 974	
Sri Lanka (DA) [2]					Wage earners - Ouvriers - Obreros						E.G./h. - Rupee
Total men and women - Total hommes et femmes - Total hombres y mujeres											
ISIC 2 - CITI 2 - CIIU 2											
Total	22.03	24.86	27.10	31.93	33.21	35.47	36.87	39.85	45.36	49.88	
Men - Hommes - Hombres											
ISIC 2 - CITI 2 - CIIU 2											
Total	22.29	25.28	27.48	32.09	33.61	35.79	37.08	39.95	46.09	55.15	
Women - Femmes - Mujeres											
ISIC 2 - CITI 2 - CIIU 2											
Total	18.10	20.36	22.59	28.03	28.90	31.17	35.09	39.08	42.95	44.61	
Sri Lanka (DA) [2]					Wage earners - Ouvriers - Obreros						E.G./d.j. - Rupee
Total men and women - Total hommes et femmes - Total hombres y mujeres											
ISIC 2 - CITI 2 - CIIU 2											
Total	199.20	222.48	230.66	273.10	306.28	308.98	336.49	356.11	412.19	432.55	
Men - Hommes - Hombres											
ISIC 2 - CITI 2 - CIIU 2											
Total	203.91	222.61	233.12	278.13	311.22	312.06	338.06	357.47	418.96	489.15	
Women - Femmes - Mujeres											
ISIC 2 - CITI 2 - CIIU 2											
Total	165.75	185.58	201.31	235.07	252.98	270.00	327.87	346.17	394.36	375.95	
Taiwan, China (DA)					Employees - Salariés - Asalariados						E.G./m. - New dollar
Total men and women - Total hommes et femmes - Total hombres y mujeres											
ISIC 2 - CITI 2 - CIIU 2											ISIC 3 - CITI 3 - CIIU 3
Total	37 686	38 792	38 277	38 208 ⎮	.	40 657	41 858	42 393	43 169	43 105	Total
Men - Hommes - Hombres											
ISIC 2 - CITI 2 - CIIU 2											ISIC 3 - CITI 3 - CIIU 3
Total	44 092	45 211	44 616	44 122 ⎮	.	46 866	48 024	48 521	49 400	49 219	Total
Women - Femmes - Mujeres											
ISIC 2 - CITI 2 - CIIU 2											ISIC 3 - CITI 3 - CIIU 3
Total	28 586	29 751	29 319	29 795 ⎮	.	31 931	33 110	33 749	34 401	34 389	Total
Thailand (BA)					Employees - Salariés - Asalariados						R.T./m. - Baht
Total men and women - Total hommes et femmes - Total hombres y mujeres											
ISIC 3 - CITI 3 - CIIU 3											
Total	.	.	6 064.6	6 795.3	6 432.2	6 129.0	6 407.4	6 941.6	6 999.2	.	

Explanatory notes: see p. 877.   Notes explicatives: voir p. 879.   Notas explicativas: véase p. 882.

[1] Methodology revised; data not strictly comparable. [2] March and Sep. of each year.   [1] Méthodologie révisée; les données ne sont pas strictement comparables. [2] Mars et sept. de chaque année.   [1] Metodología revisada; los datos no son estrictamente comparables. [2] Marzo y sept. de cada año.

WAGES · SALAIRES · SALARIOS

In manufacturing · Dans les industries manufacturières · En las industrias manufactureras

	1999	2000	2001	2002	2003	2004	2005	2006	2007	2008
West Bank and Gaza Strip (BA) [1][2]					Employees - Salariés - Asalariados					E.G./d.j. - New shekel
Total men and women - Total hommes et femmes - Total hombres y mujeres										
ISIC 3 - CITI 3 - CIIU 3										
Total	65.4	68.8	68.0	70.1	68.5	66.8	74.0	77.7	71.1	81.4
Men - Hommes - Hombres										
ISIC 3 - CITI 3 - CIIU 3										
Total	69.3	73.2	73.5	74.7	71.7	70.9	77.8	81.8	76.4	86.6
Women - Femmes - Mujeres										
ISIC 3 - CITI 3 - CIIU 3										
Total	32.4	36.0	35.2	36.8	41.6	30.8	40.8	44.5	40.4	43.4

EUROPE-EUROPE-EUROPA

	1999	2000	2001	2002	2003	2004	2005	2006	2007	2008
Albania (CA)					Employees - Salariés - Asalariados					E.G./m. - Lek
Total men and women - Total hommes et femmes - Total hombres y mujeres										
ISIC 3 - CITI 3 - CIIU 3										
Total	10 734	11 708	14 056	14 334	16 572	17 559	18 333	19 750	.	.
Andorre (F)					Employees - Salariés - Asalariados					E.G./m. - Euro
Total men and women - Total hommes et femmes - Total hombres y mujeres										
ISIC 3 - CITI 3 - CIIU 3										
Total	1 189.3	1 260.5	1 334.2	1 424.3	1 508.9	1 585.9	1 680.3	1 801.6	1 902.5	.
15	.	.	.	.	1 341.9	1 335.3	1 422.0	1 497.5	1 525.2	.
16	.	.	.	.	1 572.3	1 702.3	1 736.1	1 870.5	2 153.3	.
17	.	.	.	.	1 061.8	1 174.5	1 228.4	1 307.0	1 376.6	.
18	.	.	.	.	821.1	687.6	937.5	1 612.5	1 696.7	.
19	.	.	.	.						.
20	.	.	.	.	1 547.5	1 647.6	1 771.9	1 889.1	1 968.8	.
21	.	.	.	.						.
22	.	.	.	.	1 424.2	1 476.4	1 555.6	1 663.5	1 761.8	.
23	.	.	.	.						.
24	.	.	.	.	1 286.5	1 297.4	1 394.1	1 457.8	1 477.2	.
25	.	.	.	.	1 343.4	1 535.4	1 690.3	1 142.1	1 280.0	.
26	.	.	.	.	2 120.2	2 283.2	2 547.3	2 735.5	2 700.3	.
27	.	.	.	.	1 655.5	2 007.7	1 322.2	1 724.8	1 143.0	.
28	.	.	.	.	1 983.0	1 753.8	1 867.3	2 060.2	2 171.3	.
29	.	.	.	.	1 652.1	1 846.1	1 897.0	2 091.1	2 135.2	.
30	.	.	.	.						.
31	.	.	.	.	800.0	800.0	891.7	1 304.1	1 334.8	.
32	.	.	.	.	1 834.0	2 000.0	2 228.1	2 361.2	2 273.3	.
33	.	.	.	.	1 180.1	1 004.0	1 441.0	1 769.4	1 782.6	.
34	.	.	.	.						.
35	.	.	.	.	1 203.0	1 203.0	1 303.3	1 203.0		.
36	.	.	.	.	1 256.2	1 377.5	1 588.0	1 674.2	1 730.1	.
37	.	.	.	.	2 094.3	2 059.9	2 170.7	2 310.5	2 491.1	.
Men - Hommes - Hombres										
ISIC 3 - CITI 3 - CIIU 3										
Total	.	.	.	.	1 680.0	1 778.2	1 894.8	2 024.5	2 108.9	.
Women - Femmes - Mujeres										
ISIC 3 - CITI 3 - CIIU 3										
Total	.	.	.	.	1 165.3	1 215.5	1 263.0	1 367.4	1 503.1	.

Explanatory notes: see p. 877.   Notes explicatives: voir p. 879.   Notas explicativas: véase p. 882.

[1] Persons aged 15 years and over. [2] Net earnings.   [1] Personnes âgées de 15 ans et plus. [2] Gains nets.   [1] Personas de 15 años y más. [2] Ganancias netas.

Austria (DB) [1] — Employees - Salariés - Asalariados — E.G./h. - Euro

Total men and women - Total hommes et femmes - Total hombres y mujeres
ISIC 3 - CITI 3 - CIIU 3   ISIC 4 - CITI 4 - CIIU 4

	1999	2000	2001	2002	2003	2004	2005	2006	2007		2008	
Total [2]	12.38	12.68	13.03	13.44	13.75	14.00	14.40	14.85	15.25	|	15.80	Total [2]
15	10.47	10.68	10.93	11.27	11.32	11.36	11.57	11.94	12.14	|	12.21	10
16	17.11	17.74	18.58	19.36	20.20	20.60	21.18	22.54	23.47	|	15.70	11
17	10.57	10.93	11.22	11.54	11.63	11.89	12.32	12.77	13.03	|	23.55	12
18	7.90	8.10	8.33	8.72	8.86	9.09	9.35	9.71	9.94	|	13.36	13
19	8.00	8.27	8.44	8.73	9.09	9.36	9.49	9.69	9.88	|	10.85	14
20	9.97	10.16	10.50	10.84	11.18	11.44	11.71	11.97	12.29	|	10.10	15
21	13.70	13.99	14.35	14.83	15.22	15.45	15.76	16.12	16.51	|	12.77	16
22	14.81	15.09	15.52	16.12	16.21	16.47	16.77	17.18	17.32	|	16.88	17
23	23.40	24.13	25.03	26.79	27.66	25.25	27.07	28.40	29.58	|	16.36	18
24	15.04	15.27	15.56	16.04	16.48	16.76	17.26	18.00	18.54	|	29.72	19
25	11.59	11.94	12.12	12.30	12.70	12.98	13.28	13.66	14.01	|	18.70	20
26	12.69	12.89	13.17	13.47	13.86	14.11	14.40	14.65	15.17	|	18.78	21
27	13.66	14.06	14.51	14.81	15.19	15.50	16.05	16.49	16.93	|	14.29	22
28	11.73	12.00	12.40	12.66	13.09	13.27	13.61	14.02	14.25	|	15.56	23
29	13.22	13.58	13.91	14.25	14.57	14.97	15.52	16.13	16.48	|	17.39	24
30	11.23	11.28	11.52	12.61	14.95	14.95	15.28	15.62	16.31	|	14.71	25
31	12.78	12.99	13.35	13.86	14.22	14.25	14.70	15.14	15.78	|	19.12	26
32	16.69	16.81	17.24	18.52	18.45	18.95	19.39	20.24	20.46	|	17.78	27
33	12.67	12.75	13.19	13.75	14.08	14.54	15.17	15.63	16.09	|	17.09	28
34	13.14	13.58	13.75	14.15	14.45	14.62	15.07	15.58	16.26	|	16.92	29
35	15.04	15.24	15.63	16.22	16.81	17.00	15.84	16.18	16.28	|	18.18	30
36	9.63	9.96	10.31	10.63	10.93	11.18	11.62	11.90	12.57	|	12.75	31
37	10.90	11.80	11.96	12.07	12.55	12.78	12.85	13.05	13.55	|	14.19	32
										|	18.34	33

Belarus (D) [3][4] — Employees - Salariés - Asalariados — E.G./m. - B. roubles

	1999	2000	2001	2002	2003	2004	2005	2006	2007	2008
Total men and women — ISIC 3 - CITI 3 - CIIU 3										
Total	44 148	103 [5]	187	255	337	467	616	728	881	1 091
Men - Hommes - Hombres — ISIC 3 - CITI 3 - CIIU 3										
Total	49 370	118 [5]	214	290	338	539	711	828	1 010	1 284
Women - Femmes - Mujeres — ISIC 3 - CITI 3 - CIIU 3										
Total	38 685	88 [5]	157	216	280	384	502	608	723	859

Belgique (DA) [6] — Employees - Salariés - Asalariados — E.G./h. - Euro

Total men and women - Total hommes et femmes - Total hombres y mujeres
ISIC 3 - CITI 3 - CIIU 3

	1999	2000	2001	2002	2003	2004	2005	2006	2007	2008
Total	13.0	13.4	14.0	14.3	14.9	15.6	16.1	16.4	16.6	.
15	11.8	12.2	12.7	12.9	13.3	13.8	14.3	14.6	15.0	.
16	12.7	13.5	13.9	14.2	14.5	14.7	15.0	15.5	16.1	.
17	10.6	11.2	11.4	11.7	12.2	13.0	13.3	14.0	13.9	.
18	9.9	10.1	10.7	11.3	11.8	12.6	12.8	13.2	12.9	.
19	11.2	11.8	12.0	12.5	13.3	13.9	14.2	14.3	14.5	.
20	10.6	11.0	11.2	11.7	12.2	12.5	12.7	13.0	13.4	.
21	13.4	13.9	14.2	15.0	15.6	16.0	16.2	16.5	16.9	.
22	14.0	14.2	14.8	15.6	15.9	16.3	16.8	16.9	17.6	.
23	20.2	20.5	20.9	21.4	22.3	23.6	23.9	24.7	24.9	.
24	17.3	17.8	18.2	18.9	19.2	19.7	20.2	20.8	20.9	.
25	12.6	12.9	13.5	13.7	14.2	15.0	15.4	16.1	16.4	.
26	12.5	13.1	13.5	14.2	14.6	14.9	15.4	15.7	15.9	.
27	14.9	15.1	15.9	16.7	17.1	17.4	17.9	18.3	18.5	.
28	11.4	11.8	12.4	12.7	13.1	13.6	14.0	14.5	14.9	.
29	12.8	13.3	14.2	14.5	14.9	15.1	15.7	15.8	16.4	.
30	12.3	12.7	13.1	13.6	14.0	14.2	15.0	15.6	15.9	.
31	13.1	13.7	14.3	14.8	15.2	15.4	15.8	16.4	16.7	.
32	16.0	16.3	16.8	17.5	17.8	18.3	19.0	19.3	19.5	.
33	13.7	14.2	14.6	14.9	15.2	15.5	15.9	16.7	16.9	.
34	13.1	13.4	13.8	14.4	14.8	15.4	15.8	16.3	16.7	.
35	13.6	13.9	14.7	14.8	14.8	15.1	15.3	15.5	15.8	.
36	10.3	10.9	10.9	11.4	11.7	12.2	12.4	12.6	12.8	.
37	9.9	10.1	10.6	11.0	11.3	11.6	12.5	12.7	13.2	.

Explanatory notes: see p. 877.

[1] Per hour paid. [2] Incl. mining and quarrying. [3] Figures in thousands. [4] Dec. of each year. [5] New denomination of the rouble: 1 new rouble = 1000 old roubles. [6] Oct. of each year.

Notes explicatives: voir p. 879.

[1] Par heure rémunérée. [2] Y compris les industries extractives. [3] Données en milliers. [4] Déc. de chaque année. [5] Nouvelle dénomination du rouble: 1 nouveau rouble = 1000 anciens roubles. [6] Oct. de chaque année.

Notas explicativas: véase p. 882.

[1] Por hora pagada. [2] Incl. las minas y canteras. [3] Cifras en millares. [4] Dic. de cada año. [5] Nueva denominación del rublo: 1 nuevo rublo = 1000 antiguos rublos. [6] Oct. de cada año.

WAGES

SALAIRES

SALARIOS

In manufacturing

Dans les industries manufacturières

En las industrias manufactureras

	1999	2000	2001	2002	2003	2004	2005	2006	2007	2008

Belgique (DA) [1]   Employees - Salariés - Asalariados   E.G./h. - Euro

Men - Hommes - Hombres
ISIC 3 - CITI 3 - CIIU 3

	1999	2000	2001	2002	2003	2004	2005	2006	2007	2008
Total	13.6	14.0	14.5	14.9	15.5	16.1	16.6	16.9	17.2	.
15	12.5	12.9	13.3	13.6	14.1	14.6	15.1	15.4	15.7	.
16	14.8	15.1	15.6	16.3	16.8	17.6	18.3	19.0	19.1	.
17	11.6	12.1	12.6	13.1	13.8	14.2	14.6	15.0	15.0	.
18	14.9	15.1	15.6	15.9	16.3	16.8	16.9	17.3	14.3	.
19	12.8	13.2	13.7	14.4	14.8	15.3	15.8	16.2	16.4	.
20	10.8	11.1	11.3	11.7	12.3	12.6	12.7	13.0	13.4	.
21	13.9	14.5	15.0	15.0	15.7	16.1	16.4	17.0	17.5	.
22	14.8	15.2	15.8	16.7	16.9	17.3	17.8	17.9	18.6	.
23	20.9	21.3	21.7	22.2	23.0	24.4	25.0	25.7	26.0	.
24	17.6	18.2	18.5	19.1	19.7	20.3	21.3	21.8	21.9	.
25	13.1	13.4	13.7	14.1	14.8	15.5	15.9	16.3	16.8	.
26	12.6	13.3	13.7	14.3	14.9	15.1	15.6	15.9	16.1	.
27	15.0	15.2	15.9	16.7	17.1	17.4	17.9	18.3	18.5	.
28	11.5	11.9	12.4	12.8	13.3	13.7	14.1	14.5	15.0	.
29	13.0	13.5	14.4	14.7	15.1	15.8	15.9	15.9	16.5	.
30	14.0	14.4	14.8	15.3	15.9	16.4	16.7	17.4	17.7	.
31	14.1	14.6	14.8	15.1	15.8	16.3	16.8	17.2	17.6	.
32	18.0	18.4	18.9	19.2	19.5	19.8	20.4	20.8	21.0	.
33	14.5	14.8	15.2	15.7	16.2	16.9	17.4	17.8	18.1	.
34	13.3	13.5	14.0	14.6	15.0	15.6	16.0	16.5	16.9	.
35	13.6	13.9	14.7	14.8	14.9	15.1	15.4	15.6	15.8	.
36	10.7	10.9	11.2	11.7	11.9	12.3	12.5	12.8	13.1	.
37	10.3	10.5	11.1	11.3	11.7	12.4	12.9	13.2	13.5	.

Women - Femmes - Mujeres
ISIC 3 - CITI 3 - CIIU 3

	1999	2000	2001	2002	2003	2004	2005	2006	2007	2008
Total	10.9	11.4	12.2	12.3	12.7	13.6	14.0	14.5	14.7	.
15	10.3	10.7	11.1	11.3	11.5	12.2	12.6	13.0	13.3	.
16	10.9	11.3	11.7	12.2	12.5	13.1	13.3	13.6	14.2	.
17	9.1	9.6	10.1	10.3	10.8	11.3	11.7	12.2	12.4	.
18	8.9	9.0	9.5	10.0	10.4	11.0	11.5	12.3	12.5	.
19	9.3	9.8	10.1	10.6	11.0	11.6	11.9	12.2	12.5	.
20	9.7	10.0	10.3	10.8	11.3	11.8	12.1	12.7	13.0	.
21	11.8	12.1	12.5	13.0	13.3	13.6	14.1	14.3	14.4	.
22	11.6	12.0	12.5	13.0	13.8	14.4	14.9	15.1	15.6	.
23	16.0	16.4	17.2	17.8	18.3	19.5	19.8	20.1	20.4	.
24	13.5	14.2	14.8	15.1	15.9	16.2	17.2	18.0	18.2	.
25	10.9	11.1	11.7	12.0	12.6	13.5	13.9	14.3	14.8	.
26	11.7	12.0	12.4	12.7	12.9	13.1	13.4	13.9	14.5	.
27	12.8	13.7	14.1	14.7	15.4	16.9	17.6	18.2	18.3	.
28	10.5	10.9	11.4	11.6	12.3	12.9	13.1	13.9	14.2	.
29	11.5	12.0	12.1	12.8	13.3	13.7	14.4	14.8	15.3	.
30	9.9	10.1	10.9	11.2	11.7	12.1	12.9	13.4	13.4	.
31	11.0	11.3	11.8	12.2	12.5	12.9	13.4	13.9	14.3	.
32	11.9	12.5	13.2	13.6	14.1	14.6	15.0	15.3	15.4	.
33	11.0	11.7	12.0	12.5	13.1	13.7	14.2	14.4	14.6	.
34	12.4	12.9	13.1	13.6	14.0	14.3	14.5	14.9	15.1	.
35	12.6	12.8	13.2	13.9	14.5	15.0	15.2	15.4	15.8	.
36	9.2	9.8	10.1	10.4	10.9	11.3	11.9	12.0	12.1	.
37	8.9	9.3	9.5	9.9	10.2	10.5	10.8	11.3	11.5	.

Belgique (DA) [1]   Employees - Salariés - Asalariados   E.G./m. - Euro

Total men and women - Total hommes et femmes - Total hombres y mujeres
ISIC 3 - CITI 3 - CIIU 3

	1999	2000	2001	2002	2003	2004	2005	2006	2007	2008
Total	2 189	2 261	2 350	2 391	2 520	2 609	2 660	2 695	2 740	.
15	1 915	2 010	2 061	2 084	2 162	2 239	2 301	2 320	2 368	.
16	2 000	2 065	2 104	2 166	2 217	2 226	2 256	2 295	2 332	.
17	1 762	1 870	1 905	1 928	2 023	2 125	2 143	2 236	2 257	.
18	1 607	1 653	1 752	1 823	1 882	1 965	2 003	2 080	2 130	.
19	1 849	1 964	1 986	2 009	2 045	2 256	2 290	2 415	2 439	.
20	1 819	1 835	1 892	1 968	2 069	2 085	2 111	2 141	2 159	.
21	2 183	2 237	2 261	2 296	2 367	2 534	2 551	2 632	2 680	.
22	2 198	2 214	2 417	2 452	2 540	2 618	2 673	2 716	2 778	.
23	3 519	3 552	3 592	3 612	3 631	4 047	4 122	4 152	4 140	.
24	2 793	2 966	3 027	3 030	3 206	3 281	3 443	3 484	3 509	.
25	2 114	2 253	2 234	2 344	2 427	2 496	2 536	2 640	2 677	.
26	2 105	2 222	2 242	2 359	2 446	2 524	2 556	2 575	2 650	.
27	2 433	2 467	2 528	2 640	2 789	2 853	2 926	3 128	3 138	.
28	1 904	1 984	2 086	2 129	2 209	2 280	2 322	2 433	2 472	.
29	2 154	2 247	2 350	2 422	2 528	2 554	2 584	2 617	2 661	.
30	2 067	2 105	2 240	2 300	2 347	2 369	2 461	2 550	2 525	.
31	2 164	2 215	2 223	2 394	2 453	2 507	2 541	2 680	2 652	.
32	2 782	2 827	2 867	3 023	3 074	3 080	3 202	3 247	3 278	.
33	2 093	2 208	2 261	2 264	2 368	2 446	2 579	2 776	2 725	.
34	2 283	2 284	2 401	2 483	2 515	2 666	2 676	2 726	2 783	.
35	2 253	2 297	2 392	2 437	2 589	2 642	2 753	2 781	2 854	.
36	1 733	1 825	1 843	1 923	1 976	2 014	2 043	2 052	2 091	.
37	1 648	1 761	1 869	1 915	1 946	1 982	2 036	2 070	2 160	.

Explanatory notes: see p. 877.   Notes explicatives: voir p. 879.   Notas explicativas: véase p. 882.

[1] Oct. of each year.   [1] Oct. de chaque année.   [1] Oct. de cada año.

WAGES

In manufacturing

SALAIRES

Dans les industries manufacturières

SALARIOS

En las industrias manufactureras

5B

	1999	2000	2001	2002	2003	2004	2005	2006	2007	2008

Belgique (DA) [1] — Employees - Salariés - Asalariados — E.G./m. - Euro

Men - Hommes - Hombres
ISIC 3 - CITI 3 - CIIU 3

	1999	2000	2001	2002	2003	2004	2005	2006	2007	2008
Total	2 312	2 378	2 464	2 513	2 653	2 737	2 784	2 815	2 869	.
15	2 065	2 170	2 217	2 242	2 348	2 407	2 459	2 498	2 534	.
16	2 441	2 530	2 551	2 583	2 610	2 681	2 730	2 791	2 793	.
17	1 944	2 035	2 065	2 095	2 207	2 329	2 386	2 467	2 479	.
18	2 459	2 562	2 591	2 642	2 691	2 760	2 742	2 852	2 868	.
19	2 167	2 261	2 349	2 427	2 473	2 579	2 672	2 792	2 816	.
20	1 868	1 873	1 934	2 001	2 119	2 124	2 139	2 163	2 199	.
21	2 267	2 341	2 385	2 393	2 454	2 628	2 690	2 716	2 787	.
22	2 400	2 447	2 587	2 639	2 710	2 795	2 860	2 928	2 987	.
23	3 674	3 709	3 712	3 736	3 760	4 235	4 284	4 330	4 334	.
24	2 970	3 139	3 203	3 232	3 429	3 509	3 662	3 703	3 749	.
25	2 208	2 270	3 367	2 383	2 541	2 608	2 655	2 757	2 775	.
26	2 132	2 265	2 277	2 388	2 494	2 564	2 600	2 641	2 698	.
27	2 436	2 478	2 542	2 667	2 805	2 978	3 044	3 137	3 156	.
28	1 935	2 018	2 125	2 164	2 254	2 308	2 354	2 461	2 510	.
29	2 194	2 283	2 382	2 468	2 572	2 594	2 636	2 653	2 697	.
30	2 174	2 224	2 489	2 616	2 663	2 754	2 789	2 833	2 851	.
31	2 277	2 295	2 325	2 496	2 549	2 633	2 691	2 765	2 815	.
32	3 042	3 141	3 216	3 277	3 317	3 363	3 478	3 547	3 559	.
33	2 242	2 455	2 483	2 578	2 604	2 698	2 890	2 978	3 004	.
34	2 330	2 332	2 449	2 531	2 653	2 718	2 762	2 772	2 837	.
35	2 262	2 331	2 400	2 534	2 611	2 658	2 773	2 816	2 877	.
36	1 812	1 897	1 922	2 015	2 056	2 119	2 156	2 166	2 192	.
37	1 737	1 814	1 917	1 995	2 006	2 067	2 120	2 159	2 217	.

Women - Femmes - Mujeres
ISIC 3 - CITI 3 - CIIU 3

	1999	2000	2001	2002	2003	2004	2005	2006	2007	2008
Total	1 739	1 830	1 945	1 992	2 051	2 160	2 218	2 251	2 279	.
15	1 572	1 655	1 707	1 717	1 752	1 877	1 931	1 932	1 987	.
16	1 651	1 732	1 761	1 811	1 842	1 861	1 914	1 972	2 032	.
17	1 488	1 565	1 659	1 667	1 742	1 814	1 843	1 892	1 920	.
18	1 424	1 486	1 529	1 596	1 684	1 731	1 811	1 908	1 954	.
19	1 470	1 520	1 554	1 643	1 780	1 853	1 952	1 991	2 038	.
20	1 460	1 616	1 610	1 752	1 782	1 845	1 928	1 960	1 962	.
21	1 722	1 771	1 810	1 938	2 018	2 111	2 161	2 210	2 234	.
22	1 836	1 923	1 973	2 037	2 163	2 210	2 270	2 328	2 377	.
23	2 614	2 692	2 837	2 945	3 072	3 221	3 297	3 344	3 348	.
24	2 176	2 344	2 446	2 453	2 568	2 650	2 825	2 881	2 893	.
25	1 765	1 838	1 883	1 938	2 060	2 125	2 186	2 229	2 280	.
26	1 856	1 863	1 920	2 066	2 083	2 114	2 161	2 198	2 241	.
27	2 169	2 277	2 310	2 401	2 543	2 596	2 695	2 776	2 832	.
28	1 651	1 691	1 780	1 829	1 858	2 039	2 089	2 171	2 176	.
29	1 847	1 967	2 092	2 151	2 165	2 212	2 262	2 337	2 384	.
30	1 599	1 677	1 720	1 770	1 825	1 895	1 980	2 053	2 075	.
31	1 733	1 822	1 882	1 971	2 012	2 059	2 105	2 149	2 181	.
32	1 926	1 984	2 097	2 160	2 294	2 351	2 426	2 488	2 520	.
33	1 753	1 812	1 850	1 922	1 957	2 005	2 054	2 097	2 135	.
34	1 906	1 953	2 043	2 049	2 156	2 216	2 324	2 375	2 415	.
35	2 085	2 120	2 174	2 231	2 275	2 358	2 407	2 423	2 430	.
36	1 470	1 575	1 618	1 676	1 754	1 821	1 844	1 847	1 866	.
37	1 406	1 478	1 508	1 590	1 642	1 661	1 708	1 777	1 835	.

Belgique (DA) [1] [2] — Employees - Salariés - Asalariados — E.G./h. - Euro

Total men and women - Total hommes et femmes - Total hombres y mujeres
ISIC 3 - CITI 3 - CIIU 3

	1999	2000	2001	2002	2003	2004	2005	2006	2007	2008
Total	13	13	14	14	15	16	16	16	.	.
15	12	12	13	13	14	14	15	15	.	.
16	13	14	15	14	15	15	15	16	.	.
17	11	11	12	12	12	13	13	14	.	.
18	10	10	11	12	10	13	13	14	.	.
19	11	12	12	13	13	14	14	15	.	.
20	11	11	11	12	12	12	13	13	.	.
21	13	14	14	14	15	16	16	17	.	.
22	14	14	15	16	16	16	17	17	.	.
23	20	21	21	21	21	24	24	25	.	.
24	16	17	18	18	19	19	20	21	.	.
25	13	13	14	13	14	15	15	16	.	.
26	13	13	14	14	15	15	15	15	.	.
27	15	14	14	15	16	17	17	18	.	.
28	11	12	12	13	13	14	14	14	.	.
29	13	13	14	15	15	16	16	16	.	.
30	14	12	13	14	17	14	15	16	.	.
31	13	13	13	14	15	17	16	17	.	.
32	17	16	17	19	18	19	20	20	.	.
33	13	13	14	14	14	15	16	17	.	.
34	13	13	14	14	15	16	17	15	.	.
35	14	14	15	15	16	16	17	.	.	.
36	10	11	11	11	12	12	13	13	.	.
37	10	11	11	12	11	12	14	13	.	.

Explanatory notes: see p. 877.
[1] Oct. of each year. [2] Full-time employees only.

Notes explicatives: voir p. 879.
[1] Oct. de chaque année. [2] Salariés à plein temps seulement.

Notas explicativas: véase p. 882.
[1] Oct. de cada año. [2] Asalariados a tiempo completo solamente.

	WAGES	SALAIRES	SALARIOS
	In manufacturing	Dans les industries manufacturières	En las industrias manufactureras

	1999	2000	2001	2002	2003	2004	2005	2006	2007	2008
Belgique (DA) [1] [2]					Employees - Salariés - Asalariados					E.G./h. - Euro
Men - Hommes - Hombres										
ISIC 3 - CITI 3 - CIIU 3										
Total	14	14	14	15	16	16	17	17	.	.
15	13	13	13	14	14	15	15	15	.	.
16	15	15	17	16	16	18	17	18	.	.
17	12	12	12	12	13	14	14	15	.	.
18	15	17	18	17	13	21	17	18	.	.
19	13	13	14	14	14	15	15	16	.	.
20	11	11	11	12	12	13	12	13	.	.
21	14	14	15	15	15	17	16	17	.	.
22	15	15	16	17	17	17	18	18	.	.
23	21	21	21	21	21	24	25	26	.	.
24	17	18	19	19	20	20	21	22	.	.
25	13	13	14	14	15	15	16	16	.	.
26	13	13	14	14	15	15	16	15	.	.
27	15	14	14	15	16	17	17	18	.	.
28	11	12	12	13	13	14	14	15	.	.
29	13	13	14	15	15	16	16	16	.	.
30	15	13	14	15	18	16	16	18	.	.
31	14	14	14	15	16	18	16	17	.	.
32	19	17	19	21	20	20	21	21	.	.
33	13	14	15	15	15	16	17	18	.	.
34	13	13	14	15	16	16	17	17	.	.
35	14	14	15	15	16	16	17	16	.	.
36	11	11	11	12	12	13	13	13	.	.
37	10	11	11	12	12	12	14	13	.	.
Women - Femmes - Mujeres										
ISIC 3 - CITI 3 - CIIU 3										
Total	11	11	12	12	13	14	14	15	.	.
15	11	11	11	12	12	13	13	13	.	.
16	11	12	13	13	13	13	13	14	.	.
17	9	10	10	10	11	11	11	12	.	.
18	9	9	10	10	9	11	12	13	.	.
19	9	10	10	12	11	11	13	12	.	.
20	10	10	10	12	11	12	13	13	.	.
21	11	11	12	12	12	13	13	14	.	.
22	12	12	13	13	14	15	15	15	.	.
23	16	15	17	18	17	20	20	20	.	.
24	14	14	15	15	16	16	17	18	.	.
25	11	11	13	12	13	14	13	14	.	.
26	12	11	13	13	13	14	14	14	.	.
27	13	13	14	14	15	16	17	19	.	.
28	11	11	11	12	12	13	13	14	.	.
29	12	12	12	13	13	15	14	15	.	.
30	10	10	11	11	13	11	11	13	.	.
31	11	12	12	12	13	14	13	14	.	.
32	12	12	13	13	14	15	17	15	.	.
33	11	11	12	11	12	12	13	14	.	.
34	11	12	13	13	14	13	15	15	.	.
35	13	13	15	13	14	15	15	16	.	.
36	9	10	10	10	11	11	12	12	.	.
37	9	9	10	10	10	11	12	11	.	.
Bosnia and Herzegovina (DA) [3]					Employees - Salariés - Asalariados					E.G./m. - Marka
Total men and women - Total hommes et femmes - Total hombres y mujeres										
ISIC 3 - CITI 3 - CIIU 3										
Total	.	.	.	.	.	.	.	672.78	.	.
15	.	.	.	.	.	.	.	740.57	.	.
16	.	.	.	.	.	.	.	2 326.43	.	.
17	.	.	.	.	.	.	.	508.08	.	.
18	.	.	.	.	.	.	.	440.87	.	.
19	.	.	.	.	.	.	.	495.73	.	.
20	.	.	.	.	.	.	.	502.29	.	.
21	.	.	.	.	.	.	.	715.01	.	.
22	.	.	.	.	.	.	.	782.24	.	.
23	.	.	.	.	.	.	.	776.33	.	.
24	.	.	.	.	.	.	.	886.65	.	.
25	.	.	.	.	.	.	.	568.44	.	.
26	.	.	.	.	.	.	.	1 177.09	.	.
27	.	.	.	.	.	.	.	596.30	.	.
28	.	.	.	.	.	.	.	590.13	.	.
29	.	.	.	.	.	.	.	1 023.70	.	.
30	.	.	.	.	.	.	.	693.97	.	.
31	.	.	.	.	.	.	.	787.86	.	.
32	.	.	.	.	.	.	.	719.20	.	.
33	.	.	.	.	.	.	.	728.22	.	.
34	.	.	.	.	.	.	.	632.61	.	.
35	.	.	.	.	.	.	.	521.14	.	.
36	.	.	.	.	.	.	.	668.33	.	.
37	.	.	.	.	.	.	.	1 318.81	.	.

Explanatory notes: see p. 877.

[1] Full-time employees only. [2] Oct. of each year. [3] Data refer to the Federation of Bosnia and Herzegovina.

Notes explicatives: voir p. 879.

[1] Salariés à plein temps seulement. [2] Oct. de chaque année. [3] Les données se réfèrent à la Fédération de Bosnie-Herzégovine.

Notas explicativas: véase p. 882.

[1] Asalariados a tiempo completo solamente. [2] Oct. de cada año. [3] Los datos se refieren a la Federación de Bosnia y Herzegovina.

SALAIRES

Dans les industries manufacturières

SALARIOS

En las industrias manufactureras

5B

	1999	2000	2001	2002	2003	2004	2005	2006	2007	2008

Bulgaria (CA) — Employees - Salariés - Asalariados — E.G./m. - Leva

Total men and women - Total hommes et femmes - Total hombres y mujeres
ISIC 4 - CITI 4 - CIIU 4

	1999	2000	2001	2002	2003	2004	2005	2006	2007	2008
Total	.	.	.	.	.	.	288	319	381	471
15	179	190	193	201	212	230	257	284	346	433
16	387	459	476	461	535	612	717	804	1 033	1 234
17	152	177	185	196	210	229	258	287	343	420
18	125	137	147	155	163	177	192	214	244	292
19	132	142	146	157	160	170	182	209	243	290
20	137	153	160	172	189	199	224	249	304	382
21	192	206	222	257	263	273	296	330	388	459
22	224	263	292	289	308	311	343	369	435	550
23	481	540	580	618	.	.	.	.	.	.
24	287	318	333	350	375	394	432	483	565	663
25	191	196	200	215	215	227	241	258	296	357
26	231	247	258	281	303	317	334	376	449	575
27	306	366	385	450	471	529	565	646	772	933
28	175	192	196	204	215	231	254	283	335	435
29	206	232	248	268	285	310	339	376	469	608
30	199	228	250	303	294	324	330	367	505	629
31	193	219	233	236	258	275	316	339	438	524
32	208	250	309	319	330	323	317	354	480	535
33	180	197	213	231	247	268	311	358	458	608
34	193	212	216	225	239	260	295	322	403	462
35	249	273	282	300	321	364	456	532	624	762
36	140	152	160	168	180	194	219	236	276	322
37	164	216	143	160	207	240	236	238	445	908

Men - Hommes - Hombres
ISIC 3 - CITI 3 - CIIU 3 [1]   ISIC 4 - CITI 4 - CIIU 4

	1999	2000	2001	2002	2003	2004	2005	2006	2007	2008
Total	232	257	271	284	293	311 |	343	377	451	. Total
15	189	205	213	220	234	254 |				
16	449	553	571	560	658	672 |				
17	173	208	212	222	241	260 |				
18	150	184	179	201	211	218 |				
19	145	167	169	186	183	180 |				
20	138	165	163	173	191	200 |				
21	215	233	248	285	293	314 |				
22	267	307	349	335	352	351 |				
23	500	566	601	658	.	. |				
24	313	345	362	380	402	424 |				
25	204	216	222	227	226	244 |				
26	250	262	277	295	321	330 |				
27	322	385	405	513	492	553 |				
28	181	201	202	209	221	236 |				
29	214	243	268	280	300	325 |				
30	221	254	273	362	314	337 |				
31	204	238	264	266	284	311 |				
32	238	298	374	397	399	395 |				
33	190	217	232	242	258	281 |				
34	199	220	220	228	238	263 |				
35	260	291	298	318	339	389 |				
36	137	153	163	169	184	197 |				
37	164	218	145	163	222	263 |				

Women - Femmes - Mujeres
ISIC 3 - CITI 3 - CIIU 3 [1]   ISIC 4 - CITI 4 - CIIU 4

	1999	2000	2001	2002	2003	2004	2005	2006	2007	2008
Total	172	181	185	192	203	216 |	235	262	312	. Total
15	166	172	172	180	189	203 |				
16	334	373	393	379	434	548 |				
17	141	162	172	184	197	214 |				
18	121	131	143	148	156	171 |				
19	127	134	139	148	153	166 |				
20	136	134	153	171	184	196 |				
21	169	176	191	223	228	227 |				
22	189	225	241	247	271	275 |				
23	443	487	535	521	.	. |				
24	256	284	299	316	344	359 |				
25	177	174	174	199	202	201 |				
26	200	216	218	247	258	281 |				
27	273	317	324	259	407	453 |				
28	161	171	181	190	196	213 |				
29	187	208	199	237	245	270 |				
30	176	199	220	234	269	310 |				
31	178	194	193	199	227	233 |				
32	178	205	241	241	264	240 |				
33	168	175	192	218	233	252 |				
34	172	188	202	213	244	250 |				
35	214	210	219	224	245	251 |				
36	144	149	154	165	175	190 |				
37	162	209	137	148	161	163 |				

Explanatory notes: see p. 877.
[1] Employees under labour contract.

Notes explicatives: voir p. 879.
[1] Salariés sous contrat de travail.

Notas explicativas: véase p. 882.
[1] Asalariados bajo contrato de trabajo.

WAGES	SALAIRES	SALARIOS
In manufacturing	Dans les industries manufacturières	En las industrias manufactureras

	1999	2000	2001	2002	2003	2004	2005	2006	2007	2008

Bulgaria (CA) Employees - Salariés - Asalariados E.G./m. - Leva

Total men and women - Total hommes et femmes - Total hombres y mujeres
ISIC 4 - CITI 4 - CIIU 4

Total										
10							288.0	319.0	381.0	471.0
11							237.0	261.0	315.0	394.0
12							352.0	397.0	502.0	634.0
13							717.0	804.0	1 033.0	1 234.0
14							251.0	279.0	336.0	403.0
15							198.0	221.0	254.0	304.0
16							181.0	208.0	243.0	289.0
17							224.0	249.0	304.0	380.0
18							288.0	321.0	375.0	448.0
20							336.0	315.0	424.0	604.0
21							391.0	435.0	523.0	626.0
22							510.0	578.0	649.0	742.0
23							240.0	258.0	295.0	357.0
24							334.0	376.0	449.0	575.0
25							559.0	636.0	759.0	918.0
26							270.0	292.0	351.0	462.0
28							340.0	379.0	484.0	552.0
29							344.0	389.0	473.0	608.0
30							275.0	271.0	419.0	489.0
31							493.0	559.0	660.0	820.0
32							209.0	224.0	261.0	301.0
33							243.0	267.0	322.0	376.0
							353.0	400.0	502.0	642.0

Men - Hommes - Hombres
ISIC 4 - CITI 4 - CIIU 4

Total										
10							343.0	377.0	451.0	
11							262.0	286.0	346.0	
12							385.0	443.0	552.0	
13							811.0	906.0	1 113.0	
14							285.0	325.0	398.0	
15							253.0	279.0	317.0	
16							197.0	222.0	269.0	
17							229.0	252.0	309.0	
18							332.0	359.0	427.0	
20							383.0	359.0	492.0	
21							447.0	494.0	592.0	
22							547.0	629.0	686.0	
23							250.0	266.0	308.0	
24							343.0	386.0	460.0	
25							576.0	656.0	782.0	
26							276.0	297.0	357.0	
27							400.0	430.0	544.0	
28							360.0	412.0	500.0	
29							359.0	404.0	490.0	
30							316.0	263.0	465.0	
31							531.0	611.0	718.0	
32							214.0	225.0	258.0	
33							284.0	292.0	343.0	
							371.0	417.0	527.0	

Women - Femmes - Mujeres
ISIC 4 - CITI 4 - CIIU 4

Total										
10							235.0	262.0	312.0	
11							214.0	237.0	286.0	
12							300.0	327.0	428.0	
13							618.0	694.0	943.0	
14							230.0	250.0	300.0	
15							190.0	213.0	245.0	
16							176.0	204.0	236.0	
17							212.0	240.0	291.0	
18							238.0	275.0	317.0	
20							276.0	264.0	338.0	
21							314.0	351.0	425.0	
22							481.0	539.0	620.0	
23							224.0	243.0	275.0	
24							306.0	346.0	415.0	
25							500.0	569.0	683.0	
26							257.0	278.0	336.0	
27							278.0	327.0	425.0	
28							262.0	292.0	372.0	
29							300.0	343.0	418.0	
30							233.0	279.0	382.0	
31							331.0	340.0	418.0	
32							199.0	221.0	268.0	
33							218.0	250.0	307.0	
							288.0	332.0	399.0	

Explanatory notes: see p. 877.   Notes explicatives: voir p. 879.   Notas explicativas: véase p. 882.

In manufacturing   Dans les industries manufacturières   En las industrias manufactureras

	1999	2000	2001	2002	2003	2004	2005	2006	2007	2008
Croatia (DA) [1]					Employees - Salariés - Asalariados					E.G./m. - Kuna

Total men and women - Total hommes et femmes - Total hombres y mujeres
ISIC 3 - CITI 3 - CIIU 3

	1999	2000	2001	2002	2003	2004	2005	2006	2007	2008
Total	3 869	4 100	4 465	4 794	4 952	5 189	5 452	5 833	6 161	.
15	4 511	4 717	5 084	5 426	5 438	5 688	5 919	6 092	6 468	.
16	5 840	6 342	6 274	7 135	8 059	9 878	10 319	10 956	11 279	.
17	2 403	2 584	2 720	3 068	3 439	3 346	3 603	3 742	3 934	.
18	2 554	2 626	2 751	2 806	2 919	3 005	3 122	3 187	3 413	.
19	2 153	2 290	2 389	2 491	2 762	2 918	3 024	3 334	3 388	.
20	2 646	2 773	2 914	3 050	3 273	3 368	3 544	3 749	3 938	.
21	3 605	3 849	4 017	4 328	4 414	4 763	4 755	5 237	5 499	.
22	5 372	5 579	6 087	6 686	6 376	6 733	7 060	7 404	7 879	.
23	5 604	5 793	6 415	6 527	7 058	7 663	8 440	9 232	10 637	.
24	5 540	6 126	6 536	6 969	6 986	7 186	7 371	8 214	8 542	.
25	2 950	3 321	3 615	3 913	4 301	4 369	4 777	5 017	5 251	.
26	3 991	4 261	4 599	5 058	5 469	5 800	6 097	6 383	6 847	.
27	3 127	3 516	3 386	3 683	3 887	4 266	4 502	5 108	5 459	.
28	3 363	3 518	3 814	4 159	4 463	4 697	4 781	5 391	5 731	.
29	3 191	3 810	4 233	4 535	4 761	5 172	5 464	5 954	6 205	.
30	3 862	5 760	6 362	7 323	7 102	7 115	8 075	8 726	9 052	.
31	4 848	5 329	5 936	6 454	6 358	6 645	7 253	7 916	8 385	.
32	5 052	5 422	7 774	8 495	9 164	8 873	9 435	9 644	9 300	.
33	4 432	4 119	4 528	5 146	5 203	5 496	5 821	6 060	6 477	.
34	3 605	4 355	4 326	4 483	4 424	4 719	5 272	5 723	6 314	.
35	4 140	4 784	5 800	5 905	5 800	6 050	6 440	6 842	7 002	.
36	2 607	2 727	3 087	3 284	3 661	3 832	3 884	4 244	4 449	.
37	3 845	4 240	4 641	5 365	5 355	5 778	5 916	6 271	6 508	.

Men - Hommes - Hombres
ISIC 3 - CITI 3 - CIIU 3

	1999	2000	2001	2002	2003	2004	2005	2006	2007	2008
Total	.	.	.	.	5 412	5 680	5 969	6 377	6 734	.
15	.	.	.	.	5 775	6 050	6 377	6 534	6 944	.
16	.	.	.	.	8 960	11 010	11 136	11 403	11 583	.
17	.	.	.	.	4 094	4 084	4 449	4 832	4 874	.
18	.	.	.	.	3 942	4 038	4 195	4 381	4 871	.
19	.	.	.	.	3 305	3 552	3 785	4 146	4 067	.
20	.	.	.	.	3 383	3 473	3 683	3 880	4 113	.
21	.	.	.	.	4 716	5 060	5 023	5 527	5 767	.
22	.	.	.	.	6 819	7 143	7 429	7 900	8 451	.
23	.	.	.	.	7 159	7 779	8 554	9 390	10 730	.
24	.	.	.	.	7 077	7 286	7 330	8 075	8 428	.
25	.	.	.	.	4 460	4 535	5 082	5 231	5 488	.
26	.	.	.	.	5 539	5 896	6 202	6 484	6 986	.
27	.	.	.	.	3 937	4 303	4 568	5 197	5 529	.
28	.	.	.	.	4 516	4 749	4 829	5 465	5 814	.
29	.	.	.	.	4 828	5 299	5 606	6 099	6 366	.
30	.	.	.	.	7 414	7 511	8 349	8 926	9 276	.
31	.	.	.	.	7 098	7 350	7 943	8 670	9 329	.
32	.	.	.	.	10 117	10 278	11 178	10 901	11 476	.
33	.	.	.	.	5 181	5 461	6 069	6 439	6 810	.
34	.	.	.	.	4 647	5 127	5 997	6 139	6 903	.
35	.	.	.	.	5 860	6 119	6 511	6 923	7 085	.
36	.	.	.	.	3 813	4 020	4 081	4 454	4 656	.
37	.	.	.	.	5 477	6 006	6 152	6 540	6 982	.

Women - Femmes - Mujeres
ISIC 3 - CITI 3 - CIIU 3

	1999	2000	2001	2002	2003	2004	2005	2006	2007	2008
Total	.	.	.	.	4 196	4 359	4 560	4 874	5 148	.
15	.	.	.	.	4 932	5 146	5 258	5 446	5 793	.
16	.	.	.	.	6 695	8 372	9 122	9 948	10 608	.
17	.	.	.	.	3 138	3 032	3 271	3 340	3 567	.
18	.	.	.	.	2 763	2 832	2 948	2 990	3 187	.
19	.	.	.	.	2 606	2 743	2 830	3 125	3 227	.
20	.	.	.	.	2 977	3 082	3 175	3 390	3 492	.
21	.	.	.	.	3 824	4 089	4 146	4 524	4 831	.
22	.	.	.	.	5 857	6 255	6 618	6 835	7 232	.
23	.	.	.	.	6 827	7 417	8 174	8 879	10 430	.
24	.	.	.	.	6 844	7 020	7 440	8 437	8 722	.
25	.	.	.	.	3 905	3 953	4 053	4 443	4 606	.
26	.	.	.	.	5 183	5 390	5 649	5 957	6 285	.
27	.	.	.	.	3 642	4 072	4 194	4 693	5 137	.
28	.	.	.	.	4 146	4 385	4 481	4 894	5 154	.
29	.	.	.	.	4 412	4 485	4 670	5 119	5 256	.
30	.	.	.	.	6 272	6 059	7 291	8 145	8 300	.
31	.	.	.	.	4 784	5 143	5 705	6 283	6 308	.
32	.	.	.	.	7 569	6 959	7 242	7 757	6 902	.
33	.	.	.	.	5 234	5 553	5 452	5 512	5 949	.
34	.	.	.	.	4 016	3 967	4 061	4 750	5 174	.
35	.	.	.	.	5 286	5 434	5 801	6 142	6 303	.
36	.	.	.	.	3 349	3 457	3 477	3 777	4 004	.
37	.	.	.	.	4 860	4 959	5 051	5 463	5 212	.

Explanatory notes: see p. 877.   Notes explicatives: voir p. 879.   Notas explicativas: véase p. 882.

[1] Excl. employees in craft and trade.   [1] Non compris les salariés dans l'artisanat et dans le commerce.   [1] Excl. los asalariados en el artesanado y el comercio.

In manufacturing   **Dans les industries manufacturières**   **En las industrias manufactureras**

Cyprus (DA) [1][2][3]   Employees - Salariés - Asalariados   E.G./h. - Pound

Total men and women - Total hommes et femmes - Total hombres y mujeres
ISIC 3 - CITI 3 - CIIU 3

	1999	2000	2001	2002	2003	2004	2005	2006	2007	2008
Total	3.86	4.02	4.25	4.45	4.64	4.83	4.93	5.01		
15	3.98	4.07	4.10	4.28	4.49	4.92	5.07	4.48		
16	5.67	5.07	5.21	5.97	5.93	6.24	7.80	4.42		
17	3.18	3.56	3.55	2.72	2.78	2.93	2.96	3.16		
18	2.74	2.90	3.07	3.08	3.24	3.02	3.11	3.90		
19	3.28	3.53	3.40	4.11	4.05	3.98	4.10	4.49		
20	4.14	4.29	4.18	4.82	5.04	5.28	5.39	4.57		
21	3.68	3.76	3.93	4.02	4.30	4.47	4.50	4.06		
22	5.06	5.21	5.31	4.68	4.97	5.02	5.26	5.18		
23	10.03	10.23	10.63	11.59	12.27	10.51	9.89			
24	3.81	4.00	4.14	4.28	4.47	4.61	4.65			
25	3.81	4.00	4.18	4.54	4.89	4.99	5.32	4.98		
26	5.74	5.85	5.94	6.28	6.46	6.79	6.84	5.97		
27	4.63	4.95	4.61	5.64	5.77	6.00	4.25	7.39		
28	4.06	4.44	4.56	4.69	4.85	5.05	4.97	5.55		
29	3.85	4.04	4.34	4.90	5.00	5.05	5.28	5.14		
31	4.07	4.33	4.29	4.01	4.17	4.16	3.95	5.51		
32								5.79		
33	3.33	3.44	3.45	3.06	3.29	3.68	3.60	3.71		
34	3.99	4.38	4.73	4.66	4.69	4.98	5.06	3.76		
35	5.05	5.17	5.04	5.28	4.44	4.54	4.73	4.70		
36	3.49	3.60	3.61	4.18	4.41	4.47	4.57	4.59		
37	3.08	2.99	2.51	3.81	3.84	3.72	4.11	4.75		

Men - Hommes - Hombres
ISIC 3 - CITI 3 - CIIU 3

	1999	2000	2001	2002	2003	2004	2005	2006	2007	2008
Total	4.66	4.83	4.94	5.24	5.43	5.68	5.77	5.68		
15	4.66	4.77	4.92	5.20	5.36	5.92	6.11	5.39		
16	7.32	6.41	6.46	7.25	7.40	7.83	9.08	5.84		
17	4.75	4.97	4.84	3.85	3.89	4.14	4.31	3.94		
18	4.41	5.08	5.26	5.32	5.75	4.58	4.89	5.43		
19	4.36	4.66	4.47	5.28	5.12	4.99	5.12	5.59		
20	4.25	4.39	4.31	4.95	5.17	5.42	5.56	4.72		
21	4.52	4.58	4.76	5.02	5.40	5.58	5.61	4.54		
22	5.76	5.91	6.02	5.47	5.83	5.83	5.95	6.06		
23	10.11	10.30	10.73	11.78	12.41	10.83	10.12			
24	4.61	4.91	5.00	5.10	5.28	5.37	5.48			
25	4.28	4.49	4.64	5.09	5.46	5.61	5.90	5.75		
26	6.12	6.20	6.23	6.58	6.75	7.11	7.16	6.65		
27	4.81	5.14	4.72	5.77	5.90	6.22	4.20	7.68		
28	4.22	4.60	4.73	4.80	4.96	5.19	5.07	5.73		
29	4.02	4.20	4.52	5.14	5.22	5.56	5.52	5.27		
31	4.45	4.75	4.77	4.42	4.52	4.51	4.20	5.80		
32								6.04		
33	3.93	4.02	4.46	3.84	3.99	4.46	4.09	4.19		
34	4.32	4.76	5.28	5.09	5.19	5.51	5.63	4.35		
35	5.29	5.41	5.18	5.28	4.44	4.54	4.73	5.24		
36	3.80	3.88	3.90	4.56	4.77	4.84	4.91	4.90		
37	3.11	3.00	2.39	3.88	3.91	3.76	4.16	5.30		

Women - Femmes - Mujeres
ISIC 3 - CITI 3 - CIIU 3

	1999	2000	2001	2002	2003	2004	2005	2006	2007	2008
Total	2.79	2.94	3.16	3.19	3.39	3.50	3.60	3.70		
15	2.87	2.94	3.02	3.07	3.34	3.59	3.67	3.30		
16	4.04	3.75	4.26	5.00	4.81	5.03	6.48	2.92		
17	2.03	3.06	3.16	2.38	2.44	2.57	2.55	2.70		
18	2.51	2.60	2.76	2.77	2.89	2.80	2.86	3.62		
19	2.81	3.03	2.58	3.22	3.23	3.21	3.33	3.57		
20	3.04	3.21	3.07	3.73	3.97	4.09	3.98	3.16		
21	2.57	2.68	2.89	2.78	2.93	3.10	3.10	3.37		
22	4.15	4.30	4.52	3.80	4.01	4.12	4.49	4.18		
23	8.79	9.13	9.55	9.46	10.68	7.01	7.31			
24	2.94	2.99	3.29	3.47	3.65	3.85	3.83	4.22		
25	2.76	2.92	3.03	3.18	3.47	3.47	3.88	4.40		
26	3.52	3.83	4.08	4.36	4.60	4.78	4.80	5.53		
27	3.34	3.56	3.75	4.69	4.79	4.27	4.67	4.50		
28	2.98	3.36	3.55	4.03	4.21	4.24	4.37	4.30		
29	3.03	3.26	3.40	3.65	3.84	3.87	4.03	3.97		
31	3.08	3.22	3.22	3.12	3.40	3.41	3.40	4.98		
32								3.11		
33	2.61	2.75	2.69	2.48	2.76	3.09	3.23	3.03		
34	2.85	3.08	3.21	3.48	3.31		3.50	3.51		
35	2.37	2.51	2.56					4.12		
36	2.54	2.76	2.91	3.24	3.52	3.58	3.71	4.27		
37	2.09	2.75	3.73	3.09	3.19	3.36	3.65	4.25		

Explanatory notes: see p. 877.   Notes explicatives: voir p. 879.   Notas explicativas: véase p. 882.

[1] Adults. [2] Incl. family allowances and the value of payments in kind. [3] Oct. of each year.

[1] Adultes. [2] Y compris les allocations familiales et la valeur des paiements en nature. [3] Oct. de chaque année.

[1] Adultos. [2] Incl. las asignaciones familiares y el valor de los pagos en especie. [3] Oct. de cada año.

| In manufacturing | Dans les industries manufacturières | En las industrias manufactureras |

	1999	2000	2001	2002	2003	2004	2005	2006	2007	2008

Cyprus (DA) [1] [2] [3] — Wage earners - Ouvriers - Obreros — E.G./h. - Pound

Total men and women - Total hommes et femmes - Total hombres y mujeres
ISIC 3 - CITI 3 - CIIU 3

	1999	2000	2001	2002	2003	2004	2005	2006	2007	2008
Total	.	.	3.72	3.94	4.13	4.22	4.32	4.85	.	.
15	.	.	3.55	3.79	4.14	4.18	4.36	4.36	.	.
16	.	.	2.89	2.94	2.97	3.35	.	.	.	.
17	.	.	3.03	2.44	2.52	2.67	2.78	2.59	.	.
18	.	.	2.67	2.84	2.96	2.81	3.00	3.10	.	.
19	.	.	2.79	3.50	3.63	3.45	3.53	4.28	.	.
20	.	.	3.69	3.95	4.21	4.41	4.52	4.58	.	.
21	.	.	3.10	3.27	3.57	3.60	3.88	3.98	.	.
22	.	.	4.73	3.71	3.71	4.07	4.24	4.52	.	.
24	.	.	3.98	4.32	4.31	4.31	4.60	3.68	.	.
25	.	.	3.86	4.06	4.44	4.47	5.00	4.91	.	.
26	.	.	5.18	5.45	5.42	5.72	5.70	6.28	.	.
27	.	.	4.22	5.20	5.32	5.69	3.93	4.84	.	.
28	.	.	4.13	4.23	4.46	4.64	4.44	5.12	.	.
29	.	.	3.97	4.75	4.92	5.00	5.00	5.25	.	.
31	.	.	3.61	3.24	3.63	3.39	3.26	.	.	.
34	.	.	4.29	4.30	4.64	4.80	5.05	4.31	.	.
35	.	.	4.34	4.50	5.73	5.48	4.97	4.66	.	.
36	.	.	3.36	3.96	4.16	4.27	4.45	4.61	.	.
37	.	.	3.60	3.77	3.90	3.97	4.36	.	.	.

Men - Hommes - Hombres
ISIC 3 - CITI 3 - CIIU 3

	1999	2000	2001	2002	2003	2004	2005	2006	2007	2008
Total	.	.	4.25	4.62	4.84	4.99	5.06	5.34	.	.
15	.	.	4.35	5.25	5.66	5.72	5.84	6.36	.	.
17	.	.	3.60	3.39	3.39	4.15	5.47	3.56	.	.
18	.	.	4.37	5.30	5.76	4.94	6.04	4.65	.	.
19	.	.	3.44	4.05	4.52	4.06	4.05	5.20	.	.
20	.	.	3.75	4.03	4.30	4.51	4.65	4.65	.	.
21	.	.	3.96	4.41	4.86	4.94	5.48	4.71	.	.
22	.	.	5.39	4.58	4.68	5.07	5.20	5.40	.	.
24	.	.	4.52	4.81	4.87	4.75	5.13	3.68	.	.
25	.	.	4.35	4.46	4.87	4.88	5.42	5.43	.	.
26	.	.	5.30	5.55	5.54	5.88	5.86	6.29	.	.
27	.	.	4.22	5.20	5.32	5.69	3.93	4.92	.	.
28	.	.	4.21	4.30	4.53	4.72	4.51	5.21	.	.
29	.	.	4.05	4.86	5.03	5.13	5.07	5.44	.	.
31	.	.	3.94	3.84	4.40	4.00	3.62	.	.	.
34	.	.	4.48	4.48	4.84	5.01	5.31	4.91	.	.
35	.	.	4.34	4.50	5.73	5.48	4.97	4.90	.	.
36	.	.	3.54	4.23	4.40	4.53	4.73	4.81	.	.
37	.	.	3.60	3.77	3.90	3.97	4.36	.	.	.

Women - Femmes - Mujeres
ISIC 3 - CITI 3 - CIIU 3

	1999	2000	2001	2002	2003	2004	2005	2006	2007	2008
Total	.	.	2.78	2.72	2.86	2.86	2.99	3.22	.	.
15	.	.	2.85	2.50	2.80	2.83	3.06	2.84	.	.
16	.	.	2.89	2.94	2.97	3.35	.	.	.	.
17	.	.	2.95	2.30	2.39	2.46	2.40	2.21	.	.
18	.	.	2.55	2.66	2.76	2.66	2.78	2.93	.	.
19	.	.	2.40	3.17	3.10	3.09	3.22	3.63	.	.
20	.	.	2.99	3.01	3.09	3.16	2.92	3.22	.	.
21	.	.	2.38	2.32	2.49	2.47	2.55	3.12	.	.
22	.	.	3.90	2.60	2.49	2.80	3.02	3.17	.	.
24	.	.	2.96	3.37	3.25	3.47	3.60	.	.	.
25	.	.	2.72	3.14	3.44	3.53	4.05	3.69	.	.
26	.	.	3.63	4.15	3.78	3.60	3.63	6.09	.	.
27	.	.	.	.	.	.	.	4.23	.	.
28	.	.	3.22	3.38	3.70	3.73	3.65	3.93	.	.
29	.	.	3.15	3.69	3.78	3.68	4.28	3.41	.	.
31	.	.	3.11	2.34	2.49	2.48	2.72	.	.	.
34	.	.	2.91	2.99	3.19	3.28	3.14	3.44	.	.
35	.	.	.	.	.	.	.	3.49	.	.
36	.	.	2.54	2.74	3.09	3.11	3.17	3.83	.	.

Explanatory notes: see p. 877.

[1] Adults. [2] Incl. family allowances and the value of payments in kind. [3] Oct. of each year.

Notes explicatives: voir p. 879.

[1] Adultes. [2] Y compris les allocations familiales et la valeur des paiements en nature. [3] Oct. de chaque année.

Notas explicativas: véase p. 882.

[1] Adultos. [2] Incl. las asignaciones familiares y el valor de los pagos en especie. [3] Oct. de cada año.

5B WAGES / SALAIRES / SALARIOS

In manufacturing / Dans les industries manufacturières / En las industrias manufactureras

Cyprus (DA) [1] [2] [3]
Wage earners - Ouvriers - Obreros
E.G./w.s. - Pound

Total men and women - Total hommes et femmes - Total hombres y mujeres
ISIC 3 - CITI 3 - CIIU 3

	1999	2000	2001	2002	2003	2004	2005	2006	2007	2008
Total	139.19	141.93	152.42	157.34	165.74	169.41	171.75	200.62	.	.
15	140.15	146.10	144.41	151.97	167.04	160.89	168.18	173.72		
16	102.12	89.93	94.68	96.26	107.77	104.39				
17	108.58	127.06	121.92	96.11	97.51	104.80	106.33	97.99		
18	100.06	102.32	101.83	112.03	117.74	106.76	117.34	118.72		
19	114.91	127.19	106.08	131.64	137.87	137.03	140.91	159.29		
20	142.49	142.49	146.88	150.67	158.94	166.59	171.82	187.84		
21	105.30	112.37	127.18	127.36	135.07	136.51	146.80	155.49		
22	202.64	241.02	236.73	137.28	143.67	151.09	160.57	166.78		
24	143.91	145.88	165.34	178.67	183.23	178.04	191.29	140.37		
25	146.96	143.41	150.37	159.54	173.37	174.59	195.60	197.32		
26	256.44	215.03	224.03	235.78	226.53	249.20	243.30	286.04		
27	138.62	155.92	162.90	229.71	211.71	229.91	149.16	197.18		
28	149.79	156.40	172.61	170.20	192.55	202.05	179.91	211.91		
29	137.34	150.94	150.96	187.76	186.33	195.56	202.31	202.99		
31	132.96	146.09	138.41	127.36	136.57	132.12	122.00			
34	140.35	149.13	176.00	164.34	181.72	188.08	199.11	168.93		
35	184.97	191.15	179.33	181.15	260.75	236.21	178.11	173.69		
36	133.58	142.82	136.61	154.95	163.43	168.71	177.42	182.47		
37	133.45	139.30	136.88	150.92	155.94	158.67	174.46			

Men - Hommes - Hombres
ISIC 3 - CITI 3 - CIIU 3

	1999	2000	2001	2002	2003	2004	2005	2006	2007	2008
Total	185.85	172.45	176.64	186.29	194.91	203.27	202.86	223.09	.	.
15	172.24	176.47	180.00	215.39	225.27	222.96	224.96	246.68		
16	122.58									
17	159.28	178.07	133.04	142.73	141.49	174.67	207.99	135.33		
18	167.53	172.37	168.86	214.75	226.27	187.63	234.68	176.81		
19	137.90	148.84	132.01	153.95	171.74	171.16	169.56	197.47		
20	145.35	144.85	149.23	153.68	162.09	170.39	176.78	190.66		
21	137.86	147.82	164.32	174.31	184.69	187.64	208.11	185.18		
22	249.25	296.72	286.37	169.04	182.64	192.61	197.50	202.20		
24	180.42	174.24	186.44	197.82	207.67	195.97	213.05	140.37		
25	168.80	161.14	170.07	174.42	192.12	190.84	216.17	220.49		
26	268.86	223.29	230.02	241.44	232.80	257.34	250.88	287.87		
27	138.62	155.92	162.90	229.71	211.71	229.91	149.16	201.47		
28	152.84	160.05	176.12	172.71	194.74	206.39	183.22	216.67		
29	139.64	154.48	154.41	192.13	189.93	201.07	205.59	209.59		
31	146.59	161.73	156.22	152.62	166.52	158.89	134.53			
34	150.58	160.41	184.83	171.19	189.60	196.60	209.80	189.86		
35	184.97	191.15	179.33	181.15	260.75	236.21	178.11	182.37		
36	144.16	151.64	145.32	165.96	173.12	179.49	189.81	192.61		
37	133.45	139.30	136.88	150.92	155.94	158.67	174.46			

Women - Femmes - Mujeres
ISIC 3 - CITI 3 - CIIU 3

	1999	2000	2001	2002	2003	2004	2005	2006	2007	2008
Total	100.16	107.18	109.04	105.51	113.49	108.77	115.55	125.08	.	.
15	104.08	111.99	113.11	96.21	115.84	106.32	118.26	118.39		
16	102.12	89.93	94.68	96.26	107.77	104.39				
17	98.22	116.63	120.31	89.36	91.15	94.69	91.62	83.34		
18	95.28	97.35	97.00	104.63	109.92	100.93	108.89	112.41		
19	106.56	119.33	90.62	118.34	117.68	116.68	123.83	132.66		
20	106.45	112.76	117.97	113.68	120.15	119.88	110.86	135.11		
21	84.64	89.87	96.09	88.07	93.53	93.71	95.49	120.86		
22	147.35	174.95	174.04	97.18	94.46	98.65	113.93	107.69		
24	109.69	119.31	125.02	142.08	136.52	143.77	149.70			
25	102.91	107.66	105.12	125.36	130.30	137.25	148.36	143.43		
26	127.20	129.06	144.00	160.09	142.66	140.29	142.01	228.49		
27								162.08		
28	114.39	114.05	131.48	140.81	166.88	151.14	141.08	150.55		
29	113.61	114.48	116.07	143.56	149.94	139.81	169.12	139.77		
31	107.11	116.44	111.94	89.83	92.05	92.34	103.38			
34	104.09	109.12	110.78	113.76	123.49	125.11	120.14	138.74		
35								131.74		
36	86.96	105.60	97.34	105.32	119.75	120.09	121.56	141.89		

Explanatory notes: see p. 877.

[1] Adults. [2] Incl. family allowances and the value of payments in kind. [3] Oct. of each year.

Notes explicatives: voir p. 879.

[1] Adultes. [2] Y compris les allocations familiales et la valeur des paiements en nature. [3] Oct. de chaque année.

Notas explicativas: véase p. 882.

[1] Adultos. [2] Incl. las asignaciones familiares y el valor de los pagos en especie. [3] Oct. de cada año.

WAGES

In manufacturing

SALAIRES

Dans les industries manufacturières

SALARIOS

En las industrias manufactureras

5B

	1999	2000	2001	2002	2003	2004	2005	2006	2007	2008

Cyprus (DA) [1][2][3] — Salaried employees - Employés - Empleados — E.G./m. - Pound

Total men and women - Total hommes et femmes - Total hombres y mujeres
ISIC 3 - CITI 3 - CIIU 3

	1999	2000	2001	2002	2003	2004	2005	2006	2007	2008
Total	776.00	806.00	814.54	842.02	876.56	928.36	936.84	887.24	.	.
15	760.00	768.00	762.98	794.59	811.39	898.45	912.31	784.41	.	.
16	1 132.00	1 086.00	939.70	1 073.27	1 068.33	1 172.54	1 284.31	751.08	.	.
17	662.00	674.00	725.50	527.71	541.90	569.52	557.69	659.86	.	.
18	565.00	657.00	631.03	587.20	619.28	560.16	548.03	804.86	.	.
19	625.00	638.00	734.36	844.40	791.73	803.90	837.62	793.25	.	.
20	978.00	1 025.00	967.17	1 183.61	1 206.44	1 283.71	1 286.34	802.68	.	.
21	712.00	714.00	739.00	751.22	792.51	828.46	819.16	671.42	.	.
22	945.00	991.00	971.04	860.85	934.53	957.50	987.35	1 002.24	.	.
23	1 789.00	1 897.00	2 001.11	2 163.94	2 577.99	2 282.20	1 788.76	.	.	.
24	738.00	718.00	716.26	726.24	768.62	793.07	892.64	898.99	.	.
25	692.00	756.00	769.51	865.91	933.16	939.91	974.64	1 114.19	.	.
26	1 240.00	1 250.00	1 288.69	1 362.32	1 509.50	1 578.35	1 564.12	1 586.94	.	.
27	863.00	906.00	880.38	1 082.91	1 097.46	1 100.40	793.00	1 126.72	.	.
28	756.00	876.00	908.87	954.32	960.65	1 068.37	1 024.72	875.85	.	.
29	697.00	720.00	769.40	839.35	849.93	922.71	930.35	963.26	.	.
31	772.00	813.00	782.08	751.92	776.90	839.90	776.16	1 000.95	.	.
32	.	.	.	.	.	.	.	610.53	.	.
33	563.00	584.00	579.80	519.86	589.90	653.36	630.08	641.19	.	.
34	919.00	1 044.00	875.98	851.13	791.90	868.90	849.31	905.70	.	.
35	894.00	913.00	894.07	939.06	687.35	715.60	784.59	709.70	.	.
36	623.00	651.00	676.72	760.18	796.88	799.15	794.74	909.89	.	.
37	576.00	499.00	388.95	650.28	651.28	627.35	704.59	824.88	.	.

Men - Hommes - Hombres
ISIC 3 - CITI 3 - CIIU 3

	1999	2000	2001	2002	2003	2004	2005	2006	2007	2008
Total	919.00	954.00	967.18	1 005.67	1 038.88	1 108.16	1 104.98	1 035.12	.	.
15	873.00	887.00	899.10	929.05	933.27	1 052.68	1 073.88	936.88	.	.
16	1 283.00	1 176.00	1 072.31	1 192.33	1 222.89	1 332.76	1 494.20	986.21	.	.
17	880.00	863.00	910.07	677.40	708.34	708.34	650.00	817.31	.	.
18	741.00	915.00	958.16	886.16	957.37	723.28	702.75	962.58	.	.
19	899.00	920.00	936.70	1 093.84	960.69	1 000.25	1 038.30	999.74	.	.
20	1 036.00	1 088.00	1 060.33	1 285.40	1 295.10	1 384.81	1 389.35	854.81	.	.
21	819.00	813.00	855.43	892.34	946.89	975.53	961.20	741.91	.	.
22	1 077.00	1 147.00	1 132.00	1 009.76	1 101.88	1 124.65	1 113.93	1 228.91	.	.
23	1 813.00	1 921.00	2 033.60	2 212.24	2 640.41	2 384.41	1 836.91	.	.	.
24	871.00	876.00	883.36	887.40	934.18	949.10	1 032.59	1 063.12	.	.
25	762.00	836.00	846.11	985.27	1 057.85	1 075.28	1 099.60	1 247.11	.	.
26	1 449.00	1 436.00	1 469.91	1 560.93	1 726.08	1 799.79	1 780.75	1 838.86	.	.
27	930.00	975.00	1 001.06	1 225.02	1 238.03	1 282.37	804.47	1 214.94	.	.
28	826.00	955.00	1 018.62	1 044.30	1 044.24	1 187.64	1 107.65	908.00	.	.
29	763.00	777.00	820.13	900.73	903.51	993.19	1 002.05	1 037.48	.	.
31	829.00	887.00	861.33	790.60	789.23	871.52	806.56	1 055.10	.	.
32	.	.	.	.	.	.	.	689.34	.	.
33	668.00	685.00	748.05	658.53	731.95	803.80	729.84	749.60	.	.
34	1 042.00	1 182.00	1 098.01	1 020.61	955.29	1 049.66	1 030.41	958.66	.	.
35	1 003.00	1 021.00	928.44	939.06	687.35	715.60	784.59	.	.	.
36	710.00	732.00	788.88	891.55	928.71	918.20	892.19	983.24	.	.
37	586.00	500.00	362.30	664.32	663.23	632.73	713.21	851.43	.	.

Women - Femmes - Mujeres
ISIC 3 - CITI 3 - CIIU 3

	1999	2000	2001	2002	2003	2004	2005	2006	2007	2008
Total	545.00	556.00	593.22	604.33	641.07	667.51	692.89	654.75	.	.
15	539.00	535.00	559.90	593.98	629.56	668.36	671.27	575.07	.	.
16	867.00	927.00	801.98	949.63	907.82	1 006.16	1 066.35	502.51	.	.
17	486.00	521.00	608.13	432.53	436.07	481.25	499.00	534.91	.	.
18	495.00	554.00	537.21	501.46	522.31	513.38	503.66	758.54	.	.
19	463.00	472.00	510.40	568.31	604.72	586.57	615.50	575.50	.	.
20	607.00	623.00	568.73	748.25	827.22	851.29	845.77	540.75	.	.
21	490.00	507.00	556.32	529.80	550.29	597.72	596.30	565.68	.	.
22	766.00	779.00	796.94	699.77	753.52	776.70	850.43	758.16	.	.
23	1 434.00	1 542.00	1 641.01	1 628.59	1 886.13	1 149.39	1 255.14	.	.	.
24	584.00	533.00	572.67	587.75	626.34	658.98	772.37	755.19	.	.
25	511.00	548.00	564.51	546.50	599.48	577.64	640.22	815.41	.	.
26	612.00	688.00	722.96	742.28	833.36	887.07	887.84	896.09	.	.
27	550.00	586.00	616.38	772.05	789.97	702.33	767.91	777.86	.	.
28	502.00	591.00	617.90	715.78	739.05	752.16	804.85	739.02	.	.
29	521.00	566.00	584.01	615.01	654.11	665.10	668.29	691.62	.	.
31	572.00	556.00	548.78	638.04	740.62	746.83	686.66	822.72	.	.
32	.	.	.	.	.	.	.	512.02	.	.
33	437.00	464.00	454.15	416.30	483.82	541.01	555.58	505.68	.	.
34	546.00	624.00	560.29	610.16	559.59	611.87	591.81	640.90	.	.
35	402.00	427.00	438.60					709.70	.	.
36	463.00	504.00	532.29	591.02	627.11	645.84	669.25	761.34	.	.
37	362.00	474.00	613.55	531.90	550.56	582.02	631.89	736.03	.	.

Explanatory notes: see p. 877.

[1] Adults. [2] Incl. family allowances and the value of payments in kind. [3] Oct. of each year.

Notes explicatives: voir p. 879.

[1] Adultes. [2] Y compris les allocations familiales et la valeur des paiements en nature. [3] Oct. de chaque année.

Notas explicativas: véase p. 882.

[1] Adultos. [2] Incl. las asignaciones familiares y el valor de los pagos en especie. [3] Oct. de cada año.

WAGES — SALAIRES — SALARIOS

In manufacturing — Dans les industries manufacturières — En las industrias manufactureras

	1999	2000	2001	2002	2003	2004	2005	2006	2007	2008

Czech Republic (DA) — Employees - Salariés - Asalariados — E.G./m. - Koruna

Total men and women - Total hommes et femmes - Total hombres y mujeres
ISIC 3 - CITI 3 - CIIU 3

	1999	2000	2001	2002	2003	2004	2005	2006	2007	2008
Total	.	12 780	.	14 589	15 329	16 560	17 337	18 482	.	.
15-16	.	12 149	.	13 805	14 218	15 384	15 875	16 499	.	.
17	.	9 907	.	11 103	11 634	12 318	12 780	13 631	.	.
18	.	7 712	.	8 757	8 767	9 638	10 034	10 427	.	.
19	.	8 521	.	9 692	10 072	11 058	11 415	11 290	.	.
20	.	10 089	.	11 481	11 647	12 484	13 017	13 775	.	.
21	.	13 807	.	15 485	16 208	17 466	17 658	19 149	.	.
22	.	14 968	.	17 318	17 773	18 723	19 766	20 679	.	.
23	.	19 177	.	22 523	24 477	25 502	27 607	29 399	.	.
24	.	15 972	.	18 319	18 572	20 131	21 396	22 973	.	.
25	.	13 328	.	14 958	15 575	16 832	17 689	18 453	.	.
26	.	13 764	.	15 383	18 596	17 713	18 382	19 764	.	.
27	.	14 796	.	16 724	18 089	19 474	19 975	21 153	.	.
28	.	12 634	.	14 360	14 995	15 801	16 752	17 877	.	.
29	.	13 489	.	15 620	16 338	17 859	18 585	19 777	.	.
30	.	13 166	.	13 487	15 142	16 624	18 649	18 904	.	.
31	.	12 536	.	14 368	15 082	16 100	16 586	18 125	.	.
32	.	12 855	.	15 447	16 679	18 300	18 753	20 763	.	.
33	.	13 208	.	14 709	15 573	16 987	17 534	19 430	.	.
34	.	16 301	.	17 948	19 151	20 357	21 405	22 365	.	.
35	.	14 140	.	16 150	16 833	19 308	19 071	20 878	.	.
36	.	10 466	.	11 925	12 320	13 237	13 845	14 748	.	.
37	.	12 628	.	14 529	15 302	16 311	16 334	17 503	.	.

Denmark (CA) [1][2] — Employees - Salariés - Asalariados — E.G./h. - Krone

Total men and women - Total hommes et femmes - Total hombres y mujeres
ISIC 3 - CITI 3 - CIIU 3

	1999	2000	2001	2002	2003	2004	2005	2006	2007	2008
Total	182.34	188.59	199.10	207.02	215.34	217.15	226.63	235.63	248.81	.
15	176.38	183.79	191.60	199.27	208.72	210.71	218.08	226.10	238.31	.
16	162.56	188.87	206.19	205.50	217.05	224.25	235.50	246.50	258.90	.
17	163.38	171.12	179.40	187.97	189.93	196.35	201.10	207.29	220.46	.
18	153.68	163.89	177.44	183.24	191.51	202.88	214.66	217.63	240.52	.
19	156.40	166.82	172.42	191.35	196.61	224.93	200.77	212.49	234.97	.
20	163.04	168.19	178.11	182.06	189.43	189.94	208.31	207.52	216.24	.
21	193.29	194.86	208.77	212.76	224.79	222.30	224.93	228.66	238.35	.
22	218.78	227.59	235.45	243.65	247.78	250.19	257.73	264.79	279.31	.
23	249.15	266.74	285.34	304.26	302.91	296.15	304.24	339.29		.
24	212.15	228.22	244.42	256.44	265.91	264.97	282.67	292.15	296.62	.
25	180.08	182.11	190.49	198.09	201.99	206.53	216.64	228.68	246.32	.
26	177.58	183.84	194.52	200.89	205.69	210.97	217.26	229.36	246.74	.
27	174.14	176.32	185.00	191.64	202.17	202.08	207.33	215.97	234.36	.
28	176.41	178.86	189.26	195.76	201.95	204.78	210.74	220.55	231.70	.
29	177.56	184.03	193.41	202.56	213.91	212.11	220.35	229.52	246.34	.
30	221.97	220.66	226.20	215.70	235.21	233.19	271.39	253.90	256.24	.
31	186.59	185.73	193.03	206.48	209.02	211.44	221.42	231.91	252.03	.
32	167.96	188.91	181.90	185.97	198.40	203.13	225.35	233.05	254.84	.
33	195.22	195.95	211.62	220.82	235.62	229.67	247.82	258.06	277.75	.
34	173.58	171.55	182.19	191.86	201.87	200.59	206.90	220.94	232.43	.
35	192.49	194.94	201.56	215.63	223.08	230.05	244.99	245.24	264.26	.
36	165.17	167.10	176.62	184.53	193.60	195.45	201.51	212.16	228.26	.
37	185.67	189.88	197.24	203.46	215.96	240.46	221.23	225.20	238.73	.

Men - Hommes - Hombres
ISIC 3 - CITI 3 - CIIU 3

	1999	2000	2001	2002	2003	2004	2005	2006	2007	2008
Total	192.24	197.59	207.70	215.25	223.82	226.08	235.50	244.60	258.48	.
15	187.21	194.32	202.25	209.56	219.91	224.72	230.37	239.04	250.72	.
16	199.84	213.21	241.37	235.61	239.29	253.97	255.45	268.43	286.06	.
17	181.17	188.58	197.53	205.89	206.38	216.25	220.39	226.12	240.10	.
18	195.45	202.90	217.28	219.66	236.91	251.51	276.34	269.45	294.46	.
19	165.70	182.63	184.42	204.56	209.57		217.98	238.62	260.56	.
20	165.45	170.54	180.69	184.42	192.05	191.65	210.88	210.67	219.16	.
21	202.11	202.54	215.64	220.28	233.69	232.00	232.90	238.81	246.03	.
22	238.40	246.47	254.33	264.02	265.98	271.53	280.22	284.53	298.81	.
23	257.29	275.11	292.98	315.28	314.51	305.47	315.84	354.25		.
24	224.39	241.10	257.08	266.92	276.99	272.87	296.05	304.70	306.16	.
25	192.80	192.87	202.05	210.52	213.07	219.75	230.34	242.33	260.11	.
26	181.20	187.56	199.16	205.15	208.97	215.05	221.36	233.15	251.73	.
27	177.88	180.45	190.13	196.68	207.69	206.97	212.77	220.48	237.31	.
28	181.92	183.30	193.67	200.20	206.62	209.27	214.69	225.03	236.11	.
29	186.53	192.05	200.67	209.17	220.43	219.59	227.39	236.72	253.80	.
30	249.38	244.73	257.14	243.17	261.05	253.02	297.30	259.77	272.28	.
31	202.26	200.81	204.37	220.06	220.48	223.06	235.08	246.40	270.41	.
32	197.10	220.16	210.25	215.37	227.86	230.00	257.09	266.53	290.50	.
33	224.75	231.45	247.86	252.32	269.26	267.21	285.83	293.72	312.62	.
34	177.87	173.65	184.01	193.73	204.08	203.35	210.43	224.96	236.56	.
35	195.84	198.43	204.55	217.83	226.48	236.22	249.50	249.23	268.27	.
36	171.86	172.87	183.82	192.31	200.70	202.81	208.87	219.98	237.32	.
37	187.72	191.98	198.14	204.86	215.46	247.39	226.63	229.98	243.95	.

Explanatory notes: see p. 877.

[1] Excl. young people aged less than 18 years and trainees.
[2] Private sector.

Notes explicatives: voir p. 879.

[1] Non compris les jeunes gens âgés de moins de 18 ans et les apprentis. [2] Secteur privé.

Notas explicativas: véase p. 882.

[1] Excl. los jovenenes de menos de 18 años y los aprendices.
[2] Sector privado.

In manufacturing   Dans les industries manufacturières   En las industrias manufactureras

	1999	2000	2001	2002	2003	2004	2005	2006	2007	2008

Denmark (CA) [1][2]   Employees - Salariés - Asalariados   E.G./h. - Krone

Women - Femmes - Mujeres
ISIC 3 - CITI 3 - CIIU 3

	1999	2000	2001	2002	2003	2004	2005	2006	2007	2008
Total	160.30	166.74	178.77	186.83	194.52	196.80	204.72	213.44	223.72	.
15	153.83	160.20	169.54	176.61	184.52	186.84	191.63	198.82	210.72	.
16	138.81	161.04	169.31	172.74	187.05	187.33	206.07	212.84	226.90	.
17	142.48	148.41	156.69	163.35	166.97	169.86	173.21	182.31	193.52	.
18	136.96	144.16	156.06	161.79	166.28	176.85	182.03	187.89	204.29	.
19	142.38	143.55	152.53	167.41	164.03	.	178.99	188.23	209.94	.
20	151.87	156.01	165.73	171.22	177.67	180.65	196.86	194.36	204.63	.
21	161.61	167.31	181.58	184.67	192.07	191.60	197.06	197.86	212.00	.
22	188.50	195.73	205.18	212.75	218.20	218.54	222.22	232.59	247.61	.
23	192.54	207.20	224.76	228.10	252.64	.	256.70	281.93	.	.
24	197.43	212.33	229.40	244.08	252.67	256.07	267.18	277.31	282.46	.
25	158.49	161.95	167.52	174.15	180.91	180.09	190.81	203.15	220.97	.
26	159.52	166.92	172.59	179.58	188.72	191.26	196.45	208.62	219.73	.
27	156.06	156.42	162.36	171.87	178.58	181.18	184.47	196.95	219.52	.
28	154.09	157.27	167.80	174.15	179.61	181.66	189.83	197.99	209.19	.
29	150.92	156.47	167.66	176.25	187.23	185.24	193.23	201.07	217.25	.
30	165.51	157.14	156.01	154.83	179.09	175.51	201.64	200.44	220.25	.
31	151.39	152.38	163.19	170.53	177.98	180.87	185.99	196.00	205.82	.
32	140.88	144.73	148.20	156.99	163.87	166.28	176.36	183.76	198.53	.
33	155.87	157.88	168.46	179.84	190.11	185.47	199.55	210.02	225.63	.
34	156.86	161.61	173.80	180.90	191.83	187.99	191.64	202.08	214.56	.
35	165.64	164.56	175.32	193.29	195.32	192.95	210.32	210.95	226.51	.
36	153.73	155.09	162.43	169.75	179.88	179.84	186.40	196.35	211.21	.
37	170.50	174.05	190.39	193.78	.	.	192.35	196.90	217.83	.

España (DA) [3]   Employees - Salariés - Asalariados   E.G./h. - Euro

Total men and women - Total hommes et femmes - Total hombres y mujeres
ISIC 3 - CITI 3 - CIIU 3

	1999	2000	2001	2002	2003	2004	2005	2006	2007	2008
Total	9.75	10.04	10.46	10.97	11.50	12.00	12.40	12.90	13.35	14.05
15	8.86	8.93	9.40	9.99	10.50	10.60	10.80	11.20	11.41	11.58
16	15.60	16.31	16.54	19.26	19.50	20.00	21.10	23.05	25.33	27.35
17	6.96	7.84	8.16	8.32	8.89	9.22	9.46	10.07	10.31	10.71
18	6.20	6.01	6.33	6.77	7.12	7.66	7.97	8.17	8.78	9.80
19	5.73	5.95	6.22	6.59	6.79	7.09	7.52	7.94	8.15	8.75
20	6.81	7.19	7.38	7.49	7.36	7.96	8.57	9.12	9.51	10.30
21	10.69	11.14	11.89	12.27	12.40	14.00	13.50	14.20	15.34	15.88
22	11.03	12.13	12.07	12.42	12.80	13.70	13.90	13.93	13.75	14.26
23	21.39	22.53	23.11	24.47	26.70	26.50	26.60	28.48	29.61	28.94
24	14.08	13.95	14.79	15.83	16.90	17.40	18.50	18.71	19.71	20.93
25	11.11	11.36	11.07	11.77	12.70	12.90	13.10	13.72	13.93	14.74
26	9.70	9.83	10.40	10.72	11.40	11.40	11.80	12.33	12.98	14.04
27	13.22	13.31	13.69	14.17	15.20	15.60	16.20	17.42	17.38	17.90
28	8.51	8.93	9.54	10.02	10.40	10.90	11.30	11.48	12.26	13.17
29	9.83	10.57	11.09	11.92	12.20	12.90	12.80	13.52	14.18	14.99
30	13.52	13.85	14.31	13.76	15.70	14.30	13.30	12.62	12.01	12.56
31	10.64	10.40	11.09	11.65	12.10	13.00	13.60	14.44	14.21	15.78
32	12.01	12.68	13.22	12.73	13.30	14.50	16.50	16.28	17.25	15.31
33	9.59	10.70	12.05	12.11	12.40	13.50	13.10	13.96	14.67	14.82
34	12.26	13.01	13.02	13.56	14.50	14.70	15.50	16.15	16.44	17.10
35	12.18	12.21	12.56	13.55	14.40	15.10	15.30	16.72	17.68	17.82
36	7.18	7.37	7.58	7.84	8.26	8.60	9.09	9.73	10.11	10.62
37	8.14	8.33	8.96	9.17	9.57	9.93	9.87	10.44	11.57	12.26

Explanatory notes: see p. 877.

[1] Excl. young people aged less than 18 years and trainees. [2] Private sector. [3] Incl. overtime payments and irregular gratuities.

Notes explicatives: voir p. 879.

[1] Non compris les jeunes gens âgés de moins de 18 ans et les apprentis. [2] Secteur privé. [3] Y compris la rémunération des heures supplémentaires et les gratifications versées irrégulièrement.

Notas explicativas: véase p. 882.

[1] Excl. los jovenenes de menos de 18 años y los aprendices. [2] Sector privado. [3] Incl. los pagos por horas extraordinarias y las gratificaciones pagadas irregularmente.

WAGES

In manufacturing

SALAIRES

Dans les industries manufacturières

SALARIOS

En las industrias manufactureras

España (DA) [1] — Employees - Salariés - Asalariados

Total men and women - Total hommes et femmes - Total hombres y mujeres
ISIC 3 - CITI 3 - CIIU 3

E.G./h. - Euro

	1999	2000	2001	2002	2003	2004	2005	2006	2007	2008
Total	8.45	8.67	9.02	9.47	9.78	10.10	10.50	10.96	11.39	12.01
15	7.63	7.71	8.05	8.60	8.89	8.99	9.26	9.72	9.96	10.12
16	11.20	11.56	12.87	14.39	14.70	14.80	15.60	16.59	17.31	18.49
17	6.34	6.90	7.31	7.33	7.65	7.94	8.05	8.72	8.99	9.37
18	5.56	5.37	5.61	5.88	6.08	6.62	6.73	7.07	7.65	8.24
19	5.52	5.68	5.89	6.20	6.38	6.72	7.09	7.49	7.69	8.23
20	6.11	6.35	6.50	6.74	6.57	7.02	7.48	7.93	8.40	9.10
21	9.52	10.08	10.41	10.85	10.90	12.30	11.80	12.19	13.30	13.75
22	9.04	9.81	9.93	10.24	10.70	11.10	11.50	11.82	11.75	12.15
23	17.13	17.48	17.70	18.64	19.70	20.30	19.90	21.44	22.39	22.70
24	11.81	11.55	11.83	12.81	13.30	13.40	14.30	14.55	15.02	16.23
25	9.11	9.36	9.29	9.90	10.50	10.70	10.90	11.39	11.76	12.54
26	8.40	8.42	8.91	9.14	9.59	9.65	10.10	10.51	11.11	11.74
27	11.10	11.26	11.94	12.41	13.10	13.40	13.80	14.33	14.74	15.36
28	7.73	8.07	8.40	8.95	9.16	9.57	9.94	10.21	10.84	11.46
29	8.72	9.33	9.83	10.32	10.50	10.80	11.00	11.61	12.23	13.13
30	12.78	12.51	13.15	12.40	13.90	12.10	11.50	11.01	10.84	11.37
31	9.15	9.09	9.62	10.13	10.50	10.90	11.30	12.01	12.04	13.41
32	10.52	10.58	11.16	10.88	11.10	11.70	12.90	12.86	13.76	13.01
33	8.18	9.31	10.52	10.65	11.20	12.10	12.00	12.72	13.23	13.54
34	10.52	11.10	11.32	11.89	12.40	12.60	13.10	13.71	14.00	14.62
35	10.52	10.66	11.20	11.77	12.30	12.60	12.80	13.89	14.99	15.06
36	6.50	6.59	6.81	6.99	7.25	7.54	8.03	8.50	8.82	9.39
37	7.35	7.41	7.62	7.96	8.10	8.28	8.58	9.08	9.66	10.46

Estonia (DA) — Employees - Salariés - Asalariados

Total men and women - Total hommes et femmes - Total hombres y mujeres
ISIC 3 - CITI 3 - CIIU 3

E.G./m. - Kroon

	1999	2000	2001	2002	2003	2004	2005	2006	2007	2008
Total	4 374	4 844	5 337	5 884	6 403	7 012	7 760	9 158	11 048	12 366
15	4 564	4 788	5 269	5 798	6 314	6 879	7 578	8 955	10 558	12 003
15-16	4 564	4 788	5 269	5 798	6 314	6 879	7 578	8 955	10 558	12 003
17	3 443	4 031	4 236	4 661	4 878	5 266	5 682	6 361	7 493	8 987
18	3 339	3 745	4 126	4 487	4 706	5 077	5 242	5 893	6 834	7 623
19	3 499	3 810	4 084	4 702	5 105	5 048	5 279	6 101	7 440	8 239
20	4 186	4 783	5 481	6 141	6 607	7 084	8 013	9 433	11 395	12 289
21	5 468	5 743	6 200	6 775	7 397	8 265	8 910	10 168	12 997	14 553
22	7 956	8 484	9 425	10 243	10 672	11 875	12 654	13 705	15 670	16 669
23-24	4 396	4 917	5 567	6 012	6 594	7 423	8 309	9 830	12 309	13 897
25	3 815	4 737	5 474	6 679	7 162	7 564	8 053	9 194	11 365	12 208
26	5 320	6 436	7 090	7 891	8 801	9 762	10 993	13 358	15 710	15 152
27-28	4 748	5 526	6 153	6 501	7 334	7 707	8 407	10 295	13 050	14 532
29	4 261	4 974	5 559	6 144	6 675	7 919	8 965	10 805	13 520	15 002
30										
31	5 493	6 147	7 033	8 648	8 941	8 572	8 889	10 458	11 630	12 829
32	4 182	4 607	4 710	5 654	6 365	6 407	6 858	7 979	9 291	10 625
33	4 587	5 458	5 685	6 149	6 670	7 478	9 506	10 690	11 917	13 093
34-35	5 284	5 785	6 483	7 253	7 771	8 451	9 288	11 213	12 658	14 389
36	3 891	4 386	4 810	5 168	5 616	6 351	7 012	8 072	9 532	10 693
37										

Finland (DA) [2] [3] — Wage earners - Ouvriers - Obreros

Total men and women - Total hommes et femmes - Total hombres y mujeres
ISIC 3 - CITI 3 - CIIU 3

E.G./h. - Euro

	1999	2000	2001	2002	2003	2004	2005	2006	2007	2008
Total										
15							13.85	14.53	15.14	
16							13.55	14.05	14.48	
17	9.07	9.59	10.23	10.66	11.05 [4]	11.44 |	12.21 [5]	13.41	14.29	
18							9.82	10.03	10.43	
18-19	7.62	7.94	8.26	8.49	8.85 [4]	9.17				
19							9.99	10.31	10.77	
20	10.95	11.47	12.01	12.46	12.81 [4]	13.16 |	12.61 [5]	13.00	13.36	
21	13.58	14.30	14.95	15.53	16.14 [4]	16.70 |	17.79 [5]	18.42	19.10	
22	11.26	11.57	11.95	12.30	12.86 [4]	13.10 |	13.71 [5]	14.42	14.97	
23							21.72	22.31	20.58	
24	11.34	12.13	12.81	13.28	13.57 [4]	14.19 |	16.12 [5]	16.41	17.05	
25							13.29	14.31	15.27	
26	10.88	11.35	11.94	12.16	12.54 [4]	12.75 |	13.52 [5]	14.27	15.04	
27	13.73	14.55	14.86	15.41	15.96 [4]	16.47 |	15.37 [5]	16.41	17.29	
28							12.62	13.29	14.10	
29							14.04	14.85	15.64	
30								10.60		
31										
32							14.16	14.41	15.09	
33							12.42	12.50	12.78	
34							12.78	13.86	13.09	
35							13.54	14.20	15.46	
36	9.31	9.80	9.96	10.32	10.68 [4]	11.07 |	13.59	14.38	15.05	
37							12.06 [5]	11.61	12.09	
							12.70	12.88	13.52	

Explanatory notes: see p. 877.

[1] Excl. irregular gratuities. [2] Private sector. [3] Fourth quarter of each year. [4] From 2003: excl. seasonal and end-of-year bonuses. [5] Prior to 2005: data collected from organised employers only; data are not comparable.

Notes explicatives: voir p. 879.

[1] Non compris les gratifications versées irrégulièrement. [2] Secteur privé. [3] Quatrième trimestre de chaque année. [4] A partir de 2003: non compris les primes saisonnières et de fin d'année. [5] Avant 2005: données collectées auprès des employeurs organisés seulement; les données ne sont pas comparables.

Notas explicativas: véase p. 882.

[1] Excl. las gratificaciones pagadas irregularmente. [2] Sector privado. [3] Cuarto trimestre de cada año. [4] A partir de 2003: excl. las primas temporales y de fin de año. [5] Antes de 2005: datos recopilados de empleadores organizados sólo. datos no son comparables.

WAGES
In manufacturing

SALAIRES
Dans les industries manufacturières

SALARIOS
En las industrias manufactureras

5B

Finland (DA) [1] [2] — Wage earners - Ouvriers - Obreros — E.G./h. - Euro

Men - Hommes - Hombres
ISIC 3 - CITI 3 - CIIU 3

	1999	2000	2001	2002	2003	2004	2005	2006	2007	2008
Total	.	.	.	.	.	.	14.40	15.10	15.69	.
15	.	.	.	.	.	.	14.32	14.81	15.38	.
16	.	.	.	.	.	.	.	.	.	.
17	10.41	11.04	11.80	12.30	12.78 [3]	13.16 [|]	14.41 [4]	15.58	16.28	.
18	.	.	.	.	.	.	11.23	11.67	11.75	.
18-19	.	.	.	.	9.72 [3]	10.06	.	.	.	.
19	.	.	.	.	.	.	10.81	11.12	11.66	.
20	11.15	11.66	12.18	12.60	13.01 [3]	13.32 [|]	12.71 [4]	13.08	13.45	.
21	13.86	14.59	15.25	15.83	16.44 [3]	17.00 [|]	18.26 [4]	18.87	19.50	.
22	11.90	12.27	12.68	13.04	13.56 [3]	13.80 [|]	14.43 [4]	15.24	15.88	.
23	.	.	.	.	.	.	21.85	22.46	20.68	.
24	12.17	12.99	13.70	14.15	14.45 [3]	15.01 [|]	17.02 [4]	17.42	18.04	.
25	.	.	.	.	.	.	13.82	14.99	15.86	.
26	11.07	11.52	12.09	12.30	12.70 [3]	12.93 [|]	13.67 [4]	14.44	15.26	.
27	13.86	14.68	14.98	15.53	16.09 [3]	16.60 [|]	15.57 [4]	16.56	17.44	.
28	.	.	.	.	.	.	12.81	13.53	14.37	.
29	.	.	.	.	.	.	14.29	15.16	15.96	.
30	.	.	.	.	.	.	.	.	.	.
31	.	.	.	.	.	.	14.72	15.13	15.57	.
32	.	.	.	.	.	.	12.90	12.96	13.21	.
33	.	.	.	.	.	.	13.76	14.94	13.98	.
34	.	.	.	.	.	.	13.74	14.49	15.77	.
35	.	.	.	.	.	.	13.87	14.51	15.23	.
36	9.49	10.01	10.13	10.51	10.89 [3]	11.28 [|]	12.41 [4]	11.90	12.44	.
37	.	.	.	.	.	.	12.77	13.33	13.58	.

Women - Femmes - Mujeres
ISIC 3 - CITI 3 - CIIU 3

	1999	2000	2001	2002	2003	2004	2005	2006	2007	2008
Total	.	.	.	.	.	.	12.17	12.59	13.13	.
15	.	.	.	.	.	.	12.54	13.09	13.37	.
16	.	.	.	.	.	.	.	.	.	.
17	8.34	8.74	9.33	9.68	10.00 [3]	10.34 [|]	10.84 [4]	11.83	12.79	.
18	.	.	.	.	.	.	9.60	9.79	10.21	.
18-19	7.45	7.77	8.07	8.29	8.62 [3]	8.91	.	.	.	.
19	.	.	.	.	.	.	9.47	9.87	10.26	.
20	10.24	10.80	11.38	11.94	12.04 [3]	12.53 [|]	12.10 [4]	12.59	12.92	.
21	12.02	12.66	13.21	13.74	14.32 [3]	14.82 [|]	15.44 [4]	16.05	16.83	.
22	9.98	10.22	10.52	10.77	11.29 [3]	11.56 [|]	12.21 [4]	12.70	13.07	.
23	.	.	.	.	.	.	17.98	18.20	17.76	.
24	9.14	9.69	10.14	10.76	11.18 [3]	11.59 [|]	12.53 [4]	12.88	13.70	.
25	.	.	.	.	.	.	12.03	12.51	13.58	.
26	9.97	10.40	11.15	11.37	11.56 [3]	11.67 [|]	12.54 [4]	13.16	13.58	.
27	.	.	.	.	14.54 [3]	15.00 [|]	13.29 [4]	14.74	15.53	.
28	.	.	.	.	.	.	11.50	11.66	12.28	.
29	.	.	.	.	.	.	11.95	12.41	13.08	.
30	.	.	.	.	.	.	11.68	10.60	.	.
31	.	.	.	.	.	.	13.13	13.06	14.08	.
32	.	.	.	.	.	.	.	12.07	12.46	.
33	.	.	.	.	.	.	11.18	11.45	11.70	.
34	.	.	.	.	.	.	12.56	12.40	13.42	.
35	.	.	.	.	.	.	11.56	12.73	13.18	.
36	8.80	9.25	9.49	9.80	10.10 [3]	10.50 [|]	11.28 [4]	11.04	11.35	.
37	.	.	.	.	.	.	11.90	10.62	12.98	.

Explanatory notes: see p. 877.

[1] Private sector. [2] Fourth quarter of each year. [3] From 2003: excl. seasonal and end-of-year bonuses. [4] Prior to 2005: data collected from organised employers only; data are not comparable.

Notes explicatives: voir p. 879.

[1] Secteur privé. [2] Quatrième trimestre de chaque année. [3] A partir de 2003: non compris les primes saisonnières et de fin d'année. [4] Avant 2005: données collectées auprès des employeurs organisés seulement; les données ne sont pas comparables.

Notas explicativas: véase p. 882.

[1] Sector privado. [2] Cuarto trimestre de cada año. [3] A partir de 2003: excl. las primas temporales y de fin de año. [4] Antes de 2005: datos recopilados de empleadores organizados sólo. datos no son comparables.

5B

WAGES	SALAIRES	SALARIOS
In manufacturing	Dans les industries manufacturières	En las industrias manufactureras

	1999	2000	2001	2002	2003	2004	2005	2006	2007	2008

Finland (DA) [1] [2]   Employees - Salariés - Asalariados   E.G./m. - Euro

Total men and women - Total hommes et femmes - Total hombres y mujeres
ISIC 3 - CITI 3 - CIIU 3

	1999	2000	2001	2002	2003	2004	2005	2006	2007	2008
Total	12 510	13 124	2 275 [3]	2 357	2 463 [4]	2 564	2 641	2 788	2 915	.
15	11 148	11 748	2 068 [3]	2 141	2 292 [4]	2 371	2 479	2 559	2 645	.
16	12 338	12 975	2 155 [3]	2 384	2 565 [4]					.
17	9 904	10 743	1 931 [3]	1 966	2 060 [4]	2 176	2 195	2 416	2 574	.
18	8 754	8 989	1 573 [3]	1 657	1 751 [4]	1 857	1 865	1 926	2 088	.
19	8 327	8 776	1 531 [3]	1 582	1 672 [4]	1 733	1 746	1 824	1 919	.
20	10 877	11 180	1 950 [3]	2 036	2 083 [4]	2 161	2 271	2 324	2 373	.
21	14 648	15 404	2 700 [3]	2 763	2 856 [4]	2 923	3 086	3 184	3 318	.
22	13 026	13 443	2 345 [3]	2 342	2 496 [4]	2 578	2 659	2 783	2 895	.
23	15 047	16 150	2 892 [3]	3 223	3 126 [4]	3 405	3 654	3 784	3 730	.
24	13 377	14 413	2 485 [3]	2 658	2 695 [4]	2 826	2 941	2 987	3 133	.
25	11 528	11 737	2 117 [3]	2 220	2 308 [4]	2 352	2 405	2 609	2 759	.
26	11 931	12 364	2 133 [3]	2 229	2 290 [4]	2 345	2 482	2 616	2 746	.
27	13 356	13 962	2 422 [3]	2 485	2 604 [4]	2 708	2 756	2 931	3 070	.
28	11 428	11 942	1 968 [3]	2 036	2 117 [4]	2 228	2 309	2 466	2 596	.
29	12 966	13 763	2 351 [3]	2 410	2 541 [4]	2 659	2 718	2 866	3 039	.
30	14 280	9 781	1 868 [3]	1 737	2 760 [4]	2 855	2 589	2 933	3 254	.
31	13 066	13 253	2 301 [3]	2 423	2 411 [4]	2 528	2 803	2 869	3 023	.
32	13 882	15 021	2 612 [3]	2 817	3 008 [4]	3 122	2 813	3 320	3 601	.
33	12 446	13 788	2 446 [3]	2 406	2 577 [4]	2 692	2 866	3 051	3 268	.
34	11 644	12 586	2 148 [3]	2 277	2 281 [4]	2 365	2 437	2 487	2 764	.
35	11 981	12 727	2 236 [3]	2 217	2 406 [4]	2 463	2 566	2 721	2 834	.
36	9 772	10 334	1 757 [3]	1 822	1 921 [4]	2 002	2 171	2 152	2 213	.
37	11 244	11 072	1 974 [3]	1 899	2 032 [4]	2 295	2 384	2 384	2 597	.

Men - Hommes - Hombres
ISIC 3 - CITI 3 - CIIU 3

	1999	2000	2001	2002	2003	2004	2005	2006	2007	2008
Total	13 305	13 939	2 402 [3]	2 475	2 581 [4]	2 685	2 772	2 921	3 048	.
15	12 328	12 986	2 261 [3]	2 358	2 493 [4]	2 567	2 665	2 742	2 844	.
16	14 228	15 009	2 401 [3]	2 723	2 973 [4]					.
17	11 739	12 792	2 287 [3]	2 352	2 450 [4]	2 542	2 617	2 840	2 962	.
18	11 715	11 897	1 993 [3]	2 159	2 304 [4]	2 436	2 438	2 458	2 702	.
19	9 402	9 562	1 694 [3]	1 750	1 861 [4]	1 929	1 909	2 003	2 122	.
20	11 203	11 366	1 982 [3]	2 066	2 114 [4]	2 190	2 303	2 357	2 401	.
21	15 359	16 138	2 828 [3]	2 868	2 985 [4]	3 051	3 227	3 319	3 450	.
22	14 234	14 728	2 543 [3]	2 510	2 704 [4]	2 776	2 854	3 003	3 134	.
23	15 499	16 602	3 011 [3]	3 338	3 282 [4]	3 664	3 834	3 987	3 893	.
24	14 740	15 767	2 749 [3]	2 901	2 919 [4]	3 042	3 163	3 223	3 373	.
25	12 463	12 483	2 243 [3]	2 350	2 427 [4]	2 484	2 528	2 759	2 902	.
26	12 297	12 638	2 171 [3]	2 254	2 321 [4]	2 371	2 516	2 653	2 795	.
27	13 663	14 216	2 473 [3]	2 533	2 660 [4]	2 763	2 802	2 971	3 125	.
28	11 675	12 228	2 022 [3]	2 083	2 160 [4]	2 277	2 362	2 530	2 655	.
29	13 365	14 220	2 420 [3]	2 469	2 606 [4]	2 737	2 799	2 953	3 134	.
30	15 826	9 997	1 901 [3]	1 875	2 907 [4]	2 973	2 666	3 006	3 281	.
31	13 826	14 245	2 509 [3]	2 569	2 569 [4]	2 688	2 989	3 075	3 192	.
32	15 234	16 474	2 826 [3]	3 098	3 275 [4]	3 401	3 088	3 608	3 919	.
33	13 761	15 124	2 654 [3]	2 559	3 723 [4]	2 891	3 085	3 231	3 439	.
34	11 876	12 834	2 222 [3]	2 349	2 341 [4]	2 438	2 478	2 546	2 834	.
35	12 201	12 927	2 272 [3]	2 246	2 443 [4]	2 498	2 630	2 760	2 878	.
36	10 139	10 811	1 805 [3]	1 878	1 981 [4]	2 064	2 248	2 234	2 295	.
37			[3]		2 049 [4]	2 349	2 415	2 453	2 645	.

Women - Femmes - Mujeres
ISIC 3 - CITI 3 - CIIU 3

	1999	2000	2001	2002	2003	2004	2005	2006	2007	2008
Total	10 683	11 239	1 969 [3]	2 063	2 160 [4]	2 252	2 315	2 447	2 568	.
15	9 937	10 512	1 871 [3]	1 935	2 070 [4]	2 151	2 270	2 354	2 428	.
16	10 658	11 231	1 931 [3]	2 049	2 210 [4]					.
17	8 777	9 482	1 706 [3]	1 734	1 808 [4]	1 910	1 926	2 109	2 282	.
18	8 316	8 595	1 517 [3]	1 584	1 657 [4]	1 748	1 757	1 830	1 950	.
19	7 790	8 308	1 442 [3]	1 497	1 556 [4]	1 605	1 638	1 722	1 788	.
20	9 793	10 489	1 825 [3]	1 920	1 954 [4]	2 042	2 130	2 184	2 254	.
21	12 186	12 871	2 260 [3]	2 372	2 430 [4]	2 496	2 626	2 726	2 857	.
22	11 775	12 125	2 135 [3]	2 158	2 282 [4]	2 368	2 444	2 554	2 651	.
23	12 710	13 731	2 260 [3]	2 650	2 713 [4]	2 759	2 800	3 004	3 087	.
24	11 236	12 260	2 082 [3]	2 302	2 337 [4]	2 477	2 579	2 646	2 779	.
25	9 979	10 427	1 877 [3]	1 983	2 062 [4]	2 075	2 140	2 274	2 436	.
26	10 572	11 245	1 967 [3]	2 115	2 145 [4]	2 221	2 325	2 453	2 529	.
27	11 581	12 291	2 130 [3]	2 238	2 311 [4]	2 422	2 522	2 716	2 783	.
28	10 030	10 396	1 717 [3]	1 808	1 905 [4]	1 975	2 060	2 128	2 291	.
29	10 798	11 275	1 974 [3]	2 061	2 176 [4]	2 249	2 294	2 423	2 575	.
30	12 113	9 666	1 849 [3]	1 489	2 440 [4]	2 587	2 299	2 535	3 107	.
31	10 998	11 226	1 917 [3]	2 055	2 048 [4]	2 122	2 376	2 430	2 630	.
32	11 742	12 661	2 212 [3]	2 345	2 496 [4]	2 999	2 382	2 777	2 983	.
33	10 636	11 388	2 043 [3]	2 119	2 261 [4]	2 327	2 408	2 605	2 860	.
34	10 397	11 386	1 844 [3]	1 949	1 937 [4]	2 077	2 263	2 170	2 389	.
35	10 302	11 062	1 939 [3]	1 968	2 083 [4]	2 178	2 135	2 375	2 498	.
36	9 033	9 521	1 653 [3]	1 716	1 792 [4]	1 876	2 012	1 997	2 050	.
37			[3]		[4]	2 008	2 172	2 091	2 325	.

Explanatory notes: see p. 877.

[1] Full-time employees. [2] Fourth quarter of each year. [3] Prior to 2001: FIM; 1 Euro = 5.94573 FIM. [4] From 2003: excl. seasonal and end-of-year bonuses.

Notes explicatives: voir p. 879.

[1] Salariés à plein temps. [2] Quatrième trimestre de chaque année. [3] Avant 2001: FIM; 1 Euro = 5,94573 FIM. [4] A partir de 2003: non compris les primes saisonnières et de fin d'année.

Notas explicativas: véase p. 882.

[1] Asalariados a tiempo completo. [2] Cuarto trimestre de cada año. [3] Antes de 2001: FIM; 1 Euro = 5,94573 FIM. [4] A partir de 2003: excl. las primas temporales y de fin de año.

	1999	2000	2001	2002	2003	2004	2005	2006	2007	2008

France (F) [1]   Employees - Salariés - Asalariados   E.G./h. - Euro

Total men and women - Total hommes et femmes - Total hombres y mujeres
ISIC 3 - CITI 3 - CIIU 3

	1999	2000	2001	2002	2003	2004	2005	2006	2007	2008
Total	13.40	14.10	14.70	15.30	15.90	16.40	16.77	17.30	17.90	.
15	11.20	11.70	12.10	12.70	13.10	13.60	13.74	14.10	14.50	.
16	17.70	19.80	20.20	21.30	20.90	23.10	24.51	23.40	24.80	.
17	10.60	11.30	11.80	12.30	12.90	13.20	13.65	14.10	14.80	.
18	9.90	10.50	11.10	11.90	12.70	13.20	13.68	14.10	14.60	.
19	10.40	10.90	11.10	11.70	12.00	12.70	12.82	13.50	13.90	.
20	10.10	10.70	11.30	11.70	12.00	12.50	13.04	13.10	13.80	.
21	13.50	14.20	14.80	15.50	16.10	16.70	16.94	17.30	17.90	.
22	15.20	15.90	16.60	17.20	17.90	18.40	18.72	19.20	19.90	.
23	20.60	22.20	23.10	23.60	23.30	24.20	25.39	27.20	27.60	.
24	17.90	19.10	19.90	20.30	21.10	21.70	22.33	23.30	24.20	.
25	12.20	12.70	13.30	13.90	14.50	15.00	15.34	15.60	16.20	.
26	12.70	13.60	14.00	14.70	15.20	15.50	15.88	16.30	17.20	.
27	14.50	15.00	15.70	15.80	16.40	17.00	17.00	18.30	19.20	.
28	12.10	12.50	13.10	13.60	14.00	14.40	14.68	15.10	15.50	.
29	13.80	14.50	15.10	15.60	16.30	16.90	17.30	17.70	18.20	.
30	20.80	21.00	21.80	23.50	25.40	25.00	26.16	27.70	27.70	.
31	13.60	14.30	15.10	15.80	16.50	17.00	17.35	18.10	18.80	.
32	16.10	16.80	18.40	19.70	20.00	20.40	20.80	21.00	22.00	.
33	15.10	15.90	16.70	17.50	18.10	18.60	19.31	19.90	20.70	.
34	14.30	14.80	15.20	16.00	17.00	17.50	17.95	18.50	19.10	.
35	17.60	18.20	18.80	19.20	20.10	20.70	21.23	22.30	22.60	.
36	11.10	11.60	12.10	12.70	13.10	13.70	13.96	14.30	14.70	.
37	10.60	11.10	11.60	12.40	12.90	13.30	13.75	14.20	15.00	.

Men - Hommes - Hombres
ISIC 3 - CITI 3 - CIIU 3

	1999	2000	2001	2002	2003	2004	2005	2006	2007	2008
Total	14.30	15.00	15.60	16.20	16.80	17.30	17.65	18.20	18.80	.
15	12.20	12.80	13.20	13.90	14.30	14.80	14.89	15.30	15.80	.
16	18.00	20.40	21.20	22.60	22.00	24.30	25.64	24.10	25.90	.
17	12.10	12.80	13.40	14.00	14.80	15.00	15.36	15.90	16.70	.
18	13.50	14.10	15.00	16.40	17.20	17.90	18.42	18.70	19.30	.
19	12.50	13.10	13.10	14.00	14.50	15.30	15.70	16.40	16.90	.
20	10.30	10.80	11.40	11.80	12.20	12.70	13.21	13.20	14.00	.
21	14.40	15.10	15.60	16.30	17.10	17.60	17.79	18.10	18.80	.
22	16.20	17.10	17.80	18.50	19.10	19.70	19.89	20.40	21.00	.
23	21.40	22.90	23.90	24.20	24.00	24.90	26.02	28.00	28.40	.
24	19.20	20.50	21.30	21.60	22.60	23.10	23.73	24.70	25.60	.
25	12.90	13.50	14.10	14.70	15.30	15.90	16.19	16.40	17.00	.
26	13.10	14.00	14.40	15.20	15.60	15.90	16.30	16.70	17.60	.
27	14.70	15.20	16.00	16.00	16.60	17.20	17.20	18.50	19.50	.
28	12.30	12.80	13.40	13.90	14.30	14.70	14.93	15.40	15.80	.
29	14.20	14.90	15.60	16.10	16.80	17.40	17.76	18.20	18.70	.
30	22.70	23.20	24.60	26.10	27.40	27.10	28.27	30.00	30.00	.
31	15.00	15.70	16.60	17.30	18.10	18.50	18.83	19.60	20.30	.
32	18.40	19.20	20.80	22.00	22.40	22.90	23.29	23.70	24.60	.
33	16.70	17.50	18.40	19.30	20.00	20.60	21.27	21.90	22.80	.
34	14.60	15.20	15.50	16.30	17.40	17.90	18.37	19.00	19.50	.
35	18.10	18.60	19.20	19.60	20.50	21.10	21.67	22.80	23.20	.
36	11.70	12.10	12.70	13.30	13.70	14.30	14.57	14.80	15.20	.
37	10.70	11.30	12.00	12.80	13.30	13.60	14.05	14.60	15.30	.

Women - Femmes - Mujeres
ISIC 3 - CITI 3 - CIIU 3

	1999	2000	2001	2002	2003	2004	2005	2006	2007	2008
Total	11.20	11.80	12.40	13.00	13.50	14.00	14.48	15.00	15.60	.
15	9.40	9.80	10.20	10.70	11.10	11.60	11.85	12.20	12.60	.
16	16.50	17.90	17.40	17.90	18.10	19.80	21.64	21.40	21.70	.
17	8.80	9.30	9.80	10.30	10.60	11.10	11.65	12.00	12.70	.
18	8.80	9.50	9.90	10.50	11.20	11.70	12.17	12.50	13.00	.
19	9.00	9.50	9.90	10.30	10.60	11.20	11.23	11.90	12.40	.
20	9.40	9.90	10.40	10.80	11.30	11.60	12.19	12.40	13.00	.
21	11.00	11.70	12.30	12.90	13.30	13.70	14.23	14.40	14.90	.
22	13.40	14.00	14.70	15.30	16.00	16.50	17.01	17.40	18.30	.
23	17.10	18.50	19.60	20.30	19.80	20.80	21.97	23.60	23.70	.
24	15.70	16.90	17.80	18.20	18.80	19.50	20.17	21.20	22.10	.
25	10.00	10.50	11.00	11.50	12.20	12.50	13.00	13.30	13.90	.
26	10.90	11.40	11.90	12.70	13.30	13.60	14.04	14.60	15.40	.
27	12.80	13.10	13.80	14.20	14.70	15.10	15.55	16.50	17.40	.
28	10.80	11.10	11.50	12.10	12.50	12.70	13.26	13.60	14.00	.
29	11.70	12.10	12.70	13.20	14.00	14.40	15.07	15.50	16.00	.
30	15.80	15.70	16.00	17.80	20.90	20.40	21.33	22.40	22.50	.
31	10.70	11.40	12.20	12.60	13.20	13.70	14.13	14.80	15.60	.
32	11.90	12.60	13.80	15.10	15.20	15.40	15.80	15.70	16.70	.
33	11.80	12.30	13.10	13.70	14.40	14.60	15.21	15.70	16.40	.
34	12.40	12.80	13.30	14.10	14.90	15.40	15.87	16.40	17.10	.
35	14.80	15.30	16.10	16.90	17.70	18.20	18.79	19.60	20.00	.
36	9.80	10.40	10.90	11.40	11.80	12.40	12.59	13.10	13.50	.
37	10.00	10.00	10.20	10.60	11.10	11.70	12.40	12.90	13.70	.

Explanatory notes: see p. 877.   Notes explicatives: voir p. 879.   Notas explicativas: véase p. 882.

[1] Incl. managerial staff and intermediary occupations.   [1] Y compris les cadres et les professions intermédiaires.   [1] Incl. el personal directivo y las ocupaciones intermediarias.

5B — WAGES / SALAIRES / SALARIOS

In manufacturing / Dans les industries manufacturières / En las industrias manufactureras

France (F) — Wage earners - Ouvriers - Obreros — E.G./h. - Euro

Total men and women - Total hommes et femmes - Total hombres y mujeres
ISIC 3 - CITI 3 - CIIU 3

	1999	2000	2001	2002	2003	2004	2005	2006	2007	2008
Total	9.70	10.20	10.60	11.50	12.00	12.30	12.56	12.90	13.30	.
15	9.10	9.50	9.90	10.80	11.20	11.50	11.69	12.10	12.40	
16	12.10	13.10	13.20	16.90	14.70	18.30	19.43	16.10	18.50	
17	8.20	8.70	9.10	9.80	10.20	10.50	10.76	11.10	11.60	
18	7.50	8.00	8.20	8.90	9.40	9.60	9.86	10.20	10.50	
19	8.20	8.60	9.00	9.80	10.00	10.50	10.58	11.10	11.50	
20	8.10	8.60	9.00	9.80	10.10	10.40	10.74	11.00	11.40	
21	10.60	11.00	11.60	12.60	13.10	13.60	13.76	14.00	14.50	
22	11.00	11.60	12.20	12.80	13.20	13.50	13.71	14.00	14.10	
23	14.90	15.70	16.80	18.40	18.90	19.70	20.42	21.30	22.10	
24	11.40	12.00	12.40	13.50	14.10	14.30	14.90	15.60	16.00	
25	9.40	9.80	10.20	11.00	11.50	11.80	12.19	12.30	12.80	
26	9.90	10.50	10.80	12.00	12.40	12.80	12.92	13.30	13.90	
27	10.90	11.40	12.10	12.80	13.30	13.70	13.80	14.80	15.40	
28	9.50	9.90	10.40	11.10	11.50	11.80	12.05	12.40	12.80	
29	10.30	10.70	11.20	12.00	12.40	12.80	13.03	13.40	13.80	
30	9.10	9.50	9.60	10.90	11.20	11.90	13.49	13.40	13.00	
31	9.70	10.10	10.60	11.60	12.20	12.50	12.76	13.30	13.70	
32	9.30	9.80	10.60	11.80	11.90	12.40	12.29	12.20	12.80	
33	9.40	9.80	10.30	11.00	11.50	11.80	12.30	12.70	13.00	
34	10.90	11.50	11.80	12.90	13.60	13.80	14.04	14.40	14.70	
35	11.50	12.00	12.30	14.10	14.40	14.60	14.84	15.30	15.70	
36	8.80	9.20	9.60	10.30	10.60	11.00	11.18	11.70	12.00	
37	8.30	8.80	9.20	10.10	10.50	10.80	11.16	11.60	12.00	

Men - Hommes - Hombres
ISIC 3 - CITI 3 - CIIU 3

	1999	2000	2001	2002	2003	2004	2005	2006	2007	2008
Total	10.10	10.60	11.10	12.00	12.40	12.80	13.01	13.40	13.80	.
15	9.50	9.90	10.30	11.30	11.60	11.90	12.12	12.50	12.90	
16	12.60	13.40	13.70	17.60	15.30	18.70	19.79	16.40	18.80	
17	8.80	9.30	9.80	10.50	11.10	11.30	11.53	12.00	12.40	
18	8.70	9.20	9.40	10.10	10.70	10.90	11.11	11.20	11.60	
19	8.70	9.20	9.70	10.50	10.80	11.20	11.15	11.70	12.00	
20	8.20	8.60	9.10	9.90	10.20	10.50	10.86	11.10	11.50	
21	11.10	11.50	12.10	13.10	13.70	14.20	14.31	14.60	15.10	
22	11.60	12.30	12.90	13.50	13.90	14.10	14.36	14.60	14.80	
23	15.10	15.90	16.90	18.60	19.10	19.90	20.64	21.60	22.30	
24	12.00	12.70	13.10	14.20	14.90	15.00	15.62	16.30	16.70	
25	9.80	10.20	10.70	11.40	11.90	12.30	12.61	12.80	13.20	
26	10.10	10.70	11.10	12.30	12.60	12.90	13.19	13.50	14.20	
27	11.00	11.50	12.20	13.00	13.50	13.90	13.96	15.00	15.60	
28	9.70	10.00	10.50	11.30	11.60	11.90	12.19	12.60	13.00	
29	10.40	10.80	11.30	12.20	12.60	13.00	13.19	13.60	14.00	
30	9.70	10.00	10.20	11.70	11.90	12.90	14.00	14.40	13.80	
31	10.30	10.70	11.30	12.30	12.80	13.10	13.37	13.90	14.20	
32	10.00	10.60	11.30	12.40	12.60	13.20	13.18	13.10	13.60	
33	9.90	10.40	11.00	11.50	12.00	12.40	12.92	13.30	13.60	
34	11.10	11.70	12.10	13.10	13.90	14.10	14.35	14.70	15.10	
35	11.80	12.30	12.60	14.40	14.70	14.90	15.19	15.70	16.10	
36	9.00	9.40	9.90	10.50	10.80	11.20	11.43	11.90	12.20	
37	8.40	8.90	9.30	10.30	10.70	11.00	11.35	11.80	12.20	

Women - Femmes - Mujeres
ISIC 3 - CITI 3 - CIIU 3

	1999	2000	2001	2002	2003	2004	2005	2006	2007	2008
Total	8.30	8.70	9.10	10.00	10.30	10.70	10.99	11.30	11.70	.
15	8.00	8.40	8.90	9.70	10.00	10.30	10.57	10.90	11.10	
16	10.10	12.00	11.70	13.90	12.30	16.40	17.30	13.60	16.50	
17	7.50	7.90	8.30	8.90	9.20	9.50	9.83	10.10	10.60	
18	7.30	7.70	8.00	8.60	9.00	9.30	9.54	9.90	10.30	
19	7.90	8.30	8.60	9.50	9.70	10.00	10.33	10.80	11.20	
20	7.50	7.90	8.30	8.80	9.20	9.40	9.69	10.00	10.40	
21	8.30	8.70	9.10	10.00	10.50	10.70	11.02	11.20	11.50	
22	9.10	9.50	9.90	10.80	11.20	11.50	11.82	12.00	12.10	
23	10.10	12.30	13.60	14.40	14.60	14.90	15.28	15.80	16.90	
24	9.70	10.30	10.60	11.70	12.20	12.60	13.05	13.70	14.10	
25	8.10	8.50	8.90	9.70	10.10	10.00	10.94	11.10	11.40	
26	8.40	8.60	9.10	9.90	10.20	10.50	10.87	11.10	11.70	
27	8.70	9.00	9.60	10.90	10.80	11.10	11.27	11.70	12.10	
28	8.20	8.50	9.00	9.60	9.90	10.20	10.82	10.80	11.20	
29	8.90	9.10	9.70	10.30	10.70	11.10	11.53	11.70	12.00	
30	8.50	9.10	9.20	10.20	10.30	11.00	12.97	12.50	12.30	
31	8.70	9.20	9.60	10.50	11.10	11.30	11.67	12.20	12.70	
32	8.80	9.20	9.90	11.30	11.30	11.60	11.50	11.50	12.10	
33	8.40	8.80	9.30	10.10	10.70	10.90	11.31	11.70	12.20	
34	9.50	10.00	10.40	11.60	11.80	11.90	12.22	12.60	12.90	
35	8.20	8.50	8.70	10.30	11.30	11.00	11.03	11.30	11.90	
36	8.10	8.60	8.90	9.60	9.80	10.20	10.47	11.00	11.20	
37	7.20	7.30	7.70	8.30	8.50	8.90	9.33	9.80	10.10	

Explanatory notes: see p. 877.   Notes explicatives: voir p. 879.   Notas explicativas: véase p. 882.

In manufacturing   **Dans les industries manufacturières**   **En las industrias manufactureras**

	1999	2000	2001	2002	2003	2004	2005	2006	2007	2008	

Germany (DA)   Employees - Salariés - Asalariados   E.G./h. - Euro

Total men and women - Total hommes et femmes - Total hombres y mujeres
ISIC 3 - CITI 3 - CIIU 3

	1999	2000	2001	2002	2003	2004	2005	2006	2007	2008
Total	.	.	.	.	.	.	.	.	19.09	19.51
15	.	.	.	.	.	.	.	.	13.49	13.67
16	.	.	.	.	.	.	.	.	23.46	24.17
17	.	.	.	.	.	.	.	.	14.72	14.92
18	.	.	.	.	.	.	.	.	16.08	16.43
19	.	.	.	.	.	.	.	.	15.72	16.61
20	.	.	.	.	.	.	.	.	14.60	14.73
21	.	.	.	.	.	.	.	.	17.23	17.59
22	.	.	.	.	.	.	.	.	20.52	20.91
23	.	.	.	.	.	.	.	.	26.66	27.57
24	.	.	.	.	.	.	.	.	22.16	22.72
25	.	.	.	.	.	.	.	.	15.92	16.11
26	.	.	.	.	.	.	.	.	15.87	16.22
27	.	.	.	.	.	.	.	.	19.97	20.65
28	.	.	.	.	.	.	.	.	16.65	16.96
29	.	.	.	.	.	.	.	.	20.55	20.96
30	.	.	.	.	.	.	.	.	23.51	24.18
31	.	.	.	.	.	.	.	.	20.04	20.33
32	.	.	.	.	.	.	.	.	21.78	22.49
33	.	.	.	.	.	.	.	.	20.34	20.84
34	.	.	.	.	.	.	.	.	23.01	23.67
35	.	.	.	.	.	.	.	.	22.25	22.91
36	.	.	.	.	.	.	.	.	15.58	15.88
37	.	.	.	.	.	.	.	.	13.16	13.33

Men - Hommes - Hombres
ISIC 3 - CITI 3 - CIIU 3

	1999	2000	2001	2002	2003	2004	2005	2006	2007	2008
Total	.	.	.	.	.	.	.	.	20.01	20.46
15	.	.	.	.	.	.	.	.	15.21	15.45
16	.	.	.	.	.	.	.	.	25.50	26.21
17	.	.	.	.	.	.	.	.	16.33	16.61
18	.	.	.	.	.	.	.	.	21.06	21.30
19	.	.	.	.	.	.	.	.	18.30	19.40
20	.	.	.	.	.	.	.	.	14.82	14.95
21	.	.	.	.	.	.	.	.	18.03	18.41
22	.	.	.	.	.	.	.	.	21.97	22.36
23	.	.	.	.	.	.	.	.	27.29	28.22
24	.	.	.	.	.	.	.	.	23.22	23.80
25	.	.	.	.	.	.	.	.	16.75	16.96
26	.	.	.	.	.	.	.	.	16.20	16.55
27	.	.	.	.	.	.	.	.	20.16	20.83
28	.	.	.	.	.	.	.	.	17.00	17.33
29	.	.	.	.	.	.	.	.	20.95	21.33
30	.	.	.	.	.	.	.	.	25.11	25.82
31	.	.	.	.	.	.	.	.	21.65	21.96
32	.	.	.	.	.	.	.	.	23.88	24.55
33	.	.	.	.	.	.	.	.	22.38	22.91
34	.	.	.	.	.	.	.	.	23.37	24.03
35	.	.	.	.	.	.	.	.	22.45	23.10
36	.	.	.	.	.	.	.	.	16.34	16.60
37	.	.	.	.	.	.	.	.	13.37	13.53

Women - Femmes - Mujeres
ISIC 3 - CITI 3 - CIIU 3

	1999	2000	2001	2002	2003	2004	2005	2006	2007	2008
Total	.	.	.	.	.	.	.	.	15.27	15.61
15	.	.	.	.	.	.	.	.	10.61	10.77
16	.	.	.	.	.	.	.	.	19.09	19.86
17	.	.	.	.	.	.	.	.	11.91	12.02
18	.	.	.	.	.	.	.	.	13.67	14.06
19	.	.	.	.	.	.	.	.	12.90	13.55
20	.	.	.	.	.	.	.	.	12.68	12.86
21	.	.	.	.	.	.	.	.	13.98	14.22
22	.	.	.	.	.	.	.	.	17.56	17.98
23	.	.	.	.	.	.	.	.	23.01	23.90
24	.	.	.	.	.	.	.	.	19.08	19.60
25	.	.	.	.	.	.	.	.	12.75	12.87
26	.	.	.	.	.	.	.	.	13.85	14.18
27	.	.	.	.	.	.	.	.	17.96	18.68
28	.	.	.	.	.	.	.	.	14.28	14.53
29	.	.	.	.	.	.	.	.	17.70	18.19
30	.	.	.	.	.	.	.	.	17.98	18.48
31	.	.	.	.	.	.	.	.	15.22	15.34
32	.	.	.	.	.	.	.	.	16.01	16.61
33	.	.	.	.	.	.	.	.	15.26	15.59
34	.	.	.	.	.	.	.	.	19.96	20.60
35	.	.	.	.	.	.	.	.	20.54	21.25
36	.	.	.	.	.	.	.	.	12.92	13.29
37	.	.	.	.	.	.	.	.	11.82	12.05

Explanatory notes: see p. 877.   Notes explicatives: voir p. 879.   Notas explicativas: véase p. 882.

5B

WAGES	SALAIRES	SALARIOS
In manufacturing	Dans les industries manufacturières	En las industrias manufactureras

	1999	2000	2001[1]	2002	2003	2004	2005	2006[2]	2007	2008

Germany (DA) Wage earners - Ouvriers - Obreros E.G./h. - Euro

Total men and women - Total hommes et femmes - Total hombres y mujeres
ISIC 3 - CITI 3 - CIIU 3

	1999	2000	2001	2002	2003	2004	2005	2006	2007	2008
Total	27.53	27.78	14.42	14.72	15.09	15.40	15.60	15.74	.	.
15	23.30	23.27	12.11	12.38	12.70	12.94	13.12	13.27	.	.
16	28.28	29.21	14.08	15.70	16.05	16.53	16.24	16.03	.	.
17	20.98	20.82	10.84	11.11	11.25	11.56	11.59	11.69	.	.
18	18.90	18.88	9.83	10.09	10.25	10.45	10.55	10.86	.	.
19	19.48	19.61	10.05	10.28	10.50	10.57	10.60	10.71	.	.
20	23.88	23.62	12.21	12.42	12.56	12.74	12.75	12.78	.	.
21	26.07	26.75	13.88	14.18	14.53	14.84	15.00	15.28	.	.
22	30.53	30.70	15.95	16.19	16.39	16.49	16.56	16.41	.	.
23	32.88	33.98	17.86	18.14	19.00	19.40	19.35	19.82	.	.
24	28.55	29.37	15.22	15.54	15.85	15.93	16.13	16.24	.	.
25	24.16	24.50	12.69	13.06	13.34	13.52	13.69	13.80	.	.
26	24.31	24.48	12.71	12.96	13.29	13.44	13.51	13.66	.	.
27	28.83	30.05	15.55	15.93	16.23	16.63	16.85	17.23	.	.
28	25.49	25.66	13.28	13.60	13.86	14.05	14.21	14.37	.	.
29	28.77	29.19	15.14	15.49	15.92	16.32	16.55	16.73	.	.
30	26.05	25.18	13.12	13.49	13.59	13.41	13.40	13.45	.	.
31	26.51	26.36	13.65	14.06	14.41	14.73	14.91	15.07	.	.
32	26.08	26.44	13.66	13.92	14.24	14.37	14.46	14.55	.	.
33	25.98	25.80	13.31	13.59	13.95	14.27	14.50	14.62	.	.
34	35.21	35.24	18.08	18.01	18.58	19.24	19.56	19.59	.	.
35	28.64	29.16	15.31	15.76	16.13	16.33	16.67	16.91	.	.
36	23.82	23.82	12.40	12.67	12.91	13.07	13.18	13.26	.	.
37	20.18	20.51	10.85	11.28	11.38	11.67	11.77	11.94	.	.

Men - Hommes - Hombres
ISIC 3 - CITI 3 - CIIU 3

	1999	2000	2001	2002	2003	2004	2005	2006	2007	2008
Total	28.79	29.10	15.09	15.37	15.74	16.04	16.24	16.37	.	.
15	25.02	25.14	13.09	13.35	13.67	13.89	14.07	14.24	.	.
16	30.92	31.85	15.55	17.01	17.46	18.02	17.58	17.20	.	.
17	22.89	23.15	12.06	12.32	12.45	12.75	12.78	12.90	.	.
18	22.14	22.39	11.65	11.85	12.05	12.14	12.15	12.63	.	.
19	21.52	21.43	11.24	11.51	11.70	11.77	11.79	11.85	.	.
20	24.32	24.03	12.41	12.61	12.75	12.91	12.91	12.93	.	.
21	27.29	28.07	14.53	14.81	15.15	15.46	15.60	15.88	.	.
22	32.20	32.56	16.86	17.11	17.30	17.41	17.46	17.31	.	.
23	33.26	34.36	18.06	18.34	19.19	19.58	19.52	19.98	.	.
24	29.74	30.86	15.98	16.32	16.64	16.66	16.82	16.93	.	.
25	25.44	25.72	13.33	13.68	13.98	14.18	14.35	14.44	.	.
26	24.96	25.06	13.02	13.26	13.59	13.75	13.82	13.95	.	.
27	29.13	30.33	15.69	16.06	16.36	16.76	16.98	17.35	.	.
28	26.19	26.39	13.67	13.99	14.24	14.45	14.59	14.75	.	.
29	29.39	29.68	15.40	15.74	16.16	16.56	16.77	16.95	.	.
30	27.65	27.13	14.09	14.52	14.67	14.35	14.32	14.38	.	.
31	28.36	28.39	14.69	15.06	15.40	15.69	15.87	16.05	.	.
32	28.37	28.55	14.77	14.95	15.27	15.43	15.55	15.66	.	.
33	27.81	27.93	14.44	14.75	15.14	15.47	15.69	15.82	.	.
34	35.67	35.88	18.39	18.30	18.86	19.53	19.85	19.88	.	.
35	28.94	29.44	15.46	15.90	16.29	16.49	16.83	17.06	.	.
36	25.24	25.12	13.08	13.33	13.58	13.76	13.85	13.91	.	.
37	20.54	21.06	11.09	11.48	11.56	11.85	11.52	12.08	.	.

Women - Femmes - Mujeres
ISIC 3 - CITI 3 - CIIU 3

	1999	2000	2001	2002	2003	2004	2005	2006	2007	2008
Total	21.44	21.39	11.10	11.37	11.64	11.89	12.02	12.10	.	.
15	17.93	18.01	9.40	9.65	9.90	10.13	10.26	10.38	.	.
16	24.33	25.19	11.75	13.43	13.47	13.78	13.84	13.83	.	.
17	17.87	17.17	8.91	9.14	9.27	9.43	9.47	9.53	.	.
18	18.10	18.02	9.38	9.62	9.74	9.93	10.03	10.12	.	.
19	17.25	17.06	8.96	9.13	9.33	9.37	9.40	9.55	.	.
20	19.31	19.26	9.91	10.10	10.18	10.42	10.45	10.53	.	.
21	19.73	19.76	10.32	10.59	10.87	11.07	11.20	11.40	.	.
22	23.64	23.34	12.18	12.34	12.43	12.35	12.34	12.28	.	.
23	24.22	26.02	13.55	13.75	14.65	15.26	15.58	16.24	.	.
24	21.69	21.63	11.23	11.60	11.92	12.25	12.57	12.70	.	.
25	19.14	19.70	10.21	10.47	10.63	10.78	10.83	10.94	.	.
26	18.83	19.29	9.99	10.27	10.52	10.59	10.73	10.88	.	.
27	22.52	22.66	11.76	12.14	12.38	12.65	12.50	13.18	.	.
28	20.91	21.15	10.91	11.17	11.42	11.64	11.68	11.75	.	.
29	23.26	23.97	12.38	12.67	13.08	13.43	13.65	13.83	.	.
30	23.23	21.98	11.43	11.59	11.53	11.55	11.48	11.46	.	.
31	23.00	22.32	11.54	11.84	12.19	12.49	12.61	12.67	.	.
32	23.32	23.65	12.19	12.43	12.67	12.75	12.77	12.88	.	.
33	22.30	22.17	11.44	11.65	11.90	12.15	12.37	12.40	.	.
34	29.79	28.77	14.94	15.00	15.53	16.13	16.33	16.28	.	.
35	23.11	23.69	12.37	12.80	13.08	13.20	13.44	13.68	.	.
36	19.55	19.48	10.15	10.44	10.62	10.68	10.74	10.80	.	.
37	14.88	14.58	7.95	8.37	8.54	8.62	8.91	9.22	.	.

Explanatory notes: see p. 877. Notes explicatives: voir p. 879. Notas explicativas: véase p. 882.

[1] Prior to 2001: DEM; 1 Euro = 1.95583 DEM. [2] Series discontinued. [1] Avant 2001: DEM; 1 Euro = 1,95583 DEM. [2] Série arrêtée. [1] Antes de: DEM; 1 Euro = 1,95583 DEM. [2] Serie interrumpida.

	1999	2000	2001	2002	2003	2004	2005	2006	2007	2008
Gibraltar (CA) [1] [2]					Wage earners - Ouvriers - Obreros					E.G./w.s. - Pound
Total men and women - Total hommes et femmes - Total hombres y mujeres										
ISIC 2 - CITI 2 - CIIU 2										
Total	320.01	291.57	299.49	311.25	323.75	400.58	419.09	.	.	.
Men - Hommes - Hombres										
ISIC 2 - CITI 2 - CIIU 2										ISIC 3 - CITI 3 - CIIU 3
Total	332.55	299.82	306.40	339.48	333.23	414.25	433.32 |	447.42	437.20	. Total
Women - Femmes - Mujeres										
ISIC 2 - CITI 2 - CIIU 2										ISIC 3 - CITI 3 - CIIU 3
Total	210.39	213.83	233.90	237.05	235.47	249.73	259.98 |	253.71	267.90	. Total
Gibraltar (CA) [1] [2]					Wage earners - Ouvriers - Obreros					E.G./h. - Pound
Total men and women - Total hommes et femmes - Total hombres y mujeres										
ISIC 3 - CITI 3 - CIIU 3										
Total	6.83	6.44	6.56	7.02	7.21	7.96	8.42	8.85	8.76	.
Men - Hommes - Hombres										
ISIC 3 - CITI 3 - CIIU 3										
Total	7.01	6.56	6.65	7.15	7.22	8.14	8.56	9.05	8.92	.
Women - Femmes - Mujeres										
ISIC 3 - CITI 3 - CIIU 3										
Total	5.25	5.26	5.73	5.74	5.92	5.99	6.86	6.91	7.22	.
Greece (DA)					Employees - Salariés - Asalariados					E.G./m. - Euro
Total men and women - Total hommes et femmes - Total hombres y mujeres										
ISIC 3 - CITI 3 - CIIU 3										
Total	.	.	.	.	.	.	.	1 801	.	.
Hungary (DA) [3] [4]					Employees - Salariés - Asalariados					E.G./m. - Forint
Total men and women - Total hommes et femmes - Total hombres y mujeres										
ISIC 3 - CITI 3 - CIIU 3										
Total	76 099	88 551	101 700	114 297	124 770	136 992	147 234	156 813	171 564	184 185
15	71 725	84 231	97 549	107 511	114 510	122 586	128 515	133 756	144 225	153 942
16	151 757	186 138	213 365	249 961	271 009	335 593	326 169	317 664	307 981	324 195
17	53 612	61 491	71 429	79 260	82 068	88 402	93 617	108 323	111 114	121 692
18	44 757	50 639	57 690	65 335	68 127	71 971	77 503	82 180	89 266	97 727
19	46 301	53 573	62 173	69 269	73 055	80 249	87 592	90 897	102 457	110 897
20	46 181	53 513	63 856	72 572	77 877	84 913	91 137	99 685	107 967	121 141
21	103 183	115 347	132 442	139 821	142 659	154 721	164 839	171 421	197 430	213 269
22	77 688	91 077	104 137	110 046	125 012	144 867	152 287	170 080	188 526	207 260
23	154 350	188 535	220 488	251 113	330 556	384 683	407 130	465 322	470 483	497 474
24	122 076	140 798	160 474	179 305	195 994	216 147	242 180	260 348	275 048	297 350
25	76 551	88 709	105 491	118 966	130 154	139 306	147 804	155 847	166 807	173 593
26	83 097	94 214	107 757	123 883	134 303	142 883	156 011	167 102	183 005	197 791
27	96 649	117 557	132 305	148 154	163 038	187 697	198 330	221 194	227 627	230 585
28	65 455	76 424	86 773	95 700	105 160	111 853	117 108	123 378	140 935	151 557
29	78 611	89 445	101 183	116 200	126 382	139 794	148 955	155 411	168 091	181 710
30	81 393	91 063	101 105	123 263	126 009	157 972	164 419	179 198	197 384	208 148
31	84 797	97 698	109 331	122 447	131 886	143 938	150 678	160 430	175 111	183 502
32	82 040	96 571	112 711	126 711	139 769	146 474	158 303	169 722	185 310	194 956
33	77 648	90 245	103 432	106 521	121 661	136 888	146 321	151 278	165 797	176 401
34	99 774	116 631	136 112	156 038	163 938	179 974	193 170	199 210	217 954	227 693
35	94 434	110 592	124 029	136 746	142 440	169 623	171 579	201 044	215 596	220 136
36	52 172	56 528	66 701	78 553	81 659	86 887	93 085	100 314	116 366	123 793
37	75 220	87 193	91 428	106 464	100 214	107 610	113 207	122 960	132 398	142 855

Explanatory notes: see p. 877.

[1] Excl. part-time workers and juveniles. [2] Oct. of each year. [3] Full-time employees. [4] Enterprises with 5 or more employees.

Notes explicatives: voir p. 879.

[1] Non compris les travailleurs à temps partiel et les jeunes. [2] Oct. de chaque année. [3] Salariés à plein temps. [4] Entreprises occupant 5 salariés et plus.

Notas explicativas: véase p. 882.

[1] Excl. los trabajadores a tempo parcial y los jóvenes. [2] Oct. de cada año. [3] Asalariados a tiempo completo. [4] Empresas con 5 y más asalariados.

	WAGES	SALAIRES	SALARIOS
	In manufacturing	Dans les industries manufacturières	En las industrias manufactureras

	1999	2000	2001	2002	2003	2004	2005	2006	2007	2008

Hungary (DA) [1] [2] — Employees - Salariés - Asalariados — E.G./m. - Forint

Men - Hommes - Hombres
ISIC 3 - CITI 3 - CIIU 3

	1999	2000	2001	2002	2003	2004	2005	2006	2007	2008
Total	86 866	100 351	115 830	127 916	140 244	153 396	164 230	175 199	191 595	.
15	79 087	92 953	107 553	117 141	125 176	134 849	139 602	146 080	156 867	.
16	175 324	217 822	240 845	284 952	306 428	395 133	363 068	372 128	343 916	.
17	64 810	71 628	83 354	88 141	92 631	93 526	102 989	118 638	128 001	.
18	55 445	66 330	74 418	77 616	86 728	87 173	100 738	96 212	109 763	.
19	54 701	65 389	75 852	78 358	85 309	94 696	105 710	108 982	121 992	.
20	46 776	54 194	64 143	71 987	77 774	85 325	90 984	99 568	108 608	.
21	118 486	133 031	151 725	155 298	168 862	184 490	191 923	198 560	217 490	.
22	88 262	100 549	120 917	118 551	138 112	152 925	166 814	185 586	209 059	.
23	160 895	194 482	227 640	258 184	343 385	398 572	423 072	485 896	487 255	.
24	128 249	151 281	173 169	190 846	212 376	233 461	261 995	285 777	300 769	.
25	85 134	98 376	116 971	133 723	143 983	155 169	162 902	173 145	189 008	.
26	90 246	101 068	115 891	131 550	143 957	151 844	163 536	175 281	192 848	.
27	98 161	121 489	136 174	152 572	167 261	194 515	204 793	226 845	238 916	.
28	66 993	78 381	87 900	96 907	106 921	113 860	118 819	126 125	143 460	.
29	82 378	94 045	105 703	121 209	132 477	148 314	156 377	162 643	177 717	.
30	91 381	104 618	121 235	144 937	147 306	186 784	199 435	215 384	233 737	.
31	103 227	113 552	132 340	144 011	157 154	168 828	184 943	201 994	217 058	.
32	109 026	119 456	143 620	153 438	176 950	179 218	194 091	215 473	229 106	.
33	89 649	101 418	114 562	118 314	135 907	154 790	161 826	168 516	187 155	.
34	106 790	125 321	147 972	169 339	175 428	195 104	209 755	218 606	241 219	.
35	98 802	115 375	129 061	139 750	146 311	173 628	173 169	206 386	224 595	.
36	54 032	55 893	66 822	78 686	80 969	85 331	93 068	99 386	117 249	.
37	72 884	86 082	88 959	108 745	99 180	110 847	119 129	122 671	136 070	.

Women - Femmes - Mujeres
ISIC 3 - CITI 3 - CIIU 3

	1999	2000	2001	2002	2003	2004	2005	2006	2007	2008
Total	61 898	72 962	82 761	94 882	102 585	112 946	121 082	128 302	139 856	.
15	61 332	71 974	83 884	94 231	100 190	106 441	113 067	116 758	127 016	.
16	121 453	146 352	177 044	203 320	221 695	256 683	265 520	245 523	249 068	.
17	47 483	55 698	64 771	73 697	75 751	84 708	87 851	102 862	101 983	.
18	42 954	48 026	55 994	63 157	65 170	69 272	73 842	79 638	84 940	.
19	43 161	49 123	57 292	65 589	68 351	74 382	79 629	82 531	94 022	.
20	44 122	51 066	62 759	75 019	78 288	83 309	91 764	100 221	105 150	.
21	79 680	88 105	103 111	113 199	105 937	117 846	125 941	135 443	165 142	.
22	68 069	82 033	89 114	101 049	116 672	136 002	136 804	153 757	167 691	.
23	138 447	173 060	199 885	231 199	293 746	346 977	363 866	406 887	421 902	.
24	113 840	127 425	143 781	163 345	174 269	193 960	216 673	228 095	241 576	.
25	64 760	74 435	88 336	96 626	108 517	116 694	124 736	130 851	134 515	.
26	68 533	79 867	90 199	106 494	111 105	120 724	135 425	145 438	157 069	.
27	91 212	102 635	118 163	132 196	148 349	164 872	176 097	201 468	192 986	.
28	58 746	67 588	81 268	89 796	96 930	102 366	108 819	109 984	128 657	.
29	63 995	73 166	85 330	97 217	106 545	112 183	122 272	130 527	136 393	.
30	71 581	76 852	81 995	102 129	105 338	125 745	122 142	137 070	149 819	.
31	66 074	83 486	89 706	102 885	107 406	119 164	117 376	122 162	135 244	.
32	64 183	78 998	85 055	97 987	107 385	115 847	125 373	126 997	143 220	.
33	60 423	72 603	85 732	88 781	100 954	107 416	121 756	123 651	135 283	.
34	77 274	90 398	101 105	118 064	130 134	136 423	147 360	150 885	163 221	.
35	71 229	84 355	97 131	121 504	124 424	149 462	162 647	176 112	164 661	.
36	48 388	57 856	66 464	78 262	83 237	90 215	93 120	102 153	114 606	.
37	83 053	90 900	100 531	99 346	104 312	96 205	92 735	125 672	117 896	.

Iceland (DA) — Employees - Salariés - Asalariados — E.G./h. - Krona

Total men and women - Total hommes et femmes - Total hombres y mujeres
ISIC 3 - CITI 3 - CIIU 3

	1999	2000	2001	2002	2003	2004	2005	2006	2007	2008
Total	986	1 083	1 219	1 336	1 404	1 494	1 622	1 762	1 946	2 033
15	898	972	1 089	1 167	1 234	1 316	1 426	1 569	1 769	1 857

Men - Hommes - Hombres
ISIC 3 - CITI 3 - CIIU 3

	1999	2000	2001	2002	2003	2004	2005	2006	2007	2008
Total	1 132	1 242	1 383	1 496	1 568	1 670	1 812	1 961	2 131	2 216
15	1 040	1 128	1 244	1 324	1 408	1 513	1 649	1 813	2 028	2 135

Women - Femmes - Mujeres
ISIC 3 - CITI 3 - CIIU 3

	1999	2000	2001	2002	2003	2004	2005	2006	2007	2008
Total	760	833	941	1 074	1 122	1 200	1 312	1 425	1 597	1 675
15	744	810	909	976	1 019	1 084	1 171	1 279	1 440	1 523

Iceland (DA) [3] — Employees - Salariés - Asalariados — E.G./m. - Krona

Total men and women - Total hommes et femmes - Total hombres y mujeres
ISIC 3 - CITI 3 - CIIU 3

	1999	2000	2001	2002	2003	2004	2005	2006	2007	2008
Total	210 000	228 000	253 000	269 000	283 000	304 000	331 000	361 000	390 000	407 000
15	196 000	214 000	235 000	248 000	267 000	285 000	306 000	335 000	375 000	398 000

Explanatory notes: see p. 877.

[1] Full-time employees. [2] Enterprises with 5 or more employees. [3] Full-time adult employees.

Notes explicatives: voir p. 879.

[1] Salariés à plein temps. [2] Entreprises occupant 5 salariés et plus. [3] Salariés adultes à plein temps.

Notas explicativas: véase p. 882.

[1] Asalariados a tiempo completo. [2] Empresas con 5 y más asalariados. [3] Asalariados adultos a tiempo completo.

	1999	2000	2001	2002	2003	2004	2005	2006	2007	2008	

Iceland (DA) [1] — Employees - Salariés - Asalariados — E.G./m. - Krona

Men - Hommes - Hombres
ISIC 3 - CITI 3 - CIIU 3

	1999	2000	2001	2002	2003	2004	2005	2006	2007	2008
Total	238 000	256 000	282 000	297 000	312 000	335 000	365 000	398 000	426 000	443 000
15	225 000	246 000	264 000	277 000	300 000	323 000	348 000	382 000	425 000	453 000

Women - Femmes - Mujeres
ISIC 3 - CITI 3 - CIIU 3

	1999	2000	2001	2002	2003	2004	2005	2006	2007	2008
Total	145 000	160 000	180 000	200 000	212 000	231 000	254 000	272 000	303 000	318 000
15	145 000	160 000	182 000	190 000	203 000	216 000	235 000	253 000	283 000	303 000

Ireland (DA) [2][3] — Wage earners - Ouvriers - Obreros — E.G./h. - Euro

Total men and women - Total hommes et femmes - Total hombres y mujeres
ISIC 3 - CITI 3 - CIIU 3

	1999	2000	2001	2002	2003	2004	2005	2006	2007	2008
Total	9.80	10.50	11.61	12.50	12.85	13.56	13.95	14.45	.	.

Ireland (DA) [4] — Employees - Salariés - Asalariados — E.G./w.s. - Euro

Total men and women - Total hommes et femmes - Total hombres y mujeres [5]
ISIC 3 - CITI 3 - CIIU 3

	1999	2000	2001	2002	2003	2004	2005	2006	2007	2008
Total	462.26	498.19	543.91	569.77	603.54	632.82	659.38	678.26	.	.
15-16	445.35	499.29	553.78	575.11	595.26	619.73	648.11	646.95	.	.
17-18	315.23	349.43	394.98	412.53	421.19	446.03	476.42	499.65	.	.
19	297.36	324.95	383.85	401.83	396.79	400.22	444.80	475.86	.	.
20	391.36	415.55	453.66	477.65	505.84	526.05	541.72	563.93	.	.
21-22	562.69	572.45	616.22	637.10	680.32	710.99	741.49	760.20	.	.
24	552.53	587.71	635.84	677.00	721.44	776.52	814.29	849.82	.	.
25	418.79	451.19	463.82	491.99	525.27	544.04	578.79	591.79	.	.
26	500.52	518.27	534.76	574.11	609.60	629.83	657.41	684.39	.	.
27-28	453.53	471.06	500.91	544.16	561.17	584.52	617.72	646.95	.	.
29	427.32	461.91	498.40	523.08	548.20	577.21	600.89	632.15	.	.
30-33	449.53	486.50	537.61	556.26	597.30	628.96	647.51	668.51	.	.
34-35	529.32	571.80	578.98	599.10	667.08	672.35	694.24	694.84	.	.

Ireland (DA) [4] — Wage earners - Ouvriers - Obreros — E.G./h. - Euro

Total men and women - Total hommes et femmes - Total hombres y mujeres
ISIC 3 - CITI 3 - CIIU 3

	1999	2000	2001	2002	2003	2004	2005	2006	2007	2008
Total	9.79	10.40	11.47	12.29	12.87	13.45	13.94	.	.	.
15-16	9.77	10.56	11.99	12.91	13.10	13.41	13.82	.	.	.
17-18	7.70	8.44	9.52	10.04	10.32	10.57	11.05	.	.	.
19	7.19	7.51	8.54	8.73	9.02	.	9.85	.	.	.
20	.	.	.	10.88	11.37	11.67	12.08	.	.	.
21-22	11.29	11.79	12.58	13.33	14.32	14.73	15.31	.	.	.
23,36-37	9.16	9.62	10.99	11.23	11.70	12.08	12.63	.	.	.
24	11.76	12.39	13.72	14.80	15.51	17.01	17.98	.	.	.
25	9.71	10.05	10.57	11.25	11.82	12.49	13.23	.	.	.
26	10.68	11.24	11.73	12.55	13.26	13.38	14.02	.	.	.
27-28	10.02	10.29	11.03	12.17	12.42	12.91	13.63	.	.	.
29	9.46	10.14	10.97	11.36	12.08	12.67	13.30	.	.	.
30-33	8.89	9.46	10.39	11.04	11.80	12.56	12.74	.	.	.
34-35	11.18	11.90	12.80	14.18	15.15	15.83	16.35	.	.	.

Men - Hommes - Hombres
ISIC 3 - CITI 3 - CIIU 3

	1999	2000	2001	2002	2003	2004	2005	2006	2007	2008
Total	10.74	11.35	12.41	13.26	13.76	14.36	14.81	15.26	.	.
15-16	10.43	11.27	12.76	13.69	13.73	14.12	14.53	14.60	.	.
17-18	9.10	9.78	10.83	11.29	11.39	11.54	11.81	12.24	.	.
19	7.99	7.87	8.79	8.97	9.31	8.90	9.93	11.09	.	.
20	9.08	9.65	10.44	11.10	11.60	11.85	12.23	12.72	.	.
21-22	12.55	12.99	13.85	14.57	15.61	15.95	16.52	17.03	.	.
24	12.95	13.74	15.05	16.29	16.97	18.67	19.71	20.66	.	.
25	10.40	10.66	11.14	11.83	12.38	13.00	13.74	13.91	.	.
26	11.05	11.58	12.12	12.94	13.60	13.66	14.29	14.84	.	.
27-28	10.44	10.71	11.42	12.55	12.82	13.30	14.00	14.74	.	.
29	10.19	10.88	11.70	12.08	12.80	13.35	13.92	14.69	.	.
30-33	9.87	10.42	11.50	12.12	12.83	13.83	13.73	14.43	.	.
34-35	11.71	12.67	13.55	15.20	16.17	17.08	17.54	17.58	.	.

Explanatory notes: see p. 877.
[1] Full-time adult employees. [2] Incl. juveniles. [3] Sep. of each year. [4] Establishments with 10 or more persons employed. [5] Adult and non-adult rates of pay.

Notes explicatives: voir p. 879.
[1] Salariés adultes à plein temps. [2] Y compris les jeunes gens. [3] Sept. de chaque année. [4] Etablissements occupant 10 personnes et plus. [5] Salariés rémunérés sur la base de taux de salaires pour adultes et non-adultes.

Notas explicativas: véase p. 882.
[1] Asalariados adultos a tiempo completo. [2] Incl. los jóvenes. [3] Sept. de cada año. [4] Establecimientos con 10 y más trabajadores. [5] Asalariados pagados sobre la base de tasas de salarios para adultos y no adultos.

WAGES / SALAIRES / SALARIOS

In manufacturing / **Dans les industries manufacturières** / **En las industrias manufactureras**

Ireland (DA) [1][2] — Wage earners - Ouvriers - Obreros

Women - Femmes - Mujeres — ISIC 3 - CITI 3 - CIIU 3 — E.G./h. - Euro

	1999	2000	2001	2002	2003	2004	2005	2006	2007	2008
Total	8.00	8.55	9.43	10.06	10.74	11.13	11.63	12.28		
15-16	7.85	8.53	9.69	10.43	11.03	11.10	11.48	11.64		
17-18	6.81	7.20	8.00	8.53	8.99	9.22	9.91	10.20		
19	6.28	6.91	8.10	8.38	8.49	8.95	9.83	11.09		
20	10.07	11.51	11.64	10.40	9.60	9.95	10.27	10.71		
21-22	8.23	8.88	9.45	10.02	10.66	11.07	11.80	11.98		
23,36-37	7.67	8.11	9.34	9.58	10.02	10.48	11.14	11.33		
24	9.17	9.48	10.71	11.31	11.98	12.74	13.24	14.30		
25	7.54	8.05	8.60	8.95	9.34	10.07	10.64	10.72		
26	8.57	9.28	9.33	9.94	10.96	11.90	11.25	11.98		
27-28	7.07	7.42	8.11	8.70	8.95	9.57	10.41	11.98		
29	7.12	7.50	8.17	8.47	8.94	9.57	10.41	10.70		
30-33	8.13	8.64	9.40	10.06	10.84	11.30	11.75	12.67		
34-35	9.55	9.54	10.33	10.91	11.54	10.93	11.68	12.72		

Ireland (DA) [1][2] — Wage earners - Ouvriers - Obreros

Total men and women - Total hommes et femmes - Total hombres y mujeres — ISIC 3 - CITI 3 - CIIU 3 — E.G./w.s. - Euro

	1999	2000	2001	2002	2003	2004	2005	2006	2007	2008
Total	396.55	423.24	456.97	483.02	511.78	534.24	557.57	575.21		
15-16	391.82	423.87	481.78	505.32	516.38	527.76	553.46	548.50		
17-18	282.21	311.24	348.82	358.75	364.00	381.34	407.23	420.82		
19	264.01	284.04	331.83	346.34	337.92	332.33	358.45	385.27		
20	363.45	381.50	421.43	449.64	474.24	492.27	502.90	521.00		
21-22	465.82	473.56	504.71	520.75	560.00	571.50	584.39	613.94		
23,36-37	353.56	373.90	426.92	429.10	445.48	472.36	491.99	513.16		
24	493.42	516.22	557.74	595.09	630.93	690.19	733.57	761.64		
25	382.80	407.25	413.56	435.12	464.58	482.19	522.29	535.56		
26	473.86	491.18	501.53	540.16	563.30	587.49	610.23	634.60		
27-28	417.03	428.83	452.55	503.08	515.53	535.54	576.26	598.06		
29	385.28	416.64	439.67	454.05	484.32	515.79	535.10	567.78		
30-33	353.86	382.34	402.35	423.82	463.87	486.76	496.96	528.67		
34-35	491.80	534.64	531.30	552.82	623.15	627.86	650.37	649.78		

Men - Hommes - Hombres — ISIC 3 - CITI 3 - CIIU 3

	1999	2000	2001	2002	2003	2004	2005	2006	2007	2008
Total	452.97	477.73	512.38	538.38	564.90	588.91	609.91	624.45		
15-16	435.27	468.37	533.06	554.77	561.53	574.02	601.28	590.69		
17-18	358.54	387.20	420.77	432.38	433.11	442.77	454.91	473.42		
19	304.84	301.19	352.12	369.51	361.22	353.07	383.44	400.22		
20	381.07	397.15	438.40	463.67	488.41	502.70	513.64	530.76		
21-22	534.34	537.64	572.14	584.40	624.60	634.52	646.61	678.94		
24	560.37	591.41	631.68	669.48	706.13	780.28	826.72	859.29		
25	418.79	440.31	444.38	466.26	495.22	510.64	552.38	565.93		
26	500.72	515.78	527.62	570.17	589.48	614.15	633.70	655.07		
27-28	441.53	454.29	475.77	526.49	539.37	560.07	601.02	622.37		
29	423.73	456.46	478.92	492.80	523.79	556.49	572.75	603.54		
30-33	411.55	438.73	459.84	484.25	525.32	559.16	552.04	583.11		
34-35	532.88	576.01	581.39	595.70	674.79	679.34	698.20	688.26		

Women - Femmes - Mujeres — ISIC 3 - CITI 3 - CIIU 3

	1999	2000	2001	2002	2003	2004	2005	2006	2007	2008
Total	298.17	324.72	347.32	365.19	393.78	406.83	430.23	451.13		
15-16	278.21	308.03	346.40	366.91	388.16	393.06	416.76	425.51		
17-18	236.08	248.87	274.41	282.04	290.21	306.99	342.90	357.59		
19	220.26	251.29	283.72	297.26	291.78	292.68	328.05	376.05		
20	340.22	375.25	399.28	383.41	348.05	371.29	362.94	389.18		
21-22	314.08	332.85	354.96	366.90	392.95	401.54	419.34	432.01		
24	306.61	367.87	406.38	432.50	461.68	479.67	502.01	520.62		
25	277.42	301.90	314.23	319.90	341.78	364.06	381.16	386.21		
26	325.72	351.97	345.02	356.04	393.06	382.26	388.32	388.30		
27-28	248.04	259.28	281.98	293.37	307.65	329.60	365.47	383.63		
29	264.89	282.88	302.35	310.52	325.58	354.23	352.21	383.54		
30-33	311.70	337.91	352.54	370.47	407.52	419.83	444.82	474.89		
34-35	343.57	409.71	363.39	414.17	444.36	426.21	460.75	478.86		

Isle of Man (DA) [3] — Employees - Salariés - Asalariados

Total men and women - Total hommes et femmes - Total hombres y mujeres — ISIC 3 - CITI 3 - CIIU 3 — E.G./h. - Pound

	1999	2000	2001	2002	2003	2004	2005	2006	2007	2008
Total	9.08	8.53	9.02	10.26	9.65	10.35	10.56	11.00	12.00	12.88

Men - Hommes - Hombres — ISIC 3 - CITI 3 - CIIU 3

	1999	2000	2001	2002	2003	2004	2005	2006	2007	2008
Total	9.45	9.19	9.15	10.91	10.95	10.25	10.87	11.10	12.70	12.58

Explanatory notes: see p. 877.
[1] Wage-earners on adult rates of pay. [2] Establishments with 10 or more persons employed. [3] June of each year.

Notes explicatives: voir p. 879.
[1] Ouvriers rémunérés sur la base de taux de salaire pour adultes. [2] Etablissements occupant 10 personnes et plus. [3] Juin de chaque année.

Notas explicativas: véase p. 882.
[1] Obreros remunerados sobre la base de tasas de salarios para adultos. [2] Establecimientos con 10 y más trabajadores. [3] Junio de cada año.

	1999	2000	2001	2002	2003	2004	2005	2006	2007	2008	
Isle of Man (DA) [1]				Employees - Salariés - Asalariados							E.G./h. - Pound
Women - Femmes - Mujeres											
ISIC 3 - CITI 3 - CIIU 3											
Total	7.52	6.76	8.51	7.72	7.52	10.67	9.22	10.70	9.00	14.20	
Isle of Man (DA) [1]				Employees - Salariés - Asalariados							E.G./w.s. - Pound
Total men and women - Total hommes et femmes - Total hombres y mujeres											
ISIC 3 - CITI 3 - CIIU 3											
Total	377.05	366.94	361.40	392.03	409.56	412.44	441.00	445.80	482.40	539.99	
Men - Hommes - Hombres											
ISIC 3 - CITI 3 - CIIU 3											
Total	408.91	407.28	381.54	417.32	504.51	455.38	468.00	463.20	518.20	545.39	
Women - Femmes - Mujeres											
ISIC 3 - CITI 3 - CIIU 3											
Total	241.11	258.21	278.31	292.82	253.85	265.24	325.00	401.10	323.00	.	
Italy (FE)				Wage earners - Ouvriers - Obreros							R.T./h.
Indices, total - Indices, total - Índices, total											
ISIC 3 - CITI 3 - CIIU 3											
Total	110.9	113.1 |	89.2 [2]	91.7	94.0	96.7	99.4	102.7	105.6	109.1	
Italy (FE)				Salaried employees - Employés - Empleados							R.T./h.
Indices, total - Indices, total - Índices, total											
ISIC 3 - CITI 3 - CIIU 3											
Total	112.1	114.4 |	89.0 [2]	91.5	93.9	96.9	99.5	103.0	106.0	109.8	
Jersey (DA) [1][3][4]				Employees - Salariés - Asalariados							E.G./w.s. - Pound
Total men and women - Total hommes et femmes - Total hombres y mujeres											
ISIC 3 - CITI 3 - CIIU 3											
Total	400	420	450	460	480	500	530	530	550	.	
Latvia (DA) [5]				Employees - Salariés - Asalariados							E.G./m. - Lat
Total men and women - Total hommes et femmes - Total hombres y mujeres											
ISIC 3 - CITI 3 - CIIU 3											
Total	128.97	135.13	140.34	145.51	159.26	176.36	200.26	239.62	315.03	394.04	
15	141.23	142.16	145.11	147.64	156.61	172.96	187.26	226.33	297.74	379.48	
16	.	.	.	.	.	.	.	.	.	.	
17	131.03	140.41	143.37	144.93	155.58	175.76	174.75	210.20	264.94	308.84	
18	109.53	108.83	114.94	113.72	123.13	132.12	147.95	179.03	220.98	284.55	
19	85.53	90.51	95.75	89.21	104.37	107.36	127.88	160.45	209.62	259.07	
20	114.75	124.18	121.01	131.17	149.09	164.44	184.36	219.43	283.30	357.90	
21	121.37	168.84	156.60	158.59	190.47	206.68	244.83	287.28	390.48	436.49	
22	194.57	181.53	210.01	211.66	222.02	239.03	285.79	313.34	388.88	463.52	
23	.	.	.	.	.	.	.	.	.	.	
24	126.36	170.65	170.62	185.35	204.10	230.37	293.86	326.60	441.72	532.58	
25	105.85	111.19	108.29	121.99	125.59	172.50	192.78	230.48	329.94	375.75	
26	117.43	128.49	140.09	156.12	169.95	182.03	242.51	283.30	422.52	482.86	
27	208.32	218.27	223.92	238.90	248.50	288.87	304.68	364.87	462.13	590.55	
28	107.59	111.59	131.23	133.69	152.73	163.51	193.62	243.57	310.46	401.90	
29	119.70	133.18	135.71	133.51	146.45	159.28	198.93	240.54	327.45	400.55	
30	127.03	200.92	145.80	131.56	263.11	291.46	306.44	359.79	692.12	648.53	
31	116.54	145.29	153.42	167.32	228.79	222.70	274.02	309.49	442.06	568.87	
32	111.97	111.78	118.71	113.00	142.62	182.67	233.39	308.75	416.79	464.81	
33	160.12	178.06	138.98	142.58	188.63	214.48	224.90	278.83	346.25	423.61	
34	111.22	88.56	133.08	139.47	166.40	180.03	228.40	297.27	431.24	542.71	
35	112.85	120.65	148.71	160.68	166.97	181.84	211.15	267.05	316.00	448.36	
36	115.48	116.35	126.10	126.23	136.51	155.62	169.12	210.52	267.41	292.67	
37	97.64	99.04	100.30	111.91	115.03	145.59	166.07	214.93	264.50	360.99	

Explanatory notes: see p. 877.

[1] June of each year. [2] Index of hourly wage rates (Dec.2005=100). [3] Approximate levels since survey aims at measuring changes; excl. bonuses. [4] Full-time equivalent employees. [5] First quarter of each year.

Notes explicatives: voir p. 879.

[1] Juin de chaque année. [2] Indice des taux de salaire horaire (déc.2005=100). [3] Niveaux approximatifs étant donné que l'enquête vise à mesurer l'évolution; non compris les primes. [4] Salariés en équivalents à plein temps. [5] Premier trimestre de chaque année.

Notas explicativas: véase p. 882.

[1] Junio de cada año. [2] Indice de las tasas de salario por hora (dic.2005=100). [3] Niveles aproximativos ya que la encuesta tiene por objectivo medir cambios; excl. las primas. [4] Asalariados en equivalentes a tiempo completo. [5] Primer trimestre de cada año.

	WAGES			SALAIRES			SALARIOS		
	In manufacturing			**Dans les industries manufacturières**			**En las industrias manufactureras**		

	1999	2000	2001	2002	2003	2004	2005	2006	2007	2008
Latvia (DA) [1]					**Employees - Salariés - Asalariados**					**E.G./m. - Lat**
Men - Hommes - Hombres										
ISIC 3 - CITI 3 - CIIU 3										
Total	137.48	146.00	150.86	157.28	172.78	192.14	217.93	263.07	350.27	430.19
15	163.81	170.75	170.89	178.46	185.08	209.89	220.58	274.04	363.62	443.52
16										
17	175.41	173.38	162.75	179.84	192.35	207.52	196.31	260.36	354.80	356.97
18	129.62	126.46	132.32	144.02	164.79	176.38	202.63	219.06	298.36	379.26
19	96.98	89.56	108.54	89.77	111.41	104.84	129.05	193.53	191.75	282.82
20	112.76	123.93	119.97	129.20	149.30	165.82	183.45	220.88	290.15	363.19
21	132.74	201.96	178.04	180.42	212.24	235.24	285.69	324.62	471.42	486.95
22	212.68	192.05	256.28	227.01	238.11	251.44	307.81	332.06	408.11	484.07
23										
24	141.45	166.42	172.86	186.63	216.48	245.49	348.42	343.32	480.89	571.85
25	115.36	120.41	115.45	127.72	131.43	179.66	196.49	249.83	353.86	390.85
26	129.91	141.36	156.11	172.51	183.51	195.34	258.81	300.57	456.38	512.23
27	217.26	229.30	235.72	253.59	262.37	302.74	319.38	377.84	472.06	602.93
28	110.06	114.24	136.23	134.84	157.30	165.38	200.46	255.23	324.21	411.17
29	124.59	143.14	144.45	143.06	158.37	168.42	216.25	262.72	341.61	433.47
30	135.49	209.16	154.73	125.94	281.81	298.87	305.86	367.74	754.04	661.33
31	127.34	165.54	171.81	196.12	270.28	271.36	329.16	379.37	536.04	682.70
32	128.25	126.60	141.38	125.54	163.19	197.53	291.47	364.34	501.52	566.12
33	172.98	197.12	145.22	155.37	206.90	229.79	256.98	307.63	369.12	486.57
34	113.00	91.53	134.77	141.07	169.94	182.43	224.90	303.00	441.30	549.91
35	121.41	127.64	157.81	170.04	174.15	194.44	222.10	279.27	335.89	473.67
36	116.56	120.79	132.03	128.52	138.98	162.44	174.15	217.42	275.75	297.14
37	97.20	98.08	97.97	113.91	116.88	150.78	171.35	221.16	268.59	369.85
Women - Femmes - Mujeres										
ISIC 3 - CITI 3 - CIIU 3										
Total	118.52	122.92	127.13	131.05	141.96	155.85	177.27	208.95	269.73	346.68
15	123.03	120.72	124.85	125.13	134.48	145.04	162.19	192.21	251.41	332.85
16										
17	110.74	125.65	134.12	130.26	139.24	160.84	165.29	187.44	228.31	289.62
18	106.94	106.94	112.82	110.47	118.80	127.36	142.33	172.93	210.71	273.06
19	78.71	91.03	88.41	88.72	100.57	109.00	127.22	142.90	216.91	248.01
20	123.86	125.28	125.35	138.58	148.08	159.30	187.55	214.64	262.24	342.46
21	104.73	127.04	123.31	127.20	157.06	163.50	193.77	234.42	277.36	366.63
22	181.65	174.79	174.53	200.12	210.95	229.96	270.71	298.47	373.18	449.41
23										
24	115.24	174.57	168.43	184.03	193.02	216.37	250.02	313.54	412.34	501.98
25	86.83	97.54	94.72	108.31	111.69	154.65	182.71	194.06	280.42	339.90
26	95.36	102.93	110.34	121.73	140.09	147.74	206.01	243.09	324.89	399.10
27	175.88	177.52	179.86	184.14	196.69	232.58	246.05	315.01	426.84	544.87
28	99.30	103.79	113.55	128.89	135.21	156.47	168.28	207.45	259.08	362.06
29	105.99	105.95	113.01	108.73	118.18	136.60	154.95	182.43	294.86	319.51
30	105.72	176.34	126.17	194.04	205.88	264.76	309.05	326.26	479.40	602.84
31	101.80	116.03	129.65	130.88	171.96	167.13	202.70	228.66	333.03	430.34
32	91.79	92.81	91.52	95.52	114.57	161.95	157.52	212.66	303.41	341.47
33	128.12	137.06	125.45	118.29	155.98	183.35	178.90	231.32	305.80	340.93
34	95.62	74.75	125.19	129.00	144.24	166.28	253.66	264.05	391.41	518.16
35	84.05	94.99	109.64	122.00	137.25	133.42	164.64	220.41	243.79	362.72
36	113.35	110.76	116.33	121.65	131.77	143.00	159.18	198.28	251.10	285.05
37	99.39	104.27	107.64	104.56	104.98	123.27	146.46	185.66	248.66	329.18
Liechtenstein (F) [2]					**Employees - Salariés - Asalariados**					**E.G./m. - Swiss franc**
Total men and women - Total hommes et femmes - Total hombres y mujeres										
ISIC 3 - CITI 3 - CIIU 3										
15-20 [3]							4 481			
21-22							6 199			
24-26							4 968			
27-28							5 355			
29-35							6 909			
36-37 [4]							6 257			
Men - Hommes - Hombres										
ISIC 3 - CITI 3 - CIIU 3										
15-20 [3]							5 196			
21-22							6 587			
24-26							5 731			
27-28							5 483			
29-35							7 493			
36-37 [4]							6 558			

Explanatory notes: see p. 877.

Notes explicatives: voir p. 879.

Notas explicativas: véase p. 882.

[1] First quarter of each year. [2] Median. [3] Incl. mining and quarrying. [4] Incl. electricity, gas and water.

[1] Premier trimestre de chaque année. [2] Médiane. [3] Y compris les industries extractives. [4] Y compris l'électricité, le gaz et l'eau.

[1] Primer trimestre de cada año. [2] Mediana. [3] Incl. las minas y canteras. [4] Incl. electricidad, gas y agua.

WAGES SALAIRES SALARIOS 5B

In manufacturing
Dans les industries manufacturières
En las industrias manufactureras

	1999	2000	2001	2002	2003	2004	2005	2006	2007	2008
Liechtenstein (F) [1]				Employees - Salariés - Asalariados						E.G./m. - Swiss franc

Women - Femmes - Mujeres
ISIC 3 - CITI 3 - CIIU 3

	1999	2000	2001	2002	2003	2004	2005	2006	2007	2008
15-20 [2]	.	.	.	.	.	.	4 167	.	.	.
21-22	.	.	.	.	.	.	.	.	.	.
24-26	.	.	.	.	.	.	4 489	.	.	.
27-28	.	.	.	.	.	.	4 683	.	.	.
29-35	.	.	.	.	.	.	5 277	.	.	.
36-37 [3]	.	.	.	.	.	.	.	.	.	.

	1999	2000	2001	2002	2003	2004	2005	2006	2007	2008
Lithuania (DA) [4][5]				Employees - Salariés - Asalariados						E.G./h. - Litas

Total men and women - Total hommes et femmes - Total hombres y mujeres
ISIC 3 - CITI 3 - CIIU 3

	1999	2000	2001	2002	2003	2004	2005	2006	2007	2008
Total	6.16 [6]	6.21	6.33	6.48	6.60	6.87	7.61	8.94	11.01	12.82
15-16	6.01 [6]	6.11	6.15	6.38	6.57	6.79	7.25	8.50	10.46	12.23
17	.	5.88	6.09	6.17	6.03	6.21	6.67	7.67	9.17	10.42
17-18	5.03 [6]	5.22	5.29	5.35	5.35	5.44	6.00	6.95	8.15	9.24
18	.	4.70	4.76	4.82	5.00	5.02	5.62	6.52	7.51	8.61
19	4.53 [6]	5.07	5.23	5.41	5.36	5.58	6.16	6.77	7.81	8.92
20	5.25 [6]	4.60	5.31	4.87	5.01	5.15	6.04	6.88	8.76	10.37
21-22	7.94 [6]	7.60	7.66	8.14	8.20	8.59	9.06	9.17	11.10	13.01
24	8.16 [6]	8.56	8.74	9.13	9.51	10.38	12.06	15.03	18.62	21.87
25	6.19 [6]	5.32	5.47	5.73	6.54	6.79	7.97	9.51	12.23	14.09
26	6.29 [6]	6.51	6.71	6.88	7.20	7.64	8.70	11.17	13.76	15.30
27-28	5.45 [6]	5.21	6.10	5.82	6.15	6.43	7.80	9.28	12.16	13.26
29	5.44 [6]	5.58	5.83	6.43	6.93	7.31	8.24	10.16	12.43	13.84
30-33	7.33 [6]	7.14	7.66	7.76	7.36	7.68	8.11	9.67	11.46	13.68
34-35	7.16 [6]	7.95	7.74	8.07	8.50	8.67	10.32	11.77	14.26	17.50
35	.	8.08	7.86	8.13	8.61	8.75	10.68	11.82	14.45	18.13
36-37	5.26 [6]	5.76	5.45	5.61	6.26	6.31	7.11	8.43	10.46	11.85

Men - Hommes - Hombres
ISIC 3 - CITI 3 - CIIU 3

	1999	2000	2001	2002	2003	2004	2005	2006	2007	2008
Total	6.90 [6]	6.92	7.11	7.24	7.48	7.74	8.58	10.16	12.70	14.88
15-16	6.61 [6]	6.77	7.09	7.31	7.46	7.86	8.29	10.00	12.60	15.05
17	.	6.66	6.91	7.12	6.91	7.16	7.86	9.25	11.07	12.90
17-18	5.98 [6]	6.43	6.45	6.63	6.67	6.88	7.52	9.01	10.52	12.30
18	.	5.92	5.61	5.74	6.31	6.44	7.01	8.59	9.51	11.33
19	5.18 [6]	5.69	5.79	6.20	6.42	6.66	7.56	8.14	9.86	11.59
20	5.20 [6]	4.54	5.26	4.79	4.87	5.07	5.98	6.86	8.91	10.65
21-22	8.45 [6]	8.36	8.27	8.86	8.84	9.60	10.23	10.09	13.01	15.20
24	9.60 [6]	9.57	9.68	10.01	10.41	11.41	13.34	17.12	21.35	24.69
25	6.85 [6]	5.73	5.87	6.02	6.89	7.06	8.48	10.05	13.03	15.18
26	6.80 [6]	6.95	7.00	7.13	7.45	7.98	9.05	11.55	14.43	16.03
27-28	5.68 [6]	5.36	6.31	5.97	6.31	6.48	7.94	9.58	12.68	13.63
29	5.80 [6]	5.92	6.13	6.71	7.24	7.61	8.67	10.81	13.40	15.17
30-33	8.60 [6]	8.30	8.91	9.25	9.01	9.55	10.08	11.93	14.55	17.26
34-35	7.73 [6]	8.50	8.09	8.36	8.80	8.93	10.65	12.26	14.85	18.52
35	.	8.65	8.23	8.43	8.93	9.04	11.12	12.35	15.10	19.08
36-37	5.43 [6]	5.90	5.55	5.69	6.40	6.46	7.39	8.86	11.10	12.56

Women - Femmes - Mujeres
ISIC 3 - CITI 3 - CIIU 3

	1999	2000	2001	2002	2003	2004	2005	2006	2007	2008
Total	5.35 [6]	5.47	5.51	5.67	5.79	5.92	6.50	7.52	9.01	10.41
15-16	5.43 [6]	5.49	5.17	5.53	5.73	5.84	6.33	7.25	8.80	10.13
17	.	5.54	5.74	5.76	5.63	5.79	6.15	6.98	8.28	9.27
17-18	4.76 [6]	4.92	5.03	5.06	5.07	5.13	5.66	6.50	7.60	8.58
18	.	4.55	4.66	4.71	4.84	4.85	5.44	6.28	7.27	8.30
19	4.19 [6]	4.69	4.93	4.98	4.83	5.01	5.36	5.98	6.81	7.64
20	5.50 [6]	4.89	5.47	5.14	5.54	5.44	6.26	6.96	8.34	9.71
21-22	7.48 [6]	6.92	7.09	7.47	7.62	7.66	8.07	8.41	9.60	11.25
24	6.28 [6]	7.19	7.54	7.91	8.22	8.85	10.07	11.77	14.42	17.01
25	4.92 [6]	4.44	4.51	4.96	5.57	6.00	6.61	8.12	10.13	11.66
26	5.57 [6]	5.51	5.93	6.21	6.50	6.71	7.59	9.89	11.53	12.92
27-28	4.53 [6]	4.66	5.26	5.23	5.47	6.13	7.09	7.88	9.86	11.64
29	4.62 [6]	4.78	5.11	5.61	6.00	6.42	6.97	8.43	9.98	10.91
30-33	5.91 [6]	6.03	6.32	6.29	5.99	6.17	6.52	7.92	9.13	10.66
34-35	5.50 [6]	6.09	6.33	6.83	7.14	7.45	8.82	9.61	11.67	13.41
35	.	6.16	6.38	6.85	7.18	7.45	8.85	9.60	11.73	14.10
36-37	4.89 [6]	5.50	5.23	5.45	5.95	6.00	6.59	7.70	9.47	10.77

Explanatory notes: see p. 877.

Notes explicatives: voir p. 879.

Notas explicativas: véase p. 882.

[1] Median. [2] Incl. mining and quarrying. [3] Incl. electricity, gas and water. [4] Excl. individual unincorporated enterprises. [5] All employees converted into full-time units. [6] April.

[1] Médiane. [2] Y compris les industries extractives. [3] Y compris l'électricité, le gaz et l'eau. [4] Non compris les entreprises individuelles non constituées en société. [5] Ensemble des salariés convertis en unités à plein temps. [6] Avril.

[1] Mediana. [2] Incl. las minas y canteras. [3] Incl. electricidad, gas y agua. [4] Excl. las empresas individuales no constituidas en sociedad. [5] Todos los asalariados convertidos en unidades a tiempo completo. [6] Abril.

5B

WAGES

In manufacturing

SALAIRES

Dans les industries manufacturières

SALARIOS

En las industrias manufactureras

	1999	2000	2001	2002	2003	2004	2005	2006	2007	2008

Lithuania (DA) [1] — Employees - Salariés - Asalariados — E.G./m. - Litas

Total men and women - Total hommes et femmes - Total hombres y mujeres
ISIC 3 - CITI 3 - CIIU 3

	1999	2000	2001	2002	2003	2004	2005	2006	2007	2008
Total	963	955	963	982	1 016	1 085	1 184	1 387	1 727	2 035
15	959	917	933	954	989	1 013	1 101	1 283	1 607	
15-16	974	934	954	976	1 014	1 043	1 132	1 312	1 630	1 947
16										
17	892	921	957	938	947	1 018	1 046	1 205	1 456	1 647
17-18	797	797	796	806	813	862	921	1 060	1 269	1 467
18	726	718	702	740	746	783	854	977	1 182	1 374
19	749	768	812	800	827	898	934	1 026	1 174	1 408
20	691	664	656	686	712	766	895	1 066	1 349	1 581
21	1 042	1 073	1 116	1 175	1 243	1 348	1 360	1 584	1 886	
22	1 238	1 171	1 279	1 312	1 271	1 385	1 392	1 424	1 711	
23										
24	1 450	1 505	1 471	1 521	1 617	1 734	1 941	2 405	3 009	3 575
25	835	879	899	886	992	1 090	1 271	1 512	1 923	2 272
26	1 034	975	1 008	1 049	1 112	1 214	1 352	1 690	2 111	2 349
27	929	1 099	1 205	979	1 065	1 433	1 463	1 601	2 115	
27-28	860	883	891	866	980	1 055	1 208	1 470	1 936	2 214
28	847	850	846	851	973	1 222	1 192	1 463	1 922	
29	912	961	939	1 068	1 130	1 222	1 337	1 648	2 018	2 252
30	722	677	894	883	871	965	1 112	1 320	1 726	
31	920	1 033	1 078	1 032	1 032	1 138	1 185	1 471	1 740	
32	1 183	1 298	1 379	1 432	1 285	1 377	1 404	1 648	1 958	
33	1 111	1 135	1 172	1 269	1 289	1 441	1 473	1 699	2 016	
34	938	640	626	763	945	1 019	1 166	1 559	2 041	
34-35	1 213	1 264	1 388	1 344	1 390	1 456	1 659	1 893	2 310	2 874
35	1 281	1 303	1 425	1 379	1 417	1 486	1 737	1 947	2 361	
36	870	821	802	847	938	1 016	1 115	1 295	1 616	
37	985	858	775	771	819	1 027	1 204	1 511	2 092	

Luxembourg (CA) [2] — Wage earners - Ouvriers - Obreros — E.G./h. - Euro

Total men and women - Total hommes et femmes - Total hombres y mujeres
ISIC 3 - CITI 3 - CIIU 3

	1999	2000	2001	2002	2003	2004	2005	2006	2007	2008
Total	12.22	12.54	12.62	13.10	13.49	14.18	14.68	14.67	14.82	15.08
15	9.64	9.82	10.04	10.31	10.60	11.18	11.70	11.62	11.75	11.89
17	14.28	14.87	14.82	15.37	15.80	16.84	17.17	16.68	16.78	16.96
20	10.29	10.76	11.13	11.54	11.86	12.54	12.83	12.99	13.34	13.64
22	12.89	13.24	13.44	14.13	14.62	15.31	15.56	15.56	16.17	16.57
24	11.16	11.11	11.45	11.91	12.04	12.79	13.20	13.27	12.73	13.04
25	14.08	14.95	14.87	15.36	15.13	15.71	16.17	16.13	16.19	16.39
26	10.68	11.33	11.85	12.22	12.62	13.76	14.40	14.30	14.59	15.01
27	15.32	15.72	15.32	15.84	16.32	17.15	17.92	18.24	18.53	19.02
28	11.80	12.20	12.27	12.77	13.28	13.78	14.27	14.21	14.50	14.67
29	12.94	13.26	13.44	13.80	14.24	14.92	15.55	15.34	15.63	15.26
31	11.50	12.20	11.87	12.28	12.95	13.15	13.77	13.33	13.72	14.28
33	9.10	10.11	9.92	10.24	10.73	11.42	11.89	11.97	12.22	12.57
34	9.52	10.04	10.44	10.70	11.17	11.50	11.83	11.78	11.95	12.32
36	10.16	10.59	10.29	10.86	11.88	12.36	12.56	12.60	13.05	13.61
37	11.28	11.77	11.60	11.99	12.45	12.85	13.56	13.52	13.63	14.29

Men - Hommes - Hombres
ISIC 3 - CITI 3 - CIIU 3

	1999	2000	2001	2002	2003	2004	2005	2006	2007	2008
Total	12.74	13.06	13.11	13.61	14.02	14.71	15.19	15.18	15.31	15.57
15	10.41	10.51	10.68	11.02	11.26	11.86	12.42	12.30	12.41	12.52
17	14.70	15.27	15.32	15.80	16.22	17.30	17.73	17.40	17.25	17.41
20	10.39	10.78	11.20	11.60	11.90	12.58	12.87	13.03	13.38	13.67
22	13.66	13.91	14.20	14.80	15.16	15.87	16.26	16.20	16.70	17.08
24	11.43	11.48	11.80	12.31	12.57	13.22	13.64	13.73	13.17	13.54
25	14.15	15.05	14.95	15.45	15.31	15.91	16.34	16.30	16.34	16.52
26	10.96	11.53	12.07	12.44	12.78	13.90	14.43	14.43	14.71	15.12
27	15.34	15.74	15.34	15.88	16.36	17.18	17.95	18.27	18.57	19.06
28	11.87	12.25	12.35	12.84	13.36	13.86	14.35	14.29	14.58	14.77
29	13.09	13.41	13.58	13.95	14.38	15.09	15.73	15.55	15.81	15.26
31	11.70	12.37	12.02	12.41	13.10	13.32	13.98	13.46	13.89	14.44
33	10.34	11.08	11.18	11.65	12.05	12.72	13.03	13.19	13.56	13.90
34	9.77	10.24	10.66	10.91	11.50	11.74	12.08	11.98	12.16	12.51
36	10.29	10.59	10.29	11.12	12.07	12.54	12.63	12.71	13.16	13.74
37	11.38	11.77	11.60	12.10	12.66	13.18	13.89	14.03	14.10	14.60

Explanatory notes: see p. 877.

[1] All employees converted into full-time units. [2] Oct. of each year.

Notes explicatives: voir p. 879.

[1] Ensemble des salariés convertis en unités à plein temps. [2] Oct. de chaque année.

Notas explicativas: véase p. 882.

[1] Todos los asalariados convertidos en unidades a tiempo completo. [2] Oct. de cada año.

	1999	2000	2001	2002	2003	2004	2005	2006	2007	2008

Luxembourg (CA) [1]   Wage earners - Ouvriers - Obreros   E.G./h. - Euro

Women - Femmes - Mujeres
ISIC 3 - CITI 3 - CIIU 3

	1999	2000	2001	2002	2003	2004	2005	2006	2007	2008
Total	8.70	9.35	9.47	9.80	10.22	10.58	11.07	10.96	11.12	11.35
15	7.64	8.03	8.40	8.51	8.89	9.39	9.82	9.85	10.03	10.24
17	8.43	9.10	9.00	9.11	9.41	9.72	10.02	10.08	10.23	10.56
20	9.02	10.04	9.84	10.57	11.05	11.70	12.07	11.91	12.29	12.35
22	9.64	10.31	10.59	11.28	12.05	12.57	12.55	12.67	13.22	13.59
24	9.79	9.69	10.06	10.25	10.30	10.99	11.30	11.38	10.98	11.20
25	10.83	10.66	11.28	11.42	11.28	11.27	11.65	11.79	12.16	12.52
26	9.57	10.16	10.59	10.04	11.70	12.45	14.04	12.61	12.92	13.41
27	10.78	10.93	11.25	11.55	11.68	12.49	13.10	13.21	13.21	13.67
28	9.37	9.77	9.89	10.17	10.55	10.75	11.40	11.44	11.94	11.90
29	9.22	9.74	9.47	9.74	10.38	11.15	11.54	11.28	12.09	11.86
31	9.42	10.56	10.31	10.41	10.86	10.67	10.90	11.23	11.75	12.05
33	8.45	9.62	9.22	9.43	9.94	10.54	11.10	11.13	11.24	11.54
34	7.96	8.63	8.97	9.18	9.34	9.57	10.05	10.07	10.23	10.34
36	9.47	9.97	9.42	9.88	9.79	10.51	11.52	11.85	11.62	12.15
37	7.29	7.36	9.87	8.49	8.88	8.44	8.75	8.79	9.18	9.62

Luxembourg (CA) [1]   Salaried employees - Employés - Empleados   E.G./m. - Euro

Total men and women - Total hommes et femmes - Total hombres y mujeres
ISIC 3 - CITI 3 - CIIU 3

	1999	2000	2001	2002	2003	2004	2005	2006	2007	2008
Total	3 680	3 727	3 816	3 941	4 090	4 189	4 334	4 374	4 506	4 650
15	2 943	3 136	3 177	3 215	3 259	3 455	3 518	3 418	3 630	3 515
17	3 720	3 878	4 074	4 222	4 361	4 548	4 605	4 945	5 034	5 138
20	3 267	3 473	3 319	3 588	3 855	3 876	3 910	3 866	3 845	3 873
22	3 255	3 295	3 394	3 519	3 690	3 745	3 903	3 874	4 023	4 138
24	3 370	3 408	3 457	3 477	3 613	3 568	3 714	3 775	3 225	3 332
25	4 179	4 166	4 263	4 400	4 362	4 446	4 657	4 561	4 667	4 681
26	3 416	3 497	3 641	3 671	3 793	3 923	4 023	4 124	4 262	4 406
27	4 287	4 393	4 469	4 723	4 940	5 217	5 473	5 566	5 663	5 926
28	3 386	3 498	3 540	3 583	3 769	3 747	3 884	3 945	4 123	4 176
29	3 669	3 785	3 912	4 061	4 200	4 213	4 143	4 174	4 371	4 331
31	3 215	3 664	3 405	3 439	3 486	3 449	3 558	3 542	3 658	3 772
32	.	.	.	.	.	.	.	.	.	.
33	2 809	2 933	3 099	3 200	3 409	3 575	3 883	3 856	4 018	4 324
34	2 868	2 999	3 125	3 361	3 463	3 578	3 654	3 784	3 782	3 935
36	2 576	2 702	2 643	2 884	2 768	2 955	2 948	2 844	3 171	3 727
37	3 449	3 759	3 765	3 906	4 012	4 156	4 340	3 974	4 049	4 132

Men - Hommes - Hombres
ISIC 3 - CITI 3 - CIIU 3

	1999	2000	2001	2002	2003	2004	2005	2006	2007	2008
Total	3 944	3 995	4 104	4 251	4 412	4 510	4 663	4 710	4 876	5 007
15	3 417	3 673	3 777	3 860	3 916	4 184	4 196	4 129	4 388	4 120
17	3 751	3 920	4 150	4 334	4 454	4 661	4 711	5 057	5 133	5 302
20	3 631	3 834	3 648	3 981	4 290	4 332	4 337	4 264	4 336	4 292
22	3 683	3 710	3 813	3 951	4 138	4 220	4 319	4 322	4 533	4 692
24	3 617	3 652	3 695	3 706	3 865	3 802	4 015	4 202	3 697	3 776
25	4 312	4 261	4 389	4 543	4 522	4 658	4 871	4 801	4 889	4 918
26	3 689	3 714	3 957	3 982	4 079	4 425	4 321	4 403	4 577	4 730
27	4 466	4 578	4 654	4 971	5 226	5 458	5 727	5 815	5 974	6 293
28	3 625	3 748	3 806	3 855	4 037	4 014	4 146	4 190	4 419	4 463
29	3 887	4 008	4 109	4 236	4 447	4 443	4 412	4 438	4 633	4 573
31	3 524	3 937	3 679	3 756	3 871	3 699	3 818	3 835	3 843	3 948
33	3 050	3 160	3 350	3 497	3 718	3 903	4 165	4 190	4 473	4 791
34	3 087	3 182	3 380	3 670	3 747	3 829	3 827	4 000	3 980	4 297
36	2 961	3 159	2 968	3 155	2 972	3 104	3 145	3 021	3 355	3 539
37	4 014	4 313	4 389	4 777	4 670	5 003	5 031	4 635	4 787	4 715

Women - Femmes - Mujeres
ISIC 3 - CITI 3 - CIIU 3

	1999	2000	2001	2002	2003	2004	2005	2006	2007	2008
Total	2 535	2 621	2 710	2 782	2 911	3 030	3 185	3 229	3 280	3 489
15	2 064	2 182	2 198	2 177	2 247	2 297	2 430	2 328	2 484	2 582
17	3 405	3 507	3 476	3 397	3 682	3 812	3 922	4 327	4 491	4 587
20	2 037	2 109	2 238	2 329	2 380	2 451	2 590	2 694	2 544	2 702
22	2 535	2 596	2 709	2 772	2 888	2 928	3 105	3 076	3 175	3 291
24	2 437	2 505	2 600	2 622	2 697	2 742	2 754	2 662	2 413	2 479
25	3 147	3 429	3 360	3 422	3 446	3 442	3 682	3 433	3 582	3 606
26	2 397	2 496	2 550	2 605	2 766	2 839	2 976	3 105	3 154	3 276
27	2 908	3 107	3 209	3 340	3 561	4 006	4 262	4 474	4 338	4 643
28	2 254	2 299	2 400	2 447	2 598	2 661	2 794	2 880	2 993	3 063
29	2 564	2 586	2 835	3 046	2 888	3 055	2 944	3 001	3 089	3 127
31	2 202	2 663	2 638	2 419	2 204	2 466	2 521	2 389	2 814	3 042
33	1 992	2 126	2 265	2 276	2 437	2 452	2 724	2 683	2 625	2 817
34	1 801	1 932	1 978	2 184	2 198	2 041	2 130	2 534	2 715	2 616
36	2 069	2 106	2 248	2 494	2 554	2 767	2 735	2 654	3 025	3 877
37	2 317	2 319	2 371	2 222	2 613	2 463	2 321	2 360	2 408	2 545

Explanatory notes: see p. 877.   Notes explicatives: voir p. 879.   Notas explicativas: véase p. 882.

[1] Oct. of each year.   [1] Oct. de chaque année.   [1] Oct. de cada año.

5B · WAGES · SALAIRES · SALARIOS

In manufacturing · Dans les industries manufacturières · En las industrias manufactureras

	1999	2000	2001	2002	2003	2004	2005	2006	2007	2008	

Macedonia, The Former Yugoslav Rep. of (DA) [1] — Employees - Salariés - Asalariados — E.G./m. - Denar

Total men and women - Total hommes et femmes - Total hombres y mujeres
ISIC 2 - CITI 2 - CIIU 2   ISIC 3 - CITI 3 - CIIU 3

ISIC 2	1999	2000	2001	2002	2003	2004	2005	2006	2007	2008	ISIC 3
311-312	11 596	11 720	12 350	9 944	10 028	10 486	10 298	10 624	11 653	12 613	Total
313	15 690	17 864	18 407	14 127	14 727	15 500	14 405	14 696	14 665	15 260	15
314	11 626	11 291	11 554	12 345	12 524	12 945	13 146	12 243	12 098	12 461	16
321	6 440	6 430	6 624	6 674	6 915	6 614	6 736	7 482	7 950	8 277	17
322	5 655	5 676	5 556	5 453	5 271	5 476	5 148	5 341	6 455	7 124	18
323	3 201	4 238		4 222	2 359	2 541	2 233	3 470	4 983	7 338	19
324	4 183	5 201	4 598	8 242	7 350	7 844	8 284	8 554	8 667	8 679	20
331	5 355	8 157	4 396	11 780	11 360	11 838	12 053	11 714	12 902	14 557	21
332	5 873	6 297	6 035	14 532	13 427	14 187	14 415	14 905	15 100	15 520	22
341	7 800	8 634	10 962	17 639	18 789	19 475	20 255	20 397	24 704	26 772	23
342	8 295	9 537	9 250	12 509	18 409	19 633	21 700	22 251	23 702	27 398	24
351	8 504	7 957	6 852	7 405	6 660	5 517	5 256	4 805	6 346	8 513	25
352	15 102	16 778	17 974	14 568	14 840	15 506	15 774	15 797	18 268	20 952	26
353	12 581	13 170	15 868	12 582	13 390	13 405	14 714	15 536	17 573	18 450	27
371	9 429	10 724	12 349	8 617	9 605	8 677	8 277	8 981	8 882	9 374	28
381	8 064	8 226	8 071	10 479	11 728	12 058	12 362	13 026	12 964	12 911	29
382	13 121	13 397	15 746	11 357	12 086	13 616	14 770	16 669	20 872	22 476	30
383	8 372	8 939	9 179	10 961	12 289	11 714	10 741	10 560	10 476	12 188	31
384	7 348	8 477	8 994	7 288	7 860	7 970	7 964	8 492	11 424	14 213	32
				17 337	17 471	18 016	17 737	18 945	20 342	20 416	33
				7 849	8 951	8 429	8 162	8 851	9 881	11 289	34
				11 470	11 942	12 581	12 897	13 298	13 185	13 978	35
				7 032	7 451	6 812	6 365	7 341	6 919	7 958	36
				.	7 305	6 465	8 082	7 210	7 936	8 872	37

Malta (BA) [2][3] — Total employment - Emploi total - Empleo total — E.G./h. - Lira

Total men and women - Total hommes et femmes - Total hombres y mujeres
ISIC 3 - CITI 3 - CIIU 3

ISIC 3	1999	2000	2001	2002	2003	2004	2005	2006	2007	2008
Total	.	2.1	2.2	2.3	2.3	2.3	2.4	2.6	2.6	6.4
15	.	2.0	2.0	2.1	2.0	2.3	2.4	2.5	2.5	6.1
16	.	2.4								11.3
17	.	1.8								6.9
18	.	1.8	1.8	1.8	1.9	1.9	2.0	2.4	2.3	5.9
19	.	1.6								4.8
20	.	1.9								4.7
21	.	2.2								6.0
22	.	2.6	2.4		2.7	2.6	2.7	2.7	2.8	7.1
23	.	1.6								11.7
24	.	2.3								7.1
25	.	2.2	2.2	2.1		2.4	2.5			6.5
26	.	2.3			2.3	2.3	2.5	2.6	2.6	5.6
27	.	1.8				1.9	2.0	2.0	2.2	4.8
28	.	2.6				2.4	2.2	2.2	2.3	6.2
29	.	2.2				2.2	2.3	2.2	2.5	6.2
30	.	2.1								
31	.	2.3						2.8	4.7	20.5
32	.	2.3	2.4	2.6	2.3	2.5	2.6	2.6	2.7	7.0
33	.	1.6				2.3	2.4	2.4	2.7	6.7
34	.	2.2							2.6	5.7
35	.	2.3	2.5	2.6	2.7	2.7	2.8	2.9	3.0	4.8
36	.	2.0	2.1	2.0	2.2	2.2	2.0	2.4		7.2
37	.	1.8								5.8

Men - Hommes - Hombres
ISIC 3 - CITI 3 - CIIU 3

ISIC 3	1999	2000	2001	2002	2003	2004	2005	2006	2007	2008
Total	.	2.2	2.3	2.4	2.4	2.4	2.5	2.6	2.7	6.6
15	.	2.0		2.1	2.0	2.3	2.3	2.6	2.5	6.2
16	.	2.4								11.3
17	.	2.2								7.4
18	.	2.4								6.2
19	.	1.8			1.9					4.8
20	.	1.7								4.3
21	.	2.4								5.7
22	.	2.6								7.3
23	.	1.6				2.7	2.8	2.6	2.8	
24	.	2.4				2.4	2.6	3.0	3.2	6.9
25	.	2.4				2.3	2.6	2.8	2.8	6.9
26	.	2.3				1.9	2.0	2.0	2.1	5.6
27	.	1.8								4.7
28	.	2.7				2.3				6.0
29	.	2.2								6.6
30	.	1.8								
31	.	2.5						3.0	2.8	20.5
32	.	2.8			2.6	2.8	2.8	2.8	3.0	7.6
33	.	1.9				2.7	3.0			7.1
34	.	2.5								6.4
35	.	2.3	2.5	2.6	2.6	2.7	2.8	2.9	3.0	4.8
36	.	1.9	2.2	2.1	2.3	2.2	2.0	2.5	2.4	7.1
37	.	1.8								6.0

Explanatory notes: see p. 877.

[1] Net earnings. [2] Persons aged 15 years and over. [3] Dec. of each year. [4] Euros; 1 Euro=0.429300 MTL.

Notes explicatives: voir p. 879.

[1] Gains nets. [2] Personnes âgées de 15 ans et plus. [3] Déc. de chaque année. [4] Euros; 1 Euro=0.429300 MTL.

Notas explicativas: véase p. 882.

[1] Ganancias netas. [2] Personas de 15 años y más. [3] Dic. de cada año. [4] Euros; 1 Euro=0.429300MTL.

WAGES — SALAIRES — SALARIOS

In manufacturing — **Dans les industries manufacturières** — **En las industrias manufactureras**

	1999	2000	2001	2002	2003	2004	2005	2006	2007	2008
Malta (BA) [1][2]				Total employment - Emploi total - Empleo total						E.G./h. - Lira

Women - Femmes - Mujeres
ISIC 3 - CITI 3 - CIIU 3

	1999	2000	2001	2002	2003	2004	2005	2006	2007	2008
Total	.	1.8	1.9	2.1	2.2	2.2	2.2	2.3	2.3	5.8 [3]
15	.	2.2	1.7	.	.	2.4	2.9	2.2	2.2	5.3 [3]
16	.	.	.	.	.	.	.	.	.	
17	.	1.5	.	.	.	.	.	.	.	4.7 [3]
18	.	1.7	1.6	1.7	.	2.0	1.9	2.2	2.0	5.6 [3]
19	.	1.4	.	.	.	.	.	.	.	
20	.	3.3	.	.	.	.	.	.	.	6.7 [3]
21	.	1.6	.	.	.	2.6	1.6	.	.	7.7 [3]
22	.	2.3	.	.	.	2.5	2.5	.	.	6.4 [3]
23	.	.	.	.	.	.	.	.	.	
24	.	2.1	.	.	.	.	.	.	.	7.5 [3]
25	.	1.7	.	.	.	.	.	.	.	5.6 [3]
26	.	1.9	.	.	.	.	.	.	.	5.6 [3]
27	.	.	.	.	.	.	.	.	.	
28	.	1.2	.	.	.	.	.	.	.	8.3 [3]
29	.	2.4	.	.	.	.	.	.	.	5.3 [3]
30	.	2.4	.	.	.	.	.	.	.	
31	.	1.7	.	.	.	.	.	.	.	5.4 [3]
32	.	2.0	2.1	.	2.0	2.2	2.2	2.4	2.3	6.0 [3]
33	.	1.4	.	.	.	2.0	2.1	2.2	2.4	5.2 [3]
34	.	1.6	.	.	.	.	.	.	.	4.8 [3]
35	.	.	.	.	.	.	.	.	.	9.5 [3]
36	.	2.2	.	.	.	.	.	.	.	5.1 [3]

Moldova, Republic of (CA) [4]				Employees - Salariés - Asalariados						E.G./m. - Leu

Total men and women - Total hommes et femmes - Total hombres y mujeres
ISIC 3 - CITI 3 - CIIU 3

	1999	2000	2001	2002	2003	2004	2005	2006	2007	2008
Total	492.6	677.7	813.1	971.8	1 216.1	1 417.8	1 651.6	1 914.5	2 314.1	2 762.8
15	498.7	682.7	808.8	979.0	1 203.1	1 368.3	1 603.1	1 789.2	2 196.6	2 669.0
16	1 155.3	1 887.3	1 611.7	1 391.0	2 384.1	2 713.3	3 137.8	3 381.1	3 851.6	4 267.6
17	452.9	526.3	698.8	801.9	1 043.0	1 275.5	1 587.2	2 036.5	2 470.5	2 730.5
18	439.7	596.1	689.8	855.2	983.8	1 178.3	1 321.9	1 564.3	1 840.5	2 056.5
19	435.4	531.5	612.1	688.2	1 024.8	1 291.9	1 459.5	1 746.8	2 102.9	2 414.7
20	296.8	383.0	473.4	588.3	761.8	862.6	968.0	1 289.4	1 644.9	1 926.5
21	479.0	649.1	803.0	1 014.4	1 573.2	1 670.2	1 915.3	2 283.0	2 573.7	2 847.4
22	670.8	904.1	1 058.4	1 355.8	1 824.2	2 102.4	2 424.2	2 757.8	3 644.8	4 125.5
23	.	.	.	.	.	.	.	1 938.7	.	2 815.2
24	615.3	768.3	853.8	1 079.4	1 156.9	1 252.1	1 529.4	1 840.4	2 195.1	3 162.9
25	366.7	576.9	678.3	825.0	908.6	1 065.2	1 458.7	1 765.0	2 220.8	2 407.4
26	552.7	730.9	1 185.8	1 508.8	1 865.2	2 220.2	2 595.2	3 049.1	3 643.6	4 403.2
27	519.8	833.9	989.9	1 347.0	2 063.3	1 566.5	2 754.4	3 327.4	3 700.3	3 524.7
28	335.9	500.5	609.6	776.7	1 032.4	1 314.9	1 505.1	2 011.0	2 526.0	3 117.2
29	393.9	598.6	763.4	943.8	1 218.7	1 492.5	1 688.9	2 098.9	2 431.5	2 836.7
30	314.5	397.1	576.0	707.1	783.2	944.9	1 117.1	1 555.3	2 660.7	3 836.2
31	376.1	358.3	436.4	585.3	736.4	1 073.5	1 259.6	1 553.6	2 199.3	3 790.0
32	451.9	687.1	980.4	1 002.5	1 188.0	1 625.6	2 314.6	2 835.2	3 273.3	3 757.4
33	444.4	531.9	624.2	828.9	1 106.2	1 348.5	1 444.2	1 776.4	2 276.8	2 500.5
34	.	.	196.3	243.4	237.3	1 535.7	2 291.7	1 132.1	934.9	1 374.0
35	490.8	633.7	678.8	918.5	1 099.8	1 356.4	2 273.2	2 729.0	3 960.1	4 410.1
36	479.8	658.7	721.7	824.5	985.9	1 101.2	1 288.5	1 436.0	1 739.7	2 259.8
37	1 472.8	1 995.7	1 750.1	1 196.4	1 836.7	2 045.0	2 782.1	3 966.2	5 071.4	5 447.1

Montenegro (DA)				Employees - Salariés - Asalariados						E.G./m. - New Dinar

Total men and women - Total hommes et femmes - Total hombres y mujeres
ISIC 3 - CITI 3 - CIIU 3

	1999	2000	2001	2002	2003	2004	2005	2006	2007	2008
Total	.	.	.	.	.	.	.	.	530	615

Explanatory notes: see p. 877.

[1] Persons aged 15 years and over. [2] Dec. of each year. [3] Euros; 1 Euro=0.429300 MTL. [4] Enterprises with 20 or more employees.

Notes explicatives: voir p. 879.

[1] Personnes âgées de 15 ans et plus. [2] Déc. de chaque année. [3] Euros; 1 Euro=0.429300 MTL. [4] Entreprises occupant 20 salariés et plus.

Notas explicativas: véase p. 882.

[1] Personas de 15 años y más. [2] Dic. de cada año. [3] Euros; 1 Euro=0.429300MTL. [4] Empresas con 20 y más asalariados.

	1999	2000	2001	2002	2003	2004	2005	2006	2007	2008
Netherlands (DA) [1] [2]				Employees - Salariés - Asalariados						E.G./h. - Euro

Total men and women - Total hommes et femmes - Total hombres y mujeres
ISIC 3 - CITI 3 - CIIU 3

	1999	2000	2001	2002	2003	2004	2005	2006	2007	2008
Total	33.32	34.42	16.52 [3]	17.14	17.78	18.24	18.50	.	.	.
15-16	33.37	34.57	16.63 [3]	17.23	17.74	18.43	18.45	.	.	.
17	30.69	31.57	15.20 [3]	15.59	16.97	16.75	17.44	.	.	.
18	25.78	29.46	14.34 [3]	14.65	15.16	15.26	17.28	.	.	.
19	27.52	29.05	13.97 [3]	14.33	14.77	15.43	14.58	.	.	.
20	28.10	30.46	14.19 [3]	14.92	15.60	16.28	16.61	.	.	.
21	37.42	38.15	18.71 [3]	19.22	20.01	20.11	20.71	.	.	.
22	36.98	38.42	18.82 [3]	19.88	20.62	21.02	20.97	.	.	.
23	55.99	54.67	26.29 [3]	26.97	27.32	27.87	28.30	.	.	.
24	42.21	43.13	21.05 [3]	21.94	22.89	23.36	23.68	.	.	.
25	32.02	33.17	15.43 [3]	16.47	16.69	17.13	17.78	.	.	.
26	33.16	33.53	16.47 [3]	17.28	17.88	18.01	18.14	.	.	.
27	40.55	40.11	18.71 [3]	19.59	20.34	20.62	20.83	.	.	.
28	31.34	32.20	15.56 [3]	15.59	16.24	16.65	17.02	.	.	.
29	33.91	35.58	16.94 [3]	17.23	18.13	18.94	19.41	.	.	.
30-31	33.83	35.59	16.89 [3]	18.03	18.46	18.63	19.40	.	.	.
32-33	34.95	37.08	17.91 [3]	18.84	20.25	20.56	21.02	.	.	.
34	33.35	34.18	16.53 [3]	17.02	17.38	17.68	18.24	.	.	.
35	34.77	36.01	17.21 [3]	18.14	18.26	19.33	19.50	.	.	.
36-37	24.99	25.75	12.12 [3]	12.64	12.96	13.15	13.18	.	.	.

Men - Hommes - Hombres
ISIC 3 - CITI 3 - CIIU 3

	1999	2000	2001	2002	2003	2004	2005	2006	2007	2008
Total	34.69	35.83	17.20 [3]	17.81	18.45	18.87	19.13	.	.	.
15-16	35.85	37.41	17.97 [3]	18.68	18.99	19.68	19.69	.	.	.
17	33.88	33.99	16.63 [3]	16.71	17.98	18.06	18.65	.	.	.
18	.	.	17.26 [3]	17.35	19.71	19.73	21.92	.	.	.
19	29.56	31.61	15.02 [3]	15.05	15.78	16.13	15.64	.	.	.
20	28.42	30.68	14.31 [3]	15.10	15.81	16.40	16.71	.	.	.
21	38.73	39.36	19.29 [3]	19.82	20.50	20.50	21.23	.	.	.
22	39.38	40.67	19.95 [3]	20.82	21.88	21.91	21.86	.	.	.
23	56.51	56.41	27.10 [3]	27.85	27.95	28.50	28.85	.	.	.
24	44.27	45.42	22.25 [3]	23.11	24.22	24.53	24.95	.	.	.
25	33.23	34.47	16.11 [3]	17.04	17.28	17.79	18.38	.	.	.
26	33.67	34.08	16.73 [3]	17.49	18.13	18.27	18.38	.	.	.
27	41.13	40.68	18.95 [3]	19.85	20.57	20.82	21.03	.	.	.
28	31.78	32.74	15.83 [3]	15.79	16.41	16.80	17.15	.	.	.
29	34.65	36.21	17.25 [3]	17.54	18.46	19.28	19.77	.	.	.
30-31	35.58	37.04	17.71 [3]	18.82	19.09	19.31	20.06	.	.	.
32-33	37.20	39.46	18.90 [3]	19.97	21.47	21.71	22.21	.	.	.
34	33.81	34.56	16.78 [3]	17.23	17.58	17.85	18.43	.	.	.
35	35.04	36.46	17.49 [3]	18.52	18.50	19.58	19.73	.	.	.
36-37	25.65	26.56	12.45 [3]	13.01	13.35	13.52	13.52	.	.	.

Women - Femmes - Mujeres
ISIC 3 - CITI 3 - CIIU 3

	1999	2000	2001	2002	2003	2004	2005	2006	2007	2008
Total	26.90	27.96	13.53 [3]	14.14	14.73	15.36	15.61	.	.	.
15-16	25.88	26.49	13.08 [3]	13.22	14.21	14.79	14.83	.	.	.
17	24.67	25.43	11.86 [3]	12.62	14.39	13.52	14.32	.	.	.
18	23.57	24.25	12.00 [3]	12.93	12.42	12.57	14.24	.	.	.
19	.	.	11.83 [3]	12.54	12.27	13.66	11.87	.	.	.
20	.	.	12.76 [3]	12.77	13.54	14.83	15.54	.	.	.
21	29.18	30.79	14.84 [3]	15.26	16.73	17.52	17.11	.	.	.
22	31.58	33.37	16.28 [3]	17.74	17.83	19.09	19.05	.	.	.
23	.	.	18.84 [3]	19.33	21.12	22.96	24.11	.	.	.
24	32.06	33.31	16.14 [3]	17.12	17.52	18.64	18.82	.	.	.
25	25.96	26.17	11.80 [3]	13.40	13.47	13.85	14.52	.	.	.
26	28.14	28.00	13.86 [3]	15.05	15.16	15.29	16.04	.	.	.
27	32.82	32.07	15.48 [3]	16.15	17.16	17.83	18.10	.	.	.
28	26.17	26.67	12.99 [3]	13.37	14.35	15.00	15.55	.	.	.
29	27.30	29.52	13.89 [3]	14.28	14.91	15.65	15.92	.	.	.
30-31	25.08	27.93	12.81 [3]	13.96	14.68	14.68	15.64	.	.	.
32-33	26.83	28.15	14.24 [3]	14.42	14.45	15.79	16.19	.	.	.
34	28.83	29.90	13.96 [3]	14.89	14.96	15.58	15.96	.	.	.
35	30.61	30.22	14.21 [3]	14.12	15.42	16.50	16.76	.	.	.
36-37	22.08	22.63	10.95 [3]	11.36	11.67	11.91	12.00	.	.	.

Explanatory notes: see p. 877.

[1] Excl. overtime payments. [2] Dec. of each year. [3] Prior to 2001: NLG; 1 Euro = 2.20371 NLG.

Notes explicatives: voir p. 879.

[1] Non compris la rémunération des heures supplémentaires. [2] Déc. de chaque année. [3] Avant 2001: NLG; 1 Euro = 2,20371 NLG.

Notas explicativas: véase p. 882.

[1] Excl. los pagos por horas extraordinarias. [2] Dic. de cada año. [3] Antes de 2001: NLG; 1 Euro = 2,20371 NLG.

WAGES

In manufacturing

SALAIRES

Dans les industries manufacturières

SALARIOS

En las industrias manufactureras

5B

	1999	2000	2001	2002	2003	2004	2005	2006	2007	2008

Netherlands (DA) [1] [2] [3]   Employees - Salariés - Asalariados   E.G./m. - Euro

Total men and women - Total hommes et femmes - Total hombres y mujeres
ISIC 3 - CITI 3 - CIIU 3

	1999	2000	2001	2002	2003	2004	2005	2006	2007	2008
Total	4 797	4 958	2 392 [4]	2 487	2 572	2 637	2 689	.	.	.
15-16	4 915	5 070	2 431 [4]	2 551	2 601	2 717	2 741	.	.	.
17	4 485	4 610	2 211 [4]	2 318	2 477	2 483	2 571	.	.	.
18	3 873	4 450	2 263 [4]	2 248	2 190	2 231	2 698	.	.	.
19	4 069	4 355	2 093 [4]	2 132	2 218	2 300	2 213	.	.	.
20	3 971	4 300	2 006 [4]	2 142	2 199	2 294	2 361	.	.	.
21	5 207	5 321	2 631 [4]	2 698	2 783	2 828	2 903	.	.	.
22	5 313	5 505	2 698 [4]	2 852	2 954	3 031	3 039	.	.	.
23	7 888	7 831	3 760 [4]	3 867	3 896	4 058	4 122	.	.	.
24	6 009	6 145	3 013 [4]	3 155	3 293	3 347	3 410	.	.	.
25	4 637	4 816	2 270 [4]	2 402	2 426	2 491	2 610	.	.	.
26	4 766	4 783	2 352 [4]	2 455	2 552	2 558	2 622	.	.	.
27	5 638	5 571	2 626 [4]	2 757	2 841	2 890	2 925	.	.	.
28	4 489	4 637	2 247 [4]	2 259	2 336	2 383	2 447	.	.	.
29	4 858	5 091	2 437 [4]	2 492	2 630	2 732	2 791	.	.	.
30-31	4 860	5 099	2 447 [4]	2 593	2 668	2 696	2 807	.	.	.
32-33	5 134	5 499	2 635 [4]	2 763	2 967	3 007	3 094	.	.	.
34	4 733	4 873	2 360 [4]	2 442	2 484	2 544	2 626	.	.	.
35	4 938	5 100	2 442 [4]	2 579	2 616	2 741	2 775	.	.	.
36-37	3 552	3 676	1 732 [4]	1 809	1 852	1 865	1 893	.	.	.

Men - Hommes - Hombres
ISIC 3 - CITI 3 - CIIU 3

	1999	2000	2001	2002	2003	2004	2005	2006	2007	2008
Total	4 932	5 099	2 458 [4]	2 549	2 634	2 692	2 740	.	.	.
15-16	5 120	5 329	2 553 [4]	2 669	2 712	2 812	2 828	.	.	.
17	4 799	4 854	2 356 [4]	2 402	2 561	2 587	2 640	.	.	.
18	.	.	2 577 [4]	2 480	2 560	2 663	3 307	.	.	.
19	4 277	4 613	2 204 [4]	2 182	2 316	2 360	2 270	.	.	.
20	3 994	4 310	2 017 [4]	2 163	2 217	2 304	2 366	.	.	.
21	5 340	5 434	2 683 [4]	2 747	2 816	2 855	2 940	.	.	.
22	5 545	5 746	2 816 [4]	2 937	3 069	3 110	3 120	.	.	.
23	7 937	8 012	3 851 [4]	3 963	3 961	4 110	4 162	.	.	.
24	6 224	6 382	3 140 [4]	3 270	3 413	3 463	3 519	.	.	.
25	4 769	4 949	2 325 [4]	2 468	2 483	2 563	2 667	.	.	.
26	4 818	4 845	2 377 [4]	2 471	2 574	2 581	2 635	.	.	.
27	5 691	5 616	2 648 [4]	2 778	2 857	2 906	2 940	.	.	.
28	4 534	4 697	2 273 [4]	2 276	2 352	2 399	2 457	.	.	.
29	4 936	5 154	2 467 [4]	2 523	2 662	2 764	2 824	.	.	.
30-31	5 061	5 275	2 543 [4]	2 677	2 724	2 760	2 852	.	.	.
32-33	5 386	5 719	2 740 [4]	2 881	3 099	3 111	3 208	.	.	.
34	4 792	4 919	2 390 [4]	2 467	2 504	2 560	2 643	.	.	.
35	4 979	5 155	2 473 [4]	2 619	2 643	2 766	2 797	.	.	.
36-37	3 632	3 765	1 744 [4]	1 856	1 895	1 901	1 930	.	.	.

Women - Femmes - Mujeres
ISIC 3 - CITI 3 - CIIU 3

	1999	2000	2001	2002	2003	2004	2005	2006	2007	2008
Total	3 870	4 001	1 944 [4]	2 039	2 123	2 221	2 282	.	.	.
15-16	3 887	3 899	1 938 [4]	2 000	2 124	2 254	2 303	.	.	.
17	3 563	3 709	1 707 [4]	1 937	2 107	1 974	2 170	.	.	.
18	.	.	1 812 [4]	1 997	1 842	1 764	1 978	.	.	.
19	.	.	1 684 [4]	1 914	1 809	1 993	1 857	.	.	.
20	.	.	1 810 [4]	1 740	1 875	1 944	2 239	.	.	.
21	4 106	4 375	2 124 [4]	2 201	2 435	2 564	2 477	.	.	.
22	4 536	4 689	2 284 [4]	2 534	2 526	2 735	2 724	.	.	.
23	.	.	2 651 [4]	2 738	3 019	3 455	3 674	.	.	.
24	4 560	4 716	2 283 [4]	2 463	2 551	2 626	2 727	.	.	.
25	3 706	3 745	1 782 [4]	1 862	1 935	1 953	2 107	.	.	.
26	.	3 905	1 962 [4]	2 193	2 185	2 171	2 428	.	.	.
27	.	4 610	2 186 [4]	2 321	2 523	2 554	2 593	.	.	.
28	3 761	3 757	1 880 [4]	1 895	2 033	2 084	2 248	.	.	.
29	3 890	4 230	1 976 [4]	2 017	2 141	2 233	2 275	.	.	.
30-31	3 527	3 869	1 771 [4]	1 956	2 054	2 088	2 323	.	.	.
32-33	3 874	4 110	2 070 [4]	2 071	2 190	2 308	2 351	.	.	.
34	4 004	4 154	1 928 [4]	2 087	2 125	2 232	2 300	.	.	.
35	4 075	4 173	2 023 [4]	2 004	2 175	2 325	2 356	.	.	.
36-37	3 065	3 190	1 502 [4]	1 571	1 642	1 681	1 691	.	.	.

Explanatory notes: see p. 877.

[1] Full-time employees only. [2] Excl. overtime payments. [3] Dec. of each year. [4] Prior to 2001: NLG; 1 Euro = 2.20371 NLG.

Notes explicatives: voir p. 879.

[1] Salariés à plein temps seulement. [2] Non compris la rémunération des heures supplémentaires. [3] Déc. de chaque année. [4] Avant 2001: NLG; 1 Euro = 2,20371 NLG.

Notas explicativas: véase p. 882.

[1] Asalariados a tiempo completo solamente. [2] Excl. los pagos por horas extraordinarias. [3] Dic. de cada año. [4] Antes de 2001: NLG; 1 Euro = 2,20371 NLG.

WAGES
In manufacturing

SALAIRES
Dans les industries manufacturières

SALARIOS
En las industrias manufactureras

	1999	2000	2001	2002	2003	2004	2005	2006	2007	2008

Norway (DA) [1][2][3] — Employees - Salariés - Asalariados — E.G./m. - Krone

Total men and women - Total hommes et femmes - Total hombres y mujeres
ISIC 3 - CITI 3 - CIIU 3

	1999	2000	2001	2002	2003	2004	2005	2006	2007	2008
Total	22 441	23 388	24 426	25 991	26 944	27 920	28 908	30 162	31 983	33 977
15-16	20 134	20 940	21 869	23 352	24 017	25 172	25 972	27 092	28 207	29 852
17-19	19 118	19 931	20 816	21 859	23 116	24 225	24 689	25 584	27 181	29 039
20	19 223	20 032	20 826	22 061	22 943	24 135	24 617	25 640	26 660	28 694
21	21 811	22 829	23 708	24 862	26 024	26 893	28 112	28 943	31 300	32 295
22	25 268	26 368	27 459	28 502	29 283	30 432	31 610	32 864	34 532	37 006
23	28 604	29 340	.	.	.	.	.	.	.	.
23.25-26 [4]	23 095	23 843	25 215	26 918	27 892	28 652	29 694	30 942	33 004	34 555
24 [5]	26 472	27 619	28 910	30 832	32 192	32 994	34 048	35 837	37 146	39 346
25-26 [4]	23 095	23 843	25 215	26 918	27 892	28 652	29 694	30 942	33 004	.
27	23 383	24 538	25 359	27 075	27 987	28 681	29 869	30 423	33 057	34 984
28-34 [6]	23 330	24 348	25 487	27 257	28 137	28 865	29 558	31 010	33 255	35 077
35 [7]	22 940	23 875	24 981	26 716	28 365	29 244	30 613	31 827	34 211	36 029
36-37	19 979	20 801	21 744	23 156	23 945	24 927	26 095	27 125	28 265	30 178

Men - Hommes - Hombres
ISIC 3 - CITI 3 - CIIU 3

	1999	2000	2001	2002	2003	2004	2005	2006	2007	2008
Total	.	.	.	.	27 625	28 588	29 513	30 767	32 710	34 638
15-16	.	.	.	.	25 060	26 229	27 098	28 211	29 449	31 113
17-19	.	.	.	.	24 887	26 232	26 356	27 126	29 476	31 713
20	.	.	.	.	23 134	24 325	24 736	25 707	26 784	28 865
21	.	.	.	.	26 469	27 145	28 442	29 295	31 724	32 631
22	.	.	.	.	30 432	31 881	32 839	34 293	35 979	38 662
23.25-26 [4]	.	.	.	.	28 054	28 916	29 833	31 022	33 136	34 702
24 [5]	.	.	.	.	.	.	.	.	.	.
25-26 [4]	.	.	.	.	28 054	28 916	29 833	31 022	33 136	34 702
27	.	.	.	.	28 222	28 851	30 028	30 599	33 270	35 260
28-34 [6]	.	.	.	.	28 688	29 413	30 048	31 545	33 784	35 599
35 [7]	.	.	.	.	28 543	29 385	30 738	31 932	34 455	36 010
36-37	.	.	.	.	24 434	25 402	26 571	27 576	29 078	30 956

Women - Femmes - Mujeres
ISIC 3 - CITI 3 - CIIU 3

	1999	2000	2001	2002	2003	2004	2005	2006	2007	2008
Total	.	.	.	.	24 260	25 290	26 432	27 649	29 124	31 301
15-16	.	.	.	.	21 695	22 812	23 514	24 571	25 649	27 135
17-19	.	.	.	.	20 769	21 437	22 353	23 480	24 550	25 665
20	.	.	.	.	21 456	22 578	23 641	25 131	25 654	27 336
21	.	.	.	.	23 792	25 540	26 337	27 088	29 028	30 487
22	.	.	.	.	26 887	27 571	29 116	30 145	31 920	34 159
23.25-26 [4]	.	.	.	.	27 252	27 639	29 163	30 610	32 477	33 973
24 [5]	.	.	.	.	30 732	31 723	33 140	34 764	36 219	38 043
25	.	.	.	.	.	.	.	.	.	.
27	.	.	.	.	26 220	27 437	28 619	29 104	31 489	33 083
28-34 [6]	.	.	.	.	24 616	25 432	26 362	27 647	29 976	31 914
35 [7]	.	.	.	.	26 644	27 836	29 375	30 854	32 308	36 172
36-37	.	.	.	.	22 590	23 631	24 670	25 847	25 928	27 821

Poland (DA) [8] — Employees - Salariés - Asalariados — E.G./m. - Zloty

Total men and women - Total hommes et femmes - Total hombres y mujeres
ISIC 3 - CITI 3 - CIIU 3

	1999	2000	2001	2002	2003	2004	2005	2006	2007	2008
Total	1 598.90	1 756.40	1 866.50	1 911.50	1 980.73	2 053.65	2 123.63	2 245.95	2 450.66	.
15	1 453.52	1 604.51	1 725.04	1 741.33	1 797.04	1 854.49	1 919.66	2 004.22	2 208.00	.
16	3 225.85	3 412.35	3 681.13	3 906.90	4 314.09	4 384.01	4 617.89	4 639.46	4 782.13	.
17	1 271.64	1 372.35	1 462.25	1 502.57	1 522.21	1 548.92	1 586.10	1 676.32	1 821.82	.
18	963.43	1 032.79	1 081.02	1 091.96	1 154.02	1 190.70	1 188.30	1 235.68	1 327.02	.
19	1 085.17	1 164.66	1 214.18	1 234.54	1 258.87	1 301.87	1 323.79	1 404.62	1 517.93	.
20	1 224.11	1 323.45	1 344.13	1 377.16	1 437.17	1 458.22	1 508.28	1 582.11	1 755.99	.
21	1 904.04	2 033.17	2 181.70	2 285.98	2 428.00	2 580.91	2 423.06	2 509.18	2 691.83	.
22	2 164.72	2 368.61	2 494.00	2 702.98	2 694.90	2 722.91	2 864.39	2 937.41	3 032.27	.
23	3 059.78	3 451.98	3 736.23	3 859.01	4 017.60	4 317.87	4 634.10	4 932.52	5 394.14	.
24	2 284.82	2 569.14	2 839.99	2 987.03	3 065.74	3 171.71	3 283.77	3 387.18	3 548.49	.
25	1 644.15	1 772.62	1 850.90	1 932.40	1 995.79	2 047.61	2 112.00	2 223.02	2 404.90	.
26	1 637.43	1 809.23	1 915.82	1 954.15	2 043.34	2 118.32	2 204.69	2 337.05	2 598.12	.
27	2 060.90	2 186.91	2 328.66	2 348.98	2 440.50	2 598.17	2 680.10	2 971.24	3 235.65	.
28	1 535.69	1 698.04	1 781.55	1 810.24	1 887.56	1 967.70	2 022.18	2 158.18	2 436.50	.
29	1 680.17	1 881.19	2 018.76	2 088.67	2 202.65	2 307.84	2 423.41	2 567.49	2 791.86	.
30	2 886.96	2 959.03	2 987.69	3 010.48	3 381.70	3 511.19	3 139.02	3 139.98	3 280.49	.
31	1 831.19	1 963.70	2 057.22	2 102.63	2 191.55	2 270.43	2 313.20	2 415.42	2 629.72	.
32	2 079.50	2 429.03	2 814.47	3 057.99	2 973.02	2 804.21	2 919.74	2 899.48	2 762.90	.
33	1 849.42	2 099.03	2 247.21	2 248.90	2 299.59	2 304.80	2 391.88	2 543.58	2 850.77	.
34	1 896.52	2 066.37	2 145.61	2 218.09	2 376.46	2 554.77	2 597.97	2 777.42	3 044.64	.
35	1 922.15	2 172.83	2 349.37	2 247.35	2 272.95	2 489.52	2 542.54	2 754.48	3 018.57	.
36	1 243.86	1 370.23	1 403.65	1 432.81	1 517.19	1 540.95	1 585.58	1 701.31	1 863.66	.
37	1 994.35	2 253.86	2 281.23	2 125.90	2 106.77	2 192.13	2 144.60	2 187.39	2 354.31	.

Explanatory notes: see p. 877.

Notes explicatives: voir p. 879.

Notas explicativas: véase p. 882.

[1] Only remuneration in cash; excl. overtime payments. [2] Full-time employees. [3] Oct. of each year. [4] Other chemical and non-metallic mineral products. [5] Basic chemicals. [6] Machinery, equipment and transport. [7] Ships, oil platforms and modules. [8] Incl. the value of payments in kind.

[1] Seulement rémunération en espèces; non compris les paiements pour heures supplémentaires. [2] Salariés à plein temps. [3] Oct. de chaque année. [4] Autres produits chimiques et minéraux non métalliques. [5] Produits chimiques de base. [6] Machines, équipement et transport. [7] Bateaux, plate-formes de pétrole et modules. [8] Y compris la valeur des paiements en nature.

[1] Sólo remuneración en efectivo; excl. los pagos por horas extraordinarias. [2] Asalariados a tiempo completo. [3] Oct. de cada año. [4] Otros productos químicos y minerales no metálicos. [5] Productos químicos básicos. [6] Maquinaría, equípo y transporte. [7] Buques, plataformas petroleras y módulos. [8] Incl. el valor de los pagos en especie.

WAGES

SALAIRES

SALARIOS

5B

In manufacturing

Dans les industries manufacturières

En las industrias manufactureras

	1999	2000	2001	2002	2003	2004	2005	2006	2007	2008

Poland (DA) [1] [2] — Employees - Salariés - Asalariados — E.G./m. - Zloty

Total men and women - Total hommes et femmes - Total hombres y mujeres
ISIC 3 - CITI 3 - CIIU 3

	1999	2000	2001	2002	2003	2004	2005	2006	2007	2008
Total	1 660.9	1 827.6	1 938.9	2 000.0	2 058.7	2 140.7	2 202.0	2 337.0	2 562.0	2 805.0
15	1 514.3	1 679.9	1 797.2	1 826.0	1 861.9	1 920.3	1 972.0	2 068.0	2 289.0	2 483.0
16	3 225.9	3 412.4	3 683.5	3 912.0	4 318.7	4 390.6	4 626.0	4 654.0	4 790.0	4 959.0
17	1 300.3	1 400.2	1 492.1	1 537.0	1 554.7	1 589.5	1 616.0	1 719.0	1 865.0	2 028.0
18	991.8	1 063.2	1 104.4	1 122.0	1 166.8	1 210.3	1 216.0	1 273.0	1 380.0	1 533.0
19	1 140.8	1 229.5	1 262.9	1 275.0	1 287.6	1 352.1	1 380.0	1 467.0	1 590.0	1 722.0
20	1 324.6	1 417.9	1 452.2	1 498.0	1 517.7	1 569.4	1 590.0	1 692.0	1 920.0	2 099.0
21	1 950.3	2 102.4	2 256.1	2 355.0	2 503.0	2 467.5	2 504.0	2 588.0	2 783.0	3 044.0
22	2 309.7	2 565.6	2 800.3	2 921.0	2 983.2	3 046.0	3 120.0	3 238.0	3 411.0	3 636.0
23	3 063.7	3 459.1	3 739.8	3 875.0	4 034.1	4 343.4	4 654.0	4 963.0	5 430.0	5 917.0
24	2 307.3	2 601.7	2 858.6	3 028.0	3 115.7	3 226.2	3 326.0	3 442.0	3 602.0	3 907.0
25	1 704.4	1 845.2	1 948.4	2 017.0	2 074.4	2 119.3	2 190.0	2 300.0	2 521.0	2 749.0
26	1 730.2	1 920.8	2 006.9	2 108.0	2 152.2	2 242.1	2 316.0	2 461.0	2 752.0	3 018.0
27	2 065.4	2 194.1	2 334.3	2 358.0	2 453.5	2 610.5	2 697.0	2 992.0	3 254.0	3 560.0
28	1 606.7	1 785.9	1 852.8	1 913.0	1 978.6	2 064.5	2 126.0	2 281.0	2 559.0	2 784.0
29	1 702.8	1 903.7	2 045.1	2 121.0	2 235.3	2 355.9	2 462.0	2 622.0	2 846.0	3 145.0
30	2 982.2	3 168.9	3 115.0	3 040.0	3 641.4	3 828.6	3 796.0	3 340.0	3 501.0	4 000.0
31	1 851.9	1 994.2	2 082.6	2 138.7	2 222.6	2 297.0	2 340.0	2 446.0	2 671.0	2 884.0
32	2 122.7	2 461.2	2 865.4	3 148.0	3 031.0	2 850.3	2 980.0	2 956.0	2 780.0	2 857.0
33	1 927.9	2 139.1	2 313.7	2 367.0	2 410.4	2 416.1	2 514.0	2 655.0	2 977.0	3 337.0
34	1 911.8	2 082.8	2 159.8	2 231.0	2 389.7	2 573.8	2 612.0	2 485.0	3 060.0	3 340.0
35	1 935.9	2 190.0	2 372.2	2 263.0	2 290.1	2 526.4	2 574.0	2 777.0	3 074.0	3 407.0
36	1 314.3	1 429.4	1 460.6	1 518.0	1 580.9	1 638.1	1 649.0	1 772.0	1 970.0	2 175.0
37	2 117.7	2 396.6	2 420.3	2 256.0	2 248.6	2 334.1	2 272.0	2 354.0	2 605.0	2 951.0

Portugal (DA) — Employees - Salariés - Asalariados — E.G./m. - Euro

Total men and women - Total hommes et femmes - Total hombres y mujeres
ISIC 3 - CITI 3 - CIIU 3

	1999	2000	2001	2002	2003	2004	2005	2006	2007	2008
Total	.	126 923	133 939	705 [3]	775	806	837	868	893	932
15-16	.	135 169	147 640	768 [3]	790	794	819	852	870	906
17-18	.	95 999	101 448	537 [3]	570	588	613	637	650	687
19	.	94 327	98 505	517 [3]	557	580	587	592	609	642
20	.	112 056	118 124	621 [3]	666	708	727	760	764	791
21-22	.	184 134	192 068	1 021 [3]	1 089	1 129	1 176	1 199	1 195	1 238
23	.	271 681	321 646	1 862 [3]	2 479	2 518	2 528	2 591	2 712	2 864
24	.	220 175	226 635	1 233 [3]	1 365	1 416	1 450	1 510	1 551	1 615
25	.	144 869	148 527	815 [3]	895	916	975	1 049	1 102	1 134
26	.	140 994	150 618	786 [3]	870	881	916	949	979	1 011
27-28	.	132 836	135 925	728 [3]	742	775	825	855	869	904
29	.	155 283	166 324	860 [3]	917	974	991	1 038	1 075	1 122
30-33	.	165 306	171 241	930 [3]	1 048	1 075	1 120	1 162	1 182	1 232
34-35	.	180 550	190 425	975 [3]	1 079	1 099	1 129	1 156	1 184	1 205
36-37	.	96 138	100 848	509 [3]	597	627	646	678	706	725

Men - Hommes - Hombres
ISIC 3 - CITI 3 - CIIU 3

	1999	2000	2001	2002	2003	2004	2005	2006	2007	2008
Total	.	151 422	159 822	840 [3]	905	934	968	1 008	1 026	1 065
15-16	.	159 472	175 124	915 [3]	936	940	975	1 016	1 020	1 064
17-18	.	130 723	139 221	718 [3]	751	764	765	829	840	882
19	.	111 361	116 984	615 [3]	664	693	695	685	709	749
20	.	117 356	123 579	655 [3]	688	731	754	792	792	814
23	.	276 253	328 981	1 888 [3]	2 550	2 592	2 606	2 713	2 836	2 976
24	.	240 663	245 357	1 359 [3]	1 502	1 550	1 583	1 712	1 744	1 813
25	.	162 762	167 438	921 [3]	992	1 013	1 069	1 146	1 218	1 240
26	.	155 828	165 856	867 [3]	944	967	991	1 023	1 051	1 083
27-28	.	137 368	141 354	756 [3]	763	796	850	899	897	926
29	.	162 701	174 430	909 [3]	959	1 015	1 032	1 094	1 117	1 170
34-35	.	189 494	201 659	1 031 [3]	1 143	1 174	1 230	1 242	1 269	1 291
36	.	99 447	104 483	523 [3]	615	643	661	698	734	761

Women - Femmes - Mujeres
ISIC 3 - CITI 3 - CIIU 3

	1999	2000	2001	2002	2003	2004	2005	2006	2007	2008
Total	.	98 574	103 835	547 [3]	596	622	648	675	696	729
15-16	.	104 248	112 433	584 [3]	607	617	637	669	697	715
17-18	.	84 005	88 462	470 [3]	489	498	521	545	554	593
19	.	82 596	85 913	451 [3]	472	488	492	518	530	551
20	.	97 283	103 317	528 [3]	595	637	657	653	682	713
21-22	.	142 084	153 906	836 [3]	891	946	996	994	1 004	1 054
23	.	254 635	295 367	1 631 [3]	2 221	2 258	2 270	2 427	2 394	2 580
24	.	178 937	189 452	990 [3]	1 115	1 161	1 225	1 278	1 244	1 285
25	.	110 307	111 641	599 [3]	681	703	743	803	825	873
27-28	.	110 590	111 343	600 [3]	636	684	713	720	748	805
29	.	127 444	134 757	687 [3]	735	801	825	870	914	923
30-33	.	134 957	138 764	738 [3]	801	827	839	868	893	925
34-35	.	137 939	143 596	749 [3]	819	818	819	869	931	943
36-37	.	87 719	91 882	476 [3]	557	583	608	622	643	645

Explanatory notes: see p. 877.

[1] Economic units with 10 or more persons employed; prior to 1999, economic units with more than 5 persons employed. [2] Incl. the value of payments in kind. [3] Prior to 2002: PTE; 1 Euro= 200.482 PTE.

Notes explicatives: voir p. 879.

[1] Unités économiques occupant 10 travailleurs et plus; avant 1999, unités économiques occupant plus de 5 personnes. [2] Y compris la valeur des paiements en nature. [3] Avant 2002: PTE; 1 Euro= 200,482 PTE.

Notas explicativas: véase p. 882.

[1] Unidades económicas con 10 y más trabajadores; antes de 1999, unidades económicas con más de 5 trabajadores. [2] Incl. el valor de los pagos en especie. [3] Antes de 2002: PTE; 1 Euro= 200,482 PTE.

5B

WAGES	SALAIRES	SALARIOS
In manufacturing	Dans les industries manufacturières	En las industrias manufactureras

	1999	2000	2001	2002	2003	2004	2005	2006	2007	2008

Portugal (DA) — Wage earners - Ouvriers - Obreros — E.G./h. - Euro

Total men and women - Total hommes et femmes - Total hombres y mujeres
ISIC 3 - CITI 3 - CIIU 3

	1999	2000	2001	2002	2003	2004	2005	2006	2007	2008
Total	718.00	620.00	673.00	375.00	3.67	3.83	3.88	3.98	4.08	4.25
15	749.00									
15-16		660.00	701.00	381.00	3.73	3.92	3.86	4.06	4.06	4.27
16	1 053.00									
17	601.00									
17-18		489.00	526.00	290.00	2.86	2.93	2.96	3.01	3.13	3.28
18	490.00									
19	538.00	502.00	535.00	292.00	2.87	2.98	2.98	3.00	3.11	3.28
20	632.00	578.00	623.00	345.00	3.34	3.55	3.58	3.76	3.72	3.88
21	1 070.00									
21-22		848.00	911.00	502.00	4.94	5.08	5.28	5.39	5.36	5.48
22	1 031.00									
23	2 041.00	806.00	1 509.00	1 279.00	12.81	12.88	13.35	13.63	13.70	13.54
24	1 249.00	889.00	975.00	550.00	5.50	5.61	5.50	5.60	6.04	6.12
25	834.00	727.00	791.00	442.00	4.29	4.47	4.64	4.94	5.08	5.24
26	801.00	732.00	801.00	452.00	4.50	4.48	4.60	4.71	4.86	4.97
27	818.00									
27-28		705.00	727.00	379.00	3.75	3.91	4.07	4.16	4.26	4.45
28	715.00									
29	873.00	807.00	866.00	476.00	4.66	4.82	4.85	4.97	5.10	5.33
30	1 570.00									
30-33		739.00	808.00	455.00	4.43	4.73	4.89	4.90	4.89	5.09
31	771.00									
32	1 258.00									
33	833.00									
34	924.00									
34-35		922.00	980.00	532.00	5.18	5.42	5.40	5.46	5.50	5.60
35	1 244.00									
36	550.00									
36-37		512.00	558.00	313.00	3.09	3.12	3.26	3.37	3.42	3.57
37	930.00									

Men - Hommes - Hombres
ISIC 3 - CITI 3 - CIIU 3

	1999	2000	2001	2002	2003	2004	2005	2006	2007	2008
Total	856.00	731.00	784.00	430.00	4.22	4.39	4.46	4.58	4.65	4.82
15	892.00									
15-16		765.00	804.00	430.00	4.23	4.43	4.43	4.66	4.62	4.84
16	1 123.00									
17	713.00									
17-18		600.00	641.00	351.00	3.45	3.55	3.60	3.67	3.83	3.93
18	806.00									
19	640.00	558.00	594.00	323.00	3.17	3.29	3.25	3.29	3.41	3.62
20	664.00	607.00	651.00	357.00	3.46	3.66	3.69	3.91	3.83	4.00
21	1 213.00									
21-22		954.00	1 027.00	567.00	5.59	5.70	5.83	5.93	5.88	6.01
22	1 105.00									
23	2 052.00	806.00	1 509.00	1 279.00	12.81	12.92	13.41	13.66	13.72	13.60
24	1 360.00	993.00	1 082.00	607.00	6.06	6.19	6.38	6.37	6.73	6.77
25	940.00	807.00	880.00	493.00	4.78	4.98	5.10	5.43	5.63	5.73
26	877.00	799.00	870.00	487.00	4.84	4.88	4.94	5.05	5.21	5.31
27	843.00									
27-28		726.00	748.00	390.00	3.86	4.02	4.21	4.33	4.42	4.58
28	730.00									
29	904.00	841.00	900.00	493.00	4.85	4.99	5.01	5.10	5.26	5.54
30	1 775.00									
30-33		865.00	926.00	508.00	4.87	5.39	5.66	5.68	5.45	5.77
31	1 000.00									
32	1 593.00									
33	957.00									
34	980.00									
34-35		971.00	1 041.00	571.00	5.54	5.87	5.95	5.93	5.91	6.01
35	1 276.00									
36	566.00									
36-37		525.00	571.00	320.00	3.16	3.17	3.35	3.48	3.51	3.70
37	1 030.00									

Explanatory notes: see p. 877. Notes explicatives: voir p. 879. Notas explicativas: véase p. 882.

[1] Prior to 2003: PTE; 1 Euro= 200.482 PTE. [1] Avant 2003: PTE; 1 Euro= 200,482 PTE. [1] Antes de 2003: PTE; 1 Euro= 200,482 PTE.

WAGES · SALAIRES · SALARIOS

5B

In manufacturing · Dans les industries manufacturières · En las industrias manufactureras

	1999	2000	2001	2002	2003	2004	2005	2006	2007	2008

Portugal (DA) — Wage earners - Ouvriers - Obreros — E.G./h. - Euro

Women - Femmes - Mujeres
ISIC 3 - CITI 3 - CIIU 3

	1999	2000	2001	2002	2003	2004	2005	2006	2007	2008
Total	554.00	500.00	536.00	294.00	2.89 [1]	3.00	3.02	3.09	3.19	3.33
15	562.00				[1]					
15-16		531.00	567.00	309.00	3.01 [1]	3.19	3.13	3.29	3.37	3.47
16	797.00				[1]					
17	506.00				[1]					
17-18		455.00	485.00	264.00	2.63 [1]	2.64	2.67	2.71	2.82	3.01
18	458.00				[1]					
19	469.00	467.00	493.00	266.00	2.63 [1]	2.72	2.75	2.78	2.89	3.00
20	543.00	480.00	531.00	304.00	2.92 [1]	3.18	3.22	3.28	3.33	3.48
21	705.00				[1]					
21-22		572.00	611.00	334.00	3.32 [1]	3.36	3.49	3.64	3.65	3.74
22	890.00				[1]					
23	1 910.00		860.00	1 072.00	11.13 [1]	8.33	9.50	10.75	12.80	10.77
24	1 016.00	665.00	720.00	400.00	4.04 [1]	3.98	3.86	3.86	4.34	4.41
25	619.00	568.00	597.00	320.00	3.14 [1]	3.29	3.29	3.56	3.65	3.87
26	635.00	579.00	621.00	341.00	3.38 [1]	3.38	3.38	3.64	3.71	3.79
27	665.00				[1]					
27-28		565.00	584.00	306.00	2.98 [1]	3.19	3.19	3.18	3.28	3.45
28	631.00				[1]					
29	742.00	644.00	668.00	351.00	3.36 [1]	3.60	3.60	3.94	3.84	3.81
30	979.00				[1]					
30-33		672.00	734.00	412.00	4.07 [1]	4.21	4.21	4.33	4.38	4.45
31	627.00				[1]					
32	987.00				[1]					
33	681.00				[1]					
34	723.00				[1]					
34-35		616.00	642.00	339.00	3.29 [1]	3.51	3.51	3.81	4.11	4.18
35	917.00				[1]					
36	509.00				[1]					
36-37		473.00	520.00	294.00	2.91 [1]	2.96	2.96	3.05	3.16	3.22
37	733.00				[1]					

Roumanie (DA) — Employees - Salariés - Asalariados — E.G./m. - Leu

Total men and women - Total hommes et femmes - Total hombres y mujeres
ISIC 3 - CITI 3 - CIIU 3

	1999	2000	2001	2002	2003	2004	2005	2006	2007	2008
Total	1 712 748	2 535 223	3 734 701	4 632 583	5 804 147	7 196 971	829 [2]	950	1 146	.
15	1 552 084	2 188 316	3 315 862	4 027 417	5 237 672	6 374 250	744 [2]	863	1 059	.
16	3 646 710	6 732 686	9 829 065	11 597 497	14 581 812	19 760 605	2 322 [2]	2 941	2 964	.
17	1 303 467	1 926 885	2 772 127	3 483 310	4 596 163	5 833 585	654 [2]	740	908	.
18	1 292 384	1 834 560	2 497 708	3 011 536	4 085 262	5 324 011	595 [2]	654	804	.
19	1 181 740	1 643 930	2 421 646	3 029 981	4 155 761	5 106 858	597 [2]	655	801	.
20	1 212 145	1 717 222	2 277 549	2 775 949	3 800 164	4 652 844	566 [2]	605	777	.
21	1 680 971	2 701 558	4 104 141	5 012 734	6 371 825	7 454 289	877 [2]	1 034	1 191	.
22	1 790 758	3 199 498	4 625 948	5 881 848	6 598 525	7 793 194	886 [2]	954	1 177	.
23	3 374 359	5 208 705	8 423 731	12 074 595	13 808 464	16 027 990	1 968 [2]	2 366	2 560	.
24	2 369 429	3 723 858	5 879 771	7 425 171	8 910 098	10 810 093	1 249 [2]	1 560	1 829	.
25	1 837 351	2 593 611	4 150 708	5 098 597	6 176 967	7 459 132	808 [2]	946	1 122	.
26	1 821 344	2 826 853	4 024 570	5 219 227	6 512 106	8 274 008	966 [2]	1 127	1 396	.
27	2 375 864	3 907 706	6 092 044	7 394 106	8 602 751	11 502 811	1 265 [2]	1 475	1 719	.
28	1 578 137	2 386 479	3 506 715	4 360 662	5 976 471	7 617 074	921 [2]	1 035	1 250	.
29	1 903 020	2 842 902	4 465 295	5 746 052	6 872 914	8 588 396	980 [2]	1 136	1 339	.
30	1 974 540	3 082 377	3 524 022	4 410 916	7 848 129	9 551 850	590 [2]	1 006	1 160	.
31	1 955 234	2 790 961	4 108 019	5 175 380	6 741 645	7 923 930	877 [2]	1 021	1 172	.
32	2 659 043	4 347 680	6 644 002	9 064 680	9 683 660	13 719 384	1 658 [2]	1 866	1 958	.
33	1 975 888	2 776 622	4 192 286	5 407 063	6 570 966	8 341 459	1 090 [2]	1 119	1 260	.
34	1 944 575	2 904 114	4 447 914	5 796 573	7 330 494	9 072 291	1 077 [2]	1 293	1 567	.
35	2 222 502	3 518 329	5 292 797	7 090 335	8 820 032	10 535 659	1 218 [2]	1 378	1 611	.
36	1 339 546	1 897 223	2 737 810	3 443 325	4 422 363	5 569 108	641 [2]	750	884	.
37	1 538 123	2 273 916	3 169 766	3 951 288	5 102 517	6 313 358	772 [2]	926	1 054	.

Explanatory notes: see p. 877. — Notes explicatives: voir p. 879. — Notas explicativas: véase p. 882.

[1] Prior to 2003: PTE; 1 Euro= 200.482 PTE. [2] New denomination: 1 leu = 10 000 old lei.
[1] Avant 2003: PTE: 1 Euro= 200,482 PTE. [2] Nouvelle dénomination: 1 leu = 10 000 anciens lei.
[1] Antes de 2003: PTE; 1 Euro= 200,482 PTE. [2] Nueva denominación: 1 leu = 10 000 antiguos lei.

5B WAGES — SALAIRES — SALARIOS

In manufacturing — Dans les industries manufacturières — En las industrias manufactureras

Roumanie (DA) — Employees - Salariés - Asalariados — E.G./m. - Leu

Men - Hommes - Hombres
ISIC 3 - CITI 3 - CIIU 3

	1999	2000	2001	2002	2003	2004	2005[1]	2006	2007	2008
Total	.	.	.	.	6 662 800	8 167 249	945	1 087	1 302	.
15	.	.	.	.	5 857 297	7 031 483	830	952	1 180	.
16	.	.	.	.	17 483 765	22 288 311	2 740	2 936	3 257	.
17	.	.	.	.	5 450 033	6 519 245	763	830	1 069	.
18	.	.	.	.	4 725 932	6 220 944	661	739	942	.
19	.	.	.	.	4 529 010	5 353 709	627	723	878	.
20	.	.	.	.	3 839 247	4 632 207	558	602	776	.
21	.	.	.	.	7 047 097	8 132 541	951	1 160	1 349	.
22	.	.	.	.	7 158 501	7 712 848	957	994	1 236	.
23	.	.	.	.	14 158 518	16 276 963	2 000	2 495	2 701	.
24	.	.	.	.	9 283 078	11 259 882	1 315	1 612	1 872	.
25	.	.	.	.	6 576 500	7 929 939	853	1 020	1 179	.
26	.	.	.	.	6 855 318	8 617 118	986	1 160	1 429	.
27	.	.	.	.	8 791 003	11 699 342	1 290	1 498	1 758	.
28	.	.	.	.	6 073 712	7 750 759	936	1 051	1 266	.
29	.	.	.	.	7 051 632	8 845 783	1 005	1 166	1 374	.
30	.	.	.	.	8 985 893	9 986 013	578	1 056	1 252	.
31	.	.	.	.	7 683 299	8 750 592	999	1 196	1 336	.
32	.	.	.	.	12 005 194	16 002 326	2 100	2 299	2 306	.
33	.	.	.	.	6 965 033	8 989 383	1 194	1 216	1 372	.
34	.	.	.	.	7 771 827	9 552 840	1 127	1 347	1 703	.
35	.	.	.	.	8 989 065	10 681 018	1 242	1 393	1 631	.
36	.	.	.	.	4 443 585	5 609 316	648	752	906	.
37	.	.	.	.	5 088 882	6 326 660	791	967	1 058	.

Women - Femmes - Mujeres
ISIC 3 - CITI 3 - CIIU 3

	1999	2000	2001	2002	2003	2004	2005[1]	2006	2007	2008
Total	.	.	.	.	4 915 058	6 203 325	710	807	976	.
15	.	.	.	.	4 599 805	5 700 740	658	773	933	.
16	.	.	.	.	10 964 285	15 998 085	1 656	2 951	2 253	.
17	.	.	.	.	4 338 646	5 630 551	622	712	858	.
18	.	.	.	.	3 978 863	5 192 316	584	640	782	.
19	.	.	.	.	4 032 534	5 023 567	587	634	776	.
20	.	.	.	.	3 689 147	4 715 296	589	614	778	.
21	.	.	.	.	5 336 120	6 403 142	762	852	978	.
22	.	.	.	.	6 047 363	7 884 844	820	914	1 109	.
23	.	.	.	.	13 107 804	15 518 930	1 903	2 105	2 251	.
24	.	.	.	.	8 359 500	10 109 432	1 147	1 487	1 764	.
25	.	.	.	.	5 609 129	6 776 075	736	834	1 024	.
26	.	.	.	.	5 901 533	7 642 653	925	1 055	1 318	.
27	.	.	.	.	7 883 147	10 708 961	1 169	1 378	1 558	.
28	.	.	.	.	5 590 801	7 077 130	865	968	1 183	.
29	.	.	.	.	6 352 487	7 821 652	904	1 042	1 228	.
30	.	.	.	.	6 363 527	8 526 301	622	887	1 019	.
31	.	.	.	.	5 856 170	7 231 386	783	891	1 053	.
32	.	.	.	.	7 560 644	11 634 320	1 307	1 514	1 668	.
33	.	.	.	.	5 926 018	7 404 099	928	982	1 077	.
34	.	.	.	.	6 611 288	8 260 309	994	1 206	1 372	.
35	.	.	.	.	8 055 501	9 819 695	1 105	1 294	1 505	.
36	.	.	.	.	4 385 112	5 501 986	630	748	852	.
37	.	.	.	.	5 170 214	6 257 298	700	790	1 035	.

Explanatory notes: see p. 877.
[1] New denomination: 1 leu = 10 000 old lei.

Notes explicatives: voir p. 879.
[1] Nouvelle dénomination: 1 leu = 10 000 anciens lei.

Notas explicativas: véase p. 882.
[1] Nueva denominación: 1 leu = 10 000 antiguos lei.

In manufacturing / Dans les industries manufacturières / En las industrias manufactureras

	1999	2000	2001	2002	2003	2004	2005	2006	2007	2008

Russian Federation (DA) — Employees - Salariés - Asalariados — E.G./m. - Rouble

Total men and women - Total hommes et femmes - Total hombres y mujeres
ISIC 3 - CITI 3 - CIIU 3

	1999	2000	2001	2002	2003	2004	2005	2006	2007	2008
Total	.	.	.	.	.	.	8 421	10 199	12 879	16 050
15	.	.	.	.	.	.	7 150	8 642	10 885	13 714
16	.	.	.	.	.	.	21 807	25 377	31 750	38 062
17	.	.	.	.	.	.	4 360	5 260	6 963	9 092
18	.	.	.	.	.	.	3 607	4 693	6 270	7 957
19	.	.	.	.	.	.	4 695	5 649	7 537	9 522
20	.	.	.	.	.	.	5 895	6 950	8 816	11 301
21	.	.	.	.	.	.	9 675	11 286	13 276	16 786
22	.	.	.	.	.	.	9 289	10 748	14 046	18 014
23	.	.	.	.	.	.	19 397	22 320	28 565	34 913
24	.	.	.	.	.	.	9 928	11 599	14 616	18 220
25	.	.	.	.	.	.	6 879	8 768	11 083	13 464
26	.	.	.	.	.	.	7 922	9 984	13 193	16 372
27	.	.	.	.	.	.	12 126	14 254	17 651	20 929
28	.	.	.	.	.	.	7 295	9 007	11 818	15 007
29	.	.	.	.	.	.	8 380	10 418	13 480	16 940
30	.	.	.	.	.	.	7 636	9 533	13 742	18 208
31	.	.	.	.	.	.	8 307	10 312	12 845	16 357
32	.	.	.	.	.	.	7 968	10 039	12 217	15 524
33	.	.	.	.	.	.	8 312	10 486	14 023	17 509
34	.	.	.	.	.	.	8 683	10 713	13 138	16 068
35	.	.	.	.	.	.	9 884	11 941	14 646	18 228
36	.	.	.	.	.	.	5 954	7 732	9 865	12 203
37	.	.	.	.	.	.	7 952	10 280	11 040	14 254

San Marino (E) — Employees - Salariés - Asalariados — E.G./m. - Euro

Total men and women - Total hommes et femmes - Total hombres y mujeres
ISIC 3 - CITI 3 - CIIU 3

	1999	2000	2001	2002	2003	2004	2005	2006	2007	2008
Total	.	.	3 289 004 ¦	1 868 ¦	1 922	1 900	1 934	2 021	.	.
15	.	.	3 384 854 ¦	1 655 ¦	1 867	1 620	1 747	1 858	.	.
17	.	.	3 794 500 ¦	1 271 ¦	1 696	1 730	1 624	1 619	.	.
18	.	.	2 684 770 ¦	1 681 ¦	1 691	1 737	2 056	1 928	.	.
19	.	.	3 189 924 ¦	1 671 ¦	1 777	1 704	1 963	1 795	.	.
20	.	.	3 170 583 ¦	1 890 ¦	1 925	1 924	1 919	1 996	.	.
21	.	.	4 264 147 ¦	2 095 ¦	2 208	2 044	2 160	2 145	.	.
22	.	.	3 810 027 ¦	2 152 ¦	2 128	1 791	2 017	2 011	.	.
24	.	.	1 606 228 ¦	1 833 ¦	1 879	1 894	1 950	2 062	.	.
25	.	.	5 266 639 ¦	1 960 ¦	1 912	2 198	2 131	2 243	.	.
26	.	.	3 408 559 ¦	2 011 ¦	2 004	2 050	2 085	2 116	.	.
28-31,33	.	.	¦	2 387 ¦	2 059	1 942	.	.	.	.
32	.	.	3 289 216 ¦	1 872 ¦	1 660	1 657			.	.
33	.	.					2 522	1 984	.	.
34	.	.	4 224 825 ¦	2 056 ¦	2 564	1 928	2 522	1 984	.	.
35	.	.					994	2 420	.	.
36	.	.	3 331 380 ¦	1 875 ¦	1 842	1 895	1 813	1 894	.	.

Serbia (DA) [2] — Employees - Salariés - Asalariados — E.G./m. - New Dinar

Total men and women - Total hommes et femmes - Total hombres y mujeres
ISIC 3 - CITI 3 - CIIU 3

	1999	2000	2001	2002	2003	2004	2005	2006	2007	2008
Total	.	.	.	.	12 996	16 065	20 366	25 830	30 620	.
15	.	.	.	.	18 262	20 892	26 177	32 535	36 750	.
16	.	.	.	.	41 964	51 836	73 012	87 069	98 325	.
17	.	.	.	.	4 695	5 205	7 237	9 330	13 276	.
18	.	.	.	.	3 163	4 127	5 665	8 531	12 079	.
19	.	.	.	.	5 978	8 114	12 148	15 028	17 517	.
20	.	.	.	.	5 780	6 922	8 363	12 210	16 145	.
21	.	.	.	.	14 782	16 144	17 736	20 208	25 556	.
22	.	.	.	.	15 890	20 076	24 167	30 952	36 218	.
23	.	.	.	.	27 651	32 803	42 308	48 014	56 178	.
24	.	.	.	.	20 473	25 468	30 562	39 346	47 731	.
25	.	.	.	.	13 352	17 697	22 908	28 304	32 786	.
26	.	.	.	.	15 152	17 500	20 955	26 117	30 443	.
27	.	.	.	.	15 491	20 791	26 741	35 979	43 375	.
28	.	.	.	.	12 389	13 769	17 370	21 405	24 278	.
29	.	.	.	.	9 588	13 082	17 028	23 113	28 661	.
30	.	.	.	.	21 893	28 392	35 496	47 125	52 482	.
31	.	.	.	.	13 181	16 299	19 912	23 367	29 243	.
32	.	.	.	.	9 806	15 663	17 606	17 844	18 955	.
33	.	.	.	.	9 439	12 027	14 604	17 156	17 369	.
34	.	.	.	.	11 756	15 355	18 500	21 060	22 828	.
35	.	.	.	.	10 264	13 274	17 222	21 037	24 999	.
36	.	.	.	.	9 418	10 272	12 888	17 828	20 552	.
37	.	.	.	.	7 287	9 056	14 081	18 743	26 230	.

Explanatory notes: see p. 877.   Notes explicatives: voir p. 879.   Notas explicativas: véase p. 882.

[1] Prior to 2002: ITL; 1 Euro=1936.27 ITL. [2] Excl. Kosovo and Metohia.   [1] Avant 2002: ITL; 1 Euro=1936,27 ITL. [2] N.c. Kosovo et Metohia.   [1] Antes de 2002: ITL; 1 Euro=1936,27 ITL. [2] Excl. Kosovo y Metohia.

WAGES / SALAIRES / SALARIOS

In manufacturing / Dans les industries manufacturières / En las industrias manufactureras

	1999	2000	2001	2002	2003	2004	2005	2006	2007	2008

Slovakia (CA) [1] — Employees - Salariés - Asalariados — E.G./m. - Koruna

Total men and women - Total hommes et femmes - Total hombres y mujeres
ISIC 3 - CITI 3 - CIIU 3

	1999	2000	2001	2002	2003	2004	2005	2006	2007	2008
Total	10 758	11 722	12 908	13 837	14 873	16 378	17 604	18 817	20 024	21 449
15	10 419	11 381	12 566	13 627	14 463	16 163	16 599	18 014	19 443	20 870
16					25 481					
17	7 587	8 504	9 340	9 797	10 315	11 477	12 362	13 214	14 148	14 588
18	7 151	7 836	8 401	8 673	9 088	10 012	10 158	10 824	11 664	12 599
19	7 662	8 513	9 236	9 803	10 298	11 183	11 845	12 624	13 405	14 250
20	8 707	9 714	10 076	10 847	11 564	12 826	13 149	14 403	16 361	17 292
21	12 674	14 338	15 714	18 262	18 602	20 260	21 871	23 748	25 637	26 929
22	14 098	15 289	17 199	18 303	19 443	21 163	23 218	24 795	25 762	27 674
23	16 837	19 206	21 544	26 726	33 021	37 480	61 496	46 639	47 941	51 162
24	12 730	14 403	16 113	17 757	18 233	19 613	21 755	24 575	26 266	27 175
25	12 949	15 066	15 884	17 470	19 022	20 464	20 757	21 982	22 535	22 504
26	12 024	13 317	14 712	15 701	16 729	18 346	19 434	21 262	23 539	26 136
27	14 832	17 029	18 968	20 268	23 053	26 268	28 571	30 720	31 705	32 589
28	11 136	12 267	13 050	13 778	14 494	16 050	17 542	19 183	20 731	22 645
29	10 639	11 919	13 134	14 489	16 028	18 024	19 410	20 849	22 347	24 593
30	11 161	12 443	13 636	14 491	16 840	17 161	19 307	19 650	22 713	22 963
31	10 291	10 981	11 861	12 318	13 112	14 478	15 550	16 972	18 163	18 996
32	9 967	11 928	13 261	14 577	14 743	15 852	16 399	19 015	19 937	21 557
33	12 795	15 076	15 837	15 909	16 298	18 869	20 687	22 898	22 672	23 898
34	14 087	17 270	19 324	20 251	20 889	22 599	25 675	26 569	28 218	29 378
35	11 074	11 667	14 270	14 687	16 044	20 162	20 323	21 670	23 081	26 616
36	9 068	10 128	11 356	12 601	13 688	15 265	16 464	17 401	18 937	19 326
37	12 483	20 626	21 100	21 722	22 708	23 382	24 555	24 136	24 510	29 779

Slovenia (D) — Employees - Salariés - Asalariados — E.G./m. - Euro

Total men and women - Total hommes et femmes - Total hombres y mujeres
ISIC 3 - CITI 3 - CIIU 3

	1999	2000	2001	2002	2003	2004	2005	2006	2007	2008
Total	144 110	161 296	178 596	196 220	211 060	226 029	238 985 [2]	252 162	1 124 [3]	1 208
15	164 747	177 265	195 334	213 393	225 127	236 296	235 956 [2]	244 666	1 091 [3]	1 167
16							[2]		[3]	
17	110 670	126 505	130 574	153 881	165 733	176 573	185 578 [2]	195 564	860 [3]	915
18	99 729	108 392	121 614	128 514	135 697	144 950	148 709 [2]	156 513	679 [3]	714
19	109 761	123 586	138 495	149 127	158 674	168 981	174 754 [2]	182 923	800 [3]	889
20	122 446	134 379	146 857	159 277	169 335	183 645	192 288 [2]	206 020	937 [3]	1 021
21	147 451	171 693	193 958	212 825	224 386	234 674	250 553 [2]	259 321	1 157 [3]	1 237
22	204 221	224 681	237 393	257 295	272 118	295 558	303 986 [2]	316 633	1 384 [3]	1 485
23	162 564	181 421	198 820	216 214	245 456	273 047	300 348 [2]	308 316	1 312 [3]	1 612
24	217 614	248 995	287 302	312 906	347 143	362 724	393 741 [2]	403 257	1 812 [3]	1 932
25	148 568	162 797	180 130	194 186	206 041	221 921	235 667 [2]	249 082	1 118 [3]	1 207
26	146 607	162 923	176 069	192 067	203 940	220 337	235 594 [2]	249 942	1 141 [3]	1 229
27	147 593	169 362	185 779	208 428	224 258	241 173	261 325 [2]	280 198	1 231 [3]	1 284
28	141 644	160 230	174 072	192 198	205 958	221 188	231 009 [2]	244 922	1 089 [3]	1 163
29	139 970	157 585	174 688	194 091	212 237	231 056	244 767 [2]	260 388	1 155 [3]	1 245
30	186 096	194 523	225 347	252 382	272 138	295 263	298 951 [2]	333 410	1 542 [3]	1 701
31	146 492	164 268	181 353	199 831	210 216	221 603	232 092 [2]	244 786	1 097 [3]	1 157
32	149 722	165 929	184 359	210 424	228 318	246 344	283 194 [2]	284 257	1 223 [3]	1 334
33	145 832	160 271	177 322	192 858	207 535	215 006	229 842 [2]	240 133	1 062 [3]	1 164
34	153 785	173 975	190 417	210 795	219 888	234 463	250 116 [2]	262 976	1 147 [3]	1 224
35	144 383	165 783	179 901	197 261	212 203	228 242	244 959 [2]	268 518	1 178 [3]	1 300
36	121 173	133 273	146 566	160 460	171 030	184 270	190 412 [2]	198 476	893 [3]	970
37	173 134	198 336	216 192	228 800	246 397	277 957	279 237 [2]	293 675	1 313 [3]	1 421

Suisse (DA) [4] — Employees - Salariés - Asalariados — E.G./m. - Franc

Total men and women - Total hommes et femmes - Total hombres y mujeres
ISIC 3 - CITI 3 - CIIU 3

	1999	2000	2001	2002	2003	2004	2005	2006	2007	2008
Total		5 862		6 155		6 349		6 527		
15		5 158		5 407		5 449		5 458		
16		7 506		7 974		10 223		10 193		
17		4 683		4 992		5 264		5 434		
18		4 128		4 216		4 465		4 806		
19		4 434		4 845		4 844		4 866		
20		5 134		5 238		5 424		5 507		
21		5 676		5 900		6 127		6 497		
22		6 379		6 509		6 613		6 765		
23-24		7 390		7 625		8 087		8 478		
24										
25		5 337		5 572		5 747		5 930		
26		5 482		5 819		5 820		6 050		
27-28		5 396		5 627		5 775		5 899		
28										
29										
29,34-35		6 222		6 465		6 551		6 779		
30-32		6 322		6 704		6 846		6 989		
31										
33		5 610		6 182		6 423		6 565		
36-37		5 241		5 468		5 636		5 746		

Explanatory notes: see p. 877.

Notes explicatives: voir p. 879.

Notas explicativas: véase p. 882.

[1] Excl. enterprises with less than 20 employees. [2] Beginning 2005, methodology revised: excl. family allowances and the value of payments in kind. [3] Prior to 2007: SIT; 1 Euro = 239.64 SIT. [4] Standardised monthly earnings (40 hours x 4,3 weeks).

[1] Non compris les entreprises occupant moins de 20 salariés. [2] A partir de 2005, méthodologie révisée: non compris les allocations familiales et la valeur des paiments en nature. [3] Avant 2007: SIT; 1 Euro = 239,64 SIT. [4] Gains mensuels standardisés (40 heures x 4,3semaines).

[1] Excl. las empresas con menos de 20 asalariados. [2] A partir de 2005: metodología revisada: excl. las asignaciones familiares y el valor de los pagos en especie. [3] Antes de 2007: SIT; 1 Euro = 239,64 SIT. [4] Ganancias medias estandardizadas (40 horas x 4,3 semanas).

WAGES — SALAIRES — SALARIOS

In manufacturing — Dans les industries manufacturières — En las industrias manufactureras

	1999	2000	2001	2002	2003	2004	2005	2006	2007	2008

Suisse (DA) [1] — Employees - Salariés - Asalariados — E.G./m. - Franc

Men - Hommes - Hombres — ISIC 3 - CITI 3 - CIIU 3

	1999	2000	2001	2002	2003	2004	2005	2006	2007	2008
Total	.	6 296	.	6 552	.	6 726	.	6 915	.	.
15	.	5 591	.	5 834	.	5 827	.	5 856	.	.
16	.	8 448	.	9 016	.	11 466	.	11 270	.	.
17	.	5 588	.	5 778	.	6 067	.	6 194	.	.
18	.	6 074	.	6 204	.	5 969	.	6 421	.	.
19	.	5 295	.	5 797	.	5 747	.	5 839	.	.
20	.	5 170	.	5 289	.	5 462	.	5 542	.	.
21	.	6 219	.	6 311	.	6 528	.	6 981	.	.
22	.	7 022	.	7 055	.	7 163	.	7 297	.	.
23-24	.	7 884	.	8 050	.	8 529	.	8 960	.	.
24	.	.	.	.	.	.	.	.	.	.
25	.	5 816	.	6 009	.	6 154	.	6 363	.	.
26	.	5 567	.	5 938	.	5 957	.	6 162	.	.
27-28	.	5 608	.	5 834	.	5 977	.	6 113	.	.
28	.	.	.	.	.	.	.	.	.	.
29	.	.	.	.	.	.	.	.	.	.
29,34-35	.	6 463	.	6 690	.	6 750	.	6 997	.	.
30-32	.	6 980	.	7 313	.	7 494	.	7 675	.	.
31	.	.	.	.	.	.	.	.	.	.
33	.	6 549	.	7 036	.	7 293	.	7 481	.	.
36-37	.	5 525	.	5 727	.	5 957	.	6 023	.	.

Women - Femmes - Mujeres — ISIC 3 - CITI 3 - CIIU 3

	1999	2000	2001	2002	2003	2004	2005	2006	2007	2008
Total	.	4 550	.	4 926	.	5 162	.	5 353	.	.
15	.	4 214	.	4 438	.	4 531	.	4 561	.	.
16	.	5 074	.	5 810	.	7 490	.	7 803	.	.
17	.	3 678	.	4 113	.	4 239	.	4 459	.	.
18	.	3 453	.	3 547	.	3 851	.	4 206	.	.
19	.	3 630	.	4 064	.	4 149	.	4 058	.	.
20	.	4 630	.	4 669	.	4 941	.	5 074	.	.
21	.	4 012	.	4 543	.	4 807	.	4 991	.	.
22	.	5 078	.	5 382	.	5 525	.	5 747	.	.
23-24	.	6 105	.	6 501	.	6 993	.	7 444	.	.
24	.	.	.	.	.	.	.	.	.	.
25	.	4 040	.	4 272	.	4 574	.	4 729	.	.
26	.	4 839	.	5 039	.	4 962	.	5 335	.	.
27-28	.	4 275	.	4 558	.	4 704	.	4 842	.	.
28	.	.	.	.	.	.	.	.	.	.
29	.	.	.	.	.	.	.	.	.	.
29,34-35	.	4 695	.	5 092	.	5 293	.	5 383	.	.
30-32	.	4 466	.	4 839	.	4 892	.	4 994	.	.
31	.	.	.	.	.	.	.	.	.	.
33	.	4 309	.	4 806	.	4 986	.	5 131	.	.
36-37	.	4 273	.	4 596	.	4 646	.	4 854	.	.

Sweden (DA) [2][3] — Wage earners - Ouvriers - Obreros — E.G./h. - Krona

Total men and women - Total hommes et femmes - Total hombres y mujeres
ISIC 3 - CITI 3 - CIIU 3 [4]   ISIC 4 - CITI 4 - CIIU 4

	1999	2000	2001	2002	2003	2004	2005	2006	2007	2008	
Total	106.85	111.30	114.90	118.20	122.00	126.10	129.90	133.80	139.50 |	145.20	Total
15-16	99.77	105.00	106.70	112.30	115.00	119.00	122.40	127.20	132.40 |	139.00	10-12
17-19	94.25	99.10	103.00	104.50	110.20	113.70	117.20	120.00	124.90 |	131.40	13-15
20	103.34	106.50	111.40	114.70	118.40	122.90	126.60	129.80	135.80 |	139.60	16
21	122.16	126.00	131.70	134.00	139.70	143.50	149.20	154.30	161.00 |	166.40	17
22	107.76	113.60	117.50	122.10	122.80	133.30	134.60	138.30	142.10 |	150.70	18
23	.	136.20	153.60	153.60	162.00	162.90	150.80	167.00	158.50 |	174.80	19
23-24	116.63	121.00	128.20	132.70	136.70	140.60	144.40	150.00	153.60 |	160.90	20
24	.	119.80	126.10	131.00	135.00	139.00	144.20	148.40	153.20 |	162.10	21
25	105.09	108.90	111.60	113.60	118.70	122.20	125.00	129.50	135.30 |	140.30	22
26	107.82	110.20	115.10	117.70	122.60	126.30	126.20	129.90	137.90 |	148.40	23
27	122.96	126.50	132.80	135.10	136.50	140.40	143.60	149.30	153.80 |	158.50	24
28	102.36	104.60	111.10	112.70	118.00	121.00	124.20	127.00	134.70 |	139.30	25
29	105.19	109.10	111.70	115.10	119.90	124.40	129.40	133.60	140.20 |	.	26
30	.	100.20	102.40	104.80	110.30	113.90	118.10	118.60	123.60 |	142.60	26-28
30-33	102.86	108.40	107.20	109.50	116.90	120.60	124.50	126.60	132.00 |	156.50	29-30
31	.	105.50	103.90	108.80	117.60	120.40	125.30	126.60	133.20 |	123.10	31-32
32	.	113.10	113.10	110.70	116.20	122.90	123.80	129.30	134.10 |	143.80	33
33	.	103.40	107.40	110.50	118.00	120.00	125.30	126.90	134.40 |		
34	.	119.80	122.70	125.20	130.00	133.90	139.70	144.60	149.80 |		
34-35	112.17	118.80	121.30	124.40	129.20	133.20	138.70	144.00	148.90 |		
35	.	113.70	115.80	121.00	125.10	128.70	132.80	140.80	143.80 |		
36-37	99.01	104.20	105.90	108.20	106.30	110.10	111.60	115.00	119.10 |		

Explanatory notes: see p. 877.

[1] Standardised monthly earnings (40 hours x 4,3 weeks). [2] Private sector; Sep. of each year. [3] Excl. holidays, sick-leave and overtime payments. [4] Adults; prior to 1998: 2nd quarter of each year; 1998-2000: Sept.-Oct. of each year.

Notes explicatives: voir p. 879.

[1] Gains mensuels standardisés (40 heures x 4,3semaines). [2] Secteur privé; sept. de chaque année. [3] Non compris les versements pour les vacances, congés maladie ainsi que la rémunération des heures supplémentaires. [4] Adultes; avant 1998: 2ème trimestre de chaque année; 1998-2000: sept.-oct. de chaque année.

Notas explicativas: véase p. 882.

[1] Ganancias medias estandardizadas (40 horas x 4,3 semanas). [2] Sector privado; sept. de cada ano. [3] Excl. los pagos por vacancias, licencias de enfermedad, y pagos por horas extraordinarias. [4] Adultos; antes de 1998: segundo trimestre de cada año; 1998-2000:sept-oct. de cada año.

Sweden (DA) [1] [2]   Wage earners - Ouvriers - Obreros   E.G./h. - Krona

Men - Hommes - Hombres

ISIC 3 - CITI 3 - CIIU 3 [3]   ISIC 4 - CITI 4 - CIIU 4

ISIC 3	1999	2000	2001	2002	2003	2004	2005	2006	2007	2008	ISIC 4
Total	108.69	113.30	116.90	120.20	124.10	128.40	132.20	136.10	142.10	147.70	Total
15-16	102.53	108.50	109.70	115.10	118.30	122.30	126.10	130.70	136.30	143.80	10-12
17-19	98.35	105.20	108.20	109.40	115.10	119.00	124.10	125.50	131.60	136.90	13-15
20	103.60	106.70	111.70	115.10	118.90	123.30	126.90	130.20	136.30	140.10	16
21	124.04	128.10	134.00	136.20	141.80	145.90	151.40	156.60	163.40	168.50	17
22	111.26	117.40	120.80	125.80	126.90	138.20	138.90	143.50	147.20	156.00	18
23	.	137.50	155.10	155.10	162.00	164.10	152.30	168.60	160.10	175.00	19
23-24	119.36	124.50	132.00	136.50	140.60	144.40	148.60	154.80	157.60	163.30	20
24	.	123.10	129.60	134.60	138.50	142.60	148.40	153.20	157.30	169.90	21
25	108.28	111.80	114.30	116.60	121.90	125.50	128.20	132.30	138.70	144.30	22
26	108.79	111.40	116.50	119.30	124.20	128.70	127.40	130.80	139.30	149.90	23
27	123.84	127.10	133.20	135.70	136.90	140.60	143.90	149.70	154.30	159.40	24
28	103.59	106.10	111.80	113.70	118.80	121.80	124.90	127.80	135.90	140.30	25
29	106.03	110.10	112.70	116.20	120.90	125.50	130.50	134.70	141.40	.	26
30	.	100.20	105.30	107.50	114.00	116.50	120.70	121.50	126.50	144.90	26-28
30-33	104.08	110.00	109.10	112.20	119.80	123.10	127.70	129.50	135.30	157.80	29-30
31	.	108.00	106.30	111.90	120.70	123.00	128.00	129.60	136.20	125.60	31-32
32	.	114.40	114.60	113.20	118.90	124.70	127.00	131.70	137.60	144.60	33
33	.	105.50	109.40	112.80	120.30	123.10	128.80	129.60	133.70	.	
34	.	120.60	123.70	126.60	131.40	135.50	141.10	145.70	151.20	.	
34-35	112.83	119.50	122.20	125.60	130.30	134.60	139.90	144.90	150.20	.	
35	.	114.30	116.50	121.70	125.70	129.30	133.80	141.10	145.10	.	
36-37	100.77	106.00	107.70	109.50	107.90	112.00	114.10	117.40	122.00	.	

Women - Femmes - Mujeres

ISIC 3 - CITI 3 - CIIU 3 [3]   ISIC 4 - CITI 4 - CIIU 4

ISIC 3	1999	2000	2001	2002	2003	2004	2005	2006	2007	2008	ISIC 4
Total	99.56	103.40	106.60	109.40	112.90	116.80	119.90	124.10	128.60	134.40	Total
15-16	93.07	97.00	100.10	105.50	107.40	111.90	114.20	119.50	124.00	129.80	10-12
17-19	89.69	92.20	96.10	98.80	103.20	105.90	108.10	112.00	116.10	124.50	13-15
20	101.78	104.20	108.80	111.60	114.10	119.60	124.30	126.20	131.70	135.60	16
21	110.84	113.80	118.50	121.10	127.30	129.90	136.30	139.90	147.00	153.50	17
22	98.00	102.50	106.50	109.90	111.70	118.50	121.10	123.30	128.40	133.20	18
23-24	108.22	111.10	116.00	122.00	125.40	128.90	132.30	136.20	141.20	.	19
24	.	111.00	115.80	121.80	125.20	128.80	132.30	135.90	141.20	148.20	20
25	97.77	102.40	105.70	107.60	111.50	114.60	116.70	122.00	126.50	152.90	21
26	101.52	103.50	106.80	109.30	112.10	114.40	119.50	122.70	127.30	130.20	22
27	115.76	121.60	129.10	130.10	132.70	138.70	141.00	145.90	150.10	135.50	23
28	95.61	97.50	105.30	105.10	111.50	115.50	118.80	121.10	126.00	152.20	24
29	97.91	100.90	104.30	105.90	111.00	114.90	120.00	124.90	129.70	132.30	25
30	.	96.60	98.90	100.90	105.20	110.30	115.00	114.90	119.40	.	26
30-33	100.91	105.50	104.00	104.20	111.20	115.10	117.50	120.50	124.90	131.90	26-28
31	.	98.60	99.20	100.80	109.00	112.10	116.20	117.60	123.40	150.20	29-30
32	.	111.20	111.20	106.90	112.20	119.80	119.00	126.00	128.70	118.00	31-32
33	.	101.00	103.40	106.50	114.20	114.60	118.30	121.40	124.60	131.30	33
34	.	115.10	117.30	118.20	123.30	125.90	132.70	139.20	143.10	.	
34-35	108.00	114.10	116.20	117.70	122.80	125.60	131.80	139.00	142.10	.	
35	.	105.80	107.80	112.70	118.30	122.70	122.30	136.00	132.80	.	
36-37	94.18	97.90	100.80	103.70	103.10	106.00	105.90	109.40	112.70	.	

Turkey (DA)   Employees - Salariés - Asalariados   E.G./m. - Lira

Total men and women - Total hommes et femmes - Total hombres y mujeres

ISIC 3 - CITI 3 - CIIU 3

ISIC 3	1999	2000	2001	2002	2003	2004	2005	2006	2007	2008
Total	.	.	.	680 172	865 658	1 023 118	1 108 419	.	.	.
15				647 313	866 616	1 042 093	1 166 726			
16				1 390 740	2 585 986	2 027 618	2 432 244			
17				504 993	617 441	791 633	848 801			
18				409 598	513 946	634 954	709 976			
19				387 032	461 762	608 294	663 893			
20				383 623	457 039	609 349	640 815			
21				1 042 618	1 385 155	1 202 316	1 364 547			
22				635 481	675 872	885 769	966 376			
23				2 237 982	3 238 796	4 688 009	4 387 090			
24				1 855 976	2 054 524	2 241 766	2 260 442			
25				636 797	784 911	975 979	1 074 073			
26				708 510	894 012	1 054 122	1 169 903			
27				976 229	1 456 469	1 696 531	1 918 316			
28				472 724	628 483	769 296	837 187			
29				820 856	962 021	1 132 099	1 147 353			
30				891 678	1 224 857	1 415 983	979 009			
31				776 299	1 041 804	120 273	1 437 151			
32				1 151 675	1 541 100	1 800 126	2 000 529			
33				634 003	692 224	902 528	1 069 911			
34				1 143 780	1 443 900	1 683 651	1 760 043			
35				1 141 084	1 351 888	1 354 450	1 221 084			
36				42 765	524 454	642 116	688 206			
37				41 437	451 884	718 062	650 221			

Explanatory notes: see p. 877.   Notes explicatives: voir p. 879.   Notas explicativas: véase p. 882.

[1] Private sector; Sep. of each year. [2] Excl. holidays, sick-leave and overtime payments. [3] Adults; prior to 1998: 2nd quarter of each year; 1998-2000: Sept-Oct. of each year.

[1] Secteur privé; sept. de chaque année. [2] Non compris les versements pour les vacances, congés maladie ainsi que la rémunération des heures supplémentaires. [3] Adultes; avant 1998: 2ème trimestre de chaque année; 1998-2000: sept.-oct. de chaque année.

[1] Sector privado; sept. de cada ano. [2] Excl. los pagos por vacancias, licencias de enfermedad, y pagos por horas extraordinarias. [3] Adultos; antes de 1998: segundo trimestre de cada año; 1998-2000:sept-oct. de cada año.

In manufacturing — Dans les industries manufacturières — En las industrias manufactureras

	1999	2000	2001	2002	2003	2004	2005	2006	2007	2008

Ukraine (CA)   Employees - Salariés - Asalariados   E.G./m. - Hryvnia

Total men and women - Total hommes et femmes - Total hombres y mujeres
ISIC 3 - CITI 3 - CIIU 3

	1999	2000	2001	2002	2003	2004	2005	2006	2007	2008
Total	191.3	270.7	368.3	441.3	552.9	700.0	905.1	1 137.3	1 456.4	1 849.0
15	.	268.2	349.5	407.1	478.0	573.5	755.0	958.8	1 193.2	1 579.6
16	.	1 301.8	1 550.7	1 739.3	2 062.6	2 639.9	3 033.8	3 600.7	4 289.9	5 641.7
17	.	137.2	187.6	224.0	272.5	397.4	516.4	650.8	823.2	1 078.8
18	.	184.1	241.4	275.0	336.5	427.7	525.8	644.3	791.0	980.3
19	.	152.7	210.1	271.4	373.6	443.8	552.8	690.8	853.9	1 032.7
20	.	191.4	283.7	351.0	450.2	560.9	707.0	878.7	1 078.1	1 346.8
21	.	343.1	439.9	520.2	610.9	779.7	1 000.9	1 206.6	1 466.7	1 809.5
22	.	426.5	532.4	606.9	699.2	811.2	995.6	1 311.2	1 585.0	2 006.5
23	.	489.6	634.4	824.4	951.1	1 173.5	1 470.4	1 697.4	2 144.9	2 689.2
24	.	318.0	421.2	470.8	581.3	748.1	1 012.0	1 260.5	1 586.3	2 047.2
25	.	255.9	343.5	413.8	518.7	648.8	814.0	1 020.5	1 251.3	1 598.0
26	.	231.5	314.0	384.2	489.6	624.8	824.3	1 067.3	1 440.4	1 818.4
27	.	466.9	584.9	663.0	837.1	1 065.9	1 387.7	1 679.7	2 173.2	2 618.0
28	.	190.4	274.4	353.4	447.8	579.8	753.6	982.3	1 268.9	1 573.9
29	.	226.2	332.2	388.3	492.6	638.9	831.8	1 067.9	1 379.6	1 790.5
30	.	140.7	259.6	314.8	408.3	439.8	584.7	813.4	1 442.9	2 172.8
31	.	190.0	290.5	345.3	445.5	587.1	771.2	981.6	1 309.9	1 661.4
32	.	122.5	185.7	251.1	343.6	498.1	677.0	916.4	1 230.0	1 671.2
33	.	187.1	275.7	330.7	412.8	533.6	710.7	917.0	1 149.6	1 461.5
34	.	225.2	291.6	355.0	520.2	695.9	860.9	1 171.4	1 582.5	1 957.6
35	.	273.0	370.0	463.0	547.7	706.4	865.0	1 116.7	1 464.1	1 881.7
36	.	172.3	232.8	313.3	405.8	531.3	653.6	797.2	993.5	1 286.6
37	.	363.2	421.7	443.5	532.3	701.9	828.4	997.3	1 250.7	1 668.2

Men - Hommes - Hombres
ISIC 3 - CITI 3 - CIIU 3

	1999	2000	2001	2002	2003	2004	2005	2006	2007	2008
Total	.	.	.	509.0	640.8	809.0	1 042.3	1 302.1	1 667.0	2 103.2
15	.	.	.	440.1	518.9	619.6	828.7	1 053.9	1 308.0	1 741.3
16	.	.	.	2 033.4	2 476.8	3 042.1	3 441.4	3 887.4	4 609.4	5 832.9
17	.	.	.	262.0	322.7	461.4	592.8	745.3	931.5	1 215.9
18	.	.	.	271.4	336.2	454.5	566.7	718.4	898.8	1 047.3
19	.	.	.	327.4	450.6	514.0	623.3	808.5	974.1	1 148.5
20	.	.	.	362.2	464.8	576.6	737.7	904.4	1 118.9	1 397.1
21	.	.	.	602.2	694.4	885.8	1 132.2	1 342.5	1 650.3	2 014.6
22	.	.	.	665.2	779.5	892.1	1 119.5	1 434.0	1 735.6	2 183.2
23	.	.	.	909.2	1 052.3	1 292.4	1 616.3	1 859.7	2 369.7	2 967.3
24	.	.	.	525.3	653.7	844.1	1 143.8	1 421.1	1 770.8	2 278.2
25	.	.	.	466.3	590.1	715.1	897.4	1 122.8	1 354.7	1 737.3
26	.	.	.	430.6	550.0	698.1	912.0	1 181.2	1 591.0	1 976.8
27	.	.	.	756.7	962.9	1 222.8	1 581.1	1 910.3	2 459.2	2 958.5
28	.	.	.	397.3	496.1	646.3	831.4	1 071.7	1 368.5	1 708.1
29	.	.	.	429.3	547.7	709.9	929.0	1 188.7	1 539.4	1 993.3
30	.	.	.	391.0	480.6	495.0	616.3	875.7	1 601.5	2 548.5
31	.	.	.	411.6	527.6	688.0	890.2	1 116.7	1 491.7	1 886.5
32	.	.	.	302.3	408.7	586.5	805.9	1 084.5	1 451.9	1 946.2
33	.	.	.	366.8	455.2	599.0	786.5	1 021.9	1 278.8	1 642.1
34	.	.	.	387.3	560.0	748.7	936.4	1 272.7	1 745.9	2 152.5
35	.	.	.	538.4	670.5	809.5	978.5	1 258.0	1 658.8	2 117.3
36	.	.	.	330.8	423.8	554.9	670.2	823.5	1 053.5	1 363.2
37	.	.	.	468.6	567.8	748.0	886.2	1 052.2	1 315.3	1 752.2

Women - Femmes - Mujeres
ISIC 3 - CITI 3 - CIIU 3

	1999	2000	2001	2002	2003	2004	2005	2006	2007	2008
Total	.	.	.	358.9	443.5	562.9	727.0	920.0	1 175.3	1 503.5
15	.	.	.	376.2	439.8	530.4	686.5	868.7	1 084.9	1 423.1
16	.	.	.	1 328.7	1 467.2	1 999.6	2 348.7	3 060.1	3 621.0	5 232.5
17	.	.	.	208.9	250.8	368.7	479.6	603.0	767.5	1 007.5
18	.	.	.	275.7	336.5	423.2	518.9	631.6	772.9	969.2
19	.	.	.	242.6	333.3	404.2	511.6	628.9	786.4	972.0
20	.	.	.	322.2	411.9	520.5	637.9	816.6	983.0	1 237.3
21	.	.	.	402.1	482.1	609.7	783.9	973.3	1 160.2	1 447.4
22	.	.	.	564.1	640.0	750.3	897.3	1 212.4	1 467.5	1 869.3
23	.	.	.	666.7	764.1	950.6	1 195.2	1 388.8	1 729.1	2 182.1
24	.	.	.	407.3	497.1	637.1	855.8	1 067.8	1 360.3	1 768.4
25	.	.	.	343.0	420.5	552.9	686.2	860.6	1 082.5	1 372.4
26	.	.	.	318.0	399.9	511.0	682.1	873.2	1 169.7	1 513.5
27	.	.	.	501.1	612.3	784.5	1 036.0	1 257.5	1 644.2	1 982.1
28	.	.	.	279.2	365.0	460.9	604.7	801.0	1 062.1	1 288.4
29	.	.	.	322.2	402.8	519.9	664.2	853.3	1 089.0	1 411.9
30	.	.	.	228.1	324.3	369.3	540.4	718.8	1 217.0	1 567.6
31	.	.	.	270.9	349.7	468.1	630.0	818.0	1 086.4	1 393.1
32	.	.	.	204.4	281.7	409.1	542.9	732.6	988.1	1 361.0
33	.	.	.	288.3	364.8	459.3	624.4	799.0	1 004.9	1 254.5
34	.	.	.	302.1	454.8	602.0	724.6	990.7	1 298.9	1 622.5
35	.	.	.	351.6	430.6	549.3	686.5	906.7	1 180.7	1 536.9
36	.	.	.	289.4	379.7	496.0	626.4	756.3	900.8	1 169.6
37	.	.	.	372.8	427.5	563.3	644.0	827.6	1 047.6	1 412.4

Explanatory notes: see p. 877.   Notes explicatives: voir p. 879.   Notas explicativas: véase p. 882.

5B

	WAGES	SALAIRES	SALARIOS
	In manufacturing	Dans les industries manufacturières	En las industrias manufactureras

	1999	2000	2001	2002	2003	2004	2005	2006	2007	2008
United Kingdom (BA) [1]				Employees - Salariés - Asalariados						E.G./h. - Pound

Total men and women - Total hommes et femmes - Total hombres y mujeres
ISIC 3 - CITI 3 - CIIU 3

	1999	2000	2001	2002	2003	2004	2005	2006	2007	2008
Total	8.34	8.90	9.31	9.91	10.27	10.49	11.16	11.37	11.74	12.32

Men - Hommes - Hombres
ISIC 3 - CITI 3 - CIIU 3

Total	8.97	9.55	9.90	10.44	10.83	10.95	11.57	11.80	12.33	12.89

Women - Femmes - Mujeres
ISIC 3 - CITI 3 - CIIU 3

Total	6.59	7.09	7.62	8.36	8.62	9.17	9.96	10.05	10.05	10.73

United Kingdom (BA) [1]				Employees - Salariés - Asalariados						E.G./w.s. - Pound

Total men and women - Total hommes et femmes - Total hombres y mujeres
ISIC 3 - CITI 3 - CIIU 3

Total	355	377	395	414	431	437	467	477	491	513

Men - Hommes - Hombres
ISIC 3 - CITI 3 - CIIU 3

Total	382	405	421	438	456	462	486	495	517	521

Women - Femmes - Mujeres
ISIC 3 - CITI 3 - CIIU 3

Total	264	283	301	326	340	348	393	406	401	425

United Kingdom (DA) [2][3][4]				Employees - Salariés - Asalariados						E.G./h. - Pound

Total men and women - Total hommes et femmes - Total hombres y mujeres
ISIC 3 - CITI 3 - CIIU 3

	1999	2000	2001	2002	2003	2004	2005	2006	2007	2008
Total	9.76	10.10	10.66	11.12	11.65	12.03	12.51	12.96	13.19	.
15	8.96	9.21	9.42	10.00	10.45	10.80	11.25	11.35	11.49	.
16	17.97	16.05	15.52	16.76	16.12	21.59	24.00	24.17	22.81	.
17	7.50	7.97	8.33	8.72	9.16	9.53	9.81	10.40	10.76	.
18	6.45	7.06	7.71	7.48	8.05	8.68	9.18	10.06	10.51	.
19	7.47	7.60	8.32	8.98	8.54	8.73	9.73	10.16	9.42	.
20	7.22	8.01	8.47	8.59	8.97	9.42	9.29	9.58	10.51	.
21	9.47	9.57	10.30	10.88	10.93	11.69	11.90	12.63	12.45	.
22	11.46	12.27	12.88	13.23	13.50	14.00	14.26	14.63	15.19	.
23	12.26	13.12	14.05	15.91	16.75	17.07	20.31	20.52	22.28	.
24	12.63	12.97	13.19	14.02	15.29	14.68	15.74	16.16	16.04	.
25	8.71	8.84	9.37	9.77	10.08	10.19	10.42	10.92	11.32	.
26	8.91	8.78	9.69	9.79	10.39	10.86	11.44	11.66	12.36	.
27	9.76	10.34	10.56	10.97	11.64	11.92	12.28	12.76	12.62	.
28	8.76	8.88	9.29	9.50	9.92	10.57	10.77	11.09	11.75	.
29	9.85	10.31	10.71	11.12	11.45	11.83	12.21	12.68	13.12	.
30	11.38	11.19	12.50	11.88	12.60	12.72	13.45	13.71	14.65	.
31	9.25	9.50	9.93	10.47	11.30	11.56	12.05	12.51	13.14	.
32	10.24	10.45	12.55	12.71	12.96	14.63	14.01	15.18	14.57	.
33	10.10	10.97	11.96	12.34	12.21	13.16	13.59	14.27	14.95	.
34	10.68	10.94	11.42	12.00	12.70	13.46	13.37	14.11	14.31	.
35	11.20	11.73	12.11	12.69	13.90	13.99	15.09	15.73	15.24	.
36	7.77	8.10	8.31	9.16	9.58	9.93	10.67	10.89	11.09	.
37	8.54	7.93	7.80	7.90	8.16	8.15	8.45	9.01	10.50	.

Explanatory notes: see p. 877.

[1] Full-time employees. [2] April; full-time employees on adult rates. [3] Results with imputation and weighting. [4] Incl. overtime payments.

Notes explicatives: voir p. 879.

[1] Salariés à plein temps. [2] Avril; salariés à plein temps rémunérés sur la base de taux de salaires pour adultes. [3] Résultats après imputation et pondération. [4] Y compris la rémunération des heures supplémentaires.

Notas explicativas: véase p. 882.

[1] Asalariados a tiempo completo. [2] Abril; asalariados a tiempo completo pagados sobre la base de tasas de salarios para adultos. [3] Resultados después imputación y ponderación. [4] Incl. los pagos por horas extraordinarias.

WAGES

In manufacturing

SALAIRES

Dans les industries manufacturières

SALARIOS

En las industrias manufactureras

5B

	1999	2000	2001	2002	2003	2004	2005	2006	2007	2008

United Kingdom (DA) [1] [2] [3]   Employees - Salariés - Asalariados   E.G./h. - Pound

Men - Hommes - Hombres
ISIC 3 - CITI 3 - CIIU 3

	1999	2000	2001	2002	2003	2004	2005	2006	2007	2008
Total	10.31	10.62	11.21	11.62	12.13	12.50	12.97	13.43	13.71	.
15	9.63	9.75	10.02	10.70	11.07	11.30	11.70	11.89	12.11	.
16	19.93	16.97	16.52	17.53	17.02	24.35	28.18	.	.	.
17	8.24	8.86	9.35	9.58	10.08	10.27	10.81	11.50	11.73	.
18	8.10	8.69	9.44	8.50	9.47	9.48	10.37	11.47	12.47	.
19	7.92	8.24	8.61	9.40	9.09	9.47	9.83	11.35	10.66	.
20	7.23	8.14	8.47	8.74	9.05	9.48	9.33	9.58	10.58	.
21	9.93	10.09	10.76	11.36	11.37	12.27	12.38	12.99	13.07	.
22	12.25	13.40	13.82	13.86	14.33	14.93	15.34	15.31	16.35	.
23	12.89	13.64	14.44	16.44	17.14	17.56	20.83	21.45	23.87	.
24	13.76	13.85	14.40	15.02	16.21	15.76	16.65	17.21	16.90	.
25	9.21	9.35	9.90	10.21	10.49	10.56	10.84	11.42	11.78	.
26	9.38	9.19	10.19	10.24	10.82	11.30	11.80	12.02	12.73	.
27	10.00	10.57	10.77	11.22	11.82	12.05	12.40	12.84	12.66	.
28	9.02	9.11	9.54	9.74	10.20	10.81	11.02	11.37	11.98	.
29	10.13	10.59	10.99	11.41	11.73	12.10	12.50	12.99	13.47	.
30	12.09	11.80	13.32	12.38	13.35	12.71	13.58	14.16	15.43	.
31	10.09	10.32	10.74	11.31	12.32	12.55	12.98	13.32	14.23	.
32	11.31	11.77	13.93	14.20	14.41	16.04	15.27	16.79	15.85	.
33	10.88	11.90	13.07	13.43	13.21	14.22	14.44	15.29	16.07	.
34	10.88	11.18	11.71	12.28	13.02	13.72	13.61	14.41	14.52	.
35	11.45	11.95	12.32	12.86	14.03	14.15	15.34	15.96	15.60	.
36	8.09	8.34	8.63	9.67	9.88	10.12	11.18	11.39	11.48	.
37	8.30	.	.	7.98	.	8.57	8.57	8.89	10.54	.

Women - Femmes - Mujeres
ISIC 3 - CITI 3 - CIIU 3

	1999	2000	2001	2002	2003	2004	2005	2006	2007	2008
Total	7.68	8.02	8.52	9.04	9.64	10.02	10.52	10.78	10.99	.
15	7.13	7.55	7.76	8.02	8.79	9.45	9.94	9.90	9.78	.
16	12.18	12.80	12.11	13.60	13.77	12.97	14.15	17.78	17.39	.
17	6.11	6.15	6.33	6.63	7.07	7.73	7.05	7.57	8.40	.
18	5.73	6.18	6.74	6.91	7.08	8.09	8.52	9.24	9.41	.
19	6.40	6.47	7.82	8.11	7.44	7.32	.	7.45	7.22	.
20	7.14	6.80	8.49	7.11	8.20	8.90	8.86	9.54	9.81	.
21	7.68	7.63	8.39	8.91	9.26	9.48	10.05	10.88	9.81	.
22	9.80	9.93	10.81	11.73	11.72	11.96	12.06	13.27	12.98	.
23	10.03	10.68	12.03	12.93	14.09	13.99	17.96	16.67	16.92	.
24	9.63	10.54	10.28	11.72	13.18	12.16	13.49	13.92	13.98	.
25	6.54	6.57	7.19	7.63	7.84	8.27	8.26	8.47	8.90	.
26	6.62	6.88	7.31	7.59	8.00	8.41	8.93	9.20	9.53	.
27	7.06	7.78	8.15	8.33	9.36	10.32	10.75	11.71	11.95	.
28	6.59	6.96	7.33	7.45	7.51	8.44	8.59	8.70	10.02	.
29	7.71	8.04	8.50	8.72	9.04	9.51	9.82	9.86	10.07	.
30	9.43	9.45	10.58	10.54	10.49	12.76	13.12	12.20	11.45	.
31	6.40	6.75	7.19	7.82	7.97	7.95	8.59	9.39	9.13	.
32	7.46	7.07	8.71	8.80	8.98	10.64	9.96	9.79	9.88	.
33	7.75	8.21	8.66	9.05	9.08	9.67	10.34	10.53	11.45	.
34	8.80	8.89	8.83	9.40	9.77	10.72	10.92	11.26	12.04	.
35	8.59	9.45	10.00	10.73	12.46	12.31	12.47	13.32	11.29	.
36	6.68	7.22	7.17	7.18	8.25	9.22	8.80	8.79	9.35	.
37	.	.	.	5.69	.	6.95	6.84	10.71	.	.

United Kingdom (DA) [1] [2] [3]   Employees - Salariés - Asalariados   E.G./w.s. - Pound

Total men and women - Total hommes et femmes - Total hombres y mujeres
ISIC 3 - CITI 3 - CIIU 3

	1999	2000	2001	2002	2003	2004	2005	2006	2007	2008
Total	402.70	417.20	439.90	455.60	476.50	493.10	508.00	524.20	539.30	.
15	380.30	389.70	397.10	420.40	440.50	452.40	470.70	467.30	478.10	.
16	673.90	588.70	590.50	647.30	621.60	806.00	869.00	870.60	828.40	.
17	306.30	328.90	341.80	359.00	373.40	390.50	404.10	428.30	439.50	.
18	251.40	276.50	299.60	291.90	314.80	338.90	359.90	385.70	424.80	.
19	303.90	309.60	330.50	358.60	339.40	346.70	386.70	411.30	374.70	.
20	313.70	346.70	369.00	371.20	390.10	406.20	392.40	409.40	451.00	.
21	397.00	401.30	428.20	450.90	449.10	481.70	482.30	498.50	504.40	.
22	451.10	480.10	504.80	516.10	526.00	544.10	550.10	562.70	585.70	.
23	492.60	537.30	569.90	632.90	656.50	675.30	791.00	784.80	870.40	.
24	496.30	507.80	517.90	550.50	595.00	570.80	609.20	623.50	627.80	.
25	366.70	370.80	393.40	410.20	422.00	423.40	425.70	454.90	467.10	.
26	377.90	372.40	409.00	408.80	443.30	459.30	483.60	495.30	524.70	.
27	402.70	433.20	440.80	453.60	482.50	490.60	506.60	527.00	532.20	.
28	376.80	384.80	401.70	405.90	423.00	452.80	457.50	468.80	500.60	.
29	407.90	428.70	446.80	458.20	474.00	490.60	502.70	523.00	545.80	.
30	451.70	446.50	495.80	468.00	501.40	511.40	529.20	537.00	570.20	.
31	376.40	388.10	406.50	420.70	455.50	476.20	484.40	496.10	533.70	.
32	409.80	419.80	497.70	498.20	512.30	576.10	553.50	579.30	580.70	.
33	400.20	432.50	478.40	490.20	484.00	526.30	532.40	589.30	585.60	.
34	445.20	462.10	478.40	500.10	518.60	557.00	535.80	566.70	587.30	.
35	466.80	481.60	500.30	508.30	552.70	559.70	601.70	623.90	619.40	.
36	324.80	340.10	349.30	384.10	394.90	414.10	439.40	442.30	456.40	.
37	382.50	377.00	362.40	364.20	375.40	371.70	387.80	417.40	465.50	.

Explanatory notes: see p. 877.

[1] April; full-time employees on adult rates. [2] Results with imputation and weighting. [3] Incl. overtime payments.

Notes explicatives: voir p. 879.

[1] Avril; salariés à plein temps rémunérés sur la base de taux de salaires pour adultes. [2] Résultats après imputation et pondération. [3] Y compris la rémunération des heures supplémentaires.

Notas explicativas: véase p. 882.

[1] Abril; asalariados a tiempo completo pagados sobre la base de tasas de salarios para adultos. [2] Resultados después imputación y ponderación. [3] Incl. los pagos por horas extraordinarias.

	1999	2000	2001	2002	2003	2004	2005	2006	2007	2008

United Kingdom (DA) [1] [2] [3]   Employees - Salariés - Asalariados   E.G./w.s. - Pound

Men - Hommes - Hombres
ISIC 3 - CITI 3 - CIIU 3

	1999	2000	2001	2002	2003	2004	2005	2006	2007	2008
Total	431.70	445.60	464.90	482.90	503.02	519.40	533.80	551.40	568.70	.
15	417.70	420.70	421.10	458.20	475.80	481.20	498.10	497.50	510.70	
16	753.80	626.30	633.50	688.60	680.30	919.10	1 024.20	.		
17	344.30	375.00	390.20	402.30	418.80	432.20	457.90	482.50	494.40	
18	318.70	347.40	364.90	346.30	388.10	380.30	409.40	456.20	540.70	
19	329.40	343.20	340.00	377.20	375.50	385.70	369.90	458.00	437.80	
20	317.80	356.40	371.00	381.80	398.90	412.60	398.50	413.40	458.60	
21	424.30	432.20	453.50	479.50	475.60	512.40	509.50	523.00	537.20	
22	494.10	535.80	540.20	551.50	569.90	590.00	603.10	603.40	641.00	
23	523.80	563.10	590.70	657.50	672.80	698.00	815.60	824.30	941.00	
24	545.30	547.70	567.30	597.80	638.40	619.10	651.20	668.10	673.20	
25	392.90	396.30	417.30	433.40	444.40	444.40	448.40	482.20	492.20	
26	404.80	395.70	433.80	434.20	471.00	485.70	505.90	517.90	547.40	
27	416.40	446.70	451.40	467.60	493.80	498.60	515.60	535.70	537.30	
28	393.50	399.80	414.90	420.20	439.50	468.90	473.90	484.10	517.50	
29	423.50	444.20	458.90	474.70	490.60	506.60	518.20	541.30	565.70	
30	482.70	472.60	531.80	488.20	531.10	510.20	535.50	564.10	599.80	
31	414.90	427.10	442.10	458.20	501.00	523.20	529.00	534.20	581.70	
32	453.80	474.70	553.40	558.80	571.60	634.10	604.40	647.00	632.20	
33	434.10	473.00	521.10	538.80	527.30	574.40	570.80	639.30	635.80	
34	456.60	476.60	490.80	514.40	533.80	570.30	547.60	581.80	600.40	
35	480.60	493.80	510.20	517.60	560.90	569.40	614.20	636.40	636.70	
36	345.40	356.70	364.70	412.40	412.80	430.60	469.30	471.70	479.30	
37	374.70	.	366.90	370.80	.	378.30	398.40	418.80	473.60	

Women - Femmes - Mujeres
ISIC 3 - CITI 3 - CIIU 3

	1999	2000	2001	2002	2003	2004	2005	2006	2007	2008
Total	299.30	312.10	332.20	350.80	372.80	388.10	404.30	415.90	423.80	.
15	285.80	301.50	310.30	320.40	351.60	378.10	396.30	390.50	392.70	
16	445.30	459.00	449.30	492.20	485.90	468.00	505.20	584.80	618.60	
17	239.40	240.60	247.10	260.10	276.30	298.40	270.60	308.30	318.50	
18	222.50	239.70	256.00	263.60	268.20	309.50	332.70	348.70	366.50	
19	247.70	253.90	303.40	320.00	275.00	277.30	.	313.00	271.90	
20	277.60	264.30	329.00	279.10	318.10	349.00	334.70	368.40	384.40	
21	300.50	295.20	324.80	343.50	356.60	371.40	384.50	416.90	375.20	
22	367.90	372.10	408.50	438.10	438.10	447.80	448.80	491.70	484.50	
23	387.60	421.10	466.20	499.20	547.60	538.10	682.00	649.20	641.00	
24	370.70	401.70	394.90	446.10	499.60	461.20	508.90	525.60	526.30	
25	260.80	263.00	287.50	304.40	308.70	323.70	317.70	329.90	345.20	
26	259.60	273.00	286.90	295.10	308.20	325.80	343.50	357.60	369.20	
27	265.70	295.70	308.80	317.50	352.90	389.00	404.50	435.00	462.20	
28	255.70	274.00	288.50	294.30	292.90	327.30	330.60	344.80	383.50	
29	298.30	312.10	329.70	335.60	346.10	366.90	381.70	379.60	387.50	
30	367.80	373.80	413.50	413.30	417.40	514.40	512.30	474.40	447.80	
31	252.20	264.60	284.70	305.80	312.60	313.70	328.90	367.10	361.90	
32	296.90	281.70	342.00	341.20	351.20	414.20	391.30	380.40	392.40	
33	301.30	316.80	338.10	349.40	352.40	374.90	391.50	399.70	435.30	
34	343.60	347.40	348.80	370.50	383.00	421.40	420.10	439.80	457.40	
35	334.30	365.10	389.80	406.40	469.70	466.50	474.90	508.00	438.10	
36	261.30	284.60	281.80	283.40	321.50	357.60	338.70	343.10	361.60	
37	.	.	.	214.70	.	273.00	265.80	404.90	397.40	

Explanatory notes: see p. 877.

[1] April; full-time employees on adult rates. [2] Results with imputation and weighting. [3] Incl. overtime payments.

Notes explicatives: voir p. 879.

[1] Avril; salariés à plein temps rémunérés sur la base de taux de salaires pour adultes. [2] Résultats après imputation et pondération. [3] Y compris la rémunération des heures supplémentaires.

Notas explicativas: véase p. 882.

[1] Abril; asalariados a tiempo completo pagados sobre la base de tasas de salarios para adultos. [2] Resultados después imputación y ponderación. [3] Incl. los pagos por horas extraordinarias.

	1999	2000	2001	2002	2003	2004	2005	2006	2007	2008

OCEANIA-OCÉANIE-OCEANIA

Australia (DA) [1] [2] Employees - Salariés - Asalariados E.G./h. - Dollar

Total men and women - Total hommes et femmes - Total hombres y mujeres
ISIC 3 - CITI 3 - CIIU 3

	1999	2000	2001	2002	2003	2004	2005	2006	2007	2008
Total	.	18.16	.	20.45	.	22.77	.	25.36	.	.
15	.	18.11	.	20.57	.	22.29	.	23.45	.	.
16	.	22.90	.	.	.	.	.	.	.	.
17	.	.	.	16.15	.	18.02	.	17.60	.	.
17,21,22,24	.	19.19	.	21.16	.	24.34	.	27.03	.	.
18	.	.	.	16.58	.	18.53	.	24.20	.	.
18-19	.	14.28	.	16.92	.	17.91	.	24.20	.	.
19	.	.	.	.	.	16.67	.	.	.	.
20	.	15.56	.	17.60	.	18.67	.	21.43	.	.
21	.	.	.	21.62	.	25.58	.	31.53	.	.
22	.	.	.	23.41	.	24.41	.	27.16	.	.
23	.	28.57	.	.	.	36.20	.	47.60	.	.
24	.	.	.	22.36	.	25.87	.	26.25	.	.
25	.	16.57	.	18.94	.	25.55	.	24.60	.	.
26	.	17.78	.	22.17	.	24.02	.	24.13	.	.
27	.	.	.	25.05	.	27.61	.	32.35	.	.
27-29	.	18.46	.	20.59	.	23.05	.	26.34	.	.
28	.	.	.	19.22	.	21.57	.	24.05	.	.
29	.	.	.	19.60	.	22.04	.	24.47	.	.
30	.	18.50	.	.	.	19.89	.	26.90	.	.
31	.	16.10	.	21.45	.	18.44	.	26.10	.	.
32	.	18.33	.	18.35	.	22.93	.	20.90	.	.
33	.	19.42	.	22.30	.	24.19	.	24.03	.	.
34	.	18.34	.	20.00	.	22.72	.	24.67	.	.
35	.	18.46	.	24.10	.	24.00	.	29.87	.	.
36	.	15.24	.	17.95	.	20.27	.	19.27	.	.
37	.	23.05	.	24.55	.	31.75	.	32.53	.	.

Men - Hommes - Hombres
ISIC 3 - CITI 3 - CIIU 3

	1999	2000	2001	2002	2003	2004	2005	2006	2007	2008
Total	.	19.13	.	20.82	.	23.40	.	26.11	.	.
15	.	18.91	.	21.12	.	22.88	.	24.01	.	.
16	.	23.80	.	.	.	.	.	.	.	.
17	.	.	.	17.44	.	.	.	21.00	.	.
17,21,22,24	.	20.27	.	21.93	.	26.13	.	28.54	.	.
18	.	.	.	17.75	.	19.51	.	30.20	.	.
18-19	.	15.02	.	17.75	.	18.40	.	30.20	.	.
19	.	.	.	.	.	16.73	.	.	.	.
20	.	16.13	.	17.88	.	18.83	.	21.67	.	.
21	.	.	.	26.80	.	26.49	.	32.97	.	.
22	.	.	.	23.50	.	25.69	.	28.74	.	.
23	.	30.55	.	.	.	36.78	.	49.00	.	.
24	.	.	.	22.47	.	26.34	.	27.42	.	.
25	.	17.60	.	19.02	.	21.29	.	26.23	.	.
26	.	19.35	.	20.42	.	23.72	.	24.05	.	.
27	.	.	.	25.26	.	27.94	.	32.10	.	.
27-29	.	18.89	.	20.69	.	23.99	.	26.38	.	.
28	.	.	.	19.00	.	22.03	.	23.95	.	.
29	.	.	.	19.95	.	22.34	.	24.94	.	.
30	.	18.80	.	.	.	20.22	.	28.40	.	.
31	.	17.00	.	21.40	.	18.91	.	28.00	.	.
32	.	19.25	.	19.40	.	24.62	.	22.00	.	.
33	.	21.77	.	25.00	.	26.85	.	26.17	.	.
34	.	18.53	.	20.43	.	23.20	.	24.67	.	.
35	.	20.13	.	23.93	.	24.29	.	30.37	.	.
36	.	15.90	.	17.50	.	20.43	.	19.80	.	.
37	.	22.38	.	25.00	.	27.75	.	32.23	.	.

Explanatory notes: see p. 877.

[1] Full-time adult non-managerial employees. [2] May of each year.

Notes explicatives: voir p. 879.

[1] Salariés adultes à plein temps, non compris les cadres dirigeants. [2] Mai de chaque année.

Notas explicativas: véase p. 882.

[1] Asalariados adultos a tiempo completo, excl. el personal directivo. [2] Mayo de cada año.

5B

WAGES	SALAIRES	SALARIOS
In manufacturing	Dans les industries manufacturières	En las industrias manufactureras

	1999	2000	2001	2002	2003	2004	2005	2006	2007	2008

Australia (DA) [1] [2] — Employees - Salariés - Asalariados — E.G./h. - Dollar

Women - Femmes - Mujeres
ISIC 3 - CITI 3 - CIIU 3

	1999	2000	2001	2002	2003	2004	2005	2006	2007	2008
Total	.	16.80	.	18.45	.	19.91	.	23.62	.	.
15	.	17.22	.	18.61	.	19.97	.	21.22	.	.
16	.	22.00	.	.	.	.	.	.	.	.
17	.	.	.	16.14	.	12.31	.	14.90	.	.
17,21,22,24	.	17.36	.	18.84	.	21.03	.	23.82	.	.
18	.	.	.	15.20	.	18.10	.	21.10	.	.
18-19	.	13.53	.	15.20	.	17.04	.	21.10	.	.
19	.	.	.	.	.	13.86	.	.	.	.
20	.	14.40	.	16.02	.	17.29	.	21.15	.	.
21	.	.	.	18.23	.	18.87	.	23.70	.	.
22	.	.	.	21.02	.	21.54	.	26.70	.	.
23	.	24.60	.	.	.	33.44	.	36.00	.	.
24	.	.	.	19.30	.	24.60	.	23.90	.	.
25	.	15.34	.	14.68	.	16.71	.	21.20	.	.
26	.	15.81	.	18.70	.	21.26	.	26.95	.	.
27	.	.	.	25.50	.	23.39	.	29.07	.	.
27-29	.	17.77	.	19.79	.	20.28	.	26.72	.	.
28	.	.	.	16.77	.	19.37	.	29.70	.	.
29	.	.	.	17.10	.	19.71	.	22.34	.	.
30	.	.	.	.	.	19.60	.	.	.	.
31	.	14.75	.	16.90	.	16.39	.	17.60	.	.
32	.	17.40	.	15.90	.	19.54	.	18.20	.	.
33	.	17.07	.	18.30	.	20.14	.	21.70	.	.
34	.	18.10	.	18.50	.	20.96	.	27.35	.	.
35	.	16.23	.	25.95	.	27.26	.	26.30	.	.
36	.	14.58	.	16.13	.	16.09	.	17.33	.	.
37	.	22.50	.	23.33	.	19.87	.	26.45	.	.

New Zealand (DA) [3] [4] [5] — Employees - Salariés - Asalariados — E.G./h. - Dollar

Total men and women - Total hommes et femmes - Total hombres y mujeres
ISIC 3 - CITI 3 - CIIU 3

	1999	2000	2001	2002	2003	2004	2005	2006	2007	2008
Total	.	16.97	17.50	18.10	18.50	19.29	19.58	20.51	21.45	22.41
15-16	.	17.41	17.58	17.94	18.70	19.32	19.70	20.72	21.59	22.03
17	.	13.90	14.82	15.39	15.48	16.50	16.18	17.29	17.54	18.45
18	.	12.45	13.07	12.28	12.19	13.68	13.61	13.91	15.25	15.30
19	.	14.38	14.37	15.46	16.13	15.98	15.64	16.53	17.17	17.95
20	.	14.95	15.33	15.92	16.51	17.40	17.91	18.34	19.26	21.43
21	.	22.27	21.78	22.97	22.89	23.43	25.66	29.66	32.78	30.05
22	.	18.99	20.36	20.65	21.26	21.71	22.40	24.07	24.14	25.59
23	.	19.50	18.40	20.71	22.87	25.80	24.21	.	.	.
24	.	19.27	20.19	21.07	21.94	23.39	23.92	24.33	26.65	27.90
25	.	16.15	16.30	17.40	18.27	19.00	18.44	20.19	20.84	22.62
26	.	16.38	16.92	17.77	17.50	18.98	18.77	19.64	20.76	20.43
27	.	18.97	21.82	21.76	21.92	22.16	22.70	23.84	30.31	30.22
28	.	15.96	16.63	17.48	17.85	18.99	18.96	19.27	20.54	21.64
29	.	16.80	17.53	18.41	18.65	20.18	20.78	21.24	21.95	23.45
30	.	18.23	18.20	20.18	19.11	24.56	.	.	.	.
31	.	17.07	18.80	19.70	19.49	19.16	18.21	19.05	20.30	19.39
32	.	18.23	18.20	20.18	19.11	18.77	19.09	21.19	22.31	22.59
33	.	18.36	19.80	21.48	21.08	22.70	23.03	26.22	22.95	23.15
34	.	14.58	15.22	17.20	18.03	18.52	19.27	18.43	19.08	19.86
35	.	20.14	20.70	21.39	20.84	21.42	22.26	21.89	22.91	23.86
36	.	14.12	14.06	14.89	15.19	15.89	15.97	16.65	18.05	19.71

Men - Hommes - Hombres
ISIC 3 - CITI 3 - CIIU 3

	1999	2000	2001	2002	2003	2004	2005	2006	2007	2008
Total	.	17.87	18.28	19.06	19.54	20.24	20.54	21.52	22.54	23.55
15-16	.	18.49	18.43	18.76	20.48	20.46	20.77	21.98	22.90	23.27
17	.	15.72	16.19	16.76	18.07	18.47	17.86	19.46	19.60	21.13
18	.	16.41	16.59	16.57	16.39	18.18	18.06	18.95	20.50	20.15
19	.	15.35	16.09	16.21	15.90	16.62	16.25	17.29	17.63	18.58
20	.	15.04	15.57	15.83	17.01	17.67	18.27	18.51	19.47	21.76
21	.	23.22	23.13	24.73	22.73	24.09	27.03	31.43	35.19	32.02
22	.	20.56	21.28	21.78	23.45	23.69	24.53	26.45	26.42	27.79
23	.	19.52	18.57	20.85	23.64	26.03	24.20	.	29.13	.
24	.	20.39	21.33	22.46	23.35	24.90	25.41	26.77	29.00	30.37
25	.	16.96	16.93	18.05	18.83	19.70	19.08	20.96	21.75	23.65
26	.	16.37	16.89	17.68	17.61	18.98	18.70	19.57	20.67	20.30
27	.	19.17	22.33	22.28	22.49	22.37	22.76	23.53	30.85	30.45
28	.	16.30	16.95	17.72	18.23	19.41	19.21	19.63	20.98	22.06
29	.	17.08	18.02	18.78	19.56	20.43	21.09	21.61	22.26	23.90
30	.	20.48	20.33	22.46	20.64	20.94	.	.	.	.
31	.	18.21	20.27	21.02	20.95	20.93	19.71	20.35	21.64	20.54
32	.	20.48	20.33	22.46	20.64	20.94	21.14	23.55	24.78	25.09
33	.	19.33	22.22	24.29	23.44	25.19	26.01	31.58	25.58	25.41
34	.	14.80	15.60	17.45	18.24	18.71	19.49	18.63	19.26	19.99
35	.	20.31	20.94	21.59	21.00	21.62	22.45	22.13	23.25	24.06
36	.	14.54	14.33	15.30	15.50	16.27	16.20	16.65	18.61	20.37

Explanatory notes: see p. 877.

[1] Full-time adult non-managerial employees. [2] May of each year. [3] Full-time equivalent employees. [4] Establishments with the equivalent of more than 0.5 full-time paid employees. [5] Feb. of each year.

Notes explicatives: voir p. 879.

[1] Salariés adultes à plein temps, non compris les cadres dirigeants. [2] Mai de chaque année. [3] Salariés en équivalents à plein temps. [4] Etablissements occupant plus de l'équivalent de 0.5 salarié à plein temps. [5] Fév. de chaque année.

Notas explicativas: véase p. 882.

[1] Asalariados adultos a tiempo completo, excl. el personal directivo. [2] Mayo de cada año. [3] Asalariados en equivalentes a tiempo completo. [4] Establecimientos con más del equivalente de 0.5 asalariado a tiempo completo. [5] Febr. de cada año.

WAGES

In manufacturing

SALAIRES

Dans les industries manufacturières

SALARIOS

En las industrias manufactureras

5B

	1999	2000	2001	2002	2003	2004	2005	2006	2007	2008	
New Zealand (DA) [1] [2] [3]					Employees - Salariés - Asalariados						E.G./h. - Dollar
Women - Femmes - Mujeres											
ISIC 3 - CITI 3 - CIIU 3											
Total	.	14.44	14.93	15.30	15.51	16.55	16.84	17.62	18.47	19.16	
15-16	.	14.79	15.06	15.58	16.20	16.83	17.32	18.01	18.79	19.45	
17	.	12.09	12.63	13.01	13.00	14.45	14.53	15.00	15.64	16.08	
18	.	11.39	11.92	11.46	11.51	12.78	12.71	12.81	14.22	14.36	
19	.	12.19	12.59	13.53	13.30	14.28	13.94	14.53	15.51	15.50	
20	.	14.20	14.38	14.90	14.63	15.51	15.45	17.19	17.67	19.16	
21	.	16.65	17.59	17.18	17.16	20.13	19.06	21.59	22.94	21.09	
22	.	17.00	17.90	18.00	18.12	19.20	19.82	21.15	21.50	22.70	
23	.	19.24	16.50	19.01	16.27	23.78	24.23	24.03	.	23.39	
24	.	16.87	17.81	17.72	18.08	19.94	20.42	19.38	22.41	23.01	
25	.	13.36	14.04	14.89	15.83	16.11	16.06	17.39	17.97	19.33	
26	.	16.49	17.24	18.85	16.51	18.96	19.62	20.87	22.04	22.50	
27	.	16.98	16.97	17.68	17.57	20.08	22.00	28.00	24.46	27.05	
28	.	14.23	14.76	15.87	15.72	16.59	17.53	17.24	18.02	18.98	
29	.	14.64	15.43	15.69	15.39	18.42	18.47	18.51	19.62	20.09	
30	.	13.60	13.11	14.43	.	.	.	.	.	.	
31	.	13.88	14.39	15.36	15.48	15.02	14.82	16.16	17.39	17.12	
32	.	13.60	13.11	14.43	15.55	14.27	14.64	16.22	17.19	17.24	
33	.	16.57	15.58	16.73	16.34	18.13	18.25	19.27	19.54	.	
34	.	13.43	13.32	15.28	16.33	17.08	17.14	16.38	17.04	18.63	
35	.	18.06	17.99	18.84	18.73	18.94	19.98	19.01	20.73	22.44	
36	.	13.11	13.28	13.71	14.29	14.81	15.30	16.65	16.70	17.55	

Explanatory notes: see p. 877.

[1] Full-time equivalent employees. [2] Establishments with the equivalent of more than 0.5 full-time paid employees. [3] Feb. of each year.

Notes explicatives: voir p. 879.

[1] Salariés en équivalents à plein temps. [2] Etablissements occupant plus de l'équivalent de 0.5 salarié à plein temps. [3] Fév. de chaque année.

Notas explicativas: véase p. 882.

[1] Asalariados en equivalentes a tiempo completo. [2] Establecimientos con más del equivalente de 0.5 asalariado a tiempo completo. [3] Febr. de cada año.

Labor cost

Coût de la main-d'œuvre

Costo de la mano de obra

Labour cost

Labour cost is defined as follows in the Resolution concerning statistics of labour cost adopted by the Eleventh International Conference of Labour Statisticians (Geneva, 1966): [1]

3. For the purposes of labour cost statistics, labour cost is the cost incurred by the employer in the employment of labour. The statistical concept of labour cost comprises remuneration for work performed, payments in respect of time paid for but not worked, bonuses and gratuities, the cost of food, drink and other payments in kind, cost of workers' housing borne by employers, employers' social security expenditures, cost to the employer for vocational training, welfare services and miscellaneous items, such as transport of workers, work clothes and recruitment, together with taxes regarded as labour cost...

Compensation of employees was defined in the United Nations System of National Accounts, 1967 (SNA)[2] as follows:

7.11. The compensation of employees comprises all payments by producers of wages and salaries to their employees, in kind as well as in cash, and of contributions in respect of their employees to social security and to private pension, casualty insurance, life insurance and similar schemes...

Labour cost and compensation of employees are thus closely related concepts, with many common elements. The major part of labour cost comprises compensation of employees, while the remainder consists of employers' expenditure for vocational training and welfare services (such as canteens and assimilated services, educational, cultural and recreational facilities and services, grants to credit unions and the cost of assimilated services for employees), the cost of recruitment and other miscellaneous items (such as work clothes, travel between the home and the place of work and vice versa, etc.) and taxes regarded as labour cost. The concept of compensation of employees includes fees paid to members of boards of directors (which are excluded from the labour cost concept) and excludes outlays by employers such as expenditures on amenities at the place of work, medical examinations, sports and other recreational activities and reimbursements by employers of the expenses of work clothing and tools which are incurred by their employees.

The SNA was revised in 1993,[3] and the components of compensation of employees were, in general, extended to cover a number of welfare services such as sports, recreation, holidays facilities, etc., and other miscellaneous items (e.g. work clothes which employees choose to wear frequently outside of the workplace as well as at work, transportation to and from work, car parking). Labour cost and compensation of employees have thus become even more closely related concepts. However, most statistics of compensation of employees published in this chapter are still based on the 1967 SNA guidelines.

The statistics presented in this chapter relate to *average labour cost per employee*, or, in some cases, to *average compensation of employees*. While the level and composition of labour cost tend to vary between wage earners and salaried employees, in many cases it is not possible to distinguish between labour costs for these two groups of employees. Therefore, with a few exceptions, the figures cover all paid employees, that is, wage earners and salaried employees, of both sexes, without distinction as to age, occupation, experience, level of skill, etc. Data are provided separately for each country as a whole, and in general they represent the average for a calendar year. Where the coverage does not correspond to the above, the differences are indicated in footnotes.

The type of statistics shown for each country is indicated in the table by the following codes:

(LC) *Labour cost*

(CR) *Compensation of employees*

(h.) *per hour*

(d.j.) *per day*

(m.) *per month*

(y.a.) *per year*

For various reasons, national definitions of labour cost and compensation of employees often differ from the recommended international standard definitions. In certain countries, some items of labour cost (for example the full cost or part of the cost of social security and vocational training) are not chargeable to employers, but represent expenditures by the State for social or other reasons. As a rule, however, the State contributes along with the employer and the employee to finance the wage-related social security schemes, although the extent of State, employer and employee participation varies from country to country.[4] Taxes of a social character paid by employers are counted by some countries as labour cost, especially payroll taxes or employment taxes. The national concepts of labour cost may also differ as a result of variations in the national practices with regard to pension, health or life insurance schemes, etc., as well as taxes and subsidies relating to employment. Some of the differences in costs may therefore be explained by the fact that in some countries certain social costs are financed through general taxation and hence are excluded from labour cost, while in others they are financed through direct contributions by employers.

The statistics shown may also reflect differences in the sources, coverage and methods used for measuring labour cost. Labour cost data are obtained mainly through establishment surveys, that is either *labour cost surveys or industrial censuses or surveys*, although in some countries *official estimates* of labour cost are made on the basis of data from a number of sources, such as current surveys of earnings, administrative records of social security organizations, employers' organizations, etc.

The main objective of *labour cost surveys* is to compile measures of the level, composition and evolution of labour cost to the employer. The data are used, inter alia, for the analysis of the structure of labour cost, and the relationships between the different components. The principal objective of *industrial censuses and surveys* is to estimate the gross and net input and output of industry (including compensation of employees) and other measures which can be used for the study of the structure of industry and the analysis of the various factors influencing the industry. *Official estimates* are generally used as a measure of the evolution of total labour cost over time, and are usually calculated at quarterly or yearly intervals.

Labour cost surveys are generally sample surveys of establishments or enterprises, covering establishments above a certain size (usually those employing more than a given number of workers), and are conducted at intervals of three or more years. As a rule, they cover wage earners and salaried employees, while persons working at home, directors paid by fees, persons paid by commission only and working proprietors are usually excluded. In general, the emphasis of labour cost surveys is on the compilation of detailed data concerning labour cost and its components, together with information on the corresponding employment as well as the characteristics of the establishments. In some countries labour cost surveys are also used for collecting supplementary information on establishment practices and policies which have a bearing on the level, composition and evolution of labour cost, such as the systems of payments for time not worked, social security and pension schemes and methods of financing them, payroll taxes, etc.

Data on *compensation of employees* are generally obtained through industrial censuses or surveys, normally conducted at yearly intervals, and covering establishments or enterprises above a given size. The statistics on compensation of employees are usually compiled with respect to wage earners and salaried employees. In some cases, however, working proprietors and persons paid only by commission are covered as well as paid employees. In addition to data on compensation of employees, these surveys provide information on other inputs to production, such as materials, fuel, etc., output, value added, stocks, inventories, assets, capital formation, etc. In general, only aggregate estimates are required, so that data are not usually compiled separately on the various components of compensation of employees, nor on the different characteristics of employees.

The statistical series compiled through these surveys may be influenced by changes over time in the industrial structure, the structure of employment and levels of activity, as well as the growth or decline of establishments. Furthermore, such data may be subject to bias, owing to the exclusion of establishments or enterprises below a certain size.

When using the data to make comparisons, at either the national or the international level, it should be borne in mind that there may be variations in the definitions, scope, coverage and methods used in compiling the data, as well as in the presentation of the data. In particular, when making comparisons between countries, account should be taken of a number of factors which have a bearing on labour cost, such as the financing of social security, as well as the systems of taxes or subsidies, etc.

Care should also be taken when using the figures along with data from other chapters of the *Yearbook* or from other sources. This should only be done in cases where there is close correspondence between the definitions and the scope and coverage of the data, the methods used for compiling the data, and the ways in which the data are presented.

For further information, see ILO: *An integrated system of wages statistics, a manual on methods* (Geneva, 1979) and *Sources and Methods: Labour statistics*, Vol. 2: Employment, wages, hours of works and labour cost (establishment surveys), second edition (Geneva, 1995).

Table 6A

Labour cost in manufacturing

This table presents data on average labour cost per employee in manufacturing as a whole and by major industry group or division. The type of source of the series is shown as a code in parentheses following the name of the country, and the codes are listed on page XVI. As far as possible, the different industries have been arranged according to the *International Standard Industrial Classification of all Economic Activities (ISIC) Revision 2, 3 or 4* (see Appendix) with the corresponding codes. Any differences are indicated in footnotes.

Notes

[1] For the full text of the resolution, see ILO: *Current international recommendations on labour statistics* (Geneva, 2000) or the ILO Department of Statistics' web site (www.ilo.org/public/english/bureau/stat).

[2] For the full text, see United Nations: *A System of National Accounts*, Studies in Methods, Series F, No. 2, Rev. 3 (New York, 1967).

[3] For the full text, see «*System of National Accounts*, 1993», prepared under the auspices of the Inter-Secretariat Working Group on National Accounts (Brussels/ Luxembourg, New York, Paris, Washington, D.C., 1993).

[4] For further information concerning national social security systems and their financing, see ILO: *The cost of social security*, Fourteenth international inquiry, 1987-89 (Geneva, 1995).

Coût de la main d'œuvre

Le *coût de la main-d'œuvre* est défini comme suit dans la résolution concernant les statistiques du coût de la main-d'œuvre adoptée par la onzième Conférence internationale des statisticiens du travail (Genève, 1966)[1]:

3. Aux fins des statistiques du coût de la main-d'œuvre, celui-ci s'entend du coût supporté par l'employeur pour l'emploi de main-d'œuvre. La notion statistique du coût de la main-d'œuvre englobe la rémunération du travail accompli, les versements pour les heures rémunérées mais non effectuées, les primes et gratifications, le coût de la nourriture, des boissons et des autres avantages en nature, les coûts relatifs au logement du personnel supportés par l'employeur, les dépenses de sécurité sociale à la charge de l'employeur, le coût pour l'employeur de la formation professionnelle, les services sociaux et divers postes, tels que le transport des travailleurs, les vêtements de travail et le recrutement, ainsi que les impôts considérés comme coûts de main-d'œuvre...

La *rémunération des salariés* a été définie comme suit dans le système de comptabilité nationale, 1967 (SCN) adopté par les Nations Unies[2]:

7.11. La rémunération des salariés comprend tous les paiements effectués par les producteurs sous forme de salaires et traitements en nature aussi bien qu'en espèces, versés à leur personnel et sous forme de cotisations versées au bénéfice de ce personnel à la sécurité sociale, aux systèmes privés de retraite, d'assurance accident, d'assurance vie et aux systèmes analogues...

Le coût de la main-d'œuvre et la rémunération des salariés sont donc des notions très voisines qui ont de nombreux éléments en commun. Le coût de la main-d'œuvre comprend surtout la rémunération des salariés, les autres postes étant le coût pour l'employeur de la formation professionnelle, les services sociaux (comme les cantines et les services assimilés, les installations des services de caractère éducatif, culturel ou récréatif, les contributions aux mutuelles de crédit et le coût des services connexes dont bénéficient les travailleurs), le coût du recrutement et divers autres postes tels que les vêtements de travail, les frais de transport des travailleurs entre le domicile et le lieu de travail, etc.), ainsi que les impôts considérés comme coûts de main-d'œuvre. La notion de rémunération des salariés englobe les jetons de présence des administrateurs (qui n'entrent pas dans le «coût de la main-d'œuvre») et elle exclut les dépenses engagées par l'employeur, telles que les frais d'aménagement du lieu de travail, les examens médicaux, les activités sportives et autres activités de loisirs, ainsi que le remboursement par l'employeur des dépenses supportées par son personnel pour l'achat de vêtements et d'outils de travail.

Le SCN a été révisé en 1993[3] et les éléments constitutifs de la rémunération des salariés ont été en général étendus pour couvrir un certain nombre de services sociaux tels que les installations sportives, récréatives, les centres de vacances, etc. ainsi que divers autres avantages (vêtements de travail portés par les salariés à l'extérieur du lieu de travail et sur le lieu de travail, frais de transport entre le domicile et le lieu de travail, stationnement). Le coût de la main-d'œuvre et la rémunération des salariés sont ainsi devenus des notions plus étroitement liées. Cependant la plupart des statistiques sur la rémunération des salariés publiées dans ce chapitre sont encore basées sur les directives du SCN de 1967.

Les statistiques figurant dans le présent chapitre se rapportent au *coût moyen de la main-d'œuvre par salarié*, ou, dans certains cas, à la *rémunération moyenne des salariés*. Le niveau et la composition du coût de la main-d'œuvre varient généralement selon qu'il s'agit d'ouvriers ou d'employés, mais il n'est souvent pas possible de distinguer les coûts de la main-d'œuvre afférents à chacune de ces deux catégories de travailleurs.

En conséquence, à quelques exceptions près, les chiffres indiqués dans le présent chapitre visent tous les salariés, c'est-à-dire les ouvriers et les employés des deux sexes, sans distinction d'âge, de profession, d'expérience, de niveau de qualification, etc. Des données sont présentées séparément pour chaque pays pris dans son ensemble et elles représentent en général la moyenne pendant une année civile. Lorsqu'il n'en est pas ainsi, la portée des statistiques est précisée dans les notes de bas de page.

Le type de statistiques présenté pour chaque pays est indiqué dans le tableau par une des rubriques suivantes:

(L.C.) *Coût de la main-d'œuvre*

(C.R.) *Rémunération des salariés*

(h.) *par heure*

(d.j.) *par jour*

(m.) *par mois*

(y.a.) *par an*

Pour de multiples raisons, les définitions du coût de la main-d'œuvre et de la rémunération des salariés adoptées par les divers pays diffèrent souvent des définitions internationales types recommandées. Dans divers pays, certains éléments du coût de la main-d'œuvre (par exemple les cotisations de sécurité sociale ou les frais de formation professionnelle, en totalité ou en partie) ne sont pas à la charge de l'employeur, mais représentent des dépenses supportées par l'Etat à des fins sociales ou autres. En général, toutefois, l'Etat participe, de concert avec l'employeur et le salarié, au financement des régimes de sécurité sociale rattachés aux salaires, bien que les quotes-parts de l'Etat, de l'employeur et du salarié varient d'un pays à un autre[4]. Les impôts de caractère social payés par les employeurs sont considérés dans certains pays comme faisant partie intégrante du coût de la main-d'œuvre, notamment ceux qui sont basés sur l'emploi ou sur les bordereaux de salaires. Les concepts nationaux du coût de la main-d'œuvre peuvent aussi varier du fait des différences existant entre les pays quant aux régimes de pensions, d'assurance santé et d'assurance vie, etc., et en ce qui concerne les impôts et les subventions liés à l'emploi. Les variations des coûts entre pays peuvent ainsi tenir en partie au fait que diverses dépenses sociales sont financées dans certains pays par l'intermédiaire du régime général d'imposition et qu'elles n'entrent donc pas dans le coût de la main-d'œuvre, alors que dans d'autres pays elles sont financées par des contributions directes de l'employeur.

Les différences entre les statistiques nationales s'expliquent aussi par la diversité de sources, de portée et de méthodes utilisées pour déterminer le coût de la main-d'œuvre. Les principales sources de données sur le coût de la main-d'œuvre comprennent les enquêtes auprès des établissements — *enquêtes sur le coût de la main-d'œuvre ou enquêtes ou recensements industriels* — bien que, dans certains pays, les *estimations officielles* du coût de la main-d'œuvre soient faites sur la base de données provenant de sources multiples (enquêtes courantes sur les gains, dossiers administratifs des organismes de sécurité sociale, organisations d'employeurs, etc.).

Les enquêtes sur le coût de la *main-d'œuvre* ont pour principal objet de rassembler des données sur le niveau, la composition et l'évolution du coût de la main-d'œuvre pour l'employeur. Ces données sont notamment utilisées pour analyser la structure du coût de la main-d'œuvre et les rapports existant entre ses différents éléments constitutifs. *Les recensements et enquêtes industriels* ont pour principal objet d'évaluer la consommation et la production brutes et nettes de l'industrie (y compris la rémunération des salariés) et de faire d'autres estimations qui permettent d'étudier la structure de l'industrie et les divers facteurs qui influent sur l'industrie. Les *estimations officielles* servent, en règle générale comme indicateurs de l'évolution du coût total de la main-d'œuvre, et sont calculées aux intervalles d'un trimestre ou d'une année.

Les enquêtes sur le coût de la *main-d'œuvre* sont généralement des enquêtes par sondage auprès des établissements ou des entreprises, qui portent sur les établissements au-dessus d'une certaine taille (d'ordinaire, ceux dont l'effectif dépasse un nombre donné de travailleurs), et qui sont menées tous les trois ans ou à des intervalles de temps plus grands. En règle générale, ces enquêtes visent les ouvriers et les employés, en excluant les travailleurs à domicile, les administrateurs recevant des jetons de présence, les personnes payées uniquement à la commission et les propriétaires exploitants. Généralement, on rassemble des données détaillées concernant le coût de la main-d'œuvre et ses éléments constitutifs, ainsi que des informations sur la structure de l'emploi correspondant et les caractéristiques des établissements. Dans certains pays, les enquêtes sur le coût de la main-d'œuvre servent également à recueillir des informations supplémentaires sur les pratiques et les méthodes adoptées par les établissements, qui influent sur le niveau, la composition et l'évolution du coût de la main-d'œuvre, comme le système de rémunération des heures non effectuées, les régimes de sécurité sociale et de pensions, et les modes de financement de ces régimes, les impôts basés sur les bordereaux de salaires, etc.

Les données sur la *rémunération des salariés* sont généralement obtenues au moyen de recensements ou d'enquêtes industriels, organisés chaque année ou à des intervalles de temps plus espacés, et qui visent les établissements ou entreprises au-dessus d'une taille donnée. Ces informations se rapportent d'ordinaire aux ouvriers et aux employés. Néanmoins, dans certains cas, les propriétaires exploitants et les personnes payées uniquement à la commission sont couverts aussi bien que les salariés. Outre les données sur la rémunération des salariés, ces enquêtes fournissent des renseignements sur d'autres facteurs de production, comme les matières premières, les combustibles, etc., la production, la valeur ajoutée, les stocks, les effectifs, l'actif, la formation de capital, etc. On n'a besoin généralement que d'estimations globales de sorte que, en principe, on ne rassemble pas de données distinctes sur les divers éléments constitutifs de la rémunération des salariés, ni sur les différentes caractéristiques des salariés.

Les séries statistiques obtenues au moyen d'enquêtes sur le coût de la main-d'œuvre ou de recensements ou d'enquêtes industriels peuvent varier d'une période à une autre en fonction de la structure industrielle, de la structure de l'emploi et des taux d'activité, ainsi que de la croissance ou du déclin des établissements. De plus, ces données peuvent subir un écart systématique et être faussées à cause de l'exclusion d'établissements qui sont en deçà d'une certaine taille.

Il conviendra de ne pas perdre de vue, en utilisant les données pour faire des comparaisons au niveau national ou international, les différences qui peuvent exister quant aux définitions, à la portée, au champ d'application et aux méthodes retenues pour le rassemblement de ces données

et pour leur présentation. Il convient de se rappeler, lorsqu'on utilise ces données pour faire des comparaisons entre pays, que de nombreux facteurs influent sur le coût de la main-d'œuvre, comme le financement des systèmes de sécurité sociale, les systèmes d'imposition ou de subventions, etc.

Il y a lieu de prendre beaucoup de soin en utilisant les chiffres concurremment avec des données figurant dans d'autres chapitres de cet annuaire ou d'autres sources. Cela ne peut être fait que lorsqu'il existe une correspondance très proche entre les définitions, la portée et les méthodes d'établissement des séries, et la présentation des données.

Pour des renseignements complémentaires, voir BIT: *Un système intégré de statistiques des salaires: manuel de méthodologie* (Genève, 1980), et *Sources et méthodes: statistiques du travail*, vol. 2 «Emploi, salaires, durée du travail et coût de la main-d'œuvre (enquêtes auprès des établissements)», deuxième édition (Genève, 1995).

Tableau 6A

Coût de la main-d'œuvre dans les industries manufacturières

Ce tableau présente les données sur le coût moyen de la main-d'œuvre par salarié pour l'ensemble des industries manufacturières et par grand groupe ou branche d'industrie. Le type de source des séries apparaît sous la forme d'un code entre parenthèses placé après le nom du pays et les codes sont énumérés page XVI. Dans la mesure du possible, les différentes industries manufacturières ont été ordonnées conformément à la *Classification internationale type, par industrie, de toutes les branches d'activité économique (CITI) Révisions 2, 3 ou 4* (voir annexe) avec les numéros de code correspondants. Les divergences sont indiquées en notes de bas de page.

Notes

[1] Pour le texte intégral de la résolution, voir BIT: *Recommandations internationales en vigueur sur les statistiques du travail* (Genève, 2000) ou le site Web du Département de statistique du BIT (www.ilo.org/public/french/bureau/stat).

[2] Pour le texte intégral, voir Nations Unies: *Système de comptabilité nationale*, Etudes méthodologiques, série F, n₀ 2, rév. 3 (New York, 1970).

[3] Pour le texte intégral, voir «*Système de comptabilité nationale, 1993*», préparé sous les auspices du Groupe de travail intersecrétariat sur la comptabilité nationale (Bruxelles/Luxembourg, New York, Paris, Washington, DC, 1993).

[4] Pour des renseignements complémentaires concernant les régimes nationaux de sécurité sociale et leur financement, voir BIT: *Le coût de la sécurité sociale*, Quatorzième enquête internationale, 1987-1989 (Genève, 1995).

Costo de la mano de obra

La Resolución sobre las estadísticas del costo de la mano de obra, adoptada por la undécima Conferencia Internacional de Estadísticos del Trabajo (Ginebra, 1966), contiene la siguiente definición del *costo de la mano de obra*[1]:

3. A los efectos de las estadísticas del costo de la mano de obra, este costo es el que corre a cargo del empleador que ocupa la mano de obra. El concepto estadístico del costo de la mano de obra debería abarcar la remuneración por el trabajo cumplido, la remuneración por tiempo no trabajado, las primas y gratificaciones, los gastos en concepto de comidas, bebidas, combustible y otros pagos en especie, los costos de vivienda de los trabajadores a cargo de los empleadores, los gastos de seguridad social de los empleadores, los gastos de formación profesional a cargo de los empleadores, el costo de los servicios de bienestar y los costos no clasificados en otros grupos, como los gastos de transporte de los trabajadores, el suministro de ropa de trabajo y los gastos de contratación, así como los impuestos considerados como costos de la mano de obra...

En el Sistema de Cuentas Nacionales, 1967 (SCN), de las Naciones Unidas se definió la *remuneración de los asalariados* del modo siguiente[2]:

7.11. La remuneración de los empleados incluye todos los pagos realizados por los productores de sueldos y salarios a sus empleados, tanto en especie como en dinero, así como las contribuciones en favor de sus empleados a la seguridad social y a las cajas privadas de pensiones, los seguros de riesgos, los seguros de vida y otros regímenes análogos...

Así, el costo de la mano de obra y la remuneración de los asalariados son conceptos estrechamente relacionados, con muchos elementos comunes. La mayor parte del costo de la mano de obra corresponde a la remuneración de los asalariados, y la parte restante a los gastos a cargo de los empleadores, tales como la formación profesional, servicios de bienestar (cantinas y servicios similares, instalaciones y servicios educativos, culturales y recreativos, subvenciones a mutuales de crédito, el costo de servicios similares para el personal, etc.), gastos de contratación y otras partidas diversas (ropa de trabajo, viajes entre el domicilio y el lugar de trabajo, etc.) y los impuestos considerados como costo de la mano de obra. El concepto de la remuneración de los asalariados incluye los estipendios a los miembros de juntas directivas (que quedan excluidos del concepto de costo de la mano de obra), y excluyen los gastos realizados por los empleadores en conceptos tales como instalaciones de bienestar en el lugar de trabajo, exámenes médicos, deportes y otras actividades recreativas, así como el reembolso por los empleadores de los gastos realizados por sus empleados en ropa y herramientas de trabajo.

El SCN fue revisado en 1993[3], ampliándose generalmente los elementos de la remuneración de los empleados para abarcar diversos servicios de bienestar, tales como deportes, esparcimiento, establecimientos de vacaciones, etc., así como los no clasificados en otro sitio (por ejemplo, la ropa de trabajo que los asalariados suelen usar tanto fuera como dentro de los lugares de trabajo, el transporte de ida y vuelta al lugar de trabajo, el estacionamiento de coches o aparcamiento). De esta forma el concepto de remuneración de los empleados se ha relacionado más estrechamente al de costo de la mano de obra. Sin embargo, en la presente publicación, la mayoría de las estadísticas de este capítulo sobre la remuneración de los asalariados aún se basan en el Sistema de Cuentas Nacionales de 1967.

Las estadísticas que figuran en este capítulo se refieren al *costo medio de la mano de obra por asalariado* o, en ciertos casos, a la *remuneración media de los asalariados* (esta expresión corresponde a *remuneración de los empleados* utilizada en el SCN de las Naciones Unidas). Aunque el nivel y composición del costo de la mano de obra tienden a variar entre obreros y empleados, en muchos casos no es posible establecer distinción entre los costos de la mano de obra respecto de estos dos grupos de asalariados. Por tanto, con algunas excepciones, las cifras ofrecidas en este capítulo se refieren a todos los asalariados, es decir, obreros y empleados de uno y otro sexo, y sin distinción por razón de edad, ocupación, experiencia, nivel de calificaciones, etc. Los datos figuran separadamente para cada país en su conjunto, y en general se refieren a promedios del año civil. Cuando el alcance no corresponde a lo indicado arriba, las diferencias se señalan por medio de notas a pie de página.

El tipo de estadísticas presentado para cada país figura en el cuadro con los siguientes códigos:

(LC) *Costo de la mano de obra*

(CR) *Remuneración de los asalariados*

(h.) *por hora*

(d.j.) *por día*

(m.) *por mes*

(y.a.) *por año*

Por diversas razones, las definiciones nacionales sobre el costo de la mano de obra y la remuneración de los asalariados suelen diferir de las definiciones internacionales recomendadas. En ciertos países no recaen sobre los empleadores algunos elementos del costo de la mano de obra, por ejemplo la totalidad o parte del costo de la seguridad social y de la formación profesional, sino que representan gastos estatales por consideraciones sociales o de otro tipo. Sin embargo, en general el Estado contribuye, junto con el empleador y el asalariado, a financiar los programas de seguridad social relacionados con el salario, aunque la medida de la participación estatal, del empleador o del trabajador varía de un país a otro[4].

En ciertos países se consideran los impuestos de carácter social pagados por los empleadores como costo de la mano de obra, especialmente los impuestos sobre la nómina o por volumen de empleo. Los conceptos nacionales del costo de la mano de obra también pueden diferir a causa de las variaciones de la práctica nacional en lo que respecta a sistemas de pensiones, seguros de vida, etc., así como en lo referente a los impuestos y subsidios relacionados con el empleo. Algunas de las diferencias al respecto entre países se pueden explicar por el hecho de que en algunos de ellos determinados costos sociales se financian a través del sistema impositivo general, y por tanto quedan excluidos del costo de la mano de obra, mientras que en otros se financian mediante contribuciones directas por parte de los empleadores. Las estadísticas reflejan también variedades de ámbito y de métodos utilizados para medir el costo de la mano de obra. Las principales fuentes de datos al respecto son las encuestas de establecimientos, ya se trate de *encuestas sobre costo de la mano de obra* o de *censos* o *encuestas industriales*, aunque en algunos países se hacen *estimaciones oficiales* de los costos de la mano de obra sobre la base de datos obtenidos de diversas fuentes, tales como las encuestas frecuentes de ganancias (salarios), registros administrativos de las organizaciones de seguridad social, de las organizaciones de empleadores, etc.

El principal objetivo de las encuestas sobre *costo de la mano de obra* es recopilar datos sobre el nivel, composición y evolución de los costos de la mano de obra que recaen sobre el empleador. Esos datos se utilizan, entre otras cosas, para el análisis de la estructura del costo de la mano de obra y para mostrar las relaciones entre sus diferentes componentes. El principal objetivo de los *censos y encuestas industriales* es calcular el consumo y la producción brutos y netos del sector industrial (incluyendo la remuneración de los asalariados) y obtener otras medidas que se pueden utilizar para el estudio de la estructura industrial y el análisis de los diversos factores que influyen en la industria. Las *estimaciones oficiales* se usan generalmente para medir la evolución del costo total de la mano de obra a través del tiempo, y es usual hacerlas a intervalos trimestrales o anuales.

En general, las encuestas sobre *costo de la mano* de obra son encuestas por muestreo de establecimientos o empresas que sobrepasan cierto tamaño (normalmente aquellos en que está empleado más de un determinado número de trabajadores), y se llevan a cabo a intervalos de tres años o más. Normalmente, incluyen obreros y empleados, mientras que quedan al margen las personas que trabajan a domicilio, los directivos remunerados mediante honorarios, las personas pagadas únicamente por comisión y los propietarios que trabajan en su empresa. En general, las encuestas sobre costo de la mano de obra se proponen principalmente recopilar datos detallados sobre el costo de la mano de obra y sus componentes, además de información sobre el empleo correspondiente y sobre las características de los establecimientos. En algunos países se utilizan también las encuestas sobre costo de la mano de obra para obtener información suplementaria respecto a las prácticas y políticas empresariales que repercuten sobre el nivel, composición y evolución de dichos costos, tales como el sistema de remuneración por tiempo no trabajado, los sistemas de seguridad social y pensiones y la manera de financiarlos, impuestos sobre la nómina, etc.

Los datos sobre la *remuneración de los asalariados* se obtienen generalmente mediante censos y encuestas industriales realizados por lo regular a intervalos anuales, y referidos a los establecimientos o empresas que superan un determinado tamaño. Las estadísticas sobre remuneración de los asalariados se compilan en general únicamente en relación con los obreros y empleados; algunas veces, sin embargo, abarcan también a los propietarios que trabajan en su empresa, así como a las personas remuneradas exclusivamente mediante comisiones. Además de los datos relativos a la remuneración de los asalariados, estas encuestas facilitan información sobre otros insumos de la producción, tales como materiales, combustibles, etc., producción, valor agregado, existencias, inventarios, activos, formación de capital, etc. Por regla general, sólo se necesitan estimaciones sobre agregados, y por lo tanto no es corriente recopilar datos separados sobre los diversos componentes de la remuneración de los asalariados ni sobre las diferentes características de los asalariados.

Las modificaciones de la estructura industrial, de la estructura del empleo y de los niveles de actividad, así como el crecimiento o el declive de los establecimientos, pueden repercutir sobre las series estadísticas recopiladas mediante estas encuestas. Además, a causa de la exclusión de los establecimientos o empresas que no alcanzan determinado tamaño, tales estadísticas pueden adolecer de ciertos sesgos.

Al utilizar los datos para establecer comparaciones a nivel nacional o internacional, debe tenerse presente que pueden existir variaciones en cuanto a conceptos, ámbito, alcance y métodos utilizados en la recopilación de los datos, así como en la presentación de éstos. Al hacer comparaciones entre países hay que tener en cuenta, en particular, los factores que ejercen influencia sobre el costo de la mano de obra, tales como la manera de financiar la seguridad social, los sistemas de impuestos o subsidios, etc.

Debe procederse con cuidado en caso de utilizar las cifras conjuntamente con las de otros capítulos de este anuario o con los datos procedentes de otras fuentes. Esto podría hacerse sólo si existe una correspondencia estrecha entre las definiciones, ámbito, métodos utilizados para recopilar los datos y manera de presentarlos de esas estadísticas.

Para más información, véase OIT: *Un sistema integrado de estadísticas de salarios: Manual metodológico* (Ginebra, 1992) (La edición española puede solicitarse al Departamento de Estadística de la OIT), y *Fuentes y Métodos: Estadísticas del trabajo*, vol. 2: «Empleo, salarios, horas de trabajo y costo de la mano de obra (encuestas de establecimientos)», segunda edición (Ginebra, 1995).

Cuadro 6A

Costo de la mano de obra en las industrias manufactureras

Este cuadro contiene datos sobre el costo medio de la mano de obra por asalariado de las industrias manufactureras, en su conjunto y por grandes divisiones o agrupaciones. La fuente de las series se indica mediante un código entre paréntesis, a continuación del nombre del país; los códigos se enumeran en la página XVI. En la medida de lo posible, las diferentes industrias se han dispuesto según la *Clasificación Internacional Industrial Uniforme de Todas las Actividades Económicas (CIIU) Revisiones 2, 3 o 4* (véase Apéndice), con sus códigos correspondientes. Toda diferencia se señala en notas de pie de página.

Notas

[1] Para el texto completo de la Resolución, véase OIT: *Recomendaciones internacionales de actualidad en estadísticas del trabajo* (Ginebra, 2000) o el sitio Web del Departamento de Estadística de la OIT (www.ilo.org/public/spanish/bureau/stat).

[2] Para el texto completo, véase Naciones Unidas: *Un sistema de cuentas nacionales*, Estudios de métodos, serie F, núm. 2, Rev. 3 (Nueva York, 1970).

[3] Para el texto completo, en inglés, véase «*System of National Accounts, 1993*» *(Sistema de Cuentas Nacionales, de 1993)*, elaborado por el Grupo de Trabajo Intersecretarías sobre Cuentas Nacionales (Bruselas/Luxemburgo, Nueva York, Paris, Washington D.C., 1993) [Inter-Secretariat Working Group on National Accounts; (Brussels/Luwembourg, New York, Paris, Washington, D.C., 1993)].

[4] Para más información sobre los sistemas nacionales de seguridad social y su financiación, véase OIT: *El costo de la seguridad social*, decimocuarta encuesta internacional, 1987-1989 (Ginebra, 1995).

LABOUR COST
In manufacturing

COÛT DE LA MAIN-D OEUVRE
Dans les industries manufacturières

COSTO DE LA MANO DE OBRA
En las industrias manufactureras

6A

	1999	2000	2001	2002	2003	2004	2005	2006	2007	2008

AFRICA-AFRIQUE-AFRICA

Mauritius (CB) [1]   Employees - Salariés - Asalariados   CR/y.a. - Rupee
ISIC 3 - CITI 3 - CIIU 3

	1999	2000	2001	2002	2003	2004	2005	2006	2007	2008
Total	79 327.3	85 279.5	92 024.7	108 082.8	113 615.3	128 053.5	137 081.6	157 181.8	.	.
17	71 737.5	57 399.3	66 679.0	90 081.8	87 637.4	104 169.4	118 690.2	144 886.8	.	.
18	64 536.2	72 884.4	79 747.2	85 911.4	97 986.0	104 072.2	110 845.7	111 876.6	.	.
19	66 497.5	76 350.9	70 254.2	72 094.1	90 795.7	84 818.9	95 319.9	115 043.4	.	.
20	72 583.2	102 096.0	112 953.4	111 975.1	87 507.4	101 245.7	106 089.5	117 502.2	.	.
21	117 211.9	88 634.1	90 287.3	103 216.5	110 209.5	128 253.4	141 563.6	208 209.0	.	.
22	140 217.4	155 986.2	154 400.7	158 917.0	163 573.8	187 357.0	194 056.7	170 116.6	.	.
23-24	138 652.1	136 062.0	157 435.9	161 155.9	174 652.0	209 595.9	224 228.7	247 737.4	.	.
25-26	135 445.3	147 032.9	154 059.4	160 177.9	196 284.0	236 999.7	250 947.7	276 627.4	.	.
27	134 189.0	120 796.6	134 359.0	142 671.8	152 656.8	186 069.5	206 979.8	240 896.4	.	.
28	97 965.2	108 247.0	122 575.3	137 412.0	137 316.6	124 319.3	121 185.1	119 104.6	.	.
29-30	172 690.8	219 646.5	146 100.9	162 388.4	200 848.4	302 695.8	317 667.4	292 523.4	.	.
31-32	100 512.8	115 939.3	89 387.1	92 525.6	104 893.3	154 992.1	147 598.1	134 693.9	.	.
33	49 858.9	57 077.4	67 027.0	56 940.4	61 216.5	84 831.5	65 107.5	92 022.4	.	.
34-35	99 188.6	130 202.1	200 000.0	122 450.2	180 921.1	210 977.2	180 074.5	138 883.0	.	.
36	82 654.8	80 512.5	81 318.0	94 061.3	84 492.4	100 382.0	108 808.5	146 374.4	.	.

AMERICA-AMÉRIQUE-AMERICA

Argentina (DB)   Wage-earners - Ouvriers - Obreros   CR/m. - Peso
ISIC 3 - CITI 3 - CIIU 3

	1999	2000	2001	2002	2003	2004	2005	2006	2007	2008
Total	808.65	818.07	797.17	811.92	990.88	1 221.70	1 500.20	1 882.78	.	.
15	719.42	715.29	699.46	736.11	867.90	1 106.80	1 363.60	1 699.54	.	.
16	1 294.24	1 179.08	1 057.70	1 012.60	1 327.50	148.40	1 561.40	1 954.94	.	.
17	593.87	590.98	541.16	535.04	700.30	906.44	1 085.80	1 354.27	.	.
18	422.17	426.66	426.32	406.77	555.09	741.72	868.15	1 063.66	.	.
19	589.89	579.43	521.27	559.02	693.29	876.73	1 071.00	1 283.20	.	.
20	483.67	478.09	455.99	468.20	621.78	804.93	999.22	1 241.62	.	.
21	933.37	934.74	916.92	946.34	1 120.10	1 347.80	1 569.90	1 916.40	.	.
22	1 158.00	1 177.61	1 182.66	1 134.90	1 290.00	1 557.10	1 823.40	2 209.80	.	.
23	2 049.97	2 117.54	2 136.94	2 293.70	2 793.82	3 115.80	3 579.60	4 275.98	.	.
24	1 114.44	1 127.22	1 106.26	1 132.80	1 350.00	1 626.70	1 916.50	2 460.16	.	.
25	834.93	834.10	788.97	812.48	1 004.20	1 304.10	1 607.00	1 982.79	.	.
26	875.75	840.35	823.85	843.15	1 034.90	1 233.40	1 489.90	1 864.22	.	.
27	1 066.83	1 113.93	1 127.48	1 228.20	1 455.10	1 848.50	2 214.36	2 956.24	.	.
28	717.85	748.64	738.67	715.55	914.22	1 151.50	1 398.80	1 791.07	.	.
29	852.99	866.73	856.22	885.27	1 074.70	1 323.90	1 609.20	2 032.55	.	.
30	932.77	954.11	993.87	1 073.60	1 285.70	1 541.50	1 658.00	1 927.38	.	.
31	836.04	827.76	810.12	799.88	956.17	1 212.00	1 504.30	1 943.08	.	.
32	1 380.22	1 496.60	1 359.18	1 172.60	1 351.50	1 766.50	2 062.60	2 628.01	.	.
33	743.44	769.11	734.33	711.01	816.24	1 028.80	1 234.90	1 538.62	.	.
34	1 034.83	1 127.11	1 102.68	1 095.00	1 407.00	1 752.10	2 143.50	2 676.35	.	.
35	847.55	850.40	843.15	796.78	966.49	1 259.90	1 509.70	1 956.75	.	.
36	594.91	580.62	575.72	525.90	702.36	894.80	1 087.90	1 380.98	.	.

Brasil (DB)   All persons engaged - Ensemble de l'effectif occupé - Todo el efectivo ocupado   CR/m. - Real
ISIC 3 - CITI 3 - CIIU 3

	1999	2000	2001	2002	2003	2004	2005	2006	2007	2008
15	985	1 008	1 054	1 166	1 225	1 226	1 360	.	.	.
16	2 220	2 464	2 314	2 692	3 416	2 860	2 668	.	.	.
17	837	919	990	1 057	1 165	1 229	1 323	.	.	.
18	489	500	521	543	627	630	724	.	.	.
19	544	573	636	688	816	845	928	.	.	.
20	516	543	622	679	792	845	1 005	.	.	.
21	1 632	1 798	1 895	1 977	2 350	2 432	2 666	.	.	.
22	1 616	1 802	1 931	1 926	2 030	2 139	2 155	.	.	.
23	2 280	2 816	3 319	3 355	4 083			.	.	.
24	2 557	2 662	2 953	3 154	3 422	3 528	3 837	.	.	.
25	1 206	1 258	1 329	1 455	1 700	1 736	1 851	.	.	.
26	931	954	1 019	1 096	1 285	1 347	1 471	.	.	.
27	2 032	2 126	2 393	2 680	2 965	3 297	3 430	.	.	.
28	1 087	1 101	1 225	1 289	1 437	1 523	1 678	.	.	.
29	1 618	1 691	1 820	1 911	2 075	2 271	2 534	.	.	.
30	2 203	2 962	3 256	3 597	3 366	3 278	2 959	.	.	.
31	1 724	1 682	1 849	1 938	2 293	2 206	2 456	.	.	.
32	2 220	2 336	3 328	2 997	2 953	2 843	3 282	.	.	.
33	1 353	1 511	1 566	1 714	1 845	2 091	2 305	.	.	.
34	2 404	2 450	2 673	2 810	3 181	3 199	3 533	.	.	.
35	1 948	2 175	2 524	2 676	3 022	3 424	3 500	.	.	.
36	686	720	802	844	938	1 025	1 085	.	.	.
37	992	931	852	879	877	947	1 091	.	.	.

Explanatory notes: see p. 1039.   Notes explicatives: voir p. 1041.   Notas explicativas: véase p. 1043.

[1] Establishments with 10 or more persons employed.   [1] Etablissements occupant 10 personnes et plus.   [1] Establecimientos con 10 y más trabajadores.

LABOUR COST
In manufacturing

COÛT DE LA MAIN-D OEUVRE
Dans les industries manufacturières

COSTO DE LA MANO DE OBRA
En las industrias manufactureras

	1999	2000	2001	2002	2003	2004	2005	2006	2007	2008

Colombia (DA) [1][2]
ISIC 2 - CITI 2 - CIIU 2

Employees - Salariés - Asalariados

CR/m. - Peso
ISIC 3 - CITI 3 - CIIU 3

	1999	2000	2001	2002	2003	2004	2005	2006	2007	2008	
Total	1 178.4	1 259.4	1 373.0	1 471.9	1 552.3	1 644.2	1 733.9				Total
311-312	1 082.3	1 321.2	1 388.6	1 531.9	1 587.6	1 719.5	1 776.7				15
313	1 948.0	2 160.3	2 116.0	2 585.9	3 167.9	3 380.5	3 238.0				16
314	1 991.7	1 079.3	1 178.2	1 254.0	1 440.2	1 428.6	1 501.5				17
321	905.2	646.0	707.5	763.3	813.9	907.0	957.4				18
322	564.9	683.7	758.3	836.8	878.0	930.1	959.6				19
323	728.0	914.4	939.5	1 010.1	1 065.3	1 154.7	1 241.7				20
324	601.5	1 749.4	1 819.6	1 944.7	2 097.3	2 209.1	2 353.1				21
331	832.0	1 279.0	1 399.1	1 506.2	1 626.8	1 778.4	1 947.7				22
332	588.4	4 823.3	6 722.6	7 048.7	8 043.8	5 519.2	5 488.5				23
341	1 715.6	1 889.5	2 105.1	2 236.9	2 391.8	2 473.6	2 365.4				24
342	1 173.3	1 241.8	1 366.8	1 421.7	1 460.8	1 609.3	1 700.7				25
351	2 116.8	1 433.5	1 484.9	1 593.5	1 718.6	1 793.2	1 840.1				26
352	1 659.0	1 701.0	1 929.6	1 991.3	2 138.4	2 204.3	2 461.4				27
353	7 991.0	1 110.4	1 214.5	1 233.8	1 242.0	1 365.0	1 409.3				28
354	1 693.1	997.3	1 105.2	1 198.0	1 269.1	1 353.5	1 431.6				29
355	1 527.5	1 232.3	1 356.4	1 429.4	1 622.9	1 805.8	973.3				31
356	1 024.5	780.4	955.3	1 059.8	1 137.9	1 274.9	1 417.5				32
361	1 287.0	905.0	1 010.5	1 116.8	1 165.0	1 238.3	1 364.3				33
362	1 599.8	1 739.7	1 867.6	1 837.8	1 884.4	1 991.5	2 136.8				34
369	1 216.8	1 236.5	1 358.0	1 513.9	1 566.0	1 673.9	1 841.9				35
371	1 695.5	938.4	882.5	1 105.4	1 106.9	1 217.0	1 287.5				36
372	1 306.2										
381	960.8										
382	902.8										
383	1 287.0										
384	1 273.8										
385	1 008.7										
390	822.3										

Chile (DA) [3]
ISIC 2 - CITI 2 - CIIU 2

Employees - Salariés - Asalariados

LC/m. - Peso

	1999	2000	2001	2002	2003	2004	2005	2006	2007	2008
Total	316 073	325 729	331 352	342 689	348 379	356 965				
31	280 255	299 476	308 686	315 853	322 965	326 861				
32	193 273	182 811	182 443	186 770	188 175	189 066				
33	220 297	219 258	214 482	213 965	219 813	223 998				
34	600 351	614 185	622 858	653 489	686 713	700 110				
35	489 764	511 748	517 522	540 654	541 028	581 102				
36	368 237	370 096	373 369	385 162	373 875	391 617				
37	295 499	304 003	314 504	331 188	341 566	338 614				
38	199 545	215 934	207 548	212 916	207 467	177 020				

Ecuador (CB) [1][2]
ISIC 3 - CITI 3 - CIIU 3

Employees - Salariés - Asalariados

CR/y.a. - US dollar

	1999	2000	2001	2002	2003	2004	2005	2006	2007	2008
Total	49 505.7	4 160.9 [4]	6 003.7	6 473.4	7 284.6	7 995.8				
15	51 381.9	4 055.0 [4]	5 617.6	5 756.4	6 713.9	7 121.9				
16	72 502.0	10 335.0 [4]	10 740.4	14 070.2	11 532.7	14 086.9				
17	31 733.8	2 834.0 [4]	4 272.5	4 798.9	5 312.3	5 647.2				
18	19 625.0	1 685.6 [4]	2 782.7	3 582.4	4 170.4	4 316.4				
19	26 364.8	2 476.1 [4]	3 733.3	4 679.6	5 510.7	5 304.9				
20	36 686.1	3 170.5 [4]	4 708.5	5 306.7	5 666.6	6 561.7				
21	56 955.0	4 578.3 [4]	6 620.6	6 922.9	7 857.1	9 469.0				
22	48 637.4	3 814.8 [4]	6 479.0	8 198.3	9 106.4	10 797.7				
23		13 780.7 [4]	22 324.7	23 633.9	26 293.0	33 444.4				
24	69 890.1	6 065.6 [4]	8 452.2	9 176.2	9 902.8	10 528.7				
25	46 651.1	4 288.6 [4]	5 783.4	6 776.4	7 291.4	7 269.2				
26	66 502.5	5 928.7 [4]	7 336.5	7 577.4	8 422.7	10 541.1				
27	44 787.2	5 468.8 [4]	7 027.7	8 303.0	8 780.2	12 944.6				
28	50 531.1	4 267.9 [4]	6 535.9	7 202.7	7 830.7	9 055.5				
29	33 336.6	2 922.0 [4]	5 297.9	5 856.5	6 517.4	6 125.3				
31	50 593.7	4 661.6 [4]	5 285.3	6 113.3	6 895.0	7 606.6				
32	27 901.6	3 615.7 [4]	5 806.7	10 132.8	9 126.3	10 406.4				
33	22 820.0	1 978.5 [4]	2 782.2	3 804.4	5 866.5	6 317.2				
34	75 366.0	4 539.0 [4]	7 872.7	7 573.4	7 977.6	7 428.7				
35	45 961.3	2 150.4 [4]	7 268.5	7 562.1	7 208.5	7 773.5				
36	30 449.0	2 338.6 [4]	4 126.2	4 499.7	5 249.7	5 080.1				

Guyana (DA)
ISIC 3 - CITI 3 - CIIU 3

Employees - Salariés - Asalariados

LC/y.a. - Dollar

	1999	2000	2001	2002	2003	2004	2005	2006	2007	2008
Total					416 122	463 231		504 824	345 090	

Explanatory notes: see p. 1039.

[1] Figures in thousands. [2] Establishments with 10 or more persons employed. [3] April of each year. [4] Prior to March 2000: sucres; 25,000 sucres =1 US dollar.

Notes explicatives: voir p. 1041.

[1] Données en milliers. [2] Etablissements occupant 10 personnes et plus. [3] Avril de chaque année. [4] Avant mars 2000: sucres; 25 000 sucres = 1 dollar EU.

Notas explicativas: véase p. 1043.

[1] Cifras en millares. [2] Establecimientos con 10 y más trabajadores. [3] Abril de cada año. [4] Antes marzo 2000: sucres; 25 000 sucres = 1 dólar EU.

1046

ILO YEARBOOK OF LABOUR STATISTICS 2009   *ANNUAIRE DES STATISTIQUES DU TRAVAIL DU BIT 2009*   *ANUARIO DE ESTADISTICAS DEL TRABAJO DEL OIT 2009*

LABOUR COST

In manufacturing

COÛT DE LA MAIN-D OEUVRE

Dans les industries manufacturières

COSTO DE LA MANO DE OBRA

En las industrias manufactureras

6A

	1999	2000	2001	2002	2003	2004	2005	2006	2007	2008

México (DB) — Employees - Salariés - Asalariados — CR/h. - Nuevo peso
ISIC 3 - CITI 3 - CIIU 3

	1999	2000	2001	2002	2003	2004	2005	2006	2007	2008
Total	37.69	43.59	49.51	53.06	56.34	58.47	60.37	62.96	66.15	69.97
15	33.15	38.64	43.26	47.69	50.78	52.48	53.65	55.69	58.00	60.32
16	68.71	77.91	92.68	108.00	116.34	127.36	114.17	139.00	142.92	221.01
17	23.60	27.51	30.75	33.33	35.35	36.11	37.38	39.39	39.49	41.31
18	17.14	20.28	22.69	24.13	25.11	27.32	29.03	30.99	32.26	35.71
19	19.95	23.08	26.82	27.54	29.85	31.83	31.76	35.84	37.28	39.27
20	18.43	21.29	24.92	26.64	29.92	29.38	31.11	31.88	35.01	37.12
21	34.20	39.10	43.90	45.57	47.09	49.05	51.38	52.61	54.11	56.44
22	37.50	42.55	47.84	51.35	54.73	57.36	59.90	63.12	64.96	68.78
23	55.65	62.30	65.70	71.41	78.58	80.12	81.61	87.43	89.74	96.08
24	65.99	77.08	88.28	93.70	99.40	103.40	107.50	112.57	118.44	124.61
25	35.73	40.91	41.55	41.85	45.52	47.72	49.27	51.30	53.95	55.59
26	37.58	41.90	49.73	53.58	57.06	58.54	61.44	64.65	67.20	73.09
27	42.90	48.07	54.00	55.79	59.20	60.50	63.56	66.93	69.23	71.05
28	35.06	40.84	45.69	49.44	55.04	57.58	59.98	61.82	66.86	68.68
29	37.46	43.21	48.20	51.37	55.70	56.78	58.74	60.62	63.89	65.91
30	45.01	47.59	61.59	74.01	68.05	60.30	54.83	52.47	57.83	55.75
31	35.58	39.59	46.20	49.57	50.80	54.03	57.17	58.95	60.57	63.36
32	50.09	50.94	60.34	60.97	61.17	64.93	69.56	72.24	73.84	76.32
33	27.99	32.03	34.47	38.66	40.29	40.46	41.17	43.46	47.44	52.33
34	48.40	57.79	68.11	73.10	77.09	79.05	78.24	80.43	86.79	95.14
35	32.97	39.01	46.19	52.04	57.36	62.08	67.43	67.09	79.14	84.59
36	22.19	25.91	29.90	32.86	35.92	38.27	39.07	40.16	43.73	45.53

Nicaragua (DA) — Employees - Salariés - Asalariados — CR/h. - Córdoba
ISIC 2 - CITI 2 - CIIU 2

	1999	2000	2001	2002	2003	2004	2005	2006	2007	2008
Total	16.00	17.09	17.34	17.36	17.38	17.42	17.61	17.86	.	.
31	16.00	16.90	16.89	16.73	16.73	16.44	16.44	17.91	.	.
32	9.00	9.66	9.69	10.22	10.49	12.09	12.47	11.72	.	.
33	16.00	17.07	18.55	18.97	18.97	18.90	18.90	18.76	.	.
34	22.00	28.07	28.68	26.68	28.68	29.30	29.74	29.48	.	.
35	15.00	17.37	18.23	18.32	18.32	19.95	19.50	19.95	.	.
36	24.00	24.20	25.64	25.87	25.87	24.70	24.92	24.18	.	.
37	.	.	.	.	.	.	.	.	.	.
38	14.00	15.35	15.67	15.67	15.68	16.98	18.11	18.49	.	.
39	.	6.52	6.52	6.52	7.25	7.92	9.77	10.38	.	.

Perú (DA) [1 2 3] — Wage-earners - Ouvriers - Obreros — CR/d.j. - Nuevo sol
ISIC 3 - CITI 3 - CIIU 3

	1999	2000	2001	2002	2003	2004	2005	2006	2007	2008
Total	39.36	41.93	41.77 [4]	43.22 [5]	41.84	43.19	45.88	44.29	42.77	46.92
15	43.82	44.44	47.79 [4]	52.32 [5]	42.30	41.52	52.61	45.11	44.82	53.37
16	30.77	45.45	22.02 [4]	. [5]	.	79.32	76.19	.	.	.
17	30.89	34.68	35.37 [4]	35.85 [5]	34.00	35.98	34.67	35.44	35.22	38.40
18	23.48	28.00	27.00 [4]	29.19 [5]	29.35	31.56	33.17	34.20	31.67	35.79
19	24.57	26.10	26.44 [4]	27.87 [5]	25.52	24.50	24.58	29.27	34.46	33.31
20	21.00	23.91	25.01 [4]	. [5]	26.40	28.06	29.66	31.43	30.97	41.63
21	32.94	36.36	41.23 [4]	41.24 [5]	39.53	41.28	45.01	46.26	44.27	47.80
22	40.55	42.10	45.01 [4]	43.94 [5]	52.14	63.63	57.63	57.04	63.01	58.93
23	.	.	.	.	64.17	62.25	63.00	61.70	100.00	102.53
24	47.21	49.23	47.83 [4]	47.61 [5]	40.29	42.50	41.21	42.03	45.03	46.67
25	42.25	39.46	38.58 [4]	38.02 [5]	51.85	51.54	65.15	67.75	64.71	66.88
26	61.35	65.81	56.34 [4]	57.12 [5]	70.03	66.47	55.73	59.01	53.15	59.25
27	52.29	54.87	63.89 [4]	64.87 [5]	.	59.16	86.52	89.38	68.92	62.59
28	33.15	35.69	37.88 [4]	43.36 [5]	42.56	42.61	41.93	44.45	43.77	45.45
29	35.87	37.47	35.53 [4]	41.16 [5]	41.94	35.32	34.02	35.90	41.37	42.74
31	48.91	52.55	61.34 [4]	59.91 [5]	48.28	52.01	57.86	52.67	49.29	53.36
34	35.82	35.24	40.10 [4]	36.02 [5]	35.28	40.50	37.50	41.54	41.80	50.14
35	37.27	38.53	42.64 [4]	43.53 [5]	44.63	47.14	79.92	50.62	50.17	57.13
36	37.51	43.70	40.96 [4]	50.48 [5]	37.03	40.84	37.78	38.79	41.52	42.28

Explanatory notes: see p. 1039.

[1] Figures at the desaggregated level are not representative because of the small sample size. [2] Urban areas. [3] Second quarter. [4] Average of the first three quarters. [5] Metropolitan Lima.

Notes explicatives: voir p. 1041.

[1] Chiffres non représentatifs au niveau desagrégé en raison de la faible taille de l'échantillonage. [2] Régions urbaines. [3] Deuxième trimestre. [4] Moyenne des trois premiers trimestres. [5] Lima métropolitaine.

Notas explicativas: véase p. 1043.

[1] Cifras no reprentativas al nivel de desagregación debidas al pequeño tamaño muestral. [2] Areas urbanas. [3] Segundo trimestre. [4] Promedio de los tres primeros trimestres. [5] Lima metropolitana.

6A

LABOUR COST	COÛT DE LA MAIN-D OEUVRE	COSTO DE LA MANO DE OBRA
In manufacturing	Dans les industries manufacturières	En las industrias manufactureras

	1999	2000	2001	2002	2003	2004	2005	2006	2007	2008

Perú (DA) [1]   Employees - Salariés - Asalariados   CR/m. - Nuevo sol
ISIC 3 - CITI 3 - CIIU 3

	1999	2000	2001	2002	2003	2004	2005	2006	2007	2008
Total	2 147.94	2 269.49	2 208.27 [2]	2 303.11 [3]	2 134.25	2 184.85	2 203.13	2 136.48	2 046.65	2 295.16
15	2 600.21	2 687.97	2 610.27 [2]	2 841.89 [3]	2 246.90	2 183.36	2 631.44	2 497.22	2 345.34	3 034.57
16	2 887.04	1 796.95	941.07 [2]			3 290.09	3 431.69	1 056.51	1 035.60	
17	1 387.82	1 398.18	1 397.63 [2]	1 385.40 [3]	1 420.98	1 528.65	1 350.59	1 393.79	1 384.95	1 495.76
18	905.13	1 029.58	1 026.36 [2]	1 051.80 [3]	1 050.11	1 116.35	1 202.64	1 194.80	1 178.21	1 327.82
19	852.12	917.78	969.26 [2]	1 021.54 [3]	829.55	742.43	751.47	894.76	1 187.50	1 157.58
20	698.09	764.61	823.12 [2]	[3]	907.51	967.84	1 028.14	1 076.94	1 072.52	1 297.25
21	1 766.81	1 780.26	1 830.25 [2]	2 019.12 [3]	2 166.90	2 214.84	2 399.19	2 432.78	2 328.61	2 280.78
22	2 339.02	2 679.36	2 852.40 [2]	3 125.18 [3]	2 766.76	3 139.51	2 782.12	2 761.87	2 836.86	2 798.63
23	5 302.33	5 579.58	5 848.36 [2]	5 856.09 [3]		3 463.81	3 727.79	4 419.97	7 461.75	9 126.80
24	3 378.28	3 549.54	3 630.60 [2]	3 511.78 [3]	3 140.47	3 287.91	2 932.81	2 909.27	2 751.71	2 892.77
25	1 731.89	1 760.07	1 706.94 [2]	1 647.90 [3]	2 309.18	2 338.85	2 616.94	2 575.54	2 643.14	2 797.47
26	2 445.97	2 588.19	2 402.17 [2]	2 490.30 [3]	2 716.90	2 565.82	2 494.40	2 624.80	2 378.45	2 642.34
27	2 053.39	2 239.80	2 606.58 [2]	2 308.56 [3]		2 923.35	3 688.60	3 695.42	3 145.97	3 112.09
28	1 380.90	1 771.28	1 658.30 [2]	1 824.03 [3]	1 725.90	1 729.67	1 473.28	1 614.06	1 673.17	1 682.37
29	2 098.59	2 647.49	2 168.35 [2]	2 351.58 [3]	1 432.21	1 335.81	1 277.06	1 277.99	1 525.76	1 683.25
31	1 803.61	1 996.89	2 241.34 [2]	2 247.88 [3]	2 327.99	2 555.93	2 410.20	2 424.80	1 999.41	2 194.96
33						1 079.28				
34	1 309.83	1 332.42	1 420.31 [2]	1 277.78 [3]	1 301.81	1 611.78	1 380.72	1 505.23	1 551.03	1 802.31
35	1 292.32	1 374.25	1 468.56 [2]	1 596.46 [3]	1 758.56	1 805.43	1 945.60	2 085.94	2 158.16	2 674.70
36	1 477.19	1 679.75	1 782.88 [2]	2 113.46 [3]	1 697.16	1 715.57	2 171.38	2 035.73	1 582.94	1 702.30

United States (E) [4] [5]   Employees - Salariés - Asalariados   CR/h. - Dollar
ISIC 3 - CITI 3 - CIIU 3

	1999	2000	2001	2002	2003	2004	2005	2006	2007	2008
Total	23.6	24.6	25.9	27.0	28.2	28.9	29.7	30.0	30.6	
15-16			20.3	21.3	22.2	22.9	23.4	22.8		
17			17.2	17.7	18.4	19.2	19.3	19.2		
17-18			16.2	16.8	17.8	18.5	18.9	18.8		
18			14.7	15.4	16.6	17.3	18.0	18.0		
19			18.6	18.3	19.5	20.2	21.0	21.6		
20			17.3	17.9	18.1	18.6	19.5	19.7		
21			27.5	29.4	30.7	31.1	31.4	31.0		
23			37.6	40.4	41.1	43.4	45.6	47.9		
24			36.3	37.3	39.0	40.6	42.9	43.1		
25			21.9	22.7	23.4	24.2	24.6	24.2		
26			22.6	23.5	24.3	24.8	25.4	25.2		
27			27.7	28.6	29.9	30.7	31.4	31.3		
28			22.0	22.7	23.1	23.6	24.3	24.6		
29			27.4	28.6	29.6	29.8	30.5	30.8		
30,32			40.1	41.5	43.3	45.5	47.9	49.1		
31 [6]			25.5	26.2	27.3	28.6	29.4	29.9		
34			31.0	32.3	34.7	34.3	34.6	34.9		
34-35			31.4	33.4	35.6	35.8	36.0	36.9		
353			35.5	39.9	42.3	43.3	42.8	45.3		
361			17.9	17.9	18.7	19.0	19.6	20.1		

ASIA-ASIE-ASIA

Azerbaijan (DA)   Employees - Salariés - Asalariados   LC/h. - Manat
ISIC 3 - CITI 3 - CIIU 3

	1999	2000	2001	2002	2003	2004	2005	2006	2007	2008
Total										1.7
15										1.0
16										1.5
17										1.0
18										0.9
19										1.2
20										1.1
21										0.9
22										0.9
23										3.2
24										1.5
25										1.2
26										2.0
27										2.5
28										2.5
29										1.5
30										1.6
31										1.2
32										1.1
33										1.4
34										1.2
35										2.9
36										0.9
37										1.4

Explanatory notes: see p. 1039.

[1] Figures at the desaggregated level are not representative because of the small sample size. [2] Average of the first three quarters. [3] Metropolitan Lima. [4] National classification not strictly compatible with ISIC. [5] Excl. cost of payments in kind, vocational training, welfare servies and other costs. [6] Textile mill products only.

Notes explicatives: voir p. 1041.

[1] Chiffres non représentatifs au niveau desagrégé en raison de la faible taille de l'échantillonage. [2] Moyenne des trois premiers trimestres. [3] Lima métropolitaine. [4] Classification nationale non strictement compatible avec la CITI. [5] Non compris les coûts relatifs aux paiments en nature, a la formation professionnelle, aux services sociaux et autres coûts. [6] Seulement filature et tissage de textiles.

Notas explicativas: véase p. 1043.

[1] Cifras no reprentativas al nivel de desagregación debidas al pequeño tamaño muestral. [2] Promedio de los tres primeros trimestres. [3] Lima metropolitana. [4] Clasificación nacional no estrictamente compatible con la CIIU. [5] Excl. los pagos en especie, gastos de formacion profesional, de servicios de bienestar y otros gastos. [6] Hilado y tejido de textiles solamente.

LABOUR COST

In manufacturing

COÛT DE LA MAIN-D OEUVRE

Dans les industries manufacturières

COSTO DE LA MANO DE OBRA

En las industrias manufactureras

6A

	1999	2000	2001	2002	2003	2004	2005	2006	2007	2008

Azerbaijan (DA) — Employees - Salariés - Asalariados — LC/m. - Manat
ISIC 3 - CITI 3 - CIIU 3

	1999	2000	2001	2002	2003	2004	2005	2006	2007	2008
Total	.	.	.	.	.	663 126	149 [1]	178	245	313
15	.	.	.	.	.	329 364	81 [1]	96	152	188
16	.	.	.	.	.	1 013 615	201 [1]	214	295	278
17	.	.	.	.	.	283 519	80 [1]	91	118	190
18	.	.	.	.	.	131 730	35 [1]	57	127	172
19	.	.	.	.	.	262 638	68 [1]	74	153	201
20	.	.	.	.	.	155 084	45 [1]	88	156	199
21	.	.	.	.	.	263 745	59 [1]	106	156	175
22	.	.	.	.	.	347 422	86 [1]	96	134	161
23	.	.	.	.	.	970 681	229 [1]	335	471	602
24	.	.	.	.	.	703 346	153 [1]	200	226	263
25	.	.	.	.	.	338 016	75 [1]	95	155	222
26	.	.	.	.	.	923 840	154 [1]	176	232	340
27	.	.	.	.	.	1 007 521	239 [1]	275	334	419
28	.	.	.	.	.	1 172 865	231 [1]	269	379	472
29	.	.	.	.	.	527 047	124 [1]	152	225	774
30	.	.	.	.	.	268 536	96 [1]	103	239	276
31	.	.	.	.	.	347 635	104 [1]	117	167	223
32	.	.	.	.	.	382 882	71 [1]	84	164	214
33	.	.	.	.	.	392 292	91 [1]	135	201	257
34	.	.	.	.	.	512 597	82 [1]	142	187	236
35	.	.	.	.	.	1 058 423	268 [1]	319	377	538
36	.	.	.	.	.	237 220	54 [1]	70	111	157
37	.	.	.	.	.	572 337	77 [1]	155	287	262

Georgia (CA) — Employees - Salariés - Asalariados — LC/m. - Lari
ISIC 3 - CITI 3 - CIIU 3

	1999	2000	2001	2002	2003	2004	2005	2006	2007	2008
Total	117.9	128.2	139.4	192.3	203.5	236.9	259.1	.	.	.
15	93.3	101.3	108.6	160.6	178.7	209.5	233.7	.	.	.
16	86.7	89.1	354.4	518.6	482.2	953.3	822.0	.	.	.
17	76.4	88.6	102.7	155.1	94.0	121.3	135.3	.	.	.
18	58.5	87.0	129.4	133.2	126.1	155.0	137.6	.	.	.
19	59.1	65.8	69.2	81.8	72.8	79.4	109.1	.	.	.
20	56.4	66.2	77.7	92.5	94.6	90.1	111.6	.	.	.
21	107.0	120.7	136.2	135.7	62.4	138.9	134.7	.	.	.
22	78.9	91.8	116.3	118.0	109.0	97.2	158.3	.	.	.
23	488.8	309.8	321.7	180.8	116.8	207.6	250.1	.	.	.
24	148.1	205.4	209.5	247.3	273.2	284.4	314.6	.	.	.
25	143.3	202.8	210.7	170.7	109.9	216.6	232.2	.	.	.
26	141.7	159.3	161.3	244.2	290.2	256.0	196.5	.	.	.
27	99.5	157.0	159.4	201.0	221.0	279.3	322.5	.	.	.
28	111.9	93.5	103.6	174.5	161.7	207.1	274.7	.	.	.
29	124.4	151.5	161.4	106.1	104.7	129.3	298.6	.	.	.
30	36.8	75.4	78.4	121.5	179.0	142.0	.	.	.	.
31	126.7	130.4	132.2	115.4	132.3	169.2	171.3	.	.	.
32	65.8	68.3	69.3	67.2	70.0	39.2	162.9	.	.	.
33	26.1	42.7	51.7	78.5	94.7	94.1	188.0	.	.	.
34	135.6	92.9	94.7	147.5	160.5	102.8	122.7	.	.	.
35	181.3	190.1	193.2	287.4	286.2	350.8	355.8	.	.	.
36	98.6	84.9	85.0	110.3	135.0	121.8	149.0	.	.	.
37	82.3	80.8	88.1	124.5	103.9	218.4	269.1	.	.	.

Hong Kong, China (D) [2][3] — Employees - Salariés - Asalariados — CR/y.a. - Dollar
ISIC 3 - CITI 3 - CIIU 3

	1999	2000	2001	2002	2003	2004	2005	2006	2007	2008
Total	173 929	179 247	183 392	178 664	171 989	176 951	172 434	189 033	176 595	.
15	163 626	160 340	156 063	154 166	156 697	163 272	136 611	168 051	144 780	.
16	228 215	227 017	229 610	223 140	233 700	257 494	273 050	364 015	266 474	.
17	146 761	148 779	154 964	155 186	153 248	163 300	136 913	161 199	179 080	.
18	114 190	129 301	124 422	117 513	104 216	101 380	116 884	147 179		.
19	120 329	113 632	132 489	135 437	124 744	147 490	165 311	176 721	153 639	.
20	136 891	133 557	151 449	131 077	107 305	109 259	122 943	122 296	119 761	.
21	183 347	168 680	173 030	177 146	157 719	123 057	133 828	144 927	197 846	.
22	214 971	214 939	222 267	220 279	216 603	217 969	227 775	230 099	201 552	.
23	345 019	402 304	350 436	352 836	272 488	247 517	279 595	263 104	237 026	.
24	210 388	226 886	222 172	205 945	196 624	202 231	169 801	214 288	164 421	.
25	144 224	148 661	159 604	159 295	163 410	146 143	143 493	173 441	212 010	.
26	243 666	229 292	247 512	210 068	208 809	236 081	206 850	265 690	268 378	.
27-28	175 392	175 171	183 618	174 127	164 867	211 143	167 766	145 318	167 019	.
29,31	168 795	211 008	215 152	207 067	180 738	225 584	163 758	172 125	156 653	.
30	205 959	167 787	194 222	171 783	156 834	159 960	167 343	214 190		.
32	188 884	194 154	196 111	210 241	184 784	184 729	192 482	153 494	175 077	.
33	186 575	184 851	203 412	195 982	174 674	167 692	219 538	173 875	208 565	.
34	196 024	198 388	194 256	206 289	166 112	190 100	182 448	164 678	187 893	.
35	261 650	259 065	272 099	272 920	265 329	265 703	292 043	275 388	284 436	.
36	162 814	166 828	178 333	148 338	149 510	143 212	170 631	164 299	205 553	.

Explanatory notes: see p. 1039.

[1] New denomination of AZM; 1 AZN=5000 AZM. [2] Excl. outworkers. [3] Incl. government manufacturing.

Notes explicatives: voir p. 1041.

[1] Nouvelle dénomination de l'AZM; 1 AZN = 5000 AZM. [2] Non compris les personnes travaillant hors de l'établissement. [3] Y compris les industries manufacturières d'Etat.

Notas explicativas: véase p. 1043.

[1] Nueva denominación del AZM; 1 AZN = 5000 AZM. [2] Excl. las personas que trabajan fuera del establecimiento. [3] Incl. las industrias manufactureras del Estado.

LABOUR COST
In manufacturing

COÛT DE LA MAIN-D OEUVRE
Dans les industries manufacturières

COSTO DE LA MANO DE OBRA
En las industrias manufactureras

India (DB)
ISIC 2 - CITI 2 - CIIU 2 [1]

Employees - Salariés - Asalariados

LC/d.j. - Rupee

ISIC	1999	2000	2001	2002	2003	2004	2005	ISIC 3 - CITI 3 - CIIU 3 [1][2]
311-312 [3]	173.74 2|	167.20	177.58	184.33	193.57	196.00	200.03	15
313	204.14 2|	65.31	79.09	74.69	77.42	81.18	83.51	16
313-314			175.95	184.30	192.36	203.07	212.40	207.46	17
314	55.83 2|	137.20	148.99	159.43	176.76	176.03	191.61	18
321	175.01 2|	161.85	162.40	163.91	172.48	181.24	181.95	19
322 [4]	102.61 2|	129.27	126.96	145.08	143.10	154.89	155.07	20
323	137.43 3|	202.45	234.42	250.42	251.47	264.95	279.64	21
323-324			268.59	322.29	348.33	358.53	383.75	397.38	22
324	150.08 2|	483.42	746.04	721.55	383.75	739.01	765.86	23
33			343.16	348.77	379.29	408.41	437.00	441.29	24
331	131.76 2|	212.68	221.17	240.19	260.48	267.87	277.84	25
332	333.97 2|	199.99	220.73	225.21	193.20	244.85	245.03	26
34			307.42	366.81	396.82	447.47	501.71	481.32	27
341	229.87 2|	246.95	267.27	278.39	281.62	292.71	294.92	28
342	373.98 2|	393.03	398.06	432.49	439.13	470.27	474.20	29
351	475.33 2|	340.42	489.54	493.59	593.28	570.10	575.27	30
351-352			353.71	433.65	408.43	456.88	481.66	446.21	31
352	294.13 2|	337.68	388.05	464.87	503.62	540.97	543.66	32
353	599.66 2|	397.30	356.03	448.30	454.77	491.71	474.37	33
353-356			403.68	443.67	500.85	502.92	532.88	533.66	34
354	299.84 2|	325.56	322.56	370.84	401.52	427.57	451.27	35
355	266.46 2|	207.70	236.80	245.81	270.10	283.64	297.96	36
356	196.34 2|	91.64	140.34	128.64	236.76	216.39	203.20	37
36									
361	209.61 2|							
362	242.24 2|							
37									
371	350.00 2|							
372	285.70 2|							
381	301.00 2|							
382	356.38 2|							
383	417.10 2|							
384	377.37 2|							
385	340.45 2|							
385.390									
39	358.70 2|							

Israel (DB)
ISIC 3 - CITI 3 - CIIU 3

Employees - Salariés - Asalariados

LC/h. - New shekel

ISIC	1999	2000	2001	2002	2003	2004	2005	2006	2007
Total	49	53	57	57	59	60	62	65	67
15-16	36	39	42	43	43	44	45	46	46
17	31	33	36	36	37	39	42	45	47
18 [5]	27	28	30	31	33	33	32	33	31
19 [6]	30	33	31	31	31	29	36	39	40
20	34	37	39	40	40	40	40	41	44
21	42	44	46	45	46	48	50	52	54
22	38	40	43	43	46	47	49	50	52
23-24	64	67	72	74	73	73	78	78	85
25	39	40	43	43	45	47	48	51	53
26	43	45	48	49	52	51	53	55	59
27 [7]	48	50	55	52	53	55	52	54	54
28	39	41	43	44	45	46	47	50	51
29	55	59	61	62	64	63	66	69	72
31	52	54	55	56	57	61	60	59	63
32	83	81	85	87	84	82	81	85	90
33	88	92	103	100	104	107	104	108	111
34-35	67	73	74	77	85	87	87	88	96

Kazakhstan (CA)
ISIC 3 - CITI 3 - CIIU 3

Employees - Salariés - Asalariados

LC/y.a. - Tenge

	1999	2000	2001	2002	2003	2004	2005	2006	2007	2008
Total		105 744	112 559	122 910	137 586	166 854	199 825	248 246	317 919	375 721

Explanatory notes: see p. 1039.

[1] Year ending in March of the year indicated. [2] Establishments with 200 or more persons employed. [3] Excl. prepared animal feeds and other food products. [4] Incl. made-up textile products. [5] Excl. manufacture of articles of fur. [6] Incl. manufacture of articles of fur. [7] Incl. recycling.

Notes explicatives: voir p. 1041.

[1] Année se terminant en mars de l'année indiquée. [2] Etablissements occupant 200 personnes et plus. [3] Non compris les produits pour l'alimentation des animaux et les autres produits alimentaires. [4] Y compris la confection d'ouvrages en tissu. [5] Non compris la fabrication d'articles en fourrure. [6] Y compris la fabrication d'articles en fourrure. [7] Y compris la récupération.

Notas explicativas: véase p. 1043.

[1] Año que termina en marzo del año indicado. [2] Establecimientos con 200 y más trabajadores. [3] Excl. los alimentos preparados para animales y productos alimenticios diversos. [4] Incl. los artículos confeccionados de materiales textiles. [5] Excl. la fabricación de prendas de piel. [6] Incl. la fabricación de prendas de piel. [7] Incl. el reciclaje.

LABOUR COST
In manufacturing

COÛT DE LA MAIN-D OEUVRE
Dans les industries manufacturières

COSTO DE LA MANO DE OBRA
En las industrias manufactureras

6A

	1999	2000	2001	2002	2003	2004	2005	2006	2007	2008

Korea, Republic of (DA) [1][2]
ISIC 3 - CITI 3 - CIIU 3 — Employees - Salariés - Asalariados — LC/m. - Won

	1999	2000	2001	2002	2003	2004	2005	2006	2007	2008
Total	2 116.5	2 450.8	2 403.9	2 684.4	2 927.9 |	3 238.2 [3]	3 357.2	3 610.0	3 812.2	.
15	1 933.2	2 145.5	2 324.8	2 498.8	2 673.5 |	2 755.5 [3]	2 874.0	3 094.0	2 777.2	.
16	8 865.0	4 497.3	4 471.6	4 386.2	4 839.3 |	5 189.6 [3]	5 684.0	6 161.0	5 590.2	.
17	1 524.0	1 687.5	1 772.1	2 177.6	2 378.9 |	2 423.3 [3]	2 644.0	2 907.0	2 726.1	.
18	1 319.1	1 399.4	1 462.2	1 606.3	1 744.1 |	1 945.5 [3]	2 113.3	2 325.0	2 365.2	.
19	1 468.2	1 508.6	1 637.6	1 933.4	2 086.7 |	2 241.5 [3]	2 401.0	2 751.0	2 649.2	.
20	1 660.5	1 829.2	2 081.1	2 322.7	2 596.3 |	2 651.9 [3]	2 463.0	2 720.0	3 010.7	.
21	2 502.2	2 445.7	2 890.2	2 808.4	3 160.5 |	3 071.5 [3]	3 445.0	3 352.0	3 422.8	.
22	2 342.8	3 371.8	2 762.5	2 771.5	2 937.5 |	2 805.6 [3]	2 877.0	3 125.0	2 969.9	.
23	3 797.6	3 651.7	4 196.1	4 923.7	5 014.2 |	7 054.5 [3]	6 920.0	7 236.0	8 231.4	.
24	2 675.8	2 814.1	2 993.1	3 058.5	3 617.0 |	3 773.4 [3]	3 906.0	4 089.0	4 644.4	.
25	1 762.1	2 012.9	2 146.5	2 401.6	2 609.3 |	2 547.1 [3]	2 738.0	2 904.0	3 148.0	.
26	2 207.7	2 205.7	2 552.6	2 652.0	2 884.2 |	3 283.7 [3]	3 697.0	3 669.0	3 619.4	.
27	2 401.0	5 628.2	2 431.9	2 839.1	3 306.6 |	4 169.0 [3]	4 157.0	4 520.0	4 656.6	.
28	1 719.8	1 978.0	2 057.7	2 253.1	2 427.2 |	2 355.6 [3]	2 528.0	2 804.0	2 786.3	.
29	2 100.8	2 423.8	2 638.7	2 969.0	2 949.0 |	3 106.9 [3]	3 247.0	3 560.0	3 540.4	.
30	1 818.2	2 493.3	2 273.8	2 332.0	2 671.9 |	2 957.9 [3]	2 916.0	3 030.0	2 965.8	.
31	1 952.7	1 961.9	2 097.3	2 757.5	2 861.4 |	2 552.4 [3]	2 725.0	2 995.0	3 441.1	.
32	2 036.8	2 157.3	2 242.2	2 637.8	2 895.4 |	3 638.3 [3]	3 670.0	3 963.0	4 142.7	.
33	2 018.8	2 220.3	2 300.1	2 082.9	2 211.0 |	2 481.6 [3]	2 658.0	2 666.0	2 682.9	.
34	2 254.3	2 519.4	2 706.4	3 011.1	3 442.7 |	4 082.5 [3]	4 186.0	4 346.0	4 681.7	.
35	2 738.9	2 881.9	2 711.9	3 615.3	3 687.6 |	4 666.9 [3]	4 746.0	5 190.0	5 570.5	.
36	1 588.0	1 680.2	1 948.7	2 138.5	2 696.7 |	2 155.5 [3]	2 357.0	2 541.0	3 037.8	.
37	1 786.3	1 923.2	2 146.5	2 082.9	2 167.3 |	2 789.5 [3]	2 726.0	2 828.0	2 436.2	.

Korea, Republic of (DA) [2]
ISIC 3 - CITI 3 - CIIU 3 — Employees - Salariés - Asalariados — LC/m. - Won

	1999	2000	2001	2002	2003	2004	2005	2006	2007	2008
Total	2 124.5	2 462.3	2 414.6	2 695.9	2 941.8 |	3 412.1	3 518.0	3 865.0	4 011.7	.
15	1 938.2	2 154.6	2 334.3	2 509.5	2 685.9 |	2 860.0	2 980.0	3 263.0	2 867.4	.
16	8 881.7	4 503.7	4 474.7	4 391.1	4 844.0 |	5 189.6	5 729.0	6 159.0	5 590.2	.
17	1 528.2	1 698.0	1 781.7	2 193.2	2 401.4 |	2 529.5	2 772.0	3 088.0	2 884.5	.
18	1 323.1	1 407.9	1 467.6	1 604.2	1 746.1 |	2 009.9	2 155.0	2 390.0	2 376.3	.
19	1 471.5	1 507.0	1 635.4	1 936.9	2 092.6 |	2 263.6	2 471.0	2 867.0	2 824.5	.
20	1 669.4	1 842.5	2 091.8	2 337.8	2 622.3 |	2 879.5	2 739.0	3 172.0	3 398.7	.
21	2 520.1	2 466.4	2 937.5	2 833.4	3 199.4 |	3 395.2	3 816.0	3 885.0	3 727.6	.
22	2 370.1	3 423.3	2 799.4	2 812.9	2 972.3 |	2 925.1	2 970.0	3 318.0	3 033.5	.
23	3 803.2	3 657.1	4 201.2	4 929.7	5 021.7 |	7 236.4	7 106.0	7 536.0	8 536.8	.
24	2 681.7	2 827.8	3 004.8	3 063.3	3 630.7 |	3 923.8	4 037.0	4 333.0	4 848.3	.
25	1 784.8	2 031.7	2 166.6	2 416.5	2 627.3 |	2 689.6	2 924.0	3 149.0	3 309.3	.
26	2 217.7	2 217.8	2 568.2	2 667.0	2 906.4 |	3 582.5	4 063.0	4 205.0	3 876.5	.
27	2 402.2	5 636.3	2 433.0	2 840.3	3 308.0 |	4 378.0	4 330.0	4 744.0	4 819.0	.
28	1 740.3	2 014.8	2 086.9	2 288.7	2 464.7 |	2 376.6	2 508.0	2 919.0	2 970.1	.
29	2 114.2	2 439.5	2 657.5	2 991.0	2 967.7 |	3 278.0	3 348.0	3 779.0	3 702.5	.
30	1 820.5	2 498.4	2 283.9	2 336.8	2 684.4 |	3 018.9	2 834.0	3 110.0	3 223.8	.
31	1 957.9	1 969.8	2 108.6	2 777.7	2 885.6 |	2 649.8	2 815.0	3 199.0	3 544.6	.
32	2 038.9	2 158.2	2 245.3	2 640.5	2 898.6 |	3 729.6	3 760.0	4 092.0	4 208.2	.
33	2 026.9	2 235.5	2 316.9	2 090.1	2 225.7 |	2 531.4	2 863.0	3 008.0	3 076.2	.
34	2 255.3	2 520.2	2 708.1	3 012.3	3 444.8 |	4 181.7	4 271.0	4 480.0	4 791.7	.
35	2 742.2	2 883.0	2 712.6	3 618.3	3 687.6 |	4 748.2	4 828.0	5 248.0	5 700.0	.
36	1 602.9	1 696.5	1 969.4	2 170.2	2 751.5 |	2 321.2	2 473.0	2 680.0	3 120.7	.
37	1 704.9	1 881.3	2 113.2	2 119.4	2 202.2 |	2 900.7	2 641.0	1 771.0	2 336.2	.

Kyrgyzstan (CA)
ISIC 3 - CITI 3 - CIIU 3 — Employees - Salariés - Asalariados — LC/m. - Som

	1999	2000	2001	2002	2003	2004	2005	2006	2007	2008
Total [4]	1 720.4	2 702.1	3 167.0	3 624.6	4 097.6	4 821.0	5 341.8	8 388.0	7 546.2	.
15	.	.	.	.	.	.	3 760.1	4 026.3	4 775.2	.
16	.	.	.	.	.	.	13 689.7	13 947.0	16 510.8	.
17	.	.	.	.	.	.	2 642.9	2 839.5	3 106.1	.
18	.	.	.	.	.	.	1 038.5	1 349.3	1 794.2	.
19	.	.	.	.	.	.	2 384.7	2 561.5	2 398.9	.
20	.	.	.	.	.	.	2 244.9	2 340.7	3 200.7	.
21	.	.	.	.	.	.	3 914.8	4 167.2	5 421.5	.
22	.	.	.	.	.	.	3 920.0	4 131.6	4 660.5	.
23	.	.	.	.	.	.	12 182.1	13 804.7	14 888.9	.
24	.	.	.	.	.	.	3 927.3	4 666.9	5 258.5	.
25	.	.	.	.	.	.	2 102.7	3 294.7	3 583.0	.
26	.	.	.	.	.	.	5 826.8	6 524.1	7 399.8	.
27	.	.	.	.	.	.	20 551.6	44 404.0	30 056.8	.
28	.	.	.	.	.	.	3 130.0	3 480.3	3 817.0	.
29	.	.	.	.	.	.	5 037.0	5 943.3	7 310.8	.
30	.	.	.	.	.	.	1 923.6	2 002.9	2 383.6	.
31	.	.	.	.	.	.	4 398.5	4 782.2	6 213.4	.
32	.	.	.	.	.	.	4 062.8	5 956.0	6 958.6	.
33	.	.	.	.	.	.	4 012.4	5 982.9	6 187.7	.
34	.	.	.	.	.	.	5 006.6	3 654.0	6 279.1	.
35	.	.	.	.	.	.	1 944.8	3 665.0	4 244.5	.
36	.	.	.	.	.	.	1 739.6	1 916.3	2 240.1	.
37	.	.	.	.	.	.	2 110.8	2 006.5	1 434.4	.

Explanatory notes: see p. 1039.

[1] Establishments with 10 or more permanent employees. [2] Figures in thousands. [3] From 2004: methodology revised; data not strictly comparable. [4] Incl. major divisions 2 and 4.

Notes explicatives: voir p. 1041.

[1] Etablissements occupant 10 salariés permanents ou plus. [2] Données en milliers. [3] A partir de 2004: méthodologie révisée. Les données ne sont pas strictement comparables. [4] Y compris les branches 2 et 4.

Notas explicativas: véase p. 1043.

[1] Establecimientos con 10 y más asalariados permanentes. [2] Cifras en millares. [3] A partir de 2004: metodología revisada. Los datos no son estrictamente comparables. [4] Incl. las grandes divisiones 2 y 4.

6A

LABOUR COST
In manufacturing

COÛT DE LA MAIN-D OEUVRE
Dans les industries manufacturières

COSTO DE LA MANO DE OBRA
En las industrias manufactureras

Philippines (DB) [1]
ISIC 3 - CITI 3 - CIIU 3 — Employees - Salariés - Asalariados — CR/m. - Peso

	1999	2000	2001	2002	2003	2004	2005	2006	2007	2008
Total	8 794.0 [2]		10 410.0		11 749.0		13 646.0			
15	9 812.0 [2]		11 768.0		13 117.0		15 504.0			
16	9 021.0 [2]		9 986.0		12 614.0		19 022.0			
17	6 744.0 [2]		7 998.0		9 276.0		10 429.0			
18	6 035.0 [2]		6 864.0		7 524.0		8 720.0			
19	5 384.0 [2]		6 435.0		6 567.0		6 224.0			
20	4 803.0 [2]		6 610.0		6 399.0		8 001.0			
21	9 202.0 [2]		10 117.0		11 935.0		11 901.0			
22	11 775.0 [2]		10 275.0		11 982.0		12 298.0			
23	38 357.0 [2]		58 862.0		61 661.0		90 591.0			
24	18 220.0 [2]		18 705.0		22 313.0		26 188.0			
25	9 083.0 [2]		8 368.0		9 488.0		10 693.0			
26	7 192.0 [2]		11 714.0		14 722.0		17 553.0			
27	8 883.0 [2]		9 911.0		11 174.0		13 112.0			
28	7 318.0 [2]		9 298.0		10 119.0		10 720.0			
29	9 023.0 [2]		9 037.0		10 415.0		14 085.0			
30	8 792.0 [2]		12 138.0		12 900.0		13 387.0			
31	9 176.0 [2]		9 701.0		11 091.0		13 887.0			
32	9 463.0 [2]		12 447.0		13 624.0		15 097.0			
33	7 886.0 [2]		9 742.0		10 917.0		15 020.0			
34	14 106.0 [2]		16 426.0		17 051.0		17 282.0			
35	9 390.0 [2]		12 863.0		18 444.0		29 639.0			
36	6 112.0 [2]		6 784.0		8 617.0		8 881.0			
37	3 959.0 [2]		4 925.0		6 288.0		6 474.0			

Singapore (DB)
ISIC 3 - CITI 3 - CIIU 3 — Employees - Salariés - Asalariados — CR/y.a. - Dollar

	1999	2000	2001	2002	2003	2004	2005	2006	2007	2008
Total	33 106	36 136	36 696	36 290	36 915	37 660	38 692	39 944	41 077	
15										
15-16	28 496	30 481	30 832	29 303	29 033	30 109	28 994	28 856	29 152	
16										
17	25 131	27 858	26 853	23 747	25 027	23 064	25 397	28 694		
18	18 430	19 038	18 498	18 510	18 175	18 205	19 809	19 561	20 080	
19	25 395	25 478	29 230	28 260	29 557	30 147	30 811	29 331	29 925	
20	25 243	28 092	26 662	24 327	23 948	24 179	24 546	25 585	24 122	
21	31 603	32 826	33 202	33 326	33 303	34 459	35 445	34 301	34 102	
22	35 727	38 496	39 222	36 603	37 942	37 176	39 362	40 644	42 697	
23	92 999	102 704	110 708	123 996	119 633	112 788	113 618	119 625	131 382	
24	62 435	65 202	69 353	65 237	64 955	68 760	67 096	69 990	72 588	
25	26 040	27 629	27 920	28 254	28 682	29 200	30 192	32 362	31 443	
26	29 853	30 903	30 806	31 540	32 878	34 179	32 428	32 391	35 231	
27	42 620	46 983	44 898	48 172	48 228	47 469	44 641	46 825	47 155	
28	27 186	28 966	29 503	28 959	29 636	29 878	30 363	31 631	31 814	
29	33 162	35 004	35 752	37 025	37 039	37 951	39 647	40 291	40 955	
30	26 688	32 113	32 615	33 992	33 290	31 812	32 886	39 192	41 406	
31	33 607	36 411	36 501	38 661	37 120	37 007	36 836	38 302	40 728	
32	35 852	40 758	40 208	41 020	42 789	43 712	46 135	45 558	49 017	
33	34 804	34 895	36 805	36 291	37 151	38 301	40 726	43 243	41 999	
34	43 178	43 588	44 702	40 886	40 688	42 675	42 671	43 582	50 240	
35	34 531	35 400	35 178	33 049	34 099	35 651	35 599	36 191	35 569	
36	25 119	27 099	26 538	25 485	26 205	24 246	25 292	24 889	24 469	
37	29 773	33 687	34 273	40 896						

Thailand (DB)
ISIC 3 - CITI 3 - CIIU 3 — Employees - Salariés - Asalariados — LC/m. - Baht

	1999	2000	2001	2002	2003	2004	2005	2006	2007	2008
Total	6 394.83	10 286.09				22 421.30				
15	5 142.30	7 449.03								
16	2 763.58	11 957.61								
17	5 525.35	7 466.93								
18	6 731.09	7 238.29								
19	5 714.67	6 527.33								
20	5 068.93	6 085.48								
21	6 730.47	10 156.95								
22	7 759.10	11 391.13								
23	12 646.63	19 403.72								
24	9 929.39	12 840.83								
25	7 231.51	8 195.36								
26	4 601.57	9 361.01								
27	7 709.89	11 955.47								
28	6 738.20	7 810.18								
29	7 779.83	10 932.36								
30	11 807.66	14 536.32								
31	9 259.77	10 725.97								
32	9 970.81	10 464.29								
33	9 080.63	8 788.91								
34	7 305.47	14 564.07								
35	6 305.36	9 207.01								
36	5 529.73	6 474.07								
37	8 399.82	9 047.53								

Explanatory notes: see p. 1039.

[1] Establishments with 20 or more persons employed. [2] Before 1999: establishments with 10 or more persons employed.

Notes explicatives: voir p. 1041.

[1] Etablissements occupant 20 personnes et plus. [2] Avant 1999: établissements occupant 10 personnes et plus.

Notas explicativas: véase p. 1043.

[1] Establecimientos con 20 y más trabajadores. [2] Antes de 1999: establecimientos con 10 y más trabajadores.

LABOUR COST

In manufacturing

COÛT DE LA MAIN-D OEUVRE

Dans les industries manufacturières

COSTO DE LA MANO DE OBRA

En las industrias manufactureras

6A

EUROPE-EUROPE-EUROPA

Austria (DA) — Employees - Salariés - Asalariados — LC/h. - Euro
ISIC 3 - CITI 3 - CIIU 3

	1999	2000	2001	2002	2003	2004	2005	2006	2007	2008
Total	.	23.85 [1]	.	.	.	26.79	.	.	.	.
15	.	23.35 [1]	.	.	.	22.03	.	.	.	.
17	.	20.08 [1]	.	.	.	22.87	.	.	.	.
18	.	13.85 [1]	.	.	.	16.72	.	.	.	.
19	.	14.54 [1]	.	.	.	16.16	.	.	.	.
20	.	18.57 [1]	.	.	.	21.06	.	.	.	.
21	.	27.04 [1]	.	.	.	32.07	.	.	.	.
22	.	[1]	.	.	.	29.28	.	.	.	.
23	.	62.43 [1]	.	.	.		.	.	.	.
24	.	28.18 [1]	.	.	.	32.50	.	.	.	.
25	.	23.28 [1]	.	.	.	23.97	.	.	.	.
26	.	25.42 [1]	.	.	.	28.50	.	.	.	.
27	.	26.83 [1]	.	.	.	31.07	.	.	.	.
28	.	21.37 [1]	.	.	.	25.14	.	.	.	.
29	.	24.65 [1]	.	.	.	28.35	.	.	.	.
30	.	[1]	.	.	.	26.30	.	.	.	.
31	.	23.80 [1]	.	.	.	27.07	.	.	.	.
32	.	32.06 [1]	.	.	.	39.22	.	.	.	.
33	.	23.74 [1]	.	.	.	25.83	.	.	.	.
34	.	25.93 [1]	.	.	.	28.09	.	.	.	.
35	.	25.18 [1]	.	.	.	31.30	.	.	.	.
36	.	19.00 [1]	.	.	.	20.65	.	.	.	.
37	.	19.14 [1]	.	.	.	26.09	.	.	.	.

Austria (DA) — Employees - Salariés - Asalariados — LC/y.a. - Euro
ISIC 3 - CITI 3 - CIIU 3

	1999	2000	2001	2002	2003	2004	2005	2006	2007	2008
Total	.	40 566 [1]	.	.	.	44 204	.	.	.	.
15	.	38 241 [1]	.	.	.	37 117	.	.	.	.
16	.	[1]	.	.	.		.	.	.	.
17	.	32 864 [1]	.	.	.	36 262	.	.	.	.
18	.	22 011 [1]	.	.	.	25 259	.	.	.	.
19	.	24 386 [1]	.	.	.	27 175	.	.	.	.
20	.	31 516 [1]	.	.	.	35 940	.	.	.	.
21	.	45 345 [1]	.	.	.	51 702	.	.	.	.
22	.	[1]	.	.	.	48 552	.	.	.	.
23	.	101 725 [1]	.	.	.		.	.	.	.
24	.	48 088 [1]	.	.	.	53 942	.	.	.	.
25	.	38 430 [1]	.	.	.	38 430	.	.	.	.
26	.	42 941 [1]	.	.	.	47 257	.	.	.	.
27	.	45 872 [1]	.	.	.	49 533	.	.	.	.
28	.	37 019 [1]	.	.	.	42 086	.	.	.	.
29	.	43 606 [1]	.	.	.	47 424	.	.	.	.
30	.	[1]	.	.	.	45 042	.	.	.	.
31	.	40 961 [1]	.	.	.	44 515	.	.	.	.
32	.	54 089 [1]	.	.	.	61 645	.	.	.	.
33	.	39 624 [1]	.	.	.	41 505	.	.	.	.
34	.	42 998 [1]	.	.	.	46 606	.	.	.	.
35	.	44 866 [1]	.	.	.	53 908	.	.	.	.
36	.	32 194 [1]	.	.	.	33 926	.	.	.	.
37	.	32 837 [1]	.	.	.	40 490	.	.	.	.

Belarus (DA) [2] — Employees - Salariés - Asalariados — LC/m. - B. roubles
ISIC 3 - CITI 3 - CIIU 3

	1999	2000	2001	2002	2003	2004	2005	2006	2007	2008
Total	.	113.4 [3]	.	.	436.3	587.6	760.6	955.2	1 117.4	1 432.8

Explanatory notes: see p. 1039.

[1] Before 2000: ATS;1 Euro = 13.7603 ATS. [2] Figures in thousands. [3] New denomination of the rouble: 1 new rouble = 1000 old roubles.

Notes explicatives: voir p. 1041.

[1] Avant 2000: ATS; 1 Euro = 13,7603 ATS. [2] Données en milliers. [3] Nouvelle dénomination du rouble: 1 nouveau rouble = 1000 anciens roubles.

Notas explicativas: véase p. 1043.

[1] Antes de 2000: ATS; 1 Euro = 13,7603 ATS. [2] Cifras en millares. [3] Nueva denominación del rublo: 1 nuevo rublo = 1000 antiguos rublos.

6A

LABOUR COST	COÛT DE LA MAIN-D OEUVRE	COSTO DE LA MANO DE OBRA
In manufacturing	Dans les industries manufacturières	En las industrias manufactureras

	1999	2000	2001	2002	2003	2004	2005	2006	2007	2008

Belgique (DA) [1]
ISIC 3 - CITI 3 - CIIU 3 — Employees - Salariés - Asalariados — LC/h. - Euro

	1999	2000	2001	2002	2003	2004	2005	2006	2007	2008
Total	.	28	30	31	33	32	.	.	.	
15	.	25	.	.	.	28	.	.	.	
16	.	30	.	.	.	.	.	.	.	
17	.	21	.	.	.	24	.	.	.	
18	.	18	.	.	.	20	.	.	.	
19	.	21	.	.	.	26	.	.	.	
20	.	21	.	.	.	25	.	.	.	
21	.	28	.	.	.	33	.	.	.	
22	.	30	.	.	.	32	.	.	.	
23	.	48	.	.	.	53	.	.	.	
24	.	38	.	.	.	42	.	.	.	
25	.	28	.	.	.	31	.	.	.	
26	.	27	.	.	.	31	.	.	.	
27	.	34	.	.	.	39	.	.	.	
28	.	24	.	.	.	28	.	.	.	
29	.	28	.	.	.	32	.	.	.	
30	.	25	.	.	.	.	.	.	.	
31	.	27	.	.	.	33	.	.	.	
32	.	34	.	.	.	35	.	.	.	
33	.	28	.	.	.	29	.	.	.	
34	.	28	.	.	.	34	.	.	.	
35	.	32	.	.	.	.	.	.	.	
36	.	21	.	.	.	24	.	.	.	
37	.	20	.	.	.	.	.	.	.	

Bulgaria (CA)
ISIC 3 - CITI 3 - CIIU 3 — Employees - Salariés - Asalariados — CR/h. - Leva — ISIC 4 - CITI 4 - CIIU 4

	1999	2000	2001	2002	2003	2004	2005	2006	2007	2008	CIIU 4
Total	.	2.29	2.34	2.39	2.47	2.59 I	2.75	2.90	3.35	.	Total
15	.	1.85	1.88	1.89	2.00	2.14 I	2.12	2.24	2.64	.	10
16	.	5.02	5.06	4.92	5.70	7.02 I	3.28	3.49	4.37	.	11
17	.	1.79	1.90	1.99	2.10	2.26 I	7.62	8.26	10.39	.	12
18	.	1.36	1.46	1.52	1.58	1.71 I	2.46	2.56	2.96	.	13
19	.	1.48	1.50	1.55	1.58	1.69 I	1.87	2.00	2.22	.	14
20	.	1.50	1.52	1.62	1.77	1.87 I	1.74	1.87	2.12	.	15
21	.	2.18	2.32	2.57	2.58	2.59 I	2.03	2.16	2.56	.	16
22	.	2.46	2.69	2.66	2.81	2.84 I	2.63	2.82	3.24	.	17
23	.	6.47	6.68	7.31	.	I	3.12	2.82	3.60	.	18
24	.	3.55	3.63	3.75	3.99	4.06 I	3.91	4.13	4.68	.	20
25	.	1.99	2.01	2.11	2.08	2.11 I	4.98	5.11	5.76	.	21
26	.	2.65	2.74	2.86	3.08	3.10 I	2.20	2.25	2.55	.	22
27	.	4.19	4.38	5.04	5.28	5.73 I	3.15	3.38	3.86	.	23
28	.	1.99	1.96	1.99	2.11	2.18 I	5.83	6.24	7.15	.	24
29	.	2.56	2.67	2.84	3.01	3.14 I	2.60	2.72	3.10	.	25
30	.	2.31	2.57	2.79	2.81	2.93 I	3.31	3.54	4.24	.	26
31	.	2.39	2.51	2.57	2.81	2.90 I	3.08	3.25	3.97	.	27
32	.	2.74	3.25	3.23	3.38	3.41 I	3.25	3.53	4.16	.	28
33	.	2.04	2.12	2.25	2.41	2.61 I	2.91	2.86	3.54	.	29
34	.	2.23	2.15	2.25	2.46	2.48 I	4.62	5.13	6.15	.	30
35	.	2.88	3.05	3.19	3.39	3.64 I	1.89	1.95	2.20	.	31
36	.	1.50	1.56	1.56	1.71	1.80 I	2.30	2.39	2.78	.	32
37	.	1.86	1.21	1.34	1.77	2.01 I					

Croatia (CA)
ISIC 3 - CITI 3 - CIIU 3 — Employees - Salariés - Asalariados — LC/h. - Kuna

	1999	2000	2001	2002	2003	2004	2005	2006	2007	2008
Total	.	.	.	.	.	46.3	48.9	52.6	55.4	.
15	.	.	.	.	.	52.6	54.8	56.4	59.9	.
16	.	.	.	.	.	80.4	84.0	89.2	91.8	.
17	.	.	.	.	.	33.4	36.0	37.4	39.3	.
18	.	.	.	.	.	27.1	28.2	28.8	30.8	.
19	.	.	.	.	.	26.3	27.3	30.0	30.5	.
20	.	.	.	.	.	32.0	33.6	35.6	37.4	.
21	.	.	.	.	.	41.7	41.6	45.8	48.1	.
22	.	.	.	.	.	60.4	63.3	66.4	70.6	.
23	.	.	.	.	.	70.3	77.5	84.7	97.6	.
24	.	.	.	.	.	65.4	67.1	74.8	77.8	.
25	.	.	.	.	.	39.5	43.2	45.4	47.5	.
26	.	.	.	.	.	50.6	53.2	55.7	59.8	.
27	.	.	.	.	.	39.3	41.5	47.0	50.3	.
28	.	.	.	.	.	42.7	43.4	49.0	52.0	.
29	.	.	.	.	.	45.3	47.9	52.2	54.4	.
30	.	.	.	.	.	66.1	75.1	81.1	84.1	.
31	.	.	.	.	.	56.7	61.8	67.5	71.5	.
32	.	.	.	.	.	81.7	86.9	88.8	85.7	.
33	.	.	.	.	.	58.9	62.4	65.0	69.5	.
34	.	.	.	.	.	44.5	49.7	54.0	59.5	.
35	.	.	.	.	.	51.6	54.9	58.4	59.7	.
36	.	.	.	.	.	33.1	33.6	36.7	38.5	.
37	.	.	.	.	.	56.4	57.7	61.2	63.5	.

Explanatory notes: see p. 1039.

[1] Establishments with 10 or more persons employed.

Notes explicatives: voir p. 1041.

[1] Etablissements occupant 10 personnes et plus.

Notas explicativas: véase p. 1043.

[1] Establecimientos con 10 y más trabajadores.

LABOUR COST

In manufacturing

COÛT DE LA MAIN-D OEUVRE

Dans les industries manufacturières

COSTO DE LA MANO DE OBRA

En las industrias manufactureras

6A

	1999	2000	2001	2002	2003	2004	2005	2006	2007	2008

Cyprus (DB) — Employees - Salariés - Asalariados — CR/y.a. - Pound
ISIC 3 - CITI 3 - CIIU 3

	1999	2000	2001	2002	2003	2004	2005	2006	2007	2008
Total	7 802	8 201	8 582	9 147	9 605	10 042	10 506	.	.	.
15	8 157	8 210	8 540	8 989	9 509	9 829	10 213	.	.	.
16	15 537	14 004	14 122	14 480	15 215	15 289	19 946	.	.	.
17	5 378	6 016	6 257	6 846	6 900	7 223	7 493	.	.	.
18	5 157	5 527	5 616	5 953	5 877	5 938	6 901	.	.	.
19	7 008	7 326	7 167	8 256	8 034	7 563	8 111	.	.	.
20	7 003	7 585	7 670	8 336	8 324	9 089	9 674	.	.	.
21	8 574	8 284	8 506	9 013	10 197	10 616	10 286	.	.	.
22	9 436	9 834	10 319	10 484	11 217	11 537	11 731	.	.	.
23	29 923	26 952	27 720	28 594	31 321	29 973		.	.	.
24	9 062	9 706	10 234	10 783	10 979	11 831	11 823	.	.	.
25	8 175	8 735	8 936	9 346	10 326	10 647	11 579	.	.	.
26	10 582	10 630	11 036	11 742	12 836	13 827	14 329	.	.	.
27	10 615	11 457	11 696	14 002	14 208	13 542	12 297	.	.	.
28	7 341	7 531	7 995	8 650	9 153	10 007	9 777	.	.	.
29	8 121	8 004	8 734	9 247	9 618	8 955	10 073	.	.	.
31	7 722	8 044	8 457	9 078	9 107	7 667	10 295	.	.	.
32	5 400	5 600	6 750	5 500	5 250	8 246	8 063	.	.	.
33	7 302	7 213	7 403	7 632	7 886	9 579	8 769	.	.	.
34	7 470	7 596	8 241	8 789	8 645	10 534	10 459	.	.	.
35	9 372	8 944	8 699	11 716	9 872	8 676	9 647	.	.	.
36	7 031	7 199	7 707	8 131	8 888	8 000	8 906	.	.	.
37	7 144	6 879	7 906	7 413	7 867	.	9 220	.	.	.

Czech Republic (DA) — Employees - Salariés - Asalariados — LC/h. - Koruna
ISIC 3 - CITI 3 - CIIU 3

	1999	2000	2001	2002	2003	2004	2005	2006	2007	2008
Total	117.08	127.06	146.33	155.03	163.66	173.51	179.68	189.39	204.67	.
15-16	112.41	123.65	143.52	142.47	159.10	165.57	168.82	170.42	189.24	.
17	94.64	99.40	116.74	121.84	127.97	134.50	138.09	146.18	159.14	.
18	75.48	88.22	98.93	95.02	102.49	108.95	110.94	116.34	121.73	.
19	84.22	94.68	98.15	110.38	110.89	118.84	119.65	132.02	133.84	.
20	96.47	107.33	111.99	130.48	132.75	129.28	140.86	147.80	151.50	.
21	122.64	134.91	155.15	167.32	169.90	175.78	184.13	198.74	192.39	.
22	139.95	143.08	172.11	179.22	178.68	197.95	216.54	219.98	214.90	.
23	181.98	195.78	236.93	249.40	264.95	288.21	298.04	324.67	322.87	.
24	144.79	155.33	177.64	192.71	205.57	215.08	219.52	236.18	255.89	.
25	120.88	135.33	146.01	157.47	165.36	173.01	174.26	182.20	193.70	.
26	125.84	131.76	150.42	169.10	170.78	177.00	195.51	197.52	218.51	.
27	139.89	145.40	167.36	173.52	195.68	206.34	207.31	220.29	237.36	.
28	112.69	128.71	140.50	148.47	155.44	163.49	169.15	179.93	198.26	.
29	119.31	125.67	145.88	164.71	164.66	181.35	179.65	199.08	212.65	.
30	121.00	126.82	160.54	144.87	148.72	157.46	173.71	185.39	193.34	.
31	115.22	125.59	153.70	149.77	162.44	170.95	172.96	179.73	192.26	.
32	110.94	113.26	150.10	165.41	162.57	183.50	205.21	187.13	218.64	.
33	115.43	121.64	136.04	151.88	158.27	166.43	172.02	200.31	215.04	.
34	145.43	155.32	183.02	182.37	195.45	207.79	210.41	227.84	245.36	.
35	122.73	142.03	158.92	165.93	177.88	187.56	197.13	204.10	225.04	.
36	92.65	107.39	119.30	131.25	134.38	139.23	144.50	156.30	163.85	.
37	105.90	125.85	143.24	149.58	164.08	168.55	164.28	160.22	200.23	.

Denmark (DA) [1] — Employees - Salariés - Asalariados — LC/h. - Krone
ISIC 3 - CITI 3 - CIIU 3

	1999	2000	2001	2002	2003	2004	2005	2006	2007	2008
Total	.	.	.	210.23	219.30	221.61	231.76	241.26	255.05	.

España (DA) — Employees - Salariés - Asalariados — LC/h. - Euro
ISIC 3 - CITI 3 - CIIU 3

	1999	2000	2001	2002	2003	2004	2005	2006	2007	2008
Total	15.05 [2]	15.12	14.20	14.90	15.50	16.10	16.80	17.51	18.18	19.11
15	.	13.75	12.73	13.60	14.10	14.30	14.50	15.25	15.43	15.59
16	.	17.40	23.52	29.30	26.20	27.50	28.20	30.98	33.40	37.13
17	.	10.80	10.90	11.20	11.90	12.40	12.90	13.65	14.61	14.39
18	.	8.32	8.30	8.92	9.56	10.20	10.80	10.88	11.74	13.12
19	.	9.10	8.39	8.88	9.16	9.72	10.20	10.67	10.95	11.97
20	.	10.62	10.00	10.30	10.20	11.00	11.80	12.64	13.16	14.36
21	.	15.84	15.90	16.60	16.40	18.50	18.00	19.10	20.44	21.14
22	.	16.50	15.63	16.20	16.80	17.90	18.20	18.40	18.34	19.40
23	.	33.03	32.31	33.60	33.80	33.80	35.00	37.12	38.88	38.28
24	.	20.44	20.00	21.30	22.10	22.70	24.30	24.51	26.29	27.68
25	.	15.86	14.77	15.80	17.00	17.20	17.70	18.34	18.94	19.75
26	.	14.04	14.16	14.50	15.70	15.70	16.40	17.03	17.89	19.72
27	.	20.29	18.77	19.40	20.50	21.20	21.90	23.34	23.25	23.98
28	.	13.81	12.90	13.50	14.30	15.00	15.70	16.01	16.95	18.19
29	.	16.39	15.00	16.00	16.60	17.30	17.50	18.40	19.31	20.55
30	.	22.50	19.70	19.10	20.70	18.80	17.60	16.82	16.21	17.00
31	.	15.13	15.10	15.80	16.80	17.80	18.60	19.74	19.35	21.49
32	.	19.36	17.80	17.80	17.70	19.90	21.50	22.26	23.19	20.82
33	.	22.18	16.63	16.90	16.90	18.20	17.80	18.71	19.68	20.02
34	.	18.63	18.03	18.80	19.70	19.90	20.90	22.23	23.24	23.44
35	.	18.84	17.58	18.50	19.60	20.70	21.30	22.60	23.82	23.98
36	.	10.86	10.15	10.60	11.30	11.80	12.40	13.29	13.67	14.65
37	.	12.65	11.92	12.30	12.80	13.50	13.50	14.33	15.57	16.57

Explanatory notes: see p. 1039. Notes explicatives: voir p. 1041. Notas explicativas: véase p. 1043.

[1] Private sector. [2] Official estimates. [1] Secteur privé. [2] Estimations officielles. [1] Sector privado. [2] Estimaciones oficiales.

6A — LABOUR COST / COÛT DE LA MAIN-D OEUVRE / COSTO DE LA MANO DE OBRA

In manufacturing / Dans les industries manufacturières / En las industrias manufactureras

	1999	2000	2001	2002	2003	2004	2005	2006	2007	2008

Estonia (DA) [1] — Employees - Salariés - Asalariados — LC/h. - Kroon
ISIC 3 - CITI 3 - CIIU 3

	1999	2000	2001	2002	2003	2004	2005	2006	2007	2008
Total	.	42.31	.	.	.	61.14	.	.	.	.
15	.	42.66	.	.	.	58.77	.	.	.	.
15-16										
17	.	35.60	.	.	.	49.04	.	.	.	.
18	.	35.09	.	.	.	44.11	.	.	.	.
19	.	35.10	.	.	.	48.08	.	.	.	.
20	.	34.53	.	.	.	57.60	.	.	.	.
21	.	51.04	.	.	.	68.25	.	.	.	.
22	.	62.74	.	.	.	95.66	.	.	.	.
23-24										
24	.	49.46	.	.	.	73.34	.	.	.	.
25	.	44.36	.	.	.	66.88	.	.	.	.
26	.	52.03	.	.	.	82.51	.	.	.	.
27-28	.		.	.	.	43.15	.	.	.	.
28	.	45.90	.	.	.	59.77	.	.	.	.
29	.	43.73	.	.	.	69.35	.	.	.	.
30	.		.	.	.	90.29	.	.	.	.
31	.	57.84	.	.	.	76.83	.	.	.	.
32	.	43.93	.	.	.	60.88	.	.	.	.
33	.	48.77	.	.	.	71.35	.	.	.	.
34-35	.		.	.	.	80.42	.	.	.	.
35	.	44.38	.	.	.	71.46	.	.	.	.
36	.	36.59	.	.	.	57.26	.	.	.	.
37	.		.	.	.	72.06	.	.	.	.

Finland (CB) — Employees - Salariés - Asalariados — CR/h. - Euro
ISIC 3 - CITI 3 - CIIU 3

	1999	2000	2001	2002	2003	2004	2005	2006	2007	2008
Total	20.67	21.78	23.00	23.98	24.80	25.93	26.84	.	.	.
15	18.47	19.25	20.61	21.26				.	.	.
15-16	18.72	19.33	20.69	21.34	22.15	23.24	24.02	.	.	.
16	25.10	27.47	29.48	29.92				.	.	.
17	16.75	17.81	18.94	19.88	19.89	21.23	21.76	.	.	.
18	14.16	15.37	15.99	17.10	16.37	17.97	18.72	.	.	.
19	14.31	15.31	15.68	15.53	14.76	16.25	17.18	.	.	.
20	17.40	18.57	19.49	20.06	20.66	21.32	22.12	.	.	.
21	27.26	28.90	30.30	31.76	32.59	34.14	35.71	.	.	.
22	21.78	22.90	23.82	24.36	25.45	26.51	26.58	.	.	.
23	27.82	26.79	28.95	32.12	31.05	33.06	32.53	.	.	.
24	23.11	24.41	26.26	27.38	28.38	29.68	30.20	.	.	.
25	19.01	20.29	20.81	21.14	23.11	23.22	24.17	.	.	.
26	18.91	19.78	20.92	21.19	22.13	22.73	24.30	.	.	.
27	22.97	24.95	25.69	27.45	27.99	29.32	29.93	.	.	.
28	18.10	19.36	20.06	20.72	21.18	22.13	22.85	.	.	.
29	21.49	22.35	23.74	24.18	25.08	26.20	27.11	.	.	.
30	20.94	23.23	21.09	19.83	21.13	21.96	25.32	.	.	.
31	20.18	20.74	22.59	24.79	23.46	24.49	26.21	.	.	.
32	22.16	23.30	25.21	27.82	29.69	32.52	34.90	.	.	.
33	21.47	22.61	23.89	24.62	25.36	26.00	27.55	.	.	.
34	18.96	19.90	20.92	21.91	23.13	23.34	23.57	.	.	.
35	21.69	22.23	22.40	24.10	25.81	25.86	25.55	.	.	.
36	15.88	17.17	18.30	18.62	19.21	19.57	20.74	.	.	.
37	16.98	18.16	18.14	19.88	20.33	21.21	22.12	.	.	.

France (DA) [2] — Employees - Salariés - Asalariados — LC/h. - Euro
ISIC 3 - CITI 3 - CIIU 3

	1999	2000	2001	2002	2003	2004	2005	2006	2007	2008
Total	.	23.99	.	.	.	29.01	.	.	.	.
15	.	20.15	.	.	.	23.59	.	.	.	.
16	.	27.35	.	.	.	[3]	.	.	.	.
17	.	18.98	.	.	.	22.43	.	.	.	.
18	.	27.57	.	.	.	22.66	.	.	.	.
19	.	18.32	.	.	.	22.10	.	.	.	.
20	.	18.79	.	.	.	21.50	.	.	.	.
21	.	23.44	.	.	.	29.90	.	.	.	.
22	.	23.91	.	.	.	32.88	.	.	.	.
23	.	32.50	.	.	.	45.26	.	.	.	.
24	.	31.19	.	.	.	36.91	.	.	.	.
25	.	19.34	.	.	.	26.61	.	.	.	.
26	.	24.21	.	.	.	28.30	.	.	.	.
27	.	23.49	.	.	.	29.96	.	.	.	.
28	.	20.49	.	.	.	25.37	.	.	.	.
29	.	25.43	.	.	.	26.69	.	.	.	.
30	.	26.53	.	.	.	34.35	.	.	.	.
31	.	29.60	.	.	.	29.40	.	.	.	.
32	.	26.54	.	.	.	38.62	.	.	.	.
33	.	25.94	.	.	.	37.55	.	.	.	.
34	.	24.77	.	.	.	32.91	.	.	.	.
35	.	27.92	.	.	.	36.94	.	.	.	.
36	.	20.49	.	.	.	23.08	.	.	.	.
37	.	19.49	.	.	.	23.83	.	.	.	.

Explanatory notes: see p. 1039.

[1] Excl. cost of workers' housing and welfare services. [2] Enterprises with 10 or more persons employed. [3] Confidential.

Notes explicatives: voir p. 1041.

[1] Non compris les couts relatifs au logement du personnel et aux services sociaux. [2] Entreprises occupant 10 personnes et plus. [3] Confidentiel.

Notas explicativas: véase p. 1043.

[1] Excl. los gastos de vivienda de los trabajaodores y de los servicios de bienestar. [2] Empresas con 10 y más trabajadores. [3] Confidencial.

LABOUR COST
In manufacturing

COÛT DE LA MAIN-D OEUVRE
Dans les industries manufacturières

COSTO DE LA MANO DE OBRA
En las industrias manufactureras

	1999	2000	2001	2002	2003	2004	2005	2006	2007	2008
Germany (DA) [1]				Employees - Salariés - Asalariados						LC/h. - Euro
ISIC 3 - CITI 3 - CIIU 3										
Total	26.20 [2]	27.63	28.40 [2]	29.20 [2]	29.80 [2]	29.95	30.30 [2]	31.60 [2]	32.10 [2]	32.90
15	.	18.58	.	.	.	19.90	.	.	.	.
16	.	33.57	.	.	.	42.00	.	.	.	.
17	.	19.46	.	.	.	21.85	.	.	.	.
18	.	19.16	.	.	.	22.03	.	.	.	.
19	.	17.71	.	.	.	21.72	.	.	.	.
20	.	20.58	.	.	.	20.97	.	.	.	.
21	.	25.47	.	.	.	27.13	.	.	.	.
22	.	29.21	.	.	.	29.49	.	.	.	.
23	.	39.67	.	.	.	42.96	.	.	.	.
24	.	35.50	.	.	.	37.50	.	.	.	.
25	.	22.87	.	.	.	24.48	.	.	.	.
26	.	23.58	.	.	.	25.60	.	.	.	.
27	.	29.54	.	.	.	31.63	.	.	.	.
28	.	23.46	.	.	.	24.80	.	.	.	.
29	.	28.89	.	.	.	31.56	.	.	.	.
30	.	34.43	.	.	.	36.07	.	.	.	.
31	.	29.85	.	.	.	34.78	.	.	.	.
32	.	33.74	.	.	.	36.07	.	.	.	.
33	.	26.59	.	.	.	28.87	.	.	.	.
34	.	36.87	.	.	.	40.28	.	.	.	.
35	.	33.32	.	.	.	35.98	.	.	.	.
36	.	22.05	.	.	.	22.94	.	.	.	.
37	.	18.86	.	.	.	20.80	.	.	.	.
Hungary (DA) [3]				Employees - Salariés - Asalariados						LC/m. - Forint
ISIC 3 - CITI 3 - CIIU 3										
Total	123 663	139 520	154 660	171 180	185 012	200 644	218 122	236 347	254 919	274 038
15	116 565	133 571	147 512	160 576	169 729	181 052	208 019	219 019	217 426	232 608
16	236 105	309 440	352 874	409 031	443 559	667 367	569 668	551 591	475 994	501 434
17	90 395	97 951	106 562	116 474	119 078	125 581	139 343	162 905	160 419	167 139
18	69 260	79 196	88 282	98 404	101 690	104 304	110 140	122 081	132 437	135 677
19	72 728	83 296	93 252	102 634	107 159	120 313	127 321	135 831	153 683	162 486
20	77 975	87 872	98 576	110 140	115 788	124 415	131 676	146 606	157 463	173 347
21	152 874	181 754	196 379	201 766	200 501	204 330	204 277	214 697	266 433	308 989
22	139 024	150 527	162 087	165 856	179 177	201 390	250 925	276 120	258 828	294 138
23	.	295 976	345 813	388 147	508 603	579 008	612 672	693 179	697 852	773 974
24	200 006	227 251	256 264	283 335	312 847	349 850	388 846	399 916	431 144	465 767
25	121 711	142 646	159 459	177 841	192 397	200 188	213 654	225 029	245 189	257 734
26	132 629	149 714	165 076	186 671	200 502	209 743	233 179	254 042	273 170	295 607
27	157 085	188 223	202 866	223 658	243 727	277 840	291 018	321 468	341 850	345 244
28	106 164	123 257	134 219	143 692	153 004	166 197	186 127	202 469	211 630	229 025
29	128 412	139 370	154 261	175 326	190 581	206 621	223 010	233 060	244 597	266 056
30	138 959	139 730	147 590	178 299	183 129	228 481	251 109	266 008	292 828	316 684
31	131 849	149 520	161 876	178 074	190 037	206 042	224 973	240 311	263 608	275 723
32	131 699	148 294	169 298	187 696	205 154	212 765	253 132	278 248	279 202	290 898
33	124 616	144 650	156 801	163 226	181 197	198 317	243 574	247 058	234 198	259 581
34	159 831	176 758	202 309	229 610	242 001	261 819	288 099	300 939	330 796	346 441
35	130 529	167 181	185 395	201 514	208 019	251 274	263 585	304 073	323 062	336 984
36	82 899	89 529	102 479	117 768	122 504	127 651	144 455	160 522	164 679	177 667
37	.	142 434	144 778	163 787	155 638	154 957	185 514	205 481	196 180	200 198
Iceland (DA) [4][5]				Employees - Salariés - Asalariados						CR/h. - Krona
ISIC 3 - CITI 3 - CIIU 3										
Total	1 109	1 226	1 384	1 530	1 621	1 725	1 883	2 052	2 276	2 379
15	1 009	1 100	1 237	1 336	1 427	1 519	1 652	1 821	2 062	2 170
Iceland (DA) [5][6]				Employees - Salariés - Asalariados						CR/m. - Krona
ISIC 3 - CITI 3 - CIIU 3										
Total	250 000	272 000	306 000	324 000	345 000	368 000	405 000	443 000	473 000	476 000
15	221 000	243 000	267 000	284 000	310 000	330 000	356 000	389 000	437 000	465 000

Explanatory notes: see p. 1039.

[1] Enterprises with 10 or more persons employed. [2] Official estimates. [3] Enterprises with 5 or more employees. [4] Full-time employees. [5] Cash payments excluding overtime and employers#social security contributions. [6] Full-time adult employees.

Notes explicatives: voir p. 1041.

[1] Entreprises occupant 10 personnes et plus. [2] Estimations officielles. [3] Entreprises occupant 5 salariés et plus. [4] Salariés à plein temps. [5] Paiements en espèces n.c. la rémunération des heures supplémentaires et les cotisations des employeurs à la sécurité sociale. [6] Salariés adultes à plein temps.

Notas explicativas: véase p. 1043.

[1] Empresas con 10 y más trabajadores. [2] Estimaciones oficiales. [3] Empresas con 5 y más asalariados. [4] Asalariados a tiempo completo. [5] Pagos en dinero excl. los pagos por horas extraordinarias y las contribucciones de los empleadores a la seguridad social. [6] Asalariados adultos a tiempo completo.

6A

LABOUR COST

In manufacturing

COÛT DE LA MAIN-D OEUVRE

Dans les industries manufacturières

COSTO DE LA MANO DE OBRA

En las industrias manufactureras

	1999	2000	2001	2002	2003	2004	2005	2006	2007	2008

Italy (DA) — Employees - Salariés - Asalariados — LC/h. - Euro
ISIC 3 - CITI 3 - CIIU 3

	1999	2000	2001	2002	2003	2004	2005	2006	2007	2008
15	15.91	16.06	16.58	17.09	.	.	.	.	.	.
16	19.03	19.85	21.18	16.05	.	.	.	.	.	.
17	13.70	14.45	14.80	15.64	16.28	16.45	17.20	.	.	.
18	10.76	11.52	11.67	12.02	12.46	13.42	13.86	.	.	.
19	11.81	11.84	12.00	13.24	13.85	14.51	14.86	.	.	.
20	11.75	12.02	12.30	12.68	13.45	13.96	14.46	.	.	.
21	17.03	17.77	18.43	19.09	19.60	20.08	20.97	.	.	.
22	18.62	19.84	19.74	20.01	21.39	22.06	22.98	.	.	.
23	27.72	28.52	28.64	31.40	28.14	33.20	32.39	.	.	.
24	24.32	25.50	25.71	27.17	29.40	28.72	29.61	.	.	.
25	15.72	16.52	16.51	17.47	18.02	18.53	19.78	.	.	.
26	16.11	16.69	16.80	17.49	18.26	19.22	19.84	.	.	.
27	19.22	19.70	19.71	20.05	20.98	21.98	22.73	.	.	.
28	14.00	14.50	14.80	15.21	16.40	17.22	17.70	.	.	.
29	17.57	18.10	18.54	19.59	20.73	21.36	22.79	.	.	.
30	25.41	19.31	19.53	20.20	20.56	21.59	21.10	.	.	.
31	16.90	16.75	17.09	17.97	18.24	19.16	20.20	.	.	.
32	19.54	21.57	20.02	21.52	23.34	24.79	23.98	.	.	.
33	16.43	18.17	17.49	19.81	19.72	20.80	21.45	.	.	.
34	18.86	19.86	20.15	21.05	21.62	22.60	23.27	.	.	.
35	19.72	19.87	20.77	21.38	21.79	22.22	23.39	.	.	.
36	12.57	12.95	13.45	14.11	14.65	15.13	15.64	.	.	.
37	13.63	13.42	14.24	14.38	14.90	16.12	17.44	.	.	.

Latvia (CA) — Employees - Salariés - Asalariados — LC/h. - Lat
ISIC 3 - CITI 3 - CIIU 3

	1999	2000	2001	2002	2003	2004	2005	2006	2007	2008
Total	1.150	1.172	1.220	1.300	1.421	1.562	1.787	2.193	2.865	3.492
15	.	1.265	1.256	1.298	1.381	1.496	1.655	2.081	2.689	3.328
16	.	.	.	.	.	.	.	.	.	.
17	.	1.356	1.318	1.406	1.489	1.640	1.634	2.016	2.408	2.856
18	.	0.960	0.985	1.024	1.103	1.166	1.341	1.635	1.980	2.481
19	.	0.841	0.847	0.837	0.865	0.968	1.086	1.398	1.917	2.147
20	.	1.056	1.070	1.158	1.326	1.476	1.633	1.964	2.604	3.067
21	.	1.378	1.390	1.406	1.636	1.827	2.185	2.584	3.484	3.807
22	.	1.820	1.724	1.773	1.884	2.006	2.412	2.709	3.302	4.079
23	.	.	.	.	.	.	.	.	.	.
24	.	1.543	1.509	1.685	1.908	2.119	2.525	3.235	4.209	5.226
25	.	0.875	0.912	1.084	1.206	1.495	1.723	2.157	2.953	3.233
26	.	1.270	1.201	1.346	1.430	1.608	2.263	2.660	3.683	4.184
27	.	1.743	1.896	2.046	2.125	2.301	2.533	3.241	4.231	4.856
28	.	1.030	1.078	1.192	1.346	1.445	1.735	2.199	2.808	3.549
29	.	1.178	1.180	1.288	1.430	1.536	1.815	2.211	2.877	3.732
30	.	1.549	1.176	1.075	2.265	2.539	2.431	3.202	4.842	5.964
31	.	1.495	1.494	1.776	2.025	2.181	2.568	2.948	4.109	5.122
32	.	1.014	1.059	1.034	1.411	1.632	2.008	2.964	3.435	4.190
33	.	1.333	1.228	1.337	1.603	1.800	2.061	2.489	3.107	3.772
34	.	1.125	1.146	1.253	1.410	1.673	1.943	2.803	3.782	4.963
35	.	1.241	1.325	1.447	1.496	1.651	2.001	2.443	3.287	4.176
36	.	0.986	1.045	1.075	1.176	1.341	1.503	1.852	2.360	2.485
37	.	0.849	0.925	0.928	1.017	1.214	1.406	1.830	2.386	3.197

Lithuania (DA) — Employees - Salariés - Asalariados — LC/h. - Litas
ISIC 3 - CITI 3 - CIIU 3

	1999	2000	2001	2002	2003	2004	2005	2006	2007	2008
Total	.	9.38	.	.	.	10.07	11.20	13.22	16.32	.
15	.	9.53	.	.	.	9.40	.	.	.	.
16	.	.	.	.	.	.	.	.	.	.
17	.	9.12	.	.	.	8.99	.	.	.	.
18	.	6.72	.	.	.	7.55	.	.	.	.
19	.	7.40	.	.	.	8.57	.	.	.	.
20	.	6.60	.	.	.	7.49	.	.	.	.
21	.	9.78	.	.	.	11.60	.	.	.	.
22	.	11.31	.	.	.	12.09	.	.	.	.
23	.	.	.	.	.	.	.	.	.	.
24	.	13.47	.	.	.	16.03	.	.	.	.
25	.	8.16	.	.	.	10.84	.	.	.	.
26	.	9.53	.	.	.	11.21	.	.	.	.
27	.	9.85	.	.	.	11.05	.	.	.	.
28	.	7.69	.	.	.	9.60	.	.	.	.
29	.	8.72	.	.	.	10.85	.	.	.	.
30	.	12.00	.	.	.	9.75	.	.	.	.
31	.	9.70	.	.	.	9.90	.	.	.	.
32	.	11.31	.	.	.	12.25	.	.	.	.
33	.	10.03	.	.	.	12.78	.	.	.	.
34	.	8.34	.	.	.	8.53	.	.	.	.
35	.	12.27	.	.	.	13.72	.	.	.	.
36	.	7.66	.	.	.	8.89	.	.	.	.
37	.	8.23	.	.	.	9.65	.	.	.	.

Explanatory notes: see p. 1039.   Notes explicatives: voir p. 1041.   Notas explicativas: véase p. 1043.

LABOUR COST

In manufacturing

COÛT DE LA MAIN-D OEUVRE

Dans les industries manufacturières

COSTO DE LA MANO DE OBRA

En las industrias manufactureras

6A

	1999	2000	2001	2002	2003	2004	2005	2006	2007	2008

Luxembourg (CA) [1]
ISIC 3 - CITI 3 - CIIU 3

Employees - Salariés - Asalariados · LC/h. - Euro

Total	921.00 [2]|	22.56 [3]	22.89 [2]	23.87 [2]	24.67 [2]	27.86	28.88	29.78	30.65	31.46
15	632.00 [2]|	15.46 [3]	15.85 [2]	16.20 [2]	16.53 [2]	17.88	18.40	18.93	19.60	19.74
17	1 334.00 [2]|	. [3]		. [4]		. [4]		.	.	.
20	713.00 [2]|	17.99 [3]	18.29 [2]	19.32 [2]	20.00 [2]	24.32	25.63	26.34	26.94	27.56
22	915.00 [2]|	22.47 [3]	23.12 [2]	24.23 [2]	25.22 [2]	28.80	29.94	30.77	31.95	33.26
24	861.00 [2]|	23.23 [3]	24.19 [2]	24.76 [2]	25.11 [2]	21.32	22.22	22.47	21.44	21.60
25	1 159.00 [2]|	28.51 [3]	28.47 [2]	29.42 [2]	28.83 [2]	30.68	31.57	31.80	31.96	31.98
26	821.00 [2]|	20.25 [3]	20.96 [2]	21.80 [2]	22.67 [2]	25.56	26.56	27.50	28.60	29.30
27	1 068.00 [2]|	25.01 [3]	24.91 [2]	26.21 [2]	27.23 [2]	36.30	38.55	40.72	42.31	44.16
28	818.00 [2]|	19.41 [3]	19.64 [2]	20.37 [2]	21.23 [2]	23.78	24.37	25.21	26.01	26.58
29	930.00 [2]|	25.35 [3]	26.02 [2]	27.17 [2]	28.23 [2]	24.92	25.48	25.63	27.00	27.45
31	817.00 [2]|	20.40 [3]	19.28 [2]	19.67 [2]	20.34 [2]	.	.	.	.	.
33	663.00 [2]|	16.77 [3]	17.06 [2]	17.82 [2]	18.90 [2]	22.15	23.57	22.92	25.91	26.81
34	647.00 [2]|	. [3]		. [4]		. [4]		.	.	.
36	694.00 [2]|	15.86 [3]	15.18 [2]	16.29 [2]	17.17 [2]	.	.	.	.	.
37	708.00 [2]|	. [3]								

Macedonia, The Former Yugoslav Rep. of (DA)
ISIC 3 - CITI 3 - CIIU 3

Employees - Salariés - Asalariados · LC/h. - Denar

Total	.	.	.	144	.	124	.	136	.	.
15	.	.	.	193	.	167	.	183	.	.
16	.	.	.	172	.	155	.	173	.	.
17	.	.	.	93	.	90	.	97	.	.
18	.	.	.	79	.	78	.	86	.	.
19	.	.	.	53	.	58	.	70	.	.
20	.	.	.	80	.	84	.	89	.	.
21	.	.	.	152	.	131	.	144	.	.
22	.	.	.	144	.	159	.	172	.	.
23	.	.	.	261	.	294	.	312	.	.
24	.	.	.	265	.	189	.	295	.	.
25	.	.	.	109	.	93	.	87	.	.
26	.	.	.	217	.	235	.	261	.	.
27	.	.	.	166	.	212	.	224	.	.
28	.	.	.	120	.	104	.	123	.	.
29	.	.	.	133	.	179	.	158	.	.
30	.	.	.	160	.	211	.	220	.	.
31	.	.	.	173	.	140	.	164	.	.
32	.	.	.	109	.	116	.	128	.	.
33	.	.	.	234	.	203	.	167	.	.
34	.	.	.	122	.	107	.	156	.	.
35	.	.	.	172	.	161	.	183	.	.
36	.	.	.	70	.	81	.	85	.	.
37	.	.	.	96	.	88	.	95	.	.

Moldova, Republic of (CA) [5]
ISIC 3 - CITI 3 - CIIU 3

Employees - Salariés - Asalariados · LC/m. - Leu

Total	685.7	921.5	1 120.2	1 310.4	1 635.6	1 915.4	2 216.8	2 522.4	3 019.0	3 588.8
15	697.2	928.5	1 151.8	1 356.2	1 673.0	1 914.8	2 235.4	2 491.7	3 026.4	3 651.1
16	1 762.0	2 753.2	2 371.6	2 088.6	3 555.7	4 244.8	4 564.1	4 937.7	5 609.8	6 388.3
17	645.4	717.8	954.5	998.8	1 321.9	1 611.1	1 991.4	2 453.1	2 883.3	3 145.8
18	612.4	795.8	930.5	1 156.8	1 313.5	1 568.5	1 747.1	1 988.0	2 328.3	2 594.2
19	619.0	736.5	835.9	916.8	1 337.8	1 701.2	1 909.6	2 201.2	2 643.3	3 019.2
20	.	.	440.4	620.6	672.1	798.4	865.5	1 060.8	1 238.7	1 286.2
21	698.0	919.9	1 100.5	1 333.2	2 146.4	2 226.4	2 545.0	2 893.6	3 197.7	3 497.7
22	909.0	1 195.6	1 412.3	1 793.8	2 430.9	2 834.2	3 231.3	3 597.8	4 673.3	5 273.8
23	.	.	.	.	.	.	.	2 586.2	.	3 468.6
24	911.4	1 050.6	1 166.4	1 497.9	1 495.6	1 870.3	2 347.9	2 921.5	3 937.0	5 897.9
25	492.7	801.4	886.5	1 060.6	1 194.5	1 421.5	1 930.2	2 266.0	2 829.0	2 977.4
26	791.1	1 001.7	1 587.6	1 995.6	2 420.3	2 906.1	3 378.1	3 883.8	4 609.5	5 539.3
27	715.1	1 111.2	1 324.4	1 773.7	2 699.9	2 074.2	3 586.7	4 268.8	4 585.9	4 149.9
28	423.9	634.5	786.5	992.6	1 328.8	1 688.3	1 899.8	2 519.5	3 097.1	3 894.5
29	520.3	817.5	983.0	1 223.3	1 580.2	1 892.7	2 134.4	2 583.0	2 982.3	3 436.9
30	438.7	548.6	770.9	963.8	1 031.2	1 246.0	1 466.9	2 016.9	3 430.2	4 821.8
31	.	451.9	565.6	715.7	873.5	1 391.6	1 631.3	1 954.7	2 744.8	4 540.4
32	633.8	927.4	1 314.0	1 351.7	1 606.4	2 176.3	2 957.7	3 514.0	3 617.6	4 815.6
33	604.9	739.9	862.6	1 129.3	1 503.9	1 824.5	1 943.6	2 330.1	2 956.0	3 201.9
34	.	.	302.6	378.4	366.4	1 995.2	2 956.4	1 449.2	1 186.1	1 747.5
35	643.0	831.4	889.2	1 082.7	1 413.9	1 754.5	2 982.4	3 464.9	5 154.5	5 493.7
36	644.8	869.0	921.6	1 014.2	1 214.8	1 365.8	1 615.7	1 768.8	2 169.6	2 744.1
37	2 141.4	2 720.9	2 509.0	1 575.4	2 419.8	2 661.9	3 636.0	5 130.0	6 488.6	6 863.7

Explanatory notes: see p. 1039.

[1] Establishments with 10 or more persons employed. [2] Official estimates. [3] Prior to 2000: LUF; 1 Euro = 40.3399 LUF. [4] Confidential. [5] Enterprises with 20 or more employees.

Notes explicatives: voir p. 1041.

[1] Etablissements occupant 10 personnes et plus. [2] Estimations officielles. [3] Avant 2000: LUF; 1 Euro = 40,3399 LUF. [4] Confidentiel. [5] Entreprises occupant 20 salariés et plus.

Notas explicativas: véase p. 1043.

[1] Establecimientos con 10 y más trabajadores. [2] Estimaciones oficiales. [3] Antes de 2000: LUF; 1 Euro = 40,3399 LUF. [4] Confidencial. [5] Empresas con 20 y más asalariados.

LABOUR COST
In manufacturing

COÛT DE LA MAIN-D OEUVRE
Dans les industries manufacturières

COSTO DE LA MANO DE OBRA
En las industrias manufactureras

	1999	2000	2001	2002	2003	2004	2005	2006	2007	2008
Poland (DA) [1] ISIC 3 - CITI 3 - CIIU 3				Employees - Salariés - Asalariados						LC/m. - Zloty
Total	2 256 [2]	2 401	2 549 [3]	2 629 [3]	2 694 [3]	2 749	2 882 [4]	3 058 [4]	3 354 [4]	.
15	.	2 183	2 321 [3]	2 358 [3]	2 393 [3]	2 371	2 550 [4]	2 675 [4]	2 960 [4]	.
16	.	.	.	.	.	.	.	.	.	.
17	.	1 852	1 950 [3]	2 005 [3]	2 020 [3]	2 054	2 096 [4]	2 230 [4]	2 420 [4]	.
18	.	1 320	1 385 [3]	1 408 [3]	1 445 [3]	1 501	1 518 [4]	1 590 [4]	1 723 [4]	.
19	.	1 594	1 604 [3]	1 619 [3]	1 621 [3]	1 713	1 747 [4]	1 858 [4]	2 013 [4]	.
20	.	1 859	1 938 [3]	2 001 [3]	2 013 [3]	2 027	2 065 [4]	2 198 [4]	2 494 [4]	.
21	.	2 699	2 885 [3]	3 012 [3]	3 192 [3]	3 033	3 198 [4]	3 305 [4]	3 554 [4]	.
22	.	.	.	.	.	3 765	4 245 [4]	4 406 [4]	4 642 [4]	.
23	.	.	.	.	.	5 705	6 150 [4]	6 556 [4]	7 172 [4]	.
24	.	3 418	3 792 [3]	4 017 [3]	4 125 [3]	4 158	4 358 [4]	4 511 [4]	4 721 [4]	.
25	.	2 356	2 502 [3]	2 590 [3]	2 645 [3]	2 757	2 870 [4]	3 014 [4]	3 304 [4]	.
26	.	2 583	2 623 [3]	2 755 [3]	2 803 [3]	2 967	3 038 [4]	3 228 [4]	3 609 [4]	.
27	.	2 821	3 012 [3]	3 042 [3]	3 159 [3]	3 418	3 592 [4]	3 988 [4]	4 337 [4]	.
28	.	2 322	2 450 [3]	2 531 [3]	2 602 [3]	2 722	3 829 [4]	3 037 [4]	3 408 [4]	.
29	.	2 458	2 663 [3]	2 764 [3]	2 906 [3]	3 115	3 241 [4]	3 455 [4]	3 752 [4]	.
30	.	.	.	.	.	.	.	.	.	.
31	.	2 811	2 837 [3]	2 913 [3]	3 019 [3]	2 990	3 068 [4]	3 207 [4]	3 501 [4]	.
32	.	3 376	3 833 [3]	4 221 [3]	4 044 [3]	3 597	3 828 [4]	3 798 [4]	3 572 [4]	.
33	.	.	2 314 [3]	2 367 [3]	2 393 [3]	3 100	3 265 [4]	3 449 [4]	3 868 [4]	.
34	.	2 727	2 865 [3]	2 960 [3]	3 165 [3]	3 279	3 453 [4]	3 682 [4]	4 047 [4]	.
35	.	2 814	3 108 [3]	2 965 [3]	2 997 [3]	3 297	3 383 [4]	3 645 [4]	4 041 [4]	.
36	.	1 928	1 953 [3]	2 031 [3]	2 106 [3]	2 107	2 146 [4]	2 307 [4]	2 565 [4]	.
37	.	3 214	3 172 [3]	2 957 [3]	2 922 [3]	3 172	3 020 [4]	3 131 [4]	3 466 [4]	.
Portugal (DA) [5] ISIC 3 - CITI 3 - CIIU 3				Employees - Salariés - Asalariados						LC/h. - Euro
Total	1 335.00	1 413.00	1 486.45	7.77 [6]	8.16	8.57	8.81	9.05 [3]	9.29 [3]	9.54
15	.	.	.	.	.	.	.	.	.	.
15-16	1 353.00	1 491.00	1 552.96	8.04 [6]	8.36	8.69	8.80	9.12 [3]	9.45 [3]	9.79
16	.	.	.	.	.	.	.	.	.	.
17	.	.	.	.	.	.	.	.	.	.
17-18	963.00	1 021.00	1 055.72	5.43 [6]	5.60	5.78	5.97	6.10 [3]	6.24 [3]	6.38
18	.	.	.	.	.	.	.	.	.	.
19	992.00	1 038.00	1 066.50	5.45 [6]	5.59	5.73	5.68	5.73 [3]	5.78 [3]	5.83
20	1 130.00	1 195.00	1 273.70	6.75 [6]	7.18	7.64	7.78	8.13 [3]	8.49 [3]	8.87
21	.	.	.	.	.	.	.	.	.	.
21-22	2 154.00	2 251.00	2 366.59	12.37 [6]	12.98	13.62	14.01	14.33 [3]	14.66 [3]	15.00
22	.	.	.	.	.	.	.	.	.	.
23	4 586.00	5 619.00	5 855.67	30.33 [6]	31.55	32.82	32.95	33.31 [3]	33.68 [3]	34.05
24	2 478.00	2 553.00	2 657.32	13.75 [6]	14.28	14.84	15.19	15.22 [3]	15.26 [3]	15.30
25	1 447.00	1 485.00	1 583.16	8.39 [6]	8.93	9.50	10.04	10.88 [3]	11.80 [3]	12.80
26	1 520.00	1 631.00	1 713.51	8.95 [6]	9.38	9.84	10.18	10.47 [3]	10.76 [3]	11.06
27	.	.	.	.	.	.	.	.	.	.
28	.	.	.	.	.	.	.	.	.	.
29	1 557.00	1 676.00	1 740.80	8.99 [6]	9.32	9.66	9.73	10.10 [3]	10.49 [3]	10.90
30	.	.	.	.	.	.	.	.	.	.
30-33	1 721.00	1 785.00	1 874.47	9.78 [6]	10.26	10.75	11.09	11.40 [3]	11.71 [3]	12.03
31	.	.	.	.	.	.	.	.	.	.
32	.	.	.	.	.	.	.	.	.	.
33	.	.	.	.	.	.	.	.	.	.
34	.	.	.	.	.	.	.	.	.	.
34-35	1 732.00	1 832.00	1 952.26	10.34 [6]	11.00	11.70	11.87	12.08 [3]	12.29 [3]	12.50
35	.	.	.	.	.	.	.	.	.	.
36	.	.	.	.	.	.	.	.	.	.
36-37	1 052.00	1 106.00	1 197.21	6.44 [6]	6.96	7.52	7.72	8.05 [3]	8.40 [3]	8.77
37	.	.	.	.	.	.	.	.	.	.

Explanatory notes: see p. 1039.

[1] Enterprises with 10 or more persons employed. [2] Official estimates; enterprises with more than 5 employees. [3] Official estimates. [4] Official estimates; enterprises with more than 9 employees. [5] Establishments with 10 or more persons employed. [6] Prior to 2002: PTE; 1 Euro= 200.482 PTE.

Notes explicatives: voir p. 1041.

[1] Entreprises occupant 10 personnes et plus. [2] Estimations officielles; entreprises occupant plus de 5 salariés. [3] Estimations officielles. [4] Estimations officielles; entreprises occupant plus de 9 salariés. [5] Etablissements occupant 10 personnes et plus. [6] Avant 2002: PTE; 1 Euro= 200,482 PTE.

Notas explicativas: véase p. 1043.

[1] Empresas con 10 y más trabajadores. [2] Estimaciones oficiales; empresas con más de 5 asalariados. [3] Estimaciones oficiales. [4] Estimaciones oficiales; empresas con más de 9 asalariados. [5] Establecimientos con 10 y más trabajadores. [6] Antes de 2002: PTE; 1 Euro= 200,482 PTE.

LABOUR COST

In manufacturing

COÛT DE LA MAIN-D OEUVRE

Dans les industries manufacturières

COSTO DE LA MANO DE OBRA

En las industrias manufactureras

6A

	1999	2000	2001	2002	2003	2004	2005	2006	2007	2008
Roumanie (DA) ISIC 3 - CITI 3 - CIIU 3				Employees - Salariés - Asalariados						LC/h. - Leu
Total	.	22 104	31 971	40 187	46 613	55 969	6 [1]	7	9	.
15	.	18 637	28 837	35 603	41 880	50 345	5 [1]	7	8	.
16	.	52 427	80 438	88 932	112 644	149 640	18 [1]	23	23	.
17	.	16 731	23 706	30 439	36 831	45 722	5 [1]	6	7	.
18	.	15 635	21 673	26 977	32 327	40 145	4 [1]	5	6	.
19	.	14 586	21 005	27 002	33 216	39 211	4 [1]	5	6	.
20	.	14 917	19 961	23 825	29 836	36 011	4 [1]	5	6	.
21	.	24 035	35 991	44 543	52 812	57 832	6 [1]	8	9	.
22	.	31 065	42 272	53 248	51 808	59 327	6 [1]	7	9	.
23	.	49 095	78 807	110 844	117 206	125 261	15 [1]	17	19	.
24	.	32 735	47 457	60 950	71 157	81 615	9 [1]	12	14	.
25	.	23 434	35 956	45 546	50 414	58 730	6 [1]	7	9	.
26	.	25 414	34 313	46 116	52 973	65 165	7 [1]	9	11	.
27	.	35 474	55 325	67 680	75 126	97 474	10 [1]	13	15	.
28	.	21 216	30 133	38 026	47 853	59 260	7 [1]	8	9	.
29	.	23 997	36 736	47 944	55 297	66 466	7 [1]	9	10	.
30	.	29 121	30 063	39 030	62 480	71 376	4 [1]	8	9	.
31	.	24 460	35 079	45 821	54 803	62 369	6 [1]	8	9	.
32	.	39 417	52 753	70 529	78 348	105 262	12 [1]	15	15	.
33	.	23 243	33 872	44 795	48 250	59 706	8 [1]	8	10	.
34	.	26 070	39 307	49 755	60 897	74 556	8 [1]	10	12	.
35	.	32 278	44 801	59 694	70 538	80 740	9 [1]	10	12	.
36	.	16 646	23 658	30 470	35 264	42 752	5 [1]	6	7	.
37	.	21 168	28 818	35 243	40 136	49 223	5 [1]	7	8	.
Roumanie (DA) ISIC 3 - CITI 3 - CIIU 3				Employees - Salariés - Asalariados						LC/y.a. - Leu
Total	31 638 888	46 811 052	67 411 836	82 583 532	96 027 984	116 934 264	13 404 [1]	15 288	18 252	.
15	28 280 952	39 926 484	60 863 460	72 967 644	87 043 260	104 622 156	12 228 [1]	14 160	17 088	.
16	61 595 604	113 170 464	173 675 148	189 489 936	248 860 824	313 893 372	36 588 [1]	48 780	49 032	.
17	23 486 844	35 880 348	50 666 184	63 408 312	76 057 908	94 693 428	10 512 [1]	11 664	14 100	.
18	22 780 128	33 277 068	45 722 280	55 769 904	66 585 144	84 346 680	9 444 [1]	10 284	12 540	.
19	21 519 780	30 803 952	44 424 276	55 657 080	68 572 968	81 506 196	9 564 [1]	10 296	12 480	.
20	22 755 144	31 908 384	41 097 528	48 100 056	61 186 704	74 176 392	9 000 [1]	9 660	12 216	.
21	31 756 908	52 100 952	76 493 928	92 618 028	108 243 408	121 455 960	14 520 [1]	16 692	18 756	.
22	38 531 352	65 677 632	88 419 840	106 098 132	107 952 852	122 771 652	14 124 [1]	14 676	18 384	.
23	66 947 400	101 118 372	162 803 904	227 710 332	236 553 624	261 900 300	32 052 [1]	35 244	40 080	.
24	42 866 124	68 486 952	101 148 696	125 347 848	145 315 596	173 030 520	19 992 [1]	24 684	28 776	.
25	34 818 624	48 889 020	74 837 088	91 603 728	103 326 264	122 596 536	13 116 [1]	15 180	17 880	.
26	33 670 908	52 918 428	72 433 068	93 781 140	108 523 608	136 420 548	15 648 [1]	18 432	22 368	.
27	46 439 364	76 713 264	114 593 892	135 723 516	152 261 568	203 523 060	21 876 [1]	26 688	30 672	.
28	29 431 092	45 110 892	63 030 528	77 256 264	97 604 616	123 059 028	14 460 [1]	16 788	19 332	.
29	34 561 932	50 778 948	77 794 308	99 437 580	113 789 568	138 736 656	15 900 [1]	18 372	21 396	.
30	44 705 340	56 048 052	62 068 476	79 349 616	127 771 044	147 616 080	9 072 [1]	16 380	18 912	.
31	35 689 824	51 731 304	74 348 964	94 188 816	113 753 664	132 190 524	14 016 [1]	16 320	18 732	.
32	49 788 096	77 480 724	113 022 468	150 679 308	157 881 120	214 359 840	26 076 [1]	29 520	30 768	.
33	37 509 180	51 234 876	75 426 228	91 232 880	100 066 128	123 812 532	17 412 [1]	17 340	19 932	.
34	36 151 212	53 384 268	81 609 084	103 947 492	126 638 232	157 629 180	18 276 [1]	21 204	25 344	.
35	41 533 212	66 444 936	97 107 204	124 170 384	145 926 804	170 142 396	19 944 [1]	22 260	25 824	.
36	27 696 636	35 297 136	49 749 888	62 573 844	72 845 844	89 219 076	10 356 [1]	11 904	14 028	.
37	30 266 796	43 902 600	59 659 548	71 883 396	83 398 620	100 838 208	12 312 [1]	14 628	16 704	.
Russian Federation (DA) ISIC 3 - CITI 3 - CIIU 3				Employees - Salariés - Asalariados						LC/h. - Rouble
Total	.	.	.	.	.	.	81.6	.	123.6	.
15-16	.	.	.	.	.	.	68.7	.	103.0	.
17-18	.	.	.	.	.	.	38.9	.	66.4	.
19	.	.	.	.	.	.	44.5	.	72.5	.
20	.	.	.	.	.	.	59.4	.	91.0	.
21-22	.	.	.	.	.	.	85.5	.	139.6	.
24	.	.	.	.	.	.	91.2	.	132.1	.
27-28	.	.	.	.	.	.	106.0	.	152.7	.
29	.	.	.	.	.	.	78.3	.	127.6	.
30-33	.	.	.	.	.	.	74.2	.	116.0	.
34-35	.	.	.	.	.	.	88.0	.	126.8	.
San Marino (E) ISIC 3 - CITI 3 - CIIU 3				Employees - Salariés - Asalariados						CR/h. - Euro
Total	.	.	32 125.71	17.04 [2]	17.76	17.28	.	.	.	.
18	.	.	30 840.66	16.37 [2]	.	.	.	.	.	.
24	.	.	32 556.11	17.24 [2]	.	.	.	.	.	.
28	.	.	32 622.56	17.28 [2]	.	.	.	.	.	.
29	.	.	32 483.51	17.27 [2]	.	.	.	.	.	.

Explanatory notes: see p. 1039.

Notes explicatives: voir p. 1041.

Notas explicativas: véase p. 1043.

[1] New denomination: 1 leu = 10 000 old lei. [2] Prior to 2002: ITL; 1 Euro=1936.27 ITL.

[1] Nouvelle dénomination: 1 leu = 10 000 anciens lei. [2] Avant 2002: ITL; 1 Euro=1936,27 ITL.

[1] Nueva denominación: 1 leu = 10 000 antiguos lei. [2] Antes de 2002: ITL; 1 Euro=1936,27 ITL.

LABOUR COST

In manufacturing

COÛT DE LA MAIN-D OEUVRE

Dans les industries manufacturières

COSTO DE LA MANO DE OBRA

En las industrias manufactureras

	1999	2000	2001	2002	2003	2004	2005	2006	2007	2008

Slovakia (DA)   Employees - Salariés - Asalariados   LC/h. - Koruna
ISIC 3 - CITI 3 - CIIU 3

	1999	2000	2001	2002	2003	2004	2005	2006	2007	2008
Total	114.16	130.06	136.56	148.73	160.94	173.71	177.88	189.70	210.70	.
15	116.91	123.76	127.42	140.02	153.09	165.50	152.72	169.60	190.50	.
16	194.86		210.45	232.95	340.95	429.26	385.46	.	457.60	.
17	86.69	92.84	91.82	105.30	108.17	116.39	141.06	128.00	145.60	.
18	78.75	89.60	89.84	97.06	101.25	103.87	110.20	110.90	129.20	.
19	92.53	86.91	94.54	108.14	112.49	109.01	127.21	142.40	134.90	.
20	86.97	94.31	98.73	121.29	116.22	121.74	134.24	154.00	156.80	.
21	128.14	133.21	134.10	208.60	186.05	201.87	206.49	246.80	251.00	.
22	124.33	144.39	154.79	159.57	170.90	162.36	194.53	201.40	209.70	.
23	160.26	190.03	237.80	307.23	390.04	454.71	581.18	574.60	541.50	.
24	139.31	139.56	161.43	186.63	203.52	201.74	215.44	236.80	272.70	.
25	122.49	157.05	156.24	165.88	175.94	177.76	182.95	204.80	219.40	.
26	125.81	138.94	153.91	169.77	158.84	190.65	185.13	202.40	229.00	.
27	126.25	173.50	192.84	234.12	282.93	257.51	308.61	329.10	367.50	.
28	117.18	132.33	136.66	142.67	170.84	159.01	164.69	183.50	199.80	.
29	117.81	128.19	131.01	147.83	159.24	159.22	173.03	190.10	210.80	.
30	110.68	131.25	159.34	167.54	169.80	161.48	198.78	226.60	213.70	.
31	110.34	102.60	116.06	126.77	148.31	169.72	165.57	167.00	176.40	.
32	89.44	109.53	131.32	134.32	155.96	187.22	176.35	206.80	200.60	.
33	130.26	125.56	141.68	160.59	167.73	180.55	178.33	209.20	227.70	.
34	108.30	115.83	246.44	191.08	164.66	150.91	212.47	232.50	253.20	.
35	126.42	135.88	160.43	173.33	173.19	192.15	210.26	215.90	222.70	.
36	92.68	105.33	112.80	109.38	144.27	155.79	149.69	149.00	160.40	.
37	101.72	120.96	135.20	130.81	221.11	303.83	297.52	230.10	346.10	.

Slovenia (DA)   Employees - Salariés - Asalariados   LC/h. - Euro
ISIC 3 - CITI 3 - CIIU 3

	1999	2000	2001	2002	2003	2004	2005	2006	2007	2008
Total	.	.	1 941 [1]	2 011 [1]	2 240 [1]	2 273	2 357 [1]	2 441 [1]	11 [2]	.

Slovenia (DA)   Employees - Salariés - Asalariados   LC/m. - Euro
ISIC 3 - CITI 3 - CIIU 3

	1999	2000	2001	2002	2003	2004	2005	2006	2007	2008
Total	225 290 [1]	240 807	268 656 [1]	294 860 [1]	316 302 [1]	329 109	348 548 [1]	365 089 [1]	1 617 [2]	.

Suisse (E)   Employees - Salariés - Asalariados   LC/h. - Franc
ISIC 3 - CITI 3 - CIIU 3

	1999	2000	2001	2002	2003	2004	2005	2006	2007	2008
Total	.	47	.	50	.	50	.	52	.	.

Sweden (DB) [3] [4]   Wage-earners - Ouvriers - Obreros   CR/h. - Krona
ISIC 3 - CITI 3 - CIIU 3

	1999	2000	2001	2002	2003	2004	2005	2006	2007	2008
Total	181.70	187.91	193.66	200.31	208.09	213.42	219.08	225.43	232.01	239.08
15-16	170.29	177.66	184.73	188.39	195.19	200.40	204.16	211.93	218.03	226.53
17-19	157.74	164.97	168.26	175.25	181.06	188.18	193.90	197.96	202.69	208.12
20	170.89	176.85	182.51	190.04	196.79	202.75	209.14	214.13	221.52	227.32
21	213.43	220.49	226.66	232.92	241.26	247.01	256.48	262.66	270.64	277.62
22	191.36	195.39	201.49	209.02	217.14	221.35	226.80	232.08	237.85	242.29
23-24	197.79	203.50	213.59	226.00	237.33	239.87	245.33	248.39	255.17	262.53
25	173.14	179.71	185.43	189.42	197.90	204.25	210.92	215.24	224.02	229.00
26	177.03	184.24	190.16	196.67	207.65	212.91	217.73	222.98	232.18	242.41
27	202.43	209.97	216.84	223.11	230.06	235.02	238.64	246.59	253.62	261.81
28	171.20	176.41	182.07	187.23	195.47	200.75	206.79	210.84	217.41	226.16
29	176.24	182.49	187.98	194.73	202.15	206.77	213.02	219.48	225.91	232.72
30-33	176.84	184.32	187.85	191.67	196.13	201.88	207.66	210.92	213.91	221.26
34-35	189.82	197.30	202.38	211.71	219.02	224.77	230.01	242.21	250.39	258.62
36-37	166.61	171.22	175.27	181.73	192.34	195.83	199.35	208.02	214.79	221.03

Explanatory notes: see p. 1039.

[1] Official estimates. [2] Prior to 2007: SIT; 1 Euro = 239.64 SIT; official estimates. [3] Private sector. [4] Excl. cost of medical care and health services.

Notes explicatives: voir p. 1041.

[1] Estimations officielles. [2] Avant 2007: SIT; 1 Euro = 239,64 SIT; estimations officielles. [3] Secteur privé. [4] Non compris le coût des services médicaux et sanitaires.

Notas explicativas: véase p. 1043.

[1] Estimaciones oficiales. [2] Antes de 2007: SIT; 1 Euro = 239,64 SIT; estimaciones oficiales. [3] Sector privado. [4] Excl. los gastos de asistencia médica y servicios sanitarios.

LABOUR COST
In manufacturing

COÛT DE LA MAIN-D OEUVRE
Dans les industries manufacturières

COSTO DE LA MANO DE OBRA
En las industrias manufactureras

6A

Sweden (E) [1]

Employees - Salariés - Asalariados — LC/h. - Krona

ISIC 3 - CITI 3 - CIIU 3

	1999	2000	2001	2002	2003	2004	2005	2006	2007	2008
Total	225.66	239.02	251.85	263.27	270.80	292.33	300.39	310.87	323.06	345.29
15	212.60	210.07	221.58	229.26	236.97	251.68	259.55	268.57	278.42	287.45
16	275.62	301.91	297.59	349.19	367.21	408.43	417.20	443.00	449.90	514.80
17	184.75	195.53	203.18	214.46	218.00	234.24	247.06	252.83	257.84	265.80
18	171.79	173.42	176.34	185.64	199.24	227.11	237.88	243.99	257.59	277.69
19	175.02	185.58	195.38	198.91	207.51	229.44	231.74	242.64	250.59	261.09
20	190.84	198.48	209.33	217.48	224.29	237.71	244.50	250.63	261.06	269.66
21	247.25	253.68	262.40	272.31	282.38	284.32	295.85	305.60	313.00	322.81
22	232.06	256.05	269.16	278.00	287.42	279.89	286.94	295.39	309.10	322.11
23	259.90	285.35	303.56	315.20	340.65	365.24	379.63	379.69	399.64	428.68
24	282.41	282.99	300.64	319.27	336.56	372.41	382.96	395.13	404.94	431.72
25	204.59	210.32	222.93	228.22	241.03	244.33	252.41	257.41	270.67	278.79
26	219.06	215.12	221.50	233.12	245.33	262.41	266.91	273.33	288.27	299.33
27	233.93	255.69	267.56	277.25	285.72	289.01	296.41	307.52	321.77	335.00
28	197.01	200.48	209.42	215.26	226.27	245.76	254.54	258.92	270.14	286.83
29	230.57	238.76	254.11	264.12	278.32	286.81	294.71	305.13	316.49	337.23
30	232.12	233.00	277.37	278.04	273.33	251.30	266.27	276.72	285.49	286.48
31	204.52	225.11	243.66	266.87	279.74	312.32	315.16	325.36	330.24	345.52
32	246.80	317.53	339.89	361.96	388.37	456.38	478.92	503.22	518.21	529.35
33	248.58	275.42	297.14	297.98	306.49	318.48	330.48	330.50	330.24	349.44
34	228.15	239.29	251.34	265.70	275.62	309.41	317.03	335.46	352.30	365.01
35	235.54	268.56	278.52	294.55	311.68	308.48	327.44	355.39	372.15	388.42
36	182.57	203.26	209.55	220.80	232.81	231.95	239.21	246.70	257.43	266.23

Ukraine (CA)

Employees - Salariés - Asalariados — LC/m. - Hryvnia

ISIC 3 - CITI 3 - CIIU 3

	1999	2000	2001	2002	2003	2004	2005	2006	2007	2008
Total	293.33	.	528.02	.	.	.	.	1 610.24	.	.
15	339.91	.	509.44	.	.	.	.	1 357.23	.	.
16	.	.	.	.	.	.	.	.	.	.
17	161.45	.	308.50	.	.	.	.	898.00	.	.
18	161.45	.	308.50	.	.	.	.	.	.	.
19	149.37	.	307.83	.	.	.	.	956.48	.	.
20	177.65	.	335.25	.	.	.	.	1 252.47	.	.
21	293.33	.	707.93	.	.	.	.	1 500.66	.	.
22	.	.	.	.	.	.	.	.	.	.
23	535.25	.	1 055.30	.	.	.	.	2 713.52	.	.
24	401.58	.	651.38	.	.	.	.	1 934.44	.	.
25	305.70	.	510.40	.	.	.	.	1 367.99	.	.
26	274.57	.	416.98	.	.	.	.	1 549.19	.	.
27	370.09	.	846.11	.	.	.	.	2 132.37	.	.
29	260.18	.	407.52	.	.	.	.	1 654.60	.	.
30	242.27	.	412.55	.	.	.	.	1 409.13	.	.
31	.	.	.	.	.	.	.	.	.	.
32	.	.	.	.	.	.	.	.	.	.
33	.	.	.	.	.	.	.	1 725.33	.	.
34	278.21	.	535.19	.	.	.	.	.	.	.
35	.	.	.	.	.	.	.	1 183.65	.	.
36	236.92	.	393.58	.	.	.	.	.	.	.
37	.	.	.	.	.	.	.	.	.	.

United Kingdom (DA)

Employees - Salariés - Asalariados — LC/h. - Pound

ISIC 3 - CITI 3 - CIIU 3

	1999	2000	2001	2002	2003	2004	2005	2006	2007	2008
Total	.	14.22	.	.	.	16.69	.	.	.	.
15	.	12.57	.	.	.	15.50	.	.	.	.
16	.	25.52	.	.	.	29.24	.	.	.	.
17	.	10.85	.	.	.	13.22	.	.	.	.
18	.	9.18	.	.	.	10.71	.	.	.	.
19	.	9.88	.	.	.	11.59	.	.	.	.
20	.	11.00	.	.	.	11.98	.	.	.	.
21	.	14.11	.	.	.	16.25	.	.	.	.
22	.	17.10	.	.	.	18.27	.	.	.	.
23	.	19.14	.	.	.	20.95	.	.	.	.
24	.	19.30	.	.	.	20.00	.	.	.	.
25	.	12.45	.	.	.	14.86	.	.	.	.
26	.	12.40	.	.	.	14.35	.	.	.	.
27	.	14.55	.	.	.	15.43	.	.	.	.
28	.	12.45	.	.	.	14.35	.	.	.	.
29	.	14.94	.	.	.	16.96	.	.	.	.
30	.	16.61	.	.	.	16.11	.	.	.	.
31	.	13.99	.	.	.	16.15	.	.	.	.
32	.	15.90	.	.	.	18.96	.	.	.	.
33	.	16.06	.	.	.	18.12	.	.	.	.
34	.	15.98	.	.	.	19.46	.	.	.	.
35	.	16.81	.	.	.	21.95	.	.	.	.
36	.	11.41	.	.	.	16.48	.	.	.	.
37	.	10.84	.	.	.	12.37	.	.	.	.

Explanatory notes: see p. 1039.

[1] Private sector.

Notes explicatives: voir p. 1041.

[1] Secteur privé.

Notas explicativas: véase p. 1043.

[1] Sector privado.

LABOUR
COST

In manufacturing

COÛT DE LA
MAIN-D OEUVRE

Dans les industries
manufacturières

COSTO DE LA
MANO DE OBRA

En las industrias
manufactureras

	1999	2000	2001	2002	2003	2004	2005	2006	2007	2008

OCEANIA-OCÉANIE-OCEANIA

New Zealand (FD) [1]
ISIC 3 - CITI 3 - CIIU 3

Employees - Salariés - Asalariados

CR/y.a. - Dollar

	1999	2000	2001	2002	2003	2004	2005	2006	2007	2008
Total	38 600	37 100 [2]	36 800	39 200	40 000	42 500	44 100			
15	37 100	35 500 [2]	34 200	36 800	38 500	41 800	43 900			
16	53 800	54 500 [2]	78 800	100 700	101 700	113 300	123 800			
17	32 700	29 200 [2]	30 000	31 900	31 700	31 600	32 300			
18-19	29 400	26 600 [2]	26 000	26 400	27 300	25 900	28 400			
20	35 700	33 700 [2]	32 000	33 500	35 000	37 100	37 700			
21	56 500	96 500 [2]	57 700	62 900	70 200	66 800	77 400			
22	42 300	40 100 [2]	40 300	40 900	39 400	44 800	45 300			
23	59 400	47 500 [2]	61 800	50 600	49 600	51 300	51 800			
24	48 300	48 300 [2]	54 300	56 600	55 100	57 100	60 500			
25	37 900	35 500 [2]	34 200	39 100	42 400	45 000	46 400			
26	47 000	42 000 [2]	42 300	47 100	47 000	49 200	48 800			
27	55 700	53 800 [2]	57 900	57 900	57 400	60 900	64 700			
28	37 700	36 400 [2]	38 000	39 800	39 700	42 000	40 900			
29	37 100	32 900 [2]	33 200	37 400	36 600	37 900	40 000			
30										
30-32		34 900 [2]	38 200	42 500	46 700	50 400	54 500			
31-32	33 400	[2]								
33	34 800	35 700 [2]	39 400	32 200	37 700	41 000	47 400			
34	44 100	30 500 [2]	31 800	42 100	38 200	38 400	38 300			
35	40 200	44 600 [2]	46 600	46 400	47 000	52 300	50 900			
36	28 700	26 300 [2]	25 900	27 000	27 800	28 600	30 700			

Explanatory notes: see p. 1039.

[1] Estimations based on National Accounts. [2] Methodology revised; data not strictly comparable.

Notes explicatives: voir p. 1041.

[1] Estimations basées sur la Comptabilité nationale. [2] Méthodologie révisée; les données ne sont pas strictement comparables.

Notas explicativas: véase p. 1043.

[1] Estimaciones basadas en la Contabilidad Nacional. [2] Metodología revisada; los datos no son estrictamente comparables.

Consumer prices

Prix à la consommation

Precios al consumidor

Consumer prices

The Resolution concerning consumer price indices, adopted by the Seventeenth International Conference of Labour Statisticians (ICLS) (Geneva, 2003)[1], states the following:

"1.   The CPI is a current social and economic indicator that is constructed to measure changes over time in the general level of prices of consumer goods and services that households acquire, use or pay for consumption.

2.   The index aims to measure the change in consumer prices over time. This may be done by measuring the cost of purchasing a fixed basket of consumer goods and services of constant quality and similar characteristics, with the products in the basket being selected to be representative of households' expenditure during a year or other specified period. Such an index is called a fixed-basket price index.

3.   The index may also aim to measure the effects of price changes on the cost of achieving a constant standard of living (i.e. level of utility or welfare). This concept is called a cost-of-living index (COLI). A fixed basket price index, or another appropriate design, may be employed as an approximation to a COLI."

A consumer price index is usually estimated as a series of summary measures of the period-to-period proportional change in the prices of a fixed set of consumer goods and services of constant quantity and characteristics, acquired, used or paid for by the reference population. Each summary measure is constructed as a weighted average of a large number of elementary aggregate indices. Each of the elementary aggregate indices is estimated using a sample of prices for a defined set of goods and services obtained in, or by residents of, a specific region from a given set of outlets or other sources of consumption goods and services.

Consumer price indices are used for a variety of purposes, including:

a)   general economic and social analysis and policy determination;
b)   negotiation or indexation, or both, by government (notably of taxes, social security benefits, civil service remuneration and pensions, licence fees, fines and public debt interest or principal) and in private contracts (e.g. wages, salaries, insurance premia and service charges) and in judicial decisions (e.g. alimony payments);
c)   establishing "real" changes, or the relationship between money and the goods or services for which it can be exchanged (e.g. for the deflation of current value aggregates in the national accounts and of retail sales); and
d)   price movement comparisons done for business purposes, including inflation accounting.

Sub-indices rather than the all-items index may be suitable for some of the above uses.

Weights are the relative expenditure or consumption shares of the elementary aggregates estimated from available data. In this connection, the Seventeenth ICLS recommended the following:

"23.   The two main sources for deriving the weights are the results from household expenditure surveys (HESs) and national accounts estimates on household consumption expenditure. The results from HES are appropriate for an index defined to cover the consumption expenditures of reference population groups resident within the country, while national account estimates are suitable for an index defined to cover consumption expenditures within the country. ...

24.   The information from the main source (HESs or national accounts) should be supplemented with all other available information on the expenditure pattern. Sources of such information that can be used for disaggregating the expenditures are surveys of sales in retail outlets, point-of-purchase surveys, surveys of production, export and import data and administrative sources. Based on these data the weights for certain products may be further disaggregated by region and type of outlet. ..."

The Seventeenth ICLS also recommended that the prices used for the computation of the indices should be the:

"54.   ... actual transaction prices, including indirect taxes and nonconditional discounts, that would be paid, agreed or costed (accepted) by the reference population. ... Tips for services, where compulsory, should be treated as part of the price paid.

55.   Exceptional prices charged for stale, shopsoiled, damaged, or otherwise imperfect goods sold at clearance prices should be excluded, unless the sale of such products is a permanent and widespread phenomenon. Sale prices, discounts, cut prices and special offers should be included when applicable to all customers without there being significant limits to the quantities that can be purchased by each customer.

52.   Prices should be collected in all types of outlets that are important, including Internet sellers, open-air markets and informal markets, and in free markets as well as price-controlled markets. ..."

The scope of consumer price indices can vary between countries, in terms not only of the types of households or population groups covered, but also the geographic coverage.

National practices also differ as regards the treatment of certain issues relating to the computation of consumer price indices, including seasonal items, quality changes, new products, durable goods and owner-occupied housing. There are differences in the methods used for collecting prices and for compiling the indices. As a result, care should be taken when using the consumer price indices presented in these tables, particularly for the purposes of collective bargaining, indexation or deflation. The indices should only be used if the coverage of the consumer price index corresponds closely to that of the subject of negotiation, indexation or deflation.

Information on the scope, definitions and methods used for compiling the consumer price indices presented in this chapter is given in ILO: *Sources and Methods: Labour*

Statistics, Volume 1: Consumer price indices, Third edition (Geneva, 1992) and on the ILO's statistical web site at laborsta.ilo.org.

Tables 7A to 7F

Table 7A presents the general consumer price index for all groups of consumption items combined.

Table 7B relates to an all-items index excluding rent. Rent has been excluded from the all-items index to make the rates of price change more comparable across countries, although it does not eliminate all the difficulties encountered when making such comparisons. This index is intended to mean primarily an index without rent (actual and/or imputed). However, if such an index is not available at the national level or if it is too difficult to compute one, then for practical purposes countries provide one that excludes the housing component. If this is the case, a footnote indicates the particular exclusions (for example, the whole housing group, electricity, gas and other fuels, expenditure on maintenance and repairs of dwelling, etc.).

Table 7C relates to a food index including non-alcoholic beverages only. Where alcoholic beverages and/or tobacco are included, this is indicated in footnotes.

Tables 7D to 7F give three other major group indices, respectively for "Electricity, gas and other fuels", "Clothing (including footwear)" and "Rent". These group indices, along with the food index, are components of the general index. For most countries, the general index and the general index excluding rent cover, in addition to these four group indices, all other main groups of expenditure, i.e. "alcoholic beverages and tobacco", "furniture, household equipment and routine household maintenance", "health", "transport", "communication", "recreation and culture", "education", "restaurants and hotels" and "miscellaneous goods and services". Indices relating to these latter groups are not shown separately in the *Yearbook*, because of the variations between countries in the composition of the groups.

The general and the group indices shown in the tables refer to annual averages, although these are compiled in most cases monthly and in a few cases quarterly or biannually. Annual averages are derived from the original series

As the original base periods of the national series vary, a uniform base period (2000) has been adopted for the presentation of the data. As many as possible of the series have been recalculated by dividing the index for each date shown by the index for the year 2000 and multiplying the quotient by 100. Where data are available only for periods subsequent to 2000, the indices are generally presented with the first available calendar year as base. This operation does not involve any change in the weighting systems, etc., used by the countries.

If a new series is sufficiently comparable with the former series, the two are linked to form a continuous historical time series. If a series has been discontinued and has been replaced by another which cannot be reconciled with the former by linking or some other estimation techniques, the break is indicated by a footnote.

Note

[1] For the full text of the resolution, see ILO: *Seventeenth International Conference of Labour Statisticians, Report of the Conference* (Geneva, 2004) or the ILO Department of Statistics' web site: http://www.ilo.org/stat.

Prix à la consommation

La résolution concernant les indices des prix à la consommation adoptée par la dix-septième Conférence internationale des statisticiens du travail (CIST) (Genève, 2003)[1] stipule ce qui suit:
« 1.   L'IPC est un indicateur social et économique couramment utilisé pour mesurer les variations au cours du temps du niveau général des prix des biens et services acquis, utilisés ou payés par les ménages pour leur consommation.
2.   L'indice vise à mesurer les variations dans le temps des prix à la consommation. Cela peut être réalisé en mesurant le coût d'achat d'un panier fixe de biens et de services dont la qualité est constante et les caractéristiques similaires aux produits du panier choisis pour être représentatifs des dépenses des ménages pendant une année ou une autre période spécifiée. Un tel indice s'appelle indice des prix d'un panier fixe.
3.   L'indice peut également viser à mesurer les effets des variations de prix sur le coût que représente l'accès à un niveau de vie constant (niveau d'utilité ou de bien-être). Ce concept est dénommé indice du coût de la vie (ICV). Un indice des prix d'un panier fixe, ou une autre mesure appropriée, peut être utilisé en tant qu'approximation d'un ICV. »
Un indice est généralement estimé à partir d'une suite de mesures synthétiques des variations relatives, d'une période à l'autre, des prix d'un ensemble fixe de biens et de services de consommation constants en quantité et par leurs caractéristiques, acquis, utilisés ou payés par la population de référence. Chaque mesure synthétique est obtenue comme une moyenne pondérée d'un grand nombre d'indices de prix d'agrégats élémentaires. L'indice de chaque agrégat élémentaire est estimé au moyen d'un échantillon de prix pour un ensemble fixe de biens et de services que se procurent les individus de la population de référence dans une région donnée, ou qui habitent cette région, auprès d'un ensemble spécifié de points de vente ou auprès d'autres fournisseurs de biens et de services de consommation.
Les indices des prix à la consommation sont utilisés à diverses fins telles que:

a)   l'analyse générale de la situation économique et sociale et la prise de décisions concernant les politiques correspondantes;
b)   la négociation ou l'indexation, ou les deux, par les pouvoirs publics (en particulier des impôts, des prestations et cotisations sociales, des rémunérations et des pensions de la fonction publique, des patentes, des amendes et des emprunts publics (intérêts ou principal), dans les contrats entre particuliers (par exemple des salaires et traitements, des primes d'assurance et du coût des services) et dans les décisions de justice (par exemple des pensions alimentaires);
c)   la mesure des changements en termes réels ou des rapports entre l'argent et les biens ou les services contre lesquels il peut être changé (par exemple la déflation de la valeur aux prix courants des agrégats de la comptabilité nationale et la déflation des ventes au détail);
d)   les comparaisons des variations de prix à des fins commerciales, y compris la réévaluation comptable.

Des indices partiels peuvent être appropriés pour certaines des utilisations précédentes, en lieu et place de l'indice d'ensemble.
Les pondérations représentent les parts relatives des dépenses ou de la consommation des agrégats élémentaires, estimées sur la base des données disponibles. A cet égard, la dix-septième CIST a recommandé ce qui suit:
« 23.   Les deux principaux éléments permettant de dériver les pondérations sont les résultats obtenus à partir d'enquêtes sur les dépenses des ménages, ainsi que les estimations des dépenses de consommation des ménages de la comptabilité nationale. Les résultats d'une enquête sur les dépenses des ménages sont appropriés pour un indice que l'on a défini de manière à couvrir les dépenses de consommation des groupes de population de référence résidant dans le pays, alors que les estimations s'appuyant sur la comptabilité nationale conviennent à un indice défini pour couvrir les dépenses de consommation à l'intérieur du pays. ...

24.   Les informations provenant de la source principale (enquêtes sur les dépenses des ménages ou comptabilité nationale) devraient être complétées par toute autre information disponible sur le schéma de dépenses. Les sources d'informations de ce type qui peuvent servir à désagréger les dépenses sont les enquêtes sur les points de vente au détail ou les points d'achat, les enquêtes sur la production, les données d'exportation et d'importation, et les sources administratives. Sur la base de ces données, les pondérations pour certains produits peuvent être encore ventilées par région et par type de point de vente... »
La dix-septième CIST a en outre recommandé que les prix servant au calcul des indices devraient être :
« 54.   ... les prix correspondant à des transactions effectives – y compris les impôts indirects et les rabais inconditionnels – qui seraient payées, convenues ou chiffrées (acceptées) par la population de référence.   ...
Les pourboires versés pour le service, lorsqu'ils sont obligatoires, doivent être traités comme faisant partie du prix payé.
55. Les prix exceptionnels payés pour des produits endommagés, défraîchis ou qui ont perdu de leur qualité pour d'autres raisons et qui sont vendus pour liquider les stocks devraient être exclus des relevés, à moins qu'il ne s'agisse d'un phénomène permanent et largement répandu pour la vente de ces produits. Les prix des produits soldés, au rabais ou faisant l'objet de campagnes spéciales de promotion devraient être inclus lorsqu'ils s'appliquent à tous les consommateurs et lorsqu'il n'y a pas de limite significative aux quantités que chaque client peut acheter.
52.   Les prix doivent être collectés dans tous les types de points de vente qui sont importants, y compris les commerçants sur la toile (Internet), les marchés en plein air et les marchés informels, ainsi que sur les marchés libres et les marchés dont les prix sont contrôlés.... »
Le champ d'application des indices des prix à la consommation peut varier d'un pays à un autre, non seulement quant aux types de ménages ou groupes de population couverts, mais aussi quant à sa portée géographique.
Les pratiques nationales varient également en ce qui concerne le traitement de certains éléments retenus dans le calcul des indices des prix à la consommation tels qu'articles saisonniers, changements de qualité, nouveaux articles, biens durables et logements occupés par leur propriétaire.

Les méthodes de collecte des prix ou de calcul des indices sont également différentes. A ce titre, les indices des prix à la consommation publiés dans ces tableaux doivent être utilisés avec précaution, notamment en matière de négociations collectives et dans les calculs d'indexation ou de déflation. Ces indices ne peuvent être utilisés que si le champ d'application de l'indice des prix à la consommation correspond étroitement à celui du sujet de négociation, de l'indexation ou de la déflation.

Des informations sur le champ, les définitions et les méthodes utilisées dans le calcul des indices des prix à la consommation, diffusés dans ce chapitre, sont publiées dans Sources et méthodes: statistiques du travail, volume 1 : Indices des prix à la consommation, troisième édition (Genève, BIT, 1992) et sur le site Web des statistiques du BIT à l'adresse suivante : http://laborsta.ilo.org.

Tableaux 7A à 7F

Le tableau 7A présente les indices généraux des prix à la consommation pour tous les groupes d'articles de consommation combinés.

Le tableau 7B se réfère à un indice non compris le loyer. Le loyer a été exclu de l'indice général afin de rendre les taux de variation des prix plus comparables entre les pays, bien que cela n'élimine pas toutes les difficultés rencontrées en faisant de telles comparaisons. Cet indice s'entend principalement comme étant un indice sans loyer, qu'il soit réel et/ou imputé. Toutefois, si un tel indice n'est pas disponible au niveau national, ou s'il est trop difficile de le calculer, pour des raisons pratiques, les pays transmettent un indice qui exclut l'ensemble du groupe logement. Dans un tel cas, une note de bas de page signale les exclusions spécifiques (par exemple l'ensemble du groupe logement, électricité, gaz et autres combustibles, dépenses pour l'entretien et la réparation du logement, etc.).

Le tableau 7C se réfère à un indice «Alimentation», y compris les boissons non alcoolisées seulement. Dans le cas où les boissons alcoolisées et/ou le tabac sont compris dans le groupe «alimentation», l'utilisateur sera informé par un appel de note.

Les tableaux 7D à 7F présentent trois autres groupes principaux d'indices concernant respectivement: «Électricité, gaz et autres combustibles», «Habillement (y compris les chaussures)» et «Loyer». Les indices de ces groupes, y compris celui de l'alimentation, sont des composantes de l'indice général. En plus de ces quatre groupes d'indices, dans la majorité des pays l'indice général et l'indice général non compris l'habitation comprennent tous les autres principaux groupes de dépenses tels que : «Boissons alcoolisées et tabac»; «Ameublement, équipement ménager et entretien courant du foyer»; «Santé»; «Transport»; «Communications»; «Loisirs et culture»; «Education»; «Restaurants et hôtels»; et «Autres biens et services». Les indices relatifs à ces derniers groupes ne sont pas présentés séparément dans l'Annuaire, en raison des variations dans la composition des groupes d'un pays à un autre.

Les indices généraux et les indices de groupes présentés dans les tableaux correspondent aux moyennes annuelles bien que, dans la plupart des cas, les indices soient calculés mensuellement et pour quelques cas trimestriellement ou semestriellement. Les données annuelles sont calculées à partir des séries originales.

Comme la période de base originale des séries nationales varie elle aussi, on a adopté une période de base uniforme (2000) pour la présentation des données. Le plus grand nombre possible des séries ont été recalculées en divisant l'indice se rapportant à chacune des dates indiquées par l'indice pour l'année 2000 et en multipliant le quotient par 100. Lorsqu'on ne dispose de données que pour des périodes postérieures à 2000, les indices sont généralement présentés en prenant pour période de base la première année civile pour laquelle existent des données. Ces opérations n'impliquent aucune modification des systèmes de pondération, etc., utilisés par les pays.

Lorsqu'une nouvelle série est suffisamment comparable avec la précédente, elle est enchaînée avec celle-ci pour obtenir une série temporelle continue. Lorsqu'une série est interrompue et remplacée par une autre série qui ne peut être liée à la précédente soit par enchaînement soit par d'autres techniques d'estimation, une note de bas de page indique la rupture.

Note

[1] Pour le texte intégral de la résolution, voir BIT : Dix-septième Conférence internationale des statisticiens du travail, Rapport de la Conférence (Genève, 2003) ou le site Web du Département de statistique du BIT : http://www.ilo.org/stat

Precios al consumidor

La Resolución sobre índices de los precios al consumidor adoptada por la decimoséptima Conferencia Internacional de Estadísticos del Trabajo (CIET) (Ginebra, 2003)[1], estipula lo siguiente:

«1. El IPC es un indicador social y económico de coyuntura, construido para medir los cambios experimentados a lo largo del tiempo en relación con el nivel general de precios de los bienes y servicios de consumo que los hogares pagan, adquieren o utilizan para ser consumidos.

2. El índice mide también los cambios experimentados a lo largo del tiempo de los precios de consumo. Esto se puede realizar midiendo el precio de una canasta fija de bienes y servicios de calidad y características semejantes a los artículos de la canasta seleccionados para ser representativos de los gastos de los hogares durante un año o durante otro período específico. Este índice se conoce con el nombre de índice de precios de una canasta fija.

3. El índice también puede apuntar a medir los efectos que la variación de los precios puede tener en el costo necesario para lograr un nivel de vida constante (es decir, nivel de utilidad o bienestar). Este concepto se denomina índice del costo de la vida (ICV). Un índice de precios de una canasta fija, u otra medida apropiada, puede ser utilizado como una aproximación de un ICV. »

Por lo general, la estimación de un índice de los precios al consumidor se lleva a cabo coma una serie de mediciones de las variaciones relativas, de un periodo a otro, de los precios de un conjunto fijo, constante en cantidades y características, de bienes y servicios de consuma adquiridos, consumidos o pagados par la población de referencia. Cada medición es calculada coma una media ponderada de un gran número de índices de agregados elementales. Los índices de cada agregado elemental son estimados utilizando una muestra de precios de un grupo determinado de bienes o servicios obtenidos en, o par residentes de, una región especifica, a partir de un conjunto establecido de puntos de venta u otras fuentes de información.

Los índices de precios al consumidor se utilizan con diversos fines, tal como:

a) análisis generales de tipo económico y social y decisiones de políticas;

b) negociación, indización, o ambas casas, por el gobierno (especialmente de impuestos, contribuciones y beneficios de la seguridad social, remuneraciones y pensiones de los funcionarios, tasa, multas, de la deuda pública y sus intereses), en los contratos privados (sueldos, salarios, primas de seguro y servicios) y en decisiones judiciales (pensiones alimentarias);

c) la medición de los cambios «reales», o las relaciones entre el dinero y los bienes o servicios por los cuales puede ser intercambiado (v.g. para la deflación del valor agregado actual en las cuentas nacionales y de las ventas al par menor); y

d) comparaciones en las variaciones de los precios realizadas con propósitos comerciales, incluida la revaluación contable.

Para algunas de las aplicaciones mencionadas anteriormente pueden ser más convenientes los índices parciales que el índice general de todos los bienes y servicios.

Las ponderaciones son las proporciones de los gastos o del consumo correspondientes a los agregados elementales estimadas sobre la base de la información disponible. A este respecto, la decimoséptima CIET ha recomendado lo siguiente:

«23. ... Las dos principales fuentes para deducir las ponderaciones son los resultados de las encuestas de gastos de los hogares y las estimaciones de las cuentas nacionales sobre el gasto en consumo de los hogares. Los resultados de las encuestas de gastos de los hogares son indicados para un índice concebido para abarcar los gastos de consumo de los grupos de población de referencia residentes dentro del país, mientras que las estimaciones de las cuentas nacionales son adecuadas para la elaboración de índices relativos a los gastos de consumo dentro del país.

...

24. La información procedente de la fuente principal (encuestas de gastos de los hogares o cuentas nacionales) debería complementarse con toda información disponible sobre las pautas de gasto. Las fuentes de tal información que pueden utilizarse para desglosar los gastos son las encuestas de ventas en establecimientos minoristas, las encuestas relativas a los lugares de compra, las encuestas de producción, los datos sobre exportaciones e importaciones y las fuentes administrativas. Tomando como base estos datos, es posible desglosar aún más las ponderaciones correspondientes a ciertos artículos, por región y tipo de punto de venta... »

La decimoséptima CIET ha recomendado además que los precios que sirven para el cálculo de los índices sean:

«54. ...los precios de las transacciones efectivas, incluidos los impuestos indirectos y los descuentos no condicionados, que la población de referencia pagaría, acordaría o calcularía (aceptaría)..... Las propinas pagadas por los servicios, cuando sean obligatorias, deberían considerarse como parte del precio pagado.

55. No deberían incluirse los precios cobrados excepcionalmente por ventas a precios de liquidación de mercancías viejas, echadas a perder durante el almacenamiento, averiadas o deterioradas por cualquier otro motivo, salvo que la venta de estos productos constituya un fenómeno permanente y generalizado. En cambio, deberían incluirse los precios de los saldos, los descuentos, los precios reducidos y las ofertas especiales cuando se apliquen a todos los consumidores sin que se limiten de manera importante las cantidades que cada cliente puede comprar.

52. Los precios deberían recolectarse en todos los tipos de puntos de venta importantes, incluidos los vendedores por Internet, los mercados al aire libre y los mercados informales, así como en los mercados libres y en los mercados de precio controlado... »

El campo de aplicación de los índices de los precios al consumidor puede variar de un país a otro, no sólo con respecto a los tipos de hogares o grupos de población cubiertos, sino también en cuanto a su alcance geográfico.

Las practicas nacionales varían también en lo que se refiere al tratamiento de ciertos elementos que se tienen en cuenta en el cálculo de los índices de los precios al consumidor, tales como artículos estacionales, cambios de calidad, nuevos artículos, bienes duraderos y viviendas ocupadas par su propietario. Los métodos de recolección de los precios o de cálculo de los índices también son diferentes. Par esta razón, los índices de los precios al consumidor publicados en estos cuadros se deben utilizar con precaución, especialmente en materia de negociaciones colectivas y en los cálculos de indización o de deflación. Estos índices sólo pueden utilizarse si el campo de aplicación del índice de los precios al consumidor corresponde estrechamente al del tema de negociación, de indización o de deflación.

Se publican informaciones sobre el campo, las definiciones y los métodos utilizados en el cálculo de los índices de los precios al consumidor difundidos en este capítulo en Fuentes y Métodos: Estadísticas del trabajo, vol. 1: «Índices de los precios al consumidor», tercera edición (OIT, Ginebra, 1992) y en el sitio Web de las estadísticas de la OIT: http://laborsta.ilo.org.

Cuadros 7A a 7F

El cuadro 7A presenta los Índices generales de los precios al consumidor de todos los grupos de artículos de consumo en su conjunto.

El cuadro 7B se refiere a un índice general excluyendo el alquiler. La exclusión del alquiler del índice general permite mejorar la comparabilidad de las tasas de cambio de los precios entre los países, si bien no elimina todas las dificultades que surgen cuando se hacen tales comparaciones. Este índice es primordialmente un índice que excluye el alquiler (real y/o asignado). Sin embargo, si tal índice no estuviera disponible a nivel nacional o si su cálculo fuera muy difícil, entonces, par razones prácticas, los países proveen un índice que excluye el componente de vivienda. En tal caso, una nota a pie de pagina señala las exclusiones particulares (por ejemplo, todo el grupo de la vivienda, electricidad, gas y otros combustibles, los gastos de conservación y reparación de la vivienda, etcétera).

El cuadro 7C se refiere a un índice «Alimentación» incluyendo las bebidas no alcohólicas solamente. Si las bebidas alcohólicas y/o el tabaco son incluidas en el grupo «Alimentación», una nota a pie de pagina señala estos casos.

Los cuadros 7D a 7F presentan otros tres grupos principales de índices correspondientes, respectivamente, a: «Electricidad, gas y otros combustibles», «Vestido (Incl. Calzado» y «Alquiler». Los índices de estos grupos, incluyendo el índice de la alimentación, constituyen componentes del índice general. Además de los cuatro grupos de índices, el índice general y el índice general excluyendo la habitación, en la mayoría de los casos, comprenden todos los otros grupos principales de gastos: es decir «Bebidas alcohólicas y tabaco»; «Muebles, artículos para el hogar y para la conservación ordinaria del hogar»; «Sanidad» ; «Transporte» ; Comunicaciones» ; «Ocio y cultura» ; «Educación»; y «Restaurantes y hoteles», y «Otros bienes y servicios». Los índices relativos a estos últimos grupos no se presentan par separados en el Anuario par causa de las variaciones que existen de un país a otro en la composición de los mismos.

Los índices generales y los índices de grupos presentados en los cuadros corresponden a los promedios anuales, aunque en la mayor parte de los casos dichos índices se calculan mensualmente, y en algunos otros trimestral o semestralmente. Las cifras anuales se calculan tomando coma base las series originales.

En vista de que también varía el período escogido como base en las diferentes series nacionales, se ha adoptado un periodo de base uniforme (2000) para la presentación de los datos. En la medida de lo posible, se han calculado nuevamente en su mayor parte estas series dividiendo el índice de cada fecha indicada por el índice del año 2000 y multiplicando el cociente par 100. Cuando se dispone de datos sólo para los años posteriores a 2000, generalmente se presentan los índices escogiendo coma base el primer año civil accesible. Esta operación no implica ninguna modificación en el procedimiento de ponderación, etc., utilizado por los distintos países.

Cuando una nueva serie es suficientemente comparable con la anterior, se enlazan las dos series para formar una serie temporal continua.

Cuando ha habido interrupción en una serie y ha sido reemplazada por otra serie que no se puede combinar con la anterior sea por enlace sea por otras estimaciones técnicas, se indica la ruptura en una nota explicativa al pie de la página.

Nota

[1] Para el texto completo de la resolución, véase OIT: Decimoséptima Conferencia Internacional de Estadísticas del Trabajo, Informe de la Conferencia (Ginebra, 2003) o el sitio Web del Departamento de Estadística de la OIT, http://www.ilo.org/stat.

CONSUMER PRICES

General indices

PRIX À LA CONSOMMATION

Indices généraux

PRECIOS AL CONSUMIDOR

Indices generales

7A

(2000=100)

Country Pays País	1999	2000	2001	2002	2003	2004	2005	2006	2007	2008
AFRICA - AFRIQUE - AFRICA										
Algérie B	100.6	100.0	103.5	105.8	109.5	114.5	116.7	118.8	123.5	128.9
Angola (Luanda) B	23.5	100.0	252.6	527.6 ׀	1 045.8	1 501.2	1 846.0	2 091.6	2 347.7 ׀	2 640.5
Bénin (Cotonou) B	95.9	100.0	103.9	106.5	108.1	109.0	114.9	119.2	120.8	130.3
Botswana B	92.2	100.0	106.6	115.1	125.8	134.4	146.1	163.0 ׀	174.5	196.6
Burkina Faso (Ouagadougou) B	100.3	100.0	104.9	107.3	109.5	109.0	116.0	118.8	118.5	131.1
Burundi (Bujumbura) B	79.6	100.0	108.1	106.7	118.1	127.9	144.8	148.6	161.0	...
Cameroun B	98.8	100.0	104.4	107.4	108.1 ₂	108.4	110.5	116.2	117.2	123.5
Cap-Vert B	102.5	100.0	99.6	105.4	106.5	104.5	104.9	110.6	115.5 ׀	123.4
République centrafricaine (Bangui) ³ B	97.1	100.0	103.7	105.2	110.9	108.6	111.7	119.1	120.3	131.5
Congo (Brazzaville, Afric.) B	100.9	100.0	100.1	104.4	103.8	106.4	109.6	116.8	119.9	128.7
Côte d'Ivoire (Abidjan, Afric.) B	97.5	100.0	104.4	107.6	111.1	112.7	117.1	119.9	122.2	130.0
Egypt B	97.4 ׀	100.0	102.2	105.0	109.5	127.4 ׀	133.7	143.9	157.6 ׀	186.4
Ethiopia ⁴ B	.	.	*100.0*	*101.6*	*119.6*	*123.6*	*138.0*	*156.6*	*184.8* ׀	*266.8*
Addis Ababa B	98.1	100.0	94.5 ׀	93.7	100.7	105.8	113.7	129.6	...	...
Gabon (Libreville, Afric.) B	99.5	100.0	102.1	102.3	104.4	104.9	104.9	109.1	112.7 ׀	118.5
Gambia (Banjul,Kombo St. Mary) B	99.2	100.0	104.5	113.5	132.8	151.7	156.5	159.7 ׀	168.3	175.8
Ghana B	79.9	100.0	132.9	151.8	193.3	217.7	250.7	278.0	331.9 ׀	386.8
Guinea Ecuatorial (Malabo) B	.	100.0	108.8	117.0	125.5	130.9	.	144.5	...	...
Guinée (Conakry) B	93.5	100.0	105.4	108.4	122.4	141.1 ׀	185.3	249.6	306.6	362.9
Guinée-Bissau (Bissau) ⁵ B	.	.	.	.	*100.0*	*100.9*	*104.3*	*106.4*	*111.2*	*122.9*
Kenya (Nairobi) ⁶ B	94.5	100.0 ׀	103.6	105.3	116.7	133.5	149.1	178.3	195.1	249.6
Lesotho ³ B	94.2	100.0	106.9	120.1	129.0	135.5	140.1	148.4	160.6	177.8
Madagascar (Cinq régions) B	.	100.0	107.4	125.1	123.0	139.9	165.9	183.7	202.6	221.4

Explanations and sources: see p. 1067.

Explications et sources: voir p. 1069.

Explicaciones y fuentes: véase p. 1071.

¹ Series linked to former series. ² Prior to Dec. 2003: Douala and Yaoundé only. ³ Excl. "Rent". ⁴ Index base 2001=100. ⁵ Index base 2003=100. ⁶ Low income group.

¹ Série enchaînée à la précédente. ² Avant déc. 2003: Douala et Yaoundé seulement. ³ Non compris le groupe "Loyer". ⁴ Indice base 2001=100. ⁵ Indice base 2003=100. ⁶ Familles à revenu modique.

¹ Serie enlazada con la anterior. ² Antes de dic. 2003: Douala y Yaoundé solamente. ³ Excl. el grupo "Alquiler". ⁴ Indice base 2001=100. ⁵ Indice base 2003=100. ⁶ Familias de ingresos módicos.

(2000=100)

Country Pays País	1999	2000	2001	2002	2003	2004	2005	2006	2007	2008
Malawi										
B	77.2	100.0 [1]	122.7	140.8	154.3	172.0	198.5	226.1	244.1	265.4
Mali (Bamako)										
B	100.7	100.0	105.1	110.4	109.1	105.6	112.3	114.1	115.7	126.3
Maroc										
B	98.2	100.0	100.6	103.4	104.6	106.2	107.2	110.8	113.0	117.4
Mauritanie										
B	96.8	100.0	104.7	108.9	114.4	124.2 [1]	139.3	147.9	158.7	170.4
Mauritius										
B	96.0	100.0	105.4	112.2 [1]	116.5	122.1	128.1	139.5	154.9 [2]	166.5
Mozambique										
B	91.6	100.0	111.2	130.4	145.4	162.0	173.3	196.9	214.9	246.5
Maputo										
B	88.7	100.0	109.1	127.4	144.5	162.7	173.2 [1]	196.1	212.1	...
Namibia [3]										
B	.	.	.	100.0	107.1	111.6	114.1	119.9	127.9	141.1
Windhoek										
B	91.5	100.0	109.3	121.7	130.4	135.5	...	...	...	...
Niger (Niamey, Afric.) [4]										
B	97.2	100.0	104.0	106.7	105.1	105.2	113.5	113.6	113.6	126.5
Nigeria										
B	93.5	100.0	118.9	134.2	153.1 [1]	176.0	207.4	224.5	236.6	263.9
Réunion										
B	98.2	100.0	102.3	105.1	106.3	108.1	110.4	113.2	114.8	118.2
Rwanda (Kigali)										
B	96.2	100.0	103.4	105.4	113.2 [1]	126.7	138.3	150.6	164.2	189.5
Sénégal (Dakar)										
B	99.3	100.0	103.0	105.4	105.3	105.9	107.7	110.0	116.4	123.1
Seychelles										
B	94.2	100.0	106.0 [1]	106.2	109.7	114.0	115.0	114.6	122.1 [1]	167.3
Sierra Leone [5]										
B	.	.	.	100.0	114.9	131.8	142.5	160.8	182.6	
Freetown										
B	100.9	100.0	102.2	98.8	106.3	121.4	136.0	149.0	166.4	...
South Africa										
B	95.0	100.0 [1]	105.7	115.4	122.1	123.8	128.0	134.0	143.5	160.0
Saint Helena										
B	98.6	100.0 [1]	103.5	104.2	108.1	112.5	115.8	120.8	126.4	136.5
Swaziland										
B	91.0	100.0	107.7	120.2	129.0	133.5	139.9	147.3	159.2 [1]	179.8
Tanzania (Tanganyika)										
B	94.4	100.0	105.1	109.9 [1]	115.8	121.3	127.4	136.6	146.2	161.2
Tanzania (Zanzibar) [6]										
B	88.7 [7]	96.2 [8]	100.0	105.2	114.7	124.0	136.1	...	...	...
Tchad (N'Djamena)										
B	96.7	100.0	112.4	117.5 [1]	115.4	109.3	117.8	127.5	115.9	127.7 [1]
Togo (Lomé)										
B	98.2	100.0	103.9	107.1	106.0	106.5	113.7	116.3	117.3	127.5
Tunisie										
B	97.1	100.0 [1]	102.0	104.8	107.6	111.5	113.8	118.9	122.6	128.8

Explanations and sources: see p. 1067.

[1] Series linked to former series. [2] July-Dec.; series linked to former series. [3] Index base 2002=100. [4] Excl. "Rent". [5] Index base 2003=100. [6] Index base 2001=100. [7] Half-year average. [8] 10 months'average.

Explications et sources: voir p. 1069.

[1] Série enchaînée à la précédente. [2] Juillet-déc.; série enchaînée à la précédente. [3] Indice base 2002=100. [4] Non compris le groupe "Loyer". [5] Indice base 2003=100. [6] Indice base 2001=100. [7] Moyenne de six mois. [8] Moyenne de 10 mois.

Explicaciones y fuentes: véase p. 1071.

[1] Serie enlazada con la anterior. [2] Julio-dic.: serie enlazada con la anterior. [3] Indice base 2002=100. [4] Excl. el grupo "Alquiler". [5] Indice base 2003=100. [6] Indice base 2001=100. [7] Promedio de la mitad del año. [8] Promedio de 10 meses.

CONSUMER PRICES

General indices

PRIX À LA CONSOMMATION

Indices généraux

PRECIOS AL CONSUMIDOR

Indices generales

7A

Country Pays País	1999	2000	2001	2002	2003	2004	2005	2006	2007	(2000=100) 2008
Uganda B	96.8	100.0	101.9	101.6	110.5	114.5	124.1	133.3	141.4 ₁	158.5
Zambia B	79.3	100.0	121.4	148.4	180.1	212.5	251.4	274.1	303.3	341.1
Zimbabwe ² B	0.1	0.1	0.2 ₁	0.4	1.9	8.4	28.3	316.6	21 602	...

AMERICA - AMÉRIQUE - AMERICA

Country Pays País	1999	2000	2001	2002	2003	2004	2005	2006	2007	2008
Anguilla B	*92.5*	*100.0* |	*100.0* ³	*100.5*	*103.8*	*108.3*	*113.5*	*122.7*	*129.1*	*137.9*
Argentina (Buenos Aires) ⁴ B	100.9	100.0 ₁	98.9	124.5	141.3	147.5	161.7	179.4	195.2 ₁	211.9
Aruba B	96.1	100.0	102.9 ₁	106.3	110.2	113.0	116.8	121.0	128.3	139.0 ₁
Bahamas (New Providence) B	98.4	100.0	102.1	104.2	107.4	108.6	110.8	112.8	115.6	120.8
Barbados B	97.6	100.0	102.6 ₁	103.0	104.6	106.1	112.5	120.8	125.7	135.8
Belize B	99.4	100.0	101.2	103.4	106.1	109.3	113.1	118.2	120.9	128.6
Bermuda B	97.4	100.0	102.9	105.3	108.6	112.5	116.0	119.5 ₁	124.1	130.0
Bolivia ⁵ B	95.6	100.0	101.6	102.5	105.9	110.6	116.6	121.6	132.2	150.7 ₁
Brasil B	93.4	100.0	106.8	115.9	132.9	141.7	151.4	157.8	163.5	172.8
Canada B	97.4	100.0	102.6	104.8	107.8	109.8	112.2	114.4	116.9 ₁	119.6
Cayman Islands B	97.4	100.0	101.1	103.6	104.2	108.8	116.8	117.7	121.1	126.1
Colombia ⁶ B	91.3	100.0	108.6	116.5	125.0	132.5	139.6	145.2	153.4	166.0
Costa Rica ⁷ B	90.1	100.0	111.3	121.5	132.9	149.3	169.9	189.4 ₁	207.1	234.9
Cuba B	99.7	100.0	111.9	106.1	108.2	105.9	108.9	114.5	122.5	124.5
Chile (Santiago) B	96.3	100.0	103.6	106.1	109.1	110.3	113.6	117.5	122.7	133.4
Dominica B	*99.1*	*100.0* |	*100.0* ³	*100.2*	*101.6*	*104.1*	*105.8*	*108.6*	*112.1*	*119.2*
República Dominicana B	92.8	100.0	108.9	114.6	146.1	221.2	230.5	247.9	263.1	291.1
Ecuador B	51.0	100.0	137.7	154.9	167.1	171.7	175.5 ₁	181.2	185.4	200.9
El Salvador ⁵ B	97.8	100.0	103.7	105.7	107.9	112.7	118.0	122.8	128.4	137.7
Greenland B	98.3	100.0	103.0	107.2	109.0	112.0	113.3	116.2	118.5	126.3

Explanations and sources: see p. 1067.

¹ Series linked to former series. ² Due to lack of space, multiply each figure by 1000. ³ Series (base 2001=100) replacing former series. ⁴ Metropolitan areas. ⁵ Urban areas. ⁶ Low income group. ⁷ Central area.

Explications et sources: voir p. 1069.

¹ Série enchaînée à la précédente. ² En raison du manque de place, multiplier chaque chiffre par 1000. ³ Série (base 2001=100) remplaçant la précédente. ⁴ Régions métropolitaines. ⁵ Régions urbaines. ⁶ Familles à revenu modique. ⁷ Région centrale.

Explicaciones y fuentes: véase p. 1071.

¹ Serie enlazada con la anterior. ² Por falta de espacio, multiplicar cada indice por 1000. ³ Serie (base 2001=100) que substituye a la anterior. ⁴ Areas metropolitanas. ⁵ Areas urbanas. ⁶ Familias de ingresos módicos. ⁷ Región central.

CONSUMER PRICES	PRIX À LA CONSOMMATION	PRECIOS AL CONSUMIDOR
General indices	Indices généraux	Indices generales

(2000=100)

Country Pays País	1999	2000	2001	2002	2003	2004	2005	2006	2007	2008
Grenada B	97.9	100.0	103.2 [1]	104.3	106.6	109.0	...	...	...	...
Guadeloupe B	100.0	100.0	102.6	105.0	107.1	108.6	112.1	114.3	115.8	118.4
Guatemala (Guatemala) B	94.4	100.0	107.3 [1]	116.0	122.5	131.8	143.8	153.2	163.7	182.3
Guyana (Georgetown) B	94.3	100.0	102.7	108.2	114.6	120.0	128.3	136.9	153.6	166.0
Guyane française B	98.6	100.0	101.6	103.1	105.2	106.4	108.2	110.4	114.2	118.2
Haïti [2] B	87.8	100.0	114.0	125.3	174.5	214.3	255.4 [1]	286.9	311.3	359.6
Honduras B	94.3	100.0 [1]	109.6	118.0	127.1	137.5	149.5	157.9	168.9	188.1
Jamaica B	92.4	100.0	107.0	114.6	126.4	143.6	165.5	179.8	196.8 [1]	240.1
Martinique B	99.0	100.0	102.1	104.2	106.4	108.6	111.2	113.9	116.7	119.9
México B	91.3	100.0	106.4	111.7 [1]	116.8	122.3	127.15	131.77	137.0	144.0
Netherlands Antilles (Curaçao) B	94.5	100.0	101.8	102.1	103.8	105.2	109.4	113.0	116.4 [1]	124.4
Nicaragua [3] B	100.0		113.5	117.7	124.0	134.5	147.4	160.9	178.8	214.2
Panamá [4] [5] B					100.0	100.4	103.3	105.9	110.3	119.9
Paraguay (Asunción) B	91.8	100.0	107.3	118.5	135.4	141.3	149.5	165.4	178.8	196.9 [1]
Perú (Lima) [2] B	96.4	100.0	102.0	102.2 [1]	104.5	108.3	110.1	112.3	114.3	120.9
Puerto Rico B	67.2	71.5	76.6	81.3	87.6	98.1	111.7	128.0	136.7 [1]	149.8
Saint Lucia B	96.4	100.0	101.8	105.0	106.0	107.6	111.8	114.4	...	...
Saint-Pierre-et-Miquelon B	92.2	100.0	102.3	102.5	104.8	106.9	114.0	...	...	...
Saint Vincent and the Grenadines (St. Vincent) B	99.8	100.0	100.8 [1]	101.5	101.8	104.8	108.7	112.0	119.8	131.8
Suriname (Paramaribo) [6] B	45.3	77.4 [7]	100.0 [1]	115.9		156.9 [8]	171.4	190.7	203.0	232.8
Trinidad and Tobago B	96.6	100.0	105.6	109.9	114.2 [1]	118.3	126.5	137.0	147.9	165.7
United States [9] B	96.7	100.0	102.8	104.5	106.9	109.7	113.4	117.1	120.41	125.03
Uruguay (Montevideo) B	95.5	100.0	104.4	118.9	142.0	155.0	162.3	172.7	186.7	201.4

Explanations and sources: see p. 1067.

[1] Series linked to former series. [2] Metropolitan areas. [3] Index base 1999=100. [4] Urban areas. [5] Index base 2003=100. [6] Index base 2001=100. [7] April-Dec. [8] March-Dec. [9] All Urban Consumers.

Explications et sources: voir p. 1069.

[1] Série enchaînée à la précédente. [2] Régions métropolitaines. [3] Indices base 1999=100. [4] Régions urbaines. [5] Indice base 2003=100. [6] Indice base 2001=100. [7] Avril-déc. [8] Mars-déc. [9] Tous les consommateurs urbains.

Explicaciones y fuentes: véase p. 1071.

[1] Serie enlazada con la anterior. [2] Areas metropolitanas. [3] Indice base 1999=100. [4] Areas urbanas. [5] Indice base 2003=100. [6] Indice base 2001=100. [7] Abril-dic. [8] Marzo-dic. [9] Todos los consumidores urbanos.

CONSUMER PRICES

General indices

PRIX À LA CONSOMMATION

Indices généraux

PRECIOS AL CONSUMIDOR

Indices generales

7A

(2000=100)

Country Pays País	1999	2000	2001	2002	2003	2004	2005	2006	2007	2008
Venezuela, Rep. Bolivariana de (Caracas) B	86.0	100.0 ᵢ	112.5	137.8	180.6	219.9	255.0	289.8	343.9	452.1 ᵢ
Virgin Islands (British) B	97.3	100.0	103.1	103.5	107.2	108.3	110.4	...	...	...
ASIA - ASIE - ASIA										
Armenia B	100.8	100.0	103.1	104.2 ᵢ	109.2	116.3	117.0 ᵢ	121.1	126.5	137.8
Azerbaijan B	98.2	100.0	101.5	104.4	106.7	113.9	124.8	135.2	157.7	190.6
Bahrain B	100.7	100.0	98.8	98.3	100.0	102.3	104.9	107.1 ᵢ	110.6	114.4
Bangladesh ² B	97.9	100.0	101.5	105.4	111.5 ᵢ	118.4	126.7	135.3	147.6	160.7
Bhutan B	96.1	100.0	103.4	106.0	107.6	110.9 ᵢ	116.8	122.6	129.0	139.8
Brunei Darussalam B	98.8	100.0	100.6	98.3 ᵢ	98.6	99.5	100.5	100.7	101.0	103.8
Cambodia (Phnom Penh) B	100.8	100.0	99.4 ᵢ	102.7	103.9	107.9	114.1	119.5	126.5	151.4
China 	99.9	100.0	100.7	99.9	101.1	105.0	106.9	108.5	113.7	...
Georgia ³ B	96.1	100.0	104.7	110.5	115.8	122.4	132.5	144.6	158.0	173.8 ᵢ
Hong Kong, China B	103.8 ǀ	100.0 ⁴	98.4	95.4	93.0	92.6	93.6 ᵢ	95.5	97.4	101.6
India *Agricultural workers* ⁵ B	99.0	100.0	100.0	102.6	106.8	109.8	113.4	121.2	130.9	143.0
Industrial workers B	96.1	100.0	103.9	108.2	112.5	116.6	121.5	128 ᵢ	136	147
Urban non-manual employees B	95.1	100.0	105.5	109.8	113.7	118.0	123.2	130.6	139.1	149.7
Delhi, Industrial workers B	93.4	100.0	102.9	107.0	110.9	116.3	126.1	126 ᵢ	132	141
Indonesia B	96.4 ⁶	100.0	111.5	124.7	133.0	141.3 ᵢ	156.0	176.5	187.8 ᵢ	207.2
Iran, Islamic Rep. of B	87.4 ᵢ	100.0	111.3	127.3	148.2	170.1	192.9	215.9	246.1 ᵢ	309.1
Iraq B	95.3	100.0	116.4	138.9	185.5	235.6	322.6	494.3	646.8	664.0
Israel B	98.9	100.0 ᵢ	101.1	106.9 ᵢ	107.6	107.2	108.6	111.0 ᵢ	111.5	116.6
Japan B	100.7	100.0 ᵢ	99.3	98.4	98.1	98.1	97.8	98.1	98.1	99.5
Jordan B	99.3	100.0	101.8	103.6 ᵢ	105.3	108.9	112.7	119.7	126.2	145.0
Kazakhstan B	88.4	100.0	108.4	114.7	122.1	130.5	140.3	152.4	168.8	197.5
Korea, Republic of B	97.8	100.0 ᵢ	104.1	106.9	110.7	114.7	117.8 ᵢ	120.4	123.5	129.2

Explanations and sources: see p. 1067.

Explications et sources: voir p. 1069.

Explicaciones y fuentes: véase p. 1071.

¹ Series linked to former series. ² Government officials. ³ 5 cities. ⁴ Series replacing former series. ⁵ Excl. "Rent". ⁶ Beginnig November 1999: excluded Dili.

¹ Série enchaînée à la précédente. ² Fonctionnaires. ³ 5 villes. ⁴ Série remplaçant la précédente. ⁵ Non compris le groupe "Loyer". ⁶ A partir de novembre 1999: non compris Dili.

¹ Serie enlazada con la anterior. ² Funcionarios. ³ 5 ciudades. ⁴ Serie que substituye a la anterior. ⁵ Excl. el grupo "Alquiler". ⁶ A partir de noviembre 1999: excluye Dili.

CONSUMER PRICES	PRIX À LA CONSOMMATION	PRECIOS AL CONSUMIDOR
General indices	Indices généraux	Indices generales

(2000=100)

Country Pays País	1999	2000	2001	2002	2003	2004	2005	2006	2007	2008
Kuwait B	98.2	100.0 ı	101.8	102.3	103.2	104.5	108.8	112.1	118.3	130.8
Kyrgyzstan B	84.2	100.0	106.9	109.1	112.5	117.1	122.2	129.0	...	...
République dém. pop. lao B	81.2	100.0 ı	107.7	119.3	137.7	152.1	163.0	174.1	182.0	...
Macau, China B	101.6 [2]	100.0 ı	98.0	95.4	93.9	94.9	99.0 ı	104.1	109.9	119.4
Malaysia B	98.5	100.0 ı	101.4	103.2	104.4	105.9	109.1 ı	113.0	115.3	121.5
Maldives (Male) B	101.2	100.0	100.7	101.6	98.7	105.0	108.5	110.0 ı	117.5	131.6
Mongolia (Ulan Bator) B	89.6	100.0	106.3 ı	107.3	112.8	122.1	137.6	.	157.7 ı	...
Myanmar B	100.1	100.0	121.1	190.2	259.8	271.6	297.1	356.5	481.3	610.3
Nepal B	97.7	100.0	102.7	105.9	112.0	115.2	123.2	132.6	140.5	156.9
Oman (Muscat) B	101.2	100.0	99.0	98.3	97.9	98.3	100.2 ı	103.3	108.5	122.5
Pakistan B	95.8	100.0	103.2	107.4 ı	110.5	118.7	129.5	139.7	150.3	180.8
Philippines B	95.9	100.0 ı	106.8	110.1	113.9	120.6	129.8	137.9	141.8	155.0
Qatar B	98.4	100.0 ı	101.5	101.6	104.0	111.0	120.9	135.2	153.6	176.9
Saudi Arabia [3] B	100.6	100.0	99.2	98.6	97.2	99.5 ı	100.2	102.4	106.7	117.2
Singapore B	98.7	100.0	101.0	100.6	101.1	102.8 ı	103.2	104.2	106.4	113.4
Sri Lanka (Colombo) B	94.2	100.0	114.2	125.1	133.0	143.0	159.7	181.5 ı	*163.1* [4]	*199.9*
Syrian Arab Republic B	100.8	100.0	100.4	101.4	108.8 ı	113.5	121.9	134.1 ı	140.1	161.4
Taiwan, China B	98.8	100.0	100.0 ı	99.8	99.5	101.1	103.5	104.1	105.9 ı	109.7
Thailand B	98.5	100.0 ı	101.6	102.3	104.1	107.0 ı	111.8	117.0	119.6	126.1
United Arab Emirates B	98.6	100.0 ı	102.8	105.8	109.1	114.6	121.7	133.0	147.8	166.0 ı
Viet Nam B	101.6	100.0	99.7	103.7	107.0	115.0	125.5 ı	133.4 ı	143.8	177.0
West Bank and Gaza Strip B	97.3	100.0	101.2	107.0	111.7	115.1	119.1	123.5	126.9	139.2 ı
Yemen, Republic of B	95.6	100.0	111.9	125.6	139.2	156.6	174.5	211.6	232.8	249.1 ı

Explanations and sources: see p. 1067.

[1] Series linked to former series. [2] Series (base 2000=100) replacing former series; prior to 1999: excl. Rent. . [3] All cities. [4] Series (base 2002=100) replacing former series.

Explications et sources: voir p. 1069.

[1] Série enchaînée à la précédente. [2] Série (base 2000=100) remplaçant la précédente; avant 1999: non compris le groupe "Loyer". [3] Ensemble des villes. [4] Série (base 2002=100) remplaçant la précédente.

Explicaciones y fuentes: véase p. 1071.

[1] Serie enlazada con la anterior. [2] Serie (base 2000=100) que substiuye a la anteior; antes de 1999: excl. el grupo "Alquiler". [3] Todas las ciudades. [4] Serie (base 2002=100) que substituye a la anterior.

(2000=100)

Country Pays País	1999	2000	2001	2002	2003	2004	2005	2006	2007	2008
EUROPE - EUROPE - EUROPA										
Albania B	100.0	100.0 ¹	103.1	108.4	110.8	114.0	116.7	119.5	123.0	127.1 ¹
Andorre ² ³ B	.	.	*100.0*	*104.5*	*107.5*	*111.1*	*114.6*	*118.2*	*122.8*	*125.3*
Austria B	97.7	100.0 ¹	102.7	104.5	105.9	108.1	110.6	112.3 ¹	114.7	118.3
Belarus B	37.2	100.0	161.1	229.8	295.0	348.3	384.3	411.2	445.9	512.0
Belgique B	97.5	100.0	102.5	104.2	105.8	108.0 ¹	111.0	113.0	115.1	120.3
Bosnia and Herzegovina ⁴ B	.	.	.	.	.	.	100.0	106.1	107.7	115.7
Bulgaria B	90.6	100.0	107.4	113.6	116.3	123.4	129.6	139.0	150.7	169.3
Croatia B	95.0	100.0	104.5 ¹	106.3	108.2	110.4	114.0 ¹	117.7	121.1	128.4
Cyprus B	96.0	100.0	102.0	104.8	109.2	111.7	114.5	117.4 ¹	120.2	125.8
Czech Republic B	96.2	100.0 ¹	104.7	106.6	106.6	109.7	111.7	114.6	117.9	125.4
Denmark B	97.1	100.0 ¹	102.4	104.8	107.0	108.3	110.2	112.3	114.2	118.1
España B	96.7	100.0 ❘	*100.0* ⁵	*103.5*	*106.7*	*109.9*	*113.6*	*117.6* ¹	*120.9*	*125.8*
Estonia B	96.2	100.0	105.8	109.5	111.0	114.4	119.0	124.4	132.5	146.3
Faeroe Islands B	96.1	100.0	104.9	105.2 ¹	106.5	107.2	109.3	111.0	114.9	122.2
Finland B	96.7	100.0 ¹	102.6	104.2	105.1	105.3	106.2	107.9 ¹	110.6	115.0
France B	98.3	100.0	101.7	103.6	105.8	108.0	109.9	111.8	113.4	116.6
Germany B	98.1	100.0 ¹	102.0	103.4	104.5	106.2	108.3	110.1	112.5 ¹	115.4
Gibraltar B	98.9 ¹	100.0	101.8	102.5	105.2	107.6	110.9	113.8	116.9	121.2
Greece B	96.9 ¹	100.0	103.4	107.1	110.9	114.1	118.2 ¹	122.0	125.5	130.7
Hungary B	91.1	100.0	109.2	115.0	120.3	128.5	133.1	138.3	149.3	158.4
Iceland ⁶ B	95.2	100.0	106.7	111.8	114.2	117.8	122.6	130.9	137.5	154.5
Ireland B	94.7	100.0	104.8 ¹	109.7	113.5	116.0	118.8	123.5	129.5 ¹	134.8
Isle of Man B	97.3	100.0 ¹	101.7	104.1	107.3	112.8	117.5	121.0	125.9	132.4
Italy ⁷ B	97.5	100.0	102.8	105.4	108.2	110.5	112.4	114.7	116.9	120.7
Jersey ⁸ ⁹ B	95.7	100.0 ¹	103.9	108.3	112.9	118.3	122.6	126.2	131.6	139.0

Explanations and sources: see p. 1067.

¹ Series linked to former series. ² Dec. of each year. ³ Index base 2001=100. ⁴ Index base: 2005=100. ⁵ Series (base 2001=100) replacing former series. ⁶ Annual averages are based on the months Feb.-Dec. and of January of the following year. ⁷ Excl. tobacco. ⁸ June of each year. ⁹ Index base June 2000=100.

Explications et sources: voir p. 1069.

¹ Série enchaînée à la précédente. ² Déc. de chaque année. ³ Indice base 2001=100. ⁴ Base de l'indice: 2005=100. ⁵ Série (base 2001=100) remplaçant la précédente. ⁶ Les moyennes annuelles sont basées sur les mois de fév.-déc. et de janvier de l'année suivante. ⁷ Non compris le tabac. ⁸ Juin de chaque année. ⁹ Indice base juin 2000=100.

Explicaciones y fuentes: véase p. 1071.

¹ Serie enlazada con la anterior. ² Dic. de cada año. ³ Indice base 2001=100. ⁴ Base del indice: 2005=100. ⁵ Serie (base 2001=100) que substituye a la anterior. ⁶ La media anual esta basada sobre Feb.-Dic. y de enero del año siguiente. ⁷ Excl. el tabaco. ⁸ Junio de cada año. ⁹ Indice base junio 2000=100.

CONSUMER PRICES	PRIX À LA CONSOMMATION	PRECIOS AL CONSUMIDOR
General indices	Indices généraux	Indices generales

(2000=100)

Country / Pays / País	1999	2000	2001	2002	2003	2004	2005	2006	2007	2008
Kosovo (Serbia) [1] B				98.8 [2]	100.0	98.9	97.6	98.2	102.6	112.1
Latvia B	97.4	100.0 [3]	102.5	104.5	107.5	114.2	121.9	129.9	143.0	165.0
Lithuania B	99.1	100.0 [3]	101.3	101.6	100.4	101.6	104.3 [3]	108.2	114.4	126.9
Luxembourg B	96.9	100.0	102.7	104.8	106.9	109.3	112.0 [3]	115.0	117.7	121.7
Macedonia, The Former Yugoslav Rep. of B	94.5	100.0	105.5	107.4	108.7	108.2	108.8	112.3	114.8	124.4
Malta B	97.6	100.0	102.9	105.1	105.8 [3]	108.7	112.0	115.0	116.5	121.4
Moldova, Republic of B	76.2	100.0	109.8	115.6	129.2	145.3	162.7	183.5	206.2	232.5
Netherlands B	97.5	100.0 [3]	104.2	107.6	109.9	111.2	113.1	114.4	116.2 [3]	119.1
Norway B	97.0	100.0	103.0	104.4	106.9	107.4	109.1	111.6	112.4	116.7
Poland B	90.9	100.0	105.5	107.5	108.4	112.2	114.6	115.7	118.6	123.6
Portugal [4] B	97.2	100.0	104.3	108.0 [3]	111.6	114.2	116.7	120.4	123.3	126.4
Roumanie B	68.6	100.0	134.5	164.8	189.9	212.5	231.7	246.9	258.8	279.1
Russian Federation B	82.8	100.0	121.5 [3]	140.6	159.9	177.3	199.7	219.1	238.8	272.5
San Marino B	96.8	100.0			100.0 [5]	101.4	103.1	105.3	107.9	112.6
Serbia B	59.4	100.0	195.0	233.0	256.1	284.2	330.0	368.6	392.4	442.8
Slovakia B	89.3	100.0	107.1 [3]	110.7	120.2	129.2	132.8	138.7	142.5	149.0
Slovenia [6] B	91.8	100.0	108.4	116.5	123.0	127.4	130.6 [3]	133.8	138.6	146.5
Suisse B	98.5	100.0 [3]	101.0	101.7	102.3	103.1	104.4	105.4 [3]	106.1	108.8
Sweden B	99.11	100.00	102.41	104.62	106.64	107.03	107.52	108.98	111.39	115.22
Turkey B	64.5	100.0	154.4	223.8	280.4	310.1	329.5 [3]	361.1	392.7	433.7
Ukraine B	78.0	100.0	112.0	112.8	118.7	129.4	146.9	160.2	180.8	226.4
United Kingdom B	97.1	100.0	101.8	103.5	106.5	109.6	112.7	116.3	121.3	126.1

OCEANIA - OCÉANIE - OCEANIA

Country / Pays / País	1999	2000	2001	2002	2003	2004	2005	2006	2007	2008
American Samoa [4] B	98.1	100.0	101.2	103.4	108.4	116.1	122.1	125.7	...	...
Australia B	95.7	100.0	104.4	107.6	110.5	113.1	116.1	120.2	123.1	128.3

Explanations and sources: see p. 1067.
[1] Index base 2003=100. [2] May-Dec. [3] Series linked to former series. [4] Excl. "Rent". [5] Series (base 2003=100) replacing former series. [6] Urban areas.

Explications et sources: voir p. 1069.
[1] Indice base 2003=100. [2] Mai-déc. [3] Série enchaînée à la précédente. [4] Non compris le groupe "Loyer". [5] Série (base 2003=100) remplaçant la précédente. [6] Régions urbaines.

Explicaciones y fuentes: véase p. 1071.
[1] Indice base 2003=100. [2] Mayo-dic. [3] Serie enlazada con la anterior. [4] Excl. el grupo "Alquiler". [5] Serie (base 2003=100) que substituye a la anterior. [6] Areas urbanas.

CONSUMER PRICES

General indices

PRIX À LA CONSOMMATION

Indices généraux

PRECIOS AL CONSUMIDOR

Indices generales

(2000=100)

Country Pays País	1999	2000	2001	2002	2003	2004	2005	2006	2007	2008
Cook Islands (Rarotonga) B	97.0	100.0	108.7	112.4	114.6	115.6	118.5	122.4	125.5 [1]	135.4
Fiji B	98.9	100.0	104.3	105.0	109.4	112.5	115.1	118.1	123.7 [1]	133.3
Guam B	98.0	100.0	98.7	99.4	102.0	108.1	116.3	129.8	138.6	147.1 [1]
Kiribati (Tarawa) B	99.6	100.0	106.0	109.4	111.4	110.3	110.0	108.3	112.9	125.3
Marshall Islands (Majuro) B	98.4	100.0	101.8	103.0	100.1	102.3	106.9	111.5	115.0	135.2
New Zealand B	97.5	100.0	102.6	105.4	107.2	109.7	113.0	116.8 [1]	119.6	124.4
Niue B	96.6	100.0	106.8	109.7	112.3 [1]	116.6 [2]	117.0	119.7	127.8	139.3
Norfolk Island B	96.4	100.0	103.1	105.9	109.1	118.6	125.2	134.4	...	...
Northern Mariana Islands (Saipan) B	98.0	100.0	99.2	99.4	98.4 [1]	99.3	99.8	104.7	111.9	117.2
Nouvelle-Calédonie (Nouméa) B	98.5	100.0	102.3	104.1	105.4	106.2	107.6	110.7	111.8	115.1
Papua New Guinea B	86.5	100.0	109.3	122.2	140.2	143.2	145.7	149.2	150.6	166.8
Polynésie française B	99.0	100.0	101.0	103.9	104.3 [1]	104.8	105.8	108.7	110.9	114.4 [1]
Samoa [3] B	98.9 [1]	100.0	103.7	112.2	112.3	130.5 [1]	133.0	138.1	145.7	162.4
Solomon Islands (Honiara) B	93.6	100.0	107.8	119.5	129.4	138.7	149.3	161.2	178.1 [1]	208.9
Tonga [3] B	93.7	100.0	108.3	119.5 [1]	133.5	148.1	160.4	172.0	180.8	198.9
Tuvalu (Funafuti) B	96.2	100.0	101.5	106.7 [1]	110.2	113.3	117.0	119.0	121.6 [1]	...
Vanuatu B	97.5 [1]	100.0	103.6	105.7	108.8	110.4	111.7	114.0	118.5	124.2

Explanations and sources: see p. 1067.

[1] Series linked to former series. [2] Average of the last three quarters. [3] Excl. "Rent".

Explications et sources: voir p. 1069.

[1] Série enchaînée à la précédente. [2] Moyenne des trois derniers trimestres. [3] Non compris le groupe "Loyer".

Explicaciones y fuentes: véase p. 1071.

[1] Serie enlazada con la anterior. [2] Promedio de los tres últimos trimestres. [3] Excl. el grupo "Alquiler".

PRIX À LA CONSOMMATION

Indices généraux, non compris le logement

PRECIOS AL CONSUMIDOR

Indices generales, excluyendo la vivienda

7B

(2000=100)

Country / Pays / País	1999	2000	2001	2002	2003	2004	2005	2006	2007	2008
AFRICA - AFRIQUE - AFRICA										
République centrafricaine (Bangui) B	97.1	100.0	103.7	105.2	110.9	108.6	111.7	119.1	120.3	131.5
Côte d'Ivoire (Abidjan, Afric.) [1]	.	.	.	100.0	105.6	103.4	105.8	106.8	...	...
Lesotho B	94.2	100.0	106.9	120.1	129.0	135.5	140.1	148.4	160.6	177.8
Madagascar (Cinq régions) [2]	.	100.0	106.1	123.4	119.6	136.7	164.1	179.3	198.1	216.6
Mauritius	95.9	100.0	105.5	97.4 [3]	100.0	104.8	110.0	119.9	94.3 [4]	100.0
Niger (Niamey, Afric.) B	97.2	100.0	104.0	106.7	105.1	105.2	113.5	113.6	113.6	126.5
Sénégal (Dakar)	99.7	100.0	103.1	105.6	105.5	106.6	107.9	110.5	117.1	...
South Africa [5]	92.7	100.0 [6]	106.3	115.6	122.3	127.4	132.2	138.4	147.4	165.1
Tunisie	.	100.0 [7]	101.9	104.7	107.5	111.4	113.6	118.7	122.5	...
AMERICA - AMÉRIQUE - AMERICA										
Argentina (Buenos Aires) [8]	100.7	100.0 [6]	98.8	127.1	145.0	151.4	165.6	183.6	...	...
Aruba [9]	.	.	100.0	103.1	106.3	109.2	111.7	114.4	120.1	128.7
Bermuda [10] B	.	.	.	.	.	.	.	100.0 [11]	104.0	...
Canada [2] [12] [13]	97.7	100.0	102.1	104.9	107.5	109.3	100.0	112.9	114.8 [6]	...
Colombia [14]	90.9	100.0	109.3	118.2	127.0	134.5	142.2	148.1	157.4	171.6
Costa Rica [15]	90.3	100.0	109.9	120.2	132.1	147.7	168.5	...	...	...
Netherlands Antilles (Curaçao) B	93.8	100.0	101.7	101.8	103.8	105.1	109.0	100.0 [11]	103.1	111.2
Panamá [16] [17]	.	.	.	100.0	100.6	103.6	106.1	110.5	...	
Puerto Rico	93.9	100.0	107.1	113.6	122.6	137.3	156.3	.	100.0 [18]	109.4
United States [12] [19]	96.7	100.0	102.4	103.1	105.4	108.2	112.3	115.8	118.67	123.99
Uruguay (Montevideo)	95.4	100.0	104.4	119.4	142.3	155.2	162.2	172.1	185.9	199.6

Explanations and sources: see p. 1067.

[1] Index base 2002=100. [2] Excl. Water, Electricity, Gas and Other Fuels. [3] July-Dec.; series (base 2003=100) replacing former series. [4] July-Dec.; series (base 2008=100) replacing former series. [5] Excl. "Housing". [6] Series linked to former series. [7] Series (base 2000=100) replacing former series. [8] Metropolitan areas. [9] Index base 2001=100. [10] Index base: 2006=100. [11] Series (base 2006=100) replacing former series. [12] Excl. also expenditure on insurance, maintenance and repairs. [13] Excl. also property taxes, mortgage interest and replacement costs. [14] Low income group. [15] Central area. [16] Urban areas. [17] Index base 2003=100. [18] Series (base 2007=100) replacing former series. [19] All Urban Consumers.

Explications et sources: voir p. 1069.

[1] Indice base 2002=100. [2] Non compris l'eau, l'électricité, le gaz et autres combustibles. [3] Juillet-Déc.; série (base 2003=100) remplaçant la précédente. [4] Juillet-Déc.; série (base 2008=100) remplaçant la précédente. [5] Non compris le groupe "Logement". [6] Série enchaînée à la précédente. [7] Série (base 2000=100) remplaçant la précédente. [8] Régions métropolitaines. [9] Indice base 2001=100. [10] Base de l'indice: 2006=100. [11] Série (base 2006=100) remplaçant la précédente. [12] Non compris aussi les dépenses pour l'assurance, l'entretien et la réparation. [13] Non compris aussi les impôts sur la propriété, intérêts hypothécaires et coûts de remplacement. [14] Familles à revenu modique. [15] Région centrale. [16] Régions urbaines. [17] Indice base 2003=100. [18] Série (base 2007=100) remplaçant la précédente. [19] Tous les consommateurs urbains.

Explicaciones y fuentes: véase p. 1071.

[1] Indice base 2002=100. [2] Excl. el agua, la electricidad, el gas y otros combustibles. [3] Julio-dic.; serie (base 2003=100) que sustituye a la anterior. [4] Julio-dic.; serie (base 2008=100) que sustituye a la anterior. [5] Excl. el grupo "Vivienda". [6] Serie enlazada con la anterior. [7] Serie (base 2000=100) que substituye a la anterior. [8] Areas metropolitanas. [9] Indice base 2001=100. [10] Base del índice: 2006=100. [11] Serie (base 2006=100) que substituye a la anterior. [12] Excl. también los gastos de seguridad, conservación y reparación. [13] Excl. también los impuestos de propiedad, interés por hipoteca y costo de reemplazo. [14] Familias de ingresos módicos. [15] Región central. [16] Areas urbanas. [17] Indice base 2003=100. [18] Serie (base 2007=100) que substituye a la anterior. [19] Todos los consumidores urbanos.

7B	CONSUMER PRICES General indices, excluding housing			PRIX À LA CONSOMMATION Indices généraux, non compris le logement			PRECIOS AL CONSUMIDOR Indices generales, excluyendo la vivienda (2000=100)			
Country Pays País	1999	2000	2001	2002	2003	2004	2005	2006	2007	2008
ASIA - ASIE - ASIA										
Armenia	100.8	100.0	103.1	104.3 ı	109.2	116.2	116.9 ı	120.9	126.2	137.6
Cambodia (Phnom Penh)	101.8	100.0 ı	*100.0* [2]	*101.2*	*102.7*	*107.7*	*115.4*	*122.5*	*131.9*	...
Georgia [3]	96.1	100.0	104.6	110.5	115.8	122.4	132.4	144.3	156.2	...
Hong Kong, China [4]	*161.2* ı	100.0 [5]	99.0	97.1	95.5	96.8	98.0 ı	98.8	100.9	105.3
India *Agricultural workers* B	99.0	100.0	100.0	102.6	106.8	109.8	113.4	121.2	130.9	143.0
Industrial workers	96.1	100.0	103.2	107.0	110.9	114.5	118.0	126 ı	135	148
Delhi, Industrial workers	92.7	100.0	102.8	106.9	110.9	115.0	118.0	125.5 ı	134.7	144.0
Iran, Islamic Rep. of	87.8	100.0	107.9	121.8	139.9	158.3	178.1	...	...	...
Israel	98.1	100.0 ı	100.4	104.5 ı	107.0	107.2	109.1	111.6 ı	112.9	118.5
Japan [6]	100.9	100.0 ı	99.1	98.0	97.7	97.7	97.3	97.6	97.7	99.2
Korea, Republic of	97.5	100.0 ı	104.1	106.5	110.2	114.5 ı	118.1 [7]	121.1	124.1	130.3
Macau, China	101.2 ı	100.0	98.1	95.6	94.2	95.5	99.2	102.7	106.8	114.8
Malaysia [8]					*100.0* [9]	*101.6*	*105.0*	*109.3*	...	...
Oman (Muscat) [10]	101.4	100.0	98.6	97.9	97.3	97.8	101.2 ı	104.9	110.1	123.0
Philippines	96.0	100.0 ı	106.7	109.5	113.2	120.4	130.4	139.2	143.4	158.0
Singapore	98.2	100.0	101.0	100.7	101.5	103.5 ı	104.1	105.1	107.4	113.3
Sri Lanka (Colombo)	94.2	100.0	114.2	125.1	133.0	143.1	159.8	...	...	...
Syrian Arab Republic [11]							*100.0*	*110.5*	*112.3*	*127.4*
EUROPE - EUROPE - EUROPA										
Albania	100.0	100.0	103.1	108.6	112.0	114.8	117.1	119.2	...	...
Austria	97.7	100.0 ı	102.7	104.5	105.8	107.9	110.4	111.9 ı	114.4	...
Belgique	98.0	100.0	102.4	104.3	106.0	108.1	110.6	111.9	...	...
Bulgaria	87.3	100.0	107.4	113.6	116.3	123.4	129.6	139.1	150.8	169.4
Czech Republic	96.5	100.0 ı	104.1	105.5	105.2	107.5	107.1	108.8	114.7	118.1

Explanations and sources: see p. 1067.

Explications et sources: voir p. 1069.

Explicaciones y fuentes: véase p. 1071.

[1] Series linked to former series. [2] Series (base 2001=100) replacing former series. [3] 5 cities. [4] Index base: 1990=100. [5] Series (base 2000=100) replacing former series. [6] Excl. rental value of owner occupied dwellings. [7] Series replacing former series; prior to 2005: Excl. Rent. [8] Index base 2003=100. [9] Series (base 2003=100) replacing former series. [10] Excl. Water, Electricity, Gas and Other Fuels. [11] Index base: 2005=100.

[1] Série enchaînée à la précédente. [2] Série (base 2001=100) remplaçant la précédente. [3] 5 villes. [4] Indices base: 1990=100. [5] Série (base 2000=100) remplaçant la précédente. [6] Non compris la valeur locative des logements occupés par leurs propriétaires. [7] Série remplaçant la précédente; avant 2005: non compris le loyer. [8] Indice base 2003=100. [9] Série (base 2003=100) remplaçant la précédente. [10] Non compris l'eau, l'électricité, le gaz et autres combustibles. [11] Base de l'indice: 2005=100.

[1] Serie enlazada con la anterior. [2] Serie (base 2001=100) que substituye a la anterior. [3] 5 ciudades. [4] Indices base: 1990=100. [5] Serie (base 2000=100) que substituye a la anterior. [6] Excl. el valor locativo de la vivienda ocupada por su propietario. [7] Serie base que substituye a la anterior; antes de 2005: excl. el alquiler. [8] Indice base 2003=100. [9] Serie (base 2003=100) que substituye a la anterior. [10] Excl. el agua, la electricidad, el gas y otros combustibles. [11] Base del índice: 2005=100.

CONSUMER PRICES

General indices, excluding housing

PRIX À LA CONSOMMATION

Indices généraux, non compris le logement

PRECIOS AL CONSUMIDOR

Indices generales, excluyendo la vivienda

(2000=100)

Country Pays País	1999	2000	2001	2002	2003	2004	2005	2006	2007	2008
Denmark	97.2	100.0 ¹	102.3	104.7	106.7	107.6	109.4	111.4	113.1	117.3
España	96.7	100.0 ¦	100.0 ²	103.5	106.6	109.9	113.5	117.5 ¹	120.7	125.6
Estonia	95.8	100.0	105.2	107.8	108.8	111.9	116.2	120.4	126.1	137.5
Finland	96.7	100.0 ¹	102.5	104.0	104.8	104.8	105.6	106.4 ¹	108.2	112.1
France	98.2	100.0	103.6	101.7	105.8	107.9	109.7	111.4	111.7	114.9
Germany	98.5	100.0	102.2	103.6	104.7	106.7	109.1	111.0 ¹	113.9	117.4
Gibraltar ³	98.4	100.0	101.3	102.8	105.8	108.0	110.3	113.5	115.6	120.5
Greece	96.9 ¹	100.0	103.3	107.0	110.7	113.8	117.8 ¹	121.5	124.9	130.0
Hungary ⁴	91.0	100.0	109.1	114.9	120.2	128.4	133.0	138.1	157.3	166.9
Iceland ⁵	96.5	100.0	106.8	111.7	112.5	114.9	116.0	121.6	124.6	139.8
Ireland	95.0	100.0	104.0 ¹	109.1	113.7	116.1	118.3	121.3	124.2 ¹	128.2
Isle of Man	97.8	100.0 ¹	101.8	105.2	108.3	113.5	118.3	122.0	125.9	133.7
Italy	97.5	100.0	102.9	105.4	108.2	110.3	112.3	114.5	116.5	120.4
Jersey ⁶ ⁷	.	100.0	103.8	108.4	113.4	117.3	120.2	123.9	126.7	134.0
Latvia	97.4	100.0 ¹	102.5	104.5	107.6	114.2	121.9	129.8	142.7	164.6
Lithuania	100.0	100.0	100.8	101.1	99.7	100.7	103.1	106.8	112.8	125.5
Luxembourg ⁸	96.9	100.0	102.6	104.7	106.9	109.4	111.5 ¹	114.0	116.4	119.6
Macedonia, The Former Yugoslav Rep. of	94.6	100.0	105.3	107.1	108.3	107.9	108.4	112.0	114.3	123.9
Malta ⁹	.	.	.	.	.	100.0	102.8	105.5	106.7	...
Netherlands	97.6	100.0 ¹	104.4	107.9	110.0	110.9	112.6	113.6	117.8 ¹	123.1
Poland ¹⁰	91.2	100.0	105.1	106.8	107.5	111.3	113.5	114.5	117.2	122.1
Portugal B	97.2	100.0	104.3	108.0 ¹	111.6	114.2	116.7	120.4	123.3	126.4
Roumanie	68.6	100.0	134.5	164.8	189.9	212.5	231.7	246.9	258.8	279.1
Slovenia ¹¹	91.4	100.0	108.4	116.4	122.6	126.9	129.7 ¹	132.8	137.6	145.3

Explanations and sources: see p. 1067.

¹ Series linked to former series. ² Series (base 2001=100) replacing former series. ³ Excl. housing, water, electriciy and other fuels. ⁴ Excl. rental value of owner occupied dwellings. ⁵ Annual averages are based on the months Feb.-Dec. and of January of the following year. ⁶ June of each year. ⁷ Index base June 2000=100. ⁸ Excl. Water, Electricity, Gas and Other Fuels. ⁹ Index base: 2004=100. ¹⁰ Excl. water supply. ¹¹ Urban areas.

Explications et sources: voir p. 1069.

¹ Série enchaînée à la précédente. ² Série (base 2001=100) remplaçant la précédente. ³ Non compris le logement, l'eau, l'électricité autres combustibles. ⁴ Non compris la valeur locative des logements occupés par leurs propriétaires. ⁵ Les moyennes annuelles sont basées sur les mois de fév.-déc. et de janvier de l'année suivante. ⁶ Juin de chaque année. ⁷ Indice base juin 2000=100. ⁸ Non compris l'eau, l'électricité, le gaz et autres combustibles. ⁹ Base de l'indice: 2004=100. ¹⁰ Non compris l'approvisionnement de l'eau. ¹¹ Régions urbaines.

Explicaciones y fuentes: véase p. 1071.

¹ Serie enlazada con la anterior. ² Serie (base 2001=100) que substituye a la anterior. ³ Excl. la vivienda, el agua, la electricidad y otros combustibles. ⁴ Excl. el valor locativo de la vivienda ocupada por su propietario. ⁵ Le media anual esta basada sobre Feb.-Dic. y de enero del año siguiente. ⁶ Junio de cada año. ⁷ Indice base junio 2000=100. ⁸ Excl. el agua, la electricidad, el gas y otros combustibles. ⁹ Base del indice: 2004=100. ¹⁰ Excl. el suministro del agua. ¹¹ Areas urbanas.

CONSUMER PRICES		PRIX À LA CONSOMMATION			PRECIOS AL CONSUMIDOR				
General indices, excluding housing		Indices généraux, non compris le logement			Indices generales, excluyendo la vivienda				
									(2000=100)

Country Pays País	1999	2000	2001	2002	2003	2004	2005	2006	2007	2008
Suisse	98.5	100.0 ¹	100.5	101.0	101.8	102.5	103.6	104.5 ¹	104.9	107.4
Sweden	99.09	100.00	101.80	103.72	104.72	105.22	105.75	106.21	108.73	113.32
United Kingdom	98.5	100.0	101.5	102.9	104.7	106.0	107.7	110.5	113.6	118.6
OCEANIA - OCÉANIE - OCEANIA										
American Samoa B	98.1	100.0	101.2	103.4	108.4	116.1	122.1	125.7	...	...
Australia	96.2	100.0	104.3	107.4	109.9	112.1	114.7	118.8	121.1	125.4
New Zealand	97.3	100.0	103.6	106.3	107.2	108.5	111.1	114.2 ¹	116.2	120.5
Samoa B	98.9 ¹	100.0	103.7	112.2	112.3	130.5 ¹	133.0	138.1	145.7	162.4
Tonga B	93.7	100.0	108.3	119.5 ¹	133.5	148.1	160.4	172.0	180.8	198.9

Explanations and sources: see p. 1067.	Explications et sources: voir p. 1069.	Explicaciones y fuentes: véase p. 1071.
¹ Series linked to former series.	¹ Série enchaînée à la précédente.	¹ Serie enlazada con la anterior.

CONSUMER PRICES

Food indices, including non-alcoholic beverages

PRIX À LA CONSOMMATION

Indices de l'alimentation, y compris les boissons non alcoolisées

PRECIOS AL CONSUMIDOR

Indices de la alimentación, incluyendo las bebidas no alcohólicas

7C

(2000=100)

Country Pays País	1999	2000	2001	2002	2003	2004	2005	2006	2007	2008
AFRICA - AFRIQUE - AFRICA										
Algérie B	102.2	100.0	104.4	106.2	111.0	116.4	116.6	119.3	126.7	134.6
Angola (Luanda) B	25.7	100.0	251.1 ¹	508.6	1 062.4 ¹	1 587.5	1 957.0	2 292.4	2 617.7	3 103.8
Bénin (Cotonou) ² B	98.8	100.0	102.3	108.0	105.5	104.7	114.4	113.8	112.6	132.9
Botswana B	95.5	100.0	102.6	112.2	125.0	130.9	137.9	155.2 ¹	172.7	207.7
Burkina Faso (Ouagadougou) B	106.1	100.0	108.8	112.2	110.3	104.9	120.2	120.0	117.9	145.4
Burundi (Bujumbura) B	77.2	100.0	100.6	95.5	107.5	119.0	139.4	139.5	151.6	...
Cameroun B	97.8	100.0	107.0	112.1	111.4 ³	109.2	110.3	117.9	119.1	130.0
Cap-Vert B	101.8	100.0	105.3	. ⎟	100.0 ⁴	96.5	96.4	102.7	107.9	117.7
République centrafricaine (Bangui) B	96.3	100.0	104.7	106.8	112.4	107.2	110.9	118.9	121.1	134.9
Congo (Brazzaville, Afric.) B	105.5	100.0	98.3	102.9	96.9	90.8	95.6	105.3	...	...
Côte d'Ivoire (Abidjan, Afric.) ² B	100.0	100.0	105.7	111.6	116.1	111.6	114.3	117.5	123.8	137.8
Egypt ⁵ B	97.6 ¹	100.0	101.1	105.3	112.3 ⎟	100.0 ⁶	105.0	115.7	130.6 ¹	162.0
Ethiopia ⁷ B	.	.	100.0	102.6	130.9	134.8	153.3	175.2	214.3 ¹	343.0
Addis Ababa B	101.1	100.0	87.6 ¹	85.7	98.8	102.4	111.2	132.9	...	...
Gabon (Libreville, Afric.) ⁸ B	99.5	100.0	105.0	105.2	107.1	105.1	105.5	112.2 ⎟	100.0 ⁹	107.8
Gambia (Banjul, Kombo St. Mary) B	99.8	100.0	99.3	117.2	141.2	164.0	169.2	172.2 ¹	185.8	197.1
Ghana B	89.4	100.0	123.2	145.6	181.6	211.8	244.7	267.2	300.6 ¹	346.2
Guinea Ecuatorial (Malabo) ¹⁰ B	178.2 ⎟	100.0 ¹¹	111.5	122.2	130.0	135.7	.	153.6	...	...
Guinée (Conakry) B	96.2	100.0	.	114.4 ¹²	138.8	168.3	230.6	328.6	422.2	509.2
Guinée-Bissau (Bissau) ² B	93.2	100.0	.	. ⎟	100.0 ⁴	101.1	104.7	105.2	111.3	129.1
Kenya (Nairobi) ¹³ B	96.8	100.0 ¹	102.4	103.9	120.9	143.8	164.8	210.8	233.8	315.9

Explanations and sources: see p. 1067.

¹ Series linked to former series. ² Incl. alcoholic beverages and tobacco. ³ Prior to Dec. 2003: Douala and Yaoundé only. ⁴ Series (base 2003=100) replacing former series. ⁵ Incl. tobacco. ⁶ Series (base 2004=100) replacing former series; prior to 2004: incl. tobacco. ⁷ Index base 2001=100. ⁸ Incl. beverages and tobacco. ⁹ Series (base 2007=100) replacing former series; prior to 2007: incl. beverages and tobacco. ¹⁰ Index base: 1990=100. ¹¹ Series (base 2000=100) replacing former series. ¹² July-Dec.; series linked to former series. ¹³ Low income group.

Explications et sources: voir p. 1069.

¹ Série enchaînée à la précédente. ² Y compris les boissons alcoolisées et le tabac. ³ Avant déc. 2003: Douala et Yaoundé seulement. ⁴ Série (base 2003=100) remplaçant la précédente. ⁵ Y compris le tabac. ⁶ Série (base 2004=100) remplaçant la précédente; avant 2004: y compris le tabac. ⁷ Indice base 2001=100. ⁸ Y compris les boissons et le tabac. ⁹ Série (base 2007=100) remplaçant la précédente; avant 2007: y compris les boissons et le tabac. ¹⁰ Indices base: 1990=100. ¹¹ Série (base 2000=100) remplaçant la précédente. ¹² Juillet-déc.; série enchaînée à la précédente. ¹³ Familles à revenu modique.

Explicaciones y fuentes: véase p. 1071.

¹ Serie enlazada con la anterior. ² Incl. las bebidas alcohólicas y el tabaco. ³ Antes de dic. 2003: Douala y Yaoundé solamente. ⁴ Serie (base 2003=100) que substituye a la anterior. ⁵ Incl. el tabaco. ⁶ Serie base (2004=100) que substituye a la anterior: antes de 2004: incl. el tabaco. ⁷ Indice base 2001=100. ⁸ Incl. las bebidas y el tabaco. ⁹ Serie base (2007=100) que substituye a la anterior: antes de 2007: incl. las bebidas y el tabaco. ¹⁰ Indices base: 1990=100. ¹¹ Serie (base 2000=100) que substituye a la anterior. ¹² Julio-dic.: serie enlazada con la anterior. ¹³ Familias de ingresos módicos.

CONSUMER PRICES	PRIX À LA CONSOMMATION	PRECIOS AL CONSUMIDOR
Food indices, including non-alcoholic beverages	Indices de l'alimentation, y compris les boissons non alcoolisées	Indices de la alimentación, incluyendo las bebidas no alcohólicas

(2000=100)

Country Pays País	1999	2000	2001	2002	2003	2004	2005	2006	2007	2008
Lesotho [1] B	95.6	100.0	106.5	134.8	142.4	148.1	152.0	165.9	189.9	220.0
Madagascar (Cinq régions) [2] B	.	100.0	101.9	117.2	112.9	134.7	170.2	180.8	202.1	223.2
Malawi B	83.5	100.0 [3]	117.6	136.4	143.6	154.4	181.0	209.1	224.7	240.3
Mali (Bamako) [4] B	104.7	100.0	108.0	115.8	111.1	103.3	115.1	114.6	117.3	132.6
Maroc [5] B	98.5	100.0	99.0	103.2	104.6	106.2	106.5	110.7	114.3	122.1
Mauritanie B	96.3	100.0	106.5	111.3	117.9 [6]	131.2 [3]	149.3	157.3	173.9	190.6
Mauritius B	98.7	100.0	104.0	112.2 [3]	115.4	122.3	129.5	142.4	168.9 [7]	190.7
Mozambique B	93.1	100.0	110.6	132.3	148.8	164.9	173.9	203.6	224.6	...
Maputo B	89.4	100.0	107.9	126.4	147.9	169.9 [3]	175.7	205.6	224.0	...
Namibia [8] B	.	.	.	*100.0*	*109.5*	*110.4*	*112.0*	*119.3*	*133.8*	*156.6*
Windhoek B	93.5	100.0	111.5	133.2	144.1	147.1	...	...	...	...
Niger (Niamey, Afric.) [5] B	97.0	100.0	107.1	111.9	106.7	105.1	120.7	118.4	117.6	141.8
Nigeria B	97.6	100.0	128.0	144.8	153.8 [3]	175.8	216.3	228.3	232.6	270.0
Réunion B	99.3	100.0	101.5	108.3	107.5	107.5	108.8	111.2	114.0	121.5
Rwanda (Kigali) B	99.1	100.0	106.0	104.7	119.2 [3]	141.7	156.1	171.5	185.0	215.2
Sénégal (Dakar) [5] B	101.1	100.0	104.9	110.1	109.4	110.3	114.5	116.0	124.4	136.4
Seychelles B	98.6	100.0	104.9 [3]	105.6	108.2	109.2	110.3	114.3	125.6 [3]	173.8
Sierra Leone [9] B	.	.	.	*100.0*	*120.1*	*137.6*	*141.0*	*159.3*	*186.4*	
Freetown B	100.4	100.0	105.2	104.4	112.2	.	146.0	156.6	173.8	...
South Africa [1] B	92.8	100.0 [3]	105.4	122.0	131.9	134.9	137.9	147.8	163.1	190.0
Saint Helena B	99.4	100.0 [3]	102.5	99.0	102.7	108.8	112.7	117.0	117.2	131.2
Swaziland	93.7	100.0	106.5	129.8	145.7	155.7	169.2	194.1 [3]	228.3	271.5
Tanzania (Tanganyika) B	93.6	100.0	106.1	110.5 [3]	117.8	127.5	133.5	142.9	152.9	172.2
Tanzania (Zanzibar) [10] B	*95.0* [1]	*96.1* [12]	*100.0*	*106.9*	*116.7*	*128.6*	*143.7*	...	...	...
Tchad (N'Djamena) B	92.9	100.0	119.3	125.8 [3]	122.6	116.0	129.2	144.0	129.9 [3]	151.2

Explanations and sources: see p. 1067.

[1] Food only. [2] Incl. beverages and tobacco. [3] Series linked to former series. [4] Beginning January 1998: incl. beverages and tobacco. [5] Incl. tobacco. [6] Jan.-Nov. [7] July-Dec.; series linked to former series. [8] Index base 2002=100. [9] Index base 2003=100. [10] Index base 2001=100. [11] Half-year average. [12] 10 months'average.

Explications et sources: voir p. 1069.

[1] Alimentation seulement. [2] Y compris les boissons et le tabac. [3] Série enchaînée à la précédente. [4] A partir de janvier 1998: y compris les boissons et le tabac. [5] Y compris le tabac. [6] janv.-nov. [7] Juillet-déc.; série enchaînée à la précédente. [8] Indice base 2002=100. [9] Indice base 2003=100. [10] Indice base 2001=100. [11] Moyenne de six mois. [12] Moyenne de 10 mois.

Explicaciones y fuentes: véase p. 1071.

[1] Alimentación solamente. [2] Incl. las bebidas y el tabaco. [3] Serie enlazada con la anterior. [4] A partir de enero 1998: incl. las bebidas y el tabaco. [5] Incl. el tabaco. [6] enero-nov. [7] Julio-dic.: serie enlazada con la anterior. [8] Indice base 2002=100. [9] Indice base 2003=100. [10] Indice base 2001=100. [11] Promedio de la mitad del año. [12] Promedio de 10 meses.

CONSUMER PRICES

Food indices, including non-alcoholic beverages

PRIX À LA CONSOMMATION

Indices de l'alimentation, y compris les boissons non alcoolisées

PRECIOS AL CONSUMIDOR

Indices de la alimentación, incluyendo las bebidas no alcohólicas

(2000=100)

Country Pays País	1999	2000	2001	2002	2003	2004	2005	2006	2007	2008
Togo (Lomé) [1] B	103.5	100.0	105.2	109.3	103.1	101.9	113.0	111.7	114.9	138.3
Tunisie B	95.6	100.0 [2]	102.0	106.1	109.7	115.1	115.2	121.4	124.8	132.6
Uganda B	99.0	100.0	96.6	92.5	106.7	111.4	126.1	139.1	142.8 [2]	171.1
Zambia [1] B	81.6	100.0	118.9	151.1	184.5	214.7	254.5	267.1	281.1	319.9
Zimbabwe [3] B	0.1	0.1	0.2 [2]	0.4	1.8	8.6	27.9	316.0	23 620	...

AMERICA - AMÉRIQUE - AMERICA

Country	1999	2000	2001	2002	2003	2004	2005	2006	2007	2008
Anguilla B	98.9	100.0	*100.0* [4]	*100.5*	*98.0*	*102.1*	*105.4*	*112.4*	*119.4*	*137.5*
Argentina (Buenos Aires) [5] B	102.7	100.0 [2]	98.1	132.0	157.3	165.1	183.3	205.5	228.5 [2]	243.9
Aruba B	98.2	100.0	103.3 [2]	106.7	110.1	114.4	118.7	124.1	137.6	156.8 [2]
Bahamas (New Providence) B	98.4	100.0	102.1	104.1	104.7	107.8	111.2	116.4	120.5	128.6
Barbados B	97.5	100.0	105.2 [2]	107.1	110.1	115.0	123.1	132.8	142.2	161.4
Belize [6] B	99.4	100.0	100.5	101.6	104.2	106.9	111.8	116.6	122.7	139.0
Bermuda B	97.8	100.0	102.0	103.5	105.6	108.2	111.4	113.6 [2]	117.6	124.1
Bolivia [7] B	97.9	100.0	100.6	99.7	103.2	109.3	115.7	122.2	138.9	174.5
Brasil [8] B	95.1	100.0	106.7	117.0	140.8	146.5	151.0	151.0	161.2	182.3
Canada B	98.7	100.0	104.5	107.2	109.1	111.3	114.1	116.8	119.9 [2]	124.1
Cayman Islands B	98.3	100.0	103.5	105.7	109.1	113.9	117.0	120.1	126.3	133.4
Colombia [9] B	91.7	100.0	108.7	118.4	127.2	134.6	143.1	150.5	162.5	182.6
Costa Rica [6] [10] B	91.1	100.0	110.8	121.8	133.3	151.6	176.5	.	*100.00* [11]	*123.89*
Cuba [12] B	99.7	100.0	114.3	113.5	110.2	107.0	110.3	117.8	124.7	126.3
Chile (Santiago) B	98.6	100.0	100.8	102.9	105.8	104.4	107.4	110.6	120.5	139.8
Dominica B	100.3	100.0	*100.0* [4]	*101.5*	*101.9*	*104.8*	*107.4*	*111.8*	*117.7*	*131.5*
República Dominicana [1] B	99.6	100.0	106.1	110.7	140.1	237.0	233.2	242.8	258.8	295.7

Explanations and sources: see p. 1067.

[1] Incl. alcoholic beverages and tobacco. [2] Series linked to former series. [3] Due to lack of space, multiply each figure by 1000. [4] Series (base 2001=100) replacing former series. [5] Metropolitan areas. [6] Incl. tobacco. [7] Urban areas. [8] Incl. alcoholic beverages. [9] Low income group. [10] Central area. [11] Series (base 2007=100) replacing former series; prior to 2007: incl. alcoholic beverages and tobacco. [12] Incl. alcoholic beverages; excl. tobacco.

Explications et sources: voir p. 1069.

[1] Y compris les boissons alcoolisées et le tabac. [2] Série enchaînée à la précédente. [3] En raison du manque de place, multiplier chaque chiffre par 1000. [4] Série (base 2001=100) remplaçant la précédente. [5] Régions métropolitaines. [6] Y compris le tabac. [7] Régions urbaines. [8] Y compris les boissons alcoolisées. [9] Familles à revenu modique. [10] Région centrale. [11] Série (base 2007=100) remplaçant la précédente; avant 2007: y compris les boissons alcoolisées et le tabac. [12] Y compris les boissons alcoolisées; non compris le tabac.

Explicaciones y fuentes: véase p. 1071.

[1] Incl. las bebidas alcohólicas y el tabaco. [2] Serie enlazada con la anterior. [3] Por falta de espacio, multiplicar cada indice por 1000. [4] Serie (base 2001=100) que substituye a la anterior. [5] Areas metropolitanas. [6] Incl. el tabaco. [7] Areas urbanas. [8] Incl. las bebidas alcohólicas. [9] Familias de ingresos módicos. [10] Región central. [11] Serie (base 2007=100) que substituye a la anterior; antes de 2007: incl. las bebidas alcohólicas y el tabaco. [12] Incl. las bebidas alcohólicas; excl. el tabaco.

CONSUMER PRICES

Food indices, including non-alcoholic beverages

PRIX À LA CONSOMMATION

Indices de l'alimentation, y compris les boissons non alcoolisées

PRECIOS AL CONSUMIDOR

Indices de la alimentación, incluyendo las bebidas no alcohólicas

(2000=100)

Country Pays País	1999	2000	2001	2002	2003	2004	2005	2006	2007	2008
Ecuador [1] B	45.4	100.0	132.0	142.5	146.0	147.7	100.0 [2]	106.0	109.5	128.4
El Salvador [3] B	99.7	100.0	104.6	106.6	108.6	115.5	122.6	126.3	134.2	150.5
Greenland [4] B	97.3	100.0	103.4	107.6	109.8	111.4	114.5	117.4	120.9	130.5
Grenada [1] B	99.2	100.0	101.8 [5]	101.4	102.1	105.3	...	...	...	...
Guadeloupe B	101.2	100.0	105.3	108.0	111.7	113.1	116.1	115.7	118.1	122.9
Guatemala (Guatemala) B	95.8	100.0	110.0 [6]	121.5	128.5	141.7	160.5	171.9	188.9	217.5
Guyana (Georgetown) [7] B	96.0	100.0	100.6	104.4	108.5	113.3	121.7	130.0	150.3	172.3
Guyane française B	98.5	100.0	102.7	105.3	109.3	109.8	110.5	111.4	113.6	119.0
Haïti [1] [8] B	91.1	100.0	115.5	127.4	174.2	223.2	263.2 [6]	300.1	324.5	388.6
Honduras B	95.2	100.0 [6]	108.7	112.8	117.0	124.9	137.5	143.7	159.2	189.3
Jamaica B	93.4	100.0	103.4	109.7	120.2	136.5	161.4	172.0	194.8 [9]	254.6
Martinique B	100.2 [1]	100.0	103.8	108.8	112.5	114.6	118.3	120.5	124.5	131.2
México [1] B	94.1	100.0	105.4	109.6 [6]	115.1	122.9	129.41	134.15	142.6	154.1
Netherlands Antilles (Curaçao) B	94.1	100.0	103.4	107.3	109.5	114.7	123.3	133.0	145.0 [6]	171.6
Nicaragua [11] B		100.0	112.1	115.7	120.7	133.6	149.0	162.5	188.9	242.8
Panamá [3] [12] B					100.0	101.3	105.6	107.0	114.2	131.3
Paraguay (Asunción) B	92.3	100.0	103.8	114.4	139.3	149.7	156.2	182.5	213.2	246.1 [6]
Perú (Lima) [8] B	99.3	100.0	100.5	100.2 [6]	101.0	106.6	107.6	110.2	113.0	123.3
Puerto Rico B	91.7	100.0	114.1	127.8	145.8	176.3	212.1	257.1	281.0 [6]	331.5
Saint Lucia B	98.8	100.0	103.2	101.9	104.1	104.9	112.3	116.0	...	...
Saint-Pierre-et-Miquelon B	94.5	100.0	103.5	106.1	106.7	104.9	109.7	...	...	...
Saint Vincent and the Grenadines (St. Vincent) B	101.1	100.0	101.0 [6]	101.6	100.9	105.6	111.3	115.3	123.9	142.1
Suriname (Paramaribo) [13] B	48.6	80.5 [14]	100.0 [6]	118.1		157.8 [15]	174.2	182.7	198.0	246.8

Explanations and sources: see p. 1067.

[1] Incl. alcoholic beverages and tobacco. [2] Series (base 2005=100) replacing former series; prior to 2005 incl. alcoholic beverages and tobacco. [3] Urban areas. [4] Prior to 1996: incl. tobacco. [5] Series replacing former series; prior to 2001: incl. alcoholic beverages and tobacco. [6] Series linked to former series. [7] Incl. tobacco. [8] Metropolitan areas. [9] Series replacing former series; prior to 2007: incl. alcoholic beverages. [10] Series replacing former series; prior to 1999: incl. tobacco. [11] Index base 1999=100. [12] Index base 2003=100. [13] Index base 2001=100. [14] April-Dec. [15] March-Dec.

Explications et sources: voir p. 1069.

[1] Y compris les boissons alcoolisées et le tabac. [2] Série (base 2005=100) remplaçant la précédente; avant 2005 y compris les boissons alcoolisées et le tabac. [3] Régions urbaines. [4] Avant 1996: y compris le tabac. [5] Série remplaçant la précédente; avant 2001: y compris les boissons alcoolisées et le tabac. [6] Série enchaînée à la précédente. [7] Y compris le tabac. [8] Régions métropolitaines. [9] Série remplaçant la précédente; avant 2007: y compris les boissons alcoolisées. [10] Série remplaçant la précédente; avant 1999: y compris le tabac. [11] Indices base 1999=100. [12] Indice base 2003=100. [13] Indice base 2001=100. [14] Avril-déc. [15] Mars-déc.

Explicaciones y fuentes: véase p. 1071.

[1] Incl. las bebidas alcohólicas y el tabaco. [2] Serie (base 2005=100) que substituye a la anterior; antes de 2005 incl. las bebidas alcohólicas y el tabaco. [3] Areas urbanas. [4] Antes de 1996: incl. el tabaco. [5] Serie que substituye a la anterior; antes de 2001: incl. las bebidas alcohólicas y el tabaco. [6] Serie enlazada con la anterior. [7] Incl. el tabaco. [8] Areas metropolitanas. [9] Serie que substituye a la anterior; antes de 2007: incl. las bebidas alcohólicas. [10] Serie base que substituye a la anterior: antes de 1999: incl. el tabaco. [11] Indice base 1999=100. [12] Indice base 2003=100. [13] Indice base 2001=100. [14] Abril-dic. [15] Marzo-dic.

CONSUMER PRICES / PRIX À LA CONSOMMATION / PRECIOS AL CONSUMIDOR

Food indices, including non-alcoholic beverages

Indices de l'alimentation, y compris les boissons non alcoolisées

Indices de la alimentación, incluyendo las bebidas no alcohólicas

(2000=100)

Country / Pays / País	1999	2000	2001	2002	2003	2004	2005	2006	2007	2008
Trinidad and Tobago B	92.3	100.0	114.0	125.6	142.9 [1]	161.1	198.1	244.1	286.6	360.9
United States [2] B	97.8	100.0	103.2	105.0	107.3	111.0	113.6	116.3	120.93	127.60
Uruguay (Montevideo) B	94.6	100.0	103.1	117.2	142.5	159.2	165.7	176.0	202.5	230.3
Venezuela, Rep. Bolivariana de (Caracas) B	93.3	100.0 [1]	116.1	149.0	205.2	274.6	332.5	399.3	506.3	738.0 [1]
Virgin Islands (British) B	99.7	100.0	104.3	105.3	107.1	108.4	112.1	...	...	...

ASIA - ASIE - ASIA

Country / Pays / País	1999	2000	2001	2002	2003	2004	2005	2006	2007	2008
Armenia B	106.3	100.0	104.7	107.0 [1]	114.4	125.8	126.8 [1]	132.0	140.9	156.5
Azerbaijan [3] B	97.7	100.0	102.7	106.5	109.9	120.9	134.1	150.2	174.6	224.4
Bahrain [3] B	101.3	100.0	98.6	97.6	96.2	98.3	101.3	103.3 [1]	108.0	119.8
Bangladesh [4] B	98.0	100.0	100.8	103.4	110.1 [1]	118.3	127.8	137.5	151.9	168.7
Bhutan B	99.1	100.0	101.5	103.6	104.5	102.9 [1]	108.8	114.2	123.5	138.2
Brunei Darussalam B	100.0	100.0	100.5	100.8 [1]	100.0	101.7	102.2	102.5	104.7	109.9
Cambodia (Phnom Penh) [5] B	103.5	100.0	98.0 [1]	99.7	101.2	107.6	116.6	124.2	136.6	181.7
China	102.7	100.0	100.0	99.4	102.8	113.0	116.2	118.9	133.5	...
Georgia [3] [6] B	98.7	100.0	106.6	114.6	122.7	132.2	149.6	167.1	183.4	204.0 [1]
Hong Kong, China B	102.2 [1]	100.0 [7]	99.2	97.1	95.7	96.7	98.4 [1]	100.1	104.4	115.0
India *Agricultural workers* B	101.0	100.0	97.7	100.3	104.9	107.8	111.1	119.2	130.3	143.3
Industrial workers B	98.2	100.0	102.2	104.9	108.4	111.5	115.0	125 [1]	137	152
Urban non-manual employees [3] B	98.7	100.0	102.9	105.3	107.7	111.2	114.9	123.4	134.0	148.4
Delhi, Industrial workers B	96.2	100.0	101.2	102.6	107.8	112.3	114.5	118.4 [1]	130.5	143.7
Indonesia B	105.0 [8]	100.0	108.5	120.2	121.2	128.3 [1]	140.3	161.9	180.4 [1]	210.9
Iran, Islamic Rep. of [3] B	89.3 [1]	100.0	106.6	124.0	145.9	164.8	186.3	205.5 [1]	*100.0 [9]*	*131.0*
Iraq B	103.2	100.0	108.2	118.0	137.5	149.5	182.9	237.4	270.4	300.0
Israel B	97.7	100.0 [1]	102.5	105.4 [1]	108.4	108.0	109.9	115.1 [1]	119.5	133.2

Explanations and sources: see p. 1067.

Explications et sources: voir p. 1069.

Explicaciones y fuentes: véase p. 1071.

[1] Series linked to former series. [2] All Urban Consumers. [3] Incl. tobacco. [4] Government officials. [5] Beginning 1997: including tobacco. [6] 5 cities. [7] Series replacing former series. [8] Beginnig November 1999: excluded Dili. [9] Series (base 2007=100) replacing former series; prior to 2007: incl. tobacco.

[1] Série enchaînée à la précédente. [2] Tous les consommateurs urbains. [3] Y compris le tabac. [4] Fonctionnaires. [5] A partir de 1997: y compris le tabac. [6] 5 villes. [7] Série remplaçant la précédente. [8] A partir de novembre 1999: non compris Dili. [9] Série (base 2007=100) remplaçant la précédente; avant 2007: y compris le tabac.

[1] Serie enlazada con la anterior. [2] Todos los consumidores urbanos. [3] Incl. el tabaco. [4] Funcionarios. [5] A partir de 1997: el tabaco. [6] 5 ciudades. [7] Serie que substituye a la anterior. [8] A partir de noviembre 1999: excluye Dili. [9] Serie (base 2007=100) que substituye a la anterior; antes de 2007: incl. el tabaco.

7C CONSUMER PRICES / PRIX À LA CONSOMMATION / PRECIOS AL CONSUMIDOR

Food indices, including non-alcoholic beverages

Indices de l'alimentation, y compris les boissons non alcoolisées

Indices de la alimentación, incluyendo las bebidas no alcohólicas

(2000=100)

Country / Pays / País	1999	2000	2001	2002	2003	2004	2005	2006	2007	2008
Japan B	102.0	100.0 [1]	99.4	98.6	98.4	99.3	98.4	98.9	99.2	101.7
Jordan B	100.7	100.0	100.3	100.5 [1]	103.1	107.8	113.4	121.8	133.1	158.2
Kazakhstan [2] B	86.2	100.0	111.5	119.0	127.3	137.1	148.2	161.0	180.7	223.1
Korea, Republic of B	99.2	100.0 [1]	103.5	107.7	112.4	119.5 [1]	128.6 [3]	129.2	132.4	139.1
Kuwait B	99.0	99.8 [1]	100.4	101.1	106.6	110.0	119.4	124.0	129.9	145.0
Kyrgyzstan B	84.4	100.0	105.7	105.9	108.9	112.4	118.3	128.7	...	...
République dém. pop. lao B	84.7	100.0 [1]	106.6	117.0	134.8	148.8	160.2	...	...	...
Macau, China B	101.5	100.0 [1]	98.6	96.5	95.2	97.4	101.3 [1]	105.0	113.6	133.2
Malaysia B	98.1	100.0 [1]	100.7	101.4	102.7	105.0	108.8 [1]	112.5	115.9	126.1
Maldives (Male) [2] B	105.0	100.0	102.1	105.7	99.3	115.2	117.6 [1]	*104.0* [4]	*120.8*	*143.9*
Mongolia (Ulan Bator) [2] B	87.0 [1] [1]	100.0	101.5	98.5	105.5	118.5	139.4	...	...	...
Myanmar B	102.6	100.0	119.5	201.2	274.3	277.5	303.2	365.7	493.9	638.3
Nepal B	102.8	100.0	101.3	104.4	110.1	112.9	120.3	129.1	139.6	158.8
Oman (Muscat) [5] B	101.3	100.0	99.4	98.3	98.2	98.5	102.7 [1]	108.3	118.9	144.9
Pakistan B	96.9	100.0	101.8	105.9 [1]	108.6	120.2	132.1	143.3	158.8	202.6
Philippines [2] B	98.0	100.0 [1]	104.7	107.1	109.4	116.3	123.8	130.6	134.9	152.3
Qatar [5] B	99.6	100.0 [1]	99.8	101.1	100.7	104.4	107.7	115.1	123.6	148.2
Saudi Arabia [5] [6] B	100.9	100.0	100.6	100.0	96.9	104.4 [1]	107.5	113.3	121.2	138.3
Singapore B	99.4	100.0	100.5	100.5	101.1	103.2 [1]	104.6	106.2	109.4	117.8
Sri Lanka (Colombo) B	95.7	100.0	115.2	127.5	134.9	145.5	163.0	184.6 [1]	*163.4* [7]	*213.3*
Syrian Arab Republic B	102.1	100.0	100.2	99.6	107.2 [1]	112.8	122.5	138.1 [1]	150.6	181.8
Taiwan, China B	99.8	100.0	99.0 [1]	98.8	98.7	103.1	110.7	110.0	113.1 [1]	122.8
Thailand B	101.1	100.0 [1]	100.7	101.0	104.7	109.4 [1]	114.9	120.1	125.0	139.4

Explanations and sources: see p. 1067.

[1] Series linked to former series. [2] Incl. alcoholic beverages and tobacco. [3] Series replacing former series; prior to 2005: incl. alcoholic beverages. [4] Series (base 2005=100) replacing former series; prior to 2005 incl. alcoholic beverages and tobacco. [5] Incl. tobacco. [6] All cities. [7] Series (base 2002=100) replacing former series.

Explications et sources: voir p. 1069.

[1] Série enchaînée à la précédente. [2] Y compris les boissons alcoolisées et le tabac. [3] Série remplaçant la précédente; avant 2005: y compris les boissons alcoolisées. [4] Série (base 2005=100) remplaçant la précédente; avant 2005 y compris les boissons alcoolisées et le tabac. [5] Y compris le tabac. [6] Ensemble des villes. [7] Série (base 2002=100) remplaçant la précédente.

Explicaciones y fuentes: véase p. 1071.

[1] Serie enlazada con la anterior. [2] Incl. las bebidas alcohólicas y el tabaco. [3] Serie base que substituye a la anterior; antes d 2005: incl. las bebidas alcohólicas. [4] Serie (base 2005=100) que substituye a la anterior; antes de 2005 incl. las bebidas alcohólicas y el tabaco. [5] Incl. el tabaco. [6] Todas las ciudades. [7] Serie (base 2002=100) que substituye a la anterior.

CONSUMER PRICES

PRIX À LA CONSOMMATION

PRECIOS AL CONSUMIDOR

7C

Food indices, including non-alcoholic beverages

Indices de l'alimentation, y compris les boissons non alcoolisées

Indices de la alimentación, incluyendo las bebidas no alcohólicas

(2000=100)

Country / Pays / País	1999	2000	2001	2002	2003	2004	2005	2006	2007	2008
United Arab Emirates [1] B	99.5	100.0 [2]	101.0	102.4	104.7	112.0	117.0	123.5	130.4		116.3 [3]
Viet Nam [4] B	104.0	100.0	98.6	106.1	108.7	119.8		136.2 [5]	144.8 [2]	156.0	192.1
West Bank and Gaza Strip B	98.4	100.0	99.5	102.1	106.8	109.1	113.3	118.8	124.3	147.4 [2]
Yemen, Republic of B	95.0	100.0	115.7	121.2	141.4	168.3	199.9	269.5	317.9	323.2 [2]

EUROPE - EUROPE - EUROPA

Country / Pays / País	1999	2000	2001	2002	2003	2004	2005	2006	2007	2008
Albania [6] [7] B	431.9		100.0 [8]	103.7	110.2	115.0	114.9	114.3	115.6	119.0	125.5 [2]
Andorre [1] [9] [10] B	.	.	100.0	106.2	109.9	111.9	113.1	116.2	119.8	123.2
Austria [11] B	98.9	100.0 [2]	103.3	105.2	107.3	109.5	111.0		112.5 [12]	117.1	124.5
Belarus B	37.75	100.0	156.8	217.9	267.6	320.1	358.2	380.1	417.4	491.1
Belgique B	99.1	100.0	104.2	106.5	108.7	110.4 [2]	112.5	115.0	119.1	126.1
Bosnia and Herzegovina [13] B	.	.	.	.	.	.	100.0	108.3	111.4	124.8
Bulgaria B	90.7 [1]	100.0	106.5	106.5	105.4	112.5	117.0	123.4	140.0	163.4
Croatia B	99.6	100.0	102.1 [2]	102.3	104.0	105.5	110.4 [2]	113.1	116.9	128.6
Cyprus B	94.8 [1]	100.0	104.1	108.9	114.4	119.0	120.9	126.7 [2]	133.7	143.8
Czech Republic [16] B	98.2	100.0 [2]	104.3	104.3	104.0	109.0	110.3	111.5	118.0	127.9
Denmark B	97.7	100.0 [2]	103.9	106.1	107.7	106.6	107.3	110.2	115.1	123.8
España B	98.0	100.0		100.0 [17]	104.7	109.0	113.2	116.3	121.5 [2]	126.0	133.4
Estonia B	97.6	100.0	108.3	111.6	109.6	114.2	118.3	124.2	135.8	155.1
Faeroe Islands B	97.5	100.0	106.2	108.9 [2]	109.4	109.9	111.1	114.1	118.9	127.1
Finland B	99.0	100.0 [2]	104.4	107.4	108.1	108.9	109.2	110.7 [2]	113.0	122.7
France B	98.0	100.0	105.1	107.8	110.2	110.9	111.0	112.7	114.3	119.9
Germany B	100.5	100.0 [2]	104.5	105.3	105.2	104.8	105.3	107.3	111.5 [2]	118.3
Gibraltar B	99.2 [2]	100.0	103.5	107.1	111.3	115.1	117.4	120.4	124.4	132.1

Explanations and sources: see p. 1067.

[1] Incl. beverages and tobacco. [2] Series linked to former series. [3] Series (base 2007=100) replacing former series; prior to 2007: incl. alcoholic beverages and tobacco. [4] Incl. alcoholic beverages and tobacco. [5] Series replacing former series; prior to 2005: incl. alcoholic beverages and tobacco. [6] Incl. tobacco. [7] Index base: 1992=100. [8] Series (base 2000=100) replacing former series; prior to 2000: incl. alcoholic beverages and tobacco. [9] Dec. of each year. [10] Index base 2001=100. [11] Incl. alcoholic beverages. [12] Series replacing former series; prior to 2006: incl. alcoholic beverages. [13] Index base: 2005=100. [14] Series base 2000=100) replacing former series. [15] Series (base 2000=100) replacing former series; prior to 1999: incl. alcoholic beverages and tobacco. [16] Incl. tobacco, beverages and public catering. [17] Series (base 2001=100) replacing former series.

Explications et sources: voir p. 1069.

[1] Y compris les boissons et le tabac. [2] Série enchaînée à la précédente. [3] Série (base 2007=100) remplaçant la précédente; avant 2007: y compris les boissons alcoolisées et le tabac. [4] Y compris les boissons alcoolisées et le tabac. [5] Série remplaçant la précédente; avant 2005: y compris les boissons alcoolisées et le tabac. [6] Y compris le tabac. [7] Indices base: 1992=100. [8] Série (base 2000=100) remplaçant la précédente; avant 2000: y compris les boissons alcoolisées et le tabac. [9] Déc. de chaque année. [10] Indice base 2001=100. [11] Y compris les boissons alcoolisées. [12] Série remplaçant la précédente; avant 2006: y compris les boissons alcoolisées. [13] Base de l'indice: 2005=100. [14] Série (base 2000=100) remplaçant la précédente. [15] Série (base 2000=100) remplaçant la précédente; avant 1999: y compris les boissons alcoolisées et le tabac. [16] Y compris le tabac, les boissons et la restauration. [17] Série (base 2001=100) remplaçant la précédente.

Explicaciones y fuentes: véase p. 1071.

[1] Incl. las bebidas y el tabaco. [2] Serie enlazada con la anterior. [3] Serie (base 2007=100) que substituye a la anterior; antes de 2007: incl. las bebidas alcohólicas y el tabaco. [4] Incl. las bebidas alcohólicas y el tabaco. [5] Serie que substituye a la anterior: antes de 2005: incl. las bebidas alcohólicas y el tabaco. [6] Incl. el tabaco. [7] Indices base: 1992=100. [8] Serie base (2000=100) que substituye a la anterior: antes de 2000: incl. las bebidas acohólicas y el tabaco. [9] Dic. de cada año. [10] Indice base 2001=100. [11] Incl. las bebidas alcohólicas. [12] Serie base que substituye a la anterior; antes d 2006: incl. las bebidas alcohólicas. [13] Base del indice: 2005=100. [14] Serie (base 2000=100) que substituye a la anterior. [15] Serie base (2000=100) que substituye a la anterior: antes de 1999: incl. las bebidas acohólicas y el tabaco. [16] Incl. el tabaco, las bebidas y la restauración. [17] Serie (base 2001=100) que substituye a la anterior.

	CONSUMER PRICES			PRIX À LA CONSOMMATION			PRECIOS AL CONSUMIDOR			
	Food indices, including non-alcoholic beverages			Indices de l'alimentation, y compris les boissons non alcoolisées			Indices de la alimentación, incluyendo las bebidas no alcohólicas			
										(2000=100)
Country Pays País	1999	2000	2001	2002	2003	2004	2005	2006	2007	2008
Greece B	98.1 [1]	100.0	105.1	110.7	116.2	116.8	117.5 [1]	121.9	125.9	132.6
Hungary B	91.6	100.0	113.8	119.9	123.2	131.2	134.5	144.8	161.5	177.9
Iceland [2] B	96.2	100.0	107.4	111.1	108.4	109.7	106.7	115.7	113.8	132.3
Ireland B	96.4	100.0	107.0 [1]	110.7	112.3	111.9	111.2	112.7	116.0 [1]	123.5
Isle of Man B	97.0	100.0 [1]	104.9	113.0	119.6	126.3	131.0	135.1	141.2	152.3
Italy B	98.4 [3]	100.0	104.1	107.9	111.3	113.7	113.7	115.6	119.0	125.4
Jersey [4] [5] B	100.3	100.0 [1]	105.1	107.3	109.6	114.0	114.4	117.0	122.1	137.9
Kosovo (Serbia) [6] B				97.6 [7]	100.0	98.9	96.5	99.7	100.7	116.8
Latvia B	99.4	100.0 [1]	104.8	108.4	111.2	119.5	130.5 [8]	141.1	160.1	189.4
Lithuania B	102.5	100.0 [1]	103.5	102.8	99.0	101.2	105.3 [1]	111.7	124.3	144.1
Luxembourg B	98.0	100.0	104.8	108.9	111.0	113.0	114.8 [1]	117.6	121.5	128.1
Macedonia, The Former Yugoslav Rep. of B	100.4	100.0	106.9	108.8	107.3	104.0	102.7	105.0	109.1	125.8
Malta B	98.5	100.0	106.0	107.4	109.2 [1]	109.5	111.4	113.6	118.5	128.1
Moldova, Republic of B	73.3	100.0	110.7	115.5	131.2	147.9	168.0	183.4	203.4	234.8
Netherlands B	99.2	100.0 [1]	107.0	110.5	111.7	107.8	106.5	108.3	109.4 [1]	115.6
Norway B	98.2	100.0	98.1	96.5	99.7	101.5	103.1	104.6	107.3	111.9
Poland [9] B	91.2	100.0	105.1	104.6	103.0	108.6	110.6	111.2	115.9	122.5
Portugal B	97.9	100.0	106.5	108.1 [1]	110.9	112.1	111.3	114.2	117.0	121.1
Roumanie B	69.6	100.0	135.7 [1]	160.5	184.1	201.5	213.8	222.0	230.6	251.9
Russian Federation B	85.1	100.0	121.7 [1]	136.5	151.8	167.4	190.3	208.4	227.2	274.6
San Marino B	98.9	100.0			100.0 [10]	103.3	108.9	115.0	120.7	130.4
Serbia B	53.9	100.0	191.9	209.8	211.5	235.1	280.9	310.1	328.7	397.4
Slovakia B	94.9	100.0	105.8 [1]	107.3	111.0	116.4	114.7	116.4	121.0	130.3
Slovenia [11] B	94.8	100.0	109.0	117.5	123.1	124.2	124.3 [1]	127.1	137.0	150.8

Explanations and sources: see p. 1067.

[1] Series linked to former series. [2] Annual averages are based on the months Feb.-Dec. and of January of the following year. [3] Prior to 1999: incl. alcoholic beverages. [4] June of each year. [5] Index base June 2000=100. [6] Index base 2003=100. [7] May-Dec. [8] Series replacing former series; prior to 2005: incl. alcoholic beverages and tobacco. [9] Incl. alcoholic beverages. [10] Series (base 2003=100) replacing former series. [11] Urban areas.

Explications et sources: voir p. 1069.

[1] Série enchaînée à la précédente. [2] Les moyennes annuelles sont basées sur les mois de fév.-déc. et de janvier de l'année suivante. [3] Avant 1999: y compris les boissons alcoolisées. [4] Juin de chaque année. [5] Indice base juin 2000=100. [6] Indice base 2003=100. [7] Mai-déc. [8] Série remplaçant la précédente; avant 2005: y compris les boissons alcoolisées et le tabac. [9] Y compris les boissons alcoolisées. [10] Série (base 2003=100) remplaçant la précédente. [11] Régions urbaines.

Explicaciones y fuentes: véase p. 1071.

[1] Serie enlazada con la anterior. [2] Le media anual esta basada sobre Feb.-Dic. y de enero del año siguiente. [3] Antes de 1999: incl. las bebidas alcohólicas. [4] Junio de cada año. [5] Indice base junio 2000=100. [6] Indice base 2003=100. [7] Mayo-dic. [8] Serie que substituye a la anterior: antes de 2005: incl. las bebidas acohólicas y el tabaco. [9] Incl. las bebidas alcohólicas. [10] Serie (base 2003=100) que substituye a la anterior. [11] Areas urbanas.

Food indices, including non-alcoholic beverages

Indices de l'alimentation, y compris les boissons non alcoolisées

Indices de la alimentación, incluyendo las bebidas no alcohólicas

(2000=100)

Country Pays País	1999	2000	2001	2002	2003	2004	2005	2006	2007	2008
Suisse B	98.5		100.0		102.1	104.4	105.7	106.3	105.5	105.4	106.0	109.3
Sweden B	100.00	100.00	102.87	106.21	106.55	106.09	105.36	106.16	108.31	115.80
Turkey [2] B	66.8	100.0	150.3	225.3	290.0	316.1	112.1 [3]	123.0	138.2	155.9
Ukraine [4] B	74.3	100.0	114.4	114.4	121.5	135.1	157.5	166.5	182.4	247.0
United Kingdom B	100.3	100.0	103.3	104.0	105.4	106.0	107.3	109.6	114.6	125.2

OCEANIA - OCÉANIE - OCEANIA

	1999	2000	2001	2002	2003	2004	2005	2006	2007	2008
American Samoa B	100.5	100.0	101.6	103.1	109.7	123.5	130.4	132.2	...	...
Australia B	97.6	100.0	106.5	110.4	114.4	117.1	120.0	129.2	132.3	138.5
Cook Islands (Rarotonga) [5] B	96.8	100.0	109.4	116.9	119.9	120.9	122.3	125.2	125.5 [6]	132.9
Fiji B	103.3	100.0	104.1	104.6	111.0	115.2	117.1	119.2	130.8 [6]	145.8
Guam B	98.3	100.0	106.0	112.6	118.9	130.1	140.8	150.0	154.6	168.6 [6]
Kiribati (Tarawa) B	.	100.0 [6]	106.1	109.7	112.8	112.8	112.7	108.3	114.4	133.4
Marshall Islands (Majuro) B	100.2	100.0	100.3	102.7	102.5	106.0	106.3	109.4	110.8	129.4
New Zealand B	98.7	100.0	106.0	109.4	109.4	110.3	113.1	116.2 [6]	120.6	130.2
Niue B	94.9	100.0	111.2	115.1	118.3 [6]	121.2 [7]	122.0	127.2	134.9	150.0
Norfolk Island B	97.2	100.0	104.5	112.4	118.4	123.4	129.9	137.3	...	...
Northern Mariana Islands (Saipan) B	100.6	100.0	96.6	93.0	90.7 [6]	94.9	93.9	91.4	96.0	103.7
Nouvelle-Calédonie (Nouméa) B	99.4	100.0	102.6	105.0	107.0	108.2	109.7	113.0	114.5	119.1
Papua New Guinea B	88.0	100.0	109.6	128.3	145.3	146.1	151.2	159.3	160.3	187.0
Polynésie française B	99.2	100.0	102.2	107.4	108.2 [6]	110.6	113.2	117.5	121.0	126.6 [6]
Samoa B	100.1 [6]	100.0	105.1	117.3	115.1	146.2 [6]	146.7	152.5	164.3	187.5
Solomon Islands (Honiara) B	93.1	100.0	108.9	122.1	125.0	136.8	145.1	156.7	168.1 [6]	208.7
Tonga B	99.7	100.0	111.8	130.6 [6]	143.1	156.1	165.5	170.4	182.9	197.7

Explanations and sources: see p. 1067.

[1] Series (base 2000=100) replacing former series; prior to 2000: food only. [2] Incl. tobacco. [3] Series (base 2003=100) replacing former series; prior to 2005 incl. alcoholic beverages and tobacco. [4] Incl. alcoholic beverages and tobacco. [5] Excl. beverages. [6] Series linked to former series. [7] Average of the last three quarters.

Explications et sources: voir p. 1069.

[1] Série (base 2000=100) remplaçant la précédente; avant 2000: alimentation seulement. [2] Y compris le tabac. [3] Série (base 2003=100) remplaçant la précédente; avant 2005 y compris les boissons alcoolisées et le tabac. [4] Y compris les boissons alcoolisées et le tabac. [5] Non compris les boissons. [6] Série enchaînée à la précédente. [7] Moyenne des trois derniers trimestres.

Explicaciones y fuentes: véase p. 1071.

[1] Serie (base 2000=100) que substituye a la anterior; antes de 2000: alimentación solamente. [2] Incl. el tabaco. [3] Serie (base 2003=100) que substituye a la anterior; antes de 2005 incl. las bebidas alcohólicas y el tabaco. [4] Incl. las bebidas alcohólicas y el tabaco. [5] Excl. las bebidas. [6] Serie enlazada con la anterior. [7] Promedio de los tres últimos trimestres.

	CONSUMER PRICES			PRIX À LA CONSOMMATION			PRECIOS AL CONSUMIDOR		
	Food indices, including non-alcoholic beverages			Indices de l'alimentation, y compris les boissons non alcoolisées			Indices de la alimentación, incluyendo las bebidas no alcohólicas		
									(2000=100)	
Country Pays País	1999	2000	2001	2002	2003	2004	2005	2006	2007	2008
Tuvalu (Funafuti) B	99.0	100.0	105.3	109.4 ¹	117.4	120.8	127.4	129.2	128.6 ¹	...
Vanuatu B	98.0 ¹	100.0	102.2	102.7	105.0	108.5	108.1	111.8	116.1	125.4

Explanations and sources: see p. 1067.

¹ Series linked to former series.

Explications et sources: voir p. 1069.

¹ Série enchaînée à la précédente.

Explicaciones y fuentes: véase p. 1071.

¹ Serie enlazada con la anterior.

CONSUMER PRICES

Electricity, gas and
other fuels indices

PRIX À LA CONSOMMATION

Indices de l'électricité,
gaz et autres combustibles

PRECIOS AL CONSUMIDOR

Indices de la electricidad,
gas y otros combustibles

7D

(2000=100)

Country Pays País	1999	2000	2001	2002	2003	2004	2005	2006	2007	2008
AFRICA - AFRIQUE - AFRICA										
Botswana	81.9	100.0	108.5	115.1	118.0	125.2	147.1	.	254.5 [1]	288.9
Cameroun [2]	98.7	100.0	101.4	102.5	108.7	111.4	113.5	119.3	120.4	124.6
République centrafricaine (Bangui)	94.3	100.0	102.2	104.2	103.4	98.9	96.9	104.9	104.9	111.5
Congo (Brazzaville, Afric.) [3]	99.5	100.0	116.6	114.0	106.8	110.3	112.5	127.4	...	...
Côte d'Ivoire (Abidjan, Afric.) [4]	.	.	. [1]	100.0 [5]	113.1	110.7	113.6	114.0	...	...
Gambia (Banjul,Kombo St. Mary) [6]	61.2	.	.	71.2	81.9	100.0	105.1	...	...	...
Kenya (Nairobi) [7]	82.6	100.0	115.1	114.9	121.4	142.6	176.4	197.0	.	274.6
Lesotho	95.2	100.0	112.2	124.8	135.0	142.4	153.2	166.0	179.4	210.5
Madagascar (Cinq régions)	.	100.0	107.1	122.8	117.6	134.7	156.5	207.3	214.9	234.7
Maroc [3]	98.9	100.0	102.3	103.9	105.0	107.4	108.5	111.7	116.2	116.5
Mauritius	94.5	100.0	115.1 [1]	100.0 [8]	100.0	100.2	102.8	124.0	133.3 [9]	139.8
Réunion	89.6	94.0	92.7	93.1	93.8	93.6	94.6	98.5	99.0	102.0
Sénégal (Dakar)	92.7	100.0	103.6	108.0	112.7	114.9	113.7	112.0	123.2	...
South Africa	93.2	100.0 [1]	107.5	114.5	121.4	129.0	135.7	141.9	153.3	182.8
Saint Helena	99.9	100.0 [1]	79.5 [10]	100.0	113.4	121.8	131.8	137.6	139.2	149.1
Swaziland	40.1	100.0	103.3	105.6	114.0	119.2	123.9	...	...	...
Tanzania (Tanganyika) [3]	93.5	100.0	102.9	117.9 [1]	122.7	131.4	148.0	160.6	170.5	188.7
Tchad (N'Djamena)	92.0	100.0	101.7	119.6 [1]	126.8	115.4	130.6	149.0	...	...
Tunisie	99.3	100.0 [1]	103.5	105.0	109.5	115.0	125.3	134.4	139.7	146.7
AMERICA - AMÉRIQUE - AMERICA										
Anguilla	96.7	100.0 [1]	100.0 [11]	94.2	100.8	105.0	119.8	135.2	134.4	161.5
Argentina (Buenos Aires) [12]	100.0	100.0 [1]	98.7	103.1	112.9	113.8	118.6	115.9	...	...
Aruba [13]	.	.	100.0	110.6	109.0	112.1	137.3	132.1	175.8	126.5

Explanations and sources: see p. 1067.

[1] Series linked to former series. [2] Incl. "rent" and household items. [3] Incl. water. [4] Index base 2002=100. [5] Series (base 2002=100) replacing former series. [6] Index base: 2004=100. [7] Low income group. [8] July-Dec.; series (base 2003=100) replacing former series. [9] July-Dec.; series linked to former series. [10] Series (base 1st quarter 2002=100) replacing former series. [11] Series (base 2001=100) replacing former series. [12] Metropolitan areas. [13] Index base 2001=100.

Explications et sources: voir p. 1069.

[1] Série enchaînée à la précédente. [2] Y compris le groupe "loyer" et les articles de ménage. [3] Y compris l'eau. [4] Indice base 2002=100. [5] Série (base 2002=100) remplaçant la précédente. [6] Base de l'indice: 2004=100. [7] Familles à revenu modique. [8] Juillet-Déc.; série (base 2003=100) remplaçant la précédente. [9] Juillet-déc.; série enchaînée à la précédente. [10] Série (base 1er trimestre 2002=100) replaçant la précédente. [11] Série (base 2001=100) remplaçant la précédente. [12] Régions métropolitaines. [13] Indice base 2001=100.

Explicaciones y fuentes: véase p. 1071.

[1] Serie enlazada con la anterior. [2] Incl. el grupo "alquiler" y artículos domésticos. [3] Incl. el agua. [4] Indice base 2002=100. [5] Serie (base 2002=100) que substituye a la anterior. [6] Base del indice: 2004=100. [7] Familias de ingresos módicos. [8] Julio-dic.; serie (base 2003=100) que sustituye a la anterior. [9] Julio-dic.: serie enlazada con la anterior. [10] Serie (base primer trimestre de 2002=100) que substituye a la anterior. [11] Serie (base 2001=100) que substituye a la anterior. [12] Areas metropolitanas. [13] Indice base 2001=100.

7D

CONSUMER PRICES	PRIX À LA CONSOMMATION	PRECIOS AL CONSUMIDOR
Electricity, gas and other fuels indices	Indices de l'électricité, gaz et autres combustibles	Indices de la electricidad, gas y otros combustibles

(2000=100)

Country Pays País	1999	2000	2001	2002	2003	2004	2005	2006	2007	2008
Barbados [1]	110.3	.	119.1 |	100.0 [2]	103.8	98.8	106.3	122.7	118.8	128.3
Belize	96.5	100.0	107.2	103.5	111.6	122.7	132.1	...	...	...
Bermuda	92.4	100.0	98.8	98.0	102.7	104.6	110.5	120.7 [3]	127.4	167.9
Bolivia [4]	87.9	100.0	104.4	108.9	114.2	118.8	123.0	124.1	125.5	...
Canada [5]	90.7	100.0	108.9	106.0	115.5	119.2	127.0	133.4	134.2 [3]	143.6
Colombia [6] [7]	79.0	100.0	123.0	132.3	154.9	166.0	176.2	186.5	195.7	214.3
Costa Rica [8]	86.4	100.0	131.7	146.3	160.1	198.0	239.1	...	...	...
Cuba [9]	99.5	100.0	88.0	88.6	93.1	93.8	103.9	113.9	133.8	...
Dominica [10]	.	. |	100.0 [11]	103.7	115.6	124.3	140.2	149.9	157.9	173.6
Ecuador	71.1	100.0	165.0	203.9	.	. |	100.0 [12]	100.1	100.2	100.3
El Salvador [4]	84.8	100.0	129.3	125.3	128.8	126.9	133.4	145.1	152.4	149.9
Greenland	99.9 [3]	100.0	107.1	111.1	110.5	110.9	117.2	137.0	142.2	142.0
Grenada	93.5	100.0	106.1	104.2	108.3	111.8	...	...		...
Guadeloupe	95.7	100.0	104.7	104.9	105.2	108.4	121.8	133.6	133.9	139.0
Guatemala (Guatemala) [10]	.	. |	100.0 [11]	103.6	109.4	118.5	126.3	134.9	140.8	155.6
Guyane française	91.4	100.0	94.5	99.6	100.2	102.1	110.2	115.6	121.6	133.4
Honduras [1] [13]	340.0 |	100.0 [14]	108.6	124.8	140.8	154.8	167.3	178.3	188.8	206.2
Jamaica [13]	92.7	100.0	110.7	114.9	129.9	151.1	177.7	198.1	216.6 [3]	278.6
Martinique	95.8	100.0	106.4	105.3	105.5	108.6	117.8	127.6	131.1	137.4
México	79.9	100.0	108.9	117.2	135.8	149.1	160.62	173.10	178.2	190.7
Netherlands Antilles (Curaçao)	81.3	100.0	103.1	105.5	120.6	121.2	141.6	147.1	151.1 [3]	174.8
Perú (Lima) [15]	84.2	100.0	107.8	102.5 [3]	113.4	121.8	129.7	132.5	132.9	...
Puerto Rico	86.5	100.0	101.2	100.6	105.6	110.9	136.5	157.2	171.8 [3]	206.6

Explanations and sources: see p. 1067.

[1] Index base: 1990=100. [2] Series (base 2002=100) replacing former series. [3] Series linked to former series. [4] Urban areas. [5] Incl. water. [6] Low income group. [7] Incl. certain household equipment. [8] Central area. [9] Incl. the materials to repair the housings. [10] Index base 2001=100. [11] Series (base 2001=100) replacing former series. [12] Series (base 2005=100) replacing former series. [13] Fuel only. [14] Series (base 2000=100) replacing former series; beginning 2000: incl. housing. [15] Metropolitan areas.

Explications et sources: voir p. 1069.

[1] Indices base: 1990=100. [2] Série (base 2002=100) remplaçant la précédente. [3] Série enchaînée à la précédente. [4] Régions urbaines. [5] Y compris l'eau. [6] Familles à revenu modique. [7] Y compris certains biens d'équipement de ménage. [8] Région centrale. [9] Y compris les matériaux pour réparer les logements. [10] Indice base 2001=100. [11] Série (base 2001=100) remplaçant la précédente. [12] Série (base 2005=100) remplaçant la précédente. [13] Combustible seulement. [14] Série (base 2000=100) remplaçant la précédente; à partir de 2000: y compris le logement. [15] Régions métropolitaines.

Explicaciones y fuentes: véase p. 1071.

[1] Indices base: 1990=100. [2] Serie (base 2002=100) que substituye a la anterior. [3] Serie enlazada con la anterior. [4] Areas urbanas. [5] Incl. el agua. [6] Familias de ingresos módicos. [7] Incl. ciertos enseres domésticos. [8] Región central. [9] Incl. los materiales para reparar las viviendas. [10] Indice base 2001=100. [11] Serie (base 2001=100) que substituye a la anterior. [12] Serie (base 2005=100) que substituye a la anterior. [13] Combustible solamente. [14] Serie base (2000=100) que substituye a la anterior: a partir de 2000: incl. la vivienda. [15] Areas metropolitanas.

CONSUMER PRICES

Electricity, gas and other fuels indices

PRIX À LA CONSOMMATION

Indices de l'électricité, gaz et autres combustibles

PRECIOS AL CONSUMIDOR

Indices de la electricidad, gas y otros combustibles

(2000=100)

Country Pays País	1999	2000	2001	2002	2003	2004	2005	2006	2007	2008
Saint Lucia	91.5	100.0	98.7	97.1	100.0	103.5	111.5	117.2	...	...
Saint Vincent and the Grenadines (St. Vincent)	98.1	100.0	103.6 ₁	104.0	106.0	108.1	128.5	142.0	150.3	166.9
Trinidad and Tobago	97.4	100.0	100.3	101.2	101.8 ₁	103.2	103.9	105.3	107.1	119.8
United States ²	92.4	100.0	110.3	103.6	112.5	117.6	131.6	144.2	148.00	163.52
Uruguay (Montevideo)	93.1	100.0	105.4	125.4	175.4	199.8	209.6	226.1	241.0	260.1
ASIA - ASIE - ASIA										
Armenia	99.0	100.0	99.8	99.9 ₁	102.1	103.8	106.0 ₁	107.6	106.3	114.3
Azerbaijan	95.6	100.0	99.9	99.9	99.9	109.6	191.1	217.6	434.4	435.9
Bahrain ³	100.0	100.0	72.6	72.6	72.4	72.5	72.4	...	...	...
Georgia ⁴	81.8	100.0	105.7	114.2	114.9	122.6	125.9	159.2	181.1	...
Hong Kong, China ⁵	*144.1*	100.0 ⁶	98.0	91.3	92.5	103.1	107.3 ₁	109.6	108.8	101.7
India										
Agricultural workers	92.2	100.0	108.5	113.1	117.0	120.1	123.3	130.7	139.9	152.7
Industrial workers	85.1	100.0	109.2	120.5	128.3	138.6	136.1	140 ₁	144	154
Urban non-manual employees	80.4	100.0	115.6	125.1	131.0	137.2	146.4	151.4	161.5	170.9
Delhi, Industrial workers	78.2	100.0	115.1	129.6	129.6	139.9	158.0	171.5 ₁	171.5	174.9
Iran, Islamic Rep. of ³	77.7 ₁	100.0	112.3	129.7	149.6	166.4	176.4	179.5	...	...
Iraq	111.4	100.0	98.4	97.9	516.9	339.9	676.7	1 935.5	3 320.9	2 609.9
Israel	94.2	100.0 ₁	99.8	115.0 ₁	127.9	134.4	146.7	145.9 ₁	147.7	168.7
Japan ⁷	98.4	100.0 ₁	100.6	99.4	98.9	99.0	99.8	103.4	104.2	110.5
Jordan	100.0	100.0	103.5	112.3 ₁	117.3	123.3	134.4	167.0	173.3	266.9
Kazakhstan	91.8	100.0	105.2	110.4	115.7	121.0	...	...	...	...
Korea, Republic of ³	87.6	100.0 ₁	111.1	107.1	113.1	119.4	122.5 ⁸	132.0	135.3	146.5
Kyrgyzstan	75.0	100.0	124.5	149.8	153.1	160.1	177.8	188.5	...	...
Macau, China	95.3	100.0 ₁	100.6	95.0	98.5	99.9	110.9 ₁	119.9	114.6	96.1
Malaysia	98.5 ₁	100.0	101.3	101.3	100.0 ⁹	100.5	101.9	105.7	...	...

Explanations and sources: see p. 1067.

¹ Series linked to former series. ² All Urban Consumers. ³ Incl. water. ⁴ 5 cities. ⁵ Index base: 1990=100. ⁶ Series (base 2000=100) replacing former series. ⁷ Incl. water and sewerage. ⁸ Series replacing former series; prior to 2005: incl. water. ⁹ Series (base 2003=100) replacing former series.

Explications et sources: voir p. 1069.

¹ Série enchaînée à la précédente. ² Tous les consommateurs urbains. ³ Y compris l'eau. ⁴ 5 villes. ⁵ Indices base: 1990=100. ⁶ Série (base 2000=100) remplaçant la précédente. ⁷ Y compris l'eau et le traitement des eaux résiduaires. ⁸ Série remplaçant la précédente; avant 2005: y compris l'eau. ⁹ Série (base 2003=100) remplaçant la précédente.

Explicaciones y fuentes: véase p. 1071.

¹ Serie enlazada con la anterior. ² Todos los consumidores urbanos. ³ Incl. el agua. ⁴ 5 ciudades. ⁵ Indices base: 1990=100. ⁶ Serie (base 2000=100) que substituye a la anterior. ⁷ Incl. el agua y el tratamiento de aguas residuales. ⁸ Serie base que substituye a la anterior; antes de 2005: incl. el agua. ⁹ Serie (base 2003=100) que substituye a la anterior.

CONSUMER PRICES

Electricity, gas and other fuels indices

PRIX À LA CONSOMMATION

Indices de l'électricité, gaz et autres combustibles

PRECIOS AL CONSUMIDOR

Indices de la electricidad, gas y otros combustibles

(2000=100)

Country Pays País	1999	2000	2001	2002	2003	2004	2005	2006	2007	2008
Maldives (Male)	97.2	100.0	101.7	100.3	99.3	97.3	103.3	112.5	...	...
Mongolia (Ulan Bator) [1]	92.1	100.0	132.5	148.8	149.4	152.1	165.2	...	...	...
Myanmar	89.8	100.0	121.2	163.3	219.3	258.1	281.6	370.0	491.7	561.9
Nepal [2]	79.4	100.0	103.9	106.3	122.8	130.0	157.4	185.4	191.4	222.9
Oman (Muscat) [2]	100.0	100.0	100.0	100.0	100.1	100.4	100.1 [3]	100.1	100.2	100.5
Pakistan	87.8	100.0	.	100.0 [4]	104.9	107.5	113.8	126.9	133.1	...
Philippines [2]	90.2	100.0 [3]	113.1	115.9	123.2	132.3	156.2	176.4	182.1	193.9
Qatar [2]	100.0	100.0	.	100.0 [5]	100.4	99.0	106.5	121.6	...	...
Saudi Arabia [6]	98.6	100.0	100.0	100.0	100.1	.	99.5 [3]	99.5	...	...
Singapore	82.5	100.0	107.0	95.7	98.8	100.7 [3]	109.4	128.3	125.8	157.5
Sri Lanka (Colombo)	84.3	100.0	114.3	124.3	143.2	157.0	178.1	228.3	286.2	...
Syrian Arab Republic [2]	99.7	100.0	100.0	111.2	119.5 [3]	120.0	122.0	123.3 [3]	130.1	173.4
Taiwan, China [2]	96.5	100.0	100.3 [3]	99.3	100.2	101.5	103.3	107.3	111.0 [3]	...
Thailand	92.7	100.0 [3]	107.8	109.3	111.1	116.0 [3]	119.0	127.1	126.4	106.2
United Arab Emirates	.	100.0	104.4	104.4	104.8	117.1	125.6	...	...	...
West Bank and Gaza Strip	89.1	100.0	105.4	112.4	116.8	122.3	129.8	135.8	140.3	160.8 [3]
EUROPE - EUROPE - EUROPA										
Albania	86.7	100.0	106.8	119.5	124.9	158.9	198.7	210.0	224.9	252.1 [3]
Andorre [7] [8]	.	.	100.0	103.7	105.8	122.6	138.1	135.1	156.0	154.9
Austria	93.9	100.0 [3]	100.4	98.0	99.0	105.3	115.1	122.4 [3]	127.2	136.7
Belarus	19.13	100.0	269.2	624.9	1 374.1	1 623.2	1 645.6	1 810.1	1 999.3	2 825.4
Belgique	89.7	100.0	102.8	99.5	98.8 [3]	103.5	112.9	123.0	...	...
Bosnia and Herzegovina [9]	.	.	.	.	.	.	100.0	115.1	117.7	128.4
Bulgaria	84.5	100.0	104.5	117.7	131.0	142.8	154.1	162.0	170.2	...

Explanations and sources: see p. 1067.

[1] Incl. "Rent". [2] Incl. water. [3] Series linked to former series. [4] Series (base 2002=100) replacing former series. [5] Series (base 2002=100) replacing former series; prior to 2002: incl. water. [6] All cities. [7] Dec. of each year. [8] Index base 2001=100. [9] Index base: 2005=100.

Explications et sources: voir p. 1069.

[1] Y compris le groupe "loyer". [2] Y compris l'eau. [3] Série enchaînée à la précédente. [4] Série (base 2002=100) remplaçant la précédente. [5] Série (base 2002=100) remplaçant la précédente; avant 2002: y compris l'eau. [6] Ensemble des villes. [7] Déc. de chaque année. [8] Indice base 2001=100. [9] Base de l'indice: 2005=100.

Explicaciones y fuentes: véase p. 1071.

[1] Incl. el grupo "alquiler". [2] Incl. el agua. [3] Serie enlazada con la anterior. [4] Serie (base 2002=100) que substituye a la anterior. [5] Serie (base 2002=100) que substituye a la anterior; antes de 2002: incl. el agua. [6] Todas las ciudades. [7] Dic. de cada año. [8] Indice base 2001=100. [9] Base del indice: 2005=100.

CONSUMER PRICES

Electricity, gas and other fuels indices

PRIX À LA CONSOMMATION

Indices de l'électricité, gaz et autres combustibles

PRECIOS AL CONSUMIDOR

Indices de la electricidad, gas y otros combustibles

7D

(2000=100)

Country Pays País	1999	2000	2001	2002	2003	2004	2005	2006	2007	2008
Croatia	90.9	100.0	112.4 [1]	114.0	119.1	122.1	126.9 [1]	132.5	132.1	141.1
Czech Republic	91.5	100.0 [1]	116.1	122.4	120.8	123.1	131.0	146.9	151.6	172.6
Denmark	90.6	100.0 [1]	102.5	105.7	107.0	108.2	115.4	121.4	121.5	130.9
España	94.5	100.0 [1]	100.0 [2]	98.9	100.2	102.1	108.5	119.2 [1]	121.4	134.1
Estonia	98.0	100.0	113.6	128.9	133.4	138.5	150.4	163.4	185.5	231.4
Faeroe Islands [3]	155.8 [4]	166.9 [4]	100.0 [2]	96.0	98.7	103.8	117.5	126.0	125.7	152.9
Finland	91.5	100.0 [1]	99.9	101.8	112.7	115.8	122.1	130.0 [1]	134.9	158.5
France [5]	93.3	100.0	101.3	100.9	103.4	105.7	113.2	121.1	123.4	135.2
Germany	90.2	100.0	109.1	108.0	111.8	116.1	129.8	143.4	148.6 [1]	165.2
Greece	88.4 [1]	100.0	100.2	102.0	106.1	110.9	131.2 [1]	147.0	147.3	172.8
Hungary	91.7	100.0	110.3	116.4	124.8	142.4	151.3	160.9	200.6	225.9
Iceland [6]	97.1	100.0	102.4	104.8	109.1	114.3	120.2	119.2	121.2	127.8
Ireland	91.7	100.0	102.4 [1]	105.4	112.7	120.7	139.7	153.2	164.7 [1]	179.1
Isle of Man	92.1	100.0 [1]	93.0	92.1	100.3	114.5	139.4	151.4	159.1	189.8
Italy	90.1	100.0	104.0	101.1	104.9	105.1	113.7	124.8	126.5	140.3
Jersey [7] [8]	88.0	100.0 [1]	103.9	99.4	102.0	108.6	124.9	142.4	157.0	197.1
Latvia	95.9	100.0 [1]	101.6	101.8	104.7	114.0	121.0	139.6	158.4	215.0
Lithuania	85.7	100.0 [1]	102.0	105.2	105.4	104.9	109.7 [1]	117.1	130.0	156.3
Luxembourg	84.3	100.0	99.2	95.0	98.0	104.1	120.9 [1]	135.0	137.5	159.3
Macedonia, The Former Yugoslav Rep. of	78.5	100.0	103.9	104.9	109.6	112.8	114.0	118.2	125.0	134.2
Malta [9]	94.1	100.0	99.6	104.8	114.4 [1]	115.9	142.6	179.7	167.7	201.0
Netherlands	87.8	100.0 [1]	115.2	121.2	130.0	134.6	153.5	168.2	170.8 [1]	175.3
Norway	91.7	100.0	124.4	122.7	161.5	149.7	147.2	183.5	150.8	189.2
Poland	91.9	100.0	110.6	117.1	121.1	124.7	129.5	138.1	143.2	157.5
Portugal	96.2	100.0	104.7	105.3 [1]	109.9	112.6	119.4	124.3	128.7	134.4

Explanations and sources: see p. 1067.

[1] Series linked to former series. [2] Series (base 2001=100) replacing former series. [3] Index base: 1986 = 100. [4] Jan. [5] Incl. water. [6] Annual averages are based on the months Feb.-Dec. and of January of the following year. [7] June of each year. [8] Index base June 2000=100. [9] Incl. water.

Explications et sources: voir p. 1069.

[1] Série enchaînée à la précédente. [2] Série (base 2001=100) remplaçant la précédente. [3] Indices base: 1986 = 100. [4] Janv. [5] Y compris l'eau. [6] Les moyennes annuelles sont basées sur les mois de fév.-déc. et de janvier de l'année suivante. [7] Juin de chaque année. [8] Indice base juin 2000=100. [9] Y compris l'eau.

Explicaciones y fuentes: véase p. 1071.

[1] Serie enlazada con la anterior. [2] Serie (base 2001=100) que substituye a la anterior. [3] Indices base: 1986 = 100. [4] Enero. [5] Incl. el agua. [6] Le media anual esta basada sobre Feb.-Dic. y de enero del año siguiente. [7] Junio de cada año. [8] Indice base junio 2000=100. [9] Incl. el agua.

| CONSUMER PRICES | | PRIX À LA CONSOMMATION | | PRECIOS AL CONSUMIDOR | | | | | |
| Electricity, gas and other fuels indices | | Indices de l'électricité, gaz et autres combustibles | | Indices de la electricidad, gas y otros combustibles | | | | | |

(2000=100)

Country Pays País	1999	2000	2001	2002	2003	2004	2005	2006	2007	2008
Roumanie	61.2	100.0	139.2	200.9	244.9	297.8	350.9	388.2	417.1	460.1
Russian Federation [1] [2]	64.9	100.0	133.6	181.2	209.0	239.1	282.0	329.2	367.2	417.6
Slovakia [3]	67.9	100.0	118.6 [4]	122.9	153.2	176.3	190.6	217.5	222.3	...
Slovenia [5]	80.3	100.0	110.5	112.2	116.7	123.8	139.0 [4]	150.4	155.2	171.6
Suisse	84.6	100.0 [4]	100.2	94.8	95.8	98.8	109.9	117.4 [4]	118.9	138.5
Sweden	97.81	100.00	114.55	119.86	146.32	147.84	149.88	167.68	166.37	186.59
Turkey	64.7	100.0	201.4	291.6	349.3	371.0	400.0 [4]	446.0	479.1	604.0
United Kingdom	100.4	100.0	100.8	104.0	106.1	113.6	129.0	160.7	172.1	204.7
OCEANIA - OCÉANIE - OCEANIA										
Australia [6]	95.1	100.0	105.6	110.0	116.0	119.7	124.2	129.4	135.4	148.2
Cook Islands (Rarotonga)	101.6	100.0	111.5	111.3	111.6	113.5	128.2	151.1	171.9 [4]	...
Fiji	95.9	100.0	105.6	102.5	105.3	114.0	130.2	138.8	137.5 [4]	154.3
New Zealand	98.8	100.0	100.6	105.6	112.3	122.7	131.8	140.2 [4]	149.5	160.2
Nouvelle-Calédonie (Nouméa)	98.2	100.0	104.2	105.6	107.0	107.4	108.0	113.1	114.7	117.1
Polynésie française	100.4	100.0	106.2	100.0 [7]	100.0	99.5	95.6	102.0	100.6	106.4 [4]

Explanations and sources: see p. 1067.

[1] Electricity only. [2] Dec. of each year; Index base Dec. 2000=100. [3] Fuel only. [4] Series linked to former series. [5] Urban areas. [6] Beginning sept. 1998: incl. water and sewerage. [7] Series (base 2002=100) replacing former series.

Explications et sources: voir p. 1069.

[1] Electricité seulement. [2] Déc. de chaque année; base des indices déc. 2000=100. [3] Combustible seulement. [4] Série enchaînée à la précédente. [5] Régions urbaines. [6] A partir de sept. 1998: y compris l'eau et le traitement des eaux résiduaires. [7] Série (base 2002=100) remplaçant la précédente.

Explicaciones y fuentes: véase p. 1071.

[1] Electricidad solamente. [2] Dic. de cada año; base de los índices dic. 2000=100. [3] Combustible solamente. [4] Serie enlazada con la anterior. [5] Areas urbanas. [6] A partir de sept. 1998: incl. el agua y el tratamiento de aguas residuales. [7] Serie (base 2002=100) que substituye a la anterior.

CONSUMER PRICES

Clothing indices, including footwear

PRIX À LA CONSOMMATION

Indices de l'habillement, y compris les chaussures

PRECIOS AL CONSUMIDOR

Indices del vestido, incl. calzado

7E

(2000=100)

Country Pays País	1999	2000	2001	2002	2003	2004	2005	2006	2007	2008
AFRICA - AFRIQUE - AFRICA										
Algérie	96.3	100.0	104.5	107.4	109.3	111.9	113.5	113.7	114.2	...
Bénin (Cotonou)	96.5	100.0	99.7	101.4	101.9	101.2	101.4	103.1	102.0	102.2
Botswana	97.3	100.0	103.8	107.8	112.4	114.8	116.9	118.1 [1]	120.0	122.2
Burkina Faso (Ouagadougou)	100.3	100.0	100.2	100.8	111.0	110.3	110.2	112.7	115.1	118.4
Burundi (Bujumbura)	85.9	100.0	86.8	90.8	105.2	117.8	126.7	125.9	119.1	...
Cameroun	102.7	100.0	99.5	100.1	100.6	100.5	101.8	100.4	100.3	100.8
Cap-Vert	96.4	100.0	.	. [1]	100.0 [2]	94.2	86.9	82.0	85.4	95.5
République centrafricaine (Bangui)	102.7	100.0	100.5	104.9	109.8	123.8	122.5	131.0	128.1	130.6
Congo (Brazzaville, Afric.)	94.3	100.0	101.2	106.3	95.5	106.7	106.6	101.8	...	...
Côte d'Ivoire (Abidjan, Afric.)	99.7	100.0	103.7	100.9	99.9	100.2	101.9	101.4	100.9	100.2
Egypt	97.6 [1]	100.0	102.1	104.3	105.9 [1]	100.0 [3]	105.0	106.8	.	121.2 [1]
Ethiopia [4] [5]	.	.	94.1	92.3	90.2	90.6	91.5	94.4	102.6	116.9
Gabon (Libreville, Afric.)	100.6	100.0	.	.	97.3	105.4	103.3	105.0	109.8 [1]	109.5
Gambia (Banjul,Kombo St. Mary) [6] [7]	69.5	.	.	86.3	96.0	100.0	101.8	102.5 [1]	104.4	107.7
Ghana	76.8	100.0	148.9	164.1	193.7	207.7	220.6	233.9	275.6 [1]	...
Guinea Ecuatorial (Malabo)	.	100.0	.	110.3	122.7	128.4	...	...	...	...
Guinée (Conakry)	96.0	100.0	. [1]	100.0 [8]	.	109.8	121.9	151.6	188.3	213.7
Guinée-Bissau (Bissau) [9]	.	.	.	.	100.0	98.9	99.0	108.0	112.0	104.0
Kenya (Nairobi) [10]	96.7	100.0	100.5	99.9	100.8	105.6	111.7	116.0	118.7	120.6
Lesotho	95.6	100.0	105.9	110.2	114.6	117.9	121.5	124.5	128.1	136.4
Madagascar (Cinq régions) [6]	.	100.0	107.7	111.3	115.4	118.8	122.0	149.6	144.4	157.5
Malawi	54.7	100.0 [1]	130.5	152.7	166.8	179.5	192.8	208.8	221.2	237.7
Mali (Bamako)	104.0	100.0	104.9	104.7	106.9	99.5	96.3	98.2	97.3	105.9
Maroc	97.7	100.0	101.4	103.0	103.9	104.9	105.6	106.8	108.2	109.9

Explanations and sources: see p. 1067.
[1] Series linked to former series. [2] Series (base 2003=100) replacing former series. [3] Series (base 2004=100) replacing former series. [4] Year ending in June of the year indicated. [5] Index base: Dec. 2006=100. [6] Incl. household linen. [7] Index base: 2004=100. [8] Series (base 2002=100) replacing former series. [9] Index base 2003=100. [10] Low income group.

Explications et sources: voir p. 1069.
[1] Série enchaînée à la précédente. [2] Série (base 2003=100) remplaçant la précédente. [3] Série (base 2004=100) remplaçant la précédente. [4] Année se terminant en juin de l'année indiquée. [5] Base de l'indice: déc. 2006=100. [6] Y compris le linge de maison. [7] Base de l'indice: 2004=100. [8] Série (base 2002=100) remplaçant la précédente. [9] Indice base 2003=100. [10] Familles à revenu modique.

Explicaciones y fuentes: véase p. 1071.
[1] Serie enlazada con la anterior. [2] Serie (base 2003=100) que substituye a la anterior. [3] Serie (base 2004=100) que substituye a la anterior. [4] Año que se termina en junio del año indicado. [5] Base del indice: dic. 2006=100. [6] Incl. la ropa de casa. [7] Base del indice: 2004=100. [8] Serie (base 2002=100) que substituye a la anterior. [9] Indice base 2003=100. [10] Familias de ingresos módicos.

CONSUMER PRICES

Clothing indices, including footwear

PRIX À LA CONSOMMATION

Indices de l'habillement, y compris les chaussures

PRECIOS AL CONSUMIDOR

Indices del vestido, incl. calzado

(2000=100)

Country Pays País	1999	2000	2001	2002	2003	2004	2005	2006	2007	2008
Mauritanie	95.7	100.0	102.2	102.9	105.4 [1]	121.2 [2]	131.1	143.5	149.7	152.5
Mauritius	97.5	100.0	101.2 I	98.9 [3]	100.0	101.6	102.9	109.7	118.1 [4]	123.0
Mozambique	97.2	100.0	108.0	119.5	120.72 [2]	123.11	124.86	128.69	...	...
Namibia [5]				100.0	104.1	104.6	103.5	100.5	103.8	...
Niger (Niamey, Afric.)	100.1	100.0	99.7	101.3	101.1	99.4	102.6	100.0	99.8	103.8
Nigeria	94.6	100.0	97.5	97.6	117.8 [2]	126.2	126.9	137.9	149.8	162.1
Réunion	100.2	100.0	98.4	98.0	99.1	100.4	101.4	103.5	103.7	103.5
Rwanda (Kigali)	93.9	100.0	102.2	109.7	111.7 [2]		119.0	118.2	119.2	...
Sénégal (Dakar)	100.3	100.0	97.6	95.2	93.4	90.3	87.3	85.9	88.4	86.3
Seychelles [6]		I	100.0 [7]	100.0	105.7	118.0	121.2	117.9	130.5 [2]	171.3
Sierra Leone [8]					100.0	113.2	128.6	125.2	120.5	...
South Africa	99.2	100.0 [2]	99.6	98.3	99.8	96.0	92.3	84.6	76.8	87.7
Saint Helena	97.8	100.0 I	96.3 [9]	102.6	103.4	111.0	119.8	122.3	107.8	113.8
Swaziland	88.7	100.0	103.2	109.2	114.4	115.2	116.9	114.6 [2]	113.9	116.0
Tanzania (Tanganyika)	97.5	100.0	103.7	110.3 [2]	111.8	104.1	106.6	114.1	120.9	122.6
Tchad (N'Djamena)	105.9	100.0	109.7	112.3 [2]	107.1	87.2	78.6	75.2	72.3 [10]	73.5
Togo (Lomé)	103.3	100.0	98.4	98.9	103.8	110.4	111.5	110.8	108.8	110.2
Tunisie	99.3	100.0 [2]	101.8	103.2	104.1	105.8	108.9	111.9	115.6	118.4
Uganda	97.0	100.0	104.0	100.5	102.7	100.5	102.3	106.8	111.9 [2]	121.5
Zimbabwe [11]	0.1	0.1	0.2 [2]	0.5	2.5	10.0	37.8	350.2	14 789	...
AMERICA - AMÉRIQUE - AMERICA										
Anguilla	67.0	100.0 I	100.0 [7]	114.1	112.3	125.1	158.1	146.0	143.4	118.4
Argentina (Buenos Aires) [12]	104.6	100.0 [2]	95.4	129.6	157.6	168.2	187.2	215.6	231.8	...

Explanations and sources: see p. 1067.

[1] Jan.-Nov. [2] Series linked to former series. [3] July-Dec.; series (base 2003=100) replacing former series. [4] July-Dec.; series linked to former series. [5] Index base 2002=100. [6] Index base 2001=100. [7] Series (base 2001=100) replacing former series. [8] Index base 2003=100. [9] Series (base 1st quarter 2002=100) replacing former series. [10] 11 months' average. Series linked to former series. [11] Due to lack of space, multiply each figure by 1000. [12] Metropolitan areas.

Explications et sources: voir p. 1069.

[1] janv.-nov. [2] Série enchaînée à la précédente. [3] Juillet-Déc.; série (base 2003=100) remplaçant la précédente. [4] Juillet-déc.; série enchaînée à la précédente. [5] Indice base 2002=100. [6] Indice base 2001=100. [7] Série (base 2001=100) remplaçant la précédente. [8] Indice base 2003=100. [9] Série (base 1er trimestre 2002=100) replaçant la précédente. [10] Moyenne de 11 mois. Série enchaînée à la précédente. [11] En raison du manque de place, multiplier chaque chiffre par 1000. [12] Régions métropolitaines.

Explicaciones y fuentes: véase p. 1071.

[1] enero-nov. [2] Serie enlazada con la anterior. [3] Julio-dic.; serie (base 2003=100) que sustituye a la anterior. [4] Julio-dic.: serie enlazada con la anterior. [5] Indice base 2002=100. [6] Indice base 2001=100. [7] Serie (base 2001=100) que substituye a la anterior. [8] Indice base 2003=100. [9] Serie (base primer trimestre de 2002=100) que substituye a la anterior. [10] Promedio de 11 meses. Serie enlazada con la anterior. [11] Por falta de espacio, multiplicar cada indice por 1000. [12] Areas metropolitanas.

CONSUMER PRICES

Clothing indices, including footwear

PRIX À LA CONSOMMATION

Indices de l'habillement, y compris les chaussures

PRECIOS AL CONSUMIDOR

Indices del vestido, incl. calzado

(2000=100)

Country Pays País	1999	2000	2001	2002	2003	2004	2005	2006	2007	2008
Aruba [1]	.	.	100.0	107.2	112.1	116.5	117.3	118.7	123.9	132.7
Bahamas (New Providence)	99.3	100.0	100.5	101.0	101.0	101.3	99.0	100.2	101.0	102.6
Barbados [2]	98.1	.	81.2	100.0 [3]	97.0	97.3	96.6	88.9	88.3	91.4
Belize	103.9	100.0	96.5	95.6	96.3	96.7	96.7	98.1	98.9	98.0
Bermuda	98.9	100.0	101.3	101.9	103.8	105.8	108.0	111.4 [4]	111.6	114.6
Bolivia [5] B	94.9	100.0	102.9	105.9	109.0	111.4	114.7	119.1	125.1	134.1 [4]
Brasil	96.3	100.0	104.1	112.5	124.1	135.2	147.3	156.1	...	...
Canada	99.8	100.0	100.5	99.7	97.9	97.7	97.3	95.5	95.4 [4]	93.5
Cayman Islands	99.8	100.0	97.7	98.1	97.0	92.8	90.7	95.2	98.8	98.9
Colombia [6]	96.8	100.0	103.8	105.8	107.2	108.9	109.6	109.7	111.4	112.0
Costa Rica [7]	95.3	100.0	103.3	108.6	113.1	118.1	124.8	.	100.00 [8]	98.06
Cuba	99.7	100.0	99.1	104.1	112.4	110.5	101.8	105.8	128.1	132.3
Chile (Santiago)	107.2	100.0	94.3	90.6	86.2	84.0	83.0	82.4	81.2	...
Dominica [2]	142.0	.	100.0 [9]	99.0	98.0	98.1	98.1	97.1	97.1	96.7
República Dominicana	96.8	100.0	104.7	108.4	117.1	163.5	178.9	192.9	205.2	219.1
Ecuador	45.6	100.0	130.6	132.5	124.6	115.9	100.0 [10]	100.6	101.5	107.9
El Salvador [5]	101.0	100.0	96.8	93.5	92.3	91.5	91.5	92.1	93.2	94.6
Greenland	99.4 [4]	100.0	101.9	103.4	104.4	104.5	106.4	105.8	103.3	107.1
Grenada	99.5	100.0	100.7	101.3	100.7	99.6	...	...	...	...
Guadeloupe	102.7	100.0	98.6	98.1	94.4	90.8	93.5	93.0	90.9	88.0
Guatemala (Guatemala)	96.9	100.0	100.0 [9]	106.7	111.8	115.9	119.9	123.5	127.1	130.8
Guyana (Georgetown) [11]	100.7 [1]	100.0	99.9 [12]	101.8 [12]	102.6 [12]	102.6	102.6	102.9	117.4	116.1
Guyane française	100.9	100.0	99.1	95.7	93.3	90.2	89.4	85.8	81.0	78.5

Explanations and sources: see p. 1067.

[1] Index base 2001=100. [2] Index base: 1990=100. [3] Series (base 2002=100) replacing former series. [4] Series linked to former series. [5] Urban areas. [6] Low income group. [7] Central area. [8] Series (base 2007=100) replacing former series. [9] Series (base 2001=100) replacing former series. [10] Series (base 2005=100) replacing former series. [11] Excl. footwear. [12] Dec. of each year.

Explications et sources: voir p. 1069.

[1] Indice base 2001=100. [2] Indices base: 1990=100. [3] Série (base 2002=100) remplaçant la précédente. [4] Série enchaînée à la précédente. [5] Régions urbaines. [6] Familles à revenu modique. [7] Région centrale. [8] Série (base 2007=100) remplaçant la précédente. [9] Série (base 2001=100) remplaçant la précédente. [10] Série (base 2005=100) remplaçant la précédente. [11] Non compris la chaussure. [12] Déc. de chaque année.

Explicaciones y fuentes: véase p. 1071.

[1] Indice base 2001=100. [2] Indices base: 1990=100. [3] Serie (base 2002=100) que substituye a la anterior. [4] Serie enlazada con la anterior. [5] Areas urbanas. [6] Familias de ingresos módicos. [7] Región central. [8] Serie (base 2007=100) que substituye a la anterior. [9] Serie (base 2001=100) que substituye a la anterior. [10] Serie (base 2005=100) que substituye a la anterior. [11] Excl. el calzado. [12] Dic. de cada año.

7E	CONSUMER PRICES		PRIX À LA CONSOMMATION			PRECIOS AL CONSUMIDOR			
	Clothing indices, including footwear		Indices de l'habillement, y compris les chaussures			Indices del vestido, incl. calzado			
									(2000=100)

Country Pays País	1999	2000	2001	2002	2003	2004	2005	2006	2007	2008
Haïti [1]	81.1	100.0	112.6	123.4	155.1	179.4	203.4 [2]	225.9	250.0	278.4
Honduras	95.0	100.0 [2]	108.7	119.7	128.6	137.0	144.6	153.6	163.7	172.7
Jamaica	94.9	100.0	104.2	107.2	112.9	118.3	124.3	133.8	144.6 [2]	172.4
Martinique	100.7	100.0	100.0	100.0	98.3	98.2	97.8	97.2	98.1	98.6
México	90.6	100.0	105.8	108.9 [2]	109.8	110.9	112.07	113.49	115.0	117.0
Netherlands Antilles (Curaçao)	98.4	100.0	98.8	96.9	97.2	97.0	96.4	96.8	97.8 [2]	99.8
Nicaragua [3]	100.0	.	107.3	109.5	112.0	114.6	117.8	122.3	129.5	140.0
Panamá [4] [5]					100.0	97.1	97.1	96.3	94.9	...
Paraguay (Asunción) B	96.8	100.0	103.1	108.4	117.0	122.5	128.6	137.1	141.5	146.0 [2]
Perú (Lima) [1]	90.3	100.0	102.5	103.9 [2]	104.6	105.9	107.5	109.1	111.9	...
Puerto Rico	100.4	100.0	98.1	97.0	95.5	95.2	95.1	95.5	100.7 [2]	106.5
Saint Lucia	92.9	100.0	100.2	100.3	100.3	105.3	105.3	105.3	...	...
Saint Vincent and the Grenadines (St. Vincent)	96.5	100.0	98.7 [2]	97.7	97.1	97.2	97.0	97.4	109.8	111.7
Suriname (Paramaribo) [6]	18 638	.	100.0 [7]	96.3	.	.	128.2	131.2	133.3	136.6
Trinidad and Tobago	101.7	100.0	98.7	96.4	95.3 [2]	90.1	88.6	88.1	90.0	92.4
United States [8]	101.3	100.0	98.2	95.7	93.3	92.9	92.2	92.2	91.819	91.749
Uruguay (Montevideo)	103.7	100.0	100.1	108.0	127.5	138.5	145.2	148.9	151.8	156.3
Venezuela, Rep. Bolivariana de (Caracas)	91.6	100.0 [2]	103.7	114.9	142.9	168.6	187.2	203.3	232.5	283.1 [2]
ASIA - ASIE - ASIA										
Armenia	103.9	100.0	98.9	101.3 [2]	102.8	101.8	99.7 [2]	102.2	105.9	113.0
Azerbaijan	99.1	100.0	101.3	105.2	107.6	110.0	111.9	117.0	160.4	266.9
Bahrain	101.5	100.0	101.8	101.9	102.4	103.8	103.2	102.5 [2]	104.6	106.7
Bangladesh [9] [10]								100.0	106.5	110.8

Explanations and sources: see p. 1067.

[1] Metropolitan areas. [2] Series linked to former series. [3] Index base 1999=100. [4] Urban areas. [5] Index base 2003=100. [6] Index base: 1990=100. [7] Series (base 2001=100) replacing former series. [8] All Urban Consumers. [9] Government officials. [10] Index base: July 2006=100.

Explications et sources: voir p. 1069.

[1] Régions métropolitaines. [2] Série enchaînée à la précédente. [3] Indices base 1999=100. [4] Régions urbaines. [5] Indice base 2003=100. [6] Indices base: 1990=100. [7] Série (base 2001=100) remplaçant la précédente. [8] Tous les consommateurs urbains. [9] Fonctionnaires. [10] Base de l'indice: juillet 2006=100.

Explicaciones y fuentes: véase p. 1071.

[1] Areas metropolitanas. [2] Serie enlazada con la anterior. [3] Indice base 1999=100. [4] Areas urbanas. [5] Indice base 2003=100. [6] Indices base: 1990=100. [7] Serie (base 2001=100) que substituye a la anterior. [8] Todos los consumidores urbanos. [9] Funcionarios. [10] Base del indice: julio 2006=100.

CONSUMER PRICES

Clothing indices, including footwear

PRIX À LA CONSOMMATION

Indices de l'habillement, y compris les chaussures

PRECIOS AL CONSUMIDOR

Indices del vestido, incl. calzado

7E

(2000=100)

Country Pays País	1999	2000	2001	2002	2003	2004	2005	2006	2007	2008
Bhutan	92.1	100.0	106.8	.	.	100.0 [1]	104.2	110.6	120.1	...
Brunei Darussalam	94.3	100.0	99.1	97.4 [2]	94.6	92.7	91.2	89.8	89.1	89.4
Cambodia (Phnom Penh)	102.7	100.0	100.0 [3]	92.9	91.7	90.9	94.3	98.0	101.1	101.5
China	100.8	100.0	98.1	97.6	96.8	95.4	93.7	93.2	92.6	...
Georgia [4]	100.2	100.0	100.9	100.3	98.8	99.7	101.5	106.1	101.3	...
Hong Kong, China [5]	140.9	100.0 [6]	95.4	96.1	93.6	99.6	101.5 [2]	102.5	106.8	107.7
India										
Agricultural workers	96.8	100.0	104.9	108.1	111.4	115.6	118.5	121.8	124.7	129.9
Industrial workers	95.9	100.0	101.3	104.7	106.6	108.9	111.4	114 [2]	118	123
Urban non-manual employees	96.4	100.0	103.3	105.8	108.8	111.3	113.5	117.0	121.4	126.6
Delhi, Industrial workers	97.1	100.0	99.2	100.5	100.0	102.1	106.3	109.1 [2]	111.1	115.1
Indonesia	93.8 [7]	100.0	109.2	114.3	119.2	125.9 [2]	...	...	...	...
Iran, Islamic Rep. of	91.5 [2]	100.0	105.4	109.2	116.9	127.3	140.0	151.8	168.6 [2]	203.8
Iraq	103.1	100.0	104.8	108.0	112.8	108.7	118.9	144.5	156.6	161.5
Israel	100.1	100.0 [2]	96.2	91.4 [2]	86.3	83.0	78.0	77.1 [2]	74.8	73.7
Japan	101.1	100.0 [2]	97.8	95.6	93.8	93.6	94.3	95.1	95.6	96.1
Jordan	99.4	100.0	101.1	100.5 [2]	97.2	94.9	94.5	97.1	103.3	110.9
Kazakhstan	90.9	100.0	106.9	114.8	124.1	132.2	...	...	...	...
Korea, Republic of	98.5	100.0 [2]	103.1	106.3	110.1	110.5	111.6 [2]	114.6	117.6	120.6
Kuwait	101.7	100.0 [2]	105.8	105.6	108.0	111.0	118.1	122.8	128.6	137.9
Kyrgyzstan	92.6	100.0	103.7	105.2	106.6	107.0	108.1	109.4	...	...
Macau, China	105.8	100.0 [2]	95.3	85.5	74.9	77.4	76.7 [2]	73.1	74.0	79.3
Malaysia	101.8	100.0 [2]	97.4	95.2	93.3	91.6	90.7 [2]	89.5	88.2	87.8
Maldives (Male)	102.9	100.0	99.0	95.2	95.0	93.0	93.1	93.7 [2]	92.3	94.7
Mongolia (Ulan Bator)	98.9	100.0	103.9	105.5	108.8	109.9	111.9	...	...	...
Myanmar	100.4	100.0	132.5	195.8	272.8	300.5	299.6	337.6	462.9	583.4
Nepal [8]	97.4	100.0	103.0	104.4	106.3	108.4	111.5	114.1	116.6	121.8

Explanations and sources: see p. 1067.

[1] Series (base 2004=100) replacing former series. [2] Series linked to former series. [3] Series (base 2001=100) replacing former series. [4] 5 cities. [5] Index base: 1990=100. [6] Series (base 2000=100) replacing former series. [7] Beginnig November 1999: excluded Dili. [8] Excl. footwear.

Explications et sources: voir p. 1069.

[1] Série (base 2004=100) remplaçant la précédente. [2] Série enchaînée à la précédente. [3] Série (base 2001=100) remplaçant la précédente. [4] 5 villes. [5] Indices base: 1990=100. [6] Série (base 2000=100) remplaçant la précédente. [7] A partir de novembre 1999: non compris Dili. [8] Non compris la chaussure.

Explicaciones y fuentes: véase p. 1071.

[1] Serie (base 2004=100) que substituye a la anterior. [2] Serie enlazada con la anterior. [3] Serie (base 2001=100) que substituye a la anterior. [4] 5 ciudades. [5] Indices base: 1990=100. [6] Serie (base 2000=100) que substituye a la anterior. [7] A partir de noviembre 1999: excluye Dili. [8] Excl. el calzado.

CONSUMER PRICES
PRIX À LA CONSOMMATION
PRECIOS AL CONSUMIDOR

Clothing indices, including footwear

Indices de l'habillement, y compris les chaussures

Indices del vestido, incl. calzado

(2000=100)

Country Pays País	1999	2000	2001	2002	2003	2004	2005	2006	2007	2008
Oman (Muscat)	99.6	100.0	99.4	99.6	97.5	95.6	99.2 ı	98.8	99.1	103.3
Pakistan	96.3	100.0	ı	100.0 ²	104.1	105.9	110.3	114.6	122.9	...
Philippines	97.5	100.0 ı	104.1	107.7	111.4	114.4	118.4	122.0	124.8	130.1
Qatar	96.3	100.0 ı	102.6	103.8	103.5	106.9	104.4	117.4	132.2	147.8
Saudi Arabia ³	105.6	100.0	97.4	95.8	95.3	104.2 ı	93.2	92.6	90.4	90.7
Singapore	100.8	100.0	100.4	100.7	101.1	101.2 ı	101.2	101.9	102.7	104.2
Sri Lanka (Colombo) ⁴	98.9	100.0	104.2	108.9	111.6	112.7	117.6	122.2 ı	140.7 ⁵	154.8
Syrian Arab Republic	100.1	100.0	100.5	96.5	102.9 ı	104.0	109.0	124.9 ı	127.0	139.0
Taiwan, China	99.7	100.0	98.3 ı	98.9	100.3	103.4	103.3	100.8	103.9 ı	...
Thailand	99.0	100.0 ı	101.0	101.4	101.5	101.7 ı	102.1	102.3	102.5	102.8
United Arab Emirates	99.4	100.0 ı	104.0	104.9	106.6	112.0	114.8	119.2	127.6	153.0 ı
West Bank and Gaza Strip	97.9	100.0	98.0	101.9	102.1	101.2	102.8	103.5	102.7	102.4 ı
Yemen, Republic of	95.8	100.0	103.9	112.1	115.8	118.8	121.9	120.0	126.2 ı	141.6

EUROPE - EUROPE - EUROPA

Country Pays País	1999	2000	2001	2002	2003	2004	2005	2006	2007	2008
Albania	102.8	100.0	95.0	89.7	85.8	83.8	81.7	83.2	78.7	76.4 ı
Andorre ⁶ ⁷	.	.	100.0	106.3	107.8	109.0	111.0	112.7	114.7	112.8
Austria	99.8	100.0 ı	101.6	102.7	103.9	104.4	104.3	104.0 ı	106.2	107.8
Belarus	44.77	100.0	146.6	178.1	201.2	214.1	218.8	223.0	227.5	233.6
Belgique	99.4	100.0	100.9	102.1	103.2 ı	104.0	104.3	106.5	...	...
Bosnia and Herzegovina ⁸	.	.	.	.	.	.	100.0	99.2	96.1	94.1
Bulgaria	104.2	100.0	100.3	100.1	97.9	98.3	99.2	102.6	109.8	121.1
Croatia	93.8	100.0	103.6 ı	105.5	105.6	105.0	105.6 ı	108.0	113.6	116.6
Cyprus	100.5	100.0	93.3	90.0	91.1	90.4	88.5	88.2 ı	88.4	87.3
Czech Republic	102.0	100.0 ı	98.6	96.1	91.4	87.7	83.1	78.1	77.5	76.6

Explanations and sources: see p. 1067.

¹ Series linked to former series. ² Series (base 2002=100) replacing former series. ³ All cities. ⁴ Excl. footwear. ⁵ Series (base 2002=100) replacing former series; prior 2007: excl. footwear. ⁶ Dec. of each year. ⁷ Index base 2001=100. ⁸ Index base: 2005=100.

Explications et sources: voir p. 1069.

¹ Série enchaînée à la précédente. ² Série (base 2002=100) remplaçant la précédente. ³ Ensemble des villes. ⁴ Non compris la chaussure. ⁵ Série (base 2002=100) remplaçant la précédente; avant 2007: non compris les chaussures. ⁶ Déc. de chaque année. ⁷ Indice base 2001=100. ⁸ Base de l'indice: 2005=100.

Explicaciones y fuentes: véase p. 1071.

¹ Serie enlazada con la anterior. ² Serie (base 2002=100) que substituye a la anterior. ³ Todas las ciudades. ⁴ Excl. el calzado. ⁵ Serie (base 2002=100) que substituye a la anterior; antes de 2007: excl. el calzado. ⁶ Dic. de cada año. ⁷ Indice base 2001=100. ⁸ Base del indice: 2005=100.

CONSUMER PRICES

Clothing indices, including footwear

PRIX À LA CONSOMMATION

Indices de l'habillement, y compris les chaussures

PRECIOS AL CONSUMIDOR

Indices del vestido, incl. calzado

7E

(2000=100)

Country Pays País	1999	2000	2001	2002	2003	2004	2005	2006	2007	2008
Denmark	103.0	100.0 ı	98.5	100.8	101.8	101.8	101.1	99.1	97.4	96.9
España	97.9	100.0 ı	100.0 ²	105.1	109.1	111.1	112.6	144.0 ı	145.5	146.5
Estonia	96.7	100.0	103.8	108.1	109.5	109.1	111.1	114.0	118.0	122.5
Faeroe Islands ³	.	. ı	100.0 ²	101.5	100.0	96.6	93.1	91.6	92.4	97.7
Finland	99.8	100.0 ı	100.9	100.0	99.8	100.0	99.4	97.6 ı	98.0	98.4
France	99.8	100.0	100.6	101.5	101.1	101.4	101.6	101.8	102.5	103.1
Germany	99.8	100.0 ı	100.8	101.5	100.7	100.0	98.1	97.2	98.8 ı	99.5
Gibraltar	100.4 ı	100.0	93.5	93.5	95.9	96.8	98.1	99.8	99.6	98.2
Greece	97.9 ı	100.0	103.3	107.1	109.2	113.6	119.0 ı	121.9	126.1	129.5
Hungary	94.5	100.0	105.3	109.5	112.8	116.6	116.9	116.1	117.2	117.1
Iceland ⁴	101.2	100.0	101.1	100.2	98.6	98.4	97.3	97.3	98.6	108.7
Ireland	106.0	100.0	96.5 ı	92.4	88.6	85.5	83.1	81.5	78.8 ı	75.0
Isle of Man	104.4	100.0 ı	109.5	111.6	111.3	111.6	113.5	117.6	115.5	115.9
Italy	97.8	100.0	102.9	105.9	109.0	111.5	113.2	114.7	116.3	118.3
Jersey ⁵ ⁶	99.1	100.0 ı	95.1	96.1	94.5	92.4	90.3	90.0	87.0	83.5
Kosovo (Serbia) ⁷	.	.	.	101.2 ⁸	100.0	93.7	87.3	84.6	87.1	85.8
Latvia	98.8	100.0 ı	100.9	100.1	103.7	106.4	106.2	106.2	108.7	108.7
Lithuania	100.8	100.0 ı	95.8	92.4	89.9	89.1	87.5 ı	85.4	81.2	78.0
Luxembourg	99.1	100.0	102.1	103.8	105.3	105.8	106.5 ı	106.6	107.1	107.5
Macedonia, The Former Yugoslav Rep. of	102.4	100.0	101.3	108.2	110.5	111.6	114.0	114.2	116.3	118.4
Malta	98.9	100.0	97.7	96.5	87.7 ı	85.6	85.1	83.6	83.9	87.8
Netherlands	101.0	100.0 ı	101.8	105.0	101.8	99.9	97.3	97.8	99.0 ı	99.3
Norway	104.4	100.0	99.2	93.7	83.8	78.0	74.4	71.8	68.1	65.4
Poland	94.8	100.0	101.5	100.7	98.2	94.6	89.5	83.3	77.1	71.8
Portugal	99.2	100.0	101.5	104.1 ı	105.5	104.3	103.1	103.9	106.3	108.1

Explanations and sources: see p. 1067.

¹ Series linked to former series. ² Series (base 2001=100) replacing former series. ³ Index base 2001=100. ⁴ Annual averages are based on the months Feb.-Dec. and of January of the following year. ⁵ June of each year. ⁶ Index base June 2000=100. ⁷ Index base 2003=100. ⁸ May-Dec.

Explications et sources: voir p. 1069.

¹ Série enchaînée à la précédente. ² Série (base 2001=100) remplaçant la précédente. ³ Indice base 2001=100. ⁴ Les moyennes annuelles sont basées sur les mois de fév.-déc. et de janvier de l'année suivante. ⁵ Juin de chaque année. ⁶ Indice base juin 2000=100. ⁷ Indice base 2003=100. ⁸ Mai-déc.

Explicaciones y fuentes: véase p. 1071.

¹ Serie enlazada con la anterior. ² Serie (base 2001=100) que substituye a la anterior. ³ Indice base 2001=100. ⁴ Le media anual esta basada sobre Feb.-Dic. y de enero del año siguiente. ⁵ Junio de cada año. ⁶ Indice base junio 2000=100. ⁷ Indice base 2003=100. ⁸ Mayo-dic.

CONSUMER PRICES

Clothing indices, including footwear

PRIX À LA CONSOMMATION

Indices de l'habillement, y compris les chaussures

PRECIOS AL CONSUMIDOR

Indices del vestido, incl. calzado

(2000=100)

Country Pays País	1999	2000	2001	2002	2003	2004	2005	2006	2007	2008
Roumanie	77.3	100.0	128.4	148.2	163.8	175.4	183.2	188.7	194.9	201.4
Russian Federation [1] [2]	81.4	100.0	116.2	131.1	145.2	156.8	168.5	181.7	196.5	215.9
San Marino [3]	*140.2*			*|*	*100.0* [4]	*99.7*	*100.1*	*100.2*	*100.7*	*101.3*
Serbia	64.2	100.0	187.0	217.6	235.2	252.3	271.0	301.9	316.0	335.2
Slovakia	97.0	100.0	102.4 [5]	105.6	108.4	108.9	107.9	107.7	108.5	109.5
Slovenia [6]	93.6	100.0	102.1	105.9	112.4	114.4	113.2 [5]	112.6	115.0	120.0
Suisse	106.3	100.0 [5]	94.9	92.7	92.4	89.8	89.7	91.5 [5]	91.7	95.3
Sweden	99.69	100.00	102.59	103.55	103.56	101.61	100.48	103.68	106.18	105.07
Turkey	70.4	100.0	151.7	231.3	293.9	305.3	324.6 [5]	324.3	339.0	347.4
United Kingdom	103.9	100.0	95.7	91.2	89.8	87.3	85.2	84.1	83.4	80.4

OCEANIA - OCÉANIE - OCEANIA

Country Pays País	1999	2000	2001	2002	2003	2004	2005	2006	2007	2008
American Samoa	99.7	100.0	100.3	100.2	100.6	101.0	101.0	100.6	...	...
Australia	97.1	100.0	102.3	103.6	103.5	102.4	100.7	98.9	99.8	100.0
Cook Islands (Rarotonga)	94.4	100.0	110.9	113.3	112.2	115.1	115.9	115.8	104.1 [5]	100.8
Fiji	101.2	100.0	100.9	101.9	103.1	102.0	103.0	104.5	107.5 [5]	109.8
Guam	100.9 [7]	100.0	93.9	87.4	84.2	85.8	90.3	97.1	92.6	96.4 [5]
Kiribati (Tarawa)	.	100.0 [7]	96.5	93.3	94.7	90.2	94.5	87.3	88.3	87.5
Marshall Islands (Majuro)	90.0	100.0	106.7	115.5	94.1	96.7	96.0	98.7	97.1	100.9
New Zealand	99.5	100.0	101.7	102.9	102.4	101.8	101.6	101.6 [5]	101.6	101.5
Niue	99.3	100.0	100.8	108.4 [5]	109.8	115.4 [8]	132.2	131.9	144.6	147.9
Norfolk Island	98.9	100.0	100.5	101.2	103.7	105.4	106.3	106.4	...	...
Northern Mariana Islands (Saipan)	99.3	100.0	99.9	98.3	93.0 [5]	90.0	91.3	96.2	94.6	94.0
Nouvelle-Calédonie (Nouméa)	99.6	100.0	99.6	100.6	99.3	98.4	95.2	92.9	89.0	83.4
Papua New Guinea	86.4	100.0	111.7	121.6	127.2	130.5	127.9	127.9	136.8	139.9

Explanations and sources: see p. 1067.

[1] Excl. footwear. [2] Dec. of each year; Index base Dec. 2000=100. [3] Index base: 1990=100. [4] Series (base 2003=100) replacing former series. [5] Series linked to former series. [6] Urban areas. [7] Series (base 2000=100) replacing former series. [8] Average of the last three quarters.

Explications et sources: voir p. 1069.

[1] Non compris la chaussure. [2] Déc. de chaque année; base des indices déc. 2000=100. [3] Indices base: 1990=100. [4] Série (base 2003=100) remplaçant la précédente. [5] Série enchaînée à la précédente. [6] Régions urbaines. [7] Série (base 2000=100) remplaçant la précédente. [8] Moyenne des trois derniers trimestres.

Explicaciones y fuentes: véase p. 1071.

[1] Excl. el calzado. [2] Dic. de cada año; base de los índices dic. 2000=100. [3] Indices base: 1990=100. [4] Serie (base 2003=100) que substituye a la anterior. [5] Serie enlazada con la anterior. [6] Areas urbanas. [7] Serie (base 2000=100) que substituye a la anterior. [8] Promedio de los tres últimos trimestres.

CONSUMER PRICES

Clothing indices, including footwear

PRIX À LA CONSOMMATION

Indices de l'habillement, y compris les chaussures

PRECIOS AL CONSUMIDOR

Indices del vestido, incl. calzado

(2000=100)

Country Pays País	1999	2000	2001	2002	2003	2004	2005	2006	2007	2008
Polynésie française	101.9	100.0	98.7 [1]	98.3	98.1	94.5	93.2	90.2	86.7	91.4 [1]
Samoa	100.4	100.0	99.4	98.3	96.2	93.4 [1]	85.0	81.4	78.8	80.3
Solomon Islands (Honiara)	99.2	100.0	99.5	100.6	101.2	101.6	101.7	105.0	121.4 [1]	121.8
Tonga [2]	*99.5*	.	. [1]	*100.0* [3]	*111.5*	*118.2*	*131.2*	*144.7*	*153.2*	*164.1*
Tuvalu (Funafuti)	78.8	100.0	91.7	108.3 [1]	111.8	113.8	115.5	129.8	163.3 [1]	...
Vanuatu	100.2 [1]	100.0	100.4	100.5	101.8	101.6	101.5	101.4	101.3	102.3

Explanations and sources: see p. 1067.

[1] Series linked to former series. [2] Index base: 1990=100. [3] Series (base 2002=100) replacing former series.

Explications et sources: voir p. 1069.

[1] Série enchaînée à la précédente. [2] Indices base: 1990=100. [3] Série (base 2002=100) remplaçant la précédente.

Explicaciones y fuentes: véase p. 1071.

[1] Serie enlazada con la anterior. [2] Indices base: 1990=100. [3] Serie (base 2002=100) que substituye a la anterior.

Rent indices — **Indices du loyer** — **Indices del alquiler**

(2000=100)

Country / Pays / País	1999	2000	2001	2002	2003	2004	2005	2006	2007	2008
AFRICA - AFRIQUE - AFRICA										
Algérie [1]	97.6	100.0	101.8	102.0	104.8	107.1	121.6	125.9	126.1	...
Bénin (Cotonou) [1]	93.4	100.0	103.8	107.4	112.9	114.6	123.3	131.9	131.4	137.7
Botswana [2]	87.1	100.0	113.1	125.0	138.0	153.9	163.9 |	100.0 [3]	104.7	113.2
Burkina Faso (Ouagadougou) [1]	99.4	100.0	99.2	104.9	110.0	111.0	111.3	116.4	114.8	128.7
Burundi (Bujumbura) [4]	86.2	100.0	132.4	136.9	142.3	148.7	163.2	176.6	195.5	...
Cap-Vert [1] [5]					100.0	103.5	114.0	127.8	139.9	147.6
Congo (Brazzaville, Afric.)	108.8	100.0	103.5	113.1	115.0	118.9	121.5	124.9	...	...
Côte d'Ivoire (Abidjan, Afric.) [1]	98.4	100.0	103.4	107.4	114.4	116.3	126.1	128.3	127.7	133.5
Egypt [1]	99.9 [6]	100.0	100.2	100.7	102.2 |	100.0 [7]	104.5	108.4	.	121.7 [6]
Gabon (Libreville, Afric.) [1]	99.2	100.0	.	.	104.3	101.7	100.0	102.5	113.1 [6]	123.4
Gambia (Banjul, Kombo St. Mary) [8]	307.9	.	.	330.9	349.4 |	100.0 [9]	103.3	111.3	113.5	117.5
Ghana [1]	60.7	100.0	143.6	173.9	289.7	355.0	443.2	499.4	543.9 [6]	...
Guinea Ecuatorial (Malabo) [1]		100.0		103.4	104.4	107.3	...	...	...	...
Guinée (Conakry)	96.4	100.0	. |	100.0 [10]	.	114.0	142.7	174.7	233.9	270.3
Guinée-Bissau (Bissau) [1] [5]					100.0	101.7	101.9	105.8	111.6	121.5
Kenya (Nairobi) [11]	95.4	100.0	105.2	109.4	111.6	114.5	118.6	122.1	130.4	136.6
Madagascar (Cinq régions) [12]	.	100.0	127.2	160.7	186.0	212.7	233.7	268.7	289.2	315.2
Malawi [13]	73.6	100.0 [6]	132.9	156.6	180.0	211.7	236.9	266.9	291.4	319.1
Mali (Bamako) [1]	97.3	100.0	105.0	112.1	111.9	110.1	107.5	110.1	112.3	118.2
Maroc	97.5	100.0	101.9	103.4	104.4	105.6	107.1	108.2	109.2	109.8
Mauritanie [1]	97.9	100.0	103.2	108.6	114.1 [14]	123.3 [6]	134.7	145.1	157.3	169.6

Explanations and sources: see p. 1067.

[1] Incl. water, electricity, gas and other fuels. [2] Housing; incl. water. [3] Series (base 2006=100) replacing former series. [4] Incl. "Fuel and light" and certain household equipment. [5] Index base 2003=100. [6] Series linked to former series. [7] Series (base 2004=100) replacing former series. [8] Index base: 1990=100. [9] Series (base 2004=100) replacing former series; beginning 2004: incl. water, electricity, gas and other fuels. [10] Series (base 2002=100) replacing former series; prior to 2002: excl. water, electricity and gas. [11] Low income group. [12] Incl. housing, water, electriciy and other fuels. [13] Housing. [14] Jan.-Nov.

Explications et sources: voir p. 1069.

[1] Y compris l'eau, l'électricité, le gaz et autres combustibles. [2] Logement; y compris l'eau. [3] Série (base 2006=100) remplaçant la précédente. [4] Y compris le groupe "Combustible et éclairage" et certains biens d'équipement de ménage. [5] Indice base 2003=100. [6] Série enchaînée à la précédente. [7] Série (base 2004=100) remplaçant la précédente. [8] Indices base: 1990=100. [9] Série (base 2004=100) remplaçant la précédente; a partir de 2004: y compris l'eau, l'électricité, le gaz et autres combustible [10] Série (base 2002=100) remplaçant la précédente; avant 2002: non compris l'eau, l'électricité et le gaz. [11] Familles à revenu modique. [12] Y compris le logement, l'eau, l'électricité et autres combustibles. [13] Logement. [14] janv.-nov.

Explicaciones y fuentes: véase p. 1071.

[1] Incl. el agua, la electricidad, el gas y otros combustibles. [2] Vivienda; incl. el agua. [3] Serie (base 2006=100) que substituye a la anterior. [4] Incl. "Combustible y luz" y ciertos enseres domésticos. [5] Indice base 2003=100. [6] Serie enlazada con la anterior. [7] Serie (base 2004=100) que substituye a la anterior. [8] Indices base: 1990=100. [9] Serie (base 2004=100) que substituye a la anterior; a partir de 2004: incl. el agua, la electricidad, el gas y otros combustib [10] Serie (base 2002=100) que substituye a la anterior; antes de 2002: excl. el agua, la electricitad y el gas. [11] Familias de ingresos módicos. [12] Incl. la vivienda, el agua, la electricidad y otros combustibles. [13] Vivienda. [14] enero-nov.

7F

| | CONSUMER PRICES — Rent indices | PRIX À LA CONSOMMATION — Indices du loyer | PRECIOS AL CONSUMIDOR — Indices del alquiler (2000=100) |

Country / Pays / País	1999	2000	2001	2002	2003	2004	2005	2006	2007	2008
Mauritius [1]	99.2	100.0	100.7	99.8 [2]	100.0	100.5	101.3	123.2	128.1 [3]	130.5
Namibia [1][4][5]				100.0	107.3	114.6	116.4	120.1	124.3	...
Niger (Niamey, Afric.) [4]	99.5	100.0	99.5	101.5	103.9	105.3	106.2	107.5	108.1	113.4
Nigeria [4]	81.4	100.0	99.3	116.1	155.4 [6]	187.5	210.1	245.5	270.1	286.7
Réunion	98.9	98.5	102.4	103.3	104.7	106.4	109.2	112.1	114.5	117.2
Rwanda (Kigali) [4]	96.6	100.0	101.4	104.2	106.9 [6]		145.3	171.0	200.6	...
Sénégal (Dakar)	93.2	100.0	101.6	102.9	103.0	103.4	104.6	108.2	119.1	120.8
Seychelles [4][7]			100.0 [8]	100.2	101.8	103.1	103.8	103.1	103.4 [6]	168.9
Sierra Leone [9]				100.0	116.2	140.3	182.7	178.3		...
South Africa [1]	102.8	100.0 [6]	103.7	114.0	120.9	111.2	113.4	118.2	129.7	142.2
Saint Helena	96.7	100.0	100.0 [10]	100.9	101.3	103.0	103.7	104.5	104.8	110.4
Swaziland [1]	91.6	100.0	102.2	104.9	105.7	117.5	119.6	101.3 [11]	102.5	113.0
Tanzania (Tanganyika)	94.7	100.0	103.8	105.4 [6]	106.2	110.1	124.5	131.2	136.0	139.3
Tchad (N'Djamena)	113.2	100.0	96.7	96.7 [6]	96.9	107.1	127.3	133.6	108.0 [12]	110.0
Togo (Lomé) [4]	98.0	100.0	101.0	103.7	104.8	104.9	108.1	115.8	118.1	121.3
Tunisie [13]	146.0	100.0 [14]	103.2	106.6	109.6	114.7	118.3	121.8	126.2	131.3
Uganda [4]	97.6	100.0	107.6	110.7	116.5	121.0	130.1	139.1	164.6 [6]	181.1
AMERICA - AMÉRIQUE - AMERICA										
Anguilla	86.7	100.0	100.0 [8]	100.4	85.5	83.3	89.1	98.4	103.3	105.9
Argentina (Buenos Aires) [15]	100.6	100.0 [6]	99.7	98.1	96.2	96.9	106.2	124.9	146.4	...
Aruba [7]			100.0	105.1	108.8	112.6	116.6	120.7	125.0	129.4

Explanations and sources: see p. 1067.

[1] Housing. [2] July-Dec.; series (base 2003=100) replacing former series. [3] July-Dec.; series linked to former series. [4] Incl. water, electricity, gas and other fuels. [5] Index base 2002=100. [6] Series linked to former series. [7] Index base 2001=100. [8] Series (base 2001=100) replacing former series. [9] Index base 2003=100. [10] Series (base 1st quarter 2002=100) replacing former series. [11] Series (base 2005=100) replacing former series; prior to 2006:"Housing" only. [12] 11 months' average. Series (base 2005=100) replacing former series. [13] Index base: 1990=100. [14] Series (base 2000=100) replacing former series. [15] Metropolitan areas.

Explications et sources: voir p. 1069.

[1] Logement. [2] Juillet-Déc.; série (base 2003=100) remplaçant la précédente. [3] Juillet-déc.; série enchaînée à la précédente. [4] Y compris l'eau, l'électricité, le gaz et autres combustibles. [5] Indice base 2002=100. [6] Série enchaînée à la précédente. [7] Indice base 2001=100. [8] Série (base 2001=100) remplaçant la précédente. [9] Indice base 2003=100. [10] Série (base 1er trimestre 2002=100) replaçant la précédente. [11] Série (base 2005=100) remplaçant la précédente; avant 2006:"Logement" seulement. [12] Moyenne de 11 mois. Série (base 2005=100) remplaçant la précédente. [13] Indices base: 1990=100. [14] Série (base 2000=100) remplaçant la précédente. [15] Régions métropolitaines.

Explicaciones y fuentes: véase p. 1071.

[1] Vivienda. [2] Julio-dic.; serie (base 2003=100) que sustituye a la anterior. [3] Julio-dic.; serie enlazada con la anterior. [4] Incl. el agua, la electricidad, el gas y otros combustibles. [5] Indice base 2002=100. [6] Serie enlazada con la anterior. [7] Indice base 2001=100. [8] Serie (base 2001=100) que sustituye a la anterior. [9] Indice base 2003=100. [10] Serie (base primer trimestre de 2002=100) que sustituye a la anterior antes de 2006: "Vivienda" solamente. [12] Promedio de 11 meses. Serie (base 2005=100) que substituye a la anterior. [13] Indices base: 1990=100. [14] Serie (base 2000=100) que substituye a la anterior. [15] Areas metropolitanas.

CONSUMER PRICES

Rent indices

PRIX À LA CONSOMMATION

Indices du loyer

PRECIOS AL CONSUMIDOR

Indices del alquiler

(2000=100)

Country Pays País	1999	2000	2001	2002	2003	2004	2005	2006	2007	2008
Bahamas (New Providence) [1]	99.8	100.0	100.2	100.3	101.0	101.7	103.7	105.4	105.9	109.6
Barbados [2] [3]	*133.6*	.	*141.7* |	*100.0* [4]	*99.6*	*99.3*	*109.6*	*120.3*	*125.4*	*127.1*
Belize [5]	98.5	100.0	102.1	101.0	104.7	110.1	114.7	120.3	121.9	126.3
Bermuda	98.1	100.0	102.4	104.1	106.0	108.4	111.4	116.2 [6]	118.7	121.5
Bolivia [7]	95.0	100.0	100.2	101.1	109.0	111.0	112.3	112.7	113.1	...
Brasil	95.7	100.0	107.7	120.6	136.8	148.6	158.3	165.7	...	...
Canada	98.8	100.0	101.6	103.6	105.1	106.3	107.1	108.2	109.8 [6]	111.7
Cayman Islands	99.4	100.0	98.9	100.8	97.7	105.0	127.8	120.8	119.3	124.1
Colombia [8] [9]	96.4	100.0	102.7	105.1	108.3	112.7	117.0	121.1	126.4	132.5
Costa Rica [10]	93.1	100.0	108.1	116.9	123.5	129.1	136.3	. |	*100.00* [11]	*113.91*
Chile (Santiago) [9]	94.2	100.0	106.1	109.6	115.0	118.4	122.1	127.5	135.7	...
Dominica [1] [3]	*126.4*	. |	*100.0* [12]	*99.7*	*103.4*	*108.2*	*109.8*	*111.0*	*113.8*	*117.4*
República Dominicana [9]	92.2	100.0	106.7	120.6	165.0	206.6	227.0	253.7	262.9	277.1
Ecuador	80.2	100.0	135.2	198.1	.	. |	*100.0* [13]	*108.2*	*114.5*	*119.7*
El Salvador [7]	97.0	100.0	103.0	105.0	106.0	109.0	113.3	115.1	114.8	116.9
Greenland	98.2 [6]	100.0	100.6	111.0	114.5	125.4	125.7	125.6	132.2	139.0
Grenada	98.4	100.0	103.2	102.7	104.8	106.9	...	...	...	...
Guadeloupe	98.6	100.0	101.1	102.3	103.4	104.6	106.5	108.3	111.1	117.5
Guatemala (Guatemala) [5]	94.9	100.0 |	*100.0* [14]	*105.3*	*108.7*	*112.9*	*118.8*	*125.9*	*131.6*	*137.8*
Guyana (Georgetown) [5] [15]	88.5	100.0	101.6	111.3	118.9	122.9	140.6	144.5	154.8	162.4
Guyane française	99.6	100.0	101.1	102.3	103.7	104.9	107.0	111.5	120.3	124.0
Haïti [5] [16]	85.2	100.0	111.3	121.9	170.1	198.8	226.3 [6]	272.7	309.6	350.4

Explanations and sources: see p. 1067.

[1] Incl. "Fuel and light". [2] Housing. [3] Index base: 1990=100. [4] Series (base 2002=100) replacing former series. [5] Incl. water, electricity, gas and other fuels. [6] Series linked to former series. [7] Urban areas. [8] Low income group. [9] Incl. "Fuel and light" and certain household equipment. [10] Central area. [11] Series (base 2007=100) replacing former series. [12] Series (base 2001=100) replacing former series; prior to 2001 incl. "Fuel and Light". [13] Series (base 2005=100) replacing former series. [14] Series (base 2001=100) replacing former series. [15] Dec. of each year. [16] Metropolitan areas.

Explications et sources: voir p. 1069.

[1] Y compris le groupe "Combustible et éclairage". [2] Logement. [3] Indices base: 1990=100. [4] Série (base 2002=100) remplaçant la précédente. [5] Y compris l'eau, l'électricité, le gaz et autres combustibles. [6] Série enchaînée à la précédente. [7] Régions urbaines. [8] Familles à revenu modique. [9] Y compris le groupe "Combustible et éclairage" et certains biens d'équipement de ménage. [10] Région centrale. [11] Série (base 2007=100) remplaçant la précédente. [12] Série (base 2001=100) remplaçant la précédente; avant 2001 y compris "Combustible et éclairage". [13] Série (base 2005=100) remplaçant la précédente. [14] Série (base 2001=100) remplaçant la précédente. [15] Déc. de chaque année. [16] Régions métropolitaines.

Explicaciones y fuentes: véase p. 1071.

[1] Incl. el grupo "Combustible y alumbrado". [2] Vivienda. [3] Indices base: 1990=100. [4] Serie (base 2002=100) que substituye a la anterior. [5] Incl. el agua, la electricidad, el gas y otros combustibles. [6] Serie enlazada con la anterior. [7] Areas urbanas. [8] Familias de ingresos módicos. [9] Incl. "Combustible y luz" y ciertos enseres domésticos. [10] Región central. [11] Serie (base 2007=100) que substituye a la anterior. [12] Serie (base 2001=100) que substituye a la anterior; antes de 2001 incl. "Combustible y alumbrado". [13] Serie (base 2005=100) que substituye a la anterior. [14] Serie (base 2001=100) que substituye a la anterior. [15] Dic. de cada año. [16] Areas metropolitanas.

	CONSUMER PRICES	PRIX À LA CONSOMMATION	PRECIOS AL CONSUMIDOR
	Rent indices	Indices du loyer	Indices del alquiler

(2000=100)

Country Pays País	1999	2000	2001	2002	2003	2004	2005	2006	2007	2008
Honduras [1]	401.4 |	100.0 [2]	113.9	131.6	142.7	154.3	170.6	179.2	...	...
Jamaica	88.6	100.0	129.9	145.5	157.1	246.4	289.8	327.5 |	261.1 [3]	305.3
Martinique	97.6	100.0	100.7	101.9	105.9	109.1	114.4	119.3	123.3	126.5
México [4]	89.8	100.0	106.6	114.3 [5]	120.6	125.2	129.09	133.19	137.2	141.4
Netherlands Antilles (Curaçao)	97.8	100.0	102.2	104.3	106.4	108.6	110.8	113.0	115.8 [5]	118.5
Nicaragua [6][7]		100.0	120.7	125.6	133.5	144.8	156.0	175.0	189.7	219.3
Panamá [6][8][9]				100.0	99.8	104.0	109.3	114.3	...	
Paraguay (Asunción) [10][11]	93.9	100.0	111.6	125.4	137.8	139.8	145.5	155.7	159.7	172.0 [5]
Perú (Lima) [6][12]	90.5	100.0	105.8	104.0 [5]	110.5	115.5	120.3	123.3	124.5	...
Puerto Rico	98.9	100.0	102.6	104.4	106.0	107.5	109.0	110.9	114.0 [5]	134.6
Saint Lucia	101.6	100.0	123.9	123.8	123.8	123.8	123.8	124.0	...	...
Saint Vincent and the Grenadines (St. Vincent)	99.9	100.0	100.0 [5]	102.8	103.4	102.6	103.4	103.9	105.1	107.0
Trinidad and Tobago	97.1	100.0	101.1	102.5	105.9 [5]	110.8	117.1	121.4	126.4	133.2
United States [13]	96.5	100.0	104.5	108.6	111.7	114.7	118.2	122.4	127.61	132.28
Uruguay (Montevideo)	97.2	100.0	101.9	103.0	100.8	101.7	107.4	116.5	130.9	150.5
Venezuela, Rep. Bolivariana de (Caracas)		100.0	117.1	135.9	153.4	168.1	180.3	192.5	205.1	264.4 [5]
ASIA - ASIE - ASIA										
Armenia	99.6	100.0	100.1	100.6 [5]	100.7	116.6	132.8 [5]	147.2	156.4	158.2
Bahrain	100.6	100.0	101.0	104.5	109.7	117.0	124.7	.	134.9	138.8
Bangladesh [14][15][16]								100.0	108.7	115.6
Bhutan [6][17]						100.0	109.4	114.4	117.4	...

Explanations and sources: see p. 1067.

[1] Index base: 1990=100. [2] Series (base Dec. 2000=100) replacing former series [3] Series replacing former series. [4] Incl. "Fuel and light". [5] Series linked to former series. [6] Incl. water, electricity, gas and other fuels. [7] Index base 1999=100. [8] Urban areas. [9] Index base 2003=100. [10] Incl. housing, water, electriciy and other fuels. [11] Incl. certain household equipment and cleaning products. [12] Metropolitan areas. [13] All Urban Consumers. [14] Government officials. [15] Gross rent, Fuel and Lighting. [16] Index base: July 2006=100. [17] Index base: 2004=100.

Explications et sources: voir p. 1069.

[1] Indices base: 1990=100. [2] Série (base déc. 2000=100) remplaçant la précédente. [3] Série remplaçant la précédente. [4] Y compris le groupe "Combustible et éclairage". [5] Série enchaînée à la précédente. [6] Y compris l'eau, l'électricité, le gaz et autres combustibles. [7] Indices base 1999=100. [8] Régions urbaines. [9] Indice base 2003=100. [10] Y compris le logement, l'eau, l'électricité et autres combustibles. [11] Y compris certains biens d'équipement de ménage et les produits d'entretien. [12] Régions métropolitaines. [13] Tous les consommateurs urbains. [14] Fonctionnaires. [15] Loyer brut, combustible et éclairage. [16] Base de l'indice: juillet 2006=100. [17] Base de l'indice: 2004=100.

Explicaciones y fuentes: véase p. 1071.

[1] Indices base: 1990=100. [2] Serie (base dic. 2000=100) que substituye a la anterior. [3] Serie que substituye a la anterior. [4] Incl. el grupo "Combustible y alumbrado". [5] Serie enlazada con la anterior. [6] Incl. el agua, la electricidad, el gas y otros combustibles. [7] Indice base 1999=100. [8] Areas urbanas. [9] Indice base 2003=100. [10] Incl. la vivienda, el agua, la electricidad y otros combustibles. [11] Incl. ciertos enseres domésticos y los productos de limpieza. [12] Areas metropolitanas. [13] Todos los consumidores urbanos. [14] Funcionarios. [15] Alquiler bruto, combustible y alumbrado. [16] Base del indice: julio 2006=100. [17] Base del indice: 2004=100.

CONSUMER PRICES

Rent indices

PRIX À LA CONSOMMATION

Indices du loyer

PRECIOS AL CONSUMIDOR

Indices del alquiler

7F

(2000=100)

Country Pays País	1999	2000	2001	2002	2003	2004	2005	2006	2007	2008
Brunei Darussalam [1]	101.0	100.0	100.2	98.9 [2]	98.1	97.4	97.6	96.5	95.7	95.9
Georgia [3] [4]	95.0	100.0	103.0	110.8	114.0	116.9	131.0	131.0	185.5	...
Hong Kong, China [5]	221.9 |	100.0 [6]	97.0	91.4	87.0	82.5	82.5 [2]	86.4	88.1	91.7
India										
Industrial workers	94.3	100.0	109.2	120.4	126.5	136.4	157.9	137 [2]	142	147
Urban non-manual employees	90.6	100.0	110.0	117.9	125.0	131.8	141.5	149.4	157.1	164.4
Delhi, Industrial workers	96.4	100.0	103.9	107.1	110.5	122.6	164.4	124.7 [2]	126.8	128.9
Iran, Islamic Rep. of	86.0 [2]	100.0	120.8	143.1	172.0	204.2	236.0	271.1 |	100.0 [7]	128.2
Iraq	67.0	100.0	165.1	268.2	380.0	644.9	918.6	1 240.9	1 538.1	1 765.3
Israel	102.2	100.0 [2]	103.9	115.8 [2]	110.2	107.2	106.1	107.3 [2]	105.0	108.5
Japan	99.6	100.0 [2]	100.4	100.4	100.5	100.3	100.3	100.3	100.1	100.1
Jordan	97.7	100.0	102.2	104.0 [2]	106.3	107.8	109.1	110.8	111.8	113.5
Kazakhstan	100.5	100.0	100.9	102.7	104.7	108.9	...	...	...	...
Korea, Republic of	100.5	100.0 [2]	104.1	110.1	114.0	115.8	115.6 [2]	116.1	118.1	120.8
Kyrgyzstan [8]	82.1	100.0	147.0	168.3	175.0	201.2	214.2	235.4	...	...
Macau, China	103.1	100.0	97.4	94.8	92.7	92.1	98.1 [2]	112.0	128.3	147.0
Malaysia [9]	98.5	100.0 [2]	101.3	102.0	103.0	104.0	105.3 [2]	106.8	108.2	109.9
Maldives (Male) [4] [9] [10]	.	.	.	.	.	.	. |	100.0 [11]	103.8	115.3
Myanmar	97.6	100.0	121.4	175.3	245.4	272.2	333.0	388.8	518.7	658.6
Nepal	93.5	100.0	105.2	110.9	116.4	120.9	126.2	131.9	137.3	144.2
Oman (Muscat)	100.2	100.0	99.7	99.2	99.2	99.0	96.5 [2]	98.7	106.1	127.8
Pakistan	96.5	100.0	. |	100.0 [12]	101.6	110.2	123.0	132.7	142.1	...
Philippines [4]	95.0	100.0 [2]	107.1	112.2	117.0	121.4	126.9	131.9	133.9	139.6
Qatar	110.6 |	100.0 [13]	101.5	103.4	121.9	141.7	181.9	225.3	291.4	348.6

Explanations and sources: see p. 1067.

[1] Incl. "Fuel and light" and expenditure on maintenance and repairs of dwelling. [2] Series linked to former series. [3] 5 cities. [4] Housing. [5] Index base: 1990=100. [6] Series (base 2000=100) replacing former series. [7] Series (base 2007=100) replacing former series. [8] Housing; incl. water. [9] Incl. water, electricity, gas and other fuels. [10] Index base: 2006=100. [11] Series (base 2006=100) replacing former series. [12] Series (base 2002=100) replacing former series. [13] Series replacing former series; prior 2000: rent only.

Explications et sources: voir p. 1069.

[1] Y compris le groupe "Combustible et éclairage" et les dépenses pour l'entretien et la réparation du logement. [2] Série enchaînée à la précédente. [3] 5 villes. [4] Logement. [5] Indices base: 1990=100. [6] Série (base 2000=100) remplaçant la précédente. [7] Série (base 2007=100) remplaçant la précédente. [8] Logement; y compris l'eau. [9] Y compris l'eau, l'électricité, le gaz et autres combustibles. [10] Base de l'indice: 2006=100. [11] Série (base 2006=100) remplaçant la précédente. [12] Série (base 2002=100) remplaçant la précédente. [13] Série remplaçant la précédente; avant 2000: loyer seulement.

Explicaciones y fuentes: véase p. 1071.

[1] Incl. el grupo "Combustible y alumbrado" y los gastos de conservación y reparación de la vivienda. [2] Serie enlazada con la anterior. [3] 5 ciudades. [4] Vivienda. [5] Indices base: 1990=100. [6] Serie (base 2000=100) que substituye a la anterior. [7] Serie (base 2007=100) que substituye a la anterior. [8] Vivienda; incl. el agua. [9] Incl. el agua, la electricidad, el gas y otros combustibles. [10] Base del índice: 2006=100. [11] Serie (base 2006=100) que substituye a la anterior. [12] Serie (base 2002=100) que substituye a la anterior. [13] Serie que substituye a la anterior; antes de 2000: alquiler únicamente.

7F

	CONSUMER PRICES Rent indices		PRIX À LA CONSOMMATION Indices du loyer			PRECIOS AL CONSUMIDOR Indices del alquiler				(2000=100)

Country Pays País	1999	2000	2001	2002	2003	2004	2005	2006	2007	2008
Saudi Arabia [1]	100.2	100.0	99.9	100.0	100.0	100.2 [2]	99.7	100.9	111.2	...
Singapore	100.9	100.0	100.6	99.8	98.7	98.2 [2]	98.1	98.8	100.3	113.7
Sri Lanka (Colombo)	100.0	100.0	100.0	100.0	100.0	100.0	100.0	100.0	206.6 [3]	226.8
Syrian Arab Republic	99.6	100.0	100.7	102.9	124.0 [2]	134.0	162.0	173.9 [2]	176.6	182.7
Taiwan, China	99.9	100.0	99.9 [2]	99.0	98.0	97.3	97.3	97.5	97.7 [2]	...
Thailand	100.2	100.0 [2]	99.7	99.1	97.8	97.2 [2]	97.5	97.7	97.9	98.3
United Arab Emirates	100.1	100.0 [2]	102.7	107.1	112.7	120.0	132.0	153.4	181.8	113.4 [4]
West Bank and Gaza Strip	100.0	100.0	100.3	115.6	111.6	109.7	109.9	109.0	100.8	119.5 [2]
Yemen, Republic of	96.9	100.0	105.3	116.8	129.4	132.3	139.7	146.8	152.0 [2]	189.5

EUROPE - EUROPE - EUROPA

Country Pays País	1999	2000	2001	2002	2003	2004	2005	2006	2007	2008
Albania	98.3	100.0	118.3	131.5	130.9	136.9	142.2	149.7	154.7	154.6 [2]
Andorre [5] [6] [7]			100.0	103.4	106.9	111.2	115.4	122.8	130.2	134.1
Austria [8]	98.4	100.0 [2]	102.8	104.6	109.1	113.0	116.8	119.4	121.7	123.3
Belarus	25.9	100.0	206.4	977.8	1 348.8	2 236.4	3 201.6	4 097.7	4 313.3	4 917.1
Belgique	98.5	100.0	101.9	104.5	106.8 [2]	108.8	111.0	114.9	...	...
Bulgaria	87.5	100.0	111.6	121.8	121.4	124.7	132.3	139.5	144.8	160.9
Croatia	95.7	100.0	101.7 [2]	106.2	107.8	111.1	115.5 [2]	146.6	161.9	184.2
Cyprus [9]	94.8	100.0	101.6	105.7	111.1	115.7	122.0	125.3 [2]	128.4	139.8
Czech Republic	93.8	100.0 [2]	110.8	118.4	123.6	129.8	132.5	135.7	142.5	153.9
Denmark	97.2	100.0 [2]	102.7	105.3	108.2	111.2	113.9	116.1	118.6	121.5
España	96.4	100.0	100.0 [10]	104.2	108.7	113.2	118.0	123.1 [2]	128.5	133.9
Estonia	97.4	100.0	109.8	110.4	113.6	120.0	125.8	154.1	195.3	187.4
Faeroe Islands [11]	118.4		100.0 [10]	108.6	114.1	117.3	116.9	127.5	165.2	181.6
Finland	97.3	100.0 [2]	103.9	107.1	109.6	111.7	114.8	117.4 [2]	120.3	124.9

Explanations and sources: see p. 1067.

[1] All cities. [2] Series linked to former series. [3] Series (base 2002=100) replacing former series. [4] Series (base 2007=100) replacing former series. [5] Dec. of each year. [6] Incl. water and gas. [7] Index base 2001=100. [8] Housing. [9] Housing; incl. water. [10] Series (base 2001=100) replacing former series. [11] Index base: 1986 = 100.

Explications et sources: voir p. 1069.

[1] Ensemble des villes. [2] Série enchaînée à la précédente. [3] Série (base 2002=100) remplaçant la précédente. [4] Série (base 2007=100) remplaçant la précédente. [5] Déc. de chaque année. [6] Y compris l'eau et le gaz. [7] Indice base 2001=100. [8] Logement. [9] Logement; y compris l'eau. [10] Série (base 2001=100) remplaçant la précédente. [11] Indices base: 1986 = 100.

Explicaciones y fuentes: véase p. 1071.

[1] Todas las ciudades. [2] Serie enlazada con la anterior. [3] Serie (base 2002=100) que substituye a la anterior. [4] Serie (base 2007=100) que substituye a la anterior. [5] Dic. de cada año. [6] Incl. el agua y el gas. [7] Indice base 2001=100. [8] Vivienda. [9] Vivienda; incl. el agua. [10] Serie (base 2001=100) que substituye a la anterior. [11] Indices base: 1986 = 100.

CONSUMER PRICES
Rent indices

PRIX À LA CONSOMMATION
Indices du loyer

PRECIOS AL CONSUMIDOR
Indices del alquiler

(2000=100)

Country Pays País	1999	2000	2001	2002	2003	2004	2005	2006	2007	2008
France	100.2	100.0	100.6	103.2	106.2	108.8	112.7	116.6	120.3	122.9
Germany	98.8	100.0 ı	101.2	102.6	103.8	104.8	105.9	107.0	108.3 ı	109.6
Gibraltar [2]	101.3 ı	100.0	104.3	101.5	102.3	106.4	113.5	115.3	122.6	127.2
Greece	96.2 ı	100.0	103.9	109.1	114.8	120.9	126.0 ı	131.5	137.5	142.8
Hungary	86.1	100.0	117.4	131.2	141.0	154.8	161.6	168.4	181.2	197.5
Iceland [3] [4]	88.1	100.0	105.6	111.8	122.0	131.9	153.6	173.8	196.1	221.2
Ireland [4]	91.5	100.0	115.9 ı	117.0	114.0	117.1	125.7	147.3	182.0 ı	199.4
Isle of Man	94.7	100.0 ı	112.7	120.9	136.1	144.2	150.0	153.4	157.8	163.7
Italy	97.6	100.0	102.3	104.6	107.5	110.5	113.2	116.0	119.0	122.0
Jersey [5] [6]	.	100.0	105.3	109.5	114.3	125.9	136.9	140.0	156.0	161.4
Kosovo (Serbia) [7] [8]	.	.	.	99.3 [9]	100.0	100.3	96.9	95.3	96.1	101.0
Latvia	98.1	100.0 ı	102.7	103.2	104.9	112.3	126.5	141.0	167.3	208.7
Lithuania	97.7	100.0 ı	102.4	104.3	105.2	108.6	115.0 ı	123.1	138.8	163.3
Luxembourg	97.0	100.0	103.0	105.8	107.7	109.4	112.6 ı	115.2	117.3	120.7
Macedonia, The Former Yugoslav Rep. of [4]	91.9	100.0	111.3	115.9	120.4	120.0	120.4	119.5	127.1	134.8
Malta [4]	97.5	100.0	104.3	107.6	110.8 ı	115.0	120.7	126.5	130.1	135.3
Netherlands	97.3	100.0 ı	102.6	105.5	108.8	112.2	115.0	117.7	120.1 ı	122.1
Norway [4]	95.7	100.0	104.3	109.4	113.9	116.0	118.2	120.9	122.7	126.0
Poland [10]	83.2	100.0	113.3	122.8	128.8	133.4	138.2	142.0	147.6	157.1
Portugal	96.5	100.0	104.0	109.0 ı	112.6	116.0	119.5	123.4	123.7	...
Roumanie	63.1	100.0	113.1	140.4	162.1	187.8	204.6	216.7	372.2	469.7
Russian Federation [11] [12]	72.2	100.0	166.7	251.9	330.8	427.2	581.5	684.3	769.0	883.7
San Marino [13] [14]	145.5	.	. ı	100.0 [15]	99.9	100.2	100.3	104.6	106.6
Serbia	77.3	100.0	240.9	356.1	494.7	615.9	757.6	858.3	928.0	974.2

Explanations and sources: see p. 1067.
[1] Series linked to former series. [2] Incl. housing, water, electriciy and other fuels. [3] Annual averages are based on the months Feb.-Dec. and of January of the following year. [4] Housing. [5] June of each year. [6] Index base June 2000=100. [7] Incl. water, electricity, gas and other fuels. [8] Index base 2003=100. [9] May-Dec. [10] Incl. water supply. [11] Rent for municipal housing. [12] Dec. of each year; Index base Dec. 2000=100. [13] Incl. "Fuel and light". [14] Index base: 1990=100. [15] Series (base 2003=100) replacing former series.

Explications et sources: voir p. 1069.
[1] Série enchaînée à la précédente. [2] Y compris le logement, l'eau, l'électricité et autres combustibles. [3] Les moyennes annuelles sont basées sur les mois de fév.-déc. et de janvier de l'année suivante. [4] Logement. [5] Juin de chaque année. [6] Indice base juin 2000=100. [7] Y compris l'eau, l'électricité, le gaz et autres combustibles. [8] Indice base 2003=100. [9] Mai-déc. [10] Y compris l'approvisionnement de l'eau. [11] Loyer d'un logement municipal. [12] Déc. de chaque année; base des indices déc. 2000=100. [13] Y compris le groupe "Combustible et éclairage". [14] Indices base: 1990=100. [15] Série (base 2003=100) remplaçant la précédente.

Explicaciones y fuentes: véase p. 1071.
[1] Serie enlazada con la anterior. [2] Incl. la vivienda, el agua, la electricidad y otros combustibles. [3] Le media anual esta basada sobre Feb.-Dic. y de enero del año siguiente. [4] Vivienda. [5] Junio de cada año. [6] Indice base junio 2000=100. [7] Incl. el agua, la electricidad, el gas y otros combustibles. [8] Indice base 2003=100. [9] Mayo-dic. [10] Incl. el suministro del agua. [11] Alquiler de una vivienda municipal. [12] Dic. de cada año; base de los índices dic. 2000=100. [13] Incl. el grupo "Combustible y alumbrado". [14] Indices base: 1990=100. [15] Serie (base 2003=100) que substituye a la anterior.

CONSUMER PRICES
Rent indices

PRIX À LA CONSOMMATION
Indices du loyer

PRECIOS AL CONSUMIDOR
Indices del alquiler

(2000=100)

Country Pays País	1999	2000	2001	2002	2003	2004	2005	2006	2007	2008
Slovakia [1]	75.5	100.0	117.2 [2]	122.2	158.0	198.6	209.9	214.8	223.4	209.7
Slovenia [3]	94.7	100.0	113.7	124.5	152.9	177.8	187.7 [2]	193.8	199.5	210.7
Suisse	98.5	100.0 [2]	102.8	103.9	104.2	105.5	106.9	109.1 [2]	111.6	114.3
Sweden [1]	99.25	100.00	103.94	106.85	111.47	111.66	112.06	115.97	120.63	128.87
Turkey [1]	61.0	100.0	156.8	217.4	268.9	310.1	388.1 [2]	466.2	552.1	627.5
United Kingdom	96.8	100.0	103.5	106.1	107.7	110.1	113.9	117.2	121.1	125.6
OCEANIA - OCÉANIE - OCEANIA										
American Samoa	96.3	100.0	102.2	101.2	107.8	107.5	116.2	121.2	...	...
Australia	97.0	100.0	103.2	105.7	107.7	110.4	112.9	116.5	122.9	132.4
Cook Islands (Rarotonga) [4]	100.5	100.0	116.9	117.4	122.4	124.5	130.5	147.7	159.4 [2]	173.0
Fiji [4]	99.5	100.0	101.4	103.4	105.8	107.1	108.3	111.0	114.3 [2]	115.3
Guam [5]	98.7	100.0	92.0	91.0	86.5	84.8	87.6	91.7	97.0	105.9 [2]
Kiribati (Tarawa)	.	100.0 [6]	101.8	102.2	102.7	102.4	102.5	102.4	102.4	102.5
New Zealand [7]	99.7	100.0	90.2	91.8	94.7	97.6	100.0	102.3 [2]	105.2	108.5
Niue	99.8	100.0	98.6	96.8 [2]	96.8	97.5 [8]	98.7	100.5	107.0	109.7
Northern Mariana Islands (Saipan) [5]	100.8	100.0	99.3	97.8	96.4 [2]	95.0	96.8	117.2	139.5	149.2
Nouvelle-Calédonie (Nouméa)	99.6	100.0	100.5	100.7	101.8	102.9	104.1	109.1	112.1	113.6
Papua New Guinea [1]	93.1	100.0	106.2	109.5	116.1	124.3	135.7	149.4	154.5	177.2
Polynésie française [9]	99.8	100.0	100.9	100.0 [10]	100.0	100.5	102.6	105.4	109.4	110.6 [2]
Solomon Islands (Honiara) [1]	91.8	100.0	103.7	122.4	145.3	150.7	169.1	188.9	223.3 [2]	259.9
Tonga [11]				100.0	102.1	109.1	121.8	138.2	144.1	146.5
Tuvalu (Funafuti)	98.7	100.0	101.3	120.0 [2]	134.3	135.1	139.3	143.8	141.7 [2]	...

Explanations and sources: see p. 1067.

[1] Incl. water, electricity, gas and other fuels. [2] Series linked to former series. [3] Urban areas. [4] Housing; incl. water. [5] Housing. [6] Series (base 2000=100) replacing former series. [7] Excl. rental value of owner occupied dwellings. [8] Average of the last three quarters. [9] Incl. water. [10] Series (base 2002=100) replacing former series. [11] Index base 2002=100.

Explications et sources: voir p. 1069.

[1] Y compris l'eau, l'électricité, le gaz et autres combustibles. [2] Série enchaînée à la précédente. [3] Régions urbaines. [4] Logement; y compris l'eau. [5] Logement. [6] Série (base 2000=100) remplaçant la précédente. [7] Non compris la valeur locative des logements occupés par leurs propriétaires. [8] Moyenne des trois derniers trimestres. [9] Y compris l'eau. [10] Série (base 2002=100) remplaçant la précédente. [11] Indice base 2002=100.

Explicaciones y fuentes: véase p. 1071.

[1] Incl. el agua, la electricidad, el gas y otros combustibles. [2] Serie enlazada con la anterior. [3] Areas urbanas. [4] Vivienda; incl. el agua. [5] Vivienda. [6] Serie (base 2000=100) que substituye a la anterior. [7] Excl. el valor locativo de la vivienda ocupada por su propietario. [8] Promedio de los tres últimos trimestres. [9] Incl. el agua. [10] Serie (base 2002=100) que substituye a la anterior. [11] Indice base 2002=100.

										7F

CONSUMER PRICES

Rent indices

PRIX À LA CONSOMMATION

Indices du loyer

PRECIOS AL CONSUMIDOR

Indices del alquiler

(2000=100)

Country Pays País	1999	2000	2001	2002	2003	2004	2005	2006	2007	2008
Vanuatu [1]	99.7 [2]	100.0	100.4	100.5	103.6	112.0	115.9	118.7	123.9	126.3

Explanations and sources: see p. 1067.

[1] Incl. water, electricity, gas and other fuels. [2] Series linked to former series.

Explications et sources: voir p. 1069.

[1] Y compris l'eau, l'électricité, le gaz et autres combustibles. [2] Série enchaînée à la précédente.

Explicaciones y fuentes: véase p. 1071.

[1] Incl. el agua, la electricidad, el gas y otros combustibles. [2] Serie enlazada con la anterior.

Occupational injuries

Lésions professionnelles

Lesiones profesionales

Occupational injuries

The Resolution concerning statistics of occupational injuries (resulting from occupational accidents) adopted by the Sixteenth International Conference of Labour Statisticians (ICLS) (Geneva, 1998)[1] contains the following definitions for statistical purposes:

occupational accident: an unexpected and unplanned occurrence, including acts of violence, arising out of or in connection with work which results in one or more workers incurring a personal injury, disease or death;

as occupational accidents are to be considered travel, transport or road traffic accidents in which workers are injured and which arise out of or in the course of work, i.e. while engaged in an economic activity, or at work, or carrying on the business of the employer;

occupational injury: any personal injury, disease or death resulting from an occupational accident; an occupational injury is therefore distinct from an occupational disease, which is a disease contracted as a result of an exposure over a period of time to risk factors arising from work activity;

case of occupational injury: the case of one worker incurring an occupational injury as a result of one occupational accident;

incapacity for work: inability of the victim, due to an occupational injury, to perform the normal duties of work in the job or post occupied at the time of the occupational accident.

The statistics of occupational injuries presented in this chapter conform, as far as possible, to the guidelines contained in the Sixteenth ICLS Resolution. The data should cover all workers regardless of their status in employment (i.e. both employees and the self-employed, including employers and own-account workers), and the whole country, all branches of economic activity and all sectors of the economy.

The following are generally excluded: cases of occupational disease (an occupational disease is a disease contracted as a result of an exposure over a period of time to risk factors arising from work activity) and cases of injury due to commuting accidents (a commuting accident is an accident occurring on the habitual route, in either direction, between the place of work or work-related training and (i) the worker's principal or secondary residence; (ii) the place where the worker usually takes his or her meals; or (iii) the place where he or she usually receives his or her remuneration; which results in death or personal injury).

The type of statistics shown for a particular country depends on the source used. Data on occupational injuries are most frequently obtained from occupational accident reporting systems (e.g. to a labour inspectorate) or occupational injury compensation schemes, although surveys of establishments and of households are used in a few countries. The type of source determines the coverage of the statistics. In many countries, the coverage of reporting requirements or injury compensation, and thus the coverage of the statistics, is limited to certain types of workers (employees only in many cases), certain economic activities, cases of injury with more than a certain number of days of incapacity, etc. The type of source is shown as a code following the country name in the tables (see page XVI for explanations), and the type of injuries covered (reported or compensated) is indicated at the head of the series for each country.

The statistics presented relate to cases of occupational injury due to occupational accidents that occurred during the calendar year indicated. Total days lost as a result of a case of injury are included in the statistics for the calendar year in which the occupational accident took place.

Care should be taken when using the data provided in this chapter, particularly when making international comparisons. The sources, methods of data collection, coverage and classifications used differ between countries. For example, coverage may be limited to certain types of workers (employees, insured persons, full-time workers, etc.), certain economic activities, establishments employing more than a given number of workers, cases of injury losing more than a certain number of days of work, etc. Descriptions of the national sources, scope, definitions and methods used for compiling the statistics presented in this chapter are given in ILO: Sources and Methods: Labour Statistics, Volume 8 - Occupational Injuries (Geneva, 1999) and Volume 9 - Transition Countries (Geneva, 1999). A synoptic table showing the main points of coverage follows these explanatory notes. Additional information is also provided in the footnotes to the tables.

Workers in the reference group are those workers in the particular group under consideration and covered by the source of the statistics of occupational injuries (e.g. those of a specific sex or in a specific economic activity, occupation, region, age group, or any combination of these, or those covered by a particular compensation scheme). The number of workers in the reference group varies between countries and economic activities and from one period to another, because of differences or changes in the size and composition of employment and other factors. The differences in numbers are taken into account by using comparative measures, such as frequency, incidence and severity rates.

A rise or fall in the number of cases of occupational injury over a period of time may reflect not only changes in conditions of work and the work environment, but also modifications in reporting procedures or data collection methods, or revisions to laws or regulations governing the reporting or compensation of occupational injuries in the country concerned.

Table 8A

Cases of injury with lost workdays, by economic activity

This table shows the number of cases of occupational injury with lost workdays, as follows:

- *Total cases*: all cases of occupational injury with lost workdays, i.e. the total of fatal cases and of non-fatal cases.

- *Fatal cases*: the number of workers fatally injured as a result of occupational accidents, where death occurred within one year of the day of the accident.

- *Non-fatal cases (temporary and permanent incapacity)*: the number of cases of occupational injury where the workers injured were unable to work temporarily or permanently from the day after the day of the accident.

- *Cases of temporary incapacity*: the number of cases of occupational injury where the workers injured were unable to work from the day after the day of the accident, but were able to perform again the normal duties of work in the job or post occupied at the time of the occupational accident causing the injury within a period of one year from the day of the accident.

Table 8B

Rates of occupational injuries, by economic activity

This table shows frequency or incidence rates of fatal and non-fatal occupational injuries.

Frequency rates are generally calculated as the number of new cases of injury (fatal and non-fatal) during the calendar year (as given in Table 8A) divided by the total number of hours worked by workers in the reference group during the year, multiplied by 1,000,000. Incidence rates are calculated as the number of new cases of injury (fatal and non-fatal) during the calendar year divided by the number of workers in the reference group during the year, multiplied by 100,000.

The type of rate (per 1,000,000 hours worked, per 100,000 workers employed, per 100,000 employees, per 100,000 workers insured, etc.) is indicated at the beginning of the data for each country.

Table 8C

Days lost, by economic activity

This table presents the number of days lost by cases of occupational injury with temporary incapacity for work (as given in Table 8A). In a few cases, they also include days lost by cases with permanent incapacity, which may include estimates. The days lost are generally the calendar days during which the injured worker was temporarily unable to work, excluding the day of the accident, up to a maximum of one year. In some countries, however, particularly those where the source of the statistics is an accident compensation scheme, days lost are expressed in workdays. Temporary absences from work of less than one day for medical treatment are not included.

Note

[1] For the full text of the resolution, see ILO: *Current international recommendations on labour statistics* (Geneva, 2000) or the ILO Department of Statistics' web site (www.ilo.org/public/english/bureau/stat).

Lésions professionnelles

La résolution concernant les statistiques des lésions professionnelles (résultant des accidents du travail) adoptée par la seizième Conférence internationale des statisticiens du travail (CIST) (Genève, 1998)[1] donne les définitions suivantes des fins statistiques:

— *accident du travail*: tout événement inattendu et imprévu, y compris les actes de violence, survenant du fait du travail ou à l'occasion de celui-ci et qui entraîne, pour un ou plusieurs travailleurs, une lésion corporelle, une maladie ou la mort;

sont considérés comme des accidents du travail, les accidents de voyage, de transport ou de circulation dans lesquels les travailleurs sont blessés et qui surviennent à cause ou au cours du travail, c'est-à-dire lorsqu'ils exercent une activité économique, sont au travail ou s'occupent des affaires de l'employeur;

— *lésion professionnelle*: lésion corporelle, maladie ou décès provoqués par un accident du travail; la lésion professionnelle est donc distincte de la maladie professionnelle, qui est une maladie contractée à la suite d'une exposition des facteurs de risque découlant de l'activité professionnelle;

— *cas de lésion professionnelle*: cas d'un seul travailleur victime d'une lésion professionnelle résultant d'un seul accident du travail;

— *incapacité de travail*: incapacité de la personne blessée, due à la lésion professionnelle dont elle a été victime, d'exécuter les tâches normales correspondant à l'emploi ou au poste qu'elle occupait au moment où s'est produit l'accident du travail.

Les statistiques des lésions professionnelles présentées dans ce chapitre sont conformes, dans la mesure du possible, aux recommandations de la seizième CIST. Les données devraient couvrir tous les travailleurs, quelle que soit leur situation dans la profession (c'est-à-dire les salariés et les travailleurs indépendants, y compris les employeurs et les travailleurs à leur propre compte), l'ensemble du pays, toutes les branches d'activité économique ainsi que tous les secteurs de l'économie.

En général, sont exclus: les cas de maladie professionnelle (une maladie professionnelle est une maladie contractée à la suite d'une exposition à des facteurs de risque découlant d'une activité professionnelle pendant une période de temps) et les cas de lésions résultant des accidents de trajet (un accident de trajet est un accident survenant sur le trajet habituellement emprunté par le travailleur, quelle que soit la direction dans laquelle il se déplace, entre son lieu de travail ou de formation liée à son activité professionnelle et: (i) sa résidence principale ou secondaire, (ii) le lieu où il prend normalement ses repas, ou (iii) le lieu où il reçoit normalement son salaire, et qui entraîne la mort ou des lésions corporelles).

En principe, la source utilisée détermine le type de statistiques présentées pour chaque pays. Les sources les plus fréquentes de données dans ce domaine sont les systèmes de déclaration d'accident du travail (par exemple les services d'inspection du travail) ou les régimes d'indemnisation des lésions professionnelles, bien que les enquêtes auprès des établissements ou des ménages soient utilisées dans quelques pays. Le type de source détermine la portée des statistiques. Dans la plupart des pays, la portée des obligations de déclarer ou d'indemniser les lésions, et ainsi la portée des statistiques, est limitée à certains types de travailleurs (salariés, le plus souvent) ou certaines activités économiques ou à des cas de lésion avec incapacité pendant plus d'un nombre de jours précisé, etc. Le type de source apparaît sous la forme d'un code placé après le nom du pays dans les tableaux (pour les explications, voir la page XVI), et le type de lésions couvertes (déclarées ou indemnisées) est précisé au début de chaque série pour chaque pays.

Les statistiques présentées se réfèrent aux cas de lésion professionnelle résultant des accidents du travail survenant pendant l'année civile indiquée. Le total des journées perdues à cause d'un cas de lésion est compris dans les statistiques correspondant à l'année civile au cours de laquelle l'accident du travail a eu lieu.

Les données fournies dans ce chapitre doivent être utilisées avec précaution, en particulier s'il s'agit de procéder à des comparaisons internationales. Les sources, les méthodes de collecte de données, la portée et les classifications utilisées peuvent varier d'un pays à un autre. Par exemple, la portée pourrait ne concerner que certains types de travailleurs (salariés, personnes assurées, travailleurs à plein temps, etc.), certaines activités économiques, les établissements occupant plus d'un certain nombre de travailleurs, les cas de lésion ayant entraîné une incapacité de travail supérieure à un seuil minimum de jours, etc. Les descriptions des sources nationales, de la portée, des définitions, et des méthodes utilisées lors de la compilation des statistiques diffusées dans ce chapitre sont publiées dans BIT: Sources et Méthodes: Statistiques du travail, Volume 8 Lésions professionnelles (Genève, 1999) et Volume 9 Pays en transition (Genève,1999). Le tableau synoptique qui se trouve après ces notes explicatives indique les points essentiels de la portée de chaque série. D'autres renseignements sont fournis dans les notes de bas de page des tableaux.

Les travailleurs du groupe de référence sont les travailleurs du groupe particulier examiné qui sont couverts par la source des statistiques des lésions professionnelles (par exemple les hommes ou les femmes, les travailleurs d'une activité économique, d'une profession, d'une région, d'un groupe d'âge, etc., ou une combinaison de ceux-ci, ou les travailleurs couverts par un régime d'assurance particulier). Le nombre de travailleurs du groupe de référence varie d'un pays à l'autre, d'une activité économique à l'autre et à travers le temps, à cause de plusieurs facteurs dont les différences et les variations de taille et de structure de l'emploi. Ces différences sont prises en compte lors de l'utilisation des mesures comparatives telles que les taux de fréquence, d'incidence ou de gravité.

Les variations à la hausse ou à la baisse du nombre de cas de lésion professionnelle sur un certain laps de temps peuvent refléter non seulement une évolution des conditions du travail et de son environnement, mais aussi des modifications portant sur les méthodes de déclaration des accidents ou de collecte de données, ou encore des révisions de la législation relative à la déclaration et à l'indemnisation des lésions professionnelles dans le pays concerné.

Tableau 8A

Cas de lésion avec perte de journées de travail, par activité économique

Ce tableau donne le nombre de cas de lésion professionnelle avec perte de journées de travail, comme suit:

— *Ensemble des cas*: l'ensemble des cas de lésion professionnelle entraînant la perte des journées de travail, c'est-à-dire le total des cas mortels et des cas non mortels.

— *Cas mortels*: le nombre de travailleurs blessés mortellement dans les accidents du travail, lorsque la mort survient dans l'année suivant le jour de l'accident.

— *Cas non mortels (incapacité temporaire ou permanente)*: le nombre de cas de lésion professionnelle entraînant une incapacité temporaire ou permanente de travailler à partir du jour suivant le jour de l'accident.

— *Cas d'incapacité temporaire*: le nombre de cas de lésion professionnelle où les travailleurs blessés n'ont pas pu travailler à partir du jour suivant le jour de l'accident, mais ont pu reprendre le travail et exécuter les tâches normales correspondant à l'emploi ou au poste occupé au moment où s'est produit l'accident du travail, dans un délai d'un an après le jour de l'accident.

Tableau 8B

Taux des lésions professionnelles, par activité économique

Ce tableau donne les taux de fréquence ou d'incidence des lésions professionnelles mortelles et des lésions professionnelles non mortelles. Les taux de fréquence sont calculés en général comme le nombre de cas nouveaux de lésions (cas mortels ou cas non mortels) durant l'année (tel que présenté dans le tableau 8A) divisé par le nombre total des heures effectuées par les travailleurs du groupe de référence durant l'année, et multiplié par 1 000 000. Les taux d'incidence sont calculés comme le nombre de cas nouveaux de lésions (cas mortels ou cas non mortels) durant l'année, divisé par le nombre de travailleurs du groupe de référence et multiplié par 100 000.

Le type de taux (par 1 000 000 heures effectuées, par 100 000 travailleurs occupés, par 100 000 salariés, par 100 000 travailleurs assurés, etc.) est indiqué au début de chaque série.

Tableau 8C

Journées perdues, par activité économique

Ce tableau donne le nombre total des journées perdues par les cas de lésion professionnelle avec incapacité temporaire de travailler (tel que présenté dans le tableau 8A). Les séries relatives à certains pays comprennent également des estimations des journées perdues par les cas d'incapacité permanente. En général, les journées perdues sont les jours civils pendant lesquels le travailleur blessé était temporairement dans l'incapacité de travailler, non compris le jour de l'accident, jusqu'à un maximum d'un an. Le nombre des journées perdues présenté pour quelques pays est exprimé en journées de travail, en particulier si la source des statistiques est un régime d'indemnisation d'accidents. Les absences temporaires de travail de moins d'un jour pour traitement médical ne sont pas prises en compte.

Note

[1] Pour le texte intégral de la résolution, voir BIT: *Recommandations internationales en vigueur sur les statistiques du travail* (Genève, 2000) ou le site Web du Département de statistique du BIT (www.ilo.org/public/french/bureau/stat).

Lesiones profesionales

La Resolución sobre estadísticas de lesiones profesionales (ocasionadas por accidentes del trabajo) adoptada por la decimosexta Conferencia Internacional de Estadísticos del Trabajo (CIET) (Ginebra, 1998)[1] contiene las siguientes definiciones para los efectos de las estadísticas:

accidente de trabajo: hecho imprevisto y no intencionado, incluidos los actos de violencia, que se deriva del trabajo o está en relación con el mismo y causa una lesión, una enfermedad o la muerte a uno o a más trabajadores; se considerarán accidentes del trabajo los accidentes de viaje, de transporte o de tránsito por la vía pública en que los trabajadores resultan lesionados y que se originan con ocasión o en el curso del trabajo, es decir, que se producen mientras realizan alguna actividad económica, se encuentran en el lugar de trabajo o efectúan tareas encomendadas por el empleador;

lesión profesional: toda lesión corporal, enfermedad o muerte causadas por un accidente de trabajo; la lesión profesional es, por lo tanto, distinta de la enfermedad profesional, que es aquella contraída como resultado de la exposición a factores de riesgo inherentes a la actividad laboral;

caso de lesión profesional: el caso de un trabajador que sufre una lesión profesional causada por un accidente de trabajo;

incapacidad laboral: incapacidad de la víctima, a causa de una lesión profesional, para realizar las tareas habituales de su trabajo, correspondientes al empleo o puesto ocupado en el momento de sufrir el accidente.

Las estadísticas de lesiones profesionales de este capítulo se conforman en la medida de lo posible a las recomendaciones de la decimosexta CIET. Los datos deberían abarcar a todos los trabajadores, independientemente de su situación en el empleo (por ejemplo, asalariados o trabajadores independientes, incluyendo empleadores y trabajadores por cuenta propia), todo el país, todas las ramas de actividad económica y todos los sectores de la economía.

En general, se excluyen los siguientes casos: casos de enfermedad profesional (una enfermedad profesional es aquella contraída como resultado de la exposición a factores de riesgo inherentes a la actividad laboral) y casos de lesión provocados por accidente de trayecto (un accidente de trayecto es un accidente que ocurre en el camino habitual, en cualquier dirección, que recorre el trabajador entre el lugar de trabajo o el lugar de formación relacionada con su trabajo y: i) su residencia principal o secundaria; ii) el lugar en que suele tomar sus comidas; o iii) el lugar en que suele cobrar su remuneración, y que le ocasiona la muerte o lesiones corporales).

Los tipos de estadísticas presentadas para los países se determinan por la fuente de los datos. Estos provienen en general de sistemas de declaración de accidentes del trabajo (por ejemplo, a la inspección del trabajo) o de los regímenes de indemnización de lesiones profesionales; no obstante las encuestas de establecimientos y de hogares se utilizan en ciertos países. El tipo de fuente define el alcance de las estadísticas. En muchos países, el alcance de las obligaciones de declarar un accidente del trabajo o de indemnizar las lesiones profesionales, así como el alcance de las estadísticas, puede limitarse a ciertos grupos de trabajadores (a los asalariados lo más frecuente), a ciertas actividades económicas, a los casos de lesión con un mínimo de días de incapacidad, etc. El tipo de fuente se

indica a continuación del nombre del país en los cuadros mediante un código (para las explicaciones, véase la página XVI), y el tipo de lesiones abarcadas (declaradas o indemnizadas) se indica en el título de cada serie.

Las estadísticas de este capítulo se refieren a los casos de lesión profesional acaecidos durante el año indicado. El total de días perdidos como consecuencia de los mismos se incluye en las estadísticas relativas al año en que ocurre el accidente.

La información en este capítulo ha de utilizarse cuidadosamente, sobre todo al efectuar comparaciones internacionales. Las fuentes, métodos de recolección y alcance de datos y clasificaciones utilizadas pueden variar de un país a otro. Así, por ejemplo, su alcance puede limitarse a ciertos grupos de trabajadores (asalariados, trabajadores asegurados, trabajadores a tiempo completo, etc.), a ciertas actividades económicas, a establecimientos que emplean más de un cierto número de trabajadores, a casos de lesión con incapacidad de más de un cierto número de días, etc. Las descripciones de las fuentes, ámbito, definiciones y métodos utilizados en cada país para elaborar las estadísticas que se muestran en este capítulo figuran en OIT: Fuentes y Métodos: Estadísticas del Trabajo, volumen 8: «Lesiones profesionales» (Ginebra, 1999), y volumen 9: «Países en transición» (Ginebra, 1999). A continuación de estas notas explicativas se encuentra un cuadro sinóptico que contiene los puntos principales del alcance. En los cuadros se indica información adicional en notas a pie de página.

Los trabajadores en el grupo de referencia son aquellos trabajadores integrantes del grupo que se examina y que es abarcado por la fuente estadística de lesiones profesionales (como, por ejemplo, los hombres o las mujeres, una actividad económica, ocupación, región o grupo de edad específico, o en cualesquiera combinaciones de estas categorías, o los que están incluidos en un régimen de seguro específico). El número de trabajadores en el grupo de referencia varía según los países, la actividad económica y los períodos, debido a razones diferentes, incluyendo las diferencias de tamaño y composición del empleo. Estas diferencias se toman en cuenta utilizando medidas comparativas, como tasas de frecuencia, de incidencia o de gravedad.

Un aumento o una disminución del número de casos de lesión profesional ocurridos durante un período puede reflejar no sólo la modificación de las condiciones o del medio ambiente de trabajo, sino también la de los procedimientos de declaración o de recolección de datos, o de las leyes y reglamentos de declaración o indemnización de lesiones profesionales en el país de que se trata.

Cuadro 8A

Casos de lesión profesional con pérdida de días de trabajo, por actividad económica

Este cuadro muestra el número total de casos de lesión profesional con pérdida de días de trabajo:

- *Todos los casos*: todos los casos de lesión profesional con pérdida de días de trabajo, es decir, el total de casos mortales y casos no mortales.

- *Casos mortales*: el número de trabajadores lesionados mortalmente como resultado de accidentes de trabajo, en los cuales la muerte ocurre dentro del período de un año a contar a partir del día en que se produjo el accidente de trabajo.

- *Casos no mortales (incapacidad temporal o permanente)*: el número de casos de lesión profesional en los cuales el trabajador lesionado no puede trabajar temporalmente o permanentemente a partir del día siguiente a aquél del accidente.

- *Casos de incapacidad temporal*: el número de casos de lesión profesional en los cuales el trabajador lesionado no puede trabajar a partir del día siguiente a aquél del accidente, pero puede más tarde realizar las tareas habituales de su trabajo, correspondientes al empleo o puesto ocupado en el momento de sufrir el accidente, dentro un período de un año a partir del día del accidente.

Cuadro 8B

Tasas de lesiones profesionales, por actividad económica

Este cuadro contiene tasas de frecuencia o de incidencia de lesiones profesionales mortales y no mortales.

Las tasas de frecuencia se calculan en general como el número de nuevos casos de lesión (mortal y no mortal) durante el año (presentado en el cuadro 8A) dividido entre el total de horas trabajadas por los trabajadores del grupo de referencia durante el año, y multiplicado por 1 000 000. Las tasas de incidencia se calculan como el número de nuevos casos de lesión durante el año divido entre el total de trabajadores del grupo de referencia durante el año, y multiplicado por 100 000.

El tipo de tasa (por 1 000 000 horas trabajadas, por 100 000 trabajadores empleados, por 100 000 asalariados, por 100 000 trabajadores asegurados, etc.) se indica al comienzo de cada serie.

Cuadro 8C

Días perdidos

Este cuadro presenta el número total de días perdidos por casos de lesión profesional con incapacidad temporal (indicado en el cuadro 8A). Para ciertos países, se incluyen las estimaciones de días perdidos por casos de incapacidad permanente. Se miden en general en días civiles durante los cuales el trabajador lesionado fue incapaz temporalmente de trabajar, no incluido el día del accidente, hasta un año como máximo. Los datos para ciertos países, particularmente cuando la fuente es un régimen de indemnización de accidentes, se miden en días de trabajo. Las ausencias del trabajo de menos de un día para seguir un tratamiento médico no se incluyen.

Nota

[1] Para el texto completo de la resolución, veáse OIT: *Recomendaciones internacionales de actualidad en estadísticas del trabajo* (Ginebra, 2000) o el sitio Web del Departamento de Estadística de la OIT (www.ilo.org/public/spanish/bureau/stat).

Synoptic table   Tableau synoptique   Cuadro sinóptico

Country, area or territory Pays, zone ou territoire País, área o territorio	Type of data and source Type de données et source Tipo de datos y fuente	Minimum period of absence Période d'absence minimum Período mínimo de ausencia	Maximum period for death Période maximale du décès Período máximo para defunción	Workers - Travailleurs - Trabajadores Type / Tipo	Workers % of total emp. % emploi total % empl. total	Economic activities Activités économiques Actividades económicas	Occupational diseases Maladies profess-ionnelles Enferme-dades profesio-nales	Commuting accidents Accidents de trajet Accidentes de trayecto	Days lost Journées perdues Días perdidas	Reference year Année de référ-ence Año de refer-encia
1	2	3	4	5	6	7	8	9	10	11
Africa - Afrique - Africa										
Algérie	C/Ins	...	...	...	...	All	Incl.	Incl.	WD	C 1
Benin	R/Ins	...	...	...	...	All	Excl.	Incl.	...	C 1
Burkina faso	R/Ins	none	none	I	...	All.	Excl.	Incl.	WD	C
Mauritius (Up to 2002)	R/Ins	3 days	30 days	E	...	All x P	Incl.	Incl.	.	C 1
Mauritius	R/Ins	1 day	1 year	E		All	Incl.	Incl.	.	C 1
Nigeria	R/Inc	...	...	...	...	D,E	...	...	...	C
Seychelles	R/Not	none	none	E	...	All	Excl.	Excl.	.	C
Sierra Leone	C/Census	...	...	E	...	All	...	...	...	...
Togo	R/Ins	...	...	E	...	All x Agr,PA,F	Incl.	Incl.	WD	C
Tunisie	C/Ins	4 days	...	E	...	All x P	Excl.	Excl.	WD	C
Uganda	R/Ins	...	...	I	...	L	...	...	...	C
Uganda (2)	R/Ins	...	...	I	...	A,D,G-K,M-O	...	...	...	C
Zimbabwe	R/Ins	1 day	1 year	IE	..	All x PA,D,Inf	Incl.	Excl.	WD(TPD)	C 1
America - Amérique - America										
Argentina	R/Ins	1 day	1 year	IE	...	All	Incl.	Incl.	WD	C 1
Canada	C/Ins	1 day	none	E, SE	...	All x AF	Incl.	Excl.	WD(TPD)	C 2
Costa Rica	C/Ins	none	none	I	...	All	Incl.	Incl.	WD	C
Chile	R/...	...	...	IE	...	All	...	Incl.	CD	C
Cuba	R/Not	none	none	E	...	All	Incl.	Excl.	WD	C
Dominican Republic	C/Ins	...	...	...	...	...	...	...	...	C
El Salvador	C/Ins	none	none	IE	...	All x P (P from 1998)	Excl.	Incl.	WD	C
México	R/Ins	1 day	none	IE	...	All	Incl.	Incl.	WD(TI)	C 1
Panamá	C/Ins	none	none	E	...	All	Excl.	Incl.	.	C 1
Puerto Rico (2)	R/Survey	1 day	1 year	E	...	All x PA,Agr.	Excl.	Excl.	WD	C 1
Puerto Rico	R/Census	.	...	E,SE	...	...	...	...	.	...
Trinidad and To-bago	R/Not	...	...	E,SE	...	All	Excl.	Excl.	.	C
United States (2)	R/Survey	1 day	.	E	...	All x G	Incl.	Excl.	WD(TI)	C 1
United States	R/Census	.	none	E,SE	...	All	Incl.	Excl.	.	C 1
Asia - Asie - Asía										
Armenia	R/Not	...	...	...	...	...	...	...	...	...
Azerbaijan	R/Not	1 day	...	E	...	...	Excl.	Excl.	WD(TI)	C
Bahrain	R/Ins	none	none	E,SE	...	All	Incl.	Incl.	WD(TI)	C 1
Hong Kong (China)	R/Not	4 days	none	E	...	All	Excl.	Incl.	WD(TI)	C 1
India	R/Not	...	...	E	...	Mines	Excl.	Excl.	.	C

1131

Synoptic table   Tableau synoptique   Cuadro sinóptico

Country, area or territory / Pays, zone ou territoire / País, área o territorio	Type of data and source / Type de données et source / Tipo de datos y fuente	Minimum period of absence / Période d'absence minimum / Período mínimo de ausencia	Maximum period for death / Période maximale du décès / Período máximo para defunción	Coverage / Portée / Alcance — Workers/Travailleurs/Trabajadores — Type/Tipo	Coverage — Workers — % of total emp. / % emploi total / % empl. total	Coverage — Economic activities / Activités économiques / Actividades económicas	Coverage — Occupational diseases / Maladies professionnelles / Enfermedades profesionales	Coverage — Commuting accidents / Accidents de trajet / Accidentes de trayecto	Days lost / Journées perdues / Días perdidas	Reference year / Année de référence / Año de referencia
1	2	3	4	5	6	7	8	9	10	11
Israel	C/Ins	3 days	same year	E,SE	...	All	Incl.	Incl.	WD	C
Japan	R/Not	4 days	...	E	...	All	Excl.	Excl.	.	C
Jordan	R/Ins	1 day	none	E	...	All x AF	Incl.	Incl.	WD(TPD)	C 1
Korea, Rep. of (3)	C/Ins	...	...	I	...	All	Incl.	Incl.	WD	C
Kyrgyzstan	R/Not	none	none	E	...	All	Excl.(up to 1998)	Incl.	WD	C
Macau (China)	R/Not	none	none	E	...	All x P	Excl.	Incl.	CD(TI PI)	C 2
Myanmar (5)	R/Not	2 days	...	E,SE	...	M	Excl.	Excl.	.	C
Singapore	R/Not	4 days	none	E	...	All	Excl.	Excl.	WD(TPD)	C 1
Sri Lanka	R/Not	3 days	1 year	E	...	M,E,TSC,C	Incl.	Excl.	WD(TPD)	C 1
Rép. arabe syrienne	C/Ins	...	...	I	...	All	Incl.	Incl.	.	C
Taiwan, China	R/...	...	...	...	...	All	...	...	.	C
Thailand	C/Ins	3 days	...	I	...	All	Incl.	Incl.	.	C
Europe - Europe - Europa										
Austria	R/Ins	none	none	E, SE	...	All	Excl.	Excl.	.	C 3
Belarus	R/Not	1 day	same year	E	...	All	Excl.	Excl.	WD(TI)	C
Belgique	C/Ins	1 day	none	IE	...	All x P,AF	Excl.	Incl.	CD(TPD)	C 2
Bulgaria	R/Not	...	...	E,SE	...	All	Incl.	Incl.	.	C
Croatia	C/Ins	none	immediate	E,SE	...	All	Excl.	Incl.	WD(TI)	C 2
Cyprus (from 2002)	R/Not	4 days	1 year	E	...	All	Excl.	Excl.	.	C
Czech Republic	R/Not	1 day	none	E,SE	...	All x AF,Pol	Excl.	Excl.	CD(TI)	C 1
España	R/Not	1 day	1 month	I	...	All x PA,AF	Excl.	Excl.	CD(TI)	C 1
Estonia	C/Ins	1 day	1 year	I	...	All x AF,Pol	Incl.	Incl.	CD(TPD)	C 1
Finland	C/Ins	3 days	1 year	E	...	All	Non-fatal	Excl.	CD(TI)	C 1
France	C/Ins	1 day	varies	E	...	All x P	Excl.	Excl.	CD(TI)	C 3
Germany	C/Ins	4 days	1 month	E,SE	...	All	Excl.	Incl.	CD	C
Hungary	R/Not	4 days	1 year	E,SE	...	All	Excl.	Excl.	CD	C
Iceland	R/Not	2 days	...	E	...	All	Incl.	Excl.	.	C
Ireland	R/Not	4 days	none	E,SE	...	All	Excl.	Excl.	CD	C
Isle of Man	R/Not	4 days	1 year	E	...	All x SF,AT	Excl.	Excl.	.	C
Italy	C/Ins	3 days	none	I	...	All	Excl.	Incl.	CD(TI)	C
Latvia	R/Survey	1 day	none	E	...	All	Excl.	Excl.	WD	C
Lithuania	R/Not	1 day	none	E,SE	...	All x AF	Excl.	Incl.	CD(TPD)	C 1
Luxembourg	C/Ins	none	1 year	I	...	All	Incl.	Incl.	CD	C 1
Malta	C/Ins	4 days	...	E,SE	...	All	Incl.	Excl.	WD	C
Moldova, Rep. of	R/Not	1 day	none	E	...	All	Excl.	Excl.	WD(TPD)	C

Synoptic table				Tableau synoptique					Cuadro sinóptico	
Country, area or territory	Type of data and source	Minimum period of absence	Maximum period for death	Coverage					Days lost	Reference year
				Workers		Economic activities	Occupational diseases	Commuting accidents		
				Type	% of total emp.					
Pays, zone ou territoire	Type de données et source	Période d'absence minimum	Période maximale du décès	Portée					Journées perdues	Année de référence
				Travailleurs		Activités économiques	Maladies professionnelles	Accidents de trajet		
				Type	% emploi total					
País, área o territorio	Tipo de datos y fuente	Período mínimo de ausencia	Período máximo para defunción	Alcance					Días perdidas	Año de referencia
				Trabajadores		Actividades económicas	Enfermedades profesionales	Accidentes de trayecto		
				Tipo	% empl. total					
1	2	3	4	5	6	7	8	9	10	11
Norway	R/Not	none	none	E (7)	...	All	Excl.	Excl.	CD(IT)	C 1
Poland	R/Not	none	6 months	E,SE	...	All x Agr	Excl.	Excl.	CD(TI)	C 1
Portugal	R/Not	none	one year	E,SE	...	Al x PA,AF	Excl.	Excl.	CD(TI PI)	C 3
Roumanie	R/Not	3 days	same year	E,SE	...	All x AF,P	Excl.	Incl.	CD(TPD)	C 2
Russian Federation	R/Not	1 day	none	E	...	AllxLowrates	Excl.	Incl.	WD(TPD)	C 1
San Marino	R/Not	...	...	E	...	All	Excl.	Excl.	.	C
Slovakia	R/Not	1 day	none	IE	...	All	Excl.	Excl.	CD(TI)	C
Slovenia	R/Not	1 day	1 month	I	...	All	Excl.	Incl.	WD(TI)	C 1
Suisse	C/Ins	3 days	same year	IE	...	All	Incl.	Excl.	.	C 2
Sweden	R/Ins	1 day	none	E,SE	...	All	Excl.	Excl.	WD(TPD)	C 1
Turkey	R/Ins	...	...	IE	...	All	Incl.	Excl.	WD	C
Ukraine	R/Not	1 day	4 months	E	...	All xAF	Excl.	Excl.	WD(TI D)	C 1
United Kingdom	R/Not	3 days	1 year	E,SE	...	All x SF,AT	Excl.	Excl.	.	F 1
Oceania - Océanie - Oceania										
Australia (7)	C/Ins	5 work-days	3 years	E	...	All x AF	Incl.	Excl.	WD(TI)	F 3
New Zealand	C/ins	7 days	1 year	E	...	All	Incl.	Incl.	...	F
Papua New Guinea	C/Ins	...	...	E	...	All	...	...	...	...

Notes

(1) Establishments with 50 or more workers.

(2) Establishments with 10 or more workers.

(3) Establishments with 10 or more workers and using power, and those with 20 or more workers and without power.

(4) Establishments using power or with 20 or more employees.

(5) Excluding Victoria and Australian Capital Territory.

Notes

(1) Etablissements occupant 50 travailleurs et plus.

(2) Etablissements occupant 10 travailleurs et plus.

(3) Etablissements de 10 salariés ou plus lorsqu'ils utilisent l'électricité et dans le cas contraire, établissements de 20 salariés ou plus.

(4) Etablissements utilisant électricité et occupant 20 salariés et plus.

(5) Non compris Victoria et Australian Capital Territory.

Notas

(1) Establecimientos con 50 trabajadores o más.

(2) Establecimientos con 10 trabajadores o más.

(3) Establecimientos con 10 trabajadores o más y que utilizan electricidad, y los con 20 trabajadores o más sin electricidad.

(4) Establecimientos que utilizan electricidad o los con 20 asalariados o más.

(5) Excl. Victoria y Australian Capital Territory.

Explanations

Type of data and source (col. 2)	R	reported injuries	/Not	notification system
	C	compensated injuries	/Ins	insurance scheme
			/Survey	survey of establishments or establishment reporting
			/Census	census of occupational fatalities

Minimum period of absence from work (col. 3)	workdays		none	
	day(s)			

Maximum period for death after accident (col.4)	days		immediate	
	month(s)		same year	
	year(s)		none	
			varies	

Coverage

Workers (col. 5)	E	employees	I	insured persons
	SE	self-employed persons	IE	insured employees

Economic activities (col. 7)	All	all economic activities		
	x	excluding		
	AF	armed forces	Lowrates	activities with low rates of injuries
	Agr	agriculture	M	manufacturing
	ASO	air, sea and offshore accidents	MQ	mining and quarrying
	AT	air transport	P	public sector
	C	construction	PA	public administration
	D	domestic services	Pr	private sector
	E	electricity, gas and water	Pol	police
	F	financial services	SF	sea fishing
	G	Government	TRH	wholesale and retail trade, restaurants and hotels
	Inf	Informal sector	TSC	transport, storage and communication

Occupational diseases (col. 8)	Incl.	occupational diseases included	Excl.	occupational diseases excluded
	Non-fatal	non-fatal occupational diseases included		

Commuting accidents (col. 9)	Incl.	commuting accidents included	Excl.	commuting accidents excluded

Time lost (col. 10)	WD	workdays	measured for:	
	CD	calendar days	(TI)	cases of temporary incapacity only
	weeks		(TI PI)	cases of temporary and permanent incapacity
	none	time lost not measured	(TID)	cases of temporary incapacity and death
			(TPD)	all cases of occupational injury (temporary and permanent incapacity and death)

Reference year (col. 11)	C	calendar year	1	injuries incl. in statistics for year of accident
	F	financial year	2	injuries incl. in statistics for year of notification or submission of claims
			3	injuries incl. in statistics for year in which compensation was paid.

Explications

Type de données et source	R	lésions déclarées	/Not	système de déclaration
	C	lésions indemnisées	/Ins	régime d'indemnisation
			/Survey	enquête auprès des établissements ou rapports des établissements
(col. 2)			/Census	recensement des lésions mortelles
Période d'absence du travail minimum	workdays	journées de travail	none	aucune
(col. 3)	day(s)	jour(s)		
Période maximale du décès après l'accident	days	jours	immediate	immédiate
	month(s)	mois	same year	même année
	year(s)	année(s)	none	aucune
(col.4)			varies	varie

Portée

Travailleurs	E	salariés	I	personnes assurées
(col. 5)	SE	travailleurs indépendants	IE	salariés assurés
Activités économiques	All	ensemble des activités économiques		
	x	non compris		
(col. 6)	AF	forces armées	Lowrates	activités avec des taux de lésions bas
	Agr	agriculture	M	industries manufacturières
	ASO	accidents en mer ou dans les airs	MQ	industries extractives
	AT	transports aériens	P	secteur public
	C	bâtiment et travaux publics	PA	administration publique
	D	services domestics	Pr	secteur privé
	E	électricité, gaz et eau	Pol	police
	F	services financiers	SF	pêche en mer
	G	gourvenement	TRH	commerce de gros et de détail, restaurants et hôtels
	Inf	secteur informel	TSC	transports, entrepôts et communications
Maladies professionnelles (col. 8)	Incl.	maladies professionnelles comprises	Excl.	non compris les maladies professionnelles
	Non-fatal	y compris les maladies professionnelles non mortelles		
Accidents de trajet (col. 9)	Incl.	accidents de trajet compris	Excl.	non compris les accidents de trajet
Temps perdu	WD	journées de travail	mesuré pour:	
	CD	jours calendriers	(TI)	cas d'incapacité temporaire uniquement
	weeks	semaines	(TI PI)	cas d'incapacité temporaire et permanente
(col. 10)			(TID)	cas d'incapacité temporaire et décès
			(TPD)	tous les cas de lésion professionnelles (incapacité temporaire et permanente et décès)
Année de référence	C	année civile	1	lésions comprises dans les statistiques de l'année de l'accident
	F	année fiscale	2	lésions comprises dans les statistiques de l'année de déclaration ou de soumission de la demande d'indemnisation
(col. 11)			3	lésions comprises dans les statistiques de l'année de versement de l'indemnisation

1136

Explicaciones

Tipos de datos y fuente (col. 2)	R	lesiones declaradas	/Not	sistema de declaración
	C	lesiones indemnizadas	/Ins	regímen de indemnización
			/Survey	encuesta de establecimientos o informes de establecimientos
			/Census	censo de lesiones mortales

Período mínimo de ausencia del trabajo (co. 3)	workdays	días de trabajo	none	ningún
	day(s)	día(s)		

Período máximo para defunción (col.4)	days	días	immediate	inmediato
	month(s)	mes(es)	same year	mismo año
	year(s)	año(s)	none	ningún
			varies	varia

Alcance

Trabajadores (col. 5)	E	asalariados	I	personas aseguradas
	SE	trabajadores independientes	IE	asalariados asegurados

Actividades económicas (col. 7)	All	todas las actividades económicas		
	x	excluyendo		
	AF	fuerzas armadas	Lowrates	actividades con tasas de lesiones bajas
	Agr	agricultura	M	industrias manufactureras
	ASO	accidentes en el aéreo o en el mar	MQ	minas y canteras
	AT	transporte aéreo	P	sector público
	C	construcción	PA	administración pública
	D	servicios domesticos	Pr	sector privado
	E	electricidad, gas y agua	Pol	policia
	F	servicios financieros	SF	pesca de mar
	G	gobierno	TRH	comercio al por mayor y al por menor y restaurantes y hoteles
	Inf	sector informal	TSC	transportes, almacenamiento y comunicaciones

Enfermedades profesionales (col. 8)	Incl.	enfermedades profesionales incluidas	Excl.	enfermedades profesionales excluidas
	Non-fatal	enfermedades profesionales no mortales incluidas		

Accidentes de trayecto (col. 9)	Incl.	accidentes de trayecto incluidos	Excl.	accidentes de trayecto excluidos

Tiempo perdido (col. 10)	WD	días de trabajo	medido para:	
	CD	días civiles	(TI)	casos de incapacidad temporal únicamente
	weeks	semanas	(TI PI)	casos de incapacidad temporal y permanente
			(TID)	casos de incapacidad temporal y defunción
			(TPD)	todos los casos de lesión profesional (incapacidad temporal y permanente y defunción)

Año de referencia (col. 11)	C	año civil	1	lesiones comprendidas en las estadísticas del año del accidente
	F	año fical	2	lesiones comprendidas en las estadísticas del año de de declaración o de solicitud de indemnización
			3	lesiones comprendidas en las estadísticas del año de pago de la indemnización

1137

OCCUPATIONAL INJURIES

Cases of injury with lost workdays, by economic activity

LÉSIONS PROFESSIONNELLES

Cas de lésion avec perte de journées de travail, par activité économique

LESIONES PROFESIONALES

Casos de lesión con pérdida de días de trabajo, por actividad económica

	1999	2000	2001	2002	2003	2004	2005	2006	2007	2008

AFRICA-AFRIQUE-AFRICA

Algérie (FA) — Compensated injuries - Lésions indemnisées - Lesiones indemnizadas

Fatal cases - Cas mortels - Casos mortales

Total men and women - Total hommes et femmes - Total hombres y mujeres
ISIC 3 - CITI 3 - CIIU 3

	1999	2000	2001	2002	2003	2004	2005	2006	2007	2008
Total	798	731	683	721	723	697	.	.	.	.
D	183	160	139	121	146	166				
E	3	4	4	5	6	12				
F	178	180	173	234	225	241				
G	16	18	16	14	22	25				
I [1]	39	43	35	32	58	58				
X	383	370	355	289	316	240				

Non-fatal cases (temporary + permanent incapacity) - Cas non mortels (incapacité temporaire + permanente) - Casos no mortales (incapacidad temporal + permanente)

Total men and women - Total hommes et femmes - Total hombres y mujeres
ISIC 3 - CITI 3 - CIIU 3

	1999	2000	2001	2002	2003	2004	2005	2006	2007	2008
Total	42 145	41 305	38 803	42 147	45 762	39 726	.	.	.	.
D	12 629	12 381	10 684	10 572	11 100	10 989				
E	289	290	267	263	374	346				
F	4 900	5 026	4 279	4 897	5 550	5 730				
G	627	632	534	532	594	586				
I [1]	1 355	1 246	1 079	1 038	1 000	1 034				
X	7 021	7 293	6 474	7 164	8 739	6 238				

Cases of temporary incapacity - Cas d'incapacité temporaire - Casos de incapacidad temporal

Total men and women - Total hommes et femmes - Total hombres y mujeres
ISIC 3 - CITI 3 - CIIU 3

	1999	2000	2001	2002	2003	2004	2005	2006	2007	2008
Total	37 920	36 906	33 379	35 951	38 297	.	.	.	.	.
D	10 952	10 580	8 515							
E	248	249	211	209	290	278				
F	3 969	4 103	3 148	3 751	4 216	4 380				
G	527	532	402	391	438	461				
I [1]	1 101	982	745	748	639	766				
X	5 799	6 023	4 872	5 444	6 641	4 444				

Total cases (fatal + non-fatal) - Ensemble des cas (mortels + non mortels) - Todos los casos (mortales + no mortales)

Total men and women - Total hommes et femmes - Total hombres y mujeres
ISIC 3 - CITI 3 - CIIU 3

	1999	2000	2001	2002	2003	2004	2005	2006	2007	2008
Total	42 943	42 036	39 486	42 868	46 485	40 423	.	.	.	.
D	12 812	12 541	10 823	10 693	11 246	11 155				
E	292	294	271	268	380	358				
F	5 078	5 206	4 452	5 131	5 775	5 971				
G	642	650	550	546	616	611				
I [1]	1 394	1 289	1 114	1 070	1 058	1 092				
X	7 404	7 663	6 829	7 453	9 055	6 478				

Bénin (FA) — Reported injuries - Lésions déclarées - Lesiones declaradas

Fatal cases - Cas mortels - Casos mortales

Total men and women - Total hommes et femmes - Total hombres y mujeres
ISIC 3 - CITI 3 - CIIU 3

	1999	2000	2001	2002	2003	2004	2005	2006	2007	2008
Total	.	.	.	9	4	.	.	.	.	.

Total cases (fatal + non-fatal) - Ensemble des cas (mortels + non mortels) - Todos los casos (mortales + no mortales)

Total men and women - Total hommes et femmes - Total hombres y mujeres
ISIC 3 - CITI 3 - CIIU 3

	1999	2000	2001	2002	2003	2004	2005	2006	2007	2008
Total	.	.	.	792	744	.	.	.	.	.

Botswana (FF) [2] — Reported injuries - Lésions déclarées - Lesiones declaradas

Fatal cases - Cas mortels - Casos mortales

Total men and women - Total hommes et femmes - Total hombres y mujeres
ISIC 3 - CITI 3 - CIIU 3

	1999	2000	2001	2002	2003	2004	2005	2006	2007	2008
Total	.	.	.	.	.	81	30	48	48	

Explanatory notes: see p. 1125.
[1] Excl. communications. [2] Cases reported during the year indicated.

Notes explicatives: voir p. 1127.
[1] Non compris les communications. [2] Cas déclarés pendant l'année indiquée.

Notas explicativas: véase p. 1129.
[1] Excl. las comunicaciones. [2] Casos declarados durante el año indicado.

OCCUPATIONAL INJURIES

Cases of injury with lost workdays, by economic activity

LÉSIONS PROFESSIONNELLES

Cas de lésion avec perte de journées de travail, par activité économique

LESIONES PROFESIONALES

Casos de lesión con pérdida de días de trabajo, por actividad económica

	1999	2000	2001	2002	2003	2004	2005	2006	2007	2008

Botswana (FF) [1]   Reported injuries - Lésions déclarées - Lesiones declaradas

Non-fatal cases (temporary + permanent incapacity) - Cas non mortels (incapacité temporaire + permanente) - Casos no mortales (incapacidad temporal + permanente)

Total men and women - Total hommes et femmes - Total hombres y mujeres
ISIC 3 - CITI 3 - CIIU 3

Total							1 149	454	974	1 194

Cases of temporary incapacity - Cas d'incapacité temporaire - Casos de incapacidad temporal

Total men and women - Total hommes et femmes - Total hombres y mujeres
ISIC 3 - CITI 3 - CIIU 3

Total							266	148	275	362

Total cases (fatal + non-fatal) - Ensemble des cas (mortels + non mortels) - Todos los casos (mortales + no mortales)

Total men and women - Total hommes et femmes - Total hombres y mujeres
ISIC 3 - CITI 3 - CIIU 3

Total							1 230	484	1 022	1 242

Burkina Faso (FA)   Reported injuries - Lésions déclarées - Lesiones declaradas

Total cases (fatal + non-fatal) - Ensemble des cas (mortels + non mortels) - Todos los casos (mortales + no mortales)

Total men and women - Total hommes et femmes - Total hombres y mujeres
ISIC 3 - CITI 3 - CIIU 3

Total	4 118	3 988	3 369	3 233	3 089	2 268	3 548	2 143	1 512	

Men - Hommes - Hombres
ISIC 3 - CITI 3 - CIIU 3

Total					2 803	2 094	3 293	1 959	1 366	

Women - Femmes - Mujeres
ISIC 3 - CITI 3 - CIIU 3

Total					286	174	255	184	146	

Mauritius (FA) [2]   Reported injuries - Lésions déclarées - Lesiones declaradas

Fatal cases - Cas mortels - Casos mortales

Total men and women - Total hommes et femmes - Total hombres y mujeres [3]
ISIC 3 - CITI 3 - CIIU 3

	1999	2000	2001	2002	2003	2004	2005	2006	2007	2008
Total	5	7	4	7 [4]	5	7	4	1	1	3
A	1	1	1	0 [4]	0	1	0	0	0	0
B	0	0	0	0 [4]	0	0	0	0	0	0
C	0	0	0	0 [4]	0	0	0	0	0	0
D	0	0	1	1 [4]	0	0	0	0	0	1
E	0	0	0	0 [4]	0	0	0	0	0	0
F	0	1	1	0 [4]	1	3	0	0	1	0
G	1	3	0	0 [4]	0	1	0	0	0	0
H	0	0	0	1 [4]	0	1	1	0	0	0
I	0	0	0	1 [4]	1	0	1	0	0	2
J	0	0	0	0 [4]	0	0	0	0	0	0
K	0	0	0	0 [4]	0	0	2	0	0	0
M				[4]	0	0	0	0	0	0
N				[4]	0	0	0	0	0	0
O	2	0	0	2 [4]	1	1	0	0	0	0
P	1	2	1	2 [4]	2	0	0	1	0	0

Explanatory notes: see p. 1125.

[1] Cases reported during the year indicated. [2] Excl. public sector and parastatal bodies. [3] Up to 2002: deaths occurring within 30 days of accident. [4] Not strictly comparable.

Notes explicatives: voir p. 1127.

[1] Cas déclarés pendant l'année indiquée. [2] Non compris le secteur public et les organismes paraétatiques. [3] Jusqu'à 2002: les décès survenant pendant les 30 jours qui suivent l'accident. [4] Non strictement comparable.

Notas explicativas: véase p. 1129.

[1] Casos declarados durante el año indicado. [2] Excl. el sector público y los organismos paraestatales. [3] Hasta 2002: los fallecimientos que se produzcan durante los 30 días posteriores al accidente. [4] No estrictamente comparable.

OCCUPATIONAL INJURIES

Cases of injury with lost workdays, by economic activity

LÉSIONS PROFESSIONNELLES

Cas de lésion avec perte de journées de travail, par activité économique

LESIONES PROFESIONALES

Casos de lesión con pérdida de días de trabajo, por actividad económica

	1999	2000	2001	2002	2003	2004	2005	2006	2007	2008
Mauritius (FA) [1]				Reported injuries - Lésions déclarées - Lesiones declaradas						

Fatal cases - Cas mortels - Casos mortales

Men - Hommes - Hombres [2]
ISIC 3 - CITI 3 - CIIU 3

	1999	2000	2001	2002	2003	2004	2005	2006	2007	2008
Total	.	.	.	.	.	6	4	1	1	2
A	.	.	.	.	.	1	0	0	0	0
B	.	.	.	.	.	0	0	0	0	0
C	.	.	.	.	.	0	0	0	0	0
D	.	.	.	.	.	0	0	0	0	0
E	.	.	.	.	.	0	0	0	0	0
F	.	.	.	.	.	3	0	0	1	0
G	.	.	.	.	.	1	0	0	0	0
H	.	.	.	.	.	0	1	0	0	0
I	.	.	.	.	.	0	1	0	0	2
J	.	.	.	.	.	0	0	0	0	0
K	.	.	.	.	.	0	2	0	0	0
M	.	.	.	.	.	0	0	0	0	0
N	.	.	.	.	.	0	0	0	0	0
O	.	.	.	.	.	1	0	0	0	0
P	.	.	.	.	.	0	0	1	0	0

Women - Femmes - Mujeres [2]
ISIC 3 - CITI 3 - CIIU 3

	1999	2000	2001	2002	2003	2004	2005	2006	2007	2008
Total	.	.	.	.	.	1	0	0	0	1
A	.	.	.	.	.	0	0	0	0	0
B	.	.	.	.	.	0	0	0	0	0
C	.	.	.	.	.	0	0	0	0	0
D	.	.	.	.	.	0	0	0	0	1
E	.	.	.	.	.	0	0	0	0	0
F	.	.	.	.	.	0	0	0	0	0
G	.	.	.	.	.	0	0	0	0	0
H	.	.	.	.	.	1	0	0	0	0
I	.	.	.	.	.	0	0	0	0	0
J	.	.	.	.	.	0	0	0	0	0
K	.	.	.	.	.	0	0	0	0	0
L	.	.	.	.	.	0	0	0	0	0
M	.	.	.	.	.	0	0	0	0	0
N	.	.	.	.	.	0	0	0	0	0
O	.	.	.	.	.	0	0	0	0	0
P	.	.	.	.	.	0	0	0	0	0

Non-fatal cases (temporary + permanent incapacity) - Cas non mortels (incapacité temporaire + permanente) - Casos no mortales (incapacidad temporal + permanente)

Total men and women - Total hommes et femmes - Total hombres y mujeres [3]
ISIC 3 - CITI 3 - CIIU 3

	1999	2000	2001	2002	2003	2004	2005	2006	2007	2008
Total	5 201	4 554	4 268	3 627 [4]	2 816	3 433	2 873	2 739	2 742	1 751
A	.	.	2 135	1 194 [4]	894	1 132	1 184	812	813	425
B	.	.	0	0 [4]	1	2	1	3	3	5
C	.	.	0	0 [4]	0	0	0	0	0	0
D	.	.	755	684 [4]	611	598	506	467	446	378
E	.	.	3	2 [4]	5	16	10	2	5	3
F	.	.	699	975 [4]	651	967	515	867	820	397
G	.	.	122	155 [4]	140	196	163	142	225	201
H	.	.	62	60 [4]	61	90	75	57	54	41
I	.	.	238	332 [4]	293	318	300	272	264	174
J	.	.	0	0 [4]	3	2	1	0	1	2
K	.	.	0	0 [4]	33	69	88	45	52	83
M	.	.	.	1 [4]	3	4	4	10	7	6
N	.	.	.	0 [4]	11	20	13	23	22	20
O	.	.	136	117 [4]	60	14	10	14	19	14
P	.	.	118	105 [4]	50	5	3	25	11	2
X	.	.	0	0 [4]	0	0	0	0	0	0

Men - Hommes - Hombres [3]
ISIC 3 - CITI 3 - CIIU 3

	1999	2000	2001	2002	2003	2004	2005	2006	2007	2008
Total	.	.	.	.	.	3 079	2 541	2 450	2 477	1 556
A	.	.	.	.	.	944	1 006	671	691	385
B	.	.	.	.	.	2	1	2	2	4
C	.	.	.	.	.	0	0	0	0	0
D	.	.	.	.	.	516	428	415	397	320
E	.	.	.	.	.	9	8	1	5	2
F	.	.	.	.	.	958	507	867	820	393
G	.	.	.	.	.	163	146	123	180	154
H	.	.	.	.	.	80	59	45	43	26
I	.	.	.	.	.	303	281	234	245	163
J	.	.	.	.	.	1	1	0	1	2
K	.	.	.	.	.	67	84	41	50	77
M	.	.	.	.	.	3	0	5	2	2
N	.	.	.	.	.	19	13	19	21	16
O	.	.	.	.	.	12	7	11	14	10
P	.	.	.	.	.	2	0	16	6	2

Explanatory notes: see p. 1125.

[1] Excl. public sector and parastatal bodies. [2] Up to 2002: deaths occurring within 30 days of accident. [3] Up to 2002: incapacity of 3 days or more. [4] Not strictly comparable.

Notes explicatives: voir p. 1127.

[1] Non compris le secteur public et les organismes paraétatiques. [2] Jusqu'à 2002: les décès survenant pendant les 30 jours qui suivent l'accident. [3] Jusqu'à 2002: incapacité de 3 jours et plus. [4] Non strictement comparable.

Notas explicativas: véase p. 1129.

[1] Excl. el sector público y los organismos paraestatales. [2] Hasta 2002: los fallecimientos que se produzcan durante los 30 días posteriores al accidente. [3] Hasta 2002: incapacidad de 3 días y más. [4] No estrictamente comparable.

	OCCUPATIONAL INJURIES	**LÉSIONS PROFESSIONNELLES**	**LESIONES PROFESIONALES**
	Cases of injury with lost workdays, by economic activity	Cas de lésion avec perte de journées de travail, par activité économique	Casos de lesión con pérdida de días de trabajo, por actividad económica

	1999	2000	2001	2002	2003	2004	2005	2006	2007	2008

Mauritius (FA) [1] — Reported injuries - Lésions déclarées - Lesiones declaradas

Non-fatal cases (temporary + permanent incapacity) - Cas non mortels (incapacité temporaire + permanente) - Casos no mortales (incapacidad temporal + permanente)

Women - Femmes - Mujeres [2]
ISIC 3 - CITI 3 - CIIU 3

	1999	2000	2001	2002	2003	2004	2005	2006	2007	2008
Total	.	.	.	.	.	354	332	289	265	195
A	.	.	.	.	.	188	178	141	122	40
B	.	.	.	.	.	0	0	1	1	1
C	.	.	.	.	.	0	0	0	0	0
D	.	.	.	.	.	82	78	52	49	58
E	.	.	.	.	.	7	2	1	0	1
F	.	.	.	.	.	9	8	0	0	4
G	.	.	.	.	.	33	17	19	45	47
H	.	.	.	.	.	10	16	12	11	15
I	.	.	.	.	.	15	19	38	19	11
J	.	.	.	.	.	1	0	0	0	0
K	.	.	.	.	.	2	4	4	2	6
M	.	.	.	.	.	1	4	5	5	4
N	.	.	.	.	.	1	0	4	1	4
O	.	.	.	.	.	2	3	3	5	4
P	.	.	.	.	.	3	3	9	5	0

Cases of temporary incapacity - Cas d'incapacité temporaire - Casos de incapacidad temporal

Total men and women - Total hommes et femmes - Total hombres y mujeres [3]
ISIC 3 - CITI 3 - CIIU 3

	1999	2000	2001	2002	2003	2004	2005	2006	2007	2008
Total	4 276	4 377	3 856	2 732 [4]	.	2 738	2 274	1 943	.	.
A	2 385	2 377	1 931	1 115 [4]	.	.	.	.	.	.
B	0	0	0	0 [4]	.	.	.	.	.	.
C	0	0	0	0 [4]	.	.	.	.	.	.
D	561	488	718	622 [4]	.	.	.	.	.	.
E	2	5	3	2 [4]	.	.	.	.	.	.
F	668	686	651	953 [4]	.	.	.	.	.	.
G	103	100	88	141 [4]	.	.	.	.	.	.
H	37	50	44	58 [4]	.	.	.	.	.	.
I	210	242	201	295 [4]	.	.	.	.	.	.
J	0	0	0	0 [4]	.	.	.	.	.	.
K	3	0	0	0 [4]	.	.	.	.	.	.
M	.	.	.	1 [4]	.	.	.	.	.	.
N	.	.	.	0 [4]	.	.	.	.	.	.
O	206	92	115	105 [4]	.	.	.	.	.	.
P	101	136	105	100 [4]	.	.	.	.	.	.
X	.	201	0	0 [4]	.	.	.	.	.	.

Men - Hommes - Hombres [3]
ISIC 3 - CITI 3 - CIIU 3

	1999	2000	2001	2002	2003	2004	2005	2006	2007	2008
Total	.	.	.	.	.	2 498	2 023	1 823	.	.

Women - Femmes - Mujeres [3]
ISIC 3 - CITI 3 - CIIU 3

	1999	2000	2001	2002	2003	2004	2005	2006	2007	2008
Total	.	.	.	.	.	240	251	120	.	.

Total cases (fatal + non-fatal) - Ensemble des cas (mortels + non mortels) - Todos los casos (mortales + no mortales)

Total men and women - Total hommes et femmes - Total hombres y mujeres
ISIC 3 - CITI 3 - CIIU 3

	1999	2000	2001	2002	2003	2004	2005	2006	2007	2008
Total	5 206	4 561	4 272	3 634 [4]	2 821	3 440	2 877	2 740	2 743	1 754
A	2 386	2 386	2 136	1 194 [4]	894	1 133	1 184	812	813	425
B	0	0	0	0 [4]	1	2	1	3	3	5
C	0	0	0	0 [4]	0	0	0	0	0	0
D	561	488	756	685 [4]	611	598	506	467	446	379
E	2	5	3	2 [4]	5	16	10	2	5	3
F	668	687	700	975 [4]	652	970	515	867	821	397
G	104	103	122	155 [4]	140	197	163	142	225	201
H	37	50	62	61 [4]	61	91	76	57	54	41
I	210	242	238	333 [4]	294	318	301	272	264	176
J	0	0	0	0 [4]	3	2	1	0	1	2
K	3	0	0	0 [4]	33	69	90	45	52	83
M	.	.	.	1 [4]	3	4	4	10	7	6
N	.	.	.	0 [4]	11	20	13	23	22	20
O	208	92	136	119 [4]	61	15	10	14	19	14
P	102	138	119	107 [4]	52	5	3	26	1	2
X	925 [5]	370 [5]	0	0 [4]	0	0	0	0	0	0

Explanatory notes: see p. 1125.

[1] Excl. public sector and parastatal bodies. [2] Up to 2002: incapacity of 3 days or more. [3] Incapacity of 3 days or more. [4] Not strictly comparable. [5] Incl. cases of permanent incapacity.

Notes explicatives: voir p. 1127.

[1] Non compris le secteur public et les organismes paraétatiques. [2] Jusqu'à 2002: incapacité de 3 jours et plus. [3] Incapacité de 3 jours et plus. [4] Non strictement comparable. [5] Y compris les cas d'incapacité permanente.

Notas explicativas: véase p. 1129.

[1] Excl. el sector público y los organismos paraestatales. [2] Hasta 2002: incapacidad de 3 días y más. [3] Incapacidad de 3 días y más. [4] No estrictamente comparable. [5] Incl. los casos de incapacidad permanente.

OCCUPATIONAL INJURIES

Cases of injury with
lost workdays,
by economic activity

LÉSIONS PROFESSIONNELLES

Cas de lésion avec perte
de journées de travail,
par activité économique

LESIONES PROFESIONALES

Casos de lesión con pérdida
de días de trabajo,
por actividad económica

	1999	2000	2001	2002	2003	2004	2005	2006	2007	2008

Mauritius (FA) [1]   Reported injuries - Lésions déclarées - Lesiones declaradas

Total cases (fatal + non-fatal) - Ensemble des cas (mortels + non mortels) - Todos los casos (mortales + no mortales)

Men - Hommes - Hombres
ISIC 3 - CITI 3 - CIIU 3

	1999	2000	2001	2002	2003	2004	2005	2006	2007	2008
Total	.	.	.	.	.	3 085	2 545	2 451	2 478	1 558
A	.	.	.	.	.	945	1 006	671	691	385
B	.	.	.	.	.	2	1	2	2	4
C	.	.	.	.	.	0	0	0	0	0
D	.	.	.	.	.	516	428	415	397	320
E	.	.	.	.	.	9	8	1	5	2
F	.	.	.	.	.	961	507	867	821	393
G	.	.	.	.	.	164	146	123	180	154
H	.	.	.	.	.	80	60	45	43	26
I	.	.	.	.	.	303	282	234	245	165
J	.	.	.	.	.	1	1	0	1	2
K	.	.	.	.	.	67	86	41	50	77
M	.	.	.	.	.	3	0	5	2	2
N	.	.	.	.	.	19	13	19	21	16
O	.	.	.	.	.	13	7	11	14	10
P	.	.	.	.	.	2	0	17	14	2

Women - Femmes - Mujeres
ISIC 3 - CITI 3 - CIIU 3

	1999	2000	2001	2002	2003	2004	2005	2006	2007	2008
Total	.	.	.	.	.	355	332	289	265	196
A	.	.	.	.	.	188	178	141	122	40
B	.	.	.	.	.	0	0	1	1	1
C	.	.	.	.	.	0	0	0	0	0
D	.	.	.	.	.	82	78	52	49	59
E	.	.	.	.	.	7	2	1	0	1
F	.	.	.	.	.	9	8	0	0	4
G	.	.	.	.	.	33	17	19	45	47
H	.	.	.	.	.	11	16	12	11	15
I	.	.	.	.	.	15	19	38	19	11
J	.	.	.	.	.	1	0	0	0	0
K	.	.	.	.	.	2	4	4	2	6
M	.	.	.	.	.	1	4	5	5	4
N	.	.	.	.	.	1	0	4	1	4
O	.	.	.	.	.	2	3	3	5	4
P	.	.	.	.	.	3	3	9	5	0

Nigeria (F)   Reported injuries - Lésions déclarées - Lesiones declaradas

Fatal cases - Cas mortels - Casos mortales

Total men and women - Total hommes et femmes - Total hombres y mujeres
ISIC 3 - CITI 3 - CIIU 3

	1999	2000	2001	2002	2003	2004	2005	2006	2007	2008
Total	.	.	.	.	.	1	.	5	.	.
D	.	.	.	.	.	1	.	.	.	.
E	.	.	.	.	.	0	.	.	.	.

Non-fatal cases (temporary + permanent incapacity) - Cas non mortels (incapacité temporaire + permanente) - Casos no mortales (incapacidad temporal + permanente)

Total men and women - Total hommes et femmes - Total hombres y mujeres
ISIC 3 - CITI 3 - CIIU 3

	1999	2000	2001	2002	2003	2004	2005	2006	2007	2008
Total	.	.	.	.	.	52	.	.	.	.
D	.	.	.	.	.	50	.	.	.	.
E	.	.	.	.	.	2	.	.	.	.

Total cases (fatal + non-fatal) - Ensemble des cas (mortels + non mortels) - Todos los casos (mortales + no mortales)

Total men and women - Total hommes et femmes - Total hombres y mujeres
ISIC 3 - CITI 3 - CIIU 3

	1999	2000	2001	2002	2003	2004	2005	2006	2007	2008
Total	.	.	.	.	.	53	.	.	.	.
D	.	.	.	.	.	51	.	.	.	.
E	.	.	.	.	.	2	.	.	.	.

Sierra Leone (A)   Compensated injuries - Lésions indemnisées - Lesiones indemnizadas

Total cases (fatal + non-fatal) - Ensemble des cas (mortels + non mortels) - Todos los casos (mortales + no mortales)

Total men and women - Total hommes et femmes - Total hombres y mujeres
ISIC 3 - CITI 3 - CIIU 3

	1999	2000	2001	2002	2003	2004	2005	2006	2007	2008
Total	.	.	.	.	.	5 446	.	.	.	.

Men - Hommes - Hombres
ISIC 3 - CITI 3 - CIIU 3

	1999	2000	2001	2002	2003	2004	2005	2006	2007	2008
Total	.	.	.	.	.	3 794	.	.	.	.

Explanatory notes: see p. 1125.

[1] Excl. public sector and parastatal bodies.

Notes explicatives: voir p. 1127.

[1] Non compris le secteur public et les organismes paraétatiques.

Notas explicativas: véase p. 1129.

[1] Excl. el sector público y los organismos paraestatales.

	OCCUPATIONAL INJURIES	LÉSIONS PROFESSIONNELLES	LESIONES PROFESIONALES
	Cases of injury with lost workdays, by economic activity	Cas de lésion avec perte de journées de travail, par activité économique	Casos de lesión con pérdida de días de trabajo, por actividad económica

	1999	2000	2001	2002	2003	2004	2005	2006	2007	2008

Sierra Leone (A) — Compensated injuries - Lésions indemnisées - Lesiones indemnizadas

Total cases (fatal + non-fatal) - Ensemble des cas (mortels + non mortels) - Todos los casos (mortales + no mortales)

Women - Femmes - Mujeres
ISIC 3 - CITI 3 - CIIU 3

	1999	2000	2001	2002	2003	2004	2005	2006	2007	2008
Total	.	.	.	.	.	1 652	.	.	.	.

Togo (FA) — Reported injuries - Lésions déclarées - Lesiones declaradas

Fatal cases - Cas mortels - Casos mortales

Total men and women - Total hommes et femmes - Total hombres y mujeres
ISIC 2 - CITI 2 - CIIU 2

	1999	2000	2001	2002	2003	2004	2005	2006	2007	2008
Total	9	7	10	7	10	10	.	.	.	.
2	2	1	2	1	2	0	.	.	.	.
3	3	2	3	2	3	4	.	.	.	.
4	0	1	1	1	1	2	.	.	.	.
5	0	0	0	0	0	0	.	.	.	.
6.8	0	0	0	0	0	1	.	.	.	.
7	0	0	0	1	0	1	.	.	.	.
9	2	2	3	1	2	2	.	.	.	.
0	1	1	1	1	2	0	.	.	.	.

Non-fatal cases (temporary + permanent incapacity) - Cas non mortels (incapacité temporaire + permanente) - Casos no mortales (incapacidad temporal + permanente)

Total men and women - Total hommes et femmes - Total hombres y mujeres
ISIC 2 - CITI 2 - CIIU 2

	1999	2000	2001	2002	2003	2004	2005	2006	2007	2008
Total	966	1 002	850	780	707	297	.	.	.	.
2	204	174	150	180	109	1	.	.	.	.
3	329	308	250	208	235	130	.	.	.	.
4	51	79	70	57	54	47	.	.	.	.
5	22	25	14	2	24	4	.	.	.	.
6.8	8	17	9	27	11	16	.	.	.	.
7	22	20	20	11	7	45	.	.	.	.
9	251	276	263	158	137	47	.	.	.	.
0	80	106	75	137	130	7	.	.	.	.

Total cases (fatal + non-fatal) - Ensemble des cas (mortels + non mortels) - Todos los casos (mortales + no mortales)

Total men and women - Total hommes et femmes - Total hombres y mujeres
ISIC 2 - CITI 2 - CIIU 2

	1999	2000	2001	2002	2003	2004	2005	2006	2007	2008
Total	975	1 009	860	787	717	307	.	.	.	.
2	206	175	152	181	111	1	.	.	.	.
3	332	310	253	211	238	134	.	.	.	.
4	51	80	71	58	55	49	.	.	.	.
5	22	25	14	2	24	4	.	.	.	.
6.8	8	17	9	27	11	17	.	.	.	.
7	22	20	20	12	7	46	.	.	.	.
9	253	278	266	159	139	49	.	.	.	.
0	81	107	76	138	132	7	.	.	.	.

Tunisie (FA) — Compensated injuries - Lésions indemnisées - Lesiones indemnizadas

Fatal cases - Cas mortels - Casos mortales

Total men and women - Total hommes et femmes - Total hombres y mujeres
ISIC 3 - CITI 3 - CIIU 3

	1999	2000	2001	2002	2003	2004	2005	2006	2007	2008
Total	133	156	172	160	184	155	.	.	.	.
A	9	4	13	13	11	17	.	.	.	.
B	6	19	16	7	18	6	.	.	.	.
C	7	5	7	5	2	4	.	.	.	.
D	31	34	28	46	36	27	.	.	.	.
E-F	50	56	74	51	63	57	.	.	.	.
G.J	10	9	8	13	5	14	.	.	.	.
H	3	4	3	6	3	3	.	.	.	.
I	8	10	7	7	24	10	.	.	.	.
K-Q	9	15	16	12	22	17	.	.	.	.

Explanatory notes: see p. 1125.　　　　Notes explicatives: voir p. 1127.　　　　Notas explicativas: véase p. 1129.

OCCUPATIONAL INJURIES

Cases of injury with lost workdays, by economic activity

LÉSIONS PROFESSIONNELLES

Cas de lésion avec perte de journées de travail, par activité économique

LESIONES PROFESIONALES

Casos de lesión con pérdida de días de trabajo, por actividad económica

8A

	1999	2000	2001	2002	2003	2004	2005	2006	2007	2008

Tunisie (FA)   Compensated injuries - Lésions indemnisées - Lesiones indemnizadas

Non-fatal cases (temporary + permanent incapacity) - Cas non mortels (incapacité temporaire + permanente) - Casos no mortales (incapacidad temporal + permanente)

Total men and women - Total hommes et femmes - Total hombres y mujeres [1]
ISIC 3 - CITI 3 - CIIU 3

Total	39 878	41 142	45 326	44 773	41 656	43 162	.	.	.	.
A	1 087	1 075	1 064	875	867	1 161	.	.	.	.
B	294	308	290	265	283	283	.	.	.	.
C	577	634	610	652	588	578	.	.	.	.
D	22 611	22 720	24 735	24 754	22 622	22 939	.	.	.	.
E-F	6 883	7 039	7 513	7 239	6 544	6 620	.	.	.	.
G,J	2 012	2 098	2 274	2 469	2 381	2 554	.	.	.	.
H	2 046	2 159	2 129	1 918	1 859	1 976	.	.	.	.
I	1 673	1 600	1 718	1 632	1 544	1 518	.	.	.	.
K-Q	2 695	3 509	4 993	4 969	4 968	5 533	.	.	.	.

Cases of temporary incapacity - Cas d'incapacité temporaire - Casos de incapacidad temporal

Total men and women - Total hommes et femmes - Total hombres y mujeres
ISIC 3 - CITI 3 - CIIU 3

Total	37 716	38 741	42 581	41 959	38 976	40 589	.	.	.	.
A	1 034	1 022	984	796	790	1 095	.	.	.	.
B	261	278	259	232	252	252	.	.	.	.
C	541	578	545	604	532	508	.	.	.	.
D	21 412	21 482	23 260	23 179	21 177	21 565	.	.	.	.
E-F	6 500	6 574	6 979	6 758	6 092	6 148	.	.	.	.
G,J	1 900	1 957	2 147	2 299	2 229	2 395	.	.	.	.
H	1 964	2 078	2 046	1 850	1 780	1 917	.	.	.	.
I	1 545	1 446	1 571	1 494	1 405	1 408	.	.	.	.
K-Q	2 559	3 326	4 790	4 747	4 719	5 301	.	.	.	.

Total cases (fatal + non-fatal) - Ensemble des cas (mortels + non mortels) - Todos los casos (mortales + no mortales)

Total men and women - Total hommes et femmes - Total hombres y mujeres
ISIC 3 - CITI 3 - CIIU 3

Total	40 011	41 298	45 498	44 933	41 840	43 317	.	.	.	.
A	1 096	1 079	1 077	888	878	1 178	.	.	.	.
B	300	327	306	305	332	320	.	.	.	.
C	584	639	617	705	646	652	.	.	.	.
D	22 642	22 754	24 763	26 375	24 103	24 340	.	.	.	.
E-F	6 933	7 095	7 587	7 290	7 059	7 149	.	.	.	.
G,J	2 022	2 107	2 282	2 652	2 538	2 727	.	.	.	.
H	2 049	2 163	2 132	1 992	1 941	2 038	.	.	.	.
I	1 681	1 610	1 725	1 777	1 707	1 638	.	.	.	.
K-Q	2 704	3 524	5 009	5 203	5 239	5 782	.	.	.	.

Uganda (F) [2]   Reported injuries - Lésions déclarées - Lesiones declaradas

Total cases (fatal + non-fatal) - Ensemble des cas (mortels + non mortels) - Todos los casos (mortales + no mortales)

Total men and women - Total hommes et femmes - Total hombres y mujeres
ISIC 3 - CITI 3 - CIIU 3

L	.	.	.	.	.	112	33	.	.	.

Uganda (F) [3]   Compensated injuries - Lésions indemnisées - Lesiones indemnizadas

Total cases (fatal + non-fatal) - Ensemble des cas (mortels + non mortels) - Todos los casos (mortales + no mortales)

Total men and women - Total hommes et femmes - Total hombres y mujeres
ISIC 3 - CITI 3 - CIIU 3

Total	.	.	.	310	369	323	.	.	.	.
A	.	.	.	6	3	1	.	.	.	.
D	.	.	.	67	69	37	.	.	.	.
G-K,M-O	.	.	.	227	297	285	.	.	.	.

Explanatory notes: see p. 1125.

[1] Incapacity of 4 days or more. [2] Government employees. [3] Private sector.

Notes explicatives: voir p. 1127.

[1] Incapacité de 4 jours et plus. [2] Salariés de l'Etat. [3] Secteur privé.

Notas explicativas: véase p. 1129.

[1] Incapacidad de 4 días y más. [2] Asalariados del Estado. [3] Sector privado.

	OCCUPATIONAL INJURIES		LÉSIONS PROFESSIONNELLES			LESIONES PROFESIONALES			
	Cases of injury with lost workdays, by economic activity		Cas de lésion avec perte de journées de travail, par activité économique			Casos de lesión con pérdida de días de trabajo, por actividad económica			

	1999	2000	2001	2002	2003	2004	2005	2006	2007	2008

Zimbabwe (FA) [1]   Reported injuries - Lésions déclarées - Lesiones declaradas

Fatal cases - Cas mortels - Casos mortales

Total men and women - Total hommes et femmes - Total hombres y mujeres
ISIC 3 - CITI 3 - CIIU 3

	1999	2000	2001	2002	2003	2004	2005	2006	2007	2008
Total	169	96	101				82	71	62	
A							18	17	5	
C							14	14	14	
D							6	10	12	
E								2	7	
F							2	3	4	
G							9	4	3	
I							19	15	8	
J-K							1	1	0	
L							4	2	1	
O							9	3	8	

Non-fatal cases (temporary + permanent incapacity) - Cas non mortels (incapacité temporaire + permanente) - Casos no mortales (incapacidad temporal + permanente)

Total men and women - Total hommes et femmes - Total hombres y mujeres [2]
ISIC 3 - CITI 3 - CIIU 3

	1999	2000	2001	2002	2003	2004	2005	2006	2007	2008
Total	15 585	13 929	13 954	7 743	13 751	10 380	8 431	7 420	5 454	
A				1 142	1 835	1 335	979	868	459	
C				752	1 612	1 080	969	665	536	
D				2 739	5 576	4 207	3 452	2 897	2 410	
E				262	412	289	149	171	149	
F				437	618	499	373	345	221	
G				612	977	791	767	766	500	
I				725	1 103	858	658	612	412	
J-K				89	127	118	148	91	40	
L				378	619	452	369	399	249	
O				602	872	751	567	606	470	
X				5	0	0	0	0	8	

AMERICA-AMÉRIQUE-AMERICA

Argentina (FA) [3]   Reported injuries - Lésions déclarées - Lesiones declaradas

Fatal cases - Cas mortels - Casos mortales

Total men and women - Total hommes et femmes - Total hombres y mujeres
ISIC 2 - CITI 2 - CIIU 2

	1999	2000	2001	2002	2003	2004	2005	2006	2007	2008
Total	1 069	915		680	718	804	857	995	1 020	
1	138	78		70	82	108	115	116	104	
2	8	8		10	11	18	13	9	11	
3	186	161		123	99	140	170	184	167	
4	28	15		12	13	13	10	10	8	
5	164	113		49	75	99	108	158	163	
6	151	122		74	99	91	95	106	110	
7	144	128		105	101	98	124	149	149	
8	85	81		70	75	66	65	78	92	
9	162	208		165	163	169	156	183	216	
0	3	1		2	0	2	1	2	0	

Non-fatal cases (temporary + permanent incapacity) - Cas non mortels (incapacité temporaire + permanente) - Casos no mortales (incapacidad temporal + permanente)

Total men and women - Total hommes et femmes - Total hombres y mujeres
ISIC 2 - CITI 2 - CIIU 2

	1999	2000	2001	2002	2003	2004	2005	2006	2007	2008
Total	399 552	381 266		278 980	342 889	429 428	488 805	538 630	597 682	
1	26 990	25 194		23 335	28 154	34 033	35 413	38 322	37 822	
2	2 109	1 851		1 360	1 746	2 156	2 506	2 763	3 322	
3	126 634	106 046		68 093	89 952	113 128	123 085	128 256	139 159	
4	4 254	4 003		3 449	3 527	3 563	3 663	3 605	3 638	
5	56 286	39 558		14 816	24 697	40 424	57 759	73 404	83 129	
6	55 841	58 911		43 171	50 814	63 250	71 272	80 255	87 907	
7	31 196	33 161		25 147	30 900	34 718	37 593	41 101	45 607	
8	21 328	25 200		20 588	25 718	34 106	39 799	43 722	52 938	
9	74 094	86 741		75 373	86 836	103 712	117 258	126 801	143 722	
0	820	601		302	302	338	316	283	260	

Explanatory notes: see p. 1125.   Notes explicatives: voir p. 1127.   Notas explicativas: véase p. 1129.

[1] Year ending in March of the year indicated. [2] Incl. non-fatal cases without lost workdays. [3] Year ending in June of the year indicated.

[1] Année se terminant en mars de l'année indiquée. [2] Y compris les cas non mortels sans perte de journées de travail. [3] Année se terminant en juin de l'année indiquée.

[1] Año que termina en marzo del año indicado. [2] Incl. los casos no mortales sin pérdida de días de trabajo. [3] Año que se termina en junio del año indicado.

OCCUPATIONAL INJURIES

Cases of injury with lost workdays, by economic activity

LÉSIONS PROFESSIONNELLES

Cas de lésion avec perte de journées de travail, par activité économique

LESIONES PROFESIONALES

Casos de lesión con pérdida de días de trabajo, por actividad económica

	1999	2000	2001	2002	2003	2004	2005	2006	2007	2008

Argentina (FA) [1] — Reported injuries - Lésions déclarées - Lesiones declaradas

Cases of temporary incapacity - Cas d'incapacité temporaire - Casos de incapacidad temporal

Total men and women - Total hommes et femmes - Total hombres y mujeres
ISIC 2 - CITI 2 - CIIU 2

	1999	2000	2001	2002	2003	2004	2005	2006	2007	2008
Total	.	.	.	262 476	321 264	401 697	455 272	502 068	544 144	.
1	.	.	.	21 799	26 198	31 439	32 640	35 348	34 165	.
2	.	.	.	1 279	1 633	2 024	2 293	2 523	2 990	.
3	.	.	.	63 696	82 977	104 406	112 714	116 809	123 749	.
4	.	.	.	3 269	3 292	3 294	3 377	3 351	3 236	.
5	.	.	.	13 846	23 285	38 038	54 087	68 943	76 572	.
6	.	.	.	40 873	48 157	59 983	67 337	75 967	81 430	.
7	.	.	.	26 126	28 541	32 233	34 618	38 032	41 021	.
8	.	.	.	19 330	24 170	32 404	37 673	41 145	49 291	.
9	.	.	.	71 657	82 506	97 569	110 104	119 572	131 287	.
0	.	.	.	284	291	307	301	268	236	.

Total cases (fatal + non-fatal) - Ensemble des cas (mortels + non mortels) - Todos los casos (mortales + no mortales)

Total men and women - Total hommes et femmes - Total hombres y mujeres
ISIC 2 - CITI 2 - CIIU 2

	1999	2000	2001	2002	2003	2004	2005	2006	2007	2008
Total	400 621	382 181	.	279 660	343 607	430 232	489 662	539 625	598 702	.
1	27 128	25 272	.	23 405	28 236	34 141	35 528	38 438	37 926	.
2	2 117	1 859	.	1 370	1 757	2 174	2 519	2 772	3 333	.
3	126 820	106 207	.	68 216	90 051	113 268	123 255	128 440	139 326	.
4	4 282	4 018	.	3 461	3 540	3 576	3 673	3 615	3 646	.
5	56 450	39 671	.	14 865	24 772	40 523	57 867	73 562	83 292	.
6	55 992	59 033	.	43 245	50 913	63 341	71 367	80 361	88 017	.
7	31 340	33 289	.	28 252	31 001	34 816	37 717	41 250	45 756	.
8	21 413	25 281	.	20 658	25 793	34 172	39 864	43 800	53 028	.
9	74 256	86 949	.	75 538	86 999	103 881	117 414	126 984	143 938	.
0	823	602	.	304	302	340	317	285	260	.

Canada (FA) [2] — Compensated injuries - Lésions indemnisées - Lesiones indemnizadas

Fatal cases - Cas mortels - Casos mortales

Total men and women - Total hommes et femmes - Total hombres y mujeres
ISIC 3 - CITI 3 - CIIU 3

	1999	2000	2001	2002	2003	2004	2005	2006	2007	2008
Total	833	882	919	934	963	928	1 097	976	1 055	.
A	48	59	53	59	36	35	59	40	36	.
B	7	16	8	10	10	14	12	6	8	.
C	74	98	95	97	99	88	103	76	85	.
D	189	209	192	227	202	202	230	200	252	.
E	19	12	15	15	20	17	23	24	17	.
F	164	148	185	179	210	192	236	202	221	.
G	50	67	62	63	51	49	82	71	54	.
H	7	6	9	11	8	7	13	7	9	.
I	116	132	128	104	127	132	131	139	125	.
J	4	0	0	0	2	2	1	0	2	.
K	19	24	33	39	20	34	26	28	34	.
L	39	32	63	48	77	64	65	81	97	.
M	6	5	13	14	10	8	13	13	14	.
N	13	8	16	14	21	15	6	17	14	.
O	21	26	20	20	35	30	33	23	23	.
P	0	0	0	0	0	0	1	0	3	.
Q	0	0	0	0	0	0	0	0	0	.
X	57	40	27	34	35	39	63	49	61	.

Men - Hommes - Hombres
ISIC 3 - CITI 3 - CIIU 3

	1999	2000	2001	2002	2003	2004	2005	2006	2007	2008
Total	794	851	880	894	926	891	1 069	933	1 001	.
A	46	58	52	56	35	34	59	39	31	.
B	7	15	8	9	9	14	12	6	8	.
C	73	94	93	97	99	87	101	75	82	.
D	180	206	188	219	199	196	225	194	241	.
E	19	12	14	15	19	17	23	24	17	.
F	163	147	183	174	208	191	235	200	217	.
G	46	62	57	63	49	45	76	66	50	.
H	4	5	6	10	8	7	11	4	4	.
I	113	128	126	101	123	124	129	136	121	.
J	2	0	0	0	0	0	1	0	2	.
K	18	20	29	35	19	34	23	25	32	.
L	38	31	56	45	71	63	64	80	94	.
M	4	5	12	14	9	8	13	10	12	.
N	10	6	10	7	11	8	5	8	6	.
O	18	24	20	19	32	26	31	19	21	.
P	0	0	0	0	0	0	0	0	2	.
Q	0	0	0	0	0	0	0	0	0	.
X	53	38	26	30	35	37	61	47	61	.

Explanatory notes: see p. 1125.

[1] Year ending in June of the year indicated. [2] Total may differ from the sum of data by sex due to difficulties in coding certain cases.

Notes explicatives: voir p. 1127.

[1] Année se terminant en juin de l'année indiquée. [2] Le total peut différer de la somme des données par sexe en raison de difficultés de codification de quelques cas.

Notas explicativas: véase p. 1129.

[1] Año que se termina en junio del año indicado. [2] El total puede diferir de la suma de los datos por sexo debido a dificultades de codificación de algunos casos.

OCCUPATIONAL INJURIES	LÉSIONS PROFESSIONNELLES	LESIONES PROFESIONALES
Cases of injury with lost workdays, by economic activity	Cas de lésion avec perte de journées de travail, par activité économique	Casos de lesión con pérdida de días de trabajo, por actividad económica

	1999	2000	2001	2002	2003	2004	2005	2006	2007	2008

Canada (FA) [1]

Compensated injuries - Lésions indemnisées - Lesiones indemnizadas

Fatal cases - Cas mortels - Casos mortales

Women - Femmes - Mujeres
ISIC 3 - CITI 3 - CIIU 3

	1999	2000	2001	2002	2003	2004	2005	2006	2007	2008
Total	33	25	38	36	37	36	28	43	54	.
A	1	1	1	3	1	1	0	1	5	
B	0	0	0	1	1	0	0	0	5	
C	0	3	2	0	0	1	2	0	0	
D	8	0	4	8	3	6	5	1	3	
E	0	0	1	0	1	6	0	6	11	
F	1	0	2	5	2	1	1	0	0	
G	3	5	5	0	2	4	6	2	4	
H	3	1	3	1	0	0	6	5	4	
I	2	3	2	2	4	8	2	3	5	
J	2	0	0	0	2	2	0	3	4	
K	1	3	4	3	1	1	3	0	0	
L	1	1	7	3	6	1	1	3	2	
M	2	0	1	0	1	0	0	1	3	
N	3	2	6	7	10	7	0	3	2	
O	3	2	0	1	3	3	1	9	8	
P	0	0	0	0	0	0	2	4	2	
Q	0	0	0	0	0	0	1	0	1	
X	3	1	0	2	0	2	2	0	0	

Non-fatal cases (temporary + permanent incapacity) - Cas non mortels (incapacité temporaire + permanente) - Casos no mortales (incapacidad temporal + permanente)

Total men and women - Total hommes et femmes - Total hombres y mujeres
ISIC 3 - CITI 3 - CIIU 3

	1999	2000	2001	2002	2003	2004	2005	2006	2007	2008
Total	379 395	392 502	373 216	359 174	348 854	340 502	337 930	329 357	317 522	.
A	11 790	8 955	8 138	7 757	7 155	6 905	6 680	6 081	5 593	
B	762	847	959	861	775	752	823	739	635	
C	3 607	3 865	3 606	3 271	3 438	3 195	3 342	3 353	3 277	
D	111 865	114 969	104 517	96 074	89 376	84 466	80 193	73 950	65 440	
E	2 629	2 634	2 625	2 898	2 719	2 396	2 386	2 033	1 926	
F	28 976	31 211	30 971	30 753	30 842	31 791	32 642	33 225	33 689	
G	59 493	63 274	61 087	60 126	58 857	57 508	56 988	55 234	53 465	
H	21 622	23 654	22 392	21 740	19 871	19 303	19 085	18 998	17 846	
I	28 444	31 010	29 713	31 083	30 208	29 566	29 607	29 729	29 178	
J	899	972	681	659	610	650	591	618	574	
K	11 905	12 535	11 485	11 576	11 606	11 811	12 327	11 511	10 790	
L	17 958	20 299	19 925	22 930	21 819	20 996	20 935	22 111	20 840	
M	7 202	7 489	7 508	8 563	8 621	8 656	8 377	8 634	8 393	
N	35 123	37 754	38 890	39 539	41 621	40 949	41 261	41 957	41 419	
O	12 448	13 494	12 781	12 532	12 378	12 538	12 609	12 498	11 880	
P	811	375	282	230	285	245	227	165	161	
Q	0	32	17	27	15	16	21	26	23	
X	23 861	19 883	17 639	8 555	8 658	8 759	9 836	8 495	12 393	

Men - Hommes - Hombres
ISIC 3 - CITI 3 - CIIU 3

	1999	2000	2001	2002	2003	2004	2005	2006	2007	2008
Total	261 217	275 768	258 677	246 532	237 654	230 304	227 096	218 595	208 470	.
A	8 284	7 500	6 559	6 195	5 746	5 533	5 356	4 738	4 335	
B	643	797	885	780	703	678	727	653	543	
C	3 419	3 743	3 471	3 130	3 260	3 059	3 217	3 222	3 115	
D	90 671	94 270	85 254	77 998	72 272	68 449	64 975	59 943	53 085	
E	2 406	2 477	2 444	2 682	2 505	2 208	2 184	1 842	1 722	
F	26 788	30 312	30 036	29 839	29 839	30 792	31 529	31 914	32 276	
G	41 110	44 565	42 510	41 939	40 657	39 396	38 824	37 199	35 752	
H	8 616	9 670	9 224	8 973	8 110	7 643	7 515	7 468	6 868	
I	23 972	27 297	25 958	26 535	25 784	25 134	24 982	24 873	24 243	
J	236	265	150	155	147	139	146	128	123	
K	8 313	9 092	8 470	8 237	8 307	8 414	8 800	8 090	7 445	
L	13 132	14 286	13 731	15 423	15 689	14 923	14 718	15 208	14 243	
M	3 323	3 688	3 662	3 981	3 953	3 789	3 543	3 650	3 469	
N	6 725	6 978	7 362	7 614	7 717	7 248	7 213	7 234	7 016	
O	7 851	8 411	8 076	7 854	7 686	7 714	7 615	7 540	7 246	
P	66	52	40	25	19	22	15	13	12	
Q	0	24	11	18	10	9	9	13	13	
X	15 662	12 445	10 834	5 154	5 250	5 154	5 728	4 865	6 964	

Explanatory notes: see p. 1125.

[1] Total may differ from the sum of data by sex due to difficulties in coding certain cases.

Notes explicatives: voir p. 1127.

[1] Le total peut différer de la somme des données par sexe en raison de difficultés de codification de quelques cas.

Notas explicativas: véase p. 1129.

[1] El total puede diferir de la suma de los datos por sexo debido a dificultades de codificación de algunos casos.

OCCUPATIONAL INJURIES

Cases of injury with lost workdays, by economic activity

LÉSIONS PROFESSIONNELLES

Cas de lésion avec perte de journées de travail, par activité économique

LESIONES PROFESIONALES

Casos de lesión con pérdida de días de trabajo, por actividad económica

	1999	2000	2001	2002	2003	2004	2005	2006	2007	2008

Canada (FA) [1] Compensated injuries - Lésions indemnisées - Lesiones indemnizadas

Non-fatal cases (temporary + permanent incapacity) - Cas non mortels (incapacité temporaire + permanente) - Casos no mortales (incapacidad temporal + permanente)

Women - Femmes - Mujeres
ISIC 3 - CITI 3 - CIIU 3

	1999	2000	2001	2002	2003	2004	2005	2006	2007	2008
Total	103 718	115 436	113 153	111 100	109 747	109 138	109 912	109 861	108 125	.
A	2 856	1 422	1 534	1 526	1 366	1 349	1 298	1 327	1 237	.
B	76	46	73	80	72	74	95	86	90	.
C	100	101	111	103	123	90	112	100	129	.
D	18 382	20 431	18 956	17 836	16 877	15 889	15 095	13 902	12 253	.
E	142	151	174	210	208	183	195	184	196	.
F	646	728	770	719	802	846	999	1 193	1 260	.
G	16 125	18 473	18 353	17 896	17 973	17 937	18 004	17 840	17 541	.
H	11 944	13 864	13 021	12 594	11 581	11 530	11 445	11 422	10 866	.
I	2 867	3 616	3 665	4 436	4 317	4 329	4 545	4 781	4 871	.
J	604	706	529	502	459	510	445	489	450	.
K	3 194	3 405	2 966	3 296	3 255	3 367	3 495	3 394	3 313	.
L	4 046	5 913	6 104	7 403	6 077	6 039	6 183	6 861	6 547	.
M	3 433	3 775	3 818	4 542	4 627	4 842	4 811	4 962	4 902	.
N	26 765	30 673	31 397	31 778	33 772	33 587	33 942	34 613	34 303	.
O	4 026	5 025	4 643	4 599	4 612	4 763	4 935	4 917	4 585	.
P	706	323	240	205	266	222	212	152	148	.
Q	0	8	6	9	5	7	12	11	10	.
X	7 806	7 422	6 793	3 366	3 355	3 574	4 089	3 627	5 424	.

Total cases (fatal + non-fatal) - Ensemble des cas (mortels + non mortels) - Todos los casos (mortales + no mortales)

Total men and women - Total hommes et femmes - Total hombres y mujeres
ISIC 3 - CITI 3 - CIIU 3

	1999	2000	2001	2002	2003	2004	2005	2006	2007	2008
Total	380 228	393 384	374 135	360 108	349 817	341 430	339 027	330 333	318 577	.
A	11 838	9 014	8 191	7 816	7 190	6 940	6 739	6 121	5 629	.
B	769	863	967	871	785	766	835	745	643	.
C	3 681	3 963	3 701	3 368	3 537	3 283	3 445	3 429	3 362	.
D	112 054	115 178	104 709	96 301	89 578	84 668	80 423	74 150	65 692	.
E	2 648	2 646	2 640	2 913	2 739	2 413	2 409	2 057	1 943	.
F	29 140	31 359	31 156	30 932	31 052	31 983	32 878	33 427	33 910	.
G	59 543	63 341	61 149	60 189	58 900	57 557	57 070	55 305	53 519	.
H	21 629	23 660	22 401	21 751	19 879	19 310	19 098	19 005	17 855	.
I	28 560	31 142	29 841	31 187	30 335	29 698	29 738	29 868	29 303	.
J	903	972	681	659	612	652	592	618	576	.
K	11 924	12 559	11 518	11 615	11 626	11 845	12 353	11 539	10 824	.
L	17 997	20 331	19 988	22 978	21 896	21 060	21 000	22 192	20 937	.
M	7 208	7 494	7 521	8 577	8 631	8 664	8 390	8 647	8 407	.
N	35 136	37 762	38 906	39 553	41 642	40 964	41 267	41 974	41 433	.
O	12 469	13 520	12 801	12 552	12 413	12 568	12 642	12 521	11 903	.
P	811	375	282	230	285	245	228	165	164	.
Q	0	32	17	27	15	16	21	26	23	.
X	23 918	19 923	17 666	8 589	8 693	8 798	9 899	8 544	12 454	.

Men - Hommes - Hombres
ISIC 3 - CITI 3 - CIIU 3

	1999	2000	2001	2002	2003	2004	2005	2006	2007	2008
Total	262 011	276 619	259 557	247 426	238 580	231 195	228 165	219 528	209 471	.
A	8 330	7 558	6 611	6 251	5 781	5 567	5 415	4 777	4 366	.
B	650	812	893	789	712	692	739	659	551	.
C	3 492	3 837	3 564	3 227	3 359	3 146	3 318	3 297	3 197	.
D	90 851	94 476	85 442	78 217	72 471	68 645	65 200	60 137	53 326	.
E	2 425	2 489	2 458	2 697	2 524	2 225	2 207	1 866	1 739	.
F	26 951	30 459	30 219	30 013	30 047	30 983	31 764	32 114	32 493	.
G	41 156	44 627	42 567	42 002	40 706	39 441	38 900	37 265	35 802	.
H	8 620	9 675	9 230	8 983	8 118	7 650	7 526	7 472	6 872	.
I	24 085	27 425	26 084	26 636	25 907	25 258	25 111	25 009	24 364	.
J	238	265	150	155	147	139	147	128	125	.
K	8 331	9 112	8 499	8 272	8 326	8 448	8 823	8 115	7 477	.
L	13 170	14 317	13 787	15 468	15 760	14 986	14 782	15 288	14 337	.
M	3 327	3 693	3 674	3 995	3 962	3 797	3 556	3 660	3 481	.
N	6 735	6 984	7 372	7 621	7 728	7 256	7 218	7 242	7 022	.
O	7 869	8 435	8 096	7 873	7 718	7 740	7 646	7 559	7 267	.
P	66	52	40	25	19	22	15	13	14	.
Q	0	24	11	18	10	9	9	15	13	.
X	15 715	12 483	10 860	5 184	5 285	5 191	5 789	4 912	7 025	.

Explanatory notes: see p. 1125.

Notes explicatives: voir p. 1127.

Notas explicativas: véase p. 1129.

[1] Total may differ from the sum of data by sex due to difficulties in coding certain cases.

[1] Le total peut différer de la somme des données par sexe en raison de difficultés de codification de quelques cas.

[1] El total puede diferir de la suma de los datos por sexo debido a dificultades de codificación de algunos casos.

	OCCUPATIONAL INJURIES	LÉSIONS PROFESSIONNELLES	LESIONES PROFESIONALES
	Cases of injury with lost workdays, by economic activity	Cas de lésion avec perte de journées de travail, par activité économique	Casos de lesión con pérdida de días de trabajo, por actividad económica

	1999	2000	2001	2002	2003	2004	2005	2006	2007	2008

Canada (FA) ¹ — Compensated injuries - Lésions indemnisées - Lesiones indemnizadas

Total cases (fatal + non-fatal) - Ensemble des cas (mortels + non mortels) - Todos los casos (mortales + no mortales)

Women - Femmes - Mujeres
ISIC 3 - CITI 3 - CIIU 3

	1999	2000	2001	2002	2003	2004	2005	2006	2007	2008
Total	103 751	115 461	113 191	111 136	109 784	109 174	109 940	109 904	108 179	.
A	2 857	1 423	1 535	1 529	1 367	1 350	1 298	1 328	1 242	.
B	76	46	73	81	73	74	95	86	90	.
C	100	104	113	103	123	91	114	101	132	.
D	18 390	20 434	18 960	17 844	16 880	15 895	15 100	13 908	12 264	.
E	142	151	175	210	209	183	195	184	196	.
F	647	728	772	724	804	847	1 000	1 195	1 264	.
G	16 128	18 478	18 358	17 896	17 975	17 941	18 010	17 845	17 545	.
H	11 947	13 865	13 024	12 595	11 581	11 530	11 447	11 425	10 871	.
I	2 869	3 619	3 667	4 438	4 321	4 337	4 547	4 784	4 875	.
J	606	706	529	502	461	512	445	489	450	.
K	3 195	3 408	2 970	3 299	3 256	3 367	3 498	3 397	3 315	.
L	4 047	5 914	6 111	7 406	6 083	6 040	6 184	6 862	6 550	.
M	3 435	3 775	3 819	4 542	4 628	4 842	4 811	4 965	4 904	.
N	26 768	30 675	31 403	31 785	33 742	33 594	33 943	34 622	34 311	.
O	4 029	5 027	4 643	4 600	4 615	4 766	4 937	4 921	4 587	.
P	706	323	240	205	266	222	213	152	149	.
Q	0	8	6	9	5	7	12	11	10	.
X	7 809	7 423	6 793	3 368	3 355	3 576	4 091	3 629	5 424	.

Costa Rica (FA) — Compensated injuries - Lésions indemnisées - Lesiones indemnizadas

Fatal cases - Cas mortels - Casos mortales

Total men and women - Total hommes et femmes - Total hombres y mujeres
ISIC 2 - CITI 2 - CIIU 2

	1999	2000	2001	2002	2003	2004	2005	2006	2007	2008
Total	84	71	74	60	55	50	60	.	.	.
1	13	13	.	.	.	.	.	.	.	.
2	1	0	.	.	.	.	.	.	.	.
3	17	18	.	.	.	.	.	.	.	.
4	2	2	.	.	.	.	.	.	.	.
5	9	9	.	.	.	.	.	.	.	.
6	11	11	.	.	.	.	.	.	.	.
7	10	3	.	.	.	.	.	.	.	.
8	4	2	.	.	.	.	.	.	.	.
9	17	13	.	.	.	.	.	.	.	.
0	0	0	.	.	.	.	.	.	.	.

Non-fatal cases (temporary + permanent incapacity) - Cas non mortels (incapacité temporaire + permanente) - Casos no mortales (incapacidad temporal + permanente)

Total men and women - Total hommes et femmes - Total hombres y mujeres
ISIC 2 - CITI 2 - CIIU 2

	1999	2000	2001	2002	2003	2004	2005	2006	2007	2008
Total	120 195	118 575	110 175	110 711	103 321	105 880	109 348	.	.	.
1	36 041	34 843	.	.	.	.	.	.	.	.
2	539	532	.	.	.	.	.	.	.	.
3	28 789	26 895	.	.	.	.	.	.	.	.
4	3 191	2 923	.	.	.	.	.	.	.	.
5	13 411	12 845	.	.	.	.	.	.	.	.
6	12 861	13 506	.	.	.	.	.	.	.	.
7	4 667	4 877	.	.	.	.	.	.	.	.
8	3 024	3 217	.	.	.	.	.	.	.	.
9	16 321	17 864	.	.	.	.	.	.	.	.
0	1 351	1 073	.	.	.	.	.	.	.	.

Cases of temporary incapacity - Cas d'incapacité temporaire - Casos de incapacidad temporal

Total men and women - Total hommes et femmes - Total hombres y mujeres
ISIC 2 - CITI 2 - CIIU 2

	1999	2000	2001	2002	2003	2004	2005	2006	2007	2008
Total	.	.	.	100 214	.	.	98 098	.	.	.

Total cases (fatal + non-fatal) - Ensemble des cas (mortels + non mortels) - Todos los casos (mortales + no mortales)

Total men and women - Total hommes et femmes - Total hombres y mujeres
ISIC 2 - CITI 2 - CIIU 2

	1999	2000	2001	2002	2003	2004	2005	2006	2007	2008
Total	120 279	118 646	110 249	110 771	103 376	105 980	109 408	.	.	.
1	36 054	34 856	29 664	28 968	28 676	29 102	29 539	.	.	.
2	540	532	355	276	195	280	314	.	.	.
3	28 806	26 913	22 918	21 156	17 801	17 778	17 433	.	.	.
4	3 193	2 925	3 253	3 342	2 682	2 950	3 288	.	.	.
5	13 420	12 854	13 808	14 333	12 840	12 612	13 934	.	.	.
6	12 872	13 517	13 558	14 495	13 155	13 463	14 336	.	.	.
7	4 677	4 880	4 681	4 512	4 265	4 366	4 429	.	.	.
8	3 028	3 219	3 244	3 858	3 839	3 849	4 335	.	.	.
9	16 338	17 877	18 014	19 831	19 489	21 188	21 434	.	.	.
0	1 351	1 073	754	0	434	342	306	.	.	.

Explanatory notes: see p. 1125.

¹ Total may differ from the sum of data by sex due to difficulties in coding certain cases.

Notes explicatives: voir p. 1127.

¹ Le total peut différer de la somme des données par sexe en raison de difficultés de codification de quelques cas.

Notas explicativas: véase p. 1129.

¹ El total puede diferir de la suma de los datos por sexo debido a dificultades de codificación de algunos casos.

OCCUPATIONAL INJURIES

Cases of injury with
lost workdays,
by economic activity

LÉSIONS PROFESSIONNELLES

Cas de lésion avec perte
de journées de travail,
par activité économique

LESIONES PROFESIONALES

Casos de lesión con pérdida
de días de trabajo,
por actividad económica

8A

	1999	2000	2001	2002	2003	2004	2005	2006	2007	2008

Cuba (F)   Reported injuries - Lésions déclarées - Lesiones declaradas

Fatal cases - Cas mortels - Casos mortales

Total men and women - Total hommes et femmes - Total hombres y mujeres
ISIC 3 - CITI 3 - CIIU 3

Total	143	103	96	111	94	109	93	82	47	75

Non-fatal cases (temporary + permanent incapacity) - Cas non mortels (incapacité temporaire + permanente) - Casos no mortales (incapacidad temporal + permanente)

Total men and women - Total hommes et femmes - Total hombres y mujeres
ISIC 3 - CITI 3 - CIIU 3

Total	13 793	10 839	9 992	8 308	7 434	6 194	5 528	5 940	6 015	6 064

Total cases (fatal + non-fatal) - Ensemble des cas (mortels + non mortels) - Todos los casos (mortales + no mortales)

Total men and women - Total hommes et femmes - Total hombres y mujeres
ISIC 3 - CITI 3 - CIIU 3

Total	13 936	10 942	10 088	8 416	7 528	6 303	5 621	6 022	6 062	6 139

Chile (FA) [1]   Reported injuries - Lésions déclarées - Lesiones declaradas

Fatal cases - Cas mortels - Casos mortales

Total men and women - Total hommes et femmes - Total hombres y mujeres
ISIC 3 - CITI 3 - CIIU 3

Total	266	305	264	301	312	261	.	.	.	.

Non-fatal cases (temporary + permanent incapacity) - Cas non mortels (incapacité temporaire + permanente) - Casos no mortales (incapacidad temporal + permanente)

Total men and women - Total hommes et femmes - Total hombres y mujeres
ISIC 3 - CITI 3 - CIIU 3

Total	179 626	194 065	195 888	203 590	202 138	205 736	.	.	.	.

Men - Hommes - Hombres
ISIC 3 - CITI 3 - CIIU 3

Total	141 888	153 063	154 978	160 215	157 740	160 714	.	.	.	.

Women - Femmes - Mujeres
ISIC 3 - CITI 3 - CIIU 3

Total	37 738	41 002	40 910	43 375	44 398	45 022	.	.	.	.

Cases of temporary incapacity - Cas d'incapacité temporaire - Casos de incapacidad temporal

Total men and women - Total hommes et femmes - Total hombres y mujeres
ISIC 3 - CITI 3 - CIIU 3

Total	179 395	193 885	195 659	203 361	201 884	205 491	.	.	.	.

Men - Hommes - Hombres
ISIC 3 - CITI 3 - CIIU 3

Total	141 668	152 898	154 771	160 007	157 516	160 493	.	.	.	.

Women - Femmes - Mujeres
ISIC 3 - CITI 3 - CIIU 3

Total	37 727	40 987	40 888	43 354	44 368	44 998	.	.	.	.

Total cases (fatal + non-fatal) - Ensemble des cas (mortels + non mortels) - Todos los casos (mortales + no mortales)

Total men and women - Total hommes et femmes - Total hombres y mujeres
ISIC 3 - CITI 3 - CIIU 3

Total	179 892	194 370	196 152	203 891	202 450	205 997	.	.	.	.

República Dominicana (FA)   Compensated injuries - Lésions indemnisées - Lesiones indemnizadas

Fatal cases - Cas mortels - Casos mortales

Total men and women - Total hommes et femmes - Total hombres y mujeres
ISIC 3 - CITI 3 - CIIU 3

Total	.	.	.	.	.	.	.	88	.	.

Explanatory notes: see p. 1125.
[1] Incl. commuting accidents.

Notes explicatives: voir p. 1127.
[1] Y compris les accidents de trajet.

Notas explicativas: véase p. 1129.
[1] Incl. accidentes del trayecto.

OCCUPATIONAL INJURIES

Cases of injury with lost workdays, by economic activity

LÉSIONS PROFESSIONNELLES

Cas de lésion avec perte de journées de travail, par activité économique

LESIONES PROFESIONALES

Casos de lesión con pérdida de días de trabajo, por actividad económica

	1999	2000	2001	2002	2003	2004	2005	2006	2007	2008

República Dominicana (FA)   Compensated injuries - Lésions indemnisées - Lesiones indemnizadas

Non-fatal cases (temporary + permanent incapacity) - Cas non mortels (incapacité temporaire + permanente) - Casos no mortales (incapacidad temporal + permanente)

Total men and women - Total hommes et femmes - Total hombres y mujeres
ISIC 3 - CITI 3 - CIIU 3

	1999	2000	2001	2002	2003	2004	2005	2006	2007	2008
Total								1 708		

Total cases (fatal + non-fatal) - Ensemble des cas (mortels + non mortels) - Todos los casos (mortales + no mortales)

Total men and women - Total hommes et femmes - Total hombres y mujeres
ISIC 3 - CITI 3 - CIIU 3

	1999	2000	2001	2002	2003	2004	2005	2006	2007	2008
Total								1 896		

México (FA)   Reported injuries - Lésions déclarées - Lesiones declaradas

Fatal cases - Cas mortels - Casos mortales

Total men and women - Total hommes et femmes - Total hombres y mujeres
ISIC 3 - CITI 3 - CIIU 3

	1999	2000	2001	2002	2003	2004	2005	2006	2007	2008
Total	1 449 [1]	1 740 [1]	1 502 [1]	1 361 [1]	1 427 [1]	1 364 [1]	1 367 [1]	1 328 [1]	1 279 [1]	1 412
A-B										56
A										46
B										10
C										28
D										252
E										42
F										234
G										303
G-H										303
H										37
I										224
J										7
J-K										17
K										10
L										80
L-Q										80
M										4
N										6
O										129
P										0
Q										0
X										37

Men - Hommes - Hombres
ISIC 3 - CITI 3 - CIIU 3

	1999	2000	2001	2002	2003	2004	2005	2006	2007	2008
Total				1 263 [1]	1 341 [1]	1 258 [1]	1 272 [1]	1 247 [1]	1 207 [1]	1 320
A										46
B										10
C										28
D										230
E										39
F										231
G										245
H										31
I										217
J										7
K										9
L										73
M										2
N										6
O										113
P										0
Q										0
X										33

Explanatory notes: see p. 1125.
[1] Data for IMSS only.

Notes explicatives: voir p. 1127.
[1] Données relatives à l'IMSS seulement.

Notas explicativas: véase p. 1129.
[1] Datos relativos al IMSS solamente.

OCCUPATIONAL INJURIES
Cases of injury with lost workdays, by economic activity

LÉSIONS PROFESSIONNELLES
Cas de lésion avec perte de journées de travail, par activité économique

LESIONES PROFESIONALES
Casos de lesión con pérdida de días de trabajo, por actividad económica

	1999	2000	2001	2002	2003	2004	2005	2006	2007	2008

México (FA)   Reported injuries - Lésions déclarées - Lesiones declaradas

Fatal cases - Cas mortels - Casos mortales

Women - Femmes - Mujeres
ISIC 3 - CITI 3 - CIIU 3

	1999	2000	2001	2002	2003	2004	2005	2006	2007	2008
Total	.	.	.	98 ı	86 ı	106 ı	95 ı	81 ı	72 ı	92
A	.	.	.	.	.	.	.	.	.	0
B	.	.	.	.	.	.	.	.	.	0
C	.	.	.	.	.	.	.	.	.	0
D	.	.	.	.	.	.	.	.	.	22
E	.	.	.	.	.	.	.	.	.	3
F	.	.	.	.	.	.	.	.	.	3
G	.	.	.	.	.	.	.	.	.	21
H	.	.	.	.	.	.	.	.	.	6
I	.	.	.	.	.	.	.	.	.	7
J	.	.	.	.	.	.	.	.	.	0
K	.	.	.	.	.	.	.	.	.	1
L	.	.	.	.	.	.	.	.	.	7
M	.	.	.	.	.	.	.	.	.	2
N	.	.	.	.	.	.	.	.	.	0
O	.	.	.	.	.	.	.	.	.	16
P	.	.	.	.	.	.	.	.	.	0
Q	.	.	.	.	.	.	.	.	.	0
X	.	.	.	.	.	.	.	.	.	4

Non-fatal cases (temporary + permanent incapacity) - Cas non mortels (incapacité temporaire + permanente) - Casos no mortales (incapacidad temporal + permanente)

Total men and women - Total hommes et femmes - Total hombres y mujeres
ISIC 3 - CITI 3 - CIIU 3

	1999	2000	2001	2002	2003	2004	2005	2006	2007	2008
Total	423 505 ı	450 089 ı	413 748 ı	387 806 ı	358 784 ı	360 793 ı	373 239 ı	387 827 ı	450 102 ı	508 952
A-B	11 428 ı	11 026 ı	10 532 ı	9 297 ı	8 235 ı	7 717 ı	8 096 ı	8 391 ı	5 473 ı	8 338
A	.	.	.	.	.	.	.	.	.	8 226
B	.	.	.	.	.	.	.	.	.	112
C	5 063 ı	4 879 ı	5 004 ı	4 637 ı	4 841 ı	4 057 ı	4 045 ı	3 861 ı	2 628 ı	4 766
D	160 478 ı	172 151 ı	148 711 ı	134 349 ı	119 837 ı	116 235 ı	118 241 ı	122 166 ı	64 560 ı	112 151
E	3 992 ı	4 587 ı	4 276 ı	4 103 ı	3 990 ı	3 929 ı	4 746 ı	4 877 ı	2 356 ı	4 001
F	43 479 ı	44 999 ı	39 244 ı	35 395 ı	33 551 ı	34 520 ı	35 430 ı	36 943 ı	24 872 ı	40 148
G	71 314 ı	78 745 ı	76 970 ı	76 841 ı	72 856 ı	74 434 ı	76 424 ı	.	.	93 213
G-H	71 314	78 745	76 970	76 841	72 856	74 434	76 424	79 908 ı	50 404 ı	121 387
H	.	.	.	.	.	.	.	.	.	28 174
I	23 939 ı	26 070 ı	24 080 ı	23 542 ı	22 936 ı	23 031 ı	22 975 ı	23 794 ı	13 858 ı	23 959
J	.	.	.	.	.	.	.	.	.	2 236
J-K	62 039 ı	70 354 ı	67 803 ı	67 690 ı	64 069 ı	67 284 ı	67 728 ı	70 755 ı	36 164 ı	3 690
K	.	.	.	.	.	.	.	.	.	1 454
L	.	.	.	.	.	.	.	.	.	18 011
L-Q	32 361 ı	35 289 ı	32 761 ı	31 316 ı	28 186 ı	29 348 ı	29 567 ı	30 901 ı	25 583 ı	18 021
M	.	.	.	.	.	.	.	.	.	50 881
N	.	.	.	.	.	.	.	.	.	4 305
O	.	.	.	.	.	.	.	.	.	45 007
P	.	.	.	.	.	.	.	.	.	21
Q	.	.	.	.	.	.	.	.	.	10
X	9 412 ı	5 989 ı	4 367 ı	636 ı	283 ı	238 ı	5 987 ı	6 231 ı	224 204 ı	118 070

Men - Hommes - Hombres
ISIC 3 - CITI 3 - CIIU 3

	1999	2000	2001	2002	2003	2004	2005	2006	2007	2008
Total	319 319 ı	336 256 ı	303 055 ı	281 372 ı	260 867 ı	260 244 ı	267 812 ı	273 900 ı	260 860 ı	377 885
A	.	.	.	.	.	.	.	.	.	7 071
B	.	.	.	.	.	.	.	.	.	71
C	.	.	.	.	.	.	.	.	.	4 665
D	.	.	.	.	.	.	.	.	.	78 967
E	.	.	.	.	.	.	.	.	.	3 512
F	.	.	.	.	.	.	.	.	.	37 590
G	.	.	.	.	.	.	.	.	.	63 725
H	.	.	.	.	.	.	.	.	.	14 311
I	.	.	.	.	.	.	.	.	.	20 914
J	.	.	.	.	.	.	.	.	.	1 011
K	.	.	.	.	.	.	.	.	.	1 211
L	.	.	.	.	.	.	.	.	.	8 465
M	.	.	.	.	.	.	.	.	.	1 425
N	.	.	.	.	.	.	.	.	.	1 009
O	.	.	.	.	.	.	.	.	.	26 932
P	.	.	.	.	.	.	.	.	.	10
Q	.	.	.	.	.	.	.	.	.	6
X	.	.	.	.	.	.	.	.	.	106 990

Explanatory notes: see p. 1125.

Notes explicatives: voir p. 1127.

Notas explicativas: véase p. 1129.

¹ Data for IMSS only.

¹ Données relatives à l'IMSS seulement.

¹ Datos relativos al IMSS solamente.

8A OCCUPATIONAL INJURIES — LÉSIONS PROFESSIONNELLES — LESIONES PROFESIONALES

Cases of injury with lost workdays, by economic activity
Cas de lésion avec perte de journées de travail, par activité économique
Casos de lesión con pérdida de días de trabajo, por actividad económica

México (FA) — Reported injuries - Lésions déclarées - Lesiones declaradas

Non-fatal cases (temporary + permanent incapacity) - Cas non mortels (incapacité temporaire + permanente) - Casos no mortales (incapacidad temporal + permanente)

Women - Femmes - Mujeres
ISIC 3 - CITI 3 - CIIU 3

	1999	2000	2001	2002	2003	2004	2005	2006	2007	2008
Total[1]	104 186	117 833	110 693	106 434	97 917	100 549	105 427	113 927	119 545	131 067
A										1 155
B										41
C										101
D										33 184
E										489
F										2 558
G										29 488
H										13 863
I										3 045
J										1 225
K										243
L										9 546
M										3 663
N										3 296
O										18 075
P										11
Q										4
X										11 080

Cases of temporary incapacity - Cas d'incapacité temporaire - Casos de incapacidad temporal

Total men and women - Total hommes et femmes - Total hombres y mujeres
ISIC 3 - CITI 3 - CIIU 3

	1999	2000	2001	2002	2003	2004	2005	2006	2007	2008
Total[1]	406 731	427 972	393 742	367 379	335 820	338 962	352 546	368 500	368 500	489 953

Men - Hommes - Hombres
ISIC 3 - CITI 3 - CIIU 3

	1999	2000	2001	2002	2003	2004	2005	2006	2007	2008
Total[1]				263 327	240 470	240 912	249 458	256 805	245 442	361 542

Women - Femmes - Mujeres
ISIC 3 - CITI 3 - CIIU 3

	1999	2000	2001	2002	2003	2004	2005	2006	2007	2008
Total[1]				104 052	95 350	98 050	103 088	111 695	117 321	128 411

Total cases (fatal + non-fatal) - Ensemble des cas (mortels + non mortels) - Todos los casos (mortales + no mortales)

Total men and women - Total hommes et femmes - Total hombres y mujeres
ISIC 3 - CITI 3 - CIIU 3

	1999	2000	2001	2002	2003	2004	2005	2006	2007	2008
Total[1]	424 954	451 829	415 250	389 167	360 211	362 157	374 606	389 155	451 381	510 364

Men - Hommes - Hombres
ISIC 3 - CITI 3 - CIIU 3

	1999	2000	2001	2002	2003	2004	2005	2006	2007	2008
Total[1]				282 635	262 208	261 502	269 084	275 147	262 067	379 205

Women - Femmes - Mujeres
ISIC 3 - CITI 3 - CIIU 3

	1999	2000	2001	2002	2003	2004	2005	2006	2007	2008
Total[1]				106 532	98 003	100 655	105 522	114 008	119 617	131 159

Panamá (FA) — Compensated injuries - Lésions indemnisées - Lesiones indemnizadas

Fatal cases - Cas mortels - Casos mortales

Total men and women - Total hommes et femmes - Total hombres y mujeres
ISIC 3 - CITI 3 - CIIU 3

	1999	2000	2001	2002	2003	2004	2005	2006	2007	2008
Total	47	44	51	40	52	39	47	69	62	
A	1	1	0	0	2	2	0	2	3	
B	0	0	2	1	0	0	0	1	1	
C	0	0	0	0	0	1	0	2	1	
D	4	5	5	6	3	3	4	5	6	
E	2	3	2	1	1	1	2	0	0	
F	13	6	8	2	15	6	6	17	19	
G	8	10	6	6	10	6	8	11	8	
H	0	1	4	0	1	2	6	4	2	
I	0	5	1	5	2	1	6	3	2	
J	7	3	2	2	1	0	4	0	0	
K	8	7	10	8	5	7	1	9	10	
L	3	1	10	6	8	8	5	10	8	
M	1	0	0	1	0	1	2	2	1	
N	0	1	0	2	2	1	1	2	0	
O	1	1	1	1	2	1	2	1	0	
P	0	0	0	0	0	0	0	0	1	

Explanatory notes: see p. 1125.
[1] Data for IMSS only.

Notes explicatives: voir p. 1127.
[1] Données relatives à l'IMSS seulement.

Notas explicativas: véase p. 1129.
[1] Datos relativos al IMSS solamente.

	1999	2000	2001	2002	2003	2004	2005	2006	2007	2008
Panamá (FA)				Compensated injuries - Lésions indemnisées - Lesiones indemnizadas						

Fatal cases - Cas mortels - Casos mortales

Men - Hommes - Hombres
ISIC 3 - CITI 3 - CIIU 3

	1999	2000	2001	2002	2003	2004	2005	2006	2007	2008
Total	44	41	49	36	49	39	45	60	57	.
A	1	1	0	0	2	2	0	2	3	.
B	0	0	2	1	0	0	0	1	1	.
C	0	0	0	0	0	1	0	2	1	.
D	4	5	5	6	3	3	4	5	6	.
E	2	3	2	0	1	1	2	0	0	.
F	13	6	8	2	15	6	6	16	19	.
G	7	8	6	6	8	6	8	9	6	.
H	0	1	4	0	0	2	5	2	2	.
I	0	5	1	5	2	1	4	3	2	.
J	0	1	2	1	1	0	1	0	0	.
K	7	3	10	7	5	7	5	9	10	.
L	7	7	9	6	8	8	8	9	7	.
M	0	0	0	1	0	0	0	1	0	.
N	2	0	0	0	2	1	2	0	0	.
O	1	1	0	1	2	1	0	1	0	.

Women - Femmes - Mujeres
ISIC 3 - CITI 3 - CIIU 3

	1999	2000	2001	2002	2003	2004	2005	2006	2007	2008
Total	3	3	2	4	3	0	2	9	5	.
A	0	0	0	0	0	0	0	0	0	.
B	0	0	0	0	0	0	0	0	0	.
C	0	0	0	0	0	0	0	0	0	.
D	0	0	0	0	0	0	0	0	0	.
E	0	0	0	1	0	0	0	0	0	.
F	0	0	0	0	0	0	0	1	0	.
G	1	2	0	0	2	0	0	2	2	.
H	0	0	0	0	1	0	1	2	0	.
I	0	0	0	0	0	0	0	0	0	.
J	0	0	0	1	0	0	0	0	0	.
K	0	0	0	1	0	0	0	0	0	.
L	1	0	1	0	0	0	0	1	1	.
M	0	1	0	0	0	0	1	1	1	.
N	1	0	0	1	0	0	0	2	0	.
O	0	0	1	0	0	0	0	0	1	.

Cases of temporary incapacity - Cas d'incapacité temporaire - Casos de incapacidad temporal

Total men and women - Total hommes et femmes - Total hombres y mujeres
ISIC 3 - CITI 3 - CIIU 3

	1999	2000	2001	2002	2003	2004	2005	2006	2007	2008
Total	16 248	13 829	13 816	13 432	11 960	11 188	10 365	9 355	9 471	.
A	3 632	3 304	3 614	3 475	2 922	2 731	2 420	2 052	2 152	.
B	115	114	105	116	96	97	101	81	76	.
C	41	23	26	14	14	16	9	12	19	.
D	3 684	3 210	2 825	2 690	2 342	2 143	2 066	1 791	1 757	.
E	233	168	143	142	124	122	116	124	117	.
F	2 125	1 621	1 130	1 177	1 335	1 504	1 084	1 325	1 456	.
G	2 681	2 426	2 340	2 334	1 993	1 945	1 747	1 595	1 664	.
H	482	400	362	362	295	315	324	294	275	.
I	480	467	489	448	400	313	464	432	356	.
J	126	70	76	71	72	69	65	46	34	.
K	768	406	425	479	439	380	380	387	366	.
L	825	1 009	1 260	1 519	1 367	1 043	1 125	886	851	.
M	159	114	165	163	113	98	135	86	83	.
N	684	345	658	183	203	194	179	102	119	.
O	213	152	198	259	245	218	150	142	146	.
P	0	0	0	0	0	0	0	0	0	.

Men - Hommes - Hombres
ISIC 3 - CITI 3 - CIIU 3

	1999	2000	2001	2002	2003	2004	2005	2006	2007	2008
Total	14 226	12 533	11 982	11 477	10 279	9 672	8 799	8 328	8 404	.
A	3 495	3 205	3 427	3 294	2 811	2 649	2 349	1 981	2 056	.
B	100	108	99	104	93	77	87	75	68	.
C	41	23	25	14	13	16	9	12	18	.
D	3 450	3 015	2 651	2 505	2 182	2 019	1 922	1 703	1 669	.
E	203	148	125	127	106	98	107	118	110	.
F	2 106	1 602	1 105	1 159	1 320	1 487	1 073	1 314	1 440	.
G	2 230	2 098	1 963	1 889	1 556	1 541	1 412	1 354	1 401	.
H	328	287	233	216	201	209	189	185	178	.
I	424	443	437	405	357	278	411	403	326	.
J	67	41	40	29	23	27	30	21	13	.
K	682	363	348	388	375	322	315	339	326	.
L	640	870	1 055	1 022	921	672	699	642	605	.
M	59	52	63	60	43	33	50	37	33	.
N	239	157	273	63	73	69	42	32	44	.
O	162	121	138	202	205	175	104	112	117	.

Explanatory notes: see p. 1125.   Notes explicatives: voir p. 1127.   Notas explicativas: véase p. 1129.

ILO YEARBOOK OF LABOUR STATISTICS 2009   *ANNUAIRE DES STATISTIQUES DU TRAVAIL DU BIT 2009*   *ANUARIO DE ESTADISTICAS DEL TRABAJO DEL OIT 2009*   **1155**

OCCUPATIONAL INJURIES	LÉSIONS PROFESSIONNELLES	LESIONES PROFESIONALES
Cases of injury with lost workdays, by economic activity	Cas de lésion avec perte de journées de travail, par activité économique	Casos de lesión con pérdida de días de trabajo, por actividad económica

	1999	2000	2001	2002	2003	2004	2005	2006	2007	2008

Panamá (FA) — Compensated injuries - Lésions indemnisées - Lesiones indemnizadas

Cases of temporary incapacity - Cas d'incapacité temporaire - Casos de incapacidad temporal

Women - Femmes - Mujeres
ISIC 3 - CITI 3 - CIIU 3

	1999	2000	2001	2002	2003	2004	2005	2006	2007	2008
Total	2 022	1 296	1 834	1 955	1 681	1 516	1 566	1 027	1 067	.
A	137	99	187	181	111	82	71	71	96	.
B	15	6	6	12	3	20	14	6	8	.
C	0	0	1	0	1	0	0	0	0	.
D	234	195	174	185	160	124	144	88	88	.
E	30	20	18	15	18	24	9	6	7	.
F	19	19	25	18	15	17	11	11	16	.
G	451	328	377	445	437	404	335	241	263	.
H	154	113	129	146	94	106	135	109	97	.
I	56	24	52	43	43	35	53	29	30	.
J	59	29	36	42	49	42	35	25	21	.
K	86	43	77	91	64	58	65	48	40	.
L	185	139	205	497	446	371	426	244	246	.
M	100	62	102	103	70	65	85	49	50	.
N	445	188	385	120	130	125	137	70	75	.
O	51	31	60	57	40	43	46	30	29	.

Puerto Rico (CA) — Reported injuries - Lésions déclarées - Lesiones declaradas

Fatal cases - Cas mortels - Casos mortales

Total men and women - Total hommes et femmes - Total hombres y mujeres
ISIC 3 - CITI 3 - CIIU 3

	1999	2000	2001	2002	2003	2004	2005	2006	2007	2008
Total [1]	45	41	53	38	29	55	51	.	.	.
A-B [2]	0	0	0	0	0	0	0	.	.	.
C	0	0	0	0	0	0	0	.	.	.
D	0	3	5	0	0	0	0	.	.	.
E.I.L	9	8	7	11	9	.	.	.	.	.
F	16	9	14	15	6	16	14	.	.	.
G	.	.	.	.	.	5	5	.	.	.
G-H	11	6	9	.	3	.	.	.	.	.
H	.	.	.	.	.	.	6	.	.	.
I	0	0	6	4	.	5	6	.	.	.
J-K	0	0	0	0	0	0	.	.	.	.
K	.	.	.	.	.	.	0	.	.	.
L	.	.	.	.	.	10	7	.	.	.
M	.	.	.	.	.	.	0	.	.	.
M-O	7	11	8	4	.	.	.	.	.	.
O	.	.	.	.	.	.	7	.	.	.
X	2	4	.	.	.	.	6	.	.	.

Men - Hommes - Hombres
ISIC 3 - CITI 3 - CIIU 3

	1999	2000	2001	2002	2003	2004	2005	2006	2007	2008
Total [1]	.	.	.	.	29	54	.	.	.	.
E.I.L	.	.	.	.	9	0	.	.	.	.
F	.	.	.	.	6	16	.	.	.	.
G	.	.	.	.	3	5	.	.	.	.
H	.	.	.	.	.	5	.	.	.	.
I	.	.	.	.	.	5	.	.	.	.
L	.	.	.	.	.	10	.	.	.	.

Women - Femmes - Mujeres
ISIC 3 - CITI 3 - CIIU 3

	1999	2000	2001	2002	2003	2004	2005	2006	2007	2008
Total	.	.	.	.	0	1	.	.	.	.

Puerto Rico (DA) — Reported injuries - Lésions déclarées - Lesiones declaradas

Non-fatal cases (temporary + permanent incapacity) - Cas non mortels (incapacité temporaire + permanente) - Casos no mortales (incapacidad temporal + permanente)

Total men and women - Total hommes et femmes - Total hombres y mujeres
ISIC 3 - CITI 3 - CIIU 3

	1999	2000	2001	2002	2003	2004	2005	2006	2007	2008
Total	34 480	26 817	27 329	25 111	27 160	29 700	33 600	.	.	.
A-B [2]	181	99	181	260	210	.	100	.	.	.
C	54	72	56	56	40	.	.	.	.	.
D	5 025	4 799	4 376	4 259	3 560	4 000	3 700	.	.	.
E	.	.	.	.	1 330	.	.	.	.	.
F	.	1 848	1 756	2 181	1 660	2 100	0	.	.	.
G [3]	.	.	.	6 578	3 210	3 600	3 400	.	.	.
G-H	5 378	5 659	6 094	.	.	.	.	.	.	.
H	.	.	.	.	2 560	2 200	2 400	.	.	.
I [4]	960	1 065	.	692	390	500	600	.	.	.
J-K	.	.	.	1 334	.	.	.	.	.	.
K	.	.	.	.	490	500	400	.	.	.
L	13 038	9 220	.	5 485	9 580	9 500	5 000	.	.	.
M [5]	.	.	.	.	390	400	1 100	.	.	.
M-O	.	.	.	4 267	.	.	.	.	.	.
N [4]	.	.	.	.	1 930	.	.	.	.	.
O	.	.	.	.	.	.	1 100	.	.	.

Explanatory notes: see p. 1125.

[1] Incl. activities not shown separately. [2] Excl. farms with fewer than 11 employees. [3] Retail trade. [4] Private sector. [5] Public sector.

Notes explicatives: voir p. 1127.

[1] Y compris les activités non indiquées séparément. [2] Non compris les fermes avec moins de 11 salariés. [3] Commerce de détail. [4] Secteur privé. [5] Secteur public.

Notas explicativas: véase p. 1129.

[1] Incl. las actividades no indicadas por separado. [2] Excl. granjas con menos de 11 asalariados. [3] Comercio al por menor. [4] Sector privado. [5] Sector público.

OCCUPATIONAL INJURIES
Cases of injury with lost workdays, by economic activity

LÉSIONS PROFESSIONNELLES
Cas de lésion avec perte de journées de travail, par activité économique

LESIONES PROFESIONALES
Casos de lesión con pérdida de días de trabajo, por actividad económica

	1999	2000	2001	2002	2003	2004	2005	2006	2007	2008

Trinidad and Tobago (FF) — Reported injuries - Lésions déclarées - Lesiones declaradas

Fatal cases - Cas mortels - Casos mortales

Total men and women - Total hommes et femmes - Total hombres y mujeres
ISIC 2 - CITI 2 - CIIU 2

	1999	2000	2001	2002	2003	2004	2005	2006	2007	2008
Total	4	5	3	1	3	3	18	11	.	.
1	0	1	2	0	0	0	0	0	.	.
2	0	1	0	1	0	1	0	0	.	.
3	1	1	0	0	1	1	6	1	.	.
4	1	0	0	0	0	0	1	3	.	.
5	0	2	1	0	1	0	3	2	.	.
6	0	0	0	0	0	1	0	0	.	.
7	2	0	0	0	1	0	6	1	.	.
8	0	0	0	0	0	0	0	0	.	.
9	0	0	0	0	0	0	2	2	.	.
0	0	0	0	0	0	0	0	0	.	.

Non-fatal cases (temporary + permanent incapacity) - Cas non mortels (incapacité temporaire + permanente) - Casos no mortales (incapacidad temporal + permanente)

Total men and women - Total hommes et femmes - Total hombres y mujeres
ISIC 2 - CITI 2 - CIIU 2

	1999	2000	2001	2002	2003	2004	2005	2006	2007	2008
Total	421	444	487	536	352	231	245	377	.	.
1	116	84	114	123	45	0	0	0	.	.
2	41	47	52	30	15	15	24	33	.	.
3	227	286	292	363	246	148	175	257	.	.
4	1	4	2	0	1	0	0	2	.	.
5	4	4	4	1	2	1	3	10	.	.
6	1	0	0	2	9	15	7	11	.	.
7	31	19	23	17	34	54	34	44	.	.
8	0	0	0	0	0	0	2	18	.	.
9	0	0	0	0	0	1	0	2	.	.
0	0	0	0	0	0	0	0	0	.	.

Total cases (fatal + non-fatal) - Ensemble des cas (mortels + non mortels) - Todos los casos (mortales + no mortales)

Total men and women - Total hommes et femmes - Total hombres y mujeres
ISIC 2 - CITI 2 - CIIU 2

	1999	2000	2001	2002	2003	2004	2005	2006	2007	2008
Total	425	449	490	537	355	234	263	388	.	.
1	116	85	116	123	45	0	0	0	.	.
2	41	48	52	31	15	16	24	35	.	.
3	228	287	292	363	247	149	181	258	.	.
4	2	4	2	0	1	0	1	5	.	.
5	4	6	5	1	3	1	6	12	.	.
6	1	0	0	2	9	16	7	11	.	.
7	33	19	23	17	35	54	40	45	.	.
8	0	0	0	0	0	0	2	18	.	.
9	0	0	0	0	0	1	2	4	.	.
0	0	0	0	0	0	0	0	0	.	.

United States (CA) — Reported injuries - Lésions déclarées - Lesiones declaradas

Fatal cases - Cas mortels - Casos mortales

Total men and women - Total hommes et femmes - Total hombres y mujeres [1]
ISIC 2 - CITI 2 - CIIU 2   ISIC 3 - CITI 3 - CIIU 3 [2]

ISIC 2	1999	2000	2001	2002	2003	2004	2005	2006	2007	2008	ISIC 3
Total	6 054	5 920	5 915	5 534	5 575	5 764	5 734	5 840	5 657	.	Total
1	814	720	741	790	709	669	715	655	585	.	A-B
2	122	156	170	122	141	152	159	192	183	.	C
3	722	668	598	564	420	463	393	456	400	.	D
5	1 191	1 155	1 226	1 125	32	51	30	53	34	.	E
6 [3]	513	594	538	488	1 131	1 234	1 192	1 239	1 204	.	F
7 [4]	1 008	957	915	910	535	582	609	581	555	.	G [5]
8 [6]	107	79	86	88	187	148	136	185	164	.	H
9 [7]	736	769	772	682	872	895	950	926	969	.	I
0	841	822	869	765	45	46	42	44	46	.	J
					537	520	539	541	549	.	K [8]
					532	535	520	520	545	.	L
					41	44	46	49	34	.	M
					102	113	104	129	115	.	N
					282	306	287	263	271	.	O-P [9]
					9	6	12	7		.	X

Explanatory notes: see p. 1125.

[1] Total may differ from the sum of the data for individual activities. [2] Total and category L also include government sector excluded from the other categories. [3] Retail trade. [4] Incl. public utilities. [5] Excl. repairs and maintenance. [6] Excl. business services. [7] Incl. restaurants and hotels and business services; excl. sanitary, repair and installation services. [8] Incl. sanitary services. [9] Excl. sanitary services; incl. repairs and maintenance.

Notes explicatives: voir p. 1127.

[1] Le total peut différer de la somme des données des activités individuelles. [2] Total et catégorie L comprennent en plus le secteur gouvernemental non compris dans les autres catégories. [3] Commerce de détail. [4] Y compris les services publics. [5] Non compris la réparation et l'entretien. [6] Non compris les services aux entreprises. [7] Y compris les restaurants, hôtels et services aux entreprises; non compris les services sanitaires, de réparation et d'installation. [8] Y compris les services sanitaires. [9] Non compris les services sanitaires; y compris la réparation et l'entretien.

Notas explicativas: véase p. 1129.

[1] El total puede diferir de la suma de los datos por las actividades individuales. [2] Total y categoría L incluyen egualmante el sector gubernamental excluido de las otras categorías. [3] Comercio al por menor. [4] Incl. los servicios públicos. [5] Excl. reparacíon y mantenimiento. [6] Excl. servicios para las empresas. [7] Incl. restaurantes, hoteles y servicios paraempresas; excl. servicios de saneamiento, dereparación y de instalación. [8] Incl. los servicios de saneamiento. [9] Excl. servicios de saneamiento; incl. reparacíon y mantenimiento.

OCCUPATIONAL INJURIES

LÉSIONS PROFESSIONNELLES

LESIONES PROFESIONALES

Cases of injury with lost workdays, by economic activity

Cas de lésion avec perte de journées de travail, par activité économique

Casos de lesión con pérdida de días de trabajo, por actividad económica

	1999	2000	2001	2002	2003	2004	2005	2006	2007	2008

United States (CA) [1]   Reported injuries - Lésions déclarées - Lesiones declaradas

Fatal cases - Cas mortels - Casos mortales

Men - Hommes - Hombres [2]
ISIC 3 - CITI 3 - CIIU 3

	1999	2000	2001	2002	2003	2004	2005	2006	2007	2008
Total	.	.	.	.	5 129	5 349	5 328	5 396	5 228	.
A-B					682	651	680	630	556	
C					136	152	158	191	183	
D					397	435	358	435	377	
E					32	51	30	50	34	
F					1 113	1 218	1 171	1 224	1 192	
G [3]					476	527	545	523	504	
H					137	114	106	147	135	
I					826	850	897	872	913	
J					27	30	36	33	31	
K [4]					488	490	512	505	507	
L					465	461	458	451	473	
M					35	37	38	38	28	
N					51	61	65	62	53	
O-P [5]					256	266	263	229	239	
X					8	4	11	6	.	

Women - Femmes - Mujeres [2]
ISIC 3 - CITI 3 - CIIU 3

	1999	2000	2001	2002	2003	2004	2005	2006	2007	2008
Total	.	.	.	.	446	415	406	444	429	.
A-B					27	18	35	25	29	
C					5	.	.	.	.	
D					23	28	35	21	23	
E					0	.	.	3	.	
F					18	16	21	15	12	
G [3]					59	55	64	58	51	
H					50	34	30	38	29	
I					46	45	53	54	56	
J					18	16	6	11	15	
K [4]					49	30	27	36	42	
L					67	74	62	69	72	
M					6	7	8	11	6	
N					51	52	39	67	62	
O-P [5]					26	40	24	34	32	
X					1	0	.	.	.	

United States (DA) [6]   Reported injuries - Lésions déclarées - Lesiones declaradas

Non-fatal cases (temporary + permanent incapacity) - Cas non mortels (incapacité temporaire + permanente) - Casos no mortales (incapacidad temporal + permanente)

Total men and women - Total hommes et femmes - Total hombres y mujeres
ISIC 2 - CITI 2 - CIIU 2 [7] | ISIC 3 - CITI 3 - CIIU 3 [8]

	1999	2000	2001	2002	2003	2004	2005	2006	2007	2008	
Total [9]	2 575 900	2 587 000	2 409 400 [10]		1 315 920	1 259 320	1 234 680	1 183 500	1 158 870	.	Total [9]
1 [9]	47 500	52 400	53 500 [10]		18 430	19 750	18 870	16 890	16 980	.	A-B [9]
2	14 200	17 000	13 900 [10]		7 960	9 350	9 020	9 410	9 920	.	C
3	744 600	727 700	614 500 [10]		225 800	226 090	209 130	200 970	187 200	.	D
5	240 200	246 100	237 600 [10]		6 600	7 740	7 230	6 210	6 620	.	E
6 [11]	631 300	622 400	588 100 [10]		155 420	153 200	157 070	153 180	135 350	.	F
7 [12]	274 300	274 600	276 400 [10]		263 720	259 900	256 050	238 500	242 020	.	G [3]
8 [13]	45 800	45 900	45 000 [10]		87 640	77 620	75 670	81 930	76 510	.	H
9 [14]	578 000	601 100	580 500 [10]		156 530	141 160	138 130	128 360	129 690	.	I
					15 590	12 920	14 090	12 600	16 130	.	J
					127 280	112 510	115 990	110 640	107 580	.	K [4]
					11 370	10 070	10 500	10 390	10 680	.	M
					188 410	179 910	175 900	171 820	171 020	.	N
					51 190	49 100	47 020	42 620	49 170	.	O-P [5]

Explanatory notes: see p. 1125.

[1] Total and category L also include government sector excluded from the other categories. [2] Total may differ from the sum of the data for individual activities. [3] Excl. repairs and maintenance. [4] Incl. sanitary services. [5] Excl. sanitary services; incl. repairs and maintenance. [6] Private sector. [7] Figures rounded to nearest 100. [8] Figures rounded to nearest 10. [9] Excl. farms with fewer than 11 employees. [10] Not strictly comparable. [11] Excl. hotels and lodging-places. [12] Incl. electricity, gas and water. [13] Excl. business services. [14] Incl. restaurants and hotels and business services; excl. sanitary, repair and installation services.

Notes explicatives: voir p. 1127.

[1] Total et catégorie L comprennent en plus le secteur gouvernemental non compris dans les autres catégories. [2] Le total peut différer de la somme des données des activités individuelles. [3] Non compris la réparation et l'entretien. [4] Y compris les services sanitaires. [5] Non compris les services sanitaires; y compris la réparation et l'entretien. [6] Secteur privé. [7] Chiffres arrondis au 100 le plus proche. [8] Chiffres arrondis au 10 le plus proche. [9] Non compris les fermes avec moins de 11 salariés. [10] Non strictement comparable. [11] Non compris les hôtels et établissements analogues. [12] Y compris l'électricité, le gaz et l'eau. [13] Non compris les services aux entreprises. [14] Y compris les restaurants, hôtels et services aux entreprises; non compris les services sanitaires, de réparation et d'installation.

Notas explicativas: véase p. 1129.

[1] Total y categoría L incluyen egualmante el sector gubernamental excluido de las otras categorías. [2] El total puede diferir de la suma de los datos por las actividades individuales. [3] Excl. reparacíon y mantenimiento. [4] Incl. los servicios de saneamiento. [5] Excl. servicios de saneamiento; incl. reparacíon y mantenimiento. [6] Sector privado. [7] Cifras redondeadas al 100 más próximo. [8] Cifras redondeadas al 10 más próximo. [9] Excl. granjas con menos de 11 asalariados. [10] No estrictamente comparable. [11] Excl. hoteles y lugares de alojamiento. [12] Incl. electricidad, gas y agua. [13] Excl. servicios para las empresas. [14] Incl. restaurantes, hoteles y servicios paraempresas; excl. servicios de saneamiento, dereparación y de instalación.

OCCUPATIONAL INJURIES

LÉSIONS PROFESSIONNELLES

LESIONES PROFESIONALES

8A

Cases of injury with lost workdays, by economic activity

Cas de lésion avec perte de journées de travail, par activité économique

Casos de lesión con pérdida de días de trabajo, por actividad económica

	1999	2000	2001	2002	2003	2004	2005	2006	2007	2008

United States (DA) [1] Reported injuries - Lésions déclarées - Lesiones declaradas

Non-fatal cases (temporary + permanent incapacity) - Cas non mortels (incapacité temporaire + permanente) - Casos no mortales (incapacidad temporal + permanente)

Men - Hommes - Hombres [2]
ISIC 3 - CITI 3 - CIIU 3

	1999	2000	2001	2002	2003	2004	2005	2006	2007	2008
Total [3]	.	.	.	.	851 790	829 300	814 250	775 900	744 860	.
A-B [3]	.	.	.	.	15 200	16 200	15 540	13 560	13 830	.
C	.	.	.	.	7 810	9 200	8 790	9 180	9 670	.
D	.	.	.	.	171 260	173 380	163 220	157 290	145 960	.
E	.	.	.	.	5 850	6 880	6 470	5 610	5 840	.
F	.	.	.	.	152 260	149 430	153 750	148 530	131 840	.
G [4]	.	.	.	.	176 800	178 650	173 830	161 580	159 990	.
H	.	.	.	.	38 420	35 700	34 510	37 820	34 760	.
I	.	.	.	.	118 740	107 650	104 180	97 010	96 930	.
J	.	.	.	.	3 410	2 740	2 510	3 160	3 070	.
K [5]	.	.	.	.	87 540	76 940	80 560	76 150	73 500	.
M	.	.	.	.	5 470	4 740	4 790	4 650	4 780	.
N	.	.	.	.	34 760	34 670	34 290	32 150	30 830	.
O-P [6]	.	.	.	.	34 280	33 130	31 810	29 190	33 870	.

Women - Femmes - Mujeres [2]
ISIC 3 - CITI 3 - CIIU 3

	1999	2000	2001	2002	2003	2004	2005	2006	2007	2008
Total [3]	.	.	.	.	459 090	425 470	415 880	403 740	409 040	.
A-B [3]	.	.	.	.	3 220	3 550	3 330	3 320	3 120	.
C	.	.	.	.	150	150	230	230	250	.
D	.	.	.	.	55 410	52 660	45 740	43 440	41 010	.
E	.	.	.	.	750	860	760	590	780	.
F	.	.	.	.	3 150	3 670	3 320	4 650	3 480	.
G [4]	.	.	.	.	86 580	81 000	81 840	76 880	81 750	.
H	.	.	.	.	49 190	41 850	41 160	44 110	41 750	.
I	.	.	.	.	33 390	29 450	30 050	27 820	28 420	.
J	.	.	.	.	12 180	10 180	11 580	9 440	13 060	.
K [5]	.	.	.	.	39 680	35 570	35 430	34 480	34 060	.
M	.	.	.	.	5 900	5 330	5 710	5 740	5 900	.
N	.	.	.	.	153 600	145 220	141 580	139 640	140 140	.
O-P [6]	.	.	.	.	16 900	15 970	15 160	13 420	15 300	.

ASIA-ASIE-ASIA

Armenia (F) Reported injuries - Lésions déclarées - Lesiones declaradas

Fatal cases - Cas mortels - Casos mortales

Total men and women - Total hommes et femmes - Total hombres y mujeres
ISIC 3 - CITI 3 - CIIU 3

	1999	2000	2001	2002	2003	2004	2005	2006	2007	2008
Total	5	17	16	15	27	22	17	17	15	12

Men - Hommes - Hombres
ISIC 3 - CITI 3 - CIIU 3

	1999	2000	2001	2002	2003	2004	2005	2006	2007	2008
Total	4	17	16	15	26	17	16	16	14	11

Women - Femmes - Mujeres
ISIC 3 - CITI 3 - CIIU 3

	1999	2000	2001	2002	2003	2004	2005	2006	2007	2008
Total	1	0	0	0	1	5	1	1	1	1

Non-fatal cases (temporary + permanent incapacity) - Cas non mortels (incapacité temporaire + permanente) - Casos no mortales (incapacidad temporal + permanente)

Total men and women - Total hommes et femmes - Total hombres y mujeres
ISIC 3 - CITI 3 - CIIU 3

	1999	2000	2001	2002	2003	2004	2005	2006	2007	2008
Total	250	55	63	95	68	63	58	83	74	64

Men - Hommes - Hombres
ISIC 3 - CITI 3 - CIIU 3

	1999	2000	2001	2002	2003	2004	2005	2006	2007	2008
Total	219	53	61	93	65	61	50	78	72	61

Women - Femmes - Mujeres
ISIC 3 - CITI 3 - CIIU 3

	1999	2000	2001	2002	2003	2004	2005	2006	2007	2008
Total	31	2	2	2	3	2	8	5	2	2

Total cases (fatal + non-fatal) - Ensemble des cas (mortels + non mortels) - Todos los casos (mortales + no mortales)

Total men and women - Total hommes et femmes - Total hombres y mujeres
ISIC 3 - CITI 3 - CIIU 3

	1999	2000	2001	2002	2003	2004	2005	2006	2007	2008
Total	255	72	79	110	95	85	75	100	89	76

Men - Hommes - Hombres
ISIC 3 - CITI 3 - CIIU 3

	1999	2000	2001	2002	2003	2004	2005	2006	2007	2008
Total	223	70	77	108	91	78	66	94	86	73

Explanatory notes: see p. 1125.

[1] Private sector. [2] Figures rounded to nearest 10. [3] Excl. farms with fewer than 11 employees. [4] Excl. repairs and maintenance. [5] Incl. sanitary services. [6] Excl. sanitary services; incl. repairs and maintenance.

Notes explicatives: voir p. 1127.

[1] Secteur privé. [2] Chiffres arrondis au 10 le plus proche. [3] Non compris les fermes avec moins de 11 salariés. [4] Non compris la réparation et l'entretien. [5] Y compris les services sanitaires. [6] Non compris les services sanitaires; y compris la réparation et l'entretien.

Notas explicativas: véase p. 1129.

[1] Sector privado. [2] Cifras redondeadas al 10 más próximo. [3] Excl. granjas con menos de 11 asalariados. [4] Excl. reparación y mantenimiento. [5] Incl. los servicios de saneamiento. [6] Excl. servicios de saneamiento; incl. reparacíon y mantenimiento.

8A

OCCUPATIONAL INJURIES	LÉSIONS PROFESSIONNELLES	LESIONES PROFESIONALES
Cases of injury with lost workdays, by economic activity	Cas de lésion avec perte de journées de travail, par activité économique	Casos de lesión con pérdida de días de trabajo, por actividad económica

	1999	2000	2001	2002	2003	2004	2005	2006	2007	2008

Armenia (F)   Reported injuries - Lésions déclarées - Lesiones declaradas

Total cases (fatal + non-fatal) - Ensemble des cas (mortels + non mortels) - Todos los casos (mortales + no mortales)

Women - Femmes - Mujeres
ISIC 3 - CITI 3 - CIIU 3

	1999	2000	2001	2002	2003	2004	2005	2006	2007	2008
Total	32	2	2	2	4	7	9	6	3	3

Azerbaijan (FF)   Reported injuries - Lésions déclarées - Lesiones declaradas

Fatal cases - Cas mortels - Casos mortales

Total men and women - Total hommes et femmes - Total hombres y mujeres
ISIC 3 - CITI 3 - CIIU 3

	1999	2000	2001	2002	2003	2004	2005	2006	2007	2008
Total	34	37	27	59	52	72	54	81	128	72
A	1	0	0	0	2	2	1	0	2	2
C	.	.	.	.	6	9	5	16	1	1
D	15	17	13	15	12	8	3	13	16	14
E	.	.	.	.	8	13	10	8	8	4
F	2	0	0	6	7	18	14	17	68	30
G	.	.	.	.	1	5	5	3	4	5
H	.	.	.	.	0	0	0	0	0	0
I	2	4	5	18	10	3	5	8	2	1
J	.	.	.	.	0	0	0	0	0	1
K	.	.	.	.	1	3	1	2	1	1
L	.	.	.	.	1	8	7	11	21	7
M	.	.	.	.	2	0	0	0	1	3
N	.	.	.	.	0	2	3	1	0	1
O	.	.	.	.	2	1	0	2	4	2

Men - Hommes - Hombres
ISIC 3 - CITI 3 - CIIU 3

	1999	2000	2001	2002	2003	2004	2005	2006	2007	2008
Total	.	.	27	57	51	72	51	78	126	72
A	.	.	0	0	2	2	1	0	2	2
C	.	.	.	.	6	9	5	15	1	1
D	.	.	13	14	12	8	3	11	16	14
E	.	.	.	.	8	13	10	8	8	4
F	.	.	0	6	7	18	14	17	68	30
G	.	.	.	.	1	5	5	3	4	5
H	.	.	.	.	0	0	0	0	0	0
I	.	.	5	17	10	3	4	8	2	1
J	.	.	.	.	0	0	0	0	0	1
K	.	.	.	.	1	3	1	2	1	1
L	.	.	.	.	1	8	7	11	21	7
M	.	.	.	.	2	0	0	0	1	3
N	.	.	.	.	0	2	1	1	0	1
O	.	.	.	.	1	1	0	2	2	2

Women - Femmes - Mujeres
ISIC 3 - CITI 3 - CIIU 3

	1999	2000	2001	2002	2003	2004	2005	2006	2007	2008
Total	.	.	0	2	1	0	3	3	2	0
A	.	.	0	0	0	0	0	0	0	0
C	.	.	.	.	0	0	0	1	0	0
D	.	.	0	1	0	0	0	2	0	0
E	.	.	.	.	0	0	0	0	0	0
F	.	.	0	0	0	0	0	0	0	0
G	.	.	.	.	0	0	0	0	0	0
I	.	.	0	1	0	0	1	0	0	0
J	.	.	.	.	0	0	0	0	0	0
K	.	.	.	.	0	0	0	0	0	0
L	.	.	.	.	0	0	0	0	0	0
M	.	.	.	.	0	0	0	0	0	0
N	.	.	.	.	0	0	2	0	0	0
O	.	.	.	.	1	0	0	0	2	0

Non-fatal cases (temporary + permanent incapacity) - Cas non mortels (incapacité temporaire + permanente) - Casos no mortales (incapacidad temporal + permanente)

Total men and women - Total hommes et femmes - Total hombres y mujeres
ISIC 3 - CITI 3 - CIIU 3

	1999	2000	2001	2002	2003	2004	2005	2006	2007	2008
Total	113	140	88	120	136	168	135	192	202	212
A	17	0	0	4	4	1	5	2	3	6
C	.	.	.	.	28	47	32	49	5	23
D	69	106	69	80	59	65	33	51	42	45
E	.	.	.	.	9	10	6	2	1	8
F	1	1	4	3	9	12	26	39	101	50
G	.	.	.	.	3	4	4	12	3	8
H	.	.	.	.	0	0	0	0	0	0
I	10	7	9	10	17	11	7	12	6	15
J	.	.	.	.	0	0	0	0	0	0
K	.	.	.	.	1	1	11	7	1	3
L	.	.	.	.	5	12	7	15	37	39
M	.	.	.	.	0	0	4	1	0	2
N	.	.	.	.	0	2	0	1	1	0
O	.	.	.	.	0	3	0	1	2	13

Explanatory notes: see p. 1125.   Notes explicatives: voir p. 1127.   Notas explicativas: véase p. 1129.

Cases of injury with lost workdays, by economic activity

Cas de lésion avec perte de journées de travail, par activité économique

Casos de lesión con pérdida de días de trabajo, por actividad económica

	1999	2000	2001	2002	2003	2004	2005	2006	2007	2008

Azerbaijan (FF) — Reported injuries - Lésions déclarées - Lesiones declaradas

Non-fatal cases (temporary + permanent incapacity) - Cas non mortels (incapacité temporaire + permanente) - Casos no mortales (incapacidad temporal + permanente)

Men - Hommes - Hombres
ISIC 3 - CITI 3 - CIIU 3

	1999	2000	2001	2002	2003	2004	2005	2006	2007	2008
Total	.	.	85	100	133	152	126	184	192	196
A	.	.	0	4	4	1	4	1	3	6
C	.	.	.	.	28	44	31	46	4	23
D	.	.	67	67	56	55	29	48	40	44
E	.	.	.	.	9	10	6	2	1	8
F	.	.	4	3	9	12	26	39	101	50
G	.	.	.	.	3	4	4	12	3	8
H	.	.	.	.	0	0	0	0	0	0
I	.	.	9	8	17	10	6	12	6	9
J	.	.	.	.	0	0	0	0	0	0
K	.	.	.	.	1	1	10	7	1	1
L	.	.	.	.	5	11	7	14	32	32
M	.	.	.	.	0	0	3	1	0	2
N	.	.	.	.	0	1	0	1	1	0
O	.	.	.	.	1	3	0	1	0	13

Women - Femmes - Mujeres
ISIC 3 - CITI 3 - CIIU 3

	1999	2000	2001	2002	2003	2004	2005	2006	2007	2008
Total	.	.	3	20	3	16	9	8	10	16
A	.	.	0	4	0	0	1	1	0	0
C	.	.	.	.	0	3	1	3	1	0
D	.	.	2	13	3	10	4	3	2	1
E	.	.	.	.	0	0	0	0	0	0
F	.	.	0	0	0	0	0	0	0	0
G	.	.	.	.	0	0	0	0	0	0
H	.	.	.	.	0	0	0	0	0	0
I	.	.	0	2	0	1	1	0	0	6
J	.	.	.	.	0	0	0	0	0	0
K	.	.	.	.	0	0	1	0	0	2
L	.	.	.	.	0	1	0	1	5	7
M	.	.	.	.	0	0	1	0	0	0
N	.	.	.	.	0	1	0	0	0	0
O	.	.	.	.	0	0	0	0	2	0

Total cases (fatal + non-fatal) - Ensemble des cas (mortels + non mortels) - Todos los casos (mortales + no mortales)

Total men and women - Total hommes et femmes - Total hombres y mujeres
ISIC 3 - CITI 3 - CIIU 3

	1999	2000	2001	2002	2003	2004	2005	2006	2007	2008
Total	147	177	115	179	188	240	189	273	330	284
A	18	0	0	4	6	3	6	2	5	8
C	.	.	.	.	34	56	37	65	6	24
D	84	123	81	95	71	73	36	64	58	59
E	.	.	.	.	17	23	16	10	9	12
F	3	1	4	9	16	30	40	56	169	80
G	.	.	.	.	4	9	9	15	7	13
H	.	.	.	.	0	0	0	0	0	0
I	12	11	14	28	27	14	12	20	8	16
J	.	.	.	.	0	0	0	0	0	1
K	.	.	.	.	2	4	12	9	2	4
L	.	.	.	.	6	20	14	26	58	46
M	.	.	.	.	2	0	4	1	1	5
N	.	.	.	.	0	4	3	2	1	1
O	.	.	.	.	3	4	0	3	6	15

Men - Hommes - Hombres
ISIC 3 - CITI 3 - CIIU 3

	1999	2000	2001	2002	2003	2004	2005	2006	2007	2008
Total	.	.	112	157	184	224	177	262	318	268
A	.	.	0	4	6	3	5	1	5	8
C	.	.	.	.	34	53	36	61	5	24
D	.	.	80	81	68	63	32	59	56	58
E	.	.	.	.	17	23	16	10	9	12
F	.	.	4	9	16	30	40	56	169	80
G	.	.	.	.	4	9	9	15	7	13
H	.	.	.	.	0	0	0	0	0	0
I	.	.	14	25	27	13	10	20	8	10
J	.	.	.	.	0	0	0	0	0	1
K	.	.	.	.	2	4	11	9	2	2
L	.	.	.	.	6	19	14	25	53	39
M	.	.	.	.	2	0	3	1	1	5
N	.	.	.	.	0	3	1	2	1	1
O	.	.	.	.	2	4	0	3	2	15

Explanatory notes: see p. 1125.　　Notes explicatives: voir p. 1127.　　Notas explicativas: véase p. 1129.

OCCUPATIONAL INJURIES
Cases of injury with lost workdays, by economic activity

LÉSIONS PROFESSIONNELLES
Cas de lésion avec perte de journées de travail, par activité économique

LESIONES PROFESIONALES
Casos de lesión con pérdida de días de trabajo, por actividad económica

Azerbaijan (FF)

Reported injuries - Lésions déclarées - Lesiones declaradas

Total cases (fatal + non-fatal) - Ensemble des cas (mortels + non mortels) - Todos los casos (mortales + no mortales)

Women - Femmes - Mujeres
ISIC 3 - CITI 3 - CIIU 3

	1999	2000	2001	2002	2003	2004	2005	2006	2007	2008
Total	.	.	3	22	4	16	12	11	12	16
A	.	.	0	4	0	0	1	1	0	0
C	.	.			0	3	1	4	1	0
D	.	.	2	14	3	10	4	5	2	1
E	.	.			0	0	0	0	0	0
F	.	.	0	0	0	0	0	0	0	1
G	.	.			0	0	0	0	0	0
H	.	.			0	0	0	0	0	0
I	.	.			0	0	0	0	0	0
J	.	.	0	3	0	1	2	0	0	6
K	.	.			0	0	0	0	0	0
L	.	.			0	0	1	0	0	2
M	.	.			0	1	0	1	5	7
N	.	.			0	0	1	0	0	0
O	.	.			0	1	2	0	0	0
	.	.			1	0	0	0	4	0

Bahrain (FA)

Reported injuries - Lésions déclarées - Lesiones declaradas

Fatal cases - Cas mortels - Casos mortales

Total men and women - Total hommes et femmes - Total hombres y mujeres
ISIC 2 - CITI 2 - CIIU 2

	1999	2000	2001	2002	2003	2004	2005	2006	2007
Total	16	16	10	14	21	13	29	25	22
1	0	0	0	1	0	1	0	4	0
2	0	0	0	0	0	0	0	0	0
3	4	3	0	3	7	5	3	5	0
4	1	1	0	0	0	0	0	1	5
5	7	3	5	5	11	7	17	9	0
6	1	0	1	2	1	1	6	4	9
7	2	8	1	1	0	0	1	0	6
8	0	1	0	0	0	0	0	0	1
9	1	0	3	2	2	0	2	1	

ISIC 3 - CITI 3 - CIIU 3

Total	23
A	0
B	1
C	0
D	3
E	0
F	10
G	5
H	1
I	2
J	0
K	1
L	0
M	0
N	0
O	0
P	0
Q	0
X	0

Non-fatal cases (temporary + permanent incapacity) - Cas non mortels (incapacité temporaire + permanente) - Casos no mortales (incapacidad temporal + permanente)

Total men and women - Total hommes et femmes - Total hombres y mujeres
ISIC 2 - CITI 2 - CIIU 2

	1999	2000	2001	2002	2003	2004	2005	2006	2007
Total	1 478	1 673	1 682	1 640	1 637	1 572	1 966	1 588	985
1	19	18	22	22	20	24	23	18	7
2	0	0	0	0	0	0	0	0	0
3	359	393	411	571	557	540	598	519	329
4	62	66	63	24	22	16	19	7	2
5	560	613	674	561	584	535	739	572	426
6	140	230	182	201	173	170	230	187	88
7	98	111	98	84	109	111	148	117	48
8	40	48	44	36	34	48	43	35	27
9	200	194	187	141	138	128	166	133	58

ISIC 3 - CITI 3 - CIIU 3

Total	952
A	3
B	1
C	17
D	321
E	0
F	127
G	358
H	24
I	54
J	20
K	23
L	0
M	2
N	1
O	1
P	0
Q	0
X	0

Explanatory notes: see p. 1125.

Notes explicatives: voir p. 1127.

Notas explicativas: véase p. 1129.

OCCUPATIONAL INJURIES

Cases of injury with lost workdays, by economic activity

LÉSIONS PROFESSIONNELLES

Cas de lésion avec perte de journées de travail, par activité économique

LESIONES PROFESIONALES

Casos de lesión con pérdida de días de trabajo, por actividad económica

	1999	2000	2001	2002	2003	2004	2005	2006	2007		2008	

Bahrain (FA) — Reported injuries - Lésions déclarées - Lesiones declaradas

Total cases (fatal + non-fatal) - Ensemble des cas (mortels + non mortels) - Todos los casos (mortales + no mortales)

Total men and women - Total hommes et femmes - Total hombres y mujeres
ISIC 2 - CITI 2 - CIIU 2   ISIC 3 - CITI 3 - CIIU 3

	1999	2000	2001	2002	2003	2004	2005	2006	2007		2008	
Total	1 494	1 689	1 692	1 654	1 658	1 585	1 995	1 613	1 007		975	Total
1	19	18	22	23	20	25	23	22	7		3	A
2	0	0	1	0	0	0	0	0	0		2	B
3	363	396	411	574	564	545	601	524	334		17	C
4	63	67	63	24	22	16	19	8	2		324	D
5	567	616	679	566	595	542	756	581	435		0	E
6	141	230	183	203	174	171	236	191	94		137	F
7	100	119	99	85	109	111	149	118	49		363	G
8	40	49	44	36	34	48	43	35	27		25	H
9	201	194	190	143	140	128	168	134	59		56	I
											20	J
											24	K
											0	L
											2	M
											1	N
											1	O
											0	P
											0	Q
											0	X

Hong Kong, China (FF) — Reported injuries - Lésions déclarées - Lesiones declaradas

Fatal cases - Cas mortels - Casos mortales

Total men and women - Total hommes et femmes - Total hombres y mujeres
ISIC 2 - CITI 2 - CIIU 2

	1999	2000	2001	2002	2003	2004	2005	2006	2007	2008
Total	235	199	176	210	171	187	187	187	172	.
1	1	0	0	1	0	2	1	0	0	.
2	0	1	0	0	0	0	0	0	0	.
3	40	35	26	16	19	29	14	21	21	.
4 [1]	0	0	2	0	1	1	0	0	1	.
5 [2]	64	47	42	47	33	22	41	20	37	.
6	9	16	12	19	10	19	15	26	16	.
7	41	25	37	37	26	27	33	29	26	.
8	42	43	38	55	40	49	52	55	46	.
9 [3]	38	32	19	35	42	38	31	36	25	.
0	0	0	0	0	0	0	0	0	0	.

Non-fatal cases (temporary + permanent incapacity) - Cas non mortels (incapacité temporaire + permanente) - Casos no mortales (incapacidad temporal + permanente)

Total men and women - Total hommes et femmes - Total hombres y mujeres [4]
ISIC 2 - CITI 2 - CIIU 2

	1999	2000	2001	2002	2003	2004	2005	2006	2007	2008
Total	58 606	57 893	53 543	46 813	41 851	43 838	44 080	46 750	43 807	.
1	106	90	145	157	155	164	147	162	176	.
2	14	7	11	7	1	2	2	0	0	.
3	6 752	6 950	5 953	5 088	3 985	4 229	4 096	4 207	3 946	.
4 [1]	61	70	68	43	58	53	65	50	32	.
5 [2]	14 110	11 991	9 282	6 322	4 513	3 896	3 626	3 479	3 098	.
6	17 263	17 626	16 922	14 743	13 049	14 205	13 911	14 639	13 900	.
7	5 653	5 595	5 077	4 675	4 093	4 613	4 891	5 462	4 997	.
8	3 891	4 296	4 484	4 298	4 454	5 080	5 224	5 856	5 726	.
9 [3]	10 670	11 215	11 577	11 454	11 523	11 566	12 105	12 885	11 928	.
0	86	53	24	26	20	30	13	10	4	.

Total cases (fatal + non-fatal) - Ensemble des cas (mortels + non mortels) - Todos los casos (mortales + no mortales)

Total men and women - Total hommes et femmes - Total hombres y mujeres
ISIC 2 - CITI 2 - CIIU 2

	1999	2000	2001	2002	2003	2004	2005	2006	2007	2008
Total	58 841	58 092	53 719	47 023	42 022	44 025	44 267	46 937	43 979	.
1	107	90	145	158	155	166	148	162	176	.
2	14	8	11	7	1	2	2	0	0	.
3	6 792	6 985	5 979	5 104	4 004	4 258	4 110	4 228	3 946	.
4 [1]	61	70	70	43	59	54	65	50	33	.
5 [2]	14 174	12 038	9 324	6 369	4 546	3 918	3 667	3 499	3 135	.
6	17 272	17 642	16 934	14 762	13 059	14 224	13 926	14 665	13 916	.
7	5 694	5 620	5 114	4 712	4 119	4 640	4 924	5 491	5 023	.
8	3 933	4 339	4 522	4 353	4 494	5 129	5 276	5 911	5 772	.
9 [3]	10 708	11 247	11 596	11 489	11 565	11 604	12 136	12 921	11 953	.
0	86	53	24	26	20	30	13	10	4	.

Explanatory notes: see p. 1125.
[1] Excl. water. [2] Manual workers. [3] Incl. water. [4] Incapacity of 4 days or more.

Notes explicatives: voir p. 1127.
[1] Non compris l'eau. [2] Travailleurs manuels. [3] Y compris l'eau. [4] Incapacité de 4 jours et plus.

Notas explicativas: véase p. 1129.
[1] Excl. el agua. [2] Trabajadores manuales. [3] Incl. el agua. [4] Incapacidad de 4 días y más.

8A

OCCUPATIONAL INJURIES	LÉSIONS PROFESSIONNELLES	LESIONES PROFESIONALES
Cases of injury with lost workdays, by economic activity	Cas de lésion avec perte de journées de travail, par activité économique	Casos de lesión con pérdida de días de trabajo, por actividad económica

	1999	2000	2001	2002	2003	2004	2005	2006	2007	2008

India (FF) — Reported injuries - Lésions déclarées - Lesiones declaradas

Fatal cases - Cas mortels - Casos mortales

Per 100,000 employees - Pour 100 000 salariés - Por 100 000 asalariados

Men - Hommes - Hombres
ISIC 3 - CITI 3 - CIIU 3

C	202	198	218	149	170	157	167	203	151	196

Women - Femmes - Mujeres
ISIC 3 - CITI 3 - CIIU 3

C	8	1	4	12	5	3	2	5	0	5

Total men and women - Total hommes et femmes - Total hombres y mujeres
ISIC 3 - CITI 3 - CIIU 3

C	210	199	222	161	175	160	169	208	151	201

Non-fatal cases (temporary + permanent incapacity) - Cas non mortels (incapacité temporaire + permanente) - Casos no mortales (incapacidad temporal + permanente)

Per 100,000 employees - Pour 100 000 salariés - Por 100 000 asalariados

Men - Hommes - Hombres
ISIC 3 - CITI 3 - CIIU 3

C	895	897	924	870	768	1 188	1 247	974	1 057	778

Women - Femmes - Mujeres
ISIC 3 - CITI 3 - CIIU 3

C	6	4	4	4	7	6	4	5	0	6

Total men and women - Total hommes et femmes - Total hombres y mujeres
ISIC 3 - CITI 3 - CIIU 3

C	901	901	928	874	775	1 194	1 251	979	1 057	784

Total cases (fatal + non-fatal) - Ensemble des cas (mortels + non mortels) - Todos los casos (mortales + no mortales)

Per 100,000 employees - Pour 100 000 salariés - Por 100 000 asalariados

Men - Hommes - Hombres
ISIC 3 - CITI 3 - CIIU 3

C	1 097	1 095	1 142	1 019	938	1 345	1 414	1 177	1 208	974

Women - Femmes - Mujeres
ISIC 3 - CITI 3 - CIIU 3

C	14	5	8	16	12	9	6	10	0	11

Total men and women - Total hommes et femmes - Total hombres y mujeres
ISIC 3 - CITI 3 - CIIU 3

C	1 111	1 100	1 150	1 035	950	1 354	1 420	1 187	1 208	985

Israel (FA) — Compensated injuries - Lésions indemnisées - Lesiones indemnizadas

Fatal cases - Cas mortels - Casos mortales

Total men and women - Total hommes et femmes - Total hombres y mujeres [1]
ISIC 2 - CITI 2 - CIIU 2

Total	114	120	100	91	88	88	82	84	76	89

Non-fatal cases (temporary + permanent incapacity) - Cas non mortels (incapacité temporaire + permanente) - Casos no mortales (incapacidad temporal + permanente)

Total men and women - Total hommes et femmes - Total hombres y mujeres [2]
ISIC 2 - CITI 2 - CIIU 2

Total	73 690	76 185	69 087	70 025	61 539	65 776	63 856	64 296	67 657	69 734

Explanatory notes: see p. 1125.
[1] Only deaths resulting from accidents occurring during the same year. [2] Incapacity of 3 days or more.

Notes explicatives: voir p. 1127.
[1] Seulement les décès dus à des accidents survenus pendant la même année. [2] Incapacité de 3 jours et plus.

Notas explicativas: véase p. 1129.
[1] Solamente los fallecimientos resultados a accidentes ocurridos en el mismo año. [2] Incapacidad de 3 días y más.

OCCUPATIONAL INJURIES

Cases of injury with lost workdays, by economic activity

LÉSIONS PROFESSIONNELLES

Cas de lésion avec perte de journées de travail, par activité économique

LESIONES PROFESIONALES

Casos de lesión con pérdida de días de trabajo, por actividad económica

	1999	2000	2001	2002	2003	2004	2005	2006	2007	2008

Japan (FF)   Reported injuries - Lésions déclarées - Lesiones declaradas

Fatal cases - Cas mortels - Casos mortales

Total men and women - Total hommes et femmes - Total hombres y mujeres
ISIC 3 - CITI 3 - CIIU 3

	1999	2000	2001	2002	2003	2004	2005	2006	2007	2008
Total [1]	1 992	1 889	1 790	1 658	1 628	1 620	1 514	1 472	1 357	1 268
A	85	73	70	65	73	59	60	77	65	43
B	23	16	22	19	17	23	18	16	15	25
C	24	26	24	17	14	16	16	16	13	8
D	342	318	323	275	293	289	254	261	260	260
E	2	5	3	0	1	4	2	7	4	1
F [2]	794	731	644	607	548	594	497	508	461	430
G [3]	177	195	177	146	158	145	172	151	129	118
H	33	27	48	27	28	20	17	24	25	24
I	312	313	298	291	293	295	294	245	237	186
J-K	21	10	17	16	11	12	10	8	4	7
L	0	0	0	0	0	0	0	0	0	1
M	12	5	4	4	16	5	10	5	4	5
N	7	5	8	9	15	10	9	12	15	8
O	160	165	152	182	163	148	155	142	125	152

Non-fatal cases (temporary + permanent incapacity) - Cas non mortels (incapacité temporaire + permanente) - Casos no mortales (incapacidad temporal + permanente)

Total men and women - Total hommes et femmes - Total hombres y mujeres [4]
ISIC 3 - CITI 3 - CIIU 3

	1999	2000	2001	2002	2003	2004	2005	2006	2007	2008
Total [1]	133 844	132 566	132 287	124 702	124 455	121 475	119 121	120 048	120 068	118 023
A	5 326	5 309	5 200	4 918	4 011	4 802	4 531	4 299	4 366	4 479
B	836	815	799	797	780	754	672	634	677	565
C	773	732	700	608	641	565	534	450	414	354
D	38 108	37 410	35 882	32 571	32 140	30 903	29 719	29 336	29 056	27 999
E	104	78	120	107	100	89	80	81	81	80
F [2]	33 877	33 020	32 113	30 183	28 787	27 913	26 759	26 401	25 647	23 952
G [3]	15 875	15 598	16 534	16 321	16 651	16 228	16 299	15 869	17 258	17 166
H	1 474	1 352	1 447	1 411	1 366	1 336	1 282	1 399	1 398	1 418
I	16 737	17 057	17 485	16 351	16 588	16 338	16 522	17 115	17 161	16 854
J-K	1 075	1 165	1 173	1 014	1 119	1 018	987	1 026	977	1 114
M-N	3 198	3 477	3 912	4 056	4 571	4 669	4 874	4 934	5 494	5 810
O	16 461	16 553	16 922	16 365	16 726	16 860	16 862	18 504	17 539	18 232

Total cases (fatal + non-fatal) - Ensemble des cas (mortels + non mortels) - Todos los casos (mortales + no mortales)

Total men and women - Total hommes et femmes - Total hombres y mujeres
ISIC 3 - CITI 3 - CIIU 3

	1999	2000	2001	2002	2003	2004	2005	2006	2007	2008
Total [1]	135 836	134 455	134 077	126 360	126 083	123 095	120 635	121 520	121 425	119 291
A	5 411	5 382	5 270	4 983	4 084	4 861	4 591	4 376	4 431	4 522
B	859	831	821	816	797	777	690	650	692	590
C	797	758	724	625	655	581	550	466	427	362
D	38 450	37 728	36 205	32 846	32 433	31 192	29 973	29 597	29 316	28 259
E	106	83	123	107	101	93	82	88	85	81
F [2]	34 671	33 751	32 757	30 790	29 335	28 507	27 256	26 909	26 108	24 382
G [3]	16 052	15 793	16 711	16 467	16 809	16 373	16 471	16 020	17 387	17 284
H	1 507	1 379	1 495	1 438	1 394	1 356	1 299	1 423	1 423	1 442
I	17 049	17 370	17 783	16 642	16 881	16 633	16 816	17 360	17 398	17 040
J-K	1 096	1 175	1 190	1 030	1 130	1 030	997	1 034	981	1 121
M-N	3 217	3 487	3 924	4 069	4 602	4 684	4 893	4 951	5 494	5 823
O	16 621	16 718	17 074	16 547	16 889	17 008	17 017	18 646	17 664	18 384

Jordan (FA)   Reported injuries - Lésions déclarées - Lesiones declaradas

Fatal cases - Cas mortels - Casos mortales

Total men and women - Total hommes et femmes - Total hombres y mujeres
ISIC 3 - CITI 3 - CIIU 3

	1999	2000	2001	2002	2003	2004	2005	2006	2007	2008
Total	36	.	35	49	70	52	63	87	.	.

Non-fatal cases (temporary + permanent incapacity) - Cas non mortels (incapacité temporaire + permanente) - Casos no mortales (incapacidad temporal + permanente)

Total men and women - Total hommes et femmes - Total hombres y mujeres
ISIC 3 - CITI 3 - CIIU 3

	1999	2000	2001	2002	2003	2004	2005	2006	2007	2008
Total	19 723	.	13 637	11 297	12 558	12 807	13 689	15 301	.	.

Explanatory notes: see p. 1125.

[1] Excl. general construction. [2] General construction only. [3] Excl. repair of motor vehicles, motor cycles and personal and household goods. [4] Incapacity of 4 days or more.

Notes explicatives: voir p. 1127.

[1] Non compris la construction générale. [2] Construction générale seulement. [3] Non compris réparation de véhicules automobiles, de motocycles et de biens personnels etdomestiques. [4] Incapacité de 4 jours et plus.

Notas explicativas: véase p. 1129.

[1] Excl. construcción general. [2] Construcción general solamente. [3] Excl. reparación de vehículos automotores, motocicletas, efectos personals y enseres domesticos. [4] Incapacidad de 4 días y más.

8A

OCCUPATIONAL INJURIES	LÉSIONS PROFESSIONNELLES	LESIONES PROFESIONALES
Cases of injury with lost workdays, by economic activity	Cas de lésion avec perte de journées de travail, par activité économique	Casos de lesión con pérdida de días de trabajo, por actividad económica

	1999	2000	2001	2002	2003	2004	2005	2006	2007	2008
Jordan (FA)				Reported injuries - Lésions déclarées - Lesiones declaradas						

Cases of temporary incapacity - Cas d'incapacité temporaire - Casos de incapacidad temporal

Total men and women - Total hommes et femmes - Total hombres y mujeres
ISIC 3 - CITI 3 - CIIU 3

| Total | | | 13 612 | 10 705 | 11 948 | 12 237 | 12 923 | 14 299 | | |

Total cases (fatal + non-fatal) - Ensemble des cas (mortels + non mortels) - Todos los casos (mortales + no mortales)

Total men and women - Total hommes et femmes - Total hombres y mujeres
ISIC 3 - CITI 3 - CIIU 3

| Total | 19 759 | | 13 672 | 11 346 | 12 628 | 12 859 | 13 752 | 15 388 | | |

| **Kazakhstan (FF)** | | | | Reported injuries - Lésions déclarées - Lesiones declaradas | | | | | | |

Fatal cases - Cas mortels - Casos mortales

Total men and women - Total hommes et femmes - Total hombres y mujeres
ISIC 3 - CITI 3 - CIIU 3

| Total | 277 | 256 | 282 | 325 | 294 | 345 | 357 | 414 | 341 | 341 |

Men - Hommes - Hombres
ISIC 3 - CITI 3 - CIIU 3

| Total | 253 | 236 | 272 | 307 | 275 | 318 | 235 | 390 | 322 | 236 |

Women - Femmes - Mujeres
ISIC 3 - CITI 3 - CIIU 3

| Total | 24 | 20 | 10 | 18 | 19 | 27 | 32 | 24 | 19 | 15 |

Non-fatal cases (temporary + permanent incapacity) - Cas non mortels (incapacité temporaire + permanente) - Casos no mortales (incapacidad temporal + permanente)

Total men and women - Total hommes et femmes - Total hombres y mujeres
ISIC 3 - CITI 3 - CIIU 3

| Total | 3 753 | 3 228 | 3 248 | 3 513 | 3 395 | 3 348 | 3 333 | 3 197 | 2 829 | 2 702 |

Men - Hommes - Hombres
ISIC 3 - CITI 3 - CIIU 3

| Total | 3 093 | 2 702 | 2 734 | 3 944 | 2 797 | 2 814 | 2 768 | 2 651 | 2 328 | 2 223 |

Women - Femmes - Mujeres
ISIC 3 - CITI 3 - CIIU 3

| Total | 660 | 526 | 514 | 569 | 598 | 534 | 565 | 546 | 501 | 479 |

Total cases (fatal + non-fatal) - Ensemble des cas (mortels + non mortels) - Todos los casos (mortales + no mortales)

Total men and women - Total hommes et femmes - Total hombres y mujeres
ISIC 3 - CITI 3 - CIIU 3

| Total | 4 030 | 3 484 | 3 530 | 3 838 | 3 689 | 3 693 | 3 690 | 3 611 | 3 170 | 3 043 |

Men - Hommes - Hombres
ISIC 3 - CITI 3 - CIIU 3

| Total | 3 093 | 2 702 | 2 734 | 2 944 | 2 797 | 2 814 | 2 768 | 2 651 | 2 328 | 2 223 |

Women - Femmes - Mujeres
ISIC 3 - CITI 3 - CIIU 3

| Total | 660 | 526 | 514 | 569 | 598 | 534 | 565 | 546 | 501 | 479 |

| **Korea, Republic of (FA)** | | | | Compensated injuries - Lésions indemnisées - Lesiones indemnizadas | | | | | | |

Fatal cases - Cas mortels - Casos mortales

Total men and women - Total hommes et femmes - Total hombres y mujeres
ISIC 3 - CITI 3 - CIIU 3

Total	1 412	1 353	1 298	1 271	1 408	1 417	1 288	1 238	1 267	1 332
A	21	9	15	17	20	30	20	14	19	23
B	9	27	13	21	18	5	1	0	1	3
C	38	27	38	27	33	29	16	13	15	10
D	397	443	380	334	385	364	383	368	374	383
E	6	8	2	9	6	2	3	4	4	3
F	500	489	506	526	589	610	484	510	494	565
G-H,K,M-P,X [1]	232	206	221	218	240	272	283	238	261	234
I	182	130	114	109	108	101	86	86	94	105
J	27	14	9	10	9	4	12	5	5	6

Explanatory notes: see p. 1125.	Notes explicatives: voir p. 1127.	Notas explicativas: véase p. 1129.
[1] Incl. hunting.	[1] Y compris la chasse.	[1] Incl. caza.

OCCUPATIONAL INJURIES

Cases of injury with lost workdays, by economic activity

LÉSIONS PROFESSIONNELLES

Cas de lésion avec perte de journées de travail, par activité économique

LESIONES PROFESIONALES

Casos de lesión con pérdida de días de trabajo, por actividad económica

8A

	1999	2000	2001	2002	2003	2004	2005	2006	2007	2008

Kyrgyzstan (FF)   Reported injuries - Lésions déclarées - Lesiones declaradas

Fatal cases - Cas mortels - Casos mortales

Total men and women - Total hommes et femmes - Total hombres y mujeres
ISIC 3 - CITI 3 - CIIU 3

	1999	2000	2001	2002	2003	2004	2005	2006	2007	2008
Total	37	40	39	37	26	41	24	22	.	.
A	3	2	4	5	1	4	0	0	.	.
B	0	0	0	0	0	0	0	0	.	.
C	2	9	3	6	2	0	1	6	.	.
D	7	3	3	9	7	7	4	7	.	.
E	7	5	4	6	5	6	7	3	.	.
F	4	6	8	1	1	7	4	2	.	.
G	1	1	2	2	1	0	2	0	.	.
H	0	0	1	0	1	0	0	0	.	.
I	5	2	3	1	2	3	1	1	.	.
J	0	0	0	0	0	1	0	0	.	.
K	0	6	1	0	1	1	3	1	.	.
L	6	5	9	6	3	12	1	2	.	.
M	0	0	1	0	0	0	0	0	.	.
N	2	1	0	1	0	0	1	0	.	.
O	0	0	0	0	2	0	0	0	.	.
P	0	0	0	0	0	0	0	0	.	.

Non-fatal cases (temporary + permanent incapacity) - Cas non mortels (incapacité temporaire + permanente) - Casos no mortales (incapacidad temporal + permanente)

Total men and women - Total hommes et femmes - Total hombres y mujeres
ISIC 3 - CITI 3 - CIIU 3

	1999	2000	2001	2002	2003	2004	2005	2006	2007	2008
Total	338	269	241	228	182	194	203	148	.	.
A	37	23	26	13	24	14	6	6	.	.
B	0	0	0	0	0	0	0	0	.	.
C	24	19	13	14	8	8	21	12	.	.
D	99	85	74	78	47	51	58	63	.	.
E	22	9	14	17	17	11	16	22	.	.
F	31	14	30	19	19	4	10	11	.	.
G	20	4	6	4	5	2	15	2	.	.
H	0	0	0	0	0	1	1	0	.	.
I	35	41	20	20	14	35	25	14	.	.
J	3	1	2	0	7	9	3	0	.	.
K	7	20	10	19	9	6	7	4	.	.
L	26	19	13	10	17	34	12	8	.	.
M	5	8	5	2	1	4	4	1	.	.
N	20	24	21	25	10	12	23	3	.	.
O	9	2	7	7	4	3	2	2	.	.
P	0	0	0	0	0	0	0	0	.	.

Total cases (fatal + non-fatal) - Ensemble des cas (mortels + non mortels) - Todos los casos (mortales + no mortales)

Total men and women - Total hommes et femmes - Total hombres y mujeres
ISIC 3 - CITI 3 - CIIU 3

	1999	2000	2001	2002	2003	2004	2005	2006	2007	2008
Total	375	309	280	265	208	235	227	170	.	.
A	40	25	30	18	25	18	6	6	.	.
B	0	0	0	0	0	0	0	0	.	.
C	26	28	16	20	10	8	22	18	.	.
D	106	88	77	87	54	58	62	70	.	.
E	29	14	18	23	22	17	23	25	.	.
F	35	20	38	20	20	11	14	13	.	.
G	21	5	8	6	6	2	17	2	.	.
H	0	0	1	0	1	1	1	0	.	.
I	40	43	23	21	16	38	26	15	.	.
J	3	1	2	0	7	10	3	0	.	.
K	7	26	11	19	10	7	10	5	.	.
L	32	24	22	16	20	46	13	10	.	.
M	5	8	6	2	1	4	4	1	.	.
N	22	25	21	26	10	12	24	3	.	.
O	9	2	7	7	6	3	2	2	.	.
P	0	0	0	0	0	0	0	0	.	.

Explanatory notes: see p. 1125.   Notes explicatives: voir p. 1127.   Notas explicativas: véase p. 1129.

OCCUPATIONAL INJURIES

Cases of injury with lost workdays, by economic activity

LÉSIONS PROFESSIONNELLES

Cas de lésion avec perte de journées de travail, par activité économique

LESIONES PROFESIONALES

Casos de lesión con pérdida de días de trabajo, por actividad económica

Macau, China (FF) [1] Reported injuries - Lésions déclarées - Lesiones declaradas

Fatal cases - Cas mortels - Casos mortales

Total men and women - Total hommes et femmes - Total hombres y mujeres
ISIC 3 - CITI 3 - CIIU 3

	1999	2000	2001	2002	2003	2004	2005	2006	2007	2008
Total	2	6	6	8	9	2	15	6	15	12
A	0	0	0	0	0	0	0	0	0	0
B	0	0	0	0	0	0	0	0	0	0
C	0	0	0	0	0	0	0	0	0	0
D	0	1	1	1	1	0	1	0	0	0
E	0	0	0	1	0	0	0	0	1	0
F	0	0	1	4	6	2	12	5	7	7
G	0	2	1	0	0	0	0	0	0	0
H	0	0	0	1	0	0	0	0	0	0
I	1	0	0	0	2	0	0	0	1	1
J	0	0	0	0	0	0	0	0	0	0
K	0	2	2	1	0	0	0	0	0	1
L	0	0	0	0	0	0	0	0	0	0
M	0	0	0	0	0	0	0	0	0	0
N	0	0	0	0	0	0	0	0	0	0
O	1	1	1	0	0	0	2	1	6	3
P	0	0	0	0	0	0	0	0	0	0
Q	0	0	0	0	0	0	0	0	0	0

Men - Hommes - Hombres
ISIC 3 - CITI 3 - CIIU 3

	1999	2000	2001	2002	2003	2004	2005	2006	2007	2008
Total	2	4	6	8	7	2	14	5	14	10
A	0	0	0	0	0	0	0	0	0	0
B	.	.	.	.	0	0	0	0	0	0
C	0	0	0	0	0	0	0	0	0	0
D	0	1	1	1	1	0	0	0	0	0
E	0	0	0	1	0	0	0	0	0	0
F	0	0	1	4	4	2	12	5	6	7
G	0	1	1	0	0	0	0	0	0	0
H	0	0	0	1	0	0	0	0	0	0
I	1	0	0	0	2	0	0	0	1	0
J	0	0	0	0	0	0	0	0	0	0
K	0	1	2	1	0	0	0	0	0	1
L	0	0	0	0	0	0	0	0	0	0
M	0	0	0	0	0	0	0	0	0	0
N	0	0	0	0	0	0	0	0	0	0
O	1	1	1	0	0	0	2	0	6	2
P	0	0	0	0	0	0	0	0	0	0
Q	0	0	0	0	0	0	0	0	0	0

Women - Femmes - Mujeres
ISIC 3 - CITI 3 - CIIU 3

	1999	2000	2001	2002	2003	2004	2005	2006	2007	2008
Total	0	2	0	0	2	0	1	1	1	2
A	.	.	.	.	0	0	0	0	0	0
B	.	.	.	.	0	0	0	0	0	0
C	0	0	0	0	0	0	0	0	0	0
D	0	0	0	0	0	0	1	0	0	0
E	0	0	0	0	0	0	0	0	0	0
F	0	0	0	0	2	0	0	0	1	0
G	0	1	0	0	0	0	0	0	0	0
H	0	0	0	0	0	0	0	0	0	0
I	0	0	0	0	0	0	0	0	0	1
J	0	0	0	0	0	0	0	0	0	0
K	0	1	0	0	0	0	0	0	0	0
L	0	0	0	0	0	0	0	0	0	0
M	0	0	0	0	0	0	0	0	0	0
N	0	0	0	0	0	0	0	0	0	0
O	0	0	0	0	0	0	0	1	0	1
P	0	0	0	0	0	0	0	0	0	0
Q	0	0	0	0	0	0	0	0	0	0

Explanatory notes: see p. 1125.

[1] Private sector.

Notes explicatives: voir p. 1127.

[1] Secteur privé.

Notas explicativas: véase p. 1129.

[1] Sector privado.

OCCUPATIONAL INJURIES

Cases of injury with lost workdays, by economic activity

LÉSIONS PROFESSIONNELLES

Cas de lésion avec perte de journées de travail, par activité économique

LESIONES PROFESIONALES

Casos de lesión con pérdida de días de trabajo, por actividad económica

	1999	2000	2001	2002	2003	2004	2005	2006	2007	2008

Macau, China (FF) [1]   Reported injuries - Lésions déclarées - Lesiones declaradas

Non-fatal cases (temporary + permanent incapacity) - Cas non mortels (incapacité temporaire + permanente) - Casos no mortales (incapacidad temporal + permanente)

Total men and women - Total hommes et femmes - Total hombres y mujeres [2]
ISIC 3 - CITI 3 - CIIU 3

	1999	2000	2001	2002	2003	2004	2005	2006	2007	2008
Total	3 216	3 602	3 645	3 847	4 093	4 603	4 941	2 773	3 000	2 037
A	1	0	3	0	7	2	4	0	2	0
B	0	0	0	0	0	0	0	0	0	0
C	0	0	0	0	0	0	0	0	0	0
D	785	880	791	791	792	753	649	333	279	169
E	14	11	27	14	15	26	8	1	7	1
F	346	324	355	301	512	739	849	667	396	173
G	494	468	501	498	488	539	594	321	337	244
H	638	766	767	852	872	900	1 005	787	661	477
I	181	268	270	302	251	307	343	141	173	80
J	26	27	33	29	34	34	34	12	10	8
K	61	109	134	132	189	234	273	131	189	200
L	10	23	40	61	84	88	105	34	54	9
M	72	87	71	114	135	168	159	39	48	39
N	19	20	28	28	28	43	62	42	38	29
O	555	599	602	704	658	749	809	240	791	583
P	14	20	23	21	28	21	47	25	16	25
Q	0	0	0	0	0	0	0	0	0	0

Men - Hommes - Hombres [2]
ISIC 3 - CITI 3 - CIIU 3

	1999	2000	2001	2002	2003	2004	2005	2006	2007	2008
Total	2 001	2 168	2 196	2 309	2 458	2 748	2 974	1 711	1 714	1 159
A	1	0	3	0	6	1	4	0	1	0
B	.	.	.	.	0	0	0	0	0	0
C	0	0	0	0	0	0	0	0	0	0
D	379	380	331	338	342	318	265	181	144	95
E	13	10	26	11	11	25	8	0	7	1
F	315	297	321	279	476	666	772	604	343	165
G	324	308	320	318	322	329	378	216	207	161
H	355	400	428	462	440	460	511	374	316	233
I	126	189	168	203	163	214	266	126	145	64
J	11	14	12	13	12	13	19	4	4	3
K	44	74	83	78	100	119	144	67	90	108
L	8	14	27	42	64	55	71	20	35	7
M	18	20	18	26	38	44	48	7	13	11
N	5	3	8	5	3	11	17	5	11	6
O	401	441	451	534	480	493	470	106	398	305
P	1	0	0	0	1	0	1	1	0	0
Q	0	0	0	0	0	0	0	0	0	0
X	.	18	0	0	0	0	0	0	0	0

Women - Femmes - Mujeres [2]
ISIC 3 - CITI 3 - CIIU 3

	1999	2000	2001	2002	2003	2004	2005	2006	2007	2008
Total	1 215	1 433	1 449	1 538	1 635	1 855	1 967	1 062	1 286	878
A	.	.	.	.	1	1	0	0	0	0
B	.	.	.	.	0	0	0	0	0	0
C	0	0	0	0	0	0	0	0	0	0
D	406	492	460	453	450	435	384	152	135	74
E	1	1	1	3	4	1	0	1	0	0
F	31	21	34	22	36	73	77	63	53	8
G	170	156	181	180	166	210	216	105	130	83
H	283	366	339	390	432	440	494	413	345	244
I	55	79	102	99	88	93	77	15	28	16
J	15	13	21	16	22	21	15	8	6	5
K	17	33	51	54	89	115	129	64	99	92
L	2	9	13	19	20	33	34	14	19	2
M	54	67	53	88	97	124	111	32	35	28
N	14	17	20	23	25	32	45	37	27	23
O	154	155	151	170	178	256	339	134	393	278
P	13	20	23	21	27	21	46	24	16	25
Q	0	0	0	0	0	0	0	0	0	0
X	.	4	0	0	0	0	0	0	0	0

Explanatory notes: see p. 1125.

Notes explicatives: voir p. 1127.

Notas explicativas: véase p. 1129.

[1] Private sector. [2] Up to 2005: Incl. non-fatal cases without lost workdays.

[1] Secteur privé. [2] Jusqu'à 2005: Y compris les cas non mortels sans pertes de journées de travail.

[1] Sector privado. [2] Hasta 2005: Incl. los casos no mortales sin pérdida de días de trabajo.

OCCUPATIONAL INJURIES

Cases of injury with lost workdays, by economic activity

LÉSIONS PROFESSIONNELLES

Cas de lésion avec perte de journées de travail, par activité économique

LESIONES PROFESIONALES

Casos de lesión con pérdida de días de trabajo, por actividad económica

Macau, China (FF) [1] Reported injuries - Lésions déclarées - Lesiones declaradas

Cases of temporary incapacity - Cas d'incapacité temporaire - Casos de incapacidad temporal

Total men and women - Total hommes et femmes - Total hombres y mujeres [2]
ISIC 3 - CITI 3 - CIIU 3

	1999	2000	2001	2002	2003	2004	2005	2006	2007	2008
Total	3 209	3 586	3 639	3 836	4 086	4 594	4 936	2 766	2 971	2 035
A	1	0	3	0	7	2	4	0	1	0
B	0	0	0	0	0	0	0	0	0	0
C	0	0	0	0	0	0	0	0	0	0
D	785	874	789	786	792	750	648	333	279	169
E	14	11	27	14	15	26	8	1	7	1
F	341	318	352	300	507	736	846	663	381	172
G	493	466	501	498	488	538	593	320	337	244
H	638	766	767	850	872	898	1 005	786	661	477
I	181	268	270	300	251	307	343	140	171	79
J	26	27	33	29	34	34	34	12	10	8
K	61	109	133	132	187	234	273	131	187	200
L	10	23	40	60	84	88	105	34	54	9
M	72	87	71	114	135	168	159	39	48	39
N	18	20	28	28	28	43	62	42	38	29
O	555	597	602	704	658	749	809	240	781	583
P	14	20	23	21	28	21	47	25	16	25
Q	0	0	0	0	0	0	0	0	0	0

Men - Hommes - Hombres [2]
ISIC 3 - CITI 3 - CIIU 3

	1999	2000	2001	2002	2003	2004	2005	2006	2007	2008
Total	.	2 154 [3]	2 192	2 301	2 452	2 741	2 970	1 706	1 689	1 157
A	.	0	3	0	6	1	4	0	1	0
B	.				0	0	0	0	0	0
C	.	0	0	0	0	0	0	0	0	0
D	.	376	331	334	342	315	265	181	144	95
E	.	10	26	11	11	25	8	0	7	1
F	.	291	318	278	471	663	769	601	329	164
G	.	306	320	318	322	328	377	215	207	161
H	.	400	428	461	440	460	511	374	316	233
I	.	189	168	202	163	214	266	125	143	63
J	.	14	12	13	12	13	19	4	4	3
K	.	74	82	78	99	119	144	67	88	108
L	.	14	27	41	64	55	71	20	35	7
M	.	20	18	26	38	44	48	7	13	11
N	.	3	8	5	3	11	17	5	11	6
O	.	439	451	534	480	493	470	106	391	305
P	.	0	0	0	1	0	1	1	0	0
Q	.	0	0	0	0	0	0	0	0	0
X	.	18	0	0	0	0	0	0	0	0

Women - Femmes - Mujeres [2]
ISIC 3 - CITI 3 - CIIU 3

	1999	2000	2001	2002	2003	2004	2005	2006	2007	2008
Total	.	1 431	1 447	1 535	1 634	1 853	1 966	1 060	1 282	878
A	.				1	1	0	0	0	0
B	.				0	0	0	0	0	0
C	.	0	0	0	0	0	0	0	0	0
D	.	490	458	452	450	435	383	152	135	74
E	.	1	1	3	4	1	0	1	0	0
F	.	21	34	22	36	73	77	62	52	8
G	.	156	181	180	166	210	216	105	130	83
H	.	366	339	389	432	438	494	412	345	244
I	.	79	102	98	88	93	77	15	28	16
J	.	13	21	16	22	21	15	8	6	5
K	.	33	51	54	88	115	129	64	99	92
L	.	9	13	19	20	33	34	14	19	2
M	.	67	53	88	97	124	111	32	35	28
N	.	17	20	23	25	32	45	37	27	23
O	.	155	151	170	178	256	339	134	390	278
P	.	20	23	21	27	21	46	24	16	25
Q	.	0	0	0	0	0	0	0	0	0
X	.	4	0	0	0	0	0	0	0	0

Explanatory notes: see p. 1125.

[1] Private sector. [2] Up to 2005: Incl. non-fatal cases without lost workdays. [3] Incl. one case of occupational disease.

Notes explicatives: voir p. 1127.

[1] Secteur privé. [2] Jusqu'à 2005: Y compris les cas non mortels sans pertes de journées de travail. [3] Y compris un cas de maladie professionnelle.

Notas explicativas: véase p. 1129.

[1] Sector privado. [2] Hasta 2005: Incl. los casos no mortales sin pérdida de días de trabajo. [3] Incl. un caso de enfermedad profesional.

OCCUPATIONAL INJURIES

Cases of injury with lost workdays, by economic activity

LÉSIONS PROFESSIONNELLES

Cas de lésion avec perte de journées de travail, par activité économique

LESIONES PROFESIONALES

Casos de lesión con pérdida de días de trabajo, por actividad económica

	1999	2000	2001	2002	2003	2004	2005	2006	2007	2008

Macau, China (FF) [1] Reported injuries - Lésions déclarées - Lesiones declaradas

Total cases (fatal + non-fatal) - Ensemble des cas (mortels + non mortels) - Todos los casos (mortales + no mortales)

Total men and women - Total hommes et femmes - Total hombres y mujeres [2]
ISIC 3 - CITI 3 - CIIU 3

	1999	2000	2001	2002	2003	2004	2005	2006	2007	2008
Total	3 218	3 608 [3]	3 651	3 855	4 102	4 605	4 956	2 779	3 015	2 049
A	1	0	3	0	7	2	4	0	1	0
B	0	0	0	0	0	0	0	0	0	0
C	0	0	0	0	0	0	0	0	0	0
D	785	881	792	792	793	753	650	333	279	169
E	14	11	27	15	15	26	8	1	8	1
F	346	324 [4]	356	305	518	741	861	672	403	180
G	494	470	502	498	488	539	594	321	337	244
H	638	766	767	853	872	900	1 005	787	661	477
I	182	268	270	302	253	307	343	141	174	81
J	26	27	33	29	34	34	34	12	10	8
K	61	111	136	133	189	234	273	131	189	201
L	10	23	40	61	84	88	105	34	54	9
M	72	87	71	114	135	168	159	39	48	39
N	19	20	28	28	28	43	62	42	38	29
O	556	600	603	704	658	749	811	241	797	586
P	14	20	23	21	28	21	47	25	16	25
Q	0	0	0	0	0	0	0	0	0	0

Men - Hommes - Hombres [2]
ISIC 3 - CITI 3 - CIIU 3

	1999	2000	2001	2002	2003	2004	2005	2006	2007	2008
Total	2 003	2 172	2 202	2 317	2 465	2 750	2 988	1 716	1 728	1 169
A	1	0	3	0	6	1	4	0	1	0
B	.	.	.	.	0	0	0	0	0	0
C	0	0	0	0	0	0	0	0	0	0
D	379	381	332	339	343	318	265	181	144	95
E	13	10	26	12	11	25	8	0	8	1
F	315	297 [4]	322	283	480	668	784	609	349	172
G	324	309	321	318	322	329	378	216	207	161
H	355	400	428	463	440	460	511	374	316	233
I	127	189	168	203	165	214	266	126	146	64
J	11	14	12	13	12	13	19	4	4	3
K	44	75	85	79	100	119	144	67	90	109
L	8	14	27	42	64	55	71	20	35	7
M	18	20	18	26	38	44	48	7	13	11
N	5	3	8	5	3	11	17	5	11	6
O	402	442	452	534	480	493	472	106	404	307
P	1	0	0	0	1	0	1	1	0	0
Q	0	0	0	0	0	0	0	0	0	0
X	.	18	0	0	0	0	0	0	0	0

Women - Femmes - Mujeres [2]
ISIC 3 - CITI 3 - CIIU 3

	1999	2000	2001	2002	2003	2004	2005	2006	2007	2008
Total	1 215	1 435	1 449	1 538	1 637	1 855	1 968	1 063	1 287	880
A	.	.	.	.	1	1	0	0	0	0
B	.	.	.	.	0	0	0	0	0	0
C	0	0	0	0	0	0	0	0	0	0
D	406	492	460	453	450	435	385	152	135	74
E	1	1	1	3	4	1	0	1	0	0
F	31	21	34	22	38	73	77	63	54	8
G	170	157	181	180	166	210	216	105	130	83
H	283	366	339	390	432	440	494	413	345	244
I	55	79	102	99	88	93	77	15	28	17
J	15	13	21	16	22	21	15	8	6	5
K	17	34	51	54	89	115	129	64	99	92
L	2	9	13	19	20	33	34	14	19	2
M	54	67	53	88	97	124	111	32	35	28
N	14	17	20	23	25	32	45	37	27	23
O	154	155	151	170	178	256	339	135	393	279
P	13	20	23	21	27	21	46	24	16	25
Q	0	0	0	0	0	0	0	0	0	0
X	.	4	0	0	0	0	0	0	0	0

Myanmar (FF) [5] Reported injuries - Lésions déclarées - Lesiones declaradas

Fatal cases - Cas mortels - Casos mortales

Total men and women - Total hommes et femmes - Total hombres y mujeres
ISIC 3 - CITI 3 - CIIU 3

	1999	2000	2001	2002	2003	2004	2005	2006	2007	2008
Total	15	16	15	10	13	12	7	.	25	32
C	0	1	1	1	0	3	1	.	4	7
D	13	15	14	8	12	6	5	.	18	16
E	0	0	0	1	0	0	0	.	0	2
G	2	0	0	0	1	3	1	.	3	7

Explanatory notes: see p. 1125.

[1] Private sector. [2] Up to 2005: Incl. non-fatal cases without lost workdays. [3] Incl. one case of occupational disease and one case of injury of sex unknown. [4] Incl. one case of occupational disease. [5] Year ending in March of the year indicated.

Notes explicatives: voir p. 1127.

[1] Secteur privé. [2] Jusqu'à 2005: Y compris les cas non mortels sans pertes de journées de travail. [3] Y compris un cas de maladie professionnelle et un cas de lésion de sexe inconnu. [4] Y compris un cas de maladie professionnelle. [5] Année se terminant en mars de l'année indiquée.

Notas explicativas: véase p. 1129.

[1] Sector privado. [2] Hasta 2005: Incl. los casos no mortales sin pérdida de días de trabajo. [3] Incl. un caso de enfermedad profesional y un caso de lesión de sexo desconocido. [4] Incl. un caso de enfermedad profesional. [5] Año que termina en marzo del año indicado.

8A OCCUPATIONAL INJURIES — LÉSIONS PROFESSIONNELLES — LESIONES PROFESIONALES

Cases of injury with lost workdays, by economic activity

Cas de lésion avec perte de journées de travail, par activité économique

Casos de lesión con pérdida de días de trabajo, por actividad económica

Myanmar (FF) [1]

Reported injuries - Lésions déclarées - Lesiones declaradas

Fatal cases - Cas mortels - Casos mortales

Men - Hommes - Hombres
ISIC 3 - CITI 3 - CIIU 3

	1999	2000	2001	2002	2003	2004	2005	2006	2007	2008
Total	14	15	.	9	.	10	4	.	24	30
C	0	1	.	1	.	3	1	.	4	7
D	12	14	.	7	.	4	3	.	17	14
E	0	0	.	1	.	0	0	.	0	2
G	2	0	.	0	.	3	0	.	3	7

Women - Femmes - Mujeres
ISIC 3 - CITI 3 - CIIU 3

	1999	2000	2001	2002	2003	2004	2005	2006	2007	2008
Total	1	1	.	1	.	2	3	.	1	2
C	0	0	.	0	.	0	0	.	0	0
D	1	1	.	1	.	2	3	.	1	2
E	0	0	.	0	.	0	0	.	0	0
G	0	0	.	0	.	0	0	.	0	0

Non-fatal cases (temporary + permanent incapacity) - Cas non mortels (incapacité temporaire + permanente) - Casos no mortales (incapacidad temporal + permanente)

Total men and women - Total hommes et femmes - Total hombres y mujeres [2]
ISIC 3 - CITI 3 - CIIU 3

	1999	2000	2001	2002	2003	2004	2005	2006	2007	2008
Total	440	423	400	455	294	329	183	.	118	151
C	37	47	33	22	33	24	14	.	13	13
D	293	286	352	347	192	245	127	.	85	101
E	12	2	15	4	4	17	6	.	4	19
G	98	88	0	82	65	43	36	.	16	18

Men - Hommes - Hombres [2]
ISIC 3 - CITI 3 - CIIU 3

	1999	2000	2001	2002	2003	2004	2005	2006	2007	2008
Total	390	374	.	319	.	250	140	.	89	115
C	37	46	.	22	.	24	14	.	13	13
D	243	238	.	211	.	170	97	.	57	69
E	12	2	.	4	.	13	6	.	3	15
G	98	88	.	82	.	43	23	.	16	18

Women - Femmes - Mujeres [2]
ISIC 3 - CITI 3 - CIIU 3

	1999	2000	2001	2002	2003	2004	2005	2006	2007	2008
Total	50	49	.	136	.	79	43	.	29	36
C	0	1	.	0	.	0	0	.	0	0
D	50	48	.	136	.	75	40	.	28	32
E	0	0	.	0	.	4	3	.	1	4
G	0	0	.	0	.	0	0	.	0	0

Total cases (fatal + non-fatal) - Ensemble des cas (mortels + non mortels) - Todos los casos (mortales + no mortales)

Total men and women - Total hommes et femmes - Total hombres y mujeres
ISIC 3 - CITI 3 - CIIU 3

	1999	2000	2001	2002	2003	2004	2005	2006	2007	2008
Total	455	439	415	465	307	341	190	.	143	183
C	37	48	34	23	33	27	15	.	17	20
D	306	301	366	355	204	251	132	.	103	117
E	12	2	15	5	4	17	6	.	4	21
G	100	88	0	82	66	46	37	.	19	25

Men - Hommes - Hombres
ISIC 3 - CITI 3 - CIIU 3

	1999	2000	2001	2002	2003	2004	2005	2006	2007	2008
Total	404	419	.	328	.	260	144	.	113	145
C	37	47	.	23	.	27	15	.	17	20
D	255	282	.	218	.	174	100	.	74	83
E	12	2	.	5	.	13	6	.	3	17
G	100	88	.	82	.	46	23	.	19	25

Women - Femmes - Mujeres
ISIC 3 - CITI 3 - CIIU 3

	1999	2000	2001	2002	2003	2004	2005	2006	2007	2008
Total	51	50	.	137	.	81	46	.	30	38
C	0	1	.	0	.	0	0	.	0	0
D	51	49	.	137	.	77	43	.	29	34
E	0	0	.	0	.	4	3	.	1	4
G	0	0	.	0	.	0	0	.	0	0

Explanatory notes: see p. 1125.
[1] Year ending in March of the year indicated. [2] Incapacity of 2 days or more.

Notes explicatives: voir p. 1127.
[1] Année se terminant en mars de l'année indiquée. [2] Incapacité de 2 jours et plus.

Notas explicativas: véase p. 1129.
[1] Año que termina en marzo del año indicado. [2] Incapacidad de 2 días y más.

OCCUPATIONAL INJURIES
Cases of injury with lost workdays, by economic activity

LÉSIONS PROFESSIONNELLES
Cas de lésion avec perte de journées de travail, par activité économique

LESIONES PROFESIONALES
Casos de lesión con pérdida de días de trabajo, por actividad económica

	1999	2000	2001	2002	2003	2004	2005	2006	2007	2008

Singapore (FF) Reported injuries - Lésions déclarées - Lesiones declaradas

Fatal cases - Cas mortels - Casos mortales

Total men and women - Total hommes et femmes - Total hombres y mujeres
ISIC 3 - CITI 3 - CIIU 3

	1999	2000	2001	2002	2003	2004	2005	2006	2007	2008
Total	69	74	52	64	55	51	44	62	63	67
A	0	0	0	0	0	0	0	0	0	0
C	0	0	0	0	0	0	0	0	0	0
D	18	18	20	21	21	22	15	18	27	26
E	0	0	1	0	0	0	0	0	0	0
F	48	49	27	38	31	24	22	24	24	25
G	0	0	1	0	0	0	2	1	1	1
H	1	0	0	0	1	0	0	0	5	6
I	2	4	3	4	1	4	3	12	0	0
J	.	.	.	.	.	.	.	.	0	0
K	0	1	0	0	0	1	2	4	0	0
L	0	0	0	0	0	0	0	0	0	0
M	.	.	.	.	.	.	.	0	0	2
N	0	0	0	0	0	0	0	0	0	0
O	0	2	0	1	1	0	0	2	3	0
P	0	0	0	0	0	0	0	0	1	2
X	0	0	0	0	0	0	0	0	2	5

Non-fatal cases (temporary + permanent incapacity) - Cas non mortels (incapacité temporaire + permanente) - Casos no mortales (incapacidad temporal + permanente)

Total men and women - Total hommes et femmes - Total hombres y mujeres [1]
ISIC 3 - CITI 3 - CIIU 3

	1999	2000	2001	2002	2003	2004	2005	2006	2007	2008
Total	3 884	3 445	3 738	3 324	3 124	3 232	3 355	9 199	9 955	11 005
A	0	0	0	0	0	0	0	0	0	0
C	0	0	0	0	0	0	0	0	0	0
D	2 219	1 923	2 049	1 757	1 694	1 777	1 815	3 383	3 362	3 353
E	26	21	13	13	12	14	7	0	0	0
F	1 459	1 346	1 428	1 299	1 162	1 192	1 278	2 391	2 436	2 839
G	1	2	1	3	4	2	4	445	425	457
H	5	5	2	3	14	24	28	578	592	779
I	118	105	193	196	166	172	161	592	0	0
J	.	.	.	.	.	.	.	82	695	733
K	5	7	12	11	6	9	16	412	24	22
L	0	0	0	0	0	0	0	0	94	93
M	.	.	.	.	.	.	.	40	149	134
N	0	0	0	0	1	0	0	173	170	209
O	48	34	40	42	65	42	46	81	169	125
P	0	0	0	0	0	0	0	0	733	856
X	3	2	0	0	0	0	0	0	1 106	1 405

Cases of temporary incapacity - Cas d'incapacité temporaire - Casos de incapacidad temporal

Total men and women - Total hommes et femmes - Total hombres y mujeres [1]
ISIC 3 - CITI 3 - CIIU 3

	1999	2000	2001	2002	2003	2004	2005	2006	2007	2008
Total	3 741	3 334	3 655	3 233	3 037	3 139	3 263	9 031	9 792	10 873
A	0	0	0	0	0	0	0	0	0	0
C	0	0	0	0	0	0	0	0	0	0
D	2 127	1 854	1 997	1 696	1 642	1 709	1 746	3 382	3 272	3 285
E	25	20	13	13	12	14	7	0	0	0
F	1 414	1 309	1 404	1 273	1 133	1 173	1 258	2 364	2 401	2 804
G	1	2	1	3	3	1	4	437	422	452
H	4	5	2	3	14	24	28	573	585	773
I	117	103	187	194	162	167	158	582	0	0
J	.	.	.	.	.	.	.	82	693	730
K	5	6	12	11	6	9	16	407	24	22
L	0	0	0	0	0	0	0	0	94	93
M	.	.	.	.	.	.	.	40	148	134
N	0	0	0	0	1	0	0	173	170	208
O	46	33	39	40	64	42	46	81	166	124
P	0	0	0	0	0	0	0	0	729	850
X	2	2	0	0	0	0	0	0	1 088	1 398

Explanatory notes: see p. 1125.

Notes explicatives: voir p. 1127.

Notas explicativas: véase p. 1129.

[1] Incapacity of 4 days or more.

[1] Incapacité de 4 jours et plus.

[1] Incapacidad de 4 días y más.

	OCCUPATIONAL INJURIES	LÉSIONS PROFESSIONNELLES	LESIONES PROFESIONALES
	Cases of injury with lost workdays, by economic activity	Cas de lésion avec perte de journées de travail, par activité économique	Casos de lesión con pérdida de días de trabajo, por actividad económica

	1999	2000	2001	2002	2003	2004	2005	2006	2007	2008

Singapore (FF) Reported injuries - Lésions déclarées - Lesiones declaradas

Total cases (fatal + non-fatal) - Ensemble des cas (mortels + non mortels) - Todos los casos (mortales + no mortales)

Total men and women - Total hommes et femmes - Total hombres y mujeres
ISIC 3 - CITI 3 - CIIU 3

	1999	2000	2001	2002	2003	2004	2005	2006	2007	2008
Total	3 953	3 519	3 790	3 388	3 179	3 283	3 399	9 261	10 018	11 072
A	0	0	0	0	0	0	0	0	0	0
C	0	0	0	0	0	0	0	0	0	0
D	2 237	1 941	2 069	1 778	1 715	1 799	1 830	3 401	3 389	3 279
E	26	21	14	13	12	14	7	0	0	0
F	1 507	1 395	1 455	1 337	1 193	1 216	1 300	2 415	2 460	2 864
G	1	2	2	3	4	2	6	446	426	458
H	6	5	2	3	15	24	28	578	599	785
I	120	109	196	200	167	176	164	604	0	0
J	.	.	.	.	.	.	.	82	695	733
K	5	8	12	11	6	10	18	416	24	22
L	0	0	0	0	0	0	0	0	94	93
M	.	.	.	.	.	.	.	40	149	136
N	0	0	0	0	1	0	0	173	170	209
O	48	36	40	43	66	42	46	83	172	125
P	0	0	0	0	0	0	0	0	734	858
X	3	2	0	0	0	0	0	0	1 108	1 410

Sri Lanka (FF) Reported injuries - Lésions déclarées - Lesiones declaradas

Fatal cases - Cas mortels - Casos mortales

Total men and women - Total hommes et femmes - Total hombres y mujeres
ISIC 3 - CITI 3 - CIIU 3

	1999	2000	2001	2002	2003	2004	2005	2006	2007	2008
Total	37	41	27	36	42	42	52	84	77	49
C	1	3	0	0	7	3	0	0	5	1
D	19	15	17	15	9	11	15	45	32	22
E	1	1	0	0	0	10	12	7	10	7
F	10	10	10	7	15	8	19	24	27	17
G	.	.	.	.	.	3	0	0	0	0
H	0	2	0	0	0	1	0	1	0	0
I	6	8	0	6	5	5	6	7	3	2
O	.	.	.	.	.	1	0	0	0	0

Non-fatal cases (temporary + permanent incapacity) - Cas non mortels (incapacité temporaire + permanente) - Casos no mortales (incapacidad temporal + permanente)

Total men and women - Total hommes et femmes - Total hombres y mujeres [1]
ISIC 3 - CITI 3 - CIIU 3

	1999	2000	2001	2002	2003	2004	2005	2006	2007	2008
Total	2 142	2 119	2 157	1 754	1 492	1 411	1 388	1 740	1 755	1 525
C	1	3	9	7	2	0	1	64	136	7
D	1 908	1 744	1 942	1 316	1 105	1 137	1 260	1 523	1 420	1 143
E	23	22	10	10	17	29	23	18	15	25
F	103	85	66	68	46	25	34	23	43	40
G	.	.	.	.	.	0	0	0	0	0
H	13	4	8	6	9	3	6	10	16	6
I	94	111	122	109	65	59	65	102	125	78
O	.	.	.	.	.	0	0	0	0	0

Cases of temporary incapacity - Cas d'incapacité temporaire - Casos de incapacidad temporal

Total men and women - Total hommes et femmes - Total hombres y mujeres [1]
ISIC 3 - CITI 3 - CIIU 3

	1999	2000	2001	2002	2003	2004	2005	2006	2007	2008
Total	2 073	2 065	2 119	1 722	1 464	1 382	1 372	1 696	1 703	1 467
C	1	3	9	7	2	0	1	64	136	7
D	1 839	1 690	1 905	1 284	1 077	1 116	1 244	1 479	1 368	1 119
E	23	22	10	10	17	28	23	18	15	25
F	103	85	65	68	46	23	34	23	43	37
G	.	.	.	.	.	0	0	0	0	0
H	13	4	8	6	9	3	6	10	16	6
I	94	111	122	109	65	58	65	102	125	78
O	.	.	.	.	.	0	0	0	0	0

Explanatory notes: see p. 1125.

[1] Incapacity of 3 days or more.

Notes explicatives: voir p. 1127.

[1] Incapacité de 3 jours et plus.

Notas explicativas: véase p. 1129.

[1] Incapacidad de 3 días y más.

OCCUPATIONAL INJURIES

Cases of injury with
lost workdays,
by economic activity

LÉSIONS PROFESSIONNELLES

Cas de lésion avec perte
de journées de travail,
par activité économique

LESIONES PROFESIONALES

Casos de lesión con pérdida
de días de trabajo,
por actividad económica

8A

	1999	2000	2001	2002	2003	2004	2005	2006	2007	2008

Sri Lanka (FF) — Reported injuries - Lésions déclarées - Lesiones declaradas

Total cases (fatal + non-fatal) - Ensemble des cas (mortels + non mortels) - Todos los casos (mortales + no mortales)

Total men and women - Total hommes et femmes - Total hombres y mujeres
ISIC 3 - CITI 3 - CIIU 3

	1999	2000	2001	2002	2003	2004	2005	2006	2007	2008
Total	2 179	2 160	2 184	1 790	1 534	1 453	1 440	1 824	1 832	1 574
C	2	6	9	7	9	3	1	64	141	8
D	1 927	1 759	1 959	1 331	1 114	1 148	1 275	1 568	1 452	1 165
E	24	23	10	10	17	39	35	25	25	32
F	113	95	76	75	61	33	53	47	70	57
G	.	.	.	.	.	3	0	0	0	0
H	13	6	8	6	9	4	6	11	16	6
I	100	119	122	115	70	64	71	109	128	80
O	.	.	.	.	.	1	0	0	0	0

Syrian Arab Republic (FF) — Compensated injuries - Lésions indemnisées - Lesiones indemnizadas

Fatal cases - Cas mortels - Casos mortales

Total men and women - Total hommes et femmes - Total hombres y mujeres
ISIC 2 - CITI 2 - CIIU 2

	1999	2000	2001	2002	2003	2004	2005	2006	2007	2008
Total	267	332	185	383	174	205	612	.	.	.

Non-fatal cases (temporary + permanent incapacity) - Cas non mortels (incapacité temporaire + permanente) - Casos no mortales (incapacidad temporal + permanente)

Total men and women - Total hommes et femmes - Total hombres y mujeres [1]
ISIC 2 - CITI 2 - CIIU 2

	1999	2000	2001	2002	2003	2004	2005	2006	2007	2008
Total	11 467	12 242	13 956	14 867	15 585	17 482	9 733	.	.	.

Total cases (fatal + non-fatal) - Ensemble des cas (mortels + non mortels) - Todos los casos (mortales + no mortales)

Total men and women - Total hommes et femmes - Total hombres y mujeres [1]
ISIC 2 - CITI 2 - CIIU 2

	1999	2000	2001	2002	2003	2004	2005	2006	2007	2008
Total	11 734	12 574	14 141	15 250	15 759	17 687	10 345	8 215	.	.

Taiwan, China (FF) — Reported injuries - Lésions déclarées - Lesiones declaradas

Fatal cases - Cas mortels - Casos mortales

Total men and women - Total hommes et femmes - Total hombres y mujeres
ISIC 2 - CITI 2 - CIIU 2

	1999	2000	2001	2002	2003	2004	2005	2006	2007	2008
Total	650	602	543	507	401	366	382	.	.	.
1	93	91	65	76	64	57	39	.	.	.
2	6	4	0	3	3	2	1	.	.	.
3	219	181	186	159	110	84	106	.	.	.
4	8	3	4	3	4	5	4	.	.	.
5	146	156	144	128	118	89	118	.	.	.
6	57	53	51	49	32	39	37	.	.	.
7	48	59	44	45	36	34	41	.	.	.
8	26	20	22	19	11	15	15	.	.	.
9	47	35	27	25	23	41	21	.	.	.

Non-fatal cases (temporary + permanent incapacity) - Cas non mortels (incapacité temporaire + permanente) - Casos no mortales (incapacidad temporal + permanente)

Total men and women - Total hommes et femmes - Total hombres y mujeres
ISIC 2 - CITI 2 - CIIU 2

	1999	2000	2001	2002	2003	2004	2005	2006	2007	2008
Total	33 059	38 260	37 843	35 819	36 087	37 789	36 966	.	.	.
1	386	436	482	432	437	443	361	.	.	.
2	96	88	58	48	34	32	38	.	.	.
3	17 381	19 977	19 067	17 707	17 669	18 240	17 474	.	.	.
4	39	37	24	34	16	27	21	.	.	.
5	8 111	9 211	9 168	8 698	8 739	9 059	8 782	.	.	.
6	3 426	4 158	4 517	4 576	4 836	5 245	5 482	.	.	.
7	1 733	1 860	1 886	1 715	1 677	1 778	1 765	.	.	.
8	450	599	605	477	535	588	606	.	.	.
9	1 437	1 894	2 036	2 132	2 144	2 377	2 437	.	.	.

Explanatory notes: see p. 1125.
[1] Incl. non-fatal cases without lost workdays.

Notes explicatives: voir p. 1127.
[1] Y compris les cas non mortels sans perte de journées de travail.

Notas explicativas: véase p. 1129.
[1] Incl. los casos no mortales sin pérdida de días de trabajo.

8A

OCCUPATIONAL INJURIES	LÉSIONS PROFESSIONNELLES	LESIONES PROFESIONALES
Cases of injury with lost workdays, by economic activity	Cas de lésion avec perte de journées de travail, par activité économique	Casos de lesión con pérdida de días de trabajo, por actividad económica

	1999	2000	2001	2002	2003	2004	2005	2006	2007	2008

Taiwan, China (FF) — Reported injuries - Lésions déclarées - Lesiones declaradas

Cases of temporary incapacity - Cas d'incapacité temporaire - Casos de incapacidad temporal

Total men and women - Total hommes et femmes - Total hombres y mujeres
ISIC 2 - CITI 2 - CIIU 2

	1999	2000	2001	2002	2003	2004	2005	2006	2007	2008
Total	28 244	33 053	33 004	31 363	32 113	34 094	33 605	.	.	.
1	297	351	384	347	348	378	311	.	.	.
2	80	71	50	36	20	29	32	.	.	.
3	14 306	16 715	16 126	15 055	15 251	15 995	15 390	.	.	.
4	26	19	13	21	9	20	16	.	.	.
5	7 420	8 488	8 435	8 008	8 174	8 512	8 254	.	.	.
6	2 967	3 617	4 015	4 077	4 383	4 791	5 109	.	.	.
7	1 507	1 637	1 656	1 526	1 509	1 646	1 631	.	.	.
8	394	506	521	405	475	537	576	.	.	.
9	1 247	1 649	1 804	1 888	1 944	2 186	2 286	.	.	.

Total cases (fatal + non-fatal) - Ensemble des cas (mortels + non mortels) - Todos los casos (mortales + no mortales)

Total men and women - Total hommes et femmes - Total hombres y mujeres
ISIC 2 - CITI 2 - CIIU 2

	1999	2000	2001	2002	2003	2004	2005	2006	2007	2008
Total	33 709	38 862	38 386	36 326	36 488	38 155	37 348	.	.	.
1	479	527	547	508	501	500	400	.	.	.
2	102	92	58	51	37	34	39	.	.	.
3	17 600	20 158	19 253	17 866	17 779	18 324	17 580	.	.	.
4	47	40	28	37	20	32	25	.	.	.
5	8 257	9 367	9 312	8 826	8 857	9 148	8 900	.	.	.
6	3 483	4 211	4 568	4 625	4 868	5 284	5 519	.	.	.
7	1 781	1 919	1 930	1 760	1 713	1 812	1 806	.	.	.
8	476	619	627	496	546	603	621	.	.	.
9	1 484	1 929	2 063	2 157	2 167	2 418	2 458	.	.	.

Thailand (FA) — Compensated injuries - Lésions indemnisées - Lesiones indemnizadas

Fatal cases - Cas mortels - Casos mortales

Total men and women - Total hommes et femmes - Total hombres y mujeres
ISIC 3 - CITI 3 - CIIU 3

	1999	2000	2001	2002	2003	2004	2005	2006	2007	2008
Total	610	616	597	650	787	861	1 444	808	741	.
A	21	36	13	20	34	19	24	23	20	.
C	18	19	11	13	15	18	24	18	20	.
D	232	172	190	213	237	222	203	218	191	.
E	29	23	24	21	36	46	31	32	34	.
F	108	104	97	105	109	127	220	132	126	.
G	86	94	101	105	167	145	151	149	110	.
H	6	8	6	13	12	96	529	17	24	.
I	73	99	104	110	131	116	137	117	135	.
J	10	8	.	10	10	11	41	28	19	.
J.M	.	.	7	.	.	.	.	.	.	.
K	22	45	13	33	33	53	79	48	60	.
N	1	1	1	1	1	0	0	6	0	.
O	4	7	29	6	2	8	5	20	2	.
X	0	0	1	0	0	0	0	0	0	.

Non-fatal cases (temporary + permanent incapacity) - Cas non mortels (incapacité temporaire + permanente) - Casos no mortales (incapacidad temporal + permanente)

Total men and women - Total hommes et femmes - Total hombres y mujeres [1]
ISIC 3 - CITI 3 - CIIU 3

	1999	2000	2001	2002	2003	2004	2005	2006	2007	2008
Total	51 415	50 115	50 093	52 450	56 202	56 691	57 085	55 335	53 800	.
A	5 232	5 755	5 440	5 806	5 690	5 490	4 821	4 289	3 767	.
C	567	509	482	454	508	516	484	436	396	.
D	32 291	31 983	37 061	32 552	34 216	33 980	33 630	33 032	31 470	.
E	460	394	196	487	493	543	491	499	533	.
F	4 814	3 548	3 397	3 538	3 748	4 367	4 590	4 501	4 760	.
G	3 249	3 361	3 596	4 299	5 560	5 636	6 186	6 005	6 198	.
H	1 172	1 196	1 275	1 332	1 406	1 377	1 743	1 455	1 575	.
I	1 624	1 526	1 591	1 754	1 993	2 100	2 258	2 142	2 028	.
J	207	201	.	246	320	343	360	408	409	.
J.M	.	.	235	.	.	.	.	.	.	.
K	1 343	1 212	540	1 532	1 849	1 918	2 084	2 061	2 189	.
N	205	182	161	171	154	163	133	180	160	.
O	251	220	1 016	279	265	258	305	325	307	.
X	0	28	225	0	0	0	0	2	8	.

Explanatory notes: see p. 1125.   Notes explicatives: voir p. 1127.   Notas explicativas: véase p. 1129.

[1] Incapacity of 3 days or more.   [1] Incapacité de 3 jours et plus.   [1] Incapacidad de 3 días y más.

OCCUPATIONAL INJURIES
Cases of injury with lost workdays, by economic activity

LÉSIONS PROFESSIONNELLES
Cas de lésion avec perte de journées de travail, par activité économique

LESIONES PROFESIONALES
Casos de lesión con pérdida de días de trabajo, por actividad económica

8A

	1999	2000	2001	2002	2003	2004	2005	2006	2007	2008
Thailand (FA)				Compensated injuries - Lésions indemnisées - Lesiones indemnizadas						

Cases of temporary incapacity - Cas d'incapacité temporaire - Casos de incapacidad temporal

Total men and women - Total hommes et femmes - Total hombres y mujeres [1]
ISIC 3 - CITI 3 - CIIU 3

	1999	2000	2001	2002	2003	2004	2005	2006	2007	2008
Total	51 403	50 099	50 066	52 436	56 185	56 668	57 066	55 314	53 784	.
A	5 232	5 755	5 439	5 805	5 690	5 490	4 820	4 289	3 767	.
C	566	509	482	454	506	515	484	436	396	.
D	32 285	31 979	31 925	32 548	34 212	33 984	33 625	33 026	31 466	.
E	459	393	385	486	492	541	490	499	532	.
F	4 812	3 540	3 390	3 534	3 744	4 362	4 584	4 496	4 754	.
G	3 249	3 359	3 595	4 299	5 557	5 633	6 184	6 004	6 196	.
H	1 172	1 196	1 275	1 332	1 406	1 376	1 743	1 453	1 575	.
I	1 622	1 525	1 589	1 753	1 990	2 097	2 258	2 137	2 027	.
J	207	201	235	246	320	343	359	408	409	.
K	1 343	1 212	1 378	1 529	1 849	1 917	2 081	2 061	2 188	.
N	205	182	161	171	154	163	133	180	160	.
O	251	220	212	279	265	257	305	323	307	.
X	0	28	0	0	0	0	0	2	8	.

Total cases (fatal + non-fatal) - Ensemble des cas (mortels + non mortels) - Todos los casos (mortales + no mortales)

Total men and women - Total hommes et femmes - Total hombres y mujeres
ISIC 3 - CITI 3 - CIIU 3

	1999	2000	2001	2002	2003	2004	2005	2006	2007	2008
Total	52 025	50 731	50 690	53 100	56 989	57 552	58 529	56 143	54 541	.
A	5 253	5 791	5 466	5 826	5 724	5 509	4 845	4 312	3 787	.
C	585	528	493	467	523	534	508	454	416	.
D	32 523	32 155	37 251	32 765	34 453	34 202	33 833	33 250	31 661	.
E	489	417	220	508	529	589	522	531	567	.
F	4 922	3 652	3 494	3 643	3 857	4 494	4 810	4 633	4 886	.
G	3 335	3 455	3 697	4 404	5 727	5 881	6 337	6 154	6 308	.
H	1 178	1 204	1 281	1 345	1 418	1 473	2 272	1 472	1 599	.
I	1 697	1 625	1 695	1 864	2 124	2 216	2 395	2 259	2 163	.
J	217	209	.	256	330	354	401	436	428	.
J,M	.	.	242	.	.	.	.	.	.	.
K	1 365	1 257	553	1 565	1 882	1 981	2 163	2 109	2 249	.
N	206	183	162	172	155	163	133	186	160	.
O	255	227	1 045	285	267	266	310	345	309	.
X	0	28	226	0	0	0	0	2	8	.

EUROPE-EUROPE-EUROPA

	1999	2000	2001	2002	2003	2004	2005	2006	2007	2008
Austria (FA)				Reported injuries - Lésions déclarées - Lesiones declaradas						

Fatal cases - Cas mortels - Casos mortales

Total men and women - Total hommes et femmes - Total hombres y mujeres
ISIC 3 - CITI 3 - CIIU 3

	1999	2000	2001	2002	2003	2004	2005	2006	2007	2008
Total	129	135	122	120	103	132	124	107	108	.
A-B	9	10	6	13	11	.	.	.	.	.
A	.	.	.	.	.	10	8	7	9	.
B	.	.	.	.	.	0	0	0	0	.
C	3	1	4	3	2	3	2	1	0	.
D	26	26	24	32	14	22	21	16	19	.
E	2	1	2	4	2	2	1	1	0	.
F	41	48	32	36	34	31	39	41	31	.
G	8	11	10	8	8	12	9	9	11	.
H	4	7	2	1	0	2	1	0	0	.
I	15	21	27	16	17	25	17	16	17	.
J	3	1	0	0	1	2	0	1	0	.
K	8	6	7	11	7	11	11	7	12	.
L	6	3	1	3	2	6	5	3	5	.
M	0	0	0	0	1	0	1	0	0	.
N	0	2	2	0	0	1	2	0	1	.
O	6	5	5	3	4	4	6	5	3	.
P	0	0	0	0	0	1	1	0	0	.
Q	0	0	0	0	0	0	0	0	0	.

Explanatory notes: see p. 1125.

[1] Incapacity of 3 days or more.

Notes explicatives: voir p. 1127.

[1] Incapacité de 3 jours et plus.

Notas explicativas: véase p. 1129.

[1] Incapacidad de 3 días y más.

<table>
<tr><th>OCCUPATIONAL INJURIES</th><th>LÉSIONS PROFESSIONNELLES</th><th>LESIONES PROFESIONALES</th></tr>
<tr><td>Cases of injury with lost workdays, by economic activity</td><td>Cas de lésion avec perte de journées de travail, par activité économique</td><td>Casos de lesión con pérdida de días de trabajo, por actividad económica</td></tr>
</table>

	1999	2000	2001	2002	2003	2004	2005	2006	2007	2008

Austria (FA) — Reported injuries - Lésions déclarées - Lesiones declaradas

Fatal cases - Cas mortels - Casos mortales

Men - Hommes - Hombres
ISIC 3 - CITI 3 - CIIU 3

	1999	2000	2001	2002	2003	2004	2005	2006	2007	2008
Total	.	.	.	.	.	128	116	102	105	.
A						10	8	7	8	
B						0	0	0	0	
C						3	2	1	0	
D						22	21	13	19	
E						2	1	1	0	
F						31	39	40	31	
G						11	7	8	10	
H						1	0	0	0	
I						25	16	16	17	
J						2	0	1	0	
K						10	9	7	12	
L						6	4	3	5	
M						0	1	0	0	
N						0	1	0	0	
O						4	6	5	3	
P						1	1	0	0	
Q						0	0	0	0	

Women - Femmes - Mujeres
ISIC 3 - CITI 3 - CIIU 3

	1999	2000	2001	2002	2003	2004	2005	2006	2007	2008
Total	.	.	.	.	.	4	8	5	3	.
A						0	0	0	1	
B						0	0	0	0	
C						0	0	0	0	
D						0	0	3	0	
E						0	0	0	0	
F						0	0	1	0	
G						1	2	1	1	
H						1	1	0	0	
I						0	1	0	0	
J						0	0	0	0	
K						1	2	0	0	
L						0	1	0	0	
M						0	0	0	0	
N						1	1	0	1	
O						0	0	0	0	
P						0	0	0	0	
Q						0	0	0	0	

Non-fatal cases (temporary + permanent incapacity) - Cas non mortels (incapacité temporaire + permanente) - Casos no mortales (incapacidad temporal + permanente)

Total men and women - Total hommes et femmes - Total hombres y mujeres
ISIC 3 - CITI 3 - CIIU 3

	1999	2000	2001	2002	2003	2004	2005	2006	2007	2008
Total	.	.	.	.	.	70 581	68 945	70 394	66 064	.
A						1 140	1 035	1 026	1 001	
B						2	2	4	4	
C						259	321	316	255	
D						22 649	21 233	21 531	19 661	
E						558	564	537	412	
F						16 458	16 055	16 506	15 504	
G						9 975	10 661	10 644	10 177	
H						2 346	2 023	2 093	2 038	
I						3 894	3 842	4 014	3 493	
J						275	243	237	217	
K						5 820	6 149	6 869	6 722	
L						1 676	1 616	1 646	1 475	
M						522	541	545	441	
N						2 748	2 457	2 562	2 527	
O						2 249	2 184	2 371	2 117	
P						18	20	22	15	
Q						2	7	11	5	

Men - Hommes - Hombres
ISIC 3 - CITI 3 - CIIU 3

	1999	2000	2001	2002	2003	2004	2005	2006	2007	2008
Total	.	.	.	.	.	58 485	57 044	58 702	54 002	.
A						999	908	897	853	
B						2	2	4	4	
C						255	315	313	250	
D						20 101	18 779	19 076	17 370	
E						538	539	529	398	
F						16 237	15 860	16 327	15 322	
G						6 650	7 146	7 038	6 500	
H						1 189	1 048	1 058	1 036	
I						3 484	3 442	3 644	3 127	
J						148	127	103	112	
K						4 701	4 971	5 646	5 414	
L						1 345	1 295	1 320	1 122	
M						149	166	139	130	
N						988	813	836	818	
O						1 696	1 623	1 759	1 540	
P						3	4	5	3	
Q						0	6	8	3	

Explanatory notes: see p. 1125.   Notes explicatives: voir p. 1127.   Notas explicativas: véase p. 1129.

OCCUPATIONAL INJURIES
LÉSIONS PROFESSIONNELLES
LESIONES PROFESIONALES

8A

Cases of injury with lost workdays, by economic activity

Cas de lésion avec perte de journées de travail, par activité économique

Casos de lesión con pérdida de días de trabajo, por actividad económica

	1999	2000	2001	2002	2003	2004	2005	2006	2007	2008

Austria (FA) — Reported injuries - Lésions déclarées - Lesiones declaradas

Non-fatal cases (temporary + permanent incapacity) - Cas non mortels (incapacité temporaire + permanente) - Casos no mortales (incapacidad temporal + permanente)

Women - Femmes - Mujeres
ISIC 3 - CITI 3 - CIIU 3

	1999	2000	2001	2002	2003	2004	2005	2006	2007	2008
Total	.	.	.	.	.	12 096	11 901	12 232	12 062	.
A	.	.	.	.	.	141	127	129	148	.
B	.	.	.	.	.	0	0	0	0	.
C	.	.	.	.	.	4	6	3	5	.
D	.	.	.	.	.	2 548	2 454	2 455	2 291	.
E	.	.	.	.	.	20	25	8	14	.
F	.	.	.	.	.	221	195	179	182	.
G	.	.	.	.	.	3 325	3 515	3 606	3 677	.
H	.	.	.	.	.	1 157	975	1 035	1 002	.
I	.	.	.	.	.	410	400	370	366	.
J	.	.	.	.	.	127	116	134	105	.
K	.	.	.	.	.	1 119	1 178	1 223	1 308	.
L	.	.	.	.	.	331	321	326	353	.
M	.	.	.	.	.	373	375	406	311	.
N	.	.	.	.	.	1 760	1 644	1 726	1 709	.
O	.	.	.	.	.	553	561	612	577	.
P	.	.	.	.	.	15	16	17	12	.
Q	.	.	.	.	.	2	1	3	2	.

Cases of temporary incapacity - Cas d'incapacité temporaire - Casos de incapacidad temporal

Total men and women - Total hommes et femmes - Total hombres y mujeres
ISIC 3 - CITI 3 - CIIU 3

	1999	2000	2001	2002	2003	2004	2005	2006	2007	2008
Total	.	.	.	.	.	66 846	64 851	66 461	62 523	.
A	.	.	.	.	.	1 006	919	892	876	.
B	.	.	.	.	.	2	2	3	4	.
C	.	.	.	.	.	233	292	289	236	.
D	.	.	.	.	.	21 651	20 116	20 543	18 750	.
E	.	.	.	.	.	534	529	510	392	.
F	.	.	.	.	.	15 377	14 934	15 417	14 461	.
G	.	.	.	.	.	9 577	10 250	10 178	9 802	.
H	.	.	.	.	.	2 254	1 940	2 030	1 981	.
I	.	.	.	.	.	3 604	3 488	3 666	3 217	.
J	.	.	.	.	.	245	210	218	191	.
K	.	.	.	.	.	5 545	5 787	6 517	6 373	.
L	.	.	.	.	.	1 583	1 500	1 542	1 395	.
M	.	.	.	.	.	471	493	508	393	.
N	.	.	.	.	.	2 642	2 342	2 452	2 422	.
O	.	.	.	.	.	2 114	2 033	2 206	2 014	.
P	.	.	.	.	.	16	17	19	11	.
Q	.	.	.	.	.	2	7	11	5	.

Men - Hommes - Hombres
ISIC 3 - CITI 3 - CIIU 3

	1999	2000	2001	2002	2003	2004	2005	2006	2007	2008
Total	.	.	.	.	.	55 267	53 511	55 335	50 961	.
A	.	.	.	.	.	873	802	773	737	.
B	.	.	.	.	.	2	2	3	4	.
C	.	.	.	.	.	229	286	286	231	.
D	.	.	.	.	.	19 203	17 777	18 203	16 568	.
E	.	.	.	.	.	514	506	502	378	.
F	.	.	.	.	.	15 165	14 749	15 251	14 288	.
G	.	.	.	.	.	6 367	6 854	6 709	6 231	.
H	.	.	.	.	.	1 148	1 014	1 022	1 009	.
I	.	.	.	.	.	3 212	3 112	3 328	2 868	.
J	.	.	.	.	.	126	105	93	93	.
K	.	.	.	.	.	4 479	4 660	5 354	5 118	.
L	.	.	.	.	.	1 270	1 205	1 244	1 059	.
M	.	.	.	.	.	132	146	127	114	.
N	.	.	.	.	.	949	778	805	796	.
O	.	.	.	.	.	1 595	1 506	1 623	1 461	.
P	.	.	.	.	.	3	3	4	3	.
Q	.	.	.	.	.	0	6	8	3	.

Women - Femmes - Mujeres
ISIC 3 - CITI 3 - CIIU 3

	1999	2000	2001	2002	2003	2004	2005	2006	2007	2008
Total	.	.	.	.	.	11 579	11 340	11 666	11 562	.
A	.	.	.	.	.	133	117	119	139	.
B	.	.	.	.	.	0	0	0	0	.
C	.	.	.	.	.	4	6	3	5	.
D	.	.	.	.	.	2 448	2 339	2 340	2 182	.
E	.	.	.	.	.	20	23	8	14	.
F	.	.	.	.	.	212	185	166	173	.
G	.	.	.	.	.	3 210	3 396	3 469	3 571	.
H	.	.	.	.	.	1 106	926	1 008	972	.
I	.	.	.	.	.	392	376	338	349	.
J	.	.	.	.	.	119	105	125	98	.
K	.	.	.	.	.	1 066	1 127	1 163	1 255	.
L	.	.	.	.	.	313	295	298	336	.
M	.	.	.	.	.	339	347	381	279	.
N	.	.	.	.	.	1 693	1 564	1 647	1 626	.
O	.	.	.	.	.	519	527	583	553	.
P	.	.	.	.	.	13	14	15	8	.
Q	.	.	.	.	.	2	1	3	2	.

Explanatory notes: see p. 1125.   Notes explicatives: voir p. 1127.   Notas explicativas: véase p. 1129.

ILO YEARBOOK OF LABOUR STATISTICS 2009   *ANNUAIRE DES STATISTIQUES DU TRAVAIL DU BIT 2009*   *ANUARIO DE ESTADISTICAS DEL TRABAJO DEL OIT 2009*

1179

OCCUPATIONAL INJURIES

Cases of injury with lost workdays, by economic activity

LÉSIONS PROFESSIONNELLES

Cas de lésion avec perte de journées de travail, par activité économique

LESIONES PROFESIONALES

Casos de lesión con pérdida de días de trabajo, por actividad económica

	1999	2000	2001	2002	2003	2004	2005	2006	2007	2008

Austria (FA) — Reported injuries - Lésions déclarées - Lesiones declaradas

Total cases (fatal + non-fatal) - Ensemble des cas (mortels + non mortels) - Todos los casos (mortales + no mortales)

Total men and women - Total hommes et femmes - Total hombres y mujeres
ISIC 3 - CITI 3 - CIIU 3

	1999	2000	2001	2002	2003	2004	2005	2006	2007	2008
Total	.	.	.	.	.	70 713	69 069	70 501	66 172	.
A	.	.	.	.	.	1 150	1 043	1 033	1 010	.
B	.	.	.	.	.	2	2	4	4	.
C	.	.	.	.	.	262	323	317	255	.
D	.	.	.	.	.	22 671	21 254	21 547	19 680	.
E	.	.	.	.	.	560	565	538	412	.
F	.	.	.	.	.	16 489	16 094	16 547	15 535	.
G	.	.	.	.	.	9 987	10 670	10 653	10 188	.
H	.	.	.	.	.	2 348	2 024	2 093	2 038	.
I	.	.	.	.	.	3 919	3 859	4 030	3 510	.
J	.	.	.	.	.	277	243	238	217	.
K	.	.	.	.	.	5 831	6 160	6 876	6 234	.
L	.	.	.	.	.	1 682	1 621	1 649	1 480	.
M	.	.	.	.	.	522	542	545	441	.
N	.	.	.	.	.	2 749	2 459	2 562	2 528	.
O	.	.	.	.	.	2 253	2 190	2 376	2 120	.
P	.	.	.	.	.	19	21	22	15	.
Q	.	.	.	.	.	2	7	11	5	.

Men - Hommes - Hombres
ISIC 3 - CITI 3 - CIIU 3

	1999	2000	2001	2002	2003	2004	2005	2006	2007	2008
Total	.	.	.	.	.	58 613	57 160	58 804	54 107	.
A	.	.	.	.	.	1 009	916	904	861	.
B	.	.	.	.	.	2	2	4	4	.
C	.	.	.	.	.	258	317	314	250	.
D	.	.	.	.	.	20 123	18 800	19 089	17 389	.
E	.	.	.	.	.	540	540	530	398	.
F	.	.	.	.	.	16 268	15 899	16 367	15 353	.
G	.	.	.	.	.	6 661	7 153	7 046	6 510	.
H	.	.	.	.	.	1 190	1 048	1 058	1 036	.
I	.	.	.	.	.	3 509	3 458	3 660	3 144	.
J	.	.	.	.	.	150	127	104	112	.
K	.	.	.	.	.	4 711	4 980	5 653	5 426	.
L	.	.	.	.	.	1 351	1 299	1 323	1 127	.
M	.	.	.	.	.	149	167	139	130	.
N	.	.	.	.	.	988	814	836	818	.
O	.	.	.	.	.	1 700	1 629	1 764	1 543	.
P	.	.	.	.	.	4	5	5	3	.
Q	.	.	.	.	.	0	6	8	3	.

Women - Femmes - Mujeres
ISIC 3 - CITI 3 - CIIU 3

	1999	2000	2001	2002	2003	2004	2005	2006	2007	2008
Total	.	.	.	.	.	12 100	11 909	12 237	12 065	.
A	.	.	.	.	.	141	127	129	149	.
B	.	.	.	.	.	0	0	0	0	.
C	.	.	.	.	.	4	6	3	5	.
D	.	.	.	.	.	2 548	2 454	2 458	2 291	.
E	.	.	.	.	.	20	25	8	14	.
F	.	.	.	.	.	221	195	180	182	.
G	.	.	.	.	.	3 326	3 517	3 607	3 678	.
H	.	.	.	.	.	1 158	976	1 035	1 002	.
I	.	.	.	.	.	410	401	370	366	.
J	.	.	.	.	.	127	116	134	105	.
K	.	.	.	.	.	1 120	1 180	1 223	1 308	.
L	.	.	.	.	.	331	322	326	353	.
M	.	.	.	.	.	373	375	406	311	.
N	.	.	.	.	.	1 761	1 645	1 726	1 710	.
O	.	.	.	.	.	553	561	612	577	.
P	.	.	.	.	.	15	16	17	12	.
Q	.	.	.	.	.	2	1	3	2	.

Belarus (CA) — Reported injuries - Lésions déclarées - Lesiones declaradas

Fatal cases - Cas mortels - Casos mortales

Total men and women - Total hommes et femmes - Total hombres y mujeres
ISIC 3 - CITI 3 - CIIU 3

	1999	2000	2001	2002	2003	2004	2005	2006	2007	2008
Total	298	258	234	228	214	248	235	228	214	185

Men - Hommes - Hombres
ISIC 3 - CITI 3 - CIIU 3

	1999	2000	2001	2002	2003	2004	2005	2006	2007	2008
Total	281	231	222	210	194	233	219	217	202	172

Women - Femmes - Mujeres
ISIC 3 - CITI 3 - CIIU 3

	1999	2000	2001	2002	2003	2004	2005	2006	2007	2008
Total	17	27	12	18	20	15	16	11	12	13

Explanatory notes: see p. 1125. Notes explicatives: voir p. 1127. Notas explicativas: véase p. 1129.

OCCUPATIONAL INJURIES
Cases of injury with lost workdays, by economic activity

LÉSIONS PROFESSIONNELLES
Cas de lésion avec perte de journées de travail, par activité économique

LESIONES PROFESIONALES
Casos de lesión con pérdida de días de trabajo, por actividad económica

	1999	2000	2001	2002	2003	2004	2005	2006	2007	2008

Belarus (CA) — Reported injuries - Lésions déclarées - Lesiones declaradas

Non-fatal cases (temporary + permanent incapacity) - Cas non mortels (incapacité temporaire + permanente) - Casos no mortales (incapacidad temporal + permanente)

Total men and women - Total hommes et femmes - Total hombres y mujeres
ISIC 3 - CITI 3 - CIIU 3

	1999	2000	2001	2002	2003	2004	2005	2006	2007	2008
Total	10 335	7 960	6 973	5 767	5 428	5 240	4 295	3 709	3 329	2 815

Men - Hommes - Hombres
ISIC 3 - CITI 3 - CIIU 3

	1999	2000	2001	2002	2003	2004	2005	2006	2007	2008
Total	7 895	5 817	5 151	4 312	3 983	3 877	3 125	2 676	2 436	1 985

Women - Femmes - Mujeres
ISIC 3 - CITI 3 - CIIU 3

	1999	2000	2001	2002	2003	2004	2005	2006	2007	2008
Total	2 440	2 143	1 822	1 455	1 445	1 363	1 170	1 033	893	830

Total cases (fatal + non-fatal) - Ensemble des cas (mortels + non mortels) - Todos los casos (mortales + no mortales)

Total men and women - Total hommes et femmes - Total hombres y mujeres
ISIC 3 - CITI 3 - CIIU 3

	1999	2000	2001	2002	2003	2004	2005	2006	2007	2008
Total	10 633	8 218	7 207	5 995	5 642	5 488	4 530	3 937	3 543	3 000

Men - Hommes - Hombres
ISIC 3 - CITI 3 - CIIU 3

	1999	2000	2001	2002	2003	2004	2005	2006	2007	2008
Total	8 176	6 048	5 373	4 522	4 177	4 110	3 344	2 893	2 638	2 157

Women - Femmes - Mujeres
ISIC 3 - CITI 3 - CIIU 3

	1999	2000	2001	2002	2003	2004	2005	2006	2007	2008
Total	2 457	2 170	1 834	1 473	1 465	1 378	1 186	1 044	905	843

Belgique (FA) [1] — Compensated injuries - Lésions indemnisées - Lesiones indemnizadas

Fatal cases - Cas mortels - Casos mortales

Total men and women - Total hommes et femmes - Total hombres y mujeres
ISIC 3 - CITI 3 - CIIU 3

	1999	2000	2001	2002	2003	2004	2005	2006	2007	2008
Total	64	78	69 [2]	.	.	108	.	.	.	.
A	0	0	0 [2]	.	.	1	.	.	.	.
B	0	0	0 [2]	.	.	0	.	.	.	.
C	0	0	0 [2]	.	.	0	.	.	.	.
D	8	18	18 [2]	.	.	26	.	.	.	.
E	1	2	2 [2]	.	.	1	.	.	.	.
F	18	22	4 [2]	.	.	28	.	.	.	.
G	3	0	1 [2]	.	.	7	.	.	.	.
H	0	0	0 [2]	.	.	1	.	.	.	.
I	18	15	11 [2]	.	.	31	.	.	.	.
J	0	0	4 [2]	.	.	0	.	.	.	.
K	3	8	2 [2]	.	.	8	.	.	.	.
L	9	7	3 [2]	.	.	1	.	.	.	.
M	1	2	1 [2]	.	.	1	.	.	.	.
N	1	1	2 [2]	.	.	1	.	.	.	.
O	2	3	1 [2]	.	.	1	.	.	.	.
P	0	0	0 [2]	.	.	0	.	.	.	.
Q	0	0	0 [2]	.	.	0	.	.	.	.
X	.	.	. [2]	.	.		.	.	.	.

Men - Hommes - Hombres
ISIC 3 - CITI 3 - CIIU 3

	1999	2000	2001	2002	2003	2004	2005	2006	2007	2008
Total	.	.	.	.	.	104	.	.	.	.
A	.	.	.	.	.	1	.	.	.	.
B	.	.	.	.	.	0	.	.	.	.
C	.	.	.	.	.	0	.	.	.	.
D	.	.	.	.	.	26	.	.	.	.
E	.	.	.	.	.	1	.	.	.	.
F	.	.	.	.	.	28	.	.	.	.
G	.	.	.	.	.	6	.	.	.	.
H	.	.	.	.	.	1	.	.	.	.
I	.	.	.	.	.	30	.	.	.	.
J	.	.	.	.	.	0	.	.	.	.
K	.	.	.	.	.	8	.	.	.	.
L	.	.	.	.	.	1	.	.	.	.
M	.	.	.	.	.	1	.	.	.	.
N	.	.	.	.	.	0	.	.	.	.
O	.	.	.	.	.	1	.	.	.	.
P	.	.	.	.	.	0	.	.	.	.
Q	.	.	.	.	.	0	.	.	.	.
X	.	.	.	.	.	0	.	.	.	.

Explanatory notes: see p. 1125.

[1] Private sector: from 1992: incl. commuting accidents. [2] Not strictly comparable.

Notes explicatives: voir p. 1127.

[1] Secteur privé: à partir de 1992: y compris les accidents de trajet. [2] Non strictement comparable.

Notas explicativas: véase p. 1129.

[1] Sector privado: a partir de 1992: incl. accidentes del trayecto. [2] No estrictamente comparable.

8A

OCCUPATIONAL INJURIES	LÉSIONS PROFESSIONNELLES	LESIONES PROFESIONALES
Cases of injury with lost workdays, by economic activity	Cas de lésion avec perte de journées de travail, par activité économique	Casos de lesión con pérdida de días de trabajo, por actividad económica

	1999	2000	2001	2002	2003	2004	2005	2006	2007	2008

Belgique (FA) [1]

Compensated injuries - Lésions indemnisées - Lesiones indemnizadas

Fatal cases - Cas mortels - Casos mortales

Women - Femmes - Mujeres
ISIC 3 - CITI 3 - CIIU 3

	1999	2000	2001	2002	2003	2004	2005	2006	2007	2008
Total						4				
A						0				
B						0				
C						0				
D						0				
E						0				
F						0				
G						1				
H						0				
I						1				
J						0				
K						0				
L						0				
M						0				
N						1				
O						0				
P						0				
Q						1				
X						0				

Non-fatal cases (temporary + permanent incapacity) - Cas non mortels (incapacité temporaire + permanente) - Casos no mortales (incapacidad temporal + permanente)

Total men and women - Total hommes et femmes - Total hombres y mujeres
ISIC 3 - CITI 3 - CIIU 3

	1999	2000	2001	2002	2003	2004	2005	2006	2007	2008
Total	95 923	101 395	96 321 [2]			93 969				
A	107	154	152 [2]			1 130				
B	2	7	6 [2]			12				
C	24	11	19 [2]			437				
D	31 313	29 923	30 645 [2]			29 664				
E	971	961	1 007 [2]			199				
F	11 076	19	9 598 [2]			14 655				
G	7 572	10 324	9 485 [2]			15 226				
H	1 524	1 686	1 551 [2]			2 750				
I	9 992	14 888	11 886 [2]			10 088				
J	435	1 183	1 477 [2]			507				
K	3 816	4 944	4 458 [2]			7 246				
L	13 715	13 585	11 889 [2]			341				
M	2 175	2 049	2 299 [2]			723				
N	8 025	8 547	9 166 [2]			6 820				
O	5 099	2 435	2 710 [2]			2 656				
P	2	2	8 [2]			153				
Q	75	67	51 [2]			18				
X			[2]			1 344				

Men - Hommes - Hombres
ISIC 3 - CITI 3 - CIIU 3

	1999	2000	2001	2002	2003	2004	2005	2006	2007	2008
Total						74 961				
A						961				
B						8				
C						434				
D						26 288				
E						182				
F						14 507				
G						11 054				
H						1 417				
I						9 175				
J						242				
K						5 393				
L						239				
M						303				
N						2 195				
O						1 477				
P						52				
Q						8				
X						1 026				

Explanatory notes: see p. 1125.

[1] Private sector: from 1992: incl. commuting accidents. [2] Not strictly comparable.

Notes explicatives: voir p. 1127.

[1] Secteur privé: à partir de 1992: y compris les accidents de trajet. [2] Non strictement comparable.

Notas explicativas: véase p. 1129.

[1] Sector privado: a partir de 1992: incl. accidentes del trayecto. [2] No estrictamente comparable.

OCCUPATIONAL INJURIES
Cases of injury with lost workdays, by economic activity

LÉSIONS PROFESSIONNELLES
Cas de lésion avec perte de journées de travail, par activité économique

LESIONES PROFESIONALES
Casos de lesión con pérdida de días de trabajo, por actividad económica

8A

	1999	2000	2001	2002	2003	2004	2005	2006	2007	2008

Belgique (FA) [1]   Compensated injuries - Lésions indemnisées - Lesiones indemnizadas

Non-fatal cases (temporary + permanent incapacity) - Cas non mortels (incapacité temporaire + permanente) - Casos no mortales (incapacidad temporal + permanente)

Women - Femmes - Mujeres
ISIC 3 - CITI 3 - CIIU 3

	1999	2000	2001	2002	2003	2004	2005	2006	2007	2008
Total	.	.	.	.	.	19 005	.	.	.	.
A	.	.	.	.	.	169	.	.	.	.
B	.	.	.	.	.	4	.	.	.	.
C	.	.	.	.	.	3	.	.	.	.
D	.	.	.	.	.	3 374	.	.	.	.
E	.	.	.	.	.	17	.	.	.	.
F	.	.	.	.	.	148	.	.	.	.
G	.	.	.	.	.	4 172	.	.	.	.
H	.	.	.	.	.	1 333	.	.	.	.
I	.	.	.	.	.	913	.	.	.	.
J	.	.	.	.	.	265	.	.	.	.
K	.	.	.	.	.	1 852	.	.	.	.
L	.	.	.	.	.	102	.	.	.	.
M	.	.	.	.	.	420	.	.	.	.
N	.	.	.	.	.	4 625	.	.	.	.
O	.	.	.	.	.	1 179	.	.	.	.
P	.	.	.	.	.	101	.	.	.	.
Q	.	.	.	.	.	10	.	.	.	.
X	.	.	.	.	.	318	.	.	.	.

Cases of temporary incapacity - Cas d'incapacité temporaire - Casos de incapacidad temporal

Total men and women - Total hommes et femmes - Total hombres y mujeres
ISIC 3 - CITI 3 - CIIU 3

	1999	2000	2001	2002	2003	2004	2005	2006	2007	2008
Total	92 630	97 731	92 662 [2]	.	.	83 458	.	.	.	.
A	103	150	147 [2]	.	.	965	.	.	.	.
B	2	6	6 [2]	.	.	12	.	.	.	.
C	23	11	18 [2]	.	.	379	.	.	.	.
D	30 095	28 620	29 345 [2]	.	.	26 885	.	.	.	.
E	946	940	980 [2]	.	.	176	.	.	.	.
F	10 253	18	8 676 [2]	.	.	12 554	.	.	.	.
G	7 341	9 964	9 105 [2]	.	.	13 729	.	.	.	.
H	1 463	1 629	1 509 [2]	.	.	2 487	.	.	.	.
I	9 523	14 404	11 431 [2]	.	.	8 691	.	.	.	.
J	433	1 179	1 475 [2]	.	.	435	.	.	.	.
K	3 535	4 617	4 175 [2]	.	.	6 589	.	.	.	.
L	13 670	13 557	11 846 [2]	.	.	292	.	.	.	.
M	2 150	2 043	2 284 [2]	.	.	630	.	.	.	.
N	7 927	8 387	9 027 [2]	.	.	6 049	.	.	.	.
O	5 078	2 408	2 665 [2]	.	.	2 315	.	.	.	.
P	2	2	8 [2]	.	.	127	.	.	.	.
Q	75	67	51 [2]	.	.	14	.	.	.	.
X	.	.	. [2]	.	.	1 129	.	.	.	.

Men - Hommes - Hombres
ISIC 3 - CITI 3 - CIIU 3

	1999	2000	2001	2002	2003	2004	2005	2006	2007	2008
Total	.	.	.	.	.	66 476	.	.	.	.
A	.	.	.	.	.	819	.	.	.	.
B	.	.	.	.	.	8	.	.	.	.
C	.	.	.	.	.	378	.	.	.	.
D	.	.	.	.	.	23 782	.	.	.	.
E	.	.	.	.	.	164	.	.	.	.
F	.	.	.	.	.	12 427	.	.	.	.
G	.	.	.	.	.	9 944	.	.	.	.
H	.	.	.	.	.	1 293	.	.	.	.
I	.	.	.	.	.	7 912	.	.	.	.
J	.	.	.	.	.	209	.	.	.	.
K	.	.	.	.	.	4 910	.	.	.	.
L	.	.	.	.	.	209	.	.	.	.
M	.	.	.	.	.	262	.	.	.	.
N	.	.	.	.	.	1 967	.	.	.	.
O	.	.	.	.	.	1 269	.	.	.	.
P	.	.	.	.	.	48	.	.	.	.
Q	.	.	.	.	.	5	.	.	.	.
X	.	.	.	.	.	870	.	.	.	.

Explanatory notes: see p. 1125.

[1] Private sector: from 1992: incl. commuting accidents. [2] Not strictly comparable.

Notes explicatives: voir p. 1127.

[1] Secteur privé: à partir de 1992: y compris les accidents de trajet. [2] Non strictement comparable.

Notas explicativas: véase p. 1129.

[1] Sector privado: a partir de 1992: incl. accidentes del trayecto. [2] No estrictamente comparable.

8A

	OCCUPATIONAL INJURIES	LÉSIONS PROFESSIONNELLES	LESIONES PROFESIONALES
	Cases of injury with lost workdays, by economic activity	Cas de lésion avec perte de journées de travail, par activité économique	Casos de lesión con pérdida de días de trabajo, por actividad económica

	1999	2000	2001	2002	2003	2004	2005	2006	2007	2008

Belgique (FA) [1]

Compensated injuries - Lésions indemnisées - Lesiones indemnizadas

Cases of temporary incapacity - Cas d'incapacité temporaire - Casos de incapacidad temporal

Women - Femmes - Mujeres
ISIC 3 - CITI 3 - CIIU 3

	1999	2000	2001	2002	2003	2004	2005	2006	2007	2008
Total						16 979				
A						146				
B						4				
C						1				
D						3 101				
E						12				
F						127				
G						3 785				
H						1 194				
I						779				
J						226				
K						1 678				
L						83				
M						368				
N						4 082				
O						1 046				
P						79				
Q						9				
X						259				

Total cases (fatal + non-fatal) - Ensemble des cas (mortels + non mortels) - Todos los casos (mortales + no mortales)

Total men and women - Total hommes et femmes - Total hombres y mujeres
ISIC 3 - CITI 3 - CIIU 3

	1999	2000	2001	2002	2003	2004	2005	2006	2007	2008
Total	95 987	101 473	96 390 [2]			94 077				
A	107	154	152 [2]			1 131				
B	2	7	6 [2]			12				
C	24	11	19 [2]			437				
D	31 321	29 941	30 663 [2]			29 690				
E	972	963	1 009 [2]			200				
F	11 094	41	9 622 [2]			14 683				
G	7 575	10 324	9 486 [2]			15 233				
H	1 524	1 686	1 551 [2]			2 751				
I	10 010	14 903	11 897 [2]			10 119				
J	435	1 183	1 481 [2]			507				
K	3 819	4 952	4 460 [2]			7 254				
L	13 724	13 592	11 891 [2]			342				
M	2 176	2 051	2 300 [2]			724				
N	8 026	8 548	9 168 [2]			6 821				
O	5 101	2 438	2 711 [2]			2 657				
P	2	2	8 [2]			154				
Q	75	67	51 [2]			18				
X			[2]			1 344				

Men - Hommes - Hombres
ISIC 3 - CITI 3 - CIIU 3

	1999	2000	2001	2002	2003	2004	2005	2006	2007	2008
Total						75 065				
A						962				
B						8				
C						434				
D						26 314				
E						183				
F						14 535				
G						11 060				
H						1 418				
I						9 205				
J						242				
K						5 401				
L						240				
M						304				
N						2 195				
O						1 478				
P						52				
Q						8				
X						1 026				

Explanatory notes: see p. 1125.
[1] Private sector: from 1992: incl. commuting accidents. [2] Not strictly comparable.

Notes explicatives: voir p. 1127.
[1] Secteur privé: à partir de 1992: y compris les accidents de trajet. [2] Non strictement comparable.

Notas explicativas: véase p. 1129.
[1] Sector privado: a partir de 1992: incl. accidentes del trayecto. [2] No estrictamente comparable.

OCCUPATIONAL INJURIES

Cases of injury with lost workdays, by economic activity

LÉSIONS PROFESSIONNELLES

Cas de lésion avec perte de journées de travail, par activité économique

LESIONES PROFESIONALES

Casos de lesión con pérdida de días de trabajo, por actividad económica

	1999	2000	2001	2002	2003	2004	2005	2006	2007	2008

Belgique (FA) [1]   Compensated injuries - Lésions indemnisées - Lesiones indemnizadas

Total cases (fatal + non-fatal) - Ensemble des cas (mortels + non mortels) - Todos los casos (mortales + no mortales)

Women - Femmes - Mujeres
ISIC 3 - CITI 3 - CIIU 3

	1999	2000	2001	2002	2003	2004	2005	2006	2007	2008
Total	.	.	.	.	.	19 009	.	.	.	.
A	.	.	.	.	.	169	.	.	.	.
B	.	.	.	.	.	4	.	.	.	.
C	.	.	.	.	.	3	.	.	.	.
D	.	.	.	.	.	3 374	.	.	.	.
E	.	.	.	.	.	17	.	.	.	.
F	.	.	.	.	.	148	.	.	.	.
G	.	.	.	.	.	4 173	.	.	.	.
H	.	.	.	.	.	1 333	.	.	.	.
I	.	.	.	.	.	914	.	.	.	.
J	.	.	.	.	.	265	.	.	.	.
K	.	.	.	.	.	1 852	.	.	.	.
L	.	.	.	.	.	102	.	.	.	.
M	.	.	.	.	.	420	.	.	.	.
N	.	.	.	.	.	4 626	.	.	.	.
O	.	.	.	.	.	1 179	.	.	.	.
P	.	.	.	.	.	102	.	.	.	.
Q	.	.	.	.	.	10	.	.	.	.
X	.	.	.	.	.	318	.	.	.	.

Bulgaria (FD)   Reported injuries - Lésions déclarées - Lesiones declaradas

Fatal cases - Cas mortels - Casos mortales

Total men and women - Total hommes et femmes - Total hombres y mujeres
ISIC 3 - CITI 3 - CIIU 3

	1999	2000	2001	2002	2003	2004	2005	2006	2007	2008
Total	89	138	138	115	114	130	130	169	179	.
A	7	16	11	11	16	12	6	7	9	.
B	0	0	0	0	0	0	0	0	0	.
C	4	15	7	11	8	7	8	7	12	.
D	37	27	37	31	25	35	36	34	31	.
E	11	9	6	8	4	3	7	6	14	.
F	7	22	15	18	17	27	29	32	37	.
G	3	9	20	10	11	17	15	35	21	.
H	2	2	2	0	3	1	2	0	1	.
I	17	20	21	13	13	14	16	20	22	.
J	0	2	0	0	1	2	1	2	1	.
K	1	5	6	0	5	9	4	7	18	.
L	0	6	5	4	3	1	3	7	4	.
M	0	1	4	4	6	0	1	4	0	.
N	0	1	1	4	1	0	1	1	4	.
O	0	3	3	1	1	2	1	7	5	.
Q	.	.	.	.	0	0	0	0	0	.

Men - Hommes - Hombres
ISIC 3 - CITI 3 - CIIU 3

	1999	2000	2001	2002	2003	2004	2005	2006	2007	2008
Total	.	.	.	.	99	120	120	143	153	.
A	.	.	.	.	14	11	3	6	7	.
B	.	.	.	.	0	0	0	0	0	.
C	.	.	.	.	8	7	8	6	12	.
D	.	.	.	.	21	29	34	25	25	.
E	.	.	.	.	4	3	7	6	14	.
F	.	.	.	.	17	27	28	32	37	.
G	.	.	.	.	11	16	15	29	18	.
H	.	.	.	.	2	1	2	0	0	.
I	.	.	.	.	12	14	15	18	17	.
J	.	.	.	.	0	1	1	2	1	.
K	.	.	.	.	5	8	4	6	14	.
L	.	.	.	.	1	1	1	3	3	.
M	.	.	.	.	3	0	0	4	0	.
N	.	.	.	.	1	0	1	0	2	.
O	.	.	.	.	0	2	1	6	3	.
P	.	.	.	.	0	0	0	0	0	.
Q	.	.	.	.	0	0	0	0	0	.

Explanatory notes: see p. 1125.

[1] Private sector: from 1992: incl. commuting accidents.

Notes explicatives: voir p. 1127.

[1] Secteur privé: à partir de 1992: y compris les accidents de trajet.

Notas explicativas: véase p. 1129.

[1] Sector privado: a partir de 1992: incl. accidentes del trayecto.

8A

OCCUPATIONAL INJURIES	LÉSIONS PROFESSIONNELLES	LESIONES PROFESIONALES
Cases of injury with lost workdays, by economic activity	Cas de lésion avec perte de journées de travail, par activité économique	Casos de lesión con pérdida de días de trabajo, por actividad económica

	1999	2000	2001	2002	2003	2004	2005	2006	2007	2008

Bulgaria (FD) — Reported injuries - Lésions déclarées - Lesiones declaradas

Fatal cases - Cas mortels - Casos mortales

Women - Femmes - Mujeres
ISIC 3 - CITI 3 - CIIU 3

	1999	2000	2001	2002	2003	2004	2005	2006	2007	2008
Total					15	10	10	26	26	
A					2	1	3	1	2	
B					0	0	0	0	0	
C					0	0	0	1	0	
D					4	6	2	9	6	
E					0	0	0	0	0	
F					0	0	1	0	0	
G					0	1	0	6	3	
H					1	0	0	0	1	
I					1	0	1	2	5	
J					1	1	0	0	0	
K					0	1	0	1	4	
L					2	0	2	4	1	
M					3	0	1	0	0	
N					0	0	0	1	2	
O					1	0	0	1	2	
P					0	0	0	0	0	
Q					0	0	0	0	0	

Non-fatal cases (temporary + permanent incapacity) - Cas non mortels (incapacité temporaire + permanente) - Casos no mortales (incapacidad temporal + permanente)

Total men and women - Total hommes et femmes - Total hombres y mujeres
ISIC 3 - CITI 3 - CIIU 3

	1999	2000	2001	2002	2003	2004	2005	2006	2007	2008
Total	7 762	6 800	5 778	5 436	4 762	4 275	4 181	3 927	3 632	
A	506	272	213	157	175	120	86	97	67	
B	0	0	1	2	0	0	1	0	0	
C	913	715	668	633	505	318	343	286	245	
D	4 158	2 728	2 376	2 220	1 798	1 544	1 525	1 361	1 271	
E	341	325	289	274	257	227	216	184	137	
F	493	429	427	398	295	325	332	358	362	
G	183	166	157	150	209	231	242	295	340	
H	78	91	72	67	60	59	55	56	62	
I	960	667	598	532	509	455	462	433	370	
J	0	43	40	28	56	92	33	38	29	
K	42	82	82	83	200	217	202	198	188	
L	0	584	219	280	268	290	253	260	212	
M	0	238	216	199	108	121	115	95	106	
N	3	346	275	289	207	181	205	172	140	
O	85	114	145	124	115	94	110	94	100	
Q					0	1	1	0	0	

Men - Hommes - Hombres
ISIC 3 - CITI 3 - CIIU 3

	1999	2000	2001	2002	2003	2004	2005	2006	2007	2008
Total					3 315	2 955	2 809	2 697	2 450	
A					125	94	69	72	53	
B					0	0	1	0	0	
C					469	297	319	269	231	
D					1 319	1 124	1 079	973	870	
E					196	172	163	131	108	
F					277	309	318	345	344	
G					145	164	175	223	234	
H					20	18	19	26	33	
I					359	332	326	300	257	
J					41	75	15	15	9	
K					127	132	115	125	133	
L					101	107	82	98	62	
M					28	34	21	17	23	
N					35	33	44	39	25	
O					73	64	62	64	65	
P					0	0	0	0	0	
Q					0	0	1	0	3	

Women - Femmes - Mujeres
ISIC 3 - CITI 3 - CIIU 3

	1999	2000	2001	2002	2003	2004	2005	2006	2007	2008
Total					1 447	1 320	1 372	1 230	1 182	
A					50	26	17	25	14	
B					0	0	0	0	0	
C					36	21	24	17	14	
D					479	420	446	388	401	
E					61	55	53	53	29	
F					18	16	14	13	18	
G					64	67	67	72	106	
H					40	41	36	30	29	
I					150	123	136	133	113	
J					15	17	18	23	20	
K					73	85	87	73	55	
L					167	183	171	162	150	
M					80	87	94	78	83	
N					172	148	161	133	115	
O					42	30	48	30	35	
P					0	0	0	0	0	
Q					0	1	0	0	0	

Explanatory notes: see p. 1125.   Notes explicatives: voir p. 1127.   Notas explicativas: véase p. 1129.

OCCUPATIONAL INJURIES

Cases of injury with lost workdays, by economic activity

LÉSIONS PROFESSIONNELLES

Cas de lésion avec perte de journées de travail, par activité économique

LESIONES PROFESIONALES

Casos de lesión con pérdida de días de trabajo, por actividad económica

	1999	2000	2001	2002	2003	2004	2005	2006	2007	2008

Bulgaria (FD)   **Reported injuries - Lésions déclarées - Lesiones declaradas**

Cases of temporary incapacity - Cas d'incapacité temporaire - Casos de incapacidad temporal

Total men and women - Total hommes et femmes - Total hombres y mujeres
ISIC 3 - CITI 3 - CIIU 3

	1999	2000	2001	2002	2003	2004	2005	2006	2007	2008
Total	.	.	.	.	4 659	4 190	4 098	3 846	3 556	.
A	.	.	.	.	165	116	84	95	64	.
B	.	.	.	.	0	0	1	0	0	.
C	.	.	.	.	502	316	341	283	242	.
D	.	.	.	.	1 766	1 510	1 488	1 332	1 242	.
E	.	.	.	.	255	218	215	183	136	.
F	.	.	.	.	272	310	315	348	350	.
G	.	.	.	.	201	223	233	277	333	.
H	.	.	.	.	57	59	55	55	62	.
I	.	.	.	.	503	450	459	453	359	.
J	.	.	.	.	56	91	32	38	29	.
K	.	.	.	.	192	214	196	196	186	.
L	.	.	.	.	265	289	250	259	210	.
M	.	.	.	.	104	120	114	94	105	.
N	.	.	.	.	206	181	205	171	138	.
O	.	.	.	.	115	92	109	93	97	.
Q	.	.	.	.	0	1	1	0	3	.

Men - Hommes - Hombres
ISIC 3 - CITI 3 - CIIU 3

	1999	2000	2001	2002	2003	2004	2005	2006	2007	2008
Total	.	.	.	.	3 230	2 885	2 745	2 632	2 391	.
A	.	.	.	.	116	90	67	70	51	.
B	.	.	.	.	0	0	1	0	0	.
C	.	.	.	.	466	295	317	266	228	.
D	.	.	.	.	1 300	1 097	1 055	949	850	.
E	.	.	.	.	194	164	162	131	107	.
F	.	.	.	.	254	294	301	335	332	.
G	.	.	.	.	137	160	168	208	229	.
H	.	.	.	.	17	18	19	26	33	.
I	.	.	.	.	353	327	324	292	246	.
J	.	.	.	.	41	74	14	15	9	.
K	.	.	.	.	119	130	110	124	131	.
L	.	.	.	.	100	106	81	97	60	.
M	.	.	.	.	25	34	20	17	23	.
N	.	.	.	.	35	33	44	39	25	.
O	.	.	.	.	73	63	61	63	64	.
P	.	.	.	.	0	0	0	0	0	.
Q	.	.	.	.	0	0	1	0	3	.

Women - Femmes - Mujeres
ISIC 3 - CITI 3 - CIIU 3

	1999	2000	2001	2002	2003	2004	2005	2006	2007	2008
Total	.	.	.	.	1 429	1 305	1 353	1 214	1 165	.
A	.	.	.	.	49	26	17	25	13	.
B	.	.	.	.	0	0	0	0	0	.
C	.	.	.	.	36	21	24	17	14	.
D	.	.	.	.	466	413	433	383	392	.
E	.	.	.	.	61	54	53	52	29	.
F	.	.	.	.	18	16	14	13	18	.
G	.	.	.	.	64	63	65	69	104	.
H	.	.	.	.	40	41	36	29	29	.
I	.	.	.	.	150	123	135	130	113	.
J	.	.	.	.	15	17	18	23	20	.
K	.	.	.	.	73	84	86	72	55	.
L	.	.	.	.	165	183	169	162	150	.
M	.	.	.	.	79	86	94	77	82	.
N	.	.	.	.	171	148	161	132	113	.
O	.	.	.	.	42	29	48	30	33	.
P	.	.	.	.	0	0	0	0	0	.
Q	.	.	.	.	0	1	0	0	0	.

Explanatory notes: see p. 1125.   Notes explicatives: voir p. 1127.   Notas explicativas: véase p. 1129.

8A

OCCUPATIONAL INJURIES	LÉSIONS PROFESSIONNELLES	LESIONES PROFESIONALES
Cases of injury with lost workdays, by economic activity	Cas de lésion avec perte de journées de travail, par activité économique	Casos de lesión con pérdida de días de trabajo, por actividad económica

	1999	2000	2001	2002	2003	2004	2005	2006	2007	2008

Bulgaria (FD) · **Reported injuries - Lésions déclarées - Lesiones declaradas**

Total cases (fatal + non-fatal) - Ensemble des cas (mortels + non mortels) - Todos los casos (mortales + no mortales)

Total men and women - Total hommes et femmes - Total hombres y mujeres
ISIC 3 - CITI 3 - CIIU 3

	1999	2000	2001	2002	2003	2004	2005	2006	2007	2008
Total	7 851	6 938	5 916	5 551	4 876	4 405	4 311	4 096	3 811	.
A	513	288	224	168	191	132	92	104	76	
B	0	0	1	2	0	0	1	0	0	
C	917	730	675	644	513	325	351	293	257	
D	4 195	2 755	2 413	2 251	1 823	1 579	1 561	1 395	1 302	
E	352	334	295	282	261	230	223	190	151	
F	500	451	442	416	312	352	361	390	399	
G	186	175	177	160	220	248	257	330	361	
H	80	93	74	67	63	60	57	56	63	
I	977	687	619	545	522	469	478	453	392	
J	0	45	40	28	57	94	34	40	30	
K	43	87	88	83	205	226	206	205	206	
L	0	590	224	284	271	291	256	267	216	
M	0	239	220	203	114	121	116	99	106	
N	3	347	276	293	208	181	206	173	144	
O	85	117	148	125	116	96	111	101	105	
Q					0	1	1	0	3	

Men - Hommes - Hombres
ISIC 3 - CITI 3 - CIIU 3

	1999	2000	2001	2002	2003	2004	2005	2006	2007	2008
Total	.	.	.	.	3 414	3 075	2 929	2 840	2 603	.
A					139	105	72	78	60	
B					0	0	1	0	0	
C					477	304	327	275	243	
D					1 340	1 153	1 113	998	895	
E					200	175	170	137	122	
F					294	336	346	377	381	
G					156	180	190	252	252	
H					22	19	21	26	33	
I					371	346	341	318	274	
J					41	76	16	17	10	
K					132	140	119	131	147	
L					102	108	83	101	65	
M					31	34	21	21	23	
N					36	33	45	39	27	
O					73	66	63	70	68	
P					0	0	0	0	0	
Q					0	0	1	0	3	

Women - Femmes - Mujeres
ISIC 3 - CITI 3 - CIIU 3

	1999	2000	2001	2002	2003	2004	2005	2006	2007	2008
Total	.	.	.	.	1 462	1 330	1 382	1 256	1 208	.
A					52	27	20	26	16	
B					0	0	0	0	0	
C					36	21	24	18	14	
D					483	426	448	397	407	
E					61	55	53	53	29	
F					18	16	15	13	18	
G					64	68	67	78	109	
H					41	41	36	30	30	
I					151	123	137	135	118	
J					16	18	18	23	20	
K					73	86	87	74	59	
L					169	183	173	166	151	
M					83	87	95	78	83	
N					172	148	161	134	117	
O					43	30	48	31	37	
P					0	0	0	0	0	
Q					0	1	0	0	0	

Explanatory notes: see p. 1125.   Notes explicatives: voir p. 1127.   Notas explicativas: véase p. 1129.

OCCUPATIONAL INJURIES

Cases of injury with lost workdays, by economic activity

LÉSIONS PROFESSIONNELLES

Cas de lésion avec perte de journées de travail, par activité économique

LESIONES PROFESIONALES

Casos de lesión con pérdida de días de trabajo, por actividad económica

8A

	1999	2000	2001	2002	2003	2004	2005	2006	2007	2008

Croatia (FA)   Compensated injuries - Lésions indemnisées - Lesiones indemnizadas

Fatal cases - Cas mortels - Casos mortales

Total men and women - Total hommes et femmes - Total hombres y mujeres [1]
ISIC 3 - CITI 3 - CIIU 3

	1999	2000	2001	2002	2003	2004	2005	2006	2007	2008
Total	32	41	42	44	47	38	62	76	74	79
A	1	6	2	4	8	3	11	7	5	4
B	0	0	0	1	0	0	2	0	0	3
C	0	0	0	0	3	1	2	1	0	0
D	6	4	7	9	11	9	11	13	11	9
E [2]	2	0	0	2	1	2	1	6	1	0
F	6	9	15	7	5	13	20	29	22	35
G	1	4	6	2	4	1	5	8	4	5
H	0	1	0	0	0	0	0	0	2	2
I	3	7	3	5	5	3	4	6	4	8
J	0	1	2	1	0	1	0	0	0	2
K	1	1	0	3	0	4	2	1	2	2
L	8	4	5	5	9	1	2	5	9	5
M	1	0	1	1	0	0	1	0	2	1
N	3	3	0	2	0	0	0	0	1	1
O	0	1	1	2	1	0	1	0	10	2
P	0	0	0	0	0	0	0	0	0	0
Q	0	0	0	0	0	0	0	0	0	0

Men - Hommes - Hombres [1]
ISIC 3 - CITI 3 - CIIU 3

	1999	2000	2001	2002	2003	2004	2005	2006	2007	2008
Total	.	37	37	40	45	36	60	71	67	76
A	.	6	2	4	7	3	10	7	5	4
B	.	0	0	1	0	0	2	0	0	3
C	.	0	0	0	3	1	2	1	0	0
D	.	4	7	8	11	9	11	12	10	8
E	.	0	0	2	1	2	1	6	1	0
F	.	8	15	7	5	12	20	29	22	35
G	.	3	5	2	3	1	5	5	3	4
H	.	0	0	0	0	0	0	0	2	2
I	.	7	1	5	5	3	3	6	4	8
J	.	1	0	0	0	1	0	0	0	2
K	.	1	0	3	0	3	2	1	1	2
L	.	4	5	5	9	1	2	4	8	5
M	.	0	1	1	0	0	1	0	1	1
N	.	2	0	0	0	0	0	0	0	0
O	.	1	1	2	1	0	1	0	10	2
P	.	0	0	0	0	0	0	0	0	0
Q	.	0	0	0	0	0	0	0	0	0

Women - Femmes - Mujeres [1]
ISIC 3 - CITI 3 - CIIU 3

	1999	2000	2001	2002	2003	2004	2005	2006	2007	2008
Total	.	4	5	4	2	2	2	5	6	3
A	.	0	0	0	1	0	1	0	0	0
B	.	0	0	0	0	0	0	0	0	0
C	.	0	0	0	0	0	0	0	0	0
D	.	0	0	1	0	0	0	1	1	1
E	.	0	0	0	0	0	0	0	0	0
F	.	1	0	0	0	1	0	0	0	0
G	.	1	1	0	1	0	0	3	1	1
H	.	1	0	0	0	0	0	0	0	0
I	.	0	2	0	0	0	1	0	0	0
J	.	0	2	1	0	0	0	0	0	0
K	.	0	0	0	0	1	0	0	1	0
L	.	0	0	0	0	0	0	1	1	0
M	.	0	0	0	0	0	0	0	1	0
N	.	1	0	2	0	0	0	0	1	1
O	.	0	0	0	0	0	0	0	0	0
P	.	0	0	0	0	0	0	0	0	0
Q	.	0	0	0	0	0	0	0	0	0

Explanatory notes: see p. 1125.

[1] Deaths occurring within one day of accident. [2] Excl. electricity and gas.

Notes explicatives: voir p. 1127.

[1] Décès survenant pendant le jour qui suit l'accident. [2] Non compris l'électricité et le gaz.

Notas explicativas: véase p. 1129.

[1] Fallecimientos que se producen durante el día posterior al accidente. [2] Excl. electricidad y gas.

OCCUPATIONAL INJURIES
Cases of injury with lost workdays, by economic activity

LÉSIONS PROFESSIONNELLES
Cas de lésion avec perte de journées de travail, par activité économique

LESIONES PROFESIONALES
Casos de lesión con pérdida de días de trabajo, por actividad económica

Croatia (FA) — Compensated injuries - Lésions indemnisées - Lesiones indemnizadas

Non-fatal cases (temporary + permanent incapacity) - Cas non mortels (incapacité temporaire + permanente) - Casos no mortales (incapacidad temporal + permanente)

Total men and women - Total hommes et femmes - Total hombres y mujeres
ISIC 3 - CITI 3 - CIIU 3

	1999	2000	2001	2002	2003	2004	2005	2006	2007	2008
Total	22 782	22 014	21 705	21 140	22 995	21 912	22 676	24 767	24 743	25 183
A	1 129	1 166	1 285	1 129	1 212	1 081	1 053	1 003	895	1 037
B	32	21	16	23	25	33	18	26	20	19
C	155	127	117	86	93	116	115	128	147	123
D[1]	8 409	8 100	7 767	7 464	7 835	7 459	7 406	8 337	7 942	7 757
E[1]	747	732	673	613	652	622	644	576	553	560
F	2 523	2 172	2 087	2 284	2 655	2 725	2 645	3 143	2 924	3 360
G	1 411	1 417	1 632	1 741	2 001	1 962	2 235	2 442	2 567	3 187
H	443	514	560	506	624	665	724	833	799	902
I	2 094	2 149	1 925	1 900	1 867	1 755	1 750	1 766	1 715	1 833
J	315	278	229	242	302	307	333	360	307	324
K	484	529	577	556	655	650	777	937	957	1 077
L	2 503	2 406	2 260	2 047	1 995	1 788	1 907	1 925	1 807	1 609
M	531	492	525	540	709	664	811	810	770	854
N	1 285	1 202	1 251	1 256	1 539	1 414	1 504	1 682	1 674	1 680
O	702	680	752	726	820	667	749	795	763	857
P	13	22	17	9	0	0	1	0	0	1
Q	6	7	32	21	9	4	4	4	1	3

Men - Hommes - Hombres
ISIC 3 - CITI 3 - CIIU 3

	1999	2000	2001	2002	2003	2004	2005	2006	2007	2008
Total		16 618	16 385	15 772	16 775	16 212	16 383	17 934	17 118	17 609
A		1 022	1 116	996	1 056	964	909	860	768	848
B		19	16	22	24	32	18	25	19	13
C		123	116	80	86	113	112	124	143	117
D		6 412	6 304	5 973	6 302	6 115	6 074	6 832	6 443	6 294
E		664	602	556	590	553	574	515	418	507
F		2 094	2 037	2 212	2 598	2 661	2 583	3 068	2 836	3 282
G		859	990	1 082	1 256	1 184	1 350	1 427	1 497	1 757
H		220	245	226	246	297	334	376	369	373
I		1 752	1 559	1 520	1 508	1 483	1 413	1 462	1 393	1 473
J		83	73	64	89	77	79	104	89	85
K		406	429	429	461	447	521	656	667	707
L		1 998	1 878	1 568	1 429	1 303	1 346	1 352	1 297	1 078
M		121	129	131	146	122	177	159	175	165
N		329	319	347	379	383	398	439	471	394
O		495	530	539	599	475	491	533	515	514
P		15	12	8	0	0	1	0	0	0
Q		6	30	19	6	3	3	2	1	2

Women - Femmes - Mujeres
ISIC 3 - CITI 3 - CIIU 3

	1999	2000	2001	2002	2003	2004	2005	2006	2007	2008
Total		5 396	5 320	5 368	6 220	5 700	6 293	6 827	6 723	7 574
A		144	169	133	156	117	144	143	127	189
B		2	0	1	1	1	0	1	1	6
C		4	1	6	7	3	3	4	4	6
D		1 688	1 463	1 491	1 533	1 344	1 332	1 505	1 499	1 463
E		68	71	57	62	69	70	61	58	53
F		78	50	72	57	64	62	75	88	78
G		558	642	659	745	778	885	1 015	1 070	1 430
H		294	315	280	378	368	390	457	430	529
I		397	366	377	359	272	338	304	322	360
J		195	156	178	213	230	254	256	218	239
K		123	148	127	194	203	256	281	290	370
L		408	382	479	566	485	561	574	570	531
M		371	396	409	563	542	634	651	595	689
N		873	932	909	1 160	1 031	1 106	1 243	1 203	1 286
O		185	222	187	221	192	258	262	248	343
P		7	5	1	0	0	0	0	0	1
Q		1	2	2	3	1	1	2	0	1

Explanatory notes: see p. 1125.
[1] Excl. electricity and gas.

Notes explicatives: voir p. 1127.
[1] Non compris l'électricité et le gaz.

Notas explicativas: véase p. 1129.
[1] Excl. electricidad y gas.

OCCUPATIONAL INJURIES

Cases of injury with lost workdays, by economic activity

LÉSIONS PROFESSIONNELLES

Cas de lésion avec perte de journées de travail, par activité économique

LESIONES PROFESIONALES

Casos de lesión con pérdida de días de trabajo, por actividad económica

	1999	2000	2001	2002	2003	2004	2005	2006	2007	2008

Croatia (FA)   Compensated injuries - Lésions indemnisées - Lesiones indemnizadas

Total cases (fatal + non-fatal) - Ensemble des cas (mortels + non mortels) - Todos los casos (mortales + no mortales)

Total men and women - Total hommes et femmes - Total hombres y mujeres
ISIC 3 - CITI 3 - CIIU 3

	1999	2000	2001	2002	2003	2004	2005	2006	2007	2008
Total	22 814	22 055	21 747	21 184	23 042	21 950	22 738	24 843	24 816	25 262
A	1 130	1 172	1 287	1 133	1 220	1 084	1 064	1 010	900	1 041
B	32	21	16	24	25	33	20	26	20	22
C	155	127	117	86	96	117	117	129	147	123
D	8 415	8 104	7 774	7 473	7 846	7 468	7 417	8 350	7 953	7 766
E [1]	749	732	673	615	653	624	645	582	554	560
F	2 529	2 181	2 102	2 291	2 660	2 738	2 665	3 172	2 946	3 395
G	1 412	1 421	1 638	1 743	2 005	1 963	2 240	2 450	2 571	3 192
H	443	515	560	506	624	665	724	833	801	904
I	2 097	2 156	1 928	1 905	1 872	1 758	1 754	1 772	1 719	1 841
J	315	279	231	243	302	308	333	360	307	326
K	485	530	577	559	655	654	779	938	959	1 079
L	2 511	2 410	2 265	2 052	2 004	1 789	1 909	1 930	1 816	1 614
M	532	492	526	541	709	664	812	810	772	855
N	1 288	1 205	1 251	1 258	1 539	1 414	1 504	1 682	1 675	1 681
O	702	681	753	728	821	667	750	795	1 675	859
P	13	22	17	9	0	0	1	0	0	1
Q	6	7	32	21	9	4	4	4	1	3

Men - Hommes - Hombres
ISIC 3 - CITI 3 - CIIU 3

	1999	2000	2001	2002	2003	2004	2005	2006	2007	2008
Total	.	16 655	16 422	15 812	16 820	16 248	16 443	18 005	17 185	17 685
A	.	1 028	1 118	1 000	1 063	967	919	867	773	852
B	.	19	16	23	24	32	20	25	19	16
C	.	123	116	80	89	114	114	125	143	117
D	.	6 416	6 311	5 981	6 313	6 124	6 085	6 844	6 453	6 302
E	.	664	602	558	591	555	575	521	419	507
F	.	2 102	2 052	2 219	2 603	2 673	2 603	3 097	2 858	3 317
G	.	862	995	1 084	1 259	1 185	1 355	1 432	1 500	1 761
H	.	220	245	226	246	297	334	376	371	375
I	.	1 759	1 560	1 525	1 513	1 486	1 416	1 468	1 397	1 481
J	.	84	73	64	89	78	79	104	89	87
K	.	407	429	432	461	450	523	657	668	709
L	.	2 002	1 883	1 573	1 438	1 304	1 348	1 356	1 245	1 083
M	.	121	130	132	146	122	178	159	176	166
N	.	331	319	347	379	383	398	439	471	394
O	.	496	531	541	600	475	492	533	525	516
P	.	15	12	8	0	0	1	0	0	0
Q	.	6	30	19	6	3	3	2	1	2

Women - Femmes - Mujeres
ISIC 3 - CITI 3 - CIIU 3

	1999	2000	2001	2002	2003	2004	2005	2006	2007	2008
Total	.	5 400	5 325	5 372	6 222	5 702	6 295	6 832	6 729	7 577
A	.	144	169	133	157	117	145	143	127	189
B	.	2	0	1	1	1	0	1	1	6
C	.	4	1	6	7	3	3	4	4	6
D	.	1 688	1 463	1 492	1 533	1 344	1 332	1 506	1 500	1 464
E	.	68	71	57	62	69	70	61	58	53
F	.	79	50	72	57	65	62	75	88	78
G	.	559	643	659	746	778	885	1 018	1 071	1 431
H	.	295	315	280	378	368	390	457	430	529
I	.	397	368	377	359	272	339	304	322	360
J	.	195	158	179	213	230	254	256	218	239
K	.	123	148	127	194	204	256	281	291	370
L	.	408	382	479	566	485	561	575	571	531
M	.	371	396	409	563	542	634	651	596	689
N	.	874	932	911	1 160	1 031	1 106	1 243	1 204	1 287
O	.	185	222	187	221	192	258	262	248	343
P	.	7	5	1	0	0	0	0	0	1
Q	.	1	2	2	3	1	1	2	0	1

Explanatory notes: see p. 1125.   Notes explicatives: voir p. 1127.   Notas explicativas: véase p. 1129.

[1] Excl. electricity and gas.   [1] Non compris l'électricité et le gaz.   [1] Excl. electricidad y gas.

	OCCUPATIONAL INJURIES	LÉSIONS PROFESSIONNELLES	LESIONES PROFESIONALES
	Cases of injury with lost workdays, by economic activity	Cas de lésion avec perte de journées de travail, par activité économique	Casos de lesión con pérdida de días de trabajo, por actividad económica

1999	2000	2001	2002	2003	2004	2005	2006	2007	2008

Cyprus (FF) — Reported injuries - Lésions déclarées - Lesiones declaradas

Fatal cases - Cas mortels - Casos mortales

Total men and women - Total hommes et femmes - Total hombres y mujeres
ISIC 3 - CITI 3 - CIIU 3   ISIC 4 - CITI 4 - CIIU 4

	1999	2000	2001	2002	2003	2004	2005	2006	2007	2008	
Total				17	8	14	13	18	15	12	Total
A				0	1	0	0	1	2	1	A
B				0	0	0	0	0	0	0	B
C				0	0	1	0	0	1	4	C
D				5	4	5	2	3	2	0	D
E				0	0	0	0	0	0	0	E
F				6	1	6	6	9	4	5	F
G				3	0	1	3	2	2	1	G
H				1	0	1	1	1	1	1	H
I				0	1	0	0	0	2	0	I
J				0	0	0	0	0	0	0	J
K				0	1	0	0	1	0	0	K
L				2	0	0	1	0	1	0	L
M				0	0	0	0	0	0	0	M
N				0	0	0	0	0	0	0	N
O				0	0	0	0	1	0	0	O
P				0	0	0	0	0	0	0	P
Q				0	0	0	0	0	0	0	Q
										0	R
										0	S
										0	T
										0	U

Men - Hommes - Hombres
ISIC 3 - CITI 3 - CIIU 3   ISIC 4 - CITI 4 - CIIU 4

	1999	2000	2001	2002	2003	2004	2005	2006	2007	2008	
Total				15	8	14	13	18	15	11	Total
A				0	1	0	0	1	2	0	A
B				0	0	0	0	0	0	0	B
C				0	0	1	0	0	1	4	C
D				4	4	5	2	3	2	0	D
E				0	0	0	0	0	0	0	E
F				5	1	6	6	9	4	5	F
G				3	0	1	3	2	2	1	G
H				1	0	1	1	1	1	1	H
I				0	1	0	0	0	2	0	I
J				0	0	0	0	0	0	0	J
K				0	1	0	0	1	0	0	K
L				2	0	0	1	0	1	0	L
M				0	0	0	0	0	0	0	M
N				0	0	0	0	0	0	0	N
O				0	0	0	0	1	0	0	O
P				0	0	0	0	0	0	0	P
Q				0	0	0	0	0	0	0	Q
										0	R
										0	S
										0	T
										0	U

Women - Femmes - Mujeres
ISIC 3 - CITI 3 - CIIU 3   ISIC 4 - CITI 4 - CIIU 4

	1999	2000	2001	2002	2003	2004	2005	2006	2007	2008	
Total				2	0	0	0	0	0	1	Total
A				0	0	0	0	0	0	1	A
B				0	0	0	0	0	0	0	B
C				0	0	0	0	0	0	0	C
D				1	0	0	0	0	0	0	D
E				0	0	0	0	0	0	0	E
F				1	0	0	0	0	0	0	F
G				0	0	0	0	0	0	0	G
H				0	0	0	0	0	0	0	H
I				0	0	0	0	0	0	0	I
J				0	0	0	0	0	0	0	J
K				0	0	0	0	0	0	0	K
L				0	0	0	0	0	0	0	L
M				0	0	0	0	0	0	0	M
N				0	0	0	0	0	0	0	N
O				0	0	0	0	0	0	0	O
P				0	0	0	0	0	0	0	P
Q				0	0	0	0	0	0	0	Q
										0	R
										0	S
										0	T
										0	U

Explanatory notes: see p. 1125.   Notes explicatives: voir p. 1127.   Notas explicativas: véase p. 1129.

OCCUPATIONAL INJURIES
Cases of injury with lost workdays, by economic activity

LÉSIONS PROFESSIONNELLES
Cas de lésion avec perte de journées de travail, par activité économique

LESIONES PROFESIONALES
Casos de lesión con pérdida de días de trabajo, por actividad económica

Cyprus (FF) — Reported injuries - Lésions déclarées - Lesiones declaradas

Non-fatal cases (temporary + permanent incapacity) - Cas non mortels (incapacité temporaire + permanente) - Casos no mortales (incapacidad temporal + permanente)

Total men and women - Total hommes et femmes - Total hombres y mujeres
ISIC 3 - CITI 3 - CIIU 3 [1] / ISIC 4 - CITI 4 - CIIU 4

	1999	2000	2001	2002	2003	2004	2005	2006	2007	2008	
Total	.	.	.	1 653	2 078	2 158	2 162	2 089	2 090	2 355	Total
A	.	.	.	28	52	52	54	43	44	49	A
B	.	.	.	0	2	1	2	3	3	17	B
C	.	.	.	16	11	20	11	11	12	546	C
D	.	.	.	507	656	633	605	522	519	13	D
E	.	.	.	20	19	28	28	18	24	41	E
F	.	.	.	471	553	592	573	534	559	644	F
G	.	.	.	165	221	272	289	287	274	299	G
H	.	.	.	219	306	256	261	331	327	113	H
I	.	.	.	69	76	100	111	94	112	333	I
J	.	.	.	0	10	11	17	22	21	14	J
K	.	.	.	22	33	35	38	22	30	23	K
L	.	.	.	71	71	77	104	105	80	7	L
M	.	.	.	5	9	6	14	10	14	19	M
N	.	.	.	10	12	10	10	26	31	26	N
O	.	.	.	50	46	65	45	60	40	112	O
P	.	.	.	0	0	0	0	1	0	15	P
Q	.	.	.	0	1	0	0	0	0	33	Q
R										19	R
S										16	S
T										14	T
U										2	U

Men - Hommes - Hombres
ISIC 3 - CITI 3 - CIIU 3 [1] / ISIC 4 - CITI 4 - CIIU 4

	1999	2000	2001	2002	2003	2004	2005	2006	2007	2008	
Total	.	.	.	1 421	1 729	1 826	1 777	1 681	1 655	1 889	Total
A	.	.	.	24	47	45	45	33	35	44	A
B	.	.	.	0	2	1	2	3	3	17	B
C	.	.	.	16	11	20	11	11	12	464	C
D	.	.	.	449	568	555	524	448	451	12	D
E	.	.	.	19	18	27	26	17	24	40	E
F	.	.	.	466	548	586	563	525	550	634	F
G	.	.	.	141	178	213	227	222	189	208	G
H	.	.	.	120	158	134	137	178	169	97	H
I	.	.	.	59	68	88	96	81	88	172	I
J	.	.	.	0	8	6	9	8	7	11	J
K	.	.	.	19	24	25	22	15	19	14	K
L	.	.	.	61	56	64	77	89	66	5	L
M	.	.	.	1	3	2	1	1	4	9	M
N	.	.	.	2	2	4	3	5	7	15	N
O	.	.	.	44	38	56	34	41	31	101	O
P	.	.	.	0	0	0	0	1	0	6	P
Q	.	.	.	0	0	0	0	0	0	11	Q
R										17	R
S										10	S
T										1	T
U										1	U

Women - Femmes - Mujeres
ISIC 3 - CITI 3 - CIIU 3 [1] / ISIC 4 - CITI 4 - CIIU 4

	1999	2000	2001	2002	2003	2004	2005	2006	2007	2008	
Total	.	.	.	232	349	332	385	408	435	466	Total
A	.	.	.	4	5	7	9	10	9	5	A
B	.	.	.	0	0	0	0	0	0	0	B
C	.	.	.	0	0	0	0	0	0	82	C
D	.	.	.	58	88	78	81	71	68	1	D
E	.	.	.	1	1	1	2	1	0	1	E
F	.	.	.	5	5	6	10	9	9	10	F
G	.	.	.	24	43	59	62	65	85	91	G
H	.	.	.	99	148	122	124	153	158	16	H
I	.	.	.	10	8	12	15	13	24	161	I
J	.	.	.	0	2	5	8	14	14	3	J
K	.	.	.	3	9	10	16	7	11	9	K
L	.	.	.	10	15	13	27	16	14	2	L
M	.	.	.	4	6	4	13	9	10	10	M
N	.	.	.	8	10	6	7	21	24	11	N
O	.	.	.	6	8	9	11	19	9	11	O
P	.	.	.	0	0	0	0	0	0	9	P
Q	.	.	.	0	1	0	0	0	0	22	Q
R										2	R
S										6	S
T										13	T
U										1	U

Explanatory notes: see p. 1125. Notes explicatives: voir p. 1127. Notas explicativas: véase p. 1129.

[1] Incapacity of 4 days or more. [1] Incapacité de 4 jours et plus. [1] Incapacidad de 4 días y más.

OCCUPATIONAL INJURIES

Cases of injury with lost workdays, by economic activity

LÉSIONS PROFESSIONNELLES

Cas de lésion avec perte de journées de travail, par activité économique

LESIONES PROFESIONALES

Casos de lesión con pérdida de días de trabajo, por actividad económica

	1999	2000	2001	2002	2003	2004	2005	2006	2007	2008

Cyprus (FF)

Reported injuries - Lésions déclarées - Lesiones declaradas

Total cases (fatal + non-fatal) - Ensemble des cas (mortels + non mortels) - Todos los casos (mortales + no mortales)

Total men and women - Total hommes et femmes - Total hombres y mujeres
ISIC 3 - CITI 3 - CIIU 3

	1999	2000	2001	2002	2003	2004	2005	2006	2007	2008
Total	.	.	.	1 670	2 086	2 172	2 175	2 107	2 105	.
A	.	.	.	28	53	52	54	44	46	.
B	.	.	.	0	2	1	2	3	3	.
C	.	.	.	16	11	21	11	11	13	.
D	.	.	.	512	660	638	607	525	521	.
E	.	.	.	20	19	28	28	18	24	.
F	.	.	.	477	554	598	579	543	563	.
G	.	.	.	168	221	273	292	289	276	.
H	.	.	.	220	306	257	262	332	328	.
I	.	.	.	69	77	100	111	94	114	.
J	.	.	.	0	10	11	17	22	21	.
K	.	.	.	22	34	35	38	23	30	.
L	.	.	.	73	71	77	105	105	81	.
M	.	.	.	5	9	6	14	10	14	.
N	.	.	.	10	12	10	10	26	31	.
O	.	.	.	50	46	65	45	61	40	.
P	.	.	.	0	0	0	0	1	0	.
Q	.	.	.	0	1	0	0	0	0	.

Men - Hommes - Hombres
ISIC 3 - CITI 3 - CIIU 3

	1999	2000	2001	2002	2003	2004	2005	2006	2007	2008
Total	.	.	.	1 436	1 737	1 840	1 790	1 699	1 670	.
A	.	.	.	24	48	45	45	34	37	.
B	.	.	.	0	2	1	2	3	3	.
C	.	.	.	16	11	21	11	11	13	.
D	.	.	.	453	572	560	526	451	453	.
E	.	.	.	19	18	27	26	17	24	.
F	.	.	.	471	549	592	569	534	554	.
G	.	.	.	144	178	214	230	224	191	.
H	.	.	.	121	158	135	138	179	170	.
I	.	.	.	59	69	88	96	81	90	.
J	.	.	.	0	8	6	9	8	7	.
K	.	.	.	19	25	25	22	16	19	.
L	.	.	.	63	56	64	78	89	67	.
M	.	.	.	1	3	2	1	1	4	.
N	.	.	.	2	2	4	3	5	7	.
O	.	.	.	44	38	56	34	42	31	.
P	.	.	.	0	0	0	0	1	0	.
Q	.	.	.	0	0	0	0	0	0	.

Women - Femmes - Mujeres
ISIC 3 - CITI 3 - CIIU 3

	1999	2000	2001	2002	2003	2004	2005	2006	2007	2008
Total	.	.	.	234	349	332	385	408	435	.
A	.	.	.	4	5	7	9	10	9	.
B	.	.	.	0	0	0	0	0	0	.
C	.	.	.	0	0	0	0	0	0	.
D	.	.	.	59	88	78	81	71	68	.
E	.	.	.	1	1	1	2	1	0	.
F	.	.	.	6	5	6	10	1	0	.
G	.	.	.	24	43	59	62	9	9	.
H	.	.	.	99	148	122	124	65	85	.
I	.	.	.	10	8	12	15	153	158	.
J	.	.	.	0	2	5	8	13	24	.
K	.	.	.	3	9	10	16	14	14	.
L	.	.	.	10	15	13	27	7	11	.
M	.	.	.	4	6	4	13	16	14	.
N	.	.	.	8	10	6	7	9	10	.
O	.	.	.	6	8	9	11	21	24	.
P	.	.	.	0	0	0	0	19	9	.
Q	.	.	.	0	1	0	0	0	0	.

Explanatory notes: see p. 1125.

Notes explicatives: voir p. 1127.

Notas explicativas: véase p. 1129.

OCCUPATIONAL INJURIES
Cases of injury with lost workdays, by economic activity

LÉSIONS PROFESSIONNELLES
Cas de lésion avec perte de journées de travail, par activité économique

LESIONES PROFESIONALES
Casos de lesión con pérdida de días de trabajo, por actividad económica

Reported injuries - Lésions déclarées - Lesiones declaradas

Czech Republic (FD)

Fatal cases - Cas mortels - Casos mortales

Total men and women - Total hommes et femmes - Total hombres y mujeres
ISIC 3 - CITI 3 - CIIU 3

	1999	2000	2001	2002	2003	2004	2005	2006	2007	2008
Total	191	223	231	206	199	185	163	152	188	174
A-B	.	21	.	.	.	.	.	.	.	.
A	13	.	14	22	19	19	18	12	18	15
B	0	.	0	0	0	0	0	2	0	0
C	8	.	14	11	15	19	6	3	6	5
C-D	.	66	.	.	.	.	.	.	.	.
D	35	.	58	53	42	28	48	29	48	49
E	9	4	7	4	5	14	1	1	1	1
F	26	46	52	46	51	36	34	44	54	46
G	5	14	22	13	16	15	16	13	9	13
H	0	1	2	1	1	1	0	2	0	0
I	14	43	34	32	25	24	21	27	34	25
J	2	.	2	2	3	1	0	0	0	3
J-K	.	17	.	.	.	.	.	.	.	.
K	4	.	13	9	10	16	8	9	9	6
L	7	7	1	3	2	2	1	3	1	4
M	1	1	2	3	3	4	2	2	0	0
N	4	2	4	3	3	1	3	0	2	0
O	3	1	3	5	3	5	5	5	6	7
X	60	0	3	0	1	0	0	0	0	0

Men - Hommes - Hombres
ISIC 3 - CITI 3 - CIIU 3

	1999	2000	2001	2002	2003	2004	2005	2006	2007	2008
Total	182	216	222	197	189	176	150	148	177	166
A-B	.	21	.	.	.	.	.	.	.	.
A	12	.	14	21	19	18	17	12	16	15
B	0	.	0	0	0	0	0	2	0	0
C	8	.	13	11	15	19	6	3	6	5
C-D	.	64	.	.	.	.	.	.	.	.
D	35	.	58	51	41	27	45	29	44	49
E	8	4	7	2	5	14	1	1	1	1
F	25	45	52	46	51	36	34	44	54	45
G	5	14	20	13	13	14	11	13	8	13
H	0	1	1	1	1	0	0	2	0	0
I	13	42	34	32	25	23	20	27	32	20
J	1	.	1	1	1	2	1	0	0	1
J-K	.	15	.	.	.	.	.	.	.	.
K	4	.	11	9	8	16	7	8	8	6
L	7	7	1	3	2	2	0	2	1	4
M	1	1	1	2	2	1	1	1	0	0
N	1	1	3	3	2	1	2	0	2	0
O	3	1	3	3	3	5	5	4	5	7
X	59	0	3	0	1	0	0	0	0	0

Women - Femmes - Mujeres
ISIC 3 - CITI 3 - CIIU 3

	1999	2000	2001	2002	2003	2004	2005	2006	2007	2008
Total	9	7	9	9	10	9	13	4	11	8
A-B	.	0	.	.	.	.	.	.	.	.
A	1	.	0	1	0	0	1	0	2	0
B	0	.	0	0	0	0	0	0	0	0
C	0	.	1	0	0	0	0	0	0	0
C-D	.	2	.	.	.	.	.	.	.	.
D	0	.	0	2	1	1	3	0	4	0
E	1	0	0	2	0	0	0	0	0	0
F	1	1	0	0	0	1	5	0	1	0
G	0	0	2	0	3	1	0	0	0	0
H	0	0	1	0	0	1	1	0	2	5
I	1	1	0	0	0	0	0	0	0	2
J	1	.	1	1	1	.	.	.	.	.
J-K	.	2	.	.	.	.	.	.	.	.
K	0	.	2	0	2	0	1	1	0	0
L	0	0	1	0	1	2	0	1	0	0
M	0	0	1	0	1	1	1	0	0	0
N	3	1	1	1	1	0	0	1	1	0
O	0	0	0	2	0	0	0	0	0	0
X	1	0	.	0	0	.	.	.	.	.

Explanatory notes: see p. 1125.

Notes explicatives: voir p. 1127.

Notas explicativas: véase p. 1129.

OCCUPATIONAL INJURIES

Cases of injury with lost workdays, by economic activity

LÉSIONS PROFESSIONNELLES

Cas de lésion avec perte de journées de travail, par activité économique

LESIONES PROFESIONALES

Casos de lesión con pérdida de días de trabajo, por actividad económica

Czech Republic (FD) — Reported injuries - Lésions déclarées - Lesiones declaradas

Non-fatal cases (temporary + permanent incapacity) - Cas non mortels (incapacité temporaire + permanente) - Casos no mortales (incapacidad temporal + permanente)

Total men and women - Total hommes et femmes - Total hombres y mujeres
ISIC 3 - CITI 3 - CIIU 3

	1999	2000	2001	2002	2003	2004	2005	2006	2007	2008
Total	95 780	92 683	93 049	90 867	83 019	81 688	82 042	82 296	77 233	71 281
A-B		7 516								
A	8 341		7 278	6 971	6 194	5 746	5 360	5 025	4 392	4 270
B	47		47	41	48	40	59	47	24	43
C	2 453		1 764	1 715	1 465	1 543	1 420	901	857	762
C-D		39 050								
D	37 423		38 252	36 663	33 758	33 561	33 699	33 269	33 009	32 764
E	937	869	867	838	779	680	683	622	484	384
F	7 734	6 825	6 100	5 545	5 183	5 045	4 875	4 791	4 375	5 537
G	5 537	5 238	5 237	5 459	5 012	5 064	5 459	6 034	5 712	7 523
H	996	1 028	956	841	827	819	813	873	910	1 803
I	5 870	5 297	5 438	5 470	5 321	5 289	5 695	6 193	5 473	5 980
J	250		226	247	188	142	143	151	124	197
J-K		2 397								
K	2 200		2 481	2 904	2 456	2 413	2 934	3 158	2 905	3 895
L	3 176	3 026	2 695	2 515	1 919	1 794	1 779	1 887	1 642	1 944
M	1 040	1 089	1 272	1 329	1 527	1 548	1 464	1 550	1 383	1 768
N	2 256	2 166	2 330	2 464	2 274	2 330	2 453	2 509	2 277	2 419
O	1 399	1 408	1 437	1 525	1 459	1 531	1 654	1 596	1 499	1 917
X	16 121	16 774	16 669	16 340	14 609	14 143	13 552	13 690	12 167	75

Men - Hommes - Hombres
ISIC 3 - CITI 3 - CIIU 3

	1999	2000	2001	2002	2003	2004	2005	2006	2007	2008
Total	74 282	72 081	70 844	68 567	62 284	60 859	60.869	60 990	57 311	52 289
A-B		5 547								
A	6 130		5 331	5 024	4 436	4 104	3 801	3 571	3 088	2 999
B	39		41	36	43	34	56	42	20	37
C	2 376		1 700	1 667	1 419	1 494	1 380	864	823	734
C-D		31 114								
D	29 223		29 530	28 190	25 985	25 723	25 845	25 590	25 452	25 317
E	822	778	762	736	694	608	602	551	427	342
F	7 549	6 683	5 831	5 335	4 991	4 796	4 598	4 524	4 148	5 168
G	3 847	3 536	3 383	3 425	2 980	3 003	3 128	3 505	3 234	4 700
H	638	594	568	427	406	396	409	448	465	1 224
I	4 455	4 003	4 038	4 151	3 849	3 801	4 142	4 491	4 101	4 478
J	76		102	112	53	43	48	58	40	94
J-K		1 688								
K	1 609		1 745	1 995	1 743	1 657	2 053	2 221	1 927	2 733
L	1 963	1 918	1 548	1 473	1 327	1 220	1 214	1 274	1 164	1 360
M	354	384	464	533	391	433	376	416	366	722
N	665	680	736	756	670	663	711	767	686	803
O	1 128	1 122	1 138	1 233	1 130	1 184	1 313	1 271	1 185	1 518
X	13 408	14 034	13 927	13 474	12 167	11 700	11 193	11 397	10 185	60

Women - Femmes - Mujeres
ISIC 3 - CITI 3 - CIIU 3

	1999	2000	2001	2002	2003	2004	2005	2006	2007	2008
Total	21 498	20 602	22 205	22 300	20 735	20 829	21 173	21 306	19 922	18 992
A-B		1 969								
A	2 211		1 947	1 947	1 758	1 642	1 559	1 454	1 304	1 271
B	8		6	5	5	6	3	5	4	6
C	77		64	48	46	49	40	37	34	28
C-D		7 936								
D	8 200		8 722	8 473	7 773	7 838	7 854	7 679	7 557	7 447
E	115	91	105	102	85	72	81	71	57	42
F	185	142	269	210	192	249	277	267	227	369
G	1 690	1 702	1 854	2 034	2 032	2 061	2 331	2 529	2 478	2 823
H	358	434	388	414	421	423	404	425	445	579
I	1 415	1 294	1 400	1 319	1 472	1 488	1 553	1 702	1 372	1 502
J	174		124	135	135	99	95	93	84	103
J-K		709								
K	591		736	909	713	756	881	937	978	1 162
L	1 213	1 108	1 147	1 042	592	574	565	613	478	584
M	686	705	808	796	1 136	1 115	1 088	1 134	1 017	1 046
N	1 591	1 486	1 594	1 708	1 604	1 667	1 742	1 742	1 591	1 616
O	271	286	299	292	329	347	341	325	314	399
X	2 713	2 740	2 742	2 866	2 442	2 443	2 359	2 293	1 982	15

Explanatory notes: see p. 1125.　　　Notes explicatives: voir p. 1127.　　　Notas explicativas: véase p. 1129.

OCCUPATIONAL INJURIES
Cases of injury with lost workdays, by economic activity

LÉSIONS PROFESSIONNELLES
Cas de lésion avec perte de journées de travail, par activité économique

LESIONES PROFESIONALES
Casos de lesión con pérdida de días de trabajo, por actividad económica

	1999	2000	2001	2002	2003	2004	2005	2006	2007	2008

Czech Republic (FD)   Reported injuries - Lésions déclarées - Lesiones declaradas

Total cases (fatal + non-fatal) - Ensemble des cas (mortels + non mortels) - Todos los casos (mortales + no mortales)

Total men and women - Total hommes et femmes - Total hombres y mujeres
ISIC 3 - CITI 3 - CIIU 3

	1999	2000	2001	2002	2003	2004	2005	2006	2007	2008
Total	95 971	92 906	93 280	91 073	83 218	81 873	82 205	82 448	77 421	71 455
A-B	.	7 537	.	.	.	.	.	.	.	.
A	8 354	.	7 292	6 993	6 213	5 765	5 378	5 037	4 410	4 285
B	47	.	47	41	48	40	59	49	24	43
C	2 461	.	1 778	1 726	1 480	1 562	1 426	904	863	767
C-D	.	39 116	.	.	.	.	.	.	.	.
D	37 458	.	38 310	36 716	33 800	33 589	33 747	33 298	33 057	32 813
E	946	873	874	842	784	694	684	623	485	385
F	7 760	6 871	6 152	5 591	5 234	5 081	4 909	4 835	4 429	5 583
G	5 542	5 252	5 259	5 472	5 028	5 079	5 475	6 047	5 721	7 536
H	996	1 029	958	842	828	820	813	875	910	1 803
I	5 884	5 340	5 472	5 502	5 346	5 313	5 716	6 220	5 507	6 005
J	252	.	228	249	191	143	143	151	124	200
J-K	.	2 414	.	.	.	.	.	.	.	.
K	2 204	.	2 494	2 913	2 466	2 429	2 942	3 167	2 914	3 901
L	3 183	3 033	2 696	2 518	1 921	1 796	1 780	1 890	1 643	1 948
M	1 041	1 090	1 274	1 331	1 530	1 552	1 466	1 552	1 383	1 768
N	2 260	2 168	2 334	2 467	2 277	2 331	2 456	2 509	2 279	2 419
O	1 402	1 409	1 440	1 530	1 462	1 536	1 659	1 601	1 505	1 924
X	16 181	16 774	16 672	16 340	14 610	14 143	13 552	13 690	12 167	75

Men - Hommes - Hombres
ISIC 3 - CITI 3 - CIIU 3

	1999	2000	2001	2002	2003	2004	2005	2006	2007	2008
Total	74 464	72 297	71 066	68 764	62 473	61 035	61 019	61 138	57 488	52 455
A-B	.	5 568	.	.	.	.	.	.	.	.
A	6 142	.	5 345	5 045	4 455	4 122	3 818	3 583	3 104	3 014
B	39	.	41	36	43	34	56	44	20	37
C	2 384	.	1 713	1 678	1 434	1 513	1 386	867	829	739
C-D	.	31 178	.	.	.	.	.	.	.	.
D	29 258	.	29 588	28 241	26 026	25 750	25 890	25 619	25 496	25 366
E	830	782	769	738	699	622	603	552	428	343
F	7 574	6 728	5 883	5 381	5 042	4 832	4 632	4 568	4 202	5 213
G	3 852	3 550	3 403	3 438	2 993	3 017	3 139	3 518	3 242	4 713
H	638	595	569	428	407	396	409	450	465	1 224
I	4 468	4 045	4 072	4 183	3 874	3 824	4 162	4 518	4 133	4 498
J	77	.	103	113	55	44	48	58	40	95
J-K	.	1 703	.	.	.	.	.	.	.	.
K	1 613	.	1 756	2 004	1 751	1 673	2 060	2 229	1 935	2 739
L	1 970	1 925	1 549	1 476	1 328	1 220	1 215	1 276	1 165	1 364
M	355	385	465	535	393	435	377	417	366	722
N	666	681	739	758	672	664	713	767	688	803
O	1 131	1 123	1 141	1 236	1 133	1 189	1 318	1 275	1 190	1 525
X	13 467	14 034	13 930	13 474	12 168	11 700	11 193	11 397	10 185	60

Women - Femmes - Mujeres
ISIC 3 - CITI 3 - CIIU 3

	1999	2000	2001	2002	2003	2004	2005	2006	2007	2008
Total	21 507	20 609	22 214	22 309	20 745	20 838	21 186	21 310	19 933	19 000
A-B	.	1 969	.	.	.	.	.	.	.	.
A	2 212	.	1 947	1 948	1 758	1 643	1 560	1 454	1 306	1 271
B	8	.	6	5	5	6	3	5	4	6
C	77	.	65	48	46	49	40	37	34	28
C-D	.	7 938	.	.	.	.	.	.	.	.
D	8 200	.	8 722	8 475	7 774	7 839	7 857	7 679	7 561	7 447
E	116	91	105	104	85	72	81	71	57	42
F	186	143	269	210	192	249	277	267	227	370
G	1 690	1 702	1 856	2 034	2 035	2 062	2 336	2 529	2 479	2 823
H	358	434	389	414	421	424	404	425	445	579
I	1 416	1 295	1 400	1 319	1 472	1 489	1 554	1 702	1 374	1 507
J	175	.	125	136	136	99	95	93	84	105
J-K	.	711	.	.	.	.	.	.	.	.
K	591	.	738	909	715	756	882	938	979	1 162
L	1 213	1 108	1 147	1 042	593	576	565	614	478	584
M	686	705	809	796	1 137	1 117	1 089	1 135	1 017	1 046
N	1 594	1 487	1 595	1 709	1 605	1 667	1 743	1 742	1 591	1 616
O	271	286	299	294	329	347	341	326	315	399
X	2 714	2 740	2 742	2 866	2 442	2 443	2 359	2 293	1 982	15

Explanatory notes: see p. 1125.   Notes explicatives: voir p. 1127.   Notas explicativas: véase p. 1129.

8A

OCCUPATIONAL INJURIES	LÉSIONS PROFESSIONNELLES	LESIONES PROFESIONALES
Cases of injury with lost workdays, by economic activity	Cas de lésion avec perte de journées de travail, par activité économique	Casos de lesión con pérdida de días de trabajo, por actividad económica

España (FA) — Reported injuries - Lésions déclarées - Lesiones declaradas

Fatal cases - Cas mortels - Casos mortales

Total men and women - Total hommes et femmes - Total hombres y mujeres [1]
ISIC 3 - CITI 3 - CIIU 3

	1999	2000	2001	2002	2003	2004	2005	2006	2007	2008
Total	1 104	1 136	1 030	805	722	695	662	682	572	530
A	85	66	74	42	28	34	40	29	42	34
B	47	53	36	19	16	20	8	18	22	16
C	29	29	21	16	24	18	14	17	12	13
D	209	198	188	136	113	121	112	122	84	84
E	6	9	7	3	10	11	4	17	6	5
F	294	292	269	246	247	217	248	235	219	183
G	93	97	86	88	59	50	52	49	28	39
H	23	19	13	6	8	6	5	2	8	4
I	180	202	177	162	126	156	127	123	103	89
J	8	6	11	2	4	1	1	3	0	2
K	46	53	49	30	40	23	19	33	23	31
L,Q	28	49	49	26	24	19	13	13	8	10
M	8	9	8	1	1	1	3	2	3	2
N	20	23	10	9	10	4	1	5	3	0
O	22	25	28	19	12	13	15	14	11	18
P	6	6	4	0	0	1	0	0	0	0

Men - Hommes - Hombres [1]
ISIC 3 - CITI 3 - CIIU 3

	1999	2000	2001	2002	2003	2004	2005	2006	2007	2008
Total	1 078	1 102	1 003	785	692	671	647	660	550	513
A	83	63	71	40	27	31	39	27	39	34
B	47	53	36	19	16	20	7	18	20	16
C	29	29	21	16	24	18	14	17	12	13
D	206	190	184	133	109	116	108	119	81	83
E	6	9	7	3	10	11	4	17	6	5
F	293	291	268	246	242	216	248	234	216	182
G	90	92	80	85	53	47	50	45	24	37
H	21	14	10	6	6	4	5	2	7	4
I	176	201	177	159	125	152	124	118	101	83
J	8	5	10	2	3	1	1	3	0	2
K	43	49	46	28	37	21	18	29	21	28
L,Q	27	48	47	24	21	17	11	12	8	9
M	7	8	8	1	1	1	2	2	2	1
N	16	19	9	5	6	3	1	4	2	0
O	21	25	25	18	12	12	15	13	11	16
P	5	6	4	0	0	1	0	0	0	0

Women - Femmes - Mujeres [1]
ISIC 3 - CITI 3 - CIIU 3

	1999	2000	2001	2002	2003	2004	2005	2006	2007	2008
Total	26	34	27	20	30	24	15	22	22	17
A	2	3	3	2	1	3	1	2	3	0
B	0	0	0	0	0	0	1	0	2	0
C	0	0	0	0	0	0	0	0	0	0
D	3	8	4	3	4	5	4	3	3	1
E	0	0	0	0	0	0	0	0	0	0
F	1	1	1	0	5	1	0	1	3	1
G	3	5	6	3	6	3	2	4	4	2
H	2	5	3	0	2	2	0	0	1	0
I	4	1	0	3	1	4	3	5	2	6
J	0	1	1	0	1	0	0	0	0	0
K	3	4	3	2	3	2	1	4	2	3
L,Q	1	1	2	2	3	2	2	1	0	1
M	1	1	0	0	0	0	1	0	1	1
N	4	4	1	4	4	1	0	1	1	0
O	1	0	3	1	0	1	0	1	0	2
P	1	0	0	0	0	0	0	0	0	0

Explanatory notes: see p. 1125.
[1] Deaths occurring within one month of accident.

Notes explicatives: voir p. 1127.
[1] Les décès survenant pendant le mois qui suit l'accident.

Notas explicativas: véase p. 1129.
[1] Los fallecimientos que se produzcan durante el mes posterior al accidente.

OCCUPATIONAL INJURIES

Cases of injury with lost workdays, by economic activity

LÉSIONS PROFESSIONNELLES

Cas de lésion avec perte de journées de travail, par activité économique

LESIONES PROFESIONALES

Casos de lesión con pérdida de días de trabajo, por actividad económica

	1999	2000	2001	2002	2003	2004	2005	2006	2007	2008

España (FA) — Reported injuries - Lésions déclarées - Lesiones declaradas

Non-fatal cases (temporary + permanent incapacity) - Cas non mortels (incapacité temporaire + permanente) - Casos no mortales (incapacidad temporal + permanente)

Total men and women - Total hommes et femmes - Total hombres y mujeres
ISIC 3 - CITI 3 - CIIU 3

	1999	2000	2001	2002	2003	2004	2005	2006	2007	2008
Total	868 057	931 796	945 570	935 198	872 610	869 583	888 987	909 675	922 951	802 778
A	41 895	38 266	34 413	32 758	30 611	30 842	30 506	30 266	30 850	29 662
B	5 612	4 985	4 573	4 484	3 998	4 070	3 664	3 570	3 496	3 222
C	15 818	15 405	14 278	12 555	11 932	10 719	9 321	8 595	8 258	6 937
D	244 346	253 640	247 903	236 011	221 943	229 060	227 865	230 872	231 889	199 333
E	3 511	3 505	3 421	3 354	3 637	4 513	4 743	4 481	4 506	4 062
F	215 751	238 952	250 008	249 820	230 258	223 600	238 023	249 860	249 812	186 153
G	108 982	121 964	124 273	125 884	118 533	117 004	118 736	119 151	120 468	109 360
H	47 117	52 673	53 224	51 541	48 553	50 040	51 033	52 452	53 404	51 103
I	42 976	48 611	49 007	48 964	49 397	53 482	55 424	57 399	59 570	53 543
J	1 977	2 105	2 155	2 131	2 140	2 177	2 207	2 231	2 055	2 083
K	62 663	67 696	71 064	73 375	54 179	39 507	40 098	41 705	44 028	40 689
L,Q	34 223	35 047	36 532	36 874	36 977	37 374	38 142	37 689	37 693	37 440
M	5 216	5 482	5 816	5 782	6 597	6 748	6 902	7 363	7 616	8 131
N	20 453	22 859	26 401	27 785	28 624	29 376	31 026	31 629	34 758	36 540
O	16 541	19 554	21 413	22 900	24 629	30 181	30 544	31 566	33 316	33 264
P	976	1 052	1 089	980	602	890	753	846	1 232	1 256

Men - Hommes - Hombres
ISIC 3 - CITI 3 - CIIU 3

	1999	2000	2001	2002	2003	2004	2005	2006	2007	2008
Total	724 174	767 242	770 488	762 262	695 397	691 893	708 965	721 682	721 660	608 866
A	33 035	30 024	26 968	25 959	23 525	23 887	23 917	23 255	23 291	22 532
B	5 348	4 668	4 270	4 189	3 714	3 776	3 460	3 358	3 211	2 962
C	15 238	14 914	13 946	12 246	11 388	10 356	8 978	8 263	7 948	6 676
D	217 599	223 145	217 144	206 625	191 647	196 458	196 904	198 163	196 771	169 612
E	3 392	3 350	3 288	3 223	3 423	4 303	4 520	4 271	4 326	3 843
F	211 344	233 417	244 959	244 714	225 566	220 976	235 416	246 899	246 918	183 685
G	82 161	89 735	89 913	90 845	82 306	80 937	81 802	81 250	80 980	71 782
H	26 650	28 947	27 976	27 656	23 902	23 930	23 854	23 829	23 423	22 139
I	39 372	44 157	44 348	44 274	43 646	47 111	48 266	49 605	50 755	44 855
J	1 263	1 284	1 323	1 307	1 074	1 015	973	987	897	867
K	39 768	41 262	41 881	44 655	31 604	23 759	24 356	25 468	26 290	23 677
L,Q	26 036	26 423	26 870	27 296	26 213	26 370	27 065	26 452	25 918	25 453
M	2 666	2 722	2 817	2 827	2 588	2 428	2 308	2 379	2 449	2 402
N	6 933	7 775	8 363	9 493	7 780	7 401	7 693	7 500	7 623	7 962
O	12 603	14 608	15 578	16 212	16 576	18 684	19 000	19 534	20 174	19 695
P	766	811	844	741	445	502	453	469	686	724

Women - Femmes - Mujeres
ISIC 3 - CITI 3 - CIIU 3

	1999	2000	2001	2002	2003	2004	2005	2006	2007	2008
Total	143 883	164 554	175 082	172 936	177 213	177 690	180 022	187 993	201 291	193 912
A	8 860	8 242	7 445	6 799	7 086	6 955	6 589	7 011	7 559	7 130
B	264	317	303	295	284	294	204	212	285	260
C	580	491	332	309	544	363	343	332	310	261
D	26 747	30 495	30 759	29 386	30 296	32 602	30 961	32 709	35 118	29 721
E	119	155	133	131	214	210	223	210	180	219
F	4 407	5 535	5 049	5 106	4 692	2 624	2 607	2 961	2 894	2 468
G	26 821	32 229	34 360	35 039	36 227	36 067	36 934	37 901	39 488	37 578
H	20 467	23 726	25 248	23 885	24 651	26 110	27 179	28 623	29 981	28 964
I	3 604	4 454	4 659	4 690	5 751	6 371	7 158	7 794	8 815	8 688
J	714	821	832	824	1 066	1 162	1 234	1 244	1 158	1 216
K	22 895	26 434	29 183	28 720	22 575	15 748	15 742	16 237	17 738	17 012
L,Q	8 187	8 624	9 662	9 578	10 764	11 004	11 077	11 237	11 775	11 987
M	2 550	2 760	2 999	2 955	4 009	4 320	4 594	4 984	5 167	5 729
N	13 520	15 084	18 038	18 292	20 844	21 975	23 333	24 129	27 135	28 578
O	3 938	4 946	5 835	6 688	8 053	11 497	11 544	12 032	13 142	13 569
P	210	241	245	239	157	388	300	377	546	532

Cases of temporary incapacity - Cas d'incapacité temporaire - Casos de incapacidad temporal

Total men and women - Total hommes et femmes - Total hombres y mujeres
ISIC 3 - CITI 3 - CIIU 3

	1999	2000	2001	2002	2003	2004	2005	2006	2007	2008
Total	863 671	927 079	938 320	918 141	870 659	867 192	886 500	907 849	920 495	.
A	41 717	38 018	33 946	31 875	.	.	.	.	.	.
B	5 577	4 947	4 532	4 452	.	.	.	.	.	.
C	15 752	15 338	14 187	12 423	.	.	.	.	.	.
D	242 746	252 156	245 998	232 317	.	.	.	.	.	.
E	3 499	3 475	3 379	3 218	.	.	.	.	.	.
F	214 578	237 645	248 023	244 948	.	.	.	.	.	.
G	108 588	121 483	123 424	123 485	.	.	.	.	.	.
H	46 974	52 502	52 903	50 657	.	.	.	.	.	.
I	42 752	48 337	48 460	47 670	.	.	.	.	.	.
J	1 963	2 100	2 136	2 073	.	.	.	.	.	.
K	62 411	67 447	70 592	72 140	.	.	.	.	.	.
L,Q	34 089	34 854	36 310	36 260	.	.	.	.	.	.
M	5 201	5 457	5 772	5 632	.	.	.	.	.	.
N	20 397	22 780	26 285	27 466	.	.	.	.	.	.
O	16 461	19 494	21 290	22 566	.	.	.	.	.	.
P	966	1 046	1 083	959	.	.	.	.	.	.

Explanatory notes: see p. 1125.   Notes explicatives: voir p. 1127.   Notas explicativas: véase p. 1129.

OCCUPATIONAL INJURIES	LÉSIONS PROFESSIONNELLES	LESIONES PROFESIONALES
Cases of injury with lost workdays, by economic activity	Cas de lésion avec perte de journées de travail, par activité économique	Casos de lesión con pérdida de días de trabajo, por actividad económica

España (FA) — Reported injuries - Lésions déclarées - Lesiones declaradas

Cases of temporary incapacity - Cas d'incapacité temporaire - Casos de incapacidad temporal

Men - Hommes - Hombres
ISIC 3 - CITI 3 - CIIU 3

	1999	2000	2001	2002	2003	2004	2005	2006	2007	2008
Total	720 214	763 068	764 393	748 270	693 666	689 821	706 755	720 073	719 561	.
A	32 877	29 810	26 593	25 252	.	.	.	.	.	.
B	5 313	4 630	4 231	4 157	.	.	.	.	.	.
C	15 173	14 848	13 857	12 130	.	.	.	.	.	.
D	216 103	221 759	215 406	203 320	.	.	.	.	.	.
E	3 380	3 321	3 248	3 093	.	.	.	.	.	.
F	210 182	232 128	242 994	239 937	.	.	.	.	.	.
G	81 830	89 353	89 271	89 104	.	.	.	.	.	.
H	26 565	28 828	27 815	27 163	.	.	.	.	.	.
I	39 156	43 901	43 915	43 235	.	.	.	.	.	.
J	1 251	1 281	1 309	1 274	.	.	.	.	.	.
K	39 590	41 106	41 592	43 906	.	.	.	.	.	.
L,Q	25 928	26 278	26 703	26 833	.	.	.	.	.	.
M	2 657	2 711	2 796	2 767	.	.	.	.	.	.
N	6 918	7 751	8 331	9 374	.	.	.	.	.	.
O	12 531	14 557	15 492	16 002	.	.	.	.	.	.
P	760	806	840	723	.	.	.	.	.	.

Women - Femmes - Mujeres
ISIC 3 - CITI 3 - CIIU 3

	1999	2000	2001	2002	2003	2004	2005	2006	2007	2008
Total	143 457	164 011	173 927	169 871	176 993	177 371	179 745	187 776	200 934	.
A	8 840	8 208	7 353	6 623	.	.	.	.	.	.
B	264	317	301	295	.	.	.	.	.	.
C	579	490	330	293	.	.	.	.	.	.
D	26 643	30 397	30 592	28 997	.	.	.	.	.	.
E	119	154	131	125	.	.	.	.	.	.
F	4 396	5 517	5 029	5 011	.	.	.	.	.	.
G	26 758	32 130	34 153	34 381	.	.	.	.	.	.
H	20 409	23 674	25 088	23 494	.	.	.	.	.	.
I	3 596	4 436	4 545	4 435	.	.	.	.	.	.
J	712	819	827	799	.	.	.	.	.	.
K	22 821	26 341	29 000	28 234	.	.	.	.	.	.
L,Q	8 161	8 576	9 607	9 427	.	.	.	.	.	.
M	2 544	2 746	2 976	2 865	.	.	.	.	.	.
N	13 479	15 029	17 954	18 092	.	.	.	.	.	.
O	3 930	4 937	5 798	6 564	.	.	.	.	.	.
P	206	240	243	236	.	.	.	.	.	.

Total cases (fatal + non-fatal) - Ensemble des cas (mortels + non mortels) - Todos los casos (mortales + no mortales)

Total men and women - Total hommes et femmes - Total hombres y mujeres
ISIC 3 - CITI 3 - CIIU 3

	1999	2000	2001	2002	2003	2004	2005	2006	2007	2008
Total	869 161	932 932	946 600	936 003	873 332	870 278	889 649	910 357	923 523	803 308
A	41 980	38 332	34 487	32 800	30 639	30 876	30 546	30 295	30 892	29 696
B	5 659	5 038	4 609	4 503	4 014	4 090	3 672	3 588	3 518	3 238
C	15 847	15 434	14 299	12 571	11 956	10 737	9 335	8 612	8 270	6 950
D	244 555	253 838	248 091	236 147	222 056	229 181	227 977	230 994	231 973	199 417
E	3 517	3 514	3 428	3 357	3 647	4 524	4 747	4 498	4 512	4 067
F	216 045	239 244	250 277	250 066	230 505	223 817	238 271	250 095	250 031	186 336
G	109 075	122 061	124 359	125 972	118 592	117 054	118 788	119 200	120 496	109 399
H	47 140	52 692	53 237	51 547	48 561	50 046	51 038	52 454	53 412	51 107
I	43 156	48 813	49 184	49 126	49 523	53 638	55 551	57 522	59 673	53 632
J	1 985	2 111	2 166	2 133	2 144	2 178	2 208	2 234	2 055	2 085
K	62 709	67 749	71 113	73 405	54 219	39 530	40 117	41 738	44 051	40 720
L,Q	34 251	35 096	36 581	36 900	37 001	37 393	38 155	37 702	37 701	37 450
M	5 224	5 491	5 824	5 783	6 598	6 749	6 905	7 365	7 619	8 133
N	20 473	22 882	26 411	27 794	28 634	29 380	31 027	31 634	34 761	36 540
O	16 563	19 579	21 441	22 919	24 641	30 194	30 559	31 580	33 327	33 282
P	982	1 058	1 093	980	602	891	753	846	1 232	1 256

Men - Hommes - Hombres
ISIC 3 - CITI 3 - CIIU 3

	1999	2000	2001	2002	2003	2004	2005	2006	2007	2008
Total	725 252	768 344	771 491	763 047	696 089	692 564	709 612	722 342	722 210	609 379
A	33 118	30 087	27 039	25 999	23 552	23 918	23 917	23 282	23 330	22 566
B	5 395	4 721	4 306	4 208	3 730	3 796	3 467	3 376	3 231	2 978
C	15 267	14 943	13 967	12 262	11 412	10 374	8 992	8 280	7 960	6 689
D	217 805	223 335	217 328	206 758	191 756	196 574	197 012	198 282	196 852	169 695
E	3 398	3 359	3 295	3 226	3 433	4 314	4 524	4 288	4 332	3 848
F	211 637	233 708	245 227	244 960	225 808	221 192	235 664	247 133	247 134	183 867
G	82 251	89 827	89 993	90 930	82 359	80 984	81 852	81 295	81 004	71 819
H	26 671	28 961	27 986	27 662	23 908	23 934	23 859	23 831	23 430	22 143
I	39 548	44 358	44 525	44 433	43 791	47 263	48 390	49 723	50 856	44 938
J	1 271	1 289	1 333	1 309	1 077	1 016	974	990	897	869
K	39 811	41 311	41 927	44 683	31 641	23 780	24 374	25 497	26 311	23 705
L,Q	26 063	26 471	26 917	27 320	26 234	26 387	27 076	26 464	25 926	25 462
M	2 673	2 730	2 825	2 828	2 589	2 429	2 310	2 381	2 451	2 403
N	6 949	7 794	8 372	9 498	7 786	7 404	7 694	7 504	7 625	7 962
O	12 624	14 633	15 603	16 230	16 588	18 696	19 015	19 547	20 185	19 711
P	771	817	848	741	445	503	453	469	686	724

Explanatory notes: see p. 1125.   Notes explicatives: voir p. 1127.   Notas explicativas: véase p. 1129.

OCCUPATIONAL INJURIES

Cases of injury with lost workdays, by economic activity

LÉSIONS PROFESSIONNELLES

Cas de lésion avec perte de journées de travail, par activité économique

LESIONES PROFESIONALES

Casos de lesión con pérdida de días de trabajo, por actividad económica

8A

	1999	2000	2001	2002	2003	2004	2005	2006	2007	2008

España (FA) — Reported injuries - Lésions déclarées - Lesiones declaradas

Total cases (fatal + non-fatal) - Ensemble des cas (mortels + non mortels) - Todos los casos (mortales + no mortales)

Women - Femmes - Mujeres
ISIC 3 - CITI 3 - CIIU 3

	1999	2000	2001	2002	2003	2004	2005	2006	2007	2008
Total	143 909	164 588	175 109	172 956	177 243	177 714	180 037	188 015	201 313	193 929
A	8 862	8 245	7 448	6 801	7 087	6 958	6 590	7 013	7 562	7 130
B	264	317	303	295	284	294	205	212	287	260
C	580	491	332	309	544	363	343	332	310	261
D	26 750	30 503	30 763	29 389	30 300	32 607	30 965	32 712	35 121	29 722
E	119	155	133	131	214	210	223	210	180	219
F	4 408	5 536	5 050	5 106	4 697	2 625	2 607	2 962	2 897	2 469
G	26 824	32 234	34 366	35 042	36 233	36 070	36 936	37 905	39 492	37 580
H	20 469	23 731	25 251	23 885	24 653	26 112	27 179	28 623	29 982	28 964
I	3 608	4 455	4 659	4 693	5 752	6 375	7 161	7 799	8 817	8 694
J	714	822	833	824	1 067	1 162	1 234	1 244	1 158	1 216
K	22 898	26 438	29 186	28 722	22 578	15 750	15 743	16 241	17 740	17 015
L,Q	8 188	8 625	9 664	9 580	10 767	11 006	11 079	11 238	11 775	11 988
M	2 551	2 761	2 999	2 955	4 009	4 320	4 595	4 984	5 168	5 730
N	13 524	15 088	18 039	18 296	20 848	21 976	23 333	24 130	27 136	28 578
O	3 939	4 946	5 838	6 689	8 053	11 498	11 544	12 033	13 142	13 571
P	211	241	245	239	157	388	300	377	546	532

Estonia (FA) — Compensated injuries - Lésions indemnisées - Lesiones indemnizadas

Fatal cases - Cas mortels - Casos mortales

Total men and women - Total hommes et femmes - Total hombres y mujeres

ISIC 3 - CITI 3 - CIIU 3 · ISIC 4 - CITI 4 - CIIU 4

	1999	2000	2001	2002	2003	2004	2005	2006	2007		2008	
Total	52	27	36	35	31	34	24	28	21		21	Total
A	13	3	3	3	2	2	1	2	2		1	A
B	0	0	0	0	0	0	0	0	0		4	B
C	3	0	1	2	1	0	1	2	1		4	C
D	6	9	13	6	8	5	4	9	4		0	D
E	4	3	2	0	1	2	1	0	0		0	E
F	4	4	6	9	4	5	1	6	5		6	F
G	1	2	4	5	2	2	4	2	4		0	G
H	0	0	0	0	0	2	0	0	0		3	H
I	0	5	2	5	8	7	6	0	2		0	I
J	7	0	0	0	0	0	2	0	0		0	J
K	1	0	0	2	3	4	1	3	1		0	K
L	3	0	2	2	1	3	0	4	2		1	L
M	6	0	0	0	1	1	0	0	0		0	M
N	0	0	2	0	0	0	1	0	0		1	N
O	1	1	1	1	0	1	2	0	0		1	O
X	3	0	0	0	0	0	0	0			0	P
	0										0	Q
											0	R
											0	S

Men - Hommes - Hombres

ISIC 3 - CITI 3 - CIIU 3 · ISIC 4 - CITI 4 - CIIU 4

	1999	2000	2001	2002	2003	2004	2005	2006	2007		2008	
Total	46	25	32	32	31	24	20	23	21		19	Total
A	11	3	3	3	2	1	1	2	2		1	A
B	0	0	0	0	0	0	0	0	0		4	B
C	3	0	1	1	1	4	1	2	1		4	C
D	5	8	12	6	8	2	4	7	4		0	D
E	4	3	2	0	1	4	1	0	0		0	E
F	3	4	6	9	4	0	3	6	5		6	F
G	1	2	3	5	2	2	0	2	4		0	G
H	0	0	0	0	8	7	5	0	2		3	H
I	7	4	2	3	0	0	2	0	0		0	I
J	0	0	0	0	3	1	1	2	1		0	J
K	3	0	0	2	1	2	0	2	2		0	K
L	6	0	2	2	1	1	1	0	0		0	L
M	0	0	0	0	0	0	0	0	0		0	M
N	0	0	0	0	1	1	1	0			1	N
O	3	1	1	1							0	O
											0	P
											0	Q
											0	R
											0	S

Explanatory notes: see p. 1125.

Notes explicatives: voir p. 1127.

Notas explicativas: véase p. 1129.

OCCUPATIONAL INJURIES / LÉSIONS PROFESSIONNELLES / LESIONES PROFESIONALES

Cases of injury with lost workdays, by economic activity

Cas de lésion avec perte de journées de travail, par activité économique

Casos de lesión con pérdida de días de trabajo, por actividad económica

Estonia (FA)

Compensated injuries - Lésions indemnisées - Lesiones indemnizadas

Fatal cases - Cas mortels - Casos mortales

Women - Femmes - Mujeres — ISIC 3 - CITI 3 - CIIU 3

	1999	2000	2001	2002	2003	2004	2005	2006	2007
Total	6	2	4	3	0	10	4	5	0
A	2	0	0	0	0	1	0	0	0
B	0	0	0	0	0	0	0	0	0
C	0	0	0	1	0	0	0	0	0
D	1	1	1	0	0	0	0	0	0
E	0	0	0	0	0	0	0	2	0
F	1	0	0	0	0	0	0	0	0
G	0	0	1	0	0	1	0	0	0
H	0	0	0	0	0	2	1	0	0
I	0	1	0	2	0	1	0	0	0
J	1	0	0	0	0	0	0	0	0
K	0	0	0	0	0	0	1	0	0
L	0	0	0	0	0	3	0	1	0
M	0	0	0	0	0	1	0	2	0
N	0	0	0	0	0	0	0	0	0
O	1	0	2	0	0	0	0	0	0

2008 — ISIC 4 - CITI 4 - CIIU 4:

Total	A	B	C	D	E	F	G	H	I	J	K	L	M	N	O	P	Q	R	S
2	0	0	0	0	0	0	2	0	0	0	0	0	1	0	0	0	0	0	0

Non-fatal cases (temporary + permanent incapacity) - Cas non mortels (incapacité temporaire + permanente) - Casos no mortales (incapacidad temporal + permanente)

Total men and women - Total hommes et femmes - Total hombres y mujeres — ISIC 3 - CITI 3 - CIIU 3

	1999	2000	2001	2002	2003	2004	2005	2006	2007
Total	3 046	2 934	3 257	3 080	3 199	3 292	3 401	3 623	3 686
A	570	321	266	196	189	194	219	196	184
B	21	8	5	4	4	3	4	4	2
C	108	83	72	58	46	60	47	44	2
D	921	1 125	1 303	1 306	1 362	1 455	1 360	1 430	1 491
E	59	67	49	44	40	32	29	37	21
F	310	222	234	241	260	250	299	373	417
G	181	186	288	278	332	299	360	382	370
H	36	25	55	57	63	58	74	86	77
I	275	290	294	257	242	258	254	293	283
J	11	14	17	5	18	5	12	12	8
K	104	118	149	149	193	164	193	190	195
L	158	193	206	213	211	243	277	286	310
M	80	88	129	93	88	95	82	93	83
N	128	120	99	79	69	88	101	106	96
O	84	74	91	100	82	88	90	91	91
X	0	0	0	0	0	0	0	0	0

2008 — ISIC 4 - CITI 4 - CIIU 4:

Total	A	B	C	D	E	F	G	H	I	J	K	L	M	N	O	P	Q	R	S
4 038	186	38	1 463	16	50	473	402	290	130	17	28	21	127	95	366	104	131	65	30

Men - Hommes - Hombres — ISIC 3 - CITI 3 - CIIU 3

	1999	2000	2001	2002	2003	2004	2005	2006	2007
Total	2 044	1 962	2 016	2 134	2 242	2 325	2 321	2 490	2 499
A	368	218	142	121	116	106	121	116	107
B	19	7	5	4	4	2	4	4	2
C	87	71	61	50	41	58	43	42	48
D	648	782	864	936	987	1 052	974	975	1 019
E	50	56	33	39	36	29	25	37	14
F	287	214	218	225	250	245	289	361	404
G	120	119	164	190	212	205	222	252	224
H	10	7	14	14	24	14	23	18	17
I	199	190	199	180	174	210	189	212	204
J	1	5	6	3	12	2	2	9	3
K	73	84	87	102	135	121	131	136	133
L	97	136	126	167	157	180	213	236	230
M	15	19	25	19	26	27	15	19	20
N	22	18	23	15	10	16	19	16	16
O	48	36	49	69	58	58	51	57	58

2008 — ISIC 4 - CITI 4 - CIIU 4:

Total	A	B	C	D	E	F	G	H	I	J	K	L	M	N	O	P	Q	R	S
2 652	104	33	995	15	37	451	224	203	31	8	13	17	101	59	276	16	22	38	9

Explanatory notes: see p. 1125. — Notes explicatives: voir p. 1127. — Notas explicativas: véase p. 1129.

	1999	2000	2001	2002	2003	2004	2005	2006	2007		2008	

Estonia (FA) — Compensated injuries - Lésions indemnisées - Lesiones indemnizadas

Non-fatal cases (temporary + permanent incapacity) - Cas non mortels (incapacité temporaire + permanente) - Casos no mortales (incapacidad temporal + permanente)

Women - Femmes - Mujeres

ISIC 3 - CITI 3 - CIIU 3 / ISIC 4 - CITI 4 - CIIU 4

	1999	2000	2001	2002	2003	2004	2005	2006	2007		2008	
Total	1 002	972	1 241	946	957	967	1 080	1 133	1 187	|	1 386	Total
A	202	103	124	75	73	88	98	80	77	|	82	A
B	2	1	0	0	0	1	0	0	0	|	5	B
C	21	12	11	8	5	2	4	2	5	|	468	C
D	273	343	439	370	375	403	386	455	472	|	1	D
E	9	11	16	5	4	3	4	0	7	|	13	E
F	23	8	16	16	10	5	10	12	13	|	22	F
G	61	67	124	88	120	94	138	130	146	|	178	G
H	26	18	41	43	39	44	51	68	60	|	87	H
I	76	100	95	77	68	48	65	81	79	|	99	I
J	10	9	11	2	6	3	10	3	5	|	9	J
K	31	34	62	47	58	43	62	54	62	|	15	K
L	61	57	80	46	54	63	64	50	80	|	10	L
M	65	69	104	74	62	68	67	74	63	|	26	M
N	106	102	76	64	59	72	82	90	80	|	36	N
O	36	38	42	31	24	30	39	34	38	|	90	O
										|	88	P
										|	109	Q
										|	27	R
										|	21	S

Cases of temporary incapacity - Cas d'incapacité temporaire - Casos de incapacidad temporal

Total men and women - Total hommes et femmes - Total hombres y mujeres
ISIC 4 - CITI 4 - CIIU 4
Total 0

Men - Hommes - Hombres
ISIC 4 - CITI 4 - CIIU 4
Total 0

Women - Femmes - Mujeres
ISIC 4 - CITI 4 - CIIU 4
Total 0

Total cases (fatal + non-fatal) - Ensemble des cas (mortels + non mortels) - Todos los casos (mortales + no mortales)

Total men and women - Total hommes et femmes - Total hombres y mujeres

ISIC 3 - CITI 3 - CIIU 3 / ISIC 4 - CITI 4 - CIIU 4

	1999	2000	2001	2002	2003	2004	2005	2006	2007		2008	
Total	3 098	2 961	3 293	3 115	3 230	3 326	3 425	3 651	3 707	|	4 059	Total
A	583	324	269	199	191	196	220	198	186	|	187	A
B	21	8	5	4	4	3	4	4	2	|	42	B
C	111	83	73	60	47	60	48	46	54	|	1 467	C
D	927	1 134	1 316	1 312	1 370	1 460	1 364	1 439	1 495	|	16	D
E	63	70	51	44	41	34	30	37	21	|	50	E
F	314	226	240	250	264	255	300	379	422	|	479	F
G	182	188	292	283	334	301	364	384	374	|	402	G
H	36	25	55	57	63	60	74	86	77	|	293	H
I	282	295	296	262	250	265	260	293	285	|	130	I
J	12	14	17	5	18	5	14	12	8	|	17	J
K	107	118	149	151	196	168	194	193	196	|	28	K
L	164	193	208	215	212	246	277	290	312	|	28	L
M	80	88	129	93	89	96	82	93	83	|	127	M
N	129	120	101	79	69	88	102	106	96	|	96	N
O	87	75	92	101	82	89	92	91	91	|	367	O
X	0	0	0	0	0	0	0	0	0	|	104	P
										|	131	Q
										|	65	R
										|	30	S

Men - Hommes - Hombres

ISIC 3 - CITI 3 - CIIU 3 / ISIC 4 - CITI 4 - CIIU 4

	1999	2000	2001	2002	2003	2004	2005	2006	2007		2008	
Total	2 090	1 987	2 048	2 166	2 273	2 349	2 341	2 513	2 520	|	2 671	Total
A	379	221	145	124	118	107	122	118	109	|	105	A
B	19	7	5	4	4	2	4	4	2	|	37	B
C	90	71	62	51	42	58	44	44	49	|	999	C
D	653	790	876	942	995	1 056	978	982	1 023	|	15	D
E	54	59	35	39	37	31	26	37	14	|	37	E
F	290	218	224	234	254	249	290	367	409	|	457	F
G	121	121	167	195	214	205	225	254	228	|	224	G
H	10	7	14	14	24	15	23	18	17	|	206	H
I	206	194	201	183	182	217	194	212	206	|	31	I
J	1	5	6	3	12	2	4	9	3	|	8	J
K	76	84	87	104	138	122	132	138	134	|	13	K
L	103	136	128	169	158	182	213	238	232	|	17	L
M	15	19	25	19	27	28	15	19	20	|	101	M
N	22	18	23	15	10	16	20	16	16	|	59	N
O	51	37	50	70	58	59	51	57	58	|	277	O
										|	16	P
										|	22	Q
										|	38	R
										|	9	S

Explanatory notes: see p. 1125.   Notes explicatives: voir p. 1127.   Notas explicativas: véase p. 1129.

OCCUPATIONAL INJURIES	LÉSIONS PROFESSIONNELLES	LESIONES PROFESIONALES
Cases of injury with lost workdays, by economic activity	Cas de lésion avec perte de journées de travail, par activité économique	Casos de lesión con pérdida de días de trabajo, por actividad económica

	1999	2000	2001	2002	2003	2004	2005	2006	2007		2008	

Estonia (FA) — Compensated injuries - Lésions indemnisées - Lesiones indemnizadas

Total cases (fatal + non-fatal) - Ensemble des cas (mortels + non mortels) - Todos los casos (mortales + no mortales)

Women - Femmes - Mujeres
ISIC 3 - CITI 3 - CIIU 3 — ISIC 4 - CITI 4 - CIIU 4

	1999	2000	2001	2002	2003	2004	2005	2006	2007		2008	
Total	1 008	974	1 245	949	957	977	1 084	1 138	1 187	|	1 388	Total
A	204	103	124	75	73	89	98	80	77	|	82	A
B	2	1	0	0	0	1	0	0	0	|	5	B
C	21	12	11	9	5	2	4	2	5	|	468	C
D	274	344	440	370	375	404	386	457	472	|	1	D
E	9	11	16	5	4	3	4	0	7	|	13	E
F	24	8	16	16	10	6	10	12	13	|	22	F
G	61	67	125	88	120	96	139	130	146	|	178	G
H	26	18	41	43	39	45	51	68	60	|	87	H
I	76	101	95	79	68	48	66	81	79	|	99	I
J	11	9	11	2	6	3	10	3	5	|	9	J
K	31	34	62	47	58	46	62	55	62	|	15	K
L	61	57	80	46	54	64	64	52	80	|	11	L
M	65	69	104	74	62	68	67	74	63	|	26	M
N	107	102	78	64	59	72	82	90	80	|	37	N
O	36	38	42	31	24	30	41	34	38	|	90	O
										|	88	P
										|	109	Q
										|	27	R
										|	21	S

Finland (FA) — Compensated injuries - Lésions indemnisées - Lesiones indemnizadas

Fatal cases - Cas mortels - Casos mortales

Total men and women - Total hommes et femmes - Total hombres y mujeres
ISIC 3 - CITI 3 - CIIU 3

	1999	2000	2001	2002	2003	2004	2005	2006	2007	2008
Total	42	47	43	37	43	44	51	47	37	.
A	2	1	1	0	0	0	0	1	0	.
B	1	0	0	0	0	0	2	0	0	.
C	2	0	0	1	2	0	2	0	0	.
D	11	17	10	9	10	11	6	7	5	.
E	0	0	1	0	1	1	0	1	0	.
F	9	9	11	5	15	10	12	9	8	.
G	2	2	2	2	2	1	5	1	2	.
H	0	0	1	2	0	0	1	0	0	.
I	5	7	10	8	10	8	15	13	8	.
J	0	0	0	0	0	0	0	0	0	.
K	1	2	2	3	2	5	2	4	2	.
L	5	4	2	2	1	7	1	5	6	.
M	0	0	0	1	0	0	0	2	0	.
N	0	0	0	2	0	0	1	1	0	.
O	4	1	1	1	0	0	3	1	3	.
P	0	0	0	1	0	0	1	1	0	.
Q	0	0	0	0	0	0	0	0	0	.
X	0	4	1	0	0	0	0	0	0	.

Men - Hommes - Hombres
ISIC 3 - CITI 3 - CIIU 3

	1999	2000	2001	2002	2003	2004	2005	2006	2007	2008
Total	39	46	41	35	43	40	46	43	32	.
A	2	1	0	0	0	0	0	1	0	.
B	1	0	0	0	0	0	2	0	0	.
C	2	0	0	1	2	0	2	0	0	.
D	11	17	10	9	10	10	6	7	5	.
E	0	0	1	0	1	1	0	1	0	.
F	9	9	11	5	15	9	12	9	8	.
G	2	2	2	2	2	1	5	1	2	.
H	0	0	1	2	0	0	1	0	0	.
I	4	7	10	7	10	6	12	13	7	.
J	0	0	0	0	0	0	0	0	0	.
K	1	2	1	3	2	5	2	4	2	.
L	3	3	2	2	1	7	1	3	3	.
M	0	0	0	0	0	0	0	2	0	.
N	0	0	0	2	0	0	1	0	0	.
O	4	1	1	1	0	0	1	0	2	.
P	0	0	0	1	0	0	1	1	0	.
Q	0	0	0	0	0	0	0	0	0	.
X	0	4	1	0	0	0	0	0	0	.

Explanatory notes: see p. 1125.　　　Notes explicatives: voir p. 1127.　　　Notas explicativas: véase p. 1129.

OCCUPATIONAL INJURIES

Cases of injury with lost workdays, by economic activity

LÉSIONS PROFESSIONNELLES

Cas de lésion avec perte de journées de travail, par activité économique

LESIONES PROFESIONALES

Casos de lesión con pérdida de días de trabajo, por actividad económica

Finland (FA)

Compensated injuries - Lésions indemnisées - Lesiones indemnizadas

Fatal cases - Cas mortels - Casos mortales

Women - Femmes - Mujeres

ISIC 3 - CITI 3 - CIIU 3

	1999	2000	2001	2002	2003	2004	2005	2006	2007	2008
Total	3	1	2	2	0	4	5	4	5	.
A	0	0	0	0	0	0	0	0	0	.
B	0	0	0	0	0	0	0	0	0	.
C	0	0	0	0	0	0	0	0	0	.
D	0	0	0	0	0	1	0	0	0	.
E	0	0	0	0	0	1	0	0	0	.
F	0	0	0	0	0	0	0	0	0	.
G	0	0	0	0	0	0	0	0	0	.
H	0	0	0	0	0	0	0	0	1	.
I	1	0	0	1	0	2	3	0	0	.
J	0	0	0	0	0	0	0	0	0	.
K	0	0	1	0	0	0	0	2	3	.
L	2	1	0	0	0	0	0	0	0	.
M	0	0	0	1	0	0	0	1	0	.
N	0	0	0	0	0	0	2	1	1	.
O	0	0	0	0	0	0	0	0	0	.
P	0	0	0	0	0	0	0	0	0	.
Q	0	0	0	0	0	0	0	0	0	.
X	0	0	1	0	0	0	0	0	0	.

Non-fatal cases (temporary + permanent incapacity) - Cas non mortels (incapacité temporaire + permanente) - Casos no mortales (incapacidad temporal + permanente)

Total men and women - Total hommes et femmes - Total hombres y mujeres [1]

ISIC 3 - CITI 3 - CIIU 3

	1999	2000	2001	2002	2003	2004	2005	2006	2007	2008
Total	58 365	58 056	58 276	57 767	56 268	56 042	60 707	61 707	62 095	.
A	1 036	929	919	1 020	948	967	1 142	1 265	1 329	.
B	32	25	22	36	25	23	26	32	30	.
C	170	173	160	169	140	143	150	145	153	.
D	19 237	19 113	18 880	17 506	16 759	15 966	16 205	16 336	15 960	.
E	401	371	369	307	314	301	329	305	294	.
F	9 827	10 126	10 142	9 979	9 243	9 037	10 156	9 986	10 451	.
G	4 910	4 892	4 842	5 226	5 120	5 196	5 726	5 836	5 832	.
H	1 429	1 512	1 457	1 457	1 436	1 420	1 618	1 645	1 662	.
I	6 363	6 055	5 923	5 917	6 077	6 543	7 082	7 154	6 195	.
J	180	131	154	111	137	120	120	128	148	.
K	3 395	3 442	3 628	3 837	4 115	4 240	4 856	5 508	6 583	.
L	8 081	7 958	8 468	8 845	8 525	8 511	9 225	9 296	8 937	.
M	603	581	580	610	475	453	497	511	605	.
N	1 142	1 183	1 082	1 132	1 331	1 338	1 582	1 783	1 844	.
O	1 242	1 287	1 382	1 352	1 336	1 426	1 512	1 470	1 474	.
P	153	172	161	167	197	236	331	301	298	.
Q	4	0	4	0	6	0	0	3	1	.
X	160	106	103	96	84	122	150	3	225	.

Men - Hommes - Hombres [1]

ISIC 3 - CITI 3 - CIIU 3

	1999	2000	2001	2002	2003	2004	2005	2006	2007	2008
Total	44 637	44 253	44 120	43 171	41 830	41 441	44 528	45 114	45 146	.
A	879	766	767	802	750	711	846	895	949	.
B	24	19	18	29	23	22	23	24	27	.
C	162	168	156	165	139	139	146	142	147	.
D	16 271	16 137	15 920	14 774	14 200	13 603	13 877	14 069	13 681	.
E	372	341	338	290	296	290	314	289	283	.
F	9 653	9 932	9 950	9 794	9 061	8 842	9 959	9 759	10 207	.
G	3 402	3 412	3 333	3 585	3 411	3 431	3 816	3 885	3 759	.
H	516	525	510	552	528	486	569	523	552	.
I	5 527	5 296	5 198	5 108	5 269	5 687	6 113	6 150	5 473	.
J	50	40	40	39	56	58	37	42	71	.
K	2 361	2 372	2 520	2 612	2 872	2 925	3 387	3 917	4 660	.
L	3 809	3 701	3 735	3 842	3 657	3 571	3 630	3 649	3 379	.
M	338	291	333	322	247	236	273	271	336	.
N	250	273	243	260	310	270	317	374	359	.
O	796	780	865	802	782	870	840	873	832	.
P	120	122	119	126	157	202	277	247	254	.
Q	2	0	3	0	4	0	0	3	1	.
X	105	78	72	69	68	98	104	2	137	.

Explanatory notes: see p. 1125.

[1] Incapacity of 3 days or more.

Notes explicatives: voir p. 1127.

[1] Incapacité de 3 jours et plus.

Notas explicativas: véase p. 1129.

[1] Incapacidad de 3 días y más.

8A

OCCUPATIONAL INJURIES	LÉSIONS PROFESSIONNELLES	LESIONES PROFESIONALES
Cases of injury with lost workdays, by economic activity	Cas de lésion avec perte de journées de travail, par activité économique	Casos de lesión con pérdida de días de trabajo, por actividad económica

Finland (FA) — Compensated injuries - Lésions indemnisées - Lesiones indemnizadas

Non-fatal cases (temporary + permanent incapacity) - Cas non mortels (incapacité temporaire + permanente) - Casos no mortales (incapacidad temporal + permanente)

Women - Femmes - Mujeres [1]
ISIC 3 - CITI 3 - CIIU 3

	1999	2000	2001	2002	2003	2004	2005	2006	2007	2008
Total	13 728	13 803	14 156	14 596	14 438	14 601	16 179	16 593	16 949	.
A	157	163	152	218	198	256	296	370	380	.
B	8	6	4	7	2	1	3	8	3	.
C	8	5	4	4	1	4	4	3	3	.
D	2 966	2 976	2 960	2 732	2 559	2 363	2 328	2 267	2 279	.
E	29	30	31	17	18	11	15	16	11	.
F	174	194	192	185	182	195	197	227	244	.
G	1 508	1 480	1 509	1 641	1 709	1 765	1 910	1 951	2 073	.
H	913	987	947	905	908	934	1 049	1 122	1 110	.
I	836	759	725	809	808	856	969	1 004	722	.
J	130	91	114	72	81	62	83	86	77	.
K	1 034	1 070	1 108	1 225	1 243	1 315	1 469	1 591	1 923	.
L	4 272	4 257	4 733	5 003	4 868	4 940	5 595	5 647	5 558	.
M	265	290	247	288	228	217	224	240	269	.
N	892	910	839	872	1 021	1 068	1 265	1 409	1 485	.
O	446	507	517	550	554	556	672	597	642	.
P	33	50	42	41	40	34	54	54	44	.
Q	2	0	1	0	2	0	0	0	0	.
X	55	28	31	27	16	24	46	1	88	.

Cases of temporary incapacity - Cas d'incapacité temporaire - Casos de incapacidad temporal

Total men and women - Total hommes et femmes - Total hombres y mujeres
ISIC 3 - CITI 3 - CIIU 3

	1999	2000	2001	2002	2003	2004	2005	2006	2007	2008
Total	.	.	.	.	.	.	60 567	61 573	61 970	.
A	.	.	.	.	.	.	1 140	1 258	1 323	.
B	.	.	.	.	.	.	25	32	30	.
C	.	.	.	.	.	.	150	144	152	.
D	.	.	.	.	.	.	16 172	16 304	15 934	.
E	.	.	.	.	.	.	324	305	294	.
F	.	.	.	.	.	.	10 122	9 953	10 406	.
G	.	.	.	.	.	.	5 718	5 828	5 825	.
H	.	.	.	.	.	.	1 616	1 645	1 661	.
I	.	.	.	.	.	.	7 054	7 130	6 184	.
J	.	.	.	.	.	.	119	128	147	.
K	.	.	.	.	.	.	4 847	5 494	6 570	.
L	.	.	.	.	.	.	9 217	9 290	8 928	.
M	.	.	.	.	.	.	496	511	603	.
N	.	.	.	.	.	.	1 581	1 782	1 843	.
O	.	.	.	.	.	.	1 507	1 465	1 474	.
P	.	.	.	.	.	.	329	300	296	.
Q	.	.	.	.	.	.	0	3	1	.
X	.	.	.	.	.	.	150	3	225	.

Men - Hommes - Hombres
ISIC 3 - CITI 3 - CIIU 3

	1999	2000	2001	2002	2003	2004	2005	2006	2007	2008
Total	.	.	.	.	.	.	44 410	44 994	45 036	.
A	.	.	.	.	.	.	844	889	945	.
B	.	.	.	.	.	.	22	24	27	.
C	.	.	.	.	.	.	146	141	146	.
D	.	.	.	.	.	.	13 849	14 039	13 656	.
E	.	.	.	.	.	.	309	289	283	.
F	.	.	.	.	.	.	9 925	9 726	10 162	.
G	.	.	.	.	.	.	3 811	3 877	3 752	.
H	.	.	.	.	.	.	567	522	552	.
I	.	.	.	.	.	.	6 088	6 128	5 462	.
J	.	.	.	.	.	.	36	42	71	.
K	.	.	.	.	.	.	3 382	3 908	4 650	.
L	.	.	.	.	.	.	3 626	3 644	3 376	.
M	.	.	.	.	.	.	272	271	334	.
N	.	.	.	.	.	.	317	373	359	.
O	.	.	.	.	.	.	837	870	832	.
P	.	.	.	.	.	.	275	246	252	.
Q	.	.	.	.	.	.	0	3	1	.
X	.	.	.	.	.	.	104	2	137	.

Explanatory notes: see p. 1125.
[1] Incapacity of 3 days or more.

Notes explicatives: voir p. 1127.
[1] Incapacité de 3 jours et plus.

Notas explicativas: véase p. 1129.
[1] Incapacidad de 3 días y más.

OCCUPATIONAL INJURIES
Cases of injury with lost workdays, by economic activity

LÉSIONS PROFESSIONNELLES
Cas de lésion avec perte de journées de travail, par activité économique

LESIONES PROFESIONALES
Casos de lesión con pérdida de días de trabajo, por actividad económica

8A

	1999	2000	2001	2002	2003	2004	2005	2006	2007	2008

Finland (FA) — Compensated injuries - Lésions indemnisées - Lesiones indemnizadas

Cases of temporary incapacity - Cas d'incapacité temporaire - Casos de incapacidad temporal

Women - Femmes - Mujeres
ISIC 3 - CITI 3 - CIIU 3

	1999	2000	2001	2002	2003	2004	2005	2006	2007	2008
Total	.	.	.	.	.	.	16 157	16 579	16 934	.
A	.	.	.	.	.	.	296	369	378	.
B	.	.	.	.	.	.	3	8	3	.
C	.	.	.	.	.	.	4	3	6	.
D	.	.	.	.	.	.	2 323	2 265	2 278	.
E	.	.	.	.	.	.	15	16	11	.
F	.	.	.	.	.	.	197	227	244	.
G	.	.	.	.	.	.	1 907	1 951	2 073	.
H	.	.	.	.	.	.	1 049	1 121	1 109	.
I	.	.	.	.	.	.	966	1 002	722	.
J	.	.	.	.	.	.	83	86	76	.
K	.	.	.	.	.	.	1 465	1 586	1 920	.
L	.	.	.	.	.	.	5 591	5 646	5 552	.
M	.	.	.	.	.	.	224	240	269	.
N	.	.	.	.	.	.	1 264	1 409	1 484	.
O	.	.	.	.	.	.	670	595	642	.
P	.	.	.	.	.	.	54	54	44	.
Q	.	.	.	.	.	.	0	0	0	.
X	.	.	.	.	.	.	46	1	88	.

Total cases (fatal + non-fatal) - Ensemble des cas (mortels + non mortels) - Todos los casos (mortales + no mortales)

Total men and women - Total hommes et femmes - Total hombres y mujeres
ISIC 3 - CITI 3 - CIIU 3

	1999	2000	2001	2002	2003	2004	2005	2006	2007	2008
Total	58 407	58 103	58 319	57 804	56 311	56 086	60 758	61 754	62 132	.
A	1 038	930	920	1 020	948	967	1 142	1 266	1 329	.
B	33	25	22	36	25	23	28	32	30	.
C	172	173	160	170	142	143	152	145	153	.
D	19 248	19 130	18 890	17 515	16 769	15 977	16 211	16 343	15 965	.
E	401	371	370	307	315	302	329	306	294	.
F	9 836	10 135	10 153	9 984	9 258	9 047	10 168	9 995	10 459	.
G	4 912	4 894	4 844	5 228	5 122	5 197	5 723	5 829	5 827	.
H	1 429	1 512	1 458	1 459	1 436	1 420	1 619	1 645	1 662	.
I	6 368	6 062	5 933	5 925	6 087	6 551	7 097	7 167	6 203	.
J	180	131	154	111	137	120	120	128	148	.
K	3 396	3 444	3 630	3 840	4 117	4 245	4 858	5 512	6 585	.
L	8 086	7 962	8 470	8 847	8 526	8 518	9 226	9 301	8 943	.
M	603	581	580	611	475	453	497	513	605	.
N	1 142	1 183	1 082	1 134	1 331	1 338	1 583	1 784	1 844	.
O	1 246	1 288	1 383	1 353	1 336	1 426	1 515	1 471	1 477	.
P	153	172	161	168	197	236	332	302	298	.
Q	4	0	4	0	6	0	0	3	1	.
X	160	120	105	96	84	122	150	3	225	.

Men - Hommes - Hombres
ISIC 3 - CITI 3 - CIIU 3

	1999	2000	2001	2002	2003	2004	2005	2006	2007	2008
Total	44 676	44 299	44 161	43 206	41 873	41 481	44 574	45 157	45 178	.
A	881	767	768	802	750	711	846	896	949	.
B	25	19	18	29	23	22	25	24	27	.
C	164	168	156	166	141	139	148	142	147	.
D	16 282	16 154	15 930	14 783	14 210	13 613	13 883	14 076	13 686	.
E	372	341	339	290	297	291	314	290	283	.
F	9 662	9 941	9 961	9 799	9 076	8 851	9 971	9 768	10 215	.
G	3 404	3 414	3 335	3 587	3 413	3 432	3 816	3 878	3 754	.
H	516	525	511	554	528	486	570	523	552	.
I	5 531	5 303	5 208	5 115	5 279	5 693	6 125	6 163	5 480	.
J	50	40	40	39	56	58	37	42	71	.
K	2 362	2 374	2 521	2 615	2 874	2 930	3 389	3 921	4 662	.
L	3 812	3 704	3 737	3 844	3 658	3 578	3 631	3 652	3 382	.
M	338	291	333	322	247	236	273	273	336	.
N	250	273	243	262	310	270	318	374	359	.
O	800	781	866	803	782	870	841	873	834	.
P	120	122	119	127	157	202	278	248	254	.
Q	2	0	3	0	4	0	0	3	1	.
X	105	82	73	69	68	98	104	2	137	.

Explanatory notes: see p. 1125.   Notes explicatives: voir p. 1127.   Notas explicativas: véase p. 1129.

	OCCUPATIONAL INJURIES	LÉSIONS PROFESSIONNELLES	LESIONES PROFESIONALES
	Cases of injury with lost workdays, by economic activity	Cas de lésion avec perte de journées de travail, par activité économique	Casos de lesión con pérdida de días de trabajo, por actividad económica

	1999	2000	2001	2002	2003	2004	2005	2006	2007	2008

Finland (FA)   Compensated injuries - Lésions indemnisées - Lesiones indemnizadas

Total cases (fatal + non-fatal) - Ensemble des cas (mortels + non mortels) - Todos los casos (mortales + no mortales)

Women - Femmes - Mujeres
ISIC 3 - CITI 3 - CIIU 3

	1999	2000	2001	2002	2003	2004	2005	2006	2007	2008
Total	13 731	13 804	14 158	14 598	14 438	14 605	16 184	16 597	16 954	.
A	157	163	152	218	198	256	296	370	380	.
B	8	6	4	7	2	1	3	8	3	.
C	8	5	4	4	1	4	4	3	6	.
D	2 966	2 976	2 960	2 732	2 559	2 364	2 328	2 267	2 279	.
E	29	30	31	17	18	11	15	16	11	.
F	174	194	192	185	182	196	197	227	244	.
G	1 508	1 480	1 509	1 641	1 709	1 765	1 907	1 951	2 073	.
H	913	987	947	905	908	934	1 049	1 122	1 110	.
I	837	759	725	810	808	858	972	1 004	723	.
J	130	91	114	72	81	62	83	86	77	.
K	1 034	1 070	1 109	1 225	1 243	1 315	1 469	1 591	1 923	.
L	4 274	4 258	4 733	5 003	4 868	4 940	5 595	5 649	5 561	.
M	265	290	247	289	228	217	224	240	269	.
N	892	910	839	872	1 021	1 068	1 265	1 410	1 485	.
O	446	507	517	550	554	556	674	598	643	.
P	33	50	42	41	40	34	54	54	44	.
Q	2	0	1	0	2	0	0	0	0	.
X	55	28	32	27	16	24	46	1	88	.

France (FA) [1]   Compensated injuries - Lésions indemnisées - Lesiones indemnizadas

Fatal cases - Cas mortels - Casos mortales

Total men and women - Total hommes et femmes - Total hombres y mujeres
ISIC 3 - CITI 3 - CIIU 3

	1999	2000	2001	2002	2003	2004	2005	2006	2007	2008
Total	717	730	730	686	661	626	474	537	622	.
A	.	.	.	.	.	.	1	1	1	.
B	.	.	.	.	.	.	0	0	0	.
C	.	.	.	.	.	.	3	5	4	.
D	179	163	.	.	.	.	88	100	118	.
E [2]	1	2	.	.	.	.	4	1	2	.
F	155	191	.	.	.	.	96	135	163	.
G [3]	55	60	.	.	.	.	49	59	60	.
H	16	11	.	.	.	.	15	9	10	.
I [4]	132	128	.	.	.	.	95	81	98	.
J	.	.	.	.	.	.	4	3	6	.
J-K,O-P,X [5]	179	175	.	.	.	.	.	.	.	.
K	.	.	.	.	.	.	71	76	93	.
L	.	.	.	.	.	.	5	14	10	.
M	.	.	.	.	.	.	3	4	6	.
N	.	.	.	.	.	.	12	23	16	.
O	.	.	.	.	.	.	21	19	20	.
P	.	.	.	.	.	.	0	0	0	.
Q	.	.	.	.	.	.	0	0	0	.
X	.	.	.	.	.	.	7	7	15	.

Men - Hommes - Hombres
ISIC 3 - CITI 3 - CIIU 3

	1999	2000	2001	2002	2003	2004	2005	2006	2007	2008
Total	664	689	.	.	.	.	449	504	580	.
A	.	.	.	.	.	.	1	1	1	.
B	.	.	.	.	.	.	0	0	0	.
C	.	.	.	.	.	.	3	5	4	.
D	170	154	.	.	.	.	86	97	112	.
E [2]	1	2	.	.	.	.	4	1	2	.
F	155	190	.	.	.	.	96	134	163	.
G [3]	46	55	.	.	.	.	45	54	53	.
H	13	11	.	.	.	.	11	7	9	.
I [4]	125	120	.	.	.	.	91	77	92	.
J	.	.	.	.	.	.	2	3	5	.
J-K,O-P,X [5]	154	157	.	.	.	.	.	.	.	.
K	.	.	.	.	.	.	68	73	84	.
L	.	.	.	.	.	.	5	11	7	.
M	.	.	.	.	.	.	2	1	6	.
N	.	.	.	.	.	.	9	14	9	.
O	.	.	.	.	.	.	19	19	19	.
P	.	.	.	.	.	.	0	0	0	.
Q	.	.	.	.	.	.	0	0	0	.
X	.	.	.	.	.	.	7	7	14	.

Explanatory notes: see p. 1125.

[1] Cases recognized for compensation during the year. [2] Excl. agents of public gas and electricity services. [3] Excl. food trade. [4] Excl. transport by rail and by sea and communications. [5] Interoccupational group.

Notes explicatives: voir p. 1127.

[1] Cas reconnus pour indemnisation dans l'année. [2] Non compris les agents des services publics du gaz et de l'électricité. [3] Non compris les commerces alimentaires. [4] Non compris les transports par chemin de fer ou par mer et les communications. [5] Groupe interprofessionnel.

Notas explicativas: véase p. 1129.

[1] Casos recogidos para indemnización en el año. [2] Excl. los agentes de los servicios públicos de electricidad y gas. [3] Excl. comercio alimenticio. [4] Excl. transportes ferroviarios y marítimos y las comunicaciones. [5] Grupo interocupacional.

OCCUPATIONAL INJURIES

Cases of injury with lost workdays, by economic activity

LÉSIONS PROFESSIONNELLES

Cas de lésion avec perte de journées de travail, par activité économique

LESIONES PROFESIONALES

Casos de lesión con pérdida de días de trabajo, por actividad económica

	1999	2000	2001	2002	2003	2004	2005	2006	2007	2008

France (FA) [1] Compensated injuries - Lésions indemnisées - Lesiones indemnizadas

Fatal cases - Cas mortels - Casos mortales

Women - Femmes - Mujeres
ISIC 3 - CITI 3 - CIIU 3

	1999	2000	2001	2002	2003	2004	2005	2006	2007	2008
Total	53	41	.	.	.	.	25	33	42	.
D	9	9					2	3	6	
E [2]	0	0					0	0	0	
F	0	1					0	1	0	
G [3]	9	5					4	5	7	
H	3	0					4	2	1	
I [4]	7	8					4	4	6	
J	.	.					2	0	1	
J-K,O-P,X [5]	25	18								
K							3	3	9	
L							0	3	3	
M							1	3	0	
N							3	9	7	
O							2	0	1	
P							0	0	0	
Q							0	0	0	
X							0	0	1	

Non-fatal cases (temporary + permanent incapacity) - Cas non mortels (incapacité temporaire + permanente) - Casos no mortales (incapacidad temporal + permanente)

Total men and women - Total hommes et femmes - Total hombres y mujeres
ISIC 3 - CITI 3 - CIIU 3

	1999	2000	2001	2002	2003	2004	2005	2006	2007	2008
Total	700 458	743 435	737 499	759 980	721 227	692 004	699 217	700 772	720 150	.
A							765	888	869	
B	.	.					72	51	60	
C							1 396	1 336	1 271	
D	244 638	256 025					144 509	137 199	136 264	
E [2]	2 089	2 135					1 782	1 640	1 615	
F	119 673	125 980					96	135	163	
G [3]	45 535	47 931					113 903	112 434	112 250	
H	41 532	42 415					40 025	40 085	41 330	
I [4]	59 020	62 368					63 425	63 796	64 276	
J	.	.					3 119	3 061	2 934	
J-K,O-P,X [5]	187 971	206 581								
K							104 944	108 018	112 552	
L							14 461	14 155	14 306	
M							6 150	5 676	6 059	
N							55 987	59 339	64 088	
O							25 385	25 639	25 696	
P							18	12	0	
Q							56	53	52	
X							10 551	10 581	17 368	

Men - Hommes - Hombres
ISIC 3 - CITI 3 - CIIU 3

	1999	2000	2001	2002	2003	2004	2005	2006	2007	2008
Total	548 407	577 586	.	.	.	.	515 684	513 420	521 614	.
A							646	715	685	
B							59	38	51	
C	.					.	1 370	1 316	1 249	
D	199 290	206 518					120 021	113 811	112 701	
E [2]	2 027	2 073					1 723	1 581	1 539	
F	118 803	125 167					111 783	115 891	118 016	
G [3]	33 876	35 439					77 110	75 317	74 448	
H	23 562	23 326					20 587	20 453	20 665	
I [4]	54 929	57 569					52 723	52 922	53 110	
J							1 134	1 088	1 040	
J-K,O-P,X [5]	115 920	127 494								
K							78 470	80 594	83 515	
L							6 336	6 239	6 220	
M							2 707	2 415	2 378	
N							14 360	14 676	15 386	
O							18 343	18 175	17 843	
P							12	8	0	
Q							39	39	34	
X							8 266	8 142	12 734	

Explanatory notes: see p. 1125.

[1] Cases recognized for compensation during the year. [2] Excl. agents of public gas and electricity services. [3] Excl. food trade. [4] Excl. transport by rail and by sea and communications. [5] Interoccupational group.

Notes explicatives: voir p. 1127.

[1] Cas reconnus pour indemnisation dans l'année. [2] Non compris les agents des services publics du gaz et de l'électricité. [3] Non compris les commerces alimentaires. [4] Non compris les transports par chemin de fer ou par mer et les communications. [5] Groupe interprofessionnel.

Notas explicativas: véase p. 1129.

[1] Casos recogidos para indemnización en el año. [2] Excl. los agentes de los servicios públicos de electricidad y gas. [3] Excl. comercio alimenticio. [4] Excl. transportes ferroviarios y marítimos y las comunicaciones. [5] Grupo interocupacional.

OCCUPATIONAL INJURIES
Cases of injury with lost workdays, by economic activity

LÉSIONS PROFESSIONNELLES
Cas de lésion avec perte de journées de travail, par activité économique

LESIONES PROFESIONALES
Casos de lesión con pérdida de días de trabajo, por actividad económica

	1999	2000	2001	2002	2003	2004	2005	2006	2007	2008

France (FA) [1] — Compensated injuries - Lésions indemnisées - Lesiones indemnizadas

Non-fatal cases (temporary + permanent incapacity) - Cas non mortels (incapacité temporaire + permanente) - Casos no mortales (incapacidad temporal + permanente)

Women - Femmes - Mujeres
ISIC 3 - CITI 3 - CIIU 3

	1999	2000	2001	2002	2003	2004	2005	2006	2007	2008
Total	152 051	165 849					183 533	187 352	198 536	
A							119	173	184	
B							13	13	9	
C							26	20	22	
D	45 348	49 507					24 488	23 388	23 563	
E [2]	62	62					59	59	76	
F	870	813					886	918	1 144	
G [3]	11 659	12 492					36 793	37 117	37 802	
H	17 970	19 089					19 438	19 632	20 665	
I [4]	4 091	4 799					10 702	10 874	11 166	
J							1 985	1 973	1 894	
J-K.O-P.X [5]	72 051	79 087								
K							26 474	27 424	29 037	
L							8 125	7 916	8 086	
M							3 443	3 261	3 681	
N							41 627	44 663	48 702	
O							7 042	7 464	7 853	
P							6	4	0	
Q							22	14	18	
X							2 285	2 439	4 634	

Cases of temporary incapacity - Cas d'incapacité temporaire - Casos de incapacidad temporal

Total men and women - Total hommes et femmes - Total hombres y mujeres
ISIC 3 - CITI 3 - CIIU 3

	1999	2000	2001	2002	2003	2004	2005	2006	2007	2008
Total	655 921	695 339	694 421	712 971	672 453	640 233	647 279	654 176	673 724	
A							722	848	824	
B							67	44	54	
C							1 264	1 187	1 136	
D	229 573	239 863					133 002	127 336	126 639	
E [2]	1 915	1 948					1 610	1 490	1 485	
F	109 946	115 913					102 859	107 984	110 377	
G [3]	42 468	44 661					106 316	105 824	105 636	
H	39 660	40 544					37 923	38 154	39 378	
I [4]	55 134	58 006					58 603	59 416	60 023	
J							2 750	2 721	2 648	
J-K.O-P.X [5]	177 225	194 404								
K							97 176	100 848	105 366	
L							13 380	13 120	13 407	
M							5 617	5 149	5 624	
N							52 288	55 817	60 447	
O							23 708	24 171	24 279	
P							17	12	0	
Q							49	47	49	
X							9 928	10 008	16 352	

Men - Hommes - Hombres
ISIC 3 - CITI 3 - CIIU 3

	1999	2000	2001	2002	2003	2004	2005	2006	2007	2008
Total	512 809	539 297					476 656	478 769	487 275	
A							611	680	647	
B							55	32	48	
C							1 240	1 170	1 116	
D	186 692	193 065					110 479	105 604	104 676	
E [2]	1 857	1 889					1 555	1 434	1 413	
F	109 152	115 187					102 043	107 147	109 302	
G [3]	31 584	33 033					71 829	70 740	70 024	
H	22 513	22 309					19 501	19 490	19 722	
I [4]	51 354	53 541					48 533	49 133	49 462	
J							981	947	918	
J-K.O-P.X [5]	109 657	120 273								
K							72 943	75 520	78 397	
L							5 899	5 867	5 877	
M							2 488	2 186	2 183	
N							13 449	13 909	14 577	
O							17 221	17 147	16 921	
P							11	8	0	
Q							28	37	32	
X							7 790	7 718	11 960	

Explanatory notes: see p. 1125.

[1] Cases recognized for compensation during the year. [2] Excl. agents of public gas and electricity services. [3] Excl. food trade. [4] Excl. transport by rail and by sea and communications. [5] Interoccupational group.

Notes explicatives: voir p. 1127.

[1] Cas reconnus pour indemnisation dans l'année. [2] Non compris les agents des services publics du gaz et de l'électricité. [3] Non compris les commerces alimentaires. [4] Non compris les transports par chemin de fer ou par mer et les communications. [5] Groupe interprofessionnel.

Notas explicativas: véase p. 1129.

[1] Casos recogidos para indemnización en el año. [2] Excl. los agentes de los servicios públicos de electricidad y gas. [3] Excl. comercio alimenticio. [4] Excl. transportes ferroviarios y marítimos y las comunicaciones. [5] Grupo interocupacional.

OCCUPATIONAL INJURIES

Cases of injury with lost workdays, by economic activity

LÉSIONS PROFESSIONNELLES

Cas de lésion avec perte de journées de travail, par activité économique

LESIONES PROFESIONALES

Casos de lesión con pérdida de días de trabajo, por actividad económica

France (FA) [1] — Compensated injuries - Lésions indemnisées - Lesiones indemnizadas

Cases of temporary incapacity - Cas d'incapacité temporaire - Casos de incapacidad temporal

Women - Femmes - Mujeres

ISIC 3 - CITI 3 - CIIU 3	1999	2000	2001	2002	2003	2004	2005	2006	2007	2008
Total	143 112	156 042	.	.	.	.	170 623	175 407	186 449	.
A	.	.	.	.	.	.	111	168	177	.
B	.	.	.	.	.	.	12	12	6	.
C	.	.	.	.	.	.	24	17	20	.
D	42 881	46 798	.	.	.	.	22 523	21 732	21 963	.
E [2]	58	59	.	.	.	.	55	56	72	.
F	794	726	.	.	.	.	816	837	1 075	.
G [3]	10 884	11 628	.	.	.	.	34 487	35 084	35 612	.
H	17 147	18 235	.	.	.	.	18 422	18 664	19 656	.
I [4]	3 780	4 465	.	.	.	.	10 070	10 283	10 561	.
J	.	.	.	.	.	.	1 769	1 774	1 730	.
J-K,O-P,X [5]	67 568	74 131	.	.	.	.	24 233	25 328	26 969	.
K	.	.	.	.	.	.	7 481	7 253	7 530	.
L	.	.	.	.	.	.	3 129	2 963	3 441	.
M	.	.	.	.	.	.	38 839	41 908	45 870	.
N	.	.	.	.	.	.	6 487	7 024	7 358	.
O	.	.	.	.	.	.	6	4	0	.
P	.	.	.	.	.	.	21	10	17	.
Q	.	.	.	.	.	.	2 138	2 290	4 392	.
X	.	.	.	.	.	.	.	.	.	.

Total cases (fatal + non-fatal) - Ensemble des cas (mortels + non mortels) - Todos los casos (mortales + no mortales)

Total men and women - Total hommes et femmes - Total hombres y mujeres

ISIC 3 - CITI 3 - CIIU 3	1999	2000	2001	2002	2003	2004	2005	2006	2007	2008
Total	701 175	744 165	738 229	760 666	721 888	692 630	699 691	701 309	720 772	.
A	.	.	.	.	.	.	766	889	870	.
B	.	.	.	.	.	.	72	51	60	.
C	.	.	.	.	.	.	1 399	1 341	1 275	.
D	244 817	256 188	.	.	.	.	144 597	137 299	136 382	.
E [2]	2 090	2 137	.	.	.	.	1 786	1 641	1 617	.
F	119 828	126 171	.	.	.	.	112 765	116 944	119 323	.
G [3]	45 590	47 991	.	.	.	.	113 952	112 493	112 310	.
H	41 548	42 426	.	.	.	.	40 040	40 094	41 340	.
I [4]	59 152	62 496	.	.	.	.	63 520	63 877	64 374	.
J	.	.	.	.	.	.	3 123	3 064	2 940	.
J-K,O-P,X [5]	188 150	206 756	.	.	.	.	105 015	108 094	112 645	.
K	.	.	.	.	.	.	14 466	14 169	14 316	.
L	.	.	.	.	.	.	6 153	5 680	6 065	.
M	.	.	.	.	.	.	55 999	59 362	64 104	.
N	.	.	.	.	.	.	25 406	25 658	25 716	.
O	.	.	.	.	.	.	18	12	0	.
P	.	.	.	.	.	.	56	53	52	.
Q	.	.	.	.	.	.	10 558	10 588	17 383	.
X	.	.	.	.	.	.	.	.	.	.

Men - Hommes - Hombres

ISIC 3 - CITI 3 - CIIU 3	1999	2000	2001	2002	2003	2004	2005	2006	2007	2008
Total	549 071	578 275	.	.	.	.	516 133	513 924	522 194	.
A	.	.	.	.	.	.	647	716	686	.
C	.	.	.	.	.	.	1 373	1 321	1 253	.
D	199 460	206 672	.	.	.	.	120 107	113 908	112 813	.
E [2]	2 028	2 075	.	.	.	.	1 727	1 582	1 541	.
F	118 958	125 357	.	.	.	.	111 879	116 025	118 179	.
G [3]	33 922	35 494	.	.	.	.	77 155	75 371	74 501	.
H	23 575	23 337	.	.	.	.	20 598	20 460	20 674	.
I [4]	55 054	57 689	.	.	.	.	52 814	52 999	53 202	.
J	.	.	.	.	.	.	1 136	1 091	1 045	.
J-K,O-P,X [5]	116 074	127 651	.	.	.	.	78 538	80 667	83 599	.
K	.	.	.	.	.	.	6 341	6 250	6 227	.
L	.	.	.	.	.	.	2 709	2 416	2 384	.
M	.	.	.	.	.	.	14 369	14 690	15 395	.
N	.	.	.	.	.	.	18 362	18 194	17 862	.
O	.	.	.	.	.	.	12	8	0	.
P	.	.	.	.	.	.	34	39	34	.
Q	.	.	.	.	.	.	8 273	8 149	12 748	.
X	.	.	.	.	.	.	.	.	.	.

Explanatory notes: see p. 1125.

[1] Cases recognized for compensation during the year. [2] Excl. agents of public gas and electricity services. [3] Excl. food trade. [4] Excl. transport by rail and by sea and communications. [5] Interoccupational group.

Notes explicatives: voir p. 1127.

[1] Cas reconnus pour indemnisation dans l'année. [2] Non compris les agents des services publics du gaz et de l'électricité. [3] Non compris les commerces alimentaires. [4] Non compris les transports par chemin de fer ou par mer et les communications. [5] Groupe interprofessionnel.

Notas explicativas: véase p. 1129.

[1] Casos recogidos para indemnización en el año. [2] Excl. los agentes de los servicios públicos de electricidad y gas. [3] Excl. comercio alimenticio. [4] Excl. transportes ferroviarios y marítimos y las comunicaciones. [5] Grupo interocupacional.

8A

OCCUPATIONAL INJURIES	LÉSIONS PROFESSIONNELLES	LESIONES PROFESIONALES
Cases of injury with lost workdays, by economic activity	Cas de lésion avec perte de journées de travail, par activité économique	Casos de lesión con pérdida de días de trabajo, por actividad económica

France (FA) [1]

Compensated injuries - Lésions indemnisées - Lesiones indemnizadas

Total cases (fatal + non-fatal) - Ensemble des cas (mortels + non mortels) - Todos los casos (mortales + no mortales)

Women - Femmes - Mujeres
ISIC 3 - CITI 3 - CIIU 3

	1999	2000	2001	2002	2003	2004	2005	2006	2007	2008
Total	152 104	165 890					183 558	187 385	198 578	
A										
B							119	173	184	
C							13	13	9	
D	45 357	49 516					26	20	22	
E [2]	62	62					24 490	23 391	23 569	
F	870	814					59	59	76	
G [3]	11 668	12 497					886	919	1 144	
H	17 973	19 089					36 797	37 122	37 809	
I [4]	4 098	4 807					19 442	19 634	20 666	
J							1 987	1 973	1 895	
J-K.O-P.X [5]	72 076	79 105					1 987	1 973	1 895	
K										
L							26 477	27 427	29 046	
M							8 125	7 919	8 089	
N							3 444	3 264	3 681	
O							41 630	44 672	48 709	
P							7 044	7 464	7 854	
Q							6	4	0	
X							22	14	18	
							2 285	2 439	4 635	

France (FA) [1]

Compensated injuries - Lésions indemnisées - Lesiones indemnizadas

Fatal cases - Cas mortels - Casos mortales

Total men and women - Total hommes et femmes - Total hombres y mujeres
ISIC 3 - CITI 3 - CIIU 3

	1999	2000	2001	2002	2003	2004	2005	2006	2007	2008
A	60			119	97	108	111	92	96	

Men - Hommes - Hombres
ISIC 3 - CITI 3 - CIIU 3

	1999	2000	2001	2002	2003	2004	2005	2006	2007	2008
A				100	88	96	103	79	88	

Women - Femmes - Mujeres
ISIC 3 - CITI 3 - CIIU 3

	1999	2000	2001	2002	2003	2004	2005	2006	2007	2008
A				19	9	13	8	13	8	

Non-fatal cases (temporary + permanent incapacity) - Cas non mortels (incapacité temporaire + permanente) - Casos no mortales (incapacidad temporal + permanente)

Total men and women - Total hommes et femmes - Total hombres y mujeres
ISIC 3 - CITI 3 - CIIU 3

	1999	2000	2001	2002	2003	2004	2005	2006	2007	2008
A	53 442	51 942	53 114	52 537	50 970	48 541	47 585	46 556	45 903	

Men - Hommes - Hombres
ISIC 3 - CITI 3 - CIIU 3

	1999	2000	2001	2002	2003	2004	2005	2006	2007	2008
A		42 069	42 260	41 025	39 445	37 784	36 709	35 474	34 822	

Women - Femmes - Mujeres
ISIC 3 - CITI 3 - CIIU 3

	1999	2000	2001	2002	2003	2004	2005	2006	2007	2008
A		9 873	10 854	11 512	11 525	10 757	10 876	11 082	11 081	

Cases of temporary incapacity - Cas d'incapacité temporaire - Casos de incapacidad temporal

Total men and women - Total hommes et femmes - Total hombres y mujeres
ISIC 3 - CITI 3 - CIIU 3

	1999	2000	2001	2002	2003	2004	2005	2006	2007	2008
A	47 553			44 914	43 166	40 637	40 452	39 471	39 205	

Men - Hommes - Hombres
ISIC 3 - CITI 3 - CIIU 3

	1999	2000	2001	2002	2003	2004	2005	2006	2007	2008
A	39 919			35 262	33 685	32 042	31 547	30 402	30 143	

Women - Femmes - Mujeres
ISIC 3 - CITI 3 - CIIU 3

	1999	2000	2001	2002	2003	2004	2005	2006	2007	2008
A	7 634			9 652	9 481	8 595	8 905	9 069	9 062	

Total cases (fatal + non-fatal) - Ensemble des cas (mortels + non mortels) - Todos los casos (mortales + no mortales)

Total men and women - Total hommes et femmes - Total hombres y mujeres
ISIC 3 - CITI 3 - CIIU 3

	1999	2000	2001	2002	2003	2004	2005	2006	2007	2008
A	53 502			52 656	51 067	48 650	47 696	46 648	45 999	

Explanatory notes: see p. 1125.

[1] Cases recognized for compensation during the year. [2] Excl. agents of public gas and electricity services. [3] Excl. food trade. [4] Excl. transport by rail and by sea and communications. [5] Interoccupational group.

Notes explicatives: voir p. 1127.

[1] Cas reconnus pour indemnisation dans l'année. [2] Non compris les agents des services publics du gaz et de l'électricité. [3] Non compris les commerces alimentaires. [4] Non compris les transports par chemin de fer ou par mer et les communications. [5] Groupe interprofessionnel.

Notas explicativas: véase p. 1129.

[1] Casos recogidos para indemnización en el año. [2] Excl. los agentes de los servicios públicos de electricidad y gas. [3] Excl. comercio alimenticio. [4] Excl. transportes ferroviarios y marítimos y las comunicaciones. [5] Grupo interocupacional.

OCCUPATIONAL INJURIES

Cases of injury with lost workdays, by economic activity

LÉSIONS PROFESSIONNELLES

Cas de lésion avec perte de journées de travail, par activité économique

LESIONES PROFESIONALES

Casos de lesión con pérdida de días de trabajo, por actividad económica

8A

	1999	2000	2001	2002	2003	2004	2005	2006	2007	2008

France (FA) [1] — Compensated injuries - Lésions indemnisées - Lesiones indemnizadas

Total cases (fatal + non-fatal) - Ensemble des cas (mortels + non mortels) - Todos los casos (mortales + no mortales)

Men - Hommes - Hombres
ISIC 3 - CITI 3 - CIIU 3

	1999	2000	2001	2002	2003	2004	2005	2006	2007	2008
A	44 943	.	.	41 125	39 533	37 880	36 812	35 553	34 910	.

Women - Femmes - Mujeres
ISIC 3 - CITI 3 - CIIU 3

	1999	2000	2001	2002	2003	2004	2005	2006	2007	2008
A	8 559	.	.	11 531	11 534	10 770	10 884	11 095	11 089	.

Germany (FA) [2] — Compensated injuries - Lésions indemnisées - Lesiones indemnizadas

Fatal cases - Cas mortels - Casos mortales

Total men and women - Total hommes et femmes - Total hombres y mujeres [3]
ISIC 3 - CITI 3 - CIIU 3

	1999	2000	2001	2002	2003	2004	2005	2006	2007	2008
Total	1 293	1 153	1 107	1 071	1 029	949	863	941	812	.
A	228	243	244	219	214	238	209	233	199	.
B	4	1	2	4	0	2	4	6	0	.
C	32	25	18	18	17	13	6	7	6	.
D	218	198	190	176	158	136	132	131	112	.
E	2	2	4	6	6	9	5	15	3	.
F	227	196	165	194	178	137	138	154	152	.
G	87	76	69	65	69	65	61	70	59	.
H	20	6	7	15	16	16	8	14	20	.
I	297	258	291	174	167	158	143	163	134	.
J	1	3	3	28	20	19	21	2	3	.
K	2	2	1	38	59	43	43	51	45	.
L	13	23	9	26	32	29	9	45	24	.
M	6	2	1	14	6	2	4	2	2	.
N	83	57	54	22	16	27	18	13	15	.
O	62	44	44	31	30	22	31	23	27	.
P	5	4	2	4	3	4	4	1	3	.
Q	0	0	0	0	0	0	0	0	0	.
X	6	13	3	37	38	29	27	11	8	.

Men - Hommes - Hombres [3]
ISIC 3 - CITI 3 - CIIU 3

	1999	2000	2001	2002	2003	2004	2005	2006	2007	2008
Total	1 170	1 051	1 006	951	946	860	786	872	757	.
A	206	225	214	190	201	211	194	219	182	.
B	4	1	2	4	0	2	4	6	0	.
C	31	25	18	18	17	13	6	7	6	.
D	205	183	182	162	147	129	128	123	109	.
E	2	2	4	6	6	9	5	15	3	.
F	219	194	160	194	178	135	137	152	151	.
G	78	61	67	58	61	56	50	60	56	.
H	17	6	3	10	12	11	5	10	17	.
I	286	248	279	161	160	150	139	155	126	.
J	0	2	3	14	9	10	8	2	2	.
K	1	1	1	32	49	40	38	48	41	.
L	11	22	8	23	28	27	7	36	20	.
M	5	1	1	7	4	1	3	0	2	.
N	43	29	23	13	8	16	12	9	10	.
O	53	36	37	22	26	20	26	22	24	.
P	3	2	1	2	3	3	3	0	2	.
Q	0	0	0	0	0	0	0	0	0	.
X	6	13	3	35	37	27	21	8	6	.

Women - Femmes - Mujeres [3]
ISIC 3 - CITI 3 - CIIU 3

	1999	2000	2001	2002	2003	2004	2005	2006	2007	2008
Total	123	102	101	120	83	89	77	69	55	.
A	22	18	30	29	13	27	15	14	17	.
B	0	0	0	0	0	0	0	0	0	.
C	1	0	0	0	0	0	0	0	0	.
D	13	15	8	14	11	7	4	8	3	.
E	0	0	0	0	0	0	1	2	1	.
F	8	2	5	0	0	2	11	10	3	.
G	9	15	2	7	8	9	3	4	3	.
H	3	0	4	5	4	5	4	8	8	.
I	11	10	12	13	7	8	13	0	1	.
J	1	1	0	14	11	9	5	3	4	.
K	1	1	0	6	10	3	2	9	4	.
L	2	1	1	3	4	2	1	2	0	.
M	1	1	0	7	2	1	6	4	5	.
N	40	28	31	9	8	11	5	1	3	.
O	9	8	7	2	4	2	1	1	1	.
P	2	2	1	0	0	1	0	0	2	.
Q	0	0	0	0	0	0	0	3		.
X	0	0	0	2	1	2	6			.

Explanatory notes: see p. 1125.

[1] Cases recognized for compensation during the year. [2] Total may differ from the sum of data by sex due to difficulties in coding certain cases. [3] Deaths occurring within one month of accident.

Notes explicatives: voir p. 1127.

[1] Cas reconnus pour indemnisation dans l'année. [2] Le total peut différer de la somme des données par sexe en raison de difficultés de codification de quelques cas. [3] Les décès survenant pendant le mois qui suit l'accident.

Notas explicativas: véase p. 1129.

[1] Casos recogidos para indemnización en el año. [2] El total puede diferir de la suma de los datos por sexo debido a dificultades de codificación de algunos casos. [3] Los fallecimientos que se produzcan durante el mes posterior al accidente.

OCCUPATIONAL INJURIES

Cases of injury with lost workdays, by economic activity

LÉSIONS PROFESSIONNELLES

Cas de lésion avec perte de journées de travail, par activité économique

LESIONES PROFESIONALES

Casos de lesión con pérdida de días de trabajo, por actividad económica

Germany (FA) [1]

Compensated injuries - Lésions indemnisées - Lesiones indemnizadas

Non-fatal cases (temporary + permanent incapacity) - Cas non mortels (incapacité temporaire + permanente) - Casos no mortales (incapacidad temporal + permanente)

Total men and women - Total hommes et femmes - Total hombres y mujeres [2]
ISIC 3 - CITI 3 - CIIU 3

	1999	2000	2001	2002	2003	2004	2005	2006	2007	2008
Total	1 558 770	1 512 570	1 394 485	1 305 701	1 142 775	1 088 672	1 029 520	1 046 575	1 054 984	.
A	152 004	148 271	134 764	125 379	114 523	107 084	101 240	101 441	98 601	.
B	362	305	328	281	277	279	198	290	262	.
C	16 181	13 160	10 761	5 434	4 731	4 289	3 921	3 704	3 256	.
D	390 787	377 297	355 807	308 572	278 414	261 403	248 404	249 775	257 849	.
E	1 059	833	774	5 948	5 755	5 215	5 056	4 573	4 459	.
F	288 597	260 499	220 534	198 986	171 685	155 338	139 695	143 017	135 670	.
G	114 321	113 798	105 546	113 874	97 488	98 868	94 716	93 986	94 494	.
H	56 243	61 098	56 943	45 240	43 662	42 889	42 873	43 394	41 344	.
I	209 524	200 289	194 162	99 116	71 897	78 312	66 637	69 819	68 522	.
J	8 977	9 832	9 254	47 847	45 115	45 265	44 068	4 636	4 628	.
K	7 507	7 709	7 355	65 832	61 753	63 481	65 159	78 100	84 130	.
L	52 456	53 422	51 371	57 564	53 505	35 212	40 814	79 213	73 983	.
M	37 360	38 277	36 305	50 526	44 339	41 148	36 735	33 764	37 039	.
N	109 635	113 491	105 866	86 551	71 631	73 196	65 886	63 628	63 303	.
O	97 783	99 965	91 973	49 724	41 760	40 372	39 246	39 758	41 756	.
P	1 423	1 495	1 465	1 471	1 231	1 062	1 228	992	1 198	.
Q	0	0	0	65	105	24	51	11	211	.
X	14 554	12 829	11 278	43 290	33 874	34 286	32 730	36 475	44 280	.

Men - Hommes - Hombres [2]
ISIC 3 - CITI 3 - CIIU 3

	1999	2000	2001	2002	2003	2004	2005	2006	2007	2008
Total	1 225 113	1 177 045	1 081 401	1 000 038	873 421	832 178	783 339	801 667	813 825	.
A	117 108	114 944	104 013	98 296	90 022	84 169	79 474	79 711	78 494	.
B	335	281	309	256	250	247	155	276	230	.
C	15 921	12 900	10 551	5 312	4 626	4 127	3 757	3 569	3 240	.
D	338 190	323 559	305 764	266 019	239 697	226 850	211 990	214 245	223 167	.
E	1 016	803	774	5 577	5 378	4 735	4 594	214 245	223 167	.
F	274 898	247 088	208 504	193 100	166 038	151 627	136 070	138 465	132 007	.
G	85 635	85 179	78 184	79 960	67 805	68 395	66 416	65 800	65 711	.
H	26 373	29 486	27 528	24 621	23 251	24 469	23 673	23 438	22 612	.
I	180 762	173 536	167 713	84 414	65 994	67 250	61 662	64 128	62 831	.
J	4 152	4 784	4 391	20 575	19 784	19 574	19 123	2 008	2 130	.
K	3 287	3 628	3 269	51 864	49 110	49 990	51 274	62 822	68 156	.
L	36 738	38 100	36 880	41 141	34 941	25 002	26 648	43 281	40 505	.
M	16 960	17 025	16 704	27 148	25 049	24 260	20 678	18 995	21 447	.
N	39 241	41 002	38 196	29 535	23 371	24 530	22 466	21 729	21 754	.
O	73 288	74 659	68 451	36 686	30 678	29 708	29 393	29 195	31 311	.
P	423	427	393	539	486	362	329	463	432	.
Q	0	0	0	49	105	24	51	11	211	.
X	10 787	9 645	8 650	34 946	26 834	26 409	25 588	29 344	35 549	.

Women - Femmes - Mujeres [2]
ISIC 3 - CITI 3 - CIIU 3

	1999	2000	2001	2002	2003	2004	2005	2006	2007	2008
Total	332 309	333 250	313 084	304 606	267 213	253 913	244 032	244 908	241 159	.
A	34 876	33 280	30 722	27 083	24 501	22 465	21 766	21 729	20 106	.
B	27	24	19	25	27	32	43	14	32	.
C	260	260	210	123	105	139	164	135	16	.
D	52 475	53 671	50 001	42 523	38 650	34 439	36 354	35 529	34 682	.
E	43	21	0	371	377	480	463	386	380	.
F	13 455	13 138	11 865	5 768	5 538	3 599	3 535	4 552	3 663	.
G	28 639	28 570	27 303	33 853	29 633	30 457	28 270	28 186	28 783	.
H	29 820	31 507	29 376	20 619	20 412	18 420	19 200	19 955	18 732	.
I	28 712	26 724	26 419	14 701	5 903	11 062	4 976	5 691	5 691	.
J	4 815	5 020	4 853	26 890	25 011	25 299	24 639	2 628	2 498	.
K	4 180	4 053	4 057	13 741	12 541	13 343	13 666	15 278	16 015	.
L	15 718	15 322	14 491	16 423	18 564	10 210	14 166	35 932	33 478	.
M	20 360	21 072	19 582	23 299	19 188	16 680	15 940	14 769	15 593	.
N	70 224	72 118	67 418	56 995	48 025	48 177	43 103	41 899	41 549	.
O	23 949	24 258	23 087	12 970	10 992	10 591	9 736	10 564	10 445	.
P	999	1 068	1 072	932	745	700	899	529	765	.
Q	0	0	0	16	0	0	0	0		.
X	3 757	3 146	2 609	8 274	7 000	7 819	7 113	7 132	8 731	.

Explanatory notes: see p. 1125.

[1] Total may differ from the sum of data by sex due to difficulties in coding certain cases. [2] Incapacity of 4 days or more.

Notes explicatives: voir p. 1127.

[1] Le total peut différer de la somme des données par sexe en raison de difficultés de codification de quelques cas. [2] Incapacité de 4 jours et plus.

Notas explicativas: véase p. 1129.

[1] El total puede diferir de la suma de los datos por sexo debido a dificultades de codificación de algunos casos. [2] Incapacidad de 4 días y más.

	1999	2000	2001	2002	2003	2004	2005	2006	2007	2008

Germany (FA) [1] Compensated injuries - Lésions indemnisées - Lesiones indemnizadas

Total cases (fatal + non-fatal) - Ensemble des cas (mortels + non mortels) - Todos los casos (mortales + no mortales)

Total men and women - Total hommes et femmes - Total hombres y mujeres
ISIC 3 - CITI 3 - CIIU 3

	1999	2000	2001	2002	2003	2004	2005	2006	2007	2008
Total	1 560 063	1 513 723	1 395 592	1 306 772	1 142 775	1 088 672	1 029 520	1 047 516	1 055 796	.
A	152 232	148 514	135 008	125 598	114 737	107 322	101 449	101 674	98 800	.
B	366	306	330	285	277	281	202	296	262	.
C	16 213	13 185	10 779	5 452	4 748	4 302	3 927	3 711	3 262	.
D	391 005	377 495	355 997	308 748	278 572	261 539	248 536	249 906	257 961	.
E	1 061	835	778	5 954	5 761	5 224	5 061	4 588	4 462	.
F	288 824	260 695	220 699	199 180	171 863	155 475	139 833	143 171	135 822	.
G	114 408	113 874	105 615	113 939	97 557	98 933	94 777	94 056	94 553	.
H	56 263	61 104	56 950	45 255	43 678	42 905	42 881	43 408	41 364	.
I	209 821	200 547	194 453	99 290	72 064	78 470	66 780	69 982	68 656	.
J	8 978	9 835	9 257	47 875	45 135	45 284	44 089	4 638	4 631	.
K	7 509	7 711	7 356	65 870	61 812	63 524	65 202	78 151	84 175	.
L	52 469	53 445	51 380	57 590	53 537	35 241	40 823	79 258	74 007	.
M	37 366	38 279	36 306	50 540	44 345	41 150	36 739	33 766	37 041	.
N	109 718	113 548	105 920	86 573	71 647	73 223	65 904	63 641	63 318	.
O	97 845	100 009	92 017	49 755	41 790	40 394	39 277	39 781	41 783	.
P	1 428	1 499	1 467	1 475	1 234	1 066	1 232	993	1 201	.
Q	0	0	0	65	105	24	51	11	211	.
X	14 560	12 842	11 281	43 327	33 912	34 315	32 757	36 486	44 288	.

Men - Hommes - Hombres
ISIC 3 - CITI 3 - CIIU 3

	1999	2000	2001	2002	2003	2004	2005	2006	2007	2008
Total	1 226 283	1 178 096	1 082 407	1 000 989	874 367	833 038	784 125	802 539	814 582	.
A	117 314	115 169	104 227	98 486	90 223	84 830	79 668	79 930	78 676	.
B	339	282	311	260	250	249	159	282	230	.
C	15 952	12 925	10 569	5 330	4 643	4 140	3 763	3 576	3 246	.
D	338 395	323 742	305 946	266 181	239 844	226 979	212 118	214 368	223 276	.
E	1 018	805	778	5 583	5 384	4 744	4 599	4 202	4 082	.
F	275 117	247 282	208 664	193 294	166 216	151 762	136 207	138 465	132 007	.
G	85 713	85 240	78 251	80 018	67 866	68 451	66 466	65 860	65 767	.
H	26 390	29 492	27 531	24 631	23 263	24 480	23 678	23 448	22 629	.
I	181 048	173 784	167 992	84 575	66 154	67 400	61 801	64 283	62 957	.
J	4 152	4 786	4 394	20 589	19 793	19 584	19 131	2 010	2 132	.
K	3 288	3 629	3 270	51 896	49 159	50 030	51 312	62 870	68 156	.
L	36 749	38 122	36 888	41 164	34 969	25 029	26 655	43 317	40 525	.
M	16 965	17 026	16 705	27 155	25 053	24 261	20 681	18 995	21 449	.
N	39 284	41 031	38 219	29 548	23 379	24 546	22 478	21 738	21 764	.
O	73 341	74 695	68 488	36 708	30 704	29 728	29 419	29 217	31 335	.
P	426	429	394	541	489	365	332	463	434	.
Q	0	0	0	49	105	24	51	11	211	.
X	10 793	9 658	8 653	34 981	26 871	26 436	25 609	29 352	35 555	.

Women - Femmes - Mujeres
ISIC 3 - CITI 3 - CIIU 3

	1999	2000	2001	2002	2003	2004	2005	2006	2007	2008
Total	332 432	333 352	313 185	304 726	267 296	254 002	244 109	244 977	241 214	.
A	34 898	33 298	30 752	27 112	24 514	22 492	21 781	21 743	20 123	.
B	27	24	19	25	27	32	43	14	32	.
C	261	260	210	123	105	139	164	135	16	.
D	52 488	53 686	50 009	42 537	38 661	34 446	36 358	35 537	34 685	.
E	43	21	0	371	377	480	463	386	380	.
F	13 463	13 140	11 870	5 768	5 538	3 601	3 536	4 554	3 664	.
G	28 648	28 585	27 305	33 860	29 641	30 466	28 281	28 196	28 786	.
H	29 823	31 507	29 380	20 624	20 416	18 425	19 203	19 959	18 735	.
I	28 723	26 734	26 431	14 714	5 910	11 070	4 980	5 699	5 699	.
J	4 816	5 021	4 853	26 904	25 022	25 308	24 652	2 628	2 499	.
K	4 181	4 054	4 057	13 747	12 551	13 346	13 671	15 281	16 019	.
L	15 720	15 323	14 492	16 426	18 568	10 212	14 168	35 941	33 482	.
M	20 361	21 073	19 582	23 306	19 190	16 681	15 941	14 771	15 593	.
N	70 264	72 146	67 449	57 004	48 033	48 188	43 109	41 903	41 554	.
O	23 958	24 266	23 094	12 979	10 996	10 593	9 741	10 565	10 448	.
P	1 001	1 070	1 073	934	745	701	900	530	766	.
Q	0	0	0	16	0	0	0	0	0	.
X	3 757	3 146	2 609	8 276	7 001	7 821	7 119	7 135	8 733	.

Explanatory notes: see p. 1125.

Notes explicatives: voir p. 1127.

Notas explicativas: véase p. 1129.

[1] Total may differ from the sum of data by sex due to difficulties in coding certain cases.

[1] Le total peut différer de la somme des données par sexe en raison de difficultés de codification de quelques cas.

[1] El total puede diferir de la suma de los datos por sexo debido a dificultades de codificación de algunos casos.

8A

OCCUPATIONAL INJURIES

Cases of injury with lost workdays, by economic activity

LÉSIONS PROFESSIONNELLES

Cas de lésion avec perte de journées de travail, par activité économique

LESIONES PROFESIONALES

Casos de lesión con pérdida de días de trabajo, por actividad económica

	1999	2000	2001	2002	2003	2004	2005	2006	2007	2008	

Hungary (FF) — Reported injuries - Lésions déclarées - Lesiones declaradas

Fatal cases - Cas mortels - Casos mortales

Total men and women - Total hommes et femmes - Total hombres y mujeres
ISIC 3 - CITI 3 - CIIU 3 / ISIC 4 - CITI 4 - CIIU 4

	1999	2000	2001	2002	2003	2004	2005	2006	2007		2008	
Total	154	151	124	163	133	160	125	123	118	|	116	Total
A-B	.	.	.	.	.	.	.	16	14	|	11	A
A	20	15	14	12	16	13	15	.	.	|	0	B
B	0	1	0	0	0	0	0	.	.	|	18	C
C	0	0	0	0	0	0	1	0	.	|	2	D
D	29	31	25	26	18	38	24	17	18	|	4	E
E	3	5	3	4	1	0	1	2	2	|	41	F
F	47	35	32	49	35	55	39	35	45	|	11	G
G	15	17	11	14	19	16	11	9	4	|	15	H
H	5	4	1	4	0	1	2	2	1	|	1	I
I	15	21	18	29	23	18	14	14	18	|	0	J
J	2	0	2	7	0	0	0	0	1	|	0	K
K	9	9	3	11	9	6	7	8	7	|	2	L
L	2	1	10	4	4	3	3	6	4	|	0	M
M	3	7	2	1	3	2	1	4	0	|	4	N
N	1	3	1	1	0	3	2	5	2	|	0	O
O	3	2	2	1	2	5	5	5	2	|	2	P
Q	0	0	0	0	0	0	0	0	.	|	3	Q
X	0	0	0	0	0	0	0	0	.	|	1	R
										|	1	S
										|	0	T
										|	0	U

Men - Hommes - Hombres
ISIC 3 - CITI 3 - CIIU 3 / ISIC 4 - CITI 4 - CIIU 4

	1999	2000	2001	2002	2003	2004	2005	2006	2007		2008	
Total	149	143	115	149	129	151	121	115	116	|	107	Total
A-B	.	.	.	.	.	.	.	16	14	|	10	A
A	20	15	14	11	16	13	15	.	.	|	0	B
B	0	1	0	0	0	0	0	.	.	|	15	C
C	0	0	0	0	0	0	1	0	0	|	2	D
D	28	30	24	24	18	34	23	16	17	|	4	E
E	3	5	3	4	1	0	1	2	2	|	41	F
F	47	35	31	49	35	55	39	35	45	|	10	G
G	15	16	11	10	18	14	10	8	4	|	14	H
H	4	4	0	3	0	1	2	2	1	|	1	I
I	14	19	17	28	22	18	14	14	17	|	0	J
J	1	0	0	2	0	0	0	0	1	|	0	K
K	9	9	3	11	9	5	7	7	7	|	2	L
L	2	1	8	4	4	3	2	4	4	|	0	M
M	3	5	2	1	3	2	1	3	0	|	3	N
N	0	2	0	1	0	2	2	4	2	|	0	O
O	3	1	2	1	2	4	4	4	2	|	1	P
Q	0	0	0	0	0	0	0	0	.	|	3	Q
X	0	0	0	0	0	0	0	0	.	|	1	R
										|	0	S
										|	0	T
										|	0	U

Women - Femmes - Mujeres
ISIC 3 - CITI 3 - CIIU 3 / ISIC 4 - CITI 4 - CIIU 4

	1999	2000	2001	2002	2003	2004	2005	2006	2007		2008	
Total	5	8	9	14	4	9	4	8	2	|	9	Total
A-B	.	.	.	.	.	.	.	0	0	|	1	A
A	0	0	0	1	0	0	0	.	.	|	0	B
B	0	0	0	0	0	0	0	.	.	|	3	C
C	0	0	0	0	0	0	0	0	0	|	0	D
D	1	1	1	2	3	4	1	1	1	|	0	E
E	0	0	0	0	0	0	0	0	0	|	0	F
F	0	0	1	0	0	0	0	0	0	|	1	G
G	0	1	0	4	1	2	1	1	0	|	1	H
H	1	0	1	1	0	0	0	0	0	|	0	I
I	1	2	1	1	1	0	0	0	1	|	0	J
J	1	0	2	5	0	0	0	0	0	|	0	K
K	0	0	0	0	0	1	0	1	0	|	0	L
L	0	0	2	0	0	0	1	2	0	|	0	M
M	0	2	0	0	0	0	0	1	0	|	1	N
N	1	1	1	0	0	1	0	1	0	|	0	O
O	0	1	0	0	0	1	1	1	0	|	0	P
Q	0	0	0	0	0	0	0	0	.	|	0	Q
X	0	0	0	0	0	0	0	0	.	|	0	R
										|	1	S
										|	0	T
										|	0	U

Explanatory notes: see p. 1125.   Notes explicatives: voir p. 1127.   Notas explicativas: véase p. 1129.

OCCUPATIONAL INJURIES

LÉSIONS PROFESSIONNELLES

LESIONES PROFESIONALES

Cases of injury with lost workdays, by economic activity

Cas de lésion avec perte de journées de travail, par activité économique

Casos de lesión con pérdida de días de trabajo, por actividad económica

	1999	2000	2001	2002	2003	2004	2005	2006	2007		2008	

Hungary (FF) — Reported injuries - Lésions déclarées - Lesiones declaradas

Non-fatal cases (temporary + permanent incapacity) - Cas non mortels (incapacité temporaire + permanente) - Casos no mortales (incapacidad temporal + permanente)

Total men and women - Total hommes et femmes - Total hombres y mujeres

ISIC 3 - CITI 3 - CIIU 3 [1] · ISIC 4 - CITI 4 - CIIU 4

ISIC 3	1999	2000	2001	2002	2003	2004	2005	2006	2007		2008	ISIC 4
Total	26 543	27 063	25 412	25 121	25 612	23 712	23 846	22 562	20 804	|	22 101	Total
A-B	.	.	.	.	.	.	.	1 048	893	|	862	A
A	2 183	2 179	1 737	1 623	1 594	1 317	1 227	.	.	|	14	B
B	12	19	0	0	0	0	0	.	.	|	9 213	C
C	25	40	29	22	27	16	21	14	9	|	117	D
D	12 146	12 530	11 941	11 849	11 416	10 306	9 877	9 136	8 823	|	555	E
E	597	584	453	437	483	422	435	372	258	|	1 273	F
F	1 610	1 510	1 536	1 413	1 369	1 292	1 341	1 410	1 253	|	2 681	G
G	1 959	2 285	2 306	2 322	2 606	2 476	2 728	2 850	2 614	|	2 647	H
H	555	629	559	450	444	497	515	507	475	|	563	I
I	3 106	2 788	2 608	2 683	2 889	2 817	2 800	2 671	2 399	|	146	J
J	78	109	82	85	81	88	82	93	106	|	174	K
K	720	785	776	861	924	867	943	833	833	|	181	L
L	543	449	496	513	587	534	613	626	522	|	195	M
M	899	986	882	825	890	838	931	827	813	|	519	N
N	1 377	1 380	1 349	1 354	1 534	1 490	1 490	1 380	1 181	|	583	O
O	696	769	658	684	771	752	843	795	625	|	873	P
Q	36	17	0	0	0	0	0	0	.	|	1 204	Q
X	1	4	0	0	0	0	0	0	.	|	173	R
										|	125	S
										|	1	T
										|	2	U

Men - Hommes - Hombres

ISIC 3 - CITI 3 - CIIU 3 [1] · ISIC 4 - CITI 4 - CIIU 4

ISIC 3	1999	2000	2001	2002	2003	2004	2005	2006	2007		2008	ISIC 4
Total	19 595	19 857	18 474	17 950	18 060	16 461	16 411	15 593	14 415	|	14 960	Total
A-B	.	.	.	.	.	.	.	874	752	|	723	A
A	1 855	1 815	1 434	1 383	1 340	1 103	1 045	.	.	|	10	B
B	11	13	0	0	0	0	0	.	.	|	6 870	C
C	19	35	28	17	27	14	18	14	8	|	99	D
D	9 420	9 673	9 142	9 000	8 551	7 656	7 336	6 814	6 700	|	515	E
E	509	488	387	373	419	358	356	313	217	|	1 230	F
F	1 523	1 461	1 454	1 375	1 333	1 257	1 303	1 374	1 226	|	1 507	G
G	1 278	1 518	1 469	1 439	1 581	1 468	1 575	1 662	1 500	|	2 010	H
H	265	328	312	174	179	227	205	205	194	|	245	I
I	2 530	2 249	2 127	2 123	2 314	2 204	2 189	2 140	1 838	|	105	J
J	25	33	28	15	17	30	19	28	27	|	71	K
K	520	554	523	582	633	581	651	546	567	|	125	L
L	276	240	240	223	249	227	271	298	213	|	140	M
M	306	364	337	227	244	218	238	242	224	|	298	N
N	504	490	505	507	566	544	566	478	462	|	254	O
O	529	583	488	512	608	574	639	605	487	|	206	P
Q	25	11	0	0	0	0	0	0	.	|	387	Q
X	0	2	0	0	0	0	0	0	.	|	103	R
										|	60	S
										|	1	T
										|	1	U

Women - Femmes - Mujeres

ISIC 3 - CITI 3 - CIIU 3 [1] · ISIC 4 - CITI 4 - CIIU 4

ISIC 3	1999	2000	2001	2002	2003	2004	2005	2006	2007		2008	ISIC 4
Total	6 948	7 206	6 938	7 171	7 552	7 251	7 435	6 969	6 310	|	7 141	Total
A-B	.	.	.	.	.	.	.	174	141	|	139	A
A	328	364	303	240	254	214	182	.	.	|	4	B
B	1	6	0	0	0	0	0	.	.	|	2 343	C
C	6	5	1	5	0	2	3	0	1	|	18	D
D	2 726	2 857	2 799	2 849	2 862	2 650	2 541	2 322	2 123	|	40	E
E	88	96	66	64	64	64	79	59	41	|	43	F
F	87	49	82	38	36	35	38	36	27	|	1 174	G
G	681	767	837	883	1 025	1 008	1 153	1 188	1 114	|	637	H
H	290	301	247	276	265	270	310	302	281	|	318	I
I	576	539	481	560	575	613	611	531	561	|	41	J
J	53	76	54	70	64	58	63	65	0	|	103	K
K	200	231	253	279	291	286	292	287	266	|	56	L
L	267	209	256	290	338	307	342	328	309	|	55	M
M	593	622	545	598	646	620	693	585	589	|	221	N
N	873	890	844	847	968	946	924	902	719	|	329	O
O	167	186	170	172	163	178	204	190	138	|	667	P
Q	11	6	0	0	0	0	0	0	.	|	817	Q
X	1	2	0	0	0	0	0	0	.	|	70	R
										|	65	S
										|	0	T
										|	1	U

Explanatory notes: see p. 1125.

Notes explicatives: voir p. 1127.

Notas explicativas: véase p. 1129.

[1] Incapacity of 4 workdays or more.

[1] Incapacité de 4 journées de travail et plus.

[1] Incapacidad de 4 días de trabajo y más.

OCCUPATIONAL INJURIES

Cases of injury with lost workdays, by economic activity

LÉSIONS PROFESSIONNELLES

Cas de lésion avec perte de journées de travail, par activité économique

LESIONES PROFESIONALES

Casos de lesión con pérdida de días de trabajo, por actividad económica

Hungary (FF) — Reported injuries - Lésions déclarées - Lesiones declaradas

Cases of temporary incapacity - Cas d'incapacité temporaire - Casos de incapacidad temporal

Total men and women - Total hommes et femmes - Total hombres y mujeres

ISIC 3 - CITI 3 - CIIU 3 [1] · ISIC 4 - CITI 4 - CIIU 4

Code	1999	2000	2001	2002	2003	2004	2005	2006	2007		2008		Code
Total	26 408	26 948	25 313	25 069	25 566	23 659	23 918	22 518	20 762	|	22 044	|	Total
A-B								1 045	891	|	859	|	A
A	2 167	2 175	1 730	1 620	1 587	1 312	1 226			|	14	|	B
B	12	18	0	0	0	0	0			|	9 176	|	C
C	25	39	28	22	27	16	21	14	9	|	116	|	D
D	12 089	12 467	11 896	11 808	11 387	10 281	9 864	9 118	8 797	|	554	|	E
E	596	582	451	437	483	420	435	372	258	|	1 268	|	F
F	1 587	1 495	1 520	1 410	1 367	1 283	1 339	1 404	1 249	|	2 678	|	G
G	1 949	2 274	2 294	2 320	2 604	2 473	2 724	2 846	2 613	|	2 644	|	H
H	552	629	557	450	443	496	515	505	474	|	562	|	I
I	3 095	2 778	2 603	2 682	2 886	2 812	2 796	2 664	2 395	|	146	|	J
J	78	109	82	85	81	88	82	93	106	|	174	|	K
K	716	782	775	861	923	867	941	831	829	|	181	|	L
L	541	449	495	513	586	534	613	626	522	|	194	|	M
M	898	983	880	824	889	837	931	827	813	|	519	|	N
N	1 376	1 380	1 348	1 354	1 532	1 490	1 489	1 380	1 181	|	583	|	O
O	690	767	654	683	771	750	842	793	625	|	873	|	P
Q	36	17	0	0	0	0	0	0		|	1 204	|	Q
X	1	4	0	0	0	0	0	0		|	173	|	R
										|	123	|	S
										|	1	|	T
										|	2	|	U

Men - Hommes - Hombres

ISIC 3 - CITI 3 - CIIU 3 [1] · ISIC 4 - CITI 4 - CIIU 4

Code	1999	2000	2001	2002	2003	2004	2005	2006	2007		2008		Code
Total	19 480	19 748	18 385	17 902	18 017	16 415	16 366	15 556	14 376	|	14 912	|	Total
A-B								871	750	|	720	|	A
A	1 839	1 812	1 427	1 380	1 334	1 099	1 044			|	10	|	B
B	11	12	0	0	0	0	0			|	6 838	|	C
C	19	34	27	17	27	14	18	14	8	|	98	|	D
D	9 376	9 614	9 102	8 963	8 524	7 635	7 306	6 799	6 676	|	515	|	E
E	508	486	385	373	419	356	356	313	217	|	1 225	|	F
F	1 501	1 446	1 438	1 372	1 331	1 248	1 301	1 368	1 222	|	1 504	|	G
G	1 270	1 507	1 459	1 437	1 579	1 465	1 571	1 658	1 499	|	2 007	|	H
H	263	328	311	174	179	227	205	205	193	|	245	|	I
I	2 520	2 239	2 124	2 122	2 311	2 200	2 186	2 134	1 834	|	105	|	J
J	25	33	28	15	17	30	19	28	27	|	71	|	K
K	517	551	522	582	632	581	649	544	564	|	125	|	L
L	275	240	239	223	248	227	271	298	213	|	139	|	M
M	305	361	335	226	243	217	238	242	224	|	298	|	N
N	503	490	504	507	565	544	564	478	462	|	254	|	O
O	523	582	484	511	608	572	638	604	487	|	206	|	P
Q	25	11	0	0	0	0	0	0		|	387	|	Q
X	0	2	0	0	0	0	0	0		|	103	|	R
										|	60	|	S
										|	1	|	T
										|	1	|	U

Women - Femmes - Mujeres

ISIC 3 - CITI 3 - CIIU 3 [1] · ISIC 4 - CITI 4 - CIIU 4

Code	1999	2000	2001	2002	2003	2004	2005	2006	2007		2008		Code
Total	6 928	7 200	6 928	7 167	7 549	7 244	7 427	6 962	6 386	|	7 132	|	Total
A-B								174	141	|	139	|	A
A	328	363	303	240	253	213	182			|	4	|	B
B	1	6	0	0	0	0	0			|	2 338	|	C
C	6	5	1	5	0	2	3	0		|	18	|	D
D	2 713	2 853	2 794	2 845	2 863	2 646	2 534	2 319	2 121	|	39	|	E
E	88	96	66	64	64	64	79	59	41	|	43	|	F
F	86	49	82	38	36	35	38	36	27	|	1 174	|	G
G	679	767	835	883	1 025	1 008	1 153	1 188	1 114	|	637	|	H
H	289	301	246	276	264	269	310	300	281	|	317	|	I
I	575	539	479	560	575	612	610	530	561	|	41	|	J
J	53	76	54	70	64	58	63	65	79	|	103	|	K
K	199	231	253	279	291	286	292	287	265	|	56	|	L
L	266	209	256	290	338	307	342	328	309	|	55	|	M
M	593	622	545	598	646	620	693	585	589	|	221	|	N
N	873	890	844	847	967	946	924	902	719	|	329	|	O
O	167	185	170	172	163	178	204	189	138	|	667	|	P
Q	11	6	0	0	0	0	0	0		|	817	|	Q
X	1	2	0	0	0	0	0	0		|	70	|	R
										|	63	|	S
										|	0	|	T
										|	1	|	U

Explanatory notes: see p. 1125. · Notes explicatives: voir p. 1127. · Notas explicativas: véase p. 1129.

[1] Incapacity of 4 workdays or more. · [1] Incapacité de 4 journées de travail et plus. · [1] Incapacidad de 4 días de trabajo y más.

OCCUPATIONAL INJURIES

Cases of injury with lost workdays, by economic activity

LÉSIONS PROFESSIONNELLES

Cas de lésion avec perte de journées de travail, par activité économique

LESIONES PROFESIONALES

Casos de lesión con pérdida de días de trabajo, por actividad económica

8A

Hungary (FF) — Reported injuries - Lésions déclarées - Lesiones declaradas

Total cases (fatal + non-fatal) - Ensemble des cas (mortels + non mortels) - Todos los casos (mortales + no mortales)

Total men and women - Total hommes et femmes - Total hombres y mujeres

ISIC 3 - CITI 3 - CIIU 3 · ISIC 4 - CITI 4 - CIIU 4

ISIC 3	1999	2000	2001	2002	2003	2004	2005	2006	2007	2008	ISIC 4
Total	26 697	27 214	25 536	25 284	25 745	23 872	23 971	22 685	20 922	22 217	Total
A-B	.	.	.	.	.	.	.	1 064	907	873	A
A	2 203	2 194	1 751	1 635	1 610	1 330	1 242	.	.	14	B
B	12	20	0	0	0	0	0	.	.	9 231	C
C	25	40	29	22	27	16	22	14	9	119	D
D	12 175	12 561	11 966	11 875	11 434	10 344	9 901	9 153	8 841	559	E
E	600	589	456	441	484	422	436	374	260	1 314	F
F	1 657	1 545	1 568	1 462	1 404	1 347	1 380	1 445	1 298	2 692	G
G	1 974	2 302	2 317	2 336	2 625	2 492	2 739	2 859	2 618	2 662	H
H	560	633	560	454	444	498	517	509	476	564	I
I	3 121	2 809	2 626	2 712	2 912	2 835	2 814	2 685	2 417	146	J
J	80	109	84	92	81	88	82	93	107	174	K
K	729	794	779	872	933	873	950	841	840	183	L
L	545	450	506	517	591	537	616	632	526	195	M
M	902	993	884	826	893	840	932	831	813	523	N
N	1 378	1 383	1 350	1 355	1 534	1 493	1 492	1 385	1 183	583	O
O	699	771	660	685	773	757	848	800	627	875	P
Q	36	17	0	0	0	0	0	0	0	1 207	Q
X	1	4	0	0	0	0	0	0	.	174	R
										126	S
										1	T
										2	U

Men - Hommes - Hombres

ISIC 3 - CITI 3 - CIIU 3 · ISIC 4 - CITI 4 - CIIU 4

ISIC 3	1999	2000	2001	2002	2003	2004	2005	2006	2007	2008	ISIC 4
Total	19 744	20 000	18 589	18 099	18 189	16 612	16 532	15 708	14 531	15 067	Total
A-B	.	.	.	.	.	.	.	890	766	733	A
A	1 875	1 830	1 448	1 394	1 356	1 116	1 060	.	.	10	B
B	11	14	0	0	0	0	0	.	.	6 885	C
C	19	35	28	17	27	14	19	14	8	101	D
D	9 448	9 703	9 166	9 024	8 569	7 690	7 359	6 830	6 717	519	E
E	512	493	390	377	420	358	357	315	219	1 271	F
F	1 570	1 496	1 485	1 424	1 368	1 312	1 342	1 409	1 271	1 517	G
G	1 293	1 534	1 480	1 449	1 599	1 482	1 585	1 670	1 504	2 024	H
H	269	332	312	177	179	229	207	207	195	246	I
I	2 544	2 268	2 144	2 151	2 336	2 222	2 203	2 154	1 855	105	J
J	26	33	28	17	17	30	19	28	28	71	K
K	529	563	526	593	642	586	658	553	574	127	L
L	278	241	248	227	253	230	273	302	217	140	M
M	309	369	339	228	247	220	239	245	224	301	N
N	504	492	505	508	566	546	568	482	464	254	O
O	532	584	490	513	610	578	643	609	489	207	P
Q	25	11	0	0	0	0	0	0	0	390	Q
X	0	2	0	0	0	0	0	0	.	104	R
										60	S
										1	T
										1	U

Women - Femmes - Mujeres

ISIC 3 - CITI 3 - CIIU 3 · ISIC 4 - CITI 4 - CIIU 4

ISIC 3	1999	2000	2001	2002	2003	2004	2005	2006	2007	2008	ISIC 4
Total	6 953	7 214	6 947	7 185	7 556	7 260	7 439	6 977	6 312	7 150	Total
A-B	.	.	.	.	.	.	.	174	141	140	A
A	328	364	303	241	254	214	182	.	.	4	B
B	1	6	0	0	0	0	0	.	.	2 346	C
C	6	5	1	5	0	2	3	0	1	18	D
D	2 727	2 858	2 800	2 851	2 865	2 654	2 542	2 323	2 124	40	E
E	88	96	66	64	64	64	79	59	41	43	F
F	87	49	83	38	36	35	38	36	27	1 175	G
G	681	768	837	887	1 026	1 010	1 154	1 189	1 114	638	H
H	291	301	248	277	265	270	310	302	281	318	I
I	577	541	482	561	576	613	611	531	562	41	J
J	54	76	56	75	64	58	63	65	.	103	K
K	200	231	253	279	291	287	292	288	266	56	L
L	267	209	258	290	338	307	343	330	309	55	M
M	593	624	545	598	646	620	693	586	589	222	N
N	874	891	845	847	968	947	924	903	719	329	O
O	167	187	170	172	163	179	205	191	138	668	P
Q	11	6	0	0	0	0	0	0	0	817	Q
X	1	2	0	0	0	0	0	0	.	70	R
										66	S
										0	T
										1	U

Explanatory notes: see p. 1125. Notes explicatives: voir p. 1127. Notas explicativas: véase p. 1129.

8A

OCCUPATIONAL INJURIES	LÉSIONS PROFESSIONNELLES	LESIONES PROFESIONALES
Cases of injury with lost workdays, by economic activity	Cas de lésion avec perte de journées de travail, par activité économique	Casos de lesión con pérdida de días de trabajo, por actividad económica

	1999	2000	2001	2002	2003	2004	2005	2006	2007	2008

Iceland (F)

Reported injuries - Lésions déclarées - Lesiones declaradas

Fatal cases - Cas mortels - Casos mortales

Total men and women - Total hommes et femmes - Total hombres y mujeres
ISIC 3 - CITI 3 - CIIU 3

	1999	2000	2001	2002	2003	2004	2005	2006	2007	2008
Total	6	4	1	0	4	2	3	6	.	.
A	1	1	0	0	2	0	0	0	.	.
B	0	0	0	0	0	0	0	0	.	.
C	0	0	0	0	0	0	0	0	.	.
D	2	0	1	0	1	0	0	0	.	.
E	0	0	0	0	1	0	2	0	.	.
F	0	3	0	0	0	0	0	0	.	.
G	0	0	0	0	1	2	1	4	.	.
H	0	0	0	0	0	0	0	0	.	.
I	2	0	0	0	0	0	0	0	.	.
J	0	0	0	0	0	0	0	1	.	.
K	0	0	0	0	0	0	0	0	.	.
L	0	0	0	0	0	0	0	0	.	.
M	0	0	0	0	0	0	0	0	.	.
N	1	0	0	0	0	0	0	0	.	.
O	0	0	0	0	0	0	0	0	.	.
Q	0	0	0	0	0	0	0	1	.	.
X	0	0	0	0	0	0	0	0	.	.

Men - Hommes - Hombres
ISIC 3 - CITI 3 - CIIU 3

	1999	2000	2001	2002	2003	2004	2005	2006	2007	2008
Total	.	.	.	.	.	.	3	6		
A	.	.	.	.	.	.	0	0		
B	.	.	.	.	.	.	0	0		
C	.	.	.	.	.	.	0	0		
D	.	.	.	.	.	.	0	0		
E	.	.	.	.	.	.	2	0		
F	.	.	.	.	.	.	0	0		
G	.	.	.	.	.	.	1	4		
H	.	.	.	.	.	.	0	0		
I	.	.	.	.	.	.	0	0		
J	.	.	.	.	.	.	0	1		
K	.	.	.	.	.	.	0	0		
L	.	.	.	.	.	.	0	0		
M	.	.	.	.	.	.	0	0		
N	.	.	.	.	.	.	0	0		
O	.	.	.	.	.	.				
Q	.	.	.	.	.	.	0	1		
X	.	.	.	.	.	.	0	0		
	.	.	.	.	.	.	0	0		

Women - Femmes - Mujeres
ISIC 3 - CITI 3 - CIIU 3

	1999	2000	2001	2002	2003	2004	2005	2006	2007	2008
Total							0	0		

Non-fatal cases (temporary + permanent incapacity) - Cas non mortels (incapacité temporaire + permanente) - Casos no mortales (incapacidad temporal + permanente)

Total men and women - Total hommes et femmes - Total hombres y mujeres [1]
ISIC 3 - CITI 3 - CIIU 3

	1999	2000	2001	2002	2003	2004	2005	2006	2007	2008
Total	1 301	1 393	1 318	1 294	1 304	1 674	1 432	1 619	.	.
A	26	41	56	42	20	19	12	12	.	.
B	7	6	10	18	15	6	4	6	.	.
C	0	0	0	0	0	0	0	0	.	.
D	478	440	454	429	496	435	358	449	.	.
E	29	46	34	38	38	34	13	14	.	.
F	179	214	204	173	183	657	565	576	.	.
G	105	140	103	111	113	113	91	105	.	.
H	10	8	18	19	13	14	21	13	.	.
I	190	190	173	179	176	158	139	134	.	.
J	1	3	1	2	0	0	3	2	.	.
K	10	7	2	17	10	10	5	8	.	.
L	114	139	111	117	97	77	63	76	.	.
M	21	13	22	31	21	23	22	24	.	.
N	72	125	102	96	97	101	129	165	.	.
O	30	19	26	20	23	25	0	29	.	.
Q	27	0	0	0	0	0	6	3	.	.
X	2	2	2	2	2	2	1	3	.	.

Explanatory notes: see p. 1125.
[1] Incapacity of 2 days or more.

Notes explicatives: voir p. 1127.
[1] Incapacité de 2 jours et plus.

Notas explicativas: véase p. 1129.
[1] Incapacidad de 2 días y más.

OCCUPATIONAL INJURIES	LÉSIONS PROFESSIONNELLES	LESIONES PROFESIONALES
Cases of injury with lost workdays, by economic activity	**Cas de lésion avec perte de journées de travail, par activité économique**	**Casos de lesión con pérdida de días de trabajo, por actividad económica**

	1999	2000	2001	2002	2003	2004	2005	2006	2007	2008

Iceland (F)   **Reported injuries - Lésions déclarées - Lesiones declaradas**

Non-fatal cases (temporary + permanent incapacity) - Cas non mortels (incapacité temporaire + permanente) - Casos no mortales (incapacidad temporal + permanente)

Men - Hommes - Hombres [1]
ISIC 3 - CITI 3 - CIIU 3

	1999	2000	2001	2002	2003	2004	2005	2006	2007	2008
Total	.	.	.	.	.	.	1 004	1 140	.	.
A	.	.	.	.	.	.	8	7	.	.
B	.	.	.	.	.	.	1	5	.	.
C	.	.	.	.	.	.	0	0	.	.
D	.	.	.	.	.	.	263	337	.	.
E	.	.	.	.	.	.	12	12	.	.
F	.	.	.	.	.	.	448	485	.	.
G	.	.	.	.	.	.	63	68	.	.
H	.	.	.	.	.	.	7	7	.	.
I	.	.	.	.	.	.	89	84	.	.
J	.	.	.	.	.	.	1	2	.	.
K	.	.	.	.	.	.	4	5	.	.
L	.	.	.	.	.	.	46	55	.	.
M	.	.	.	.	.	.	3	7	.	.
N	.	.	.	.	.	.	.	43	.	.
O [2]	.	.	.	.	.	.	53	20	.	.
Q	.	.	.	.	.	.	5	1	.	.
X	.	.	.	.	.	.	1	2	.	.

Women - Femmes - Mujeres [1]
ISIC 3 - CITI 3 - CIIU 3

	1999	2000	2001	2002	2003	2004	2005	2006	2007	2008
Total	.	.	.	.	.	.	428	479	.	.
A	.	.	.	.	.	.	4	5	.	.
B	.	.	.	.	.	.	3	1	.	.
C	.	.	.	.	.	.	0	0	.	.
D	.	.	.	.	.	.	95	112	.	.
E	.	.	.	.	.	.	1	2	.	.
F	.	.	.	.	.	.	117	91	.	.
G	.	.	.	.	.	.	28	37	.	.
H	.	.	.	.	.	.	14	6	.	.
I	.	.	.	.	.	.	50	50	.	.
J	.	.	.	.	.	.	2	0	.	.
K	.	.	.	.	.	.	1	3	.	.
L	.	.	.	.	.	.	17	21	.	.
M	.	.	.	.	.	.	19	17	.	.
N	.	.	.	.	.	.	.	122	.	.
O [2]	.	.	.	.	.	.	76	9	.	.
Q	.	.	.	.	.	.	1	2	.	.
X	.	.	.	.	.	.	0	1	.	.

Total cases (fatal + non-fatal) - Ensemble des cas (mortels + non mortels) - Todos los casos (mortales + no mortales)

Total men and women - Total hommes et femmes - Total hombres y mujeres
ISIC 3 - CITI 3 - CIIU 3

	1999	2000	2001	2002	2003	2004	2005	2006	2007	2008
Total	1 307	1 397	1 318	1 294	1 308	1 676	1 435	1 625	.	.
A	27	42	56	42	22	19	12	12	.	.
B	7	6	10	18	15	6	4	6	.	.
C	0	0	0	0	0	0	0	0	.	.
D	480	440	454	429	497	435	360	449	.	.
E	29	46	34	38	38	34	13	14	.	.
F	179	217	204	173	184	659	566	580	.	.
G	105	140	103	111	113	113	91	105	.	.
H	10	8	18	19	13	14	21	13	.	.
I	192	190	173	179	176	158	139	135	.	.
J	1	3	1	2	0	0	3	2	.	.
K	10	7	2	17	10	10	5	8	.	.
L	114	139	111	117	97	77	63	76	.	.
M	21	13	22	31	21	23	22	24	.	.
N	73	125	102	96	97	101	129	165	.	.
O	30	19	26	20	23	25	0	30	.	.
Q	27	0	0	0	0	0	6	3	.	.
X	2	2	2	2	2	2	1	3	.	.

Men - Hommes - Hombres
ISIC 3 - CITI 3 - CIIU 3

	1999	2000	2001	2002	2003	2004	2005	2006	2007	2008
Total	.	.	.	.	.	.	1 007	1 146	.	.
A	.	.	.	.	.	.	8	7	.	.
B	.	.	.	.	.	.	1	5	.	.
C	.	.	.	.	.	.	0	0	.	.
D	.	.	.	.	.	.	265	337	.	.
E	.	.	.	.	.	.	12	12	.	.
F	.	.	.	.	.	.	449	489	.	.
G	.	.	.	.	.	.	63	68	.	.
H	.	.	.	.	.	.	7	7	.	.
I	.	.	.	.	.	.	89	85	.	.
J	.	.	.	.	.	.	1	2	.	.
K	.	.	.	.	.	.	4	5	.	.
L	.	.	.	.	.	.	46	55	.	.
M	.	.	.	.	.	.	3	7	.	.
N	.	.	.	.	.	.	.	43	.	.
O [2]	.	.	.	.	.	.	53	21	.	.
Q	.	.	.	.	.	.	5	1	.	.
X	.	.	.	.	.	.	1	2	.	.

Explanatory notes: see p. 1125.   Notes explicatives: voir p. 1127.   Notas explicativas: véase p. 1129.

[1] Incapacity of 2 days or more. [2] Incl. category N.   [1] Incapacité de 2 jours et plus. [2] Y compris la catégorie N.   [1] Incapacidad de 2 días y más. [2] Incl. la categoría N.

	OCCUPATIONAL INJURIES	LÉSIONS PROFESSIONNELLES	LESIONES PROFESIONALES
	Cases of injury with lost workdays, by economic activity	Cas de lésion avec perte de journées de travail, par activité économique	Casos de lesión con pérdida de días de trabajo, por actividad económica

	1999	2000	2001	2002	2003	2004	2005	2006	2007	2008

Iceland (F)   Reported injuries - Lésions déclarées - Lesiones declaradas

Total cases (fatal + non-fatal) - Ensemble des cas (mortels + non mortels) - Todos los casos (mortales + no mortales)

Women - Femmes - Mujeres
ISIC 3 - CITI 3 - CIIU 3

	1999	2000	2001	2002	2003	2004	2005	2006	2007	2008
Total							428	479		
A							4	5		
B							3	1		
C							0	0		
D							95	112		
E							1	2		
F							117	91		
G							28	37		
H							14	6		
I							50	50		
J							2	0		
K							1	3		
L							17	21		
M							19	17		
N							.	122		
O [1]							76	9		
Q							1	2		
X							0	1		

Ireland (BA) [2]   Reported injuries - Lésions déclarées - Lesiones declaradas

Non-fatal cases (temporary + permanent incapacity) - Cas non mortels (incapacité temporaire + permanente) - Casos no mortales (incapacidad temporal + permanente)

Total men and women - Total hommes et femmes - Total hombres y mujeres [3]
ISIC 3 - CITI 3 - CIIU 3

	1999	2000	2001	2002	2003	2004	2005	2006	2007	2008
Total	14 900	12 600	.	24 800	22 400	21 600	23 900	24 400	28 800	.
A-B	1 800	1 100	.	2 000	1 500	2 100	1 900	1 100	1 300	.
C-E	4 000	3 300	.	6 500	5 600	3 200	4 500	4 700	6 400	.
F	2 300	2 100	.	4 800	5 400	5 300	5 700	5 800	5 800	.
G	1 200	1 400	.	2 300	2 700	2 100	2 300	1 200	3 700	.
H	900	700	.	900	1 200	700	1 760	400	1 300	.
I	1 300	1 200	.	1 600	1 300	2 200	1 000	3 800	1 900	.
J-K	700	800	.	1 500	600	800	600	200	2 000	.
L	700	700	.	1 300	1 300	1 300	1 900	1 600	900	.
M	.	.	.	-	-	-	600	400	800	.
N	.	.	.	-	-	-	2 700	3 900	2 200	.
O-Q	500	400	.	1 200	0	600	1 000	1 300	2 400	.

Men - Hommes - Hombres [3]
ISIC 3 - CITI 3 - CIIU 3

	1999	2000	2001	2002	2003	2004	2005	2006	2007	2008
Total	11 400	9 400	.	17 400	18 100	17 800	18 800	.	.	.
A-B	-	-	.	-	-	-	-	.	.	.
C-E	-	-	.	4 900	-	-	-	.	.	.
F	-	-	.	-	-	-	-	.	.	.
G	-	900	.	1 300	1 800	1 800	1 600	.	.	.
H	-	-	.	-	-	-	1 000	.	.	.
I	1 100	1 100	.	-	-	1 500	-	.	.	.
J-K	-	-	.	-	-	-	-	.	.	.
L	600	-	.	700	-	-	-	.	.	.
M	-	-	.	-	-	-	-	.	.	.
N	-	-	.	-	-	-	600	.	.	.
O-Q	-	-	.	-	-	-	-	.	.	.

Women - Femmes - Mujeres [3]
ISIC 3 - CITI 3 - CIIU 3

	1999	2000	2001	2002	2003	2004	2005	2006	2007	2008
Total	3 500	3 200	.	7 400	4 300	5 700	5 100	.	.	.
A-B	-	-	.	-	-	-	-	.	.	.
C-E	-	-	.	1 700	-	-	-	.	.	.
F	-	-	.	-	-	-	-	.	.	.
G	-	600	.	1 000	900	600	700	.	.	.
H	600	-	.	-	-	-	700	.	.	.
I	-	-	.	-	-	700	-	.	.	.
J-K	-	-	.	-	-	-	-	.	.	.
L	0	0	.	600	-	-	-	.	.	.
M	-	-	.	-	-	-	-	.	.	.
N	1 000	-	.	-	-	-	2 100	.	.	.
O-Q	-	-	.	-	-	-	-	.	.	.

Explanatory notes: see p. 1125.

[1] Incl. category N. [2] Figures rounded to nearest 100. [3] Incapacity of 4 workdays or more.

Notes explicatives: voir p. 1127.

[1] Y compris la catégorie N. [2] Chiffres arrondis au 100 le plus proche. [3] Incapacité de 4 journées de travail et plus.

Notas explicativas: véase p. 1129.

[1] Incl. la categoría N. [2] Cifras redondeadas al 100 más próximo. [3] Incapacidad de 4 días de trabajo y más.

OCCUPATIONAL INJURIES

Cases of injury with lost workdays, by economic activity

LÉSIONS PROFESSIONNELLES

Cas de lésion avec perte de journées de travail, par activité économique

LESIONES PROFESIONALES

Casos de lesión con pérdida de días de trabajo, por actividad económica

8A

	1999	2000	2001	2002	2003	2004	2005	2006	2007	2008

Ireland (FF) — Reported injuries - Lésions déclarées - Lesiones declaradas

Fatal cases - Cas mortels - Casos mortales

Total men and women - Total hommes et femmes - Total hombres y mujeres
ISIC 3 - CITI 3 - CIIU 3

	1999	2000	2001	2002	2003	2004	2005	2006	2007	2008
Total	69	70	66	61	68	50	74	51	67	57
A-B	.	.	.	.	20	16	20	20	21	22
A	23	16	25	13	19	0	0	0	0	0
B	2	7	2	3	0	0	0	0	0	0
C	3	3	5	2	1	0	0	0	0	0
C-E	.	.	.	.	10	3	13	6	6	9
D	8	9	3	7	6	0	0	0	0	0
E	0	1	0	2	2	0	0	0	0	0
F	18	18	21	21	20	16	23	13	14	15
G	1	3	1	1	4	4	8	3	1	3
H	0	0	0	0	0	0	0	0	0	0
I	8	4	5	7	9	6	5	4	7	3
J	0	0	0	0	0	0	0	0	0	0
J-K	.	.	.	.	0	1	1	2	2	1
K	2	3	1	1	0	0	0	0	0	0
L	2	5	2	3	1	0	2	1	4	2
M	0	0	0	0	0	1	0	0	0	0
M-N	.	.	.	.	0	2	0	1	0	0
N	1	1	1	0	0	1	0	1	0	0
O	1	0	0	1	4	0	0	0	0	0
O-Q	.	.	.	.	4	2	2	1	4	2

Isle of Man (FF) — Reported injuries - Lésions déclarées - Lesiones declaradas

Fatal cases - Cas mortels - Casos mortales

Total men and women - Total hommes et femmes - Total hombres y mujeres
ISIC 3 - CITI 3 - CIIU 3

	1999	2000	2001	2002	2003	2004	2005	2006	2007	2008
Total	0	2	2	0	0	0	1	0	0	1

Non-fatal cases (temporary + permanent incapacity) - Cas non mortels (incapacité temporaire + permanente) - Casos no mortales (incapacidad temporal + permanente)

Total men and women - Total hommes et femmes - Total hombres y mujeres [1]
ISIC 3 - CITI 3 - CIIU 3

	1999	2000	2001	2002	2003	2004	2005	2006	2007	2008
Total	182	170	142	165	211	159	146	174	180	159

Total cases (fatal + non-fatal) - Ensemble des cas (mortels + non mortels) - Todos los casos (mortales + no mortales)

Total men and women - Total hommes et femmes - Total hombres y mujeres
ISIC 3 - CITI 3 - CIIU 3

	1999	2000	2001	2002	2003	2004	2005	2006	2007	2008
Total	182	172	144	165	211	159	146	174	180	159

Italy (FA) — Compensated injuries - Lésions indemnisées - Lesiones indemnizadas

Fatal cases - Cas mortels - Casos mortales

Total men and women - Total hommes et femmes - Total hombres y mujeres [2]
ISIC 3 - CITI 3 - CIIU 3

	1999	2000	2001	2002	2003	2004	2005	2006	2007	2008
Total	1 188	1 155	1 077	934	976	930	918	987	847	744
A	158	161	138	140	116	152	124	122	97	109
B	1	2	1	2	4	5	3	3	3	2
C	8	8	9	12	9	11	6	13	7	6
D	273	256	236	194	231	204	185	203	204	159
E	6	5	9	3	6	5	5	6	6	4
F	278	267	272	230	279	243	239	274	219	168
G	123	92	83	66	71	62	78	91	73	49
H	23	21	19	11	12	17	22	21	17	10
I	185	175	177	142	137	130	137	128	116	108
J	8	8	4	5	5	2	9	1	5	1
K	52	57	47	52	48	44	45	50	39	33
L	10	11	14	13	11	6	15	6	8	13
M	3	4	1	3	1	1	1	2	1	0
N	9	9	9	5	3	10	4	20	7	6
O	29	39	21	19	16	18	19	24	20	17
P	1	2	2	0	1	2	3	1	1	1
X	21	38	35	37	26	18	23	22	24	58

Explanatory notes: see p. 1125.

[1] Incapacity of 4 days or more. [2] Total may differ from the sum of data by sex due to difficulties in coding certain cases.

Notes explicatives: voir p. 1127.

[1] Incapacité de 4 jours et plus. [2] Le total peut différer de la somme des données par sexe en raison de difficultés de codification de quelques cas.

Notas explicativas: véase p. 1129.

[1] Incapacidad de 4 días y más. [2] El total puede diferir de la suma de los datos por sexo debido a dificultades de codificación de algunos casos.

8A

OCCUPATIONAL INJURIES	LÉSIONS PROFESSIONNELLES	LESIONES PROFESIONALES
Cases of injury with lost workdays, by economic activity	Cas de lésion avec perte de journées de travail, par activité économique	Casos de lesión con pérdida de días de trabajo, por actividad económica

	1999	2000	2001	2002	2003	2004	2005	2006	2007	2008

Italy (FA) — Compensated injuries - Lésions indemnisées - Lesiones indemnizadas

Fatal cases - Cas mortels - Casos mortales

Men - Hommes - Hombres
ISIC 3 - CITI 3 - CIIU 3

	1999	2000	2001	2002	2003	2004	2005	2006	2007	2008
Total	1 103	1 075	1 017	892	930	889	877	945	805	715
A	144	146	131	136	111	144	118	121	92	106
B	1	2	1	2	4	5	3	3	3	2
C	8	8	9	12	9	11	6	13	7	6
D	256	234	222	187	220	198	175	199	195	151
E	6	4	7	3	5	5	5	6	6	4
F	278	267	271	228	277	242	238	271	219	167
G	107	87	77	62	67	56	74	87	68	47
H	18	16	14	9	9	13	18	17	13	8
I	182	173	172	141	136	127	135	125	115	105
J	6	6	3	4	3	2	8	1	4	1
K	41	49	44	44	38	39	40	45	34	31
L	6	8	12	7	8	5	13	6	8	13
M	2	1	1	2	1	1	1	1	1	0
N	4	4	5	3	2	6	3	11	1	4
O	24	32	18	16	13	18	18	20	17	14
P	0	1	0	0	1	1	0	0	0	0
X	20	37	30	36	26	16	22	19	22	56

Women - Femmes - Mujeres
ISIC 3 - CITI 3 - CIIU 3

	1999	2000	2001	2002	2003	2004	2005	2006	2007	2008
Total	85	80	60	42	46	41	41	42	42	29
A	14	15	7	4	5	8	6	1	5	3
B	0	0	0	0	0	0	0	0	0	0
C	0	0	0	0	0	0	0	0	0	0
D	17	22	14	7	11	6	10	4	9	8
E	0	1	2	0	1	0	0	0	0	0
F	0	0	1	2	2	1	1	3	0	1
G	16	5	6	4	4	6	4	4	5	2
H	5	5	5	2	3	4	4	4	4	2
I	3	2	5	1	1	3	2	3	1	3
J	2	2	1	1	2	0	1	0	1	0
K	11	8	3	8	10	5	5	5	5	2
L	4	3	2	6	3	1	2	0	0	0
M	1	3	0	1	0	0	0	1	0	0
N	5	5	4	2	1	4	1	9	6	2
O	5	7	3	3	3	0	1	4	3	3
P	1	1	2	0	0	1	3	1	1	1
X	1	1	5	0	0	2	1	3	2	2

Non-fatal cases (temporary + permanent incapacity) - Cas non mortels (incapacité temporaire + permanente) - Casos no mortales (incapacidad temporal + permanente)

Total men and women - Total hommes et femmes - Total hombres y mujeres [1]
ISIC 3 - CITI 3 - CIIU 3

	1999	2000	2001	2002	2003	2004	2005	2006	2007	2008
Total	641 027	651 751	623 894	593 155	588 114	576 963	555 462	543 552	525 612	487 856
A	75 241	70 757	64 769	60 176	59 596	58 301	56 199	53 778	48 848	44 772
B	399	365	362	420	393	376	422	333	327	325
C	2 005	2 049	1 893	1 699	1 631	1 546	1 554	1 407	1 323	1 114
D	228 122	227 623	217 760	198 643	190 067	179 975	171 263	166 943	159 715	139 912
E	5 393	5 543	4 779	4 351	4 058	3 985	4 030	3 633	3 190	2 819
F	89 814	89 908	87 067	86 604	90 065	89 924	86 624	84 181	81 154	69 881
G	59 529	59 651	57 548	56 839	56 411	57 221	56 028	54 151	53 646	49 637
H	23 040	24 361	23 723	23 023	24 372	24 113	24 252	23 675	23 999	21 671
I	54 046	56 569	57 275	54 779	54 061	54 302	54 371	52 774	52 623	48 928
J	3 083	3 515	3 802	3 629	2 293	2 321	2 309	2 172	2 155	2 018
K	30 942	33 912	37 382	38 920	39 206	39 370	29 933	33 842	32 993	32 448
L	18 061	18 541	18 153	17 315	17 904	17 820	17 827	16 247	15 046	14 141
M	1 805	3 378	1 791	1 854	1 779	1 896	2 059	1 799	1 863	1 647
N	17 935	20 020	19 661	19 557	19 944	20 342	21 052	20 971	20 690	20 055
O	22 992	23 378	19 609	19 461	20 204	20 401	21 595	21 895	22 577	21 064
P	916	940	954	1 028	1 576	1 658	1 672	1 771	1 752	2 111
X	7 704	11 241	12 486	10 310	4 554	3 590	5 008	3 980	3 711	15 313

Men - Hommes - Hombres [1]
ISIC 3 - CITI 3 - CIIU 3

	1999	2000	2001	2002	2003	2004	2005	2006	2007	2008
Total	520 244	522 663	498 322	472 197	467 720	456 936	436 774	426 601	410 407	377 359
A	55 118	52 159	47 927	44 872	44 861	44 013	42 467	40 825	36 934	34 271
B	390	356	347	404	376	359	396	310	309	308
C	2 004	2 031	1 872	1 678	1 610	1 532	1 534	1 378	1 284	1 097
D	200 467	198 628	190 447	173 849	166 804	158 234	150 283	146 894	140 951	123 808
E	4 762	4 892	4 371	3 959	3 719	3 675	3 630	3 244	2 834	2 501
F	89 446	89 274	86 268	85 623	89 140	89 079	85 471	83 268	80 306	69 188
G	47 685	46 799	44 999	43 899	42 557	42 962	41 569	39 931	39 084	35 790
H	11 456	12 216	11 512	11 257	11 779	11 593	11 436	11 205	11 237	9 994
I	47 655	49 101	49 503	47 217	46 705	46 485	45 882	44 534	43 959	40 544
J	2 021	2 204	2 423	2 254	1 266	1 314	1 254	1 152	1 114	1 007
K	20 300	21 633	24 680	25 828	25 734	25 955	18 274	21 150	20 549	20 221
L	9 522	9 728	9 316	8 942	9 236	8 844	8 735	7 939	7 129	6 739
M	1 066	1 825	993	914	848	860	864	795	807	618
N	5 789	6 166	5 880	5 833	5 733	5 693	5 924	5 585	5 344	5 108
O	16 898	16 976	13 695	13 776	14 445	14 480	15 039	15 531	15 809	14 588
P	126	112	106	155	246	187	212	203	203	231
X	5 539	8 563	9 103	7 190	2 651	1 693	3 804	2 657	2 554	11 346

Explanatory notes: see p. 1125. Notes explicatives: voir p. 1127. Notas explicativas: véase p. 1129.

[1] Incapacity of 4 workdays or more. [1] Incapacité de 4 journées de travail et plus. [1] Incapacidad de 4 días de trabajo y más.

OCCUPATIONAL INJURIES
Cases of injury with lost workdays, by economic activity

LÉSIONS PROFESSIONNELLES
Cas de lésion avec perte de journées de travail, par activité économique

LESIONES PROFESIONALES
Casos de lesión con pérdida de días de trabajo, por actividad económica

8A

	1999	2000	2001	2002	2003	2004	2005	2006	2007	2008

Italy (FA) — Compensated injuries - Lésions indemnisées - Lesiones indemnizadas

Non-fatal cases (temporary + permanent incapacity) - Cas non mortels (incapacité temporaire + permanente) - Casos no mortales (incapacidad temporal + permanente)

Women - Femmes - Mujeres [1]
ISIC 3 - CITI 3 - CIIU 3

	1999	2000	2001	2002	2003	2004	2005	2006	2007	2008
Total	121 836	129 088	125 572	120 958	120 394	120 027	118 688	116 951	115 205	110 497
A	20 274	18 598	16 842	15 304	14 735	14 288	13 732	12 953	11 914	10 501
B	9	9	15	16	17	17	26	23	18	17
C	10	18	21	21	21	14	20	29	39	17
D	27 954	28 995	27 313	24 794	23 263	21 741	20 795	20 049	18 764	16 104
E	640	651	408	392	339	310	395	389	356	318
F	557	634	799	981	925	845	914	913	848	693
G	11 916	12 852	12 549	12 940	13 854	14 259	14 381	14 220	14 562	13 847
H	11 611	12 145	12 211	11 766	12 593	12 520	12 794	12 470	12 762	11 677
I	6 503	7 468	7 772	7 562	7 356	7 817	8 352	8 240	8 664	8 384
J	1 072	1 311	1 379	1 375	1 027	1 007	1 046	1 020	1 041	1 011
K	10 689	12 279	12 702	13 092	13 472	13 415	11 614	12 692	12 444	12 227
L	8 577	8 813	8 837	8 373	8 668	8 976	9 077	8 308	7 917	7 402
M	742	1 553	798	940	931	1 036	1 194	1 004	1 056	1 029
N	12 176	13 854	13 781	13 724	14 211	14 649	15 128	15 386	15 346	14 947
O	6 130	6 402	5 914	5 685	5 749	5 921	6 556	6 364	6 768	6 476
P	790	828	848	873	1 330	1 471	1 460	1 568	1 549	1 880
X	2 186	2 678	3 383	3 120	1 903	1 897	1 204	1 323	1 157	3 967

Cases of temporary incapacity - Cas d'incapacité temporaire - Casos de incapacidad temporal

Total men and women - Total hommes et femmes - Total hombres y mujeres
ISIC 3 - CITI 3 - CIIU 3

	1999	2000	2001	2002	2003	2004	2005	2006	2007	2008
Total	612 038	633 374	607 544	574 894	561 390	548 525	525 084	513 582	496 354	464 890
A	69 716	67 761	61 308	56 422	55 534	53 895	51 631	49 271	44 837	41 503
B	377	350	346	402	370	347	397	311	304	297
C	1 867	1 943	1 784	1 584	1 524	1 423	1 422	1 284	1 211	1 037
D	220 157	222 471	212 037	192 535	183 345	172 969	163 935	159 880	152 639	134 711
E	5 192	5 380	4 622	4 192	3 886	3 805	3 803	3 435	3 031	2 679
F	83 809	86 159	82 367	81 334	83 860	83 256	79 501	77 271	74 421	65 092
G	57 267	58 247	55 868	54 929	54 308	54 796	53 430	51 787	51 205	47 710
H	22 406	23 962	23 232	22 454	23 760	23 394	23 439	22 901	23 269	21 097
I	51 649	55 060	55 324	52 579	51 471	51 589	51 286	49 906	49 838	46 702
J	2 960	3 418	3 647	3 491	2 158	2 180	2 147	2 046	2 033	1 923
K	29 866	33 195	36 422	37 755	37 906	37 921	28 510	32 395	31 591	31 312
L	17 397	17 866	17 642	16 755	17 201	17 081	16 260	15 509	14 386	13 616
M	1 737	3 184	1 740	1 788	1 706	1 806	1 969	1 703	1 769	1 579
N	17 419	19 669	19 268	19 090	19 401	19 770	20 441	20 349	20 084	19 536
O	22 104	22 844	19 042	18 781	19 340	19 519	20 591	20 913	21 479	20 191
P	801	884	869	910	1 389	1 480	1 474	1 546	1 537	1 897
X	7 314	10 981	12 026	9 893	4 231	3 294	4 848	3 075	2 720	14 008

Men - Hommes - Hombres
ISIC 3 - CITI 3 - CIIU 3

	1999	2000	2001	2002	2003	2004	2005	2006	2007	2008
Total	495 840	507 259	485 438	457 701	445 173	432 984	411 698	401 908	386 292	358 489
A	51 154	49 958	45 372	42 053	41 768	40 689	39 022	37 378	33 848	31 731
B	368	341	331	387	353	330	372	290	288	282
C	1 866	1 927	1 764	1 564	1 504	1 409	1 402	1 259	1 174	1 021
D	193 255	194 019	185 327	168 396	160 698	151 939	143 853	140 524	134 584	119 058
E	4 580	4 742	4 224	3 809	3 558	3 509	3 420	3 069	2 688	2 373
F	83 467	85 539	81 595	80 387	82 979	82 453	78 635	76 405	73 613	64 431
G	45 788	45 636	43 618	42 308	40 853	40 957	39 513	38 030	37 104	34 214
H	11 101	11 992	11 261	10 961	11 445	11 204	11 039	10 797	10 863	9 695
I	45 434	47 713	47 746	45 235	44 356	44 031	43 245	41 976	41 448	38 559
J	1 936	2 132	2 316	2 160	1 174	1 219	1 165	1 072	1 036	953
K	19 547	21 147	24 004	24 938	24 819	24 946	17 308	20 163	19 587	19 445
L	9 108	9 322	9 019	8 610	8 834	8 427	8 042	7 530	6 771	6 443
M	1 024	1 714	960	876	806	819	819	751	763	586
N	5 577	6 014	5 727	5 646	5 505	5 468	5 668	5 356	5 128	4 911
O	16 239	16 582	13 303	13 310	13 813	13 851	14 330	14 804	15 022	13 971
P	112	101	95	141	211	165	189	174	181	212
X	5 284	8 380	8 776	6 920	2 497	1 568	3 676	2 330	2 194	10 604

Women - Femmes - Mujeres
ISIC 3 - CITI 3 - CIIU 3

	1999	2000	2001	2002	2003	2004	2005	2006	2007	2008
Total	117 251	126 115	122 106	117 193	116 217	115 541	113 386	111 674	110 062	106 401
A	18 713	17 803	15 936	14 369	13 766	13 206	12 609	11 893	10 989	9 772
B	9	9	15	15	17	17	25	21	16	15
C	10	16	20	20	20	14	20	25	37	16
D	27 201	28 452	26 710	24 139	22 647	21 030	20 082	19 356	18 055	15 653
E	621	638	398	383	328	296	383	366	343	306
F	531	620	772	947	881	803	866	866	808	661
G	11 551	12 611	12 250	12 621	13 455	14 265	13 917	13 757	14 101	13 496
H	11 332	11 970	11 971	11 493	12 315	12 190	12 400	12 104	12 406	11 402
I	6 327	7 347	7 578	7 344	7 115	7 558	8 041	7 930	8 390	8 143
J	1 034	1 286	1 331	1 331	984	961	982	974	997	970
K	10 366	12 048	12 418	12 817	13 087	12 975	11 202	12 232	12 004	11 867
L	8 327	8 544	8 623	8 145	8 367	8 654	8 218	7 979	7 615	7 173
M	716	1 470	780	912	900	987	1 150	952	1 006	993
N	11 872	13 655	13 541	13 444	13 896	14 302	14 773	14 993	14 956	14 625
O	5 901	6 262	5 739	5 471	5 527	5 668	6 261	6 109	6 457	6 220
P	689	783	774	769	1 178	1 315	1 285	1 372	1 356	1 685
X	2 051	2 601	3 250	2 973	1 734	1 726	1 172	745	526	3 404

Explanatory notes: see p. 1125.
[1] Incapacity of 4 workdays or more.

Notes explicatives: voir p. 1127.
[1] Incapacité de 4 journées de travail et plus.

Notas explicativas: véase p. 1129.
[1] Incapacidad de 4 días de trabajo y más.

OCCUPATIONAL INJURIES	LÉSIONS PROFESSIONNELLES	LESIONES PROFESIONALES
Cases of injury with lost workdays, by economic activity	Cas de lésion avec perte de journées de travail, par activité économique	Casos de lesión con pérdida de días de trabajo, por actividad económica

	1999	2000	2001	2002	2003	2004	2005	2006	2007	2008

Italy (FA)   Compensated injuries - Lésions indemnisées - Lesiones indemnizadas

Total cases (fatal + non-fatal) - Ensemble des cas (mortels + non mortels) - Todos los casos (mortales + no mortales)

Total men and women - Total hommes et femmes - Total hombres y mujeres
ISIC 3 - CITI 3 - CIIU 3

	1999	2000	2001	2002	2003	2004	2005	2006	2007	2008
Total	642 215	652 906	624 971	594 089	589 090	577 893	556 380	544 539	526 459	488 600
A	75 399	70 918	64 907	60 316	59 712	58 453	56 323	53 900	48 945	44 881
B	400	367	363	422	397	381	425	336	330	327
C	2 013	2 057	1 902	1 711	1 640	1 557	1 560	1 420	1 330	1 120
D	228 395	227 879	217 996	198 837	190 298	180 179	171 078	167 146	159 919	140 071
E	5 399	5 548	4 788	4 354	4 064	3 990	4 025	3 639	3 196	2 823
F	90 092	90 175	87 339	86 834	90 344	90 167	86 385	84 455	81 373	70 049
G	59 652	59 743	57 631	56 905	56 482	57 283	55 950	54 242	53 719	49 686
H	23 063	24 382	23 742	23 034	24 384	24 130	24 230	23 696	24 016	21 681
I	54 231	56 744	57 452	54 921	54 198	54 432	54 234	52 902	52 739	49 036
J	3 091	3 523	3 806	3 634	2 298	2 323	2 300	2 173	2 160	2 019
K	30 994	33 969	37 429	38 972	39 254	39 414	29 888	33 892	33 032	32 481
L	18 071	18 552	18 167	17 328	17 915	17 826	17 812	16 253	15 054	14 154
M	1 808	3 382	1 792	1 857	1 780	1 897	2 058	1 801	1 864	1 647
N	17 944	20 029	19 670	19 562	19 947	20 352	21 056	20 991	20 697	20 061
O	23 021	23 417	19 630	19 480	20 220	20 419	21 614	21 919	22 597	21 081
P	917	942	956	1 028	1 577	1 660	1 675	1 772	1 753	2 112
X	7 725	11 279	12 521	10 347	4 580	3 608	5 031	4 002	3 735	15 371

Men - Hommes - Hombres
ISIC 3 - CITI 3 - CIIU 3

	1999	2000	2001	2002	2003	2004	2005	2006	2007	2008
Total	521 347	523 738	499 339	473 089	468 650	457 825	437 651	427 546	411 212	378 074
A	55 262	52 305	48 058	45 008	44 972	44 157	42 585	40 946	37 026	34 377
B	391	358	348	406	380	364	399	313	312	310
C	2 012	2 039	1 881	1 690	1 619	1 543	1 540	1 371	1 291	1 103
D	200 723	198 862	190 669	174 036	167 024	158 432	150 458	147 093	141 146	123 959
E	4 724	4 896	4 378	3 962	3 724	3 680	3 635	3 250	2 840	2 505
F	89 724	89 541	86 539	85 851	89 417	89 321	85 709	83 539	80 525	69 355
G	47 792	46 886	45 076	43 961	42 624	43 018	41 643	40 018	39 152	35 837
H	11 474	12 232	11 526	11 266	11 788	11 606	11 454	11 222	11 250	10 002
I	47 837	49 274	49 675	47 358	46 841	46 612	46 017	44 659	44 074	40 649
J	2 027	2 210	2 426	2 258	1 269	1 316	1 262	1 153	1 118	1 008
K	20 341	21 682	24 724	25 872	25 772	25 994	18 314	21 195	20 583	20 252
L	9 528	9 736	9 328	8 949	9 244	8 849	8 748	7 945	7 137	6 752
M	1 068	1 826	994	916	849	861	865	796	808	618
N	5 793	6 170	5 885	5 836	5 735	5 699	5 927	5 596	5 345	5 112
O	16 922	17 008	13 713	13 792	14 468	14 498	15 057	15 551	15 826	14 602
P	126	113	106	155	247	188	212	203	203	231
X	5 559	8 600	9 133	7 226	2 677	1 709	3 826	2 676	2 576	11 402

Women - Femmes - Mujeres
ISIC 3 - CITI 3 - CIIU 3

	1999	2000	2001	2002	2003	2004	2005	2006	2007	2008
Total	121 921	129 168	125 632	121 000	120 440	120 068	118 729	116 993	115 247	110 526
A	20 288	18 613	16 849	15 308	14 740	14 296	13 738	12 954	11 919	10 504
B	9	9	15	16	17	17	26	23	18	17
C	10	18	21	21	21	14	20	29	39	17
D	27 971	29 017	27 327	24 801	23 274	21 747	20 805	20 053	18 773	16 112
E	640	652	410	392	340	310	395	389	356	318
F	557	634	800	983	927	846	915	916	848	694
G	11 932	12 857	12 555	12 944	13 858	14 265	14 385	14 224	14 567	13 849
H	11 616	12 150	12 216	11 768	12 596	12 524	12 798	12 474	12 766	11 679
I	6 506	7 470	7 777	7 563	7 357	7 820	8 354	8 243	8 665	8 387
J	1 074	1 313	1 380	1 376	1 029	1 007	1 047	1 020	1 042	1 011
K	10 700	12 287	12 705	13 100	13 482	13 420	11 619	12 697	12 449	12 229
L	8 581	8 816	8 839	8 379	8 671	8 977	9 079	8 308	7 917	7 402
M	743	1 556	798	941	931	1 036	1 194	1 005	1 056	1 029
N	12 181	13 859	13 785	13 726	14 212	14 653	15 129	15 395	15 352	14 949
O	6 135	6 409	5 917	5 688	5 752	5 921	6 557	6 368	6 771	6 479
P	791	829	850	873	1 330	1 472	1 463	1 569	1 550	1 881
X	2 187	2 679	3 388	3 121	1 903	1 899	1 205	1 326	1 159	3 969

Explanatory notes: see p. 1125.   Notes explicatives: voir p. 1127.   Notas explicativas: véase p. 1129.

OCCUPATIONAL INJURIES

Cases of injury with lost workdays, by economic activity

LÉSIONS PROFESSIONNELLES

Cas de lésion avec perte de journées de travail, par activité économique

LESIONES PROFESIONALES

Casos de lesión con pérdida de días de trabajo, por actividad económica

	1999	2000	2001	2002	2003	2004	2005	2006	2007	2008

Latvia (DA) Reported injuries - Lésions déclarées - Lesiones declaradas

Fatal cases - Cas mortels - Casos mortales

Total men and women - Total hommes et femmes - Total hombres y mujeres
ISIC 3 - CITI 3 - CIIU 3

	1999	2000	2001	2002	2003	2004	2005	2006	2007	2008
Total	66	43	72	56	41	61	56	53	58	.
A	5	5	5	12	3	3	3	8	3	.
B	7	1	0	0	0	7	1	0	1	.
C	2	1	0	1	0	0	0	1	0	.
D	14	16	27	15	11	18	9	17	9	.
E	2	1	2	1	0	1	6	1	2	.
F	8	4	4	9	11	11	15	10	21	.
G	7	7	9	5	6	5	2	0	4	.
H	0	0	1	0	0	0	0	1	1	.
I	13	2	14	6	4	10	10	8	14	.
J	0	1	0	0	0	0	1	0	0	.
K	2	0	1	1	0	3	1	2	1	.
L	3	2	4	2	2	1	1	0	1	.
M	1	1	1	1	1	0	1	2	0	.
N	1	0	0	0	0	0	0	0	0	.
O	1	2	4	3	3	2	6	3	1	.
Q					0	0	0	0	0	.
X	0	0	0	0	0	0	0	0	.	.

Non-fatal cases (temporary + permanent incapacity) - Cas non mortels (incapacité temporaire + permanente) - Casos no mortales (incapacidad temporal + permanente)

Total men and women - Total hommes et femmes - Total hombres y mujeres
ISIC 3 - CITI 3 - CIIU 3

	1999	2000	2001	2002	2003	2004	2005	2006	2007	2008
Total	1 077	817	1 349	1 348	1 322	1 341	1 526	1 719	1 812	.
A	47	41	70	149	77	85	79	70	69	.
B	0	0	5	4	2	2	3	3	0	.
C	11	3	0	8	10	9	9	9	11	.
D	385	397	601	536	543	464	525	594	584	.
E	62	27	43	47	35	25	34	36	51	.
F	54	69	152	121	136	156	157	212	230	.
G	57	27	49	54	86	101	105	152	174	.
H	1	13	0	3	9	11	20	14	28	.
I	242	94	216	185	188	196	251	286	261	.
J	2	1	6	10	6	3	8	1	9	.
K	29	11	45	12	17	26	23	23	33	.
L	142	84	40	58	48	79	58	68	67	.
M	11	9	45	40	33	38	88	54	59	.
N	15	31	48	60	87	84	111	128	148	.
O	19	10	29	61	45	61	55	66	86	.
Q					0	1	0	3	2	.
X	0	0	0	0	0	0	0	0	.	.

Total cases (fatal + non-fatal) - Ensemble des cas (mortels + non mortels) - Todos los casos (mortales + no mortales)

Total men and women - Total hommes et femmes - Total hombres y mujeres
ISIC 3 - CITI 3 - CIIU 3

	1999	2000	2001	2002	2003	2004	2005	2006	2007	2008
Total	1 143	860	1 421	1 404	1 363	1 402	1 582	1 772	1 870	.
A	52	46	75	161	80	88	82	78	72	.
B	7	1	5	4	2	9	4	3	1	.
C	13	4	0	9	10	9	9	10	11	.
D	399	413	628	551	554	482	534	611	593	.
E	64	28	45	48	35	26	40	37	53	.
F	62	73	156	130	147	167	172	222	251	.
G	64	34	58	59	92	106	107	152	178	.
H	1	13	1	3	9	11	20	15	29	.
I	255	96	230	191	192	206	261	294	275	.
J	2	2	6	10	6	3	9	1	9	.
K	31	11	46	13	17	29	24	25	34	.
L	145	86	44	60	50	80	59	68	68	.
M	12	10	46	41	34	38	89	56	59	.
N	16	31	48	60	87	84	111	128	148	.
O	20	12	33	64	48	63	61	69	87	.
Q					0	1	0	3	2	.
X	0	0	0	0	0	0	0	0	.	.

Explanatory notes: see p. 1125. Notes explicatives: voir p. 1127. Notas explicativas: véase p. 1129.

OCCUPATIONAL INJURIES

Cases of injury with lost workdays, by economic activity

LÉSIONS PROFESSIONNELLES

Cas de lésion avec perte de journées de travail, par activité économique

LESIONES PROFESIONALES

Casos de lesión con pérdida de días de trabajo, por actividad económica

	1999	2000	2001	2002	2003	2004	2005	2006	2007	2008

Lithuania (FF) [1]   Reported injuries - Lésions déclarées - Lesiones declaradas

Fatal cases - Cas mortels - Casos mortales

Total men and women - Total hommes et femmes - Total hombres y mujeres
ISIC 3 - CITI 3 - CIIU 3

	1999	2000	2001	2002	2003	2004	2005	2006	2007	2008
Total	74	66	86	83	118	94	118	108	101	77
A	14	7	5	7	15	8	11	9	13	9
B	0	0	1	2	3	0	2	2	2	0
C	1	2	2	1	1	2	1	0	1	2
D	12	7	20	19	16	17	29	13	21	13
E	6	5	3	4	7	4	5	4	4	0
F	19	14	23	23	22	32	33	29	23	21
G	8	4	7	5	21	8	5	9	4	3
H	0	0	0	0	0	0	0	1	1	0
I	11	22	16	14	24	16	24	29	21	22
J	0	0	0	3	0	0	0	0	2	0
K	1	1	0	0	2	2	1	4	4	2
L	1	2	1	1	1	1	1	1	1	4
M	1	0	1	0	2	3	0	4	1	0
N	0	0	1	1	0	0	0	0	3	0
O	0	2	5	3	4	1	6	2	0	1
P	.	.	1	0	0	0	0	1	0	0
Q	0	0	0	0	0	0	0	0	0	0
X	0	0	0	0	0	0	0	0	0	0

Men - Hommes - Hombres
ISIC 3 - CITI 3 - CIIU 3

	1999	2000	2001	2002	2003	2004	2005	2006	2007	2008
Total	69	62	83	79	115	88	111	102	97	69
A	14	7	5	7	14	8	11	2	12	9
B	0	0	1	2	3	0	2	2	2	0
C	1	2	2	1	1	2	1	0	1	2
D	10	6	20	18	15	17	26	13	20	12
E	6	5	3	4	7	4	5	4	4	0
F	19	14	23	23	22	31	33	28	23	21
G	6	3	5	5	21	5	5	8	4	2
H	0	0	0	0	0	0	0	1	0	0
I	10	22	16	12	24	15	23	29	20	19
J	0	0	0	2	0	0	0	0	2	0
K	1	0	0	0	2	2	1	4	3	2
L	1	2	1	1	1	1	1	1	1	1
M	1	0	0	0	1	2	0	3	1	0
N	0	0	1	0	0	0	0	0	3	0
O	0	1	5	3	4	1	3	0	0	1
P	.	.	1	0	0	0	0	0	0	0
Q	0	0	0	0	0	0	0	0	0	0
X	0	0	0	0	0	0	0	0	0	0

Women - Femmes - Mujeres
ISIC 3 - CITI 3 - CIIU 3

	1999	2000	2001	2002	2003	2004	2005	2006	2007	2008
Total	5	4	3	4	3	6	7	6	4	8
A	0	0	0	0	1	0	0	0	1	0
B	0	0	0	0	0	0	0	0	0	0
C	0	0	0	0	0	0	0	0	0	0
D	2	1	0	1	1	0	3	0	1	1
E	0	0	0	0	0	0	0	0	0	0
F	0	0	0	0	0	1	0	1	0	0
G	2	1	2	0	0	3	0	1	0	1
H	0	0	0	0	0	0	0	0	1	0
I	1	0	0	1	0	1	1	0	0	3
J	0	0	0	1	0	0	0	0	0	0
K	0	1	0	0	0	0	0	0	1	0
L	0	0	0	0	0	0	0	0	0	3
M	0	0	1	0	1	1	0	1	0	0
N	0	0	0	1	0	0	0	0	0	0
O	0	1	0	0	0	0	3	2	0	0
P	.	.	0	0	0	0	0	1	0	0
Q	0	0	0	0	0	0	0	0	0	0
X	0	0	0	0	0	0	0	0	0	0

Explanatory notes: see p. 1125.

[1] Total may differ from the sum of data by sex due to difficulties in coding certain cases.

Notes explicatives: voir p. 1127.

[1] Le total peut différer de la somme des données par sexe en raison de difficultés de codification de quelques cas.

Notas explicativas: véase p. 1129.

[1] El total puede diferir de la suma de los datos por sexo debido a dificultades de codificación de algunos casos.

OCCUPATIONAL INJURIES

Cases of injury with lost workdays, by economic activity

LÉSIONS PROFESSIONNELLES

Cas de lésion avec perte de journées de travail, par activité économique

LESIONES PROFESIONALES

Casos de lesión con pérdida de días de trabajo, por actividad económica

	1999	2000	2001	2002	2003	2004	2005	2006	2007	2008

Lithuania (FF) [1] **Reported injuries - Lésions déclarées - Lesiones declaradas**

Non-fatal cases (temporary + permanent incapacity) - Cas non mortels (incapacité temporaire + permanente) - Casos no mortales (incapacidad temporal + permanente)

Total men and women - Total hommes et femmes - Total hombres y mujeres
ISIC 3 - CITI 3 - CIIU 3

	1999	2000	2001	2002	2003	2004	2005	2006	2007	2008
Total	2 942	2 731	2 496	2 512	2 601	2 610	3 240	3 473	3 577	.
A	236	170	139	128	121	99	120	110	109	.
B	7	5	5	1	2	8	6	3	3	.
C	21	23	22	20	20	18	22	26	19	.
D	1 178	1 137	993	1 005	934	956	1 188	1 260	1 221	.
E	125	118	80	75	69	53	64	59	60	.
F	428	330	330	386	430	411	564	632	679	.
G	152	157	161	169	211	216	276	350	338	.
H	22	22	20	28	23	35	46	44	65	.
I	313	297	299	265	264	282	411	389	456	.
J	18	25	26	14	19	13	6	15	16	.
K	29	32	39	43	56	69	93	100	112	.
L	54	56	67	72	72	73	91	89	71	.
M	109	115	121	106	140	132	111	130	135	.
N	146	139	131	127	135	149	142	152	183	.
O	104	105	63	71	105	94	98	113	71	.
P	.	.	0	2	0	0	2	0	0	.
Q	0	0	0	0	0	2	0	1	1	.
X	0	0	0	0	0	0	0	0	0	.

Men - Hommes - Hombres
ISIC 3 - CITI 3 - CIIU 3

	1999	2000	2001	2002	2003	2004	2005	2006	2007	2008
Total	2 153	1 950	1 786	1 838	1 854	1 898	2 343	2 457	2 479	.
A	186	127	105	106	97	83	86	71	73	.
B	6	4	4	1	2	8	6	3	3	.
C	20	21	18	20	17	17	17	23	16	.
D	869	829	730	747	683	729	852	884	821	.
E	107	104	72	62	59	44	52	50	53	.
F	406	322	324	381	419	397	548	604	653	.
G	110	111	114	119	150	164	206	241	226	.
H	12	12	10	14	5	12	11	10	19	.
I	237	220	230	214	207	225	326	308	374	.
J	10	7	13	4	2	1	3	5	3	.
K	21	19	29	30	42	46	68	62	70	.
L	30	32	41	42	38	32	44	51	31	.
M	44	42	33	27	38	38	25	35	32	.
N	33	32	25	26	24	39	31	38	34	.
O	62	69	38	43	71	61	66	72	71	.
P	.	.	0	2	0	0	2	0	0	.
Q	0	0	0	0	0	2	0	0	0	.
X	0	0	0	0	0	0	0	0	0	.

Women - Femmes - Mujeres
ISIC 3 - CITI 3 - CIIU 3

	1999	2000	2001	2002	2003	2004	2005	2006	2007	2008
Total	789	781	710	674	747	712	897	1 016	1 098	.
A	50	43	34	22	24	16	34	39	36	.
B	1	1	1	0	0	0	0	0	0	.
C	1	2	4	0	3	1	5	3	3	.
D	309	308	263	258	251	227	336	376	400	.
E	18	14	8	13	10	9	12	9	7	.
F	22	8	6	5	11	14	16	28	26	.
G	42	46	47	50	61	52	70	109	112	.
H	10	10	10	14	18	23	35	34	46	.
I	76	77	69	51	57	57	85	81	82	.
J	8	18	13	10	17	12	3	10	13	.
K	8	13	10	13	14	23	25	38	42	.
L	24	24	26	30	34	41	47	38	40	.
M	65	73	88	79	102	94	86	95	103	.
N	113	107	106	101	111	110	111	114	149	.
O	42	37	25	28	34	33	32	41	38	.
P	.	.	0	0	0	0	0	0	0	.
Q	0	0	0	0	0	0	0	1	1	.
X	0	0	0	0	0	0	0	0	0	.

Explanatory notes: see p. 1125.

[1] Total may differ from the sum of data by sex due to difficulties in coding certain cases.

Notes explicatives: voir p. 1127.

[1] Le total peut différer de la somme des données par sexe en raison de difficultés de codification de quelques cas.

Notas explicativas: véase p. 1129.

[1] El total puede diferir de la suma de los datos por sexo debido a dificultades de codificación de algunos casos.

8A

OCCUPATIONAL INJURIES	LÉSIONS PROFESSIONNELLES	LESIONES PROFESIONALES
Cases of injury with lost workdays, by economic activity	Cas de lésion avec perte de journées de travail, par activité économique	Casos de lesión con pérdida de días de trabajo, por actividad económica

Lithuania (FF) [1]

Reported injuries - Lésions déclarées - Lesiones declaradas

Total cases (fatal + non-fatal) - Ensemble des cas (mortels + non mortels) - Todos los casos (mortales + no mortales)

Total men and women - Total hommes et femmes - Total hombres y mujeres
ISIC 3 - CITI 3 - CIIU 3

	1999	2000	2001	2002	2003	2004	2005	2006	2007	2008
Total	3 016	2 797	2 582	2 595	2 719	2 704	3 358	3 581	3 678	.
A	250	177	144	135	136	107	131	119	122	.
B	7	5	6	3	5	8	8	5	5	.
C	22	25	24	21	21	20	23	26	20	.
D	1 190	1 144	1 037	1 024	950	973	1 217	1 273	1 242	.
E	131	123	83	79	76	57	69	63	64	.
F	447	344	353	409	452	443	594	661	702	.
G	160	161	168	174	232	224	280	359	342	.
H	22	22	20	28	23	35	46	45	66	.
I	324	319	315	279	288	298	435	418	474	.
J	18	25	26	17	19	13	6	15	16	.
K	30	33	39	43	58	71	94	104	116	.
L	55	58	68	73	73	74	92	90	72	.
M	110	115	122	106	142	135	111	134	136	.
N	146	139	132	128	135	149	142	152	186	.
O	104	107	68	74	109	95	104	115	71	.
P	.	.	1	2	0	0	2	1	0	.
Q	0	0	0	0	0	0	0	1	1	.
X	0	0	0	0	0	2	0	1	1	.

Men - Hommes - Hombres
ISIC 3 - CITI 3 - CIIU 3

	1999	2000	2001	2002	2003	2004	2005	2006	2007	2008
Total	2 222	2 012	1 869	1 917	1 969	1 986	2 454	2 559	2 576	.
A	200	134	110	113	111	91	97	80	85	.
B	6	4	5	3	5	8	8	5	5	.
C	21	23	20	21	18	19	18	23	17	.
D	879	835	750	765	698	746	878	897	841	.
E	113	109	75	66	66	48	57	54	57	.
F	425	336	347	404	441	428	581	632	676	.
G	116	114	119	124	171	169	211	249	230	.
H	12	12	10	14	5	12	11	11	19	.
I	247	242	246	227	231	240	349	337	394	.
J	10	7	13	6	2	1	3	5	5	.
K	22	19	29	30	44	48	69	66	73	.
L	31	34	42	43	39	33	45	52	32	.
M	45	42	33	27	39	40	25	38	33	.
N	33	32	26	26	24	39	31	38	37	.
O	62	70	43	46	75	62	69	72	71	.
P	.	.	1	2	0	0	2	0	0	.
Q	0	0	0	0	0	0	2	0	0	.
X	0	0	0	0	0	2	0	0	0	.

Women - Femmes - Mujeres
ISIC 3 - CITI 3 - CIIU 3

	1999	2000	2001	2002	2003	2004	2005	2006	2007	2008
Total	794	785	713	678	750	718	904	1 022	1 102	.
A	50	43	34	22	25	16	34	39	37	.
B	1	1	1	0	0	0	0	0	0	.
C	1	2	4	0	3	1	5	3	3	.
D	311	309	263	259	251	227	339	376	401	.
E	18	14	8	13	10	9	12	9	7	.
F	22	8	6	5	11	15	16	29	26	.
G	44	47	49	50	61	55	70	110	112	.
H	10	10	10	14	18	23	35	34	47	.
I	77	77	69	52	57	58	86	81	82	.
J	8	18	13	11	17	12	3	10	13	.
K	8	14	10	13	14	23	25	38	43	.
L	24	24	26	30	34	41	47	38	40	.
M	65	73	89	79	103	95	86	96	103	.
N	113	107	106	101	111	110	111	114	149	.
O	42	38	25	28	34	33	35	43	38	.
P	.	.	0	0	0	0	0	1	0	.
Q	0	0	0	0	0	0	0	1	1	.
X	0	0	0	0	0	0	0	1	1	.

Explanatory notes: see p. 1125.

[1] Total may differ from the sum of data by sex due to difficulties in coding certain cases.

Notes explicatives: voir p. 1127.

[1] Le total peut différer de la somme des données par sexe en raison de difficultés de codification de quelques cas.

Notas explicativas: véase p. 1129.

[1] El total puede diferir de la suma de los datos por sexo debido a dificultades de codificación de algunos casos.

OCCUPATIONAL INJURIES

Cases of injury with lost workdays, by economic activity

LÉSIONS PROFESSIONNELLES

Cas de lésion avec perte de journées de travail, par activité économique

LESIONES PROFESIONALES

Casos de lesión con pérdida de días de trabajo, por actividad económica

8A

	1999	2000	2001	2002	2003	2004	2005	2006	2007	2008

Luxembourg (FA) [1]   Compensated injuries - Lésions indemnisées - Lesiones indemnizadas

Fatal cases - Cas mortels - Casos mortales

Total men and women - Total hommes et femmes - Total hombres y mujeres
ISIC 3 - CITI 3 - CIIU 3

	1999	2000	2001	2002	2003	2004	2005	2006	2007	2008
Total	7	16	16	18	16	6	.	.	.	10
A		.		1	1	0	.	.	.	1
B	.	.	.	0	0	0	.	.	.	0
C	.	.	.	0	0	0	.	.	.	0
D	.	.	.	1	2	1	.	.	.	1
E	.	.	.	0	0	0	.	.	.	0
F	.	.	.	2	6	2	.	.	.	0
G	.	.	.	4	2	0	.	.	.	0
H	.	.	.	0	0	0	.	.	.	1
I	.	.	.	4	2	3	.	.	.	3
J	.	.	.	1	0	0	.	.	.	0
K	.	.	.	3	2	0	.	.	.	2
L	.	.	.	1	0	0	.	.	.	1
M	.	.	.	0	0	0	.	.	.	0
N	.	.	.	0	1	0	.	.	.	0
O	.	.	.	0	0	0	.	.	.	0
P	.	.	.	0	0	0	.	.	.	0
Q	.	.	.	0	0	0	.	.	.	0
X	.	.	.	1	0	0	.	.	.	1

Men - Hommes - Hombres
ISIC 3 - CITI 3 - CIIU 3

	1999	2000	2001	2002	2003	2004	2005	2006	2007	2008
Total	.	.	.	14	15	6	.	.	.	10
A	.	.	.	1	1	0	.	.	.	1
B	.	.	.	0	0	0	.	.	.	0
C	.	.	.	0	0	0	.	.	.	0
D	.	.	.	1	2	1	.	.	.	1
E	.	.	.	0	0	0	.	.	.	0
F	.	.	.	2	6	2	.	.	.	0
G	.	.	.	2	2	0	.	.	.	0
H	.	.	.	0	0	0	.	.	.	1
I	.	.	.	3	2	3	.	.	.	3
J	.	.	.	0	0	0	.	.	.	0
K	.	.	.	3	1	0	.	.	.	2
L	.	.	.	1	0	0	.	.	.	1
M	.	.	.	0	0	0	.	.	.	0
N	.	.	.	0	1	0	.	.	.	0
O	.	.	.	0	0	0	.	.	.	0
P	.	.	.	0	0	0	.	.	.	0
Q	.	.	.	0	0	0	.	.	.	0
X	.	.	.	1	0	0	.	.	.	1

Women - Femmes - Mujeres
ISIC 3 - CITI 3 - CIIU 3

	1999	2000	2001	2002	2003	2004	2005	2006	2007	2008
Total	.	.	.	4	1	0	.	.	.	0
A	.	.	.	0	0	0	.	.	.	0
B	.	.	.	0	0	0	.	.	.	0
C	.	.	.	0	0	0	.	.	.	0
D	.	.	.	0	0	0	.	.	.	0
E	.	.	.	0	0	0	.	.	.	0
F	.	.	.	0	0	0	.	.	.	0
G	.	.	.	2	0	0	.	.	.	0
H	.	.	.	0	0	0	.	.	.	0
I	.	.	.	1	0	0	.	.	.	0
J	.	.	.	1	0	0	.	.	.	0
K	.	.	.	0	1	0	.	.	.	0
L	.	.	.	0	0	0	.	.	.	0
M	.	.	.	0	0	0	.	.	.	0
N	.	.	.	0	0	0	.	.	.	0
O	.	.	.	0	0	0	.	.	.	0
P	.	.	.	0	0	0	.	.	.	0
Q	.	.	.	0	0	0	.	.	.	0
X	.	.	.	0	0	0	.	.	.	0

Explanatory notes: see p. 1125.

[1] Up to 2001: excl. agriculture and forestry.

Notes explicatives: voir p. 1127.

[1] Jusqu'à 2001: non compris agriculture et sylviculture.

Notas explicativas: véase p. 1129.

[1] Hasta 2001: excl. agricultura y silvicultura.

OCCUPATIONAL INJURIES	LÉSIONS PROFESSIONNELLES	LESIONES PROFESIONALES
Cases of injury with lost workdays, by economic activity	Cas de lésion avec perte de journées de travail, par activité économique	Casos de lesión con pérdida de días de trabajo, por actividad económica

	1999	2000	2001	2002	2003	2004	2005	2006	2007	2008

Luxembourg (FA) [1]   Compensated injuries - Lésions indemnisées - Lesiones indemnizadas

Non-fatal cases (temporary + permanent incapacity) - Cas non mortels (incapacité temporaire + permanente) - Casos no mortales (incapacidad temporal + permanente)

Total men and women - Total hommes et femmes - Total hombres y mujeres
ISIC 3 - CITI 3 - CIIU 3

	1999	2000	2001	2002	2003	2004	2005	2006	2007	2008
Total	20 394	21 128	21 605	20 295	19 368	20 827	.	.	.	10 617
A				533	515	813				196
B				0	0	0				1
C				39	30	35				25
D				3 056	2 860	2 924				1 286
E				61	59	54				31
F				5 094	4 953	5 565				3 541
G				2 587	2 440	2 372				1 199
H				1 021	1 006	1 034				486
I				1 768	1 639	1 787				992
J				547	536	210				69
K				2 496	2 454	2 395				1 588
L				1 491	1 391	1 619				275
M				39	27	30				8
N				722	732	1 413				589
O				145	123	290				152
P				0	0	78				62
Q				0	0	42				27
X				696	603	166				83

Men - Hommes - Hombres
ISIC 3 - CITI 3 - CIIU 3

	1999	2000	2001	2002	2003	2004	2005	2006	2007	2008
Total				16 062	15 265	16 883	.	.	.	8 912
A				439	434	681				174
B				0	0	0				1
C				39	30	35				25
D				2 651	2 497	2 712				1 156
E				60	58	54				31
F				5 050	4 909	5 535				3 522
G				1 858	1 707	1 779				944
H				545	527	525				225
I				1 603	1 469	1 659				953
J				239	235	107				31
K				1 787	1 748	1 796				1 212
L				1 051	1 035	1 220				198
M				13	9	7				2
N				166	161	417				228
O				39	28	191				102
P				0	0	9				8
Q				0	0	22				26
X				522	418	134				67

Women - Femmes - Mujeres
ISIC 3 - CITI 3 - CIIU 3

	1999	2000	2001	2002	2003	2004	2005	2006	2007	2008
Total				4 233	4 103	3 944	.	.	.	1 705
A				94	81	132				22
B				0	0	0				0
C				0	0	0				0
D				405	363	212				130
E				1	1	0				0
F				44	44	30				19
G				729	733	593				255
H				476	479	509				261
I				165	170	128				39
J				308	301	103				38
K				709	706	599				376
L				440	356	399				77
M				26	18	23				6
N				556	571	996				361
O				106	95	99				50
P				0	0	69				54
Q				0	0	20				1
X				174	185	32				16

Explanatory notes: see p. 1125.   Notes explicatives: voir p. 1127.   Notas explicativas: véase p. 1129.

[1] Up to 2001: excl. agriculture and forestry.   [1] Jusqu'à 2001: non compris agriculture et sylviculture.   [1] Hasta 2001: excl. agricultura y silvicultura.

OCCUPATIONAL INJURIES

Cases of injury with lost workdays, by economic activity

LÉSIONS PROFESSIONNELLES

Cas de lésion avec perte de journées de travail, par activité économique

LESIONES PROFESIONALES

Casos de lesión con pérdida de días de trabajo, por actividad económica

8A

	1999	2000	2001	2002	2003	2004	2005	2006	2007	2008
Luxembourg (FA) [1]				**Compensated injuries - Lésions indemnisées - Lesiones indemnizadas**						

Total cases (fatal + non-fatal) - Ensemble des cas (mortels + non mortels) - Todos los casos (mortales + no mortales)

Total men and women - Total hommes et femmes - Total hombres y mujeres
ISIC 3 - CITI 3 - CIIU 3

	1999	2000	2001	2002	2003	2004	2005	2006	2007	2008
Total	20 401	21 144	21 621	20 313	19 384	20 833	.	.	.	10 627
A		.		534	516	813			.	197
B		.		0	0	0			.	1
C		.		39	30	35			.	25
D		.		3 057	2 862	2 925			.	1 287
E		.		61	59	54			.	31
F		.		5 096	4 959	5 567			.	3 541
G		.		2 591	2 442	2 372			.	1 199
H		.		1 021	1 006	1 034			.	487
I		.		1 772	1 641	1 790			.	995
J		.		548	536	210			.	69
K		.		2 499	2 456	2 395			.	1 590
L		.		1 492	1 391	1 619			.	276
M		.		39	27	30			.	8
N		.		722	733	1 413			.	589
O		.		145	123	290			.	152
P		.		0	0	78			.	62
Q		.		0	0	42			.	27
X		.		697	603	166			.	84

Men - Hommes - Hombres
ISIC 3 - CITI 3 - CIIU 3

	1999	2000	2001	2002	2003	2004	2005	2006	2007	2008
Total	.	.	.	16 076	15 280	16 889	.	.	.	8 922
A				440	435	681			.	175
B				0	0	0			.	1
C				39	30	35			.	25
D				2 652	2 499	2 713			.	1 157
E				60	58	54			.	31
F				5 052	4 915	5 537			.	3 522
G				1 860	1 709	1 779			.	944
H				545	527	525			.	226
I				1 606	1 471	1 662			.	956
J				239	235	107			.	31
K				1 790	1 749	1 796			.	1 214
L				1 052	1 035	1 220			.	199
M				13	9	7			.	2
N				166	162	417			.	228
O				39	28	191			.	102
P				0	0	9			.	8
Q				0	0	22			.	26
X				523	418	134			.	68

Women - Femmes - Mujeres
ISIC 3 - CITI 3 - CIIU 3

	1999	2000	2001	2002	2003	2004	2005	2006	2007	2008
Total	.	.	.	4 237	4 104	3 944	.	.	.	1 705
A				94	81	132			.	22
B				0	0	0			.	0
C				0	0	0			.	0
D				405	363	212			.	130
E				1	1	0			.	0
F				44	44	30			.	19
G				731	733	593			.	255
H				476	479	509			.	261
I				166	170	128			.	39
J				309	301	103			.	38
K				709	707	599			.	376
L				440	356	399			.	77
M				26	18	23			.	6
N				556	571	996			.	361
O				106	95	99			.	50
P				0	0	69			.	54
Q				0	0	20			.	1
X				174	185	32			.	16

Explanatory notes: see p. 1125.

Notes explicatives: voir p. 1127.

Notas explicativas: véase p. 1129.

[1] Up to 2001: excl. agriculture and forestry.

[1] Jusqu'à 2001: non compris agriculture et sylviculture.

[1] Hasta 2001: excl. agricultura y silvicultura.

8A

OCCUPATIONAL INJURIES	LÉSIONS PROFESSIONNELLES	LESIONES PROFESIONALES
Cases of injury with lost workdays, by economic activity	Cas de lésion avec perte de journées de travail, par activité économique	Casos de lesión con pérdida de días de trabajo, por actividad económica

Malta (FA) — Compensated injuries - Lésions indemnisées - Lesiones indemnizadas

Fatal cases - Cas mortels - Casos mortales

Total men and women - Total hommes et femmes - Total hombres y mujeres
ISIC 3 - CITI 3 - CIIU 3

	1999	2000	2001	2002	2003	2004	2005	2006	2007	2008
Total	9	5	6	4	12	12	6	8	7	3
A	.	.	0	0	0	1	0	1	0	0
B	.	.	0	0	0	0	0	0	0	0
C	.	.	0	1	0	0	0	0	0	1
D	.	.	1	0	1	0	1	2	1	0
E	.	.	0	0	0	0	0	0	1	0
F	.	.	1	3	8	10	3	4	4	1
G	.	.	0	0	1	0	1	0	1	1
H	.	.	0	0	0	0	1	0	0	0
I	.	.	0	0	0	1	0	0	0	0
J	.	.	0	0	0	0	0	0	0	0
K	.	.	1	0	1	0	0	0	0	0
L	.	.	3	0	0	0	0	0	0	0
M	.	.	0	0	0	0	0	0	0	0
N	.	.	0	0	0	0	0	0	0	0
O	.	.	0	0	1	0	0	0	0	0
P	.	.	0	0	0	0	0	1	0	0
Q	.	.	0	0	0	0	0	0	0	0
X	.	.	0	0	0	0	0	0	0	0

Men - Hommes - Hombres
ISIC 3 - CITI 3 - CIIU 3

	1999	2000	2001	2002	2003	2004	2005	2006	2007	2008
Total	.	.	5	4	12	11	6	7	7	3
A	.	.	0	0	0	0	0	1	0	0
B	.	.	0	0	0	0	0	0	0	0
C	.	.	0	1	0	0	0	0	0	1
D	.	.	1	0	1	0	1	2	1	0
E	.	.	0	0	0	0	0	0	1	0
F	.	.	1	3	8	10	3	4	4	1
G	.	.	0	0	1	0	1	0	1	1
H	.	.	0	0	0	0	1	0	0	0
I	.	.	0	0	0	1	0	0	0	0
J	.	.	0	0	0	0	0	0	0	0
K	.	.	0	0	1	0	0	0	0	0
L	.	.	3	0	0	0	0	0	0	0
M	.	.	0	0	0	0	0	0	0	0
N	.	.	0	0	0	0	0	0	0	0
O	.	.	0	0	1	0	0	0	0	0
P	.	.	0	0	0	0	0	0	0	0
Q	.	.	0	0	0	0	0	0	0	0
X	.	.	0	0	0	0	0	0	0	0

Women - Femmes - Mujeres
ISIC 3 - CITI 3 - CIIU 3

	1999	2000	2001	2002	2003	2004	2005	2006	2007	2008
Total	.	.	1	0	0	1	0	1	0	0
A	.	.	0	0	0	1	0	0	0	0
B	.	.	0	0	0	0	0	0	0	0
C	.	.	0	0	0	0	0	0	0	0
D	.	.	0	0	0	0	0	0	0	0
E	.	.	0	0	0	0	0	0	0	0
F	.	.	0	0	0	0	0	0	0	0
G	.	.	0	0	0	0	0	0	0	0
H	.	.	0	0	0	0	0	0	0	0
I	.	.	0	0	0	0	0	0	0	0
J	.	.	0	0	0	0	0	0	0	0
K	.	.	1	0	0	0	0	0	0	0
L	.	.	0	0	0	0	0	0	0	0
M	.	.	0	0	0	0	0	0	0	0
N	.	.	0	0	0	0	0	0	0	0
O	.	.	0	0	0	0	0	0	0	0
P	.	.	0	0	0	0	0	1	0	0
Q	.	.	0	0	0	0	0	0	0	0
X	.	.	0	0	0	0	0	0	0	0

Explanatory notes: see p. 1125. — Notes explicatives: voir p. 1127. — Notas explicativas: véase p. 1129.

	1999	2000	2001	2002	2003	2004	2005	2006	2007	2008

Malta (FA) Compensated injuries - Lésions indemnisées - Lesiones indemnizadas

Non-fatal cases (temporary + permanent incapacity) - Cas non mortels (incapacité temporaire + permanente) - Casos no mortales (incapacidad temporal + permanente)

Total men and women - Total hommes et femmes - Total hombres y mujeres [1]
ISIC 3 - CITI 3 - CIIU 3

	1999	2000	2001	2002	2003	2004	2005	2006	2007	2008
Total	5 265	5 157	5 114	4 936	4 746	4 111	4 002	4 366	4 328	4 023
A	.	.	42	46	41	55	55	55	46	63
B	.	.	5	7	8	12	15	15	11	15
C	.	.	9	17	19	22	25	37	32	44
D	.	.	1 987	1 733	1 726	1 423	1 425	1 472	1 432	1 197
E	.	.	145	161	161	154	145	136	145	128
F	.	.	471	533	571	627	659	698	689	652
G	.	.	214	217	245	289	318	364	402	357
H	.	.	268	278	347	384	286	315	303	314
I	.	.	285	357	384	383	356	388	489	468
J	.	.	19	11	33	12	16	7	10	9
K	.	.	84	99	172	175	128	198	209	209
L	.	.	178	155	211	198	174	240	171	172
M	.	.	228	215	64	62	57	70	58	63
N	.	.	34	23	200	218	241	285	237	236
O	.	.	79	52	80	56	72	60	60	57
P	.	.	0	0	0	0	0	1	0	0
Q	.	.	1	0	1	4	5	3	5	3
X	.	.	1 065	1 032	483	37	25	22	29	36

Men - Hommes - Hombres [1]
ISIC 3 - CITI 3 - CIIU 3

	1999	2000	2001	2002	2003	2004	2005	2006	2007	2008
Total	.	.	4 562	4 438	4 208	3 611	3 496	3 848	3 829	3 499
A	.	.	42	42	39	53	55	53	44	63
B	.	.	5	7	8	12	15	15	11	15
C	.	.	9	17	19	22	25	37	32	43
D	.	.	1 830	1 581	1 574	1 300	1 309	1 364	1 333	1 099
E	.	.	144	157	160	153	141	135	144	128
F	.	.	465	528	562	626	655	696	685	648
G	.	.	197	199	228	264	288	338	367	317
H	.	.	208	231	257	289	216	253	237	247
I	.	.	256	323	351	348	328	354	457	439
J	.	.	9	10	21	8	12	5	5	7
K	.	.	74	82	146	147	98	168	169	168
L	.	.	157	141	190	177	161	217	153	149
M	.	.	116	128	27	31	29	33	19	21
N	.	.	2	6	94	98	85	111	91	79
O	.	.	68	46	75	46	56	50	53	44
P	.	.	0	0	0	0	0	0	0	0
Q	.	.	1	0	1	2	3	1	3	2
X	.	.	979	940	456	35	20	18	26	30

Women - Femmes - Mujeres [1]
ISIC 3 - CITI 3 - CIIU 3

	1999	2000	2001	2002	2003	2004	2005	2006	2007	2008
Total	.	.	552	498	538	500	506	518	499	524
A	.	.	0	4	2	2	0	2	2	0
B	.	.	0	0	0	0	0	0	0	0
C	.	.	0	0	0	0	0	0	0	1
D	.	.	157	152	152	123	116	108	99	98
E	.	.	1	4	1	1	4	1	1	0
F	.	.	6	5	9	1	4	2	4	4
G	.	.	17	18	17	25	30	26	35	40
H	.	.	60	47	90	95	70	62	66	67
I	.	.	29	34	33	35	28	34	32	29
J	.	.	10	1	12	4	4	2	5	2
K	.	.	10	17	26	28	30	30	40	41
L	.	.	21	14	21	21	13	23	18	23
M	.	.	112	87	37	31	28	37	39	42
N	.	.	32	17	106	120	156	174	146	157
O	.	.	11	6	5	10	16	10	7	13
P	.	.	0	0	0	0	0	1	0	0
Q	.	.	0	0	0	2	2	2	2	1
X	.	.	86	92	27	2	5	4	3	6

Explanatory notes: see p. 1125.

[1] Incapacity of 4 days or more.

Notes explicatives: voir p. 1127.

[1] Incapacité de 4 jours et plus.

Notas explicativas: véase p. 1129.

[1] Incapacidad de 4 días y más.

	OCCUPATIONAL INJURIES	LÉSIONS PROFESSIONNELLES	LESIONES PROFESIONALES
	Cases of injury with lost workdays, by economic activity	**Cas de lésion avec perte de journées de travail, par activité économique**	**Casos de lesión con pérdida de días de trabajo, por actividad económica**

	1999	2000	2001	2002	2003	2004	2005	2006	2007	2008

Malta (FA) — Compensated injuries - Lésions indemnisées - Lesiones indemnizadas

Cases of temporary incapacity - Cas d'incapacité temporaire - Casos de incapacidad temporal

Total men and women - Total hommes et femmes - Total hombres y mujeres [1]
ISIC 3 - CITI 3 - CIIU 3

	1999	2000	2001	2002	2003	2004	2005	2006	2007	2008
Total			5 114	4 936	4 746	4 111	4 002	4 366	4 328	4 023
A			42	46	41	55	55	55	46	63
B			5	7	8	12	15	15	11	15
C			9	17	19	22	25	37	32	44
D			1 987	1 733	1 726	1 423	1 425	1 472	1 432	1 197
E			145	161	161	154	145	136	145	128
F			471	533	571	627	659	698	689	652
G			214	217	245	289	318	364	402	357
H			268	278	347	384	286	315	303	314
I			285	357	384	383	356	388	489	468
J			19	11	33	12	16	7	10	9
K			84	99	172	175	128	198	209	209
L			178	155	211	198	174	240	171	172
M			228	215	64	62	57	70	58	63
N			34	23	200	218	241	285	237	236
O			79	52	80	56	72	60	60	57
P			0	0	0	0	0	1	0	0
Q			1	0	1	4	5	3	5	3
X			1 065	1 032	483	37	25	22	29	36

Men - Hommes - Hombres [1]
ISIC 3 - CITI 3 - CIIU 3

	1999	2000	2001	2002	2003	2004	2005	2006	2007	2008
Total			4 562	4 438	4 208	3 611	3 496	3 848	3 829	3 499
A			42	42	39	53	55	53	44	63
B			5	7	8	12	15	15	11	15
C			9	17	19	22	25	37	32	43
D			1 830	1 581	1 574	1 309	1 300	1 364	1 333	1 099
E			144	157	160	153	141	135	144	128
F			465	528	562	626	655	696	685	648
G			197	199	228	264	288	338	367	317
H			208	231	257	289	216	253	237	247
I			256	323	351	348	328	354	457	439
J			9	10	21	8	12	5	5	7
K			74	82	146	147	98	168	169	168
L			157	141	190	177	161	217	153	149
M			116	128	27	31	29	33	19	21
N			2	6	94	98	85	111	91	79
O			68	46	75	46	56	50	53	44
P			0	0	0	0	0	0	0	0
Q			1	0	1	2	3	1	3	2
X			979	940	456	35	20	18	26	30

Women - Femmes - Mujeres [1]
ISIC 3 - CITI 3 - CIIU 3

	1999	2000	2001	2002	2003	2004	2005	2006	2007	2008
Total			552	498	538	500	506	518	499	524
A			0	4	2	2	0	2	2	0
B			0	0	0	0	0	0	0	0
C			0	0	0	0	0	0	0	1
D			157	152	152	123	116	108	99	98
E			1	4	1	1	4	1	1	0
F			6	5	9	1	4	2	4	4
G			17	18	17	25	30	26	35	40
H			60	47	90	95	70	62	66	67
I			29	34	33	35	28	34	32	29
J			10	1	12	4	4	2	5	2
K			10	17	26	28	30	30	40	41
L			21	14	21	21	13	23	18	23
M			112	87	37	31	28	37	39	42
N			32	17	106	120	156	174	146	157
O			11	6	5	10	16	10	7	13
P			0	0	0	0	0	1	0	0
Q			0	0	0	2	2	2	2	1
X			86	92	27	2	5	4	3	6

Explanatory notes: see p. 1125.
[1] Incapacity of 4 days or more.

Notes explicatives: voir p. 1127.
[1] Incapacité de 4 jours et plus.

Notas explicativas: véase p. 1129.
[1] Incapacidad de 4 días y más.

OCCUPATIONAL INJURIES
Cases of injury with lost workdays, by economic activity

LÉSIONS PROFESSIONNELLES
Cas de lésion avec perte de journées de travail, par activité économique

LESIONES PROFESIONALES
Casos de lesión con pérdida de días de trabajo, por actividad económica

Malta (FA) — **Compensated injuries - Lésions indemnisées - Lesiones indemnizadas**

Total cases (fatal + non-fatal) - Ensemble des cas (mortels + non mortels) - Todos los casos (mortales + no mortales)

Total men and women - Total hommes et femmes - Total hombres y mujeres
ISIC 2 - CITI 2 - CIIU 2 ... ISIC 3 - CITI 3 - CIIU 3

1999	2000	2001	2002	2003	2004	2005	2006	2007	2008	
5 274	5 162	5 120	4 940	4 758	4 123	4 008	4 374	4 335	4 026	Total
		42	46	41	56	55	56	46	63	A
		5	7	8	12	15	15	11	15	B
		9	18	19	22	25	37	32	45	C
		1 988	1 733	1 727	1 423	1 426	1 474	1 433	1 197	D
		145	161	161	154	145	136	146	128	E
		472	536	579	637	662	702	693	653	F
		214	217	246	289	319	364	403	358	G
		268	278	347	384	287	315	303	314	H
		285	357	384	384	356	388	489	468	I
		19	11	33	12	16	7	10	9	J
		85	99	173	175	128	198	209	209	K
		181	155	211	198	174	240	171	172	L
		228	215	64	62	57	70	58	63	M
		34	23	200	218	241	285	237	236	N
		79	52	81	56	72	60	60	57	O
		0	0	0	0	0	2	0	0	P
		1	0	1	4	5	3	5	3	Q
		1 065	1 032	483	37	25	22	29	36	X

Men - Hommes - Hombres
ISIC 2 - CITI 2 - CIIU 2 ... ISIC 3 - CITI 3 - CIIU 3

1999	2000	2001	2002	2003	2004	2005	2006	2007	2008	
4 749	.	4 567	4 442	4 220	3 622	3 502	3 855	3 836	3 502	Total
		42	42	39	53	55	54	44	63	A
		5	7	8	12	15	15	11	15	B
		9	18	19	22	25	37	32	44	C
		1 831	1 581	1 575	1 300	1 310	1 366	1 334	1 099	D
		144	157	160	153	141	135	145	128	E
		466	531	570	636	658	700	689	649	F
		197	199	229	264	289	338	368	318	G
		208	231	257	289	217	253	237	247	H
		256	323	351	349	328	354	457	439	I
		9	10	21	8	12	5	5	7	J
		74	82	147	147	98	168	169	168	K
		160	141	190	177	161	217	153	149	L
		116	128	27	31	29	33	19	21	M
		2	6	94	98	85	111	91	79	N
		68	46	76	46	56	50	53	44	O
		0	0	0	0	0	0	0	0	P
		1	0	1	2	3	1	3	2	Q
		979	940	456	35	20	18	26	30	X

Women - Femmes - Mujeres
ISIC 2 - CITI 2 - CIIU 2 ... ISIC 3 - CITI 3 - CIIU 3

1999	2000	2001	2002	2003	2004	2005	2006	2007	2008	
525	.	553	498	538	501	506	519	499	524	Total
		0	4	2	3	0	2	2	0	A
		0	0	0	0	0	0	0	0	B
		0	0	0	0	0	0	0	1	C
		157	152	152	123	116	108	99	98	D
		1	4	1	1	4	1	1	0	E
		6	5	9	1	4	2	4	4	F
		17	18	17	25	30	26	35	40	G
		60	47	90	95	70	62	66	67	H
		29	34	33	35	28	34	32	29	I
		10	1	12	4	4	2	5	2	J
		11	17	26	28	30	30	40	41	K
		21	14	21	21	13	23	18	23	L
		112	87	37	31	28	37	39	42	M
		32	17	106	120	156	174	146	157	N
		11	6	5	10	16	10	7	13	O
		0	0	0	0	0	2	0	0	P
		0	0	0	2	2	2	2	1	Q
		86	92	27	2	5	4	3	6	X

Explanatory notes: see p. 1125.   Notes explicatives: voir p. 1127.   Notas explicativas: véase p. 1129.

8A OCCUPATIONAL INJURIES / LÉSIONS PROFESSIONNELLES / LESIONES PROFESIONALES

Cases of injury with lost workdays, by economic activity

Cas de lésion avec perte de journées de travail, par activité économique

Casos de lesión con pérdida de días de trabajo, por actividad económica

Moldova, Republic of (CA) [1]

Reported injuries - Lésions déclarées - Lesiones declaradas

Fatal cases - Cas mortels - Casos mortales

Total men and women - Total hommes et femmes - Total hombres y mujeres
ISIC 3 - CITI 3 - CIIU 3

	1999	2000	2001	2002	2003	2004	2005	2006	2007	2008
Total	45	52	39	41	43	38	49	38	54	40
A	15	12	14	9	9	10	16	5	2	7
B	1	0	0	0	0	0	0	0	1	0
C	0	1	1	0	1	1	0	0	2	2
D	12	9	9	7	7	7	8	4	11	7
E	1	3	1	5	4	3	4	1	5	2
F	1	3	1	3	7	5	4	10	13	5
G	3	2	3	1	3	1	4	4	0	5
H	0	0	0	0	0	0	0	0	0	1
I	4	3	5	2	2	0	6	4	0	4
J	0	0	0	0	0	5	0	4	10	0
K	1	2	0	1	2	0	1	0	0	0
L	7	16	1	10	2	0	3	1	2	1
M	0	0	3	0	3	1	2	1	2	1
N	0	1	0	2	0	1	0	3	3	2
O	0	0	1	1	3	2	0	5	3	3

Non-fatal cases (temporary + permanent incapacity) - Cas non mortels (incapacité temporaire + permanente) - Casos no mortales (incapacidad temporal + permanente)

Total men and women - Total hommes et femmes - Total hombres y mujeres
ISIC 3 - CITI 3 - CIIU 3

	1999	2000	2001	2002	2003	2004	2005	2006	2007	2008
Total	827	615	603	565	619	682	633	628	541	500
A	189	118	85	84	82	104	51	38	43	42
B	0	0	0	0	0	0	0	0	0	0
C	6	5	2	14	6	10	8	14	0	0
D	217	157	204	169	246	250	241	220	16	12
E	35	34	44	70	93	44	52	60	182	159
F	28	26	22	25	22	22	33	47	34	31
G	11	12	13	16	13	35	32	19	41	37
H	...	...	3	2	2	2	1	3	19	33
I	40	49	50	40	55	69	33	55	2	3
J	13	11	2	1	2	4	18	18	42	50
K	25	27	31	14	20	63	70	47	14	14
L	213	131	108	89	20	19	30	31	24	33
M	16	12	17	12	28	16	18	23	52	28
N	24	27	17	23	23	33	43	41	12	7
O	10	6	5	7	6	11	3	12	52	40

Total cases (fatal + non-fatal) - Ensemble des cas (mortels + non mortels) - Todos los casos (mortales + no mortales)

Total men and women - Total hommes et femmes - Total hombres y mujeres
ISIC 3 - CITI 3 - CIIU 3

	1999	2000	2001	2002	2003	2004	2005	2006	2007	2008
Total	872	667	642	606	662	720	682	666	595	540
A	204	130	99	93	91	114	67	43	45	49
B	1	0	0	0	0	0	0	0	1	0
C	6	6	3	14	7	11	8	14	2	2
D	229	166	213	176	253	257	249	224	18	14
E	36	37	45	75	97	47	56	61	193	166
F	29	29	23	28	29	27	37	57	39	33
G	14	14	16	17	16	36	36	23	54	42
H	...	...	3	2	2	2	1	3	19	38
I	44	52	55	42	57	74	39	59	2	4
J	13	11	2	1	2	4	18	18	52	54
K	26	29	31	15	22	65	71	48	14	14
L	220	147	109	99	22	19	33	32	26	33
M	16	12	20	12	31	17	20	26	54	29
N	24	28	17	25	23	34	43	41	14	8
O	10	6	6	7	10	13	3	17	55	42

Explanatory notes: see p. 1125.

[1] Enterprises with 20 or more employees, state-owned and municipal enterprises, institutions and organisations.

Notes explicatives: voir p. 1127.

[1] Entreprises occupant 20 salariés et plus, entreprises d'Etat et municipales, institutions et organisations.

Notas explicativas: véase p. 1129.

[1] Empresas con 20 y más asalariados, empresas estatales y municipales, instituciones y organisaciones.

OCCUPATIONAL INJURIES

Cases of injury with lost workdays, by economic activity

LÉSIONS PROFESSIONNELLES

Cas de lésion avec perte de journées de travail, par activité économique

LESIONES PROFESIONALES

Casos de lesión con pérdida de días de trabajo, por actividad económica

Netherlands (FA)

Reported injuries - Lésions déclarées - Lesiones declaradas

Fatal cases - Cas mortels - Casos mortales

Total men and women - Total hommes et femmes - Total hombres y mujeres [1]

ISIC 3 - CITI 3 - CIIU 3

	1999	2000	2001	2002	2003	2004	2005	2006	2007	2008
Total	94	110	116	89	108	93	73	84	86	92
A-B	18	23	18	16	13	15	13	14	17	20
C-E	13	17	19	15	27	13	20	6	10	11
F	29	29	38	35	29	30	17	28	32	38
G,J-K	2	1	5	5	5	4	5	5	3	1
H	0	2	0	1	0	0	1	1	0	0
I	18	26	22	11	12	13	11	19	12	11
L	0	6	4	0	5	1	1	1	3	2
M,N,P,Q	9	2	5	2	7	3	1	0	7	8
O	5	4	5	4	10	14	4	10	2	1

Men - Hommes - Hombres [1]

ISIC 3 - CITI 3 - CIIU 3

	1999	2000	2001	2002	2003	2004	2005	2006	2007	2008
Total	92	108	114	87	105	89	71	78	83	89
A-B	18	22	17	16	12	15	13	10	15	19
C-E	12	17	19	14	27	13	19	6	10	11
F	29	29	37	35	29	30	17	27	32	37
G,J-K	2	1	5	4	5	3	5	5	2	1
H	0	2	0	1	0	0	0	0	0	0
I	18	26	22	11	11	13	11	19	12	10
L	0	6	4	0	5	1	1	1	3	2
M,N,P,Q	8	2	5	2	6	3	1	0	7	8
O	5	3	5	4	10	11	4	10	2	1

Women - Femmes - Mujeres [1]

ISIC 3 - CITI 3 - CIIU 3

	1999	2000	2001	2002	2003	2004	2005	2006	2007	2008
Total	2	2	2	2	3	4	2	6	3	3
A-B	0	1	1	0	1	0	0	4	2	1
C-E	1	0	0	1	0	0	1	0	0	0
F	0	0	1	0	0	1	0	0	1	1
G,J-K	0	0	0	1	0	0	1	1	1	0
H	0	0	0	0	0	0	0	0	0	1
I	0	0	0	0	1	0	0	0	0	0
L	0	0	0	0	0	0	0	0	0	0
M,N,P,Q	1	0	0	0	1	0	0	0	0	0
O	0	1	0	0	0	3	0	0	0	0

Norway (FF)

Reported injuries - Lésions déclarées - Lesiones declaradas

Fatal cases - Cas mortels - Casos mortales

Total men and women - Total hommes et femmes - Total hombres y mujeres

ISIC 3 - CITI 3 - CIIU 3

	1999	2000	2001	2002	2003	2004	2005	2006	2007	2008
Total	58	57	37	39	49	38	48	31	38	51
A	10	17	9	5	14	11	16	4	4	12
B [2]	2	1	0	0	0	0	1	0	1	1
C [3]	1	4	4	0	3	3	2	5	2	3
D	9	10	9	8	6	2	5	1	8	10
E	1	1	2	0	0	1	0	8	0	1
F	13	6	4	4	13	2	11	8	5	6
G	5	2	2	2	4	1	2	2	1	2
H	0	0	0	4	0	0	0	1	0	0
I [4]	7	12	5	0	9	9	7	3	9	8
J	0	0	0	0	0	0	0	5	0	0
K	2	1	0	0	1	2	0	0	3	2
L	4	2	2	0	0	1	0	5	4	1
M	1	0	0	1	0	1	0	0	0	0
N	0	1	0	1	0	0	0	2	1	1
O	3	0	0	1	1		0	0	0	4
O,Q	3	0	0		0	0	0	0	0	0
P	0	0	0		0	0	0	0	0	0
Q	·	·	·		1	0	0	0	0	0
X	·	·	·							

Explanatory notes: see p. 1125.

[1] Excl. road traffic accidents. [2] Excl. sea fishing. [3] Excl. offshore oil extraction. [4] Excl. maritime transport.

Notes explicatives: voir p. 1127.

[1] Non compris les accidents de la circulation. [2] Non compris la pêche en mer. [3] Non compris l'extraction du pétrole en mer. [4] Non compris les transports maritimes.

Notas explicativas: véase p. 1129.

[1] Excl. los accidentes de la circulación. [2] Excl. la pesca de altura y costera. [3] Excl. la extracción del petróleo en el mar. [4] Excl. el transporte marítimo.

8A OCCUPATIONAL INJURIES

Cases of injury with lost workdays, by economic activity

LÉSIONS PROFESSIONNELLES

Cas de lésion avec perte de journées de travail, par activité économique

LESIONES PROFESIONALES

Casos de lesión con pérdida de días de trabajo, por actividad económica

Norway (FF)

Reported injuries - Lésions déclarées - Lesiones declaradas

Fatal cases - Cas mortels - Casos mortales

Men - Hommes - Hombres
ISIC 3 - CITI 3 - CIIU 3

	1999	2000	2001	2002	2003	2004	2005	2006	2007	2008
Total	54	54	36	36	47	36	.	.	.	.
A	10	15	9	5	13	10	.	.	.	.
B[1]	2	1	0	0	0	0	.	.	.	.
C[2]	1	4	4	0	3	0	.	.	.	.
D	8	10	8	7	6	3	.	.	.	.
E	1	1	2	0	2	2	.	.	.	.
F	13	6	4	13	0	1	.	.	.	.
G	5	2	2	4	9	2	.	.	.	.
H	0	0	0	2	4	1	.	.	.	.
I[3]	7	12	5	4	0	0	.	.	.	.
J	0	0	0	0	8	9	.	.	.	.
K	1	1	0	0	0	0	.	.	.	.
L	4	2	2	0	1	2	.	.	.	.
M	0	0	0	0	0	1	.	.	.	.
N	0	0	0	0	1	0	.	.	.	.
O	2	0	0	0	0	0	.	.	.	.
O.Q	2	0	0	1	0	5	.	.	.	.
P	0	0	0	0			.	.	.	.
Q					0	0	.	.	.	.
X					1	0	.	.	.	.

Women - Femmes - Mujeres
ISIC 3 - CITI 3 - CIIU 3

	1999	2000	2001	2002	2003	2004	2005	2006	2007	2008
Total	4	3	1	3	2	2	.	.	.	.
A	0	2	0	0	1	1	.	.	.	.
B[1]	0	0	0	0	0	0	.	.	.	.
C[2]	0	0	0	0	0	0	.	.	.	.
D	1	0	1	1	0	0	.	.	.	.
E	0	0	0	0	0	0	.	.	.	.
F	0	0	0	0	0	0	.	.	.	.
G	0	0	0	0	0	0	.	.	.	.
H	0	0	0	0	0	0	.	.	.	.
I[3]	0	0	0	0	0	0	.	.	.	.
J	0	0	0	0	1	0	.	.	.	.
K	1	0	0	0	0	0	.	.	.	.
L	0	0	0	0	0	0	.	.	.	.
M	1	0	0	1	0	1	.	.	.	.
N	0	1	0	1	0	0	.	.	.	.
O	1	0	0	0	0	1	.	.	.	.
O.Q	1	0	0	0	0	0	.	.	.	.
P	0	0	0	0			.	.	.	.
Q					0	0	.	.	.	.
X					0	0	.	.	.	.

Non-fatal cases (temporary + permanent incapacity) - Cas non mortels (incapacité temporaire + permanente) - Casos no mortales (incapacidad temporal + permanente)

Total men and women - Total hommes et femmes - Total hombres y mujeres
ISIC 3 - CITI 3 - CIIU 3

	1999	2000	2001	2002	2003	2004	2005	2006	2007	2008
Total	33 499	31 706	28 683	26 950	23 767	22 557	20 541	18 439	19 081	16 630
A	440	450	398	330	305	269	265	225	188	215
B[1]	110	82	86	79	63	73	86	59	61	82
C[2]	249	229	222	224	166	154	150	91	163	155
D	8 974	8 187	7 458	6 619	5 520	4 841	4 295	3 804	4 020	3 730
E	550	457	400	341	285	272	260	196	180	190
F	3 657	3 607	3 301	3 027	2 807	2 679	2 419	2 137	2 273	2 051
G	1 976	2 041	1 823	1 635	1 483	1 417	1 305	1 141	1 122	968
H	566	494	498	480	351	306	288	288	286	249
I[3]	2 790	2 586	2 141	1 948	1 730	1 780	1 608	1 577	1 553	1 384
J	122	114	100	87	53	44	38	48	36	24
K	948	958	877	985	777	786	729	665	805	703
L	2 698	2 590	2 050	2 269	1 989	1 858	1 636	1 345	1 461	1 134
M	2 775	2 990	2 686	2 668	2 448	2 411	2 167	1 907	2 286	1 680
N	6 429	5 924	5 743	5 442	5 099	5 106	4 733	4 440	4 118	3 568
O	628	626	564	599	516	454	434	384	369	324
P	5	2	5	2	0	4	6	4	4	0
Q	2	2	1	1	1	0	0	1	0	1
X	580	367	330	214	172	122	131	127	156	120

Explanatory notes: see p. 1125.

[1] Excl. sea fishing. [2] Excl. offshore oil extraction. [3] Excl. maritime transport.

Notes explicatives: voir p. 1127.

[1] Non compris la pêche en mer. [2] Non compris l'extraction du pétrole en mer. [3] Non compris les transports maritimes.

Notas explicativas: véase p. 1129.

[1] Excl. la pesca de altura y costera. [2] Excl. la extracción del petróleo en el mar. [3] Excl. el transporte marítimo.

OCCUPATIONAL INJURIES

Cases of injury with lost workdays, by economic activity

LÉSIONS PROFESSIONNELLES

Cas de lésion avec perte de journées de travail, par activité économique

LESIONES PROFESIONALES

Casos de lesión con pérdida de días de trabajo, por actividad económica

8A

	1999	2000	2001	2002	2003	2004	2005	2006	2007	2008

Norway (FF)   Reported injuries - Lésions déclarées - Lesiones declaradas

Non-fatal cases (temporary + permanent incapacity) - Cas non mortels (incapacité temporaire + permanente) - Casos no mortales (incapacidad temporal + permanente)

Men - Hommes - Hombres
ISIC 3 - CITI 3 - CIIU 3

	1999	2000	2001	2002	2003	2004	2005	2006	2007	2008
Total	21 786	20 396	18 362	16 864	14 597	13 731	.	.	.	.
A	354	361	316	265	245	222	.	.	.	.
B [1]	93	64	72	61	52	61	.	.	.	.
C [2]	236	215	204	196	152	139	.	.	.	.
D	7 744	6 947	6 419	5 626	4 670	4 135	.	.	.	.
E	523	423	367	324	266	257	.	.	.	.
F	3 541	3 485	3 202	2 924	2 724	2 597	.	.	.	.
G	1 467	1 478	1 333	1 197	1 072	1 011	.	.	.	.
H	250	220	216	187	150	123	.	.	.	.
I [3]	2 111	1 984	1 601	1 530	1 338	1 363	.	.	.	.
J	50	49	33	33	21	22	.	.	.	.
K	646	671	632	682	524	568	.	.	.	.
L	1 575	1 462	1 172	1 126	1 086	1 011	.	.	.	.
M	970	1 051	850	862	800	747	.	.	.	.
N	1 488	1 343	1 344	1 217	1 046	1 100	.	.	.	.
O	441	449	419	405	369	322	.	.	.	.
P	4	2	4	1	0	3	.	.	.	.
Q	1	2	0	1	1	0	.	.	.	.
X	292	190	178	127	79	50	.	.	.	.

Women - Femmes - Mujeres
ISIC 3 - CITI 3 - CIIU 3

	1999	2000	2001	2002	2003	2004	2005	2006	2007	2008
Total	11 713	11 310	10 321	10 086	9 170	8 826	.	.	.	.
A	86	89	82	65	60	47	.	.	.	.
B [1]	17	18	14	18	11	12	.	.	.	.
C [2]	13	14	18	28	14	15	.	.	.	.
D	1 230	1 240	1 039	993	850	704	.	.	.	.
E	27	34	33	17	19	14	.	.	.	.
F	116	122	99	103	83	80	.	.	.	.
G	509	563	490	438	411	405	.	.	.	.
H	316	274	282	293	201	183	.	.	.	.
I [3]	679	602	540	418	392	408	.	.	.	.
J	72	65	67	54	32	22	.	.	.	.
K	302	287	245	303	253	216	.	.	.	.
L	1 123	1 128	878	1 043	903	846	.	.	.	.
M	1 805	1 939	1 836	1 806	1 648	1 663	.	.	.	.
N	4 941	4 581	4 399	4 225	4 053	4 006	.	.	.	.
O	187	177	145	194	147	132	.	.	.	.
P	1	0	1	1	0	1	.	.	.	.
Q	1	0	1	0	0	0	.	.	.	.
X	288	177	152	.	93	72	.	.	.	.

Total cases (fatal + non-fatal) - Ensemble des cas (mortels + non mortels) - Todos los casos (mortales + no mortales)

Total men and women - Total hommes et femmes - Total hombres y mujeres
ISIC 3 - CITI 3 - CIIU 3

	1999	2000	2001	2002	2003	2004	2005	2006	2007	2008
Total	33 557	31 763	28 720	26 989	23 816	22 595	20 589	18 470	19 119	16 681
A	450	467	407	335	319	280	271	229	192	227
B [1]	112	83	86	79	63	73	87	59	62	83
C [2]	250	233	226	224	169	157	151	91	165	158
D	8 983	8 197	7 467	6 627	5 526	4 843	4 300	3 809	4 028	3 740
E	551	458	402	341	285	273	260	197	180	191
F	3 670	3 613	3 305	3 040	2 816	2 681	2 430	2 145	2 278	2 057
G	1 981	2 043	1 825	1 639	1 487	1 418	1 312	1 143	1 123	970
H	566	494	498	482	351	306	288	289	286	249
I [3]	2 797	2 598	2 146	1 952	1 739	1 789	1 615	1 580	1 562	1 392
J	122	114	100	87	53	44	38	48	36	24
K	950	959	877	985	778	788	729	670	808	705
L	2 702	2 592	2 052	2 269	1 989	1 859	1 638	1 345	1 465	1 135
M	2 776	2 990	2 686	2 669	2 449	2 412	2 167	1 907	2 286	1 680
N	6 429	5 925	5 743	5 443	5 099	5 106	4 733	4 442	4 119	3 569
O	631	626	564	600	517	459	436	384	369	328
P	5	2	5	2	0	4	6	4	4	0
Q	2	2	1	1	1	0	0	1	0	1
X	580	367	330	214	173	122	131	127	156	120

Explanatory notes: see p. 1125.

[1] Excl. sea fishing. [2] Excl. offshore oil extraction. [3] Excl. maritime transport.

Notes explicatives: voir p. 1127.

[1] Non compris la pêche en mer. [2] Non compris l'extraction du pétrole en mer. [3] Non compris les transports maritimes.

Notas explicativas: véase p. 1129.

[1] Excl. la pesca de altura y costera. [2] Excl. la extracción del petróleo en el mar. [3] Excl. el transporte marítimo.

	OCCUPATIONAL INJURIES Cases of injury with lost workdays, by economic activity	LÉSIONS PROFESSIONNELLES Cas de lésion avec perte de journées de travail, par activité économique	LESIONES PROFESIONALES Casos de lesión con pérdida de días de trabajo, por actividad económica

	1999	2000	2001	2002	2003	2004	2005	2006	2007	2008

Norway (FF) — Reported injuries - Lésions déclarées - Lesiones declaradas

Total cases (fatal + non-fatal) - Ensemble des cas (mortels + non mortels) - Todos los casos (mortales + no mortales)

Men - Hommes - Hombres
ISIC 3 - CITI 3 - CIIU 3

	1999	2000	2001	2002	2003	2004	2005	2006	2007	2008
Total	21 840	20 450	18 398	16 900	14 644	13 767	.	.	.	.
A	364	376	325	270	258	232	.	.	.	.
B [1]	95	65	72	61	52	61	.	.	.	.
C [2]	237	219	208	196	155	142	.	.	.	.
D	7 752	6 957	6 427	5 633	4 676	4 137	.	.	.	.
E	524	424	369	324	266	258	.	.	.	.
F	3 554	3 491	3 206	2 937	2 733	2 599	.	.	.	.
G	1 472	1 480	1 335	1 201	1 076	1 012	.	.	.	.
H	250	220	216	189	150	123	.	.	.	.
I [3]	2 118	1 996	1 606	1 534	1 346	1 372	.	.	.	.
J	50	49	33	33	21	22	.	.	.	.
K	647	672	632	682	525	570	.	.	.	.
L	1 579	1 464	1 174	1 126	1 086	1 012	.	.	.	.
M	970	1 051	850	862	801	747	.	.	.	.
N	1 488	1 343	1 344	1 217	1 046	1 100	.	.	.	.
O	443	449	419	406	370	327	.	.	.	.
P	4	2	4	1	0	3	.	.	.	.
Q	1	2	0	1	1	0	.	.	.	.
X	292	190	178	127	80	50	.	.	.	.

Women - Femmes - Mujeres
ISIC 3 - CITI 3 - CIIU 3

	1999	2000	2001	2002	2003	2004	2005	2006	2007	2008
Total	11 717	11 313	10 322	10 089	9 172	8 828	.	.	.	.
A	86	91	82	65	61	48	.	.	.	.
B [1]	17	18	14	18	11	12	.	.	.	.
C [2]	13	14	18	28	14	15	.	.	.	.
D	1 231	1 240	1 040	994	850	704	.	.	.	.
E	27	34	33	17	19	14	.	.	.	.
F	116	122	99	103	83	80	.	.	.	.
G	509	563	490	438	411	405	.	.	.	.
H	316	274	282	293	201	183	.	.	.	.
I [3]	679	602	540	418	393	408	.	.	.	.
J	72	65	67	54	32	22	.	.	.	.
K	303	287	245	303	253	216	.	.	.	.
L	1 123	1 128	878	1 043	903	846	.	.	.	.
M	1 806	1 939	1 836	1 807	1 648	1 664	.	.	.	.
N	4 941	4 582	4 399	4 226	4 053	4 006	.	.	.	.
O	188	177	145	194	147	132	.	.	.	.
P	1	0	1	1	0	1	.	.	.	.
Q	1	0	1	0	0	0	.	.	.	.
X	288	177	152	.	93	72	.	.	.	.

Poland (FF) — Reported injuries - Lésions déclarées - Lesiones declaradas

Fatal cases - Cas mortels - Casos mortales

Total men and women - Total hommes et femmes - Total hombres y mujeres [4]
ISIC 3 - CITI 3 - CIIU 3

	1999	2000	2001	2002	2003	2004	2005	2006	2007	2008
Total [5]	523	594	554	515	515	490	468	493	479	523
A [5]	16	11	15	20	12	21	25	16	23	28
B	3	3	5	1	5	2	1	0	0	1
C	33	41	31	44	41	19	24	29	26	30
D	117	161	138	112	121	122	106	129	122	107
E	25	9	14	13	17	20	10	12	22	15
F	120	145	114	96	88	93	106	113	92	122
G	64	66	84	79	69	50	41	43	54	58
H	3	3	5	1	4	4	2	0	1	2
I	54	67	63	60	58	72	65	72	61	80
J	13	9	9	3	1	7	7	4	4	7
K	31	24	32	34	40	29	33	30	30	27
L	12	18	16	17	20	17	21	14	9	9
M	10	20	10	10	15	15	12	12	11	10
N	7	8	7	9	10	3	5	10	4	8
O	15	9	11	16	14	16	10	13	20	19
Q	0	0	0	0	0	0	0	0	0	0

Explanatory notes: see p. 1125.

[1] Excl. sea fishing. [2] Excl. offshore oil extraction. [3] Excl. maritime transport. [4] Deaths occurring within six months of accident. [5] Excl. private farms in agriculture.

Notes explicatives: voir p. 1127.

[1] Non compris la pêche en mer. [2] Non compris l'extraction du pétrole en mer. [3] Non compris les transports maritimes. [4] Les décès survenant pendant les six mois qui suivent l'accident. [5] Non compris les fermes privées dans l'agriculture.

Notas explicativas: véase p. 1129.

[1] Excl. la pesca de altura y costera. [2] Excl. la extracción del petróleo en el mar. [3] Excl. el transporte marítimo. [4] Los fallecimientos que se produzcan durante los seis meses que siguen el accidente. [5] Excl. las granjas privadas en la agricultura.

OCCUPATIONAL INJURIES

Cases of injury with lost workdays, by economic activity

LÉSIONS PROFESSIONNELLES

Cas de lésion avec perte de journées de travail, par activité économique

LESIONES PROFESIONALES

Casos de lesión con pérdida de días de trabajo, por actividad económica

	1999	2000	2001	2002	2003	2004	2005	2006	2007	2008

Poland (FF)　　　　Reported injuries - Lésions déclarées - Lesiones declaradas

Fatal cases - Cas mortels - Casos mortales

Men - Hommes - Hombres [1]
ISIC 3 - CITI 3 - CIIU 3

	1999	2000	2001	2002	2003	2004	2005	2006	2007	2008
Total [2]	490	552	514	483	481	451	443	467	447	498
A [2]	16	10	15	20	12	19	23	16	23	27
B	3	3	5	1	5	2	1	0	0	1
C	33	39	31	44	41	19	24	29	25	30
D	108	154	124	106	113	112	101	117	117	105
E	24	9	14	12	17	20	9	12	21	15
F	117	142	114	94	88	92	106	113	91	121
G	60	58	78	72	63	48	37	40	48	54
H	1	1	3	1	2	3	1	0	1	2
I	52	65	62	58	56	66	64	71	58	79
J	10	6	5	3	0	5	5	3	2	6
K	27	24	27	30	33	23	29	29	27	24
L	11	12	14	16	17	14	16	11	6	8
M	8	14	8	7	13	10	12	7	8	4
N	5	6	4	6	8	3	5	6	3	4
O	15	9	10	13	13	15	10	13	17	18
P	0	0	0	0	0	0	0	0	0	0
Q	0	0	0	0	0	0	0	0	0	0

Women - Femmes - Mujeres [1]
ISIC 3 - CITI 3 - CIIU 3

	1999	2000	2001	2002	2003	2004	2005	2006	2007	2008
Total [2]	33	42	40	32	34	39	25	26	32	25
A [2]	0	1	0	0	0	2	2	0	0	1
B	0	0	0	0	0	0	0	0	0	0
C	0	2	0	0	0	0	0	0	1	0
D	9	7	14	6	8	10	5	10	5	2
E	1	0	0	1	0	1	1	0	1	0
F	3	3	0	2	0	1	0	0	1	1
G	4	8	6	7	6	2	4	3	6	4
H	2	2	2	0	2	1	1	0	0	0
I	2	2	1	2	2	6	1	1	3	1
J	3	3	4	0	1	2	2	1	2	1
K	4	0	5	4	7	6	4	1	3	3
L	1	6	2	1	3	3	5	3	3	1
M	2	6	2	3	2	5	0	3	3	6
N	2	2	3	3	2	0	0	4	1	4
O	0	0	1	3	1	1	0	0	3	1
P	0	0	0	0	0	0	0	0	0	0
Q	0	0	0	0	0	0	0	0	0	0

Non-fatal cases (temporary + permanent incapacity) - Cas non mortels (incapacité temporaire + permanente) - Casos no mortales (incapacidad temporal + permanente)

Total men and women - Total hommes et femmes - Total hombres y mujeres
ISIC 3 - CITI 3 - CIIU 3

	1999	2000	2001	2002	2003	2004	2005	2006	2007	2008
Total [2]	95 288	90 723	80 743	75 455	80 307	82 290	79 348	89 701	92 824	97 109
A [2]	2 340	1 970	1 738	1 662	1 624	1 610	1 559	1 709	1 612	1 770
B	110	89	57	81	52	52	43	54	38	33
C	5 383	3 938	3 274	3 174	3 263	3 119	2 792	2 868	2 955	3 060
D	39 398	37 379	32 617	29 585	31 434	33 607	32 112	36 600	39 307	40 299
E	2 223	2 047	1 968	1 886	2 058	1 900	1 826	1 992	1 912	1 727
F	11 531	10 943	9 306	7 615	7 075	6 812	6 422	7 588	8 562	9 508
G	7 422	7 954	7 417	7 258	7 994	8 020	7 973	9 197	9 827	11 070
H	699	919	777	776	842	912	856	929	1 099	1 165
I	6 383	6 134	5 623	4 933	5 474	5 330	5 441	6 090	6 116	6 274
J	782	800	615	624	733	740	737	780	716	786
K	3 884	4 013	3 935	4 443	5 322	5 024	4 811	5 569	5 296	5 581
L	2 295	2 374	2 515	2 773	3 090	3 227	3 206	3 223	3 231	3 350
M	2 547	2 450	2 407	2 335	2 605	3 275	3 262	3 575	3 425	3 664
N	8 306	7 737	6 650	6 495	6 774	6 628	6 377	7 129	6 477	6 360
O	1 984	1 976	1 844	1 815	1 967	2 034	1 931	2 398	2 250	2 460
P	1	0	0	0	0	0	0	0	1	1
Q	1	0	0	0	0	0	0	0	0	1

Men - Hommes - Hombres
ISIC 3 - CITI 3 - CIIU 3

	1999	2000	2001	2002	2003	2004	2005	2006	2007	2008
Total [2]	72 374	68 718	60 631	55 677	58 763	60 401	57 927	65 500	67 917	70 442
A [2]	1 988	1 652	1 475	1 367	1 352	1 311	1 251	1 375	1 285	1 399
B	98	82	53	77	51	46	38	50	30	31
C	5 299	3 871	3 219	3 112	3 197	3 064	2 746	2 809	2 901	3 028
D	32 218	30 908	26 904	24 413	25 957	27 904	26 624	30 264	31 909	32 452
E	1 940	1 810	1 758	1 689	1 831	1 723	1 615	1 781	1 752	1 564
F	11 276	10 679	9 098	7 426	6 894	6 624	6 274	7 420	8 386	9 283
G	5 187	5 580	5 143	4 934	5 484	5 338	5 116	5 886	6 163	6 940
H	316	415	348	353	370	422	396	399	478	512
I	5 184	5 076	4 607	4 018	4 385	4 422	4 534	5 087	5 107	5 176
J	248	260	181	196	245	237	249	248	229	254
K	2 602	2 637	2 552	2 874	3 328	3 326	3 283	3 750	3 574	3 525
L	1 324	1 358	1 367	1 425	1 634	1 649	1 640	1 716	1 698	1 694
M	990	919	891	805	849	1 070	1 034	1 096	1 052	1 132
N	2 245	2 072	1 693	1 658	1 785	1 798	1 744	1 869	1 689	1 679
O	1 458	1 399	1 342	1 330	1 401	1 467	1 383	1 750	1 664	1 773
P	1	0	0	0	0	0	0	0	0	0

Explanatory notes: see p. 1125.　　Notes explicatives: voir p. 1127.　　Notas explicativas: véase p. 1129.

[1] Deaths occurring within six months of accident. [2] Excl. private farms in agriculture.

[1] Les décès survenant pendant les six mois qui suivent l'accident. [2] Non compris les fermes privées dans l'agriculture.

[1] Los fallecimientos que se produzcan durante los seis meses que siguen el accidente. [2] Excl. las granjas privadas en la agricultura.

8A   OCCUPATIONAL INJURIES / LÉSIONS PROFESSIONNELLES / LESIONES PROFESIONALES

Cases of injury with lost workdays, by economic activity

Cas de lésion avec perte de journées de travail, par activité économique

Casos de lesión con pérdida de días de trabajo, por actividad económica

Poland (FF)

Reported injuries - Lésions déclarées - Lesiones declaradas

Non-fatal cases (temporary + permanent incapacity) - Cas non mortels (incapacité temporaire + permanente) - Casos no mortales (incapacidad temporal + permanente)

Women - Femmes - Mujeres
ISIC 3 - CITI 3 - CIIU 3

	1999	2000	2001	2002	2003	2004	2005	2006	2007	2008
Total[1]	22 914	22 005	20 112	19 778	21 544	21 889	21 421	24 201	24 907	26 667
A[1]	352	318	263	295	272	299	308	334	327	371
B	12	7	4	4	1	6	5	4	8	2
C	84	67	55	62	66	55	46	59	54	32
D	7 180	6 471	5 713	5 172	5 477	5 703	5 488	6 336	7 398	7 847
E	283	237	210	197	227	177	211	211	160	163
F	255	264	208	189	181	188	148	168	176	225
G	2 235	2 374	2 274	2 324	2 510	2 682	2 857	3 311	3 664	4 130
H	383	504	429	423	472	490	460	530	621	653
I	1 199	1 058	1 016	915	1 089	908	907	1 003	1 009	1 098
J	534	540	434	428	488	503	488	532	487	532
K	1 282	1 376	1 383	1 569	1 994	1 698	1 528	1 819	1 722	2 056
L	971	1 016	1 148	1 348	1 456	1 578	1 566	1 507	1 533	1 656
M	1 557	1 531	1 516	1 530	1 756	2 205	2 228	2 479	2 373	2 532
N	6 061	5 665	4 957	4 837	4 989	4 830	4 633	5 260	4 788	4 681
O	526	577	502	485	566	567	548	648	586	687

Total cases (fatal + non-fatal) - Ensemble des cas (mortels + non mortels) - Todos los casos (mortales + no mortales)

Total men and women - Total hommes et femmes - Total hombres y mujeres
ISIC 3 - CITI 3 - CIIU 3

	1999	2000	2001	2002	2003	2004	2005	2006	2007	2008
Total[1]	95 811	91 317	81 297	75 970	80 822	82 780	79 816	90 194	93 303	97 632
A[1]	2 356	1 981	1 753	1 682	1 636	1 631	1 584	1 725	1 635	1 798
B	113	92	62	82	57	54	44	54	38	34
C	5 416	3 979	3 305	3 218	3 304	3 138	2 816	2 897	2 981	3 090
D	39 515	37 540	32 755	29 697	31 555	33 729	32 218	36 727	39 429	40 406
E	2 248	2 056	1 982	1 899	2 075	1 920	1 836	2 004	1 934	1 742
F	11 651	11 088	9 420	7 711	7 163	6 905	6 528	7 701	8 654	9 630
G	7 486	8 020	7 501	7 337	8 063	8 070	8 014	9 240	9 881	11 128
H	702	922	782	777	846	916	858	929	1 100	1 167
I	6 437	6 201	5 686	4 993	5 532	5 402	5 506	6 162	6 177	6 354
J	795	809	624	627	734	747	744	784	720	793
K	3 915	4 037	3 967	4 477	5 362	5 053	4 844	5 599	5 326	5 608
L	2 307	2 392	2 531	2 790	3 110	3 244	3 227	3 237	3 240	3 359
M	2 557	2 470	2 417	2 345	2 620	3 290	3 274	3 585	3 436	3 674
N	8 313	7 745	6 657	6 504	6 784	6 631	6 382	7 139	6 481	6 368
O	1 999	1 985	1 855	1 831	1 981	2 050	1 941	2 411	2 270	2 479
P	1	0	0	0	0	0	0	0	0	1
Q	0	0	0	0	0	0	0	0	1	1

Men - Hommes - Hombres
ISIC 3 - CITI 3 - CIIU 3

	1999	2000	2001	2002	2003	2004	2005	2006	2007	2008
Total[1]	72 864	69 270	61 145	56 160	59 244	60 852	58 370	65 967	68 364	70 940
A[1]	2 004	1 662	1 490	1 387	1 364	1 330	1 274	1 391	1 308	1 426
B	101	85	58	78	56	48	39	50	30	32
C	5 332	3 910	3 250	3 156	3 238	3 083	2 770	2 838	2 926	3 058
D	32 326	31 062	27 028	24 519	26 070	28 016	26 725	30 381	32 026	32 557
E	1 964	1 819	1 772	1 701	1 848	1 743	1 624	1 793	1 773	1 579
F	11 393	10 821	9 212	7 520	6 982	6 716	6 380	7 533	8 477	9 404
G	5 247	5 638	5 221	5 006	5 547	5 386	5 153	5 926	6 211	6 994
H	317	416	351	354	372	425	397	399	479	514
I	5 236	5 141	4 669	4 076	4 441	4 488	4 598	5 158	5 165	5 255
J	258	266	186	199	245	242	254	251	231	260
K	2 629	2 661	2 579	2 904	3 361	3 349	3 312	3 779	3 601	3 549
L	1 335	1 370	1 381	1 441	1 651	1 663	1 656	1 727	1 704	1 702
M	998	933	899	812	862	1 080	1 046	1 103	1 060	1 136
N	2 250	2 078	1 697	1 664	1 793	1 801	1 749	1 875	1 692	1 683
O	1 473	1 408	1 352	1 343	1 414	1 482	1 393	1 763	1 681	1 791
P	1	0	0	0	0	0	0	0	0	0

Women - Femmes - Mujeres
ISIC 3 - CITI 3 - CIIU 3

	1999	2000	2001	2002	2003	2004	2005	2006	2007	2008
Total[1]	22 947	22 047	20 152	19 810	21 578	21 928	21 446	24 227	24 939	26 692
A[1]	352	319	263	295	272	301	310	334	327	372
B	12	7	4	4	1	6	5	4	8	2
C	84	69	55	62	66	55	46	59	55	32
D	7 189	6 478	5 727	5 178	5 485	5 713	5 493	6 346	7 403	7 849
E	284	237	210	198	227	177	212	211	161	163
F	258	267	208	191	181	189	148	168	177	226
G	2 239	2 382	2 280	2 331	2 516	2 684	2 861	3 314	3 670	4 134
H	385	506	431	423	474	491	461	530	621	653
I	1 201	1 060	1 017	917	1 091	914	908	1 004	621	653
J	537	543	438	428	489	505	490	533	489	533
K	1 286	1 376	1 388	1 573	2 001	1 704	1 532	1 820	1 725	2 059
L	972	1 022	1 150	1 349	1 459	1 581	1 571	1 510	1 536	1 657
M	1 559	1 537	1 518	1 533	1 758	2 210	2 228	2 482	2 376	2 538
N	6 063	5 667	4 960	4 840	4 991	4 830	4 633	5 264	4 789	4 685
O	526	577	503	488	567	568	548	648	589	688
P	0	0	0	0	0	0	0	0	1	1

Explanatory notes: see p. 1125.
[1] Excl. private farms in agriculture.

Notes explicatives: voir p. 1127.
[1] Non compris les fermes privées dans l'agriculture.

Notas explicativas: véase p. 1129.
[1] Excl. las granjas privadas en la agricultura.

	OCCUPATIONAL INJURIES Cases of injury with lost workdays, by economic activity	LÉSIONS PROFESSIONNELLES Cas de lésion avec perte de journées de travail, par activité économique	LESIONES PROFESIONALES Casos de lesión con pérdida de días de trabajo, por actividad económica

	1999	2000	2001	2002	2003	2004	2005	2006	2007	2008

Poland (FF)   Reported injuries - Lésions déclarées - Lesiones declaradas

Fatal cases - Cas mortels - Casos mortales

Total men and women - Total hommes et femmes - Total hombres y mujeres
ISIC 3 - CITI 3 - CIIU 3

	1999	2000	2001	2002	2003	2004	2005	2006	2007	2008
A [1]	257	216	220	209	211	173	128	123	94	.

Non-fatal cases (temporary + permanent incapacity) - Cas non mortels (incapacité temporaire + permanente) - Casos no mortales (incapacidad temporal + permanente)

Total men and women - Total hommes et femmes - Total hombres y mujeres
ISIC 3 - CITI 3 - CIIU 3

	1999	2000	2001	2002	2003	2004	2005	2006	2007	2008
A [1]	31 649	30 727	29 627	30 511	31 455	27 860	20 741	20 528	18 629	.

Total cases (fatal + non-fatal) - Ensemble des cas (mortels + non mortels) - Todos los casos (mortales + no mortales)

Total men and women - Total hommes et femmes - Total hombres y mujeres
ISIC 3 - CITI 3 - CIIU 3

	1999	2000	2001	2002	2003	2004	2005	2006	2007	2008
A [1]	31 906	30 943	29 847	30 720	31 666	28 033	20 869	20 651	18 723	.

Portugal (FA)   Reported injuries - Lésions déclarées - Lesiones declaradas

Fatal cases - Cas mortels - Casos mortales

Total men and women - Total hommes et femmes - Total hombres y mujeres
ISIC 3 - CITI 3 - CIIU 3

	1999	2000	2001	2002	2003	2004	2005	2006	2007	2008
Total [2]	236	368	365	357	312	306	300	253	.	.
A	21	25	27	39	22	20	21	23	.	.
B	3	8	6	6	3	12	7	15	.	.
C	3	9	16	5	8	12	6	3	.	.
D	52	78	59	75	52	55	56	43	.	.
E	0	3	1	4	1	3	1	3	.	.
F	83	102	139	109	113	110	111	83	.	.
G	30	42	32	32	38	27	24	21	.	.
H	4	9	6	4	4	1	2	5	.	.
I	20	33	32	38	34	38	32	33	.	.
J	2	1	0	0	1	1	0	1	.	.
K	11	16	26	22	17	14	20	12	.	.
L	4	6	9	6	9	3	11	4	.	.
M	0	1	0	1	1	1	1	1	.	.
N	1	2	2	1	1	0	1	2	.	.
O	1	4	7	7	3	7	1	3	.	.
P	1	1	1	3	0	1	3	0	.	.
Q	.	0	1	0	0	0	0	0	.	.
X	0	28	1	5	5	1	3	1	.	.

Men - Hommes - Hombres
ISIC 3 - CITI 3 - CIIU 3

	1999	2000	2001	2002	2003	2004	2005	2006	2007	2008
Total [2]	228	347	352	340	293	298	287	298	.	.
A	19	25	25	35	20	19	20	19	.	.
B	3	8	6	6	3	12	7	12	.	.
C	3	9	16	5	8	12	6	12	.	.
D	51	69	57	73	47	53	52	53	.	.
E	0	3	1	4	1	3	1	3	.	.
F	83	102	139	109	113	110	111	110	.	.
G	29	39	29	29	34	27	22	27	.	.
H	4	9	3	2	4	1	1	1	.	.
I	20	33	32	38	33	37	31	37	.	.
J	2	1	0	0	1	1	0	1	.	.
K	9	11	24	21	16	11	20	11	.	.
L	3	5	9	6	7	3	10	3	.	.
M	0	1	0	1	1	1	1	1	.	.
N	1	1	2	0	0	0	1	0	.	.
O	0	4	6	7	3	6	1	6	.	.
P	1	0	1	0	0	1	0	1	.	.
Q	.	0	1	0	0	0	0	0	.	.
X	.	27	1	4	2	1	3	1	.	.

Explanatory notes: see p. 1125.

[1] Private farms. [2] Excl. public administration and services and defence.

Notes explicatives: voir p. 1127.

[1] Fermes privées. [2] Non compris l'administration publique, les services publics et la défense.

Notas explicativas: véase p. 1129.

[1] Granjas privadas. [2] Excl. la administración pública, los servicios públicos y defensa.

	OCCUPATIONAL INJURIES Cases of injury with lost workdays, by economic activity	**LÉSIONS PROFESSIONNELLES** Cas de lésion avec perte de journées de travail, par activité économique	**LESIONES PROFESIONALES** Casos de lesión con pérdida de días de trabajo, por actividad económica

	1999	2000	2001	2002	2003	2004	2005	2006	2007	2008

Portugal (FA)   Reported injuries - Lésions déclarées - Lesiones declaradas

Fatal cases - Cas mortels - Casos mortales

Women - Femmes - Mujeres
ISIC 3 - CITI 3 - CIIU 3

	1999	2000	2001	2002	2003	2004	2005	2006	2007	2008
Total [1]	8	21	13	17	13	8	13	8	.	.
A	2	0	2	4	1	1	1	1	.	.
B	0	0	0	0	0	0	0	0	.	.
C	0	0	0	0	0	0	0	0	.	.
D	1	9	2	2	4	2	4	2	.	.
E	0	0	0	0	0	0	0	0	.	.
F	0	0	0	0	0	0	0	0	.	.
G	1	3	3	3	2	0	2	0	.	.
H	0	0	3	2	0	0	1	0	.	.
I	0	0	0	0	1	1	1	1	.	.
J	0	0	0	0	0	0	0	0	.	.
K	2	5	2	1	1	3	0	3	.	.
L	1	1	0	0	2	0	1	0	.	.
M	0	0	0	0	0	0	0	0	.	.
N	0	1	0	1	1	0	0	0	.	.
O	0	1	0	1	0	0	1	0	1	.
P	0	1	0	3	0	0	3	0	.	.
Q	.	0	0	0	0	0	0	0	.	.
X	.	1	0	1	1	0	0	0	.	.

Non-fatal cases (temporary + permanent incapacity) - Cas non mortels (incapacité temporaire + permanente) - Casos no mortales (incapacidad temporal + permanente)

Total men and women - Total hommes et femmes - Total hombres y mujeres [2]
ISIC 3 - CITI 3 - CIIU 3

	1999	2000	2001	2002	2003	2004	2005	2006	2007	2008
Total [1]	169 554	179 867	187 051	176 884	171 661	171 037	166 642	173 274	.	.
A	5 524	5 903	5 905	5 408	5 660	5 522	4 926	5 238	.	.
B	1 694	1 505	895	1 457	1 307	1 703	1 316	1 339	.	.
C	2 009	2 027	2 269	2 192	1 810	1 798	1 584	1 512	.	.
D	72 079	65 806	69 659	63 138	59 258	54 673	53 726	54 000	.	.
E	579	916	809	692	665	589	891	865	.	.
F	38 821	40 734	43 923	42 008	40 613	40 858	38 908	39 660	.	.
G	22 623	24 416	25 957	25 533	25 173	26 026	24 864	27 163	.	.
H	5 888	6 576	6 243	6 299	6 339	7 631	7 216	8 427	.	.
I	6 310	7 253	7 615	7 336	7 606	7 154	7 137	7 857	.	.
J	658	520	456	403	318	412	404	419	.	.
K	7 466	7 747	7 862	8 228	7 950	9 392	9 513	10 141	.	.
L	133	3 849	5 056	4 129	3 644	4 418	4 855	5 370	.	.
M	1 034	924	1 046	864	912	921	951	1 303	.	.
N	2 422	2 841	3 669	3 662	3 820	4 018	4 837	5 084	.	.
O	1 553	3 325	3 384	3 530	3 546	3 584	3 391	3 278	.	.
P	761	1 018	740	749	855	781	664	679	.	.
Q	.	3	31	0	12	7	4	11	.	.
X	.	4 504	1 532	1 256	2 173	1 550	1 455	928	.	.

Men - Hommes - Hombres [2]
ISIC 3 - CITI 3 - CIIU 3

	1999	2000	2001	2002	2003	2004	2005	2006	2007	2008
Total [1]	139 148	146 020	150 387	141 236	137 496	135 763	131 498	135 763	.	.
A	4 170	4 592	4 600	4 171	4 409	4 229	3 782	4 229	.	.
B	1 557	1 419	800	1 378	1 174	1 577	1 245	1 577	.	.
C	1 925	1 784	2 229	2 151	1 735	1 765	1 549	1 765	.	.
D	58 646	53 207	55 671	50 265	47 959	44 305	43 030	44 305	.	.
E	562	870	784	605	627	555	779	555	.	.
F	38 482	40 153	43 302	41 275	39 914	40 209	38 336	40 209	.	.
G	17 448	18 708	19 594	19 054	18 900	18 957	18 619	18 957	.	.
H	2 708	2 056	2 649	2 647	2 716	3 254	3 042	3 254	.	.
I	5 838	6 456	6 950	6 410	6 726	6 383	6 241	6 383	.	.
J	421	338	285	256	188	225	234	225	.	.
K	5 192	5 127	4 851	5 348	5 321	6 311	6 625	6 311	.	.
L	117	3 209	4 112	3 300	2 823	3 449	3 751	3 449	.	.
M	459	331	296	246	230	236	267	236	.	.
N	542	634	765	704	638	839	874	839	.	.
O	995	2 369	2 522	2 445	2 447	2 251	2 035	2 251	.	.
P	86	104	44	38	57	43	40	43	.	.
Q	.	.	17	0	6	7	2	7	.	.
X	.	1	916	943	1 626	1 168	1 047	1 168	.	.

Explanatory notes: see p. 1125.

[1] Excl. public administration and services and defence. [2] Incl. non-fatal cases without lost workdays.

Notes explicatives: voir p. 1127.

[1] Non compris l'administration publique, les services publics et la défense. [2] Y compris les cas non mortels sans perte de journées de travail.

Notas explicativas: véase p. 1129.

[1] Excl. la administración pública, los servicios públicos y defensa. [2] Incl. los casos no mortales sin pérdida de días de trabajo.

OCCUPATIONAL INJURIES

Cases of injury with lost workdays, by economic activity

LÉSIONS PROFESSIONNELLES

Cas de lésion avec perte de journées de travail, par activité économique

LESIONES PROFESIONALES

Casos de lesión con pérdida de días de trabajo, por actividad económica

	1999	2000	2001	2002	2003	2004	2005	2006	2007	2008

Portugal (FA) Reported injuries - Lésions déclarées - Lesiones declaradas

Non-fatal cases (temporary + permanent incapacity) - Cas non mortels (incapacité temporaire + permanente) - Casos no mortales (incapacidad temporal + permanente)

Women - Femmes - Mujeres [1]
ISIC 3 - CITI 3 - CIIU 3

	1999	2000	2001	2002	2003	2004	2005	2006	2007	2008
Total [2]	30 406	33 683	36 025	35 308	33 755	35 063	34 926	35 063	.	.
A	1 354	1 302	1 293	1 228	1 241	1 292	1 144	1 292	.	.
B	137	85	94	77	132	125	71	125	.	.
C	84	56	40	38	68	32	35	32	.	.
D	13 433	12 543	13 904	12 797	11 228	10 332	10 696	10 332	.	.
E	17	46	22	85	38	33	112	33	.	.
F	339	542	575	656	620	629	572	629	.	.
G	5 175	5 690	6 338	6 437	6 247	7 059	6 245	7 059	.	.
H	3 180	3 614	3 590	3 647	3 615	4 372	4 174	4 372	.	.
I	472	790	637	921	860	761	896	761	.	.
J	237	182	171	144	129	186	170	186	.	.
K	2 274	2 615	3 002	2 863	2 612	3 066	2 888	3 066	.	.
L	16	639	944	820	818	968	1 104	968	.	.
M	575	593	750	618	680	684	684	684	.	.
N	1 880	2 205	2 900	2 952	3 173	3 177	3 963	3 177	.	.
O	558	954	862	1 083	1 089	1 330	1 356	1 330	.	.
P	675	913	695	711	798	738	624	738	.	.
Q	.	2	14	0	6	0	2	0	.	.
X	912	194	231	401	279	190	279		.	.

Total cases (fatal + non-fatal) - Ensemble des cas (mortels + non mortels) - Todos los casos (mortales + no mortales)

Total men and women - Total hommes et femmes - Total hombres y mujeres [1]
ISIC 3 - CITI 3 - CIIU 3

	1999	2000	2001	2002	2003	2004	2005	2006	2007	2008
Total [2]	169 790	180 235	187 416	177 241	171 973	171 343	166 942	173 527	.	.
A	5 545	5 928	5 932	5 447	5 682	5 542	4 947	5 261	.	.
B	1 697	1 513	901	1 463	1 310	1 715	1 323	1 354	.	.
C	2 012	2 036	2 285	2 197	1 818	1 810	1 590	1 515	.	.
D	72 131	65 884	69 718	63 213	59 310	54 728	53 782	54 043	.	.
E	579	919	810	696	666	592	892	868	.	.
F	38 904	40 836	44 062	42 117	40 726	40 968	39 019	39 743	.	.
G	22 653	24 458	25 989	25 565	25 211	26 053	24 888	27 184	.	.
H	5 892	6 585	6 249	6 303	6 343	7 632	7 218	8 432	.	.
I	6 330	7 286	7 647	7 374	7 640	7 192	7 169	7 890	.	.
J	660	521	456	403	319	413	404	420	.	.
K	7 477	7 763	7 888	8 250	7 967	9 406	9 533	10 153	.	.
L	137	3 855	5 065	4 135	3 653	4 421	4 866	5 374	.	.
M	1 034	925	1 046	865	913	922	952	1 304	.	.
N	2 423	2 843	3 671	3 663	3 821	4 018	4 838	5 086	.	.
O	1 554	3 329	3 391	3 537	3 549	3 591	3 392	3 281	.	.
P	762	1 019	741	753	855	782	667	679	.	.
Q	.	3	32	0	12	7	4	11	.	.
X	.	4 532	1 533	1 261	2 178	1 551	1 458	929	.	.

Men - Hommes - Hombres [1]
ISIC 3 - CITI 3 - CIIU 3

	1999	2000	2001	2002	2003	2004	2005	2006	2007	2008
Total [2]	139 376	146 367	150 739	141 576	137 789	136 061	131 785	136 061	.	.
A	4 189	4 617	4 625	4 206	4 429	4 248	3 802	4 248	.	.
B	1 560	1 427	806	1 384	1 177	1 589	1 252	1 589	.	.
C	1 928	1 793	2 245	2 156	1 743	1 777	1 555	1 777	.	.
D	58 697	53 276	55 728	50 338	48 006	44 358	43 082	44 358	.	.
E	562	873	785	609	628	558	780	558	.	.
F	38 565	40 255	43 441	41 384	40 027	40 319	38 447	40 319	.	.
G	17 477	18 747	19 623	19 083	18 934	18 984	18 641	18 984	.	.
H	2 712	2 065	2 652	2 649	2 720	3 255	3 043	3 255	.	.
I	5 858	6 489	6 982	6 448	6 759	6 420	6 272	6 420	.	.
J	423	339	285	256	189	226	234	226	.	.
K	5 201	5 138	4 875	5 369	5 337	6 322	6 645	6 322	.	.
L	120	3 214	4 121	3 306	2 830	3 452	3 761	3 452	.	.
M	459	332	296	247	231	237	268	237	.	.
N	543	635	767	704	638	839	875	839	.	.
O	995	2 373	2 528	2 452	2 450	2 257	2 036	2 257	.	.
P	87	104	45	38	57	44	40	44	.	.
Q	.	.	18	0	6	7	2	7	.	.
X	.	28	917	947	1 628	1 169	1 050	1 169	.	.

Explanatory notes: see p. 1125.

[1] Incl. non-fatal cases without lost workdays. [2] Excl. public administration and services and defence.

Notes explicatives: voir p. 1127.

[1] Y compris les cas non mortels sans perte de journées de travail. [2] Non compris l'administration publique, les services publics et la défense.

Notas explicativas: véase p. 1129.

[1] Incl. los casos no mortales sin pérdida de días de trabajo. [2] Excl. la administración pública, los servicios públicos y defensa.

OCCUPATIONAL INJURIES
Cases of injury with lost workdays, by economic activity

LÉSIONS PROFESSIONNELLES
Cas de lésion avec perte de journées de travail, par activité économique

LESIONES PROFESIONALES
Casos de lesión con pérdida de días de trabajo, por actividad económica

Portugal (FA)

Reported injuries - Lésions déclarées - Lesiones declaradas

Total cases (fatal + non-fatal) - Ensemble des cas (mortels + non mortels) - Todos los casos (mortales + no mortales)

Women - Femmes - Mujeres [1]
ISIC 3 - CITI 3 - CIIU 3

	1999	2000	2001	2002	2003	2004	2005	2006	2007	2008
Total [2]	30 414	33 704	36 038	35 325	33 768	35 071	34 939	35 071	.	.
A	1 356	1 302	1 295	1 232	1 242	1 293	1 145	1 293		
B	137	85	94	77	132	125	71	125		
C	84	56	40	38	68	32	35	32		
D	13 434	12 552	13 906	12 799	11 232	10 334	10 700	10 334		
E	17	46	22	85	38	33	112	33		
F	339	542	575	656	620	629	572	629		
G	5 176	5 693	6 341	6 440	6 249	7 059	6 247	7 059		
H	3 180	3 614	3 593	3 649	3 615	4 372	4 175	4 372		
I	472	790	637	921	861	762	897	762		
J	237	182	171	144	129	186	170	186		
K	2 276	2 620	3 004	2 864	2 613	3 069	2 888	3 069		
L	17	640	944	820	820	968	1 105	968		
M	575	593	750	618	680	684	684	684		
N	1 880	2 206	2 900	2 953	3 174	3 177	3 963	3 177		
O	559	954	863	1 083	1 089	1 331	1 356	1 331		
P	675	914	695	714	798	738	627	738		
Q	.	2	14	0	6	0	2	0		
X	.	913	194	232	402	279	190	279		

Roumanie (FF)

Reported injuries - Lésions déclarées - Lesiones declaradas

Fatal cases - Cas mortels - Casos mortales

Total men and women - Total hommes et femmes - Total hombres y mujeres [3]
ISIC 3 - CITI 3 - CIIU 3 (1999–2006); ISIC 4 - CITI 4 - CIIU 4 (2007–2008)

	1999	2000	2001	2002	2003	2004	2005	2006	2007	2008	
Total	454	490	456	442	423	432	531	422	474	419	Total
A	57	51	40	40	50	37	49	32	50	44	A
B	1	0	1	0	1	0	0	1	2	22	B
C	59	62	53	55	30	31	26	28	12	78	C
D	127	144	140	150	110	134	158	121	113	10	D
E	22	22	18	18	11	12	16	12	14	18	E
F	86	92	86	75	100	89	125	92	128	111	F
G	24	17	31	20	39	33	38	32	42	29	G
H	5	4	1	1	1	10	2	1	5	48	H
I	38	45	46	43	43	48	75	52	60	3	I
J	2	3	2	3	1	5	4	1	3	6	J
K	10	12	9	10	15	18	14	21	20	4	K
L	11	17	3	11	6	3	5	13	12	0	L
M	1	9	2	3	3	1	7	3	3	9	M
N	4	3	2	5	3	8	4	4	2	19	N
O	7	9	22	8	10	3	8	9	8	5	O
P	0	0	0	0	0	0	0	0	0	6	P
Q	0	0	0	0	0	0	0	0	0	3	Q
X	0	0	0	0	0	0	0	0	0	3	R
										0	S
										0	T
										0	U
										0	X

Men - Hommes - Hombres [3]
ISIC 3 - CITI 3 - CIIU 3 (1999–2006); ISIC 4 - CITI 4 - CIIU 4 (2007–2008)

	1999	2000	2001	2002	2003	2004	2005	2006	2007	2008	
Total	426	448	427	413	399	394	477	386	438	390	Total
A	57	49	40	40	49	37	46	32	49	44	A
B	1	0	1	0	1	0	0		2	22	B
C	59	61	52	53	30	30	24	28	12	69	C
D	112	123	127	136	100	120	127	108	96	8	D
E	21	21	17	18	10	12	15	11	13	14	E
F	83	91	86	74	99	88	125	91	127	111	F
G	21	15	26	19	38	28	31	28	39	27	G
H	5	2	1	0	0	5	2	0	2	45	H
I	37	43	41	42	42	45	71	46	57	3	I
J	1	3	2	2	1	3	2	1	1	6	J
K	9	11	7	10	13	17	14	20	19	2	K
L	9	13	3	9	6	3	6	10	10	0	L
M	1	5	1	1	2	1	3	1	3	7	M
N	4	3	2	2	1	3	3	2	2	19	N
O	6	8	21	7	7	2	8	7	6	5	O
										4	P
										0	Q
										1	R
										3	S
										0	T
										0	U
										0	X

Explanatory notes: see p. 1125.

[1] Incl. non-fatal cases without lost workdays. [2] Excl. public administration and services and defence. [3] Deaths occurring within the same reference year as accident.

Notes explicatives: voir p. 1127.

[1] Y compris les cas non mortels sans perte de journées de travail. [2] Non compris l'administration publique, les services publics et la défense. [3] Décès survenant pendant la même année de référence que l'accident.

Notas explicativas: véase p. 1129.

[1] Incl. los casos no mortales sin pérdida de días de trabajo. [2] Excl. la administración pública, los servicios públicos y defensa. [3] Fallecimientos que se producen durante el mismo año de referencia que el accidente.

OCCUPATIONAL INJURIES

Cases of injury with lost workdays, by economic activity

LÉSIONS PROFESSIONNELLES

Cas de lésion avec perte de journées de travail, par activité économique

LESIONES PROFESIONALES

Casos de lesión con pérdida de días de trabajo, por actividad económica

8A

	1999	2000	2001	2002	2003	2004	2005	2006	2007		2008	

Roumanie (FF) — Reported injuries - Lésions déclarées - Lesiones declaradas

Fatal cases - Cas mortels - Casos mortales

Women - Femmes - Mujeres [1]

ISIC 3 - CITI 3 - CIIU 3 / ISIC 4 - CITI 4 - CIIU 4

	1999	2000	2001	2002	2003	2004	2005	2006	2007		2008	
Total	28	42	29	29	24	38	54	36	36	|	29	Total
A	0	2	0	0	1	0	3	0	1	|	0	B
B	0	0	0	0	0	0	0	0	0	|	9	C
C	0	1	1	2	0	1	2	0	0	|	2	D
D	15	21	13	14	10	14	31	13	17	|	4	E
E	1	1	1	0	1	0	1	1	1	|	0	F
F	3	1	0	1	1	1	0	1	1	|	2	G
G	3	2	5	1	1	5	7	4	3	|	3	H
H	0	2	0	1	1	5	0	3	3	|	0	I
I	1	2	5	1	1	3	4	6	3	|	0	J
J	1	0	0	1	0	2	2	0	2	|	2	K
K	1	1	2	0	2	1	0	1	1	|	0	L
L	2	4	0	2	0	0	2	3	2	|	2	M
M	0	4	1	2	1	0	1	2	0	|	0	N
N	0	0	0	3	2	5	1	2	0	|	0	O
O	0	1	1	1	3	1	0	2	2	|	2	P
										|	3	Q
										|	0	R
										|	0	S
										|	0	T
										|	0	U
										|	0	X

Non-fatal cases (temporary + permanent incapacity) - Cas non mortels (incapacité temporaire + permanente) - Casos no mortales (incapacidad temporal + permanente)

Total men and women - Total hommes et femmes - Total hombres y mujeres

ISIC 3 - CITI 3 - CIIU 3 [2] / ISIC 4 - CITI 4 - CIIU 4 [1]

	1999	2000	2001	2002	2003	2004	2005	2006	2007		2008	
Total	6 137	6 143	6 373	5 942	5 553	5 264	4 500	4 595	4 393	|	4 534	Total
A	372	262	245	200	198	192	113	122	122	|	142	A
B	1	2	2	1	3	2	0	0	1	|	330	B
C	1 711	1 799	1 834	1 635	1 322	820	533	450	371	|	1 852	C
D	2 710	2 673	2 774	2 669	2 549	2 602	2 317	2 341	1 973	|	100	D
E	157	132	147	122	116	125	147	125	140	|	119	E
F	545	569	586	527	576	599	571	608	652	|	740	F
G	74	85	106	123	156	205	213	249	285	|	446	G
H	19	16	32	29	37	45	38	43	39	|	307	H
I	406	372	402	368	329	351	279	269	360	|	58	I
J	8	12	9	11	17	14	5	17	22	|	30	J
K	51	68	70	66	84	94	92	118	160	|	21	K
L	44	46	46	44	46	49	35	60	68	|	10	L
M	14	26	25	28	22	22	28	33	37	|	58	M
N	33	35	42	39	44	55	58	76	78	|	129	N
O	49	46	53	80	54	89	71	84	85	|	72	O
P	0	0	0	0	0	0	0	0	0	|	29	P
Q	0	0	0	0	0	0	0	0	0	|	71	Q
X	0	0	0	0	0	0	0	0	0	|	14	R
										|	6	S
										|	0	T
										|	0	U
										|	0	X

Men - Hommes - Hombres

ISIC 3 - CITI 3 - CIIU 3 [2] / ISIC 4 - CITI 4 - CIIU 4 [1]

	1999	2000	2001	2002	2003	2004	2005	2006	2007		2008	
Total	5 267	5 290	5 462	5 088	4 693	4 342	3 669	3 711	3 506	|	3 582	Total
A	336	233	221	184	179	180	106	111	109	|	127	A
B	1	2	2	1	3	2	0	0	1	|	323	B
C	1 673	1 778	1 809	1 598	1 299	800	523	438	363	|	1 401	C
D	2 119	2 075	2 163	2 111	1 971	1 998	1 745	1 792	1 489	|	87	D
E	136	115	128	104	100	104	131	108	118	|	97	E
F	521	549	562	504	557	583	559	590	644	|	725	F
G	60	66	80	99	124	156	163	201	211	|	281	G
H	11	8	19	16	18	26	18	23	20	|	242	H
I	342	307	329	296	257	272	229	215	266	|	31	I
J	1	5	1	5	7	3	2	3	4	|	26	J
K	40	57	56	57	69	84	83	92	137	|	7	K
L	26	37	31	30	36	28	25	35	42	|	8	L
M	7	12	11	14	14	14	17	14	14	|	41	M
N	13	9	14	15	18	21	21	27	24	|	101	N
O	38	37	36	54	41	71	47	62	64	|	40	O
										|	8	P
										|	26	Q
										|	7	R
										|	4	S
										|	0	T
										|	0	U
										|	0	X

Explanatory notes: see p. 1125.

[1] Deaths occurring within the same reference year as accident.
[2] Prior to 1997: incapacity of 3 days or more.

Notes explicatives: voir p. 1127.

[1] Décès survenant pendant la même année de référence que l'accident. [2] Avant 1997: incapacité de 3 jours et plus.

Notas explicativas: véase p. 1129.

[1] Fallecimientos que se producen durante el mismo año de referencia que el accidente. [2] Antes de 1997: incapacidad de 3 días y más.

8A

OCCUPATIONAL INJURIES	LÉSIONS PROFESSIONNELLES	LESIONES PROFESIONALES
Cases of injury with lost workdays, by economic activity	Cas de lésion avec perte de journées de travail, par activité économique	Casos de lesión con pérdida de días de trabajo, por actividad económica

	1999	2000	2001	2002	2003	2004	2005	2006	2007	2008	

Roumanie (FF) — Reported injuries - Lésions déclarées - Lesiones declaradas

Non-fatal cases (temporary + permanent incapacity) - Cas non mortels (incapacité temporaire + permanente) - Casos no mortales (incapacidad temporal + permanente)

Women - Femmes - Mujeres
ISIC 3 - CITI 3 - CIIU 3 [1]   ISIC 4 - CITI 4 - CIIU 4 [2]

	1999	2000	2001	2002	2003	2004	2005	2006	2007	2008	
Total	870	853	911	854	860	922	831	884	887	952	Total
A	36	29	24	16	19	12	7	11	13	15	A
B	0	0	0	0	0	0	0	0	0	7	B
C	38	21	25	37	23	20	10	12	8	451	C
D	591	598	611	558	578	604	572	549	484	13	D
E	21	17	19	18	16	21	16	17	22	22	E
F	24	20	24	23	19	16	12	18	8	15	F
G	14	19	26	24	32	49	50	48	74	165	G
H	8	8	13	13	19	19	20	20	19	65	H
I	64	65	73	72	72	79	50	54	94	27	I
J	7	7	8	6	10	11	3	14	18	4	J
K	11	11	14	9	15	10	10	26	23	14	K
L	18	9	15	14	10	21	10	25	26	2	L
M	7	14	14	14	8	8	11	19	23	17	M
N	20	26	28	24	26	34	37	49	54	28	N
O	11	9	17	26	13	18	24	22	21	32	O
P										21	P
Q										45	Q
R										7	R
S										2	S
T										0	T
U										0	U
X										0	X

Cases of temporary incapacity - Cas d'incapacité temporaire - Casos de incapacidad temporal

Total men and women - Total hommes et femmes - Total hombres y mujeres
ISIC 3 - CITI 3 - CIIU 3 [1]   ISIC 4 - CITI 4 - CIIU 4 [2]

	1999	2000	2001	2002	2003	2004	2005	2006	2007	2008	
Total	5 865	5 899	6 089	5 741	5 265	4 811	4 302	4 399	3 760	3 318	Total
A	277	239	229	184	173	179	109	109	99	97	A
B	1	2	1	2	3	2	0	0	1	268	B
C	1 690	1 784	1 819	1 621	1 314	813	531	445	358	1 420	C
D	2 596	2 554	2 635	2 567	2 426	2 406	2 212	2 242	1 728	68	D
E	151	128	140	115	107	116	143	122	125	92	E
F	503	525	536	495	500	490	529	574	506	482	F
G	62	76	90	117	140	171	199	236	235	324	G
H	16	14	32	27	35	42	37	41	21	215	H
I	382	358	376	356	315	304	268	251	320	39	I
J	7	12	8	11	16	13	5	17	16	16	J
K	47	64	65	65	80	84	88	117	114	16	K
L	42	45	44	42	42	43	33	58	56	8	L
M	10	24	24	25	21	21	25	32	35	39	M
N	32	34	40	37	42	52	56	74	69	90	N
O	48	40	49	78	51	75	67	81	77	55	O
P	0	0	0	0	0	0	0	0	0	23	P
Q	0	0	0	0	0	0	0	0	0	53	Q
R										9	R
S										4	S
T										0	T
U										0	U
X										0	X

Men - Hommes - Hombres
ISIC 3 - CITI 3 - CIIU 3 [1]   ISIC 4 - CITI 4 - CIIU 4 [2]

	1999	2000	2001	2002	2003	2004	2005	2006	2007	2008	
Total	5 032	5 083	5 224	4 918	4 449	3 965	3 512	3 543	2 988	2 572	Total
A	244	212	205	168	155	167	102	98	90	85	A
B	1	2	2	1	3	2	0	0	1	262	B
C	1 652	1 763	1 794	1 585	1 292	793	521	433	351	1 053	C
D	2 030	1 982	2 051	2 032	1 878	1 844	1 671	1 714	1 300	59	D
E	130	111	122	97	92	97	127	105	107	71	E
F	480	506	515	472	484	474	518	556	499	469	F
G	49	60	70	94	110	131	151	190	176	189	G
H	9	8	19	15	16	24	17	21	12	170	H
I	318	295	304	286	246	235	219	198	229	22	I
J	1	5	1	5	6	2	2	3	14	14	J
K	36	53	52	56	65	76	80	91	96	6	K
L	25	36	29	28	33	25	23	34	33	7	L
M	6	10	11	13	13	14	16	14	13	27	M
N	13	9	14	14	16	20	21	26	21	74	N
O	37	31	35	52	40	61	44	60	57	30	O
P										8	P
Q										18	Q
R										5	R
S										3	S
T										0	T
U										0	U
X										0	X

Explanatory notes: see p. 1125.
[1] Prior to 1997: incapacity of 3 days or more. [2] Deaths occurring within the same reference year as accident.

Notes explicatives: voir p. 1127.
[1] Avant 1997: incapacité de 3 jours et plus. [2] Décès survenant pendant la même année de référence que l'accident.

Notas explicativas: véase p. 1129.
[1] Antes de 1997: incapacidad de 3 días y más. [2] Fallecimientos que se producen durante el mismo año de referencia que el accidente.

OCCUPATIONAL INJURIES

Cases of injury with lost workdays, by economic activity

LÉSIONS PROFESSIONNELLES

Cas de lésion avec perte de journées de travail, par activité économique

LESIONES PROFESIONALES

Casos de lesión con pérdida de días de trabajo, por actividad económica

8A

	1999	2000	2001	2002	2003	2004	2005	2006	2007	2008	

Roumanie (FF) — Reported injuries - Lésions déclarées - Lesiones declaradas

Cases of temporary incapacity - Cas d'incapacité temporaire - Casos de incapacidad temporal

Women - Femmes - Mujeres
ISIC 3 - CITI 3 - CIIU 3 [1]   ISIC 4 - CITI 4 - CIIU 4 [2]

	1999	2000	2001	2002	2003	2004	2005	2006	2007	2008	
Total	833	816	865	823	816	846	790	856	772	746	Total
A	33	27	24	16	18	12	7	11	9	12	A
B	0	0	0	0	0	0	0	0	0	6	B
C	38	21	25	36	22	20	10	12	7	367	C
D	566	572	584	535	548	562	541	528	428	9	D
E	21	17	18	18	15	19	16	17	18	21	E
F	23	19	21	23	16	16	11	18	7	13	F
G	13	16	20	23	30	40	48	46	59	135	G
H	7	6	13	12	19	18	20	20	9	45	H
I	64	63	72	70	69	69	49	53	91	17	I
J	6	7	7	6	10	11	3	14	13	2	J
K	11	11	13	9	15	8	9	26	18	10	K
L	17	9	15	14	9	18	10	24	23	1	L
M	4	14	13	12	8	7	9	18	22	12	M
N	19	25	26	23	26	32	26	48	48	16	N
O	11	9	14	26	11	14	23	21	20	25	O
P										15	P
Q										35	Q
R										4	R
S										1	S
T										0	T
U										0	U
X										0	X

Total cases (fatal + non-fatal) - Ensemble des cas (mortels + non mortels) - Todos los casos (mortales + no mortales)

Total men and women - Total hommes et femmes - Total hombres y mujeres
ISIC 3 - CITI 3 - CIIU 3   ISIC 4 - CITI 4 - CIIU 4 [2]

	1999	2000	2001	2002	2003	2004	2005	2006	2007	2008	
Total	6 591	6 633	6 829	6 384	5 976	5 696	5 031	5 017	4 867	4 953	Total
A	372	313	285	240	248	229	162	154	172	186	A
B	2	2	3	1	4	2	0	1	3	352	B
C	1 770	1 861	1 887	1 690	1 352	851	559	478	383	1 930	C
D	2 837	2 817	2 914	2 819	2 659	2 736	2 475	2 462	2 086	110	D
E	179	154	165	140	127	137	163	137	154	137	E
F	631	661	672	602	676	688	696	700	780	851	F
G	98	102	137	143	195	238	251	281	327	475	G
H	24	20	33	30	38	55	40	44	44	355	H
I	444	417	448	411	372	399	354	321	420	61	I
J	10	15	11	14	18	19	9	18	25	36	J
K	61	80	79	76	99	112	106	139	180	25	K
L	55	63	49	55	52	52	40	73	80	10	L
M	15	35	27	31	25	23	35	36	40	67	M
N	37	38	44	44	47	63	62	80	80	148	N
O	56	55	75	88	64	92	79	93	93	77	O
P	0	0	0	0	0	0	0	0	0	35	P
Q	0	0	0	0	0	0	0	0	0	74	Q
X	0	0	0	0	0	0	0	0	0	15	R
										9	S
										0	T
										0	U
										0	X

Men - Hommes - Hombres
ISIC 3 - CITI 3 - CIIU 3   ISIC 4 - CITI 4 - CIIU 4 [2]

	1999	2000	2001	2002	2003	2004	2005	2006	2007	2008	
Total	5 693	5 738	5 889	5 501	5 092	4 736	4 146	4 097	3 944	3 972	Total
A	336	282	261	224	228	217	152	143	158	171	A
B	2	2	3	1	4	2	0	1	3	345	B
C	1 732	1 839	1 861	1 651	1 329	830	547	466	375	1 470	C
D	2 231	2 198	2 290	2 247	2 071	2 118	1 872	1 900	1 585	95	D
E	157	136	145	122	110	116	146	119	131	111	E
F	604	640	648	578	656	671	684	681	771	836	F
G	81	81	106	118	162	184	194	229	250	308	G
H	16	10	20	16	18	31	20	23	22	287	H
I	379	350	370	338	299	317	300	261	323	34	I
J	2	8	3	7	8	6	4	4	5	32	J
K	49	68	63	67	82	101	97	112	156	9	K
L	35	50	34	39	42	31	28	45	52	8	L
M	8	17	12	15	16	15	23	15	17	48	M
N	17	12	16	17	19	24	24	29	26	120	N
O	44	45	57	61	48	73	55	69	70	45	O
P										12	P
Q										26	Q
R										8	R
S										7	S
T										0	T
U										0	U
X										0	X

Explanatory notes: see p. 1125.

[1] Prior to 1997: incapacity of 3 days or more. [2] Deaths occurring within the same reference year as accident.

Notes explicatives: voir p. 1127.

[1] Avant 1997: incapacité de 3 jours et plus. [2] Décès survenant pendant la même année de référence que l'accident.

Notas explicativas: véase p. 1129.

[1] Antes de 1997: incapacidad de 3 días y más. [2] Fallecimientos que se producen durante el mismo año de referencia que el accidente.

	OCCUPATIONAL INJURIES	LÉSIONS PROFESSIONNELLES	LESIONES PROFESIONALES
	Cases of injury with lost workdays, by economic activity	Cas de lésion avec perte de journées de travail, par activité économique	Casos de lesión con pérdida de días de trabajo, por actividad económica

	1999	2000	2001	2002	2003	2004	2005	2006	2007	2008	

Roumanie (FF) — Reported injuries - Lésions déclarées - Lesiones declaradas

Total cases (fatal + non-fatal) - Ensemble des cas (mortels + non mortels) - Todos los casos (mortales + no mortales)

Women - Femmes - Mujeres
ISIC 3 - CITI 3 - CIIU 3

ISIC 4 - CITI 4 - CIIU 4 [1]

	1999	2000	2001	2002	2003	2004	2005	2006	2007		2008	
Total	898	895	940	883	884	960	885	920	923	|	981	Total
A	36	31	24	16	20	12	10	11	14	|	15	A
B	0	0	0	0	0	0	0	0	0	|	7	B
C	38	22	26	39	23	21	12	12	8	|	460	C
D	606	619	624	572	588	618	603	562	501	|	15	D
E	22	18	20	18	17	21	17	18	23	|	26	E
F	27	21	24	24	20	17	12	19	9	|	15	F
G	17	21	31	25	33	54	57	52	77	|	167	G
H	8	10	13	14	20	24	20	21	22	|	68	H
I	65	67	78	73	73	82	54	60	97	|	27	I
J	8	7	8	7	10	13	5	14	20	|	4	J
K	12	12	16	9	17	11	9	27	24	|	16	K
L	20	13	15	16	10	21	12	28	28	|	2	L
M	7	18	15	16	9	8	12	21	23	|	19	M
N	20	26	28	27	28	39	38	51	54	|	28	N
O	12	10	18	27	16	19	24	24	22	|	32	O
										|	23	P
										|	48	Q
										|	7	R
										|	2	S
										|	0	T
										|	0	U
										|	0	X

Russian Federation (DA) [2] — Reported injuries - Lésions déclarées - Lesiones declaradas

Fatal cases - Cas mortels - Casos mortales

Total men and women - Total hommes et femmes - Total hombres y mujeres [3]
ISIC 3 - CITI 3 - CIIU 3

	1999	2000	2001	2002	2003	2004	2005	2006	2007	2008
Total	4 260	4 400	4 370	3 920	3 540	3 290	3 090	2 900	2 990	2 550

Men - Hommes - Hombres [3]
ISIC 3 - CITI 3 - CIIU 3

	1999	2000	2001	2002	2003	2004	2005	2006	2007	2008
Total	4 000	4 150	4 090	3 660	3 330	3 060	2 880	2 680	2 820	2 360

Women - Femmes - Mujeres [3]
ISIC 3 - CITI 3 - CIIU 3

	1999	2000	2001	2002	2003	2004	2005	2006	2007	2008
Total	260	260	280	260	210	230	210	220	170	190

Non-fatal cases (temporary + permanent incapacity) - Cas non mortels (incapacité temporaire + permanente) - Casos no mortales (incapacidad temporal + permanente)

Total men and women - Total hommes et femmes - Total hombres y mujeres [3]
ISIC 3 - CITI 3 - CIIU 3

	1999	2000	2001	2002	2003	2004	2005	2006	2007	2008
Total	148 850	147 390	140 350	123 790	103 150	84 470	74 650	67 810	63 070	55 760

Men - Hommes - Hombres [3]
ISIC 3 - CITI 3 - CIIU 3

	1999	2000	2001	2002	2003	2004	2005	2006	2007	2008
Total	115 220	112 570	106 380	92 310	75 940	61 790	54 470	49 030	45 000	39 280

Women - Femmes - Mujeres [3]
ISIC 3 - CITI 3 - CIIU 3

	1999	2000	2001	2002	2003	2004	2005	2006	2007	2008
Total	33 630	34 820	33 970	31 470	27 210	22 680	20 180	18 780	18 060	16 480

Total cases (fatal + non-fatal) - Ensemble des cas (mortels + non mortels) - Todos los casos (mortales + no mortales)

Total men and women - Total hommes et femmes - Total hombres y mujeres [3]
ISIC 3 - CITI 3 - CIIU 3

	1999	2000	2001	2002	2003	2004	2005	2006	2007	2008
Total	153 110	151 790	144 720	127 710	106 690	87 760	77 740	70 710	66 060	58 310

Men - Hommes - Hombres [3]
ISIC 3 - CITI 3 - CIIU 3

	1999	2000	2001	2002	2003	2004	2005	2006	2007	2008
Total	119 220	116 720	110 470	95 970	79 270	64 850	57 350	51 710	47 820	41 640

Women - Femmes - Mujeres [3]
ISIC 3 - CITI 3 - CIIU 3

	1999	2000	2001	2002	2003	2004	2005	2006	2007	2008
Total	33 890	35 070	34 250	31 730	27 420	22 910	20 390	19 000	18 230	16 670

San Marino (FF) — Reported injuries - Lésions déclarées - Lesiones declaradas

Fatal cases - Cas mortels - Casos mortales

Total men and women - Total hommes et femmes - Total hombres y mujeres
ISIC 3 - CITI 3 - CIIU 3

	1999	2000	2001	2002	2003	2004	2005
Total	0	0	0	0	0	0	0

Explanatory notes: see p. 1125.

[1] Deaths occurring within the same reference year as accident. [2] Excl. activities with low injury rates. [3] Figures rounded to nearest 10.

Notes explicatives: voir p. 1127.

[1] Décès survenant pendant la même année de référence que l'accident. [2] Non compris les activités avec les taux de lésion bas. [3] Chiffres arrondis au 10 le plus proche.

Notas explicativas: véase p. 1129.

[1] Fallecimientos que se producen durante el mismo año de referencia que el accidente. [2] Excl. las actividades con tasas de lesion bajas. [3] Cifras redondeadas al 10 más próximo.

OCCUPATIONAL INJURIES / LÉSIONS PROFESSIONNELLES / LESIONES PROFESIONALES

Cases of injury with lost workdays, by economic activity
Cas de lésion avec perte de journées de travail, par activité économique
Casos de lesión con pérdida de días de trabajo, por actividad económica

	1999	2000	2001	2002	2003	2004	2005	2006	2007	2008

San Marino (FF) — Reported injuries - Lésions déclarées - Lesiones declaradas

Non-fatal cases (temporary + permanent incapacity) - Cas non mortels (incapacité temporaire + permanente) - Casos no mortales (incapacidad temporal + permanente)

Total men and women - Total hommes et femmes - Total hombres y mujeres
ISIC 3 - CITI 3 - CIIU 3

	1999	2000	2001	2002	2003	2004	2005	2006	2007	2008
Total	1 074	1 109	864	761	859	659	682	866	573	.
A	9	8	4	6	7	4	5	3	2	.
D	428	439	311	343	310	260	273	374	260	.
E	0	0	0	0	0	0	0	0	0	.
F	307	169	124	119	84	64	102	140	79	.
G	74	57	59	134	105	43	97	142	87	.
H	20	30	22	0	0	0	7	2	8	.
I	19	8	9	7	4	3	15	12	7	.
J	2	5	10	9	1	2	2	5	4	.
K	6	0	0	0	0	0	35	49	35	.
L	.	43	42	49	54	35	97	118	80	.
O	.	98	84	47	75	42	0	21	11	.
X	67	192	153	47	219	0	49	0	0	.

Total cases (fatal + non-fatal) - Ensemble des cas (mortels + non mortels) - Todos los casos (mortales + no mortales)

Total men and women - Total hommes et femmes - Total hombres y mujeres
ISIC 3 - CITI 3 - CIIU 3

	1999	2000	2001	2002	2003	2004	2005	2006	2007	2008
Total	1 074	1 109	864	761	859	659	682	866	573	.
A	9	8	4	6	7	4	5	3	2	.
D	428	439	311	343	310	260	273	374	260	.
F	307	169	124	119	84	64	102	140	79	.
G	74	57	59	134	105	43	97	142	87	.
H	20	30	22	0	0	0	7	2	8	.
I	19	8	9	7	4	3	15	12	7	.
J	2	5	10	9	1	2	2	5	4	.
K	6	0	0	0	0	0	35	49	35	.
L	.	43	42	49	54	35	97	118	80	.
O	.	98	84	47	75	42	0	21	11	.
X	67	192	153	47	219	0	49	0	0	.

Slovakia (CA) — Reported injuries - Lésions déclarées - Lesiones declaradas

Fatal cases - Cas mortels - Casos mortales

Total men and women - Total hommes et femmes - Total hombres y mujeres
ISIC 3 - CITI 3 - CIIU 3

	1999	2000	2001	2002	2003	2004	2005	2006	2007	2008
Total	115	88	100	87	94	79	76	95	97	80
A	15	8	15	9	9	9	5	8	9	13
B	0	0	0	0	0	0	0	0	0	0
C	1	0	2	3	0	3	0	5	0	0
D	22	23	11	14	13	10	13	14	25	16
E	6	3	2	3	3	9	1	3	0	2
F	11	7	13	7	9	3	10	7	25	18
G	5	6	4	9	8	3	1	5	19	9
H	1	0	0	0	0	0	0	0	0	0
I	4	6	16	7	12	7	14	10	13	9
J	2	0	0	0	0	2	0	0	0	0
K	2	6	3	3	3	2	1	2	5	5
L	39	28	32	29	36	28	30	38	0	1
M	3	0	1	2	1	2	0	0	0	3
N	1	1	1	1	0	0	0	1	0	0
O	3	0	0	0	0	1	1	2	1	4
P	0	0	0	0	0	0	0	0	0	0
Q	0	0	0	0	0	0	0	0	0	0
X	0	0	0	0	0	0	0	0	0	0

Men - Hommes - Hombres
ISIC 3 - CITI 3 - CIIU 3

	1999	2000	2001	2002	2003	2004	2005	2006	2007	2008
Total	105	83	98	82	89	72	74	93	85	78
A	14	8	15	8	9	9	4	8	9	13
B	0	0	0	0	0	0	0	0	0	0
C	1	0	2	3	0	3	0	5	0	0
D	20	22	11	13	13	10	13	14	17	16
E	6	3	2	3	3	9	1	2	0	2
F	11	7	13	7	9	3	10	7	25	18
G	3	6	2	7	6	2	1	5	16	9
H	1	0	0	0	0	0	0	0	0	0
I	4	6	16	7	12	4	14	10	12	8
J	2	0	0	0	0	2	0	0	0	0
K	1	5	3	3	3	2	1	2	5	5
L	36	25	32	29	33	27	29	38	0	1
M	2	0	1	1	1	0	0	0	0	2
N	1	1	1	1	0	0	0	1	0	0
O	3	0	0	0	0	1	1	1	1	4
P	0	0	0	0	0	0	0	0	0	0
Q	0	0	0	0	0	0	0	0	0	0
X	0	0	0	0	0	0	0	0	0	0

Explanatory notes: see p. 1125.   Notes explicatives: voir p. 1127.   Notas explicativas: véase p. 1129.

	OCCUPATIONAL INJURIES	LÉSIONS PROFESSIONNELLES	LESIONES PROFESIONALES
	Cases of injury with lost workdays, by economic activity	Cas de lésion avec perte de journées de travail, par activité économique	Casos de lesión con pérdida de días de trabajo, por actividad económica

	1999	2000	2001	2002	2003	2004	2005	2006	2007	2008

Slovakia (CA) — Reported injuries - Lésions déclarées - Lesiones declaradas

Fatal cases - Cas mortels - Casos mortales

Women - Femmes - Mujeres
ISIC 3 - CITI 3 - CIIU 3

	1999	2000	2001	2002	2003	2004	2005	2006	2007	2008
Total	10	5	2	5	5	7	2	2	12	2
A	1	0	0	1	0	0	1	0	0	0
B	0	0	0	0	0	0	0	0	0	0
C	0	0	0	0	0	0	0	0	0	0
D	2	1	0	1	0	0	0	0	8	0
E	0	0	0	0	0	0	0	1	0	0
F	0	0	0	0	0	0	0	0	0	0
G	2	0	2	2	2	1	0	0	3	0
H	0	0	0	0	0	0	0	0	0	0
I	0	0	0	0	0	3	0	0	1	1
J	0	0	0	0	0	0	0	0	0	0
K	1	1	0	0	0	0	0	0	0	0
L	3	3	0	0	3	1	1	0	0	0
M	1	0	0	1	0	2	0	0	0	1
N	0	0	0	0	0	0	0	0	0	0
O	0	0	0	0	0	0	0	1	0	0
P	0	0	0	0	0	0	0	0	0	0
Q	0	0	0	0	0	0	0	0	0	0
X	0	0	0	0	0	0	0	0	0	0

Non-fatal cases (temporary + permanent incapacity) - Cas non mortels (incapacité temporaire + permanente) - Casos no mortales (incapacidad temporal + permanente)

Total men and women - Total hommes et femmes - Total hombres y mujeres
ISIC 3 - CITI 3 - CIIU 3

	1999	2000	2001	2002	2003	2004	2005	2006	2007	2008
Total	24 023	22 116	20 889	19 439	17 443	13 396	12 958	13 826	14 990	12 524
A	3 550	3 019	2 775	2 504	2 027	1 272	1 052	1 005	719	634
B	0	1	1	1	0	2	3	1	1	2
C	874	704	660	581	626	470	308	677	417	351
D	8 730	8 094	7 602	7 240	6 552	5 316	5 119	5 075	5 985	5 511
E	353	323	289	283	257	214	164	160	105	84
F	1 656	1 477	1 322	1 254	1 115	887	816	740	1 174	1 099
G	890	995	961	1 020	966	773	688	760	1 300	1 329
H	198	159	144	118	145	72	65	82	223	197
I	1 425	1 446	1 226	1 111	1 003	803	775	789	836	829
J	96	80	66	61	60	83	43	102	66	72
K	512	498	587	550	382	339	250	344	568	540
L	4 299	3 949	4 010	3 518	3 068	2 210	2 766	3 161	516	452
M	381	332	279	327	393	340	297	352	303	347
N	718	720	645	603	549	308	387	344	323	352
O	341	319	322	268	206	228	225	234	308	313
P	0	0	0	0	0	0	0	0	0	0
Q	0	0	0	0	0	0	0	0	160	119
X	0	0	0	0	0	0	0	0	1 986	293

Men - Hommes - Hombres
ISIC 3 - CITI 3 - CIIU 3

	1999	2000	2001	2002	2003	2004	2005	2006	2007	2008
Total	18 568	16 991	16 343	14 852	13 294	10 268	9 687	10 274	11 229	8 957
A	2 855	2 357	2 220	2 053	1 617	1 049	802	783	553	482
B	0	1	0	1	0	0	2	1	1	2
C	866	699	652	576	621	471	304	671	410	338
D	6 783	6 382	6 039	5 545	5 073	4 105	3 876	3 767	4 526	4 140
E	321	283	265	255	232	202	150	142	97	79
F	1 609	1 445	1 295	1 223	1 104	878	796	732	1 142	1 072
G	580	731	606	593	606	479	416	402	806	762
H	96	70	54	54	71	29	30	24	91	84
I	1 127	1 085	1 024	896	774	611	578	544	671	632
J	45	28	26	23	16	20	12	28	24	26
K	402	380	491	436	298	263	169	253	414	357
L	3 278	2 969	3 131	2 719	2 445	1 814	2 226	2 593	364	305
M	144	101	93	116	105	100	70	82	70	75
N	189	205	193	151	162	63	90	79	76	75
O	273	255	254	211	170	182	166	183	242	227
P	0	0	0	0	0	0	0	0	0	0
Q	0	0	0	0	0	0	0	0	118	84
X	0	0	0	0	0	0	0	0	1 624	217

Explanatory notes: see p. 1125.   Notes explicatives: voir p. 1127.   Notas explicativas: véase p. 1129.

OCCUPATIONAL INJURIES

Cases of injury with lost workdays, by economic activity

LÉSIONS PROFESSIONNELLES

Cas de lésion avec perte de journées de travail, par activité économique

LESIONES PROFESIONALES

Casos de lesión con pérdida de días de trabajo, por actividad económica

8A

	1999	2000	2001	2002	2003	2004	2005	2006	2007	2008

Slovakia (CA)   Reported injuries - Lésions déclarées - Lesiones declaradas

Non-fatal cases (temporary + permanent incapacity) - Cas non mortels (incapacité temporaire + permanente) - Casos no mortales (incapacidad temporal + permanente)

Women - Femmes - Mujeres
ISIC 3 - CITI 3 - CIIU 3

	1999	2000	2001	2002	2003	2004	2005	2006	2007	2008
Total	5 455	5 125	4 546	4 587	4 149	3 128	3 271	3 552	3 761	3 567
A	695	662	555	451	419	232	250	222	166	152
B	0	0	1	0	0	0	1	0	0	0
C	8	5	8	5	5	2	4	6	7	13
D	1 947	1 712	1 563	1 695	1 492	1 221	1 243	1 308	1 459	1 371
E	32	40	24	28	28	21	14	18	8	5
F	47	32	27	31	20	12	20	8	32	27
G	310	264	355	427	338	297	272	358	494	567
H	102	89	90	64	74	43	35	58	132	113
I	298	361	202	215	241	199	197	245	165	197
J	51	52	40	38	44	65	31	74	42	46
K	110	118	96	114	87	78	81	91	154	183
L	1 021	980	879	799	659	424	540	568	152	147
M	237	231	186	211	289	242	227	270	233	272
N	529	515	452	452	387	245	297	265	247	277
O	68	64	68	57	36	47	59	51	66	86
P	0	0	0	0	0	0	0	0	0	0
Q	0	0	0	0	0	0	0	0	42	35
X	0	0	0	0	0	0	0	0	362	76

Cases of temporary incapacity - Cas d'incapacité temporaire - Casos de incapacidad temporal

Total men and women - Total hommes et femmes - Total hombres y mujeres
ISIC 3 - CITI 3 - CIIU 3

	1999	2000	2001	2002	2003	2004	2005	2006	2007	2008
Total	24 023	22 116	20 889	19 439	17 349	13 317	12 958	13 826	14 990	12 524
A	3 550	3 019	2 775	2 504	2 027	1 272	1 052	1 005	719	634
B	0	1	1	1	0	2	3	1	1	2
C	874	704	660	581	626	470	308	677	417	351
D	8 730	8 094	7 602	7 240	6 552	5 316	5 119	5 075	5 985	5 511
E	353	323	289	283	257	214	164	160	105	86
F	1 656	1 477	1 322	1 254	1 115	887	816	740	1 174	1 099
G	890	995	961	1 020	966	773	688	760	1 300	1 329
H	198	159	144	118	145	72	65	82	223	197
I	1 425	1 446	1 226	1 111	1 003	803	775	789	836	829
J	96	80	66	61	60	83	43	102	66	72
K	512	498	587	550	382	339	250	344	568	540
L	4 299	3 949	4 010	3 518	3 068	2 210	2 766	3 161	516	452
M	381	332	279	327	393	340	297	352	303	347
N	718	720	645	603	549	308	387	344	323	352
O	341	319	322	268	206	228	225	234	308	313
P	0	0	0	0	0	0	0	0	0	0
Q	0	0	0	0	0	0	0	0	160	119
X	0	0	0	0	0	0	0	0	1 986	293

Men - Hommes - Hombres
ISIC 3 - CITI 3 - CIIU 3

	1999	2000	2001	2002	2003	2004	2005	2006	2007	2008
Total	18 568	16 991	16 343	14 852	13 294	10 268	9 687	10 274	11 229	8 957
A	2 855	2 357	2 220	2 053	1 617	1 049	802	783	553	482
B	0	1	0	1	0	0	2	1	1	2
C	866	699	652	576	621	471	304	671	410	338
D	6 783	6 382	6 039	5 545	5 073	4 105	3 876	3 767	4 526	4 140
E	321	283	265	255	232	202	150	142	97	79
F	1 609	1 445	1 295	1 223	1 104	878	796	732	1 142	1 072
G	580	731	606	593	606	479	416	402	806	762
H	96	70	54	54	71	29	30	24	91	84
I	1 127	1 085	1 024	896	774	611	578	544	671	632
J	45	28	26	23	16	20	12	28	24	26
K	402	380	491	436	298	263	169	253	414	357
L	3 278	2 969	3 131	2 719	2 445	1 814	2 226	2 593	364	305
M	144	101	93	116	105	100	70	82	70	75
N	189	205	193	151	162	63	90	79	76	75
O	273	255	254	211	170	182	166	183	242	227
P	0	0	0	0	0	0	0	0	0	0
Q	0	0	0	0	0	0	0	0	118	84
X	0	0	0	0	0	0	0	0	1 624	217

Explanatory notes: see p. 1125.   Notes explicatives: voir p. 1127.   Notas explicativas: véase p. 1129.

OCCUPATIONAL INJURIES

Cases of injury with lost workdays, by economic activity

LÉSIONS PROFESSIONNELLES

Cas de lésion avec perte de journées de travail, par activité économique

LESIONES PROFESIONALES

Casos de lesión con pérdida de días de trabajo, por actividad económica

	1999	2000	2001	2002	2003	2004	2005	2006	2007	2008

Slovakia (CA) — Reported injuries - Lésions déclarées - Lesiones declaradas

Cases of temporary incapacity - Cas d'incapacité temporaire - Casos de incapacidad temporal

Women - Femmes - Mujeres
ISIC 3 - CITI 3 - CIIU 3

	1999	2000	2001	2002	2003	2004	2005	2006	2007	2008
Total	5 455	5 125	4 546	4 587	4 149	3 128	3 271	3 552	3 761	3 567
A	695	662	555	451	419	232	250	222	166	152
B	0	0	1	0	0	0	1	0	0	0
C	8	5	8	5	5	2	4	6	7	13
D	1 947	1 712	1 563	1 695	1 492	1 221	1 243	1 308	1 459	1 371
E	32	40	24	28	28	21	14	18	8	5
F	47	32	27	31	20	12	20	8	32	27
G	310	264	355	427	338	297	272	358	494	567
H	102	89	90	64	74	43	35	58	132	113
I	298	361	202	215	241	199	197	245	165	197
J	51	52	40	38	44	65	31	74	42	46
K	110	118	96	114	87	78	81	91	154	183
L	1 021	980	879	799	659	424	540	568	152	147
M	237	231	186	211	289	242	227	270	233	272
N	529	515	452	452	387	245	297	265	247	277
O	68	64	68	57	36	47	59	51	66	86
P	0	0	0	0	0	0	0	0	0	0
Q	0	0	0	0	0	0	0	0	42	35
X	0	0	0	0	0	0	0	0	362	76

Total cases (fatal + non-fatal) - Ensemble des cas (mortels + non mortels) - Todos los casos (mortales + no mortales)

Total men and women - Total hommes et femmes - Total hombres y mujeres
ISIC 3 - CITI 3 - CIIU 3

	1999	2000	2001	2002	2003	2004	2005	2006	2007	2008
Total	24 138	22 204	20 989	19 526	17 537	13 475	13 034	13 921	15 087	12 604
A	3 565	3 027	2 790	2 513	2 036	1 281	1 057	1 013	728	647
B	0	1	1	1	0	2	3	1	1	2
C	875	704	662	584	626	473	308	682	417	351
D	8 752	8 117	7 613	7 254	6 565	5 326	5 132	5 089	6 010	5 527
E	359	326	291	286	260	223	165	163	105	86
F	1 667	1 484	1 335	1 261	1 124	890	826	747	1 199	1 117
G	895	1 001	965	1 029	974	776	689	765	1 319	1 338
H	199	159	144	118	145	72	65	82	223	197
I	1 429	1 452	1 242	1 118	1 015	810	789	799	849	838
J	98	80	66	61	60	85	43	102	66	72
K	514	504	590	553	385	341	251	346	573	545
L	4 338	3 977	4 042	3 547	3 104	2 238	2 796	3 199	516	453
M	384	332	280	329	394	342	297	352	303	350
N	719	721	646	604	549	308	387	345	323	352
O	344	319	322	268	206	229	226	236	309	317
P	0	0	0	0	0	0	0	0	0	0
Q	0	0	0	0	0	0	0	0	160	119
X	0	0	0	0	0	0	0	0	1 986	293

Men - Hommes - Hombres
ISIC 3 - CITI 3 - CIIU 3

	1999	2000	2001	2002	2003	2004	2005	2006	2007	2008
Total	18 673	17 074	16 441	14 934	13 383	10 340	9 761	10 367	11 314	9 035
A	2 869	2 365	2 235	2 061	1 626	1 058	806	791	562	495
B	0	1	0	1	0	0	2	1	1	2
C	867	699	654	579	621	474	304	676	410	338
D	6 803	6 404	6 050	5 558	5 086	4 115	3 889	3 781	4 543	4 156
E	327	286	267	258	235	211	151	144	97	81
F	1 620	1 452	1 308	1 230	1 113	881	806	739	1 167	1 090
G	583	737	608	600	612	481	417	407	822	771
H	97	70	54	54	71	29	30	24	91	84
I	1 131	1 091	1 040	903	786	615	592	554	683	640
J	47	28	26	23	16	22	12	28	24	26
K	403	385	494	439	301	265	170	255	419	362
L	3 314	2 994	3 163	2 748	2 478	1 841	2 255	2 631	364	306
M	146	101	94	117	106	100	70	82	70	77
N	190	206	194	152	162	63	90	80	76	75
O	276	255	254	211	170	183	167	184	243	231
P	0	0	0	0	0	0	0	0	0	0
Q	0	0	0	0	0	0	0	0	118	84
X	0	0	0	0	0	0	0	0	1 624	217

Explanatory notes: see p. 1125.

Notes explicatives: voir p. 1127.

Notas explicativas: véase p. 1129.

OCCUPATIONAL INJURIES

Cases of injury with lost workdays, by economic activity

LÉSIONS PROFESSIONNELLES

Cas de lésion avec perte de journées de travail, par activité économique

LESIONES PROFESIONALES

Casos de lesión con pérdida de días de trabajo, por actividad económica

	1999	2000	2001	2002	2003	2004	2005	2006	2007	2008

Slovakia (CA) — Reported injuries - Lésions déclarées - Lesiones declaradas

Total cases (fatal + non-fatal) - Ensemble des cas (mortels + non mortels) - Todos los casos (mortales + no mortales)

Women - Femmes - Mujeres
ISIC 3 - CITI 3 - CIIU 3

	1999	2000	2001	2002	2003	2004	2005	2006	2007	2008
Total	5 465	5 130	4 548	4 592	4 154	3 135	3 273	3 554	3 773	3 569
A	696	662	555	452	419	232	251	222	166	152
B	0	0	1	0	0	0	1	0	0	0
C	8	5	8	5	5	2	4	6	7	13
D	1 949	1 713	1 563	1 696	1 492	1 221	1 243	1 308	1 467	1 371
E	32	40	24	28	28	21	14	19	8	5
F	47	32	27	31	20	12	20	8	32	27
G	312	264	357	429	340	298	272	358	497	567
H	102	89	90	64	74	43	35	58	132	113
I	298	361	202	215	241	202	197	245	166	198
J	51	52	40	38	44	65	31	74	42	46
K	111	119	96	114	87	78	81	91	154	183
L	1 024	983	879	799	662	425	541	568	152	147
M	238	231	186	212	289	244	227	270	233	273
N	529	515	452	452	387	245	297	265	247	277
O	68	64	68	57	36	47	59	52	66	86
P	0	0	0	0	0	0	0	0	0	0
Q	0	0	0	0	0	0	0	0	42	35
X	0	0	0	0	0	0	0	0	362	76

Slovenia (FF) — Reported injuries - Lésions déclarées - Lesiones declaradas

Fatal cases - Cas mortels - Casos mortales

Total men and women - Total hommes et femmes - Total hombres y mujeres
ISIC 3 - CITI 3 - CIIU 3

	1999	2000	2001	2002	2003	2004	2005	2006	2007	2008
Total	27	26	34	32	40	21	21	32	43	.
A	2	0	4	2	2	2	4	2	3	.
B	0	0	0	0	0	0	0	0	0	.
C	0	0	5	0	4	0	0	1	1	.
D	6	10	4	10	7	6	5	9	10	.
E	1	2	0	0	1	1	0	0	0	.
F	6	8	11	7	15	6	7	10	16	.
G	2	1	2	3	4	1	3	0	3	.
H	0	0	0	1	0	0	0	0	0	.
I	4	2	3	5	5	1	1	5	3	.
J	0	0	0	0	0	0	0	1	2	.
K	2	0	1	2	0	1	1	2	1	.
L	1	2	1	0	0	1	0	1	3	.
M	0	0	0	1	0	0	0	0	0	.
N	0	1	1	1	0	2	0	0	1	.
O	0	0	2	0	2	0	0	0	0	.
P	0	0	0	0	0	0	0	0	0	.
Q	0	0	0	0	0	0	0	0	0	.
X	3	0	0	0	0	0	0	0	0	.

Non-fatal cases (temporary + permanent incapacity) - Cas non mortels (incapacité temporaire + permanente) - Casos no mortales (incapacidad temporal + permanente)

Total men and women - Total hommes et femmes - Total hombres y mujeres [1]
ISIC 3 - CITI 3 - CIIU 3

	1999	2000	2001	2002	2003	2004	2005	2006	2007	2008
Total	41 036	40 369	40 270	40 762	41 295	42 052	37 038	36 900	36 700	.
A	1 256	1 106	1 004	1 054	949	961	898	843	856	.
B	13	18	9	15	8	12	13	7	6	.
C	727	624	603	454	488	405	379	329	316	.
D	16 196	15 901	16 388	16 380	16 008	15 706	13 936	13 602	13 600	.
E	708	739	758	773	705	735	682	682	552	.
F	4 955	5 254	5 325	5 129	5 076	5 438	4 639	4 641	5 231	.
G	3 565	3 862	3 720	3 808	3 851	3 723	3 436	3 545	3 668	.
H	827	941	1 107	1 218	1 264	1 215	1 188	1 149	1 150	.
I	2 039	2 268	2 301	2 630	2 867	2 955	2 476	2 504	2 460	.
J	299	361	382	448	449	482	435	439	354	.
K	1 392	1 534	1 658	1 725	2 041	2 072	1 852	2 017	1 953	.
L	1 995	2 165	2 341	2 513	2 791	3 278	2 716	2 603	2 317	.
M	1 281	1 293	1 258	1 332	1 487	1 529	1 358	1 349	1 265	.
N	1 982	2 210	2 400	2 019	1 937	2 088	1 703	1 836	1 721	.
O	679	789	853	890	873	892	827	841	758	.
P	2	2	2	1	0	0	0	0	0	.
Q	0	0	0	0	0	0	0	0	0	.
X	3 120	1 302	161	368	501	561	500	513	493	.

Explanatory notes: see p. 1125.   Notes explicatives: voir p. 1127.   Notas explicativas: véase p. 1129.

[1] Incl. commuting accidents.   [1] Y compris les accidents de trajet.   [1] Incl. accidentes del trayecto.

8A

OCCUPATIONAL INJURIES	LÉSIONS PROFESSIONNELLES	LESIONES PROFESIONALES
Cases of injury with lost workdays, by economic activity	Cas de lésion avec perte de journées de travail, par activité économique	Casos de lesión con pérdida de días de trabajo, por actividad económica

	1999	2000	2001	2002	2003	2004	2005	2006	2007	2008

Slovenia (FF) — Reported injuries - Lésions déclarées - Lesiones declaradas

Total cases (fatal + non-fatal) - Ensemble des cas (mortels + non mortels) - Todos los casos (mortales + no mortales)

Total men and women - Total hommes et femmes - Total hombres y mujeres
ISIC 3 - CITI 3 - CIIU 3

	1999	2000	2001	2002	2003	2004	2005	2006	2007	2008
Total	41 063	40 395	40 304	40 794	41 335	42 073	37 059	36 931	36 743	.
A	1 258	1 106	1 008	1 056	951	963	902	845	859	.
B	13	18	9	15	8	12	13	7	6	.
C	727	624	608	454	492	405	379	330	317	.
D	16 202	15 911	16 392	16 389	16 015	15 712	13 941	13 611	13 610	.
E	709	741	758	773	706	736	682	682	552	.
F	4 961	5 262	5 336	5 136	5 091	5 444	4 646	4 651	5 247	.
G	3 567	3 863	3 722	3 811	3 855	3 724	3 439	3 545	3 671	.
H	827	941	1 107	1 219	1 264	1 215	1 188	1 149	1 150	.
I	2 043	2 270	2 304	2 635	2 872	2 956	2 477	2 509	2 463	.
J	299	361	382	448	449	482	435	440	356	.
K	1 394	1 534	1 659	1 727	2 041	2 073	1 853	2 019	1 954	.
L	1 996	2 167	2 342	2 513	2 791	3 279	2 716	2 604	2 320	.
M	1 281	1 293	1 258	1 333	1 487	1 529	1 358	1 349	1 265	.
N	1 982	2 211	2 401	2 020	1 937	2 090	1 703	1 836	1 722	.
O	679	789	855	890	875	892	827	841	758	.
P	2	2	2	1	0	0	0	0	0	.
Q	0	0	0	0	0	0	0	0	0	.
X	3 123	1 302	161	368	501	561	500	513	493	.

Suisse (FA) — Compensated injuries - Lésions indemnisées - Lesiones indemnizadas

Fatal cases - Cas mortels - Casos mortales

Total men and women - Total hommes et femmes - Total hombres y mujeres [1]
ISIC 3 - CITI 3 - CIIU 3

	1999	2000	2001	2002	2003	2004	2005	2006	2007	2008
Total	83	82	72	53	46	67	45	51	59	.
A	5	1	7	3	1	5	1	3	0	.
B	0	0	0	0	0	0	0	0	0	.
C-D	12	27	14	18	11	18	12	14	7	.
E	0	1	1	1	2	0	1	0	1	.
F	20	18	21	15	14	16	13	13	13	.
G	4	5	4	1	4	4	1	3	5	.
H	2	1	0	0	0	2	0	0	0	.
I	19	18	10	8	5	8	6	9	10	.
J	0	0	0	0	2	2	0	0	0	.
K	3	4	1	3	4	5	2	4	7	.
L	0	0	0	0	0	0	0	0	0	.
M	0	0	1	0	0	0	0	0	0	.
N	1	0	0	0	0	1	1	0	0	.
O	4	1	1	0	0	0	0	0	0	.
P	1	0	0	0	0	0	0	0	0	.
Q	0	0	0	0	0	0	0	0	0	.
X	12	6	12	4	3	6	8	5	16	.

Non-fatal cases (temporary + permanent incapacity) - Cas non mortels (incapacité temporaire + permanente) - Casos no mortales (incapacidad temporal + permanente)

Total men and women - Total hommes et femmes - Total hombres y mujeres [2]
ISIC 3 - CITI 3 - CIIU 3

	1999	2000	2001	2002	2003	2004	2005	2006	2007	2008
Total	91 250	90 849	91 217	88 703	85 059	83 645	84 220	85 773	86 313	.
A	3 108	3 300	3 145	3 011	2 928	2 865	2 980	2 842	2 702	.
B	7	5	7	6	8	7	6	4	4	.
C-D	25 804	25 297	25 705	24 256	22 411	21 247	20 613	20 665	20 638	.
E	537	529	466	504	436	474	445	411	389	.
F	21 178	21 172	20 922	20 575	19 883	19 685	19 699	20 109	19 458	.
G	9 647	9 460	9 612	9 766	9 375	8 980	8 824	9 149	8 871	.
H	5 563	5 569	5 898	5 649	5 323	5 184	5 116	5 317	5 303	.
I	5 367	5 531	5 505	5 443	5 140	5 144	5 010	5 366	5 235	.
J	359	357	337	317	311	319	284	285	319	.
K	7 779	8 423	8 172	7 638	7 494	7 628	8 542	9 777	9 920	.
L	239	242	253	242	215	228	220	273	246	.
M	72	63	49	44	66	61	69	68	48	.
N	1 577	1 536	1 554	1 743	1 756	1 772	1 838	1 812	1 949	.
O	2 814	3 003	3 039	3 058	3 047	3 199	3 159	3 333	3 383	.
P	200	159	161	165	180	183	166	179	156	.
Q	3	1	0	3	1	1	1	2	6	.
X	6 996	6 202	6 392	6 283	6 485	6 668	7 248	6 181	7 686	.

Explanatory notes: see p. 1125.

[1] Only deaths resulting from accidents occurring during the same year. [2] Incapacity of 3 days or more.

Notes explicatives: voir p. 1127.

[1] Seulement les décès dus à des accidents survenus pendant la même année. [2] Incapacité de 3 jours et plus.

Notas explicativas: véase p. 1129.

[1] Solamente los fallecimientos resultados a accidentes ocurridos en el mismo año. [2] Incapacidad de 3 días y más.

OCCUPATIONAL INJURIES

Cases of injury with lost workdays, by economic activity

LÉSIONS PROFESSIONNELLES

Cas de lésion avec perte de journées de travail, par activité économique

LESIONES PROFESIONALES

Casos de lesión con pérdida de días de trabajo, por actividad económica

	1999	2000	2001	2002	2003	2004	2005	2006	2007	2008

Suisse (FA) — Compensated injuries - Lésions indemnisées - Lesiones indemnizadas

Total cases (fatal + non-fatal) - Ensemble des cas (mortels + non mortels) - Todos los casos (mortales + no mortales)

Total men and women - Total hommes et femmes - Total hombres y mujeres
ISIC 3 - CITI 3 - CIIU 3

	1999	2000	2001	2002	2003	2004	2005	2006	2007	2008
Total	91 333	90 931	91 289	88 756	85 105	83 712	84 265	85 824	86 372	.
A	3 113	3 301	3 152	3 014	2 929	2 870	2 981	2 845	2 702	.
B	7	5	7	6	8	7	6	4	4	.
C-D	25 816	25 324	25 719	24 274	22 422	21 265	20 625	20 679	20 645	.
E	537	530	467	505	438	474	446	411	390	.
F	21 198	21 190	20 943	20 590	19 897	19 701	19 712	20 122	19 471	.
G	9 651	9 465	9 616	9 767	9 379	8 984	8 825	9 152	8 876	.
H	5 565	5 570	5 898	5 649	5 323	5 186	5 116	5 317	5 303	.
I	5 386	5 549	5 515	5 451	5 145	5 152	5 016	5 376	5 245	.
J	359	357	337	317	313	321	284	285	319	.
K	7 782	8 427	8 173	7 641	7 498	7 633	8 544	9 781	9 927	.
L	239	242	253	242	215	228	220	273	246	.
M	72	63	50	44	66	61	69	68	48	.
N	1 578	1 536	1 554	1 743	1 756	1 773	1 839	1 812	1 949	.
O	2 818	3 004	3 040	3 058	3 047	3 199	3 159	3 333	3 383	.
P	201	159	161	165	180	183	166	179	156	.
Q	3	1	0	3	1	1	1	2	6	.
X	7 008	6 208	6 404	6 287	6 488	6 674	7 256	6 186	7 702	.

Sweden (FA) — Reported injuries - Lésions déclarées - Lesiones declaradas

Fatal cases - Cas mortels - Casos mortales

Total men and women - Total hommes et femmes - Total hombres y mujeres
ISIC 3 - CITI 3 - CIIU 3

	1999	2000	2001	2002	2003	2004	2005	2006	2007	2008
Total	67	59	56	60	56	57	67	68	75	.
A	16	14	10	11	4	9	15	9	17	.
B	1	2	2	1	1	3	1	1	0	.
C	1	0	1	1	0	0	0	1	1	.
D	13	5	8	8	9	7	10	11	7	.
E	1	0	1	0	0	1	0	0	0	.
F	8	13	12	12	10	6	11	11	16	.
G	5	4	5	0	4	4	3	7	2	.
H	0	0	1	1	0	1	0	1	0	.
I	13	12	14	17	9	14	12	13	9	.
J	0	0	0	0	0	0	0	0	0	.
K	2	3	0	7	7	4	7	6	5	.
L	3	4	1	1	10	5	5	5	10	.
M	2	0	0	0	1	0	0	0	1	.
N	0	0	0	1	0	1	1	1	1	.
O	1	2	1	0	1	2	2	2	5	.
P	0	0	0	0	0	0	0	0	1	.
Q	0	0	0	0	0	0	0	0	0	.
X	1	0	0	0	0	0	0	0	1	.

Men - Hommes - Hombres
ISIC 3 - CITI 3 - CIIU 3

	1999	2000	2001	2002	2003	2004	2005	2006	2007	2008
Total	62	56	51	56	54	47	61	66	68	.
A	16	14	9	11	4	9	14	9	17	.
B	1	2	2	1	1	2	1	1	0	.
C	1	0	1	1	0	0	0	1	1	.
D	11	4	6	7	8	7	10	10	7	.
E	1	0	1	0	0	1	0	0	0	.
F	7	13	12	12	10	6	11	11	16	.
G	4	4	5	0	4	3	2	7	2	.
H	0	0	1	1	0	0	0	1	0	.
I	13	10	13	17	8	12	11	13	6	.
J	0	0	0	0	0	0	0	0	0	.
K	1	3	0	5	7	3	5	5	4	.
L	3	4	0	1	10	3	5	5	10	.
M	2	0	0	0	1	0	0	0	1	.
N	0	0	0	0	0	1	0	1	1	.
O	1	2	1	0	1	0	2	2	3	.
P	0	0	0	0	0	0	0	0	0	.
Q	0	0	0	0	0	0	0	0	0	.
X	1	0	0	0	0	0	0	0	0	.

Explanatory notes: see p. 1125.

Notes explicatives: voir p. 1127.

Notas explicativas: véase p. 1129.

OCCUPATIONAL INJURIES

Cases of injury with lost workdays, by economic activity

LÉSIONS PROFESSIONNELLES

Cas de lésion avec perte de journées de travail, par activité économique

LESIONES PROFESIONALES

Casos de lesión con pérdida de días de trabajo, por actividad económica

Sweden (FA)

Fatal cases - Cas mortels - Casos mortales — Reported injuries - Lésions déclarées - Lesiones declaradas

Women - Femmes - Mujeres
ISIC 3 - CITI 3 - CIIU 3

	1999	2000	2001	2002	2003	2004	2005	2006	2007	2008
Total	5	3	5	4	2	10	6	2	7	.
A	0	0	1	0	0	0	1	0	0	.
B	0	0	0	0	0	1	0	0	0	.
C	0	0	0	0	0	0	0	0	0	.
D	2	1	2	1	1	0	0	0	0	.
E	0	0	0	0	0	0	0	1	0	.
F	1	0	0	0	0	0	0	0	0	.
G	1	0	0	0	0	0	0	0	0	.
H	0	0	0	0	0	1	0	0	0	.
I	0	0	0	0	1	1	1	0	0	.
J	0	2	1	0	0	2	1	0	3	.
K	1	0	0	0	0	0	0	0	0	.
L	0	0	0	2	0	1	2	1	1	.
M	0	0	0	0	0	2	0	0	0	.
N	0	0	0	1	0	0	0	0	0	.
O	0	0	0	0	0	1	1	1	0	.
P	0	0	0	0	0	0	1	0	2	.
Q	0	0	0	0	0	0	0	0	0	.
X	0	0	0	0	0	0	0	0	1	.

Non-fatal cases (temporary + permanent incapacity) - Cas non mortels (incapacité temporaire + permanente) - Casos no mortales (incapacidad temporal + permanente)

Total men and women - Total hommes et femmes - Total hombres y mujeres [1]
ISIC 3 - CITI 3 - CIIU 3

	1999	2000	2001	2002	2003	2004	2005	2006	2007	2008
Total	37 761	39 275	37 405	37 628	34 536	32 648	31 673	32 216	29 675	.
A	888	981	896	651	518	419	520	450	382	.
B	26	22	18	11	7	10	6	6	10	.
C	201	212	206	185	159	122	141	151	136	.
D	10 593	11 429	10 319	10 715	9 664	8 927	8 357	8 183	7 755	.
E	248	199	195	174	172	157	151	131	113	.
F	3 429	3 392	3 547	3 622	3 322	3 045	3 048	3 250	3 217	.
G	2 443	2 564	2 593	2 448	2 189	2 116	2 011	2 032	1 939	.
H	538	530	503	544	493	431	436	460	481	.
I	3 532	3 424	3 547	3 455	3 277	3 231	3 088	3 174	2 807	.
J	186	199	292	248	244	196	240	222	243	.
K	2 131	2 225	2 420	2 422	2 202	2 112	2 183	2 214	2 346	.
L	2 076	1 989	2 112	2 021	1 940	1 627	1 578	1 618	1 424	.
M	1 967	2 154	1 987	2 817	2 656	2 710	2 540	2 670	2 388	.
N	8 292	8 777	7 567	7 015	6 517	6 478	6 223	6 564	5 418	.
O	1 076	1 038	1 091	1 067	966	890	940	902	848	.
P	0	1	0	0	0	0	0	0	0	.
Q	0	0	1	0	1	1	0	0	0	.
X	.	.	.	233	209	176	211	189	169	.

Men - Hommes - Hombres [1]
ISIC 3 - CITI 3 - CIIU 3

	1999	2000	2001	2002	2003	2004	2005	2006	2007	2008
Total	23 003	23 659	23 209	22 830	20 762	19 440	18 875	18 951	17 791	.
A	745	822	759	520	416	333	411	363	301	.
B	25	22	18	11	7	10	6	5	10	.
C	193	206	197	178	150	114	130	136	124	.
D	8 658	9 274	8 418	8 742	7 866	7 319	6 813	6 663	6 234	.
E	230	186	176	162	154	145	139	112	103	.
F	3 368	3 344	3 482	3 547	3 242	2 952	2 968	3 163	3 115	.
G	1 589	1 668	1 728	1 612	1 428	1 387	1 303	1 335	1 233	.
H	228	236	209	235	192	187	167	187	183	.
I	2 737	2 648	2 790	2 692	2 557	2 552	2 455	2 503	2 199	.
J	49	58	93	51	46	46	64	63	73	.
K	1 473	1 537	1 717	1 589	1 466	1 405	1 482	1 512	1 626	.
L	1 309	1 233	1 398	1 206	1 143	1 029	932	964	822	.
M	571	559	513	539	481	499	500	444	447	.
N	1 015	1 057	922	882	845	778	760	814	675	.
O	736	721	729	709	631	558	596	556	545	.
P	0	1	0	0	0	0	0	0	0	.
Q	0	0	1	0	1	0	0	0	0	.
X	77	87	.	155	137	126	149	131	101	.

Explanatory notes: see p. 1125.

[1] Incl. cases of dental injury; also from 1997, cases with acute hearing loss/psychological reaction, but without absence.

Notes explicatives: voir p. 1127.

[1] Y.c. cas de lésion dentaire; et dès 1997, cas avec perte d'ouïe/ réaction psychologique aigües mais sans absence.

Notas explicativas: véase p. 1129.

[1] Incl. a los casos de lesión dental; y desde 1997 los con perdida de oído/reacción psicológicas agudas pero sin ausencia.

OCCUPATIONAL INJURIES	LÉSIONS PROFESSIONNELLES	LESIONES PROFESIONALES	8A
Cases of injury with lost workdays, by economic activity	Cas de lésion avec perte de journées de travail, par activité économique	Casos de lesión con pérdida de días de trabajo, por actividad económica	

	1999	2000	2001	2002	2003	2004	2005	2006	2007	2008

Sweden (FA)   Reported injuries - Lésions déclarées - Lesiones declaradas

Non-fatal cases (temporary + permanent incapacity) - Cas non mortels (incapacité temporaire + permanente) - Casos no mortales (incapacidad temporal + permanente)

Women - Femmes - Mujeres [1]
ISIC 3 - CITI 3 - CIIU 3

	1999	2000	2001	2002	2003	2004	2005	2006	2007	2008
Total	14 758	15 616	14 196	14 798	13 774	13 208	12 798	13 265	11 884	.
A	143	159	137	131	102	86	109	87	81	.
B	1	0	0	0	0	0	0	0	0	.
C	8	6	9	7	9	8	11	15	12	.
D	1 935	2 155	1 901	1 973	1 798	1 608	1 544	1 520	1 521	.
E	18	13	19	12	18	12	12	19	10	.
F	61	48	65	75	80	93	80	87	102	.
G	854	896	865	836	761	729	708	697	706	.
H	310	294	294	309	301	244	269	273	298	.
I	795	776	757	763	720	679	633	671	608	.
J	137	141	199	197	198	150	176	159	170	.
K	658	688	703	833	736	707	701	702	720	.
L	767	756	714	815	797	598	646	654	602	.
M	1 396	1 595	1 474	2 278	2 175	2 211	2 040	2 226	1 940	.
N	7 277	7 720	6 645	6 133	5 672	5 700	5 463	5 750	4 743	.
O	340	317	362	358	335	332	344	346	303	.
P	0	0	0	0	0	0	0	0	0	.
Q	0	0	0	0	0	1	0	0	0	.
X	58	52	.	78	72	50	62	58	68	.

Total cases (fatal + non-fatal) - Ensemble des cas (mortels + non mortels) - Todos los casos (mortales + no mortales)

Total men and women - Total hommes et femmes - Total hombres y mujeres [1]
ISIC 3 - CITI 3 - CIIU 3

	1999	2000	2001	2002	2003	2004	2005	2006	2007	2008
Total	37 828	39 334	37 461	37 688	34 536	32 648	31 740	32 284	29 750	.
A	904	995	906	662	522	428	535	459	399	.
B	27	24	20	12	8	13	7	7	10	.
C	202	212	207	186	159	122	141	152	137	.
D	10 606	11 434	10 327	10 723	9 673	8 934	8 367	8 194	7 762	.
E	249	199	196	174	172	158	151	131	113	.
F	3 437	3 405	3 559	3 634	3 332	3 051	3 059	3 261	3 233	.
G	2 448	2 568	2 598	2 448	2 193	2 120	2 014	2 039	1 941	.
H	538	530	504	545	493	432	436	461	481	.
I	3 545	3 436	3 561	3 472	3 286	3 245	3 100	3 187	2 816	.
J	186	199	292	248	244	196	240	222	243	.
K	2 133	2 228	2 420	2 429	2 209	2 116	2 190	2 220	2 351	.
L	2 079	1 993	2 113	2 022	1 950	1 632	1 583	1 623	1 434	.
M	1 969	2 154	1 987	2 817	2 656	2 710	2 540	2 670	2 388	.
N	8 292	8 777	7 567	7 016	6 517	6 479	6 224	6 565	5 419	.
O	1 077	1 040	1 092	1 067	967	892	942	904	853	.
P	0	1	0	0	0	0	0	0	0	.
Q	0	0	1	0	1	1	0	0	0	.
X	.	.	.	233	209	176	211	189	170	.

Men - Hommes - Hombres [1]
ISIC 3 - CITI 3 - CIIU 3

	1999	2000	2001	2002	2003	2004	2005	2006	2007	2008
Total	23 065	23 715	23 260	22 886	20 816	19 487	18 936	19 017	17 859	.
A	761	836	768	531	420	342	425	372	318	.
B	26	24	20	12	8	12	7	6	10	.
C	194	206	198	179	150	114	130	137	125	.
D	8 669	9 278	8 424	8 749	7 874	7 326	6 823	6 673	6 241	.
E	231	186	177	162	154	146	139	112	103	.
F	3 375	3 357	3 494	3 559	3 252	2 958	2 979	3 174	3 131	.
G	1 593	1 672	1 733	1 612	1 432	1 390	1 305	1 342	1 235	.
H	228	236	210	236	192	187	167	188	183	.
I	2 750	2 658	2 803	2 709	2 565	2 564	2 466	2 516	2 205	.
J	49	58	93	51	46	46	64	63	73	.
K	1 474	1 540	1 717	1 594	1 473	1 408	1 487	1 517	1 630	.
L	1 312	1 237	1 398	1 207	1 153	1 032	937	969	832	.
M	573	559	513	539	482	499	500	444	448	.
N	1 015	1 057	922	882	845	778	760	815	676	.
O	737	723	730	709	632	559	598	558	548	.
P	0	1	0	0	0	0	0	0	0	.
Q	0	0	1	0	1	0	0	0	0	.
X	78	87	.	155	137	126	149	131	101	.

Explanatory notes: see p. 1125.

[1] Incl. cases of dental injury; also from 1997, cases with acute hearing loss/psychological reaction, but without absence.

Notes explicatives: voir p. 1127.

[1] Y.c. cas de lésion dentaire; et dès 1997, cas avec perte d'ouïe/ réaction psychologique aigües mais sans absence.

Notas explicativas: véase p. 1129.

[1] Incl. a los casos de lesión dental; y desde 1997 los con perdida de oído/reacción psicológicas agudas pero sin ausencia.

8A

	OCCUPATIONAL INJURIES	LÉSIONS PROFESSIONNELLES	LESIONES PROFESIONALES
	Cases of injury with lost workdays, by economic activity	Cas de lésion avec perte de journées de travail, par activité économique	Casos de lesión con pérdida de días de trabajo, por actividad económica

	1999	2000	2001	2002	2003	2004	2005	2006	2007	2008

Sweden (FA) — Reported injuries - Lésions déclarées - Lesiones declaradas

Total cases (fatal + non-fatal) - Ensemble des cas (mortels + non mortels) - Todos los casos (mortales + no mortales)

Women - Femmes - Mujeres [1]
ISIC 3 - CITI 3 - CIIU 3

	1999	2000	2001	2002	2003	2004	2005	2006	2007	2008
Total	14 763	15 619	14 201	14 802	13 776	13 218	12 804	13 267	11 891	.
A	143	159	138	131	102	86	110	87	81	
B	1	0	0	0	0	1	0	1	0	
C	8	6	9	7	9	8	11	15	12	
D	1 937	2 156	1 903	1 974	1 799	1 608	1 544	1 521	1 521	
E	18	13	19	12	18	12	12	19	10	
F	62	48	65	75	80	93	80	87	102	
G	855	896	865	836	761	730	709	697	706	
H	310	294	294	309	301	245	269	273	298	
I	795	778	758	763	721	681	634	671	611	
J	137	141	199	197	198	150	176	159	170	
K	659	688	703	835	736	708	703	703	721	
L	767	756	715	815	797	600	646	654	602	
M	1 396	1 595	1 474	2 278	2 175	2 211	2 040	2 226	1 940	
N	7 277	7 720	6 645	6 134	5 672	5 701	5 464	5 750	4 743	
O	340	317	362	358	335	333	344	346	305	
P	0	0	0	0	0	0	0	0	0	
Q	0	0	0	0	0	1	0	0	0	
X	58	52	.	78	72	50	62	58	69	

Turkey (FA) — Reported injuries - Lésions déclarées - Lesiones declaradas

Fatal cases - Cas mortels - Casos mortales

Total men and women - Total hommes et femmes - Total hombres y mujeres
ISIC 2 - CITI 2 - CIIU 2

	1999	2000	2001	2002	2003	2004	2005	2006	2007	2008
Total	1 333	1 291	1 008	878	811	843	1 096	1 601		
1	13	17	23	14	9	8	22	16		
2	328	93	96	69	82	68	121	80		
3	214	243	219	182	186	201	241	251		
4	44	43	35	36	29	25	32	34		
5	407	379	341	319	274	263	290	397		
6	72	52	66	52	61	52	62	70		
7	170	147	146	133	91	112	169	168		
8	5	5	4	1	2	2	5	2		
9	80	194	60	60	47	55	66	74		
0	0	118	18	12	30	57	88	509		

Men - Hommes - Hombres
ISIC 2 - CITI 2 - CIIU 2

	1999	2000	2001	2002	2003	2004	2005	2006	2007	2008
Total	.	.	991	864	796	832	1 081	1 587		
1			23	13	9	8	22	16		
2			96	69	81	68	121	80		
3			207	172	175	195	237	245		
4			35	36	29	25	32	34		
5			341	319	274	263	290	397		
6			64	52	61	52	59	69		
7			145	133	91	112	167	168		
8			4	1	2	0	5	2		
9			58	57	44	54	62	72		
0			18	12	30	55	86	504		

Women - Femmes - Mujeres
ISIC 2 - CITI 2 - CIIU 2

	1999	2000	2001	2002	2003	2004	2005	2006	2007	2008
Total	.	.	17	14	15	11	15	14		
1			0	1	0	0	0	0		
2			0	0	1	0	0	0		
3			12	10	11	6	4	6		
4			0	0	0	0	0	0		
5			0	0	0	0	0	0		
6			2	0	0	0	3	1		
7			1	0	0	0	2	0		
8			0	0	0	2	0	0		
9			2	3	3	1	4	2		
0			0	0	0	2	2	5		

Explanatory notes: see p. 1125.

[1] Incl. cases of dental injury; also from 1997, cases with acute hearing loss/psychological reaction, but without absence.

Notes explicatives: voir p. 1127.

[1] Y.c. cas de lésion dentaire; et dès 1997, cas avec perte d'ouïe/ réaction psychologique aigües mais sans absence.

Notas explicativas: véase p. 1129.

[1] Incl. a los casos de lesión dental; y desde 1997 los con perdida de oído/reacción psicológicas agudas pero sin ausencia.

OCCUPATIONAL INJURIES

Cases of injury with lost workdays, by economic activity

LÉSIONS PROFESSIONNELLES

Cas de lésion avec perte de journées de travail, par activité économique

LESIONES PROFESIONALES

Casos de lesión con pérdida de días de trabajo, por actividad económica

8A

	1999	2000	2001	2002	2003	2004	2005	2006	2007	2008

Turkey (FA) — Reported injuries - Lésions déclarées - Lesiones declaradas

Non-fatal cases (temporary + permanent incapacity) - Cas non mortels (incapacité temporaire + permanente) - Casos no mortales (incapacidad temporal + permanente)

Total men and women - Total hommes et femmes - Total hombres y mujeres
ISIC 2 - CITI 2 - CIIU 2

	1999	2000	2001	2002	2003	2004	2005	2006	2007	2008
Total	3 407	1 848	2 183	2 087	1 596	1 693	1 639	2 267	.	.
1	19	24	21	20	14	16	12	21	.	.
2	1 047	360	382	318	198	334	314	448	.	.
3	1 264	733	914	943	709	676	632	963	.	.
4	53	31	55	47	33	31	29	46	.	.
5	721	399	517	446	356	349	324	428	.	.
6	70	73	73	78	68	44	50	84	.	.
7	145	107	111	122	111	90	86	137	.	.
8	3	1	2	4	1	3	0	1	.	.
9	85	90	72	89	62	54	53	113	.	.
0	0	30	36	20	44	96	139	26	.	.

Men - Hommes - Hombres
ISIC 2 - CITI 2 - CIIU 2

	1999	2000	2001	2002	2003	2004	2005	2006	2007	2008
Total	.	.	2 118	2 021	1 547	1 644	1 592	2 210	.	.
1	.	.	19	17	13	15	11	20	.	.
2	.	.	382	318	198	334	314	448	.	.
3	.	.	870	901	684	638	612	928	.	.
4	.	.	55	46	33	31	29	46	.	.
5	.	.	516	445	355	348	324	427	.	.
6	.	.	67	72	60	41	45	77	.	.
7	.	.	108	118	107	90	81	131	.	.
8	.	.	2	3	1	3	0	1	.	.
9	.	.	63	81	55	51	48	107	.	.
0	.	.	36	20	41	93	128	25	.	.

Women - Femmes - Mujeres
ISIC 2 - CITI 2 - CIIU 2

	1999	2000	2001	2002	2003	2004	2005	2006	2007	2008
Total	.	.	65	66	49	49	47	57	.	.
1	.	.	2	3	1	1	1	1	.	.
2	.	.	0	0	0	0	0	0	.	.
3	.	.	44	42	25	38	20	35	.	.
4	.	.	0	1	0	0	0	0	.	.
5	.	.	1	1	1	1	0	1	.	.
6	.	.	6	6	8	3	5	7	.	.
7	.	.	3	4	4	0	5	6	.	.
8	.	.	0	1	0	0	0	0	.	.
9	.	.	9	8	7	3	5	6	.	.
0	.	.	0	0	3	3	11	1	.	.

Total cases (fatal + non-fatal) - Ensemble des cas (mortels + non mortels) - Todos los casos (mortales + no mortales)

Total men and women - Total hommes et femmes - Total hombres y mujeres
ISIC 2 - CITI 2 - CIIU 2

	1999	2000	2001	2002	2003	2004	2005	2006	2007	2008
Total	4 740	3 139	3 191	2 965	2 407	2 536	2 735	3 868	.	.
1	32	41	44	34	23	24	34	37	.	.
2	1 375	453	478	387	280	402	435	528	.	.
3	1 478	976	1 133	1 125	895	877	873	1 214	.	.
4	97	74	90	83	62	56	61	80	.	.
5	1 128	778	858	765	630	612	614	825	.	.
6	142	125	139	130	129	96	112	154	.	.
7	315	254	257	255	202	202	255	305	.	.
8	8	6	6	5	3	5	5	3	.	.
9	165	284	132	149	109	109	119	187	.	.
0	0	148	54	32	74	153	227	535	.	.

Men - Hommes - Hombres
ISIC 2 - CITI 2 - CIIU 2

	1999	2000	2001	2002	2003	2004	2005	2006	2007	2008
Total	.	.	3 109	2 885	2 343	2 476	2 673	3 797	.	.
1	.	.	42	30	22	23	33	36	.	.
2	.	.	478	387	279	402	435	528	.	.
3	.	.	1 077	1 073	859	833	849	1 173	.	.
4	.	.	90	82	62	56	61	80	.	.
5	.	.	857	764	629	611	614	824	.	.
6	.	.	131	124	121	93	104	146	.	.
7	.	.	253	251	198	202	248	299	.	.
8	.	.	6	4	3	3	5	3	.	.
9	.	.	121	138	99	105	110	179	.	.
0	.	.	54	32	71	148	214	529	.	.

Explanatory notes: see p. 1125.   Notes explicatives: voir p. 1127.   Notas explicativas: véase p. 1129.

OCCUPATIONAL INJURIES
Cases of injury with lost workdays, by economic activity

LÉSIONS PROFESSIONNELLES
Cas de lésion avec perte de journées de travail, par activité économique

LESIONES PROFESIONALES
Casos de lesión con pérdida de días de trabajo, por actividad económica

	1999	2000	2001	2002	2003	2004	2005	2006	2007	2008

Turkey (FA) — Reported injuries - Lésions déclarées - Lesiones declaradas

Total cases (fatal + non-fatal) - Ensemble des cas (mortels + non mortels) - Todos los casos (mortales + no mortales)

Women - Femmes - Mujeres
ISIC 2 - CITI 2 - CIIU 2

	1999	2000	2001	2002	2003	2004	2005	2006	2007	2008
Total	·	·	82	80	64	60	62	71	·	·
1			2	4	1	1	1	1		
2			0	0	1	1	1	1		
3			0	0	1	0	0	0		
4			56	52	36	44	24	41		
5			0	1	0	0	0	0		
6			1	1	1	1	0	1		
7			8	6	8	3	8	8		
8			4	4	4	0	7	6		
9			0	1	0	2	0	0		
0			11	11	10	4	9	8		
			0	0	3	5	13	6		

Ukraine (FF) — Reported injuries - Lésions déclarées - Lesiones declaradas

Fatal cases - Cas mortels - Casos mortales

Total men and women - Total hommes et femmes - Total hombres y mujeres [1]
ISIC 3 - CITI 3 - CIIU 3

	1999	2000	2001	2002	2003	2004	2005	2006	2007	2008
Total	1 321	1 239	1 325	1 227	1 128	1 068	989	972	1 069	927

Men - Hommes - Hombres [1]
ISIC 3 - CITI 3 - CIIU 3

	1999	2000	2001	2002	2003	2004	2005	2006	2007	2008
Total	1 227	·	1 242	1 136	1 065	996	907	898	982	860

Women - Femmes - Mujeres [1]
ISIC 3 - CITI 3 - CIIU 3

	1999	2000	2001	2002	2003	2004	2005	2006	2007	2008
Total	94	·	83	91	63	72	82	74	87	67

Non-fatal cases (temporary + permanent incapacity) - Cas non mortels (incapacité temporaire + permanente) - Casos no mortales (incapacidad temporal + permanente)

Total men and women - Total hommes et femmes - Total hombres y mujeres
ISIC 3 - CITI 3 - CIIU 3

	1999	2000	2001	2002	2003	2004	2005	2006	2007	2008
Total	41 987	33 049	32 616	26 581	24 563	22 208	20 186	18 769	17 709	15 564

Men - Hommes - Hombres
ISIC 3 - CITI 3 - CIIU 3

	1999	2000	2001	2002	2003	2004	2005	2006	2007	2008
Total	35 803	·	27 285	21 967	19 987	18 016	16 062	14 791	14 164	12 294

Women - Femmes - Mujeres
ISIC 3 - CITI 3 - CIIU 3

	1999	2000	2001	2002	2003	2004	2005	2006	2007	2008
Total	6 184	·	5 331	4 614	4 576	4 192	4 124	3 978	3 545	3 270

Total cases (fatal + non-fatal) - Ensemble des cas (mortels + non mortels) - Todos los casos (mortales + no mortales)

Total men and women - Total hommes et femmes - Total hombres y mujeres
ISIC 3 - CITI 3 - CIIU 3

	1999	2000	2001	2002	2003	2004	2005	2006	2007	2008
Total	43 308	34 288	33 941	27 808	25 691	23 276	21 175	19 741	18 778	16 491

Men - Hommes - Hombres
ISIC 3 - CITI 3 - CIIU 3

	1999	2000	2001	2002	2003	2004	2005	2006	2007	2008
Total	37 030	·	28 527	23 103	21 052	19 012	16 969	15 689	15 146	13 154

Women - Femmes - Mujeres
ISIC 3 - CITI 3 - CIIU 3

	1999	2000	2001	2002	2003	2004	2005	2006	2007	2008
Total	6 278	·	5 414	4 705	4 639	4 264	4 206	4 052	3 632	3 337

Explanatory notes: see p. 1125.
[1] Deaths occurring within 4 months of accident.

Notes explicatives: voir p. 1127.
[1] Décès survenant pendant les 4 mois qui suivent l'accident.

Notas explicativas: véase p. 1129.
[1] Fallecimientos que se produzcan durante los 4 meses posteriores al accidente.

OCCUPATIONAL INJURIES

Cases of injury with lost workdays, by economic activity

LÉSIONS PROFESSIONNELLES

Cas de lésion avec perte de journées de travail, par activité économique

LESIONES PROFESIONALES

Casos de lesión con pérdida de días de trabajo, por actividad económica

8A

	1999	2000	2001	2002	2003	2004	2005	2006	2007	2008

United Kingdom (FF) [1][2] Reported injuries - Lésions déclarées - Lesiones declaradas

Fatal cases - Cas mortels - Casos mortales

Total men and women - Total hommes et femmes - Total hombres y mujeres
ISIC 3 - CITI 3 - CIIU 3

	1999	2000	2001	2002	2003	2004	2005	2006	2007	2008
Total	173	219	210	191	174	179	173	203	.	.
A	13	13	20	14	6	16	13	15	.	.
B	0	0	0	2	0	0	0	1	.	.
C	4	9	9	3	7	2	5	9	.	.
D	45	47	48	43	27	45	43	39	.	.
E	2	0	5	2	3	0	1	1	.	.
F	65	75	62	60	55	58	46	59	.	.
G	6	13	12	14	14	8	12	6	.	.
H	1	4	1	1	5	2	2	4	.	.
I	19	34	23	27	32	20	21	33	.	.
J	0	1	0	2	0	0	1	0	.	.
K	7	6	11	8	8	6	16	8	.	.
L	2	3	4	5	5	9	2	6	.	.
M	0	2	2	0	1	1	1	3	.	.
N	0	2	2	0	4	0	2	3	.	.
O	.	.	.	10	7	12	8	17	.	.
O-Q	9	10	11	.	.	.	.	17	.	.
P	.	.	.	0	0	0	0	0	.	.
Q	.	.	.	0	0	0	0	0	.	.

Men - Hommes - Hombres
ISIC 3 - CITI 3 - CIIU 3

	1999	2000	2001	2002	2003	2004	2005	2006	2007	2008
Total	172	213	206	184	167	172	166	198	.	.
A	13	12	19	13	6	16	13	14	.	.
B	0	0	0	2	0	0	0	1	.	.
C	4	9	9	3	7	2	5	9	.	.
D	44	44	48	41	27	40	43	39	.	.
E	2	0	5	2	3	0	1	1	.	.
F	65	75	62	60	55	58	46	58	.	.
G	6	12	12	14	14	7	11	6	.	.
H	1	4	1	0	3	2	1	3	.	.
I	19	34	22	27	32	20	20	33	.	.
J	0	1	0	0	0	0	1	0	.	.
K	7	6	11	8	8	5	16	8	.	.
L	2	2	4	5	5	9	1	5	.	.
M	0	2	1	0	0	1	0	3	.	.
N	0	2	1	0	2	0	1	1	.	.
O	.	.	.	9	5	12	7	17	.	.
O-Q	9	10	11	.	.	.	.	17	.	.
P	.	.	.	0	0	0	0	0	.	.
Q	.	.	.	0	0	0	0	0	.	.

Women - Femmes - Mujeres
ISIC 3 - CITI 3 - CIIU 3

	1999	2000	2001	2002	2003	2004	2005	2006	2007	2008
Total	1	6	4	7	7	7	7	5	.	.
A	0	1	1	1	0	0	0	1	.	.
B	0	0	0	0	0	0	0	0	.	.
C	0	0	0	0	0	0	0	0	.	.
D	1	3	0	2	0	5	0	0	.	.
E	0	0	0	0	0	0	0	0	.	.
F	0	0	0	0	0	0	0	0	.	.
G	0	1	0	0	0	1	1	0	.	.
H	0	0	0	1	2	0	1	1	.	.
I	0	0	1	0	0	0	1	0	.	.
J	0	0	0	2	0	0	0	0	.	.
K	0	0	0	0	0	1	0	0	.	.
L	0	1	0	0	0	0	1	1	.	.
M	0	0	1	0	1	0	1	0	.	.
N	0	0	1	0	2	0	1	2	.	.
O	.	.	.	1	2	0	1	0	.	.
O-Q	0	0	0	.	.	.	.	0	.	.
P	.	.	.	0	0	0	0	0	.	.
Q	.	.	.	0	0	0	0	0	.	.

Explanatory notes: see p. 1125.

[1] Total may differ from the sum of data by sex due to difficulties in coding certain cases. [2] Year beginning in April of year indicated; prior to 1994: excl. Northern Ireland.

Notes explicatives: voir p. 1127.

[1] Le total peut différer de la somme des données par sexe en raison de difficultés de codification de quelques cas. [2] Année commençant en avril de l'année indiquée; avant 1994: non compris l'Irlande du Nord.

Notas explicativas: véase p. 1129.

[1] El total puede diferir de la suma de los datos por sexo debido a dificultades de codificación de algunos casos. [2] Año que comienza en abril del año indicado; antes de 1994: excl. Irlanda del Norte.

OCCUPATIONAL INJURIES
Cases of injury with lost workdays, by economic activity

LÉSIONS PROFESSIONNELLES
Cas de lésion avec perte de journées de travail, par activité économique

LESIONES PROFESIONALES
Casos de lesión con pérdida de días de trabajo, por actividad económica

United Kingdom (FF) [1] [2] — Reported injuries - Lésions déclarées - Lesiones declaradas

Non-fatal cases (temporary + permanent incapacity) - Cas non mortels (incapacité temporaire + permanente) - Casos no mortales (incapacidad temporal + permanente)

Total men and women - Total hommes et femmes - Total hombres y mujeres [3]
ISIC 3 - CITI 3 - CIIU 3

	1999	2000	2001	2002	2003	2004	2005	2006	2007	2008
Total	167 789	165 289	161 466	159 608	164 767	155 020	150 911	145 857	.	.
A	2 086	1 978	2 163	1 871	1 465	1 401	1 344	1 277	.	.
B	39	38	37	25	35	43	26	31	.	.
C	1 687	1 792	1 703	1 365	1 154	957	810	817	.	.
D	48 479	46 685	43 189	40 782	37 204	33 222	30 353	27 741	.	.
E	1 294	1 108	1 041	987	1 099	1 033	943	963	.	.
F	14 775	13 837	13 320	13 145	12 417	11 514	11 500	11 132	.	.
G	18 817	18 214	17 793	18 983	19 810	19 305	18 748	17 841	.	.
H	4 327	4 130	4 150	4 366	5 085	5 248	5 261	5 178	.	.
I	23 831	25 914	25 859	26 804	28 037	26 264	25 681	24 202	.	.
J	735	726	1 060	1 133	1 221	1 221	993	1 006	.	.
K	5 083	4 554	6 608	6 934	10 689	9 917	9 732	9 548	.	.
L	18 045	18 243	17 640	17 137	22 479	20 778	20 922	20 548	.	.
M	6 459	6 319	6 036	5 827	4 001	3 846	3 942	4 347	.	.
N	16 174	15 709	15 271	14 910	15 950	15 978	16 580	16 989	.	.
O	.	.	.	5 267	4 095	4 185	4 055	4 205	.	.
O-Q	5 958	6 042	5 596	.	.	.	.	4 237	.	.
P	.	.	.	60	23	102	20	25	.	.
Q	.	.	.	12	3	6	1	7	.	.
X	0	0	0	0	0	0	0	0	.	.

Men - Hommes - Hombres [3]
ISIC 3 - CITI 3 - CIIU 3

	1999	2000	2001	2002	2003	2004	2005	2006	2007	2008
Total	124 938	123 184	120 407	118 496	120 020	111 887	107 535	102 899	.	.
A	1 729	1 624	1 793	1 551	1 225	1 193	1 132	1 106	.	.
B	38	33	34	24	32	41	25	27	.	.
C	1 673	1 774	1 665	1 349	1 131	940	797	800	.	.
D	41 725	40 407	37 385	35 314	32 156	28 942	26 483	24 336	.	.
E	1 237	1 055	969	927	1 042	972	896	890	.	.
F	14 439	13 542	12 952	12 823	12 201	11 281	11 266	10 918	.	.
G	11 800	11 429	11 225	11 878	12 264	12 163	11 626	10 928	.	.
H	2 079	1 983	2 072	2 269	2 504	2 551	2 594	2 592	.	.
I	21 286	23 048	22 959	23 879	24 948	23 246	22 651	21 500	.	.
J	225	208	370	336	374	389	277	294	.	.
K	3 551	3 181	4 787	5 050	8 095	7 575	7 338	7 137	.	.
L	13 621	13 722	13 242	12 780	14 940	13 516	13 406	12 970	.	.
M	2 305	2 212	2 187	2 028	1 575	1 508	1 440	1 616	.	.
N	4 904	4 567	4 540	4 399	4 430	4 468	2 990	4 754	.	.
O	.	.	.	3 839	3 053	3 042	2 990	3 007	.	.
O-Q	4 326	4 399	4 227	.	.	.	.	3 031	.	.
P	.	.	.	46	18	56	17	17	.	.
Q	.	.	.	4	2	4	1	7	.	.

Women - Femmes - Mujeres [3]
ISIC 3 - CITI 3 - CIIU 3

	1999	2000	2001	2002	2003	2004	2005	2006	2007	2008
Total	42 809	42 037	41 047	41 100	44 734	41 300	43 361	42 562	.	.
A	357	354	370	320	210	208	212	171	.	.
B	1	5	3	1	3	2	1	4	.	.
C	14	18	38	16	23	17	13	17	.	.
D	6 753	6 278	5 801	5 468	5 048	4 280	3 868	3 404	.	.
E	57	53	72	60	57	61	47	73	.	.
F	335	295	368	322	216	233	234	50	.	.
G	6 996	6 745	6 568	7 105	7 546	7 142	7 122	6 714	.	.
H	2 243	2 139	2 078	2 097	2 581	2 697	2 667	2 586	.	.
I	2 531	2 852	2 891	2 914	3 076	2 985	3 017	2 674	.	.
J	510	518	690	797	847	832	716	712	.	.
K	1 532	1 370	1 821	1 883	2 594	2 342	2 394	2 410	.	.
L	4 424	4 521	4 398	4 357	7 539	7 262	7 516	7 578	.	.
M	4 154	4 107	3 849	3 799	2 426	2 338	2 502	2 729	.	.
N	11 270	11 140	10 731	10 511	11 520	11 510	11 984	12 234	.	.
O	.	.	.	1 428	1 042	1 143	1 065	1 198	.	.
O-Q	1 632	1 642	1 369	.	.	.	.	1 206	.	.
P	.	.	.	14	5	46	3	8	.	.
Q	.	.	.	8	1	2	0	0	.	.

Explanatory notes: see p. 1125.

[1] Total may differ from the sum of data by sex due to difficulties in coding certain cases. [2] Year beginning in April of year indicated; prior to 1994: excl. Northern Ireland. [3] Incapacity of 4 workdays or more.

Notes explicatives: voir p. 1127.

[1] Le total peut différer de la somme des données par sexe en raison de difficultés de codification de quelques cas. [2] Année commençant en avril de l'année indiquée; avant 1994: non compris l'Irlande du Nord. [3] Incapacité de 4 journées de travail et plus.

Notas explicativas: véase p. 1129.

[1] El total puede diferir de la suma de los datos por sexo debido a dificultades de codificación de algunos casos. [2] Año que comienza en abril del año indicado; antes de 1994: excl. Irlanda del Norte. [3] Incapacidad de 4 días de trabajo y más.

OCCUPATIONAL INJURIES

Cases of injury with lost workdays, by economic activity

LÉSIONS PROFESSIONNELLES

Cas de lésion avec perte de journées de travail, par activité économique

LESIONES PROFESIONALES

Casos de lesión con pérdida de días de trabajo, por actividad económica

United Kingdom (FF) [1][2] — Reported injuries - Lésions déclarées - Lesiones declaradas

Total cases (fatal + non-fatal) - Ensemble des cas (mortels + non mortels) - Todos los casos (mortales + no mortales)

Total men and women - Total hommes et femmes - Total hombres y mujeres

ISIC 3 - CITI 3 - CIIU 3

	1999	2000	2001	2002	2003	2004	2005	2006	2007	2008
Total	167 962	165 508	161 676	159 799	164 941	155 199	151 084	146 060	.	.
A	2 099	1 991	2 183	1 885	1 471	1 417	1 357	1 292		
B	39	38	37	27	35	43	26	32		
C	1 691	1 801	1 712	1 368	1 161	959	815	826		
D	48 524	46 732	43 237	40 825	37 231	33 267	30 396	27 780		
E	1 296	1 108	1 046	989	1 102	1 033	944	964		
F	14 840	13 912	13 382	13 205	12 472	11 572	11 546	11 190		
G	18 823	18 227	17 805	18 997	19 824	19 313	18 760	17 847		
H	4 328	4 134	4 151	4 367	5 090	5 250	5 263	5 182		
I	23 850	25 948	25 882	26 831	28 069	26 284	25 702	24 235		
J	735	727	1 060	1 135	1 221	1 221	994	1 006		
K	5 090	4 560	6 619	6 942	10 697	9 923	9 748	9 556		
L	18 047	18 246	17 644	17 142	22 484	20 787	20 924	20 554		
M	6 459	6 321	6 038	5 827	4 002	3 847	3 943	4 350		
N	16 174	15 711	15 273	14 910	15 954	15 978	16 582	16 992		
O				5 277	4 102	4 197	4 063	4 222		
O-Q	5 967	6 052	5 607					4 254		
P				60	23	102	20	25		
Q				12	3	6	1	7		
X	0	0	0	0	0	0	0	0		

Men - Hommes - Hombres

ISIC 3 - CITI 3 - CIIU 3

	1999	2000	2001	2002	2003	2004	2005	2006	2007	2008
Total	125 110	123 397	120 613	118 680	120 187	112 059	107 701	103 097	.	.
A	1 742	1 636	1 812	1 564	1 231	1 209	1 145	1 120		
B	38	33	34	26	32	41	25	28		
C	1 677	1 783	1 674	1 352	1 138	942	802	809		
D	41 769	40 451	37 433	35 355	32 183	28 982	26 526	24 375		
E	1 239	1 055	974	929	1 045	972	897	891		
F	14 504	13 617	13 014	12 883	12 256	11 339	11 312	10 976		
G	11 806	11 441	11 237	11 892	12 278	12 170	11 637	10 934		
H	2 080	1 987	2 073	2 269	2 507	2 553	2 595	2 595		
I	21 305	23 082	22 981	23 906	24 980	23 266	22 671	21 533		
J	225	209	370	336	374	389	278	294		
K	3 558	3 187	4 798	5 058	8 103	7 580	7 354	7 145		
L	13 623	13 724	13 246	12 785	14 945	13 525	13 407	12 975		
M	2 305	2 214	2 188	2 028	1 575	1 509	1 440	1 619		
N	4 904	4 569	4 541	4 399	4 432	4 468	2 991	4 755		
O				3 848	3 058	3 054	2 997	3 024		
O-Q	4 335	4 409	4 238					3 048		
P				46	18	56	17	17		
Q				4	2	4	1	7		

Women - Femmes - Mujeres

ISIC 3 - CITI 3 - CIIU 3

	1999	2000	2001	2002	2003	2004	2005	2006	2007	2008
Total	42 810	42 043	41 051	41 107	44 741	41 307	43 368	42 567	.	.
A	357	355	371	321	210	208	212	172		
B	1	5	3	1	3	2	1	4		
C	14	18	38	16	23	17	13	17		
D	6 754	6 281	5 801	5 470	5 048	4 285	3 868	3 404		
E	57	53	72	60	57	61	47	73		
F	335	295	368	322	216	233	234	214		
G	6 996	6 746	6 568	7 105	7 546	7 143	7 123	6 714		
H	2 243	2 139	2 078	2 098	2 583	2 697	2 668	2 586		
I	2 531	2 852	2 892	2 914	3 076	2 985	3 018	2 674		
J	510	518	690	799	847	832	716	712		
K	1 532	1 370	1 821	1 883	2 594	2 343	2 394	2 410		
L	4 424	4 522	4 398	4 357	7 539	7 262	7 517	7 579		
M	4 154	4 107	3 850	3 799	2 427	2 338	2 503	2 729		
N	11 270	11 140	10 732	10 511	11 522	11 510	11 985	12 236		
O				1 429	1 044	1 143	1 066	1 198		
O-Q	1 632	1 642	1 369					1 206		
P				14	5	46	3	8		
Q				8	1	2	0	0		

Explanatory notes: see p. 1125.

[1] Total may differ from the sum of data by sex due to difficulties in coding certain cases. [2] Year beginning in April of year indicated; prior to 1994: excl. Northern Ireland. [3] Financial year ending in year indicated; excl. Victoria and Australian Capital Territory.

Notes explicatives: voir p. 1127.

[1] Le total peut différer de la somme des données par sexe en raison de difficultés de codification de quelques cas. [2] Année commençant en avril de l'année indiquée; avant 1994: non compris l'Irlande du Nord. [3] Année fiscale se terminant en l'année indiquée; non compris Victoria et Australian Capital Territory.

Notas explicativas: véase p. 1129.

[1] El total puede diferir de la suma de los datos por sexo debido a dificultades de codificación de algunos casos. [2] Año que comienza en abril del año indicado; antes de 1994: excl. Irlanda del Norte. [3] Año fiscal que se termina en el año indicado; excl. Victoria y Australian Capital Territory.

OCCUPATIONAL INJURIES

Cases of injury with lost workdays, by economic activity

LÉSIONS PROFESSIONNELLES

Cas de lésion avec perte de journées de travail, par activité économique

LESIONES PROFESIONALES

Casos de lesión con pérdida de días de trabajo, por actividad económica

OCEANIA-OCÉANIE-OCEANIA

Australia (FA) [1] [2]

Fatal cases - Cas mortels - Casos mortales

Compensated injuries - Lésions indemnisées - Lesiones indemnizadas

Total men and women - Total hommes et femmes - Total hombres y mujeres
ISIC 3 - CITI 3 - CIIU 3

	1999	2000	2001	2002	2003	2004	2005	2006	2007	2008
Total	212	216	213	200	193	177	179	190	187	.
A-B	12	13	26	9	13	6	5	15	6	.
C	12	13	16	9	12	6	4	12	6	.
D	18	28	35	26	25	25	20	27	29	.
E	2	3	2	2	1	2	2	5	0	.
F	36	35	35	26	25	25	20	27	29	.
G	25	18	18	18	18	22	16	12	17	.
H	5	3	2	2	2	1	3	4	3	.
I	47	43	45	53	54	39	46	42	47	.
J	2	1	3	1	1	1	0	0	0	.
K	17	14	14	15	13	13	13	24	11	.
L	4	6	5	3	12	8	8	5	12	.
M	3	7	4	4	3	2	2	4	2	.
M-N	.	.	.	.	.	.	.	.	.	.
N-O	15	17	21	26	13	13	16	12	15	.
X	5	0	0	1	0	0	1	0	0	.

Men - Hommes - Hombres
ISIC 3 - CITI 3 - CIIU 3

	1999	2000	2001	2002	2003	2004	2005	2006	2007	2008
Total	199	199	198	187	176	164	167	177	166	.
A-B	21	26	27	18	23	22	25	22	11	.
C	12	13	16	9	11	6	5	12	6	.
D	18	28	34	26	24	24	18	27	29	.
E	2	2	2	2	1	2	2	5	0	.
F	36	35	34	26	24	24	18	27	29	.
G	22	15	15	17	17	20	15	11	14	.
H	4	2	2	2	2	1	2	3	2	.
I	45	42	44	50	54	37	45	41	45	.
J	1	0	3	1	1	0	0	0	0	.
K	16	13	11	13	12	11	12	19	10	.
L	4	4	5	2	10	8	7	5	6	.
M	3	6	3	3	1	1	2	3	1	.
N-O	10	13	17	23	9	9	13	9	13	.
X	5	0	0	1	0	0	1	0	0	.

Women - Femmes - Mujeres
ISIC 3 - CITI 3 - CIIU 3

	1999	2000	2001	2002	2003	2004	2005	2006	2007	2008
Total	13	17	15	13	17	13	12	13	21	.
A-B	0	2	1	1	1	1	1	1	2	.
C	0	0	0	0	2	0	0	0	0	.
D	0	0	1	0	1	1	0	0	0	.
E	0	1	0	0	1	1	2	0	0	.
F	0	0	1	0	0	0	0	0	0	.
G	3	3	3	1	1	1	2	0	0	.
H	1	1	0	0	0	1	1	1	3	.
I	2	1	1	3	0	2	1	1	1	.
J	1	1	0	0	0	2	1	1	2	.
K	1	1	3	2	1	0	0	0	1	.
L	0	2	0	1	1	2	1	5	0	.
M	0	1	1	1	2	0	0	0	6	.
N-O	5	4	4	3	4	4	3	1	1	.
X	0	0	0	0	0	0	0	3	2	.

Explanatory notes: see p. 1125.

[1] Financial year ending in year indicated; excl. Victoria and Australian Capital Territory. [2] Total may differ from the sum of data by sex due to difficulties in coding certain cases.

Notes explicatives: voir p. 1127.

[1] Année fiscale se terminant en l'année indiquée; non compris Victoria et Australian Capital Territory. [2] Le total peut différer de la somme des données par sexe en raison de difficultés de codification de quelques cas.

Notas explicativas: véase p. 1129.

[1] Año fiscal que se termina en el año indicado; excl. Victoria y Australian Capital Territory. [2] El total puede diferir de la suma de los datos por sexo debido a dificultades de codificación de algunos casos.

1268

ILO YEARBOOK OF LABOUR STATISTICS 2009   *ANNUAIRE DES STATISTIQUES DU TRAVAIL DU BIT 2009*   *ANUARIO DE ESTADISTICAS DEL TRABAJO DEL OIT 2009*

OCCUPATIONAL INJURIES
Cases of injury with lost workdays, by economic activity

LÉSIONS PROFESSIONNELLES
Cas de lésion avec perte de journées de travail, par activité économique

LESIONES PROFESIONALES
Casos de lesión con pérdida de días de trabajo, por actividad económica

8A

	1999	2000	2001	2002	2003	2004	2005	2006	2007	2008

Australia (FA) [1] [2]   Compensated injuries - Lésions indemnisées - Lesiones indemnizadas

Non-fatal cases (temporary + permanent incapacity) - Cas non mortels (incapacité temporaire + permanente) - Casos no mortales (incapacidad temporal + permanente)

Total men and women - Total hommes et femmes - Total hombres y mujeres [3]
ISIC 3 - CITI 3 - CIIU 3

	1999	2000	2001	2002	2003	2004	2005	2006	2007	2008
Total	128 820	127 280	118 170	114 800	107 400	106 340	105 430	95 710	97 370	.
A-B	5 440	5 540	5 100	5 090	4 690	4 400	4 140	3 760	3 790	.
C	2 150	1 960	1 850	1 900	1 830	1 880	1 960	1 820	2 040	.
D	29 290	28 230	11 470	10 440	10 110	11 010	11 010	10 030	10 590	.
E	910	880	710	690	480	530	530	420	480	.
F	11 740	12 010	11 470	10 440	10 110	11 010	11 010	10 030	10 590	.
G	18 885	20 430	19 030	17 890	16 020	15 580	15 320	14 310	14 430	.
H	6 070	6 290	5 930	5 770	5 710	5 550	5 500	4 930	5 120	.
I	11 985	11 660	11 050	11 070	10 120	9 730	9 360	8 830	8 920	.
J	990	1 700	930	970	890	850	720	750	750	.
K	8 500	8 660	8 230	8 310	8 330	8 560	8 870	8 080	7 720	.
L	3 525	3 690	3 440	3 920	6 720	6 270	6 180	4 850	4 790	.
M	4 675	5 120	4 540	4 450	3 500	3 660	3 820	3 730	3 850	.
N-O	21 690	21 270	20 470	20 110	17 010	17 340	17 550	15 700	16 290	.
X	0	600	150	130	100	50	40	180	230	.

Men - Hommes - Hombres [3]
ISIC 3 - CITI 3 - CIIU 3

	1999	2000	2001	2002	2003	2004	2005	2006	2007	2008
Total	90 985	90 650	82 660	79 910	75 070	74 070	73 100	66 540	67 410	.
A-B	4 600	4 670	4 300	4 230	3 960	3 640	3 410	3 040	3 080	.
C	2 075	1 910	1 800	1 840	1 760	1 800	1 890	1 760	1 950	.
D	25 010	24 050	11 260	10 220	9 920	10 780	10 790	9 790	10 370	.
E	885	850	680	650	460	500	480	380	440	.
F	11 540	11 800	11 260	10 220	9 920	10 780	10 790	9 790	10 370	.
G	13 010	13 540	12 310	11 630	10 380	10 030	9 830	9 240	9 160	.
H	2 995	3 090	2 920	2 850	2 840	2 650	2 640	2 340	2 430	.
I	10 580	10 360	9 690	9 750	8 960	8 630	8 260	7 750	7 850	.
J	275	250	200	240	250	190	180	180	190	.
K	6 005	6 100	5 710	5 740	5 920	6 170	6 570	6 010	5 700	.
L	2 480	2 660	2 490	2 840	4 080	3 750	3 710	2 890	2 940	.
M	2 025	2 280	1 830	1 670	1 320	1 330	1 350	1 300	1 320	.
N-O	8 560	8 600	8 040	7 810	6 450	6 480	6 420	5 840	5 850	.
X	955	510	110	100	80	40	30	150	180	.

Women - Femmes - Mujeres [3]
ISIC 3 - CITI 3 - CIIU 3

	1999	2000	2001	2002	2003	2004	2005	2006	2007	2008
Total	35 835	36 630	35 510	34 890	32 330	32 280	32 330	29 170	29 950	.
A-B	840	880	810	860	730	760	730	720	710	.
C	70	40	50	60	70	80	70	60	90	.
D	4 285	4 190	220	220	190	230	220	230	230	.
E	30	30	30	40	30	40	50	30	30	.
F	200	210	220	220	190	230	220	230	230	.
G	5 875	6 880	6 720	6 270	5 650	5 550	5 490	5 070	5 270	.
H	3 075	3 210	3 010	2 920	2 870	2 900	2 860	2 590	2 680	.
I	1 405	1 310	1 360	1 320	1 160	1 100	1 100	1 080	1 080	.
J	705	680	730	730	640	660	540	570	560	.
K	2 495	2 560	2 530	2 570	2 410	2 390	2 300	2 060	2 010	.
L	945	1 040	950	1 090	2 630	2 520	2 480	1 960	1 850	.
M	2 650	2 830	2 720	2 790	2 180	2 330	2 470	2 430	2 530	.
N-O	13 130	12 680	12 430	12 300	10 560	10 850	11 130	9 850	10 440	.
X	135	0	40	40	30	10	10	40	50	.

Cases of temporary incapacity - Cas d'incapacité temporaire - Casos de incapacidad temporal

Total men and women - Total hommes et femmes - Total hombres y mujeres [3]
ISIC 3 - CITI 3 - CIIU 3

	1999	2000	2001	2002	2003	2004	2005	2006	2007	2008
Total	105 705	105 040	94 790	93 070	87 060	86 230	86 960	80 190	83 850	.
A-B	4 445	4 510	4 180	4 130	3 850	3 630	3 410	3 110	3 270	.
C	1 675	1 500	1 270	1 290	1 250	1 300	1 470	1 400	1 630	.
D	24 250	23 160	8 840	8 130	7 930	8 620	8 730	8 060	8 820	.
E	720	690	500	490	350	390	410	350	390	.
F	9 445	9 460	8 840	8 130	7 930	8 620	8 730	8 060	8 820	.
G	15 980	17 140	15 450	14 630	13 150	12 540	12 560	11 900	12 300	.
H	5 140	5 250	4 800	4 710	4 730	4 600	4 640	4 250	4 510	.
I	10 445	9 940	9 050	9 250	8 430	8 020	7 860	7 530	7 780	.
J	785	1 480	730	800	730	680	590	620	660	.
K	7 075	7 230	6 620	6 830	6 740	6 970	7 350	6 790	6 590	.
L	2 845	2 990	2 790	3 300	5 670	5 310	5 320	4 220	4 270	.
M	3 975	4 390	3 800	3 730	2 900	3 090	3 300	3 260	3 420	.
N-O	17 970	17 560	16 810	16 820	14 190	14 710	15 150	13 680	14 620	.
X	965	480	60	80	70	40	20	140	160	.

Explanatory notes: see p. 1125.

[1] Financial year ending in year indicated; excl. Victoria and Australian Capital Territory. [2] Total may differ from the sum of data by sex due to difficulties in coding certain cases. [3] Incapacity of 6 workdays or more.

Notes explicatives: voir p. 1127.

[1] Année fiscale se terminant en l'année indiquée; non compris Victoria et Australian Capital Territory. [2] Le total peut différer de la somme des données par sexe en raison de difficultés de codification de quelques cas. [3] Incapacité de 6 journées de travail et plus.

Notas explicativas: véase p. 1129.

[1] Año fiscal que se termina en el año indicado; excl. Victoria y Australian Capital Territory. [2] El total puede diferir de la suma de los datos por sexo debido a dificultades de codificación de algunos casos. [3] Incapacidad de 6 días de trabajo y más.

8A

OCCUPATIONAL INJURIES	LÉSIONS PROFESSIONNELLES	LESIONES PROFESIONALES
Cases of injury with lost workdays, by economic activity	Cas de lésion avec perte de journées de travail, par activité économique	Casos de lesión con pérdida de días de trabajo, por actividad económica

	1999	2000	2001	2002	2003	2004	2005	2006	2007	2008

Australia (FA) [1] [2]　　　　Compensated injuries - Lésions indemnisées - Lesiones indemnizadas

Cases of temporary incapacity - Cas d'incapacité temporaire - Casos de incapacidad temporal

Men - Hommes - Hombres [3]
ISIC 3 - CITI 3 - CIIU 3

	1999	2000	2001	2002	2003	2004	2005	2006	2007	2008
Total	76 385	75 150	66 110	64 560	60 660	59 650	59 780	55 420	57 550	.
A-B	3 795	3 820	3 530	3 430	3 270	3 000	2 800	2 500	2 660	.
C	1 630	1 470	1 240	1 250	1 210	1 250	1 430	1 360	1 560	.
D	20 835	19 900	8 680	7 970	7 800	8 440	8 560	7 880	8 630	.
E	700	660	480	460	330	350	370	320	360	.
F	9 300	9 310	8 680	7 970	7 800	8 440	8 560	7 880	8 630	.
G	11 100	11 360	9 970	9 500	8 460	8 070	8 020	7 720	7 820	.
H	2 605	2 640	2 430	2 370	2 410	2 260	2 250	2 040	2 160	.
I	9 210	8 820	7 920	8 110	7 430	7 060	6 890	6 580	6 820	.
J	215	200	160	200	200	140	130	150	160	.
K	5 140	5 190	4 650	4 830	4 880	5 110	5 510	5 120	4 890	.
L	2 015	2 110	1 980	2 350	3 400	3 130	3 140	2 500	2 590	.
M	1 760	2 000	1 500	1 390	1 090	1 120	1 130	1 100	1 150	.
N-O	7 240	7 270	6 650	6 600	5 430	5 500	5 590	5 120	5 250	.
X	845	410	50	50	50	30	20	120	130	.

Women - Femmes - Mujeres [3]
ISIC 3 - CITI 3 - CIIU 3

	1999	2000	2001	2002	2003	2004	2005	2006	2007	2008
Total	29 325	29 890	28 680	28 510	26 390	26 580	27 180	24 770	26 300	.
A-B	650	690	650	700	580	630	600	600	620	.
C	45	30	40	50	40	50	50	40	70	.
D	3 415	3 260	160	160	130	180	170	180	180	.
E	20	20	20	30	20	30	40	30	30	.
F	150	160	160	160	130	180	170	180	180	.
G	4 880	5 770	5 490	5 130	4 690	4 470	4 530	4 180	4 480	.
H	2 535	2 610	2 370	2 340	2 320	2 340	2 380	2 210	2 350	.
I	1 230	1 120	1 130	1 140	1 000	960	970	950	960	.
J	570	550	580	610	530	540	460	480	500	.
K	1 935	2 040	1 970	1 990	1 870	1 860	1 840	1 670	1 700	.
L	830	880	810	940	2 260	2 180	2 180	1 720	1 680	.
M	2 215	2 390	2 300	2 340	1 820	1 980	2 160	2 140	2 280	.
N-O	10 730	10 300	10 150	10 220	8 760	9 210	9 560	8 550	9 370	.
X	120	0	10	30	20	10	0	20	30	.

Total cases (fatal + non-fatal) - Ensemble des cas (mortels + non mortels) - Todos los casos (mortales + no mortales)

Total men and women - Total hommes et femmes - Total hombres y mujeres
ISIC 3 - CITI 3 - CIIU 3

	1999	2000	2001	2002	2003	2004	2005	2006	2007	2008
Total	129 032	127 496	118 380	115 000	107 590	106 520	105 610	95 900	97 550	.
A-B	5 460	5 568	5 130	5 110	4 710	4 430	4 160	3 780	3 810	.
C	2 160	1 973	1 870	1 910	1 840	1 880	1 970	1 830	2 040	.
D	29 310	28 258	11 510	10 460	10 130	11 040	11 030	10 050	10 620	.
E	915	883	710	690	480	540	530	420	480	.
F	11 775	12 045	11 510	10 460	10 130	11 040	11 030	10 050	10 620	.
G	19 025	20 448	19 050	17 910	16 040	15 600	15 340	14 320	14 450	.
H	6 075	6 293	5 930	5 770	5 710	5 550	5 510	4 930	5 120	.
I	12 035	11 703	11 090	11 120	10 180	9 770	9 410	8 870	8 970	.
J	990	1 701	930	980	890	850	720	750	750	.
K	8 515	8 674	8 250	8 320	8 340	8 580	8 890	8 100	7 730	.
L	3 530	3 696	3 440	3 930	6 730	6 270	6 190	4 850	4 800	.
M	4 680	5 127	4 550	4 460	3 500	3 670	3 830	3 740	3 850	.
N-O	21 705	21 287	20 490	20 140	17 020	17 350	17 560	15 710	16 310	.
X	1 095	600	150	130	100	50	40	180	230	.

Men - Hommes - Hombres
ISIC 3 - CITI 3 - CIIU 3

	1999	2000	2001	2002	2003	2004	2005	2006	2007	2008
Total	91 185	90 849	82 860	80 090	75 250	74 230	73 270	66 720	67 580	.
A-B	4 620	4 696	4 320	4 250	4 990	3 660	3 440	3 060	3 090	.
C	2 085	1 923	1 820	1 850	1 770	1 810	1 900	1 770	1 960	.
D	25 030	24 078	11 290	10 240	9 940	10 800	10 810	9 820	10 400	.
E	885	852	680	660	460	500	490	390	440	.
F	11 575	11 835	11 290	10 240	9 940	10 800	10 810	9 820	10 400	.
G	13 030	13 555	12 320	11 640	10 390	10 050	9 850	9 250	9 170	.
H	3 000	3 092	2 920	2 850	2 840	2 650	2 640	2 340	2 440	.
I	10 625	10 402	9 730	9 800	9 010	8 670	8 300	7 790	7 890	.
J	275	250	200	240	250	190	180	180	190	.
K	6 020	6 113	5 720	5 750	5 930	6 190	6 580	6 030	5 710	.
L	2 485	2 664	2 500	2 840	4 090	3 750	3 710	2 890	2 950	.
M	2 030	2 286	1 830	1 670	1 320	1 340	1 350	1 300	1 320	.
N-O	8 570	8 613	8 060	7 830	6 450	6 490	6 430	5 850	5 870	.
X	960	510	110	100	80	40	30	150	180	.

Explanatory notes: see p. 1125.

[1] Financial year ending in year indicated; excl. Victoria and Australian Capital Territory. [2] Total may differ from the sum of data by sex due to difficulties in coding certain cases. [3] Incapacity of 6 workdays or more.

Notes explicatives: voir p. 1127.

[1] Année fiscale se terminant en l'année indiquée; non compris Victoria et Australian Capital Territory. [2] Le total peut différer de la somme des données par sexe en raison de difficultés de codification de quelques cas. [3] Incapacité de 6 journées de travail et plus.

Notas explicativas: véase p. 1129.

[1] Año fiscal que se termina en el año indicado; excl. Victoria y Australian Capital Territory. [2] El total puede diferir de la suma de los datos por sexo debido a dificultades de codificación de algunos casos. [3] Incapacidad de 6 días de trabajo y más.

OCCUPATIONAL INJURIES

Cases of injury with lost workdays, by economic activity

LÉSIONS PROFESSIONNELLES

Cas de lésion avec perte de journées de travail, par activité économique

LESIONES PROFESIONALES

Casos de lesión con pérdida de días de trabajo, por actividad económica

	1999	2000	2001	2002	2003	2004	2005	2006	2007	2008
Australia (FA) [1] [2]				**Compensated injuries - Lésions indemnisées - Lesiones indemnizadas**						

Total cases (fatal + non-fatal) - Ensemble des cas (mortels + non mortels) - Todos los casos (mortales + no mortales)

Women - Femmes - Mujeres
ISIC 3 - CITI 3 - CIIU 3

	1999	2000	2001	2002	2003	2004	2005	2006	2007	2008
Total	35 850	36 647	35 520	34 900	32 340	32 290	32 340	29 180	29 980	.
A-B	840	882	810	860	730	760	730	720	710	.
C	70	40	50	60	70	80	70	60	90	.
D	4 285	4 190	220	220	190	230	230	230	230	.
E	30	31	30	40	30	40	50	30	30	.
F	200	210	220	220	190	230	230	230	230	.
G	5 875	6 883	6 730	6 270	5 650	5 550	5 490	5 070	5 270	.
H	3 075	3 211	3 010	2 920	2 870	2 900	2 860	2 590	2 680	.
I	1 410	1 311	1 360	1 320	1 160	1 100	1 110	1 080	1 080	.
J	705	681	730	730	640	660	540	570	560	.
K	2 495	2 561	2 530	2 570	2 410	2 390	2 300	2 070	2 010	.
L	945	1 042	950	1 090	2 630	2 520	2 480	1 960	1 860	.
M	2 650	2 831	2 720	2 790	2 180	2 330	2 470	2 440	2 530	.
N-O	13 135	12 684	12 430	12 310	10 570	10 860	11 130	9 860	10 440	.
X	135	0	40	40	30	10	10	40	50	.

New Zealand (FA) [3] **Reported injuries - Lésions déclarées - Lesiones declaradas**

Fatal cases - Cas mortels - Casos mortales

Total men and women - Total hommes et femmes - Total hombres y mujeres
ISIC 3 - CITI 3 - CIIU 3

	1999	2000	2001	2002	2003	2004	2005	2006	2007	2008
Total	41 [4]	63	74	82	88	82	109	98	84	77
A	8 [4]	21	22	19	20	11	22	16	10	12
B	. [5]	. [5]	. [5]	. [5]	. [5]	0	4 [5]	0	0	0
C	. [5]	0	. [5]	. [5]	0	. [5]	. [5]	. [5]	0	0
D	. [5]	4	8	15	14	11	16	18	12	16
E	0 [4]	. [5]	0	. [5]	. [5]	. [5]	0	0	0 [5]	0
F	6 [4]	15	12	16	21	18	28	32	26	15
G	. [5]	. [5]	. [5]	. [5]	4	. [5]	5 [5]	6 [5]	0 [5]	0
H	. [5]	0	4	0	0	. [5]	0	0	0	0
I	7 [4]	6	9	8	13	14	16	4	4 [5]	7
J	0 [4]	0	0 [5]	0	0	. [5]	. [5]	. [5]	0	0
K	0 [4]	. [5]	. [5]	5	. [5]	. [5]	. [5]	4	4	0
L	. [5]	. [5]	.	. [5]	. [5]	4	. [5]	. [5]	6	0
M	0 [4]	0	0	0	0	. [5]	0	0	0 [5]	0
N	0 [4]	0		. [5]	. [5]	0	0	0 [5]	0	0
O	. [5]	. [5]	4	. [5]	. [5]	4 [5]	. [5]	.	0	0
P	0 [4]	0	0	0	0	0	0	0	0	0
Q	0 [4]	0	0	0	0	0	.	.	0	0
X	6 [4]	4	. [5]	5	5	6	9	7	14	14

Men - Hommes - Hombres
ISIC 3 - CITI 3 - CIIU 3

	1999	2000	2001	2002	2003	2004	2005	2006	2007	2008
Total	39 [4]	61	70	79	84	78	105	96	82	73
A	7 [4]	20	21	18	20	11	21	16	10	10
B	. [5]	. [5]	. [5]	. [5]	. [5]	0	4 [5]	0	0	0
C	. [5]	0	. [5]	. [5]	0	. [5]	. [5]	. [5]	0 [5]	0
D	. [5]	4	7	15	13	11	16	18	12	16
E	0 [4]	. [5]	0	. [5]	. [5]	. [5]	0	0	0 [5]	0
F	6 [4]	15	12	16	21	18	28	32	26	15
G	. [5]	. [5]	. [5]	. [5]	0	. [5]	5 [5]	5 [5]	0 [5]	0
H	. [5]	0	. [5]	0	0	. [5]	0	0	0	0
I	7 [4]	6	9	8	12	13	16	4 [5]	0 [5]	7
J	0 [4]	0	0	0 [5]	0	0 [5]	0 [5]	0 [5]	0	0
K	0 [4]	. [5]	. [5]	4	. [5]	. [5]	. [5]	4	4	0
L	. [5]	. [5]	. [5]	. [5]	. [5]	4	0 [5]	0 [5]	6	0
M	0 [4]	0	0	0	0	. [5]	0	0	0 [5]	0
N	0 [4]	0	.	. [5]	. [5]	0	0	0 [5]	0	0
O	. [5]	. [5]	4	. [5]	. [5]	. [5]	. [5]	.	0	0
P	0 [4]	0	0	0	0	0	0	0	0	0
Q	.	.	0	.	.	.	.	.	0	0
X	6 [4]	. [5]	. [5]	4	4	6	6	7	13	12

Explanatory notes: see p. 1125.

[1] Financial year ending in year indicated; excl. Victoria and Australian Capital Territory. [2] Total may differ from the sum of data by sex due to difficulties in coding certain cases. [3] Year beginning in July of year indicated. [4] Data may be incomplete. [5] Data included in totals only for reasons of confidentiality.

Notes explicatives: voir p. 1127.

[1] Année fiscale se terminant en l'année indiquée; non compris Victoria et Australian Capital Territory. [2] Le total peut différer de la somme des données par sexe en raison de difficultés de codification de quelques cas. [3] Année commençant en juillet de l'année indiquée. [4] Les données peuvent être incomplètes. [5] Données incluses uniquement dans le total pour des raisons de confidentialité.

Notas explicativas: véase p. 1129.

[1] Año fiscal que se termina en el año indicado; excl. Victoria y Australian Capital Territory. [2] El total puede diferir de la suma de los datos por sexo debido a dificultades de codificación de algunos casos. [3] Año que comienza en julio del año indicado. [4] Datos pueden ser incompletados. [5] Datos incluidos en el total solamente por razón de confidencialidad.

	OCCUPATIONAL INJURIES	LÉSIONS PROFESSIONNELLES	LESIONES PROFESIONALES
	Cases of injury with lost workdays, by economic activity	Cas de lésion avec perte de journées de travail, par activité économique	Casos de lesión con pérdida de días de trabajo, por actividad económica

	1999	2000	2001	2002	2003	2004	2005	2006	2007	2008

New Zealand (FA) [1] — Reported injuries - Lésions déclarées - Lesiones declaradas

Fatal cases - Cas mortels - Casos mortales

Women - Femmes - Mujeres
ISIC 3 - CITI 3 - CIIU 3

	1999	2000	2001	2002	2003	2004	2005	2006	2007	2008
Total	. [2]	. [2]	4	. [2]	4	4 [2]	4	0 [2]	0 [2]	4
A	. [2]	. [2]	. [2]	. [2]	0	0	. [2]	0	0	0
B	0 [3]	0	0	0	0	0	0	0	0	0
C	. [3]	0	0	0	0	0	0	0	0	0
D	. [2]	0	0	. [2]	0	. [2]	0	0	0	0
E	.	0	0	0	0	0	0	0	0	0
F	0 [3]	0	0	0	0	0	0	0	0	0
G	0 [3]	0	0	0	. [2]	0	0	0	0	0
H	0 [3]	0	. [2]	0	0	. [2]	0	0	0	0
I	0 [3]	0	0	0	. [2]	. [2]	0	0	0 [2]	0
J	0 [3]	0	0	0	0	0	0	0	0	0
K	0 [3]	0	0	. [2]	0	0	0	0	0	0
L	0 [3]	0		0	0	0	0	0	0	0
M	0 [3]	0	0	0	0	0	0	0	0	0
N	0 [3]	0	0	0	0	0	0	0	0	0
O	0 [3]	0	0	0	0	0	. [2]	0	0	0
P	. [3]	0	0	0	0	0	0	0	0	0
Q	0 [3]	0	0	0	0	0		0	0	0
X	0 [3]	. [2]	. [2]	. [2]	. [2]	0	. [2]	0 [2]	0 [2]	0

Non-fatal cases (temporary + permanent incapacity) - Cas non mortels (incapacité temporaire + permanente) - Casos no mortales (incapacidad temporal + permanente)

Total men and women - Total hommes et femmes - Total hombres y mujeres [4]
ISIC 3 - CITI 3 - CIIU 3

	1999	2000	2001	2002	2003	2004	2005	2006	2007	2008
Total	3 182 [3]	20 750	22 847	24 561	25 600	26 212	26 534	26 814	25 861	23 890
A	973 [3]	3 313	3 644	3 957	3 944	3 797	3 597	3 467	2 934	2 511
B	105 [3]	240	265	233	181	152	153	129	104	88
C	4 [3]	89	109	91	100	122	95	81	107	92
D	325 [3]	5 037	5 740	6 108	6 390	6 827	6 552	6 693	6 034	5 046
E	. [3]	94	93	93	70	76	85	89	60	49
F	848 [3]	2 882	2 855	3 121	3 501	3 764	4 037	4 045	3 929	3 346
G	204 [3]	2 177	2 263	2 410	2 707	2 515	2 694	2 722	2 535	4 239
H	72 [3]	705	788	849	852	848	827	840	772	666
I	228 [3]	1 744	1 829	1 919	2 039	2 016	2 272	2 207	2 150	1 725
J	17 [3]	53	37	48	43	51	58	65	87	72
K	145 [3]	1 019	1 087	1 231	1 318	1 364	1 508	1 760	1 609	1 245
L	18 [3]	443	588	580	482	558	477	520	522	395
M	13 [3]	353	415	427	368	386	432	406	372	300
N	45 [3]	1 216	1 397	1 566	1 537	1 454	1 588	1 545	1 454	1 260
O	145 [3]	775	811	975	946	1 021	948	984	956	734
P	. [2]	. [2]	4	. [2]	. [2]	. [2]	. [2]	0	0	0
Q	0 [3]	. [2]	. [2]	0	0	0	.	0	0	0
X	36 [3]	608	921	952	1 119	1 259	1 210	1 261	2 236	2 122

Men - Hommes - Hombres [4]
ISIC 3 - CITI 3 - CIIU 3

	1999	2000	2001	2002	2003	2004	2005	2006	2007	2008
Total	2 743 [3]	16 196	17 720	18 854	19 706	20 339	20 382	19 962	19 286	17 020
A	838 [3]	2 809	3 047	3 283	3 255	3 158	2 971	2 830	2 370	2 027
B	99 [3]	219	235	211	166	144	142	116	98	81
C	4 [3]	88	106	88	98	115	94	80	104	91
D	279 [3]	4 327	4 949	5 198	5 400	5 768	5 482	5 225	4 827	3 965
E	. [3]	88	88	87	65	71	82	82	59	47
F	840 [3]	2 837	2 819	3 068	3 449	3 692	3 952	3 881	3 805	3 218
G	166 [3]	1 579	1 635	1 741	1 944	1 850	1 938	1 931	1 756	2 265
H	37 [3]	295	324	350	372	356	374	334	302	292
I	206 [3]	1 555	1 619	1 664	1 752	1 725	1 884	1 790	1 696	1 360
J	4 [3]	10	12	18	19	19	29	27	36	33
K	106 [3]	708	772	907	926	988	1 094	1 283	1 186	908
L	15 [3]	343	472	457	346	412	332	368	373	284
M	5 [3]	141	146	126	137	129	156	134	105	108
N	7 [3]	158	195	217	231	210	256	214	205	190
O	105 [3]	568	598	693	676	739	677	720	673	528
P	. [2]	0	. [2]	0	. [2]	. [2]	0	0	0	0
Q	.		0		.		.		0	
X	28 [3]	471	701	746	867	962	919	947	1 691	1 623

Explanatory notes: see p. 1125.

[1] Year beginning in July of year indicated. [2] Data included in totals only for reasons of confidentiality. [3] Data may be incomplete. [4] Incapacity of 6 days or more.

Notes explicatives: voir p. 1127.

[1] Année commençant en juillet de l'année indiquée. [2] Données incluses uniquement dans le total pour des raisons de confidentialité. [3] Les données peuvent être incomplètes. [4] Incapacité de 6 jours et plus.

Notas explicativas: véase p. 1129.

[1] Año que comienza en julio del año indicado. [2] Datos incluidos en el total solamente por razón de confidencialidad. [3] Datos pueden ser incompletados. [4] Incapacidad de 6 días y más.

OCCUPATIONAL INJURIES

Cases of injury with lost workdays, by economic activity

LÉSIONS PROFESSIONNELLES

Cas de lésion avec perte de journées de travail, par activité économique

LESIONES PROFESIONALES

Casos de lesión con pérdida de días de trabajo, por actividad económica

8A

	1999	2000	2001	2002	2003	2004	2005	2006	2007	2008

New Zealand (FA) [1][2]   **Reported injuries - Lésions déclarées - Lesiones declaradas**

Non-fatal cases (temporary + permanent incapacity) - Cas non mortels (incapacité temporaire + permanente) - Casos no mortales (incapacidad temporal + permanente)

Women - Femmes - Mujeres [3]
ISIC 3 - CITI 3 - CIIU 3

	1999	2000	2001	2002	2003	2004	2005	2006	2007	2008
Total	439 [4]	4 554	5 127	5 707	5 894	5 873	6 152	6 852	6 575	6 870
A	135 [4]	504	597	674	689	639	626	637	564	484
B	6 [4]	21	30	22	15	8	11	13	6	7
C	. [4]	.	. [5]	. [5]	. [5]	7	0 [5]	0 [5]	0 [5]	0
D	46 [4]	710	791	910	990	1 059	1 070	1 468	1 207	1 081
E	. [4]	6	5	6	5	5	. [5]	7	0	0
F	8 [4]	45	36	53	52	72	85	164	124	128
G	38 [4]	598	628	669	763	665	756	791	779	1 974
H	35 [4]	410	464	499	480	492	453	506	470	374
I	22 [4]	189	210	255	287	291	388	417	454	365
J	13 [4]	43	25	30	24	32	29	38	51	39
K	39 [4]	311	315	324	392	376	414	477	423	337
L	. [4]	100	116	123	136	146	145	152	149	111
M	8 [4]	212	269	301	231	257	276	272	267	192
N	38 [4]	1 058	1 202	1 349	1 306	1 244	1 332	1 331	1 249	1 070
O	40 [4]	207	213	282	270	282	271	264	283	206
P	. [4]	. [5]	. [5]	. [5]	0	. [5]	. [5]	0	0	0
Q	0 [4]	. [5]	. [5]	0	0	0	.	.	0	0
X	8 [4]	137	220	206	252	297	291	314	545	499

Cases of temporary incapacity - Cas d'incapacité temporaire - Casos de incapacidad temporal

Total men and women - Total hommes et femmes - Total hombres y mujeres [3]
ISIC 3 - CITI 3 - CIIU 3

	1999	2000	2001	2002	2003	2004	2005	2006	2007	2008
Total	3 179 [4]	20 726	22 827	24 537	25 576	26 193	26 520	26 786	25 833	23 870
A	972 [4]	3 304	3 639	3 951	3 941	3 793	3 597	3 461	2 927	2 507
B	105 [4]	239	265	232	181	152	153	129	104	88
C	4 [4]	88	109	91	100	122	95	81	106	92
D	325 [4]	5 036	5 736	6 105	6 386	6 825	6 550	6 691	6 032	5 046
E	. [4]	94	93	92	70	76	85	88	60	49
F	847 [4]	2 878	2 851	3 117	3 500	3 760	4 032	4 041	3 923	3 343
G	203 [4]	2 176	2 263	2 408	2 705	2 513	2 692	2 721	2 534	4 233
H	72 [4]	705	787	848	852	848	827	840	772	665
I	228 [4]	1 741	1 827	1 917	2 034	2 015	2 271	2 204	2 147	1 720
J	17 [4]	53	37	48	43	51	58	65	87	72
K	145 [4]	1 018	1 087	1 230	1 317	1 363	1 506	1 758	1 606	1 245
L	18 [4]	443	587	580	482	558	477	518	522	395
M	13 [4]	353	415	427	368	385	432	405	371	299
N	45 [4]	1 216	1 397	1 566	1 537	1 454	1 588	1 544	1 454	1 260
O	145 [4]	774	809	973	943	1 018	947	980	955	734
P	. [5]	. [5]	4	. [5]	. [5]	. [5]	. [5]	0	0	0
Q	0 [4]	. [5]	. [5]	0	0	0	.	.	0	0
X	36 [4]	606	920	951	1 114	1 258	1 209	1 260	2 233	2 122

Men - Hommes - Hombres [3]
ISIC 3 - CITI 3 - CIIU 3

	1999	2000	2001	2002	2003	2004	2005	2006	2007	2008
Total	2 741 [4]	16 173	17 702	18 833	19 684	20 324	20 371	19 939	19 259	17 001
A	838 [4]	2 801	3 042	3 278	3 252	3 154	2 971	2 825	2 364	2 023
B	99 [4]	218	235	210	166	144	142	116	98	81
C	4 [4]	87	106	88	98	115	94	80	103	91
D	279 [4]	4 326	4 945	5 195	5 396	5 766	5 481	5 224	4 825	3 965
E	. [4]	88	88	86	65	71	82	81	59	47
F	839 [4]	2 833	2 815	3 064	3 448	3 688	3 947	3 877	3 799	3 215
G	165 [4]	1 578	1 635	1 739	1 942	1 848	1 936	1 930	1 755	2 260
H	37 [4]	295	324	350	372	356	374	334	302	291
I	206 [4]	1 552	1 617	1 662	1 747	1 724	1 883	1 787	1 693	1 355
J	4 [4]	10	12	18	19	19	29	27	36	33
K	106 [4]	707	772	906	925	987	1 093	1 281	1 183	908
L	15 [4]	343	471	457	346	412	332	367	373	284
M	5 [4]	141	146	126	137	129	156	134	104	107
N	7 [4]	158	195	217	231	210	256	213	205	190
O	105 [4]	567	597	692	674	739	676	717	672	528
P	. [4]	0	. [5]	0	. [5]	. [5]	0	0	0	0
Q	.	.	0	.	.	.	.	.	0	0
X	28 [4]	469	700	745	863	961	919	946	1 688	1 623

Explanatory notes: see p. 1125.

[1] Incl. cases of temporary incapacity with absence from work of more than one year. [2] Year beginning in July of year indicated. [3] Incapacity of 6 days or more. [4] Data may be incomplete. [5] Data included in totals only for reasons of confidentiality.

Notes explicatives: voir p. 1127.

[1] Y compris les cas d'incapacité temporaire avec abscence du travail de plus d'une année. [2] Année commençant en juillet de l'année indiquée. [3] Incapacité de 6 jours et plus. [4] Les données peuvent être incomplètes. [5] Données incluses uniquement dans le total pour des raisons de confidentialité.

Notas explicativas: véase p. 1129.

[1] Incl. los cases de incapacidad temporal con ausencia del trabajo de más de un año. [2] Año que comienza en julio del año indicado. [3] Incapacidad de 6 días y más. [4] Datos pueden ser incompletados. [5] Datos incluidos en el total solamente por razón de confidencialidad.

OCCUPATIONAL INJURIES / LÉSIONS PROFESSIONNELLES / LESIONES PROFESIONALES

Cases of injury with lost workdays, by economic activity

Cas de lésion avec perte de journées de travail, par activité économique

Casos de lesión con pérdida de días de trabajo, por actividad económica

New Zealand (FA) [1] — Reported injuries - Lésions déclarées - Lesiones declaradas

Cases of temporary incapacity - Cas d'incapacité temporaire - Casos de incapacidad temporal

Women - Femmes - Mujeres [2]
ISIC 3 - CITI 3 - CIIU 3

	1999	2000	2001	2002	2003	2004	2005	2006	2007	2008
Total	438[3]	4 553	5 125	5 704	5 892	5 869	6 149	6 847	6 574	6 869
A	134[3]	503	597	673	689	639	626	636	563	484
B	6[3]	21	30	22	15	8	11	13	6	7
C	.	.	.	.[4]	.	7	0[4]	0[4]	0[4]	0
D	46[3]	710	791	910	990	1 059	1 069	1 467	1 207	1 081
E	.	6	5	6	5	5	.[4]	7	0[4]	0
F	8[3]	45	36	53	52	72	85	164	124	128
G	38[3]	598	628	669	763	665	756	791	779	1 973
H	35[3]	410	463	498	480	492	453	506	470	374
I	22[3]	189	210	255	287	291	388	417	454	365
J	13[3]	43	25	30	24	32	29	38	51	39
K	39[3]	311	315	324	392	376	413	477	423	337
L	.	100	116	123	136	146	145	151	149	111
M	8[3]	212	269	301	231	256	276	271	267	192
N	38[3]	1 058	1 202	1 349	1 306	1 244	1 332	1 331	1 249	1 070
O	40[3]	207	212	281	269	279	271	263	283	206
P	.[3]		.[4]		.[4]		.[4]		0	0
Q	0[3]	.[4]	.[4]	0	0	0	.[4]	.	0	0
X	8[3]	137	220	206	251	297	290	314	545	499

Total cases (fatal + non-fatal) - Ensemble des cas (mortels + non mortels) - Todos los casos (mortales + no mortales)

Total men and women - Total hommes et femmes - Total hombres y mujeres [5]
ISIC 3 - CITI 3 - CIIU 3

	1999	2000	2001	2002	2003	2004	2005	2006	2007	2008
Total	3 223[3]	20 813	22 921	24 643	25 688	26 294	26 643	26 912	25 945	23 967
A	981[3]	3 334	3 666	3 976	3 964	3 808	3 619	3 483	2 944	2 523
B	107[3]	242[4]	267[4]	235[4]	183[4]	152	157[4]	129	104	89
C	6[3]	89	112[4]	92[4]	100	125[4]	98[4]	84	107	93
D	327[3]	5 041	5 748	6 123	6 404	6 838	6 568	6 711	6 046	5 062
E	.[3]	95	93	94[4]	72[4]	78[4]	85	90	62	50
F	854[3]	2 897	2 867	3 137	3 522	3 782	4 065	4 077	3 955	3 361
G	207[3]	2 180[4]	2 264[4]	2 413[4]	2 711	2 518[4]	2 699[4]	2 728	2 538	4 240
H	73[4]	705	792	849	852	850[4]	827	840	772	667
I	235[3]	1 750	1 838	1 927	2 052	2 030	2 288	2 211	2 154	1 732
J	17[3]	53	37	48[4]	43	52[4]	59[4]	67	87	72
K	145[3]	1 022[4]	1 090[4]	1 236	1 319[4]	1 366[4]	1 509[4]	1 764	1 613	1 247
L	21[3]	446[4]	591	582[4]	484[4]	562	480[4]	523	528	396
M	13[3]	353	415	427	368	387[4]	432	406	375	301
N	45[3]	1 216	1 398	1 568[4]	1 538[4]	1 454	1 588	1 545	1 454	1 262
O	146[3]	776[4]	815	978[4]	949[4]	1 025[4]	949[4]	986	956	736
P	.[4]	.[4]	4	.[4]	.[4]	.[4]		0	0	0
Q	0[3]	.[4]	.[4]	0	0	0	.		0	0
X	42[3]	612	923[4]	957	1 124	1 265	1 219	1 268	2 250	2 136

Men - Hommes - Hombres [5]
ISIC 3 - CITI 3 - CIIU 3

	1999	2000	2001	2002	2003	2004	2005	2006	2007	2008
Total	2 782[3]	16 257	17 790	18 933	19 790	20 417	20 487	20 058	19 368	17 093
A	845[3]	2 829	3 068	3 301	3 275	3 169	2 992	2 846	2 380	2 037
B	101[4]	221[4]	237[4]	213[4]	168[4]	144	146[4]	116	98	82
C	6[3]	88	109[4]	89[4]	98	118[4]	97[4]	83	104	92
D	280[4]	4 331	4 956	5 213	5 413	5 779	5 498	5 243	4 839	3 981
E	.[3]	89[4]	88	88[4]	67[4]	73[4]	82	83	61	48
F	846[3]	2 852	2 831	3 084	3 470	3 710	3 980	3 913	3 831	3 233
G	169[4]	1 582[4]	1 636[4]	1 744[4]	1 947	1 853[4]	1 943[4]	1 936	1 759	2 266
H	38[4]	295	327[4]	350	372	357[4]	374	334	302	293
I	213[3]	1 561	1 628	1 672	1 764	1 738	1 900	1 794	1 699	1 367
J	4[3]	10	12	18[4]	19	20[4]	30[4]	29	36	33
K	106[3]	711[4]	775[4]	911	927[4]	990[4]	1 095[4]	1 287	1 190	910
L	18[3]	346[4]	474[4]	459[4]	348[4]	416	335[4]	371	379	285
M	5[3]	141	146	126	137	130[4]	156	134	108	109
N	7[3]	158	196	219[4]	232[4]	210	256	214	205	192
O	106[4]	569[4]	602	696[4]	679[4]	741[4]	678[4]	721	673	530
P	.[4]	0	.[4]	0	.[4]	.[4]	0	0	0	0
Q	.[3]		0				.		0	0
X	34[3]	474[4]	703[4]	750	871	968	925	954	1 704	1 635

Explanatory notes: see p. 1125.

[1] Year beginning in July of year indicated. [2] Incapacity of 6 days or more. [3] Data may be incomplete. [4] Data included in totals only for reasons of confidentiality. [5] Incl. cases of temporary incapacity with absence from work of more than one year.

Notes explicatives: voir p. 1127.

[1] Année commençant en juillet de l'année indiquée. [2] Incapacité de 6 jours et plus. [3] Les données peuvent être incomplètes. [4] Données incluses uniquement dans le total pour des raisons de confidentialité. [5] Y compris les cas d'incapacité temporaire avec abscence du travail de plus d'une année.

Notas explicativas: véase p. 1129.

[1] Año que comienza en julio del año indicado. [2] Incapacidad de 6 días y más. [3] Datos pueden ser incompletados. [4] Datos incluidos en el total solamente por razón de confidencialidad. [5] Incl. los cases de incapacidad temporal con ausencia del trabajo de más de un año.

OCCUPATIONAL INJURIES

Cases of injury with lost workdays, by economic activity

LÉSIONS PROFESSIONNELLES

Cas de lésion avec perte de journées de travail, par activité économique

LESIONES PROFESIONALES

Casos de lesión con pérdida de días de trabajo, por actividad económica

8A

	1999	2000	2001	2002	2003	2004	2005	2006	2007	2008
New Zealand (FA) [1]				Reported injuries - Lésions déclarées - Lesiones declaradas						

Total cases (fatal + non-fatal) - Ensemble des cas (mortels + non mortels) - Todos los casos (mortales + no mortales)

Women - Femmes - Mujeres [2]
ISIC 3 - CITI 3 - CIIU 3

	1999	2000	2001	2002	2003	2004	2005	2006	2007	2008
Total	441 [3]	4 556 [3]	5 131	5 710 [3]	5 898	5 877 [3]	6 156	6 854	6 577	6 874
A	136 [3]	505 [3]	598 [3]	675 [3]	689	639	627 [3]	637	564	486
B	6 [4]	21	30	22	15	8	11	13	6	7
C	. [4]	.	. [3]	. [3]	. [3]	7	. [3]	0 [3]	0 [3]	0
D	47 [4]	710	792 [3]	910	991 [3]	1 059	1 070	1 468	1 207	1 081
E	. [4]	6	5	6	5	5	. [3]	7	0 [3]	0
F	8 [4]	45	36	53	52	72	85	164	124	128
G	38 [4]	598	628	669	764 [3]	665	756	792	779	1 974
H	35 [4]	410	465 [3]	499	480	493 [3]	453	506	470	374
I	22 [4]	189	210	255	288 [3]	292 [3]	388	417	455	365
J	13 [4]	43	25	30	24	32	29	38	51	39
K	39 [4]	311	315	325 [3]	392	376	414	477	423	337
L	. [4]	100	117 [3]	123	136	146	145	152	149	111
M	8 [4]	212	269	301	231	257	276	272	267	192
N	38 [4]	1 058	1 202	1 349	1 306	1 244	1 332	1 331	1 249	1 070
O	40 [4]	207	213	282	270	284 [3]	271	265	283	206
P	. [4]	. [3]	. [3]	. [3]	0	. [3]	. [3]	0	0	0
Q	0 [4]	. [3]	. [3]	0	0	0	.	.	0	0
X	8 [4]	138 [3]	220	207 [3]	253 [3]	297 [3]	294 [3]	314	546	501

Explanatory notes: see p. 1125.

[1] Year beginning in July of year indicated. [2] Incl. cases of temporary incapacity with absence from work of more than one year. [3] Data included in totals only for reasons of confidentiality. [4] Data may be incomplete.

Notes explicatives: voir p. 1127.

[1] Année commençant en juillet de l'année indiquée. [2] Y compris les cas d'incapacité temporaire avec abscence du travail de plus d'une année. [3] Données incluses uniquement dans le total pour des raisons de confidentialité. [4] Les données peuvent être incomplètes.

Notas explicativas: véase p. 1129.

[1] Año que comienza en julio del año indicado. [2] Incl. los cases de incapacidad temporal con ausencia del trabajo de más de un año. [3] Datos incluidos en el total solamente por razón de confidencialidad. [4] Datos pueden ser incompletados.

OCCUPATIONAL INJURIES

Rates of occupational injuries, by economic activity

LÉSIONS PROFESSIONNELLES

Taux de lésions professionnelles, par activité économique

LESIONES PROFESIONALES

Tasas de lesiones profesionales, por actividad económica

	1999	2000	2001	2002	2003	2004	2005	2006	2007	2008

AFRICA-AFRIQUE-AFRICA

Algérie (FA) — **Compensated injuries - Lésions indemnisées - Lesiones indemnizadas**

Rates of fatal injuries - Taux de lésions mortelles - Tasas de lesiones mortales

Per 100,000 workers insured - Pour 100 000 travailleurs assurés - Por 100 000 trabajadores asegurados

Total men and women - Total hommes et femmes - Total hombres y mujeres
ISIC 3 - CITI 3 - CIIU 3

	1999	2000	2001	2002	2003	2004	2005	2006	2007	2008
Total	32.6	27.3	23.2	20.9	19.0	17.6	.	.	.	.

Rates of non-fatal injuries - Taux de lésions non mortelles - Tasas de lesiones no mortales

Per 100,000 workers insured - Pour 100 000 travailleurs assurés - Por 100 000 trabajadores asegurados

Total men and women - Total hommes et femmes - Total hombres y mujeres
ISIC 3 - CITI 3 - CIIU 3

	1999	2000	2001	2002	2003	2004	2005	2006	2007	2008
Total	1 723.8	1 541.5	1 320.2	1 220.4	1 325.0	1 002.7	.	.	.	.

Mauritius (FA) [1] — **Reported injuries - Lésions déclarées - Lesiones declaradas**

Rates of non-fatal injuries - Taux de lésions non mortelles - Tasas de lesiones no mortales

Per 100,000 workers insured - Pour 100 000 travailleurs assurés - Por 100 000 trabajadores asegurados

Total men and women - Total hommes et femmes - Total hombres y mujeres [2]
ISIC 3 - CITI 3 - CIIU 3

	1999	2000	2001	2002	2003	2004	2005	2006	2007	2008
Total	.	.	1 300 |	1 250 [3]	.	.	.	.	845	525
A	.	.	.	.	.	.	.	.	4 584	2 237
B	.	.	.	.	.	.	.	.	93	162
C	.	.	.	.	.	.	.	.	0	0
D	.	.	.	.	.	.	.	.	434	393
E	.	.	.	.	.	.	.	.	374	194
F	.	.	.	.	.	.	.	.	3 524	1 688
G	.	.	.	.	.	.	.	.	448	376
H	.	.	.	.	.	.	.	.	160	116
I	.	.	.	.	.	.	.	.	1 192	725
J	.	.	.	.	.	.	.	.	9	15
K	.	.	.	.	.	.	.	.	172	237
L	.	.	.	.	.	.	.	.	0	0
M	.	.	.	.	.	.	.	.	63	52
N	.	.	.	.	.	.	.	.	613	518
O	.	.	.	.	.	.	.	.	148	106
P	.	.	.	.	.	.	.	.	5 419	1 070

Men - Hommes - Hombres [2]
ISIC 3 - CITI 3 - CIIU 3

	1999	2000	2001	2002	2003	2004	2005	2006	2007	2008
Total	.	.	. |	.	.	.	.	.	1 240	761
A	.	.	.	.	.	.	.	.	5 198	2 763
B	.	.	.	.	.	.	.	.	124	242
C	.	.	.	.	.	.	.	.	0	0
D	.	.	.	.	.	.	.	.	747	642
E	.	.	.	.	.	.	.	.	511	178
F	.	.	.	.	.	.	.	.	388	1 873
G	.	.	.	.	.	.	.	.	605	495
H	.	.	.	.	.	.	.	.	182	107
I	.	.	.	.	.	.	.	.	1 444	890
J	.	.	.	.	.	.	.	.	17	30
K	.	.	.	.	.	.	.	.	255	335
L	.	.	.	.	.	.	.	.	0	0
M	.	.	.	.	.	.	.	.	46	45
N	.	.	.	.	.	.	.	.	1 925	1 379
O	.	.	.	.	.	.	.	.	182	129
P	.	.	.	.	.	.	.	.	5 085	1 887

Explanatory notes: see p. 1125.

[1] Excl. public sector and parastatal bodies. [2] Up to 2002: incapacity of 3 days or more. [3] Not strictly comparable.

Notes explicatives: voir p. 1127.

[1] Non compris le secteur public et les organismes paraétatiques. [2] Jusqu'à 2002: incapacité de 3 jours et plus. [3] Non strictement comparable.

Notas explicativas: véase p. 1129.

[1] Excl. el sector público y los organismos paraestatales. [2] Hasta 2002: incapacidad de 3 días y más. [3] No estrictamente comparable.

OCCUPATIONAL INJURIES

LÉSIONS PROFESSIONNELLES

LESIONES PROFESIONALES

Rates of occupational injuries, by economic activity

Taux de lésions professionnelles, par activité économique

Tasas de lesiones profesionales, por actividad económica

	1999	2000	2001	2002	2003	2004	2005	2006	2007	2008

Mauritius (FA) [1]   Reported injuries - Lésions déclarées - Lesiones declaradas

Rates of non-fatal injuries - Taux de lésions non mortelles - Tasas de lesiones no mortales

Per 100,000 workers insured - Pour 100 000 travailleurs assurés - Por 100 000 trabajadores asegurados

Women - Femmes - Mujeres [2]
ISIC 3 - CITI 3 - CIIU 3

	1999	2000	2001	2002	2003	2004	2005	2006	2007	2008
Total	.	.	I	.	.	.	.	.	213	151
A	.	.	.	.	.	.	.	.	2 747	790
B	.	.	.	.	.	.	.	.	62	70
C	.	.	.	.	.	.	.	.	0	0
D	.	.	.	.	.	.	.	.	99	125
E	.	.	.	.	.	.	.	.	0	234
F	.	.	.	.	.	.	.	.	0	157
G	.	.	.	.	.	.	.	.	220	211
H	.	.	.	.	.	.	.	.	109	137
I	.	.	.	.	.	.	.	.	367	193
J	.	.	.	.	.	.	.	.	0	0
K	.	.	.	.	.	.	.	.	19	50
L	.	.	.	.	.	.	.	.	0	0
M	.	.	.	.	.	.	.	.	74	56
N	.	.	.	.	.	.	.	.	40	148
O	.	.	.	.	.	.	.	.	96	73
P	.	.	.	.	.	.	.	.	5 882	0

Togo (FA)   Reported injuries - Lésions déclarées - Lesiones declaradas

Rates of fatal injuries - Taux de lésions mortelles - Tasas de lesiones mortales

Per 100,000 employees - Pour 100 000 salariés - Por 100 000 asalariados

Total men and women - Total hommes et femmes - Total hombres y mujeres
ISIC 2 - CITI 2 - CIIU 2

	1999	2000	2001	2002	2003	2004	2005	2006	2007	2008
Total	15.1	11.7	16.8	11.3	15.0	16.3	.	.	.	.
2	80.3	41.6	82.9	43.8	87.4	0.0	.	.	.	.
3	74.9	46.4	74.4	75.8	60.8	57.8	.	.	.	.
4	0.0	0.0	38.8	45.4	42.7	54.7	.	.	.	.
5	0.0	0.0	0.0	0.0	0.0	0.0	.	.	.	.
6.8	0.0	0.0	0.0	0.0	0.0	10.7	.	.	.	.
7	0.0	0.0	0.0	23.0	0.0	22.9	.	.	.	.
9	5.8	6.2	9.1	2.5	4.9	6.7	.	.	.	.

Rates of non-fatal injuries - Taux de lésions non mortelles - Tasas de lesiones no mortales

Per 100,000 employees - Pour 100 000 salariés - Por 100 000 asalariados

Total men and women - Total hommes et femmes - Total hombres y mujeres
ISIC 2 - CITI 2 - CIIU 2

	1999	2000	2001	2002	2003	2004	2005	2006	2007	2008
Total	1 623	1 680	1 429	1 253	1 057	484	.	.	.	.
2	8 193	7 241	6 216	7 877	4 766	1 333	.	.	.	.
3	8 217	7 143	6 199	7 888	4 759	1 878	.	.	.	.
4	2 024	3 123	2 713	2 587	2 307	1 284	.	.	.	.
5	923	1 115	748	172	1 426	172	.	.	.	.
6.8	125	245	155	488	184	171	.	.	.	.
7	433	351	382	253	150	1 029	.	.	.	.
9	728	853	797	394	335	157	.	.	.	.

Tunisie (FA)   Compensated injuries - Lésions indemnisées - Lesiones indemnizadas

Rates of fatal injuries - Taux de lésions mortelles - Tasas de lesiones mortales

Per 100,000 workers insured - Pour 100 000 travailleurs assurés - Por 100 000 trabajadores asegurados

Total men and women - Total hommes et femmes - Total hombres y mujeres
ISIC 3 - CITI 3 - CIIU 3

	1999	2000	2001	2002	2003	2004	2005	2006	2007	2008
Total	13.4	14.9	15.9	14.3	16.0	13.1	.	.	.	.
A	13.0	5.8	20.2	19.6	18.8	28.7	.	.	.	.
B	30.9	98.3	79.2	38.4	85.7	28.3	.	.	.	.
C	34.3	25.5	37.5	27.9	11.0	22.0	.	.	.	.
D	7.5	7.8	6.3	9.6	7.1	5.2	.	.	.	.
E-F	43.1	46.0	57.3	38.1	49.3	46.5	.	.	.	.
G-J	8.1	6.8	5.8	9.6	3.6	10.0	.	.	.	.
H	3.9	5.8	5.0	9.1	4.6	4.3	.	.	.	.
I	12.3	16.3	11.3	11.8	47.0	19.2	.	.	.	.
K-Q	10.0	12.6	10.8	8.6	13.6	9.1	.	.	.	.

Explanatory notes: see p. 1125.

[1] Excl. public sector and parastatal bodies. [2] Up to 2002: incapacity of 3 days or more.

Notes explicatives: voir p. 1127.

[1] Non compris le secteur public et les organismes paraétatiques. [2] Jusqu'à 2002: incapacité de 3 jours et plus.

Notas explicativas: véase p. 1129.

[1] Excl. el sector público y los organismos paraestatales. [2] Hasta 2002: incapacidad de 3 días y más.

OCCUPATIONAL INJURIES

Rates of occupational injuries, by economic activity

LÉSIONS PROFESSIONNELLES

Taux de lésions professionnelles, par activité économique

LESIONES PROFESIONALES

Tasas de lesiones profesionales, por actividad económica

8B

	1999	2000	2001	2002	2003	2004	2005	2006	2007	2008

Tunisie (FA)   Compensated injuries - Lésions indemnisées - Lesiones indemnizadas

Rates of non-fatal injuries - Taux de lésions non mortelles - Tasas de lesiones no mortales

Per 100,000 workers insured - Pour 100 000 travailleurs assurés - Por 100 000 trabajadores asegurados

Total men and women - Total hommes et femmes - Total hombres y mujeres [1]
ISIC 3 - CITI 3 - CIIU 3

	1999	2000	2001	2002	2003	2004	2005	2006	2007	2008
Total	4 004	3 937	4 180	4 005	3 627	3 639	.	.	.	.
A	1 574	1 567	1 653	1 319	1 484	1 958	.	.	.	.
B	1 512	1 593	1 436	1 453	1 347	1 335	.	.	.	.
C	2 829	3 237	3 269	3 632	3 224	3 184	.	.	.	.
D	5 445	5 229	5 565	5 142	4 482	4 445	.	.	.	.
E-F	5 932	5 784	5 814	5 407	5 119	5 399	.	.	.	.
G,J	1 634	1 591	1 651	1 827	1 701	1 820	.	.	.	.
H	2 634	3 137	3 546	2 903	2 863	2 826	.	.	.	.
I	2 563	2 600	2 782	2 740	3 021	2 910	.	.	.	.
K-Q	3 003	2 948	3 377	3 567	3 065	2 969	.	.	.	.

Zimbabwe (FA) [2]   Reported injuries - Lésions déclarées - Lesiones declaradas

Rates of fatal injuries - Taux de lésions mortelles - Tasas de lesiones mortales

Per 100,000 workers insured - Pour 100 000 travailleurs assurés - Por 100 000 trabajadores asegurados

Total men and women - Total hommes et femmes - Total hombres y mujeres
ISIC 3 - CITI 3 - CIIU 3

	1999	2000	2001	2002	2003	2004	2005	2006	2007	2008
Total	.	.	.	.	.	.	6.2	7.5	6.3	.
A	.	.	.	.	.	.	6.0	9.0	2.6	.
C	.	.	.	.	.	.	18.7	29.0	28.1	.
D	.	.	.	.	.	.	2.1	4.8	5.7	.
E	.	.	.	.	.	.	.	15.6	57.1	.
F	.	.	.	.	.	.	2.3	6.4	8.1	.
G	.	.	.	.	.	.	3.6	2.2	1.6	.
I	.	.	.	.	.	.	24.4	25.3	13.4	.
J-K	.	.	.	.	.	.	1.6	2.6	0.0	.
L	.	.	.	.	.	.	9.8	5.2	2.7	.
O	.	.	.	.	.	.	6.4	2.3	6.0	.

Men - Hommes - Hombres
ISIC 3 - CITI 3 - CIIU 3

	1999	2000	2001	2002	2003	2004	2005	2006	2007	2008
Total	.	.	.	.	.	.	6.8	8.8	7.4	.
A	.	.	.	.	.	.	5.9	11.7	3.3	.
C	.	.	.	.	.	.	19.6	28.5	29.8	.
D	.	.	.	.	.	.	2.0	5.4	5.9	.
E	.	.	.	.	.	.	.	16.9	61.7	.
F	.	.	.	.	.	.	2.4	6.6	8.4	.
G	.	.	.	.	.	.	4.7	2.2	2.2	.
I	.	.	.	.	.	.	26.6	27.9	12.9	.
J-K	.	.	.	.	.	.	2.4	4.0	0.0	.
L	.	.	.	.	.	.	9.5	6.9	0.0	.
O	.	.	.	.	.	.	7.3	2.9	7.5	.

Women - Femmes - Mujeres
ISIC 3 - CITI 3 - CIIU 3

	1999	2000	2001	2002	2003	2004	2005	2006	2007	2008
Total	.	.	.	.	.	.	3.1	1.2	1.7	.
A	.	.	.	.	.	.	6.1	0.0	0.0	.
C	.	.	.	.	.	.	0.0	39.3	0.0	.
D	.	.	.	.	.	.	3.0	0.0	4.1	.
G	.	.	.	.	.	.	0.0	2.3	0.0	.
I	.	.	.	.	.	.	0.0	0.0	18.2	.
J-K	.	.	.	.	.	.	0.0	0.0	0.0	.
L	.	.	.	.	.	.	1.6	0.0	10.9	.
O	.	.	.	.	.	.	3.4	0.0	0.0	.

Rates of non-fatal injuries - Taux de lésions non mortelles - Tasas de lesiones no mortales

Per 100,000 workers insured - Pour 100 000 travailleurs assurés - Por 100 000 trabajadores asegurados

Total men and women - Total hommes et femmes - Total hombres y mujeres [3]
ISIC 3 - CITI 3 - CIIU 3

	1999	2000	2001	2002	2003	2004	2005	2006	2007	2008
Total	.	.	.	703	1 251	747	635	780	556	.
A	.	.	.	482	798	416	326	462	234	.
C	.	.	.	1 555	3 244	1 436	1 293	1 379	1 078	.
D	.	.	.	1 093	2 224	1 374	1 207	1 390	1 137	.
E	.	.	.	1 872	2 971	1 981	1 068	1 338	1 215	.
F	.	.	.	715	1 057	559	434	736	446	.
G	.	.	.	332	522	323	311	425	273	.
I	.	.	.	1 045	1 604	1 063	845	1 034	691	.
J-K	.	.	.	186	259	197	242	233	84	.
L	.	.	.	984	1 613	1 086	901	1 043	671	.
O	.	.	.	466	660	480	405	463	350	.

Explanatory notes: see p. 1125.

[1] Incapacity of 4 days or more. [2] Year ending in March of the year indicated. [3] Incl. non-fatal cases without lost workdays.

Notes explicatives: voir p. 1127.

[1] Incapacité de 4 jours et plus. [2] Année se terminant en mars de l'année indiquée. [3] Y compris les cas non mortels sans perte de journées de travail.

Notas explicativas: véase p. 1129.

[1] Incapacidad de 4 días y más. [2] Año que termina en marzo del año indicado. [3] Incl. los casos no mortales sin pérdida de días de trabajo.

OCCUPATIONAL INJURIES	LÉSIONS PROFESSIONNELLES	LESIONES PROFESIONALES
Rates of occupational injuries, by economic activity	Taux de lésions professionnelles, par activité économique	Tasas de lesiones profesionales, por actividad económica

	1999	2000	2001	2002	2003	2004	2005	2006	2007	2008

Zimbabwe (FA) [1] Reported injuries - Lésions déclarées - Lesiones declaradas

Rates of non-fatal injuries - Taux de lésions non mortelles - Tasas de lesiones no mortales

Per 100,000 workers insured - Pour 100 000 travailleurs assurés - Por 100 000 trabajadores asegurados

Men - Hommes - Hombres [2]
ISIC 3 - CITI 3 - CIIU 3

	1999	2000	2001	2002	2003	2004	2005	2006	2007	2008
Total						839	717	873	631	
A						437	342	467	238	
C						1 495	1 342	1 436	1 115	
D						1 492	1 326	1 498	1 219	
E						2 087	1 108	1 413	1 279	
F						569	444	749	460	
G						391	352	495	325	
I						1 134	909	1 121	745	
J-K						262	319	317	121	
L						1 083	963	1 114	739	
O						536	469	508	394	

Women - Femmes - Mujeres [2]
ISIC 3 - CITI 3 - CIIU 3

	1999	2000	2001	2002	2003	2004	2005	2006	2007	2008
Total						298	236	350	222	
A						338	267	444	221	
C						358	354	354	440	
D						480	314	525	504	
E						509	527	415	403	
F						246	116	373	57	
G						96	167	209	120	
I						304	138	182	164	
J-K						65	81	79	18	
L						1 096	697	822	459	
O						246	169	281	180	

AMERICA-AMÉRIQUE-AMERICA

Argentina (FA) [3] Reported injuries - Lésions déclarées - Lesiones declaradas

Rates of fatal injuries - Taux de lésions mortelles - Tasas de lesiones mortales

Per 100,000 workers insured - Pour 100 000 travailleurs assurés - Por 100 000 trabajadores asegurados

Total men and women - Total hommes et femmes - Total hombres y mujeres
ISIC 2 - CITI 2 - CIIU 2

	1999	2000	2001	2002	2003	2004	2005	2006	2007	2008
Total	21.6	18.6		15.2	15.2	15.0	14.3	14.9	14.1	
1	55.2	33.5		32.2	32.8	38.3	37.0	35.2	30.7	
2	32.2	33.1		41.8	41.4	60.1	37.9	23.9	26.8	
3	20.0	19.3		17.8	13.2	16.2	17.7	17.6	14.9	
4	47.1	23.8		19.3	21.3	20.8	16.6	16.2	12.7	
5	58.0	47.2		39.4	47.4	44.9	35.8	41.6	36.3	
6	21.3	17.5		11.7	14.7	11.7	10.7	10.6	10.1	
7	38.6	34.3		31.9	29.1	25.3	28.9	31.7	29.3	
8	18.4	16.6		15.0	15.8	12.5	10.7	11.3	11.9	
9	8.8	10.7		8.6	8.3	7.7	6.5	6.9	7.5	
0				47.2		32.6	26.9	53.8		

Rates of non-fatal injuries - Taux de lésions non mortelles - Tasas de lesiones no mortales

Per 100,000 workers insured - Pour 100 000 travailleurs assurés - Por 100 000 trabajadores asegurados

Total men and women - Total hommes et femmes - Total hombres y mujeres
ISIC 2 - CITI 2 - CIIU 2

	1999	2000	2001	2002	2003	2004	2005	2006	2007	2008
Total	8 075	7 747		6 240	7 270	8 020	8 150	8 070	8 250	
1	10 793	10 812		10 750	11 270	12 050	11 400	11 620	11 170	
2	8 487	7 665		5 690	6 580	7 190	7 300	7 320	8 080	
3	13 598	12 715		9 890	11 970	13 120	12 830	12 250	12 440	
4	7 162	6 337		5 540	5 790	5 710	6 060	5 850	5 790	
5	19 901	16 536		11 930	15 620	18 310	19 130	19 320	18 490	
6	7 862	8 433		6 820	7 570	8 090	8 000	8 050	8 100	
7	8 351	8 895		8 560	8 900	8 950	8 770	8 740	8 970	
8	4 604	5 162		4 410	5 430	6 460	6 530	6 340	6 860	
9	4 030	4 441		3 930	4 410	4 730	4 880	4 770	5 010	
0				7 130	6 830	5 510	8 510	7 620	6 970	

Explanatory notes: see p. 1125.

[1] Year ending in March of the year indicated. [2] Incl. non-fatal cases without lost workdays. [3] Year ending in June of the year indicated.

Notes explicatives: voir p. 1127.

[1] Année se terminant en mars de l'année indiquée. [2] Y compris les cas non mortels sans perte de journées de travail. [3] Année se terminant en juin de l'année indiquée.

Notas explicativas: véase p. 1129.

[1] Año que termina en marzo del año indicado. [2] Incl. los casos no mortales sin pérdida de días de trabajo. [3] Año que se termina en junio del año indicado.

OCCUPATIONAL INJURIES

Rates of occupational injuries, by economic activity

LÉSIONS PROFESSIONNELLES

Taux de lésions professionnelles, par activité économique

LESIONES PROFESIONALES

Tasas de lesiones profesionales, por actividad económica

Canada (FA)

Compensated injuries - Lésions indemnisées - Lesiones indemnizadas

Rates of fatal injuries - Taux de lésions mortelles - Tasas de lesiones mortales

Per 100,000 employees - Pour 100 000 salariés - Por 100 000 asalariados

Total men and women - Total hommes et femmes - Total hombres y mujeres
ISIC 3 - CITI 3 - CIIU 3

	1999	2000	2001	2002	2003	2004	2005	2006	2007	2008
Total	5.8	6.0	6.1	6.1	6.1	5.8	6.8	5.9	6.3	.
A	9.9	12.9	13.5	14.9	9.0	8.9	14.4	9.9	9.2	.
B	21.3	48.2	26.9	34.5	34.1	46.5	38.8	19.7	27.8	.
C	47.9	61.1	53.0	56.9	55.6	46.9	48.9	31.6	33.4	.
D	8.6	9.3	8.6	9.9	8.8	8.8	10.4	9.4	12.3	.
E	17.0	10.6	12.3	11.5	15.3	12.8	18.4	19.7	12.3	.
F	21.6	18.5	22.5	20.9	23.3	20.4	23.3	19.1	19.7	.
G	2.0	2.6	2.4	2.4	1.9	1.8	2.9	2.5	1.8	.
H	0.8	0.6	1.0	1.1	0.8	0.7	1.3	0.7	0.8	.
I	10.6	11.7	11.1	9.3	11.1	11.4	11.4	11.9	10.5	.
J	0.6	0.0	0.0	0.0	0.3	0.3	0.1	0.0	0.3	.
K	1.1	1.4	1.9	2.2	1.1	1.8	1.3	1.3	1.6	.
L	5.1	4.2	8.1	6.1	9.4	7.8	7.8	9.7	11.3	.
M	0.6	0.5	1.3	1.4	1.0	0.8	1.2	1.1	1.2	.
N	0.9	0.5	1.0	0.9	1.2	0.9	0.3	1.0	0.8	.
O	3.3	3.9	3.0	2.8	4.7	4.0	4.4	3.0	2.9	.
P	0.0	0.0	0.0	0.0	0.0	0.0	1.6	0.0	5.0	.
Q	0.0	0.0	0.0	0.0	0.0	0.0	0.0	0.0	0.0	.

Men - Hommes - Hombres
ISIC 3 - CITI 3 - CIIU 3

	1999	2000	2001	2002	2003	2004	2005	2006	2007	2008
Total	10.2	10.7	11.0	10.9	11.1	10.5	12.4	10.7	11.3	.
A	13.3	17.4	17.8	19.4	11.8	11.8	20.0	13.4	11.0	.
B	24.6	55.4	32.9	36.1	36.1	55.8	46.0	23.2	33.8	.
C	55.6	71.0	62.1	68.4	66.8	55.9	57.5	39.0	39.9	.
D	11.4	12.7	11.7	13.4	12.3	11.9	14.2	12.8	16.5	.
E	22.5	13.6	15.3	15.2	18.6	17.4	24.7	25.9	17.2	.
F	23.9	20.5	24.9	22.5	25.8	22.8	26.0	21.3	21.9	.
G	3.3	4.4	3.9	4.4	3.3	3.0	5.0	4.2	3.2	.
H	1.1	1.3	1.6	2.6	2.0	1.7	2.7	1.0	0.9	.
I	14.8	16.4	15.9	13.0	15.7	15.7	16.3	16.7	14.5	.
J	0.9	0.0	0.0	0.0	0.0	0.0	0.4	0.0	0.7	.
K	2.0	2.1	3.0	3.5	1.9	3.2	2.1	2.2	2.7	.
L	9.3	7.7	13.6	10.7	16.8	14.8	15.0	18.8	21.9	.
M	1.2	1.5	3.5	4.1	2.4	2.3	3.4	2.4	2.9	.
N	3.8	2.1	3.6	2.4	3.7	2.5	1.6	2.6	1.9	.
O	6.6	8.7	7.1	6.2	10.3	8.2	9.9	6.1	6.4	.
P	0.0	0.0	0.0	0.0	0.0	0.0	0.0	0.0		0.0
Q	0.0	0.0	0.0	0.0	0.0	0.0	0.0	0.0	0.0	

Women - Femmes - Mujeres
ISIC 3 - CITI 3 - CIIU 3

	1999	2000	2001	2002	2003	2004	2005	2006	2007	2008
Total	0.5	0.4	0.5	0.5	0.5	0.5	0.4	0.6	0.7	.
A	0.7	0.8	1.0	2.8	0.9	0.9	0.0	0.9	4.5	.
B	0.0	0.0	0.0	24.4	22.7	0.0	0.0	0.0	0.0	.
C	0.0	10.8	6.8	0.0	0.0	3.1	5.7	2.1	6.1	.
D	1.2	0.5	0.6	1.2	0.5	0.9	0.8	1.0	1.9	.
E	0.0	0.0	3.2	0.0	3.5	0.0	0.0	1.7	0.0	.
F	1.3	0.0	2.3	6.0	2.1	0.9	0.9	0.4	3.0	.
G	0.3	0.4	0.4	0.0	0.2	0.3	0.5	0.4	0.3	.
H	0.5	0.2	0.6	0.2	0.0	0.0	0.3	0.5	0.8	.
I	0.6	0.9	0.5	0.6	1.1	2.2	0.6	0.8	1.1	.
J	0.5	0.0	0.0	0.0	0.5	0.5	0.0	0.0	0.0	.
K	0.1	0.4	0.5	0.4	0.1	0.0	0.3	0.3	0.2	.
L	0.3	0.3	2.0	0.8	1.5	0.3	0.2	0.2	0.7	.
M	0.3	0.0	0.2	0.0	0.2	0.0	0.0	0.4	0.3	.
N	0.3	0.2	0.5	0.5	0.7	0.5	0.1	0.6	0.5	.
O	0.8	0.5	0.0	0.2	0.7	0.7	0.5	0.9	0.4	.
P	0.0	0.0	0.0	0.0	0.0	0.0	0.0	1.7	0.0	1.8
Q	0.0	0.0	0.0	0.0	0.0	0.0	0.0	0.0	0.0	.

Explanatory notes: see p. 1125.

Notes explicatives: voir p. 1127.

Notas explicativas: véase p. 1129.

OCCUPATIONAL INJURIES
Rates of occupational injuries, by economic activity

LÉSIONS PROFESSIONNELLES
Taux de lésions professionnelles, par activité économique

LESIONES PROFESIONALES
Tasas de lesiones profesionales, por actividad económica

Canada (FA)

Compensated injuries - Lésions indemnisées - Lesiones indemnizadas

Rates of non-fatal injuries - Taux de lésions non mortelles - Tasas de lesiones no mortales

Per 100,000 employees - Pour 100 000 salariés - Por 100 000 asalariados

Total men and women - Total hommes et femmes - Total hombres y mujeres
ISIC 3 - CITI 3 - CIIU 3

	1999	2000	2001	2002	2003	2004	2005	2006	2007	2008
Total	2 637	2 659	2 497	2 346	2 227	2 135	2 090	1 998	1 883	.
A	2 431	1 963	2 068	1 960	1 779	1 749	1 634	1 500	1 423	.
B	2 323	2 551	3 229	2 969	2 645	2 498	2 663	2 423	2 205	.
C	2 333	2 411	2 013	1 918	1 931	1 703	1 586	1 394	1 287	.
D	5 080	5 101	4 688	4 194	3 914	3 685	3 633	3 492	3 200	.
E	2 347	2 317	2 146	2 212	2 085	1 797	1 904	1 666	1 396	.
F	3 818	3 894	3 769	3 588	3 428	3 371	3 224	3 134	3 003	.
G	2 380	2 474	2 331	2 263	2 164	2 075	2 007	1 910	1 814	.
H	2 360	2 529	2 371	2 207	1 974	1 907	1 900	1 872	1 669	.
I	2 607	2 753	2 567	2 782	2 650	2 557	2 566	2 536	2 439	.
J	145	159	107	102	94	95	84	83	76	.
K	717	723	648	639	617	613	619	552	500	.
L	2 371	2 663	2 565	2 900	2 666	2 547	2 521	2 651	2 417	.
M	746	769	765	849	838	836	757	745	709	.
N	2 509	2 518	2 520	2 437	2 743	2 362	2 379	2 350	2 244	.
O	1 951	2 046	1 903	1 744	1 668	1 661	1 700	1 639	1 477	.
P	838	478	443	313	378	376	367	279	271	.
Q	0	1 185	708	1 174	789	0	840	788	720	.

Men - Hommes - Hombres
ISIC 3 - CITI 3 - CIIU 3

	1999	2000	2001	2002	2003	2004	2005	2006	2007	2008
Total	3 352	3 460	3 219	3 013	2 848	2 716	2 642	2 505	2 345	.
A	2 393	2 250	2 251	2 144	1 939	1 918	1 811	1 632	1 543	.
B	2 264	2 941	3 642	3 133	2 823	2 701	2 785	2 521	2 291	.
C	2 606	2 827	2 319	2 206	2 201	1 965	1 833	1 676	1 517	.
D	5 743	5 797	5 308	4 783	4 462	4 169	4 109	3 949	3 624	.
E	2 844	2 812	2 677	2 723	2 458	2 260	2 343	1 991	1 739	.
F	3 922	4 225	4 083	3 857	3 701	3 684	3 482	3 396	3 263	.
G	2 973	3 182	2 944	2 903	2 737	2 599	2 532	2 391	2 267	.
H	2 331	2 547	2 413	2 300	1 984	1 900	1 868	1 857	1 583	.
I	3 132	3 490	3 275	3 408	3 287	3 187	3 153	3 054	2 912	.
J	110	121	66	64	63	56	57	47	45	.
K	908	954	870	822	809	790	800	701	617	.
L	3 229	3 537	3 326	3 678	3 713	3 515	3 457	3 569	3 315	.
M	957	1 072	1 075	1 156	1 076	1 069	934	889	838	.
N	2 575	2 467	2 645	2 640	2 576	2 283	2 326	2 313	2 178	.
O	2 882	3 056	2 863	2 565	2 468	2 430	2 426	2 418	2 192	.
P	1 179	1 182	1 081	532	396	595	319	310	414	.
Q	0	0	0	0	0	0	0	652	0	.

Women - Femmes - Mujeres
ISIC 3 - CITI 3 - CIIU 3

	1999	2000	2001	2002	2003	2004	2005	2006	2007	2008
Total	1 572	1 700	1 637	1 559	1 499	1 462	1 451	1 416	1 355	.
A	2 058	1 158	1 502	1 430	1 291	1 268	1 150	1 154	1 103	.
B	1 689	742	1 352	1 951	1 636	1 480	1 979	1 870	1 800	.
C	427	362	379	360	411	281	318	207	261	.
D	2 950	3 255	3 040	2 701	2 542	2 443	2 411	2 317	2 112	.
E	518	588	561	646	730	514	607	624	501	.
F	851	866	893	861	858	788	934	991	950	.
G	1 443	1 597	1 559	1 476	1 456	1 428	1 378	1 335	1 280	.
H	2 185	2 494	2 317	2 117	1 937	1 890	1 901	1 864	1 710	.
I	880	1 050	1 004	1 309	1 215	1 177	1 257	1 336	1 340	.
J	149	180	129	124	112	117	98	105	93	.
K	429	436	371	408	382	390	392	365	348	.
L	1 154	1 650	1 677	1 993	1 535	1 511	1 527	1 682	1 514	.
M	556	600	596	684	699	711	662	663	637	.
N	2 350	2 521	2 482	2 383	2 441	2 372	2 383	2 350	2 251	.
O	1 101	1 307	1 192	1 116	1 071	1 089	1 154	1 090	968	.
P	774	436	400	298	377	361	371	276	261	.
Q	0	421	375	0	0	0	706	0	0	.

Costa Rica (FA)

Compensated injuries - Lésions indemnisées - Lesiones indemnizadas

Rates of fatal injuries - Taux de lésions mortelles - Tasas de lesiones mortales

Per 100,000 workers insured - Pour 100 000 travailleurs assurés - Por 100 000 trabajadores asegurados

Total men and women - Total hommes et femmes - Total hombres y mujeres
ISIC 2 - CITI 2 - CIIU 2

	1999	2000	2001	2002	2003	2004	2005	2006	2007	2008
Total	11.6	9.6	9.5	7.5	7.0	6.1	6.4	.	.	.
1	9.4	10.6	.	.	.	.	.	.	.	.
2	90.5	0.0	.	.	.	.	.	.	.	.
3	13.8	12.4	.	.	.	.	.	.	.	.
4	11.5	9.7	.	.	.	.	.	.	.	.
5	31.5	26.8	.	.	.	.	.	.	.	.
6	5.9	7.8	.	.	.	.	.	.	.	.
7	43.4	9.5	.	.	.	.	.	.	.	.
8	9.8	3.7	.	.	.	.	.	.	.	.
9	10.5	6.8	.	.	.	.	.	.	.	.

Explanatory notes: see p. 1125. Notes explicatives: voir p. 1127. Notas explicativas: véase p. 1129.

| | | | | | | | | | | 8B |

OCCUPATIONAL INJURIES

Rates of occupational injuries, by economic activity

LÉSIONS PROFESSIONNELLES

Taux de lésions professionnelles, par activité économique

LESIONES PROFESIONALES

Tasas de lesiones profesionales, por actividad económica

	1999	2000	2001	2002	2003	2004	2005	2006	2007	2008

Costa Rica (FA) Compensated injuries - Lésions indemnisées - Lesiones indemnizadas

Rates of non-fatal injuries - Taux de lésions non mortelles - Tasas de lesiones no mortales

Per 100,000 workers insured - Pour 100 000 travailleurs assurés - Por 100 000 trabajadores asegurados

Total men and women - Total hommes et femmes - Total hombres y mujeres
ISIC 2 - CITI 2 - CIIU 2

	1999	2000	2001	2002	2003	2004	2005	2006	2007	2008
Total	16 602	15 994	14 213	13 838	13 330	1 302	11 802	.	.	.
1	25 937	28 306	.	.	.	.	.	.	.	.
2	48 778	49 534	.	.	.	.	.	.	.	.
3	23 325	18 492	.	.	.	.	.	.	.	.
4	18 381	14 141	.	.	.	.	.	.	.	.
5	46 956	38 309	.	.	.	.	.	.	.	.
6	6 887	9 603	.	.	.	.	.	.	.	.
7	20 246	15 441	.	.	.	.	.	.	.	.
8	7 423	5 927	.	.	.	.	.	.	.	.
9	10 050	9 380	.	.	.	.	.	.	.	.

Cuba (F) Reported injuries - Lésions déclarées - Lesiones declaradas

Rates of fatal injuries - Taux de lésions mortelles - Tasas de lesiones mortales

Per 1,000,000 hours worked - Pour 1 000 000 heures effectuées - Por 1 000 000 horas trabajadas

Total men and women - Total hommes et femmes - Total hombres y mujeres
ISIC 3 - CITI 3 - CIIU 3

	1999	2000	2001	2002	2003	2004	2005	2006	2007	2008
Total	0.025	0.018	0.016	0.018	0.015	0.017	0.014	0.012	0.007	0.011

Rates of non-fatal injuries - Taux de lésions non mortelles - Tasas de lesiones no mortales

Per 1,000,000 hours worked - Pour 1 000 000 heures effectuées - Por 1 000 000 horas trabajadas

Total men and women - Total hommes et femmes - Total hombres y mujeres
ISIC 3 - CITI 3 - CIIU 3

	1999	2000	2001	2002	2003	2004	2005	2006	2007	2008
Total	2.387	1.914	1.677	1.359	1.209	0.992	0.850	0.868	0.869	0.878

México (FA) Reported injuries - Lésions déclarées - Lesiones declaradas

Rates of fatal injuries - Taux de lésions mortelles - Tasas de lesiones mortales

Per 100,000 workers insured - Pour 100 000 travailleurs assurés - Por 100 000 trabajadores asegurados

Total men and women - Total hommes et femmes - Total hombres y mujeres
ISIC 3 - CITI 3 - CIIU 3

	1999	2000	2001	2002	2003	2004	2005	2006	2007	2008
Total	12 [1]	14 [1]	12 [1]	11 [1]	12 [1]	11 [1]	11 [1]	10 [1]	9 [1]	10

Men - Hommes - Hombres
ISIC 3 - CITI 3 - CIIU 3

	1999	2000	2001	2002	2003	2004	2005	2006	2007	2008
Total	.	.	.	19 [1]	20 [1]	17 [1]	16 [1]	16 [1]	19 [1]	17

Women - Femmes - Mujeres
ISIC 3 - CITI 3 - CIIU 3

	1999	2000	2001	2002	2003	2004	2005	2006	2007	2008
Total	.	.	.	2 [1]	2 [1]	2 [1]	2 [1]	1 [1]	1 [1]	1

Rates of non-fatal injuries - Taux de lésions non mortelles - Tasas de lesiones no mortales

Per 100,000 workers insured - Pour 100 000 travailleurs assurés - Por 100 000 trabajadores asegurados

Total men and women - Total hommes et femmes - Total hombres y mujeres
ISIC 3 - CITI 3 - CIIU 3

	1999	2000	2001	2002	2003	2004	2005	2006	2007	2008
Total	3 575 [1]	3 624 [1]	3 384 [1]	3 202 [1]	2 968 [1]	2 922 [1]	2 931 [1]	2 856 [1]	3 120 [1]	3 569

Men - Hommes - Hombres
ISIC 3 - CITI 3 - CIIU 3

	1999	2000	2001	2002	2003	2004	2005	2006	2007	2008
Total	4 337 [1]	4 268 [1]	3 956 [1]	4 130 [1]	3 836 [1]	3 421 [1]	3 414 [1]	3 613 [1]	4 094 [1]	.

Women - Femmes - Mujeres
ISIC 3 - CITI 3 - CIIU 3

	1999	2000	2001	2002	2003	2004	2005	2006	2007	2008
Total	.	.	.	2 009 [1]	1 852 [1]	2 121 [1]	2 156 [1]	1 899 [1]	1 484 [1]	2 081

Explanatory notes: see p. 1125.   Notes explicatives: voir p. 1127.   Notas explicativas: véase p. 1129.

[1] Data for IMSS only.   [1] Données relatives à l'IMSS seulement.   [1] Datos relativos al IMSS solamente.

8B

OCCUPATIONAL INJURIES
Rates of occupational injuries, by economic activity

LÉSIONS PROFESSIONNELLES
Taux de lésions professionnelles, par activité économique

LESIONES PROFESIONALES
Tasas de lesiones profesionales, por actividad económica

	1999	2000	2001	2002	2003	2004	2005	2006	2007	2008

Puerto Rico (DA) — Reported injuries - Lésions déclarées - Lesiones declaradas

Rates of non-fatal injuries - Taux de lésions non mortelles - Tasas de lesiones no mortales

Per 100,000 full-time equivalent employees - Pour l'équivalent de 100 000 salariés à plein temps - Por la equivalencia de 100 000 asalariados a tiempo completo

Total men and women - Total hommes et femmes - Total hombres y mujeres
ISIC 3 - CITI 3 - CIIU 3

	1999	2000	2001	2002	2003	2004	2005	2006	2007	2008
Total[1]	4 400	3 500	4 100	4 300	3 700	.	4 300	.	.	.
A-B[1]	3 400	3 100	7 200	4 900	3 900	.	3 300	.	.	.
C	3 700	4 700	4 300	4 200	2 900	.	.	.	.	.
D	5 200	3 800	4 000	4 300	3 300	.	3 300	.	.	.
E	.	.	.	.	9 600	.	.	.	.	.
F	6 100	2 900	3 700	4 300	2 600	.	.	.	.	.
G[2]	.	.	.	.	3 200	.	3 200	.	.	.
G-H	3 600	3 500	4 100	.	.	.	.	.	.	.
H	.	.	.	.	5 800	.	5 100	.	.	.
I[3]	3 900	3 500	.	2 700	2 800	.	4 500	.	.	.
J-K	.	.	.	3 000	.	.	.	.	.	.
K	.	.	.	.	3 900	.	3 300	.	.	.
L	8 700	.	.	5 900	6 700	.	5 400	.	.	.
M[4]	.	.	.	.	4 600	.	8 900	.	.	.
M-O	6 600	2 500	.	.	3 200	.	.	.	.	.
N[3]	.	.	.	.	3 200	.	.	.	.	.
O[3]	.	.	.	.	.	.	3 000	.	.	.

Trinidad and Tobago (FF) — Reported injuries - Lésions déclarées - Lesiones declaradas

Rates of fatal injuries - Taux de lésions mortelles - Tasas de lesiones mortales

Per 100,000 workers employed - Pour 100 000 travailleurs occupés - Por 100 000 trabajadores empleados

Total men and women - Total hommes et femmes - Total hombres y mujeres
ISIC 2 - CITI 2 - CIIU 2

	1999	2000	2001	2002	2003	2004	2005	2006	2007	2008
Total	0.8	0.9	0.5	0.1	0.5	0.5	3.1	1.9	.	.
1	0.0	2.8	4.9	0.0	0.0	0.0	0.0	0.0	.	.
2	0.0	6.1	0.0	5.5	0.0	4.9	0.0	4.9	.	.
3	1.8	1.8	0.0	0.0	1.8	1.7	10.8	1.8	.	.
4	1.8	0.0	0.0	0.0	0.0	0.0	14.5	39.0	.	.
5	0.0	3.2	1.4	0.0	1.4	0.0	3.2	2.1	.	.
6	0.0	0.0	0.0	0.0	0.0	0.9	0.0	0.0	.	.
7	2.3	0.0	0.0	0.0	2.4	0.0	14.4	2.3	.	.
8	0.0	0.0	0.0	0.0	0.0	0.0	0.0	0.0	.	.
9	0.0	0.0	0.0	0.0	0.0	0.0	1.1	1.1	.	.

Rates of non-fatal injuries - Taux de lésions non mortelles - Tasas de lesiones no mortales

Per 100,000 workers employed - Pour 100 000 travailleurs occupés - Por 100 000 trabajadores empleados

Total men and women - Total hommes et femmes - Total hombres y mujeres
ISIC 2 - CITI 2 - CIIU 2

	1999	2000	2001	2002	2003	2004	2005	2006	2007	2008
Total	86	88	95	102	65	41	43	64	.	.
1	349	231	283	341	113	0	0	0	.	.
2	255	285	313	167	88	75	118	161	.	.
3	430	521	4 635	651	447	252	315	463	.	.
4	2	58	27	0	13	0	0	26	.	.
5	6	6	6	1	2	1	7	10	.	.
6	6	0	0	2	9	15	81	103	.	.
7	37	49	59	41	81	129	4	37	.	.
8	0	0	0	0	0	0	4	37	.	.
9	0	0	0	0	0	1	0	1	.	.
0	0	0	0	0	0	0	0	0	.	.

United States (CA) — Reported injuries - Lésions déclarées - Lesiones declaradas

Rates of fatal injuries - Taux de lésions mortelles - Tasas de lesiones mortales

Per 100,000 workers employed - Pour 100 000 travailleurs occupés - Por 100 000 trabajadores empleados

Total men and women - Total hommes et femmes - Total hombres y mujeres
ISIC 2 - CITI 2 - CIIU 2   ISIC 3 - CITI 3 - CIIU 3 [5]

	1999	2000	2001	2002	2003	2004	2005	2006	2007	2008	ISIC 3
Total	4	4	4	4	4	4	4	4	4	.	Total
1	24	21	23	23	31	31	33	30	28	.	A-B
2	22	30	30	24	27	28	26	28	25	.	C
3	4	3	3	3	3	3	2	3	3	.	D
5	14	13	13	12	4	6	4	6	4	.	E
7[6]	13	12	11	11	12	12	11	11	11	.	F
8[7]	1	1	1	1	2	2	2	2	2	.	H
9[8]	2	2	2	2	1	1	1	1	1	.	J
					3	3	2	2	3	.	L
					1	1	1	1	1	.	M
					1	1	1	1	1	.	N

Explanatory notes: see p. 1125.

[1] Excl. farms with fewer than 11 employees. [2] Retail trade. [3] Private sector. [4] Public sector. [5] Total and category L also include government sector excluded from the other categories. [6] Incl. public utilities. [7] Excl. business services. [8] Incl. restaurants and hotels and business services; excl. sanitary, repair and installation services.

Notes explicatives: voir p. 1127.

[1] Non compris les fermes avec moins de 11 salariés. [2] Commerce de détail. [3] Secteur privé. [4] Secteur public. [5] Total et catégorie L comprennent en plus le secteur gouvernemental non compris dans les autres catégories. [6] Y compris les services publics. [7] Non compris les services aux entreprises. [8] Y compris les restaurants, hôtels et services aux entreprises; non compris les services sanitaires, de réparation et d'installation.

Notas explicativas: véase p. 1129.

[1] Excl. granjas con menos de 11 asalariados. [2] Comercio al por menor. [3] Sector privado. [4] Sector público. [5] Total y categoría L incluyen egualmante el sector gubernamental excluido de las otras categorías. [6] Incl. los servicios públicos. [7] Excl. servicios para las empresas. [8] Incl. restaurantes, hoteles y servicios paraempresas; excl. servicios de saneamiento, dereparación y de instalación.

OCCUPATIONAL INJURIES

Rates of occupational injuries, by economic activity

LÉSIONS PROFESSIONNELLES

Taux de lésions professionnelles, par activité économique

LESIONES PROFESIONALES

Tasas de lesiones profesionales, por actividad económica

	1999	2000	2001	2002	2003	2004	2005	2006	2007	2008

United States (CA) [1]   Reported injuries - Lésions déclarées - Lesiones declaradas

Rates of fatal injuries - Taux de lésions mortelles - Tasas de lesiones mortales

Per 100,000 workers employed - Pour 100 000 travailleurs occupés - Por 100 000 trabajadores empleados

Men - Hommes - Hombres
ISIC 3 - CITI 3 - CIIU 3

Total	.	.	.	.	7	7	7	7	7	.

Women - Femmes - Mujeres
ISIC 3 - CITI 3 - CIIU 3

Total	.	.	.	.	1	1	1	1	1	.

United States (DA) [2]   Reported injuries - Lésions déclarées - Lesiones declaradas

Rates of non-fatal injuries - Taux de lésions non mortelles - Tasas de lesiones no mortales

Per 200,000 hours worked - Pour 200 000 heures effectuées - Por 200 000 horas trabajadas

Total men and women - Total hommes et femmes - Total hombres y mujeres
ISIC 2 - CITI 2 - CIIU 2   ISIC 3 - CITI 3 - CIIU 3

	1999	2000	2001	2002	2003	2004	2005	2006	2007	2008	
Total	5.9	5.8	5.4	5.0	1.5	1.4	1.4	1.3	1.2	.	Total [3]
1	7.0	6.8	7.0	6.0	2.1	2.3	2.1	1.9	1.8	.	A-B [3]
2	4.1	4.6	3.9	3.8	1.4	1.6	1.5	1.4	1.4	.	C
3	8.0	7.8	7.0	6.4	1.6	1.6	1.5	1.4	1.3	.	D
5	8.4	8.2	7.8	6.9	1.2	1.4	1.3	1.2	1.2	.	E
6	6.0	5.8	5.4	5.1	2.6	2.4	2.4	2.2	1.9	.	F
7	7.0	6.7	6.6	5.8	1.3	1.1	1.0	1.1	1.0	.	H
8	1.6	1.6	1.5	1.5	0.3	0.2	0.3	0.2	0.3	.	J
9	4.6	4.6	4.4	4.3	0.3	.	.	.	.	.	K [4]
					0.8	0.7	0.7	0.7	0.7	.	M
					1.7	1.6	1.6	1.5	1.4	.	N

ASIA-ASIE-ASIA

Azerbaijan (FF)   Reported injuries - Lésions déclarées - Lesiones declaradas

Rates of fatal injuries - Taux de lésions mortelles - Tasas de lesiones mortales

Per 1,000 employees - Pour 1 000 salariés - Por 1 000 asalariados

Total men and women - Total hommes et femmes - Total hombres y mujeres
ISIC 3 - CITI 3 - CIIU 3

	1999	2000	2001	2002	2003	2004	2005	2006	2007	2008
Total	0.04	0.04	0.03	0.06	0.06	0.08	0.06	0.08	0.13	0.07
A	0.13	0.00	0.00	0.00	0.43	0.78	0.24	0.00	0.18	0.16
C					0.10	0.15	0.08	0.23	0.14	0.08
D	0.10	0.10	0.09	0.12	0.33	0.19	0.07	0.23	0.32	0.30
E					0.36	0.52	0.70	0.72	0.57	0.11
F	0.09	0.00	0.00	0.31	0.23	0.83	0.59	0.37	1.46	0.48
G					0.12	0.50	0.98	0.28	0.43	0.71
H					0.00	0.00	0.00	0.00	0.00	0.00
I	0.10	0.08	0.10	0.32	0.17	0.06	0.22	0.15	0.03	0.02
J					0.00	0.00	0.00	0.00	0.00	0.13
K					0.05	0.34	0.02	0.09	0.05	0.05
L					0.00	0.02	0.02	0.03	0.04	0.02
M					0.01	0.00	0.00	0.00	0.00	0.01
N					0.00	0.49	1.21	0.19	0.00	0.12
O					0.03	0.10	0.00	0.13	0.08	0.03

Men - Hommes - Hombres
ISIC 3 - CITI 3 - CIIU 3

	1999	2000	2001	2002	2003	2004	2005	2006	2007	2008
Total	.	.	0.05	0.10	0.11	0.16	0.11	0.15	0.24	0.14
A	.	.	0.00	0.00	0.78	1.26	0.31	0.00	0.25	0.20
C	.	.			0.14	0.20	0.10	0.28	0.16	0.09
D	.	.	0.13	0.15	0.52	0.28	0.10	0.29	0.46	0.42
E	.	.			0.45	0.65	0.81	0.93	0.71	0.13
F	.	.	0.00	0.37	0.26	0.90	0.66	0.42	1.65	0.53
G	.	.			0.17	0.64	1.19	0.37	0.56	0.91
H	.	.			0.00	0.00	0.00	0.00	0.00	0.00
I	.	.	0.13	0.41	0.22	0.08	0.25	0.19	0.04	0.02
J	.	.			0.00	0.00	0.00	0.00	0.00	0.22
K	.	.			0.10	0.57	0.03	0.17	0.10	0.09
L	.	.			0.01	0.05	0.04	0.08	0.10	0.04
M	.	.			0.01	0.00	0.00	0.00	0.01	0.04
N	.	.			0.00	1.39	0.86	0.77	0.00	0.28
O	.	.			0.04	0.18	0.00	0.23	0.10	0.08

Women - Femmes - Mujeres
ISIC 3 - CITI 3 - CIIU 3

	1999	2000	2001	2002	2003	2004	2005	2006	2007	2008
Total	.	.	0.00	0.00	0.00	0.00	0.01	0.01	0.00	0.00

Explanatory notes: see p. 1125.

Notes explicatives: voir p. 1127.

Notas explicativas: véase p. 1129.

[1] Total and category L also include government sector excluded from the other categories. [2] Private sector. [3] Excl. farms with fewer than 11 employees. [4] Incl. sanitary services.

[1] Total et catégorie L comprennent en plus le secteur gouvernemental non compris dans les autres catégories. [2] Secteur privé. [3] Non compris les fermes avec moins de 11 salariés. [4] Y compris les services sanitaires.

[1] Total y categoría L incluyen egualmante el sector gubernamental excluido de las otras categorías. [2] Sector privado. [3] Excl. granjas con menos de 11 asalariados. [4] Incl. los servicios de saneamiento.

OCCUPATIONAL INJURIES

Rates of occupational injuries, by economic activity

LÉSIONS PROFESSIONNELLES

Taux de lésions professionnelles, par activité économique

LESIONES PROFESIONALES

Tasas de lesiones profesionales, por actividad económica

	1999	2000	2001	2002	2003	2004	2005	2006	2007	2008

Azerbaijan (FF) — Reported injuries - Lésions déclarées - Lesiones declaradas

Rates of non-fatal injuries - Taux de lésions non mortelles - Tasas de lesiones no mortales

Per 1,000 employees - Pour 1 000 salariés - Por 1 000 asalariados

Total men and women - Total hommes et femmes - Total hombres y mujeres
ISIC 3 - CITI 3 - CIIU 3

	1999	2000	2001	2002	2003	2004	2005	2006	2007	2008
Total	0.12	0.14	0.09	0.12	0.16	0.19	0.15	0.20	0.20	0.21
A	2.13	0.00	0.00	0.41	0.86	0.39	1.20	0.14	0.27	0.47
C					0.48	0.78	0.49	0.71	0.68	1.89
D	0.40	0.63	0.47	0.62	1.60	0.05	0.72	0.92	0.83	0.97
E					0.41	0.40	0.42	0.18	0.07	0.22
F	0.04	0.06	0.18	0.16	0.29	0.56	1.10	0.84	2.20	0.80
G					0.37	0.40	0.78	1.12	0.32	1.14
H					0.00	0.00	0.00	0.00	0.00	0.00
I	0.49	0.14	0.18	0.18	0.28	0.23	0.31	0.23	0.10	0.28
J					0.00	0.00	0.00	0.00	0.00	0.00
K					0.05	0.11	0.27	0.32	0.05	0.14
L					0.02	0.03	0.02	0.04	0.08	0.09
M					0.00	0.00	0.02	0.00	0.00	0.01
N					0.00	0.49	0.00	0.19	0.13	0.00
O					0.02	0.29	0.00	0.06	0.08	0.20

Men - Hommes - Hombres
ISIC 3 - CITI 3 - CIIU 3

	1999	2000	2001	2002	2003	2004	2005	2006	2007	2008
Total			0.15	0.17	0.29	0.34	0.27	0.36	0.37	0.39
A			0.00	0.62	1.56	0.63	1.24	0.09	0.38	0.61
C					0.64	0.98	0.62	0.86	0.62	2.18
D			0.66	0.71	2.44	1.95	0.95	1.26	1.14	1.32
E					0.51	0.50	0.48	0.23	0.09	0.26
F			0.22	0.19	0.34	0.60	1.23	0.96	2.45	0.89
G					0.50	0.51	0.95	1.48	0.42	1.46
H					0.00	0.00	0.00	0.00	0.00	0.00
I			0.24	0.19	0.38	0.27	0.37	0.29	0.13	0.21
J					0.00	0.00	0.00	0.00	0.00	0.00
K					0.10	0.19	0.34	0.59	0.10	0.09
L					0.05	0.07	0.04	0.10	0.16	0.17
M					0.00	0.00	0.03	0.01	0.00	0.03
N					0.00	0.69	0.00	0.77	0.31	0.00
O					0.04	0.53	0.00	0.11	0.00	0.53

Women - Femmes - Mujeres
ISIC 3 - CITI 3 - CIIU 3

	1999	2000	2001	2002	2003	2004	2005	2006	2007	2008
Total			0.01	0.04	0.01	0.04	0.02	0.02	0.02	0.03
A			0.00	1.19	0.00	0.00	1.05	0.31	0.00	0.00
C					0.00	0.20	0.06	0.19	1.05	0.00
D			0.04	0.38	0.22	0.68	0.26	0.17	0.13	0.08
E					0.00	0.00	0.00	0.00	0.00	0.00
F			0.00	0.00	0.00	0.00	0.00	0.00	0.00	0.00
G					0.00	0.00	0.00	0.00	0.00	0.00
H					0.00	0.00	0.00	0.00	0.00	0.00
I			0.00	0.14	0.00	0.10	0.16	0.00	0.00	0.54
J					0.00	0.00	0.00	0.00	0.00	0.00
K					0.00	0.00	0.10	0.00	0.00	0.20
L					0.00	0.00	0.00	0.01	0.02	0.03
M					0.00	0.00	0.01	0.00	0.00	0.00
N					0.00	0.38	0.00	0.00	0.00	0.00
O					0.00	0.00	0.00	0.00	0.06	0.00

Bahrain (FA) — Reported injuries - Lésions déclarées - Lesiones declaradas

Rates of fatal injuries - Taux de lésions mortelles - Tasas de lesiones mortales

Per 100,000 workers employed - Pour 100 000 travailleurs occupés - Por 100 000 trabajadores empleados

Total men and women - Total hommes et femmes - Total hombres y mujeres
ISIC 2 - CITI 2 - CIIU 2   /   ISIC 3 - CITI 3 - CIIU 3

	1999	2000	2001	2002	2003	2004	2005	2006	2007			
Total	10.7	10.0	5.9	7.5	10.0	5.0	10.0	8.0	7.0	|	5	Total
1	0.0	0.0	0.0	69.5	0.0	47.0	0.0	94.9	0.0	|	0	A
2	0.0	0.0	0.0	0.0	0.0	0.0	0.0	0.0	0.0	|	24	B
3	11.0	7.3	0.0	5.9	13.0	9.0	5.0	8.0	8.0	|	0	C
4	28.0	28.9	0.0	0.0	0.0	0.0	0.0	74.0	0.0	|	4	D
5	16.3	6.7	10.6	9.5	17.0	9.0	19.0	9.0	9.0	|	0	E
6	3.5	0.0	2.9	5.2	2.0	2.0	8.0	5.0	7.0	|	8	F
7	19.3	76.3	9.7	9.7	0.0	0.0	8.0	7.0	7.0	|	5	G
8	0.0	11.0	0.0	0.0	0.0	0.0	0.0	0.0	0.0	|	4	H
9	5.7	0.0	15.8	8.8	8.0	0.0	5.0	2.0	2.0	|	11	I
										|	0	J
										|	3	K
										|	0	L
										|	0	M
										|	0	N
										|	0	O
										|	0	P
										|	0	Q
										|	0	X

Explanatory notes: see p. 1125.   Notes explicatives: voir p. 1127.   Notas explicativas: véase p. 1129.

OCCUPATIONAL INJURIES

Rates of occupational injuries, by economic activity

LÉSIONS PROFESSIONNELLES

Taux de lésions professionnelles, par activité économique

LESIONES PROFESIONALES

Tasas de lesiones profesionales, por actividad económica

8B

	1999	2000	2001	2002	2003	2004	2005	2006	2007	2008

Bahrain (FA) — Reported injuries - Lésions déclarées - Lesiones declaradas

Rates of non-fatal injuries - Taux de lésions non mortelles - Tasas de lesiones no mortales

Per 100,000 workers employed - Pour 100 000 travailleurs occupés - Por 100 000 trabajadores empleados

Total men and women - Total hommes et femmes - Total hombres y mujeres

ISIC 2 - CITI 2 - CIIU 2   ISIC 3 - CITI 3 - CIIU 3

	1999	2000	2001	2002	2003	2004	2005	2006	2007	2008	
Total	.	.	.	.	775	633	659	490	296 |	221	Total
1	.	.	.	.	1 347	1 137	597	427	156 |	147	A
2	.	.	.	.	0	0	0	0	0 |	24	B
3	.	.	.	.	1 061	948	964	831	513 |	807	C
4	.	.	.	.	1 474	1 062	1 427	514	146 |	424	D
5	.	.	.	.	912	681	836	582	418 |	0	E
6	.	.	.	.	390	310	314	239	112 |	99	F
7	.	.	.	.	993	914	1 133	861	353 |	337	G
8	.	.	.	.	324	398	292	207	160 |	85	H
9	.	.	.	.	535	431	402	274	120 |	298	I
									|	134	J
									|	71	K
									|	0	L
									|	37	M
									|	95	N
									|	11	O
									|	0	P
									|	0	Q
									|	0	X

Hong Kong, China (FF) — Reported injuries - Lésions déclarées - Lesiones declaradas

Rates of fatal injuries - Taux de lésions mortelles - Tasas de lesiones mortales

Per 100,000 employees - Pour 100 000 salariés - Por 100 000 asalariados

Total men and women - Total hommes et femmes - Total hombres y mujeres

ISIC 2 - CITI 2 - CIIU 2

	1999	2000	2001	2002	2003	2004	2005	2006	2007	2008
Total	9.7	8.0	7.1	8.6	7.2	7.7	7.5	7.3	6.6	.
2	0.0	429.2	0.0	0.0	0.0	0.0	0.0	.	0.0	
3	16.1	15.1	12.7	8.3	11.0	17.3	8.5	13.1	13.4	.
4 [1]	0.0	0.0	24.3	0.0	12.0	12.2	0.0	0.0	12.6	.
5 [2]	90.2	59.0	52.3	64.2	51.5	34.6	69.2	37.8	73.7	.
6	0.9	1.6	1.2	1.9	1.0	1.9	1.5	2.5	1.5	.
7	23.5	14.0	20.2	20.5	15.1	15.1	18.0	15.7	13.7	.
8	10.3	10.0	8.7	12.8	9.5	11.2	11.4	11.5	9.1	.
9 [3]	7.2	6.0	3.4	6.2	7.3	6.5	5.2	5.7	3.9	.

Rates of non-fatal injuries - Taux de lésions non mortelles - Tasas de lesiones no mortales

Per 100,000 employees - Pour 100 000 salariés - Por 100 000 asalariados

Total men and women - Total hommes et femmes - Total hombres y mujeres [4]

ISIC 2 - CITI 2 - CIIU 2

	1999	2000	2001	2002	2003	2004	2005	2006	2007	2008
Total	2 419	2 323	2 150	1 913	1 759	1 804	1 774	1 833	1 682	.
2	3 888	3 004	5 612	5 147	794	1 320	1 581	0	0	.
3	2 724	2 995	2 808	2 636	2 302	2 518	2 487	2 621	2 513	.
4	685	837	826	516	694	645	809	627	405	.
5	19 889	15 064	11 559	8 634	7 039	6 134	6 118	6 581	6 173	.
6	1 351	1 709	1 661	1 481	1 352	1 431	1 366	1 410	1 317	.
7	3 236	3 123	2 768	2 596	2 377	2 583	2 669	2 948	2 638	.
8	955	1 002	1 029	1 000	1 056	1 162	1 145	1 222	1 133	.
9	2 028	2 105	2 099	2 019	2 006	1 991	2 033	2 056	1 866	.

India (FF) — Reported injuries - Lésions déclarées - Lesiones declaradas

Rates of fatal injuries - Taux de lésions mortelles - Tasas de lesiones mortales

Per 100,000 employees - Pour 100 000 salariés - Por 100 000 asalariados

Total men and women - Total hommes et femmes - Total hombres y mujeres

ISIC 3 - CITI 3 - CIIU 3

	1999	2000	2001	2002	2003	2004	2005	2006	2007	2008
C	32	31	37	28	31	28	30	38	27	.

Men - Hommes - Hombres

ISIC 3 - CITI 3 - CIIU 3

	1999	2000	2001	2002	2003	2004	2005	2006	2007	2008
C	32	33	38	27	31	29	31	39	.	.

Women - Femmes - Mujeres

ISIC 3 - CITI 3 - CIIU 3

	1999	2000	2001	2002	2003	2004	2005	2006	2007	2008
C	22	3	15	44	18	11	8	19	.	.

Explanatory notes: see p. 1125.

[1] Excl. water. [2] Manual workers. [3] Incl. water. [4] Incapacity of 4 days or more.

Notes explicatives: voir p. 1127.

[1] Non compris l'eau. [2] Travailleurs manuels. [3] Y compris l'eau. [4] Incapacité de 4 jours et plus.

Notas explicativas: véase p. 1129.

[1] Excl. el agua. [2] Trabajadores manuales. [3] Incl. el agua. [4] Incapacidad de 4 días y más.

8B

OCCUPATIONAL INJURIES	LÉSIONS PROFESSIONNELLES	LESIONES PROFESIONALES
Rates of occupational injuries, by economic activity	Taux de lésions professionnelles, par activité économique	Tasas de lesiones profesionales, por actividad económica

	1999	2000	2001	2002	2003	2004	2005	2006	2007	2008

India (FF) — Reported injuries - Lésions déclarées - Lesiones declaradas

Rates of non-fatal injuries - Taux de lésions non mortelles - Tasas de lesiones no mortales

Per 100,000 employees - Pour 100 000 salariés - Por 100 000 asalariados

Total men and women - Total hommes et femmes - Total hombres y mujeres
ISIC 3 - CITI 3 - CIIU 3

	1999	2000	2001	2002	2003	2004	2005	2006	2007	2008
C	137	141	155	150	135	210	224	180	166	

Men - Hommes - Hombres
ISIC 3 - CITI 3 - CIIU 3

	1999	2000	2001	2002	2003	2004	2005	2006	2007	2008
C	144	148	162	157	141	220	234	188		

Women - Femmes - Mujeres
ISIC 3 - CITI 3 - CIIU 3

	1999	2000	2001	2002	2003	2004	2005	2006	2007	2008
C	17	12	15	15	26	22	15	19		

Japan (FF) — Reported injuries - Lésions déclarées - Lesiones declaradas

Rates of fatal injuries - Taux de lésions mortelles - Tasas de lesiones mortales

Per 1,000,000 hours worked - Pour 1 000 000 heures effectuées - Por 1 000 000 horas trabajadas

Total men and women - Total hommes et femmes - Total hombres y mujeres [1]
ISIC 3 - CITI 3 - CIIU 3

	1999	2000	2001	2002	2003	2004	2005	2006	2007	2008
Total [2]	0.01	0.01	0.01	0.01	0.01	0.01	0.01	0.01	0.01	0.00
A [3]	0.00	0.00	0.00	0.00	0.00					
C	0.04	0.19	0.06	0.00	0.08	0.09	0.00	0.00	0.00	0.00
D	0.01	0.01	0.01	0.01	0.00	0.01	0.01	0.01	0.01	0.01
E	0.00	0.00	0.00	0.00	0.00	0.00	0.00	0.00	0.00	0.01
F [4]	0.03	0.08	0.04	0.01	0.01	0.06	0.01	0.04	0.04	0.04
G [5]	0.00	0.01	0.01	0.00	0.00	0.01	0.00	0.00	0.00	0.00
I	0.02	0.02	0.02	0.01	0.01					
O	0.01	0.01	0.02	0.01	0.01					

Jordan (FA) — Reported injuries - Lésions déclarées - Lesiones declaradas

Rates of fatal injuries - Taux de lésions mortelles - Tasas de lesiones mortales

Per 1,000,000 hours worked - Pour 1 000 000 heures effectuées - Por 1 000 000 horas trabajadas

Total men and women - Total hommes et femmes - Total hombres y mujeres
ISIC 3 - CITI 3 - CIIU 3

	1999	2000	2001	2002	2003	2004	2005	2006	2007	2008
Total			0.069	0.052	0.062	0.039	0.025	0.055		

Rates of non-fatal injuries - Taux de lésions non mortelles - Tasas de lesiones no mortales

Per 1,000,000 hours worked - Pour 1 000 000 heures effectuées - Por 1 000 000 horas trabajadas

Total men and women - Total hommes et femmes - Total hombres y mujeres
ISIC 3 - CITI 3 - CIIU 3

	1999	2000	2001	2002	2003	2004	2005	2006	2007	2008
Total			14.880	11.310	14.780	10.270	9.630	9.640		

Kazakhstan (FF) — Reported injuries - Lésions déclarées - Lesiones declaradas

Rates of fatal injuries - Taux de lésions mortelles - Tasas de lesiones mortales

Per 100,000 workers employed - Pour 100 000 travailleurs occupés - Por 100 000 trabajadores empleados

Total men and women - Total hommes et femmes - Total hombres y mujeres
ISIC 3 - CITI 3 - CIIU 3

	1999	2000	2001	2002	2003	2004	2005	2006	2007	2008
Total	9.7	11.3	9.7	10.7	9.3	10.4	10.3	11.3	8.7	8.2

Men - Hommes - Hombres
ISIC 3 - CITI 3 - CIIU 3

	1999	2000	2001	2002	2003	2004	2005	2006	2007	2008
Total	16.4	19.4	17.2	17.2	15.9	17.7	17.2	17.8	15.0	14.1

Women - Femmes - Mujeres
ISIC 3 - CITI 3 - CIIU 3

	1999	2000	2001	2002	2003	2004	2005	2006	2007	2008
Total	1.8	1.9	0.8	1.4	1.3	1.8	2.0	1.6	1.1	0.8

Rates of non-fatal injuries - Taux de lésions non mortelles - Tasas de lesiones no mortales

Per 100,000 workers employed - Pour 100 000 travailleurs occupés - Por 100 000 trabajadores empleados

Total men and women - Total hommes et femmes - Total hombres y mujeres
ISIC 3 - CITI 3 - CIIU 3

	1999	2000	2001	2002	2003	2004	2005	2006	2007	2008
Total	132	142	112	116	107	101	96	87	73	65

Explanatory notes: see p. 1125.

[1] Establishments with 100 or more regular employees. [2] Excl. general construction. [3] Forestry only. [4] General construction only. [5] Excl. repair of motor vehicles, motor cycles and personal and household goods.

Notes explicatives: voir p. 1127.

[1] Etablissements de 100 salariés stables et plus. [2] Non compris la construction générale. [3] Sylviculture seulement. [4] Construction générale seulement. [5] Non compris réparation de véhicules automobiles, de motocycles et de biens personnels etdomestiques.

Notas explicativas: véase p. 1129.

[1] Establecimientos de 100 y más asalariados etables. [2] Excl. construcción general. [3] Silvicultura solamente. [4] Construcción general solamente. [5] Excl. reparación de vehículos automotores, motocicletas, efectos personals y enseres domesticos.

	1999	2000	2001	2002	2003	2004	2005	2006	2007	2008

Kazakhstan (FF)   Reported injuries - Lésions déclarées - Lesiones declaradas

Rates of non-fatal injuries - Taux de lésions non mortelles - Tasas de lesiones no mortales

Per 100,000 workers employed - Pour 100 000 travailleurs occupés - Por 100 000 trabajadores empleados

Men - Hommes - Hombres
ISIC 3 - CITI 3 - CIIU 3

	1999	2000	2001	2002	2003	2004	2005	2006	2007	2008
Total	200	222	173	165	162	157	147	121	109	96

Women - Femmes - Mujeres
ISIC 3 - CITI 3 - CIIU 3

	1999	2000	2001	2002	2003	2004	2005	2006	2007	2008
Total	51	50	39	46	42	35	36	37	29	26

Korea, Republic of (FA)   Compensated injuries - Lésions indemnisées - Lesiones indemnizadas

Rates of fatal injuries - Taux de lésions mortelles - Tasas de lesiones mortales

Per 1,000,000 hours worked - Pour 1 000 000 heures effectuées - Por 1 000 000 horas trabajadas

Total men and women - Total hommes et femmes - Total hombres y mujeres
ISIC 3 - CITI 3 - CIIU 3

	1999	2000	2001	2002	2003	2004	2005	2006	2007	2008
Total	0.08	0.06	0.05	0.05	0.06	0.06	0.05	0.05	0.04	0.05
A [1]	0.10	0.05	0.06	0.06	0.08	0.13	0.08	0.06	0.08	0.11
B	1.81	6.23	2.83	4.88	4.23	6.18	1.45	0.00	0.16	0.28
C	0.81	0.57	0.87	0.66	0.84	0.79	0.44	0.37	0.41	0.32
D	0.06	0.06	0.05	0.05	0.05	0.05	0.05	0.05	0.05	0.05
E	0.05	0.06	0.02	0.07	0.05	0.02	0.03	0.03	0.03	0.03
F	0.12	0.09	0.09	0.08	0.10	0.13	0.10	0.09	0.08	0.09
G-H,K,M-P,X [2]	0.05	0.03	0.02	0.03	0.03	0.03	0.03	0.02	0.02	0.02
I	0.12	0.08	0.07	0.07	0.07	0.06	0.05	0.05	0.06	0.07
J	0.03	0.02	0.01	0.01	0.01	0.00	0.01	0.01	0.01	0.01

Kyrgyzstan (FF)   Reported injuries - Lésions déclarées - Lesiones declaradas

Rates of fatal injuries - Taux de lésions mortelles - Tasas de lesiones mortales

Per 100,000 workers employed - Pour 100 000 travailleurs occupés - Por 100 000 trabajadores empleados

Total men and women - Total hommes et femmes - Total hombres y mujeres
ISIC 3 - CITI 3 - CIIU 3

	1999	2000	2001	2002	2003	2004	2005	2006	2007	2008
Total	6	7	7	7	5	8	5	5	.	.
A	3	3	8	12	3	8	0	0	.	.
B	0	0	0	0	0	0	0	0	.	.
C	30	102	58	77	26	0	14	157	.	.
D	9	4	4	14	12	12	7	12	.	.
E	37	24	25	27	22	27	33	14	.	.
F	14	19	31	4	5	34	22	10	.	.
G	5	4	11	10	7	0	14	0	.	.
H	0	0	42	0	67	0	0	0	.	.
I	11	4	8	3	6	9	3	3	.	.
J	0	0	0	0	0	16	0	0	.	.
K	0	23	4	0	5	4	13	4	.	.
L	4	4	7	4	2	9	1	2	.	.
M	0	0	2	0	0	0	0	0	.	.
N	3	1	0	2	0	0	2	0	.	.
O	0	0	0	0	14	0	0	0	.	.
P	0	0	0	0	0	0	0	0	.	.

Rates of non-fatal injuries - Taux de lésions non mortelles - Tasas de lesiones no mortales

Per 100,000 workers employed - Pour 100 000 travailleurs occupés - Por 100 000 trabajadores empleados

Total men and women - Total hommes et femmes - Total hombres y mujeres
ISIC 3 - CITI 3 - CIIU 3

	1999	2000	2001	2002	2003	2004	2005	2006	2007	2008
Total	57	47	46	45	38	38	39	32	.	.
A	3	41	55	31	70	29	13	30	.	.
B	0	0	0	0	0	0	0	0	.	.
C	359	216	250	180	104	102	285	315	.	.
D	125	111	101	119	78	87	107	110	.	.
E	115	43	87	77	74	50	76	101	.	.
F	106	43	117	81	89	19	54	55	.	.
G	91	17	32	20	35	15	104	9	.	.
H	0	0	0	0	0	38	36	0	.	.
I	79	90	51	54	41	102	63	49	.	.
J	56	17	36	0	132	145	43	0	.	.
K	25	77	43	85	41	27	31	17	.	.
L	19	14	10	7	13	25	9	7	.	.
M	12	15	9	4	2	7	6	2	.	.
N	32	34	31	40	16	19	36	5	.	.
O	64	13	44	48	27	17	8	11	.	.

Explanatory notes: see p. 1125.   Notes explicatives: voir p. 1127.   Notas explicativas: véase p. 1129.

[1] Excl. hunting. [2] Incl. hunting.   [1] Non compris la chasse. [2] Y compris la chasse.   [1] Excl. la caza. [2] Incl. caza.

8B

OCCUPATIONAL INJURIES	LÉSIONS PROFESSIONNELLES	LESIONES PROFESIONALES
Rates of occupational injuries, by economic activity	Taux de lésions professionnelles, par activité économique	Tasas de lesiones profesionales, por actividad económica

	1999	2000	2001	2002	2003	2004	2005	2006	2007	2008
Myanmar (FF) [1]					**Reported injuries - Lésions déclarées - Lesiones declaradas**					

Rates of fatal injuries - Taux de lésions mortelles - Tasas de lesiones mortales

Per 100,000 employees - Pour 100 000 salariés - Por 100 000 asalariados

Total men and women - Total hommes et femmes - Total hombres y mujeres
ISIC 3 - CITI 3 - CIIU 3

	1999	2000	2001	2002	2003	2004	2005	2006	2007	2008
Total	.	.	.	.	3	3	2	.	7	8
C	0	10	10	10	0	28	9	.	36	58
D	5	5	4	2	4	2	2	.	6	5
E	0	0	0	22	0	0	0	.	0	48
G	13	0	0	0	5	9	3	.	12	40

Men - Hommes - Hombres
ISIC 3 - CITI 3 - CIIU 3

	1999	2000	2001	2002	2003	2004	2005	2006	2007	2008
Total	.	.	.	.	.	5	2	.	12	14
C	0	10	.	10	.	28	11	.	36	58
D	8	9	.	4	.	2	2	.	7	7
E	0	0	.	22	.	0	0	.	0	67
G	11	0	.	0	.	9	0	.	12	40

Women - Femmes - Mujeres
ISIC 3 - CITI 3 - CIIU 3

	1999	2000	2001	2002	2003	2004	2005	2006	2007	2008
Total	.	.	.	.	.	1	2	.	1	2
C	0	2	.	0	.	0	0	.	0	0
D	1	0	.	1	.	1	2	.	1	1
E	0	0	.	0	.	0	0	.	0	0
G	0	0	.	0	.	0	0	.	0	0

Rates of non-fatal injuries - Taux de lésions non mortelles - Tasas de lesiones no mortales

Per 100,000 employees - Pour 100 000 salariés - Por 100 000 asalariados

Total men and women - Total hommes et femmes - Total hombres y mujeres [2]
ISIC 3 - CITI 3 - CIIU 3

	1999	2000	2001	2002	2003	2004	2005	2006	2007	2008
Total	.	.	.	.	77	84	52	.	33	40
C	485	487	348	215	323	224	132	.	117	107
D	108	88	100	101	56	79	41	.	26	29
E	306	46	337	88	90	360	130	.	108	457
G	616	423	0	366	296	133	113	.	62	102

Men - Hommes - Hombres [2]
ISIC 3 - CITI 3 - CIIU 3

	1999	2000	2001	2002	2003	2004	2005	2006	2007	2008
Total	.	.	.	.	.	117	72	.	49	54
C	485	172	.	215	.	224	160	.	117	107
D	161	158	.	131	.	102	80	.	24	36
E	306	183	.	88	.	340	167	.	109	508
G	518	441	.	366	.	133	138	.	62	102

Women - Femmes - Mujeres [2]
ISIC 3 - CITI 3 - CIIU 3

	1999	2000	2001	2002	2003	2004	2005	2006	2007	2008
Total	.	.	.	.	.	54	29	.	11	22
C	0	0	.	0	.	0	0	.	0	0
D	41	34	.	75	.	52	25	.	31	20
E	0	0	.	0	.	445	270	.	109	333
G	0	0	.	0	.	0	.	.	0	0

	1999	2000	2001	2002	2003	2004	2005	2006	2007	2008
Singapore (FF)					**Reported injuries - Lésions déclarées - Lesiones declaradas**					

Rates of fatal injuries - Taux de lésions mortelles - Tasas de lesiones mortales

Per 1,000,000 hours worked - Pour 1 000 000 heures effectuées - Por 1 000 000 horas trabajadas

Total men and women - Total hommes et femmes - Total hombres y mujeres
ISIC 3 - CITI 3 - CIIU 3

	1999	2000	2001	2002	2003	2004	2005	2006	2007	2008
Total	0.0	0.0	0.0	0.0	0.0	0.0	0.0	0.0	.	.
A	0.0	0.0	0.0	0.0	0.0	0.0	0.0	0.0	.	.
B	0.0	0.0	0.0	0.0	0.0	0.0	0.0	0.0	.	.
C	0.0	0.0	0.0	0.0	0.0	0.0	0.0	0.0	.	.
D	0.0	0.0	0.0	0.0	0.0	0.0	0.0	0.0	.	.
E	0.0	0.0	0.2	0.0	0.0	0.0	0.0	0.0	.	.
F	0.1	0.0	0.1	0.1	0.1	0.1	0.1	0.0	.	.
G	0.0	0.0	0.3	0.0	0.0	0.0	0.4	0.0	.	.
H	0.1	0.0	0.0	0.0	0.1	0.0	0.0	0.0	.	.
I	0.0	0.0	0.0	0.0	0.0	0.0	0.0	0.0	.	.
K	0.0	0.0	0.0	0.0	0.0	0.1	0.1	0.0	.	.
L	0.0	0.0	0.0	0.0	0.0	0.0	0.0	0.0	.	.
M	.	.	.	.	.	.	.	0.0	.	.
N	0.0	0.0	0.0	0.0	0.0	0.0	0.0	0.0	.	.
O	0.0	0.0	0.0	0.0	0.0	0.0	0.0	0.0	.	.
P	0.0	0.0	0.0	0.0	0.0	0.0	0.0	0.0	.	.

Explanatory notes: see p. 1125.   Notes explicatives: voir p. 1127.   Notas explicativas: véase p. 1129.

[1] Year ending in March of the year indicated. [2] Incapacity of 2 days or more.

[1] Année se terminant en mars de l'année indiquée. [2] Incapacité de 2 jours et plus.

[1] Año que termina en marzo del año indicado. [2] Incapacidad de 2 días y más.

OCCUPATIONAL INJURIES

Rates of occupational injuries, by economic activity

LÉSIONS PROFESSIONNELLES

Taux de lésions professionnelles, par activité économique

LESIONES PROFESIONALES

Tasas de lesiones profesionales, por actividad económica

8B

	1999	2000	2001	2002	2003	2004	2005	2006	2007	2008

Singapore (FF)   Reported injuries - Lésions déclarées - Lesiones declaradas

Rates of fatal injuries - Taux de lésions mortelles - Tasas de lesiones mortales

Per 100,000 workers employed - Pour 100 000 travailleurs occupés - Por 100 000 trabajadores empleados

Total men and women - Total hommes et femmes - Total hombres y mujeres [1]
ISIC 3 - CITI 3 - CIIU 3

	1999	2000	2001	2002	2003	2004	2005	2006	2007	2008
Total	.	.	.	.	.	.	.	.	2.9	2.8
D	.	.	.	.	.	.	.	.	3.7	2.9
F	.	.	.	.	.	.	.	.	8.1	6.9
G	.	.	.	.	.	.	.	.	0.3	0.2
H	.	.	.	.	.	.	.	.	2.7	3.0
J	.	.	.	.	.	.	.	.	0.0	0.0
K	.	.	.	.	.	.	.	.	0.0	0.0
L	.	.	.	.	.	.	.	.	0.0	0.0
M	.	.	.	.	.	.	.	.	0.0	2.9
N	.	.	.	.	.	.	.	.	0.0	0.0
O	.	.	.	.	.	.	.	.	2.4	0.0
P-Q	.	.	.	.	.	.	.	.	0.2	0.3

Rates of non-fatal injuries - Taux de lésions non mortelles - Tasas de lesiones no mortales

Per 1,000,000 hours worked - Pour 1 000 000 heures effectuées - Por 1 000 000 horas trabajadas

Total men and women - Total hommes et femmes - Total hombres y mujeres [1]
ISIC 3 - CITI 3 - CIIU 3

	1999	2000	2001	2002	2003	2004	2005	2006	2007	2008
Total	2.4	2.1	2.3	2.2	2.2	2.2	2.1	1.9	.	.
D	2.1	1.8	0.0	1.9	1.8	1.8	1.7	2.5	.	.
E	4.4	3.3	2.0	2.2	2.0	2.3	1.7	0.0	.	.
F	2.7	2.5	2.9	2.9	2.8	3.0	3.0	3.5	.	.
G	0.3	0.9	0.3	1.7	2.4	0.5	0.7	0.5	.	.
H	0.6	0.7	0.2	0.3	1.4	2.0	3.2	1.9	.	.
I	1.6	0.8	1.5	1.5	1.4	1.4	1.9	1.4	.	.
K	0.8	0.6	0.9	0.8	0.4	0.5	0.8	0.6	.	.
L	0.0	0.0	0.0	0.0	0.0	0.0	0.0	0.0	.	.
M	.	.	.	.	.	.	.	0.4	.	.
N	0.0	0.0	0.0	0.0	0.6	0.0	0.0	1.1	.	.
O	1.2	0.9	0.9	1.0	1.6	0.9	1.2	0.4	.	.

Per 100,000 workers employed - Pour 100 000 travailleurs occupés - Por 100 000 trabajadores empleados

Total men and women - Total hommes et femmes - Total hombres y mujeres [1]
ISIC 3 - CITI 3 - CIIU 3

	1999	2000	2001	2002	2003	2004	2005	2006	2007	2008
Total	.	.	.	.	.	.	.	.	460.0	469.0
D	.	.	.	.	.	.	.	.	665.0	633.0
F	.	.	.	.	.	.	.	.	831.0	796.0
G	.	.	.	.	.	.	.	.	111.0	114.0
H	.	.	.	.	.	.	.	.	324.0	397.0
J	.	.	.	.	.	.	.	.	429.0	409.0
K	.	.	.	.	.	.	.	.	30.0	26.0
L	.	.	.	.	.	.	.	.	63.0	58.0
M	.	.	.	.	.	.	.	.	243.0	199.0
N	.	.	.	.	.	.	.	.	113.0	124.0
O	.	.	.	.	.	.	.	.	139.0	93.0
P-Q	.	.	.	.	.	.	.	.	132.0	145.0

Sri Lanka (FF)   Reported injuries - Lésions déclarées - Lesiones declaradas

Rates of fatal injuries - Taux de lésions mortelles - Tasas de lesiones mortales

Per 1,000,000 hours worked - Pour 1 000 000 heures effectuées - Por 1 000 000 horas trabajadas

Total men and women - Total hommes et femmes - Total hombres y mujeres
ISIC 3 - CITI 3 - CIIU 3

	1999	2000	2001	2002	2003	2004	2005	2006	2007	2008
Total	0.072	0.009	0.007	0.008	0.010	0.007	0.009	0.014	0.012	0.008
C	0.060	0.020	0.068	0.000	0.054	0.022	0.000	0.000	0.036	0.007
D	0.094	0.008	0.010	0.009	0.006	0.005	0.006	0.018	0.030	0.009
E	0.131	0.021	0.000	0.000	0.000	0.157	0.109	0.106	0.157	0.106
F	0.149	0.016	0.019	0.013	0.028	0.012	0.028	0.029	0.032	0.019
G	.	.	.	.	.	0.002	0.000	0.000	0.000	0.000
H	.	0.001	0.000	0.000	0.000	0.004	0.000	0.003	0.000	0.000
I	0.075	0.015	0.000	0.009	0.008	0.007	0.008	0.009	0.033	0.021
O	.	.	.	.	.	0.005	0.000	0.000	0.000	0.000

Explanatory notes: see p. 1125.

[1] Incapacity of 4 days or more.

Notes explicatives: voir p. 1127.

[1] Incapacité de 4 jours et plus.

Notas explicativas: véase p. 1129.

[1] Incapacidad de 4 días y más.

8B

OCCUPATIONAL INJURIES	LÉSIONS PROFESSIONNELLES	LESIONES PROFESIONALES
Rates of occupational injuries, by economic activity	Taux de lésions professionnelles, par activité économique	Tasas de lesiones profesionales, por actividad económica

	1999	2000	2001	2002	2003	2004	2005	2006	2007	2008

Sri Lanka (FF) — Reported injuries - Lésions déclarées - Lesiones declaradas

Rates of non-fatal injuries - Taux de lésions non mortelles - Tasas de lesiones no mortales

Per 1,000,000 hours worked - Pour 1 000 000 heures effectuées - Por 1 000 000 horas trabajadas

Total men and women - Total hommes et femmes - Total hombres y mujeres
ISIC 3 - CITI 3 - CIIU 3

	1999	2000	2001	2002	2003	2004	2005	2006	2007	2008
Total	4.182	0.445	0.526	0.411	0.364	0.235	0.231	0.279	0.274	0.244
C	0.060	0.020	0.068	0.051	0.015	0.000	0.060	0.447	0.988	0.049
D	9.426	0.897	1.199	0.780	0.682	0.483	0.535	0.622	1.342	0.467
E	3.018	0.457	0.164	0.157	0.279	0.456	0.362	0.273	0.236	0.379
F	1.537	0.138	0.123	0.121	0.086	0.039	0.050	0.028	0.050	0.045
G						0.000	0.000	0.000	0.000	0.000
H	0.093	0.003	0.007	0.005	0.008	0.011	0.022	0.036	0.062	0.022
I	1.175	0.208	0.191	0.164	0.102	0.078	0.086	0.131	1.366	0.819
O						0.000	0.000	0.000	0.000	0.000

Taiwan, China (FF) — Reported injuries - Lésions déclarées - Lesiones declaradas

Rates of fatal injuries - Taux de lésions mortelles - Tasas de lesiones mortales

Per 100,000 workers insured - Pour 100 000 travailleurs assurés - Por 100 000 trabajadores asegurados

Total men and women - Total hommes et femmes - Total hombres y mujeres
ISIC 2 - CITI 2 - CIIU 2

	1999	2000	2001	2002	2003	2004	2005	2006	2007	2008
Total	8.5	7.7	6.9	6.5	5.0	4.4	4.5	.	.	.
1	30.1	28.3	19.4	21.7	17.8	15.7	10.7	.	.	.
2	72.9	51.7	.	48.9	52.4	35.6	19.0	.	.	.
3	7.8	6.3	6.7	5.9	4.1	3.0	3.8	.	.	.
4	26.8	10.1	13.7	10.4	13.9	17.7	14.2	.	.	.
5	20.3	22.3	21.0	18.8	17.5	13.1	17.2	.	.	.
6	4.3	3.8	3.6	3.2	2.0	2.3	2.1	.	.	.
7	9.2	11.2	8.3	8.9	7.2	6.7	7.9	.	.	.
8	.	.	5.9	6.4	4.8	4.3	4.9	.	.	.
9	.	.	1.9	1.7	1.5	2.6	1.3	.	.	.

Rates of non-fatal injuries - Taux de lésions non mortelles - Tasas de lesiones no mortales

Per 100,000 workers insured - Pour 100 000 travailleurs assurés - Por 100 000 trabajadores asegurados

Total men and women - Total hommes et femmes - Total hombres y mujeres
ISIC 2 - CITI 2 - CIIU 2

	1999	2000	2001	2002	2003	2004	2005	2006	2007	2008
Total	433	489	486	456	445	453	433	.	.	.
1	125	135	141	122	121	122	99	.	.	.
2	1 166	1 138	912	820	612	581	739	.	.	.
3	623	701	709	656	644	649	625	.	.	.
4	130	125	83	119	56	96	14	.	.	.
5	1 129	1 318	1 355	1 281	1 296	1 327	1 262	.	.	.
6	257	300	321	306	310	317	315	.	.	.
7	332	354	360	340	338	354	343	.	.	.
8	68	84	81	68	73	76	74	.	.	.
9	114	147	150	153	144	156	155	.	.	.

Thailand (FA) — Compensated injuries - Lésions indemnisées - Lesiones indemnizadas

Rates of fatal injuries - Taux de lésions mortelles - Tasas de lesiones mortales

Per 100,000 workers insured - Pour 100 000 travailleurs assurés - Por 100 000 trabajadores asegurados

Total men and women - Total hommes et femmes - Total hombres y mujeres
ISIC 3 - CITI 3 - CIIU 3

	1999	2000	2001	2002	2003	2004	2005	2006	2007	2008
Total	11.5	11.3	0.1	9.9	11.2	11.7	18.7	10.1	9.1	.

Rates of non-fatal injuries - Taux de lésions non mortelles - Tasas de lesiones no mortales

Per 100,000 workers insured - Pour 100 000 travailleurs assurés - Por 100 000 trabajadores asegurados

Total men and women - Total hommes et femmes - Total hombres y mujeres [1]
ISIC 3 - CITI 3 - CIIU 3

	1999	2000	2001	2002	2003	2004	2005	2006	2007	2008
Total	966	925	903	802	799	767	739	692	658	.

Explanatory notes: see p. 1125.	Notes explicatives: voir p. 1127.	Notas explicativas: véase p. 1129.
[1] Incapacity of 3 days or more.	[1] Incapacité de 3 jours et plus.	[1] Incapacidad de 3 días y más.

Rates of occupational injuries, by economic activity

Taux de lésions professionnelles, par activité économique

Tasas de lesiones profesionales, por actividad económica

	1999	2000	2001	2002	2003	2004	2005	2006	2007	2008

EUROPE-EUROPE-EUROPA

Austria (FA)   **Reported injuries - Lésions déclarées - Lesiones declaradas**

Rates of fatal injuries - Taux de lésions mortelles - Tasas de lesiones mortales

Per 100,000 employees - Pour 100 000 salariés - Por 100 000 asalariados

Total men and women - Total hommes et femmes - Total hombres y mujeres
ISIC 3 - CITI 3 - CIIU 3

	1999	2000	2001	2002	2003	2004	2005	2006	2007	2008
Total	4.9	5.3	4.5	4.7	3.9	5.0	4.6	3.9	3.9	.
A-B	34.8	39.0	23.5	50.3	41.8	.	.	.	.	.
A	.	.	.	.	.	37.7	29.9	26.0	32.0	.
B	.	.	.	.	.	0.0	0.0	0.0	0.0	.
C	21.5	7.3	29.8	22.6	15.1	23.0	15.4	7.9	0.0	.
D	4.2	4.2	3.9	5.3	2.4	3.8	3.7	2.8	3.2	.
E	6.6	3.4	7.0	14.6	7.7	7.7	3.8	4.0	0.0	.
F	15.6	18.6	12.9	15.0	14.3	13.2	16.6	17.1	12.5	.
G	1.6	2.2	2.0	1.6	1.6	2.4	1.8	1.8	2.1	.
H	2.7	4.7	1.3	0.6	0.0	1.3	0.6	0.0	0.0	.
I	11.3	15.2	19.5	8.6	13.1	18.8	12.7	11.8	12.4	.
J	2.8	0.9	0.0	0.0	0.9	1.8	0.0	0.9	3.5	.
K	3.4	2.4	2.6	3.9	2.4	3.7	3.6	2.1	3.5	.
L	2.1	1.1	0.4	1.1	0.8	2.7	2.2	1.3	2.3	.
M	0.0	0.0	0.0	0.0	2.1	0.0	2.4	0.0	0.0	.
N	0.0	1.4	1.3	0.0	0.0	0.6	1.2	0.0	0.6	.
O	4.4	3.6	3.5	2.1	2.8	2.8	4.1	3.4	2.0	.
P	0.0	0.0	0.0	0.0	0.0	29.6	29.9	0.0	0.0	.
Q	0.0	0.0	0.0	0.0	0.0	0.0	0.0	0.0	0.0	.

Men - Hommes - Hombres
ISIC 3 - CITI 3 - CIIU 3

	1999	2000	2001	2002	2003	2004	2005	2006	2007	2008
Total	.	.	.	.	.	8.7	7.9	6.8	6.9	.
A	.	.	.	.	.	58.7	46.8	41.1	44.6	.
B	.	.	.	.	.	0.0	0.0	0.0	0.0	.
C	.	.	.	.	.	26.4	17.7	9.1	0.0	.
D	.	.	.	.	.	5.3	5.1	3.1	4.5	.
E	.	.	.	.	.	9.2	4.6	4.9	0.0	.
F	.	.	.	.	.	15.1	19.0	19.1	14.4	.
G	.	.	.	.	.	4.6	2.9	3.2	4.0	.
H	.	.	.	.	.	1.6	0.0	0.0	0.0	.
I	.	.	.	.	.	26.6	17.1	16.9	17.7	.
J	.	.	.	.	.	3.6	0.0	1.8	0.0	.
K	.	.	.	.	.	6.7	5.8	4.1	6.6	.
L	.	.	.	.	.	7.2	4.8	3.7	6.3	.
M	.	.	.	.	.	14.4	13.4	0.0	0.0	.
N	.	.	.	.	.	0.0	2.5	0.0	0.0	.
O	.	.	.	.	.	7.3	10.8	8.8	5.2	.
P	.	.	.	.	.	316.5	319.5	0.0	0.0	.
Q	.	.	.	.	.	0.0	0.0	0.0	0.0	.

Women - Femmes - Mujeres
ISIC 3 - CITI 3 - CIIU 3

	1999	2000	2001	2002	2003	2004	2005	2006	2007	2008
Total	.	.	.	.	.	0.3	0.7	0.4	0.2	.
A	.	.	.	.	.	0.0	0.0	0.0	0.0	.
B	.	.	.	.	.	0.0	0.0	0.0	0.0	.
C	.	.	.	.	.	0.0	0.0	0.0	0.0	.
D	.	.	.	.	.	0.0	0.0	2.4	0.0	.
E	.	.	.	.	.	0.0	0.0	0.0	0.0	.
F	.	.	.	.	.	0.0	0.0	3.3	0.0	.
G	.	.	.	.	.	0.4	0.8	0.4	0.4	.
H	.	.	.	.	.	1.0	1.0	0.0	0.0	.
I	.	.	.	.	.	0.0	2.5	0.0	0.0	.
J	.	.	.	.	.	0.0	0.0	0.0	0.0	.
K	.	.	.	.	.	0.7	1.3	0.0	0.0	.
L	.	.	.	.	.	0.0	0.7	0.0	0.0	.
M	.	.	.	.	.	0.0	0.0	0.0	0.0	.
N	.	.	.	.	.	0.8	0.8	0.0	0.7	.
O	.	.	.	.	.	0.0	0.0	0.0	0.0	.
P	.	.	.	.	.	0.0	0.0	0.0	0.0	.
Q	.	.	.	.	.	0.0	0.0	0.0	0.0	.

Explanatory notes: see p. 1125.   Notes explicatives: voir p. 1127.   Notas explicativas: véase p. 1129.

	OCCUPATIONAL INJURIES	LÉSIONS PROFESSIONNELLES	LESIONES PROFESIONALES
	Rates of occupational injuries, by economic activity	Taux de lésions professionnelles, par activité économique	Tasas de lesiones profesionales, por actividad económica

	1999	2000	2001	2002	2003	2004	2005	2006	2007	2008

Austria (FA)   Reported injuries - Lésions déclarées - Lesiones declaradas

Rates of non-fatal injuries - Taux de lésions non mortelles - Tasas de lesiones no mortales

Per 100,000 employees - Pour 100 000 salariés - Por 100 000 asalariados

Total men and women - Total hommes et femmes - Total hombres y mujeres
ISIC 3 - CITI 3 - CIIU 3

	1999	2000	2001	2002	2003	2004	2005	2006	2007	2008
Total						3 890	3 847	3 925	3 584	
A						5 989	5 588	5 811	5 348	
B						7 229	4 124	3 077	4 908	
C						3 109	3 221	3 004	2 486	
D						5 090	4 900	4 908	4 386	
E						3 371	3 352	3 308	3 034	
F						9 282	9 235	9 570	8 647	
G						2 939	3 141	3 135	2 966	
H						2 430	2 093	2 125	2 058	
I						4 311	4 299	4 522	3 981	
J						498	424	463	386	
K						2 990	3 043	3 152	2 900	
L						1 421	1 469	1 569	1 508	
M						2 399	2 624	2 665	2 289	
N						4 529	4 361	4 323	3 846	
O						2 634	2 612	2 830	2 525	
P						1 184	1 198	1 504	799	
Q						364	548	767	552	

Men - Hommes - Hombres
ISIC 3 - CITI 3 - CIIU 3

	1999	2000	2001	2002	2003	2004	2005	2006	2007	2008
Total						5 560	5 486	5 611	5 069	
A						7 959	7 497	7 858	6 939	
B						4 839	2 817	4 348	6 957	
C						3 509	3 614	3 397	2 812	
D						6 245	5 976	5 988	5 342	
E						3 900	3 821	3 925	3 469	
F						10 473	10 431	10 829	9 780	
G						3 983	4 235	4 206	3 897	
H						3 148	2 764	2 756	2 650	
I						5 421	5 422	5 754	5 060	
J						522	418	400	378	
K						4 653	4 700	4 878	4 390	
L						2 733	2 853	3 055	2 755	
M						2 198	2 378	2 092	1 993	
N						5 741	5 261	5 113	4 614	
O						3 083	2 912	5 345	4 696	
P						2 215	2 556	2 821	1 425	
Q						452	374	1 046	688	

Women - Femmes - Mujeres
ISIC 3 - CITI 3 - CIIU 3

	1999	2000	2001	2002	2003	2004	2005	2006	2007	2008
Total						1 829	1 831	1 855	1 761	
A						969	891	2 286	2 548	
B						0	0	0	0	
C						363	591	417	353	
D						2 082	2 083	2 642	1 894	
E						753	1 041	392	833	
F						1 093	1 009	927	928	
G						1 959	2 115	2 136	2 106	
H						1 968	1 659	1 713	1 671	
I						1 660	1 657	1 644	1 438	
J						473	430	527	394	
K						1 301	1 325	1 298	1 270	
L						645	665	720	795	
M						2 495	2 743	2 944	2 434	
N						4 158	4 088	4 086	3 619	
O						1 184	1 182	1 274	1 193	
P						1 078	1 058	1 364	727	
Q						282	286	500	426	

Belarus (CA)   Reported injuries - Lésions déclarées - Lesiones declaradas

Rates of fatal injuries - Taux de lésions mortelles - Tasas de lesiones mortales

Per 100,000 workers employed - Pour 100 000 travailleurs occupés - Por 100 000 trabajadores empleados

Total men and women - Total hommes et femmes - Total hombres y mujeres
ISIC 3 - CITI 3 - CIIU 3

	1999	2000	2001	2002	2003	2004	2005	2006	2007	2008
Total	7.4	6.4	5.8	5.9	5.6	6.4	6.1	5.8	5.4	5.1

Men - Hommes - Hombres
ISIC 3 - CITI 3 - CIIU 3

	1999	2000	2001	2002	2003	2004	2005	2006	2007	2008
Total	14.4	12.0	11.5	11.4	10.7	12.7	11.8	11.5	10.6	10.2

Women - Femmes - Mujeres
ISIC 3 - CITI 3 - CIIU 3

	1999	2000	2001	2002	2003	2004	2005	2006	2007	2008
Total	0.8	1.3	0.6	0.9	1.0	0.7	0.8	0.5	0.6	0.7

Explanatory notes: see p. 1125.   Notes explicatives: voir p. 1127.   Notas explicativas: véase p. 1129.

OCCUPATIONAL INJURIES

Rates of occupational injuries, by economic activity

LÉSIONS PROFESSIONNELLES

Taux de lésions professionnelles, par activité économique

LESIONES PROFESIONALES

Tasas de lesiones profesionales, por actividad económica

8B

	1999	2000	2001	2002	2003	2004	2005	2006	2007	2008

Belarus (CA)   **Reported injuries - Lésions déclarées - Lesiones declaradas**

Rates of non-fatal injuries - Taux de lésions non mortelles - Tasas de lesiones no mortales

Per 100,000 workers employed - Pour 100 000 travailleurs occupés - Por 100 000 trabajadores empleados

Total men and women - Total hommes et femmes - Total hombres y mujeres
ISIC 3 - CITI 3 - CIIU 3

	1999	2000	2001	2002	2003	2004	2005	2006	2007	2008
Total	256	199	174	150	143	136	111	95	84	78

Men - Hommes - Hombres
ISIC 3 - CITI 3 - CIIU 3

Total	403	303	266	234	220	211	168	142	128	118

Women - Femmes - Mujeres
ISIC 3 - CITI 3 - CIIU 3

Total	117	103	88	72	73	69	58	51	43	43

Bulgaria (FD)   **Reported injuries - Lésions déclarées - Lesiones declaradas**

Rates of fatal injuries - Taux de lésions mortelles - Tasas de lesiones mortales

Per 100,000 workers insured - Pour 100 000 travailleurs assurés - Por 100 000 trabajadores asegurados

Total men and women - Total hommes et femmes - Total hombres y mujeres
ISIC 3 - CITI 3 - CIIU 3

	1999	2000	2001	2002	2003	2004	2005	2006	2007	2008
Total	8.3	7.3	7.3	6.0	5.2	6.0	5.8	7.2	7.1	.
A	8.4	17.9	13.9	14.1	21.3	17.3	8.8	10.4	13.2	.
B	0.0	0.0	0.0	0.0	0.0	0.0	0.0	0.0	0.0	.
C	8.8	37.1	19.0	32.6	24.5	23.9	30.0	25.8	40.4	.
D	7.1	4.8	6.6	5.4	4.6	6.7	6.8	6.1	5.3	.
E	19.1	15.2	10.1	13.5	6.9	5.4	12.8	11.5	27.8	.
F	8.9	22.4	15.5	18.9	14.9	22.4	20.3	19.1	18.4	.
G	3.7	4.3	9.0	4.2	2.9	4.4	3.6	7.8	4.2	.
H	9.7	4.0	3.6	0.0	4.2	1.4	2.7	0.0	1.1	.
I	11.2	12.2	12.9	8.0	7.7	8.4	9.6	13.0	13.3	.
J	0.0	7.2	0.0	0.0	2.8	5.4	2.6	4.8	2.1	.
K	4.8	5.6	6.0	0.0	2.7	4.7	1.9	3.1	7.3	.
L	0.0	6.7	5.2	4.1	1.5	0.5	1.5	3.4	2.0	.
M	0.0	0.5	2.0	2.0	5.0	0.0	0.8	3.3	0.0	.
N	0.0	0.7	0.8	3.0	0.8	0.0	0.8	0.8	3.3	.
O	0.0	4.7	4.6	1.5	1.4	2.6	1.3	8.3	5.5	.
Q	.	.	.	.	.	0.0	0.0	0.0	0.0	.

Men - Hommes - Hombres
ISIC 3 - CITI 3 - CIIU 3

Total	.	.	.	.	9.3	11.2	10.8	12.1	12.0	.
A	.	.	.	.	28.2	23.9	6.7	13.6	15.7	.
B	.	.	.	.	0.0	0.0	0.0	0.0	0.0	.
C	.	.	.	.	30.5	29.4	36.6	27.1	49.8	.
D	.	.	.	.	7.9	11.4	13.1	9.1	8.7	.
E	.	.	.	.	9.3	7.2	17.3	15.5	36.7	.
F	.	.	.	.	17.9	26.8	23.0	22.4	21.5	.
G	.	.	.	.	6.3	8.8	7.6	13.4	7.4	.
H	.	.	.	.	7.8	3.9	7.2	0.0	0.0	.
I	.	.	.	.	11.0	12.9	13.6	17.8	15.4	.
J	.	.	.	.	0.0	7.3	7.0	13.6	6.2	.
K	.	.	.	.	5.6	8.3	3.8	5.1	10.5	.
L	.	.	.	.	1.3	1.2	1.3	3.9	4.2	.
M	.	.	.	.	9.0	0.0	0.0	12.5	0.0	.
N	.	.	.	.	3.6	0.0	3.7	0.0	7.3	.
O	.	.	.	.	0.0	5.6	2.8	15.5	7.2	.
Q	.	.	.	.	0.0	0.0	0.0	0.0	0.0	.

Women - Femmes - Mujeres
ISIC 3 - CITI 3 - CIIU 3

Total	.	.	.	.	1.3	0.9	0.9	2.2	2.1	.
A	.	.	.	.	7.8	4.3	13.0	4.3	8.6	.
B	.	.	.	.	0.0	0.0	0.0	0.0	0.0	.
C	.	.	.	.	0.0	0.0	0.0	20.0	0.0	.
D	.	.	.	.	1.4	2.2	0.7	3.2	2.0	.
E	.	.	.	.	0.0	0.0	0.0	0.0	0.0	.
F	.	.	.	.	0.0	0.0	4.6	0.0	0.0	.
G	.	.	.	.	0.0	0.5	0.0	2.6	1.2	.
H	.	.	.	.	2.2	0.0	0.0	0.0	1.8	.
I	.	.	.	.	1.7	0.0	1.8	3.8	9.0	.
J	.	.	.	.	4.4	4.3	0.0	0.0	0.0	.
K	.	.	.	.	0.0	1.0	0.0	0.9	3.5	.
L	.	.	.	.	1.5	0.0	1.6	3.1	0.8	.
M	.	.	.	.	3.4	0.0	1.1	0.0	0.0	.
N	.	.	.	.	0.0	0.0	0.0	1.1	2.1	.
O	.	.	.	.	2.6	0.0	0.0	2.2	4.0	.
Q	.	.	.	.	0.0	0.0	0.0	0.0	0.0	.

Explanatory notes: see p. 1125.   Notes explicatives: voir p. 1127.   Notas explicativas: véase p. 1129.

	OCCUPATIONAL INJURIES			LÉSIONS PROFESSIONNELLES			LESIONES PROFESIONALES		
	Rates of occupational injuries, by economic activity			Taux de lésions professionnelles, par activité économique			Tasas de lesiones profesionales, por actividad económica		

	1999	2000	2001	2002	2003	2004	2005	2006	2007	2008

Bulgaria (FD) — Reported injuries - Lésions déclarées - Lesiones declaradas

Rates of non-fatal injuries - Taux de lésions non mortelles - Tasas de lesiones no mortales

Per 100,000 workers insured - Pour 100 000 travailleurs assurés - Por 100 000 trabajadores asegurados

Total men and women - Total hommes et femmes - Total hombres y mujeres
ISIC 3 - CITI 3 - CIIU 3

	1999	2000	2001	2002	2003	2004	2005	2006	2007	2008
Total	721	358	304	282	218	196	187	167	144	.
A	605	304	269	201	233	173	126	144	99	.
B	0	0	280	456	0	0	135	0	0	.
C	2 007	1 771	1 809	1 857	1 549	1 084	1 288	1 054	824	.
D	799	485	423	387	329	295	289	245	218	.
E	591	548	488	464	444	406	396	352	272	.
F	625	438	440	418	258	270	232	214	180	.
G	228	79	70	63	55	60	59	66	68	.
H	377	182	129	115	84	83	73	68	69	.
I	632	406	366	328	303	272	277	282	223	.
J	0	154	146	101	154	249	85	91	62	.
K	202	92	82	79	109	112	98	87	76	.
L	0	650	229	289	130	140	127	126	108	.
M	0	110	107	100	90	100	95	79	82	.
N	199	246	208	219	169	151	172	143	116	.
O	550	180	224	183	157	123	140	112	109	.
Q						104	105	0	360	.

Men - Hommes - Hombres
ISIC 3 - CITI 3 - CIIU 3

	1999	2000	2001	2002	2003	2004	2005	2006	2007	2008
Total	.	.	.	.	311	276	252	228	192	.
A	.	.	.	.	252	204	153	163	119	.
B	.	.	.	.	0	0	202	0	0	.
C	.	.	.	.	1 788	1 246	1 459	1 215	959	.
D	.	.	.	.	498	440	414	352	301	.
E	.	.	.	.	457	414	403	338	283	.
F	.	.	.	.	292	306	262	242	200	.
G	.	.	.	.	83	91	89	103	97	.
H	.	.	.	.	78	70	68	86	99	.
I	.	.	.	.	330	305	295	297	233	.
J	.	.	.	.	299	544	104	102	56	.
K	.	.	.	.	141	137	110	105	100	.
L	.	.	.	.	132	134	109	128	87	.
M	.	.	.	.	84	102	64	53	70	.
N	.	.	.	.	128	121	161	141	91	.
O	.	.	.	.	209	179	174	165	155	.
Q	.	.	.	.	0	0	249	0	809	.

Women - Femmes - Mujeres
ISIC 3 - CITI 3 - CIIU 3

	1999	2000	2001	2002	2003	2004	2005	2006	2007	2008
Total	.	.	.	.	129	119	122	105	95	.
A	.	.	.	.	196	112	74	109	60	.
B	.	.	.	.	0	0	0	0	0	.
C	.	.	.	.	567	382	503	341	248	.
D	.	.	.	.	170	157	167	139	137	.
E	.	.	.	.	408	382	376	393	237	.
F	.	.	.	.	93	82	65	53	61	.
G	.	.	.	.	31	33	31	31	41	.
H	.	.	.	.	88	91	76	57	51	.
I	.	.	.	.	253	210	241	253	203	.
J	.	.	.	.	66	73	74	86	65	.
K	.	.	.	.	79	88	86	68	48	.
L	.	.	.	.	129	143	138	126	121	.
M	.	.	.	.	92	99	107	88	86	.
N	.	.	.	.	182	160	175	144	123	.
O	.	.	.	.	110	73	112	66	70	.
Q	.	.	.	.	0	183	0	0	0	.

Explanatory notes: see p. 1125.   Notes explicatives: voir p. 1127.   Notas explicativas: véase p. 1129.

OCCUPATIONAL INJURIES

Rates of occupational injuries, by economic activity

LÉSIONS PROFESSIONNELLES

Taux de lésions professionnelles, par activité économique

LESIONES PROFESIONALES

Tasas de lesiones profesionales, por actividad económica

8B

	1999	2000	2001	2002	2003	2004	2005	2006	2007	2008

Croatia (FA)   **Compensated injuries - Lésions indemnisées - Lesiones indemnizadas**

Rates of fatal injuries - Taux de lésions mortelles - Tasas de lesiones mortales

Per 100,000 workers employed - Pour 100 000 travailleurs occupés - Por 100 000 trabajadores empleados

Total men and women - Total hommes et femmes - Total hombres y mujeres [1]
ISIC 3 - CITI 3 - CIIU 3

	1999	2000	2001	2002	2003	2004	2005	2006	2007	2008
Total	2.5	3.1	3.2	3.3	3.4	2.7	4.3	5.0	4.7	5.2
A	2.7	16.9	5.7	11.5	22.2	8.6	31.6	21.0	15.1	10.4
B	0.0	0.0	0.0	61.2	0.0	0.0	122.2	0.0	0.0	87.8
C	0.0	0.0	0.0	0.0	60.7	19.1	38.1	19.2	0.0	0.0
D	2.1	1.5	2.6	3.4	4.2	3.4	4.2	4.9	4.1	3.1
E [2]	7.3	0.0	0.0	7.4	3.7	7.3	3.6	22.5	3.9	0.0
F	8.2	13.0	21.9	9.6	6.2	15.6	23.1	31.0	22.0	28.6
G	0.7	2.6	3.8	1.2	2.2	0.5	2.5	4.0	1.8	2.0
H	0.0	0.0	2.6	0.0	0.0	0.0	0.0	0.0	4.5	2.9
I	3.5	8.1	3.5	5.9	5.9	3.5	4.7	7.2	4.9	9.1
J	0.0	3.3	6.7	3.3	0.0	3.1	0.0	0.0	0.0	4.9
K	1.8	1.7	0.0	4.7	0.0	5.4	2.5	1.1	1.8	1.6
L	6.3	3.1	4.0	4.1	7.6	0.9	1.8	4.5	8.1	4.5
M	1.3	0.0	1.2	1.2	0.0	0.0	1.1	0.0	2.0	1.0
N	4.1	4.2	0.0	2.8	0.0	0.0	0.0	0.0	1.3	1.1
O	0.0	3.1	3.0	5.8	2.6	0.0	2.3	0.0	21.4	3.2
P	0.0	0.0	0.0	0.0	0.0	0.0	0.0	0.0	0.0	0.0
Q	0.0	0.0	0.0	0.0	0.0	0.0	0.0	0.0	0.0	0.0

Men - Hommes - Hombres [1]
ISIC 3 - CITI 3 - CIIU 3

	1999	2000	2001	2002	2003	2004	2005	2006	2007	2008
Total	.	5.2	5.1	5.5	5.8	4.6	7.5	8.6	7.9	9.1
A	.	23.8	8.0	16.2	27.5	12.3	41.1	29.8	21.8	14.9
B	.	0.0	0.0	86.2	0.0	0.0	173.2	0.0	0.0	109.7
C	.	0.0	0.0	0.0	69.1	21.7	44.0	22.5	0.0	0.0
D	.	2.5	4.4	5.0	6.8	5.6	6.8	7.2	5.9	4.4
E	.	0.0	0.0	9.3	4.6	9.2	4.6	28.2	4.9	0.0
F	.	13.5	25.5	11.0	7.1	16.6	26.7	35.6	25.4	32.6
G	.	4.1	6.5	2.4	3.3	1.1	5.1	4.9	2.8	3.4
H	.	0.0	0.0	0.0	0.0	0.0	0.0	0.0	10.0	6.2
I	.	11.2	1.6	8.3	8.3	5.0	5.0	10.3	7.1	12.7
J	.	11.9	0.0	0.0	0.0	10.5	0.0	0.0	0.0	16.2
K	.	2.9	0.0	7.7	0.0	6.5	4.1	1.7	1.5	2.6
L	.	4.9	6.2	6.6	12.3	1.5	3.1	6.2	12.7	8.0
M	.	0.0	4.7	4.7	0.0	0.0	4.5	0.0	4.2	4.2
N	.	12.9	0.0	0.0	0.0	0.0	0.0	0.0	0.0	0.0
O	.	5.8	5.6	10.9	5.0	0.0	4.6	0.0	44.9	7.0
P	.	0.0	0.0	0.0	0.0	0.0	0.0	0.0	0.0	0.0
Q	.	0.0	0.0	0.0	0.0	0.0	0.0	0.0	0.0	0.0

Women - Femmes - Mujeres [1]
ISIC 3 - CITI 3 - CIIU 3

	1999	2000	2001	2002	2003	2004	2005	2006	2007	2008
Total	.	0.5	0.9	0.7	0.3	0.3	0.3	0.7	0.8	0.4
A	.	0.0	0.0	0.0	9.5	0.0	9.6	0.0	0.0	0.0
B	.	0.0	0.0	0.0	0.0	0.0	0.0	0.0	0.0	0.0
C	.	0.0	0.0	0.0	0.0	0.0	0.0	0.0	0.0	0.0
D	.	0.0	0.0	1.0	0.0	0.0	0.0	1.0	1.0	0.9
E	.	0.0	0.0	0.0	0.0	0.0	0.0	0.0	0.0	0.0
F	.	9.9	0.0	0.0	0.0	9.2	0.0	0.0	0.0	0.0
G	.	1.2	1.2	0.0	1.1	0.0	0.0	2.8	0.9	0.8
H	.	4.6	0.0	0.0	0.0	0.0	0.0	0.0	0.0	0.0
I	.	0.0	8.0	0.0	0.0	0.0	4.0	0.0	0.0	0.0
J	.	0.0	9.4	4.6	0.0	0.0	0.0	0.0	0.0	0.0
K	.	0.0	0.0	0.0	0.0	3.5	0.0	0.0	2.5	0.0
L	.	0.0	0.0	0.0	0.0	0.0	0.0	2.1	2.1	0.0
M	.	0.0	0.0	0.0	0.0	0.0	0.0	0.0	1.3	0.0
N	.	1.8	0.0	3.5	0.0	0.0	0.0	0.0	1.6	1.4
O	.	0.0	0.0	0.0	0.0	0.0	0.0	0.0	0.0	0.0
P	.	0.0	0.0	0.0	0.0	0.0	0.0	0.0	0.0	0.0
Q	.	0.0	0.0	0.0	0.0	0.0	0.0	0.0	0.0	0.0

Explanatory notes: see p. 1125.

[1] Deaths occurring within one day of accident. [2] Excl. electricity and gas.

Notes explicatives: voir p. 1127.

[1] Décès survenant pendant le jour qui suit l'accident. [2] Non compris l'électricité et le gaz.

Notas explicativas: véase p. 1129.

[1] Fallecimientos que se producen durante el día posterior al accidente. [2] Excl. electricidad y gas.

OCCUPATIONAL INJURIES / LÉSIONS PROFESSIONNELLES / LESIONES PROFESIONALES

Rates of occupational injuries, by economic activity

Taux de lésions professionnelles, par activité économique

Tasas de lesiones profesionales, por actividad económica

	1999	2000	2001	2002	2003	2004	2005	2006	2007	2008

Croatia (FA) — Compensated injuries - Lésions indemnisées - Lesiones indemnizadas

Rates of non-fatal injuries - Taux de lésions non mortelles - Tasas de lesiones no mortales

Per 100,000 workers employed - Pour 100 000 travailleurs occupés - Por 100 000 trabajadores empleados

Total men and women - Total hommes et femmes - Total hombres y mujeres
ISIC 3 - CITI 3 - CIIU 3

	1999	2000	2001	2002	2003	2004	2005	2006	2007	2008
Total	1 751	1 698	1 662	1 595	1 659	1 551	1 564	1 645	1 540	1 656
A	3 096	3 276	3 634	3 253	3 367	3 098	3 030	2 973	2 704	2 697
B	2 121	1 404	1 028	1 407	1 481	2 005	1 100	1 554	1 207	556
C	4 549	4 022	3 601	1 907	1 881	2 204	2 189	2 462	2 557	2 266
D	2 988	2 959	2 899	2 839	2 965	2 853	2 840	3 135	2 945	2 697
E	2 723	2 654	2 421	2 278	2 407	2 276	2 343	2 155	2 148	2 197
F	3 431	3 134	3 046	3 116	3 282	3 277	3 055	3 352	2 929	2 744
G	916	916	1 037	1 045	1 096	1 034	1 133	1 165	1 166	1 279
H	1 179	1 351	1 484	1 348	1 610	1 689	1 807	1 983	1 810	1 330
I	2 419	2 470	2 230	2 240	2 194	2 071	2 069	2 114	2 117	2 074
J	1 015	918	769	790	941	937	961	974	606	787
K	861	915	968	870	923	876	982	998	884	867
L	1 961	1 875	1 794	1 694	1 686	1 571	1 702	1 722	1 623	1 451
M	663	602	633	638	814	741	879	852	779	861
N	1 735	1 680	1 757	1 743	2 087	1 884	1 965	2 146	2 093	1 886
O	2 268	2 135	2 281	2 089	2 134	1 623	1 717	1 739	3 563	1 353
P	0	0	0	0	0	0	10	0	0	10
Q	2 439	1 707	7 095	4 268	1 952	725	614	611	143	249

Men - Hommes - Hombres
ISIC 3 - CITI 3 - CIIU 3

	1999	2000	2001	2002	2003	2004	2005	2006	2007	2008
Total	.	2 324	2 272	2 147	2 167	2 066	2 048	2 162	2 011	2 102
A	.	4 061	4 458	4 037	4 144	3 946	3 732	3 657	3 343	3 166
B	.	1 834	1 465	1 896	2 022	2 771	1 558	2 137	1 616	475
C	.	4 562	4 147	2 013	1 980	2 457	2 466	2 787	3 156	2 552
D	.	3 936	3 925	3 742	3 881	3 772	3 737	4 116	3 818	3 473
E	.	3 009	2 705	2 585	2 726	2 534	2 620	2 420	2 040	2 499
F	.	3 538	3 460	3 481	3 683	3 680	3 443	3 771	3 272	3 061
G	.	1 161	1 293	1 314	1 377	1 252	1 385	1 389	1 400	1 472
H	.	1 352	1 511	1 389	1 438	1 721	1 874	1 993	1 863	1 163
I	.	2 813	2 538	2 510	2 492	2 466	2 369	2 508	2 483	2 342
J	.	991	869	727	959	805	775	953	751	687
K	.	1 184	1 196	1 103	1 053	9 759	1 071	1 123	984	936
L	.	2 426	2 334	2 062	1 956	1 914	2 059	2 113	2 057	1 729
M	.	580	611	611	672	554	789	694	741	690
N	.	2 127	2 066	2 214	2 355	2 332	2 375	2 561	2 699	2 070
O	.	2 861	2 984	2 933	3 007	2 287	2 256	2 385	2 311	1 800
P	.	0	0	0	0	0	131	0	0	0
Q	.	3 158	14 423	7 916	2 643	1 167	920	573	255	308

Women - Femmes - Mujeres
ISIC 3 - CITI 3 - CIIU 3

	1999	2000	2001	2002	2003	2004	2005	2006	2007	2008
Total	.	928	910	909	1 011	906	968	1 010	965	1 110
A	.	1 381	1 636	1 325	1 483	1 120	1 384	1 399	1 254	1 621
B	.	435	0	211	200	204	0	199	208	881
C	.	868	221	1 121	1 169	451	421	533	501	712
D	.	1 522	1 364	1 444	1 505	1 354	1 356	1 506	1 486	1 376
E	.	1 234	1 283	1 056	1 138	1 252	1 254	1 120	1 105	1 018
F	.	772	518	739	550	591	536	604	670	512
G	.	692	794	782	815	817	886	950	944	1 102
H	.	1 350	1 466	1 316	1 747	1 682	1 753	1 975	1 769	1 480
I	.	1 606	1 470	1 554	1 460	1 105	1 354	1 205	1 295	1 412
J	.	890	730	815	934	992	1 038	983	776	830
K	.	522	623	508	917	715	839	792	717	760
L	.	887	839	1 069	1 307	1 060	1 202	1 208	1 182	1 093
M	.	610	640	647	862	802	908	903	792	915
N	.	1 556	1 671	1 612	2 012	1 758	1 850	2 030	1 836	1 836
O	.	1 271	1 460	1 142	1 195	944	1 180	1 121	1 015	987
P	.	0	0	0	0	0	0	0	0	11
Q	.	455	823	794	1 282	339	308	654	0	181

Explanatory notes: see p. 1125.　　Notes explicatives: voir p. 1127.　　Notas explicativas: véase p. 1129.

OCCUPATIONAL INJURIES

Rates of occupational injuries, by economic activity

LÉSIONS PROFESSIONNELLES

Taux de lésions professionnelles, par activité économique

LESIONES PROFESIONALES

Tasas de lesiones profesionales, por actividad económica

	1999	2000	2001	2002	2003	2004	2005	2006	2007	2008

Cyprus (FF) — Reported injuries - Lésions déclarées - Lesiones declaradas

Rates of fatal injuries - Taux de lésions mortelles - Tasas de lesiones mortales

Per 100,000 employees - Pour 100 000 salariés - Por 100 000 asalariados

Total men and women - Total hommes et femmes - Total hombres y mujeres
ISIC 3 - CITI 3 - CIIU 3

	1999	2000	2001	2002	2003	2004	2005	2006	2007	2008
Total	.	.	.	7	3	5	5	6	5	.
A	.	.	.	0	29	0	0	22	44	.
B	.	.	.	0	0	0	0	0	0	.
C	.	.	.	0	0	268	0	0	195	.
D	.	.	.	16	14	18	6	10	7	.
E	.	.	.	0	0	0	0	0	0	.
F	.	.	.	25	4	21	21	30	12	.
G	.	.	.	8	0	3	7	4	4	.
H	.	.	.	5	0	4	5	5	5	.
I	.	.	.	0	7	0	0	0	11	.
J	.	.	.	0	0	0	0	0	0	.
K	.	.	.	0	6	0	0	6	0	.
L	.	.	.	8	0	0	4	0	3	.
M	.	.	.	0	0	0	0	0	0	.
N	.	.	.	0	0	0	0	0	0	.
O	.	.	.	0	0	0	0	7	0	.
P	.	.	.	0	0	0	0	0	0	.
Q	.	.	.	0	0	0	0	0	0	.

Men - Hommes - Hombres
ISIC 3 - CITI 3 - CIIU 3

	1999	2000	2001	2002	2003	2004	2005	2006	2007	2008
Total	.	.	.	12	6	11	9	12	10	.
A	.	.	.	0	42	0	0	27	54	.
B	.	.	.	0	0	0	0	0	0	.
C	.	.	.	0	0	268	0	0	211	.
D	.	.	.	22	24	31	10	16	10	.
E	.	.	.	0	0	0	0	0	0	.
F	.	.	.	23	4	22	22	34	14	.
G	.	.	.	16	0	5	14	8	8	.
H	.	.	.	10	0	10	12	13	13	.
I	.	.	.	0	12	0	0	0	20	.
J	.	.	.	0	0	0	0	0	0	.
K	.	.	.	0	15	0	0	15	0	.
L	.	.	.	13	0	0	6	0	5	.
M	.	.	.	0	0	0	0	0	0	.
N	.	.	.	0	0	0	0	0	0	.
O	.	.	.	0	0	0	0	15	0	.
P	.	.	.	0	0	0	0	0	0	.
Q	.	.	.	0	0	0	0	0	0	.

Women - Femmes - Mujeres
ISIC 3 - CITI 3 - CIIU 3

	1999	2000	2001	2002	2003	2004	2005	2006	2007	2008
Total	.	.	.	2	0	0	0	0	0	.
A	.	.	.	0	0	0	0	0	0	.
B	.	.	.	0	0	0	0	0	0	.
C	.	.	.	0	0	0	0	0	0	.
D	.	.	.	8	0	0	0	0	0	.
E	.	.	.	0	0	0	0	0	0	.
F	.	.	.	48	0	0	0	0	0	.
G	.	.	.	0	0	0	0	0	0	.
H	.	.	.	0	0	0	0	0	0	.
I	.	.	.	0	0	0	0	0	0	.
J	.	.	.	0	0	0	0	0	0	.
K	.	.	.	0	0	0	0	0	0	.
L	.	.	.	0	0	0	0	0	0	.
M	.	.	.	0	0	0	0	0	0	.
N	.	.	.	0	0	0	0	0	0	.
O	.	.	.	0	0	0	0	0	0	.
P	.	.	.	0	0	0	0	0	0	.
Q	.	.	.	0	0	0	0	0	0	.

Explanatory notes: see p. 1125.   Notes explicatives: voir p. 1127.   Notas explicativas: véase p. 1129.

	OCCUPATIONAL INJURIES	LÉSIONS PROFESSIONNELLES	LESIONES PROFESIONALES
	Rates of occupational injuries, by economic activity	Taux de lésions professionnelles, par activité économique	Tasas de lesiones profesionales, por actividad económica

	1999	2000	2001	2002	2003	2004	2005	2006	2007	2008

Cyprus (FF)   Reported injuries - Lésions déclarées - Lesiones declaradas

Rates of non-fatal injuries - Taux de lésions non mortelles - Tasas de lesiones no mortales

Per 100,000 employees - Pour 100 000 salariés - Por 100 000 asalariados

Total men and women - Total hommes et femmes - Total hombres y mujeres [1]
ISIC 3 - CITI 3 - CIIU 3

	1999	2000	2001	2002	2003	2004	2005	2006	2007	2008
Total				681	832	840	809	745	694	
A				743	1 496	1 598	1 397	937	966	
B				0	866	498	1 626	2 609	2 326	
C				4 520	2 594	5 362	1 652	1 719	2 335	
D				1 644	2 309	2 242	1 956	1 759	1 742	
E				664	534	714	1 029	617	873	
F				1 967	2 063	2 046	1 977	1 804	1 676	
G				411	570	700	673	640	549	
H				997	1 365	1 054	1 259	1 777	1 685	
I				504	512	619	755	560	603	
J				0	67	80	105	124	118	
K				162	201	217	231	121	125	
L				299	291	327	395	351	257	
M				27	46	30	69	45	58	
N				101	104	81	80	206	222	
O				465	409	562	355	415	322	
P				0	0	0	0	7	0	
Q				0	42	0	0	0	0	

Men - Hommes - Hombres [1]
ISIC 3 - CITI 3 - CIIU 3

	1999	2000	2001	2002	2003	2004	2005	2006	2007	2008
Total				1 127	1 359	1 385	1 262	1 145	1 069	
A				939	1 967	1 940	1 406	892	950	
B				0	866	526	1 626	2 609	2 326	
C				4 520	3 006	5 362	1 861	1 771	2 532	
D				2 446	3 432	3 402	2 658	2 373	2 335	
E				732	568	811	1 191	678	1 016	
F				2 131	2 257	2 169	2 100	1 993	1 868	
G				736	998	1 158	1 039	930	754	
H				1 233	1 736	1 363	1 626	2 287	2 196	
I				714	784	851	1 031	801	888	
J				0	137	117	117	96	86	
K				380	367	390	358	225	195	
L				408	365	394	430	443	337	
M				17	50	32	19	18	58	
N				81	90	165	102	162	201	
O				684	540	869	522	597	480	
P				0	0	0	0	332	0	
Q				0	0	0	0	0	0	

Women - Femmes - Mujeres [1]
ISIC 3 - CITI 3 - CIIU 3

	1999	2000	2001	2002	2003	2004	2005	2006	2007	2008
Total				199	285	267	304	305	297	
A				330	460	749	1 353	1 124	1 032	
B				0	0	0	0	0	0	
C				0	0	0	0	0	0	
D				464	738	654	722	658	650	
E				239	255	169	372	244	0	
F				240	198	314	459	275	230	
G				115	206	288	294	310	342	
H				809	1 111	844	1 007	1 411	1 349	
I				185	129	206	278	195	277	
J				0	22	57	93	150	145	
K				35	91	103	156	61	77	
L				113	166	178	322	163	121	
M				32	45	30	86	54	59	
N				108	108	60	73	220	229	
O				139	189	176	178	250	150	
P				0	0	0	0	0	0	
Q				0	122	0	0	0	0	

Explanatory notes: see p. 1125.   Notes explicatives: voir p. 1127.   Notas explicativas: véase p. 1129.

[1] Incapacity of 4 days or more.   [1] Incapacité de 4 jours et plus.   [1] Incapacidad de 4 días y más.

OCCUPATIONAL INJURIES

Rates of occupational injuries, by economic activity

LÉSIONS PROFESSIONNELLES

Taux de lésions professionnelles, par activité économique

LESIONES PROFESIONALES

Tasas de lesiones profesionales, por actividad económica

8B

	1999	2000	2001	2002	2003	2004	2005	2006	2007	2008

Czech Republic (FD) Reported injuries - Lésions déclarées - Lesiones declaradas

Rates of fatal injuries - Taux de lésions mortelles - Tasas de lesiones mortales

Per 100,000 workers insured - Pour 100 000 travailleurs assurés - Por 100 000 trabajadores asegurados

Total men and women - Total hommes et femmes - Total hombres y mujeres
ISIC 3 - CITI 3 - CIIU 3

	1999	2000	2001	2002	2003	2004	2005	2006	2007	2008
Total	4.2	4.9	5.2	4.6	4.5	4.2	3.7	3.4	4.1	3.8
A-B	.	12.6	.	.	.	.	.	.	.	.
A	7.2	.	9.2	15.3	14.2	15.2	15.1	10.5	16.9	10.5
B	0.0	.	0.6	0.0	0.0	0.0	0.0	161.0	0.0	0.0
C	12.9	.	25.5	21.0	31.3	41.7	13.6	7.8	14.6	12.8
C-D	.	5.9	.	.	.	.	.	.	.	.
D	3.3	.	5.4	5.0	4.1	2.7	4.6	2.7	4.4	3.8
E	11.9	5.6	10.2	6.1	7.8	22.6	1.7	1.8	1.9	2.0
F	13.8	26.7	32.4	30.2	33.7	24.1	22.5	29.3	36.1	15.3
G	1.9	5.4	8.7	5.1	6.2	5.8	5.7	4.3	2.8	2.1
H	0.0	2.4	4.7	2.4	2.3	2.3	0.0	4.2	0.0	0.0
I	5.0	15.8	13.0	12.2	9.2	9.1	8.2	10.4	12.7	7.3
J	2.6	.	2.9	3.0	4.5	1.6	0.0	0.0	0.0	3.7
J-K	.	6.0	.	.	.	.	.	.	.	.
K	2.0	.	6.2	4.1	4.5	7.1	3.1	3.2	2.8	1.2
L	2.2	2.3	0.4	1.1	1.0	1.0	0.5	1.4	0.5	1.7
M	0.5	0.5	1.0	0.9	1.2	1.6	0.8	0.8	0.0	0.0
N	1.8	0.9	1.8	1.3	1.3	0.4	1.2	0.0	0.8	0.0
O	3.3	1.1	3.2	5.2	3.0	4.9	4.8	4.8	5.6	4.2
X	4.5	0.0	0.2	0.0	0.0	0.0	0.0	0.0	0.0	0.0

Men - Hommes - Hombres
ISIC 3 - CITI 3 - CIIU 3

	1999	2000	2001	2002	2003	2004	2005	2006	2007	2008
Total	7.5	9.0	9.4	8.3	8.0	7.6	6.4	6.2	7.3	6.8
A-B	.	19.6	.	.	.	.	.	.	.	.
A	10.6	.	14.3	22.6	21.9	22.2	21.9	16.1	23.0	16.6
B	0.0	.	0.0	0.0	0.0	0.0	0.0	195.0	0.0	0.0
C	15.1	.	27.8	24.5	36.7	48.9	16.0	9.2	16.9	15.0
C-D	.	9.6	.	.	.	.	.	.	.	.
D	5.6	.	9.2	8.1	6.6	4.4	7.2	4.6	6.7	6.3
E	14.5	7.6	13.8	4.1	10.5	30.4	2.3	2.4	2.6	2.7
F	15.8	31.3	38.9	36.4	40.3	28.7	26.9	35.4	43.8	21.2
G	4.3	12.4	17.9	11.8	11.7	12.5	9.4	10.1	6.0	4.3
H	0.0	5.9	5.4	5.9	5.6	0.0	0.0	10.1	0.0	0.0
I	7.6	25.2	20.8	19.6	14.9	14.0	12.4	16.5	18.9	9.5
J	4.1	.	4.6	4.7	9.7	4.7	0.0	0.0	0.0	3.4
J-K	.	11.7	.	.	.	.	.	.	.	.
K	3.9	.	10.3	7.7	6.5	13.1	4.9	5.2	4.9	2.2
L	7.8	7.2	1.1	3.4	1.3	0.0	1.3	2.6	1.3	4.3
M	1.6	1.5	1.5	2.8	2.7	2.8	1.4	1.4	0.0	0.0
N	2.2	2.1	6.3	4.1	4.1	2.0	3.8	0.0	3.5	0.0
O	6.3	2.1	6.2	6.0	5.8	9.4	9.3	7.3	9.1	7.7
X	8.0	0.0	0.4	0.0	0.0	0.0	0.0	0.0	0.0	0.0

Women - Femmes - Mujeres
ISIC 3 - CITI 3 - CIIU 3

	1999	2000	2001	2002	2003	2004	2005	2006	2007	2008
Total	0.4	0.3	0.4	0.4	0.5	0.4	0.6	0.2	0.5	0.4
A-B	.	0.0	.	.	.	.	.	.	.	.
A	1.5	.	0.0	1.9	0.0	2.3	2.4	0.0	5.5	0.0
B	0.0	.	0.0	0.0	0.0	0.0	0.0	0.0	0.0	0.0
C	0.0	.	12.2	0.0	0.0	0.0	0.0	0.0	0.0	0.0
C-D	.	0.4	.	.	.	.	.	.	.	.
D	0.0	.	0.0	0.5	0.2	0.2	0.7	0.0	0.9	0.0
E	4.9	0.0	0.0	11.6	0.0	0.0	0.0	0.0	0.0	0.0
F	3.2	3.5	0.0	0.0	0.0	0.0	0.0	0.0	0.0	1.1
G	0.0	0.0	1.4	0.0	2.0	0.7	3.1	0.0	0.5	0.0
H	0.0	0.0	4.2	0.0	0.0	3.7	0.0	0.0	0.0	0.0
I	0.9	0.9	0.0	0.0	0.0	1.0	1.0	0.0	2.0	3.8
J	1.9	.	2.1	2.2	2.2	0.0	0.0	0.0	0.0	3.9
J-K	.	1.3	.	.	.	.	.	.	.	.
K	0.0	.	1.9	0.0	2.0	0.0	0.9	0.8	0.7	0.0
L	0.0	0.0	0.0	0.0	0.8	1.5	0.0	0.8	0.0	0.0
M	0.0	0.0	0.7	0.0	0.5	1.1	0.6	0.6	0.0	0.0
N	1.7	0.6	0.6	0.5	0.5	0.0	0.5	0.0	0.0	0.0
O	0.0	0.0	0.0	4.4	0.0	0.0	0.0	2.0	1.9	0.0
X	0.2	0.0	0.0	0.0	0.0	0.0	0.0	0.0	0.0	0.0

Explanatory notes: see p. 1125. Notes explicatives: voir p. 1127. Notas explicativas: véase p. 1129.

OCCUPATIONAL INJURIES

Rates of occupational injuries, by economic activity

LÉSIONS PROFESSIONNELLES

Taux de lésions professionnelles, par activité économique

LESIONES PROFESIONALES

Tasas de lesiones profesionales, por actividad económica

	1999	2000	2001	2002	2003	2004	2005	2006	2007	2008

Czech Republic (FD) — Reported injuries - Lésions déclarées - Lesiones declaradas

Rates of non-fatal injuries - Taux de lésions non mortelles - Tasas de lesiones no mortales

Per 100,000 workers insured - Pour 100 000 travailleurs assurés - Por 100 000 trabajadores asegurados

Total men and women - Total hommes et femmes - Total hombres y mujeres
ISIC 3 - CITI 3 - CIIU 3

	1999	2000	2001	2002	2003	2004	2005	2006	2007	2008
Total	2 092	2 052	2 075	2 034	1 872	1 861	1 847	1 830	1 680	1 559
A-B		4 519								
A	4 621		4 759	4 834	4 614	4 610	4 502	4 391	4 132	2 983
B	2 693		3 161	2 822	3 279	2 817	4 581	3 784	2 226	2 645
C	3 942		3 269	3 268	3 053	3 384	3 223	2 345	2 090	1 953
C-D		3 501								
D	3 504		3 356	3 453	3 256	3 263	3 231	3 153	3 034	2 515
E	1 240	1 228	1 268	1 280	1 212	1 096	1 164	1 108	927	774
F	4 108	3 961	3 797	3 645	3 429	3 376	3 221	3 189	2 921	1 845
G	2 099	2 042	2 081	2 145	1 932	1 956	1 957	1 983	1 794	1 197
H	2 361	2 528	2 257	2 059	1 916	1 843	1 813	1 832	1 812	1 138
I	2 104	1 943	2 073	2 084	1 966	2 009	2 214	2 396	2 049	1 752
J	325		328	371	285	223	223	235	178	244
J-K		851								
K	1 093		1 179	1 331	1 109	1 073	1 144	1 137	919	793
L	1 022	985	954	884	918	860	860	906	787	807
M	543	544	618	623	592	619	585	611	538	560
N	1 024	980	1 030	1 065	973	998	1 018	1 023	910	807
O	1 526	1 525	1 531	1 590	1 472	1 492	1 583	1 521	1 401	1 145
X	1 217	1 270	1 258	1 236	1 091	1 065	1 026	1 040	926	633

Men - Hommes - Hombres
ISIC 3 - CITI 3 - CIIU 3

	1999	2000	2001	2002	2003	2004	2005	2006	2007	2008
Total	3 057	3 016	2 985	2 900	2 627	2 613	2 577	2 553	2 354	2 156
A-B		5 185								
A	5 398		5 430	5 407	5 114	5 065	4 899	4 782	4 431	3 322
B	2 855		3 525	3 166	3 601	2 977	5 283	4 102	2 262	3 223
C	4 496		3 634	3 709	3 474	3 844	3 676	2 647	2 321	2 195
C-D		4 667								
D	4 683		4 680	4 491	4 204	4 171	4 114	4 021	3 851	3 241
E	1 492	1 489	1 507	1 525	1 457	1 320	1 377	1 307	1 101	937
F	4 784	4 645	4 361	4 218	3 945	3 824	3 641	3 642	3 362	2 439
G	3 289	3 144	3 033	3 101	2 693	2 676	2 664	2 714	2 409	1 549
H	3 828	3 482	3 089	2 524	2 279	2 240	2 191	2 252	2 140	1 565
I	2 601	2 404	2 475	2 538	2 290	2 318	2 559	2 747	2 429	2 127
J	313		467	530	258	204	220	265	172	322
J-K		1 321								
K	1 580		1 633	1 715	1 426	1 353	1 448	1 438	1 170	1 015
L	2 002	1 969	1 742	1 647	1 682	1 553	1 573	1 651	1 529	1 458
M	566	570	705	753	535	612	526	563	486	671
N	1 435	1 457	1 543	1 536	1 362	1 314	1 357	1 408	1 206	1 004
O	2 387	2 385	2 339	2 465	2 200	2 233	2 452	2 327	2 149	1 675
X	1 817	1 903	1 884	1 833	1 606	1 603	1 531	1 563	1 395	708

Women - Femmes - Mujeres
ISIC 3 - CITI 3 - CIIU 3

	1999	2000	2001	2002	2003	2004	2005	2006	2007	2008
Total	1 001	968	1 052	1 061	1 004	1 011	1 017	1 011	921	884
A-B		3 319								
A	3 302		3 556	3 795	3 702	3 765	3 760	3 658	3 563	2 404
B	2 110		1 852	1 582	1 852	2 158	1 316	2 294	2 062	1 255
C	821		781	636	645	728	613	639	612	503
C-D		1 769								
D	1 847		1 962	1 952	1 856	1 902	1 894	1 834	1 770	1 428
E	562	491	590	593	511	450	541	508	424	319
F	607	500	998	819	780	1 036	1 106	1 026	861	418
G	1 151	1 182	1 324	1 412	1 366	1 405	1 443	1 444	1 346	868
H	1 555	1 838	1 619	1 731	1 660	1 580	1 543	1 531	1 562	722
I	1 313	1 219	1 412	1 333	1 435	1 499	1 628	1 791	1 397	1 149
J	331		263	297	297	232	224	220	182	200
J-K		462								
K	594		711	893	719	738	768	759	645	524
L	570	528	592	534	455	441	436	467	360	396
M	532	531	577	559	615	622	609	631	560	502
N	915	852	893	937	870	911	924	913	822	735
O	610	631	662	637	689	699	670	646	606	519
X	462	470	468	489	420	409	400	390	339	446

Explanatory notes: see p. 1125.   Notes explicatives: voir p. 1127.   Notas explicativas: véase p. 1129.

OCCUPATIONAL INJURIES
Rates of occupational injuries, by economic activity

LÉSIONS PROFESSIONNELLES
Taux de lésions professionnelles, par activité économique

LESIONES PROFESIONALES
Tasas de lesiones profesionales, por actividad económica

España (FA) — Reported injuries - Lésions déclarées - Lesiones declaradas

Rates of fatal injuries - Taux de lésions mortelles - Tasas de lesiones mortales

Per 100,000 workers insured - Pour 100 000 travailleurs assurés - Por 100 000 trabajadores asegurados

Total men and women - Total hommes et femmes - Total hombres y mujeres [1]
ISIC 3 - CITI 3 - CIIU 3

	1999	2000	2001	2002	2003	2004	2005	2006	2007	2008
Total	9.5	9.2	8.0	6.1	5.3	4.9	4.5	4.4	3.6	3.3
A	7.1	5.6	6.3	3.6	2.4	3.0	3.6	2.7	3.9	3.3
B	77.9	89.3	62.3	34.3	29.4	38.4	15.9	37.4	47.8	36.1
C	59.6	59.9	44.0	34.5	52.9	40.2	32.0	38.4	29.4	33.9
D	9.7	8.8	8.2	6.0	5.0	5.3	5.0	5.4	3.6	3.7
E	7.8	11.8	9.3	3.9	13.0	14.3	5.1	21.4	7.8	6.3
F	25.6	22.9	19.7	17.0	16.4	13.5	14.0	12.1	11.0	10.6
G	5.2	5.1	4.3	4.2	2.7	2.2	2.1	1.9	1.1	1.5
H	3.6	2.8	1.8	0.8	1.0	0.7	0.6	0.2	0.8	0.4
I	31.5	32.5	27.1	24.1	18.1	21.4	16.6	15.2	12.0	10.3
J	2.3	1.7	3.0	0.6	1.1	0.3	0.3	0.8	0.0	0.5
K	3.9	4.0	3.4	2.0	2.5	1.3	1.0	1.6	1.1	1.5
L,Q	3.1	5.3	5.1	2.6	2.3	1.8	1.2	1.2	0.8	0.9
M	2.0	2.2	1.8	0.2	0.2	0.2	0.6	0.4	0.5	0.3
N	3.0	3.3	1.4	1.2	1.3	0.5	0.1	0.5	0.3	0.0
O	4.8	5.1	5.3	3.4	2.1	2.1	2.3	2.1	1.6	2.6
P	15.7	16.0	10.8	0.0	0.0	2.7	0.0	0.0	0.0	0.0

Men - Hommes - Hombres [1]
ISIC 3 - CITI 3 - CIIU 3

	1999	2000	2001	2002	2003	2004	2005	2006	2007	2008
Total	14.9	14.6	12.9	9.8	8.5	8.0	7.4	7.3	5.9	5.7
A	.	.	.	.	4.0	4.8	6.2	4.5	6.7	6.0
B	.	.	.	.	35.7	45.9	16.8	45.1	52.4	43.5
C	.	.	.	.	58.2	44.2	35.3	42.6	32.2	37.3
D	.	.	.	.	6.5	6.9	6.5	7.1	4.7	5.0
E	.	.	.	.	15.6	17.2	6.1	26.1	9.4	7.7
F	.	.	.	.	17.5	14.5	15.2	13.1	11.8	11.6
G	.	.	.	.	4.5	3.8	3.8	3.3	1.8	2.8
H	.	.	.	.	1.6	1.1	1.2	0.5	1.6	0.9
I	.	.	.	.	23.5	27.4	21.4	19.4	15.8	12.9
J	.	.	.	.	1.4	0.5	0.5	1.4	0.0	0.9
K	.	.	.	.	5.0	2.7	2.1	3.0	2.1	2.8
L,Q	.	.	.	.	4.2	3.3	2.1	2.2	1.5	1.7
M	.	.	.	.	0.6	0.6	1.1	1.1	0.9	0.4
N	.	.	.	.	2.8	1.4	0.4	1.7	0.7	0.0
O	.	.	.	.	4.3	4.1	4.9	4.0	3.4	4.9
P	.	.	.	.	0.0	3.8	0.0	0.0	0.0	0.0

Women - Femmes - Mujeres [1]
ISIC 3 - CITI 3 - CIIU 3

	1999	2000	2001	2002	2003	2004	2005	2006	2007	2008
Total	0.6	0.7	0.5	0.4	0.5	0.4	0.2	0.3	0.3	0.2
A	.	.	.	.	0.2	0.6	0.2	0.4	0.6	0.0
B	.	.	.	.	0.0	0.0	11.8	0.0	25.4	0.0
C	.	.	.	.	0.0	0.0	0.0	0.0	0.0	0.0
D	.	.	.	.	0.7	0.9	0.7	0.5	0.5	0.2
E	.	.	.	.	0.0	0.0	0.0	0.0	0.0	0.0
F	.	.	.	.	4.0	0.8	0.0	0.6	1.9	0.7
G	.	.	.	.	0.6	0.3	0.2	0.3	0.3	0.2
H	.	.	.	.	0.5	0.5	0.0	0.0	0.2	0.0
I	.	.	.	.	0.6	2.3	1.6	2.5	0.9	2.7
J	.	.	.	.	0.7	0.0	0.0	0.0	0.0	0.0
K	.	.	.	.	0.4	0.2	0.1	0.4	0.2	0.3
L,Q	.	.	.	.	0.6	0.4	0.4	0.2	0.0	0.2
M	.	.	.	.	0.0	0.0	0.3	0.0	0.2	0.2
N	.	.	.	.	0.7	0.2	0.0	0.1	0.1	0.0
O	.	.	.	.	0.0	0.3	0.0	0.3	0.0	0.5
P	.	.	.	.	0.0	0.0	0.0	0.0	0.0	0.0

Explanatory notes: see p. 1125.

[1] Deaths occurring within one month of accident.

Notes explicatives: voir p. 1127.

[1] Les décès survenant pendant le mois qui suit l'accident.

Notas explicativas: véase p. 1129.

[1] Los fallecimientos que se produzcan durante el mes posterior al accidente.

OCCUPATIONAL INJURIES

Rates of occupational injuries, by economic activity

LÉSIONS PROFESSIONNELLES

Taux de lésions professionnelles, par activité économique

LESIONES PROFESIONALES

Tasas de lesiones profesionales, por actividad económica

	1999	2000	2001	2002	2003	2004	2005	2006	2007	2008

España (FA)   Reported injuries - Lésions déclarées - Lesiones declaradas

Rates of non-fatal injuries - Taux de lésions non mortelles - Tasas de lesiones no mortales

Per 100,000 workers insured - Pour 100 000 travailleurs assurés - Por 100 000 trabajadores asegurados

Total men and women - Total hommes et femmes - Total hombres y mujeres
ISIC 3 - CITI 3 - CIIU 3

	1999	2000	2001	2002	2003	2004	2005	2006	2007	2008
Total	7 428	7 549	7 342	7 035	6 371	6 121	5 999	5 868	5 748	5 055
A	3 502	3 236	2 929	2 788	2 575	2 688	2 740	2 813	2 900	2 885
B	9 305	8 403	7 915	8 085	7 355	7 805	7 302	7 417	7 591	7 273
C	32 496	31 802	29 905	27 069	26 294	23 956	21 315	19 413	20 220	18 069
D	11 325	11 297	10 856	10 358	9 787	10 095	10 083	10 209	9 936	8 772
E	4 539	4 611	4 530	4 382	4 742	5 861	6 064	5 645	5 825	5 140
F	18 769	18 747	18 287	17 275	15 267	13 866	13 471	12 886	12 575	10 824
G	6 072	6 355	6 153	5 951	5 390	5 024	4 856	4 671	4 656	4 220
H	7 434	7 827	7 414	6 824	6 212	6 066	5 771	5 565	5 353	5 027
I	7 510	7 820	7 508	7 282	7 098	7 335	7 226	7 095	6 940	6 172
J	561	589	593	583	582	581	576	567	523	517
K	5 309	5 156	4 975	4 863	3 410	2 304	2 150	2 043	2 058	1 903
L,Q	3 812	3 762	3 782	3 730	3 571	3 528	3 494	3 352	3 539	3 542
M	1 303	1 316	1 329	1 277	1 422	1 414	1 387	1 397	1 215	1 226
N	3 054	3 285	3 648	3 627	3 573	3 476	3 480	3 338	3 109	2 984
O	3 620	3 981	4 070	4 138	4 217	4 931	4 732	4 626	4 873	4 787
P	2 545	2 801	2 930	2 620	1 630	2 438	2 100	2 404	3 044	3 015

Men - Hommes - Hombres
ISIC 3 - CITI 3 - CIIU 3

	1999	2000	2001	2002	2003	2004	2005	2006	2007	2008
Total	9 990	10 171	9 931	9 483	8 560	8 272	8 125	7 966	7 796	6 801
A					3 473	3 686	3 828	3 874	3 984	3 999
B					8 274	8 663	8 298	8 419	8 410	8 048
C					27 633	25 418	22 669	20 722	21 335	19 145
D					11 337	11 599	11 770	11 865	11 439	10 128
E					5 332	6 727	6 992	6 564	6 795	5 954
F					16 300	14 869	14 469	13 875	13 512	11 713
G					7 032	6 589	6 268	6 038	6 080	5 443
H					6 533	6 313	5 946	5 716	5 473	5 087
I					8 209	8 500	8 331	8 163	7 924	6 970
J					491	466	442	445	412	396
K					4 292	3 012	2 784	2 661	2 657	2 404
L,Q					5 187	5 137	5 127	4 917	4 899	4 831
M					1 512	1 417	1 273	1 257	1 131	1 061
N					3 619	3 399	3 319	3 104	2 715	2 663
O					5 917	6 443	6 183	6 078	6 255	6 024
P					1 630	1 880	1 725	1 832	2 348	2 416

Women - Femmes - Mujeres
ISIC 3 - CITI 3 - CIIU 3

	1999	2000	2001	2002	2003	2004	2005	2006	2007	2008
Total	3 242	3 429	3 419	3 290	3 181	3 042	2 955	2 918	2 960	2 799
A					1 386	1 393	1 348	1 474	1 578	1 534
B					2 998	3 435	2 405	2 571	3 620	3 469
C					13 055	9 068	8 315	7 545	8 645	7 415
D					5 248	5 667	5 275	5 531	5 724	4 972
E					1 712	1 612	1 643	1 467	1 314	1 512
F					3 773	2 075	1 864	1 856	1 818	1 629
G					3 522	3 277	3 240	3 145	3 145	2 953
H					5 930	5 856	5 626	5 445	5 262	4 982
I					3 500	3 644	3 815	3 872	4 047	3 880
J					714	741	757	724	660	659
K					2 648	1 700	1 590	1 497	1 542	1 476
L,Q					2 030	2 016	1 965	1 916	2 197	2 260
M					1 370	1 412	1 453	1 476	1 259	1 312
N					3 556	3 503	3 536	3 418	3 241	3 088
O					2 650	3 569	3 413	3 334	3 639	3 688
P					1 628	3 958	3 122	3 932	4 855	4 551

Explanatory notes: see p. 1125.   Notes explicatives: voir p. 1127.   Notas explicativas: véase p. 1129.

OCCUPATIONAL INJURIES

Rates of occupational injuries, by economic activity

LÉSIONS PROFESSIONNELLES

Taux de lésions professionnelles, par activité économique

LESIONES PROFESIONALES

Tasas de lesiones profesionales, por actividad económica

8B

Estonia (FA) — Compensated injuries - Lésions indemnisées - Lesiones indemnizadas

Rates of fatal injuries - Taux de lésions mortelles - Tasas de lesiones mortales

Per 100,000 workers insured - Pour 100 000 travailleurs assurés - Por 100 000 trabajadores asegurados

Total men and women - Total hommes et femmes - Total hombres y mujeres

ISIC 3 - CITI 3 - CIIU 3

	1999	2000	2001	2002	2003	2004	2005	2006	2007		2008	ISIC 4 - CITI 4 - CIIU 4
Total	8.5	4.4	6.2	6.0	5.2	5.7	4.0	4.3	3.2	I	3.2	Total
A	25.4	7.1	8.0	7.7	5.8	6.4	3.4	6.7	6.9	I	0.0	A
B	0.0	0.0	0.0	0.0	0.0	0.0	0.0	0.0	0.0	I	66.7	B
C	34.9	0.0	17.2	35.1	17.5	0.0	17.0	38.5	18.1	I	3.0	C
D	4.7	6.5	9.7	4.7	6.0	3.6	2.9	6.6	3.0	I	0.0	D
E	21.9	19.1	17.5	0.0	9.8	16.7	8.0	0.0	0.0	I	0.0	E
F	10.0	9.4	15.3	23.1	9.3	10.7	2.1	9.6	6.2	I	7.4	F
G	1.1	2.4	4.8	5.8	2.5	2.5	5.0	2.3	4.5	I	0.0	G
H	0.0	0.0	0.0	0.0	0.0	12.4	0.0	0.0	0.0	I	0.0	H
I	12.7	8.3	3.7	9.2	14.2	13.6	11.0	0.0	3.4	I	0.0	I
J	11.4	0.0	0.0	0.0	0.0	0.0	29.0	0.0	0.0	I	0.0	J
K	7.4	0.0	0.0	4.5	6.8	10.2	2.2	6.2	2.0	I	0.0	K
L	15.2	0.0	5.8	6.0	2.9	8.1	0.0	10.3	5.1	I	9.8	L
M	0.0	0.0	0.0	0.0	1.8	1.8	0.0	0.0	0.0	I	0.0	M
N	2.9	0.0	6.5	0.0	0.0	0.0	2.9	0.0	0.0	I	5.8	N
O	10.2	3.2	3.3	3.3	0.0	3.5	6.5	0.0	0.0	I	2.6	O
										I	0.0	P
										I	0.0	Q
										I	0.0	R
										I	0.0	S

Men - Hommes - Hombres

ISIC 3 - CITI 3 - CIIU 3

	1999	2000	2001	2002	2003	2004	2005	2006	2007		2008	ISIC 4 - CITI 4 - CIIU 4
Total	14.6	8.0	10.9	10.8	10.3	8.0	6.7	7.1	6.4	I	5.7	Total
A	35.0	10.6	11.3	11.2	8.6	4.7	5.3	10.2	10.3	I	5.7	A
B	0.0	0.0	0.0	0.0	0.0	0.0	0.0	0.0	0.0	I	75.5	B
C	39.5	0.0	22.7	20.0	20.0	0.0	18.5	42.5	20.4	I	5.5	C
D	7.1	10.4	16.0	8.3	10.9	5.3	5.5	9.4	5.5	I	0.0	D
E	31.3	26.3	22.0	0.0	12.5	23.5	10.6	0.0	0.0	I	0.0	E
F	8.3	10.4	16.5	25.2	10.0	9.5	2.3	10.3	6.8	I	8.2	F
G	2.7	5.4	8.8	14.0	6.1	0.0	9.1	5.6	11.1	I	0.0	G
H	0.0	0.0	0.0	0.0	0.0	23.3	0.0	0.0	0.0	I	8.2	H
I	17.2	9.6	5.4	8.3	21.8	19.8	13.0	0.0	5.1	I	0.0	I
J	0.0	0.0	0.0	0.0	0.0	0.0	166.7	0.0	0.0	I	0.0	J
K	13.3	0.0	0.0	7.8	11.0	4.4	3.7	7.6	3.9	I	0.0	K
L	29.0	0.0	11.0	11.8	5.3	10.9	0.0	10.6	11.1	I	0.0	L
M	0.0	0.0	0.0	0.0	9.4	9.6	0.0	0.0	0.0	I	0.0	M
N	0.0	0.0	0.0	0.0	0.0	0.0	20.4	0.0	0.0	I	0.0	N
O	28.3	8.6	9.5	9.7	0.0	9.4	0.0	0.0	0.0	I	5.8	O
										I	0.0	P
										I	0.0	Q
										I	0.0	R
										I	0.0	S

Women - Femmes - Mujeres

ISIC 3 - CITI 3 - CIIU 3

	1999	2000	2001	2002	2003	2004	2005	2006	2007		2008	ISIC 4 - CITI 4 - CIIU 4
Total	2.0	0.7	1.4	1.0	0.0	3.4	1.3	1.5	0.0	I	0.6	Total
A	10.1	0.0	0.0	0.0	0.0	9.7	0.0	0.0	0.0	I	0.0	A
B	0.0	0.0	0.0	0.0	0.0	0.0	0.0	0.0	0.0	I	0.0	B
C	0.0	0.0	0.0	142.9	0.0	0.0	0.0	0.0	0.0	I	0.0	C
D	1.7	1.6	1.7	0.0	0.0	1.5	0.0	3.2	0.0	I	0.0	D
E	0.0	0.0	0.0	0.0	0.0	0.0	0.0	0.0	0.0	I	0.0	E
F	25.6	0.0	0.0	0.0	0.0	21.3	0.0	0.0	0.0	I	0.0	F
G	0.0	0.0	2.0	0.0	0.0	4.3	2.1	0.0	0.0	I	0.0	G
H	0.0	0.0	0.0	0.0	0.0	8.4	0.0	0.0	0.0	I	0.0	H
I	0.0	5.3	0.0	10.9	0.0	0.0	6.0	0.0	0.0	I	0.0	I
J	18.5	0.0	0.0	0.0	0.0	0.0	0.0	0.0	0.0	I	0.0	J
K	0.0	0.0	0.0	0.0	0.0	17.8	0.0	4.6	0.0	I	0.0	K
L	0.0	0.0	0.0	0.0	0.0	5.4	0.0	9.9	0.0	I	18.2	L
M	0.0	0.0	0.0	0.0	0.0	0.0	0.0	0.0	0.0	I	0.0	M
N	3.3	0.0	7.7	0.0	0.0	0.0	0.0	0.0	0.0	I	11.6	N
O	0.0	0.0	0.0	0.0	0.0	0.0	9.7	0.0	0.0	I	0.0	O
										I	0.0	P
										I	0.0	Q
										I	0.0	R
										I	0.0	S

Explanatory notes: see p. 1125.   Notes explicatives: voir p. 1127.   Notas explicativas: véase p. 1129.

8B

OCCUPATIONAL INJURIES	LÉSIONS PROFESSIONNELLES	LESIONES PROFESIONALES
Rates of occupational injuries, by economic activity	Taux de lésions professionnelles, par activité économique	Tasas de lesiones profesionales, por actividad económica

Estonia (FA) — Compensated injuries - Lésions indemnisées - Lesiones indemnizadas

Rates of non-fatal injuries - Taux de lésions non mortelles - Tasas de lesiones no mortales

Per 100,000 workers insured - Pour 100 000 travailleurs assurés - Por 100 000 trabajadores asegurados

Total men and women - Total hommes et femmes - Total hombres y mujeres

ISIC 3 - CITI 3 - CIIU 3 … ISIC 4 - CITI 4 - CIIU 4

ISIC 3	1999	2000	2001	2002	2003	2004	2005	2006	2007	2008	ISIC 4
Total	495	482	564	526	538	553	560	561	562	615	Total
A	1 113	764	713	505	549	618	745	656	639	0	A
B	677	258	185	211	182	83	143	182	95	633	B
C	1 256	1 051	1 241	1 018	807	750	797	846	964	1 084	C
D	717	816	972	1 019	1 016	1 033	975	1 048	1 106	195	D
E	322	427	430	419	392	267	232	298	221	2	E
F	777	522	595	620	606	534	614	594	515	584	F
G	203	220	345	322	411	374	447	431	420	435	G
H	277	118	316	318	362	358	335	386	338	581	H
I	500	479	547	472	431	501	465	476	485	551	I
J	125	173	236	63	237	63	174	164	85	111	J
K	255	282	390	336	435	416	416	395	394	269	K
L	400	530	592	642	612	659	747	744	791	265	L
M	147	188	253	167	155	174	149	158	152	620	M
N	365	403	320	250	190	235	289	283	264	549	N
O	286	240	299	332	270	306	290	265	256	953	O
										174	P
										421	Q
										439	R
										203	S

Men - Hommes - Hombres

ISIC 3 - CITI 3 - CIIU 3 … ISIC 4 - CITI 4 - CIIU 4

ISIC 3	1999	2000	2001	2002	2003	2004	2005	2006	2007	2008	ISIC 4
Total	648	625	686	717	741	777	772	747	757	802	Total
A	1 172	773	536	451	498	502	637	589	551	591	A
B	679	233	200	235	182	65	160	200	125	623	B
C	1 145	1 127	1 386	1 000	820	892	796	936	979	1 359	C
D	920	1 016	1 155	1 296	1 341	1 401	1 331	1 314	1 402	234	D
E	391	491	363	453	450	341	266	363	171	2 846	E
F	797	556	601	630	627	582	654	621	550	614	F
G	319	322	480	531	648	614	673	710	624	594	G
H	526	149	452	311	667	326	489	429	425	556	H
I	488	456	534	499	474	595	488	504	522	620	I
J	29	135	231	125	462	91	167	529	120	96	J
K	323	387	437	400	493	535	480	515	515	406	K
L	469	768	692	982	826	978	1 217	1 255	1 278	362	L
M	130	241	260	176	243	260	165	194	227	1 122	M
N	440	514	460	294	179	286	388	333	364	686	N
O	453	310	467	670	479	542	495	528	513	1 614	O
										131	P
										786	Q
										809	R
										231	S

Women - Femmes - Mujeres

ISIC 3 - CITI 3 - CIIU 3 … ISIC 4 - CITI 4 - CIIU 4

ISIC 3	1999	2000	2001	2002	2003	2004	2005	2006	2007	2008	ISIC 4
Total	334	330	437	328	328	326	352	351	365	426	Total
A	1 020	746	1 148	630	658	854	942	784	819	1 065	A
B	667	1 000	0	0	0	200	0	0	0	0	B
C	2 100	750	786	1 143	714	133	800	400	.	757	C
D	470	564	740	661	619	612	583	732	760	56	D
E	164	256	696	250	182	86	129	0	538	1 300	E
F	590	200	552	500	333	106	222	255	173	0	F
G	118	141	251	174	249	201	289	245	280	293	G
H	234	110	287	321	283	370	295	374	319	649	H
I	535	532	579	418	349	296	411	415	409	649	I
J	185	200	244	36	120	53	175	54	72	532	J
K	170	169	337	250	341	254	323	249	262	129	K
L	324	305	479	284	348	341	327	248	377	208	L
M	151	178	251	165	134	154	146	152	138	182	M
N	352	389	293	242	192	225	272	275	250	226	N
O	191	197	212	157	131	165	188	145	156	419	O
										423	P
										185	Q
										384	R
										267	S
										191	

Explanatory notes: see p. 1125.   Notes explicatives: voir p. 1127.   Notas explicativas: véase p. 1129.

OCCUPATIONAL INJURIES

Rates of occupational injuries, by economic activity

LÉSIONS PROFESSIONNELLES

Taux de lésions professionnelles, par activité économique

LESIONES PROFESIONALES

Tasas de lesiones profesionales, por actividad económica

8B

	1999	2000	2001	2002	2003	2004	2005	2006	2007	2008

Finland (FA) — Compensated injuries - Lésions indemnisées - Lesiones indemnizadas

Rates of fatal injuries - Taux de lésions mortelles - Tasas de lesiones mortales

Per 100,000 employees - Pour 100 000 salariés - Por 100 000 asalariados

Total men and women - Total hommes et femmes - Total hombres y mujeres
ISIC 3 - CITI 3 - CIIU 3

	1999	2000	2001	2002	2003	2004	2005	2006	2007	2008
Total	2.1	2.3	2.1	1.8	2.1	2.1	2.4	2.2	1.7	.
A	5.1	2.5	2.7	0.0	0.0	0.0	0.0	3.0	0.0	.
B	0.0	0.0	0.0	0.0	0.0	0.0	333.3	0.0	0.0	.
C	50.0	0.0	0.0	28.6	47.6	0.0	43.5	0.0	0.0	.
D	2.6	3.9	2.3	2.1	2.4	2.7	1.5	1.7	1.2	.
E	0.0	0.0	4.6	0.0	5.0	5.4	0.0	6.0	0.0	.
F	7.5	7.5	9.3	4.2	12.7	8.5	9.8	7.3	5.9	.
G	0.8	0.9	0.9	0.8	0.8	0.4	1.9	0.4	0.7	.
H	0.0	0.0	1.5	2.8	0.0	0.0	1.5	0.0	0.0	.
I	3.3	4.7	6.5	5.4	6.6	5.4	10.0	8.1	5.2	.
J	0.0	0.0	0.0	0.0	0.0	0.0	0.0	0.0	0.0	.
K	0.5	1.0	0.9	1.3	0.9	2.2	0.8	1.6	0.8	.
L	4.3	3.5	1.8	1.7	0.8	6.0	0.9	4.4	5.1	.
M	0.0	0.0	0.0	0.6	0.0	0.0	0.0	1.2	0.0	.
N	0.0	0.0	0.0	0.6	0.0	0.0	0.3	0.3	0.0	.
O	4.2	1.0	1.0	1.0	0.0	0.0	2.8	0.9	2.7	.
P	0.0	0.0	0.0	30.3	0.0	0.0	13.7	14.3	0.0	.
Q	0.0	0.0	0.0	0.0	0.0	0.0	0.0	0.0	0.0	.

Men - Hommes - Hombres
ISIC 3 - CITI 3 - CIIU 3

	1999	2000	2001	2002	2003	2004	2005	2006	2007	2008
Total	0.0	4.6	4.0	3.4	4.2	3.9	4.4	4.1	3.0	.
A	3.9	3.7	4.0	0.0	0.0	0.0	0.0	4.3	0.0	.
B	166.6	0.0	0.0	0.0	0.0	0.0	500.0	0.0	0.0	.
C	62.5	0.0	0.0	30.3	51.3	0.0	48.8	0.0	0.0	.
D	9.7	5.5	3.2	2.9	3.4	3.4	2.1	2.3	1.6	.
E	0.0	0.0	6.1	0.0	6.5	6.9	0.0	7.9	0.0	.
F	8.1	8.1	10.0	4.6	13.7	8.3	10.5	7.9	6.4	.
G	1.7	1.8	1.7	1.7	1.7	0.8	4.0	0.8	1.6	.
H	0.0	0.0	5.5	11.4	0.0	0.0	6.2	0.0	0.0	.
I	4.0	6.7	9.1	6.7	9.3	5.7	11.3	11.5	6.5	.
J	0.0	0.0	0.0	0.0	0.0	0.0	0.0	0.0	0.0	.
K	1.0	1.8	0.8	2.4	1.6	4.0	1.6	3.0	1.4	.
L	5.2	5.6	3.8	3.5	1.8	12.7	1.9	5.6	5.6	.
M	0.0	0.0	0.0	0.0	0.0	0.0	0.0	3.6	0.0	.
N	0.0	0.0	0.0	5.4	0.0	0.0	2.5	0.0	0.0	.
O	10.4	2.5	2.2	2.2	0.0	0.0	2.2	0.0	4.5	.
P	0.0	0.0	0.0	.	0.0	0.0	29.4	37.0	0.0	.
Q	0.0	0.0	0.0	0.0	0.0	0.0	0.0	0.0	0.0	.

Women - Femmes - Mujeres
ISIC 3 - CITI 3 - CIIU 3

	1999	2000	2001	2002	2003	2004	2005	2006	2007	2008
Total	0.5	0.1	0.2	0.2	0.0	0.4	0.5	0.4	0.5	.
A	0.0	0.0	0.0	0.0	0.0	0.0	0.0	0.0	0.0	.
B	0.0	0.0	0.0	0.0	0.0	0.0	0.0	0.0	0.0	.
C	0.0	0.0	0.0	0.0	0.0	0.0	0.0	0.0	0.0	.
D	0.0	0.0	0.0	0.0	0.0	0.8	0.0	0.0	0.0	.
E	0.0	0.0	0.0	0.0	0.0	0.0	0.0	0.0	0.0	.
F	0.0	0.0	0.0	0.0	0.0	12.0	0.0	0.0	0.0	.
G	0.0	0.0	0.0	0.0	0.0	0.0	0.0	0.0	0.0	.
H	0.0	0.0	0.0	0.0	0.0	0.0	0.0	0.0	0.0	.
I	2.2	0.0	0.0	2.2	0.0	4.7	6.9	0.0	2.2	.
J	0.0	0.0	0.0	0.0	0.0	0.0	0.0	0.0	0.0	.
K	0.0	0.0	1.0	0.0	0.0	0.0	0.0	0.0	0.0	.
L	0.0	1.7	0.0	0.0	0.0	0.0	0.0	3.3	4.7	.
M	0.0	0.0	0.0	0.9	0.0	0.0	0.0	0.0	0.0	.
N	0.0	0.0	0.0	0.0	0.0	0.0	0.0	0.3	0.0	.
O	0.0	0.0	0.0	0.0	0.0	0.0	3.3	1.6	1.5	.
P	0.0	0.0	0.0	0.0	0.0	0.0	0.0	0.0	0.0	.
Q	0.0	0.0	0.0	0.0	0.0	0.0	0.0	0.0	0.0	.

Explanatory notes: see p. 1125.   Notes explicatives: voir p. 1127.   Notas explicativas: véase p. 1129.

	OCCUPATIONAL INJURIES	LÉSIONS PROFESSIONNELLES	LESIONES PROFESIONALES
	Rates of occupational injuries, by economic activity	Taux de lésions professionnelles, par activité économique	Tasas de lesiones profesionales, por actividad económica

	1999	2000	2001	2002	2003	2004	2005	2006	2007	2008

Finland (FA)   Compensated injuries - Lésions indemnisées - Lesiones indemnizadas

Rates of non-fatal injuries - Taux de lésions non mortelles - Tasas de lesiones no mortales

Per 100,000 employees - Pour 100 000 salariés - Por 100 000 asalariados

Total men and women - Total hommes et femmes - Total hombres y mujeres [1]
ISIC 3 - CITI 3 - CIIU 3

	1999	2000	2001	2002	2003	2004	2005	2006	2007	2008
Total	2 956	2 879	2 829	2 793	2 730	2 715	2 887	2 892	2 845	.
A	2 656	2 364	2 484	2 965	2 944	2 869	3 266	3 824	4 187	.
B	5 333	2 778	2 000	6 000	8 333	7 667	4 167	4 000	3 000	.
C	4 250	5 088	6 667	4 829	3 333	3 405	3 261	3 064	3 800	.
D	4 465	4 369	4 256	4 011	4 006	3 884	3 926	3 912	3 789	.
E	1 831	1 671	1 708	1 498	1 570	1 618	1 761	1 837	1 849	.
F	8 169	8 417	8 580	8 450	7 833	7 704	8 276	8 105	7 685	.
G	2 115	2 100	2 069	2 179	2 095	2 090	2 216	2 256	2 177	.
H	2 175	2 333	2 130	2 058	2 176	2 195	2 452	2 441	2 275	.
I	4 391	4 086	3 854	3 987	4 038	4 442	4 703	4 467	4 034	.
J	401	273	316	244	282	252	264	290	304	.
K	1 826	1 714	1 683	1 698	1 806	1 837	2 026	2 218	2 494	.
L	6 942	6 981	7 567	7 553	7 218	7 293	8 371	8 106	7 644	.
M	393	360	356	380	290	268	298	306	368	.
N	368	376	328	339	402	399	451	499	515	.
O	1 305	1 324	1 381	1 316	1 269	1 357	1 418	1 356	1 311	.
P	3 643	4 195	4 879	5 061	4 378	3 746	4 507	4 286	4 111	.
Q	800	0	500	0	2 000	0	0	333	111	.

Men - Hommes - Hombres [1]
ISIC 3 - CITI 3 - CIIU 3

	1999	2000	2001	2002	2003	2004	2005	2006	2007	2008
Total	4 514	4 378	4 273	4 212	4 087	4 043	4 280	4 281	4 189	.
A	3 381	2 827	3 068	3 580	3 425	3 038	3 488	3 799	4 163	.
B	4 000	3 167	2 571	14 500	11 500	7 333	5 500	4 800	3 857	.
C	5 063	6 222	7 429	5 000	3 564	3 658	3 561	3 279	3 946	.
D	5 433	5 253	5 129	4 838	4 759	4 668	4 746	4 695	4 479	.
E	2 102	1 971	2 048	1 835	1 922	2 000	2 161	2 276	2 358	.
F	8 657	8 900	9 029	8 969	8 298	8 112	8 721	8 487	8 104	.
G	3 008	3 006	2 883	3 131	2 915	2 822	3 029	3 129	2 920	.
H	2 804	3 035	2 802	3 136	3 451	3 115	3 500	3 283	3 209	.
I	5 533	5 078	4 751	4 921	4 906	5 432	5 711	5 442	5 062	.
J	382	290	270	305	438	426	269	321	477	.
K	2 373	2 135	2 123	2 098	2 309	2 325	2 665	2 941	3 324	.
L	6 624	6 854	7 008	6 812	6 496	6 493	6 987	6 786	6 358	.
M	645	549	620	608	452	428	477	489	607	.
N	712	805	681	701	840	692	801	926	952	.
O	2 073	1 960	1 935	1 782	1 722	1 938	1 832	1 973	1 853	.
P	0	.	.	.	.	6 733	8 088	9 111	7 875	.
Q	0	.	.	.	.	0	0	750	200	.

Women - Femmes - Mujeres [1]
ISIC 3 - CITI 3 - CIIU 3

	1999	2000	2001	2002	2003	2004	2005	2006	2007	2008
Total	1 393	1 372	1 378	1 399	1 392	1 406	1 524	1 537	1 535	.
A	1 208	1 336	1 256	1 832	1 941	2 485	2 766	3 884	4 247	.
B	0	2 000	1 333	2 333	2 000	1 064	1 000	2 667	1 000	.
C	889	714	1 333	2 000	333	1 000	800	600	3 000	.
D	2 260	7 284	2 222	2 085	2 134	1 976	1 934	1 923	1 972	.
E	690	612	608	362	391	262	357	421	282	.
F	1 977	2 230	2 400	2 079	2 068	2 349	2 318	2 768	2 440	.
G	1 267	1 240	1 274	1 310	1 341	1 390	1 443	1 452	1 490	.
H	1 934	2 078	1 886	1 701	1 791	1 902	2 111	2 181	1 987	.
I	1 858	1 733	1 637	1 814	1 875	2 009	2 226	2 132	1 590	.
J	409	267	336	220	226	182	263	277	227	.
K	1 195	1 193	1 143	1 207	1 202	1 252	1 305	1 382	1 555	.
L	7 253	7 083	8 077	8 229	7 877	8 006	9 607	9 271	8 716	.
M	263	268	226	268	208	191	204	215	247	.
N	324	324	285	294	347	360	407	445	464	.
O	785	883	933	952	923	924	1 107	931	953	.
P	825	1 250	1 355	1 367	976	1 030	1 350	1 256	1 073	.
Q	667	0	200	0	2 000	0	0	0	0	.

Explanatory notes: see p. 1125.   Notes explicatives: voir p. 1127.   Notas explicativas: véase p. 1129.

[1] Incapacity of 3 days or more.   [1] Incapacité de 3 jours et plus.   [1] Incapacidad de 3 días y más.

OCCUPATIONAL INJURIES
LÉSIONS PROFESSIONNELLES
LESIONES PROFESIONALES

8B

Rates of occupational injuries, by economic activity
Taux de lésions professionnelles, par activité économique
Tasas de lesiones profesionales, por actividad económica

	1999	2000	2001	2002	2003	2004	2005	2006	2007	2008

France (FA) [1]   Compensated injuries - Lésions indemnisées - Lesiones indemnizadas

Rates of fatal injuries - Taux de lésions mortelles - Tasas de lesiones mortales

Per 100,000 workers insured - Pour 100 000 travailleurs assurés - Por 100 000 trabajadores asegurados

Total men and women - Total hommes et femmes - Total hombres y mujeres
ISIC 3 - CITI 3 - CIIU 3

	1999	2000	2001	2002	2003	2004	2005	2006	2007	2008
Total	4.5	4.4	4.2	3.8	3.7	3.5	2.7	3.0	3.4	.
A	.	.	.	.	.	.	5.9	6.1	5.8	.
B	.	.	.	.	.	.	0.0	0.0	0.0	.
C	.	.	.	.	.	.	11.2	19.2	15.6	.
D	3.8	.	.	.	.	.	2.6	3.1	3.7	.
E [2]	1.7	.	.	.	.	.	6.8	1.6	3.2	.
F	13.8	.	.	.	.	.	7.8	10.2	12.0	.
G [3]	3.3	.	.	.	.	.	1.7	2.1	2.1	.
H	2.2	.	.	.	.	.	1.7	1.1	1.1	.
I [4]	16.3	.	.	.	.	.	9.1	8.0	9.1	.
J	.	.	.	.	.	.	0.7	0.5	1.0	.
J-K,O-P,X [5]	2.7	.	.	.	.	.				
K	.	.	.	.	.	.	2.0	2.1	2.6	.
L	.	.	.	.	.	.	0.5	1.3	0.9	.
M	.	.	.	.	.	.	0.7	0.9	1.1	.
N	.	.	.	.	.	.	0.7	1.4	0.9	.
O	.	.	.	.	.	.	2.4	2.1	2.1	.
P	.	.	.	.	.	.	0.0	0.0	0.0	.
Q	.	.	.	.	.	.	0.0	0.0	0.0	.
X	.	.	.	.	.	.	3.2	4.0	4.7	.

Rates of non-fatal injuries - Taux de lésions non mortelles - Tasas de lesiones no mortales

Per 100,000 workers insured - Pour 100 000 travailleurs assurés - Por 100 000 trabajadores asegurados

Total men and women - Total hommes et femmes - Total hombres y mujeres
ISIC 3 - CITI 3 - CIIU 3

	1999	2000	2001	2002	2003	2004	2005	2006	2007	2008
Total	4 432.2	.	4 279.3	4 300.0	4 090.2	3 948.9	3 910.0	3 939.8	3 943.1	.
A	.	.	.	.	.	.	4 514.3	5 441.5	5 000.0	.
B	.	.	.	.	.	.	5 955.3	4 377.7	5 769.2	.
C	.	.	.	.	.	.	5 208.0	5 120.3	4 959.8	.
D	5 154.7	.	.	.	.	.	4 310.8	4 194.5	4 223.8	.
E	3 611.5	.	.	.	.	.	3 033.7	2 694.3	2 553.6	.
F	10 676.7	.	.	.	.	.	9 115.1	8 828.9	8 751.7	.
G	2 703.7	.	.	.	.	.	3 918.9	3 953.0	3 964.1	.
H	5 655	.	.	.	.	.	4 649	4 700	4 697	.
I [4]	7 306.5	.	.	.	.	.	6 066.0	6 288.1	5 989.2	.
J	.	.	.	.	.	.	521.5	509.2	484.4	.
J-K,O-P,X [5]	2 825	.	.	.	.	.				
K	.	.	.	.	.	.	2 970.4	3 021.1	3 128.0	.
L	.	.	.	.	.	.	1 313.9	1 327.6	1 321.9	.
M	.	.	.	.	.	.	1 468.8	1 297.0	1 144.8	.
N	.	.	.	.	.	.	3 462.2	3 662.2	3 797.6	.
O	.	.	.	.	.	.	2 888.3	2 871.4	2 697.8	.
P	.	.	.	.	.	.	2 870.8	2 109.0	0.0	.
Q	.	.	.	.	.	.	993.4	889.7	866.5	.
X	.	.	.	.	.	.	4 777.0	5 987.8	5 387.0	.

France (FA) [1]   Compensated injuries - Lésions indemnisées - Lesiones indemnizadas

Rates of fatal injuries - Taux de lésions mortelles - Tasas de lesiones mortales

Per 100,000 workers insured - Pour 100 000 travailleurs assurés - Por 100 000 trabajadores asegurados

Total men and women - Total hommes et femmes - Total hombres y mujeres
ISIC 3 - CITI 3 - CIIU 3

	1999	2000	2001	2002	2003	2004	2005	2006	2007	2008
A	4	.	.	7	6	6	6	6	6	.

Men - Hommes - Hombres
ISIC 3 - CITI 3 - CIIU 3

	1999	2000	2001	2002	2003	2004	2005	2006	2007	2008
A	.	.	.	9	8	9	10	8	9	.

Women - Femmes - Mujeres
ISIC 3 - CITI 3 - CIIU 3

	1999	2000	2001	2002	2003	2004	2005	2006	2007	2008
A	.	.	.	3	1	2	1	2	1	.

Rates of non-fatal injuries - Taux de lésions non mortelles - Tasas de lesiones no mortales

Per 100,000 workers insured - Pour 100 000 travailleurs assurés - Por 100 000 trabajadores asegurados

Total men and women - Total hommes et femmes - Total hombres y mujeres
ISIC 3 - CITI 3 - CIIU 3

	1999	2000	2001	2002	2003	2004	2005	2006	2007	2008
A	3 514	.	.	4 710	4 573	4 356	4 234	4 272	4 596	.

Explanatory notes: see p. 1125.

[1] Cases recognized for compensation during the year. [2] Excl. agents of public gas and electricity services. [3] Excl. food trade. [4] Excl. transport by rail and by sea and communications. [5] Interoccupational group.

Notes explicatives: voir p. 1127.

[1] Cas reconnus pour indemnisation dans l'année. [2] Non compris les agents des services publics du gaz et de l'électricité. [3] Non compris les commerces alimentaires. [4] Non compris les transports par chemin de fer ou par mer et les communications. [5] Groupe interprofessionnel.

Notas explicativas: véase p. 1129.

[1] Casos recogidos para indemnización en el año. [2] Excl. los agentes de los servicios públicos de electricidad y gas. [3] Excl. comercio alimenticio. [4] Excl. transportes ferroviarios y marítimos y las comunicaciones. [5] Grupo interocupacional.

OCCUPATIONAL INJURIES	LÉSIONS PROFESSIONNELLES	LESIONES PROFESIONALES
Rates of occupational injuries, by economic activity	Taux de lésions professionnelles, par activité économique	Tasas de lesiones profesionales, por actividad económica

	1999	2000	2001	2002	2003	2004	2005	2006	2007	2008

France (FA) [1]   Compensated injuries - Lésions indemnisées - Lesiones indemnizadas

Rates of non-fatal injuries - Taux de lésions non mortelles - Tasas de lesiones no mortales

Per 100,000 workers insured - Pour 100 000 travailleurs assurés - Por 100 000 trabajadores asegurados

Men - Hommes - Hombres
ISIC 3 - CITI 3 - CIIU 3

	1999	2000	2001	2002	2003	2004	2005	2006	2007	2008
A				5 816	5 624	5 381	5 208	5 216	5 609	

Women - Femmes - Mujeres
ISIC 3 - CITI 3 - CIIU 3

	1999	2000	2001	2002	2003	2004	2005	2006	2007	2008
A				2 937	2 888	2 741	2 716	2 819	3 055	

Germany (FA)   Compensated injuries - Lésions indemnisées - Lesiones indemnizadas

Rates of fatal injuries - Taux de lésions mortelles - Tasas de lesiones mortales

Per 100,000 full-time equivalent workers - Pour l'équivalent de 100 000 travailleurs à plein temps - Por la equivalencia de 100 000 trabajadores a tiempo completo

Total men and women - Total hommes et femmes - Total hombres y mujeres [2]
ISIC 3 - CITI 3 - CIIU 3

	1999	2000	2001	2002	2003	2004	2005	2006	2007	2008
Total	3.42	3.05	2.95	2.92	2.83	2.57	2.38	2.54	2.16	

Rates of non-fatal injuries - Taux de lésions non mortelles - Tasas de lesiones no mortales

Per 100,000 full-time equivalent workers - Pour l'équivalent de 100 000 travailleurs à plein temps - Por la equivalencia de 100 000 trabajadores a tiempo completo

Total men and women - Total hommes et femmes - Total hombres y mujeres [3]
ISIC 3 - CITI 3 - CIIU 3

	1999	2000	2001	2002	2003	2004	2005	2006	2007	2008
Total	4 128	4 001	3 713	3 554	3 138	2 948	2 835	2 825	2 803	

Hungary (FF)   Reported injuries - Lésions déclarées - Lesiones declaradas

Rates of fatal injuries - Taux de lésions mortelles - Tasas de lesiones mortales

Per 100,000 employees - Pour 100 000 salariés - Por 100 000 asalariados

Total men and women - Total hommes et femmes - Total hombres y mujeres
ISIC 3 - CITI 3 - CIIU 3 | | | | | | | | | ISIC 4 - CITI 4 - CIIU 4

	1999	2000	2001	2002	2003	2004	2005	2006	2007	2008	
Total	4.06	3.98	3.21	4.21	3.39	4.10	3.20	3.13	3.01	2.99	Total
A-B	.	.	.	.	.	.	.	8.39	7.65	6.50	A
A	7.43	9.17	5.84	4.98	7.43	6.34	7.73	.	.	0.00	B
B	0.00	51.00	0.00	0.00	0.00	0.00	0.00	.	.	2.11	C
C	0.00	0.00	0.00	0.00	0.00	0.00	6.71	0.00	0.00	5.93	D
D	3.12	2.88	2.61	2.71	1.03	4.25	2.76	1.96	2.06	8.51	E
E	3.33	5.23	3.77	5.39	1.47	0.00	1.55	2.96	3.12	13.14	F
F	18.58	22.42	11.73	18.08	11.69	17.82	12.38	10.88	13.62	1.91	G
G	2.90	4.07	2.00	2.54	3.43	2.93	1.88	1.55	0.68	5.81	H
H	3.76	3.72	0.69	2.91	0.00	0.67	1.30	1.27	0.64	0.64	I
I	4.87	6.68	5.78	9.36	7.59	6.08	4.91	4.65	5.97	0.00	J
J	2.47	0.00	2.53	9.30	0.00	0.00	0.00	0.00	1.19	0.00	K
K	4.89	4.01	1.36	4.73	3.38	2.20	2.54	2.83	2.49	9.85	L
L	0.71	0.25	3.45	1.42	1.35	1.00	1.01	2.01	1.40	0.00	M
M	0.98	2.03	0.64	0.31	0.91	0.60	0.31	1.24	0.00	3.82	N
N	0.42	1.04	0.42	0.42	0.00	1.11	0.76	1.86	0.77	0.00	O
O	1.76	1.97	1.21	0.62	1.14	2.93	2.81	2.86	1.09	0.64	P
Q	0.00	.	0.00	0.00	0.00	0.00	0.00	0.00	0.00	1.22	Q
										1.53	R
										1.14	S
										0.00	T
										0.00	U

Men - Hommes - Hombres
ISIC 3 - CITI 3 - CIIU 3 | | | | | | | | | ISIC 4 - CITI 4 - CIIU 4

	1999	2000	2001	2002	2003	2004	2005	2006	2007	2008	
Total	.	.	5.39	7.05	6.07	7.13	5.72	5.38	5.41	5.07	Total
A-B	.	.	.	.	.	.	.	11.25	9.94	7.78	A
A	.	.	7.80	6.21	9.60	8.23	10.32	.	.	0.00	B
B	.	.	0.00	0.00	0.00	0.00	0.00	.	.	2.84	C
C	.	.	0.00	0.00	0.00	0.00	7.94	0.00	0.00	7.75	D
D	.	.	4.30	4.25	3.29	6.34	4.33	3.01	3.19	11.14	E
E	.	.	4.97	7.19	1.99	0.00	2.09	4.11	4.17	14.28	F
F	.	.	12.34	19.58	12.72	19.35	13.27	11.67	14.64	3.67	G
G	.	.	4.08	3.79	6.73	5.26	3.74	2.97	1.44	7.22	H
H	.	.	0.00	4.80	0.00	1.60	2.82	2.89	1.48	1.44	I
I	.	.	7.54	12.32	10.02	8.35	6.59	6.40	7.59	0.00	J
J	.	.	0.00	8.62	0.00	0.00	0.00	0.00	3.72	0.00	K
K	.	.	2.46	8.57	6.27	3.35	4.58	4.44	4.58	18.18	L
L	.	.	5.09	2.71	2.64	1.99	1.37	2.65	2.88	0.00	M
M	.	.	2.86	1.44	4.20	2.98	1.38	4.16	0.00	4.86	N
N	.	.	0.00	1.77	0.00	3.26	3.42	6.67	3.51	0.00	O
O	.	.	2.64	1.37	2.57	5.13	5.11	5.24	2.38	1.43	P
Q	.	.	0.00	0.00	0.00	0.00	0.00	0.00	0.00	5.60	Q
										2.92	R
										0.00	S
										0.00	T
										0.00	U

Explanatory notes: see p. 1125.

[1] Cases recognized for compensation during the year. [2] Deaths occurring within one month of accident. [3] Incapacity of 4 days or more.

Notes explicatives: voir p. 1127.

[1] Cas reconnus pour indemnisation dans l'année. [2] Les décès survenant pendant le mois qui suit l'accident. [3] Incapacité de 4 jours et plus.

Notas explicativas: véase p. 1129.

[1] Casos recogidos para indemnización en el año. [2] Los fallecimientos que se produzcan durante el mes posterior al accidente. [3] Incapacidad de 4 días y más.

OCCUPATIONAL INJURIES
Rates of occupational injuries, by economic activity

LÉSIONS PROFESSIONNELLES
Taux de lésions professionnelles, par activité économique

LESIONES PROFESIONALES
Tasas de lesiones profesionales, por actividad económica

8B

Hungary (FF) — Reported injuries - Lésions déclarées - Lesiones declaradas

Rates of fatal injuries - Taux de lésions mortelles - Tasas de lesiones mortales

Per 100,000 employees - Pour 100 000 salariés - Por 100 000 asalariados

Women - Femmes - Mujeres

ISIC 3 - CITI 3 - CIIU 3   ISIC 4 - CITI 4 - CIIU 4

ISIC 3	1999	2000	2001	2002	2003	2004	2005	2006	2007	2008	ISIC 4
Total	.	.	0.52	0.80	0.23	0.50	0.22	0.44	0.11	0.51	Total
A-B								0.00	0.00	2.46	A
A	.	.	0.00	1.56	0.00	0.00	0.00	.	.	0.00	B
B	.	.	0.00	0.00	0.00	0.00	0.00	.	.	0.92	C
C	.	.	0.00	0.00	0.00	0.00	0.00	0.00	0.00	0.00	D
D	.	.	0.25	0.51	0.79	1.12	0.30	0.30	0.30	0.00	E
E	.	.	0.00	0.00	0.00	0.00	0.00	0.00	0.00	0.00	F
F	.	.	4.65	0.00	0.00	0.00	0.00	0.00	0.00	0.33	G
G	.	.	0.00	1.39	0.35	0.72	0.31	0.32	0.00	1.56	H
H	.	.	1.42	1.34	0.00	0.00	0.00	0.00	0.00	0.00	I
I	.	.	1.16	1.21	1.19	0.00	0.00	0.00	1.29	0.00	J
J	.	.	3.66	9.60	0.00	0.00	0.00	0.00	0.00	0.00	K
K	.	.	0.00	0.00	0.00	0.81	0.00	0.80	0.00	0.00	L
L	.	.	1.50	0.00	0.00	0.00	0.66	1.35	0.00	0.00	M
M	.	.	0.00	0.00	0.00	0.00	0.00	0.40	0.00	2.32	N
N	.	.	0.55	0.00	0.00	0.48	0.00	0.48	0.00	0.00	O
O	.	.	0.00	0.00	0.00	1.08	1.01	1.02	0.00	0.41	P
Q	.	.	0.00	0.00	0.00	0.00	0.00	0.00	0.00	0.00	Q
										0.00	R
										1.70	S
										0.00	T
										0.00	U

Rates of non-fatal injuries - Taux de lésions non mortelles - Tasas de lesiones no mortales

Per 100,000 employees - Pour 100 000 salariés - Por 100 000 asalariados

Total men and women - Total hommes et femmes - Total hombres y mujeres

ISIC 3 - CITI 3 - CIIU 3 [1]   ISIC 4 - CITI 4 - CIIU 4

ISIC 3	1999	2000	2001	2002	2003	2004	2005	2006	2007	2008	ISIC 4
Total	699	714	658	649	656	608	611	574	530	570	Total
A-B								549	488	509	A
A	815	1 319	725	673	748	643	632	.	.	165	B
B	632	971	0	0	0	0	0	.	.	1 080	C
C	102	470	223	149	211	113	141	93	62	347	D
D	1 307	1 166	1 249	1 234	1 235	1 153	1 136	1 056	1 012	1 181	E
E	664	611	570	589	710	662	673	550	402	408	F
F	636	967	563	521	469	419	426	438	379	465	G
G	378	547	420	421	475	454	466	490	442	1 025	H
H	417	585	391	328	318	334	334	323	304	358	I
I	1 008	886	839	866	960	951	981	886	795	151	J
J	96	160	104	113	111	110	102	116	126	185	K
K	392	349	353	370	351	318	342	295	294	892	L
L	193	111	171	182	200	179	206	209	183	134	M
M	293	286	285	259	271	252	280	256	257	495	N
N	576	480	574	563	584	553	567	512	454	203	O
O	410	756	399	423	442	441	474	455	340	279	P
Q	2 400	.	0	0	0	0	0	0	0	490	Q
										265	R
										142	S
										48	T
										400	U

Men - Hommes - Hombres

ISIC 3 - CITI 3 - CIIU 3 [1]   ISIC 4 - CITI 4 - CIIU 4

ISIC 3	1999	2000	2001	2002	2003	2004	2005	2006	2007	2008	ISIC 4
Total	.	.	867	850	855	777	776	730	673	709	Total
A-B								615	534	563	A
A	.	.	800	782	814	698	719	.	.	128	B
B	.	.	0	0	0	0	0	.	.	1 302	C
C	.	.	246	127	245	124	143	108	63	384	D
D	.	.	1 640	1 595	1 566	1 428	1 382	1 284	1 256	1 435	E
E	.	.	642	671	836	775	743	643	452	428	F
F	.	.	579	549	497	442	443	458	399	553	G
G	.	.	545	545	598	551	589	616	542	1 036	H
H	.	.	428	278	300	363	290	296	287	352	I
I	.	.	944	934	1 064	1 023	1 030	978	821	162	J
J	.	.	115	65	75	117	71	101	100	233	K
K	.	.	430	453	447	389	426	346	371	1 136	L
L	.	.	153	151	167	150	185	197	153	214	M
M	.	.	483	327	346	303	327	335	309	483	N
N	.	.	918	896	906	887	960	797	811	181	O
O	.	.	645	701	783	737	816	793	580	294	P
Q	.	.	0	0	0	0	0	0	0	722	Q
										300	R
										250	T
										333	U

Explanatory notes: see p. 1125.

[1] Incapacity of 4 workdays or more.

Notes explicatives: voir p. 1127.

[1] Incapacité de 4 journées de travail et plus.

Notas explicativas: véase p. 1129.

[1] Incapacidad de 4 días de trabajo y más.

OCCUPATIONAL INJURIES
Rates of occupational injuries, by economic activity

LÉSIONS PROFESSIONNELLES
Taux de lésions professionnelles, par activité économique

LESIONES PROFESIONALES
Tasas de lesiones profesionales, por actividad económica

	1999	2000	2001	2002	2003	2004	2005	2006	2007		2008	

Hungary (FF) — Reported injuries - Lésions déclarées - Lesiones declaradas

Rates of non-fatal injuries - Taux de lésions non mortelles - Tasas de lesiones no mortales

Per 100,000 employees - Pour 100 000 salariés - Por 100 000 asalariados

Women - Femmes - Mujeres
ISIC 3 - CITI 3 - CIIU 3 [1]

ISIC 4 - CITI 4 - CIIU 4

ISIC 3	1999	2000	2001	2002	2003	2004	2005	2006	2007		2008	ISIC 4
Total	.	.	401	408	429	407	416	387	358	|	404	Total
A-B								358	335	|	342	A
A	.	.	504	375	523	456	374	.	.	|	571	B
B			0	0	0	0	0		.	|	720	C
C	.	.	62	357	0	69	130	0	53	|	228	D
D			700	720	758	741	750	694	627	|	360	E
E			344	344	356	366	473	312	253	|	173	F
F			381	184	148	143	179	167	116	|	386	G
G			300	306	359	361	362	380	354	|	991	H
H			352	369	332	313	371	344	318	|	363	I
I			562	680	688	761	838	644	722	|	129	J
J			99	134	127	107	117	124	139	|	162	K
K			258	267	238	232	237	229	205	|	596	L
L			193	216	235	208	226	221	211	|	69	M
M			227	241	251	238	276	233	241	|	513	N
N			469	460	473	455	452	431	353	|	223	O
O			192	194	168	192	205	193	138	|	274	P
Q			0	0	0	0	0	0	0	|	425	Q
										|	227	R
										|	111	S
										|	0	T
										|	333	U

Ireland (FF) — Reported injuries - Lésions déclarées - Lesiones declaradas

Rates of fatal injuries - Taux de lésions mortelles - Tasas de lesiones mortales

Per 100,000 workers employed - Pour 100 000 travailleurs occupés - Por 100 000 trabajadores empleados

Total men and women - Total hommes et femmes - Total hombres y mujeres
ISIC 3 - CITI 3 - CIIU 3

	1999	2000	2001	2002	2003	2004	2005	2006	2007	2008
Total	4.3	4.2	3.8	3.0	3.2	2.5	3.3	2.2	2.8	2.5
A-B				12.2	13.0	13.3	14.7	15.5	17.7	15.5
A	16.9									
B	0.0									
C	52.6									
C-E				2.3	3.4	1.0	4.2	2.1	2.1	3.2
D	2.8									
E	0.0									
F	12.6	10.8		11.0	8.0	6.6	8.3	4.3	5.0	5.6
G	0.5	1.2		0.4	1.6	1.5	1.8	0.7	0.3	1.0
H	0.0	0.0		0.0	0.0	0.0	0.0	0.0	0.0	0.0
I	8.3	3.9		5.3	7.0	5.2	4.2	2.6	5.8	2.5
J	0.0									
J-K				0.0	0.0	0.4	0.4	0.7	0.7	0.4
K	1.5									
L	2.7	6.4		3.4	1.1	0.0	2.0	1.0	3.8	1.9
M	0.0			0.0	0.0	0.8	0.0	0.0	0.0	0.0
N	0.8			0.0	0.0	0.5	0.0	0.0	0.0	0.0
O	1.1	0.0		1.0						
O-Q				1.0	3.8	1.7	1.6	0.8	3.2	1.6

Rates of non-fatal injuries - Taux de lésions non mortelles - Tasas de lesiones no mortales

Per 1,000 workers employed - Pour 1 000 travailleurs occupés - Por 1 000 trabajadores empleados

Total men and women - Total hommes et femmes - Total hombres y mujeres
ISIC 3 - CITI 3 - CIIU 3

	1999	2000	2001	2002	2003	2004	2005	2006	2007	2008
Total				12.2	11.3	12.0	11.6	13.5		
A-B				12.6	18.7	16.5	9.5	10.7		
C-E				18.8	10.8	15.8	16.2	22.2		
F				26.7	22.7	22.5	20.2	21.2		
G				10.3	7.8	8.0	4.1	12.0		
H				10.6	6.2	15.9	3.3	9.7		
I				11.5	19.0	8.3	30.0	15.5		
J-K				2.6	3.2	2.2	0.7	6.8		
L				14.5	13.5	18.4	15.2	9.0		
M				4.2	3.3	4.5	2.1	6.0		
N				10.7	15.6	13.8	18.4	10.0		
O-Q				12.2	11.3	12.0	11.6	20.0		

Isle of Man (FF) — Reported injuries - Lésions déclarées - Lesiones declaradas

Rates of fatal injuries - Taux de lésions mortelles - Tasas de lesiones mortales

Per 100,000 workers employed - Pour 100 000 travailleurs occupés - Por 100 000 trabajadores empleados

Total men and women - Total hommes et femmes - Total hombres y mujeres
ISIC 3 - CITI 3 - CIIU 3

	1999	2000	2001	2002	2003	2004	2005	2006	2007	2008
Total	0	6	5	0	0	0	3	0	0	2

Explanatory notes: see p. 1125.

Notes explicatives: voir p. 1127.

Notas explicativas: véase p. 1129.

[1] Incapacity of 4 workdays or more.

[1] Incapacité de 4 journées de travail et plus.

[1] Incapacidad de 4 días de trabajo y más.

	1999	2000	2001	2002	2003	2004	2005	2006	2007	2008

Isle of Man (FF)
Reported injuries - Lésions déclarées - Lesiones declaradas

Rates of non-fatal injuries - Taux de lésions non mortelles - Tasas de lesiones no mortales

Per 100,000 workers employed - Pour 100 000 travailleurs occupés - Por 100 000 trabajadores empleados

Total men and women - Total hommes et femmes - Total hombres y mujeres [1]
ISIC 3 - CITI 3 - CIIU 3

	1999	2000	2001	2002	2003	2004	2005	2006	2007	2008
Total	535	500	364	423	548	407	374	427	441	390

Italy (FA)
Compensated injuries - Lésions indemnisées - Lesiones indemnizadas

Rates of fatal injuries - Taux de lésions mortelles - Tasas de lesiones mortales

Per 100,000 workers insured - Pour 100 000 travailleurs assurés - Por 100 000 trabajadores asegurados

Total men and women - Total hommes et femmes - Total hombres y mujeres
ISIC 3 - CITI 3 - CIIU 3

	1999	2000	2001	2002	2003	2004	2005	2006	2007	2008
Total	7	7	6	5	5	5	5	5	4	.
A	15	15	12	12	11	14	12	11	9	.
B	5	10	4	7	13	17	11	11	11	.
C	17	17	19	27	16	19	10	22	11	.
D	6	5	5	4	5	4	4	4	4	.
E	2	2	4	1	3	2	2	3	3	.
F	22	20	18	15	17	14	14	15	11	.
G	6	4	4	3	3	2	3	3	3	.
H	4	4	3	2	2	2	3	3	2	.
I	16	14	14	11	10	9	10	9	8	.
J	1	1	0	1	1	0	1	0	1	.
K	4	5	3	3	3	2	2	2	2	.
L	1	1	1	1	1	1	1	1	1	.
M	2	1	1	2	1	1	1	1	1	.
N	1	1	1	1	0	1	2	2	1	.
O	3	5	3	2	2	2	1	3	2	.
P	.	.	.	.	0	1	1	0	0	.

Rates of non-fatal injuries - Taux de lésions non mortelles - Tasas de lesiones no mortales

Per 100,000 workers insured - Pour 100 000 travailleurs assurés - Por 100 000 trabajadores asegurados

Total men and women - Total hommes et femmes - Total hombres y mujeres
ISIC 3 - CITI 3 - CIIU 3

	1999	2000	2001	2002	2003	2004	2005	2006	2007	2008
Total	4 020	3 891	3 515	3 311	3 193	3 097	2 848	2 744	2 647	.
A	7 039	5 794	5 403	5 085	5 499	5 248	5 231	4 755	4 557	.
B	2 121	1 809	1 422	1 532	1 323	1 246	1 612	1 259	1 225	.
C	4 237	4 222	3 930	3 819	2 872	2 721	2 581	2 327	2 142	.
D	4 786	4 588	4 237	3 937	3 737	3 586	3 510	3 420	3 264	.
E	2 130	2 445	1 961	1 821	1 700	1 742	1 815	1 647	1 590	.
F	6 968	6 504	5 828	5 610	5 337	5 263	4 983	4 656	4 246	.
G	2 924	2 778	2 445	2 351	2 231	2 220	2 130	2 076	2 014	.
H	4 198	4 155	3 710	3 477	3 421	3 301	3 362	3 224	3 120	.
I	4 573	5 026	4 565	4 353	3 868	3 909	3 931	3 830	3 843	.
J	366	400	466	441	287	296	291	285	282	.
K	2 481	2 277	2 110	2 087	2 096	2 011	1 501	1 671	1 584	.
L	1 892	1 969	1 770	1 709	1 700	1 616	1 751	1 558	1 575	.
M	1 280	2 552	1 260	1 197	985	1 108	1 181	1 016	1 056	.
N	2 500	2 373	2 506	2 453	2 402	2 338	2 442	2 352	2 371	.
O	2 761	3 172	2 444	2 339	2 369	2 308	2 434	2 334	2 294	.
P	.	.	.	.	293	336	339	326	373	.

Latvia (DA)
Reported injuries - Lésions déclarées - Lesiones declaradas

Rates of fatal injuries - Taux de lésions mortelles - Tasas de lesiones mortales

Per 100,000 employees - Pour 100 000 salariés - Por 100 000 asalariados

Total men and women - Total hommes et femmes - Total hombres y mujeres
ISIC 3 - CITI 3 - CIIU 3

	1999	2000	2001	2002	2003	2004	2005	2006	2007	2008
Total	.	.	.	6.9	4.9	6.9	6.0	5.5	5.7	.
A	.	.	.	65.8	16.1	14.8	14.4	38.1	14.1	.
B	.	.	.	0.0	0.0	427.4	61.2	0.0	59.5	.
C	.	.	.	54.3	0.0	0.0	0.0	35.5	0.0	.
D	.	.	.	9.7	7.0	10.9	5.5	10.5	5.7	.
E	.	.	.	5.5	0.0	5.4	33.2	5.9	12.5	.
F	.	.	.	20.0	23.0	20.8	24.6	13.8	24.6	.
G	.	.	.	3.4	3.9	3.0	1.1	0.0	2.1	.
H	.	.	.	0.0	0.0	0.0	0.0	3.3	3.1	.
I	.	.	.	8.4	5.5	12.9	12.4	9.7	16.5	.
J	.	.	.	0.0	0.0	0.0	4.7	0.0	0.0	.
K	.	.	.	1.7	0.0	4.4	1.2	2.2	1.0	.
L	.	.	.	2.9	2.9	1.4	1.3	0.0	1.3	.
M	.	.	.	1.0	1.0	0.0	1.0	2.0	0.0	.
N	.	.	.	0.0	0.0	0.0	0.0	0.0	0.0	.
O	.	.	.	7.0	6.5	4.2	11.9	6.0	1.7	.
X	.	.	.	0.0	.	.	0.0	0.0	0.0	.

Explanatory notes: see p. 1125.	Notes explicatives: voir p. 1127.	Notas explicativas: véase p. 1129.
[1] Incapacity of 4 days or more.	[1] Incapacité de 4 jours et plus.	[1] Incapacidad de 4 días y más.

OCCUPATIONAL INJURIES — **LÉSIONS PROFESSIONNELLES** — **LESIONES PROFESIONALES**

Rates of occupational injuries, by economic activity — Taux de lésions professionnelles, par activité économique — Tasas de lesiones profesionales, por actividad económica

	1999	2000	2001	2002	2003	2004	2005	2006	2007	2008

Latvia (DA) — Reported injuries - Lésions déclarées - Lesiones declaradas

Rates of non-fatal injuries - Taux de lésions non mortelles - Tasas de lesiones no mortales

Per 100,000 employees - Pour 100 000 salariés - Por 100 000 asalariados

Total men and women - Total hommes et femmes - Total hombres y mujeres
ISIC 3 - CITI 3 - CIIU 3

	1999	2000	2001	2002	2003	2004	2005	2006	2007	2008
Total	.	.	.	165	157	151	163	178	179	.
A	.	.	.	817	413	419	379	334	324	.
B	.	.	.	264	122	122	184	192	0	.
C	.	.	.	435	547	363	347	319	378	.
D	.	.	.	347	343	282	321	368	368	.
E	.	.	.	258	182	134	188	211	318	.
F	.	.	.	269	285	295	257	293	270	.
G	.	.	.	37	56	61	59	84	91	.
H	.	.	.	16	46	48	72	46	87	.
I	.	.	.	258	256	253	311	346	307	.
J	.	.	.	56	34	15	38	5	38	.
K	.	.	.	21	27	38	28	26	33	.
L	.	.	.	83	69	110	77	90	86	.
M	.	.	.	41	33	38	87	53	57	.
N	.	.	.	112	165	158	203	234	260	.
O	.	.	.	142	98	128	109	131	148	.
X	.	.	.	0	.	.	.	.	.	.

Lithuania (FF) — Reported injuries - Lésions déclarées - Lesiones declaradas

Rates of fatal injuries - Taux de lésions mortelles - Tasas de lesiones mortales

Per 100,000 employees - Pour 100 000 salariés - Por 100 000 asalariados

Total men and women - Total hommes et femmes - Total hombres y mujeres
ISIC 3 - CITI 3 - CIIU 3

	1999	2000	2001	2002	2003	2004	2005	2006	2007	2008
Total	7.0	8.6	8.9	8.1	11.3	9.0	10.9	9.6	8.7	6.6
A	28.4	19.2	15.5	22.7	51.1	28.8	38.0	30.5	44.7	32.3
B	0.0	104.0	117.9	157.7	235.5	0.0	119.0	117.2	122.1	0.0
C	31.5	67.0	77.8	37.0	36.2	65.1	31.4	0.0	32.1	68.4
D	5.4	3.2	9.3	8.6	7.1	7.7	13.0	5.9	9.6	6.3
E	15.8	14.3	9.7	13.3	24.4	14.9	19.4	16.3	17.0	0.0
F	27.3	24.2	39.7	36.0	30.9	43.1	40.6	31.8	22.1	19.9
G	5.4	2.7	4.6	3.2	12.9	4.7	2.7	4.6	1.9	1.4
H	0.0	0.0	0.0	0.0	0.0	0.0	0.0	3.6	3.2	0.0
I	13.8	28.4	21.3	18.3	31.0	20.9	30.1	34.0	23.0	23.2
J	0.0	0.0	0.0	21.2	0.0	0.0	0.0	0.0	12.0	0.0
K	2.1	2.2	0.0	0.0	3.7	3.4	1.6	5.5	4.9	2.4
L	1.5	2.8	1.4	1.4	1.4	1.4	1.3	1.3	1.3	4.9
M	0.7	0.0	0.7	0.0	1.4	2.0	0.0	2.7	0.7	0.0
N	0.0	0.0	1.1	1.1	0.0	0.0	0.0	0.0	3.5	0.0
O	0.0	4.4	11.5	7.0	9.3	2.6	14.4	4.6	0.0	2.2

Men - Hommes - Hombres
ISIC 3 - CITI 3 - CIIU 3

	1999	2000	2001	2002	2003	2004	2005	2006	2007	2008
Total	13.5	12.9	17.4	16.2	23.3	17.7	21.6	19.1	17.5	12.6
A	41.3	27.8	22.6	33.1	72.9	44.1	58.8	47.9	66.1	51.4
B	0.0	0.0	104.5	197.4	295.6	0.0	144.8	144.8	149.8	0.0
C	40.1	84.0	95.1	44.3	43.9	78.4	37.9	0.0	38.8	83.1
D	8.7	5.4	18.1	15.9	13.6	15.4	23.1	11.6	18.1	11.5
E	20.9	19.0	12.7	17.5	32.2	19.7	25.8	21.9	23.2	0.0
F	31.6	28.0	46.1	41.0	35.6	47.9	46.7	35.2	25.5	23.2
G	8.4	4.6	6.9	6.5	27.6	6.3	5.9	9.0	4.3	2.2
H	0.0	0.0	0.0	0.0	0.0	0.0	0.0	16.9	0.0	0.0
I	18.2	42.7	32.7	25.4	46.0	28.8	42.2	49.5	33.6	29.4
J	0.0	0.0	0.0	40.8	0.0	0.0	0.0	0.0	45.6	0.0
K	4.1	0.0	0.0	0.0	7.5	6.9	3.2	11.3	7.6	4.9
L	2.5	5.0	2.6	2.7	2.4	2.5	2.4	2.4	2.4	2.4
M	3.0	0.0	0.0	0.0	2.7	5.5	0.0	8.7	3.0	0.0
N	0.0	0.0	6.3	0.0	0.0	0.0	0.0	0.0	21.2	0.0
O	0.0	4.7	22.6	14.0	20.6	5.9	16.5	0.0	0.0	5.4

Women - Femmes - Mujeres
ISIC 3 - CITI 3 - CIIU 3

	1999	2000	2001	2002	2003	2004	2005	2006	2007	2008
Total	0.9	0.7	0.6	0.7	0.5	1.1	1.2	1.0	0.7	1.3
A	0.0	0.0	0.0	0.0	9.8	0.0	0.0	0.0	9.1	0.0
B	0.0	0.0	0.0	0.0	0.0	0.0	0.0	0.0	0.0	0.0
C	0.0	0.0	0.0	0.0	0.0	0.0	0.0	0.0	0.0	0.0
D	1.9	0.9	0.0	0.9	0.9	0.0	2.7	0.0	0.9	1.0
E	0.0	0.0	0.0	0.0	0.0	0.0	0.0	0.0	0.0	0.0
F	0.0	0.0	0.0	0.0	0.0	10.4	0.0	8.5	0.0	0.0
G	2.6	1.2	2.5	0.0	0.0	3.3	0.0	0.9	0.0	0.8
H	0.0	0.0	0.0	0.0	0.0	0.0	0.0	0.0	4.1	0.0
I	4.0	0.0	0.0	4.0	0.0	4.1	4.0	0.0	0.0	9.9
J	0.0	0.0	0.0	10.8	0.0	0.0	0.0	0.0	0.0	0.0
K	0.0	4.4	0.0	0.0	0.0	0.0	0.0	0.0	2.3	0.0
L	0.0	0.0	0.0	0.0	0.0	0.0	0.0	0.0	0.0	7.6
M	0.0	0.0	0.9	0.0	0.9	0.9	0.0	0.9	0.0	0.0
N	0.0	0.0	0.0	1.3	0.0	0.0	0.0	0.0	0.0	0.0
O	0.0	4.2	0.0	0.0	0.0	0.0	12.8	8.0	0.0	0.0

Explanatory notes: see p. 1125.　　　Notes explicatives: voir p. 1127.　　　Notas explicativas: véase p. 1129.

OCCUPATIONAL INJURIES

Rates of occupational injuries, by economic activity

LÉSIONS PROFESSIONNELLES

Taux de lésions professionnelles, par activité économique

LESIONES PROFESIONALES

Tasas de lesiones profesionales, por actividad económica

	1999	2000	2001	2002	2003	2004	2005	2006	2007	2008

Lithuania (FF)   Reported injuries - Lésions déclarées - Lesiones declaradas

Rates of non-fatal injuries - Taux de lésions non mortelles - Tasas de lesiones no mortales

Per 100,000 employees - Pour 100 000 salariés - Por 100 000 asalariados

Total men and women - Total hommes et femmes - Total hombres y mujeres
ISIC 3 - CITI 3 - CIIU 3

	1999	2000	2001	2002	2003	2004	2005	2006	2007	2008
Total	278	268	248	245	250	249	300	310	307	.
A	479	465	431	415	412	356	415	373	375	.
B	758	532	522	79	157	393	357	176	183	.
C	661	771	856	740	724	586	690	813	609	.
D	532	522	461	453	417	433	532	570	559	.
E	330	337	258	248	240	197	248	240	255	.
F	615	571	570	604	605	553	694	693	652	.
G	103	106	107	107	129	127	151	179	163	.
H	115	116	103	138	106	156	187	157	210	.
I	392	383	397	347	341	368	516	456	499	.
J	119	173	183	99	133	93	41	100	96	.
K	60	69	82	85	103	116	148	137	137	.
L	80	80	96	102	97	99	121	116	90	.
M	72	76	81	71	95	88	75	88	94	.
N	147	144	139	138	152	171	167	178	212	.
O	219	233	145	166	243	245	235	258	239	.

Men - Hommes - Hombres
ISIC 3 - CITI 3 - CIIU 3

	1999	2000	2001	2002	2003	2004	2005	2006	2007	2008
Total	420	407	374	378	375	383	456	460	448	.
A	548	504	474	501	505	458	460	378	402	.
B	808	527	514	99	197	467	434	217	225	.
C	802	882	856	886	747	666	645	878	875	.
D	754	753	661	658	618	661	756	790	743	.
E	373	395	306	271	272	217	269	274	307	.
F	676	644	650	679	678	613	775	760	723	.
G	155	170	157	155	197	207	245	272	243	.
H	228	210	182	235	98	229	195	169	303	.
I	432	427	470	418	396	432	599	526	599	.
J	175	132	255	82	43	23	70	121	68	.
K	86	80	115	120	153	158	220	176	177	.
L	76	79	107	113	92	80	107	123	75	.
M	130	117	94	84	101	105	72	101	96	.
N	218	208	159	168	161	265	218	269	240	.
O	280	321	172	200	365	360	363	386	366	.

Women - Femmes - Mujeres
ISIC 3 - CITI 3 - CIIU 3

	1999	2000	2001	2002	2003	2004	2005	2006	2007	2008
Total	145	145	134	125	136	129	159	173	180	.
A	326	378	336	226	236	165	332	364	329	.
B	0	0	0	0	0	0	0	0	0	.
C	146	332	855	0	617	193	906	527	552	.
D	291	286	250	238	221	205	303	344	371	.
E	195	162	107	177	143	136	185	141	111	.
F	231	103	75	64	118	146	151	238	188	.
G	55	55	60	62	70	57	71	102	98	.
H	73	76	72	97	109	134	184	154	187	.
I	304	296	261	202	226	232	338	302	283	.
J	85	197	143	108	176	124	29	92	106	.
K	33	57	45	51	50	76	78	101	99	.
L	86	80	82	89	104	123	139	107	105	.
M	55	64	76	68	93	82	76	85	93	.
N	134	132	136	132	150	152	156	160	206	.
O	166	157	118	131	143	154	136	163	145	.

Explanatory notes: see p. 1125.   Notes explicatives: voir p. 1127.   Notas explicativas: véase p. 1129.

OCCUPATIONAL INJURIES

Rates of occupational injuries, by economic activity

LÉSIONS PROFESSIONNELLES

Taux de lésions professionnelles, par activité économique

LESIONES PROFESIONALES

Tasas de lesiones profesionales, por actividad económica

	1999	2000	2001	2002	2003	2004	2005	2006	2007	2008

Luxembourg (FA) [1]   **Compensated injuries - Lésions indemnisées - Lesiones indemnizadas**

Rates of fatal injuries - Taux de lésions mortelles - Tasas de lesiones mortales

Per 1,000,000 hours worked - Pour 1 000 000 heures effectuées - Por 1 000 000 horas trabajadas

Total men and women - Total hommes et femmes - Total hombres y mujeres
ISIC 3 - CITI 3 - CIIU 3

Total	.	.	.	.	.	.	.	.	.	0.0
A	.	.	.	.	.	.	.	.	.	0.4
B	.	.	.	.	.	.	.	.	.	0.0
C	.	.	.	.	.	.	.	.	.	0.0
D	.	.	.	.	.	.	.	.	.	0.0
E	.	.	.	.	.	.	.	.	.	0.0
F	.	.	.	.	.	.	.	.	.	0.0
G	.	.	.	.	.	.	.	.	.	0.0
H	.	.	.	.	.	.	.	.	.	0.1
I	.	.	.	.	.	.	.	.	.	0.1
J	.	.	.	.	.	.	.	.	.	0.0
K	.	.	.	.	.	.	.	.	.	0.0
L	.	.	.	.	.	.	.	.	.	0.0
M	.	.	.	.	.	.	.	.	.	0.0
N	.	.	.	.	.	.	.	.	.	0.0
O	.	.	.	.	.	.	.	.	.	0.0
P	.	.	.	.	.	.	.	.	.	0.0
Q	.	.	.	.	.	.	.	.	.	0.0
X	.	.	.	.	.	.	.	.	.	0.1

Men - Hommes - Hombres
ISIC 3 - CITI 3 - CIIU 3

Total	.	.	.	.	.	.	.	.	.	0.0
A	.	.	.	.	.	.	.	.	.	0.4
B	.	.	.	.	.	.	.	.	.	0.0
C	.	.	.	.	.	.	.	.	.	0.0
D	.	.	.	.	.	.	.	.	.	0.0
E	.	.	.	.	.	.	.	.	.	0.0
F	.	.	.	.	.	.	.	.	.	0.0
G	.	.	.	.	.	.	.	.	.	0.0
H	.	.	.	.	.	.	.	.	.	0.1
I	.	.	.	.	.	.	.	.	.	0.1
J	.	.	.	.	.	.	.	.	.	0.0
K	.	.	.	.	.	.	.	.	.	0.0
L	.	.	.	.	.	.	.	.	.	0.0
M	.	.	.	.	.	.	.	.	.	0.0
N	.	.	.	.	.	.	.	.	.	0.0
O	.	.	.	.	.	.	.	.	.	0.0
P	.	.	.	.	.	.	.	.	.	0.0
Q	.	.	.	.	.	.	.	.	.	0.0
X	.	.	.	.	.	.	.	.	.	0.1

Women - Femmes - Mujeres
ISIC 3 - CITI 3 - CIIU 3

Total	.	.	.	.	.	.	.	.	.	0.0
A	.	.	.	.	.	.	.	.	.	0.0
B	.	.	.	.	.	.	.	.	.	0.0
C	.	.	.	.	.	.	.	.	.	0.0
D	.	.	.	.	.	.	.	.	.	0.0
E	.	.	.	.	.	.	.	.	.	0.0
F	.	.	.	.	.	.	.	.	.	0.0
G	.	.	.	.	.	.	.	.	.	0.0
H	.	.	.	.	.	.	.	.	.	0.0
I	.	.	.	.	.	.	.	.	.	0.0
J	.	.	.	.	.	.	.	.	.	0.0
K	.	.	.	.	.	.	.	.	.	0.0
L	.	.	.	.	.	.	.	.	.	0.0
M	.	.	.	.	.	.	.	.	.	0.0
N	.	.	.	.	.	.	.	.	.	0.0
O	.	.	.	.	.	.	.	.	.	0.0
P	.	.	.	.	.	.	.	.	.	0.0
Q	.	.	.	.	.	.	.	.	.	0.0
X	.	.	.	.	.	.	.	.	.	0.0

Explanatory notes: see p. 1125.   Notes explicatives: voir p. 1127.   Notas explicativas: véase p. 1129.

[1] Up to 2001: excl. agriculture and forestry.   [1] Jusqu'à 2001: non compris agriculture et sylviculture.   [1] Hasta 2001: excl. agricultura y silvicultura.

OCCUPATIONAL INJURIES

Rates of occupational injuries, by economic activity

LÉSIONS PROFESSIONNELLES

Taux de lésions professionnelles, par activité économique

LESIONES PROFESIONALES

Tasas de lesiones profesionales, por actividad económica

	1999	2000	2001	2002	2003	2004	2005	2006	2007	2008

Luxembourg (FA) [1]   Compensated injuries - Lésions indemnisées - Lesiones indemnizadas

Rates of fatal injuries - Taux de lésions mortelles - Tasas de lesiones mortales

Per 100,000 workers insured - Pour 100 000 travailleurs assurés - Por 100 000 trabajadores asegurados

Total men and women - Total hommes et femmes - Total hombres y mujeres
ISIC 3 - CITI 3 - CIIU 3

	1999	2000	2001	2002	2003	2004	2005	2006	2007	2008
Total	2.1	4.6	.	5.7	4.9	1.9	.	.	.	.
A			.	67.5	66.4	0.0	.	.	.	.
B	.	.	.	0.0	0.0	0.0	.	.	.	.
C	.	.	.	0.0	0.0	0.0	.	.	.	.
D	.	.	.	2.7	5.5	2.9	.	.	.	.
E	.	.	.	0.0	0.0	0.0	.	.	.	.
F	.	.	.	6.5	19.0	6.4	.	.	.	.
G	.	.	.	9.8	4.8	0.0	.	.	.	.
H	.	.	.	0.0	0.0	0.0	.	.	.	.
I	.	.	.	15.9	7.6	11.7	.	.	.	.
J	.	.	.	2.9	0.0	0.0	.	.	.	.
K	.	.	.	7.5	4.8	0.0	.	.	.	.
L	.	.	.	2.3	0.0	0.0	.	.	.	.
M	.	.	.	0.0	0.0	0.0	.	.	.	.
N	.	.	.	0.0	5.4	0.0	.	.	.	.
O	.	.	.	0.0	0.0	0.0	.	.	.	.
P	.	.	.	0.0	0.0	0.0	.	.	.	.
Q	.	.	.	0.0	0.0	0.0	.	.	.	.
X	.	.	.	5.0	0.0	0.0	.	.	.	.

Men - Hommes - Hombres
ISIC 3 - CITI 3 - CIIU 3

	1999	2000	2001	2002	2003	2004	2005	2006	2007	2008
Total	.	.	.	7.2	7.5	3.1	.	.	.	.
A	.	.	.	83.6	80.9	0.0	.	.	.	.
B	.	.	.	0.0	0.0	0.0	.	.	.	.
C	.	.	.	0.0	0.0	0.0	.	.	.	.
D	.	.	.	3.3	6.7	3.6	.	.	.	.
E	.	.	.	0.0	0.0	0.0	.	.	.	.
F	.	.	.	6.9	20.3	7.0	.	.	.	.
G	.	.	.	8.8	8.7	0.0	.	.	.	.
H	.	.	.	0.0	0.0	0.0	.	.	.	.
I	.	.	.	9.5	9.1	14.4	.	.	.	.
J	.	.	.	0.0	0.0	0.0	.	.	.	.
K	.	.	.	13.0	4.1	0.0	.	.	.	.
L	.	.	.	4.3	0.0	0.0	.	.	.	.
M	.	.	.	0.0	0.0	0.0	.	.	.	.
N	.	.	.	0.0	25.4	0.0	.	.	.	.
O	.	.	.	0.0	0.0	0.0	.	.	.	.
P	.	.	.	0.0	0.0	0.0	.	.	.	.
Q	.	.	.	0.0	0.0	0.0	.	.	.	.
X	.	.	.	9.0	0.0	0.0	.	.	.	.

Women - Femmes - Mujeres
ISIC 3 - CITI 3 - CIIU 3

	1999	2000	2001	2002	2003	2004	2005	2006	2007	2008
Total	.	.	.	3.2	0.7	0.0	.	.	.	.
A	.	.	.	0.0	0.0	0.0	.	.	.	.
B	.	.	.	0.0	0.0	0.0	.	.	.	.
C	.	.	.	0.0	0.0	0.0	.	.	.	.
D	.	.	.	0.0	0.0	0.0	.	.	.	.
E	.	.	.	0.0	0.0	0.0	.	.	.	.
F	.	.	.	0.0	0.0	0.0	.	.	.	.
G	.	.	.	11.0	0.0	0.0	.	.	.	.
H	.	.	.	0.0	0.0	0.0	.	.	.	.
I	.	.	.	23.6	0.0	0.0	.	.	.	.
J	.	.	.	6.4	0.0	0.0	.	.	.	.
K	.	.	.	0.0	5.6	0.0	.	.	.	.
L	.	.	.	0.0	0.0	0.0	.	.	.	.
M	.	.	.	0.0	0.0	0.0	.	.	.	.
N	.	.	.	0.0	0.0	0.0	.	.	.	.
O	.	.	.	0.0	0.0	0.0	.	.	.	.
P	.	.	.	0.0	0.0	0.0	.	.	.	.
Q	.	.	.	0.0	0.0	0.0	.	.	.	.
X	.	.	.	0.0	0.0	0.0	.	.	.	.

Explanatory notes: see p. 1125.   Notes explicatives: voir p. 1127.   Notas explicativas: véase p. 1129.

[1] Up to 2001: excl. agriculture and forestry.   [1] Jusqu'à 2001: non compris agriculture et sylviculture.   [1] Hasta 2001: excl. agricultura y silvicultura.

	1999	2000	2001	2002	2003	2004	2005	2006	2007	2008

Luxembourg (FA) [1]   **Compensated injuries - Lésions indemnisées - Lesiones indemnizadas**

Rates of non-fatal injuries - Taux de lésions non mortelles - Tasas de lesiones no mortales

Per 1,000,000 hours worked - Pour 1 000 000 heures effectuées - Por 1 000 000 horas trabajadas

Total men and women - Total hommes et femmes - Total hombres y mujeres
ISIC 3 - CITI 3 - CIIU 3

	1999	2000	2001	2002	2003	2004	2005	2006	2007	2008
Total	.	.	.	.	.	.	.	.	.	19
A	.	.	.	.	.	.	.	.	.	71
B	.	.	.	.	.	.	.	.	.	198
C	.	.	.	.	.	.	.	.	.	44
D	.	.	.	.	.	.	.	.	.	22
E	.	.	.	.	.	.	.	.	.	17
F	.	.	.	.	.	.	.	.	.	58
G	.	.	.	.	.	.	.	.	.	18
H	.	.	.	.	.	.	.	.	.	24
I	.	.	.	.	.	.	.	.	.	19
J	.	.	.	.	.	.	.	.	.	1
K	.	.	.	.	.	.	.	.	.	21
L	.	.	.	.	.	.	.	.	.	4
M	.	.	.	.	.	.	.	.	.	2
N	.	.	.	.	.	.	.	.	.	18
O	.	.	.	.	.	.	.	.	.	11
P	.	.	.	.	.	.	.	.	.	10
Q	.	.	.	.	.	.	.	.	.	13
X	.	.	.	.	.	.	.	.	.	5

Men - Hommes - Hombres
ISIC 3 - CITI 3 - CIIU 3

	1999	2000	2001	2002	2003	2004	2005	2006	2007	2008
Total	.	.	.	.	.	.	.	.	.	25
A	.	.	.	.	.	.	.	.	.	77
B	.	.	.	.	.	.	.	.	.	198
C	.	.	.	.	.	.	.	.	.	49
D	.	.	.	.	.	.	.	.	.	23
E	.	.	.	.	.	.	.	.	.	20
F	.	.	.	.	.	.	.	.	.	62
G	.	.	.	.	.	.	.	.	.	24
H	.	.	.	.	.	.	.	.	.	22
I	.	.	.	.	.	.	.	.	.	21
J	.	.	.	.	.	.	.	.	.	1
K	.	.	.	.	.	.	.	.	.	26
L	.	.	.	.	.	.	.	.	.	5
M	.	.	.	.	.	.	.	.	.	1
N	.	.	.	.	.	.	.	.	.	25
O	.	.	.	.	.	.	.	.	.	16
P	.	.	.	.	.	.	.	.	.	28
Q	.	.	.	.	.	.	.	.	.	22
X	.	.	.	.	.	.	.	.	.	6

Women - Femmes - Mujeres
ISIC 3 - CITI 3 - CIIU 3

	1999	2000	2001	2002	2003	2004	2005	2006	2007	2008
Total	.	.	.	.	.	.	.	.	.	9
A	.	.	.	.	.	.	.	.	.	44
B	.	.	.	.	.	.	.	.	.	0
C	.	.	.	.	.	.	.	.	.	0
D	.	.	.	.	.	.	.	.	.	15
E	.	.	.	.	.	.	.	.	.	0
F	.	.	.	.	.	.	.	.	.	5
G	.	.	.	.	.	.	.	.	.	10
H	.	.	.	.	.	.	.	.	.	27
I	.	.	.	.	.	.	.	.	.	6
J	.	.	.	.	.	.	.	.	.	1
K	.	.	.	.	.	.	.	.	.	13
L	.	.	.	.	.	.	.	.	.	3
M	.	.	.	.	.	.	.	.	.	3
N	.	.	.	.	.	.	.	.	.	15
O	.	.	.	.	.	.	.	.	.	7
P	.	.	.	.	.	.	.	.	.	9
Q	.	.	.	.	.	.	.	.	.	1
X	.	.	.	.	.	.	.	.	.	3

Explanatory notes: see p. 1125.

[1] Up to 2001: excl. agriculture and forestry.

Notes explicatives: voir p. 1127.

[1] Jusqu'à 2001: non compris agriculture et sylviculture.

Notas explicativas: véase p. 1129.

[1] Hasta 2001: excl. agricultura y silvicultura.

OCCUPATIONAL INJURIES

Rates of occupational injuries, by economic activity

LÉSIONS PROFESSIONNELLES

Taux de lésions professionnelles, par activité économique

LESIONES PROFESIONALES

Tasas de lesiones profesionales, por actividad económica

8B

	1999	2000	2001	2002	2003	2004	2005	2006	2007	2008

Luxembourg (FA) [1]   Compensated injuries - Lésions indemnisées - Lesiones indemnizadas

Rates of non-fatal injuries - Taux de lésions non mortelles - Tasas de lesiones no mortales

Per 100,000 workers insured - Pour 100 000 travailleurs assurés - Por 100 000 trabajadores asegurados

Total men and women - Total hommes et femmes - Total hombres y mujeres
ISIC 3 - CITI 3 - CIIU 3

	1999	2000	2001	2002	2003	2004	2005	2006	2007	2008
Total	6 196	6 136	.	6 433	5 962	6 563	.	.	.	.
A	.	.	.	.	.	17 207	.	.	.	.
B	.	.	.	0	0	0	.	.	.	.
C	.	.	.	.	.	10 638	.	.	.	.
D	.	.	.	8 461	7 925	8 429	.	.	.	.
E	.	.	.	6 106	5 734	5 158	.	.	.	.
F	.	.	.	.	.	17 871	.	.	.	.
G	.	.	.	6 362	5 918	5 953	.	.	.	.
H	.	.	.	7 525	7 142	7 564	.	.	.	.
I	.	.	.	7 044	6 263	6 984	.	.	.	.
J	.	.	.	1 592	1 577	617	.	.	.	.
K	.	.	.	6 276	5 890	5 826	.	.	.	.
L	.	.	.	3 449	3 090	3 947	.	.	.	.
M	.	.	.	2 413	1 513	1 737	.	.	.	.
N	.	.	.	3 998	3 980	6 885	.	.	.	.
O	.	.	.	1 486	1 145	3 520	.	.	.	.
P	.	.	.	0	0	906	.	.	.	.
Q	.	.	.	0	0	2 437	.	.	.	.
X	.	.	.	3 541	2 835	1 790	.	.	.	.

Men - Hommes - Hombres
ISIC 3 - CITI 3 - CIIU 3

	1999	2000	2001	2002	2003	2004	2005	2006	2007	2008
Total	.	.	.	8 356	7 704	8 696	.	.	.	.
A	.	.	.	.	.	20 950	.	.	.	.
B	.	.	.	0	0	0	.	.	.	.
C	.	.	.	.	.	10 638	.	.	.	.
D	.	.	.	8 941	8 423	9 734	.	.	.	.
E	.	.	.	6 952	6 539	5 876	.	.	.	.
F	.	.	.	.	.	19 435	.	.	.	.
G	.	.	.	8 246	7 446	8 316	.	.	.	.
H	.	.	.	8 204	7 701	7 700	.	.	.	.
I	.	.	.	7 682	6 709	7 970	.	.	.	.
J	.	.	.	1 267	1 251	531	.	.	.	.
K	.	.	.	7 773	7 332	8 345	.	.	.	.
L	.	.	.	4 574	4 236	4 674	.	.	.	.
M	.	.	.	1 958	1 184	1 064	.	.	.	.
N	.	.	.	4 318	4 104	8 791	.	.	.	.
O	.	.	.	3 764	2 351	4 382	.	.	.	.
P	.	.	.	0	0	0	.	.	.	.
Q	.	.	.	0	0	0	.	.	.	.
X	.	.	.	4 730	3 477	2 305	.	.	.	.

Women - Femmes - Mujeres
ISIC 3 - CITI 3 - CIIU 3

	1999	2000	2001	2002	2003	2004	2005	2006	2007	2008
Total	.	.	.	3 435	3 238	3 202	.	.	.	.
A	.	.	.	.	.	8 953	.	.	.	.
B	.	.	.	.	.	0	.	.	.	.
C	.	.	.	0	0	0	.	.	.	.
D	.	.	.	6 262	5 632	3 104	.	.	.	.
E	.	.	.	735	704	0	.	.	.	.
F	.	.	.	2 188	2 088	1 128	.	.	.	.
G	.	.	.	4 021	4 004	3 213	.	.	.	.
H	.	.	.	6 873	6 613	7 428	.	.	.	.
I	.	.	.	3 900	3 979	2 683	.	.	.	.
J	.	.	.	1 989	1 981	740	.	.	.	.
K	.	.	.	4 225	3 961	3 058	.	.	.	.
L	.	.	.	2 173	1 730	2 674	.	.	.	.
M	.	.	.	2 731	1 758	2 150	.	.	.	.
N	.	.	.	3 912	3 946	6 313	.	.	.	.
O	.	.	.	1 215	995	2 551	.	.	.	.
P	.	.	.	0	0	801	.	.	.	.
Q	.	.	.	0	0	2 532	.	.	.	.
X	.	.	.	2 019	2 000	924	.	.	.	.

Explanatory notes: see p. 1125.   Notes explicatives: voir p. 1127.   Notas explicativas: véase p. 1129.

[1] Up to 2001: excl. agriculture and forestry.   [1] Jusqu'à 2001: non compris agriculture et sylviculture.   [1] Hasta 2001: excl. agricultura y silvicultura.

8B

OCCUPATIONAL INJURIES

Rates of occupational injuries, by economic activity

LÉSIONS PROFESSIONNELLES

Taux de lésions professionnelles, par activité économique

LESIONES PROFESIONALES

Tasas de lesiones profesionales, por actividad económica

	1999	2000	2001	2002	2003	2004	2005	2006	2007	2008

Malta (FA)   **Compensated injuries - Lésions indemnisées - Lesiones indemnizadas**

Rates of fatal injuries - Taux de lésions mortelles - Tasas de lesiones mortales

Per 100,000 workers employed - Pour 100 000 travailleurs occupés - Por 100 000 trabajadores empleados

Total men and women - Total hommes et femmes - Total hombres y mujeres
ISIC 2 - CITI 2 - CIIU 2   ISIC 3 - CITI 3 - CIIU 3

	1999	2000	2001	2002	2003	2004	2005	2006	2007	2008	
Total	6.72	3.67	4.3	2.8	8.2	8.1	4.0	5.2	4.5	1.9	Total
			0.0	0.0	0.0	49.1	0.0	50.6	0.0	0.0	A
			0.0	0.0	0.0	0.0	0.0	0.0	0.0	0.0	B
			0.0	137.0	0.0	0.0	0.0	0.0	0.0	148.8	C
			3.2	0.0	3.6	0.0	3.7	7.5	3.9	0.0	D
			0.0	0.0	0.0	0.0	0.0	0.0	31.5	0.0	E
			9.0	25.2	71.3	87.4	24.4	35.0	33.7	7.5	F
			0.0	0.0	4.5	0.0	4.3	0.0	4.1	4.0	G
			0.0	0.0	0.0	0.0	7.4	0.0	0.0	0.0	H
			0.0	0.0	0.0	9.1	0.0	0.0	0.0	0.0	I
			0.0	0.0	0.0	0.0	0.0	0.0	0.0	0.0	J
			11.0	0.0	13.7	0.0	0.0	0.0	0.0	0.0	K
			27.7	0.0	0.0	0.0	0.0	0.0	0.0	0.0	L
			0.0	0.0	0.0	0.0	0.0	0.0	0.0	0.0	M
			0.0	0.0	0.0	0.0	0.0	0.0	0.0	0.0	N
			0.0	0.0	15.5	0.0	0.0	0.0	0.0	0.0	O
			0.0	0.0	0.0	0.0	0.0	480.8	0.0	0.0	P
			0.0	0.0	0.0	0.0	0.0	0.0	0.0	0.0	Q
			0.0	0.0	0.0	0.0	0.0	0.0	0.0	0.0	X

Men - Hommes - Hombres
ISIC 3 - CITI 3 - CIIU 3

	1999	2000	2001	2002	2003	2004	2005	2006	2007	2008
Total	.	.	4.9	4.0	11.9	10.7	5.7	6.7	6.8	2.8
A	.	.	0.0	0.0	0.0	0.0	0.0	56.1	0.0	0.0
B	.	.	0.0	0.0	0.0	0.0	0.0	0.0	0.0	0.0
C	.	.	0.0	137.0	0.0	0.0	0.0	0.0	0.0	162.1
D	.	.	4.4	0.0	4.8	0.0	4.7	10.2	5.2	0.0
E	.	.	0.0	0.0	0.0	0.0	0.0	0.0	33.3	0.0
F	.	.	9.1	26.2	73.9	89.5	24.8	36.2	34.6	7.7
G	.	.	0.0	0.0	7.0	0.0	6.3	0.0	6.2	5.8
H	.	.	0.0	0.0	0.0	0.0	12.2	0.0	0.0	0.0
I	.	.	0.0	0.0	0.0	11.3	0.0	0.0	0.0	0.0
J	.	.	0.0	0.0	0.0	0.0	0.0	0.0	0.0	0.0
K	.	.	0.0	0.0	19.4	0.0	0.0	0.0	0.0	0.0
L	.	.	35.5	0.0	0.0	0.0	0.0	0.0	0.0	0.0
M	.	.	0.0	0.0	0.0	0.0	0.0	0.0	0.0	0.0
N	.	.	0.0	0.0	0.0	0.0	0.0	0.0	0.0	0.0
O	.	.	0.0	0.0	21.0	0.0	0.0	0.0	0.0	0.0
P	.	.	0.0	0.0	0.0	0.0	0.0	0.0	0.0	0.0
Q	.	.	0.0	0.0	0.0	0.0	0.0	0.0	0.0	0.0
X	.	.	0.0	0.0	0.0	0.0	0.0	0.0	0.0	0.0

Women - Femmes - Mujeres
ISIC 3 - CITI 3 - CIIU 3

	1999	2000	2001	2002	2003	2004	2005	2006	2007	2008
Total	.	.	2.6	0.0	0.0	2.2	0.0	2.1	0.0	0.0
A	.	.	0.0	0.0	0.0	492.6	0.0	0.0	0.0	0.0
B	.	.	0.0	0.0	0.0	0.0	0.0	0.0	0.0	0.0
C	.	.	0.0	0.0	0.0	0.0	0.0	0.0	0.0	0.0
D	.	.	0.0	0.0	0.0	0.0	0.0	0.0	0.0	0.0
E	.	.	0.0	0.0	0.0	0.0	0.0	0.0	0.0	0.0
F	.	.	0.0	0.0	0.0	0.0	0.0	0.0	0.0	0.0
G	.	.	0.0	0.0	0.0	0.0	0.0	0.0	0.0	0.0
H	.	.	0.0	0.0	0.0	0.0	0.0	0.0	0.0	0.0
I	.	.	0.0	0.0	0.0	0.0	0.0	0.0	0.0	0.0
J	.	.	0.0	0.0	0.0	0.0	0.0	0.0	0.0	0.0
K	.	.	57.6	0.0	0.0	0.0	0.0	0.0	0.0	0.0
L	.	.	0.0	0.0	0.0	0.0	0.0	0.0	0.0	0.0
M	.	.	0.0	0.0	0.0	0.0	0.0	0.0	0.0	0.0
N	.	.	0.0	0.0	0.0	0.0	0.0	0.0	0.0	0.0
O	.	.	0.0	0.0	0.0	0.0	0.0	0.0	0.0	0.0
P	.	.	0.0	0.0	0.0	0.0	0.0	476.2	0.0	0.0
Q	.	.	0.0	0.0	0.0	0.0	0.0	0.0	0.0	0.0
X	.	.	0.0	0.0	0.0	0.0	0.0	0.0	0.0	0.0

Explanatory notes: see p. 1125.   Notes explicatives: voir p. 1127.   Notas explicativas: véase p. 1129.

Rates of occupational injuries, by economic activity

Taux de lésions professionnelles, par activité économique

Tasas de lesiones profesionales, por actividad económica

	1999	2000	2001	2002	2003	2004	2005	2006	2007	2008	

Malta (FA) **Compensated injuries - Lésions indemnisées - Lesiones indemnizadas**

Rates of non-fatal injuries - Taux de lésions non mortelles - Tasas de lesiones no mortales

Per 100,000 workers employed - Pour 100 000 travailleurs occupés - Por 100 000 trabajadores empleados

Total men and women - Total hommes et femmes - Total hombres y mujeres

ISIC 2 - CITI 2 - CIIU 2 / ISIC 3 - CITI 3 - CIIU 3 [1]

	1999	2000	2001	2002	2003	2004	2005	2006	2007	2008	
Total	3 929	3 789	3 649	3 475	3 228	2 776	2 651	2 862	2 777	2 506	Total
			1 771	1 793	1 648	2 701	1 850	2 795	1 952	2 481	A
			681	2 303	1 429	2 429	2 874	6 522	3 526	2 641	B
			1 919	2 329	1 836	2 218	5 165	6 903	6 273	6 548	C
			6 405	6 257	6 139	5 076	5 329	5 557	5 525	5 038	D
			4 715	4 296	3 912	5 224	4 378	4 643	4 561	3 693	E
			4 222	4 485	5 092	5 478	5 370	6 137	5 808	4 874	F
			1 112	1 082	1 106	1 339	1 382	1 449	1 647	1 421	G
			2 352	2 397	2 931	2 912	2 116	2 851	2 368	2 516	H
			2 227	2 913	3 396	3 486	2 922	3 256	4 504	3 604	I
			353	197	620	293	253	96	164	166	J
			1 512	1 439	2 358	2 052	1 480	2 041	1 742	1 771	K
			1 643	1 267	1 593	1 298	1 459	1 601	1 165	1 150	L
			2 221	1 913	590	514	506	553	456	467	M
			337	236	1 903	1 968	2 289	2 708	2 210	2 090	N
			1 591	995	1 242	1 179	1 014	1 142	838	697	O
			0	0	0	0	0	476	0	0	P
			377	0	730	849	2 564	1 000	2 551	1 038	Q
			0	0	0	0	0	0	0	0	X

Men - Hommes - Hombres [1]

ISIC 3 - CITI 3 - CIIU 3

	1999	2000	2001	2002	2003	2004	2005	2006	2007	2008
Total	.	.	4 477	4 438	4 160	3 513	3 318	3 707	3 696	3 225
A	.	.	1 914	1 762	1 693	2 891	2 036	2 993	1 896	2 643
B	.	.	729	2 465	1 429	2 429	2 874	6 522	3 526	2 846
C	.	.	1 919	2 329	1 987	2 218	5 165	9 046	7 637	6 969
D	.	.	8 002	8 416	7 626	6 435	6 167	6 968	6 890	5 878
E	.	.	4 875	4 728	4 191	5 596	4 711	4 715	4 802	3 868
F	.	.	4 248	4 608	5 191	5 604	5 422	6 332	5 925	4 962
G	.	.	1 416	1 342	1 591	1 659	1 811	1 950	2 290	1 826
H	.	.	2 528	2 748	3 474	3 457	2 639	3 530	3 086	3 146
I	.	.	2 347	3 328	4 053	3 937	3 252	3 946	5 503	4 421
J	.	.	341	346	787	304	367	119	170	277
K	.	.	1 936	1 562	2 833	2 432	1 564	2 553	2 525	2 215
L	.	.	1 860	1 528	1 918	1 559	1 762	1 973	1 397	1 464
M	.	.	2 737	2 873	659	767	741	727	372	425
N	.	.	34	121	1 854	1 957	1 761	2 263	1 913	1 563
O	.	.	1 952	1 404	1 572	1 563	1 556	1 647	1 312	1 007
P	.	.	0	0	0	0	0	0	0	0
Q	.	.	752	0	0	837	1 538	422	2 098	1 754
X	.	.	0	0	0	0	0	0	0	0

Women - Femmes - Mujeres [1]

ISIC 3 - CITI 3 - CIIU 3

	1999	2000	2001	2002	2003	2004	2005	2006	2007	2008
Total	.	.	1 443	1 185	1 173	1 104	1 110	1 063	980	1 007
A	.	.	0	2 198	1 081	985	0	1 015	5 000	0
B	.	.	0	0	0	0	0	0	0	0
C	.	.	0	0	0	0	0	0	0	1 818
D	.	.	1 925	1 705	2 033	1 571	2 104	1 562	1 506	1 936
E	.	.	826	937	336	467	1 254	1 562	1 506	0
F	.	.	2 857	1 177	2 320	362	2 083	524	1 329	1 250
G	.	.	318	344	217	441	422	334	418	515
H	.	.	1 895	1 472	2 026	1 969	1 313	1 598	1 290	1 447
I	.	.	1 537	1 335	1 246	1 630	1 336	1 155	1 254	948
J	.	.	364	37	453	274	131	65	158	69
K	.	.	576	1 043	1 215	1 128	1 257	962	754	973
L	.	.	877	466	629	538	466	576	483	481
M	.	.	1 858	1 283	548	386	381	455	513	492
N	.	.	755	355	1 949	1 977	2 736	3 096	2 448	2 518
O	.	.	742	308	300	553	457	451	224	341
P	.	.	0	0	0	0	0	481	0	0
Q	.	.	0	0	0	862	0	3 571	3 774	571
X	.	.	0	0	0	0	0	0	0	0

Explanatory notes: see p. 1125.

Notes explicatives: voir p. 1127.

Notas explicativas: véase p. 1129.

[1] Incapacity of 4 days or more.

[1] Incapacité de 4 jours et plus.

[1] Incapacidad de 4 días y más.

OCCUPATIONAL INJURIES

Rates of occupational injuries, by economic activity

LÉSIONS PROFESSIONNELLES

Taux de lésions professionnelles, par activité économique

LESIONES PROFESIONALES

Tasas de lesiones profesionales, por actividad económica

	1999	2000	2001	2002	2003	2004	2005	2006	2007	2008

Moldova, Republic of (CA) [1]   Reported injuries - Lésions déclarées - Lesiones declaradas

Rates of fatal injuries - Taux de lésions mortelles - Tasas de lesiones mortales

Per 100,000 employees - Pour 100 000 salariés - Por 100 000 asalariados

Total men and women - Total hommes et femmes - Total hombres y mujeres
ISIC 3 - CITI 3 - CIIU 3

	1999	2000	2001	2002	2003	2004	2005	2006	2007	2008
Total	5.4	6.5	5.0	5.3	5.6	4.9	6.4	4.7	7.1	5.3
A	5.7	6.4	8.0	5.5	6.2	7.4	13.3	5.1	2.3	1.3
B	146.6	0.0	0.0	0.0	0.0	0.0	0.0	0.0	138.0	0.0
C	0.0	41.0	46.2	0.0	45.8	43.4	36.9	0.0	60.0	62.6
D	10.7	7.7	7.7	6.0	5.8	5.7	6.4	3.3	8.9	6.0
E	4.3	14.6	4.8	25.0	20.4	16.2	21.2	5.4	26.7	10.9
F	4.1	11.8	4.3	13.4	32.0	21.0	15.0	32.9	42.0	16.2
G	7.6	2.8	4.5	1.5	4.1	1.2	4.6	4.4	0.0	4.8
I	7.9	5.8	9.6	3.8	3.7	8.7	10.4	7.0	17.0	6.7
K	3.6	6.1	0.0	2.7	5.4	5.2	2.4	2.2	4.5	0.0
L	14.4	32.0	2.0	18.5	3.7	0.0	5.7	1.9	3.7	1.9
M			2.4	0.0	2.4	0.8	1.6	2.4	1.6	0.8
N	0.0	1.5	0.0	3.0	0.0	1.6	0.0	0.0	4.7	3.1
O			4.3	4.4	12.2	7.7	0.0	17.4	3.5	10.6

Rates of non-fatal injuries - Taux de lésions non mortelles - Tasas de lesiones no mortales

Per 100,000 employees - Pour 100 000 salariés - Por 100 000 asalariados

Total men and women - Total hommes et femmes - Total hombres y mujeres
ISIC 3 - CITI 3 - CIIU 3

	1999	2000	2001	2002	2003	2004	2005	2006	2007	2008
Total	100	77	78	73	81	88	82	82	71	66
A	72	63	49	51	56	77	42	39	50	55
C	228	205	93	670	275	434	295	452	481	376
D	194	134	175	145	205	203	193	179	147	136
E	154	165	212	351	473	237	275	323	182	168
F	115	102	94	111	101	92	124	155	132	120
G	28	17	19	24	18	43	37	21	19	32
H			48	28	25	23	11	29	18	25
I	80	94	96	75	101	121	57	96	72	84
J	183	147	22	10	19	35	149	142	94	84
K	91	82	89	39	54	164	170	105	54	71
L	440	262	212	165	37	34	57	58	96	53
M	12	10	14	10	22	13	14	18	9	6
N	33	39	25	34	36	52	68	64	81	62
O	53	26	22	26	28	43	11	42	28	39

Norway (FF) [2]   Reported injuries - Lésions déclarées - Lesiones declaradas

Rates of fatal injuries - Taux de lésions mortelles - Tasas de lesiones mortales

Per 100,000 workers employed - Pour 100 000 travailleurs occupés - Por 100 000 trabajadores empleados

Total men and women - Total hommes et femmes - Total hombres y mujeres
ISIC 3 - CITI 3 - CIIU 3

	1999	2000	2001	2002	2003	2004	2005	2006	2007	2008
Total	2.5	2.5	1.6	1.7	2.1	1.7	2.1	1.3	1.6	2.0
A	11.9	22.1	12.5	7.2	20.9	17.5	25.0	6.0	7.1	21.4
B [3]	46.0	23.1	0.0	0.0	0.0	0.0	23.6	0.0	20.9	20.4
C [4]	3.0	12.1	11.1	0.0	9.3	9.1	3.0	0.0	5.1	7.1
D	3.0	3.4	3.1	2.8	2.1	0.8	2.0	2.0	2.9	3.5
E	5.6	5.0	11.1	0.0	0.0	6.3	0.0	6.0	0.0	5.6
F	8.9	4.1	2.6	8.3	5.6	1.3	7.0	5.0	2.8	3.3
G	1.5	0.6	0.6	1.2	1.1	0.3	2.0	1.0	0.3	0.5
H	0.0	0.0	0.0	2.9	0.0	0.0	0.0	1.0	0.0	0.0
I [5]	4.1	7.1	2.9	2.5	6.0	6.0	4.0	2.0	5.7	5.1
J	0.0	0.0	0.0	0.0	0.0	0.0	0.0	0.0	0.0	0.0
K	1.0	0.5	0.0	0.0	0.4	0.9	0.0	2.0	1.1	0.6
L	2.6	1.3	1.3	0.0	0.0	0.7	1.0	0.0	2.6	0.6
M	0.6	0.0	0.0	0.5	0.5	0.5	0.0	0.0	0.0	0.0
N	0.0	0.2	0.0	0.2	0.0	0.0	0.0	0.0	0.2	0.2
O	3.3	0.0	0.0	1.1	1.0	5.2	2.0	0.0	0.0	3.7
P	0.0	0.0	0.0	0.0	0.0	0.0	0.0	0.0	0.0	0.0

Explanatory notes: see p. 1125.

[1] Enterprises with 20 or more employees, state-owned and municipal enterprises, institutions and organisations. [2] Cases reported during the year indicated. [3] Excl. sea fishing. [4] Excl. offshore oil extraction. [5] Excl. maritime transport.

Notes explicatives: voir p. 1127.

[1] Entreprises occupant 20 salariés et plus, entreprises d'Etat et municipales, institutions et organisations. [2] Cas déclarés pendant l'année indiquée. [3] Non compris la pêche en mer. [4] Non compris l'extraction du pétrole en mer. [5] Non compris les transports maritimes.

Notas explicativas: véase p. 1129.

[1] Empresas con 20 y más asalariados, empresas estatales y municipales, instituciones y organisaciones. [2] Casos declarados en el año indicado. [3] Excl. la pesca de altura y costera. [4] Excl. la extracción del petróleo en el mar. [5] Excl. el transporte marítimo.

OCCUPATIONAL INJURIES	**LÉSIONS PROFESSIONNELLES**	**LESIONES PROFESIONALES**
Rates of occupational injuries, by economic activity	Taux de lésions professionnelles, par activité économique	Tasas de lesiones profesionales, por actividad económica

8B

	1999	2000	2001	2002	2003	2004	2005	2006	2007	2008

Norway (FF) [1] — Reported injuries - Lésions déclarées - Lesiones declaradas

Rates of non-fatal injuries - Taux de lésions non mortelles - Tasas de lesiones no mortales

Per 100,000 workers employed - Pour 100 000 travailleurs occupés - Por 100 000 trabajadores empleados

Total men and women - Total hommes et femmes - Total hombres y mujeres
ISIC 3 - CITI 3 - CIIU 3

	1999	2000	2001	2002	2003	2004	2005	2006	2007	2008
Total	1 482	1 400	1 260	1 179	1 047	993	899	780	781	662
A	524	584	553	478	455	444	422	357	336	383
B [2]	2 531	1 895	1 910	1 794	1 427	1 702	2 032	1 323	1 273	1 676
C [3]	755	694	617	640	519	485	438	2 275	418	369
D	2 991	2 823	2 608	2 290	1 986	1 828	1 639	1 404	1 451	1 304
E	3 056	2 285	2 222	2 436	1 677	1 706	1 729	1 225	1 059	1 056
F	2 505	2 454	2 172	1 928	1 765	1 676	1 537	1 280	1 263	1 121
G	585	590	552	492	440	411	309	323	313	225
H	786	677	743	706	501	437	386	424	427	297
I [4]	1 632	1 539	1 267	1 210	1 161	1 201	1 018	1 011	983	887
J	226	233	204	171	113	92	84	89	66	53
K	474	467	392	446	345	353	300	260	299	204
L	1 763	1 650	1 358	1 565	1 335	1 291	1 083	941	949	700
M	1 550	1 625	1 414	1 419	1 316	1 237	1 196	988	1 063	893
N	1 619	1 474	1 377	1 237	1 159	1 137	1 065	945	865	711
O	690	688	600	651	561	483	470	392	351	297
P	100	50	250	67	0	200	513	133	133	0

Poland (FF) — Reported injuries - Lésions déclarées - Lesiones declaradas

Rates of fatal injuries - Taux de lésions mortelles - Tasas de lesiones mortales

Per 100,000 workers employed - Pour 100 000 travailleurs occupés - Por 100 000 trabajadores empleados

Total men and women - Total hommes et femmes - Total hombres y mujeres [5]
ISIC 3 - CITI 3 - CIIU 3

	1999	2000	2001	2002	2003	2004	2005	2006	2007	2008
Total [6]	.	5.2	5.1	4.9	4.9	4.7	4.4	4.6	4.3	4.6
A [6]	.	6.1	9.0	12.8	8.5	16.2	19.3	12.3	17.2	20.7
B	.	26.9	57.3	14.9	79.4	33.6	19.0	0.0	0.0	22.9
C	.	17.5	14.1	20.7	20.0	9.8	12.8	15.8	14.4	16.9
D	.	5.8	5.3	4.5	5.0	4.9	4.2	5.0	4.6	4.0
E	.	3.7	5.8	5.4	7.2	8.7	4.5	5.5	10.2	7.1
F	.	17.0	14.7	13.6	13.6	15.4	17.5	17.2	12.5	16.1
G	.	3.2	4.2	4.0	3.4	2.5	2.0	2.1	2.5	2.6
H	.	1.4	2.3	0.5	1.9	1.9	0.9	0.0	0.4	0.8
I	.	8.3	8.4	8.3	8.1	10.2	9.3	10.0	8.1	10.4
J	.	2.6	3.1	1.0	0.4	2.6	2.5	1.3	1.3	2.1
K	.	3.0	3.8	3.9	4.4	3.1	3.5	3.1	2.9	2.5
L	.	3.2	2.7	2.8	3.3	2.8	3.3	2.2	1.4	1.3
M	.	2.2	1.1	1.1	1.6	1.5	1.2	1.0	1.1	1.0
N	.	0.9	0.8	1.0	1.3	0.4	0.7	1.4	0.6	1.1
O	.	2.3	3.0	4.5	3.8	4.3	2.6	3.3	5.0	4.7
P	.	0.0	0.0	0.0	0.0	0.0	0.0	0.0	0.0	0.0

Portugal (FA) — Reported injuries - Lésions déclarées - Lesiones declaradas

Rates of fatal injuries - Taux de lésions mortelles - Tasas de lesiones mortales

Per 100,000 workers insured - Pour 100 000 travailleurs assurés - Por 100 000 trabajadores asegurados

Total men and women - Total hommes et femmes - Total hombres y mujeres
ISIC 3 - CITI 3 - CIIU 3

	1999	2000	2001	2002	2003	2004	2005	2006	2007	2008
Total [7]	7.4	8.7	8.3	8.1	7.1	7.0	7.0	6.0	.	.
A	10.7	4.2	4.3	6.3	3.5	3.4	3.6	3.9	.	.
B	20.1	41.7	29.1	28.7	16.2	56.1	37.5	92.9	.	.
C	22.9	56.3	96.4	28.8	55.9	82.5	31.4	17.1	.	.
D	5.1	7.2	5.4	7.1	5.1	5.5	5.8	4.4	.	.
E	0.0	10.4	2.6	10.0	2.8	9.6	4.0	11.5	.	.
F	18.9	17.2	23.7	17.6	19.4	20.1	20.0	15.0	.	.
G	5.9	5.8	4.2	4.1	4.9	3.5	3.1	2.8	.	.
H	2.0	3.5	2.3	1.5	1.5	0.4	0.7	1.8	.	.
I	13.1	18.3	15.9	18.6	15.9	17.7	14.5	13.8	.	.
J	2.5	1.1	0.0	0.0	1.1	1.0	0.0	1.1	.	.
K	6.6	7.8	11.3	9.1	6.5	4.8	7.1	4.1	.	.
L	0.0								.	.
M	0.0		.	.	.	.	.	.	.	.
N	1.3								.	.
O	0.7	2.6	4.7	4.3	1.9	4.5	0.6	1.8	.	.
P	0.8	0.7	0.7	1.9	0.0	0.7	2.0	0.0	.	.
Q		.	58.8	0.0	0.0	0.0	0.0	0.0	.	.

Explanatory notes: see p. 1125.

[1] Cases reported during the year indicated. [2] Excl. sea fishing. [3] Excl. offshore oil extraction. [4] Excl. maritime transport. [5] Deaths occurring within six months of accident. [6] Excl. private farms in agriculture. [7] Excl. public administration and services and defence.

Notes explicatives: voir p. 1127.

[1] Cas déclarés pendant l'année indiquée. [2] Non compris la pêche en mer. [3] Non compris l'extraction du pétrole en mer. [4] Non compris les transports maritimes. [5] Les décès survenant pendant les six mois qui suivent l'accident. [6] Non compris les fermes privées dans l'agriculture. [7] Non compris l'administration publique, les services publics et la défense.

Notas explicativas: véase p. 1129.

[1] Casos declarados en el año indicado. [2] Excl. la pesca de altura y costera. [3] Excl. la extracción del petróleo en el mar. [4] Excl. el transporte marítimo. [5] Los fallecimientos que se produzcan durante los seis meses que siguen el accidente. [6] Excl. las granjas privadas en la agricultura. [7] Excl. la administración pública, los servicios públicos y defensa.

OCCUPATIONAL INJURIES

Rates of occupational injuries, by economic activity

LÉSIONS PROFESSIONNELLES

Taux de lésions professionnelles, par activité économique

LESIONES PROFESIONALES

Tasas de lesiones profesionales, por actividad económica

	1999	2000	2001	2002	2003	2004	2005	2006	2007	2008

Portugal (FA) — Reported injuries - Lésions déclarées - Lesiones declaradas

Rates of fatal injuries - Taux de lésions mortelles - Tasas de lesiones mortales

Per 100,000 workers insured - Pour 100 000 travailleurs assurés - Por 100 000 trabajadores asegurados

Men - Hommes - Hombres
ISIC 3 - CITI 3 - CIIU 3

	1999	2000	2001	2002	2003	2004	2005	2006	2007	2008
Total [1]	12.5	14.3	14.0	13.4	11.7	12.0	11.7	12.0	.	.
A	19.9	8.7	8.3	11.7	6.4	6.3	7.0	6.3		
B	20.5	44.1	31.2	30.3	17.3	63.9	42.5	63.9		
C	24.4	60.0	101.9	30.8	62.7	90.6	33.5	90.6		
D	9.3	11.6	9.4	12.4	8.2	9.2	9.3	9.2		
E	0.0	11.8	3.1	11.7	3.3	11.4	4.9	11.4		
F	19.7	17.8	24.7	18.4	20.3	21.1	21.0	21.1		
G	9.8	9.6	6.6	6.5	7.8	6.2	5.1	6.2		
H	5.3	9.1	2.9	1.9	3.9	0.9	0.9	0.9		
I	17.2	23.0	20.2	23.2	19.6	22.5	18.9	22.5		
J	3.9	1.8	0.0	0.0	1.9	1.6	0.0	1.6		
K	12.0	10.5	20.1	17.1	12.7	7.2	13.3	7.2		
L	500.0	.	.	.	.	.	.	.		
M	0.0	.	.	.	.	.	.	.		
N	7.4	.	.	.	.	.	.	.		
O	0.0	5.6	9.3	10.4	4.3	8.4	1.5	8.4		
P	58.8	0.0	66.7	0.0	0.0	47.1	0.0	47.1		
Q	.	.	100.0	0.0	0.0	0.0	0.0	0.0		
X	.	.	.	266.3	156.1	87.8	.	.		

Women - Femmes - Mujeres
ISIC 3 - CITI 3 - CIIU 3

	1999	2000	2001	2002	2003	2004	2005	2006	2007	2008
Total [1]	0.6	1.1	0.7	0.9	0.7	0.4	0.7	0.4	.	.
A	2.0	0.0	0.6	1.2	0.3	0.3	0.3	0.3		
B	0.0	0.0	0.0	0.0	0.0	0.0	0.0	0.0		
C	0.0	0.0	0.0	0.0	0.0	0.0	0.0	0.0		
D	0.2	1.8	0.4	0.4	0.9	0.5	1.0	0.5		
E	0.0	0.0	0.0	0.0	0.0	0.0	0.0	0.0		
F	0.0	0.0	0.0	0.0	0.0	0.0	0.0	0.0		
G	0.5	0.9	0.9	0.9	0.6	0.0	0.6	0.0		
H	0.0	0.0	1.9	1.2	0.0	0.0	0.6	0.0		
I	0.0	0.0	0.0	0.0	2.2	2.0	1.8	2.0		
J	0.0	0.0	0.0	0.0	0.0	0.0	0.0	0.0		
K	2.2	4.9	1.8	0.8	0.7	2.2	0.0	2.2		
L	90.9	.	.	.	.	.	.	.		
M	0.0	.	.	.	.	.	.	.		
N	0.0	.	.	.	.	.	.	.		
O	1.4	0.0	1.2	0.0	0.0	1.2	2.0	1.2		
P	0.0	0.6	0.0	2.0	0.0	0.0	2.0	0.0		

Rates of non-fatal injuries - Taux de lésions non mortelles - Tasas de lesiones no mortales

Per 100,000 workers insured - Pour 100 000 travailleurs assurés - Por 100 000 trabajadores asegurados

Total men and women - Total hommes et femmes - Total hombres y mujeres
ISIC 3 - CITI 3 - CIIU 3

	1999	2000	2001	2002	2003	2004	2005	2006	2007	2008
Total [1]	5 320	4 260	4 276	4 016	3 931	3 947	3 867	3 996	.	.
A	2 827	989	943	878	908	925	838	891		
B	11 369	7 839	4 345	6 979	7 056	7 956	7 043	8 291		
C	15 336	12 668	13 669	12 627	12 645	12 364	8 299	8 596		
D	7 113	6 086	6 367	6 001	5 816	5 455	5 547	5 508		
E	1 892	3 170	2 140	1 737	1 842	1 886	3 584	3 315		
F	8 833	6 863	7 494	6 794	6 959	7 455	7 022	7 171		
G	4 442	3 377	3 377	3 298	3 249	3 328	3 217	3 616		
H	2 916	2 594	2 417	2 354	2 442	2 875	2 616	3 010		
I	4 143	4 021	3 785	3 584	3 559	3 336	3 233	3 279		
J	826	590	509	479	366	426	424	465		
K	4 492	3 772	3 412	3 390	3 033	3 214	3 353	3 443		
L	8 867	.	.	.	.	.	.	.		
M	3 143	.	.	.	.	.	.	.		
N	3 225	.	.	.	.	.	.	.		
O	1 150	2 190	2 273	2 171	2 273	2 280	2 138	1 988		
P	618	693	516	481	541	530	440	446		
Q	0	130	1 824	0	628	324	154	379		

Explanatory notes: see p. 1125.

Notes explicatives: voir p. 1127.

Notas explicativas: véase p. 1129.

[1] Excl. public administration and services and defence.

[1] Non compris l'administration publique, les services publics et la défense.

[1] Excl. la administración pública, los servicios públicos y defensa.

OCCUPATIONAL INJURIES

Rates of occupational injuries, by economic activity

LÉSIONS PROFESSIONNELLES

Taux de lésions professionnelles, par activité économique

LESIONES PROFESIONALES

Tasas de lesiones profesionales, por actividad económica

8B

	1999	2000	2001	2002	2003	2004	2005	2006	2007	2008

Portugal (FA) — Reported injuries - Lésions déclarées - Lesiones declaradas

Rates of non-fatal injuries - Taux de lésions non mortelles - Tasas de lesiones no mortales

Per 100,000 workers insured - Pour 100 000 travailleurs assurés - Por 100 000 trabajadores asegurados

Men - Hommes - Hombres
ISIC 3 - CITI 3 - CIIU 3

	1999	2000	2001	2002	2003	2004	2005	2006	2007	2008
Total [1]	7 643	6 035	5 990	5 583	5 516	5 448	5 354	5 448	.	.
A	4 357	1 616	1 525	1 394	1 422	1 400	1 352	1 400	.	.
B	10 664	7 839	4 167	6 965	6 784	8 400	7 556	8 400	.	.
C	15 650	1 893	14 197	13 265	13 659	13 320	8 644	13 320	.	.
D	10 737	8 954	9 173	8 570	8 362	7 710	7 664	7 710	.	.
E	2 036	3 425	2 420	1 781	2 055	2 109	3 813	2 109	.	.
F	9 123	7 036	7 710	6 976	7 182	7 705	7 251	7 705	.	.
G	5 897	4 622	4 487	4 302	4 327	6 332	4 280	4 332	.	.
H	3 592	2 079	2 602	2 531	2 673	3 062	2 798	3 062	.	.
I	5 033	4 508	4 399	3 922	4 006	3 874	3 807	3 874	.	.
J	817	618	517	558	358	370	423	370	.	.
K	6 941	4 939	4 063	4 356	4 227	4 125	4 402	4 125	.	.
L	19 500	.	.	.	.	.	.	.	.	.
M	5 100	.	.	.	.	.	.	.	.	.
N	4 015	.	.	.	.	.	.	.	.	.
O	1 618	3 318	3 916	3 616	3 473	3 162	2 982	3 162	.	.
P	5 059	5 474	2 933	1 714	2 209	2 025	2 364	2 025	.	.
Q	.	.	1 700	0	423	597	153	597	.	.

Women - Femmes - Mujeres
ISIC 3 - CITI 3 - CIIU 3

	1999	2000	2001	2002	2003	2004	2005	2006	2007	2008
Total [1]	2 226	1 869	1 933	1 884	1 807	1 896	1 885	1 896	.	.
A	1 370	416	395	388	397	439	379	439	.	.
B	-	7 727	6 714	7 071	11 253	4 753	3 216	4 753	.	.
C	-	5 600	4 444	3 325	4 379	2 479	2 997	2 479	.	.
D	2 889	2 576	2 854	2 748	2 525	2 417	2 627	2 417	.	.
E	531	1 314	407	1 445	686	671	2 528	671	.	.
F	1 873	2 377	2 347	2 461	2 359	2 404	2 257	2 404	.	.
G	2 426	1 788	1 896	1 943	1 853	2 050	1 848	2 050	.	.
H	2 518	2 336	2 294	2 238	2 291	2 747	2 498	2 747	.	.
I	1 290	2 124	1 471	2 234	1 912	1 531	1 577	1 531	.	.
J	812	545	496	377	378	519	426	519	.	.
K	2 488	2 574	2 702	2 387	1 923	2 202	2 168	2 202	.	.
L	1 455	.	.	.	.	.	.	.	.	.
M	2 246	.	.	.	.	.	.	.	.	.
N	3 057	.	.	.	.	.	.	.	.	.
O	758	1 187	1 021	1 141	1 275	1 546	1 501	1 547	.	.
P	555	630	490	463	513	508	418	508	.	.
Q	.	182	2 000	0	1 217	0	154	0	.	.

Roumanie (FF) — Reported injuries - Lésions déclarées - Lesiones declaradas

Rates of fatal injuries - Taux de lésions mortelles - Tasas de lesiones mortales

Per 100,000 employees - Pour 100 000 salariés - Por 100 000 asalariados

Total men and women - Total hommes et femmes - Total hombres y mujeres
ISIC 3 - CITI 3 - CIIU 3

ISIC 4 - CITI 4 - CIIU 4 [2]

	1999	2000	2001	2002	2003	2004	2005	2006	2007		2008	
Total	7	8	7	7	7	7	9	7	8	I	7	Total
A	8	8	7	7	11	9	12	8	14	I	13	A
B	10	0	10	0	9	0	0	8	17	I	19	B
C	28	29	25	28	16	18	16	19	9	I	4	C
D	6	6	6	7	5	6	7	6	5	I	8	D
E	11	11	9	9	6	7	9	7	8	I	18	E
F	19	20	19	18	25	24	34	25	34	I	26	F
G	4	2	4	3	5	5	5	5	6	I	5	G
H	5	4	1	1	1	10	2	1	5	I	14	H
I	7	9	10	9	9	11	17	12	13	I	2	I
J	2	2	2	2	1	4	4	1	2	I	6	J
K	6	7	5	6	9	11	8	12	11	I	3	K
L	8	13	2	8	4	2	3	9	8	I	0	L
M	-	2	0	1	0	0	1	1	1	I	7	M
N	1	1	1	2	1	3	1	1	1	I	16	N
O	4	5	12	4	5	2	5	5	5	I	3	O
P	0	0	0	0	0	0	0	0	0	I	1	P
Q	0	0	0	0	0	0	0	0	0	I	1	Q
										I	1	R
										I	6	S
										I	0	T
										I	0	U
										I	0	X

Explanatory notes: see p. 1125.

[1] Excl. public administration and services and defence. [2] Deaths occurring within the same reference year as accident.

Notes explicatives: voir p. 1127.

[1] Non compris l'administration publique, les services publics et la défense. [2] Décès survenant pendant la même année de référence que l'accident.

Notas explicativas: véase p. 1129.

[1] Excl. la administración pública, los servicios públicos y defensa. [2] Fallecimientos que se producen durante el mismo año de referencia que el accidente.

OCCUPATIONAL INJURIES	LÉSIONS PROFESSIONNELLES	LESIONES PROFESIONALES
Rates of occupational injuries, by economic activity	Taux de lésions professionnelles, par activité économique	Tasas de lesiones profesionales, por actividad económica

	1999	2000	2001	2002	2003	2004	2005	2006	2007	2008	

Roumanie (FF) — Reported injuries - Lésions déclarées - Lesiones declaradas

Rates of non-fatal injuries - Taux de lésions non mortelles - Tasas de lesiones no mortales

Per 100,000 employees - Pour 100 000 salariés - Por 100 000 asalariados

Total men and women - Total hommes et femmes - Total hombres y mujeres
ISIC 3 - CITI 3 - CIIU 3 .... ISIC 4 - CITI 4 - CIIU 4 [1]

	1999	2000	2001	2002	2003	2004	2005	2006	2007	2008	
Total	95	94	99	94	91	89	76	78	76	79	Total
A	54	39	40	37	43	46	28	32	34	41	A
B	10	21	20	10	27	23	0	0	8	280	B
C	804	831	863	820	722	473	333	306	285	92	C
D	125	120	124	120	118	120	107	107	93	82	D
E	77	65	72	63	64	71	84	71	83	122	E
F	118	123	133	129	143	160	156	168	174	174	F
G	11	12	14	17	21	29	30	35	42	71	G
H	18	15	28	26	34	44	37	41	36	87	H
I	79	75	84	79	71	79	62	60	80	46	I
J	6	10	7	9	14	12	4	14	18	29	J
K	32	40	41	39	53	57	55	69	91	18	K
L	32	34	35	32	33	35	24	39	44	28	L
M	3	5	5	6	5	5	6	7	8	48	M
N	12	12	15	14	16	20	21	27	28	111	N
O	28	25	28	45	29	51	41	49	52	47	O
P	0	0	0	0	0	0	0	0	0	7	P
Q	0	0	0	0	0	0	0	0	0	25	Q
R										21	R
S										13	S
T										0	T
U										0	U
X										0	X

Russian Federation (DA) [2] — Reported injuries - Lésions déclarées - Lesiones declaradas

Rates of fatal injuries - Taux de lésions mortelles - Tasas de lesiones mortales

Per 100,000 employees - Pour 100 000 salariés - Por 100 000 asalariados

Total men and women - Total hommes et femmes - Total hombres y mujeres
ISIC 3 - CITI 3 - CIIU 3

	1999	2000	2001	2002	2003	2004	2005	2006	2007	2008
Total	14.4	14.9	15.0	13.8	13.1	12.9	12.4	11.9	12.4	10.9

Men - Hommes - Hombres
ISIC 3 - CITI 3 - CIIU 3

	1999	2000	2001	2002	2003	2004	2005	2006	2007	2008
Total	24.2	25.0	25.0	23.2	22.3	21.7	21.1	20.2	21.2	18.4

Women - Femmes - Mujeres
ISIC 3 - CITI 3 - CIIU 3

	1999	2000	2001	2002	2003	2004	2005	2006	2007	2008
Total	2.0	2.0	2.2	2.0	1.7	2.0	1.9	2.0	1.6	1.8

Rates of non-fatal injuries - Taux de lésions non mortelles - Tasas de lesiones no mortales

Per 100,000 employees - Pour 100 000 salariés - Por 100 000 asalariados

Total men and women - Total hommes et femmes - Total hombres y mujeres
ISIC 3 - CITI 3 - CIIU 3

	1999	2000	2001	2002	2003	2004	2005	2006	2007	2008
Total	500	499	482	436	381	331	300	277	262	238

Men - Hommes - Hombres
ISIC 3 - CITI 3 - CIIU 3

	1999	2000	2001	2002	2003	2004	2005	2006	2007	2008
Total	697	679	651	585	508	438	399	370	339	306

Women - Femmes - Mujeres
ISIC 3 - CITI 3 - CIIU 3

	1999	2000	2001	2002	2003	2004	2005	2006	2007	2008
Total	259	269	265	250	225	198	180	169	167	155

San Marino (FF) — Reported injuries - Lésions déclarées - Lesiones declaradas

Rates of fatal injuries - Taux de lésions mortelles - Tasas de lesiones mortales

Per 100,000 employees - Pour 100 000 salariés - Por 100 000 asalariados

Total men and women - Total hommes et femmes - Total hombres y mujeres
ISIC 3 - CITI 3 - CIIU 3

	1999	2000	2001	2002	2003	2004	2005	2006	2007	2008
Total	.	0	0	0	0	0	0		.	.

Explanatory notes: see p. 1125.

[1] Deaths occurring within the same reference year as accident.
[2] Excl. activities with low injury rates.

Notes explicatives: voir p. 1127.

[1] Décès survenant pendant la même année de référence que l'accident. [2] Non compris les activités avec les taux de lésion bas.

Notas explicativas: véase p. 1129.

[1] Fallecimientos que se producen durante el mismo año de referencia que el accidente. [2] Excl. las actividades con tasas de lesion bajas.

OCCUPATIONAL INJURIES / LÉSIONS PROFESSIONNELLES / LESIONES PROFESIONALES

8B

Rates of occupational injuries, by economic activity / Taux de lésions professionnelles, par activité économique / Tasas de lesiones profesionales, por actividad económica

	1999	2000	2001	2002	2003	2004	2005	2006	2007	2008

San Marino (FF) — Reported injuries - Lésions déclarées - Lesiones declaradas

Rates of non-fatal injuries - Taux de lésions non mortelles - Tasas de lesiones no mortales

Per 100,000 employees - Pour 100 000 salariés - Por 100 000 asalariados

Total men and women - Total hommes et femmes - Total hombres y mujeres
ISIC 3 - CITI 3 - CIIU 3

	1999	2000	2001	2002	2003	2004	2005	2006	2007	2008
Total	.	6 986	5 117	4 479	5 018	3 726	3 800	4 652	.	.
A	.	33 333	16 667	23 077	26 923	16 666	14 285	7 895	.	.
D	.	7 704	5 206	5 783	5 144	4 240	4 551	6 128	.	.
F	.	13 328	9 219	8 880	6 087	4 456	7 088	9 414	.	.
G	.	.	2 986	5 317	4 208	1 680	4 435	5 917	.	.
H	.	.	4 555	.	.	.	4 666	1 342	.	.
I	.	2 381	2 486	1 917	1 033	740	3 521	2 581	.	.
J	.	899	1 637	1 404	148	270	253	589	.	.
K	.	.	.	.	.	.	1 755	2 327	.	.
L	.	.	1 821	1 587	1 338	862	2 424	2 939	.	.
M	.	.	0	0	.	.	.	.	.	.
N	.	.	4 636	0	.	.	.	.	.	.
O	.	.	3 154	2 379	3 585	1 804	.	2 450	.	.

Slovakia (CA) — Reported injuries - Lésions déclarées - Lesiones declaradas

Rates of fatal injuries - Taux de lésions mortelles - Tasas de lesiones mortales

Per 100,000 workers insured - Pour 100 000 travailleurs assurés - Por 100 000 trabajadores asegurados

Total men and women - Total hommes et femmes - Total hombres y mujeres
ISIC 3 - CITI 3 - CIIU 3

	1999	2000	2001	2002	2003	2004	2005	2006	2007	2008
Total	5	4	5	4	5	4	4	5	4	4
A	13	8	16	11	12	15	9	15	2	26
B	0	0	0	0	0	0	0	0	0	0
C	7	0	17	29	0	34	0	65	0	0
D	5	6	3	4	3	3	4	4	5	3
E	13	6	4	6	7	22	3	9	0	7
F	14	11	22	12	17	6	20	15	23	16
G	5	6	4	9	8	3	1	5	8	3
H	6	0	0	0	0	0	0	0	0	0
I	3	5	13	6	11	7	14	10	9	6
J	6	0	0	0	0	7	0	0	0	0
K	3	9	4	4	5	3	1	3	3	3
L	5	3	4	3	4	3	3	4	0	1
M	3	0	0	2	1	1	0	0	0	2
N	1	1	1	1	0	0	0	1	0	0
O	8	0	0	0	0	3	3	6	2	6
P	0	0	0	0	0	0	0	0	0	0
Q	0	0	0	0	0	0	0	0	0	0
X	0	0	0	0	0	0	0	0	0	0

Men - Hommes - Hombres
ISIC 3 - CITI 3 - CIIU 3

	1999	2000	2001	2002	2003	2004	2005	2006	2007	2008
Total	9	8	9	8	8	7	7	9	6	8
A	18	11	23	13	17	20	10	22	12	37
B	0	0	0	0	0	0	0	0	0	0
C	8	0	20	33	0	39	0	74	0	0
D	8	10	5	6	6	5	6	7	4	6
E	16	8	6	8	9	28	3	7	0	9
F	17	12	25	14	19	7	23	17	11	19
G	7	13	5	16	14	5	3	13	12	7
H	15	0	0	0	0	0	0	0	0	0
I	5	7	20	9	16	6	22	16	10	8
J	20	0	0	0	0	22	0	0	0	0
K	2	12	7	7	8	5	3	5	6	6
L	8	6	7	6	7	5	5	7	0	2
M	6	0	3	3	3	0	0	0	0	5
N	5	5	5	5	0	0	0	6	0	0
O	13	0	0	0	0	5	5	5	3	11
P	0	0	0	0	0	0	0	0	0	0
Q	0	0	0	0	0	0	0	0	0	0

Explanatory notes: see p. 1125. Notes explicatives: voir p. 1127. Notas explicativas: véase p. 1129.

8B

OCCUPATIONAL INJURIES	LÉSIONS PROFESSIONNELLES	LESIONES PROFESIONALES
Rates of occupational injuries, by economic activity	Taux de lésions professionnelles, par activité économique	Tasas de lesiones profesionales, por actividad económica

	1999	2000	2001	2002	2003	2004	2005	2006	2007	2008

Slovakia (CA) — Reported injuries - Lésions déclarées - Lesiones declaradas

Rates of fatal injuries - Taux de lésions mortelles - Tasas de lesiones mortales

Per 100,000 workers insured - Pour 100 000 travailleurs assurés - Por 100 000 trabajadores asegurados

Women - Femmes - Mujeres
ISIC 3 - CITI 3 - CIIU 3

	1999	2000	2001	2002	2003	2004	2005	2006	2007	2008
Total	1	1	0	1	1	1	0	0	1	2
A	3	0	0	4	0	0	6	0	0	0
B	0	0	0	0	0	0	0	0	0	0
C	0	0	0	0	0	0	0	0	0	0
D	1	1	0	1	0	0	0	0	4	0
E	0	0	0	0	0	0	0	13	0	0
F	0	0	0	0	0	0	0	0	0	0
G	4	0	4	4	3	2	0	0	2	0
H	0	0	0	0	0	0	0	0	0	0
I	0	0	0	0	0	8	0	0	2	2
J	0	0	0	0	0	0	0	0	0	0
K	4	4	0	0	0	0	0	0	0	0
L	1	1	0	0	1	0	0	0	0	0
M	2	0	0	1	0	2	0	0	0	1
N	0	0	0	0	0	0	0	0	0	0
O	0	0	0	0	0	0	0	7	0	0
P	0	0	0	0	0	0	0	0	0	0
Q	0	0	0	0	0	0	0	0	0	0

Rates of non-fatal injuries - Taux de lésions non mortelles - Tasas de lesiones no mortales

Per 100,000 workers insured - Pour 100 000 travailleurs assurés - Por 100 000 trabajadores asegurados

Total men and women - Total hommes et femmes - Total hombres y mujeres
ISIC 3 - CITI 3 - CIIU 3

	1999	2000	2001	2002	2003	2004	2005	2006	2007	2008
Total	1 137	1 071	1 021	956	801	659	635	678	648	657
A	3 122	2 985	2 970	2 924	2 720	2 060	1 838	1 929	1 415	1 283
B	0	1 408	1 389	1 961	0	4 545	7 692	2 777	1 219	2 531
C	5 800	5 285	5 644	5 623	6 097	5 317	3 817	8 809	4 254	3 545
D	2 059	1 998	1 915	1 839	1 601	1 420	1 412	1 444	1 279	1 181
E	729	683	616	606	595	520	433	460	366	298
F	2 163	2 267	2 197	2 218	2 049	1 760	1 638	1 568	1 073	987
G	922	1 006	1 002	1 003	954	790	746	811	523	504
H	1 099	939	915	786	976	550	513	672	419	360
I	1 086	1 171	1 017	954	882	770	790	804	595	562
J	275	235	194	193	195	270	144	344	155	170
K	734	705	782	773	572	490	373	464	384	345
L	512	462	466	408	376	250	288	323	325	296
M	381	357	299	310	277	240	213	256	183	213
N	663	678	618	591	561	330	430	390	240	262
O	846	831	843	719	556	620	624	685	446	437
P	0	0	0	0	0	0	0	0	0	0
Q	0	0	0	0	0	0	0	0	0	287
X	0	0	0	0	0	0	0	0	0	2 395

Men - Hommes - Hombres
ISIC 3 - CITI 3 - CIIU 3

	1999	2000	2001	2002	2003	2004	2005	2006	2007	2008
Total	1 633	1 530	1 497	1 366	1 228	932	874	942	849	925
A	3 674	3 368	3 396	3 428	2 987	2 363	1 960	2 116	728	1 374
B	0	1 818	0	2 632	0	0	6 896	3 703	1 219	3 508
C	6 579	5 986	6 363	6 340	6 942	6 033	4 305	9 986	2 645	4 062
D	2 826	2 756	2 639	2 452	2 172	1 883	1 837	1 836	1 122	1 508
E	849	766	730	695	676	599	502	523	290	356
F	2 439	2 563	2 498	2 504	2 327	2 014	1 841	1 788	509	1 125
G	1 399	1 561	1 459	1 340	1 366	1 158	1 086	1 038	623	624
H	1 459	1 142	954	1 008	1 361	624	689	588	242	419
I	1 295	1 339	1 289	1 152	1 019	885	897	846	544	614
J	426	276	258	252	181	201	134	314	140	217
K	960	909	1 084	1 014	745	639	425	586	495	402
L	746	663	699	594	535	351	407	479	460	552
M	421	343	318	375	284	268	192	200	203	177
N	890	983	930	743	836	344	494	449	275	279
O	1 214	1 191	1 210	1 021	836	892	843	956	654	618
P	0	0	0	0	0	0	0	0	0	0
Q	0	0	0	0	0	0	0	0	59	408
X	0	0	0	0	0	0	0	0	406	3 928

Explanatory notes: see p. 1125.   Notes explicatives: voir p. 1127.   Notas explicativas: véase p. 1129.

OCCUPATIONAL INJURIES

LÉSIONS PROFESSIONNELLES

LESIONES PROFESIONALES

8B

Rates of occupational injuries, by economic activity

Taux de lésions professionnelles, par activité économique

Tasas de lesiones profesionales, por actividad económica

	1999	2000	2001	2002	2003	2004	2005	2006	2007	2008

Slovakia (CA)   **Reported injuries - Lésions déclarées - Lesiones declaradas**

Rates of non-fatal injuries - Taux de lésions non mortelles - Tasas de lesiones no mortales

Per 100,000 workers insured - Pour 100 000 travailleurs assurés - Por 100 000 trabajadores asegurados

Women - Femmes - Mujeres
ISIC 3 - CITI 3 - CIIU 3

	1999	2000	2001	2002	2003	2004	2005	2006	2007	2008
Total	560	537	478	486	443	340	351	374	363	381
A	1 933	2 127	1 983	1 753	1 932	1 310	1 533	1 470	712	1 060
B	0	0	5 882	0	0	0	10 000	0	0	0
C	420	304	554	403	378	180	396	621	777	822
D	1 059	988	930	1 012	846	780	821	894	631	714
E	306	389	227	280	301	240	174	237	115	83
F	446	366	327	404	272	170	303	127	248	167
G	562	509	652	745	586	520	505	652	289	400
H	894	824	894	663	768	510	421	714	204	326
I	676	852	495	558	619	550	586	723	392	442
J	211	217	167	169	200	300	149	357	137	152
K	394	411	324	406	321	270	296	294	247	270
L	256	242	214	199	180	110	130	130	187	150
M	360	364	290	283	275	230	220	265	180	226
N	608	604	541	553	493	330	414	376	194	257
O	384	377	395	344	215	280	361	339	146	246
P	0	0	0	0	0	0	0	0	0	0
Q	0	0	0	0	0	0	0	0	7	168
X	0	0	0	0	0	0	0	0	362	1 133

Slovenia (FF)   **Reported injuries - Lésions déclarées - Lesiones declaradas**

Rates of fatal injuries - Taux de lésions mortelles - Tasas de lesiones mortales

Per 100,000 workers insured - Pour 100 000 travailleurs assurés - Por 100 000 trabajadores asegurados

Total men and women - Total hommes et femmes - Total hombres y mujeres
ISIC 3 - CITI 3 - CIIU 3

	1999	2000	2001	2002	2003	2004	2005	2006	2007	2008
Total	3.5	3.3	4.3	4.0	5.1	2.6	2.6	3.8	5.0	.
A	7.6	0.0	17.2	8.9	9.3	9.7	19.7	10.2	15.5	.
B	0.0	0.0	0.0	0.0	0.0	0.0	0.0	0.0	0.0	.
C	0.0	0.0	96.2	0.0	87.0	0.0	0.0	26.0	27.1	.
D	2.4	4.1	1.7	3.7	2.9	2.5	2.2	3.9	4.3	.
E	8.5	17.0	0.0	0.0	8.6	8.6	0.0	0.0	0.0	.
F	9.8	12.8	17.6	11.3	24.2	9.6	10.8	14.1	19.7	.
G	1.8	0.9	1.9	2.8	3.9	0.9	2.7	0.0	2.5	.
H	0.0	0.0	0.0	3.6	0.0	0.0	0.0	0.0	0.0	.
I	8.0	4.0	6.0	9.8	9.3	2.0	1.9	9.4	5.4	.
J	0.0	0.0	0.0	0.0	0.0	0.0	0.0	4.5	8.8	.
K	3.9	0.0	1.8	3.4	0.0	1.6	1.5	2.7	1.3	.
L	2.3	4.4	2.1	0.0	0.0	1.9	0.0	1.9	5.7	.
M	0.0	0.0	0.0	1.8	0.0	0.0	0.0	0.0	0.0	.
N	0.0	1.8	1.7	2.1	0.0	4.1	0.0	0.0	1.9	.
O	0.0	0.0	7.2	0.0	6.9	0.0	0.0	0.0	0.0	.
P	0.0	0.0	0.0	0.0	0.0	0.0	0.0	0.0	0.0	.
Q	0.0	0.0	0.0	0.0	0.0	0.0	0.0	0.0	0.0	.

Rates of non-fatal injuries - Taux de lésions non mortelles - Tasas de lesiones no mortales

Per 100,000 workers insured - Pour 100 000 travailleurs assurés - Por 100 000 trabajadores asegurados

Total men and women - Total hommes et femmes - Total hombres y mujeres [1]
ISIC 3 - CITI 3 - CIIU 3

	1999	2000	2001	2002	2003	2004	2005	2006	2007	2008
Total	5 246	5 092	5 080	5 153	5 214	5 238	4 565	4 437	4 250	.
A	4 790	4 357	4 319	4 695	4 426	4 663	4 428	4 289	4 436	.
B	4 643	6 818	3 502	5 769	3 065	4 918	5 138	2 966	2 632	.
C	11 319	11 225	11 607	9 298	10 609	9 703	9 342	8 566	8 568	.
D	6 744	6 524	6 828	6 725	6 681	6 655	6 042	5 929	5 898	.
E	5 983	6 290	6 490	6 593	6 062	6 322	5 821	5 791	4 681	.
F	8 119	8 374	8 505	8 315	8 196	8 688	7 188	6 560	6 455	.
G	3 287	3 625	3 502	3 588	3 770	3 447	3 144	3 149	3 092	.
H	3 008	3 330	3 926	4 384	4 368	4 247	4 074	3 861	3 796	.
I	4 088	4 547	4 590	5 171	5 341	5 893	4 823	4 733	4 404	.
J	1 542	1 795	1 875	2 163	2 193	2 295	2 022	1 990	1 555	.
K	2 711	2 921	3 035	2 973	3 373	3 228	2 719	2 725	2 465	.
L	4 618	4 793	5 032	5 283	5 666	6 341	5 189	4 952	4 376	.
M	2 369	2 352	2 256	2 353	2 572	2 571	2 230	2 164	2 007	.
N	3 705	3 940	4 168	4 211	3 986	4 239	3 369	3 550	3 252	.
O	2 555	2 884	3 070	3 119	3 026	3 013	2 708	2 690	2 334	.
P	10 000	13 333	15 385	6 667	0	0	0	0	0	.

Explanatory notes: see p. 1125.   Notes explicatives: voir p. 1127.   Notas explicativas: véase p. 1129.

[1] Incl. commuting accidents.   [1] Y compris les accidents de trajet.   [1] Incl. accidentes del trayecto.

8B

OCCUPATIONAL INJURIES	LÉSIONS PROFESSIONNELLES	LESIONES PROFESIONALES
Rates of occupational injuries, by economic activity	Taux de lésions professionnelles, par activité économique	Tasas de lesiones profesionales, por actividad económica

	1999	2000	2001	2002	2003	2004	2005	2006	2007	2008

Suisse (FA) — Compensated injuries - Lésions indemnisées - Lesiones indemnizadas

Rates of fatal injuries - Taux de lésions mortelles - Tasas de lesiones mortales

Per 100,000 workers insured - Pour 100 000 travailleurs assurés - Por 100 000 trabajadores asegurados

Total men and women - Total hommes et femmes - Total hombres y mujeres [1]
ISIC 3 - CITI 3 - CIIU 3

	1999	2000	2001	2002	2003	2004	2005	2006	2007	2008
Total	2.4	2.3	2.0	1.5	1.3	1.9	1.3	1.4	1.6	.
A	11.7	2.1	14.6	7.2	2.4	11.8	2.4	6.9	0.0	
B	0.0	0.0	0.0	0.0	0.0	0.0	0.0	0.0	0.0	
C-D	1.5	3.2	1.6	2.2	1.4	2.2	1.5	1.7	0.8	
E	0.0	4.2	4.5	4.5	8.6	0.0	0.0	0.0	4.0	
F	7.8	6.9	7.9	5.6	5.3	5.9	4.8	4.5	4.5	
G	0.9	1.0	0.8	0.2	0.8	0.8	0.2	0.6	1.0	
H	1.3	0.6	0.0	0.0	0.0	0.4	0.0	0.0	0.0	
I	12.5	11.2	6.1	5.3	3.3	5.3	4.0	5.9	6.5	
J	0.0	0.0	0.0	0.0	0.9	1.0	0.0	0.0	0.0	
K	0.8	1.0	0.2	0.7	1.0	1.2	0.5	0.9	1.4	
L	0.0	0.0	0.0	0.0	0.0	0.0	0.0	0.0	0.0	
M	0.0	0.0	14.2	0.0	0.0	0.0	0.0	0.0	0.0	
N	0.6	0.0	0.0	0.0	0.0	0.2	0.2	0.0	0.0	
O	3.2	0.8	0.5	0.0	0.0	0.0	0.0	0.0	0.0	
P	5.6	0.0	0.0	0.0	0.0	0.0	0.0	0.0	0.0	
Q	0.0	0.0	0.0	0.0	0.0	0.0	0.0	0.0	0.0	
X		1.1	2.5	0.8	0.6	1.0	1.4	0.9	2.6	.

Rates of non-fatal injuries - Taux de lésions non mortelles - Tasas de lesiones no mortales

Per 100,000 workers insured - Pour 100 000 travailleurs assurés - Por 100 000 trabajadores asegurados

Total men and women - Total hommes et femmes - Total hombres y mujeres [2]
ISIC 3 - CITI 3 - CIIU 3

	1999	2000	2001	2002	2003	2004	2005	2006	2007	2008
Total	2 685	2 580	2 546	2 534	2 447	2 342	2 377	2 349	2 270	.
A	7 277	6 778	6 570	7 202	6 997	6 758	7 196	6 501	6 513	
B	3 431	2 128	4 321	3 371	4 545	3 933	3 750	2 151	2 186	
D	3 131	2 977	2 988	2 918	2 783	2 612	2 578	2 538	2 471	
E	2 636	2 203	2 095	2 262	1 879	2 051	1 866	1 772	1 563	
F	8 257	8 132	7 880	7 748	7 520	7 284	7 205	7 028	6 761	
G	2 056	1 913	1 882	1 953	1 905	1 792	1 770	1 824	1 731	
H	3 526	3 425	3 510	3 463	3 278	3 189	3 211	3 289	3 154	
I	3 539	3 456	3 371	3 586	3 415	3 380	3 376	3 517	3 401	
J	168	160	153	140	145	145	145	145	145	
K	2 079	2 198	2 018	1 896	1 887	1 846	2 001	2 172	2 040	
L	365	362	421	557	480	462	432	515	312	
M	984	874	697	588	960	872	960	1 049	749	
N	1 000	939	948	1 054	1 047	990	986	963	970	
O	2 248	2 361	1 613	2 137	2 112	2 279	2 232	2 285	2 283	
P	1 117	912	864	860	859	906	729	759	608	
Q	708	244	0	677	215	222	193	380	775	
X		1 165	1 327	1 218	1 206	1 135	1 307	1 053	1 266	.

Sweden (FA) — Reported injuries - Lésions déclarées - Lesiones declaradas

Rates of fatal injuries - Taux de lésions mortelles - Tasas de lesiones mortales

Per 100,000 workers employed - Pour 100 000 travailleurs occupés - Por 100 000 trabajadores empleados

Total men and women - Total hommes et femmes - Total hombres y mujeres
ISIC 3 - CITI 3 - CIIU 3

	1999	2000	2001	2002	2003	2004	2005	2006	2007	2008
Total	1.7	1.5	1.4	1.4	1.3	1.4	1.6	1.6	1.7	.
A	20.9	18.3	13.5	15.1	5.3	11.9	19.6	11.7	22.8	.
B	95.8	182.1	168.1	83.8	76.7	243.5	76.0	71.0	0.0	.
C	12.4	0.0	13.8	14.0	0.0	0.0	0.0	13.3	12.8	.
D	1.7	0.7	1.4	1.1	1.2	1.1	1.6	1.7	1.1	.
E	3.8	0.0	4.3	0.0	0.0	4.2	0.0	0.0	0.0	.
F	3.7	9.1	5.1	5.0	4.2	2.5	4.4	4.1	5.6	.
G	1.0	0.8	1.0	0.0	0.8	0.8	0.6	1.3	0.4	.
H	0.0	0.0	1.0	1.0	0.0	0.9	0.0	0.9	0.0	.
I	5.0	4.4	5.2	6.3	3.4	5.3	4.5	4.9	3.3	.
J	0.0	0.0	0.0	0.0	0.0	0.0	0.0	0.0	0.0	.
K	0.4	0.6	0.0	1.4	1.4	0.7	1.2	1.0	0.7	.
L	1.4	1.8	0.4	0.4	4.2	2.1	2.1	2.0	4.1	.
M	0.7	0.0	0.0	0.0	0.2	0.0	0.0	0.0	0.2	.
N	0.0	0.0	0.0	0.1	0.0	0.1	0.1	0.1	0.1	.
O	0.6	1.1	0.5	0.0	0.5	1.0	1.0	1.0	2.4	.
P	0.0	0.0	0.0	0.0	0.0	0.0	0.0	0.0	0.0	.
Q	0.0	0.0	0.0	0.0	0.0	0.0	0.0	0.0	0.0	.
X	0.0	0.0	0.0	0.0	0.0	0.0	0.0	0.0	1.0	.

Explanatory notes: see p. 1125. | Notes explicatives: voir p. 1127. | Notas explicativas: véase p. 1129.

[1] Only deaths resulting from accidents occurring during the same year. [2] Incapacity of 3 days or more.

[1] Seulement les décès dus à des accidents survenus pendant la même année. [2] Incapacité de 3 jours et plus.

[1] Solamente los fallecimientos resultados a accidentes ocurridos en el mismo año. [2] Incapacidad de 3 días y más.

	1999	2000	2001	2002	2003	2004	2005	2006	2007	2008

Sweden (FA) — Reported injuries - Lésions déclarées - Lesiones declaradas

Rates of fatal injuries - Taux de lésions mortelles - Tasas de lesiones mortales

Per 100,000 workers employed - Pour 100 000 travailleurs occupés - Por 100 000 trabajadores empleados

Men - Hommes - Hombres
ISIC 3 - CITI 3 - CIIU 3

	1999	2000	2001	2002	2003	2004	2005	2006	2007	2008
Total	3.0	2.6	2.4	2.6	2.5	2.2	2.8	3.0	3.0	.
A	27.0	23.6	15.7	19.4	6.5	14.7	22.6	14.7	28.5	.
B	103.4	197.6	181.5	91.4	82.9	175.6	82.5	77.5	0.0	.
C	14.2	0.0	15.6	15.8	0.0	0.0	0.0	15.1	14.8	.
D	2.0	0.7	1.1	1.3	1.5	1.4	2.1	2.1	1.4	.
E	4.9	0.0	5.7	0.0	0.0	5.6	0.0	0.0	0.0	.
F	3.5	9.2	5.5	5.4	4.6	2.7	4.7	4.4	6.1	.
G	1.5	1.5	1.8	0.0	1.4	1.0	0.7	2.4	0.7	.
H	0.0	0.0	2.3	2.3	0.0	0.0	0.0	1.9	0.0	.
I	7.0	5.2	6.7	8.7	4.1	6.1	5.6	6.6	3.0	.
J	0.0	0.0	0.0	0.0	0.0	0.0	0.0	0.0	0.0	.
K	0.4	1.0	0.0	1.7	2.4	0.9	1.4	1.3	1.0	.
L	2.9	3.8	0.0	0.9	9.0	2.7	4.6	4.5	9.0	.
M	2.1	0.0	0.0	0.0	0.9	0.0	0.0	0.0	0.9	.
N	0.0	0.0	0.0	0.0	0.0	0.0	0.0	0.9	0.8	.
O	1.2	2.4	1.2	0.0	1.1	1.1	2.1	2.1	3.1	.
P	0.0	0.0	0.0	0.0	0.0	0.0	0.0	0.0	0.0	.
Q	0.0	0.0	0.0	0.0	0.0	0.0	0.0	0.0	0.0	.
X	2.1	0.0	0.0	0.0	0.0	0.0	0.0	0.0	0.0	.

Women - Femmes - Mujeres
ISIC 3 - CITI 3 - CIIU 3

	1999	2000	2001	2002	2003	2004	2005	2006	2007	2008
Total	0.3	0.2	0.3	0.2	0.1	0.5	0.3	0.1	0.3	.
A	0.0	0.0	6.0	0.0	0.0	0.0	6.8	0.0	0.0	.
B	0.0	0.0	0.0	0.0	0.0	1 075.3	0.0	0.0	0.0	.
C	0.0	0.0	0.0	0.0	0.0	0.0	0.0	0.0	0.0	.
D	1.0	0.5	1.0	0.5	0.5	0.0	0.0	0.6	0.0	.
E	0.0	0.0	0.0	0.0	0.0	0.0	0.0	0.0	0.0	.
F	5.8	0.0	0.0	0.0	0.0	0.0	0.0	0.0	0.0	.
G	0.5	0.0	0.0	0.0	0.0	0.4	0.4	0.0	0.0	.
H	0.0	0.0	0.0	0.0	0.0	1.7	0.0	0.0	0.0	.
I	0.0	2.5	1.3	0.0	1.4	2.9	1.5	0.0	4.3	.
J	0.0	0.0	0.0	0.0	0.0	0.0	0.0	0.0	0.0	.
K	0.5	0.0	0.0	1.0	0.0	0.4	0.9	0.4	0.4	.
L	0.0	0.0	0.8	0.0	0.0	1.6	0.0	0.0	0.0	.
M	0.0	0.0	0.0	0.0	0.0	0.0	0.0	0.0	0.0	.
N	0.0	0.0	0.0	0.2	0.0	0.2	0.2	0.0	0.0	.
O	0.0	0.0	0.0	0.0	0.0	0.9	0.0	0.0	1.7	.
P	0.0	0.0	0.0	0.0	0.0	0.0	0.0	0.0	0.0	.
Q	0.0	0.0	0.0	0.0	0.0	0.0	0.0	0.0	0.0	.
X	0.0	0.0	0.0	0.0	0.0	0.0	0.0	.	3.3	.

Rates of non-fatal injuries - Taux de lésions non mortelles - Tasas de lesiones no mortales

Per 100,000 workers employed - Pour 100 000 travailleurs occupés - Por 100 000 trabajadores empleados

Total men and women - Total hommes et femmes - Total hombres y mujeres
ISIC 3 - CITI 3 - CIIU 3

	1999	2000	2001	2002	2003	2004	2005	2006	2007	2008
Total	954	970	912	907	828	782	757	751	674	.
A	1 161	1 303	1 211	896	686	554	678	587	512	.
B	2 490	2 186	1 513	922	537	812	456	426	717	.
C	2 498	2 887	2 850	2 590	2 219	1 746	1 923	2 003	1 744	.
D	1 413	1 488	1 377	1 426	1 313	1 355	1 302	1 277	1 209	.
E	942	810	831	730	619	662	645	554	488	.
F	1 581	1 490	1 499	1 518	1 408	1 259	1 212	1 208	1 126	.
G	511	520	532	491	428	415	395	391	363	.
H	552	510	493	534	454	397	398	403	389	.
I	1 347	1 260	1 314	1 280	1 236	1 212	1 165	1 192	1 034	.
J	221	230	341	278	281	246	303	270	289	.
K	465	456	474	492	447	365	368	353	347	.
L	968	910	945	866	821	685	668	656	577	.
M	665	707	628	658	612	623	574	592	526	.
N	1 139	1 200	1 005	1 052	956	951	908	937	762	.
O	622	589	597	558	486	443	462	432	400	.
P	.	.	.	0	0	0	0	0	0	.
Q	.	.	.	0	408	407	0	0	0	.
X	.	.	.	289	298	263	.	.	321	.

Explanatory notes: see p. 1125. Notes explicatives: voir p. 1127. Notas explicativas: véase p. 1129.

OCCUPATIONAL INJURIES
LÉSIONS PROFESSIONNELLES
LESIONES PROFESIONALES

Rates of occupational injuries, by economic activity
Taux de lésions professionnelles, par activité économique
Tasas de lesiones profesionales, por actividad económica

	1999	2000	2001	2002	2003	2004	2005	2006	2007	2008

Sweden (FA) — Reported injuries - Lésions déclarées - Lesiones declaradas

Rates of non-fatal injuries - Taux de lésions non mortelles - Tasas de lesiones no mortales

Per 100,000 workers employed - Pour 100 000 travailleurs occupés - Por 100 000 trabajadores empleados

Men - Hommes - Hombres
ISIC 3 - CITI 3 - CIIU 3

	1999	2000	2001	2002	2003	2004	2005	2006	2007	2008
Total	1 109	1 110	1 088	1 057	959	893	866	848	774	.
A	1 256	1 409	1 321	917	675	543	664	592	505	
B	2 585	2 372	1 633	1 005	580	878	495	387	786	
C	2 732	3 166	3 079	2 813	2 375	1 830	2 002	2 059	1 829	
D	1 561	1 640	1 525	1 574	1 444	1 478	1 410	1 380	1 285	
E	1 126	990	1 004	919	733	815	789	635	595	
F	1 686	1 590	1 597	1 610	1 487	1 321	1 278	1 274	1 181	
G	588	610	637	582	502	484	454	458	413	
H	546	530	478	534	398	375	335	362	327	
I	1 467	1 370	1 446	1 373	1 312	1 292	1 253	1 264	1 088	
J	132	150	246	132	121	133	185	172	192	
K	541	527	567	541	495	403	413	399	399	
L	1 246	1 180	1 322	1 096	1 032	926	858	860	739	
M	599	577	517	502	443	460	452	393	395	
N	1 047	1 070	894	861	783	705	682	705	570	
O	910	880	860	791	680	595	633	580	560	
P				0	0	0	0	0	0	
Q	.			0	1 190	0	0	0	0	
X				364	445	427			447	

Women - Femmes - Mujeres
ISIC 3 - CITI 3 - CIIU 3

	1999	2000	2001	2002	2003	2004	2005	2006	2007	2008
Total	783	810	721	744	687	661	639	645	565	
A	834	933	828	821	733	603	737	568	540	
B	1 299	0	0	0	0	0	0	0		
C	815	719	1 084	858	1 059	1 055	1 314	0	1 174	
D	993	1 063	963	1 006	940	981	974	962	974	
E	305	220	320	194	265	202	206	317	172	
F	356	270	350	409	445	503	418	421	465	
G	411	420	400	377	335	327	318	306	299	
H	557	500	505	534	500	415	451	437	440	
I	1 052	980	985	1 033	1 025	984	928	984	874	
J	292	290	415	391	406	332	394	350	371	
K	354	350	339	419	375	309	299	283	267	
L	701	670	606	661	635	473	506	486	445	
M	697	768	679	711	668	677	615	658	570	
N	1 153	1 220	1 023	1 087	988	998	952	982	801	
O	369	336	369	353	317	311	314	306	264	
P				0	0	0	0	0	0	
Q				0	0	637	0	0	0	
X				204	183	134			226	

Turkey (FA) — Reported injuries - Lésions déclarées - Lesiones declaradas

Rates of fatal injuries - Taux de lésions mortelles - Tasas de lesiones mortales

Per 100,000 workers insured - Pour 100 000 travailleurs assurés - Por 100 000 trabajadores asegurados

Total men and women - Total hommes et femmes - Total hombres y mujeres
ISIC 2 - CITI 2 - CIIU 2

	1999	2000	2001	2002	2003	2004	2005	2006	2007	2008
Total	22.9	24.6	20.6	16.8	14.4	13.6	15.8	20.5	.	.
1	16.7	25.9	35.0	21.3	13.4	11.5	29.8	20.1		
2	338.3	94.5	171.1	81.7	98.7	78.7	124.5	74.2		
3	10.2	12.1	12.2	9.1	8.4	8.3	9.5	9.2		
4	20.6	21.2	17.0	17.7	14.2	12.1	15.3	17.7		
5	38.0	48.6	50.0	44.7	39.9	35.0	31.1	33.5		
6	10.3	8.1	10.9	8.2	8.7	6.5	6.9	6.9		
7	45.2	40.9	43.4	38.1	24.2	26.0	34.0	29.9		
8	5.1	5.3	4.6	1.2	2.3	2.2	4.9	1.7		
9	7.2	19.2	5.9	5.5	4.0	4.1	4.2	4.0		

Men - Hommes - Hombres
ISIC 2 - CITI 2 - CIIU 2

	1999	2000	2001	2002	2003	2004	2005	2006	2007	2008
Total	.	.	25.3	20.7	17.9	16.9	19.7	25.6	.	.
1			40.4	22.7	15.4	13.0	34.3	23.3		
2			119.4	83.0	99.6	80.4	126.9	75.7		
3			14.6	11.1	10.0	10.2	11.7	11.2		
4			18.0	19.2	15.3	13.0	16.7	19.2		
5			52.5	46.2	41.8	36.5	32.3	34.9		
6			14.1	10.8	11.7	8.8	8.9	9.3		
7			49.4	43.0	27.7	29.6	38.3	34.0		
8			7.6	1.9	3.9	0.0	8.6	3.0		
9			8.1	7.4	5.4	5.8	5.9	5.9		

Explanatory notes: see p. 1125.   Notes explicatives: voir p. 1127.   Notas explicativas: véase p. 1129.

OCCUPATIONAL INJURIES

Rates of occupational injuries, by economic activity

LÉSIONS PROFESSIONNELLES

Taux de lésions professionnelles, par activité économique

LESIONES PROFESIONALES

Tasas de lesiones profesionales, por actividad económica

8B

	1999	2000	2001	2002	2003	2004	2005	2006	2007	2008

Turkey (FA) — Reported injuries - Lésions déclarées - Lesiones declaradas

Rates of fatal injuries - Taux de lésions mortelles - Tasas de lesiones mortales

Per 100,000 workers insured - Pour 100 000 travailleurs assurés - Por 100 000 trabajadores asegurados

Women - Femmes - Mujeres
ISIC 2 - CITI 2 - CIIU 2

	1999	2000	2001	2002	2003	2004	2005	2006	2007	2008
Total	.	.	1.7	1.3	1.3	0.9	1.0	0.9	.	.
1	.	.	0.0	11.6	0.0	0.0	0.0	0.0	.	.
2	.	.	0.0	0.0	58.4	0.0	0.0	0.0	.	.
3	.	.	3.1	2.2	2.3	1.2	0.8	1.1	.	.
4	.	.	0.0	0.0	0.0	0.0	0.0	0.0	.	.
5	.	.	0.0	0.0	0.0	0.0	0.0	0.0	.	.
6	.	.	1.3	0.0	0.0	0.0	1.3	0.4	.	.
7	.	.	2.3	0.0	0.0	0.0	3.3	0.0	.	.
8	.	.	0.0	0.0	0.0	5.6	0.0	0.0	.	.
9	.	.	0.7	0.9	0.8	0.2	0.8	0.3	.	.

Rates of non-fatal injuries - Taux de lésions non mortelles - Tasas de lesiones no mortales

Per 100,000 workers insured - Pour 100 000 travailleurs assurés - Por 100 000 trabajadores asegurados

Total men and women - Total hommes et femmes - Total hombres y mujeres
ISIC 2 - CITI 2 - CIIU 2

	1999	2000	2001	2002	2003	2004	2005	2006	2007	2008
Total	68	35	45	40	28	27	24	29	.	.
1	28	37	32	30	24	23	16	26	.	.
2	1 227	366	466	376	238	387	323	416	.	.
3	66	37	51	47	32	28	25	35	.	.
4	27	15	27	23	16	15	14	24	.	.
5	95	51	76	63	52	46	35	36	.	.
6	11	11	12	12	10	6	6	8	.	.
7	44	30	33	35	30	21	17	24	.	.
8	3	1	2	5	1	3	0	1	.	.
9	9	9	7	8	5	4	3	6	.	.

Men - Hommes - Hombres
ISIC 2 - CITI 2 - CIIU 2

	1999	2000	2001	2002	2003	2004	2005	2006	2007	2008
Total	.	.	54	48	35	33	29	36	.	.
1	.	.	33	30	22	24	17	29	.	.
2	.	.	475	383	243	395	329	424	.	.
3	.	.	61	58	39	33	30	42	.	.
4	.	.	28	25	18	16	15	26	.	.
5	.	.	79	64	54	48	36	37	.	.
6	.	.	15	15	12	7	7	10	.	.
7	.	.	37	38	33	24	19	27	.	.
8	.	.	4	6	2	5	0	2	.	.
9	.	.	9	11	7	6	5	9	.	.

Women - Femmes - Mujeres
ISIC 2 - CITI 2 - CIIU 2

	1999	2000	2001	2002	2003	2004	2005	2006	2007	2008
Total	.	.	7	6	4	4	3	4	.	.
1	.	.	23	35	12	13	10	9	.	.
2	.	.	0	0	0	0	0	0	.	.
3	.	.	11	9	5	8	4	6	.	.
4	.	.	0	7	0	0	0	0	.	.
5	.	.	3	4	3	3	0	2	.	.
6	.	.	4	4	4	2	2	3	.	.
7	.	.	7	10	9	0	8	9	.	.
8	.	.	0	4	0	0	0	0	.	.
9	.	.	3	3	2	1	1	1	.	.

Ukraine (FF) — Reported injuries - Lésions déclarées - Lesiones declaradas

Rates of fatal injuries - Taux de lésions mortelles - Tasas de lesiones mortales

Per 100,000 workers employed - Pour 100 000 travailleurs occupés - Por 100 000 trabajadores empleados

Total men and women - Total hommes et femmes - Total hombres y mujeres
ISIC 3 - CITI 3 - CIIU 3

	1999	2000	2001	2002	2003	2004	2005	2006	2007	2008
Total	9.2	9.5	10.5	10.0	9.4	8.9	8.4	8.3	9.3	8.0

Men - Hommes - Hombres
ISIC 3 - CITI 3 - CIIU 3

	1999	2000	2001	2002	2003	2004	2005	2006	2007	2008
Total	17.1	.	19.5	18.7	18.2	17.0	15.7	15.7	17.8	15.6

Women - Femmes - Mujeres
ISIC 3 - CITI 3 - CIIU 3

	1999	2000	2001	2002	2003	2004	2005	2006	2007	2008
Total	1.3	.	1.3	1.5	1.0	1.2	1.4	1.2	1.5	1.1

Rates of non-fatal injuries - Taux de lésions non mortelles - Tasas de lesiones no mortales

Per 100,000 workers employed - Pour 100 000 travailleurs occupés - Por 100 000 trabajadores empleados

Total men and women - Total hommes et femmes - Total hombres y mujeres
ISIC 3 - CITI 3 - CIIU 3

	1999	2000	2001	2002	2003	2004	2005	2006	2007	2008
Total	294	253	258	216	205	186	172	160	155	135

Men - Hommes - Hombres
ISIC 3 - CITI 3 - CIIU 3

	1999	2000	2001	2002	2003	2004	2005	2006	2007	2008
Total	499	.	428	362	341	306	279	258	257	223

Explanatory notes: see p. 1125.   Notes explicatives: voir p. 1127.   Notas explicativas: véase p. 1129.

8B

	OCCUPATIONAL INJURIES	LÉSIONS PROFESSIONNELLES	LESIONES PROFESIONALES
	Rates of occupational injuries, by economic activity	Taux de lésions professionnelles, par activité économique	Tasas de lesiones profesionales, por actividad económica

	1999	2000	2001	2002	2003	2004	2005	2006	2007	2008

Ukraine (FF) — Reported injuries - Lésions déclarées - Lesiones declaradas

Rates of non-fatal injuries - Taux de lésions non mortelles - Tasas de lesiones no mortales

Per 100,000 workers employed - Pour 100 000 travailleurs occupés - Por 100 000 trabajadores empleados

Women - Femmes - Mujeres
ISIC 3 - CITI 3 - CIIU 3

	1999	2000	2001	2002	2003	2004	2005	2006	2007	2008
Total	87	.	85	74	75	69	69	66	60	55

United Kingdom (FF) [1] — Reported injuries - Lésions déclarées - Lesiones declaradas

Rates of fatal injuries - Taux de lésions mortelles - Tasas de lesiones mortales

Per 100,000 employees - Pour 100 000 salariés - Por 100 000 asalariados

Total men and women - Total hommes et femmes - Total hombres y mujeres
ISIC 3 - CITI 3 - CIIU 3

	1999	2000	2001	2002	2003	2004	2005	2006	2007	2008
Total	0.7	0.9	0.8	0.7	0.7	0.7	0.6	0.7	.	.
A	4.4	4.6	7.8	6.2	2.7	6.8	5.8	6.4	.	.
B	0.0	0.0	0.0	23.4	0.0	0.0	0.0	14.9	.	.
C	5.6	12.3	12.3	4.6	11.7	3.5	8.8	15.4	.	.
D	1.1	1.2	1.3	1.2	0.8	1.4	1.4	1.3	.	.
E	1.6	0.0	3.7	1.5	2.5	0.0	1.0	1.0	.	.
F	5.7	6.4	5.3	5.1	4.4	4.9	3.7	4.5	.	.
G	1.0	0.3	0.3	0.3	0.3	0.2	0.3	0.1	.	.
H	0.1	0.2	0.1	0.1	0.3	0.1	0.1	0.2	.	.
I	1.3	2.2	1.5	1.7	2.0	1.3	1.3	2.1	.	.
J	0.0	0.1	0.0	0.2	0.0	0.0	0.1	0.0	.	.
K	0.2	0.2	0.3	0.2	0.2	0.1	0.4	0.2	.	.
L	0.1	0.2	0.3	0.3	0.3	0.6	0.1	0.4	.	.
M	0.0	0.1	0.1	0.0	0.0	0.0	0.0	0.1	.	.
N	0.0	0.1	37.4	0.0	0.1	0.0	0.1	0.1	.	.
O				0.7	0.5	0.9	0.6	1.2	.	.
O-Q	0.7	0.8	0.8					1.2	.	.

Men - Hommes - Hombres
ISIC 3 - CITI 3 - CIIU 3

	1999	2000	2001	2002	2003	2004	2005	2006	2007	2008
Total	1.3	1.6	1.6	1.4	1.3	1.3	1.2	1.4	.	.
A	6.2	6.0	10.7	7.9	3.8	10.1	8.6	8.5	.	.
B	0.0	0.0	0.0	27.7	0.0	0.0	0.0	17.1	.	.
C	6.4	13.9	14.2	5.3	13.2	4.0	10.2	17.9	.	.
D	1.5	1.6	1.8	1.6	1.1	1.7	1.9	1.8	.	.
E	2.2	0.0	5.8	2.3	3.6	0.0	1.5	1.4	.	.
F	6.7	7.6	6.2	6.0	5.2	5.7	4.4	5.3	.	.
G	0.3	0.6	0.6	0.6	0.6	0.3	0.5	0.3	.	.
H	0.2	0.6	0.2	0.0	0.4	0.3	0.1	0.4	.	.
I	1.8	3.0	2.0	2.4	2.8	1.8	1.7	2.9	.	.
J	0.0	0.2	.	0.0	0.0	0.0	0.2	0.0	.	.
K	0.4	0.3	.	0.4	0.4	0.2	0.7	0.3	.	.
L	0.3	0.3	.	0.7	0.7	1.3	0.1	0.7	.	.
M	0.0	0.3	0.2	0.0	0.0	0.2	0.0	0.5	.	.
N	0.0	0.4	0.2	0.0	0.4	0.0	1.0	0.2	.	.
O				1.3	0.8	1.8	1.0	2.4	.	.
O-Q	1.5	1.6	1.7					2.4	.	.

Women - Femmes - Mujeres
ISIC 3 - CITI 3 - CIIU 3

	1999	2000	2001	2002	2003	2004	2005	2006	2007	2008
Total	-	-	0.0	0.1	0.1	0.1	0.1	0.0	.	.
A	0.0	1.2	1.3	1.7	0.0	0.0	0.0	1.4	.	.
B	0.0	0.0	0.0	0.0	0.0	0.0	0.0	0.0	.	.
C	0.0	0.0	0.0	0.0	0.0	0.0	0.0	0.0	.	.
D	0.1	0.3	0.0	0.2	0.0	0.6	0.0	0.0	.	.
E	0.0	0.0	0.0	0.0	0.0	0.0	0.0	0.0	.	.
F	0.0	0.0	0.0	0.0	0.0	0.0	0.0	0.0	.	.
G	0.0	0.0	0.0	0.0	0.0	0.0	0.0	0.0	.	.
H	0.0	0.0	0.0	0.0	0.2	0.0	0.1	0.1	.	.
I	0.0	0.0	0.2	0.0	0.0	0.0	0.2	0.0	.	.
J	0.0	0.0	0.0	0.4	0.0	0.0	0.0	0.0	.	.
K	0.0	0.0	0.0	0.0	0.0	0.5	0.0	0.0	.	.
L	0.0	0.1	0.0	0.0	0.0	0.0	0.1	0.1	.	.
M	0.0	0.0	0.1	0.0	0.1	0.0	0.1	0.0	.	.
N	0.0	0.0	0.0	0.1	0.1	0.0	0.0	0.1	.	.
O				0.1	0.3	0.0	0.1	0.0	.	.
O-Q	0.0	0.0	0.0					0.0	.	.

Explanatory notes: see p. 1125.

[1] Year beginning in April of year indicated; prior to 1994: excl. Northern Ireland.

Notes explicatives: voir p. 1127.

[1] Année commençant en avril de l'année indiquée; avant 1994: non compris l'Irlande du Nord.

Notas explicativas: véase p. 1129.

[1] Año que comienza en abril del año indicado; antes de 1994: excl. Irlanda del Norte.

OCCUPATIONAL INJURIES

Rates of occupational injuries, by economic activity

LÉSIONS PROFESSIONNELLES

Taux de lésions professionnelles, par activité économique

LESIONES PROFESIONALES

Tasas de lesiones profesionales, por actividad económica

	1999	2000	2001	2002	2003	2004	2005	2006	2007	2008

United Kingdom (FF) [1]   Reported injuries - Lésions déclarées - Lesiones declaradas

Rates of non-fatal injuries - Taux de lésions non mortelles - Tasas de lesiones no mortales

Per 100,000 employees - Pour 100 000 salariés - Por 100 000 asalariados

Total men and women - Total hommes et femmes - Total hombres y mujeres
ISIC 3 - CITI 3 - CIIU 3

	1999	2000	2001	2002	2003	2004	2005	2006	2007	2008
Total	666	645	623	614	630	585	562	515	.	.
A	709	697	841	833	667	595	599	545	.	.
B	325	387	388	292	504	682	435	461	.	.
C	2 376	2 442	2 321	2 086	1 923	1 653	1 417	1 400	.	.
D	1 209	1 191	1 157	1 153	1 117	1 036	995	942	.	.
E	1 035	1 038	767	742	911	982	970	925	.	.
F	1 296	1 189	1 134	1 122	994	968	926	868	.	.
G	429	413	394	415	432	418	405	389	.	.
H	263	250	245	250	283	288	287	284	.	.
I	1 584	1 687	1 640	1 698	1 774	1 672	1 604	1 541	.	.
J	68	68	99	103	111	113	93	96	.	.
K	140	118	166	175	265	238	218	207	.	.
L	1 292	1 302	1 238	1 179	1 505	1 362	1 377	1 352	.	.
M	317	298	280	263	176	167	165	182	.	.
N	617	579	552	526	548	495	498	504	.	.
O	.	.	.	383	301	302	287	296	.	.
O-Q	474	470	420	.	.	.	.	298	.	.

Men - Hommes - Hombres
ISIC 3 - CITI 3 - CIIU 3

	1999	2000	2001	2002	2003	2004	2005	2006	2007	2008
Total	979	946	922	902	906	841	798	723	.	.
A	823	816	1 011	942	788	751	750	673	.	.
B	380	410	434	332	551	774	490	461	.	.
C	2 656	2 741	2 623	2 377	2 129	1 880	1 628	1 593	.	.
D	1 439	1 426	1 383	1 365	1 297	1 216	1 161	1 104	.	.
E	1 374	1 366	1 123	1 070	1 255	1 306	1 349	1 263	.	.
F	1 490	1 368	1 293	1 274	1 147	1 111	1 070	1 006	.	.
G	560	543	518	540	549	540	512	483	.	.
H	315	298	305	309	326	328	329	326	.	.
I	1 984	2 063	2 056	2 103	2 216	2 038	1 929	1 857	.	.
J	43	42	77	64	74	79	53	59	.	.
K	191	157	228	239	366	330	302	281	.	.
L	2 051	1 917	1 820	1 737	1 982	1 887	1 886	1 806	.	.
M	407	350	347	318	243	229	225	255	.	.
N	1 075	955	964	926	897	732	430	1 059	.	.
O	.	.	.	572	462	449	430	432	.	.
O-Q	714	713	653	.	.	.	.	435	.	.

Women - Femmes - Mujeres
ISIC 3 - CITI 3 - CIIU 3

	1999	2000	2001	2002	2003	2004	2005	2006	2007	2008
Total	344	334	320	320	347	327	324	301	.	.
A	420	417	464	532	349	272	289	245	.	.
B	50	283	178	75	266	200	114	463	.	.
C	156	208	384	184	334	216	158	209	.	.
D	608	578	564	575	578	518	502	460	.	.
E	158	180	146	129	151	199	153	217	.	.
F	196	170	213	196	116	134	124	25	.	.
G	307	292	280	300	321	302	302	289	.	.
H	227	217	205	208	251	258	256	251	.	.
I	586	680	628	658	677	694	707	647	.	.
J	92	89	118	138	143	143	128	129	.	.
K	87	75	97	102	142	125	120	117	.	.
L	604	660	631	606	1 019	897	930	945	.	.
M	283	0	252	241	149	142	143	156	.	.
N	521	0	467	446	477	439	449	452	.	.
O	.	.	.	203	149	161	149	165	.	.
O-Q	251	245	200	.	.	.	.	166	.	.

Explanatory notes: see p. 1125.

[1] Year beginning in April of year indicated; prior to 1994: excl. Northern Ireland. [2] Financial year ending in year indicated; excl. Victoria and Australian Capital Territory.

Notes explicatives: voir p. 1127.

[1] Année commençant en avril de l'année indiquée; avant 1994: non compris l'Irlande du Nord. [2] Année fiscale se terminant en l'année indiquée; non compris Victoria et Australian Capital Territory.

Notas explicativas: véase p. 1129.

[1] Año que comienza en abril del año indicado; antes de 1994: excl. Irlanda del Norte. [2] Año fiscal que se termina en el año indicado; excl. Victoria y Australian Capital Territory.

8B

	OCCUPATIONAL INJURIES	LÉSIONS PROFESSIONNELLES	LESIONES PROFESIONALES
	Rates of occupational injuries, by economic activity	Taux de lésions professionnelles, par activité économique	Tasas de lesiones profesionales, por actividad económica

	1999	2000	2001	2002	2003	2004	2005	2006	2007	2008

OCEANIA-OCÉANIE-OCEANIA

Australia (FA) [1] Compensated injuries - Lésions indemnisées - Lesiones indemnizadas

Rates of fatal injuries - Taux de lésions mortelles - Tasas de lesiones mortales

Per 100,000 employees - Pour 100 000 salariés - Por 100 000 asalariados

Total men and women - Total hommes et femmes - Total hombres y mujeres
ISIC 3 - CITI 3 - CIIU 3

	1999	2000	2001	2002	2003	2004	2005	2006	2007	2008
Total	2.0	2.0	2.6	2.4	2.3	2.0	1.9	2.1	2.0	.
A-B	11.1	14.4	13.9	8.8	13.2	12.3	14.1	12.8	7.2	.
C	15.0	17.0	21.3	11.8	15.7	6.6	5.0	9.8	4.7	.
D	1.0	2.0	3.3	2.6	2.5	2.8	2.0	2.8	3.0	.
E	3.0	4.0	3.0	3.1	1.4	2.7	2.7	6.0	0.0	.
F	8.0	7.0	8.0	5.9	5.5	4.9	3.6	4.7	4.5	.
G	1.0	1.0	1.0	1.1	1.1	1.3	0.9	0.7	0.9	.
H	1.0	0.0	0.4	0.4	0.4	0.2	0.6	0.8	0.6	.
I	9.0	8.0	8.6	10.8	11.0	7.3	8.4	7.3	8.0	.
J	0.0	0.0	0.9	0.3	0.3	0.3	0.0	0.0	0.0	.
K	2.0	1.0	1.5	1.5	1.3	1.2	1.2	2.2	1.0	.
L	1.0	1.0	1.2	0.7	2.7	1.7	1.7	1.1	2.4	.
M	0.0	1.0	0.6	0.6	0.4	0.3	0.3	0.5	0.3	.
N-O	1.0	1.0	1.5	1.8	0.9	0.9	1.0	0.7	0.9	.

Men - Hommes - Hombres
ISIC 3 - CITI 3 - CIIU 3

	1999	2000	2001	2002	2003	2004	2005	2006	2007	2008
Total	4.0	4.0	4.5	4.3	4.0	3.6	3.6	3.7	3.3	.
A-B	15.0	18.0	18.7	11.7	17.4	16.4	18.9	17.0	8.5	.
C	17.0	19.0	24.0	13.3	15.0	7.5	5.7	11.5	5.4	.
D	2.0	3.0	4.4	3.6	3.2	3.3	2.5	3.7	4.0	.
E	3.0	3.0	3.6	3.9	1.8	3.4	3.3	7.6	0.0	.
F	9.0	8.0	8.8	6.8	6.1	5.4	3.8	5.4	5.1	.
G	2.0	1.0	1.9	2.0	2.0	2.3	1.7	1.2	1.6	.
H	2.0	1.0	0.9	1.0	1.0	0.5	0.9	1.5	0.9	.
I	13.0	11.0	11.7	14.0	15.0	9.7	11.5	9.9	10.7	.
J	0.0	0.0	2.2	0.7	0.0	0.7	0.0	0.0	0.0	.
K	3.0	2.0	2.1	2.5	2.2	2.0	2.1	3.2	1.6	.
L	2.0	2.0	2.4	0.8	4.3	3.4	2.9	2.1	2.5	.
M	1.0	3.0	1.4	1.4	0.5	0.4	0.9	1.3	0.4	.
N-O	2.0	3.0	3.9	5.1	2.0	1.9	2.7	1.8	2.5	.
X	0.1	0.0	0.0	0.0	0.0	0.0	0.0	.	.	.

Women - Femmes - Mujeres
ISIC 3 - CITI 3 - CIIU 3

	1999	2000	2001	2002	2003	2004	2005	2006	2007	2008
Total	0.0	0.0	0.4	0.3	0.4	0.3	0.3	0.3	0.5	.
A-B	0.0	3.0	1.8	1.6	2.0	1.9	1.9	2.0	3.8	.
C	0.0	0.0	0.0	0.0	21.5	0.0	0.0	0.0	0.0	.
D	0.0	0.0	0.4	0.0	0.4	0.4	0.8	0.0	0.0	.
E	0.0	8.0	0.0	0.0	0.0	0.0	0.0	0.0	0.0	.
F	0.0	0.0	1.9	0.0	1.7	1.6	2.8	0.0	0.0	.
G	0.0	0.0	0.4	0.1	0.1	0.2	0.1	0.1	0.3	.
H	0.0	0.0	0.0	0.0	0.0	0.0	0.3	0.3	0.3	.
I	0.0	0.0	0.7	2.3	0.0	1.3	0.6	0.6	1.2	.
J	0.0	0.0	0.0	0.0	0.5	0.0	0.0	0.0	0.0	.
K	0.0	0.0	0.7	0.4	0.2	0.4	0.2	1.0	0.2	.
L	0.0	1.0	0.0	0.5	0.9	0.0	0.4	0.0	2.3	.
M	0.0	0.0	0.2	0.2	0.4	0.2	0.0	0.2	0.2	.
N-O	0.0	0.0	0.4	0.3	0.4	0.4	0.3	0.3	0.2	.
O	0.9	0.8	0.8	0.0	0.4	.	.	.	.	.

Rates of non-fatal injuries - Taux de lésions non mortelles - Tasas de lesiones no mortales

Per 100,000 employees - Pour 100 000 salariés - Por 100 000 asalariados

Total men and women - Total hommes et femmes - Total hombres y mujeres
ISIC 3 - CITI 3 - CIIU 3

	1999	2000	2001	2002	2003	2004	2005	2006	2007	2008
Total	1 660	1 620	1 440	1 390	1 270	1 230	1 190	1 040	1 030	.
A-B	2 870	2 860	2 540	2 370	2 580	2 360	2 250	2 090	2 090	.
C	2 820	2 630	2 460	2 480	2 210	2 060	1 960	1 480	1 580	.
D	2 960	2 760	1 090	1 050	1 000	1 120	1 110	1 030	1 080	.
E	1 430	1 390	1 070	1 060	670	720	710	500	590	.
F	2 860	2 640	2 620	2 380	2 230	2 180	2 000	1 750	1 650	.
G	1 190	1 260	1 160	1 070	920	890	850	780	770	.
H	1 480	1 470	1 240	1 220	1 220	1 150	1 050	980	960	.
I	2 480	2 290	2 110	2 260	2 060	1 830	1 710	1 540	1 510	.
J	320	540	280	290	260	260	210	210	200	.
K	1 000	950	860	860	830	820	850	730	670	.
L	980	1 100	850	900	1 490	1 370	1 310	1 030	960	.
M	780	840	690	660	490	500	540	500	510	.
N-O	1 700	1 610	1 490	1 410	1 150	1 160	1 130	960	960	.

Explanatory notes: see p. 1125. Notes explicatives: voir p. 1127. Notas explicativas: véase p. 1129.

[1] Financial year ending in year indicated; excl. Victoria and Australian Capital Territory. [1] Année fiscale se terminant en l'année indiquée; non compris Victoria et Australian Capital Territory. [1] Año fiscal que se termina en el año indicado; excl. Victoria y Australian Capital Territory.

OCCUPATIONAL INJURIES

Rates of occupational injuries, by economic activity

LÉSIONS PROFESSIONNELLES

Taux de lésions professionnelles, par activité économique

LESIONES PROFESIONALES

Tasas de lesiones profesionales, por actividad económica

8B

	1999	2000	2001	2002	2003	2004	2005	2006	2007	2008

Australia (FA) [1]   Compensated injuries - Lésions indemnisées - Lesiones indemnizadas

Rates of non-fatal injuries - Taux de lésions non mortelles - Tasas de lesiones no mortales

Per 100,000 employees - Pour 100 000 salariés - Por 100 000 asalariados

Men - Hommes - Hombres
ISIC 3 - CITI 3 - CIIU 3

	1999	2000	2001	2002	2003	2004	2005	2006	2007	2008
Total	2 210	2 141	1 895	1 831	1 685	1 621	1 562	1 385	1 354	.
A-B	3 390	3 350	2 970	2 750	3 000	2 710	2 580	2 340	2 380	.
C	3 020	2 890	2 690	2 720	2 390	2 250	2 160	1 680	1 750	.
D	3 390	3 200	1 460	1 400	1 320	1 490	1 480	1 360	1 420	.
E	1 690	1 630	1 230	1 270	810	850	790	570	690	.
F	3 180	2 930	2 920	2 660	2 520	2 420	2 250	1 940	1 830	.
G	1 540	1 590	1 580	1 390	1 200	1 150	1 100	1 040	1 040	.
H	1 680	1 700	1 370	1 490	1 480	1 290	1 200	1 150	1 090	.
I	3 050	2 780	2 570	2 720	2 490	2 270	2 120	1 870	1 860	.
J	210	190	150	170	170	130	120	110	110	.
K	1 300	1 240	1 110	1 110	1 110	1 110	1 160	1 000	910	.
L	1 290	1 480	1 180	1 190	1 740	1 580	1 550	1 200	1 220	.
M	1 050	1 160	870	790	600	580	610	550	570	.
N-O	2 050	2 060	1 860	1 750	1 420	1 400	1 330	1 170	1 130	.

Women - Femmes - Mujeres
ISIC 3 - CITI 3 - CIIU 3

	1999	2000	2001	2002	2003	2004	2005	2006	2007	2008
Total	1 030	1 010	930	900	800	790	770	670	660	.
A-B	1 560	1 610	1 440	1 410	1 470	1 450	1 410	1 450	1 370	.
C	930	470	580	680	750	730	570	330	510	.
D	1 700	1 540	80	80	70	90	80	90	90	.
E	250	270	270	280	200	270	360	170	170	.
F	430	400	410	410	320	380	310	330	300	.
G	790	900	850	780	670	660	630	560	570	.
H	1 330	1 310	1 130	1 050	1 040	1 050	940	870	860	.
I	1 030	960	940	1 000	870	730	700	680	640	.
J	410	380	380	380	340	360	280	290	270	.
K	650	610	570	570	520	500	480	400	380	.
L	600	670	500	560	1 220	1 130	1 060	840	720	.
M	650	680	610	600	450	470	510	470	490	.
N-O	1 530	1 400	1 320	1 260	1 030	1 060	1 040	870	890	.

Explanatory notes: see p. 1125.

[1] Financial year ending in year indicated; excl. Victoria and Australian Capital Territory.

Notes explicatives: voir p. 1127.

[1] Année fiscale se terminant en l'année indiquée; non compris Victoria et Australian Capital Territory.

Notas explicativas: véase p. 1129.

[1] Año fiscal que se termina en el año indicado; excl. Victoria y Australian Capital Territory.

OCCUPATIONAL INJURIES
Days lost, by economic activity

LÉSIONS PROFESSIONNELLES
Journées perdues, par activité économique

LESIONES PROFESIONALES
Días perdidos, por actividad económica

8C

	1999	2000	2001	2002	2003	2004	2005	2006	2007	2008

AFRICA-AFRIQUE-AFRICA

Algérie (FA)

Compensated injuries - Lésions indemnisées - Lesiones indemnizadas

Total men and women - Total hommes et femmes - Total hombres y mujeres
ISIC 3 - CITI 3 - CIIU 3

	1999	2000	2001	2002	2003	2004	2005	2006	2007	2008
Total	1 045 667	1 072 700	965 094	1 047 422	1 248 337	1 259 511	.	.	.	.
D	400 856	404 826	348 660	386 033	419 370	.	.	.	.	.
E	9 841	11 257	9 633	10 059	16 071	16 369	.	.	.	.
F	228 050	223 497	208 471	239 919	286 841	291 701	.	.	.	.
G	23 458	21 682	25 835	20 651	25 918	23 486	.	.	.	.
I [1]	60 291	58 262	52 935	50 053	59 677	60 371	.	.	.	.
X	325 200	352 029	318 525	340 707	440 460	315 670	.	.	.	.

Togo (FA)

Reported injuries - Lésions déclarées - Lesiones declaradas

Total men and women - Total hommes et femmes - Total hombres y mujeres
ISIC 2 - CITI 2 - CIIU 2

	1999	2000	2001	2002	2003	2004	2005	2006	2007	2008
Total	7 701	6 663	6 032	3 535	3 767	5 768	.	.	.	.
2	1 630	1 139	1 062	931	581	27	.	.	.	.
3	2 619	2 046	1 772	1 076	1 252	2 431	.	.	.	.
4	404	525	495	295	291	884	.	.	.	.
5	172	165	103	10	126	81	.	.	.	.
6,8	66	113	60	140	58	502	.	.	.	.
7	176	132	145	57	39	835	.	.	.	.
9	1 993	1 838	1 864	317	729	884	.	.	.	.
0	641	704	531	709	691	124	.	.	.	.

Tunisie (FA)

Compensated injuries - Lésions indemnisées - Lesiones indemnizadas

Total men and women - Total hommes et femmes - Total hombres y mujeres
ISIC 3 - CITI 3 - CIIU 3

	1999	2000	2001	2002	2003	2004	2005	2006	2007	2008
Total	855 646	982 553	1 108 871	1 132 357	1 065 338	1 059 962	.	.	.	.
A	24 273	24 957	31 044	33 149	33 746	32 012	.	.	.	.
B	10 188	8 971	12 841	10 977	9 359	11 866	.	.	.	.
C	16 977	19 159	25 372	21 777	23 471	22 608	.	.	.	.
D	430 297	471 758	547 422	584 266	549 669	540 513	.	.	.	.
E-F	156 662	199 910	211 755	208 291	182 516	180 825	.	.	.	.
G,J	58 566	66 693	69 375	67 653	68 012	71 206	.	.	.	.
H	42 217	43 374	46 796	43 189	38 860	40 203	.	.	.	.
I	52 680	68 858	66 865	63 667	56 337	51 485	.	.	.	.
K-Q	63 786	78 873	97 401	99 388	103 368	109 244	.	.	.	.

AMERICA-AMÉRIQUE-AMERICA

Argentina (FA) [2]

Reported injuries - Lésions déclarées - Lesiones declaradas

Total men and women - Total hommes et femmes - Total hombres y mujeres
ISIC 2 - CITI 2 - CIIU 2

	1999	2000	2001	2002	2003	2004	2005	2006	2007	2008
Total	7 426 709	7 771 910	.	6 381 975	7 748 171	10 245 610	12 022 892	14 765 377	17 818 104	.
1	695 110	627 279	.	574 236	727 106	938 782	982 500	1 167 028	1 229 124	.
2	40 921	41 724	.	32 026	41 652	61 810	66 533	78 543	102 980	.
3	2 161 329	1 883 896	.	1 388 588	1 818 168	2 367 651	2 669 291	3 182 282	3 843 657	.
4	91 138	86 865	.	78 742	89 058	96 149	106 087	110 696	117 210	.
5	970 498	775 817	.	317 413	501 250	873 567	1 258 062	1 751 026	2 212 644	.
6	1 020 680	1 069 238	.	874 089	998 620	1 327 310	1 559 506	1 954 825	2 342 279	.
7	614 143	770 044	.	683 815	760 721	892 363	1 035 520	1 245 961	1 518 891	.
8	403 528	554 630	.	486 141	575 671	761 489	869 189	1 118 725	1 421 482	.
9	1 409 682	1 948 618	.	1 939 405	2 219 576	2 915 440	3 466 071	4 144 408	5 011 124	.
0	19 680	13 799	.	7 520	8 591	11 049	6 167	6 692	7 277	.

Explanatory notes: see p. 1125.
[1] Excl. communications. [2] Year ending in June of the year indicated.

Notes explicatives: voir p. 1127.
[1] Non compris les communications. [2] Année se terminant en juin de l'année indiquée.

Notas explicativas: véase p. 1129.
[1] Excl. las comunicaciones. [2] Año que se termina en junio del año indicado.

8C

OCCUPATIONAL INJURIES	LÉSIONS PROFESSIONNELLES	LESIONES PROFESIONALES
Days lost, by economic activity	Journées perdues, par activité économique	Días perdidos, por actividad económica

	1999	2000	2001	2002	2003	2004	2005	2006	2007	2008

Costa Rica (FA) — Compensated injuries - Lésions indemnisées - Lesiones indemnizadas

Total men and women - Total hommes et femmes - Total hombres y mujeres
ISIC 2 - CITI 2 - CIIU 2

	1999	2000	2001	2002	2003	2004	2005	2006	2007	2008
Total	1 502 509	1 631 386	1 543 506	1 539 664	1 329 688	1 297 594	1 513 206	.	.	.
1	465 307	508 267	462 559	450 364	397 512	387 377	449 616			
2	8 297	7 467	.	4 750	2 619	4 283	6 492			
3	375 392	394 692	243 578	315 013	256 299	245 209	273 267			
4	14 340	15 095	13 320	12 959	10 957	12 048	14 309			
5	185 170	196 424	216 729	227 845	192 578	189 976	239 113			
6	188 273	220 306	224 304	241 475	205 467	201 525	238 610			
7	86 366	94 724	85 878	83 628	78 799	77 020	87 509			
8	45 570	47 154	48 742	59 763	58 025	54 820	71 316			
9	122 507	141 045	139 353	143 989	125 913	123 944	132 974			
0	11 287	6 212	2 572	0	.	1 392	0			

Cuba (F) — Reported injuries - Lésions déclarées - Lesiones declaradas

Total men and women - Total hommes et femmes - Total hombres y mujeres
ISIC 3 - CITI 3 - CIIU 3

	1999	2000	2001	2002	2003	2004	2005	2006	2007	2008
Total	577 423	489 469	456 926	398 703	363 016	314 087	289 281	301 885	311 656	302 563

Chile (FA) [1] — Reported injuries - Lésions déclarées - Lesiones declaradas

Total men and women - Total hommes et femmes - Total hombres y mujeres
ISIC 3 - CITI 3 - CIIU 3

	1999	2000	2001	2002	2003	2004	2005	2006	2007	2008
Total	2 383 406	2 552 589	2 535 008	2 599 085	2 533 460	2 498 468	.	.	.	.
A-B	322 265	351 504	369 729	385 048	386 944	367 501				
C	29 113	27 383	28 312	30 514	30 619	29 983				
D	641 032	657 991	633 395	634 440	604 043	573 162				
E	18 867	20 898	15 810	18 426	17 863	16 926				
F	377 607	400 693	428 002	439 632	407 247	439 080				
G-H	250 423	274 142	261 513	272 883	261 983	257 566				
I	289 403	304 165	293 174	292 220	278 012	285 523				
J	90 745	107 267	109 406	116 306	129 484	141 799				
K-P	362 707	407 639	395 590	409 541	417 255	386 883				
X	1 244	907	77	75	10	45				

Men - Hommes - Hombres
ISIC 3 - CITI 3 - CIIU 3

	1999	2000	2001	2002	2003	2004	2005	2006	2007	2008
Total	1 993 992	2 132 506	2 131 689	2 183 726	2 115 309	2 104 257	.	.	.	.
A-B	285 428	309 127	320 931	330 207	328 342	308 675				
C	28 737	26 951	28 104	30 209	30 305	29 419				
D	563 220	577 788	558 340	558 301	535 306	510 086				
E	17 671	19 326	14 695	17 553	16 964	16 036				
F	370 612	393 732	421 186	432 687	401 057	432 966				
G-H	186 188	202 632	194 373	207 409	195 938	191 399				
I	275 952	291 173	280 455	280 716	265 983	275 708				
J	61 889	74 988	78 734	85 259	94 900	104 778				
K-P	203 085	235 978	234 802	241 310	246 504	235 145				
X	1 210	811	69	75	10	45				

Women - Femmes - Mujeres
ISIC 3 - CITI 3 - CIIU 3

	1999	2000	2001	2002	2003	2004	2005	2006	2007	2008
Total	389 414	420 083	403 319	415 359	418 151	394 211	.	.	.	.
A-B	36 837	42 377	48 798	54 841	58 602	58 826				
C	376	432	208	305	314	564				
D	77 812	80 203	75 055	76 139	68 737	63 076				
E	1 196	1 572	1 115	873	899	890				
F	6 995	6 961	6 816	6 945	6 190	6 114				
G-H	64 235	71 510	67 140	65 474	66 045	66 167				
I	13 451	12 992	12 719	11 504	12 029	9 815				
J	28 856	32 279	30 672	31 047	34 584	37 021				
K-P	159 622	171 661	160 788	168 231	170 751	151 738				
X	34	96	8	0	0	0				

ASIA-ASIE-ASIA

Armenia (F) — Reported injuries - Lésions déclarées - Lesiones declaradas

Total men and women - Total hommes et femmes - Total hombres y mujeres
ISIC 3 - CITI 3 - CIIU 3

	1999	2000	2001	2002	2003	2004	2005	2006	2007	2008
Total	5 415	3 053	5 701	3 828	4 191	3 478	2 557	3 010	4 294	3 264

Explanatory notes: see p. 1125.	Notes explicatives: voir p. 1127.	Notas explicativas: véase p. 1129.
[1] Incl. commuting accidents.	[1] Y compris les accidents de trajet.	[1] Incl. accidentes del trayecto.

	1999	2000	2001	2002	2003	2004	2005	2006	2007	2008	

Bahrain (FA)   Reported injuries - Lésions déclarées - Lesiones declaradas

Total men and women - Total hommes et femmes - Total hombres y mujeres

ISIC 2 - CITI 2 - CIIU 2   ISIC 3 - CITI 3 - CIIU 3

	1999	2000	2001	2002	2003	2004	2005	2006	2007		2008	
Total	22 847	28 666	27 902	33 438	35 533	37 623	53 257	63 296	22 984	I	19 879	Total
1	304	371	338	163	282	282	509	217	208	I	7	A
2	0	0	4	0	0	0	0	0	0	I	2	B
3	5 653	7 936	7 694	10 756	10 939	12 673	14 564	11 889	7 662	I	396	C
4	906	653	1 132	507	309	259	259	189	156	I	6 087	D
5	8 955	11 082	11 054	12 450	13 091	12 940	20 906	12 717	8 966	I	0	E
6	3 191	3 795	3 315	4 492	4 568	4 559	6 721	5 782	2 719	I	4 150	F
7	1 361	1 295	1 553	1 773	2 840	2 893	3 972	2 686	1 037	I	6 083	G
8	550	691	717	575	647	1 441	1 637	752	738	I	414	H
9	1 927	2 843	2 095	2 722	2 857	2 576	4 689	29 064	1 498	I	1 578	I
										I	461	J
										I	610	K
										I	0	L
										I	66	M
										I	2	N
										I	23	O
										I	0	P
										I	0	Q
										I	0	X

Hong Kong, China (FF)   Reported injuries - Lésions déclarées - Lesiones declaradas

Total men and women - Total hommes et femmes - Total hombres y mujeres

ISIC 2 - CITI 2 - CIIU 2

	1999	2000	2001	2002	2003	2004	2005	2006	2007	2008
Total	540 454	530 250	535 225	490 849	411 677	420 929	408 423	424 529	390 369	.
1	1 214	1 032	1 166	2 087	2 218	2 339	1 316	1 503	1 699	.
2	259	97	69	91	13	5	0	0	0	.
3	64 291	64 853	66 794	62 070	45 889	45 841	45 061	43 568	40 436	.
4 [1]	337	580	281	628	548	423	503	386	337	.
5 [2]	175 510	152 240	137 632	105 439	72 946	58 987	50 364	45 758	47 179	.
6	132 412	135 024	141 612	131 085	110 248	122 486	118 944	124 159	111 842	.
7	54 141	56 710	56 851	55 822	49 546	50 574	52 181	57 898	48 415	.
8	33 197	38 666	42 077	41 633	42 942	47 872	48 674	50 597	51 826	.
9 [3]	79 096	81 050	88 745	91 995	87 329	92 405	91 368	100 662	88 637	.
0	0	0	0	0	0	0	0	13	0	.

Israel (FA)   Compensated injuries - Lésions indemnisées - Lesiones indemnizadas

Total men and women - Total hommes et femmes - Total hombres y mujeres

ISIC 2 - CITI 2 - CIIU 2

	1999	2000	2001	2002	2003	2004	2005	2006	2007	2008
Total	2 747 215	2 863 296	2 765 654	2 594 111	2 084 364	2 204 345	2 109 993	2 170 751	2 291 149	2 408 514

Kazakhstan (FF)   Reported injuries - Lésions déclarées - Lesiones declaradas

Total men and women - Total hommes et femmes - Total hombres y mujeres

ISIC 3 - CITI 3 - CIIU 3

	1999	2000	2001	2002	2003	2004	2005	2006	2007	2008
Total	181 578	156 243	149 559	171 594	167 764	167 520	172 261	169 181	150 529	148 424

Kyrgyzstan (FF)   Reported injuries - Lésions déclarées - Lesiones declaradas

Total men and women - Total hommes et femmes - Total hombres y mujeres

ISIC 3 - CITI 3 - CIIU 3

	1999	2000	2001	2002	2003	2004	2005	2006	2007	2008
Total	22 637	16 672	21 446	12 012	9 467	10 074	9 663	6 544	.	.
A	2 162	3 075	1 540	1 003	1 033	769	241	408	.	.
B	0	0	0	0	0	0	0	0	.	.
C	1 667	1 314	3 738	451	389	756	1 371	896	.	.
D	9 727	3 017	4 331	2 944	2 968	2 587	2 732	2 379	.	.
E	1 596	992	655	1 171	924	450	420	665	.	.
F	2 113	1 292	2 914	1 363	977	232	293	355	.	.
G	148	118	126	356	228	56	618	54	.	.
H	0	0	0	0	0	11	55	0	.	.
I	2 772	1 821	1 021	1 293	1 111	1 652	948	634	.	.
J	58	56	199	0	177	394	187	0	.	.
K	260	1 197	697	1 425	150	510	323	392	.	.
L	958	1 352	1 662	578	912	1 973	508	251	.	.
M	180	534	225	15	22	236	176	178	.	.
N	402	1 819	3 871	963	412	302	1 611	282	.	.
O	594	85	467	450	164	146	180	50	.	.
P	0	0	0	0	0	0	0	0	.	.

Explanatory notes: see p. 1125.   Notes explicatives: voir p. 1127.   Notas explicativas: véase p. 1129.

[1] Excl. water. [2] Manual workers. [3] Incl. water.   [1] Non compris l'eau. [2] Travailleurs manuels. [3] Y compris l'eau.   [1] Excl. el agua. [2] Trabajadores manuales. [3] Incl. el agua.

OCCUPATIONAL INJURIES
Days lost, by economic activity

LÉSIONS PROFESSIONNELLES
Journées perdues, par activité économique

LESIONES PROFESIONALES
Días perdidos, por actividad económica

	1999	2000	2001	2002	2003	2004	2005	2006	2007	2008

Macau, China (FF) [1] Reported injuries - Lésions déclarées - Lesiones declaradas

Total men and women - Total hommes et femmes - Total hombres y mujeres
ISIC 3 - CITI 3 - CIIU 3

	1999	2000	2001	2002	2003	2004	2005	2006	2007	2008
Total	19 966	21 104	18 145	17 262	24 686	26 477	27 384	35 886	59 702	27 955
A	30	0	6	0	64	0	4	0	4	0
B	0	0	0	0	0	0	0	0	0	0
C	0	0	0	0	0	0	0	0	0	0
D	4 009	5 001	3 081	3 132	4 055	3 941	2 711	3 980	4 107	1 731
E	26	1	48	42	12	20	5	16	86	67
F	5 512	4 452	4 260	3 622	6 886	6 703	9 553	12 602	15 685	5 188
G	2 416	2 429	2 457	2 154	2 604	3 067	2 926	3 297	5 202	2 999
H	3 602	3 546	3 797	3 808	4 349	5 015	5 126	7 564	6 872	4 175
I	906	1 277	982	1 133	1 219	1 510	1 546	2 401	5 305	2 038
J	61	201	19	198	66	43	179	45	337	35
K	458	411	1 195	1 043	1 553	1 078	1 416	1 753	3 570	2 940
L	4	22	110	151	85	113	270	263	630	29
M	70	249	398	233	346	631	513	472	669	491
N	158	177	114	104	252	164	569	743	882	361
O	2 685	3 211	1 644	1 630	3 063	4 182	2 486	2 637	16 127	7 625
P	29	127	34	12	132	10	80	113	226	276
Q	0	0	0	0	0	0	0	0	0	0

Men - Hommes - Hombres
ISIC 3 - CITI 3 - CIIU 3

	1999	2000	2001	2002	2003	2004	2005	2006	2007	2008
Total	.	13 248	11 677	10 831	17 356	16 709	18 547	23 202	39 319	17 322
A	.	0	6	0	64	0	4	0	4	0
B	.	0	.	.	0	0	0	0	0	0
C	.	0	0	0	0	0	0	0	0	0
D	.	3 111	1 748	1 604	2 562	1 771	1 191	2 419	2 050	1 141
E	.	1	41	19	11	19	5	0	86	67
F	.	4 162	4 027	3 514	6 395	6 027	8 904	11 189	13 807	5 098
G	.	1 441	1 578	1 346	1 755	2 045	2 066	2 493	3 531	1 646
H	.	1 517	1 570	1 839	2 017	2 522	2 251	2 844	2 509	1 676
I	.	999	637	777	974	931	1 421	1 938	4 637	1 449
J	.	191	4	58	35	29	161	7	23	14
K	.	341	847	573	1 002	683	679	1 035	1 445	1 637
L	.	14	76	102	56	90	197	103	385	16
M	.	52	179	56	177	81	151	93	71	112
N	.	29	28	47	4	16	52	96	430	33
O	.	1 390	936	896	2 304	2 495	1 446	984	10 341	4 433
P	.	0	0	0	0	0	19	1	0	0
Q	.	0	0	0	0	0	0	0	0	0

Women - Femmes - Mujeres
ISIC 3 - CITI 3 - CIIU 3

	1999	2000	2001	2002	2003	2004	2005	2006	2007	2008
Total	.	7 856	6 468	6 431	7 330	9 768	8 837	12 684	20 383	10 633
A	.	.	.	.	0	0	0	0	0	0
B	.	.	.	.	0	0	0	0	0	0
C	.	0	0	0	0	0	0	0	0	0
D	.	1 890	1 333	1 528	1 493	2 170	1 520	1 561	2 057	590
E	.	0	7	23	1	1	0	16	0	0
F	.	290	233	108	491	676	649	1 413	1 878	90
G	.	988	879	808	849	1 022	860	804	1 671	1 353
H	.	2 029	2 227	1 969	2 332	2 493	2 875	4 720	4 363	2 499
I	.	278	345	356	245	579	125	463	668	589
J	.	10	15	140	31	14	18	38	314	21
K	.	70	348	470	551	395	737	718	2 125	1 303
L	.	8	34	49	29	23	73	160	245	13
M	.	197	219	177	169	550	362	379	598	379
N	.	148	86	57	248	148	517	647	452	328
O	.	1 821	708	734	759	1 687	1 040	1 653	5 786	3 192
P	.	127	34	12	132	10	61	112	226	276
Q	.	0	0	0	0	0	0	0	0	0

Singapore (FF) Reported injuries - Lésions déclarées - Lesiones declaradas

Total men and women - Total hommes et femmes - Total hombres y mujeres
ISIC 3 - CITI 3 - CIIU 3

	1999	2000	2001	2002	2003	2004	2005	2006	2007	2008
Total	58 581	49 240	54 914	48 147	48 275	51 451	50 655	179 082	.	.
A	0	0	0	0	0	0	0	0	.	.
C	0	0	0	0	0	0	0	0	.	.
D	29 135	24 073	28 919	23 967	25 117	26 343	26 191	60 867	.	.
E	236	205	174	156	165	199	138	0	.	.
F	26 793	23 027	23 030	21 261	19 966	21 581	20 532	52 054	.	.
G	60	69	18	68	15	8	32	8 324	.	.
H	39	38	14	37	121	214	412	8 217	.	.
I	1 509	1 203	2 051	2 019	2 044	2 347	2 313	12 049	.	.
J	.	.	.	.	.	.	.	1 346	.	.
K	67	53	182	219	81	117	215	8 264	.	.
L	0	0	0	0	0	0	0	0	.	.
M	.	.	.	.	.	.	.	1 143	.	.
N	0	0	0	0	13	0	0	3 005	.	.
O	701	521	526	420	753	671	822	1 695	.	.
P	0	0	0	0	0	0	0	0	.	.
X	41	51	0	0	0	0	0	0	.	.

Explanatory notes: see p. 1125.   Notes explicatives: voir p. 1127.   Notas explicativas: véase p. 1129.

[1] Private sector.   [1] Secteur privé.   [1] Sector privado.

OCCUPATIONAL INJURIES

LÉSIONS PROFESSIONNELLES

LESIONES PROFESIONALES

8C

Days lost, by economic activity

Journées perdues, par activité économique

Días perdidos, por actividad económica

	1999	2000	2001	2002	2003	2004	2005	2006	2007	2008

Sri Lanka (FF)   Reported injuries - Lésions déclarées - Lesiones declaradas

Total men and women - Total hommes et femmes - Total hombres y mujeres
ISIC 3 - CITI 3 - CIIU 3

	1999	2000	2001	2002	2003	2004	2005	2006	2007	2008
Total	35 254	36 302	28 302	25 423	27 546	15 996	13 847	23 365	25 021	18 526
C	8	43	71	107	28	0	8	404	623	84
D	32 231	31 224	24 302	13 560	18 163	12 917	12 555	21 509	22 954	15 727
E	189	428	107	324	128	324	355	294	224	196
F	1 172	2 146	2 102	450	1 848	324	345	191	312	1 626
G	.	.	.	.	.	0	0	0	0	0
H	126	34	78	72	76	46	61	86	92	74
I	1 528	2 427	1 642	2 300	2 123	740	659	881	816	619
O	.	.	.	.	.	0	0	0	0	0

EUROPE-EUROPE-EUROPA

Austria (FA)   Reported injuries - Lésions déclarées - Lesiones declaradas

Total men and women - Total hommes et femmes - Total hombres y mujeres
ISIC 3 - CITI 3 - CIIU 3

	1999	2000	2001	2002	2003	2004	2005	2006	2007	2008
Total	.	.	.	.	.	1 613 998	1 594 144	1 583 695	1 513 780	.
A	.	.	.	.	.	37 839	33 773	33 248	35 021	.
B	.	.	.	.	.	49	23	173	43	.
C	.	.	.	.	.	7 490	7 775	8 780	7 672	.
D	.	.	.	.	.	476 502	454 030	437 666	416 417	.
E	.	.	.	.	.	11 592	12 596	10 307	8 654	.
F	.	.	.	.	.	429 301	417 932	416 156	402 316	.
G	.	.	.	.	.	191 536	197 513	200 085	190 737	.
H	.	.	.	.	.	45 944	38 830	38 255	36 271	.
I	.	.	.	.	.	111 478	117 198	118 358	103 971	.
J	.	.	.	.	.	6 828	5 905	5 666	5 718	.
K	.	.	.	.	.	133 474	147 103	153 197	155 732	.
L	.	.	.	.	.	39 032	40 636	36 514	35 181	.
M	.	.	.	.	.	11 926	12 486	12 274	12 046	.
N	.	.	.	.	.	57 182	52 908	52 893	53 576	.
O	.	.	.	.	.	53 033	54 524	59 273	49 572	.
P	.	.	.	.	.	774	829	757	798	.
Q	.	.	.	.	.	18	83	93	55	.

Men - Hommes - Hombres
ISIC 3 - CITI 3 - CIIU 3

	1999	2000	2001	2002	2003	2004	2005	2006	2007	2008
Total	.	.	.	.	.	1 371 856	1 352 687	1 337 667	1 270 798	.
A	.	.	.	.	.	35 179	30 794	30 367	31 725	.
B	.	.	.	.	.	49	23	173	43	.
C	.	.	.	.	.	7 388	7 653	8 726	7 151	.
D	.	.	.	.	.	425 740	403 101	388 546	369 326	.
E	.	.	.	.	.	11 411	12 060	10 201	8 394	.
F	.	.	.	.	.	424 427	414 496	411 789	398 774	.
G	.	.	.	.	.	134 442	136 912	136 293	128 929	.
H	.	.	.	.	.	22 296	19 284	20 391	17 730	.
I	.	.	.	.	.	101 261	107 427	108 203	94 627	.
J	.	.	.	.	.	3 873	3 689	2 538	3 142	.
K	.	.	.	.	.	109 755	121 958	126 578	127 709	.
L	.	.	.	.	.	31 736	32 444	28 388	26 740	.
M	.	.	.	.	.	3 687	3 597	3 488	3 208	.
N	.	.	.	.	.	19 532	16 686	15 351	15 105	.
O	.	.	.	.	.	40 978	42 167	46 454	38 125	.
P	.	.	.	.	.	102	315	122	58	.
Q	.	.	.	.	.	0	81	59	12	.

Women - Femmes - Mujeres
ISIC 3 - CITI 3 - CIIU 3

	1999	2000	2001	2002	2003	2004	2005	2006	2007	2008
Total	.	.	.	.	.	242 142	241 457	246 028	242 982	.
A	.	.	.	.	.	2 660	2 979	2 881	3 296	.
B	.	.	.	.	.	0	0	0	0	.
C	.	.	.	.	.	102	122	54	521	.
D	.	.	.	.	.	50 762	50 929	49 120	47 091	.
E	.	.	.	.	.	181	536	106	260	.
F	.	.	.	.	.	4 874	3 436	4 367	3 542	.
G	.	.	.	.	.	57 094	60 601	63 792	61 808	.
H	.	.	.	.	.	23 648	19 546	17 864	18 541	.
I	.	.	.	.	.	10 217	9 771	10 155	9 344	.
J	.	.	.	.	.	2 955	2 216	3 128	2 576	.
K	.	.	.	.	.	23 719	25 145	26 619	28 023	.
L	.	.	.	.	.	7 296	8 192	8 126	8 441	.
M	.	.	.	.	.	8 239	8 889	8 786	8 838	.
N	.	.	.	.	.	37 650	36 222	37 542	38 471	.
O	.	.	.	.	.	12 055	12 357	12 819	11 447	.
P	.	.	.	.	.	672	514	635	740	.
Q	.	.	.	.	.	18	2	34	43	.

Explanatory notes: see p. 1125.   Notes explicatives: voir p. 1127.   Notas explicativas: véase p. 1129.

8C

OCCUPATIONAL INJURIES
Days lost, by economic activity

LÉSIONS PROFESSIONNELLES
Journées perdues, par activité économique

LESIONES PROFESIONALES
Días perdidos, por actividad económica

	1999	2000	2001	2002	2003	2004	2005	2006	2007	2008
Belarus (CA)				Reported injuries - Lésions déclarées - Lesiones declaradas						
Total men and women - Total hommes et femmes - Total hombres y mujeres										
ISIC 3 - CITI 3 - CIIU 3										
Total	300 539	276 957	224 469	187 114	191 994	178 154	155 915	134 559	120 603	108 720
Men - Hommes - Hombres										
ISIC 3 - CITI 3 - CIIU 3										
Total	236 444	218 587	172 967	143 299	144 453	140 693	117 856	103 363	93 996	825 116
Women - Femmes - Mujeres										
ISIC 3 - CITI 3 - CIIU 3										
Total	64 095	58 370	51 502	43 845	47 541	37 461	38 059	31 196	26 607	26 204
Belgique (FA) [1]				Compensated injuries - Lésions indemnisées - Lesiones indemnizadas						
Total men and women - Total hommes et femmes - Total hombres y mujeres										
ISIC 3 - CITI 3 - CIIU 3										
Total	2 260 384	2 393 436	2 282 239 [2]	.	.	1 311 065				
A	2 065	3 056	2 767 [2]	.	.	16 329				
B	16	183	89 [2]	.	.	370				
C	355	193	519 [2]	.	.	6 840				
D	600 929	604 407	617 101 [2]	.	.	398 629				
E	21 574	21 102	23 686 [2]	.	.	2 410				
F	287 480	634	278 874 [2]	.	.	221 218				
G	147 866	188 691	176 738 [2]	.	.	205 801				
H	29 589	32 252	26 704 [2]	.	.	38 390				
I	238 080	546 532	424 084 [2]	.	.	154 218				
J	7 581	17 298	25 035 [2]	.	.	6 205				
K	91 252	112 276	108 609 [2]	.	.	97 628				
L	326 565	294 838	292 552 [2]	.	.	4 205				
M	51 050	49 406	61 060 [2]	.	.	9 898				
N	159 555	178 534	188 118 [2]	.	.	90 133				
O	289 910	81 562	54 409 [2]	.	.	35 058				
P	7	8	311 [2]	.	.	2 909				
Q	662	1 444	1 583 [2]	.	.	135				
X	0	0	0 [2]	.	.	20 689				
Men - Hommes - Hombres										
ISIC 3 - CITI 3 - CIIU 3										
Total	.	.	.	.	.	1 048 127				
A	.	.	.	.	.	13 104				
B	.	.	.	.	.	291				
C	.	.	.	.	.	6 831				
D	.	.	.	.	.	351 822				
E	.	.	.	.	.	2 273				
F	.	.	.	.	.	218 894				
G	.	.	.	.	.	149 948				
H	.	.	.	.	.	18 697				
I	.	.	.	.	.	142 076				
J	.	.	.	.	.	3 023				
K	.	.	.	.	.	71 581				
L	.	.	.	.	.	3 043				
M	.	.	.	.	.	3 822				
N	.	.	.	.	.	26 502				
O	.	.	.	.	.	19 760				
P	.	.	.	.	.	1 075				
Q	.	.	.	.	.	24				
X	.	.	.	.	.	15 361				
Women - Femmes - Mujeres										
ISIC 3 - CITI 3 - CIIU 3										
Total	.	.	.	.	.	262 876				
A	.	.	.	.	.	3 225				
B	.	.	.	.	.	79				
C	.	.	.	.	.	9				
D	.	.	.	.	.	46 772				
E	.	.	.	.	.	137				
F	.	.	.	.	.	2 324				
G	.	.	.	.	.	55 853				
H	.	.	.	.	.	19 693				
I	.	.	.	.	.	12 142				
J	.	.	.	.	.	3 182				
K	.	.	.	.	.	26 020				
L	.	.	.	.	.	1 162				
M	.	.	.	.	.	6 076				
N	.	.	.	.	.	63 631				
O	.	.	.	.	.	15 298				
P	.	.	.	.	.	1 834				
Q	.	.	.	.	.	111				
X	.	.	.	.	.	5 328				

Explanatory notes: see p. 1125.

[1] Private sector: from 1992: incl. commuting accidents. [2] Not strictly comparable.

Notes explicatives: voir p. 1127.

[1] Secteur privé: à partir de 1992: y compris les accidents de trajet. [2] Non strictement comparable.

Notas explicativas: véase p. 1129.

[1] Sector privado: a partir de 1992: incl. accidentes del trayecto. [2] No estrictamente comparable.

OCCUPATIONAL INJURIES

Days lost, by economic activity

LÉSIONS PROFESSIONNELLES

Journées perdues, par activité économique

LESIONES PROFESIONALES

Días perdidos, por actividad económica

8C

	1999	2000	2001	2002	2003	2004	2005	2006	2007	2008

Bulgaria (FD) — Reported injuries - Lésions déclarées - Lesiones declaradas

Total men and women - Total hommes et femmes - Total hombres y mujeres
ISIC 3 - CITI 3 - CIIU 3

	1999	2000	2001	2002	2003	2004	2005	2006	2007	2008
Total	232 062	323 485	268 750	293 250	269 335	260 858	268 286	260 180	238 869	.
A	14 568	15 086	9 982	9 050	9 296	7 617	6 705	7 015	5 989	.
B	0	0	7	124	0	0	50	0	0	.
C	24 131	33 207	32 318	32 758	24 996	19 550	19 351	17 952	14 915	.
D	120 612	118 618	101 823	111 334	94 486	90 570	89 622	85 888	80 823	.
E	11 031	16 175	17 235	16 703	14 197	15 905	11 272	12 128	8 732	.
F	16 809	24 093	24 077	24 795	24 029	26 046	31 236	30 880	31 612	.
G	6 837	8 948	7 837	8 598	15 665	14 587	19 790	21 677	22 997	.
H	1 887	2 929	2 705	2 658	2 282	2 308	1 721	3 354	3 288	.
I	32 676	34 296	28 725	31 202	30 897	28 014	31 013	28 943	24 242	.
J	0	2 442	2 050	1 674	2 709	4 071	3 433	1 697	1 613	.
K	1 233	4 031	4 795	6 357	11 791	13 170	15 461	12 508	.	.
L	0	29 549	9 532	15 631	14 071	15 896	13 501	15 503	11 766	.
M	0	13 541	9 469	11 794	8 426	6 956	7 370	8 296	6 409	.
N	58	15 190	11 115	13 931	10 482	9 851	11 716	9 406	7 413	.
O	2 220	5 380	7 080	6 641	6 008	6 286	6 015	4 933	6 375	.
Q	.	.	.	.	.	31	30	0	0	.

Men - Hommes - Hombres
ISIC 3 - CITI 3 - CIIU 3

	1999	2000	2001	2002	2003	2004	2005	2006	2007	2008
Total	.	.	.	.	192 519	189 029	184 033	181 687	170 583	.
A	.	.	.	.	7 248	6 726	5 694	5 246	4 491	.
B	.	.	.	.	0	50	0	0	0	.
C	.	.	.	.	23 405	17 914	17 415	16 283	13 694	.
D	.	.	.	.	68 681	67 972	61 541	62 481	56 636	.
E	.	.	.	.	11 442	12 199	8 659	8 241	7 103	.
F	.	.	.	.	23 058	25 202	30 191	29 830	30 700	.
G	.	.	.	.	10 693	10 370	15 054	17 298	16 669	.
H	.	.	.	.	722	829	464	949	1 659	.
I	.	.	.	.	24 022	20 922	22 671	20 279	18 926	.
J	.	.	.	.	2 009	3 462	1 972	524	591	.
K	.	.	.	.	8 416	9 378	9 026	7 406	8 820	.
L	.	.	.	.	5 373	6 313	4 001	6 598	4 930	.
M	.	.	.	.	2 193	1 841	1 999	1 629	1 132	.
N	.	.	.	.	1 574	1 667	1 867	2 015	822	.
O	.	.	.	.	3 683	4 234	3 399	2 908	4 283	.
P	.	.	.	.	0	0	0	0	0	.
Q	.	.	.	.	0	0	30	0	127	.

Women - Femmes - Mujeres
ISIC 3 - CITI 3 - CIIU 3

	1999	2000	2001	2002	2003	2004	2005	2006	2007	2008
Total	.	.	.	.	76 816	71 829	84 253	78 493	68 286	.
A	.	.	.	.	2 048	891	1 011	1 769	1 498	.
B	.	.	.	.	0	0	0	0	0	.
C	.	.	.	.	1 591	1 636	1 936	1 669	1 221	.
D	.	.	.	.	25 805	22 598	28 081	23 407	24 187	.
E	.	.	.	.	2 755	3 706	2 613	3 887	1 629	.
F	.	.	.	.	971	844	1 045	1 050	912	.
G	.	.	.	.	4 972	4 217	4 736	4 379	6 328	.
H	.	.	.	.	1 560	1 479	1 257	2 405	1 629	.
I	.	.	.	.	6 875	7 092	8 342	8 664	5 316	.
J	.	.	.	.	700	609	1 461	1 173	1 022	.
K	.	.	.	.	3 375	3 792	6 435	5 102	3 748	.
L	.	.	.	.	8 698	9 583	9 500	8 905	6 836	.
M	.	.	.	.	6 233	5 115	5 371	6 667	5 277	.
N	.	.	.	.	8 908	8 184	9 849	7 391	6 591	.
O	.	.	.	.	2 325	2 052	2 616	2 025	2 092	.
P	.	.	.	.	0	0	0	0	0	.
Q	.	.	.	.	0	31	0	0	0	.

Czech Republic (FD) — Reported injuries - Lésions déclarées - Lesiones declaradas

Total men and women - Total hommes et femmes - Total hombres y mujeres
ISIC 3 - CITI 3 - CIIU 3

	1999	2000	2001	2002	2003	2004	2005	2006	2007	2008
Total	3 781 345	3 780 854	3 787 692	3 788 076	3 599 340	3 565 634	3 702 310	3 766 313	3 600 581	3 548 355
A-B	.	322 141	.	.	.	.	.	.	.	.
A	350 384	.	314 486	316 703	305 011	274 733	269 318	269 565	240 861	246 377
B	1 617	.	1 711	1 457	1 981	1 812	2 524	2 264	1 189	1 669
C	183 693	.	139 483	131 368	122 036	106 363	98 308	81 600	87 897	73 858
C-D	.	1 493 647	.	.	.	.	.	.	.	.
D	1 325 814	.	1 395 150	1 356 121	1 310 217	1 299 682	1 362 546	1 345 968	1 338 996	1 524 199
E	41 167	39 988	40 817	40 684	37 332	33 877	36 689	33 029	26 759	21 474
F	331 262	313 378	280 045	259 395	239 433	246 237	245 642	246 346	227 221	317 878
G	200 999	188 852	188 448	193 540	184 964	190 908	213 750	241 359	231 212	341 691
H	32 836	34 478	33 877	27 885	27 753	28 000	29 695	31 650	35 537	85 141
I	246 980	248 264	242 373	258 898	263 666	263 787	290 900	334 478	294 350	342 702
J	11 276	.	8 641	9 607	7 812	5 702	7 546	6 456	6 244	9 684
J-K	.	107 557	.	.	.	.	.	.	.	.
K	88 594	.	115 806	119 552	106 074	107 392	131 581	135 769	122 880	185 893
L	112 424	117 152	97 569	94 871	72 465	72 366	68 881	77 643	69 550	87 829
M	42 511	48 689	48 817	60 142	63 051	62 695	67 565	69 461	65 769	82 388
N	86 579	85 673	90 413	102 405	90 941	97 826	109 471	114 921	111 334	122 163
O	54 187	56 889	59 420	66 901	64 335	63 849	76 839	77 713	70 851	99 011
X	671 022	724 146	730 636	748 547	702 269	710 405	691 055	698 091	669 931	6 398

Explanatory notes: see p. 1125.   Notes explicatives: voir p. 1127.   Notas explicativas: véase p. 1129.

ILO YEARBOOK OF LABOUR STATISTICS 2009   *ANNUAIRE DES STATISTIQUES DU TRAVAIL DU BIT 2009*   *ANUARIO DE ESTADISTICAS DEL TRABAJO DEL OIT 2009*

1345

OCCUPATIONAL INJURIES
Days lost, by economic activity

LÉSIONS PROFESSIONNELLES
Journées perdues, par activité économique

LESIONES PROFESIONALES
Días perdidos, por actividad económica

	1999	2000	2001	2002	2003	2004	2005	2006	2007	2008
Czech Republic (FD)				Reported injuries - Lésions déclarées - Lesiones declaradas						
Men - Hommes - Hombres										
ISIC 3 - CITI 3 - CIIU 3										
Total	2 889 991	2 920 247	2 882 449	2 862 219	2 726 999	2 671 670	2 745 964	2 779 873	2 675 636	2 426 986
A-B		230 978								
A	245 607		221 293	223 777	211 758	189 234	184 423	184 426	163 261	169 329
B	1 250		1 462	1 204	1 606	1 627	2 361	1 990	854	1 452
C	178 683		135 778	128 645	119 821	103 809	95 977	78 810	84 889	71 492
C-D		1 183 124								
D	1 004 727		1 063 065	1 031 874	998 825	985 734	1 024 438	1 009 154	1 015 944	1 145 821
E	35 688	35 633	36 188	35 182	33 690	29 901	32 827	29 537	23 810	20 016
F	316 787	300 959	267 809	249 446	230 230	235 278	232 908	233 915	216 964	294 483
G	131 288	122 676	119 699	120 240	115 726	115 130	125 801	139 064	129 017	217 450
H	20 484	18 541	19 320	12 746	12 831	12 826	13 631	15 168	18 485	59 323
I	184 192	186 363	178 705	192 488	192 473	185 528	209 257	241 873	218 733	262 232
J	4 439		3 647	4 041	2 246	1 922	2 360	2 253	1 816	4 031
J-K		70 491								
K	57 746		70 589	79 461	72 359	74 357	88 807	93 050	77 292	129 285
L	66 710	71 986	54 733	52 214	47 022	45 276	44 574	48 876	46 554	59 562
M	14 607	17 982	17 187	22 190	17 190	18 296	17 959	19 716	17 805	34 969
N	24 346	25 466	27 105	31 857	27 702	26 658	31 936	35 589	32 013	41 110
O	41 191	43 902	46 722	50 434	49 870	50 406	59 296	61 493	55 602	78 369
X	562 246	612 146	619 147	626 420	593 650	595 688	579 409	584 959	572 597	5 923
Women - Femmes - Mujeres										
ISIC 3 - CITI 3 - CIIU 3										
Total	891 354	860 607	905 243	925 857	872 341	893 964	956 346	986 440	924 945	953 508
A-B		91 163								
A	104 777		93 193	92 926	93 253	85 499	84 895	85 139	77 600	77 048
B	367		249	253	375	185	163	274	335	217
C	5 010		3 705	2 723	2 215	2 554	2 331	2 790	3 008	2 366
C-D		310 523								
D	321 087		332 085	324 247	311 392	313 948	338 108	336 814	323 052	378 378
E	5 479	4 355	4 629	5 502	3 642	3 976	3 862	3 492	2 949	1 458
F	14 475	12 419	12 236	9 949	9 203	10 959	12 734	12 431	10 257	23 395
G	69 711	66 176	68 749	73 300	69 238	75 778	87 949	102 295	102 195	124 241
H	12 352	15 937	14 557	15 139	14 922	15 174	16 064	16 482	17 052	25 818
I	62 788	61 901	63 668	66 410	71 193	78 259	81 643	92 605	75 617	80 470
J	6 837		4 994	5 566	5 566	3 780	5 186	4 203	4 428	5 653
J-K		37 066								
K	30 848		45 217	40 091	33 715	33 035	42 774	42 719	45 588	1 162
L	45 714	45 166	42 836	42 657	25 443	27 090	24 307	28 767	22 996	28 267
M	27 904	30 707	31 630	37 952	45 861	44 399	49 606	49 745	47 964	47 419
N	62 233	60 207	63 308	70 548	63 239	71 168	77 535	79 332	79 321	81 053
O	12 996	12 987	12 698	16 467	14 465	13 443	17 543	16 220	15 249	20 642
X	108 776	112 000	111 489	122 127	108 619	114 717	111 646	113 132	97 334	475
España (FA)				Reported injuries - Lésions déclarées - Lesiones declaradas						
Total men and women - Total hommes et femmes - Total hombres y mujeres										
ISIC 3 - CITI 3 - CIIU 3										
Total	19 284 914	20 164 872	20 984 804	20 959 780	20 452 104	19 181 427	20 150 964	20 392 326	21 560 983	
A	1 095 776	927 697	843 419	814 872	781 879	790 283	792 561	795 391	822 835	
B	180 850	171 243	153 520	158 793	136 646	144 626	136 970	122 912	133 017	
C	360 562	339 717	383 467	334 116	318 291	255 794	235 744	200 897	208 907	
D	5 072 409	5 112 817	5 226 981	5 065 888	4 999 834	4 766 311	4 922 237	4 933 992	5 140 169	
E	92 392	83 636	81 353	81 887	92 173	115 716	113 263	111 956	117 434	
F	4 697 718	5 018 010	5 361 123	5 396 862	5 349 420	4 817 420	5 276 610	5 481 268	5 775 448	
G	2 289 133	2 451 695	2 532 935	2 649 973	2 590 711	2 342 610	2 467 066	2 458 134	2 585 741	
H	992 993	1 109 499	1 134 710	1 104 917	1 071 816	1 012 848	1 068 441	1 069 775	1 134 703	
I	1 076 668	1 190 212	1 225 530	1 224 436	1 273 236	1 305 654	1 379 711	1 424 368	1 521 950	
J	53 392	63 102	61 326	63 453	57 857	58 815	60 084	61 299	62 422	
K	1 375 393	1 460 062	1 577 893	1 622 200	1 259 941	883 520	917 425	950 054	1 051 660	
L,Q	827 376	890 063	917 685	939 344	946 954	936 477	986 081	965 091	1 000 317	
M	131 977	136 377	147 260	144 073	164 484	167 923	173 093	185 737	197 856	
N	605 454	711 815	792 213	800 529	801 311	871 296	869 227	876 492	958 670	
O	401 458	466 236	513 853	529 304	589 862	689 896	730 891	729 767	813 169	
P	31 363	32 691	31 536	29 133	17 689	22 238	21 560	25 193	36 685	
Men - Hommes - Hombres										
ISIC 3 - CITI 3 - CIIU 3										
Total	15 948 033	16 392 489	16 948 021	16 952 764	16 238 707	15 100 777	15 978 601	16 056 076	16 808 290	
A	864 918	735 899	664 191	647 137	599 796	606 223	624 231	610 679	618 924	
B	171 359	159 833	141 958	147 226	126 786	136 157	130 352	116 415	120 960	
C	349 034	328 400	374 763	326 671	304 335	247 072	227 586	192 819	201 353	
D	4 509 351	4 477 915	4 569 273	4 423 322	4 313 389	4 081 051	4 245 564	4 217 859	4 360 137	
E	89 453	80 278	77 913	79 281	86 255	110 542	108 611	106 711	113 088	
F	4 595 422	4 895 644	5 245 395	5 281 830	5 237 072	4 755 008	5 213 258	5 409 933	5 704 375	
G	1 731 648	1 809 315	1 845 117	1 922 494	1 805 364	1 620 727	1 712 274	1 679 599	1 745 295	
H	555 315	597 566	587 897	586 367	519 811	474 444	494 150	485 698	498 355	
I	980 533	1 082 738	1 115 052	1 110 997	1 127 950	1 157 954	1 213 586	1 241 919	1 305 281	
J	34 364	40 412	39 520	39 885	30 495	29 866	28 905	28 227	29 481	
K	853 229	856 296	908 627	966 560	727 758	520 646	546 645	566 318	628 124	
L,Q	620 313	662 857	662 384	684 828	664 283	647 818	684 036	665 909	689 045	
M	64 750	65 134	69 429	67 490	63 600	58 599	58 736	60 380	63 525	
N	196 092	228 051	248 603	271 274	216 955	214 786	215 246	207 827	206 194	
O	307 705	346 672	374 026	375 991	401 529	426 791	462 078	451 134	503 626	
P	24 547	25 479	23 873	21 411	13 329	13 093	13 343	14 649	20 527	

Explanatory notes: see p. 1125.   Notes explicatives: voir p. 1127.   Notas explicativas: véase p. 1129.

OCCUPATIONAL INJURIES

Days lost, by economic activity

LÉSIONS PROFESSIONNELLES

Journées perdues, par activité économique

LESIONES PROFESIONALES

Días perdidos, por actividad económica

8C

	1999	2000	2001	2002	2003	2004	2005	2006	2007	2008

España (FA) — Reported injuries - Lésions déclarées - Lesiones declaradas

Women - Femmes - Mujeres
ISIC 3 - CITI 3 - CIIU 3

	1999	2000	2001	2002	2003	2004	2005	2006	2007	2008
Total	3 336 881	3 772 383	4 036 783	4 007 016	4 213 397	4 080 650	4 172 363	4 336 250	4 752 693	.
A	230 858	191 798	179 228	167 735	182 083	184 060	168 330	184 712	203 911	.
B	9 491	11 410	11 562	11 567	9 860	8 469	6 618	6 497	12 057	.
C	11 528	11 317	8 704	7 445	13 956	8 722	8 158	8 078	7 554	.
D	563 058	634 902	657 708	642 566	686 445	685 260	676 673	716 133	780 032	.
E	2 939	3 358	3 440	2 606	5 918	5 174	4 652	5 245	4 346	.
F	102 296	122 366	115 728	115 032	112 348	62 412	63 352	71 335	71 073	.
G	557 485	642 380	687 818	727 479	785 347	721 883	754 792	778 535	840 446	.
H	437 678	511 933	546 813	518 550	552 005	538 404	574 291	584 077	636 348	.
I	96 135	107 474	110 478	113 439	145 286	147 700	166 125	182 449	216 669	.
J	19 028	22 690	21 806	23 568	27 362	28 949	31 179	33 072	32 941	.
K	522 164	603 766	669 266	655 640	532 183	362 874	370 780	383 736	423 536	.
L,Q	207 063	227 206	255 301	254 516	282 671	288 659	302 045	299 182	311 272	.
M	67 227	71 243	77 831	76 583	100 884	109 324	114 357	125 357	134 331	.
N	409 362	483 764	543 610	529 255	584 356	656 510	653 981	668 665	752 476	.
O	93 753	119 564	139 827	153 313	188 333	263 105	268 813	278 633	309 543	.
P	6 816	7 212	7 663	7 722	4 360	9 145	8 217	10 544	16 158	.

Finland (FA) — Compensated injuries - Lésions indemnisées - Lesiones indemnizadas

Total men and women - Total hommes et femmes - Total hombres y mujeres
ISIC 3 - CITI 3 - CIIU 3

	1999	2000	2001	2002	2003	2004	2005	2006	2007	2008
Total	1 192 156	1 213 249	1 247 819	1 047 768	1 040 348	1 165 970	1 232 796	1 309 645	1 303 116	.
A	28 954	27 325	28 634	24 936	25 984	24 500	27 927	30 415	33 329	.
B	874	469	695	988	515	424	448	924	559	.
C	5 053	9 407	3 911	3 796	3 973	3 501	3 731	3 745	3 608	.
D	342 318	347 532	350 120	283 527	282 684	298 356	297 630	306 708	293 841	.
E	8 708	8 051	9 068	5 800	6 817	.	.	.	.	.
F	233 194	251 256	258 169	200 815	189 599	202 255	236 296	241 612	255 886	.
G	90 703	87 942	86 027	82 873	78 584	88 661	95 635	100 917	110 602	.
H	21 468	24 224	22 057	20 753	21 970	22 121	25 995	27 223	29 184	.
I	152 142	152 612	149 356	127 172	129 695	159 720	168 739	175 909	146 823	.
J	3 056	2 554	3 246	1 725	2 799	2 660	2 713	3 551	3 303	.
K	65 421	71 653	76 925	69 126	73 886	83 246	94 922	117 863	132 450	.
L	167 466	162 420	178 978	159 703	156 776	189 870	183 972	204 688	187 081	.
M	14 454	13 154	13 097	10 999	10 842	10 498	11 372	13 303	14 806	.
N	21 285	21 160	22 386	20 392	21 186	26 512	27 904	35 526	34 225	.
O	28 325	28 466	32 740	27 855	26 603	32 757	35 888	33 275	34 047	.
P	5 002	6 234	7 441	5 085	5 633	8 608	8 250	7 409	9 461	.
Q	41	0	32	0	80	0	0	89	41	.
X	3 692	3 790	4 937	2 223	2 722	5 132	4 300	31	5 387	.

France (FA) [1] — Compensated injuries - Lésions indemnisées - Lesiones indemnizadas

Total men and women - Total hommes et femmes - Total hombres y mujeres
ISIC 3 - CITI 3 - CIIU 3

	1999	2000	2001	2002	2003	2004	2005	2006	2007	2008
Total	28 114 114	30 684 007	31 897 526	35 123 699	36 097 299	35 096 561	33 251 840	34 726 602	35 871 141	.
A	.	.	.	.	.	.	33 371	37 536	43 166	.
B	.	.	.	.	.	.	3 688	3 382	3 804	.
C	.	.	.	.	.	.	76 528	71 796	72 397	.
D	8 636 417	9 363 399	.	.	.	.	6 173 635	6 143 163	6 106 989	.
E [2]	83 860	86 782	.	.	.	.	77 145	71 995	73 872	.
F	5 838 099	6 234 215	.	.	.	.	5 866 493	6 186 558	6 238 483	.
G [3]	1 836 130	1 994 303	.	.	.	.	5 091 477	5 308 580	5 354 763	.
H	1 425 063	1 523 788	.	.	.	.	1 736 960	1 809 037	1 871 356	.
I [4]	2 850 393	3 081 407	.	.	.	.	3 368 621	3 533 757	3 565 084	.
J	.	.	.	.	.	.	175 374	176 834	162 179	.
J-K,O-P,X [5]	7 444 152	8 400 113	.	.	.	.	.	.	.	.
K	.	.	.	.	.	.	5 322 728	5 746 726	5 958 213	.
L	.	.	.	.	.	.	630 430	613 850	610 714	.
M	.	.	.	.	.	.	291 289	271 955	288 472	.
N	.	.	.	.	.	.	2 769 701	3 057 303	3 349 880	.
O	.	.	.	.	.	.	1 164 927	1 237 733	1 239 459	.
P	.	.	.	.	.	.	940	208	0	.
Q	.	.	.	.	.	.	2 555	2 821	3 257	.
X	.	.	.	.	.	.	465 978	453 368	929 053	.

Explanatory notes: see p. 1125.

[1] Cases recognized for compensation during the year. [2] Excl. agents of public gas and electricity services. [3] Excl. food trade. [4] Excl. transport by rail and by sea and communications. [5] Interoccupational group.

Notes explicatives: voir p. 1127.

[1] Cas reconnus pour indemnisation dans l'année. [2] Non compris les agents des services publics du gaz et de l'électricité. [3] Non compris les commerces alimentaires. [4] Non compris les transports par chemin de fer ou par mer et les communications. [5] Groupe interprofessionnel.

Notas explicativas: véase p. 1129.

[1] Casos recogidos para indemnización en el año. [2] Excl. los agentes de los servicios públicos de electricidad y gas. [3] Excl. comercio alimenticio. [4] Excl. transportes ferroviarios y marítimos y las comunicaciones. [5] Grupo interocupacional.

ILO YEARBOOK OF LABOUR STATISTICS 2009 — *ANNUAIRE DES STATISTIQUES DU TRAVAIL DU BIT 2009* — *ANUARIO DE ESTADISTICAS DEL TRABAJO DEL OIT 2009*

1347

OCCUPATIONAL INJURIES
Days lost, by economic activity

LÉSIONS PROFESSIONNELLES
Journées perdues, par activité économique

LESIONES PROFESIONALES
Días perdidos, por actividad económica

	1999	2000	2001	2002	2003	2004	2005	2006	2007	2008

France (FA)¹ — Compensated injuries - Lésions indemnisées - Lesiones indemnizadas

Men - Hommes - Hombres
ISIC 3 - CITI 3 - CIIU 3

	1999	2000	2001	2002	2003	2004	2005	2006	2007	2008
Total	21 905 493	23 702 746	.	.	.	.	23 953 934	24 812 597	25 260 288	.
A			.	.	.	.	25 878	29 373	30 069	.
B			.	.	.	.	2 686	2 627	2 856	.
C			.	.	.	.	74 763	70 659	71 903	.
D	6 890 923	7 386 825	.	.	.	.	4 943 555	4 918 164	4 870 682	.
E²	81 633	84 335	.	.	.	.	75 140	70 047	71 009	.
F	5 789 102	6 187 909	.	.	.	.	5 812 572	6 129 797	6 169 241	.
G³	1 342 122	1 437 247	.	.	.	.	3 312 541	3 401 354	3 380 652	.
H	765 380	792 767	.	.	.	.	847 148	862 901	874 814	.
I⁴	2 648 826	2 846 068	.	.	.	.	2 863 752	3 006 310	3 016 793	.
J			.	.	.	.	74 350	71 955	60 527	.
J-K.O-P.X⁵	4 387 507	4 967 595	.	.	.	.				.
K			.	.	.	.	3 776 684	4 067 448	4 190 681	.
L			.	.	.	.	251 654	238 907	238 252	.
M			.	.	.	.	124 706	118 896	111 523	.
N			.	.	.	.	597 263	629 822	659 304	.
O			.	.	.	.	809 819	848 007	834 289	.
P			.	.	.	.	648	98	0	.
Q			.	.	.	.	1 237	1 734	2 349	.
X			.	.	.	.	359 538	344 498	675 344	.

Women - Femmes - Mujeres
ISIC 3 - CITI 3 - CIIU 3

	1999	2000	2001	2002	2003	2004	2005	2006	2007	2008
Total	6 208 621	6 981 261	.	.	.	.	9 297 906	9 914 005	10 610 853	.
A			.	.	.	.	7 493	8 163	13 097	.
B			.	.	.	.	1 002	755	948	.
C			.	.	.	.	1 765	1 137	494	.
D	1 745 494	1 976 574	.	.	.	.	1 230 080	1 224 999	1 236 307	.
E²	2 227	2 447	.	.	.	.	2 005	1 948	2 863	.
F	48 997	46 306	.	.	.	.	53 921	56 761	69 242	.
G³	494 008	557 056	.	.	.	.	1 778 936	1 907 226	1 974 111	.
H	659 683	731 021	.	.	.	.	889 812	946 136	996 542	.
I⁴	201 567	235 339	.	.	.	.	504 869	527 447	548 291	.
J			.	.	.	.	101 024	104 879	101 652	.
J-K.O-P.X⁵	3 056 645	3 432 518	.	.	.	.				.
K			.	.	.	.	1 546 044	1 679 278	1 767 532	.
L			.	.	.	.	378 776	374 943	372 462	.
M			.	.	.	.	166 583	153 059	176 949	.
N			.	.	.	.	2 172 438	2 427 481	2 690 576	.
O			.	.	.	.	355 108	389 726	405 170	.
P			.	.	.	.	292	110	0	.
Q			.	.	.	.	1 318	1 087	908	.
X			.	.	.	.	106 440	108 870	253 709	.

France (FA)¹ — Compensated injuries - Lésions indemnisées - Lesiones indemnizadas

Total men and women - Total hommes et femmes - Total hombres y mujeres
ISIC 3 - CITI 3 - CIIU 3

	1999	2000	2001	2002	2003	2004	2005	2006	2007	2008
A	2 065 755	2 653 411	2 894 044	3 127 158	3 273 644	2 982 024	3 003 507	2 952 519	2 955 792	.

Men - Hommes - Hombres
ISIC 3 - CITI 3 - CIIU 3

	1999	2000	2001	2002	2003	2004	2005	2006	2007	2008
A	1 707 259	2 036 015	2 163 203	2 246 280	2 316 560	2 124 264	2 097 753	2 046 641	2 020 622	.

Women - Femmes - Mujeres
ISIC 3 - CITI 3 - CIIU 3

	1999	2000	2001	2002	2003	2004	2005	2006	2007	2008
A	358 496	617 396	730 841	880 878	957 084	857 760	905 754	905 878	935 170	.

Italy (FA) — Compensated injuries - Lésions indemnisées - Lesiones indemnizadas

Total men and women - Total hommes et femmes - Total hombres y mujeres
ISIC 3 - CITI 3 - CIIU 3

	1999	2000	2001	2002	2003	2004	2005	2006	2007	2008
Total	13 721 283	15 595 055	14 521 610	13 657 574	13 567 682	13 475 090	13 109 116	13 117 697	12 697 446	11 967 950
A	1 750 156	1 951 271	1 748 813	1 646 210	1 604 824	1 578 227	1 515 068	1 489 127	1 364 596	1 295 833
B	10 022	9 614	9 723	13 023	11 287	11 255	13 064	10 205	10 411	9 658
C	44 831	52 914	47 494	42 963	39 001	39 202	38 177	34 906	36 617	30 736
D	4 434 241	4 925 999	4 566 875	4 228 296	4 021 963	3 848 177	3 757 386	3 723 442	3 584 068	3 168 212
E	123 478	139 986	114 780	108 369	99 492	100 856	97 585	91 366	79 178	71 553
F	1 956 884	2 320 490	2 124 195	2 128 867	2 141 806	2 183 149	2 107 326	2 108 347	2 021 282	1 805 290
G	1 213 437	1 369 281	1 271 059	1 257 931	1 240 636	1 261 870	1 242 562	1 223 334	1 201 200	1 135 448
H	442 559	513 664	479 882	476 770	497 813	499 895	504 517	508 356	516 513	465 768
I	1 305 010	1 515 622	1 501 866	1 441 436	1 400 156	1 430 342	1 416 309	1 419 822	1 403 740	1 313 690
J	62 693	80 705	81 432	78 961	51 063	49 282	47 949	46 506	46 762	42 151
K	688 552	831 001	868 962	606 302	890 207	907 285	739 434	830 841	810 279	789 103
L	387 764	434 346	423 863	406 253	426 498	420 866	415 352	405 112	380 458	351 980
M	35 480	84 247	40 886	40 462	38 428	39 259	43 558	41 127	39 974	37 826
N	385 229	470 649	447 881	454 870	468 293	480 805	497 910	514 852	514 712	490 250
O	499 892	559 537	472 964	471 112	484 859	488 966	523 011	549 597	573 289	537 074
P	23 589	32 152	28 775	28 957	41 808	45 483	45 788	51 439	49 496	64 739
X	165 011	271 425	292 160	226 792	109 548	90 171	104 120	69 318	64 871	358 639

Explanatory notes: see p. 1125.

¹ Cases recognized for compensation during the year. ² Excl. agents of public gas and electricity services. ³ Excl. food trade. ⁴ Excl. transport by rail and by sea and communications. ⁵ Interoccupational group.

Notes explicatives: voir p. 1127.

¹ Cas reconnus pour indemnisation dans l'année. ² Non compris les agents des services publics du gaz et de l'électricité. ³ Non compris les commerces alimentaires. ⁴ Non compris les transports par chemin de fer ou par mer et les communications. ⁵ Groupe interprofessionnel.

Notas explicativas: véase p. 1129.

¹ Casos recogidos para indemnización en el año. ² Excl. los agentes de los servicios públicos de electricidad y gas. ³ Excl. comercio alimenticio. ⁴ Excl. transportes ferroviarios y marítimos y las comunicaciones. ⁵ Grupo interocupacional.

	1999	2000	2001	2002	2003	2004	2005	2006	2007	2008
Italy (FA)				Compensated injuries - Lésions indemnisées - Lesiones indemnizadas						
Men - Hommes - Hombres										
ISIC 3 - CITI 3 - CIIU 3										
Total	10 931 708	12 366 557	11 490 826	11 032 387	10 670 338	10 556 050	10 209 297	10 192 937	9 817 183	9 184 100
A	1 263 842	1 407 151	1 252 309	1 191 294	1 169 553	1 155 339	1 105 862	1 096 311	996 766	954 861
B	9 913	9 364	9 384	12 706	10 692	10 688	12 264	9 663	9 637	9 158
C	45 428	52 561	46 754	42 228	38 478	38 956	37 622	34 393	35 606	30 449
D	3 882 057	4 251 819	3 954 622	3 666 260	3 497 127	3 352 165	3 268 111	3 238 324	3 134 477	2 774 561
E	108 861	121 444	104 130	97 098	90 473	92 224	86 803	81 443	69 812	64 034
F	1 973 562	2 301 605	2 102 295	2 102 378	2 117 782	2 162 680	2 084 410	2 086 195	1 998 046	1 787 338
G	970 296	1 072 345	991 844	967 962	935 582	945 572	923 044	901 656	875 967	819 558
H	214 615	251 056	227 023	225 955	232 748	234 909	231 029	235 192	237 104	208 532
I	1 147 471	1 309 093	1 289 972	1 239 657	1 201 148	1 216 455	1 187 387	1 190 315	1 164 900	1 075 559
J	41 211	50 524	53 076	49 211	29 295	28 060	25 204	24 742	23 272	20 838
K	449 855	527 030	562 657	591 683	579 398	585 128	450 411	509 428	496 061	482 937
L	202 878	225 511	211 429	204 915	214 446	201 627	206 110	195 690	176 387	162 484
M	20 266	43 524	21 644	19 299	18 172	16 977	17 019	17 249	16 429	13 161
N	118 371	139 002	129 354	131 480	124 675	128 011	129 985	129 673	126 367	122 934
O	362 397	400 201	321 604	331 592	342 752	343 056	360 096	385 099	399 303	373 199
P	2 580	3 334	2 835	4 519	6 408	4 557	5 247	5 502	5 046	6 751
X	118 105	200 993	209 894	154 150	61 609	39 646	78 693	52 062	52 003	277 746
Women - Femmes - Mujeres										
ISIC 3 - CITI 3 - CIIU 3										
Total	2 765 986	3 196 346	3 030 784	2 625 187	2 897 344	2 919 040	2 899 819	2 924 760	2 880 263	2 783 850
A	502 435	544 120	496 504	454 916	435 271	422 888	409 206	392 816	367 830	340 972
B	109	250	339	317	595	567	800	542	774	500
C	408	353	740	735	523	246	555	513	1 011	287
D	609 771	674 180	612 253	562 036	524 836	496 012	489 275	485 118	449 591	393 651
E	15 967	18 542	10 650	11 271	9 019	8 632	10 782	9 923	9 366	7 519
F	13 857	18 885	21 900	26 489	24 024	20 469	22 916	22 152	23 236	17 952
G	255 645	296 936	279 215	289 969	305 054	316 298	319 518	321 678	325 233	315 890
H	232 548	262 608	252 859	250 815	265 065	264 986	273 488	273 164	279 409	257 236
I	173 704	206 529	211 894	201 779	199 008	213 887	228 922	229 507	238 840	238 131
J	22 602	30 181	28 356	29 750	21 768	21 222	22 745	21 764	23 490	21 313
K	247 286	303 971	306 305	14 619	310 809	322 157	289 023	321 413	314 218	306 166
L	189 224	208 835	212 434	201 338	212 052	219 239	209 242	209 422	204 071	189 496
M	15 944	40 723	19 242	21 163	20 256	22 282	26 539	23 878	23 545	24 665
N	271 794	331 647	318 527	323 390	343 618	352 794	367 925	385 179	388 345	367 316
O	143 299	159 336	151 360	139 520	142 107	145 910	162 915	164 498	173 986	163 875
P	21 009	28 818	25 940	24 438	35 400	40 926	40 541	45 937	44 450	57 988
X	50 384	70 432	82 266	72 642	47 939	50 525	25 427	17 256	12 868	80 893
Latvia (DA)				Reported injuries - Lésions déclarées - Lesiones declaradas						
Total men and women - Total hommes et femmes - Total hombres y mujeres										
ISIC 3 - CITI 3 - CIIU 3										
Total	21 800	26 000	34 048	36 011	52 080	48 128	35 317	47 242	38 274	.
Lithuania (FF)				Reported injuries - Lésions déclarées - Lesiones declaradas						
Total men and women - Total hommes et femmes - Total hombres y mujeres [1]										
ISIC 3 - CITI 3 - CIIU 3										
Total	70 905	65 463	80 574	110 481	106 594	106 620	129 446	121 569	109 092	.
A	4 660	3 202	4 586	3 750	5 156	3 912	5 357	3 904	3 453	.
B	209	144	233	45	82	658	387	85	285	.
C	755	1 018	1 624	560	1 374	794	592	1 560	1 269	.
D	28 482	24 738	30 330	42 252	37 669	41 272	45 412	44 735	39 476	.
E	3 396	3 664	2 932	3 268	2 792	2 516	2 325	2 930	1 808	.
F	10 284	7 955	10 790	20 564	17 820	19 340	28 813	25 457	24 002	.
G	3 089	4 232	6 992	7 224	8 345	7 966	10 145	8 612	7 471	.
H	420	719	814	728	943	886	766	706	638	.
I	8 938	8 603	8 557	13 250	10 867	10 650	18 263	13 850	15 218	.
J	406	523	875	784	715	618	57	185	187	.
K	640	870	1 206	2 193	2 332	2 084	2 720	1 974	2 483	.
L	1 250	1 953	2 100	3 456	2 970	2 370	2 335	2 488	1 008	.
M	2 079	2 355	3 342	3 498	5 767	4 224	2 732	4 263	3 914	.
N	4 039	3 248	3 722	5 842	5 462	5 646	6 035	6 049	4 399	.
O	2 258	2 239	2 434	3 053	4 300	3 550	3 439	4 771	3 481	.
P	.	.	37	14	0	0	68	0	0	.
Q	0	0	0	0	0	134	0	0	0	.
X	0	0	0	0	0	0	0	0	0	.

Explanatory notes: see p. 1125.
Notes explicatives: voir p. 1127.
Notas explicativas: véase p. 1129.

[1] Days lost by all cases of non-fatal injury.
[1] Journées perdues par l'ensemble des cas de lésion non mortelle.
[1] Días perdidos por todos los casos de lesión no mortal.

8C

	OCCUPATIONAL INJURIES	LÉSIONS PROFESSIONNELLES	LESIONES PROFESIONALES
	Days lost, by economic activity	Journées perdues, par activité économique	Días perdidos, por actividad económica

	1999	2000	2001	2002	2003	2004	2005	2006	2007	2008

Malta (FA) — Compensated injuries - Lésions indemnisées - Lesiones indemnizadas

Total men and women - Total hommes et femmes - Total hombres y mujeres
ISIC 3 - CITI 3 - CIIU 3

	1999	2000	2001	2002	2003	2004	2005	2006	2007	2008
Total	.	.	81 363	76 851	79 299	71 537	69 227	80 827	83 697	80 934
A	.	.	958	622	846	1 059	1 310	1 448	1 052	1 886
B	.	.	24	221	217	219	342	333	176	308
C	.	.	301	151	437	611	670	831	802	1 340
D	.	.	19 601	26 137	20 219	20 980	18 207	24 049	22 297	20 287
E	.	.	2 179	2 751	2 488	2 336	2 839	2 272	3 309	3 035
F	.	.	9 610	7 666	12 912	15 047	16 031	17 606	17 534	17 781
G	.	.	3 016	3 627	4 898	6 623	6 962	7 906	8 221	7 699
H	.	.	4 697	4 208	4 681	5 977	4 791	4 869	5 060	4 862
I	.	.	4 975	5 504	7 811	8 281	7 081	9 485	12 439	11 265
J	.	.	299	62	571	234	303	236	363	247
K	.	.	1 654	2 094	2 850	3 128	3 126	3 253	4 068	4 103
L	.	.	2 109	2 192	2 808	2 698	2 737	3 075	3 087	2 835
M	.	.	2 764	3 224	1 110	1 291	968	1 362	712	1 161
N	.	.	306	313	2 677	1 856	2 112	3 010	3 262	2 911
O	.	.	1 335	928	1 320	999	1 562	963	1 200	1 149
P	.	.	0	0	0	0	0	61	0	0
Q	.	.	17	0	0	42	176	64	106	47
X	.	.	27 518	17 151	13 454	156	10	4	9	18

Men - Hommes - Hombres
ISIC 3 - CITI 3 - CIIU 3

	1999	2000	2001	2002	2003	2004	2005	2006	2007	2008
Total	.	.	74 364	68 728	71 651	64 458	62 421	73 421	75 782	73 884
A	.	.	958	599	819	1 038	1 310	1 396	1 052	1 886
B	.	.	24	221	217	219	342	333	176	308
C	.	.	301	151	437	611	670	831	802	1 331
D	.	.	18 143	23 965	18 795	19 301	16 931	22 184	20 891	18 888
E	.	.	2 158	2 668	2 463	2 336	2 797	2 268	3 297	3 035
F	.	.	9 499	7 500	12 872	14 946	15 925	17 523	17 508	17 705
G	.	.	2 891	3 357	4 760	6 286	6 270	7 320	7 870	7 158
H	.	.	3 787	3 440	3 100	4 530	3 226	3 879	3 785	3 798
I	.	.	4 328	5 046	7 139	7 645	6 725	8 807	11 731	10 766
J	.	.	179	62	367	92	224	196	166	228
K	.	.	1 457	1 570	2 625	2 470	2 504	2 854	3 314	3 284
L	.	.	1 780	1 910	2 595	2 381	2 384	2 744	2 758	2 622
M	.	.	1 630	1 634	537	833	695	786	297	351
N	.	.	56	76	775	744	920	1 368	1 039	1 386
O	.	.	1 249	751	1 313	853	1 358	886	996	1 080
P	.	.	0	0	0	0	0	0	0	0
Q	.	.	17	0	0	18	131	42	91	40
X	.	.	25 907	15 778	12 837	155	9	4	9	18

Women - Femmes - Mujeres
ISIC 3 - CITI 3 - CIIU 3

	1999	2000	2001	2002	2003	2004	2005	2006	2007	2008
Total	.	.	6 999	8 123	7 648	7 079	6 806	7 406	7 915	7 050
A	.	.	0	23	27	21	0	52	0	0
B	.	.	0	0	0	0	0	0	0	0
C	.	.	0	0	0	0	0	0	0	9
D	.	.	1 458	2 172	1 424	1 679	1 276	1 865	1 406	1 399
E	.	.	21	83	25	0	42	4	12	0
F	.	.	111	166	40	101	106	83	26	76
G	.	.	125	270	138	337	692	586	351	541
H	.	.	910	768	1 581	1 447	1 565	990	1 275	1 064
I	.	.	647	458	672	636	356	678	708	499
J	.	.	120	0	204	142	79	40	197	19
K	.	.	197	524	225	658	622	399	754	819
L	.	.	329	282	213	317	353	331	329	213
M	.	.	1 134	1 590	573	458	273	576	415	810
N	.	.	250	237	1 902	1 112	1 192	1 642	2 223	1 525
O	.	.	86	177	7	146	204	77	204	69
P	.	.	0	0	0	0	0	61	0	0
Q	.	.	0	0	0	24	45	22	15	7
X	.	.	1 611	1 373	617	1	1	0	0	0

Moldova, Republic of (CA) [1] — Reported injuries - Lésions déclarées - Lesiones declaradas

Total men and women - Total hommes et femmes - Total hombres y mujeres
ISIC 3 - CITI 3 - CIIU 3

	1999	2000	2001	2002	2003	2004	2005	2006	2007	2008
Total	30 101	23 313	21 015	21 817	20 398	19 958	22 169	21 967	20 005	18 985
A	8 359	4 862	3 608	2 725	3 352	3 184	2 462	1 904	2 294	1 915
B	0	0	0	0	0	0	0	0	0	.
C	135	251	171	320	80	348	256	607	900	886
D	7 738	5 801	7 557	9 228	6 888	6 449	7 853	7 432	5 881	6 228
E	1 802	1 252	1 202	2 243	2 070	1 986	2 056	2 326	1 338	772
F	1 078	1 226	735	1 207	784	1 250	2 129	2 528	2 501	1 530
G	334	946	810	626	788	685	1 060	735	775	1 051
H	.	.	82	562	853	324	13	58	62	41
I	2 276	2 196	2 033	1 643	2 126	2 227	1 427	1 796	1 818	2 547
J	250	368	20	12	35	60	420	267	219	286
K	805	1 000	845	398	616	1 142	1 344	813	594	854
L	5 963	4 044	2 316	1 520	542	472	984	919	1 700	1 217
M	448	325	1 087	318	1 330	648	574	867	562	263
N	505	899	429	848	667	609	1 360	1 220	1 221	1 018
O	408	143	120	167	267	574	231	495	140	377

Explanatory notes: see p. 1125. Notes explicatives: voir p. 1127. Notas explicativas: véase p. 1129.

[1] Enterprises with 20 or more employees, state-owned and municipal enterprises, institutions and organisations.
[1] Entreprises occupant 20 salariés et plus, entreprises d'Etat et municipales, institutions et organisations.
[1] Empresas con 20 y más asalariados, empresas estatales y municipales, instituciones y organisaciones.

OCCUPATIONAL INJURIES
Days lost, by economic activity

LÉSIONS PROFESSIONNELLES
Journées perdues, par activité économique

LESIONES PROFESIONALES
Días perdidos, por actividad económica

	1999	2000	2001	2002	2003	2004	2005	2006	2007	2008

Poland (FF) — Reported injuries - Lésions déclarées - Lesiones declaradas

Total men and women - Total hommes et femmes - Total hombres y mujeres
ISIC 3 - CITI 3 - CIIU 3

	1999	2000	2001	2002	2003	2004	2005	2006	2007	2008
Total [1]	4 385 412	4 107 344	3 707 979	3 540 166	3 825 081	3 872 979	3 666 934	4 147 170	4 084 929	3 638 805
A [1]	107 730	93 921	87 892	80 766	91 472	82 343	79 470	86 295	79 442	75 394
B	4 955	4 602	3 574	4 752	3 600	3 418	1 933	2 682	1 798	989
C	370 377	278 546	229 716	238 608	222 208	219 786	186 559	193 749	133 250	183 997
D	1 674 046	1 575 883	1 412 025	1 303 884	1 410 609	1 483 739	1 416 635	1 602 534	1 671 820	1 426 468
E	105 189	93 502	90 206	90 778	99 120	91 084	87 193	94 587	87 355	67 775
F	613 616	579 941	513 895	428 710	407 265	393 944	372 638	442 410	466 065	427 286
G	318 528	338 514	313 184	318 621	356 870	355 985	338 162	388 826	395 404	369 773
H	25 542	34 705	26 847	28 340	32 197	36 997	33 529	35 101	37 804	35 161
I	316 216	291 206	273 777	238 845	277 430	264 995	263 323	312 785	295 124	247 625
J	33 099	30 540	23 164	25 884	30 608	30 757	29 055	30 118	26 175	25 752
K	183 320	182 789	179 555	205 546	256 728	236 035	219 579	244 422	232 305	204 673
L	96 643	100 891	105 960	117 302	136 538	137 115	138 565	139 636	136 474	120 318
M	111 677	106 691	100 428	103 153	116 897	151 408	137 604	156 942	142 444	134 450
N	332 044	304 047	262 554	268 142	291 012	287 363	271 934	301 896	276 270	225 399
O	92 359	91 566	85 202	86 835	92 527	98 010	90 755	115 187	103 154	93 546
P	71	0	0	0	0	0	0	0	45	109
Q	.	.	.	.	.	.	.	.	.	90

Men - Hommes - Hombres
ISIC 3 - CITI 3 - CIIU 3

	1999	2000	2001	2002	2003	2004	2005	2006	2007	2008
Total [1]	3 439 508	3 225 078	2 896 068	2 714 257	2 889 082	2 932 192	2 772 932	3 133 200	3 088 192	2 735 082
A [1]	91 635	79 453	75 564	67 090	77 682	68 066	64 867	72 052	67 095	61 083
B	4 499	4 225	3 388	4 591	3 516	3 074	1 619	2 514	1 422	960
C	364 961	274 770	227 352	234 601	217 876	216 422	183 312	190 639	130 684	181 884
D	1 379 084	1 318 340	1 181 103	1 091 399	1 175 177	1 248 710	1 186 802	1 337 874	1 379 698	1 163 163
E	92 117	83 252	81 912	82 106	89 011	83 279	77 364	85 258	80 931	62 233
F	600 843	566 104	503 617	419 116	397 012	384 034	364 378	433 031	458 099	418 670
G	230 590	247 631	226 977	226 949	256 431	249 108	233 837	262 430	261 451	244 691
H	11 292	15 596	12 108	12 994	12 229	16 995	16 530	15 446	16 062	16 340
I	261 220	243 433	225 443	196 443	226 503	221 240	221 867	266 317	247 605	208 497
J	12 156	11 595	6 794	8 819	11 087	10 252	10 690	10 200	8 430	8 844
K	123 434	122 723	120 522	134 482	165 300	157 866	152 292	165 927	159 640	134 249
L	57 361	62 475	62 314	62 338	73 370	72 361	72 725	77 248	75 856	65 613
M	45 460	41 328	39 174	35 308	37 228	49 549	43 411	49 900	47 481	42 216
N	97 653	89 301	66 292	72 288	80 811	80 173	77 415	78 566	75 977	59 947
O	67 132	64 852	63 508	65 733	65 849	71 063	65 823	85 798	77 761	66 692
P	71	0	0	0	0	0	0	0	0	0

Women - Femmes - Mujeres
ISIC 3 - CITI 3 - CIIU 3

	1999	2000	2001	2002	2003	2004	2005	2006	2007	2008
Total [1]	945 904	882 266	811 911	825 909	935 999	940 787	894 002	1 013 970	996 737	903 723
A [1]	16 095	14 468	12 328	13 676	13 790	14 277	14 603	14 243	12 347	14 311
B	456	377	186	161	84	344	314	168	376	29
C	5 416	3 776	2 364	4 007	4 332	3 364	3 247	3 110	2 566	2 113
D	294 962	257 543	230 922	212 485	235 432	235 029	229 833	264 660	292 122	263 305
E	13 072	10 250	8 294	8 672	10 109	7 805	9 829	9 329	6 424	5 542
F	12 773	13 837	10 278	9 594	10 253	9 910	8 260	9 379	7 966	8 616
G	87 938	90 883	86 207	91 672	100 439	106 877	104 325	126 396	133 953	125 082
H	14 250	19 109	14 739	15 346	19 968	20 002	16 999	19 655	21 742	18 821
I	54 996	47 773	48 334	42 402	50 927	43 755	41 456	46 468	47 519	39 128
J	20 943	18 945	16 370	17 065	19 521	20 505	18 365	19 918	17 745	16 908
K	59 886	60 066	59 033	71 064	91 428	78 169	67 287	78 495	72 665	70 424
L	39 282	38 416	43 646	54 964	63 168	64 754	65 840	62 388	60 618	54 705
M	66 217	65 363	61 254	67 845	79 669	101 859	94 193	107 042	94 963	92 234
N	234 391	214 746	196 262	195 854	210 201	207 190	194 519	223 330	200 293	165 452
O	25 227	26 714	21 694	21 102	26 678	26 947	24 932	29 389	25 393	26 854
P	0	0	0	0	0	0	0	0	45	109

Explanatory notes: see p. 1125.

[1] Excl. private farms in agriculture.

Notes explicatives: voir p. 1127.

[1] Non compris les fermes privées dans l'agriculture.

Notas explicativas: véase p. 1129.

[1] Excl. las granjas privadas en la agricultura.

OCCUPATIONAL INJURIES — LÉSIONS PROFESSIONNELLES — LESIONES PROFESIONALES

Days lost, by economic activity — Journées perdues, par activité économique — Días perdidos, por actividad económica

Roumanie (FF) — Reported injuries - Lésions déclarées - Lesiones declaradas

Total men and women - Total hommes et femmes - Total hombres y mujeres
ISIC 3 - CITI 3 - CIIU 3 / ISIC 4 - CITI 4 - CIIU 4 [1]

	1999	2000	2001	2002	2003	2004	2005	2006	2007	2008	
Total	349 867	3 344 774	361 057	346 511	319 535	298 598	276 065	288 217	243 136	186 236	Total
A	21 712	19 379	18 829	13 807	14 064	13 522	10 294	8 683	7 303	6 843	A
B	12	62	213	62	265	182	0	0	209	14 913	B
C	77 595	77 328	81 325	76 847	65 278	43 514	30 479	26 192	21 366	82 435	C
D	161 393	158 052	162 985	161 107	151 783	151 334	139 310	142 275	111 061	4 061	D
E	10 224	8 327	8 281	7 491	6 985	7 240	10 858	9 369	7 616	5 214	E
F	39 269	38 647	42 163	38 588	37 301	38 082	39 201	43 960	40 679	31 283	F
G	3 946	5 827	6 288	7 665	8 930	8 723	9 991	15 395	13 625	14 990	G
H	658	1 188	1 359	1 114	1 146	957	919	1 182	947	9 982	H
I	23 723	22 948	25 283	23 057	18 212	17 894	18 301	16 180	18 744	972	I
J	894	346	656	909	1 036	647	264	1 149	532	485	J
K	2 100	3 722	3 311	3 575	4 620	5 307	5 677	6 942	7 449	580	K
L	2 505	3 232	2 251	3 310	2 702	2 469	1 765	3 618	2 924	699	L
M	667	1 622	1 887	1 681	1 019	1 686	1 696	2 520	2 014	1 949	M
N	2 545	2 266	2 404	3 100	2 750	2 813	3 447	6 264	4 385	4 911	N
O	2 701	2 150	2 463	4 198	3 444	4 228	3 863	4 485	4 282	2 916	O
P	0	0	0	0	0	0	0	0	0	1 169	P
Q	0	0	0	0	0	0	0	0	0	2 178	Q
R										466	R
S										190	S
T										0	T
U										0	U
X										0	X

Men - Hommes - Hombres
ISIC 3 - CITI 3 - CIIU 3 / ISIC 4 - CITI 4 - CIIU 4 [1]

	1999	2000	2001	2002	2003	2004	2005	2006	2007	2008	
Total	297 152	295 233	306 574	294 680	271 231	251 261	232 675	234 355	198 987	150 481	Total
A	19 396	17 539	17 036	12 406	12 691	12 941	9 819	7 984	6 223	6 343	A
B	12	62	213	62	265	182	0	0	209	14 070	B
C	75 137	76 010	79 734	74 449	63 804	42 075	29 883	25 014	20 627	61 703	C
D	126 493	123 553	126 271	127 854	119 085	118 288	108 743	109 329	84 965	3 922	D
E	8 266	7 637	7 140	6 524	6 143	5 968	9 823	8 043	6 467	4 204	E
F	37 246	37 273	40 466	36 838	36 231	37 102	38 541	42 420	40 332	30 674	F
G	3 117	4 648	5 069	6 557	7 434	7 360	7 931	12 743	10 922	10 290	G
H	385	683	810	609	479	547	488	695	793	8 384	H
I	20 476	19 420	21 606	19 013	14 758	14 384	15 516	13 173	15 386	556	I
J	180	84	34	652	294	48	67	92	141	466	J
K	1 677	3 306	2 628	3 208	3 760	4 898	5 444	5 727	6 360	77	K
L	1 332	2 667	1 489	1 930	2 083	1 562	1 259	2 276	1 479	668	L
M	333	462	649	763	590	1 163	1 105	1 422	706	1 405	M
N	926	697	762	954	987	1 110	1 722	1 912	1 175	3 988	N
O	2 253	1 514	1 907	2 861	2 627	3 633	2 334	3 525	3 202	2 029	O
P										532	P
Q										690	Q
R										330	R
S										150	S
T										0	T
U										0	U
X										0	X

Women - Femmes - Mujeres
ISIC 3 - CITI 3 - CIIU 3 / ISIC 4 - CITI 4 - CIIU 4 [1]

	1999	2000	2001	2002	2003	2004	2005	2006	2007	2008	
Total	52 715	49 541	53 884	51 831	48 304	47 337	43 390	53 862	44 149	35 755	Total
A	2 316	1 840	1 793	1 401	1 373	581	475	702	1 080	500	A
B	0	0	0	0	0	0	0	0	0	843	B
C	2 458	1 318	1 591	2 398	1 474	1 439	596	1 178	739	20 732	C
D	34 900	34 499	36 714	33 253	32 698	33 046	30 567	32 946	26 096	139	D
E	1 958	690	1 141	967	842	1 272	1 035	1 326	1 149	1 010	E
F	2 023	1 374	1 697	1 750	1 070	980	660	1 540	347	609	F
G	829	1 179	1 219	1 108	1 496	1 363	2 060	2 652	2 703	4 700	G
H	273	505	549	505	667	410	431	487	154	1 598	H
I	3 247	3 528	3 677	4 044	3 454	3 510	2 785	3 007	3 358	416	I
J	714	262	622	257	742	599	197	1 057	391	19	J
K	423	416	683	367	860	409	233	1 215	1 089	503	K
L	1 173	565	762	1 380	619	907	506	1 342	1 445	31	L
M	334	1 160	1 238	918	429	523	591	1 098	1 308	544	M
N	1 619	1 569	1 642	2 146	1 763	1 703	1 725	4 352	3 210	923	N
O	448	636	556	1 337	817	595	1 529	960	1 080	887	O
P										637	P
Q										1 488	Q
R										136	R
S										40	S
T										0	T
U										0	U
X										0	X

Russian Federation (DA) [2] — Reported injuries - Lésions déclarées - Lesiones declaradas

Total men and women - Total hommes et femmes - Total hombres y mujeres [3]
ISIC 3 - CITI 3 - CIIU 3

	1999	2000	2001	2002	2003	2004	2005	2006	2007	2008
Total	4 275 030	4 295 150	4 110 830	3 679 750	3 258 730	2 755 230	2 499 450	2 324 460	2 718 670	2 720 560

Explanatory notes: see p. 1125.
[1] Deaths occurring within the same reference year as accident. [2] Excl. activities with low injury rates. [3] Figures rounded to nearest 10.

Notes explicatives: voir p. 1127.
[1] Décès survenant pendant la même année de référence que l'accident. [2] Non compris les activités avec les taux de lésion bas. [3] Chiffres arrondis au 10 le plus proche.

Notas explicativas: véase p. 1129.
[1] Fallecimientos que se producen durante el mismo año de referencia que el accidente. [2] Excl. las actividades con tasas de lesion bajas. [3] Cifras redondeadas al 10 más próximo.

OCCUPATIONAL INJURIES

Days lost, by economic activity

LÉSIONS PROFESSIONNELLES

Journées perdues, par activité économique

LESIONES PROFESIONALES

Días perdidos, por actividad económica

8C

	1999	2000	2001	2002	2003	2004	2005	2006	2007	2008

Slovakia (CA) — Reported injuries - Lésions déclarées - Lesiones declaradas

Total men and women - Total hommes et femmes - Total hombres y mujeres
ISIC 3 - CITI 3 - CIIU 3

	1999	2000	2001	2002	2003	2004	2005	2006	2007	2008
Total	942 700	855 713	835 945	800 189	741 436	589 281	622 068	692 560	688 468	544 214
A	149 724	128 955	117 590	116 397	98 648	63 936	59 574	55 491	37 578	29 834
B	0	109	30	17	0	151	255	34	34	138
C	36 153	29 563	28 999	27 734	30 701	25 376	16 297	37 935	21 704	18 965
D	301 537	279 846	273 152	261 042	247 754	195 948	201 690	212 119	246 449	225 946
E	16 469	14 480	14 186	12 952	11 247	10 116	8 945	7 978	6 330	3 296
F	80 190	67 295	60 975	58 501	51 758	46 509	43 531	43 267	65 490	57 554
G	35 945	35 054	31 141	34 297	34 681	31 906	29 746	32 365	52 620	52 762
H	7 105	5 593	5 670	3 950	4 314	2 829	2 137	3 651	9 644	9 053
I	61 603	59 605	51 714	48 119	47 679	38 704	40 060	43 776	44 207	37 655
J	4 105	3 471	2 467	2 118	2 552	2 490	1 426	2 686	2 847	2 529
K	20 209	21 697	24 607	22 955	15 776	13 341	12 897	14 507	26 213	23 293
L	172 378	153 560	174 976	162 076	143 025	118 124	159 488	190 525	20 630	16 354
M	16 803	14 404	12 839	13 554	18 510	16 098	16 179	18 791	15 492	18 242
N	27 674	27 952	25 030	24 515	25 065	13 473	19 403	18 048	14 347	16 722
O	12 805	14 129	12 569	11 962	9 726	10 280	10 440	11 387	13 612	13 825
P	0	0	0	0	0	0	0	0	0	0
Q	0	0	0	0	0	0	0	0	6 736	5 097
X	0	0	0	0	0	0	0	0	104 535	12 949

Men - Hommes - Hombres
ISIC 3 - CITI 3 - CIIU 3

	1999	2000	2001	2002	2003	2004	2005	2006	2007	2008
Total	727 687	658 392	656 845	617 356	568 743	450 798	471 049	524 901	524 146	392 359
A	119 177	99 158	91 684	94 945	78 475	51 507	45 764	41 598	29 805	22 686
B	0	109	0	17	0	0	199	34	34	138
C	35 733	29 436	28 815	27 628	30 483	25 303	16 133	37 620	21 318	18 141
D	231 510	217 632	216 258	198 740	192 648	150 130	151 283	154 524	184 429	167 102
E	15 007	12 514	12 372	11 939	10 211	9 003	8 449	7 152	5 748	3 100
F	78 148	65 578	59 369	57 375	50 272	45 388	42 472	42 859	63 621	56 497
G	24 081	25 631	19 579	20 374	22 882	19 716	19 330	18 787	33 285	31 026
H	2 891	2 852	2 610	1 759	2 090	1 243	877	959	4 273	4 108
I	47 666	47 686	43 504	38 645	34 244	27 554	29 635	30 065	36 343	30 176
J	1 414	1 486	1 214	776	443	631	562	797	638	814
K	15 353	16 298	20 958	17 940	13 361	10 067	8 626	10 796	19 465	15 794
L	133 563	116 639	139 703	126 394	113 043	94 065	131 338	159 847	13 151	10 603
M	5 605	4 210	4 049	4 855	5 077	5 109	3 757	5 030	4 051	4 560
N	7 784	7 744	7 177	6 595	7 503	3 281	5 269	6 001	3 935	3 778
O	9 755	11 419	9 553	9 374	8 011	7 644	7 355	8 832	10 930	10 052
P	0	0	0	0	0	0	0	0	0	0
Q	0	0	0	0	0	0	0	0	5 356	3 584
X	0	0	0	0	0	0	0	0	87 764	10 200

Women - Femmes - Mujeres
ISIC 3 - CITI 3 - CIIU 3

	1999	2000	2001	2002	2003	2004	2005	2006	2007	2008
Total	215 013	197 321	179 100	182 833	172 693	138 489	151 019	167 959	164 322	151 855
A	30 547	29 797	25 906	21 452	20 173	12 429	13 810	13 893	7 773	7 148
B	0	0	30	0	0	0	56	0	0	0
C	420	127	184	106	218	73	164	315	386	824
D	70 027	62 214	56 894	62 302	55 106	45 818	50 407	57 595	62 020	58 844
E	1 462	1 966	1 814	1 013	1 036	1 113	496	826	582	196
F	2 042	1 717	1 606	1 126	1 486	1 121	1 059	408	1 869	1 057
G	11 864	9 423	11 562	13 923	11 799	12 190	10 416	13 578	19 335	21 736
H	4 214	2 741	3 060	2 191	2 224	1 586	1 260	2 692	5 371	4 945
I	13 937	11 919	8 210	9 474	13 435	11 150	10 425	13 711	7 864	7 479
J	2 691	1 985	1 253	1 342	2 109	1 859	864	1 889	2 209	1 715
K	4 856	5 399	3 649	5 015	2 415	3 274	4 271	3 711	6 748	7 499
L	38 815	36 921	35 273	35 682	29 982	24 059	28 150	30 678	7 479	5 751
M	11 198	10 194	8 790	8 699	13 433	10 989	12 422	13 761	11 441	13 682
N	19 890	20 208	17 853	17 920	17 562	10 192	14 134	12 047	10 412	12 944
O	3 050	2 710	3 016	2 588	1 715	2 636	3 085	2 555	2 682	3 773
P	0	0	0	0	0	0	0	0	0	0
Q	0	0	0	0	0	0	0	0	1 380	1 513
X	0	0	0	0	0	0	0	0	16 771	2 749

Explanatory notes: see p. 1125.　　　　Notes explicatives: voir p. 1127.　　　　Notas explicativas: véase p. 1129.

8C

	OCCUPATIONAL INJURIES	LÉSIONS PROFESSIONNELLES	LESIONES PROFESIONALES
	Days lost, by economic activity	Journées perdues, par activité économique	Días perdidos, por actividad económica

	1999	2000	2001	2002	2003	2004	2005	2006	2007	2008
Slovenia (FF)				Reported injuries - Lésions déclarées - Lesiones declaradas						

Total men and women - Total hommes et femmes - Total hombres y mujeres
ISIC 3 - CITI 3 - CIIU 3

	1999	2000	2001	2002	2003	2004	2005	2006	2007	2008
Total	976 489	969 541	970 297	995 419	1 017 730	1 026 057	878 790	891 063	903 296	.
A	41 799	35 873	31 826	33 135	34 457	36 230	29 272	30 066	29 276	.
B	217	336	184	315	255	216	329	192	175	.
C	19 269	19 334	18 192	14 089	14 581	12 180	10 884	9 238	8 368	.
D	341 971	333 793	351 156	359 919	353 892	346 121	303 342	296 651	304 203	.
E	15 473	18 194	16 702	17 589	14 995	17 534	15 805	16 862	12 969	.
F	131 672	138 001	145 208	142 236	143 672	151 948	127 146	130 224	148 892	.
G	85 755	94 515	89 148	92 394	95 512	87 640	77 256	80 659	85 652	.
H	19 126	23 539	28 192	28 801	30 499	28 719	27 220	26 468	24 946	.
I	58 502	67 858	64 470	75 496	80 214	80 813	68 356	70 026	70 001	.
J	7 177	8 523	9 755	10 970	10 671	10 403	9 071	10 114	8 362	.
K	35 762	37 336	42 678	44 825	50 402	48 124	41 693	45 909	45 981	.
L	47 286	52 332	56 239	57 372	66 055	77 091	61 699	59 870	88 542	.
M	28 452	29 966	27 901	28 224	31 939	32 942	27 723	28 819	26 039	.
N	46 591	52 955	54 698	44 867	44 176	46 005	36 167	40 665	39 136	.
O	18 366	19 274	21 006	22 673	22 088	23 782	22 559	22 347	19 683	.
P	50	64	44	26	0	0	0	0	0	.
Q	0	0	0	0	0	0	0	0	0	.
X	79 021	37 648	12 898	22 488	24 322	26 309	20 268	22 953	23 771	.

	1999	2000	2001	2002	2003	2004	2005	2006	2007	2008
Sweden (FA)				Reported injuries - Lésions déclarées - Lesiones declaradas						

Total men and women - Total hommes et femmes - Total hombres y mujeres
ISIC 3 - CITI 3 - CIIU 3

	1999	2000	2001	2002	2003	2004	2005	2006	2007	2008
Total	1 242 260	1 354 914	1 696 221	1 597 172	1 505 477	1 210 647	.	.	.	.
A	47 960	51 043	56 643	41 572	39 054	25 753	.	.	.	.
B	1 856	1 139	862	1 464	968	516	.	.	.	.
C	5 641	5 317	9 264	7 462	7 757	2 846	.	.	.	.
D	284 741	315 707	398 750	384 680	328 547	282 538	.	.	.	.
E	7 426	7 028	8 121	5 992	3 488	3 448	.	.	.	.
F	139 767	142 582	186 999	206 664	213 941	165 046	.	.	.	.
G	91 097	105 802	127 959	117 270	119 366	88 467	.	.	.	.
H	19 625	21 642	28 937	29 521	27 391	18 573	.	.	.	.
I	141 109	149 972	194 745	188 402	182 437	149 186	.	.	.	.
J	3 356	4 608	6 522	4 673	4 709	2 744	.	.	.	.
K	75 461	94 646	120 247	125 798	120 077	96 855	.	.	.	.
L	59 146	52 640	75 025	69 083	68 725	39 662	.	.	.	.
M	56 648	59 143	74 541	84 006	86 948	74 296	.	.	.	.
N	262 284	295 285	344 520	266 570	243 813	217 979	.	.	.	.
O	39 942	42 737	57 545	52 527	50 572	37 040	.	.	.	.
P	0	0	0	0	0	0	.	.	.	.
Q	0	0	120	0	41	30	.	.	.	.
X	6 201	5 623	.	11 488	7 643	5 668	.	.	.	.

Men - Hommes - Hombres
ISIC 3 - CITI 3 - CIIU 3

	1999	2000	2001	2002	2003	2004	2005	2006	2007	2008
Total	774 246	836 908	1 063 142	1 042 482	979 752	782 115	.	.	.	.
A	39 865	41 965	47 703	32 461	34 038	23 248	.	.	.	.
B	1 846	1 139	862	1 464	968	516	.	.	.	.
C	5 449	5 157	9 001	6 358	7 694	2 802	.	.	.	.
D	231 485	258 445	318 267	314 838	267 261	232 792	.	.	.	.
E	6 994	6 757	7 409	5 193	3 303	3 089	.	.	.	.
F	138 853	140 810	183 113	203 746	210 389	161 345	.	.	.	.
G	59 562	71 799	88 463	88 033	80 394	61 670	.	.	.	.
H	8 160	10 168	13 180	12 848	9 999	10 874	.	.	.	.
I	118 868	121 701	167 794	156 586	151 869	129 000	.	.	.	.
J	807	1 119	1 912	1 020	710	806	.	.	.	.
K	54 290	66 282	83 246	86 545	85 890	66 583	.	.	.	.
L	35 802	32 434	45 846	39 489	41 641	27 569	.	.	.	.
M	16 753	15 703	21 183	17 479	17 766	12 454	.	.	.	.
N	26 167	28 994	33 163	29 704	27 849	21 917	.	.	.	.
O	25 858	30 666	38 990	38 708	35 980	22 867	.	.	.	.
P	0	0	0	0	0	0	.	.	.	.
Q	0	0	120	0	41	0	.	.	.	.
X	3 487	3 769	.	8 010	3 960	4 583	.	.	.	.

Explanatory notes: see p. 1125.   Notes explicatives: voir p. 1127.   Notas explicativas: véase p. 1129.

OCCUPATIONAL INJURIES

Days lost, by economic activity

LÉSIONS PROFESSIONNELLES

Journées perdues, par activité économique

LESIONES PROFESIONALES

Días perdidos, por actividad económica

8C

	1999	2000	2001	2002	2003	2004	2005	2006	2007	2008

Sweden (FA) — Reported injuries - Lésions déclarées - Lesiones declaradas

Women - Femmes - Mujeres
ISIC 3 - CITI 3 - CIIU 3

	1999	2000	2001	2002	2003	2004	2005	2006	2007	2008
Total	468 014	518 006	633 079	554 690	525 725	428 532	.	.	.	.
A	8 095	9 078	8 940	9 111	5 016	2 505	.	.	.	.
B	10	0	0	0	0	0	.	.	.	.
C	192	160	263	1 104	63	44	.	.	.	.
D	53 256	57 262	80 483	69 842	61 286	49 746	.	.	.	.
E	432	271	712	799	185	359	.	.	.	.
F	914	1 772	3 886	2 918	3 552	3 701	.	.	.	.
G	31 535	34 003	39 496	29 237	38 972	26 797	.	.	.	.
H	11 465	11 474	15 757	16 673	17 392	7 699	.	.	.	.
I	22 241	28 271	26 951	31 816	30 568	20 186	.	.	.	.
J	2 549	3 489	4 610	3 653	3 999	1 938	.	.	.	.
K	21 171	28 364	37 001	39 253	34 187	30 272	.	.	.	.
L	23 344	20 206	29 179	29 594	27 084	12 093	.	.	.	.
M	39 895	43 440	53 358	66 527	69 182	61 842	.	.	.	.
N	236 117	266 291	311 357	236 866	215 964	196 062	.	.	.	.
O	14 084	12 071	18 555	13 819	14 592	14 173	.	.	.	.
P	0	0	0	0	0	0	.	.	.	.
Q	0	0	0	0	0	30	.	.	.	.
X	2 714	1 854	.	3 478	3 683	1 085	.	.	.	.

Turkey (FA) — Reported injuries - Lésions déclarées - Lesiones declaradas

Total men and women - Total hommes et femmes - Total hombres y mujeres [1]
ISIC 2 - CITI 2 - CIIU 2

	1999	2000	2001	2002	2003	2004	2005	2006	2007	2008
Total	1 879 205	1 697 695	1 852 502	1 831 252	2 111 432	1 983 410	1 745 616	1 849 010	.	.
1	0	16 844	20 992	18 809	19 689	16 507	13 346	13 515	.	.
2	143 744	166 498	175 672	166 038	143 764	133 873	148 618	158 491	.	.
3	1 022 529	942 660	1 003 495	986 443	1 221 391	1 175 621	1 023 054	1 057 445	.	.
4	53 815	47 403	53 420	47 110	52 527	45 370	32 843	30 929	.	.
5	367 516	281 835	311 019	305 284	323 767	280 237	229 048	251 409	.	.
6	68 035	59 882	73 240	67 327	86 168	86 548	76 480	86 003	.	.
7	135 538	105 954	123 777	129 683	146 685	136 423	133 197	145 861	.	.
8	2 119	753	1 719	2 869	1 392	1 086	1 245	1 667	.	.
9	85 909	75 849	89 077	107 669	113 385	105 617	87 488	103 416	.	.
0	0	17	91	20	2 664	2 128	297	274	.	.

Men - Hommes - Hombres [1]
ISIC 2 - CITI 2 - CIIU 2

	1999	2000	2001	2002	2003	2004	2005	2006	2007	2008
Total	.	.	1 798 188	1 766 938	2 022 702	1 892 458	1 677 338	1 776 186	.	.
1	.	.	20 172	18 332	17 461	15 449	12 525	12 679	.	.
2	.	.	175 593	165 665	143 602	133 644	148 346	158 413	.	.
3	.	.	967 859	942 773	1 159 551	1 111 459	974 486	1 010 678	.	.
4	.	.	53 264	46 899	52 272	44 702	32 586	30 361	.	.
5	.	.	310 379	302 572	320 905	278 008	227 755	250 336	.	.
6	.	.	69 197	64 766	80 674	81 345	71 258	79 058	.	.
7	.	.	120 375	125 811	141 624	131 020	128 984	141 756	.	.
8	.	.	1 571	2 819	1 390	1 030	1 179	1 667	.	.
9	.	.	79 687	97 293	102 594	93 673	79 922	90 981	.	.
0	.	.	91	8	2 629	2 128	297	257	.	.

Women - Femmes - Mujeres [1]
ISIC 2 - CITI 2 - CIIU 2

	1999	2000	2001	2002	2003	2004	2005	2006	2007	2008
Total	.	.	54 314	64 314	88 730	90 952	68 278	72 824	.	.
1	.	.	820	477	2 228	1 058	821	836	.	.
2	.	.	79	373	162	229	272	78	.	.
3	.	.	35 636	43 670	61 840	64 162	48 568	46 767	.	.
4	.	.	156	211	255	668	257	568	.	.
5	.	.	640	2 712	2 862	2 229	1 293	1 073	.	.
6	.	.	4 043	2 561	5 494	5 203	5 222	6 945	.	.
7	.	.	3 402	3 872	5 061	5 403	4 213	4 105	.	.
8	.	.	148	50	2	56	66	0	.	.
9	.	.	9 390	10 376	10 791	11 944	7 566	12 435	.	.
0	.	.	0	12	35	0	0	17	.	.

Ukraine (FF) — Reported injuries - Lésions déclarées - Lesiones declaradas

Total men and women - Total hommes et femmes - Total hombres y mujeres [2]
ISIC 3 - CITI 3 - CIIU 3

	1999	2000	2001	2002	2003	2004	2005	2006	2007	2008
Total	1 250 563	.	1 028 583	893 434	853 730	839 475	769 425	745 897	706 009	653 110

Explanatory notes: see p. 1125.

[1] Incl. days lost by cases of permanent incapacity. [2] Incl. days lost by cases of fatal injury. [3] Financial year ending in year indicated; excl. Victoria and Australian Capital Territory.

Notes explicatives: voir p. 1127.

[1] Y compris les journées perdues par les cas d'incapacité permanente. [2] Y compris les jours perdus par les cas de lésion mortelle. [3] Année fiscale se terminant en l'année indiquée; non compris Victoria et Australian Capital Territory.

Notas explicativas: véase p. 1129.

[1] Incl. los díos perdidos por los casos de incapacidad permanente. [2] Incl. los días perdidos por los casos de lesión mortal. [3] Año fiscal que se termina en el año indicado; excl. Victoria y Australian Capital Territory.

OCCUPATIONAL INJURIES	LÉSIONS PROFESSIONNELLES	LESIONES PROFESIONALES
Days lost, by economic activity	Journées perdues, par activité économique	Días perdidos, por actividad económica

	1999	2000	2001	2002	2003	2004	2005	2006	2007	2008

OCEANIA-OCÉANIE-OCEANIA

Australia (FA) [1]   Compensated injuries - Lésions indemnisées - Lesiones indemnizadas

Total men and women - Total hommes et femmes - Total hombres y mujeres
ISIC 3 - CITI 3 - CIIU 3

	1999	2000	2001	2002	2003	2004
Total	4 534 685	4 267 635	6 554 040	6 012 300	5 256 990	4 222 860
A-B	206 785	181 020	340 365	279 325	268 345	206 360
C	93 155	83 060	131 825	130 885	88 055	85 130
D	1 085 300	1 001 800	1 420 625	1 136 845	912 735	669 625
E	21 520	19 775	20 685	28 425	22 650	18 315
F	455 145	417 185	615 990	506 880	494 030	400 765
G	673 035	630 285	990 195	878 150	720 150	598 830
H	179 060	171 220	295 145	276 445	245 390	213 300
I	460 790	413 810	648 960	627 480	507 640	431 765
J	37 515	46 135	51 385	51 130	49 705	36 170
K	392 580	423 395	580 360	551 035	516 740	396 015
L	135 965	108 585	163 005	197 825	205 175	145 490
M	116 350	122 840	225 900	243 225	220 345	168 650
N-O	673 225	645 230	1 067 090	1 104 265	1 004 260	852 180
X	4 260	3 305	2 500	380	1 770	865

Men - Hommes - Hombres
ISIC 3 - CITI 3 - CIIU 3

	1999	2000	2001	2002	2003	2004
Total	2 824 880	2 687 950	4 112 110	3 675 905	3 217 250	2 612 825
A-B	3 795	3 840	3 910	3 710	3 450	3 160
C	92 130	80 485	130 125	127 280	85 585	82 560
D	699 495	643 285	1 012 000	813 615	671 645	496 915
E	21 145	18 075	20 005	26 005	21 110	16 060
F	443 085	411 235	600 875	490 120	479 810	388 035
G	432 615	407 515	594 865	535 735	436 550	366 505
H	64 220	64 935	130 335	119 335	98 410	84 005
I	404 020	345 230	560 105	536 570	441 580	372 635
J	6 675	14 920	8 675	10 585	8 650	6 735
K	228 005	247 350	332 130	305 380	276 510	227 765
L	50 080	43 970	67 335	88 335	95 675	73 070
M	29 760	48 360	75 705	83 420	79 115	60 820
N	92 108	103 524	99 467	112 584	75 560	
N-O	200 390	229 485	340 480	332 835	316 585	276 155
O	171 287	189 031	203 092	187 299	142 069	
X	2 740	2 275	2 495	195	1 770	865

Women - Femmes - Mujeres
ISIC 3 - CITI 3 - CIIU 3

	1999	2000	2001	2002	2003	2004
Total	1 709 805	1 579 685	2 441 930	2 336 400	2 039 740	1 610 035
A-B	56 270	50 195	103 390	72 830	64 090	45 665
C	1 025	2 570	1 700	3 605	2 475	2 565
D	385 800	358 515	408 625	323 235	241 095	172 105
E	380	1 700	680	2 425	1 535	2 260
F	12 060	5 950	15 115	16 760	14 215	12 730
G	240 415	222 770	395 330	342 415	283 600	232 325
H	114 840	106 285	164 810	157 105	146 980	129 295
I	56 775	68 575	88 855	90 910	66 060	59 130
J	30 840	31 215	42 715	40 545	41 055	29 435
K	164 575	176 045	248 230	245 650	240 230	168 250
L	85 890	64 615	95 665	109 490	109 505	72 415
M	86 590	74 475	150 195	159 805	141 225	107 825
N	461 769	427 769	518 482	525 213	347 095	
N-O	472 835	415 745	426 615	771 435	687 675	576 020
O	102 615	92 473	108 329	108 758	75 715	
X	1 520	1 030	10	185	0	0

New Zealand (FA) [2]   Reported injuries - Lésions déclarées - Lesiones declaradas

Total men and women - Total hommes et femmes - Total hombres y mujeres
ISIC 3 - CITI 3 - CIIU 3

	1999	2000	2001	2002	2003	2004	2005	2006	2007	2008
Total	277 751 [3]	1 381 319	1 494 949	1 627 892	1 739 584	1 791 296	1 918 758	1 977 625	1 940 682	1 340 451
A	80 038 [3]	240 835	268 353	310 692	311 404	299 670	289 182	296 042	259 806	167 337
B	7 303 [3]	18 808	18 960	20 895	18 101	13 870	18 148	14 143	9 455	6 295
C	507 [3]	6 702	8 802	7 474	8 053	9 763	9 284	6 813	10 195	5 667
D	31 146 [3]	305 426	348 432	362 530	408 375	437 842	429 299	460 843	427 716	262 594
E	118 [3]	6 403	5 908	5 044	4 253	5 346	7 499	5 789	5 112	2 592
F	74 645 [3]	220 947	214 514	237 981	264 435	290 021	336 325	329 026	345 143	210 915
G	19 370 [3]	144 400	152 069	163 506	185 147	178 810	203 188	198 767	203 184	245 650
H	7 255 [3]	41 646	46 817	52 487	53 896	50 414	57 841	60 288	58 979	33 302
I	16 630 [3]	118 742	133 190	132 663	148 571	148 624	167 549	172 280	169 110	100 682
J	2 265 [3]	3 511	3 577	3 351	2 611	3 809	3 516	5 479	6 095	3 647
K	13 210 [3]	71 521	69 878	82 737	88 690	94 448	105 740	131 969	122 976	77 111
L	2 663 [3]	22 631	26 684	27 731	25 584	29 704	32 711	31 226	31 506	19 531
M	1 269 [3]	24 912	27 190	32 393	23 746	23 505	35 508	30 322	29 792	15 839
N	5 114 [3]	88 508	96 474	101 234	113 064	112 217	127 933	125 291	112 449	71 048
O	13 143 [3]	52 198	56 736	67 771	64 465	72 554	69 075	69 003	75 289	39 832
P	7 [3]	296	137	14	32	22	7	0	0	0
Q	0 [3]	28	80	0	0	0		0	0	0
X	3 068 [3]	13 805	17 148	19 389	19 157	20 677	25 953	40 344	73 875	78 409

Explanatory notes: see p. 1125.

[1] Financial year ending in year indicated; excl. Victoria and Australian Capital Territory. [2] Year beginning in July of year indicated. [3] Data may be incomplete.

Notes explicatives: voir p. 1127.

[1] Année fiscale se terminant en l'année indiquée; non compris Victoria et Australian Capital Territory. [2] Année commençant en juillet de l'année indiquée. [3] Les données peuvent être incomplètes.

Notas explicativas: véase p. 1129.

[1] Año fiscal que se termina en el año indicado; excl. Victoria y Australian Capital Territory. [2] Año que comienza en julio del año indicado. [3] Datos pueden ser incompletados.

OCCUPATIONAL INJURIES

Days lost, by economic activity

LÉSIONS PROFESSIONNELLES

Journées perdues, par activité économique

LESIONES PROFESIONALES

Días perdidos, por actividad económica

8C

	1999	2000	2001	2002	2003	2004	2005	2006	2007	2008
New Zealand (FA) [1]				Reported injuries - Lésions déclarées - Lesiones declaradas						
Men - Hommes - Hombres										
ISIC 3 - CITI 3 - CIIU 3										
Total	235 464 [2]	1 067 855	1 144 522	1 233 615	1 315 488	1 379 508	1 457 244	1 456 541	1 438 451	950 303
A	67 630 [2]	200 798	224 088	251 403	250 241	241 510	238 450	236 954	204 890	132 464
B	6 591 [2]	17 609	16 623	19 125	16 863	12 726	16 517	12 525	9 177	5 878
C	507 [2]	6 641	8 665	6 726	7 323	9 006	9 215	6 558	9 668	5 608
D	26 619 [2]	259 590	292 301	302 774	335 378	362 131	354 183	355 494	338 095	204 562
E	118 [2]	5 812	5 580	4 910	3 575	4 966	7 088	5 252	5 082	2 556
F	74 097 [2]	215 241	212 048	233 859	258 847	283 653	329 486	315 735	334 589	201 988
G	16 741 [2]	101 534	104 896	113 532	130 707	135 583	145 175	137 818	136 540	125 643
H	3 182 [2]	16 938	20 060	21 517	23 727	20 545	24 357	20 969	21 565	15 231
I	14 179 [2]	106 583	114 064	113 576	127 975	128 372	138 783	141 150	137 447	81 138
J	527 [2]	1 056	1 931	1 737	712	1 886	1 443	2 255	3 023	1 790
K	10 136 [2]	50 986	50 297	57 604	59 655	65 289	73 160	93 928	86 874	56 856
L	2 210 [2]	16 864	19 323	20 553	16 817	20 139	21 306	19 304	23 797	14 125
M	611 [2]	10 464	8 441	11 032	9 971	8 950	12 504	10 331	8 282	5 123
N	1 385 [2]	10 864	11 790	13 806	14 519	15 531	18 531	17 253	13 133	9 637
O	8 952 [2]	35 615	41 579	46 382	44 309	53 099	47 075	50 740	49 944	27 722
P	7 [2]	0	126	0	32	15	0	0	0	0
Q	. [2]	.	0	.	.	.	.	.	0	0
X	1 972 [2]	11 260	12 710	15 079	14 837	16 107	19 971	30 275	56 345	59 982
Women - Femmes - Mujeres										
ISIC 3 - CITI 3 - CIIU 3										
Total	42 287 [2]	313 464	350 427	394 277	424 096	411 788	461 514	521 084	502 231	390 148
A	12 408 [2]	40 037	44 265	59 289	61 163	58 160	50 732	59 088	54 916	34 873
B	712 [2]	1 199	2 337	1 770	1 238	1 144	1 631	1 618	278	417
C	. [2]	61	137	748	730	757	69	255	527	59
D	4 527 [2]	45 836	56 131	59 756	72 997	75 711	75 116	105 349	89 621	58 032
E	. [2]	591	328	134	678	380	411	537	30	36
F	548 [2]	5 706	2 466	4 122	5 588	6 368	6 839	13 291	10 554	8 927
G	2 629 [2]	42 866	47 173	49 974	54 440	43 227	58 013	60 949	66 644	120 007
H	4 073 [2]	24 708	26 757	30 970	30 169	29 869	33 484	39 319	37 414	18 071
I	2 451 [2]	12 159	19 126	19 087	20 596	20 252	28 766	31 130	31 663	19 544
J	1 738 [2]	2 455	1 646	1 614	1 899	1 923	2 073	3 224	3 072	1 857
K	3 074 [2]	20 535	19 581	25 133	29 035	29 159	32 580	38 041	36 102	20 255
L	453 [2]	5 767	7 361	7 178	8 767	9 565	11 405	11 922	7 709	5 406
M	658 [2]	14 448	18 749	21 361	13 775	14 555	23 004	19 991	21 510	10 716
N	3 729 [2]	77 644	84 684	87 428	98 545	96 686	109 402	108 038	99 316	61 411
O	4 191 [2]	16 583	15 157	21 389	20 156	19 455	22 000	18 263	25 345	12 110
P	. [2]	296	11	14	0	7	7	0	0	0
Q	0 [2]	28	80	0	0	0	.	.	0	0
X	1 096 [2]	2 545	4 438	4 310	4 320	4 570	5 982	10 069	17 530	18 427

Explanatory notes: see p. 1125.

[1] Year beginning in July of year indicated. [2] Data may be incomplete.

Notes explicatives: voir p. 1127.

[1] Année commençant en juillet de l'année indiquée. [2] Les données peuvent être incomplètes.

Notas explicativas: véase p. 1129.

[1] Año que comienza en julio del año indicado. [2] Datos pueden ser incompletados.

Strikes and lockouts

Grèves et lock-out

Huelgas y cierres patronales

Strikes and lockouts

The Resolution concerning statistics of strikes, lockouts and other action due to labour disputes, adopted by the Fifteenth International Conference of Labour Statisticians (Geneva, 1993), [1] gives the following definitions for statistical purposes:

A *strike* is a temporary work stoppage effected by one or more groups of workers with a view to enforcing or resisting demands or expressing grievances, or supporting other workers in their demands or grievances.

A *lockout* is a total or partial temporary closure of one or more places of employment, or the hindering of the normal work activities of employees, by one or more employers with a view to enforcing or resisting demands or expressing grievances, or supporting other employers in their demands or grievances.

Workers involved in a strike: Workers directly involved in a strike are those who participated directly by stopping work. *Workers indirectly involved* in a strike are those employees of the establishments involved, or self-employed workers in the group involved, who did not participate directly by stopping work but who were prevented from working because of the strike.

Workers involved in a lockout: Workers *directly involved* in a lockout are those employees of the establishments involved who were directly concerned by the labour dispute and who were prevented from working by the lockout. Workers *indirectly involved* in a lockout are those employees of the establishments involved who were not directly concerned by the labour dispute but who were prevented from working by the lockout.

A *labour dispute* is a state of disagreement over a particular issue or group of issues over which there is conflict between workers and employers, or about which grievance is expressed by workers or employers, or about which workers or employers support other workers or employers in their demands or grievances.

The national definitions may differ from these, depending on the source of the statistics. In general, they are drawn from the administrative records of conciliation services, services concerned with labour relations, etc. The data may come from several sources, including strike notices, newspaper reports and direct enquiries addressed to employers or to workers' organizations. The type of source is shown as a code following the country name (see page XVI for explanations).

The data presented in this chapter cover strikes and lockouts together, as most countries do not distinguish between these two types of action in their statistics. In general, the series cover all types of strikes and lockouts and all economic activities, and relate to action in progress during the calendar year, i.e. strikes and lockouts beginning during the year and those continuing from the previous year. Any differences from the above are indicated in footnotes. If the statistics cover only strikes and lockouts above a certain size (in terms of the number of workers involved, duration or the amount of time not worked, or a combination of two or more of these), the limit is also indicated in a footnote.

The international recommendations state that all work stoppages due to a single labour dispute should be counted as one strike or lockout, as long as the period between stoppages is not more than two months. Different criteria are used in some countries to identify a single strike or lockout; e.g. each stoppage in each establishment may be considered to be one strike or lockout. In these cases, the number of strikes and lockouts and the number of workers involved are often higher than they would have been if the international recommendations had been followed, and the total number of workers involved sometimes exceeds the total employment in the economic activity concerned.

When using these data, it should be borne in mind that the number of workers exposed to the risk of strikes and lockouts varies between economic activities and countries, and from one period to another. For this reason, it is useful to calculate relative measures such as the severity rate, in which the amount of time not worked because of strikes and lockouts is related to the total number of workers.

Descriptions of the national sources, scope, definitions and methods used for compiling the statistics presented in this chapter are given in ILO: Sources and Methods: Labour Statistics, Volume 7: Strikes and lockouts, (Geneva, 1993) and Volume 9: Transition Countries, (Geneva, 1999).

Table 9A

Strikes and lockouts, by economic activity

This table presents the number of strikes and lockouts in progress during the year indicated, i.e. those beginning during the year plus those continuing from the previous year.

If a strike or lockout covers several economic activities, the information about it is usually given under each of the activities involved. As a result, the total number of strikes and lockouts shown for the total (all economic activities together) may be less that the sum for the component activities.

Table 9B

Workers involved, by economic activity

This table presents the number of workers involved in strikes and lockouts in progress during the year indicated, which usually includes those involved indirectly as well as those involved directly.

Table 9C

Days not worked, by economic activity

This table presents the number of days not worked as a result of strikes and lockouts in progress during the year indicated. It is usually measured in terms of the sum of the actual working days during which work would normally have been carried out by each worker involved had there been no stoppage.

Table 9D

Rates of days not worked, by economic activity

This table presents the severity rates of strikes and lockouts, generally calculated in terms of the number of days not worked per 1,000 workers. The type of rate is indicated by a code after the country name, as follows:

(1) per 1,000 employees;

(2) per 1,000 persons employed;

(3) other.

Note

[1] For the full text of the resolution, see ILO: *Current international recommendations on labour statistics* (Geneva, 2000) or the ILO Department of Statistics' Web site (www.ilo.org/public/english/bureau/stat).

Grèves et lock-out

La résolution concernant les statistiques des conflits du travail: grèves, lock-out et autres actions de revendication, adoptée par la quinzième Conférence internationale des statisticiens du travail (CIST) (Genève, 1993)[1] donne les définitions suivantes à des fins statistiques:

Une *grève* est un arrêt temporaire de travail déclenché par un ou des groupes de travailleurs en vue d'imposer ou de s'opposer à une exigence ou de formuler des doléances, ou de soutenir d'autres travailleurs dans leurs revendications ou doléances.

Un *lock-out* est la fermeture temporaire totale ou partielle d'un ou plusieurs lieux de travail, ou les mesures prises par un ou plusieurs employeurs pour empêcher les travailleurs d'exécuter normalement leur travail, en vue d'imposer ou de s'opposer à une exigence ou de soutenir les revendications ou les doléances d'autres employeurs.

Travailleurs impliqués dans une grève: Les travailleurs directement impliqués dans une grève sont ceux qui y ont participé délibérément en cessant le travail. Les travailleurs indirectement impliqués dans une grève sont les salariés des établissements impliqués ou les travailleurs indépendants inclus dans le groupe impliqué, qui n'ont pas participé délibérément à la grève en cessant le travail mais qui ont été contraints de cesser le travail du fait de la grève.

Travailleurs impliqués dans un lock-out: Les travailleurs directement impliqués dans un lock-out sont ceux qui, dans les établissements impliqués, étaient directement concernés par le conflit du travail et ont été empêchés de travailler par le lock-out. Les travailleurs indirectement impliqués dans un lock-out sont ceux qui, dans les établissements impliqués, n'étaient pas directement concernés par le conflit du travail, mais qui ont été contraints de cesser le travail du fait du lock-out.

Un conflit du travail est un désaccord qui porte sur un problème ou un groupe de problèmes à propos duquel ou desquels il existe un différend entre des travailleurs et des employeurs, ou à propos duquel ou desquels une revendication a été formulée par des travailleurs ou des employeurs, ou à propos duquel ou desquels des travailleurs ou des employeurs soutiennent les revendications ou les doléances d'autres travailleurs ou employeurs.

Les définitions nationales peuvent différer de ces définitions selon la source statistique utilisée. En général, les données statistiques proviennent de rapports administratifs des services d'arbitrage, des services impliqués dans les relations du travail, etc. Les données peuvent être extraites de diverses sources, dont des avis de grève, des articles de presse et des enquêtes directes auprès des employeurs et des organisations de travailleurs. Le type de source apparaît sous forme d'un code placé après le nom du pays (pour les explications, voir la page XVI).

Les données présentées dans ce chapitre englobent les grèves et les lock-out sans distinction, car la plupart des pays n'établissent pas de statistiques séparées pour ces deux types d'action. En général, les séries couvrent tous les types de grèves et lock-out ainsi que toutes les branches d'activité économique et se réfèrent aux actions en cours durant l'année civile en question, c'est-à-dire aux grèves et lock-out qui sont survenus au cours de l'année ou qui étaient déjà engagés avant l'année considérée. Toute divergence

éventuelle (par rapport à cette façon de procéder) est indiquée en note de bas de page. Si les statistiques ne couvrent que les grèves et lock-out d'une certaine importance (en termes de nombre de travailleurs impliqués, de durée de l'action ou de temps de travail non effectué ou encore d'une combinaison de deux ou plus de ces caractéristiques), le seuil limite est également précisé en note de bas de page.

Les recommandations internationales précisent que tous les arrêts de travail dus à un même conflit du travail devraient être comptabilisés comme une grève ou un lock-out, tant que la période entre deux arrêts de travail n'excède pas deux mois. Certains pays utilisent différents critères pour identifier un même arrêt de travail; par exemple, chaque arrêt dans un établissement peut être considéré comme une grève ou un lock-out. De ce fait, le nombre de grèves ou de lock-out ainsi que le nombre de travailleurs impliqués sont souvent plus élevés qu'ils ne l'auraient été si on avait suivi les recommandations internationales et le nombre total de travailleurs impliqués excède parfois l'emploi total dans l'activité économique concernée.

En utilisant ces données, il ne faut pas perdre de vue que le nombre de travailleurs exposés au risque de grèves ou de lock-out varie en fonction des différentes branches d'activité économique, des pays et d'une période à l'autre. Pour cette raison, il est utile d'adopter des mesures comparatives telles que le taux de gravité qui rapporte le temps non travaillé suite à une grève ou un lock-out au nombre total de travailleurs.

Les descriptions des sources nationales, de la portée, des définitions et des méthodes utilisées lors de la compilation des statistiques diffusées dans ce chapitre sont publiées dans BIT: *Sources et méthodes: statistiques du travail*, volume 7: «Grèves et lock-out», (Genève, 1993) et volume 9: «Pays en transition» (Genève, 1999).

Tableau 9A

Grèves et lock-out, par activité économique

Ce tableau présente le nombre de grèves et de lock-out en cours pendant l'année indiquée, c'est-à-dire ceux survenus pendant l'année plus ceux déjà engagés l'année précédente.

Si une grève ou un lock-out couvre plusieurs branches d'activité économique, l'information à ce sujet est généralement précisée pour chacune des branches concernées. Par conséquent le nombre total de grèves et de lock-out apparaissant pour l'ensemble (toutes branches d'activité économique confondues) peut être inférieur à la somme des chiffres pour chaque branche.

Tableau 9B

Travailleurs impliqués, par activité économique

Ce tableau présente le nombre de travailleurs impliqués dans les grèves et les lock-out en cours pendant l'année indiquée, qui comprend généralement ceux qui étaient indirectement impliqués en plus de ceux qui étaient directement impliqués.

Tableau 9C

Journées non effectuées, par activité économique

Ce tableau présente le nombre de journées non effectuées à cause des grèves et des lock-out en cours pendant l'année indiquée. Il se mesure généralement en termes de la somme des jours ouvrables qui auraient normalement été effectués par chaque travailleur impliqué si l'arrêt de travail n'était pas intervenu.

Tableau 9D

Taux de journées non effectuées, par activité économique

Ce tableau présente les taux de gravité des grèves et des lock-out, qui sont généralement calculés en termes de nombre de jours non travaillés pour 1 000 travailleurs. Le type de taux apparaît sous forme d'un code placé après le nom du pays, comme suit:

(1) pour 1 000 salariés;
(2) pour 1 000 personnes occupées;
(3) autre.

Note

[1] Pour le texte intégral de la résolution, se reporter à BIT: *Recommandations internationales en vigueur sur les statistiques du travail* (Genève, 2000) ou au site Web du Département de statistique du BIT (www.ilo.org/public/french/bureau/stat).

Huelgas y cierres patronales

La Resolución sobre las estadísticas de huelgas, cierres patronales y otras acciones causadas por conflictos laborales, adoptada por la decimoquinta Conferencia Internacional de Estadísticos del Trabajo (Ginebra, 1993)[1], da, a efectos estadísticos, las definiciones siguientes:

Se entiende por *huelga* una interrupción temporal del trabajo efectuada por uno o varios grupos de trabajadores con objeto de obtener reivindicaciones o rechazar exigencias o expresar quejas o de apoyar las reivindicaciones o las quejas de otros trabajadores.

Se entiende por *cierre patronal* el cierre temporal, ya sea parcial o total, de uno o varios centros de trabajo decidido por uno o varios empleadores o el impedimento por parte de éstos del desarrollo de la actividad laboral de sus trabajadores con objeto de lograr una reivindicación o rechazar exigencias o de apoyar las reivindicaciones o las quejas de otros empleadores.

Trabajadores implicados en una huelga: los trabajadores *directamente implicados* en una huelga son los que participaron directamente interrumpiendo el trabajo. Los trabajadores *indirectamente implicados* en una huelga son los asalariados de los establecimientos implicados o los trabajadores independientes que pertenecen al grupo implicado, que no participaron directamente interrumpiendo su trabajo, pero que no pudieron trabajar a causa de la huelga.

Trabajadores implicados en un cierre patronal: los trabajadores *directamente implicados* en un cierre patronal son los asalariados de los establecimientos implicados a los que el conflicto de trabajo afectó directamente y que no pudieron trabajar a causa del cierre patronal. Los trabajadores *indirectamente implicados* en un cierre patronal son los asalariados de los establecimientos implicados a los que el conflicto de trabajo no afectó directamente, pero que no pudieron trabajar a causa del cierre patronal.

Un *conflicto de trabajo o conflicto laboral* es una situación de desacuerdo referente a una cuestión o conjunto de cuestiones con relación a la cual o a las cuales existe una discrepancia entre trabajadores y empleadores, o acerca de la cual o las cuales los trabajadores o empleadores expresan una reivindicación o queja o dan su apoyo a las reivindicaciones o quejas de otros trabajadores o empleadores.

Las definiciones que utilizan los países pueden variar de las anteriores según sea la fuente de las estadísticas. Estas provienen por lo general de registros administrativos de los servicios de conciliación u otros interesados en las relaciones laborales, etc. Los datos pueden provenir de diversas fuentes, comprendidos los avisos de huelgas, informes periodísticos y averiguación directa a empleadores o organizaciones de trabajadores. El tipo de fuente se indica a continuación del nombre del país mediante un código (para las explicaciones, véase la página XVI).

Los datos que se presentan en este capítulo abarcan indistintamente las huelgas y los conflictos laborales, pues las estadísticas de la mayoría de los países no hacen distinción entre estas dos clases de acción reivindicativa. En general, las series abarcan toda clase de huelgas y cierres patronales, así como toda actividad económica, y se refieren tanto a las acciones en curso durante el año como a las que continúan las iniciadas el año anterior. Toda diferencia con respecto a lo antes expresado se señala en notas de pie de página. Si las estadísticas sólo abarcan huelgas y cierres patronales de cierta entidad, es decir que superan ciertos límites relativos al número de trabajadores implicados,

duración, total del tiempo no trabajado o una combinación de dos o más de éstos; dichos límites también se indican en notas de pie de página.

Según las recomendaciones internacionales, todas las interrupciones del trabajo que se deban a un mismo conflicto laboral deben considerarse como una sola huelga o cierre patronal siempre que el lapso entre estas interrupciones no supere dos meses. En algunos países se utilizan criterios distintos para considerar como único un cierre patronal o una huelga; por ejemplo, cada interrupción del trabajo de cada establecimiento puede considerarse como un mismo y único cierre patronal o huelga. En tales casos, el número de huelgas y cierres patronales y el de trabajadores implicados suelen ser más elevados que los que se habrían podido obtener siguiendo las recomendaciones, al punto que algunas veces el número de trabajadores implicados supera el total del empleo de la rama de actividad económica interesada.

Al utilizar estos datos cabe tener presente que el número de trabajadores expuestos al riesgo de una huelga o un cierre patronal varía según la actividad económica o el país considerado y de un período a otro. Por tal motivo es útil calcular medidas relativas, como las tasas de gravedad, en las cuales el total del tiempo no trabajado como consecuencia de huelgas y cierres patronales se relaciona con el número total de trabajadores.

Las descripciones de las fuentes, ámbito, definiciones y métodos utilizados en el plano nacional para elaborar las estadísticas que se muestran en este capítulo figuran en OIT: *Fuentes y Métodos: Estadísticas del Trabajo*, volumen 7: «Huelgas y cierres patronales» (Ginebra, 1993), y volumen 9: «Países en transición» (Ginebra, 1999).

Cuadro 9A

Huelgas y cierres patronales, por actividad económica

Este cuadro presenta el número de huelgas y cierres patronales que tuvieron lugar durante el año indicado, es decir, los comenzados en el año y también los que continúan del año anterior.

Si una huelga o un cierre patronal abarca varias actividades económicas, la información pertinente se da, habitualmente, para cada una de las actividades afectadas. En consecuencia el número total de huelgas y cierres patronales que se presenta para la actividad económica en su conjunto puede ser inferior a la suma de los datos de cada actividad.

Cuadro 9B

Trabajadores implicados, por actividad económica

Este cuadro presenta el número de trabajadores implicados en las huelgas y los cierres patronales que tuvieron lugar en el año indicado, que incluye por lo general los implicados indirectamente además de los implicados directamente.

Cuadro 9C

Días no trabajados, por actividad económica

Este cuadro presenta el número de días no trabajados como consecuencia de las huelgas y los cierres patronales que tuvieron lugar durante el año indicado. Se suele medir en términos de la suma de días laborables que hubieran sido normalmente trabajados por cada trabajador implicado de no haberse producido la interrupción de la actividad.

Cuadro 9D

Tasas de días no trabajados, por actividad económica

Este cuadro presenta las tasas de gravedad de huelgas y cierres patronales, que se calculan por lo general en términos de días no trabajados por 1 000 trabajadores. El tipo de tasa se indica mediante un código que sigue al nombre del país, de esta forma:
(1) por 1 000 asalariados;
(2) por 1 000 personas ocupadas;
(3) otra.

Nota

[1] Para el texto completo de la Resolución, veáse OIT: *Recomendaciones internacionales de actualidad en estadísticas del trabajo* (Ginebra, 2000) o el sitio Web del Departamento de Estadística de la OIT (www.ilo.org/public/spanish/bureau/stat).

STRIKES AND LOCKOUTS	GRÈVES ET LOCK-OUT	HUELGAS Y CIERRES PATRONALES
Strikes and lockouts, by economic activity	Grèves et lock-out, par activité économique	Huelgas y cierres patronales, por actividad económica

	1999	2000	2001	2002	2003	2004	2005	2006	2007	2008

AFRICA-AFRIQUE-AFRICA

Algérie (FG) [1]
ISIC 3 - CITI 3 - CIIU 3

	1999	2000	2001	2002	2003	2004	2005	2006	2007	2008
Total	173	187	176	175	23	35	.	.	.	.
A-B	10	6	8	7	0	1				
C	6	5	5	5	0	0				
D	45	50	58	54	0	8				
E [2]	0	0	0	0	0	0				
F	52	56	29	31	0	11				
G	4	5	2	3	0	0				
H	0	0	1	4	0	0				
I	6	10	4	5	1	2				
J-K	0	0	3	5	0	0				
L	6	7	14	7	6	5				
M	16	30	18	33	7	5				
N	3	6	9	8	8	1				
Q	11	5	3	7	0	1				
X	14	7	22	6	1	1				

Mauritius (FG)
ISIC 3 - CITI 3 - CIIU 3

	1999	2000	2001	2002	2003	2004	2005	2006	2007	2008
Total	19	25	25	29	46	47	17	13	29	15
A	1	1	0	1	0	0	0	0	0	0
B	0	0	1	0	0	0	0	0	0	0
C	0	0	0	0	0	0	0	0	0	0
D	14	21	20	25	41	43	17	13	29	10
E	0	0	0	0	0	0	0	0	0	0
F	2	0	2	0	3	3	0	0	0	4
G	0	2	1	1	1	1	0	0	0	0
H	1	0	0	1	0	0	0	0	0	0
I	0	1	1	0	1	0	0	0	0	0
J	0	0	0	0	0	0	0	0	0	0
K	0	0	0	0	0	0	0	0	0	0
L	0	0	0	0	0	0	0	0	0	0
M	0	0	0	1	0	0	0	0	0	0
N	0	0	0	0	0	0	0	0	0	0
O	0	0	0	0	0	0	0	0	0	0
X	1	0	0	0	0	0	0	0	0	1

Nigeria (FG) [3]
ISIC 2 - CITI 2 - CIIU 2

	1999	2000	2001	2002	2003	2004	2005	2006	2007	2008
Total	52	49	24	52	77	36	149	189	.	.
1	0	2	0	0	0	0	1	1	.	.
2	1	4	0	1	0	0	0	2	.	.
3	4	8	2	1	5	10	17	11	.	.
4	0	0	0	0	0	0	9	9	.	.
5	0	3	1	1	0	2	2	2	.	.
6	1	2	0	1	3	0	4	1	.	.
7	2	2	1	0	3	1	6	3	.	.
8	2	2	2	1	0	2	.	12	.	.
9	17	24	15	26	1	4	7	12	.	.
0	0	0	0	0	16	7	11	22	.	.

South Africa (FG)
ISIC 3 - CITI 3 - CIIU 3

	1999	2000	2001	2002	2003	2004	2005	2006	2007	2008
Total	107	80	83	47	62	49	102	99	75	57
A	8	15	6	1	5	5	6	5	3	2
C	14	11	7	5	8	9	16	7	17	7
D	30	16	22	9	14	13	27	9	16	10
E	2	3	1	1	3	1	2	1	1	0
F	3	3	5	3	2	0	2	2	3	2
G	12	6	2	11	8	4	11	7	4	4
I	9	6	14	4	12	4	14	15	9	7
J	1	3	0	0	1	2	3	5	3	5
O	28	17	26	13	9	11	21	48	19	20

Saint Helena (FG)
ISIC 3 - CITI 3 - CIIU 3

	1999	2000	2001	2002	2003	2004	2005	2006	2007	2008
Total	0	0	0	0	0	0	0	.	.	.

Explanatory notes: see p. 1361.

[1] Strikes only. [2] Incl. sanitary services. [3] Year beginning in April of year indicated.

Notes explicatives: voir p. 1363.

[1] Grèves seulement. [2] Y compris les services sanitaires. [3] Année commençant en avril de l'année indiquée.

Notas explicativas: véase p. 1365.

[1] Huelgas solamente. [2] Incl. los servicios de saneamiento. [3] Año que comienza en abril del año indicado.

9A

STRIKES AND LOCKOUTS	GRÈVES ET LOCK-OUT	HUELGAS Y CIERRES PATRONALES
Strikes and lockouts, by economic activity	Grèves et lock-out, par activité économique	Huelgas y cierres patronales, por actividad económica

	1999	2000	2001	2002	2003	2004	2005	2006	2007	2008
Tunisie (FG)										
ISIC 3 - CITI 3 - CIIU 3										
Total	308	411	380	345	395	391	466	392	382	.
A	17	17	17	29	16	18	18	15	14	.
B	3	2	1	1	0	0	0	2	4	.
C	18	22	6	15	19	11	17	20	13	.
D	182	297	230	229	251	273	254	213	201	.
E	1	4	6	3	8	1	5	1	3	.
F	60	36	59	36	28	31	70	49	26	.
G	1	1	4	2	2	0	8	3	12	.
H	8	4	8	6	23	13	19	21	23	.
I	9	7	14	14	9	9	9	7	7	.
J	.	.	.	1	0	3	3	.	6	.
L [1]	2	1	4	1	8	6	3	.	11	.
M	.	.	.	2	6	2	15	8	10	.
N	.	.	.	2	0	6	15	4	9	.
O	6	13	24	4	24	18	30	47	43	.
X	1	7	7	0	1	0	0	0	0	.
Uganda (F)										
ISIC 3 - CITI 3 - CIIU 3										
Total	6	5	3	5	1	3				
AMERICA-AMÉRIQUE-AMERICA										
Argentina (F) [2]										
ISIC 3 - CITI 3 - CIIU 3										
Total	.	.	.	.	.	.	.	770	838	839
A	.	.	.	.	.	.	.	3	4	2
B	.	.	.	.	.	.	.	0	1	5
C	.	.	.	.	.	.	.	18	28	18
D	.	.	.	.	.	.	.	60	67	87
E	.	.	.	.	.	.	.	33	27	34
F	.	.	.	.	.	.	.	28	17	26
G	.	.	.	.	.	.	.	14	15	13
H	.	.	.	.	.	.	.	2	2	2
I	.	.	.	.	.	.	.	124	108	107
J	.	.	.	.	.	.	.	5	16	6
K	.	.	.	.	.	.	.	2	6	5
L	.	.	.	.	.	.	.	247	296	296
M	.	.	.	.	.	.	.	88	127	120
N	.	.	.	.	.	.	.	147	145	164
O	.	.	.	.	.	.	.	26	26	21
Aruba (F)										
ISIC 3 - CITI 3 - CIIU 3										
Total	.	.	.	.	.	3	1	1	3	.
D	.	.	.	.	.	.	.	0	0	.
E	.	.	.	.	.	2	0	1	0	.
F	.	.	.	.	.	0	0	0	0	.
G	.	.	.	.	.	0	0	0	1	.
H	.	.	.	.	.	0	0	0	0	.
I	.	.	.	.	.	0	0	0	0	.
J	.	.	.	.	.	0	0	0	0	.
K	.	.	.	.	.	.	.	.	1	.
N	.	.	.	.	.	0	0	0	1	.
X	.	.	.	.	.	1	1	0	0	.
Brasil (FH) [3]										
ISIC 3 - CITI 3 - CIIU 3										
Total	508	532	439	281	333	304				

Explanatory notes: see p. 1361.

[1] Incl. category N and state education. [2] Work stoppages beginning in the year indicated. [3] Strikes only.

Notes explicatives: voir p. 1363.

[1] Y compris la catégorie N et l'éducation publique. [2] Arrêts du travail commençant pendant l'année indiquée. [3] Grèves seulement.

Notas explicativas: véase p. 1365.

[1] Incl. la categoría N y la educación pública. [2] Interrupciones del trabajo que empiezan en el año indicado. [3] Huelgas solamente.

STRIKES AND LOCKOUTS

Strikes and lockouts, by economic activity

GRÈVES ET LOCK-OUT

Grèves et lock-out, par activité économique

HUELGAS Y CIERRES PATRONALES

Huelgas y cierres patronales, por actividad económica

9A

	1999	2000	2001	2002	2003	2004	2005	2006	2007	2008
Canada (FG) [1]										
ISIC 3 - CITI 3 - CIIU 3										
Total	413	378	381	294	266	297	260	151	206	187
A	8	5	5	2	5	2	1	1	0	0
B	0	0	0	0	1	0	0	0	0	0
C	8	10	14	3	5	4	4	3	6	3
D	124	130	122	98	92	96	64	61	46	54
E	7	1	5	2	1	4	1	0	3	3
F	8	7	6	8	0	8	6	1	16	4
G	43	34	39	39	33	32	30	15	10	35
H	21	19	17	28	13	15	31	8	9	22
I	30	33	32	24	24	24	15	13	25	11
J	10	13	4	0	6	3	2	3	2	1
K	14	10	13	8	4	8	16	2	5	5
L	36	23	19	19	17	21	8	11	10	9
M	23	27	31	14	17	17	47	8	17	15
N	52	42	44	19	29	30	21	11	32	12
O	28	22	31	30	20	35	13	14	25	13
X	0	0	0	0	0	0	0	0	0	0
Chile (FG) [2]										
ISIC 2 - CITI 2 - CIIU 2										
Total	108	125	88	117	92	125	101	134	146	159
1	2	4	2	1	1	4	5	8	11	3
2	4	8	2	4	5	12	8	3	17	5
3	53	45	41	48	35	52	32	44	38	48
4	0	0	1	0	0	1	1	1	2	1
5	3	3	2	3	5	0	2	6	10	10
6	11	11	13	7	7	10	13	20	17	27
7	13	6	5	15	10	5	9	13	12	16
8	3	7	7	12	7	5	5	8	7	6
9	19	41	15	27	22	36	26	31	32	43
0	0	0	0	0	0	0	0	0	0	0
República Dominicana (F)										
ISIC 3 - CITI 3 - CIIU 3										
Total	0	1	1	0	0	0	0	1	0	0
I	0	1	1	0	0	0	0	1	0	0
Ecuador (FG)										
ISIC 3 - CITI 3 - CIIU 3										
Total	8	11	4	17	17	11	8	16	8	11
A	0	2	1	7	3	2	0	1	0	7
B	0	0	0	3	0	0	0	0	0	0
C	1	3	0	0	0	0	0	0	0	0
D	1	1	0	1	5	1	5	2	3	2
E	1	3	0	2	1	0	0	0	2	0
F	0	0	0	0	1	0	0	8	1	1
G	0	0	0	0	1	2	1	0	0	0
H	0	0	0	0	1	0	0	0	0	0
I	3	1	1	1	1	0	0	0	0	1
J	1	0	0	0	0	0	0	0	0	0
K	0	1	0	2	0	1	1	0	0	0
L	1	0	1	1	3	4	1	4	2	0
M	0	0	0	0	0	0	0	0	0	0
N	0	0	1	0	0	0	0	1	0	0
O	0	0	0	0	1	1	0	0	0	0

El Salvador (FG)

ISIC 2 - CITI 2 - CIIU 2   ISIC 3 - CITI 3 - CIIU 3

	1999	2000	2001	2002	2003	2004	2005	2006	2007	2008	
Total	36	38	19	25	17	27	25 |	17	11	12	Total
1	0	0	0	0	0	0	0 |	0	0	0	A
2	0	0	0	0	0	0	0 |	0	0	0	B
3	4	3	8	3	1	9	8 |	0	0	0	C
4	2	2	0	0	0	2	0 |	8	4	8	D
5	2	6	0	1	0	1	1 |	0	0	0	E
6	0	0	0	0	0	0	2 |	0	0	0	F
7	1	4	5	0	1	3	2 |	0	2	0	G
8	0	0	0	0	0	0	0 |	0	0	0	H
9	27	23	6	21	15	12	12 |	3	3	0	I
							|	0	0	0	J
							|	1	0	0	K
							|	1	1	3	L
							|	1	1	0	M
							|	2	0	1	N
							|	1	0	0	O

Explanatory notes: see p. 1361.

[1] Strikes lasting at least half a day with more than 10 days lost.
[2] Strikes only.

Notes explicatives: voir p. 1363.

[1] Grèves d'une durée d'une demi-journée au moins et dans lesquelles 10 jours de travail sont perdus. [2] Grèves seulement.

Notas explicativas: véase p. 1365.

[1] Huelgas con duración de media jornada laboral por lo menos y con más de 10 días perdidos. [2] Huelgas solamente.

ILO YEARBOOK OF LABOUR STATISTICS 2009   *ANNUAIRE DES STATISTIQUES DU TRAVAIL DU BIT 2009*   *ANUARIO DE ESTADISTICAS DEL TRABAJO DEL OIT 2009*

1369

STRIKES AND LOCKOUTS
Strikes and lockouts, by economic activity

GRÈVES ET LOCK-OUT
Grèves et lock-out, par activité économique

HUELGAS Y CIERRES PATRONALES
Huelgas y cierres patronales, por actividad económica

	1999	2000	2001	2002	2003	2004	2005	2006	2007	2008
Guyana (FG)										
ISIC 2 - CITI 2 - CIIU 2										
Total	244	268	243	226	225	229	163	208	177	.
1	224	0	232	0	0	227	160	0	174	.
2	3	.	.	.	.	.	.	.	.	.
4	.	.	1	.	.	.	.	.	.	.
9	11	0	2	0	0	1	0	0	1	.
0	6	.	.	.	.	.	.	.	.	.
Jamaica (FG)										
ISIC 2 - CITI 2 - CIIU 2										
Total	43	28	14	19	29	16	7	.	.	.
1	1	4	1	4	3	2	0			
2	0	0	1	1	4	0	0			
3	14	10	2	2	1	1	2			
4	0	1	3	1	0	1	1			
5	2	0	2	0	1	0	0			
6	0	1	0	1	0	1	0			
7	4	3	2	0	3	4	3			
8	4	4	0	3	2	1	0			
9	18	5	3	7	15	2	1			
México (FG) [1] [2]										
ISIC 3 - CITI 3 - CIIU 3										
Total	32	26	35	45	44	38	50	55	28	21
A	0	0	0	0	0	0	0	0	0	0
B	0	0	0	0	0	0	0	0	0	0
C	0	2	0	6	1	7	1	2	3	1
D	25	20	31	29	35	23	36	38	13	8
E	0	0	0	0	0	0	0	0	0	0
F	0	0	0	1	0	0	0	3	4	2
G	0	1	0	0	0	0	0	0	0	0
H	0	0	0	0	0	0	0	0	0	0
I	5	2	2	4	4	7	8	10	4	4
J	1	0	0	1	1	0	0	0	1	0
K	0	0	0	0	0	0	0	0	0	0
M	1	0	1	3	1	1	2	0	1	3
N	0	0	0	0	0	0	0	0	0	0
O	0	1	1	1	2	0	3	2	2	3
Panamá (FG)										
ISIC 3 - CITI 3 - CIIU 3										
Total	9	2	10	4	3	1	1	3	4	.
A	0	0	3	0	1	0	0	0	0	.
B	0	0	0	0	0	0	0	0	0	.
C	1	0	0	4	0	0	0	0	0	.
D	0	0	2	0	0	0	0	1	0	.
E	0	0	0	0	0	0	0	0	0	.
F	6	0	3	0	1	0	1	1	3	.
G	0	0	0	0	1	0	0	0	1	.
H	0	1	0	0	0	0	0	1	0	.
I	0	1	1	0	0	1	0	0	0	.
J	0	0	0	0	0	0	0	0	0	.
K	0	0	1	0	0	0	0	0	0	.
L	0	0	0	0	0	0	0	0	0	.
M	0	0	0	0	0	0	0	0	0	.
N	2	0	0	0	0	0	0	0	0	.
O	2	0	0	0	0	0	0	0	0	.
Perú (FG) [3]										
ISIC 3 - CITI 3 - CIIU 3										
Total	71	37	40	64	68	107	65	67	73	63
A	1	0	2	1	2	1	0	0	2	1
B	3	0	0	0	0	0	0	0	0	0
C	12	9	15	20	4	21	12	10	29	39
D	17	7	11	10	21	26	7	6	8	8
E	1	5	0	4	8	16	14	12	3	2
F	13	6	9	4	6	5	4	9	9	4
G	0	0	0	0	2	0	0	2	0	0
H	0	0	1	0	0	0	0	0	0	0
I	22	9	0	11	12	14	7	13	13	3
J	0	0	0	0	0	0	0	0	1	0
K	0	0	1	9	3	3	2	7	2	1
L	0	1	1	1	6	13	6	6	4	1
M	1	0	0	0	1	1	3	1	2	2
N	0	0	0	1	2	6	9	1	0	0
O	0	0	0	0	1	1	1	0	0	0
P				3	0	0	0	0	0	0
X	1	0	0	0	0	0	0	0	0	1

Explanatory notes: see p. 1361.

[1] Strikes only, beginning in the year indicated. [2] Excl. enterprises covered by local jurisdiction. [3] Strikes only; private sector.

Notes explicatives: voir p. 1363.

[1] Grèves seulement, commençant pendant l'année indiquée. [2] Non compris les entreprises sous juridiction locale. [3] Grèves seulement; secteur privé.

Notas explicativas: véase p. 1365.

[1] Huelgas solamente, que empiezan en el año indicado. [2] Excl. las empresas de jurisdicción local. [3] Huelgas solamente; sector privado.

STRIKES AND LOCKOUTS

Strikes and lockouts,
by economic activity

GRÈVES ET LOCK-OUT

Grèves et lock-out,
par activité économique

HUELGAS Y CIERRES PATRONALES

Huelgas y cierres patronales,
por actividad económica

9A

	1999	2000	2001	2002	2003	2004	2005	2006	2007	2008
Puerto Rico (FG) [1]										
ISIC 3 - CITI 3 - CIIU 3										
Total	1	4	4	2	0	1	0	0	1	2
A	0	0	0	0	0	0	0	0	0	0
B	0	0	0	0	0	0	0	0	0	0
C	0	0	0	0	0	0	0	0	0	0
D	0	1	1	1	0	0	0	0	0	0
E	0	0	0	0	0	0	0	0	0	0
F	0	0	1	0	0	0	0	0	0	0
G	1	0	.	1	0	0	0	0	0	0
G,I	.	.	1						0	0
H	0	1	1	0	0	0	0	0	1	0
H,M-O	.	.	.	.	.	.	.	.		
I	0	1	.	0	0	0	0	0	0	2
J	0	0	0	0	0	0	0	0	0	0
K	0	1	0	0	0	0	0	0	0	0
L	0	0	0	0	0	1	0	0	0	0
M	0	0	.	0	0	0	0	0	0	0
N	0	0	.	0	0	0	0	0	0	0
O	0	0	.	0	0	0	0	0	0	0
Trinidad and Tobago (FG)										
ISIC 2 - CITI 2 - CIIU 2										
Total	8	38	76	22	31	22	.	.	.	.
1	0	2	0	0	0	0	.	.	.	.
2	0	0	1	20	29	15	.	.	.	.
3	1	1	0	0	1	3	.	.	.	.
4	0	0	0	0	0	0	.	.	.	.
5	0	0	0	0	0	1	.	.	.	.
6	0	0	0	0	0	1	.	.	.	.
7	3	10	73	2	1	2	.	.	.	.
8	0	25	0	0	0	0	.	.	.	.
9	3	0	2	0	0	0	.	.	.	.
0	0	0	0	0	0	0	.	.	.	.
United States (H) [2][3]										
ISIC 3 - CITI 3 - CIIU 3										
Total	17	39	29	19	14	17	22	23	23	16
A	0	0	0	0	0	0	0	0	0	0
B	0	0	0	0	0	0	0	0	0	0
C	0	0	0	0	0	0	1	0	1	0
D	5	10	5	5	3	4	6	7	6	6
E	0	0	2	1	0	1	1	0	0	0
F	2	4	8	3	1	0	6	5	2	1
G	1	1	2	0	3	1	0	1	0	0
H	1	1	0	0	0	3	1	0	0	0
I	2	3	1	3	2	3	4	2	5	1
J	0	0	0	0	0	0	0	0	0	0
K	0	5	0	1	0	0	0	0	1	1
L	0	2	1	1	1	0	0	4	0	0
M	5	4	3	2	2	0	3	2	4	3
N	1	9	7	3	0	5	0	1	2	3
O	0	0	0	0	2	0	0	1	2	1
X	0	0	0	0	0	0	0	0	.	0
Uruguay (Z)										
ISIC 3 - CITI 3 - CIIU 3										
Total	.	.	.	.	.	.	.	.	.	150
A	.	.	.	.	.	.	.	.	.	3
B	.	.	.	.	.	.	.	.	.	0
C	.	.	.	.	.	.	.	.	.	1
D	.	.	.	.	.	.	.	.	.	35
E	.	.	.	.	.	.	.	.	.	4
F	.	.	.	.	.	.	.	.	.	13
G	.	.	.	.	.	.	.	.	.	4
H	.	.	.	.	.	.	.	.	.	0
I	.	.	.	.	.	.	.	.	.	20
J	.	.	.	.	.	.	.	.	.	4
K	.	.	.	.	.	.	.	.	.	8
L	.	.	.	.	.	.	.	.	.	25
M	.	.	.	.	.	.	.	.	.	11
N	.	.	.	.	.	.	.	.	.	14
O	.	.	.	.	.	.	.	.	.	8
P	.	.	.	.	.	.	.	.	.	0
Q	.	.	.	.	.	.	.	.	.	0
X	.	.	.	.	.	.	.	.	.	.

Explanatory notes: see p. 1361.

[1] Strikes and lockouts ending during the 12 months beginning in July of the year indicated. [2] Work stoppages beginning in the year indicated. [3] Excl. work stoppages involving fewer than 1,000 workers and lasting less than a full day or shift. [4] Incl. stoppages involving fewer than 10 workers or lasting less than one day.

Notes explicatives: voir p. 1363.

[1] Grèves et lock-out se terminant pendant les 12 mois commençant en juillet de l'année indiquée. [2] Arrêts du travail commençant pendant l'année indiquée. [3] Non compris arrêts de travail impliquant moins de 1000 travailleurs; durée inférieure à 1 jour ou à 1 poste de travail. [4] Y compris les arrêts impliquant moins de 10 travailleurs ou de moins d'un jour.

Notas explicativas: véase p. 1365.

[1] Huelgas y cierres patronales que terminan dentro de los 12 meses que comienzan en julio del año indicado. [2] Interrupciones del trabajo que empiezan en el año indicado. [3] Excl. las interrupciones del trabajo que implican menos de 1000 trabajadores y que duran menos de 1 día o turno completo. [4] Incl. las interrupciones con menos de 10 trabajadores o de menos de un día.

9A

	STRIKES AND LOCKOUTS	GRÈVES ET LOCK-OUT	HUELGAS Y CIERRES PATRONALES
	Strikes and lockouts, by economic activity	Grèves et lock-out, par activité économique	Huelgas y cierres patronales, por actividad económica

	1999	2000	2001	2002	2003	2004	2005	2006	2007	2008

ASIA-ASIE-ASIA

Hong Kong, China (FG) [1]
ISIC 3 - CITI 3 - CIIU 3

	1999	2000	2001	2002	2003	2004	2005	2006	2007	2008
Total [2]	3	5	1	0	1	2	1	3	3	4
A	0	0	0	0	0	0	0	0	0	0
B	0	0	0	0	0	0	0	0	0	0
C	0	0	0	0	0	0	0	0	0	0
D	0	0	0	0	0	0	0	0	0	3
E	0	0	0	0	0	0	0	0	0	0
F	1	3	0	0	1	0	0	0	1	0
G	0	1	0	0	0	0	0	0	0	0
H	0	0	0	0	0	0	0	0	0	0
I	2	0	0	0	0	0	1	3	2	1
J	0	0	0	0	0	0	0	0	0	0
K	0	1	1	0	0	0	0	0	0	0
M	0	0	0	0	0	0	0	0	0	0
N	0	0	0	0	0	0	0	0	0	0
O	0	0	0	0	0	2	0	0	0	0

India (H) [3][4]
ISIC 2 - CITI 2 - CIIU 2   ISIC 3 - CITI 3 - CIIU 3

	1999	2000	2001	2002	2003	2004	2005	2006	2007	2008	
Total	927	771	674	579	552	477	456	430	389	392	Total
1	28	31	30	58	50	55	30	34	33	14	A
2	114	1	0	0	0	0	0	0	0	20	B
3	599	91	101	38	23	21	18	18	11	0	C
4	6	505	400	379	353	307	290	259	236	204	D
5	2	8	8	1	7	1	10	9	6	5	E
6	23	3	2	0	3	6	3	1	1	1	F
7	7	16	4	0	1	2	2	5	1	0	G
8	18	8	10	5	8	10	9	7	7	4	H
9	55	12	10	6	3	4	5	12	23	25	I
0	75	14	14	25	24	15	26	46	38	76	J
		3	6	1	2	1	5	1	3	1	K
		4	5	5	7	2	8	3	0	3	L
		1	0	0	0	0	0	0	0	1	M
		4	4	4	3	4	3	1	2	0	N
		69	80	57	69	49	47	33	27	37	O
		1	0	0	0	0	0	1	1	1	P

Israel (FG) [5]
ISIC 3 - CITI 3 - CIIU 3

	1999	2000	2001	2002	2003	2004	2005	2006	2007	2008
Total	66	54	62	47	60	49	57	35	30	14
A	0	0	0	2	2	0	0	0	0	0
B	0	0	0	0	0	0	0	0	0	0
C-D	19	9	11	10	3	6	10	2	4	5
E	1	0	0	0	0	0	0	0	0	0
F	0	1	3	3	1	0	0	1	0	0
G	1	0	1	3	0	0	2	0	0	0
H	0	1	2	0	1	0	0	1	1	0
I	5	7	7	8	12	5	6	6	7	2
J	2	1	1	0	6	11	10	5	2	1
K	0	0	1	0	0	0	0	0	0	0
L	27	20	28	12	23	20	21	16	8	2
M	3	8	6	6	1	3	3	1	5	3
N	2	6	1	2	6	3	2	2	1	1
O	6	1	1	1	5	1	3	1	1	0
P	0	0	0	0	0	0	0	0	0	0
Q	0	0	0	0	0	0	0	0	0	0
X	0	0	0	0	0	0	0	0	1	0

Explanatory notes: see p. 1361.

[1] Incl. stoppages involving fewer than 10 workers or lasting less than one day. [2] Excl. government sector. [3] Excl. work stoppages involving fewer than 10 workers. [4] Excl. political and sympathetic strikes. [5] Excl. work stoppages in which less than 10 workdays not worked.

Notes explicatives: voir p. 1363.

[1] Y compris les arrêts impliquant moins de 10 travailleurs ou de moins d'un jour. [2] Non compris le secteur gouvernemental. [3] Non compris les arrêts du travail impliquant moins de 10 travailleurs. [4] Non compris les grèves politiques et les grèves de solidarité. [5] Non compris les arrêts de travail de moins de 10 journées de travail non effectuées.

Notas explicativas: véase p. 1365.

[1] Incl. las interrupciones con menos de 10 trabajadores o de menos de un día. [2] Excl. el sector gubernamental. [3] Excl. las interrupciones del trabajo que implican menos de 10 trabajadores. [4] Excl. huelgas políticas y huelgas de solidaridad. [5] Excl. las interrupciones de trabajo de menos de 10 días de trabajo no trabajados.

STRIKES AND LOCKOUTS

Strikes and lockouts, by economic activity

GRÈVES ET LOCK-OUT

Grèves et lock-out, par activité économique

HUELGAS Y CIERRES PATRONALES

Huelgas y cierres patronales, por actividad económica

9A

	1999	2000	2001	2002	2003	2004	2005	2006	2007	2008	

Japan (FG) [1]
ISIC 2 - CITI 2 - CIIU 2   ISIC 3 - CITI 3 - CIIU 3

Code	1999	2000	2001	2002	2003	2004	2005	2006	2007	2008	Code
Total	154	118	90	74	47	51	50	46	54	.	Total
1	0	0	0	0	.	0	0	0	0	.	A
2	0	0	0	0	.	0	0	0	0	.	B
3	51	52	35	27	.	0	0	2	0	.	C
4	0	0	0	1	.	22	7	9	12	.	D
5	1	2	2	1	.	0	0	1	0	.	E
6 [2]	7	4	6	2	.	0	0	0	1	.	F
7	51	31	15	19	.	1	5	1	1	.	G [3]
8 [4]	2	0	0	0	.	1	0	0	0	.	H
9 [5]	42	29	0	24	.	14	17	23	26	.	I
0	0	0	0	0	.	0	0	0	1	.	J
						1	0	0	0	.	K
						0	0	0	0	.	L
						2	1	2	3	.	M
						3	13	3	5	.	N
						7	7	5	5	.	O

Jordan (FG)
ISIC 3 - CITI 3 - CIIU 3

Code	1999	2000	2001	2002	2003	2004	2005	2006	2007	2008
Total	0	0	0	0	0	0	0	.	.	.

Korea, Republic of (FG)
ISIC 3 - CITI 3 - CIIU 3

Code	1999	2000	2001	2002	2003	2004	2005	2006	2007	2008
Total	198	250	235	322	320	462	287	138	115	108
A	0	0	1	.	.	.	.	.	.	.
B	0	0	0	.	.	.	.	.	.	.
C	0	1	0	.	.	.	.	.	.	.
D	116	121	117	.	.	.	.	.	.	.
E	0	2	4	.	.	.	.	.	.	.
F	5	4	6	.	.	.	.	.	.	.
G	1	6	4	.	.	.	.	.	.	.
H	6	6	2	.	.	.	.	.	.	.
I	26	27	38	.	.	.	.	.	.	.
J	0	18	12	.	.	.	.	.	.	.
K	24	15	8	.	.	.	.	.	.	.
L	0	0	0	.	.	.	.	.	.	.
M	4	15	13	.	.	.	.	.	.	.
N	10	19	8	.	.	.	.	.	.	.
O	6	16	22	.	.	.	.	.	.	.

Myanmar (F)
ISIC 3 - CITI 3 - CIIU 3

Code	1999	2000	2001	2002	2003	2004	2005	2006	2007	2008
Total	13	10	18	11	28	9	4	6	7	6
D	13	10	18	11	28	9	4	6	7	6

Philippines (H) [6]
ISIC 2 - CITI 2 - CIIU 2   ISIC 3 - CITI 3 - CIIU 3

Code	1999	2000	2001	2002	2003	2004	2005	2006	2007	2008	Code
Total	58	60	43	36	38	25	26	12	6	5	Total
1	0	2	0	0	3	1	1	1	0	1	A
2	1	0	0	0	0	0	0	0	0	0	B
3	31	33	0	0	1	0	1	0	1	0	C
4	0	2	28	21	22	16	20	7	3	3	D
5	0	1	3	1	2	0	0	0	0	0	E
6 [7]	4	2	1	0	0	0	0	0	0	0	F
7	14	9	2	1	2	1	1	0	0	0	G
8	1	3	4	2	0	1	1	0	0	0	H
9 [8]	7	8	2	7	4	4	2	4	1	1	I
			0	0	1	0	0	0	0	0	J
			0	1	0	0	0	0	0	0	K
			0	0	0	0	0	0	0	0	L
			2	2	1	2	0	0	0	0	M
			0	0	1	0	0	0	1	0	N
			1	1	1	0	0	0	0	0	O

Singapore (FG)
ISIC 3 - CITI 3 - CIIU 3

Code	1999	2000	2001	2002	2003	2004	2005	2006	2007	2008
Total	0	0	0	0	0	0	0	0	0	0

Explanatory notes: see p. 1361.

[1] Excl. work stoppages lasting less than half a day. [2] Excl. hotels. [3] Excl. repair of motor vehicles, motor cycles and personal and household goods. [4] Excl. business services. [5] Incl. business services and hotels. [6] Excl. work stoppages lasting less than a full day or shift. [7] Excl. restaurants and hotels. [8] Incl. restaurants and hotels.

Notes explicatives: voir p. 1363.

[1] Non compris les arrêts du travail de durée inférieure à une demi-journée. [2] Non compris les hôtels. [3] Non compris réparation de véhicules automobiles, de motocycles et de biens personnels etdomestiques. [4] Non compris les services aux entreprises. [5] Y compris les services aux entreprises et les hôtels. [6] Non compris les arrêts du travail dont la durée est inférieure à une journée ou à un poste de travail. [7] Non compris les restaurants et les hôtels. [8] Y compris les restaurants et hôtels.

Notas explicativas: véase p. 1365.

[1] Excl. las interrupciones del trabajo de duración inferior a medio día. [2] Excl. hoteles. [3] Excl. reparación de vehículos automotores, motocicletas, efectos personals y enseres domesticos. [4] Excl. servicios para las empresas. [5] Incl. servicios para empresas y hoteles. [6] Excl. las interrupciones del trabajo de duración menor de un día o turno completo. [7] Excl. restaurantes y hoteles. [8] Incl. restaurantes y hoteles.

9A — STRIKES AND LOCKOUTS / GRÈVES ET LOCK-OUT / HUELGAS Y CIERRES PATRONALES

Strikes and lockouts, by economic activity
Grèves et lock-out, par activité économique
Huelgas y cierres patronales, por actividad económica

	1999	2000	2001	2002	2003	2004	2005	2006	2007	2008
Sri Lanka (FD) [1][2][3]										
ISIC 2 - CITI 2 - CIIU 2										
Total	125	87	92	104	98	90	57	52	25	51
1 [4]	42	24	31	43	45	44	17	18	8	34
2	0	0	0	0	0	0	0	0	0	
3	83	63	61	61	53	46	40	34	17	17
Thailand (H)										
ISIC 3 - CITI 3 - CIIU 3										
Total	16	13	5	6	5	2	9	2	5	.
A	0	0	0	0	0	0	0	0	0	.
B	0	0	0	0	0	0	0	0	0	.
C	0	0	0	0	0	0	0	0	0	.
D	16	13	5	6	5	2	6	2	5	.
E	0	0	0	0	0	0	0	0	0	.
F	0	0	0	0	0	0	0	0	0	.
G-H	0	0	0	0	0	0	3	0	0	.
I	0	0	0	0	0	0	0	0	0	.
J-K	0	0	0	0	0	0	0	0	0	.
L-O	0	0	0	0	0	0	0	0	0	.

EUROPE-EUROPE-EUROPA

	1999	2000	2001	2002	2003	2004	2005	2006	2007	2008
Austria (FH)										
ISIC 3 - CITI 3 - CIIU 3										
Total	0	4	0	4	.	.	0	0	0	0
Belarus (FH)										
ISIC 2 - CITI 2 - CIIU 2										
Total	0	0	0	0	0	0	.	.	.	.

Cyprus (H)
ISIC 2 - CITI 2 - CIIU 2 ..... ISIC 3 - CITI 3 - CIIU 3

	1999	2000	2001	2002	2003	2004	2005	2006	2007	2008	
Total	21	6	25	23	18	13	11	10	.	.	Total
1	0	1	3	1	0	0	1	0	.	.	A
2	0	0	0	1	0	0	0	0	.	.	B
3	2	0	1	0	0	0	0	0	.	.	C
4	0	0	0	2	0	3	3	1	.	.	D
5	2	1	7	3	0	0	2	0	.	.	E
6	4	2	3	2	5	1	1	1	.	.	F
7	7	1	0	2	0	0	0	1	.	.	G
8	0	0	5	1	2	1	0	1	.	.	H
9	6	1	6	7	1	0	0	3	.	.	I
				2	0	1	4	0	.	.	J
				0	0	0	0	0	.	.	K
				0	0	0	0	3	.	.	L
				0	0	0	0	0	.	.	M
				0	0	0	0	0	.	.	N
				2	10	7	0	0	.	.	O

	1999	2000	2001	2002	2003	2004	2005	2006	2007	2008
Denmark (FH) [5]										
ISIC 3 - CITI 3 - CIIU 3										
Total	1 079	1 081	840	1 349	681	804	534	476	862	335
A-C	0	2	3	1	1	0	0	2	0	0
D	628	675	497	725	365	437	229	161	306	138
E	9	3	8	2	4	0	0	0	0	0
F	72	102	99	126	84	81	63	95	103	33
G	45	68	38	67	31	30	32	39	106	40
H	11	7	10	13	7	13	18	7	4	1
I	92	120	93	137	90	121	117	59	214	68
J	0	0	0	0	0	0	0	0	0	0
K	0	0	0	0	0	0	0	0	0	0
L	0	0	0	0	0	0	0	0	0	0
M	0	0	0	0	0	0	0	0	0	0
N	0	0	0	0	0	0	0	0	0	0
O	0	0	0	0	0	0	0	0	0	0
X	222	104	92	278	99	122	75	113	129	55

Explanatory notes: see p. 1361.

[1] Number of strikes that ended during the year; excl. political strikes. [2] Incl. work stoppages lasting less than one day only if more than 50 workdays not worked. [3] Excl. work stoppages involving fewer than 5 workers. [4] Plantations. [5] Up to 1995: excl. work stoppages in which less than 100 work-days not worked.

Notes explicatives: voir p. 1363.

[1] Nombre de grèves qui se sont terminées pendant l'année; non compris les grèves politiques. [2] Y compris les arrêts du travail d'une durée inférieure à une journée si plus de 50 journées de travail non effectuées. [3] Non compris les arrêts du travail impliquant moins de 5 travailleurs. [4] Plantations. [5] Jusqu'à 1995: non compris les arrêts du travail de moins de 100 journées de travail non effectuées.

Notas explicativas: véase p. 1365.

[1] Número de huelgas que terminaron durante el año; excl. las huelgas políticas. [2] Incl. las interrupciones del trabajo de menos de un día si no se han trabajado más de 50 días. [3] Excl. las interrupciones del trabajo que implican menos de 5 trabajadores. [4] Plantaciones. [5] Hasta 1995: excl. las interrupciones del trabajo de menos de 100 días no trabajados.

Strikes and lockouts, by economic activity

Grèves et lock-out, par activité économique

Huelgas y cierres patronales, por actividad económica

	1999	2000	2001	2002	2003	2004	2005	2006	2007	2008
España (FG) [1]										
ISIC 3 - CITI 3 - CIIU 3										
Total	749	750	737	688	678	708	685	783	752	811
A	6	4	5	15	3	14	13	5	5	12
B	0	3	1	0	2	0	1	0	0	2
C	64	45	38	16	17	14	19	12	14	13
D	237	299	319	252	326	303	297	359	363	320
E	11	3	10	12	3	6	8	10	8	7
F	12	36	30	11	5	9	12	24	16	20
G	18	26	16	16	21	18	12	25	22	36
H	15	11	9	16	9	8	14	13	8	20
I	106	100	111	135	102	112	100	120	94	107
J	14	3	5	3	3	5	4	8	3	0
K	38	39	40	56	38	38	34	43	41	74
L	26	48	23	20	25	63	52	46	34	37
M	29	45	28	29	16	19	18	36	21	34
N	126	35	50	48	47	50	65	48	57	60
O	42	47	41	52	59	47	36	34	64	67
P	1	0	6	0	0	0	0	0	0	0
X [2]	4	6	5	7	2	2	0	0	2	2
Estonia (FG)										
ISIC 3 - CITI 3 - CIIU 3										
Total	0	0	0	.	1	1	0			.
Finland (FH)										
ISIC 3 - CITI 3 - CIIU 3										
Total	65	96	84	76	112	84	365	97	91	92
A	0	2	0	0	2	0	0	0	0	0
B	0	0	0	0	0	0	0	0	0	0
C	0	0	0	0	0	0	0	0	2	1
D	49	63	63	62	95	70	346	83	69	80
E	1	0	5	1	1	1	1	5	0	0
F	5	0	0	3	2	0	2	1	2	1
G	0	2	0	1	1	0	1	0	6	0
H	1	0	0	0	0	0	0	0	0	0
I	3	26	6	3	8	7	7	5	5	10
J	5	2	0	2	3	1	0	0	0	0
K	0	0	4	3	2	4	1	0	5	0
L	0	0	0	0	0	0	2	1	0	0
M-N	0	1	1	0	0	0	0	0	1	0
N	.	.	.	.	.	.	.	.	1	0
O	1	0	5	1	0	1	4	0	0	0
X	0	0	0	0	0	0	1	2	1	0
Hungary (H) [3]										
ISIC 3 - CITI 3 - CIIU 3										
Total	5	5	6	4	7	8	11	16	22	8
A	0	0	0	0	0	0	0	0	0	0
B	0	0	0	0	0	0	0	0	0	0
C	0	0	0	0	0	0	0	0	0	0
D	1	2	3	3	5	3	9	7	4	0
E	1	0	0	0	0	1	0	1	2	0
F	0	0	0	0	0	0	0	0	1	0
G	0	0	0	0	0	0	0	2	1	1
H	0	0	0	0	0	0	0	0	0	0
I	2	2	0	0	2	1	2	1	7	5
J	0	0	0	0	0	0	0	0	0	0
K	0	0	0	0	0	0	0	1	1	1
L	0	0	0	0	0	0	0	1	0	0
M	0	0	0	0	0	0	0	1	2	0
N	1	1	1	1	0	3	0	0	2	1
O	0	0	2	0	0	0	0	2	2	0
Iceland (H)										
ISIC 3 - CITI 3 - CIIU 3										
Total	0	7	17	0	0	1	.	.	.	.

Explanatory notes: see p. 1361.

[1] Prior to 1990: strikes only; excl. the Basque country. [2] General strikes. [3] 1991-95: Work stoppages in which 800 hours or more not worked; beginning 1996: stoppages involving 10 workers or more.

Notes explicatives: voir p. 1363.

[1] Avant 1990: grèves seulement; non compris le Pays basque. [2] Grèves générales. [3] 1991-95: Arrêts de travail avec 800 h. de travail non effectuées au moins; dès 1996: ceux impliquant 10 travailleurs ou plus.

Notas explicativas: véase p. 1365.

[1] Antes de 1990: huelgas solamente; excl. el País Vasco. [2] Huelgas generales. [3] 1991-95: Interrupciones del trabajo de 800 horas no trabajadas y más: desde 1996: las que implican 10 trabajadores o más.

STRIKES AND LOCKOUTS / GRÈVES ET LOCK-OUT / HUELGAS Y CIERRES PATRONALES

Strikes and lockouts, by economic activity

Grèves et lock-out, par activité économique

Huelgas y cierres patronales, por actividad económica

Ireland (H) [1]
ISIC 3 - CITI 3 - CIIU 3

	1999	2000	2001	2002	2003	2004	2005	2006	2007	2008
Total	32	39	26	27	24	11	15	10	6	12
A-B	1	0	0	0	0	0	1	0	0	0
C	0	1	0	0	0	1	1	0	0	0
D	4	11	9	5	5	2	2	3	2	3
E	2	0	0	0	0	0	1	0	0	0
F	4	2	2	1	1	0	3	2	0	1
G	1	2	1	2	1	1	2	0	1	1
H	1	1	0	1	0	0	0	0	0	0
I	6	12	10	4	5	3	3	1	2	3
J-K	.	.	.	.	1	2	0	1	0	0
L	1	5	0	1	2	1	1	1	1	1
M	4	3	1	3	3	0	0	0	0	0
N	7	2	3	7	11	0	0	2	0	1
O	.	.	.	2	0	0	0	0	0	0
O-Q	0	0	0	.	3	1	1	0	0	2
P	.	.	.	0	0	0	0	0	0	0
Q	.	.	.	1	0	0	0	0	0	0

Isle of Man (FG)
ISIC 3 - CITI 3 - CIIU 3

	1999	2000	2001	2002	2003	2004	2005	2006	2007	2008
Total	1	0	0	0	0	0	0	0	0	.
A	0	0	0	0	0	0	0	0	0	.
B	0	0	0	0	0	0	0	0	0	.
C	0	0	0	0	0	0	0	0	0	.
D	0	0	0	0	0	0	0	0	0	.
E	0	0	0	0	0	0	0	0	0	.
F	1	0	0	0	0	0	0	0	0	.
G	0	0	0	0	0	0	0	0	0	.
H	0	0	0	0	0	0	0	0	0	.
I	0	0	0	0	0	0	0	0	0	.
J	0	0	0	0	0	0	0	0	0	.
K	0	0	0	0	0	0	0	0	0	.
L	0	0	0	0	0	0	0	0	0	.
M	0	0	0	0	0	0	0	0	0	.
N	0	0	0	0	0	0	0	0	0	.
O	0	0	0	0	0	0	0	0	0	.

Italy (H)
ISIC 3 - CITI 3 - CIIU 3

	1999	2000	2001	2002	2003	2004	2005	2006	2007	2008
Total	753	966	746	616	710	745	654	587	667	621
A-B	10	31	12	12	19	17	18	14	18	13
C	13	5	8	6	4	3	5	6	0	1
D	264	368	273	287	330	407	376	301	325	273
E	34	32	29	18	14	15	6	8	4	6
F	28	20	22	12	7	9	18	16	13	9
G	24	23	12	9	18	15	15	12	24	18
H	2	4	4	2	9	4	2	3	3	4
I	170	200	148	92	118	112	77	82	110	96
J	28	39	21	20	10	9	8	11	12	12
K,O	48	70	77	58	73	70	57	59	63	95
L	77	95	70	52	59	40	50	39	57	55
M	25	46	32	13	27	17	6	7	11	11
N	30	31	33	31	11	27	16	29	27	28
X	0	2	5	4	11	0	0	0	0	0

Latvia (D)
ISIC 3 - CITI 3 - CIIU 3

	1999	2000	2001	2002	2003	2004	2005	2006	2007	2008
Total	.	.	.	.	.	.	0	0	0	14
D	.	.	.	.	.	.	0	0	0	0
I	.	.	.	.	.	.	0	0	0	0
L	.	.	.	.	.	.	0	0	0	0
M	.	.	.	.	.	.	0	0	0	0
N	.	.	.	.	.	.	0	0	0	14
O	.	.	.	.	.	.	0	0	0	0

Liechtenstein (H)
ISIC 3 - CITI 3 - CIIU 3

	1999	2000	2001	2002	2003	2004	2005	2006	2007	2008
Total	0	0	0	0	0	0	0	0	.	.

Lithuania (D)
ISIC 3 - CITI 3 - CIIU 3

	1999	2000	2001	2002	2003	2004	2005	2006	2007	2008
Total	.	56	34	0	0	0	1	0	161	112
D	.	0	2	0	0	0	0	0	0	0
I	.	4	0	0	0	0	0	0	0	0
M	.	52	32	0	0	0	0	0	161	112
O	.	.	.	.	.	.	1	0	0	0

Explanatory notes: see p. 1361.

[1] Work stoppages lasting at least one day or with at least 10 days not worked.

Notes explicatives: voir p. 1363.

[1] Arrêts de travail d'un jour au moins ou avec un minimum de 10 jours de travail non effectués.

Notas explicativas: véase p. 1365.

[1] Interrupciones del trabajo de un día por lo menos o de un mínimo de 10 días no trabajados.

STRIKES AND LOCKOUTS

GRÈVES ET LOCK-OUT

HUELGAS Y CIERRES PATRONALES

Strikes and lockouts, by economic activity

Grèves et lock-out, par activité économique

Huelgas y cierres patronales, por actividad económica

	1999	2000	2001	2002	2003	2004	2005	2006	2007	2008
Malta (H)										
ISIC 3 - CITI 3 - CIIU 3										
Total	.	12	13	5	8	6	8	8	5	4
A	.	0	0	0	0	0	0	0	0	0
B	.	0	0	0	0	0	0	0	0	0
C	.	0	0	0	0	0	0	0	0	0
D	.	3	0	1	1	1	1	1	0	0
E	.	0	1	1	1	0	1	0	0	0
F	.	0	1	0	0	0	0	0	0	0
G	.	0	0	0	0	0	0	1	0	0
H	.	1	0	0	1	0	0	0	0	0
I	.	4	5	1	4	3	3	2	3	0
J	.	1	0	0	0	0	0	0	0	0
K	.	0	0	1	0	0	0	1	0	0
L	.	2	0	1	0	0	2	1	0	1
M	.	0	2	0	0	0	0	1	2	2
N	.	1	4	0	1	1	1	0	0	0
O	.	0	0	0	0	1	0	1	0	1
Netherlands (H)										
ISIC 3 - CITI 3 - CIIU 3										
Total	24	23	16	16	14	12	28	31	20	21
A	0	0	0	0	0	.	.	0	0	0
B	0	0	0	0	0	0	0	0	0	0
C	0	0	0	0	0	0	0	0	0	0
D	7	7	5 [1]	4	4	6	11 [2]	12	4	9 [1]
E	0	0	.	0	0	0	0	0	0	0
F	2	0	0	1	0	0	.	0	0	0
G	0	4 [3]	.	0	.	0	0	0	0	0
H	0	.	0	0	0	0	0	0	0	0
I	11 [4]	8	10 [5]	9 [4]	8 [6]	3	7 [5]	16 [6]	7	9
J	0	0	0	0	0	0	0	0	0	0
K	.	.	0	.	.	0	6	0	4	0
L	3	4 [7]	0	2 [8]	2 [9]	0	0	3 [10]	5	3
M	1	.	.	0	0	0	0	0	0	0
N	0	0	3 [7]	.	0	0	0	0	0	0
O	0	.	.	0	0	0	0	0	0	0
X	.	.	.	.	.	3 [11]	4 [11]	0	0	0
Norway (FH) [12]										
ISIC 3 - CITI 3 - CIIU 3										
Total	15	29	3	16	5	12	2	12	4	10
A	0	0	0	0	0	0	0	0	0	0
B	0	0	0	0	0	0	0	0	0	0
C	.	.	.	.	.	.	1	1	0	0
D	.	.	.	.	.	.	0	0	0	1
E	0	0	0	0	0	0	0	1	0	0
F	0	.	0	.	0	.	1	1	0	0
G	.	.	0	.	.	.	0	1	0	1
H	.	.	.	.	0	.	0	0	0	0
I	.	.	0	.	0	.	0	4	0	3
J	0	0	0	0	0	0	0	1	0	0
K	.	.	0	0	0	0	0	0	1	1
L	0	0	0	0	0	0	0	1	0	0
M	.	.	0	0	.	.	0	0	1	1
N	0	.	0	.	0	0	0	0	1	3
O	0	.	0	.	0	0	0	2	1	0
Poland (FG)										
ISIC 3 - CITI 3 - CIIU 3										
Total	920	44	11	1	24	2	8	27	1 736	12 765
A	0	0	0	0	0	0	0	0	0	0
B	0	0	0	0	0	0	0	0	0	0
C	0	0	0	0	0	0	0	1	0	1
D	21	4	4	1	15	0	5	2	26	4
E	3	2	2	0	0	0	0	0	0	1
F	0	0	0	0	0	0	0	0	0	1
G	1	0	0	0	0	0	0	0	0	0
H	0	0	0	0	0	0	0	0	0	2
I	6	4	0	0	2	2	2	0	53	51
J	0	0	0	0	0	0	0	0	0	0
K	6	0	0	0	7	0	0	0	1	7
L	0	0	0	0	0	0	0	0	0	0
M	881	0	0	0	0	0	0	0	1 543	12 609
N	1	34	5	0	0	0	1	24	113	80
O	1	0	0	0	0	0	0	0	0	9

Explanatory notes: see p. 1361.

[1] Incl. category E. [2] Incl. category F. [3] Incl. categories H and K. [4] Incl. category K. [5] Including category G. [6] Incl. categories G and K. [7] Incl. categories M and O. [8] Incl. category N. [9] Incl. category O. [10] Incl. categories N and O. [11] Incl. categories A and O. [12] Excl. work stoppages lasting less than one day.

Notes explicatives: voir p. 1363.

[1] Y compris la catégorie E. [2] Y compris catégorie F. [3] Y compris les catégories H et K. [4] Y compris la catégorie K. [5] Y compris la catégorie G. [6] Y compris les catégories G et K. [7] Y compris les catégories M et O. [8] Y compris la catégorie N. [9] Y compris la catégorie O. [10] Y compris les catégories N et O. [11] Y compris les catégories A et O. [12] Non compris les arrêts du travail dont la durée est inférieure à une journée.

Notas explicativas: véase p. 1365.

[1] Incl. la categoría E. [2] Incl. categoría F. [3] Incl. las categorías H y K. [4] Incl. la categoría K. [5] Incl. la categoría G. [6] Incl. las categorías G y K. [7] Incl. las categorías M y O. [8] Incl. la categoría N. [9] Incl. la categoría O. [10] Incl. las categorías N y O. [11] Incl. las categorías A y O. [12] Excl. las interrupciones del trabajo de menos de un día de duración.

9A

STRIKES AND LOCKOUTS

Strikes and lockouts, by economic activity

GRÈVES ET LOCK-OUT

Grèves et lock-out, par activité économique

HUELGAS Y CIERRES PATRONALES

Huelgas y cierres patronales, por actividad económica

	1999	2000	2001	2002	2003	2004	2005	2006	2007	2008
Portugal (FG) [1]										
ISIC 3 - CITI 3 - CIIU 3										
Total [2]	200	250	208	250	170	122	126	155	99	.
A	0	0	0	0	0	0	0	0	0	.
B	2	2	0	1	1	0	0	0	0	.
C	1	10	1	4	1	0	3	1	3	.
D	132	122	97	140	85	67	78	79	44	.
E	4	2	3	3	1	2	3	2	3	.
F	4	0	1	3	1	2	4	2	7	.
G	19	13	8	11	6	5	3	6	7	.
H	6	6	11	15	3	11	5	9	7	.
I	27	67	54	58	58	26	31	47	33	.
J	1	0	0	0	0	2	0	1	3	.
K	5	24	25	32	20	16	11	21	16	.
M [2]	0	0	2	3	1	0	5	3	3	.
N	3	4	3	6	1	0	1	0	2	.
O	5	10	13	7	2	6	9	3	7	.
Roumanie (FG) [1]										
ISIC 3 - CITI 3 - CIIU 3										
Total	85	10	5	13	9	11	8	2	12	8
A	8	0	0	0	0	1	0	0	1	0
B	0	0	0	0	0	0	0	0	0	0
C	1	1	0	2	0	1	0	0	0	6
D	40	6	4	9	7	6	5	2	7	1
E	1	0	0	0	1	0	0	0	1	0
F	2	0	0	0	0	1	0	0	0	0
G	0	0	0	0	0	0	0	0	0	0
H	0	0	0	0	0	0	0	0	0	1
I	11	0	1	1	1	2	3	0	3	0
J	0	0	0	0	0	0	0	0	0	0
K	0	0	0	0	0	0	0	0	0	0
L	0	0	0	0	0	0	0	0	0	0
M	16	1	0	0	0	0	0	0	0	0
N	6	1	0	1	0	0	0	0	0	0
O	0	1	0	0	0	0	0	0	0	0
X	0	0	0	0	0	0	0	0	0	0
Russian Federation (FG) [3]										
ISIC 3 - CITI 3 - CIIU 3										
Total	7 285	817	291	80	67	5 933	2 575	6	7	4
A	.	.	.	.	.	.	7	0	0	2
C-E	21	7	4	.	.	.	.	0	0	0
D	.	.	.	.	.	.	.	2	3	0
E	.	.	.	.	.	.	1	1	0	0
F	5	.	.	.	.	.	1	0	0	1
I	6	4	.	.	.	.	1	1	4	0
K	.	.	.	.	.	.	.	1	0	0
M	7 130	789	280	.	.	.	2 478	0	0	0
N	49	3	.	.	.	.	27	0	0	0
O	.	9	6	.	.	.	60	3	0	0
X	74	5	1	.	.	.	.	0	0	0
San Marino (H)										
ISIC 2 - CITI 2 - CIIU 2										
Total	3	3	2	13	7	1	2	.	.	.
3 [4]	.	2	0	5	5	1	2	.	.	.
4	.	0	0	0	0	0	0	.	.	.
5	.	0	0	0	0	0	0	.	.	.
6	.	0	0	0	0	0	0	.	.	.
7	.	0	0	0	0	0	0	.	.	.
8	.	0	0	0	0	0	0	.	.	.
9	.	1	1	3	1	0	0	.	.	.
0	.	.	1 [5]	5 [5]	1	0	0	.	.	.
Slovakia (FG)										
ISIC 3 - CITI 3 - CIIU 3										
Total	0	0	0	0	2	0	0	4	1	1

Explanatory notes: see p. 1361.

[1] Strikes only. [2] Excl. public administration. [3] Excl. work stoppages lasting less than one day. [4] Incl. generalized strikes. [5] Generalized strikes.

Notes explicatives: voir p. 1363.

[1] Grèves seulement. [2] Non compris l'administration publique. [3] Non compris les arrêts du travail dont la durée est inférieure à une journée. [4] Y compris les grèves généralisées. [5] Grèves généralisées.

Notas explicativas: véase p. 1365.

[1] Huelgas solamente. [2] Excl. la administración pública. [3] Excl. las interrupciones del trabajo de menos de un día de duración. [4] Incl. las huelgas generalizadas. [5] Huelgas generalizadas.

STRIKES AND LOCKOUTS

Strikes and lockouts, by economic activity

GRÈVES ET LOCK-OUT

Grèves et lock-out, par activité économique

HUELGAS Y CIERRES PATRONALES

Huelgas y cierres patronales, por actividad económica

9A

Suisse (H) [1]
ISIC 3 - CITI 3 - CIIU 3

	1999	2000	2001	2002	2003	2004	2005	2006	2007	2008
Total	5	8	3	4	9	8	5	3	2	8
A	0	0	0	0	0	0	0	0	0	0
B	0	0	0	0	0	0	0	0	0	0
C	0	0	0	0	0	0	0	0	0	0
D	1	2	0	0	2	4	3	1	0	2
E	0	0	0	0	0	0	0	0	0	0
F	1	0	0	2	2	2	0	0	2	3
G	0	0	1	0	0	0	0	0	0	0
H	0	0	0	0	0	0	0	0	0	0
I	0	1	0	1	1	0	2	1	0	1
J	1	0	0	0	0	0	0	0	0	0
K	0	0	0	0	2	0	0	0	0	0
L	2	1	0	0	1	2	0	0	0	2
M	0	0	1	1	1	0	0	0	0	0
N	0	1	1	0	0	0	0	0	0	0
O	0	3	0	0	0	0	0	1	0	0
X	0	0	0	0	0	0	0	0	0	0

Sweden (H) [2]
ISIC 3 - CITI 3 - CIIU 3

	1999	2000	2001	2002	2003	2004	2005	2006	2007	2008
Total	10	2	20	10	11	9	14	9	14	5
A	0	0	0	0	0	0	0	0	0	0
B	0	0	0	0	0	0	0	0	0	0
C	1	0	0	0	0	0	0	0	0	0
D	1	0	6	3	0	3	1	3	5	1
E	0	0	2	0	0	0	2	0	0	0
F	1	1	3	1	2	4	1	0	2	0
G	0	0	0	0	0	0	0	0	0	0
H	0	0	0	1	0	0	0	0	0	0
I	3	1	6	2	5	1	4	1	2	3
J	1	0	0	0	0	0	0	0	0	0
K	0	0	0	0	0	0	2	0	1	0
L	2	0	0	1	0	0	0	0	0	0
M	1	0	0	2	1	0	1	1	2	0
N	0	0	1	0	0	0	0	2	1	1
O	0	0	2	0	3	1	3	1	1	0
X	.	.	.	.	.	.	.	1	.	.

Turkey (FG) [3]
ISIC 3 - CITI 3 - CIIU 3

	1999	2000	2001	2002	2003	2004	2005	2006	2007	2008
Total	34	52	35	27	23	30	34	26	15	15
A	0	0	0	0	0	0	0	0	0	0
B	0	0	0	0	0	0	0	0	0	0
C	2	3	2	1	2	1	1	0	0	0
D	16	19	26	11	12	22	25	18	10	14
E	0	0	0	0	1	0	0	0	0	0
F	0	0	0	1	1	1	0	0	0	0
G	0	0	0	0	0	0	0	0	0	0
H	3	4	3	3	2	3	5	1	1	0
I	11	7	0	4	5	2	3	4	3	0
J	0	0	0	0	0	0	0	0	0	0
K	0	0	0	0	0	0	0	0	0	0
L	0	0	0	0	0	0	0	0	0	0
M	0	0	0	0	0	0	0	0	0	0
N	0	0	0	0	0	0	0	0	0	0
O	2	19	4	7	0	1	0	3	1	1

Ukraine (FG) [4]
ISIC 2 - CITI 2 - CIIU 2 (1999–2001) · ISIC 3 - CITI 3 - CIIU 3 (2002–2008)

	1999	2000	2001	2002	2003	2004	2005	2006	2007	2008	
Total	290	73	31	97	15	4	4	13	5	1	Total
2	50	34	8	0	0	0	0	0	0	0	A
3 [5]	5	2	3	0	0	0	0	0	0	0	B
5	10	7	7	4	7	1	2	2	1	0	C
7	1	.	.	1	3	0	0	5	1	0	D
9 [6]	224	30	13	0	1	1	1	1	1	0	E
				1	1	0	0	3	0	1	F
				0	0	0	0	0	0	0	G
				0	0	0	0	0	0	0	H
				1	3	2	0	1	1	0	I
				0	0	0	0	0	0	0	J
				0	0	0	0	1	0	0	K
				0	0	0	0	0	0	0	L
				86	0	0	0	0	0	0	M
				2	0	0	0	0	0	0	N
				2	0	0	1	0	1	0	O

Explanatory notes: see p. 1361.

[1] Excl. work stoppages lasting less than one day. [2] Work stoppages in which at least 8 hours not worked. [3] Strikes only. [4] One strike represents one establishment on strike. [5] Incl. electricity, gas and water. [6] All activities not shown elsewhere.

Notes explicatives: voir p. 1363.

[1] Non compris les arrêts du travail dont la durée est inférieure à une journée. [2] Arrêts de travail avec un minimum de 8 heures de travail non effectuées. [3] Grèves seulement. [4] Une grève représente un établissement en grève. [5] Y compris l'électricité, le gaz et l'eau. [6] Toutes les activités non indiquées ailleurs.

Notas explicativas: véase p. 1365.

[1] Excl. las interrupciones del trabajo de menos de un día de duración. [2] Interrupciones del trabajo de un mínimo de 8 horas no trabajadas. [3] Huelgas solamente. [4] Una huelga representa un establecimiento en huelga. [5] Incl. electricidad, gas y agua. [6] Todas las actividades no indicadas en otra parte.

STRIKES AND LOCKOUTS / GRÈVES ET LOCK-OUT / HUELGAS Y CIERRES PATRONALES

Strikes and lockouts, by economic activity

Grèves et lock-out, par activité économique

Huelgas y cierres patronales, por actividad económica

	1999	2000	2001	2002	2003	2004	2005	2006	2007	2008
United Kingdom (H) [1][2]										
ISIC 3 - CITI 3 - CIIU 3										
Total	205	226	207	162	138	135	116	158	152	144
A-B	0	0	0	0	0	0	0	0	1	2
C	0	2	1	1	0	1	1	1	0	1
D	37	38	32	33	43	30	19	25	22	2
E	0	1	2	1	1	2	1	1	0	0
F	20	16	9	3	4	1	3	5	4	4
G	0	1	2	3	1	1	0	4	0	3
H	4	3	5	5	1	0	1	0	0	0
I	91	116	94	51	45	46	42	30	55	28
J	0	0	1	0	0	1	2	0	0	0
K	4	1	1	4	2	2	7	9	6	7
L	17	7	22	20	10	19	13	18	20	16
M	21	18	16	16	15	16	22	53	21	40
N	4	10	12	14	7	4	1	4	12	4
O	8	13	10	11	9	12	5	8	11	18

OCEANIA-OCÉANIE-OCEANIA

	1999	2000	2001	2002	2003	2004	2005	2006	2007	2008
Australia (H) [3]										
ISIC 3 - CITI 3 - CIIU 3										
Total	731	700	675	767	643	692	472	202	135	177
A-B	.[4]	0	.[4]	3	.	.[4]	0	.[4]	.[4]	0
C	89	54	47	55	46	29	31	13	5	5
D	209	239	221	210	160	156	136	79	48	39
E	19	9	16	16	7	13	15	6	3	10
F	248	221	225	292	311	375	221	54	29	41
G-H	15	28	24	31	16	5	8	3	3	3
I	85	84	67	70	57	38	48	39	22	27
J-K	27	23	31	28	11	22	18	9	3	1
L	14	11	14	24	8	33	10	7	.[4]	23
M	26	22	4	.[4]	9	10	10	6	6	17
N [5]	15	12	17	20	17	10	15	9	10	9
O	14	22	31	30	17	3	14	13	8	3
X	0	0	0	0	0	0	0	0	0	0
New Zealand (FG) [6][7][8]										
ISIC 3 - CITI 3 - CIIU 3										
Total	32	21	42	46	28	34	60	42	31	.
A	0	0	0	1	0	1	0	0	0	.
B	0	0	1	0	0	0	0	0	0	.
C	0	0	0	0	1	1	1	0	1	.
D	7	5	17	14	8	13	20	13	11	.
E	0	0	0	0	0	0	0	2	0	.
F	1	1	3	0	1	2	1	4	1	.
G	1	1	2	0	2	0	2	2	2	.
H	0	0	0	1	0	1	1	1	1	.
I	6	2	3	6	2	3	6	3	4	.
J	1	0	0	1	0	2	2	0	0	.
K	1	0	4	1	1	1	0	1	1	.
L	0	3	5	4	1	3	5	5	1	.
M	8	1	3	6	2	3	6	1	2	.
N	5	8	3	11	8	4	10	7	5	.
O	2	0	1	1	2	0	6	3	2	.

Explanatory notes: see p. 1361.

[1] Incl. stoppages involving fewer than 10 workers or lasting less than one day if 100 or more workdays not worked. [2] Excl. political strikes. [3] Excl. work stoppages in which less than 10 workdays not worked. [4] Data included in totals only for reasons of confidentiality. [5] Incl. community services. [6] Excl. work stoppages in which less than 10 workdays not worked (from 2000, 5 workdays). [7] Incl. partial strikes and lockouts. [8] Prior to 1988: excl. public sector stoppages.

Notes explicatives: voir p. 1363.

[1] Y compris les arrêts impliquant moins de 10 travailleurs ou de moins d'un jour si plus de 100 journées de travail non effectuées. [2] Non compris les grèves politiques. [3] Non compris les arrêts de travail de moins de 10 journées de travail non effectuées. [4] Données incluses uniquement dans le total pour des raisons de confidentialité. [5] Y compris les services à la collectivité. [6] Non compris les arrêts de travail de moins de 10 journées de travail non effectuées (à partir de 2000, 5 journées de travail). [7] Y compris les grèves et lock-out partiels. [8] Avant 1988: non compris les arrêts du travail du secteur public.

Notas explicativas: véase p. 1365.

[1] Incl. las interrupciones con menos de 10 trabajadores o de menos de un día si hubo más de 100 días de trabajo no trabajados. [2] Excl. las huelgas políticas. [3] Excl. las interrupciones de trabajo de menos de 10 días de trabajo no trabajados. [4] Datos incluidos en el total solamente por razón de confidencialidad. [5] Incl. servicios comunales. [6] Excl. las interrupciones de trabajo de menosde 10 días de trabajo no trabajados (desde 2000, 5 días de trabajo). [7] Incl. huelgas y cierres patronales parciales. [8] Antes de 1988: excl. las interrupciones del sector público.

STRIKES AND LOCKOUTS — GRÈVES ET LOCK-OUT — HUELGAS Y CIERRES PATRONALES — 9B

Workers involved, by economic activity — Travailleurs impliqués, par activité économique — Trabajadores implicados, por actividad económica

	1999	2000	2001	2002	2003	2004	2005	2006	2007	2008

AFRICA-AFRIQUE-AFRICA

Algérie (FG) [1]
ISIC 3 - CITI 3 - CIIU 3

	1999	2000	2001	2002	2003	2004	2005	2006	2007	2008
Total	33 989	65 152	50 229	81 851	83 919	56 861	.	.	.	.
A-B	359	221	389	1 148	0	330	.	.	.	.
C	519	2 890	1 414	771	0	0	.	.	.	.
D	7 982	18 834	22 192	17 420	0	14 148	.	.	.	.
E [2]	0	0	0	0	0	0	.	.	.	.
F	13 523	6 212	3 462	4 939	0	1 796	.	.	.	.
G	282	218	78	197	0	0	.	.	.	.
H	0	0	65	5 764	0	0	.	.	.	.
I	337	7 308	1 254	12 620	7 815	3 298	.	.	.	.
J-K	0	0	170	381	0	0	.	.	.	.
L	421	158	3 212	285	11 016	2 330	.	.	.	.
M	4 590	26 480	14 752	32 178	29 626	26 674	.	.	.	.
N	806	972	1 558	1 926	30 397	4 950	.	.	.	.
Q	4 207	674	168	3 815	0	3 285	.	.	.	.
X	963	1 185	1 515	407	5 065	50	.	.	.	.

Mauritius (FG) [3]
ISIC 3 - CITI 3 - CIIU 3

	1999	2000	2001	2002	2003	2004	2005	2006	2007	2008
Total	881	3 905	1 796	4 034	3 177	2 958	3 640	1 478	4 687	2 148
A	96	1 050	0	147	0	0	0	0	0	0
B	0	0	56	0	0	0	0	0	0	0
C	0	0	0	0	0	0	0	0	0	0
D	650	2 714	1 553	3 808	2 996	2 935	3 640	1 478	4 687	835
E	0	0	0	0	0	0	0	0	0	0
F	75	0	119	0	99	13	0	0	0	813
G	0	123	40	50	18	10	0	0	0	0
H	19	0	0	16	0	0	0	0	0	0
I	0	18	28	0	64	0	0	0	0	0
J	0	0	0	0	0	0	0	0	0	0
K	0	0	0	0	0	0	0	0	0	0
L	0	0	0	0	0	0	0	0	0	0
M	0	0	0	13	0	0	0	0	0	0
N	0	0	0	0	0	0	0	0	0	0
O	0	0	0	0	0	0	0	0	0	0
X	41	0	0	0	0	0	0	0	0	500

Nigeria (FG) [3][4]
ISIC 2 - CITI 2 - CIIU 2

	1999	2000	2001	2002	2003	2004	2005	2006	2007	2008
Total	173 858	344 722	57 188	49 155	249 697	127 377	280 606	208 589	.	.
1	0	0	0	0	1 500	0	880	1 081	.	.
2	950	330	0	298	0	0	6 436	4 287	.	.
3	300	27 910	3 030	138	1 023	8 483	10 778	4 784	.	.
4	0	0	0	0	0	0	1 272	879	.	.
5	0	423	280	300	0	516	256	31 535	.	.
6	0	200	0	180	35	0	58	28 266	.	.
7	185	235	82	0	4 240	120	4 371	167	.	.
8	41	236	370	0	0	18 805			.	.
9	172 382	315 388	53 426	58 231	9 381	36 263	227 377	30 654	.	.
0	0	0	0	0	207 776	63 190	29 178	106 936	.	.

South Africa (FG) [3]
ISIC 3 - CITI 3 - CIIU 3

	1999	2000	2001	2002	2003	2004	2005	2006	2007	2008
Total	555 435	1 142 428	90 392	66 250	83 533	395 301	399 291	250 787	608 919	118 979
A	5 819	2 221	806	400	2 958	3 230	7 554	2 820	2 753	411
C	64 271	170 193	12 367	21 647	23 078	44 922	165 791	85 396	161 193	46 911
D	52 999	63 850	32 678	5 303	18 021	16 690	55 649	14 555	98 839	24 669
E	438	23	2 126	16	4 576	20	406	6 447	69	0
F	12 390	17 113	1 124	329	8 730	0	4 006	78	7 052	857
G	2 245	11 761	45	1 363	14 118	637	46 634	63 553	466	6 454
I	62 566	118 770	11 042	3 430	8 840	1 440	54 271	35 723	3 470	15 241
J	120	10	.	0	12	1 963	2 018	16 488	3 003	999
O	354 587	758 487	30 204	33 762	3 200	326 399	62 962	25 727	332 074	23 437

Saint Helena (FG)
ISIC 3 - CITI 3 - CIIU 3

	1999	2000	2001	2002	2003	2004	2005	2006	2007	2008
Total	0	0	0	0	0	0	0	.	.	.

Explanatory notes: see p. 1361.

[1] Strikes only. [2] Incl. sanitary services. [3] Excl. workers indirectly involved. [4] Year beginning in April of year indicated.

Notes explicatives: voir p. 1363.

[1] Grèves seulement. [2] Y compris les services sanitaires. [3] Non compris les travailleurs indirectement impliqués. [4] Année commençant en avril de l'année indiquée.

Notas explicativas: véase p. 1365.

[1] Huelgas solamente. [2] Incl. los servicios de saneamiento. [3] Excl. los trabajadores indirectamente implicados. [4] Año que comienza en abril del año indicado.

STRIKES AND LOCKOUTS
Workers involved, by economic activity

GRÈVES ET LOCK-OUT
Travailleurs impliqués, par activité économique

HUELGAS Y CIERRES PATRONALES
Trabajadores implicados, por actividad económica

	1999	2000	2001	2002	2003	2004	2005	2006	2007	2008
Tunisie (FG) [1]										
ISIC 3 - CITI 3 - CIIU 3										
Total	31 989	35 886	38 242	33 386	46 893	44 637	78 953	115 443	98 210	.
A	1 741	3 252	1 805	1 921	1 202	2 916	667	821	1 907	.
B	167	97	65	15	0	0	0	150	639	.
C	2 876	1 038	248	604	5 900	517	797	1 625	1 797	.
D	17 996	27 980	23 528	25 045	32 663	30 022	40 708	45 161	43 757	.
E	176	150	221	215	288	16	631	27	703	.
F	7 684	1 561	4 722	2 953	2 957	3 137	5 720	2 465	2 805	.
G	81	66	258	49	83	0	536	77	8 168	.
H	277	294	316	210	1 423	530	1 024	776	1 228	.
I	630	418	778	772	339	483	1 089	444	1 572	.
J	.	.	.	21	0	2 324	1 327	.	1 892	.
L [2]	26	70	2 773	61	673	3 465	250	.	1 011	.
M	.	.	.	449	251	19	23 309	46 702	14 772	.
N	.	.	.	915	0	397	868	9 382	10 440	.
O	121	323	2 044	156	1 100	811	2 027	7 459	7 519	.
X	214	637	1 484	0	12	0	0	.	.	.
Uganda (F)										
ISIC 3 - CITI 3 - CIIU 3										
Total	1 184	872	554	1 816	1 200	1 412				

AMERICA-AMÉRIQUE-AMERICA

	1999	2000	2001	2002	2003	2004	2005	2006	2007	2008
Argentina (F) [3]										
ISIC 3 - CITI 3 - CIIU 3										
Total	2 497 746	6 760 850	.	.	.	.	.	1 185 076	1 119 272	1 931 373
A	.	.	.	.	.	.	.	7 552	816	6 500
B	.	.	.	.	.	.	.	0	260	707
C	.	.	.	.	.	.	.	16 384	16 013	16 308
D	.	.	.	.	.	.	.	116 281	39 656	415 283
E	.	.	.	.	.	.	.	11 723	4 635	10 863
F	.	.	.	.	.	.	.	8 044	56 931	266 680
G	.	.	.	.	.	.	.	39 048	13 843	49 901
H	.	.	.	.	.	.	.	112	6 533	5 223
I	.	.	.	.	.	.	.	57 906	50 085	78 611
J	.	.	.	.	.	.	.	2 971	23 407	11 213
K	.	.	.	.	.	.	.	74	2 489	342
L	.	.	.	.	.	.	.	258 446	238 931	303 744
M	.	.	.	.	.	.	.	490 450	570 774	606 094
N	.	.	.	.	.	.	.	133 838	117 376	156 254
O	.	.	.	.	.	.	.	8 357	7 828	3 650
Aruba (F) [1]										
ISIC 3 - CITI 3 - CIIU 3										
Total	.	.	.	.	.	324	40	40	222	
E	.	.	.	.	.	308	0	40	0	
F	.	.	.	.	.	0	0	0	0	
G	.	.	.	.	.	0	0	0	15	
H	.	.	.	.	.	0	0	0	0	
I	.	.	.	.	.	0	0	0	0	
J	.	.	.	.	.	0	0	0	0	
K	.	.	.	.	.	.	.	.	7	
N	.	.	.	.	.	0	0	0	200	
X	.	.	.	.	.	16	40	0	0	
Brasil (FH) [4]										
ISIC 3 - CITI 3 - CIIU 3										
Total	1 319 826	3 579 155	3 836 579	1 241 329	1 263 697	1 289 332				

Explanatory notes: see p. 1361.

[1] Excl. workers indirectly involved. [2] Incl. category N and state education. [3] Work stoppages beginning in the year indicated. [4] Strikes only.

Notes explicatives: voir p. 1363.

[1] Non compris les travailleurs indirectement impliqués. [2] Y compris la catégorie N et l'éducation publique. [3] Arrêts du travail commençant pendant l'année indiquée. [4] Grèves seulement.

Notas explicativas: véase p. 1365.

[1] Excl. los trabajadores indirectamente implicados. [2] Incl. la categoría N y la educación pública. [3] Interrupciones del trabajo que empiezan en el año indicado. [4] Huelgas solamente.

	1999	2000	2001	2002	2003	2004	2005	2006	2007	2008
Canada (FG) [1] [2]										
ISIC 3 - CITI 3 - CIIU 3										
Total	159 626	142 672	221 145	165 590	78 765	259 229	199 007	42 314	65 552	41 291
A	2 027	1 197	936	200	660	462	594	198	0	0
B	0	0	0	0	0	0	0	0	0	0
C	2 676	5 002	4 231	591	3 747	2 671	1 695	857	1 433	1 149
D	25 239	32 606	18 059	22 614	22 440	14 283	11 894	10 978	11 930	5 881
E	3 214	5	842	73	37	520	850	0	187	347
F	1 014	937	12 777	472	0	6 088	158	18	16 329	60
G	2 439	9 642	2 940	9 047	9 881	6 650	6 782	1 005	749	1 818
H	4 195	3 285	981	3 550	913	1 565	3 149	282	386	2 091
I	31 965	5 876	9 291	5 662	6 996	19 663	22 127	9 510	10 325	14 287
J	218	1 060	145	0	208	69	47	164	176	85
K	859	1 450	5 446	1 218	663	621	1 525	84	286	102
L	6 028	35 942	51 021	52 922	1 692	150 492	40 983	4 793	7 006	1 048
M	29 047	31 607	33 295	59 405	12 088	4 865	98 979	10 764	9 071	11 847
N	48 439	10 435	76 983	6 270	17 294	45 799	8 578	711	3 147	417
O	2 366	3 628	4 198	3 566	2 146	5 931	1 646	2 950	4 527	2 159
X	0	0	0	0	0	0	0	0	0	0
Chile (FG) [2] [3]										
ISIC 2 - CITI 2 - CIIU 2										
Total	10 667	13 227	11 591	14 662	10 443	13 013	11 209	15 602	17 294	17 473
1	135	320	355	96	35	89	171	829	980	366
2	236	810	410	590	2 748	2 383	1 083	2 137	1 692	642
3	6 448	4 764	4 321	3 763	4 206	5 834	3 725	4 568	3 364	4 555
4	0	0	138	0	0	202	108	42	119	95
5	47	90	251	130	169	0	651	875	866	1 442
6	554	726	564	1 161	501	625	1 950	1 823	2 303	4 802
7	1 521	679	1 145	5 689	352	783	1 176	1 418	3 166	1 197
8	204	762	1 930	877	617	205	206	997	2 257	1 105
9	1 522	5 076	2 477	2 326	1 815	2 892	2 139	2 913	2 547	3 269
0	0	0	0	0	0	0	0	0	0	0
Ecuador (FG)										
ISIC 3 - CITI 3 - CIIU 3										
Total	1 873	1 766	536	2 257	1 670	500	963	1 066	1 525	574
A	0	582	49	990	215	169	0	137	0	344
B	0	0	0	112	0	0	0	0	0	0
C	31	135	0	0	0	0	0	0	0	0
D	1 379	607	0	27	927	34	566	73	211	164
E	31	155	0	493	264	0	0	0	518	0
F	0	0	0	0	43	0	0	0	111	31
G	0	0	0	0	7	62	243	0	0	0
H	0	0	0	0	31	0	0	0	0	0
I	292	198	198	40	50	0	0	74	0	35
J	88	0	0	0	0	0	0	0	0	0
K	0	89	0	435	0	58	40	0	0	0
L	52	0	269	160	99	143	114	326	685	0
M	0	0	0	0	0	0	0	0	0	0
N	0	0	20	0	0	0	0	424	0	0
O	0	0	0	0	34	34	0	32	0	0
El Salvador (FG)											
ISIC 2 - CITI 2 - CIIU 2											ISIC 3 - CITI 3 - CIIU 3
Total	68 901	17 684	19 395	8 909	9 953	8 584	5 961	8 597	2 436	5 006	Total
1	0	0	0	0	0	0	0	0	0	0	A
2	0	0	0	0	0	0	0	0	0	0	B
3	595	563	3 350	1 225	1 880	3 185	812	0	0	0	C
4	250	850	0	0	0	3 092	0	3 551	2 008	4 666	D
5	1 180	671	0	250	0	27	50	0	0	0	E
6	0	0	0	0	0	0	36	0	0	0	F
7	150	5 546	2 096	0	60	215	244	0	12	0	G
8	0	0	0	0	0	0	0	0	0	0	H
9	66 726	10 054	13 949	7 434	8 013	2 065	4 819	768	307	0	I
								0	0	0	J
								30	0	0	K
								50	35	40	L
								1 500	74	0	M
								2 570	0	300	N
								128	0	0	O

Explanatory notes: see p. 1361.

[1] Strikes lasting at least half a day with more than 10 days lost. [2] Excl. workers indirectly involved. [3] Strikes only.

Notes explicatives: voir p. 1363.

[1] Grèves d'une durée d'une demi-journée au moins et dans lesquelles 10 jours de travail sont perdus. [2] Non compris les travailleurs indirectement impliqués. [3] Grèves seulement.

Notas explicativas: véase p. 1365.

[1] Huelgas con duración de media jornada laboral por lo menos y con más de 10 días perdidos. [2] Excl. los trabajadores indirectamente implicados. [3] Huelgas solamente.

9B

STRIKES AND LOCKOUTS	GRÈVES ET LOCK-OUT	HUELGAS Y CIERRES PATRONALES
Workers involved, by economic activity	Travailleurs impliqués, par activité économique	Trabajadores implicados, por actividad económica

	1999	2000	2001	2002	2003	2004	2005	2006	2007	2008
Jamaica (FG)										
ISIC 2 - CITI 2 - CIIU 2										
Total	31 992	9 385	3 275	2 400	25 568	863	680	.		
1	26	1 485	1 000	1 312	367	70	0	.		
2	0	0	150	170	106	0	0	.		
3	1 576	532	71	147	70	200	300	.		
4	0	0	137	0	0	0	40	.		
5	0	0	1 580	0	106	0	0	.		
6	0	0	0	0	0	0	0	.		
7	104	3 150	200	0	500	400	320	.		
8	3 125	2 215	0	158	1 500	150	0	.		
9	27 161	2 030	137	613	22 919	70	20	.		
México (FG) [1] [2] [3]										
ISIC 3 - CITI 3 - CIIU 3										
Total	50 195	60 015	23 234	22 660	11 797	24 628	12 208	59 788	10 601	13 242
A	0	0	0	0	0	0	0	0	0	0
B	0	0	0	0	0	0	0	0	0	0
C	0	636	0	4 143	1 119	3 516	94	981	2 205	350
D	48 514	57 709	19 829	5 993	6 739	14 799	6 527	57 588	1 864	1 393
E	0	0	0	0	0	0	0	0	0	0
F	0	0	0	460	0	0	0	149	150	610
G	0	120	0	0	0	0	0	0	0	0
H	0	0	0	0	0	0	0	0	0	0
I	687	1 546	1 540	548	887	437	856	1 024	962	1 527
J	60	0	0	43	36	0	0	0	41	0
K	0	0	0	0	0	0	0	0	0	0
M	934	0	1 859	11 467	3 000	5 876	4 180	0	5 364	7 521
N	0	0	0	0	0	0	0	0	0	0
O	0	4	6	6	16	0	551	46	15	1 841
Nicaragua (FG) [4]										
ISIC 2 - CITI 2 - CIIU 2										
Total	73	0	0	0	.	51	.	.	.	.
1 [5]	0	0	0	0						
2	0	0	0	0						
3	.	0	0	0						
4	.	0	0	0						
5	0	0	0	0						
6	0	0	0	0						
7	0	0	0	0						
8	0	0	0	0						
9	0	0	0	0						
Panamá (FG) [6]										
ISIC 3 - CITI 3 - CIIU 3										
Total	34 804	26	4 172	2 454	650	7	20	395	690	.
A	0	0	3 580	0	125	0	0	0	0	.
B	0	0	0	0	0	0	0	0	0	.
C	150	0	0	2 454	0	0	0	0	0	.
D	0	0	171	0	0	0	0	335	0	.
E	0	0	0	0	0	0	0	0	0	.
F	33 280	0	170	0	25	0	20	21	650	.
G	0	0	0	0	500	0	0	0	40	.
H	0	15	0	0	0	0	0	39	0	.
I	0	11	187	0	0	7	0	0	0	.
J	0	0	0	0	0	0	0	0	0	.
K	0	0	64	0	0	0	0	0	0	.
L	0	0	0	0	0	0	0	0	0	.
M	0	0	0	0	0	0	0	0	0	.
N	1 374	0	0	0	0	0	0	0	0	.
O	0	0	0	0	0	0	0	0	0	.

Explanatory notes: see p. 1361.

[1] Strikes only, beginning in the year indicated. [2] Excl. workers indirectly involved and workers in positions of trust; union members only. [3] Excl. enterprises covered by local jurisdiction. [4] Strikes only. [5] Excl. hunting, forestry and fishing. [6] Excl. workers indirectly involved.

Notes explicatives: voir p. 1363.

[1] Grèves seulement, commençant pendant l'année indiquée. [2] Non compris les travailleurs indirectement impliqués et les travailleurs de confiance; travailleurs syndiqués seulement. [3] Non compris les entreprises sous juridiction locale. [4] Grèves seulement. [5] Non compris la chasse, la sylviculture et la pêche. [6] Non compris les travailleurs indirectement impliqués.

Notas explicativas: véase p. 1365.

[1] Huelgas solamente, que empiezan en el año indicado. [2] Excl. trabajadores indirectamente implicados y trabajadores de confianza; trabajadores sindicados solamente. [3] Excl. las empresas de jurisdicción local. [4] Huelgas solamente. [5] Excl. caza, silvicultura y pesca. [6] Excl. los trabajadores indirectamente implicados.

STRIKES AND LOCKOUTS
Workers involved, by economic activity

GRÈVES ET LOCK-OUT
Travailleurs impliqués, par activité économique

HUELGAS Y CIERRES PATRONALES
Trabajadores implicados, por actividad económica

Perú (FG) [1]
ISIC 3 - CITI 3 - CIIU 3

	1999	2000	2001	2002	2003	2004	2005	2006	2007	2008
Total	52 080	5 280	11 050	22 925	37 323	29 273	19 022	19 565	48 096	34 011
A	52	0	1 303	67	400	139	0	0	800	800
B	912	0	0	0	0	0	0	0	0	0
C	3 369	1 323	2 121	7 712	1 554	9 020	3 475	2 841	41 676	28 136
D	1 690	1 220	6 128	3 583	9 099	7 208	4 684	702	1 089	610
E	31	514	0	1 724	768	3 761	2 387	5 686	518	913
F	6 398	1 175	1 359	3 306	19 047	569	882	550	790	577
G	0	0	0	0	13	0	0	306	0	0
H	0	0	73	0	0	0	0	0	0	0
I	3 225	928	0	2 537	2 313	3 430	922	4 971	2 736	908
J	0	0	0	0	0	0	0	0	8	0
K	0	0	30	1 642	2 483	1 984	33	3 387	100	57
L	0	120	36	11	1 325	1 811	889	956	386	341
M	9	0	0	0	245	42	224	148	53	143
N	0	0	0	77	37	1 197	5 480	18	0	100
O	0	0	0	0	39	112	46	0	0	0
P	.	.	.	2 266	0	0	0	0	0	0
X	36 394	0	0	0	0	0	0	0	0	1 426

Puerto Rico (FG) [2]
ISIC 3 - CITI 3 - CIIU 3

	1999	2000	2001	2002	2003	2004	2005	2006	2007	2008
Total	110	251	246	66	0	4 500	0	0	44	126
A	0	0	0	0	0	0	0	0	0	0
B	0	0	0	0	0	0	0	0	0	0
C	0	0	0	0	0	0	0	0	0	0
D	0	80	80	40	0	0	0	0	0	0
E	0	0	0	0	0	0	0	0	0	0
F	0	0	75	0	0	0	0	0	0	0
G	110	0		26	0	0	0	0	0	0
G,I	.	.	51	.	.	.	.	.	0	0
H	.	40	40	0	0	0	0	0	44	0
H,M-O	.	.	.	.	.	.	.	.	.	.
I	0	51	.	0	0	0	0	0	0	126
J	0	0	0	0	0	0	0	0	0	0
K	0	80	0	0	0	0	0	0	0	0
L	0	0	0	0	0	4 500	0	0	0	0
M	0	0	.	0	0	0	0	0	0	0
N	0	0		0	0	0	0	0	0	0
O	0	0	.	0	0	0	0	0	0	0

Trinidad and Tobago (FG)
ISIC 2 - CITI 2 - CIIU 2

	1999	2000	2001	2002	2003	2004	2005	2006	2007	2008
Total	9 185	3 126	6 941	6 858	10 134	7 469	.	.	.	.
1	0	39	0	0	0	0	.	.	.	.
2	105	0	1 215	6 026	9 065	3 420	.	.	.	.
3	2 390	703	0	0	387	1 404	.	.	.	.
4	0	0	0	0	0	0	.	.	.	.
5	0	0	0	0	0	2 500	.	.	.	.
6	0	0	0	0	0	0	.	.	.	.
7	6 168	1 151	5 644	832	682	145	.	.	.	.
8	0	1 233	0	0	0	0	.	.	.	.
9	522	0	82	0	0	0	.	.	.	.
0	0	0	0	0	0	0	.	.	.	.

United States (H) [3] [4] [5]
ISIC 3 - CITI 3 - CIIU 3

	1999	2000	2001	2002	2003	2004	2005	2006	2007	2008
Total	72 600	393 700	99 100	45 900	129 200	173 300	99 700	76 600	192 900	82 700
A	0	0	0	0	0	0	0	0	0	0
B	0	0	0	0	0	0	0	0	0	0
C	0	0	0	0	0	0	1 400	0	1 200	0
D	19 000	42 800	11 900	11 400	22 800	10 500	27 500	24 400	90 700	43 000
E	0	0	2 100	3 500	0	1 300	1 900	0	0	0
F	2 600	10 800	13 000	5 700	4 000	0	10 100	12 800	4 000	2 900
G	7 100	1 400	3 100	0	80 700	2 000	0	1 400	0	0
H	12 000	1 100	0	0	0	17 100	2 400	0	0	0
I	4 600	94 300	3 300	13 500	7 500	106 200	45 400	5 600	62 800	1 300
J	0	0	0	0	0	0	0	0	0	0
K	0	157 000	0	1 800	0	0	0	0	10 500	10 500
L	0	48 200	24 900	3 800	5 000	0	0	19 000	0	0
M	26 100	14 700	21 800	2 300	4 400	0	11 000	10 900	6 700	11 400
N	1 200	23 400	19 000	3 900	0	36 200	0	1 200	10 000	11 800
O	0	0	0	0	4 800	0	0	1 300	7 000	1 800
X	0	0	0	0	0	0	0	0	.	0

Explanatory notes: see p. 1361.

[1] Strikes only; private sector. [2] Strikes and lockouts ending during the 12 months beginning in July of the year indicated. [3] Work stoppages beginning in the year indicated. [4] Excl. work stoppages involving fewer than 1,000 workers and lasting less than a full day or shift. [5] Figures rounded to nearest 100.

Notes explicatives: voir p. 1363.

[1] Grèves seulement; secteur privé. [2] Grèves et lock-out se terminant pendant les 12 mois commençant en juillet de l'année indiquée. [3] Arrêts du travail commençant pendant l'année indiquée. [4] Non compris arrêts de travail impliquant moins de 1000 travailleurs; durée inférieure à 1 jour ou à 1 poste de travail. [5] Chiffres arrondis au 100 le plus proche.

Notas explicativas: véase p. 1365.

[1] Huelgas solamente; sector privado. [2] Huelgas y cierres patronales que terminan dentro de los 12 meses que comienzan en julio del año indicado. [3] Interrupciones del trabajo que empiezan en el año indicado. [4] Excl. las interrupciones del trabajo que implican menos de 1000 trabajadores y que duran menos de 1 día o turno completo. [5] Cifras redondeadas al 100 más próximo.

9B

	STRIKES AND LOCKOUTS	GRÈVES ET LOCK-OUT	HUELGAS Y CIERRES PATRONALES
	Workers involved, by economic activity	Travailleurs impliqués, par activité économique	Trabajadores implicados, por actividad económica

	1999	2000	2001	2002	2003	2004	2005	2006	2007	2008

Uruguay (Z)
ISIC 3 - CITI 3 - CIIU 3

	2008
A	763 983
B	761
C	0
D	58 343
E	11 634
F	424 638
G	19 848
H	0
I	38 278
J	23 000
K	5 686
L	54 100
M	106 490
N	19 810
O	900
P	
Q	
X	

ASIA-ASIE-ASIA

Hong Kong, China (FG) [1] [2]
ISIC 3 - CITI 3 - CIIU 3

	1999	2000	2001	2002	2003	2004	2005	2006	2007	2008
Total [3]	152	381	130	0	300	143	200	67	849	1 337
A	0	0	0	0	0	0	0	0	0	0
B	0	0	0	0	0	0	0	0	0	0
C	0	0	0	0	0	0	0	0	0	0
D	0	0	0	0	0	0	0	0	0	587
E	0	0	0	0	0	0	0	0	0	0
F	21	208	0	0	300	0	0	0	800	0
G	0	73	0	0	0	0	0	0	0	0
H	0	0	0	0	0	0	0	0	0	0
I	131	0	0	0	0	0	200	67	49	750
J	0	0	0	0	0	0	0	0	0	0
K	0	100	130	0	0	0	0	0	0	0
M	0	0	0	0	0	0	0	0	0	0
N	0	0	0	0	0	0	0	0	0	0
O	0	0	0	0	0	143	0	0	0	0

India (H) [4] [5]
ISIC 2 - CITI 2 - CIIU 2 / ISIC 3 - CITI 3 - CIIU 3

ISIC 2	1999	2000	2001	2002	2003	2004	2005	2006	2007	2008	ISIC 3
Total	1 310 695	1 418 299	687 778	1 079 434	1 815 945	2 072 221	2 913 601	1 810 348	724 574	1 483 593	Total
1	382 257	18 689	21 629	41 474	259 306	64 545	264 290	34 940	32 429	12 893	A
2	82 215	72	0	0	0	0	0	0	0	74 534	B
3	345 960	392 369	350 484	167 158	790 746	320 446	383 069	150 064	13 184	0	C
4	3 558	289 545	213 929	652 369	466 419	415 394	623 185	162 021	391 765	355 030	D
5	146	3 119	10 976	1 684	1 636	97	6 313	3 177	46 783	77 411	E
6	3 869	298	703	0	903	2 286	111			0	F
7	1 021	6 591	1 766	0	455	1 067	9 512	3 683	50	0	G
8	457 967	682	571	137	317	388	252	214	316	105	H
9	6 917	673 081	36 578	9 990	31 501	8 134	44 652	46 009	134 101	104 180	I
0	26 785	12 803	24 931	189 931	246 191	1 252 463	1 544 909	1 369 161	103 901	845 543	J
		158	468	136	140	40	317	60	314	86	K
		1 208	1 486	1 637	7 918	3 068	34 169	39 244	0	3 459	L
		0	0	0	0	0	0	0	0	208	M
		702	309	1 629	51	663	129	289	407	0	N
		18 969	23 948	13 289	10 362	3 630	2 693	1 452	1 290	10 110	O
		13	0	0	0	0	0	34	34	34	P

Explanatory notes: see p. 1361.

[1] Incl. stoppages involving fewer than 10 workers or lasting less than one day. [2] Excl. workers indirectly involved. [3] Excl. government sector. [4] Excl. work stoppages involving fewer than 10 workers. [5] Excl. political and sympathetic strikes.

Notes explicatives: voir p. 1363.

[1] Y compris les arrêts impliquant moins de 10 travailleurs ou de moins d'un jour. [2] Non compris les travailleurs indirectement impliqués. [3] Non compris le secteur gouvernemental. [4] Non compris les arrêts du travail impliquant moins de 10 travailleurs. [5] Non compris les grèves politiques et les grèves de solidarité.

Notas explicativas: véase p. 1365.

[1] Incl. las interrupciones con menos de 10 trabajadores o de menos de un día. [2] Excl. los trabajadores indirectamente implicados. [3] Excl. el sector gubernamental. [4] Excl. las interrupciones del trabajo que implican menos de 10 trabajadores. [5] Excl. huelgas políticas y huelgas de solidaridad.

STRIKES AND LOCKOUTS

Workers involved, by economic activity

GRÈVES ET LOCK-OUT

Travailleurs impliqués, par activité économique

HUELGAS Y CIERRES PATRONALES

Trabajadores implicados, por actividad económica

9B

	1999	2000	2001	2002	2003	2004	2005	2006	2007	2008
Israel (FG) [1]										
ISIC 3 - CITI 3 - CIIU 3										
Total	292 583	297 882	426 560	1 647 810	1 258 904	722 875	103 666	125 730	386 075	19 275
A	0	0	0	193	462	0	0	0	0	0
B	0	0	0	0	0	0	0	0	0	0
C-D	7 023	1 079	4 700	6 191	136	1 132	4 082	1 750	2 490	2 380
E	2 600	0	0	0	0	0	0	0	0	0
F	0	40	760	150	4 800	0	0	180	0	0
G	250	0	11	2 650	0	0	3 650	0	0	0
H	0	30	130	0	6 500	0	0	180	45	0
I	5 209	8 190	4 253	17 555	19 123	4 626	1 037	778	8 245	3 865
J	2 000	540	600	0	40 658	12 037	27 600	4 800	6 500	80
K	0	0	300	0	0	0	0	0	0	0
L	171 183	115 158	298 940	1 467 521	1 178 055	605 680	14 009	114 580	308 300	3 500
M	100 037	148 285	109 850	124 970	60	57 500	44 150	2 000	59 800	9 200
N	650	19 560	7 000	28 500	6 050	41 800	9 030	1 440	450	250
O	3 631	5 000	16	80	3 060	100	108	22	50	0
P	0	0	0	0	0	0	0	0	0	0
Q	0	0	0	0	0	0	0	0	0	0
X	0	0	0	0	0	0	0	0	195	0

	1999	2000	2001	2002	2003	2004	2005	2006	2007	2008	
Japan (FG) [2][3]											ISIC 3 - CITI 3 - CIIU 3
ISIC 2 - CITI 2 - CIIU 2											
Total	25 673	15 322	12 172	7 015	4 447	6 998	4 119	5 766	20 825	.	Total
1	0	0	0	0	.	0	0	0	0	.	A
2	0	0	0	0	.	0	0	0	0	.	B
3	5 821	5 042	5 429	1 002	.	0	0	4	0	.	C
4	0	0	0	30	.	1 921	613	667	679	.	D
5	14	207	19	20	.	0	0	15	0	.	E
6 [4]	632	159	194	13	.	0	0	0	5	.	F
7	14 085	6 169	3 559	3 132	.	15	106	54	66	.	G [5]
8 [6]	8	0	0	0	.	4	0	0	0	.	H
9 [7]	5 113	3 745	0	2 818	.	2 795	2 483	2 696	8 235	.	I
0	0	0	0	0	.	0	0	0	51	.	J
						10	0	0	0	.	K
						0	0	0	0	.	L
						44	1	9	52	.	M
						1 074	255	1 071	137	.	N
						1 135	661	1 250	11 600	.	O

	1999	2000	2001	2002	2003	2004	2005	2006	2007	2008
Jordan (FG)										
ISIC 3 - CITI 3 - CIIU 3										
Total	0	0	0	0	0	0	0	.	.	.

	1999	2000	2001	2002	2003	2004	2005	2006	2007	2008
Korea, Republic of (FG) [3]										
ISIC 3 - CITI 3 - CIIU 3										
Total	92 026	177 969	88 548	93 859	137 241	184 969	117 912	131 359	93 385	114 290
A	0	0	9	.	.	.	.	.	.	.
B	0	0	0	.	.	.	.	.	.	.
C	0	13	0	.	.	.	.	.	.	.
D	57 179	126 557	54 232	.	.	.	.	.	.	.
E	0	483	3 670	.	.	.	.	.	.	.
F	554	831	3 463	.	.	.	.	.	.	.
G	1 320	344	1 449	.	.	.	.	.	.	.
H	828	2 112	493	.	.	.	.	.	.	.
I	12 796	10 498	8 263	.	.	.	.	.	.	.
J	0	26 619	12 073	.	.	.	.	.	.	.
K	15 085	2 533	1 075	.	.	.	.	.	.	.
L	0	0	0	.	.	.	.	.	.	.
M	710	291	1 469	.	.	.	.	.	.	.
N	1 237	4 415	974	.	.	.	.	.	.	.
O	2 317	3 273	1 378	.	.	.	.	.	.	.

	1999	2000	2001	2002	2003	2004	2005	2006	2007	2008
Myanmar (F)										
ISIC 3 - CITI 3 - CIIU 3										
Total	2 000	4 875	7 226	4 550	12 979	3 723	1 250	1 109	1 019	1 087
D	2 000	4 875	7 226	4 550	12 979	3 723	1 250	1 109	1 019	1 087

Explanatory notes: see p. 1361.

[1] Excl. work stoppages in which less than 10 workdays not worked. [2] Excl. work stoppages lasting less than half a day. [3] Excl. workers indirectly involved. [4] Excl. hotels. [5] Excl. repair of motor vehicles, motor cycles and personal and household goods. [6] Excl. business services. [7] Incl. business services and hotels.

Notes explicatives: voir p. 1363.

[1] Non compris les arrêts de travail de moins de 10 journées de travail non effectuées. [2] Non compris les arrêts du travail de durée inférieure à une demi-journée. [3] Non compris les travailleurs indirectement impliqués. [4] Non compris les hôtels. [5] Non compris réparation de véhicules automobiles, de motocycles et de biens personnels etdomestiques. [6] Non compris les services aux entreprises. [7] Y compris les services aux entreprises et les hôtels.

Notas explicativas: véase p. 1365.

[1] Excl. las interrupciones de trabajo de menos de 10 días de trabajo no trabajados. [2] Excl. las interrupciones del trabajo de duración inferior a medio día. [3] Excl. los trabajadores indirectamente implicados. [4] Excl. hoteles. [5] Excl. reparación de vehículos automotores, motocicletas, efectos personals y enseres domesticos. [6] Excl. servicios para las empresas. [7] Incl. servicios para empresas y hoteles.

	STRIKES AND LOCKOUTS	GRÈVES ET LOCK-OUT	HUELGAS Y CIERRES PATRONALES
	Workers involved, by economic activity	Travailleurs impliqués, par activité économique	Trabajadores implicados, por actividad económica

	1999	2000	2001	2002	2003	2004	2005	2006	2007	2008	

Philippines (H) [1][2]
ISIC 2 - CITI 2 - CIIU 2   ISIC 3 - CITI 3 - CIIU 3

	1999	2000	2001	2002	2003	2004	2005	2006	2007	2008	
Total	15 517	21 442	7 919	18 240	10 035	11 197	8 496	1 415	915	1 115	Total
1	0	516	0	0	403	60	400	31	0	500	A
2	961	0	0	0	0	0	0	0	0	0	B
3	6 690	9 227	0	0	1 692	0	1 687	0	200	0	C
4	0	3 146	4 925	7 869	5 277	8 669	5 618	1 013	405	515	D
5	0	350	227	71	168	0	0	0	0	0	E
6 [3]	1 726	904	290	0	0	0	0	0	0	0	F
7	3 795	4 988	74	200	842	65	21	0	0	0	G
8	800	499	582	512	0	42	70	0	0	0	H
9 [4]	1 545	1 812	727	8 370	989	2 124	700	371	180	100	I
			0	0	151	0	0	0	0	0	J
			0	1 000	0	0	0	0	0	0	K
			0	0	0	0	0	0	0	0	L
			1 070	145	400	237	0	0	0	0	M
			0	0	64	0	0	0	130	0	N
			24	73	49	0	0	0	0	0	O

Singapore (FG)
ISIC 3 - CITI 3 - CIIU 3

	1999	2000	2001	2002	2003	2004	2005	2006	2007	2008
Total	0	0	0	0	0	0	0	0	0	0

Sri Lanka (FD) [2][5][6]
ISIC 2 - CITI 2 - CIIU 2

	1999	2000	2001	2002	2003	2004	2005	2006	2007	2008
Total	42 346	25 858	42 344	27 717	42 561	33 346	53 565	209 804	7 547	37 931
1 [7]	16 018	8 408	26 069	12 088	17 779	15 832	4 283	196 520	1 468	34 014
2	0	0	0	0	0	0	0	0	0	0
3	26 328	17 450	16 275	15 629	24 782	17 514	49 282	13 284	6 079	3 917

Thailand (H)
ISIC 3 - CITI 3 - CIIU 3

	1999	2000	2001	2002	2003	2004	2005	2006	2007	2008
Total	7 867	5 969	526	1 907	3 576	193	2 578	900	620	.
A	0	0	0	0	0	0	0	0	0	
B	0	0	0	0	0	0	0	0	0	
C	0	0	0	0	0	0	0	0	0	
D	7 867	5 969	526	1 907	3 576	193	795	900	620	
E	0	0	0	0	0	0	0	0	0	
F	0	0	0	0	0	0	0	0	0	
G-H	0	0	0	0	0	0	1 283	0	0	
I	0	0	0	0	0	0	0	0	0	
J-K	0	0	0	0	0	0	0	0	0	
L-O	0	0	0	0	0	0	0	0	0	

EUROPE-EUROPE-EUROPA

Austria (FH) [2]
ISIC 3 - CITI 3 - CIIU 3

	1999	2000	2001	2002	2003	2004	2005	2006	2007	2008
Total	0	19 439	0	6 305	779 182	30	0	0	0	0

Belarus (FH)
ISIC 2 - CITI 2 - CIIU 2

	1999	2000	2001	2002	2003	2004	2005	2006	2007	2008
Total	0	0	0	0	0	0	.	.	.	

Explanatory notes: see p. 1361.

[1] Excl. work stoppages lasting less than a full day or shift. [2] Excl. workers indirectly involved. [3] Excl. restaurants and hotels. [4] Incl. restaurants and hotels. [5] Incl. work stoppages lasting less than one day only if more than 50 workdays not worked. [6] Excl. work stoppages involving fewer than 5 workers. [7] Plantations.

Notes explicatives: voir p. 1363.

[1] Non compris les arrêts du travail dont la durée est inférieure à une journée ou à un poste de travail. [2] Non compris les travailleurs indirectement impliqués. [3] Non compris les restaurants et les hôtels. [4] Y compris les restaurants et hôtels. [5] Y compris les arrêts du travail d'une durée inférieure à une journée si plus de 50 journées de travail non effectuées. [6] Non compris les arrêts du travail impliquant moins de 5 travailleurs. [7] Plantations.

Notas explicativas: véase p. 1365.

[1] Excl. las interrupciones del trabajo de duración menor de un día o turno completo. [2] Excl. los trabajadores indirectamente implicados. [3] Excl. restaurantes y hoteles. [4] Incl. restaurantes y hoteles. [5] Incl. las interrupciones del trabajo de menos de un día si no se han trabajado más de 50 días. [6] Excl. las interrupciones del trabajo que implican menos de 5 trabajadores. [7] Plantaciones.

STRIKES AND LOCKOUTS
Workers involved, by economic activity

GRÈVES ET LOCK-OUT
Travailleurs impliqués, par activité économique

HUELGAS Y CIERRES PATRONALES
Trabajadores implicados, por actividad económica

9B

Cyprus (H)
ISIC 2 - CITI 2 - CIIU 2 (1999–2001) · ISIC 3 - CITI 3 - CIIU 3 (2002–2008)

Label	1999	2000	2001	2002	2003	2004	2005	2006	2007	2008
Total / Total	2 108	180	1 699	3 496	3 535	6 479	13 895	25 955	·	·
1 / A	0			40	0	0	12	0	·	·
2 / B	0	·	·	20	0	0	0	0	·	·
3 / C	67	·	·	0	0	5 500	8 063	8	·	·
4 / D	0	·	·	89	0	0	2 577	0	·	·
5 / E	150	·	·	2 034	0	12	13	25 000	·	·
6 / F	280	·	·	330	115	0	0	150	·	·
7 / G	1 025	·	·	52	0	30	0	25	·	·
8 / H	0	·	·	100	2 847	0	0	360	·	·
9 / I	586	·	·	679	50	500	3 230	0	·	·
J				58	0	0	0	0	·	·
K				0	0	0	0	412	·	·
L				0	0	0	0	0	·	·
M				0	0	0	0	0	·	·
N				0	0	0	0	0	·	·
O				94	523	437	0	0	·	·

Denmark (FH) [1]
ISIC 3 - CITI 3 - CIIU 3

Label	1999	2000	2001	2002	2003	2004	2005	2006	2007	2008
Total	75 170	75 656	54 664	110 854	44 365	75 710	32 833	79 128	61 113	·
A-C	0	50	98	4	4	0	0	57	0	·
D	47 546	49 010	40 120	64 325	28 594	51 790	19 344	10 305	24 599	·
E	382	170	363	196	203	0	0	0	0	·
F	1 534	2 273	2 032	3 454	2 302	2 781	1 665	1 642	2 751	·
G	1 305	4 424	1 602	4 094	814	1 413	1 130	1 772	4 097	·
H	438	355	457	1 187	275	569	529	979	479	·
I	5 979	10 292	4 562	8 155	4 036	11 524	5 027	4 246	8 407	·
J	0	0	0	0	0	0	0	0	0	·
K	0	0	0	0	0	0	0	0	0	·
L	0	0	0	0	0	0	0	0	0	·
M	0	0	0	0	0	0	0	0	0	·
N	0	0	0	0	0	0	0	0	0	·
O	0	0	0	0	0	0	0	0	0	·
X	17 986	9 082	5 430	3 039	8 137	7 633	5 138	60 127	20 780	·

España (FG) [2][3]
ISIC 3 - CITI 3 - CIIU 3

Label	1999	2000	2001	2002	2003	2004	2005	2006	2007	2008
Total	1 132 655	2 067 287	1 244 634	4 534 274	728 975	555 909	404 759	499 551	497 022	543 008
A	611	5 100	613	2 911	51	117 324	1 467	177	321	4 536
B	0	8 300	1 343	0	1 050	2 749	4 911	0	0	4 483
C	41 194	10 189	21 527	2 223	2 749	5 593	15 323	2 539	1 724	1 466
D	61 965	103 089	338 838	73 333	148 568	179 104	180 821	157 776	102 084	152 655
E	2 230	88	790	767	546	2 957	626	531	1 070	161
F	191 464	698 082	565 923	586	344	12 204	802	152 969	90 323	60 518
G	6 612	611 625	1 905	790	2 360	40 056	581	21 893	1 289	2 429
H	1 226	854	799	1 835	851	1 162	4 058	1 188	279	1 922
I	129 181	146 537	65 638	94 566	44 203	18 524	84 653	29 874	31 077	92 655
J	2 146	16	697	185	1 326	164	482	875	1 419	0
K	4 462	7 033	2 726	4 569	8 137	69 587	5 600	8 783	19 949	42 723
L	9 110	400 705	10 198	5 910	5 994	10 105	20 488	17 228	29 083	24 430
M	59 805	28 580	60 240	70 741	1 305	74 914	48 824	57 936	54 521	72 266
N	18 455	6 468	23 422	5 836	14 506	11 707	32 428	44 714	27 865	41 867
O	5 672	5 051	3 030	10 081	6 343	3 960	3 695	3 068	15 460	11 027
P	62	0	587	0	0	0	0	0	0	0
X [4]	598 460	35 570	146 358	4 259 941	490 642	8 548		0	120 558	29 870

Estonia (FG)
ISIC 3 - CITI 3 - CIIU 3

Label	1999	2000	2001	2002	2003	2004	2005	2006	2007	2008
Total	0	0	0	·	13 260	·	0			

Explanatory notes: see p. 1361.
[1] Up to 1995: excl. work stoppages in which less than 100 work-days not worked. [2] Prior to 1990: strikes only; excl. the Basque country. [3] Excl. workers indirectly involved. [4] General strikes.

Notes explicatives: voir p. 1363.
[1] Jusqu'à 1995: non compris les arrêts du travail de moins de 100 journées de travail non effectuées. [2] Avant 1990: grèves seulement; non compris le Pays basque. [3] Non compris les travailleurs indirectement impliqués. [4] Grèves générales.

Notas explicativas: véase p. 1365.
[1] Hasta 1995: excl. las interrupciones del trabajo de menos de 100 días no trabajados. [2] Antes de 1990: huelgas solamente; excl. el País Vasco. [3] Excl. los trabajadores indirectamente implicados. [4] Huelgas generales.

ILO YEARBOOK OF LABOUR STATISTICS 2009 — ANNUAIRE DES STATISTIQUES DU TRAVAIL DU BIT 2009 — ANUARIO DE ESTADISTICAS DEL TRABAJO DEL OIT 2009

1389

STRIKES AND LOCKOUTS
Workers involved, by economic activity

GRÈVES ET LOCK-OUT
Travailleurs impliqués, par activité économique

HUELGAS Y CIERRES PATRONALES
Trabajadores implicados, por actividad económica

	1999	2000	2001	2002	2003	2004	2005	2006	2007	2008
Finland (FH) ISIC 3 - CITI 3 - CIIU 3										
Total	14 993	84 092	21 715	70 867	91 866	25 211	106 796	48 276	89 729	15 992
A	0	1 200	0	0	315	0	0	0	0	0
B	0	0	0	0	0	0	0	0	0	0
C	0	0	0	0	0	0	0	0	0	0
D	10 605	59 379	9 828	10 738	70 169	21 183	100 814	33 679	74	44
E	80		311	155	122	17	7		26 281	14 876
F	250	0	10	52 513	48		57	203	0	
G		950	22	143	100	0	24	685	0	200
H	10		0	0	0		0	0	6 365	0
I	2 046	22 312	2 950	4 203	12 168	3 403	3 339	0	0	0
J	1 961	51	0	2 211	9 044	92		13 052	965	872
K	0	0	381	242	215	396	70	0	0	0
L	0	0	0	0	0	0	539	0	90	0
M-N	0	200	3 452	0	0	0	0	657	0	0
N									52 000	0
O	41	0	4 761	662	0	120	1 946	0	52 000	0
X	0	0	0	0	0	0			0	0
									3 954	
Germany (FG) [1][2] ISIC 3 - CITI 3 - CIIU 3										
Total [3]	187 749	7 428	60 948	428 283	39 692	101 419	17 097	168 723	106 483	154 052
A	0	0	0	0	0	0	0	0	0	
B	0	0	0	0	0	0	0	0	0	
C	0	0	0	0	0	0	0	0	0	
D	172 179	3 432	56 649	399 041	37 394	97 910	12 053	134 501	77 653	
E		187	0	25		155	32	0	0	
F	0	0	0	13 850	0	0	0	0	0	
G	4 255	1 572	950	5 707	1 460	0	0	0	696	
H	0	0	0	0	0	294	1 752	912	11 698	
I	2 451	1 085	3 349	4 671	46	1 173	109	0	0	
J	8 738	0	0	3 541	0	0	0	272	16 242	
K [3]	0	0	0	692	58	700	0	169	0	
L	69	0	0	429	18	58	33	482	0	
M	23	1 071	0	257	20	58	1 644	12 882	100	
N	34	0	0	70	0	0	568	1 307	0	
O	0	81	0	0	696	1 106	835	10 180	0	
Q						23	71	6 571	0	
								0		
Hungary (H) [4] ISIC 3 - CITI 3 - CIIU 3										
Total	16 685	26 978	21 128	4 573	10 831	6 276	1 425	24 665	60 805	8 633
A	0	0	0	0	0	0	0	0	0	0
B	0	0	0	0	0	0	0	0	0	0
C	0	0	0	0	0	0	0	0	0	0
D	113	449	748	1 873	916	235	1 095	2 742	1 281	0
E	933	0	0	0	0	61	0	253	4 817	0
F	0	0	0	0	0	0	0		723	0
G	0	0	0	0	0	0	0	6 120	35	11
H	0	0	0	0	0	0	0			
I	12 139	15 151	0	0	9 915	250	330	0	13 599	0
J	0	0	0	0	0	0	0	33	0	8 131
K	0	0	0	0	0	0	0	0	0	0
L	0	0	0	0	0	0	0	84	229	126
M	0	0	0	0	0	0	0	16	0	0
N	3 500	11 378	180	2 700	0	5 730	0	15 000	31 200	0
O		0	20 200	0	0	0	0	0	8 801	365
								417	120	0
Iceland (H) [2] ISIC 3 - CITI 3 - CIIU 3										
Total	0	1 713	8 948	0	0	4 256				

Explanatory notes: see p. 1361.

[1] Incl. work stoppages lasting less than one day if more than 100 workdays not worked. [2] Excl. workers indirectly involved. [3] Excl. public administration. [4] 1991-95: Work stoppages in which 800 hours or more not worked; beginning 1996: stoppages involving 10 workers or more.

Notes explicatives: voir p. 1363.

[1] Y compris les arrêts du travail d'une durée inférieure à une journée si plus de 100 journées de travail non effectuées. [2] Non compris les travailleurs indirectement impliqués. [3] Non compris l'administration publique. [4] 1991-95: Arrêts de travail avec 800 h. de travail non effectuées au moins; dès 1996: ceux impliquant 10 travailleurs ou plus.

Notas explicativas: véase p. 1365.

[1] Incl. las interrupciones del trabajo de menos de un día si no se han trabajado más de 100 días. [2] Excl. los trabajadores indirectamente implicados. [3] Excl. la administración pública. [4] 1991-95: Interrupciones del trabajo de 800 horas no trabajadas y más: desde 1996: las que implican 10 trabajadores o más.

STRIKES AND LOCKOUTS

Workers involved, by economic activity

GRÈVES ET LOCK-OUT

Travailleurs impliqués, par activité économique

HUELGAS Y CIERRES PATRONALES

Trabajadores implicados, por actividad económica

9B

	1999	2000	2001	2002	2003	2004	2005	2006	2007	2008
Ireland (H) [1]										
ISIC 3 - CITI 3 - CIIU 3										
Total	36 505	28 192	32 168	3 553	3 567	10 227	3 291	1 186	1 436	356
A-B	26	0	0	0	0	0	8	0	0	0
C	0	240	0	0	0	250	240	0	0	0
D	317	1 458	1 840	808	530	1 320	49	332	400	94
E	375	0	0	0	0	0	1 000	0	0	0
F	2 076	215	158	12	20	0	458	239	0	42
G	219	54	8 565	149	400	21	223	0	450	22
H	40	74	0	35	0	0	0	0	0	0
I	599	6 608	4 796	734	1 081	8 345	1 215	40	479	76
J-K	.	.	.	.	200	220	0	280	0	0
L	40	409	0	454	287	26	86	270	107	6
M	1 040	16 687	16 604	48	580	0	0	0	0	0
N	31 761	2 447	205	1 264	383	0	0	25	0	65
O	.	.	.	44	0	0	0	0	0	0
O-Q	0	0	0	.	76	45	12	0	0	51
P	.	.	.	0	0	0	0	0	0	0
Q	.	.	.	5	0	0	0	0	0	0
Isle of Man (FG)										
ISIC 3 - CITI 3 - CIIU 3										
Total	120	0	0	0	0	0	0	0	0	.
A	0	0	0	0	0	0	0	0	0	.
B	0	0	0	0	0	0	0	0	0	.
C	0	0	0	0	0	0	0	0	0	.
D	0	0	0	0	0	0	0	0	0	.
E	0	0	0	0	0	0	0	0	0	.
F	120	0	0	0	0	0	0	0	0	.
G	0	0	0	0	0	0	0	0	0	.
H	0	0	0	0	0	0	0	0	0	.
I	0	0	0	0	0	0	0	0	0	.
J	0	0	0	0	0	0	0	0	0	.
K	0	0	0	0	0	0	0	0	0	.
L	0	0	0	0	0	0	0	0	0	.
M	0	0	0	0	0	0	0	0	0	.
N	0	0	0	0	0	0	0	0	0	.
O	0	0	0	0	0	0	0	0	0	.
Italy (H) [2]										
ISIC 3 - CITI 3 - CIIU 3										
Total	935 000	687 000	1 125 000	5 442 000	2 560 700	709 480	960 854	466 855	906 292	669 153
A-B	3 000	3 000	1 500	6 000	9 600	9 741	8 013	3 329	22 301	6 664
C	900	1 000	1 200	11 000	1 400	1 905	308	473	0	40
D	635 700	232 000	624 600	445 000	503 700	234 815	684 063	291 861	571 509	248 567
E	18 300	15 000	16 600	6 400	2 600	3 774	3 097	3 918	405	2 446
F	4 700	5 000	420 800	2 000	1 800	1 130	11 862	49 272	5 523	52 295
G	78 000	22 000	63 600	2 300	36 900	17 292	1 176	2 435	72 793	84 113
H	0	.	.	.	2 900	169	410	479	556	3 105
I	81 400	141 000	86 600	83 700	92 400	58 775	57 700	62 645	77 920	59 226
J	47 800	11 000	9 200	42 500	6 300	61 620	1 766	5 337	1 029	5 532
K,O	11 300	10 000	10 500	25 200	8 000	5 283	9 139	19 839	23 736	10 453
L	44 600	20 000	135 700	178 400	137 000	197 121	116 518	15 317	86 940	85 993
M	3 100	191 000	47 800	75 600	17 900	71 646	31 025	2 810	23 660	95 226
N	6 200	8 000	25 400	10 600	87 200	46 209	35 777	9 140	19 920	15 493
X	0	19 000	60 200	4 552 900	1 653 000	.	.	0	0	0
Latvia (D) [3]										
ISIC 3 - CITI 3 - CIIU 3										
Total	.	.	.	.	.	.	0	0	0	812
D	.	.	.	.	.	.	0	0	0	0
I	.	.	.	.	.	.	0	0	0	0
L	.	.	.	.	.	.	0	0	0	0
M	.	.	.	.	.	.	0	0	0	0
N	.	.	.	.	.	.	0	0	0	812
O	.	.	.	.	.	.	0	0	0	0
Liechtenstein (H)										
ISIC 3 - CITI 3 - CIIU 3										
Total	0	0	0	0	0	0	0	0	.	.

Explanatory notes: see p. 1361.

[1] Work stoppages lasting at least one day or with at least 10 days not worked. [2] Figures rounded to nearest 100. [3] Excl. workers indirectly involved.

Notes explicatives: voir p. 1363.

[1] Arrêts de travail d'un jour au moins ou avec un minimum de 10 jours de travail non effectués. [2] Chiffres arrondis au 100 le plus proche. [3] Non compris les travailleurs indirectement impliqués.

Notas explicativas: véase p. 1365.

[1] Interrupciones del trabajo de un día por lo menos o de un mínimo de 10 días no trabajados. [2] Cifras redondeadas al 100 más próximo. [3] Excl. los trabajadores indirectamente implicados.

STRIKES AND LOCKOUTS
Workers involved, by economic activity

GRÈVES ET LOCK-OUT
Travailleurs impliqués, par activité économique

HUELGAS Y CIERRES PATRONALES
Trabajadores implicados, por actividad económica

	1999	2000	2001	2002	2003	2004	2005	2006	2007	2008
Lithuania (D)										
ISIC 3 - CITI 3 - CIIU 3										
Total	.	3 303	1 703	0	0	0	70	0	7 033	7 961
D	.	0	. [1]	0	0	0	0	0	0	0
I	.	985	0	0	0	0	0	0	0	0
M	.	2 318	1 465	0	0	0	0	0	7 033	7 961
O	.						70	0	0	0
Malta (H)										
ISIC 3 - CITI 3 - CIIU 3										
Total	.	5 305	1 659	678	1 945	523	972	7 023	1 106	1 522
A	.	0	0	0	0	0	0	0	0	0
B	.	0	0	0	0	0	0	0	0	0
C	.	0	0	0	0	0	0	0	0	0
D	.	278	0	200	125	35	6	13	0	0
E	.	0	31	300	700	0	60	0	0	0
F	.	0	60	0	0	0	0	0	0	0
G	.	0	0	0	0	0	0	12	0	0
H	.	95	0	0	63	0	0	0	0	0
I	.	600	1 255	70	937	408	728	820	679	0
J	.	1 700	0	0	0	0	0	0	0	0
K	.	0	0	8	0	0	0	70	0	0
L	.	2 602	0	100	0	0	58	18	0	254
M	.	0	60	0	0	0	0	6 000	427	1 258
N	.	30	253	0	120	40	120	0	0	0
O	.	0	0	0	0	40	0	90	0	10
Netherlands (H)										
ISIC 3 - CITI 3 - CIIU 3										
Total	58 900	10 300	37 400	29 600	10 800	104 200	29 000	11 300	20 700	51 900
A	0	0	0	0	0	0	0	0	0	0
B	0	0	0	0	0	0	0	0	0	0
C	0	0	0	0	0	0	0	0	0	0
D	1 900	1 100	9 100 [2]	2 500	600	8 200	9 400 [3]	2 100	2 800	6 200 [2]
E	0	0			0	0	0	0	0	0
F	2 700	0	0	20 200	0	0	0	0	0	0
G	0	200 [4]			0		0	0	0	0
H	0		0			0	0	0	0	0
I	1 500 [5]	4 100	7 900 [6]	4 900 [5]	7 600 [7]	600	1 800 [6]	6 000 [7]	2 600	26 300
J	0	0		0	0	0	0	0	0	0
K			0				0	2 100	1 200	0
L	8 700	4 800 [8]	0	1 100 [9]	2 500 [10]	0	0	3 100 [11]	14 100	19 400
M	44 100			0	0	0	0	0	0	0
N	0	0	20 400 [8]		0	0	0	0	0	0
O	0				0	0	0	0	0	0
X						95 400 [12]	15 700 [12]	0	0	0
Norway (FH) [13] [14]										
ISIC 3 - CITI 3 - CIIU 3										
Total	651	93 889	29	9 865	95	9 873	591	29 109	519	12 963
A	0	0	0	0	0	0	0	0	0	0
B	0	0	0	0	0	0	0	0	0	0
C	160	2 490	0	400	78	752	139	87	0	0
D	57	57 714	5	4 353	3	5 867	0	0	0	727
E	0	0	0	0	0	0	0	2 747	0	0
F	0	18 825	0	139	0	451	452	16 000	0	0
G	253	2 048	0	8	12	7	0	1	0	4
H	14	2 446	24	3 040	0	27	0	0	0	0
I	129	3 980	0	64	0	1 710	0	1 651	0	626
J	0	0	0	0	0	0	0	5 300	0	0
K	27	2 545	0	0	0	0	0	0	9	87
L	0	0	0	0	0	0	0	588	0	0
M	11	17	0	0	2	1 059	0	0	12	10 262
N	0	3 721	0	1 561	0	0	0	0	496	1 257
O	0	103	0	300	0	0	0	2 735	2	0

Explanatory notes: see p. 1361.

[1] Data included in totals only for reasons of confidentiality. [2] Incl. category E. [3] Incl. category F. [4] Incl. categories H and K. [5] Incl. category K. [6] Including category G. [7] Incl. categories G and K. [8] Incl. categories M and O. [9] Incl. category N. [10] Incl. category O. [11] Incl. categories N and O. [12] Incl. categories A and O. [13] Excl. work stoppages lasting less than one day. [14] Excl. workers indirectly involved.

Notes explicatives: voir p. 1363.

[1] Données incluses uniquement dans le total pour des raisons de confidentialité. [2] Y compris la catégorie E. [3] Y compris catégorie F. [4] Y compris les catégories H et K. [5] Y compris la catégorie K. [6] Y compris la catégorie G. [7] Y compris les catégories G et K. [8] Y compris les catégories M et O. [9] Y compris la catégorie N. [10] Y compris la catégorie O. [11] Y compris les catégories N et O. [12] Y compris les catégories A et O. [13] Non compris les arrêts du travail dont la durée est inférieure à une journée. [14] Non compris les travailleurs indirectement impliqués.

Notas explicativas: véase p. 1365.

[1] Datos incluidos en el total solamente por razón de confidencialidad. [2] Incl. la categoría E. [3] Incl. categoría F. [4] Incl. las categorías H y K. [5] Incl. la categoría K. [6] Incl. la categoría G. [7] Incl. las categorías G y K. [8] Incl. las categorías M y O. [9] Incl. la categoría N. [10] Incl. la categoría O. [11] Incl. las categorías N y O. [12] Incl. las categorías A y O. [13] Excl. las interrupciones del trabajo de menos de un día de duración. [14] Excl. los trabajadores indirectamente implicados.

STRIKES AND LOCKOUTS
Workers involved, by economic activity

GRÈVES ET LOCK-OUT
Travailleurs impliqués, par activité économique

HUELGAS Y CIERRES PATRONALES
Trabajadores implicados, por actividad económica

Poland (FG)
ISIC 3 - CITI 3 - CIIU 3

	1999	2000	2001	2002	2003	2004	2005	2006	2007	2008
Total	27 149	7 858	1 383	13	3 034	217	1 592	24 647	59 909	209 030
A	0	0	0	0	0	0	0	0	0	0
B	0	0	0	0	0	0	0	0	0	0
C	0	0	0	0	0	0	0	20 685	0	1 155
D	6 135	1 967	871	13	2 848	0	1 363	503	23 616	2 144
E	393	250	83	0	0	0	0	0	0	166
F	0	0	0	0	0	0	0	0	0	39
G	18	0	0	0	0	0	0	0	0	0
H	0	0	0	0	0	0	0	0	0	9
I	1 338	515	0	0	37	217	217	0	1 779	11 521
J	0	0	0	0	0	0	0	0	0	0
K	271	0	0	0	149	0	0	0	55	118
L	0	0	0	0	0	0	0	0	0	0
M	18 933	0	0	0	0	0	0	0	26 419	190 677
N	45	5 126	429	0	0	0	12	3 459	8 040	3 048
O	16	0	0	0	0	0	0	0	0	153

Portugal (FG) [1] [2]
ISIC 3 - CITI 3 - CIIU 3

	1999	2000	2001	2002	2003	2004	2005	2006	2007	2008
Total [3]	33 500	38 830	26 058	80 168	30 330	31 906	21 740	33 493	29 164	.
A	0	0	0	0	0	0	0	0	0	.
B	400	47	0	162	57	0	0	0	0	.
C	200	894	66	819	113	0	272	28	368	.
D	20 100	13 947	10 562	36 282	10 486	10 183	11 259	12 275	12 094	.
E	300	297	37	3 023	384	211	159	106	615	.
F	200	0	22	106	12	131	176	39	337	.
G	1 100	298	228	1 833	75	327	43	172	1 044	.
H	500	121	261	1 407	120	437	437	375	1 226	.
I	9 700	20 705	12 150	30 048	17 651	6 220	4 066	16 087	9 792	.
J	. [4]	0	0	0	0	13 356	0	2 271	1 292	.
K	700	1 896	1 318	3 714	846	644	3 471	1 881	1 575	.
M [3]	0	0	78	222	1	0	65	79	112	.
N	.	85	1 035	1 966	453	0	688	0	18	.
O	8 000	540	301	586	132	397	1 104	180	691	.

Roumanie (FG) [1]
ISIC 3 - CITI 3 - CIIU 3

	1999	2000	2001	2002	2003	2004	2005	2006	2007	2008
Total	232 217	24 964	1 848	35 195	27 045	13 720	2 892	1 254	8 081	16 730
A	1 605	0	0	0	0	530	0	0	500	0
B	0	0	0	0	0	0	0	0	0	0
C	13 000	340	0	3 086	0	6 250	0	0	0	15 630
D	36 533	2 444	1 816	6 919	23 595	5 884	2 135	1 254	5 921	650
E	373	0	0	0	1 200	0	0	0	1 000	0
F	443	0	0	0	0	256	0	0	0	0
G	0	0	0	0	0	0	0	0	0	0
H	0	0	0	0	0	0	0	0	0	450
I	76 943	0	32	24 000	2 250	800	757	0	660	0
J	0	0	0	0	0	0	0	0	0	0
K	0	0	0	0	0	0	0	0	0	0
L	0	0	0	0	0	0	0	0	0	0
M	98 064	20 000	0	0	0	0	0	0	0	0
N	5 256	1 780	0	1 190	0	0	0	0	0	0
O	0	400	0	0	0	0	0	0	0	0
X	0	0	0	0	0	0	0	0	0	0

Russian Federation (FG) [5]
ISIC 3 - CITI 3 - CIIU 3

	1999	2000	2001	2002	2003	2004	2005	2006	2007	2008
Total	238 400	31 000	13 000	3 900	5 736	195 533	84 574	522	2 894	1 920
A	.	.	.	.	.	.	148	0	0	178
C-E	8 700	1 900	400	.	.	.	.	.	.	.
D	.	.	.	.	.	.	.	.	1 684	0
E	.	.	.	.	.	.	85	252	0	0
F	1 300	.	.	.	.	.	32	0	0	440
I	900	2 300	.	.	.	.	24	82	1 210	0
K	.	.	.	.	.	.	.	82	0	0
M	215 200	23 900	11 600	.	.	.	79 899	0	0	0
N	3 800	700	.	.	.	.	2 772	0	0	0
O	.	2 100	1 000	.	.	.	1 614	106	0	0
X	8 600	200	-	.	.	.	.	0	0	0

Explanatory notes: see p. 1361.

[1] Strikes only. [2] Excl. workers indirectly involved. [3] Excl. public administration. [4] Data included in those for the other activities involved. [5] Excl. work stoppages lasting less than one day.

Notes explicatives: voir p. 1363.

[1] Grèves seulement. [2] Non compris les travailleurs indirectement impliqués. [3] Non compris l'administration publique. [4] Données comprises dans celles des autres activités impliqués. [5] Non compris les arrêts du travail dont la durée est inférieure à une journée.

Notas explicativas: véase p. 1365.

[1] Huelgas solamente. [2] Excl. los trabajadores indirectamente implicados. [3] Excl. la administración pública. [4] Datos comprendidos en los de las otras actividades implicadas. [5] Excl. las interrupciones del trabajo de menos de un día de duración.

9B

	STRIKES AND LOCKOUTS	GRÈVES ET LOCK-OUT	HUELGAS Y CIERRES PATRONALES
	Workers involved, by economic activity	Travailleurs impliqués, par activité économique	Trabajadores implicados, por actividad económica

	1999	2000	2001	2002	2003	2004	2005	2006	2007	2008
San Marino (H) ISIC 2 - CITI 2 - CIIU 2										
Total	3 500	3 500	5 015	71 300	2 148	70	4 000	.	.	.
3 [1]	.	200	0	40 000	133	70	4 000			
4	.	0	0	0	0	0	0			
5	.	0	0	0	0	0	0			
6	.	0	0	0	0	0	0			
7	.	0	0	0	0	0	0			
8	.	0	0	0	0	0	0			
9	.	3 300	15	5 300	15	0	0			
0	.	.	5 000 [2]	26 000 [2]	2 000	0	0			
Slovakia (FG) ISIC 3 - CITI 3 - CIIU 3										
Total	0	0	0	0	18 326	0	0	1 333	72	445
Suisse (H) [3] ISIC 3 - CITI 3 - CIIU 3										
Total	2 255	3 894	20 098	21 947	8 111	24 399	338	635	5 083	10 160
A	0	0	0	0	0	0	0	0	0	0
B	0	0	0	0	0	0	0	0	0	0
C	0	0	0	0	0	0	0	0	0	0
D	75	18	0	0	119	601	208	275	0	93
E	0	0	0	0	0	0	0	0	0	0
F	400	0	0	20 797	47	2 540	0	0	5 083	630
G	0	0	45	0	0	0	0	0	0	0
H	0	0	0	0	0	0	0	0	0	0
I	0	120	0	800	233	0	130	240	0	352
J	560	0	0	0	0	0	0	0	0	0
K	0	0	0	0	112	0	0	0	0	0
L	1 220	962	0	0	1 200	21 258	0	0	0	9 085
M	0	0	53	350	6 400	0	0	0	0	0
N	0	2 245	20 000	0	0	0	0	0	0	0
O	0	549	0	0	0	0	0	120	0	0
X	0	0	0	0	0	0	0	0	0	0
Sweden (H) [4][5] ISIC 3 - CITI 3 - CIIU 3										
Total	9 481	163	9 831	711	80 538	2 449	604	1 740	3 635	12 766
A	0	0	0	0	0	0	0	0	0	0
B	0	0	0	0	0	0	0	0	0	0
C	723	0	0	0	0	0	0	0	0	0
D	18	0	337	384	0	201	50	230	1 151	6
E	0	0	4	0	0	0	101	0	0	0
F	181	75	4 465	230	2 576	1 991	200	0	1 022	0
G	0	0	0	0	0	0	0	0	0	0
H	0	0	0	2	0	0	0	0	0	0
I	8 473	88	5 018	54	3 230	250	222	1 500	1 450	2 528
J	43	0	0	0	0	0	0	0	0	0
K	0	0	0	0	0	0	2	0	6	0
L	3	0	0	1	0	0	0	0	0	0
M	40	0	0	40	20	0	20	1	2	0
N	0	0	2	0	0	0	0	15	1	10 000
O	0	0	5	0	74 712	7	9	3	3	0
X								0		0
Turkey (FG) [6] ISIC 3 - CITI 3 - CIIU 3										
Total	3 263	18 705	9 911	4 618	1 535	3 557	3 529	2 061	25 920	5 040
A	0	0	0	0	0	0	0	0	0	0
B	0	0	0	0	0	0	0	0	0	0
C	779	326	261	0	801	0	0	0	0	0
D	2 261	6 475	8 913	1 866	686	3 258	2 843	1 076	1 636	4 430
E	0	0	0	0	8	0	0	0	0	0
F	0	0	0	0	0	0	0	0	0	0
G	0	0	0	0	0	0	0	0	0	0
H	0	9	0	0	0	0	233	30	19	0
I	156	16	0	17	40	16	453	37	24 016	0
J	0	0	0	0	0	0	0	0	0	0
K	0	0	0	0	0	0	0	0	0	0
L	0	0	0	0	0	0	0	0	0	0
M	0	0	0	0	0	0	0	0	0	0
N	0	0	0	0	0	0	0	0	0	0
O	67	11 879	737	2 735	0	283	0	918	249	610

Explanatory notes: see p. 1361.

[1] Incl. generalized strikes. [2] Generalized strikes. [3] Excl. work stoppages lasting less than one day. [4] Work stoppages in which at least 8 hours not worked. [5] Excl. workers indirectly involved. [6] Strikes only.

Notes explicatives: voir p. 1363.

[1] Y compris les grèves généralisées. [2] Grèves généralisées. [3] Non compris les arrêts du travail dont la durée est inférieure à une journée. [4] Arrêts de travail avec un minimum de 8 heures de travail non effectuées. [5] Non compris les travailleurs indirectement impliqués. [6] Grèves seulement.

Notas explicativas: véase p. 1365.

[1] Incl. las huelgas generalizadas. [2] Huelgas generalizadas. [3] Excl. las interrupciones del trabajo de menos de un día de duración. [4] Interrupciones del trabajo de un mínimo de 8 horas no trabajadas. [5] Excl. los trabajadores indirectamente implicados. [6] Huelgas solamente.

STRIKES AND LOCKOUTS
Workers involved, by economic activity

GRÈVES ET LOCK-OUT
Travailleurs impliqués, par activité économique

HUELGAS Y CIERRES PATRONALES
Trabajadores implicados, por actividad económica

Ukraine (FG)
ISIC 2 - CITI 2 - CIIU 2   ISIC 3 - CITI 3 - CIIU 3

	1999	2000	2001	2002	2003	2004	2005	2006	2007	2008	
Total	42 029	20 649	6 776	9 344	5 448	997	630	2 266	849	354	Total
2	25 244	18 520	5 063	0	0	0	0	0	0	0	A
3 [1]	1 059	859	509	0	0	0	0	0	0	0	B
5	987	375	397	1 822	3 713	486	581	826	25	0	C
7	578	.	.	253	1 002	0	0	681	277	0	D
9 [2]	14 161	890	807	0	35	22	6	23	310	0	E
				45	34	0	0	17	0	354	F
				0	0	0	0	0	0	0	G
				0	0	0	0	0	0	0	H
				250	664	489	0	362	210	0	I
				0	0	0	0	0	0	0	J
				0	0	0	0	357	0	0	K
				0	0	0	0	0	0	0	L
				6 766	0	0	0	0	0	0	M
				140	0	0	0	0	0	0	N
				68	0	0	43	0	27	0	O

United Kingdom (H) [3][4][5]
ISIC 3 - CITI 3 - CIIU 3

	1999	2000	2001	2002	2003	2004	2005	2006	2007	2008
Total	140 900	183 200	179 900	942 900	150 600	292 700	92 600	713 300	744 800	511 200
A-B	0	0	0	0	0	0	0	0	0	100
C	0	900	300	0	0	500	1	1 100	0	800
D	30 600	28 200	16 700	10 100	18 200	13 600	3 300	10 700	13 500	4 900
E	0	500	2 200	300	400	300	5 500	0	0	0
F	17 900	15 800	2 900	16 800	1 900	-	900	1 800	800	2 700
G	0	100	100	200	700	100	0	500	0	400
H	1 400	12 200	800	73 900	.	0	700	0	0	0
I	42 100	39 100	69 100	33 300	52 200	11 900	12 700	14 400	399 300	19 000
J	0	0	100	0	0	-	2 300	0	0	0
K	1 100	-	200	1 700	300	700	1 900	1 300	1 500	500
L	17 400	28 900	46 200	171 000	56 100	206 500	15 300	653 500	317 400	370 300
M	28 300	16 600	33 700	388 100	15 200	55 200	43 400	27 700	8 700	110 300
N	400	27 600	6 300	144 300	3 200	1 000	400	1 600	2 100	500
O	1 800	13 200	1 200	103 300	3 300	2 900	6 100	600	1 600	1 600

OCEANIA-OCÉANIE-OCEANIA

Australia (H) [5][6]
ISIC 3 - CITI 3 - CIIU 3

	1999	2000	2001	2002	2003	2004	2005	2006	2007	2008
Total	461 100	325 400	225 700	159 700	275 600	194 000	241 000	122 700	36 000	172 900
A-B	1 000	0	200	1 200	.	100	0	0	600	0
C	21 200	23 100	4 500	6 400	10 900	3 100	5 200	1 100	700	800
D	114 100	63 100	89 800	30 300	36 900	26 800	43 500	22 100	5 500	5 200
E	6 800	2 000	4 300	3 100	500	1 900	4 100	800	700	12 300
F	124 400	58 300	69 200	73 700	91 600	86 700	69 000	16 300	4 700	8 500
G-H	1 600	3 600	3 700	7 500	2 400	1 800	328	100	100	0
I	25 700	20 400	12 000	12 400	11 300	22 300	11 300	9 200	2 100	7 900
J-K	3 400	18 300	6 700	2 100	1 600	11 600	2 400	600	0	0
L	2 700	4 100	5 600	10 900	5 400	11 800	9 200	900	200	4 100
M	147 100	126 400	18 300	0	107 500	25 900	91 600	67 000	17 300	132 400
N [7]	2 800	1 700	6 600	5 400	4 400	1 200	2 600	900	3 800	1 400
O	10 200	4 500	4 700	6 800	3 200	700	1 800	3 600	400	100

New Zealand (FG) [8][9]
ISIC 3 - CITI 3 - CIIU 3

	1999	2000	2001	2002	2003	2004	2005	2006	2007	2008
Total	10 747	2 632	22 022	23 309	5 098	6 127	17 752	10 079	4 090	.
A	0	0	0	0	0	. [10]	0	0	0	.
B	0	0	. [10]	0	0	0	0	0	0	.
C	0	0	0	0	. [10]	. [10]	. [10]	0	. [10]	.
D	2 028	1 285	2 273	1 504	696	2 325	1 763	1 706	341	.
E	0	0	0	0	. [10]	. [10]	0	. [10]	0	.
F	. [10]	. [10]	90	0	. [10]	. [10]	. [10]	754	. [10]	.
G	. [10]	. [10]	. [10]	0	. [10]	0	. [10]	. [10]	. [10]	.
H	0	0	0	. [10]	0	. [10]	. [10]	. [10]	. [10]	.
I	3 424	. [10]	515	1 414	. [10]	1 042	2 275	274	422	.
J	. [10]	0	0	. [10]	0	. [10]	. [10]	0	0	.
K	. [10]	0	320	. [10]	. [10]	. [10]	0	. [10]	. [10]	.
L	0	383	3 574	397	. [10]	85	3 304	2 343	. [10]	.
M	848	. [10]	11 638	17 249	. [10]	1 015	4 215	. [10]	. [10]	.
N	2 464	484	3 413	814	2 994	447	1 057	3 579	1 708	.
O	. [10]	0	. [10]	. [10]	. [10]	. [10]	0	452	505	.

Explanatory notes: see p. 1361.

[1] Incl. electricity, gas and water. [2] All activities not shown elsewhere. [3] Incl. stoppages involving fewer than 10 workers or lasting less than one day if 100 or more workdays not worked. [4] Excl. political strikes. [5] Figures rounded to nearest 100. [6] Excl. work stoppages in which less than 10 workdays not worked. [7] Incl. community services. [8] Excl. work stoppages in which less than 10 workdays not worked (from 2000, 5 workdays). [9] Prior to 1988: excl. public sector stoppages. [10] Data included in totals only for reasons of confidentiality.

Notes explicatives: voir p. 1363.

[1] Y compris l'électricité, le gaz et l'eau. [2] Toutes les activités non indiquées ailleurs. [3] Y compris les arrêts impliquant moins de 10 travailleurs ou de moins d'un jour si plus de 100 journées de travail non effectuées. [4] Non compris les grèves politiques. [5] Chiffres arrondis au 100 le plus proche. [6] Non compris les arrêts de travail de moins de 10 journées de travail non effectuées. [7] Y compris les services à la collectivité. [8] Non compris les arrêts de travail de moins de 10 journées de travail non effectuées (à partir de 2000, 5 journées de travail). [9] Avant 1988: non compris les arrêts du travail du secteur public. [10] Données incluses uniquement dans le total pour des raisons de confidentialité.

Notas explicativas: véase p. 1365.

[1] Incl. electricidad, gas y agua. [2] Todas las actividades no indicadas en otra parte. [3] Incl. las interrupciones con menos de 10 trabajadores o de menos de un día si hubo más de 100 días de trabajo no trabajados. [4] Excl. las huelgas políticas. [5] Cifras redondeadas al 100 más próximo. [6] Excl. las interrupciones de trabajo de menos de 10 días de trabajo no trabajados. [7] Incl. servicios comunales. [8] Excl. las interrupciones de trabajo de menosde 10 días de trabajo no trabajados (desde 2000, 5 días de trabajo). [9] Antes de 1988: excl. las interrupciones del sector público. [10] Datos incluidos en el total solamente por razón de confidencialidad.

STRIKES AND LOCKOUTS

Days not worked, by economic activity

GRÈVES ET LOCK-OUT

Journées non effectuées, par activité économique

HUELGAS Y CIERRES PATRONALES

Días no trabajados, por actividad económica

AFRICA-AFRIQUE-AFRICA

	1999	2000	2001	2002	2003	2004	2005	2006	2007	2008
Algérie (FG) ¹										
ISIC 3 - CITI 3 - CIIU 3										
Total	242 665	436 555	237 776	533 764	181 045	628 838	.	.	.	.
A-B	9 362	2 200	2 914	11 079	0	37				
C	587	3 026	3 187	1 786	0	0				
D	55 635	74 806	102 613	136 266	0	18 282				
E ²	0	0	0	0	0	0				
F	129 243	168 208	52 453	49 949	0	30 485				
G	4 592	1 986	1 372	531	0	0				
H	0	0	65	23 598	0	0				
I	546	33 942	5 255	13 239	31 260	4 904				
J-K	0	0	1 174	781	0	0				
L	7 637	1 889	7 713	1 277	12 100	564 397				
M	9 432	130 829	43 161	267 209	70 877	6 618				
N	383	10 856	12 747	6 704	61 743	1 500				
Q	11 581	2 950	1 066	17 426	0	568				
X	13 667	5 863	4 056	3 919	5 065	2 047				
Mauritius (FG)										
ISIC 3 - CITI 3 - CIIU 3										
Total	2 779	4 531	6 720	7 440	7 734	114	10 310	4 290	15 214	15 482
A	192	658	0	147	0	0	0	0	0	0
B	0	0	448	0	0	0	0	0	0	0
C	0	0	0	0	0	0	0	0	0	0
D	2 422	3 758	5 997	7 252	5 948	105	10 310	4 290	15 214	2 025
E	0	0	0	0	0	0	0	0	0	0
F	110	0	211	0	969	6	0	0	0	9 457
G	0	104	40	16	6	4	0	0	0	0
H	29	0	0	13	0	0	0	0	0	0
I	0	11	24	0	810	0	0	0	0	0
J	0	0	0	0	0	0	0	0	0	0
K	0	0	0	0	0	0	0	0	0	0
L	0	0	0	0	0	0	0	0	0	0
M	0	0	0	13	0	0	0	0	0	0
N	0	0	0	0	0	0	0	0	0	0
O	0	0	0	0	0	0	0	0	0	0
X	27	0	0	0	0	0	0	0	0	4 000
Nigeria (FG) ³										
ISIC 2 - CITI 2 - CIIU 2										
Total	3 158 087	6 287 733	1 030 199	2 578 692	5 690 952	2 737 399	4 308 013	7 785 993	.	.
South Africa (FG)										
ISIC 3 - CITI 3 - CIIU 3										
Total	2 625 535	1 669 966	953 610	615 723	919 780	1 286 003	2 627 953	4 152 563	9 528 945	497 436
A	93 678	10 466	13 073	4 400	28 833	59 714	102 000	43 574	30 728	9 081
C	266 581	364 210	229 042	94 547	279 176	544 658	932 711	115 926	536 740	82 535
D	225 623	127 273	412 745	41 894	202 534	105 020	306 291	199 029	695 156	72 073
E	838	1 282	5 568	16	22 196	200	379	19 341	345	0
F	113 197	18 075	5 902	3 111	71 270	0	10 190	934	50 548	15 415
G	93 843	104 537	108	15 416	249 099	3 777	332 697	1 273 414	18 299	15 817
I	443 363	121 781	188 597	4 660	48 717	72 644	551 286	164 629	25 881	106 622
J	360	20	0	0	180	35 428	10 389	1 302 592	9 947	13 082
O	1 388 052	922 322	98 575	451 679	17 775	464 562	382 010	1 033 124	8 161 301	182 811
X	0	0	0	0	0	0	0	0	0	0
Saint Helena (FG)										
ISIC 3 - CITI 3 - CIIU 3										
Total	0	0	0	0	0	0	0	.	.	.

Explanatory notes: see p. 1361.

¹ Strikes only. ² Incl. sanitary services. ³ Year beginning in April of year indicated.

Notes explicatives: voir p. 1363.

¹ Grèves seulement. ² Y compris les services sanitaires. ³ Année commençant en avril de l'année indiquée.

Notas explicativas: véase p. 1365.

¹ Huelgas solamente. ² Incl. los servicios de saneamiento. ³ Año que comienza en abril del año indicado.

STRIKES AND LOCKOUTS

Days not worked, by economic activity

GRÈVES ET LOCK-OUT

Journées non effectuées, par activité économique

HUELGAS Y CIERRES PATRONALES

Días no trabajados, por actividad económica

	1999	2000	2001	2002	2003	2004	2005	2006	2007	2008
Tunisie (FG)										
ISIC 3 - CITI 3 - CIIU 3										
Total	36 790	47 549	50 590	47 282	53 338	66 816	84 496	89 644	107 515	.
A	1 294	3 704	2 532	5 301	1 373	1 197	1 322	1 411	2 789	.
B	268	59	390	47	0	0	0	43	318	.
C	2 568	1 163	239	449	5 400	558	997	1 615	2 979	.
D	21 833	38 587	25 923	33 609	36 475	54 733	53 668	26 851	53 524	.
E	45	518	403	348	346	14	656	22	699	.
F	8 299	1 635	8 100	3 168	4 564	3 216	6 650	4 598	3 791	.
G	105	156	155	32	27	0	615	57	11 063	.
H	686	50	240	83	1 304	263	791	682	1 617	.
I	838	642	1 043	3 203	1 178	355	1 222	550	1 529	.
J	.	.	.	42	0	2 216	1 485	.	4 021	.
L [1]	.	17	1 993	56	631	3 360	139	.	2 005	.
M	.	.	.	86	235	2	14 583	36 343	9 157	.
N	.	.	.	776	0	266	485	9 298	7 630	.
O	426	672	7 209	82	1 804	636	1 873	7 372	6 420	.
X	428	346	2 363	0	1	0	0	0	0	.
Uganda (F)										
ISIC 3 - CITI 3 - CIIU 3										
Total	10 481	2 376	1 084	4 086	3 600	3 936	.	.	.	.

AMERICA-AMÉRIQUE-AMERICA

	1999	2000	2001	2002	2003	2004	2005	2006	2007	2008
Argentina (F) [2]										
ISIC 3 - CITI 3 - CIIU 3										
Total	6 248 966	12 392 241	.	.	.	.	.	6 332 096	8 400 398	8 623 434
A	.	.	.	.	.	.	.	15 671	4 638	45 580
B	.	.	.	.	.	.	.	0	260	7 348
C	.	.	.	.	.	.	.	69 126	164 743	64 371
D	.	.	.	.	.	.	.	156 860	210 344	478 976
E	.	.	.	.	.	.	.	29 665	17 551	55 527
F	.	.	.	.	.	.	.	12 399	13 554	44 966
G	.	.	.	.	.	.	.	45 484	28 303	95 824
H	.	.	.	.	.	.	.	12	13 132	5 207
I	.	.	.	.	.	.	.	143 885	294 157	136 867
J	.	.	.	.	.	.	.	15 397	161 111	22 157
K	.	.	.	.	.	.	.	628	2 891	674
L	.	.	.	.	.	.	.	1 095 739	1 671 295	1 692 894
M	.	.	.	.	.	.	.	3 716 328	4 295 672	4 543 214
N	.	.	.	.	.	.	.	988 933	1 475 175	1 421 711
O	.	.	.	.	.	.	.	41 869	47 572	8 118
Aruba (F) [2]										
ISIC 3 - CITI 3 - CIIU 3										
Total	.	.	.	.	.	1 556	40	10	52	.
D	.	.	.	.	.	0	0	0	0	.
E	.	.	.	.	.	1 540	0	10	0	.
F	.	.	.	.	.	0	0	0	0	.
G	.	.	.	.	.	0	0	0	42	.
H	.	.	.	.	.	0	0	0	0	.
I	.	.	.	.	.	0	0	0	0	.
J	.	.	.	.	.	0	0	0	0	.
K	.	.	.	.	.	.	.	.	4	.
N	.	.	.	.	.	0	0	0	6	.
X	.	.	.	.	.	16	40	0	0	.
Brasil (FH) [3]										
ISIC 3 - CITI 3 - CIIU 3										
Total	5 934 657	224 999 551	828 380 168	49 673 223	294 318 831	150 183 670	.	.	.	.

Explanatory notes: see p. 1361.

[1] Incl. category N and state education. [2] Computed on the basis of an eight-hour working day. [3] Strikes only.

Notes explicatives: voir p. 1363.

[1] Y compris la catégorie N et l'éducation publique. [2] Calculées sur la base de journées de travail de huit heures. [3] Grèves seulement.

Notas explicativas: véase p. 1365.

[1] Incl. la categoría N y la educación pública. [2] Calculados en base a días de trabajo de ocho horas. [3] Huelgas solamente.

STRIKES AND LOCKOUTS / GRÈVES ET LOCK-OUT / HUELGAS Y CIERRES PATRONALES

Days not worked, by economic activity

Journées non effectuées, par activité économique

Días no trabajados, por actividad económica

Canada (FG) [1]
ISIC 3 - CITI 3 - CIIU 3

	1999	2000	2001	2002	2003	2004	2005	2006	2007	2008
Total	2 440 630	1 644 100	2 202 500	2 985 940	1 730 342	3 184 948	4 147 580	7 929 236	1 770 707	875 640
A	118 350	36 570	25 570	35 800	38 800	190	8 190	29 110	0	0
B	0	0	0	0	31 570	0	0	0	0	0
C	150 580	167 460	117 290	74 940	209 010	103 910	61 050	45 060	45 580	51 910
D	456 610	497 770	558 660	555 110	606 660	547 310	446 870	340 583	652 015	281 590
E	178 350	70	17 380	2 960	790	19 700	60 260	0	3 120	5 070
F	6 420	17 630	69 910	11 390	0	91 420	11 320	2 550	222 282	1 930
G	79 500	91 350	87 040	132 470	251 410	227 750	234 700	43 310	19 630	77 280
H	61 230	78 060	39 910	8 060	39 100	43 530	70 710	24 230	15 280	66 900
I	490 610	82 680	370 840	451 280	241 710	593 833	1 574 120	33 920	158 700	114 820
J	21 560	24 190	20 540	0	4 670	4 030	2 170	11 690	10 670	12 850
K	41 060	38 210	34 200	63 800	22 700	14 390	6 510	650	2 570	1 100
L	210 190	218 980	219 390	1 201 770	17 607	994 790	608 440	31 370	289 250	20 310
M	181 990	214 850	373 940	299 390	227 420	54 185	909 110	144 210	124 520	107 840
N	315 450	87 290	214 800	84 920	51 435	310 520	117 760	16 760	48 640	10 720
O	128 730	88 990	53 030	64 140	19 030	179 390	36 370	69 500	178 450	123 320
X	0	0	0	0	0	0	0	0	0	0

Chile (FG) [2]
ISIC 2 - CITI 2 - CIIU 2

	1999	2000	2001	2002	2003	2004	2005	2006	2007	2008
Total	103 232	114 306	127 157	207 224	73 467	172 858	99 931	195 344	163 770	202 178
1	2 817	4 696	914	576	18	1 594	1 036	5 270	3 487	1 582
2	808	10 469	2 882	2 600	20 057	29 175	7 028	52 269	22 003	13 201
3	57 346	41 308	68 301	35 855	27 853	93 075	46 203	49 051	47 325	74 053
4	0	0	1 242	0	0	1 616	108	672	726	570
5	88	639	2 404	866	1 310	0	2 198	11 418	12 392	11 494
6	5 061	3 544	6 815	13 795	3 638	5 765	13 475	28 191	21 421	34 998
7	12 106	3 553	2 204	120 224	3 549	9 903	11 260	13 947	15 054	12 922
8	1 684	5 686	13 114	14 217	4 378	4 096	3 215	14 081	21 808	22 197
9	23 322	44 411	29 281	19 091	12 664	27 634	15 410	20 445	19 555	31 161
0	0	0	0	0	0	0	0	0	0	0

Ecuador (FG)
ISIC 3 - CITI 3 - CIIU 3

	1999	2000	2001	2002	2003	2004	2005	2006	2007	2008
Total	51 361	115 558	19 259	98 400	112 574	64 210	25 290	91 676	68 439	36 672
A	0	63 460	7 889	56 509	17 416	35 428	0	48 635	0	22 052
B	0	0	0	12 324	0	0	0	0	0	0
C	713	12 812	0	0	0	0	0	0	0	0
D	8 274	13 354	0	1 053	63 731	4 148	9 152	3 922	28 846	14 022
E	1 178	16 229	0	20 624	20 592	0	0	0	8 232	0
F	0	0	0	0	2 322	0	0	0	23 643	248
G	0	0	0	0	63	10 390	1 944	0	0	0
H	0	0	0	0	124	0	0	0	0	0
I	36 040	1 782	10 692	320	400	0	0	4 884	0	350
J	5 104	0	0	0	0	0	0	0	0	0
K	0	7 921	0	3 250	0	58	2 680	0	0	0
L	52	0	538	4 320	3 574	11 534	11 514	14 463	7 718	0
M	0	0	0	0	0	0	0	0	0	0
N	0	0	140	0	0	0	0	15 688	0	0
O	0	0	0	0	4 352	2 652	0	3 904	0	0

El Salvador (FG)
ISIC 2 - CITI 2 - CIIU 2 (1999–2005) ‖ ISIC 3 - CITI 3 - CIIU 3 (2006–2008)

(ISIC 2)	1999	2000	2001	2002	2003	2004	2005	‖	2006	2007	2008	(ISIC 3)
Total	626 388	621 186	40 561	72 813	153 962	49 986	46 701	‖	97 093	3 883	7 213	Total
1	0	0	0	0	0	0	0	‖	0	0	0	A
2	0	0	0	0	0	0	0	‖	0	0	0	B
3	3 915	9 155	17 750	7 525	470	37 944	3 448	‖	0	0	0	C
4	100	850	0	0	0	6 684	0	‖	17 583	1 974	5 073	D
5	2 900	3 829	0	5 250	0	135	50	‖	0	0	0	E
6	0	0	0	0	0	0	36	‖	0	0	0	F
7	450	7 316	6 321	0	23	220	207	‖	0	80	0	G
8	0	0	0	0	0	0	0	‖	0	0	0	H
9	619 023	600 036	16 490	60 038	153 469	5 003	42 960	‖	1 586	914	0	I
								‖	0	0	0	J
								‖	30	0	0	K
								‖	50	175	1 840	L
								‖	15 000	740	0	M
								‖	62 780	0	300	N
								‖	64	0	0	O

Guyana (FG)
ISIC 2 - CITI 2 - CIIU 2

	1999	2000	2001	2002	2003	2004	2005	2006	2007	2008
Total	158 424	56 175	60 755	70 544	53 577	83 760	85 186	120 032	66 299	.
1	35 136	0	54 890	0	0	82 880	83 536	0	66 175	.
2	2 045	.	.	.	.	.	.	.	.	.
4	.	.	1 818	.	.	.	.	.	0	.
9	121 199	0	2 430	0	0	0	0	0	124	.
0	44	.	.	.	.	.	.	.	.	.

Explanatory notes: see p. 1361.
[1] Strikes lasting at least half a day with more than 10 days lost.
[2] Strikes only.

Notes explicatives: voir p. 1363.
[1] Grèves d'une durée d'une demi-journée au moins et dans lesquelles 10 jours de travail sont perdus. [2] Grèves seulement.

Notas explicativas: véase p. 1365.
[1] Huelgas con duración de media jornada laboral por lo menos y con más de 10 días perdidos. [2] Huelgas solamente.

STRIKES AND LOCKOUTS — GRÈVES ET LOCK-OUT — HUELGAS Y CIERRES PATRONALES

Days not worked, by economic activity — **Journées non effectuées, par activité économique** — **Días no trabajados, por actividad económica**

	1999	2000	2001	2002	2003	2004	2005	2006	2007	2008
Jamaica (FG)										
ISIC 2 - CITI 2 - CIIU 2										
Total	69 025	22 580	13 178	4 963	65 976	1 553	1 340	.	.	.
1	26	9 738	3 000	3 932	1 805	420	0			
2	0	0	300	170	2 800	0	0			
3	5 099	1 975	177	90	210	400	500			
4	0	0	197	0	0	0	40			
5	0	0	9 160	0	106	0	0			
6	0	0	0	0	0	0	0			
7	168	3 112	250	0	500	500	780			
8	3 395	4 245	0	158	500	150	0			
9	60 337	3 510	94	613	60 055	420	20			
México (FG) [1][2]										
ISIC 3 - CITI 3 - CIIU 3										
Total	65 663	847 201	246 186	371 347	107 604	178 791	222 408	661 401	200 856	286 430
A	0	0	0	0	0	0	0	0	0	0
B	0	0	0	0	0	0	0	0	0	0
C	0	5 538	0	75 066	12 729	46 932	1 551	491	3 308	5 775
D	50 512	819 662	240 368	62 383	79 154	55 658	112 683	641 195	27 582	8 601
E	0	0	0	0	0	0	0	0	0	0
F	0	0	0	1 150	0	0	0	1 722	1 313	16 089
G	0	1 260	0	0	0	0	0	0	0	0
H	0	0	0	0	0	0	0	0	0	0
I	12 242	20 631	131	8 102	3 408	5 689	9 618	17 820	22 658	37 609
J	690	0	0	43	36	0	0	0	1 087	0
K	0	0	0	0	0	0	0	0	0	0
M	2 218	0	5 577	224 524	12 000	70 512	93 450	0	144 828	206 221
N	0	0	0	0	0	0	0	0	0	0
O	0	110	110	79	278	0	5 106	615	80	12 135
Nicaragua (FG) [3]										
ISIC 2 - CITI 2 - CIIU 2										
Total	73	0	0	0	.	51	.	.	.	.
1 [4]	0	0	0	0						
2	0	0	0	0						
3	0	0	0	0						
4	0	0	0	0						
5	0	0	0	0						
6	0	0	0	0						
7	0	0	0	0						
8	0	0	0	0						
9	73	0	0	0						
Panamá (FG) [5]										
ISIC 3 - CITI 3 - CIIU 3										
Total	14 852	30 168	340 623	3 372	49 000	952	540	2 109	110 610	.
A	0	0	312 320	0	12 000	0	0	0	0	
B	0	0	0	0	0	0	0	0	0	
C	1 200	0	0	3 372	0	0	0	0	0	
D	0	0	5 472	0	0	0	0	2 010	0	
E	0	0	0	0	0	0	0	0	0	
F	2 660	0	17 290	0	1 000	0	540	21	108 170	
G	0	0	0	0	36 000	0	0	0	2 440	
H	0	25 680	0	0	0	0	0	78	0	
I	0	4 488	4 005	0	0	952	0	0	0	
J	0	0	0	0	0	0	0	0	0	
K	0	0	1 536	0	0	0	0	0	0	
L	0	0	0	0	0	0	0	0	0	
M	0	0	0	0	0	0	0	0	0	
N	10 992	0	0	0	0	0	0	0	0	
O	0	0	0	0	0	0	0	0	0	

Explanatory notes: see p. 1361.

[1] Strikes only, beginning in the year indicated. [2] Excl. enterprises covered by local jurisdiction. [3] Strikes only. [4] Excl. hunting, forestry and fishing. [5] Computed on the basis of an eight-hour working day.

Notes explicatives: voir p. 1363.

[1] Grèves seulement, commençant pendant l'année indiquée. [2] Non compris les entreprises sous juridiction locale. [3] Grèves seulement. [4] Non compris la chasse, la sylviculture et la pêche. [5] Calculées sur la base de journées de travail de huit heures.

Notas explicativas: véase p. 1365.

[1] Huelgas solamente, que empiezan en el año indicado. [2] Excl. las empresas de jurisdicción local. [3] Huelgas solamente. [4] Excl. caza, silvicultura y pesca. [5] Calculados en base a días de trabajo de ocho horas.

STRIKES AND LOCKOUTS

Days not worked, by economic activity

GRÈVES ET LOCK-OUT

Journées non effectuées, par activité économique

HUELGAS Y CIERRES PATRONALES

Días no trabajados, por actividad económica

9C

	1999	2000	2001	2002	2003	2004	2005	2006	2007	2008
Perú (FG) [1][2]										
ISIC 3 - CITI 3 - CIIU 3										
Total	90 532	22 711	61 116	111 815	881 362	582 328	478 738	446 584	2 216 520	1 520 960
A	936	0	25 952	67	2 000	1 112	0	0	6 400	12 800
B	1 056	0	0	0	0	0	0	0	0	0
C	7 913	2 322	8 751	47 096	43 200	179 184	118 808	82 632	2 057 232	1 418 424
D	2 330	2 415	21 953	16 984	163 368	283 040	56 712	17 832	24 368	40 856
E	23	612	0	1 724	4 774	31 848	22 064	42 958	9 776	9 112
F	7 857	2 158	4 321	11 860	577 112	7 544	16 112	20 440	25 792	7 680
G	0	0	0	0	776	0	0	2 448	0	0
H	0	0	73	0	0	0	0	0	0	0
I	34 012	14 963	0	29 070	15 340	37 880	13 774	86 458	87 632	9 576
J	0	0	0	0	0	0	0	0	64	0
K	0	0	30	4 926	56 168	15 872	640	185 184	800	1 368
L	0	240	36	11	10 888	14 488	16 480	7 304	4 032	8 192
M	9	0	0	0	1 960	336	1 792	1 184	424	1 144
N	0	0	0	77	464	10 128	231 988	144	0	400
O	0	0	0	0	5 312	896	368	0	0	0
P	.	.				0	0	0	0	0
X	36 394	0	0	0	0	0	0	0	0	11 408
Puerto Rico (FG) [3]										
ISIC 3 - CITI 3 - CIIU 3										
Total	15 730	10 365	73 120	67 768	0	290 250	0	0	88	504
A	0	0	0	0	0	0	0	0	0	0
B	0	0	0	0	0	0	0	0	0	0
C	0	0	0	0	0	0	0	0	0	0
D	0	5 040	40 320	27 520	0	0	0	0	0	0
E	0	0	0	0	0	0	0	0	0	0
F	0	0	3 000	0	0	0	0	0	0	0
G	15 730	0	.	40 248	0	0	0	0	0	0
G,I	.	.	22 440	.	.	.	.	.	0	0
H	0	920	7 360	0	0	0	0	0	88	0
H,M-O	.	.	.	.						
I	0	2 805	.	0	0	0	0	0	0	504
J	0	0	0	0	0	0	0	0	0	0
K	0	1 600	0	0	0	0	0	0	0	0
L	0	0	0	0	0	290 250	0	0	0	0
M	0	0	.	.	.	0	0	0	0	0
N	0	0	.	0	0	0	0	0	0	0
O	0	0	.	0	0	0	0	0	0	0
Trinidad and Tobago (FG)										
ISIC 2 - CITI 2 - CIIU 2										
Total	23 332	880	13 544	11 873	52 568	1 583 373	0	.	.	.
1	0	227	0	0	0	0	0	.	.	.
2	33	0	6 075	11 572	36 103	7 064	0	.	.	.
3	3 206	17	0	0	97	292 667	0	.	.	.
4	0	0	0	0	0	0	0	.	.	.
5	0	0	0	0	0	1 275 000	0	.	.	.
6	0	0	0	0	0	0	0	.	.	.
7	20 052	262	7 465	301	16 368	8 642	0	.	.	.
8	0	374	0	0	0	0	0	.	.	.
9	41	0	4	0	0	0	0	.	.	.
0	0	0	0	0	0	0	0	.	.	.
United States (H) [4][5]										
ISIC 3 - CITI 3 - CIIU 3										
Total	1 995 800	20 419 400	1 151 300	659 600	4 077 400	1 017 200	1 348 000	2 687 500	1 264 800	1 954 100
A	0	0	0	0	0	0	0	0	0	0
B	0	0	0	0	0	0	0	0	0	0
C	0	0	0	0	0	0	134 100	0	9 600	0
D	1 777 700	1 508 400	183 600	209 800	82 800	75 300	577 600	1 576 800	561 400	1 537 900
E	0	0	102 000	35 000	0	20 800	22 800	0	0	0
F	6 800	75 000	115 000	65 800	28 000	0	74 800	36 200	18 400	5 800
G	35 500	1 400	81 300	0	3 689 000	104 000	0	23 800	0	0
H	24 000	6 800	0	0	0	396 700	7 200	0	0	0
I	38 400	1 158 300	116 600	186 500	178 700	282 400	520 500	820 600	104 800	6 500
J	0	0	0	0	0	0	0	0	0	0
K	0	17 445 300	0	32 400	0	0	0	0	409 500	304 500
L	0	48 200	242 500	3 800	25 000	0	0	61 600	0	0
M	101 400	41 300	190 600	46 100	44 800	0	11 000	118 500	83 100	55 000
N	12 000	134 700	119 700	80 200	0	138 000	0	24 000	25 000	31 800
O	0	0	0	0	29 100	0	0	26 000	53 000	12 600
X	0	0	0	0	0	0	0	0	.	0

Explanatory notes: see p. 1361.

[1] Strikes only; private sector. [2] Computed on the basis of an eight-hour working day. [3] Strikes and lockouts ending during the 12 months beginning in July of the year indicated. [4] Excl. work stoppages involving fewer than 1,000 workers and lasting less than a full day or shift. [5] Figures rounded to nearest 100.

Notes explicatives: voir p. 1363.

[1] Grèves seulement; secteur privé. [2] Calculées sur la base de journées de travail de huit heures. [3] Grèves et lock-out se terminant pendant les 12 mois commençant en juillet de l'année indiquée. [4] Non compris arrêts de travail impliquant moins de 1000 travailleurs; durée inférieure à 1 jour ou à 1 poste de travail. [5] Chiffres arrondis au 100 le plus proche.

Notas explicativas: véase p. 1365.

[1] Huelgas solamente; sector privado. [2] Calculados en base a días de trabajo de ocho horas. [3] Huelgas y cierres patronales que terminan dentro de los 12 meses que comienzan en julio del año indicado. [4] Excl. las interrupciones del trabajo que implican menos de 1000 trabajadores y que duran menos de 1 día o turno completo. [5] Cifras redondeadas al 100 más próximo.

STRIKES AND LOCKOUTS / GRÈVES ET LOCK-OUT / HUELGAS Y CIERRES PATRONALES

Days not worked, by economic activity — **Journées non effectuées, par activité économique** — **Días no trabajados, por actividad económica**

Uruguay (Z)
ISIC 3 - CITI 3 - CIIU 3

	1999	2000	2001	2002	2003	2004	2005	2006	2007	2008
Total	.	.	.	.	.	.	.	.	.	876 600
A	.	.	.	.	.	.	.	.	.	10 136
B	.	.	.	.	.	.	.	.	.	
C	.	.	.	.	.	.	.	.	.	4 950
D	.	.	.	.	.	.	.	.	.	90 524
E	.	.	.	.	.	.	.	.	.	13 964
F	.	.	.	.	.	.	.	.	.	281 277
G	.	.	.	.	.	.	.	.	.	19 262
H	.	.	.	.	.	.	.	.	.	0
I	.	.	.	.	.	.	.	.	.	72 126
J	.	.	.	.	.	.	.	.	.	22 966
K	.	.	.	.	.	.	.	.	.	8 347
L	.	.	.	.	.	.	.	.	.	84 444
M	.	.	.	.	.	.	.	.	.	224 235
N	.	.	.	.	.	.	.	.	.	38 011
O	.	.	.	.	.	.	.	.	.	6 358
P	.	.	.	.	.	.	.	.	.	
Q	.	.	.	.	.	.	.	.	.	
X	.	.	.	.	.	.	.	.	.	0

ASIA-ASIE-ASIA

Hong Kong, China (FG) [1]
ISIC 3 - CITI 3 - CIIU 3

	1999	2000	2001	2002	2003	2004	2005	2006	2007	2008
Total [2]	299	934	780	0	150	351	100	54	8 027	1 408
A	0	0	0	0	0	0	0	0	0	0
B	0	0	0	0	0	0	0	0	0	0
C	0	0	0	0	0	0	0	0	0	0
D	0	0	0	0	0	0	0	0	0	1 174
E	0	0	0	0	0	0	0	0	0	0
F	168	208	0	0	150	0	0	0	8 010	0
G	0	626	0	0	0	0	0	0	0	0
H	0	0	0	0	0	0	0	0	0	0
I	131	0	0	0	0	0	100	54	17	234
J	0	0	0	0	0	0	0	0	0	0
K	0	100	780	0	0	0	0	0	0	0
M	0	0	0	0	0	0	0	0	0	0
N	0	0	0	0	0	0	0	0	0	0
O	0	0	0	0	0	351	0	0	0	0

India (H) [3][4]
ISIC 2 - CITI 2 - CIIU 2 .... ISIC 3 - CITI 3 - CIIU 3

ISIC 2	1999	2000	2001	2002	2003	2004	2005	2006	2007	2008	ISIC 3
Total	26 786 856	28 763 121	23 766 809	26 585 919	30 255 911	23 866 367	29 664 999	20 324 378	27 166 752	16 683 942	Total
1	3 698 805	570 641	852 911	1 809 841	2 925 665	2 413 520	5 478 409	3 000 658	2 868 860	2 760 018	A
2	248 301	2 448	0	0	0	0	0	0	0	253 630	B
3	18 039 943	1 508 564	1 303 489	692 220	7 632 966	2 180 333	2 360 643	223 378	114 903	0	C
4	113 248	16 456 101	19 099 286	22 379 992	17 638 417	17 261 723	19 327 293	14 170 651	23 432 883	12 004 578	D
5	338	64 481	38 410	1 684	32 782	1 380	51 569	25 566	92 912	115 663	E
6	312 525	3 047	14 521	0	6 321	69 804	12 801	0			F
7	18 744	159 926	44 554	0	455	5 657	21 507	22 059	2 050	0	G
8	683 550	70 507	48 845	35 461	54 722	85 263	66 724	48 611	38 296	32 050	H
9	188 830	8 531 406	455 178	90 863	53 156	56 650	98 423	58 595	170 991	139 149	I
0	3 482 572	26 075	48 369	189 836	246 320	1 252 463	1 556 501	2 366 510	115 286	1 050 911	J
		42 645	69 198	13 056	31 320	9 960	16 534	360	27 758	860	K
		11 836	50 158	9 393	24 634	4 322	63 555	40 091	0	3 459	L
		0	0	0	0	0	0	0	0	4 992	M
		15 689	8 252	92 940	4 458	11 228	19 494	1 734	1 257	0	N
		1 298 624	1 733 638	1 270 633	1 604 695	514 064	591 546	358 107	291 186	308 228	O
		1 131	0	0	0	0	0	8 058	10 370	10 404	P

Explanatory notes: see p. 1361.

[1] Incl. stoppages involving fewer than 10 workers or lasting less than one day. [2] Excl. government sector. [3] Excl. work stoppages involving fewer than 10 workers. [4] Excl. political and sympathetic strikes.

Notes explicatives: voir p. 1363.

[1] Y compris les arrêts impliquant moins de 10 travailleurs ou de moins d'un jour. [2] Non compris le secteur gouvernemental. [3] Non compris les arrêts du travail impliquant moins de 10 travailleurs. [4] Non compris les grèves politiques et les grèves de solidarité.

Notas explicativas: véase p. 1365.

[1] Incl. las interrupciones con menos de 10 trabajadores o de menos de un día. [2] Excl. el sector gubernamental. [3] Excl. las interrupciones del trabajo que implican menos de 10 trabajadores. [4] Excl. huelgas políticas y huelgas de solidaridad.

STRIKES AND LOCKOUTS

Days not worked, by economic activity

GRÈVES ET LOCK-OUT

Journées non effectuées, par activité économique

HUELGAS Y CIERRES PATRONALES

Días no trabajados, por actividad económica

Israel (FG) [1]
ISIC 3 - CITI 3 - CIIU 3

	1999	2000	2001	2002	2003	2004	2005	2006	2007	2008
Total	1 640 890	2 011 263	2 039 973	1 488 120	2 725 159	1 224 423	244 236	136 189	2 548 627	87 151
A	0	0	0	245	162	0	0	0	0	0
B	0	0	0	0	0	0	0	0	0	0
C-D	40 636	20 888	21 030	8 068	256	5 484	49 714	3 050	7 237	5 880
E	124 800	0	0	0	0	0	0	0	0	0
F	0	40	8 400	280	9 600	0	0	90	0	0
G	500	0	11	24 550	0	0	3 575	0	0	0
H	0	450	220	0	6 500	0	0	360	585	0
I	11 212	48 082	9 149	63 655	41 100	24 222	18 537	407	14 460	1 441
J	2 000	202	600	0	12 859	28 689	68 600	9 500	6 500	80
K	0	0	300	0	0	0	0	0	0	0
L	1 344 206	192 730	1 601 097	1 261 962	2 637 340	1 071 003	70 442	119 845	319 500	6 700
M	110 074	804 550	280 150	94 220	120	53 125	24 200	2 000	2 199 200	72 550
N	32 625	929 320	119 000	34 500	13 550	41 800	9 060	915	900	500
O	14 199	15 000	16	640	3 672	100	108	22	50	0
P	0	0	0	0	0	0	0	0	0	0
Q	0	0	0	0	0	0	0	0	0	0
X	0	0	0	0	0	0	0	0	195	0

Japan (FG) [2]
ISIC 2 - CITI 2 - CIIU 2   ISIC 3 - CITI 3 - CIIU 3

	1999	2000	2001	2002	2003	2004	2005	2006	2007	2008	
Total	87 069	35 050	29 101	12 262	6 727	9 755	5 629	7 914	33 236	.	Total
1	0	0	0	0	.	0	0	0	0	.	A
2	0	0	0	0	.	0	0	0	0	.	B
3	9 820	12 779	7 202	2 172	.	0	0	10	0	.	C
4	0	0	0	90	.	3 175	868	667	713	.	D
5	28	414	59	20	.	0	0	15	0	.	E
6 [3]	1 492	342	723	13	.	0	0	0	50	.	F
7	68 724	15 951	14 810	6 519	.	15	136	54	82	.	G [4]
8 [5]	260	0	0	0	.	177	0	0	0	.	H
9 [6]	6 745	5 564	0	3 448	.	3 022	3 063	4 765	10 200	.	I
0	0	0	0	0	.	0	0	0	250	.	J
						10	0	0	0	.	K
						0	0	0	0	.	L
						44	8	23	367	.	M
						1 074	405	1 077	198	.	N
						2 238	1 149	1 303	21 376	.	O

Jordan (FG)
ISIC 3 - CITI 3 - CIIU 3

	1999	2000	2001	2002	2003	2004	2005	2006	2007	2008
Total	0	0	0	0	0	0	0	.	.	.

Korea, Republic of (FG)
ISIC 3 - CITI 3 - CIIU 3

	1999	2000	2001	2002	2003	2004	2005	2006	2007	2008
Total	1 366 281	1 893 563	1 083 079	1 580 424	1 298 663	1 198 779	847 697	1 200 567	536 285	809 402
A	0	0	279	.	.	.	.	.	.	.
B	0	0	0	.	.	.	.	.	.	.
C	0	726	0	.	.	.	.	.	.	.
D	897 173	1 046 493	744 040	.	.	.	.	.	.	.
E	0	1 932	6 640	.	.	.	.	.	.	.
F	27 743	21 946	19 994	.	.	.	.	.	.	.
G	1 320	6 150	7 634	.	.	.	.	.	.	.
H	8 574	85 824	4 413	.	.	.	.	.	.	.
I	125 270	107 792	94 347	.	.	.	.	.	.	.
J	0	472 200	136 661	.	.	.	.	.	.	.
K	244 028	55 979	15 245	.	.	.	.	.	.	.
L	0	0	0	.	.	.	.	.	.	.
M	16 548	5 822	27 604	.	.	.	.	.	.	.
N	7 253	40 074	12 354	.	.	.	.	.	.	.
O	38 372	48 625	13 868	.	.	.	.	.	.	.

Myanmar (F)
ISIC 3 - CITI 3 - CIIU 3

	1999	2000	2001	2002	2003	2004	2005	2006	2007	2008
Total	2 000	4 875	7 226	4 550	12 979	3 723	1 250	1 109	1 019	1 087
D	2 000	4 875	7 226	4 550	12 979	3 723	1 250	1 109	1 019	1 087

Explanatory notes: see p. 1361.

[1] Excl. work stoppages in which less than 10 workdays not worked. [2] Excl. work stoppages lasting less than half a day. [3] Excl. hotels. [4] Excl. repair of motor vehicles, motor cycles and personal and household goods. [5] Excl. business services. [6] Incl. business services and hotels.

Notes explicatives: voir p. 1363.

[1] Non compris les arrêts de travail de moins de 10 journées de travail non effectuées. [2] Non compris les arrêts du travail de durée inférieure à une demi-journée. [3] Non compris les hôtels. [4] Non compris réparation de véhicules automobiles, de motocycles et de biens personnels etdomestiques. [5] Non compris les services aux entreprises. [6] Y compris les services aux entreprises et les hôtels.

Notas explicativas: véase p. 1365.

[1] Excl. las interrupciones de trabajo de menos de 10 días de trabajo no trabajados. [2] Excl. las interrupciones del trabajo de duración inferior a medio día. [3] Excl. hoteles. [4] Excl. reparación de vehículos automotores, motocicletas, efectos personals y enseres domesticos. [5] Excl. servicios para las empresas. [6] Incl. servicios para empresas y hoteles.

STRIKES AND LOCKOUTS

Days not worked, by economic activity

GRÈVES ET LOCK-OUT

Journées non effectuées, par activité économique

HUELGAS Y CIERRES PATRONALES

Días no trabajados, por actividad económica

	1999	2000	2001	2002	2003	2004	2005	2006	2007	2008	
Philippines (H) [1]											
ISIC 2 - CITI 2 - CIIU 2											ISIC 3 - CITI 3 - CIIU 3
Total	229 248	319 233	206 493	358 152	150 465	53 434	123 329	43 519	12 112	38 711	Total
1	0	10 064	0	0	1 926	2 040	1 200	155	0	13 500	A
2	2 883	0	0	0	0	0	0	0	0	0	B
3	172 246	243 401	0	0	3 384	0	10 122	0	600	0	C
4	950 [2]	3 532	149 998	271 100	75 533	41 872	57 706	37 081	5 832	13 711	D
5	0	2 100	7 689	568	1 176	0	0	0	0	0	E
6 [3]	16 389	11 618	2 320	0	0	0	0	0	0	0	F
7	20 408	25 826	1 374	4 800	14 079	130	231	0	0	0	G
8	8 000	6 601	36 852	6 748	0	294	70	0	0	0	H
9 [4]	8 372	16 091	4 454	63 770	44 168	7 524	54 000	6 283	5 420	11 500	I
			0	0	151	0	0	0	0	0	J
			0	10 000	0	0	0	0	0	0	K
			0	0	0	0	0	0	0	0	L
			2 990	290	2 800	1 574	0	0	0	0	M
			0	0	192	0	0	0	260	0	N
			816	876	7 056	0	0	0	0	0	O
Singapore (FG)											
ISIC 3 - CITI 3 - CIIU 3											
Total	0	0	0	0	0	0	0	0	0	0	
Sri Lanka (FD) [5] [6]											
ISIC 2 - CITI 2 - CIIU 2											
Total	304 246	64 481	69 997	70 350	87 172	81 100	158 352	4 895 148	39 237	65 665	
1 [7]	41 195	23 540	32 548	40 038	45 421	40 779	8 370	4 821 394	5 489	41 525	
2	0	0	0	0	0	0	0	0	0		
3	263 051	40 941	37 449	30 312	41 751	40 321	149 982	73 754	33 748	24 130	
Thailand (H)											
ISIC 3 - CITI 3 - CIIU 3											
Total	142 913	225 788	6 067	23 902	24 051	472	45 857	24 000	11 601	.	
A	0	0	0	0	0	0	0	0	0	.	
B	0	0	0	0	0	0	0	0	0	.	
C	0	0	0	0	0	0	0	0	0	.	
D	142 913	225 788	6 067	23 902	24 051	472	29 659	24 000	11 601	.	
E	0	0	0	0	0	0	0	0	0	.	
F	0	0	0	0	0	0	0	0	0	.	
G-H	0	0	0	0	0	0	16 198	0	0	.	
I	0	0	0	0	0	0	0	0	0	.	
J-K	0	0	0	0	0	0	0	0	0	.	
L-O	0	0	0	0	0	0	0	0	0	.	

EUROPE-EUROPE-EUROPA

	1999	2000	2001	2002	2003	2004	2005	2006	2007	2008
Austria (FH) [8]										
ISIC 3 - CITI 3 - CIIU 3										
Total	0	2 947	0	9 306	1 305 466	178	0	0	0	0
Belarus (FH)										
ISIC 2 - CITI 2 - CIIU 2										
Total	0	0	0	0	0	0	.	.	.	.

Explanatory notes: see p. 1361.

[1] Excl. work stoppages lasting less than a full day or shift. [2] Concerns one strike continuing from previous year. [3] Excl. restaurants and hotels. [4] Incl. restaurants and hotels. [5] Incl. work stoppages lasting less than one day only if more than 50 workdays not worked. [6] Excl. work stoppages involving fewer than 5 workers. [7] Plantations. [8] Computed on the basis of an eight-hour working day.

Notes explicatives: voir p. 1363.

[1] Non compris les arrêts du travail dont la durée est inférieure à une journée ou à un poste de travail. [2] Concerne une grève continuant de l'année précédente. [3] Non compris les restaurants et les hôtels. [4] Y compris les restaurants et hôtels. [5] Y compris les arrêts du travail d'une durée inférieure à une journée si plus de 50 journées de travail non effectuées. [6] Non compris les arrêts du travail impliquant moins de 5 travailleurs. [7] Plantations. [8] Calculées sur la base de journées de travail de huit heures.

Notas explicativas: véase p. 1365.

[1] Excl. las interrupciones del trabajo de duración menor de un día o turno completo. [2] Concierne a una huelga que se continúa del año anterior. [3] Excl. restaurantes y hoteles. [4] Incl. restaurantes y hoteles. [5] Incl. las interrupciones del trabajo de menos de un día si no se han trabajado más de 50 días. [6] Excl. las interrupciones del trabajo que implican menos de 5 trabajadores. [7] Plantaciones. [8] Calculados en base a días de trabajo de ocho horas.

STRIKES AND LOCKOUTS

Days not worked, by economic activity

GRÈVES ET LOCK-OUT

Journées non effectuées, par activité économique

HUELGAS Y CIERRES PATRONALES

Días no trabajados, por actividad económica

	1999	2000	2001	2002	2003	2004	2005	2006	2007	2008
Belgique (H)										
ISIC 3 - CITI 3 - CIIU 3										
Total	76 310	264 919	460 177	60 954	239 344	166 287	669 982	.	.	.
A	0	83	104	6	18	1	175	.	.	.
B	1 632	0	0	0	0	0	0	.	.	.
C	0	668	6 948	4	728	544	2 762	.	.	.
D	37 645	69 229	89 368	31 747	130 459	64 700	334 862	.	.	.
E	188	370	11 079	761	16 296	446	4 629	.	.	.
F	262	7 438	18 647	363	1 049	1 298	28 089	.	.	.
G	3 146	8 982	16 137	5 244	9 911	1 887	38 755	.	.	.
H	219	479	380	295	150	88	3 916	.	.	.
I	12 591	63 747	30 390	7 953	45 124	44 497	112 403	.	.	.
J	14 037	5 288	11 867	2 129	1 680	1 050	12 333	.	.	.
K	902	2 202	5 882	6 300	21 201	2 580	22 498	.	.	.
L	17	1 277	3 648	22	2 066	883	14 211	.	.	.
M	197	95 601	252 462	416	368	858	18 429	.	.	.
N	4 883	8 414	12 610	5 346	9 310	39 980	69 842	.	.	.
O	416	1 097	619	367	814	7 467	7 044	.	.	.
P	0	0	0	0	0	0	2	.	.	.
Q	156	0	1	0	0	6	25	.	.	.
X	19	44	35	1	171	0	5	.	.	.

Cyprus (H)
ISIC 2 - CITI 2 - CIIU 2 — (2002 onward: ISIC 3 - CITI 3 - CIIU 3)

(ISIC 2)	1999	2000	2001	2002	2003	2004	2005	2006	2007	2008	(ISIC 3)
Total	26 037	1 136	4 778	7 051	6 901	9 053	13 967	26 898	.	.	Total
1	0	600	1 821	40	0	0	12	0	.	.	A
2	0	0	0	40	0	0	0	0	.	.	B
3	67	0	140	0	0	0	0	0	.	.	C
4	0	0	0	317	0	7 500	8 135	40	.	.	D
5	300	360	891	2 289	0	0	2 577	0	.	.	E
6	19 510	78	57	2 130	620	60	13	25 000	.	.	F
7	5 455	28	0	104	0	0	0	900	.	.	G
8	0	0	1 237	200	5 659	30	0	25	.	.	H
9	705	70	632	1 262	50	0	0	360	.	.	I
				575	0	500	3 230	0	.	.	J
				0	0	0	0	0	.	.	K
				0	0	0	0	573	.	.	L
				0	0	0	0	0	.	.	M
				0	0	0	0	0	.	.	N
				94	572	963	0	0	.	.	O

	1999	2000	2001	2002	2003	2004	2005	2006	2007	2008
Denmark (FH) [1] [2]										
ISIC 3 - CITI 3 - CIIU 3										
Total	91 800	124 800	59 700	193 600	55 100	76 400	51 300	85 800	91 700	.
A-C	0	100	100	0	0	0	0	0	0	.
D	58 400	70 300	40 400	70 100	30 400	54 000	23 800	11 000	39 900	.
E	600	100	500	200	200	0	0	0	0	.
F	2 900	3 600	3 400	5 000	5 000	3 400	3 000	2 700	4 200	.
G	2 200	6 400	2 300	5 500	1 000	1 900	800	1 700	6 500	.
H	300	200	200	2 800	100	500	300	600	0	.
I	6 300	17 600	6 200	8 600	3 900	8 600	6 000	5 700	19 000	.
J	0	0	0	0	0	0	0	0	0	.
K	0	0	0	0	0	0	0	0	0	.
L	0	0	0	0	0	0	0	0	0	.
M	0	0	0	0	0	0	0	0	0	.
N	0	0	0	0	0	0	0	0	0	.
O	0	0	0	0	0	0	0	0	0	.
X	21 200	26 300	6 600	101 400	14 500	8 000	17 200	64 200	22 100	.
España (FG) [3]										
ISIC 3 - CITI 3 - CIIU 3										
Total	1 504 589	3 616 907	1 923 758	4 945 091	792 101	4 472 576	951 495	927 712	1 187 654	1 510 219
A	1 232	8 555	10 510	12 060	44	3 217 720	18 700	675	2 471	16 965
B	0	83 305	5 372	0	3 150	0	19 645	0	0	10 241
C	117 509	25 912	30 177	13 456	8 632	14 752	26 123	5 915	2 685	4 548
D	173 564	581 974	889 673	226 309	452 873	457 610	309 647	363 267	290 719	376 961
E	6 051	272	1 887	4 707	1 041	24 135	1 686	2 140	8 004	565
F	191 604	1 446 934	569 130	16 524	5 491	317 957	1 571	158 685	320 703	1 794
G	12 968	515 094	5 251	2 189	3 045	111 749	1 310	30 675	8 932	21 770
H	2 674	2 106	3 131	5 867	8 197	2 334	10 423	1 672	1 087	3 615
I	221 732	401 462	99 383	196 869	135 109	66 891	248 537	82 604	111 085	425 410
J	1 461	16	123	50	418	76	863	995	1 728	0
K	9 864	42 699	36 975	13 893	22 802	97 855	9 699	33 760	81 688	231 245
L	10 006	405 180	10 280	7 861	6 889	17 094	32 858	47 221	82 529	199 335
M	70 489	41 809	61 491	75 567	1 771	86 645	90 163	68 557	60 077	90 687
N	74 503	11 266	62 689	90 298	29 581	26 371	167 421	123 541	78 371	87 824
O	12 162	14 253	12 102	19 560	15 637	27 879	12 849	7 947	17 017	38 325
P	310	0	4 182	0	0	0	0	0	0	0
X [4]	598 460	36 070	121 402	4 259 881	97 421	3 508	0	0	120 558	934

Explanatory notes: see p. 1361.

[1] Up to 1995: excl. work stoppages in which less than 100 work-days not worked. [2] Figures rounded to nearest 100. [3] Prior to 1990: strikes only; excl. the Basque country. [4] General strikes.

Notes explicatives: voir p. 1363.

[1] Jusqu'à 1995: non compris les arrêts du travail de moins de 100 journées de travail non effectuées. [2] Chiffres arrondis au 100 le plus proche. [3] Avant 1990: grèves seulement; non compris le Pays basque. [4] Grèves générales.

Notas explicativas: véase p. 1365.

[1] Hasta 1995: excl. las interrupciones del trabajo de menos de 100 días no trabajados. [2] Cifras redondeadas al 100 más próximo. [3] Antes de 1990: huelgas solamente; excl. el País Vasco. [4] Huelgas generales.

9C

STRIKES AND LOCKOUTS

Days not worked, by economic activity

GRÈVES ET LOCK-OUT

Journées non effectuées, par activité économique

HUELGAS Y CIERRES PATRONALES

Días no trabajados, por actividad económica

	1999	2000	2001	2002	2003	2004	2005	2006	2007	2008
Estonia (FG)										
ISIC 3 - CITI 3 - CIIU 3										
Total	0	0	0	.	10 993	.	0	.	.	.
Finland (FH)										
ISIC 3 - CITI 3 - CIIU 3										
Total	18 954	253 838	60 652	74 985	66 136	42 385	672 904	85 075	94 579	16 352
A	0	20 100	0	0	10 138	0	0	0	0	0
B	0	0	0	0	0	0	0	0	0	0
C	0	0	0	0	0	0	0	0	30	26
D	11 251	162 843	8 825	11 899	39 350	23 960	658 859	50 685	27 552	15 429
E	80	0	289	58	40	9	21	120	0	0
F	293	0	4	50 026	41	0	1 047	650	0	100
G	0	119	8	75	83	0	6	0	36 802	0
H	10	0	0	0	0	0	0	0	0	0
I	6 171	70 700	3 680	1 776	12 213	15 752	6 988	33 374	978	797
J	1 026	51	0	8 598	4 214	163	0	0	0	797
K	0	0	754	2 204	57	221	298	0	56	0
L	0	0	0	0	0	0	4 815	246	0	0
M-N	0	25	46 339	0	0	0	0	0	0	0
N									0	0
O	123	0	753	348	0	2 280	870	0	0	0
X	0	0	0	0	0	0	0	.	29 162	0
France (DA) [1]										
ISIC 3 - CITI 3 - CIIU 3										
Total	.	.	.	.	.	.	1 997 000	1 421 400	1 553 000	
D							642 300	381 400	339 100	
E							133 600	243 600	134 300	
F							19 200	12 900	13 900	
G							87 000	26 700	36 800	
H							26 600	10 100	6 500	
I							851 700	604 600	908 400	
J							103 400	39 800	22 400	
K							73 400	55 400	49 500	
M							8 500	5 000	300	
N							24 400	23 600	27 900	
O							26 900	18 300	13 900	
France (FG) [2]										
ISIC 3 - CITI 3 - CIIU 3										
L [3]	579 691	1 459 204	925 596	605 355	3 659 607	373 900	1 116 000	952 000	610 900	
Germany (FG) [4]										
ISIC 3 - CITI 3 - CIIU 3										
Total [5]	78 785	10 776	26 833	310 149	163 281	50 673	18 633	428 739	286 368	131 679
A	0	0	0	0	0	0	0	0	0	.
B	0	0	0	0	0	0	0	0	0	.
C	0	0	0	0	0	0	0	0	0	.
D	63 288	4 883	21 068	240 762	159 253	48 315	13 307	76 951	36 054	.
E	0	187	0	75	0	155	32	55	0	.
F	0	0	0	53 976	0	0	0	0	8 159	.
G	4 339	2 058	950	6 331	1 585	335	2 140	529	32 434	.
H	0	0	0	0	0	0	0	1 084	0	.
I	1 077	591	4 815	3 714	92	1 173	217	1 130	209 227	.
J	9 801	0	0	3 095	0	0	0	169	0	.
K	0	0	0	1 428	458	100	33	1 270	0	.
L [5]	69	0	0	224	36	58	1 585	139 508	0	.
M	47	141	0	474	20	0	564	15 280	0	.
N	164	0	0	70	0	514	684	151 843	0	.
O	0	2 916	0	0	1 837	23	71	23 390	0	.
P								17 530	0	.

Explanatory notes: see p. 1361.

[1] Localized strikes (the call to strike concerns only one establishment). [2] Localized and generalized strikes. [3] Public administration. [4] Incl. work stoppages lasting less than one day if more than 100 workdays not worked. [5] Excl. public administration.

Notes explicatives: voir p. 1363.

[1] Grèves localisées (le mot d'ordre de grève est interne à l'établissement). [2] Grèves localisées et généralisées. [3] Administration publique. [4] Y compris les arrêts du travail d'une durée inférieure à une journée si plus de 100 journées de travail non effectuées. [5] Non compris l'administration publique.

Notas explicativas: véase p. 1365.

[1] Huelgas localizadas (la contraseña de huelga afecta a un establecimiento). [2] Huelgas localizadas y generalizadas. [3] Administración pública. [4] Incl. las interrupciones del trabajo de menos de un día si no se han trabajado más de 100 días. [5] Excl. la administración pública.

STRIKES AND LOCKOUTS

Days not worked, by economic activity

GRÈVES ET LOCK-OUT

Journées non effectuées, par activité économique

HUELGAS Y CIERRES PATRONALES

Días no trabajados, por actividad económica

	1999	2000	2001	2002	2003	2004	2005	2006	2007	2008
Hungary (H) [1] [2]										
ISIC 3 - CITI 3 - CIIU 3										
Total	241 959	149 845	7 685	1 377	2 426	19 067	963	6 501	27 848	.
A	0	0	0	0	0	0	0	0	0	.
B	0	0	0	0	0	0	0	0	0	.
C	0	0	0	0	0	0	0	0	0	.
D	223	112	2 555	477	907	223	873	1 023	675	.
E	1 866	0	0	0	0	61	0	32	1 202	.
F	0	0	0	0	0	0	0	0	181	.
G	0	0	0	0	0	0	0	1 522	31	.
H	0	0	0	0	0	0	0	0	0	.
I	232 870	146 179	0	0	1 519	639	90	8	4 881	.
J	0	0	0	0	0	0	0	0	0	.
K	0	0	0	0	0	0	0	17	57	.
L	0	0	0	0	0	0	0	48	0	.
M	0	0	0	0	0	0	0	3 750	18 600	.
N	7 000	3 554	80	900	0	18 143	0	0	2 200	.
O	0	0	5 050	0	0	0	0	101	21	.
Iceland (H)										
ISIC 3 - CITI 3 - CIIU 3										
Total	0	47 093	207 663	0	0	140 448	.	.	.	.
Ireland (H) [3]										
ISIC 3 - CITI 3 - CIIU 3										
Total	215 587	97 046	114 613	21 257	37 482	20 784	26 665	7 352	6 038	4 179
A-B	1 144	0	0	0	0	0	552	0	0	0
C	0	3 120	0	0	0	416	240	0	0	0
D	8 823	13 458	14 512	8 989	3 479	2 393	935	1 114	2 700	2 051
E	616	0	0	0	0	0	2 143	0	0	0
F	22 182	1 015	3 160	12	33	0	881	4 769	0	175
G	714	798	6 531	886	161	1 335	90	0	186	14
H	900	64	0	368	0	0	0	0	0	0
I	2 201	27 908	15 724	2 958	1 899	12 340	21 653	57	2 315	644
J-K	.	.	.	.	143	2 280	0	280	0	0
L	80	2 375	0	973	12 412	1 030	123	663	837	12
M	1 268	45 863	74 286	348	540	0	0	0	0	0
N	177 571	2 445	400	5 465	15 778	0	0	469	0	329
O	.	.	.	1 093	0	0	0	0	0	0
O-Q	0	0	0	.	3 113	990	48	0	0	954
P	.	.	.	0	0	0	0	0	0	0
Q	.	.	.	165	0	0	0	0	0	0
Isle of Man (FG)										
ISIC 3 - CITI 3 - CIIU 3										
Total	480	0	0	0	0	0	0	0	0	.
A	0	0	0	0	0	0	0	0	0	.
B	0	0	0	0	0	0	0	0	0	.
C	0	0	0	0	0	0	0	0	0	.
D	0	0	0	0	0	0	0	0	0	.
E	0	0	0	0	0	0	0	0	0	.
F	480	0	0	0	0	0	0	0	0	.
G	0	0	0	0	0	0	0	0	0	.
H	0	0	0	0	0	0	0	0	0	.
I	0	0	0	0	0	0	0	0	0	.
J	0	0	0	0	0	0	0	0	0	.
K	0	0	0	0	0	0	0	0	0	.
L	0	0	0	0	0	0	0	0	0	.
M	0	0	0	0	0	0	0	0	0	.
N	0	0	0	0	0	0	0	0	0	.
O	0	0	0	0	0	0	0	0	0	.

Explanatory notes: see p. 1361.

[1] 1991-95: Work stoppages in which 800 hours or more not worked; beginning 1996: stoppages involving 10 workers or more. [2] Computed on the basis of an eight-hour working day. [3] Work stoppages lasting at least one day or with at least 10 days not worked.

Notes explicatives: voir p. 1363.

[1] 1991-95: Arrêts de travail avec 800 h. de travail non effectuées au moins; dès 1996: ceux impliquant 10 travailleurs ou plus. [2] Calculées sur la base de journées de travail de huit heures. [3] Arrêts de travail d'un jour au moins ou avec un minimum de 10 jours de travail non effectués.

Notas explicativas: véase p. 1365.

[1] 1991-95: Interrupciones del trabajo de 800 horas no trabajadas y más: desde 1996: las que implican 10 trabajadores o más. [2] Calculados en base a días de trabajo de ocho horas. [3] Interrupciones del trabajo de un día por lo menos o de un mínimo de 10 días no trabajados.

STRIKES AND LOCKOUTS

Days not worked, by economic activity

GRÈVES ET LOCK-OUT

Journées non effectuées, par activité économique

HUELGAS Y CIERRES PATRONALES

Días no trabajados, por actividad económica

	1999	2000	2001	2002	2003	2004	2005	2006	2007	2008
Italy (H) [1] [2]										
ISIC 3 - CITI 3 - CIIU 3										
Total	909 100	884 100	1 026 000	4 861 000	1 961 700	698 571	906 857	554 713	929 714	722 714
A-B	3 300	164 000	2 000	7 400	11 300	10 429	12 714	20 714	27 571	15 000
C	1 100	1 300	1 500	8 300	700	2 000	429	2 571	0	46
D	585 400	310 600	607 400	425 700	433 000	257 571	629 000	349 571	502 286	314 143
E	17 100	10 600	9 800	7 300	2 300	2 600	3 000	4 000	429	7 286
F	6 600	6 100	52 400	4 000	2 700	860	13 571	54 714	5 714	48 714
G	93 000	25 100	56 800	2 300	43 000	33 428	1 143	2 714	99 857	84 143
H					3 000	142	714	286	857	3 429
I	73 000	235 100	65 700	79 300	103 300	70 300	58 857	61 957	135 571	72 286
J	50 600	14 600	18 700	51 400	6 700	67 142	1 714	6 386	1 286	6 143
K,O	35 600	18 000	18 100	21 700	11 100	10 140	9 286	30 943	36 857	16 000
L	32 300	23 300	110 500	173 600	116 400	140 000	121 143	10 143	72 857	57 000
M	2 900	203 100	36 400	48 800	19 100	58 000	36 000	2 857	21 000	79 571
N	8 100	9 000	25 300	42 100	66 000	45 900	19 286	7 857	25 286	19 000
X	0	10 900	20 700	3 988 700	1 143 100	.	.	0	0	0
Latvia (D)										
ISIC 3 - CITI 3 - CIIU 3										
Total	26 692	0	6	3 055	0	0	0	0	0	3 254
D	8	0	6	0	0	0	0	0	0	0
I	0	0	0	0	0	0	0	0	0	0
L	1	0	0	0	0	0	0	0	0	0
M	26 283	0	0	0	0	0	0	0	0	0
N	0	0	0	3 055	0	0	0	0	0	3 254
O	400	0	0	0	0	0	0	0	0	0
Liechtenstein (H)										
ISIC 3 - CITI 3 - CIIU 3										
Total	0	0	0	0	0	0	0	0	.	.
Lithuania (D)										
ISIC 3 - CITI 3 - CIIU 3										
Total	.	10 394	971	0	0	0	834	0	9 559	31 601
D	.	0	.³	0	0	0	0	0	0	0
I	.	725	0	0	0	0	0	0	0	0
M	.	9 669	971	0	0	0	0	0	9 559	31 601
O	.	.	.	.	.	.	834	0	0	0
Malta (H)										
ISIC 3 - CITI 3 - CIIU 3										
Total	.	4 764	2 793	744	3 306	1 652	1 341	2 935	721	1 771
A	.	0	0	0	0	0	0	0	0	0
B	.	0	0	0	0	0	0	0	0	0
C	.	0	0	0	0	0	0	0	0	0
D	.	70	0	400	273	7	492	13	0	0
E	.	0	31	38	2 406	0	60	0	0	0
F	.	0	11	0	0	0	0	0	0	0
G	.	0	0	0	0	0	0	2	0	0
H	.	248	0	0	63	0	0	0	0	0
I	.	2 378	1 794	280	548	1 630	761	1 992	614	0
J	.	1 700	0	0	0	0	0	0	0	0
K	.	0	0	1	0	0	0	70	0	0
L	.	330	660	25	0	0	13	18	0	1 016
M	.	0	15	0	0	0	0	750	107	754
N	.	38	282	0	15	10	15	0	0	0
O	.	0	0	0	0	5	0	90	0	1

Explanatory notes: see p. 1361.

[1] Computed on the basis of a seven-hour working day. [2] Figures rounded to nearest 100. [3] Data included in totals only for reasons of confidentiality.

Notes explicatives: voir p. 1363.

[1] Calculées sur la base de journées de travail de sept heures. [2] Chiffres arrondis au 100 le plus proche. [3] Données incluses uniquement dans le total pour des raisons de confidentialité.

Notas explicativas: véase p. 1365.

[1] Calculados en base a días de trabajo de siete horas. [2] Cifras redondeadas al 100 más próximo. [3] Datos incluidos en el total solamente por razón de confidencialidad.

STRIKES AND LOCKOUTS

GRÈVES ET LOCK-OUT

HUELGAS Y CIERRES PATRONALES

Days not worked, by economic activity

Journées non effectuées, par activité économique

Días no trabajados, por actividad económica

	1999	2000	2001	2002	2003	2004	2005	2006	2007	2008
Netherlands (H)										
ISIC 3 - CITI 3 - CIIU 3										
Total	75 800	9 400	45 100	245 500	15 000	62 200	41 700	15 800	26 400	120 600
A	0	0	0	0	0	0	0	0	0	0
B	0	0	0	0	0	0	0	0	0	0
C	0	0	0	0	0	0	0	0	0	0
D	4 200	3 400	8 600 [1]	3 000	1 700	11 100	18 300 [2]	6 300	4 100	9 600 [1]
E	0	0		0	0	0	0	0	0	0
F	17 700	0	0	224 200	0	0	0	0	0	0
G	0	100 [3]		0	0	0	0	0	0	0
H	0		0	0	0	0	0	0	0	0
I	900 [4]	3 300	13 000 [5]	17 200 [4]	12 500 [6]	700	2 200 [5]	8 300 [6]	7 200	82 900
J	0	0	0	0	0	0	0	0	0	0
K			0			0	2 000	0	1 000	0
L	8 900	2 600 [7]	0	1 000 [8]	800 [9]	0	0	1 200 [10]	14 200	28 100
M	44 100			0	0	0	0	0	0	0
N		0	23 500 [7]		0	0	0	0	0	0
O	0			0					0	0
X						50 400 [11]	19 200 [11]	0	0	0
Norway (FH) [12]										
ISIC 3 - CITI 3 - CIIU 3										
Total	7 148	496 568	619	150 775	962	141 179	10 998	146 758	3 954	62 568
A	0	0	0	0	0	0	0	0	0	0
B	0	0	0	0	0	0	0	0	0	0
C	3 040	12 760	0	11 282	546	41 979	2 919	2 958	0	0
D	673	285 983	100	43 995	30	39 973	0	0	0	4 259
E	0	0	0	0	0	0	0	25 669	0	0
F	0	92 875	0	4 354	0	24 412	8 079	30 000	0	0
G	762	9 937	0	178	200	63	0	4	0	12
H	46	11 608	519	69 645	0	81	0	0	0	0
I	1 744	13 335	0	932	0	33 188	0	19 436	0	2 502
J	0	0	0	0	0	0	0	36 000	0	0
K	709	13 156	0	0	0	0	0	0	56	586
L	0	0	0	0	0	0	0	2 002	0	0
M	174	323	0	0	186	1 483	0	0	180	46 846
N	0	55 973	0	19 789	0	0	0	0	3 704	8 363
O	0	618	0	600	0	0	0	30 689	14	0
Poland (FG)										
ISIC 3 - CITI 3 - CIIU 3										
Total	106 893	74 266	4 201	118	6 551	358	413	31 418	186 213	275 819
A	0	0	0	0	0	0	0	0	0	0
B	0	0	0	0	0	0	0	0	0	0
C		0	0	0	0	0	0	5 171	0	13 387
D	70 026	10 421	111	118	6 469	0	196	13 963	25 343	562
E	719	62	61	0	0	0	0	0	0	21
F	0	0	0	0	0	0	0	0	0	275
G	9	0	0	0	0	0	0	0	0	0
H	0	0	0	0	0	0	0	0	0	9
I	3 417	6 417	0	0	6	358	209	0	11 821	48 615
J	0	0	0	0	0	0	0	0	0	0
K	892	0	0	0	76	0	0	0	10	123
L	0	0	0	0	0	0	0	0	0	0
M	31 685	0	0	0	0	0	0	0	11 396	209 930
N	81	57 366	4 029	0	0	0	8	12 284	137 643	2 769
O	64	0	0	0	0	0	0	0	0	128
Portugal (FG) [13]										
ISIC 3 - CITI 3 - CIIU 3										
Total [14]	67 500	40 545	41 570	108 062	53 370	46 096	27 333	44 732	29 851	.
A	.	0	0	0	0	0	0	0	0	.
B	19 000	724	0	7 050	57	0	0	0	0	.
C	200	3 551	66	719	46	0	235	4	615	.
D	27 200	12 564	21 406	53 908	23 857	16 097	15 018	18 830	11 392	.
E	800	474	24	3 018	384	115	63	69	582	.
F	200	0	42	194	19	95	59	12	350	.
G	3 800	396	382	1 855	124	291	45	157	925	.
H	600	120	304	2 198	120	561	440	621	1 352	.
I	14 000	17 861	13 769	31 999	26 586	13 908	3 854	19 900	10 097	.
J	. [15]	0	0	0	0	13 356	0	2 771	1 291	.
K	1 200	3 692	3 437	3 782	972	743	4 078	1 937	1 595	.
M [14]	0	0	121	221	1	0	70	116	112	.
N	.	198	1 526	2 538	1 072	0	1 185	0	18	.
O	400	965	493	580	132	930	2 286	315	1 522	.

Explanatory notes: see p. 1361.

[1] Incl. category E. [2] Incl. category F. [3] Incl. categories H and K. [4] Incl. category K. [5] Including category G. [6] Incl. categories G and K. [7] Incl. categories M and O. [8] Incl. category N. [9] Incl. category O. [10] Incl. categories N and O. [11] Incl. categories A and O. [12] Excl. work stoppages lasting less than one day. [13] Strikes only. [14] Excl. public administration. [15] Data included in those for the other activities involved.

Notes explicatives: voir p. 1363.

[1] Y compris la catégorie E. [2] Y compris catégorie F. [3] Y compris les catégories H et K. [4] Y compris la catégorie K. [5] Y compris la catégorie G. [6] Y compris les catégories G et K. [7] Y compris les catégories M et O. [8] Y compris la catégorie N. [9] Y compris la catégorie O. [10] Y compris les catégories N et O. [11] Y compris les catégories A et O. [12] Non compris les arrêts du travail dont la durée est inférieure à une journée. [13] Grèves seulement. [14] Non compris l'administration publique. [15] Données comprises dans celles des autres activités impliqués.

Notas explicativas: véase p. 1365.

[1] Incl. la categoría E. [2] Incl. categoría F. [3] Incl. las categorías H y K. [4] Incl. la categoría K. [5] Incl. la categoría G. [6] Incl. las categorías G y K. [7] Incl. las categorías M y O. [8] Incl. la categoría N. [9] Incl. la categoría O. [10] Incl. las categorías N y O. [11] Incl. las categorías A y O. [12] Excl. las interrupciones del trabajo de menos de un día de duración. [13] Huelgas solamente. [14] Excl. la administración pública. [15] Datos comprendidos en los de las otras actividades implicadas.

9C	**STRIKES AND LOCKOUTS** Days not worked, by economic activity	**GRÈVES ET LOCK-OUT** Journées non effectuées, par activité économique	**HUELGAS Y CIERRES PATRONALES** Días no trabajados, por actividad económica

	1999	2000	2001	2002	2003	2004	2005	2006	2007	2008
Roumanie (FG) [1]										
ISIC 3 - CITI 3 - CIIU 3										
Total	1 402 998	565 422	1 114	34 223	11 786	21 403	12 506	24 390	494 034	138 453
A	15 752	0	0	0	0	7 023	0	0	10 000	0
B	0	0	0	0	0	0	0	0	0	0
C	236 604	85	0	15 234	0	1 904	0	0	0	134 188
D	120 910	12 375	1 043	12 692	10 033	10 621	12 316	24 390	348 234	166
E	1 492	0	0	0	1 180	0	0	0	2 000	0
F	224	0	0	0	0	280	0	0	0	0
G	0	0	0	0	0	0	0	0	0	0
H	0	0	0	0	0	0	0	0	0	4 100
I	235 042	0	71	6 000	573	1 575	189	0	133 800	0
J	0	0	0	0	0	0	0	0	0	0
K	0	0	0	0	0	0	0	0	0	0
L	0	0	0	0	0	0	0	0	0	0
M	782 522	485 000	0	0	0	0	0	0	0	0
N	10 452	67 862	0	298	0	0	0	0	0	0
O	0	100	0	0	0	0	0	0	0	0
X	0	0	0	0	0	0	0	0	0	0
Russian Federation (FG) [2]										
ISIC 3 - CITI 3 - CIIU 3										
Total	1 827 200	236 400	47 100	29 100	29 453	210 852	85 929	1 416	20 457	29 081
A	.	.	.	.	.	.	148	0	0	342
C-E	268 700	9 100	2 300	.	.	.	0	0	0	0
D	.	.	.	.	.	.	.	.	15 963	0
E	.	.	.	.	.	.	832	429	0	0
F	68 900	.	.	.	.	.	160	0	0	6 604
I	5 600	5 800	.	.	.	.	24	410	4 494	0
K	.	.	.	.	.	.	.	294	0	0
M	1 360 400	186 000	36 900	.	.	.	80 379	0	0	0
N	34 600	9 000	.	.	.	.	2 772	0	0	0
O	.	26 000	8 000	.	.	.	1 614	283	0	0
X	88 900	400	-	.	.	.	.	0	0	0
San Marino (H) [3]										
ISIC 2 - CITI 2 - CIIU 2										
Total	1 250	1 250	20 045	454 520	7 343	3 500	24 000	.	.	.
3 [4]	.	13	0	300 000	1 230	3 500	24 000	.	.	.
4	.	0	0	0	0	0	0	.	.	.
5	.	0	0	0	0	0	0	.	.	.
6	.	0	0	0	0	0	0	.	.	.
7	.	0	0	0	0	0	0	.	.	.
8	.	0	0	0	0	0	0	.	.	.
9	.	1 237	45	32 520	113	0	0	.	.	.
0	.	.	20 000 [5]	122 000 [5]	6 000	0	0	.	.	.
Slovakia (FG)										
ISIC 3 - CITI 3 - CIIU 3										
Total	0	0	0	0	4	0	0	14	6	2
Suisse (H) [2]										
ISIC 3 - CITI 3 - CIIU 3										
Total	2 675	4 757	20 098	21 447	6 141	38 915	1 392	7 870	7 083	13 844
A	0	0	0	0	0	0	0	0	0	0
B	0	0	0	0	0	0	0	0	0	0
C	0	0	0	0	0	0	0	0	0	0
D	75	48	0	0	617	4 978	682	7 150	0	226
E	0	0	0	0	0	0	0	0	0	0
F	400	0	0	20 797	200	5 524	0	0	7 083	1 390
G	0	0	45	0	0	0	0	0	0	0
H	0	0	0	0	0	0	0	0	0	0
I	0	120	0	300	847	0	710	240	0	352
J	980	0	0	0	0	0	0	0	0	0
K	0	0	0	0	939	0	0	0	0	0
L	1 220	962	0	0	263	28 413	0	0	0	4 484
M	0	0	53	350	3 275	0	0	0	0	0
N	0	2 625	20 000	0	0	0	0	0	0	0
O	0	1 002	0	0	0	0	0	480	0	0
X	0	0	0	0	0	0	0	0	0	0

Explanatory notes: see p. 1361.

[1] Strikes only. [2] Excl. work stoppages lasting less than one day. [3] Computed on the basis of an eight-hour working day. [4] Incl. generalized strikes. [5] Generalized strikes.

Notes explicatives: voir p. 1363.

[1] Grèves seulement. [2] Non compris les arrêts du travail dont la durée est inférieure à une journée. [3] Calculées sur la base de journées de travail de huit heures. [4] Y compris les grèves généralisées. [5] Grèves généralisées.

Notas explicativas: véase p. 1365.

[1] Huelgas solamente. [2] Excl. las interrupciones del trabajo de menos de un día de duración. [3] Calculados en base a días de trabajo de ocho horas. [4] Incl. las huelgas generalizadas. [5] Huelgas generalizadas.

STRIKES AND LOCKOUTS — GRÈVES ET LOCK-OUT — HUELGAS Y CIERRES PATRONALES   9C

Days not worked, by economic activity
Journées non effectuées, par activité économique
Días no trabajados, por actividad económica

Sweden (H) [1]
ISIC 3 - CITI 3 - CIIU 3

	1999	2000	2001	2002	2003	2004	2005	2006	2007	2008
Total	78 735	272	11 098	838	627 541	15 282	568	1 971	13 666	106 801
A	0	0	0	0	0	0	0	0	0	0
B	0	0	0	0	0	0	0	0	0	0
C	723	0	0	0	0	0	0	0	0	0
D	36	0	211	248	0	390	25	39	1 920	41
E	0	0	175	248	0	0	139	0	0	0
F	808	260	8 194	230	22 555	14 434	100	0	4 138	0
G	0	0	0	0	0	0	0	0	0	0
H	0	0	0	6	0	0	0	0	0	0
I	76 788	12	2 476	35	2 294	444	200	750	7 201	11 760
J	215	0	0	0	0	0	0	0	0	0
K	0	0	0	0	0	0	48	0	306	0
L	125	0	0	45	0	0	0	0	0	0
M	40	0	0	11	8	0	20	4	15	0
N	0	0	8	0	0	0	0	175	85	95 000
O	0	0	34	15	602 684	14	36	3	1	0
X	.	.	.	.	.	.	.	1 000	.	0

Turkey (FG) [2]
ISIC 3 - CITI 3 - CIIU 3

	1999	2000	2001	2002	2003	2004	2005	2006	2007	2008
Total	229 825	368 475	286 015	43 885	144 772	93 161	176 824	165 666	1 353 558	145 725
A	0	0	0	0	0	0	0	0	0	0
B	0	0	0	0	0	0	0	0	0	0
C	14 022	14 706	15 399	0	108 936	0	0	0	0	0
D	203 789	214 933	251 999	24 852	30 710	86 316	156 173	158 319	196 680	145 115
E	0	0	0	0	184	0	0	0	0	0
F	0	0	0	0	0	0	0	0	0	0
G	0	0	0	0	0	0	0	0	0	0
H	0	1 062	0	0	0	0	14 897	180	760	0
I	10 097	4 784	0	3 583	4 942	4 864	5 754	4 953	1 152 632	0
J	0	0	0	0	0	0	0	0	0	0
K	0	0	0	0	0	0	0	0	0	0
L	0	0	0	0	0	0	0	0	0	0
M	0	0	0	0	0	0	0	0	0	0
N	0	0	0	0	0	0	0	0	0	0
O	1 917	132 990	18 617	15 450	0	1 981	0	2 214	3 486	610

Ukraine (FG)
ISIC 2 - CITI 2 - CIIU 2

	1999	2000	2001
Total	443 125	280 500	36 875
2	352 403	270 175	27 600
3 [3]	21 175	1 061	3 963
5	8 871	3 705	3 250
7	2 706	.	.
9 [4]	58 018	5 558	2 000

ISIC 3 - CITI 3 - CIIU 3

	2002	2003	2004	2005	2006	2007	2008
Total	128 300	420 500	66 400	25 940	39 800	31 953	164 456
A	0	0	0	0	0	0	0
B	0	0	0	0	0	0	0
C	65 300	61 800	13 000	23 900	9 600	8 000	0
D	800	343 300	0	0	12 300	9 481	0
E	0	4 000	100	1 000	1 600	11 480	0
F	400	4 600	0	0	700	0	164 456
G	0	0	0	0	0	0	0
H	0	0	0	0	5 600	0	0
I	200	6 800	53 300	0	10 000	2 776	0
J	0	0	0	0	0	0	0
K	0	0	0	0	5 600	0	0
L	0	0	0	0	0	0	0
M	60 300	0	0	0	0	0	0
N	1 000	0	0	0	0	0	0
O	300	0	0	1 000	0	216	0

United Kingdom (H) [5][6][7]
ISIC 3 - CITI 3 - CIIU 3

	1999	2000	2001	2002	2003	2004	2005	2006	2007	2008
Total	241 800	498 800	525 100	1 323 300	499 100	≈ 904 900	223 801	754 500	1 041 100	758 861
A-B	0	0	0	0	0	0	0	0	0	100
C	0	2 300	15 100	0		4 900	1	10 500		700
D	57 300	52 300	42 800	20 900	63 300	30 500	82 800	17 900	15 600	6 800
E	0	1 000	10 200	200	400	300	5 500	1 400	0	0
F	49 300	49 400	9 800	16 800	13 900	100	1 700	15 100	2 300	2 700
G	0	100	500	800	700	900	0	600	0	700
H	9 800	39 900	3 600	61 000	.	0	21 100	0	0	0
I	50 100	97 100	107 000	95 800	125 500	43 900	32 500	40 500	657 500	24 800
J	0	0	200	0	0	-	3 000	0	0	0
K	2 300	100	200	8 400	500	600	5 200	3 900	2 200	700
L	35 500	49 800	215 900	488 300	138 400	436 700	22 600	626 000	324 700	614 300
M	25 400	49 500	42 900	376 200	131 300	379 400	43 100	31 400	30 500	103 400
N	4 800	121 600	72 600	148 200	15 400	3 800	300	4 800	4 700	1 700
O	7 300	35 800	4 300	106 600	9 700	3 900	6 000	1 700	3 500	2 900

Explanatory notes: see p. 1361.

[1] Work stoppages in which at least 8 hours not worked. [2] Strikes only. [3] Incl. electricity, gas and water. [4] All activities not shown elsewhere. [5] Incl. stoppages involving fewer than 10 workers or lasting less than one day if 100 or more workdays not worked. [6] Excl. political strikes. [7] Figures rounded to nearest 100. [8] Excl. work stoppages in which less than 10 workdays not worked.

Notes explicatives: voir p. 1363.

[1] Arrêts de travail avec un minimum de 8 heures de travail non effectuées. [2] Grèves seulement. [3] Y compris l'électricité, le gaz et l'eau. [4] Toutes les activités non indiquées ailleurs. [5] Y compris les arrêts impliquant moins de 10 travailleurs ou de moins d'un jour si plus de 100 journées de travail non effectuées. [6] Non compris les grèves politiques. [7] Chiffres arrondis au 100 le plus proche. [8] Non compris les arrêts de travail de moins de 10 journées de travail non effectuées.

Notas explicativas: véase p. 1365.

[1] Interrupciones del trabajo de un mínimo de 8 horas no trabajadas. [2] Huelgas solamente. [3] Incl. electricidad, gas y agua. [4] Todas las actividades no indicadas en otra parte. [5] Incl. las interrupciones con menos de 10 trabajadores o de menos de un día si hubo más de 100 días de trabajo no trabajados. [6] Excl. las huelgas políticas. [7] Cifras redondeadas al 100 más próximo. [8] Excl. las interrupciones de trabajo de menos de 10 días de trabajo no trabajados.

STRIKES AND LOCKOUTS / GRÈVES ET LOCK-OUT / HUELGAS Y CIERRES PATRONALES

Days not worked, by economic activity

Journées non effectuées, par activité économique

Días no trabajados, por actividad económica

	1999	2000	2001	2002	2003	2004	2005	2006	2007	2008

OCEANIA-OCÉANIE-OCEANIA

Australia (H) [1][2]
ISIC 3 - CITI 3 - CIIU 3

	1999	2000	2001	2002	2003	2004	2005	2006	2007	2008
Total	650 600	469 100	393 100	259 000	439 400	379 800	228 300	132 600	49 700	196 500
A-B	1 000	0	200	1 600	.	0	0	0	300	0
C	28 000	41 200	21 100	8 100	28 800	14 800	14 726	4 300	3 500	2 100
D	184 500	146 200	195 400	87 800	116 900	47 900	54 910	46 000	15 000	15 300
E	7 700	6 000	8 800	6 800	1 000	1 700	2 905	600	300	16 000
F	165 100	108 800	120 600	101 700	123 300	120 100	89 363	15 200	6 800	13 900
G-H	3 300	5 700	3 800	8 100	6 000	2 100	447	300	700	0
I	20 300	26 200	13 800	18 300	19 300	20 400	11 110	9 000	1 900	8 500
J-K	5 900	16 400	6 100	3 500	6 800	31 800	1 533	1 900	300	0
L	2 700	3 800	6 100	11 300	5 300	9 500	3 938	300	200	3 100
M	221 200	109 000	6 300	200	125 700	129 800	46 015	49 500	17 100	135 900
N [3]	2 900	1 100	5 200	4 700	3 500	900	1 398	300	3 300	1 600
O	7 700	4 700	5 700	7 000	2 700	700	1 888	5 000	300	0

New Zealand (FG) [4][5][6]
ISIC 3 - CITI 3 - CIIU 3

	1999	2000	2001	2002	2003	2004	2005	2006	2007	2008
Total	16 674	11 495	54 440	34 398	19 390	6 162	30 029	27 983	11 439	.
A	0	0	0	. [7]	0	. [7]	0	0	0	.
B	0	0	. [7]	0	0	0	0	0	0	.
C	0	0	0	0	. [7]	. [7]	. [7]	0	. [7]	.
D	2 396	8 962	22 416	5 036	17 806	2 044	4 480	3 056	965	.
E	0	0	0	0	0	0	0	. [7]	0	.
F	. [7]	. [7]	161	0	. [7]	. [7]	. [7]	9	. [7]	.
G	. [7]	. [7]	. [7]	0	0	0	. [7]	. [7]	. [7]	.
H	0	0	. [7]	0	. [7]	. [7]	. [7]	. [7]	. [7]	.
I	7 733	. [7]	876	108	. [7]	1 692	7 624	197	1 270	.
J	. [7]	0	0	. [7]	0	. [7]	. [7]	0	0	.
K	. [7]	0	435	. [7]	. [7]	0	. [7]		. [7]	.
L	0	184	6 546	220	. [7]	70	1 881	1 042	. [7]	.
M	910	. [7]	19 664	25 490	. [7]	551	5 256	. [7]	. [7]	.
N	3 761	1 750	3 696	1 939	367	1 116	2 145	11 873	4 067	.
O	. [7]	0	. [7]	. [7]	. [7]	. [7]	0	478	470	. [7]

Explanatory notes: see p. 1361.

[1] Excl. work stoppages in which less than 10 workdays not worked. [2] Figures rounded to nearest 100. [3] Incl. community services. [4] Excl. work stoppages in which less than 10 workdays not worked (from 2000, 5 workdays). [5] Computed on the basis of an eight-hour working day. [6] Prior to 1988: excl. public sector stoppages. [7] Data included in totals only for reasons of confidentiality.

Notes explicatives: voir p. 1363.

[1] Non compris les arrêts de travail de moins de 10 journées de travail non effectuées. [2] Chiffres arrondis au 100 le plus proche. [3] Y compris les services à la collectivité. [4] Non compris les arrêts de travail de moins de 10 journées de travail non effectuées (à partir de 2000, 5 journées de travail). [5] Calculées sur la base de journées de travail de huit heures. [6] Avant 1988: non compris les arrêts du travail du secteur public. [7] Données incluses uniquement dans le total pour des raisons de confidentialité.

Notas explicativas: véase p. 1365.

[1] Excl. las interrupciones de trabajo de menos de 10 días de trabajo no trabajados. [2] Cifras redondeadas al 100 más próximo. [3] Incl. servicios comunales. [4] Excl. las interrupciones de trabajo de menos de 10 días de trabajo no trabajados (desde 2000, 5 días de trabajo). [5] Calculados en base a días de trabajo de ocho horas. [6] Antes de 1988: excl. las interrupciones del sector público. [7] Datos incluidos en el total solamente por razón de confidencialidad.

STRIKES AND LOCKOUTS / GRÈVES ET LOCK-OUT / HUELGAS Y CIERRES PATRONALES

Rates of days not worked, by economic activity — Per thousand workers
Taux de journées non effectuées, par activité économique — Pour mille travailleurs
Tasas de días no trabajados, por actividad económica — Por mil trabajadores

	1999	2000	2001	2002	2003	2004	2005	2006	2007	2008
AFRICA-AFRIQUE-AFRICA										
Mauritius (FG) (1) [1] ISIC 3 - CITI 3 - CIIU 3										
Total	9.3	15.3	22.3	25.3	25.9	0.4	35.5	.	.	.
D	21.0	32.7	51.3	65.3	54.6	1.0	111.3	.	.	.
F	12.0	0.0	15.9	0.0	66.3	0.4	0.0	.	.	.
G	0.0	6.3	2.4	0.9	0.4	0.2	0.0	.	.	.
H	0.1	0.0	0.0	0.8	0.0	0.0	0.0	.	.	.
I	0.0	0.7	1.4	.	45.6	.	.	.	.	.
South Africa (FG) (1) ISIC 3 - CITI 3 - CIIU 3										
Total	253	142	84	54	80	107	221	334	753	36
A	85	6	8	3	15	47	87	33	29	12
C	560	920	578	239	365	926	2 189	291	1 180	263
D	151	142	459	47	82	123	185	174	395	38
E	11	23	98	0	169	2	3	188	4	0
F	200	41	13	7	80	0	13	1	52	14
G	45	65	0	10	69	2	126	425	6	5
I	823	359	556	14	55	121	930	297	45	139
J	0	0	0	0	0	32	9	1 091	8	8
O	700	789	84	386	5	204	171	473	3 533	70
AMERICA-AMÉRIQUE-AMERICA										
Argentina (F) (1) ISIC 3 - CITI 3 - CIIU 3										
Total [2]	1 047	2 083	.	.	.	.	.	563	747	767
A								.	.	.
B								0	0	0
C								0	0	0
D								101	136	310
E								0	0	0
F								15	16	53
G								27	17	56
H								0	32	13
I								191	390	181
J								296	0	0
K								20	0	0
L								903	1 365	1 383
M								3 318	3 836	4 057
N								1 500	2 237	2 156
O								75	85	15
Canada (FG) (1) [3] ISIC 3 - CITI 3 - CIIU 3										
Total	203.8	132.7	173.8	229.8	130.4	236.0	303.7	56.7	124.2	60.4
A	627.5	190.7	138.1	145.4	204.9	1.1	45.1	157.8	0.0	0.0
B	0.0	0.0	0.0	0.0	0.0	0.0	0.0	0.0	0.0	0.0
C	1 053.0	1 118.6	704.0	470.1	1 285.4	608.0	320.8	206.7	195.5	213.4
D	218.0	230.5	262.3	253.2	277.8	249.2	211.9	168.3	335.7	150.9
E	1 565.8	0.6	140.0	22.5	6.1	148.0	482.9	0.0	22.6	33.4
F	12.9	32.9	124.7	19.0	0.0	142.6	16.2	3.5	284.8	2.2
G	38.5	42.4	38.9	57.8	106.8	95.4	96.0	17.3	7.7	30.0
H	42.8	53.3	26.9	5.1	24.6	26.7	44.3	14.8	9.0	38.4
I	603.8	99.0	426.5	537.4	289.1	692.5	1 838.7	38.7	177.6	126.2
J	38.5	43.7	35.4	0.0	7.9	6.5	3.4	17.5	15.7	18.2
K	37.6	33.1	28.1	51.3	17.7	11.0	4.8	0.5	1.7	0.7
L	369.9	400.3	401.9	2 171.6	31.0	1 756.6	1 049.2	53.3	474.6	31.1
M	197.2	231.2	400.2	311.8	232.8	54.8	866.1	130.2	110.2	94.5
N	253.3	66.2	158.4	59.8	34.9	204.5	77.4	10.1	30.8	6.4
O	216.1	141.4	83.9	96.1	27.1	254.9	52.1	97.0	242.8	167.0
X	0.0	0.0	0.0	0.0	0.0	0.0	0.0	0.0	0.0	0.0
United States (H) (3) [4][5] ISIC 3 - CITI 3 - CIIU 3										
Total	0.0	0.1	.	.	0.0	.	.	.	.	.
ASIA-ASIE-ASIA										
Hong Kong, China (FG) (1) ISIC 3 - CITI 3 - CIIU 3										
Total [6]	0.1	0.3	0.3	0.0	0.1	0.1	0.0	0.0	2.6	0.5

Explanatory notes: see p. 1361.

[1] Per 1,000 employees in establishments with 10 or more workers. [2] Excl. agriculture. [3] Strikes lasting at least half a day with more than 10 days lost. [4] Time not worked as percentage of available work time. [5] Excl. work stoppages involving fewer than 1,000 workers and lasting less than a full day or shift. [6] Excl. government sector.

Notes explicatives: voir p. 1363.

[1] Pour 1 000 salariés dans les établissements de 10 travailleurs et plus. [2] Non compris l'agriculture. [3] Grèves d'une durée d'une demi-journée au moins et dans lesquelles 10 jours de travail sont perdus. [4] Temps non effectué comme pourcentage du temps de travail disponible. [5] Non compris arrêts de travail impliquant moins de 1000 travailleurs; durée inférieure à 1 jour ou à 1 poste de travail. [6] Non compris le secteur gouvernemental.

Notas explicativas: véase p. 1365.

[1] Por 1 000 asalariados en los establecimientos con 10 y más trabajadores. [2] Excl. agricultura. [3] Huelgas con duración de media jornada laboral por lo menos y con más de 10 días perdidos. [4] Tiempo no trabajado como porcentaje del tiempo de trabajo disponible. [5] Excl. las interrupciones del trabajo que implican menos de 1000 trabajadores y que duran menos de 1 día o turno completo. [6] Excl. el sector gubernamental.

STRIKES AND LOCKOUTS
Rates of days not worked, by economic activity
Per thousand workers

GRÈVES ET LOCK-OUT
Taux de journées non effectuées, par activité économique
Pour mille travailleurs

HUELGAS Y CIERRES PATRONALES
Tasas de días no trabajados, por actividad económica
Por mil trabajadores

	1999	2000	2001	2002	2003	2004	2005	2006	2007	2008
Israel (FG) (1) [1] [2]										
ISIC 3 - CITI 3 - CIIU 3										
Total	710.5	841.8	842.2	612.4	1 124.0	497.1	95.5	50.9	907.3	.
A-B	0.0	0.0	0.0	3.4	.	.	.	.	.	.
C-D	117.1	59.2	0.0	0.0	.	.	.	.	.	.
E	6 933.3	0.0	0.0	0.0	.	.	.	.	.	.
F	0.0	0.3	144.1	56.4	91.6	0.0	0.0	0.8	.	.
G	1.8	0.0	0.0	0.0	0.0	0.0	.	.	.	.
H	0.0	4.2	80.5	2.8	.	.	.	.	.	.
I	95.7	379.2	0.1	186.0	.	.	.	.	.	.
J	28.0	2.8	3.0	0.0	.	.	.	.	.	.
K	0.0	0.0	21.4	152.6	.	.	.	.	.	.
L	1 491.7	1 491.7	5.9	0.0	.	.	.	.	.	.
M	380.4	2 721.8	0.9	0.0	.	.	.	.	.	.
N	141.6	3 832.3	6 193.8	4 631.1	.	.	.	.	.	.
O	129.8	132.7	2 292.6	746.0	.	.	.	.	.	.
X	0.0	0.0	0.0	0.0	0.0	0.0	0.0	0.0	.	.
Korea, Republic of (FG) (1)										
ISIC 3 - CITI 3 - CIIU 3										
Total	109.1	141.7	79.3	111.4	90.2	80.5	55.8	77.2	33.6	49.9
Myanmar (F) (1)										
ISIC 3 - CITI 3 - CIIU 3										
Total	.	.	.	.	.	6.0	2.0	1.7	1.6	1.5
Singapore (FG) (1)										
ISIC 2 - CITI 2 - CIIU 2										
Total	0	0	0	0	0	0	0	0	.	.
Thailand (H) (1)										
ISIC 3 - CITI 3 - CIIU 3										
Total	18	32	1	3	3	0	5	3	1	.

EUROPE-EUROPE-EUROPA

	1999	2000	2001	2002	2003	2004	2005	2006	2007	2008
Austria (FH) (1)										
ISIC 3 - CITI 3 - CIIU 3										
Total	0.0	0.9	0.0	3.0	4.1	0.0	0.0	0.0	0.0	0.0
Cyprus (H) (1)										
ISIC 3 - CITI 3 - CIIU 3										
Total	.	.	.	20.1	29.0	37.2	66.2	110.3	.	.
A	.	.	.	7.5	0.0	0.0	2.3	0.0	.	.
B	.	.	.	200.0	0.0	0.0	0.0	0.0	.	.
C	.	.	.	0.0	0.0	0.0	0.0	0.0	.	.
D	.	.	.	11.4	0.0	274.7	272.9	1.3	.	.
E	.	.	.	.	0.0	0.0	996.5	0.0	.	.
F	.	.	.	95.9	26.1	2.4	0.4	984.9	.	.
G	.	.	.	2.7	0.0	0.0	0.0	18.6	.	.
H	.	.	.	8.0	229.1	1.2	0.0	0.9	.	.
I	.	.	.	67.5	2.7	0.0	0.0	24.5	.	.
J	.	.	.	40.8	0.0	34.2	216.6	0.0	.	.
K	.	.	.	0.0	0.0	0.0	0.0	0.0	.	.
L	.	.	.	0.0	0.0	0.0	0.0	49.7	.	.
M	.	.	.	0.0	0.0	0.0	0.0	0.0	.	.
N	.	.	.	0.0	0.0	0.0	0.0	0.0	.	.
O	.	.	.	8.8	53.0	88.3	0.0	0.0	.	.

Explanatory notes: see p. 1361.

[1] Excl. work stoppages in which less than 10 workdays not worked. [2] Incl. those working in Israel from West Bank and Gaza Strip.

Notes explicatives: voir p. 1363.

[1] Non compris les arrêts de travail de moins de 10 journées de travail non effectuées. [2] Y compris ceux travaillant en Israël et provenant de la rive ouest et la bande de Gaza.

Notas explicativas: véase p. 1365.

[1] Excl. las interrupciones de trabajo de menos de 10 días de trabajo no trabajados. [2] Incl. a los que trabajan en Israel y provienen de la Ribera Occidental y la Faja de Gaza.

STRIKES AND LOCKOUTS
Rates of days not worked, by economic activity
Per thousand workers

GRÈVES ET LOCK-OUT
Taux de journées non effectuées, par activité économique
Pour mille travailleurs

HUELGAS Y CIERRES PATRONALES
Tasas de días no trabajados, por actividad económica
Por mil trabajadores

9D

	1999	2000	2001	2002	2003	2004	2005	2006	2007	2008
España (FG) (2) [1]										
ISIC 3 - CITI 3 - CIIU 3										
Total	102.4	233.3	119.1	297.4	45.8	248.9	50.1	47.0	58.3	74.5
A	1.2	8.9	10.7	12.8	0.0	3 431.9	19.9	0.8	2.8	20.4
B	0.0	1 299.6	84.7	0.0	65.5	0.0	326.9	0.0	0.0	214.2
C	1 751.3	393.2	470.8	206.4	135.7	247.5	432.5	89.1	44.7	85.8
D	62.0	199.0	295.0	75.0	149.0	150.0	99.5	116.9	94.1	123.2
E	66.8	2.8	19.3	52.1	10.5	232.7	15.8	18.0	71.5	5.0
F	121.9	839.9	303.3	8.3	2.6	141.1	0.7	62.4	118.9	0.7
G	5.4	205.1	2.0	0.8	1.1	39.7	0.5	10.3	2.9	6.7
H	2.9	2.1	3.1	5.3	7.2	1.9	8.1	1.2	0.7	2.5
I	255.5	431.7	101.8	195.2	128.6	62.7	222.4	71.4	94.4	359.9
J	4.0	0.0	0.3	0.1	1.0	0.2	1.9	2.1	3.5	0.0
K	9.7	37.6	29.5	10.5	16.1	63.3	5.8	18.2	40.5	111.5
L	10.7	415.6	10.3	7.6	6.3	15.2	27.5	38.4	66.5	155.8
M	84.4	49.7	69.0	79.8	1.8	85.8	82.7	61.8	54.0	80.1
N	95.4	13.6	73.5	98.3	29.6	25.6	147.6	104.6	63.8	68.8
O	22.0	23.6	19.3	29.7	22.0	38.3	16.2	9.7	20.1	44.9
P	0.8	0.0	9.1	0.0	0.0	0.0	0.0	0.0	0.0	0.0
X [2]	40.7	2.3	7.5	256.2	5.6	0.2	0.0	0.0	.	.
Finland (FH) (1)										
ISIC 3 - CITI 3 - CIIU 3										
Total	9.5	110.0	25.6	31.0	28.0	18.0	280.3	29.9	37.9	6.5
A	0.0	142.0	0.0	0.0	102.8	0.0	0.0	0.0	0.0	0.0
B	0.0	0.0	0.0	0.0	0.0	0.0	0.0	0.0	0.0	0.0
C	0.0	0.0	0.0	0.0	0.0	0.0	0.0	0.0	5.9	5.2
D	24.4	346.0	.	25.0	110.1	55.0	1 514.6	114.5	64.0	37.0
E	2.1	0.0	.	.	2.0	0.5	0.8	7.2	0.0	0.0
F	0.8	0.0	.	345.0	0.3	0.0	6.6	4.0	0.0	0.5
G	0.0	0.4	.	.	0.3	0.0	0.1	0.0	118.0	0.0
H	0.0	0.0	0.0	0.0	0.0	0.0	0.0	0.0	0.0	0.0
I	37.6	413.0	.	9.5	70.6	92.0	40.7	184.5	5.6	5.2
J	21.4	1.1	0.0	179.0	85.4	3.3	0.0	0.0	0.0	0.0
K	0.0	0.0	.	17.0	0.3	0.8	1.1	0.0	1.1	0.0
L	0.0	0.0	0.0	0.0	0.0	0.0	43.6	2.1	0.0	0.0
M-N	0.0	-	.	0.0	0.0	0.0	0.0	0.0	0.0	0.0
O	0.0	0.0	9.0	4.0	0.0	17.0	6.0	0.0	0.0	0.0
France (DA) (2) [3]										
ISIC 3 - CITI 3 - CIIU 3										
Total	.	.	.	.	.	.	151	116	.	.
Germany (FG) (1) [4]										
ISIC 3 - CITI 3 - CIIU 3										
Total [5]	2.3	0.3	0.8	8.9	4.8	1.3	0.5	12.4	8.1	3.7
A	0.0	0.0	0.0	0.0	0.0	0.0	0.0	0.0	0.0	.
B	0.0	0.0	0.0	0.0	0.0	0.0	0.0	0.0	0.0	.
C	0.0	0.0	0.0	0.0	0.0	0.0	0.0	0.0	0.0	.
D	8.2	0.6	2.7	31.5	21.5	6.3	1.9	10.8	5.0	.
E	0.0	0.6	0.0	0.3	0.0	0.5	0.1	0.2	0.0	.
F	0.0	0.0	0.0	26.9	0.0	0.0	0.0	0.0	4.7	.
G	0.5	0.2	0.0	0.7	0.2	0.1	0.4	0.1	6.3	.
H	0.0	0.0	0.0	0.0	0.0	0.0	0.0	0.8	0.0	.
I	0.6	0.3	2.4	1.9	0.1	0.6	0.1	0.6	102.0	.
J	8.7	0.0	0.0	2.7	0.0	0.0	0.0	0.2	0.0	.
K	0.0	0.0	0.0	0.4	0.0	0.0	0.0	0.3	0.0	.
L [5]	0.0	0.0	0.0	0.1	0.0	0.0	0.6	52.4	0.0	.
M	0.0	0.0	0.0	0.1	0.0	0.0	0.3	7.0	0.0	.
N	0.0	0.0	0.0	0.0	0.0	0.1	0.2	41.4	0.0	.
O	0.0	1.9	0.0	0.0	0.0	0.0	0.0	14.1	0.0	.
Hungary (H) (1) [6]										
ISIC 3 - CITI 3 - CIIU 3										
Total	89.9	55.1	2.8	0.5	0.9	6.8	0.4	2.3	10.1	.
A	0.0	0.0	0.0	0.0	0.0	0.0	0.0	0.0	0.0	.
B	0.0	0.0	0.0	0.0	0.0	0.0	0.0	0.0	0.0	.
C	0.0	0.0	0.0	0.0	0.0	0.0	0.0	0.0	0.0	.
D	0.0	0.2	3.4	0.6	1.2	0.3	1.2	1.5	1.0	.
E	3.0	0.0	0.0	0.0	0.0	1.0	0.0	0.6	24.8	.
F	0.0	0.0	0.0	0.0	0.0	0.0	0.0	0.0	1.4	.
G	0.0	0.0	0.0	0.0	0.0	0.0	0.0	4.3	0.1	.
H	0.0	0.0	0.0	0.0	0.0	0.0	0.0	0.0	0.0	.
I	1 027.7	641.1	0.0	0.0	4.9	2.7	0.4	0.0	22.7	.
J	0.0	0.0	0.0	0.0	0.0	0.0	0.0	0.0	0.0	.
K	0.0	0.0	0.0	0.0	0.0	0.0	0.0	0.1	0.2	.
L	0.0	0.0	0.0	0.0	0.0	0.0	0.0	0.2	0.0	.
M	0.0	0.0	0.0	0.0	0.0	0.0	0.0	14.8	68.1	.
N	4.2	17.1	0.4	4.2	0.0	80.5	0.0	0.0	10.5	.
O	0.0	0.0	67.9	0.0	0.0	0.0	0.0	1.2	0.2	.

Explanatory notes: see p. 1361.

[1] Prior to 1990: strikes only; excl. the Basque country. [2] General strikes. [3] Localized strikes (the call to strike concerns only one establishment). [4] Incl. work stoppages lasting less than one day if more than 100 workdays not worked . [5] Excl. public administration. [6] 1991-95: Work stoppages in which 800 hours or more not worked; beginning 1996: stoppages involving 10 workers or more.

Notes explicatives: voir p. 1363.

[1] Avant 1990: grèves seulement; non compris le Pays basque. [2] Grèves générales. [3] Grèves localisées (le mot d'ordre de grève est interne à l'établissement). [4] Y compris les arrêts du travail d'une durée inférieure à une journée si plus de 100 journées de travail non effectuées. [5] Non compris l'administration publique. [6] 1991-95: Arrêts de travail avec 800 h. de travail non effectuées au moins; dès 1996: ceux impliquant 10 travailleurs ou plus.

Notas explicativas: véase p. 1365.

[1] Antes de 1990: huelgas solamente; excl. el País Vasco. [2] Huelgas generales. [3] Huelgas localizadas (la contraseña de huelga afecta a un establecimiento). [4] Incl. las interrupciones del trabajo de menos de un día si no se han trabajado más de 100 días. [5] Excl. la administración pública. [6] 1991-95: Interrupciones del trabajo de 800 horas no trabajadas y más: desde 1996: las que implican 10 trabajadores o más.

9D

STRIKES AND LOCKOUTS	GRÈVES ET LOCK-OUT	HUELGAS Y CIERRES PATRONALES
Rates of days not worked, by economic activity Per thousand workers	Taux de journées non effectuées, par activité économique Pour mille travailleurs	Tasas de días no trabajados, por actividad económica Por mil trabajadores

	1999	2000	2001	2002	2003	2004	2005	2006	2007	2008
Isle of Man (FG) (1) ISIC 3 - CITI 3 - CIIU 3										
Total		0	0	0	0	0	0	0	0	
Italy (H) (1) ISIC 3 - CITI 3 - CIIU 3										
Total	60.6	57.9	65.6	304.9	121.7	43.3	54.8	32.8	52.6	
A-B	7.3	363.6	4.3	16.0						
C	17.2	23.2	26.8	150.9	13.5	62.5	11.9	67.7	0.0	
D	143.7	76.5	149.6	103.8	104.9	63.3	153.9	85.8	117.9	
E	103.0	66.7	63.6	48.0	15.1	17.9	19.2	26.0	3.2	
F	7.0	6.2	50.4	3.7	2.4	0.8	11.4	46.0	4.7	
G	62.1	15.8	34.7	1.3	24.0	18.7	0.6	1.4	46.7	
H					5.5	0.2	1.1	0.4	1.1	
I	77.8	240.1	67.4	81.8	107.4	68.1	56.6	61.0	125.0	
J	88.2	26.0	33.6	90.7	11.7	129.1	3.2	11.4	2.3	
K,O	28.2	13.3	12.5	14.0						
L	16.8	12.1	56.3	88.7	61.0	97.9	85.3	7.2	52.4	
M	2.1	142.6	24.7	32.9	12.9	38.4	24.6	1.9	13.8	
N	7.4	8.2	22.4	36.8	57.3	36.6	14.8	5.9	18.5	
Latvia (D) (1) ISIC 3 - CITI 3 - CIIU 3										
Total	37.3	0.0	0.0	4.2	0.0	0.0	0.0	0.0	0.0	3.2
D	0.1	0.0	0.0	0.0	0.0	0.0	0.0	0.0	0.0	0.0
I	0.0	0.0	0.0	0.0	0.0	0.0	0.0	0.0	0.0	0.0
L	0.0	0.0	0.0	0.0	0.0	0.0	0.0	0.0	0.0	0.0
M	302.1	0.0	0.0	0.0	0.0	0.0	0.0	0.0	0.0	0.0
N	0.0	0.0	0.0	66.4	0.0	0.0	0.0	0.0	0.0	54.9
O	400.0	0.0	0.0	0.0	0.0	0.0	0.0	0.0	0.0	0.0
Liechtenstein (H) ISIC 3 - CITI 3 - CIIU 3										
Total	0	0	0	0	0	0	0	0		
Malta (H) ISIC 3 - CITI 3 - CIIU 3										
Total		33	19	5	23	12	9	19	5	11
A		0	0	0	0	0	0	0	0	0
B		0	0	0	0	0	0	0	0	0
C		0	0	0	0	0	0	0	0	0
D		2	0	14	10	0	18	1	0	0
E		0	10	10	585	0	18	0	0	0
F		0	1	0	0	0	0	0	0	0
G		0	0	0	0	0	0	0	0	0
H		23	0	0	5	0	0	0	0	0
I		212	138	22	49	148	62	167	57	0
J		324	0	0	0	0	0	0	0	0
K		0	0	0	0	0	1	1	0	0
L		27	60	2	0	0	0	59	0	68
M		0	1	0	0	0	0	59	8	56
N		4	26	0	1	1	1	0	0	0
O		0	0	0	0	1	0	0	0	0
Netherlands (H) (2) ISIC 3 - CITI 3 - CIIU 3										
Total	11	1	6	35	2	9	6	2	3	15
A	0	0	0	0	0	0	0	0	0	0
B	0	0	0	0	0	0	0	0	0	0
C	0	0	0	0	0	0	0	0	0	0
D	4	4	9 [1]	2	2	13	14 [2]	7	5	10 [1]
E	0	0	0	0	0	0	0	0	0	0
F	45	0	0	557	0	0	0	0	0	0
G	0	- [3]		0	0	0	0	0	0	0
H	0		0	0	0	0	0	0	0	0
I	1 [4]	7	8 [5]	11 [4]	5 [6]	2	1 [5]	3 [6]	16	178
J	0	0	0	0	0	0	0	0	0	0
K			0				0	2	0	0
L	19	2 [7]	0	1 [8]	1 [9]	0	0	1 [10]	7	29
M	107			0	0	0	0	0	0	0
N	0	0	14 [7]		0	0	0	0	0	0
O	0			0	0	0	0	0	0	0
X						7 [11]	3 [11]	0	0	0

Explanatory notes: see p. 1361.

[1] Incl. category E. [2] Incl. category F. [3] Incl. categories H and K. [4] Incl. category K. [5] Including category G. [6] Incl. categories G and K. [7] Incl. categories M and O. [8] Incl. category N. [9] Incl. category O. [10] Incl. categories N and O. [11] Incl. categories A and O.

Notes explicatives: voir p. 1363.

[1] Y compris la catégorie E. [2] Y compris catégorie F. [3] Y compris les catégories H et K. [4] Y compris la catégorie K. [5] Y compris la catégorie G. [6] Y compris les catégories G et K. [7] Y compris les catégories M et O. [8] Y compris la catégorie N. [9] Y compris la catégorie O. [10] Y compris les catégories N et O. [11] Y compris les catégories A et O.

Notas explicativas: véase p. 1365.

[1] Incl. la categoría E. [2] Incl. categoría F. [3] Incl. las categorías H y K. [4] Incl. la categoría K. [5] Incl. la categoría G. [6] Incl. las categorías G y K. [7] Incl. las categorías M y O. [8] Incl. la categoría N. [9] Incl. la categoría O. [10] Incl. las categorías N y O. [11] Incl. las categorías A y O.

STRIKES AND LOCKOUTS

Rates of days not worked, by economic activity
Per thousand workers

GRÈVES ET LOCK-OUT

Taux de journées non effectuées, par activité économique
Pour mille travailleurs

HUELGAS Y CIERRES PATRONALES

Tasas de días no trabajados, por actividad económica
Por mil trabajadores

9D

	1999	2000	2001	2002	2003	2004	2005	2006	2007	2008
Poland (FG) (1)										
ISIC 3 - CITI 3 - CIIU 3										
Total	11	8	-	-	1	1	0	0	2	.
A	0	0	0	0	0	0	0	0	0	.
B	0	0	0	0	0	0	0	0	0	.
C	0	0	0	0	0	0	0	0	0	.
D	26	4	-	-	3	0	0	0	1	.
E	3	0	0	0	0	0	0	0	0	.
F	0	0	0	0	0	0	0	0	0	.
G	-	0	0	0	0	0	0	0	0	.
H	0	0	0	0	0	0	0	0	0	.
I	5	10	0	0	0	1	0	0	2	.
J	0	0	0	0	0	0	0	0	0	.
K	1	0	0	0	0	0	0	0	0	.
L	0	0	0	0	0	0	0	0	0	.
M	35	0	0	0	0	0	0	0	1	.
N	0	66	5	0	0	0	0	0	21	.
O	-	0	0	0	0	0	0	0	0	.
Portugal (FG) [1]										
ISIC 3 - CITI 3 - CIIU 3										
Total [2]	31.0	18.7	17.5	43.9	21.7	18.1	10.5	16.0	10.0	.
A	.	0.0	0.0	0.0	0.0	0.0	0.0	0.0	0.0	.
B	3.7	141.8	0.0	534.1	12.7	0.0	0.0	0.0	0.0	.
C	14.0	271.0	5.0	51.0	3.0	0.0	18.0	0.2	49.0	.
D	34.0	15.8	26.3	67.2	29.7	21.5	20.2	26.0	16.0	.
E	45.0	25.1	1.4	178.3	22.7	8.2	4.4	5.0	41.0	.
F	1.0	0.0	0.2	0.7	0.1	0.3	0.2	0.0	1.0	.
G	9.0	0.9	0.8	3.9	0.2	0.6	0.1	0.3	2.0	.
H	4.0	0.9	2.0	13.7	0.7	3.2	2.4	3.0	7.0	.
I	106.0	134.5	95.1	216.1	179.6	92.5	25.9	129.0	66.0	.
J	.	0.0	0.0	0.0	0.0	167.8	0.0	27.0	16.0	.
K	8.0	25.0	17.6	16.9	4.3	3.1	14.3	6.0	4.0	.
M [2]	0.0	0.0	0.4	4.5	0.0	0.0	1.5	2.0	2.0	.
N	.	2.8	17.2	25.9	11.0	0.0	9.7	0.0	.	.
O	8.0	20.2	8.7	9.5	2.2	12.2	27.5	3.0	15.0	.
Roumanie (FG) (2) [1]										
ISIC 3 - CITI 3 - CIIU 3										
Total	294.7	122.3	0.2	7.5	2.6	4.8	4.9	.	.	.
A	48.2	0.0	0.0	0.0	0.0	0.0	0.0	.	.	.
B	0.0	0.0	0.0	0.0	0.0	0.0	0.0	.	.	.
C	1 269.9	0.5	0.0	106.4	0.0	14.3	0.0	.	.	.
D	57.7	6.2	0.5	6.7	5.2	5.3	5.5	.	.	.
E	8.4	0.0	0.0	0.0	6.3	0.0	0.0	.	.	.
F	0.7	0.0	0.0	0.0	0.0	0.9	0.0	.	.	.
G	0.0	0.0	0.0	0.0	0.0	0.0	0.0	.	.	.
H	0.0	0.0	0.0	0.0	0.0	0.0	0.0	.	.	.
I	629.8	0.0	0.2	17.2	1.7	4.9	0.6	.	.	.
J	0.0	0.0	0.0	0.0	0.0	0.0	0.0	.	.	.
K	0.0	0.0	0.0	0.0	0.0	0.0	0.0	.	.	.
L	0.0	0.0	0.0	0.0	0.0	0.0	0.0	.	.	.
M	1 883.3	1 191.1	0.0	0.0	0.0	0.0	0.0	.	.	.
N	36.9	222.5	0.0	1.0	0.0	0.0	0.0	.	.	.
O	0.0	1.0	0.0	0.0	0.0	0.0	0.0	.	.	.
Slovakia (FG) (1)										
ISIC 3 - CITI 3 - CIIU 3										
Total	0.0	0.0	0.0	0.0	0.0	0.0	0.0	0.0	0.0	0.0
Suisse (H) (2) [3]										
ISIC 3 - CITI 3 - CIIU 3										
Total	0.7	1.2	4.8	5.1	1.4	9.3	0.3	1.8	1.6	3.1
Turkey (FG) (1) [1]										
ISIC 3 - CITI 3 - CIIU 3										
Total	85.3	121.4	74.9	23.8	65.1	43.1	69.5	41.7	502.2	60.0
A	0.0	0.0	0.0	0.0	0.0	0.0	0.0	0.0	0.0	0.0
B	0.0	0.0	0.0	0.0	0.0	0.0	0.0	0.0	0.0	0.0
C	115.0	122.1	134.0	0.0	899.4	0.0	0.0	0.0	0.0	0.0
D	118.7	138.4	152.5	25.7	23.4	52.4	92.9	58.1	114.4	75.0
E	0.0	0.0	0.0	0.0	0.2	0.0	0.0	0.0	0.0	0.0
F	0.0	0.0	0.0	0.0	0.0	0.0	0.0	0.0	0.0	0.0
G	0.0	0.0	0.0	0.0	0.0	0.0	0.0	0.0	0.0	0.0
H	0.0	4.9	0.0	0.0	0.0	0.0	49.1	0.3	2.3	0.0
I	20.0	52.0	0.0	6.8	47.2	43.8	10.3	84.0	6 177.9	0.0
J	0.0	0.0	0.0	0.0	0.0	0.0	0.0	0.0	0.0	0.0
K	0.0	0.0	0.0	0.0	0.0	0.0	0.0	0.0	0.0	0.0
L	0.0	0.0	0.0	0.0	0.0	0.0	0.0	0.0	0.0	0.0
M	0.0	0.0	0.0	0.0	0.0	0.0	0.0	0.0	0.0	0.0
N	0.0	0.0	0.0	0.0	0.0	0.0	0.0	0.0	0.0	0.0
O	5.5	358.3	46.8	37.0	0.0	5.0	0.0	1.9	7.5	1.0

Explanatory notes: see p. 1361.

[1] Strikes only. [2] Excl. public administration. [3] Excl. work stoppages lasting less than one day.

Notes explicatives: voir p. 1363.

[1] Grèves seulement. [2] Non compris l'administration publique. [3] Non compris les arrêts du travail dont la durée est inférieure à une journée.

Notas explicativas: véase p. 1365.

[1] Huelgas solamente. [2] Excl. la administración pública. [3] Excl. las interrupciones del trabajo de menos de un día de duración.

9D

STRIKES AND LOCKOUTS	GRÈVES ET LOCK-OUT	HUELGAS Y CIERRES PATRONALES
Rates of days not worked, by economic activity	Taux de journées non effectuées, par activité économique	Tasas de días no trabajados, por actividad económica
Per thousand workers	Pour mille travailleurs	Por mil trabajadores

	1999	2000	2001	2002	2003	2004	2005	2006	2007	2008
United Kingdom (H) (1) [1][2]										
ISIC 3 - CITI 3 - CIIU 3										
Total	10	19	20	51	19	34	6	28	38	28
A-B	0	0	0	0	0	0	0	0	0	0
C	0	33	201	0	0	81	3	476	0	4
D	14	13	11	6	19	6	5	6	5	2
E	0	8	98	1	3	3	53	0	0	0
F	44	42	8	15	12	0	1	11	2	2
G	0	-	-	-	-	-	0	0	0	0
H	6	24	2	35	.	0	11	0	0	0
I	34	64	69	61	82	28	21	25	422	16
J	0	0	0	0	-	-	3	0	0	0
K	1	0	0	2	0	0	1	1	0	0
L	26	36	153	338	93	288	15	412	215	422
M	13	24	21	172	59	165	19	13	13	43
N	2	47	26	53	5	1	0	1	1	0
O	6	28	3	79	7	3	4	1	2	2

OCEANIA-OCÉANIE-OCEANIA

	1999	2000	2001	2002	2003	2004	2005	2006	2007	2008
Australia (H) [3]										
ISIC 3 - CITI 3 - CIIU 3										
Total	87	61	50	33	54	45	26	15	5	21
F	381	234	275	220	248	223	153	24	10	20
I	42	52	27	37	53	37	20	16	3	17
New Zealand (FG) (2) [4][5]										
ISIC 3 - CITI 3 - CIIU 3										
Total	9.5	6.7	29.8	22.7	12.5	3.4	13.0	9.6	.	.
A	0.0	0.0	0.0	.	.	.	.	.	.	.
B	0.0	0.0	. [6]	.	.	.	.	.	.	.
C	0.0	0.0	0.0	.	.	.	.	.	.	.
D	8.6	31.8	77.5	19.6	71.9	7.9	18.0	12.4	.	.
E	0.0	0.0	0.0	.	.	.	.	.	.	.
F	. [6]	. [6]	.	.	.	.	.	.	.	.
G	. [6]	. [6]	. [6]	.	.	.	.	.	.	.
H	0.0	0.0	0.0	.	.	.	.	.	.	.
I	70.1	. [6]	7.8	.	.	.	.	.	.	.
J	. [6]	0.0	0.0	.	.	.	.	.	.	.
K	. [6]	0.0	2.4	.	.	.	0.0	.	.	.
L	0.0	2.1	70.0	.	.	.	.	.	.	.
M	7.3	. [6]	143.2	.	.	.	.	.	.	.
N	27.9	12.2	23.3	.	.	.	.	.	.	.
O	. [6]	0.0	. [6]	.	.	.	.	.	.	.

Explanatory notes: see p. 1361.

[1] Incl. stoppages involving fewer than 10 workers or lasting less than one day if 100 or more workdays not worked. [2] Excl. political strikes. [3] Excl. work stoppages in which less than 10 workdays not worked. [4] Excl. work stoppages in which less than 10 workdays not worked (from 2000, 5 workdays). [5] Prior to 1988: excl. public sector stoppages. [6] Data included in totals only for reasons of confidentiality.

Notes explicatives: voir p. 1363.

[1] Y compris les arrêts impliquant moins de 10 travailleurs ou de moins d'un jour si plus de 100 journées de travail non effectuées. [2] Non compris les grèves politiques. [3] Non compris les arrêts de travail de moins de 10 journées de travail non effectuées. [4] Non compris les arrêts de travail de moins de 10 journées de travail non effectuées (à partir de 2000, 5 journées de travail). [5] Avant 1988: non compris les arrêts du travail du secteur public. [6] Données incluses uniquement dans le total pour des raisons de confidentialité.

Notas explicativas: véase p. 1365.

[1] Incl. las interrupciones con menos de 10 trabajadores o de menos de un día si hubo más de 100 días de trabajo no trabajados. [2] Excl. las huelgas políticas. [3] Excl. las interrupciones de trabajo de menos de 10 días de trabajo no trabajados. [4] Excl. las interrupciones de trabajo de menosde 10 días de trabajo no trabajados (desde 2000, 5 días de trabajo). [5] Antes de 1988: excl. las interrupciones del sector público. [6] Datos incluidos en el total solamente por razón de confidencialidad.

Classifications used in the *Yearbook*

Classifications utilisées dans *l' Annuaire*

Clasificaciones empleadas *en el Anuario*

References

Références

Referencias

Order of arrangement of countries, areas and territories

Ordre de présentation des pays, zones et territoires

Orden de presentación de los países, áreas y territorios

International Standard Industrial Classification of all Economic Activities (ISIC - Rev. 2, 1968) [1]

Major Division 1. Agriculture, Hunting, Forestry and Fishing

11		Agriculture and Hunting
	111	Agricultural and livestock production
	112	Agricultural services
	113	Hunting, trapping and game propagation
12		Forestry and Logging
	121	Forestry
	122	Logging
13	130	Fishing

Major Division 2. Mining and Quarrying

21	210	Coal Mining
22	220	Crude Petroleum and Natural Gas Production
23	230	Metal Ore Mining
29	290	Other Mining

Major Division 3. Manufacturing

31		Manufacture of Food, Beverages and Tobacco
	311-312	Food manufacturing
	313	Beverage industries
	314	Tobacco manufactures
32		Textile, Wearing Apparel and Leather Industries
	321	Manufacture of textiles
	322	Manufacture of wearing apparel, except footwear
	323	Manufacture of leather and products of leather, leather substitutes and fur, except footwear and wearing apparel
	324	Manufacture of footwear, except vulcanized or moulded rubber or plastic footwear
33		Manufacture of Wood and Wood Products, including Furniture
	331	Manufacture of wood and wood and cork products, except furniture
	332	Manufacture of furniture and fixtures, except primarily of metal
34		Manufacture of Paper and Paper Products, Printing and Publishing
	341	Manufacture of paper and paper products
	342	Printing, publishing and allied industries
35		Manufacture of Chemicals and Chemical, Petroleum, Coal, Rubber and Plastic Products
	351	Manufacture of industrial chemicals
	352	Manufacture of other chemical products
	353	Petroleum refineries
	354	Manufacture of miscellaneous products of petroleum and coal
	355	Manufacture of rubber products
	356	Manufacture of plastic products not elsewhere classified
36		Manufacture of Non-Metallic Mineral Products, except Products of Petroleum and Coal
	361	Manufacture of pottery, china and earthenware
	362	Manufacture of glass and glass products
	369	Manufacture of other non-metallic mineral products
37		Basic Metal Industries
	371	Iron and steel basic industries
	372	Non-ferrous metal basic industries
38		Manufacture of Fabricated Metal Products, Machinery and Equipment
	381	Manufacture of fabricated metal products, except machinery and equipment
	382	Manufacture of machinery except electrical
	383	Manufacture of electrical machinery apparatus, appliances and supplies
	384	Manufacture of transport equipment
	385	Manufacture of professional and scientific and measuring and controlling equipment not elsewhere classified, and of photographic and optical goods
39	390	Other Manufacturing Industries

Major Division 4. Electricity, Gas and Water

41	410	Electricity, Gas and Steam
42	420	Water Works and Supply

Major Division 5. Construction

50	500	Construction

Major Division 6. Wholesale and Retail Trade and Restaurants and Hotels

61	610	Wholesale Trade
62	620	Retail Trade
63		Restaurants and Hotels
	631	Restaurants, cafés and other eating and drinking places
	632	Hotels, rooming houses, camps and other lodging places

Major Division 7. Transport, Storage and Communication

71		Transport and Storage
	711	Land transport
	712	Water transport
	713	Air transport
	719	Services allied to transport
72	720	Communication

Major Division 8. Financing, Insurance, Real Estate and Business Services

81	810	Financial Institutions
82	820	Insurance
83		Real Estate and Business Services
	831	Real estate
	832	Business services except machinery and equipment rental and leasing
	833	Machinery and equipment rental and leasing

Major Division 9. Community, Social and Personal Services

91	910	Public Administration and Defence
92	920	Sanitary and Similar Services
93		Social and Related Community Services
	931	Education services
	932	Research and scientific institutes
	933	Medical, dental, other health and veterinary services
	934	Welfare institutions
	935	Business, professional and labour associations
	939	Other social and related community services
94		Recreational and Cultural Services
	941	Motion picture and other entertainment services
	942	Libraries, museums, botanical and zoological gardens, and other cultural services not elsewhere classified

949 Amusement and recreational services not elsewhere classified
95 Personal and Household Services
951 Repair services not elsewhere classified
952 Laundries, laundry services, and cleaning and dyeing plants
953 Domestic services
959 Miscellaneous personal services
96 960 International and Other Extra-Territorial Bodies

Major Division 0. Activities not Adequately Defined
00 000 Activities not adequately defined

Note

[1] This Classification consists of Major Divisions (one-digit codes), Divisions (two-digit codes), Major Groups (three-digit codes) and Groups (four-digit codes); the last are not shown separately in this Annex.

For full details see United Nations: *Statistical Papers,* Series M, No. 4, rev. 2 (New York, 1968).

Classification internationale type, par industrie, de toutes les branches d'activité économique (CITI - Rév. 2, 1968) [1]

Branche 1. Agriculture, chasse, sylviculture et pêche

11		Agriculture et chasse
	111	Production agricole et élevage
	112	Activités annexes de l'agriculture
	113	Chasse, piégeage et repeuplement en gibier
12		Sylviculture et exploitation forestière
	121	Sylviculture
	122	Exploitation forestière
13	130	Pêche

Branche 2. Industries extractives

21	210	Extraction du charbon
22	220	Production de pétrole brut et de gaz naturel
23	230	Extraction des minerais métalliques
29	290	Extraction d'autres minéraux

Branche 3. Industries manufacturières

31		Fabrication de produits alimentaires, boissons et tabacs
	311-312	Industries alimentaires
	313	Fabrication des boissons
	314	Industrie du tabac
32		Industries des textiles, de l'habillement et du cuir
	321	Industrie textile
	322	Fabrication d'articles d'habillement, à l'exclusion des chaussures
	323	Industrie du cuir, des articles en cuir et en succédanés du cuir, et de la fourrure, à l'exclusion des chaussures et des articles d'habillement
	324	Fabrication des chaussures, à l'exclusion des chaussures en caoutchouc vulcanisé ou moulé et des chaussures en matière plastique
33		Industrie du bois et fabrication d'ouvrages en bois, y compris les meubles
	331	Industrie du bois et fabrication d'ouvrages en bois et en liège, à l'exclusion des meubles
	332	Fabrication de meubles et d'accessoires, à l'exclusion des meubles et accessoires faits principalement en métal
34		Fabrication de papier et d'articles en papier; imprimerie et édition
	341	Fabrication de papier et d'articles en papier
	342	Imprimerie, édition et industries annexes
35		Industrie chimique et fabrication de produits chimiques, de dérivés du pétrole et du charbon, et d'ouvrages en caoutchouc et en matière plastique
	351	Industrie chimique
	352	Fabrication d'autres produits chimiques
	353	Raffineries de pétrole
	354	Fabrication de divers dérivés du pétrole et du charbon
	355	Industrie du caoutchouc
	356	Fabrication d'ouvrages en matière plastique non classés ailleurs
36		Fabrication de produits minéraux non métalliques, à l'exclusion des dérivés du pétrole et du charbon
	361	Fabrication des grès, porcelaines et faïences
	362	Industrie du verre
	369	Fabrication d'autres produits minéraux non métalliques
37		Industrie métallique de base
	371	Sidérurgie et première transformation de la fonte, du fer et de l'acier
	372	Production et première transformation des métaux non ferreux
38		Fabrication d'ouvrages en métaux, de machines et de matériel
	381	Fabrication d'ouvrages en métaux, à l'exclusion des machines et du matériel
	382	Construction de machines, à l'exclusion des machines électriques
	383	Fabrication de machines, appareils et fournitures électriques
	384	Construction de matériel de transport
	385	Fabrication de matériel médico-chirurgical, d'instruments de précision, d'appareils de mesure et de contrôle non classés ailleurs, de matériel photographique et d'instruments d'optique
39	390	Autres industries manufacturières

Branche 4. Electricité, gaz et eau

41	410	Electricité, gaz et vapeur
42	420	Installations de distribution d'eau et distribution publique de l'eau

Branche 5. Bâtiment et travaux publics

50	500	Bâtiment et travaux publics

Branche 6. Commerce de gros et de détail; restaurants et hôtels

61	610	Commerce de gros
62	620	Commerce de détail
63		Restaurants et hôtels
	631	Restaurants et débits de boissons
	632	Hôtels, hôtels meublés et établissements analogues; terrains de camping

Branche 7. Transports, entrepôts et communications

71		Transports et entrepôts
	711	Transports par la voie terrestre
	712	Transports par eau
	713	Transports aériens
	719	Services auxiliaires des transports
72	720	Communications

Branche 8. Banques, assurances, affaires immobilières et services fournis aux entreprises

81	810	Etablissements financiers
82	820	Assurances
83		Affaires immobilières et services fournis aux entreprises
	831	Affaires immobilières
	832	Services fournis aux entreprises, à l'exclusion de la location de machines et de matériel
	833	Location de machines et de matériel

Branche 9. Services fournis à la collectivité, services sociaux et services personnels

91	910	Administration publique et défense nationale
92	920	Services sanitaires et services analogues

93		Services sociaux et services connexes fournis à la collectivité
	931	Enseignement
	932	Institutions scientifiques et centres de recherche
	933	Services médicaux et dentaires et autres services sanitaires, et services vétérinaires
	934	Œuvres sociales
	935	Associations commerciales, professionnelles et syndicales
	939	Autres services sociaux et services connexes fournis à la collectivité
94		Services récréatifs et services culturels annexes
	941	Films cinématographiques et autres services récréatifs
	942	Bibliothèques, musées, jardins botaniques et zoologiques et autres services culturels non classés ailleurs
	949	Amusements et services récréatifs non classés ailleurs

95		Services fournis aux particuliers et aux ménages
	951	Services de réparation non classés ailleurs
	952	Blanchisserie, teinturerie
	953	Services domestiques
	959	Services personnels divers
96	960	Organisations internationales et autres organismes extra-territoriaux

Branche 0. Activités mal désignées

| 00 | 000 | Activités mal désignées |

Note

[1] Cette classification comprend des *branches* (codes à un chiffre), des *catégories* (codes à deux chiffres), des *classes* (codes à trois chiffres) et des *groupes* (codes à quatre chiffres); ces derniers ne sont pas présentés séparément dans cette annexe.

Pour de plus amples détails, voir Nations Unies: *Etudes statistiques,* série M, n° 4, rév. 2 (New York, 1969).

Clasificación Industrial Internacional Uniforme de Todas las Actividades Económicas (CIIU - Rev. 2, 1968) [1]

Gran división 1. Agricultura, caza, silvicultura y pesca

11		Agricultura y caza
	111	Producción agropecuaria
	112	Servicios agrícolas
	113	Caza ordinaria y mediante trampas, y repoblación de animales
12		Silvicultura y extracción de madera
	121	Silvicultura
	122	Extracción de madera
13	130	Pesca

Gran división 2. Explotación de minas y canteras

21	210	Explotación de minas de carbón
22	220	Producción de petróleo crudo y gas natural
23	230	Extracción de minerales metálicos
29	290	Extracción de otros minerales

Gran división 3. Industrias manufactureras

31		Productos alimenticios, bebidas y tabaco
	311-312	Fabricación de productos alimenticios
	313	Industrias de bebidas
	314	Industria del tabaco
32		Textiles, prendas de vestir e industrias del cuero
	321	Fabricación de textiles
	322	Fabricación de prendas de vestir, excepto calzado
	323	Industria del cuero y productos de cuero y sucedáneos de cuero y pieles, excepto el calzado y otras prendas de vestir
	324	Fabricación de calzado, excepto el de caucho vulcanizado o moldeado o de plástico
33		Industria de la madera y productos de la madera, incluidos muebles
	331	Industria de la madera y productos de madera y de corcho, excepto muebles
	332	Fabricación de muebles y accesorios, excepto los que son principalmente metálicos
34		Fabricación de papel y productos de papel; imprentas y editoriales
	341	Fabricación de papel y productos de papel
	342	Imprentas, editoriales e industrias conexas
35		Fabricación de sustancias químicas y de productos químicos, derivados del petróleo y del carbón, de caucho y plásticos
	351	Fabricación de sustancias químicas industriales
	352	Fabricación de otros productos químicos
	353	Refinerías de petróleo
	354	Fabricación de productos diversos derivados del petróleo y del carbón
	355	Fabricación de productos de caucho
	356	Fabricación de productos plásticos, n.e.p.
36		Fabricación de productos minerales no metálicos, exceptuando los derivados del petróleo y del carbón
	361	Fabricación de objetos de barro, loza y porcelana
	362	Fabricación de vidrio y productos de vidrio
	369	Fabricación de otros productos minerales no metálicos
37		Industrias metálicas básicas
	371	Industrias básicas de hierro y acero
	372	Industrias básicas de metales no ferrosos
38		Fabricación de productos metálicos, maquinaria y equipo
	381	Fabricación de productos metálicos, exceptuando maquinaria y equipo
	382	Construcción de maquinaria, exceptuando la eléctrica
	383	Construcción de maquinaria, aparatos, accesorios y suministros eléctricos
	384	Construcción de material de transporte
	385	Fabricación de equipo profesional y científico, instrumentos de medida y de control n.e.p., y de aparatos fotográficos e instrumentos de óptica
39	390	Otras industrias manufactureras

Gran división 4. Electricidad, gas y agua

41	410	Electricidad, gas y vapor
42	420	Obras hidráulicas y suministro de agua

Gran división 5. Construcción

50	500	Construcción

Gran división 6. Comercio al por mayor y al por menor y restaurantes y hoteles

61	610	Comercio al por mayor
62	620	Comercio al por menor
63		Restaurantes y hoteles
	631	Restaurantes, cafés y otros establecimientos que expenden comidas y bebidas
	632	Hoteles, casas de huéspedes, campamentos y otros lugares de alojamiento

Gran división 7. Transportes, almacenamiento y comunicaciones

71		Transporte y almacenamiento
	711	Transporte terrestre
	712	Transporte por agua
	713	Transporte aéreo
	719	Servicios conexos del transporte
72	720	Comunicaciones

Gran división 8. Establecimientos financieros, seguros, bienes inmuebles y servicios prestados a las empresas

81	810	Establecimientos financieros
82	820	Seguros
83		Bienes inmuebles y servicios prestados a las empresas
	831	Bienes inmuebles
	832	Servicios prestados a las empresas, exceptuando el alquiler y arrendamiento de maquinaria y equipo
	833	Alquiler y arrendamiento de maquinaria y equipo

Gran división 9. Servicios comunales, sociales y personales

91	910	Administración pública y defensa
92	920	Servicios de saneamiento y similares
93		Servicios sociales y otros servicios comunales conexos
	931	Instrucción pública
	932	Institutos de investigaciones y científicos
	933	Servicios médicos y odontológicos; otros servicios de sanidad y veterinaria
	934	Institutos de asistencia social

935 Asociaciones comerciales, profesionales y laborales

939 Otros servicios sociales y servicios comunales conexos

94   Servicios de diversión y esparcimiento y servicios

941 Películas cinematográficas y otros servicios de esparcimiento

942 Bibliotecas, museos, jardines botánicos y zoológicos y otros servicios culturales, n.e.p.

949 Servicios de diversión y esparcimiento, n.e.p.

95   Servicios personales y de los hogares

951 Servicios de reparación, n.e.p.

952 Lavanderías y servicios de lavandería; establecimientos de limpieza y teñido

953 Servicios domésticos

959 Servicios personales diversos

96   960 Organizaciones internacionales y otros organismos extraterritoriales

Gran división 0.   Actividades no bien especificadas

00   000 Actividades no bien especificadas

Nota

[1] Esta Clasificación se compone de *Grandes Divisiones* (clave de un dígito), *Divisiones* (clave de dos dígitos), *Agrupaciones* (clave de tres dígitos) y *Grupos* (clave de cuatro dígitos); estos últimos no están presentados separadamente en este anexo.

Para más amplios detalles, véanse Naciones Unidas: *Informes estadísticos,* serie M, núm. 4, rev. 2 (Nueva York, 1969).

International Standard Industrial Classification of all Economic Activities (ISIC - Rev. 3)[1]

Tabulation category A: Agriculture, Hunting and Forestry

01   Agriculture, Hunting and related service activities
02   Forestry, Logging and related service activities

Tabulation category B: Fishing

05   Fishing, Operation of Fish Hatcheries and Fish Farms; Service activities incidental to Fishing

Tabulation category C: Mining and Quarrying

10   Mining of Coal and Lignite; Extraction of Peat
11   Extraction of Crude Petroleum and Natural Gas; Service activities incidental to Oil and Gas extraction, excluding surveying
12   Mining of Uranium and Thorium Ores
13   Mining of Metal Ores
14   Other Mining and Quarrying

Tabulation category D: Manufacturing

15   Manufacture of Food Products and Beverages
16   Manufacture of Tobacco Products
17   Manufacture of Textiles
18   Manufacture of Wearing Apparel; Dressing and Dyeing of Fur
19   Tanning and Dressing of Leather; Manufacture of Luggage, Handbags, Saddlery, Harness and Footwear
20   Manufacture of Wood and of Products of Wood and Cork, except Furniture; Manufacture of articles of Straw and Plaiting Materials
21   Manufacture of Paper and Paper Products
22   Publishing, Printing and Reproduction of Recorded Media
23   Manufacture of Coke, Refined Petroleum Products and Nuclear Fuel
24   Manufacture of Chemicals and Chemical Products
25   Manufacture of Rubber and Plastics Products
26   Manufacture of Other Non-Metallic Mineral Products
27   Manufacture of Basic Metals
28   Manufacture of Fabricated Metal Products, except Machinery and Equipment
29   Manufacture of Machinery and Equipment NEC[2]
30   Manufacture of Office, Accounting and Computing Machinery
31   Manufacture of Electrical Machinery and Apparatus NEC[2]
32   Manufacture of Radio, Television and Communication Equipment and Apparatus
33   Manufacture of Medical, Precision and Optical Instruments, Watches and Clocks
34   Manufacture of Motor Vehicles, Trailers and Semi-Trailers
35   Manufacture of other Transport Equipment
36   Manufacture of Furniture; Manufacturing NEC[2]
37   Recycling

Tabulation category E: Electricity, Gas and Water Supply

40   Electricity, Gas, Steam and Hot Water Supply
41   Collection, Purification and Distribution of Water

Tabulation category F: Construction

45   Construction

Tabulation category G: Wholesale and Retail Trade; Repair of Motor Vehicles, Motorcycles and Personal and Household Goods

50   Sale, Maintenance and Repair of Motor Vehicles and Motorcycles; Retail Sale of Automotive Fuel

51   Wholesale Trade and Commission Trade, except of Motor Vehicles and Motorcycles
52   Retail Trade, except of Motor Vehicles and Motorcycles; Repair of Personal and Household Goods

Tabulation category H: Hotels and Restaurants

55   Hotels and Restaurants

Tabulation category I: Transport, Storage and Communications

60   Land Transport; Transport via Pipelines
61   Water Transport
62   Air Transport
63   Supporting and Auxiliary Transport Activities; Activities of Travel Agencies
64   Post and Telecommunications

Tabulation category J: Financial Intermediation

65   Financial Intermediation, except Insurance and Pension Funding
66   Insurance and Pension Funding, except Compulsory Social Security
67   Activities auxiliary to Financial Intermediation

Tabulation category K: Real Estate, Renting and Business Activities

70   Real Estate activities
71   Renting of Machinery and Equipment without Operator and of Personal and Household Goods
72   Computer and related activities
73   Research and Development
74   Other Business activities

Tabulation category L: Public Administration and Defence; Compulsory Social Security

75   Public Administration and Defence; Compulsory Social Security

Tabulation category M: Education

80   Education

Tabulation category N: Health and Social Work

85   Health and Social Work

Tabulation category O: Other Community, Social and Personal Service Activities

90   Sewage and Refuse Disposal, Sanitation and similar activities
91   Activities of Membership Organizations NEC**
92   Recreational, Cultural and Sporting activities
93   Other Service activities

Tabulation category P: Private Households with Employed Persons

95   Private Households with Employed Persons

Tabulation category Q: Extra-Territorial Organizations and Bodies

99   Extra-Territorial Organizations and Bodies

Additional category X: Not classifiable by economic activity

Notes

[1] For full details see United Nations: *Statistical Papers*, Series M, No. 4/ Rev. 3 (New York, 1990).
[2] Not elsewhere classified.

Classification internationale type, par industrie, de toutes les branches d'activité économique (CITI-Rév. 3)[1]

Catégorie de classement A: Agriculture, chasse et sylviculture

01   Agriculture, chasse et activités annexes
02   Sylviculture, exploitation forestière et activités annexes

Catégorie de classement B: Pêche

05   Pêche, pisciculture, aquaculture et activités annexes

Catégorie de classement C: Activités extractives

10   Extraction de charbon et de lignite; extraction de tourbe
11   Extraction de pétrole brut et de gaz naturel; activités annexes à l'extraction de pétrole et de gaz, sauf prospection
12   Extraction de minerais d'uranium et de thorium
13   Extraction de minerais métalliques
14   Autres activites extractives

Catégorie de classement D: Activités de fabrication

15   Fabrication de produits alimentaires et de boissons
16   Fabrication de produits à base de tabac
17   Fabrication des textiles
18   Fabrication d'articles d'habillement; préparation et teinture des fourrures
19   Apprêt et tannage des cuirs; fabrication d'articles de voyage et de maroquinerie, d'articles de sellerie et de bourrellerie; fabrication de chaussures
20   Production de bois et d'articles en bois et en liège (sauf fabrication de meubles); fabrication d'articles de vannerie et de sparterie
21   Fabrication de papier, de carton et d'articles en papier et en carton
22   Edition, imprimerie et reproduction de supports enregistrés
23   Fabrication de produits pétroliers raffinés; cokéfaction; traitement de combustibles nucléaires
24   Fabrication de produits chimiques
25   Fabrication d'articles en caoutchouc et en matières plastiques
26   Fabrication d'autres produits minéraux non métalliques
27   Fabrication de produits métallurgiques de base
28   Fabrication d'ouvrages en métaux (sauf machines et matériel)
29   Fabrication de machines et de matériel NCA[2]
30   Fabrication de machines de bureau, de machines comptables et de matériel de traitement de l'information
31   Fabrication de machines et d'appareils électriques NCA[2]
32   Fabrication d'équipements et appareils de radio, télévision et communication
33   Fabrication d'instruments médicaux, de précision et d'optique et d'horlogerie
34   Construction de véhicules automobiles, de remorques et de semi-remorques
35   Fabrication d'autres matériels de transport
36   Fabrication de meubles; activités de fabrication NCA[2]
37   Récupération

Catégorie de classement E: Production et distribution d'électricité, de gaz et d'eau

40   Production et distribution d'électricité, de gaz, de vapeur et d'eau chaude
41   Captage, épuration et distribution de l'eau

Catégorie de classement F: Construction

45   Construction

Catégorie de classement G: Commerce de gros et de détail; réparation de véhicules automobiles, de motocycles et de biens personnels et domestiques

50   Commerce, entretien et réparation de véhicules automobiles et de motocycles; commerce de détail de carburants automobiles
51   Commerce de gros et activités d'intermédiaires du commerce de gros (sauf de véhicules automobiles et de motocycles)
52   Commerce de détail; sauf de véhicules automobiles et de motocycles; réparation d'articles personnels et domestiques

Catégorie de classement H: Hôtels et restaurants

55   Hôtels et restaurants

Catégorie de classement I: Transports, entreposage et communications

60   Transports terrestres; transports par conduites
61   Transports par eau
62   Transports aériens
63   Activités annexes et auxiliaires des transports; activités d'agences de voyages
64   Postes et télécommunications

Catégorie de classement J: Intermédiation financière

65   Intermédiation financière (sauf activités d'assurance et de caisses de retraite)
66   Activités d'assurances et de caisses de retraite (sauf sécurité sociale obligatoire)
67   Activités auxiliaires de l'intermédiation financière

Catégorie de classement K: Immobilier, locations et activités de services aux entreprises

70   Activités immobilières
71   Location de machines et d'équipements sans opérateur et de biens personnels et domestiques
72   Activités informatiques et activités rattachées
73   Recherche-développement
74   Autres activités de services aux entreprises

Catégorie de classement L: Administration publique et défense; sécurité sociale obligatoire

75   Administration publique et défense; sécurité sociale obligatoire

Catégorie de classement M: Education

80   Education

Catégorie de classement N: Santé et action sociale

85   Santé et action sociale

Catégorie de classement O: Autres activités de services collectifs, sociaux et personnels

90   Assainissement et enlèvement des ordures; voirie et activités similaires
91   Activités associatives diverses
92   Activités récréatives, culturelles et sportives
93   Autres activités de services

Catégorie de classement P: Ménages privés employant du personnel domestique

95   Ménages privés employant du personnel domestique

Catégorie de classement Q: Organisations et organismes extraterritoriaux

99   Organisations et organismes extraterritoriaux

Catégorie supplémentaire X: Ne pouvant être classés selon l'activité économique

Notes

[1] Pour de plus amples détails, voir Nations Unies: *Etudes statistiques*, série M, n° 4, rév. 3 (New York, 1990).

[2] Non classés ailleurs.

Clasificación Industrial Internacional Uniforme de Todas las Actividades Económicas (CIIU - Rev. 3)[1]

Categoría de tabulación A: Agricultura, ganadería, caza y silvicultura

01   Agricultura, ganadería, caza y actividades de servicios conexas
02   Silvicultura, extracción de madera y actividades de servicios conexas

Categoría de tabulación B: Pesca

05   Pesca, explotación de criaderos de peces y granjas piscícolas; actividades de servicios relacionadas con la pesca

Categoría de tabulación C: Explotación de minas y canteras

10   Extracción de carbón y lignito; extracción de turba
11   Extracción de petróleo crudo y gas natural; actividades de tipo servicio relacionadas con la extracción de petróleo y gas, excepto las actividades de prospección
12   Extracción de minerales de uranio y torio
13   Extracción de minerales metalíferos
14   Explotación de otras minas y canteras

Categoría de tabulación D: Industrias manufactureras

15   Elaboración de productos alimenticios y bebidas
16   Elaboración de productos de tabaco
17   Fabricación de productos textiles
18   Fabricación de prendas de vestir; adobo y teñido de pieles
19   Curtido y adobo de cueros; fabricación de maletas, bolsos de mano, artículos de talabartería y guarnicionería, y calzado
20   Producción de madera y fabricación de productos de madera y corcho, excepto muebles; fabricación de artículos de paja y de materiales trenzables
21   Fabricación de papel y de productos de papel
22   Actividades de edición e impresión y de reproducción de grabaciones
23   Fabricación de coque, productos de la refinación del petróleo y combustible nuclear
24   Fabricación de sustancias y productos químicos
25   Fabricación de productos de caucho y plástico
26   Fabricación de otros productos minerales no metálicos
27   Fabricación de metales comunes
28   Fabricación de productos elaborados de metal, excepto maquinaria y equipo
29   Fabricación de maquinaria y equipo NCP[2]
30   Fabricación de maquinaria de oficina, contabilidad e informática
31   Fabricación de maquinaria y aparatos eléctricos NCP[2]
32   Fabricación de equipo y aparatos de radio, televisión y comunicaciones
33   Fabricación de instrumentos médicos, ópticos y de precisión y fabricación de relojes
34   Fabricación de vehículos automotores, remolques y semirremolques
35   Fabricación de otros tipos de equipo de transporte
36   Fabricación de muebles; industrias manufactureras NCP[2]
37   Reciclamiento

Categoría de tabulación E: Suministro de electricidad, gas y agua

40   Suministro de electricidad, gas, vapor y agua caliente
41   Captación, depuración y distribución de agua

Categoría de tabulación F: Construcción

45   Construcción

Categoría de tabulación G: Comercio al por mayor y al por menor; reparación de vehículos automotores, motocicletas, efectos personales y enseres domésticos

50   Venta, mantenimiento y reparación de vehículos automotores y motocicletas; venta al por menor de combustible para automotores
51   Comercio al por mayor y en comisión, excepto el comercio de vehículos automotores y motocicletas
52   Comercio al por menor, excepto el comercio de vehículos automotores y motocicletas; reparación de efectos personales y enseres domésticos

Categoría de tabulación H: Hoteles y restaurantes

55   Hoteles y restaurantes

Categoría de tabulación I: Transporte, almacenamiento y comunicaciones

60   Transporte por vía terrestre; transporte por tuberías
61   Transporte por vía acuática
62   Transporte por vía aérea
63   Actividades de transporte complementarias y auxiliares; actividades de agencias de viajes
64   Correo y telecomunicaciones

Categoría de tabulación J: Intermediación financiera

65   Intermediación financiera, excepto la financiación de planes de seguros y de pensiones
66   Financiación de planes de seguros y de pensiones, excepto los planes de seguridad social de afiliación obligatoria
67   Actividades auxiliares de la intermediación financiera

Categoría de tabulación K: Actividades inmobiliarias, empresariales y de alquiler

70   Actividades inmobiliarias
71   Alquiler de maquinaria y equipo sin operarios y de efectos personales y enseres domésticos
72   Informática y actividades conexas
73   Investigación y desarrollo
74   Otras actividades empresariales

Categoría de tabulación L: Administración pública y defensa; planes de seguridad social de afiliación obligatoria

75   Administración pública y defensa; planes de seguridad social de afiliación obligatoria

Categoría de tabulación M: Enseñanza

80   Enseñanza

Categoría de tabulación N: Servicios sociales y de salud

85   Servicios sociales y de salud

Categoría de tabulación O: Otras actividades de servicios comunitarios, sociales y personales

90   Eliminación de desperdicios y aguas residuales, saneamiento y actividades similares
91   Actividades de asociaciones NCP[2]

92   Actividades de esparcimiento y actividades culturales
        y deportivas
93   Otras actividades de servicios

**Categoría de tabulación P: Hogares privados con servicio
                            doméstico**
95   Hogares privados con servicio doméstico

**Categoría de tabulación Q: Organizaciones y órganos
                            extraterritoriales**
99   Organizaciones y órganos extraterritoriales

**Categoría adicional X: No pueden clasificarse según la
                          actividad económica**

Notas

¹ Para más amplios detalles, véase Naciones Unidas: *Informes estadísticos*, serie M, núm. 4/Rev. 3 (Nueva York, 1990).

² No clasificados en otra parte.

International Standard Industrial Classification of all Economic Activities (ISIC - Rev. 4)[1]

Section A: Agriculture, forestry and fishing

01	Crop and animal production, hunting and related service activities
02	Forestry and logging
03	Fishing and aquaculture

Section B: Mining and quarrying

05	Mining of coal and lignite
06	Extraction of crude petroleum and natural gas
07	Mining of metal ores
08	Other mining and quarrying
09	Mining support service activities

Section C: Manufacturing

10	Manufacture of food products
11	Manufacture of beverages
12	Manufacture of tobacco products
13	Manufacture of textiles
14	Manufacture of wearing apparel
15	Manufacture of leather and related products
16	Manufacture of wood and of products of wood and cork, except furniture; manufacture of articles of straw and plaiting materials
17	Manufacture of paper and paper products
18	Printing and reproduction of recorded media
19	Manufacture of coke and refined petroleum products
20	Manufacture of chemicals and chemical products
21	Manufacture of basic pharmaceutical products and pharmaceutical preparations
22	Manufacture of rubber and plastics products
23	Manufacture of other non-metallic mineral products
24	Manufacture of basic metals
25	Manufacture of fabricated metal products, except machinery and equipment
26	Manufacture of computer, electronic and optical products
27	Manufacture of electrical equipment
28	Manufacture of machinery and equipment n.e.c.
29	Manufacture of motor vehicles, trailers and semi-trailers
30	Manufacture of other transport equipment
31	Manufacture of furniture
32	Other manufacturing
33	Repair and installation of machinery and equipment

Section D: Electricity, gas, stream and air conditioning supply

35	Electricity, gas, steam and air conditioning supply

Section E: Water supply; sewerage, waste management and remediation activities

36	Water collection, treatment and supply
37	Sewerage
38	Waste collection, treatment and disposal activities; materials recovery
39	Remediation activities and other waste management services

Section F: Construction

41	Construction of buildings
42	Civil engineering
43	Specialized construction activities

Section G: Wholesale and retail trade; repair of motor vehicles and motorcycles

45	Wholesale and retail trade and repair of motor vehicles and motorcycles
46	Wholesale trade, except of motor vehicles and motorcycles
47	Retail trade, except of motor vehicles and motorcycles

Section H: Transportation and storage

49	Land transport and transport via pipelines
50	Water transport
51	Air transport
52	Warehousing and support activities for transportation
53	Postal and courier activities

Section I: Accommodation and food service activities

55	Accommodation
56	Food and beverage service activities

Section J: Information and communication

58	Publishing activities
59	Motion picture, video and television programme production, sound recording and music publishing activities
60	Programming and broadcasting activities
61	Telecommunications
62	Computer programming, consultancy and related activities
63	Information service activities

Section K: Financial and insurance activities

64   Financial service activities, except insurance and pension funding

65   Insurance, reinsurance and pension funding, except compulsory social security

66   Activities auxiliary to financial service and insurance activities

Section L: Real estate activities

68   Real estate activities

Section M: Professional, scientific and technical activities

69   Legal and accounting activities

70   Activities of head offices; management consultancy activities

71   Architectural and engineering activities; technical testing and analysis

72   Scientific research and development

73   Advertising and market research

74   Other professional, scientific and technical activities

75   Veterinary activities

Section N: Administrative and support service activities

77   Rental and leasing activities

78   Employment activities

79   Travel agency, tour operator, reservation service and related activities

80   Security and investigation activities

81   Services to buildings and landscape activities

82   Office administrative, office support and other business support activities

Section O: Public administration and defence; compulsory social security

84   Public administration and defence; compulsory social security

Section P: Education

85   Education

Section Q: Human health and social work activities

86   Human health activities

87   Residential care activities

88   Social work activities without accommodation

Section R: Arts, entertainment and recreation

90   Creative, arts and entertainment activities

91   Libraries, archives, museums and other cultural activities

92   Gambling and betting activities

93   Sports activities and amusement and recreation activities

Section S: Other service activities

94   Activities of membership organizations

95   Repair of computers and personal and household goods

96   Other personal service activities

Section T: Activities of households as employers; undifferentiated goods- and services-producing activities of households for own use

97   Activities of households as employers of domestic personnel

98   Undifferentiated goods- and services-producing activities of private households for own use

Section U: Activities of extraterritorial organizations and bodies

99   Activities of extraterritorial organizations and bodies

Additional section X: Not classifiable by economic activity

[1] For details see:
http://unstats.un.org/unsd/cr/registry/regcst.asp?Cl=27

Classification internationale type, par industrie, de toutes les branches d'activité économique (CITI - Rév. 4)[1]

Section A: Agriculture, sylviculture et pêche

01 Culture et production animale, chasse et activités de services connexes

02 Sylviculture et exploitation forestière

03 Pêche et aquaculture

Section B: Activités extractives

05 Extraction de charbon et de lignite

06 Extraction de pétrole brut et de gaz naturel

07 Extraction de minerais métalliques

08 Autres activités extractives

09 Activités annexes de l'extraction

Section C: Activités de fabrication

10 Fabrication de produits alimentaires et de boissons

11 Fabrication de boissons

12 Fabrication de produits à base de tabac

13 Fabrication de textiles

14 Fabrication d'articles d'habillement

15 Fabrication de cuir et d'articles de cuir

16 Production de bois et d'articles en bois et en liège (sauf fabrication de meubles); fabrication d'articles de vannerie et de sparterie

17 Fabrication de papier et d'articles en papier

18 Imprimerie et reproduction de supports enregistrés

19 Cokéfaction et fabrication de produits pétroliers raffinés

20 Fabrication de produits chimiques

21 Fabrication de préparations pharmaceutiques, de produits chimiques à usage médicinal et de produits d'herboristerie

22 Fabrication d'articles en caoutchouc et en matières plastiques

23 Fabrication d'autres produits minéraux non métalliques

24 Fabrication de produits métallurgiques de base

25 Fabrication d'ouvrages en métaux (sauf machines et matériel)

26 Fabrication d'ordinateurs, d'articles électroniques et optiques

27 Fabrication de matériels électriques

28 Fabrication de machines et de matériel, n.c.a.

29 Construction de véhicules automobiles, de remorques et semi-remorques

30 Fabrication d'autres matériels de transport

31 Fabrication de meubles

32 Autres activités de fabrication

33 Réparation et installation de machines et de matériel

Section D: Production et distribution d'électricité, de gaz, de vapeur et climatisation

35 Production et distribution d'électricité, de gaz, de vapeur et climatisation

Section E: Distribution d'eau; réseau d'assainissement; gestion des déchets et activités de remise en état

36 Collecte et traitement des eaux, distribution d'eau

37 Réseau d'assainissement

38 Collecte des déchets, activités de traitement et d'évacuation; récupération des matières

39 Activités de remise en état et autres services de traitement des déchets

Section F: Construction

41 Construction de bâtiments

42 Génie civil

43 Activités de construction spécialisées

Section G: Commerce de gros et de détail, réparations de véhicules automobiles et de motocycles

45 Commerce de gros et de détail, réparation de véhicules automobiles et de motocycles

46 Commerce de gros à l'exception des véhicules automobiles et des motocycles

47 Commerce de détail à l'exception des véhicules automobiles et des motocycles

Section H: Transport et entreposage

49 Transports terrestres, transport par conduites

50 Transports par eau

51 Transports aériens

52 Magasinage et activités annexes des transports

53 Activités de poste et de courrier

Section I: Activités d'hébergement et de restauration

55 Hébergement

56 Activités de services de restauration et de consommation de boissons

Section J: Information et communication

58 Activités d'édition

59 Activités de production de films cinématographiques et vidéo, de programmes de télévision, d'enregistrements sonores et d'édition musicale

60 Activités de programmation et de diffusion

61 Télécommunications

| 62 | Programmation informatique; conseils et activités connexes |
| 63 | Activités de services d'information |

Section K: Activités financières et d'assurances

64	Activités de services financiers, à l'exception des assurances et des caisses de retraite
65	Activités d'assurances, réassurance et de caisses de retraite, à l'exception de la sécurité sociale obligatoire
66	Activités auxiliaires des services financiers et des assurances

Section L: Activités immobilières

| 68 | Activités immobilières |

Section M: Activités professionnelles, scientifiques et techniques

69	Activités juridiques et comptables
70	Activités de bureaux principaux; activités de conseils en matière de gestion
71	Activités d'architecture et d'ingénierie; activités d'essais et d'analyses techniques
72	Recherche scientifique et développement
73	Publicité et études de marché
74	Autres activités professionnelles, scientifiques et techniques
75	Activités de services vétérinaires

Section N: Activités de services administratifs et d'appui

77	Activités de location
78	Activités relatives à l'emploi
79	Activités des agences de voyages, voyagistes, services de réservation et activités connexes
80	Activités d'enquêtes et de sécurité
81	Activités des services concernant les bâtiments, architecture paysagère
82	Activités d'appui administratif, de secrétariat, et autres activités d'appui aux entreprises

Section O: Administration publique et défense; sécurité sociale obligatoire

| 84 | Administration publique et défense; sécurité sociale obligatoire |

Section P: Éducation

| 85 | Éducation |

Section Q: Santé et activités d'action sociale

86	Activités relatives à la santé
87	Activités de soins de santé dispensés en établissement
88	Activités d'action sociale sans hébergement

Section R: Arts, spectacles et loisirs

90	Activités créatives, arts et spectacles
91	Activités des bibliothèques, archives, musées et autres activités culturelles
92	Activités de jeux de hasard et de pari
93	Activités sportives et activités de loisirs et récréatives

Section S: Autres activités de services

94	Activités des organisations associatives
95	Activités de réparation d'ordinateurs et d'articles personnels et ménagers
96	Autres activités de services personnels

Section T: Activités des ménages privés employant du personnel domestique; activités non différenciées de production de biens et de services des ménages privés pour usage propre

| 97 | Activités des ménages privés employant du personnel domestique |
| 98 | Activités non différenciées de production de biens et de services des ménages privés pour usage propre |

Section U: Activités des organisations et organismes extra-territoriaux

| 99 | Activités des organisations et organismes extra-territoriaux |

Section supplémentaire X: Ne pouvant être classés selon l'activité économique

[1] Pour plus de détails voir:
http://unstats.un.org/unsd/cr/registry/isic-4.asp

Clasificación Industrial, Internacional Uniforme de Todas las Actividades Económicas (CIIU - Rev. 4)[1]

Sección A: Agricultura, ganadería, silvicultura y pesca

01   Agricultura, ganadería, caza y actividades de servicios conexos

02   Silvicultura y extracción de madera

03   Pesca y acuicultura

Sección B: Explotación de minas y canteras

05   Extracción de carbón de piedra y lignito

06   Extracción de petróleo crudo y gas natural

07   Extracción de minerales metalíferos

08   Explotación de otras minas y canteras

09   Actividades de servicios de apoyo para la explotación de minas y canteras

Sección C: Industrias manufactureras

10   Elaboración de productos alimenticios

11   Elaboración de bebidas

12   Elaboración de productos de tabaco

13   Fabricación de productos textiles

14   Fabricación de prendas de vestir

15   Fabricación de productos de cuero y productos conexos

16   Producción de madera y fabricación de productos de madera y corcho, excepto muebles; fabricación de artículos de paja y de materiales trenzables

17   Fabricación de papel y de productos de papel

18   Impresión y reproducción de grabaciones

19   Fabricación de coque y productos de la refinación del petróleo

20   Fabricación de sustancias y productos químicos

21   Fabricación de productos farmacéuticos, sustancias químicas medicinales y productos botánicos de uso farmacéutico

22   Fabricación de productos de caucho y de plástico

23   Fabricación de otros productos minerales no metálicos

24   Fabricación de metales comunes

25   Fabricación de productos elaborados de metal, excepto maquinaria y equipo

26   Fabricación de productos de informática, de electrónica y de óptica

27   Fabricación de equipo eléctrico

28   Fabricación de maquinaria y equipo n.c.p.

29   Fabricación de vehículos automotores, remolques y semirremolques

30   Fabricación de otro equipo de transporte

31   Fabricación de muebles

32   Otras industrias manufactureras

33   Reparación e instalación de maquinaria y equipo

Sección D: Suministro de electricidad, gas, vapor y aire acondicionado

35   Suministro de electricidad, gas, vapor y aire acondicionado

Sección E: Suministro de agua; evacuación de aguas residuales, gestión de desechos y descontaminación

36   Captación, tratamiento y distribución de agua

37   Evacuación de aguas residuales

38   Recogida, tratamiento y eliminación de desechos; recuperación de materiales

39   Actividades de descontaminación y otros servicios de gestión de desechos

Sección F: Construcción

41   Construcción de edificios

42   Obras de ingeniería civil

43   Actividades especializadas de construcción

Sección G: Comercio al por mayor y al por menor; reparación de vehículos automotores y motocicletas

45   Comercio al por mayor y al por menor y reparación de vehículos automotores y motocicletas

46   Comercio al por mayor, excepto el de vehículos automotores y motocicletas

47   Comercio al por menor, excepto el de vehículos automotores y motocicletas

Sección H: Transporte y almacenamiento

49   Transporte por vía terrestre y transporte por tuberías

50   Transporte por vía acuática

51   Transporte por vía aérea

52   Almacenamiento y actividades de apoyo al transporte

53   Actividades postales y de mensajería

Sección I: Actividades de alojamiento y de servicio de comidas

55   Actividades de alojamiento

56   Actividades de servicio de comidas y bebidas

Sección J: Información y comunicaciones

58   Actividades de edición

59   Actividades de producción de películas cinematográficas, vídeos y programas de televisión, grabación de sonido y edición de música

60   Actividades de programación y transmisión

61   Telecomunicaciones

| 62 | Programación informática, consultoría de informática y actividades conexas |
| 63 | Actividades de servicios de información |

Sección K: Actividades financieras y de seguros

64	Actividades de servicios financieros, excepto las de seguros y fondos de pensiones
65	Seguros, reaseguros y fondos de pensiones, excepto planes de seguridad social de afiliación obligatoria
66	Actividades auxiliares de las actividades de servicios financieros

Sección L: Actividades inmobiliarias

| 68 | Actividades inmobiliarias |

Sección M: Actividades profesionales, científicas y técnicas

69	Actividades jurídicas y de contabilidad
70	Actividades de oficinas principales; actividades de consultoría de gestión
71	Actividades de arquitectura e ingeniería; ensayos y análisis técnicos
72	Investigación científica y desarrollo
73	Publicidad y estudios de mercado
74	Otras actividades profesionales, científicas y técnicas
75	Actividades veterinarias

Sección N: Actividades de servicios administrativos y de apoyo

77	Actividades de alquiler y arrendamiento
78	Actividades de empleo
79	Actividades de agencias de viajes y operadores turísticos y servicios de reservas y actividades conexas
80	Actividades de seguridad e investigación
81	Actividades de servicios a edificios y de paisajismo
82	Actividades administrativas y de apoyo de oficina y otras actividades de apoyo a las empresas

Sección O: Administración pública y defensa; planes de seguridad social de afiliación obligatoria

| 84 | Administración pública y defensa; planes de seguridad social de afiliación obligatoria |

Sección P: Enseñanza

| 85 | Enseñanza |

Sección Q: Actividades de atención de la salud humana y de asistencia social

86	Actividades de atención de la salud humana
87	Actividades de atención en instituciones
88	Actividades de asistencia social sin alojamiento

Sección R: Actividades artísticas, de entretenimiento y recreativas

90	Actividades creativas, artísticas y de entretenimiento
91	Actividades de bibliotecas, archivos y museos y otras actividades culturales
92	Actividades de juegos de azar y apuestas
93	Actividades deportivas, de esparcimiento y recreativas

Sección S: Otras actividades de servicios

94	Actividades de asociaciones
95	Reparación de ordenadores y de efectos personales y enseres domésticos
96	Otras actividades de servicios personales

Sección T: Actividades de los hogares como empleadores; actividades no diferenciadas de los hogares como productores de bienes y servicios para uso propio

| 97 | Actividades de los hogares como empleadores de personal doméstico |
| 98 | Actividades no diferenciadas de los hogares como productores de bienes y servicios para uso propio |

Sección U: Actividades de organizaciones y órganos extraterritoriales

| 99 | Actividades de organizaciones y órganos extraterritoriales |

Sección adicional X: No pueden clasificarse según la actividad económica

[1] Para más detalles, ver:
http://unstats.un.org/unsd/cr/registry/isic-4.asp

International Classification by Status in Employment (ICSE)

ICSE - 1958

The United Nations Statistical Commission approved in 1958 the following classification: [1]

(a) *Employer:* a person who operates his or her own economic enterprise, or engages independently in a profession or trade, and hires one or more employees. Some countries may wish to distinguish among employers according to the number of persons they employ.

(b) *Own-account worker:* a person who operates his or her own economic enterprise, or engages independently in a profession or trade, and hires no employees.

(c) *Employee:* a person who works for a public or private employer and receives remuneration in wages, salary, commission, tips, piece-rates or pay in kind.

(d) *Unpaid family worker:* usually a person who works without pay in an economic enterprise operated by a related person living in the same household. Where it is customary for young persons, in particular, to work without pay in an economic enterprise operated by a related person who does not live in the same household, the requirement of "living in the same household" may be eliminated. If there are a significant number of unpaid family workers in enterprises of which the operators are members of a producers' cooperative who are classified in category (e), these unpaid family workers should be classified in a separate subgroup.

(e) *Member of producers' cooperative:* a person who is an active member of a producers' cooperative, regardless of the industry in which it is established. Where this group is not numerically important, it may be excluded from the classification, and members of producers' cooperatives should be classified under other headings, as appropriate.

(f) *Persons not classifiable by status:* experienced workers whose status is unknown or inadequately described and unemployed persons not previously employed (i.e. new entrants). A separate group for new entrants may be included if information for this group is not already available elsewhere.

ICSE - 1993

The 15th International Conference of Labour Statisticians adopted, in January 1993, a resolution concerning the ICSE which states *[extract]:* [2]

II. THE ISCE-93 GROUPS[3]

4. The ICSE-93 consists of the following groups, which are defined in section III:

1. employees;

   among whom countries may need and be able to distinguish "employees with stable contracts" (including "regular employees");

2. employers;

3. own-account workers;

4. members of producers' cooperatives;

5. contributing family workers;

6. workers not classifiable by status.

III. GROUP DEFINITIONS

5. The groups in the ICSE-93 are defined with reference to the distinction between "paid employment" jobs on the one side and self-employment jobs on the other. Groups are defined with reference to one or more aspects of the economic risk and/or the type of authority which the explicit or implicit employment contract gives the incumbents or to which it subjects them.

6. *Paid employment jobs* are those jobs where the incumbents hold explicit (written or oral) or implicit employment contracts which give them a basic remuneration which is not directly dependent upon the revenue of the unit for which they work (this unit can be a corporation, a non-profit institution, a government unit or a household). Some or all of the tools, capital equipment, information systems and/or premises used by the incumbents may be owned by others, and the incumbents may work under direct supervision of, or according to strict guidelines set by the owner(s) or persons in the owners' employment. (Persons in "paid employment jobs" are typically remunerated by wages and salaries, but, may be paid by commission from sales, by piece-rates, bonuses or in-kind payments such as food, housing or training.)

7. *Self-employment jobs* are those jobs where the remuneration is directly dependent upon the profits (or the potential for profits) derived from the goods and services produced (where own consumption is considered to be part of profits). The incumbents make the operational decisions affecting the enterprise, or delegate such decisions while retaining responsibility for the welfare of the enterprise. (In this context "enterprise" includes one-person operations.)

8. *Employees* are all those workers who hold the type of job defined as "paid employment jobs "(cf. paragraph 6). *Employees with stable contracts* are those "employees" who have had, and continue to have, an explicit (written or oral) or implicit contract of employment, or a succession of such contracts, with the same employer on a continuous basis. "On a continuous basis" implies a period of employment which is longer than a specified minimum determined according to national cirumstances. (If interruptions are allowed in this minimum period, their maximum duration should also be determined according to national circumstances.) *Regular employees* are those "employees with stable contracts" for whom the employing organization is responsible for payment of relevant taxes and social security

contributions and/or where the contractual relationship is subject to national labour legislation.

9. *Employers* are those workers who, working on their own account or with one or a few partners, hold the type of job defined as a "self-employment job" (cf. paragraph 7), and, in this capacity, on a continuous basis (including the reference period) have engaged one or more persons to work for them in their business as "employee(s)" (cf. paragraph 8). The meaning of "engage on a continuous basis" is to be determined by national circumstances, in a way which is consistent with the definition of "employees with stable contracts" (cf. paragraph 8). (The partners may or may not be members of the same family or household.)

10. *Own-account workers* are those workers who, working on their own account or with one or more partners, hold the type of job defined as "a self-employment job" (cf. paragraph 7), and have not engaged on a continuous basis any "employees" (cf. paragraph 8) to work for them during the reference period. It should be noted that during the reference period the members of this group may have engaged "employees", provided that this is on a non-continuous basis. (The partners may or may not be members of the same family or household.)

11. *Members of producers' cooperatives* are workers who hold a "self-employment" job (cf. paragraph 7) in a cooperative producing goods and services, in which each member takes part on an equal footing with other members in determining the organization of production, sales and/or other work of the establishment, the invest- ments and the distribution of the proceeds of the establis- hment amongst their members. (It should be noted that "employees" (cf. paragraph 8) of producers' cooperatives are not to be classified to this group.)

12. *Contributing family workers* are those workers who hold a "self-employment" job (cf. paragraph 7) in a market-oriented establishment operated by a related person living in the same household, who cannot be regarded as a partner, because their degree of commit- ment to the operation of the establishment, in terms of working time or other factors to be determined by national circumstances, is not at a level comparable to that of the head of the establishment. (Where it is customary for young persons, in particular, to work without pay in an economic enterprise operated by a related person who does not live in the same household, the requirement of "living in the same household" may be eliminated.)

13. *Workers not classifiable by status* include those for whom insufficient relevant information is available, and/or who cannot be included in any of the preceding categories.

IV. STATISTICAL TREATMENT OF PARTICULAR GROUPS

14. This section outlines a possible statistical treatment of particular groups of workers. Some of the groups represent subcategories or disaggregations of one of the specific ICSE-93 categories. Others may cut across two or more of these categories. Countries may need and be able to distinguish one or more of the groups, in

particular group (a), and may also create other groups according to national requirements:

(a) *Owner-managers of incorporated enterprises* are workers who hold a job in an incorporated enterprise, in which they: (a) alone, or together with other members of their families or one or a few partners, hold controlling ownership of the enterprise; and (b) have the authority to act on its behalf as regards contracts with other organiza- tions and the hiring and dismissal of persons "in paid employment" with the same organization, subject only to national legislation regulating such matters and the rules established by the elected or appointed board of the organization. Different users of labour market, economic and social statistics may have different views on whether these workers are best classified as in "paid employment" (cf. paragraph 6) or as in "self-employment" (cf. para- graph 7), because these workers receive part of their remuneration in a way similar to persons in "paid employment" while their authority in and responsibility for the enterprise corresponds more to persons in "self- employment", and in particular to "employers". (Note, for example, that to classify them as "employees" will be consistent with their classification in the "System of National Accounts", while they may be best classified as "employers" or "own-account workers" for labour market analysis.) Countries should, therefore, according to the needs of users of their statistics and their data collection possibilities, endeavour to identify this group separately. This will also facilitate international comparisons.

Notes

[1] United Nations Statistical Office (1990): *Supplementary principles and recommen- dations for population and housing censuses.* Statistical Papers (doc. ST/ESA/STAT/SER./M/67/Add.1). United Nations, New York, 1990).

[2] ILO (1993): *Fifteenth International Conference of Labour Statisticians, Report of the Conference.* ICLS/15/D.6 (Rev. 1). International Labour Office, Geneva 1993.

[3] For linguistic convenience the group titles and definitions have been formulated in a way which corresponds to the situation where each person holds only one job during the reference period.

Classification internationale d'après la situation dans la profession (CISP)

CISP - 1958

La Commission de statistique des Nations Unies a approuvé en 1958 la classification suivante [1]:

a) *Employeur:* personne qui exploite sa propre entreprise économique ou qui exerce pour son propre compte une profession ou un métier, et qui emploie un ou plusieurs salariés. Certains pays classent aussi les employeurs selon le nombre de personnes qu'ils emploient.

b) *Personne travaillant pour son propre compte:* personne qui exploite sa propre entreprise économique ou qui exerce pour son propre compte une profession ou un métier, mais qui n'emploie aucun salarié.

c) *Salarié:* personne qui travaille pour un employeur public ou privé et qui reçoit une rémunération sous forme de traitement, salaire, commission, pourboires, salaire aux pièces ou paiement en nature.

d) *Travailleur familial non rémunéré:* personne qui travaille sans rémunération dans une entreprise exploitée par un parent vivant dans le même ménage. Lorsqu'il est fréquent que des jeunes, en particulier, accomplissent un travail non rémunéré dans une entreprise exploitée par un parent ne vivant pas dans le même ménage, on pourra supprimer le critère «vivant dans le même ménage». Si le nombre de travailleurs familiaux non rémunérés employés dans des entreprises gérées par les membres d'une coopérative de production appartenant à la catégorie qui fait l'objet de l'alinéa *e)* ci-dessous est important, ces travailleurs familiaux non rémunérés devront être classés dans un sous-groupe distinct.

e) *Membre d'une coopérative de producteurs:* personne qui est membre actif d'une coopérative de producteurs, quelle que soit la branche d'activité économique. Quand ce groupe n'est pas numériquement important, on peut ne pas le faire figurer dans la classification et répartir les membres des coopératives de producteurs entre les autres groupes, comme il convient.

f) *Personnes inclassables d'après la situation dans la profession:* travailleurs expérimentés dont la situation exacte n'est pas connue ou est mal définie, et chômeurs n'ayant jamais travaillé (nouveaux arrivants sur le marché du travail). On pourra classer les nouveaux arrivants sur le marché du travail dans un groupe distinct si des données concernant ce groupe n'existent pas déjà ailleurs.

CISP - 1993

La 15e Conférence internationale des statisticiens du travail a adopté, en janvier 1993, une résolution relative à la CISP qui dit *[extrait]* [2]:

II. GROUPES DÉFINIS DANS LA CISP-93 [3]

4. La CISP-93 comprend les groupes suivants, définis dans la section III:

1) salariés;

parmi lesquels certains pays pourraient avoir le besoin et la capacité de distinguer les «salariés titulaires d'un contrat de travail stable» (y compris les «salariés réguliers»);

2) employeurs;

3) personnes travaillant pour leur propre compte;

4) membres de coopératives de producteurs;

5) travailleurs familiaux collaborant à l'entreprise familiale;

6) travailleurs inclassables d'après la situation dans la profession.

III. DÉFINITION DES GROUPES

5. Les groupes de la CISP sont définis conformément à la distinction faite entre l'«emploi rémunéré», d'une part, et l'«emploi à titre indépendant», d'autre part. Une fois opérée cette distinction élémentaire, des groupes sont définis en fonction d'un ou de plusieurs aspects du risque économique ou de la nature du contrôle que les contrats de travail explicites ou implicites octroient aux titulaires ou auquel ils les soumettent.

6. *Emplois rémunérés:* emplois pour lesquels les titulaires ont des contrats explicites ou implicites, écrits ou oraux, qui leur donnent droit à une rémunération de base qui n'est pas directement dépendante du revenu de l'unité pour laquelle ils travaillent (cette unité pouvant être une entreprise, une institution à but non lucratif, une administration publique ou un ménage). Les outils, les équipements lourds, les systèmes d'information et/ou les locaux utilisés par les titulaires peuvent appartenir pour partie ou en totalité à d'autres; et les titulaires peuvent être placés sous la supervision directe du (des) propriétaire(s) ou de personnes employées par lui (eux) ou devoir travailler selon de strictes directives établies par lui (eux). (De manière caractéristique, les personnes dans l'«emploi rémunéré» perçoivent des traitements et des salaires, mais peuvent aussi être payées à la commission sur ventes, à la pièce, à la prime ou en nature [par exemple nourriture, logement, formation].)

7. *Emplois à titre indépendant:* emplois dont la rémunération est directement dépendante des bénéfices (réalisés ou potentiels) provenant des biens ou services produits (lorsque la consommation propre est considérée comme faisant partie des bénéfices). Les titulaires prennent les décisions de gestion affectant l'entreprise ou délèguent cette compétence mais sont tenus pour responsables de la bonne santé de leur entreprise. (Dans ce contexte, l'«entreprise» inclut les entreprises unipersonnelles.)

8. *Salariés:* ensemble des travailleurs qui occupent un emploi défini comme «emploi rémunéré» (cf. paragraphe 6 ci-dessus). Les *salariés titulaires de contrats de travail stables* sont des salariés (cf. paragraphe 8) qui ont été et sont titulaires d'un contrat de travail explicite ou impli-

cite, écrit ou oral, ou d'une série de tels contrats, avec le même employeur continûment. «Continûment» implique une période d'emploi plus longue qu'un minimum spécifié et déterminé selon les conditions nationales. (Si des interruptions sont autorisées au cours de cette période minimum, leur durée maximum doit aussi être déterminée selon les conditions nationales.) Les *salariés réguliers* sont des «salariés titulaires de contrats de travail stables» pour lesquels l'organisation employeuse est responsable du paiement des impôts et contributions à la sécurité sociale appropriés et/ou la relation contractuelle est régie par la législation du travail normale.

9. *Employeurs:* personnes qui, travaillant pour leur propre compte ou avec un ou plusieurs associés (cf. paragraphe 11), occupent le type d'emploi défini comme «emploi indépendant» (cf. paragraphe 7 ci-dessus) et qui, à ce titre, engagent sur une période continue incluant la période de référence une ou plusieurs personnes pour travailler dans leur entreprise (cf. paragraphe 8 ci-dessus). La signification de «sur une période continue» doit être déterminée selon les conditions nationales, de façon à ce qu'il y ait correspondance avec la définition «salariés titulaires de contrats de travail stables» (cf. paragraphe 8 ci-dessus). (A noter que les associés peuvent être ou ne pas être membres de la même famille ou du même ménage.)

10. *Personnes travaillant pour leur propre compte:* personnes qui, travaillant pour leur propre compte ou avec un ou plusieurs associés, occupent un emploi défini comme «emploi à titre indépendant» (cf. paragraphe 7 ci-dessus) et qui, pendant la période de référence, n'ont engagé continûment aucun «salarié» pour travailler avec eux (cf. paragraphe 8). (Les partenaires peuvent être ou ne pas être membres de la même famille ou du même ménage.)

11. *Membres de coopératives de producteurs:* personnes qui occupent un «emploi indépendant» (cf. paragraphe 7) et, à ce titre, appartiennent à une coopérative produisant des biens et des services, dans laquelle chaque membre prend part sur un pied d'égalité à l'organisation de la production et des autres activités de l'établissement, décide des investissements ainsi que de la répartition des bénéfices de l'établissement entre les membres. (Il faut noter que les «salariés» des coopératives de producteurs ne doivent pas être classés dans ce groupe.)

12. *Travailleurs familiaux collaborant à l'entreprise familiale:* personnes qui occupent un «emploi indépendant» (cf. paragraphe 7) dans une entreprise orientée vers le marché et exploitée par un parent vivant dans le même ménage, mais qui ne peut pas être considéré comme associé, parce que leur degré d'engagement, en termes de temps de travail ou d'autres facteurs à déterminer selon les conditions nationales, n'est pas comparable à celui du dirigeant de l'établissement. (Lorsqu'il est fréquent que des jeunes, en particulier, accomplissent un travail non rémunéré dans une entreprise exploitée par un parent ne vivant pas dans le même ménage, on pourra supprimer le critère «vivant dans le même ménage».)

13. *Travailleurs inclassables d'après la situation dans la profession:* personnes pour lesquelles on ne dispose pas d'informations suffisantes. (Si l'on utilise la CISP-93 pour classer les personnes à la recherche d'un emploi, elles peuvent aussi être classées dans ce groupe: *a)* si elles ne rentrent pas dans la nouvelle classification des emplois d'après la situation dans la profession (classement sur la base de l'emploi recherché) ou *b)* si elles n'occupaient pas d'emploi auparavant [classement sur la base de l'emploi antérieurement occupé].)

IV. TRAITEMENT STATISTIQUE DES GROUPES PARTICULIERS

14. Cette section de la résolution montre une possibilité de traitement statistique de groupes particuliers de travailleurs. Certains de ces groupes représentent des sous-catégories ou distributions d'une des catégories spécifiques de la CISP-93. D'autres peuvent être trouvées dans deux ou plusieurs de ces catégories. Les pays peuvent avoir le besoin et la capacité de distinguer un ou plusieurs de ces groupes, en particulier le groupe a), ils peuvent aussi créer d'autres groupes selon les besoins nationaux:

a) *Les propriétaires-gérants d'entreprises constituées en sociétés* se définissent comme les personnes qui occupent un emploi dans une entreprise constituée en société dans laquelle *a)* seules, ou avec d'autres membres de leurs familles ou un ou plusieurs associés, elles possèdent une participation majoritaire dans cette société ou cette organisation; et *b)* elles sont habilitées à agir au nom de la société ou de l'organisation en ce qui concerne les contrats avec d'autres entreprises et l'embauche et le licenciement d'autres personnes occupant un «emploi rémunéré» au sein de la même société ou organisation, à la seule condition de se conformer à la législation nationale pertinente et aux règles établies par le conseil d'administration élu ou désigné de l'organisation. Différents utilisateurs des statistiques de l'emploi et des statistiques économiques et sociales peuvent avoir des vues divergentes sur le point de savoir s'il vaut mieux classer ces travailleurs dans l'«emploi rémunéré» (cf. paragraphe 6) ou dans l'«emploi indépendant» (cf. paragraphe 7), parce qu'ils reçoivent une partie de leur rémunération de la même manière que les personnes dans l'«emploi rémunéré», alors que leur autorité dans l'entreprise et leur responsabilité vis-à-vis d'elle correspondent aux personnes dans l'«emploi indépendant», en particulier les «employeurs». (Il faut noter, par exemple, que les classer dans les «salariés» serait cohérent avec leur classement dans le «système de comptabilité nationale», tandis qu'il vaudrait mieux les classer dans les «employeurs» ou les «personnes travaillant à leur propre compte» aux fins d'analyse du marché du travail.) Les pays devraient en conséquence, selon les besoins des utilisateurs de leurs statistiques et leurs possibilités de collecte de données, s'efforcer d'identifier ce groupe séparément. Cela facilitera aussi les comparaisons internationales.

Notes

[1] Bureau de statistique des Nations Unies (1990): *Principes et recommandations complémentaires concernant les recensements de la population et de l'habitation* (doc. ST/ESA/STAT/SER. M/67/Add. 1), Nations Unies, New York, 1990.

[2] BIT (1993): *Quinzième Conférence internationale des statisticiens du travail, Rapport de la Conférence.* ICLS/15/D.6 (Rev. 1), Bureau international du Travail, Genève, 1993.

[3] Pour des raisons d'ordre pratique, les définitions données dans cette section se réfèrent à la situation où chaque personne n'a occupé qu'un emploi pendant la période de référence. Les règles de classification des personnes ayant occupé plusieurs emplois sont données dans la section IV.

Clasificación Internacional de la Situación en el Empleo (CISE)

CISE - 1958

La Comisión de Estadística de las Naciones Unidas aprobó en 1958 la clasificación siguiente [1]:

a) *Empleador:* es la persona que dirige su propia empresa económica o que ejerce por cuenta propia una profesión u oficio, y que contrata a uno o más empleados. Algunos países tal vez encuentren conveniente dividir a los empleadores según el número de personas que emplean.

b) *Trabajador por cuenta propia:* es la persona que explota su propia empresa económica o que ejerce por cuenta propia una profesión u oficio, pero que no emplea asalariado alguno.

c) *Empleado:* es la persona que trabaja para un empleador público o privado y que percibe una remuneración en forma de salario, sueldo, comisión, propinas, pago a destajo o pago en especie.

d) *Trabajador familiar no remunerado:* es, por lo general, la persona que trabaja sin remuneración en una empresa económica explotada por una persona emparentada con él y que vive en el mismo hogar. Cuando sea costumbre que los jóvenes, en especial, trabajen sin remuneración en una empresa económica dirigida por un pariente que no vive en el mismo hogar, se puede suprimir el criterio «que vive en el mismo hogar». Cuando en empresas explotadas por miembros de una cooperativa de producción clasificada en la categoría *e) infra* haya un número importante de trabajadores familiares no remunerados, estos trabajadores deberán clasificarse en un subgrupo distinto.

e) *Miembro de una cooperativa de producción:* es la persona afiliada en forma activa a una cooperativa de esa clase, cualquiera que sea la rama de actividad económica en que se encuentre establecida. Cuando no tenga importancia numérica, este grupo podrá excluirse de la clasificación, y los miembros de las cooperativas de producción se incluirán en otras categorías, según convenga.

f) *Personas no clasificables por categoría en el empleo:* son los trabajadores con experiencia cuya categoría se desconoce, o está mal definida, y las personas desempleadas que nunca han trabajado (es decir, las personas que aspiran a ingresar por vez primera en la fuerza de trabajo). Estas últimas pueden ser incluidas en un grupo separado, si no hay información a su respecto en otra parte.

CISE - 1993

La decimoquinta Conferencia Internacional de Estadísticos del Trabajo adoptó, en enero de 1993, una resolución relativa a la CISE que dice *(extracto)* [2]:

II. LOS GRUPOS DE LA CISE-93 [3]

4. La CISE-93 se compone de los siguientes grupos, que se definen en la sección III:

1. Asalariados:

   los países quizás necesiten y puedan hacer una distinción suplementaria creando un grupo separado para los «empleados con contratos estables» (incluyendo a los «empleados regulares»).

2. Empleadores.

3. Trabajadores por cuenta propia.

4. Miembros de cooperativas de productores.

5. Trabajadores familiares auxiliares.

6. Trabajadores que no pueden clasificarse según la situación en el empleo.

III. DEFINICIONES DE LOS GRUPOS

5. Los grupos de la CISE-93 se definen haciendo referencia a la distinción entre los «empleos asalariados», por un lado, y los «empleos independientes», por el otro. Los grupos y subgrupos se definen haciendo referencia a uno o más aspectos del riesgo económico y/o del tipo de autoridad que el contrato de trabajo implícito o explícito confiere a los titulares o a que los somete.

6. *Empleos asalariados:* son aquellos empleos en los que los titulares tienen contratos de trabajo implícitos o explícitos (orales o escritos), por los que reciben una remuneración básica que no depende directamente de los ingresos de la unidad para la que trabajan (esta unidad puede ser una corporación, una institución sin fines de lucro, una unidad gubernamental o un hogar). Algunos o todos los instrumentos, bienes de capital, sistemas de información y/o locales utilizados por los titulares son la propiedad de terceras personas, y los titulares pueden trabajar bajo la supervisión directa de, o de acuerdo con directrices estrictas establecidas por el(los) propietario(s) o las personas empleadas por el(los) propietario(s). (Las personas con «empleos asalariados» se remuneran típicamente con sueldos y salarios, pero también pueden remunerarse por medio de comisiones de ventas, pagos a destajo, primas o pagos en especie tales como comida, habitación o formación.)

7. *Empleos independientes:* son aquellos empleos en los que la remuneración depende directamente de los beneficios (o del potencial para realizar beneficios) derivados de los bienes o servicios producidos (en estos empleos se considera que el consumo propio forma parte de los beneficios). Los titulares toman las decisiones operacionales que afectan a la empresa, o delegan tales decisiones, pero mantienen la responsabilidad por el bienestar de la empresa. (En este contexto, la «empresa» se define de manera suficientemente amplia para incluir a las operaciones de una sola persona.)

8. *Asalariados:* son todos aquellos trabajadores que tienen el tipo de empleo definido como «empleos asalariados» (véase el párrafo 6). *Empleados con contratos estables:* son aquellos «empleados» que han tenido, y continúan teniendo, un contrato de trabajo implícito o explícito (oral o escrito), o una serie de tales contratos,

con el mismo empleador de manera continua. El significado de «de manera continua» se refiere a un período de empleo que es más largo que una duración mínima especificada, la cual se determina de acuerdo con las circunstancias nacionales. (Si este período mínimo permite que haya interrupciones, la duración máxima también debe determinarse de acuerdo con las circunstancias nacionales.) Los *empleados regulares* son aquellos «empleados con contratos estables» ante quienes la organización empleadora es responsable por el pago de las cargas fiscales y de las contribuciones de la seguridad social y/o aquellos cuya relación contractual se rige por la legislación general del trabajo.

9. *Empleadores:* son aquellos trabajadores que, trabajando por su cuenta o con uno o más socios (véase el párrafo 11), tienen el tipo de empleo definido como «empleo independiente» (véase el párrafo 7) y que, en virtud de su condición de tales, han contratado a una o a varias personas para que trabajen para ellos en su empresa como «empleados» a lo largo de un período continuo que incluye el período de referencia (véase el párrafo 8). El significado de «a lo largo de un período continuo» se debe determinar de acuerdo con las circunstancias nacionales, de tal manera que corresponda con la definición de «empleados con contratos estables» (véase el párrafo 8). (Los socios no son necesariamente miembros de la misma familia u hogar.)

10. *Trabajadores por cuenta propia:* son aquellos trabajadores que, trabajando por su cuenta o con uno o más socios (véase el párrafo 11), tienen el tipo de empleo definido como «empleo independiente» (véase el párrafo 7) y no han contratado a ningún «empleado» de manera continua para que trabaje para ellos durante el período de referencia (véase el párrafo 8). Cabe notar que durante el período de referencia los miembros de este grupo pueden haber contratado «empleados», siempre y cuando lo hagan de manera no continua. (Los socios no son necesariamente miembros de la misma familia u hogar.)

11. *Miembros de cooperativas de productores:* son los trabajadores que tienen un «empleo independiente» (véase el párrafo 7) en una cooperativa que produce bienes y servicios, en la que cada miembro participa en pie de igualdad con los demás miembros en la determinación de la organización de la producción y en las demás actividades del establecimiento, en las inversiones y en la distribución de los beneficios del establecimiento entre los miembros. (Cabe precisar que los «empleados» de cooperativas de productores no deben clasificarse en este grupo.)

12. *Trabajadores familiares auxiliares:* son aquellos trabajadores que tienen un «empleo independiente» (véase el párrafo 7) en un establecimiento con orientación de mercado, dirigido por una persona de su familia que vive en el mismo hogar, pero a la que no puede considerarse como socia, debido a que el nivel de dedicación, en términos de tiempo de trabajo u otros factores que deben determinarse de acuerdo con circunstancias nacionales, no es comparable con aquel del jefe del establecimiento. (Cuando sea costumbre que los jóvenes, en especial, trabajen sin remuneración en una empresa económica dirigida por un pariente que no vive en el mismo hogar, se puede suprimir el criterio «que vive en el mismo hogar».)

13. *Trabajadores que no se pueden clasificar según la situación en el empleo:* en este grupo se incluye a los trabajadores sobre los que no se dispone de suficiente información pertinente, y/o que no pueden ser incluidos en ninguna de las categorías anteriores.

IV. TRATAMIENTO ESTADISTICO DE GRUPOS PARTICULARES

14. Esta sección presenta un posible tratamiento estadístico de grupos particulares de trabajadores. Algunos grupos representan subcategorías o divisiones de una categoría específica de la CISE-93. Otros grupos se encuentran en dos o más de estas categorías. Los países quizás necesiten y puedan distinguir uno o varios de estos grupos, en particular el grupo a), y pueden también crear otros grupos de acuerdo con las necesidades nacionales:

a) *Gerentes-propietarios de empresas constituidas en sociedad:* son trabajadores que tienen un empleo en una empresa constituida en sociedad, en la cual ellos: a) solos o junto con otros miembros de su familia, o con uno o varios socios, tienen una participación mayoritaria en la empresa u organización; y b) tienen la autoridad para actuar en su nombre en lo que se refiere a los contratos con otras organizaciones y a la contratación y el despido de personas con «empleos asalariados» de la misma organización, sujetos solamente a la legislación nacional sobre la materia y las normas establecidas por el consejo de administración de la organización elegido o designado. Los diferentes usuarios de las estadísticas del mercado de trabajo, económicas y sociales pueden tener diferentes opiniones acerca de si estos trabajadores se clasificarían mejor entre los «empleos asalariados» (véase el párrafo 6) o entre los «empleos independientes» (véase el párrafo 7), porque estos trabajadores reciben parte de su remuneración de manera similar a las personas con «empleos asalariados» mientras que su autoridad y responsabilidad sobre la empresa corresponde mejor a las personas con «empleos independientes», especialmente a los «empleadores». (Cabe notar, por ejemplo, que el clasificarlos como «empleados» será coherente con su clasificación en el «Sistema de Contabilidad Nacional», mientras que para el análisis del mercado de trabajo conviene mejor clasificarlos como «empleadores» o «trabajadores por cuenta propia».) Por lo tanto, los países deberán tratar de identificar a este grupo separadamente, de acuerdo con las necesidades de los usuarios de sus estadísticas y con las posibilidades de recolección de datos. Esto también facilitará las comparaciones internacionales.

Notas

[1] Oficina de Estadística de las Naciones Unidas (1990): *Principios y recomendaciones complementarios para los censos de poblaciones y habitación* (doc. ST/ESA/STAT/SER.M/67/Add.1), Naciones Unidas, Nueva York, 1990.

[2] OIT (1993): *Decimoquinta Conferencia Internacional de Estadísticos del Trabajo, Informe de la Conferencia.* ICLS/15/D.6 (Rev. 1). Oficina Internacional del Trabajo, Ginebra 1993.

[3] Por comodidad, los títulos de los grupos y las definiciones se refieren a la situación en que cada persona ocupa solamente un empleo durante el período de referencia. En la sección V se enuncian las reglas de clasificación de las personas que ocupan varios empleos en dicho período.

International Standard Classification of Occupations (ISCO-1968) [1, 2]

Major Group 0/1   Professional, technical and related workers

0-1	Physical scientists and related technicians
0-2/3	Architects, engineers and related technicians
0-4	Aircraft and ships' officers
0-5	Life scientists and related technicians
0-6/7	Medical, dental, veterinary and related workers
0-8	Statisticians, mathematicians, systems analysts and related technicians
0-9	Economists
1-1	Accountants
1-2	Jurists
1-3	Teachers
1-4	Workers in religion
1-5	Authors, journalists and related writers
1-6	Sculptors, painters, photographers and related creative artists
1-7	Composers and performing artists
1-8	Athletes, sportsmen and related workers
1-9	Professional, technical and related workers not elsewhere classified

Major Group 2   Administrative and managerial workers

2-0	Legislative officials and government administrators
2-1	Managers

Major Group 3   Clerical and related workers

3-0	Clerical supervisors
3-1	Government executive officials
3-2	Stenographers, typists and card- and tape-punching machine operators
3-3	Bookkeepers, cashiers and related workers
3-4	Computing machine operators
3-5	Transport and communications supervisors
3-6	Transport conductors
3-7	Mail distribution clerks
3-8	Telephone and telegraph operators
3-9	Clerical related workers not elsewhere classified

Major Group 4   Sales workers

4-0	Managers (wholesale and retail trade)
4-1	Working proprietors (wholesale and retail trade)
4-2	Sales supervisors and buyers
4-3	Technical salesmen, commercial travellers and manufacturers' agents
4-4	Insurance, real estate, securities and business services salesmen and auctioneers
4-5	Salesmen, shop assistants and related workers
4-9	Sales workers not elsewhere classified

Major Group 5   Service workers

5-0	Managers (catering and lodging services)
5-1	Working proprietors (catering and lodging services)
5-2	Housekeeping and related service supervisors
5-3	Cooks, waiters, bartenders and related workers
5-4	Maids and related housekeeping service workers not elsewhere classified
5-5	Building caretakers, charworkers, cleaners and related workers
5-6	Launderers, dry-cleaners and pressers
5-7	Hairdressers, barbers, beauticians and related workers
5-8	Protective service workers
5-9	Service workers not elsewhere classified

Major Group 6   Agriculture, animal husbandry and forestry workers, fishermen and hunters

6-0	Farm managers and supervisors
6-1	Farmers
6-2	Agriculture and animal husbandry workers
6-3	Forestry workers
6-4	Fishermen, hunters and related workers

Major Group 7/8/9   Production and related workers, transport equipment operators and labourers

7-0	Production supervisors and general foremen
7-1	Miners, quarrymen, well drillers and related workers
7-2	Metal processers
7-3	Wood preparation workers and paper makers
7-4	Chemical processers and related workers
7-5	Spinners, weavers, knitters, dyers and related workers
7-6	Tanners, fellmongers and pelt dressers
7-7	Food and beverage processers
7-8	Tobacco preparers and tobacco product makers
7-9	Tailors, dressmakers, sewers, upholsterers and related workers
8-0	Shoemakers and leather goods makers
8-1	Cabinetmakers and related woodworkers
8-2	Stone cutters and carvers
8-3	Blacksmiths, toolmakers and machine-tool operators
8-4	Machinery fitters, machine assemblers and precision instrument makers (except electrical)
8-5	Electrical fitters and related electrical and electronics workers
8-6	Broadcasting station and sound equipment operators and cinema projectionists
8-7	Plumbers, welders, sheet metal and structural metal preparers and erectors
8-8	Jewellery and precious metal workers
8-9	Glass formers, potters and related workers
9-0	Rubber and plastics product makers
9-1	Paper and paper board products makers
9-2	Printers and related workers
9-3	Painters
9-4	Production and related workers not elsewhere classified
9-5	Bricklayers, carpenters and other construction workers
9-6	Stationary engine and related equipment operators
9-7	Material-handling and related equipment operators, dockers and freight handlers
9-8	Transport equipment operators
9-9	Labourers not elsewhere classified

Major Group X   Workers not classifiable by occupation

X-1   New workers seeking employment

X-2   Workers reporting occupations unidentifiable or
        inadequately described

X-3   Workers not reporting any occupation

Armed Forces   Members of the armed forces

Notes

[1] *Major* and *Minor groups* only. This Classification consists of *Major groups* (one-digit codes), *Minor groups* (two-digit codes), *Unit groups* (three-digit codes) and *Occupational categories* (five-digit codes).

For full details, see ILO: *International Standard Classification of Occupations, revised edition, 1968* (Geneva, 1969).

[2] The revised *International Standard Classification of Occupations* (ISCO-88), which was approved by the 14th International Conference of Labour Statisticians 1987, was published in 1990.

Classification internationale type des professions (CITP-1968) [1] [2]

Grand groupe 0/1   Personnel des professions scientifiques, techniques, libérales et assimilées

0-1   Spécialistes des sciences physico-chimiques et techniciens assimilés

0-2/3   Architectes, ingénieurs et techniciens assimilés

0-4   Pilotes, officiers de pont et officiers mécaniciens (marine et aviation)

0-5   Biologistes, agronomes et techniciens assimilés

0-6/7   Médecins, dentistes, vétérinaires et travailleurs assimilés

0-8   Statisticiens, mathématiciens, analystes de systèmes et techniciens assimilés

0-9   Economistes

1-1   Comptables

1-2   Juristes

1-3   Personnel enseignant

1-4   Membres du clergé et assimilés

1-5   Auteurs, journalistes et écrivains assimilés

1-6   Sculpteurs, peintres, photographes et artistes créateurs assimilés

1-7   Musiciens, acteurs, danseurs et artistes assimilés

1-8   Athlètes, sportifs et assimilés

1-9   Personnel des professions scientifiques, techniques, libérales et assimilées non classé ailleurs

Grand groupe 2   Directeurs et cadres administratifs supérieurs

2-0   Membres des corps législatifs et cadres supérieurs de l'administration publique

2-1   Directeurs et cadres dirigeants

Grand groupe 3   Personnel administratif et travailleurs assimilés

3-0   Chefs de groupe d'employés de bureau

3-1   Agents administratifs (administration publique)

3-2   Sténographes dactylographes et opérateurs sur machines perforatrices de cartes et de rubans

3-3   Employés de comptabilité, caissiers et travailleurs assimilés

3-4   Opérateurs sur machines à traiter l'information

3-5   Chefs de services de transports et de communications

3-6   Chefs de train et receveurs

3-7   Facteurs et messagers

3-8   Opérateurs des téléphones et télégraphes

3-9   Personnel administratif et travailleurs assimilés non classés ailleurs

Grand groupe 4   Personnel commercial et vendeurs

4-0   Directeurs (commerces de gros et de détail)

4-1   Propriétaires-gérants de commerces de gros et de détail

4-2   Chefs des ventes et acheteurs

4-3   Agents commerciaux techniciens et voyageurs de commerce

4-4   Agents d'assurances, agents immobiliers, courtiers en valeurs, agents de vente de services aux entreprises et vendeurs aux enchères.

4-5   Commis vendeurs, employés de commerce et travailleurs assimilés

4-9   Personnel commercial et vendeurs non classés ailleurs

Grand groupe 5   Travailleurs spécialisés dans les services

5-0   Directeurs d'hôtels, de cafés ou de restaurants

5-1   Propriétaires-gérants d'hôtel, de cafés ou de restaurants

5-2   Chefs de groupe d'employés de maison et travailleurs assimilés

5-3   Cuisiniers, serveurs, barmen et travailleurs assimilés

5-4   Employés de maison et travailleurs assimilés non classés ailleurs

5-5   Gardiens d'immeubles, nettoyeurs et travailleurs assimilés

5-6   Blanchisseurs, dégraisseurs et presseurs

5-7   Coiffeurs, spécialistes des soins de beauté et travailleurs assimilés

5-8   Personnel des services de protection et de sécurité

5-9   Travailleurs spécialisés dans les services non classés ailleurs

Grand groupe 6   Agriculteurs, éleveurs, forestiers, pêcheurs et chasseurs

6-0   Directeurs et chefs d'exploitation agricoles

6-1   Exploitants agricoles

6-2   Travailleurs agricoles

6-3   Travailleurs forestiers

6-4   Pêcheurs, chasseurs et travailleurs assimilés

Grand groupe 7/8/9   Ouvriers et manœuvres non agricoles et conducteurs d'engins de transport

7-0   Agents de maîtrise et assimilés

7-1   Mineurs, carriers, foreurs de puits et travailleurs assimilés

7-2   Ouvriers de la production et du traitement des métaux

7-3   Ouvriers de la première préparation des bois et de la fabrication du papier

7-4   Conducteurs de fours et d'appareils chimiques

7-5   Ouvriers du textile

7-6   Tanneurs, peaussiers, mégissiers et ouvriers de la pelleterie

7-7   Ouvriers de l'alimentation et des boissons

7-8   Ouvriers des tabacs

7-9   Tailleurs, couturiers, couseurs, tapissiers et ouvriers assimilés

8-0   Bottiers, ouvriers de la chaussure et du cuir

8-1   Ebénistes, menuisiers et travailleurs assimilés

8-2   Tailleurs et graveurs de pierres

8-3   Ouvriers du façonnage et de l'usinage des métaux

8-4   Ajusteurs-monteurs, installateurs de machines et mécaniciens de précision (électriciens exceptés)

8-5   Electriciens, électroniciens et travailleurs assimilés

8-6   Opérateurs de stations d'émissions de radio et de télévision, opérateurs d'appareils de sonorisation et projectionnistes de cinéma

8-7   Plombiers soudeurs, tôliers-chaudronniers, monteurs de charpentes et de structures métalliques

8-8   Joailliers et orfèvres

8-9   Verriers, potiers et travailleurs assimilés

9-0   Ouvriers de la fabrication d'articles en caoutchouc et en matières plastiques

9-1   Confectionneurs d'articles en papier et en carton

9-2   Compositeurs typographes et travailleurs assimilés

9-3   Peintres

9-4   Ouvriers à la production et assimilés non classés ailleurs

9-5   Maçons, charpentiers et autres travailleurs de la construction

9-6   Conducteurs de machines et d'installations fixes

9-7   Conducteurs d'engins de manutention et de terrassement, dockers et manutentionnaires

9-8   Conducteurs d'engins de transport

9-9   Manœuvres non classés ailleurs

Grand groupe X Travailleurs ne pouvant être classés selon la profession

X-1   Personnes en quête de leur premier emploi

X-2   Travailleurs ayant fait au sujet de leur profession

une déclaration imprécise ou insuffisante

X-3   Travailleurs n'ayant déclaré aucune profession

Forces armées Membres des forces armées

Notes

[1] *Grands groupes* et *sous-groupes* seulement. Cette classification comprend des *grands groupes* (codes à un chiffre), des *sous-groupes* (codes à deux chiffres), des *groupes de base* (codes à trois chiffres) et des *catégories professionnelles* (codes à cinq chiffres).

Pour de plus amples détails, voir BIT: *Classification internationale type des professions, édition révisée, 1968* (Genève, 1969).

[2] La *Classification internationale type des professions*, révisée (CITP-88), qui a été approuvée par la 14e Conférence internationale des statisticiens du travail, 1987, a paru en 1991.

Clasificación Internacional Uniforme de Ocupaciones (CIUO - 1968) [1, 2]

Gran grupo 0/1 Profesionales, técnicos y trabajadores asimilados

0-1   Especialistas en ciencias físico-químicas y técnicos asimilados

0-2/3   Arquitectos, ingenieros y técnicos asimilados

0-4   Pilotos y oficiales de cubierta y oficiales maquinistas (aviación y marina)

0-5   Biólogos, agrónomos y técnicos asimilados

0-6/7   Médicos, odontólogos, veterinarios y trabajadores asimilados

0-8   Estadígrafos, matemáticos, analistas de sistemas y técnicos asimilados

0-9   Economistas

1-1   Contadores

1-2   Juristas

1-3   Profesores

1-4   Miembros del clero y asimilados

1-5   Autores, periodistas y escritores asimilados

1-6   Escultores, pintores, fotógrafos y artistas asimilados

1-7   Músicos, artistas, empresarios y productores de espectáculos

1-8   Atletas, deportistas y trabajadores asimilados

1-9   Profesionales, técnicos y trabajadores asimilados no clasificados bajo otros epígrafes

Gran grupo 2 Directores y funcionarios públicos superiores

2-0   Miembros de los cuerpos legislativos y personal directivo de la administración pública

2-1   Directores y personal directivo

Gran grupo 3 Personal administrativo y trabajadores asimilados

3-0   Jefes de empleados de oficinas

3-1   Agentes administrativos (administración pública)

3-2   Taquígrafos, mecanógrafos y operadores de máquinas perforadoras de tarjetas y cintas

3-3   Empleados de contabilidad, cajeros y trabajadores asimilados

3-4   Operadores de máquinas para cálculos contables y estadísticos

3-5   Jefes de servicios de transportes y de comunicaciones

3-6   Jefes de tren, controladores de coches-cama y cobradores

3-7   Carteros y mensajeros

3-8   Telefonistas y telegrafistas

3-9   Personal administrativo y trabajadores asimilados no clasificados bajo otros epígrafes

Gran grupo 4 Comerciantes y vendedores

4-0   Directores (comercio al por mayor y al por menor)

4-1   Comerciantes propietarios (comercio al por mayor y al por menor)

4-2   Jefes de ventas y compradores

4-3   Agentes técnicos de ventas, viajantes de comercio y representantes de fábrica

4-4   Agentes de seguros, agentes inmobiliarios, agentes de cambio y bolsa, agentes de venta de servicios a las empresas y subastadores

4-5   Vendedores, empleados de comercio y trabajadores asimilados

4-9   Comerciantes y vendedores no clasificados bajo otros epígrafes

Gran grupo 5 Trabajadores de los servicios

5-0   Directores (servicios de hostelería, bares y similares)

5-1   Gerentes propietarios (servicios de hostelería, bares y similares)

5-2   Jefes de personal de servidumbre

5-3   Cocineros, camareros, bármanes y trabajadores asimilados

5-4   Personal de servidumbre no clasificado bajo otros epígrafes

5-5   Guardianes de edificios, personal de limpieza y trabajadores asimilados

5-6   Lavanderos, limpiadores en seco y planchadores

5-7   Peluqueros, especialistas en tratamientos de belleza y trabajadores asimilados

5-8   Personal de los servicios de protección y de seguridad

5-9   Trabajadores de los servicios no clasificados bajo otros epígrafes

Gran grupo 6 Trabajadores agrícolas y forestales, pescadores y cazadores

6-0   Directores y jefes de explotaciones agrícolas

6-1   Explotadores agrícolas

6-2   Obreros agrícolas

6-3   Trabajadores forestales

6-4   Pescadores, cazadores y trabajadores asimilados

Gran grupo 7/8/9 Obreros no agrícolas, conductores de máquinas y vehículos de transporte y trabajadores asimilados

7-0   Contramaestres y capataces mayores

7-1   Mineros, canteros, sondistas y trabajadores asimilados

7-2   Obreros metalúrgicos

7-3   Obreros del tratamiento de la madera y de la fabricación de papel

7-4   Obreros de los tratamientos químicos y trabajadores asimilados

7-5   Hilanderos, tejedores, tintoreros y trabajadores asimilados

7-6   Obreros de la preparación, curtido y tratamiento de pieles

7-7   Obreros de la preparación de alimentos y bebidas

7-8   Obreros del tabaco

7-9   Sastres, modistos, peleteros, tapiceros y trabajadores asimilados

8-0   Zapateros y guarnicioneros

8-1   Ebanistas, operadores de máquinas de labrar madera y trabajadores asimilados

8-2   Labrantes y adornistas

8-3   Obreros de la labra de metales

8-4   Ajustadores-montadores e instaladores de maquinaria e instrumentos de precisión, relojeros y mecánicos (excepto electricistas)

8-5   Electricistas, electronicistas y trabajadores asimilados

8-6   Operadores de estaciones emisoras de radio y televisión y de equipos de sonorización y de proyecciones cinematográficas

8-7	Fontaneros, soldadores, chapistas, caldereros y preparadores y montadores de estructuras metálicas
8-8	Joyeros y plateros
8-9	Vidrieros, ceramistas y trabajadores asimilados
9-0	Obreros de la fabricación de productos de caucho y plástico
9-1	Confeccionadores de productos de papel y cartón
9-2	Obreros de las artes gráficas
9-3	Pintores
9-4	Obreros manufactureros y trabajadores asimilados no clasificados bajo otros epígrafes
9-5	Obreros de la construcción
9-6	Operadores de máquinas fijas y de instalaciones similares
9-7	Obreros de la manipulación de mercancías y materiales y de movimiento de tierras
9-8	Conductores de vehículos de transporte
9-9	Peones no clasificados bajo otros epígrafes

Gran grupo X   Trabajadores que no pueden ser clasificados según la ocupación

X-1	Personas en busca de su primer empleo
X-2	Trabajadores que han declarado ocupaciones no identificables o insuficientemente descritas
X-3	Trabajadores que no han declarado ninguna ocupación

Fuerzas armadas   Miembros de las fuerzas armadas

Notas

[1] *Grandes grupos* y *Subgrupos* solamente. Esta Clasificación se compone de *Grandes grupos* (clave de un dígito), *Subgrupos* (clave de dos dígitos), *Grupos unitarios* (clave de tres dígitos) y *Categorías profesionales* (clave de cinco dígitos).

Para más amplios detalles, véase OIT: *Clasificación Internacional Uniforme de Ocupaciones, edición revisada, 1968* (Ginebra, 1970).

[2] La *Clasificación Internacional Uniforme de Ocupaciones* revisada (CIUO-88), que se aprobó por la 14.ª Conferencia Internacional de Estadísticos del Trabajo, 1987, apareció en 1991.

International Standard Classification of Occupations (ISCO-88)
Major, Sub-Major and Minor Groups

Major Group 1   Legislators, senior officials and managers

11		Legislators and senior officials
	111	Legislators
	112	Senior government officials
	113	Traditional chiefs and heads of villages
	114	Senior officials of special-interest organisations
12		Corporate managers [1]
	121	Directors and chief executives
	122	Production and operations department managers
	123	Other department managers
13		General managers [2]
	131	General managers

Major Group 2   Professionals

21		Physical, mathematical and engineering science professionals
	211	Physicists, chemists and related professionals
	212	Mathematicians, statisticians and related professionals
	213	Computing professionals
	214	Architects, engineers and related professionals
22		Life science and health professional
	221	Life science professionals
	222	Health professionals (except nursing)
	223	Nursing and midwifery professionals
23		Teaching professionals
	231	College, university and higher education teaching professionals
	232	Secondary education teaching professionals
	233	Primary and pre-primary education teaching professionals
	234	Special education teaching professionals
	235	Other teaching professionals
24		Other professionals
	241	Business professionals
	242	Legal professionals
	243	Archivists, librarians and related information professionals
	244	Social science and related professionals
	245	Writers and creative or performing artists
	246	Religious professionals

Major Group 3   Technicians and associate professionals

31		Physical and engineering science associate professionals
	311	Physical and engineering science technicians
	312	Computer associate professionals
	313	Optical and electronic equipment operators
	314	Ship and aircraft controllers and technicians
	315	Safety and quality inspectors
32		Life science and health associate professionals
	321	Life science technicians and related associate professionals
	322	Modern health associate professionals (except nursing)
	323	Nursing and midwifery associate professionals
	324	Traditional medicine practitioners and faith healers
33		Teaching associate professionals
	331	Primary education teaching associate professionals
	332	Pre-primary education teaching associate professionals
	333	Special education teaching associate professionals
	334	Other teaching associate professionals
34		Other associate professionals
	341	Finance and sales associate professionals
	342	Business services agents and trade brokers
	343	Administrative associate professionals
	344	Customs, tax and related government associate professionals
	345	Police inspectors and detectives
	346	Social work associate professionals
	347	Artistic, entertainment and sports associate professionals
	348	Religious associate professionals

Major Group 4   Clerks

41		Office clerks
	411	Secretaries and keyboard-operating clerks
	412	Numerical clerks
	413	Material-recording and transport clerks
	414	Library, mail and related clerks
	419	Other office clerks
42		Customer service clerks
	421	Cashiers, tellers and related clerks
	422	Client information clerks

Major Group 5   Service workers and shop and market sales workers

51		Personal and protective services workers
	511	Travel attendants and related workers
	512	Housekeeping and restaurant services workers
	513	Personal care and related workers
	514	Other personal service workers
	515	Astrologers, fortune-tellers and related workers
	516	Protective services workers
52		Models, salespersons and demonstrators
	521	Fashion and other models
	522	Shop salespersons and demonstrators
	523	Stall and market salespersons

Major Group 6   Skilled agricultural and fishery workers

61		Market-oriented skilled agricultural and fishery workers
	611	Market-oriented gardeners and crop growers
	612	Market-oriented animal producers and related workers
	613	Market-oriented crop and animal producers
	614	Forestry and related workers
	615	Fishery workers, hunters and trappers
62		Subsistence agricultural and fishery workers
	621	Subsistence agricultural and fishery workers

Major Group 7   Craft and related trade workers

71		Extraction and building trade workers
	711	Miners, shotfirers, stone cutters and carvers
	712	Building frame and related trades workers
	713	Building finishers and related trades workers
	714	Painters, building structure cleaners and related trades workers
72		Metal, machinery and related trades workers
	721	Metal moulders, welders, sheet-metal workers, structural-metal preparers, and related trades workers

722 Blacksmiths, tool-makers and related trades workers
723 Machinery mechanics and fitters
724 Electrical and electronic equipment mechanics and fitters
73 Precision, handicraft, printing and related trades workers
731 Precision workers in metal and related materials
732 Potters, glass-makers and related trades workers
733 Handicraft workers in wood, textile, leather and related material
734 Printing and related trades workers
74 Other craft and related trades workers
741 Food processing and related trades workers
742 Wood treaters, cabinet-makers and related trades workers
743 Textile, garment and related trades workers
744 Pelt, leather and shoemaking trades workers

Major Group 8   Plant and machine operators and assemblers
81 Stationary plant and related operators
811 Mining and mineral-processing-plant operators
812 Metal-processing-plant operators
813 Glass, ceramics and related plant-operators
814 Wood-processing-and papermaking-plant operators
815 Chemical-processing-plant operators
816 Power-production and related plant operators
817 Automated-assembly-line and industrial-robot operators
82 Machine operators and assemblers
821 Metal- and mineral-products machine operators
822 Chemical-products machine operators
823 Rubber- and plastic-products machine operators
824 Wood-products machine operators
825 Printing-, binding- and paper-products machine operators
826 Textile-, fur- and leather-products machine operators
827 Food and related products machine operators
828 Assemblers
829 Other machine operators and assemblers

83 Drivers and mobile plant operators
831 Locomotive engine drivers and related workers
832 Motor vehicle drivers
833 Agricultural and other mobile plant operators
834 Ships' deck crews and related workers

Major Group 9   Elementary occupations
91 Sales and services elementary occupations
911 Street vendors and related workers
912 Shoe cleaning and other street services elementary occupations
913 Domestic and related helpers, cleaners and launderers
914 Building caretakers, window and related cleaners
915 Messengers, porters, doorkeepers and related workers
916 Garbage collectors and related labourers
92 Agricultural, fishery and related labourers
921 Agricultural, fishery and related labourers
93 Labourers in mining, construction, manufacturing and transport
931 Mining and construction labourers
932 Manufacturing labourers
933 Transport labourers and freight handlers

Major Group 0   Armed forces
01 Armed forces
011 Armed forces

Notes

[1] This sub-major group is intended to include persons who — as directors, chief executives or specialised managers — manage enterprises requiring a total of three or more managers.

[2] This sub-major group is intended to include persons who manage enterprises on their own behalf, or on behalf of the proprietor, with some non-managerial help and assistance of no more than one other manager.

Classification internationale type des professions (CITP-88) Grands groupes, sous-grands groupes et sous-groupes

Grand groupe 1   **Membres de l'exécutif et des corps législatifs, cadres supérieurs de l'administration publique, dirigeants et cadres supérieurs d'entreprise**

11   Membres de l'exécutif et des corps législatifs, et cadres supérieurs de l'administration publique
    111   Membres de l'exécutif et des corps législatifs
    112   Cadres supérieurs de l'administration publique
    113   Chefs traditionnels et chefs de village
    114   Dirigeants et cadres supérieurs d'organisations spécialisées
12   Directeurs de société [1]
    121   Directeurs
    122   Cadres de direction, production et opérations
    123   Autres cadres de direction
13   Dirigeants et gérants [2]
    131   Dirigeants et gérants

Grand groupe 2   **Professions intellectuelles et scientifiques**

21   Spécialistes des sciences physiques, mathématiques et techniques
    211   Physiciens, chimistes et assimilés
    212   Mathématiciens, statisticiens et assimilés
    213   Spécialistes de l'informatique
    214   Architectes, ingénieurs et assimilés
22   Spécialistes des sciences de la vie et de la santé
    221   Spécialistes des sciences de la vie
    222   Médecins et assimilés (à l'exception des cadres infirmiers)
    223   Cadres infirmiers et sages-femmes
23   Spécialistes de l'enseignement
    231   Professeurs d'université et d'établissements d'enseignement supérieur
    232   Professeurs de l'enseignement secondaire
    233   Instituteurs de l'enseignement primaire et préprimaire
    234   Enseignants spécialisés dans l'éducation des handicapés
    235   Autres spécialistes de l'enseignement
24   Autres spécialistes des professions intellectuelles et scientifiques
    241   Spécialistes des fonctions administratives et commerciales des entreprises
    242   Juristes
    243   Archivistes, bibliothécaires, documentalistes et assimilés
    244   Spécialistes des sciences sociales et humaines
    245   Ecrivains et artistes créateurs et exécutants
    246   Membres du clergé

Grand groupe 3   **Professions intermédiaires**

31   Professions intermédiaires des sciences physiques et techniques
    311   Techniciens des sciences physiques et techniques
    312   Pupitreurs et autres opérateurs de matériels informatiques
    313   Techniciens d'appareils optiques et électroniques
    314   Techniciens des moyens de transport maritime et aérien
    315   Inspecteurs d'immeubles, de sécurité, d'hygiène et de qualité
32   Professions intermédiaires des sciences de la vie et de la santé
    321   Techniciens et travailleurs assimilés des sciences de la vie de la santé
    322   Professions intermédiaires de la médecine moderne (à l'exception du personnel infirmier)
    323   Personnel infirmier et sages-femmes (niveau intermédiaire)
    324   Praticiens de la médecine traditionnelle et guérisseurs
33   Professions intermédiaires de l'enseignement
    331   Professions intermédiaires de l'enseignement primaire
    332   Professions intermédiaires de l'enseignement préprimaire
    333   Professions intermédiaires de l'éducation des handicapés
    334   Autres professions intermédiaires de l'enseignement
34   Autres professions intermédiaires
    341   Professions intermédiaires des finances et de la vente
    342   Agents commerciaux et courtiers
    343   Professions intermédiaires de la gestion administrative
    344   Professions intermédiaires de l'administration publique des douanes et des impôts, et assimilés
    345   Inspecteurs de police judiciaire et détectives
    346   Professions intermédiaires du travail social
    347   Professions intermédiaires de la création artistique, du spectacle et du sport
    348   Assistants laïcs des cultes

Grand groupe 4   **Employés de type administratif**

41   Employés de bureau
    411   Secrétaires et opérateurs sur claviers
    412   Employés des services comptables et financiers
    413   Employés d'approvisionnement, d'ordonnancement et des transports
    414   Employés de bibliothèque, de service du courrier et assimilés
    419   Autres employés de bureau
42   Employés de réception, caissiers, guichetiers et assimilés
    421   Caissiers, guichetiers et assimilés
    422   Employés de réception et d'information de la clientèle

Grand groupe 5   **Personnel des services et vendeurs de magasin et de marché**

51   Personnel des services directs aux particuliers et des services de protection et de sécurité
    511   Agents d'accompagnement et assimilés
    512   Intendants et personnel des services de restauration
    513   Personnel soignant et assimilé
    514   Autre personnel des services directs aux particuliers
    515   Astrologues, diseurs de bonne aventure et assimilés
    516   Personnel des services de protection et de sécurité
52   Modèles, vendeurs et démonstrateurs
    521   Mannequins et autres modèles
    522   Vendeurs et démonstrateurs en magasin
    523   Vendeurs à l'étal et sur les marchés

Grand groupe 6 Agriculteurs et ouvriers qualifiés de l'agriculture et de la pêche

61   Agriculteurs et ouvriers qualifiés de l'agriculture et de la pêche destinées aux marchés
     611   Agriculteurs et ouvriers qualifiés des cultures destinées aux marchés
     612   Eleveurs et ouvriers qualifiés de l'élevage destiné aux marchés et assimilés
     613   Agriculteurs et ouvriers qualifiés de polyculture et d'élevage destinés aux marchés
     614   Professions du forestage et assimilées
     615   Pêcheurs, chasseurs et trappeurs
62   Agriculteurs et ouvriers de l'agriculture et de la pêche de subsistance
     621   Agriculteurs et ouvriers de l'agriculture et de la pêche de subsistance

Grand groupe 7 Artisans et ouvriers des métiers de type artisanal

71   Artisans et ouvriers des métiers de l'extraction et du bâtiment
     711   Mineurs, carriers, boutefeux ettailleurs de pierre
     712   Ouvriers du bâtiment (gros œuvre) et assimilés
     713   Ouvriers du bâtiment (finitions) et assimilés
     714   Ouvriers peintres, ravaleurs de façades et assimilés
72   Artisans et ouvriers des métiers de la métallurgie, de la construction mécanique et assimilés
     721   Mouleurs de fonderie, soudeurs, tôliers-chaudronniers, monteurs de charpentes métalliques et assimilés
     722   Forgerons, outilleurs et assimilés
     723   Mécaniciens et ajusteurs de machines
     724   Mécaniciens et ajusteurs d'appareils électriques et électroniques
73   Artisans et ouvriers de la mécanique de précision, des métiers d'art, de l'imprimerie et assimilés
     731   Mécaniciens de précision sur métaux et matériaux similaires
     732   Potiers, souffleurs de verre et assimilés
     733   Ouvriers des métiers d'artisanat sur bois, sur textile, sur cuir et sur des matériaux similaires
     734   Artisans et ouvriers de l'imprimerie et assimilés
74   Autres artisans et ouvriers des métiers de type artisanal
     741   Artisans et ouvriers de l'alimentation et assimilés
     742   Artisans et ouvriers du traitement du bois, ébénistes et assimilés
     743   Artisans et ouvriers des métiers du textile et de l'habillement et assimilés
     744   Artisans et ouvriers du travail du cuir, des peaux et de la chaussure

Grand groupe 8 Conducteurs d'installations et de machines et ouvriers de l'assemblage

81   Conducteurs d'installations et de matériels fixes et assimilés
     811   Conducteurs d'installations d'exploitation minière et d'extraction des minéraux
     812   Conducteurs d'installations de transformation des métaux
     813   Conducteurs d'installations de verrerie et de céramique et assimilés
     814   Conducteurs d'installations pour le travail du bois et de la fabrication du papier
     815   Conducteurs d'installations de traitement chimique
     816   Conducteurs d'installations de production d'énergie et assimilés
     817   Conducteurs de chaînes de montage automatiques et de robots industriels

82   Conducteurs de machines et ouvriers de l'assemblage
     821   Conducteurs de machines à travailler les métaux et les produits minéraux
     822   Conducteurs de machines pour la fabrication des produits chimiques
     823   Conducteurs de machines pour la fabrication de produits en caoutchouc et en matières plastiques
     824   Conducteurs de machines à bois
     825   Conducteurs de machines d'imprimerie, de machines à relier et de machines de papeterie
     826   Conducteurs de machines pour la fabrication de produits textiles et d'articles en fourrure et en cuir
     827   Conducteurs de machines pour la fabrication de denrées alimentaires et de produits connexes
     828   Ouvriers de l'assemblage
     829   Autres conducteurs de machines et ouvriers de l'assemblage
83   Conducteurs de véhicules et d'engins lourds de levage et de manœuvre
     831   Conducteurs de locomotives et assimilés
     832   Conducteurs de véhicules à moteur
     833   Conducteurs de matériels mobiles agricoles et d'autres engins mobiles
     834   Matelots de pont et assimilés

Grand groupe 9 Ouvriers et employés non qualifiés

91   Employés non qualifiés des services et de la vente
     911   Vendeurs ambulants et assimilés
     912   Cireurs de chaussures et autres travailleurs des petits métiers des rues
     913   Aides de ménage et autres aides, nettoyeurs et blanchisseurs
     914   Personnel du service d'immeuble, laveurs de vitres et assimilés
     915   Messagers, porteurs, gardiens, portiers et assimilés
     916   Eboueurs et manœuvres assimilés
92   Manœuvres de l'agriculture, de la pêche et assimilés
     921   Manœuvres de l'agriculture, de la pêche et assimilés
93   Manœuvres des mines, du bâtiment et des travaux publics, des industries manufacturières et des transports
     931   Manœuvres des mines, du bâtiment et des travaux publics
     932   Manœuvres des industries manufacturières
     933   Manœuvres des transports et manutentionnaires

Grand groupe 0 Forces armées

01   Forces armées
     011   Forces armées

Notes

[1] Dans ce groupe doivent être classées les personnes qui — en tant que directeur ou cadre de direction — gèrent une entreprise ou un organisme comprenant en tout et nécessairement trois cadres de direction ou davantage.

[2] Dans ce groupe doivent être classées les personnes qui assument la gestion d'une entreprise ou, le cas échéant, d'un organisme, pour leur propre compte ou pour le compte de son propriétaire avec le concours d'un seul autre cadre de direction et d'assistants subalternes.

Clasificación Internacional Uniforme de Ocupaciones (CIUO - 88)
Grandes grupos, subgrupos principales y subgrupos

Gran grupo 1 Miembros del poder ejecutivo y de los cuerpos legislativos y personal directivo de la administración pública y de empresas

11   Miembros del poder ejecutivo y de los cuerpos legislativos y personal directivo de la administración pública

    111 Miembros del poder ejecutivo y de los cuerpos legislativos

    112 Personal directivo de la administración pública

    113 Jefes de pequeñas poblaciones

    114 Dirigentes y administradores de organizaciones especializadas

12   Directores de empresa [1]

    121 Directores generales y gerentes generales de empresa

    122 Directores de departamentos de producción y operaciones

    123 Otros directores de departamentos

13   Gerentes de empresa [2]

    131 Gerentes de empresa

Gran grupo 2 Profesionales científicos e intelectuales

21   Profesionales de las ciencias físicas, químicas y matemáticas y de la ingeniería

    211 Físicos, químicos y afines

    212 Matemáticos, estadísticos y afines

    213 Profesionales de la informática

    214 Arquitectos, ingenieros y afines

22   Profesionales de las ciencias biológicas, la medicina y la salud

    221 Profesionales en ciencias biológicas y otras disciplinas relativas a los seres orgánicos

    222 Médicos y profesionales afines (excepto el personal de enfermería y partería)

    223 Personal de enfermería y partería de nivel superior

23   Profesionales de la enseñanza

    231 Profesores de universidades y otros establecimientos de la enseñanza superior

    232 Profesores de la enseñanza secundaria

    233 Maestros de nivel superior de la enseñanza primaria y preescolar

    234 Maestros e instructores de nivel superior de la enseñanza especial

    235 Otros profesionales de la enseñanza

24   Otros profesionales científicos e intelectuales

    241 Especialistas en organización y administración de empresas y afines

    242 Profesionales del derecho

    243 Archiveros, bibliotecarios, documentalistas y afines

    244 Especialistas en ciencias sociales y humanas

    245 Escritores, artistas creativos y ejecutantes

    246 Sacerdotes de distintas religiones

Gran grupo 3 Técnicos y profesionales de nivel medio

31   Técnicos y profesionales de nivel medio de las ciencias físicas y químicas, la ingeniería y afines

    311 Técnicos en ciencias físicas y químicas y en ingeniería

    312 Técnicos en programación y control informáticos

    313 Operadores de equipos ópticos y electrónicos

    314 Técnicos en navegación marítima y aeronáutica

    315 Inspectores de obras, seguridad y salud y control de calidad

32   Técnicos y profesionales de nivel medio de las ciencias biológicas, la medicina y la salud

    321 Técnicos de nivel medio en ciencias biológicas, agronomía, zootecnia y afines

    322 Profesionales de nivel medio de la medicina moderna y la salud (excepto el personal de enfermería y partería)

    323 Personal de enfermería y partería de nivel medio

    324 Practicantes de la medicina tradicional y curanderos

33   Maestros e instructores de nivel medio

    331 Maestros de nivel medio de la enseñanza primaria

    332 Maestros de nivel medio de la enseñanza preescolar

    333 Maestros de nivel medio de la enseñanza especial

    334 Otros maestros e instructores de nivel medio

34   Otros técnicos y profesionales de nivel medio

    341 Profesionales de nivel medio en operaciones financieras y comerciales

    342 Agentes comerciales y corredores

    343 Profesionales de nivel medio de servicios de administración

    344 Agentes de las administraciones públicas de aduanas, impuestos y afines

    345 Inspectores de policía y detectives

    346 Trabajadores y asistentes sociales de nivel medio

    347 Profesionales de nivel medio de actividades artísticas, espectáculos y deportes

    348 Auxiliares laicos de los cultos

Gran grupo 4 Empleados de oficina

41   Oficinistas

    411 Secretarios y operadores de máquinas de oficina

    412 Auxiliares contables y financieros

    413 Empleados encargados del registro de materiales y de transportes

    414 Empleados de bibliotecas y servicios de correos y afines

    419 Otros oficinistas

42   Empleados en trato directo con el público

    421 Cajeros, taquilleros y afines

    422 Empleados de servicios de información a la clientela

Gran grupo 5 Trabajadores de los servicios y vendedores de comercios y mercados

51   Trabajadores de los servicios personales y de los servicios de protección y seguridad

    511 Personal al servicio directo de los pasajeros

    512 Personal de intendencia y de restauración

    513 Trabajadores de los cuidados personales y afines

    514 Otros trabajadores de servicios personales a particulares

    515 Astrólogos, adivinadores y afines

    516 Personal de los servicios de protección y seguridad

52   Modelos, vendedores y demostradores

    521 Modelos de modas, arte y publicidad

    522 Vendedores y demostradores de tiendas y almacenes

    523 Vendedores de quioscos y de puestos de mercado

Gran grupo 6   Agricultores y trabajadores calificados agropecuarios y pesqueros

61   Agricultores y trabajadores calificados de explotaciones agropecuarias, forestales y pesqueras con destino al mercado

    611   Agricultores y trabajadores calificados de cultivos para el mercado

    612   Criadores y trabajadores pecuarios calificados de la cría de animales para el mercado y afines

    613   Productores y trabajadores agropecuarios calificados cuya producción se destina al mercado

    614   Trabajadores forestales calificados y afines

    615   Pescadores, cazadores y tramperos

62   Trabajadores agropecuarios y pesqueros de subsistencia

    621   Trabajadores agropecuarios y pesqueros de subsistencia

Gran grupo 7   Oficiales, operarios y artesanos de artes mecánicas y de otros oficios

71   Oficiales y operarios de las industrias extractivas y de la construcción

    711   Mineros, canteros, pegadores y labrantes de piedra

    712   Oficiales y operarios de la construcción (obra gruesa) y afines

    713   Oficiales y operarios de la construcción (trabajos de acabado) y afines

    714   Pintores, limpiadores de fachadas y afines

72   Oficiales y operarios de la metalurgia, la construcción mecánica y afines

    721   Moldeadores, soldadores, chapistas, caldereros, montadores de estructuras metálicas y afines

    722   Herreros, herramentistas y afines

    723   Mecánicos y ajustadores de máquinas

    724   Mecánicos y ajustadores de equipos eléctricos y electrónicos

73   Mecánicos de precisión, artesanos, operarios de las artes gráficas y afines

    731   Mecánicos de precisión en metales y materiales similares

    732   Alfareros, operarios de cristalerías y afines

    733   Artesanos de la madera, tejidos, cuero y materiales similares

    734   Oficiales y operarios de las artes gráficas y afines

74   Otros oficiales, operarios y artesanos de artes mecánicas y de otros oficios

    741   Oficiales y operarios del procesamiento de alimentos y afines

    742   Oficiales y operarios del tratamiento de la madera, ebanistas y afines

    743   Oficiales y operarios de los textiles y de la confección y afines

    744   Oficiales y operarios de las pieles, cuero y calzado

Gran grupo 8   Operadores de instalaciones y máquinas y montadores

81   Operadores de instalaciones fijas y afines

    811   Operadores de instalaciones mineras y de extracción y procesamiento de minerales

    812   Operadores de instalaciones de procesamiento de metales

    813   Operadores de instalaciones de vidriería, cerámica y afines

    814   Operadores de instalaciones de procesamiento de la madera y de la fabricación de papel

    815   Operadores de instalaciones de tratamientos químicos

    816   Operadores de instalaciones de producción de energía y afines

    817   Operadores de cadenas de montaje automatizadas y de robots industriales

82   Operadores de máquinas y montadores

    821   Operadores de máquinas para trabajar metales y produtos minerales

    822   Operadores de máquinas para fabricar productos químicos

    823   Operadores de máquinas para fabricar productos de caucho y de material plástico

    824   Operadores de máquinas para fabricar productos de madera

    825   Operadores de máquinas de imprenta, encuadernación y fabricación de productos de papel

    826   Operadores de máquinas para fabricar productos textiles y artículos de piel y cuero

    827   Operadores de máquinas para elaborar alimentos y productos afines

    828   Montadores

    829   Otros operadores de máquinas y montadores

83   Conductores de vehículos y operadores de equipos pesados móviles

    831   Maquinistas de locomotoras y afines

    832   Conductores de vehículos de motor

    833   Operadores de maquinaria agrícola móvil y de otras máquinas móviles

    834   Marineros de cubierta y afines

Gran grupo 9   Trabajadores no calificados

91   Trabajadores no calificados de ventas y servicios

    911   Vendedores ambulantes y afines

    912   Limpiabotas y otros trabajadores callejeros

    913   Personal doméstico y afines, limpiadores, lavanderos y planchadores

    914   Conserjes, lavadores de ventanas y afines

    915   Mensajeros, porteadores, porteros y afines

    916   Recolectores de basura y afines

92   Peones agropecuarios, forestales, pesqueros y afines

    921   Peones agropecuarios, forestales, pesqueros y afines

93   Peones de la minería, la construcción, la industria manufacturera y el transporte

    931   Peones de la minería y la construcción

    932   Peones de la industria manufacturera

    933   Peones del transporte

Gran grupo 0   Fuerzas armadas

01   Fuerzas armadas

    011   Fuerzas armadas

Notas

[1] En este subgrupo principal se incluyen las personas que — en tanto que directores o personal directivo — dirigen una empresa u organismo que comprenda por lo menos tres o más directores.

[2] En este subgrupo principal se incluyen las personas que ejercen la dirección de una empresa o de un organismo, por cuenta propia o de su propietario con la ayuda de solo un director y de asistentes subalternos.

International Standard Classification of Education (ISCED-76)

X: No schooling
Less than one year of schooling.

Level 0: Education preceding the first level
Education delivered in kindergartens, nursery schools as well as in infant classes attached to primary schools.

Level 1: First level
Programmes are designed to give the students a sound basic education in reading, writing and arithmetic along with an elementary understanding of other subjects such as national history, geography, natural science, social science, art, music and religious instruction. Children enter these programmes when they are 5 to 7 years old. Literacy programmes for adults are also to be classified under Level 1.

Level 2: Second level, first stage
The basic programmes constituting the first level are continued, but usually on a more subject-oriented pattern. Some small beginnings of specialization may be seen at this level with some students having the opportunity to direct their attention more particularly to certain types of subjects, e.g. commercial or technical subjects. Vocational programmes designed to train for a specific occupation and often associated with relatively unskilled jobs, as well as apprenticeship programmes for skilled trades and crafts that provide further education as part of the programme, are also included.

Level 3: Second level, second stage
General education continues to be an important constituent of the programmes, but separate subject presentation and more specialization are found at this level. Also to be classified under Level 3 are programmes consisting of subject matter mainly with a specific vocational emphasis or apprenticeship programmes, with an entrance requirement of eight full years of education, or a combination of basic education and vocational experience that demonstrates the ability to handle the subject matter of that level.

Level 5: Third level, first stage, leading to an award not equivalent to a first university degree
Programmes of this type are usually "practical" in orientation in that they are designed to prepare students for particular vocational fields in which they can qualify as high level technicians, teachers, nurses, production supervisors, etc.

Level 6: Third level, first stage, leading to a first university degree or equivalent qualification
Programmes of this type comprise those leading to typical first university degrees such as a "Bachelor's degree", a "Licence", etc., as well as those which lead to first professional degrees such as "Doctorates" awarded after completion of studies in medicine, engineering, law, etc.

Level 7: Third level, second stage
Programmes leading to a post-graduate university degree or equivalent qualification. Programmes of this type generally require a first university degree or equivalent qualification for admission. They are intended to reflect specialization within a given subject area.

Level 9: Education not definable by level
Programmes for which there are no entrance requirements.

?: Level not stated

Classification internationale type de l'éducation (CITE-76)

X: Non scolarisé

Moins d'une année de scolarité.

Niveau 0: Enseignement précédant le premier degré

Il est dispensé dans les jardins d'enfants, les écoles maternelles et les classes enfantines des écoles primaires.

Niveau 1: Premier degré

Les programmes visent à donner aux élèves des bases solides en lecture, écriture et arithmétique tout en leur inculquant des connaissances élémentaires en histoire nationale, géographie, sciences naturelles, sciences sociales, beaux-arts, musique et éventuellement instruction religieuse. L'âge auquel les enfants accèdent à cet enseignement se situe entre 5 et 7 ans. Les programmes d'alphabétisation des adultes doivent aussi être classés dans le niveau 1.

Niveau 2: Second degré, premier cycle

Les programmes de base continuent ceux du premier niveau avec une subdivision plus nette par sujets. On constate à ce niveau un petit début de spécialisation, les élèves ayant la possibilité de s'intéresser plus particulièrement à certaines matières (commerciales, techniques, etc.). Les programmes professionnels visant à former du personnel peu qualifié pour une profession spécifique, ainsi que les programmes orientés vers la formation de personnels qualifiés (artisans ou techniciens) comprenant une part d'instruction générale, sont aussi inclus.

Niveau 3: Second degré, deuxième cycle

L'instruction générale continue à occuper une place importante dans les programmes mais les matières sont enseignées séparément et la tendance à la spécialisation est plus marquée qu'aux niveaux précédents. Doivent aussi être classés au niveau 3 les programmes à orientation professionnelle marquée ou les programmes d'apprentissage qui requièrent huit années d'études préalables à plein temps ou bien une instruction de base jointe à l'expérience professionnelle requise pour être apte à suivre un enseignement de ce niveau.

Niveau 5: Troisième degré, premier niveau, conduisant à un titre non équivalent au premier grade universitaire

Les programmes de ce type sont généralement de caractère «pratique» en ce sens qu'ils sont conçus pour former les étudiants à des domaines professionnels particuliers dans lesquels ils peuvent se qualifier comme techniciens de haut niveau, professeur, personnel infirmier, contremaître de production, etc.

Niveau 6: Troisième degré, premier niveau, conduisant au premier grade universitaire ou à un titre équivalent

Les programmes de ce type comprennent ceux qui conduisent à des premiers diplômes universitaires types tels qu'un «Bachelor's Degree», une «licence», etc., comme ceux qui conduisent à des premiers diplômes professionnels tels que les «doctorats» acquis après la fin d'études médicales, juridiques, d'ingénierie, etc.

Niveau 7: Troisième degré, deuxième niveau, conduisant à un grade universitaire supérieur ou à un titre équivalent

Les programmes de ce type sont généralement accessibles avec un premier diplôme universitaire ou un titre équivalent. Ils sont conçus pour refléter la spécialisation dans un domaine donné.

Niveau 9: Enseignement impossible à définir selon le degré

Programmes pour lesquels il n'existe pas de conditions d'entrée.

?: Niveau inconnu

Clasificación Internacional Normalizada de la Educación (CINE-76)

X: Sin escolaridad

Menos de un año de escolaridad.

Nivel 0: Enseñanza anterior al primer grado

Se da en las guarderías infantiles, las escuelas de párvulos y las clases infantiles de las escuelas primarias.

Nivel 1: Enseñanza de primer grado

Los programas están encaminados a dar a los alumnos sólidas bases en lectura, escritura y aritmética, junto con conocimientos elementales en historia nacional, geografía, ciencias naturales, ciencias sociales, bellas artes, música y eventualmente enseñanza religiosa. Los niños entran en esta enseñanza entre los 5 y los 7 años de edad. Hay que clasificar también los programas de alfabetización de los adultos en el nivel 1.

Nivel 2: Enseñanza de segundo grado, ciclo inferior

Los programas básicos continúan los del primer grado pero con una subdivisión más clara por temas. Se observa en este grado un pequeño comienzo de especialización; los alumnos tienen la posibilidad de interesarse más particularmente por ciertas asignaturas (comerciales, técnicas, etcétera). Los programas profesionales encaminados a formar a un personal poco calificado para una profesión específica, así como los programas de aprendizaje para personal calificado (artesano o técnico) que comprenden una parte de instrucción general, también están incluidos.

Nivel 3: Enseñanza de segundo grado, ciclo superior

La instrucción general sigue ocupando una parte importante en los programas pero las asignaturas se enseñan por separado y la tendencia a la especialización es más clara que en los niveles anteriores. Hay que clasificar en el nivel 3 también los programas con una orientación profesional acentuada o los programas de aprendizaje que necesitan el cumplimiento anterior de ocho años de estudios de dedicación exclusiva o bien una instrucción básica y la experiencia profesional requerida para tener la capacidad de seguir las clases a este nivel.

Nivel 5: Enseñanza de tercer grado que no permite obtener un primer título universitario o equivalente

Los programas de este tipo tienen por lo general un carácter «práctico» ya que están encaminados a formar los estudiantes en sectores profesionales especiales en que pueden calificarse como técnicos superiores, personal enfermero, encargado de producción, etcétera.

Nivel 6: Enseñanza de tercer grado que permite obtener un primer título universitario o equivalente

Los programas de este tipo comprenden los que conducen a un primer diploma universitario tal como una Licencia, etcétera, y también los que conducen a un primer diploma profesional tal como los Doctorados obtenidos después del cumplimiento de estudios de medicina, de derecho, de ingeniería, etcétera.

Nivel 7: Enseñanza de tercer grado que permite obtener un título o diploma universitario superior

Los programas de este tipo requieren por lo general un primer diploma universitario o un título equivalente. Están encaminados a reflejar la especialización en un sector particular.

Nivel 9: Enseñanza que no puede definirse por grados

Estos programas no necesitan el cumplimiento de estudios anteriores.

?: Nivel desconocido

International Standard Classification of Education (ISCED -97) [Summary]

X: No schooling

Less than one year of schooling

Level 0: Pre-primary education

Programmes are designed primarily to introduce children, aged at least three years, to a school type environment; they are school or centre-based.

Level 1: Primary education or first stage of basic education

Programmes are designed on a unit or project basis to give students a sound basic education in reading, writing and mathematics along with an elementary understanding of other subjects such as history, geography, natural science, social science, art and music; religious instruction may also be featured. The customary or legal age of entrance is between five and seven years. This level covers in principle six years of full-time schooling. Literacy programmes for adults are also included at this level.

Level 2: Lower secondary or second stage of basic education

Programmes are designed to complete the provision of basic education begun at Level 1. They are usually on a more subject-oriented pattern, often with teachers conducting classes in their field of specialization. The end of this level often coincides with the end of compulsory education where it exists.
Programmes can be sub-classified according to the subsequent education or destination for which they have been designed:
2A: direct access to Level 3 (3A or 3B) in a sequence leading ultimately to tertiary education;
2B: direct access to Level 3C;
2C: direct access to the labour market.
Programmes at Level 2 can also be sub-divided into three categories according to their orientation: those providing (i) General education, mainly designed to lead to a deeper understanding of a subject or group of subjects, especially (but not necessarily) in preparation for further education; (ii) Pre-vocational or pre-technical education, designed as a preparation for entry into vocational or technical education programmes; (iii) Vocational or technical education, mainly designed to lead to the acquisition of skills, necessary for employment in a particular occupation or trade, the successful completion of which leads to a labour-market relevant vocational qualification.

Level 3: Upper secondary education

Educational programmes typically require the completion of 9 years full-time education (since the beginning of Level 1) and the completion of Level 2 for admission; the entrance age is thus typically 15 or 16 years. More specialization may be observed and teachers more qualified or specialized.
As at Level 2, programmes can be sub-classified according to the subsequent education or destination for which they have been designed:
3A: direct access to Level 5A;
3B: direct access to Level 5B;
3C: not designed to lead directly to Levels 5A or 5B, but rather to the labour market or to Level 4 or other Level 3 programmes.
The programme orientation categories are the same as for Level 2.

Level 4: Post-secondary non-tertiary education

Level 4 captures programmes that straddle the boundary between upper-secondary (Level 3) and post-secondary education. Due to their content they cannot be considered as tertiary programmes as they are often not significantly more advanced than Level 3 programmes but serve to broaden the knowledge of participants who have successfully completed Level 3 programmes. They have a typical full-time equivalent duration of between six months and two years. Programmes can be sub-classified into two categories according to the subsequent education or destination for which they have been designed:
4A: preparation for entry to Level 5;
4B: do not give access to Level 5 (primarily designed for labour market entry).
The programme orientation categories are the same as those for Levels 2 and 3.

Level 5: First stage of tertiary education (not leading directly to an advanced research qualification)

Entry to Level 5 programmes normally requires the successful completion of Level 3A or 3B or a similar qualification at Level 4A. Level 5 programmes are subdivided into two distinct categories:
5A: Programmes are largely theoretically based and are intended to provide sufficient qualifications for
gaining entry into advanced research programmes and professions with high skill requirements (e.g. medicine, dentistry, architecture, etc.) They have a minimum cumulative theoretical duration of three years full-time equivalent, although typically they are four or more years.
5B: Programmes are practically oriented/ occupationally specific and mainly designed to permit the acquisition of the practical skills and know-how necessary for employment in a particular occupation or trade; successful completion usually provides participants with a labour-market relevant qualification. Programmes are typically shorter than in 5A with a minimum duration of 2 years' full-time equivalent and they do not provide direct access to advanced research programmes.

Level 6: second stage of tertiary education (leading to an advanced research qualification)

Programmes are devoted to advanced study and original research and are not based on course-work only. They typically require the submission of a thesis or dissertation of publishable quality which is the product of original research and represents a significant contribution to knowledge.

?: Level not stated

Notes

[1] The full text of ISCED-97 is available in English, French, Spanish and Russian on UNESCO's website (www.uis.unesco.org).

[2] In order to maintain parallel structure to the educational and labour market destinations at Level 3, it has been proposed that Level 4 be split into 3 sub-categories, 4A, 4B and 4C. Although not formally part of ISCED-97 a sub-category 4C is used in the joint UNESCO/OECD/ EUROSTAT Data Collection on Education Systems.

Classification internationale type de l'éducation (CITE-97) [Résumé]

X: Non scolarisé

Moins d'une année de scolarité.

Niveau 0: Education préprimaire

Les programmes visent essentiellement à préparer les enfants, âgés de trois ans au moins, à un environnement scolaire; l'enseignement est dispensé dans une école ou dans un centre extérieur à la famille.

Niveau 1: Enseignement primaire ou premier cycle de l'éducation de base

S'articulant normalement autour d'une unité ou d'un projet les programmes visent à donner aux élèves un solide enseignement de base en lecture, en écriture et en mathématiques et des connaissances élémentaires dans d'autres matières telles que l'histoire, la géographie, les sciences naturelles, les sciences sociales, le dessin et la musique; une instruction religieuse peut éventuellement être prévue. L'âge habituel ou légal auquel les enfants accèdent à cet enseignement se situe entre 5 et 7 ans. La durée habituelle de scolarité est en principe de six ans à plein temps. Les programmes d'alphabétisation des adultes sont également inclus dans ce niveau.

Niveau 2: Premier cycle de l'enseignement secondaire ou deuxième cycle de l'éducation de base

Les programmes sont destinés à compléter l'éducation de base commencée au niveau 1. Ils ont généralement une structure davantage orientée vers les matières enseignées, et il est plus fréquent que plusieurs enseignants se chargent chacun d'une matière dans laquelle ils sont spécialisés. La fin de ce niveau coïncide souvent avec celle de la scolarité obligatoire dans les pays où celle-ci existe. Les programmes peuvent être classés en sous-catégories selon le type d'enseignement ou d'orientation ultérieurs pour lequel ils ont été conçus:
2A: accès direct au niveau 3 (3A ou 3B) dans une filière menant à terme à l'enseignement supérieur;
2B: accès direct au niveau 3C;
2C: accès direct au marché de travail.
Les programmes du niveau 2 peuvent aussi être répartis en trois catégories selon leur orientation, à savoir: (i) l'enseignement général, conçu principalement pour permettre aux participants de mieux comprendre une matière ou un groupe de matières afin, en particulier (mais non nécessairement), de les préparer à la poursuite d'autres études; (ii) Enseignement préprofessionel ou prétechnique, destiné à préparer les participants à recevoir un enseignement professionnel ou technique; (iii) Enseignement professionnel ou technique, destiné principalement à permettre aux participants d'acquérir les compétences qu'ils emploieront dans un métier ou une profession; ceux qui ont suivi avec succès un programme ayant cette orientation obtiennent un titre utilisable sur le marché du travail.

Niveau 3: Enseignement secondaire (deuxième cycle)

Les programmes exigent normalement l'accomplissement préalable de 9 ans d'études à plein temps (depuis le début du niveau 1) et, comme condition minimale d'admission, l'achèvement du niveau 2. L'âge d'admission est normalement de 15 ou 16 ans. On peut observer une plus grande spécialisation et les enseignants doivent souvent être plus qualifiés ou spécialisés qu'au niveau 2.
Comme pour le niveau 2, les programmes peuvent être classés en trois sous-catégories selon le type d'enseignement ou d'orientation ultérieurs pour lequel ils ont été conçus:
3A: accès direct au niveau 5A;
3B: accès direct au niveau 5B;
3C: ne sont pas conçus pour permettre d'accéder directement aux niveaux 5A ou 5B, mais mènent directement au marché du travail, à des programmes du niveau 4 ou à d'autres programmes du niveau 3.
Les programmes du niveau 3 peuvent être répartis selon les mêmes catégories d'orientation que ceux du niveau 2.

Niveau 4: Enseignement postsecondaire qui n'est pas du supérieur

Le niveau 4 regroupe des programme qui se situent à la limite entre le deuxième cycle du secondaire (niveau 3) et l'enseignement postsecondaire. Le contenu des programmes du niveau 4 ne peut être considéré comme relevant du supérieur. Souvent ces programmes ne sont pas d'un niveau sensiblement plus élevé que ceux du niveau 3, mais permettent d'élargir les connaissances des participants qui ont déjà terminé un programme au niveau 3. La durée normale des programmes est comprise entre six mois et deux ans en équivalent plein-temps. Les programmes peuvent être classés en deux sous-catégories selon le type d'enseignement ou d'orientation ultérieurs pour lequel ils ont été conçus:
4A: préparation à l'entrée au niveau 5A;
4B: ne donnent pas accès au niveau 5 (principalement conçus pour permettre un accès direct au marché du travail);
Les programmes du niveau 4 peuvent être répartis selon les mêmes catégories d'orientation que ceux des niveaux 2 et 3.

Niveau 5: premier cycle de l'enseignement supérieur (ne conduisant pas directement à un titre de chercheur de haut niveau)

L'admission aux programmes du niveau 5 exige normalement l'achèvement avec succès du niveau 3A ou 3B ou l'acquisition d'une qualification comparable au niveau 4A. Les programmes du niveau 5 sont subdivisés en deux catégories distinctes:
5A: Les programmes sont fondés principalement sur la théorie et destinés à offrir des qualifications suffisantes pour être admis à suivre des programmes de recherche de pointe ou à exercer une profession exigeant de hautes compétences (par exemple, médecine, dentisterie, architecture, etc.). Ils ont une durée cumulée minimale de trois ans en équivalent plein-temps, bien qu'ils durent habituellement quatre ans ou plus.
5B: Le contenu des programmes a une orientation pratique correspondant a une profession précise et est principalement destiné à permettre aux participants d'acquérir les compétences pratiques et le savoir-faire nécessaires pour occuper un emploi dans une profession ou un métier particulier. L'achèvement avec succès de ces programmes permet normalement aux participants d'obtenir un titre utilisable sur le marché du travail. Les qualifications correspondant aux programmes 5B sont normalement obtenues par des études plus courtes que celles de la catégorie 5A. Les programmes ont une durée minimale de deux ans en équivalent plein-temps et ne donnent pas directement accès à des programmes de formation à la recherche de pointe.

Niveau 6: Deuxième cycle de l'enseignement supérieur (conduisant à un titre de chercheur hautement qualifié)

Les programmes sont consacrés à des études approfondies et à des travaux de recherche originaux et ne sont pas fondés uniquement sur des cours. Ils exigent normalement que soit soutenue une thèse d'une qualité suffisante pour en permettre la publication, thèse qui doit être le produit d'un travail de recherche original et représenter une contribution appréciable à la connaissance.

?: Niveau inconnu

Notes

[1] Le texte intégral de la CITE-97 est disponible en français, anglais, espagnol et russe sur le site de l'UNESCO (www.uis.unesco.org).

[2] Afin de conserver une structure parallèle à celle du niveau 3 en ce qui concerne l'enseignement ultérieur et l'accès au marché du travail, il a été proposé que le niveau 4 soit classé en 3 sous-catégories, 4A, 4B et 4C. Bien que la sous-catégorie 4C ne fasse pas partie officiellement de la CITE-97 elle est utilisée par l'organisme conjoint de l'UNESCO/OCDE/ EUROSTAT pour la collecte de données sur les systèmes d'éducation.

Clasificación internacional Normalizada de la Educación (CINE-97) [Resumen]

X: Sin escolaridad

Menos de un año de escolaridad.

Nivel 0: Enseñanza preescolar

Los programas están destinados esencialmente a familiarizar a niños de por lo menos 3 años de edad con un entorno de tipo escolar; se organizan en una escuela o en un centro.

Nivel 1: Enseñanza primaria o primer ciclo de la educación básica

Basados en unidades o proyectos los programas están destinados a proporcionar una sólida educación básica en lectura, escritura y aritmética junto con conocimientos elementales en otras asignaturas como historia, geografía, ciencias naturales, ciencias sociales, arte y música; en algunos casos se imparte instrucción religiosa. La edad habitual o legal de ingreso es de 5 a 7 años. Este nivel comprende por lo general 6 años de escolarización de tiempo completo. También se incluyen en este nivel los programas de alfabetización de los adultos.

Nivel 2: Primer ciclo de enseñanza secundaria o segundo ciclo de educación básica

Los programas están destinados a completar la educación de base iniciada en el nivel 1. Suelen seguir un modelo más orientado por asignaturas: los profesores son más especializados y generalmente varios imparten enseñanza en su especialización. El final de este ciclo suele coincidir con el término de la escolarización obligatoria, donde existe. Los programas se pueden clasificar según el tipo de enseñanza ulterior o destino al que fueron asignados:

2A: acceso directo al nivel 3 (3A o 3B) en una secuencia que en último término llevaría a la educación terciaria;

2B: acceso directo al nivel 3C;

2C: acceso directo al mercado de trabajo.

Los programas de nivel 2 se subdividen también según su orientación, a saber: (i) enseñanza general, destinada principalmente a transmitir a los participantes un conocimiento más profundo de un tema o grupo de temas, en particular (pero no necesariamente), con miras a prepararlos a una educación ulterior; (ii) Educación preprofesional o pretécnica, destinada a preparar los participantes para que ingresen en la enseñanza profesional o técnica; (iii) Enseñanza profesional o técnica, destinada principalmente a que los participantes adquieran las competencias necesarias para que se les pueda emplear en una ocupación u oficio particular - los que terminan con éxito reciben la correspondiente calificación profesional para el mercado de trabajo.

Nivel 3: Segundo ciclo de enseñanza secundaria

Los programas exigen por lo general que se hayan cursado nueve años de enseñanza de tiempo completo (desde el nivel 1), siendo el requisito mínimo de ingreso la terminación de nivel 2; La edad normal de ingreso es de 15 o 16 años. Se puede observar una mayor especialización y con frecuencia es preciso que los profesores sean más calificados o especializados que en el nivel 2.

De la misma manera que el nivel 2, los programas se subdividen en tres grupos según el tipo de enseñanza ulterior o destino al que fueron asignados:

3A: acceso directo al nivel 5A;

3B: acceso directo al nivel 5B;

3C: no conducen directamente a los niveles 5A ni 5B, sino al mercado de trabajo, a los programas de nivel 4 o a otros programas de nivel 3.

Los programas de nivel 3 se subdividen también según las mismas categorías de orientación que los de nivel 2.

Nivel 4: Enseñanza postsecundaria, no terciaria

El nivel 4 comprende programas que unen el segundo ciclo de secundario (nivel 3) a la enseñanza postsecundaria. Habida cuenta de su contenido, los programas no pueden considerarse de nivel terciario. No suelen ser mucho más avanzados que los de nivel 3 pero sirven para ampliar los conocimientos de los participantes que ya han cursado un programa de nivel 3. La duración de programas, calculada en tiempo completo, suele oscilar entre 6 meses y 2 años. Se puede subdividir los programas en dos grupos según el tipo de enseñanza ulterior o destino al que fueron asignados:

4A: preparación para el ingreso al nivel 5A;

4B: no conducen al nivel 5 (destinados primariamente al ingreso directo en el mercado laboral).

Los programas de nivel 4 también se subdividen también según las mismas categorías de orientación que los de niveles 2 y 3.

Nivel 5: Primer ciclo de la educación terciaria (no conduce directamente a una calificación avanzada)

Para ingresar a programas de nivel 5 se suele exigir la aprobación del nivel 3A o 3B o una calificación similar de nivel 4A. Los programas de nivel 5 se subdividen en dos categorías distintas:

5A: Los programas son en gran parte teóricos, que están destinados a facilitar una calificación suficiente para ingresar en programas de investigación avanzada o que dan acceso al ejercicio de profesiones que requieren un alto nivel de capacitación (por ejemplo, medicina, odontología, arquitectura, etc.) Tienen una duración teórica total mínima de tres años, calculados en tiempo completo, aunque suelen durar cuatro años o más.

5B: El contenido de los programas está orientado a la práctica o es específico de una profesión y está concebido sobre todo para que los participantes adquieran las destrezas prácticas y los conocimientos necesarios para ejercer una profesión particular o un oficio. La aprobación de los correspondientes programas suele facilitar a los participantes la calificación adecuada para el mercado de trabajo. Las calificaciones del nivel 5B suelen exigir menos tiempo que las del 5A. Los programas tienen una duración mínima de 2 años calculados en tiempo completo y no facilita acceso directo a programas de investigación avanzada.

Nivel 6: Segundo ciclo de la enseñanza terciaria (conduce a una calificación de investigación avanzada)

Este nivel está reservado a los programas de enseñanza terciaria que conducen a una calificación de investigación avanzada; por consiguiente están dedicados a estudios avanzados e investigaciones originales, y no están basados únicamente en cursos. Por lo general se requiere presentar una tesis o disertación que se pueda publicar, sea fruto de una investigación original y represente una contribución significativa al conocimiento.

?: Nivel desconocido

Notes

[1] El texto completo de la CINE-97 está disponible en español, francés, inglés y ruso en el sitio de la UNESCO (www.uis.unesco.org).

[2] A fin de conservar una estructura paralela a la del nivel 3 en lo que concierne la enseñanza ulterior y el acceso al mercado de trabajo, se propone que el nivel 4 se subdivida en tres grupos, 4A, 4B y 4C. Aunque el grupo 4C oficialmente no forme parte de la CINE-97 está utilizado por el organismo conjunto de UNESCO/OCDE/EUROSTAT para la recopilación de datos sobre los Sistemas de Educación.

References – Références – Referencias

The references given below are a selected list of International Labour Office publications on methodology and practice in the field of labour statistics.

Les références présentées ci-dessous fournissent une liste sélectionnée de publications du Bureau international du Travail traitant des pratiques et des méthodes utilisées en matière de statistiques du travail.

Las referencias dadas abajo comprenden una selección de publicaciones de la Oficina Internacional del Trabajo sobre la metodología y la práctica en materia de estadísticas del trabajo.

General – Général – General

International Standard Classification of Occupations (Revised 1988) (Geneva, 1990)

Classification internationale type des professions (révisée, 1988) (Genève, 1991)

Clasificación internacional uniforme de ocupaciones (revisada, 1988) (Ginebra, 1991)

Current international recommendations on labour statistics (Geneva, 2000)

Recommandations internationales en vigueur sur les statistiques du travail (Genève, 2000)

Recomendaciones internacionales de actualidad en estadísticas del trabajo (Ginebra, 2000)

Fourteenth International Conference of Labour Statisticians, Reports I-IV ; Report of the Conference (Geneva, 1987)

Quatorzième Conférence internationale des statisticiens du travail, rapports I-IV ; rapport de la Conférence (Genève, 1987)

Decimocuarta Conferencia Internacional de Estadísticos del Trabajo, Informes I-IV ; Informe de la Conferencia (Ginebra, 1987)

Fifteenth International Conference of Labour Statisticians, Reports I-IV ; Report of the Conference (Geneva, 1993)

Quinzième Conférence internationale des statisticiens du travail, rapports I-IV ; rapport de la Conférence (Genève, 1993)

Decimoquinta Conferencia Internacional de Estadísticos del Trabajo, Informes I-IV ; Informe de la Conferencia (Ginebra, 1993)

Sixteenth International Conference of Labour Statisticans, Reports I-IV; Report of the Conference (Geneva, 1998).

Seizième Conférence internationale des statisticiens du travail, rapports I-IV ; Rapport de la Conférence (Genève, 1998)

Decimosexta Conferencia Internacional de Estadísticos del Trabajo, Informes I-IV ; Informe de la Conferencia (Ginebra, 1998)

Revision of the International Standard Classification of Occupations, Fourteenth International Conference of Labour Statisticians, see Report of the Conference

Révision de la classification internationale type des professions, quatorzième Conférence internationale des statisticiens du travail, voir rapport de la conférence

Revisión de la Clasificación internacional uniforme de ocupaciones, Decimocuarta Conferencia Internacional de Estadísticos del Trabajo, ver Informe de la Conferencia

Revision of the International Classification of Status in Employment, Fifteenth International Conference of Labour Statisticians, see Report IV and Report of the Conference

Révision de la classification internationale d'après la situation dans la profession, quinzième Conférence internationale des statisticiens du travail, voir rapport IV et rapport de la Conférence

Revisión de la Clasificación internacional de la categoría en el empleo, Decimoquinta Conferencia Internacional de Estadísticos del Trabajo, ver Informe IV e Informe de la Conferencia

Sources and Methods: Labour Statistics, Vol. 9: Transition Countries (Geneva, 1999)

Sources et méthodes: Statistiques du travail, vol. 9: Pays en transition (Genève, 1999)

Fuentes y Métodos : Estadísticas del Trabajo, vol. 9: Países en transición (Ginebra, 1999)

Total and economically active population, employment and unemployment – Population totale et population active, emploi et chômage – Población total y población económicamente activa, empleo y desempleo

Surveys on economically active population, employment, unemployment and underemployment – An ILO manual on concepts and methods (Geneva, 1990)

Enquêtes sur la population active, l'emploi, le chômage et le sous-emploi : Un manuel du BIT sur les concepts et méthodes (version française en préparation)

Encuestas de la población económicamente activa, empleo, desempleo y subempleo – Un manual de la OIT sobre conceptos y métodos (Madrid, 1993)

Measurement of Underemployment, Concepts and Methods, Eleventh International Conference of Labour Statisticians, Report IV (Geneva, 1966)

Mesure du sous-emploi, concepts et méthodes, onzième Conférence internationale des statisticiens du travail, rapport IV (Genève, 1966)

Medición del subempleo, conceptos y métodos, Undécima Conferencia Internacional de Estadísticos del Trabajo, Informe IV (Ginebra, 1966)

Labour Force, Employment, Unemployment and Underemployment, Thirteenth International Conference of Labour Statisticians, Report II (Geneva, 1982)

Main-d'œuvre, emploi, chômage et sous-emploi, treizième Conférence internationale des statisticiens du travail, rapport II (Genève, 1982)

Fuerza de trabajo, empleo, desempleo y subempleo, Decimotercera Conferencia Internacional de Estadísticos del Trabajo, Informe II (Ginebra, 1982)

Economically Active Population, 1950-2010 (Geneva, 1996) Vol. I : Asia – Vol. II : Africa – Vol. III : Latin America and the Caribbean – Vol. IV : Northern America, Europe and Oceania – Vol. V : World ; Vol. VI : Methodological Supplement (under preparation)

Population active, 1950-2010 (Genève, 1996)
Vol. I : Asie – Vol. II : Afrique – Vol. III : Amérique latine et les Caraïbes – Vol. IV : Amérique du Nord, Europe et Océanie – Vol. V : Monde ; Vol. VI : Supplément méthodologique (en cours de préparation)
Población económicamente activa, 1950-2010 (Ginebra, 1996)
Vol. I : Asia – Vol. II : Africa – Vol. III : América Latina y las Antillas – Vol. IV : América del Norte, Europa y Oceanía – Vol. V : Mundo ; Vol. VI : Suplemento metodológico (en preparación)

Sources and Methods: Labour Statistics (formerly *Statistical Sources and Methods*), Vol. 2 : Employment, wages, hours of work and labour cost (establishment surveys), second edition (Geneva, 1995); Vol. 3 : Economically active population, employment, unemployment and hours of work (Household surveys), second edition (Geneva, 1990); Vol. 4 : Employment, unemployment, wages and hours of work (administrative records and related sources) (Geneva, 1989); Vol. 5 : Total and economically active population, employment and unemployment (population censuses), second edition (Geneva, 1996). A technical guide of series published in the *Yearbook of Labour Statistics* and the *Bulletin of Labour Statistics*
Sources et méthodes : statistique du travail (précédemment *Sources et méthodes statistiques*), vol. 2 : Emploi, salaires, durée du travail et coût de la main-d'œuvre (enquêtes auprès des établissements), deuxième édition (Genève, 1995); vol. 3 : Population active, emploi, chômage et durée du travail (enquête auprès des ménages), deuxième édition (Genève, 1991); vol. 4 : Emploi, chômage, salaires et durée du travail (documents administratifs et sources assimilées) (Genève, 1989); vol. 5 : Population totale et population active, emploi et chômage (recensements de population), deuxième édition (Genève, 1996). Un guide technique des séries publiées dans l'*Annuaire des statistiques du travail* et le *Bulletin des statistiques du travail*
Fuentes y Métodos : Estadísticas del Trabajo (anteriormente *Fuentes y Métodos Estadísticos*), vol. 2 : Empleo, salarios, horas de trabajo y costo de la mano de obra (encuestas de establecimientos), segunda edición (Ginebra, 1995); vol. 3 : Población económicamente activa, empleo, desempleo y horas de trabajo (encuestas de hogares), segunda edición (Ginebra, 1991); vol. 4: Empleo, desempleo, salarios y horas de trabajo (registros administrativos y fuentes conexas) (Ginebra, 1989); vol. 5 : Población total y población económicamente activa, empleo y desempleo (censos de población), segunda edición (Ginebra, 1996). Una guía técnica de las series publicadas en el *Anuario de Estadísticas del Trabajo* y en el *Boletín de Estadísticas del Trabajo*

Year Book of Labour Statistics : Retrospective edition on population censuses, 1945-89 (Geneva, 1990).
Annuaire des statistiques du travail : édition rétrospective sur les recensements de population, 1945-89 (Genève, 1990)
Anuario de Estadísticas del Trabajo : Edición retrospectiva sobre los censos de población, 1945-89 (Ginebra, 1990)

Statistics of employment in the informal sector, Fifteenth International Conference of Labour Statisticians, see Report III and Report of the Conference
Statistiques de l'emploi dans le secteur informel, quinzième Conférence internationale des statisticiens du travail, voir rapport III et rapport de la Conférence
Estadísticas del empleo en el sector informal, Decimoquinta Conferencia Internacional de Estadísticos del Trabajo, ver Informe III e Informe de la Conferencia

Hours of work – Durée du travail – Horas de trabajo

Statistics of Hours of Work, Tenth International Conference of Labour Statisticians, Report III (Geneva, 1962)
Statistiques de la durée du travail, dixième Conférence internationale des statisticiens du travail, rapport III (Genève, 1962)
Estadísticas de la duración del trabajo, Décima Conferencia Internacional de Estadísticos del Trabajo, Informe III (Ginebra, 1962)

Sources and Methods: Labour Statistics (formerly Statistical Sources and Methods), Vol. 2 : Employment, wages, hours of work and labour cost (establishment surveys), second edition (Geneva, 1995); Vol. 3 : Economically active population, employment, unemployment and hours of work (Household surveys), second edition (Geneva, 1990); Vol. 4 : Employment, unemployment, wages and hours of work (administrative records and related sources) (Geneva, 1989). A technical guide of series published in the *Yearbook of Labour Statistics* and the *Bulletin of Labour Statistics*
Sources et méthodes statistiques du travail (précédemment Sources et méthodes statistiques), vol. 2 : Emploi, salaires , durée du travail et coût de la main-d'œuvre (enquêtes auprès des établissements), deuxième édition (Genève, 1995) ; vol. 3 : Population active, emploi, chômage et durée du travail (enquêtes auprès des ménages), deuxième édition (Genève, 1991) ; vol. 4 : Emploi, chômage, salaires et durée du travail (documents administratifs et sources assimilées) (Genève, 1989). Un guide technique des séries publiées dans l'*Annuaire des statistiques du travail* et le *Bulletin des statistiques du travail*
Fuentes y Métodos : Estadísticas del Trabajo (anteriormente *Fuentes y Métodos Estadísticos*), vol. 2 : Empleo, salarios, horas de trabajo y costo de la mano de obra (encuestas de establecimientos), segunda edición (Ginebra, 1995) ; vol. 3 : Población económicamente activa, empleo, desempleo y horas de trabajo (encuestas de hogares), segunda edición (Ginebra, 1991) ; vol. 4 : Empleo, desempleo, salarios y horas de trabajo (registros administrativos y fuentes conexas) (Ginebra, 1989). Una guía técnica de las series publicadas en el *Anuario de Estadísticas del Trabajo* y en el *Boletín de Estadísticas del Trabajo*

Wages – Salaires – Salarios

Wages and Payroll Statistics, Studies and Reports, New Series, No. 16 (Geneva, 1949)
Statistiques des bordereaux des salaires et des gains, Etudes et documents, nouvelle série, n° 16 (Genève, 1949)
Estadísticas de nóminas de salarios y de ganancias, Estudios y documentos, nueva serie, núm. 16 (Ginebra, 1949)

International Comparisons of Real Wages, Studies and Reports, New Series, No. 45 (Geneva, 1956)
Les comparaisons internationales des salaires réels, Etudes et documents, nouvelle série, n° 45 (Genève, 1956)

Statistics of Wages and Employee Income, Twelfth International Conference of Labour Statisticians, Report II (Geneva, 1973)
Statistiques des salaires et du revenu salarial, douzième Conférence internationale des statisticiens du travail, rapport II (Genève, 1973)
Estadísticas de salarios e ingresos de los trabajadores, Duodécima Conferencia Internacional de Estadísticos del Trabajo, Informe II (Ginebra, 1973)

An integrated system of wages statistics : a manual on methods (Geneva, 1979)

Un système intégré des statistiques des salaires – Manuel de méthodologie (Genève, 1980)

Sistema integrado de estadísticas de salarios: manual metodológico (Ginebra, 1992)

Um sistema integrado de estatísticas de salários: Manual de Metodología (Lisboa, 1992)

Sources and Methods : Labour Statistics (formerly *Statistical Sources and Methods*), Vol. 2 : Employment, wages, hours of work and labour cost (establishment surveys), second edition (Geneva, 1995) ; Vol. 4 : Employment, unemployment, wages and hours of work (administrative records and related sources) (Geneva, 1989)

Sources et méthodes : statistiques du travail (précédemment *Sources et méthodes statistiques*), vol. 2 : Emploi, salaires, durée du travail et coût de la main-d'œuvre (enquêtes auprès des établissements), deuxième édition (Genève, 1995) ; vol. 4 : Emploi, chômage, salaires et durée du travail (documents administratifs et sources assimilées) (Genève, 1989)

Fuentes y Métodos : Estadísticas del Trabajo (anteriormente *Fuentes y Métodos Estadísticos*), vol. 2 : Empleo, salarios, horas de trabajo y costo de la mano de obra (encuestas de establecimientos), segunda edición (Ginebra, 1995) ; vol. 4 : Empleo, desempleo, salarios y horas de trabajo (registros administrativos y fuentes conexas) (Ginebra, 1989)

Labour cost – Coût de la main-d'œuvre – Costo de la mano de obra

Statistics of Labour Cost, Eleventh International Conference of Labour Statisticians, Report II (Geneva, 1966)

Statistiques du coût de la main-d'œuvre, onzième Conférence internationale des statisticiens du travail, rapport II (Genève, 1966)

Estadísticas del costo de la mano de obra, Undécima Conferencia Internacional de Estadísticos del Trabajo, Informe II (Ginebra, 1966)

An integrated system of wages statistics: a manual on methods (Geneva, 1979)

Un système intégré des statistiques des salaires – Manuel de méthodologie (Genève, 1980)

Sistema integrado de estadísticas de salarios: manual metodológico (Ginebra, 1992)

Um sistema integrado de estatísticas de salários: Manual de Metodología (Lisboa, 1992)

Sources and Methods: Labour Statistics, Vol. 2: Employment, wages, hours of work and labour cost (establishment surveys), second edition (Geneva, 1995).

Sources et méthodes : statistiques du travail, vol. 2 : Emploi, salaires, durée du travail et coût de la main-d'œuvre (enquêtes auprès des établissements), deuxième édition (Genève, 1995)

Fuentes y Métodos : Estadísticas del Trabajo, vol. 2 : Empleo, salarios, horas de trabajo y costo de la mano de obra (encuestas de establecimientos), segunda edición (Ginebra, 1995)

The Cost of Social Security. Fourteenth international inquiry, 1987-1989 (Geneva, 1995)

Le coût de la sécurité sociale. Quatorzième enquête internationale, 1987-1989 (Genève, 1995)

El costo de la seguridad social. Decimocuarta encuesta internacional, 1987-1989 (Ginebra, 1995)

Consumer prices – Prix à la consommation – Precios al consumidor

A Contribution to the Study of International Comparisons of Cost of Living, Studies and Reports, Series N, No. 17 (Geneva, 1932)

Contribution à l'étude de la comparaison internationale du coût de la vie, Etudes et documents, série N, n° 17 (Genève, 1932)

International Comparisons of Cost of Living, Studies and Report, Series N, No. 20 (Geneva, 1934)

La comparaison internationale du coût de la vie, Etudes et documents, série N, n° 20 (Genève, 1934)

Cost-of-Living Statistics, Studies and Reports, New Series, No. 7, Part 2 (Geneva, 1948)

Statistiques du coût de la vie, Etudes et documents, nouvelle série, n° 7, partie 2 (Genève, 1948)

Estadísticas del costo de la vida, Estudios y documentos, nueva serie, núm. 7, parte 2 (Ginebra, 1948)

Computation of Consumer Price Indices (Special Problems), Tenth International Conference of Labour Statisticians, Report IV (reprint, Geneva, 1970)

Calcul des indices des prix à la consommation (problèmes particuliers), dixième Conférence internationale des statisticiens du travail, rapport IV (réimpression, Genève, 1970)

Cálculo de los índices de los precios al consumidor (Problemas especiales), Décima Conferencia Internacional de Estadísticos del Trabajo, Informe IV (Ginebra, 1962)

Consumer price indices, Fourteenth International Conference of Labour Statisticians, Report II (Geneva, 1987)

Indices des prix à la consommation, quatorzième Conférence internationale des statisticiens du travail, rapport II (Genève, 1987)

Indices de los precios al consumidor, Decimocuarta Conferencia Internacional de Estadísticos del Trabajo, Informe II (Ginebra, 1987)

Consumer price indices : An ILO manual (Geneva, 1989)

Sources and Methods : Labour Statistics, Vol. 1 : Consumer price indices, third edition (Geneva, 1992)

Sources et méthodes : statistiques du travail, vol. 1 : Indices des prix à la consommation, troisième édition (Genève, 1992)

Fuentes y Métodos : Estadísticas del Trabajo, vol. 1 : Indices de los precios al consumidor, tercera edición (Ginebra, 1992)

Household budgets – Budgets de ménage – Presupuestos del hogar

Methods of Family Living Studies, Studies and Reports, Series N, No. 23 (Geneva, 1940)

Méthodes d'enquête sur les conditions de vie des familles, Etudes et documents, série N, n° 23 (Genève, 1941)

Métodos de encuesta sobre las condiciones de vida de las familias, Estudios y documentos, serie N, núm. 23 (Montreal, 1942)

Methods of Family Living Studies, Studies and Reports, New Series, No. 17 (Geneva, 1949)

Méthodes d'enquête sur les conditions de vie des familles, Etudes et documents, nouvelle série, n° 17 (Genève, 1949)

Métodos de encuesta sobre las condiciones de vida de las familias, Estudios y documentos, nueva serie, núm. 17 (Ginebra, 1949)

Family Living Studies – A Symposium, Studies and Reports, New Series, No. 63 (Geneva, 1961)

Enquêtes sur les conditions de vie des familles : recueil de monographies, Etudes et documents, nouvelle série, n° 63 (Genève, 1961)

Encuestas sobre las condiciones de vida de las familias : Recopilación de monografías, Estudios y documentos, nueva serie, núm. 63 (Ginebra, 1961)

Scope, Methods and Uses of Family Expenditure Surveys, Twelfth International Conference of Labour Statisticians, Report III (Geneva, 1971)

Portée, méthodes et utilisation des enquêtes sur les dépenses des familles, douzième Conférence internationale des statisticiens du travail, rapport III (Genève, 1973)

Alcance, métodos y utilización de las encuestas sobre gastos familiares, Duodécima Conferencia Internacional de Estadísticos del Trabajo, Informe III (Ginebra, 1971)

Household Income and Expenditure Statistics No. 4 – 1979-91 (Geneva, 1995)

Statistiques des revenus et des dépenses des ménages n° 4 – 1979-1991 (Genève, 1995)

Estadísticas de ingresos y gastos de los hogares núm. 4 – 1979-1991 (Ginebra, 1995)

Sources and Methods: Labour Statistics, Vol. 6 : Household income and expenditure surveys (Geneva, 1994)

Sources et méthode: statistiques du travail, vol. 6 : Enquêtes sur le revenu et les dépenses des ménages (Genève, 1994)

Fuentes y Métodos: Estadísticas del Trabajo, vol. 6 : Encuestas sobre los ingresos de los hogares (Ginebra, 1994)

Occupational injuries – Lésions professionnelles – Lesiones profesionales

Occupational injuries, Thirteenth International Conference of Labour Statisticians, Report III (Geneva, 1982)

Lésions professionnelles, treizième Conférence internationale des statisticiens du travail, rapport III (Genève, 1982)

Lesiones profesionales, Decimotercera Conferencia Internacional de Estadísticos del Trabajo, Informe III (Ginebra, 1982)

Statistics of occupational injuries, Sixteenth International Conference of Labour Statisticians, Report III (Geneva, 1998).

Statistiques des lésions professionnelles, seizième Conférence internationale des statisticiens du travail, rapport III (Genève, 1998).

Estadísticas de lesiones profesionales, Decimosexta Conferencia Internacional de Estadísticos del Trabajo, Informe III (Ginebra, 1998).

Sources and Methods: Labour Statistics, Vol. 8 : Occupational injuries (Geneva, 1999)

Sources et méthodes: statistiques du travail, vol. 8 : Lésions professionnelles (Genève, 1999)

Fuentes y Métodos: Estadísticas del Trabajo, vol. 8 : Lesiones profesionales (Ginebra, 1999)

Strikes and lockouts – Grèves et lock-out – Huelgas y cierres patronales

Methods of compiling statistics of industrial disputes, Studies and reports, Series N, No. 10 (Geneva, 1926)

Les méthodes de la statistique des conflits du travail, Etudes et documents, série N, n° 10 (Genève, 1926)

National methodologies for statistics of strikes and lockouts, Meeting of Experts on Statistics of Strikes and Lockouts, Geneva 1990 ; document MESS/D.2 (English only)

Statistics of strikes, lockouts and other forms of industrial action, Fifteenth International Conference of Labour Statisticians, Report II (Geneva, 1992) and Report of the Conference (Geneva, 1993)

Statistiques des grèves, des lock-out et d'autres actions de revendication, quinzième Conférence internationale des statisticiens du travail, rapport II (Genève, 1992) et rapport de la Conférence (Genève, 1993)

Estadísticas de huelgas, cierres patronales y otros tipos de acción laboral directa, Decimoquinta Conferencia Internacional de Estadísticos del Trabajo, Informe II (Ginebra, 1992) e Informe de la Conferencia (Ginebra, 1993)

Sources and Methods : Labour Statistics, Vol. 7 : Strikes and lockouts (Geneva, 1993)

Sources et méthodes : statistiques du travail, vol. 7 : Grèves et lock-out (Genève, 1993)

Fuentes y Métodos : Estadísticas del Trabajo, vol. 7 : Huelgas y cierres patronales (Ginebra, 1993)

Order of arrangement of countries, areas and territories

Ordre de présentation des pays, zones et territoires

Orden de presentación de los países, áreas y territorios

The countries, areas and territories are listed by continent in the following order: Africa, America, Asia, Europe and Oceania. The designations employed are those in use on 31 August 2004 for statistical and other technical information.

The name of each country appears in English, French or Spanish when the national language of the country, or the language commonly used in it, is one of the three; in other cases the name of the country is given in the language used in official correspondence between the country in question and the ILO.

In the following table the name and order of listing of the countries appear under the heading *Yearbook* with a reference number for each country. The table also comprises an index in which the countries are arranged in the alphabetical order of their names in each of the three languages; by using the reference numbers the reader can quickly find the name in English, French or Spanish of a country appearing under the heading *Yearbook* or, starting from its name in any one of these languages, the country designation used in the *Yearbook.*

Les pays, zones et territoires sont présentés par continent dans l'ordre: Afrique, Amérique, Asie, Europe et Océanie. Les désignations utilisées sont celles qui étaient en usage au 31 août 2004 pour les données statistiques et les autres données techniques.

Le nom de chaque pays figure en français, en anglais ou en espagnol quand la langue nationale de ce pays ou celle qui y est communément utilisée est l'une de ces trois langues; dans les autres cas, le nom du pays figure dans la langue de correspondance officielle de ce pays avec le BIT.

Dans le tableau ci-après, la dénomination et l'ordre de présentation des pays figurent sous la rubrique *Annuaire* avec un numéro de référence pour chaque pays. Ce tableau comporte également un index où les pays sont disposés dans l'ordre alphabétique de leur dénomination dans chacune des trois langues; les numéros de référence permettent de retrouver rapidement la dénomination française, anglaise ou espagnole d'un pays figurant sous la rubrique *Annuaire* ou, inversement, de retrouver la dénomination d'un pays utilisée dans *l'Annuaire* en partant de sa dénomination dans l'une quelconque de ces langues.

Los países, áreas y territorios se presentan por continentes en este orden: Africa, América, Asia, Europa y Oceanía. Las designaciones empleadas son las vigentes al 31 de agosto de 2004 para informaciones estadísticas y otras informaciones técnicas.

El nombre de cada país figura en español, francés o inglés cuando su idioma nacional o de uso general es una de estas tres lenguas; en otros casos el nombre del país figura en la lengua que el país utiliza en su correspondencia oficial con la OIT.

En el cuadro siguiente, la denominación y el orden de presentación de los países figuran bajo la rúbrica *«Anuario»,* que va acompañada de un número de referencia para cada país. Este cuadro comprende también un índice en que los países se hallan dispuestos en el orden alfabético de su denominación en cada una de las tres lenguas; los números de referencia permiten hallar rápidamente la denominación en español, francés o inglés de un país que figura en la rúbrica *«Anuario»* o, al contrario, hallar la denominación de un país que se utiliza en el *Anuario* partiendo de la denominación en una de estas tres lenguas.

Note: The designations employed (which reflect United Nations practice) and the presentation of the material in this publication do not imply the expression of any opinion whatsoever on the part of the International Labour Office concerning the legal status of any country, territory, city or area or of its authorities, or concerning the delimitation of its frontiers or boundaries; where the designation "country" appears in the headings of tables, it covers countries, territories, cities or areas.

Note: Les désignations utilisées dans cette publication (qui s'inspirent de la pratique des Nations Unies) et la présentation des données n'impliquent de la part du Bureau international du Travail aucune prise de position quant au statut juridique de tel ou tel pays, territoire, ville ou zone ou de ses autorités ni quant au tracé de ses frontières ou limites; l'appellation «pays» figurant dans certaines rubriques des tableaux désigne des pays, des territoires, des villes ou des zones.

Nota: Las designaciones empleadas en esta publicación (que se inspiran en la práctica seguida en las Naciones Unidas) y la forma en que aparecen presentados los datos no implican juicio alguno por parte de la OIT sobre la condición jurídica de ninguno de los países, territorios, ciudades o áreas citados o de sus autoridades, ni respecto de la delimitación de sus fronteras o límites; con la palabra «país» que figura en los títulos de algunos cuadros se designa a países, territorios, ciudades o áreas.

	English	Français	Español

AFRICA — AFRIQUE — AFRICA

	English	Français	Español
1 **Algérie**	Algeria	Algérie	Argelia
2 **Angola**	Angola	Angola	Angola
3 **Bénin**	Benin	Bénin	Benin
4 **Botswana**	Botswana	Botswana	Botswana
5 **Burkina Faso**	Burkina Faso	Burkina Faso	Burkina Faso
6 **Burundi**	Burundi	Burundi	Burundi
			Cabo Verde (8)
7 **Cameroun**	Cameroon	Cameroun	Camerún
8 **Cap-Vert**	Cape Verde	Cap-Vert	*Cabo Verde*
9 **Rép. centrafricaine**	Central African Rep.	République centrafricaine	Rep. Centroafricana
10 **Congo**	Congo	Congo	Congo
11 **Côte d'Ivoire**	Côte d'Ivoire	Côte d'Ivoire	Côte d'Ivoire
	Chad (42)	—	Chad (42)
12 **Egypt**	Egypt	Egypte	Egipto
13 **Ethiopia**	Ethiopia	Ethiopie	Etiopía
14 **Gabon**	Gabon	Gabon	Gabón
15 **Gambia**	Gambia	Gambie	Gambia
16 **Ghana**	Ghana	Ghana	Ghana
17 **Guinée**	Guinea	Guinée	Guinea
18 **Guinée-Bissau**	Guinea-Bissau	Guinée-Bissau	Guinea Bissau
19 **Guinea Ecuatorial**	Equatorial Guinea	Guinée Equatoriale	Guinea Ecuatorial
20 **Kenya**	Kenya	Kenya	Kenya
21 **Lesotho**	Lesotho	Lesotho	Lesotho
22 **Madagascar**	Madagascar	Madagascar	Madagascar
23 **Malawi**	Malawi	Malawi	Malawi
24 **Mali**	Mali	Mali	Malí
25 **Maroc**	*Morocco*	Maroc	Marruecos
26 **Mauritanie**	Mauritania	Mauritanie	Mauritania
27 **Mauritius**	Mauritius	Maurice	Mauricio
28 **Mozambique**	Mozambique	Mozambique	Mozambique
	Morocco (25)	—	—
29 **Namibia**	Namibia	Namibie	Namibia
30 **Niger**	Niger	Niger	Níger
31 **Nigeria**	Nigeria	Nigéria	Nigeria
32 **Réunion**	Réunion	Réunion	Reunión
33 **Rwanda**	Rwanda	Rwanda	Rwanda
	—	Sainte-Hélène (38)	Santa Elena (38)
34 **Sénégal**	Senegal	Sénégal	Senegal
35 **Seychelles**	Seychelles	Seychelles	Seychelles
36 **Sierra Leone**	Sierra Leone	Sierra Leone	Sierra Leona
37 **South Africa**	South Africa	Afrique du Sud	Sudáfrica
38 **St. Helena**	St. Helena	*Sainte-Hélène*	*Santa Elena*
39 **Swaziland**	Swaziland	Swaziland	Swazilandia
40 **Tanzania (Tanganyika)**	Tanzania (Tanganyika)	Tanzanie (Tanganyika)	Tanzanía (Tangañika)
41 **Tanzania (Zanzibar)**	Tanzania (Zanzibar)	Tanzanie (Zanzibar)	Tanzanía (Zanzíbar)
42 **Tchad**	*Chad*	Tchad	Chad
43 **Togo**	Togo	Togo	Togo
44 **Tunisie**	Tunisia	Tunisie	Túnez
45 **Uganda**	Uganda	Ouganda	Uganda
46 **Zambia**	Zambia	Zambie	Zambia
47 **Zimbabwe**	Zimbabwe	Zimbabwe	Zimbabwe

AMERICA — AMÉRIQUE — AMERICA

	English	Français	Español
48 **Anguilla**	Anguilla	Anguilla	Anguila
49 **Antigua and Barbuda**	Antigua and Barbuda	Antigua et Barbuda	Antigua y Barbuda
	—	Antilles néerlandaises (79)	Antillas Neerlandesas (79)
50 **Argentina**	Argentina	Argentine	Argentina
51 **Aruba**	Aruba	Aruba	Aruba
52 **Bahamas**	Bahamas	Bahamas	Bahamas
53 **Barbados**	Barbados	Barbade	Barbados
54 **Belize**	Belize	Belize	Belice
55 **Bermuda**	Bermuda	Bermudes	Bermudas
56 **Bolivia**	Bolivia	Bolivie	Bolivia
57 **Brasil**	Brazil	Brésil	Brasil
	—	Iles Caïmanes (59)	Islas Caimán (59)

Trilingual - Trilingue - Trilingüe	English	Français	Español
58 **Canada**	Canada	Canada	Canadá
	Chile (62)	Chili (62)	—
59 **Cayman Islands**	Cayman Islands	*Iles Caïmanes*	*Islas Caimán*
60 **Colombia**	Colombia	Colombie	Colombia
61 **Costa Rica**	Costa Rica	Costa Rica	Costa Rica
62 **Chile**	*Chile*	*Chili*	Chile
63 **Dominica**	Dominica	Dominique	Dominica
64 **República Dominicana**	Dominican Republic	République dominicaine	República Dominicana
	—	El Salvador (66)	—
65 **Ecuador**	Ecuador	Equateur	Ecuador
66 **El Salvador**	El Salvador	*El Salvador*	El Salvador
	—	Etats-Unis (91)	Estados Unidos (91)
67 **Falkland Is. (Malvinas)**	Falkland Is. (Malvinas)	Iles Falkland (Malouines)	*Islas Malvinas (Falkland)*
	French Guiana (73)	—	—
68 **Greenland**	Greenland	Groenland	Groenlandia
69 **Grenada**	Grenada	Grenade	Granada
70 **Guadeloupe**	Guadeloupe	Guadeloupe	Guadalupe
71 **Guatemala**	Guatemala	Guatemala	Guatemala
	—	—	Guayana Francesa (73)
72 **Guyana**	Guyana	Guyana	Guyana
73 **Guyane française**	*French Guiana*	Guyane française	*Guayana Francesa*
74 **Haïti**	Haiti	Haïti	Haití
75 **Honduras**	Honduras	Honduras	Honduras
76 **Jamaica**	Jamaica	Jamaïque	Jamaica
	—	—	Islas Malvinas (Falkland)(67)
77 **Martinique**	Martinique	Martinique	Martinica
78 **México**	Mexico	Mexique	México
79 **Netherlands Antilles**	Netherlands Antilles	*Antilles néerlandaises*	*Antillas Neerlandesas*
80 **Nicaragua**	Nicaragua	Nicaragua	Nicaragua
81 **Panamá**	Panama	Panama	Panamá
82 **Paraguay**	Paraguay	Paraguay	Paraguay
83 **Perú**	Peru	Pérou	Perú
84 **Puerto Rico**	Puerto Rico	Porto Rico	Puerto Rico
85 **Saint Kitts and Nevis**	Saint Kitts and Nevis	Saint-Kitts-et-Nevis	San Kitts y Nevis
86 **Saint Lucia**	Saint Lucia	Sainte-Lucie	Santa Lucía
87 **Saint-Pierre-et-Miquelon**	St. Pierre and Miquelon	Saint-Pierre-et-Miquelon	San Pedro y Miquelón
88 **St. Vincent and the Grenadines**	St. Vincent and the Grenadines	Saint-Vincent-et les Grenadines	San Vicente y las Granadinas
89 **Suriname**	Suriname	Suriname	Suriname
90 **Trinidad and Tobago**	Trinidad and Tobago	Trinité-et-Tobago	Trinidad y Tabago
91 **United States**	United States	*Etats-Unis*	*Estados Unidos*
92 **Uruguay**	Uruguay	Uruguay	Uruguay
93 **Venezuela**	Venezuela	Venezuela	Venezuela
94 **Virgin Islands (British)**	Virgin Islands (British)	Iles Vierges (britanniques)	Islas Vírgenes (E.U.)
95 **Virgin Islands (US)**	Virgin Islands (US)	Iles Vierges (américaines)	Islas Vírgenes (EEUU)

ASIA — ASIE — ASIA

96 **Armenia**	Armenia	Armenie	Armenia
97 **Azerbaijan**	Azerbaijan	Azerbaïdjan	Azerbaiyán
	—	Arabie saoudite (126)	Arabia Saudita (126)
98 **Bahrain**	Bahrain	Bahreïn	Bahrein
99 **Bangladesh**	Bangladesh	Bangladesh	Bangladesh
100 **Bhutan**	Bhutan	Bhoutan	Bhután
101 **Brunei Darussalam**	Brunei Darussalam	Brunéi Darussalam	Brunei Darussalam
102 **Cambodge**	Cambodia	Cambodge	Camboya
103 **China**	China	Chine	China
	—	République de Corée (113)	República de Corea (113)
	—	—	Filipinas (125)
104 **Georgia**	Georgia	Georgie	Georgia
105 **Hong Kong, China**	Hong Kong, China	Hong-kong, Chine	Hong Kong, China
106 **India**	India	Inde	India
107 **Indonesia**	Indonesia	Indonésie	Indonesia
108 **Iran (Islamic Rep. of)**	Iran (Islamic Rep. of)	Iran (Rép. islamique d')	Irán (Rep. Islámica del)
109 **Israel**	Israel	Israël	Israel
110 **Japan**	Japan	Japon	Japón
111 **Jordan**	Jordan	Jordanie	Jordania
112 **Kazakhstan**	Kazakhstan	Kazakhstan	Kazajstán
	—	Kirghizistan (115)	Kirguistán (115)

Trilingual - Trilingue - Trilingüe	English	Français	Español
113 **Korea, Republic of**	Korea, Republic of	*République de Corée*	*República de Corea*
114 **Kuwait**	Kuwait	Koweït	Kuwait
115 **Kyrgyzstan**	Kyrgyzstan	*Kirghizistan*	*Kirguistán*
116 **Lao, Rép. dém. pop.**	Lao, People's Dem. Rep.	Lao, République dém. Pop.	Lao, República Dem. Pop.
117 **Macau**	Macau	Macao	Macao
118 **Malaysia**	Malaysia	Malaisie	Malasia
119 **Maldives**	Maldives	Maldives	Maldivas
120 **Mongolia**	Mongolia	Mongolie	Mongolia
121 **Myanmar**	Myanmar	Myanmar	Myanmar
122 **Nepal**	Nepal	Népal	Nepal
123 **Oman**	Oman	Oman	Omán
124 **Pakistan**	Pakistan	Pakistan	Pakistán
125 **Philippines**	Philippines	Philippines	*Filipinas*
126 **Saudi Arabia**	Saudi Arabia	*Arabie saoudite*	*Arabia Saudita*
127 **Singapore**	Singapore	Singapour	Singapur
128 **Sri Lanka**	Sri Lanka	Sri Lanka	Sri Lanka
129 **République arabe syrienne**	Syrian Arab Republic	*République arabe syrienne*	República Arabe Siria
130 **Taiwan, China**	Taiwan, China	Taïwan, Chine	Taiwan, China
131 **Thailand**	Thailand	Thaïlande	Tailandia
132 **Uzbekistan**	Uzbekistan	Ouzbékistan	Uzbekistán
133 **Viet Nam**	Viet Nam	Viet Nam	Viet Nam
134 **West Bank and Gaza strip**	West bank and Gaza strip	Rive occidentale et Bande de Gaza	Ribera occidental y Faja de Gaza

EUROPE — EUROPE — EUROPA

Trilingual - Trilingue - Trilingüe	English	Français	Español
135 **Albanie**	Albania	Albanie	Albania
	—	Allemagne (149)	Alemania (149)
136 **Austria**	Austria	Autriche	Austria
137 **Belarus**	Belarus	Bélarus	Belarús
138 **Belgique**	Belgium	Belgique	Bélgica
139 **Bulgarie**	Bulgaria	Bulgarie	Bulgaria
140 **Croatia**	Croatia	Croatie	Croacia
141 **Cyprus**	Cyprus	Chypre	Chipre
142 **Czech Republic**	Czech Republic	*République tchèque*	*República Checa*
143 **Denmark**	Denmark	Danemark	Dinamarca
	—	—	Eslovaquia (173)
	—	—	Eslovenia (174)
144 **España**	Spain	Espagne	España
145 **Estonia**	Estonia	Estonie	Estonia
146 **Faeroe Islands**	Faeroe Islands	Iles Féroé	Islas Féroé
147 **Finland**	Finland	Finlande	Finlandia
148 **France**	France	France	Francia
149 **Germany**	Germany	*Allemagne*	*Alemania*
150 **Gibraltar**	Gibraltar	Gibraltar	Gibraltar
151 **Grèce**	Greece	Grèce	Grecia
152 **Hongrie**	Hungary	Hongrie	Hungría
	—	Ile de Man (155)	—
	—	Irlande (154)	Irlanda (154)
153 **Iceland**	Iceland	Islande	Islandia
154 **Ireland**	Ireland	*Irlande*	*Irlanda*
155 **Isle of Man**	Isle of Man	*Ile de Man*	Isla de Man
156 **Italie**	Italy	Italie	Italia
157 **Jersey**	Jersey	Jersey	Jersey
158 **Latvia**	Latvia	Lettonie	Letonia
159 **Lithuania**	Lithuania	Lituanie	Lituania
160 **Luxembourg**	Luxembourg	Luxembourg	Luxemburgo
161 **Macedonia, The former Yugoslav Republic of**	Macedonia, The Former Yugoslav Republic of	Macédoine, Ex-République yougoslave de	Macedonia, Ex Republica Yugoslava de
162 **Malta**	Malta	Malte	Malta
163 **Moldova**	Moldova	Moldova	Moldova
164 **Montenegro**	Montenegro	Monténégro	Montenegro
165 **Netherlands**	Netherlands	*Pays-Bas*	*Países Bajos*
166 **Norway**	Norway	Norvège	Noruega
	—	Pays-Bas (165)	Países Bajos (165)
167 **Poland**	Poland	Pologne	Polonia
168 **Portugal**	Portugal	Portugal	Portugal
	—	—	Reino Unido (178)
169 **Roumanie**	Romania	Roumanie	Rumania
	—	Royaume-Uni (178)	—

Trilingual - Trilingue - Trilingüe	English	Français	Español
170 **Russian Federation**	Russian Federation	Russie, Fédération de	Rusia, Federación de
171 **Saint-Marin**	San Marino	Saint-Marin	San Marino
	Spain (144)	—	—
172 **Serbia**	Serbia	Serbie	Serbia
173 **Slovakia**	Slovakia	Slovaquie	*Eslovaquia*
174 **Slovenia**	Slovenia	Slovénie	*Eslovenia*
	—	Suède (176)	Suecia (176)
175 **Suisse**	*Switzerland*	Suisse	Suiza
176 **Sweden**	Sweden	Suède	Suecia
	Switzerland (175)	—	—
	—	République tchèque (142)	—
177 **Turkey**	Turkey	Turquie	Turquía
178 **United Kingdom**	United Kingdom	*Royaume-Uni*	*Reino Unido*
179 **Ukraine**	Ukraine	Ukraine	Ucrania

OCEANIA — OCÉANIE — OCEANIA

Trilingual	English	Français	Español
180 **American Samoa**	American Samoa	*Samoa américaines*	*Samoa Americana*
181 **Australia**	Australia	Australie	Australia
182 **Cook Islands**	Cook Islands	Iles Cook	Islas Cook
183 **Fiji**	Fiji	Fidji	Fiji
	French Polynesia (193)	—	—
184 **Guam**	Guam	Guam	Guam
	—	Iles Mariannes du Nord (190)	Islas Marianas del Norte(190)
185 **Kiribati**	Kiribati	Kiribati	Kiribati
	New Caledonia (191)	—	Nueva Caledonia (191)
186 **Marshall Islands**	Marshall Islands	Iles Marshall	Islas Marshall
187 **New Zealand**	New Zealand	*Nouvelle-Zélande*	*Nueva Zelandia*
188 **Niue**	Niue	Nioué	Niue
189 **Norfolk Island**	Norfolk Island	Ile Norfolk	Isla Norfolk
190 **Northern Mariana Islands**	Northern Mariana Islands	*Iles Mariannes du Nord*	*Islas Marianas del Norte*
191 **Nouvelle-Calédonie**	New Caledonia	Nouvelle-Calédonie	*Nueva Caledonia*
	—	Nouvelle-Zélande (187)	—
192 **Papua New Guinea**	Papua New Guinea	Papouasie-Nouvelle-Guinée	Papua Nueva Guinea
193 **Polynésie française**	*French Polynesia*	Polynésie française	Polinesia Francesa
194 **Samoa**	Samoa	Samoa	Samoa
	—	Samoa américaines (180)	Samoa Americana (180)
195 **Solomon Islands**	Solomon Islands	Iles Salomon	Islas Salomón
196 **Tonga**	Tonga	Tonga	Tonga
197 **Tuvalu**	Tuvalu	Tuvalu	Tuvalu
198 **Vanuatu**	Vanuatu	Vanuatu	Vanuatu

Countries, areas and territories included in each table

Pays, zones et territoires compris dans chaque tableau

Países, áreas y territorios incluidos en cada cuadro

Index

Countries, areas and territories included in each table (with corresponding page number)
Pays, zones et territoires compris dans chaque tableau (avec le numéro de page correspondant)
Países, áreas y territorios incluidos en cada cuadro (con el número de página correspondiente)

Country Pays País	1 ACTIVE POPULATION POPULATION ACTIVE POBLACION ACTIVA		2 EMPLOYMENT EMPLOI EMPLEO						3 UNEMPLOYMENT CHÔMAGE DESEMPLEO					4 HOURS OF WORK DURÉE DU TRAVAIL HORAS DE TRABAJO	
	1A	1B	2A	2B	2C	2D	2E	2F	3A	3B	3C	3D	3E	4A	4B
AFRICA-AFRIQUE-AFRICA															
Algérie	.	.	87	.			.	.	461	479	.	.		.	.
Angola	.	.	.	.	.	.	.	.	.	.	.	.		.	.
Bénin	.	.	.	.	.	.	.	.	.	.	.	.		.	.
Botswana	9	33	87	99	197	257	293	381	461	479	555	.		.	.
Burkina Faso	.	.	.	.	.	.	.	.	.	.	.	.		.	.
Burundi	.	.	.	.	.	.	.	.	.	.	.	.		.	.
Cameroun	.	.	.	.	.	.	.	.	.	.	.	.		.	.
Cap-Vert	.	.	.	.	.	.	.	.	.	.	.	.		.	.
République centrafricaine	.	.	.	.	.	.	.	.	.	.	.	.		.	.
Congo	.	.	.	.	.	.	.	.	.	.	.	.		.	.
Côte d'Ivoire	.	.	.	.	.	.	.	.	.	.	.	.		.	.
Egypt	9	.	87	100	197	257	294	.	461	479	.	605	669	727	805
Ethiopia	.	.	.	.	.	.	.	.	461	480	.	.		728	806
Gabon	.	.	.	.	.	.	.	.	.	.	.	.		.	.
Gambia	.	.	.	.	.	.	.	.	.	.	.	.		.	.
Ghana	.	.	.	.	.	.	.	.	.	.	.	.		.	.
Guinea Ecuatorial	.	.	.	.	.	.	.	.	.	.	.	.		.	.
Guinée	.	.	.	.	.	.	.	.	.	.	.	.		.	.
Guinée-Bissau	.	.	.	.	.	.	.	.	.	.	.	.		.	.
Kenya	.	.	.	.	.	.	.	.	.	.	.	.		.	.
Lesotho	.	.	.	.	.	.	.	.	.	.	.	.		.	.
Madagascar	.	.	87	101	198	257	294	.	461	480	555	.		.	.
Malawi	.	.	.	.	.	.	.	.	.	.	.	.		.	.
Mali	.	.	87	101	.	258	.	.	461	.	.	.		.	.
Maroc	9	.	87	102	198	258	.	.	461	481	555	606	669	.	.
Mauritanie	.	.	.	.	.	.	.	.	.	.	.	.		.	.
Mauritius	9	.	87	103	199	258	295	382	461	481	556	606	670	729	806
Mozambique	.	.	.	.	.	.	.	.	.	.	.	.		.	.
Namibia	.	.	87	105	200	259	.	.	.	.	.	.		.	.
Niger	.	.	.	.	.	.	.	.	.	.	.	.		.	.
Nigeria	.	.	.	.	.	.	.	.	.	.	.	.		.	.
Réunion	.	.	87	.			296	.	462	483	.	.		.	.
Rwanda	.	.	.	.	.	.	.	.	.	.	.	.		.	.
Sao Tomé-et-Principe	.	.	87	.		.	.	.	462	.	.	.		.	.
Sénégal	.	.	87	105	.	.	.	.	462	.	.	.		.	.
Seychelles	.	.	.	.	.	.	296	.	.	.	.	.		.	.
Sierra Leone	.	.	87	.	.	.	.	.	.	.	.	.		.	.
South Africa	10	33	87	106	200	259	296	.	462	483	557	607	670	.	.
Saint Helena	.	.	88	107	.	.	.	.	462	.	.	.		.	.
Sudan	.	.	88	.	.	.	.	.	462	.	.	.		.	.
Swaziland	.	.	.	.	.	.	.	.	.	.	.	.		.	.
Tanzania, United Republic of	.	.	88	108	201	.	297	.	462	484	.	.		.	.
Tanzania (Tanganyika)	.	.	.	.	.	.	.	.	.	.	.	.		.	.
Tanzania (Zanzibar)	.	.	.	.	.	.	.	.	.	.	.	.		.	.
Tchad	.	.	.	.	.	.	.	.	.	.	.	.		.	.
Togo	.	.	.	.	.	.	.	.	.	.	.	.		.	.
Tunisie	.	.	88	.	.	260	.	.	462	484	557	.		.	.
Uganda	.	.	.	.	.	.	.	.	.	.	.	.		.	.
Zambia	.	.	.	.	.	.	297	.	.	.	.	.		.	.
Zimbabwe	.	.	.	.	.	.	.	.	.	.	.	.		.	.
AMERICA-AMÉRIQUE-AMERICA															
Anguilla	.	.	.	.	.	.	.	.	.	.	.	.		.	.
Antigua and Barbuda	.	.	88	109			.	.	.	.	.	.		.	.
Argentina	10	.	88	110	201	260	298	383	462	485	558	608	671	730	807

Country Pays País	5 WAGES SALAIRES SALARIOS		6 LABOUR COST COÛT DE LA MAIN-D'ŒUVRE COSTO DE LA MANO DE HOBRA	7 CONSUMER PRICES PRIX À LA CONSOMMATION PRECIOS AL CONSUMIDOR						8 OCCUPATIONAL INJURIES LÉSIONS PROFESSIONNELLES LESIONES PROFESIONALES			9 STRIKES AND LOCKOUTS GRÈVES ET LOCK-OUT HUELGAS Y CIERRES PATRONALES			
	5A	5B	6A	7A	7B	7C	7D	7E	7F	8A	8B	8C	9A	9B	9C	9D
AFRICA-AFRIQUE-AFRICA																
Algérie	.	.	.	1073	.	1087	.	1103	1113	1139	1277	1339	1367	1381	1397	.
Angola	.	.	.	1073	.	1087	.	.	.	.	.	.	.	.	.	.
Bénin	.	.	.	1073	.	1087	.	1103	1113	1139	.	.	.	.	.	.
Botswana	885	959	.	1073	.	1087	1097	1103	1113	1139	.	.	.	.	.	.
Burkina Faso	.	.	.	1073	.	1087	.	1103	1113	1140	.	.	.	.	.	.
Burundi	.	.	.	1073	.	1087	.	1103	1113	.	.	.	.	.	.	.
Cameroun	.	.	.	1073	.	1087	1097	1103	.	.	.	.	.	.	.	.
Cap-Vert	.	.	.	1073	.	1087	.	1103	1113	.	.	.	.	.	.	.
République centrafricaine	.	.	.	1073	1083	1087	1097	1103	.	.	.	.	.	.	.	.
Congo	.	.	.	1073	.	1087	1097	1103	1113	.	.	.	.	.	.	.
Côte d'Ivoire	.	.	.	1073	1083	1087	1097	1103	1113	.	.	.	.	.	.	.
Egypt	885	960	.	1073	.	1087	.	1103	1113	.	.	.	.	.	.	.
Ethiopia	.	.	.	1073	.	1087	.	1103	.	.	.	.	.	.	.	.
Gabon	.	.	.	1073	.	1087	.	1103	1113	.	.	.	.	.	.	.
Gambia	.	.	.	1073	.	1087	1097	1103	1113	.	.	.	.	.	.	.
Ghana	.	.	.	1073	.	1087	.	1103	1113	.	.	.	.	.	.	.
Guinea Ecuatorial	.	.	.	1073	.	1087	.	1103	1113	.	.	.	.	.	.	.
Guinée	.	.	.	1073	.	1087	.	1103	1113	.	.	.	.	.	.	.
Guinée-Bissau	.	.	.	1073	.	1087	1097	1103	1113	.	.	.	.	.	.	.
Kenya	.	.	.	1073	1083	1088	1097	1103	.	.	.	.	.	.	.	.
Lesotho	.	.	.	1073	1083	1088	1097	1103	1113	.	.	.	.	.	.	.
Madagascar	.	.	.	1074	.	1088	.	1103	1113	.	.	.	.	.	.	.
Malawi	.	.	.	1074	.	1088	.	1103	1113	.	.	.	.	.	.	.
Mali	.	.	.	1074	.	1088	1097	1103	1113	.	.	.	.	.	.	.
Maroc	.	.	.	1074	.	1088	.	1104	1113	.	.	.	.	.	.	.
Mauritanie	886	961	1045	1074	1083	1088	1097	1104	1114	1140	1277	.	1367	1381	1397	1413
Mauritius	.	.	.	1074	.	1088	.	1104	.	.	.	.	.	.	.	.
Mozambique	.	.	.	1074	.	1088	.	1104	1114	.	.	.	.	.	.	.
Namibia	.	.	.	1074	1083	1088	.	1104	1114	.	.	.	.	.	.	.
Niger	.	.	.	1074	.	1088	.	1104	1114	1143	.	.	1367	1381	1397	.
Nigeria	.	.	.	1074	.	1088	1097	1104	1114	.	.	.	.	.	.	.
Réunion	.	.	.	1074	.	1088	.	1104	1114	.	.	.	.	.	.	.
Rwanda	.	.	.	.	.	.	.	.	.	.	.	.	.	.	.	.
Sao Tomé-et-Principe	.	.	.	1074	1083	1088	1097	1104	1114	.	.	.	.	.	.	.
Sénégal	887	961	.	1074	.	1088	.	1104	1114	.	.	.	.	.	.	.
Seychelles	.	.	.	1074	.	1088	.	1104	1114	1143	.	.	.	.	.	.
Sierra Leone	.	.	.	1074	1083	1088	1097	1104	1114	.	.	.	1367	1381	1397	1413
South Africa	.	.	.	1074	.	1088	1097	1104	1114	.	.	.	1367	1381	1397	.
Saint Helena	.	.	.	.	.	.	.	.	.	.	.	.	.	.	.	.
Sudan	.	.	.	1074	.	1088	1097	1104	1114	.	.	.	.	.	.	.
Swaziland	.	.	.	.	.	.	.	.	.	.	.	.	.	.	.	.
Tanzania, United Republic of	.	.	.	1074	.	1088	1097	1104	1114	.	.	.	.	.	.	.
Tanzania (Tanganyika)	.	.	.	1074	.	1088	.	.	.	.	.	.	.	.	.	.
Tanzania (Zanzibar)	.	.	.	1074	.	1088	1097	1104	1114	.	.	.	.	.	.	.
Tchad	.	.	.	1074	.	1089	.	1104	1114	1144	1278	1339	.	.	.	.
Togo	.	.	.	1074	1083	1089	1097	1104	1114	1144	1278	1339	1368	1382	1398	.
Tunisie	.	.	.	1075	.	1089	.	1104	1114	1145	.	.	1368	1382	1398	.
Uganda	.	.	.	1075	.	1089	.	.	.	.	.	.	.	.	.	.
Zambia	.	.	.	1075	.	1089	.	1104	.	1146	1279	.	.	.	.	.
Zimbabwe	.	.	.	.	.	.	.	.	.	.	.	.	.	.	.	.
AMERICA-AMÉRIQUE-AMERICA																
Anguilla	.	.	.	1075	.	1089	1097	1104	1114	.	.	.	.	.	.	.
Antigua and Barbuda	.	.	.	.	.	.	.	.	.	.	.	.	.	.	.	.
Argentina	887	962	1045	1075	1083	1089	1097	1104	1114	1146	1280	1339	1368	1382	1398	1413

Index

Countries, areas and territories included in each table (with corresponding page number)
Pays, zones et territoires compris dans chaque tableau (avec le numéro de page correspondant)
Países, áreas y territorios incluidos en cada cuadro (con el número de página correspondiente)

Country / Pays / País	1 ACTIVE POPULATION / POPULATION ACTIVE / POBLACION ACTIVA		2 EMPLOYMENT / EMPLOI / EMPLEO						3 UNEMPLOYMENT / CHÔMAGE / DESEMPLEO					4 HOURS OF WORK / DURÉE DU TRAVAIL / HORAS DE TRABAJO	
	1A	1B	2A	2B	2C	2D	2E	2F	3A	3B	3C	3D	3E	4A	4B
AMERICA-AMÉRIQUE-AMERICA															
Aruba	10	.	88	111	202	260	299	384	462	486	.	.	.	.	.
Bahamas	.	.	88	111	203	.	.	.	463	486	558	609	672	.	.
Barbados	10	.	88	.	.	.	.	.	463	.	.	.	.	.	.
Belize	10	.	88	.	.	.	.	.	463	.	559	.	.	.	.
Bermuda	.	.	88	.	203	.	300	384	.	.	.	.	.	731	809
Bolivia	10	.	88	112	204	260	.	.	463	.	.	.	.	732	810
Brasil	10	34	88	113	204	261	301	385	463	487	559	.	.	733	810
Canada	11	35	89	114	205	261	302	386	463	487	560	610	672	734	811
Cayman Islands	11	35	89	115	205	262	.	.	463	488	560	.	.	734	.
Colombia	11	.	89	116	206	262	303	387	463	488	560	610	673	735	811
Costa Rica	11	36	89	117	206	262	303	388	464	489	561	611	673	736	812
Cuba	12	36	89	117	207	263	304	.	464	490	561	.	.	737	813
Chile	12	37	89	118	207	263	305	.	464	490	562	612	674	737	813
Dominica	.	.	.	.	.	.	.	.	.	.	.	.	.	.	.
República Dominicana	12	38	89	119	208	263	305	389	464	490	562	613	675	738	813
Ecuador	12	.	89	120	208	264	306	390	464	491	562	614	675	739	814
El Salvador	12	.	89	120	209	264	307	391	464	492	.	615	676	740	815
Greenland	.	.	89	.	.	.	.	.	464	.	.	.	.	.	.
Grenada	.	.	.	.	.	.	.	.	.	.	.	.	.	.	.
Guadeloupe	.	.	89	.	.	.	.	.	464	492	.	.	.	.	.
Guatemala	.	.	89	121	.	.	.	.	464	.	.	.	.	.	.
Guyana	.	.	.	.	.	.	.	.	.	.	.	.	.	741	816
Guyane française	.	.	89	.	.	.	308	.	465	492	.	.	.	.	.
Haïti	13	.	.	.	.	.	.	.	.	.	.	.	.	.	.
Honduras	.	.	89	122	.	264	308	.	465	493	.	615	676	.	.
Jamaica	13	.	90	122	209	265	.	.	465	493	563	616	677	.	.
Martinique	13	.	90	.	.	.	308	.	465	493	.	.	.	.	.
México	13	38	90	123	210	265	309	392	465	494	563	617	678	741	816
Netherlands Antilles	14	.	90	124	211	265	.	.	465	495	564	.	.	.	.
Nicaragua	14	.	90	124	211	266	.	.	465	495	564	.	.	.	.
Panamá	14	39	90	125	212	266	310	.	465	496	565	618	678	742	817
Paraguay	14	40	90	126	212	266	310	.	465	496	565	618	679	743	817
Perú	15	40	90	127	213	267	311	393	466	497	566	619	679	744	818
Puerto Rico	15	.	90	128	214	267	.	.	466	498	.	620	680	744	819
Saint Lucia	.	.	90	129	215	.	.	.	466	498	.	.	681	.	.
Saint-Pierre-et-Miquelon	.	.	.	.	.	.	.	.	.	.	.	.	.	.	.
Saint Vincent and the Grenadines	.	.	.	.	.	.	.	.	.	.	.	.	.	.	.
Suriname	.	.	.	.	.	.	.	.	.	.	.	.	.	.	.
Trinidad and Tobago	15	41	90	130	215	268	.	.	466	498	566	620	681	.	.
Turks and Caicos Islands	15	.	90	131	216	268	313	.	466	.	.	.	.	.	.
United States	15	41	90	131	216	268	314	395	466	499	567	621	682	744	819
Uruguay	.	.	90	132	216	269	315	.	466	500	567	622	682	745	.
Venezuela, Rep. Bolivariana de	15	.	91	132	217	269	.	.	466	500	.	.	683	746	819
Virgin Islands (British)	.	.	.	.	.	.	315	.	.	.	.	.	.	.	.
Virgin Islands (US)	.	.	.	.	.	.	.	.	.	.	.	.	.	746	820
ASIA-ASIE-ASIA															
Afghanistan	.	.	91	.	.	.	.	.	.	.	.	.	.	.	.
Armenia	16	42	91	133	.	270	316	.	466	501	567	.	.	746	820
Azerbaijan	16	42	91	134	217	270	317	397	467	502	568	623	683	747	821
Bahrain	.	.	.	.	218	.	318	.	467	503	569	.	684	.	.
Bangladesh	.	.	.	.	.	.	.	.	467	.	.	.	.	.	.
Bhutan	.	.	.	.	.	.	.	.	.	.	.	.	.	.	.
Brunei Darussalam	.	.	.	.	.	.	.	.	.	.	.	.	.	.	.
Cambodia	.	.	.	.	.	.	.	.	.	.	.	.	.	.	.
China	.	.	91	135	.	.	319	.	467	.	.	.	.	748	822
Georgia	16	.	91	136	219	270	319	.	467	504	570	.	.	.	.

Country Pays País	5 WAGES SALAIRES SALARIOS		6 LABOUR COST COÛT DE LA MAIN-D'ŒUVRE COSTO DE LA MANO DE HOBRA	7 CONSUMER PRICES PRIX À LA CONSOMMATION PRECIOS AL CONSUMIDOR						8 OCCUPATIONAL INJURIES LÉSIONS PROFESSIONNELLES LESIONES PROFESIONALES			9 STRIKES AND LOCKOUTS GRÈVES ET LOCK-OUT HUELGAS Y CIERRES PATRONALES			
	5A	5B	6A	7A	7B	7C	7D	7E	7F	8A	8B	8C	9A	9B	9C	9D
AMERICA-AMÉRIQUE-AMERICA																
Aruba	.	.	.	1075	1083	1089	1097	1105	1114	.	.	.	1368	1382	1398	.
Bahamas	.	.	.	1075	.	1089	.	1105	1115	.	.	.	.	.	.	.
Barbados	.	.	.	1075	.	1089	1098	1105	1115	.	.	.	.	.	.	.
Belize	.	.	.	1075	.	1089	1098	1105	1115	.	.	.	.	.	.	.
Bermuda	887	962	.	1075	1083	1089	1098	1105	1115	.	.	.	.	.	.	.
Bolivia	888	.	.	1075	.	1089	1098	1105	1115	.	.	.	.	.	.	.
Brasil	.	.	1045	1075	.	1089	.	1105	1115	.	.	.	1368	1382	1398	.
Canada	889	962	.	1075	1083	1089	1098	1105	1115	1147	1281	.	1369	1383	1399	1413
Cayman Islands	.	.	.	1075	.	1089	.	1105	1115	.	.	.	.	.	.	.
Colombia	889	963	1046	1075	1083	1089	1098	1105	1115	.	.	.	.	.	.	.
Costa Rica	890	963	.	1075	1083	1089	1098	1105	1115	1150	1282	1340	.	.	.	.
Cuba	892	965	.	1075	.	1089	1098	1105	.	1151	1283	1340	.	.	.	.
Chile	892	966	1046	1075	.	1089	.	1105	1115	1151	.	1340	1369	1383	1399	.
Dominica	.	.	.	1075	.	1089	1098	1105	1115	.	.	.	.	.	.	.
República Dominicana	892	966	.	1075	.	1089	.	1105	1115	1151	.	.	1369	.	.	.
Ecuador	.	.	1046	1075	.	1090	1098	1105	1115	.	.	.	1369	1383	1399	.
El Salvador	893	966	.	1075	.	1090	1098	1105	1115	.	.	.	1369	1383	1399	.
Greenland	.	.	.	1075	.	1090	1098	1105	1115	.	.	.	.	.	.	.
Grenada	.	.	.	1076	.	1090	1098	1105	1115	.	.	.	.	.	.	.
Guadeloupe	.	.	.	1076	.	1090	1098	1105	1115	.	.	.	.	.	.	.
Guatemala	894	967	.	1076	.	1090	1098	1105	1115	.	.	.	.	.	.	.
Guyana	894	967	1046	1076	.	1090	.	1105	1115	.	.	.	1370	.	1399	.
Guyane française	.	.	.	1076	.	1090	1098	1105	1115	.	.	.	.	.	.	.
Haïti	.	.	.	1076	.	1090	.	1106	1115	.	.	.	.	.	.	.
Honduras	.	.	.	1076	.	1090	1098	1106	1116	.	.	.	.	.	.	.
Jamaica	.	.	.	1076	.	1090	1098	1106	1116	.	.	.	1370	1384	1400	.
Martinique	.	.	.	1076	.	1090	1098	1106	1116	.	.	.	.	.	.	.
México	894	967	1047	1076	.	1090	1098	1106	1116	1152	1283	.	1370	1384	1400	.
Netherlands Antilles	.	.	.	1076	1083	1090	1098	1106	1116	.	.	.	.	.	.	.
Nicaragua	895	968	1047	1076	.	1090	.	1106	1116	.	.	.	.	1384	1400	.
Panamá	895	968	.	1076	1083	1090	.	1106	1116	1154	.	.	1370	1384	1400	.
Paraguay	896	968	.	1076	.	1090	.	1106	1116	.	.	.	.	.	.	.
Perú	897	969	1047	1076	.	1090	1098	1106	1116	.	.	.	1370	1385	1401	.
Puerto Rico	897	969	.	1076	1083	1090	1098	1106	1116	1156	1284	.	1371	1385	1401	.
Saint Lucia	.	.	.	1076	.	1090	1099	1106	1116	.	.	.	.	.	.	.
Saint-Pierre-et-Miquelon	.	.	.	1076	.	1090	.	.	.	.	.	.	.	.	.	.
Saint Vincent and the Grenadines	.	.	.	1076	.	1090	1099	1106	1116	.	.	.	.	.	.	.
Suriname	.	.	.	1076	.	1090	.	1106	.	.	.	.	.	.	.	.
Trinidad and Tobago	.	.	.	1076	.	1091	1099	1106	1116	1157	1284	.	1371	1385	1401	.
Turks and Caicos Islands	.	.	.	.	.	.	.	.	.	.	.	.	.	.	.	.
United States	897	969	1048	1076	1083	1091	1099	1106	1116	1157	1284	.	1371	1385	1401	1413
Uruguay	898	970	.	1076	1083	1091	1099	1106	1116	.	.	.	1371	1386	1402	.
Venezuela, Rep. Bolivariana de	.	.	.	1077	.	1091	.	1106	1116	.	.	.	.	.	.	.
Virgin Islands (British)	.	.	.	1077	.	1091	.	.	.	.	.	.	.	.	.	.
Virgin Islands (US)	898	970	.	.	.	.	.	.	.	.	.	.	.	.	.	.
ASIA-ASIE-ASIA																
Afghanistan	.	.	.	.	.	.	.	.	.	.	.	.	.	.	.	.
Armenia	898	970	.	1077	1084	1091	1099	1106	1116	1159	.	1340	.	.	.	.
Azerbaijan	899	971	1048	1077	.	1091	1099	1106	.	1160	1285	.	.	.	.	.
Bahrain	900	972	.	1077	.	1091	1099	1106	1116	1162	1286	1341	.	.	.	.
Bangladesh	.	.	.	1077	.	1091	.	1106	1116	.	.	.	.	.	.	.
Bhutan	.	.	.	1077	.	1091	.	1107	1116	.	.	.	.	.	.	.
Brunei Darussalam	.	.	.	1077	.	1091	.	1107	1117	.	.	.	.	.	.	.
Cambodia	.	.	.	1077	1084	1091	.	1107	.	.	.	.	.	.	.	.
China	901	972	.	1077	.	1091	.	1107	.	.	.	.	.	.	.	.
Georgia	902	972	1049	1077	1084	1091	1099	1107	1117	.	.	.	.	.	.	.

1477

Index

Countries, areas and territories included in each table (with corresponding page number)
Pays, zones et territoires compris dans chaque tableau (avec le numéro de page correspondant)
Países, áreas y territorios incluidos en cada cuadro (con el número de página correspondiente)

Country Pays País	1 ACTIVE POPULATION POPULATION ACTIVE POBLACION ACTIVA		2 EMPLOYMENT EMPLOI EMPLEO						3 UNEMPLOYMENT CHÔMAGE DESEMPLEO					4 HOURS OF WORK DURÉE DU TRAVAIL HORAS DE TRABAJO	
	1A	1B	2A	2B	2C	2D	2E	2F	3A	3B	3C	3D	3E	4A	4B
ASIA-ASIE-ASIA															
Hong Kong, China	16	43	91	137	219	271	320	398	467	504	570	623	684	749	822
India	.	.	.	.	.	.	321	.	467	505	570	.	685	750	823
Indonesia	17	44	91	138	220	271	322	399	467	505	571	.	.	751	824
Iran, Islamic Rep. of	17	45	91	139	220	271	.	.	467	506	571	624	686	.	.
Iraq	.	.	.	.	.	.	.	.	467					.	.
Israel	17	45	91	140	221	272	323	400	468	506	572	625	686	752	824
Japan	17	45	91	141	221	272	324	401	468	507	572	626	687	753	825
Jordan	.	.	.	.	.	.	.	.	.	.	.	.	.	756	828
Kazakhstan	18	46	91	141	222	272	325	.	468	507	573	.	.	.	.
Korea, Republic of	18	.	92	142	222	273	325	.	468	508	573	627	687	756	829
Kuwait	18	.	.	.	.	.	.	.	468	.	574	.	.	.	.
Kyrgyzstan	.	.	92	143	223	273	326	402	468	508	574	628	688	757	831
République dém. pop. lao	.	.	.	.	.	.	.	.	.	.	.	.	.	.	.
Liban	18	.	92	.	223	274	.	.	468	510	575	.	689	.	.
Macau, China	19	46	92	144	224	274	328	403	468	510	575	629	689	758	831
Malaysia	19	47	92	145	224	274	329	403	469	511	576	.	.	758	831
Maldives	.	.	.	.	.	.	.	.	.	.	.	.	.	.	.
Mongolia	19	.	92	146	225	.	.	.	469	511	576	.	.	.	.
Myanmar	.	.	.	.	.	.	.	.	469	.	.	.	.	759	831
Nepal	.	.	.	.	.	.	.	.	.	.	.	.	.	.	.
Oman	.	.	.	.	.	.	.	.	.	.	.	.	.	.	.
Pakistan	.	.	92	147	225	275	330	.	469	512	576	630	690	.	.
Philippines	19	47	92	147	226	275	331	404	469	513	577	.	690	759	831
Qatar	19	.	92	149	226	.	332	.	469	513	.	.	.	762	834
Saudi Arabia	20	.	92	150	227	.	.	.	469	513	577	.	.	.	.
Singapore	20	48	92	151	227	275	333	.	469	514	578	631	691	762	835
Sri Lanka	20	48	92	152	228	276	334	406	470	514	578	.	.	763	835
Syrian Arab Republic	20	49	93	152	229	276	335	.	470	515	578	.	.	.	.
Taiwan, China	20	49	93	153	229	276	336	.	470	516	579	.	.	763	835
Tajikistan	.	.	93	.	.	.	.	.	470	516	579	.	.	.	.
Thailand	21	.	93	153	229	276	.	.	470	516	579	.	692	.	.
United Arab Emirates	21	.	93	154	230	277	336	.	470	517	580	632	692	.	.
Uzbekistan	.	.	93	.	.	.	.	.	470	.	.	.	.	.	.
Viet Nam	.	.	93	155	230	277	.	.	470	517	.	.	.	.	.
West Bank and Gaza Strip	21	49	93	156	231	278	337	408	470	518	580	.	.	764	836
Yemen, Republic of	.	.	.	.	.	.	.	.	.	.	.	.	.	.	.
EUROPE-EUROPE-EUROPA															
Albania	.	.	.	157	.	.	337	.	470	518	581	.	.	765	.
Andorre	.	.	.	.	.	.	338	409	.	.	.	.	.	.	.
Austria	22	50	93	158	232	278	338	409	471	519	581	633	693	765	837
Belarus	22	.	93	.	.	.	.	.	471	520	581	.	.	766	.
Belgique	22	50	93	159	232	278	340	411	471	520	582	635	694	766	838
Bosnia and Herzegovina	22	.	93	.	.	279	.	.	471	521	582	.	.	.	.
Bulgaria	22	51	93	160	233	279	341	412	471	521	582	636	695	768	840
Croatia	23	52	93	161	233	279	342	413	471	522	583	637	695	768	841
Cyprus	23	53	94	162	234	280	343	414	471	523	584	639	696	769	841
Czech Republic	23	53	94	163	235	280	344	415	472	524	585	641	698	770	842
Denmark	23	.	94	164	235	280	346	418	472	525	586	642	698	.	.
España	24	54	94	165	236	281	347	419	472	526	586	643	699	770	843
Estonia	24	55	94	165	236	281	347	420	472	527	587	644	700	771	844
Faeroe Islands	.	.	.	.	.	.	.	.	.	.	.	.	.	.	.
Finland	24	56	94	166	237	281	348	421	472	528	588	645	701	772	844
France	25	56	94	167	238	282	349	422	473	528	588	.	.	773	845
Germany	25	57	94	168	238	282	350	423	473	530	588	646	701	775	847
Gibraltar	.	.	94	169	.	.	351	.	473	.	.	.	.	776	849
Greece	25	58	94	169	239	283	352	424	473	531	589	647	702	776	849

Country / Pays / País	5 WAGES SALAIRES SALARIOS		6 LABOUR COST COÛT DE LA MAIN-D'ŒUVRE COSTO DE LA MANO DE HOBRA	7 CONSUMER PRICES PRIX À LA CONSOMMATION PRECIOS AL CONSUMIDOR						8 OCCUPATIONAL INJURIES LÉSIONS PROFESSIONNELLES LESIONES PROFESIONALES			9 STRIKES AND LOCKOUTS GRÈVES ET LOCK-OUT HUELGAS Y CIERRES PATRONALES			
	5A	5B	6A	7A	7B	7C	7D	7E	7F	8A	8B	8C	9A	9B	9C	9D
ASIA-ASIE-ASIA																
Hong Kong, China	902	973	1049	1077	1084	1091	1099	1107	1117	1163	1287	1341	1372	1386	1402	1413
India	903	974	1050	1077	1084	1091	1099	1107	1117	1164	1287	.	1372	1386	1402	.
Indonesia	904	975	.	1077	.	1091	.	1107	.	.	.	.	.	.	.	.
Iran, Islamic Rep. of	.	.	.	1077	1084	1091	1099	1107	1117	.	.	.	.	.	.	.
Iraq	.	.	.	1077	.	1091	1099	1107	1117	.	.	.	.	.	.	.
Israel	905	976	1050	1077	1084	1091	1099	1107	1117	1164	.	1341	1372	1387	1403	1414
Japan	905	976	.	1077	1084	1092	1099	1107	1117	1165	1288	.	1373	1387	1403	.
Jordan	906	977	.	1077	.	1092	1099	1107	1117	1165	1288	.	1373	1387	1403	.
Kazakhstan	907	978	1050	1077	.	1092	1099	1107	1117	1166	1288	1341	.	.	.	.
Korea, Republic of	908	979	1051	1077	1084	1092	1099	1107	1117	1166	1289	.	1373	1387	1403	1414
Kuwait	.	.	.	1078	.	1092	.	1107	.	.	.	.	.	.	.	.
Kyrgyzstan	910	982	1051	1078	.	1092	1099	1107	1117	1167	1289	1341	.	.	.	.
République dém. pop. lao	.	.	.	1078	.	1092	.	.	.	.	.	.	.	.	.	.
Liban	.	.	.	.	.	.	.	.	.	.	.	.	.	.	.	.
Macau, China	910	982	.	1078	1084	1092	1099	1107	1117	1168	.	1342	.	.	.	.
Malaysia	.	.	.	1078	1084	1092	1099	1107	1117	.	.	.	.	.	.	.
Maldives	.	.	.	1078	.	1092	1100	1107	1117	.	.	.	.	.	.	.
Mongolia	911	982	.	1078	.	1092	1100	1107	.	.	.	.	.	.	.	.
Myanmar	912	983	.	1078	.	1092	1100	1107	1117	1171	1290	.	1373	1387	1403	1414
Nepal	.	.	.	1078	.	1092	1100	1107	1117	.	.	.	.	.	.	.
Oman	.	.	.	1078	1084	1092	1100	1108	1117	.	.	.	.	.	.	.
Pakistan	.	.	.	1078	.	1092	1100	1108	1117	.	.	.	.	.	.	.
Philippines	912	983	1052	1078	1084	1092	1100	1108	1117	.	.	.	1373	1388	1404	.
Qatar	914	984	.	1078	.	1092	1100	1108	1117	.	.	.	.	.	.	.
Saudi Arabia	.	.	.	1078	.	1092	1100	1108	1118	.	.	.	.	.	.	.
Singapore	915	985	1052	1078	1084	1092	1100	1108	1118	1173	1290	1342	1373	1388	1404	1414
Sri Lanka	915	985	.	1078	1084	1092	1100	1108	1118	1174	1291	1343	1374	1388	1404	.
Syrian Arab Republic	.	.	.	1078	1084	1092	1100	1108	1118	1175	.	.	.	.	.	.
Taiwan, China	916	985	.	1078	.	1092	1100	1108	1118	1175	1292	.	.	.	.	.
Tajikistan	917	.	.	.	.	.	.	.	.	.	.	.	.	.	.	.
Thailand	917	985	1052	1078	.	1092	1100	1108	1118	1176	1292	.	1374	1388	1404	1414
United Arab Emirates	.	.	.	1078	.	1093	1100	1108	1118	.	.	.	.	.	.	.
Uzbekistan	.	.	.	.	.	.	.	.	.	.	.	.	.	.	.	.
Viet Nam	.	.	.	1078	.	1093	.	.	.	.	.	.	.	.	.	.
West Bank and Gaza Strip	917	986	.	1078	.	1093	1100	1108	1118	.	.	.	.	.	.	.
Yemen, Republic of	.	.	.	1078	.	1093	.	1108	1118	.	.	.	.	.	.	.
EUROPE-EUROPE-EUROPA																
Albania	918	986	.	1079	1084	1093	1100	1108	1118	.	.	.	.	.	.	.
Andorre	918	986	.	1079	.	1093	1100	1108	1118	.	.	.	.	.	.	.
Austria	919	987	1053	1079	1084	1093	1100	1108	1118	1177	1293	1343	1374	1388	1404	1414
Belarus	919	987	1053	1079	.	1093	1100	1108	1118	1180	1294	1344	1374	1388	1404	.
Belgique	920	987	1054	1079	1084	1093	1100	1108	1118	1181	.	1344	.	.	1405	.
Bosnia and Herzegovina	922	990	.	1079	.	1093	1100	1108	.	.	.	.	.	.	.	.
Bulgaria	922	991	1054	1079	1084	1093	1100	1108	1118	1185	1295	1345	.	.	.	.
Croatia	923	993	1054	1079	.	1093	1101	1108	1118	1189	1297	.	.	.	.	.
Cyprus	924	994	1055	1079	.	1093	.	1108	1118	1192	1299	.	1374	1389	1405	1414
Czech Republic	927	998	1055	1079	1084	1093	1101	1108	1118	1195	1301	1345	.	.	.	.
Denmark	927	998	1055	1079	1085	1093	1101	1109	1118	.	.	.	1374	1389	1405	.
España	928	999	1055	1079	1085	1093	1101	1109	1118	1198	1303	1346	1375	1389	1405	1415
Estonia	928	1000	1056	1079	1085	1093	1101	1109	1118	1201	1305	.	1375	1389	1406	.
Faeroe Islands	.	.	.	1079	.	1093	1101	1109	1118	.	.	.	.	.	.	.
Finland	929	1000	1056	1079	1085	1093	1101	1109	1118	1204	1307	1347	1375	1390	1406	1415
France	930	1003	1056	1079	1085	1093	1101	1109	1119	1208	1309	1347	.	.	1406	1415
Germany	931	1005	1057	1079	1085	1093	1101	1109	1119	1213	1310	.	.	1390	1406	1415
Gibraltar	932	1007	.	1079	1085	1093	.	1109	1119	.	.	.	.	.	.	.
Greece	934	1007	.	1079	1085	1094	1101	1109	1119	.	.	.	.	.	.	.

Index

Countries, areas and territories included in each table (with corresponding page number)
Pays, zones et territoires compris dans chaque tableau (avec le numéro de page correspondant)
Países, áreas y territorios incluidos en cada cuadro (con el número de página correspondiente)

Country / Pays / País	1 ACTIVE POPULATION / POPULATION ACTIVE / POBLACION ACTIVA		2 EMPLOYMENT / EMPLOI / EMPLEO						3 UNEMPLOYMENT / CHÔMAGE / DESEMPLEO					4 HOURS OF WORK / DURÉE DU TRAVAIL / HORAS DE TRABAJO	
	1A	1B	2A	2B	2C	2D	2E	2F	3A	3B	3C	3D	3E	4A	4B
EUROPE-EUROPE-EUROPA															
Hungary	25	59	94	170	239	283	353	425	473	531	589	648	703	777	850
Iceland	26	.	94	171	240	283	353	426	474	532	.	.	.	778	851
Ireland	26	59	94	172	241	284	354	427	474	532	590	.	.	779	852
Isle of Man	.	.	.	.	.	.	.	.	474	.	.	.	.	780	853
Italy	26	60	94	173	241	284	355	428	474	533	590	649	704	781	854
Jersey	.	.	95	174	.	.	.	.	474	.	.	.	.	.	.
Kosovo (Serbia)	.	.	.	.	.	.	.	.	474	.	.	.	.	.	.
Latvia	26	61	95	175	242	284	355	429	474	534	591	649	704	782	855
Liechtenstein	.	.	95	.	.	.	.	.	474	.	.	.	.	.	.
Lithuania	27	62	95	176	242	285	357	430	474	535	592	650	705	784	855
Luxembourg	27	62	95	176	.	.	358	430	475	536	593	.	.	.	.
Macedonia, The Former Yugoslav Rep. of	27	.	95	177	243	285	359	430	475	537	.	.	.	.	.
Malta	27	63	95	177	244	285	360	431	475	538	593	651	706	785	856
Moldova, Republic of	28	.	95	178	244	286	361	432	475	539	.	652	707	786	857
Montenegro	.	.	95	179	245	286	.	.	.	.	.	.	.	.	.
Netherlands	28	64	95	180	245	286	362	433	475	540	593	.	.	786	857
Norway	28	64	95	180	246	287	363	434	476	540	594	.	708	788	859
Poland	28	65	95	181	246	287	364	435	476	541	594	653	708	789	860
Portugal	29	66	95	182	247	288	365	435	476	542	595	655	709	790	861
Roumanie	29	.	95	183	248	288	366	436	476	543	595	656	709	792	863
Russian Federation	29	67	96	184	248	288	367	437	476	544	596	657	710	792	863
San Marino	29	67	96	185	249	289	368	438	477	544	597	.	.	793	864
Serbia	30	.	96	186	249	289	.	.	477	545	.	658	711	.	.
Slovakia	30	68	96	187	250	289	369	439	477	546	597	659	711	793	864
Slovenia	30	69	96	188	250	290	371	441	477	547	598	661	712	793	864
Suisse	30	70	96	189	251	290	372	.	477	548	599	662	713	795	866
Sweden	31	70	96	190	251	290	373	442	477	549	599	662	713	796	867
Turkey	31	71	96	191	252	291	374	443	478	550	600	663	714	798	869
Ukraine	31	71	96	192	253	291	375	444	478	551	601	664	715	799	870
United Kingdom	31	72	96	193	253	291	376	445	478	552	602	665	715	800	871
OCEANIA-OCÉANIE-OCEANIA															
American Samoa	.	.	.	.	.	.	.	.	.	.	.	.	.	.	.
Australia	32	73	96	194	254	292	377	447	478	553	602	666	716	801	872
Cook Islands	.	.	.	.	.	.	.	.	.	.	.	.	.	.	.
Fiji	.	.	.	.	.	.	.	.	.	.	.	.	.	.	.
Guam	.	.	.	.	.	.	377	.	.	.	.	.	.	.	.
Kiribati	.	.	.	.	.	.	.	.	.	.	.	.	.	.	.
Marshall Islands	.	.	.	.	.	.	.	.	.	.	.	.	.	.	.
New Zealand	32	73	96	195	254	292	378	448	478	553	603	667	717	802	873
Niue	.	.	.	.	.	.	.	.	.	.	.	.	.	.	.
Norfolk Island	.	.	.	.	.	.	.	.	.	.	.	.	.	.	.
Northern Mariana Islands	.	.	.	.	.	.	.	.	.	.	.	.	.	.	.
Nouvelle-Calédonie	.	.	.	.	.	.	.	.	478	.	.	.	.	.	.
Papua New Guinea	.	.	.	.	.	.	.	.	.	.	.	.	.	.	.
Polynésie française	.	.	97	.	.	.	.	.	.	.	.	.	.	803	874
Samoa	.	.	.	.	.	.	.	.	.	.	.	.	.	.	.
Solomon Islands	.	.	.	.	.	.	.	.	.	.	.	.	.	.	.
Tonga	.	.	.	.	.	.	.	.	.	.	.	.	.	.	.
Tuvalu	.	.	.	.	.	.	.	.	.	.	.	.	.	.	.
Vanuatu	.	.	.	.	.	.	.	.	.	.	.	.	.	.	.

Country / Pays / País	5 WAGES SALAIRES SALARIOS		6 LABOUR COST COÛT DE LA MAIN-D'ŒUVRE COSTO DE LA MANO DE HOBRA	7 CONSUMER PRICES PRIX À LA CONSOMMATION PRECIOS AL CONSUMIDOR						8 OCCUPATIONAL INJURIES LÉSIONS PROFESSIONNELLES LESIONES PROFESIONALES			9 STRIKES AND LOCKOUTS GRÈVES ET LOCK-OUT HUELGAS Y CIERRES PATRONALES			
	5A	5B	6A	7A	7B	7C	7D	7E	7F	8A	8B	8C	9A	9B	9C	9D
EUROPE-EUROPE-EUROPA																
Hungary	934	1007	1057	1079	1085	1094	1101	1109	1119	1216	1310	.	1375	1390	1407	1415
Iceland	935	1008	1057	1079	1085	1094	1101	1109	1119	1220	.	.	1375	1390	1407	
Ireland	935	1009	.	1079	1085	1094	1101	1109	1119	1222	1312	.	1376	1391	1407	.
Isle of Man	936	1010	.	1079	1085	1094	1101	1109	1119	1223	1312	.	1376	1391	1407	1416
Italy	938	1011	1058	1079	1085	1094	1101	1109	1119	1223	1313	1348	1376	1391	1408	1416
Jersey	938	1011	.	1079	1085	1094	1101	1109	1119	.	.	.	.	.	.	.
Kosovo (Serbia)	.	.	.	1080	.	1094	.	1109	1119	.	.	.	.	.	.	.
Latvia	939	1011	1058	1080	1085	1094	1101	1109	1119	1227	1313	1349	1376	1391	1408	1416
Liechtenstein	939	1012	.	.	.	.	.	.	.	.	.	.	1376	1391	1408	1416
Lithuania	940	1013	1058	1080	1085	1094	1101	1109	1119	1228	1314	1349	1376	1392	1408	.
Luxembourg	941	1014	1059	1080	1085	1094	1101	1109	1119	1231	1316	.	.	.	.	.
Macedonia, The Former Yugoslav Rep. of	942	1016	1059	1080	1085	1094	1101	1109	1119	.	.	.	.	.	.	.
Malta	943	1016	.	1080	1085	1094	1101	1109	1119	1234	1320	1350	1377	1392	1408	1416
Moldova, Republic of	944	1017	1059	1080	.	1094	.	.	.	1238	1322	1350	.	.	.	.
Montenegro	944	1017	.	.	.	.	.	.	.	.	.	.	.	.	.	.
Netherlands	944	1018	.	1080	1085	1094	1101	1109	1119	1239	.	.	1377	1392	1409	1416
Norway	946	1020	.	1080	.	1094	1101	1109	1119	1239	1322	.	1377	1392	1409	.
Poland	946	1020	1060	1080	1085	1094	1101	1109	1119	1242	1323	1351	1377	1393	1409	1417
Portugal	947	1021	1060	1080	1085	1094	1101	1109	1119	1245	1323	.	1378	1393	1409	1417
Roumanie	948	1023	1061	1080	1085	1094	1102	1110	1119	1248	1325	1352	1378	1393	1410	1417
Russian Federation	949	1025	1061	1080	.	1094	1102	1110	1119	1252	1326	1352	1378	1393	1410	.
San Marino	949	1025	1061	1080	.	1094	.	1110	1119	1252	1326	.	1378	1394	1410	.
Serbia	949	1025	.	1080	.	1094	.	1110	1119	.	.	.	.	.	.	.
Slovakia	949	1026	1062	1080	.	1094	1102	1110	1120	1253	1327	1353	1378	1394	1410	1417
Slovenia	950	1026	1062	1080	1085	1094	1102	1110	1120	1257	1329	1354	.	.	.	.
Suisse	950	1026	1062	1080	1086	1095	1102	1110	1120	1258	1330	.	1379	1394	1410	1417
Sweden	951	1027	1062	1080	1086	1095	1102	1110	1120	1259	1330	1354	1379	1394	1411	.
Turkey	952	1028	.	1080	.	1095	1102	1110	1120	1262	1332	1355	1379	1394	1411	1417
Ukraine	952	1029	1063	1080	.	1095	.	.	.	1264	1333	1355	1379	1395	1411	.
United Kingdom	953	1030	1063	1080	1086	1095	1102	1110	1120	1265	1334	.	1380	1395	1411	1418
OCEANIA-OCÉANIE-OCEANIA																
American Samoa	.	.	.	1080	1086	1095	.	1110	1120	.	.	.	.	.	.	.
Australia	956	1033	.	1080	1086	1095	1102	1110	1120	1268	1336	1356	1380	1395	1412	1418
Cook Islands	.	.	.	1081	.	1095	1102	1110	1120	.	.	.	.	.	.	.
Fiji	.	.	.	1081	.	1095	1102	1110	1120	.	.	.	.	.	.	.
Guam	.	.	.	1081	.	1095	.	1110	1120	.	.	.	.	.	.	.
Kiribati	.	.	.	1081	.	1095	.	1110	1120	.	.	.	.	.	.	.
Marshall Islands	.	.	.	1081	.	1095	.	1110	.	.	.	.	.	.	.	.
New Zealand	956	1034	1064	1081	1086	1095	1102	1110	1120	1271	.	1356	1380	1395	1412	1418
Niue	.	.	.	1081	.	1095	.	1110	1120	.	.	.	.	.	.	.
Norfolk Island	.	.	.	1081	.	1095	.	1110	.	.	.	.	.	.	.	.
Northern Mariana Islands	.	.	.	1081	.	1095	.	1110	1120	.	.	.	.	.	.	.
Nouvelle-Calédonie	.	.	.	1081	.	1095	1102	1110	1120	.	.	.	.	.	.	.
Papua New Guinea	.	.	.	1081	.	1095	.	1110	1120	.	.	.	.	.	.	.
Polynésie française	.	.	.	1081	.	1095	1102	1111	1120	.	.	.	.	.	.	.
Samoa	.	.	.	1081	1086	1095	.	1111	.	.	.	.	.	.	.	.
Solomon Islands	.	.	.	1081	.	1095	.	1111	1120	.	.	.	.	.	.	.
Tonga	.	.	.	1081	1086	1095	.	1111	1120	.	.	.	.	.	.	.
Tuvalu	.	.	.	1081	.	1096	.	1111	1120	.	.	.	.	.	.	.
Vanuatu	.	.	.	1081	.	1096	.	1111	1121	.	.	.	.	.	.	.